CPS

Compendium of Pharmaceuticals and Specialties

Thirty-fourth Edition

1999

The Canadian Reference for Health Professionals

CPS

Compendium of Pharmaceuticals and Specialties

Published by	Canadian Pharmacists Association Ottawa, Ontario, Canada
President	Garry Cruickshank, BScPharm
Executive Director	Leroy Fevang, BScPharm, MBA
Publisher	Leesa D. Bruce
Editor-in-Chief	M. Claire Gillis, BSc(Pharm)
Associate Editors	Louise Welbanks, BScPhm Diane Bergeron, BPharm Marline Cormier-Boyd, BSc(Pharm) Frances Hachborn, BScPhm Barbara Jovaisas, BSc(Pharm) Sandra Pagotto, BSP Carol Repchinsky, BSP
Senior Assistant Editor	Roxanne Bisson
Production Coordinator	Rita Tremblay
PRS Coordinator	Julie Lévesque
Assistant Editors	Dianne Baxter Robin McIntosh, BA
Editorial Assistant	Murielle Danis
Manager, Book Production	Darquise Leblanc
Typesetters	Bob Heathorn, Lucienne Prévost, Kathleen Régimbald

The Canadian Pharmacists Association expresses sincere thanks to Claire Gillis, Editor-in-Chief, for her guidance and commitment to CPS *over the past 15 years.*

The editors gratefully acknowledge the assistance of Sylvie Brûlé, Patricia Carruthers-Czyzewski, Nicole Castéran, Sylvie Marcotte, Sonal Purohit, Tess Radford, Kate Reid and Caroline Shaughnessy in the production of this edition.

Special thanks are extended to Ken Fremont at C.K. Productions and Mike Collinge and all the people at Webcom Limited who brought this book to completion.

The *Compendium of Pharmaceuticals and Specialties*
is available in print in English and French.
CPS on CD-ROM is available only in English.

Copies of the *Compendium of Pharmaceuticals and Specialties*
may be obtained from the Canadian Pharmacists Association,
1785 Alta Vista Drive, Ottawa, Ontario, Canada, K1G 3Y6.
Tel (613) 523-7877, (800) 917-9489 Fax (613) 523-0445
E-mail requests@cdnpharm.ca

ISSN 0069–7966
ISBN 0–919115–99–3

Design, Production and Typesetting
Graphic Communications, CPhA

Cover Design
Lucienne Prévost

Advertising Sales
Keith Health Care Inc.

All prescription drug advertisements
have been cleared by the Pharmaceutical Advertising Advisory Board.

Printed in Canada by Webcom Limited, Toronto

TABLE OF CONTENTS

PREFACE

The ***Compendium of Pharmaceuticals and Specialties*** *(CPS)* is editorially compiled and produced by the staff of the Canadian Pharmacists Association for the benefit of all health professionals.

Users are advised that the information provided in the *CPS* is not exhaustive. Other sources may contain additional necessary information for safe use of the product.

Changes to monographs contained in the *CPS* received by the publisher after established deadlines are not included in this edition.

The *CPS* editors work closely with the *CPS* Editorial Advisory Panel, the Therapeutic Products Programme, Health Canada, and the pharmaceutical industry.

The editors acknowledge the collaborative effort of the many contributors and reviewers listed on page viii.

The editors express their thanks to all manufacturers and distributors who have cooperated by supplying information, offering suggestions and reading proofs. We extend an appreciation to the users of the *CPS* who forwarded constructive suggestions for amendments to the text and revisions in the format.

The assistance of the Ottawa Valley Regional Drug Information Service, the Drug Information and Research Centre and numerous drug information centres across Canada is greatly appreciated.

EDITORIAL ADVISORY PANEL

CONTRIBUTORS/REVIEWERS

M. Ackerman, MD, FRCPC
Heart and Stroke Foundation of Canada
Emergency Cardiac Care Subcommittee
Burlington, Ontario

D.R. Anderson, MD, FRCPC
Assistant Professor of Medicine,
Dalhousie University, Halifax
Division of Hematology
Queen Elizabeth II Health Sciences Centre, Halifax

C. Bayliff, PharmD
Clinical Coordinator of Pharmacy Services
London Health Sciences Centre, Victoria Campus
London, Ontario

M. Bédard, PharmD
Drug Information Specialist
The Ottawa Hospital, General Campus

M. Bodie-Collins, RN, BScN
Travel Medicine Advisor
Travel Medicine Program
Office of Special Health Initiatives
Health Canada, Ottawa

J. Bruni, MD, FRCPC
Head, Division of Neurology
Wellesley Hospital, Toronto

P. Camfield, MD, FRCPC
Professor and Head, Department of Pediatrics
Dalhousie University
IWK Grace Health Centre, Halifax

N. Campbell, MD, FRCPC
President, Canadian Coalition for High Blood
Pressure Prevention and Control
Department of Medicine
University of Calgary

S.G. Carruthers, MD, FRCPC
Richard Ivey Professor and Chair
Department of Medicine, University of Western Ontario
Chief of Medicine
London Health Sciences Centre, London, Ontario

J. Courtemanche, BScN(Ed)
Secretary
Canadian Association of Poison Control Centres
Children's Hospital of Eastern Ontario, Ottawa

S. Cowan, BScPhm
McGill University, Montreal

P.W.F. Fischer, BSc, PhD
Chief, Nutrition Research Division
Food Directorate, Health Protection Branch
Health Canada, Ottawa

W.C. Foong, BSc(Hons), PhD
Associate Professor
Division of Oral Biology, Faculty of Dentistry
Dalhousie University, Halifax

M.J. Friedland, MD, FRCPC
Department of Anaesthesia
Trillium Health Centre, Mississauga Site
Mississauga, Ontario

R.E. Grymonpre, BScPharm, PharmD
Associate Professor, Faculty of Pharmacy
University of Manitoba, Winnipeg

A. Guberman, MD, FRCPC
Professor, Neurology Division
University of Ottawa
The Ottawa Hospital, General Campus

D.A. Haas, DDS, PhD, FRCDC
Associate Professor
Department of Anaesthesia, Faculty of Dentistry
Department of Pharmacology, Faculty of Medicine
University of Toronto

B.G. Hardy, PharmD, FCSHP, FCCP
Coordinator—Clinical Programs, Department of Pharmacy
Sunnybrook Health Sciences Centre
Associate Professor, Faculty of Pharmacy
University of Toronto

R. Hossie, BScPhm, MScPhm, PhD
Bureau of Drug Surveillance
Therapeutic Products Programme
Health Canada, Ottawa

S. Ito, MD, ABCP
Division of Clinical Pharmacology
Department of Pediatrics
Hospital for Sick Children, Toronto

M. Jones, MD, FRCPC
Director, EEG Laboratory
Neurology Division
Vancouver General Hospital

S.H. Kennedy, MD, FRCPC
Head, Mood and Anxiety Division
Clarke Institute of Psychiatry, Toronto
Professor and Head, Mood Disorders Program
University of Toronto

S. Lovell, BScPhm
Department of Pharmacy
London Health Sciences Centre, University Campus
London, Ontario

A. Massicotte, BPharm, MSc
Drug Information Centre
The Ottawa Hospital, Civic Campus

I. MacKay, BSc(Hons), MSc
Acting Head, Special Access Programme
Therapeutic Products Programme
Health Canada, Ottawa

V.J.H. Marchessault, MD, FRCPC
Chairman, National Advisory Committee on Immunization
Department of Pediatrics
Children's Hospital of Eastern Ontario, Ottawa

CONTRIBUTORS/REVIEWERS *(cont'd)*

A.E. McCarthy, MD, FRCPC, DTM&H
Director, Tropical Medicine and International Health Clinic
The Ottawa Hospital, General Campus

R.S. McLachlan, MD, FRCPC
Epilepsy Unit
London Health Sciences Centre, University Campus
London, Ontario

M.J. McQueen, MB, ChB, PhD, FCACB, FRCPC
Director, Hamilton Regional Laboratory Medicine
Director, Lipid Research Clinic
Hamilton General Hospital Campus
Professor of Pathology
McMaster University, Hamilton, Ontario

D.G. Mills, BSc, PhD
Coordinator, Drug Information Services
Department of Pharmacy
London Health Sciences Centre, London, Ontario

S. Otawa, BScPharm
Pharmacist
Mississauga, Ontario

C.J. Patterson, MD, FRCPC, FACP
Professor
Division of Geriatric Medicine
McMaster University, Hamilton, Ontario

R. Pless, MD, MSc
Head, Vaccine-associated Adverse
Events Surveillance Section
Division of Immunization
Laboratory Centre for Disease Control
Health Canada, Ottawa

N. Ramuscak, BScPhm
Clinical Pharmacist, Neurosurgery and Orthopaedics
Trillium Health Centre, Mississauga Site
Mississauga, Ontario

M.B.M. Sundaram, MD
Professor, Department of Neurology
University of Mississippi
Jackson, Mississippi USA

H. Sutcliffe, BScPharm
Acting Head, Adverse Drug Reaction Reporting Unit
Bureau of Drug Surveillance
Health Canada, Ottawa

G. Sweeney, MD
McMaster University, Hamilton, Ontario

M.P. Thirlwell, MD, FRCPC, FACP
Professor of Medicine and Oncology
McGill University, Montreal
Acting-Chief, Department of Oncology
Montreal General Hospital

D. Wong, BScPhm
Pharmacist
Scarborough, Ontario

G.B. Young, MD, FRCPC
Department of Clinical Neurological Sciences
University of Western Ontario
London Health Sciences Centre, Victoria Campus
London, Ontario

SUPPORTERS

The financial support of the following companies is gratefully acknowledged:

Abbott
Albert Pharma
Alcon
Allerex
Allergan
AltiMed
Alza
Amgen
Apotex
Ashbury Biologicals/Herbal Laboratories
Astra
Axcan Pharma
Baxter
Bayer
Bayer Consumer
BDH
Bencard
Berlex Canada
Berna Products
BioChem Vaccines
Biomatrix
Bioniche
Block Drug
Boehringer Ingelheim
Bristol
Bristol-Myers Squibb
Canderm Pharma
Cangene
Carter Horner
Chattem
CIBA Vision
Clintec
Connaught
Crystaal
Dermik Laboratories Canada
Dermtek
Desbergers
Dioptic
Dispensapharm
Dormer
Draxis Health
Duchesnay
DuPont Pharma
Endo
Fabrigen
Faulding
Ferring
Fournier
Frosst
Fujisawa
Galderma
Genpharm
Germiphene
Glaxo Wellcome
Glenwood
Hoechst Marion Roussel
Hoffmann-La Roche
ICN
Janssen-Ortho
Johnson & Johnson • Merck
Key
Knoll
Labcatal
Leo
Ligand
Lilly
Lundbeck
Mallinckrodt
May & Baker Pharma
McNeil Consumer Products
Mead Johnson
Medican Pharma
Medicis
Medisan Pharmaceuticals
Merck Sharp & Dohme
Milex
Nadeau
Nestlé, Carnation
NeXstar
Novartis Consumer Health
Novartis Nutrition
Novartis Pharmaceuticals
Novo Nordisk
Novopharm
Nu-Pharm
Nycomed
Odan
Ophtapharma
Organon
Organon Teknika
Parke-Davis
Pfizer
Pfizer Consumer
Pharmaceutical Partners
Pharmacia & Upjohn
Pharmascience
Procter & Gamble
Procter & Gamble Pharmaceuticals
Purdue Frederick
R&D Laboratories
Reed & Carnrick
Rhodiapharm
Rhône-Poulenc Rorer
RHO-Pharm
RhoxalPharma
Riva
Rivex Ophthalmics
Rivex Pharma
Roberts
Rougier
Sabex
Sanofi
Schein Pharmaceutical
Schering
Searle
Serono
Servier
Shepherd
Sigma-Tau
SmithKline Beecham
SmithKline Beecham Consumer Healthcare
Smith & Nephew
Solvay Pharma
SpectroPharm Dermatology
Squibb
Stanley
Stiefel
Sun
Swiss Herbal
Tanta
Taro
Technilab
Therapex
3M Pharmaceuticals
Trans CanaDerm
Trianon
UCB Pharma
Warner-Lambert Consumer Healthcare
Waymar
Welcker-Lyster
WestCan
Westwood-Squibb
Whitehall-Robins
Wyeth-Ayerst
Zeneca
Zila

GENERAL CONSIDERATIONS

In the *CPS* 34th edition (1999), the format of previous editions has been retained and the policy of making improvements has been continued.

Great care has been taken to ensure the accuracy and completeness of the information contained in the *CPS*. However, the editors and publishers are not responsible for errors or any consequences arising from the use of the information published herein.

Users are advised that the information provided in the *CPS* is not exhaustive. Other sources may contain additional necessary information for safe use of the product.

The *CPS* monographs in the **White Section** are based on information received from the manufacturers and the Therapeutic Products Programme, Health Canada. Included are those products and medical devices with a drug component available for use in Canada. Products registered under the Food and Drug Regulations, Division 10, which are offered to the public for self-medication, are not generally included.

The inclusion of a manufacturer's product monograph in the *CPS* does not imply that the editors or the *CPS* Editorial Advisory Panel accept, endorse or recommend these preparations as being clinically superior to similar products of any other firm. Individual products may differ in their constituents. In addition to therapeutic or drug components, products may contain nonmedicinal ingredients. Examples of nonmedicinal ingredients include diluents, lubricants, binders, buffers, antioxidants, preservatives, fillers, flavors, coloring agents and sweeteners.

Product monographs contain information on nonmedicinal ingredients. This information has been voluntarily submitted by the manufacturers and compiled by the editors. A statement may appear in the "Supplied" sections of the monographs indicating the presence or absence of a specific nonmedicinal ingredient in the product. The lack of a statement indicates no information was available to the editorial staff regarding a specific nonmedicinal ingredient. *CPS* users are urged to consult the product monograph of the product dispensed (see Clin-Info Section for further discussion on this topic).

All of the product monographs in the *CPS* are sent to the manufacturers every year for review. Monographs that have been revised extensively by the *CPS* editorial staff, the manufacturer and/or the *CPS* Editorial Advisory Panel are designated "Reviewed..." and the year when this occurred. Products that have been newly introduced on the Canadian market are designated *"New Product 1998"*.

In the monograph section, not including the general monographs, products are alphabetically listed by names that are registered trademarks of the company whose name, in full or in abbreviated form, immediately follows it. The appropriate designation ® or ™ appears beside the product name. *CPS* users are cautioned regarding the unauthorized use of any registered trade name.

The monographs present unbiased, factual information on drugs in a format useful to health care practitioners. For additional product information, readers are referred to the pertinent scientific and professional literature, to the descriptive literature of the company concerned, or to its professional personnel.

Changes to monographs contained in the *CPS* received by the publisher after established deadlines are not included in this edition.

The general monographs have been developed by the *CPS* editors and/or contributors and reviewed by the *CPS* Editorial Advisory Panel. Those included in this edition are listed on page 3. Readers should be aware that the text may contain information different from that approved by the Therapeutic Products Programme, Health Canada and that the pharmaceutical manufacturers' approval has not been requested.

The **Clin-Info Section** includes tables identifying alcohol, gluten, sulfites and tartrazine content of selected products. In addition, information on drug interactions, drug exposure during lactation and pregnancy, drugs and older individuals, drugs in dentistry, drugs to consider in patients with porphyria, antineoplastic drug therapy and clinical approaches on a variety of topics, as well as a directory of health organizations are included. The Clin-Info section contains information that is reviewed yearly by experts in their fields. For a complete lising of these topics, refer to Table of Contents on page L1.

Comments concerning the *CPS* 34th Edition (1999), its usefulness to the practitioners of the various health professions, and suggestions for the improvement of future editions are welcomed. Please use the Comment Card provided.

ERRATUM POLICY

Serious dosage errors, errors that threaten the patient's safety, or errors that could have other serious consequences will be considered for an erratum. In this event, a letter of correction or an appropriate insert will be sent to all known subscribers of the *CPS* as soon as possible.

Minor errors that do not have an impact on health care will be corrected in the next edition of the *CPS*.

In some cases, such appropriate journals as the *Canadian Pharmaceutical Journal* and the *Canadian Medical Association Journal* will be used to convey changes that are not urgent or serious.

EDITORIAL POLICY

The *CPS* contains information about products intended for human use. Products are alphabetically listed by names that are the registered trademarks of the company whose name, in full or abbreviated form, immediately follows the trademark. General monographs are shown in the monograph section under the generic name or class.

The *CPS* is not intended to be exhaustive in terms of drug products available in Canada. The *CPS* editors compile, edit and distribute appropriate monographs which have been submitted by the manufacturer for inclusion in the book.

Users are advised that the information provided in the *CPS* is not exhaustive. Other sources may contain additional necessary information for safe use of the product.

Changes to monographs contained in the *CPS* received by the publisher after established deadlines are not included in this edition.

The *CPS* contains information on proprietary and nonproprietary products intended for human use.

The information provided in the *CPS* monographs is based on the Product Monograph prepared by the pharmaceutical manufacturers and accepted by the Therapeutic Products Programme, Health Canada. Product information as published in the *CPS* is a direct equivalent of the prescribing information contained and described in Sections 2.2 to 2.12 of the Drugs Directorate, Health Protection Branch Guidelines for Product Monographs (1989). Editorial changes are limited to those required for consistency of style, clarity and presentation.

Manufacturers' product monographs accepted by Therapeutic Products Programme and containing the same therapeutic ingredient(s) may differ in their indications, contraindications, warnings, precautions, adverse effects and dosing regimens. *CPS* users are encouraged to consult the product monograph of the product dispensed to ensure specific information.

Information published in various literature sources may be valuable to *CPS* users, and the *CPS* Editorial Advisory Panel may recommend additional information.

The general monographs are developed by the *CPS* editors and/or contributors and are based on information available from the originator's Product Monograph and independent literature sources. The *CPS* Editorial Advisory Panel reviews the monographs for accuracy and appropriateness with respect to current medical practice. Readers should be aware that the text may contain information different from that approved by the Therapeutic Products Programme, Health Canada and that the pharmaceutical manufacturers' approval has not been requested.

Prescribing information for products marketed before the publication of the Trade Information Letter, No. 302, June 6, 1968, is reviewed periodically in cooperation with the appropriate pharmaceutical manufacturer, Therapeutic Products Programme and the *CPS* Editorial Advisory Panel.

The Clin-Info Section contains selected information for health care professionals based on clinical practice and a review of the literature. The editors have collaborated with the contributors to compile this information. Although the information is not intended to be all inclusive, the editors, contributors and publisher have tried to ensure its accuracy at the time of publication. Readers should be aware that the text may contain information different from that approved by Therapeutic Products Programme and that the pharmaceutical manufacturers' approval has not been requested.

Drug therapy is constantly changing; consequently, it is the responsibility of the health care professional to seek additional and confirmatory information; to evaluate its appropriateness as it relates to the actual clinical situation; and to consider new developments.

What's new in *CPS* 1999

- Product News 1999

- Changes to the Clin-Info (Lilac) section
  - New sections added to Drugs in Dentistry, Antiepileptic Drug Therapy and Drug Exposure during Pregnancy
  - New format and complete reorganization of Drug Interactions table
  - Expanded sections on Clinical Laboratory Reference Values and Immunization Schedules
  - Completely revised information on Water Treatment Methods for Travellers

- New general monograph
  - Selective Serotonin Reuptake Inhibitors

PRODUCT NEWS 1999

Here is a quick look at what's new in the *CPS* 1999! New drugs (i.e., new chemical entities) with approved indications, previously available drugs with new indications, suppliers or dosage forms, new products (e.g., new generic products) and product name changes are listed. We hope this will help you to use the *CPS* more effectively than ever! Look for the product name in the *CPS* monographs section for more information.

CPS users are cautioned that listings may not be exhaustive although every effort has been made to include all applicable products. Only information pertaining to full product monographs is highlighted here.

Brand Name	Generic Name/ Dosage Form	Manufacturer	Classification	Comments
Accolate®	Zafirlukast 20 mg tablets	Zeneca	Leukotriene Receptor Antagonist	New drug—for the prophylaxis and chronic treatment of asthma in patients 12 years of age and older
Accuretic™	Quinapril—Hydrochlorothiazide 10/12.5 mg and 20/12.5 mg tablets	Parke-Davis	ACE Inhibitor—Diuretic	New product—for the treatment of essential hypertension when combination therapy is appropriate
Acel-P™	Acellular Pertussis Vaccine Adsorbed suspension for i.m. injection	Wyeth-Ayerst	Active Immunizing Agent	New product—for primary immunization (3 doses) of children 15 months-6 years of age against disease caused by *Bordetella pertussis*; also for booster immunization as a fourth dose for children who previously received their primary immunization
Acyclovir Sodium for Injection	Acyclovir 500 mg and 1 g vials for i.v. infusion	Novopharm	Antiviral	New product
Acyclovir Sodium Injection	Acyclovir 25 mg/mL; 500 mg and 1 g vials for i.v. infusion	Faulding	Antiviral	New product
Advil®	Ibuprofen	Whitehall-Robins	Analgesic—Antipyretic	New dosage forms—200 mg gel caplets and 100 mg/5 mL children's suspension
Airomir™	Salbutamol Sulfate 100 µg/actuation, 200 dose inhalation aerosol	3M Pharmaceuticals	Bronchodilator—Beta$_2$-adrenergic Stimulant	New product—does not contain chlorofluorocarbons
Alesse™ 21 Alesse™ 28	Levonorgestrel 100 µg—Ethinyl Estradiol 20 µg per tablet	Wyeth-Ayerst	Oral Contraceptive	New product
Alphagan™	Brimonidine 0.2% ophthalmic solution	Allergan	Elevated Intraocular Pressure Therapy—Alpha Adrenergic Receptor Agonist	New drug—for control of intraocular pressure in open angle glaucoma or ocular hypertension
Amerge®	Naratriptan 1 and 2.5 mg tablets	Glaxo Wellcome	Migraine Therapy—5-HT$_1$ Receptor Agonist	New drug—for the acute treatment of migraine attacks with or without aura
Antibiotic Cold Sore Ointment	Polymyxin B Compound	Novartis Consumer Health	Cold Sore Therapy	Name change—formerly Webber Antibiotic Cold Sore Ointment
Apo®-Acyclovir	Acyclovir 200, 400 and 800 mg tablets	Apotex	Antiviral	New product
Apo®-Cefaclor	Cefaclor 125, 250 and 375 mg/mL oral suspension	Apotex	Antibiotic	New dosage form—oral suspension
Apo®-Cromolyn	Cromolyn 2% nasal spray	Apotex	Seasonal Rhinitis Therapy	New product
Apo®-Cromolyn Sterules	Cromolyn 1% inhalation solution (2 mL)	Apotex	Prophylaxis of Symptoms of Bronchial Asthma	New product
Apo®-Domperidone	Domperidone 10 mg tablets	Apotex	Upper Gastrointestinal Motility Modifier	New product
Apo®-Etodolac	Etodolac 200 and 300 mg capsules	Apotex	Anti-inflammatory	New product
Apo®-Ketoconazole	Ketoconazole 200 mg tablets	Apotex	Antifungal	New product

Brand Name	Generic Name/ Dosage Form	Manufacturer	Classification	Comments
Apo®-Loxapine	Loxapine 5, 10, 25 and 50 mg tablets	Apotex	Antipsychotic	New product
Apo®-Moclobemide	Moclobemide 100 and 150 mg tablets	Apotex	Antidepressant	New product
Apo®-Oflox	Ofloxacin 200, 300 and 400 mg tablets	Apotex	Antibacterial	New product
Apo®-Terazosin	Terazosin 1, 2, 5 and 10 mg tablets	Apotex	Antihypertensive—Symptomatic Treatment of Benign Prostatic Hyperplasia	New product
Apo®-Ticlopidine	Ticlopidine 250 mg tablets	Apotex	Platelet Inhibitor	New product
Aspirin®, Coated Daily Low Dose	Enteric-coated ASA 81 mg	Bayer Consumer	Platelet Aggregation Inhibitor	New strength
Aspirin®, Coated Super Extra Strength	Enteric-coated ASA 650 mg	Bayer Consumer	Analgesic—Anti-inflammatory—Antipyretic	New strength
Astracaine®	Articaine 40 mg/mL—Epinephrine 1:200 000	Astra	Local Anesthetic	New product—for infiltration and nerve block anesthesia in dentistry
Astracaine® Forte	Articaine 40 mg/mL—Epinephrine 1:100 000	Astra	Local Anesthetic	New product—for infiltration and nerve block anesthesia in dentistry
Atracurium Besylate Injection	Atracurium 10 mg/mL vials for i.v. use	Faulding	Neuromuscular Blocking Agent	New product
Avapro™	Irbesartan 75, 150 and 300 mg tablets	Bristol-Myers Squibb/ Sanofi Canada	Angiotensin II AT_1 Receptor Blocker	New drug—for treatment of essential hypertension
Baycol®	Cerivastatin 0.2 and 0.3 mg tablets	Bayer	Lipid Metabolism Regulator	New drug—HMG-CoA reductase inhibitor
Beano®	Alpha-D-Galactosidase 150 GalU tablets and 150 GalU/5 drops	Block Drug	Alpha Galactosidase Enzyme	New product—to prevent digestive gas
Benadryl® Junior Strength Chewable Tablets	Diphenhydramine 12.5 mg chewable tablet	Warner-Lambert Consumer Healthcare	Antihistamine	New product
Benylin® DM 12 Hour	Dextromethorphan Polistirex 30 mg/5 mL controlled-release formula syrup	Warner-Lambert Consumer Healthcare	Antitussive	New product
Benylin® DM for Children 12 Hour	Dextromethorphan Polistirex 15 mg/5 mL controlled-release formula syrup	Warner-Lambert Consumer Healthcare	Antitussive	New product
Bleomycin Sulfate USP	Bleomycin 15 units/vial (lyophilized) for i.m., s.c., i.v., intra-articular, intrapleural or intraperitoneal use	Faulding	Antineoplastic	New product
Caltrate® Plus	Calcium Carbonate—Vitamin D—Magnesium—Zinc—Copper—Manganese tablets	Whitehall-Robins	Vitamin and Mineral Supplement	New product
Cerebyx®	Fosphenytoin Sodium 75 mg/mL for i.v. infusion or i.m. administration	Parke-Davis	Antiepileptic	New product—75 mg of fosphenytoin is equivalent to 50 mg/mL phenytoin sodium
Chronovera®	Verapamil 180 mg and 240 mg controlled-onset extended-release tablets	Searle	Antihypertensive—Antianginal	New product—formulation designed to initiate release of verapamil about 4-5 hours after ingestion and then a constant release over 12 hours
Cipro®	Ciprofloxacin 5 g/100 mL and 10 g/100 mL oral suspension; 2 mg/mL minibags of 100 and 200 mL	Bayer	Antibiotic	New dosage forms
Claritin®	Loratadine 10 mg rapid dissolve tongue tablets	Schering	Histamine H_1 Receptor Antagonist	New dosage form

Brand Name	Generic Name/ Dosage Form	Manufacturer	Classification	Comments
Climara®	Estradiol-17ß transdermal system	Berlex Canada	Estrogen	New product—once weekly application
Cytovene®	Ganciclovir 250 mg capsules and 500 mg vials	Roche	Antiviral	New indication—for the prevention of CMV disease in solid organ transplant recipients
Dalacin® C Phosphate Sterile Solution	Clindamycin 150 mg/mL injection	Pharmacia & Upjohn	Antibiotic	New indication—for treatment of *Pneumocystis carinii* pneumonia in patients with AIDS (with primaquine in patients who are intolerant to or fail to respond to conventional therapy)
Demadex®	Torsemide 5, 10, 20 and 100 mg tablets and 10 mg/mL ampuls	Roche	Diuretic	New supplier—formerly Boehringer Mannheim
Deproic®	Valproic acid 250 mg/5 mL syrup	Technilab	Anticonvulsant	New dosage form
Dexiron™	Iron Dextran 50 mg/mL, 1 and 2 mL single dose vials	Genpharm	Iron Supplement	New product—for i.m. injection
Diane®-35	Cyproterone 2 mg—Ethinyl Estradiol 0.035 mg tablets, 21 day pack	Berlex Canada	Antiandrogen—Estrogen Combination Hormone	New product—for treatment of androgen-dependent acne in females; also provides reliable contraception
Diclotec	Diclofenac 50 and 100 mg suppositories	Technilab	Nonsteroidal Anti-inflammatory Drug	New product
Dimetapp® Quick Dissolve	Brompheniramine 1 mg—Phenylpropanolamine 6.25 mg quick dissolve tablets	Whitehall-Robins	Antihistamine—Decongestant	New dosage form
Diovan®	Valsartan 80 mg and 160 mg capsules	Novartis Pharmaceuticals	Angiotensin II AT_1 Receptor Blocker	New drug—for treatment of mild to moderate essential hypertension
Ditropan®	Oxybutynin 5 mg tablets and 5 mg/mL syrup	Alza	Antispasmodic	New distributor—formerly Procter & Gamble
Echinacea Angustifolia	Extract of Echinacea Angustifolia	Swiss Herbal	Herbal Medicine	New product—for relief of colds and minor flu symptoms
Echovist®	Galactose granules 3 g/vial and 20% solution, 13.5 mL/vial	Berlex Canada	Ultrasound Contrast Agent	New product—for ultrasound examination of the uterine cavity and fallopian tubes
Effexor® XR	Venlafaxine 37.5, 75 and 150 mg extended-release capsules	Wyeth-Ayerst	Antidepressant	New dosage form
Efudex®	5-Fluorouracil 5% cream	ICN	Topical Antineoplastic	New supplier—formerly Roche
Elmiron™	Pentosan Polysulfate Sodium 100 mg capsules	Alza	Interstitial Cystitis Treatment	New supplier—formerly Baker Cummins
Emadine®	Emedastine 0.05% ophthalmic solution	Alcon	Antiallergy	New drug—topical histamine H_1 antagonist
EMLA® Cream	Lidocaine 25 mg—Prilocaine 25 mg per gram	Astra	Topical Anesthetic	New indication—for topical analgesia of leg ulcers in connection with mechanical cleansing/débridement
Epiject® I.V.	Valproic Acid 100 mg/mL for i.v. injection; 5 mL single dose vials	Abbott	Anticonvulsant	New product
Euglucon®	Glyburide 2.5 mg and 5 mg tablets	Pharmascience	Hypoglycemic	New supplier—formerly Boehringer Mannheim
Evista™	Raloxifene 60 mg tablets	Lilly	Selective Estrogen Receptor Modulator	New drug—for the prevention of osteoporosis in postmenopausal women
Ex-Lax® Chocolated Pieces, Sugar Coated Pills and Extra Strength Sugar Coated Pills	Sennosides 15 mg (25 mg in extra strength)	Novartis Consumer Health	Laxative	New product

Brand Name	Generic Name/ Dosage Form	Manufacturer	Classification	Comments
Ex-Lax® Stool Softener	Docusate Sodium 100 mg caplets	Novartis Consumer Health	Laxative	New product
Famvir™	Famciclovir 125, 250 and 500 mg tablets	SmithKline Beecham	Antiviral	New indication—to treat or suppress recurrent genital herpes in immunocompetent adults
Fexicam	Piroxicam 20 mg suppositories	Technilab	Nonsteroidal Anti-inflammatory Drug	New product
Flomax®	Tamsulosin 0.4 mg SR capsules	Boehringer Ingelheim	$Alpha_{1A}$-adrenoceptor Blocker	New drug—for treatment of benign prostatic hyperplasia
Flovent®	Fluticasone 50, 100, 250 or 500 μg blisters in a plastic inhaler device	Glaxo Wellcome	Corticosteroid	New dosage form
Fosamax®	Alendronate 5, 10 and 40 mg tablets	MSD	Bone Metabolism Regulator	New indications—for prevention of osteoporosis in post-menopausal women and for prevention of fractures in post-menopausal women treated for osteoporosis New strength—5 mg tablet
Fragmin®	Dalteparin Sodium for injection	Pharmacia & Upjohn	Anticoagulant Antithrombotic	New indication—for unstable coronary artery disease i.e., unstable angina and non-Q-wave myocardial infarction
Fraxiparine™	Nadroparin Calcium 9 500 IU anti-Xa/mL prefilled syringes	Sanofi	Anticoagulant—Low Molecular Weight Heparin	New drug—for prophylaxis of thromboembolism in general and orthopedic surgeries, treatment of deep vein thrombosis and prevention of clotting during hemodialysis
Gas-X® Gas-X® Extra Strength	Simethicone 80 and 125 mg tablets	Novartis Consumer Health	Antiflatulent	New product
Gemzar®	Gemcitabine 200 mg and 1 g vials for i.v. injection	Lilly	Antineoplastic	New indication—for treatment of nonresectable (Stage II or III) or metastatic (Stage IV) adenocarcinoma of the pancreas
Hydrasense® Nasal Care	Isotonic sterile 100% Natural-source Sea Water	Schering	Emollient	New product—for clearing nasal mucus caused by colds, allergies, sinusitis, rhinitis and dry air
Imodium®	Loperamide 2 mg caplets and 2 mg lingual tablets	Janssen-Ortho/McNeil Consumer Products	Antidiarrheal	New dosage form—lingual tablets
Imogam® Rabies Pasteurized	Rabies Immune Globulin 150 IU/mL, 2 and 10 mL vials for i.m. injection	Connaught	Immunoglobulin	New product—a heat treatment step has been added to the process
Kwellada-P™	Permethrin 5% Lotion	R & C	Topical Scabicide	New product
Lescol®	Fluvastatin 20 and 40 mg capsules	Novartis Pharmaceuticals	Lipid Metabolism Regulator	New indication—to reduce the rate of progression of atherosclerosis in patients with coronary artery disease and mild to moderate elevations of cholesterol
Levaquin®	Levofloxacin 250 and 500 mg tablets and 5 and 25 mg/mL injections	Janssen-Ortho	Antibacterial	New drug—a quinolone for treatment of upper and lower respiratory tract, skin and urinary tract infections caused by susceptible organisms
Levotec	Levothyroxine 25, 50, 75, 100, 112, 125, 150, 175, 200 and 300 μg tablets	Technilab	Thyroid Supplement	New product
Levovist®	Galactose 99.9%—Palmitic Acid 0.1%; 200, 300 and 400 mg granules to be reconstituted for i.v. injection	Berlex Canada	Ultrasound Contrast Agent	New product—for Doppler sonographic blood flow imaging and B-mode contrast echocardiography

Brand Name	Generic Name/ Dosage Form	Manufacturer	Classification	Comments
Losec®	Omeprazole 10 and 20 mg tablets	Astra	Proton Pump Inhibitor	New indication—for treatment of NSAID-associated gastric and duodenal ulcers
Lovenox®	Enoxaparin 30 mg/0.3 mL prefilled syringe and 300 mg/3 mL multidose vial	Rhône-Poulenc Rorer	Antithrombotic	New indications—for prophylaxis of deep vein thrombosis in high risk abdominal, gynecological or urological surgeries and colorectal surgery; for treatment of pulmonary embolism; for treatment of unstable angina and non-Q-wave myocardial infarction New dosage form—multidose vial
Lupron Depot® 3.75 mg, 7.5 mg and 22.5 mg	Leuprolide 3.75 mg, 7.5 mg and 22.5 mg slow release injection	Abbott	Gonadotropin-releasing Hormone Analog	New product—now availabe as prefilled dual-chamber syringes as well as single dose vials with diluent
Maalox H2 Acid Controller™	Famotidine 10 mg tablets	Novartis Consumer Health	Histamine H_2 Receptor Antagonist	New product—for treatment and prevention of acid indigestion, heartburn, sour or upset stomach
Malarone™	Atovaquone 250 mg—Proguanil 100 mg tablets	Glaxo Wellcome	Antimalarial	New product—for treatment of acute, uncomplicated *Plasmodium falciparum* malaria
Maxipime™	Cefepime injection	Bristol-Myers Squibb	Antibiotic	New indication—in pediatric patients, for the treatment of the following infections when caused by susceptible organisms: lower respiratory tract, urinary tract, skin and skin structure; and as empiric therapy in febrile neutropenia
Mavik™	Trandolapril 0.5, 1 and 2 mg tablets	Knoll	ACE Inhibitor	New indication—following acute MI in stable patients with left ventricular dysfunction, to improve survival and reduce hospitalizations for heart failure
Methylprednisolone Sodium Succinate for Injection USP	Methylprednisolone 500 mg and 1 g/vial (lyophilized powder) for i.v. or i.m. injection	Faulding	Glucocorticoid	New product—includes vial of bacteriostatic water for injection for reconstitution
Micanol®	Anthralin 1% cream	Canderm Pharma	Psoriasis Treatment	New product
Micatin®	Miconazole 2% spray	McNeil Consumer Products	Topical Antifungal	New dosage form
Mirapex®	Pramipexole 0.25, 1 and 1.5 mg tablets	Boehringer Ingelheim	Antiparkinsonian	New drug—a non-ergot dopamine agonist for the treatment of Parkinson's disease
Mitomycin for Injection, USP	Mitomycin 5 and 20 mg/vial (lyophilized powder) for i.v. and intravesical use	Faulding	Antineoplastic	New product
Motrin® (Children's)	Ibuprofen 100 mg/5 mL suspension	McNeil Consumer Products	Analgesic—Antipyretic	New product
Neptazane®	Methazolamide 25 and 50 mg tablets	Wyeth-Ayerst	Carbonic Anhydrase Inhibitor	New supplier—formerly Storz
Nidagel™	Metronidazole 0.75% vaginal gel	3M Pharmaceuticals	Antibacterial	New dosing—once daily application, as well as b.i.d., now approved for bacterial vaginosis
Nitrolingual® Pumpspray	Nitroglycerin sublingual spray 0.4 mg per metered dose	Rhône-Poulenc Rorer	Antianginal	New product—does not contain chlorofluorocarbons
NovaSource™ Renal	Nutrition formula for oral or enteral use	Novartis Nutrition	Therapeutic Nutrient	New product—a calorically dense, moderate protein, low residue formula designed for dialysis patients
Novo-Cyproterone	Cyproterone 50 mg tablets	Novopharm	Antiandrogen	New product

Brand Name	Generic Name/ Dosage Form	Manufacturer	Classification	Comments
Novo-Domperidone	Domperidone 10 mg tablets	Novopharm	Upper Gastrointestinal Motility Modifier	New product
Novo-Terazosin	Terazosin 1, 2, 5 and 10 mg tablets	Novopharm	Antihypertensive	New product
Omniscan®	Gadodiamide 287 mg/mL for i.v. injection	Nycomed Imaging A.S.	Contrast Enhancement Agent for MRI	New indication—for use in MRI in adults to visualize abnormal vascularity within the thoracic, abdominal, pelvic cavities, breast, retroperitoneal space and musculoskeletal system
Oncaspar®	Pegaspargase 750 IU/mL, 5 mL vial for i.m. injection and i.v. infusion	Rhône-Poulenc Rorer	Antineoplastic	New drug—a pegylated form of L-asparaginase derived from *Escherichia coli*, indicated in the treatment of acute lymphoblastic leukemia of childhood for patients with known hypersensitivity to other forms of L-asparaginase
Optiray® 240	Loversol 509 mg/mL	Mallinckrodt	Radiopaque Medium	New indication—for subarachnoid administration for lumbar, thoracic and cervical myelography
Ostac®	Clodronate 300 mg/10 mL ampuls and 400 mg capsules	Roche	Bisphosphonate	New supplier—formerly Boehringer Mannheim
Oxeze® Turbuhaler®	Formoterol 6 and 12 µg/ metered dose dry powder inhalers	Astra	Bronchodilator	New product
Oxizole®	Oxiconazole Nitrate 1% cream and lotion	Stiefel	Topical Antifungal	New drug—for the treatment of tinea pedis due to *Trichophyton rubrum, Trichophyton mentagrophytes* or *Epidermophyton floccosum*
Paclitaxel Injection	Paclitaxel 6 mg/mL for i.v. infusion	Boehringer Ingelheim	Antineoplastic	New product
Patanol™	Olaptadine 0.1% ophthalmic solution	Alcon	Antiallergy	New drug—mast cell stabilizer and H_1 antagonist for treatment of allergic conjunctivitis
Pedialyte® Freezer Pops	Oral electrolyte maintenance solution	Abbott	Electrolyte Maintenance	New dosage form—62.5 mL freezer pops
PedvaxHIB®	Hemophilus Influenzae Type B Vaccine suspension for injection	MSD	Active Immunizing Agent	New dosage form—liquid
Peridex®	Chlorhexidine Gluconate 0.12% oral rinse	Zila Pharmaceuticals	Antigingivitis	New supplier—formerly Procter & Gamble
Pethidine Injection BP	Pethidine 10 mg/mL in 50 mL Rapiject prefilled, single-dose syringes	Faulding	Opioid Analgesic	New product
Phazyme™ Preparations	Simethicone 125 mg/5 mL	R & C	Antiflatulent	New dosage form—liquid adult formula
Phosphate-Novartis	Phosphate 500 mg tablets	Novartis Pharmaceuticals	Electrolyte Replenisher	Name change—formerly Phosphate-Sandoz
Phosphates Solution	Sodium Phosphates solution	Pharmascience	Laxative	Name change—formerly pms-Phosphates Solution
Plavix™	Clopidrogel 75 mg tablets	Sanofi/Bristol-Myers Squibb	Platelet Aggregation Inhibitor	New drug—a specific inhibitor of ADP-induced platelet aggregation, indicated for the secondary prevention of vascular ischemic events (MI, stroke, vascular death) in patients with a history of symptomatic ASHD
Pneumococcal Polysaccharide Vaccine Pneumo 23™	Pneumococcal Polysaccharide Vaccine for i.m. and s.c. injection	Connaught	Active Immunizing Agent	New product—for the prevention of infection caused by the 23 types of *Streptococcus pneumoniae* contained in the vaccine

Brand Name	Generic Name/ Dosage Form	Manufacturer	Classification	Comments
Pnu-Imune® 23	Pneumococcal Vaccine Polyvalent Solution for i.m. and s.c. injection	Wyeth-Ayerst	Active Immunizing Agent	New product—for the prevention of infection caused by the pneumococcal types included in the vaccine
Polycitra-K®	Potassium Citrate crystals and solution	Alza	Potassium Supplement	New supplier—formerly Baker Cummins
Pregnyl®	Chorionic Gonadotropin 10 000 units for i.m. injection	Organon	Human Gonadotropin	New product—for prepubertal cryptorchidism not due to anatomic obstruction, hypogonadism secondary to pituitary deficiency and for induction of ovulation and pregnancy when anovulation is not due to primary ovarian failure
Preparation H® Cooling Gel	Phenylephrine 0.25%—Hamamelis Water 50% in gel	Whitehall-Robins	Hemorrhoid Therapy	New product
Prevacid®	Lansoprazole 15 and 30 mg capsules	Abbott	H+, K+-ATPase Inhibitor	New indication—for eradication of *Helicobacter pylori*; triple therapy regimen: lansoprazole 30 mg, clarithromycin 500 mg and amoxicillin 1 g, each given b.i.d. × 14 days; dual therapy regimen: lansoprazole 30 mg and amoxicillin 1 g, both given t.i.d. × 14 days
Prinivil®	Lisinopril 5, 10 and 20 mg tablets	MSD	ACE Inhibitor	New indication—to improve survival following acute MI
Prograf®	Tacrolimus 1 and 5 mg capsules and 5 mg/mL solution for i.v. injection	Fujisawa	Immunosuppressant	New indication—for the prophylaxis of organ rejection in patients receiving allogeneic liver or kidney transplants
Propecia®	Finasteride 1 mg tablets	MSD	Type II Alpha-reductase Inhibitor	New product—new strength indicated for treatment of male pattern hair loss in men with mild to moderate hair loss of the vertex and anterior mid-scalp
Protamine Sulfate Injection	Protamine Sulfate 10 mg/mL	Pharmaceutical Partners	Heparin Antagonist	New supplier—formerly Fujisawa
Puregon™	Follitropin beta 50 or 100 IU FSH activity per ampul for i.m. or s.c. injection	Organon	Human Gonadotropin	New product—for development of multiple follicles in ovulatory patients in assisted reproduction technology program and for induction of ovulation and pregnancy in secondary ovarian failure
Pylorid®	Ranitidine Bismuth Citrate 400 mg tablets	Glaxo Wellcome	Duodenal Ulcer Therapy	New product—histamine H_2-receptor antagonist with *Helicobacter pylori* suppressive activity indicated, in combination with clarithromycin, for treatment of patients with active duodenal ulcer
Quibron®-T	Theophylline anhydrous 300 mg tablets	Bristol	Bronchodilator	New dosage form—regular release tablets
Raxar™	Grepafloxacin 200 mg tablets	Glaxo Wellcome	Antibacterial	New drug—a fluoroquinolone antibiotic for treatment of acute bronchitis, community-acquired pneumonia, uncomplicated gonorrhea and nongonococcal cervicitis and urethritis caused by susceptible organisms
Rebif™	Interferon beta-1a 3 and 12 MIU lyophilized powder for injection, 6 and 12 MIU liquid for injection	Serono	Immunomodulator	New product—for treatment of relapsing-remitting multiple sclerosis and condyloma acuminatum
Rejuva-A®	Tretinoin 0.025% cream	Stiefel	Retinoid	New product—for the treatment of photodamaged skin

Brand Name	Generic Name/ Dosage Form	Manufacturer	Classification	Comments
Reopro™	Abciximab 2 mg/mL solution for i.v. injection (5 and 20 mL)	Lilly	Chimeric Monoclonal Antiplatelet Antibody	New drug—as an adjunct to PTCA for the prevention of acute cardiac ischemic complications in patients at high risk for abrupt closure of the treated coronary vessel
Requip™	Ropinirole 0.25, 1, 2 and 5 mg tablets	SmithKline Beecham	Antiparkinsonian	New drug—a non-ergot dopamine agonist for treatment of Parkinson's disease
Resource® Fruit Beverage	Protein and calorie source, 235 mL	Novartis Nutrition	Therapeutic Nutrient	Name change—formerly Citrisource
Ridaura®	Auranofin 3 mg capsules	Pharmascience	Antirheumatic	New supplier—formerly SmithKline Beecham
Risperdal® Oral Solution	Risperidone 1 mg/mL oral solution	Janssen-Ortho	Antipsychotic	New dosage form
Salofalk®	5-Aminosalicylic Acid oral enteric-coated tablets	Axcan Pharma	Gastrointestinal Anti-inflammatory	New indication—for the prevention of relapse of Crohn's disease following bowel resection
Sandostatin®	Octreotide 50, 100 and 500 µg ampuls and 1 000 µg/5 mL multidose vials	Novartis Pharmaceuticals	Synthetic Analog of Somatostatin	New indication—for emergency management of bleeding gastroesophageal varices in patients with cirrhosis and as protection from rebleeding
Seroquel®	Quetiapine 25,100 and 200 mg tablets	Zeneca	Antipsychotic	New drug—for the management of schizophrenia
Singulair®	Montelukast 10 mg tablets and 5 mg chewable tablets	MSD	Leukotriene Receptor Antagonist	New drug—for prophylaxis and chronic treatment of asthma in adults and children at least 6 years of age
Sinutab® Nightime Extra Strength	Acetaminophen 500 mg—Pseudoephedrine 30 mg—Diphenhydramine 25 mg caplets	Warner-Lambert Consumer Healthcare	Analgesic—Decongestant—Antihistamine	New product
Slow-Mag™	Magnesium Chloride Hexahydrate 535 mg enteric-coated tablets	Roberts	Mineral Supplement	New product
St. John's Wort	Extract of St. John's Wort *(Hypercin perforatum)*	Swiss Herbal	Herbal Medicine	New product—to relieve stress and fatigue
Suprefact®	Buserelin 1 mg/mL intranasal solution	Hoechst Marion Roussel	Luteinizing Hormone-releasing Hormone	New indication—for treatment of endometriosis in patients who do not require surgery as primary therapy
Tarka®	Trandolapril—Verapamil SR 1/180 mg, 2/180 mg and 4/240 mg	Knoll	Antihypertensive	New product—for treatment of mild to moderate essential hypertension in patients for whom combination therapy is appropriate (not for initial therapy)
Tasmar™	Tolcapone 100 and 200 mg tablets	Roche	Antiparkinsonian	New drug—a COMT inhibitor to be used as an adjunct to levodopa in the treatment of Parkinson's disease
Taxol™	Paclitaxel 6 mg/mL injection	Bristol-Myers Squibb	Antineoplastic	New indication—for first-line treatment of advanced non-small cell lung cancer
Tiazac®	Diltiazem 120, 180, 240, 300 and 360 mg extended-release capsules	Crystaal	Antihypertensive—Antianginal	New indication—for management of chronic stable angina (effort-associated angina) without evidence of vasospasm, despite adequate doses of beta-blockers and/or organic nitrates
Tri-Cyclen®	Norgestimate—Ethinyl Estradiol	Janssen-Ortho	Oral Contraceptive	New indication—for treatment of moderate acne vulgaris
Trinipatch® 0.2, 0.4 and 0.6	Nitroglycerin 0.2, 0.4 and 0.6 mg/hour transdermal delivery system	Sanofi	Antianginal	New product

Brand Name	Generic Name/ Dosage Form	Manufacturer	Classification	Comments
Tylenol® Decongestant	Acetaminophen 160 mg—Pseudoephedrine 15 mg/5 mL	McNeil Consumer Products	Analgesic—Antipyretic—Decongestant	New product
Urispas®	Flavoxate 200 mg tablets	Pharmascience	Urinary Tract Antispasmodic	New indication—for the relief of vesicourethral spasms due to catheterization, cystoscopy or indwelling catheters
Vasopressin Injection	Vasopressin 20 units/mL	Pharmaceutical Partners	Antidiuretic	New supplier—formerly Fujisawa
Vaxigrip®	Inactivated Influenza Vaccine Trivalent Types A and B (Split Virion)	Connaught	Influenza Prophylaxis	New indication—for use in children 6 months of age and older (previously was 3 years of age) and new dose of 0.25 mL for children aged 6-35 months
Versed®	Midazolam 1 and 5 mg/mL for i.m. and i.v. injection	Roche	Premedicant—Sedative—Anesthetic	New indication—for use in pediatric patients
Viprinex®	Ancrod 70 IU/1 mL ampuls for s.c. injection or i.v. infusion	Knoll	Anticoagulant	Name change—formerly Arvin
Viquin Forte®	Hydroquinone 4%—Glycolic Acid 10% cream	ICN	Depigmenting Agent—Moisturizer	New product—for skin bleaching
Vivotif Berna® L Vaccine	Typhoid Vaccine Live Oral Attenuated Ty21a	Berna Products	Active Immunizing Agent	New dosage form—double-chambered foil sachets, one containing vaccine and one containing a buffer, requiring simultaneous reconstitution to a liquid for oral administration
Wartec®	Podofilox 0.5%	Pharmascience	Antimitotic	New supplier—formerly Carter Horner
Wellbutrin® SR	Bupropion 50, 100 and 150 mg sustained-release tablets	Glaxo Wellcome	Antidepressant	New drug—a new chemical class, an aminoketone, for the treatment of depression
Wellferon®	Interferon alpha-n1 3 or 10 Mu per vial for i.m. or s.c. injections	Glaxo Wellcome	Biological Response Modifier	New indication—for treatment of chronic hepatitis C infections
Zantac® 75	Ranitidine 75 mg tablets	Glaxo Wellcome	Histamine H_2-receptor Antagonist	New strength—for non-prescription treatment of dyspepsia, heartburn and hyper-acidity
Zerit™	Stavudine 1 mg/mL powder for oral solution	Bristol-Myers Squibb	Antiretroviral	New dosage form
Zilactin® Preparations	Benzyl Alcohol, Benzocaine, Lidocaine and Sunscreens; gel, liquid, teething gel and lip balm	Zila Pharmaceuticals	Protective—Topical Analgesic—Emollient	New products—for canker and cold sores, gum and lip sores and baby teething pain
Zithromax™	Azithromycin 250 mg capsules, powder for oral suspension (100 and 200 mg/5 mL; 1 g single dose), 250 and 600 mg tablets	Pfizer	Antibiotic	New indication—for treatment of community-acquired pneumonia caused by *Hemophilus influenzae, Streptococcus pneumoniae, Mycoplasma pneumoniae* or *Chlamydia pneumoniae*
Zoladex®	Goserelin 3.6 mg per syringe for s.c. injection	Zeneca	LHRH Analog	New indication—for the palliative treatment of advanced breast cancer in pre- and peri-menopausal women whose tumor contains estrogen and/or progesterone receptors
Zoloft™	Sertraline 25, 50 and 100 mg capsules	Pfizer	Antidepressant—Antipanic—Antiobsessional	New indication—for the symptomatic relief of obsessive-compulsive disorder

HOW TO USE THIS EDITION

CONSULT: FOR INFORMATION ON:	GREEN SECTION	PINK SECTION	PRS SECTION	YELLOW SECTION	LILAC SECTION	BLUE SECTION	WHITE SECTION
Antiepileptic Drug Therapy					×		
Antineoplastic Drug Therapy					×		
Body Surface Area Nomograms					×		
Cardiac Arrest					×		
Clinical Laboratory Reference Values					×		
CPS Abbreviations							× (p. 7)
CPS Nomenclature for Microorganisms							× (p. 5)
Creatinine Clearance Formula					×		
Drug Administration and Food					×		×
Drug Considerations in Porphyria					×		
Drugs in Dentistry					×		
Emergency Drug Release Special Access Program					×		
Essential Product Information:							
• Canadian Brand Name(s)	×						×
• Generic Name(s)	×						×
• US Brand Name(s)	×						
• Pharmacology/Pharmacokinetics							×
• Indications/Contraindications/ Warnings							×
• Precautions:							
• Drugs and Driving (Occupational Hazards)							×
• Drug Interactions					×		×
• Pregnancy					×		×
• Lactation					×		×
• Children							×
• Geriatrics					×		×
• Adverse Effects					× (Form/ Summary)		×
• Overdose (Poison Information)					× (Poison Control Centres)		×
• Dosage							×
• Information for the Patient						×	×
• Supplied (Product Appearance)			×				×
• Nonmedicinal Ingredients:							
• Alcohol					× (Table)		×
• Gluten					× (Table)		×
• Lactose					×		×
• Sodium							×
• Sulfites					× (Table)		×
• Tartrazine					× (Table)		×
• Energy Content							×
Health Organizations Directory					×		
Hypertension, Nonpharmacological Therapy for					×		
Immunization Schedules					×		
Malaria Prevention					×		
Manufacturer(s):							
• Address(es)				×			
• Product Line				×			
• of a particular product							×
• of same product	×						
Narcotic and Controlled Drugs (Summary of Regulations)					×		×
Oral Contraceptives						×	×
Perioperative Management of Medication					×		
Recommended Nutrient Intake and Dietary Supplementation					×		
Serum Drug Concentration Monitoring					×		
Therapeutic Classification Guide		×					
Vitamin and Mineral Food Sources					×		
Water Treatment Methods					×		

SOME FACTS ABOUT *CPS*

Since its inception in 1960, the Compendium of Pharmaceuticals and Specialties (CPS) has undergone many changes in both content and format. Every year, new drug products are added, some are deleted, and modifications are made to the design of the text itself with the view to improving its utility and accessibility.

Many of the changes we make are a result of suggestions and comments we receive from CPS users.

Some of the letters we receive contain comments or questions that we hear many times over. The following facts address a few of the more common ones.

Advertising Inserts

During the production for each of the past several years, we have experienced a 70 to 80% change in the content of the *CPS*. This reflects the number of drug information changes needed to keep the *CPS* as up to date as possible. The revenue derived from advertising has helped support the investment required to process these constant revisions.

Updates

In response to suggestions received, we investigated a three-ring binder system. This proved to be impractical, however, as the content of the *CPS* changes about 75% each year. Almost every page in the book would need replacing. The administrative effort and cost involved in providing periodic updates to the 100,000+ *CPS* owners would be prohibitive.

The availability of *CPS* in an electronic format responds to this need with a semiannual update.

Binding Problems

Some users have experienced binding problems with the book. The *CPS* has grown considerably in size over the years, and as a result, the binding has a tendency to break down with heavy use and photocopying.

Over the past few years, we have experimented with alternative gluing and binding techniques. These met with little success as the expanding size of the book was the true source of the problem. More expensive alternatives currently being considered are to publish a hardcover or two-volume format. We expect to make a decision on this for a future edition. In the meantime, we have begun to widen the margins in some sections to alleviate some of the stress put on the spine by pressing the book flat for photocopying.

Drug Prices and DINs

Physicians and pharmacists often request that drug prices and/or DINs be listed in the *CPS*. We appreciate the convenience of having prices integrated with the product information. However, we would have difficulty incorporating provincial and manufacturers' prices into one list. DIN information would have to be gathered manually, and annual updating would prove very time consuming.

Unfortunately, our staff and space resources are too limited to gather and maintain data on drug prices and DINs.

Electronic Products

The *CPS* is available on CD-ROM from Login Brothers Canada. For more information, call 1-800-665-1148.

Generic Names

We receive many requests to list drug products by generic name rather than by brand name. Brand name product monographs are listed to recognize the financial support of the pharmaceutical manufacturer. This support, and revenues derived from advertising, are critical to the financial viability of the book. Generic names can be easily located in the Brand and Generic Name Index (Green Section).

CPhA pharmacists and the *CPS* Editorial Advisory Panel continue to develop new general monographs for inclusion in the book. An alphabetical listing of available monographs appears at the beginning of the White Section.

Brand and Generic Name Index (Green Section)

A new and expanded index was introduced in the 30th edition. With few exceptions, it includes all *CPS*-listed products, whereas previously, only single- and double-entity products were included. The listing also includes products contained in the *Drug Product Database*. Products listed in the monograph section of the *CPS* are shown in ***bold*** print, and products that are underlined indicate the availability of full prescribing information. As well, many U.S. products are listed.

Some users have asked that we index the Green Section with page numbers for easier location of specific products. Our current production software does not accommodate such an index automatically and setting this up would be an onerous task for our editors. Annual maintenance would be extremely time consuming.

A key word search capability exists as a standard function of the *CPS* on CD-ROM, making access to specific monographs almost instantaneous.

Missing Products

Each year manufacturers are asked to update the list of products they included in the previous edition. Participation in the *CPS* is voluntary, and the decision to include a product monograph is solely the manufacturer's. The book is not exhaustive as, for one reason or another, manufacturers may discontinue listing certain products even though they are still being marketed. *CPS* staff actively solicit company participation in an effort to keep the book as comprehensive as possible. Users can augment these efforts by communicating directly with companies whose products are missing.

Therapeutic Guide (Pink Section)

We have received a great deal of feedback since we introduced the revised Therapeutic Guide in 1993. To provide a more scientific clinical guide, the pre-1992 format was revised, based on the World Health Organization's Anatomical Therapeutic Chemical (ATC) Classification Index.

In response to many user comments concerning the utility of this new system, we modified the format while maintaining the principles of the ATC classification index. The main anatomical groups have been eliminated, and the therapeutic categories are now listed in alphabetical order.

Several users also suggested the inclusion of brand names in the Therapeutic Guide. Unfortunately, space limitations make it impossible to list both generic and brand names in this section. The Brand and Generic Name Index (Green Section) provides a cross-reference of the two.

"Supplied" Information

Many comments have been received concerning the lack of prescribing information for certain products. We too are concerned about the number of *CPS* entries that provide no prescribing information. The decision to list either full prescribing information or a shortened, "supplied" version is the manufacturer's. *CPS* editorial staff do their best to persuade manufacturers to submit the full monograph for publication. We encourage *CPS* users who are concerned about this lack of prescribing information to write to the manufacturers involved.

Vitamin Chart

The vitamin chart has been expanded and moved to the *CPS* sister publication, *Compendium of Nonprescription Products* (*CNP*). Information on recommended nutrient intake, dietary supplementation and vitamin and mineral food sources can be found in Clin-Info (Lilac Section).

We continually look for ways to improve the CPS, and the feedback we receive from our users is very helpful in planning future editions. If you have any comments or concerns, please forward them to us on the Comment Card provided.

BRAND AND GENERIC NAME INDEX

This section is an alphabetical, cross-reference of brand and generic names. Brand Names and Generic Manufacturers underlined in bold type appear in the *CPS* Monograph Section in a detailed format. Brand Names and Generic Manufacturers in bold type, not underlined, appear in the *CPS* Monograph Section in an abbreviated format. General Monographs, developed by the Canadian Pharmacists Association (CPhA), are presented in square parentheses in bold type and appear in the *CPS* Monograph Section, in a detailed format. Brand Names in regular type are available in Canada but could not appear in the *CPS* Monograph Section due to production deadlines. Brand Names in regular type marked with a dagger(†) represent products available in the U.S. Generic names are presented in italics.

Listings by generic name are presented in the following format:

generic name. alternate generic name. **[General Monograph Name, General Monograph, CPhA]; Brand Name, Brand Name,** Brand Name; **(Generic Manufacturer), (Generic Manufacturer),** (Generic Manufacturer). †U.S. Brand Name.

Listings by brand name are presented in the following format:

Brand Name (Manufacturer). *generic name.* or
Brand Name (Manufacturer). *generic name.* or
Brand Name (Manufacturer). *generic name.* or
†U.S. Brand Name. *generic name.*

Products with more than one active ingredient will be listed as follows (This example illustrates three active ingredients with one Brand Name listing.):

generic name 1/generic name 2/generic name 3. **Brand Name.**
generic name 2/generic name 1/generic name 3. **Brand Name.**
generic name 3/generic name 1/generic name 2. **Brand Name.**
Brand Name (Manufacturer). *generic name 1/generic name 2/generic name 3.*

Various categories have been created for those products that could not be easily identified by ingredient classification: balanced salt solution, cold storage solution, denture adhesive, dermatological base, electrolytes, emollient, enteral nutrition, fat emulsion, fibrin sealant, gland extracts, glucose enzymatic test strip, herbal medicine, infant formula, insulin delivery device, intrauterine contraceptive, lubricating jelly, minerals, multiple vitamins, multiple vitamins and minerals, nonmedicated soap, oral protective emollient, pregnancy test, sea water, skin test antigens, tuberculin test.

No claim is made for therapeutic equivalence of the products listed. Therapeutic efficacy depends on the amount of drug present in each dose, the pharmaceutical form, the physical nature of the active drug used, the presence of other substances, the method of manufacture and the exercise of quality control. *CPS* users are cautioned that listings may not be exhaustive although every attempt has been made to include all applicable products.

A

Abbokinase (Abbott). *urokinase.*

Abbokinase Open-Cath (Abbott). *urokinase.*

abciximab. **ReoPro.**

Abenol (SmithKline Beecham). *acetaminophen.*

acarbose. **Prandase.**

Accolate (Zeneca). *zafirlukast.*

Accupril (Parke-Davis). *quinapril hydrochloride.*

Accuretic (Parke-Davis). *hydrochlorothiazide/quinapril hydrochloride.*

Accutane Roche (Roche). *isotretinoin.*

acebutolol hydrochloride. **Apo-Acebutolol, Monitan, Novo-Acebutolol, Nu-Acebutolol, Rhotral, Sectral.**

ACE inhibitors. **(General Monograph, CPhA).**

Acel-P (Wyeth-Ayerst). *pertussis vaccine adsorbed, acellular.*

acenocoumarin. see nicoumalone.

acenocoumarol. see nicoumalone.

acetaminophen. APAP. NAPAP. paracetamol. **[Acetaminophen, General Monograph, CPhA]; Abenol, Apo-Acetaminophen, Atasol, Children's Acetaminophen Elixir Drops, Children's Acetaminophen Oral Solution, Children's Chewable Acetaminophen, Extra Strength Acetaminophen, Pediatrix, Regular Strength Acetaminophen, Tempra, 222 AF, Tylenol; (Stanley), (Trianon).**

acetaminophen/caffeine citrate/codeine phosphate. **Atasol-8, -15, -30, Triatec-8, -8 Strong.**

acetaminophen/caffeine/codeine phosphate. **Extra Strength Acetaminophen with Codeine, Lenoltec No.1, No.2, No.3, Novo-Gesic C8, C15, C30, Regular Strength Acetaminophen with Codeine, Tylenol NO. 1 with Codeine, Tylenol NO. 2 and NO. 3 with Codeine; (Stanley).**

acetaminophen/caffeine/pheniramine maleate/phenylpropanolamine hydrochloride/pyrilamine maleate. **Triaminicin.**

acetaminophen/caffeine/pyrilamine maleate. **Midol Extra Strength.**

acetaminophen/chlorpheniramine maleate/codeine/pseudoephedrine hydrochloride. **Sinutab with Codeine.**

acetaminophen/chlorpheniramine maleate/dextromethorphan hydrobromide/pseudoephedrine hydrochloride. **NeoCitran Extra Strength (Cough, Cold & Flu), Tylenol Cold and Flu, Tylenol Cold Medication Junior Strength DM, Tylenol Cold Medication (Nighttime).**

acetaminophen/chlorpheniramine maleate/phenylephrine hydrochloride. **Dristan, Dristan Extra Strength.**

acetaminophen/chlorpheniramine maleate/pseudoephedrine hydrochloride. **Sinutab, Tylenol Allergy Sinus Medication.**

acetaminophen/chlorzoxazone. **Acetazone, Parafon Forte, Tylenol Aches and Strains Medication.**

acetaminophen/chlorzoxazone/codeine phosphate. **Acetazone Forte C8, Parafon Forte C8.**

acetaminophen/codeine phosphate. **Empracet -30, -60, Emtec-30, Lenoltec No. 4, Triatec-30, Tylenol Elixir with Codeine, Tylenol NO. 4 with Codeine.**

acetaminophen/codeine phosphate/doxylamine succinate. **Mersyndol with Codeine.**

acetaminophen/codeine phosphate/methocarbamol. **Methoxacet-C, Robaxacet-8.**

acetaminophen/dextromethorphan hydrobromide. **Tylenol Cough Caplets/Liquid Suspension.**

acetaminophen/dextromethorphan hydrobromide/guaifenesin/pseudoephedrine hydrochloride. **Benylin 4 Flu, Calmylin Cough and Flu, Robitussin Cough, Cold & Flu Liqui-Gels, Sudafed Cold & Flu.**

acetaminophen/dextromethorphan hydrobromide/pseudoephedrine hydrochloride. **Contac Cough, Cold and Flu Day, NeoCitran Extra Strength Daycaps, Sudafed Cold & Cough, Triaminic Cold & Fever, Tylenol Cold Medication (Daytime), Tylenol Cough Liquid Suspension with Decongestant.**

acetaminophen/dichloralphenazone/isometheptene mucate. †Miltride.

acetaminophen/diphenhydramine hydrochloride/pseudoephedrine hydrochloride. **Benadryl Allergy/Sinus/Headache, Contac Cough, Cold and Flu Night, Tylenol Flu Medication.**

acetaminophen/diphenhydramine/pseudoephedrine hydrochloride. **Sinutab Nightime.**

acetaminophen/methocarbamol. **Methoxacet, Robaxacet.**

acetaminophen/oxycodone hydrochloride. **Endocet, Oxycocet, Percocet, Percocet-Demi.**

acetaminophen/pamabrom/pyrilamine maleate. **Midol PMS Extra Strength, Pamprin, Pamprin Extra Strength, Pamprin PMS.**

acetaminophen/pheniramine maleate/phenylephrine hydrochloride. **NeoCitran Adult, NeoCitran Extra Strength, NeoCitran Nutrasweet.**

acetaminophen/phenylephrine hydrochloride. **NeoCitran Sinus Extra Strength.**

acetaminophen/phenylephrine hydrochloride/phenylpropanolamine hydrochloride. **Dimetapp-A Sinus.**

acetaminophen/phenylpropanolamine hydrochloride/phenyltoloxamine citrate. **Sinutab SA.**

acetaminophen/propoxyphene napsylate. †Darvocet-N 100, †Propacet 100.

acetaminophen/pseudoephedrine hydrochloride. **Dristan N.D., Dristan N.D. Extra Strength, Sinutab Non Drowsy, Sudafed Head Cold and Sinus, Tylenol Decongestant, Tylenol Sinus Medication.**

acetaminophen/pseudoephedrine hydrochloride/triprolidine hydrochloride. **Actifed Plus Extra Strength.**

acetazolamide. **Apo-Acetazolamide, Diamox.** †Ak-Zol, †Dazamide.

Acetazone (Technilab). *acetaminophen/chlorzoxazone.*

Acetazone Forte C8 (Technilab). *acetaminophen/chlorzoxazone/codeine phosphate.*

acetic acid/benzethonium chloride/hydrocortisone/1,2-propanediol diacetate. **VōSoL HC.**

acetic acid/benzethonium chloride/1,2-propanediol diacetate. **VōSoL.**

acetic acid/camphor/lemon extract oil/sodium lauryl ether sulfate. **SH-206.**

acetohexamide. **[Sulfonylureas, General Monograph, CPhA].**

acetohydroxamic acid. †Lithostat.

acetophenazine maleate. †Tindal.

Acetoxyl (Stiefel). *benzoyl peroxide.*

acetylcholine chloride/electrolytes. **Miochol-E.**

N-acetylcysteine. see acetylcysteine.

acetylcysteine. N-acetylcysteine. **Mucomyst, Parvolex.**

acetylsalicylic acid. see ASA.

†Achromycin V. *tetracycline hydrochloride.*

Acilac (Technilab). *lactulose.*

acitretin. **Soriatane.**

Acne-Aid Soap (Stiefel). *nonmedicated soap.*

Acnex (Dermtek). *salicylic acid.*

Acnomel Acne Mask (Chattem). *salicylic acid.*

Acnomel Cream (Chattem). *isopropyl alcohol/resorcinol/sulfur.*

Acnomel Vanishing Cream (Chattem). *resorcinol/sulfur.*

Act-HIB (Connaught). *haemophilus b (Hib) polysaccharide conjugate (tetanus protein conjugate) vaccine.*

Acti-B$_{12}$ (Technilab). *hydroxocobalamin.*

†Actibine. *yohimbine hydrochloride.*

†Acticort 100. *hydrocortisone.*

Actifed (Warner-Lambert Consumer Healthcare). *pseudoephedrine hydrochloride/triprolidine hydrochloride.*

Actifed Plus Extra Strength (Warner-Lambert Consumer Healthcare). *acetaminophen/pseudoephedrine hydrochloride/triprolidine hydrochloride.*

†Actigall. *ursodiol.*

†Actimmune. *interferon gamma-1b recombinant.*

Actinac (Hoechst Marion Roussel). *allantoin/butoxyethyl nicotinate/chloramphenicol/hydrocortisone acetate/sulfur.*

Actiprofen (Bayer Consumer). *ibuprofen.*

Activase rt-PA (Roche). *alteplase.*

activated attapulgite. see attapulgite, activated.

activated charcoal. see charcoal, activated.

activated dimethicone. see simethicone.

activated polymethylsiloxane. see simethicone.

Acular (Allergan). *ketorolac tromethamine.*

acyclovir. **Alti-Acyclovir, Apo-Acyclovir, Avirax, Nu-Acyclovir, Zovirax Cream, Zovirax Ointment, Zovirax Oral.**

acyclovir sodium. **Zovirax for Injection; (Abbott), (Faulding), (Novopharm).**

†Adagen. *pegademase bovine.*

Adalat (Bayer). *nifedipine.*

Adalat PA (Bayer). *nifedipine.*

Adalat XL (Bayer). *nifedipine.*

adapalene. **Differin.**

Adasept Acne Gel (Odan). *salicylic acid/sodium thiosulfate/triclosan.*

Adasept Skin Cleanser (Odan). *triclosan.*

Adeks Pediatric Drops (Axcan Pharma). *multiple vitamins/zinc sulfate.*

Adeks Tablets (Axcan Pharma). *multiple vitamins/zinc oxide.*

Adenocard (Fujisawa). *adenosine.*

adenosine. **Adenocard.**

†Adipex-P. *phentermine hydrochloride.*

adrenal cortical extract/cyanocobalamin/orchitic extract. **Heracline.**

Adrenalin (Parke-Davis). *epinephrine hydrochloride.*

adrenaline. see epinephrine.

Adriamycin PFS (Pharmacia & Upjohn). *doxorubicin hydrochloride.*

Adriamycin RDF (Pharmacia & Upjohn). *doxorubicin hydrochloride.*

Adrucil (Pharmacia & Upjohn). *fluorouracil.*

†Adsorbocarpine. *pilocarpine hydrochloride.*

Advantage 24 (Roberts). *nonoxynol-9.*

Advil (Whitehall-Robins). *ibuprofen.*

Advil Cold & Sinus (Whitehall-Robins). *ibuprofen/pseudoephedrine hydrochloride.*

Agrylin (Roberts). *anagrelide hydrochloride.*

A-Hydrocort (Abbott). *hydrocortisone sodium succinate.*

Airomir (3M Pharmaceuticals). *salbutamol sulfate.*
Akineton (Knoll). *biperiden hydrochloride.*
†Ak-Zol. *acetazolamide.*
†Alaxin. *poloxamer 188.*
Albalon-A Liquifilm (Allergan). *antazoline phosphate/naphazoline hydrochloride.*
Albert Docusate (Albert Pharma). *docusate calcium.*
Albert Glyburide (Albert Pharma). *glyburide.*
Albert Oxybutynin (Albert Pharma). *oxybutynin chloride.*
Albert Pentoxifylline (Albert Pharma). *pentoxifylline.*
Albert Tiafen (Albert Pharma). *tiaprofenic acid.*
Albert Tiafen SR (Albert Pharma). *tiaprofenic acid.*
albumin (human). normal serum albumin (human). **Plasbumin-5, Plasbumin-25.**
albuterol. see salbutamol.
Alcaine (Alcon). *proparacaine hydrochloride.*
Alcojel (Roberts). *isopropyl alcohol.*
Alcomicin (Alcon). *gentamicin sulfate.*
Aldactazide 25 (Searle). *hydrochlorothiazide/spironolactone.*
Aldactazide 50 (Searle). *hydrochlorothiazide/spironolactone.*
Aldactone (Searle). *spironolactone.*
†Aldara. *imiquimod.*
aldesleukin. **Proleukin.**
†Aldoclor. *chlorothiazide/methyldopa.*
Aldomet Injection (MSD). *methyldopa hydrochloride.*
Aldomet Tablets (MSD). *methyldopa.*
Aldoril-15 (MSD). *hydrochlorothiazide/methyldopa.*
Aldoril-25 (MSD). *hydrochlorothiazide/methyldopa.*
alendronate sodium. **Fosamax.**
Alertonic (Hoechst Marion Roussel). *pipradrol/vitamin B compound.*
Alesse 21 (Wyeth-Ayerst). *ethinyl estradiol/levonorgestrel.*
Alesse 28 (Wyeth-Ayerst). *ethinyl estradiol/levonorgestrel.*
alfacalcidol. 1α-hydroxycholecalciferol. 1α-hydroxyvitamin D_3. vitamin D. [**Vitamin D, General Monograph, CPhA**]; **One-Alpha.**
Alfenta (Janssen-Ortho). *alfentanil hydrochloride.*
alfentanil hydrochloride. **Alfenta.**
†Alferon N. *interferon alfa-n3.*
algedrate. see aluminum hydroxide.
alginic acid/aluminum hydroxide. **Gaviscon Heartburn Relief Formula Tablets, Rafton Tablets.**
alginic acid/magnesium carbonate. **Gaviscon Heartburn Relief Formula Aluminum-free Tablets.**
alimemazine tartrate. see trimeprazine tartrate.
Alimentum (Abbott). *infant formula, casein hydrolysate.*
Alkeran (Glaxo Wellcome). *melphalan.*
allantoin/butoxyethyl nicotinate/chloramphenicol/hydrocortisone acetate/sulfur. **Actinac.**
Allegra (Hoechst Marion Roussel). *fexofenadine hydrochloride.*
Allenburys Basic Soap (Roberts). *nonmedicated soap.*
Allerdryl (ICN). *diphenhydramine hydrochloride.*
†Allerest. *naphazoline hydrochloride.*
Allernix (Technilab). *diphenhydramine hydrochloride.*
allopurinol. [**Allopurinol, General Monograph, CPhA**]; **Apo-Allopurinol, Zyloprim.** †Lopurin.
Alomide (Alcon). *lodoxamide tromethamine.*
alpha-D-galactosidase. **Beano.**
Alphagan (Allergan). *brimonidine tartrate.*
alpha$_1$-proteinase inhibitor (human). **Prolastin.**
†Alphatrex. *betamethasone dipropionate.*
alprazolam. [**Benzodiazepines, General Monograph, CPhA**]; **Alti-Alprazolam, Apo-Alpraz, Gen-Alprazolam, Novo-Alprazol, Nu-Alpraz, Xanax, Xanax TS.**
alprostadil. prostaglandin E_1. **Caverject,** Muse, **Prostin VR.**
Alsoy (Nestlé, Carnation). *infant formula, soy protein isolate.*
Altace (Hoechst Marion Roussel). *ramipril.*
alteplase. **Activase rt-PA.**
Alti-Acyclovir (AltiMed). *acyclovir.*
Alti-Alprazolam (AltiMed). *alprazolam.*
Alti-Amiloride HCTZ (AltiMed). *amiloride hydrochloride/hydrochlorothiazide.*
Alti-Azathioprine (AltiMed). *azathioprine.*
Alti-Beclomethasone Aqueous Suspension (AltiMed). *beclomethasone dipropionate.*
Alti-Beclomethasone Inhalation Aerosol (AltiMed). *beclomethasone dipropionate.*
Alti-Benzydamine (AltiMed). *benzydamine hydrochloride.*
Alti-Bromazepam (AltiMed). *bromazepam.*
Alti-Captopril (AltiMed). *captopril.*
Alti-Cholestyramine Light (AltiMed). *cholestyramine resin.*
Alti-Clobetasol (AltiMed). *clobetasol 17-propionate.*
Alti-Clonazepam (AltiMed). *clonazepam.*
Alti-CPA (AltiMed). *cyproterone acetate.*
Alti-Cyclobenzaprine (AltiMed). *cyclobenzaprine hydrochloride.*
Alti-Desipramine (AltiMed). *desipramine hydrochloride.*
Alti-Diltiazem (AltiMed). *diltiazem hydrochloride.*
Alti-Diltiazem CD (AltiMed). *diltiazem hydrochloride.*
Alti-Domperidone Maleate (AltiMed). *domperidone maleate.*
Alti-Doxepin (AltiMed). *doxepin hydrochloride.*
Alti-Doxycycline (AltiMed). *doxycycline hyclate.*
Alti-Flurbiprofen (AltiMed). *flurbiprofen.*
Alti-Fluvoxamine (AltiMed). *fluvoxamine maleate.*
Alti-Ibuprofen (AltiMed). *ibuprofen.*
Alti-Ipratropium (AltiMed). *ipratropium bromide.*
Alti-Mexiletine (AltiMed). *mexiletine hydrochloride.*
Alti-Minocycline (AltiMed). *minocycline hydrochloride.*
Alti-Moclobemide (AltiMed). *moclobemide.*
Alti-MPA (AltiMed). *medroxyprogesterone acetate.*
Alti-Nadolol (AltiMed). *nadolol.*
Alti-Orciprenaline (AltiMed). *orciprenaline sulfate.*
Alti-Piroxicam (AltiMed). *piroxicam.*
Alti-Prazosin (AltiMed). *prazosin hydrochloride.*
Alti-Ranitidine (AltiMed). *ranitidine hydrochloride.*
Alti-Salbutamol (AltiMed). *salbutamol.*
Alti-Salbutamol Sulfate (AltiMed). *salbutamol sulfate.*
Alti-Sotalol (AltiMed). *sotalol hydrochloride.*
Alti-Sulfasalazine (AltiMed). *sulfasalazine.*
Alti-Terazosin (AltiMed). *terazosin hydrochloride dihydrate.*
Alti-Trazodone (AltiMed). *trazodone hydrochloride.*
Alti-Trazodone Dividose (AltiMed). *trazodone hydrochloride.*
Alti-Triazolam (AltiMed). *triazolam.*
Alti-Tryptophan (AltiMed). *l-tryptophan.*

Names **underlined** have complete prescribing information in the *CPS* Monograph Section.

Alti-Valproic (AltiMed). *valproic acid.*
Alti-Verapamil (AltiMed). *verapamil hydrochloride.*
altretamine. hexamethylmelamine. **Hexalen.**
aluminum acetate/benzethonium chloride. **Buro-Sol Otic Solution, Buro-Sol Powder.**
aluminum chlorhydroxide/methylprednisolone acetate/neomycin sulfate/sulfur. **Neo-Medrol Acne.**
aluminum chlorhydroxide/methylprednisolone acetate/sulfur. **Medrol Acne.**
aluminum dihydroxyallantoinate/cellulose/chloroxylenol. **ZeaSORB.**
aluminum hydroxide. algedrate. **Amphojel, Basaljel.**
aluminum hydroxide/alginic acid. **Gaviscon Heartburn Relief Formula Tablets, Rafton Tablets.**
aluminum hydroxide-magnesium carbonate/magnesium alginate/ magnesium carbonate. **Maalox HRF.**
aluminum hydroxide/magnesium hydroxide. **Diovol, Diovol Ex, Gelusil, Gelusil Extra Strength, Maalox, Maalox TC, Mylanta Double Strength Plain Liquid, Univol.**
aluminum hydroxide/magnesium hydroxide/oxethazaine. **Mucaine.**
aluminum hydroxide/magnesium hydroxide/simethicone. **Diovol Plus, Maalox Plus, Maalox Plus Extra Strength, Mylanta Double Strength Plain Tablet, Mylanta Extra Strength, Mylanta Regular Strength.**
aluminum hydroxide/sodium alginate. **Gaviscon Heartburn Relief Formula Liquid, Rafton Liquid.**
aluminum oxide. **Brāsivol.**
Alupent (Boehringer Ingelheim). *orciprenaline sulfate.*
†Alurate. *aprobarbital.*
amantadine hydrochloride. **Endantadine, Gen-Amantadine (Antiparkinsonian), Gen-Amantadine (Antiviral), Symmetrel (Antiparkinson), Symmetrel (Antiviral).** †Symadine.
Amatine (Knoll). *midodrine hydrochloride.*
ambenonium chloride. †Mytelase.
†Ambien. *zolpidem.*
amcinonide. **[Corticosteroids: Topical, General Monograph, CPhA]; Cyclocort.**
Amerge (Glaxo Wellcome). *naratriptan hydrochloride.*
†A-methaPred. *methylprednisolone sodium succinate.*
amethocaine hydrochloride. see tetracaine hydrochloride.
amethopterin. see methotrexate sodium.
Ametop (Smith & Nephew). *tetracaine hydrochloride.*
amfepramone. see diethylpropion hydrochloride.
Amicar (Wyeth-Ayerst). *aminocaproic acid.*
†Amidate. *etomidate.*
amifostine. **Ethyol.**
†Amigesic. *salsalate.*
amikacin sulfate. **Amikin.**
Amikin (Bristol). *amikacin sulfate.*
amiloride hydrochloride. **Midamor.**
amiloride hydrochloride/hydrochlorothiazide. **Alti-Amiloride HCTZ, Apo-Amilzide, Moduret, Novamilor, Nu-Amilzide.** †Moduretic.
amino acids. **Primene, Vamin 18 Electrolyte-Free.**
amino acids/bacitracin zinc/neomycin sulfate. **Cicatrin.**
amino acids/dextrose. **Travasol without Electrolytes.**
amino acids/dextrose/electrolytes. **Travasol with Electrolytes.**
amino acids/electrolytes. **Nutrineal PD4, Vamin N.**
amino acids/sodium propionate/urea. **Amino-Cerv.**
aminobenzoate potassium. **Potaba.**
aminocaproic acid. **Amicar.**
Amino-Cerv (Milex). *amino acids/sodium propionate/urea.*
aminoglutethimide. **Cytadren.**
aminohippurate sodium. PAH. **(MSD).**
aminophylline. theophylline ethylenediamine. **[Theophylline and its Salts, General Monograph, CPhA]; Phyllocontin, Phyllocontin-350; (Abbott).**
aminosalicylate sodium. para-aminosalicylate sodium. PAS Sodium. **[PAS Sodium, General Monograph, CPhA]; Nemasol Sodium—ICN.** †Tubasal.
5-aminosalicylic acid. mesalamine. **Asacol, Mesasal, Novo-5 ASA, Pentasa, Quintasa, Salofalk.** †Rowasa.
amiodarone hydrochloride. **Cordarone, Cordarone I.V.**
amitriptyline hydrochloride. **[Amitriptyline, General Monograph, CPhA]; Apo-Amitriptyline, Elavil.** †Endep.
amitriptyline hydrochloride/chlordiazepoxide. †Limbitrol.
amitriptyline hydrochloride/perphenazine. **Elavil Plus, Etrafon, Triavil.**
amlodipine besylate. **Norvasc.**
ammonium chloride/codeine phosphate/diphenhydramine hydrochloride. **Calmylin Original with Codeine.**
ammonium chloride/codeine phosphate/guaifenesin. **Cheracol.**
ammonium chloride/dextromethorphan hydrobromide/ diphenhydramine hydrochloride. **Calmylin #4.**
ammonium chloride/hydrocodone bitartrate/phenylephrine hydrochloride/pyrilamine maleate. **Hycomine, Hycomine-S.**
ammonium lactate. **Lac-Hydrin.**
ammonium molybdate. molybdenem. †Molypen.
amobarbital sodium. amylobarbitone sodium. **[Barbiturates, General Monograph, CPhA]; Amytal.**
amoxapine. **Asendin.**
amoxicillin trihydrate. amoxycillin trihydrate. **[Amoxicillin, General Monograph, CPhA]; Amoxil, Apo-Amoxi, Novamoxin, Nu-Amoxi.** †Trimox, †Wymox.
amoxicillin trihydrate/potassium clavulanate. **Clavulin.** †Augmentin.
Amoxil (Wyeth-Ayerst). *amoxicillin trihydrate.*
amoxycillin trihydrate. see amoxicillin trihydrate.
d-amphetamine. see dexamphetamine sulfate.
Amphojel (Axcan Pharma). *aluminum hydroxide.*
amphotericin B. **Fungizone.**
ampicillin. **Novo-Ampicillin.** †Omnipen.
ampicillin sodium. **Ampicin; (Bioniche).** †Omnipen-N, †Polycillin-N.
ampicillin sodium/sulbactam sodium. †Unasyn.
ampicillin trihydrate. **Apo-Ampi, Nu-Ampi.** †Polycillin, †Totacillin.
Ampicin (Bristol). *ampicillin sodium.*
amrinone lactate. **Inocor.**
amsacrine. **Amsa P-D.**
Amsa P-D (Parke-Davis). *amsacrine.*
amyl nitrite. **(Roberts).**
amylobarbitone sodium. see amobarbital sodium.
Amytal (Lilly). *amobarbital sodium.*
Anacin (Whitehall-Robins). *ASA/caffeine.*
Anacin Extra Strength (Whitehall-Robins). *ASA/caffeine.*
Anafranil (Novartis Pharmaceuticals). *clomipramine hydrochloride.*
anagrelide hydrochloride. **Agrylin.**
Ana-Kit (Bayer). *chlorpheniramine maleate/epinephrine.*
Analgesic Balm (Warner-Lambert Consumer Healthcare). *menthol/ methyl salicylate.*
Anandron (Hoechst Marion Roussel). *nilutamide.*
Anaprox (Roche). *naproxen sodium.*

Anaprox DS (Roche). *naproxen sodium.*
†Anaspaz. *hyoscyamine sulfate.*
anastrozole. **Arimidex.**
Anbesol (Whitehall-Robins). *benzocaine compound.*
Ancef (SmithKline Beecham). *cefazolin sodium.*
†Ancobon. *flucytosine.*
ancrod. **Viprinex.**
Andriol (Organon). *testosterone undecanoate.*
Androcur (Berlex Canada). *cyproterone acetate.*
Androcur Depot (Berlex Canada). *cyproterone acetate.*
†Android-F. *fluoxymesterone.*
†Andronate. *testosterone cypionate.*
†Andropository 100. *testosterone enanthate.*
Anectine (Glaxo Wellcome). *succinylcholine chloride.*
anethole trithione. anetholtrithion. **Sialor.**
anetholtrithion. see anethole trithione.
Anexate (Roche). *flumazenil.*
†Anhydron. *cyclothiazide.*
anileridine hydrochloride. **[Opioids, General Monograph, CPhA]; Leritine Tablets.**
anileridine phosphate. **[Opioids, General Monograph, CPhA]; Leritine Injection.**
anise oil/dill oil/fennel oil/sodium bicarbonate. **Baby's Own Gripe Water.**
anisindione. †Miradon.
anistreplase. **Eminase.**
Anodan-HC (Odan). *hydrocortisone acetate/zinc sulfate monohydrate.*
Ansaid (Pharmacia & Upjohn). *flurbiprofen.*
Antabuse (Wyeth-Ayerst). *disulfiram.*
antazoline phosphate/naphazoline hydrochloride. **Albalon-A Liquifilm, Vasocon-A.**
antazoline phosphate/naphazoline hydrochloride/zinc sulfate. **Zincfrin-A.**
antazoline sulfate/xylometazoline hydrochloride. **Ophtrivin-A.**
Anthraforte (Medican). *anthralin.*
anthralin. dihydroxyanthranol. dithranol. **Anthraforte, Anthranol, Anthrascalp, Micanol.**
Anthranol (Medican). *anthralin.*
Anthrascalp (Medican). *anthralin.*
Antibiotic Cold Sore Ointment (Novartis Consumer Health). *benzocaine/camphor/menthol/polymyxin B sulfate/tyrothricin.*
antihemophilic factor (human). **Koāte-HP.** †Hemofil M, †Humate-P.
antihemophilic factor (recombinant). **Kogenate.**
Antiphlogistine Rub A-535 (Carter Horner). *camphor/eucalyptus oil/menthol/methyl salicylate.*
Antiphlogistine Rub A-535 Capsaicin (Carter Horner). *capsaicin.*
Antiphlogistine Rub A-535 Ice (Carter Horner). *menthol.*
Antiphlogistine Rub A-535 No Odour (Carter Horner). *triethanolamine salicylate.*
antipyrine/benzocaine. **Auralgan.**
antithrombin III. †Kybernin.
antithrombin III (human). **Thrombate III.**
anti-thymocyte globulin (equine)/lymphocyte immune globulin. **Atgam.**
Antivenin (Wyeth-Ayerst). *crotalid serum (snake antivenom).*
Antivenin (Lactrodectus Mactans) (MSD). *black widow spider antivenom.*
Antivert (Pfizer). *meclizine hydrochloride/niacin.*
Anturan (Novartis Pharmaceuticals). *sulfinpyrazone.*
Anugesic-HC (Parke-Davis). *hydrocortisone acetate/pramoxine hydrochloride/zinc sulfate monohydrate.*
Anusol (Warner-Lambert Consumer Healthcare). *zinc sulfate monohydrate.*
Anusol-HC (Parke-Davis). *hydrocortisone acetate/zinc sulfate monohydrate.*
Anusol Plus (Warner-Lambert Consumer Healthcare). *pramoxine hydrochloride/zinc sulfate monohydrate.*
Anuzinc (Technilab). *zinc sulfate monohydrate.*
†Anxanil. *hydroxyzine hydrochloride.*
Anzemet (Hoechst Marion Roussel). *dolasetron mesylate.*
APAP. see acetaminophen.
†Aphrodyne. *yohimbine hydrochloride.*
A.P.L. (Wyeth-Ayerst). *gonadotropin (human) chorionic.*
Apo-Acebutolol (Apotex). *acebutolol hydrochloride.*
Apo-Acetaminophen (Apotex). *acetaminophen.*
Apo-Acetazolamide (Apotex). *acetazolamide.*
Apo-Acyclovir (Apotex). *acyclovir.*
Apo-Allopurinol (Apotex). *allopurinol.*
Apo-Alpraz (Apotex). *alprazolam.*
Apo-Amilzide (Apotex). *amiloride hydrochloride/hydrochlorothiazide.*
Apo-Amitriptyline (Apotex). *amitriptyline hydrochloride.*
Apo-Amoxi (Apotex). *amoxicillin trihydrate.*
Apo-Ampi (Apotex). *ampicillin trihydrate.*
Apo-ASA (Apotex). *ASA.*
Apo-Atenol (Apotex). *atenolol.*
Apo-Baclofen (Apotex). *baclofen.*
Apo-Benztropine (Apotex). *benztropine mesylate.*
Apo-Bisacodyl (Apotex). *bisacodyl.*
Apo-Bromazepam (Apotex). *bromazepam.*
Apo-Bromocriptine (Apotex). *bromocriptine mesylate.*
Apo-Buspirone (Apotex). *buspirone hydrochloride.*
Apo-C (Apotex). *ascorbic acid.*
Apo-Cal (Apotex). *calcium carbonate.*
Apo-Capto (Apotex). *captopril.*
Apo-Carbamazepine (Apotex). *carbamazepine.*
Apo-Cefaclor (Apotex). *cefaclor.*
Apo-Cephalex (Apotex). *cephalexin.*
Apo-Chlorax (Apotex). *chlordiazepoxide hydrochloride/clidinium bromide.*
Apo-Chlordiazepoxide (Apotex). *chlordiazepoxide hydrochloride.*
Apo-Chlorpropamide (Apotex). *chlorpropamide.*
Apo-Chlorthalidone (Apotex). *chlorthalidone.*
Apo-Cimetidine (Apotex). *cimetidine.*
Apo-Clomipramine (Apotex). *clomipramine hydrochloride.*
Apo-Clonazepam (Apotex). *clonazepam.*
Apo-Clonidine (Apotex). *clonidine hydrochloride.*
Apo-Clorazepate (Apotex). *clorazepate dipotassium.*
Apo-Cloxi (Apotex). *cloxacillin sodium.*
Apo-Cromolyn (Apotex). *sodium cromoglycate.*
Apo-Cromolyn Sterules (Apotex). *sodium cromoglycate.*
Apo-Cyclobenzaprine (Apotex). *cyclobenzaprine hydrochloride.*
Apo-Desipramine (Apotex). *desipramine hydrochloride.*
Apo-Diazepam (Apotex). *diazepam.*

Names **underlined** have complete prescribing information in the *CPS* Monograph Section.

Apo-Diclo (Apotex). *diclofenac sodium.*
Apo-Diclo SR (Apotex). *diclofenac sodium.*
Apo-Diflunisal (Apotex). *diflunisal.*
Apo-Diltiaz (Apotex). *diltiazem hydrochloride.*
Apo-Diltiaz CD (Apotex). *diltiazem hydrochloride.*
Apo-Diltiaz SR (Apotex). *diltiazem hydrochloride.*
Apo-Dimenhydrinate (Apotex). *dimenhydrinate.*
Apo-Dipyridamole FC (Apotex). *dipyridamole.*
Apo-Domperidone (Apotex). *domperidone maleate.*
Apo-Doxepin (Apotex). *doxepin hydrochloride.*
Apo-Doxy (Apotex). *doxycycline hyclate.*
Apo-Doxy-Tabs (Apotex). *doxycycline hyclate.*
Apo-Erythro Base (Apotex). *erythromycin.*
Apo-Erythro E-C (Apotex). *erythromycin.*
Apo-Erythro-ES (Apotex). *erythromycin ethylsuccinate.*
Apo-Erythro-S (Apotex). *erythromycin stearate.*
Apo-Etodolac (Apotex). *etodolac.*
Apo-Famotidine (Apotex). *famotidine.*
Apo-Fenofibrate (Apotex). *fenofibrate.*
Apo-Ferrous Gluconate (Apotex). *ferrous gluconate.*
Apo-Ferrous Sulfate (Apotex). *ferrous sulfate.*
Apo-Fluoxetine (Apotex). *fluoxetine hydrochloride.*
Apo-Fluphenazine (Apotex). *fluphenazine hydrochloride.*
Apo-Flurazepam (Apotex). *flurazepam hydrochloride.*
Apo-Flurbiprofen (Apotex). *flurbiprofen.*
Apo-Fluvoxamine (Apotex). *fluvoxamine maleate.*
Apo-Folic (Apotex). *folic acid.*
Apo-Furosemide (Apotex). *furosemide.*
Apo-Gain (Apotex). *minoxidil.*
Apo-Gemfibrozil (Apotex). *gemfibrozil.*
Apo-Glyburide (Apotex). *glyburide.*
Apo-Haloperidol (Apotex). *haloperidol.*
Apo-Hexa (Apotex). *multiple vitamins.*
Apo-Hydralazine (Apotex). *hydralazine hydrochloride.*
Apo-Hydro (Apotex). *hydrochlorothiazide.*
Apo-Hydroxyzine (Apotex). *hydroxyzine hydrochloride.*
Apo-Ibuprofen (Apotex). *ibuprofen.*
Apo-Imipramine (Apotex). *imipramine hydrochloride.*
Apo-Indapamide (Apotex). *indapamide.*
Apo-Indomethacin (Apotex). *indomethacin.*
Apo-Ipravent (Apotex). *ipratropium bromide.*
Apo-ISDN (Apotex). *isosorbide dinitrate.*
Apo-K (Apotex). *potassium chloride.*
Apo-Keto (Apotex). *ketoprofen.*
Apo-Ketoconazole (Apotex). *ketoconazole.*
Apo-Keto-E (Apotex). *ketoprofen.*
Apo-Ketorolac (Apotex). *ketorolac tromethamine.*
Apo-Keto SR (Apotex). *ketoprofen.*
Apo-Ketotifen (Apotex). *ketotifen fumarate.*
Apo-Levocarb (Apotex). *carbidopa/levodopa.*
Apo-Lisinopril (Apotex). *lisinopril.*
Apo-Loperamide (Apotex). *loperamide hydrochloride.*
Apo-Lorazepam (Apotex). *lorazepam.*
Apo-Lovastatin (Apotex). *lovastatin.*
Apo-Loxapine (Apotex). *loxapine.*
Apo-Mefenamic (Apotex). *mefenamic acid.*
Apo-Megestrol (Apotex). *megestrol acetate.*
Apo-Meprobamate (Apotex). *meprobamate.*
Apo-Metformin (Apotex). *metformin hydrochloride.*
Apo-Methazide (Apotex). *hydrochlorothiazide/methyldopa.*
Apo-Methoprazine (Apotex). *methotrimeprazine.*
Apo-Methyldopa (Apotex). *methyldopa.*
Apo-Metoclop (Apotex). *metoclopramide hydrochloride.*
Apo-Metoprolol (Apotex). *metoprolol tartrate.*
Apo-Metoprolol (Type L) (Apotex). *metoprolol tartrate.*
Apo-Metronidazole (Apotex). *metronidazole.*
Apo-Minocycline (Apotex). *minocycline hydrochloride.*
Apo-Moclobemide (Apotex). *moclobemide.*
Apo-Nadol (Apotex). *nadolol.*
Apo-Napro-Na (Apotex). *naproxen sodium.*
Apo-Napro-Na DS (Apotex). *naproxen sodium.*
Apo-Naproxen (Apotex). *naproxen.*
Apo-Nifed (Apotex). *nifedipine.*
Apo-Nifed PA (Apotex). *nifedipine.*
Apo-Nitrofurantoin (Apotex). *nitrofurantoin.*
Apo-Nizatidine (Apotex). *nizatidine.*
Apo-Norflox (Apotex). *norfloxacin.*
Apo-Nortriptyline (Apotex). *nortriptyline hydrochloride.*
Apo-Oflox (Apotex). *ofloxacin.*
Apo-Oxazepam (Apotex). *oxazepam.*
Apo-Oxtriphylline (Apotex). *oxtriphylline.*
Apo-Oxybutynin (Apotex). *oxybutynin chloride.*
Apo-Pentoxifylline SR (Apotex). *pentoxifylline.*
Apo-Pen VK (Apotex). *penicillin V potassium.*
Apo-Perphenazine (Apotex). *perphenazine.*
Apo-Phenylbutazone (Apotex). *phenylbutazone.*
Apo-Pindol (Apotex). *pindolol.*
Apo-Piroxicam (Apotex). *piroxicam.*
Apo-Prazo (Apotex). *prazosin hydrochloride.*
Apo-Prednisone (Apotex). *prednisone.*
Apo-Primidone (Apotex). *primidone.*
Apo-Procainamide (Apotex). *procainamide hydrochloride.*
Apo-Propranolol (Apotex). *propranolol hydrochloride.*
Apo-Quinidine (Apotex). *quinidine sulfate.*
Apo-Ranitidine (Apotex). *ranitidine hydrochloride.*
Apo-Salvent (Apotex). *salbutamol.*
Apo-Selegiline (Apotex). *selegiline hydrochloride.*
Apo-Sotalol (Apotex). *sotalol hydrochloride.*
Apo-Sucralfate (Apotex). *sucralfate.*
Apo-Sulfatrim (Apotex). *sulfamethoxazole/trimethoprim.*
Apo-Sulfinpyrazone (Apotex). *sulfinpyrazone.*
Apo-Sulin (Apotex). *sulindac.*
Apo-Tamox (Apotex). *tamoxifen citrate.*
Apo-Temazepam (Apotex). *temazepam.*
Apo-Tenoxicam (Apotex). *tenoxicam.*
Apo-Terazosin (Apotex). *terazosin hydrochloride dihydrate.*
Apo-Terfenadine (Apotex). *terfenadine.*
Apo-Tetra (Apotex). *tetracycline hydrochloride.*
Apo-Theo LA (Apotex). *theophylline.*
Apo-Thioridazine (Apotex). *thioridazine hydrochloride.*
Apo-Tiaprofenic (Apotex). *tiaprofenic acid.*
Apo-Ticlopidine (Apotex). *ticlopidine hydrochloride.*
Apo-Timol (Apotex). *timolol maleate.*
Apo-Timop (Apotex). *timolol maleate.*

Apo-Tolbutamide (Apotex). *tolbutamide.*
Apo-Trazodone (Apotex). *trazodone hydrochloride.*
Apo-Trazodone D (Apotex). *trazodone hydrochloride.*
Apo-Triazide (Apotex). *hydrochlorothiazide/triamterene.*
Apo-Triazo (Apotex). *triazolam.*
Apo-Trifluoperazine (Apotex). *trifluoperazine hydrochloride.*
Apo-Trihex (Apotex). *trihexyphenidyl hydrochloride.*
Apo-Trimip (Apotex). *trimipramine maleate.*
Apo-Valproic (Apotex). *valproic acid.*
Apo-Verap (Apotex). *verapamil hydrochloride.*
Apo-Zidovudine (Apotex). *zidovudine.*
Apo-Zopiclone (Apotex). *zopiclone.*
apraclonidine hydrochloride. **Iopidine.**
Apresoline (Novartis Pharmaceuticals). *hydralazine hydrochloride.*
aprobarbital. †Alurate.
aprotinin. **Trasylol.**
†Aquachloral. *chloral hydrate.*
Aquacort (Spectropharm Dermatology). *hydrocortisone.*
†Aqua Mephyton. *phytonadione.*
Aquaphor (Smith & Nephew). *petrolatum.*
Aquasite (CIBA Vision). *dextran 70/polyethylene glycol.*
Aquasol E (Novartis Consumer Health). *vitamin E.*
Aquasol E TPGS (Novartis Consumer Health). *vitamin E.*
Aquatain (Whitehall-Robins). *emollient.*
Aralen (Sanofi). *chloroquine phosphate.*
†Aramine. *metaraminol bitartrate.*
†Arduan. *pipecuronium bromide.*
Aredia (Novartis Pharmaceuticals). *pamidronate disodium.*
Aricept (Pfizer). *donepezil hydrochloride.*
Arimidex (Zeneca). *anastrozole.*
Aristocort Parenteral (Stiefel/Glades). *triamcinolone diacetate.*
Aristocort Tablets (Stiefel/Glades). *triamcinolone.*
Aristocort Topicals (Stiefel/Glades). *triamcinolone acetonide.*
Aristospan (Stiefel/Glades). *triamcinolone hexacetonide.*
Arlidin (Rhône-Poulenc Rorer). *nylidrin hydrochloride.*
Arlidin Forte (Rhône-Poulenc Rorer). *nylidrin hydrochloride.*
†Arrestin. *trimethobenzamide hydrochloride.*
Arthrotec (Searle). *diclofenac sodium/misoprostol.*
articaine hydrochloride/epinephrine. **Astracaine, Astracaine Forte, Ultracaine DS, Ultracaine DS Forte.**
†Articulose-L.A. *triamcinolone diacetate.*
Artificial Tears (Rivex Ophthalmics). *polyvinyl alcohol.*
ASA. acetylsalicylic acid. **[ASA, General Monograph, CPhA]; Apo-ASA, A.S.A., A.S.A. Enteric Coated, Asaphen, Asaphen E.C., Aspirin, Aspirin, Coated, Entrophen, MSD Enteric Coated ASA, Novasen.**
A.S.A. (WestCan). *ASA.*
ASA/butalbital/caffeine. **Fiorinal, Tecnal, Trianal.** †Lanorinal.
ASA/butalbital/caffeine/codeine phosphate. **Fiorinal-C¼, -C½, Tecnal C¼, C½, Trianal C¼ C½.**
ASA/caffeine. **Anacin, Anacin Extra Strength, Midol.**
ASA/caffeine citrate/codeine phosphate. **222, 292.**
ASA/caffeine citrate/codeine phosphate/meprobamate. **282 MEP.**
ASA/caffeine/codeine phosphate. **(WestCan).**
ASA/caffeine/orphenadrine citrate. **Norgesic, Norgesic Forte.**
ASA/caffeine/propoxyphene hydrochloride. **692.**
ASA/calcium carbonate/magnesium carbonate/magnesium oxide. **Aspirin With Stomach Guard.**
ASA/chlorpheniramine maleate. **Coricidin Cold.**
ASA/chlorpheniramine maleate/phenylpropanolamine. **Coricidin "D".**
ASA/codeine phosphate/methocarbamol. **Methoxisal-C, Robaxisal-C.**
ASA/codeine phosphate/phenobarbital. **Phenaphen with Codeine.**
Asacol (Procter & Gamble Pharmaceuticals). *5-aminosalicylic acid.*
ASA/dipyridamole. **Asasantine.**
A.S.A. Enteric Coated (WestCan). *ASA.*
ASA/methocarbamol. **Aspirin Backache, Methoxisal, Robaxisal.**
ASA/oxycodone hydrochloride. **Endodan, Oxycodan, Percodan, Percodan-Demi.**
Asaphen (Pharmascience). *ASA.*
Asaphen E.C. (Pharmascience). *ASA.*
ASA/phenylpropanolamine hydrochloride. **Coricidin Non-Drowsy.**
Asasantine (Boehringer Ingelheim). *ASA/dipyridamole.*
Ascofer (Desbergers). *ferrous ascorbate.*
ascorbic acid. cevitamic acid. vitamin C. **[Vitamin C, General Monograph, CPhA]; Apo-C, Duo-C.V.P., Redoxon, Revitalose-C-1000, Timed Release Vitamin C 500 mg, Timed Release Vitamin C 1000 mg; (Roberts), (Swiss Herbal).**
ascorbic acid/calcium carbonate/pyridoxine hydrochloride/vitamin D. **Redoxon-Cal.**
ascorbic acid/chlorpheniramine maleate/prednisone acetate. **Metreton.**
ascorbic acid/ferrous fumarate/folic acid. **Palafer CF.**
ascorbic acid/gland extracts. **Revitonus C-1000.**
ascorbic acid/inositol/thiamine. **Vitathion-A.T.P.**
ascorbic acid/magnesium carbonate/magnesium sulfate/vitamin B compound. **Redoxon-B.**
ascorbic acid/minerals/vitamin D. **Cal-Mag.**
ascorbic acid/selenium/vitamin B compound/vitamin E/zinc. **Stresstabs Plus.**
ascorbic acid/thiamine. **Penta-Thion.**
ascorbic acid/vitamin B compound. **Beminal with C Fortis, Penta/3B + C, Vita 3B + C.**
Asendin (Wyeth-Ayerst). *amoxapine.*
Asmavent (Technilab). *salbutamol sulfate.*
asparaginase. see L-asparaginase.
L-asparaginase. asparaginase. colaspase. **Kidrolase.** †Elspar.
Aspirin (Bayer Consumer). *ASA.*
Aspirin Backache (Bayer Consumer). *ASA/methocarbamol.*
Aspirin, Coated (Bayer Consumer). *ASA.*
Aspirin With Stomach Guard (Bayer Consumer). *ASA/calcium carbonate/magnesium carbonate/magnesium oxide.*
astemizole. **Hismanal.**
Astracaine (Astra). *articaine hydrochloride/epinephrine.*
Astracaine Forte (Astra). *articaine hydrochloride/epinephrine.*
Atarax (Pfizer). *hydroxyzine hydrochloride.*
Atasol (Carter Horner). *acetaminophen.*
Atasol-8, -15, -30 (Carter Horner). *acetaminophen/caffeine citrate/codeine phosphate.*
atenolol. **Apo-Atenol, Gen-Atenolol, Novo-Atenol, Nu-Atenol, PMS-Atenolol, Rho-Atenolol, Scheinpharm Atenolol, Tenolin, Tenormin.**

Names underlined have complete prescribing information in the *CPS* Monograph Section.

atenolol/chlorthalidone. **Tenoretic.**

Atgam (Pharmacia & Upjohn). *anti-thymocyte globulin (equine)/ lymphocyte immune globulin.*

Ativan (Wyeth-Ayerst). *lorazepam.*

atorvastatin calcium. **Lipitor.**

atovaquone. **Mepron.**

atovaquone/proguanil hydrochloride. **Malarone.**

atracurium besylate. **Tracrium; (Abbott), (Faulding).**

Atromid-S (Wyeth-Ayerst). *clofibrate.*

atropine sulfate. **Atropisol, Isopto Atropine, Minims Atropine; (Abbott), (Alcon), (Astra), (Bioniche), (CIBA Vision), (Dioptic), (Rivex Ophthalmics).**

atropine sulfate/attapulgite, activated/hyoscyamine sulfate/opium/ pectin/scopolamine hydrobromide. **Diban.**

atropine sulfate/diphenoxylate hydrochloride. **Lomotil.**

atropine sulfate/hyoscyamine sulfate/phenobarbital/scopolamine hydrobromide. **Donnatal.**

Atropisol (CIBA Vision). *atropine sulfate.*

Atrovent Inhalation Aerosol (Boehringer Ingelheim). *ipratropium bromide.*

Atrovent Inhalation Solution (Boehringer Ingelheim). *ipratropium bromide.*

Atrovent Nasal Spray (Boehringer Ingelheim). *ipratropium bromide.*

attapulgite, activated. activated attapulgite. **Kaopectate.**

attapulgite, activated/atropine sulfate/hyoscyamine sulfate/opium/ pectin/scopolamine hydrobromide. **Diban.**

attapulgite, activated/opium/pectin. **Donnagel-PG Capsules.**

†Augmentin. *amoxicillin trihydrate/potassium clavulanate.*

Auralgan (Whitehall-Robins). *antipyrine/benzocaine.*

auranofin. gold compound. **Ridaura.**

Aureomycin (Wyeth-Ayerst). *chlortetracycline hydrochloride.*

aurothioglucose. gold compound. **Solganal.**

Avapro (Bristol-Myers Squibb/Sanofi Canada). *irbesartan.*

AVC (Hoechst Marion Roussel). *sulfanilamide.*

Aventyl (Lilly). *nortriptyline hydrochloride.*

Avirax (Fabrigen). *acyclovir.*

Avlosulfon (Wyeth-Ayerst). *dapsone.*

Avonex (Biogen). *interferon beta-1a.*

Axid (Lilly). *nizatidine.*

†Aygestin. *norethindrone acetate.*

†Azactam. *aztreonam.*

azatadine maleate. **Optimine.**

azatadine maleate/pseudoephedrine sulfate. **Trinalin.**

azathioprine. **Alti-Azathioprine, Gen-Azathioprine, Imuran Tablets.**

azathioprine sodium. **Imuran Injection; (Novopharm).**

azidothymidine. see zidovudine.

azithromycin dihydrate. **Zithromax.**

Azmacort (Rhône-Poulenc Rorer). *triamcinolone acetonide.*

†Azo-Standard. *phenazopyridine hydrochloride.*

AZT. see zidovudine.

aztreonam. †Azactam.

†Azulfidine. *sulfasalazine.*

B

Baby's Own Gripe Water (Block Drug). *anise oil/dill oil/fennel oil/ sodium bicarbonate.*

Baby's Own Infant Drops (Block Drug). *simethicone.*

Baby's Own Ointment (Block Drug). *zinc oxide.*

Baby's Own Teething Gel (Block Drug). *benzyl alcohol.*

bacampicillin hydrochloride. **Penglobe.** †Spectrobid.

Bacid (Rhône-Poulenc Rorer). *lactobacillus acidophilus.*

Baciguent (Johnson & Johnson • Merck). *bacitracin.*

Bacillus Calmette-Guérin, intravesical. **ImmuCyst, OncoTICE, PACIS.**

Bacillus Calmette-Guérin vaccine, intradermal. tubercle bacillus. **(Connaught).**

bacitracin. **Baciguent; (Pharmacia & Upjohn).**

bacitracin/gramicidin/polymyxin B sulfate. **Polysporin Triple Antibiotic Ointment.**

bacitracin/polymyxin B sulfate. **Bioderm, Polycidin Ophthalmic Ointment, Polysporin Ointment, Polytopic Ointment.**

bacitracin zinc. zinc bacitracin. **(Roberts).**

bacitracin zinc/amino acids/neomycin sulfate. **Cicatrin.**

bacitracin zinc/hydrocortisone/neomycin sulfate/polymyxin B sulfate. **Cortisporin Ointment, Cortisporin Ophthalmic Ointment.**

bacitracin zinc/neomycin sulfate/polymyxin B sulfate. **Neosporin Ointment/Ophthalmic Ointment, Neotopic.**

bacitracin zinc/polymyxin B sulfate. **Optimyxin Ointment.**

baclofen. **Apo-Baclofen, Gen-Baclofen, Lioresal, Lioresal Intrathecal, Liotec, Novo-Baclofen, Nu-Baclo, PMS-Baclofen; (BDH).**

Bactigras (Smith & Nephew). *chlorhexidine acetate.*

†Bactocill. *oxacillin sodium.*

Bactrim Roche (Roche). *sulfamethoxazole/trimethoprim.*

Bactroban (SmithKline Beecham). *mupirocin.*

balanced salt solution. **BSS, BSS Plus, Eye-Stream.**

Balminil Camphorub (Rougier). *camphor/eucalyptol/menthol.*

Balminil Decongestant (Rougier). *pseudoephedrine hydrochloride.*

Balminil DM (Rougier). *dextromethorphan hydrobromide.*

Balminil DM Children (Rougier). *dextromethorphan hydrobromide.*

Balminil DM + Decongestant (Rougier). *dextromethorphan hydrobromide/pseudoephedrine hydrochloride.*

Balminil DM + Decongestant + Expectorant (Rougier). *dextromethorphan hydrobromide/guaifenesin/pseudoephedrine hydrochloride.*

Balminil DM + Expectorant (Rougier). *dextromethorphan hydrobromide/guaifenesin.*

Balminil Expectorant (Rougier). *guaifenesin.*

Balnetar (Westwood-Squibb). *coal tar.*

†Banthine. *methantheline bromide.*

†Barbita. *phenobarbital.*

barbiturates. **(General Monograph, CPhA).**

Barriere (Roberts). *dimethicone.*

Barriere-HC (Roberts). *hydrocortisone/silicone.*

Basaljel (Axcan Pharma). *aluminum hydroxide.*

Baycol (Bayer). *cerivastatin sodium.*

Baygam (Bayer). *immune globulin (human), i.m.*

Bayhep B (Bayer). *immune globulin, hepatitis B (human).*

Bayrab (Bayer). *immune globulin, rabies (human).*

Baytet (Bayer). *immune globulin, tetanus (human).*

Beano (Block Drug). *alpha-D-galactosidase.*

Beben (Parke-Davis). *betamethasone benzoate.*

becaplermin. †Regranax.

Beclodisk (Glaxo Wellcome). *beclomethasone dipropionate.*

Beclodisk Diskhaler (Glaxo Wellcome). *beclomethasone dipropionate.*

Becloforte (Glaxo Wellcome). *beclomethasone dipropionate.*

beclomethasone dipropionate. **[Corticosteroids: Eye Ear Nose, Corticosteroids: Inhaled, General Monographs, CPhA]; Alti-Beclomethasone Aqueous Suspension, Alti-Beclomethasone Inhalation Aerosol, Beclodisk, Beclodisk Diskhaler, Becloforte, Beclovent Inhaler, Beclovent Rotacaps, Beclovent Rotahaler, Beconase Aq, Gen-Beclo Aq., Propaderm, Rivanase Aq., Vancenase, Vanceril.**

Beclovent Inhaler (Glaxo Wellcome). *beclomethasone dipropionate.*

Beclovent Rotacaps (Glaxo Wellcome). *beclomethasone dipropionate.*

Beclovent Rotahaler (Glaxo Wellcome). *beclomethasone dipropionate.*

Beconase Aq (Glaxo Wellcome). *beclomethasone dipropionate.*

beef serum proteins/iron/liver extract/vitamin B compound. **Hormodausse.**

†Beepen-VK. *penicillin V potassium.*

belladonna/caffeine/ergotamine tartrate/pentobarbital. **Cafergot-PB.**

belladonna/ergotamine/phenobarbital. **Bellergal Spacetabs.**

Bellergal Spacetabs (Novartis Pharmaceuticals). *belladonna/ergotamine/phenobarbital.*

Beminal with C Fortis (Wyeth-Ayerst). *ascorbic acid/vitamin B compound.*

Benadryl (Warner-Lambert Consumer Healthcare). *diphenhydramine hydrochloride.*

Benadryl Allergy/Sinus/Headache (Warner-Lambert Consumer Healthcare). *acetaminophen/diphenhydramine hydrochloride/pseudoephedrine hydrochloride.*

Benadryl Cream (Warner-Lambert Consumer Healthcare). *diphenhydramine.*

benazepril hydrochloride. **[ACE Inhibitors, General Monograph, CPhA]; Lotensin.**

bendrofluazide. see bendroflumethiazide.

bendroflumethiazide. bendrofluazide. benzydroflumethiazide.

bendroflumethiazide/rauwolfia serpentina. †Rauzide.

Benemid (MSD). *probenecid.*

benoxinate. **Minims Benoxinate.**

Benoxyl (Stiefel). *benzoyl peroxide.*

benserazide hydrochloride/levodopa. **Prolopa.**

bentiromide. †Chymex.

Bentylol (Hoechst Marion Roussel). *dicyclomine hydrochloride.*

Benuryl (ICN). *probenecid.*

Benylin Codeine (Warner-Lambert Consumer Healthcare). *codeine phosphate/guaifenesin/pseudoephedrine hydrochloride.*

Benylin DM (Warner-Lambert Consumer Healthcare). *dextromethorphan hydrobromide.*

Benylin DM 12 Hour (Warner-Lambert Consumer Healthcare). *dextromethorphan hydrobromide.*

Benylin DM for Children (Warner-Lambert Consumer Healthcare). *dextromethorphan hydrobromide.*

Benylin DM-D (Adult) (Warner-Lambert Consumer Healthcare). *dextromethorphan hydrobromide/pseudoephedrine hydrochloride.*

Benylin DM-D-E (Warner-Lambert Consumer Healthcare). *dextromethorphan hydrobromide/guaifenesin/pseudoephedrine hydrochloride.*

Benylin DM-D For Children (Warner-Lambert Consumer Healthcare). *dextromethorphan hydrobromide/pseudoephedrine hydrochloride.*

Benylin DM-E (Warner-Lambert Consumer Healthcare). *dextromethorphan hydrobromide/guaifenesin.*

Benylin DM for Children (Warner-Lambert Consumer Healthcare). *dextromethorphan hydrobromide.*

Benylin DM for Children 12 Hour (Warner-Lambert Consumer Healthcare). *dextromethorphan hydrobromide.*

Benylin E (Warner-Lambert Consumer Healthcare). *guaifenesin.*

Benylin 4 Flu (Warner-Lambert Consumer Healthcare). *acetaminophen/dextromethorphan hydrobromide/guaifenesin/pseudoephedrine hydrochloride.*

Benzac AC (Galderma). *benzoyl peroxide.*

†Benzacot. *trimethobenzamide hydrochloride.*

Benzac W (Galderma). *benzoyl peroxide.*

Benzac W Wash (Galderma). *benzoyl peroxide.*

2.5 Benzagel Acne Gel (Novartis Consumer Health). *benzoyl peroxide.*

5 Benzagel Acne Gel (Novartis Consumer Health). *benzoyl peroxide.*

10 Benzagel Acne Gel (Dermik Laboratories Canada). *benzoyl peroxide.*

2.5 Benzagel Acne Lotion (Novartis Consumer Health). *benzoyl peroxide.*

5 Benzagel Acne Lotion (Novartis Consumer Health). *benzoyl peroxide.*

5 Benzagel Acne Wash (Novartis Consumer Health). *benzoyl peroxide.*

benzalkonium chloride. **Zephiran.**

benzalkonium chloride/coal tar. **Ionil-T.**

benzalkonium chloride/salicylic acid. **Ionil.**

Benzamycin (Dermik Laboratories Canada). *benzoyl peroxide/erythromycin.*

†BenzaShave. *benzoyl peroxide.*

benzethacil. see penicillin G benzathine.

benzethonium chloride/acetic acid/hydrocortisone/1,2-propanediol diacetate. **VōSoL HC.**

benzethonium chloride/acetic acid/1,2-propanediol diacetate. **VōSoL.**

benzethonium chloride/aluminum acetate. **Buro-Sol Otic Solution, Buro-Sol Powder.**

benzhexol hydrochloride. see trihexyphenidyl hydrochloride.

benzocaine. ethyl aminobenzoate. **Topicaine, Zilactin-B, Zilactin Baby.**

benzocaine/antipyrine. **Auralgan.**

benzocaine/bicetonium. **Bionet.**

benzocaine/camphor/menthol/polymyxin B sulfate/tyrothricin. **Antibiotic Cold Sore Ointment.**

benzocaine compound. **Anbesol.**

benzocaine/hydrocortisone acetate/zinc sulfate monohydrate. **Rectogel HC.**

benzocaine/magnesium sulfate. **Osmopak Plus.**

benzocaine/tetracaine hydrochloride. **Panocaine.**

benzocaine/zinc sulfate monohydrate. **Rectogel.**

benzodiazepines. **(General Monograph, CPhA).**

Names **underlined** have complete prescribing information in the *CPS* Monograph Section.

benzonatate. †Tessalon.

benzoyl peroxide. **Acetoxyl, Benoxyl, Benzac AC, Benzac W, Benzac W Wash, 2.5 Benzagel Acne Gel, 5 Benzagel Acne Gel, 10 Benzagel Acne Gel, 2.5 Benzagel Acne Lotion, 5 Benzagel Acne Lotion, 5 Benzagel Acne Wash, Desquam-X, Oxyderm, PanOxyl Aquagel, PanOxyl Gel/Bars, PanOxyl Wash, Solugel.** †BenzaShave, †Dryox, †Oxy 10, †Persa-Gel.

benzoyl peroxide/erythromycin. **Benzamycin.**

benzoyl peroxide/sulfur. **Sulfoxyl.**

benzphetamine hydrochloride. †Didrex.

benzthiazide. †Exna.

benztropine mesylate. [**Benztropine Mesylate, General Monograph, CPhA**]; **Apo-Benztropine, Cogentin.**

benzydamine hydrochloride. **Alti-Benzydamine, Novo-Benzydamine, PMS-Benzydamine, Sun-Benz, Tantum.**

benzydroflumethiazide. see bendroflumethiazide.

benzyl alcohol. **Baby's Own Teething Gel, Zilactin.**

benzylpenicillin potassium. see penicillin G potassium.

benzylpenicilloyl-polylysine. **Pre-Pen.**

bepridil hydrochloride. †Vascor.

beractant. **Survanta.**

Berotec Forte Inhalation Aerosol (Boehringer Ingelheim). *fenoterol hydrobromide.*

Berotec Inhalation Aerosol (Boehringer Ingelheim). *fenoterol hydrobromide.*

Berotec Inhalation Solution (Boehringer Ingelheim). *fenoterol hydrobromide.*

Betaderm (Taro). *betamethasone valerate.*

Betadine Topical (Purdue Frederick). *povidone-iodine.*

Betadine Vaginal (Purdue Frederick). *povidone-iodine.*

Betagan (Allergan). *levobunolol hydrochloride.*

betahistine hydrochloride. **Serc.**

Betaloc (Astra). *metoprolol tartrate.*

Betaloc Durules (Astra). *metoprolol tartrate.*

betamethasone. **Celestone.**

betamethasone acetate/betamethasone sodium phosphate. **Celestone Soluspan.**

betamethasone benzoate. [**Corticosteroids: Topical, General Monograph, CPhA**]; **Beben.** †Uticort.

betamethasone dipropionate. [**Corticosteroids: Topical, General Monograph, CPhA**]; **Diprolene Glycol, Diprosone, Taro-Sone, Topilene, Topisone.** †Alphatrex, †Maxivate.

betamethasone dipropionate/clotrimazole. **Lotriderm.** †Lotrisone.

betamethasone dipropionate/gentamicin sulfate. **Diprogen.**

betamethasone dipropionate/salicylic acid. **Diprosalic.**

betamethasone disodium phosphate. see betamethasone sodium phosphate.

betamethasone sodium phosphate. betamethasone disodium phosphate. [**Corticosteroids: Eye Ear Nose, Corticosteroids: Systemic, General Monographs, CPhA**]; **Betnesol.** †Selestoject.

betamethasone sodium phosphate/betamethasone acetate. **Celestone Soluspan.**

betamethasone sodium phosphate/gentamicin sulfate. **Garasone.**

betamethasone valerate. [**Corticosteroids: Topical, General Monograph, CPhA**]; **Betaderm, Betnovate, Celestoderm-V, Celestoderm-V/2, Ectosone Mild, Ectosone Regular, Ectosone Scalp Lotion, Prevex B, Valisone Scalp.** †Betatrex, †Beta-Val.

betamethasone valerate/gentamicin sulfate. **Valisone-G.**

†Betapace. *sotalol hydrochloride.*

†Betapen-VK. *penicillin V potassium.*

beta-phenoxyethanol. phenoxetol. **Lanohex Skin Cleanser.**

Betaseron (Berlex Canada). *interferon beta-1b.*

†Betatrex. *betamethasone valerate.*

†Beta-Val. *betamethasone valerate.*

Betaxin (Sanofi). *thiamine hydrochloride.*

betaxolol. †Kerlone.

betaxolol hydrochloride. **Betoptic S.**

bethanechol chloride. **Duvoid, Myotonachol, Urecholine.**

Betnesol (Roberts). *betamethasone sodium phosphate.*

Betnovate (Roberts). *betamethasone valerate.*

Betoptic S (Alcon). *betaxolol hydrochloride.*

bezafibrate. **Bezalip.**

Bezalip (Roche). *bezafibrate.*

Biaxin (Abbott). *clarithromycin.*

bicalutamide. **Casodex.**

bicetonium/benzocaine. **Bionet.**

Bichloracetic Acid (Glenwood). *dichloroacetic acid.*

Bicillin L-A (Wyeth-Ayerst). *penicillin G benzathine.*

BiCNU (Bristol). *carmustine.*

Biltricide (Bayer). *praziquantel.*

bioallethrin/piperonyl butoxide. **Para.**

Biobase (Odan). *ethyl alcohol.*

Biobase-G (Odan). *ethyl alcohol/glycolic acid.*

Bioderm (Odan). *bacitracin/polymyxin B sulfate.*

†Bio-Gan. *trimethobenzamide hydrochloride.*

Biolon (Ophtapharma). *sodium hyaluronate.*

Bionet (Carter Horner). *benzocaine/bicetonium.*

Bion Tears (Alcon). *dextran 70/hydroxypropyl methylcellulose.*

biperiden hydrochloride. **Akineton.**

Biquin Durules (Astra). *quinidine bisulfate.*

bisacodyl. **Apo-Bisacodyl, Dulcolax, Soflax Ex; (Technilab).**

bisacodyl/magnesium citrate. **Royvac.**

Bismutal (Technilab). *bismuth camphocarbonate/guaifenesin.*

bismuth camphocarbonate/guaifenesin. **Bismutal.**

bismuth dipropylacetate. **Neo-Laryngobis.**

bisoprolol fumarate. †Zebeta.

bisoprolol fumarate/hydrochlorothiazide. †Ziac.

bitolterol mesylate. †Tornalate.

black widow spider antivenom. **Antivenin (Lactrodectus Mactans).**

Blenoxane (Bristol). *bleomycin sulfate.*

bleomycin sulfate. **Blenoxane; (Faulding).**

Blephamide (Allergan). *prednisolone acetate/sulfacetamide sodium.*

Blocadren (Frosst). *timolol maleate.*

Bonamil (Wyeth-Ayerst). *infant formula.*

Bonamine (Pfizer). *meclizine hydrochloride.*

Bonefos (Rhône-Poulenc Rorer). *clodronate disodium.*

†Bonine. *meclizine hydrochloride.*

†Bontril. *phendimetrazine tartrate.*

boric acid. **Eyewash.**

Botox (Allergan). *botulinum toxin type A.*

botulinum toxin type A. **Botox.**

botulism antitoxin trivalent types A, B and E (equine). **(Connaught).**

Bradosol (Novartis Consumer Health). *hexylresorcinol.*

Bradosol Extra-Strength (Novartis Consumer Health). *hexylresorcinol.*

Brāsivol (Stiefel). *aluminum oxide.*

†Brethaire. *terbutaline sulfate.*

†Brethine. *terbutaline sulfate.*

Bretylate (Glaxo Wellcome). *bretylium tosylate.*

bretylium tosylate. **Bretylate; (Abbott).** †Bretylol.

bretylium tosylate/dextrose monohydrate. **(Abbott).**

†Bretylol. *bretylium tosylate.*

Brevibloc (Zeneca). *esmolol hydrochloride.*

Brevicon 0.5/35 (Searle). *ethinyl estradiol/norethindrone.*

Brevicon 1/35 (Searle). *ethinyl estradiol/norethindrone.*

†Brevital. *methohexital sodium.*

Bricanyl Tablets (Astra). *terbutaline sulfate.*

Bricanyl Turbuhaler (Astra). *terbutaline sulfate.*

Brietal Sodium (Lilly). *methohexital sodium.*

brimonidine tartrate. **Alphagan.**

bromazepam. **[Benzodiazepines, General Monograph, CPhA]; Alti-Bromazepam, Apo-Bromazepam, Gen-Bromazepam, Lectopam, Novo-Bromazepam, Nu-Bromazepam.**

bromfenac. †Duract.

bromocriptine mesylate. **Apo-Bromocriptine, Parlodel.**

brompheniramine maleate. parabromdylamine maleate. **Dimetane.**

brompheniramine maleate/codeine phosphate/guaifenesin/phenylephrine hydrochloride/phenylpropanolamine hydrochloride. **Dimetane Expectorant-C.**

brompheniramine maleate/codeine phosphate/phenylephrine hydrochloride/phenylpropanolamine hydrochloride. **Dimetapp-C.**

brompheniramine maleate/dextromethorphan hydrobromide/phenylephrine hydrochloride/phenylpropanolamine hydrochloride. **Dimetapp-DM.**

brompheniramine maleate/dextromethorphan hydrobromide/phenylpropanolamine hydrochloride. **Dimetapp Cough & Cold Liqui-Gels.**

brompheniramine maleate/guaifenesin/hydrocodone bitartrate/phenylephrine hydrochloride/phenylpropanolamine hydrochloride. **Dimetane Expectorant-DC.**

brompheniramine maleate/guaifenesin/phenylephrine hydrochloride/phenylpropanolamine hydrochloride. **Dimetane Expectorant.**

brompheniramine maleate/phenylephrine hydrochloride/phenylpropanolamine hydrochloride. **Dimetapp, Dimetapp Oral Infant Drops.**

brompheniramine maleate/phenylpropanolamine hydrochloride. **Dimetapp Chewables, Dimetapp Clear, Dimetapp Liqui-Gels, Dimetapp Quick Dissolve.**

Bronalide (Boehringer Ingelheim). *flunisolide.*

Broncho-Grippol-DM (Technilab). *dextromethorphan hydrobromide.*

Bronkaid Mistometer (Sanofi). *epinephrine.*

†Bronkometer. *isoetharine mesylate.*

†Bronkosol. *isoetharine.*

BSS (Alcon). *balanced salt solution.*

BSS Plus (Alcon). *balanced salt solution.*

budesonide. **[Corticosteroids: Eye Ear Nose, Corticosteroids: Inhaled, General Monographs, CPhA]; Entocort Capsules, Entocort Enema, Gen-Budesonide Aq., Pulmicort Nebuamp, Pulmicort Turbuhaler, Rhinocort Aqua, Rhinocort Turbuhaler.**

bumetanide. **Burinex.** †Bumex.

†Bumex. *bumetanide.*

buphenine hydrochloride. see nylidrin hydrochloride.

bupivacaine hydrochloride. **Marcaine, Sensorcaine; (Abbott).**

bupivacaine hydrochloride/epinephrine. **Sensorcaine Forte, Sensorcaine with Epinephrine.**

†Buprenex. *buprenorphine hydrochloride.*

buprenorphine hydrochloride. †Buprenex.

bupropion hydrochloride. **Wellbutrin SR,** Zyban.

Burinex (Leo). *bumetanide.*

Buro-Sol Otic Solution (TCD). *aluminum acetate/benzethonium chloride.*

Buro-Sol Powder (TCD). *aluminum acetate/benzethonium chloride.*

Buscopan (Boehringer Ingelheim). *scopolamine butylbromide.*

buserelin acetate. **Suprefact, Suprefact Depot.**

Buspar (Bristol). *buspirone hydrochloride.*

Buspirex (Technilab). *buspirone hydrochloride.*

buspirone hydrochloride. **Apo-Buspirone, Buspar, Buspirex, Bustab, Gen-Buspirone, Novo-Buspirone, Nu-Buspirone, PMS-Buspirone.**

Bustab (ICN). *buspirone hydrochloride.*

busulfan. busulphan. **Myleran.**

busulphan. see busulfan.

butabarbital sodium. secbutabarbital. secbutobarbitone. **[Barbiturates, General Monograph, CPhA]; Butisol Sodium.**

butalbital/ASA/caffeine. **Fiorinal, Tecnal, Trianal.** †Lanorinal.

butalbital/ASA/caffeine/codeine phosphate. **Fiorinal-C¼, -C½, Tecnal C¼, C½, Trianal C¼ C½.**

butamben picrate. †Butesin Picrate.

†Butesin Picrate. *butamben picrate.*

Butisol Sodium (Carter Horner). *butabarbital sodium.*

butoconazole nitrate. †Femstat.

butorphanol tartrate. **[Opioids, General Monograph, CPhA]; Stadol NS.**

butoxyethyl nicotinate/allantoin/chloramphenicol/hydrocortisone acetate/sulfur. **Actinac.**

C

Caelyx (Schering). *doxorubicin hydrochloride pegylated liposome.*

Cafergot (Novartis Pharmaceuticals). *caffeine/ergotamine tartrate.*

Cafergot-PB (Novartis Pharmaceuticals). *belladonna/caffeine/ergotamine tartrate/pentobarbital.*

caffeine/acetaminophen/codeine phosphate. **Extra Strength Acetaminophen with Codeine, Lenoltec No.1, No.2, No.3, Novo-Gesic C8, C15, C30, Regular Strength Acetaminophen with Codeine, Tylenol NO. 1 with Codeine, Tylenol NO. 2 and NO. 3 with Codeine; (Stanley).**

caffeine/acetaminophen/pheniramine maleate/phenylpropanolamine hydrochloride/pyrilamine maleate. **Triaminicin.**

caffeine/acetaminophen/pyrilamine maleate. **Midol Extra Strength.**

caffeine/ASA. **Anacin, Anacin Extra Strength, Midol.**

caffeine/ASA/butalbital. **Fiorinal, Tecnal, Trianal.** †Lanorinal.

caffeine/ASA/butalbital/codeine phosphate. **Fiorinal-C¼, -C½, Tecnal C¼, C½, Trianal C¼ C½.**

caffeine/ASA/codeine phosphate. **(WestCan).**

caffeine/ASA/orphenadrine citrate. **Norgesic, Norgesic Forte.**

Names **underlined** have complete prescribing information in the *CPS* Monograph Section.

caffeine/ASA/propoxyphene hydrochloride. **692.**

caffeine/belladonna/ergotamine tartrate/pentobarbital. **Cafergot-PB.**

caffeine citrate/acetaminophen/codeine phosphate. **Atasol-8, -15, -30, Triatec-8, -8 Strong.**

caffeine citrate/ASA/codeine phosphate. **222, 292.**

caffeine citrate/ASA/codeine phosphate/meprobamate. **282 MEP.**

caffeine citrate/diphenhydramine hydrochloride/ergotamine tartrate. **Ergodryl.**

caffeine/dimenhydrinate/ergotamine tartrate. **Gravergol.**

caffeine/ergotamine tartrate. **Cafergot.**

caffeine hydrate/cyclizine hydrochloride/ergotamine tartrate. **Megral.**

Caladryl (Warner-Lambert Consumer Healthcare). *calamine/diphenhydramine hydrochloride.*

calamine/diphenhydramine hydrochloride. **Caladryl.**

†Calan. *verapamil hydrochloride.*

†Calcibind. *cellulose sodium phosphate.*

calcifediol. 25-hydroxycholecalciferol. 25-hydroxyvitamin D_3*. vitamin D.* **[Vitamin D, General Monograph, CPhA];** †Calderol.

calciferol. see ergocalciferol.

Calcijex (Abbott). *calcitriol.*

Calcimar (Rhône-Poulenc Rorer). *calcitonin (salmon).*

calcipotriol. **Dovonex.**

Calcite 500 (Riva). *calcium carbonate.*

Calcite D 500 (Riva). *calcium carbonate/vitamin D.*

calcitonin (human). †Cibacalcin.

calcitonin (salmon). salcatonin. **Calcimar, Caltine.** †Miacalcin.

calcitriol. 1,25-dihydroxycholecalciferol. 1,25-dihydroxyvitamin D_3*. vitamin D.* **[Vitamin D, General Monograph, CPhA]; Calcijex, Rocaltrol.**

calcium. **Nu-Cal.**

Calcium 500 (Trianon). *calcium carbonate.*

calcium carbimide. calcium cyanamide.

calcium carbonate. **[Calcium Salts: Oral, General Monograph, CPhA]; Apo-Cal, Calcite 500, Calcium 500, Calsan, Caltrate 600, Os-Cal, Webber Calcium Carbonate.**

calcium carbonate/ASA/magnesium carbonate/magnesium oxide. **Aspirin With Stomach Guard.**

calcium carbonate/ascorbic acid/pyridoxine hydrochloride/vitamin D. **Redoxon-Cal.**

calcium carbonate/calcium lactate-gluconate/citric acid. **Calcium-Sandoz Forte, Calcium-Sandoz Gramcal, Gramcal.**

calcium carbonate/cholecalciferol. **Os-Cal D.**

calcium carbonate/copper/magnesium/manganese/vitamin D/zinc. **Caltrate Plus.**

calcium carbonate/etidronate disodium. **Didrocal.**

calcium carbonate/ferrous fumarate/multiple vitamins. **Prenavite.**

calcium carbonate/magnesium hydroxide/simethicone. **Diovol Plus AF.**

calcium carbonate/vitamin D. **Calcite D 500, Calcium D 500, Caltrate 600 + Vitamin D.**

calcium chloride. **[Calcium Salts: Parenteral, General Monograph, CPhA]; (Abbott), (Astra).**

calcium cyanamide. see calcium carbimide.

Calcium D 500 (Trianon). *calcium carbonate/vitamin D.*

calcium disodium edetate. **Calcium Disodium Versenate.**

Calcium Disodium Versenate (3M Pharmaceuticals). *calcium disodium edetate.*

calcium folinate. citrovorum factor. folinic acid, calcium salt. leucovorin calcium. **Lederle Leucovorin Calcium; (Faulding), (Novopharm).** †Wellcovorin.

calcium glubionate. †Neo-Calglucon.

calcium glubionate/calcium lactobionate. **Calcium-Sandoz Syrup.**

calcium glucoheptonate/calcium gluconate. **[Calcium Salts: Oral, General Monograph, CPhA]; Calcium Stanley.**

calcium gluconate. **[Calcium Salts: Oral, Calcium Salts: Parenteral, General Monographs, CPhA]; (Abbott), (Astra).**

calcium gluconate/calcium glucoheptonate. **[Calcium Salts: Oral, General Monograph, CPhA]; Calcium Stanley.**

calcium lactate-gluconate/calcium carbonate/citric acid. **Calcium-Sandoz Forte, Calcium-Sandoz Gramcal, Gramcal.**

calcium lactobionate/calcium glubionate. **Calcium-Sandoz Syrup.**

calcium pantothenate. see pantothenic acid.

calcium polystyrene sulfonate. **Resonium Calcium.**

Calcium-Sandoz Forte (Novartis Consumer Health). *calcium carbonate/calcium lactate-gluconate/citric acid.*

Calcium-Sandoz Gramcal (Novartis Consumer Health). *calcium carbonate/calcium lactate-gluconate/citric acid.*

Calcium-Sandoz Syrup (Novartis Consumer Health). *calcium glubionate/calcium lactobionate.*

Calcium Stanley (Stanley). *calcium glucoheptonate/calcium gluconate.*

†Calderol. *calcifediol.*

Caldomine-DH (Technilab). *hydrocodone bitartrate/pheniramine maleate/phenylpropanolamine hydrochloride/pyrilamine maleate.*

Cal-Mag (Swiss Herbal). *ascorbic acid/minerals/vitamin D.*

Calmurid (Galderma). *urea.*

Calmurid HC (Galderma). *hydrocortisone/urea.*

Calmydone (Technilab). *doxylamine succinate/etafedrine hydrochloride/hydrocodone bitartrate/sodium citrate.*

Calmylin #1 (Technilab). *dextromethorphan hydrobromide.*

Calmylin #2 (Technilab). *dextromethorphan hydrobromide/pseudoephedrine hydrochloride.*

Calmylin #3 (Technilab). *dextromethorphan hydrobromide/guaifenesin/pseudoephedrine hydrochloride.*

Calmylin #4 (Technilab). *ammonium chloride/dextromethorphan hydrobromide/diphenhydramine hydrochloride.*

Calmylin Ace (Technilab). *codeine phosphate/guaifenesin/pheniramine maleate.*

Calmylin Cough and Flu (Technilab). *acetaminophen/dextromethorphan hydrobromide/guaifenesin/pseudoephedrine hydrochloride.*

Calmylin Expectorant (Technilab). *guaifenesin.*

Calmylin Original with Codeine (Technilab). *ammonium chloride/codeine phosphate/diphenhydramine hydrochloride.*

Calmylin Pediatric (Technilab). *dextromethorphan hydrobromide/pseudoephedrine hydrochloride.*

Calmylin with Codeine (Technilab). *codeine phosphate/guaifenesin/pseudoephedrine hydrochloride.*

Calsan (Novartis Consumer Health). *calcium carbonate.*

Caltine (Ferring). *calcitonin (salmon).*

Caltrate 600 (Whitehall-Robins). *calcium carbonate.*

Caltrate 600 + Vitamin D (Whitehall-Robins). *calcium carbonate/vitamin D.*

Caltrate Plus (Whitehall-Robins). *calcium carbonate/copper/magnesium/manganese/vitamin D/zinc.*

camphor/acetic acid/lemon extract oil/sodium lauryl ether sulfate. **SH-206.**

camphor/benzocaine/menthol/polymyxin B sulfate/tyrothricin. **Antibiotic Cold Sore Ointment.**
camphor/diphenylpyraline hydrochloride/guaiacol carbonate. **Creo-Rectal.**
camphor/eucalyptol/menthol. **Balminil Camphorub.**
camphor/eucalyptus oil/menthol/methyl salicylate. **Antiphlogistine Rub A-535.**
camphor/menthol/pramoxine hydrochloride. **Sarna-P.**
Camptosar (Pharmacia & Upjohn). *irinotecan hydrochloride trihydrate.*
Candistatin (Westwood-Squibb). *nystatin.*
Canesten Topical (Bayer Consumer). *clotrimazole.*
Canesten Vaginal (Bayer Consumer). *clotrimazole.*
Canthacur (Pharmascience). *cantharidin.*
Canthacur-PS (Pharmascience). *cantharidin/podophyllin/salicylic acid.*
cantharidin. **Canthacur, Cantharone.**
cantharidin/podophyllin/salicylic acid. **Canthacur-PS, Cantharone Plus.**
Cantharone (Dormer). *cantharidin.*
Cantharone Plus (Dormer). *cantharidin/podophyllin/salicylic acid.*
†Cantil. *mepenzolate bromide.*
†Capitrol. *chloroxine.*
Capoten (Squibb). *captopril.*
†Capozide. *captopril/hydrochlorothiazide.*
capsaicin. **Antiphlogistine Rub A-535 Capsaicin, Zostrix, Zostrix H.P.; (Stiefel/Glades).**
captopril. [**ACE Inhibitors, General Monograph, CPhA**]; **Alti-Captopril, Apo-Capto, Capoten, Captril, Gen-Captopril, Novo-Captoril, Nu-Capto.**
captopril/hydrochlorothiazide. †Capozide.
Captril (Technilab). *captopril.*
†Carafate. *sucralfate.*
carbachol. carbamylcholine chloride. [**Carbachol, General Monograph, CPhA**]; **Carbastat, Isopto Carbachol, Miostat; (Bioniche).**
carbamazepine. **Apo-Carbamazepine, Novo-Carbamaz, Nu-Carbamazepine, Taro-Carbamazepine, Tegretol.** †Epitol.
carbamylcholine chloride. see carbachol.
Carbastat (CIBA Vision). *carbachol.*
carbenicillin indanyl sodium. †Geocillin.
carbidopa/levodopa. **Apo-Levocarb, Endo Levodopa/ Carbidopa, Nu-Levocarb, Sinemet, Sinemet CR.**
Carbocaine (Sanofi). *mepivacaine hydrochloride.*
Carbolith (ICN). *lithium carbonate.*
carboplatin. **Paraplatin-AQ; (Faulding), (Novopharm).**
carboprost tromethamine. †Hemabate.
carboxymethylcellulose sodium. **Cellufresh, Cellufresh M-D, Celluvisc.**
Cardene (Roche). *nicardipine hydrochloride.*
Cardioquin (Purdue Frederick). *quinidine polygalacturonate.*
Cardizem (Hoechst Marion Roussel). *diltiazem hydrochloride.*
Cardizem CD (Hoechst Marion Roussel). *diltiazem hydrochloride.*
Cardizem Injectable (Hoechst Marion Roussel). *diltiazem hydrochloride.*
Cardizem SR (Hoechst Marion Roussel). *diltiazem hydrochloride.*
Cardura-1 (Astra). *doxazosin mesylate.*
Cardura-2 (Astra). *doxazosin mesylate.*
Cardura-4 (Astra). *doxazosin mesylate.*
carisoprodol. isomeprobamate. **Soma.**
carmustine. **BiCNU.**
Carnitor (Sigma-Tau). *levocarnitine.*
carteolol hydrochloride. †Cartrol, †Ocupress.
†Cartrol. *carteolol hydrochloride.*
carvedilol. **Coreg.**
casanthranol/docusate sodium. **Peri-Colace.**
Casodex (Zeneca). *bicalutamide.*
†Cataflam. *diclofenac potassium.*
Catapres (Boehringer Ingelheim). *clonidine hydrochloride.*
Caverject (Pharmacia & Upjohn). *alprostadil.*
CCNU. see lomustine.
Ceclor (Lilly). *cefaclor.*
Cedocard SR (Pharmascience). *isosorbide dinitrate.*
CeeNU (Bristol). *lomustine.*
cefaclor. **Apo-Cefaclor, Ceclor, Nu-Cefaclor, PMS-Cefaclor, Scheinpharm Cefaclor.**
cefadroxil. **Duricef.**
†Cefadyl. *cephapirin sodium.*
cefamandole nafate. **Mandol.**
cefazolin sodium. **Ancef, Kefzol; (Novopharm).**
cefepime hydrochloride. **Maxipime.**
cefixime. **Suprax.**
Cefizox (SmithKline Beecham). *ceftizoxime sodium.*
cefmetazole sodium. †Zefazone.
†Cefobid. *cefoperazone sodium.*
cefonicid sodium. †Monocid.
cefoperazone sodium. †Cefobid.
Cefotan (Wyeth-Ayerst). *cefotetan disodium.*
cefotaxime sodium. **Claforan.**
cefotetan disodium. **Cefotan.**
cefoxitin sodium. **Mefoxin; (Novopharm).**
cefpodoxime proxetil. †Vantin.
cefprozil. **Cefzil.**
ceftazidime. **Ceptaz, Tazidime.** †Tazicef.
ceftazidime pentahydrate. **Fortaz.**
Ceftin (Glaxo Wellcome). *cefuroxime axetil.*
ceftizoxime sodium. **Cefizox.**
ceftriaxone sodium. **Rocephin.**
cefuroxime axetil. **Ceftin.**
cefuroxime sodium. **Kefurox, Zinacef; (Schein Pharmaceutical).**
Cefzil (Bristol-Myers Squibb). *cefprozil.*
Celestoderm-V (Schering). *betamethasone valerate.*
Celestoderm-V/2 (Schering). *betamethasone valerate.*
Celestone (Schering). *betamethasone.*
Celestone Soluspan (Schering). *betamethasone acetate/ betamethasone sodium phosphate.*
†Celexa. *citalopram.*
CellCept (Roche). *mycophenolate mofetil.*
Cellufresh (Allergan). *carboxymethylcellulose sodium.*
Cellufresh M-D (Allergan). *carboxymethylcellulose sodium.*
cellulose/aluminum dihydroxyallantoinate/chloroxylenol. **ZeaSORB.**
cellulose/glycerides/polyglycol/polysiloxane copolyol/silicones. **Spectro Derm.**
cellulose sodium phosphate. †Calcibind.

Names **underlined** have complete prescribing information in the *CPS* Monograph Section.

Celluvisc (Allergan). *carboxymethylcellulose sodium.*

Celontin (Parke-Davis). *methsuximide.*

Centrum (Whitehall-Robins). *multiple vitamins and minerals.*

Centrum Forte (Whitehall-Robins). *multiple vitamins and minerals.*

Centrum Junior Complete (Whitehall-Robins). *multiple vitamins and minerals.*

Centrum Junior Regular (Whitehall-Robins). *multiple vitamins and minerals.*

Centrum Protegra (Whitehall-Robins). *multiple vitamins and minerals.*

Centrum Select (Whitehall-Robins). *multiple vitamins and minerals.*

cephalexin. **Apo-Cephalex, Keflex, Novo-Lexin, Nu-Cephalex, PMS-Cephalexin.**

cephalexin hydrochloride monohydrate. †Keftab.

cephalothin sodium. **Ceporacin, Keflin.**

cephapirin sodium. †Cefadyl.

Ceporacin (Bioniche). *cephalothin sodium.*

Ceptaz (Glaxo Wellcome). *ceftazidime.*

Cerebyx (Parke-Davis). *fosphenytoin sodium.*

†Cerespan. *papaverine hydrochloride.*

cerivastatin sodium. **Baycol.**

Cerubidine (Rhône-Poulenc Rorer). *daunorubicin.*

Cerumenex (Purdue Frederick). *triethanolamine polypeptide oleate-condensate.*

Cerumol (Solvay Pharma). *chlorbutol/paradichlorobenzene/terebinth oil.*

Cervidil (Ferring). *dinoprostone.*

C.E.S. (ICN). *conjugated estrogens.*

Cesamet (Lilly). *nabilone.*

†Cetacort. *hydrocortisone.*

Cetamide (Alcon). *sulfacetamide sodium.*

cetirizine hydrochloride. **Reactine, Zyrtec.**

cetrimide/chlorhexidine gluconate. **Savlodil 1:100, Savlon Hospital Concentrate.**

cevitamic acid. see ascorbic acid.

charcoal, activated. activated charcoal. **Charcodote, Charcodote Aqueous, Charcodote TFS.**

Charcodote (Pharmascience). *charcoal, activated.*

Charcodote Aqueous (Pharmascience). *charcoal, activated.*

Charcodote TFS (Pharmascience). *charcoal, activated.*

†Chemet. *succimer.*

Cheracol (Roberts). *ammonium chloride/codeine phosphate/guaifenesin.*

†Chibroxin. *norfloxacin.*

Children's Acetaminophen Elixir Drops (WestCan). *acetaminophen.*

Children's Acetaminophen Oral Solution (WestCan). *acetaminophen.*

Children's Chewable Acetaminophen (WestCan). *acetaminophen.*

Children's Choice Super Multi-Vitamins and Minerals (Swiss Herbal). *multiple vitamins and minerals.*

chlophedianol hydrochloride. **Ulone.**

†Chloracol. *chloramphenicol.*

chloral hydrate. **[Chloral Hydrate, General Monograph, CPhA]; PMS-Chloral Hydrate.** †Aquachloral.

chlorambucil. **Leukeran.**

chloramphenicol. **[Chloramphenicol, General Monograph, CPhA]; Chloromycetin Injection, Diochloram, Minims Chloramphenicol, Ophtho-Chloram, Pentamycetin.** †Chloracol, †Econochlor, †Ocu-Chlor.

chloramphenicol/allantoin/butoxyethyl nicotinate/hydrocortisone acetate/sulfur. **Actinac.**

chloramphenicol/hydrocortisone acetate. **Pentamycetin/HC.**

chlorbutol/paradichlorobenzene/terebinth oil. **Cerumol.**

chlordiazepoxide/amitriptyline hydrochloride. †Limbitrol.

chlordiazepoxide hydrochloride. **[Benzodiazepines, General Monograph, CPhA]; Apo-Chlordiazepoxide, Novo-Poxide.** †Libritabs.

chlordiazepoxide hydrochloride/clidinium bromide. **Apo-Chlorax, Librax.**

chlorhexidine acetate. **Bactigras.**

chlorhexidine digluconate/silver sulfadiazine. **Flamazine C.**

chlorhexidine gluconate. **Hibidil 1:2000, Hibitane Skin Cleanser, Oro-Clense, Peridex, Spectro Gram "2".**

chlorhexidine gluconate/cetrimide. **Savlodil 1:100, Savlon Hospital Concentrate.**

chlorhexidine gluconate/coal tar. **Spectro Tar Antiseptic Shampoo.**

chloriguane. see proguanil.

chlormethine. see mechlorethamine hydrochloride.

chlormezanone. †Trancopal.

chloroguanide. see proguanil.

chloroiodoquine. see clioquinol.

Chloromycetin Injection (Parke-Davis). *chloramphenicol.*

chloroprocaine hydrochloride. **Nesacaine-CE.**

chloroquine phosphate. **Aralen.**

chlorothiazide. †Diuril.

chlorothiazide/methyldopa. **Supres.** †Aldoclor.

chloroxine. †Capitrol.

chloroxylenol/aluminum dihydroxyallantoinate/cellulose. **ZeaSORB.**

chloroxylenol/coal tar/menthol. **Denorex, Denorex Extra Strength.**

chlorphenesin. **Mycil.**

d-chlorpheniramine. see dexchlorpheniramine maleate.

chlorpheniramine/codeine/ephedrine/guaiacol carbonate/phenyltoloxamine. **Omni-Tuss.**

chlorpheniramine maleate. **Chlor-Tripolon.**

chlorpheniramine maleate/acetaminophen/codeine/pseudoephedrine hydrochloride. **Sinutab with Codeine.**

chlorpheniramine maleate/acetaminophen/dextromethorphan hydrobromide/pseudoephedrine hydrochloride. **NeoCitran Extra Strength (Cough, Cold & Flu), Tylenol Cold and Flu, Tylenol Cold Medication Junior Strength DM, Tylenol Cold Medication (Nighttime).**

chlorpheniramine maleate/acetaminophen/phenylephrine hydrochloride. **Dristan, Dristan Extra Strength.**

chlorpheniramine maleate/acetaminophen/pseudoephedrine hydrochloride. **Sinutab, Tylenol Allergy Sinus Medication.**

chlorpheniramine maleate/ASA. **Coricidin Cold.**

chlorpheniramine maleate/ASA/phenylpropanolamine. **Coricidin "D".**

chlorpheniramine maleate/ascorbic acid/prednisone acetate. **Metreton.**

chlorpheniramine maleate/dextromethorphan hydrobromide/guaifenesin/pseudoephedrine hydrochloride. **Triaminic DM Expectorant.**

chlorpheniramine maleate/dextromethorphan hydrobromide/pseudoephedrine hydrochloride. **Triaminic DM Nighttime, Triaminicol DM.**

chlorpheniramine maleate/epinephrine. **Ana-Kit.**

chlorpheniramine maleate/guaifenesin/pseudoephedrine hydrochloride. **Triaminic Expectorant.**

chlorpheniramine maleate/phenylpropanolamine hydrochloride. **Chlor-Tripolon Decongestant Syrup, Contac Cold 12 Hour Relief Extra Strength, Contac Cold 12 Hour Relief Regular Strength, Coricidin "D" Long Acting, Triaminic Cold and Allergy Syrup.**

chlorpheniramine maleate/pseudoephedrine sulfate. **Chlor-Tripolon Decongestant Tablets.**

chlorphthalidone. see chlorthalidone.

Chlorpromanyl (Technilab). *chlorpromazine hydrochloride.*

chlorpromazine hydrochloride. **[Chlorpromazine, General Monograph, CPhA]; Chlorpromanyl, Largactil; (Bioniche).** †Ormazine, †Thorazine, †Thor-Prom.

chlorpropamide. **[Sulfonylureas, General Monograph, CPhA]; Apo-Chlorpropamide, Diabinese.**

chlorprothixene. †Taractan.

chlortalidone. see chlorthalidone.

chlortetracycline hydrochloride. **[Tetracyclines, General Monograph, CPhA]; Aureomycin.**

chlorthalidone. chlorphthalidone. chlortalidone. **Apo-Chlorthalidone, Hygroton.**

chlorthalidone/atenolol. **Tenoretic.**

chlorthalidone/reserpine. †Regroton.

Chlor-Tripolon (Schering). *chlorpheniramine maleate.*

Chlor-Tripolon Decongestant Syrup (Schering). *chlorpheniramine maleate/phenylpropanolamine hydrochloride.*

Chlor-Tripolon Decongestant Tablets (Schering). *chlorpheniramine maleate/pseudoephedrine sulfate.*

Chlor-Tripolon N.D. (Schering). *loratadine/pseudoephedrine sulfate.*

chlorzoxazone. †Paraflex.

chlorzoxazone/acetaminophen. **Acetazone, Parafon Forte, Tylenol Aches and Strains Medication.**

chlorzoxazone/acetaminophen/codeine phosphate. **Acetazone Forte C8, Parafon Forte C8.**

†Cholebrine. *iocetamic acid.*

cholecalciferol. colecalciferol. vitamin D_3. **[Vitamin D, General Monograph, CPhA].**

cholecalciferol/calcium carbonate. **Os-Cal D.**

cholecystokinin. **(Ferring).**

Choledyl (Parke-Davis). *oxtriphylline.*

Choledyl Expectorant (Parke-Davis). *guaifenesin/oxtriphylline.*

Choledyl SA (Parke-Davis). *oxtriphylline.*

cholera vaccine. **(Connaught).**

cholera vaccine live oral. **Mutacol Berna.**

cholestyramine resin. **Alti-Cholestyramine Light, Novo-Cholamine, Novo-Cholamine Light, PMS-Cholestyramine, Questran, Questran Light.**

choline salicylate. **Teejel.**

choline salicylate/magnesium salicylate. **Trilisate.**

choline theophyllinate. see oxtriphylline.

Choloxin (Knoll). *dextrothyroxine sodium.*

Chronovera (Searle). *verapamil hydrochloride.*

†Chymex. *bentiromide.*

Chymodiactin (Knoll). *chymopapain.*

chymopapain. **Chymodiactin.**

†Cibacalcin. *calcitonin (human).*

†Cibalith-S. *lithium citrate.*

Cicatrin (Glaxo Wellcome). *amino acids/bacitracin zinc/neomycin sulfate.*

ciclopirox olamine. **Loprox.**

ciclosporine. see cyclosporine.

Cidomycin (Hoechst Marion Roussel). *gentamicin sulfate.*

cilastatin sodium/imipenem. **Primaxin.**

cilazapril. **[ACE Inhibitors, General Monograph, CPhA]; Inhibace.**

Ciloxan (Alcon). *ciprofloxacin hydrochloride.*

cimetidine. **Apo-Cimetidine, Gen-Cimetidine, Novo-Cimetine, Nu-Cimet, Peptol, PMS-Cimetidine, Tagamet.**

†Cinalone 40. *triamcinolone diacetate.*

cinchocaine. see dibucaine.

†Cinobac. *cinoxacin.*

†Cinonide 40. *triamcinolone acetonide.*

cinoxacin. †Cinobac.

Cipro (Bayer). *ciprofloxacin hydrochloride.*

Cipro I.V. (Bayer). *ciprofloxacin.*

ciprofloxacin. **Cipro I.V., Cipro Oral Suspension.**

ciprofloxacin hydrochloride. **Ciloxan, Cipro.**

Cipro Oral Suspension (Bayer). *ciprofloxacin.*

cis-platinum. see cisplatin.

cisapride monohydrate. **Prepulsid.** †Propulsid.

cisatracurium besylate. **Nimbex.**

cisplatin. cis-platinum. **Platinol-AQ; (Faulding).**

cis-retinoic acid. see isotretinoin.

citalopram. †Celexa.

Citanest 4% Forte (Astra). *epinephrine/prilocaine hydrochloride.*

Citanest 4% Plain (Astra). *prilocaine hydrochloride.*

citric acid/calcium carbonate/calcium lactate-gluconate. **Calcium-Sandoz Forte, Calcium-Sandoz Gramcal, Gramcal.**

citric acid/sodium citrate. **PMS-Dicitrate.**

Citrocarbonate (Roberts). *sodium bicarbonate/sodium citrate.*

Citro-Mag (Rougier). *magnesium citrate.*

Citrotein (Novartis Nutrition). *enteral nutrition.*

citrovorum factor. see calcium folinate.

cladribine. **Leustatin.**

Claforan (Hoechst Marion Roussel). *cefotaxime sodium.*

clarithromycin. **Biaxin.**

Claritin (Schering). *loratadine.*

Claritin Extra (Schering). *loratadine/pseudoephedrine sulfate.*

Clavulin (SmithKline Beecham). *amoxicillin trihydrate/potassium clavulanate.*

clemastine hydrogen fumarate. **Tavist.**

clemastine hydrogen fumarate/phenylpropanolamine hydrochloride. **Tavist-D.**

†Cleocin. *clindamycin hydrochloride.*

†Cleocin Pediatric. *clindamycin palmitate hydrochloride.*

†Cleocin T. *clindamycin phosphate.*

clidinium bromide. †Quarzan.

clidinium bromide/chlordiazepoxide hydrochloride. **Apo-Chlorax, Librax.**

Climacteron (Sabox). *estradiol benzoate/estradiol dienanthate/testosterone enanthate benzilic acid hydrazone.*

Climara (Berlex Canada). *estradiol-17β.*

†Clinda-Derm. *clindamycin phosphate.*

clindamycin hydrochloride. **Dalacin C.** †Cleocin.

Names **underlined** have complete prescribing information in the *CPS* Monograph Section.

clindamycin palmitate hydrochloride. **Dalacin C Flavored Granules.** †Cleocin Pediatric.

clindamycin phosphate. **Dalacin C Phosphate Sterile Solution, Dalacin T Topical Solution, Dalacin Vaginal Cream; (Abbott).** †Cleocin T, †Clinda-Derm.

clioquinol. chloroiodoquine. iodochlorydroxyquine. **Vioform.**

clioquinol/flumethasone pivalate. **Locacorten Vioform, Locacorten Vioform Eardrops.**

clioquinol/hydrocortisone. **Vioform Hydrocortisone.**

clobazam. **[Benzodiazepines, General Monograph, CPhA]; Frisium, Novo-Clobazam.**

clobetasol propionate. see clobetasol 17-propionate.

clobetasol 17-propionate. clobetasol propionate. **[Corticosteroids: Topical, General Monograph, CPhA]; Alti-Clobetasol, Dermasone, Dermovate, Gen-Clobetasol Cream/Ointment, Gen-Clobetasol Scalp Application, Novo-Clobetasol, PMS-Clobetasol.** †Temovate.

clobetasone butyrate. see clobetasone 17-butyrate.

clobetasone 17-butyrate. clobetasone butyrate. **[Corticosteroids: Topical, General Monograph, CPhA]; Eumovate.**

clocortolone pivalate. †Cloderm.

†Cloderm. *clocortolone pivalate.*

clodronate disodium. **Bonefos, Ostac.**

clofazimine. †Lamprene.

clofibrate. **Atromid-S.**

Clomid (Hoechst Marion Roussel). *clomiphene citrate.*

clomifene citrate. see clomiphene citrate.

clomiphene citrate. clomifene citrate. **Clomid, Serophene.** †Milophene.

clomipramine hydrochloride. **Anafranil, Apo-Clomipramine, Gen-Clomipramine, Novo-Clopamine.**

Clonapam (ICN). *clonazepam.*

clonazepam. **[Benzodiazepines, General Monograph, CPhA]; Alti-Clonazepam, Apo-Clonazepam, Clonapam, Gen-Clonazepam,** Novo-Clonazepam, **Nu-Clonazepam, PMS-Clonazepam, Rho-Clonazepam, Rivotril.** †Klonopin.

clonidine hydrochloride. **Apo-Clonidine, Catapres, Dixarit, Novo-Clonidine, Nu-Clonidine.**

clopidogrel bisulfate. **Plavix.**

Clopixol (Lundbeck). *zuclopenthixol dihydrochloride.*

Clopixol-Acuphase (Lundbeck). *zuclopenthixol acetate.*

Clopixol Depot (Lundbeck). *zuclopenthixol decanoate.*

clorazepate dipotassium. **[Benzodiazepines, General Monograph, CPhA]; Apo-Clorazepate, Novo-Clopate, Tranxene.** †Gen-XENE.

Clotrimaderm (Taro). *clotrimazole.*

clotrimazole. **Canesten Topical, Canesten Vaginal, Clotrimaderm, Scheinpharm Clotrimazole.**

clotrimazole/betamethasone dipropionate. **Lotriderm.** †Lotrisone.

cloxacillin sodium. **Apo-Cloxi, Novo-Cloxin, Nu-Cloxi, Tegopen.**

clozapine. **Clozaril.**

Clozaril (Novartis Pharmaceuticals). *clozapine.*

CoActifed (Glaxo Wellcome). *codeine phosphate/pseudoephedrine hydrochloride/triprolidine hydrochloride.*

CoActifed Expectorant (Glaxo Wellcome). *codeine phosphate/guaifenesin/pseudoephedrine hydrochloride/triprolidine hydrochloride.*

coagulant complex anti-inhibitor. **Feiba VH Immuno.**

coal tar. **Balnetar, Estar, Ionil-T Plus, Liquor Carbonis Detergens, Psorigel, Spectro Tar Skin Wash, Zetar.**

coal tar/benzalkonium chloride. **Ionil-T.**

coal tar/chlorhexidine gluconate. **Spectro Tar Antiseptic Shampoo.**

coal tar/chloroxylenol/menthol. **Denorex, Denorex Extra Strength.**

coal tar/juniper tar/pine tar/zinc pyrithione. **Multi-Tar Plus.**

coal tar/menthol/pyrithione disulfide/salicylic acid. **Polytar AF.**

coal tar/menthol/salicylic acid. **X-Tar.**

coal tar/salicylic acid. **Sebcur/T.**

coal tar/salicylic acid/sulfur. **Sebutone.**

cobalamin. see cyanocobalamin.

cobalt gluconate/manganese gluconate. **Oligosol, Manganese-Cobalt.**

cobalt gluconate/nickel gluconate/zinc gluconate. **Oligosol, Zinc-Nickel-Cobalt.**

cocaine hydrochloride. **(BDH).**

Codéine (Trianon). *codeine phosphate.*

codeine/acetaminophen/chlorpheniramine maleate/pseudoephedrine hydrochloride. **Sinutab with Codeine.**

codeine/chlorpheniramine/ephedrine/guaiacol carbonate/phenyltoloxamine. **Omni-Tuss.**

Codeine Contin (Purdue Frederick). *codeine monohydrate/codeine sulfate trihydrate.*

codeine monohydrate/codeine sulfate trihydrate. **Codeine Contin.**

codeine phosphate. methylmorphine phosphate. **[Opioids, General Monograph, CPhA]; Codéine; (Abbott), (Rougier), (Technilab).**

codeine phosphate/acetaminophen. **Empracet -30, -60, Emtec-30, Lenoltec No. 4, Triatec-30, Tylenol Elixir with Codeine, Tylenol NO. 4 with Codeine.**

codeine phosphate/acetaminophen/caffeine. **Extra Strength Acetaminophen with Codeine, Lenoltec No.1, No.2, No.3, Novo-Gesic C8, C15, C30, Regular Strength Acetaminophen with Codeine, Tylenol NO. 1 with Codeine, Tylenol NO. 2 and NO. 3 with Codeine; (Stanley).**

codeine phosphate/acetaminophen/caffeine citrate. **Atasol-8, -15, -30, Triatec-8, -8 Strong.**

codeine phosphate/acetaminophen/chlorzoxazone. **Acetazone Forte C8, Parafon Forte C8.**

codeine phosphate/acetaminophen/doxylamine succinate. **Mersyndol with Codeine.**

codeine phosphate/acetaminophen/methocarbamol. **Methoxacet-C, Robaxacet-8.**

codeine phosphate/ammonium chloride/diphenhydramine hydrochloride. **Calmylin Original with Codeine.**

codeine phosphate/ammonium chloride/guaifenesin. **Cheracol.**

codeine phosphate/ASA/butalbital/caffeine. **Fiorinal-C¼, -C½, Tecnal C¼, C½, Trianal C¼ C½.**

codeine phosphate/ASA/caffeine. **(WestCan).**

codeine phosphate/ASA/caffeine citrate. **222, 292.**

codeine phosphate/ASA/caffeine citrate/meprobamate. **282 MEP.**

codeine phosphate/ASA/methocarbamol. **Methoxisal-C, Robaxisal-C.**

codeine phosphate/ASA/phenobarbital. **Phenaphen with Codeine.**

codeine phosphate/brompheniramine maleate/guaifenesin/phenylephrine hydrochloride/phenylpropanolamine hydrochloride. **Dimetane Expectorant-C.**

codeine phosphate/brompheniramine maleate/phenylephrine hydrochloride/phenylpropanolamine hydrochloride. **Dimetapp-C.**

codeine phosphate/guaifenesin/pheniramine maleate. **Calmylin Ace, Robitussin AC, Robitussin with Codeine.**

codeine phosphate/guaifenesin/pseudoephedrine hydrochloride. **Benylin Codeine, Calmylin with Codeine.**

codeine phosphate/guaifenesin/pseudoephedrine hydrochloride/triprolidine hydrochloride. **CoActifed Expectorant, Cotridin Expectorant.**

codeine phosphate/pheniramine maleate/phenylpropanolamine hydrochloride/pyrilamine maleate. **Tussaminic C.**

codeine phosphate/phenylephrine hydrochloride. **Novahistex C.**

codeine phosphate/potassium guaiacolsulfonate/promethazine hydrochloride. **Phenergan Expectorant with Codeine.**

codeine phosphate/pseudoephedrine hydrochloride/triprolidine hydrochloride. **CoActifed, Cotridin.**

codeine sulfate trihydrate/codeine monohydrate. **Codeine Contin.**

Cogentin (MSD). *benztropine mesylate.*

Colace (Roberts). *docusate sodium.*

colaspase. see L-asparaginase.

colchicine. **[Colchicine, General Monograph, CPhA]; (Abbott), (Odan), (Welcker-Lyster).**

cold storage solution. **Viaspan.**

colecalciferol. see cholecalciferol.

Colestid (Pharmacia & Upjohn). *colestipol hydrochloride.*

colestipol hydrochloride. **Colestid.**

colfosceril palmitate. **Exosurf Neonatal.**

collagenase. **Santyl.**

Colpermin (R & C). *peppermint oil.*

Colprone (Wyeth-Ayerst). *medrogestone.*

Coly-Mycin M (Parke-Davis). *sodium colistimethate.*

Colyte (R & C). *electrolytes/polyethylene glycol.*

Combantrin (Pfizer Consumer). *pyrantel pamoate.*

Combivent Inhalation Aerosol (Boehringer Ingelheim). *ipratropium bromide/salbutamol sulfate.*

Combivent Inhalation Solution (Boehringer Ingelheim). *ipratropium bromide/salbutamol sulfate.*

†Compa-Z. *prochlorperazine edisylate.*

†Compazine. *prochlorperazine.*

Compleat Modified (Novartis Nutrition). *enteral nutrition.*

Complex 15 (Schering). *dimethicone/lecithin.*

Condyline (Canderm Pharma). *podofilox.*

Congest (Trianon). *conjugated estrogens.*

conjugated estrogens. estrogens, conjugated. **C.E.S., Congest, Premarin Intravenous, Premarin Tablets, Premarin Vaginal Cream.**

conjugated estrogens/medroxyprogesterone acetate. †Prempro.

Conray 30 (Mallinckrodt). *iothalamate meglumine.*

Conray 43 (Mallinckrodt). *iothalamate meglumine.*

Conray 60 (Mallinckrodt). *iothalamate meglumine.*

Contac Cold 12 Hour Relief Extra Strength (SmithKline Beecham Consumer Healthcare). *chlorpheniramine maleate/phenylpropanolamine hydrochloride.*

Contac Cold 12 Hour Relief Non Drowsy (SmithKline Beecham Consumer Healthcare). *pseudoephedrine hydrochloride.*

Contac Cold 12 Hour Relief Regular Strength (SmithKline Beecham Consumer Healthcare). *chlorpheniramine maleate/phenylpropanolamine hydrochloride.*

Contac Cough, Cold and Flu Day (SmithKline Beecham Consumer Healthcare). *acetaminophen/dextromethorphan hydrobromide/pseudoephedrine hydrochloride.*

Contac Cough, Cold and Flu Night (SmithKline Beecham Consumer Healthcare). *acetaminophen/diphenhydramine hydrochloride/pseudoephedrine hydrochloride.*

Cophylac (Hoechst Marion Roussel). *hydroxyephedrine hydrochloride/normethadone hydrochloride.*

Cophylac Expectorant (Hoechst Marion Roussel). *emetine hydrochloride/hydroxyephedrine hydrochloride/normethadone hydrochloride.*

copper/calcium carbonate/magnesium/manganese/vitamin D/zinc. **Caltrate Plus.**

copper gluconate. **Oligosol, Copper.**

copper gluconate/gold, colloidal/silver gluconate. **Oligosol, Copper-Gold-Silver.**

copper gluconate/manganese gluconate. **Oligosol, Manganese-Copper.**

Coptin (Axcan Pharma). *sulfadiazine/trimethoprim.*

Cordarone (Wyeth-Ayerst). *amiodarone hydrochloride.*

Cordarone I.V. (Wyeth-Ayerst). *amiodarone hydrochloride.*

†Cordran. *flurandrenolide.*

Coreg (SmithKline Beecham). *carvedilol.*

Corgard (Squibb). *nadolol.*

Coricidin Cold (Schering). *ASA/chlorpheniramine maleate.*

Coricidin "D" (Schering). *ASA/chlorpheniramine maleate/phenylpropanolamine.*

Coricidin "D" Long Acting (Schering). *chlorpheniramine maleate/phenylpropanolamine hydrochloride.*

Coricidin Non-Drowsy (Schering). *ASA/phenylpropanolamine hydrochloride.*

Coristex-DH (Technilab). *hydrocodone bitartrate/phenylephrine hydrochloride.*

Coristine-DH (Technilab). *hydrocodone bitartrate/phenylephrine hydrochloride.*

†Corlopam. *fenoldopam mesylate.*

Cortamed (Sabex). *hydrocortisone acetate.*

Cortate (Schering). *hydrocortisone.*

†Cort-Dome. *hydrocortisone.*

Cortef (Pharmacia & Upjohn). *hydrocortisone.*

Cortenema (Axcan Pharma). *hydrocortisone.*

†Corticaine. *hydrocortisone acetate.*

corticosteroids: eye, ear, nose. **(General Monograph, CPhA).**

corticosteroids: inhaled. **(General Monograph, CPhA).**

corticosteroids: systemic. **(General Monograph, CPhA).**

corticosteroids: topical. **(General Monograph, CPhA).**

Cortifoam (R & C). *hydrocortisone acetate.*

Cortimyxin (Sabex). *hydrocortisone/neomycin sulfate/polymyxin B sulfate.*

cortisol. see hydrocortisone.

cortisone acetate. **[Corticosteroids: Systemic, General Monograph, CPhA]; Cortisone Acetate-ICN, Cortone Suspension, Cortone Tablets.**

Cortisone Acetate-ICN (ICN). *cortisone acetate.*

Cortisporin Eye/Ear Suspension (Glaxo Wellcome). *hydrocortisone/neomycin sulfate/polymyxin B sulfate.*

Cortisporin Ointment (Glaxo Wellcome). *bacitracin zinc/hydrocortisone/neomycin sulfate/polymyxin B sulfate.*

Cortisporin Ophthalmic Ointment (Glaxo Wellcome). *bacitracin zinc/hydrocortisone/neomycin sulfate/polymyxin B sulfate.*

Cortisporin Otic Solution (Glaxo Wellcome). *hydrocortisone/neomycin sulfate/polymyxin B sulfate.*

Names **underlined** have complete prescribing information in the *CPS* Monograph Section.

Cortoderm (Taro). *hydrocortisone.*

Cortone Suspension (MSD). *cortisone acetate.*

Cortone Tablets (MSD). *cortisone acetate.*

†Cortril. *hydrocortisone.*

Cortrosyn (Organon). *cosyntropin.*

Cosmegen (MSD). *dactinomycin.*

cosyntropin. **Cortrosyn.**

cosyntropin/zinc hydroxide. **Synacthen Depot.**

Cotazym (Organon). *pancrelipase.*

†Cotranzine. *prochlorperazine edisylate.*

Cotridin (Technilab). *codeine phosphate/pseudoephedrine hydrochloride/triprolidine hydrochloride.*

Cotridin Expectorant (Technilab). *codeine phosphate/guaifenesin/pseudoephedrine hydrochloride/triprolidine hydrochloride.*

Coumadin (DuPont Pharma). *warfarin sodium.*

Coversyl (Servier). *perindopril erbumine.*

Cozaar (MSD). *losartan potassium.*

Creon 10 (Solvay Pharma). *pancrelipase.*

Creon 25 (Solvay Pharma). *pancrelipase.*

Creo-Rectal (Nadeau). *camphor/diphenylpyraline hydrochloride/guaiacol carbonate.*

Crixivan (MSD). *indinavir sulfate.*

Cromolyn Nasal Solution (Pharmascience). *sodium cromoglycate.*

Cromolyn Ophthalmic Solution (Pharmascience). *sodium cromoglycate.*

cromolyn sodium. see sodium cromoglycate.

crotalid serum (snake antivenom). **Antivenin.**

crotamiton. **Eurax.**

Crystapen (Buffered) (Bioniche). *penicillin G sodium.*

†Crysticillin 300 AS. *penicillin G procaine.*

†Crystodigin. *digitoxin.*

Cuplex (TCD). *lactic acid/salicylic acid.*

cupric oxide/multiple vitamins/zinc oxide. **Stresstabs with Zinc.**

Cuprimine (MSD). *penicillamine.*

cyanocobalamin. cobalamin. vitamin B_{12}. **[Vitamin B_{12}, General Monograph, CPhA]; Rubramin, Scheinpharm B12; (Abbott), (Taro).**

cyanocobalamin/adrenal cortical extract/orchitic extract. **Heracline.**

cyanocobalamin/minerals. **Oligofer.**

Cyclen (Janssen-Ortho). *ethinyl estradiol/norgestimate.*

cyclizine hydrochloride/caffeine hydrate/ergotamine tartrate. **Megral.**

cyclobenzaprine hydrochloride. **Alti-Cyclobenzaprine, Apo-Cyclobenzaprine, Flexeril, Flexitec, Gen-Cycloprine, Novo-Cycloprine, Nu-Cyclobenzaprine.** †Cycoflex.

Cyclocort (Stiefel). *amcinonide.*

Cyclogyl (Alcon). *cyclopentolate hydrochloride.*

Cyclomen (Sanofi). *danazol.*

cyclomethicone/petrolatum. **Prevex Cream.**

cyclopentolate hydrochloride. **[Cyclopentolate HCl, General Monograph, CPhA]; Cyclogyl, Diopentolate, Minims Cyclopentolate.**

cyclophosphamide. **Cytoxan, Procytox.** †Neosar.

cyclosporine. ciclosporine. **Neoral, Sandimmune I.V.**

cyclothiazide. †Anhydron.

†Cycoflex. *cyclobenzaprine hydrochloride.*

†Cycrin. *medroxyprogesterone acetate.*

Cyklokapron (Pharmacia & Upjohn). *tranexamic acid.*

Cylert (Abbott). *pemoline.*

cyproheptadine hydrochloride. **Periactin.**

cyproterone acetate. **Alti-CPA, Androcur, Androcur Depot, Novo-Cyproterone.**

cyproterone acetate/ethinyl estradiol. **Diane-35.**

Cystistat (Bioniche). *sodium hyaluronate.*

Cysto-Conray (Mallinckrodt). *iothalamate meglumine.*

Cysto-Conray II (Mallinckrodt). *iothalamate meglumine.*

†Cystospaz. *hyoscyamine.*

Cytadren (Novartis Pharmaceuticals). *aminoglutethimide.*

cytarabine. cytosine arabinoside. **Cytosar; (Faulding), (Novopharm).**

Cytosar (Pharmacia & Upjohn). *cytarabine.*

cytosine arabinoside. see cytarabine.

Cytotec (Searle). *misoprostol.*

Cytovene Capsules (Roche). *ganciclovir.*

Cytovene Injection (Roche). *ganciclovir sodium.*

Cytoxan (Bristol). *cyclophosphamide.*

D

dacarbazine. **DTIC.**

dactinomycin. **Cosmegen.**

Dagenan (Rhône-Poulenc Rorer). *sulfapyridine.*

Dairyaid (Tanta). *lactase.*

Dalacin C (Pharmacia & Upjohn). *clindamycin hydrochloride.*

Dalacin C Flavored Granules (Pharmacia & Upjohn). *clindamycin palmitate hydrochloride.*

Dalacin C Phosphate Sterile Solution (Pharmacia & Upjohn). *clindamycin phosphate.*

Dalacin T Topical Solution (Pharmacia & Upjohn). *clindamycin phosphate.*

Dalacin Vaginal Cream (Pharmacia & Upjohn). *clindamycin phosphate.*

†Dalgan. *dezocine.*

Dalmacol (Riva). *doxylamine succinate/etafedrine hydrochloride/hydrocodone bitartrate/sodium citrate.*

Dalmane (Roche). *flurazepam hydrochloride.*

dalteparin sodium. **[Heparins: Low Molecular Weight, General Monograph, CPhA]; Fragmin.**

danaparoid sodium. **Orgaran.**

danazol. **Cyclomen.** †Danocrine.

Dan-Gard (Stiefel). *zinc pyrithione.*

†Danocrine. *danazol.*

Dan-Tar Plus (Stiefel). *polytar/pyrithione disulfide.*

Dantrium Capsules (Procter & Gamble Pharmaceuticals). *dantrolene sodium.*

Dantrium Intravenous (Procter & Gamble Pharmaceuticals). *dantrolene sodium.*

dantrolene sodium. **Dantrium Capsules, Dantrium Intravenous.**

dapsone. DDS. diaphenylsulfone. **Avlosulfon.**

†Daranide. *dichlorphenamide.*

Daraprim (Glaxo Wellcome). *pyrimethamine.*

†Darvocet-N 100. *acetaminophen/propoxyphene napsylate.*

Darvon-N (Lilly). *propoxyphene napsylate.*

daunomycin. see daunorubicin.

daunorubicin. daunomycin. **Cerubidine.**

daunorubicin hydrochloride. **(Novopharm).**

DaunoXome (NeXstar). *liposomal daunorubicin.*

Daypro (Searle). *oxaprozin.*

†Dazamide. *acetazolamide.*

DDAVP Injection (Ferring). *desmopressin acetate.*
DDAVP Spray and Rhinyle Nasal Solutions (Ferring). *desmopressin acetate.*
DDAVP Tablets (Ferring). *desmopressin acetate.*
ddC. see zalcitabine.
o,p'DDD. see mitotane.
ddI. see didanosine.
DDS. see dapsone.
Decadron Phosphate Injection (MSD). *dexamethasone sodium phosphate.*
Decadron Tablets (MSD). *dexamethasone.*
Deca-Durabolin (Organon). *nandrolone decanoate.*
Declomycin (Wyeth-Ayerst). *demeclocycline hydrochloride.*
Decongest (Technilab). *xylometazoline hydrochloride.*
deferoxamine mesylate. desferrioxamine. **Desferal.**
Dehydral (TCD). *methenamine.*
dehydrocholic acid. ketocholanic acid. **Dycholium.**
†Delatest. *testosterone enanthate.*
Delatestryl (Squibb). *testosterone enanthate.*
delaviridine mesylate. Drescriptor.
Delestrogen (Squibb). *estradiol valerate.*
Delsym (Novartis Consumer Health). *dextromethorphan hydrobromide.*
†Delta-Cortef. *prednisolone.*
deltacortisone. see prednisone.
deltahydrocortisone. see prednisolone acetate.
Deltasone (Pharmacia & Upjohn). *prednisone.*
delta-9-tetrahydrocannabinol. see dronabinol.
Demadex (Roche). *torsemide.*
demecarium bromide. †Humorsol.
demeclocycline hydrochloride. **[Tetracyclines, General Monograph, CPhA]; Declomycin.**
Demerol (Sanofi). *pethidine hydrochloride.*
†Demser. *metyrosine.*
Demulen (Searle). *ethinyl estradiol/ethynodiol diacetate.*
Denorex (Whitehall-Robins). *chloroxylenol/coal tar/menthol.*
Denorex Extra Strength (Whitehall-Robins). *chloroxylenol/coal tar/menthol.*
denture adhesive. **Orahesive.**
Depakene (Abbott). *valproic acid.*
†Depakote. *divalproex sodium.*
Depen (Carter Horner). *penicillamine.*
†depGynogen. *estradiol cypionate.*
†depMedalone. *methylprednisolone acetate.*
†Depogen. *estradiol cypionate.*
Depo-Medrol (Pharmacia & Upjohn). *methylprednisolone acetate.*
Depo-Medrol with Lidocaine (Pharmacia & Upjohn). *lidocaine hydrochloride/methylprednisolone acetate.*
†Depopred. *methylprednisolone acetate.*
Depo-Provera (Pharmacia & Upjohn). *medroxyprogesterone acetate.*
†Depotest. *testosterone cypionate.*
Depo-Testosterone Cypionate (Pharmacia & Upjohn). *testosterone cypionate.*
l-deprenyl hydrochloride. see selegiline hydrochloride.
Deproic (Technilab). *valproic acid.*
Dequadin (Roberts). *dequalinium chloride.*
dequalinium chloride. **Dequadin.**
†Dermacort. *hydrocortisone.*
†Dermarest DriCort. *hydrocortisone acetate.*
Dermasone (Technilab). *clobetasol 17-propionate.*
dermatological base. **Glaxal Base, Schering Base.**
Dermazin (Pharmascience). *silver sulfadiazine.*
Dermovate (Glaxo Wellcome). *clobetasol 17-propionate.*
†Dermtex HC. *hydrocortisone.*
DES. see diethylstilbestrol sodium diphosphate.
Desenex (Novartis Consumer Health). *undecylenic acid/zinc undecylenate.*
deserpidine. †Harmonyl.
deserpidine/hydrochlorothiazide. †Oreticyl.
Desferal (Novartis Pharmaceuticals). *deferoxamine mesylate.*
desferrioxamine. see deferoxamine mesylate.
desflurane. **Suprane.**
desipramine hydrochloride. **Alti-Desipramine, Apo-Desipramine, Norpramin, Novo-Desipramine, Nu-Desipramine, PMS-Desipramine.**
deslorelin. †Somagard
desmopressin acetate. **DDAVP Injection, DDAVP Spray and Rhinyle Nasal Solutions, DDAVP Tablets, Octostim.**
Desocort (Galderma). *desonide.*
†Desogen. *desogestrel/ethinyl estradiol.*
desogestrel/ethinyl estradiol. **Marvelon, Ortho-Cept.** †Desogen.
desonide. **[Corticosteroids: Topical, General Monograph, CPhA]; Desocort, Scheinpharm Desonide, Tridesilon.** †DesOwen.
†DesOwen. *desonide.*
desoximetasone. **[Corticosteroids: Topical, General Monograph, CPhA]; Topicort.**
desoxyephedrine. see methamphetamine hydrochloride.
†Desoxyn. *methamphetamine hydrochloride.*
Desquam-X (Westwood-Squibb). *benzoyl peroxide.*
Desyrel (Bristol). *trazodone hydrochloride.*
Desyrel Dividose (Bristol). *trazodone hydrochloride.*
†Dexair. *dexamethasone sodium phosphate.*
dexamethasone. **[Corticosteroids: Eye Ear Nose, Corticosteroids: Systemic, General Monographs, CPhA]; Decadron Tablets, Dexasone, Maxidex.** †Dexone, †Hexadrol, †Mymethasone.
dexamethasone acetate. **[Corticosteroids: Eye Ear Nose, Corticosteroids: Systemic, General Monographs, CPhA];** †Solurex-LA.
dexamethasone disodium phosphate. see dexamethasone sodium phosphate.
dexamethasone/framycetin sulfate/gramicidin. **Sofracort.**
dexamethasone/neomycin sulfate/polymyxin B sulfate. **Dioptrol, Maxitrol.**
dexamethasone phosphate disodium. see dexamethasone sodium phosphate.
dexamethasone sodium phosphate. dexamethasone disodium phosphate. dexamethasone phosphate disodium. **[Corticosteroids: Eye Ear Nose, Corticosteroids: Systemic, General Monographs, CPhA]; Decadron Phosphate Injection, Diodex, Hexadrol Phosphate; (Rivex Ophthalmics).** †Dexair, †Dexotic, †Storz-Dexa.
dexamethasone/tobramycin. **Tobradex.**

Names **underlined** have complete prescribing information in the *CPS* Monograph Section.

dexamphetamine sulfate. d-amphetamine. dextroamphetamine. **Dexedrine.**

Dexasone (ICN). *dexamethasone.*

dexbrompheniramine maleate/pseudoephedrine sulfate. **Drixoral, Drixoral Night, Drixtab.**

dexchlorpheniramine maleate. d-chlorpheniramine. **Polaramine.**

Dexedrine (SmithKline Beecham). *dexamphetamine sulfate.*

dexfenfluramine. †Redux.

Dexiron (Genpharm). *iron dextran.*

†Dexone. *dexamethasone.*

†Dexotic. *dexamethasone sodium phosphate.*

dexrazoxane. **Zinecard.**

dextran 40. **Gentran 40, Rheomacrodex.**

dextran 70. **Gentran 70.**

dextran 70/dextrose. **Hyskon.**

dextran 70/hydroxypropyl methylcellulose. **Bion Tears, Tears Naturale, Tears Naturale Free, Tears Naturale II.**

dextran 70/polyethylene glycol. **Aquasite.**

dextroamphetamine. see dexamphetamine sulfate.

dextromethorphan hydrobromide. **Balminil DM, Balminil DM Children, Benylin DM, Benylin DM 12 Hour, Benylin DM for Children, Benylin DM for Children, Benylin DM for Children 12 Hour, Broncho-Grippol-DM, Calmylin #1, Delsym, Koffex DM, Novahistex DM, Novahistine DM, Robitussin Pediatric, Triaminic DM Long Lasting For Children.**

dextromethorphan hydrobromide/acetaminophen. **Tylenol Cough Caplets/Liquid Suspension.**

dextromethorphan hydrobromide/acetaminophen/chlorpheniramine maleate/pseudoephedrine hydrochloride. **NeoCitran Extra Strength (Cough, Cold & Flu), Tylenol Cold and Flu, Tylenol Cold Medication Junior Strength DM, Tylenol Cold Medication (Nighttime).**

dextromethorphan hydrobromide/acetaminophen/guaifenesin/pseudoephedrine hydrochloride. **Benylin 4 Flu, Calmylin Cough and Flu, Robitussin Cough, Cold & Flu Liqui-Gels, Sudafed Cold & Flu.**

dextromethorphan hydrobromide/acetaminophen/pseudoephedrine hydrochloride. **Contac Cough, Cold and Flu Day, NeoCitran Extra Strength Daycaps, Sudafed Cold & Cough, Triaminic Cold & Fever, Tylenol Cold Medication (Daytime), Tylenol Cough Liquid Suspension with Decongestant.**

dextromethorphan hydrobromide/ammonium chloride/diphenhydramine hydrochloride. **Calmylin #4.**

dextromethorphan hydrobromide/brompheniramine maleate/phenylephrine hydrochloride/phenylpropanolamine hydrochloride. **Dimetapp-DM.**

dextromethorphan hydrobromide/brompheniramine maleate/phenylpropanolamine hydrochloride. **Dimetapp Cough & Cold Liqui-Gels.**

dextromethorphan hydrobromide/chlorpheniramine maleate/guaifenesin/pseudoephedrine hydrochloride. **Triaminic DM Expectorant.**

dextromethorphan hydrobromide/chlorpheniramine maleate/pseudoephedrine hydrochloride. **Triaminic DM Nighttime, Triaminicol DM.**

dextromethorphan hydrobromide/guaifenesin. **Balminil DM + Expectorant, Benylin DM-E, Robitussin DM.**

dextromethorphan hydrobromide/guaifenesin/phenylpropanolamine hydrochloride. **Triaminic DM Daytime.**

dextromethorphan hydrobromide/guaifenesin/pseudoephedrine hydrochloride. **Balminil DM + Decongestant + Expectorant, Benylin DM-D-E, Calmylin #3, Novahistex DM Decongestant Expectorant, Novahistine DM Decongestant Expectorant, Robitussin Cough & Cold, Robitussin Cough & Cold Liqui-Gels.**

dextromethorphan hydrobromide/pheniramine maleate/phenylephrine hydrochloride. **NeoCitran DM.**

dextromethorphan hydrobromide/pseudoephedrine hydrochloride. **Balminil DM + Decongestant, Benylin DM-D (Adult), Benylin DM-D For Children, Calmylin #2, Calmylin Pediatric, Novahistex DM Decongestant, Novahistine DM Decongestant, Robitussin Pediatric Cough and Cold.**

dextrose. **Glucodex; (Bioniche).**

dextrose/amino acids. **Travasol without Electrolytes.**

dextrose/amino acids/electrolytes. **Travasol with Electrolytes.**

dextrose/dextran 70. **Hyskon.**

dextrose/dopamine hydrochloride. **(Abbott), (Baxter).**

dextrose/electrolytes. **Enfalac Lytren, Gastrolyte, Pedialyte, Pedialyte Freezer Pops.**

dextrose/heparin sodium. **(Abbott), (Baxter).**

dextrose/lidocaine hydrochloride. **(Baxter).**

dextrose monohydrate/bretylium tosylate. **(Abbott).**

dextrose/nitroglycerin. **(Baxter).**

dextrothyroxine sodium. d-thyroxine sodium. **Choloxin.**

dezocine. †Dalgan.

d4T. see stavudine.

†D.H.E. 45. *dihydroergotamine mesylate.*

DHT. see dihydrotachysterol.

Diaβeta (Hoechst Marion Roussel). *glyburide.*

Diabinese (Pfizer). *chlorpropamide.*

Diamicron (Servier). *gliclazide.*

diamorphine hydrochloride. **[Opioids, General Monograph, CPhA].**

Diamox (Wyeth-Ayerst). *acetazolamide.*

Diane-35 (Berlex Canada). *cyproterone acetate/ethinyl estradiol.*

diaphenylsulfone. see dapsone.

†Diapid. *lypressin.*

diatrizoate meglumine/diatrizoate sodium. **Hypaque Parenteral, MD-76.**

diatrizoate sodium/diatrizoate meglumine. **Hypaque Parenteral, MD-76.**

Dia-Vite (R&D Laboratories). *multiple vitamins.*

Diazemuls (Pharmacia & Upjohn). *diazepam.*

diazepam. **[Benzodiazepines, General Monograph, CPhA]; Apo-Diazepam, Diazemuls, Valium Roche Injection, Valium Roche Oral, Vivol.** †Valrelease, †Zetran.

diazoxide. **Hyperstat, Proglycem.**

Diban (Wyeth-Ayerst). *atropine sulfate/attapulgite, activated/hyoscyamine sulfate/opium/pectin/scopolamine hydrobromide.*

†Dibenzyline. *phenoxybenzamine hydrochloride.*

dibucaine. cinchocaine. **Nupercainal Ointment.**

dibucaine/domiphen bromide. **Nupercainal Cream.**

dibucaine hydrochloride/esculin/framycetin sulfate/hydrocortisone. **Proctosedyl.**

dibucaine hydrochloride/esculin/framycetin sulfate/hydrocortisone acetate. **Proctosone.**

Dicetel (Solvay Pharma). *pinaverium bromide.*

dichloralphenazone/acetaminophen/isometheptene mucate. †Miltride.

dichloroacetic acid. **Bichloracetic Acid.**

dichlorphenamide. †Daranide.

dichysterol. see dihydrotachysterol.

Diclectin (Duchesnay). *doxylamine succinate/pyridoxine hydrochloride.*

diclofenac potassium. **Voltaren Rapide.** †Cataflam.

diclofenac sodium. **Apo-Diclo, Apo-Diclo SR, Diclotec, Novo-Difenac, Novo-Difenac SR, Nu-Diclo, Nu-Diclo-SR, PMS-Diclofenac,** Vifenal, **Voltaren, Voltaren Ophtha.**

diclofenac sodium/misoprostol. **Arthrotec.**

Diclotec (Technilab). *diclofenac sodium.*

dicloxacillin sodium. †Dynapen.

dicyclomine hydrochloride. dicycloverine hydrochloride. **Bentylol, Formulex, Lomine.**

dicycloverine hydrochloride. see dicyclomine hydrochloride.

didanosine. ddI. **Videx.**

†Didrex. *benzphetamine hydrochloride.*

Didrocal (Procter & Gamble Pharmaceuticals). *calcium carbonate/ etidronate disodium.*

Didronel (Procter & Gamble Pharmaceuticals). *etidronate disodium.*

dienestrol. dienoestrol. **Ortho Dienestrol.**

dienoestrol. see dienestrol.

diethylpropion hydrochloride. amfepramone. **Tenuate.**

diethylstilbestrol. see diethylstilbestrol sodium diphosphate.

diethylstilbestrol sodium diphosphate. DES. diethylstilbestrol. stilboestrol. **Honvol; (Roberts).** †Stilphostrol.

Differin (Galderma). *adapalene.*

diflorasone diacetate. †Maxiflor.

Diflucan (Pfizer). *fluconazole.*

Diflucan-150 (Pfizer). *fluconazole.*

diflucortolone valerate. **[Corticosteroids: Topical, General Monograph, CPhA]; Nerisone.**

diflucortolone valerate/salicylic acid. **Nerisalic.**

diflunisal. **Apo-Diflunisal, Dolobid, Novo-Diflunisal, Nu-Diflunisal.**

difluorophate. see isoflurophate.

Digibind (Glaxo Wellcome). *digoxin immune Fab (ovine).*

digitoxin. †Crystodigin.

digoxin. **Lanoxin.** †Lanoxicaps.

digoxin immune Fab (ovine). digoxin-specific antibody fragments. **Digibind.**

digoxin-specific antibody fragments. see digoxin immune Fab (ovine).

dihydrochlorothiazide. see hydrochlorothiazide.

dihydrocodeinone bitartrate. see hydrocodone bitartrate.

Dihydroergotamine (DHE) (Novartis Pharmaceuticals). *dihydroergotamine mesylate.*

dihydroergotamine mesylate. **Dihydroergotamine (DHE), Migranal.** †D.H.E. 45.

dihydrohydroxycodeinone. see oxycodone hydrochloride.

dihydromorphinone hydrochloride. see hydromorphone hydrochloride.

dihydrotachysterol. DHT. dichysterol. vitamin D. **[Vitamin D, General Monograph, CPhA]; Hytakerol.**

dihydroxyanthranol. see anthralin.

1,25-dihydroxycholecalciferol. see calcitriol.

1,25-dihydroxyvitamin D_3. see calcitriol.

diiodohydroxyquin. see iodoquinol.

diiodohydroxyquinolone. see iodoquinol.

Dilantin (Parke-Davis). *phenytoin sodium.*

Dilantin-125 (Parke-Davis). *phenytoin (acid form).*

Dilantin Infatabs (Parke-Davis). *phenytoin (acid form).*

Dilantin-30 Pediatric (Parke-Davis). *phenytoin (acid form).*

Dilaudid (Knoll). *hydromorphone hydrochloride.*

Dilaudid-HP (Knoll). *hydromorphone hydrochloride.*

Dilaudid-HP-Plus (Knoll). *hydromorphone hydrochloride.*

Dilaudid Sterile Powder (Knoll). *hydromorphone hydrochloride.*

Dilaudid-XP (Knoll). *hydromorphone hydrochloride.*

dill oil/anise oil/fennel oil/sodium bicarbonate. **Baby's Own Gripe Water.**

†Dilor. *dyphylline.*

diltiazem hydrochloride. **Alti-Diltiazem, Alti-Diltiazem CD, Apo-Diltiaz, Apo-Diltiaz CD, Apo-Diltiaz SR, Cardizem, Cardizem CD, Cardizem Injectable, Cardizem SR, Gen-Diltiazem, Gen-Diltiazem SR, Novo-Diltazem, Novo-Diltazem SR, Nu-Diltiaz, Tiazac; (Novopharm).**

Dilusol (Dermtek). *ethyl alcohol.*

dimecamine hydrochloride. see mecamylamine hydrochloride.

dimenhydrinate. **Apo-Dimenhydrinate, Gravol, Traveltabs, Travel Tabs; (Astra), (Bioniche).**

dimenhydrinate/caffeine/ergotamine tartrate. **Gravergol.**

dimercaptosuccinic acid. see succimer.

Dimetane (Whitehall-Robins). *brompheniramine maleate.*

Dimetane Expectorant (Whitehall-Robins). *brompheniramine maleate/guaifenesin/phenylephrine hydrochloride/ phenylpropanolamine hydrochloride.*

Dimetane Expectorant-C (Whitehall-Robins). *brompheniramine maleate/codeine phosphate/guaifenesin/phenylephrine hydrochloride/phenylpropanolamine hydrochloride.*

Dimetane Expectorant-DC (Whitehall-Robins). *brompheniramine maleate/guaifenesin/hydrocodone bitartrate/phenylephrine hydrochloride/phenylpropanolamine hydrochloride.*

Dimetapp (Whitehall-Robins). *brompheniramine maleate/ phenylephrine hydrochloride/phenylpropanolamine hydrochloride.*

Dimetapp-A Sinus (Whitehall-Robins). *acetaminophen/ phenylephrine hydrochloride/phenylpropanolamine hydrochloride.*

Dimetapp-C (Whitehall-Robins). *brompheniramine maleate/codeine phosphate/phenylephrine hydrochloride/phenylpropanolamine hydrochloride.*

Dimetapp Chewables (Whitehall-Robins). *brompheniramine maleate/phenylpropanolamine hydrochloride.*

Dimetapp Clear (Whitehall-Robins). *brompheniramine maleate/ phenylpropanolamine hydrochloride.*

Dimetapp Cough & Cold Liqui-Gels (Whitehall-Robins). *brompheniramine maleate/dextromethorphan hydrobromide/ phenylpropanolamine hydrochloride.*

Dimetapp-DM (Whitehall-Robins). *brompheniramine maleate/ dextromethorphan hydrobromide/phenylephrine hydrochloride/ phenylpropanolamine hydrochloride.*

Dimetapp Liqui-Gels (Whitehall-Robins). *brompheniramine maleate/phenylpropanolamine hydrochloride.*

Dimetapp Oral Infant Drops (Whitehall-Robins). *brompheniramine maleate/phenylephrine hydrochloride/phenylpropanolamine hydrochloride.*

Dimetapp Quick Dissolve (Whitehall-Robins). *brompheniramine maleate/phenylpropanolamine hydrochloride.*

Names underlined have complete prescribing information in the *CPS* Monograph Section.

dimethicone. dimethylpolysiloxane. **Barriere.**
dimethicone/homosalate/menthol/octyl methoxycinnamate/oxybenzone. **Zilactin-Lip.**
dimethicone/lecithin. **Complex 15.**
dimethicone/perfluoropolymethylisopropyl ether/tricontanyl PVP. **Spectro Gluvs "19".**
dimethicone/petrolatum. **Moisturel.**
dimethylpolysiloxane. see dimethicone.
dimethyl sulfoxide. DMSO. methylsulfoxide. **Kemsol, Rimso-50.**
dinoprostone. prostaglandin E_2. **Cervidil, Prepidil, Prostin E_2, Prostin E_2 Vaginal Gel.**
Diocaine (Dioptic). *proparacaine hydrochloride.*
Diocarpine (Dioptic). *pilocarpine hydrochloride.*
Diochloram (Dioptic). *chloramphenicol.*
dioctyl calcium sulfosuccinate. see docusate calcium.
dioctyl sodium sulfosuccinate. see docusate sodium.
Diodex (Dioptic). *dexamethasone sodium phosphate.*
Diodoquin (Glenwood). *iodoquinol.*
Diofluor Injection (Dioptic). *fluorescein sodium.*
Diofluor Strips (Dioptic). *fluorescein sodium.*
Diogent Ointment (Dioptic). *gentamicin sulfate.*
Diogent Solution (Dioptic). *gentamicin sulfate.*
Diomycin (Dioptic). *erythromycin.*
Dionephrine (Dioptic). *phenylephrine hydrochloride.*
Diopentolate (Dioptic). *cyclopentolate hydrochloride.*
Diophenyl-T (Dioptic). *phenylephrine hydrochloride/tropicamide.*
Diopred (Dioptic). *prednisolone acetate.*
Dioptimyd (Dioptic). *prednisolone acetate/sulfacetamide sodium.*
Dioptrol (Dioptic). *dexamethasone/neomycin sulfate/polymyxin B sulfate.*
Diosulf (Dioptic). *sulfacetamide sodium.*
Diotrope (Dioptic). *tropicamide.*
Diovan (Novartis Pharmaceuticals). *valsartan.*
Diovol (Carter Horner). *aluminum hydroxide/magnesium hydroxide.*
Diovol Ex (Carter Horner). *aluminum hydroxide/magnesium hydroxide.*
Diovol Plus (Carter Horner). *aluminum hydroxide/magnesium hydroxide/simethicone.*
Diovol Plus AF (Carter Horner). *calcium carbonate/magnesium hydroxide/simethicone.*
Dipentum (Pharmacia & Upjohn). *olsalazine sodium.*
diphenhydramine. **Benadryl Cream.**
diphenhydramine/acetaminophen/pseudoephedrine hydrochloride. **Sinutab Nightime.**
diphenhydramine hydrochloride. **Allerdryl, Allernix, Benadryl, Nytol, Nytol Extra Strength, PMS-Diphenhydramine, Scheinpharm Diphenhydramine.**
diphenhydramine hydrochloride/acetaminophen/pseudoephedrine hydrochloride. **Benadryl Allergy/Sinus/Headache, Contac Cough, Cold and Flu Night, Tylenol Flu Medication.**
diphenhydramine hydrochloride/ammonium chloride/codeine phosphate. **Calmylin Original with Codeine.**
diphenhydramine hydrochloride/ammonium chloride/dextromethorphan hydrobromide. **Calmylin #4.**
diphenhydramine hydrochloride/caffeine citrate/ergotamine tartrate. **Ergodryl.**
diphenhydramine hydrochloride/calamine. **Caladryl.**
diphenidol hydrochloride. †Vontrol.
diphenoxylate hydrochloride/atropine sulfate. **Lomotil.**
†Diphenylan. *phenytoin sodium.*
diphenylhydantoin. see phenytoin.
diphenylpyraline hydrochloride/camphor/guaiacol carbonate. **Creo-Rectal.**
diphtheria antitoxin. **(Connaught).**
diphtheria toxoid. **(Connaught).**
diphtheria toxoid adsorbed/haemophilus b conjugate vaccine (tetanus protein conjugate)/pertussis vaccine (acellular)/poliomyelitis vaccine, inactivated/tetanus toxoid adsorbed. **Pentacel.**
diphtheria toxoid adsorbed/pertussis vaccine (acellular)/poliomyelitis vaccine, inactivated/tetanus toxoid adsorbed. **Quadracel.**
diphtheria toxoid adsorbed/pertussis vaccine adsorbed/poliomyelitis vaccine adsorbed, inactivated/tetanus toxoid adsorbed. **(Connaught).**
diphtheria toxoid adsorbed/pertussis vaccine (cellular)/tetanus toxoid adsorbed. **(Connaught).**
diphtheria toxoid adsorbed/poliomyelitis vaccine adsorbed, inactivated/tetanus toxoid adsorbed. **(Connaught).**
diphtheria toxoid adsorbed/tetanus toxoid adsorbed. **(BioChem Vaccines), (Connaught).**
dipivefrin hydrochloride. **DPE, Ophtho-Dipivefrin, Propine.**
dipivefrin hydrochloride/levobunolol hydrochloride. **Probeta.**
Diprivan (Zeneca). *propofol.*
Diprogen (Schering). *betamethasone dipropionate/gentamicin sulfate.*
Diprolene Glycol (Schering). *betamethasone dipropionate.*
diprophylline. see dyphylline.
Diprosalic (Schering). *betamethasone dipropionate/salicylic acid.*
Diprosone (Schering). *betamethasone dipropionate.*
dipyridamole. **Apo-Dipyridamole FC, Novo-Dipiradol, Persantine.**
dipyridamole/ASA. **Asasantine.**
Disalcid (3M Pharmaceuticals). *salsalate.*
Disipal (3M Pharmaceuticals). *orphenadrine hydrochloride.*
disopyramide. **Rythmodan.**
disopyramide phosphate. **Rythmodan-LA.**
disposable needles. **NovoFine 28G, NovoFine 30G.**
disulfiram. **Antabuse.**
dithranol. see anthralin.
Ditropan (Alza). *oxybutynin chloride.*
†Diucardin. *hydroflumethiazide.*
†Diulo. *metolazone.*
†Diuril. *chlorothiazide.*
divalproex sodium. **Epival.** †Depakote.
Dixarit (Boehringer Ingelheim). *clonidine hydrochloride.*
DMSA. see succimer.
DMSO. see dimethyl sulfoxide.
Doak-Oil (TCD). *isopropyl palmitate/mineral oil/tar distillate.*
Doak-Oil Forte (TCD). *isopropyl palmitate/mineral oil/tar distillate.*
Doan's Backache Pills (Novartis Consumer Health). *magnesium salicylate.*
dobutamine hydrochloride. **Dobutrex, Scheinpharm Dobutamine; (Abbott), (Novopharm).**
Dobutrex (Lilly). *dobutamine hydrochloride.*
docetaxel. **Taxotere.**
docusate calcium. dioctyl calcium sulfosuccinate. **Albert Docusate, PMS-Docusate Calcium, Surfak; (Taro), (Technilab).**

docusate sodium. dioctyl sodium sulfosuccinate. **Colace, Ex-Lax Stool Softener, PMS-Docusate Sodium, Selax, Soflax; (Taro), (Technilab), (Trianon).**

docusate sodium/casanthranol. **Peri-Colace.**

docusate sodium/sennosides. **Senokot•S.**

dolasetron mesylate. **Anzemet.**

Dolobid (Frosst). *diflunisal.*

domiphen bromide/dibucaine. **Nupercainal Cream.**

domperidone maleate. **Alti-Domperidone Maleate, Apo-Domperidone, Motilidone, Motilium, Novo-Domperidone, Nu-Domperidone, PMS-Domperidone.**

donepezil hydrochloride. **Aricept.**

Donnagel-PG Capsules (Wyeth-Ayerst). *attapulgite, activated/ opium/pectin.*

Donnagel-PG Suspension (Wyeth-Ayerst). *kaolin/opium/pectin.*

Donnatal (Wyeth-Ayerst). *atropine sulfate/hyoscyamine sulfate/ phenobarbital/scopolamine hydrobromide.*

dopamine hydrochloride. **Intropin.**

dopamine hydrochloride/dextrose. **(Abbott), (Baxter).**

†Dopar. *levodopa.*

Dopram (Wyeth-Ayerst). *doxapram hydrochloride.*

†Doral. *quazepam.*

dornase alfa recombinant. **Pulmozyme.**

dorzolamide hydrochloride. **Trusopt.**

Dovonex (Leo). *calcipotriol.*

doxacurium chloride. **Nuromax.**

doxapram hydrochloride. **Dopram.**

doxazosin mesylate. **Cardura-1, Cardura-2, Cardura-4.**

doxepin hydrochloride. **Alti-Doxepin, Apo-Doxepin, Novo-Doxepin, Sinequan, Zonalon.**

doxorubicin hydrochloride. **Adriamycin PFS, Adriamycin RDF; (Faulding), (Novopharm).**

doxorubicin hydrochloride pegylated liposome. Caelyx.

Doxycin (Riva). *doxycycline hyclate.*

doxycycline hyclate. **[Tetracyclines, General Monograph, CPhA]; Alti-Doxycycline, Apo-Doxy, Apo-Doxy-Tabs, Doxycin, Doxytec, Novo-Doxylin, Nu-Doxycycline, Vibra-Tabs, Vibra-Tabs C-Pak.**

doxylamine succinate/acetaminophen/codeine phosphate. **Mersyndol with Codeine.**

doxylamine succinate/etafedrine hydrochloride/hydrocodone bitartrate/sodium citrate. **Calmydone, Dalmacol, Mercodol with Decapryn.**

doxylamine succinate/pyridoxine hydrochloride. **Diclectin.**

Doxytec (Technilab). *doxycycline hyclate.*

DPE (Alcon). *dipivefrin hydrochloride.*

Drescriptor (Pharmacia & Upjohn). *delaviridine mesylate.*

Drisdol (Sanofi). *ergocalciferol.*

Dristan (Whitehall-Robins). *acetaminophen/chlorpheniramine maleate/phenylephrine hydrochloride.*

Dristan Extra Strength (Whitehall-Robins). *acetaminophen/ chlorpheniramine maleate/phenylephrine hydrochloride.*

Dristan Long Lasting Nasal Mist/Spray (Whitehall-Robins). *oxymetazoline hydrochloride.*

Dristan Nasal Mist/Spray (Whitehall-Robins). *pheniramine maleate/phenylephrine hydrochloride.*

Dristan N.D. (Whitehall-Robins). *acetaminophen/pseudoephedrine hydrochloride.*

Dristan N.D. Extra Strength (Whitehall-Robins). *acetaminophen/ pseudoephedrine hydrochloride.*

Dristan Sinus (Whitehall-Robins). *ibuprofen/pseudoephedrine hydrochloride.*

Drixoral (Schering). *dexbrompheniramine maleate/ pseudoephedrine sulfate.*

Drixoral Day (Schering). *pseudoephedrine sulfate.*

Drixoral Nasal (Schering). *oxymetazoline hydrochloride.*

Drixoral N.D. (Schering). *pseudoephedrine sulfate.*

Drixoral Night (Schering). *dexbrompheniramine maleate/ pseudoephedrine sulfate.*

Drixtab (Schering). *dexbrompheniramine maleate/ pseudoephedrine sulfate.*

dronabinol. delta-9-tetrahydrocannabinol. **Marinol.**

droperidol. **(Novopharm).**

†Dryox. *benzoyl peroxide.*

DTIC (Bayer). *dacarbazine.*

Dulcolax (Boehringer Ingelheim Self Medication Division). *bisacodyl.*

Duo-C.V.P. (Rhône-Poulenc Rorer). *ascorbic acid.*

Duofilm (Stiefel). *lactic acid/salicylic acid.*

Duoforte 27 (Stiefel). *salicylic acid.*

Duonalc (ICN). *isopropyl alcohol.*

Duonalc-E Mild (ICN). *ethyl alcohol.*

Duonalc-E Solution (ICN). *ethyl alcohol/isopropyl alcohol.*

Duoplant (Stiefel). *formalin/lactic acid/salicylic acid.*

Duovent UDV (Boehringer Ingelheim). *fenoterol hydrobromide/ ipratropium bromide.*

Duphalac (Solvay Pharma). *lactulose.*

†Duract. *bromfenac.*

†Dura-Estrin. *estradiol cypionate.*

Duragesic (Janssen-Ortho). *fentanyl.*

Duralith (Janssen-Ortho). *lithium carbonate.*

†Duramorph. *morphine sulfate.*

†Duranest. *epinephrine/etidocaine hydrochloride.*

Duratears (Alcon). *lanolin/mineral oil/white petrolatum.*

Duricef (Bristol). *cefadroxil.*

Duvoid (Roberts). *bethanechol chloride.*

Dyazide (SmithKline Beecham). *hydrochlorothiazide/triamterene.*

Dycholium (Novartis Consumer Health). *dehydrocholic acid.*

dyflos. see isoflurophate.

†DynaCirc. *isradipine.*

†Dynapen. *dicloxacillin sodium.*

dyphylline. diprophylline. †Dilor, †Lufyllin.

Dyrenium (SmithKline Beecham). *triamterene.*

E

Echinacea Angustifolia (Swiss Herbal). *herbal medicine.*

echothiophate iodide. **Phospholine Iodide.**

Echovist (Berlex Canada). *galactose.*

econazole nitrate. **Ecostatin.** †Spectazole.

†Econochlor. *chloramphenicol.*

†Econopred. *prednisolone acetate.*

Ecostatin (Westwood-Squibb). *econazole nitrate.*

Ectosone Mild (Technilab). *betamethasone valerate.*

Ectosone Regular (Technilab). *betamethasone valerate.*

Ectosone Scalp Lotion (Technilab). *betamethasone valerate.*

Edecrin (MSD). *ethacrynic acid.*

Names **underlined** have complete prescribing information in the *CPS* Monograph Section.

edrophonium chloride. **Enlon, Tensilon.**

EES (Abbott). *erythromycin ethylsuccinate.*

Effexor (Wyeth-Ayerst). *venlafaxine hydrochloride.*

Effexor XR (Wyeth-Ayerst). *venlafaxine hydrochloride.*

†Eflone. *fluorometholone acetate.*

eflornithine hydrochloride. †Ornidyl.

Efudex (ICN). *fluorouracil.*

Elavil (MSD). *amitriptyline hydrochloride.*

Elavil Plus (MSD). *amitriptyline hydrochloride/perphenazine.*

Eldepryl (Draxis Health). *selegiline hydrochloride.*

Eldisine (Lilly). *vindesine sulfate.*

Eldopaque (ICN). *hydroquinone.*

Eldoquin (ICN). *hydroquinone.*

electrolytes. **Pediatric Electrolyte, Trace Elements Solution.**

electrolytes/acetylcholine chloride. **Miochol-E.**

electrolytes/amino acids. **Nutrineal PD4, Vamin N.**

electrolytes/amino acids/dextrose. **Travasol with Electrolytes.**

electrolytes/dextrose. **Enfalac Lytren, Gastrolyte, Pedialyte, Pedialyte Freezer Pops.**

electrolytes/polyethylene glycol. **Colyte, Electropeg, GoLytely, Klean-Prep, Lyteprep, PegLyte, Pro-Lax.**

Electropeg (Technilab). *electrolytes/polyethylene glycol.*

†Elixophyllin. *theophylline.*

Elmiron (Alza). *pentosan polysulfate sodium.*

Elocom (Schering). *mometasone furoate.*

†Elspar. *L-asparaginase.*

Eltor (Hoechst Marion Roussel). *pseudoephedrine hydrochloride.*

Eltroxin (Glaxo Wellcome). *levothyroxine sodium.*

Emadine (Alcon). *emedastine difumarate.*

Emcyt (Pharmacia & Upjohn). *estramustine sodium phosphate.*

emedastine difumarate. **Emadine.**

emetine hydrochloride/hydroxyephedrine hydrochloride/normethadone hydrochloride. **Cophylac Expectorant.**

†Emgel. *erythromycin.*

Eminase (Roberts). *anistreplase.*

EMLA (Astra). *lidocaine/prilocaine.*

Emo-Cort (TCD). *hydrocortisone.*

emollient. **Aquatain.**

Empracet -30, -60 (Glaxo Wellcome). *acetaminophen/codeine phosphate.*

Emtec-30 (Technilab). *acetaminophen/codeine phosphate.*

enalaprilat. **[ACE Inhibitors, General Monograph, CPhA]; Vasotec I.V.**

enalapril maleate. **[ACE Inhibitors, General Monograph, CPhA]; Vasotec.**

enalapril maleate/hydrochlorothiazide. **Vaseretic.**

Endantadine (Endo). *amantadine hydrochloride.*

†Endep. *amitriptyline hydrochloride.*

Endocet (Endo). *acetaminophen/oxycodone hydrochloride.*

Endodan (Endo). *ASA/oxycodone hydrochloride.*

Endo Levodopa/Carbidopa (Endo). *carbidopa/levodopa.*

†Enduron. *methyclothiazide.*

Enfalac Lytren (Mead Johnson). *dextrose/electrolytes.*

Enfalac Nutramigen (Mead Johnson). *infant formula, casein hydrolysate.*

Enfalac Pregestimil (Mead Johnson). *infant formula, casein hydrolysate.*

Enfalac Prosobee (Mead Johnson). *infant formula, soy protein isolate.*

enflurane. **Ēthrane; (Abbott).**

Engerix-B (SmithKline Beecham). *hepatitis B vaccine (recombinant).*

Enlon (Zeneca). *edrophonium chloride.*

enoxaparin. **[Heparins: Low Molecular Weight, General Monograph, CPhA]; Lovenox.**

Entacyl (Roberts). *piperazine adipate.*

enteral nutrition. **Citrotein, Compleat Modified, Isocal, Isocal HN, Isocal with Fibre, Isosource, Isosource HN, Isosource VHN, Lipisorb, Lofenalac, Meritene, Novasource Renal, Nutrisource, Nutrisource HN, PediaSure, Portagen, Resource, Resource Diabetic, Resource Fruit Beverage, Resource Just For Kids, Resource Plus, Sandosource Peptide, Sustacal, Tolerex, Vivonex Pediatric, Vivonex Plus, Vivonex T.E.N.**

Entex LA (Purdue Frederick). *guaifenesin/phenylpropanolamine hydrochloride.*

Entocort Capsules (Astra). *budesonide.*

Entocort Enema (Astra). *budesonide.*

Entrophen (Johnson & Johnson • Merck). *ASA.*

Enuclene (Alcon). *tyloxapol.*

ephedrine/chlorpheniramine/codeine/guaiacol carbonate/phenyltoloxamine. **Omni-Tuss.**

ephedrine hydrochloride. **(Roberts).**

ephedrine sulfate. **(Abbott).**

†Epifoam. *hydrocortisone acetate.*

Epiject I.V. (Abbott). *valproic acid.*

E-Pilo (CIBA Vision). *epinephrine bitartrate/pilocarpine hydrochloride.*

Epi-Lyt AHA (Stiefel). *glycerin/lactic acid.*

epinephrine. adrenaline. **Bronkaid Mistometer, EpiPen, EpiPen Jr.; (Abbott), (Bioniche).**

epinephrine/articaine hydrochloride. **Astracaine, Astracaine Forte, Ultracaine DS, Ultracaine DS Forte.**

epinephrine bitartrate/pilocarpine hydrochloride. **E-Pilo.**

epinephrine/bupivacaine hydrochloride. **Sensorcaine Forte, Sensorcaine with Epinephrine.**

epinephrine/chlorpheniramine maleate. **Ana-Kit.**

epinephrine/etidocaine hydrochloride. †Duranest.

epinephrine hydrochloride. **Adrenalin, Vaponefrin.**

epinephrine/lidocaine. **(Bioniche).**

epinephrine/lidocaine hydrochloride. **Xylocaine Dental Solutions, Xylocaine Parenteral with Epinephrine.**

epinephrine/prilocaine hydrochloride. **Citanest 4% Forte.**

EpiPen (Allerex). *epinephrine.*

EpiPen Jr. (Allerex). *epinephrine.*

epirubicin hydrochloride. **Pharmorubicin PFS, Pharmorubicin RDF.**

†Epitol. *carbamazepine.*

Epival (Abbott). *divalproex sodium.*

epoetin alfa. **Eprex.** †Epogen.

†Epogen. *epoetin alfa.*

epoprostenol sodium. **Flolan.**

Eprex (Janssen-Ortho). *epoetin alfa.*

Equanil (Wyeth-Ayerst). *meprobamate.*

Ergamisol (Janssen-Ortho). *levamisole hydrochloride.*

ergocalciferol. calciferol. ergosterol. vitamin D_2. **[Vitamin D, General Monograph, CPhA]; Drisdol, Ostoforte.**

Ergodryl (Parke-Davis). *caffeine citrate/diphenhydramine hydrochloride/ergotamine tartrate.*

ergoloid mesylates. **Hydergine.** †Gerimal.
Ergomar (Rhône-Poulenc Rorer). *ergotamine tartrate.*
ergometrine maleate. see ergonovine maleate.
ergonovine maleate. ergometrine maleate. **[Ergonovine Maleate, General Monograph, CPhA]; (Abbott), (Bioniche).**
†Ergostat. *ergotamine tartrate.*
ergosterol. see ergocalciferol.
ergotamine/belladonna/phenobarbital. **Bellergal Spacetabs.**
ergotamine tartrate. **Ergomar.** †Ergostat
ergotamine tartrate/belladonna/caffeine/pentobarbital. **Cafergot-PB.**
ergotamine tartrate/caffeine. **Cafergot.**
ergotamine tartrate/caffeine citrate/diphenhydramine hydrochloride. **Ergodryl.**
ergotamine tartrate/caffeine/dimenhydrinate. **Gravergol.**
ergotamine tartrate/caffeine hydrate/cyclizine hydrochloride. **Megral.**
Erybid (Abbott). *erythromycin.*
Eryc (Parke-Davis). *erythromycin.*
†Erygel. *erythromycin.*
Erysol (Stiefel). *erythromycin/ethyl alcohol/octyl methoxycinnamate/Parsol 1789.*
†Ery-Tab. *erythromycin.*
Erythrocin (Abbott). *erythromycin stearate.*
Erythrocin I.V. (Abbott). *erythromycin lactobionate.*
†Erythrocot. *erythromycin stearate.*
Erythromid (Abbott). *erythromycin.*
erythromycin. **[Erythromycin, General Monograph, CPhA]; Apo-Erythro Base, Apo-Erythro E-C, Diomycin, Erybid, Eryc, Erythromid, Novo-Rythro Encap, PCE, PMS-Erythromycin; (Rivex Ophthalmics).** †Emgel, †Erygel, †Ery-Tab.
erythromycin/benzoyl peroxide. **Benzamycin.**
erythromycin estolate. **[Erythromycin, General Monograph, CPhA]; Ilosone.**
erythromycin/ethyl alcohol. **Sans-Acne, T-Stat.**
erythromycin/ethyl alcohol/laureth-4. **Staticin.**
erythromycin/ethyl alcohol/octyl methoxycinnamate/Parsol 1789. **Erysol.**
erythromycin ethylsuccinate. **[Erythromycin, General Monograph, CPhA]; Apo-Erythro-ES, EES.**
erythromycin ethylsuccinate/sulfisoxazole acetyl. **Pediazole.** †Sulfimycin.
erythromycin lactobionate. **[Erythromycin, General Monograph, CPhA]; Erythrocin I.V.**
erythromycin stearate. **[Erythromycin, General Monograph, CPhA]; Apo-Erythro-S, Erythrocin, Nu-Erythromycin-S.** †Erythrocot.
erythromycin/tretinoin. **Stievamycin.**
esculin/dibucaine hydrochloride/framycetin sulfate/hydrocortisone. **Proctosedyl.**
esculin/dibucaine hydrochloride/framycetin sulfate/hydrocortisone acetate. **Proctosone.**
esdepallethrin/piperonyl butoxide. **Scabene.**
†Eserine. *physostigmine sulfate.*
†Esidrix. *hydrochlorothiazide.*
†Esimil. *guanethidine monosulfate/hydrochlorothiazide.*
†Eskalith. *lithium carbonate.*
esmolol hydrochloride. **Brevibloc.**
Estar (Westwood-Squibb). *coal tar.*
esterified estrogens. estrogens, esterified. †Estratab, †Menest.
esterified estrogens/methyltestosterone. †Estratest.
Estinyl (Schering). *ethinyl estradiol.*
Estrace (Roberts). *estradiol-17β (micronized).*
Estracomb (Novartis Pharmaceuticals). *estradiol-17β/norethindrone acetate.*
Estraderm (Novartis Pharmaceuticals). *estradiol-17β.*
estradiol-17β. **Climara, Estraderm, Estring, Vivelle.**
estradiol-17β hemihydrate. Estrogel.
estradiol-17β (micronized). **Estrace.**
estradiol-17β/norethindrone acetate. **Estracomb.**
estradiol benzoate/estradiol dienanthate/testosterone enanthate benzilic acid hydrazone. **Climacteron.**
estradiol cypionate. †depGynogen, †Depogen, †Dura-Estrin, †Estrofem.
estradiol dienanthate/estradiol benzoate/testosterone enanthate benzilic acid hydrazone. **Climacteron.**
estradiol valerate. **Delestrogen.** †Valergen.
†Estragyn. *estrone.*
estramustine sodium phosphate. **Emcyt.**
†Estratab. *esterified estrogens.*
†Estratest. *esterified estrogens/methyltestosterone.*
Estring (Pharmacia & Upjohn). *estradiol-17β.*
†Estrofem. *estradiol cypionate.*
Estrogel (Schering). *estradiol-17β hemihydrate.*
estrogens, conjugated. see conjugated estrogens.
estrogens, esterified. see esterified estrogens.
estrone. ketohydroxyestrin. †Estragyn.
estropipate. piperazine estrone sulfate. **Ogen.** †Ortho-Est.
etafedrine hydrochloride/doxylamine succinate/hydrocodone bitartrate/sodium citrate. **Calmydone, Dalmacol, Mercodol with Decapryn.**
ethacrynate sodium. **Sodium Edecrin.**
ethacrynic acid. **Edecrin.**
ethambutol hydrochloride. **[Ethambutol HCl, General Monograph, CPhA]; Etibi, Myambutol.**
ethinyl estradiol. **Estinyl.**
ethinyl estradiol/cyproterone acetate. **Diane-35.**
ethinyl estradiol/desogestrel. **Marvelon, Ortho-Cept.** †Desogen.
ethinyl estradiol/ethynodiol diacetate. **Demulen.**
ethinyl estradiol/levonorgestrel. **Alesse 21, Alesse 28, Min-Ovral 21, Min-Ovral 28, Triphasil 21, Triphasil 28, Triquilar 21, Triquilar 28.** †Nordette, †Tri-Levlen.
ethinyl estradiol/norethindrone. **Brevicon 0.5/35, Brevicon 1/35, Ortho 0.5/35, Ortho 1/35, Ortho 7/7/7, Ortho 10/11, Select 1/35, Synphasic.** †Genora, †Ovcon, †Tri Norinyl.
ethinyl estradiol/norethindrone acetate. **Loestrin 1.5/30, Minestrin 1/20.**
ethinyl estradiol/norgestimate. **Cyclen, Tri-Cyclen.**
ethinyl estradiol/norgestrel. **Ovral 21, Ovral 28.** †Lo/Ovral.
ethionamide. †Trecator-SC.
†Ethmozine. *moricizine hydrochloride.*
ethopropazine hydrochloride. **Parsitan.** †Parsidol.
ethosuximide. **Zarontin.**
ethotoin. †Peganone.
Ethrane (Zeneca). *enflurane.*
ethyl alcohol. **Biobase, Dilusol, Duonalc-E Mild.**

Names **underlined** have complete prescribing information in the *CPS* Monograph Section.

ethyl alcohol/erythromycin. **Sans-Acne, T-Stat.**
ethyl alcohol/erythromycin/laureth-4. **Staticin.**
ethyl alcohol/erythromycin/octyl methoxycinnamate/Parsol 1789. **Erysol.**
ethyl alcohol/glycolic acid. **Biobase-G.**
ethyl alcohol/isopropyl alcohol. **Duonalc-E Solution.**
ethyl aminobenzoate. see benzocaine.
ethynodiol diacetate/ethinyl estradiol. **Demulen.**
Ethyol (Lilly). *amifostine.*
Etibi (ICN). *ethambutol hydrochloride.*
etidocaine hydrochloride/epinephrine. †Duranest.
etidronate disodium. **Didronel.**
etidronate disodium/calcium carbonate. **Didrocal.**
etodolac. **Apo-Etodolac, Ultradol.** †Lodine.
etomidate. †Amidate.
etoposide. **Vepesid; (BDH), (Novopharm).**
Etrafon (Schering). *amitriptyline hydrochloride/perphenazine.*
eucalyptol/camphor/menthol. **Balminil Camphorub.**
eucalyptus oil/camphor/menthol/methyl salicylate. **Antiphlogistine Rub A-535.**
Euflex (Schering). *flutamide.*
Euglucon (Roche). *glyburide.*
†Eulexin. *flutamide.*
Eumovate (Glaxo Wellcome). *clobetasone 17-butyrate.*
Eurax (Novartis Consumer Health). *crotamiton.*
evening primrose oil. **(Swiss Herbal).**
†Everone 200. *testosterone enanthate.*
Evista (Lilly). *raloxifene hydrochloride.*
†Exelderm. *sulconazole nitrate.*
Ex-Lax Chocolated Pieces (Novartis Consumer Health). *sennosides.*
Ex-Lax Extra Strength Sugar Coated Pills (Novartis Consumer Health). *sennosides.*
Ex-Lax Stool Softener (Novartis Consumer Health). *docusate sodium.*
Ex-Lax Sugar Coated Pills (Novartis Consumer Health). *sennosides.*
†Exna. *benzthiazide.*
Exosurf Neonatal (Glaxo Wellcome). *colfosceril palmitate.*
Extra Strength Acetaminophen (WestCan). *acetaminophen.*
Extra Strength Acetaminophen with Codeine (WestCan). *acetaminophen/caffeine/codeine phosphate.*
Eye Drops (Rivex Ophthalmics). *tetrahydrozoline hydrochloride.*
Eyestil (Ophtapharma). *sodium hyaluronate.*
Eye-Stream (Alcon). *balanced salt solution.*
Eyewash (Rivex Ophthalmics). *boric acid.*

F

factor IX concentrate (human). **Immunine VH.**
Factrel (Wyeth-Ayerst). *gonadorelin hydrochloride.*
famciclovir. **Famvir.**
famotidine. **Apo-Famotidine, Gen-Famotidine, Maalox H2 Acid Controller, Novo-Famotidine, Nu-Famotidine, Pepcid AC, Pepcid I.V., Pepcid Tablets, Ulcidine.**
Famvir (SmithKline Beecham). *famciclovir.*
Fansidar (Roche). *pyrimethamine/sulfadoxine.*
†Fareston. *toremifene.*
Fastin (SmithKline Beecham). *phentermine hydrochloride.*
fat emulsion. **Intralipid.**
Feiba VH Immuno (Baxter). *coagulant complex anti-inhibitor.*
Feldene (Pfizer). *piroxicam.*
felodipine. **Plendil, Renedil.**
Femara (Novartis Pharmaceuticals). *letrozole.*
†Femstat. *butoconazole nitrate.*
fennel oil/anise oil/dill oil/sodium bicarbonate. **Baby's Own Gripe Water.**
fenofibrate. **Apo-Fenofibrate, Nu-Fenofibrate.**
fenofibrate (micronized). **Lipidil Micro.** †Tricor.
fenoldopam mesylate. †Corlopam.
fenoprofen calcium. **Nalfon.**
fenoterol hydrobromide. **Berotec Forte Inhalation Aerosol, Berotec Inhalation Aerosol, Berotec Inhalation Solution.**
fenoterol hydrobromide/ipratropium bromide. **Duovent UDV.**
fentanyl. **[Opioids, General Monograph, CPhA]; Duragesic.**
fentanyl citrate. **[Opioids, General Monograph, CPhA]; (Abbott), (Faulding).**
Fer-In-Sol (Mead Johnson). *ferrous sulfate.*
Fermalac (Rougier). *lactobacillus acidophillus/lactobacillus bulgaricus/streptococcus lactis.*
Fermalac Vaginal (Rougier). *lactobacillus acidophillus/lactobacillus bulgaricus/streptococcus lactis.*
Fermentol (Carter Horner). *pepsin.*
Ferodan (Odan). *ferrous sulfate.*
Fero-Grad (Abbott). *ferrous sulfate.*
ferrous ascorbate. **[Iron Salts, General Monograph, CPhA]; Ascofer.**
ferrous fumarate. **[Iron Salts, General Monograph, CPhA]; Palafer, Scheinpharm Ferrous Fumarate.**
ferrous fumarate/ascorbic acid/folic acid. **Palafer CF.**
ferrous fumarate/calcium carbonate/multiple vitamins. **Prenavite.**
ferrous fumarate/multiple vitamins. **Flintstones Plus Iron, Stresstabs with Iron.**
ferrous gluconate. **[Iron Salts, General Monograph, CPhA]; Apo-Ferrous Gluconate.**
ferrous sulfate. **[Iron Salts, General Monograph, CPhA]; Apo-Ferrous Sulfate, Fer-In-Sol, Ferodan, Fero-Grad, Slow-Fe.**
ferrous sulfate/folic acid. **Slow-Fe Folic.**
Fertinorm HP (Serono). *urofollitropin.*
feverfew. **Tanacet 125.**
Fexicam (Technilab). *piroxicam.*
fexofenadine hydrochloride. **Allegra.**
fibrin sealant. **Tisseel Kit VH.**
filgrastim. **Neupogen.**
finasteride. **Propecia, Proscar.**
Fiorinal (Novartis Pharmaceuticals). *ASA/butalbital/caffeine.*
Fiorinal-C¼, -C½ (Novartis Pharmaceuticals). *ASA/butalbital/caffeine/codeine phosphate.*
Flagyl (Rhône-Poulenc Rorer). *metronidazole.*
Flagyl 500 Injection (Baxter). *metronidazole.*
Flagystatin (Rhône-Poulenc Rorer). *metronidazole/nystatin.*
Flamazine (Smith & Nephew). *silver sulfadiazine.*
Flamazine C (Smith & Nephew). *chlorhexidine digluconate/silver sulfadiazine.*
Flarex (Alcon). *fluorometholone acetate.*
flavoxate hydrochloride. **Urispas.**
Flaxedil (Rhône-Poulenc Rorer). *gallamine triethiodide.*
flecainide acetate. **Tambocor.**

Fleet Enema (Johnson & Johnson • Merck). *sodium phosphates.*

Fleet Enema Mineral Oil (Johnson & Johnson • Merck). *mineral oil.*

Fleet Phospho-Soda (Johnson & Johnson • Merck). *sodium phosphates.*

Flexall (Chattem). *menthol.*

Flexall Stick (Chattem). *menthol/methyl salicylate.*

Flexeril (Frosst). *cyclobenzaprine hydrochloride.*

Flexitec (Technilab). *cyclobenzaprine hydrochloride.*

Flintstones (Bayer Consumer). *multiple vitamins.*

Flintstones Complete (Bayer). *multiple vitamins and minerals.*

Flintstones Plus Iron (Bayer). *ferrous fumarate/multiple vitamins.*

Flintstones with Extra C (Bayer). *multiple vitamins.*

floctafenine. **Idarac.**

Flolan (Glaxo Wellcome). *epoprostenol sodium.*

Flomax (Boehringer Ingelheim). *tamsulosin hydrochloride.*

Flonase (Glaxo Wellcome). *fluticasone propionate.*

Florinef (Roberts). *fludrocortisone acetate.*

†Floropryl. *isoflurophate.*

Flovent (Glaxo Wellcome). *fluticasone propionate.*

Floxin (Janssen-Ortho). *ofloxacin.*

floxuridine. †FUDR.

Fluanxol Depot (Lundbeck). *flupenthixol decanoate.*

Fluanxol Tablets (Lundbeck). *flupenthixol dihydrochloride.*

fluconazole. **Diflucan, Diflucan-150.**

flucytosine. 5-fluorocytosine. †Ancobon.

Fludara (Berlex Canada). *fludarabine phosphate.*

fludarabine phosphate. **Fludara.**

fludrocortisone acetate. [**Corticosteroids: Systemic, General Monograph, CPhA**]; **Florinef.**

†Flumadine. *rimantadine hydrochloride.*

flumazenil. **Anexate.**

flumethasone. [**Corticosteroids: Topical, General Monograph CPhA**].

flumethasone pivalate/clioquinol. **Locacorten Vioform, Locacorten Vioform Eardrops.**

flumethasone pivalate/salicylic acid. **Locasalen.**

flunisolide. [**Corticosteroids: Eye Ear Nose, Corticosteroids: Inhaled, General Monographs, CPhA**]; **Bronalide, Rhinalar.** †Nasalide.

†Fluocet. *fluocinolone acetonide.*

†Fluocin. *fluocinonide.*

fluocinolone acetonide. [**Corticosteroids: Topical, General Monograph, CPhA**]; **Fluoderm, Synalar.** †Fluocet, †Flurosyn.

fluocinonide. [**Corticosteroids: Topical, General Monograph, CPhA**]; **Lidemol, Lidex, Lyderm, Lydonide, Tiamol, Topsyn.** †Fluocin, †Licon.

Fluoderm (Taro). *fluocinolone acetonide.*

Fluoracaine (Dioptic). *fluorescein sodium/proparacaine hydrochloride.*

Fluor-A-Day (Pharmascience). *sodium fluoride.*

fluorescein sodium. **Diofluor Injection, Diofluor Strips, Fluorescite, Fluorets, Minims Fluorescein.**

fluorescein sodium/lidocaine. **Minims Lidocaine/Fluorescein.**

fluorescein sodium/proparacaine hydrochloride. **Fluoracaine.**

Fluorescite (Alcon). *fluorescein sodium.*

Fluorets (Ophtapharma). *fluorescein sodium.*

5-fluorocytosine. see flucytosine.

fluorometholone. [**Corticosteroids: Eye Ear Nose, General Monograph, CPhA**]; **FML Forte, FML Liquifilm.** †Fluor-Op.

fluorometholone acetate. [**Corticosteroids: Eye Ear Nose, General Monograph, CPhA**]; **Flarex.** †Eflone.

†Fluor-Op. *fluorometholone.*

Fluoroplex (Allergan). *fluorouracil.*

5-fluorouracil. see fluorouracil.

fluorouracil. 5-fluorouracil. 5-FU. **Adrucil, Efudex, Fluoroplex.**

Fluorouracil Roche (Roche). *fluorouracil sodium.*

fluorouracil sodium. **Fluorouracil Roche.**

Fluotic (Hoechst Marion Roussel). *sodium fluoride.*

fluoxetine hydrochloride. [**Selective Serotonin Reuptake Inhibitors, General Monograph, CPhA**]; **Apo-Fluoxetine, Novo-Fluoxetine, Nu-Fluoxetine, PMS-Fluoxetine, Prozac.**

fluoxymesterone. **Halotestin.** †Android-F.

flupenthixol decanoate. **Fluanxol Depot.**

flupenthixol dihydrochloride. **Fluanxol Tablets.**

fluphenazine decanoate. [**Fluphenazine, General Monograph, CPhA**]; **Modecate Concentrate, PMS-Fluphenazine Decanoate, Rho-Fluphenazine Decanoate.**

fluphenazine enanthate. [**Fluphenazine, General Monograph, CPhA**]; **Moditen Enanthate.**

fluphenazine hydrochloride. [**Fluphenazine, General Monograph, CPhA**]; **Apo-Fluphenazine, Moditen HCl.**

flurandrenolide. [**Corticosteroids: Topical, General Monograph, CPhA**]; †Cordran.

flurazepam hydrochloride. [**Benzodiazepines, General Monograph, CPhA**]; **Apo-Flurazepam, Dalmane.**

flurazepam monohydrochloride. **Somnol.**

flurbiprofen. **Alti-Flurbiprofen, Ansaid, Apo-Flurbiprofen, Froben, Froben SR, Novo-Flurprofen, Nu-Flurbiprofen.**

flurbiprofen sodium. **Ocufen.**

†Flurosyn. *fluocinolone acetonide.*

flutamide. **Euflex, Novo-Flutamide, PMS-Flutamide.** †Eulexin.

†Flutex. *triamcinolone acetonide.*

fluticasone propionate. [**Corticosteroids: Eye Ear Nose, Corticosteroids: Inhaled, General Monographs, CPhA**]; **Flonase, Flovent.**

fluvastatin sodium. **Lescol.**

Fluviral (BioChem Vaccines). *influenza virus vaccine trivalent (whole-virion), inactivated.*

Fluviral S/F (BioChem Vaccines). *influenza virus vaccine, inactivated.*

fluvoxamine maleate. [**Selective Serotonin Reuptake Inhibitors, General Monograph, CPhA**]; **Alti-Fluvoxamine, Apo-Fluvoxamine, Luvox.**

Fluzone (Connaught). *influenza virus vaccine, inactivated.*

FML Forte (Allergan). *fluorometholone.*

FML Liquifilm (Allergan). *fluorometholone.*

folacin. see folic acid.

folate sodium. see folic acid.

†Folex. *methotrexate sodium.*

folic acid. folacin. folate sodium. pteroylglutamic acid. [**Folic Acid, General Monograph, CPhA**]; **Apo-Folic.**

folic acid/ascorbic acid/ferrous fumarate. **Palafer CF.**

folic acid/ferrous sulfate. **Slow-Fe Folic.**

folinic acid, calcium salt. see calcium folinate.

follitropin alpha (rDNA origin). **Gonal-F.**

follitropin beta. **Puregon.**

Names **underlined** have complete prescribing information in the *CPS* Monograph Section.

Follow-Up (Nestlé, Carnation). *infant formula.*
Follow-Up Soy (Nestlé, Carnation). *infant formula, soy protein isolate.*
Foradil (Novartis Pharmaceuticals). *formoterol fumarate.*
Forane (Zeneca). *isoflurane.*
formalin/lactic acid/salicylic acid. **Duoplant.**
formoterol fumarate. **Foradil.**
formoterol fumarate dihydrate. **Oxeze Turbuhaler.**
Formulex (ICN). *dicyclomine hydrochloride.*
Fortaz (Glaxo Wellcome). *ceftazidime pentahydrate.*
Fosamax (MSD). *alendronate sodium.*
foscarnet sodium. †Foscavir.
†Foscavir. *foscarnet sodium.*
fosinopril sodium. [**ACE Inhibitors, General Monograph, CPhA**]; **Monopril.**
fosphenytoin sodium. **Cerebyx.**
fractar. **Pentrax.**
Fragmin (Pharmacia & Upjohn). *dalteparin sodium.*
framycetin sulfate. **Soframycin Ophthalmic, Sofra-Tulle.**
framycetin sulfate/dexamethasone/gramicidin. **Sofracort.**
framycetin sulfate/dibucaine hydrochloride/esculin/hydrocortisone. **Proctosedyl.**
framycetin sulfate/dibucaine hydrochloride/esculin/hydrocortisone acetate. **Proctosone.**
framycetin sulfate/gramicidin. **Soframycin Ointment.**
Fraxiparine (Sanofi). *nadroparin calcium.*
Frisium (Hoechst Marion Roussel). *clobazam.*
Froben (Knoll). *flurbiprofen.*
Froben SR (Knoll). *flurbiprofen.*
frusemide. see furosemide.
5-FU. see fluorouracil.
Fucidin Cream (Leo). *fusidic acid.*
Fucidin H Cream (Leo). *fusidic acid/hydrocortisone.*
Fucidin Intertulle (Leo). *sodium fusidate.*
Fucidin I.V. (Leo). *sodium fusidate.*
Fucidin Ointment (Leo). *sodium fusidate.*
Fucidin Suspension (Leo). *fusidic acid.*
Fucidin Tablets (Leo). *sodium fusidate.*
†FUDR. *floxuridine.*
Fulvicin P/G (Schering). *griseofulvin.*
Fulvicin U/F (Schering). *griseofulvin.*
Fungizone (Squibb). *amphotericin B.*
†Furadantin. *nitrofurantoin.*
furazolidone. †Furoxone.
furosemide. frusemide. **Apo-Furosemide, Lasix, Lasix Special; (Abbott).**
†Furoxone. *furazolidone.*
fusidate diethanolamine. see fusidic acid.
fusidic acid. fusidate diethanolamine. **Fucidin Cream, Fucidin Suspension.**
fusidic acid/hydrocortisone. Fucidin H Cream.

G

gabapentin. **Neurontin.**
†Gabitril. *tiagapine.*
gadodiamide. **Omniscan.**
gadopentetate dimeglumine. **Magnevist.**
galactose. **Echovist.**
galactose/palmitic acid. **Levovist.**
gallamine triethiodide. **Flaxedil.**
gallium nitrate. †Ganite.
Gamimune N (Bayer). *immune globulin (human), i.v.*
gamma benzene hexachloride. see lindane.
ganciclovir. **Cytovene Capsules.**
ganciclovir sodium. **Cytovene Injection.**
†Ganite. *gallium nitrate.*
Garamycin Ophthalmic/Otic (Schering). *gentamicin sulfate.*
Garamycin Parenteral (Schering). *gentamicin sulfate.*
Garamycin Topical (Schering). *gentamicin sulfate.*
Garasone (Schering). *betamethasone sodium phosphate/gentamicin sulfate.*
Garatec (Technilab). *gentamicin sulfate.*
†Gastrocrom. *sodium cromoglycate.*
Gastrolyte (Rhône-Poulenc Rorer). *dextrose/electrolytes.*
†Gastrosed. *hyoscyamine sulfate.*
Gas-X (Novartis Consumer Health). *simethicone.*
Gas-X Extra Strength (Novartis Consumer Health). *simethicone.*
Gaviscon Heartburn Relief Formula Aluminum-free Tablets (SmithKline Beecham Consumer Healthcare). *alginic acid/magnesium carbonate.*
Gaviscon Heartburn Relief Formula Liquid (SmithKline Beecham Consumer Healthcare). *aluminum hydroxide/sodium alginate.*
Gaviscon Heartburn Relief Formula Tablets (SmithKline Beecham Consumer Healthcare). *alginic acid/aluminum hydroxide.*
gelatin. **Gelfilm, Gelfoam.**
Gelfilm (Pharmacia & Upjohn). *gelatin.*
Gelfoam (Pharmacia & Upjohn). *gelatin.*
Gelusil (Warner-Lambert Consumer Healthcare). *aluminum hydroxide/magnesium hydroxide.*
Gelusil Extra Strength (Warner-Lambert Consumer Healthcare). *aluminum hydroxide/magnesium hydroxide.*
gemcitabine hydrochloride. **Gemzar.**
gemfibrozil. **Apo-Gemfibrozil, Gen-Fibro, Lopid, Novo-Gemfibrozil, Nu-Gemfibrozil, PMS-Gemfibrozil; (AltiMed).**
Gemzar (Lilly). *gemcitabine hydrochloride.*
†Genabid. *papaverine hydrochloride.*
Gen-Alprazolam (Genpharm). *alprazolam.*
Gen-Amantadine (Antiparkinsonian) (Genpharm). *amantadine hydrochloride.*
Gen-Amantadine (Antiviral) (Genpharm). *amantadine hydrochloride.*
Gen-Atenolol (Genpharm). *atenolol.*
Gen-Azathioprine (Genpharm). *azathioprine.*
Gen-Baclofen (Genpharm). *baclofen.*
Gen-Beclo Aq. (Genpharm). *beclomethasone dipropionate.*
Gen-Bromazepam (Genpharm). *bromazepam.*
Gen-Budesonide Aq. (Genpharm). *budesonide.*
Gen-Buspirone (Genpharm). *buspirone hydrochloride.*
Gen-Captopril (Genpharm). *captopril.*
Gen-Cimetidine (Genpharm). *cimetidine.*
Gen-Clobetasol Cream/Ointment (Genpharm). *clobetasol 17-propionate.*
Gen-Clobetasol Scalp Application (Genpharm). *clobetasol 17-propionate.*
Gen-Clomipramine (Genpharm). *clomipramine hydrochloride.*

Gen-Clonazepam (Genpharm). *clonazepam.*
Gen-Cromoglycate Nasal Solution (Genpharm). *sodium cromoglycate.*
Gen-Cromoglycate Sterinebs (Genpharm). *sodium cromoglycate.*
Gen-Cycloprine (Genpharm). *cyclobenzaprine hydrochloride.*
Gen-Diltiazem (Genpharm). *diltiazem hydrochloride.*
Gen-Diltiazem SR (Genpharm). *diltiazem hydrochloride.*
Gen-Famotidine (Genpharm). *famotidine.*
Gen-Fibro (Genpharm). *gemfibrozil.*
Gen-Glybe (Genpharm). *glyburide.*
Gen-Indapamide (Genpharm). *indapamide hemihydrate.*
Gen-Medroxy (Genpharm). *medroxyprogesterone acetate.*
Gen-Metformin (Genpharm). *metformin hydrochloride.*
Gen-Minocycline (Genpharm). *minocycline hydrochloride.*
Gen-Minoxidil (Genpharm). *minoxidil.*
Gen-Nifedipine (Genpharm). *nifedipine.*
Gen-Nortriptyline (Genpharm). *nortriptyline hydrochloride.*
†Genoptic. *gentamicin sulfate.*
†Genora. *ethinyl estradiol/norethindrone.*
Gen-Oxybutynin (Genpharm). *oxybutynin chloride.*
Gen-Pindolol (Genpharm). *pindolol.*
Gen-Piroxicam (Genpharm). *piroxicam.*
Gen-Ranitidine (Genpharm). *ranitidine hydrochloride.*
Gen-Salbutamol Respirator Solution (Genpharm). *salbutamol sulfate.*
Gen-Salbutamol Sterinebs P.F. (Genpharm). *salbutamol sulfate.*
Gen-Selegiline (Genpharm). *selegiline hydrochloride.*
Gen-Sotalol (Genpharm). *sotalol hydrochloride.*
Gentacidin (CIBA Vision). *gentamicin sulfate.*
gentamicin sulfate. **Alcomicin, Cidomycin, Diogent Ointment, Diogent Solution, Garamycin Ophthalmic/Otic, Garamycin Parenteral, Garamycin Topical, Garatec, Gentacidin, Minims Gentamicin, Scheinpharm Gentamicin; (Novopharm), (Rivex Ophthalmics), (Technilab).** †Genoptic, †G-Mycin, †Ocu-Mycin.
gentamicin sulfate/betamethasone dipropionate. **Diprogen.**
gentamicin sulfate/betamethasone sodium phosphate. **Garasone.**
gentamicin sulfate/betamethasone valerate. **Valisone-G.**
gentamicin sulfate/sodium chloride. **(Abbott), (Baxter).**
Gen-Tamoxifen (Genpharm). *tamoxifen citrate.*
Genteal (CIBA Vision). *hydroxypropyl methylcellulose.*
Gen-Temazepam (Genpharm). *temazepam.*
Gen-Timolol (Genpharm). *timolol maleate.*
Gent-L-Tip (Baxter). *sodium biphosphate/sodium phosphate.*
Gentran 40 (Baxter). *dextran 40.*
Gentran 70 (Baxter). *dextran 70.*
Gen-Trazodone (Genpharm). *trazodone.*
Gen-Triazolam (Genpharm). *triazolam.*
Gen-Valproic (Genpharm). *valproic acid.*
Gen-Verapamil SR (Genpharm). *verapamil hydrochloride.*
†Gen-XENE. *clorazepate dipotassium.*
†Geocillin. *carbenicillin indanyl sodium.*
†Gerimal. *ergoloid mesylates.*
gland extracts/ascorbic acid. **Revitonus C-1000.**
Glaxal Base (Roberts). *dermatological base.*
glibenclamide. see glyburide.
gliclazide. **[Sulfonylureas, General Monograph, CPhA]; Diamicron, Novo-Gliclazide.**
glipizide. †Glucotrol XL.
glucagon. **(Lilly).**
Glucodex (Rougier). *dextrose.*
gluconolactone. **Neostrata AHA Cleansing Lotion, Neostrata AHA Eye Contour Cream, Neostrata AHA Lip Conditioner, Neostrata AHA Ultra Moisturizing Cream.**
Glucophage (Hoechst Marion Roussel). *metformin hydrochloride.*
glucose enzymatic test strip. **Tes-Tape.**
glucose/lidocaine hydrochloride. **Xylocaine Spinal 5%.**
†Glucotrol XL. *glipizide.*
glutaral. **Sonacide.**
glyburide. glibenclamide. **[Sulfonylureas, General Monograph, CPhA]; Albert Glyburide, Apo-Glyburide, Diaβeta, Euglucon, Gen-Glybe, Novo-Glyburide, Nu-Glyburide, PMS-Glyburide.** †Glynase PresTab, †Micronase.
glycerides/cellulose/polyglycol/polysiloxane copolyol/silicones. **Spectro Derm.**
glycerin. **(Nadeau), (Warner-Lambert Consumer Healthcare).**
glycerin/hamamelis water. **Preparation H Cleansing Pads.**
glycerin/lactic acid. **Epi-Lyt AHA.**
glycerin/sodium citrate/sodium lauryl sulfoacetate/sorbic acid/sorbitol. **Microlax.**
glyceryl guaiacolate. see guaifenesin.
glyceryl guaiacolate carbamate. see methocarbamol.
glyceryl guaiacol ether. see guaifenesin.
glyceryl trinitrate. see nitroglycerin.
glycolic acid. **Neostrata AHA Cream, Neostrata AHA Lotion, Neostrata AHA Sensitive Skin Cream, Neostrata AHA Solution, Reversa AHA.**
glycolic acid/ethyl alcohol. **Biobase-G.**
glycolic acid/hydroquinone. **Viquin Forte.**
Glycon (ICN). *metformin hydrochloride.*
glycophenylate bromide. see mepenzolate bromide.
glycopyrrolate. glycopyrronium bromide. **Robinul, Robinul Forte, Robinul Injectable.**
glycopyrronium bromide. see glycopyrrolate.
†Glynase PresTab. *glyburide.*
Glysennid (Novartis Consumer Health). *sennosides.*
GM-CSF. see sargramostim.
†G-Mycin. *gentamicin sulfate.*
gold, colloidal/copper gluconate/silver gluconate. **Oligosol, Copper-Gold-Silver.**
gold compound. see auranofin.
gold compound. see aurothioglucose.
gold compound. see sodium aurothiomalate.
gold sodium thiomalate. see sodium aurothiomalate.
GoLytely (Baxter). *electrolytes/polyethylene glycol.*
gonadorelin acetate. **Lutrepulse.**
gonadorelin hydrochloride. **Factrel.**
gonadotropin (human) chorionic. HCG. **A.P.L., Humegon, Pregnyl, Profasi HP.**
Gonal-F (Serono). *follitropin alpha (rDNA origin).*
Good Start (Nestlé, Carnation). *infant formula.*
goserelin acetate. **Zoladex, Zoladex LA.**
Gramcal (Novartis Consumer Health). *calcium carbonate/calcium lactate-gluconate/citric acid.*
gramicidin/bacitracin/polymyxin B sulfate. **Polysporin Triple Antibiotic Ointment.**

Names **underlined** have complete prescribing information in the *CPS* Monograph Section.

gramicidin/dexamethasone/framycetin sulfate. **Sofracort.**

gramicidin/framycetin sulfate. **Soframycin Ointment.**

gramicidin/lidocaine hydrochloride/polymyxin B sulfate. **Lidosporin Cream, Polysporin Antibiotic Burn Cream.**

gramicidin/neomycin sulfate/nystatin/triamcinolone acetonide. **Kenacomb, Triacomb, Viaderm-K.C.**

gramicidin/neomycin sulfate/polymyxin B sulfate. **Neosporin Cream, Neosporin Eye and Ear Solution, Optimyxin Plus Solution.**

gramicidin/polymyxin B sulfate. **Optimyxin Solution, Polycidin Eye/Ear Drops, Polysporin Cream, Eye/Ear Drops, Polytopic Cream.**

granisetron hydrochloride. **Kytril.**

Gravergol (Carter Horner). *caffeine/dimenhydrinate/ergotamine tartrate.*

Gravol (Carter Horner). *dimenhydrinate.*

grepafloxacin hydrochloride. **Raxar.**

†Grifulvin V. *griseofulvin.*

†Grisactin. *griseofulvin.*

griseofulvin. **Fulvicin P/G, Fulvicin U/F, Grisovin FP.** †Grifulvin V, †Grisactin, †Gris-PEG.

Grisovin FP (Roberts). *griseofulvin.*

†Gris-PEG. *griseofulvin.*

guaiacol carbonate/camphor/diphenylpyraline hydrochloride. **Creo-Rectal.**

guaiacol carbonate/chlorpheniramine/codeine/ephedrine/phenyltoloxamine. **Omni-Tuss.**

guaifenesin. glyceryl guaiacolate. glyceryl guaiacol ether. methoxypropanediol. methphenoxydiol. [**Guaifenesin, General Monograph, CPhA**]; **Balminil Expectorant, Benylin E, Calmylin Expectorant, Robitussin.**

guaifenesin/acetaminophen/dextromethorphan hydrobromide/pseudoephedrine hydrochloride. **Benylin 4 Flu, Calmylin Cough and Flu, Robitussin Cough, Cold & Flu Liqui-Gels, Sudafed Cold & Flu.**

guaifenesin/ammonium chloride/codeine phosphate. **Cheracol.**

guaifenesin/bismuth camphocarbonate. **Bismutal.**

guaifenesin/brompheniramine maleate/codeine phosphate/phenylephrine hydrochloride/phenylpropanolamine hydrochloride. **Dimetane Expectorant-C.**

guaifenesin/brompheniramine maleate/hydrocodone bitartrate/phenylephrine hydrochloride/phenylpropanolamine hydrochloride. **Dimetane Expectorant-DC.**

guaifenesin/brompheniramine maleate/phenylephrine hydrochloride/phenylpropanolamine hydrochloride. **Dimetane Expectorant.**

guaifenesin/chlorpheniramine maleate/dextromethorphan hydrobromide/pseudoephedrine hydrochloride. **Triaminic DM Expectorant.**

guaifenesin/chlorpheniramine maleate/pseudoephedrine hydrochloride. **Triaminic Expectorant.**

guaifenesin/codeine phosphate/pheniramine maleate. **Calmylin Ace, Robitussin AC, Robitussin with Codeine.**

guaifenesin/codeine phosphate/pseudoephedrine hydrochloride. **Benylin Codeine, Calmylin with Codeine.**

guaifenesin/codeine phosphate/pseudoephedrine hydrochloride/triprolidine hydrochloride. **CoActifed Expectorant, Cotridin Expectorant.**

guaifenesin/dextromethorphan hydrobromide. **Balminil DM + Expectorant, Benylin DM-E, Robitussin DM.**

guaifenesin/dextromethorphan hydrobromide/phenylpropanolamine hydrochloride. **Triaminic DM Daytime.**

guaifenesin/dextromethorphan hydrobromide/pseudoephedrine hydrochloride. **Balminil DM + Decongestant + Expectorant, Benylin DM-D-E, Calmylin #3, Novahistex DM Decongestant Expectorant, Novahistine DM Decongestant Expectorant, Robitussin Cough & Cold, Robitussin Cough & Cold Liqui-Gels.**

guaifenesin/hydrocodone bitartrate/pheniramine maleate/phenylpropanolamine hydrochloride/pyrilamine maleate. **Triaminic Expectorant DH.**

guaifenesin/hydrocodone bitartrate/phenylephrine hydrochloride. **Novahistex DH Expectorant.**

guaifenesin/mepyramine maleate/potassium iodide/theophylline. **Theo-Bronc.**

guaifenesin/oxtriphylline. **Choledyl Expectorant.**

guaifenesin/phenylpropanolamine hydrochloride. **Entex LA.**

guanabenz acetate. †Wytensin.

guanadrel sulfate. †Hylorel.

guanethidine monosulfate/hydrochlorothiazide. †Esimil.

guanfacine hydrochloride. †Tenex.

Gynecure (Pfizer Consumer). *tioconazole.*

Gyne-T 380 Slimline Intrauterine Copper Contraceptive (Janssen-Ortho). *intrauterine contraceptive.*

Gyne-T Intrauterine Copper Contraceptive (Janssen-Ortho). *intrauterine contraceptive.*

H

Habitrol (Novartis Consumer Health). *S(-)-nicotine.*

haemophilus b conjugate vaccine (tetanus protein conjugate)/diphtheria toxoid adsorbed/pertussis vaccine (acellular)/poliomyelitis vaccine, inactivated/tetanus toxoid adsorbed. **Pentacel.**

haemophilus b (Hib) polysaccharide conjugate (meningococcal protein conjugate) vaccine. **PedvaxHIB.**

haemophilus b (Hib) polysaccharide conjugate (tetanus protein conjugate) vaccine. **Act-HIB.**

halazepam. †Paxipam.

halcinonide. [**Corticosteroids: Topical, General Monograph, CPhA**]; **Halog.**

Halcion (Pharmacia & Upjohn). *triazolam.*

Haldol (Janssen-Ortho). *haloperidol.*

Haldol LA (Janssen-Ortho). *haloperidol decanoate.*

Halfan (SmithKline Beecham). *halofantrine hydrochloride.*

halobetasol propionate. **Ultravate.**

halofantrine hydrochloride. **Halfan.**

Halog (Westwood-Squibb). *halcinonide.*

haloperidol. **Apo-Haloperidol, Haldol, Novo-Peridol, Peridol, PMS-Haloperidol LA; (Sabex).**

haloperidol decanoate. **Haldol LA, Rho-Haloperidol Decanoate.**

Halotestin (Pharmacia & Upjohn). *fluoxymesterone.*

hamamelis water/glycerin. **Preparation H Cleansing Pads.**

hamamelis water/phenylephrine hydrochloride. **Preparation H Cooling Gel.**

†Harmonyl. *deserpidine.*

Havrix (SmithKline Beecham). *hepatitis A vaccine, inactivated.*

HCG. see gonadotropin (human) chorionic.

Healon (Pharmacia & Upjohn). *sodium hyaluronate.*

Healon GV (Pharmacia & Upjohn). *sodium hyaluronate.*

†Hemabate. *carboprost tromethamine.*

Hemarexin (Technilab). *multiple vitamins and minerals.*

Hemcort HC (Technilab). *hydrocortisone acetate/zinc sulfate monohydrate.*

†Hemofil M. *antihemophilic factor (human).*

†Hemril-HC. *hydrocortisone acetate.*

Hepalean (Organon Teknika). *heparin sodium.*

Hepalean-Lok (Organon Teknika). *heparin sodium.*

Heparin Leo (Leo). *heparin sodium.*

Heparin Lock Flush (Abbott). *heparin sodium.*

heparins: low molecular weight. **(General Monograph, CPhA).**

heparin sodium. **[Heparin: Unfractionated, General Monograph, CPhA]; Hepalean, Hepalean-Lok, Heparin Leo, Heparin Lock Flush.**

heparin sodium/dextrose. **(Abbott), (Baxter).**

heparin sodium/sodium chloride. **(Baxter).**

heparin sodium/zinc sulfate. **Lipactin.**

hepatitis A vaccine/hepatitis B vaccine. **Twinrix.**

hepatitis A vaccine, inactivated. **Havrix.**

hepatitis A vaccine, purified inactivated. **Vaqta.**

hepatitis B immune globulin (human). see immune globulin, hepatitis B (human).

hepatitis B vaccine/hepatitis A vaccine. **Twinrix.**

hepatitis B vaccine (recombinant). **Engerix-B, Recombivax HB.**

Heracline (Technilab). *adrenal cortical extract/cyanocobalamin/orchitic extract.*

Herbal Laxative (Swiss Herbal). *herbal medicine.*

herbal medicine. **Echinacea Angustifolia, Herbal Laxative, Herbal Nerve, St. John's Wort.**

Herbal Nerve (Swiss Herbal). *herbal medicine.*

Herplex (Allergan). *idoxuridine.*

Herplex-D (Allergan). *idoxuridine.*

Hexabrix (Mallinckrodt). *ioxaglate meglumine/ioxaglate sodium.*

hexachlorophene. **pHisoHex.**

†Hexadrol. *dexamethasone.*

Hexadrol Phosphate (Organon Teknika). *dexamethasone sodium phosphate.*

Hexalen (Lilly). *altretamine.*

hexamethylmelamine. see altretamine.

hexamine. see methenamine.

hexavitamins. see multiple vitamins.

hexetidine. **Steri/Sol.**

Hexit (Odan). *lindane.*

hexylresorcinol. **Bradosol, Bradosol Extra-Strength.**

Hibidil 1:2000 (Zeneca). *chlorhexidine gluconate.*

Hibitane Skin Cleanser (Zeneca). *chlorhexidine gluconate.*

†Hi-Cor. *hydrocortisone.*

Hi Potency B-Compound "50" (Swiss Herbal). *vitamin B compound.*

Hip-Rex (3M Pharmaceuticals). *methenamine hippurate.*

Hismanal (Johnson & Johnson • Merck). *astemizole.*

histamethizine. see meclizine hydrochloride.

histamine phosphate. **(Bioniche).**

Hivid (Roche). *zalcitabine.*

homatropine. **[Homatropine, General Monograph, CPhA]; Minims Homatropine.**

homatropine hydrobromide. **[Homatropine, General Monograph, CPhA]; Isopto Homatropine.**

homosalate/dimethicone/menthol/octyl methoxycinnamate/oxybenzone. **Zilactin-Lip.**

Honvol (Carter Horner). *diethylstilbestrol sodium diphosphate.*

Hormodausse (Technilab). *beef serum proteins/iron/liver extract/vitamin B compound.*

Hp-PAC (Abbott). *lansoprazole.*

Humalog (Lilly). *insulin lispro.*

†Humate-P. *antihemophilic factor (human).*

Humatin (Parke-Davis). *paromomycin sulfate.*

Humatrope (Lilly). *somatropin.*

Humegon (Organon). *gonadotropin (human) chorionic.*

†Humorsol. *demecarium bromide.*

Humulin 10/90 (Lilly). *insulin injection (human)/insulin isophane (human).*

Humulin 20/80 (Lilly). *insulin injection (human)/insulin isophane (human).*

Humulin 30/70 (Lilly). *insulin injection (human)/insulin isophane (human).*

Humulin 40/60 (Lilly). *insulin injection (human)/insulin isophane (human).*

Humulin 50/50 (Lilly). *insulin injection (human)/insulin isophane (human).*

Humulin-L (Lilly). *insulin zinc (human).*

Humulin-N (Lilly). *insulin isophane (human).*

Humulin-R (Lilly). *insulin injection (human).*

Humulin-U (Lilly). *insulin zinc, extended (human).*

hyaluronidase. **Wydase.**

†Hybolin Decanoate. *nandrolone decanoate.*

†Hybolin-Improved. *nandrolone phenpropionate.*

Hycamtin (SmithKline Beecham). *topotecan hydrochloride.*

Hycodan (DuPont Pharma). *hydrocodone bitartrate.*

Hycomine (DuPont Pharma). *ammonium chloride/hydrocodone bitartrate/phenylephrine hydrochloride/pyrilamine maleate.*

Hycomine-S (DuPont Pharma). *ammonium chloride/hydrocodone bitartrate/phenylephrine hydrochloride/pyrilamine maleate.*

Hycort (ICN). *hydrocortisone.*

†Hydeltrasol. *prednisolone sodium phosphate.*

†Hydeltra T.B.A. *prednisolone tebutate.*

Hydergine (Novartis Pharmaceuticals). *ergoloid mesylates.*

Hyderm (Taro). *hydrocortisone acetate.*

hydralazine hydrochloride. hydrallazine. **Apo-Hydralazine, Apresoline, Novo-Hylazin, Nu-Hydral.**

hydralazine hydrochloride/hydrochlorothiazide/reserpine. **Ser-Ap-Es.**

hydrallazine. see hydralazine hydrochloride.

Hydrasense Nasal Care (Schering). *sea water.*

hydrated magnesium aluminate. see magaldrate.

Hydrea (Squibb). *hydroxyurea.*

hydrochlorothiazide. dihydrochlorothiazide. **[Hydrochlorothiazide, General Monograph, CPhA]; Apo-Hydro, HydroDiuril.** †Esidrix, †Oretic.

hydrochlorothiazide/amiloride hydrochloride. **Alti-Amiloride HCTZ, Apo-Amilzide, Moduret, Novamilor, Nu-Amilzide.** †Moduretic.

hydrochlorothiazide/bisoprolol fumarate. †Ziac.

hydrochlorothiazide/captopril. †Capozide.

hydrochlorothiazide/deserpidine. †Oreticyl.

hydrochlorothiazide/enalapril maleate. **Vaseretic.**

Names **underlined** have complete prescribing information in the *CPS* Monograph Section.

hydrochlorothiazide/guanethidine monosulfate. †Esimil.

hydrochlorothiazide/hydralazine hydrochloride/reserpine. **Ser-Ap-Es.**

hydrochlorothiazide/lisinopril. **Prinzide, Zestoretic.**

hydrochlorothiazide/losartan potassium. **Hyzaar.**

hydrochlorothiazide/methyldopa. **Aldoril-15, Aldoril-25, Apo-Methazide.**

hydrochlorothiazide/pindolol. **Viskazide.**

hydrochlorothiazide/propranolol hydrochloride. **Inderide.**

hydrochlorothiazide/quinapril hydrochloride. **Accuretic.**

hydrochlorothiazide/reserpine. **Hydropres-25.**

hydrochlorothiazide/spironolactone. **Aldactazide 25, Aldactazide 50, Novo-Spirozine.**

hydrochlorothiazide/timolol maleate. **Timolide.**

hydrochlorothiazide/triamterene. **Apo-Triazide, Dyazide, Novo-Triamzide, Nu-Triazide.** †Maxzide.

hydrocodone bitartrate. dihydrocodeinone bitartrate. [**Opioids, General Monograph, CPhA**]; **Hycodan, Robidone.**

hydrocodone bitartrate/ammonium chloride/phenylephrine hydrochloride/pyrilamine maleate. **Hycomine, Hycomine-S.**

hydrocodone bitartrate/brompheniramine maleate/guaifenesin/ phenylephrine hydrochloride/phenylpropanolamine hydrochloride. **Dimetane Expectorant-DC.**

hydrocodone bitartrate/doxylamine succinate/etafedrine hydrochloride/sodium citrate. **Calmydone, Dalmacol, Mercodol with Decapryn.**

hydrocodone bitartrate/guaifenesin/pheniramine maleate/ phenylpropanolamine hydrochloride/pyrilamine maleate. **Triaminic Expectorant DH.**

hydrocodone bitartrate/guaifenesin/phenylephrine hydrochloride. **Novahistex DH Expectorant.**

hydrocodone bitartrate/pheniramine maleate/ phenylpropanolamine hydrochloride/pyrilamine maleate. **Caldomine-DH, Tussaminic DH.**

hydrocodone bitartrate/phenylephrine hydrochloride. **Coristex-DH, Coristine-DH, Novahistex DH, Novahistine DH.**

hydrocodone/phenyltoloxamine. **Tussionex.**

hydrocortisone. cortisol. [**Corticosteroids: Systemic, Corticosteroids: Topical, General Monographs, CPhA**]; **Aquacort, Cortate, Cortef, Cortenema, Cortoderm, Emo-Cort, Hycort, Prevex HC, Sarna HC.** †Acticort 100, †Cetacort, †Cort-Dome, †Cortril, †Dermacort, †Dermtex HC, †Hi-Cor, †Hydrocortone, †Hydro-Tex, †Hytone, †Nutracort, †Penecort, †Proctocort, †Synacort.

hydrocortisone-17-valerate. [**Corticosteroids: Topical, General Monograph, CPhA**]; **Westcort.**

hydrocortisone acetate. [**Corticosteroids: Topical, General Monograph, CPhA**]; **Cortamed, Cortifoam, Hyderm, Rectocort.** †Corticaine, †Dermarest DriCort, †Epifoam, †Hemril-HC.

hydrocortisone acetate/allantoin/butoxyethyl nicotinate/ chloramphenicol/sulfur. **Actinac.**

hydrocortisone acetate/benzocaine/zinc sulfate monohydrate. **Rectogel HC.**

hydrocortisone acetate/chloramphenicol. **Pentamycetin/HC.**

hydrocortisone acetate/dibucaine hydrochloride/esculin/framycetin sulfate. **Proctosone.**

hydrocortisone acetate/neomycin sulfate. **Neo-Cortef.**

hydrocortisone acetate/pramoxine hydrochloride. **Pramox-HC, Proctofoam-HC.**

hydrocortisone acetate/pramoxine hydrochloride/zinc sulfate monohydrate. **Anugesic-HC, Proctodan-HC.**

hydrocortisone acetate/urea. **Uremol-HC.**

hydrocortisone acetate/zinc sulfate monohydrate. **Anodan-HC, Anusol-HC, Hemcort HC, PMS-Egozinc-HC, Rivasol HC.**

hydrocortisone/acetic acid/benzethonium chloride/1,2-propanediol diacetate. **VōSoL HC.**

hydrocortisone/bacitracin zinc/neomycin sulfate/polymyxin B sulfate. **Cortisporin Ointment, Cortisporin Ophthalmic Ointment.**

hydrocortisone butyrate. [**Corticosteroids: Topical, General Monograph, CPhA**]; †Locoid.

hydrocortisone/clioquinol. **Vioform Hydrocortisone.**

hydrocortisone/dibucaine hydrochloride/esculin/framycetin sulfate. **Proctosedyl.**

hydrocortisone/fusidic acid. Fucidin H Cream.

hydrocortisone/neomycin sulfate/polymyxin B sulfate. **Cortimyxin, Cortisporin Eye/Ear Suspension, Cortisporin Otic Solution.**

hydrocortisone/silicone. **Barriere-HC.**

hydrocortisone sodium succinate. [**Corticosteroids: Systemic, General Monograph, CPhA**]; **A-Hydrocort, Solu-Cortef.**

hydrocortisone/urea. **Calmurid HC, Ti-U-Lac HC.**

†Hydrocortone. *hydrocortisone.*

HydroDiuril (MSD). *hydrochlorothiazide.*

hydroflumethiazide. †Diucardin, †Saluron.

Hydromorph Contin (Purdue Frederick). *hydromorphone hydrochloride.*

hydromorphone hydrochloride. dihydromorphinone hydrochloride. [**Opioids, General Monograph, CPhA**]; **Dilaudid, Dilaudid-HP, Dilaudid-HP-Plus, Dilaudid Sterile Powder, Dilaudid-XP, Hydromorph Contin, PMS-Hydromorphone; (Sabex).**

†Hydromox. *quinethazone.*

Hydropres-25 (MSD). *hydrochlorothiazide/reserpine.*

hydroquinone. **Eldopaque, Eldoquin, Neostrata HQ, Solaquin, Solaquin Forte, Ultraquin.**

hydroquinone/glycolic acid. **Viquin Forte.**

†Hydro-Tex. *hydrocortisone.*

hydroxocobalamin. vitamin B_{12a}. [**Vitamin B_{12}, General Monograph, CPhA**]; **Acti-B_{12}.**

hydroxychloroquine sulfate. **Plaquenil.**

1α-hydroxycholecalciferol. see alfacalcidol.

25-hydroxycholecalciferol. see calcifediol.

hydroxyephedrine hydrochloride/emetine hydrochloride/ normethadone hydrochloride. **Cophylac Expectorant.**

hydroxyephedrine hydrochloride/normethadone hydrochloride. **Cophylac.**

hydroxyethylcellulose/sodium chloride. **Minims Artificial Tears.**

hydroxyprogesterone caproate. †Hy/Gestrone, †Hylutin.

hydroxypropyl cellulose. **Lacrisert.**

hydroxypropyl methylcellulose. **Genteal, Isopto Tears.** †Ocucoat.

hydroxypropyl methylcellulose/dextran 70. **Bion Tears, Tears Naturale, Tears Naturale Free, Tears Naturale II.**

hydroxyurea. **Hydrea.**

1α-hydroxyvitamin D_3. see alfacalcidol.

25-hydroxyvitamin D_3. see calcifediol.

hydroxyzine hydrochloride. **Apo-Hydroxyzine, Atarax, Multipax, Novo-Hydroxyzin, PMS-Hydroxyzine.** †Anxanil, †Quiess, †Vistazine 50.

hydroxyzine pamoate. †Vistaril.

†Hy/Gestrone. *hydroxyprogesterone caproate.*

Hygroton (Novartis Pharmaceuticals). *chlorthalidone.*

hylan G-F 20. **Synvisc.**

†Hylorel. *guanadrel sulfate.*

†Hylutin. *hydroxyprogesterone caproate.*

hyoscine butylbromide. see scopolamine butylbromide.

hyoscine hydrobromide. see scopolamine hydrobromide.

hyoscyamine. †Cystospaz.

hyoscyamine sulfate. **Levsin.** †Anaspaz, †Gastrosed.

hyoscyamine sulfate/atropine sulfate/attapulgite, activated/opium/pectin/scopolamine hydrobromide. **Diban.**

hyoscyamine sulfate/atropine sulfate/phenobarbital/scopolamine hydrobromide. **Donnatal.**

Hypaque Parenteral (Nycomed Imaging A.S.). *diatrizoate meglumine/diatrizoate sodium.*

Hyperstat (Schering). *diazoxide.*

Hypotears (CIBA Vision). *polyvinyl alcohol.*

Hypotears Eye Ointment (CIBA Vision). *mineral oil/white petrolatum.*

Hyskon (Medisan Pharmaceuticals). *dextran 70/dextrose.*

Hytakerol (Sanofi). *dihydrotachysterol.*

†Hytone. *hydrocortisone.*

Hytrin (Abbott). *terazosin hydrochloride dihydrate.*

Hyzaar (MSD). *hydrochlorothiazide/losartan potassium.*

I

†Ibu. *ibuprofen.*

ibuprofen. **Actiprofen, Advil, Alti-Ibuprofen, Apo-Ibuprofen, Motrin, Motrin (Children's), Motrin IB, Novo-Profen, Nu-Ibuprofen.** †Ibu, †Rufen.

ibuprofen/pseudoephedrine hydrochloride. **Advil Cold & Sinus, Dristan Sinus.**

ICAPS (CIBA Vision). *multiple vitamins and minerals.*

ICAPS Time Release (CIBA Vision). *multiple vitamins and minerals.*

Idamycin (Pharmacia & Upjohn). *idarubicin hydrochloride.*

Idarac (Sanofi). *floctafenine.*

idarubicin hydrochloride. **Idamycin.**

idoxuridine. **Herplex, Herplex-D.**

Ifex (Bristol). *ifosfamide.*

ifosfamide. **Ifex.**

Iletin Lente (Lilly). *insulin zinc (beef and pork).*

Iletin NPH (Lilly). *insulin isophane (beef and pork).*

Iletin Regular (Lilly). *insulin injection (beef and pork).*

Iletin II Pork Lente (Lilly). *insulin zinc (pork).*

Iletin II Pork NPH (Lilly). *insulin isophane (pork).*

Iletin II Pork Regular (Lilly). *insulin injection (pork).*

Ilosone (Lilly). *erythromycin estolate.*

†Imagent GI. *perflubron.*

Imdur (Astra). *isosorbide-5-mononitrate.*

imipenem/cilastatin sodium. **Primaxin.**

imipramine hydrochloride. **Apo-Imipramine, Tofranil.** †Norfranil, †Tipramine.

imiquimod. †Aldara.

Imitrex Injection/Tablets (Glaxo Wellcome). *sumatriptan succinate.*

Imitrex Nasal Spray (Glaxo Wellcome). *sumatriptan hemisulfate.*

ImmuCyst (Connaught). *Bacillus Calmette-Guérin, intravesical.*

immune globulin, hepatitis B (human). hepatitis B immune globulin (human). **Bayhep B.**

immune globulin (human), i.m. **Baygam.**

immune globulin (human), i.v. **Gamimune N, Iveegam Immuno.**

immune globulin, rabies (human). rabies immune globulin (human). **Bayrab.**

immune globulin, rabies pasteurized (human). **Imogam Rabies.**

immune globulin, Rh_o (D) (human). Rh_o (D) immune globulin (human). **WinRho SDF.**

immune globulin, tetanus (human). tetanus immune globulin (human). **[Tetanus Immune Globulin (Human), General Monograph, CPhA]; Baytet.**

Immunine VH (Baxter). *factor IX concentrate (human).*

Imodium (Janssen-Ortho/McNeil Consumer Products). *loperamide hydrochloride.*

Imogam Rabies (Connaught). *immune globulin, rabies pasteurized (human).*

Imovane (Rhône-Poulenc Rorer). *zopiclone.*

Imovax (Connaught). *rabies vaccine, inactivated (diploid cell origin).*

Imuran Injection (Glaxo Wellcome). *azathioprine sodium.*

Imuran Tablets (Glaxo Wellcome). *azathioprine.*

indapamide. **Apo-Indapamide, Novo-Indapamide.** †Lozol.

indapamide hemihydrate. **Gen-Indapamide, Lozide, Nu-Indapamide.**

Inderal (Wyeth-Ayerst). *propranolol hydrochloride.*

Inderal-LA (Wyeth-Ayerst). *propranolol hydrochloride.*

Inderide (Wyeth-Ayerst). *hydrochlorothiazide/propranolol hydrochloride.*

indinavir sulfate. **Crixivan.**

Indocid (MSD). *indomethacin.*

Indocid P.D.A. (MSD). *indomethacin sodium.*

Indocid SR (MSD). *indomethacin.*

†Indocin. *indomethacin.*

indomethacin. **Apo-Indomethacin, Indocid, Indocid SR, Indotec, Novo-Methacin, Nu-Indo, Rhodacine.** †Indocin.

indomethacin sodium. **Indocid P.D.A.**

Indotec (Technilab). *indomethacin.*

infant formula. **Bonamil, Follow-Up, Good Start, SMA Preparations.**

infant formula, casein hydrolysate. **Alimentum, Enfalac Nutramigen, Enfalac Pregestimil.**

infant formula, lactose-free. **Similac LF.**

infant formula, low birthweight. **SMA, Preemie.**

infant formula, soy protein isolate. **Alsoy, Enfalac Prosobee, Follow-Up Soy, Isomil, Nursoy.**

Infantol (Carter Horner). *multiple vitamins.*

Inflamase Forte (CIBA Vision). *prednisolone sodium phosphate.*

Inflamase Mild (CIBA Vision). *prednisolone sodium phosphate.*

influenza virus vaccine, inactivated. **Fluviral S/F, Fluzone.**

influenza virus vaccine trivalent types A and B (split-virion), inactivated. **Vaxigrip.**

influenza virus vaccine trivalent (whole-virion), inactivated. **Fluviral.**

Infufer (Sabex). *iron dextran.*

INH. see isoniazid.

Inhibace (Roche). *cilazapril.*

Innohep (Leo). *tinzaparin sodium.*

Inocor (Sanofi). *amrinone lactate.*

inosiplex. **Isoprinosine.**

inositol/ascorbic acid/thiamine. **Vitathion-A.T.P.**

insulin delivery device. **Novolin-Pen 1.5, Novolin-Pen 3.**

insulin injection (beef and pork). **Iletin Regular.**

Names **underlined** have complete prescribing information in the *CPS* Monograph Section.

insulin injection (human). **Humulin-R, Novolin ge Toronto.**

insulin injection (human)/insulin isophane (human). **Humulin 10/90, Humulin 20/80, Humulin 30/70, Humulin 40/60, Humulin 50/50, Novolin ge 10/90, Novolin ge 20/80, Novolin ge 30/70, Novolin ge 40/60, Novolin ge 50/50.**

insulin injection (pork). **Iletin II Pork Regular.**

insulin isophane (beef and pork). **Iletin NPH.**

insulin isophane (human). **Humulin-N, Novolin ge NPH.**

insulin isophane (human)/insulin injection (human). **Humulin 10/90, Humulin 20/80, Humulin 30/70, Humulin 40/60, Humulin 50/50, Novolin ge 10/90, Novolin ge 20/80, Novolin ge 30/70, Novolin ge 40/60, Novolin ge 50/50.**

insulin isophane (pork). **Iletin II Pork NPH.**

insulin lispro. **Humalog.**

insulin zinc (beef and pork). **Iletin Lente.**

insulin zinc, extended (human). **Humulin-U, Novolin ge Ultralente.**

insulin zinc (human). **Humulin-L, Novolin ge Lente.**

insulin zinc (pork). **Iletin II Pork Lente.**

Intal (Rhône-Poulenc Rorer). *sodium cromoglycate.*

Intal Inhaler/Syncroner (Rhône-Poulenc Rorer). *sodium cromoglycate.*

Intal Spincaps/Nebulizer (Rhône-Poulenc Rorer). *sodium cromoglycate.*

interferon alfa-n3. †Alferon N.

interferon alfa-2a. **Roferon-A.**

interferon alfa-2b. **Intron A.**

interferon alpha-n1 (Ins). **Wellferon.**

interferon beta-1a. Avonex, **Rebif.**

interferon beta-1b. **Betaseron.**

interferon gamma-1b recombinant. †Actimmune.

Intralipid (Pharmacia & Upjohn). *fat emulsion.*

intrauterine contraceptive. **Gyne-T 380 Slimline Intrauterine Copper Contraceptive, Gyne-T Intrauterine Copper Contraceptive, Nova-T.**

Intron A (Schering). *interferon alfa-2b.*

Intropin (DuPont Pharma). *dopamine hydrochloride.*

†Inversine. *mecamylamine hydrochloride.*

Invirase (Roche). *saquinavir mesylate.*

iocetamic acid. †Cholebrine.

iodixanol. **Visipaque.**

iodochlorydroxyquine. see clioquinol.

iodoquinol. diiodohydroxyquin. diiodohydroxyquinolone. **Diodoquin.** †Yodoquinol.

iohexol. **Omnipaque.**

Ionamin (Rhône-Poulenc Rorer). *phentermine.*

Ionil (Galderma). *benzalkonium chloride/salicylic acid.*

Ionil-T (Galderma). *benzalkonium chloride/coal tar.*

Ionil-T Plus (Galderma). *coal tar.*

Iopidine (Alcon). *apraclonidine hydrochloride.*

iopromide. **Ultravist.**

iothalamate meglumine. meglumine iothalamate. **Conray 30, Conray 43, Conray 60, Cysto-Conray, Cysto-Conray II.**

iotrolan. **Osmovist.**

ioversol. **Optiray.**

ioxaglate meglumine/ioxaglate sodium. **Hexabrix.**

ioxaglate sodium/ioxaglate meglumine. **Hexabrix.**

ipecac. **[Ipecac Syrup, General Monograph, CPhA].**

†I-Phrine. *phenylephrine hydrochloride.*

†I-Picamide. *tropicamide.*

†Ipol. *poliovirus vaccine (inactivated enhanced potency).*

ipratropium bromide. **Alti-Ipratropium, Apo-Ipravent, Atrovent Inhalation Aerosol, Atrovent Inhalation Solution, Atrovent Nasal Spray, Novo-Ipramide, Nu-Ipratropium, PMS-Ipratropium.**

ipratropium bromide/fenoterol hydrobromide. **Duovent UDV.**

ipratropium bromide/salbutamol sulfate. **Combivent Inhalation Aerosol, Combivent Inhalation Solution.**

†I-Pred. *prednisolone sodium phosphate.*

IPV. see poliomyelitis vaccine, inactivated (diploid cell origin).

irbesartan. **Avapro.**

irinotecan hydrochloride trihydrate. **Camptosar.**

iron/beef serum proteins/liver extract/vitamin B compound. **Hormodausse.**

iron dextran. **Dexiron, Infufer.**

iron salts. **(General Monograph, CPhA).**

iron-sorbitol-citric acid complex dextrin-stabilized. **Jectofer.**

Ismo (Wyeth-Ayerst). *isosorbide-5-mononitrate.*

Isocal (Mead Johnson). *enteral nutrition.*

Isocal HN (Mead Johnson). *enteral nutrition.*

Isocal with Fibre (Mead Johnson). *enteral nutrition.*

isoetharine. †Bronkosol.

isoetharine mesylate. †Bronkometer.

isoflurane. **Forane; (Abbott), (Schein Pharmaceutical), (Technilab).**

isoflurophate. difluorophate. dyflos. †Floropryl.

isomeprobamate. see carisoprodol.

isometheptene mucate/acetaminophen/dichloralphenazone. †Miltride.

Isomil (Abbott). *infant formula, soy protein isolate.*

isoniazid. INH. isonicotinic acid hydrazide. isonicotinylhydrazide. **[Isoniazid, General Monograph, CPhA]; Isotamine, PMS-Isoniazid.** †Nydrazid.

isoniazid/pyrazinamide/rifampin. **Rifater.**

isoniazid/rifampin. †Rifamate.

isonicotinic acid hydrazide. see isoniazid.

isonicotinylhydrazide. see isoniazid.

isonipecaine. see pethidine hydrochloride.

isoprenaline. see isoproterenol hydrochloride.

Isoprinosine (Rivex Pharma). *inosiplex.*

isopropamide iodide/trifluoperazine hydrochloride. **Stelabid.**

isopropanol. see isopropyl alcohol.

isopropyl alcohol. isopropanol. **Alcojel, Duonalc.**

isopropyl alcohol/ethyl alcohol. **Duonalc-E Solution.**

isopropyl alcohol/resorcinol/sulfur. **Acnomel Cream.**

isopropylarterenol. see isoproterenol hydrochloride.

isopropylnoradrenaline. see isoproterenol hydrochloride.

isopropyl palmitate/mineral oil/tar distillate. **Doak-Oil, Doak-Oil Forte.**

isoproterenol hydrochloride. isoprenaline. isopropylarterenol. isopropylnoradrenaline. **Isuprel.**

Isoptin (Knoll). *verapamil hydrochloride.*

Isoptin I.V. (Knoll). *verapamil hydrochloride.*

Isoptin SR (Knoll). *verapamil hydrochloride.*

Isopto Atropine (Alcon). *atropine sulfate.*

Isopto Carbachol (Alcon). *carbachol.*

Isopto Carpine (Alcon). *pilocarpine hydrochloride.*

†Isopto Eserine. *physostigmine salicylate.*

Isopto Homatropine (Alcon). *homatropine hydrobromide.*

Isopto Tears (Alcon). *hydroxypropyl methylcellulose.*

Isordil (Wyeth-Ayerst). *isosorbide dinitrate.*

isosorbide dinitrate. sorbide nitrate. **Apo-ISDN, Cedocard SR, Isordil.**

isosorbide-5-mononitrate. **Imdur, Ismo.**

Isosource (Novartis Nutrition). *enteral nutrition.*

Isosource HN (Novartis Nutrition). *enteral nutrition.*

Isosource VHN (Novartis Nutrition). *enteral nutrition.*

Isotamine (ICN). *isoniazid.*

isotretinoin. cis-retinoic acid. **Accutane Roche, Isotrex.**

Isotrex (Stiefel). *isotretinoin.*

isoxsuprine hydrochloride. †Vasodilan.

isradipine. †DynaCirc.

Isuprel (Sanofi). *isoproterenol hydrochloride.*

itraconazole. **Sporanox Capsules, Sporanox Oral Solution.**

Iveegam Immuno (Baxter). *immune globulin (human), i.v.*

J

Japanese encephalitis virus vaccine (inactivated). **Je-Vax.**

Jectofer (Astra). *iron-sorbitol-citric acid complex dextrin-stabilized.*

Je-Vax (Connaught). *Japanese encephalitis virus vaccine (inactivated).*

jojoba oil/mineral oil. **Prevex Oil.**

juniper tar/coal tar/pine tar/zinc pyrithione. **Multi-Tar Plus.**

K

Kabikinase (Pharmacia & Upjohn). *streptokinase.*

†Kabolin. *nandrolone decanoate.*

Kadian (Knoll). *morphine sulfate.*

kanamycin sulfate. †Kantrex.

†Kantrex. *kanamycin sulfate.*

Kaochlor (Pharmacia & Upjohn). *potassium chloride.*

kaolin/opium/pectin. **Donnagel-PG Suspension.**

Kaon (Pharmacia & Upjohn). *potassium gluconate.*

Kaopectate (Johnson & Johnson • Merck). *attapulgite, activated.*

Kayexalate (Sanofi). *sodium polystyrene sulfonate.*

K-Dur (Key). *potassium chloride.*

Keflex (Lilly). *cephalexin.*

Keflin (Lilly). *cephalothin sodium.*

†Keftab. *cephalexin hydrochloride monohydrate.*

Kefurox (Lilly). *cefuroxime sodium.*

Kefzol (Lilly). *cefazolin sodium.*

Kemadrin (Glaxo Wellcome). *procyclidine hydrochloride.*

Kemsol (Carter Horner). *dimethyl sulfoxide.*

†Kenac. *triamcinolone acetonide.*

Kenacomb (Westwood-Squibb). *gramicidin/neomycin sulfate/nystatin/triamcinolone acetonide.*

Kenalog (Westwood-Squibb). *triamcinolone acetonide.*

Kenalog-10 (Westwood-Squibb). *triamcinolone acetonide.*

Kenalog-40 (Westwood-Squibb). *triamcinolone acetonide.*

Kenalog in Orabase (Westwood-Squibb). *triamcinolone acetonide.*

†Kenonel. *triamcinolone acetonide.*

Keralyt (Westwood-Squibb). *salicylic acid.*

†Kerlone. *betaxolol.*

Ketalar (Parke-Davis). *ketamine hydrochloride.*

ketamine hydrochloride. **Ketalar.**

ketocholanic acid. see dehydrocholic acid.

ketoconazole. **Apo-Ketoconazole, Nizoral Cream, Nizoral Shampoo, Nizoral Tablets.**

ketohydroxyestrin. see estrone.

ketoprofen. **Apo-Keto, Apo-Keto-E, Apo-Keto SR, Novo-Keto, Novo-Keto-EC, Nu-Ketoprofen, Nu-Ketoprofen-E, Nu-Ketoprofen-SR, Orafen, Orudis, Orudis E, Orudis SR, Oruvail, Rhodis, Rhodis-EC, Rhodis SR, Rhovail.**

ketorolac tromethamine. **Acular,** Apo-Ketorolac, **Novo-Ketorolac, Toradol, Toradol IM.**

ketotifen fumarate. **Apo-Ketotifen, Novo-Ketotifen, Zaditen.**

Kidrolase (Rhône-Poulenc Rorer). *L-asparaginase.*

Klean-Prep (Rivex Pharma). *electrolytes/polyethylene glycol.*

†Klonopin. *clonazepam.*

K-Lor (Abbott). *potassium chloride.*

†Klor-Con. *potassium chloride.*

K-Lyte (Roberts). *potassium citrate.*

K-Lyte/Cl (Roberts). *potassium chloride.*

Koāte-HP (Bayer). *antihemophilic factor (human).*

Koffex DM (Rougier). *dextromethorphan hydrobromide.*

Kogenate (Bayer). *antihemophilic factor (recombinant).*

†Konakion. *phytonadione.*

K-10 (SmithKline Beecham). *potassium chloride.*

Kwellada-P (R & C). *permethrin.*

†Kybernin. *antithrombin III.*

Kytril (SmithKline Beecham). *granisetron hydrochloride.*

L

labetalol hydrochloride. **Trandate.** †Normodyne.

Lac-Hydrin (Westwood-Squibb). *ammonium lactate.*

Lacri-Lube S.O.P. (Allergan). *lanolin alcohols/mineral oil/white petrolatum.*

Lacrisert (MSD). *hydroxypropyl cellulose.*

Lactaid (McNeil Consumer Products). *lactase.*

lactase. **Dairyaid, Lactaid, Lactrase.**

lactic acid/formalin/salicylic acid. **Duoplant.**

lactic acid/glycerin. **Epi-Lyt AHA.**

lactic acid/salicylic acid. **Cuplex, Duofilm.**

lactic acid/sodium pyrrolidone carboxylate. **Lacticare AHA.**

Lacticare AHA (Stiefel). *lactic acid/sodium pyrrolidone carboxylate.*

lactobacillus acidophillus/lactobacillus bulgaricus/streptococcus lactis. **Fermalac, Fermalac Vaginal.**

lactobacillus acidophilus. **Bacid.**

lactobacillus bulgaricus/lactobacillus acidophillus/streptococcus lactis. **Fermalac, Fermalac Vaginal.**

lactoflavin. see riboflavin.

lactose. **Placebo.**

Lactrase (Rivex Pharma). *lactase.*

lactulose. **Acilac, Duphalac, Laxilose, PMS-Lactulose.**

Lamictal (Glaxo Wellcome). *lamotrigine.*

Lamisil (Novartis Pharmaceuticals). *terbinafine hydrochloride.*

lamivudine. 3TC. **3TC.**

lamotrigine. **Lamictal.**

†Lamprene. *clofazimine.*

Lanohex Skin Cleanser (Rougier). *beta-phenoxyethanol.*

lanolin alcohols/mineral oil/white petrolatum. **Lacri-Lube S.O.P.**

Names underlined have complete prescribing information in the *CPS* Monograph Section.

lanolin/mineral oil/white petrolatum. **Duratears.**

†Lanorinal. *ASA/butalbital/caffeine.*

†Lanoxicaps. *digoxin.*

Lanoxin (Glaxo Wellcome). *digoxin.*

lansoprazole. Hp-PAC, **Prevacid.**

Lansoÿl (Axcan Pharma). *mineral oil.*

Lanvis (Glaxo Wellcome). *thioguanine.*

Largactil (Rhône-Poulenc Rorer). *chlorpromazine hydrochloride.*

†Largon. *propiomazine hydrochloride.*

Lariam (Roche). *mefloquine hydrochloride.*

Lasix (Hoechst Marion Roussel). *furosemide.*

Lasix Special (Hoechst Marion Roussel). *furosemide.*

latanoprost. **Xalatan.**

laureth-4/erythromycin/ethyl alcohol. **Staticin.**

Laxilose (Technilab). *lactulose.*

lecithin/dimethicone. **Complex 15.**

Lectopam (Roche). *bromazepam.*

Ledercillin VK (Wyeth-Ayerst). *penicillin V potassium.*

Lederle Leucovorin Calcium (Wyeth-Ayerst). *calcium folinate.*

lemon extract oil/acetic acid/camphor/sodium lauryl ether sulfate. **SH-206.**

Lenoltec No.1, No.2, No.3 (Technilab). *acetaminophen/caffeine/codeine phosphate.*

Lenoltec No. 4 (Technilab). *acetaminophen/codeine phosphate.*

Leritine Injection (Frosst). *anileridine phosphate.*

Leritine Tablets (Frosst). *anileridine hydrochloride.*

Lescol (Novartis Pharmaceuticals). *fluvastatin sodium.*

letrozole. **Femara.**

leucovorin calcium. see calcium folinate.

Leukeran (Glaxo Wellcome). *chlorambucil.*

†Leukine. *sargramostim.*

leuprolide acetate. **Lupron Depot 3.75 mg, Lupron/Lupron Depot 3.75 mg/7.5 mg, Lupron/Lupron Depot 7.5 mg/22.5 mg.**

Leustatin (Janssen-Ortho). *cladribine.*

levamisole hydrochloride. **Ergamisol, Novo-Levamisole.**

Levaquin (Janssen-Ortho). *levofloxacin.*

levarterenol bitartrate. see norepinephrine bitartrate.

†Levatol. *penbutolol sulfate.*

levobunolol hydrochloride. **Betagan, Novo-Levobunolol, Ophtho-Bunolol; (Rivex Ophthalmics).**

levobunolol hydrochloride/dipivefrin hydrochloride. **Probeta.**

levocabastine hydrochloride. **Livostin Eye Drops, Livostin Nasal Spray.**

levocarnitine. **Carnitor.** †VitaCarn.

levodopa. †Dopar.

levodopa/benserazide hydrochloride. **Prolopa.**

levodopa/carbidopa. **Apo-Levocarb, Endo Levodopa/Carbidopa, Nu-Levocarb, Sinemet, Sinemet CR.**

levofloxacin. **Levaquin.**

levomepromazine maleate. see methotrimeprazine maleate.

levonordefrin/mepivacaine hydrochloride. **Polocaine 2% with Levonordefrin 1:20 000.**

levonorgestrel. **Norplant.**

levonorgestrel/ethinyl estradiol. **Alesse 21, Alesse 28, Min-Ovral 21, Min-Ovral 28, Triphasil 21, Triphasil 28, Triquilar 21, Triquilar 28.** †Nordette, †Tri-Levlen.

Levophed (Sanofi). *norepinephrine bitartrate.*

Levotec (Technilab). *levothyroxine sodium.*

†Levothroid. *levothyroxine sodium.*

levothyroxine sodium. sodium levothyroxine. **Eltroxin, Levotec, Synthroid.** †Levothroid, †Levoxyl.

Levovist (Berlex Canada). *galactose/palmitic acid.*

†Levoxyl. *levothyroxine sodium.*

Levsin (Rivex Pharma). *hyoscyamine sulfate.*

Librax (Roche). *chlordiazepoxide hydrochloride/clidinium bromide.*

†Libritabs. *chlordiazepoxide hydrochloride.*

†Licon. *fluocinonide.*

Lidemol (Medicis). *fluocinonide.*

Lidex (Medicis). *fluocinonide.*

lidocaine. lignocaine. **Lidodan Ointment, Xylocaine Dental Ointment 5%, Xylocaine Ointment 5%, Xylocaine Topical 5%, Zilactin-L.**

lidocaine/epinephrine. **(Bioniche).**

lidocaine/fluorescein sodium. **Minims Lidocaine/Fluorescein.**

lidocaine hydrocarbonate. **Xylocaine CO_2.**

lidocaine hydrochloride. **Lidodan Entotracheal, Lidodan Viscous, Xylocaine Endotracheal, Xylocaine 4% Sterile Solution, Xylocaine Jelly 2%, Xylocaine Parenteral without Epinephrine, Xylocaine Topical 4%, Xylocaine Viscous 2%, Xylocard; (Abbott), (Bioniche).**

lidocaine hydrochloride/dextrose. **(Baxter).**

lidocaine hydrochloride/epinephrine. **Xylocaine Dental Solutions, Xylocaine Parenteral with Epinephrine.**

lidocaine hydrochloride/glucose. **Xylocaine Spinal 5%.**

lidocaine hydrochloride/gramicidin/polymyxin B sulfate. **Lidosporin Cream, Polysporin Antibiotic Burn Cream.**

lidocaine hydrochloride/methylprednisolone acetate. **Depo-Medrol with Lidocaine.**

lidocaine hydrochloride/polymyxin B sulfate. **Lidosporin Ear Drops.**

lidocaine/prilocaine. **EMLA.**

Lidodan Entotracheal (Odan). *lidocaine hydrochloride.*

Lidodan Ointment (Odan). *lidocaine.*

Lidodan Viscous (Odan) *lidocaine hydrochloride.*

Lidosporin Cream (Warner-Lambert Consumer Healthcare). *gramicidin/lidocaine hydrochloride/polymyxin B sulfate.*

Lidosporin Ear Drops (Warner-Lambert Consumer Healthcare). *lidocaine hydrochloride/polymyxin B sulfate.*

lignocaine. see lidocaine.

†Limbitrol. *amitriptyline hydrochloride/chlordiazepoxide.*

Lincocin (Pharmacia & Upjohn). *lincomycin hydrochloride monohydrate.*

lincomycin hydrochloride monohydrate. **Lincocin.** †Lincorex.

†Lincorex. *lincomycin hydrochloride monohydrate.*

lindane. gamma benzene hexachloride. **Hexit, PMS-Lindane.**

Lioresal (Novartis Pharmaceuticals). *baclofen.*

Lioresal Intrathecal (Novartis Pharmaceuticals). *baclofen.*

Liotec (Technilab). *baclofen.*

liotrix. †Thyrolar.

Lipactin (Novartis Consumer Health). *heparin sodium/zinc sulfate.*

Lipidil Micro (Fournier). *fenofibrate (micronized).*

Lipisorb (Mead Johnson). *enteral nutrition.*

Lipitor (Parke-Davis). *atorvastatin calcium.*

liposomal daunorubicin. **DaunoXome.**

liquid carbonis detergens. **Targel.**

liquid carbonis detergens/salicylic acid. **Targel S.A.**

liquid carbonis detergens/salicylic acid/triclosan. **Tardan.**

liquid paraffin. **Oilatum Dermatological Shower and Bath Oil.**

Liquifilm Forte (Allergan). *polyvinyl alcohol.*

Liquifilm Tears (Allergan). *polyvinyl alcohol.*

Liquor Carbonis Detergens (Odan). *coal tar.*

lisinopril. **[ACE Inhibitors, General Monograph, CPhA]; Apo-Lisinopril, Prinivil, Zestril.**

lisinopril/hydrochlorothiazide. **Prinzide, Zestoretic.**

†Lite Pred. *prednisolone sodium phosphate.*

Lithane (Pfizer). *lithium carbonate.*

lithium carbonate. **[Lithium, General Monograph, CPhA]; Carbolith, Duralith, Lithane, PMS-Lithium Carbonate.** †Eskalith.

lithium citrate. **[Lithium, General Monograph, CPhA]; PMS-Lithium Citrate.** †Cibalith-S.

†Lithostat. *acetohydroxamic acid.*

liver extract/beef serum proteins/iron/vitamin B compound. **Hormodausse.**

Livostin Eye Drops (CIBA Vision). *levocabastine hydrochloride.*

Livostin Nasal Spray (Janssen-Ortho). *levocabastine hydrochloride.*

Locacorten Vioform (Novartis Pharmaceuticals). *clioquinol/ flumethasone pivalate.*

Locacorten Vioform Eardrops (Novartis Pharmaceuticals). *clioquinol/flumethasone pivalate.*

Locasalen (Novartis Pharmaceuticals). *flumethasone pivalate/ salicylic acid.*

†Locoid. *hydrocortisone butyrate.*

†Lodine. *etodolac.*

lodoxamide tromethamine. **Alomide.**

Loestrin 1.5/30 (Parke-Davis). *ethinyl estradiol/norethindrone acetate.*

Lofenalac (Mead Johnson). *enteral nutrition.*

Lomine (Riva). *dicyclomine hydrochloride.*

Lomotil (Searle). *atropine sulfate/diphenoxylate hydrochloride.*

lomustine. CCNU. **CeeNU.**

Loniten (Pharmacia & Upjohn). *minoxidil.*

†Lo/Ovral. *ethinyl estradiol/norgestrel.*

Loperacap (ICN). *loperamide hydrochloride.*

loperamide hydrochloride. **Apo-Loperamide, Imodium, Loperacap, Novo-Loperamide, Rho-Loperamide.**

Lopid (Parke-Davis). *gemfibrozil.*

Lopresor (Novartis Pharmaceuticals). *metoprolol tartrate.*

Loprox (Hoechst Marion Roussel). *ciclopirox olamine.*

†Lopurin. *allopurinol.*

†Lorabid. *loracarbef.*

loracarbef. †Lorabid.

loratadine. **Claritin.**

loratadine/pseudoephedrine sulfate. **Chlor-Tripolon N.D., Claritin Extra.**

lorazepam. **[Benzodiazepines, General Monograph, CPhA]; Apo-Lorazepam, Ativan, Novo-Lorazem, Nu-Loraz.**

losartan potassium. **Cozaar.**

losartan potassium/hydrochlorothiazide. **Hyzaar.**

Losec (Astra). *omeprazole magnesium.*

Lotensin (Novartis Pharmaceuticals). *benazepril hydrochloride.*

Lotriderm (Schering). *betamethasone dipropionate/clotrimazole.*

†Lotrisone. *betamethasone dipropionate/clotrimazole.*

lovastatin. **Apo-Lovastatin, Mevacor.**

Lovenox (Rhône-Poulenc Rorer). *enoxaparin.*

Loxapac (Wyeth-Ayerst). *loxapine.*

loxapine. oxilapine. **Apo-Loxapine, Loxapac, PMS-Loxapine.** †Loxitane.

loxapine succinate. **Nu-Loxapine.**

†Loxitane. *loxapine.*

Lozide (Servier). *indapamide hemihydrate.*

†Lozol. *indapamide.*

lubricating jelly. **Taro Gel.**

Ludiomil (Novartis Pharmaceuticals). *maprotiline hydrochloride.*

†Lufyllin. *dyphylline.*

†Luminal. *phenobarbital.*

Lupron Depot 3.75 mg (Abbott). *leuprolide acetate.*

Lupron/Lupron Depot 3.75 mg/7.5 mg (Abbott/Tap Pharmaceuticals). *leuprolide acetate.*

Lupron/Lupron Depot 7.5 mg/22.5 mg (Abbott). *leuprolide acetate.*

Lutrepulse (Ferring). *gonadorelin acetate.*

Luvox (Solvay Pharma). *fluvoxamine maleate.*

Lyderm (Taro). *fluocinonide.*

Lydonide (Technilab). *fluocinonide.*

lymphocyte immune globulin/anti-thymocyte globulin (equine). **Atgam.**

†Lyphocin. *vancomycin hydrochloride.*

lypressin. †Diapid.

Lysodren (Bristol). *mitotane.*

Lyteprep (Therapex). *electrolytes/polyethylene glycol.*

M

Maalox (Novartis Consumer Health). *aluminum hydroxide/ magnesium hydroxide.*

Maalox HRF (Novartis Consumer Health). *aluminum hydroxide-magnesium carbonate/magnesium alginate/ magnesium carbonate.*

Maalox H2 Acid Controller (Novartis Consumer Health). *famotidine.*

Maalox Plus (Novartis Consumer Health). *aluminum hydroxide/ magnesium hydroxide/simethicone.*

Maalox Plus Extra Strength (Novartis Consumer Health). *aluminum hydroxide/magnesium hydroxide/simethicone.*

Maalox TC (Novartis Consumer Health). *aluminum hydroxide/ magnesium hydroxide.*

MacroBID (Procter & Gamble Pharmaceuticals). *nitrofurantoin/ nitrofurantoin monohydrate.*

Macrodantin (Procter & Gamble Pharmaceuticals). *nitrofurantoin.*

magaldrate. hydrated magnesium aluminate. monalium hydrate. **Riopan.**

magaldrate/simethicone. **Riopan Plus.**

Maglucate (Pharmascience). *magnesium gluconate.*

magnesium alginate/aluminum hydroxide-magnesium carbonate/ magnesium carbonate. **Maalox HRF.**

magnesium/calcium carbonate/copper/manganese/vitamin D/zinc. **Caltrate Plus.**

magnesium carbonate/alginic acid. **Gaviscon Heartburn Relief Formula Aluminum-free Tablets.**

magnesium carbonate/aluminum hydroxide-magnesium carbonate/ magnesium alginate. **Maalox HRF.**

magnesium carbonate/ASA/calcium carbonate/magnesium oxide. **Aspirin With Stomach Guard.**

Names **underlined** have complete prescribing information in the *CPS* Monograph Section.

magnesium carbonate/ascorbic acid/magnesium sulfate/vitamin B compound. **Redoxon-B.**

magnesium chloride. **Slow-Mag.**

magnesium citrate. **Citro-Mag.**

magnesium citrate/bisacodyl. **Royvac.**

magnesium glucoheptonate. **Magnesium-Rougier.**

magnesium gluconate. **Maglucate, Oligosol, Magnesium.**

magnesium hydroxide/aluminum hydroxide. **Diovol, Diovol Ex, Gelusil, Gelusil Extra Strength, Maalox, Maalox TC, Mylanta Double Strength Plain Liquid, Univol.**

magnesium hydroxide/aluminum hydroxide/oxethazaine. **Mucaine.**

magnesium hydroxide/aluminum hydroxide/simethicone. **Diovol Plus, Maalox Plus, Maalox Plus Extra Strength, Mylanta Double Strength Plain Tablet, Mylanta Extra Strength, Mylanta Regular Strength.**

magnesium hydroxide/calcium carbonate/simethicone. **Diovol Plus AF.**

magnesium oxide/ASA/calcium carbonate/magnesium carbonate. **Aspirin With Stomach Guard.**

Magnesium-Rougier (Rougier). *magnesium glucoheptonate.*

magnesium salicylate. **Doan's Backache Pills.**

magnesium salicylate/choline salicylate. **Trilisate.**

magnesium sulfate. **(Abbott).**

magnesium sulfate/ascorbic acid/magnesium carbonate/vitamin B compound. **Redoxon-B.**

magnesium sulfate/benzocaine. **Osmopak Plus.**

Magnevist (Berlex Canada). *gadopentetate dimeglumine.*

Majeptil (Rhône-Poulenc Rorer). *thioproperazine mesylate.*

Malarone (Glaxo Wellcome). *atovaquone/proguanil hydrochloride.*

Maltlevol (Carter Horner). *multiple vitamins.*

Maltlevol-M (Carter Horner). *multiple vitamins and minerals.*

Maltlevol-12 (Carter Horner). *multiple vitamins.*

Mandelamine (Parke-Davis). *methenamine mandelate.*

Mandol (Lilly). *cefamandole nafate.*

Manerix (Roche). *moclobemide.*

manganese/calcium carbonate/copper/magnesium/vitamin D/zinc. **Caltrate Plus.**

manganese gluconate. **Oligosol, Manganese.**

manganese gluconate/cobalt gluconate. **Oligosol, Manganese-Cobalt.**

manganese gluconate/copper gluconate. **Oligosol, Manganese-Copper.**

mannitol. **Osmitrol; (Abbott).**

maprotiline hydrochloride. **Ludiomil, Novo-Maprotiline.**

Marcaine (Sanofi). *bupivacaine hydrochloride.*

Marinol (Sanofi). *dronabinol.*

Marvelon (Organon). *desogestrel/ethinyl estradiol.*

Materna (Wyeth-Ayerst). *multiple vitamins and minerals.*

†Matulane. *procarbazine hydrochloride.*

Mavik (Knoll). *trandolapril.*

†Maxalt. *rizatriptan.*

Maxeran (Hoechst Marion Roussel). *metoclopramide hydrochloride.*

Maxidex (Alcon). *dexamethasone.*

†Maxiflor. *diflorasone diacetate.*

Maxipime (Bristol-Myers Squibb). *cefepime hydrochloride.*

Maxitrol (Alcon). *dexamethasone/neomycin sulfate/polymyxin B sulfate.*

†Maxivate. *betamethasone dipropionate.*

†Maxzide. *hydrochlorothiazide/triamterene.*

†Mazanor. *mazindol.*

mazindol. **Sanorex.** †Mazanor.

M.C.T. Oil (Mead Johnson). *medium chain triglycerides.*

MD-76 (Mallinckrodt). *diatrizoate meglumine/diatrizoate sodium.*

measles virus vaccine (live attenuated). **(Connaught).**

measles virus vaccine (live attenuated)/mumps virus vaccine (live attenuated)/rubella virus vaccine (live attenuated). **M-M-R II.**

measles virus vaccine (live attenuated)/rubella virus vaccine (live attenuated). **MoRu-Viraten Berna.**

mebendazole. **Vermox.**

mecamylamine hydrochloride. dimecamine hydrochloride. †Inversine.

mechlorethamine hydrochloride. chlormethine. mustine hydrochloride. nitrogen mustard. **Mustargen.**

†Meclan. *meclocycline sulfosalicylate.*

meclizine hydrochloride. histamethizine. meclozine hydrochloride. **Bonamine.** †Bonine.

meclizine hydrochloride/niacin. **Antivert.**

meclocycline sulfosalicylate. †Meclan.

meclofenamate sodium. †Meclomen.

†Meclomen. *meclofenamate sodium.*

meclozine hydrochloride. see meclizine hydrochloride.

medium chain triglycerides. **M.C.T. Oil.**

†Medralone. *methylprednisolone acetate.*

medrogestone. metrogestone. **Colprone.**

Medrol (Pharmacia & Upjohn). *methylprednisolone.*

Medrol Acne (Pharmacia & Upjohn). *aluminum chlorhydroxide/methylprednisolone acetate/sulfur.*

Medrol Veriderm (Pharmacia & Upjohn). *methylprednisolone acetate.*

medroxyprogesterone acetate. **Alti-MPA, Depo-Provera, Gen-Medroxy, Novo-Medrone, Provera.** †Cycrin.

medroxyprogesterone acetate/conjugated estrogens. †Prempro.

mefenamic acid. **Apo-Mefenamic, Nu-Mefenamic, PMS-Mefenamic Acid, Ponstan.** †Ponstel.

mefloquine hydrochloride. **Lariam.**

Mefoxin (MSD). *cefoxitin sodium.*

Megace (Bristol). *megestrol acetate.*

Megace OS (Bristol). *megestrol acetate.*

megestrol acetate. **Apo-Megestrol, Megace, Megace OS, Nu-Megestrol.**

meglumine iothalamate. see iothalamate meglumine.

meglumine ioxitalamate/sodium ioxitalamate. **Telebrix 38 Oral.**

Megral (Glaxo Wellcome). *caffeine hydrate/cyclizine hydrochloride/ergotamine tartrate.*

†Melfiat-105. *phendimetrazine tartrate.*

Mellaril (Novartis Pharmaceuticals). *thioridazine hydrochloride.*

melphalan. **Alkeran.**

menadiol sodium diphosphate. vitamin K_1. †Synkayvite.

†Menest. *esterified estrogens.*

meningococcal polysaccharide vaccine. **(Connaught).**

menotropins. **Pergonal.**

menthol. **Antiphlogistine Rub A-535 Ice, Flexall.**

menthol/benzocaine/camphor/polymyxin B sulfate/tyrothricin. **Antibiotic Cold Sore Ointment.**

menthol/camphor/eucalyptol. **Balminil Camphorub.**

menthol/camphor/eucalyptus oil/methyl salicylate. **Antiphlogistine Rub A-535.**

menthol/camphor/pramoxine hydrochloride. **Sarna-P.**

menthol/chloroxylenol/coal tar. **Denorex, Denorex Extra Strength.**
menthol/coal tar/pyrithione disulfide/salicylic acid. **Polytar AF.**
menthol/coal tar/salicylic acid. **X-Tar.**
menthol/dimethicone/homosalate/octyl methoxycinnamate/oxybenzone. **Zilactin-Lip.**
menthol/methyl salicylate. **Analgesic Balm, Flexall Stick.**
menthol/pramoxine hydrochloride. **Pramegel.**
menthol/triethanolamine salicylate. **Myoflex Ice Plus.**
menthol/zinc pyrithione. **Z-Plus.**
mepenzolate bromide. glycophenylate bromide. †Cantil.
meperidine hydrochloride. see pethidine hydrochloride.
†Mephyton. *phytonadione.*
mepivacaine hydrochloride. **Carbocaine, Polocaine 3%.**
mepivacaine hydrochloride/levonordefrin. **Polocaine 2% with Levonordefrin 1:20 000.**
meprobamate. **Apo-Meprobamate, Equanil.**
meprobamate/ASA/caffeine citrate/codeine phosphate. **282 MEP.**
†Meprolone. *methylprednisolone.*
Mepron (Glaxo Wellcome). *atovaquone.*
mepyramine maleate/guaifenesin/potassium iodide/theophylline. **Theo-Bronc.**
mercaptopurine. **Purinethol.**
Mercodol with Decapryn (Hoechst Marion Roussel). *doxylamine succinate/etafedrine hydrochloride/hydrocodone bitartrate/sodium citrate.*
†Meridia. *sibutramine.*
Meritene (Novartis Nutrition). *enteral nutrition.*
meropenem. **Merrem.**
Merrem (Zeneca). *meropenem.*
Mersyndol with Codeine (Hoechst Marion Roussel). *acetaminophen/codeine phosphate/doxylamine succinate.*
mesalamine. see 5-aminosalicylic acid.
Mesasal (SmithKline Beecham). *5-aminosalicylic acid.*
M-Eslon (Rhône-Poulenc Rorer). *morphine sulfate.*
mesna. **Uromitexan.** †Mesnex.
†Mesnex. *mesna.*
mesoridazine besylate. **Serentil.**
Mestinon (ICN). *pyridostigmine bromide.*
Mestinon-SR (ICN). *pyridostigmine bromide.*
mestranol/norethindrone. **Norinyl 1/50, Ortho-Novum 1/50.**
mesuximide. see methsuximide.
metacortandracin. see prednisone.
metacortandrolone. see prednisolone acetate.
†Metahydrin. *trichlormethiazide.*
Metamucil (Procter & Gamble). *psyllium hydrophilic mucilloid.*
Metandren (Novartis Pharmaceuticals). *methyltestosterone.*
metaproterenol sulfate. see orciprenaline sulfate.
metaraminol bitartrate. †Aramine.
metaxalone. †Skelaxin.
Meted (Medicis). *salicylic acid/sulfur.*
metformin hydrochloride. **Apo-Metformin, Gen-Metformin, Glucophage, Glycon, Novo-Metformin, Nu-Metformin, Rho-Metformin; (BDH).**
methacholine chloride. †Provocholine.
methadone hydrochloride. **[Opioids, General Monograph, CPhA]**; †Methadose.
†Methadose. *methadone hydrochloride.*
methamphetamine hydrochloride. desoxyephedrine. †Desoxyn.
methantheline bromide. †Banthine.
methazolamide. **Neptazane.**
methdilazine hydrochloride. †Tacaryl.
methenamine. hexamine. **Dehydral, Urasal.**
methenamine hippurate. **Hip-Rex.** †Urex.
methenamine mandelate. **Mandelamine.**
†Methergine. *methylergonovine maleate.*
methicillin sodium. †Staphcillin.
methimazole. thiamazole. **Tapazole.**
methocarbamol. glyceryl guaiacolate carbamate. **Robaxin, Robaxin-750, Robaxin Injectable.**
methocarbamol/acetaminophen. **Methoxacet, Robaxacet.**
methocarbamol/acetaminophen/codeine phosphate. **Methoxacet-C, Robaxacet-8.**
methocarbamol/ASA. **Aspirin Backache, Methoxisal, Robaxisal.**
methocarbamol/ASA/codeine phosphate. **Methoxisal-C, Robaxisal-C.**
methohexital sodium. methohexitone. **Brietal Sodium.** †Brevital
methohexitone. see methohexital sodium.
methotrexate. **(Faulding).**
methotrexate sodium. amethopterin. **Rheumatrex; (Faulding), (Novopharm), (Wyeth-Ayerst).** †Folex, †Mexate.
methotrimeprazine. Apo-Methoprazine.
methotrimeprazine maleate. levomepromazine maleate. **Novo-Meprazine, Nozinan, PMS-Methotrimeprazine.**
Methoxacet (Technilab). *acetaminophen/methocarbamol.*
Methoxacet-C (Technilab). *acetaminophen/codeine phosphate/methocarbamol.*
methoxamine hydrochloride. **Vasoxyl.**
Methoxisal (Technilab). *ASA/methocarbamol.*
Methoxisal-C (Technilab). *ASA/codeine phosphate/methocarbamol.*
methoxsalen. **Oxsoralen, Oxsoralen-Ultra, UltraMOP Capsules, UltraMOP Lotion.** †8-MOP.
methoxyflurane. †Penthrane.
methoxypropanediol. see guaifenesin.
methphenoxydiol. see guaifenesin.
methscopolamine bromide. †Pamine.
methsuximide. mesuximide. **Celontin.**
methyclothiazide. †Enduron.
methyldopa. **Aldomet Tablets, Apo-Methyldopa, Novo-Medopa, Nu-Medopa.**
methyldopa/chlorothiazide. **Supres.** †Aldoclor.
methyldopa hydrochloride. **Aldomet Injection.**
methyldopa/hydrochlorothiazide. **Aldoril-15, Aldoril-25, Apo-Methazide.**
methylene blue. tetramethylthionine chloride trihydrate. **(Bioniche), (Faulding).**
methylergonovine maleate. †Methergine.
methylmorphine phosphate. see codeine phosphate.
methylphenidate hydrochloride. methylphenidylacetate hydrochloride. **PMS-Methylphenidate, Riphenidate, Ritalin, Ritalin SR.**
methylphenidylacetate hydrochloride. see methylphenidate hydrochloride.

Names **underlined** have complete prescribing information in the *CPS* Monograph Section.

methylprednisolone. **[Corticosteroids: Systemic, General Monograph, CPhA]; Medrol.** †Meprolone.

methylprednisolone acetate. **[Corticosteroids: Systemic, Corticosteroids: Topical, General Monographs, CPhA]; Depo-Medrol, Medrol Veriderm.** †depMedalone, †Depopred, †Medralone.

methylprednisolone acetate/aluminum chlorhydroxide/neomycin sulfate/sulfur. **Neo-Medrol Acne.**

methylprednisolone acetate/aluminum chlorhydroxide/sulfur. **Medrol Acne.**

methylprednisolone acetate/lidocaine hydrochloride. **Depo-Medrol with Lidocaine.**

methylprednisolone acetate/neomycin sulfate. **Neo-Medrol Veriderm.**

methylprednisolone sodium succinate. **[Corticosteroids: Systemic, General Monograph, CPhA]; Solu-Medrol; (Faulding).** †A-methaPred.

methyl salicylate/camphor/eucalyptus oil/menthol. **Antiphlogistine Rub A-535.**

methyl salicylate/menthol. **Analgesic Balm, Flexall Stick.**

methylsulfoxide. see dimethyl sulfoxide.

methyltestosterone. **Metandren.** †Oreton, †Testred, †Virilon.

methyltestosterone/esterified estrogens. †Estratest.

methysergide maleate. **Sansert.**

†Meticorten. *prednisone.*

Metimyd (Schering). *prednisolone acetate/sulfacetamide sodium.*

metipranolol hydrochloride. †OptiPranolol.

metoclopramide hydrochloride. **Apo-Metoclop, Maxeran, Nu-Metoclopramide, PMS-Metoclopramide, Reglan.**

metolazone. **Zaroxolyn.** †Diulo, †Mykrox.

metoprolol succinate. †Toprol-XL.

metoprolol tartrate. **Apo-Metoprolol, Apo-Metoprolol (Type L), Betaloc, Betaloc Durules, Lopresor, Novo-Metoprol, Nu-Metop, PMS-Metoprolol-B, PMS-Metoprolol-L.**

Metreton (Schering). *ascorbic acid/chlorpheniramine maleate/ prednisone acetate.*

†Metric 21. *metronidazole.*

MetroCream (Galderma). *metronidazole.*

MetroGel (Galderma). *metronidazole.*

metrogestone. see medrogestone.

†Metro I.V. *metronidazole.*

metronidazole. **[Metronidazole, General Monograph, CPhA]; Apo-Metronidazole, Flagyl, Flagyl 500 Injection, MetroCream, MetroGel, NidaGel, Noritate, Novo-Nidazol; (Abbott).** †Metric 21, †Metro I.V., †Protostat.

metronidazole/nystatin. **Flagystatin.**

metyrosine. †Demser.

Mevacor (MSD). *lovastatin.*

†Mexate. *methotrexate sodium.*

mexiletine hydrochloride. **Alti-Mexiletine, Mexitil, Novo-Mexiletine.**

Mexitil (Boehringer Ingelheim). *mexiletine hydrochloride.*

†Mezlin. *mezlocillin sodium.*

mezlocillin sodium. †Mezlin.

†Miacalcin. *calcitonin (salmon).*

mibefradil. †Posicor.

Micanol (Canderm Pharma). *anthralin.*

Micatin (McNeil Consumer Products). *miconazole nitrate.*

miconazole nitrate. **Micatin, Micozole, Monazole 7, Monistat 3, Monistat 7, Monistat Derm.**

Micozole (Taro). *miconazole nitrate.*

Micro-K Extencaps (Wyeth-Ayerst). *potassium chloride.*

Micro-K-10 Extencaps (Wyeth-Ayerst). *potassium chloride.*

Microlax (Pharmacia & Upjohn). *glycerin/sodium citrate/sodium lauryl sulfoacetate/sorbic acid/sorbitol.*

†Micronase. *glyburide.*

Micronor (Janssen-Ortho). *norethindrone.*

Midamor (MSD). *amiloride hydrochloride.*

midazolam hydrochloride. **[Benzodiazepines, General Monograph, CPhA]; Versed.**

midodrine hydrochloride. **Amatine.**

Midol (Bayer Consumer). *ASA/caffeine.*

Midol Extra Strength (Bayer Consumer). *acetaminophen/caffeine/ pyrilamine maleate.*

Midol PMS Extra Strength (Bayer Consumer). *acetaminophen/ pamabrom/pyrilamine maleate.*

Migranal (Novartis Pharmaceuticals). *dihydroergotamine mesylate.*

†Milontin. *phensuximide.*

†Milophene. *clomiphene citrate.*

milrinone lactate. **Primacor.**

†Miltride. *acetaminophen/dichloralphenazone/isometheptene mucate.*

mineral oil. **Fleet Enema Mineral Oil, Lansoÿl, Oilatum Soap.**

mineral oil/isopropyl palmitate/tar distillate. **Doak-Oil, Doak-Oil Forte.**

mineral oil/jojoba oil. **Prevex Oil.**

mineral oil/lanolin alcohols/white petrolatum. **Lacri-Lube S.O.P.**

mineral oil/lanolin/white petrolatum. **Duratears.**

mineral oil/white petrolatum. **Hypotears Eye Ointment.**

minerals/ascorbic acid/vitamin D. **Cal-Mag.**

minerals/cyanocobalamin. **Oligofer.**

Minestrin 1/20 (Parke-Davis). *ethinyl estradiol/norethindrone acetate.*

Minims Artificial Tears (Ophtapharma). *hydroxyethylcellulose/ sodium chloride.*

Minims Atropine (Ophtapharma). *atropine sulfate.*

Minims Benoxinate (Ophtapharma). *benoxinate.*

Minims Chloramphenicol (Ophtapharma). *chloramphenicol.*

Minims Cyclopentolate (Ophtapharma). *cyclopentolate hydrochloride.*

Minims Fluorescein (Ophtapharma). *fluorescein sodium.*

Minims Gentamicin (Ophtapharma). *gentamicin sulfate.*

Minims Homatropine (Ophtapharma). *homatropine.*

Minims Lidocaine/Fluorescein (Ophtapharma). *fluorescein sodium/lidocaine.*

Minims Phenylephrine (Ophtapharma). *phenylephrine.*

Minims Pilocarpine (Ophtapharma). *pilocarpine nitrate.*

Minims Prednisolone (Ophtapharma). *prednisolone.*

Minims Sodium Chloride (Ophtapharma). *sodium chloride.*

Minims Tetracaine (Ophtapharma). *tetracaine.*

Minims Tropicamide (Ophtapharma). *tropicamide.*

Minipress (Pfizer). *prazosin hydrochloride.*

Minitran (3M Pharmaceuticals). *nitroglycerin.*

Minocin (Wyeth-Ayerst). *minocycline hydrochloride.*

minocycline hydrochloride. **[Tetracyclines, General Monograph, CPhA]; Alti-Minocycline, Apo-Minocycline, Gen-Minocycline, Minocin, Novo-Minocycline.**

Min-Ovral 21 (Wyeth-Ayerst). *ethinyl estradiol/levonorgestrel.*

Min-Ovral 28 (Wyeth-Ayerst). *ethinyl estradiol/levonorgestrel.*

Minox (Riva). *minoxidil.*

minoxidil. **Apo-Gain, Gen-Minoxidil, Loniten, Minox, Rogaine.**

Mintezol (MSD). *thiabendazole.*

Miocarpine (CIBA Vision). *pilocarpine hydrochloride.*

Miochol-E (CIBA Vision). *acetylcholine chloride/electrolytes.*

Miostat (Alcon). *carbachol.*

†Miradon. *anisindione.*

Mirapex (Boehringer Ingelheim). *pramipexole dihydrochloride.*

Mireze (Allergan). *nedocromil sodium.*

misoprostol. **Cytotec.**

misoprostol/diclofenac sodium. **Arthrotec.**

†Mithracin. *plicamycin.*

mithramycin. see plicamycin.

mitomycin. **Mutamycin; (Faulding), (Novopharm).**

mitotane. o,p'DDD. **Lysodren.**

mitoxantrone hydrochloride. **Novantrone.**

Mivacron (Glaxo Wellcome). *mivacurium chloride.*

mivacurium chloride. **Mivacron.**

M-M-R II (MSD). *measles virus vaccine (live attenuated)/mumps virus vaccine (live attenuated)/rubella virus vaccine (live attenuated).*

†Moban. *molindone hydrochloride.*

Mobiflex (Roche). *tenoxicam.*

moclobemide. **Alti-Moclobemide, Apo-Moclobemide, Manerix.**

†Moctanin. *monooctanoin.*

Modecate Concentrate (Squibb). *fluphenazine decanoate.*

Moditen Enanthate (Squibb). *fluphenazine enanthate.*

Moditen HCl (Squibb). *fluphenazine hydrochloride.*

†Modrastane. *trilostane.*

Modulon (Axcan Pharma). *trimebutine maleate.*

Moduret (MSD). *amiloride hydrochloride/hydrochlorothiazide.*

†Moduretic. *amiloride hydrochloride/hydrochlorothiazide.*

Mogadon (Roche). *nitrazepam.*

Moisturel (Westwood-Squibb). *dimethicone/petrolatum.*

molindone hydrochloride. †Moban.

molybdenem. see ammonium molybdate.

†Molypen. *ammonium molybdate.*

mometasone furoate. **[Corticosteroids: Topical, Corticosteroids: Eye Ear Nose, General Monographs, CPhA]; Elocom.**

mometasone furoate monohydrate. Nasonex.

monalium hydrate. see magaldrate.

Monazole 7 (Technilab). *miconazole nitrate.*

Monistat 3 (McNeil Consumer Products). *miconazole nitrate.*

Monistat 7 (McNeil Consumer Products). *miconazole nitrate.*

Monistat Derm (McNeil Consumer Products). *miconazole nitrate.*

Monitan (Wyeth-Ayerst). *acebutolol hydrochloride.*

†Monocid. *cefonicid sodium.*

monooctanoin. †Moctanin.

Monopril (Bristol-Myers Squibb). *fosinopril sodium.*

montelukast sodium. **Singulair.**

†8-MOP. *methoxsalen.*

moricizine hydrochloride. †Ethmozine.

morphine hydrochloride. **[Opioids, General Monograph, CPhA]; Morphitec-1, -5, -10, -20, M.O.S., M.O.S.-SR.**

morphine sulfate. **[Opioids, General Monograph, CPhA]; Kadian, M-Eslon, M.O.S.-Sulfate, MS Contin, MS•IR, Oramorph SR, Statex; (Abbott), (Faulding), (Sabex).** †Duramorph, †RMS Uniserts, †Roxanol.

Morphitec-1, -5, -10, -20 (Technilab). *morphine hydrochloride.*

MoRu-Viraten Berna (Berna Products). *measles virus vaccine (live attenuated)/rubella virus vaccine (live attenuated).*

M.O.S. (ICN). *morphine hydrochloride.*

M.O.S.-SR (ICN). *morphine hydrochloride.*

M.O.S.-Sulfate (ICN). *morphine sulfate.*

Motilidone (Technilab). *domperidone maleate.*

Motilium (Janssen-Ortho). *domperidone maleate.*

Motrin (Pharmacia & Upjohn). *ibuprofen.*

Motrin (Children's) (McNeil Consumer Products). *ibuprofen.*

Motrin IB (McNeil Consumer Products). *ibuprofen.*

MS Contin (Purdue Frederick). *morphine sulfate.*

MSD Enteric Coated ASA (Johnson & Johnson • Merck). *ASA.*

MS•IR (Purdue Frederick). *morphine sulfate.*

Mucaine (Axcan Pharma). *aluminum hydroxide/magnesium hydroxide/oxethazaine.*

Mucomyst (Roberts). *acetylcysteine.*

Multipax (Rhône-Poulenc Rorer). *hydroxyzine hydrochloride.*

multiple vitamins. hexavitamins. **Apo-Hexa, Dia-Vite, Flintstones, Flintstones with Extra C, Infantol, Maltlevol, Maltlevol-12, M.V.I.-12 (Multivitamin Infusion), Penta/3B Plus, Sopalamine/3B, Sopalamine/3B Plus C, Stresstabs.**

multiple vitamins and minerals. **Centrum, Centrum Forte, Centrum Junior Complete, Centrum Junior Regular, Centrum Protegra, Centrum Select, Children's Choice Super Multi-Vitamins and Minerals, Flintstones Complete, Hemarexin, ICAPS, ICAPS Time Release, Maltlevol-M, Materna, Natavite, One A Day Advance, Orifer.F, Suplevit, Swiss One, Timed Release Swiss One "50".**

multiple vitamins/calcium carbonate/ferrous fumarate. **Prenavite.**

multiple vitamins/cupric oxide/zinc oxide. **Stresstabs with Zinc.**

multiple vitamins/ferrous fumarate. **Flintstones Plus Iron, Stresstabs with Iron.**

multiple vitamins/zinc oxide. **Adeks Tablets.**

multiple vitamins/zinc sulfate. **Adeks Pediatric Drops, Z-BEC.**

Multi-Tar Plus (ICN). *coal tar/juniper tar/pine tar/zinc pyrithione.*

Multitest CMI (Connaught). *skin test antigens.*

Mumpsvax (MSD). *mumps virus vaccine (live attenuated).*

mumps virus vaccine (live attenuated). **Mumpsvax.**

mumps virus vaccine (live attenuated)/measles virus vaccine (live attenuated)/rubella virus vaccine (live attenuated). **M-M-R II.**

mupirocin. **Bactroban.**

muromonab-CD3. **Orthoclone OKT 3.**

Muse (Janssen-Ortho). *alprostadil.*

Mustargen (MSD). *mechlorethamine hydrochloride.*

mustine hydrochloride. see mechlorethamine hydrochloride.

Mutacol Berna (Berna Products). *cholera vaccine live oral.*

Mutamycin (Bristol). *mitomycin.*

M.V.I.-12 (Multivitamin Infusion) (Rhône-Poulenc Rorer). *multiple vitamins.*

Myambutol (Wyeth-Ayerst). *ethambutol hydrochloride.*

Mycifradin (Pharmacia & Upjohn). *neomycin sulfate.*

Myciguent (Pharmacia & Upjohn). *neomycin sulfate.*

Mycil (Roberts). *chlorphenesin.*

Names **underlined** have complete prescribing information in the *CPS* Monograph Section.

Mycobutin (Pharmacia & Upjohn). *rifabutin.*

mycophenolate mofetil. **CellCept.**

Mycostatin (Squibb). *nystatin.*

Mydfrin (Alcon). *phenylephrine hydrochloride.*

Mydriacyl (Alcon). *tropicamide.*

†Mydriafair. *tropicamide.*

†Myidone. *primidone.*

†Mykrox. *metolazone.*

Mylanta Double Strength Plain Liquid (Warner-Lambert Consumer Healthcare). *aluminum hydroxide/magnesium hydroxide.*

Mylanta Double Strength Plain Tablet (Warner-Lambert Consumer Healthcare). *aluminum hydroxide/magnesium hydroxide/simethicone.*

Mylanta Extra Strength (Warner-Lambert Consumer Healthcare). *aluminum hydroxide/magnesium hydroxide/simethicone.*

Mylanta Regular Strength (Warner-Lambert Consumer Healthcare). *aluminum hydroxide/magnesium hydroxide/simethicone.*

Myleran (Glaxo Wellcome). *busulfan.*

†Mymethasone. *dexamethasone.*

Myochrysine (Rhône-Poulenc Rorer). *sodium aurothiomalate.*

Myoflex (Bayer Consumer). *triethanolamine salicylate.*

Myoflex Ice Plus (Bayer Consumer). *menthol/triethanolamine salicylate.*

Myotonachol (Glenwood). *bethanechol chloride.*

Mysoline (Wyeth-Ayerst). *primidone.*

†Mytelase. *ambenonium chloride.*

N

nabilone. **Cesamet.**

nabumetone. **Relafen.**

nadolol. **Alti-Nadolol, Apo-Nadol, Corgard, Novo-Nadolol.**

Nadopen-V (Nadeau). *penicillin V potassium.*

Nadostine (Nadeau). *nystatin.*

nadroparin calcium. **[Heparins: Low Molecular Weight, General Monograph, CPhA]; Fraxiparine.**

nafarelin acetate. **Synarel.**

†Nafcil. *nafcillin sodium.*

nafcillin sodium. †Nafcil, †Nallpen.

naftifine hydrochloride. **Naftin.**

Naftin (Allergan). *naftifine hydrochloride.*

nalbuphine hydrochloride. **[Opioids, General Monograph, CPhA]; Nubain.**

Nalcrom (Rhône-Poulenc Rorer). *sodium cromoglycate.*

Nalfon (Lilly). *fenoprofen calcium.*

nalidixic acid. **NegGram.**

†Nallpen. *nafcillin sodium.*

naloxone hydrochloride. **Narcan.**

naltrexone hydrochloride. **ReVia.** †Trexan.

nandrolone decanoate. **Deca-Durabolin.** †Hybolin Decanoate, †Kabolin.

nandrolone phenpropionate. †Hybolin-Improved.

NAPAP. see acetaminophen.

naphazoline hydrochloride. **Naphcon Forte, Red Away, Vasocon.** †Allerest.

naphazoline hydrochloride/antazoline phosphate. **Albalon-A Liquifilm, Vasocon-A.**

naphazoline hydrochloride/antazoline phosphate/zinc sulfate. **Zincfrin-A.**

naphazoline hydrochloride/pheniramine maleate. **Naphcon-A.**

Naphcon-A (Alcon). *naphazoline hydrochloride/pheniramine maleate.*

Naphcon Forte (Alcon). *naphazoline hydrochloride.*

Naprosyn (Roche). *naproxen.*

naproxen. **Apo-Naproxen, Naprosyn, Naxen, Novo-Naprox, Nu-Naprox, Rhodiaprox.**

naproxen sodium. **Anaprox, Anaprox DS, Apo-Napro-Na, Apo-Napro-Na DS, Novo-Naprox Sodium, Novo-Naprox Sodium DS, Synflex, Synflex DS.**

†Naqua. *trichlormethiazide.*

naratriptan hydrochloride. **Amerge.**

Narcan (DuPont Pharma). *naloxone hydrochloride.*

Nardil (Parke-Davis). *phenelzine sulfate.*

Naropin (Astra). *ropivacaine hydrochloride.*

Nasacort (Rhône-Poulenc Rorer). *triamcinolone acetonide.*

Nasacort AQ (Rhône-Poulenc Rorer). *triamcinolone acetonide.*

†Nasalcrom. *sodium cromoglycate.*

†Nasalide. *flunisolide.*

Nasonex (Schering). *mometasone furoate monohydrate.*

†Natacyn. *natamycin.*

natamycin. pimaricin. †Natacyn.

Natavite (Schein Pharmaceutical). *multiple vitamins and minerals.*

Navane (Pfizer). *thiothixene.*

Navelbine (Glaxo Wellcome). *vinorelbine tartrate.*

Naxen (AltiMed). *naproxen.*

Nebcin (Lilly). *tobramycin sulfate.*

†NebuPent. *pentamidine isethionate.*

nedocromil sodium. **Mireze, Tilade.**

nefazodone hydrochloride. **Serzone.**

NegGram (Sanofi). *nalidixic acid.*

Nemasol Sodium—ICN (ICN). *aminosalicylate sodium.*

Nembutal Sodium (Abbott). *pentobarbital sodium.*

†Neo-Calglucon. *calcium glubionate.*

NeoCitran A (Novartis Consumer Health). *pheniramine maleate/phenylephrine hydrochloride.*

NeoCitran Adult (Novartis Consumer Health). *acetaminophen/pheniramine maleate/phenylephrine hydrochloride.*

NeoCitran DM (Novartis Consumer Health). *dextromethorphan hydrobromide/pheniramine maleate/phenylephrine hydrochloride.*

NeoCitran Extra Strength (Novartis Consumer Health). *acetaminophen/pheniramine maleate/phenylephrine hydrochloride.*

NeoCitran Extra Strength (Cough, Cold & Flu) (Novartis Consumer Health). *acetaminophen/chlorpheniramine maleate/dextromethorphan hydrobromide/pseudoephedrine hydrochloride.*

NeoCitran Extra Strength Daycaps (Novartis Consumer Health). *acetaminophen/dextromethorphan hydrobromide/pseudoephedrine hydrochloride.*

NeoCitran Nutrasweet (Novartis Consumer Health). *acetaminophen/pheniramine maleate/phenylephrine hydrochloride.*

NeoCitran Sinus Extra Strength (Novartis Consumer Health). *acetaminophen/phenylephrine hydrochloride.*

Neo-Cortef (Pharmacia & Upjohn). *hydrocortisone acetate/neomycin sulfate.*

Neo-Laryngobis (Technilab). *bismuth dipropylacetate.*
Neo-Medrol Acne (Pharmacia & Upjohn). *aluminum chlorhydroxide/methylprednisolone acetate/neomycin sulfate/sulfur.*
Neo-Medrol Veriderm (Pharmacia & Upjohn). *methylprednisolone acetate/neomycin sulfate.*
neomycin sulfate. **Mycifradin, Myciguent.**
neomycin sulfate/aluminum chlorhydroxide/methylprednisolone acetate/sulfur. **Neo-Medrol Acne.**
neomycin sulfate/amino acids/bacitracin zinc. **Cicatrin.**
neomycin sulfate/bacitracin zinc/hydrocortisone/polymyxin B sulfate. **Cortisporin Ointment, Cortisporin Ophthalmic Ointment.**
neomycin sulfate/bacitracin zinc/polymyxin B sulfate. **Neosporin Ointment/Ophthalmic Ointment, Neotopic.**
neomycin sulfate/dexamethasone/polymyxin B sulfate. **Dioptrol, Maxitrol.**
neomycin sulfate/gramicidin/nystatin/triamcinolone acetonide. **Kenacomb, Triacomb, Viaderm-K.C.**
neomycin sulfate/gramicidin/polymyxin B sulfate. **Neosporin Cream, Neosporin Eye and Ear Solution, Optimyxin Plus Solution.**
neomycin sulfate/hydrocortisone acetate. **Neo-Cortef.**
neomycin sulfate/hydrocortisone/polymyxin B sulfate. **Cortimyxin, Cortisporin Eye/Ear Suspension, Cortisporin Otic Solution.**
neomycin sulfate/methylprednisolone acetate. **Neo-Medrol Veriderm.**
neomycin sulfate/polymyxin B sulfate. **Neosporin Irrigating Solution.**
Neoral (Novartis Pharmaceuticals). *cyclosporine.*
†Neosar. *cyclophosphamide.*
Neosporin Cream (Glaxo Wellcome). *gramicidin/neomycin sulfate/polymyxin B sulfate.*
Neosporin Eye and Ear Solution (Glaxo Wellcome). *gramicidin/neomycin sulfate/polymyxin B sulfate.*
Neosporin Irrigating Solution (Glaxo Wellcome). *neomycin sulfate/polymyxin B sulfate.*
Neosporin Ointment/Ophthalmic Ointment (Glaxo Wellcome). *bacitracin zinc/neomycin sulfate/polymyxin B sulfate.*
neostigmine bromide. **Prostigmin Tablets.**
neostigmine methylsulfate. **Prostigmin Injection.**
Neostrata AHA Cleansing Lotion (Canderm Pharma). *gluconolactone.*
Neostrata AHA Cream (Canderm Pharma). *glycolic acid.*
Neostrata AHA Eye Contour Cream (Canderm Pharma). *gluconolactone.*
Neostrata AHA Lip Conditioner (Canderm Pharma). *gluconolactone.*
Neostrata AHA Lotion (Canderm Pharma). *glycolic acid.*
Neostrata AHA Sensitive Skin Cream (Canderm Pharma). *glycolic acid.*
Neostrata AHA Solution (Canderm Pharma). *glycolic acid.*
Neostrata AHA Ultra Moisturizing Cream (Canderm Pharma). *gluconolactone.*
Neostrata HQ (Canderm Pharma). *hydroquinone.*
Neo-Synephrine (Sanofi). *phenylephrine hydrochloride.*
Neotopic (Technilab). *bacitracin zinc/neomycin sulfate/polymyxin B sulfate.*
Neptazane (Storz). *methazolamide.*
Nerisalic (Stiefel). *diflucortolone valerate/salicylic acid.*
Nerisone (Stiefel). *diflucortolone valerate.*
Nesacaine-CE (Astra). *chloroprocaine hydrochloride.*
netilmicin sulfate. **Netromycin.**
Netromycin (Schering). *netilmicin sulfate.*
Neuleptil (Rhône-Poulenc Rorer). *pericyazine.*
Neupogen (Amgen). *filgrastim.*
Neurontin (Parke-Davis). *gabapentin.*
Neutrexin (Lilly). *trimetrexate glucuronate.*
nevirapine. Viramune.
niacin. nicotinic acid. Vitamin B_3. **[Niacin/Niacinamide, General Monograph, CPhA]; (Stanley).** †Nicobid Tempules.
niacinamide. nicotinamide. **[Niacin/Niacinamide, General Monograph, CPhA].**
niacin/meclizine hydrochloride. **Antivert.**
nicardipine hydrochloride. **Cardene.**
nickel gluconate/cobalt gluconate/zinc gluconate. **Oligosol, Zinc-Nickel-Cobalt.**
†Nicobid Tempules. *niacin.*
Nicoderm (Hoechst Marion Roussel). *nicotine.*
Nicorette (Hoechst Marion Roussel). *nicotine.*
Nicorette Plus (Hoechst Marion Roussel). *nicotine.*
nicotinamide. see niacinamide.
nicotine. **Nicoderm, Nicorette, Nicorette Plus, Nicotrol.**
S(-)-nicotine. **Habitrol.**
nicotinic acid. see niacin.
Nicotrol (Johnson & Johnson • Merck). *nicotine.*
nicoumalone. acenocoumarin. acenocoumarol. **Sintrom.**
NidaGel (3M Pharmaceuticals). *metronidazole.*
nifedipine. **Adalat, Adalat PA, Adalat XL, Apo-Nifed, Apo-Nifed PA, Gen-Nifedipine, Novo-Nifedin, Nu-Nifed, Nu-Nifedipine-PA, PMS-Nifedipine; (Schein Pharmaceutical).** †Procardia.
Nilstat (Technilab). *nystatin.*
nilutamide. **Anandron.**
Nimbex (Glaxo Wellcome). *cisatracurium besylate.*
nimodipine. **Nimotop, Nimotop I.V.**
Nimotop (Bayer). *nimodipine.*
Nimotop I.V. (Bayer). *nimodipine.*
Nipride (Roche). *sodium nitroprusside.*
Nitoman (Roche). *tetrabenazine.*
Nitrazadon (ICN). *nitrazepam.*
nitrazepam. **[Benzodiazepines, General Monograph, CPhA]; Mogadon, Nitrazadon, Rho-Nitrazepam.**
Nitro-Dur (Key). *nitroglycerin.*
nitrofurantoin. **Apo-Nitrofurantoin, Macrodantin, Novo-Furantoin.** †Furadantin.
nitrofurantoin monohydrate/nitrofurantoin. **MacroBID.**
nitrofurantoin/nitrofurantoin monohydrate. **MacroBID.**
nitrogen mustard. see mechlorethamine hydrochloride.
nitroglycerin. glyceryl trinitrate. **[Nitroglycerin, General Monograph, CPhA]; Minitran, Nitro-Dur, Nitrol, Nitrolingual Pumpspray, Nitrolingual Spray, Nitrong SR, Nitrostat, Transderm-Nitro, Tridil, Trinipatch 0.2, Trinipatch 0.4, Trinipatch 0.6; (Faulding).**
nitroglycerin/dextrose. **(Baxter).**
Nitrol (Rhône-Poulenc Rorer). *nitroglycerin.*
Nitrolingual Pumpspray (Rhône-Poulenc Rorer). *nitroglycerin.*
Nitrolingual Spray (Rhône-Poulenc Rorer). *nitroglycerin.*

Names **underlined** have complete prescribing information in the *CPS* Monograph Section.

Nitrong SR (Rhône-Poulenc Rorer). *nitroglycerin.*
†Nitropress. *nitroprusside sodium.*
nitroprusside sodium. †Nitropress.
Nitrostat (Parke-Davis). *nitroglycerin.*
Nix Creme Rinse (Warner-Lambert Consumer Healthcare). *permethrin.*
Nix Dermal Cream (Glaxo Wellcome). *permethrin.*
nizatidine. **Apo-Nizatidine, Axid.**
Nizoral Cream (Janssen-Ortho). *ketoconazole.*
Nizoral Shampoo (McNeil Consumer Products). *ketoconazole.*
Nizoral Tablets (Janssen-Ortho). *ketoconazole.*
†Nolahist. *phenindamine tartrate.*
Nolvadex (Zeneca). *tamoxifen citrate.*
Nolvadex-D (Zeneca). *tamoxifen citrate.*
nonmedicated soap. **Acne-Aid Soap, Allenburys Basic Soap.**
nonoxynol-9. **Advantage 24.**
noradrenaline bitartrate. see norepinephrine bitartrate.
Norcuron (Organon). *vecuronium bromide.*
†Nordette. *ethinyl estradiol/levonorgestrel.*
norepinephrine bitartrate. levarterenol bitartrate. noradrenaline bitartrate. **Levophed.**
norethindrone. norethisterone. **Micronor.** †Nor-QD.
norethindrone acetate. **Norlutate.** †Aygestin.
norethindrone acetate/estradiol-17β. **Estracomb.**
norethindrone acetate/ethinyl estradiol. **Loestrin 1.5/30, Minestrin 1/20.**
norethindrone/ethinyl estradiol. **Brevicon 0.5/35, Brevicon 1/35, Ortho 0.5/35, Ortho 1/35, Ortho 7/7/7, Ortho 10/11, Select 1/35, Synphasic.** †Genora, †Ovcon, †Tri-Norinyl.
norethindrone/mestranol. **Norinyl 1/50, Ortho-Novum 1/50.**
norethisterone. see norethindrone.
Norflex (3M Pharmaceuticals). *orphenadrine citrate.*
norfloxacin. Apo-Norflox, **Noroxin, Noroxin Ophthalmic,** Novo-Norfloxacin. †Chibroxin.
†Norfranil. *imipramine hydrochloride.*
Norgesic (3M Pharmaceuticals). *ASA/caffeine/orphenadrine citrate.*
Norgesic Forte (3M Pharmaceuticals). *ASA/caffeine/orphenadrine citrate.*
norgestimate/ethinyl estradiol. **Cyclen, Tri-Cyclen.**
norgestrel. †Ovrette.
norgestrel/ethinyl estradiol. **Ovral 21, Ovral 28.** †Lo/Ovral.
Norinyl 1/50 (Searle). *mestranol/norethindrone.*
Noritate (Dermik Laboratories Canada). *metronidazole.*
Norlutate (Parke-Davis). *norethindrone acetate.*
Normacol (Rivex Pharma). *sterculia.*
normal serum albumin (human). see albumin (human).
normethadone hydrochloride/emetine hydrochloride/hydroxyephedrine hydrochloride. **Cophylac Expectorant.**
normethadone hydrochloride/hydroxyephedrine hydrochloride. **Cophylac.**
†Normodyne. *labetalol hydrochloride.*
Noroxin (MSD). *norfloxacin.*
Noroxin Ophthalmic (MSD). *norfloxacin.*
Norplant (Wyeth-Ayerst). *levonorgestrel.*
Norpramin (Hoechst Marion Roussel). *desipramine hydrochloride.*
†Nor-Pred T.B.A. *prednisolone tebutate.*
†Nor-QD. *norethindrone.*
nortriptyline hydrochloride. **Apo-Nortriptyline, Aventyl, Gen-Nortriptyline, Norventyl, Novo-Nortriptyline, Nu-Nortriptyline, PMS-Nortriptyline.** †Pamelor.
Norvasc (Pfizer). *amlodipine besylate.*
Norventyl (ICN). *nortriptyline hydrochloride.*
Norvir (Abbott). *ritonavir.*
†Norzine. *thiethylperazine maleate.*
†Nostril Spray Pump. *phenylephrine hydrochloride.*
Novahistex C (Hoechst Marion Roussel). *codeine phosphate/phenylephrine hydrochloride.*
Novahistex DH (Hoechst Marion Roussel). *hydrocodone bitartrate/phenylephrine hydrochloride.*
Novahistex DH Expectorant (Hoechst Marion Roussel). *guaifenesin/hydrocodone bitartrate/phenylephrine hydrochloride.*
Novahistex DM (Hoechst Marion Roussel). *dextromethorphan hydrobromide.*
Novahistex DM Decongestant (Hoechst Marion Roussel). *dextromethorphan hydrobromide/pseudoephedrine hydrochloride.*
Novahistex DM Decongestant Expectorant (Hoechst Marion Roussel). *dextromethorphan hydrobromide/guaifenesin/pseudoephedrine hydrochloride.*
Novahistine DH (Hoechst Marion Roussel). *hydrocodone bitartrate/phenylephrine hydrochloride.*
Novahistine DM (Hoechst Marion Roussel). *dextromethorphan hydrobromide.*
Novahistine DM Decongestant (Hoechst Marion Roussel). *dextromethorphan hydrobromide/pseudoephedrine hydrochloride.*
Novahistine DM Decongestant Expectorant (Hoechst Marion Roussel). *dextromethorphan hydrobromide/guaifenesin/pseudoephedrine hydrochloride.*
Novamilor (Novopharm). *amiloride hydrochloride/hydrochlorothiazide.*
Novamoxin (Novopharm). *amoxicillin trihydrate.*
Novantrone (Wyeth-Ayerst). *mitoxantrone hydrochloride.*
Nova Rectal (Sabex). *pentobarbital sodium.*
Novasen (Novopharm). *ASA.*
Novasource Renal (Novartis Nutrition). *enteral nutrition.*
Nova-T (Berlex Canada). *intrauterine contraceptive.*
Novo-Acebutolol (Novopharm). *acebutolol hydrochloride.*
Novo-Alprazol (Novopharm). *alprazolam.*
Novo-Ampicillin (Novopharm). *ampicillin.*
Novo-Atenol (Novopharm). *atenolol.*
Novo-AZT (Novopharm). *zidovudine.*
Novo-Baclofen (Novopharm). *baclofen.*
Novo-Benzydamine (Novopharm). *benzydamine hydrochloride.*
Novo-Bromazepam (Novopharm). *bromazepam.*
Novo-Buspirone (Novopharm). *buspirone hydrochloride.*
Novocain (Sanofi). *procaine hydrochloride.*
Novo-Captoril (Novopharm). *captopril.*
Novo-Carbamaz (Novopharm). *carbamazepine.*
Novo-Cholamine (Novopharm). *cholestyramine resin.*
Novo-Cholamine Light (Novopharm). *cholestyramine resin.*
Novo-Cimetine (Novopharm). *cimetidine.*
Novo-Clobazam (Novopharm). *clobazam.*
Novo-Clobetasol (Novopharm). *clobetasol 17-propionate.*
Novo-Clonazepam (Novopharm). *clonazepam.*
Novo-Clonidine (Novopharm). *clonidine hydrochloride.*
Novo-Clopamine (Novopharm). *clomipramine hydrochloride.*

Novo-Clopate (Novopharm). *clorazepate dipotassium.*
Novo-Cloxin (Novopharm). *cloxacillin sodium.*
Novo-Cromolyn (Novopharm). *sodium cromoglycate.*
Novo-Cycloprine (Novopharm). *cyclobenzaprine hydrochloride.*
Novo-Cyproterone (Novopharm). *cyproterone acetate.*
Novo-Desipramine (Novopharm). *desipramine hydrochloride.*
Novo-Difenac (Novopharm). *diclofenac sodium.*
Novo-Difenac SR (Novopharm). *diclofenac sodium.*
Novo-Diflunisal (Novopharm). *diflunisal.*
Novo-Diltazem (Novopharm). *diltiazem hydrochloride.*
Novo-Diltazem SR (Novopharm). *diltiazem hydrochloride.*
Novo-Dipiradol (Novopharm). *dipyridamole.*
Novo-Domperidone (Novopharm). *domperidone maleate.*
Novo-Doxepin (Novopharm). *doxepin hydrochloride.*
Novo-Doxylin (Novopharm). *doxycycline hyclate.*
Novo-Famotidine (Novopharm). *famotidine.*
NovoFine 28G (Novo Nordisk). *disposable needles.*
NovoFine 30G (Novo Nordisk). *disposable needles.*
Novo-5 ASA (Novopharm). *5-aminosalicylic acid.*
Novo-Fluoxetine (Novopharm). *fluoxetine hydrochloride.*
Novo-Flurprofen (Novopharm). *flurbiprofen.*
Novo-Flutamide (Novopharm). *flutamide.*
Novo-Furantoin (Novopharm). *nitrofurantoin.*
Novo-Gemfibrozil (Novopharm). *gemfibrozil.*
Novo-Gesic C8, C15, C30 (Novopharm). *acetaminophen/caffeine/codeine phosphate.*
Novo-Gliclazide (Novopharm). *gliclazide.*
Novo-Glyburide (Novopharm). *glyburide.*
Novo-Hydroxyzin (Novopharm). *hydroxyzine hydrochloride.*
Novo-Hylazin (Novopharm). *hydralazine hydrochloride.*
Novo-Indapamide (Novopharm). *indapamide.*
Novo-Ipramide (Novopharm). *ipratropium bromide.*
Novo-Keto (Novopharm). *ketoprofen.*
Novo-Keto-EC (Novopharm). *ketoprofen.*
Novo-Ketorolac (Novopharm). *ketorolac tromethamine.*
Novo-Ketotifen (Novopharm). *ketotifen fumarate.*
Novo-Levamisole (Novopharm). *levamisole hydrochloride.*
Novo-Levobunolol (Novopharm). *levobunolol hydrochloride.*
Novo-Lexin (Novopharm). *cephalexin.*
Novolin ge 10/90 (Novo Nordisk). *insulin injection (human)/insulin isophane (human).*
Novolin ge 20/80 (Novo Nordisk). *insulin injection (human)/insulin isophane (human).*
Novolin ge 30/70 (Novo Nordisk). *insulin injection (human)/insulin isophane (human).*
Novolin ge 40/60 (Novo Nordisk). *insulin injection (human)/insulin isophane (human).*
Novolin ge 50/50 (Novo Nordisk). *insulin injection (human)/insulin isophane (human).*
Novolin ge Lente (Novo Nordisk). *insulin zinc (human).*
Novolin ge NPH (Novo Nordisk). *insulin isophane (human).*
Novolin ge Toronto (Novo Nordisk). *insulin injection (human).*
Novolin ge Ultralente (Novo Nordisk). *insulin zinc, extended (human).*
Novolin-Pen 1.5 (Novo Nordisk). *insulin delivery device.*
Novolin-Pen 3 (Novo Nordisk). *insulin delivery device.*
Novo-Loperamide (Novopharm). *loperamide hydrochloride.*
Novo-Lorazem (Novopharm). *lorazepam.*
Novo-Maprotiline (Novopharm). *maprotiline hydrochloride.*
Novo-Medopa (Novopharm). *methyldopa.*
Novo-Medrone (Novopharm). *medroxyprogesterone acetate.*
Novo-Meprazine (Novopharm). *methotrimeprazine maleate.*
Novo-Metformin (Novopharm). *metformin hydrochloride.*
Novo-Methacin (Novopharm). *indomethacin.*
Novo-Metoprol (Novopharm). *metoprolol tartrate.*
Novo-Mexiletine (Novopharm). *mexiletine hydrochloride.*
Novo-Minocycline (Novopharm). *minocycline hydrochloride.*
Novo-Mucilax (Novopharm). *psyllium hydrophilic mucilloid.*
Novo-Nadolol (Novopharm). *nadolol.*
Novo-Naprox (Novopharm). *naproxen.*
Novo-Naprox Sodium (Novopharm). *naproxen sodium.*
Novo-Naprox Sodium DS (Novopharm). *naproxen sodium.*
Novo-Nidazol (Novopharm). *metronidazole.*
Novo-Nifedin (Novopharm). *nifedipine.*
Novo-Norfloxacin (Novopharm). *norfloxacin.*
Novo-Nortriptyline (Novopharm). *nortriptyline hydrochloride.*
Novo-Oxybutynin (Novopharm). *oxybutynin chloride.*
Novo-Pen-VK (Novopharm). *penicillin V potassium.*
Novo-Peridol (Novopharm). *haloperidol.*
Novo-Pindol (Novopharm). *pindolol.*
Novo-Pirocam (Novopharm). *piroxicam.*
Novo-Poxide (Novopharm). *chlordiazepoxide hydrochloride.*
Novo-Prazin (Novopharm). *prazosin hydrochloride.*
Novo-Profen (Novopharm). *ibuprofen.*
Novo-Ranidine (Novopharm). *ranitidine hydrochloride.*
Novo-Rythro Encap (Novopharm). *erythromycin.*
Novo-Salmol (Novopharm). *salbutamol sulfate.*
Novo-Salmol Inhaler (Novopharm). *salbutamol.*
Novo-Selegiline (Novopharm). *selegiline hydrochloride.*
Novo-Sotalol (Novopharm). *sotalol hydrochloride.*
Novo-Spiroton (Novopharm). *spironolactone.*
Novo-Spirozine (Novopharm). *hydrochlorothiazide/spironolactone.*
Novo-Sucralate (Novopharm). *sucralfate.*
Novo-Sundac (Novopharm). *sulindac.*
Novo-Tamoxifen (Novopharm). *tamoxifen citrate.*
Novo-Temazepam (Novopharm). *temazepam.*
Novo-Tenoxicam (Novopharm). *tenoxicam.*
Novo-Terazosin (Novopharm). *terazosin hydrochloride.*
Novo-Tetra (Novopharm). *tetracycline hydrochloride.*
Novo-Theophyl SR (Novopharm). *theophylline.*
Novo-Tiaprofenic (Novopharm). *tiaprofenic acid.*
Novo-Timol Ophthalmic Solution (Novopharm). *timolol maleate.*
Novo-Timol Tablets (Novopharm). *timolol maleate.*
Novo-Tolmetin (Novopharm). *tolmetin sodium.*
Novo-Trazodone (Novopharm). *trazodone hydrochloride.*
Novo-Triamzide (Novopharm). *hydrochlorothiazide/triamterene.*
Novo-Trimel (Novopharm). *sulfamethoxazole/trimethoprim.*
Novo-Trimel D.S. (Novopharm). *sulfamethoxazole/trimethoprim.*
Novo-Tripramine (Novopharm). *trimipramine maleate.*
Novo-Valproic (Novopharm). *valproic acid.*
Novo-Veramil (Novopharm). *verapamil hydrochloride.*
Novo-Veramil SR (Novopharm). *verapamil hydrochloride.*
Nozinan (Rhône-Poulenc Rorer). *methotrimeprazine maleate.*

Names **underlined** have complete prescribing information in the *CPS* Monograph Section.

Nu-Acebutolol (Nu-Pharm). *acebutolol hydrochloride.*
Nu-Acyclovir (Nu-Pharm). *acyclovir.*
Nu-Alpraz (Nu-Pharm). *alprazolam.*
Nu-Amilzide (Nu-Pharm). *amiloride hydrochloride/ hydrochlorothiazide.*
Nu-Amoxi (Nu-Pharm). *amoxicillin trihydrate.*
Nu-Ampi (Nu-Pharm). *ampicillin trihydrate.*
Nu-Atenol (Nu-Pharm). *atenolol.*
Nu-Baclo (Nu-Pharm). *baclofen.*
Nubain (DuPont Pharma). *nalbuphine hydrochloride.*
Nu-Bromazepam (Nu-Pharm). *bromazepam.*
Nu-Buspirone (Nu-Pharm). *buspirone hydrochloride.*
Nu-Cal (Odan). *calcium.*
Nu-Capto (Nu-Pharm). *captopril.*
Nu-Carbamazepine (Nu-Pharm). *carbamazepine.*
Nu-Cefaclor (Nu-Pharm). *cefaclor.*
Nu-Cephalex (Nu-Pharm). *cephalexin.*
Nu-Cimet (Nu-Pharm). *cimetidine.*
Nu-Clonazepam (Nu-Pharm). *clonazepam.*
Nu-Clonidine (Nu-Pharm). *clonidine hydrochloride.*
Nu-Cloxi (Nu-Pharm). *cloxacillin sodium.*
Nu-Cotrimox (Nu-Pharm). *sulfamethoxazole/trimethoprim.*
Nu-Cromolyn (Nu-Pharm). *sodium cromoglycate.*
Nu-Cyclobenzaprine (Nu-Pharm). *cyclobenzaprine hydrochloride.*
Nu-Desipramine (Nu-Pharm). *desipramine hydrochloride.*
Nu-Diclo (Nu-Pharm). *diclofenac sodium.*
Nu-Diclo-SR (Nu-Pharm). *diclofenac sodium.*
Nu-Diflunisal (Nu-Pharm). *diflunisal.*
Nu-Diltiaz (Nu-Pharm). *diltiazem hydrochloride.*
Nu-Domperidone (Nu-Pharm). *domperidone maleate.*
Nu-Doxycycline (Nu-Pharm). *doxycycline hyclate.*
Nu-Erythromycin-S (Nu-Pharm). *erythromycin stearate.*
Nu-Famotidine (Nu-Pharm). *famotidine.*
Nu-Fenofibrate (Nu-Pharm). *fenofibrate.*
Nu-Fluoxetine (Nu-Pharm). *fluoxetine hydrochloride.*
Nu-Flurbiprofen (Nu-Pharm). *flurbiprofen.*
Nu-Gemfibrozil (Nu-Pharm). *gemfibrozil.*
Nu-Glyburide (Nu-Pharm). *glyburide.*
Nu-Hydral (Nu-Pharm). *hydralazine hydrochloride.*
Nu-Ibuprofen (Nu-Pharm). *ibuprofen.*
Nu-Indapamide (Nu-Pharm). *indapamide hemihydrate.*
Nu-Indo (Nu-Pharm). *indomethacin.*
Nu-Ipratropium (Nu-Pharm). *ipratropium bromide.*
Nu-Ketoprofen (Nu-Pharm). *ketoprofen.*
Nu-Ketoprofen-E (Nu-Pharm). *ketoprofen.*
Nu-Ketoprofen-SR (Nu-Pharm). *ketoprofen.*
Nu-Levocarb (Nu-Pharm). *carbidopa/levodopa.*
Nu-Loraz (Nu-Pharm). *lorazepam.*
Nu-Loxapine (Nu-Pharm). *loxapine succinate.*
Nu-Medopa (Nu-Pharm). *methyldopa.*
Nu-Mefenamic (Nu-Pharm). *mefenamic acid.*
Nu-Megestrol (Nu-Pharm). *megestrol acetate.*
Nu-Metformin (Nu-Pharm). *metformin hydrochloride.*
Nu-Metoclopramide (Nu-Pharm). *metoclopramide hydrochloride.*
Nu-Metop (Nu-Pharm). *metoprolol tartrate.*
Numorphan (DuPont Pharma). *oxymorphone hydrochloride.*
Nu-Naprox (Nu-Pharm). *naproxen.*
Nu-Nifed (Nu-Pharm). *nifedipine.*
Nu-Nifedipine-PA (Nu-Pharm). *nifedipine.*
Nu-Nortriptyline (Nu-Pharm). *nortriptyline hydrochloride.*
Nu-Oxybutyn (Nu-Pharm). *oxybutynin chloride.*
Nu-Pentoxifylline-SR (Nu-Pharm). *pentoxifylline.*
Nu-Pen-VK (Nu-Pharm). *penicillin V potassium.*
Nupercainal Cream (Novartis Consumer Health). *dibucaine/ domiphen bromide.*
Nupercainal Ointment (Novartis Consumer Health). *dibucaine.*
Nu-Pindol (Nu-Pharm). *pindolol.*
Nu-Pirox (Nu-Pharm). *piroxicam.*
Nu-Prazo (Nu-Pharm). *prazosin hydrochloride.*
Nu-Prochlor (Nu-Pharm). *prochlorperazine bimaleate.*
Nu-Propranolol (Nu-Pharm). *propranolol hydrochloride.*
Nu-Ranit (Nu-Pharm). *ranitidine hydrochloride.*
Nuromax (Glaxo Wellcome). *doxacurium chloride.*
Nursoy (Wyeth-Ayerst). *infant formula, soy protein isolate.*
Nu-Salbutamol Solution (Nu-Pharm). *salbutamol sulfate.*
Nu-Salbutamol Tablets (Nu-Pharm). *salbutamol sulfate.*
Nu-Selegiline (Nu-Pharm). *selegiline hydrochloride.*
Nu-Sotalol (Nu-Pharm). *sotalol hydrochloride.*
Nu-Sucralfate (Nu-Pharm). *sucralfate.*
Nu-Sulfinpyrazone (Nu-Pharm). *sulfinpyrazone.*
Nu-Sulindac (Nu-Pharm). *sulindac.*
Nu-Temazepam (Nu-Pharm). *temazepam.*
Nu-Terazosin (Nu-Pharm). *terazosin hydrochloride dihydrate.*
Nu-Tetra (Nu-Pharm). *tetracycline hydrochloride.*
Nu-Tiaprofenic (Nu-Pharm). *tiaprofenic acid.*
Nu-Ticlopidine (Nu-Pharm). *ticlopidine hydrochloride.*
Nu-Timolol (Nu-Pharm). *timolol maleate.*
†Nutracort. *hydrocortisone.*
Nu-Trazodone (Nu-Pharm). *trazodone hydrochloride.*
Nu-Trazodone-D (Nu-Pharm). *trazodone hydrochloride.*
Nu-Triazide (Nu-Pharm). *hydrochlorothiazide/triamterene.*
Nu-Trimipramine (Nu-Pharm). *trimipramine maleate.*
Nutrineal PD4 (Baxter). *amino acids/electrolytes.*
Nutrisource (Novartis Nutrition). *enteral nutrition.*
Nutrisource HN (Novartis Nutrition). *enteral nutrition.*
Nutropin (Roche). *somatropin.*
Nutropin AQ (Roche). *somatropin.*
Nu-Verap (Nu-Pharm). *verapamil hydrochloride.*
Nu-Zopiclone (Nu-Pharm). *zopiclone.*
Nyaderm (Taro). *nystatin.*
†Nydrazid. *isoniazid.*
nylidrin hydrochloride. buphenine hydrochloride. **Arlidin, Arlidin Forte.**
nystatin. **Candistatin, Mycostatin, Nadostine, Nilstat, Nyaderm, PMS-Nystatin.**
nystatin/gramicidin/neomycin sulfate/triamcinolone acetonide. **Kenacomb, Triacomb, Viaderm-K.C.**
nystatin/metronidazole. **Flagystatin.**
Nytol (Block Drug). *diphenhydramine hydrochloride.*
Nytol Extra Strength (Block Drug). *diphenhydramine hydrochloride.*
Nytol Natural Source (Block Drug). *valerian root.*

O

Occlusal (Medicis). *salicylic acid.*

Occlusal-HP (Medicis). *salicylic acid.*

Octostim (Ferring). *desmopressin acetate.*

octreotide acetate. **Sandostatin.**

octyl methoxycinnamate/dimethicone/homosalate/menthol/oxybenzone. **Zilactin-Lip.**

octyl methoxycinnamate/erythromycin/ethyl alcohol/Parsol 1789. **Erysol.**

octyl methoxycinnamate/octyl salicylate/oxybenzone. **Pro•Tec Sport.**

octyl methoxycinnamate/octyl salicylate/oxybenzone/Parsol 1789. **PreSun Ultra 30.**

octyl salicylate/octyl methoxycinnamate/oxybenzone. **Pro•Tec Sport.**

octyl salicylate/octyl methoxycinnamate/oxybenzone/Parsol 1789. **PreSun Ultra 30.**

†Ocu-Caine. *proparacaine hydrochloride.*

†Ocu-Carpine. *pilocarpine hydrochloride.*

†Ocu-Chlor. *chloramphenicol.*

Ocuclear (Schering). *oxymetazoline hydrochloride.*

†Ocucoat. *hydroxypropyl methylcellulose.*

Ocufen (Allergan). *flurbiprofen sodium.*

Ocuflox (Allergan). *ofloxacin.*

†Ocu-Mycin. *gentamicin sulfate.*

†Ocu-Phrin. *phenylephrine hydrochloride.*

†Ocupress. *carteolol hydrochloride.*

†Ocu-Tropic. *tropicamide.*

ofloxacin. **Apo-Oflox, Floxin, Ocuflox.**

Ogen (Pharmacia & Upjohn). *estropipate.*

Oilatum Dermatological Shower and Bath Oil (Stiefel). *liquid paraffin.*

Oilatum Soap (Stiefel). *mineral oil.*

olanzapine. **Zyprexa.**

Oligofer (Sabex). *cyanocobalamin/minerals.*

Oligosol, Copper (Labcatal). *copper gluconate.*

Oligosol, Copper-Gold-Silver (Labcatal). *copper gluconate/gold, colloidal/silver gluconate.*

Oligosol, Magnesium (Labcatal). *magnesium gluconate.*

Oligosol, Manganese (Labcatal). *manganese gluconate.*

Oligosol, Manganese-Copper (Labcatal). *copper gluconate/manganese gluconate.*

Oligosol, Manganese-Cobalt (Labcatal). *cobalt gluconate/manganese gluconate.*

Oligosol, Zinc-Nickel-Cobalt (Labcatal). *cobalt gluconate/nickel gluconate/zinc gluconate.*

olopatadine hydrochloride. **Patanol.**

olsalazine sodium. **Dipentum.**

omeprazole. †Prilosec.

omeprazole magnesium. **Losec.**

Omnipaque (Nycomed Imaging A.S.). *iohexol.*

†Omnipen. *ampicillin.*

†Omnipen-N. *ampicillin sodium.*

Omniscan (Nycomed Imaging A.S.). *gadodiamide.*

Omni-Tuss (Rhône-Poulenc Rorer). *chlorpheniramine/codeine/ephedrine/guaiacol carbonate/phenyltoloxamine.*

Oncaspar (Rhône-Poulenc Rorer). *pegaspargase.*

OncoTICE (Organon Teknika). *Bacillus Calmette-Guérin, intravesical.*

ondansetron hydrochloride dihydrate. **Zofran.**

One A Day Advance (Bayer Consumer). *multiple vitamins and minerals.*

One-Alpha (Leo). *alfacalcidol.*

†Ophthacet. *sulfacetamide sodium.*

†Ophthaine. *proparacaine hydrochloride.*

Ophthetic (Allergan). *proparacaine hydrochloride.*

Ophtho-Bunolol (AltiMed). *levobunolol hydrochloride.*

Ophtho-Chloram (AltiMed). *chloramphenicol.*

Ophtho-Dipivefrin (AltiMed). *dipivefrin hydrochloride.*

Ophtho-Tate (AltiMed). *prednisolone acetate.*

Ophtrivin-A (CIBA Vision). *antazoline sulfate/xylometazoline hydrochloride.*

opioids. **(General Monograph, CPhA).**

opium/atropine sulfate/attapulgite, activated/hyoscyamine sulfate/pectin/scopolamine hydrobromide. **Diban.**

opium/attapulgite, activated/pectin. **Donnagel-PG Capsules.**

opium/kaolin/pectin. **Donnagel-PG Suspension.**

Opticrom (Allergan). *sodium cromoglycate.*

Optimine (Schering). *azatadine maleate.*

Optimyxin Ointment (Sabex). *bacitracin zinc/polymyxin B sulfate.*

Optimyxin Plus Solution (Sabex). *gramicidin/neomycin sulfate/polymyxin B sulfate.*

Optimyxin Solution (Sabex). *gramicidin/polymyxin B sulfate.*

†OptiPranolol. *metipranolol hydrochloride.*

Optiray (Mallinckrodt). *ioversol.*

OPV. see poliovirus vaccine (live oral trivalent) (types 1,2&3).

Orabase (Squibb). *oral protective emollient.*

Oracort (Taro). *triamcinolone acetonide.*

Orafen (Technilab). *ketoprofen.*

Orahesive (Squibb). *denture adhesive.*

†Oralone. *triamcinolone acetonide.*

oral protective emollient. **Orabase.**

Oramorph SR (Boehringer Ingelheim). *morphine sulfate.*

Orap (Janssen-Ortho). *pimozide.*

Orascan (Germiphene). *toluidine blue O.*

†Orasone. *prednisone.*

orchitic extract/adrenal cortical extract/cyanocobalamin. **Heracline.**

Orcipren (Technilab). *orciprenaline sulfate.*

orciprenaline sulfate. metaproterenol sulfate. **Alti-Orciprenaline, Alupent, Orcipren, Tanta Orciprenaline.**

†Oretic. *hydrochlorothiazide.*

†Oreticyl. *deserpidine/hydrochlorothiazide.*

†Oreton. *methyltestosterone.*

Orgaran (Organon). *danaparoid sodium.*

Orifer.F (Hoechst Marion Roussel). *multiple vitamins and minerals.*

†Ormazine. *chlorpromazine hydrochloride.*

†Ornidyl. *eflornithine hydrochloride.*

Oro-Clense (Germiphene). *chlorhexidine gluconate.*

orphenadrine citrate. **Norflex.**

orphenadrine citrate/ASA/caffeine. **Norgesic, Norgesic Forte.**

orphenadrine hydrochloride. **Disipal.**

Ortho 0.5/35 (Janssen-Ortho). *ethinyl estradiol/norethindrone.*

Ortho 1/35 (Janssen-Ortho). *ethinyl estradiol/norethindrone.*

Ortho 7/7/7 (Janssen-Ortho). *ethinyl estradiol/norethindrone.*

Names **underlined** have complete prescribing information in the *CPS* Monograph Section.

Ortho 10/11 (Janssen-Ortho). *ethinyl estradiol/norethindrone.*
Ortho-Cept (Janssen-Ortho). *desogestrel/ethinyl estradiol.*
Orthoclone OKT 3 (Janssen-Ortho). *muromonab-CD3.*
Ortho Dienestrol (Janssen-Ortho). *dienestrol.*
†Ortho-Est. *estropipate.*
Ortho-Novum 1/50 (Janssen-Ortho). *mestranol/norethindrone.*
Orudis (Rhône-Poulenc Rorer). *ketoprofen.*
Orudis E (Rhône-Poulenc Rorer). *ketoprofen.*
Orudis SR (Rhône-Poulenc Rorer). *ketoprofen.*
Oruvail (May & Baker Pharma). *ketoprofen.*
Os-Cal (Wyeth-Ayerst). *calcium carbonate.*
Os-Cal D (Wyeth-Ayerst). *calcium carbonate/cholecalciferol.*
Osmitrol (Baxter). *mannitol.*
Osmopak Plus (Technilab). *benzocaine/magnesium sulfate.*
Osmovist (Berlex Canada). *iotrolan.*
Ostac (Roche). *clodronate disodium.*
Ostoforte (Frosst). *ergocalciferol.*
Otrivin (Novartis Consumer Health). *xylometazoline hydrochloride.*
†Ovcon. *ethinyl estradiol/norethindrone.*
Ovol (Carter Horner). *simethicone.*
Ovral 21 (Wyeth-Ayerst). *ethinyl estradiol/norgestrel.*
Ovral 28 (Wyeth-Ayerst). *ethinyl estradiol/norgestrel.*
†Ovrette. *norgestrel.*
oxacillin sodium. †Bactocill, †Prostaphlin.
oxamniquine. †Vansil.
oxaprozin. **Daypro.**
oxazepam. **[Benzodiazepines, General Monograph, CPhA]; Apo-Oxazepam, Serax.**
oxethazaine/aluminum hydroxide/magnesium hydroxide. **Mucaine.**
Oxeze Turbuhaler (Astra). *formoterol fumarate dihydrate.*
oxiconazole nitrate. **Oxizole.** †Oxistat.
oxilapine. see loxapine.
†Oxistat. *oxiconazole nitrate.*
Oxizole (Stiefel). *oxiconazole nitrate.*
oxprenolol hydrochloride. **Slow-Trasicor, Trasicor.**
Oxsoralen (ICN). *methoxsalen.*
Oxsoralen-Ultra (ICN). *methoxsalen.*
oxtriphylline. choline theophyllinate. **[Theophylline and its Salts, General Monograph, CPhA]; Apo-Oxtriphylline, Choledyl, Choledyl SA.**
oxtriphylline/guaifenesin. **Choledyl Expectorant.**
oxybenzone/dimethicone/homosalate/menthol/octyl methoxycinnamate. **Zilactin-Lip.**
oxybenzone/octyl methoxycinnamate/octyl salicylate. **Pro•Tec Sport.**
oxybenzone/octyl methoxycinnamate/octyl salicylate/Parsol 1789. **PreSun Ultra 30.**
Oxybutyn (ICN). *oxybutynin chloride.*
oxybutynin chloride. **Albert Oxybutynin, Apo-Oxybutynin, Ditropan, Gen-Oxybutynin, Novo-Oxybutynin, Nu-Oxybutyn, Oxybutyn.**
Oxycocet (Technilab). *acetaminophen/oxycodone hydrochloride.*
Oxycodan (Technilab). *ASA/oxycodone hydrochloride.*
oxycodone hydrochloride. dihydrohydroxycodeinone. **[Opioids, General Monograph, CPhA]; OxyContin, Supeudol.** †Roxicodone.
oxycodone hydrochloride/acetaminophen. **Endocet, Oxycocet, Percocet, Percocet-Demi.**
oxycodone hydrochloride/ASA. **Endodan, Oxycodan, Percodan, Percodan-Demi.**
OxyContin (Purdue Frederick). *oxycodone hydrochloride.*
Oxyderm (ICN). *benzoyl peroxide.*
oxymetazoline hydrochloride. **Dristan Long Lasting Nasal Mist/Spray, Drixoral Nasal, Ocuclear.**
oxymorphone hydrochloride. **[Opioids, General Monograph, CPhA]; Numorphan.**
†Oxy 10. *benzoyl peroxide.*
oxytetracycline hydrochloride. †Terramycin.
oxytocin. **(Abbott).** †Pitocin.

P

PACIS (Faulding). *Bacillus Calmette-Guérin, intravesical.*
paclitaxel. **Taxol; (Boehringer Ingelheim).**
PAH. see aminohippurate sodium.
Palafer (SmithKline Beecham). *ferrous fumarate.*
Palafer CF (SmithKline Beecham). *ascorbic acid/ferrous fumarate/folic acid.*
palmitic acid/galactose. **Levovist.**
Paludrine (Wyeth-Ayerst). *proguanil.*
pamabrom/acetaminophen/pyrilamine maleate. **Midol PMS Extra Strength, Pamprin, Pamprin Extra Strength, Pamprin PMS.**
2-PAM chloride. see pralidoxime chloride.
†Pamelor. *nortriptyline hydrochloride.*
pamidronate disodium. **Aredia.**
†Pamine. *methscopolamine bromide.*
Pamprin (Chattem). *acetaminophen/pamabrom/pyrilamine maleate.*
Pamprin Extra Strength (Chattem). *acetaminophen/pamabrom/pyrilamine maleate.*
Pamprin PMS (Chattem). *acetaminophen/pamabrom/pyrilamine maleate.*
Pancrease (Janssen-Ortho). *pancrelipase.*
Pancrease MT (Janssen-Ortho). *pancrelipase.*
pancrelipase. **Cotazym, Creon 10, Creon 25, Pancrease, Pancrease MT, Ultrase, Ultrase MT, Viokase.**
pancuronium bromide. **(Abbott).**
Panectyl (Rhône-Poulenc Rorer). *trimeprazine tartrate.*
†Panmycin. *tetracycline hydrochloride.*
Panocaine (Hoechst Marion Roussel). *benzocaine/tetracaine hydrochloride.*
PanOxyl Aquagel (Stiefel). *benzoyl peroxide.*
PanOxyl Gel/Bars (Stiefel). *benzoyl peroxide.*
PanOxyl Wash (Stiefel). *benzoyl peroxide.*
Pantoloc (Solvay Pharma/Byk Canada). *pantoprazole.*
pantoprazole. **Pantoloc.**
pantothenic acid. calcium pantothenate. vitamin B_5. **[Pantothenic Acid, General Monograph, CPhA].**
†Panwarfin. *warfarin sodium.*
papaverine hydrochloride. **(Frosst).** †Cerespan, †Genabid.
Para (Technilab). *bioallethrin/piperonyl butoxide.*
para-aminosalicylate sodium. see aminosalicylate sodium.
parabromdylamine maleate. see brompheniramine maleate.
paracetamol. see acetaminophen.
paradichlorobenzene/chlorbutol/terebinth oil. **Cerumol.**
†Paraflex. *chlorzoxazone.*
Parafon Forte (Johnson & Johnson • Merck). *acetaminophen/chlorzoxazone.*

Parafon Forte C8 (Johnson & Johnson • Merck). *acetaminophen/chlorzoxazone/codeine phosphate.*

†Paral. *paraldehyde.*

paraldehyde. **(Faulding).** †Paral.

Paraplatin-AQ (Bristol). *carboplatin.*

†Parathar. *teriparatide acetate.*

Parlodel (Novartis Pharmaceuticals). *bromocriptine mesylate.*

Parnate (SmithKline Beecham). *tranylcypromine sulfate.*

paromomycin sulfate. **Humatin.**

paroxetine hydrochloride. **[Selective Serotonin Reuptake Inhibitors, General Monograph, CPhA]; Paxil.**

†Parsidol. *ethopropazine hydrochloride.*

Parsitan (Rhône-Poulenc Rorer). *ethopropazine hydrochloride.*

Parsol 1789/erythromycin/ethyl alcohol/octyl methoxycinnamate. **Erysol.**

Parsol 1789/octyl methoxycinnamate/octyl salicylate/oxybenzone. **PreSun Ultra 30.**

Parvolex (Bioniche). *acetylcysteine.*

PAS Sodium. see aminosalicylate sodium.

Patanol (Alcon). *olopatadine hydrochloride.*

Paxil (SmithKline Beecham). *paroxetine hydrochloride.*

†Paxipam. *halazepam.*

PCE (Abbott). *erythromycin.*

pectin/atropine sulfate/attapulgite, activated/hyoscyamine sulfate/opium/scopolamine hydrobromide. **Diban.**

pectin/attapulgite, activated/opium. **Donnagel-PG Capsules.**

pectin/kaolin/opium. **Donnagel-PG Suspension.**

Pedialyte (Abbott). *dextrose/electrolytes.*

Pedialyte Freezer Pops (Abbott). *dextrose/electrolytes.*

Pediapred (Rhône-Poulenc Rorer). *prednisolone sodium phosphate.*

PediaSure (Abbott). *enteral nutrition.*

Pediatric Electrolyte (Pharmascience). *electrolytes.*

Pediatrix (Technilab). *acetaminophen.*

Pediazole (Abbott). *erythromycin ethylsuccinate/sulfisoxazole acetyl.*

Pedi-Dent (Stanley). *sodium fluoride.*

PedvaxHIB (MSD). *haemophilus b (Hib) polysaccharide conjugate (meningococcal protein conjugate) vaccine.*

pegademase bovine. †Adagen.

†Peganone. *ethotoin.*

pegaspargase. **Oncaspar.**

PegLyte (Pharmascience). *electrolytes/polyethylene glycol.*

pemoline. phenylisohydantoin. **Cylert.**

penbutolol sulfate. †Levatol.

†Penecort. *hydrocortisone.*

Penglobe (Astra). *bacampicillin hydrochloride.*

penicillamine. **Cuprimine, Depen.**

penicillin G benzathine. benzethacil. **[Penicillin G/Penicillin V, General Monograph, CPhA]; Bicillin L-A.**

penicillin G potassium. benzylpenicillin potassium. **[Penicillin G/Penicillin V, General Monograph, CPhA];** †Pentids, †Pfizerpen.

penicillin G procaine. **[Penicillin G/Penicillin V, General Monograph, CPhA];** †Crysticillin 300 AS.

penicillin G sodium. **[Penicillin G/Penicillin V, General Monograph, CPhA]; Crystapen (Buffered), Scheinpharm Penicillin G Sodium.**

penicillin V. phenoxymethyl penicillin. **[Penicillin G/Penicillin V, General Monograph, CPhA].**

penicillin V potassium. phenoxymethyl penicillin potassium. **[Penicillin G/Penicillin V, General Monograph, CPhA]; Apo-Pen VK, Ledercillin VK, Nadopen-V, Novo-Pen-VK, Nu-Pen-VK.** †Beepen-VK, †Betapen-VK, †Veetids.

Pentacarinat (Rhône-Poulenc Rorer). *pentamidine isethionate.*

Pentacel (Connaught). *diphtheria toxoid adsorbed/haemophilus b conjugate vaccine (tetanus protein conjugate)/pertussis vaccine (acellular)/poliomyelitis vaccine, inactivated/tetanus toxoid adsorbed.*

pentaerythritol tetranitrate. pentaerythrityl tetranitrate. †Pentylan.

pentaerythrityl tetranitrate. see pentaerythritol tetranitrate.

†Pentam 300. *pentamidine isethionate.*

pentamidine isethionate. **Pentacarinat; (Faulding).** †NebuPent, †Pentam 300.

Pentamycetin (Sabex). *chloramphenicol.*

Pentamycetin/HC (Sabex). *chloramphenicol/hydrocortisone acetate.*

Pentasa (Hoechst Marion Roussel). *5-aminosalicylic acid.*

Pentaspan (DuPont Pharma). *pentastarch.*

pentastarch. **Pentaspan.**

Penta-Thion (Sabex). *ascorbic acid/thiamine.*

Penta/3B (Sabex). *vitamin B compound.*

Penta/3B + C (Sabex). *ascorbic acid/vitamin B compound.*

Penta/3B Plus (Sabex). *multiple vitamins.*

pentazocine hydrochloride. **[Opioids, General Monograph, CPhA]; Talwin Tablets.**

pentazocine lactate. **[Opioids, General Monograph, CPhA]; Talwin Injection.**

†Penthrane. *methoxyflurane.*

†Pentids. *penicillin G potassium.*

pentobarbital/belladonna/caffeine/ergotamine tartrate. **Cafergot-PB.**

pentobarbital sodium. **[Barbiturates, General Monograph, CPhA]; Nembutal Sodium, Nova Rectal.**

pentosan polysulfate sodium. **Elmiron.**

Pentothal (Abbott). *thiopental sodium.*

pentoxifylline. **Albert Pentoxifylline, Apo-Pentoxifylline SR, Nu-Pentoxifylline-SR, Trental.**

Pentrax (Medicis). *fractar.*

†Pentylan. *pentaerythritol tetranitrate.*

Pepcid AC (Johnson & Johnson • Merck). *famotidine.*

Pepcid I.V. (MSD). *famotidine.*

Pepcid Tablets (MSD). *famotidine.*

peppermint oil. **Colpermin.**

pepsin. **Fermentol.**

Peptol (Carter Horner). *cimetidine.*

Percocet (DuPont Pharma). *acetaminophen/oxycodone hydrochloride.*

Percocet-Demi (DuPont Pharma). *acetaminophen/oxycodone hydrochloride.*

Percodan (DuPont Pharma). *ASA/oxycodone hydrochloride.*

Percodan-Demi (DuPont Pharma). *ASA/oxycodone hydrochloride.*

perflubron. †Imagent GI.

perfluoropolymethylisopropyl ether/dimethicone/tricontanyl PVP. **Spectro Gluvs "19".**

pergolide mesylate. **Permax.**

Pergonal (Serono). *menotropins.*

Names **underlined** have complete prescribing information in the *CPS* Monograph Section.

Periactin (Johnson & Johnson • Merck). *cyproheptadine hydrochloride.*

Peri-Colace (Roberts). *casanthranol/docusate sodium.*

pericyazine. propericyazine. **Neuleptil.**

Peridex (Zila Pharmaceuticals). *chlorhexidine gluconate.*

Peridol (Technilab). *haloperidol.*

perindopril erbumine. **[ACE Inhibitors, General Monograph, CPhA]; Coversyl.**

Permax (Draxis Health). *pergolide mesylate.*

permethrin. **Kwellada-P, Nix Creme Rinse, Nix Dermal Cream.**

Pernox (Westwood-Squibb). *salicylic acid/sulfur.*

perphenazine. **Apo-Perphenazine, Trilafon.**

perphenazine/amitriptyline hydrochloride. **Elavil Plus, Etrafon, Triavil.**

†Persa-Gel. *benzoyl peroxide.*

Persantine (Boehringer Ingelheim). *dipyridamole.*

pertussis vaccine (acellular)/diphtheria toxoid adsorbed/ haemophilus b conjugate vaccine (tetanus protein conjugate)/ poliomyelitis vaccine, inactivated/tetanus toxoid adsorbed. **Pentacel.**

pertussis vaccine (acellular)/diphtheria toxoid adsorbed/ poliomyelitis vaccine, inactivated/tetanus toxoid adsorbed. **Quadracel.**

pertussis vaccine adsorbed, acellular. **Acel-P.**

pertussis vaccine adsorbed/diphtheria toxoid adsorbed/ poliomyelitis vaccine adsorbed, inactivated/tetanus toxoid adsorbed. **(Connaught).**

pertussis vaccine (cellular)/diphtheria toxoid adsorbed/tetanus toxoid adsorbed. **(Connaught).**

pethidine hydrochloride. isonipecaine. meperidine hydrochloride. **[Opioids, General Monograph, CPhA]; Demerol; (Abbott), (Faulding).**

petrolatum. **Aquaphor, Prevex Lotion.**

petrolatum/cyclomethicone. **Prevex Cream.**

petrolatum/dimethicone. **Moisturel.**

†Pfizerpen. *penicillin G potassium.*

Pharmorubicin PFS (Pharmacia & Upjohn). *epirubicin hydrochloride.*

Pharmorubicin RDF (Pharmacia & Upjohn). *epirubicin hydrochloride.*

Phazyme (R & C). *simethicone.*

phenacemide. phenacetylcarbamide. †Phenurone.

phenacetylcarbamide. see phenacemide.

Phenaphen with Codeine (Wyeth-Ayerst). *ASA/codeine phosphate/phenobarbital.*

Phenazo (ICN). *phenazopyridine hydrochloride.*

†Phenazodine. *phenazopyridine hydrochloride.*

phenazopyridine hydrochloride. **Phenazo, Pyridium.** †Azo-Standard, †Phenazodine, †Pyridiate, †Urodine, †Urogesic.

†Phendiet. *phendimetrazine tartrate.*

†Phendimet. *phendimetrazine tartrate.*

phendimetrazine tartrate. †Bontril, †Melfiat-105, †Phendiet, †Phendimet, †Plegine, †Prelu-2, †PT 105, †Wehless.

phenelzine sulfate. **Nardil.**

Phenergan Cream (Novartis Consumer Health). *promethazine.*

Phenergan Expectorant with Codeine (Novartis Consumer Health). *codeine phosphate/potassium guaiacolsulfonate/ promethazine hydrochloride.*

Phenergan Injectable (Rhône-Poulenc Rorer). *promethazine hydrochloride.*

Phenergan Tablets (Novartis Consumer Health). *promethazine hydrochloride.*

phenindamine tartrate. †Nolahist.

pheniramine maleate/acetaminophen/caffeine/ phenylpropanolamine hydrochloride/pyrilamine maleate. **Triaminicin.**

pheniramine maleate/acetaminophen/phenylephrine hydrochloride. **NeoCitran Adult, NeoCitran Extra Strength, NeoCitran Nutrasweet.**

pheniramine maleate/codeine phosphate/guaifenesin. **Calmylin Ace, Robitussin AC, Robitussin with Codeine.**

pheniramine maleate/codeine phosphate/phenylpropanolamine hydrochloride/pyrilamine maleate. **Tussaminic C.**

pheniramine maleate/dextromethorphan hydrobromide/ phenylephrine hydrochloride. **NeoCitran DM.**

pheniramine maleate/guaifenesin/hydrocodone bitartrate/ phenylpropanolamine hydrochloride/pyrilamine maleate. **Triaminic Expectorant DH.**

pheniramine maleate/hydrocodone bitartrate/ phenylpropanolamine hydrochloride/pyrilamine maleate. **Caldomine-DH, Tussaminic DH.**

pheniramine maleate/naphazoline hydrochloride. **Naphcon-A.**

pheniramine maleate/phenylephrine hydrochloride. **Dristan Nasal Mist/Spray, NeoCitran A.**

pheniramine maleate/phenylpropanolamine hydrochloride/ pyrilamine maleate. **Triaminic Tablets.**

pheniramine maleate/phenylpropanolamine hydrochloride/ pyrilamine maleate/sulfadiazine/sulfamerazine/sulfamethazine. **Trisulfaminic.**

phenobarbital. phenobarbitone. **[Barbiturates, General Monograph, CPhA]; (Abbott).** †Barbita, †Luminal, †Solfoton.

phenobarbital/ASA/codeine phosphate. **Phenaphen with Codeine.**

phenobarbital/atropine sulfate/hyoscyamine sulfate/scopolamine hydrobromide. **Donnatal.**

phenobarbital/belladonna/ergotamine. **Bellergal Spacetabs.**

phenobarbital sodium. **[Barbiturates, General Monograph, CPhA].**

phenobarbitone. see phenobarbital.

phenoxetol. see beta-phenoxyethanol.

phenoxybenzamine hydrochloride. †Dibenzyline.

phenoxymethyl penicillin. see penicillin V.

phenoxymethyl penicillin potassium. see penicillin V potassium.

phensuximide. †Milontin.

†Phentercot. *phentermine hydrochloride.*

phentermine. **Ionamin.**

phentermine hydrochloride. **Fastin.** †Adipex-P, †Phentercot, †T-Diet, †Zantryl.

phentolamine mesylate. **Rogitine.** †Regitine.

†Phenurone. *phenacemide.*

phenylbutazone. **Apo-Phenylbutazone.**

phenylephrine. **Minims Phenylephrine.**

phenylephrine hydrochloride. **Dionephrine, Mydfrin, Neo-Synephrine.** †I-Phrine, †Nostril Spray Pump, †Ocu-Phrin.

phenylephrine hydrochloride/acetaminophen. **NeoCitran Sinus Extra Strength.**

phenylephrine hydrochloride/acetaminophen/chlorpheniramine maleate. **Dristan, Dristan Extra Strength.**

phenylephrine hydrochloride/acetaminophen/pheniramine maleate. **NeoCitran Adult, NeoCitran Extra Strength, NeoCitran Nutrasweet.**

phenylephrine hydrochloride/acetaminophen/phenylpropanolamine hydrochloride. **Dimetapp-A Sinus.**

phenylephrine hydrochloride/ammonium chloride/hydrocodone bitartrate/pyrilamine maleate. **Hycomine, Hycomine-S.**

phenylephrine hydrochloride/brompheniramine maleate/codeine phosphate/guaifenesin/phenylpropanolamine hydrochloride. **Dimetane Expectorant-C.**

phenylephrine hydrochloride/brompheniramine maleate/codeine phosphate/phenylpropanolamine hydrochloride. **Dimetapp-C.**

phenylephrine hydrochloride/brompheniramine maleate/dextromethorphan hydrobromide/phenylpropanolamine hydrochloride. **Dimetapp-DM.**

phenylephrine hydrochloride/brompheniramine maleate/guaifenesin/hydrocodone bitartrate/phenylpropanolamine hydrochloride. **Dimetane Expectorant-DC.**

phenylephrine hydrochloride/brompheniramine maleate/guaifenesin/phenylpropanolamine hydrochloride. **Dimetane Expectorant.**

phenylephrine hydrochloride/brompheniramine maleate/phenylpropanolamine hydrochloride. **Dimetapp, Dimetapp Oral Infant Drops.**

phenylephrine hydrochloride/codeine phosphate. **Novahistex C.**

phenylephrine hydrochloride/dextromethorphan hydrobromide/pheniramine maleate. **NeoCitran DM.**

phenylephrine hydrochloride/guaifenesin/hydrocodone bitartrate. **Novahistex DH Expectorant.**

phenylephrine hydrochloride/hamamelis water. **Preparation H Cooling Gel.**

phenylephrine hydrochloride/hydrocodone bitartrate. **Coristex-DH, Coristine-DH, Novahistex DH, Novahistine DH.**

phenylephrine hydrochloride/pheniramine maleate. **Dristan Nasal Mist/Spray, NeoCitran A.**

phenylephrine hydrochloride/tropicamide. **Diophenyl-T.**

phenylephrine hydrochloride/zinc sulfate. **Zincfrin.**

phenylisohydantoin. see pemoline.

phenylpropanolamine/ASA/chlorpheniramine maleate. **Coricidin "D".**

phenylpropanolamine hydrochloride/acetaminophen/caffeine/pheniramine maleate/pyrilamine maleate. **Triaminicin.**

phenylpropanolamine hydrochloride/acetaminophen/phenylephrine hydrochloride. **Dimetapp-A Sinus.**

phenylpropanolamine hydrochloride/acetaminophen/phenyltoloxamine citrate. **Sinutab SA.**

phenylpropanolamine hydrochloride/ASA. **Coricidin Non-Drowsy.**

phenylpropanolamine hydrochloride/brompheniramine maleate. **Dimetapp Chewables, Dimetapp Clear, Dimetapp Liqui-Gels, Dimetapp Quick Dissolve.**

phenylpropanolamine hydrochloride/brompheniramine maleate/codeine phosphate/guaifenesin/phenylephrine hydrochloride. **Dimetane Expectorant-C.**

phenylpropanolamine hydrochloride/brompheniramine maleate/codeine phosphate/phenylephrine hydrochloride. **Dimetapp-C.**

phenylpropanolamine hydrochloride/brompheniramine maleate/dextromethorphan hydrobromide. **Dimetapp Cough & Cold Liqui-Gels.**

phenylpropanolamine hydrochloride/brompheniramine maleate/dextromethorphan hydrobromide/phenylephrine hydrochloride. **Dimetapp-DM.**

phenylpropanolamine hydrochloride/brompheniramine maleate/guaifenesin/hydrocodone bitartrate/phenylephrine hydrochloride. **Dimetane Expectorant-DC.**

phenylpropanolamine hydrochloride/brompheniramine maleate/guaifenesin/phenylephrine hydrochloride. **Dimetane Expectorant.**

phenylpropanolamine hydrochloride/brompheniramine maleate/phenylephrine hydrochloride. **Dimetapp, Dimetapp Oral Infant Drops.**

phenylpropanolamine hydrochloride/chlorpheniramine maleate. **Chlor-Tripolon Decongestant Syrup, Contac Cold 12 Hour Relief Extra Strength, Contac Cold 12 Hour Relief Regular Strength, Coricidin "D" Long Acting, Triaminic Cold and Allergy Syrup.**

phenylpropanolamine hydrochloride/clemastine hydrogen fumarate. **Tavist-D.**

phenylpropanolamine hydrochloride/codeine phosphate/pheniramine maleate/pyrilamine maleate. **Tussaminic C.**

phenylpropanolamine hydrochloride/dextromethorphan hydrobromide/guaifenesin. **Triaminic DM Daytime.**

phenylpropanolamine hydrochloride/guaifenesin. **Entex LA.**

phenylpropanolamine hydrochloride/guaifenesin/hydrocodone bitartrate/pheniramine maleate/pyrilamine maleate. **Triaminic Expectorant DH.**

phenylpropanolamine hydrochloride/hydrocodone bitartrate/pheniramine maleate/pyrilamine maleate. **Caldomine-DH, Tussaminic DH.**

phenylpropanolamine hydrochloride/pheniramine maleate/pyrilamine maleate. **Triaminic Tablets.**

phenylpropanolamine hydrochloride/pheniramine maleate/pyrilamine maleate/sulfadiazine/sulfamerazine/sulfamethazine. **Trisulfaminic.**

phenyltoloxamine/chlorpheniramine/codeine/ephedrine/guaiacol carbonate. **Omni-Tuss.**

phenyltoloxamine citrate/acetaminophen/phenylpropanolamine hydrochloride. **Sinutab SA.**

phenyltoloxamine/hydrocodone. **Tussionex.**

†Phenytex. *phenytoin sodium.*

phenytoin. diphenylhydantoin. **[Phenytoin, General Monograph, CPhA].**

phenytoin (acid form). **Dilantin-125, Dilantin Infatabs, Dilantin-30 Pediatric.**

phenytoin sodium. **Dilantin; (Abbott).** †Diphenylan, †Phenytex.

pHisoHex (Sanofi). *hexachlorophene.*

Phosphate-Novartis (Novartis Pharmaceuticals). *sodium acid phosphate.*

Phosphates Solution (Pharmascience). *sodium phosphates.*

Phospholine Iodide (Wyeth-Ayerst). *echothiophate iodide.*

Photofrin (Ligand). *porfimer sodium.*

Phyllocontin (Purdue Frederick). *aminophylline.*

Phyllocontin-350 (Purdue Frederick). *aminophylline.*

phylloquinone. see phytonadione.

physostigmine salicylate. †Isopto Eserine.

physostigmine sulfate. †Eserine.

phytomenadione. see phytonadione.

phytonadione. phylloquinone. phytomenadione. vitamin K_1. **[Vitamin K, General Monograph, CPhA]; (Abbott).** †Aqua Mephyton, †Konakion, †Mephyton.

†Pilagan. *pilocarpine nitrate.*

pilocarpine hydrochloride. **Diocarpine, Isopto Carpine, Miocarpine, Pilopine HS, Salagen, Scheinpharm Pilocarpine; (Rivex Ophthalmics), (Technilab).** †Adsorbocarpine, †Ocu-Carpine, †Piloptic.

Names **underlined** have complete prescribing information in the *CPS* Monograph Section.

pilocarpine hydrochloride/epinephrine bitartrate. **E-Pilo.**
pilocarpine hydrochloride/timolol maleate. **Timpilo.**
pilocarpine nitrate. **Minims Pilocarpine.** †Pilagan.
Pilopine HS (Alcon). *pilocarpine hydrochloride.*
†Piloptic. *pilocarpine hydrochloride.*
pimaricin. see natamycin.
pimozide. **Orap.**
pinaverium bromide. **Dicetel.**
pindolol. **Apo-Pindol, Gen-Pindolol, Novo-Pindol, Nu-Pindol, Visken.**
pindolol/hydrochlorothiazide. **Viskazide.**
pine tar/coal tar/juniper tar/zinc pyrithione. **Multi-Tar Plus.**
pipecuronium bromide. †Arduan.
piperacillin sodium. **Pipracil.**
piperacillin sodium/tazobactam sodium. **Tazocin.**
piperazine adipate. **Entacyl.**
piperazine estrone sulfate. see estropipate.
piperonyl butoxide/bioallethrin. **Para.**
piperonyl butoxide/esdepallethrin. **Scabene.**
piperonyl butoxide/pyrethrins. **R & C Shampoo/Conditioner, R & C II Spray.**
Piportil L4 (Rhône-Poulenc Rorer). *pipotiazine palmitate.*
pipotiazine palmitate. **Piportil L4.**
Pipracil (Wyeth-Ayerst). *piperacillin sodium.*
pipradrol/vitamin B compound. **Alertonic.**
piroxicam. **Alti-Piroxicam, Apo-Piroxicam, Feldene, Fexicam, Gen-Piroxicam, Novo-Pirocam, Nu-Pirox.**
†Pitocin. *oxytocin.*
Pitrex (Taro). *tolnaftate.*
pivampicillin. **Pondocillin.**
pivmecillinam hydrochloride. **Selexid.**
pizotifen maleate. **Sandomigran, Sandomigran DS.**
Placebo (Odan). *lactose.*
Plaquenil (Sanofi). *hydroxychloroquine sulfate.*
Plasbumin-5 (Bayer). *albumin (human).*
Plasbumin-25 (Bayer). *albumin (human).*
Platinol-AQ (Bristol). *cisplatin.*
Plavix (Sanofi/Bristol-Myers Squibb). *clopidogrel bisulfate.*
†Plegine. *phendimetrazine tartrate.*
Plendil (Astra). *felodipine.*
plicamycin. mithramycin. †Mithracin.
PMS-Atenolol (Pharmascience). *atenolol.*
PMS-Baclofen (Pharmascience). *baclofen.*
PMS-Benzydamine (Pharmascience). *benzydamine hydrochloride.*
PMS-Buspirone (Pharmascience). *buspirone hydrochloride.*
PMS-Cefaclor (Pharmascience). *cefaclor.*
PMS-Cephalexin (Pharmascience). *cephalexin.*
PMS-Chloral Hydrate (Pharmascience). *chloral hydrate.*
PMS-Cholestyramine (Pharmascience). *cholestyramine resin.*
PMS-Cimetidine (Pharmascience). *cimetidine.*
PMS-Clobetasol (Pharmascience). *clobetasol 17-propionate.*
PMS-Clonazepam (Pharmascience). *clonazepam.*
PMS-Desipramine (Pharmascience). *desipramine hydrochloride.*
PMS-Dicitrate (Pharmascience). *citric acid/sodium citrate.*
PMS-Diclofenac (Pharmascience). *diclofenac sodium.*
PMS-Diphenhydramine (Pharmascience). *diphenhydramine hydrochloride.*
PMS-Docusate Calcium (Pharmascience). *docusate calcium.*
PMS-Docusate Sodium (Pharmascience). *docusate sodium.*
PMS-Domperidone (Pharmascience). *domperidone maleate.*
PMS-Egozinc (Pharmascience). *zinc sulfate.*
PMS-Egozinc-HC (Pharmascience). *hydrocortisone acetate/zinc sulfate monohydrate.*
PMS-Erythromycin (Pharmascience). *erythromycin.*
PMS-Fluoxetine (Pharmascience). *fluoxetine hydrochloride.*
PMS-Fluphenazine Decanoate (Pharmascience). *fluphenazine decanoate.*
PMS-Flutamide (Pharmascience). *flutamide.*
PMS-Gemfibrozil (Pharmascience). *gemfibrozil.*
PMS-Glyburide (Pharmascience). *glyburide.*
PMS-Haloperidol LA (Pharmascience). *haloperidol.*
PMS-Hydromorphone (Pharmascience). *hydromorphone hydrochloride.*
PMS-Hydroxyzine (Pharmascience). *hydroxyzine hydrochloride.*
PMS-Ipratropium (Pharmascience). *ipratropium bromide.*
PMS-Isoniazid (Pharmascience). *isoniazid.*
PMS-Lactulose (Pharmascience). *lactulose.*
PMS-Lindane (Pharmascience). *lindane.*
PMS-Lithium Carbonate (Pharmascience). *lithium carbonate.*
PMS-Lithium Citrate (Pharmascience). *lithium citrate.*
PMS-Loxapine (Pharmascience). *loxapine.*
PMS-Mefenamic Acid (Pharmascience). *mefenamic acid.*
PMS-Methotrimeprazine (Pharmascience). *methotrimeprazine maleate.*
PMS-Methylphenidate (Pharmascience). *methylphenidate hydrochloride.*
PMS-Metoclopramide (Pharmascience). *metoclopramide hydrochloride.*
PMS-Metoprolol-B (Pharmascience). *metoprolol tartrate.*
PMS-Metoprolol-L (Pharmascience). *metoprolol tartrate.*
PMS-Nifedipine (Pharmascience). *nifedipine.*
PMS-Nortriptyline (Pharmascience). *nortriptyline hydrochloride.*
PMS-Nystatin (Pharmascience). *nystatin.*
PMS-Salbutamol Respirator Solution (Pharmascience). *salbutamol sulfate.*
PMS-Sennosides (Pharmascience). *sennosides.*
PMS-Sodium Cromoglycate (Pharmascience). *sodium cromoglycate.*
PMS-Sodium Polystyrene Sulfonate (Pharmascience). *sodium polystyrene sulfonate.*
PMS-Temazepam (Pharmascience). *temazepam.*
PMS-Tiaprofenic (Pharmascience). *tiaprofenic acid.*
PMS-Timolol (Pharmascience). *timolol maleate.*
PMS-Trazodone (Pharmascience). *trazodone hydrochloride.*
PMS-Tryptophan (Pharmascience). *l-tryptophan.*
PMS-Valproic Acid (Pharmascience). *valproic acid.*
PMS-Valproic Acid E.C. (Pharmascience). *valproic acid.*
PMS-Yohimbine (Pharmascience). *yohimbine hydrochloride.*
Pneumo 23 (Connaught). *pneumococcal polysaccharide vaccine.*
pneumococcal polysaccharide vaccine. **Pneumo 23.**
pneumococcal vaccine (polyvalent). **Pneumovax 23, Pnu-Imune 23.**
Pneumovax 23 (MSD). *pneumococcal vaccine (polyvalent).*
Pnu-Imune 23 (Wyeth-Ayerst). *pneumococcal vaccine (polyvalent).*
Podofilm (Pharmascience). *podophyllum resin.*
podofilox. **Condyline, Wartec.**

podophyllin/cantharidin/salicylic acid. **Canthacur-PS, Cantharone Plus.**

podophyllum resin. **Podofilm.**

Polaramine (Schering). *dexchlorpheniramine maleate.*

poliomyelitis vaccine adsorbed, inactivated/diphtheria toxoid adsorbed/pertussis vaccine adsorbed/tetanus toxoid adsorbed. **(Connaught).**

poliomyelitis vaccine adsorbed, inactivated/diphtheria toxoid adsorbed/tetanus toxoid adsorbed. **(Connaught).**

poliomyelitis vaccine, inactivated/diphtheria toxoid adsorbed/haemophilus b conjugate vaccine (tetanus protein conjugate)/pertussis vaccine (acellular)/tetanus toxoid adsorbed. **Pentacel.**

poliomyelitis vaccine, inactivated/diphtheria toxoid adsorbed/pertussis vaccine (acellular)/tetanus toxoid adsorbed. **Quadracel.**

poliomyelitis vaccine, inactivated (diploid cell origin). IPV. **(Connaught).**

poliovirus vaccine (inactivated enhanced potency). †Ipol.

poliovirus vaccine (live oral trivalent) (types 1,2&3). OPV. **(Connaught).**

Pollinex-R (Bencard). *ragweed tyrosine adsorbate, modified.*

Polocaine 3% (Astra). *mepivacaine hydrochloride.*

Polocaine 2% with Levonordefrin 1:20 000 (Astra). *levonordefrin/mepivacaine hydrochloride.*

poloxamer 188. †Alaxin.

polycarbophil. **Replens.**

Polycidin Eye/Ear Drops (CIBA Vision). *gramicidin/polymyxin B sulfate.*

Polycidin Ophthalmic Ointment (CIBA Vision). *bacitracin/polymyxin B sulfate.*

†Polycillin. *ampicillin trihydrate.*

†Polycillin-N. *ampicillin sodium.*

Polycitra-K (Alza). *potassium citrate.*

polyethylene glycol/dextran 70. **Aquasite.**

polyethylene glycol/electrolytes. **Colyte, Electropeg, GoLytely, Klean-Prep, Lyteprep, PegLyte, Pro-Lax.**

polyethylene glycol/propylene glycol. **Rhinaris, Salinol, Secaris.**

polyglycol/cellulose/glycerides/polysiloxane copolyol/silicones. **Spectro Derm.**

polymyxin B sulfate/bacitracin. **Bioderm, Polycidin Ophthalmic Ointment, Polysporin Ointment, Polytopic Ointment.**

polymyxin B sulfate/bacitracin/gramicidin. **Polysporin Triple Antibiotic Ointment.**

polymyxin B sulfate/bacitracin zinc. **Optimyxin Ointment.**

polymyxin B sulfate/bacitracin zinc/hydrocortisone/neomycin sulfate. **Cortisporin Ointment, Cortisporin Ophthalmic Ointment.**

polymyxin B sulfate/bacitracin zinc/neomycin sulfate. **Neosporin Ointment/Ophthalmic Ointment, Neotopic.**

polymyxin B sulfate/benzocaine/camphor/menthol/tyrothricin. **Antibiotic Cold Sore Ointment.**

polymyxin B sulfate/dexamethasone/neomycin sulfate. **Dioptrol, Maxitrol.**

polymyxin B sulfate/gramicidin. **Optimyxin Solution, Polycidin Eye/Ear Drops, Polysporin Cream, Eye/Ear Drops, Polytopic Cream.**

polymyxin B sulfate/gramicidin/lidocaine hydrochloride. **Lidosporin Cream, Polysporin Antibiotic Burn Cream.**

polymyxin B sulfate/gramicidin/neomycin sulfate. **Neosporin Cream, Neosporin Eye and Ear Solution, Optimyxin Plus Solution.**

polymyxin B sulfate/hydrocortisone/neomycin sulfate. **Cortimyxin, Cortisporin Eye/Ear Suspension, Cortisporin Otic Solution.**

polymyxin B sulfate/lidocaine hydrochloride. **Lidosporin Ear Drops.**

polymyxin B sulfate/neomycin sulfate. **Neosporin Irrigating Solution.**

polymyxin B sulfate/trimethoprim sulfate. **Polytrim.**

polysiloxane cellulose complex. **Spectro Jel "609".**

polysiloxane copolyol/cellulose/glycerides/polyglycol/silicones. **Spectro Derm.**

polysorbate 80. **Tears Encore.**

Polysporin Antibiotic Burn Cream (Warner-Lambert Consumer Healthcare). *gramicidin/lidocaine hydrochloride/polymyxin B sulfate.*

Polysporin Cream, Eye/Ear Drops (Warner-Lambert Consumer Healthcare). *gramicidin/polymyxin B sulfate.*

Polysporin Ointment (Warner-Lambert Consumer Healthcare). *bacitracin/polymyxin B sulfate.*

Polysporin Triple Antibiotic Ointment (Warner-Lambert Consumer Healthcare). *bacitracin/gramicidin/polymyxin B sulfate.*

polytar. **(Stiefel).**

Polytar AF (Stiefel). *coal tar/menthol/pyrithione disulfide/salicylic acid.*

polytar/pyrithione disulfide. **Dan-Tar Plus.**

Polytopic Cream (Technilab). *gramicidin/polymyxin B sulfate.*

Polytopic Ointment (Technilab). *bacitracin/polymyxin B sulfate.*

Polytrim (Allergan). *polymyxin B sulfate/trimethoprim sulfate.*

polyvinyl alcohol. **Artificial Tears, Hypotears, Liquifilm Forte, Liquifilm Tears, Refresh, Scheinpharm Artificial Tears, Scheinpharm Artificial Tears Plus.**

polyvinyl alcohol/povidone. **Teardrops, Tears Plus.**

Pondocillin (Leo). *pivampicillin.*

Ponstan (Parke-Davis). *mefenamic acid.*

†Ponstel. *mefenamic acid.*

Pontocaine (Sanofi). *tetracaine hydrochloride.*

porfimer sodium. **Photofrin.**

Portagen (Mead Johnson). *enteral nutrition.*

†Posicor. *mibefradil.*

Postacne (Dermik Laboratories Canada). *sulfur.*

Potaba (Glenwood). *aminobenzoate potassium.*

potassium chloride. **[Potassium Salts, General Monograph, CPhA]; Apo-K, Kaochlor, K-Dur, K-Lor, K-Lyte/Cl, K-10, Micro-K Extencaps, Micro-K-10 Extencaps, Roychlor, Slow-K; (Abbott), (Astra).** †Klor-Con.

potassium citrate. **[Potassium Salts, General Monograph, CPhA]; K-Lyte, Polycitra-K.**

potassium clavulanate/amoxicillin trihydrate. **Clavulin.** †Augmentin.

potassium clavulanate/ticarcillin disodium. **Timentin.**

potassium gluconate. **[Potassium Salts, General Monograph, CPhA]; Kaon.**

potassium guaiacolsulfonate/codeine phosphate/promethazine hydrochloride. **Phenergan Expectorant with Codeine.**

potassium iodide. **Thyro-Block.**

potassium iodide/guaifenesin/mepyramine maleate/theophylline. **Theo-Bronc.**

potassium phosphates. **(Abbott).**

povidone-iodine. **Betadine Topical, Betadine Vaginal, Proviodine.**

povidone/polyvinyl alcohol. **Teardrops, Tears Plus.**

Names **underlined** have complete prescribing information in the *CPS* Monograph Section.

PPD-B (Mantoux). **Purified Protein Derivative.**

pralidoxime chloride. 2-PAM chloride. **Protopam Chloride.**

Pramegel (Medicis). *menthol/pramoxine hydrochloride.*

pramipexole dihydrochloride. **Mirapex.**

Pramox-HC (Dermtek). *hydrocortisone acetate/pramoxine hydrochloride.*

pramoxine hydrochloride/camphor/menthol. **Sarna-P.**

pramoxine hydrochloride/hydrocortisone acetate. **Pramox-HC, Proctofoam-HC.**

pramoxine hydrochloride/hydrocortisone acetate/zinc sulfate monohydrate. **Anugesic-HC, Proctodan-HC.**

pramoxine hydrochloride/menthol. **Pramegel.**

pramoxine hydrochloride/zinc sulfate monohydrate. **Anusol Plus.**

Prandase (Bayer). *acarbose.*

†Prandin. *repaglinide.*

Pravachol (Squibb). *pravastatin sodium.*

pravastatin sodium. **Pravachol.**

praziquantel. **Biltricide.**

prazosin hydrochloride. **Alti-Prazosin, Apo-Prazo, Minipress, Novo-Prazin, Nu-Prazo.**

†Predaject-50. *prednisolone acetate.*

†Predalone 50. *prednisolone acetate.*

†Predalone T.B.A. *prednisolone tebutate.*

†Predcor. *prednisolone.*

Pred Forte (Allergan). *prednisolone acetate.*

Pred Mild (Allergan). *prednisolone acetate.*

†Prednicen-M. *prednisone.*

prednisolone. **[Corticosteroids: Eye Ear Nose, Corticosteroids: Systemic, General Monographs, CPhA]; Minims Prednisolone.** †Delta-Cortef, †Predcor, †Prelone.

prednisolone acetate. deltahydrocortisone. metacortandrolone. **[Corticosteroids: Eye Ear Nose, Corticosteroids: Systemic, General Monographs, CPhA]; Diopred, Ophtho-Tate, Pred Forte, Pred Mild.** †Econopred, †Predaject-50, †Predalone 50.

prednisolone acetate/sulfacetamide sodium. **Blephamide, Dioptimyd, Metimyd.**

prednisolone phosphate sodium. see prednisolone sodium phosphate.

prednisolone sodium phosphate. prednisolone phosphate sodium. **[Corticosteroids: Eye Ear Nose, Corticosteroids: Systemic, General Monographs, CPhA]; Inflamase Forte, Inflamase Mild, Pediapred; (Rivex Ophthalmics).** †Hydeltrasol, †I-Pred, †Lite Pred.

prednisolone sodium phosphate/sulfacetamide sodium. **Vasocidin.**

prednisolone tebutate. **[Corticosteroids: Systemic, General Monograph, CPhA]**; †Hydeltra T.B.A., †Nor-Pred T.B.A., †Predalone T.B.A.

prednisone. deltacortisone. metacortandracin. **[Corticosteroids: Systemic, General Monograph, CPhA]; Apo-Prednisone, Deltasone, Winpred.** †Meticorten, †Orasone, †Prednicen-M.

prednisone acetate/ascorbic acid/chlorpheniramine maleate. **Metreton.**

Pregnyl (Organon). *gonadotropin (human) chorionic.*

†Prelone. *prednisolone.*

†Prelu-2. *phendimetrazine tartrate.*

Premarin Intravenous (Wyeth-Ayerst). *conjugated estrogens.*

Premarin Tablets (Wyeth-Ayerst). *conjugated estrogens.*

Premarin Vaginal Cream (Wyeth-Ayerst). *conjugated estrogens.*

†Prempro. *conjugated estrogens/medroxyprogesterone acetate.*

Prenavite (Roberts). *calcium carbonate/ferrous fumarate/multiple vitamins.*

Preparation H Cleansing Pads (Whitehall-Robins). *glycerin/hamamelis water.*

Preparation H Cooling Gel (Whitehall-Robins). *hamamelis water/phenylephrine hydrochloride.*

Preparation H Cream/Ointment/Suppositories (Whitehall-Robins). *shark liver oil/yeast.*

Pre-Pen (Rivex Pharma). *benzylpenicilloyl-polylysine.*

Prepidil (Pharmacia & Upjohn). *dinoprostone.*

Prepulsid (Janssen-Ortho). *cisapride monohydrate.*

Pressyn (Ferring). *vasopressin.*

PreSun Sunblock 28 (Westwood-Squibb). *titanium dioxide.*

PreSun Ultra 30 (Westwood-Squibb). *octyl methoxycinnamate/octyl salicylate/oxybenzone/Parsol 1789.*

Prevacid (Abbott). *lansoprazole.*

Prevex B (TCD). *betamethasone valerate.*

Prevex Baby Diaper Rash (TCD). *zinc oxide.*

Prevex Cream (TCD). *cyclomethicone/petrolatum.*

Prevex HC (TCD). *hydrocortisone.*

Prevex Lotion (TCD). *petrolatum.*

Prevex Oil (TCD). *jojoba oil/mineral oil.*

†Priftin. *rifapentine.*

prilocaine hydrochloride. **Citanest 4% Plain.**

prilocaine hydrochloride/epinephrine. **Citanest 4% Forte.**

prilocaine/lidocaine. **EMLA.**

†Prilosec. *omeprazole.*

primaclone. see primidone.

Primacor (Sanofi). *milrinone lactate.*

primaquine phosphate. **(Sanofi).**

Primaxin (MSD). *cilastatin sodium/imipenem.*

Primene (Clintec). *amino acids.*

primidone. primaclone. **Apo-Primidone, Mysoline.** †Myidone.

Prinivil (MSD). *lisinopril.*

Prinzide (MSD). *hydrochlorothiazide/lisinopril.*

†Pro-50. *promethazine hydrochloride.*

†Probalan. *probenecid.*

Pro-Banthine (Roberts). *propantheline bromide.*

probenecid. **Benemid, Benuryl.** †Probalan.

Probeta (Allergan). *dipivefrin hydrochloride/levobunolol hydrochloride.*

procainamide hydrochloride. **Apo-Procainamide, Procan SR, Pronestyl, Pronestyl-SR.** †Promine.

procaine hydrochloride. **Novocain.**

Procan SR (Parke-Davis). *procainamide hydrochloride.*

procarbazine hydrochloride. †Matulane.

†Procardia. *nifedipine.*

prochlorperazine. **Stemetil Suppositories.** †Compazine.

prochlorperazine bimaleate. **Nu-Prochlor, Stemetil Tablets.**

prochlorperazine edisylate. †Compa-Z, †Cotranzine, †Ultrazine-10.

prochlorperazine mesylate. **Stemetil Injectable/Liquid.**

†Proctocort. *hydrocortisone.*

Proctodan-HC (Odan). *hydrocortisone acetate/pramoxine hydrochloride/zinc sulfate monohydrate.*

Proctofoam-HC (R & C). *hydrocortisone acetate/pramoxine hydrochloride.*

Proctosedyl (Hoechst Marion Roussel). *dibucaine hydrochloride/esculin/framycetin sulfate/hydrocortisone.*

Proctosone (Technilab). *dibucaine hydrochloride/esculin/framycetin sulfate/hydrocortisone acetate.*

Procyclid (ICN). *procyclidine hydrochloride.*

procyclidine hydrochloride. **Kemadrin, Procyclid.**

Procytox (Carter Horner). *cyclophosphamide.*

Prodiem Plain (Novartis Consumer Health). *psyllium.*

Prodiem Plus (Novartis Consumer Health). *psyllium/senna.*

Profasi HP (Serono). *gonadotropin (human) chorionic.*

†Profenal. *suprofen.*

progesterone. **Prometrium.**

Proglycem (Schering). *diazoxide.*

Prograf (Fujisawa). *tacrolimus.*

proguanil. chloriguane. chloroguanide. **Paludrine.**

proguanil hydrochloride/atovaquone. **Malarone.**

Prolastin (Bayer). *$alpha_1$-proteinase inhibitor (human).*

Pro-Lax (Rivex Pharma). *electrolytes/polyethylene glycol.*

Proleukin (Ligand). *aldesleukin.*

Prolopa (Roche). *benserazide hydrochloride/levodopa.*

Proloprim (Glaxo Wellcome). *trimethoprim.*

promazine hydrochloride. **(Abbott).** †Sparine.

promethazine. **Phenergan Cream.**

promethazine hydrochloride. **Phenergan Injectable, Phenergan Tablets; (Bioniche)** †Pro-50

promethazine hydrochloride/codeine phosphate/potassium guaiacolsulfonate. **Phenergan Expectorant with Codeine.**

Prometrium (Schering). *progesterone.*

†Promine. *procainamide hydrochloride.*

Pronestyl (Squibb). *procainamide hydrochloride.*

Pronestyl-SR (Squibb). *procainamide hydrochloride.*

†Propacet 100. *acetaminophen/propoxyphene napsylate.*

Propaderm (Roberts). *beclomethasone dipropionate.*

propafenone hydrochloride. **Rythmol.**

1,2-propanediol diacetate/acetic acid/benzethonium chloride. **VōSoL.**

1,2-propanediol diacetate/acetic acid/benzethonium chloride/hydrocortisone. **VōSoL HC.**

Propanthel (ICN). *propantheline bromide.*

propantheline bromide. **Pro-Banthine, Propanthel.**

proparacaine hydrochloride. proxymetacaine hydrochloride. **Alcaine, Diocaine, Ophthetic.** †Ocu-Caine, †Ophthaine.

proparacaine hydrochloride/fluorescein sodium. **Fluoracaine.**

Propecia (MSD). *finasteride.*

propericyazine. see pericyazine.

Propine (Allergan). *dipivefrin hydrochloride.*

propiomazine hydrochloride. †Largon.

propofol. **Diprivan; (Abbott).**

propoxyphene hydrochloride/ASA/caffeine. **692.**

propoxyphene napsylate. **[Opioids, General Monograph, CPhA]; Darvon-N.**

propoxyphene napsylate/acetaminophen. †Darvocet-N 100, †Propacet 100.

propranolol hydrochloride. **Apo-Propranolol, Inderal, Inderal-LA, Nu-Propranolol.**

propranolol hydrochloride/hydrochlorothiazide. **Inderide.**

†Propulsid. *cisapride monohydrate.*

propylene glycol/polyethylene glycol. **Rhinaris, Salinol, Secaris.**

propylene glycol/triethanolamine polypeptide cocoate condensate/tyrothricin. **Soropon.**

propylthiouracil. **Propyl-Thyracil.**

Propyl-Thyracil (Frosst). *propylthiouracil.*

Proscar (MSD). *finasteride.*

prostaglandin E_1. see alprostadil.

prostaglandin E_2. see dinoprostone.

†Prostaphlin. *oxacillin sodium.*

Prostigmin Injection (ICN). *neostigmine methylsulfate.*

Prostigmin Tablets (ICN). *neostigmine bromide.*

Prostin E_2 (Pharmacia & Upjohn). *dinoprostone.*

Prostin E_2 Vaginal Gel (Pharmacia & Upjohn). *dinoprostone.*

Prostin VR (Pharmacia & Upjohn). *alprostadil.*

protamine sulfate. **(Pharmaceutical Partners), (Sabex).**

Pro•Tec Sport (Allergan). *octyl methoxycinnamate/octyl salicylate/oxybenzone.*

protirelin. **Relefact TRH.**

Protopam Chloride (Wyeth-Ayerst). *pralidoxime chloride.*

†Protostat. *metronidazole.*

protriptyline hydrochloride. **Triptil.** †Vivactil.

Protropin (Roche). *somatrem.*

†Proventil. *salbutamol.*

Provera (Pharmacia & Upjohn). *medroxyprogesterone acetate.*

Proviodine (Rougier). *povidone iodine.*

†Provocholine. *methacholine chloride.*

proxymetacaine hydrochloride. see proparacaine hydrochloride.

Prozac (Lilly). *fluoxetine hydrochloride.*

pseudoephedrine hydrochloride. **Balminil Decongestant, Contac Cold 12 Hour Relief Non Drowsy, Eltor, Sudafed Decongestant, Sudafed Decongestant 12 Hour, Triaminic Oral Pediatric Drops.**

pseudoephedrine hydrochloride/acetaminophen. **Dristan N.D., Dristan N.D. Extra Strength, Sinutab Non Drowsy, Sudafed Head Cold and Sinus, Tylenol Decongestant, Tylenol Sinus Medication.**

pseudoephedrine hydrochloride/acetaminophen/chlorpheniramine maleate. **Sinutab, Tylenol Allergy Sinus Medication.**

pseudoephedrine hydrochloride/acetaminophen/chlorpheniramine maleate/codeine. **Sinutab with Codeine.**

pseudoephedrine hydrochloride/acetaminophen/chlorpheniramine maleate/dextromethorphan hydrobromide. **NeoCitran Extra Strength (Cough, Cold & Flu), Tylenol Cold and Flu, Tylenol Cold Medication Junior Strength DM, Tylenol Cold Medication (Nighttime).**

pseudoephedrine hydrochloride/acetaminophen/dextromethorphan hydrobromide. **Contac Cough, Cold and Flu Day, NeoCitran Extra Strength Daycaps, Sudafed Cold & Cough, Triaminic Cold & Fever, Tylenol Cold Medication (Daytime), Tylenol Cough Liquid Suspension with Decongestant.**

pseudoephedrine hydrochloride/acetaminophen/dextromethorphan hydrobromide/guaifenesin. **Benylin 4 Flu, Calmylin Cough and Flu, Robitussin Cough, Cold & Flu Liqui-Gels, Sudafed Cold & Flu.**

pseudoephedrine hydrochloride/acetaminophen/diphenhydramine. **Sinutab Nighttime.**

pseudoephedrine hydrochloride/acetaminophen/diphenhydramine hydrochloride. **Benadryl Allergy/Sinus/Headache, Contac Cough, Cold and Flu Night, Tylenol Flu Medication.**

pseudoephedrine hydrochloride/acetaminophen/triprolidine hydrochloride. **Actifed Plus Extra Strength.**

pseudoephedrine hydrochloride/chlorpheniramine maleate/dextromethorphan hydrobromide. **Triaminic DM Nighttime, Triaminicol DM.**

Names **underlined** have complete prescribing information in the *CPS* Monograph Section.

pseudoephedrine hydrochloride/chlorpheniramine maleate/ dextromethorphan hydrobromide/guaifenesin. **Triaminic DM Expectorant.**

pseudoephedrine hydrochloride/chlorpheniramine maleate/ guaifenesin. **Triaminic Expectorant.**

pseudoephedrine hydrochloride/codeine phosphate/guaifenesin. **Benylin Codeine, Calmylin with Codeine.**

pseudoephedrine hydrochloride/codeine phosphate/guaifenesin/ triprolidine hydrochloride. **CoActifed Expectorant, Cotridin Expectorant.**

pseudoephedrine hydrochloride/codeine phosphate/triprolidine hydrochloride. **CoActifed, Cotridin.**

pseudoephedrine hydrochloride/dextromethorphan hydrobromide. **Balminil DM + Decongestant, Benylin DM-D (Adult), Benylin DM-D For Children, Calmylin #2, Calmylin Pediatric, Novahistex DM Decongestant, Novahistine DM Decongestant, Robitussin Pediatric Cough and Cold.**

pseudoephedrine hydrochloride/dextromethorphan hydrobromide/ guaifenesin. **Balminil DM + Decongestant + Expectorant, Benylin DM-D-E, Calmylin #3, Novahistex DM Decongestant Expectorant, Novahistine DM Decongestant Expectorant, Robitussin Cough & Cold, Robitussin Cough & Cold Liqui-Gels.**

pseudoephedrine hydrochloride/ibuprofen. **Advil Cold & Sinus, Dristan Sinus.**

pseudoephedrine hydrochloride/triprolidine hydrochloride. **Actifed.**

pseudoephedrine sulfate. **Drixoral Day, Drixoral N.D.**

pseudoephedrine sulfate/azatadine maleate. **Trinalin.**

pseudoephedrine sulfate/chlorpheniramine maleate. **Chlor-Tripolon Decongestant Tablets.**

pseudoephedrine sulfate/dexbrompheniramine maleate. **Drixoral, Drixoral Night, Drixtab.**

pseudoephedrine sulfate/loratadine. **Chlor-Tripolon N.D., Claritin Extra.**

Psorigel (Galderma). *coal tar.*

psyllium. **Prodiem Plain.**

psyllium hydrophilic mucilloid. **Metamucil, Novo-Mucilax.**

psyllium/senna. **Prodiem Plus.**

†PT 105. *phendimetrazine tartrate.*

pteroylglutamic acid. see folic acid.

Pulmicort Nebuamp (Astra). *budesonide.*

Pulmicort Turbuhaler (Astra). *budesonide.*

Pulmozyme (Roche). *dornase alfa recombinant.*

Puregon (Organon). *follitropin beta.*

Purified Protein Derivative (Connaught). *PPD-B (Mantoux).*

Purinethol (Glaxo Wellcome). *mercaptopurine.*

Pylorid (Glaxo Wellcome). *ranitidine bismuth citrate.*

pyrantel pamoate. **Combantrin.**

pyrazinamide. **Tebrazid.**

pyrazinamide/isoniazid/rifampin. **Rifater.**

pyrethrins/piperonyl butoxide. **R & C Shampoo/Conditioner, R & C II Spray.**

Pyribenzamine (Novartis Consumer Health). *tripelennamine hydrochloride.*

†Pyridiate. *phenazopyridine hydrochloride.*

Pyridium (Parke-Davis). *phenazopyridine hydrochloride.*

pyridostigmine bromide. **Mestinon, Mestinon-SR.**

pyridoxine hydrochloride. vitamin B_6. **[Vitamin B_6, General Monograph, CPhA]; (Abbott).**

pyridoxine hydrochloride/ascorbic acid/calcium carbonate/ vitamin D. **Redoxon-Cal.**

pyridoxine hydrochloride/doxylamine succinate. **Diclectin.**

pyrilamine maleate/acetaminophen/caffeine. **Midol Extra Strength.**

pyrilamine maleate/acetaminophen/caffeine/pheniramine maleate/ phenylpropanolamine hydrochloride. **Triaminicin.**

pyrilamine maleate/acetaminophen/pamabrom. **Midol PMS Extra Strength, Pamprin, Pamprin Extra Strength, Pamprin PMS.**

pyrilamine maleate/ammonium chloride/hydrocodone bitartrate/ phenylephrine hydrochloride. **Hycomine, Hycomine-S.**

pyrilamine maleate/codeine phosphate/pheniramine maleate/ phenylpropanolamine hydrochloride. **Tussaminic C.**

pyrilamine maleate/guaifenesin/hydrocodone bitartrate/ pheniramine maleate/phenylpropanolamine hydrochloride. **Triaminic Expectorant DH.**

pyrilamine maleate/hydrocodone bitartrate/pheniramine maleate/ phenylpropanolamine hydrochloride. **Caldomine-DH, Tussaminic DH.**

pyrilamine maleate/pheniramine maleate/phenylpropanolamine hydrochloride. **Triaminic Tablets.**

pyrilamine maleate/pheniramine maleate/phenylpropanolamine hydrochloride/sulfadiazine/sulfamerazine/sulfamethazine. **Trisulfaminic.**

pyrimethamine. **Daraprim.**

pyrimethamine/sulfadoxine. **Fansidar.**

pyrithione disulfide/coal tar/menthol/salicylic acid. **Polytar AF.**

pyrithione disulfide/polytar. **Dan-Tar Plus.**

pyrvinium pamoate. viprynium pamoate. **Vanquin.**

Q

Quadracel (Connaught). *diphtheria toxoid adsorbed/pertussis vaccine (acellular)/poliomyelitis vaccine, inactivated/tetanus toxoid adsorbed.*

†Quarzan. *clidinium bromide.*

quazepam. †Doral.

Quelicin Chloride (Abbott). *succinylcholine chloride.*

Questran (Bristol). *cholestyramine resin.*

Questran Light (Bristol). *cholestyramine resin.*

quetiapine fumarate. **Seroquel.**

Quibron-T (Bristol). *theophylline.*

Quibron-T/SR (Bristol). *theophylline.*

†Quiess. *hydroxyzine hydrochloride.*

quinalbarbitone. see secobarbital sodium.

quinapril hydrochloride. **[ACE Inhibitors, General Monograph, CPhA]; Accupril.**

quinapril hydrochloride/hydrochlorothiazide. **Accuretic.**

Quinate (Rougier). *quinidine gluconate.*

quinethazone. †Hydromox.

Quinidex Extentabs (Wyeth-Ayerst). *quinidine sulfate.*

quinidine bisulfate. **[Quinidine, General Monograph, CPhA]; Biquin Durules.**

quinidine gluconate. **[Quinidine, General Monograph, CPhA]; Quinate.**

quinidine phenylethylbarbiturate. **Quinobarb.**

quinidine polygalacturonate. **[Quinidine, General Monograph, CPhA]; Cardioquin.**

quinidine sulfate. **[Quinidine, General Monograph, CPhA]; Apo-Quinidine, Quinidex Extentabs; (Abbott), (Glaxo Wellcome).**

quinine sulfate. **[Quinine Sulfate, General Monograph, CPhA].**

Quinobarb (Rougier). *quinidine phenylethylbarbiturate.*

Quintasa (Ferring). *5-aminosalicylic acid.*

R

rabies immune globulin (human). see immune globulin, rabies (human).

rabies vaccine, inactivated (diploid cell origin). Imovax; **(Connaught).**

Rafton Liquid (Ferring). *aluminum hydroxide/sodium alginate.*

Rafton Tablets (Ferring). *alginic acid/aluminum hydroxide.*

ragweed tyrosine adsorbate, modified. **Pollinex-R.**

raloxifene hydrochloride. **Evista.**

raltitrexed disodium. **Tomudex.**

ramipril. **[ACE Inhibitors, General Monograph, CPhA]; Altace.**

R & C Shampoo/Conditioner (R & C). *piperonyl butoxide/pyrethrins.*

R & C II Spray (R & C). *piperonyl butoxide/pyrethrins.*

ranitidine bismuth citrate. **Pylorid.**

ranitidine hydrochloride. **Alti-Ranitidine, Apo-Ranitidine, Gen-Ranitidine, Novo-Ranidine, Nu-Ranit, Zantac, Zantac 75.**

†Raudixin. *rauwolfia serpentina.*

†Rauval. *rauwolfia serpentina.*

rauwolfia serpentina. †Raudixin, †Rauval, †Wolfina.

rauwolfia serpentina/bendroflumethiazide. †Rauzide.

†Rauzide. *bendroflumethiazide/rauwolfia serpentina.*

Raxar (Glaxo Wellcome). *grepafloxacin hydrochloride.*

Reactine (Pfizer Consumer). *cetirizine hydrochloride.*

Rebif (Serono). *interferon beta-1a.*

Recombivax HB (MSD). *hepatitis B vaccine (recombinant).*

Rectocort (Welcker-Lyster). *hydrocortisone acetate.*

Rectogel (Riva). *benzocaine/zinc sulfate monohydrate.*

Rectogel HC (Riva). *benzocaine/hydrocortisone acetate/zinc sulfate monohydrate.*

Red Away (Rivex Ophthalmics). *naphazoline hydrochloride.*

Redoxon (Roche). *ascorbic acid.*

Redoxon-B (Roche). *ascorbic acid/magnesium carbonate/magnesium sulfate/vitamin B compound.*

Redoxon-Cal (Roche). *ascorbic acid/calcium carbonate/pyridoxine hydrochloride/vitamin D.*

†Redux. *dexfenfluramine.*

Refresh (Allergan). *polyvinyl alcohol.*

†Regitine. *phentolamine mesylate.*

Reglan (Wyeth-Ayerst). *metoclopramide hydrochloride.*

†Regranax. *becaplermin.*

†Regroton. *chlorthalidone/reserpine.*

Regular Strength Acetaminophen (WestCan). *acetaminophen.*

Regular Strength Acetaminophen with Codeine (WestCan). *acetaminophen/caffeine/codeine phosphate.*

Rejuva-A (Stiefel). *tretinoin.*

Relafen (SmithKline Beecham). *nabumetone.*

Relefact TRH (Hoechst Marion Roussel). *protirelin.*

remifentanil hydrochloride. **Ultiva.**

Renedil (Hoechst Marion Roussel). *felodipine.*

Renova (Janssen-Ortho). *tretinoin.*

ReoPro (Lilly). *abciximab.*

repaglinide. †Prandin.

Replens (Roberts). *polycarbophil.*

Requip (SmithKline Beecham). *ropinirole hydrochloride.*

reserpine. **Serpasil.** †Serpalan.

reserpine/chlorthalidone. †Regroton.

reserpine/hydralazine hydrochloride/hydrochlorothiazide. **Ser-Ap-Es.**

reserpine/hydrochlorothiazide. **Hydropres-25.**

Resonium Calcium (Sanofi). *calcium polystyrene sulfonate.*

resorcinol/isopropyl alcohol/sulfur. **Acnomel Cream.**

resorcinol/sulfur. **Acnomel Vanishing Cream.**

Resource (Novartis Nutrition). *enteral nutrition.*

Resource Diabetic (Novartis Nutrition). *enteral nutrition.*

Resource Fruit Beverage (Novartis Nutrition). *enteral nutrition.*

Resource Just For Kids (Novartis Nutrition). *enteral nutrition.*

Resource Plus (Novartis Nutrition). *enteral nutrition.*

†Respbid. *theophylline.*

Restoril (Novartis Pharmaceuticals). *temazepam.*

Retin-A (Janssen-Ortho). *tretinoin.*

retinol. see vitamin A.

Retisol-A (Stiefel). *tretinoin.*

Retrovir (AZT) (Glaxo Wellcome). *zidovudine.*

Reversa AHA (Dermtek). *glycolic acid.*

ReVia (DuPont Pharma). *naltrexone hydrochloride.*

Revitalose-C-1000 (Rivex Pharma). *ascorbic acid.*

Revitonus C-1000 (Sabex). *ascorbic acid/gland extracts.*

Rheomacrodex (Medisan Pharmaceuticals). *dextran 40.*

Rheumatrex (Wyeth-Ayerst). *methotrexate sodium.*

Rhinalar (Roche). *flunisolide.*

Rhinaris (Pharmascience). *polyethylene glycol/propylene glycol.*

Rhinocort Aqua (Astra). *budesonide.*

Rhinocort Turbuhaler (Astra). *budesonide.*

Rho-Atenolol (Rhodiapharm). *atenolol.*

Rho-Clonazepam (RhoxalPharma). *clonazepam.*

Rhodacine (Rhodiapharm). *indomethacin.*

Rhodiaprox (Rhodiapharm). *naproxen.*

Rh_o (D) immune globulin (human). see immune globulin, Rh_o (D) (human).

Rhodis (Rhodiapharm). *ketoprofen.*

Rhodis-EC (Rhodiapharm). *ketoprofen.*

Rhodis SR (Rhodiapharm). *ketoprofen.*

Rho-Fluphenazine Decanoate (Rhodiapharm). *fluphenazine decanoate.*

Rho-Haloperidol Decanoate (Rhodiapharm). *haloperidol decanoate.*

Rho-Loperamide (RhoxalPharma). *loperamide hydrochloride.*

Rho-Metformin (RhoxalPharma). *metformin hydrochloride.*

Rho-Nitrazepam (RhoxalPharma). *nitrazepam.*

Rho-Salbutamol (Rhodiapharm). *salbutamol sulfate.*

Rho-Sotalol (RhoxalPharma). *sotalol hydrochloride.*

Rhotral (Rhodiapharm). *acebutolol hydrochloride.*

Rhotrimine (Rhodiapharm). *trimipramine maleate.*

Rhovail (RHO-Pharm). *ketoprofen.*

Rhovane (Rhodiapharm). *zopiclone.*

ribavirin. **Virazole (Lyophilized).**

riboflavin. lactoflavin. vitamin B_2. vitamin G. **[Vitamin B_2, General Monograph, CPhA].**

Names **underlined** have complete prescribing information in the *CPS* Monograph Section.

Ridaura (Pharmascience). *auranofin.*
rifabutin. **Mycobutin.**
Rifadin (Hoechst Marion Roussel). *rifampin.*
†Rifamate. *isoniazid/rifampin.*
rifampicin. see rifampin.
rifampin. rifampicin. **[Rifampin, General Monograph, CPhA]; Rifadin, Rimactane, Rofact.**
rifampin/isoniazid. †Rifamate.
rifampin/isoniazid/pyrazinamide. **Rifater.**
rifapentine. †Priftin.
Rifater (Hoechst Marion Roussel). *isoniazid/pyrazinamide/rifampin.*
Rimactane (Novartis Pharmaceuticals). *rifampin.*
rimantadine hydrochloride. †Flumadine.
rimexolone. **Vexol.**
Rimso-50 (Roberts). *dimethyl sulfoxide.*
Riopan (Whitehall-Robins). *magaldrate.*
Riopan Plus (Whitehall-Robins). *magaldrate/simethicone.*
Riphenidate (Technilab). *methylphenidate hydrochloride.*
Risperdal Oral Solution (Janssen-Ortho). *risperidone tartrate.*
Risperdal Tablets (Janssen-Ortho). *risperidone.*
risperidone. **Risperdal Tablets.**
risperidone tartrate. **Risperdal Oral Solution.**
Ritalin (Novartis Pharmaceuticals). *methylphenidate hydrochloride.*
Ritalin SR (Novartis Pharmaceuticals). *methylphenidate hydrochloride.*
ritodrine hydrochloride. **Yutopar.**
ritonavir. **Norvir.**
†Rituxan. *rituximab.*
rituximab. †Rituxan.
Rivanase Aq. (Riva). *beclomethasone dipropionate.*
Riva-Senna (Riva). *sennosides.*
Rivasol (Riva). *zinc sulfate monohydrate.*
Rivasol HC (Riva). *hydrocortisone acetate/zinc sulfate monohydrate.*
Rivotril (Roche). *clonazepam.*
rizatriptan. †Maxalt.
†RMS Uniserts. *morphine sulfate.*
Robaxacet (Whitehall-Robins). *acetaminophen/methocarbamol.*
Robaxacet-8 (Whitehall-Robins). *acetaminophen/codeine phosphate/methocarbamol.*
Robaxin (Whitehall-Robins). *methocarbamol.*
Robaxin-750 (Whitehall-Robins). *methocarbamol.*
Robaxin Injectable (Wyeth-Ayerst). *methocarbamol.*
Robaxisal (Whitehall-Robins). *ASA/methocarbamol.*
Robaxisal-C (Whitehall-Robins). *ASA/codeine phosphate/methocarbamol.*
Robidone (Wyeth-Ayerst). *hydrocodone bitartrate.*
Robinul (Wyeth-Ayerst). *glycopyrrolate.*
Robinul Forte (Wyeth-Ayerst). *glycopyrrolate.*
Robinul Injectable (Wyeth-Ayerst). *glycopyrrolate.*
Robitussin (Whitehall-Robins). *guaifenesin.*
Robitussin AC (Whitehall-Robins). *codeine phosphate/guaifenesin/pheniramine maleate.*
Robitussin Cough & Cold (Whitehall-Robins). *dextromethorphan hydrobromide/guaifenesin/pseudoephedrine hydrochloride.*
Robitussin Cough, Cold & Flu Liqui-Gels (Whitehall-Robins). *acetaminophen/dextromethorphan hydrobromide/guaifenesin/pseudoephedrine hydrochloride.*
Robitussin Cough & Cold Liqui-Gels (Whitehall-Robins). *dextromethorphan hydrobromide/guaifenesin/pseudoephedrine hydrochloride.*
Robitussin DM (Whitehall-Robins). *dextromethorphan hydrobromide/guaifenesin.*
Robitussin Pediatric (Whitehall-Robins). *dextromethorphan hydrobromide.*
Robitussin Pediatric Cough and Cold (Whitehall-Robins). *dextromethorphan hydrobromide/pseudoephedrine hydrochloride.*
Robitussin with Codeine (Whitehall-Robins). *codeine phosphate/guaifenesin/pheniramine maleate.*
Rocaltrol (Roche). *calcitriol.*
Rocephin (Roche). *ceftriaxone sodium.*
rocuronium bromide. **Zemuron.**
Rofact (ICN). *rifampin.*
Roferon-A (Roche). *interferon alfa-2a.*
Rogaine (Pharmacia & Upjohn). *minoxidil.*
Rogitine (Novartis Pharmaceuticals). *phentolamine mesylate.*
ropinirole hydrochloride. **Requip.**
ropivacaine hydrochloride. **Naropin.**
Rovamycine (Rhône-Poulenc Rorer). *spiramycin.*
†Rowasa. *5-aminosalicylic acid.*
†Roxanol. *morphine sulfate.*
†Roxicodone. *oxycodone hydrochloride.*
Roychlor (Waymar). *potassium chloride.*
Royflex (Waymar). *triethanolamine salicylate.*
Royvac (Waymar). *bisacodyl/magnesium citrate.*
rubella virus vaccine (live attenuated)/measles virus vaccine (live attenuated). **MoRu-Viraten Berna.**
rubella virus vaccine (live attenuated)/measles virus vaccine (live attenuated)/mumps virus vaccine (live attenuated). **M-M-R II.**
Rubramin (Squibb). *cyanocobalamin.*
†Rufen. *ibuprofen.*
Rylosol (ICN). *sotalol hydrochloride.*
Rythmodan (Hoechst Marion Roussel). *disopyramide.*
Rythmodan-LA (Hoechst Marion Roussel). *disopyramide phosphate.*
Rythmol (Knoll). *propafenone hydrochloride.*

S

Sabril (Hoechst Marion Roussel). *vigabatrin.*
Saizen (Serono). *somatropin.*
Salac (Medicis). *salicylic acid.*
Salagen (Pharmacia & Upjohn). *pilocarpine hydrochloride.*
Salazopyrin (Pharmacia & Upjohn). *sulfasalazine.*
Salazopyrin En-Tabs (Pharmacia & Upjohn). *sulfasalazine.*
salbutamol. albuterol. **Alti-Salbutamol, Apo-Salvent, Novo-Salmol Inhaler, Ventolin Inhalation Aerosol/Oral Liquid.** †Proventil.
Salbutamol Nebuamp (Astra). *salbutamol sulfate.*
salbutamol sulfate. **Airomir, Alti-Salbutamol Sulfate, Asmavent, Gen-Salbutamol Respirator Solution, Gen-Salbutamol Sterinebs P.F., Novo-Salmol, Nu-Salbutamol Solution, Nu-Salbutamol Tablets, PMS-Salbutamol Respirator Solution, Rho-Salbutamol, Salbutamol Nebuamp, Ventodisk Disk/Diskhaler, Ventolin Injection, Ventolin Nebules P.F./Respirator Solution, Ventolin Rotacaps/Rotahaler; (BDH).**
salbutamol sulfate/ipratropium bromide. **Combivent Inhalation Aerosol, Combivent Inhalation Solution.**

salcatonin. see calcitonin (salmon).

†Salflex. *salsalate.*

salicylazosulfapyridine. see sulfasalazine.

salicylic acid. **Acnex, Acnomel Acne Mask, Duoforte 27, Keralyt, Occlusal, Occlusal-HP, Salac, Sebcur, Soluver, Soluver Plus, Trans-Plantar, Trans•Ver•Sal.**

salicylic acid/benzalkonium chloride. **Ionil.**

salicylic acid/betamethasone dipropionate. **Diprosalic.**

salicylic acid/cantharidin/podophyllin. **Canthacur-PS, Cantharone Plus.**

salicylic acid/coal tar. **Sebcur/T.**

salicylic acid/coal tar/menthol. **X-Tar.**

salicylic acid/coal tar/menthol/pyrithione disulfide. **Polytar AF.**

salicylic acid/coal tar/sulfur. **Sebutone.**

salicylic acid/diflucortolone valerate. **Nerisalic.**

salicylic acid/flumethasone pivalate. **Locasalen.**

salicylic acid/formalin/lactic acid. **Duoplant.**

salicylic acid/lactic acid. **Cuplex, Duofilm.**

salicylic acid/liquid carbonis detergens. **Targel S.A.**

salicylic acid/liquid carbonis detergens/triclosan. **Tardan.**

salicylic acid/sodium thiosulfate/triclosan. **Adasept Acne Gel.**

salicylic acid/sulfur. **Meted, Pernox, Sastid, Sebulex.**

salicylic acid/triclosan. **TersAc.**

salicylsalicylic acid. see salsalate.

Saline from Otrivin (Novartis Consumer Health). *sodium chloride.*

Salinex (Technilab). *sodium chloride.*

Salinol (Technilab). *polyethylene glycol/propylene glycol.*

salmeterol xinafoate. **Serevent.**

salmonella typhi Vi capsular polysaccharide vaccine. **Typhim Vi.**

Salofalk (Axcan Pharma). *5-aminosalicylic acid.*

salsalate. salicylsalicylic acid. **Disalcid.** †Amigesic, †Salflex, †Salsitab.

†Salsitab. *salsalate.*

†Saluron. *hydroflumethiazide.*

Sandimmune I.V. (Novartis Pharmaceuticals). *cyclosporine.*

Sandomigran (Novartis Pharmaceuticals). *pizotifen maleate.*

Sandomigran DS (Novartis Pharmaceuticals). *pizotifen maleate.*

Sandosource Peptide (Novartis Nutrition). *enteral nutrition.*

Sandostatin (Novartis Pharmaceuticals). *octreotide acetate.*

Sanorex (Novartis Pharmaceuticals). *mazindol.*

Sans-Acne (Galderma). *erythromycin/ethyl alcohol.*

Sansert (Novartis Pharmaceuticals). *methysergide maleate.*

Santyl (Knoll). *collagenase.*

saquinavir mesylate. **Invirase.**

sargramostim. GM-CSF. †Leukine.

Sarna HC (Stiefel). *hydrocortisone.*

Sarna-P (Stiefel). *camphor/menthol/pramoxine hydrochloride.*

S.A.S. (ICN). *sulfasalazine.*

Sastid (Stiefel). *salicylic acid/sulfur.*

Savlodil 1:100 (Zeneca). *cetrimide/chlorhexidine gluconate.*

Savlon Hospital Concentrate (Zeneca). *cetrimide/chlorhexidine gluconate.*

Scabene (Medican). *esdepallethrin/piperonyl butoxide.*

Scheinpharm Artificial Tears (Schein Pharmaceutical). *polyvinyl alcohol.*

Scheinpharm Artificial Tears Plus (Schein Pharmaceutical). *polyvinyl alcohol.*

Scheinpharm Atenolol (Schein Pharmaceutical). *atenolol.*

Scheinpharm B12 (Schein Pharmaceutical). *cyanocobalamin.*

Scheinpharm Cefaclor (Schein Pharmaceutical). *cefaclor.*

Scheinpharm Clotrimazole (Schein Pharmaceutical). *clotrimazole.*

Scheinpharm Desonide (Schein Pharmaceutical). *desonide.*

Scheinpharm Diphenhydramine (Schein Pharmaceutical). *diphenhydramine hydrochloride.*

Scheinpharm Dobutamine (Schein Pharmaceutical). *dobutamine hydrochloride.*

Scheinpharm Ferrous Fumarate (Schein Pharmaceutical). *ferrous fumarate.*

Scheinpharm Gentamicin (Schein Pharmaceutical). *gentamicin sulfate.*

Scheinpharm Penicillin G Sodium (Schein Pharmaceutical). *penicillin G sodium.*

Scheinpharm Pilocarpine (Schein Pharmaceutical). *pilocarpine hydrochloride.*

Scheinpharm Testone-Cyp (Schein Pharmaceutical). *testosterone cypionate.*

Scheinpharm Tobramycin (Schein Pharmaceutical). *tobramycin sulfate.*

Scheinpharm Triamcine-A (Schein Pharmaceutical). *triamcinolone acetonide.*

Schering Base (Schering). *dermatological base.*

scopolamine. **[Scopolamine, General Monograph, CPhA]; Transderm-V.**

scopolamine butylbromide. hyoscine butylbromide. **[Scopolamine, General Monograph, CPhA]; Buscopan.**

scopolamine hydrobromide. hyoscine hydrobromide. **[Scopolamine, General Monograph, CPhA]; (Abbott).**

scopolamine hydrobromide/atropine sulfate/attapulgite, activated/hyoscyamine sulfate/opium/pectin. **Diban.**

scopolamine hydrobromide/atropine sulfate/hyoscyamine sulfate/phenobarbital. **Donnatal.**

sea water. **Hydrasense Nasal Care.**

Sebcur (Dermtek). *salicylic acid.*

Sebcur/T (Dermtek). *coal tar/salicylic acid.*

Sebulex (Westwood-Squibb). *salicylic acid/sulfur.*

Sebulon (Westwood-Squibb). *zinc pyrithione.*

Sebutone (Westwood-Squibb). *coal tar/salicylic acid/sulfur.*

Secaris (Pharmascience). *polyethylene glycol/propylene glycol.*

secbutabarbital. see butabarbital sodium.

secbutobarbitone. see butabarbital sodium.

secobarbital sodium. quinalbarbitone. **[Barbiturates, General Monograph, CPhA].**

secretin. **(Ferring).**

Sectral (Rhône-Poulenc Rorer). *acebutolol hydrochloride.*

Selax (Odan). *docusate sodium.*

Seldane (Hoechst Marion Roussel). *terfenadine.*

selective serotonin reuptake inhibitors. **(General Monograph, CPhA).**

Select 1/35 (Dispensapharm). *ethinyl estradiol/norethindrone.*

selegiline hydrochloride. l-deprenyl hydrochloride. **Apo-Selegiline, Eldepryl, Gen-Selegiline, Novo-Selegiline, Nu-Selegiline.**

selenious acid. †Sele-Pak, †Selepen.

selenium/ascorbic acid/vitamin B compound/vitamin E/zinc. **Stresstabs Plus.**

selenium sulfide. **Versel.**

†Sele-Pak. *selenious acid.*

Names **underlined** have complete prescribing information in the *CPS* Monograph Section.

†Selepen. *selenious acid.*

†Selestoject. *betamethasone sodium phosphate.*

Selexid (Leo). *pivmecillinam hydrochloride.*

senna/psyllium. **Prodiem Plus.**

sennosides. **Ex-Lax Chocolated Pieces, Ex-Lax Extra Strength Sugar Coated Pills, Ex-Lax Sugar Coated Pills, Glysennid, PMS-Sennosides, Riva-Senna, Senokot, X-Prep.**

sennosides/docusate sodium. **Senokot•S.**

Senokot (Purdue Frederick). *sennosides.*

Senokot•S (Purdue Frederick). *docusate sodium/sennosides.*

Sensorcaine (Astra). *bupivacaine hydrochloride.*

Sensorcaine Forte (Astra). *bupivacaine hydrochloride/epinephrine.*

Sensorcaine with Epinephrine (Astra). *bupivacaine hydrochloride/ epinephrine.*

Septra (Glaxo Wellcome). *sulfamethoxazole/trimethoprim.*

Septra DS (Glaxo Wellcome). *sulfamethoxazole/trimethoprim.*

Septra Injection (Glaxo Wellcome). *sulfamethoxazole/ trimethoprim.*

Ser-Ap-Es (Novartis Pharmaceuticals). *hydralazine hydrochloride/ hydrochlorothiazide/reserpine.*

Serax (Wyeth-Ayerst). *oxazepam.*

Serc (Solvay Pharma). *betahistine hydrochloride.*

Serentil (Novartis Pharmaceuticals). *mesoridazine besylate.*

Serevent (Glaxo Wellcome). *salmeterol xinafoate.*

Serophene (Serono). *clomiphene citrate.*

Seroquel (Zeneca). *quetiapine fumarate.*

†Serpalan. *reserpine.*

Serpasil (Novartis Pharmaceuticals). *reserpine.*

sertraline hydrochloride. **[Selective Serotonin Reuptake Inhibitors, General Monograph, CPhA]; Zoloft.**

Serzone (Bristol-Myers Squibb). *nefazodone hydrochloride.*

sevoflurane. **Sevorane.**

Sevorane (Abbott). *sevoflurane.*

shark liver oil/yeast. **Preparation H Cream/Ointment/ Suppositories.**

SH-206 (Pharmascience). *acetic acid/camphor/lemon extract oil/ sodium lauryl ether sulfate.*

Sialor (Solvay Pharma). *anethole trithione.*

sibutramine. †Meridia.

sildenafil citrate. †Viagra.

†Sildimac. *silver sulfadiazine.*

silicone/hydrocortisone. **Barriere-HC.**

silicones/cellulose/glycerides/polyglycol/polysiloxane copolyol. **Spectro Derm.**

†Silvadene. *silver sulfadiazine.*

silver gluconate/copper gluconate/gold, colloidal. **Oligosol, Copper-Gold-Silver.**

silver sulfadiazine. **Dermazin, Flamazine, SSD.** †Sildimac, †Silvadene, †Thermazene.

silver sulfadiazine/chlorhexidine digluconate. **Flamazine C.**

simethicone. activated dimethicone. activated polymethylsiloxane. **Baby's Own Infant Drops, Gas-X, Gas-X Extra Strength, Ovol, Phazyme.**

simethicone/aluminum hydroxide/magnesium hydroxide. **Diovol Plus, Maalox Plus, Maalox Plus Extra Strength, Mylanta Double Strength Plain Tablet, Mylanta Extra Strength, Mylanta Regular Strength.**

simethicone/calcium carbonate/magnesium hydroxide. **Diovol Plus AF.**

simethicone/magaldrate. **Riopan Plus.**

Similac LF (Abbott). *infant formula, lactose-free.*

simvastatin. **Zocor.**

Sinemet (DuPont Pharma). *carbidopa/levodopa.*

Sinemet CR (DuPont Pharma). *carbidopa/levodopa.*

Sinequan (Pfizer). *doxepin hydrochloride.*

Singulair (MSD). *montelukast sodium.*

Sintrom (Novartis Pharmaceuticals). *nicoumalone.*

Sinutab (Warner-Lambert Consumer Healthcare). *acetaminophen/ chlorpheniramine maleate/pseudoephedrine hydrochloride.*

Sinutab Nightime (Warner-Lambert Consumer Healthcare). *acetaminophen/diphenhydramine/pseudoephedrine hydrochloride.*

Sinutab Non Drowsy (Warner-Lambert Consumer Healthcare). *acetaminophen/pseudoephedrine hydrochloride.*

Sinutab SA (Warner-Lambert Consumer Healthcare). *acetaminophen/phenylpropanolamine hydrochloride/ phenyltoloxamine citrate.*

Sinutab with Codeine (Warner-Lambert Consumer Healthcare). *acetaminophen/chlorpheniramine maleate/codeine/ pseudoephedrine hydrochloride.*

692 (Frosst). *ASA/caffeine/propoxyphene hydrochloride.*

†Skelaxin. *metaxalone.*

skin test antigens. **Multitest CMI.**

Slo-Bid (Rhône-Poulenc Rorer). *theophylline.*

†Slo-Phyllin. *theophylline.*

Slow-Fe (Novartis Consumer Health). *ferrous sulfate.*

Slow-Fe Folic (Novartis Consumer Health). *ferrous sulfate/folic acid.*

Slow-K (Novartis Pharmaceuticals). *potassium chloride.*

Slow-Mag (Roberts). *magnesium chloride.*

Slow-Trasicor (Novartis Pharmaceuticals). *oxprenolol hydrochloride.*

SMA, Preemie (Wyeth-Ayerst). *infant formula, low birthweight.*

SMA Preparations (Wyeth-Ayerst). *infant formula.*

sodium acid phosphate. **Phosphate-Novartis.**

sodium alginate/aluminum hydroxide. **Gaviscon Heartburn Relief Formula Liquid, Rafton Liquid.**

sodium aurothiomalate. gold compound. gold sodium thiomalate. **Myochrysine.**

sodium bicarbonate. **[Sodium Bicarbonate, General Monograph, CPhA]; (Abbott), (Astra).**

sodium bicarbonate/anise oil/dill oil/fennel oil. **Baby's Own Gripe Water.**

sodium bicarbonate/sodium citrate. **Citrocarbonate.**

sodium biphosphate/sodium phosphate. **Gent-L-Tip.**

sodium chloride. **Minims Sodium Chloride, Saline from Otrivin, Salinex, Thalaris; (Abbott), (Astra), (BDH).**

sodium chloride/gentamicin sulfate. **(Abbott), (Baxter).**

sodium chloride/heparin sodium. **(Baxter).**

sodium chloride/hydroxyethylcellulose. **Minims Artificial Tears.**

sodium citrate/citric acid. **PMS-Dicitrate.**

sodium citrate/doxylamine succinate/etafedrine hydrochloride/ hydrocodone bitartrate. **Calmydone, Dalmacol, Mercodol with Decapryn.**

sodium citrate/glycerin/sodium lauryl sulfoacetate/sorbic acid/ sorbitol. **Microlax.**

sodium citrate/sodium bicarbonate. **Citrocarbonate.**

sodium colistimethate. **Coly-Mycin M.**

Names **underlined** have complete prescribing information in the *CPS* Monograph Section.

Stievamycin (Stiefel). *erythromycin/tretinoin.*

Stilamin (Serono). *somatostatin.*

stilboestrol. see diethylstilbestrol sodium diphosphate.

†Stilphostrol. *diethylstilbestrol sodium diphosphate.*

†Storz-Dexa. *dexamethasone sodium phosphate.*

Streptase (Hoechst Marion Roussel). *streptokinase.*

streptococcus lactis/lactobacillus acidophillus/lactobacillus bulgaricus. **Fermalac, Fermalac Vaginal.**

streptokinase. **Kabikinase, Streptase.**

streptomycin sulfate. **[Streptomycin, General Monograph, CPhA]; (Pfizer).**

streptozocin. **Zanosar.**

Stresstabs (Whitehall-Robins). *multiple vitamins.*

Stresstabs Plus (Whitehall-Robins). *ascorbic acid/selenium/vitamin B compound/vitamin E/zinc.*

Stresstabs with Iron (Whitehall-Robins). *ferrous fumarate/multiple vitamins.*

Stresstabs with Zinc (Whitehall-Robins). *cupric oxide/multiple vitamins/zinc oxide.*

succimer. dimercaptosuccinic acid. DMSA. †Chemet.

succinylcholine chloride. suxamethonium. **Anectine, Quelicin Chloride; (Bioniche).** †Sucostrin.

†Sucostrin. *succinylcholine chloride.*

sucralfate. **Apo-Sucralfate, Novo-Sucralate, Nu-Sucralfate, Sulcrate, Sulcrate Suspension Plus.** †Carafate.

Sudafed Cold & Cough (Warner-Lambert Consumer Healthcare). *acetaminophen/dextromethorphan hydrobromide/pseudoephedrine hydrochloride.*

Sudafed Cold & Flu (Warner-Lambert Consumer Healthcare). *acetaminophen/dextromethorphan hydrobromide/guaifenesin/pseudoephedrine hydrochloride.*

Sudafed Decongestant (Warner-Lambert Consumer Healthcare). *pseudoephedrine hydrochloride.*

Sudafed Decongestant 12 Hour (Warner-Lambert Consumer Healthcare). *pseudoephedrine hydrochloride.*

Sudafed Head Cold and Sinus (Warner-Lambert Consumer Healthcare). *acetaminophen/pseudoephedrine hydrochloride.*

Sufenta (Janssen-Ortho). *sufentanil citrate.*

sufentanil citrate. **Sufenta.**

sulbactam sodium/ampicillin sodium. †Unasyn.

sulconazole nitrate. †Exelderm.

Sulcrate (Hoechst Marion Roussel). *sucralfate.*

Sulcrate Suspension Plus (Hoechst Marion Roussel). *sucralfate.*

†Sulf-10. *sulfacetamide sodium.*

sulfabenzamide/sulfacetamide/sulfathiazole. **Sultrin.** †Sulfa-Gyn, †Sulnac, †V.V.S.

sulfacetamide sodium. **Cetamide, Diosulf, Sodium Sulamyd.** †Ophthacet, †Spectro-Sulf, †Sulf-10, †Sulfamide, †Sulten-10.

sulfacetamide sodium/prednisolone acetate. **Blephamide, Dioptimyd, Metimyd.**

sulfacetamide sodium/prednisolone sodium phosphate. **Vasocidin.**

sulfacetamide sodium/sulfur. **Sulfacet-R.**

sulfacetamide/sulfabenzamide/sulfathiazole. **Sultrin.** †Sulfa-Gyn, †Sulnac, †V.V.S.

Sulfacet-R (Dermik Laboratories Canada). *sulfacetamide sodium/sulfur.*

sulfadiazine/pheniramine maleate/phenylpropanolamine hydrochloride/pyrilamine maleate/sulfamerazine/sulfamethazine. **Trisulfaminic.**

sulfadiazine/trimethoprim. **Coptin.**

sulfadoxine/pyrimethamine. **Fansidar.**

†Sulfa-Gyn. *sulfabenzamide/sulfacetamide/sulfathiazole.*

sulfamerazine/pheniramine maleate/phenylpropanolamine hydrochloride/pyrilamine maleate/sulfadiazine/sulfamethazine. **Trisulfaminic.**

sulfamethazine/pheniramine maleate/phenylpropanolamine hydrochloride/pyrilamine maleate/sulfadiazine/sulfamerazine. **Trisulfaminic.**

sulfamethizole. †Thiosulfil Forte.

sulfamethoxazole/trimethoprim. **Apo-Sulfatrim, Bactrim Roche, Novo-Trimel, Novo-Trimel D.S., Nu-Cotrimox, Septra, Septra DS, Septra Injection.** †Sulfatrim.

†Sulfamide. *sulfacetamide sodium.*

sulfanilamide. **AVC.** †Vagitrol.

sulfapyridine. **[Sulfapyridine, General Monograph, CPhA]; Dagenan.**

sulfasalazine. salicylazosulfapyridine. sulphasalazine. **Alti-Sulfasalazine, Salazopyrin, Salazopyrin En-Tabs, S.A.S.** †Azulfidine.

sulfathiazole/sulfabenzamide/sulfacetamide. **Sultrin.** †Sulfa-Gyn, †Sulnac, †V.V.S.

†Sulfatrim. *sulfamethoxazole/trimethoprim.*

†Sulfimycin. *erythromycin ethylsuccinate/sulfisoxazole acetyl.*

sulfinpyrazone. sulphinpyrazone. **Anturan, Apo-Sulfinpyrazone, Nu-Sulfinpyrazone.**

sulfisoxazole acetyl/erythromycin ethylsuccinate. **Pediazole.** †Sulfimycin.

sulfonylureas. **(General Monograph, CPhA).**

Sulfoxyl (Stiefel). *benzoyl peroxide/sulfur.*

sulfur. **Postacne, Sulfur Soap.**

sulfur/allantoin/butoxyethyl nicotinate/chloramphenicol/hydrocortisone acetate. **Actinac.**

sulfur/aluminum chlorhydroxide/methylprednisolone acetate. **Medrol Acne.**

sulfur/aluminum chlorhydroxide/methylprednisolone acetate/neomycin sulfate. **Neo-Medrol Acne.**

sulfur/benzoyl peroxide. **Sulfoxyl.**

sulfur/coal tar/salicylic acid. **Sebutone.**

sulfur/isopropyl alcohol/resorcinol. **Acnomel Cream.**

sulfur/resorcinol. **Acnomel Vanishing Cream.**

sulfur/salicylic acid. **Meted, Pernox, Sastid, Sebulex.**

Sulfur Soap (Stiefel). *sulfur.*

sulfur/sulfacetamide sodium. **Sulfacet-R.**

sulindac. **Apo-Sulin, Novo-Sundac, Nu-Sulindac.**

†Sulnac. *sulfabenzamide/sulfacetamide/sulfathiazole.*

sulphasalazine. see sulfasalazine.

sulphinpyrazone. see sulfinpyrazone.

†Sulten-10. *sulfacetamide sodium.*

Sultrin (Janssen-Ortho). *sulfabenzamide/sulfacetamide/sulfathiazole.*

sumatriptan hemisulfate. **Imitrex Nasal Spray.**

sumatriptan succinate. **Imitrex Injection/Tablets.**

Sun-Benz (Sun). *benzydamine hydrochloride.*

Supeudol (Sabex). *oxycodone hydrochloride.*

Suplasyn (Bioniche). *sodium hyaluronate.*

Suplevit (Riva). *multiple vitamins and minerals.*

Supracaine (Hoechst Marion Roussel). *tetracaine.*

Suprane (Zeneca). *desflurane.*

Suprax (Rhône-Poulenc Rorer). *cefixime.*

Suprefact (Hoechst Marion Roussel). *buserelin acetate.*

Suprefact Depot (Hoechst Marion Roussel). *buserelin acetate.*

Supres (Frosst). *chlorothiazide/methyldopa.*
suprofen. †Profenal.
Surfak (Hoechst Marion Roussel). *docusate calcium.*
Surgam (Hoechst Marion Roussel). *tiaprofenic acid.*
Surgam SR (Hoechst Marion Roussel). *tiaprofenic acid.*
Surmontil (Rhône-Poulenc Rorer). *trimipramine maleate.*
Survanta (Abbott). *beractant.*
Sustacal (Mead Johnson). *enteral nutrition.*
suxamethonium. see succinylcholine chloride.
Swiss One (Swiss Herbal). *multiple vitamins and minerals.*
†Symadine. *amantadine hydrochloride.*
Symmetrel (Antiparkinson) (DuPont Pharma). *amantadine hydrochloride.*
Symmetrel (Antiviral) (DuPont Pharma). *amantadine hydrochloride.*
†Synacort. *hydrocortisone.*
Synacthen Depot (Novartis Pharmaceuticals). *cosyntropin/zinc hydroxide.*
Synalar (Roche). *fluocinolone acetonide.*
Synarel (Searle). *nafarelin acetate.*
Synflex (AltiMed). *naproxen sodium.*
Synflex DS (AltiMed). *naproxen sodium.*
†Synkayvite. *menadiol sodium diphosphate.*
Synphasic (Searle). *ethinyl estradiol/norethindrone.*
synthetic human parathyroid hormone 1-34. see teriparatide acetate.
Synthroid (Knoll). *levothyroxine sodium.*
Synvisc (Biomatrix/Rhône-Poulenc Rorer). *hylan G-F 20.*
†Syprine. *trientine hydrochloride.*

T

†Tacaryl. *methdilazine hydrochloride.*
tacrolimus. **Prograf.**
Tagamet (SmithKline Beecham). *cimetidine.*
Talwin Injection (Sanofi). *pentazocine lactate.*
Talwin Tablets (Sanofi). *pentazocine hydrochloride.*
Tambocor (3M Pharmaceuticals). *flecainide acetate.*
Tamofen (Rhône-Poulenc Rorer). *tamoxifen citrate.*
Tamone (Pharmacia & Upjohn). *tamoxifen citrate.*
tamoxifen citrate. **Apo-Tamox, Gen-Tamoxifen, Nolvadex, Nolvadex-D, Novo-Tamoxifen, Tamofen, Tamone.**
tamsulosin hydrochloride. **Flomax.**
Tanacet 125 (Ashbury Biologicals/Herbal Laboratories). *feverfew.*
Tanta Orciprenaline (Tanta). *orciprenaline sulfate.*
Tantum (3M Pharmaceuticals). *benzydamine hydrochloride.*
Tapazole (Lilly). *methimazole.*
†Taractan. *chlorprothixene.*
Tardan (Odan). *liquid carbonis detergens/salicylic acid/triclosan.*
tar distillate. **Tersa-Tar.**
tar distillate/isopropyl palmitate/mineral oil. **Doak-Oil, Doak-Oil Forte.**
Targel (Odan). *liquid carbonis detergens.*
Targel S.A. (Odan). *liquid carbonis detergens/salicylic acid.*
Tarka (Knoll). *trandolapril/verapamil hydrochloride.*
Taro-Carbamazepine (Taro). *carbamazepine.*
Taro Gel (Taro). *lubricating jelly.*
Taro-Sone (Taro). *betamethasone dipropionate.*
Tasmar (Roche). *tolcapone.*
Tavist (Novartis Consumer Health). *clemastine hydrogen fumarate.*
Tavist-D (Novartis Consumer Health). *clemastine hydrogen fumarate/phenylpropanolamine hydrochloride.*
Taxol (Bristol-Myers Squibb). *paclitaxel.*
Taxotere (Rhône-Poulenc Rorer). *docetaxel.*
tazarotene. **Tazorac.**
†Tazicef. *ceftazidime.*
Tazidime (Lilly). *ceftazidime.*
tazobactam sodium/piperacillin sodium. **Tazocin.**
Tazocin (Wyeth-Ayerst). *piperacillin sodium/tazobactam sodium.*
Tazorac (Allergan). *tazarotene.*
†T-Diet. *phentermine hydrochloride.*
Teardrops (CIBA Vision). *polyvinyl alcohol/povidone.*
Tears Encore (Dioptic). *polysorbate 80.*
Tears Naturale (Alcon). *dextran 70/hydroxypropyl methylcellulose.*
Tears Naturale Free (Alcon). *dextran 70/hydroxypropyl methylcellulose.*
Tears Naturale II (Alcon). *dextran 70/hydroxypropyl methylcellulose.*
Tears Plus (Allergan). *polyvinyl alcohol/povidone.*
Tebrazid (ICN). *pyrazinamide.*
Tecnal (Technilab). *ASA/butalbital/caffeine.*
Tecnal C¼, C½ (Technilab). *ASA/butalbital/caffeine/codeine phosphate.*
Teejel (Purdue Frederick). *choline salicylate.*
†Tegamide. *trimethobenzamide hydrochloride.*
Tegopen (Bristol). *cloxacillin sodium.*
Tegretol (Novartis Pharmaceuticals). *carbamazepine.*
Telebrix 38 Oral (Mallinckrodt). *meglumine ioxitalamate/sodium ioxitalamate.*
†Temaril. *trimeprazine tartrate.*
temazepam. **[Benzodiazepines, General Monograph, CPhA]; Apo-Temazepam, Gen-Temazepam, Novo-Temazepam, Nu-Temazepam, PMS-Temazepam, Restoril.**
†Temovate. *clobetasol 17-propionate.*
Tempra (Mead Johnson). *acetaminophen.*
†Tenex. *guanfacine hydrochloride.*
teniposide. **Vumon.**
Tenolin (Technilab). *atenolol.*
Tenoretic (Zeneca). *atenolol/chlorthalidone.*
Tenormin (Zeneca). *atenolol.*
tenoxicam. **Apo-Tenoxicam, Mobiflex, Novo-Tenoxicam.**
Tensilon (ICN). *edrophonium chloride.*
Tenuate (Hoechst Marion Roussel). *diethylpropion hydrochloride.*
Terazol (Janssen-Ortho). *terconazole.*
terazosin hydrochloride. **Novo-Terazosin.**
terazosin hydrochloride dihydrate. **Alti-Terazosin, Apo-Terazosin, Hytrin, Nu-Terazosin.**
terbinafine hydrochloride. **Lamisil.**
terbutaline sulfate. **Bricanyl Tablets, Bricanyl Turbuhaler.** †Brethaire, †Brethine.
terconazole. **Terazol.**
terebinth oil/chlorbutol/paradichlorobenzene. **Cerumol.**
terfenadine. **Apo-Terfenadine, Seldane.**
teriparatide acetate. synthetic human parathyroid hormone 1-34. †Parathar.

Names **underlined** have complete prescribing information in the *CPS* Monograph Section.

†Terramycin. *oxytetracycline hydrochloride.*

TersAc (TCD). *salicylic acid/triclosan.*

Tersaseptic (TCD). *triclosan.*

Tersa-Tar (TCD). *tar distillate.*

†Teslac. *testolactone.*

†Tessalon. *benzonatate.*

†Testamone 100. *testosterone.*

Tes-Tape (Lilly). *glucose enzymatic test strip.*

†Testaqua. *testosterone.*

†Testex. *testosterone propionate.*

†Testoderm. *testosterone.*

testolactone. †Teslac.

testosterone. †Testamone 100, †Testaqua, †Testoderm.

testosterone cyclopentylpropionate. see testosterone cypionate.

testosterone cypionate. testosterone cyclopentylpropionate. **Depo-Testosterone Cypionate, Scheinpharm Testone-Cyp.** †Andronate, †Depotest, †Testred Cypionate 200, †Virilon IM.

testosterone enanthate. **Delatestryl; (Taro).** †Andropository 100, †Delatest, †Everone 200, †Testrin-P.A.

testosterone enanthate benzilic acid hydrazone/estradiol benzoate/estradiol dienanthate. **Climacteron.**

testosterone propionate. **(Taro).** †Testex.

testosterone undecanoate. **Andriol.**

†Testred. *methyltestosterone.*

†Testred Cypionate 200. *testosterone cypionate.*

†Testrin-P.A. *testosterone enanthate.*

tetanus immune globulin (human). see immune globulin, tetanus (human).

tetanus toxoid adsorbed. **(BioChem Vaccines), (Connaught).**

tetanus toxoid adsorbed/diphtheria toxoid adsorbed. **(BioChem Vaccines), (Connaught).**

tetanus toxoid adsorbed/diphtheria toxoid adsorbed/haemophilus b conjugate vaccine (tetanus protein conjugate)/pertussis vaccine (acellular)/poliomyelitis vaccine, inactivated. **Pentacel.**

tetanus toxoid adsorbed/diphtheria toxoid adsorbed/pertussis vaccine (acellular)/poliomyelitis vaccine, inactivated. **Quadracel.**

tetanus toxoid adsorbed/diphtheria toxoid adsorbed/pertussis vaccine adsorbed/poliomyelitis vaccine adsorbed, inactivated. **(Connaught).**

tetanus toxoid adsorbed/diphtheria toxoid adsorbed/pertussis vaccine (cellular). **(Connaught).**

tetanus toxoid adsorbed/diphtheria toxoid adsorbed/poliomyelitis vaccine adsorbed, inactivated. **(Connaught).**

tetrabenazine. **Nitoman.**

tetracaine. **Minims Tetracaine, Supracaine.**

tetracaine hydrochloride. amethocaine hydrochloride. **Ametop, Pontocaine.**

tetracaine hydrochloride/benzocaine. **Panocaine.**

tetracycline hydrochloride. **[Tetracyclines, General Monograph, CPhA]; Apo-Tetra, Novo-Tetra, Nu-Tetra.** †Achromycin V, †Panmycin, †Topicycline.

tetrahydrozoline hydrochloride. **Eye Drops.**

tetramethylthionine chloride trihydrate. see methylene blue.

Thalaris (Technilab). *sodium chloride.*

†Theo-24. *theophylline.*

Theo-Bronc (Rougier). *guaifenesin/mepyramine maleate/potassium iodide/theophylline.*

Theochron SR (Riva). *theophylline.*

Theo-Dur (Astra). *theophylline.*

Theolair (3M Pharmaceuticals). *theophylline.*

Theolair-SR (3M Pharmaceuticals). *theophylline.*

theophylline. **[Theophylline and its Salts, General Monograph, CPhA]; Apo-Theo LA, Novo-Theophyl SR, Quibron-T, Quibron-T/SR, Slo-Bid, Theochron SR, Theo-Dur, Theolair, Theolair-SR, Theo-SR, Uniphyl; (Desbergers), (Technilab).** †Elixophyllin, †Respbid, †Slo-Phyllin, †Theo-24, †Theovent Long-Acting.

theophylline ethylenediamine. see aminophylline.

theophylline/guaifenesin/mepyramine maleate/potassium iodide. **Theo-Bronc.**

Theo-SR (Rhône-Poulenc Rorer). *theophylline.*

†Theovent Long-Acting. *theophylline.*

†Thermazene. *silver sulfadiazine.*

thiabendazole: **Mintezol.**

thiamazole. see methimazole.

thiamine/ascorbic acid. **Penta-Thion.**

thiamine/ascorbic acid/inositol. **Vitathion-A.T.P.**

thiamine hydrochloride. vitamin B_1. **[Vitamin B_1, General Monograph, CPhA]; Betaxin; (Bioniche), (Faulding).**

thiethylperazine maleate. †Norzine, †Torecan.

6-thioguanine. see thioguanine.

thioguanine. 6-thioguanine. **Lanvis.**

†Thiola. *tiopronin.*

thiopental sodium. **Pentothal.**

thioproperazine mesylate. **Majeptil.**

thioridazine hydrochloride. **Apo-Thioridazine, Mellaril.**

†Thiosulfil Forte. *sulfamethizole.*

thiotepa. **(Wyeth-Ayerst).**

thiothixene. **Navane.**

†Thorazine. *chlorpromazine hydrochloride.*

†Thor-Prom. *chlorpromazine hydrochloride.*

3TC (Glaxo Wellcome). *lamivudine.*

3TC. see lamivudine.

Thrombate III (Bayer). *antithrombin III (human).*

thrombin (bovine). **Thrombostat.**

Thrombostat (Parke-Davis). *thrombin (bovine).*

Thyro-Block (Carter Horner). *potassium iodide.*

thyroid. **(Parke-Davis).**

†Thyrolar. *liotrix.*

d-thyroxine sodium. see dextrothyroxine sodium.

tiagapine. †Gabitril.

Tiamol (Spectropharm Dermatology). *fluocinonide.*

tiaprofenic acid. **Albert Tiafen, Albert Tiafen SR, Apo-Tiaprofenic, Novo-Tiaprofenic, Nu-Tiaprofenic, PMS-Tiaprofenic, Surgam, Surgam SR.**

Tiazac (Crystaal). *diltiazem hydrochloride.*

ticarcillin disodium/potassium clavulanate. **Timentin.**

Ticlid (Roche). *ticlopidine hydrochloride.*

ticlopidine hydrochloride. **Apo-Ticlopidine, Nu-Ticlopidine, Ticlid.**

†Tigan. *trimethobenzamide hydrochloride.*

†Tiject-20. *trimethobenzamide hydrochloride.*

Tilade (Rhône-Poulenc Rorer). *nedocromil sodium.*

Tim-Ak (Dioptic). *timolol maleate.*

Timed Release Swiss One "50" (Swiss Herbal). *multiple vitamins and minerals.*

Timed Release Vitamin C 500 mg (Swiss Herbal). *ascorbic acid.*

Timed Release Vitamin C 1000 mg (Swiss Herbal). *ascorbic acid.*

Timentin (SmithKline Beecham). *potassium clavulanate/ticarcillin disodium.*

Timolide (Frosst). *hydrochlorothiazide/timolol maleate.*

timolol maleate. **Apo-Timol, Apo-Timop, Blocadren, Gen-Timolol, Novo-Timol Ophthalmic Solution, Novo-Timol Tablets, Nu-Timolol, PMS-Timolol, Tim-Ak, Timoptic, Timoptic-XE; (BDH).**

timolol maleate/hydrochlorothiazide. **Timolide.**

timolol maleate/pilocarpine hydrochloride. **Timpilo.**

Timoptic (MSD). *timolol maleate.*

Timoptic-XE (MSD). *timolol maleate.*

Timpilo (MSD). *pilocarpine hydrochloride/timolol maleate.*

Tinactin (Schering). *tolnaftate.*

Tinactin Jock Itch (Schering). *tolnaftate.*

Tinactin Plus (Schering). *tolnaftate.*

†Tindal. *acetophenazine maleate.*

tinzaparin sodium. **[Heparins: Low Molecular Weight, General Monograph, CPhA]; Innohep.**

tioconazole. **Gynecure, Trosyd AF, Trosyd J.**

tiopronin. †Thiola.

†Tipramine. *imipramine hydrochloride.*

Tisseel Kit VH (Baxter). *fibrin sealant.*

titanium dioxide. **PreSun Sunblock 28.**

Ti-U-Lac HC (Spectropharm Dermatology). *hydrocortisone/urea.*

Tobradex (Alcon). *dexamethasone/tobramycin.*

tobramycin. **Tobrex.**

tobramycin/dexamethasone. **Tobradex.**

tobramycin sulfate. **Nebcin, Scheinpharm Tobramycin.**

Tobrex (Alcon). *tobramycin.*

tocainide hydrochloride. **Tonocard.**

tocofersolan. see vitamin E.

α-tocopheryl. see vitamin E.

Tofranil (Novartis Pharmaceuticals). *imipramine hydrochloride.*

tolazamide. †Tolinase.

tolbutamide. **[Sulfonylureas, General Monograph, CPhA]; Apo-Tolbutamide.**

tolcapone. **Tasmar.**

Tolectin (Janssen-Ortho). *tolmetin sodium.*

Tolerex (Novartis Nutrition). *enteral nutrition.*

†Tolinase. *tolazamide.*

tolmetin sodium. **Novo-Tolmetin, Tolectin.**

tolnaftate. **Pitrex, Tinactin, Tinactin Jock Itch, Tinactin Plus, ZeaSORB AF.**

toluidine blue O. **Orascan.**

Tomudex (Zeneca). *raltitrexed disodium.*

Tonocard (Astra). *tocainide hydrochloride.*

Topamax (Janssen-Ortho). *topiramate.*

Topicaine (Hoechst Marion Roussel). *benzocaine.*

Topicort (Hoechst Marion Roussel). *desoximetasone.*

†Topicycline. *tetracycline hydrochloride.*

Topilene (Technilab). *betamethasone dipropionate.*

topiramate. **Topamax.**

Topisone (Technilab). *betamethasone dipropionate.*

topotecan hydrochloride. **Hycamtin.**

†Toprol-XL. *metoprolol succinate.*

Topsyn (Medicis). *fluocinonide.*

Toradol (Roche). *ketorolac tromethamine.*

Toradol IM (Roche). *ketorolac tromethamine.*

†Torecan. *thiethylperazine maleate.*

toremifene. †Fareston.

†Tornalate. *bitolterol mesylate.*

torsemide. **Demadex.**

†Totacillin. *ampicillin trihydrate.*

Trace Elements Solution (Faulding). *electrolytes.*

Tracrium (Glaxo Wellcome). *atracurium besylate.*

tramadol. †Ultram.

†Trancopal. *chlormezanone.*

Trandate (Roberts). *labetalol hydrochloride.*

trandolapril. **[ACE Inhibitors, General Monograph, CPhA]; Mavik.**

trandolapril/verapamil hydrochloride. **Tarka.**

tranexamic acid. **Cyklokapron.**

Transderm-Nitro (Novartis Pharmaceuticals). *nitroglycerin.*

Transderm-V (Novartis Pharmaceuticals). *scopolamine.*

Trans-Plantar (Westwood-Squibb). *salicylic acid.*

trans-retinoic acid. see tretinoin.

Trans•Ver•Sal (Westwood-Squibb). *salicylic acid.*

Tranxene (Abbott). *clorazepate dipotassium.*

tranylcypromine sulfate. **Parnate.**

Trasicor (Novartis Pharmaceuticals). *oxprenolol hydrochloride.*

Trasylol (Bayer). *aprotinin.*

Travasol with Electrolytes (Clintec). *amino acids/dextrose/electrolytes.*

Travasol without Electrolytes (Clintec). *amino acids/dextrose.*

Traveltabs (Stanley). *dimenhydrinate.*

Travel Tabs (WestCan). *dimenhydrinate.*

trazodone. **Gen-Trazodone.**

trazodone hydrochloride. **Alti-Trazodone, Alti-Trazodone Dividose, Apo-Trazodone, Apo-Trazodone D, Desyrel, Desyrel Dividose, Novo-Trazodone, Nu-Trazodone, Nu-Trazodone-D, PMS-Trazodone, Trazorel.** †Trazon, †Trialodine.

†Trazon. *trazodone hydrochloride.*

Trazorel (ICN). *trazodone hydrochloride.*

†Trecator-SC. *ethionamide.*

Trental (Hoechst Marion Roussel). *pentoxifylline.*

tretinoin. trans-retinoic acid. **Rejuva-A, Renova, Retin-A, Retisol-A, StieVA-A, StieVA-A Forte, Vesanoid, Vitamin A Acid, Vitinoin.**

tretinoin/erythromycin. **Stievamycin.**

†Trexan. *naltrexone hydrochloride.*

†Triacet. *triamcinolone acetonide.*

Triacomb (Technilab). *gramicidin/neomycin sulfate/nystatin/triamcinolone acetonide.*

Triaderm (Taro). *triamcinolone acetonide.*

†Trialodine. *trazodone hydrochloride.*

triamcinolone. **[Corticosteroids: Systemic, General Monograph, CPhA]; Aristocort Tablets.**

triamcinolone acetonide. **[Corticosteroids: Eye Ear Nose, Corticosteroids: Inhaled, Corticosteroids: Systemic, Corticosteroids: Topical, General Monographs, CPhA]; Aristocort Topicals, Azmacort, Kenalog, Kenalog-10, Kenalog-40, Kenalog in Orabase, Nasacort, Nasacort AQ, Oracort, Scheinpharm Triamcine-A, Triaderm.** †Cinonide 40, †Flutex, †Kenac, †Kenonel, †Oralone, †Triacet, †Triderm, †Trilog.

triamcinolone acetonide/gramicidin/neomycin sulfate/nystatin. **Kenacomb, Triacomb, Viaderm-K.C.**

Names underlined have complete prescribing information in the *CPS* Monograph Section.

triamcinolone diacetate. **[Corticosteroids: Systemic, General Monograph, CPhA]; Aristocort Parenteral; (Taro).** †Articulose-L.A., †Cinalone 40, †Triam-Forte, †Trilone.

triamcinolone hexacetonide. **[Corticosteroids: Systemic, General Monograph, CPhA]; Aristospan.**

†Triam-Forte. *triamcinolone diacetate.*

Triaminic Cold and Allergy Syrup (Novartis Consumer Health). *chlorpheniramine maleate/phenylpropanolamine hydrochloride.*

Triaminic Cold & Fever (Novartis Consumer Health). *acetaminophen/dextromethorphan hydrobromide/pseudoephedrine hydrochloride.*

Triaminic DM Daytime (Novartis Consumer Health). *dextromethorphan hydrobromide/guaifenesin/phenylpropanolamine hydrochloride.*

Triaminic DM Expectorant (Novartis Consumer Health). *chlorpheniramine maleate/dextromethorphan hydrobromide/guaifenesin/pseudoephedrine hydrochloride.*

Triaminic DM Long Lasting For Children (Novartis Consumer Health). *dextromethorphan hydrobromide.*

Triaminic DM Nighttime (Novartis Consumer Health). *chlorpheniramine maleate/dextromethorphan hydrobromide/pseudoephedrine hydrochloride.*

Triaminic Expectorant (Novartis Consumer Health). *chlorpheniramine maleate/guaifenesin/pseudoephedrine hydrochloride.*

Triaminic Expectorant DH (Novartis Consumer Health). *guaifenesin/hydrocodone bitartrate/pheniramine maleate/phenylpropanolamine hydrochloride/pyrilamine maleate.*

Triaminicin (Novartis Consumer Health). *acetaminophen/caffeine/pheniramine maleate/phenylpropanolamine hydrochloride/pyrilamine maleate.*

Triaminicol DM (Novartis Consumer Health). *chlorpheniramine maleate/dextromethorphan hydrobromide/pseudoephedrine hydrochloride.*

Triaminic Oral Pediatric Drops (Novartis Consumer Health). *pseudoephedrine hydrochloride.*

Triaminic Tablets (Novartis Consumer Health). *pheniramine maleate/phenylpropanolamine hydrochloride/pyrilamine maleate.*

triamterene. **Dyrenium.**

triamterene/hydrochlorothiazide. **Apo-Triazide, Dyazide, Novo-Triamzide, Nu-Triazide.** †Maxzide.

Trianal (Trianon). *ASA/butalbital/caffeine.*

Trianal C¼ C½ (Trianon). *ASA/butalbital/caffeine/codeine phosphate.*

Triatec-8, -8 Strong (Trianon). *acetaminophen/caffeine citrate/codeine phosphate.*

Triatec-30 (Trianon). *acetaminophen/codeine phosphate.*

Triavil (MSD). *amitriptyline hydrochloride/perphenazine.*

triazolam. **[Benzodiazepines, General Monograph, CPhA]; Alti-Triazolam, Apo-Triazo, Gen-Triazolam, Halcion.**

†Tribenzagan. *trimethobenzamide hydrochloride.*

†Trichlorex. *trichlormethiazide.*

trichlormethiazide. †Metahydrin, †Naqua, †Trichlorex.

triclosan. **Adasept Skin Cleanser, Tersaseptic.**

triclosan/liquid carbonis detergens/salicylic acid. **Tardan.**

triclosan/salicylic acid. **TersAc.**

triclosan/salicylic acid/sodium thiosulfate. **Adasept Acne Gel.**

tricontanyl PVP/dimethicone/perfluoropolymethylisopropyl ether. **Spectro Gluvs "19".**

†Tricor. *fenofibrate (micronized).*

Tri-Cyclen (Janssen-Ortho). *ethinyl estradiol/norgestimate.*

†Triderm. *triamcinolone acetonide.*

Tridesilon (Bayer). *desonide.*

Tridil (DuPont Pharma). *nitroglycerin.*

trientine hydrochloride. triethylenetetramine dihyrochloride. †Syprine.

triethanolamine polypeptide cocoate condensate/propylene glycol/tyrothricin. **Soropon.**

triethanolamine polypeptide oleate-condensate. **Cerumenex.**

triethanolamine salicylate. **Antiphlogistine Rub A-535 No Odour, Myoflex, Royflex.**

triethanolamine salicylate/menthol. **Myoflex Ice Plus.**

triethylenetetramine dihyrochloride. see trientine hydrochloride.

trifluoperazine hydrochloride. **Apo-Trifluoperazine, Stelazine.**

trifluoperazine hydrochloride/isopropamide iodide. **Stelabid.**

triflupromazine hydrochloride. †Vesprin.

trifluridine. **Viroptic.**

†Trihexane. *trihexyphenidyl hydrochloride.*

†Trihexy. *trihexyphenidyl hydrochloride.*

trihexyphenidyl hydrochloride. benzhexol hydrochloride. **[Trihexyphenidyl HCl, General Monograph, CPhA]; Apo-Trihex.** †Trihexane, †Trihexy.

†Tri-K. *trikates.*

trikates. †Tri-K.

Trilafon (Schering). *perphenazine.*

†Tri-Levlen. *ethinyl estradiol/levonorgestrel.*

Trilisate (Purdue Frederick). *choline salicylate/magnesium salicylate.*

†Trilog. *triamcinolone acetonide.*

†Trilone. *triamcinolone diacetate.*

trilostane. †Modrastane.

trimebutine maleate. **Modulon.**

trimeprazine tartrate. alimemazine tartrate. **Panectyl.** †Temaril.

trimethobenzamide hydrochloride. †Arrestin, †Benzacot, †Bio-Gan, †Stemetic, †Tegamide, †Tigan, †Tiject-20, †Tribenzagan.

trimethoprim. **Proloprim.** †Trimpex.

trimethoprim/sulfadiazine. **Coptin.**

trimethoprim/sulfamethoxazole. **Apo-Sulfatrim, Bactrim Roche, Novo-Trimel, Novo-Trimel D.S., Nu-Cotrimox, Septra, Septra DS, Septra Injection.** †Sulfatrim.

trimethoprim sulfate/polymyxin B sulfate. **Polytrim.**

trimetrexate glucuronate. **Neutrexin.**

trimipramine maleate. **Apo-Trimip, Novo-Tripramine, Nu-Trimipramine, Rhotrimine, Surmontil.**

†Trimox. *amoxicillin trihydrate.*

†Trimpex. *trimethoprim.*

Trinalin (Schering). *azatadine maleate/pseudoephedrine sulfate.*

Trinipatch 0.2 (Sanofi). *nitroglycerin.*

Trinipatch 0.4 (Sanofi). *nitroglycerin.*

Trinipatch 0.6 (Sanofi). *nitroglycerin.*

†Tri-Norinyl. *ethinyl estradiol/norethindrone.*

trioxsalen. **Trisoralen.**

tripelennamine hydrochloride. **Pyribenzamine.**

Triphasil 21 (Wyeth-Ayerst). *ethinyl estradiol/levonorgestrel.*

Triphasil 28 (Wyeth-Ayerst). *ethinyl estradiol/levonorgestrel.*

triprolidine hydrochloride/acetaminophen/pseudoephedrine hydrochloride. **Actifed Plus Extra Strength.**

triprolidine hydrochloride/codeine phosphate/guaifenesin/pseudoephedrine hydrochloride. **CoActifed Expectorant, Cotridin Expectorant.**

triprolidine hydrochloride/codeine phosphate/pseudoephedrine hydrochloride. **CoActifed, Cotridin.**

triprolidine hydrochloride/pseudoephedrine hydrochloride. **Actifed.**

Triptil (MSD). *protriptyline hydrochloride.*

Triquilar 21 (Berlex Canada). *ethinyl estradiol/levonorgestrel.*

Triquilar 28 (Berlex Canada). *ethinyl estradiol/levonorgestrel.*

Trisoralen (ICN). *trioxsalen.*

Trisulfaminic (Shepherd). *pheniramine maleate/phenylpropanolamine hydrochloride/pyrilamine maleate/sulfadiazine/sulfamerazine/sulfamethazine.*

Trombovar (Therapex). *sodium tetradecyl sulfate.*

tropicamide. **Diotrope, Minims Tropicamide, Mydriacyl; (Rivex Ophthalmics).** †I-Picamide, †Mydriafair, †Ocu-Tropic.

tropicamide/phenylephrine hydrochloride. **Diophenyl-T.**

Trosyd AF (Pfizer Consumer). *tioconazole.*

Trosyd J (Pfizer Consumer). *tioconazole.*

trovafloxin. †Trovan.

†Trovan. *trovafloxin.*

Trusopt (MSD). *dorzolamide hydrochloride.*

Tryptan (ICN). *l-tryptophan.*

l-tryptophan. **Alti-Tryptophan, PMS-Tryptophan, Tryptan.**

T-Stat (Westwood-Squibb). *erythromycin/ethyl alcohol.*

†Tubasal. *aminosalicylate sodium.*

tubercle bacillus. see Bacillus Calmette-Guérin vaccine, intradermal.

Tuberculin, Old, Tine Test (Wyeth-Ayerst). *tuberculin test.*

Tuberculin Purified Protein Derivative (Mantoux)--Tubersol (Connaught). *tuberculin test.*

tuberculin test. **Tuberculin, Old, Tine Test, Tuberculin Purified Protein Derivative (Mantoux)--Tubersol.**

Tussaminic C (Novartis Consumer Health). *codeine phosphate/pheniramine maleate/phenylpropanolamine hydrochloride/pyrilamine maleate.*

Tussaminic DH (Novartis Consumer Health). *hydrocodone bitartrate/pheniramine maleate/phenylpropanolamine hydrochloride/pyrilamine maleate.*

Tussionex (Rhône-Poulenc Rorer). *hydrocodone/phenyltoloxamine.*

Twinrix (SmithKline Beecham). *hepatitis A vaccine/hepatitis B vaccine.*

222 (Johnson & Johnson • Merck). *ASA/caffeine citrate/codeine phosphate.*

222 AF (Johnson & Johnson • Merck). *acetaminophen.*

282 MEP (Frosst). *ASA/caffeine citrate/codeine phosphate/meprobamate.*

292 (Frosst). *ASA/caffeine citrate/codeine phosphate.*

Tylenol (McNeil Consumer Products). *acetaminophen.*

Tylenol Aches and Strains Medication (McNeil Consumer Products). *acetaminophen/chlorzoxazone.*

Tylenol Allergy Sinus Medication (McNeil Consumer Products). *acetaminophen/chlorpheniramine maleate/pseudoephedrine hydrochloride.*

Tylenol Cold and Flu (McNeil Consumer Products). *acetaminophen/chlorpheniramine maleate/dextromethorphan hydrobromide/pseudoephedrine hydrochloride.*

Tylenol Cold Medication (Daytime) (McNeil Consumer Products). *acetaminophen/dextromethorphan hydrobromide/pseudoephedrine hydrochloride.*

Tylenol Cold Medication Junior Strength DM (McNeil Consumer Products). *acetaminophen/chlorpheniramine maleate/dextromethorphan hydrobromide/pseudoephedrine hydrochloride.*

Tylenol Cold Medication (Nighttime) (McNeil Consumer Products). *acetaminophen/chlorpheniramine maleate/dextromethorphan hydrobromide/pseudoephedrine hydrochloride.*

Tylenol Cough Caplets/Liquid Suspension (McNeil Consumer Products). *acetaminophen/dextromethorphan hydrobromide.*

Tylenol Cough Liquid Suspension with Decongestant (McNeil Consumer Products). *acetaminophen/dextromethorphan hydrobromide/pseudoephedrine hydrochloride.*

Tylenol Decongestant (McNeil Consumer Products). *acetaminophen/pseudoephedrine hydrochloride.*

Tylenol Elixir with Codeine (Janssen-Ortho). *acetaminophen/codeine phosphate.*

Tylenol Flu Medication (McNeil Consumer Products). *acetaminophen/diphenhydramine hydrochloride/pseudoephedrine hydrochloride.*

Tylenol NO. 1 with Codeine (McNeil Consumer Products). *acetaminophen/caffeine/codeine phosphate.*

Tylenol NO. 2 and NO. 3 with Codeine (Janssen-Ortho). *acetaminophen/caffeine/codeine phosphate.*

Tylenol NO. 4 with Codeine (Janssen-Ortho). *acetaminophen/codeine phosphate.*

Tylenol Sinus Medication (McNeil Consumer Products). *acetaminophen/pseudoephedrine hydrochloride.*

tyloxapol. **Enuclene.**

Typhim Vi (Connaught). *salmonella typhi Vi capsular polysaccharide vaccine.*

typhoid vaccine (live oral attenuated Ty21a). **Vivotif Berna, Vivotif Berna L.**

tyrothricin/benzocaine/camphor/menthol/polymyxin B sulfate. **Antibiotic Cold Sore Ointment.**

tyrothricin/propylene glycol/triethanolamine polypeptide cocoate condensate. **Soropon.**

U

Ulcidine (ICN). *famotidine.*

Ulone (3M Pharmaceuticals). *chlophedianol hydrochloride.*

Ultiva (Glaxo Wellcome). *remifentanil hydrochloride.*

Ultracaine DS (Hoechst Marion Roussel). *articaine hydrochloride/epinephrine.*

Ultracaine DS Forte (Hoechst Marion Roussel). *articaine hydrochloride/epinephrine.*

Ultradol (Procter & Gamble Pharmaceuticals). *etodolac.*

†Ultram. *tramadol.*

UltraMOP Capsules (Canderm Pharma). *methoxsalen.*

UltraMOP Lotion (Canderm Pharma). *methoxsalen.*

Ultraquin (Canderm Pharma). *hydroquinone.*

Ultrase (Axcan Pharma). *pancrelipase.*

Ultrase MT (Axcan Pharma). *pancrelipase.*

Ultravate (Westwood-Squibb). *halobetasol propionate.*

Ultravist (Berlex Canada). *iopromide.*

†Ultrazine-10. *prochlorperazine edisylate.*

†Unasyn. *ampicillin sodium/sulbactam sodium.*

undecylenic acid/zinc undecylenate. **Desenex.**

Uniphyl (Purdue Frederick). *theophylline.*

Names **underlined** have complete prescribing information in the *CPS* Monograph Section.

Univol (Carter Horner). *aluminum hydroxide/magnesium hydroxide.*
Urasal (Carter Horner). *methenamine.*
urea. **Calmurid, Uremol 10, Uremol 20, UriSec.**
urea/amino acids/sodium propionate. **Amino-Cerv.**
urea/hydrocortisone. **Calmurid HC, Ti-U-Lac HC.**
urea/hydrocortisone acetate. **Uremol-HC.**
Urecholine (Frosst). *bethanechol chloride.*
Uremol 10 (TCD). *urea.*
Uremol 20 (TCD). *urea.*
Uremol-HC (TCD). *hydrocortisone acetate/urea.*
†Urex. *methenamine hippurate.*
UriSec (Odan). *urea.*
Urispas (Pharmascience). *flavoxate hydrochloride.*
†Urodine. *phenazopyridine hydrochloride.*
urofollitropin. **Fertinorm HP.**
†Urogesic. *phenazopyridine hydrochloride.*
urokinase. **Abbokinase, Abbokinase Open-Cath.**
Uromitexan (Bristol). *mesna.*
ursodeoxycholic acid. see ursodiol.
ursodiol. ursodeoxycholic acid. **Ursofalk.** †Actigall.
Ursofalk (Axcan Pharma). *ursodiol.*
†Uticort. *betamethasone benzoate.*

V

†Vagitrol. *sulfanilamide.*
valacyclovir hydrochloride. **Valtrex.**
†Valergen. *estradiol valerate.*
valerian root. **Nytol Natural Source.**
Valisone-G (Schering). *betamethasone valerate/gentamicin sulfate.*
Valisone Scalp (Schering). *betamethasone valerate.*
Valium Roche Injection (Roche). *diazepam.*
Valium Roche Oral (Roche). *diazepam.*
valproic acid. **Alti-Valproic,** Apo-Valproic, **Depakene, Deproic, Epiject I.V., Gen-Valproic, Novo-Valproic, PMS-Valproic Acid, PMS-Valproic Acid E.C.**
†Valrelease. *diazepam.*
valsartan. **Diovan.**
Valtrex (Glaxo Wellcome). *valacyclovir hydrochloride.*
Vamin 18 Electrolyte-Free (Pharmacia & Upjohn). *amino acids.*
Vamin N (Pharmacia & Upjohn). *amino acids/electrolytes.*
Vancenase (Schering). *beclomethasone dipropionate.*
Vanceril (Schering). *beclomethasone dipropionate.*
Vancocin (Lilly). *vancomycin hydrochloride.*
†Vancoled. *vancomycin hydrochloride.*
vancomycin hydrochloride. **Vancocin.** †Lyphocin, †Vancoled.
Vanquin (Warner-Lambert Consumer Healthcare). *pyrvinium pamoate.*
†Vansil. *oxamniquine.*
†Vantin. *cefpodoxime proxetil.*
Vaponefrin (Rhône-Poulenc Rorer). *epinephrine hydrochloride.*
Vaqta (MSD). *hepatitis A vaccine, purified inactivated.*
†Vascor. *bepridil hydrochloride.*
Vaseretic (Frosst). *enalapril maleate/hydrochlorothiazide.*
Vasocidin (CIBA Vision). *prednisolone sodium phosphate/sulfacetamide sodium.*
Vasocon (CIBA Vision). *naphazoline hydrochloride.*
Vasocon-A (CIBA Vision). *antazoline phosphate/naphazoline hydrochloride.*
†Vasodilan. *isoxsuprine hydrochloride.*
vasopressin. **Pressyn; (Pharmaceutical Parnters).**
Vasotec (Frosst). *enalapril maleate.*
Vasotec I.V. (Frosst). *enalaprilat.*
Vasoxyl (Glaxo Wellcome). *methoxamine hydrochloride.*
Vaxigrip (Connaught). *influenza virus vaccine trivalent types A and B (split-virion), inactivated.*
vecuronium bromide. **Norcuron.**
†Veetids. *penicillin V potassium.*
†Velban. *vinblastine sulfate.*
Velbe (Lilly). *vinblastine sulfate.*
†Velsar. *vinblastine sulfate.*
venlafaxine hydrochloride. **Effexor, Effexor XR.**
Ventodisk Disk/Diskhaler (Glaxo Wellcome). *salbutamol sulfate.*
Ventolin Inhalation Aerosol/Oral Liquid (Glaxo Wellcome). *salbutamol.*
Ventolin Injection (Glaxo Wellcome). *salbutamol sulfate.*
Ventolin Nebules P.F./Respirator Solution (Glaxo Wellcome). *salbutamol sulfate.*
Ventolin Rotacaps/Rotahaler (Glaxo Wellcome). *salbutamol sulfate.*
Vepesid (Bristol). *etoposide.*
verapamil hydrochloride. **Alti-Verapamil, Apo-Verap, Chronovera, Gen-Verapamil SR, Isoptin, Isoptin I.V., Isoptin SR, Novo-Veramil, Novo-Veramil SR, Nu-Verap, Verelan; (Abbott).** †Calan.
verapamil hydrochloride/trandolapril. **Tarka.**
Verelan (Wyeth-Ayerst). *verapamil hydrochloride.*
Vermox (Janssen-Ortho). *mebendazole.*
Versed (Roche). *midazolam hydrochloride.*
Versel (TCD). *selenium sulfide.*
Vesanoid (Roche). *tretinoin.*
†Vesprin. *triflupromazine hydrochloride.*
Vexol (Alcon). *rimexolone.*
Viaderm-K.C. (Taro). *gramicidin/neomycin sulfate/nystatin/triamcinolone acetonide.*
†Viagra. *sildenafil citrate.*
Viaspan (DuPont Pharma). *cold storage solution.*
Vibra-Tabs (Pfizer). *doxycycline hyclate.*
Vibra-Tabs C-Pak (Pfizer). *doxycycline hyclate.*
Videx (Bristol). *didanosine.*
Vifenal (Alcon). *diclofenac sodium.*
vigabatrin. **Sabril.**
vinblastine sulfate. **Velbe; (Faulding).** †Velban, †Velsar.
†Vincasar PFS. *vincristine sulfate.*
†Vincrex. *vincristine sulfate.*
vincristine sulfate. **(Faulding), (Novopharm).** †Vincasar PFS, †Vincrex.
vindesine sulfate. **Eldisine.**
vinorelbine tartrate. **Navelbine.**
Vioform (Novartis Pharmaceuticals). *clioquinol.*
Vioform Hydrocortisone (Novartis Pharmaceuticals). *clioquinol/hydrocortisone.*
Viokase (Axcan Pharma). *pancrelipase.*
Viprinex (Knoll). *ancrod.*
viprynium pamoate. see pyrvinium pamoate.
Viquin Forte (ICN). *glycolic acid/hydroquinone.*
Viramune (Boehringer Ingelheim). *nevirapine.*
Virazole (Lyophilized) (ICN). *ribavirin.*

†Virilon. *methyltestosterone.*
†Virilon IM. *testosterone cypionate.*
Viroptic (Glaxo Wellcome). *trifluridine.*
Visipaque (Nycomed Imaging A.S.). *iodixanol.*
Viskazide (Novartis Pharmaceuticals). *hydrochlorothiazide/pindolol.*
Visken (Novartis Pharmaceuticals). *pindolol.*
†Vistaril. *hydroxyzine pamoate.*
†Vistazine 50. *hydroxyzine hydrochloride.*
†VitaCarn. *levocarnitine.*
vitamin A. retinol. **[Vitamin A, General Monograph, CPhA].**
Vitamin A Acid (Dermik Laboratories Canada). *tretinoin.*
vitamin B_1. see thiamine hydrochloride.
vitamin B_2. see riboflavin.
Vitamin B_3. see niacin.
vitamin B_5. see pantothenic acid.
vitamin B_6. see pyridoxine hydrochloride.
vitamin B_{12}. see cyanocobalamin.
vitamin B_{12a}. see hydroxocobalamin.
vitamin B compound. **Hi Potency B-Compound "50", Penta/3B, Vita 3B.**
vitamin B compound/ascorbic acid/magnesium carbonate/magnesium sulfate. **Redoxon-B.**
vitamin B compound/ascorbic acid. **Beminal with C Fortis, Penta/3B + C, Vita 3B + C.**
vitamin B compound/ascorbic acid/selenium/vitamin E/zinc. **Stresstabs Plus.**
vitamin B compound/beef serum proteins/iron/liver extract. **Hormodausse.**
vitamin B compound/pipradrol. **Alertonic.**
vitamin C. see ascorbic acid.
vitamin D. see alfacalcidol.
vitamin D. see calcifediol.
vitamin D. see calcitriol.
vitamin D. see dihydrotachysterol.
vitamin D_2. see ergocalciferol.
vitamin D_3. see cholecalciferol.
vitamin D/ascorbic acid/calcium carbonate/pyridoxine hydrochloride. **Redoxon-Cal.**
vitamin D/ascorbic acid/minerals. **Cal-Mag.**
vitamin D/calcium carbonate. **Calcite D 500, Calcium D 500, Caltrate 600 + Vitamin D.**
vitamin D/calcium carbonate/copper/magnesium/manganese/zinc. **Caltrate Plus.**
vitamin E. tocofersolan. α-tocopheryl. **[Vitamin E, General Monograph, CPhA]; Aquasol E, Aquasol E TPGS, Webber Vitamin E; (Swiss Herbal).**
vitamin E/ascorbic acid/selenium/vitamin B compound/zinc. **Stresstabs Plus.**
vitamin G. see riboflavin.
vitamin K_1. see phytonadione.
vitamin K_1. see menadiol sodium diphosphate.
Vitathion-A.T.P. (Servier). *ascorbic acid/inositol/thiamine.*
Vita 3B (Riva). *vitamin B compound.*
Vita 3B + C (Riva). *ascorbic acid/vitamin B compound.*
Vitinoin (Pharmascience). *tretinoin.*
†Vivactil. *protriptyline hydrochloride.*
Vivelle (Novartis Pharmaceuticals). *estradiol-17β.*
Vivol (Carter Horner). *diazepam.*
Vivonex Pediatric (Novartis Nutrition). *enteral nutrition.*
Vivonex Plus (Novartis Nutrition). *enteral nutrition.*
Vivonex T.E.N. (Novartis Nutrition). *enteral nutrition.*
Vivotif Berna (Berna Products). *typhoid vaccine (live oral attenuated Ty21a).*
Vivotif Berna L (Berna Products). *typhoid vaccine (live oral attenuated Ty21a).*
Voltaren (Novartis Pharmaceuticals). *diclofenac sodium.*
Voltaren Ophtha (CIBA Vision). *diclofenac sodium.*
Voltaren Rapide (Novartis Pharmaceuticals). *diclofenac potassium.*
†Vontrol. *diphenidol hydrochloride.*
VōSoL (Carter Horner). *acetic acid/benzethonium chloride/1,2-propanediol diacetate.*
VōSoL HC (Carter Horner). *acetic acid/benzethonium chloride/hydrocortisone/1,2-propanediol diacetate.*
Vumon (Bristol). *teniposide.*
†V.V.S. *sulfabenzamide/sulfacetamide/sulfathiazole.*

W

warfarin sodium. **Coumadin, Warfilone.** †Panwarin, †Sofarin.
Warfilone (Frosst). *warfarin sodium.*
Wartec (Pharmascience). *podofilox.*
Webber Calcium Carbonate (Novartis Consumer Health). *calcium carbonate.*
Webber Vitamin E (Novartis Consumer Health). *vitamin E.*
†Wehless. *phendimetrazine tartrate.*
Wellbutrin SR (Glaxo Wellcome). *bupropion hydrochloride.*
†Wellcovorin. *calcium folinate.*
Wellferon (Glaxo Wellcome). *interferon alpha-n1 (lns).*
Westcort (Westwood-Squibb). *hydrocortisone-17-valerate.*
white petrolatum/lanolin alcohols/mineral oil. **Lacri-Lube S.O.P.**
white petrolatum/lanolin/mineral oil. **Duratears.**
white petrolatum/mineral oil. **Hypotears Eye Ointment.**
Winpred (ICN). *prednisone.*
WinRho SDF (Cangene). *immune globulin, Rh_o (D) (human).*
†Wolfina. *rauwolfia serpentina.*
Wydase (Wyeth-Ayerst). *hyaluronidase.*
†Wymox. *amoxicillin trihydrate.*
†Wytensin. *guanabenz acetate.*

X

Xalatan (Pharmacia & Upjohn). *latanoprost.*
Xanax (Pharmacia & Upjohn). *alprazolam.*
Xanax TS (Pharmacia & Upjohn). *alprazolam.*
X-Prep (Purdue Frederick). *sennosides.*
X-Tar (Dormer). *coal tar/menthol/salicylic acid.*
Xylocaine CO_2 (Astra). *lidocaine hydrocarbonate.*
Xylocaine Dental Ointment 5% (Astra). *lidocaine.*
Xylocaine Dental Solutions (Astra). *epinephrine/lidocaine hydrochloride.*
Xylocaine Endotracheal (Astra). *lidocaine hydrochloride.*
Xylocaine 4% Sterile Solution (Astra). *lidocaine hydrochloride.*
Xylocaine Jelly 2% (Astra). *lidocaine hydrochloride.*
Xylocaine Ointment 5% (Astra). *lidocaine.*
Xylocaine Parenteral with Epinephrine (Astra). *epinephrine/lidocaine hydrochloride.*

Names **underlined** have complete prescribing information in the *CPS* Monograph Section.

Xylocaine Parenteral without Epinephrine (Astra). *lidocaine hydrochloride.*

Xylocaine Spinal 5% (Astra). *glucose/lidocaine hydrochloride.*

Xylocaine Topical 4% (Astra). *lidocaine hydrochloride.*

Xylocaine Topical 5% (Astra). *lidocaine.*

Xylocaine Viscous 2% (Astra). *lidocaine hydrochloride.*

Xylocard (Astra). *lidocaine hydrochloride.*

xylometazoline hydrochloride. **Decongest, Otrivin.**

xylometazoline hydrochloride/antazoline sulfate. **Ophtrivin-A.**

Y

yeast/shark liver oil. **Preparation H Cream/Ointment/ Suppositories.**

yellow fever vaccine (live 17D virus). **(Connaught).**

Yocon (Glenwood). *yohimbine hydrochloride.*

†Yodoquinol. *iodoquinol.*

yohimbine hydrochloride. **PMS-Yohimbine, Yocon; (Odan), (Rougier), (Tanta), (Welcker-Lyster).** †Actibine, †Aphrodyne, †Yohimex.

†Yohimex. *yohimbine hydrochloride.*

Yutopar (Bristol). *ritodrine hydrochloride.*

Z

Zaditen (Novartis Pharmaceuticals). *ketotifen fumarate.*

zafirlukast. **Accolate.**

zalcitabine. ddC. **Hivid.**

Zanosar (Pharmacia & Upjohn). *streptozocin.*

Zantac (Glaxo Wellcome). *ranitidine hydrochloride.*

Zantac-75 (Glaxo Wellcome). *ranitidine hydrochloride.*

†Zantryl. *phentermine hydrochloride.*

Zarontin (Parke-Davis). *ethosuximide.*

Zaroxolyn (Rhône-Poulenc Rorer). *metolazone.*

Z-BEC (Whitehall-Robins). *multiple vitamins/zinc sulfate.*

ZeaSORB (Stiefel). *aluminum dihydroxyallantoinate/cellulose/ chloroxylenol.*

ZeaSORB AF (Stiefel). *tolnaftate.*

†Zebeta. *bisoprolol fumarate.*

†Zefazone. *cefmetazole sodium.*

Zemuron (Organon). *rocuronium bromide.*

Zephiran (Sanofi). *benzalkonium chloride.*

Zerit (Bristol-Myers Squibb). *stavudine.*

Zestoretic (Zeneca). *hydrochlorothiazide/lisinopril.*

Zestril (Zeneca). *lisinopril.*

Zetar (Dermik Laboratories Canada). *coal tar.*

†Zetran. *diazepam.*

†Ziac. *bisoprolol fumarate/hydrochlorothiazide.*

zidovudine. azidothymidine. AZT. **Apo-Zidovudine, Novo-AZT, Retrovir (AZT).**

Zilactin (Zila Pharmaceuticals). *benzyl alcohol.*

Zilactin-B (Zila Pharmaceuticals). *benzocaine.*

Zilactin Baby (Zila Pharmaceuticals). *benzocaine.*

Zilactin-L (Zila Pharmaceuticals). *lidocaine.*

Zilactin-Lip (Zila Pharmaceuticals). *dimethicone/homosalate/ menthol/octyl methoxycinnamate/oxybenzone.*

Zinacef (Glaxo Wellcome). *cefuroxime sodium.*

zinc/ascorbic acid/selenium/vitamin B compound/vitamin E. **Stresstabs Plus.**

zinc bacitracin. see bacitracin zinc.

zinc/calcium carbonate/copper/magnesium/manganese/vitamin D. **Caltrate Plus.**

Zincfrin (Alcon). *phenylephrine hydrochloride/zinc sulfate.*

Zincfrin-A (Alcon). *antazoline phosphate/naphazoline hydrochloride/zinc sulfate.*

zinc gluconate/cobalt gluconate/nickel gluconate. **Oligosol, Zinc-Nickel-Cobalt.**

zinc hydroxide/cosyntropin. **Synacthen Depot.**

Zincofax (Warner-Lambert Consumer Healthcare). *zinc oxide.*

zinc oxide. **Baby's Own Ointment, Prevex Baby Diaper Rash, Zincofax.**

zinc oxide/cupric oxide/multiple vitamins. **Stresstabs with Zinc.**

zinc oxide/multiple vitamins. **Adeks Tablets.**

zinc pyrithione. **Dan-Gard, Sebulon, ZNP.**

zinc pyrithione/coal tar/juniper tar/pine tar. **Multi-Tar Plus.**

zinc pyrithione/menthol. **Z-Plus.**

zinc sulfate. **PMS-Egozinc.**

zinc sulfate/antazoline phosphate/naphazoline hydrochloride. **Zincfrin-A.**

zinc sulfate/heparin sodium. **Lipactin.**

zinc sulfate monohydrate. **Anusol, Anuzinc, Rivasol.**

zinc sulfate monohydrate/benzocaine. **Rectogel.**

zinc sulfate monohydrate/benzocaine/hydrocortisone acetate. **Rectogel HC.**

zinc sulfate monohydrate/hydrocortisone acetate. **Anodan-HC, Anusol-HC, Hemcort HC, PMS-Egozinc-HC, Rivasol HC.**

zinc sulfate monohydrate/hydrocortisone acetate/pramoxine hydrochloride. **Anugesic-HC, Proctodan-HC.**

zinc sulfate monohydrate/pramoxine hydrochloride. **Anusol Plus.**

zinc sulfate/multiple vitamins. **Adeks Pediatric Drops, Z-BEC.**

zinc sulfate/phenylephrine hydrochloride. **Zincfrin.**

zinc undecylenate/undecylenic acid. **Desenex.**

Zinecard (Pharmacia & Upjohn). *dexrazoxane.*

Zithromax (Pfizer). *azithromycin dihydrate.*

ZNP (Stiefel). *zinc pyrithione.*

Zocor (Frosst). *simvastatin.*

Zofran (Glaxo Wellcome). *ondansetron hydrochloride dihydrate.*

Zoladex (Zeneca). *goserelin acetate.*

Zoladex LA (Zeneca). *goserelin acetate.*

zolmitriptan. Zomig.

zolmitriptan. †Zomig.

Zoloft (Pfizer). *sertraline hydrochloride.*

zolpidem. †Ambien.

Zomig (Zeneca). *zolmitriptan.*

†Zomig. *zolmitriptan.*

Zonalon (Medicis). *doxepin hydrochloride.*

zopiclone. **Apo-Zopiclone, Imovane, Nu-Zopiclone, Rhovane.**

Zostrix (Medicis). *capsaicin.*

Zostrix H.P. (Medicis). *capsaicin.*

Zovirax Cream (Glaxo Wellcome). *acyclovir.*

Zovirax for Injection (Glaxo Wellcome). *acyclovir sodium.*

Zovirax Ointment (Glaxo Wellcome). *acyclovir.*

Zovirax Oral (Glaxo Wellcome). *acyclovir.*

Z-Plus (Dormer). *menthol/zinc pyrithione.*

zuclopenthixol acetate. **Clopixol-Acuphase.**

zuclopenthixol decanoate. **Clopixol Depot.**

zuclopenthixol dihydrochloride. **Clopixol.**

Zyban (Glaxo Wellcome). *bupropion hydrochloride.*
Zyloprim (Glaxo Wellcome). *allopurinol.*
Zyprexa (Lilly). *olanzapine.*
Zyrtec (UCB Pharma). *cetirizine hydrochloride.*

Names **underlined** have complete prescribing information in the *CPS* Monograph Section.

Compliments of:

MERCK FROSST

Discovering today for a better tomorrow.

When Charles Frosst, together with four associates and five thousand dollars, founded Charles E. Frosst & Co. in 1899, the Canadian pharmaceutical industry was still in its infancy. Right from the start, Frosst and his associates made it clear that their company was an innovator, rapidly introducing new products such as the famous numbered analgesics 222® (acetylsalicylic acid, codeine phosphate, caffeine tablets, USP) and N292® [acetylsalicylic acid 375mg, codeine phosphate 30mg and caffeine 15mg (from caffeine citrate), USP] - products that are still used in Canada. During the 1920s, the company became family-owned, and as it grew, it consolidated its reputation for innovation. Two of Frosst's former associates, William S. Ayerst and Frank W. Horner both went on to found other Canadian pharmaceutical companies. During the mid-Forties, Charles E. Frosst pioneered nuclear medicine in Canada by developing the country's first radio-active pharmaceutical products, for sale here and abroad. In 1965, Charles E. Frosst joined Merck & Co., Inc. of New Jersey.

The Merck family has its roots in 1668 in Darmstadt, Germany — roots that were transplanted to the New World by George Merck in 1891. The union of the two companies was logical: Merck had a branch in Montreal dating to 1911, at first as an importer and seller of pharmaceuticals and fine chemicals, and by 1930 as a manufacturer. More significantly, Merck was following the same path of innovation and discovery as its Canadian colleagues. The company was producing vitamin B1 in 1940, and penicillin by 1944, in the Commonwealth's first deep fermentation unit. Innovations followed at a rapid pace. Merck's pursuit of vitamin research led to discoveries in sulfa drugs, penicillins and corticosteroids. Its pioneering work in nuclear medicine began with a request from the National Research Council for the production of specialty compounds to be used as tracers in the study of chemicals and biological processes. In 1955, Merck merged with another manufacturer of drugs, Toronto-based Sharp & Dohme. With its headquarters in Montreal, the new company became known in 1961 as Merck Sharp & Dohme Canada Limited.

The stage was thus set for the latest chapter in a long and distinguished history, beginning with the 1965 acquisition of Charles E. Frosst & Co. by Merck & Co., Inc.

In 1968, Merck Frosst Laboratories was created to act as the service company to the two sales companies: Merck Sharp & Dohme Canada Limited and Charles E. Frosst & Co. In 1982, the three companies were restructured under the name Merck Frosst Canada Inc. and became a fully integrated pharmaceutical company that has grown and evolved into what it is today.

® Trademarks of Merck Frosst Canada Inc.

See inside

Driven by Research Excellence

Merck Frosst's roots are planted deep in the history of Canadian scientific research. This is both a historic fact and an enduring facet of the company's operations.

In the 1970s, researchers at Merck Frosst were responsible for the discovery of PrBLOCADREN® (timolol maleate tablets, Frosst Std.), which was the first and only beta-adrenergic blocking agent discovered in Canada and PrFLEXERIL® (cyclobenzaprine hychloride tablets, Frosst Std.), a muscle relaxant. Clinical trials of timolol maleate revealed that the compound had another therapeutic property. It was found to relieve elevated intraocular pressure. For millions of people around the world suffering from glaucoma, a leading cause of blindness, timolol maleate was the first breakthrough in treatment in almost half a century.

Today, the Merck Frosst Centre for Therapeutic Research is Canada's largest biomedical research facility and houses one of the fully integrated pharmaceutical research centres in the country. The Centre employs more than 225 world-class scientists who continue the company's long tradition of Canadian research excellence. The clinical research department employs more than 60 additional research professionals. The Centre's mandate is to discover novel therapies for the treatment of respiratory, inflammatory and other diseases. The Centre's researchers have spearheaded the assault on bronchial asthma with the development of a medication in a new class of therapies called leukotriene receptor antagonists. PrSINGULAIR™ (montelukast sodium) is the first asthma treatment advance in more than 20 years. More recently, progress has been made in a special program to develop new anti-inflammatory therapies, safer than current non-steroidal anti-inflammatory drugs (NSAIDs) for the treatment of osteoarthritis and rheumatoid arthritis. Another important research program currently underway arose from a Merck Frosst discovery of a series of novel cysteine proteases involved in apoptosis (programmed cell death). Regulation of this key process in the body may have important therapeutic applications in a number of diseases including cancer, neurodegenerative, stroke and cardiovascular diseases. In 1997, Merck Frosst invested over $80 million in research and development programs.

Dedicated to Quality

The Merck Manufacturing Division (MMD) employs more than 350 people. The Division manufactures tablets, capsules and liquids, sterile injectable medicines and radio-labeled pharmaceutical products. MMD manufactures more than 150 products in 290 salable sizes. Since 1992, Merck Frosst has invested more than $112 million to expand and modernize its manufacturing division. These projects demonstrate the company's continuous commitment to innovation. They result in a world-class state-of-the-art pharmaceutical manufacturing facility and position Merck Frosst as a producer of medicines for domestic and global markets.

Exercising Our Responsibility

Merck Frosst fulfills its corporate responsibility in areas that it knows best, and where it can thereby do the greatest good. Chief among these is its encouragement of medical and pharmaceutical research in Canadian universities, hospitals and other institutions; its participation in programs aimed at increasing the quality and cost-effectiveness of Canadian health care; and its support of general scientific education for young people. Similarly, the company participates in two of the federally sponsored Networks of Centres of Excellence, focused on genetic research and protein engineering.

Committed to Health Care

Although the Company's primary mission is to develop new medicines, Merck Frosst is committed to being a partner in health care. The company actively works with academia, the medical community, patients, the private sector, key stakeholders and governments across Canada to identify new ways to improve the quality and cost-effectiveness of patient care, as well as to develop and recommend effective health-care policy for Canadians.

The People of Merck Frosst

Merck Frosst is respected for its leadership by its peers and the health-care community it serves. At the same time, it recognizes that its reputation is earned and maintained through the hard work of the people it employs. This is why Merck Frosst directs so many resources to recruiting the best professionals in their field — people who are imbued with the spirit of excellence that prevails at Merck Frosst.

The Dingbats© - 1999 series

MERCK FROSST
Merck Frosst Canada Inc., Kirkland, Quebec

Printed in Canada / Imprimé au Canada

Recycled paper with 10% post-consumer waste fibre

Recyclable

THERAPEUTIC GUIDE

The Therapeutic Guide has been adapted from the Canadian version of the World Health Organization's Anatomical Therapeutic Chemical (ATC) Classification Index[1] to provide a practical clinical guide for the use of single entity drugs listed in the *CPS*.

HOW TO USE THE THERAPEUTIC GUIDE

Drugs found in this Guide are listed under several alphabetically arranged Therapeutic Categories (e.g., antihypertensives, cardiac therapy, diuretics, lipid lowering agents, etc.). Drugs are further classified under specific therapeutic, pharmacologic or chemical subheadings within a Therapeutic Category.

Drugs may be classified under more than one section if used for more than one indication. For example, some beta-blockers can be found under Cardiac Therapy and Antihypertensives. Cross references listed under a Therapeutic Category will refer users to other Therapeutic Categories where a drug is also listed.

Combinations of drugs are usually not listed, with a few exceptions (e.g., oral contraceptives).

To find the brand name of a drug, *CPS* users will have to consult the Brand and Generic Name Index (Green Section).

This guide is not intended to be exhaustive; a drug entity may not be listed under each approved indication. Users must exercise professional judgment when consulting the Therapeutic Guide. For further information on drugs listed in the Guide, readers are encouraged to consult the *CPS* product monographs.

References:
1. Patented Medicine Prices Review Board (PMPRB). ATC Classification System For Human Medicines (Canada). Ottawa, ON: PMPRB. 1995.

THERAPEUTIC GUIDE INDEX

Acne Therapy

Systemic

Antiandrogen/Estrogen Combination
cyproterone acetate/ethinyl estradiol

Antibiotics
erythromycin
erythromycin estolate
minocycline hydrochloride
tetracycline hydrochloride

Retinoids
isotretinoin

Topical

Antibiotics
clindamycin phosphate
erythromycin

Corticosteroids
methylprednisolone acetate

Peroxides
benzoyl peroxide

Retinoids
tazarotene
tretinoin

Sulfur Containing Preparations
sulfur

Various Acne Preparations for Topical Use
adapalene
aluminum oxide
povidone-iodine
salicylic acid
triclosan

Adrenocortical Agents

see also Anti-inflammatory Agents, Topical; Antipruritics; Asthma Therapy; Gout and Hyperuricemia Therapy; Immunosuppressive Agents; Nasal Preparations; Ophthalmologicals; Rheumatic Disease Therapy

Adrenal Steroid Inhibitors
aminoglutethimide

Corticosteroids, Systemic

Glucocorticoids
betamethasone sodium phosphate
cortisone acetate
dexamethasone
dexamethasone sodium phosphate
hydrocortisone
hydrocortisone sodium succinate
methylprednisolone
methylprednisolone acetate
methylprednisolone sodium succinate
prednisolone sodium phosphate
prednisone
triamcinolone
triamcinolone acetonide
triamcinolone diacetate

Mineralocorticoids
fludrocortisone acetate

Alcoholism Therapy

disulfiram
naltrexone hydrochloride

Allergy Therapy

see also Adrenocortical Agents; Anti-inflammatory Agents, Topical; Antipruritics; Nasal Preparations; Ophthalmologicals

Anaphylaxis Therapy
epinephrine

Antihistamines

Alkylamines
brompheniramine maleate
chlorpheniramine maleate
dexchlorpheniramine maleate

Ethanolamines
clemastine hydrogen fumarate
diphenhydramine hydrochloride

Ethylenediamines
tripelennamine hydrochloride

Phenothiazine Derivatives
promethazine hydrochloride
trimeprazine tartrate

Piperazine Derivatives
cetirizine hydrochloride
cyclizine lactate
hydroxyzine hydrochloride
meclizine hydrochloride

Piperidine Derivatives
astemizole
azatadine maleate
cyproheptadine hydrochloride
loratadine
terfenadine

Gastrointestinal Allergy Therapy
sodium cromoglycate

Ragweed Allergic Rhinitis Therapy

Immunotherapy
ragweed vaccine

Alzheimer's Disease Therapy

Cholinesterase Inhibitors
donepezil hydrochloride

Analgesics

see also Gout and Hyperuricemia Therapy; Mouth Preparations and Dry Mouth Therapy; Rheumatic Disease Therapy

Antimigraine Preparations

Barbiturates
butalbital

Beta-Adrenergic Blocking Agents
propranolol hydrochloride

Calcium Channel Blocking Agents, Selective
flunarizine hydrochloride

Ergot Alkaloids
dihydroergotamine mesylate
ergotamine tartrate
methysergide maleate

Serotonin (5-HT$_{1D}$)-Agonists
naratriptan hydrochloride
sumatriptan hemisulfate
sumatriptan succinate

Various Antimigraine Preparations
feverfew
pizotifen

Neuralgia Therapy

Trigeminal Neuralgia
carbamazepine

Neuralgia Therapy, Topical
capsaicin

Nonsteroidal Anti-inflammatory Drugs (NSAIDs)

Acetic Acid Derivatives (including Indole Derivatives)
diclofenac potassium
diclofenac sodium
etodolac
indomethacin
ketorolac tromethamine
sulindac
tolmetin sodium

Fenamates
floctafenine
mefenamic acid

Oxicams
piroxicam
tenoxicam

Propionic Acid Derivatives
fenoprofen calcium
flurbiprofen
ibuprofen
ketoprofen
naproxen
naproxen sodium
oxaprozin
tiaprofenic acid

Salicylic Acid Derivatives
acetylsalicylic acid (ASA)
choline magnesium trisalicylate (choline salicylate/magnesium salicylate)
diflunisal
magnesium salicylate

Various Nonsteroidal Anti-inflammatory Agents
nabumetone

Opioids

Benzomorphan Derivatives
pentazocine hydrochloride
pentazocine lactate

Diphenylpropylamine Derivatives
propoxyphene hydrochloride
propoxyphene napsylate

Morphinan Derivatives
butorphanol tartrate
nalbuphine hydrochloride

Natural Opium Alkaloids
codeine phosphate
diamorphine hydrochloride
hydromorphone hydrochloride
morphine hydrochloride
morphine sulfate
oxycodone hydrochloride
oxymorphone hydrochloride

Phenylpiperidine Derivatives
alfentanil hydrochloride
anileridine
fentanyl citrate
pethidine hydrochloride
sufentanil citrate

Para-aminophenol Derivatives

Anilides
acetaminophen

Anemia Therapy

see also Minerals; Vitamins

Erythropoietic Growth Factors
epoetin alfa

Iron Preparations

Iron Bivalent, Oral Preparations
ferrous ascorbate
ferrous fumarate
ferrous gluconate
ferrous sulfate

Iron Complex, Parenteral Preparations
iron-dextran

Iron Trivalent, Parenteral Preparations
iron-sorbitol-citric acid complex

Vitamin B_{12} and Folic Acid

Folic Acid
folic acid

Vitamin B_{12} Derivatives
cyanocobalamin
hydroxocobalamin

Various Agents for Anemia

Androgenic-Anabolic Steroids
nandrolone decanoate
nandrolone phenpropionate

Anesthetics, General

Barbiturates
methohexital sodium
thiopental sodium

Halogenated Hydrocarbons
desflurane
enflurane
halothane
isoflurane
sevoflurane

Opioid Anesthetics
alfentanil hydrochloride
anileridine
fentanyl citrate
remifentanil hydrochloride
sufentanil citrate

Various General Anesthetics
ketamine hydrochloride
midazolam hydrochloride
propofol

Anesthetics, Local

see also Antipruritics; Mouth Preparations and Dry Mouth Therapy; Ophthalmologicals; Otologicals

Amides
articaine hydrochloride
bupivacaine hydrochloride
lidocaine
lidocaine hydrocarbonate
lidocaine hydrochloride
mepivacaine hydrochloride
prilocaine hydrochloride
ropivacaine hydrochloride

Esters of Amino Benzoic Acid
benzocaine
chloroprocaine hydrochloride
cocaine hydrochloride
procaine hydrochloride
tetracaine
tetracaine hydrochloride

Antacids

see also Peptic Ulcer Therapy; Reflux Therapy

Aluminum Containing Preparations
aluminum hydroxide

Aluminum/Magnesium Containing Preparations
aluminum hydroxide/magnesium hydroxide
magaldrate

Calcium Containing Preparations
calcium carbonate

Magnesium Containing Preparations
magnesium carbonate
magnesium hydroxide

Anthelmintics

Piperazine Derivatives
piperazine

Pyrimidine Derivatives
pyrantel pamoate

Various Anthelmintics
mebendazole
praziquantel
pyrvinium pamoate
thiabendazole

Antibacterials

see also Acne Therapy; Antidiarrheal and Anti-infective Agents; Antiprotozoals; Antituberculosis Agents; Medicated Dressings; Ophthalmologicals; Otologicals; Urinary Tract Agents; Vaginal Preparations

Antibiotics

Aminoglycosides
amikacin sulfate
gentamicin sulfate
netilmicin sulfate
paromomycin sulfate
streptomycin sulfate
tobramycin sulfate

Carbapenems
imipenem/cilastatin sodium
meropenem

Cephalosporins, 1st Generation
cefadroxil
cefazolin sodium
cephalexin
cephalothin sodium

Cephalosporins, 2nd Generation
cefaclor
cefamandole nafate
cefotetan disodium
cefoxitin sodium
cefprozil
cefuroxime axetil
cefuroxime sodium

Cephalosporins, 3rd Generation
cefixime
cefotaxime sodium
ceftazidime
ceftazidime pentahydrate
ceftizoxime sodium
ceftriaxone sodium

Cephalosporins, 4th Generation
cefepime hydrochloride

Fluoroquinolones
ciprofloxacin
ciprofloxacin hydrochloride
grepafloxacin hydrochloride
levofloxacin
norfloxacin
ofloxacin

Glycopeptides
vancomycin hydrochloride

Lincosamides
clindamycin hydrochloride
clindamycin palmitate hydrochloride
clindamycin phosphate
lincomycin hydrochloride monohydrate

Macrolides
azithromycin dihydrate
clarithromycin
erythromycin
erythromycin estolate
erythromycin ethylsuccinate
erythromycin gluceptate
erythromycin lactobionate
erythromycin stearate
spiramycin

Penicillins, Aminopenicillins
amoxicillin
amoxicillin trihydrate
ampicillin
ampicillin sodium
ampicillin trihydrate
bacampicillin hydrochloride
pivampicillin
pivmecillinam hydrochloride

Penicillins, Antipseudomonal
piperacillin sodium
ticarcillin disodium

Penicillins, Penicillinase Sensitive
penicillin G benzathine
penicillin G potassium
penicillin G sodium
phenoxymethyl penicillin
phenoxymethyl penicillin benzathine
phenoxymethyl penicillin potassium

Penicillins, Penicillinase Resistant
cloxacillin sodium

Penicillins, β-lactamase Inhibitor Combinations
amoxicillin/potassium clavulanate
piperacillin sodium/tazobactam sodium
potassium clavulanate/ticarcillin disodium

Sulfonamides
sulfamethoxazole
sulfapyridine

Sulfonamide Combinations
co-trimazine (sulfadiazine/trimethoprim)
co-trimoxazole (sulfamethoxazole/trimethoprim)
erythromycin ethylsuccinate/sulfisoxazole

Trimethoprim and Derivatives
trimethoprim

Tetracyclines
demeclocycline hydrochloride
doxycycline hyclate
minocycline hydrochloride
tetracycline hydrochloride

Various Antibacterials
bacitracin
chloramphenicol
colistimethate sodium
fusidic acid
metronidazole
polymyxin B sulfate
rifabutin
sodium fusidate

Antibacterials, Topical
bacitracin
bacitracin zinc
chloramphenicol
chlorhexidine acetate
chlorhexidine gluconate
chlortetracycline hydrochloride
clioquinol
framycetin sulfate
fusidic acid

gentamicin sulfate
mupirocin
neomycin sulfate
polymyxin B sulfate
silver sulfadiazine
sodium fusidate
tetracycline hydrochloride

Anticoagulants

Heparins, Standard
heparin sodium

Heparins, Low Molecular Weight (LMWH)
dalteparin sodium
enoxaparin sodium
nadroparin calcium
tinzaparin sodium

Heparinoids
danaparoid sodium

Vitamin K Antagonists
nicoumalone
warfarin sodium

Various Anticoagulants
ancrod
antithrombin III (human)

Anticonvulsants

see also Anxiolytics; Hypnotics and Sedatives

Barbiturates and Derivatives
phenobarbital
primidone

Benzodiazepines
clobazam
clonazepam
diazepam
lorazepam
nitrazepam

Carboxylic Acid Derivatives
divalproex sodium
valproic acid

Gamma Aminobutyric Acid (GABA) Derivatives
gabapentin
vigabatrin

Hydantoin Derivatives
fosphenytoin sodium
phenytoin
phenytoin sodium

Iminostilbene Derivatives
carbamazepine

Succinimide Derivatives
ethosuximide
methsuximide

Various Anticonvulsants
lamotrigine
magnesium sulfate
paraldehyde
topiramate

Antidepressants

see also Antiobsessional Agents; Antipanic Agents; Eating Disorders; Urinary Tract Agents

Monoamine Oxidase (MAO) Inhibitors, Nonselective (Types A, B)
phenelzine sulfate
tranylcypromine sulfate

Monoamine Oxidase (MAO) Inhibitors, Selective (Type A)
moclobemide

Nonselective Monoamine Reuptake Inhibitors
amitriptyline hydrochloride
amoxapine
clomipramine hydrochloride
desipramine hydrochloride
doxepin hydrochloride
imipramine hydrochloride
maprotiline hydrochloride
nortriptyline hydrochloride
protriptyline hydrochloride
trimipramine maleate

Selective Serotonin Reuptake Inhibitors (SSRIs)
fluoxetine hydrochloride
fluvoxamine maleate
paroxetine hydrochloride
sertraline hydrochloride

Serotonin-Norepinephrine Reuptake Inhibitors
venlafaxine hydrochloride

Various Antidepressants
bupropion hydrochloride
nefazodone hydrochloride
trazodone hydrochloride
l tryptophan
venlafaxine hydrochloride

Antidiarrheal and Anti-infective Agents

see also Antibacterials; Antifungals

Antiperistaltics
diphenoxylate hydrochloride/atropine sulfate
loperamide hydrochloride

Flora Modifiers
lactobacillus acidophilus

Intestinal Adsorbents
attapulgite, activated
bismuth subsalicylate

Intestinal Anti-Infectives

Antibacterials
ciprofloxacin hydrochloride
co-trimoxazole (sulfamethoxazole/trimethoprim)
doxycycline hyclate
metronidazole
neomycin sulfate
vancomycin hydrochloride

Antifungals
nystatin

Antidotes

Acetaminophen Antidotes
acetylcysteine

Benzodiazepine Antagonists
flumazenil

Chelating Agents
calcium disodium edetate
deferoxamine mesylate

Cyanide Antidotes
amyl nitrite
sodium thiosulfate

Digoxin Antibodies
digoxin immune Fab (ovine)

Heparin Antagonists
protamine sulfate

Nonspecific Therapy for Overdoses

Adsorbents
activated charcoal

Emetics
ipecac

Opioid Antagonists
naloxone hydrochloride
naltrexone hydrochloride

Organic Phosphorus Insecticides Antidote

Cholinesterase Reactivators
pralidoxime chloride

Antiemetics and Antinauseants

see also Gastrointestinal Motility Agents; Reflux Therapy

Antihistamines
dimenhydrinate
hydroxyzine hydrochloride
promethazine hydrochloride

Anticholinergics
scopolamine

Cannabinoids
dronabinol
nabilone

Dopamine Antagonists
chlorpromazine hydrochloride
droperidol
metoclopramide hydrochloride
perphenazine
prochlorperazine
prochlorperazine mesylate
trifluoperazine hydrochloride

Serotonin ($5\text{-}HT_3$) Antagonists
dolasetron mesylate
granisetron hydrochloride
ondansetron hydrochloride dihydrate

Antiemetics and Antinauseants (Pregnancy)

doxylamine/pyridoxine

Antiflatulents

Coalescing Agents
simethicone

Antifungals

see also Antidiarrheal and Anti-infective Agents; Dermatological Preparations; Mouth Preparations and Dry Mouth Therapy; Vaginal Preparations

Antifungals, Systemic

Allylamines
terbinafine hydrochloride

Antifungal Antibiotics
amphotericin B
griseofulvin

Imidazoles
ketoconazole

Pyrimidines
flucytosine

Triazoles
fluconazole
itraconazole

Antifungals, Topical
see also Vaginal Preparations

Allylamines
naftifine hydrochloride
terbinafine hydrochloride

Antifungal Antibiotics
nystatin

Imidazoles
clotrimazole
econazole nitrate
ketoconazole
miconazole nitrate
oxiconazole nitrate
tioconazole

Various Antifungals for Topical Use
chlorphenesin
ciclopirox olamine
clioquinol
selenium sulfide
tolnaftate
undecylenic acid

Antihypertensives

see also Cardiac Therapy; Diuretics

Antiadrenergic Agents

Alpha₁-adrenergic Blocking Agents
doxazosin mesylate
prazosin hydrochloride
terazosin hydrochloride dihydrate

Alpha₁- and Alpha₂-adrenergic Blocking Agents
phentolamine mesylate

Alpha₁- and Beta-adrenergic Blocking Agents
labetalol hydrochloride

Beta-adrenergic Blocking Agents, Selective, Intrinsic Sympathomimetic Activity (ISA)
acebutolol hydrochloride

Beta-adrenergic Blocking Agents, Selective, Non-ISA
atenolol
esmolol hydrochloride
metoprolol tartrate

Beta-adrenergic Blocking Agents, Nonselective, ISA
oxprenolol hydrochloride
pindolol

Beta-adrenergic Blocking Agents, Nonselective, Non-ISA
nadolol
propranolol hydrochloride
timolol maleate

Centrally Acting Antiadrenergic Agents
clonidine hydrochloride
methyldopa
reserpine

Postganglionic Blocking Agents
guanethidine monosulfate

Arteriolar Smooth Muscle, Agents Acting on

Calcium Channel Blockers
amlodipine besylate
diltiazem hydrochloride
felodipine
nicardipine hydrochloride
nifedipine
verapamil hydrochloride

Vasodilators
diazoxide
epoprostenol sodium
hydralazine hydrochloride
minoxidil
nitroglycerin
sodium nitroprusside

Diuretics

Loop Diuretics
ethacrynate sodium
ethacrynic acid
furosemide
torsemide

Osmotic Diuretics
mannitol

Potassium Sparing Agents
amiloride hydrochloride
spironolactone
triamterene

Thiazides and Related Agents
chlorthalidone
hydrochlorothiazide
indapamide
indapamide hemihydrate
metolazone

Renin-Angiotensin System, Agents Acting on

Angiotensin Converting Enzyme (ACE) Inhibitors
benazepril hydrochloride
captopril
cilazapril
enalapril maleate
enalaprilat
fosinopril sodium
lisinopril
perindopril erbumine
quinapril hydrochloride
ramipril
trandolapril

Angiotensin II Receptor Antagonists
irbesartan
losartan potassium
valsartan

Anti-inflammatory Agents, Topical

see also Antipruritics; Asthma Therapy; Nasal Preparations; Ophthalmologicals

Corticosteroids, Topical

Corticosteroids, Weak (Group I)
hydrocortisone
hydrocortisone acetate
methylprednisolone
methylprednisolone acetate

Corticosteroids, Moderately Potent (Group II)
clobetasone 17-butyrate
desonide
flumethasone pivalate
hydrocortisone acetate
hydrocortisone 17-valerate
triamcinolone acetonide

Corticosteroids, Potent (Group III)
amcinonide
betamethasone benzoate
betamethasone dipropionate
betamethasone valerate
desoximetasone
diflucortolone valerate
fluocinolone acetonide
fluocinonide
mometasone furoate

Corticosteroids, Very Potent (Group IV)
clobetasol 17-propionate
halcinonide

Antineoplastics

see also Bladder Therapy, Local; Cancer Chemotherapy Toxicity, Prevention of; Immunostimulating Agents; Immunosuppressive Agents; Psoriasis Therapy; Rheumatic Disease Therapy

Alkylating Agents

Alkyl Sulphonates
busulfan

Ethylene Imines
thiotepa

Nitrogen Mustard Analogues
chlorambucil
cyclophosphamide
estramustine sodium phosphate
ifosfamide
mechlorethamine hydrochloride
melphalan

Nitrosoureas
carmustine
lomustine
streptozocin

Platinum-containing Compounds
carboplatin
cisplatin

Antimetabolites

Cytidine Analogues
gemcitabine hydrochloride

Folic Acid Analogues
methotrexate sodium
raltitrexed disodium

Purine Analogues
cladribine
mercaptopurine
thioguanine

Pyrimidine Analogues
cytarabine
fluorouracil

Urea Derivatives
hydroxyurea

Cytotoxic Antibiotics

Anthracyclines
daunorubicin
doxorubicin hydrochloride
epirubicin hydrochloride
idarubicin hydrochloride
liposomal daunorubicin

Actinomycins
dactinomycin

Various Cytotoxic Antibiotics
bleomycin sulfate
mitomycin
mitotane
mitoxantrone hydrochloride

Plant Alkaloids and other Natural Products

Camptothecin Derivatives
irinotecan hydrochloride

Epipodophyllotoxins
etoposide
teniposide

Taxanes
docetaxel
paclitaxel

Vinca Alkaloids and Analogues
vinblastine sulfate
vincristine sulfate
vindesine sulfate
vinorelbine tartrate

Various Antineoplastics
altretamine
amsacrine
l-asparaginase
dacarbazine
fludarabine phosphate
pegaspargase
porfimer sodium
procarbazine hydrochloride
topotecan hydrochloride
tretinoin (all-trans retinoic acid), systemic

Hormones
Estrogens
diethylstilbestrol sodium diphosphate

Gonadotropin Releasing Hormone Agonist Analogues
buserelin acetate
goserelin acetate
leuprolide acetate

Progestogens
medroxyprogesterone acetate
megestrol acetate

Hormone Antagonists
Adrenal Steroid Inhibitors
aminoglutethimide

Antiandrogens
bicalutamide
cyproterone acetate
flutamide
nilutamide

Antiestrogens
tamoxifen citrate

Nonsteroidal Aromatase Inhibitors
anastrozole
letrozole

Antiobsessional Agents
see also Antidepressants

Selective Serotonin Reuptake Inhibitors
fluoxetine hydrochloride
fluvoxamine maleate
paroxetine hydrochloride
sertraline hydrochloride

Tricyclic Derivatives
clomipramine hydrochloride

Antipanic Agents
see also Antidepressants; Anxiolytics

Benzodiazepines
alprazolam

Selective Serotonin Reuptake Inhibitors
paroxetine hydrochloride
sertraline

Antiparkinsonian Agents
Anticholinergic Agents
benztropine mesylate
biperiden hydrochloride
ethopropazine hydrochloride
orphenadrine hydrochloride
procyclidine hydrochloride
trihexyphenidyl hydrochloride

Catechol-O-Methyltransferase (COMT) Inhibitors
tolcapone

Dopaminergic Agents
Dopamine Agonists
bromocriptine mesylate
pergolide mesylate
pramipexole dihydrochloride
ropinirole hydrochloride

Dopamine Precursors
levodopa

Dopamine Precursors and Decarboxylase Inhibitors
levodopa/benserazide hydrochloride
levodopa/carbidopa

Monoamine Oxidase (MAO) Inhibitors, Selective (Type B)
selegiline hydrochloride

Various Dopaminergic Agents
amantadine hydrochloride

Antiprotozoals
see also Antibacterials

Amebicides
Aminoglycosides
paromomycin sulfate

8-Hydroxyquinoline Derivatives
iodoquinol

Nitroimidazole Derivatives
metronidazole

Antimalarials
Biguanides
proguanil

Cinchona Alkaloids
quinidine gluconate injection
quinine sulfate

Folic Acid Antagonists
pyrimethamine

Quinoline Derivatives
chloroquine phosphate
hydroxychloroquine sulfate
mefloquine hydrochloride
primaquine phosphate

Sulfonamide Combinations
sulfadoxine/pyrimethamine

Pneumocystis Carinii Therapy
atovaquone
co-trimoxazole (sulfamethoxazole/trimethoprim)
pentamidine isethionate
trimetrexate glucuronate

Various Antiprotozoals
halofantrine hydrochloride

Antipruritics
see also Adrenocortical Agents; Allergy Therapy; Anesthetics, Local; Anti-inflammatory Agents, Topical

Anesthetics, Topical
benzocaine
chloroprocaine hydrochloride
dibucaine hydrochloride
lidocaine hydrochloride
tetracaine
tetracaine hydrochloride

Antihistamines, Systemic
Alkylamines
brompheniramine maleate
chlorpheniramine maleate
dexchlorpheniramine maleate

Ethanolamines
clemastine fumarate
diphenhydramine hydrochloride

Ethylenediamines
tripelennamine hydrochloride

Phenothiazine Derivatives
promethazine hydrochloride
trimeprazine tartrate

Piperazine Derivatives
cetirizine hydrochloride
hydroxyzine hydrochloride

Piperidine Derivatives
astemizole
azatadine maleate
cyproheptadine hydrochloride
loratadine
terfenadine

Antihistamines, Topical
diphenhydramine
doxepin hyrochloride
promethazine

Various Antipruritics for Topical Use
crotamiton

Antipsychotics
Benzisoxazole Derivatives
risperidone

Butyrophenone Derivatives
droperidol
haloperidol
haloperidol decanoate

Dibenzodiazepine Derivatives
clozapine

Dibenzothiazepine Derivatives
quetiapine fumarate

Dibenzoxazepine Derivatives
loxapine

Diphenylbutylpiperidine Derivatives
fluspirilene
pimozide

Phenothiazines, Aliphatic
chlorpromazine hydrochloride
methotrimeprazine
promazine hydrochloride

Phenothiazines, Piperazine
fluphenazine decanoate
fluphenazine enanthate
fluphenazine hydrochloride
perphenazine
prochlorperazine
thioproperazine mesylate
trifluoperazine hydrochloride

Phenothiazines, Piperidine
mesoridazine besylate
pericyazine
pipotiazine palmitate
thioridazine hydrochloride

Thienobenzodiazepine Derivatives
olanzapine

Thioxanthene Derivatives
flupenthixol decanoate
flupenthixol dihydrochloride
thiothixene
zuclopenthixol acetate
zuclopenthixol decanoate
zuclopenthixol dihydrochloride

Various Antipsychotics
reserpine

Antiseptics

see also Mouth Preparations and Dry Mouth Therapy; Vaginal Preparations

Alcohols
ethyl alcohol
isopropyl alcohol

Biguanides and Amidines
chlorhexidine gluconate

Iodine Products
povidone-iodine

Phenol Derivatives
phenol
triclosan

Quaternary Ammonium Compounds
benzalkonium chloride
cetrimide

Antispasmodics

see also Urinary Tract Agents

Anticholinergic Agents

Natural Alkaloids, Tertiary Amines
atropine sulfate
hyoscine butylbromide
hyoscine hydrobromide
hyoscyamine sulfate

Synthetic Amines, Quaternary Ammonium Preparations
glycopyrrolate
pinaverium bromide
propantheline bromide

Synthetic Amines, Tertiary Amine Preparations
dicyclomine hydrochloride
oxybutynin chloride

Various Antispasmodics

Lower Gastrointestinal Tract Motility Regulators
trimebutine maleate

Antituberculosis Agents

see also Antibacterials

Aminosalicylic Acid Derivatives
para-aminosalicylate sodium (PAS sodium)

Antibiotics
cycloserine
rifampin
streptomycin sulfate

Hydrazides
isoniazid

Various Antituberculosis Agents
ethambutol hydrochloride
pyrazinamide

Combination Antituberculosis Agents
isoniazid/pyrazinamide/rifampin

Antivirals

Cyclic Amines
amantadine hydrochloride

Nucleosides
acyclovir
famciclovir
ganciclovir sodium
ribavirin
valacyclovir hydrochloride

Nucleoside Analogue Reverse Transcriptase Inhibitors (Antiretrovirals)
didanosine (ddI)
lamivudine (3TC)
stavudine (d4T)
zalcitabine (ddC)
zidovudine (AZT)

Protease Inhibitors
indinavir sulfate
ritonavir
saquinavir mesylate

Antivirals, Topical

see also Ophthalmologicals

Nucleosides
acyclovir
idoxuridine
trifluridine

Anxiolytics

see also Anticonvulsants; Antipanic Agents; Hypnotics and Sedatives

Azaspirodecanedione Derivatives
buspirone hydrochloride

Benzodiazepines
alprazolam
bromazepam
chlordiazepoxide hydrochloride
clorazepate dipotassium
diazepam
lorazepam
oxazepam

Various Anxiolytics
hydroxyzine hydrochloride
meprobamate
trifluoperazine hydrochloride

Asthma Therapy

see also Adrenocortical Agents

Adrenergics, Inhalants

Alpha- and Beta-adrenergic Agonists
epinephrine
epinephrine bitartrate
epinephrine hydrochloride, racemic

Beta-adrenergic Agonists, Nonselective
isoproterenol hydrochloride
orciprenaline sulfate

Beta-2-adrenergic Agonists, Selective
fenoterol hydrobromide
formoterol fumarate
formoterol fumarate dihydrate
salbutamol
salmeterol xinafoate
terbutaline sulfate

Adrenergics, Systemic

Alpha- and Beta-adrenergic Agonists
epinephrine

Beta-adrenergic Agonists, Nonselective
isoproterenol hydrochloride
orciprenaline sulfate

Beta-2-adrenergic Agonists, Selective
fenoterol hydrobromide
salbutamol
terbutaline sulfate

Antiallergic Agents, Inhalants
sodium cromoglycate

Antiallergic Agents, Systemic
ketotifen fumarate

Anticholinergics, Inhalants
ipratropium bromide

Combination Adrenergics and Anticholinergics, Inhalants
salbutamol/ipratropium bromide

Bronchial Anti-inflammatory Agents, Inhalants

Corticosteroids
beclomethasone dipropionate
budesonide
flunisolide
fluticasone propionate
triamcinolone acetonide

Nonsteroidal Agents
nedocromil sodium

Bronchial Anti-inflammatory Agents, Systemic

Corticosteroids
hydrocortisone sodium succinate
methylprednisolone sodium succinate
prednisone
triamcinolone

Leukotriene Receptor Antagonists, Systemic
montelukast sodium
zafirlukast

Xanthines, Systemic

Theophylline Salts
aminophylline
oxtriphylline
theophylline

Biliary Tract Therapy

Gallstone Solubilizing Agents
ursodiol

Various Bile Preparations
anethole trithione
dehydrocholic acid

Bladder Therapy, Local

Carcinoma-in-situ Therapy

Intravesical Instillations
bacillus Calmette-Guérin (BCG), strain TICE, intravesical
bacillus Calmette-Guérin (BCG), substrain Connaught, intravesical
bacillus Calmette-Guérin (BCG), substrain Montréal, intravesical
doxorubicin hydrochloride

Cystitis Therapy, Local

Anti-inflammatory Agents, Intravesical
dimethyl sulfoxide

Glycosaminoglycan Layer Replacement
pentosan polysulfate sodium
sodium hyaluronate

Bleeding Therapy

Antifibrinolytics

Amino Acids
aminocaproic acid
tranexamic acid

Proteinase Inhibitors
aprotinin

Vitamin K Analogues
phytonadione

Hemostatics

Blood Coagulation Factors
antihemophilic factor VIII (human)
antihemophilic factor IX concentrate (human)
antihemophilic factor (recombinant)

Local Hemostatics
thrombin (bovine)

Various Hemostatics
absorbable gelatin
desmopressin acetate

Cancer Chemotherapy Toxicity, Prevention of

Cardioprotective Agents
dexrazoxane

Cytoprotective Agents
amifostine

Methotrexate Rescue
calcium folinate

Urinary Tract Protective Agents
mesna

Cardiac Therapy

see also Antihypertensives; Diuretics

Angina Therapy

Beta-adrenergic Blocking Agents, Selective, Intrinsic Sympathomimetic Activity (ISA)
acebutolol hydrochloride

Beta-adrenergic Blocking Agents, Selective, Non-ISA
atenolol
metoprolol tartrate

Beta-adrenergic Blocking Agents, Nonselective, ISA
pindolol

Beta-adrenergic Blocking Agents, Nonselective, Non-ISA
nadolol
propranolol hydrochloride
timolol maleate

Calcium Channel Blockers
amlodipine besylate
diltiazem hydrochloride
nicardipine hydrochloride
nifedipine
verapamil hydrochloride

Coronary Vasodilators, Nitrates
isosorbide dinitrate
isosorbide-5-mononitrate
nitroglycerin
pentaerythritol tetranitrate

Antiarrhythmics

Cardiac Glycosides
digoxin

Class I, Type 1A
disopyramide
disopyramide phosphate
procainamide hydrochloride
quinidine bisulfate
quinidine gluconate
quinidine phenylethylbarbiturate
quinidine polygalacturonate
quinidine sulfate

Class I, Type IB
lidocaine hydrochloride
mexiletine hydochloride
tocainide hydrochloride

Class I, Type IC
flecainide acetate
propafenone hydrochloride

Class II, Beta-adrenergic Blocking Agents
esmolol hydrochloride
propranolol hydrochloride
sotalol hydrochloride

Class III
amiodarone hydrochloride
bretylium tosylate

Class IV, Calcium Channel Blockers
diltiazem hydrochloride
verapamil hydrochloride

Various Antiarrhythmics
adenosine

Cardiac Sympathomimetics
dobutamine hydrochloride
dopamine hydrochloride
epinephrine hydrochloride
isoproterenol hydrochloride
methoxamine hydrochloride
norepinephrine bitartrate
phenylephrine hydrochloride

Congestive Heart Failure Therapy

Angiotensin Converting Enzyme (ACE) Inhibitors
captopril
cilazapril
enalapril maleate
fisunopril sodium
lisinopril
quinapril hydrochloride

Beta-adrenergic Blocking Agents, Nonselective, Non-ISA
carvedilol

Cardiac Glycosides
digoxin

Diuretics
amiloride hydrochloride
bumetanide
chlorthalidone
ethacrynate sodium
ethacrynic acid
furosemide
hydrochlorothiazide
methyclothiazide
metolazone
spironolactone
torsemide
triamterene

Inotropes
amrinone lactate
dobutamine hydrochloride
dopamine hydrochloride
milrinone lactate

Various Cardiac Preparations

Patent Ductus Arteriosus Therapy, Closure
indomethacin sodium

Patent Ductus Arteriosus Therapy, Patency Maintenance
alprostadil

CNS Agents

Stimulants

Attention Deficit Hyperactivity Disorder Therapy
methylphenidate hydrochloride
pemoline

Phenylethylamine Derivatives
dexamphetamine sulfate

Various CNS Agents
ergoloid mesylates
inosiplex

Cough and Cold Preparations

see also Nasal Preparations

Antitussives

Opioids
codeine phosphate
hydrocodone bitartrate

Nonopioids
chlophedianol hydrochloride
dextromethorphan hydrobromide

Decongestants, Nasal Preparations

Sympathomimetics
oxymetazoline hydrochloride
phenylephrine hydrochloride
xylometazoline hydrochloride

Decongestants, Systemic

Sympathomimetics
ephedrine hydrochloride
phenylephrine hydrochloride
phenylpropanolamine hydrochloride
pseudoephedrine hydrochloride
pseudoephedrine sulfate

Expectorants
guaifenesin

Sore Throat Therapy, Local

Antiseptics
dequalinium chloride
hexylresorcinol

Dermatological Preparations

see also Acne Therapy; Antibacterials; Antifungals; Anti-inflammatory Agents, Topical; Antipruritics; Antiseptics; Antivirals, Topical; Emollients and Protectants; Medicated Dressings; Pediculicides and Scabicides; Psoriasis Therapy; Wound and Ulcer Treatment

Antihyperhidrotics (Antiperspirants)
methenamine

Depigmenting Agents
hydroquinone

Dermatitis Herpetiformis Therapy
dapsone
sulfapyridine

Keratolytic Agents
lactic acid
salicylic acid

Medicated Shampoos
coal tar
ketoconazole
povidone-iodine
salicylic acid
sulfur
zinc pyrithione

Neuralgia Therapy
capsaicin

Photodamaged Skin Therapy
tretinoin

Rosacea Therapy
metronidazole

Sunscreens

UVA Absorbers (Large Spectrum)
benzophenones
butyl methoxydibenzoylmethane (Parsol 1789)

UVB Absorbers (Narrow Spectrum)
ethoxyethyl p-methoxycinnamate
methylbenzylidene camphor (Parsol 5000)

octocrylene
octyl dimethyl PABA
octyl methoxycinnamate (Parsol MCX)
octyl salicylate
para-aminobenzoic acid (PABA)
phenylbenzymidazole sulfonic acid (Parsol HS)

Physical Agents
titanium dioxide
zinc oxide

Vitiligo Therapy
methoxsalen
trioxsalen

Wart and Corn Preparations
cantharidine
dichloroacetic acid
podofilox
podophyllum resin
salicylic acid

Diabetes Therapy

Insulins, Analogues
Very Rapid Acting
insulin lispro

Insulins, Beef and Pork
Rapid Acting
insulin regular

Intermediate Acting
insulin lente
insulin NPH

Insulins, Human
Rapid Acting
insulin regular, biosynthetic

Intermediate Acting
insulin lente, biosynthetic
insulin NPH, biosynthetic

Long Acting
insulin ultralente, biosynthetic

Mixed (Regular/NPH)
insulin (10/90), biosynthetic
insulin (20/80), biosynthetic
insulin (30/70), biosynthetic
insulin (40/60), biosynthetic
insulin (50/50), biosynthetic

Insulins, Pork
Rapid Acting
insulin regular

Intermediate Acting
insulin lente
insulin NPH

Oral Agents
Alpha-glucosidase Inhibitors
acarbose

Biguanides
metformin hydrochloride

Sulfonylureas
acetohexamide
chlorpropamide
gliclazide
glyburide
tolbutamide

Diagnostics, Contrast Media and Radiopharmaceuticals

Diagnostics
Adrenal Function
cosyntropin
dexamethasone sodium phosphate

Cholecystokinetic
sincalide

Diabetes
dextrose
glucagon

Fertility Disturbances
gonadorelin acetate

Gastric Secretions
histamine phosphate
methylene blue

Glycosuria
glucose enzymatic test strips

Hypersensitivity
skin test antigens

Immunotherapeutics
epinephrine

Intestinal Absorption
D-xylose

Methemoglobinemia
methylene blue

Ophthalmic
fluorescein sodium

Oral Cancer
toluidine

Pancreatic Function
cholecystokinin
secretin

Penicillin Hypersensitivity
benzylpenicilloyl

Pheochromocytoma
phentolamine

Renal Permeability
methylene blue

Thyroid Function
protirelin

Tuberculosis
tuberculin
tuberculin purified protein derivative (Mantoux)

Contrast Media
Paramagnetic Contrast Media
gadopentetate dimeglumine
gadoteridol

Ultrasound Contrast Agents
galactose
galactose/palmitic acid

Water soluble, Nephrotropic, High Osmolar X-Ray Contrast Media, Ionated
diatrizoate meglumine
diatrizoate sodium
iodipamide meglumine
iothalamate meglumine

Water soluble, Nephrotropic, Low Osmolar X-Ray Contrast Media, Ionated
iopamidol
iopromide
iotrolan
ioversol
ioxaglate meglumine
ioxaglate sodium

Radiopharmaceuticals
Technetium (Tc99m) Derivatives
tc99m mebrofenin

Diuretics

see also Antihypertensives; Cardiac Therapy

Loop Diuretics
bumetanide
ethacrynate sodium
ethacrynic acid
furosemide
torsemide

Osmotic Diuretics
mannitol

Potassium Sparing Agents
amiloride hydrochloride
spironolactone
triamterene

Thiazides and Related Agents
chlorthalidone
hydrochlorothiazide
indapamide
indapamide hemihydrate
metolazone

Eating Disorders

see also Antidepressants

Antianorexic/Anticachexic
megestrol acetate

Antibulimics
fluoxetine hydrochloride

Appetite Suppressants
Amphetamine-like Agents
diethylpropion hydrochloride
mazindol
phentermine hydrochloride

Electrolytes

see also Hypercalcemia and Paget's Disease Therapy; Hyperkalemia Therapy; Minerals

Bicarbonate Preparations
sodium bicarbonate

Calcium Preparations
Calcium Salts
calcium carbonate
calcium citrate
calcium chloride
calcium gluconate
calcium gluconogalactogluconate
calcium lactobionate

Magnesium Preparations
Magnesium Salts
magnesium chloride hexahydrate
magnesium glucoheptonate
magnesium gluconate
magnesium sulfate

Potassium Preparations
Potassium Salts
potassium acetate
potassium bicarbonate
potassium chloride
potassium citrate
potassium gluconate
potassium phosphates

Rehydration Preparations
electrolytes, oral

Sodium Preparations
Sodium Salts
sodium chloride

Emollients and Protectants

Silicone Products
dimethicone
silicone

Urea Products
urea

Zinc Products
zinc oxide
zinc sulfate monohydrate

Various Emollients and Protectants
aluminum acetate
ammonium lactate
glycolic acid
isopropanol
lactic acid
mineral oil
petrolatum

Enzymes

see also Wound and Ulcer Treatment

Digestive Enzymes

Lactose Digestive Enzymes
lactase

Pancreatic Enzymes
pancrelipase

Proteolytic Enzymes
chymopapain

Gastrointestinal Motility Agents

see also Antiemetics and Antinauseants; Reflux Therapy

Gastrointestinal Prokinetic Agents

Upper Gastrointestinal Tract Agents
domperidone maleate
metoclopramide hydrochloride

Upper and Lower Gastrointestinal Tract Agents
cisapride monohydrate

Gout and Hyperuricemia Therapy

see also Analgesics; Rheumatic Disease Therapy

Gout Therapy

Antimitotics
colchicine

Corticosteroids
dexamethasone
dexamethasone sodium phosphate
hydrocortisone sodium succinate
methylprednisolone acetate
prednisone
triamcinolone

Nonsteroidal Anti-inflammatory Drugs (NSAIDs)
indomethacin
phenylbutazone
sulindac

Hyperuricemia Therapy

Uricosurics
probenecid
sulfinpyrazone

Xanthine Oxidase Inhibitors
allopurinol

Gynecological Agents

see also Antineoplastics, Hormones; Sex Hormones; Vaginal Preparations

Endometriosis Therapy

Estrogen/Progestogen Containing Preparations
mestranol/norethindrone

Gonadotropin Inhibitors
danazol

Gonadotropin Releasing Hormone (GnRH) Analogues
nafarelin acetate

Progestogens
medroxyprogesterone acetate
norethindrone acetate

Labor Suppressants

Sympathomimetics
ritodrine hydrochloride

Oxytocics

Ergot Alkaloids
ergometrine (ergonovine) maleate

Oxytocin Derivatives
oxytocin

Prostaglandins
dinoprostone

Prolactin Inhibitors
bromocriptine mesylate

Hair Growth

Systemic

5-α-Reductase Inhibitors
finasteride

Topical
minoxidil

HIV (Human Immunodeficiency Virus) Infections and Related Disorders Therapy

see also Antibacterials; Antifungals; Antivirals; Antidiarrheal and Anti-infective Agents; Antiemetics and Antinauseants; Antituberculosis Agents; Eating Disorders; Vaccines

Prophylactic Therapy

Cytomegalovirus
ganciclovir sodium

Mycobacterium Avium Complex
azithromycin
clarithromycin
rifabutin

Mycobacterium Tuberculosis
isoniazid

Pneumocystis Carinii Pneumonia
atovaquone
co-trimoxazole (sulfamethoxazole/trimethoprim)
dapsone
pentamidine isethionate

Toxoplasma Gondii Encephalitis
co-trimoxazole (sulfamethoxazole/trimethoprim)
dapsone
pyrimethamine

Bacterial Infections

Mycobacterium Avium Complex
azithromycin
clarithromycin
ethambutol hydrochloride
rifabutin
rifampin

Fungal Infections

Candida Species
amphotericin B
fluconazole
ketoconazole
itraconazole

Cryptococcus Neoformans
amphotericin B
fluconazole

Parasitic Infections

Pneumocystis Carinii Pneumonia
atovaquone
co-trimoxazole (sulfamethoxazole/trimethoprim)
dapsone
pentamidine isethionate
trimetrexate glucuronate

Toxoplasma Gondii
atovaquone
azithromycin
clarithromycin
co-trimoxazole (sulfamethoxazole/trimethoprim)
dapsone
pyrimethamine
sulfadiazine

Viral Infections

Cytomegalovirus
ganciclovir sodium

Nucleoside Analogue Reverse Transcriptase Inhibitors (Antiretrovirals)
didanosine (ddI) lamivudine (3TC)
stavudine (d4T)
zalcitabine (ddC)
zidovudine (AZT)

Protease Inhibitors
indinavir sulfate
ritonavir
saquinavir mesylate

Related Disorders Therapy

Anemia (AZT-induced)
epoetin alfa

Kaposi's Sarcoma
liposomal daunorubicin
interferon alfa-2a
interferon alfa-2b

Weight Loss, Anorexia, Cachexia
megestrol acetate
specialized liquid nutrition

Hypercalcemia and Paget's Disease Therapy

Bone Metabolism Regulators

Antiparathyroid Hormones
calcitonin salmon

Biphosphonates
alendronate monosodium
clodronate disodium
etidronate disodium
pamidronate disodium

Hyperkalemia Therapy

see also Electrolytes

Potassium Exchange Resins

Cation Exchange Resins

sodium polystyrene sulfonate

Ion Exchange Resins

calcium polystyrene sulfonate

Hyperkinetic Movement Disorders Therapy

see also Antipsychotics; Anxiolytics

Monoamine Depleting Agents

tetrabenazine

Hypnotics and Sedatives

see also Anxiolytics

Aldehydes and Derivatives

chloral hydrate
paraldehyde

Barbiturates

amobarbital
amobarbital sodium
butabarbital sodium
pentobarbital sodium
phenobarbital
secobarbital sodium

Benzodiazepines

alprazolam
bromazepam
clorazepate dipotassium
diazepam
flurazepam hydrochloride
flurazepam monohydrochloride
lorazepam
midazolam hydrochloride
nitrazepam
oxazepam
temazepam
triazolam

Cyclopyrrolones

zopiclone

Various Hypnotics and Sedatives

ethchlorvynol
propofol

Hypothalamic and Pituitary Hormones

see also Antineoplastics, Hormones; Gynecological Agents; Sex Hormones; Thyroid Therapy

Anterior Pituitary Hormones

Adrenocorticotropic Hormones (ACTH)

cosyntropin
cosyntropin/zinc hydroxide

Growth Hormones

somatrem
somatropin

Hypothalamic Hormones

Gonadotropin Releasing Hormone (GnRH) Analogues

buserelin acetate
gonadorelin hydrochloride
goserelin acetate
leuprolide acetate
nafarelin acetate

Somatostatin and Analogues

octreotide acetate
somatostatin

Posterior Pituitary Hormones

Antidiuretic Hormone Analogues

desmopressin acetate
vasopressin

Oxytocics

oxytocin

Immune Sera and Immunoglobulins

Immune Sera

black widow spider antivenin (equine)
botulism antitoxin trivalent types A, B and E (equine)
crotalid antivenin, polyvalent (equine)
diphtheria antitoxin (equine)

Immune Globulins, Specific

hepatitis B immune globulin (human)
rabies immune globulin (human)
rabies immune globulin (pasteurized, human)
Rh_o(D) immune globulin (human)
tetanus immune globulin (human)

Immune Globulins, Standard

immune globulin (human), i.m.
immune globulin (human), i.v.

Immunostimulating Agents

Biological Response Modifiers

aldesleukin
filgrastim (G-CSF)
interferon alfa-N1
interferon alfa-2a
interferon alfa-2b

Immunomodulators

interferon beta-1a
interferon beta-1b
levamisole hydrochloride

Immunosuppressive Agents

see also Adrenocortical Agents; Antineoplastics; Rheumatic Disease Therapy

Corticosteroids, Systemic

Glucocorticoids

betamethasone sodium phosphate
cortisone acetate
dexamethasone
hydrocortisone
hydrocortisone sodium succinate
methylprednisolone
methylprednisolone sodium succinate
prednisolone
prednisone
triamcinolone diacetate

Cyclic Peptides

cyclosporine

Cytotoxic Agents

azathioprine

Immune Globulins

anti-thymocyte globulin (equine)

Monoclonal Antibodies

muromonab-CD3

Selective Immunosuppressive Agents

mycophenolate mofetil
tacrolimus

Inflammatory Bowel Disease Therapy

5-Aminosalicylic Acid Derivatives

5-aminosalicylic acid (mesalazine)
olsalazine sodium
sulfasalazine

Corticosteroids for Rectal Use

betamethasone sodium phosphate
budesonide
hydrocortisone
hydrocortisone acetate
tixocortol pivalate

Laxatives

Bulk Forming Agents

psyllium hydrophilic muciloid
sterculia gum

Hyperosmotic Laxatives, Rectal

glycerin

Lubricant, Laxatives

mineral oil

Osmotic Laxatives

lactulose
magnesium citrate
magnesium hydroxide
polyethylene glycol/electrolytes
sodium phosphates

Stimulant Laxatives

bisacodyl
sennosides

Stool Softeners

docusate calcium
docusate sodium

Lipid Lowering Agents

Cholesterol and Triglyceride Reducers

Bile Acid Sequestrants

cholestyramine resin
colestipol hydrochloride

Fibrates

bezafibrate
clofibrate
fenofibrate (micronized)
gemfibrozil

3-Hydroxy-3-Methylgluteryl(HMG)-CoA Reductase Inhibitors

atorvastatin calcium
cerivastatin sodium
fluvastatin sodium
lovastatin
pravastatin sodium
simvastatin

Niacin Derivatives

niacin

Various Cholesterol and Triglyceride Reducers

dextrothyroxine sodium

Mania Therapy

Iminostilbene Derivatives

carbamazepine

Lithium Salts

lithium carbonate
lithium citrate

Various Adjunctive Agents

l-tryptophan

Medicated Dressings

see also Wound and Ulcer Treatment

Anti-infective Dressings
framycetin sulfate
povidone-iodine
sodium fusidate

Minerals

see also Anemia Therapy; Electrolytes; Vitamins

Fluoride Replacement Therapy

Fluoride
sodium fluoride

Iron Replacement Therapy

Iron Bivalent, Oral Preparations
ferrous ascorbate
ferrous fumarate
ferrous gluconate
ferrous sulfate

Iron Trivalent, Parenteral Preparations
iron-sorbitol citric acid complex

Trace Elements

magnesium gluconate
copper gluconate

Zinc Replacement Therapy

Zinc Salts
zinc gluconate
zinc sulfate

Mouth Preparations and Dry Mouth Therapy

see also Antiseptics

Analgesic Agents

benzydamine hydrochloride
choline salicylate

Anesthetic Agents

benzocaine

Antifungals

nystatin

Antiseptics

hexetidine
povidone-iodine

Canker Sore Therapy

betamethasone sodium phosphate

Dental Caries Prophylaxis

sodium fluoride

Gingivitis Therapy

chlorhexidine gluconate

Sialagogues (Saliva Stimulators)

anethole trithione
pilocarpine hydrochloride

Muscle Relaxants

see also Anxiolytics; Hypnotics and Sedatives

Centrally Acting Agents

Antihistamine Derivatives
orphenadrine citrate

Benzodiazepines
chlordiazepoxide hydrochloride
diazepam

Carbamic Acid Esters
carisoprodol
meprobamate
methocarbamol

Gamma Aminobutyric Acid (GABA) Derivatives
baclofen

Tricyclic Derivatives
cyclobenzaprine hydrochloride

Directly Acting Agents

dantrolene sodium

Neuromuscular Blocking Agents

Depolarizing Agents, Choline Derivatives
succinylcholine chloride

Nondepolarizing Agents, Quaternary Ammonium Compounds
atracurium besylate
cisatracurium besylate
doxacurium chloride
gallamine triethiodide
mivacurium chloride
pancuronium bromide
rocuronium bromide
vecuronium bromide

Musculoskeletal Therapy

see also Gout and Hyperuricemia Therapy; Hypercalcemia and Paget's Disease Therapy; Muscle Relaxants; Rheumatic Disease Therapy

Synovial Fluid Replacement
hylan G-F 20

Nasal Preparations

see also Allergy Therapy; Cough and Cold Preparations

Antiallergic Agents

levocabastine hydrochloride
sodium cromoglycate

Anticholinergic Agents

ipratropium bromide

Anti-inflammatory Agents

Corticosteroids
beclomethasone dipropionate
budesonide
flunisolide
fluticasone propionate
triamcinolone acetonide

Decongestants

Sympathomimetics
oxymetazoline hydrochloride
phenylephrine hydrochloride
xylometazoline hydrochloride

Nasal Moisturizers/Lubricants

polyethylene glycol/propylene glycol
sea water
sodium chloride

Ophthalmologicals

Antiallergics, Ophthalmic

emedastine difumarate
levocabastine hydrochloride
lodoxamide tromethamine
nedocromil sodium
olopatadine hydrochloride
sodium cromoglycate

Anti-infectives, Ophthalmic

Antibacterials
chloramphenicol
chlortetracycline hydrochloride
ciprofloxacin hydrochloride
erythromycin
framycetin sulfate
gentamicin sulfate
norfloxacin
ofloxacin
polymyxin B sulfate
sulfacetamide sodium
tetracycline hydrochloride
tobramycin

Antivirals
idoxuridine
trifluridine

Anti-inflammatory Agents, Ophthalmic

Corticosteroids
dexamethasone sodium phosphate
fluorometholone
fluorometholone acetate
prednisolone acetate
prednisone sodium phosphate
rimexolone

Nonsteroidal Anti-inflammatory Agents
diclofenac sodium
flurbiprofen sodium
indomethacin
ketorolac tromethamine

Artificial Tears

carboxymethylcellulose sodium
dextran 70/hydroxypropyl methylcellulose
glycerin
hydroxypropyl cellulose
hydroxypropyl methylcellulose
methylcellulose
polysorbate 80
polyvinyl alcohol
sodium hyaluronate

Decongestants, Ophthalmic

Sympathomimetics
naphazoline hydrochloride
oxymetazoline hydrochloride
phenylephrine hydrochloride
tetrahydrozoline hydrochloride

Diagnostic Agents, Ophthalmic

Coloring Agents
fluorescein sodium

Glaucoma Therapy, Ophthalmic Preparations

Alpha-adrenergic Receptor Agonists
brimonidine tartrate

Beta-blocking Agents
betaxolol hydrochloride
levobunolol hydrochloride
timolol maleate

Carbonic Anhydrase Inhibitors, Systemic
acetazolamide
methazolamide

Carbonic Anhydrase Inhibitors, Topical
dorzolamide hydrochloride

Miotics, Cholinesterase Inhibitors
echothiophate iodide

Miotics, Parasympathomimetics
acetylcholine chloride
carbachol
pilocarpine hydrochloride

Prostaglandin F2 Analogues
latanoprost

Sympathomimetics
dipivefrin hydrochloride
epinephrine

Beta-blocking/Sympathomimetic Agents Combinations
dipivefrin hydrochloride/levobunolol hydrochloride

Local Anesthetics, Ophthalmic
benoxinate
proparacaine hydrochloride
tetracaine hydrochloride

Mydriatics and Cycloplegics
Anticholinergics
atropine sulfate
cyclopentolate hydrochloride
homatropine
tropicamide

Mydriatics, Sympathomimetics
phenylephrine hydrochloride

Ophthalmic Surgical Preparations
Viscoelastic Preparations
sodium hyaluronate

Enzymatic Preparations
chymotrypsin

Various Ophthalmic Surgical Preparations
absorbable gelatin

Various Ophthalmic Preparations
apraclonidine hydrochloride
boric acid
botulinum toxin type A
sodium chloride, hypertonic
tyloxapol

Osteoporosis

see also Hypercalcemia and Paget's Disease Therapy; Sex Hormones

Estrogen Receptor Modulator
Benzothiophen
raloxifene hydrochloride

Otologicals

Anesthetics, Otic
lidocaine hydrochloride

Antibiotics, Otic
chloramphenicol
gentamicin sulfate

Anti-inflammatory Agents, Otic
betamethasone sodium phosphate
dexamethasone sodium

Cerumenolytics
triethanolamine polypeptide oleate-condensate

Pancreatic Hormones

Hyperglycemic Agents
glucagon

Parasympathomimetics, Central

Cholinesterase Inhibitors
edrophonium chloride
neostigmine bromide
neostigmine methylsulfate
pyridostigmine bromide

Choline Esters
carbachol

Pediculicides and Scabicides

Pediculicides
piperonyl butoxide/pyrethrins

Pediculicides and Scabicides
lindane (gamma benzene hexachloride)
permethrin

Scabicides
esdepallethrin/piperonyl butoxide

Peptic Ulcer Therapy

see also Antacids; Reflux Therapy

Antacids
aluminum hydroxide
aluminum hydroxide/magnesium hydroxide
magaldrate

Cytoprotectives
sucralfate

Histamine H_2-receptor Antagonists
cimetidine
famotidine
nizatidine
ranitidine bismuth citrate
ranitidine hydrochloride

Prostaglandins
misoprostol

Proton Pump Inhibitors
lansoprazole
omeprazole
pantoprazole

Peripheral Vascular Disease Therapy

Peripheral Vasodilators
nylidrin hydrochloride
papaverine hydrochloride
pentoxifylline
tolazoline hydrochloride

Phosphate Binders

Aluminum Containing Preparations
aluminum hydroxide gel

Plasma Substitutes

Blood Derivatives
albumin (human)
plasma protein fraction (human)

Plasma Expanders
dextran
pentastarch

Platelet Aggregation Inhibitors

Adenosine Diphosphate Inhibitors
clopidogrel bisulfate
dipyridamole
sulfinpyrazone

Chimeric Monoclonal Antiplatelet Antibody
abciximab

Fibrinogen-Platelet Binding Inhibitors
ticlopidine hydrochloride

Thromboxane-A_2 Inhibitors
acetylsalicylic acid (ASA)

Prostatic Hyperplasia Therapy

Benign Prostatic Hyperplasia Therapy
Alpha$_1$-adrenergic Blocking Agent
doxazosin
tamsulosin hydrochloride
terazosin

5-α-Reductase Inhibitors
finasteride

Psoriasis Therapy

Psoriasis Therapy, Systemic
Cytotoxics
methotrexate sodium

Psoralens
methoxsalen

Retinoids
acitretin

Psoriasis Therapy, Topical
Antracen Derivatives
anthralin

Nonsteroidal Agents
calcipotriol

Psoralens
methoxsalen

Tars
coal tar
fractar

Various Psoriasis Preparations for Topical Use
phenol
salicylic acid

Reflux Therapy

see also Antacids; Antiemetics and Antinauseants; Gastrointestinal Motility Agents; Peptic Ulcer Therapy

Antacids
Aluminum Containing Preparations
aluminum hydroxide

Aluminum/Magnesium Containing Preparations
aluminum hydroxide/magnesium hydroxide
magaldrate

Calcium Containing Preparations
calcium carbonate

Magnesium Containing Preparations
magnesium hydroxide
magnesium carbonate

Foaming Agents
alginic acid
sodium alginate

Histamine H_2-receptor Antagonists
cimetidine
famotidine
nizatidine
ranitidine hydrochloride

Proton Pump Inhibitors
lansoprazole
omeprazole
pantoprazole

Prokinetic Agents
cisapride monohydrate

Respiratory System Agents

see also Allergy Therapy; Asthma Therapy; Cough and Cold Preparations; Nasal Preparations

Lung Surfactants
alpha$_1$-proteinase inhibitor (human)
beractant
colfosceril palmitate

Mucolytics
acetylcysteine
dornase alfa, recombinant

Rheumatic Disease Therapy

see also Adrenocortical Agents; Analgesics

Corticosteroids
betamethasone sodium phosphate
cortisone acetate
dexamethasone
dexamethasone sodium phosphate
methylprednisolone acetate
prednisolone
prednisone
triamcinolone
triamcinolone diacetate

Disease Modifying Drugs (DMARDS)
Cytotoxics
azathioprine
methotrexate sodium

Gold Preparations
aurothioglucose
sodium aurothiomalate

Other DMARDS
hydroxychloroquine sulfate
penicillamine
sulfasalazine

Various Agents for Rheumatic Disease Therapy
Joint and Muscular Pain Therapy, Topical
capsaicin
menthol
triethanolamine salicylate

Sex Hormones

see also Antineoplastics, Hormones; Gynecological Agents

Androgenic-Anabolic Steroids
fluoxymesterone
methyltestosterone
nandrolone decanoate
testosterone cypionate
testosterone enanthate
testosterone undecanoate

Estrogens
Estrogens, Oral
conjugated estrogens
esterified estrogens
estradiol-17β
estropipate
ethinyl estradiol

Estrogens, Parenteral
estradiol valerate

Estrogens, Transdermal
estradiol-17β

Estrogens, Vaginal Preparations
conjugated estrogens
dienestrol
estradiol

Progestogens
medrogestone
medroxyprogesterone acetate
megestrol acetate
norethindrone
progesterone

Various Estrogen/Progestogen Combinations
Estrogen/Progestogen Combinations, Oral
mestranol/norethindrone

Estrogen/Progestogen Combinations, Transdermal
estradiol-17β/norethindrone

Fertility Regulators
Gonadotropins
chorionic gonadotropin
follitropin alpha (rDNA origin)
follitropin beta (rec FSH)
human gonadotropin
menotropins
urofollitropin

Ovulation Stimulants, Synthetic
clomiphene citrate
gonadorelin acetate

Oral Contraceptives
Estrogens and Progestogens, Monophasic
desogestrel/ethinyl estradiol
ethinyl estradiol/ethynodiol diacetate
ethinyl estradiol/levonorgestrel
ethinyl estradiol/norethindrone
ethinyl estradiol/norethindrone acetate
ethinyl estradiol/norgestimate
ethinyl estradiol/norgestrel
mestranol/norethindrone

Estrogens and Progestogens, Biphasic
ethinyl estradiol/norethindrone

Estrogens and Progestogens, Triphasic
ethinyl estradiol/levonorgestrel
ethinyl estradiol/norethindrone
ethinyl estradiol/norgestimate

Progestogens
levonorgestrel
norethindrone

Smoking Cessation Therapy

Nicotine Replacement Therapy
Nicotine Gum
nicotine polacrilex

Nicotine Transdermal
nicotine

Subarachnoid Hemorrhage Therapy

see also Bleeding Therapy

Calcium Channel Blocking Agent
nimodipine

Fibrinolytic Inhibitor
aminocaproic acid

Thrombolytic Agents

Plasminogen Activators
Natural Enzymes
urokinase

Proteins, Derived from Bacteria
streptokinase

Proteins, Recombinant DNA Origin
alteplase
anistreplase

Other Antithrombotic Agents
anagrelide hydrochloride

Thyroid Therapy

see also Hypothalamic and Pituitary Hormones

Antithyroid Agents
methimazole
propylthiouracil

Iodine Therapy
potassium iodide

Thyroid Hormones
levothyroxine sodium
thyroid

Urinary Tract Agents

see also Antispasmodics; Cancer Chemotherapy Toxicity, Prevention of

Enuresis Therapy
Antidiuretic Hormone Analogues
desmopressin acetate

Tricyclics
imipramine hydrochloride

Urinary Analgesics
Azo Dyes
phenazopyridine hydrochloride

Urinary Antiseptics and Anti-Infectives
see also Antibacterials

Methenamine Salts
methenamine (hexamine)
methenamine hippurate
methenamine mandelate

Nitrofuran Derivatives
nitrofurantoin
nitrofurantoin monohydrate

Quinolones
nalidixic acid

Urinary Antispasmodics
Anticholinergics
hyoscine butylbromide
hyoscyamine sulfate

Smooth Muscle Relaxants
flavoxate hydrochloride
oxybutynin chloride

Urinary Retention Therapy
Parasympathomimetic Agents
bethanechol chloride

Vaccines

Bacterial Vaccines and Toxoids
Toxoids
diphtheria toxoid
diphtheria, tetanus toxoids (adsorbed)—DT
tetanus toxoid (adsorbed)

Bacterial Vaccines, Single Entity
bacillus Calmette-Guérin (BCG) vaccine (live, attenuated)
cholera vaccine (inactivated)
cholera vaccine (live, oral, attenuated)
haemophilus b oligosaccharide conjugate vaccine (diphtheria protein conjugate)—HbOC
haemophilus b polysaccharide conjugate vaccine (meningococcal protein conjugate)—PRP-OMP

haemophilus b polysaccharide conjugate vaccine (tetanus protein conjugate)—PRP-T
meningococcal polysaccharide vaccine, groups A, C, Y, W-135
pertussis vaccine (acellular, adsorbed)
pneumococcal polysaccharide vaccine
pneumococcal vaccine (polyvalent)
salmonella typhi Vi capsular polysaccharide vaccine
typhoid vaccine Ty21a (live, oral, attenuated)

Bacterial Vaccines and Toxoids, Combined

diphtheria, tetanus toxoids, pertussis (cellular) vaccine (adsorbed)—DPT

Viral Vaccines

Hepatitis Vaccines

hepatitis A vaccine (inactivated)
hepatitis A vaccine (purified, inactivated)
hepatitis B vaccine (recombinant)
hepatitis A (inactivated) and hepatitis B (recombinant) combined vaccines

Influenza Vaccines

influenza virus vaccine (inactivated)
influenza virus vaccine (trivalent, inactivated, types A and B, split-virion)
influenza virus vaccine (trivalent, inactivated, whole-virion)

Viral Vaccines, Single Entity

japanese encephalitis virus vaccine (inactivated)
measles virus vaccine (live, attenuated)
mumps virus vaccine (live, attenuated)
poliomyelitis vaccine (inactivated, diploid cell origin)—IVP
poliovirus vaccine (live, attenuated, oral, trivalent) (types 1, 2 & 3)—OPV
rabies vaccine inactivated (diploid cell origin)
yellow fever vaccine (live 17D virus)

Viral Vaccines, Combined

measles, mumps, rubella virus vaccine (live, attenuated)—MMR

Bacterial and Viral Vaccines, Combined

diphtheria, tetanus toxoids, pertussis (acellular) vaccine (adsorbed), poliomyelitis vaccine (inactivated)—DPT Polio
diphtheria, tetanus toxoids, poliomyelitis vaccine (inactivated, adsorbed) - DT Polio
diphtheria, tetanus toxoids, pertussis (acellular) vaccine (adsorbed), poliomyelitis (inactivated) and haemophilus b conjugate (tetanus protein conjugate) vaccines

Vaginal Preparations

see also Antibacterials; Antifungals

Antibacterials, Vaginal

Lincosamides

clindamycin phosphate

Antifungals, Vaginal

Antibiotics

nystatin

Imidazoles

clotrimazole
econazole nitrate
metronidazole
miconazole nitrate
tioconazole

Triazoles

terconazole

Contraceptives, Vaginal

nonoxynol-9

Trichomonas Therapy, Vaginal

Nitroimidazoles

metronidazole

Various Vaginal Anti-infectives and Antiseptics

povidone-iodine

Vascular Agents

Impotence

Alpha₂-adrenergic Blocking Agents

yohimbine

Prostaglandins

alprostadil

Primary Pulmonary Hypertension Therapy

Prostaglandins

epoprostenol sodium

Varicose Therapy

Sclerosing Agents for Local Injection

sodium tetradecyl sulfate

Vitamins

see also Anemia Therapy; Minerals

Vitamin A (Fat Soluble)

Vitamin A

retinol

Vitamin B Complex (Water Soluble)

Folic Acid

folic acid

Vitamin B_1

thiamine hydrochloride

Vitamin B_2

riboflavin

Vitamin B_3

niacin
niacinamide

Vitamin B_5

calcium pantothenate
pantothenic acid

Vitamin B_6

pyridoxine hydrochloride

Vitamin B_{12}

cyanocobalamin
hydroxocobalamin

Vitamin C (Water Soluble)

Ascorbic Acid

ascorbic acid

Vitamin D Analogues (Fat Soluble)

Vitamin D_2 Analogues

calciferol
ergocalciferol

Vitamin D_3 Analogues

alfacalcidol
calcifediol
calcitriol
cholecalciferol

Various Vitamin D Analogues

dihydrotachysterol

Vitamin E (Fat Soluble)

Tocopherols

alpha tocopherol

Vitamin K (Fat Soluble) Analogues

Vitamin K_1

phytonadione

Wound and Ulcer Treatment

see also Medicated Dressings

Debriding Agents

Proteolytic Enzymes

collagenase

Hyperosmotics

magnesium sulfate

PRODUCT RECOGNITION SECTION
SECTION D'IDENTIFICATION DES PRODUITS

This section contains full-color reproductions of products selected for inclusion by manufacturers. Products which appear in this section are cross-referenced within the product monograph in the white section.

Cette section contient la photographie en couleurs des produits choisis à cette fin par les compagnies. La section des monographies (pages blanches) comporte des renvois à ces monographies de produits.

PARTICIPATING MANUFACTURERS/COMPAGNIES PARTICIPANTES

Abbott
Allerex
Astra
Axcan Pharma
Bayer
BDH
Berlex Canada
Boehringer Ingelheim
Bristol-Myers Squibb
Carter Horner
Crystaal
Dispensapharm
DuPont Pharma
Fabrigen
Fournier
Frosst
Fujisawa
Glaxo Wellcome
Glenwood
Hoechst Marion Roussel
Janssen-Ortho
Johnson & Johnson • Merck
Key
Knoll
Leo
Lundbeck
May & Baker Pharma
McNeil Consumer Products (Produits aux Consommateurs McNeil)
MSD
Novartis Consumer Health (Novartis Santé Familiale)
Novartis Pharmaceuticals (Novartis Pharma)
Novo Nordisk
Organon
Parke-Davis
Pfizer
Pfizer Consumer (Pfizer, Soins de la santé)
Pharmacia & Upjohn
Procter & Gamble Pharmaceuticals
Purdue Frederick
Rhône-Poulenc Rorer
Roberts
Roche
Sabex
Sanofi
Schering
Searle
Servier
SmithKline Beecham
Solvay Pharma
Squibb
3M Pharmaceuticals
UCB Pharma
Warner-Lambert Consumer Healthcare (Warner-Lambert, Santé grand public)
Wyeth-Ayerst
Zeneca

	Page	Code
Atasol® 325 mg Tablets/comprimés	R10	B6
Atasol® 500 mg Forte Caplets	R14	D5
Atasol® 500 mg Forte Tablets/comprimés	R13	D2
Atasol®-8	R18	E8
Atasol®-15	R17	A4
Atasol®-30	R26	C1
Ativan® 0.5 mg	R25	A5
Ativan® 1 mg	R14	C6
Ativan® 2 mg	R13	C5
Ativan® 0.5 mg Sublingual	R25	E4
Ativan® 1 mg Sublingual	R7	A1
Ativan® 2 mg Sublingual	R26	C5
Atromid-S®/Atromide-S® 500 mg	R30	E5
Atromid-S®/Atromide-S® 1 g	R31	C3
Atrovent® Inhalation Aerosol/aérosol pour inhalation	R38	C1
Atrovent® 0.03% Nasal Spray/atomiseur nasal	R35	D4
Atrovent® 0.06% Nasal Spray/atomiseur nasal	R35	E4
Avapro™ 75 mg	R13	A6
Avapro™ 150 mg	R14	D1
Avapro™ 300 mg	R14	A5
Avirax™ 200 mg	R27	D2
Avirax™ 400 mg	R22	E6
Avirax™ 800 mg	R28	C4
Avlosulfon®	R7	C7

B

	Page	Code
Bacid®	R30	A4
Bactrim™ Roche® Adult/adulte	R10	B8
Bactrim™ Roche® DS	R14	E3
Baycol® 0.2 mg	R16	A4
Baycol® 0.3 mg	R18	B4
Beclodisk® 100 µg	R38	D3
Beclodisk® 200 µg	R38	E3
Beclovent® Inhaler/aérosol-doseur 50 µg	R38	E1
Becloforte® Inhaler/aérosol-doseur 250 µg	R38	D2
Beclovent Rotacaps® 100 µg	R29	B4
Beclovent Rotacaps® 200 µg	R31	A6
Bellergal® Spacetabs®	R17	B6
Benadryl® 25 mg	R23	D8
Benadryl® 50 mg	R31	B1
Benadryl® Allergy/Sinus/Headache	R26	C4
Benadryl® Junior Strength Chewable/formule junior comprimés à croquer	R28	E3
Benemid® 500 mg	R12	B2
Bentylol® 10 mg	R8	D1
Bentylol® 20 mg	R8	A7
Benylin® 4 Flu/grippe	R26	D4
Betaloc® 50 mg	R9	A1
Betaloc® 100 mg	R10	E8
Betaloc® Durules® 200 mg	R14	B2
Betaseron®	R34	E7
Betnesol® 0.5 mg Effervescent Tablets/comprimés effervescents	R21	E8
Bezalip® 200 mg	R10	E6
Bezalip® 400 mg	R11	E6
Biaxin® 250 mg	R19	C5
Biaxin® 500 mg	R16	D5
Biltricide®	R16	D1
Bionet® Lozenges/pastilles	R12	A5
Biquin® Durules® 250 mg	R14	B3
Blocadren® 5 mg	R7	A3
Blocadren® 10 mg	R27	D1
Bonamine™ 25 mg	R9	E6
Bonefos® 400 mg	R29	E8
Brevicon® 0.5/35(21)	R37	C7
Brevicon® 0.5/35(28)	R37	C8
Brevicon® 1/35(21)	R37	B7
Brevicon® 1/35(28)	R37	B8
Bricanyl® 2.5 mg	R9	C4
Bricanyl® 5 mg	R9	D2
Bricanyl® Turbuhaler®	R38	B5
Burinex® 1 mg	R8	A5
Burinex® 2 mg	R10	A1
Burinex® 5 mg	R10	D7
Buspar® 10 mg	R13	E3
Butisol® Sodium/Sodique 15 mg	R26	C8
Butisol® Sodium/Sodique 30 mg	R25	A8
Butisol® Sodium/Sodique 100 mg	R22	C5

C

	Page	Code
Cafergot®	R18	B7
Cafergot® Supp.	R34	E1
Cafergot®-PB Supp.	R33	D7
Calcium-Sandoz® Forte	R12	B5
Calcium-Sandoz® Syrup/sirop	R39	A3
Calsan® 500 mg Capsules	R29	E3
Calsan® 500 mg Chewable Tablets/comprimés à croquer	R16	E1
Canesten® Combi-Pak 1 Day/1 jour	R34	A3
Canesten® Combi-Pak 3 Day/3 jours	R34	B3
Canesten® 1 Day Cream Combi-Pak/1 jour	R34	C3
Canesten® 2% Vaginal Cream/crème vaginale	R34	D3
Capoten® 12.5 mg	R14	E5
Capoten® 25 mg	R12	B8
Capoten® 50 mg	R13	B7
Capoten® 100 mg	R14	C2
Cardene® 20 mg	R28	D6
Cardene® 30 mg	R32	C3
Cardizem® 30 mg	R25	C8
Cardizem® 60 mg	R16	E4
Cardizem® CD 120 mg Capsules	R32	D3
Cardizem® CD 180 mg Capsules	R32	E3
Cardizem® CD 240 mg Capsules	R32	E4
Cardizem® CD 300 mg Capsules	R32	E2
Cardizem® SR 60 mg Capsules	R33	E2
Cardizem® SR 90 mg Capsules	R33	A3
Cardizem® SR 120 mg Capsules	R33	B3
Cardura-1™	R7	D7
Cardura-2™	R14	E6
Cardura-4™	R13	A3
Casodex®	R7	E3
CeeNU® 10 mg	R28	B7
CeeNU® 40 mg	R31	C7
CeeNU® 100 mg	R31	B8
Ceftin® 125 mg/5 mL Suspension	R38	B7
Ceftin® 250 mg Sachet	R38	C7
Ceftin® 250 mg Tablets/comprimés	R15	A2
Ceftin® 500 mg Tablets/comprimés	R15	A8
Cefzil™ 250 mg	R24	A1
Cefzil™ 500 mg	R14	A4
Celestone® 0.5 mg Tablets/comprimés	R26	D8
CellCept® 250 mg	R33	B4
CellCept® 500 mg	R28	D4
Celontin® 300 mg	R32	C6
Chlor-Tripolon® 4 mg	R16	E8
Chlor-Tripolon® 12 mg	R24	E4
Chlor-Tripolon N.D.®	R11	C2
Choledyl® 200 mg	R17	D5
Choledyl® SA 400 mg	R23	C7
Choledyl® SA 600 mg	R25	C4
Choloxin® 2 mg	R17	B7
Choloxin® 4 mg	R13	D5
Chronovera® 180 mg	R27	E2
Chronovera® 240 mg	R11	B8
Cipro® 100 mg	R8	D7
Cipro® 250 mg	R11	B2
Cipro® 500 mg	R15	A7
Cipro® 750 mg	R15	B7
Cipro® I.V. 10 mg/mL	R34	A7
Claritin® 10 mg	R13	B5
Claritin® Extra	R11	B5
Clavulin®-250	R14	E1
Clavulin®-500F	R14	E1
Climara® 3.9 mg Patches	R40	A5
Climara® 7.8 mg Patches	R40	B5
Clomid® 50 mg	R10	B4
Clopixol® 10 mg	R24	E6
Clopixol® 25 mg	R24	A7
Clopixol® 40 mg	R24	B7
Clozaril® 25 mg	R16	E6
Clozaril® 100 mg	R17	E3
CoActifed®	R10	C5
Coated Aspirin® 80 mg	R26	E8
Coated Aspirin® Daily Low Dose 81 mg	R40	C5
Coated Aspirin® 325 mg	R18	A2
Coated Aspirin® Extra Strength 500 mg	R18	B2
Coated Aspirin® Super Extra Strength 650 mg	R40	D5
Cocaine HCl Topical Solution/Chlorhydrate de cocaine solution topique	R39	B6
Codeine Contin® 50 mg	R26	D7
Codeine Contin® 100 mg	R18	D8
Codeine Contin® 150 mg	R24	E5
Codeine Contin® 200 mg	R20	C2
Cogentin® 2 mg	R7	B6
Combantrin® 125 mg	R18	C8
Combantrin® Suspension	R39	C2
Combivent™ Inhalation Aerosol/aérosol pour inhalation	R38	B1
Coptin® 500 mg	R15	D5
Cordarone® 200 mg	R22	A5
Coreg™ 3.125 mg	R13	B4
Coreg™ 6.25 mg	R13	C4
Coreg™ 12.5 mg	R13	A7
Coreg™ 25 mg	R13	D8
Corgard® 40 mg	R16	C4
Corgard® 80 mg	R16	A5
Corgard® 160 mg	R28	D1
Coricidin® Cold Tablets/dragées contre le rhume	R24	D5
Coricidin "D"®	R11	D6
Coricidin "D"® Long Acting/action prolongée	R27	E1
Coricidin® Non-Drowsy/non sédatif	R23	A1
Cortef® 10 mg	R9	A7
Cortef® 20 mg	R10	D2
Cortone® 5 mg	R8	D5
Cortone® 25 mg	R9	D5
Cotazym®	R28	E8
Cotazym® ECS 8	R29	A6
Cotazym® ECS 20	R30	E1
Cotazym®-65 B	R28	B8
Coumadin® 1 mg	R22	E3
Coumadin® 2 mg	R28	E2
Coumadin® 2.5 mg	R25	B8
Coumadin® 4 mg	R27	C3
Coumadin® 5 mg	R22	E5
Coumadin® 10 mg	R9	D7
Coversyl® 2 mg	R7	D1
Coversyl® 4 mg	R14	B6
Cozaar® 25 mg	R26	E4
Cozaar® 50 mg	R26	A5
Cozaar® 100 mg	R26	B5
Creon® 10	R31	D6
Crixivan® 200 mg	R28	E7
Crixivan® 400 mg	R29	D1
Cuprimine® 125 mg	R32	D5
Cuprimine® 250 mg	R29	C6
Cyclen® Dialpak 21-day/jours	R36	A7
Cyclen® Dialpak 28-day/jours	R36	A8
Cyclen® Discreet 21-day/jours	R37	B5
Cyclen® Discreet 28-day/jours	R37	B6
Cyclomen® 50 mg	R30	E2
Cyclomen® 100 mg	R30	A2
Cyclomen® 200 mg	R30	D4
Cyklokapron® 500 mg	R15	D6
Cylert® 37.5 mg	R20	C7
Cylert® 75 mg	R21	A1
Cytadren® 250 mg	R10	C6
Cytotec® 100 µg	R7	B7
Cytotec® 200 µg	R12	A7
Cytovene®	R31	A8
Cytoxan® 25 mg	R9	A8
Cytoxan® 50 mg	R27	D3

D

	Page	Code
Dagenan®	R12	E3
Dalacin® C 150 mg	R31	C4
Dalacin® C 300 mg	R32	A5
Dalmane® 15 mg	R32	B6
Dalmane® 30 mg	R32	D7
Daraprim® 25 mg	R8	A8
Daypro™ 600 mg	R15	C6
Decadron® 0.5 mg	R12	B6
Decadron® 4 mg	R12	C6
Deltasone® 5 mg	R7	C3
Deltasone® 50 mg	R10	A8
Demadex® 5 mg	R13	D4
Demadex® 10 mg	R13	D6
Demadex® 20 mg	R14	B1
Demadex® 100 mg	R14	E8
Demerol® 50 mg	R7	D3
Demulen® 30 (21s)	R37	E1
Demulen® 30 (28s)	R37	E2
Demulen® 50 (21s)	R37	E3
Demulen® 50 (28s)	R37	E4
Depakene® 250 mg	R30	B6
Depakene® 500 mg	R29	B7
Depakene® Syrup/sirop	R39	C4
Depen® 250 mg	R14	A1
Desyrel® 50 mg	R20	C8
Desyrel® 100 mg	R11	E7
Desyrel® Dividose 150 mg	R24	A2
Dexedrine® 5 mg	R20	C3
Dexedrine® Spansule® 10 mg	R33	C2
Dexedrine® Spansule® 15 mg	R33	D2
Diaβeta® 2.5 mg	R7	D2
Diaβeta® 5 mg	R14	C7
Diabinese™ 100 mg	R19	C2
Diabinese™ 250 mg	R14	C4
Diamicron® 80 mg	R9	C3
Diamox® 250 mg	R11	B7
Diamox® Sequels® 500 mg	R30	C5
Diane®-35	R16	E3
Dicetel® 50 mg	R19	C6
Didrocal®	R28	A5
Diflucan™ 50 mg	R23	D2
Diflucan™ 100 mg	R23	E2
Diflucan-150™	R28	A8

	Page	Code
Lamisil® 1% Cream/ crème	R36	C1
Lamisil® 250 mg	R11	D1
Lanoxin® 0.0625 mg	R21	E6
Lanoxin® 0.125 mg	R16	C6
Lanoxin® 0.25 mg	R8	B3
Lansoÿl® Gel/gelée	R39	C5
Lansoÿl® Jelly Unidose/ gelée unidose	R39	D5
Lanvis® 40 mg	R17	D1
Largactil®	R34	A1
Lariam® 250 mg	R11	A8
Lasix® 20 mg	R7	A4
Lasix® 40 mg	R17	A2
Lasix® 80 mg	R18	D1
Lasix® Special/Spécial 500 mg	R17	C5
Lectopam® 1.5 mg	R9	E3
Lectopam® 3 mg	R22	D3
Lectopam® 6 mg	R25	E8
Leritine® 25 mg	R8	E6
Lescol® 20 mg	R33	C1
Lescol® 40 mg	R33	D1
Leukeran® 2 mg	R7	B3
Levaquin® 250 mg	R23	E8
Levaquin® 500 mg	R24	C1
Levaquin® 25 mg/mL	R34	C8
Librax®	R31	D7
Lincocin® 500 mg	R32	B5
Lioresal® 10 mg	R13	C7
Lioresal® D.S. 20 mg	R15	B5
Lioresal® Intrathecal 0.05 mg/mL	R35	C1
Lioresal® Intrathecal 0.5 mg/mL	R35	D1
Lioresal® Intrathecal 2 mg/mL	R35	E1
Lipidil Micro®	R30	E3
Lipitor™ 10 mg	R13	C6
Lipitor™ 20 mg	R13	B8
Lipitor™ 40 mg	R14	C3
Lithane™ 300 mg	R32	A8
Livostin® Nasal Spray/ vaporisant nasal	R35	C5
Loestrin™ 1.5/30 21-day/jours	R37	E5
Loestrin™ 1.5/30 28-day/jours	R37	E6
Lomotil® 2.5 mg	R7	C2
Loniten® 2.5 mg	R7	C8
Loniten® 10 mg	R7	D8
Lopid® 300 mg	R31	A4
Lopid® 600 mg	R14	D4
Lopresor® 50 mg	R23	C8
Lopresor® 100 mg	R27	E7
Lopresor® SR 100 mg	R18	A8
Lopresor® SR 200 mg	R17	D3
Losec® 10 mg	R20	A5
Losec® 20 mg	R20	B5
Lotensin® 5 mg	R19	D2
Lotensin® 10 mg	R19	A3
Lotensin® 20 mg	R25	E1
Lozide® 1.25 mg	R19	B6
Lozide® 2.5 mg	R22	B1
Ludiomil® 10 mg	R16	B7
Ludiomil® 25 mg	R24	D2
Ludiomil® 50 mg	R18	C5
Ludiomil® 75 mg	R24	D7
Luvox® 50 mg	R9	B6
Luvox® 100 mg	R14	D2

M

	Page	Code
Majeptil®	R19	E6
Malarone™	R40	E5
Maltlevol®-M	R18	A1
Mandelamine® 500 mg	R25	A3
Manerix® 150 mg	R21	E5
Marvelon® 21	R37	D5
Marvelon® 28	R37	D6
Maxeran® 5 mg	R12	D8
Maxeran® 10 mg	R9	C1
Medrol® 4 mg	R13	A5
Medrol® 16 mg	R13	D7
Megace® 40 mg	R27	C2
Megace® 160 mg	R14	A3
Megral®	R10	D5
Mellaril® Solution	R39	A2
Mellaril® Suspension	R39	C1
Mepron® Suspension	R39	D2
Mersyndol® with Codeine/ avec codéine	R10	A7
Mesasal® 500 mg	R20	C1
M-Eslon® 10 mg	R28	A7
M-Eslon® 15 mg	R29	B5
M-Eslon® 30 mg	R31	E1
M-Eslon® 60 mg	R30	B3
M-Eslon® 100 mg	R29	D2
M-Eslon® 200 mg	R29	E2
Metreton®	R8	A6
Mevacor® 20 mg	R27	A4
Mevacor® 40 mg	R26	D1
Micatin® Cream 2%	R36	A2
Micatin® Spray Powder/ aérosol	R36	B2
Micro-K Extencaps® 600 mg	R30	D1
Micro-K Extencaps® 750 mg	R30	C3
Micronor® 28-day/jours	R36	C3
Midamor®	R17	D6
Midol® Regular	R15	E2
Midol® PMS Extra Strength/SPM extra-fort	R15	A5
Migranal® 4 mg/mL	R35	E5
Minestrin™ 1/20 21-day/jours	R37	A5
Minestrin™ 1/20 28-day/jours	R37	A6
Minipress™ 1 mg	R20	D2
Minipress™ 2 mg	R9	E1
Minipress™ 5 mg	R13	C3
Minitran™ 0.2 mg/h Patches	R40	A3
Minitran™ 0.4 mg/h Patches	R40	B3
Minitran™ 0.6 mg/h Patches	R40	C3
Min-Ovral® 21	R37	A3
Min-Ovral® 28	R37	B3
Mintezol® 500 mg	R21	C2
Mirapex® 0.25 mg	R13	E4
Mirapex® 1 mg	R9	E7
Mirapex® 1.5 mg	R11	E1
Mobiflex® 20 mg	R19	E2
Moditen® HCl 5 mg	R9	B4
Moditen® HCl 10 mg	R24	C5
Modulon® 100 mg	R9	B3
Modulon® 200 mg	R12	A4
Moduret®	R21	E3
Mogadon® 5 mg	R7	D4
Mogadon® 10 mg	R8	B6
Monistat® 3 Ovules 400 mg	R33	B7
Monistat® 7 Supp. 100 mg	R33	C7
Monitan® 100 mg	R7	A7
Monitan® 200 mg	R13	A8
Monitan® 400 mg	R15	D3
Monopril® 10 mg	R13	E2
Monopril® 20 mg	R14	A8
Motrin® 300 mg	R11	E8
Motrin® 400 mg	R19	D7
Motrin® 600 mg	R21	A6
Motrin® (Children's) Suspension	R39	B3
Motrin® IB Caplets	R15	B2
Motrin® IB Tablets/ comprimés	R10	B5
MS Contin® 15 mg	R25	E6
MS Contin® 30 mg	R28	A2
MS Contin® 60 mg	R20	E4
MS Contin® 100 mg	R28	B2
MS Contin® 200 mg	R24	C6
MSD® Enteric Coated ASA/AAS à enrobage entéro-soluble 325 mg	R25	A1
MSD® Enteric Coated ASA/AAS à enrobage entéro-soluble 650 mg	R20	B1
MS•IR® 5 mg	R7	B8
MS•IR® 10 mg	R9	E5
MS•IR® 20 mg	R14	D6
MS•IR® 30 mg	R14	B7
Multipax® 25 mg	R26	C2
Mycifradin® 0.5 g	R11	A5
Mycostatin® 500 000 units	R24	E8
Myleran® 2 mg	R7	C6
Myoflex® Ultra	R36	A1
Mysoline® 250 mg	R10	A6
Mysoline® Pediatric/ pédiatrique	R8	E5

N

	Page	Code
Nalcrom® 100 mg	R28	D7
Naprosyn® 250 mg	R17	E8
Naprosyn® 375 mg	R23	A6
Naprosyn® 500 mg	R18	C2
Naprosyn® 500 mg Supp.	R34	B1
Naprosyn® E 250 mg	R10	C3
Naprosyn® E 375 mg	R14	A2
Naprosyn® E 500 mg	R15	E3
Naprosyn® SR 750 mg	R21	B6
Nardil® 15 mg	R24	B5
Nasacort® AQ	R35	D5
Nasacort® Nasal Aerosol	R38	A1
Navane™ 2 mg	R28	E5
Navane™ 5 mg	R30	C2
Navane™ 10 mg	R30	D3
NegGram® 500 mg	R18	D2
Neoral® 10 mg	R29	A3
Neoral® 25 mg	R29	B3
Neoral® 50 mg	R29	C3
Neoral® 100 mg	R29	D3
Neoral® Oral Solution/ solution orale	R35	B1
Neptazane® 25 mg	R12	A8
Neptazane® 50 mg	R7	E6
Neuleptil® 5 mg	R32	A3
Neuleptil® 10 mg	R32	A1
Neuleptil® 20 mg	R32	C1
Neurontin™ 100 mg	R28	C6
Neurontin™ 300 mg	R29	D6
Neurontin™ 400 mg	R30	C1
Nicotrol® 5 mg/16 h Patches	R39	A8
Nicotrol® 10 mg/16 h Patches	R39	B8
Nicotrol® 15 mg/16 h Patches	R39	C8
Nimotop® 30 mg	R29	A4
Nimotop® I.V.	R35	A1
Nitro-Dur® 0.2 mg/h Patches	R40	A1
Nitro-Dur® 0.3 mg/h Patches	R40	B1
Nitro-Dur® 0.4 mg/h Patches	R40	C1
Nitro-Dur® 0.6 mg/h Patches	R40	D1
Nitro-Dur® 0.8 mg/h Patches	R40	E1
Nitrolingual® Spray/ pulvérisateur 0.4 mg	R35	C4
Nitrong® SR 2.6 mg	R26	A2
Nitrostat® 0.3 mg	R7	B1
Nitrostat® 0.6 mg	R7	C1
Nizoral® 200 mg	R16	D4
Nizoral® 2% Cream/ crème	R36	B1
Nizoral® 2% Shampoo/ shampooing	R36	C2
Norinyl® 1/50 (21s)	R37	A7
Norinyl® 1/50 (28s)	R37	A8
Norlutate® 5 mg	R21	A8
Noroxin® 400 mg	R13	C8
Norpramin® 10 mg	R26	A6
Norpramin® 25 mg	R18	D6
Norpramin® 50 mg	R25	B7
Norpramin® 75 mg	R24	A8
Norpramin® 100 mg	R19	C7
Norvasc™ 5 mg	R12	D7
Norvasc™ 10 mg	R12	E7
Nova-T	R37	E8
NovoFine® 30G	R35	D6
Novolin® **ge** Penfill®	R35	E6
Novolin-Pen® 3	R35	C6
Nozinan® 25 mg	R17	B3

O

	Page	Code
Ogen® 0.625 mg	R18	C1
Ogen® 1.25 mg	R21	B5
Ogen® 2.5 mg	R27	D7
One A Day® Advance Fem/forme logique fem	R20	A2
Optimine®	R8	C8
Orifer®.F	R22	B6
Ortho® 0.5/35 21-day/jours	R36	B7
Ortho® 0.5/35 28-day/jours	R36	B8
Ortho® 1/35 21-day/jours	R36	C7
Ortho® 1/35 28-day/jours	R36	C8
Ortho® 7/7/7 21-day/jours	R36	D5
Ortho® 7/7/7 28-day/jours	R36	E5
Ortho® 10/11 21-day/jours	R36	C4
Ortho® 10/11 28-day/jours	R36	C5
Ortho-Cept® 21-day/jours	R36	B3
Ortho-Cept® 28-day/jours	R36	B4
Ortho-Novum® 1/50 21-day/jours	R36	D7
Ortho-Novum® 1/50 28-day/jours	R36	D8
Orudis® 50 mg Capsules	R32	C8
Orudis® 100 mg Supp.	R34	A2
Orudis® E-50 50 mg	R17	B2
Orudis® E-100 100 mg	R17	E4
Orudis® SR-200 200 mg	R11	A7
Oruvail® 150 mg	R31	C1
Oruvail® 200 mg	R33	A5
Os-Cal® 250 mg	R26	A1
Os-Cal® 500 mg	R26	B4
Os-Cal®-D 500 mg	R15	B6
Ostac® 400 mg	R29	A1
Ostoforte® 50 000 units	R29	D7
Ovol®-40	R11	B4
Ovol®-80	R12	D3
Ovol®-160	R12	A1
Ovral® 21	R37	C3
Ovral® 28	R37	D3
Oxeze® Turbuhaler® 6 µg	R38	A6
Oxeze® Turbuhaler® 12 µg	R38	B6
OxyContin® 10 mg	R7	E8
OxyContin® 20 mg	R22	B2
OxyContin® 40 mg	R17	B1
OxyContin® 80 mg	R25	D8

P

	Page	Code
Paludrine®	R8	B4
Pancrease®	R29	C1
Pancrease® MT 4	R29	D4
Pancrease® MT 10	R30	D7
Pancrease® MT 16	R30	E7
Panectyl® 2.5 mg	R21	D6
Panectyl® 5 mg	R20	D4
Pantoloc™ 40 mg	R17	D7
Parlodel® 2.5 mg Tablets/ comprimés	R13	B6
Parlodel® 5 mg Capsules/ gélules	R31	E3
Parnate® 10 mg	R24	C4
Parsitan®	R9	E8
Paxil® 10 mg	R19	D1
Paxil® 20 mg	R23	A8

	Page	Code
Synthroid® 175 µg	R28	D2
Synthroid® 200 µg	R22	A2
Synthroid® 300 µg	R25	D6

T

	Page	Code
Talwin® 50 mg	R20	D6
Tamofen® 10 mg	R8	C1
Tamofen® 20 mg	R8	D8
Tasmar™ 100 mg	R19	B3
Tasmar™ 200 mg	R19	C3
Tegretol®/Tégrétol® 200 mg	R10	A2
Tegretol®/Tégrétol® 100 mg Chewtabs/ comprimés à mâcher	R22	E4
Tegretol®/Tégrétol® 200 mg Chewtabs/ comprimés à mâcher	R23	D5
Tegretol®/Tégrétol® CR 200 mg	R20	E2
Tegretol®/Tégrétol® CR 400 mg	R21	D5
Tegretol®/Tégrétol® Suspension	R39	E2
Tenuate® 25 mg	R10	D6
Tenuate® Dospan® 75 mg	R15	C7
Terazol® 3 Dual-Pak	R34	A5
Terazol® 3 Vaginal Cream	R34	B5
Terazol® 3 Vaginal Ovules	R34	C5
Terazol® 7 Vaginal Cream	R34	D5
Theo-Dur® 100 mg	R10	D3
Theo-Dur® 200 mg	R13	E8
Theo-Dur® 300 mg	R15	A3
Theo-Dur® 450 mg	R15	D7
Theo-SR® 300 mg	R15	D4
3TC® 10 mg/mL Oral Solution/solution orale	R39	D1
3TC® 150 mg Tablets	R13	B3
Tiazac™ 120 mg	R32	A6
Tiazac™ 180 mg	R31	A7
Tiazac™ 240 mg	R31	E8
Tiazac™ 300 mg	R32	E5
Tiazac™ 360 mg	R31	D8
Ticlid® 250 mg	R14	C1
Timolide®	R27	C4
Tofranil® 25 mg	R24	C2
Tofranil® 50 mg	R24	B3
Tofranil® 75 mg	R24	E7
Tolectin® 200 mg Tablets/ comprimés	R17	D4
Tolectin® 400 mg Capsules	R30	E4
Tolectin® 600 mg Tablets/ comprimés	R20	A1
Tonocard® 400 mg	R19	C1
Topamax® 25 mg	R7	E2
Topamax® 100 mg	R18	B8
Topamax® 200 mg	R21	E1
Toradol® 10 mg	R9	C2
Trandate® 100 mg	R19	A2
Trandate® 200 mg	R14	D8
Trandate® Injection	R34	A8
Transderm-Nitro® 0.2 Patches	R40	A2
Transderm-Nitro® 0.4 Patches	R40	B2
Transderm-Nitro® 0.6 Patches	R40	C2
Trasicor® 40 mg	R8	D6
Trasicor® 80 mg	R18	D7
Trental® 400 mg	R24	B1
Triavil®	R23	B8
Tri-Cyclen® Dialpak 21-day/jours	R36	D3
Tri-Cyclen® Dialpak 28-day/jours	R36	E3
Tri-Cyclen® Discreet 21-day/jours	R37	C1
Tri-Cyclen® Discreet 28-day/jours	R37	D1
Trilafon® 2 mg	R16	B2
Trilafon® 4 mg	R16	C2
Trinalin®	R16	D2
Triphasil® 21	R36	A5
Triphasil® 28	R36	B5
Triptil® 10 mg	R8	B1
Triquilar® 21	R36	E7
Triquilar® 28	R36	E8
Trosyd™ AF	R36	D1
Trosyd™ J	R36	E1
Tussionex®	R25	D4
282 MEP®	R12	E1
292®	R21	A2
222®	R11	D5
Tylenol® 325 mg Caplets	R15	C2
Tylenol® 325 mg Tablets	R10	B7
Tylenol® 500 mg Caplets	R15	C5
Tylenol® 500 mg Tablets	R11	E5
Tylenol® Aches and Strains Medication	R28	B1
Tylenol® Allergy Sinus Extra Strength	R18	E2
Tylenol® Chewable Tablets (fruit)	R22	A7
Tylenol® Chewable Tablets sucrose-free (bubble gum)	R22	B7
Tylenol® Chewable Tablets sucrose-free (grape)	R28	B3
Tylenol® Children's Elixir	R39	D4
Tylenol® Children's Suspension Liquid (bubble gum)	R39	B4
Tylenol® Children's Suspension Liquid (grape)	R39	E5
Tylenol® Cold Medications Children's Chewable Tablets	R22	C7
Tylenol® Cold Medications Children's DM Chewable Tablets	R22	D7
Tylenol® Cold Medications Children's Suspension	R39	D3
Tylenol® Cold Medications Children's DM Suspension	R39	E3
Tylenol® Cold Medications Extra Strength Cold and Flu (honey-lemon) Powder	R38	D7
Tylenol® Cold Medications Extra Strength (Daytime) Caplets	R19	D4
Tylenol® Cold Medications Extra Strength (Nighttime) Caplets	R19	E4
Tylenol® Cold Medications Infant's Suspension	R39	C6
Tylenol® Cold Medications Jr. Strength DM Chewable Tablets	R28	D3
Tylenol® Cold Medications Regular Strength (Daytime) Caplets	R19	B4
Tylenol® Cold Medications Regular Strength (Nighttime) Caplets	R19	C4
Tylenol® Cough Medication Extra Strength Caplets	R24	D6
Tylenol® Decongestant Liquid	R39	A4
Tylenol® Flu Medication	R32	C2
Tylenol® Gelcaps 500 mg	R32	E7
Tylenol® Infant's Suspension Drops (grape)	R39	D6
Tylenol® Infant's Suspension Drops (cherry)	R39	E6
Tylenol® Jr. Strength Chewable Tablets (fruit)	R23	C1
Tylenol® Jr. Strength Chewable Tablets, sucrose-free (bubble gum)	R23	D1
Tylenol® Jr. Strength Chewable Tablets, sucrose-free (grape)	R28	C3
Tylenol® Sinus Medication Extra Strength	R26	A4
Tylenol® Sinus Medication Regular Strength	R26	C3
Tylenol® with Codeine NO. 2, 15 mg	R11	B3
Tylenol® with Codeine NO. 3, 30 mg	R11	C3
Tylenol® with Codeine NO. 4, 60 mg	R11	D3
Tylenol® with Codeine Elixir	R39	A5

U

	Page	Code
Ultrase® MT6	R29	B6
Ultrase® MT12	R29	C5
Ultrase® MT20	R32	E8
Uniphyl® 400 mg	R11	E2
Uniphyl® 600 mg	R16	C1
Urecholine® 10 mg	R11	C6
Urecholine® 25 mg	R17	C4
Ursofalk® 250 mg	R29	B1

V

	Page	Code
Valium® Roche® 5 mg	R16	A8
Valium® Roche® 10 mg	R26	B8
Valtrex® 500 mg	R28	A1
Vaseretic®	R24	E1
Vasotec® 2.5 mg	R18	A3
Vasotec® 5 mg	R12	C8
Vasotec® 10 mg	R25	D3
Vasotec® 20 mg	R21	C4
Ventodisk® 200 µg	R38	B3
Ventodisk® 400 µg	R38	C3
Ventolin® 100 µg	R38	A3
Ventolin® Oral/liquide	R39	A1
Ventolin® Rotacaps® 200 µg	R31	B7
Ventolin® Rotacaps® 400 µg	R32	B2
Vepesid® 50 mg	R30	B7
Vesanoid™ 10 mg	R29	E7
Vibramycin® I.V. 100 mL	R34	B7
Vibra-Tabs™ 100 mg	R18	C7
Vibra-Tabs™ C-Pak™	R36	D2
Videx™ 25 mg	R12	B4
Videx™ 50 mg	R12	C4
Videx™ 100 mg	R12	D4
Videx™ 150 mg	R12	E4
Viskazide® 10/25	R20	A8
Viskazide® 10/50	R20	B8
Visken® 5 mg	R8	C2
Visken® 10 mg	R8	D2
Visken® 15 mg	R10	D1
Vitathion® -A.T.P. Granules	R38	E7
Vivelle® 37.5 mg Patches	R39	D7
Vivelle® 50 mg Patches	R39	E7
Vivelle® 75 mg Patches	R39	D8
Vivelle® 100 mg Patches	R39	E8
Vivol® 2 mg	R25	C7
Vivol® 5 mg	R25	D7
Vivol® 10 mg	R25	E7
Voltaren® 25 mg	R18	D4
Voltaren® 50 mg	R18	D5
Voltaren Rapide® 50 mg	R24	B4
Voltaren® SR 75 mg	R23	E3
Voltaren® SR 100 mg	R20	E7
Voltaren® 50 mg Supp.	R33	D8
Voltaren® 100 mg Supp.	R33	E8

W

	Page	Code
Warfilone® 5 mg	R9	A4
Wellbutrin® SR 100 mg	R27	A2
Wellbutrin® SR 150 mg	R28	A3

X

	Page	Code
Xanax® 0.25 mg	R13	E5
Xanax® 0.5 mg	R21	E4
Xanax® 1 mg	R28	A4
Xanax® 2 mg	R16	A1

Y

	Page	Code
Yocon®	R10	A3

Z

	Page	Code
Zaditen® 1 mg	R7	B5
Zaditen® Syrup/sirop	R39	B1
Zantac® 75 Tablets/ comprimés	R23	D3
Zantac® 150 mg Capsules	R30	A8
Zantac® 150 mg Tablets/ comprimés	R10	A5
Zantac® 300 mg Capsules	R30	B8
Zantac® 300 mg Tablets/ comprimés	R15	E6
Zantac® Oral Solution/ solution orale	R39	B2
Zarontin® 250 mg	R30	A6
Zaroxolyn® 2.5 mg	R21	D8
Zaroxolyn® 5 mg	R26	C6
Zerit™ 15 mg	R33	A1
Zerit™ 20 mg	R30	B1
Zerit™ 30 mg	R33	B1
Zerit™ 40 mg	R30	C4
Zestoretic® 10/12.5 mg	R21	C7
Zestoretic® 20/12.5 mg	R9	A2
Zestoretic® 20/25 mg	R20	C6
Zestril® 5 mg	R21	E7
Zestril® 10 mg	R20	A7
Zestril® 20 mg	R20	B7
Zithromax™ 250 mg Capsules	R31	E2
Zithromax™ Powder for Oral Suspension/ poudre pour suspension orale	R38	E6
Zocor® 5 mg	R18	D3
Zocor® 10 mg	R23	C3
Zocor® 20 mg	R21	D3
Zocor® 40 mg	R23	B4
Zofran® 4 mg	R19	B2
Zofran® 8 mg	R19	D3
Zofran® Injection/ injectable	R34	A6
Zofran® Oral Solution/ solution orale	R39	E1
Zoloft™ 25 mg	R29	E5
Zoloft™ 50 mg	R29	D5
Zoloft™ 100 mg	R30	D5
Zovirax™ 200 mg	R27	E4
Zovirax™ 400 mg	R23	C4
Zovirax™ 800 mg	R28	C1
Zyloprim® 100 mg	R9	C8
Zyloprim® 200 mg	R9	D8
Zyloprim® 300 mg	R21	D1
Zyrtec®	R14	E7

Use code A, B, C, D, E, horizontal bar and 1 to 8 vertical bar to locate illustrated products

Utiliser le code A, B, C, D, E de la ligne horizontale et les chiffres 1 à 8 de la ligne verticale pour repérer les produits illustrés

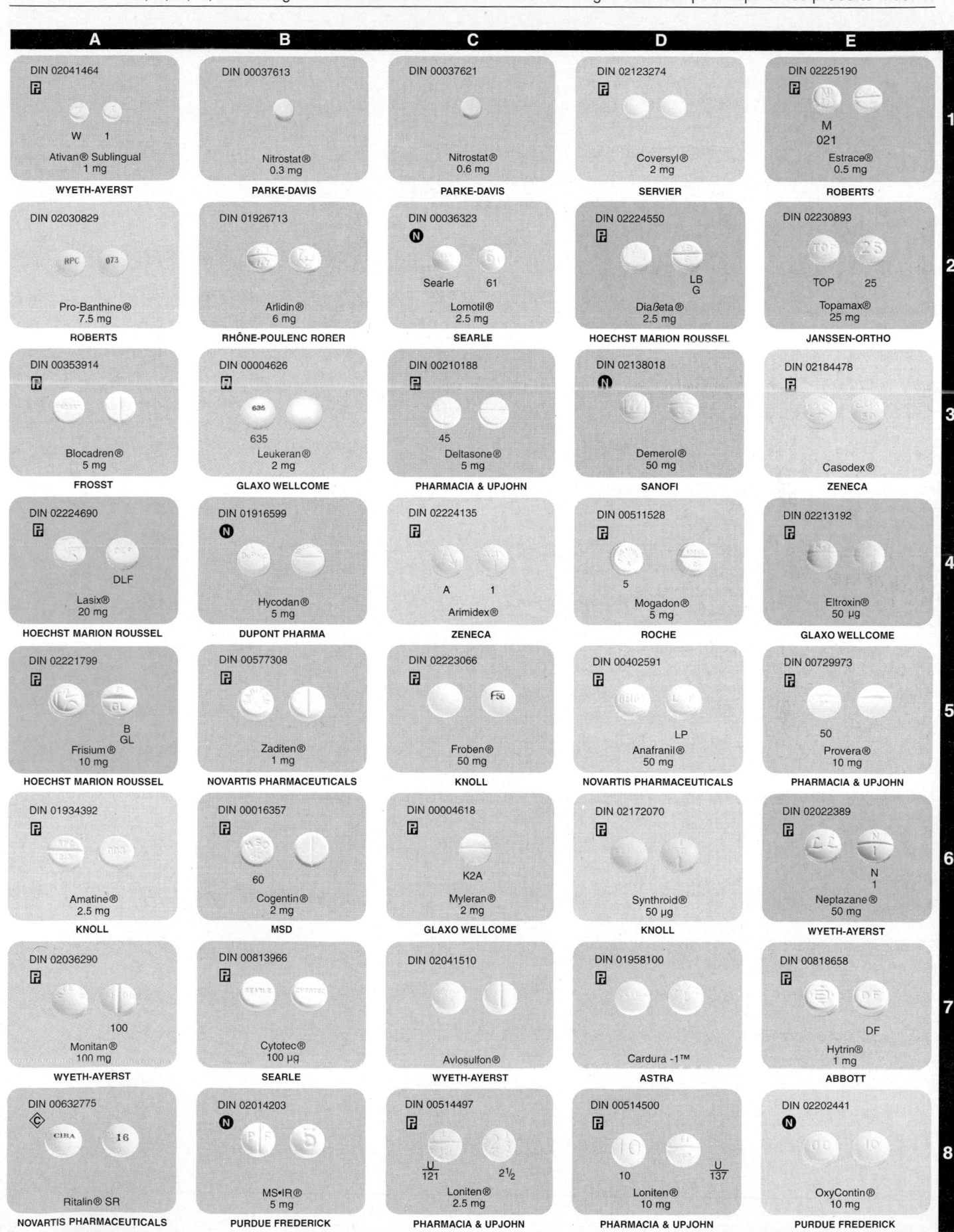

	A	B	C	D	E
1	DIN 02041464 Pr W 1 Ativan® Sublingual 1 mg **WYETH-AYERST**	DIN 00037613 Nitrostat® 0.3 mg **PARKE-DAVIS**	DIN 00037621 Nitrostat® 0.6 mg **PARKE-DAVIS**	DIN 02123274 Pr Coversyl® 2 mg **SERVIER**	DIN 02225190 Pr M 021 Estrace® 0.5 mg **ROBERTS**
2	DIN 02030829 RPC 073 Pro-Banthine® 7.5 mg **ROBERTS**	DIN 01926713 Arlidin® 6 mg **RHÔNE-POULENC RORER**	DIN 00036323 N Searle 61 Lomotil® 2.5 mg **SEARLE**	DIN 02224550 Pr LB G Diaßeta® 2.5 mg **HOECHST MARION ROUSSEL**	DIN 02230893 TOP 25 Topamax® 25 mg **JANSSEN-ORTHO**
3	DIN 00353914 Pr Blocadren® 5 mg **FROSST**	DIN 00004626 Pr 635 Leukeran® 2 mg **GLAXO WELLCOME**	DIN 00210188 Pr 45 Deltasone® 5 mg **PHARMACIA & UPJOHN**	DIN 02138018 N Demerol® 50 mg **SANOFI**	DIN 02184478 Pr Casodex® **ZENECA**
4	DIN 02224690 Pr DLF Lasix® 20 mg **HOECHST MARION ROUSSEL**	DIN 01916599 N Hycodan® 5 mg **DUPONT PHARMA**	DIN 02224135 Pr A 1 Arimidex® **ZENECA**	DIN 00511528 Pr 5 Mogadon® 5 mg **ROCHE**	DIN 02213192 Pr Eltroxin® 50 µg **GLAXO WELLCOME**
5	DIN 02221799 Pr B GL Frisium® 10 mg **HOECHST MARION ROUSSEL**	DIN 00577308 Pr Zaditen® 1 mg **NOVARTIS PHARMACEUTICALS**	DIN 02223066 Pr F50 Froben® 50 mg **KNOLL**	DIN 00402591 Pr LP Anafranil® 50 mg **NOVARTIS PHARMACEUTICALS**	DIN 00729973 Pr 50 Provera® 10 mg **PHARMACIA & UPJOHN**
6	DIN 01934392 Pr Amatine® 2.5 mg **KNOLL**	DIN 00016357 Pr 60 Cogentin® 2 mg **MSD**	DIN 00004618 Pr K2A Myleran® 2 mg **GLAXO WELLCOME**	DIN 02172070 Pr Synthroid® 50 µg **KNOLL**	DIN 02022389 Pr N 1 Neptazane® 50 mg **WYETH-AYERST**
7	DIN 02036290 Pr 100 Monitan® 100 mg **WYETH-AYERST**	DIN 00813966 Pr Cytotec® 100 µg **SEARLE**	DIN 02041510 Avlosulfon® **WYETH-AYERST**	DIN 01958100 Pr Cardura -1™ **ASTRA**	DIN 00818658 Pr DF Hytrin® 1 mg **ABBOTT**
8	DIN 00632775 C CIBA 16 Ritalin® SR **NOVARTIS PHARMACEUTICALS**	DIN 02014203 N MS•IR® 5 mg **PURDUE FREDERICK**	DIN 00514497 Pr U/121 2½ Loniten® 2.5 mg **PHARMACIA & UPJOHN**	DIN 00514500 Pr 10 U/137 Loniten® 10 mg **PHARMACIA & UPJOHN**	DIN 02202441 N OxyContin® 10 mg **PURDUE FREDERICK**

Use code A, B, C, D, E, horizontal bar and 1 to 8 vertical bar to locate illustrated products

Utiliser le code A, B, C, D, E de la ligne horizontale et les chiffres 1 à 8 de la ligne verticale pour repérer les produits illustrés

	A	B	C	D	E
1	DIN 00004758  S3A Kemadrin® 5 mg **GLAXO WELLCOME**	DIN 00322741  47 Triptil® 10 mg **MSD**	DIN 01926624  Tamofen® 10 mg **RHÔNE-POULENC RORER**	DIN 02103087 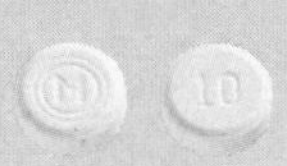 Bentylol® 10 mg **HOECHST MARION ROUSSEL**	DIN 00836311  5 Prepulsid® 5 mg **JANSSEN-ORTHO**
2	DIN 00262676  Procytox® 25 mg **CARTER HORNER**	DIN 00016497  Edecrin® 50 mg **MSD**	DIN 00417270 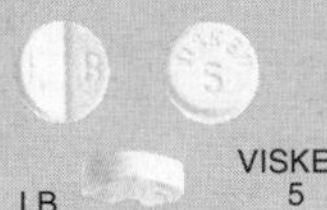 LB VISKEN 5 Visken® 5 mg **NOVARTIS PHARMACEUTICALS**	DIN 00443174 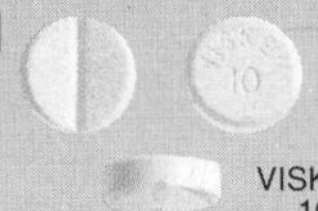 VISKEN 10 Visken® 10 mg **NOVARTIS PHARMACEUTICALS**	DIN 02172119  Synthroid® 125 µg **KNOLL**
3	DIN 02232043  Aricept™ 5 mg **PFIZER**	DIN 00004685  X3A Lanoxin® 0.25 mg **GLAXO WELLCOME**	DIN 00511552 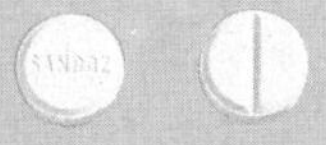 Sandomigran DS® 1 mg **NOVARTIS PHARMACEUTICALS**	DIN 02221861  Anandron® 50 mg **HOECHST MARION ROUSSEL**	DIN 00013749  Procytox® 50 mg **CARTER HORNER**
4	DIN 00176176  Hydergine® **NOVARTIS PHARMACEUTICALS**	DIN 02043068  Paludrine® **WYETH-AYERST**	DIN 00443948 N 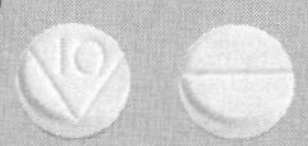 Supeudol® 10 mg **SABEX**	DIN 01926705  Arlidin® Forte 12 mg **RHÔNE-POULENC RORER**	DIN 00411892  Drixtab® **SCHERING**
5	DIN 00728284  133 Burinex® 1 mg **LEO**	DIN 00068500  M2A Actifed® **WARNER-LAMBERT CANADA**	DIN 00004715  A2A Alkeran® 2 mg **GLAXO WELLCOME**	DIN 00016438  126 Cortone® 5 mg **MSD**	DIN 02042363  Mysoline® Pediatric / pédiatrique **WYETH-AYERST**
6	DIN 00177091  Metreton® **SCHERING**	DIN 00511536  10 Mogadon® 10 mg **ROCHE**	DIN 02042622  10 Isordil® Titradose® 10 mg **WYETH-AYERST**	DIN 00402575  Trasicor® 40 mg **NOVARTIS PHARMACEUTICALS**	DIN 00010014 N  Leritine® 25 mg **FROSST**
7	DIN 02103095  Bentylol® 20 mg **HOECHST MARION ROUSSEL**	DIN 00010391  Sintrom® 4 mg **NOVARTIS PHARMACEUTICALS**	DIN 02190885  G 50 Prandase® 50 mg **BAYER**	DIN 02155931 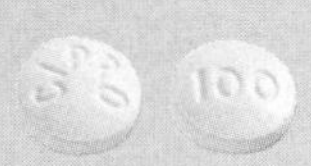 Cipro® 100 mg **BAYER**	DIN 00382841 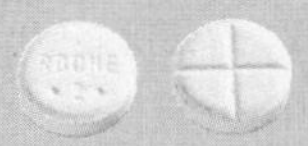 Rivotril® 2 mg **ROCHE**
8	DIN 00004774  A3A Daraprim® 25 mg **GLAXO WELLCOME**	DIN 02182912  Hismanal® **JOHNSON & JOHNSON • MERCK**	DIN 00355666  Optimine® **SCHERING**	DIN 01926632  Tamofen® 20 mg **RHÔNE-POULENC RORER**	DIN 00013781  Honvol® **CARTER HORNER**

Use code A, B, C, D, E, horizontal bar and 1 to 8 vertical bar to locate illustrated products

Utiliser le code A, B, C, D, E de la ligne horizontale et les chiffres 1 à 8 de la ligne verticale pour repérer les produits illustrés

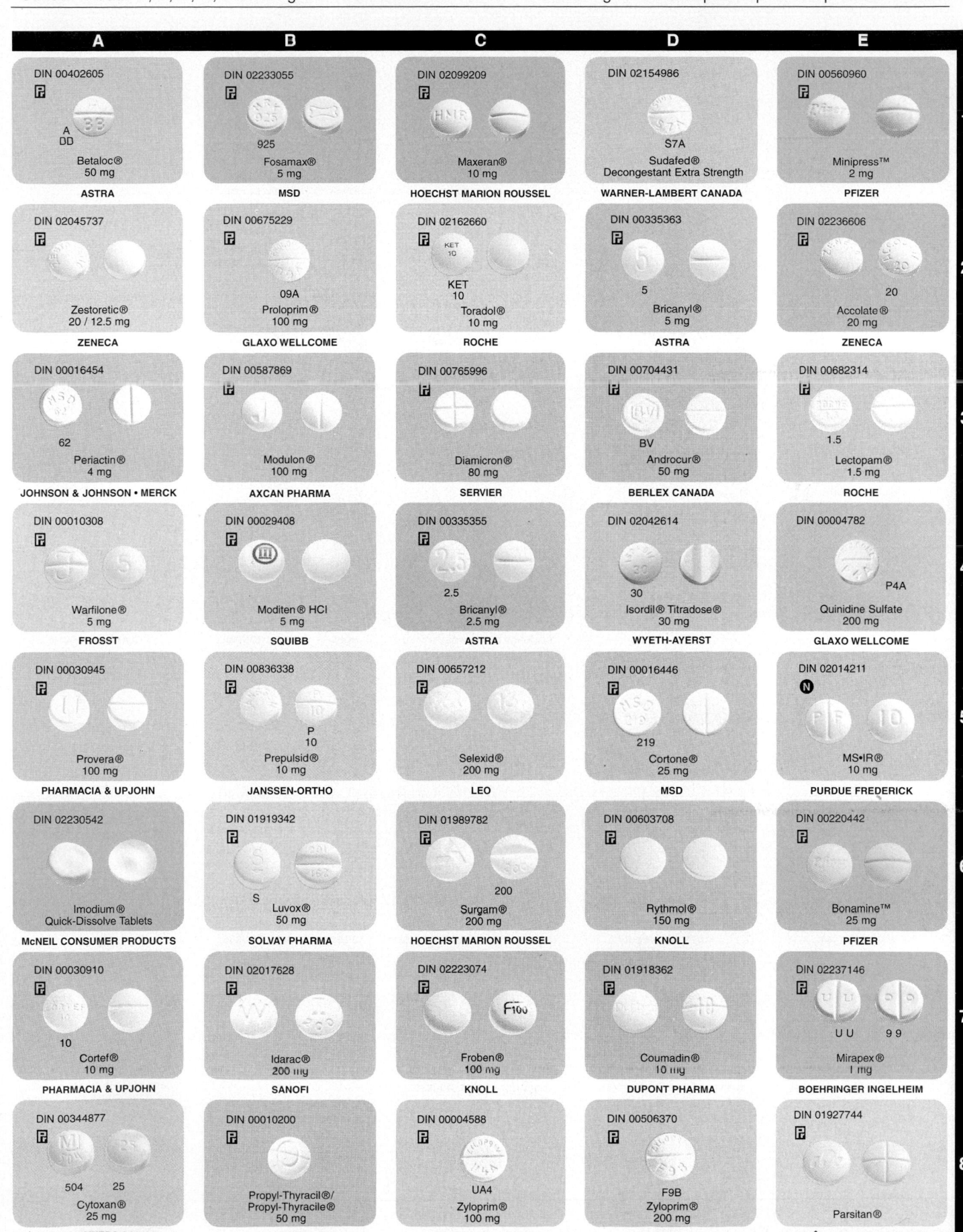

	A	B	C	D	E
1	DIN 00402605  A DD Betaloc® 50 mg **ASTRA**	DIN 02233055  925 Fosamax® 5 mg **MSD**	DIN 02099209  Maxeran® 10 mg **HOECHST MARION ROUSSEL**	DIN 02154986  S7A Sudafed® Decongestant Extra Strength **WARNER-LAMBERT CANADA**	DIN 00560960  Minipress™ 2 mg **PFIZER**
2	DIN 02045737  Zestoretic® 20 / 12.5 mg **ZENECA**	DIN 00675229  09A Proloprim® 100 mg **GLAXO WELLCOME**	DIN 02162660  KET 10 Toradol® 10 mg **ROCHE**	DIN 00335363  5 Bricanyl® 5 mg **ASTRA**	DIN 02236606 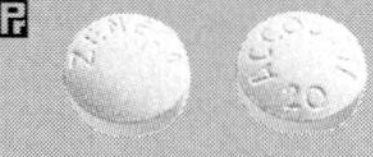 20 Accolate® 20 mg **ZENECA**
3	DIN 00016454  62 Periactin® 4 mg **JOHNSON & JOHNSON • MERCK**	DIN 00587869  Modulon® 100 mg **AXCAN PHARMA**	DIN 00765996  Diamicron® 80 mg **SERVIER**	DIN 00704431  BV Androcur® 50 mg **BERLEX CANADA**	DIN 00682314  1.5 Lectopam® 1.5 mg **ROCHE**
4	DIN 00010308  Warfilone® 5 mg **FROSST**	DIN 00029408  Moditen® HCl 5 mg **SQUIBB**	DIN 00335355  2.5 Bricanyl® 2.5 mg **ASTRA**	DIN 02042614  30 Isordil® Titradose® 30 mg **WYETH-AYERST**	DIN 00004782 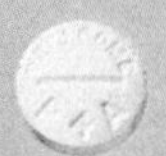 P4A Quinidine Sulfate 200 mg **GLAXO WELLCOME**
5	DIN 00030945  Provera® 100 mg **PHARMACIA & UPJOHN**	DIN 00836338  P 10 Prepulsid® 10 mg **JANSSEN-ORTHO**	DIN 00657212  Selexid® 200 mg **LEO**	DIN 00016446 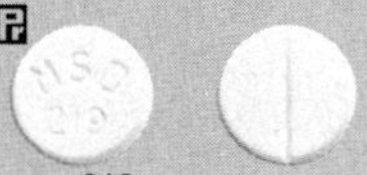 219 Cortone® 25 mg **MSD**	DIN 02014211 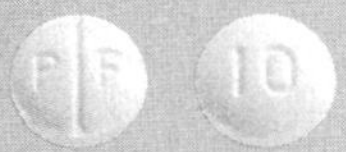 MS•IR® 10 mg **PURDUE FREDERICK**
6	DIN 02230542  Imodium® Quick-Dissolve Tablets **McNEIL CONSUMER PRODUCTS**	DIN 01919342  S Luvox® 50 mg **SOLVAY PHARMA**	DIN 01989782  200 Surgam® 200 mg **HOECHST MARION ROUSSEL**	DIN 00603708  Rythmol® 150 mg **KNOLL**	DIN 00220442  Bonamine™ 25 mg **PFIZER**
7	DIN 00030910  10 Cortef® 10 mg **PHARMACIA & UPJOHN**	DIN 02017628  Idarac® 200 mg **SANOFI**	DIN 02223074  Froben® 100 mg **KNOLL**	DIN 01918362  Coumadin® 10 mg **DUPONT PHARMA**	DIN 02237146  UU 99 Mirapex® 1 mg **BOEHRINGER INGELHEIM**
8	DIN 00344877  504 25 Cytoxan® 25 mg **BRISTOL-MYERS SQUIBB**	DIN 00010200  Propyl-Thyracil®/ Propyl-Thyracile® 50 mg **FROSST**	DIN 00004588  UA4 Zyloprim® 100 mg **GLAXO WELLCOME**	DIN 00506370  F9B Zyloprim® 200 mg **GLAXO WELLCOME**	DIN 01927744  Parsitan® **RHÔNE-POULENC RORER**

Use code A, B, C, D, E, horizontal bar and 1 to 8 vertical bar to locate illustrated products

Utiliser le code A, B, C, D, E de la ligne horizontale et les chiffres 1 à 8 de la ligne verticale pour repérer les produits illustrés

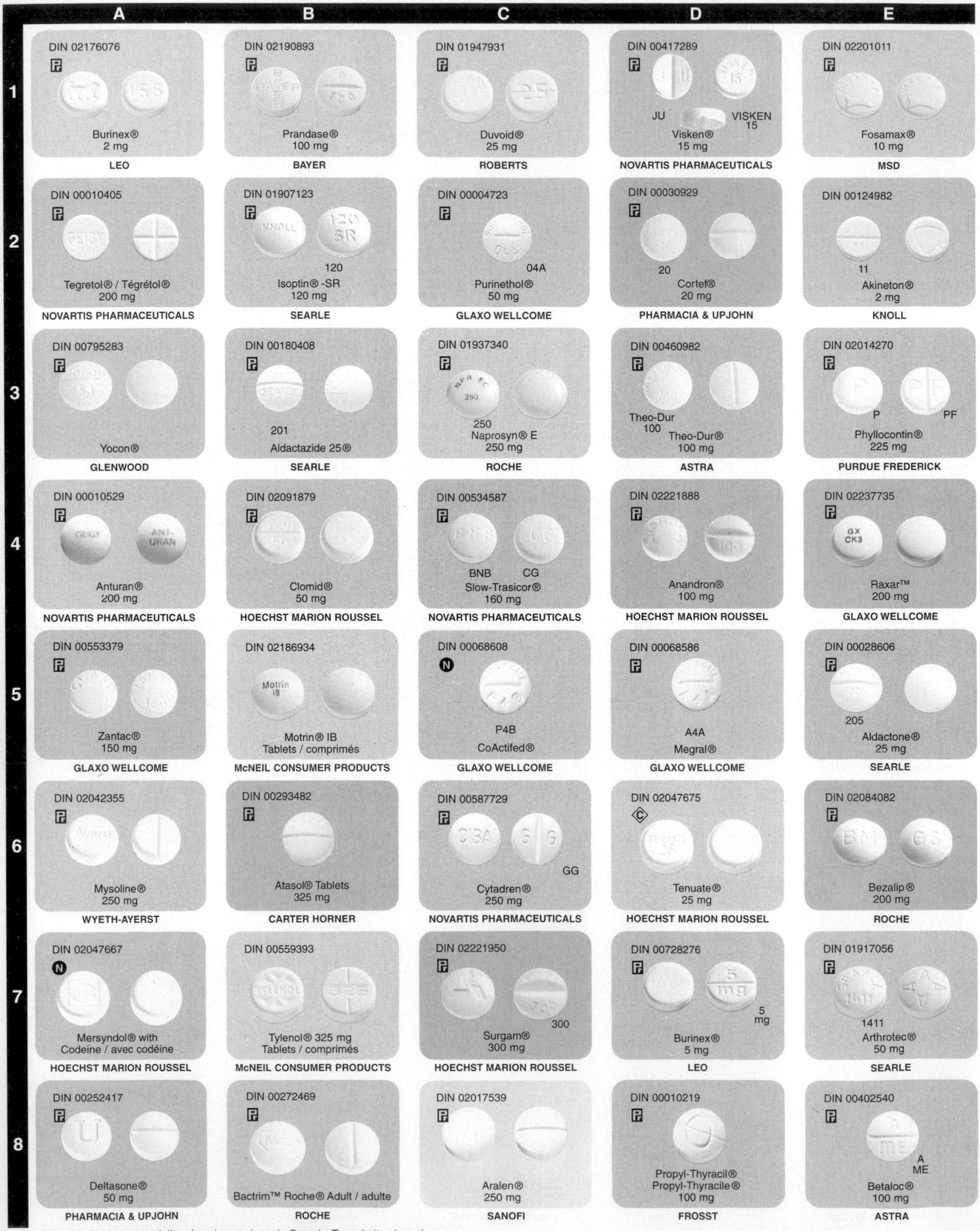

	A	B	C	D	E
1	DIN 02176076 Burinex® 2 mg **LEO**	DIN 02190893 Prandase® 100 mg **BAYER**	DIN 01947931 Duvoid® 25 mg **ROBERTS**	DIN 00417289 JU VISKEN 15 Visken® 15 mg **NOVARTIS PHARMACEUTICALS**	DIN 02201011 Fosamax® 10 mg **MSD**
2	DIN 00010405 Tegretol® / Tégrétol® 200 mg **NOVARTIS PHARMACEUTICALS**	DIN 01907123 120 Isoptin® -SR 120 mg **SEARLE**	DIN 00004723 04A Purinethol® 50 mg **GLAXO WELLCOME**	DIN 00030929 20 Cortef® 20 mg **PHARMACIA & UPJOHN**	DIN 00124982 11 Akineton® 2 mg **KNOLL**
3	DIN 00795283 Yocon® **GLENWOOD**	DIN 00180408 201 Aldactazide 25® **SEARLE**	DIN 01937340 250 Naprosyn® E 250 mg **ROCHE**	DIN 00460982 Theo-Dur 100 Theo-Dur® 100 mg **ASTRA**	DIN 02014270 P PF Phyllocontin® 225 mg **PURDUE FREDERICK**
4	DIN 00010529 Anturan® 200 mg **NOVARTIS PHARMACEUTICALS**	DIN 02091879 Clomid® 50 mg **HOECHST MARION ROUSSEL**	DIN 00534587 BNB CG Slow-Trasicor® 160 mg **NOVARTIS PHARMACEUTICALS**	DIN 02221888 Anandron® 100 mg **HOECHST MARION ROUSSEL**	DIN 02237735 Raxar™ 200 mg **GLAXO WELLCOME**
5	DIN 00553379 Zantac® 150 mg **GLAXO WELLCOME**	DIN 02186934 Motrin® IB Tablets / comprimés **McNEIL CONSUMER PRODUCTS**	DIN 00068608 P4B CoActifed® **GLAXO WELLCOME**	DIN 00068586 A4A Megral® **GLAXO WELLCOME**	DIN 00028606 205 Aldactone® 25 mg **SEARLE**
6	DIN 02042355 Mysoline® 250 mg **WYETH-AYERST**	DIN 00293482 Atasol® Tablets 325 mg **CARTER HORNER**	DIN 00587729 GG Cytadren® 250 mg **NOVARTIS PHARMACEUTICALS**	DIN 02047675 Tenuate® 25 mg **HOECHST MARION ROUSSEL**	DIN 02084082 Bezalip® 200 mg **ROCHE**
7	DIN 02047667 Mersyndol® with Codeine / avec codéine **HOECHST MARION ROUSSEL**	DIN 00559393 Tylenol® 325 mg Tablets / comprimés **McNEIL CONSUMER PRODUCTS**	DIN 02221950 300 Surgam® 300 mg **HOECHST MARION ROUSSEL**	DIN 00728276 5 mg Burinex® 5 mg **LEO**	DIN 01917056 1411 Arthrotec® 50 mg **SEARLE**
8	DIN 00252417 Deltasone® 50 mg **PHARMACIA & UPJOHN**	DIN 00272469 Bactrim™ Roche® Adult / adulte **ROCHE**	DIN 02017539 Aralen® 250 mg **SANOFI**	DIN 00010219 Propyl-Thyracil® Propyl-Thyracile® 100 mg **FROSST**	DIN 00402540 A ME Betaloc® 100 mg **ASTRA**

Use code A, B, C, D, E, horizontal bar and 1 to 8 vertical bar to locate illustrated products

Utiliser le code A, B, C, D, E de la ligne horizontale et les chiffres 1 à 8 de la ligne verticale pour repérer les produits illustrés

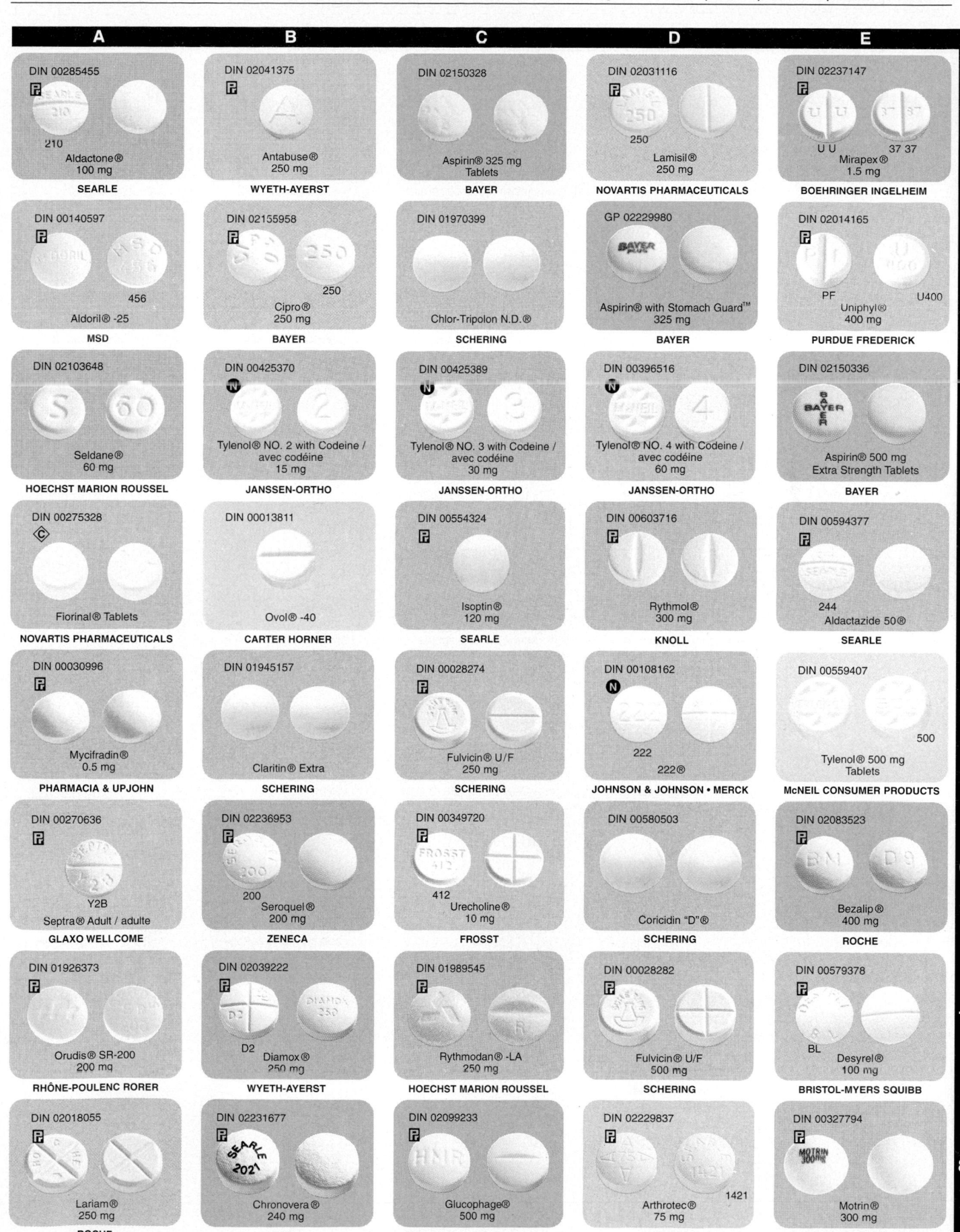

	A	B	C	D	E
1	DIN 00285455  210 Aldactone® 100 mg **SEARLE**	DIN 02041375  Antabuse® 250 mg **WYETH-AYERST**	DIN 02150328 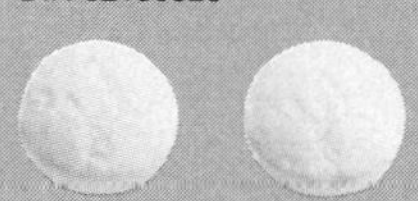 Aspirin® 325 mg Tablets **BAYER**	DIN 02031116 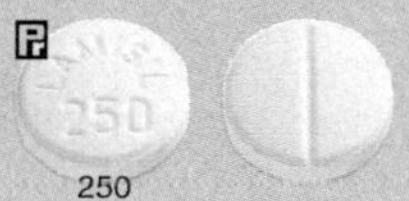 250 Lamisil® 250 mg **NOVARTIS PHARMACEUTICALS**	DIN 02237147 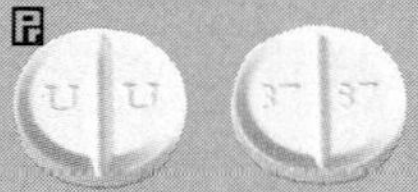 U U 37 37 Mirapex® 1.5 mg **BOEHRINGER INGELHEIM**
2	DIN 00140597 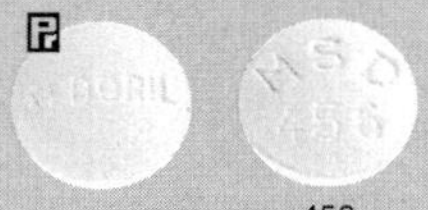 456 Aldoril® -25 **MSD**	DIN 02155958  250 Cipro® 250 mg **BAYER**	DIN 01970399  Chlor-Tripolon N.D.® **SCHERING**	GP 02229980 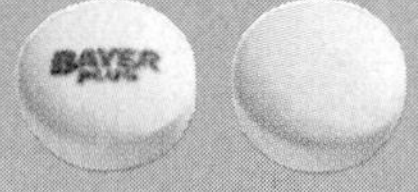 Aspirin® with Stomach Guard™ 325 mg **BAYER**	DIN 02014165 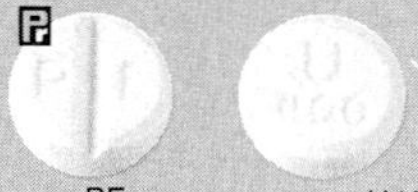 PF U400 Uniphyl® 400 mg **PURDUE FREDERICK**
3	DIN 02103648 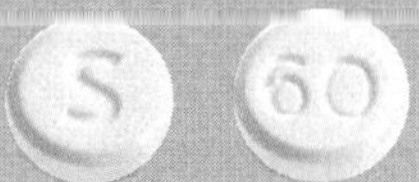 Seldane® 60 mg **HOECHST MARION ROUSSEL**	DIN 00425370 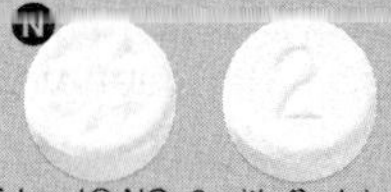 Tylenol® NO. 2 with Codeine / avec codéine 15 mg **JANSSEN-ORTHO**	DIN 00425389  Tylenol® NO. 3 with Codeine / avec codéine 30 mg **JANSSEN-ORTHO**	DIN 00396516 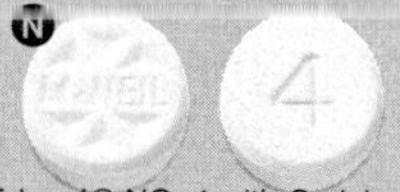 Tylenol® NO. 4 with Codeine / avec codéine 60 mg **JANSSEN-ORTHO**	DIN 02150336 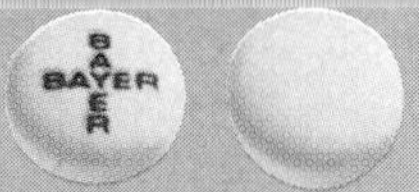 Aspirin® 500 mg Extra Strength Tablets **BAYER**
4	DIN 00275328  Fiorinal® Tablets **NOVARTIS PHARMACEUTICALS**	DIN 00013811  Ovol® -40 **CARTER HORNER**	DIN 00554324  Isoptin® 120 mg **SEARLE**	DIN 00603716 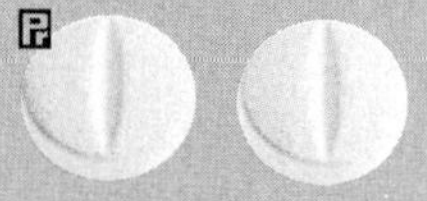 Rythmol® 300 mg **KNOLL**	DIN 00594377  244 Aldactazide 50® **SEARLE**
5	DIN 00030996  Mycifradin® 0.5 mg **PHARMACIA & UPJOHN**	DIN 01945157  Claritin® Extra **SCHERING**	DIN 00028274 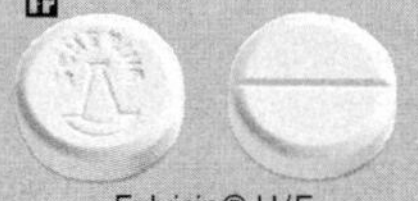 Fulvicin® U/F 250 mg **SCHERING**	DIN 00108162 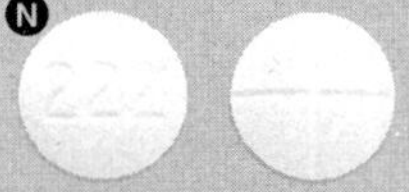 222 222® **JOHNSON & JOHNSON • MERCK**	DIN 00559407 500 Tylenol® 500 mg Tablets **McNEIL CONSUMER PRODUCTS**
6	DIN 00270636  Y2B Septra® Adult / adulte **GLAXO WELLCOME**	DIN 02236953 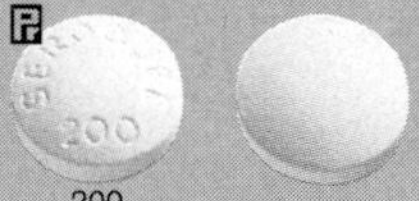 200 Seroquel® 200 mg **ZENECA**	DIN 00349720  412 Urecholine® 10 mg **FROSST**	DIN 00580503 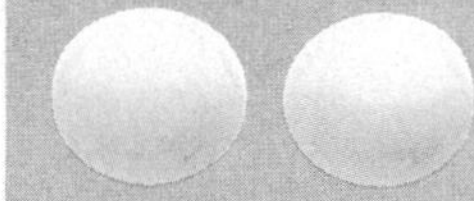 Coricidin "D"® **SCHERING**	DIN 02083523 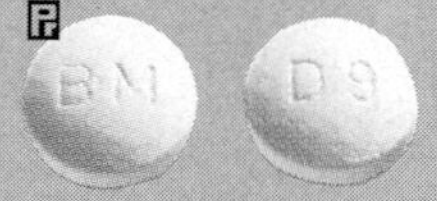 Bezalip® 400 mg **ROCHE**
7	DIN 01926373 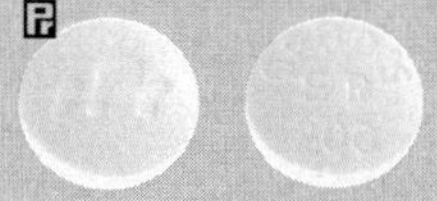 Orudis® SR-200 200 mg **RHÔNE-POULENC RORER**	DIN 02039222 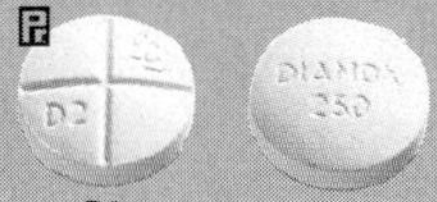 D2 Diamox® 250 mg **WYETH-AYERST**	DIN 01989545  Rythmodan® -LA 250 mg **HOECHST MARION ROUSSEL**	DIN 00028282 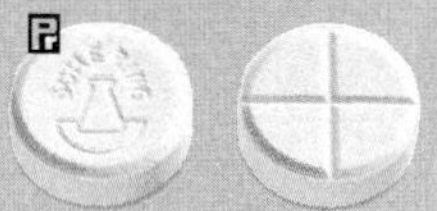 Fulvicin® U/F 500 mg **SCHERING**	DIN 00579378  BL Desyrel® 100 mg **BRISTOL-MYERS SQUIBB**
8	DIN 02018055 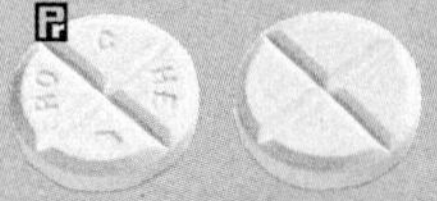 Lariam® 250 mg **ROCHE**	DIN 02231677  Chronovera® 240 mg **SEARLE**	DIN 02099233 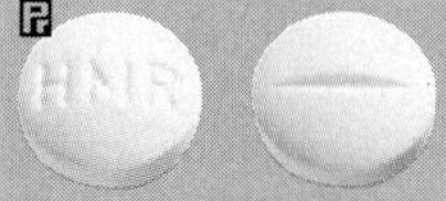 Glucophage® 500 mg **HOECHST MARION ROUSSEL**	DIN 02229837 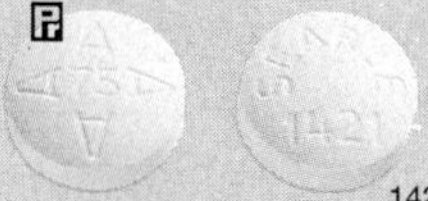 1421 Arthrotec® 75 mg **SEARLE**	DIN 00327794 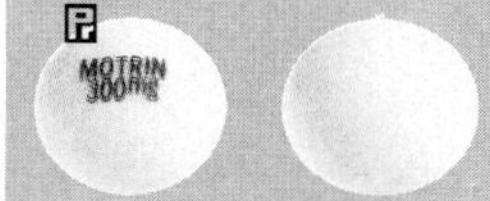 Motrin® 300 mg **PHARMACIA & UPJOHN**

Use code A, B, C, D, E, horizontal bar and 1 to 8 vertical bar to locate illustrated products

Utiliser le code A, B, C, D, E de la ligne horizontale et les chiffres 1 à 8 de la ligne verticale pour repérer les produits illustrés

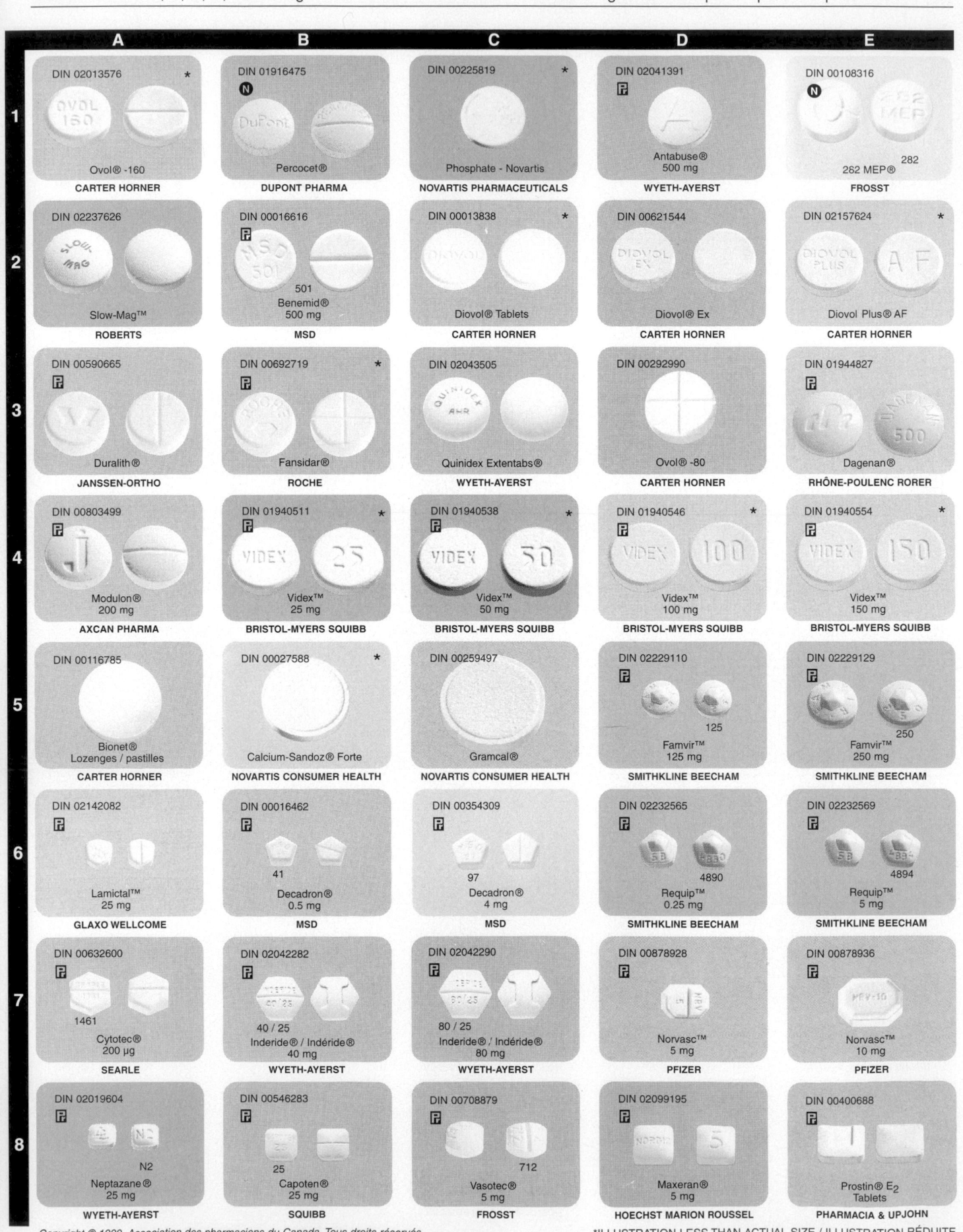

	A	B	C	D	E
1	DIN 02013576 *  Ovol® -160 **CARTER HORNER**	DIN 01916475 N 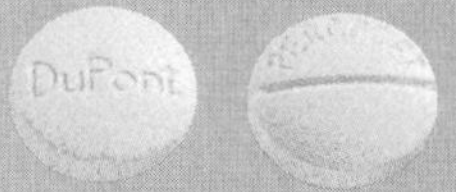 Percocet® **DUPONT PHARMA**	DIN 00225819 *  Phosphate - Novartis **NOVARTIS PHARMACEUTICALS**	DIN 02041391  Antabuse® 500 mg **WYETH-AYERST**	DIN 00108316 N 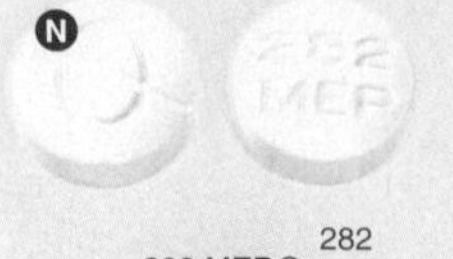 282 262 MEP® **FROSST**
2	DIN 02237626  Slow-Mag™ **ROBERTS**	DIN 00016616 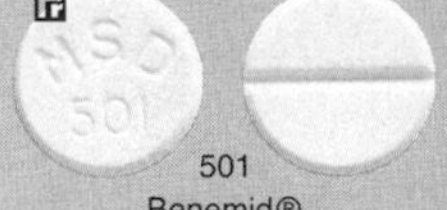 501 Benemid® 500 mg **MSD**	DIN 00013838 * 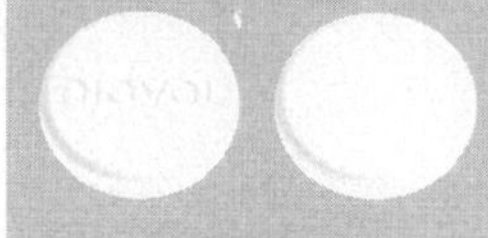 Diovol® Tablets **CARTER HORNER**	DIN 00621544 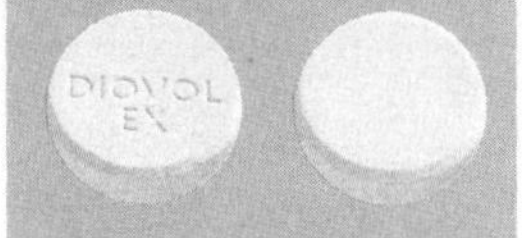 Diovol® Ex **CARTER HORNER**	DIN 02157624 * 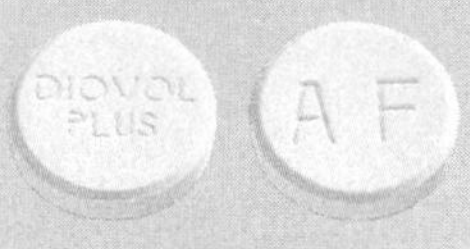 Diovol Plus® AF **CARTER HORNER**
3	DIN 00590665 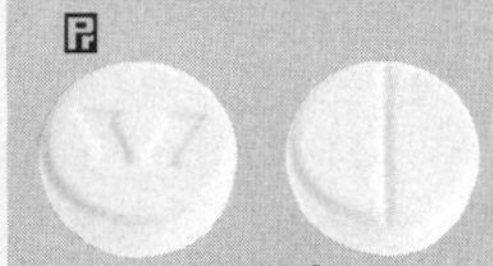 Duralith® **JANSSEN-ORTHO**	DIN 00692719 * 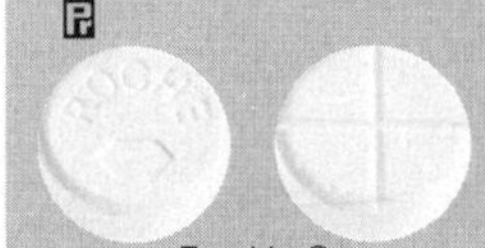 Fansidar® **ROCHE**	DIN 02043505  Quinidex Extentabs® **WYETH-AYERST**	DIN 00292990  Ovol® -80 **CARTER HORNER**	DIN 01944827 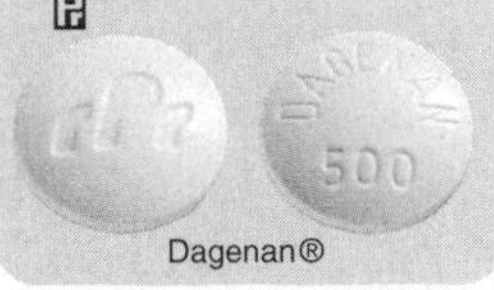 Dagenan® **RHÔNE-POULENC RORER**
4	DIN 00803499 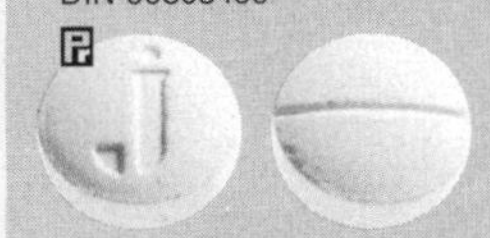 Modulon® 200 mg **AXCAN PHARMA**	DIN 01940511 * 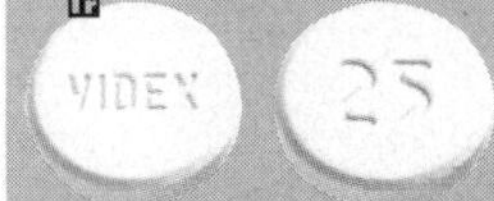 Videx™ 25 mg **BRISTOL-MYERS SQUIBB**	DIN 01940538 * 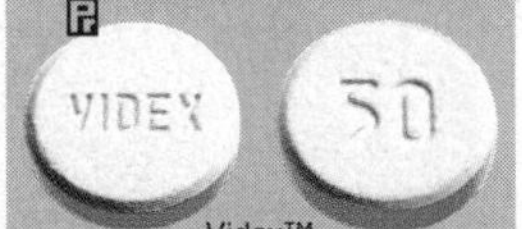 Videx™ 50 mg **BRISTOL-MYERS SQUIBB**	DIN 01940546 * 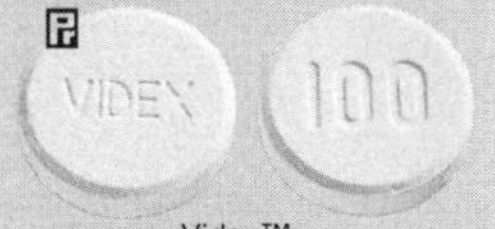 Videx™ 100 mg **BRISTOL-MYERS SQUIBB**	DIN 01940554 * 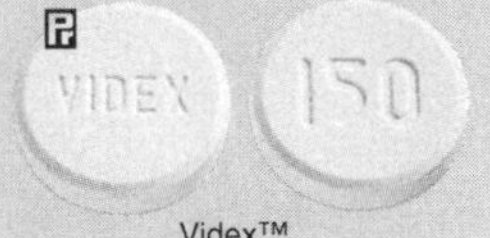 Videx™ 150 mg **BRISTOL-MYERS SQUIBB**
5	DIN 00116785 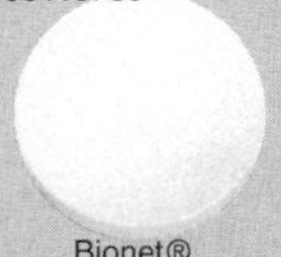 Bionet® Lozenges / pastilles **CARTER HORNER**	DIN 00027588 *  Calcium-Sandoz® Forte **NOVARTIS CONSUMER HEALTH**	DIN 00259497  Gramcal® **NOVARTIS CONSUMER HEALTH**	DIN 02229110 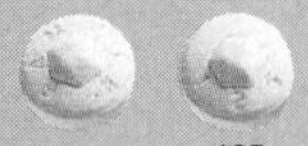 125 Famvir™ 125 mg **SMITHKLINE BEECHAM**	DIN 02229129  250 Famvir™ 250 mg **SMITHKLINE BEECHAM**
6	DIN 02142082  Lamictal™ 25 mg **GLAXO WELLCOME**	DIN 00016462  41 Decadron® 0.5 mg **MSD**	DIN 00354309  97 Decadron® 4 mg **MSD**	DIN 02232565  4890 Requip™ 0.25 mg **SMITHKLINE BEECHAM**	DIN 02232569  4894 Requip™ 5 mg **SMITHKLINE BEECHAM**
7	DIN 00632600  1461 Cytotec® 200 µg **SEARLE**	DIN 02042282 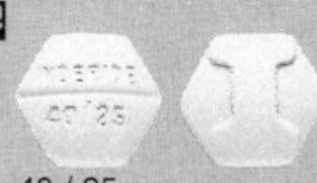 40 / 25 Inderide® / Indéride® 40 mg **WYETH-AYERST**	DIN 02042290 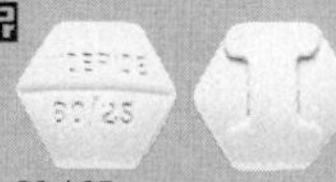 80 / 25 Inderide® / Indéride® 80 mg **WYETH-AYERST**	DIN 00878928  Norvasc™ 5 mg **PFIZER**	DIN 00878936  Norvasc™ 10 mg **PFIZER**
8	DIN 02019604  N2 Neptazane® 25 mg **WYETH-AYERST**	DIN 00546283  25 Capoten® 25 mg **SQUIBB**	DIN 00708879  712 Vasotec® 5 mg **FROSST**	DIN 02099195  Maxeran® 5 mg **HOECHST MARION ROUSSEL**	DIN 00400688  Prostin® E_2 Tablets **PHARMACIA & UPJOHN**

*ILLUSTRATION LESS THAN ACTUAL SIZE / ILLUSTRATION RÉDUITE

Use code A, B, C, D, E, horizontal bar and 1 to 8 vertical bar to locate illustrated products

Utiliser le code A, B, C, D, E de la ligne horizontale et les chiffres 1 à 8 de la ligne verticale pour repérer les produits illustrés

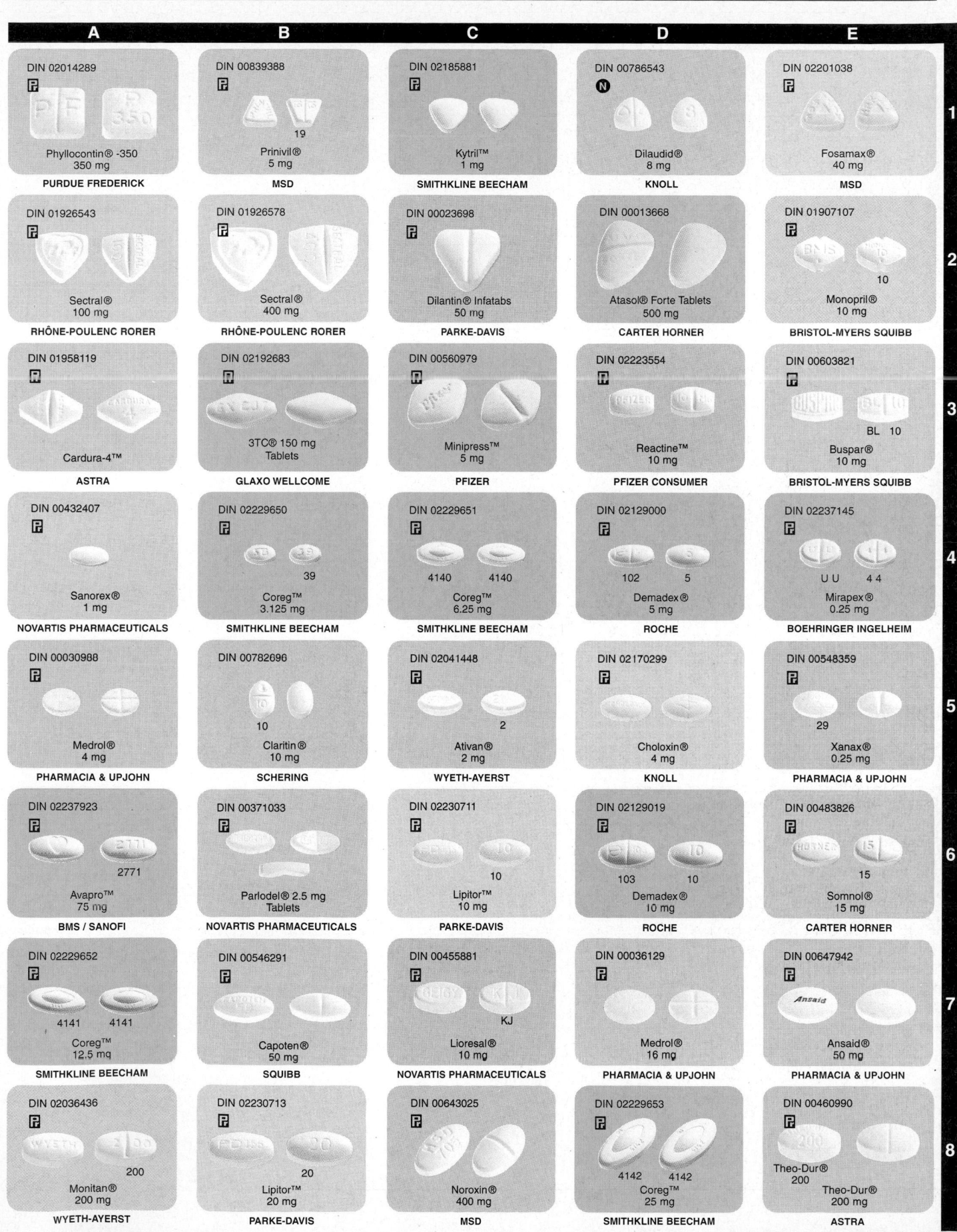

	A	B	C	D	E
1	DIN 02014289  Phyllocontin® -350 350 mg **PURDUE FREDERICK**	DIN 00839388  19 Prinivil® 5 mg **MSD**	DIN 02185881 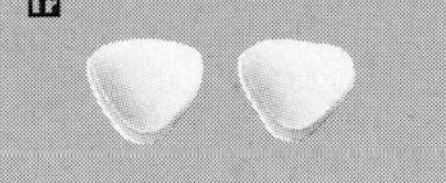 Kytril™ 1 mg **SMITHKLINE BEECHAM**	DIN 00786543  Dilaudid® 8 mg **KNOLL**	DIN 02201038  Fosamax® 40 mg **MSD**
2	DIN 01926543 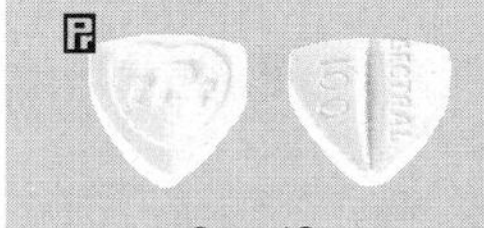 Sectral® 100 mg **RHÔNE-POULENC RORER**	DIN 01926578  Sectral® 400 mg **RHÔNE-POULENC RORER**	DIN 00023698  Dilantin® Infatabs 50 mg **PARKE-DAVIS**	DIN 00013668  Atasol® Forte Tablets 500 mg **CARTER HORNER**	DIN 01907107 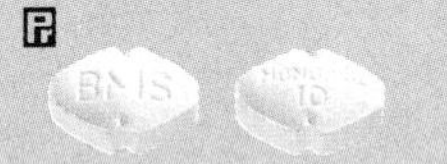 10 Monopril® 10 mg **BRISTOL-MYERS SQUIBB**
3	DIN 01958119  Cardura-4™ **ASTRA**	DIN 02192683 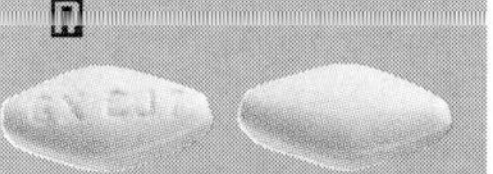 3TC® 150 mg Tablets **GLAXO WELLCOME**	DIN 00560979  Minipress™ 5 mg **PFIZER**	DIN 02223554 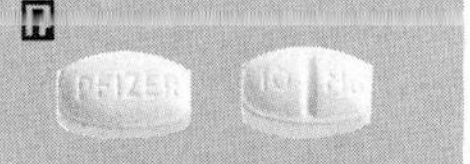 Reactine™ 10 mg **PFIZER CONSUMER**	DIN 00603821  BL 10 Buspar® 10 mg **BRISTOL-MYERS SQUIBB**
4	DIN 00432407  Sanorex® 1 mg **NOVARTIS PHARMACEUTICALS**	DIN 02229650  39 Coreg™ 3.125 mg **SMITHKLINE BEECHAM**	DIN 02229651  4140 4140 Coreg™ 6.25 mg **SMITHKLINE BEECHAM**	DIN 02129000 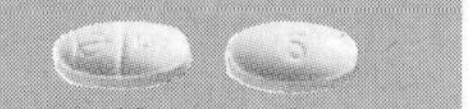 102 5 Demadex® 5 mg **ROCHE**	DIN 02237145  U U 4 4 Mirapex® 0.25 mg **BOEHRINGER INGELHEIM**
5	DIN 00030988  Medrol® 4 mg **PHARMACIA & UPJOHN**	DIN 00782696  10 Claritin® 10 mg **SCHERING**	DIN 02041448  2 Ativan® 2 mg **WYETH-AYERST**	DIN 02170299  Choloxin® 4 mg **KNOLL**	DIN 00548359  29 Xanax® 0.25 mg **PHARMACIA & UPJOHN**
6	DIN 02237923 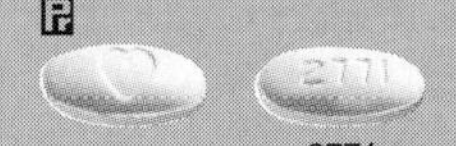 2771 Avapro™ 75 mg **BMS / SANOFI**	DIN 00371033  Parlodel® 2.5 mg Tablets **NOVARTIS PHARMACEUTICALS**	DIN 02230711  10 Lipitor™ 10 mg **PARKE-DAVIS**	DIN 02129019 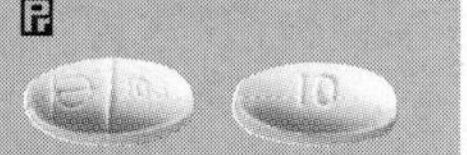 103 10 Demadex® 10 mg **ROCHE**	DIN 00483826 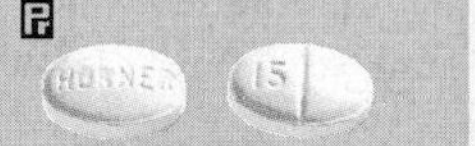 15 Somnol® 15 mg **CARTER HORNER**
7	DIN 02229652  4141 4141 Coreg™ 12.5 mg **SMITHKLINE BEECHAM**	DIN 00546291  Capoten® 50 mg **SQUIBB**	DIN 00455881  KJ Lioresal® 10 mg **NOVARTIS PHARMACEUTICALS**	DIN 00036129  Medrol® 16 mg **PHARMACIA & UPJOHN**	DIN 00647942  Ansaid® 50 mg **PHARMACIA & UPJOHN**
8	DIN 02036436  200 Monitan® 200 mg **WYETH-AYERST**	DIN 02230713 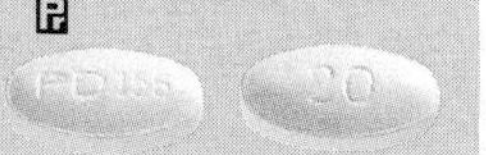 20 Lipitor™ 20 mg **PARKE-DAVIS**	DIN 00643025  Noroxin® 400 mg **MSD**	DIN 02229653 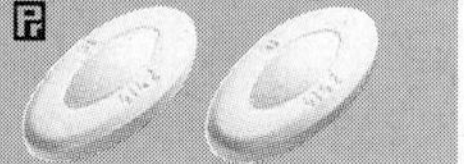 4142 4142 Coreg™ 25 mg **SMITHKLINE BEECHAM**	DIN 00460990  Theo-Dur® 200 Theo-Dur® 200 mg **ASTRA**

Use code A, B, C, D, E, horizontal bar and 1 to 8 vertical bar to locate illustrated products

Utiliser le code A, B, C, D, E de la ligne horizontale et les chiffres 1 à 8 de la ligne verticale pour repérer les produits illustrés

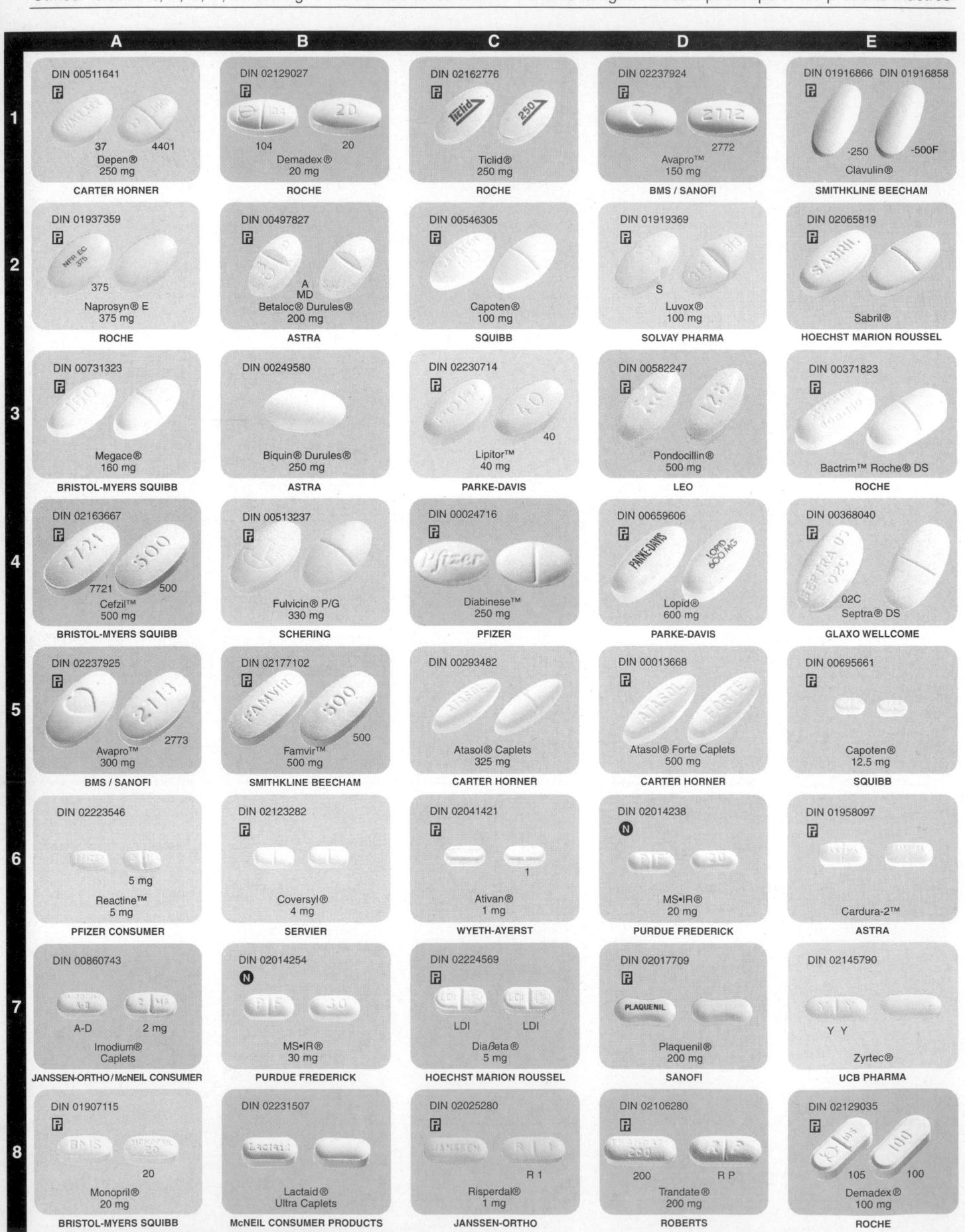

	A	B	C	D	E
1	DIN 00511641 37 4401 Depen® 250 mg **CARTER HORNER**	DIN 02129027 104 20 Demadex® 20 mg **ROCHE**	DIN 02162776 Ticlid® 250 mg **ROCHE**	DIN 02237924 2772 Avapro™ 150 mg **BMS / SANOFI**	DIN 01916866 DIN 01916858 -250 -500F Clavulin® **SMITHKLINE BEECHAM**
2	DIN 01937359 375 Naprosyn® E 375 mg **ROCHE**	DIN 00497827 A MD Betaloc® Durules® 200 mg **ASTRA**	DIN 00546305 Capoten® 100 mg **SQUIBB**	DIN 01919369 S Luvox® 100 mg **SOLVAY PHARMA**	DIN 02065819 Sabril® **HOECHST MARION ROUSSEL**
3	DIN 00731323 Megace® 160 mg **BRISTOL-MYERS SQUIBB**	DIN 00249580 Biquin® Durules® 250 mg **ASTRA**	DIN 02230714 40 Lipitor™ 40 mg **PARKE-DAVIS**	DIN 00582247 Pondocillin® 500 mg **LEO**	DIN 00371823 Bactrim™ Roche® DS **ROCHE**
4	DIN 02163667 7721 500 Cefzil™ 500 mg **BRISTOL-MYERS SQUIBB**	DIN 00513237 Fulvicin® P/G 330 mg **SCHERING**	DIN 00024716 Diabinese™ 250 mg **PFIZER**	DIN 00659606 Lopid® 600 mg **PARKE-DAVIS**	DIN 00368040 02C Septra® DS **GLAXO WELLCOME**
5	DIN 02237925 2773 Avapro™ 300 mg **BMS / SANOFI**	DIN 02177102 500 Famvir™ 500 mg **SMITHKLINE BEECHAM**	DIN 00293482 Atasol® Caplets 325 mg **CARTER HORNER**	DIN 00013668 Atasol® Forte Caplets 500 mg **CARTER HORNER**	DIN 00695661 Capoten® 12.5 mg **SQUIBB**
6	DIN 02223546 5 mg Reactine™ 5 mg **PFIZER CONSUMER**	DIN 02123282 Coversyl® 4 mg **SERVIER**	DIN 02041421 1 Ativan® 1 mg **WYETH-AYERST**	DIN 02014238 MS•IR® 20 mg **PURDUE FREDERICK**	DIN 01958097 Cardura-2™ **ASTRA**
7	DIN 00860743 A-D 2 mg Imodium® Caplets **JANSSEN-ORTHO / McNEIL CONSUMER**	DIN 02014254 MS•IR® 30 mg **PURDUE FREDERICK**	DIN 02224569 LDI LDI Diaßeta® 5 mg **HOECHST MARION ROUSSEL**	DIN 02017709 Plaquenil® 200 mg **SANOFI**	DIN 02145790 Y Y Zyrtec® **UCB PHARMA**
8	DIN 01907115 20 Monopril® 20 mg **BRISTOL-MYERS SQUIBB**	DIN 02231507 Lactaid® Ultra Caplets **McNEIL CONSUMER PRODUCTS**	DIN 02025280 R 1 Risperdal® 1 mg **JANSSEN-ORTHO**	DIN 02106280 200 R P Trandate® 200 mg **ROBERTS**	DIN 02129035 105 100 Demadex® 100 mg **ROCHE**

Use code A, B, C, D, E, horizontal bar and 1 to 8 vertical bar to locate illustrated products

Utiliser le code A, B, C, D, E de la ligne horizontale et les chiffres 1 à 8 de la ligne verticale pour repérer les produits illustrés

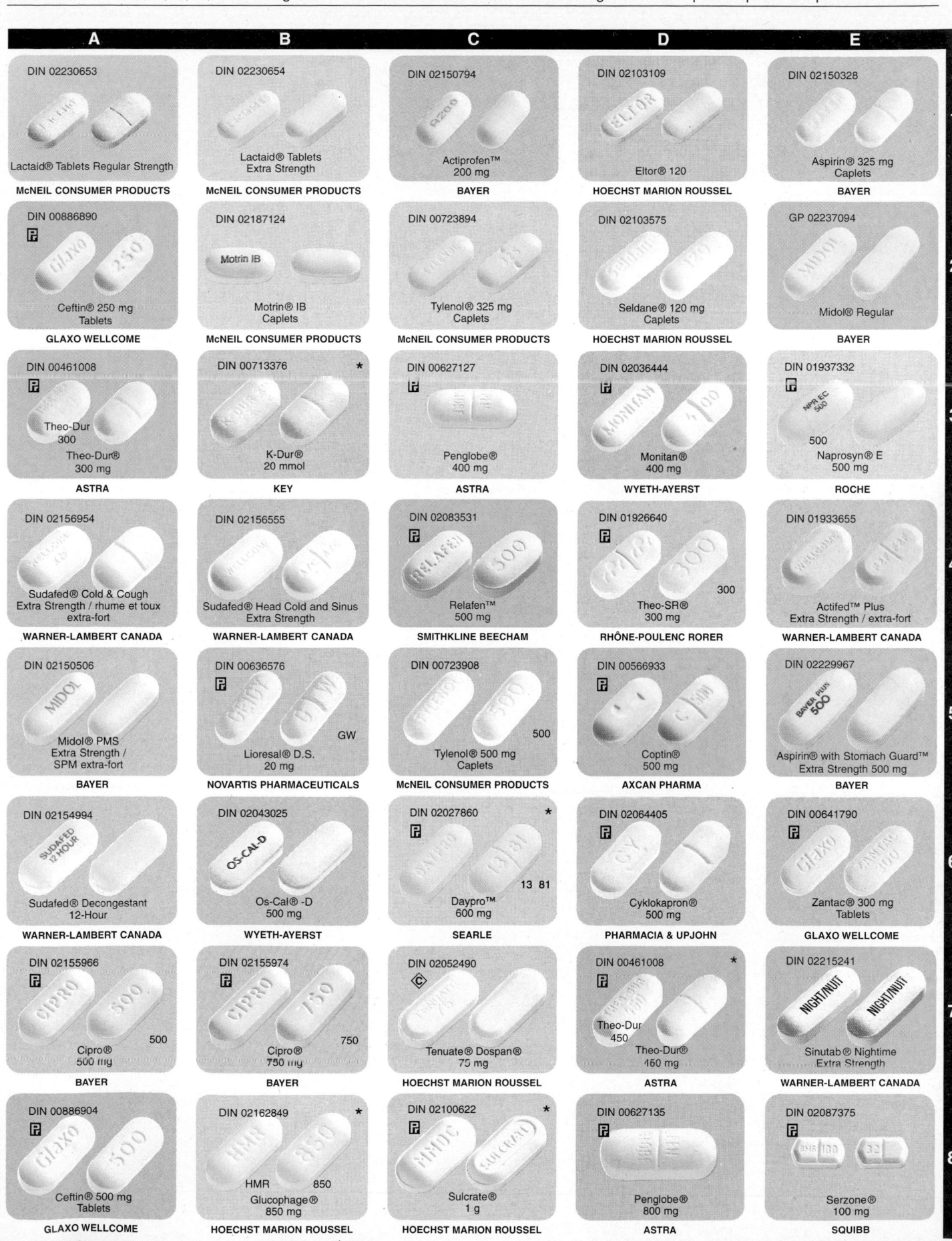

	A	B	C	D	E
1	DIN 02230653 Lactaid® Tablets Regular Strength **McNEIL CONSUMER PRODUCTS**	DIN 02230654 Lactaid® Tablets Extra Strength **McNEIL CONSUMER PRODUCTS**	DIN 02150794 Actiprofen™ 200 mg **BAYER**	DIN 02103109 Eltor® 120 **HOECHST MARION ROUSSEL**	DIN 02150328 Aspirin® 325 mg Caplets **BAYER**
2	DIN 00886890 Ceftin® 250 mg Tablets **GLAXO WELLCOME**	DIN 02187124 Motrin IB Motrin® IB Caplets **McNEIL CONSUMER PRODUCTS**	DIN 00723894 Tylenol® 325 mg Caplets **McNEIL CONSUMER PRODUCTS**	DIN 02103575 Seldane® 120 mg Caplets **HOECHST MARION ROUSSEL**	GP 02237094 Midol® Regular **BAYER**
3	DIN 00461008 Theo-Dur 300 Theo-Dur® 300 mg **ASTRA**	DIN 00713376 * K-Dur® 20 mmol **KEY**	DIN 00627127 Penglobe® 400 mg **ASTRA**	DIN 02036444 Monitan® 400 mg **WYETH-AYERST**	DIN 01937332 500 Naprosyn® E 500 mg **ROCHE**
4	DIN 02156954 Sudafed® Cold & Cough Extra Strength / rhume et toux extra-fort **WARNER-LAMBERT CANADA**	DIN 02156555 Sudafed® Head Cold and Sinus Extra Strength **WARNER-LAMBERT CANADA**	DIN 02083531 Relafen™ 500 mg **SMITHKLINE BEECHAM**	DIN 01926640 300 Theo-SR® 300 mg **RHÔNE-POULENC RORER**	DIN 01933655 Actifed™ Plus Extra Strength / extra-fort **WARNER-LAMBERT CANADA**
5	DIN 02150506 Midol® PMS Extra Strength / SPM extra-fort **BAYER**	DIN 00636576 GW Lioresal® D.S. 20 mg **NOVARTIS PHARMACEUTICALS**	DIN 00723908 500 Tylenol® 500 mg Caplets **McNEIL CONSUMER PRODUCTS**	DIN 00566933 Coptin® 500 mg **AXCAN PHARMA**	DIN 02229967 Aspirin® with Stomach Guard™ Extra Strength 500 mg **BAYER**
6	DIN 02154994 Sudafed® Decongestant 12-Hour **WARNER-LAMBERT CANADA**	DIN 02043025 Os-Cal® -D 500 mg **WYETH-AYERST**	DIN 02027860 * 13 81 Daypro™ 600 mg **SEARLE**	DIN 02064405 Cyklokapron® 500 mg **PHARMACIA & UPJOHN**	DIN 00641790 Zantac® 300 mg Tablets **GLAXO WELLCOME**
7	DIN 02155966 500 Cipro® 500 mg **BAYER**	DIN 02155974 750 Cipro® 750 mg **BAYER**	DIN 02052490 Tenuate® Dospan® 75 mg **HOECHST MARION ROUSSEL**	DIN 00461008 * Theo-Dur 450 Theo-Dur® 450 mg **ASTRA**	DIN 02215241 Sinutab® Nightime Extra Strength **WARNER-LAMBERT CANADA**
8	DIN 00886904 Ceftin® 500 mg Tablets **GLAXO WELLCOME**	DIN 02162849 * HMR 850 Glucophage® 850 mg **HOECHST MARION ROUSSEL**	DIN 02100622 * Sulcrate® 1 g **HOECHST MARION ROUSSEL**	DIN 00627135 Penglobe® 800 mg **ASTRA**	DIN 02087375 Serzone® 100 mg **SQUIBB**

*ILLUSTRATION LESS THAN ACTUAL SIZE / ILLUSTRATION RÉDUITE

Use code A, B, C, D, E, horizontal bar and 1 to 8 vertical bar to locate illustrated products

Utiliser le code A, B, C, D, E de la ligne horizontale et les chiffres 1 à 8 de la ligne verticale pour repérer les produits illustrés

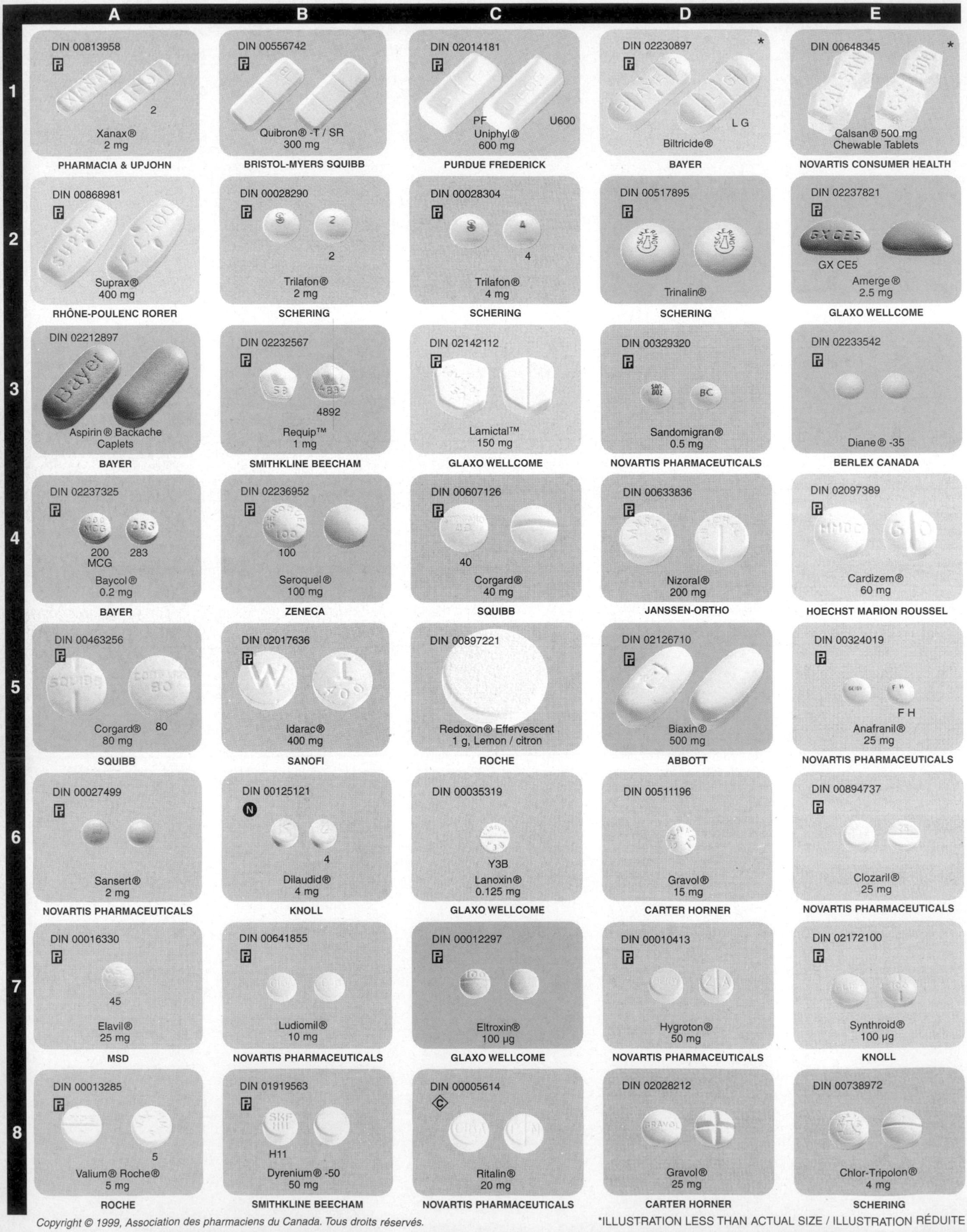

	A	B	C	D	E
1	DIN 00813958 2 Xanax® 2 mg PHARMACIA & UPJOHN	DIN 00556742 Quibron® -T / SR 300 mg BRISTOL-MYERS SQUIBB	DIN 02014181 PF U600 Uniphyl® 600 mg PURDUE FREDERICK	DIN 02230897 * L G Biltricide® BAYER	DIN 00648345 * Calsan® 500 mg Chewable Tablets NOVARTIS CONSUMER HEALTH
2	DIN 00868981 Suprax® 400 mg RHÔNE-POULENC RORER	DIN 00028290 2 Trilafon® 2 mg SCHERING	DIN 00028304 4 Trilafon® 4 mg SCHERING	DIN 00517895 Trinalin® SCHERING	DIN 02237821 GX CE5 Amerge® 2.5 mg GLAXO WELLCOME
3	DIN 02212897 Aspirin® Backache Caplets BAYER	DIN 02232567 4892 Requip™ 1 mg SMITHKLINE BEECHAM	DIN 02142112 Lamictal™ 150 mg GLAXO WELLCOME	DIN 00329320 Sandomigran® 0.5 mg NOVARTIS PHARMACEUTICALS	DIN 02233542 Diane® -35 BERLEX CANADA
4	DIN 02237325 200 MCG 283 Baycol® 0.2 mg BAYER	DIN 02236952 100 Seroquel® 100 mg ZENECA	DIN 00607126 40 Corgard® 40 mg SQUIBB	DIN 00633836 Nizoral® 200 mg JANSSEN-ORTHO	DIN 02097389 Cardizem® 60 mg HOECHST MARION ROUSSEL
5	DIN 00463256 Corgard® 80 mg 80 SQUIBB	DIN 02017636 Idarac® 400 mg SANOFI	DIN 00897221 Redoxon® Effervescent 1 g, Lemon / citron ROCHE	DIN 02126710 Biaxin® 500 mg ABBOTT	DIN 00324019 F H Anafranil® 25 mg NOVARTIS PHARMACEUTICALS
6	DIN 00027499 Sansert® 2 mg NOVARTIS PHARMACEUTICALS	DIN 00125121 4 Dilaudid® 4 mg KNOLL	DIN 00035319 Y3B Lanoxin® 0.125 mg GLAXO WELLCOME	DIN 00511196 Gravol® 15 mg CARTER HORNER	DIN 00894737 Clozaril® 25 mg NOVARTIS PHARMACEUTICALS
7	DIN 00016330 45 Elavil® 25 mg MSD	DIN 00641855 Ludiomil® 10 mg NOVARTIS PHARMACEUTICALS	DIN 00012297 Eltroxin® 100 µg GLAXO WELLCOME	DIN 00010413 Hygroton® 50 mg NOVARTIS PHARMACEUTICALS	DIN 02172100 Synthroid® 100 µg KNOLL
8	DIN 00013285 5 Valium® Roche® 5 mg ROCHE	DIN 01919563 H11 Dyrenium® -50 50 mg SMITHKLINE BEECHAM	DIN 00005614 Ritalin® 20 mg NOVARTIS PHARMACEUTICALS	DIN 02028212 Gravol® 25 mg CARTER HORNER	DIN 00738972 Chlor-Tripolon® 4 mg SCHERING

*ILLUSTRATION LESS THAN ACTUAL SIZE / ILLUSTRATION RÉDUITE

Use code A, B, C, D, E, horizontal bar and 1 to 8 vertical bar to locate illustrated products

Utiliser le code A, B, C, D, E de la ligne horizontale et les chiffres 1 à 8 de la ligne verticale pour repérer les produits illustrés

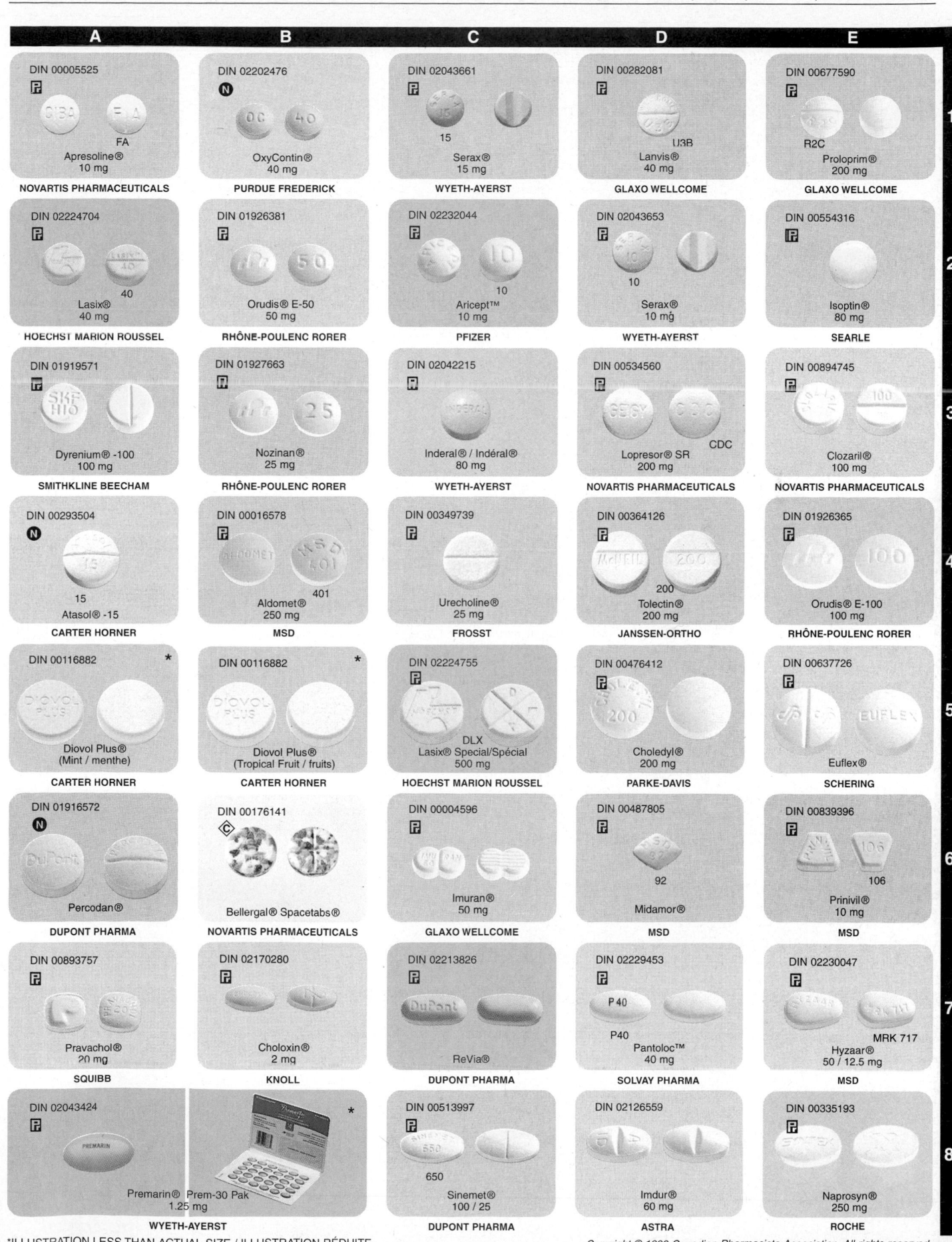

	A	B	C	D	E
1	DIN 00005525  FA Apresoline® 10 mg **NOVARTIS PHARMACEUTICALS**	DIN 02202476  OxyContin® 40 mg **PURDUE FREDERICK**	DIN 02043661  15 Serax® 15 mg **WYETH-AYERST**	DIN 00282081  U3B Lanvis® 40 mg **GLAXO WELLCOME**	DIN 00677590  R2C Proloprim® 200 mg **GLAXO WELLCOME**
2	DIN 02224704  40 Lasix® 40 mg **HOECHST MARION ROUSSEL**	DIN 01926381  Orudis® E-50 50 mg **RHÔNE-POULENC RORER**	DIN 02232044  10 Aricept™ 10 mg **PFIZER**	DIN 02043653  10 Serax® 10 mg **WYETH-AYERST**	DIN 00554316  Isoptin® 80 mg **SEARLE**
3	DIN 01919571 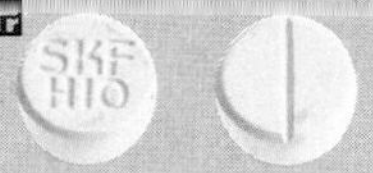 Dyrenium® -100 100 mg **SMITHKLINE BEECHAM**	DIN 01927663  Nozinan® 25 mg **RHÔNE-POULENC RORER**	DIN 02042215  Inderal® / Indéral® 80 mg **WYETH-AYERST**	DIN 00534560 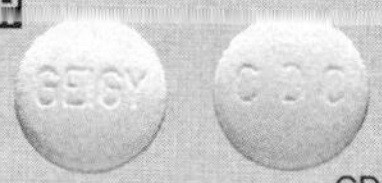 CDC Lopresor® SR 200 mg **NOVARTIS PHARMACEUTICALS**	DIN 00894745 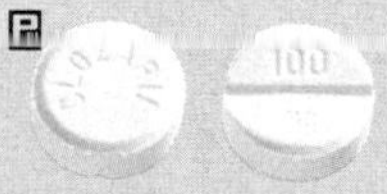 Clozaril® 100 mg **NOVARTIS PHARMACEUTICALS**
4	DIN 00293504 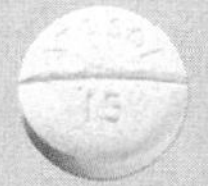 15 Atasol® -15 **CARTER HORNER**	DIN 00016578 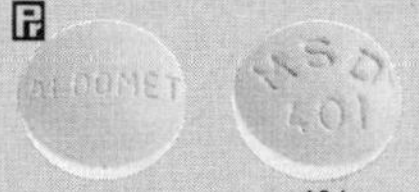 401 Aldomet® 250 mg **MSD**	DIN 00349739  Urecholine® 25 mg **FROSST**	DIN 00364126 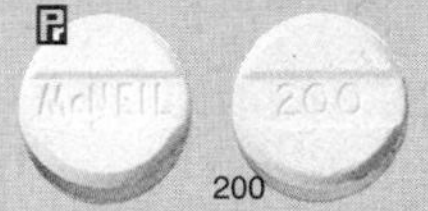 200 Tolectin® 200 mg **JANSSEN-ORTHO**	DIN 01926365 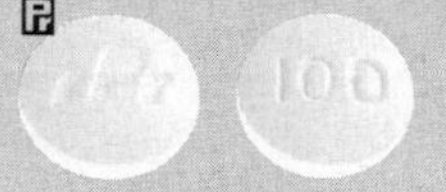 Orudis® E-100 100 mg **RHÔNE-POULENC RORER**
5	DIN 00116882 * 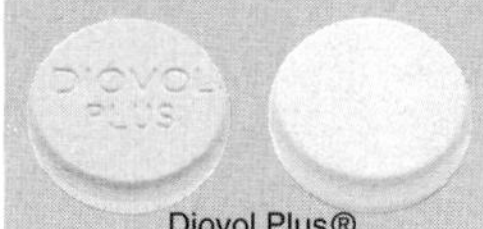 Diovol Plus® (Mint / menthe) **CARTER HORNER**	DIN 00116882 * 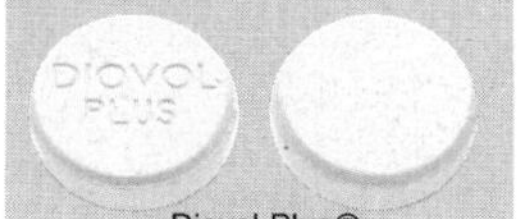 Diovol Plus® (Tropical Fruit / fruits) **CARTER HORNER**	DIN 02224755 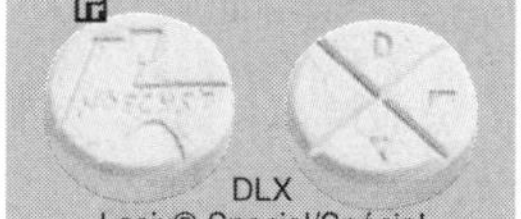 DLX Lasix® Special/Spécial 500 mg **HOECHST MARION ROUSSEL**	DIN 00476412  Choledyl® 200 mg **PARKE-DAVIS**	DIN 00637726  Euflex® **SCHERING**
6	DIN 01916572 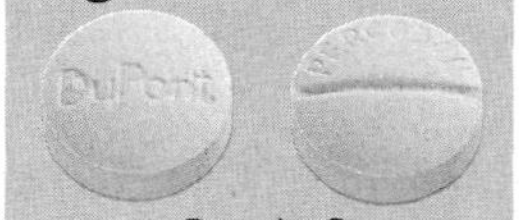 Percodan® **DUPONT PHARMA**	DIN 00176141  Bellergal® Spacetabs® **NOVARTIS PHARMACEUTICALS**	DIN 00004596  Imuran® 50 mg **GLAXO WELLCOME**	DIN 00487805  92 Midamor® **MSD**	DIN 00839396  106 Prinivil® 10 mg **MSD**
7	DIN 00893757  Pravachol® 20 mg **SQUIBB**	DIN 02170280  Choloxin® 2 mg **KNOLL**	DIN 02213826 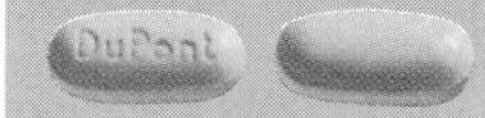 ReVia® **DUPONT PHARMA**	DIN 02229453  P40 Pantoloc™ 40 mg **SOLVAY PHARMA**	DIN 02230047  MRK 717 Hyzaar® 50 / 12.5 mg **MSD**
8	DIN 02043424 * 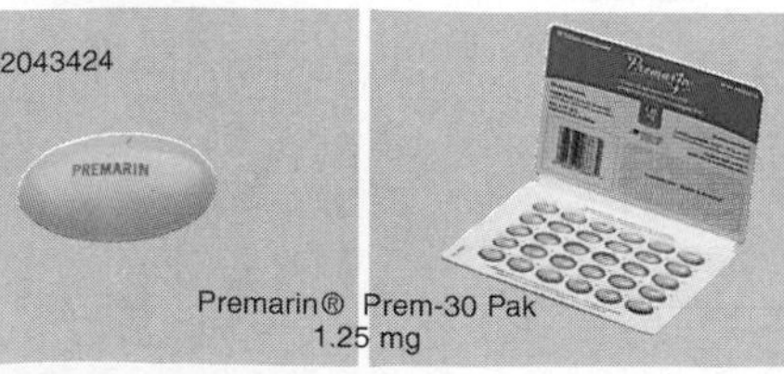 Premarin® Prem-30 Pak 1.25 mg **WYETH-AYERST**		DIN 00513997  650 Sinemet® 100 / 25 **DUPONT PHARMA**	DIN 02126559  Imdur® 60 mg **ASTRA**	DIN 00335193  Naprosyn® 250 mg **ROCHE**

*ILLUSTRATION LESS THAN ACTUAL SIZE / ILLUSTRATION RÉDUITE

Use code A, B, C, D, E, horizontal bar and 1 to 8 vertical bar to locate illustrated products

Utiliser le code A, B, C, D, E de la ligne horizontale et les chiffres 1 à 8 de la ligne verticale pour repérer les produits illustrés

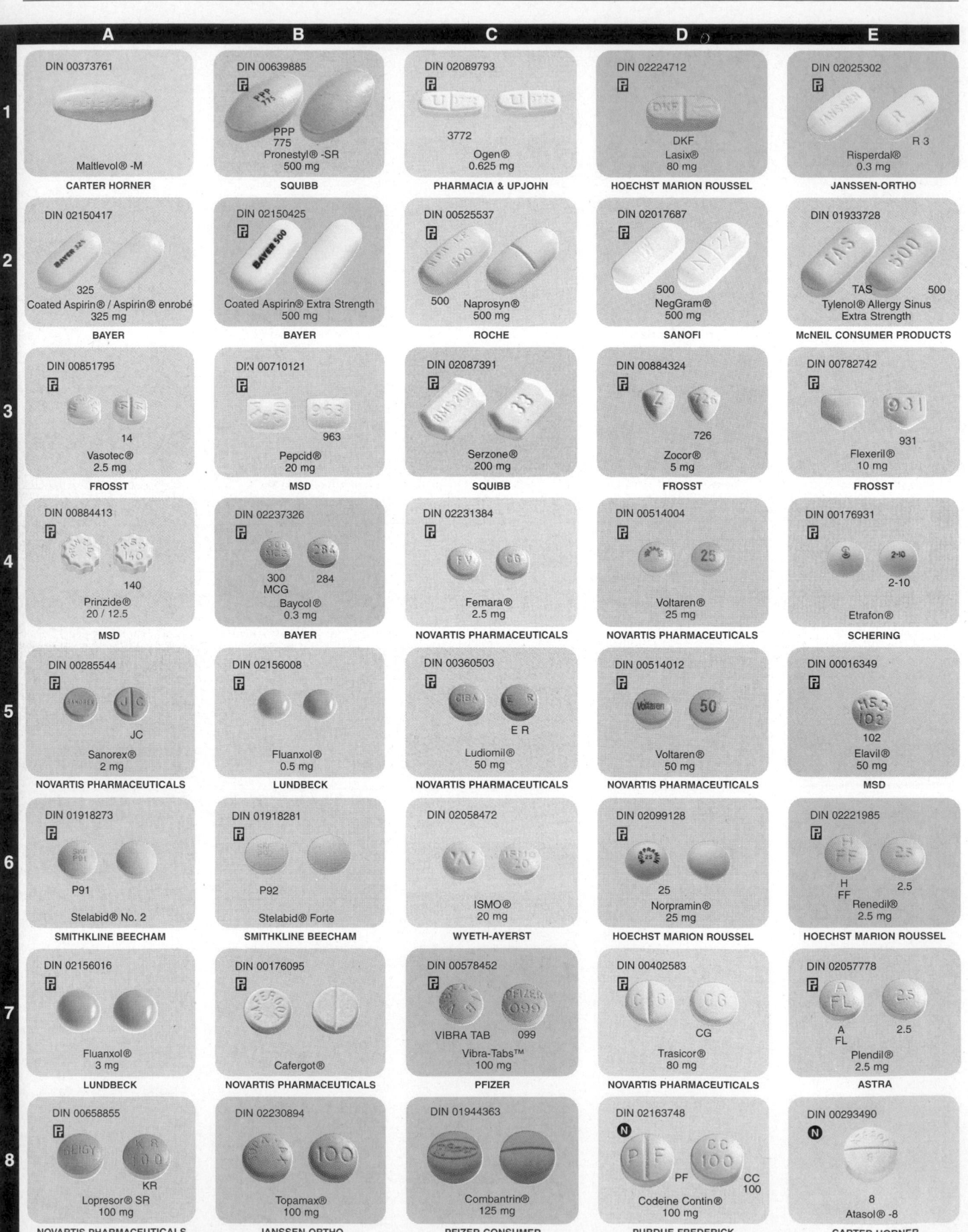

	A	B	C	D	E
1	DIN 00373761 Maltlevol® -M **CARTER HORNER**	DIN 00639885 PPP 775 Pronestyl® -SR 500 mg **SQUIBB**	DIN 02089793 3772 Ogen® 0.625 mg **PHARMACIA & UPJOHN**	DIN 02224712 DKF Lasix® 80 mg **HOECHST MARION ROUSSEL**	DIN 02025302 R 3 Risperdal® 0.3 mg **JANSSEN-ORTHO**
2	DIN 02150417 325 Coated Aspirin® / Aspirin® enrobé 325 mg **BAYER**	DIN 02150425 Coated Aspirin® Extra Strength 500 mg **BAYER**	DIN 00525537 500 Naprosyn® 500 mg **ROCHE**	DIN 02017687 500 NegGram® 500 mg **SANOFI**	DIN 01933728 TAS 500 Tylenol® Allergy Sinus Extra Strength **McNEIL CONSUMER PRODUCTS**
3	DIN 00851795 14 Vasotec® 2.5 mg **FROSST**	DIN 00710121 963 Pepcid® 20 mg **MSD**	DIN 02087391 Serzone® 200 mg **SQUIBB**	DIN 00884324 726 Zocor® 5 mg **FROSST**	DIN 00782742 931 Flexeril® 10 mg **FROSST**
4	DIN 00884413 140 Prinzide® 20 / 12.5 **MSD**	DIN 02237326 300 MCG 284 Baycol® 0.3 mg **BAYER**	DIN 02231384 Femara® 2.5 mg **NOVARTIS PHARMACEUTICALS**	DIN 00514004 Voltaren® 25 mg **NOVARTIS PHARMACEUTICALS**	DIN 00176931 2-10 Etrafon® **SCHERING**
5	DIN 00285544 JC Sanorex® 2 mg **NOVARTIS PHARMACEUTICALS**	DIN 02156008 Fluanxol® 0.5 mg **LUNDBECK**	DIN 00360503 E R Ludiomil® 50 mg **NOVARTIS PHARMACEUTICALS**	DIN 00514012 Voltaren® 50 mg **NOVARTIS PHARMACEUTICALS**	DIN 00016349 102 Elavil® 50 mg **MSD**
6	DIN 01918273 P91 Stelabid® No. 2 **SMITHKLINE BEECHAM**	DIN 01918281 P92 Stelabid® Forte **SMITHKLINE BEECHAM**	DIN 02058472 ISMO® 20 mg **WYETH-AYERST**	DIN 02099128 25 Norpramin® 25 mg **HOECHST MARION ROUSSEL**	DIN 02221985 H FF 2.5 Renedil® 2.5 mg **HOECHST MARION ROUSSEL**
7	DIN 02156016 Fluanxol® 3 mg **LUNDBECK**	DIN 00176095 Cafergot® **NOVARTIS PHARMACEUTICALS**	DIN 00578452 VIBRA TAB 099 Vibra-Tabs™ 100 mg **PFIZER**	DIN 00402583 CG Trasicor® 80 mg **NOVARTIS PHARMACEUTICALS**	DIN 02057778 A FL 2.5 Plendil® 2.5 mg **ASTRA**
8	DIN 00658855 KR Lopresor® SR 100 mg **NOVARTIS PHARMACEUTICALS**	DIN 02230894 Topamax® 100 mg **JANSSEN-ORTHO**	DIN 01944363 Combantrin® 125 mg **PFIZER CONSUMER**	DIN 02163748 PF CC 100 Codeine Contin® 100 mg **PURDUE FREDERICK**	DIN 00293490 8 Atasol® -8 **CARTER HORNER**

Use code A, B, C, D, E, horizontal bar and 1 to 8 vertical bar to locate illustrated products

Utiliser le code A, B, C, D, E de la ligne horizontale et les chiffres 1 à 8 de la ligne verticale pour repérer les produits illustrés

1

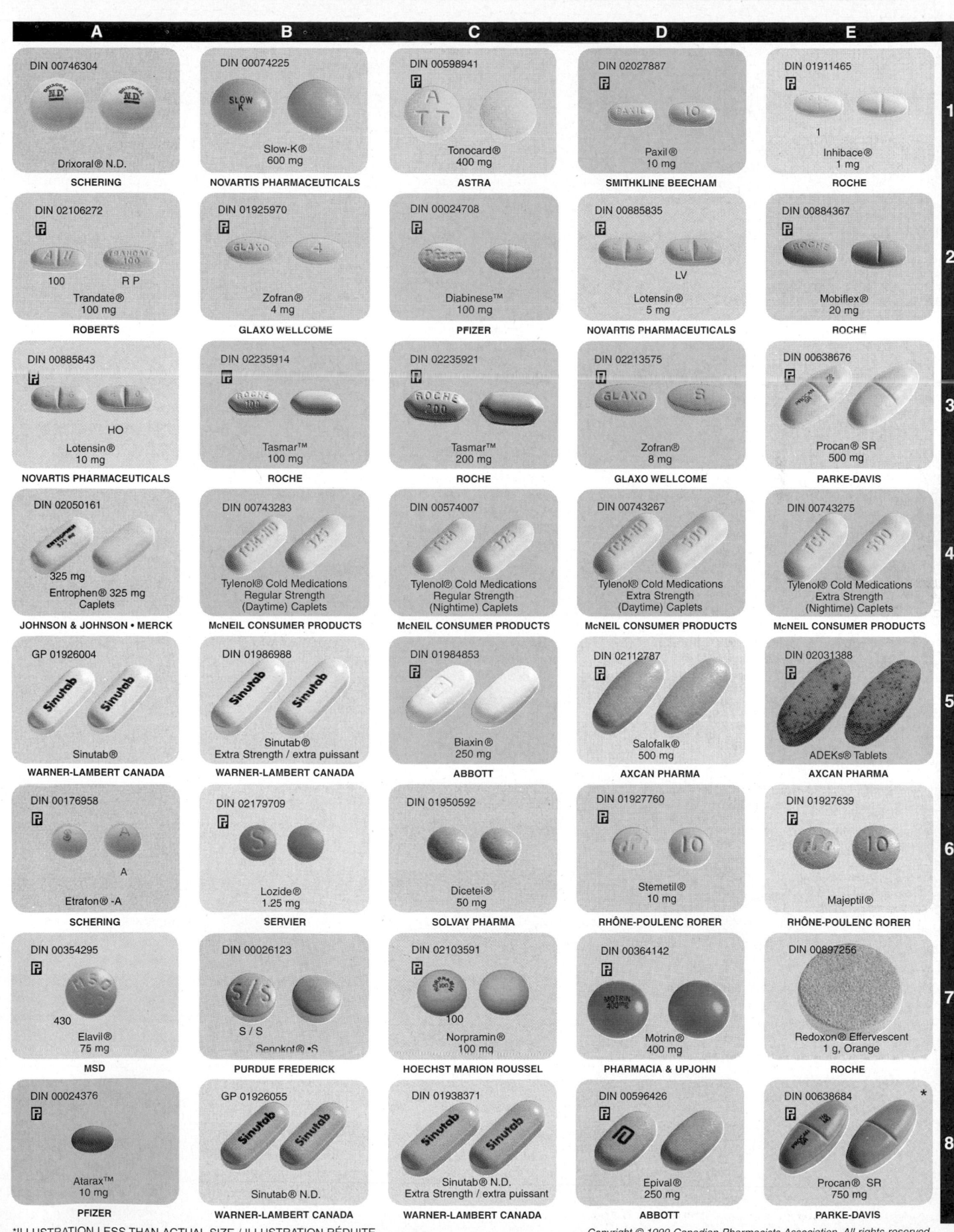

A — DIN 00746304

Drixoral® N.D.
SCHERING

B — DIN 00074225
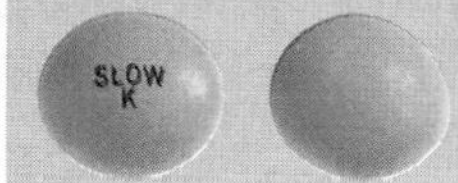
Slow-K®
600 mg
NOVARTIS PHARMACEUTICALS

C — DIN 00598941
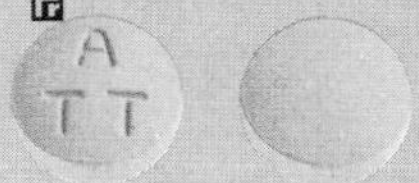
Tonocard®
400 mg
ASTRA

D — DIN 02027887
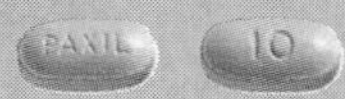
Paxil®
10 mg
SMITHKLINE BEECHAM

E — DIN 01911465

1
Inhibace®
1 mg
ROCHE

2

A — DIN 02106272

100 R P
Trandate®
100 mg
ROBERTS

B — DIN 01925970

Zofran®
4 mg
GLAXO WELLCOME

C — DIN 00024708

Diabinese™
100 mg
PFIZER

D — DIN 00885835

LV
Lotensin®
5 mg
NOVARTIS PHARMACEUTICALS

E — DIN 00884367

Mobiflex®
20 mg
ROCHE

3

A — DIN 00885843

HO
Lotensin®
10 mg
NOVARTIS PHARMACEUTICALS

B — DIN 02235914

Tasmar™
100 mg
ROCHE

C — DIN 02235921
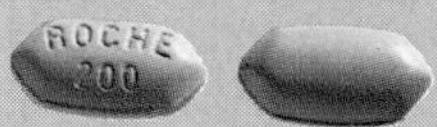
Tasmar™
200 mg
ROCHE

D — DIN 02213575
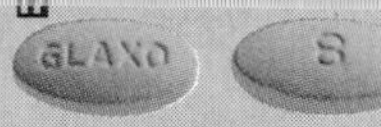
Zofran®
8 mg
GLAXO WELLCOME

E — DIN 00638676
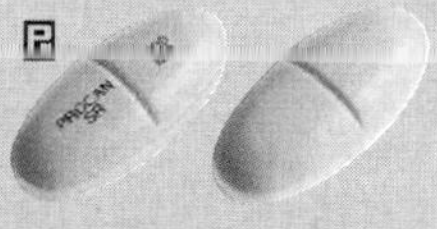
Procan® SR
500 mg
PARKE-DAVIS

4

A — DIN 02050161

325 mg
Entrophen® 325 mg
Caplets
JOHNSON & JOHNSON • MERCK

B — DIN 00743283
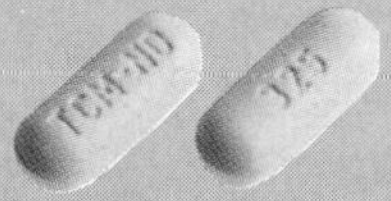
Tylenol® Cold Medications
Regular Strength
(Daytime) Caplets
McNEIL CONSUMER PRODUCTS

C — DIN 00574007
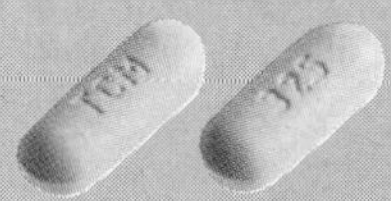
Tylenol® Cold Medications
Regular Strength
(Nightime) Caplets
McNEIL CONSUMER PRODUCTS

D — DIN 00743267
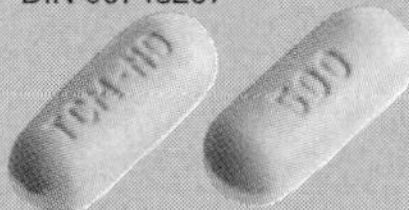
Tylenol® Cold Medications
Extra Strength
(Daytime) Caplets
McNEIL CONSUMER PRODUCTS

E — DIN 00743275
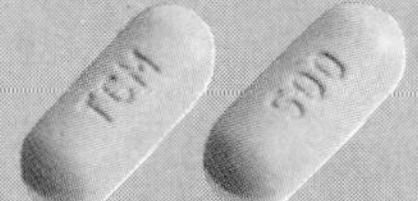
Tylenol® Cold Medications
Extra Strength
(Nightime) Caplets
McNEIL CONSUMER PRODUCTS

5

A — GP 01926004
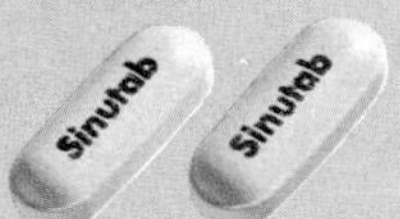
Sinutab®
WARNER-LAMBERT CANADA

B — DIN 01986988
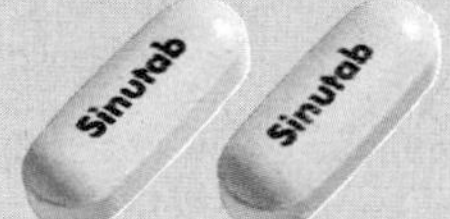
Sinutab®
Extra Strength / extra puissant
WARNER-LAMBERT CANADA

C — DIN 01984853
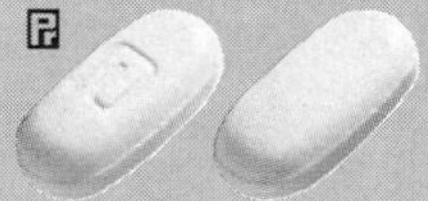
Biaxin®
250 mg
ABBOTT

D — DIN 02112787
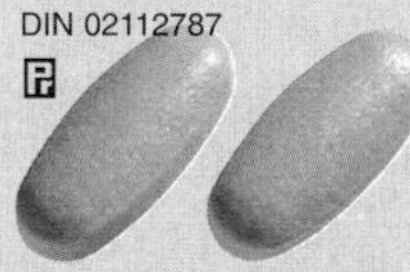
Salofalk®
500 mg
AXCAN PHARMA

E — DIN 02031388

ADEKs® Tablets
AXCAN PHARMA

6

A — DIN 00176958

A
Etrafon® -A
SCHERING

B — DIN 02179709
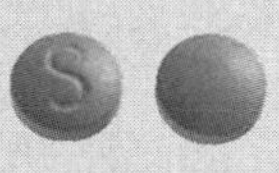
Lozide®
1.25 mg
SERVIER

C — DIN 01950592

Dicetei®
50 mg
SOLVAY PHARMA

D — DIN 01927760
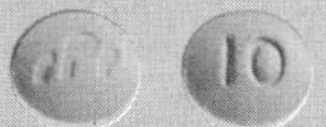
Stemetil®
10 mg
RHÔNE-POULENC RORER

E — DIN 01927639

Majeptil®
RHÔNE-POULENC RORER

7

A — DIN 00354295

430
Elavil®
75 mg
MSD

B — DIN 00026123

S / S
Senokot® •S
PURDUE FREDERICK

C — DIN 02103591
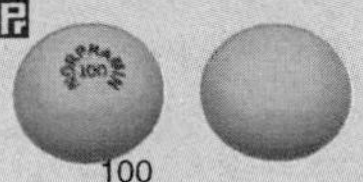
100
Norpramin®
100 mg
HOECHST MARION ROUSSEL

D — DIN 00364142
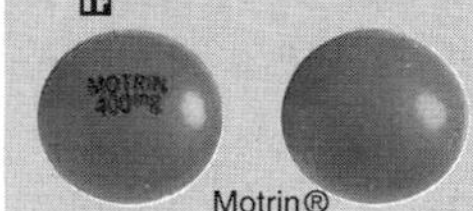
Motrin®
400 mg
PHARMACIA & UPJOHN

E — DIN 00897256

Redoxon® Effervescent
1 g, Orange
ROCHE

8

A — DIN 00024376

Atarax™
10 mg
PFIZER

B — GP 01926055
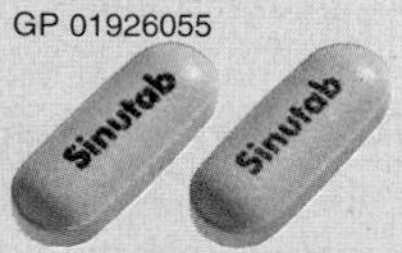
Sinutab® N.D.
WARNER-LAMBERT CANADA

C — DIN 01938371
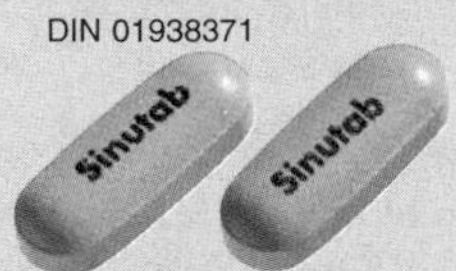
Sinutab® N.D.
Extra Strength / extra puissant
WARNER-LAMBERT CANADA

D — DIN 00596426

Epival®
250 mg
ABBOTT

E — DIN 00638684 *

Procan® SR
750 mg
PARKE-DAVIS

*ILLUSTRATION LESS THAN ACTUAL SIZE / ILLUSTRATION RÉDUITE

Use code A, B, C, D, E, horizontal bar and 1 to 8 vertical bar to locate illustrated products

Utiliser le code A, B, C, D, E de la ligne horizontale et les chiffres 1 à 8 de la ligne verticale pour repérer les produits illustrés

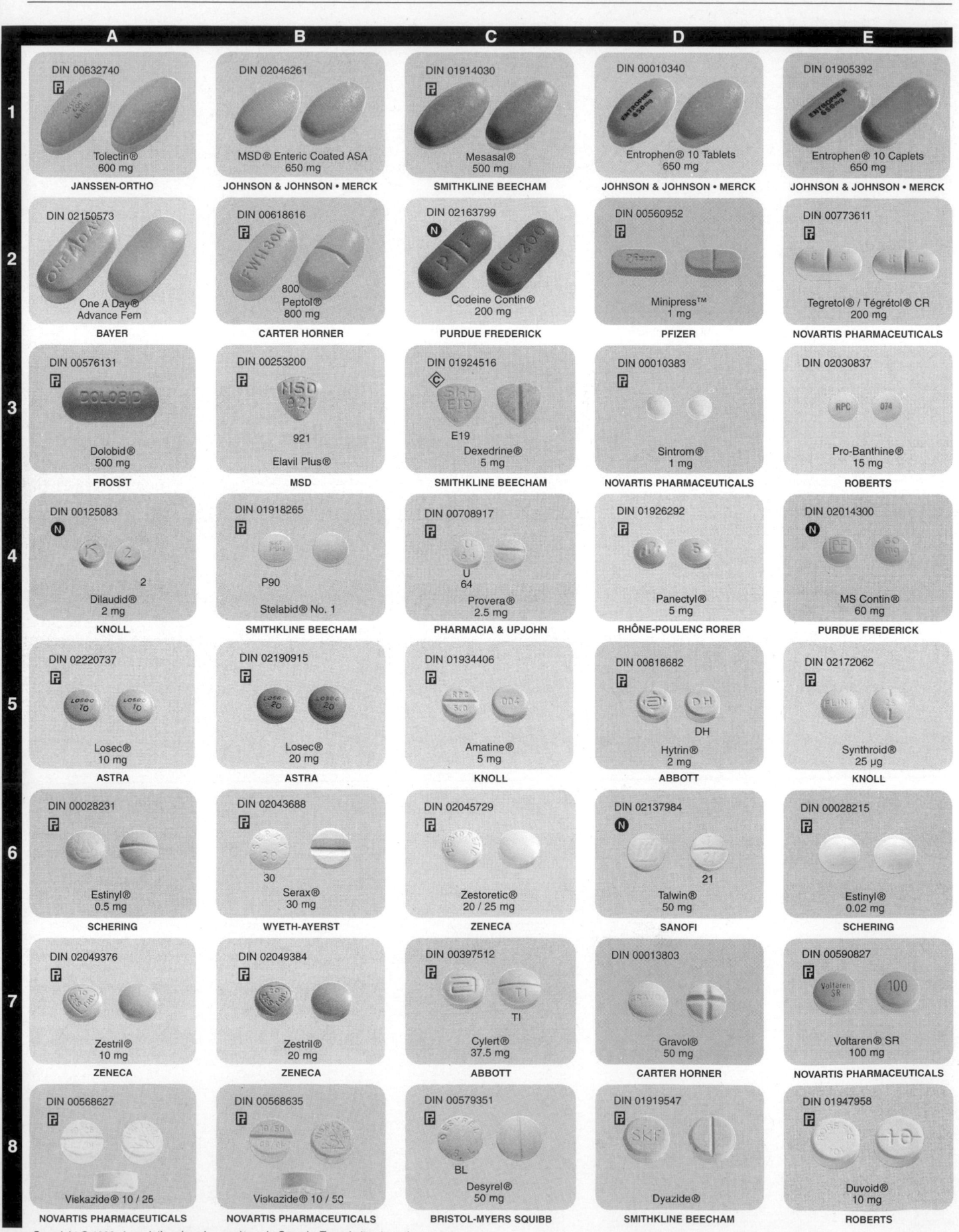

	A	B	C	D	E
1	DIN 00632740 Pr Tolectin® 600 mg **JANSSEN-ORTHO**	DIN 02046261 MSD® Enteric Coated ASA 650 mg **JOHNSON & JOHNSON • MERCK**	DIN 01914030 Pr Mesasal® 500 mg **SMITHKLINE BEECHAM**	DIN 00010340 Entrophen® 10 Tablets 650 mg **JOHNSON & JOHNSON • MERCK**	DIN 01905392 Entrophen® 10 Caplets 650 mg **JOHNSON & JOHNSON • MERCK**
2	DIN 02150573 One A Day® Advance Fem **BAYER**	DIN 00618616 Pr 800 Peptol® 800 mg **CARTER HORNER**	DIN 02163799 N Codeine Contin® 200 mg **PURDUE FREDERICK**	DIN 00560952 Pr Minipress™ 1 mg **PFIZER**	DIN 00773611 Pr Tegretol® / Tégrétol® CR 200 mg **NOVARTIS PHARMACEUTICALS**
3	DIN 00576131 Pr Dolobid® 500 mg **FROSST**	DIN 00253200 Pr 921 Elavil Plus® **MSD**	DIN 01924516 C E19 Dexedrine® 5 mg **SMITHKLINE BEECHAM**	DIN 00010383 Pr Sintrom® 1 mg **NOVARTIS PHARMACEUTICALS**	DIN 02030837 Pro-Banthine® 15 mg **ROBERTS**
4	DIN 00125083 N 2 Dilaudid® 2 mg **KNOLL**	DIN 01918265 Pr P90 Stelabid® No. 1 **SMITHKLINE BEECHAM**	DIN 00708917 Pr U 64 Provera® 2.5 mg **PHARMACIA & UPJOHN**	DIN 01926292 Pr Panectyl® 5 mg **RHÔNE-POULENC RORER**	DIN 02014300 N MS Contin® 60 mg **PURDUE FREDERICK**
5	DIN 02220737 Pr Losec® 10 mg **ASTRA**	DIN 02190915 Pr Losec® 20 mg **ASTRA**	DIN 01934406 Pr Amatine® 5 mg **KNOLL**	DIN 00818682 Pr DH Hytrin® 2 mg **ABBOTT**	DIN 02172062 Pr Synthroid® 25 µg **KNOLL**
6	DIN 00028231 Pr Estinyl® 0.5 mg **SCHERING**	DIN 02043688 Pr 30 Serax® 30 mg **WYETH-AYERST**	DIN 02045729 Pr Zestoretic® 20 / 25 mg **ZENECA**	DIN 02137984 N 21 Talwin® 50 mg **SANOFI**	DIN 00028215 Pr Estinyl® 0.02 mg **SCHERING**
7	DIN 02049376 Pr Zestril® 10 mg **ZENECA**	DIN 02049384 Pr Zestril® 20 mg **ZENECA**	DIN 00397512 Pr TI Cylert® 37.5 mg **ABBOTT**	DIN 00013803 Gravol® 50 mg **CARTER HORNER**	DIN 00590827 Pr Voltaren® SR 100 mg **NOVARTIS PHARMACEUTICALS**
8	DIN 00568627 Pr Viskazide® 10 / 25 **NOVARTIS PHARMACEUTICALS**	DIN 00568635 Pr Viskazide® 10 / 50 **NOVARTIS PHARMACEUTICALS**	DIN 00579351 Pr BL Desyrel® 50 mg **BRISTOL-MYERS SQUIBB**	DIN 01919547 Pr Dyazide® **SMITHKLINE BEECHAM**	DIN 01947958 Pr Duvoid® 10 mg **ROBERTS**

Use code A, B, C, D, E, horizontal bar and 1 to 8 vertical bar to locate illustrated products

Utiliser le code A, B, C, D, E de la ligne horizontale et les chiffres 1 à 8 de la ligne verticale pour repérer les produits illustrés

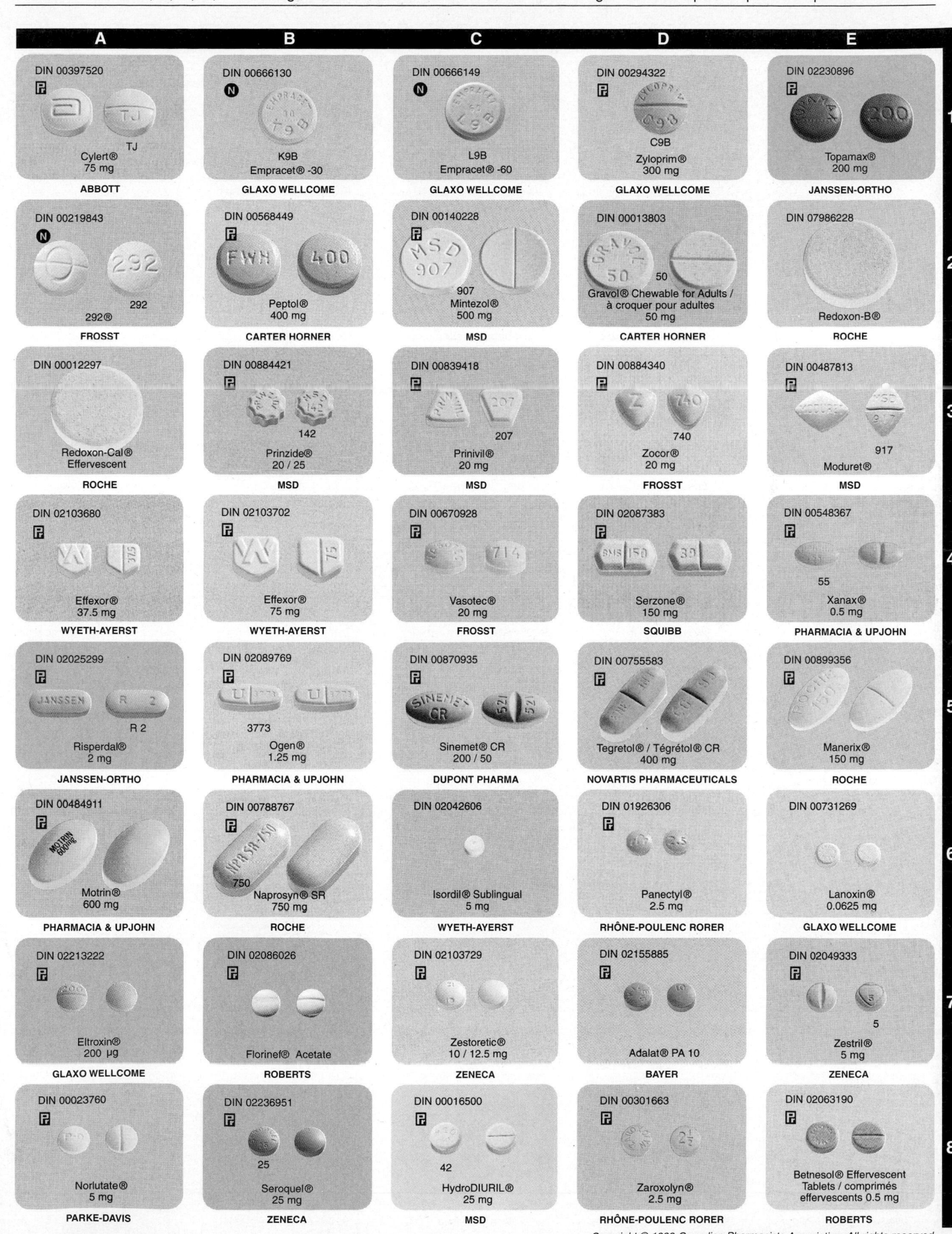

	A	B	C	D	E
1	DIN 00397520 Pr 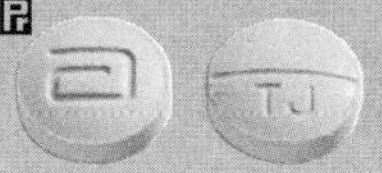 TJ Cylert® 75 mg **ABBOTT**	DIN 00666130 N 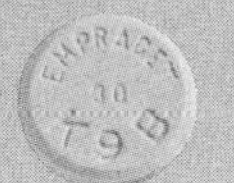 K9B Empracet® -30 **GLAXO WELLCOME**	DIN 00666149 N  L9B Empracet® -60 **GLAXO WELLCOME**	DIN 00294322 Pr  C9B Zyloprim® 300 mg **GLAXO WELLCOME**	DIN 02230896 Pr  Topamax® 200 mg **JANSSEN-ORTHO**
2	DIN 00219843 N 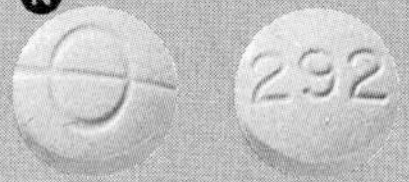 292 292® **FROSST**	DIN 00568449 Pr 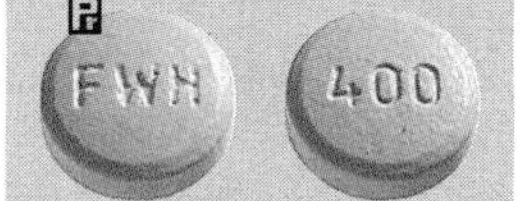 Peptol® 400 mg **CARTER HORNER**	DIN 00140228 Pr  907 Mintezol® 500 mg **MSD**	DIN 00013803  50 Gravol® Chewable for Adults / à croquer pour adultes 50 mg **CARTER HORNER**	DIN 07986228  Redoxon-B® **ROCHE**
3	DIN 00012297 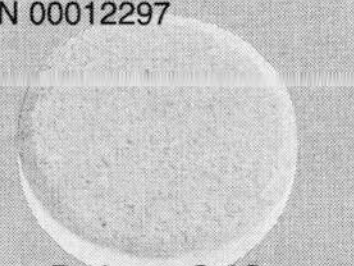 Redoxon-Cal® Effervescent **ROCHE**	DIN 00884421 Pr  142 Prinzide® 20 / 25 **MSD**	DIN 00839418 Pr  207 Prinivil® 20 mg **MSD**	DIN 00884340 Pr 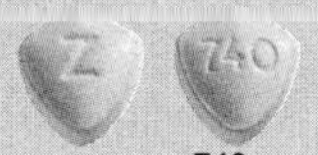 740 Zocor® 20 mg **FROSST**	DIN 00487813 Pr  917 Moduret® **MSD**
4	DIN 02103680 Pr  Effexor® 37.5 mg **WYETH-AYERST**	DIN 02103702 Pr  Effexor® 75 mg **WYETH-AYERST**	DIN 00670928 Pr  Vasotec® 20 mg **FROSST**	DIN 02087383 Pr 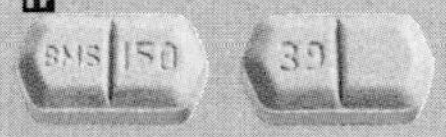 Serzone® 150 mg **SQUIBB**	DIN 00548367 Pr  55 Xanax® 0.5 mg **PHARMACIA & UPJOHN**
5	DIN 02025299 Pr 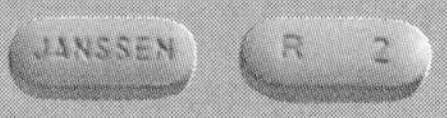 R 2 Risperdal® 2 mg **JANSSEN-ORTHO**	DIN 02089769 Pr  3773 Ogen® 1.25 mg **PHARMACIA & UPJOHN**	DIN 00870935 Pr 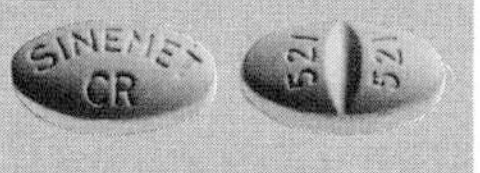 Sinemet® CR 200 / 50 **DUPONT PHARMA**	DIN 00755583 Pr 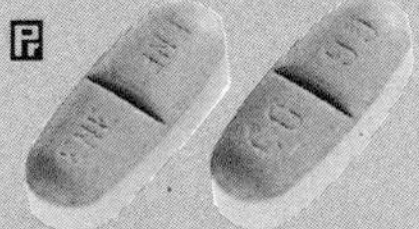 Tegretol® / Tégrétol® CR 400 mg **NOVARTIS PHARMACEUTICALS**	DIN 00899356 Pr 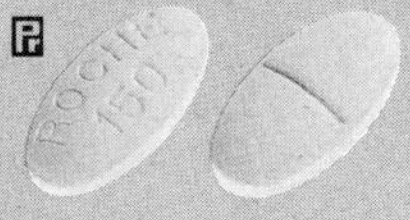 Manerix® 150 mg **ROCHE**
6	DIN 00484911 Pr  Motrin® 600 mg **PHARMACIA & UPJOHN**	DIN 00788767 Pr 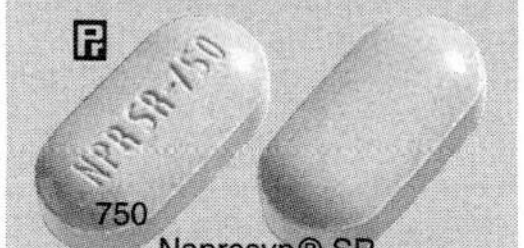 750 Naprosyn® SR 750 mg **ROCHE**	DIN 02042606  Isordil® Sublingual 5 mg **WYETH-AYERST**	DIN 01926306 Pr 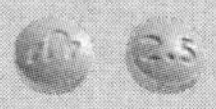 Panectyl® 2.5 mg **RHÔNE-POULENC RORER**	DIN 00731269  Lanoxin® 0.0625 mg **GLAXO WELLCOME**
7	DIN 02213222 Pr 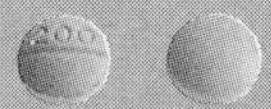 Eltroxin® 200 µg **GLAXO WELLCOME**	DIN 02086026 Pr 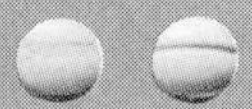 Florinef® Acetate **ROBERTS**	DIN 02103729 Pr  Zestoretic® 10 / 12.5 mg **ZENECA**	DIN 02155885 Pr  Adalat® PA 10 **BAYER**	DIN 02049333 Pr 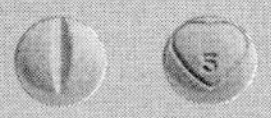 5 Zestril® 5 mg **ZENECA**
8	DIN 00023760 Pr  Norlutate® 5 mg **PARKE-DAVIS**	DIN 02236951 Pr 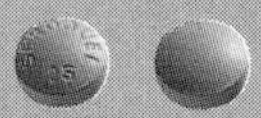 25 Seroquel® 25 mg **ZENECA**	DIN 00016500 Pr  42 HydroDIURIL® 25 mg **MSD**	DIN 00301663 Pr  Zaroxolyn® 2.5 mg **RHÔNE-POULENC RORER**	DIN 02063190 Pr 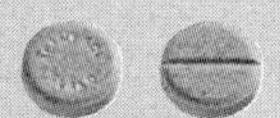 Betnesol® Effervescent Tablets / comprimés effervescents 0.5 mg **ROBERTS**

Use code A, B, C, D, E, horizontal bar and 1 to 8 vertical bar to locate illustrated products

Utiliser le code A, B, C, D, E de la ligne horizontale et les chiffres 1 à 8 de la ligne verticale pour repérer les produits illustrés

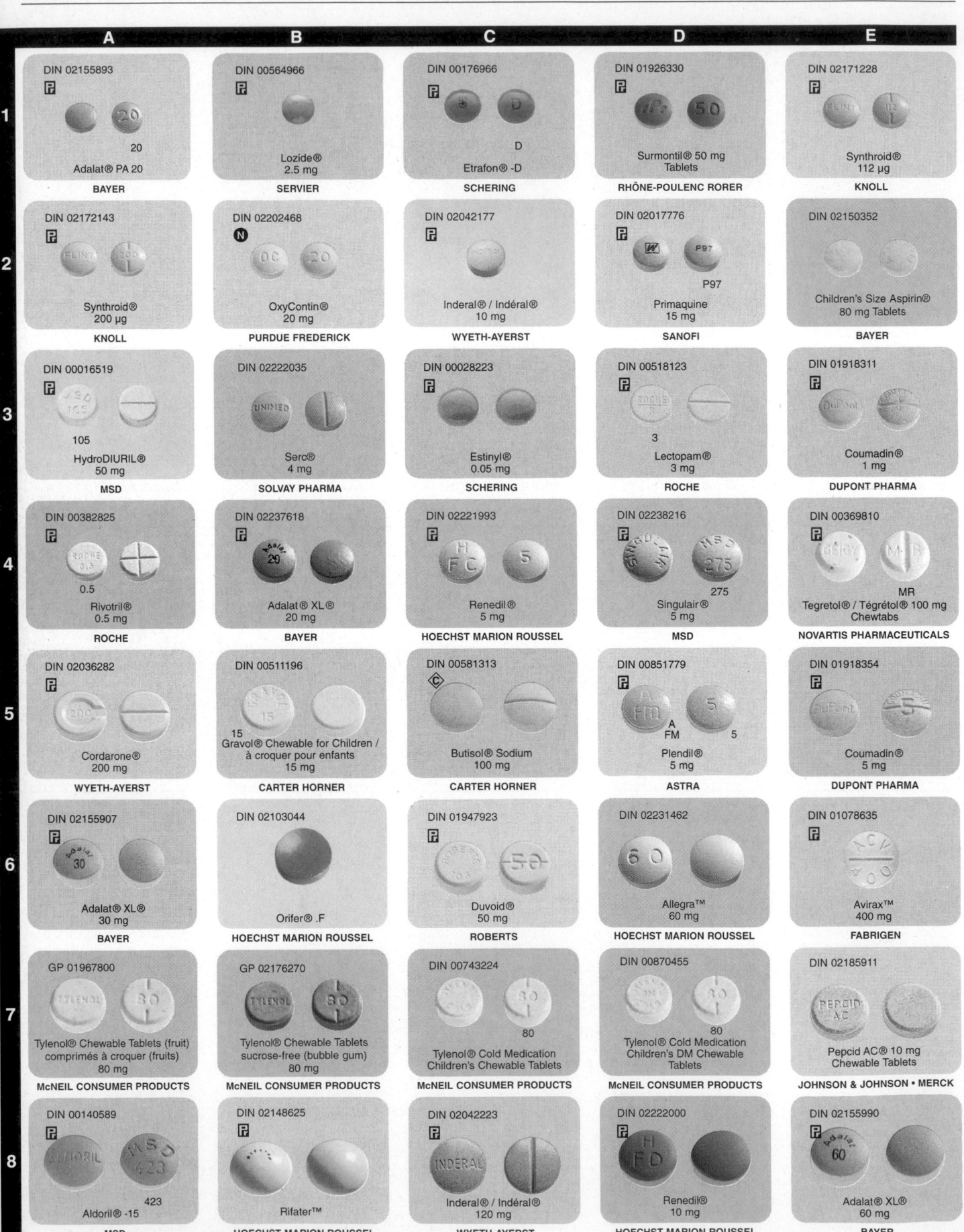

	A	B	C	D	E
1	DIN 02155893 20 Adalat® PA 20 **BAYER**	DIN 00564966 Lozide® 2.5 mg **SERVIER**	DIN 00176966 D Etrafon® -D **SCHERING**	DIN 01926330 Surmontil® 50 mg Tablets **RHÔNE-POULENC RORER**	DIN 02171228 Synthroid® 112 µg **KNOLL**
2	DIN 02172143 Synthroid® 200 µg **KNOLL**	DIN 02202468 OxyContin® 20 mg **PURDUE FREDERICK**	DIN 02042177 Inderal® / Indéral® 10 mg **WYETH-AYERST**	DIN 02017776 P97 Primaquine 15 mg **SANOFI**	DIN 02150352 Children's Size Aspirin® 80 mg Tablets **BAYER**
3	DIN 00016519 105 HydroDIURIL® 50 mg **MSD**	DIN 02222035 Serc® 4 mg **SOLVAY PHARMA**	DIN 00028223 Estinyl® 0.05 mg **SCHERING**	DIN 00518123 3 Lectopam® 3 mg **ROCHE**	DIN 01918311 Coumadin® 1 mg **DUPONT PHARMA**
4	DIN 00382825 0.5 Rivotril® 0.5 mg **ROCHE**	DIN 02237618 Adalat® XL® 20 mg **BAYER**	DIN 02221993 Renedil® 5 mg **HOECHST MARION ROUSSEL**	DIN 02238216 275 Singulair® 5 mg **MSD**	DIN 00369810 MR Tegretol® / Tégrétol® 100 mg Chewtabs **NOVARTIS PHARMACEUTICALS**
5	DIN 02036282 Cordarone® 200 mg **WYETH-AYERST**	DIN 00511196 15 Gravol® Chewable for Children / à croquer pour enfants 15 mg **CARTER HORNER**	DIN 00581313 Butisol® Sodium 100 mg **CARTER HORNER**	DIN 00851779 A FM 5 Plendil® 5 mg **ASTRA**	DIN 01918354 Coumadin® 5 mg **DUPONT PHARMA**
6	DIN 02155907 Adalat® XL® 30 mg **BAYER**	DIN 02103044 Orifer® .F **HOECHST MARION ROUSSEL**	DIN 01947923 Duvoid® 50 mg **ROBERTS**	DIN 02231462 Allegra™ 60 mg **HOECHST MARION ROUSSEL**	DIN 01078635 Avirax™ 400 mg **FABRIGEN**
7	GP 01967800 Tylenol® Chewable Tablets (fruit) comprimés à croquer (fruits) 80 mg **McNEIL CONSUMER PRODUCTS**	GP 02176270 Tylenol® Chewable Tablets sucrose-free (bubble gum) 80 mg **McNEIL CONSUMER PRODUCTS**	DIN 00743224 80 Tylenol® Cold Medication Children's Chewable Tablets **McNEIL CONSUMER PRODUCTS**	DIN 00870455 80 Tylenol® Cold Medication Children's DM Chewable Tablets **McNEIL CONSUMER PRODUCTS**	DIN 02185911 Pepcid AC® 10 mg Chewable Tablets **JOHNSON & JOHNSON • MERCK**
8	DIN 00140589 423 Aldoril® -15 **MSD**	DIN 02148625 Rifater™ **HOECHST MARION ROUSSEL**	DIN 02042223 Inderal® / Indéral® 120 mg **WYETH-AYERST**	DIN 02222000 Renedil® 10 mg **HOECHST MARION ROUSSEL**	DIN 02155990 Adalat® XL® 60 mg **BAYER**

Use code A, B, C, D, E, horizontal bar and 1 to 8 vertical bar to locate illustrated products

Utiliser le code A, B, C, D, E de la ligne horizontale et les chiffres 1 à 8 de la ligne verticale pour repérer les produits illustrés

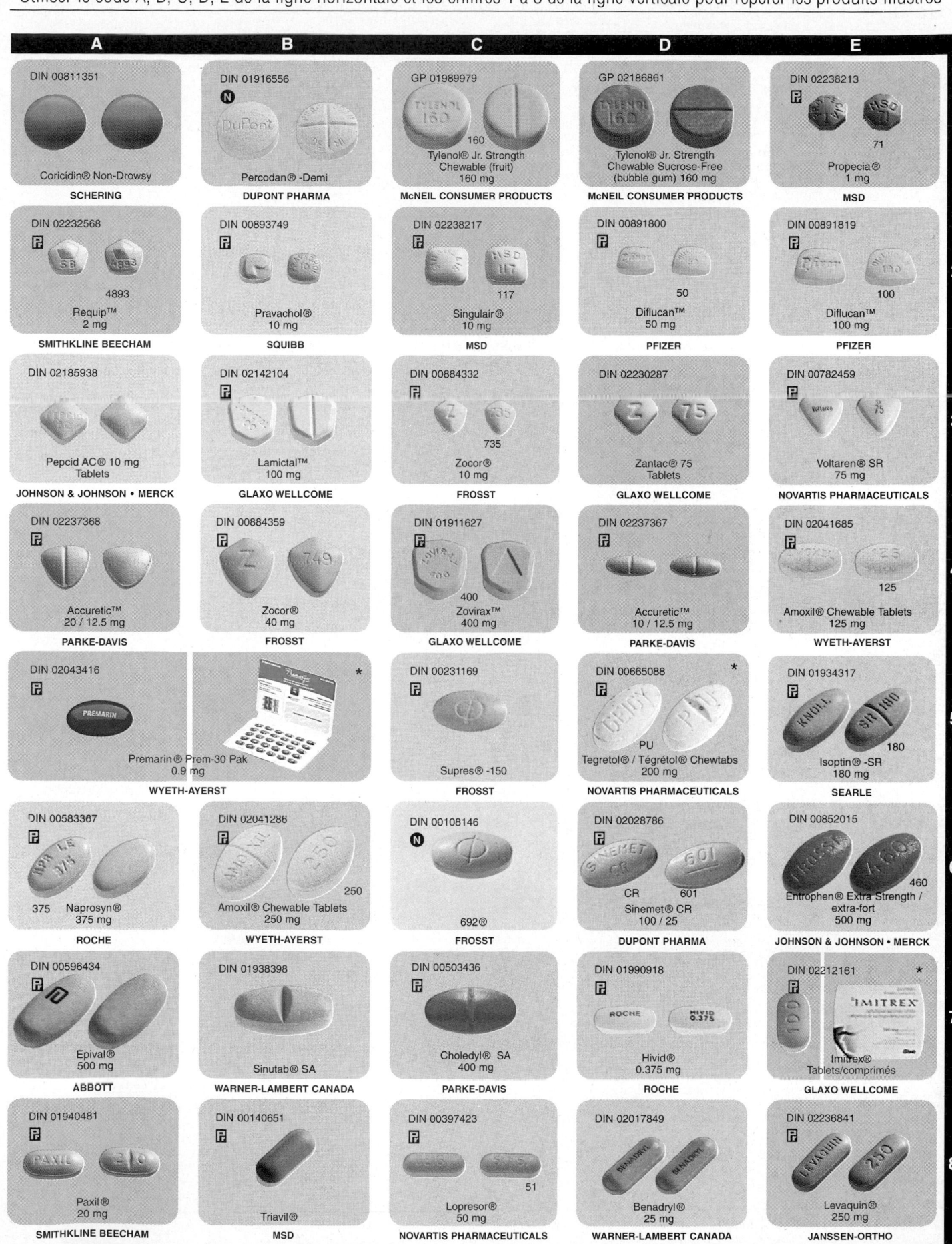

	A	B	C	D	E
1	DIN 00811351 Coricidin® Non-Drowsy **SCHERING**	DIN 01916556 N Percodan® -Demi **DUPONT PHARMA**	GP 01989979 160 Tylenol® Jr. Strength Chewable (fruit) 160 mg **McNEIL CONSUMER PRODUCTS**	GP 02186861 Tylenol® Jr. Strength Chewable Sucrose-Free (bubble gum) 160 mg **McNEIL CONSUMER PRODUCTS**	DIN 02238213 71 Propecia® 1 mg **MSD**
2	DIN 02232568 4893 Requip™ 2 mg **SMITHKLINE BEECHAM**	DIN 00893749 Pravachol® 10 mg **SQUIBB**	DIN 02238217 117 Singulair® 10 mg **MSD**	DIN 00891800 50 Diflucan™ 50 mg **PFIZER**	DIN 00891819 100 Diflucan™ 100 mg **PFIZER**
3	DIN 02185938 Pepcid AC® 10 mg Tablets **JOHNSON & JOHNSON • MERCK**	DIN 02142104 Lamictal™ 100 mg **GLAXO WELLCOME**	DIN 00884332 735 Zocor® 10 mg **FROSST**	DIN 02230287 Zantac® 75 Tablets **GLAXO WELLCOME**	DIN 00782459 Voltaren® SR 75 mg **NOVARTIS PHARMACEUTICALS**
4	DIN 02237368 Accuretic™ 20 / 12.5 mg **PARKE-DAVIS**	DIN 00884359 Zocor® 40 mg **FROSST**	DIN 01911627 400 Zovirax™ 400 mg **GLAXO WELLCOME**	DIN 02237367 Accuretic™ 10 / 12.5 mg **PARKE-DAVIS**	DIN 02041685 125 Amoxil® Chewable Tablets 125 mg **WYETH-AYERST**
5	DIN 02043416 Premarin® 0.9 mg **WYETH-AYERST**	Prem-30 Pak * **WYETH-AYERST**	DIN 00231169 Supres® -150 **FROSST**	DIN 00665088 * PU Tegretol® / Tégrétol® Chewtabs 200 mg **NOVARTIS PHARMACEUTICALS**	DIN 01934317 180 Isoptin® -SR 180 mg **SEARLE**
6	DIN 00583367 375 Naprosyn® 375 mg **ROCHE**	DIN 02041286 250 Amoxil® Chewable Tablets 250 mg **WYETH-AYERST**	DIN 00108146 N 692® **FROSST**	DIN 02028786 CR 601 Sinemet® CR 100 / 25 **DUPONT PHARMA**	DIN 00852015 460 Entrophen® Extra Strength / extra-fort 500 mg **JOHNSON & JOHNSON • MERCK**
7	DIN 00596434 Epival® 500 mg **ABBOTT**	DIN 01938398 Sinutab® SA **WARNER-LAMBERT CANADA**	DIN 00503436 Choledyl® SA 400 mg **PARKE-DAVIS**	DIN 01990918 Hivid® 0.375 mg **ROCHE**	DIN 02212161 * Imitrex® Tablets/comprimés **GLAXO WELLCOME**
8	DIN 01940481 Paxil® 20 mg **SMITHKLINE BEECHAM**	DIN 00140651 Triavil® **MSD**	DIN 00397423 51 Lopresor® 50 mg **NOVARTIS PHARMACEUTICALS**	DIN 02017849 Benadryl® 25 mg **WARNER-LAMBERT CANADA**	DIN 02236841 Levaquin® 250 mg **JANSSEN-ORTHO**

*ILLUSTRATION LESS THAN ACTUAL SIZE / ILLUSTRATION RÉDUITE

Use code A, B, C, D, E, horizontal bar and 1 to 8 vertical bar to locate illustrated products

Utiliser le code A, B, C, D, E de la ligne horizontale et les chiffres 1 à 8 de la ligne verticale pour repérer les produits illustrés

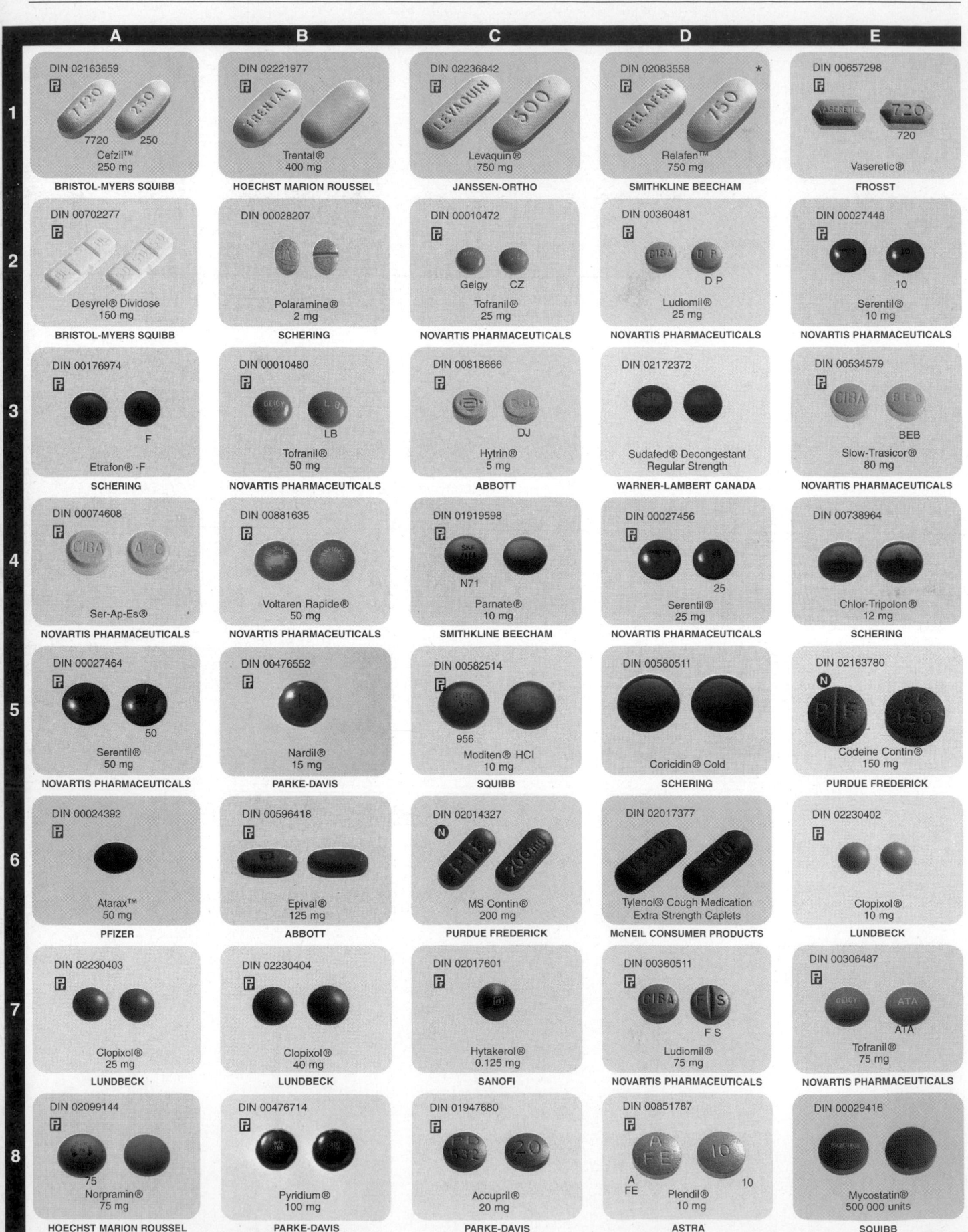

	A	B	C	D	E
1	DIN 02163659 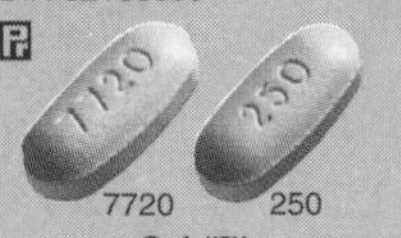 7720 250 Cefzil™ 250 mg **BRISTOL-MYERS SQUIBB**	DIN 02221977 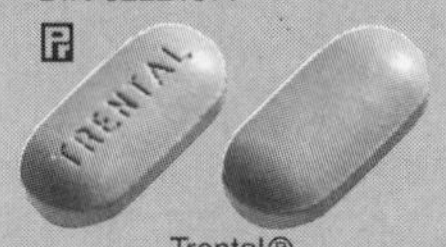 Trental® 400 mg **HOECHST MARION ROUSSEL**	DIN 02236842 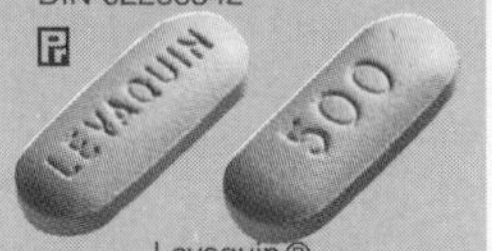 Levaquin® 750 mg **JANSSEN-ORTHO**	DIN 02083558 * 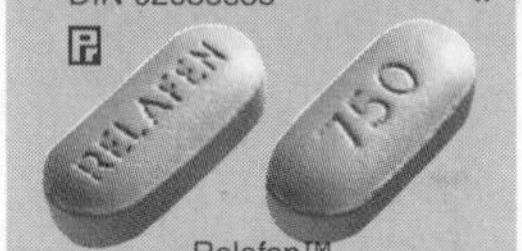 Relafen™ 750 mg **SMITHKLINE BEECHAM**	DIN 00657298  720 Vaseretic® **FROSST**
2	DIN 00702277  Desyrel® Dividose 150 mg **BRISTOL-MYERS SQUIBB**	DIN 00028207  Polaramine® 2 mg **SCHERING**	DIN 00010472  Geigy CZ Tofranil® 25 mg **NOVARTIS PHARMACEUTICALS**	DIN 00360481  D P Ludiomil® 25 mg **NOVARTIS PHARMACEUTICALS**	DIN 00027448  10 Serentil® 10 mg **NOVARTIS PHARMACEUTICALS**
3	DIN 00176974  F Etrafon® -F **SCHERING**	DIN 00010480  LB Tofranil® 50 mg **NOVARTIS PHARMACEUTICALS**	DIN 00818666 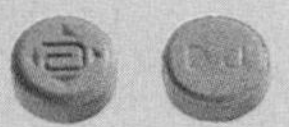 DJ Hytrin® 5 mg **ABBOTT**	DIN 02172372  Sudafed® Decongestant Regular Strength **WARNER-LAMBERT CANADA**	DIN 00534579 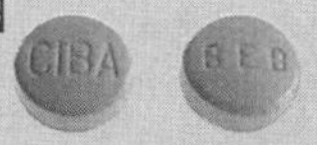 BEB Slow-Trasicor® 80 mg **NOVARTIS PHARMACEUTICALS**
4	DIN 00074608  Ser-Ap-Es® **NOVARTIS PHARMACEUTICALS**	DIN 00881635  Voltaren Rapide® 50 mg **NOVARTIS PHARMACEUTICALS**	DIN 01919598  N71 Parnate® 10 mg **SMITHKLINE BEECHAM**	DIN 00027456  25 Serentil® 25 mg **NOVARTIS PHARMACEUTICALS**	DIN 00738964  Chlor-Tripolon® 12 mg **SCHERING**
5	DIN 00027464  50 Serentil® 50 mg **NOVARTIS PHARMACEUTICALS**	DIN 00476552  Nardil® 15 mg **PARKE-DAVIS**	DIN 00582514  956 Moditen® HCl 10 mg **SQUIBB**	DIN 00580511  Coricidin® Cold **SCHERING**	DIN 02163780 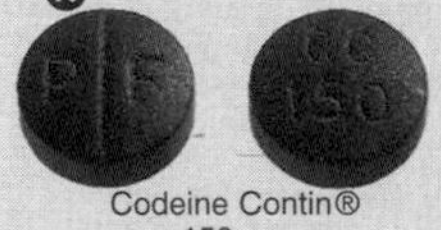 Codeine Contin® 150 mg **PURDUE FREDERICK**
6	DIN 00024392  Atarax™ 50 mg **PFIZER**	DIN 00596418  Epival® 125 mg **ABBOTT**	DIN 02014327  MS Contin® 200 mg **PURDUE FREDERICK**	DIN 02017377  Tylenol® Cough Medication Extra Strength Caplets **McNEIL CONSUMER PRODUCTS**	DIN 02230402  Clopixol® 10 mg **LUNDBECK**
7	DIN 02230403  Clopixol® 25 mg **LUNDBECK**	DIN 02230404  Clopixol® 40 mg **LUNDBECK**	DIN 02017601  Hytakerol® 0.125 mg **SANOFI**	DIN 00360511  F S Ludiomil® 75 mg **NOVARTIS PHARMACEUTICALS**	DIN 00306487  ATA Tofranil® 75 mg **NOVARTIS PHARMACEUTICALS**
8	DIN 02099144  75 Norpramin® 75 mg **HOECHST MARION ROUSSEL**	DIN 00476714  Pyridium® 100 mg **PARKE-DAVIS**	DIN 01947680  Accupril® 20 mg **PARKE-DAVIS**	DIN 00851787  A FE 10 Plendil® 10 mg **ASTRA**	DIN 00029416  Mycostatin® 500 000 units **SQUIBB**

*ILLUSTRATION LESS THAN ACTUAL SIZE / ILLUSTRATION RÉDUITE

Use code A, B, C, D, E, horizontal bar and 1 to 8 vertical bar to locate illustrated products

Utiliser le code A, B, C, D, E de la ligne horizontale et les chiffres 1 à 8 de la ligne verticale pour repérer les produits illustrés

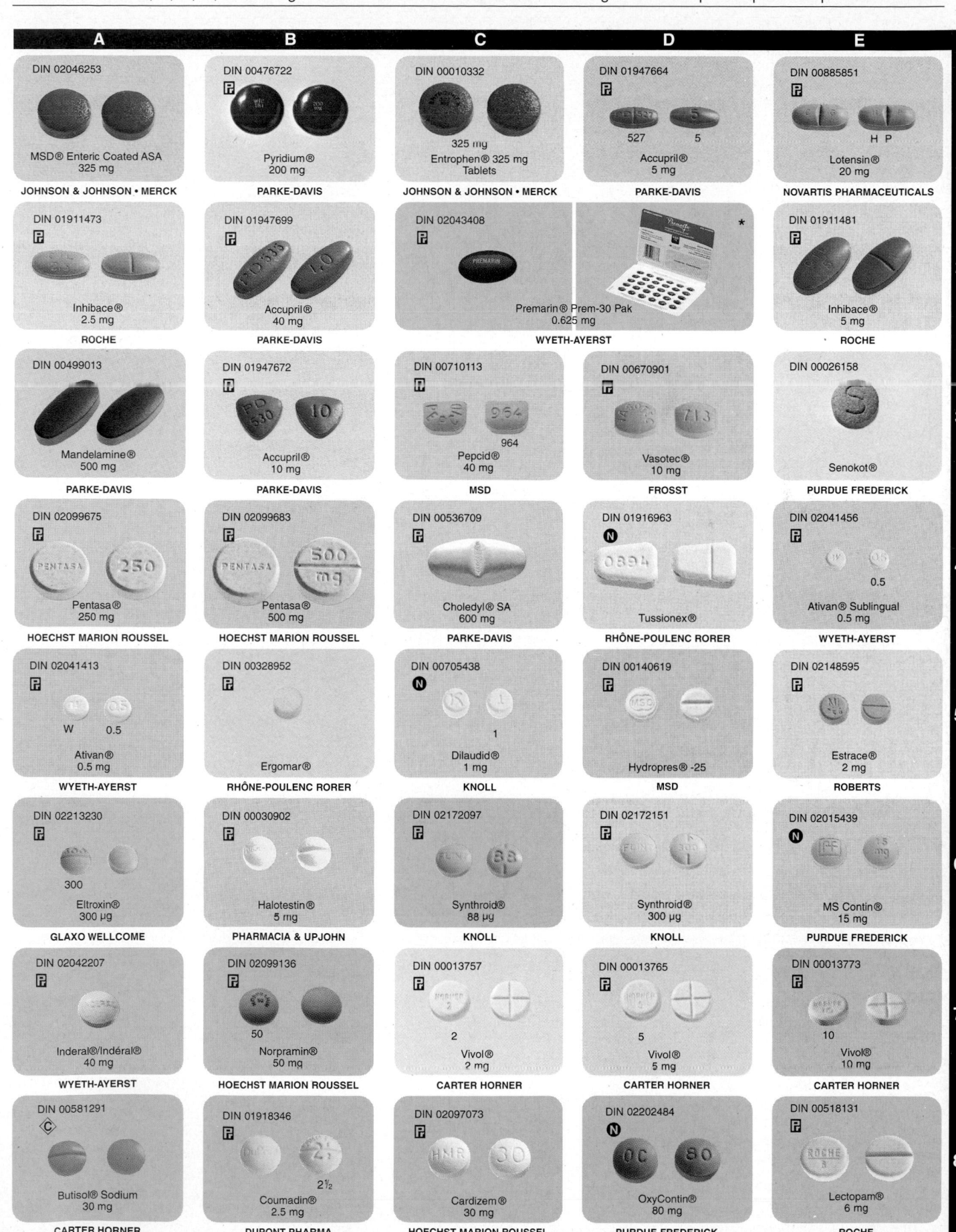

	A	B	C	D	E
1	DIN 02046253  MSD® Enteric Coated ASA 325 mg **JOHNSON & JOHNSON • MERCK**	DIN 00476722  Pyridium® 200 mg **PARKE-DAVIS**	DIN 00010332  325 mg Entrophen® 325 mg Tablets **JOHNSON & JOHNSON • MERCK**	DIN 01947664  527 5 Accupril® 5 mg **PARKE-DAVIS**	DIN 00885851  H P Lotensin® 20 mg **NOVARTIS PHARMACEUTICALS**
2	DIN 01911473  Inhibace® 2.5 mg **ROCHE**	DIN 01947699 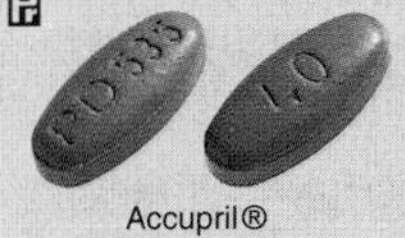 Accupril® 40 mg **PARKE-DAVIS**	DIN 02043408  * Premarin® Prem-30 Pak 0.625 mg **WYETH-AYERST**		DIN 01911481 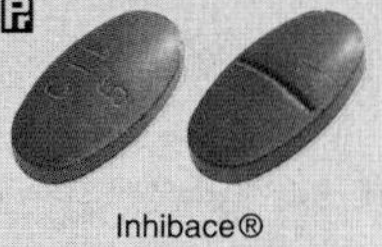 Inhibace® 5 mg **ROCHE**
3	DIN 00499013  Mandelamine® 500 mg **PARKE-DAVIS**	DIN 01947672  Accupril® 10 mg **PARKE-DAVIS**	DIN 00710113  964 Pepcid® 40 mg **MSD**	DIN 00670901 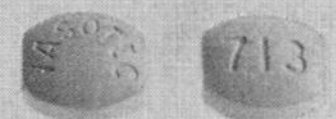 Vasotec® 10 mg **FROSST**	DIN 00026158  Senokot® **PURDUE FREDERICK**
4	DIN 02099675 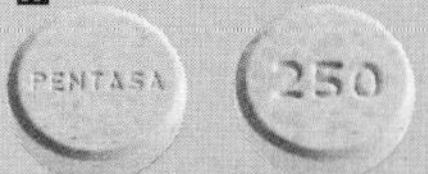 Pentasa® 250 mg **HOECHST MARION ROUSSEL**	DIN 02099683  Pentasa® 500 mg **HOECHST MARION ROUSSEL**	DIN 00536709  Choledyl® SA 600 mg **PARKE-DAVIS**	DIN 01916963 N  Tussionex® **RHÔNE-POULENC RORER**	DIN 02041456  0.5 Ativan® Sublingual 0.5 mg **WYETH-AYERST**
5	DIN 02041413  W 0.5 Ativan® 0.5 mg **WYETH-AYERST**	DIN 00328952  Ergomar® **RHÔNE-POULENC RORER**	DIN 00705438 N  1 Dilaudid® 1 mg **KNOLL**	DIN 00140619  Hydropres® -25 **MSD**	DIN 02148595  Estrace® 2 mg **ROBERTS**
6	DIN 02213230 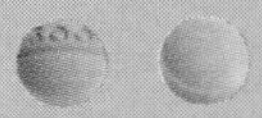 300 Eltroxin® 300 µg **GLAXO WELLCOME**	DIN 00030902 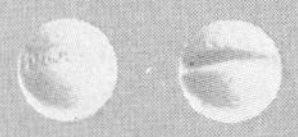 Halotestin® 5 mg **PHARMACIA & UPJOHN**	DIN 02172097 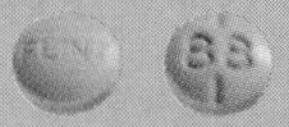 Synthroid® 88 µg **KNOLL**	DIN 02172151  Synthroid® 300 µg **KNOLL**	DIN 02015439 N  MS Contin® 15 mg **PURDUE FREDERICK**
7	DIN 02042207  Inderal®/Indéral® 40 mg **WYETH-AYERST**	DIN 02099136 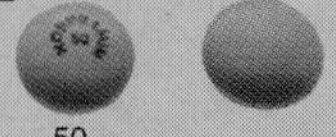 50 Norpramin® 50 mg **HOECHST MARION ROUSSEL**	DIN 00013757  2 Vivol® 2 mg **CARTER HORNER**	DIN 00013765  5 Vivol® 5 mg **CARTER HORNER**	DIN 00013773 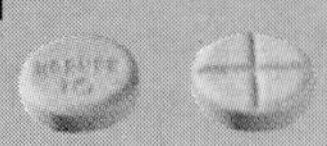 10 Vivol® 10 mg **CARTER HORNER**
8	DIN 00581291 C 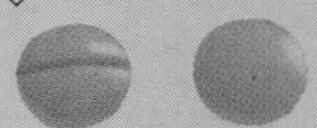 Butisol® Sodium 30 mg **CARTER HORNER**	DIN 01918346 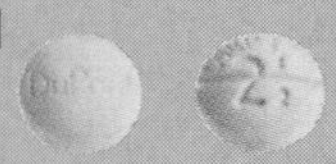 2½ Coumadin® 2.5 mg **DUPONT PHARMA**	DIN 02097073  Cardizem® 30 mg **HOECHST MARION ROUSSEL**	DIN 02202484 N 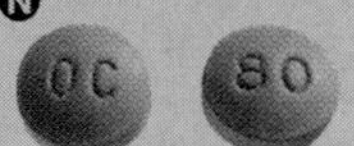 OxyContin® 80 mg **PURDUE FREDERICK**	DIN 00518131 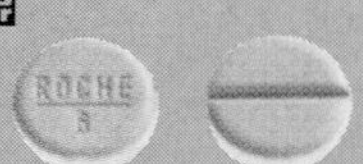 Lectopam® 6 mg **ROCHE**

*ILLUSTRATION LESS THAN ACTUAL SIZE / ILLUSTRATION RÉDUITE

Use code A, B, C, D, E, horizontal bar and 1 to 8 vertical bar to locate illustrated products

Utiliser le code A, B, C, D, E de la ligne horizontale et les chiffres 1 à 8 de la ligne verticale pour repérer les produits illustrés

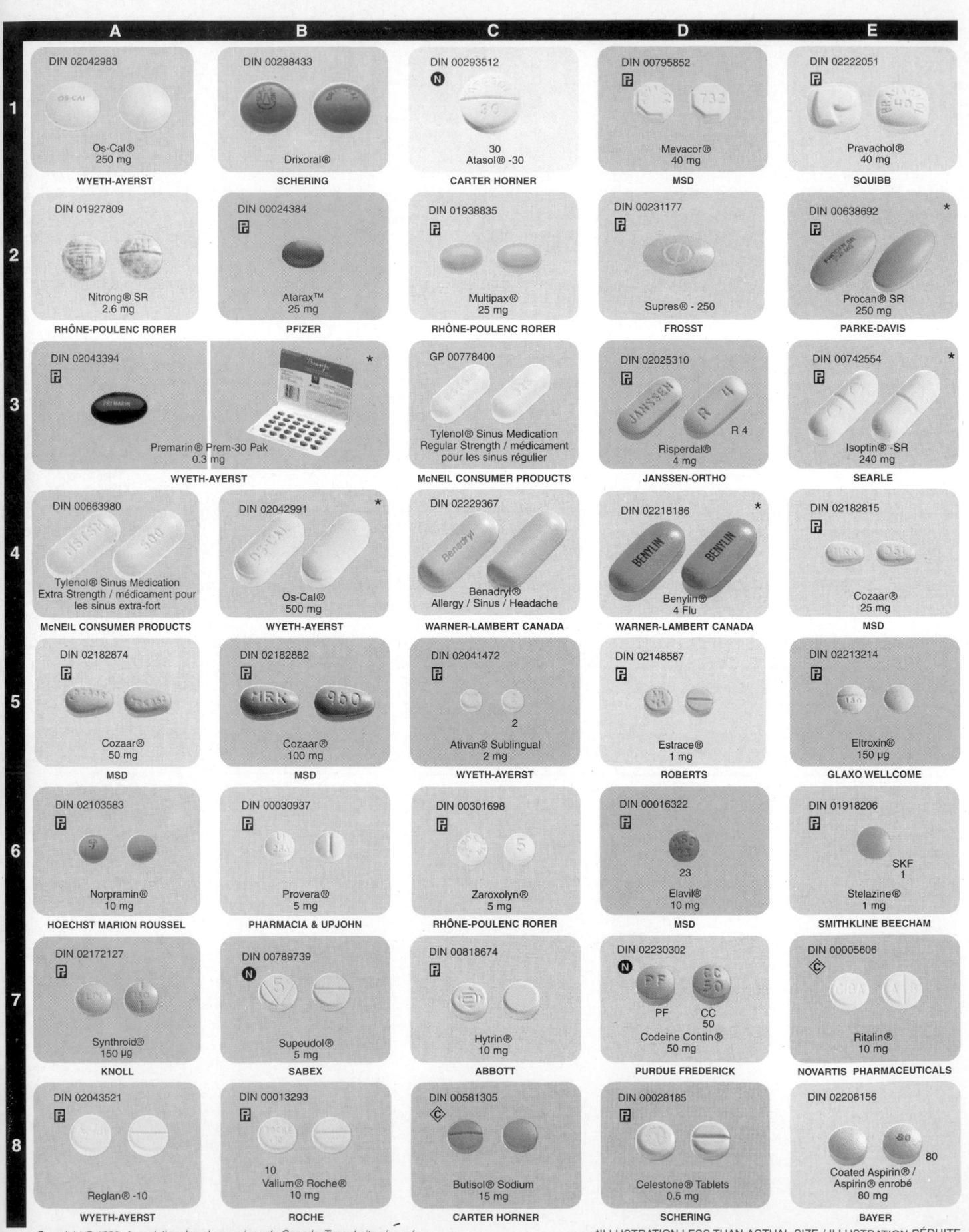

	A	B	C	D	E
1	DIN 02042983 Os-Cal® 250 mg **WYETH-AYERST**	DIN 00298433 Drixoral® **SCHERING**	DIN 00293512 Ⓝ 30 Atasol® -30 **CARTER HORNER**	DIN 00795852 Mevacor® 40 mg **MSD**	DIN 02222051 Pravachol® 40 mg **SQUIBB**
2	DIN 01927809 Nitrong® SR 2.6 mg **RHÔNE-POULENC RORER**	DIN 00024384 Atarax™ 25 mg **PFIZER**	DIN 01938835 Multipax® 25 mg **RHÔNE-POULENC RORER**	DIN 00231177 Supres® - 250 **FROSST**	DIN 00638692 * Procan® SR 250 mg **PARKE-DAVIS**
3	DIN 02043394 * Premarin® Prem-30 Pak 0.3 mg **WYETH-AYERST**		GP 00778400 Tylenol® Sinus Medication Regular Strength / médicament pour les sinus régulier **McNEIL CONSUMER PRODUCTS**	DIN 02025310 R 4 Risperdal® 4 mg **JANSSEN-ORTHO**	DIN 00742554 * Isoptin® -SR 240 mg **SEARLE**
4	DIN 00663980 Tylenol® Sinus Medication Extra Strength / médicament pour les sinus extra-fort **McNEIL CONSUMER PRODUCTS**	DIN 02042991 * Os-Cal® 500 mg **WYETH-AYERST**	DIN 02229367 Benadryl® Allergy / Sinus / Headache **WARNER-LAMBERT CANADA**	DIN 02218186 * Benylin® 4 Flu **WARNER-LAMBERT CANADA**	DIN 02182815 Cozaar® 25 mg **MSD**
5	DIN 02182874 Cozaar® 50 mg **MSD**	DIN 02182882 Cozaar® 100 mg **MSD**	DIN 02041472 2 Ativan® Sublingual 2 mg **WYETH-AYERST**	DIN 02148587 Estrace® 1 mg **ROBERTS**	DIN 02213214 Eltroxin® 150 µg **GLAXO WELLCOME**
6	DIN 02103583 Norpramin® 10 mg **HOECHST MARION ROUSSEL**	DIN 00030937 Provera® 5 mg **PHARMACIA & UPJOHN**	DIN 00301698 Zaroxolyn® 5 mg **RHÔNE-POULENC RORER**	DIN 00016322 23 Elavil® 10 mg **MSD**	DIN 01918206 SKF 1 Stelazine® 1 mg **SMITHKLINE BEECHAM**
7	DIN 02172127 Synthroid® 150 µg **KNOLL**	DIN 00789739 Ⓝ Supeudol® 5 mg **SABEX**	DIN 00818674 Hytrin® 10 mg **ABBOTT**	DIN 02230302 Ⓝ PF CC 50 Codeine Contin® 50 mg **PURDUE FREDERICK**	DIN 00005606 Ⓒ Ritalin® 10 mg **NOVARTIS PHARMACEUTICALS**
8	DIN 02043521 Reglan® -10 **WYETH-AYERST**	DIN 00013293 10 Valium® Roche® 10 mg **ROCHE**	DIN 00581305 Ⓒ Butisol® Sodium 15 mg **CARTER HORNER**	DIN 00028185 Celestone® Tablets 0.5 mg **SCHERING**	DIN 02208156 80 Coated Aspirin® / Aspirin® enrobé 80 mg **BAYER**

*ILLUSTRATION LESS THAN ACTUAL SIZE / ILLUSTRATION RÉDUITE

Use code A, B, C, D, E, horizontal bar and 1 to 8 vertical bar to locate illustrated products

Utiliser le code A, B, C, D, E de la ligne horizontale et les chiffres 1 à 8 de la ligne verticale pour repérer les produits illustrés

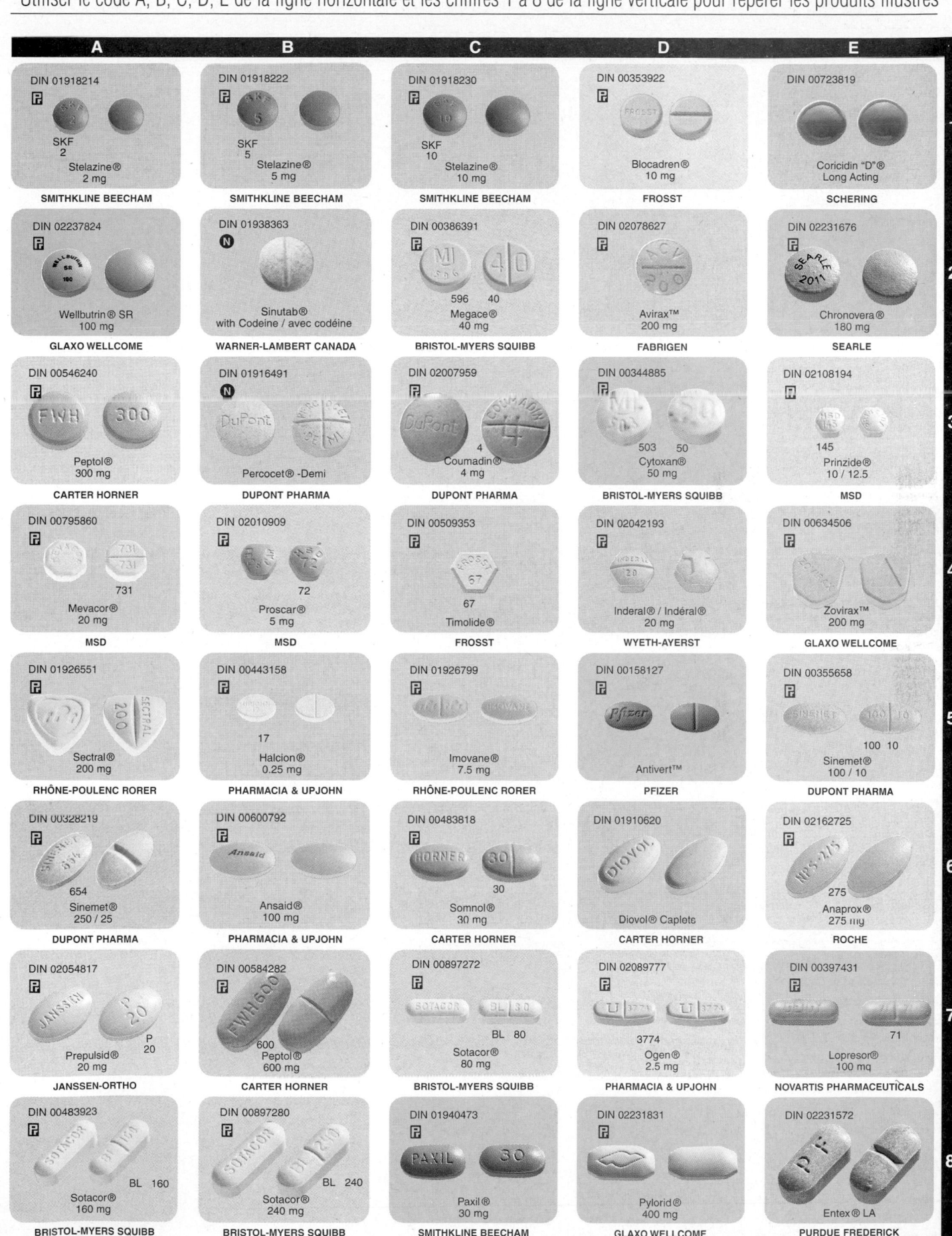

	A	B	C	D	E
1	DIN 01918214 SKF 2 Stelazine® 2 mg **SMITHKLINE BEECHAM**	DIN 01918222 SKF 5 Stelazine® 5 mg **SMITHKLINE BEECHAM**	DIN 01918230 SKF 10 Stelazine® 10 mg **SMITHKLINE BEECHAM**	DIN 00353922 Blocadren® 10 mg **FROSST**	DIN 00723819 Coricidin "D"® Long Acting **SCHERING**
2	DIN 02237824 Wellbutrin® SR 100 mg **GLAXO WELLCOME**	DIN 01938363 N Sinutab® with Codeine / avec codéine **WARNER-LAMBERT CANADA**	DIN 00386391 596 40 Megace® 40 mg **BRISTOL-MYERS SQUIBB**	DIN 02078627 Avirax™ 200 mg **FABRIGEN**	DIN 02231676 Chronovera® 180 mg **SEARLE**
3	DIN 00546240 Peptol® 300 mg **CARTER HORNER**	DIN 01916491 N Percocet® -Demi **DUPONT PHARMA**	DIN 02007959 4 Coumadin® 4 mg **DUPONT PHARMA**	DIN 00344885 503 50 Cytoxan® 50 mg **BRISTOL-MYERS SQUIBB**	DIN 02108194 145 Prinzide® 10 / 12.5 **MSD**
4	DIN 00795860 731 Mevacor® 20 mg **MSD**	DIN 02010909 72 Proscar® 5 mg **MSD**	DIN 00509353 67 Timolide® **FROSST**	DIN 02042193 Inderal® / Indéral® 20 mg **WYETH-AYERST**	DIN 00634506 Zovirax™ 200 mg **GLAXO WELLCOME**
5	DIN 01926551 Sectral® 200 mg **RHÔNE-POULENC RORER**	DIN 00443158 17 Halcion® 0.25 mg **PHARMACIA & UPJOHN**	DIN 01926799 Imovane® 7.5 mg **RHÔNE-POULENC RORER**	DIN 00158127 Antivert™ **PFIZER**	DIN 00355658 100 10 Sinemet® 100 / 10 **DUPONT PHARMA**
6	DIN 00328219 654 Sinemet® 250 / 25 **DUPONT PHARMA**	DIN 00600792 Ansaid® 100 mg **PHARMACIA & UPJOHN**	DIN 00483818 30 Somnol® 30 mg **CARTER HORNER**	DIN 01910620 Diovol® Caplets **CARTER HORNER**	DIN 02162725 275 Anaprox® 275 mg **ROCHE**
7	DIN 02054817 P 20 Prepulsid® 20 mg **JANSSEN-ORTHO**	DIN 00584282 600 Peptol® 600 mg **CARTER HORNER**	DIN 00897272 BL 80 Sotacor® 80 mg **BRISTOL-MYERS SQUIBB**	DIN 02089777 3774 Ogen® 2.5 mg **PHARMACIA & UPJOHN**	DIN 00397431 71 Lopresor® 100 mg **NOVARTIS PHARMACEUTICALS**
8	DIN 00483923 BL 160 Sotacor® 160 mg **BRISTOL-MYERS SQUIBB**	DIN 00897280 BL 240 Sotacor® 240 mg **BRISTOL-MYERS SQUIBB**	DIN 01940473 Paxil® 30 mg **SMITHKLINE BEECHAM**	DIN 02231831 Pylorid® 400 mg **GLAXO WELLCOME**	DIN 02231572 Entex® LA **PURDUE FREDERICK**

Use code A, B, C, D, E, horizontal bar and 1 to 8 vertical bar to locate illustrated products

Utiliser le code A, B, C, D, E de la ligne horizontale et les chiffres 1 à 8 de la ligne verticale pour repérer les produits illustrés

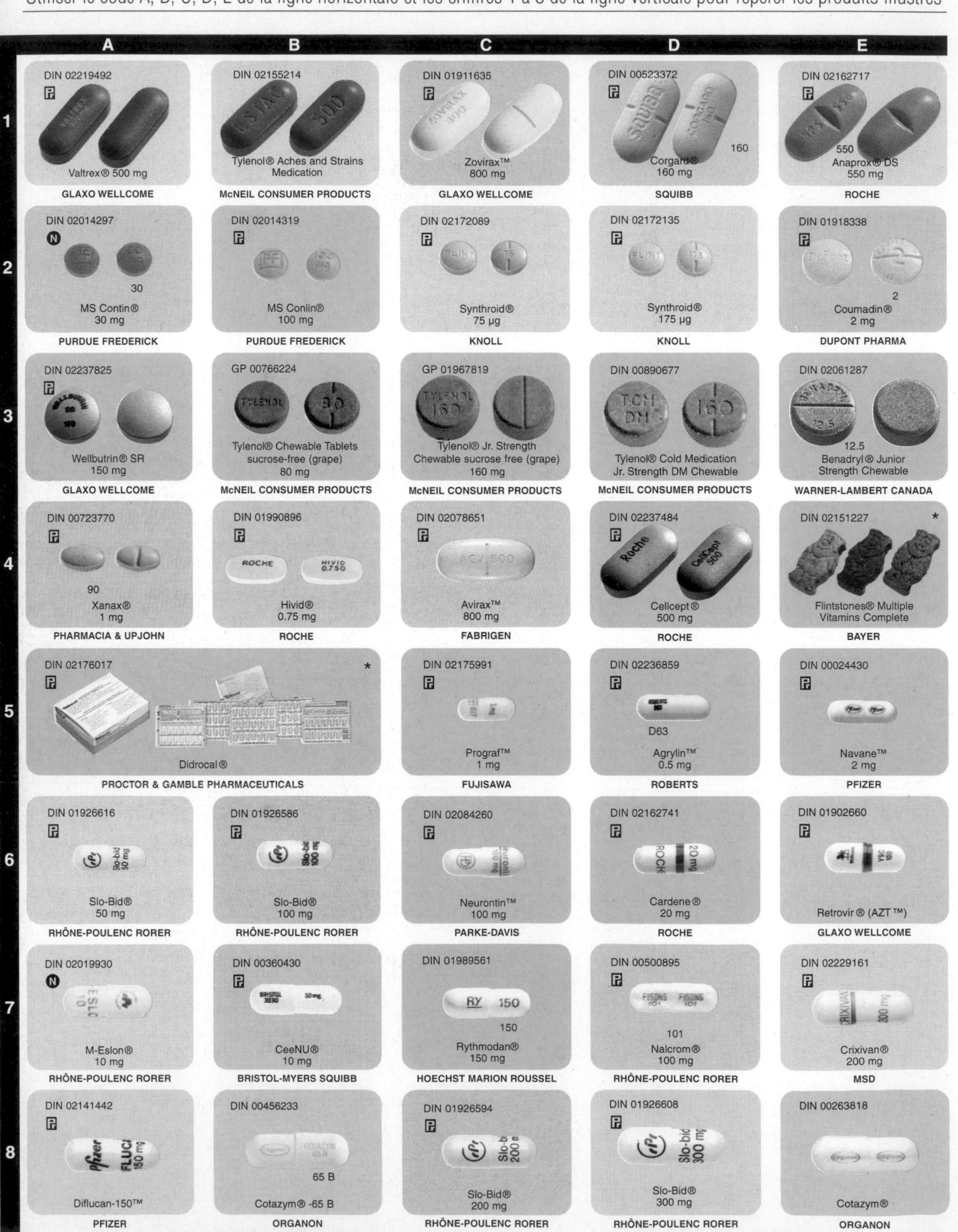

	A	B	C	D	E
1	DIN 02219492 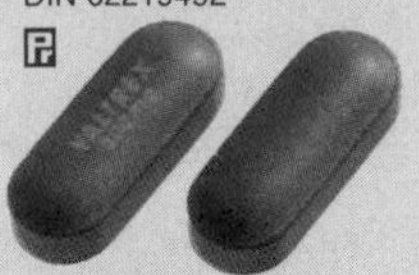 Valtrex® 500 mg **GLAXO WELLCOME**	DIN 02155214 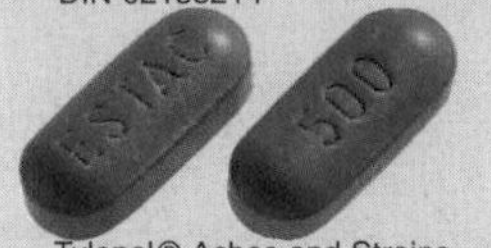 Tylenol® Aches and Strains Medication **McNEIL CONSUMER PRODUCTS**	DIN 01911635 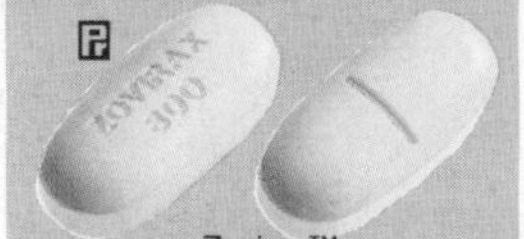 Zovirax™ 800 mg **GLAXO WELLCOME**	DIN 00523372 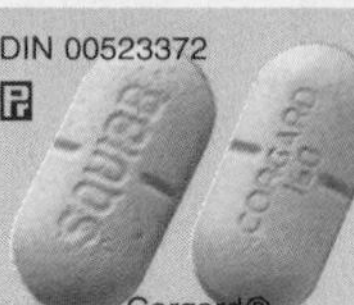 160 Corgard® 160 mg **SQUIBB**	DIN 02162717  550 Anaprox® DS 550 mg **ROCHE**
2	DIN 02014297  30 MS Contin® 30 mg **PURDUE FREDERICK**	DIN 02014319 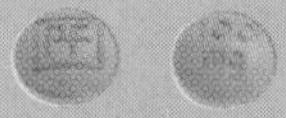 MS Conlin® 100 mg **PURDUE FREDERICK**	DIN 02172089 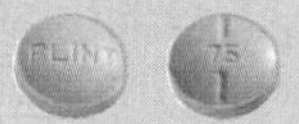 Synthroid® 75 µg **KNOLL**	DIN 02172135  Synthroid® 175 µg **KNOLL**	DIN 01918338  2 Coumadin® 2 mg **DUPONT PHARMA**
3	DIN 02237825  Wellbutrin® SR 150 mg **GLAXO WELLCOME**	GP 00766224 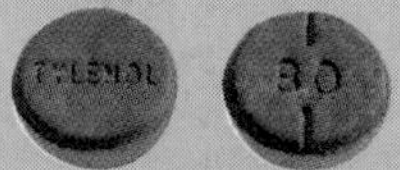 Tylenol® Chewable Tablets sucrose-free (grape) 80 mg **McNEIL CONSUMER PRODUCTS**	GP 01967819 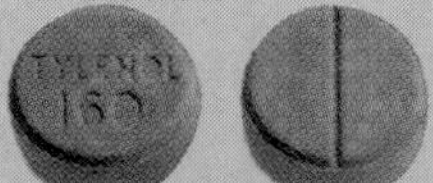 Tylenol® Jr. Strength Chewable sucrose free (grape) 160 mg **McNEIL CONSUMER PRODUCTS**	DIN 00890677 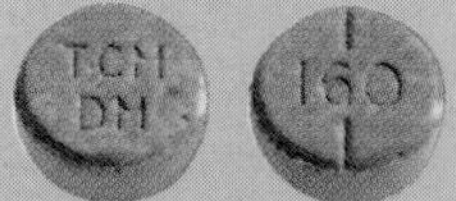 Tylenol® Cold Medication Jr. Strength DM Chewable **McNEIL CONSUMER PRODUCTS**	DIN 02061287  12.5 Benadryl® Junior Strength Chewable **WARNER-LAMBERT CANADA**
4	DIN 00723770 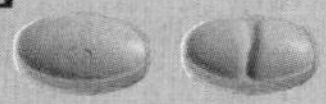 90 Xanax® 1 mg **PHARMACIA & UPJOHN**	DIN 01990896  Hivid® 0.75 mg **ROCHE**	DIN 02078651  Avirax™ 800 mg **FABRIGEN**	DIN 02237484 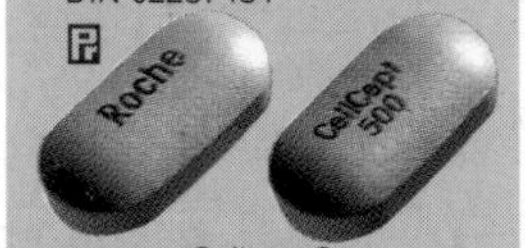 Cellcept® 500 mg **ROCHE**	DIN 02151227 *  Flintstones® Multiple Vitamins Complete **BAYER**
5	DIN 02176017 *  Didrocal® **PROCTOR & GAMBLE PHARMACEUTICALS**		DIN 02175991  Prograf™ 1 mg **FUJISAWA**	DIN 02236859  D63 Agrylin™ 0.5 mg **ROBERTS**	DIN 00024430  Navane™ 2 mg **PFIZER**
6	DIN 01926616  Slo-Bid® 50 mg **RHÔNE-POULENC RORER**	DIN 01926586  Slo-Bid® 100 mg **RHÔNE-POULENC RORER**	DIN 02084260  Neurontin™ 100 mg **PARKE-DAVIS**	DIN 02162741  Cardene® 20 mg **ROCHE**	DIN 01902660 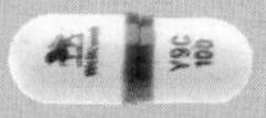 Retrovir® (AZT™) **GLAXO WELLCOME**
7	DIN 02019930  M-Eslon® 10 mg **RHÔNE-POULENC RORER**	DIN 00360430 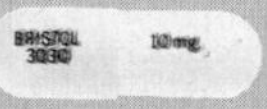 CeeNU® 10 mg **BRISTOL-MYERS SQUIBB**	DIN 01989561 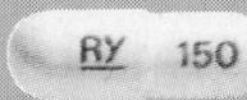 150 Rythmodan® 150 mg **HOECHST MARION ROUSSEL**	DIN 00500895  101 Nalcrom® 100 mg **RHÔNE-POULENC RORER**	DIN 02229161  Crixivan® 200 mg **MSD**
8	DIN 02141442 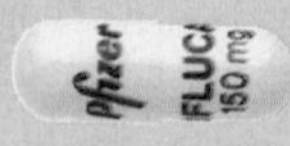 Diflucan-150™ **PFIZER**	DIN 00456233  65 B Cotazym® -65 B **ORGANON**	DIN 01926594  Slo-Bid® 200 mg **RHÔNE-POULENC RORER**	DIN 01926608  Slo-Bid® 300 mg **RHÔNE-POULENC RORER**	DIN 00263818  Cotazym® **ORGANON**

*ILLUSTRATION LESS THAN ACTUAL SIZE / ILLUSTRATION RÉDUITE

Use code A, B, C, D, E, horizontal bar and 1 to 8 vertical bar to locate illustrated products

Utiliser le code A, B, C, D, E de la ligne horizontale et les chiffres 1 à 8 de la ligne verticale pour repérer les produits illustrés

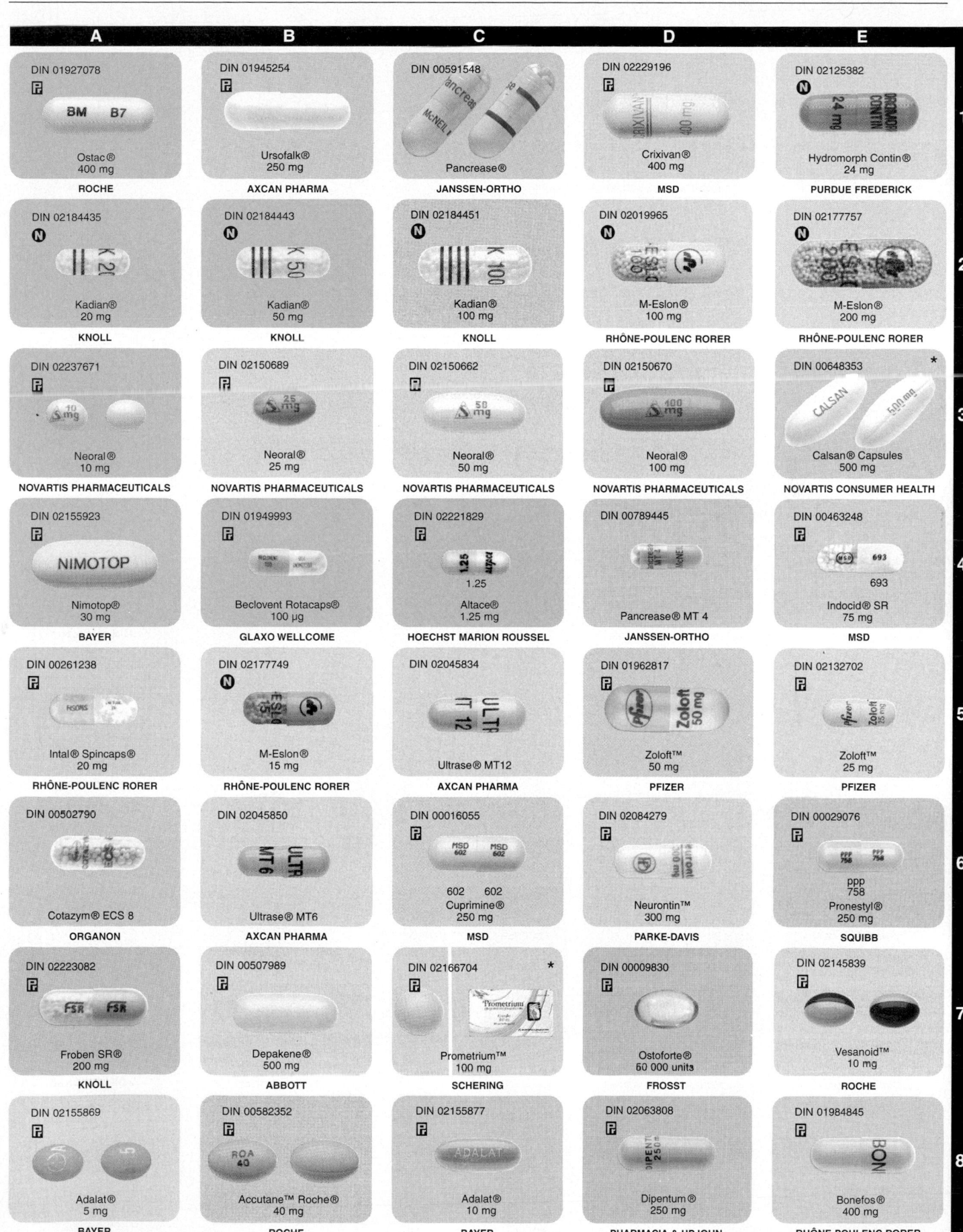

1

A1 — DIN 01927078 — Pr

Ostac® 400 mg
ROCHE

B1 — DIN 01945254 — Pr

Ursofalk® 250 mg
AXCAN PHARMA

C1 — DIN 00591548
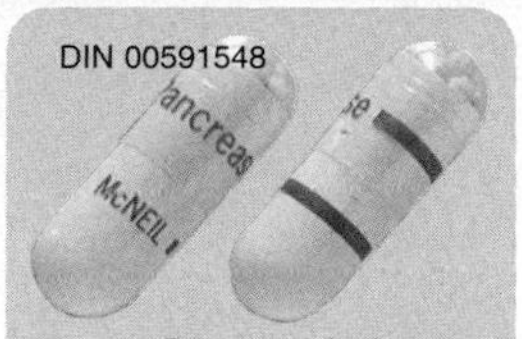
Pancrease®
JANSSEN-ORTHO

D1 — DIN 02229196 — Pr

Crixivan® 400 mg
MSD

E1 — DIN 02125382 — N
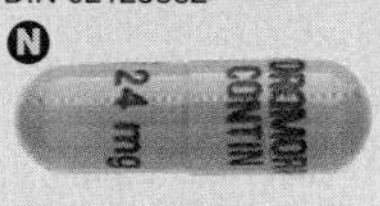

Hydromorph Contin® 24 mg
PURDUE FREDERICK

2

A2 — DIN 02184435 — N

Kadian® 20 mg
KNOLL

B2 — DIN 02184443 — N
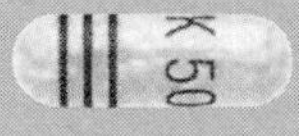

Kadian® 50 mg
KNOLL

C2 — DIN 02184451 — N

Kadian® 100 mg
KNOLL

D2 — DIN 02019965 — N

M-Eslon® 100 mg
RHÔNE-POULENC RORER

E2 — DIN 02177757 — N

M-Eslon® 200 mg
RHÔNE-POULENC RORER

3

A3 — DIN 02237671 — Pr

Neoral® 10 mg
NOVARTIS PHARMACEUTICALS

B3 — DIN 02150689 — Pr

Neoral® 25 mg
NOVARTIS PHARMACEUTICALS

C3 — DIN 02150662 — Pr

Neoral® 50 mg
NOVARTIS PHARMACEUTICALS

D3 — DIN 02150670 — Pr

Neoral® 100 mg
NOVARTIS PHARMACEUTICALS

E3 — DIN 00648353 *
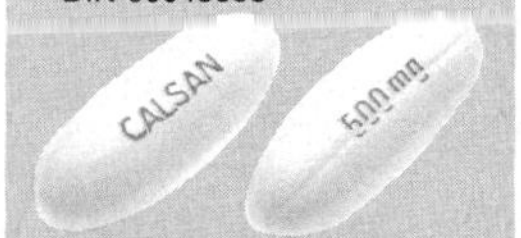

Calsan® Capsules 500 mg
NOVARTIS CONSUMER HEALTH

4

A4 — DIN 02155923 — Pr
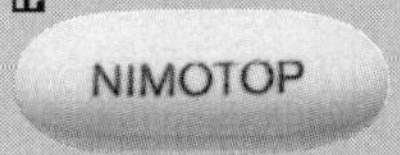

Nimotop® 30 mg
BAYER

B4 — DIN 01949993 — Pr

Beclovent Rotacaps® 100 µg
GLAXO WELLCOME

C4 — DIN 02221829 — Pr

1.25
Altace® 1.25 mg
HOECHST MARION ROUSSEL

D4 — DIN 00789445
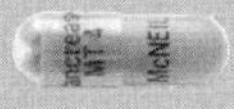
Pancrease® MT 4
JANSSEN-ORTHO

E4 — DIN 00463248 — Pr

693
Indocid® SR 75 mg
MSD

5

A5 — DIN 00261238 — Pr
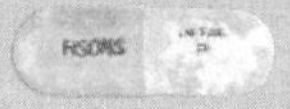
Intal® Spincaps® 20 mg
RHÔNE-POULENC RORER

B5 — DIN 02177749 — N

M-Eslon® 15 mg
RHÔNE-POULENC RORER

C5 — DIN 02045834
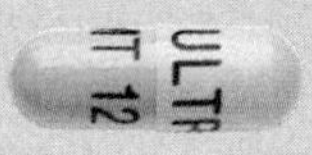
Ultrase® MT12
AXCAN PHARMA

D5 — DIN 01962817 — Pr

Zoloft™ 50 mg
PFIZER

E5 — DIN 02132702 — Pr
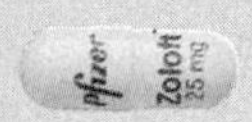
Zoloft™ 25 mg
PFIZER

6

A6 — DIN 00502790

Cotazym® ECS 8
ORGANON

B6 — DIN 02045850

Ultrase® MT6
AXCAN PHARMA

C6 — DIN 00016055 — Pr

602 602
Cuprimine® 250 mg
MSD

D6 — DIN 02084279 — Pr

Neurontin™ 300 mg
PARKE-DAVIS

E6 — DIN 00029076 — Pr

ppp 758
Pronestyl® 250 mg
SQUIBB

7

A7 — DIN 02223082 — Pr

Froben SR® 200 mg
KNOLL

B7 — DIN 00507989 — Pr

Depakene® 500 mg
ABBOTT

C7 — DIN 02166704 — Pr *

Prometrium™ 100 mg
SCHERING

D7 — DIN 00009830 — Pr

Ostoforte® 50 000 units
FROSST

E7 — DIN 02145839 — Pr

Vesanoid™ 10 mg
ROCHE

8

A8 — DIN 02155869 — Pr
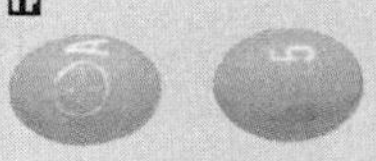
Adalat® 5 mg
BAYER

B8 — DIN 00582352 — Pr
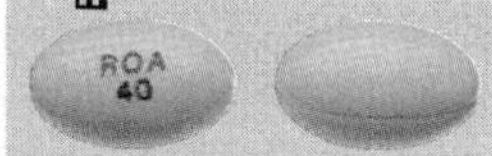

Accutane™ Roche® 40 mg
ROCHE

C8 — DIN 02155877 — Pr

Adalat® 10 mg
BAYER

D8 — DIN 02063808 — Pr

Dipentum® 250 mg
PHARMACIA & UPJOHN

E8 — DIN 01984845 — Pr

Bonefos® 400 mg
RHÔNE-POULENC RORER

*ILLUSTRATION LESS THAN ACTUAL SIZE / ILLUSTRATION RÉDUITE

Use code A, B, C, D, E, horizontal bar and 1 to 8 vertical bar to locate illustrated products

Utiliser le code A, B, C, D, E de la ligne horizontale et les chiffres 1 à 8 de la ligne verticale pour repérer les produits illustrés

1

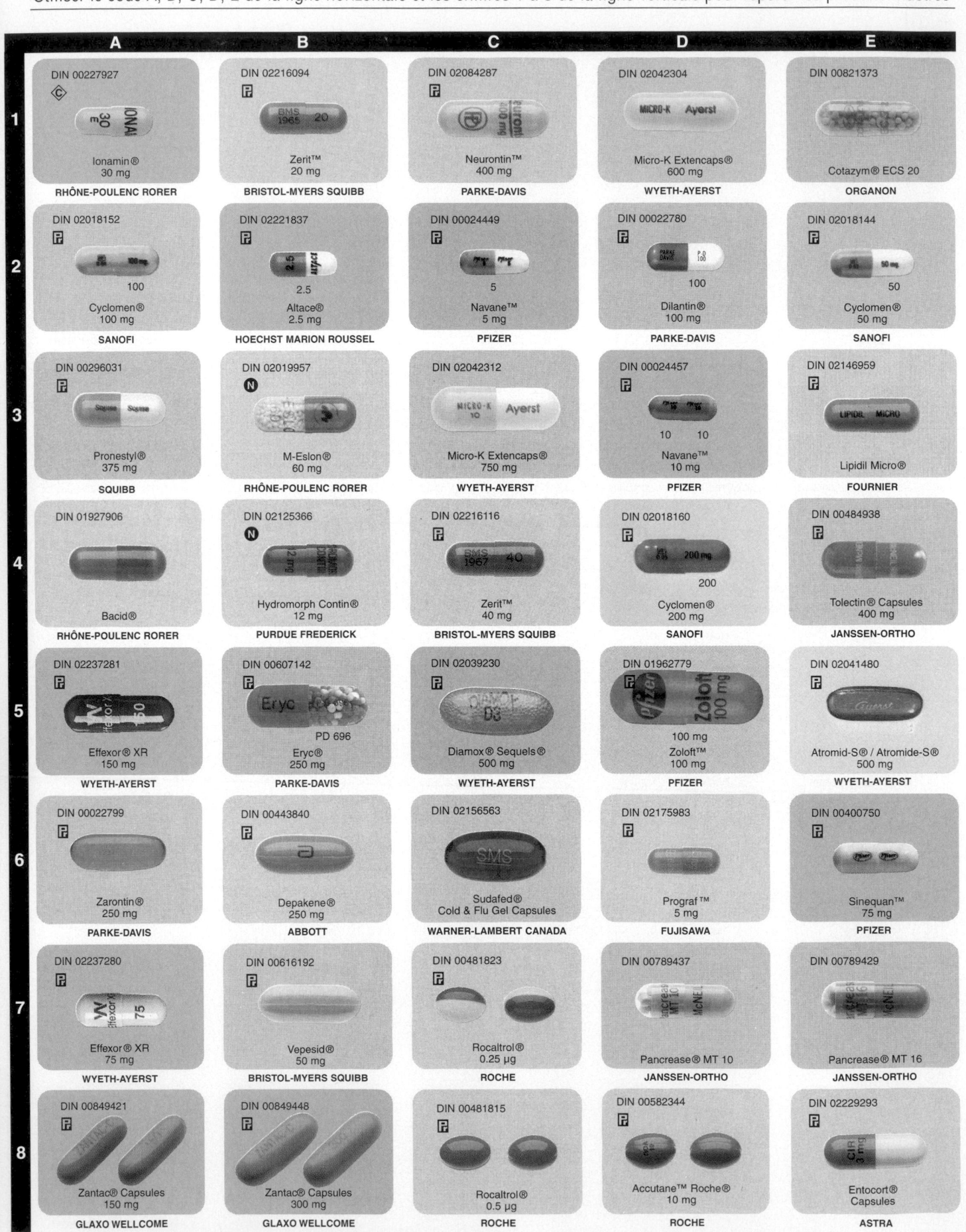

A1 — DIN 00227927 Ⓒ
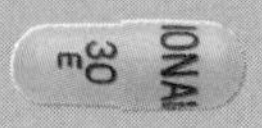
Ionamin® 30 mg
RHÔNE-POULENC RORER

B1 — DIN 02216094 Pr

Zerit™ 20 mg
BRISTOL-MYERS SQUIBB

C1 — DIN 02084287 Pr

Neurontin™ 400 mg
PARKE-DAVIS

D1 — DIN 02042304

Micro-K Extencaps® 600 mg
WYETH-AYERST

E1 — DIN 00821373

Cotazym® ECS 20
ORGANON

2

A2 — DIN 02018152 Pr

100
Cyclomen® 100 mg
SANOFI

B2 — DIN 02221837 Pr

2.5
Altace® 2.5 mg
HOECHST MARION ROUSSEL

C2 — DIN 00024449 Pr
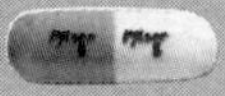
5
Navane™ 5 mg
PFIZER

D2 — DIN 00022780 Pr

100
Dilantin® 100 mg
PARKE-DAVIS

E2 — DIN 02018144 Pr

50
Cyclomen® 50 mg
SANOFI

3

A3 — DIN 00296031 Pr

Pronestyl® 375 mg
SQUIBB

B3 — DIN 02019957 Ⓝ

M-Eslon® 60 mg
RHÔNE-POULENC RORER

C3 — DIN 02042312
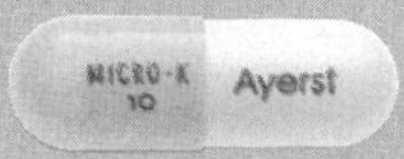
Micro-K Extencaps® 750 mg
WYETH-AYERST

D3 — DIN 00024457 Pr

10 10
Navane™ 10 mg
PFIZER

E3 — DIN 02146959 Pr

Lipidil Micro®
FOURNIER

4

A4 — DIN 01927906

Bacid®
RHÔNE-POULENC RORER

B4 — DIN 02125366 Ⓝ

Hydromorph Contin® 12 mg
PURDUE FREDERICK

C4 — DIN 02216116 Pr

Zerit™ 40 mg
BRISTOL-MYERS SQUIBB

D4 — DIN 02018160 Pr

200
Cyclomen® 200 mg
SANOFI

E4 — DIN 00484938 Pr

Tolectin® Capsules 400 mg
JANSSEN-ORTHO

5

A5 — DIN 02237281 Pr
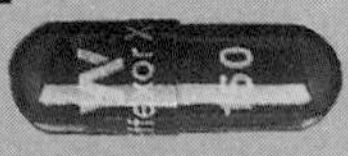
Effexor® XR 150 mg
WYETH-AYERST

B5 — DIN 00607142 Pr

PD 696
Eryc® 250 mg
PARKE-DAVIS

C5 — DIN 02039230 Pr

Diamox® Sequels® 500 mg
WYETH-AYERST

D5 — DIN 01962779 Pr

100 mg
Zoloft™ 100 mg
PFIZER

E5 — DIN 02041480 Pr

Atromid-S® / Atromide-S® 500 mg
WYETH-AYERST

6

A6 — DIN 00022799 Pr

Zarontin® 250 mg
PARKE-DAVIS

B6 — DIN 00443840 Pr

Depakene® 250 mg
ABBOTT

C6 — DIN 02156563

Sudafed® Cold & Flu Gel Capsules
WARNER-LAMBERT CANADA

D6 — DIN 02175983 Pr

Prograf™ 5 mg
FUJISAWA

E6 — DIN 00400750 Pr

Sinequan™ 75 mg
PFIZER

7

A7 — DIN 02237280 Pr
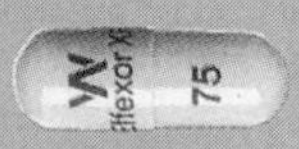
Effexor® XR 75 mg
WYETH-AYERST

B7 — DIN 00616192 Pr

Vepesid® 50 mg
BRISTOL-MYERS SQUIBB

C7 — DIN 00481823 Pr
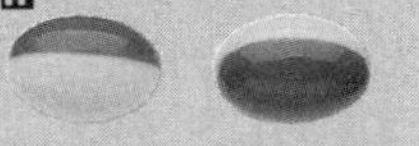
Rocaltrol® 0.25 µg
ROCHE

D7 — DIN 00789437

Pancrease® MT 10
JANSSEN-ORTHO

E7 — DIN 00789429

Pancrease® MT 16
JANSSEN-ORTHO

8

A8 — DIN 00849421 Pr
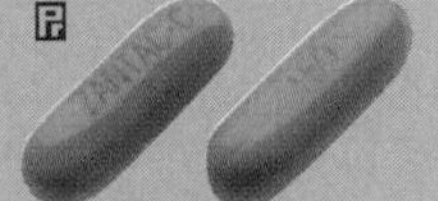
Zantac® Capsules 150 mg
GLAXO WELLCOME

B8 — DIN 00849448 Pr
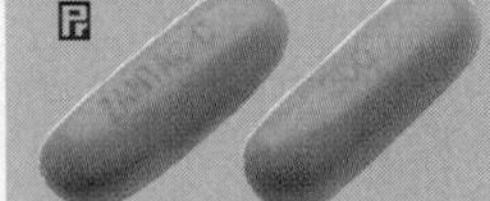
Zantac® Capsules 300 mg
GLAXO WELLCOME

C8 — DIN 00481815 Pr
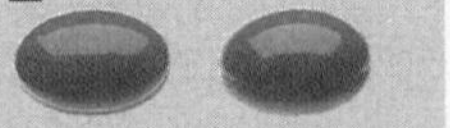
Rocaltrol® 0.5 µg
ROCHE

D8 — DIN 00582344 Pr
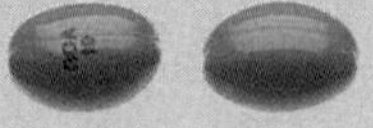
Accutane™ Roche® 10 mg
ROCHE

E8 — DIN 02229293 Pr
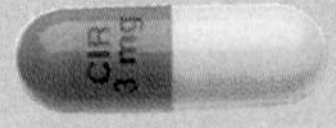
Entocort® Capsules
ASTRA

Use code A, B, C, D, E, horizontal bar and 1 to 8 vertical bar to locate illustrated products

Utiliser le code A, B, C, D, E de la ligne horizontale et les chiffres 1 à 8 de la ligne verticale pour repérer les produits illustrés

A	B	C	D	E	
DIN 00022772 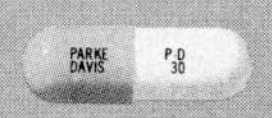 30 Dilantin® 30 mg **PARKE-DAVIS**	DIN 02019671  Benadryl® 50 mg **WARNER-LAMBERT CANADA**	DIN 01913050  Oruvail® 150 mg **MAY & BAKER PHARMA**	DIN 00024341 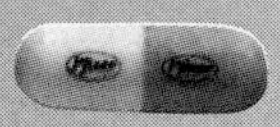 Sinequan™ 50 mg **PFIZER**	DIN 02019949  M-Eslon® 30 mg **RHÔNE-POULENC RORER**	1
DIN 02237279 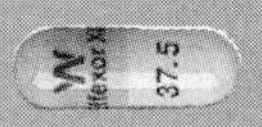 Effexor® XR 37.5 mg **WYETH-AYERST**	DIN 02236808  Diovan® 80 mg **NOVARTIS PHARMACEUTICALS**	DIN 02125331  Hydromorph Contin® 6 mg **PURDUE FREDERICK**	DIN 00024325  Sinequan™ 10 mg **PFIZER**	DIN 02091291  Zithromax™ 250 mg **PFIZER**	2
DIN 00584274 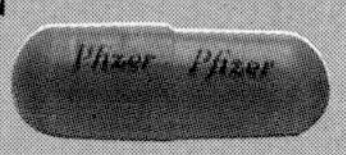 Sinequan™ 150 mg **PFIZER**	DIN 01914006 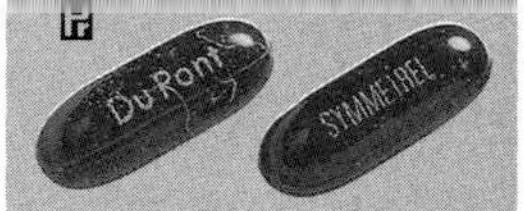 Symmetrel® 100 mg **DUPONT PHARMA**	DIN 02041499  Atromid-S® / Atromide-S® 1 g **WYETH-AYERST**	DIN 02221845  5 Altace® 5 mg **HOECHST MARION ROUSSEL**	DIN 00568643  Parlodel® Capsules 5 mg **NOVARTIS PHARMACEUTICALS**	3
DIN 00599026  Lopid® 300 mg **PARKE-DAVIS**	DIN 00525618 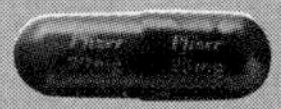 Feldene™ 20 mg **PFIZER**	DIN 00030570 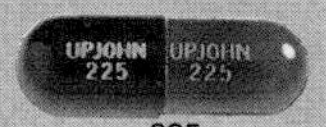 225 Dalacin® C 150 mg **PHARMACIA & UPJOHN**	DIN 02092808  Rifadin® 300 mg **HOECHST MARION ROUSSEL**	DIN 02221969  Surgam® SR 300 mg **HOECHST MARION ROUSSEL**	4
DIN 02091887  Rifadin® 150 mg **HOECHST MARION ROUSSEL**	DIN 02125390  Hydromorph Contin® 30 mg **PURDUE FREDERICK**	DIN 02224666  Surfak® 240 mg **HOECHST MARION ROUSSEL**	DIN 00782327 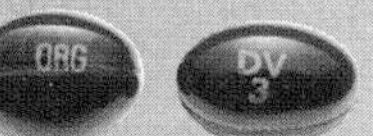 Andriol **ORGANON**	DIN 02070847  Soriatane® 10 mg **ROCHE**	5
DIN 01950002  Beclovent Rotacaps® 200 µg **GLAXO WELLCOME**	DIN 00604453  Restoril® 15 mg **NOVARTIS PHARMACEUTICALS**	DIN 00210463 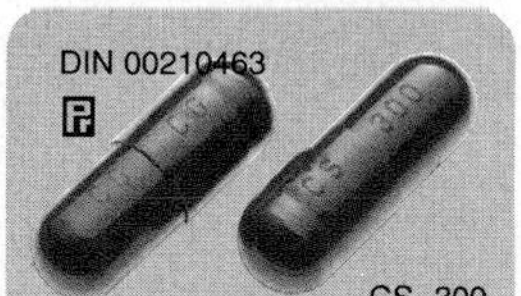 CS 300 Rimactane® 300 mg **NOVARTIS PHARMACEUTICALS**	DIN 02200104  Creon® 10 **SOLVAY PHARMA**	DIN 00507245  Duricef® 500 mg **BRISTOL-MYERS SQUIBB**	6
DIN 02231151  BVF 180 Tiazac™ 100 mg **CRYSTAAL**	DIN 02212315  Ventolin® Rotacaps® 200 µg **GLAXO WELLCOME**	DIN 00360422  3031 40 CeeNU® 40 mg **BRISTOL-MYERS SQUIBB**	DIN 00115630  Librax® **ROCHE**	DIN 02125323  Hydromorph Contin® 3 mg **PURDUE FREDERICK**	7
DIN 02186802  Cytovene® **ROCHE**	DIN 00360414  3032 100 mg CeeNU® 100 mg **BRISTOL-MYERS SQUIBB**	DIN 00116858  Gravergol® **CARTER HORNER**	DIN 02231155  BVF 360 Tiazac™ 360 mg **CRYSTAAL**	DIN 02231152  BVF 240 Tiazac™ 240 mg **CRYSTAAL**	8

Use code A, B, C, D, E, horizontal bar and 1 to 8 vertical bar to locate illustrated products

Utiliser le code A, B, C, D, E de la ligne horizontale et les chiffres 1 à 8 de la ligne verticale pour repérer les produits illustrés

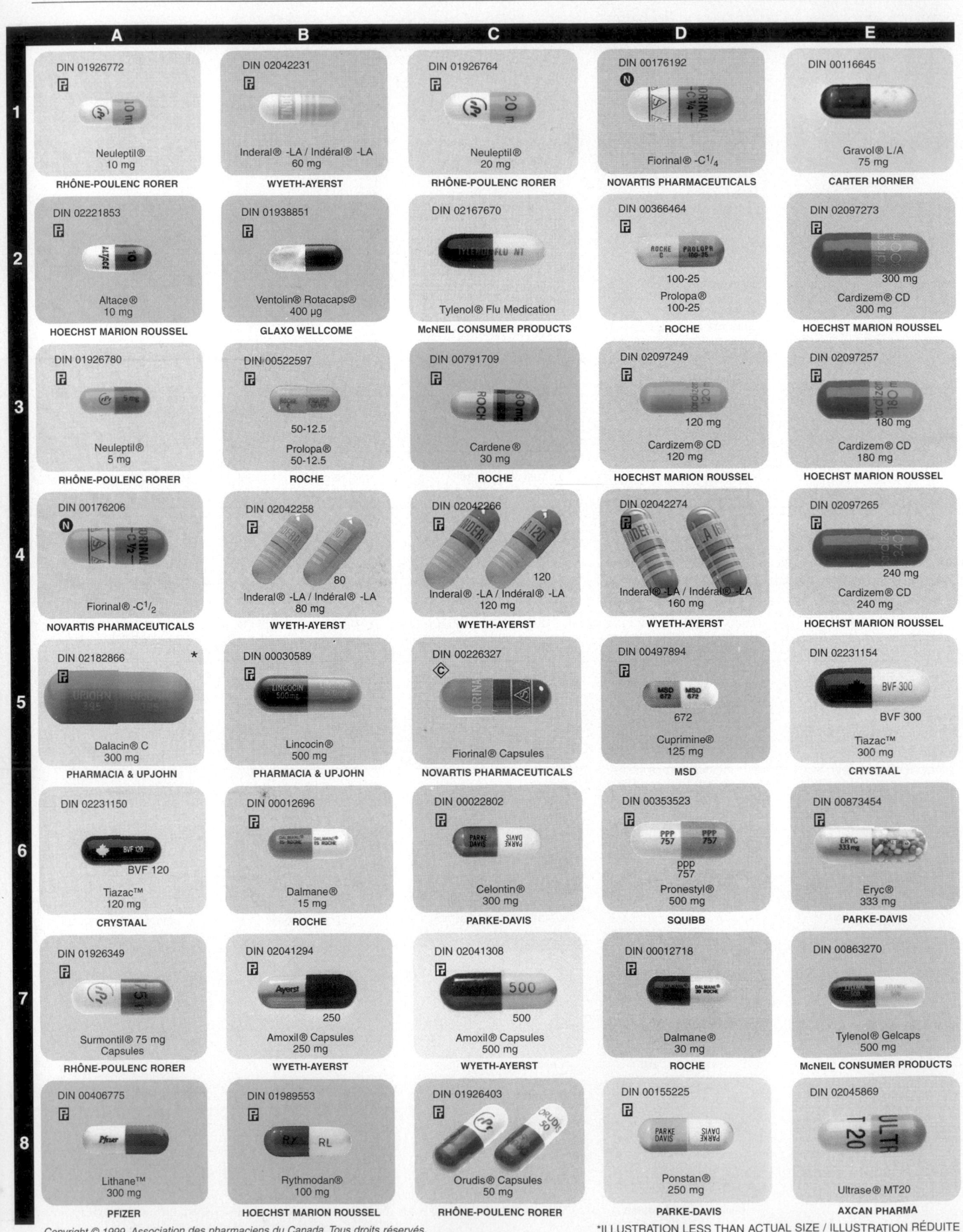

	A	B	C	D	E
1	DIN 01926772 Neuleptil® 10 mg **RHÔNE-POULENC RORER**	DIN 02042231 Inderal® -LA / Indéral® -LA 60 mg **WYETH-AYERST**	DIN 01926764 Neuleptil® 20 mg **RHÔNE-POULENC RORER**	DIN 00176192 Fiorinal® -C$^1/_4$ **NOVARTIS PHARMACEUTICALS**	DIN 00116645 Gravol® L/A 75 mg **CARTER HORNER**
2	DIN 02221853 Altace® 10 mg **HOECHST MARION ROUSSEL**	DIN 01938851 Ventolin® Rotacaps® 400 µg **GLAXO WELLCOME**	DIN 02167670 Tylenol® Flu Medication **McNEIL CONSUMER PRODUCTS**	DIN 00366464 100-25 Prolopa® 100-25 **ROCHE**	DIN 02097273 300 mg Cardizem® CD 300 mg **HOECHST MARION ROUSSEL**
3	DIN 01926780 Neuleptil® 5 mg **RHÔNE-POULENC RORER**	DIN 00522597 50-12.5 Prolopa® 50-12.5 **ROCHE**	DIN 00791709 Cardene® 30 mg **ROCHE**	DIN 02097249 120 mg Cardizem® CD 120 mg **HOECHST MARION ROUSSEL**	DIN 02097257 180 mg Cardizem® CD 180 mg **HOECHST MARION ROUSSEL**
4	DIN 00176206 Fiorinal® -C$^1/_2$ **NOVARTIS PHARMACEUTICALS**	DIN 02042258 80 Inderal® -LA / Indéral® -LA 80 mg **WYETH-AYERST**	DIN 02042266 120 Inderal® -LA / Indéral® -LA 120 mg **WYETH-AYERST**	DIN 02042274 Inderal® -LA / Indéral® -LA 160 mg **WYETH-AYERST**	DIN 02097265 240 mg Cardizem® CD 240 mg **HOECHST MARION ROUSSEL**
5	DIN 02182866 * Dalacin® C 300 mg **PHARMACIA & UPJOHN**	DIN 00030589 Lincocin® 500 mg **PHARMACIA & UPJOHN**	DIN 00226327 Fiorinal® Capsules **NOVARTIS PHARMACEUTICALS**	DIN 00497894 672 Cuprimine® 125 mg **MSD**	DIN 02231154 BVF 300 Tiazac™ 300 mg **CRYSTAAL**
6	DIN 02231150 BVF 120 Tiazac™ 120 mg **CRYSTAAL**	DIN 00012696 Dalmane® 15 mg **ROCHE**	DIN 00022802 Celontin® 300 mg **PARKE-DAVIS**	DIN 00353523 ppp 757 Pronestyl® 500 mg **SQUIBB**	DIN 00873454 Eryc® 333 mg **PARKE-DAVIS**
7	DIN 01926349 Surmontil® 75 mg Capsules **RHÔNE-POULENC RORER**	DIN 02041294 250 Amoxil® Capsules 250 mg **WYETH-AYERST**	DIN 02041308 500 Amoxil® Capsules 500 mg **WYETH-AYERST**	DIN 00012718 Dalmane® 30 mg **ROCHE**	DIN 00863270 Tylenol® Gelcaps 500 mg **McNEIL CONSUMER PRODUCTS**
8	DIN 00406775 Lithane™ 300 mg **PFIZER**	DIN 01989553 Rythmodan® 100 mg **HOECHST MARION ROUSSEL**	DIN 01926403 Orudis® Capsules 50 mg **RHÔNE-POULENC RORER**	DIN 00155225 Ponstan® 250 mg **PARKE-DAVIS**	DIN 02045869 Ultrase® MT20 **AXCAN PHARMA**

*ILLUSTRATION LESS THAN ACTUAL SIZE / ILLUSTRATION RÉDUITE

Use code A, B, C, D, E, horizontal bar and 1 to 8 vertical bar to locate illustrated products

Utiliser le code A, B, C, D, E de la ligne horizontale et les chiffres 1 à 8 de la ligne verticale pour repérer les produits illustrés

	A	B	C	D	E
1	DIN 02216086  Zerit™ 15 mg **BRISTOL-MYERS SQUIBB**	DIN 02216108  Zerit™ 30 mg **BRISTOL-MYERS SQUIBB**	DIN 02061562  Lescol® 20 mg **NOVARTIS PHARMACEUTICALS**	DIN 02061570  Lescol® 40 mg **NOVARTIS PHARMACEUTICALS**	DIN 02078759  Humatin™ 250 mg **PARKE-DAVIS**
2	DIN 00227935  Ionamin® 15 mg **RHÔNE-POULENC RORER**	DIN 02070863  Soriatane® 25 mg **ROCHE**	DIN 01924559  E13 Dexedrine® Spansule® 10 mg **SMITHKLINE BEECHAM**	DIN 01924567  E14 Dexedrine® Spansule® 15 mg **SMITHKLINE BEECHAM**	DIN 02097214  Cardizem® SR 60 mg **HOECHST MARION ROUSSEL**
3	DIN 02097222  Cardizem® SR 90 mg **HOECHST MARION ROUSSEL**	DIN 02097230  Cardizem® SR 120 mg **HOECHST MARION ROUSSEL**	DIN 02238123 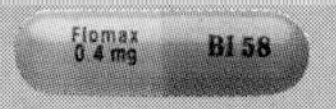 BI 58 Flomax® 0.4 mg **BOEHRINGER INGELHEIM**	DIN 02216965  Invirase™ **ROCHE**	DIN 01927817  Rovamycine® "500" **RHÔNE-POULENC RORER**
4	DIN 01926853  Flagy® 500 mg Capsules **RHÔNE-POULENC RORER**	DIN 02192748  CellCept® 250 mg **ROCHE**	DIN 01927825  Rovamycine® "250" **RHÔNE-POULENC RORER**	DIN 00156086  Ergodryl® **PARKE-DAVIS**	DIN 00465283  BMS 303 Hydrea® 500 mg **SQUIBB**
5	DIN 01913069  200 Oruvail® 200 mg **MAY & BAKER**	DIN 00024333  Sinequan™ 25 mg **PFIZER**	DIN 02047454  Sporanox® 100 mg **JANSSEN-ORTHO**	DIN 02236809  Diovan® 160 mg **NOVARTIS PHARMACEUTICALS**	DIN 00326925  Sinequan™ 100 mg **PFIZER**
6	DIN 00386472  200-50 Prolopa® 200-50 **ROCHE**	DIN 00525596  10 Feldene™ 10 mg **PFIZER**	DIN 00604461  Restoril® 30 mg **NOVARTIS PHARMACEUTICALS**	DIN 01926888 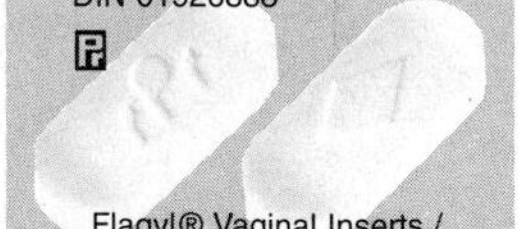 Flagyl® Vaginal Inserts / comprimés vaginaux 500 mg **RHÔNE-POULENC RORER**	DIN 01926837 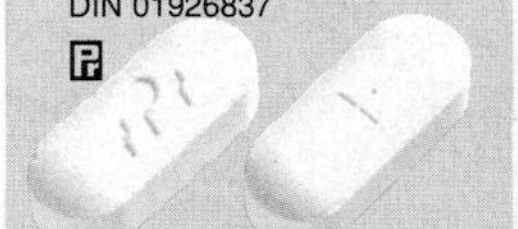 Flagystatin® Vaginal Inserts / comprimés vaginaux **RHÔNE-POULENC RORER**
7	DIN 01926829 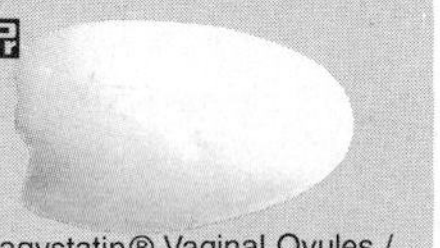 Flagystatin® Vaginal Ovules / ovules vaginaux **RHÔNE-POULENC RORER**	DIN 02126605  Monistat® 3 Ovules 400 mg **McNEIL CONSUMER PRODUCTS**	DIN 02084295  Monistat® 7 Supp. 100 mg **McNEIL CONSUMER PRODUCTS**	DIN 00176214 *  Cafergot-PB® Supp. **NOVARTIS PHARMACEUTICALS**	DIN 00632716  Feldene™ Supp. 20 mg **PFIZER**
8	DIN 00783595  Gravol® Children's Supp. / supp. pour enfants 25 mg **CARTER HORNER**	DIN 00013595  Gravol® Junior Strength Supp. / supp. pour enfants plus âgés 50 mg **CARTER HORNER**	DIN 00013609  Gravol® Adult Supp. / supp. pour adultes 100 mg **CARTER HORNER**	DIN 00632724  Voltaren® Supp. 50 mg **NOVARTIS PHARMACEUTICALS**	DIN 00632732  Voltaren® Supp. 100 mg **NOVARTIS PHARMACEUTICALS**

*ILLUSTRATION LESS THAN ACTUAL SIZE / ILLUSTRATION RÉDUITE

Use code A, B, C, D, E, horizontal bar and 1 to 8 vertical bar to locate illustrated products

Utiliser le code A, B, C, D, E de la ligne horizontale et les chiffres 1 à 8 de la ligne verticale pour repérer les produits illustrés

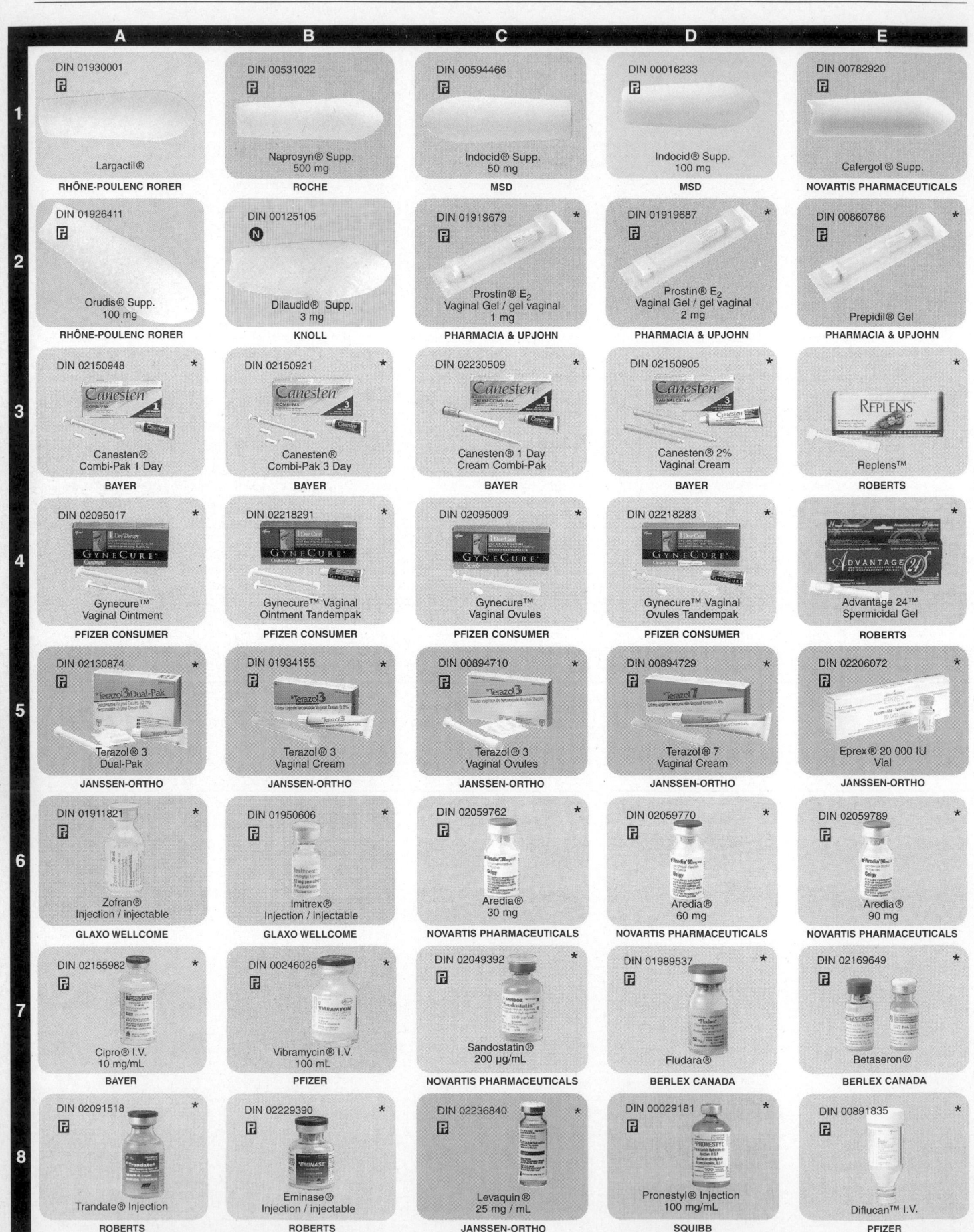

	A	B	C	D	E
1	DIN 01930001  Largactil® **RHÔNE-POULENC RORER**	DIN 00531022  Naprosyn® Supp. 500 mg **ROCHE**	DIN 00594466  Indocid® Supp. 50 mg **MSD**	DIN 00016233  Indocid® Supp. 100 mg **MSD**	DIN 00782920  Cafergot ® Supp. **NOVARTIS PHARMACEUTICALS**
2	DIN 01926411 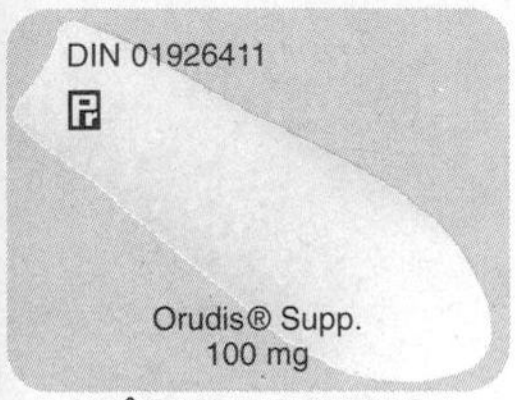 Orudis® Supp. 100 mg **RHÔNE-POULENC RORER**	DIN 00125105  Dilaudid® Supp. 3 mg **KNOLL**	DIN 01919679 * 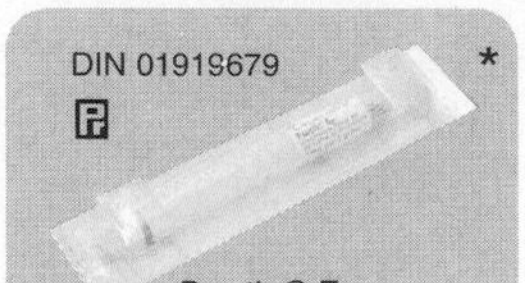 Prostin® E_2 Vaginal Gel / gel vaginal 1 mg **PHARMACIA & UPJOHN**	DIN 01919687 * 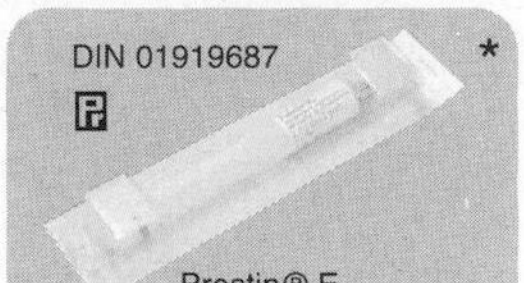 Prostin® E_2 Vaginal Gel / gel vaginal 2 mg **PHARMACIA & UPJOHN**	DIN 00860786 * 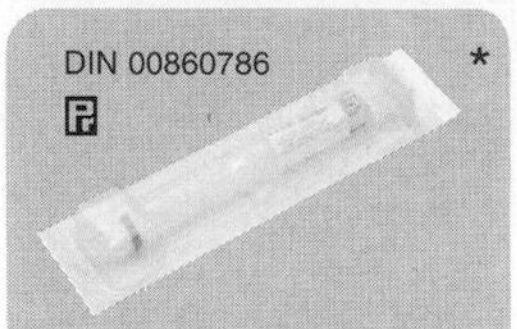 Prepidil® Gel **PHARMACIA & UPJOHN**
3	DIN 02150948 * 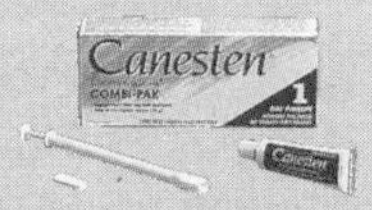 Canesten® Combi-Pak 1 Day **BAYER**	DIN 02150921 * 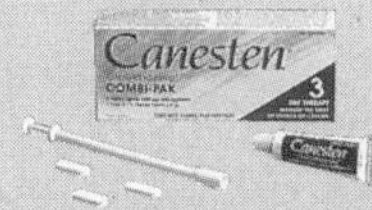 Canesten® Combi-Pak 3 Day **BAYER**	DIN 02230509 * 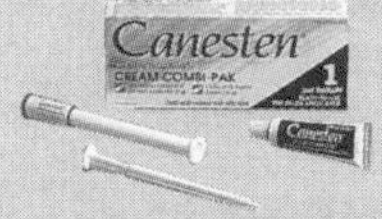 Canesten® 1 Day Cream Combi-Pak **BAYER**	DIN 02150905 * 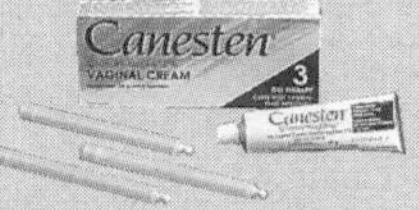 Canesten® 2% Vaginal Cream **BAYER**	*  Replens™ **ROBERTS**
4	DIN 02095017 *  Gynecure™ Vaginal Ointment **PFIZER CONSUMER**	DIN 02218291 * 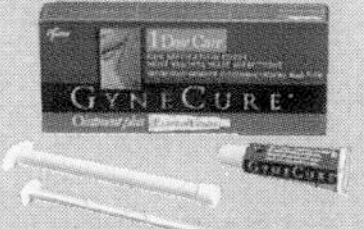 Gynecure™ Vaginal Ointment Tandempak **PFIZER CONSUMER**	DIN 02095009 *  Gynecure™ Vaginal Ovules **PFIZER CONSUMER**	DIN 02218283 *  Gynecure™ Vaginal Ovules Tandempak **PFIZER CONSUMER**	*  Advantage 24™ Spermicidal Gel **ROBERTS**
5	DIN 02130874 * 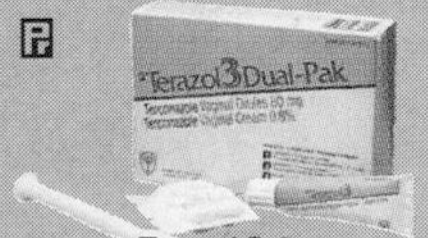 Terazol® 3 Dual-Pak **JANSSEN-ORTHO**	DIN 01934155 * 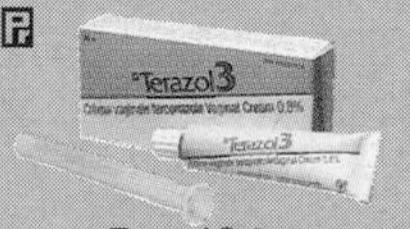 Terazol® 3 Vaginal Cream **JANSSEN-ORTHO**	DIN 00894710 * 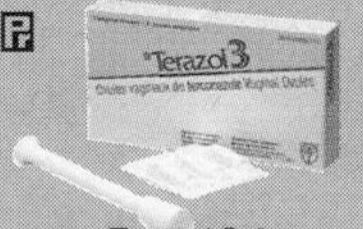 Terazol® 3 Vaginal Ovules **JANSSEN-ORTHO**	DIN 00894729 * 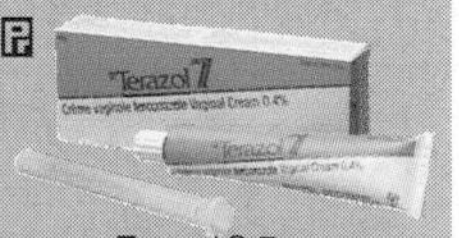 Terazol® 7 Vaginal Cream **JANSSEN-ORTHO**	DIN 02206072 *  Eprex® 20 000 IU Vial **JANSSEN-ORTHO**
6	DIN 01911821 *  Zofran® Injection / injectable **GLAXO WELLCOME**	DIN 01950606 * 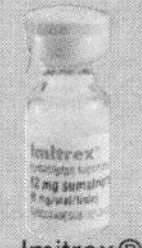 Imitrex® Injection / injectable **GLAXO WELLCOME**	DIN 02059762 * 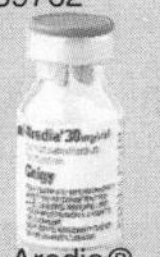 Aredia® 30 mg **NOVARTIS PHARMACEUTICALS**	DIN 02059770 * 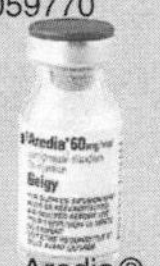 Aredia® 60 mg **NOVARTIS PHARMACEUTICALS**	DIN 02059789 * 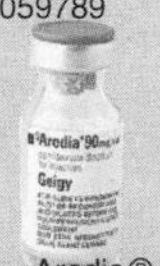 Aredia® 90 mg **NOVARTIS PHARMACEUTICALS**
7	DIN 02155982 * 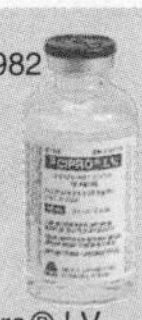 Cipro® I.V. 10 mg/mL **BAYER**	DIN 00246026 * 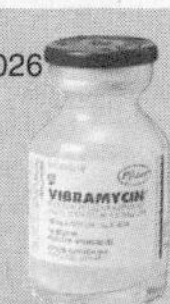 Vibramycin® I.V. 100 mL **PFIZER**	DIN 02049392 * 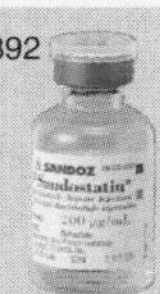 Sandostatin® 200 µg/mL **NOVARTIS PHARMACEUTICALS**	DIN 01989537 * 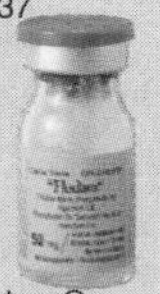 Fludara® **BERLEX CANADA**	DIN 02169649 * 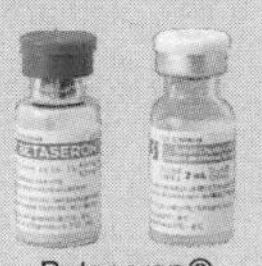 Betaseron® **BERLEX CANADA**
8	DIN 02091518 * 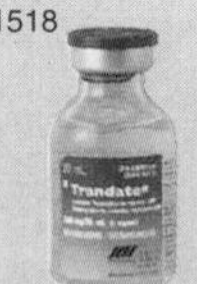 Trandate® Injection **ROBERTS**	DIN 02229390 *  Eminase® Injection / injectable **ROBERTS**	DIN 02236840 * 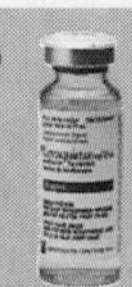 Levaquin® 25 mg / mL **JANSSEN-ORTHO**	DIN 00029181 * 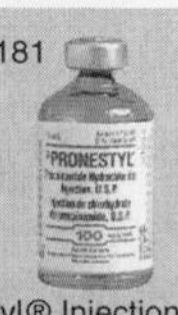 Pronestyl® Injection 100 mg/mL **SQUIBB**	DIN 00891835 *  Diflucan™ I.V. **PFIZER**

*ILLUSTRATION LESS THAN ACTUAL SIZE / ILLUSTRATION RÉDUITE

Use code A, B, C, D, E, horizontal bar and 1 to 8 vertical bar to locate illustrated products

Utiliser le code A, B, C, D, E de la ligne horizontale et les chiffres 1 à 8 de la ligne verticale pour repérer les produits illustrés

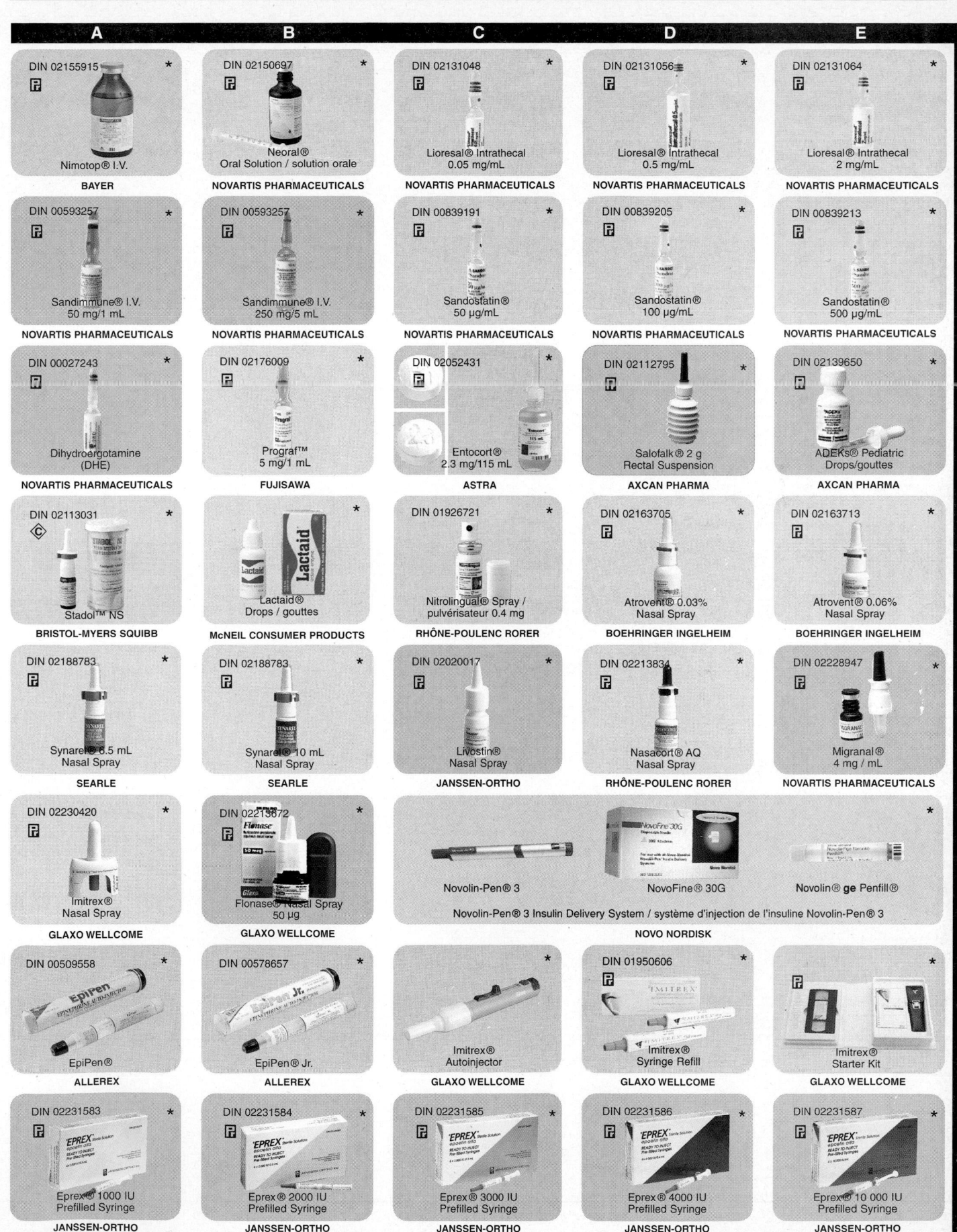

	A	B	C	D	E
1	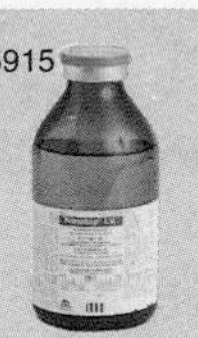 DIN 02155915 * Nimotop® I.V. **BAYER**	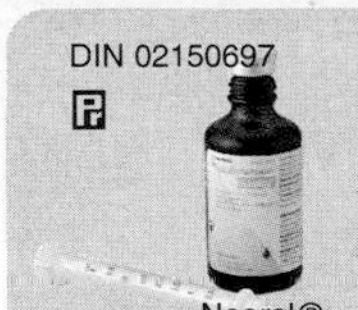 DIN 02150697 * Neoral® Oral Solution / solution orale **NOVARTIS PHARMACEUTICALS**	 DIN 02131048 * Lioresal® Intrathecal 0.05 mg/mL **NOVARTIS PHARMACEUTICALS**	 DIN 02131056 * Lioresal® Intrathecal 0.5 mg/mL **NOVARTIS PHARMACEUTICALS**	 DIN 02131064 * Lioresal® Intrathecal 2 mg/mL **NOVARTIS PHARMACEUTICALS**
2	 DIN 00593257 * Sandimmune® I.V. 50 mg/1 mL **NOVARTIS PHARMACEUTICALS**	 DIN 00593257 * Sandimmune® I.V. 250 mg/5 mL **NOVARTIS PHARMACEUTICALS**	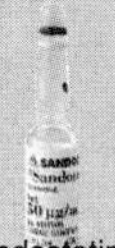 DIN 00839191 * Sandostatin® 50 µg/mL **NOVARTIS PHARMACEUTICALS**	 DIN 00839205 * Sandostatin® 100 µg/mL **NOVARTIS PHARMACEUTICALS**	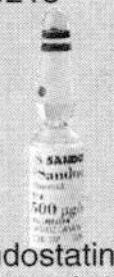 DIN 00839213 * Sandostatin® 500 µg/mL **NOVARTIS PHARMACEUTICALS**
3	 DIN 00027243 * Dihydroergotamine (DHE) **NOVARTIS PHARMACEUTICALS**	 DIN 02176009 * Prograf™ 5 mg/1 mL **FUJISAWA**	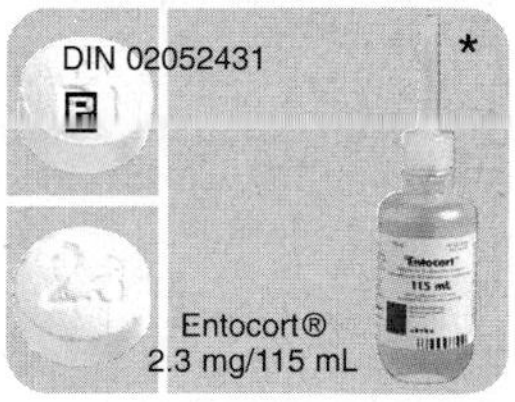 DIN 02052431 * Entocort® 2.3 mg/115 mL **ASTRA**	 DIN 02112795 * Salofalk® 2 g Rectal Suspension **AXCAN PHARMA**	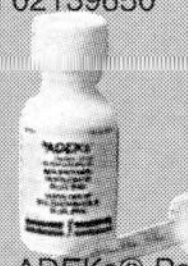 DIN 02139650 * ADEKs® Pediatric Drops/gouttes **AXCAN PHARMA**
4	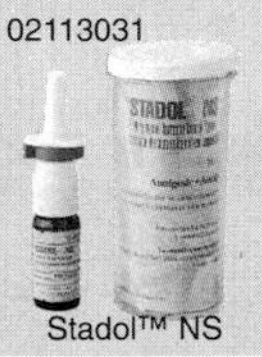 DIN 02113031 * Stadol™ NS **BRISTOL-MYERS SQUIBB**	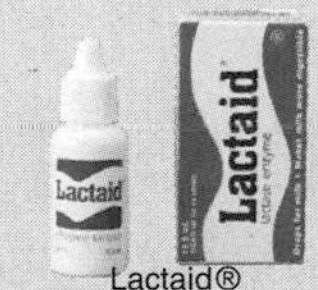 * Lactaid® Drops / gouttes **McNEIL CONSUMER PRODUCTS**	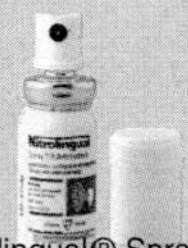 DIN 01926721 * Nitrolingual® Spray / pulvérisateur 0.4 mg **RHÔNE-POULENC RORER**	 DIN 02163705 * Atrovent® 0.03% Nasal Spray **BOEHRINGER INGELHEIM**	 DIN 02163713 * Atrovent® 0.06% Nasal Spray **BOEHRINGER INGELHEIM**
5	 DIN 02188783 * Synarel® 6.5 mL Nasal Spray **SEARLE**	 DIN 02188783 * Synarel® 10 mL Nasal Spray **SEARLE**	 DIN 02020017 * Livostin® Nasal Spray **JANSSEN-ORTHO**	 DIN 02213834 * Nasacort® AQ Nasal Spray **RHÔNE-POULENC RORER**	 DIN 02228947 * Migranal® 4 mg / mL **NOVARTIS PHARMACEUTICALS**
6	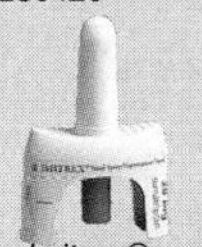 DIN 02230420 * Imitrex® Nasal Spray **GLAXO WELLCOME**	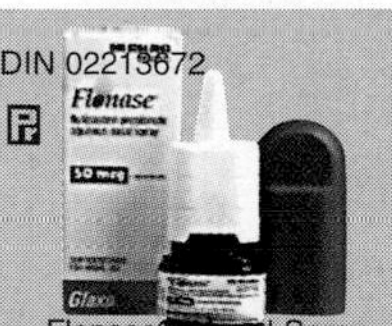 DIN 02213672 * Flonase® Nasal Spray 50 µg **GLAXO WELLCOME**	 * Novolin-Pen® 3 · NovoFine® 30G · Novolin® ge Penfill® Novolin-Pen® 3 Insulin Delivery System / système d'injection de l'insuline Novolin-Pen® 3 **NOVO NORDISK**		
7	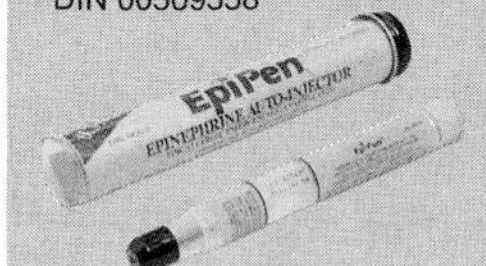 DIN 00509558 * EpiPen® **ALLEREX**	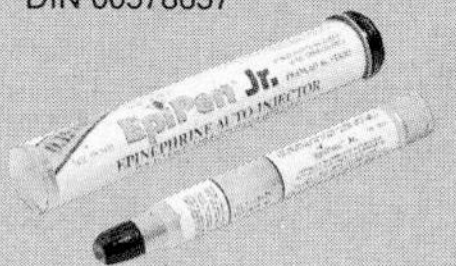 DIN 00578657 * EpiPen® Jr. **ALLEREX**	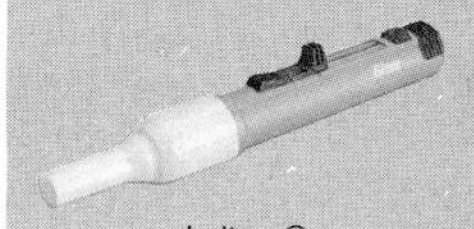 * Imitrex® Autoinjector **GLAXO WELLCOME**	 DIN 01950606 * Imitrex® Syringe Refill **GLAXO WELLCOME**	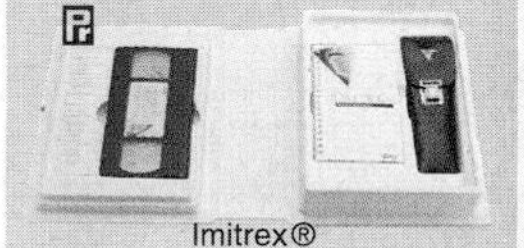 * Imitrex® Starter Kit **GLAXO WELLCOME**
8	 DIN 02231583 * Eprex® 1000 IU Prefilled Syringe **JANSSEN-ORTHO**	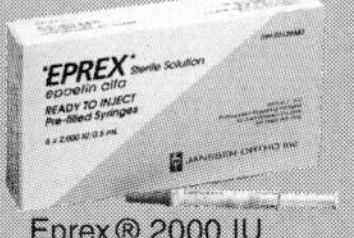 DIN 02231584 * Eprex® 2000 IU Prefilled Syringe **JANSSEN-ORTHO**	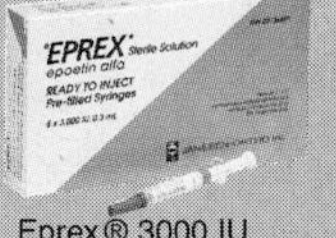 DIN 02231585 * Eprex® 3000 IU Prefilled Syringe **JANSSEN-ORTHO**	 DIN 02231586 * Eprex® 4000 IU Prefilled Syringe **JANSSEN-ORTHO**	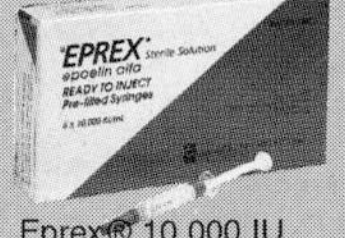 DIN 02231587 * Eprex® 10 000 IU Prefilled Syringe **JANSSEN-ORTHO**

*ILLUSTRATION LESS THAN ACTUAL SIZE / ILLUSTRATION RÉDUITE

Use code A, B, C, D, E, horizontal bar and 1 to 8 vertical bar to locate illustrated products

Utiliser le code A, B, C, D, E de la ligne horizontale et les chiffres 1 à 8 de la ligne verticale pour repérer les produits illustrés

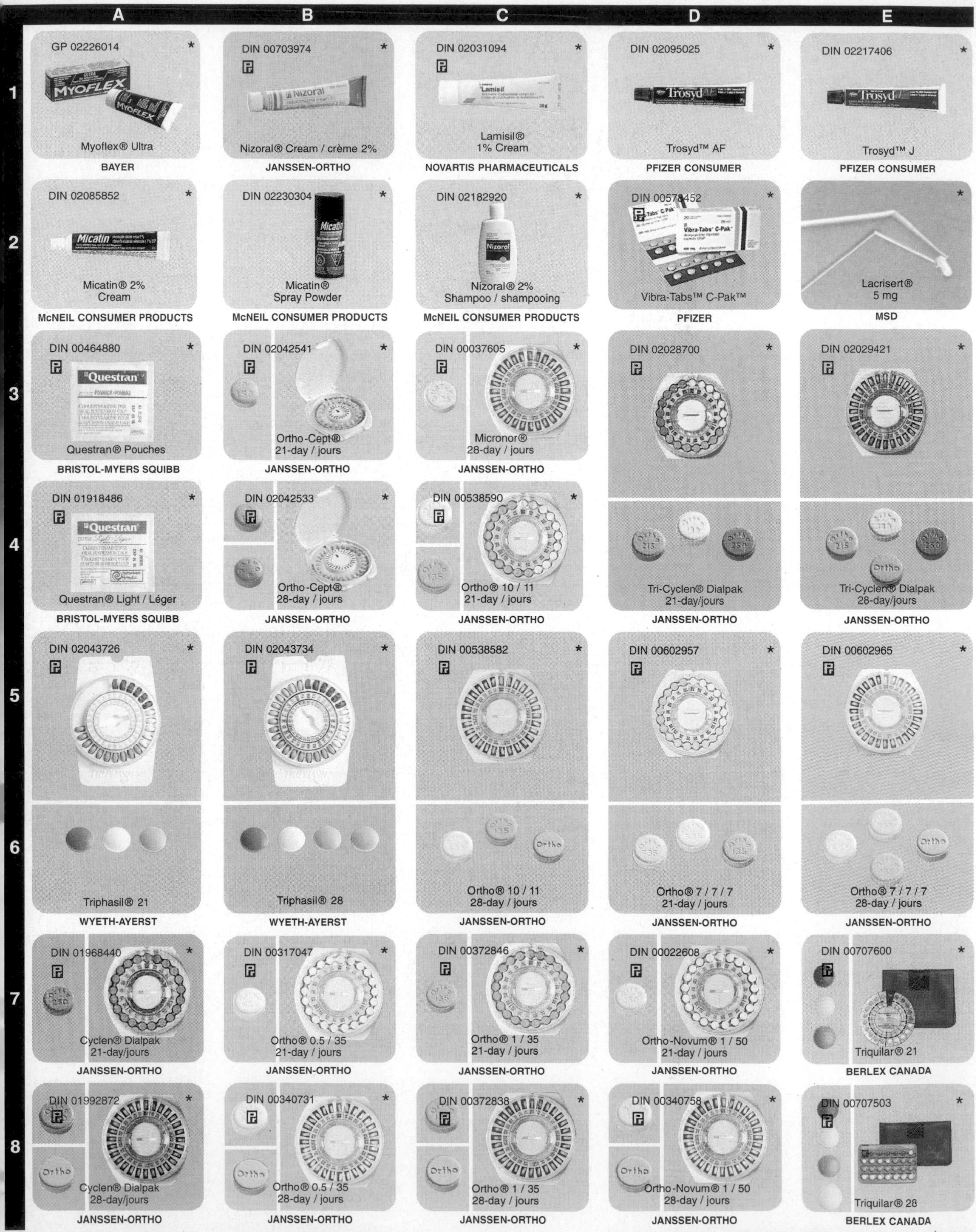

	A	B	C	D	E
1	GP 02226014 ★ — Myoflex® Ultra — BAYER	DIN 00703974 ★ — Nizoral® Cream / crème 2% — JANSSEN-ORTHO	DIN 02031094 ★ — Lamisil® 1% Cream — NOVARTIS PHARMACEUTICALS	DIN 02095025 ★ — Trosyd™ AF — PFIZER CONSUMER	DIN 02217406 ★ — Trosyd™ J — PFIZER CONSUMER
2	DIN 02085852 ★ — Micatin® 2% Cream — McNEIL CONSUMER PRODUCTS	DIN 02230304 ★ — Micatin® Spray Powder — McNEIL CONSUMER PRODUCTS	DIN 02182920 ★ — Nizoral® 2% Shampoo / shampooing — McNEIL CONSUMER PRODUCTS	DIN 00578452 ★ — Vibra-Tabs™ C-Pak™ — PFIZER	★ — Lacrisert® 5 mg — MSD
3	DIN 00464880 ★ — Questran® Pouches — BRISTOL-MYERS SQUIBB	DIN 02042541 ★ — Ortho-Cept® 21-day / jours — JANSSEN-ORTHO	DIN 00037605 ★ — Micronor® 28-day / jours — JANSSEN-ORTHO	DIN 02028700 ★ —	DIN 02029421 ★ —
4	DIN 01918486 ★ — Questran® Light / Léger — BRISTOL-MYERS SQUIBB	DIN 02042533 ★ — Ortho-Cept® 28-day / jours — JANSSEN-ORTHO	DIN 00538590 ★ — Ortho® 10 / 11 21-day / jours — JANSSEN-ORTHO	Tri-Cyclen® Dialpak 21-day/jours — JANSSEN-ORTHO	Tri-Cyclen® Dialpak 28-day/jours — JANSSEN-ORTHO
5	DIN 02043726 ★ —	DIN 02043734 ★ —	DIN 00538582 ★ —	DIN 00602957 ★ —	DIN 00602965 ★ —
6	Triphasil® 21 — WYETH-AYERST	Triphasil® 28 — WYETH-AYERST	Ortho® 10 / 11 28-day / jours — JANSSEN-ORTHO	Ortho® 7 / 7 / 7 21-day / jours — JANSSEN-ORTHO	Ortho® 7 / 7 / 7 28-day / jours — JANSSEN-ORTHO
7	DIN 01968440 ★ — Cyclen® Dialpak 21-day/jours — JANSSEN-ORTHO	DIN 00317047 ★ — Ortho® 0.5 / 35 21-day / jours — JANSSEN-ORTHO	DIN 00372846 ★ — Ortho® 1 / 35 21-day / jours — JANSSEN-ORTHO	DIN 00022608 ★ — Ortho-Novum® 1 / 50 21-day / jours — JANSSEN-ORTHO	DIN 00707600 ★ — Triquilar® 21 — BERLEX CANADA
8	DIN 01992872 ★ — Cyclen® Dialpak 28-day/jours — JANSSEN-ORTHO	DIN 00340731 ★ — Ortho® 0.5 / 35 28-day / jours — JANSSEN-ORTHO	DIN 00372838 ★ — Ortho® 1 / 35 28-day / jours — JANSSEN-ORTHO	DIN 00340758 ★ — Ortho-Novum® 1 / 50 28-day / jours — JANSSEN-ORTHO	DIN 00707503 ★ — Triquilar® 28 — BERLEX CANADA

*ILLUSTRATION LESS THAN ACTUAL SIZE / ILLUSTRATION RÉDUITE

Use code A, B, C, D, E, horizontal bar and 1 to 8 vertical bar to locate illustrated products

Utiliser le code A, B, C, D, E de la ligne horizontale et les chiffres 1 à 8 de la ligne verticale pour repérer les produits illustrés

A1–2
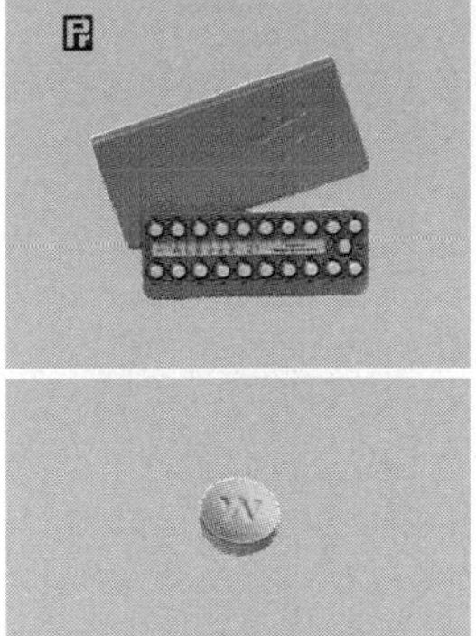
DIN 02236974 *
Alesse™ 21
WYETH-AYERST

B1–2
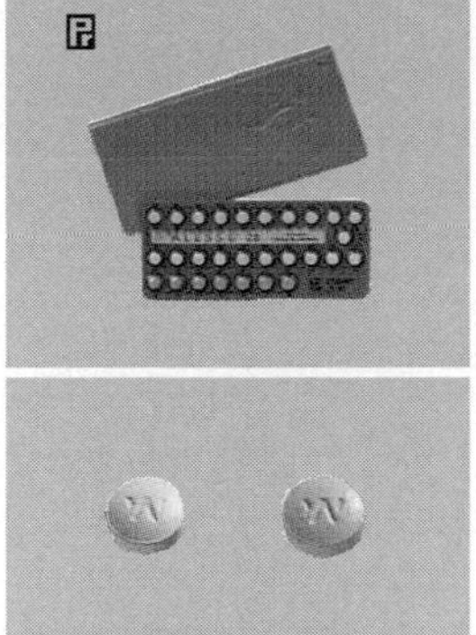
DIN 02236975 *
Alesse™ 28
WYETH-AYERST

C1–2
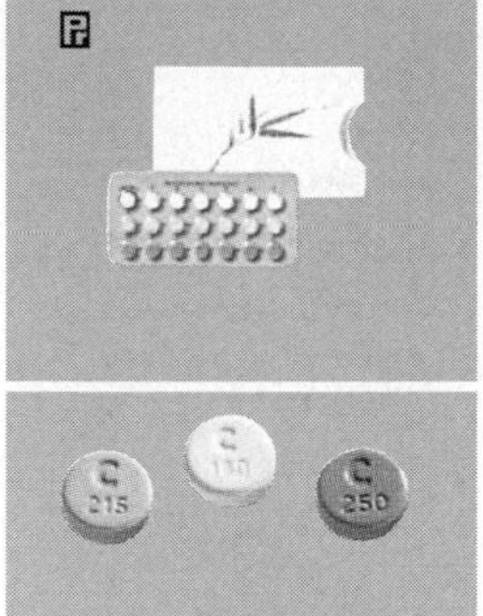
DIN 02028700 *
Tri-Cyclen® Discreet 21-day/jours
JANSSEN-ORTHO

D1–2
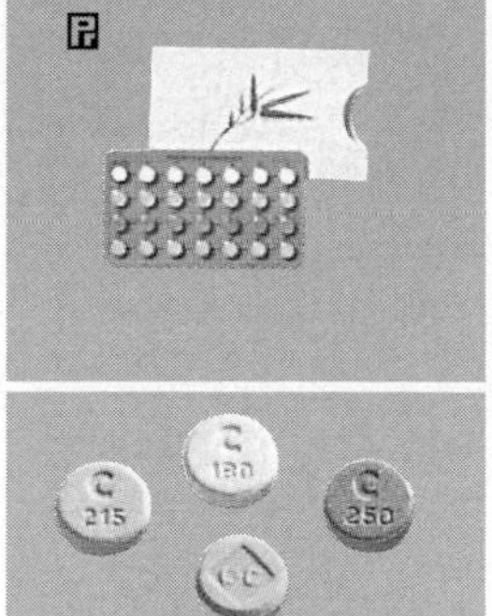
DIN 02029421 *
Tri-Cyclen® Discreet 28-day/jours
JANSSEN-ORTHO

E1
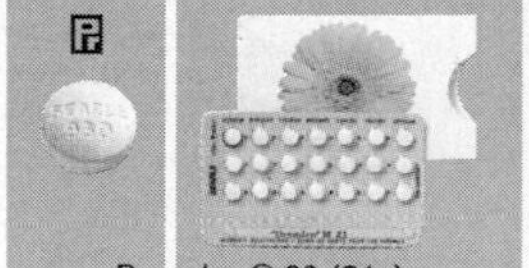
DIN 00469327 *
Demulen® 30 (21s)
SEARLE

E2
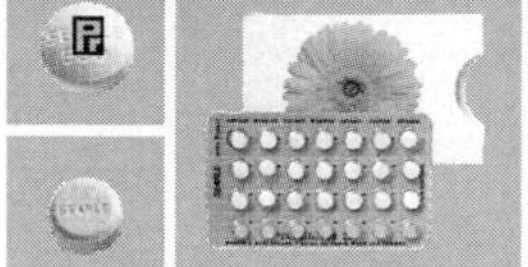
DIN 00471526 *
Demulen® 30 (28s)
SEARLE

A3–4
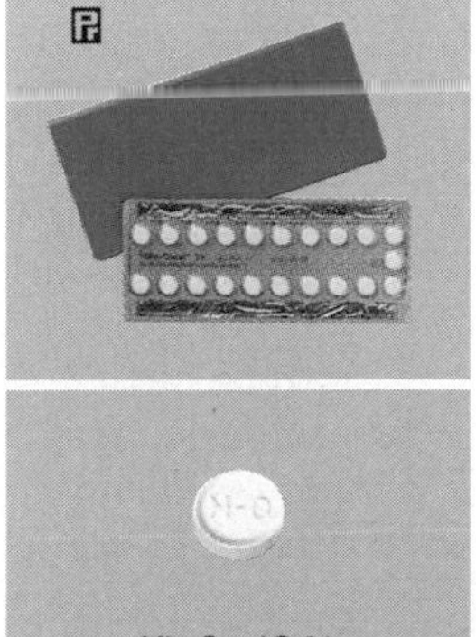
DIN 02042320 *
Min-Ovral® 21
WYETH-AYERST

B3–4
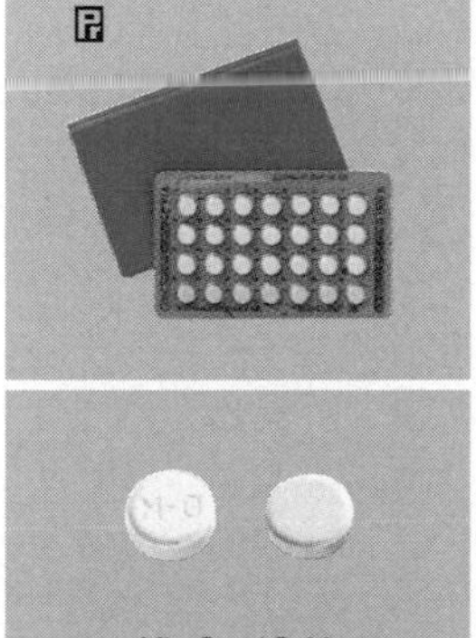
DIN 02042339 *
Min-Ovral® 28
WYETH-AYERST

C3–4
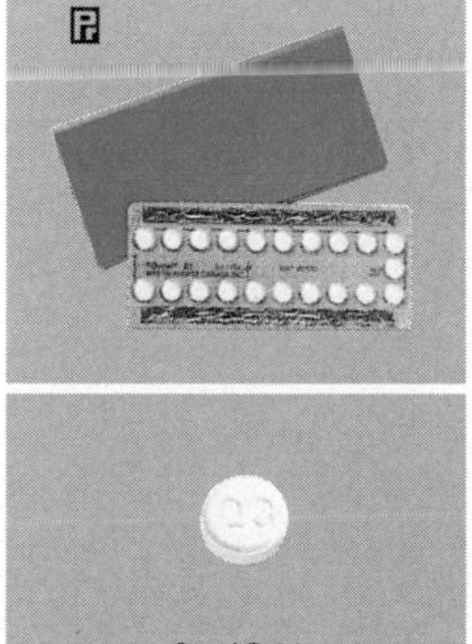
DIN 02043033 *
Ovral® 21
WYETH-AYERST

D3–4
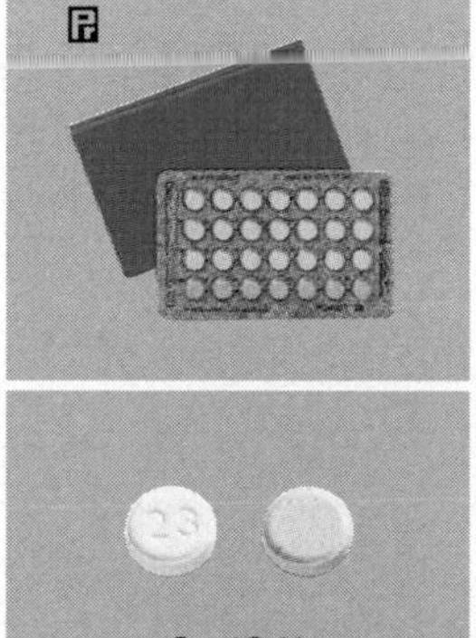
DIN 02043041 *
Ovral® 28
WYETH-AYERST

E3
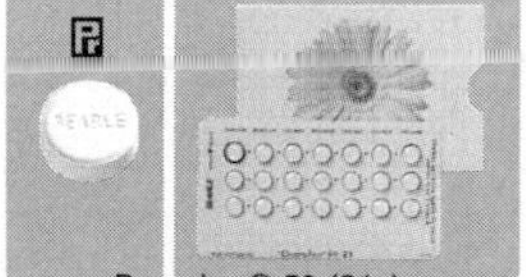
DIN 00028630 *
Demulen® 50 (21s)
SEARLE

E4
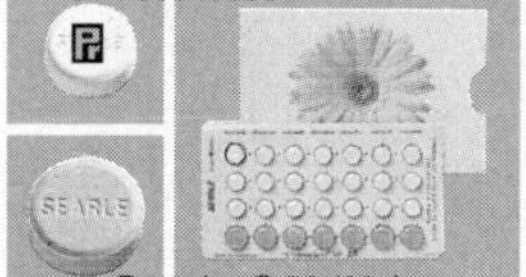
DIN 00343536 *
Demulen® 50 (28s)
SEARLE

A5
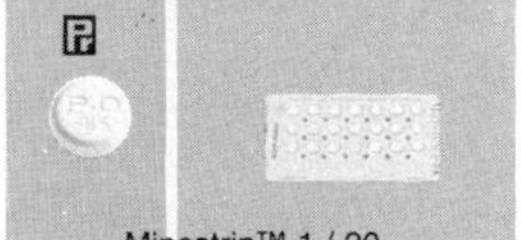
DIN 00315966 *
Minestrin™ 1 / 20 21-day / jours
PARKE-DAVIS

B5
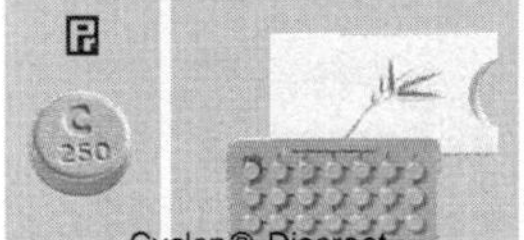
DIN 01968440 *
Cyclen® Discreet 21-day / jours
JANSSEN-ORTHO

C5
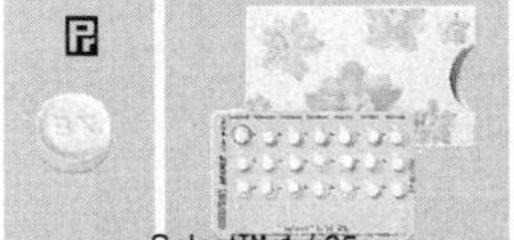
DIN 02197502 *
Select™ 1 / 35 21-day / jours
DISPENSAPHARM

D5
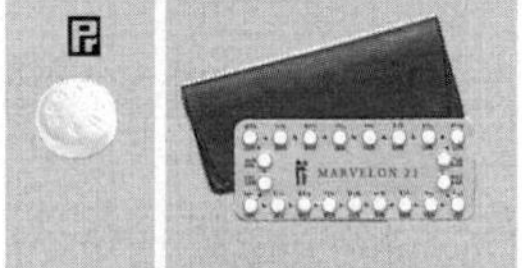
DIN 02042487 *
Marvelon® 21
ORGANON

E5
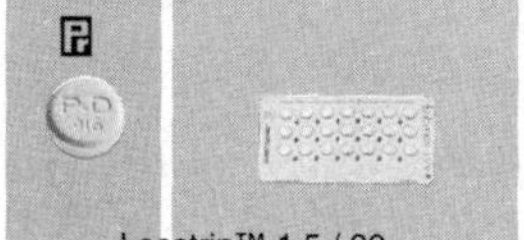
DIN 00297143 *
Loestrin™ 1.5 / 30 21-day / jours
PARKE-DAVIS

A6
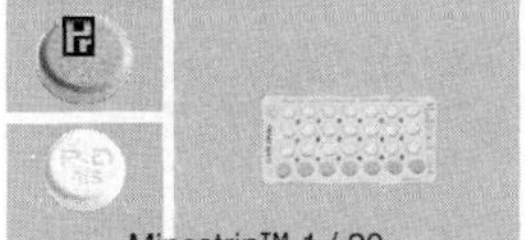
DIN 00343838 *
Minestrin™ 1 / 20 28-day / jours
PARKE-DAVIS

B6
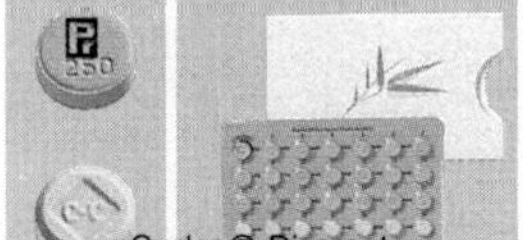
DIN 01992872 *
Cyclen® Discreet 28-day / jours
JANSSEN-ORTHO

C6
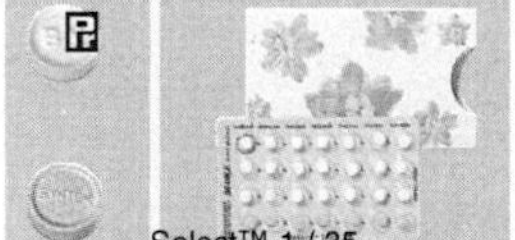
DIN 02199297 *
Select™ 1 / 35 28-day / jours
DISPENSAPHARM

D6
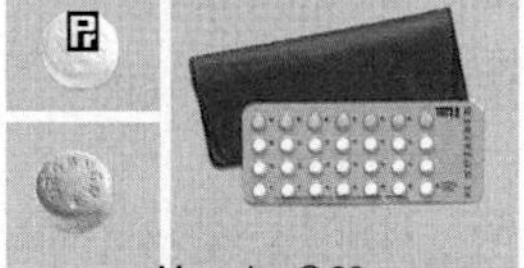
DIN 02042479 *
Marvelon® 28
ORGANON

E6
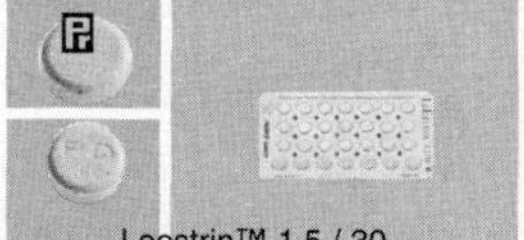
DIN 00353027 *
Loestrin™ 1.5 / 30 28-day / jours
PARKE-DAVIS

A7
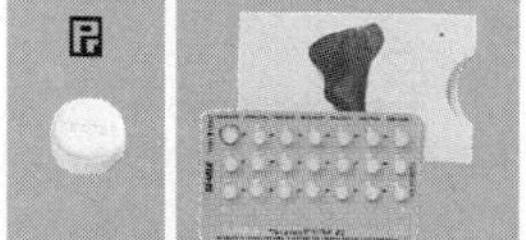
DIN 02188724 *
Norinyl® 1 / 50 (21s)
SEARLE

B7

DIN 02189054 *
Brevicon® 1 / 35 21-day / jours
SEARLE

C7
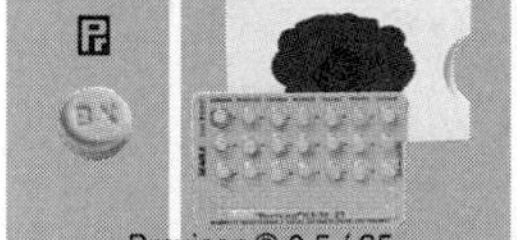
DIN 02187086 *
Brevicon® 0.5 / 35 21-day / jours
SEARLE

D7
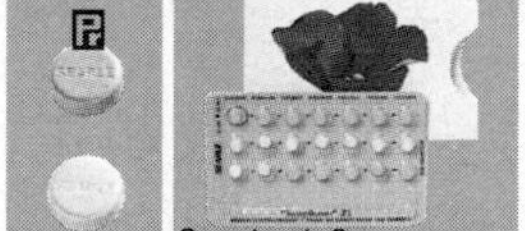
DIN 02187108 *
Synphasic® 21-day / jours
SEARLE

E7
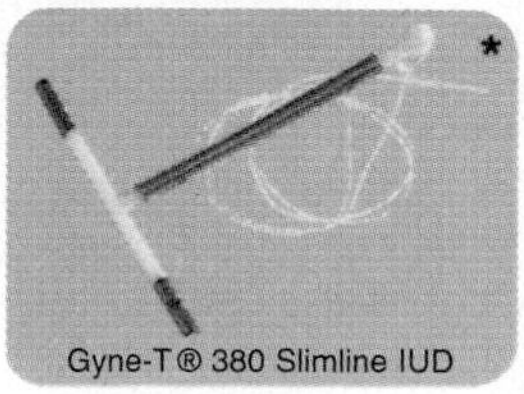
*
Gyne-T® 380 Slimline IUD
JANSSEN-ORTHO

A8
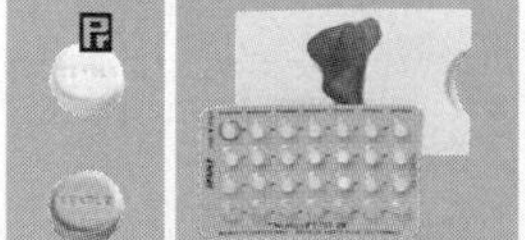
DIN 02188732 *
Norinyl® 1 / 50 (28s)
SEARLE

B8
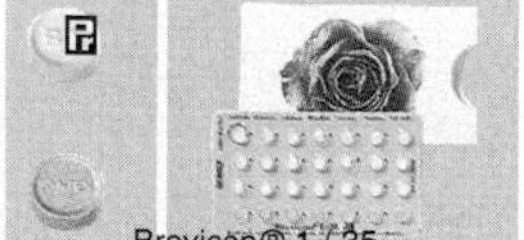
DIN 02189062 *
Brevicon® 1 / 35 28-day / jours
SEARLE

C8

DIN 02187094 *
Brevicon® 0.5 / 35 28-day / jours
SEARLE

D8
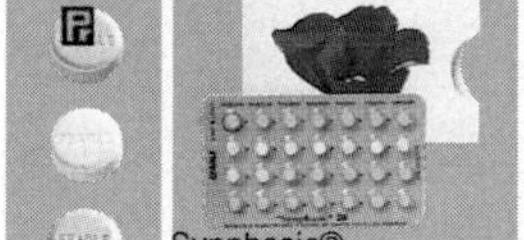
DIN 02187116 *
Synphasic® 28-day / jours
SEARLE

E8
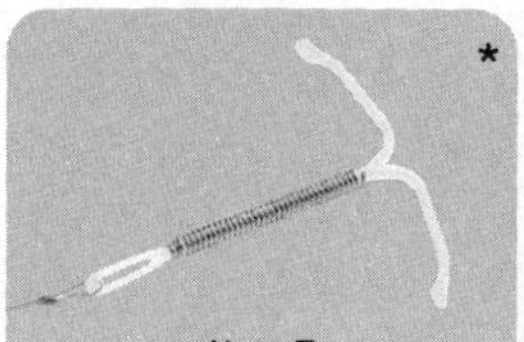
*
Nova-T
BERLEX CANADA

*ILLUSTRATION LESS THAN ACTUAL SIZE / ILLUSTRATION RÉDUITE

Use code A, B, C, D, E, horizontal bar and 1 to 8 vertical bar to locate illustrated products

Utiliser le code A, B, C, D, E de la ligne horizontale et les chiffres 1 à 8 de la ligne verticale pour repérer les produits illustrés

	A	B	C	D	E
1	DIN 01913328 * Nasacort® Nasal Aerosol RHÔNE-POULENC RORER	DIN 02163721 * Combivent™ Inhalation Aerosol BOEHRINGER INGELHEIM	DIN 00576158 * Atrovent® Inhalation Aerosol BOEHRINGER INGELHEIM	DIN 02174731 * Flovent® 25 µg GLAXO WELLCOME	DIN 00893683 * Beclovent® Inhaler 50 µg GLAXO WELLCOME
2	DIN 02174758 * Flovent® 50 µg GLAXO WELLCOME	DIN 02174766 * Flovent® 125 µg GLAXO WELLCOME	DIN 02174774 * Flovent® 250 µg GLAXO WELLCOME	DIN 02215055 * Becloforte® Inhaler 250 µg GLAXO WELLCOME	DIN 02136139 * Serevent® Inhalation Aerosol GLAXO WELLCOME
3	DIN 02213478 * Ventolin® 100 µg GLAXO WELLCOME	DIN 02214997 * Ventodisk® 200 µg GLAXO WELLCOME	DIN 02215004 * Ventodisk® 400 µg GLAXO WELLCOME	DIN 02213710 * Beclodisk® 100 µg GLAXO WELLCOME	DIN 02213729 * Beclodisk® 200 µg GLAXO WELLCOME
4	DIN 02214261 * Serevent® Diskhaler GLAXO WELLCOME	DIN 02229099 * Pulmicort® Nebuamp® 0.125 mg ASTRA	DIN 01978918 * Pulmicort® Nebuamp® 0.25 mg / mL ASTRA	DIN 01978926 * Pulmicort® Nebuamp® 0.5 mg / mL ASTRA	DIN 02237246 * Flovent® Diskus® 250 µg GLAXO WELLCOME
5	DIN 02231129 * Serevent® Diskus® 50 µg GLAXO WELLCOME	DIN 00786616 * Bricanyl® Turbuhaler® ASTRA	DIN 00852074 * Pulmicort® Turbuhaler® 100 µg ASTRA	DIN 00851752 * Pulmicort® Turbuhaler® 200 µg ASTRA	DIN 00851760 * Pulmicort® Turbuhaler® 400 µg ASTRA
6	DIN 02237225 * Oxeze® Turbuhaler® 6 µg ASTRA	DIN 02237224 * Oxeze® Turbuhaler® 12 µg ASTRA	DIN 02230898 * Foradil® 12 µg NOVARTIS PHARMACEUTICALS	DIN 02024152 * Diflucan™ Powder for Oral Suspension PFIZER	DIN 02223724 * Zithromax™ Powder for Oral Suspension PFIZER
7	DIN 02231527 Duphalac® SOLVAY PHARMA	DIN 01943049 Ceftin® 125 mg / 5 mL Oral Suspension GLAXO WELLCOME	DIN 02145286 Ceftin® 250 mg Sachet GLAXO WELLCOME	DIN 01938169 Tylenol® Cold Medications Extra Strength Cold and Flu (honey lemon) McNEIL CONSUMER PRODUCTS	DIN 00517909 Vitathion®-A.T.P. Granules SERVIER
8	DIN 00836354 * Prepulsid® Suspension JANSSEN-ORTHO		DIN 02236950 * Risperdal® Oral Solution JANSSEN-ORTHO		DIN 01913999 Symmetrel® Syrup / sirop DUPONT PHARMA

*ILLUSTRATION LESS THAN ACTUAL SIZE / ILLUSTRATION RÉDUITE

Use code A, B, C, D, E, horizontal bar and 1 to 8 vertical bar to locate illustrated products

Utiliser le code A, B, C, D, E de la ligne horizontale et les chiffres 1 à 8 de la ligne verticale pour repérer les produits illustrés

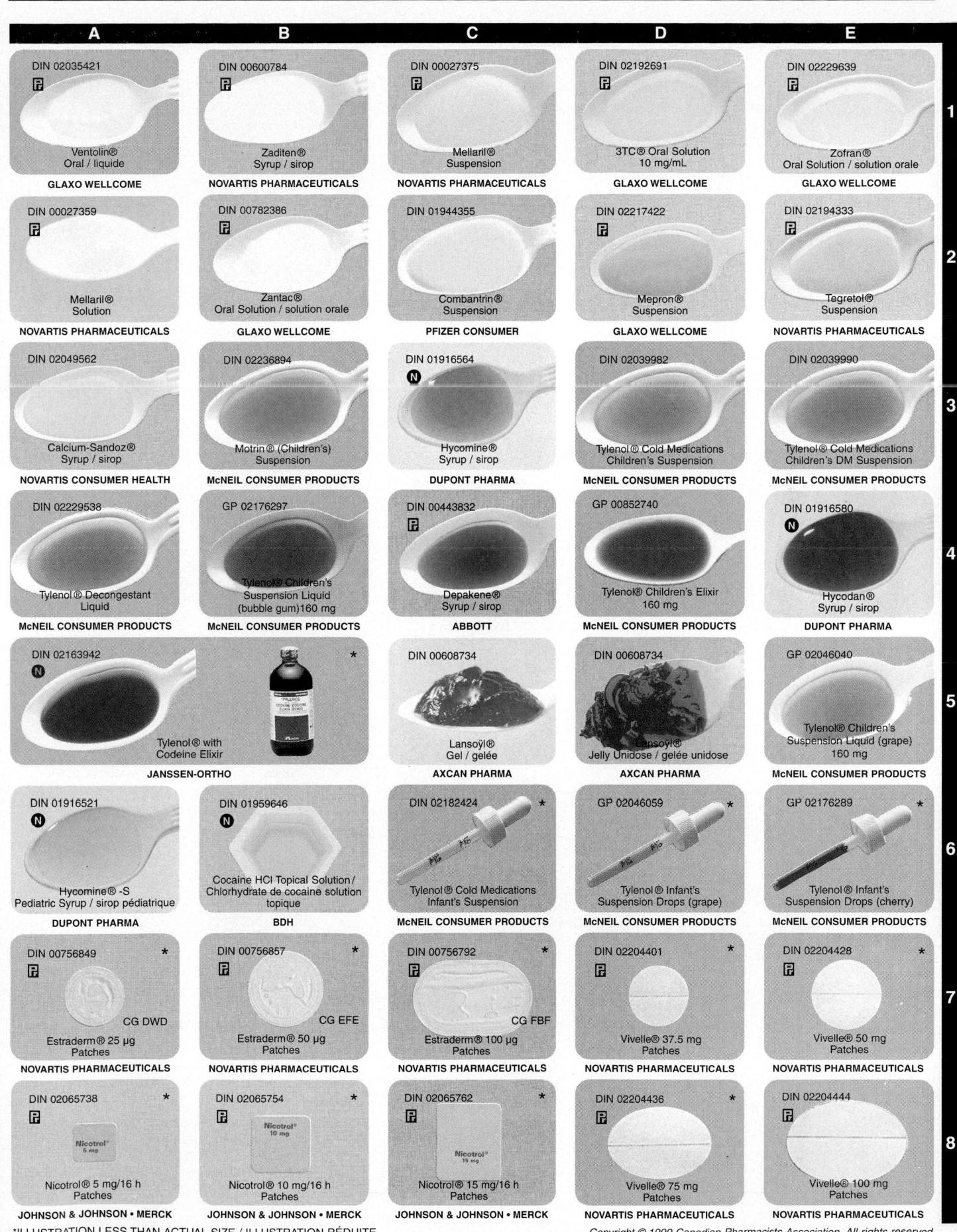

	A	B	C	D	E
1	DIN 02035421 Pr Ventolin® Oral / liquide **GLAXO WELLCOME**	DIN 00600784 Pr Zaditen® Syrup / sirop **NOVARTIS PHARMACEUTICALS**	DIN 00027375 Pr Mellaril® Suspension **NOVARTIS PHARMACEUTICALS**	DIN 02192691 Pr 3TC® Oral Solution 10 mg/mL **GLAXO WELLCOME**	DIN 02229639 Pr Zofran® Oral Solution / solution orale **GLAXO WELLCOME**
2	DIN 00027359 Pr Mellaril® Solution **NOVARTIS PHARMACEUTICALS**	DIN 00782386 Pr Zantac® Oral Solution / solution orale **GLAXO WELLCOME**	DIN 01944355 Combantrin® Suspension **PFIZER CONSUMER**	DIN 02217422 Pr Mepron® Suspension **GLAXO WELLCOME**	DIN 02194333 Pr Tegretol® Suspension **NOVARTIS PHARMACEUTICALS**
3	DIN 02049562 Calcium-Sandoz® Syrup / sirop **NOVARTIS CONSUMER HEALTH**	DIN 02236894 Motrin® (Children's) Suspension **McNEIL CONSUMER PRODUCTS**	DIN 01916564 N Hycomine® Syrup / sirop **DUPONT PHARMA**	DIN 02039982 Tylenol® Cold Medications Children's Suspension **McNEIL CONSUMER PRODUCTS**	DIN 02039990 Tylenol® Cold Medications Children's DM Suspension **McNEIL CONSUMER PRODUCTS**
4	DIN 02229538 Tylenol® Decongestant Liquid **McNEIL CONSUMER PRODUCTS**	GP 02176297 Tylenol® Children's Suspension Liquid (bubble gum)160 mg **McNEIL CONSUMER PRODUCTS**	DIN 00443832 Pr Depakene® Syrup / sirop **ABBOTT**	GP 00852740 Tylenol® Children's Elixir 160 mg **McNEIL CONSUMER PRODUCTS**	DIN 01916580 N Hycodan® Syrup / sirop **DUPONT PHARMA**
5	DIN 02163942 N * Tylenol® with Codeine Elixir **JANSSEN-ORTHO**		DIN 00608734 Lansoÿl® Gel / gelée **AXCAN PHARMA**	DIN 00608734 Lansoÿl® Jelly Unidose / gelée unidose **AXCAN PHARMA**	GP 02046040 Tylenol® Children's Suspension Liquid (grape) 160 mg **McNEIL CONSUMER PRODUCTS**
6	DIN 01916521 N Hycomine® -S Pediatric Syrup / sirop pédiatrique **DUPONT PHARMA**	DIN 01959646 N Cocaine HCl Topical Solution / Chlorhydrate de cocaine solution topique **BDH**	DIN 02182424 * Tylenol® Cold Medications Infant's Suspension **McNEIL CONSUMER PRODUCTS**	GP 02046059 * Tylenol® Infant's Suspension Drops (grape) **McNEIL CONSUMER PRODUCTS**	GP 02176289 * Tylenol® Infant's Suspension Drops (cherry) **McNEIL CONSUMER PRODUCTS**
7	DIN 00756849 * Pr CG DWD Estraderm® 25 µg Patches **NOVARTIS PHARMACEUTICALS**	DIN 00756857 * Pr CG EFE Estraderm® 50 µg Patches **NOVARTIS PHARMACEUTICALS**	DIN 00756792 * Pr CG FBF Estraderm® 100 µg Patches **NOVARTIS PHARMACEUTICALS**	DIN 02204401 * Pr Vivelle® 37.5 mg Patches **NOVARTIS PHARMACEUTICALS**	DIN 02204428 * Pr Vivelle® 50 mg Patches **NOVARTIS PHARMACEUTICALS**
8	DIN 02065738 * Pr Nicotrol® 5 mg/16 h Patches **JOHNSON & JOHNSON • MERCK**	DIN 02065754 * Pr Nicotrol® 10 mg/16 h Patches **JOHNSON & JOHNSON • MERCK**	DIN 02065762 * Pr Nicotrol® 15 mg/16 h Patches **JOHNSON & JOHNSON • MERCK**	DIN 02204436 * Pr Vivelle® 75 mg Patches **NOVARTIS PHARMACEUTICALS**	DIN 02204444 Pr Vivelle® 100 mg Patches **NOVARTIS PHARMACEUTICALS**

*ILLUSTRATION LESS THAN ACTUAL SIZE / ILLUSTRATION RÉDUITE

Use code A, B, C, D, E, horizontal bar and 1 to 8 vertical bar to locate illustrated products

Utiliser le code A, B, C, D, E de la ligne horizontale et les chiffres 1 à 8 de la ligne verticale pour repérer les produits illustrés

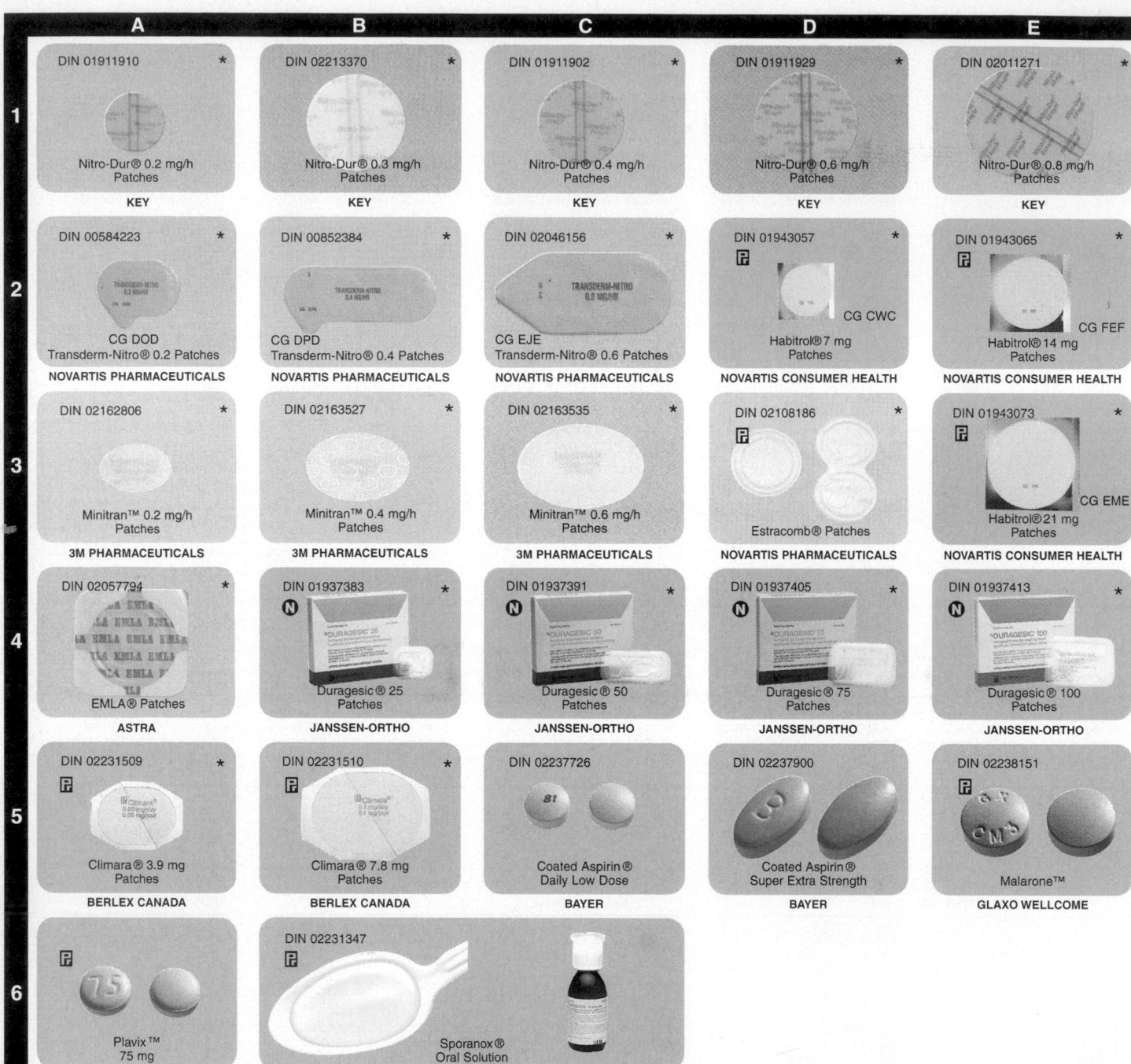

	A	B	C	D	E
1	DIN 01911910 *  Nitro-Dur® 0.2 mg/h Patches **KEY**	DIN 02213370 *  Nitro-Dur® 0.3 mg/h Patches **KEY**	DIN 01911902 *  Nitro-Dur® 0.4 mg/h Patches **KEY**	DIN 01911929 *  Nitro-Dur® 0.6 mg/h Patches **KEY**	DIN 02011271 *  Nitro-Dur® 0.8 mg/h Patches **KEY**
2	DIN 00584223 *  CG DOD Transderm-Nitro® 0.2 Patches **NOVARTIS PHARMACEUTICALS**	DIN 00852384 *  CG DPD Transderm-Nitro® 0.4 Patches **NOVARTIS PHARMACEUTICALS**	DIN 02046156 *  CG EJE Transderm-Nitro® 0.6 Patches **NOVARTIS PHARMACEUTICALS**	DIN 01943057 * Pr  CG CWC Habitrol® 7 mg Patches **NOVARTIS CONSUMER HEALTH**	DIN 01943065 * Pr  CG FEF Habitrol® 14 mg Patches **NOVARTIS CONSUMER HEALTH**
3	DIN 02162806 *  Minitran™ 0.2 mg/h Patches **3M PHARMACEUTICALS**	DIN 02163527 *  Minitran™ 0.4 mg/h Patches **3M PHARMACEUTICALS**	DIN 02163535 *  Minitran™ 0.6 mg/h Patches **3M PHARMACEUTICALS**	DIN 02108186 * Pr  Estracomb® Patches **NOVARTIS PHARMACEUTICALS**	DIN 01943073 * Pr 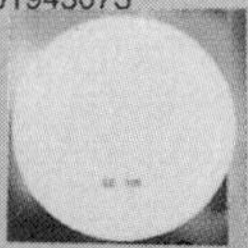 CG EME Habitrol® 21 mg Patches **NOVARTIS CONSUMER HEALTH**
4	DIN 02057794 *  EMLA® Patches **ASTRA**	DIN 01937383 * N 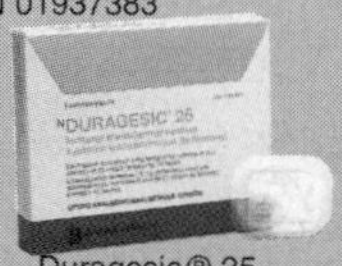 Duragesic® 25 Patches **JANSSEN-ORTHO**	DIN 01937391 * N 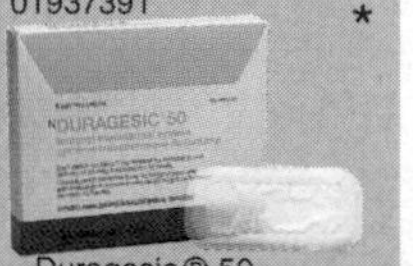 Duragesic® 50 Patches **JANSSEN-ORTHO**	DIN 01937405 * N 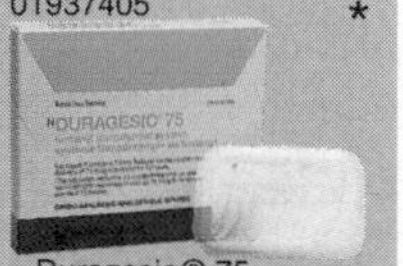 Duragesic® 75 Patches **JANSSEN-ORTHO**	DIN 01937413 * N 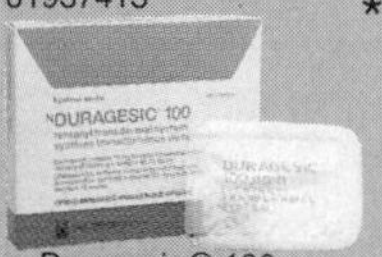 Duragesic® 100 Patches **JANSSEN-ORTHO**
5	DIN 02231509 * Pr 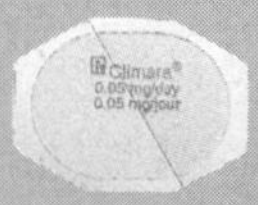 Climara® 3.9 mg Patches **BERLEX CANADA**	DIN 02231510 * Pr  Climara® 7.8 mg Patches **BERLEX CANADA**	DIN 02237726 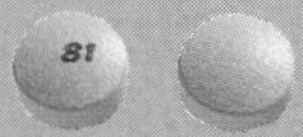 Coated Aspirin® Daily Low Dose **BAYER**	DIN 02237900  Coated Aspirin® Super Extra Strength **BAYER**	DIN 02238151 Pr  Malarone™ **GLAXO WELLCOME**
6	Pr  Plavix™ 75 mg **SANOFI / BMS**	DIN 02231347 Pr 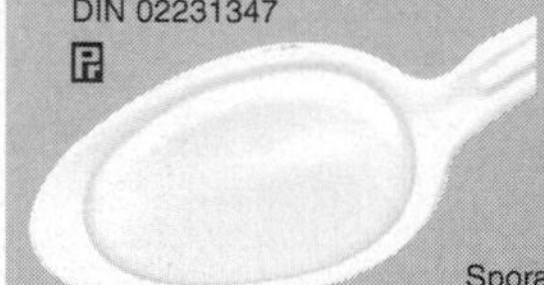  Sporanox® Oral Solution **JANSSEN-ORTHO**			
7					
8					

*ILLUSTRATION LESS THAN ACTUAL SIZE / ILLUSTRATION RÉDUITE

MANUFACTURERS' INDEX

This section provides the full name, addresses, telephone and facsimile numbers of manufacturers and Canadian distributors of pharmaceutical preparations listed in the *CPS*. For further information on products listed in this index, readers are encouraged to consult the *CPS* monographs.

ABBOTT LABORATORIES LIMITED

Executive Offices (Head Office):

8401 Trans-Canada Hwy
Saint-Laurent QC H4S 1Z1

PO Box 6150, Station A
Montréal QC H3C 3K6

Tel.: (514) 832-7000
Toll-free (Canada): 1-800-361-7852
Fax: (514) 832-7800

Montréal Order Desk:

Hospital/Institution:
Tel. (all area codes): 1-888-832-7755
Tel. (Montréal): (514) 832-7755

Retail/Pharmacy:
Tel. (all area codes): 1-800-567-2226
Tel. (Montréal): (514) 832-7333
Fax: (514) 832-7251
Toll-free Fax: 1-800-513-7337

Distribution Centres:

Dartmouth:
47 Fielding Ave.
Dartmouth NS B3B 1E3
Tel.: (902) 468-5906
Fax: (902) 468-9251

Nfld:
Prov. Medical Supplies
51 Pippy Pl., PO Box 13427
St. John's NF A1B 4B7
Tel.: (709) 754-3033
Toll-free: 1-800-563-8755
Fax: (709) 754-3014

Edmonton:
16607-116th Ave.
Edmonton AB T5M 3V1
Tel.: (403) 451-4297
Fax: (403) 455-7275

Montréal:
5685 Cypihot Rd.
Saint-Laurent QC H4S 1R3
Tel.: (514) 340-7900
Fax: (514) 337-2811

Toronto:
7115 Millcreek Dr.
Mississauga ON L5N 3R3
Tel.: (905) 821-4912
Toll-free: 1-800-263-5922
Fax: (905) 821-3284

Vancouver:
7403 Progress Way
Delta BC V4G 1E7
Tel.: (604) 940-4148
Fax: (604) 940-4102

Winnipeg:
989 A. Keewatin St.
Winnipeg MB R2X 2X4
Tel.: (204) 633-1094
Fax: (204) 694-2380

Plants:

Main Plant:
5400, Côte-de-Liesse Rd.
Montréal QC H4P 1A5
Tel.: (514) 341-6880
Fax: (514) 341-6803

Toronto Plant:
500 Oakdale Rd.
Downsview ON M3N 1W5
Tel.: (416) 745-0411
Fax: (416) 745-5895

Wolseley Plant:
551 Garnet St.
Wolseley SK S0G 5H0
Tel.: (306) 698-2518
Fax: (306) 698-2812

Customer Service (Sask. only):

Toll-free: 1-800-667-8969 (Ext. 10)

Hospital Products Division (HPD)

Dopamine HCl and Dextrose Injection
Enflurane
Gentamicin Sulfate in 0.9% Sodium Chloride Injection
Heparin Sodium in 5% Dextrose Injection
Isoflurane, USP
Meperidine
Metronidazole Injection
Morphine Sulfate
Pentothal® Sodium
Sevorane™

Small Volume Parenterals

Acyclovir Sodium for Injection
A-Hydrocort
Aminophylline
Atracurium Besylate Injection
Atropine Sulfate
Bretylium Tosylate Injection
Bretylium Tosylate and Dextrose Injection
Bupivacaine Hydrochloride Injection
Calcijex®
Calcium Chloride
Calcium Gluconate
Clindamycin Phosphate Injection
Codeine Phosphate
Dobutamine Hydrochloride Injection
Ephedrine Sulfate
Epinephrine
Ergonovine Maleate
Erythrocin™ I.V.
Fentanyl Citrate
Furosemide Injection
Heparin Lock Flush
Lidocaine Parenteral
Magnesium Sulfate
Mannitol
Meperidine
Morphine Sulfate
Nembutal® Sodium
Oxytocin Injection, USP
Pancuronium Bromide Injection
Phenobarbital
Phenytoin Sodium Injection, USP
Potassium Chloride
Potassium Phosphates Injection
Promazine Hydrochloride
Pyridoxine HCl
Quelicin® Chloride Injection
Quinidine Sulfate
Scopolamine Hydrobromide
Sodium Bicarbonate Injection
Sodium Chloride Injection, USP
Verapamil Injection
Vitamin B_{12}
Vitamin K_1

Pharmaceutical Products Division (PPD)

Abbokinase®
Abbokinase® Open-Cath®
Biaxin®
Colchicine
Cylert®
Depakene®
EES® 200
EES® 400
EES® 600
Epival®
Epiject® I.V.
Erybid™
Erythrocin®
Erythromid®
Fero-Grad®
Hytrin®
K-Lor®
Nembutal® Sodium
Norvir®
PCE®
Pediazole®
Survanta®
Tranxene®

Ross Products Division

Executive Offices (Head Office):

8401 Trans-Canada Hwy
Saint-Laurent QC H4S 1Z1

PO Box 6150, Station Centre-ville
Montréal QC H3C 3K6

Tel.: (514) 832-7000
Toll-free, area codes 416/418/506/514/519/613/705/819/902: 1-800-361-7852; area codes 204/306/403/604/709/807: 1-800-361-7894
Fax: (514) 340-9219

Alimentum®
Isomil® Preparations
Pedialyte®
Pedialyte® Freezer Pops
Pediasure™
Similac® LF

Abbott Laboratories Limited:
Diagnostic Reagents:
Diagnostic Division
7115 Millcreek Dr.
Mississauga ON L5N 3R3
Tel.: (905) 858-2450
Toll-free: 1-800-387-8378
Fax: (905) 858-2462

Cardiovascular Products

Abbokinase®
Hytrin®

Therapeutic Drug Monitoring Products

Lidocaine Parenteral
Phenobarbital
Quinidine Sulfate

Canadian Distributor for:
TAP Pharmaceuticals
North Chicago IL 60064 U.S.A.

Lupron® Depot 3.75 mg
Lupron®/Lupron Depot® 3.75 mg/7.5 mg

Lupron®/Lupron Depot® 7.5 mg/22.5 mg
Prevacid®

ALBERT PHARMA INC.

2100 Syntex Court
Mississauga ON L5N 3X4

Client Relation:

Toll-free: 1-800-337-2584
Toll-free Fax: 1-800-361-7141

Albert® Docusate *
Albert® Glyburide *
Albert® Oxybutynin *
Albert® Pentoxifylline *
Albert® Tiafen *
Albert® Tiafen SR

**Distributor: AltiMed Pharmaceutical Company*

ALCON CANADA INC.

2145 Meadowpine Blvd.
Mississauga ON L5N 6R8
Tel.: (905) 826-6700
Toll-free: 1-800-268-4574;
(Quebec): 1-800-387-8184
Fax: (905) 826-1448/567-0592

Medical Information:

Toll-free: 1-800-613-2245

Alcaine®
Alcomicin®
Alomide®
Atropine™ Ointment
Betoptic® S
Bion Tears®
BSS®
BSS® Plus
Cetamide™
Ciloxan®
Cyclogyl®
DPE™
Duratears® Naturale
Emadine®
Enuclene™
Eye-Stream®
Flarex®
Fluorescite®
Iopidine® 0.5%, 1.0%
Isopto® Atropine
Isopto® Carbachol
Isopto® Carpine
Isopto® Homatropine
Isopto® Tears
Maxidex®
Maxitrol®
Miostat®
Mydfrin®
Mydriacyl®
Naphcon®-A
Naphcon® Forte
Patanol™
Pilopine HS®
Tears Naturale®
Tears Naturale® Free
Tears Naturale® II
Tobradex®
Tobrex® Ophthalmic
Vexol™
Zincfrin®
Zincfrin®-A

ALLEREX LABORATORY LTD.

580 Terry Fox Dr., Suite 408
Kanata ON K2L 4B9
Tel.: (613) 592-8200
Fax: (613) 592-6347

EpiPen®
EpiPen® Jr.

ALLERGAN INC.

110 Cochrane Dr.
Markham ON L3R 9S1
Tel.: (905) 940-1660
Fax: (905) 940-1902

Medical Information/ Adverse Event Reporting:

Tel.: (905) 940-7164
Toll-free: 1-877-ALLERGAN (255-3746)

Information on Botox®:

1-800-433-8871

Acular®
Albalon®-A Liquifilm®
Alphagan™
Betagan®
Blephamide®
Botox®
Cellufresh®
Cellufresh® M-D™
Celluvisc™
Fluoroplex®
FML Forte®
FML® Liquifilm®
Herplex®
Herplex®-D
Lacri-Lube® S.O.P.®
Liquifilm® Forte
Liquifilm® Tears
Mireze®
Naftin® Preparations
Ocufen™
Ocuflox™
Ophthetic®
Opticrom®
Polytrim™
Pred Forte®
Pred Mild®
Probeta®
Propine®
Pro•Tec Sport™
Refresh™
Tazorac™
Tears Plus®

ALTIMED PHARMACEUTICAL COMPANY

Formerly Kenral and SynCare

2100 Syntex Court, Suite 100
Mississauga ON L5N 3X4
Tel.: (905) 821-7610
Toll-free: 1-800-266-ALTI (2584)
Fax: (905) 542-5170
Toll-free Fax: 1-800-881-5175
Web site: www.altimed.com

Customer Service:

Toll-free: 1-800-337-ALTI (2584)
Toll-free Fax: 1-800-361-7141
E-mail: clients@altimed.com

Medical Information:

E-mail: medinfo@altimed.com

Alti-Acyclovir
Alti-Alprazolam
Alti-Amiloride HCTZ
Alti-Azathioprine
Alti-Beclomethasone Aqueous Suspension
Alti-Beclomethasone Inhalation Aerosol
Alti-Benzydamine
Alti-Bromazepam
Alti-Captopril
Alti-Cholestyramine Light
Alti-Clobetasol
Alti-Clonazepam
Alti-CPA
Alti-Cyclobenzaprine
Alti-Desipramine
Alti-Diltiazem
Alti-Diltiazem CD
Alti-Domperidone
Alti-Doxepin
Alti-Doxycycline
Alti-Flurbiprofen
Alti-Fluvoxamine
Alti-Ibuprofen
Alti-Ipratropium
Alti-Mexiletine
Alti-Minocycline
Alti-Moclobemide
Alti-MPA
Alti-Nadolol
Alti-Orciprenaline
Alti-Piroxicam
Alti-Prazosin
Alti-Ranitidine
Alti-Salbutamol
Alti-Salbutamol Sulfate
Alti-Sotalol
Alti-Sulfasalazine
Alti-Terazosin
Alti-Trazodone
Alti-Trazodone Dividose
Alti-Triazolam
Alti-Tryptophan
Alti-Valproic
Alti-Verapamil
Gemfibrozil
Naxen®
Ophtho-Bunolol®
Ophtho-Chloram®
Ophtho-Dipivefrin™
Ophtho-Tate®
Synflex®
Synflex® DS

ALZA CANADA

2900 John St., Unit 1
Markham ON L3R 5G3
Tel.: (905) 475-9777
Toll-free: 1-800-668-3535
Fax: (905) 475-2996

Ditropan®
Elmiron™
Polycitra-K®

AMGEN CANADA INC.

6733 Mississauga Rd., Suite 303
Mississauga ON L5N 6J5
Tel.: (905) 542-7277
Toll-free (Canada): 1-800-665-4273;
(Quebec): 1-800-565-9654
Fax: (905) 542-7450

Order Desk:

Tel. (Toronto): (905) 847-8113
Toll-free: 1-800-563-9798
Fax: 1-800-495-3187

Neupogen®

APOTEX INC.

150 Signet Dr.
Weston ON M9L 1T9
Tel.: (416) 749-9300
Toll-free (Canada): 1-800-268-4623
Fax: (416) 749-9578

Order Desk:

Tel. (Toronto local): 749-1234
Toll-free (Ont.): 1-800-668-4823
Toll-free (Quebec and Atlantic Provinces, french speaking): 1-800-361-1685
Toll-free Fax: 1-800-665-2854

Medical Information:

Toll-free: 1-800-667-4708
E-mail: druginfo@apotex.ca

Branches:

2970, av. André
Dorval QC H9P 2P2
Tel.: (514) 421-9555
Toll-free: 1-800-361-1685
Fax: (514) 421-2120
Toll-free Fax: 1-800-665-4385

1575 Inkster Blvd.
Winnipeg MB R2X 1R2
Tel.: (204) 694-2661
Toll-free (Man., Sask., N.W. Ont.): 1-800-665-0370
Fax: (204) 694-5245

34-36 E. 69th Ave.
Vancouver BC V5X 4K6
Tel.: (604) 324-6030
Toll-free (BC & AB): 1-800-663-6716
Fax: (604) 324-0823
Toll-free Fax: 1-800-661-8105

PO Box 5355
St. John's NF A1C 5W2
Tel.: (709) 753-3362
Fax: (709) 753-0975

2712—37th Ave. N.E.
Calgary AB T1Y 5L3
Tel.: (403) 735-6195
Fax: (403) 735-6199

Apo®-Acebutolol
Apo®-Acetaminophen
Apo®-Acetazolamide
Apo®-Acyclovir
Apo®-Allopurinol
Apo®-Alpraz
Apo®-Amilzide
Apo®-Amitriptyline
Apo®-Amoxi
Apo®-Ampi
Apo®-ASA
Apo®-Atenol
Apo®-Baclofen
Apo®-Benztropine
Apo®-Bisacodyl
Apo®-Bromazepam
Apo®-Bromocriptine
Apo®-Buspirone
Apo®-C
Apo®-Cal
Apo®-Capto
Apo®-Carbamazepine
Apo®-Cefaclor
Apo®-Cephalex
Apo®-Chlorax
Apo®-Chlordiazepoxide
Apo®-Chlorpropamide
Apo®-Chlorthalidone
Apo®-Cimetidine
Apo®-Clomipramine
Apo®-Clonazepam
Apo®-Clonidine
Apo®-Clorazepate
Apo®-Cloxi
Apo®-Cromolyn
Apo®Cromolyn Sterules
Apo®-Cyclobenzaprine
Apo®-Desipramine
Apo®-Diazepam
Apo®-Diclo
Apo®-Diclo SR
Apo®-Diflunisal
Apo®-Diltiaz
Apo®-Diltiaz CD
Apo®-Diltiaz SR
Apo®-Dimenhydrinate
Apo®-Dipyridamole FC
Apo®-Domperidone
Apo®-Doxepin
Apo®-Doxy
Apo®-Doxy Tabs
Apo®-Erythro Base
Apo®-Erythro E-C
Apo®-Erythro-ES
Apo®-Erythro-S
Apo®-Etodolac
Apo®-Famotidine
Apo®-Fenofibrate
Apo®-Ferrous Gluconate
Apo®-Ferrous Sulfate
Apo®-Fluoxetine
Apo®-Fluphenazine
Apo®-Flurazepam
Apo®-Flurbiprofen
Apo®-Fluvoxamine
Apo®-Folic
Apo®-Furosemide
Apo®-Gain
Apo®-Gemfibrozil
Apo®-Glyburide
Apo®-Haloperidol
Apo®-Hexa
Apo®-Hydralazine
Apo®-Hydro
Apo®-Hydroxyzine
Apo®-Ibuprofen
Apo®-Imipramine
Apo®-Indapamide
Apo®-Indomethacin
Apo®-Ipravent
Apo®-ISDN
Apo®-K
Apo®-Keto
Apo®-Keto-E
Apo®-Keto SR
Apo®-Ketoconazole
Apo®-Ketotifen
Apo®-Levocarb
Apo®-Lisinopril
Apo®-Loperamide
Apo®-Lorazepam
Apo®-Lovastatin
Apo®-Loxapine
Apo®-Mefenamic
Apo®-Megestrol
Apo®-Meprobamate
Apo®-Metformin
Apo®-Methazide
Apo® Mothyldopa
Apo®-Metoclop
Apo®-Metoprolol
Apo®-Metoprolol (Type L)
Apo®-Metronidazole
Apo®-Minocycline
Apo®-Moclobemide
Apo®-Nadol
Apo®-Napro-Na
Apo®-Napro-Na DS
Apo®-Naproxen
Apo®-Nifed
Apo®-Nifed PA
Apo®-Nitrofurantoin
Apo®-Nizatidine
Apo®-Nortriptyline
Apo®-Oflox
Apo®-Oxazepam
Apo®-Oxtriphylline
Apo®-Oxybutynin
Apo®-Pen VK
Apo®-Pentoxifylline SR
Apo®-Perphenazine
Apo®-Phenylbutazone
Apo®-Pindol
Apo®-Piroxicam
Apo®-Prazo
Apo®-Prednisone
Apo®-Primidone
Apo®-Procainamide
Apo®-Propranolol
Apo®-Quinidine
Apo®-Ranitidine
Apo®-Salvent
Apo®-Selegiline
Apo®-Sotalol
Apo®-Sulcralfate
Apo®-Sulfatrim
Apo®-Sulfinpyrazone
Apo®-Sulin
Apo®-Tamox
Apo®-Temazepam
Apo®-Tenoxicam
Apo®-Terazosin
Apo®-Terfenadine
Apo®-Tetra
Apo®-Theo LA
Apo®-Thioridazine
Apo®-Tiaprofenic
Apo®-Ticlopidine
Apo®-Timol
Apo®-Timop
Apo®-Tolbutamide
Apo®-Trazodone
Apo®-Trazodone D
Apo®-Triazide
Apo®-Triazo
Apo®-Trifluoperazine
Apo®-Trihex
Apo®-Trimip
Apo®-Verap
Apo®-Zidovudine
Apo®-Zopiclone

ASHBURY BIOLOGICALS INC./HERBAL LABORATORIES LTD.

4700 Keele St.
Farquharson Bldg.
Toronto ON M3J 1P3
Tel.: (416) 736-5585
Toll-free: 1-800-567-5060
Fax: (416) 736-5846

Tanacet 125®

ASTRA PHARMA INC.

Head Office:

1004 Middlegate Rd.
Mississauga ON L4Y 1M4
Tel.: (905) 277-7111
Fax: (905) 270-3248

Customer Relations, Product Information & Order Processing:

Tel.: (905) 566-4015 (English)
Toll-free: 1-800-668-6000 (English);
1-800-461-3787 (French)
Fax: (905) 896-4745
Toll-free Fax: 1-800-268-0774

Medical Information:

Tel.: (905) 896-6623 (English);
(905) 896-6124 (French & English)
Toll-free: 1-800-668-6000, ext. 6623 or 6126 (English);
1-800-461-3787, ext. 6124 (French)

Astracaine®
Astracaine® Forte
Atropine Sulfate Injection USP
Betaloc®
Betaloc® Durules®
Biquin Durules®
Bricanyl® Tablets
Bricanyl® Turbuhaler®
Calcium Chloride Injection
Calcium Gluconate Injection
Cardura-1™, -2™, -4™ *
Citanest® 4% Forte
Citanest® 4% Plain
Dimenhydrinate Injection
EMLA® Cream/Patch
Entocort® Capsules
Entocort® Enema
Imdur®
Jectofer®
Losec®
Naropin®
Nesacaine®-CE
Oxeze® Turbuhaler®
Penglobe®
Plendil®
Polocaine® 3%
Polocaine® 2% with Levonordefrin 1:20 000
Potassium Chloride for Injection Concentrate USP
Pulmicort® Nebuamp®
Pulmicort® Turbuhaler®
Rhinocort® Aqua
Rhinocort® Turbuhaler®
Salbutamol Nebuamp®
Sensorcaine®
Sensorcaine® Forte
Sensorcaine® with Epinephrine
Sodium Bicarbonate Injection USP
Sodium Chloride Injection USP
Sodium Chloride Irrigation Solution USP
Theo-Dur®
Tonocard®
Xylocaine® CO_2
Xylocaine® Dental Solutions
Xylocaine® Endotracheal
Xylocaine® 4% Sterile Solution
Xylocaine® Jelly 2%
Xylocaine® Ointment 5%, Xylocaine® Dental Ointment 5%
Xylocaine® Parenteral Solutions
Xylocaine® Spinal 5%
Xylocaine® Topical 4%
Xylocaine® Topical 5%
Xylocaine® Viscous 2%
Xylocard®

**TM Pfizer Products Inc., used under license.*

AXCAN PHARMA INC.

597 Laurier Blvd.
Mont St-Hilaire QC J3H 4X8
Tel.: (514) 467-5138
Toll-free: Direct Line: 1-800-565-3255
Fax: (514) 464-9979
E-mail: axcan@axcan.com

ADEKs® Pediatric Drops
ADEKs® Tablets
Amphojel®
Basaljel®
Coptin®
Cortenema®
Lansoÿl®
Lansoÿl® Sugar-Free
Modulon®
Mucaine®
Salofalk®
Ultrase®
Ultrase® MT
Ursofalk®
Viokase®

BAKER CUMMINS INC.

see "Alza Canada"

BAXTER CORPORATION

Head Office:

4 Robert Speck Pkwy
Suite 700
Mississauga ON L4Z 3Y4
Tel.: (905) 270-1125
Toll-free: 1-800-387-8399
Fax: (905) 281-6420

Hospital Products

Dopamine HCl and 5% Dextrose Injection
Flagyl® 500 Injection
Gentamicin Sulfate Injection in 0.9% Sodium Chloride
Gentran® 40
Gentran® 70
Heparin Sodium and 0.9% Sodium Chloride Injection
Heparin Sodium in 5% Dextrose Injection
Lidocaine HCl 0.4% and 0.8% in 5% Dextrose for I.V. Infusion
Nitroglycerin in 5% Dextrose Injection
Nutrineal PD4
Osmitrol®

Pharmaceutical Products

Gent-L-Tip®
GoLytely™

Baxter Corporation, Hyland/Immuno Division

Feiba® VH Immuno
Immunine® VH
Iveegam Immuno®
Tisseel® Kit VH

BAYER INC.

77 Belfield Rd.
Toronto ON M9W 1G6
Tel.: (416) 248-0771
Toll-free: 1-800-268-1331
Fax: (416) 248-1846

Drug Safety & Medical Information (Healthcare Division):

Toll-free (Canada): 1-800-265-7382

Customer Service (Consumer Care and Healthcare Divisions):

Toll-free: 1-800-268-1432
Toll-free Fax: 1-800-567-1710

Consumer Care Division

Actiprofen™
Aspirin®
Aspirin® Backache
Aspirin® with Stomach Guard™
Canesten® Topical
Canesten® Vaginal
Coated Aspirin®
Flintstones®
Midol®
Midol® Extra Strength
Midol® PMS Extra Strength
Myoflex®
Myoflex® Ice Plus
One A Day® Advance Preparations

Healthcare Division

Adalat®
Adalat® PA 10
Adalat® PA 20
Adalat® XL®
Baycol®
Baygam™
Bayhep B™
Bayrab™
Baytet™
Biltricide®
Cipro®
Cipro® I.V.
Cipro® Oral Suspension
DTIC®
Nimotop®
Nimotop® I.V.
Prandase®
Trasylol®
Tridesilon®

(Biological Products)

Ana-Kit®
Gamimune® N
Koāte®-HP
Kogenate®
Plasbumin®-5
Plasbumin®-25
Prolastin®
Thrombate III®

BDH INC.

Health Care Group

350 Evans Ave.
Toronto ON M8Z 1K5
Tel.: (416) 255-8521
Toll-free: 1-800-268-0310
Fax: (416) 255-7453
Toll-free Fax: 1-800-551-7052

Baclofen
Cocaine HCl
Etoposide Injection
Metformin
Salbutamol
Sodium Chloride Inhalation Solution
Timolol

BENCARD ALLERGY LABORATORIES

An Allergy Therapeutics (Canada) Ltd. Company

1345 Fewster Dr.
Mississauga ON L4W 2A5
Tel.: (905) 624-6250
Toll-free: 1-800-268-2038
Fax: (905) 624-6418

Pollinex®-R

BERLEX CANADA INC.

2260, 32nd Ave.
Lachine QC H8T 3H4
Tel.: (514) 631-7400
Toll-free: 1-800-361-0240
Fax: (514) 636-9177

Order Desk:

Toll-free: 1-888-323-7539
Fax: (514) 631-3879

Androcur®
Androcur® Depot
Betaseron®
Climara®
Diane®-35
Echovist®
Fludara®
Levovist®
Magnevist®
Nova-T
Osmovist®
Triquilar® 21
Triquilar® 28
Ultravist®

BERNA PRODUCTS, CORP.

North American Headquarters:

4216 Ponce de Leon Blvd.
Coral Gables FL 33146 U.S.A.
Toll-free: 1-800-533-5899
Toll-free Fax: 1-800-392-9490

MoRu-Viraten Berna™
Mutacol Berna®
Vivotif Berna™
Vivotif Berna® L Vaccine

BIOCHEM VACCINES INC.

2323, Parc Technologique Blvd.
Sainte-Foy QC G1P 4R8
Tel.: (418) 650-0010
Fax: (418) 650-0080

Medical Information:

Tel.: (418) 650-0010

Diphtheria and Tetanus Toxoids (d2T5) Adsorbed
Fluviral®
Fluviral S/F®
Pacis™ *
Tetanus Toxoid Adsorbed

**Manufactured by BioChem Vaccines Inc. Disbributed by Faulding (Canada) Inc.*

BIOMATRIX MEDICAL CANADA INC.

275, av. Labrosse
Pointe-Claire QC H9R 1A3
Tel.: (514) 697-8851
Toll-free: 1-800-263-8851
Fax: (514) 697-3670

Synvisc® *

**Developed by Biomatrix Inc. and manufactured by Biomatrix Medical Canada Inc. Distributed by Rhône-Poulenc Rorer Canada Inc.*

BIONICHE INC.

383 Sovereign Rd.
London ON N6M 1A3
Tel.: (519) 453-0641
Toll-free: 1-800-567-2028
Fax: (519) 453-2418

Ampicillin Sodium
Atropine Injection
Carbachol
Ceporacin®
Chlorpromazine HCl Injection
Crystapen® (buffered)
Cystistat®
Dextrose 50% Injection
Dimenhydrinate Injection
Epinephrine Injection
Ergonovine Maleate Injection
Histamine
Lidocaine Parenteral
Methylene Blue
Parvolex®
Promethazine Hydrochloride Injection
Succinylcholine Chloride Injection
Suplasyn®
Thiamine HCl Injection

BLOCK DRUG COMPANY (CANADA) LTD.

7600 Danbro Cres.
Mississauga ON L5N 6L6
Tel.: (905) 542-7282
Fax: (905) 542-7785

Baby's Own™ Gripe Water
Baby's Own™ Infant Drops
Baby's Own™ Ointment
Baby's Own™ Teething Gel
Beano®
Nytol™
Nytol™ Extra Strength
Nytol™ Natural Source

BOEHRINGER INGELHEIM (CANADA) LTD.

5180 South Service Rd.
Burlington ON L7L 5H4
Tel.: (905) 639-0333
Toll-free: 1-800-263-9107
Fax: (905) 639-3769

Medical Information:

Tel.: (905) 639-4633 (4-MED)
Toll-free: 1-800-263-5103 ext. 4633 (4-MED)

Customer Service:

Toll-free: 1-800-263-BICL (2425)

Orders and Distribution Centres:

(BC, AB, SK, MB, ON, QC):
Toll-free: 1-800-263-BICL (2425)
Fax: (905) 634-4421
Toll-free Fax: 1-800-665-3405

Atlantic Provinces:
Tel.: (506) 861-0270
Toll-free: 1-800-561-3933
Fax: (506) 861-0273

Alupent® Preparations
Asasantine®
Atrovent® Inhalation Aerosol
Atrovent® Inhalation Solution
Atrovent® Nasal Spray
Berotec® Inhalation Aerosol
Berotec® Forte Inhalation Aerosol
Berotec® Inhalation Solution
Bronalide®
Buscopan®
Catapres®
Combivent® Inhalation Aerosol
Combivent® Inhalation Solution
Dixarit®
Duovent® UDV
Flomax®
Mexitil®
Mirapex®
Oramorph SR™
Paclitaxel Injection
Persantine®

BOEHRINGER INGELHEIM (CANADA) LTD., SELF MEDICATION DIVISION

5180 South Service Rd.
Burlington ON L7L 5H4
Tel.: (905) 637-7800
Toll-free: 1-800-263-9107
Fax: (905) 639-5293

Medical Information:

Tel.: (604) 261-0611
Toll-free: 1-800-958-9966

Orders and Distribution Centres:

Toll-free: 1-800-381-WELL (9355)
Fax: (905) 634-4421
Toll-free Fax: 1-800-665-3405

Dulcolax®

BOEHRINGER MANNHEIM (CANADA) LTD.

see "Hoffmann-La Roche Limited"

BRISTOL LABORATORIES OF CANADA

see "Bristol-Myers Squibb Canada Inc."

BRISTOL-MYERS SQUIBB CANADA INC.

Executive Office:

2365 Côte-de-Liesse Rd.
Montréal QC H4N 2M7
Tel.: (514) 333-3200
Fax: (514) 335-4102

General Information:

Toll-free: 1-800-267-1088

Medical Information: ext. 2269/4302
Adverse Event Reporting: ext. 2274/4215

Toll-free: 1-800-267-1088
Fax: (514) 331-8880

Order Desk:

Toll-free: 1-800-361-7124

Customer Service:

Toll-free: 1-800-267-0005

Bristol Laboratories of Canada

Amikin®
Ampicin®
BiCNU®
Blenoxane®
Buspar®
CeeNU®
Cytoxan®
Desyrel®
Desyrel® Dividose
Duricef™
Ifex®
Lysodren
Megace®
Megace® OS
Mutamycin®
Paraplatin-AQ
Platinol®-AQ
Questran®
Questran® Light
Quibron®-T
Quibron®-T/SR

Sotacor®
Tegopen®
Uromitexan™
Vepesid®
Videx™
Vumon® Parenteral
Yutopar®

Bristol-Myers Squibb

Cefzil™
Maxipime™
Monopril™
Serzone®
Stadol NS™
Taxol™
Zerit™

Bristol-Myers Squibb/Sanofi Canada

Avapro™ [a]
Plavix™ [a,b]

Squibb Canada

Capoten™
Corgard®
Delatestryl®
Delestrogen®
Fungizone® Intravenous
Hydrea®
Modecate®
Modecate® Concentrate
Moditen® Enanthate
Moditen® HCl
Mycostatin® Preparations
Orabase®
Orahesive®
Pravachol®
Pronestyl®
Pronestyl®-SR
Rubramin®

[a]*Discovered by Sanofi Research. Distributed by Bristol-Myers Squibb/Sanofi Canada.*
[b]*Contact Sanofi Canada, Inc. for product information.*

CANDERM PHARMA

5353 Thimens Blvd.
Saint-Laurent QC H4R 2H4
Tel.: (514) 334-3835
Fax: (514) 334-7078
E-mail: mail@canderm.com

Condyline™
Micanol®
NeoStrata™ AHA Preparations
UltraMOP™ Capsules
UltraMOP™ Lotion
Ultraquin™ Preparations

CANGENE CORPORATION

104 Chancellor Matheson Rd.
Winnipeg MB R3T 5Y3
Tel.: (204) 989-6850
Fax: (204) 269-7003

WinRho SDF™

CARNATION NUTRITIONAL PRODUCTS

see "Nestlé, Carnation"

CARTER HORNER INC.

Head Office:

6600 Kitimat Rd.
Mississauga ON L5N 1L9
Tel. (Toronto): (905) 826-6200
Toll-free: 1-800-387-2130
Fax: (905) 826-0389

Customer Service and Ordering:

5485 Ferrier St.
Montréal QC H4P 1M6
Tel. (Montréal): (514) 731-3931
Toll-free: 1-800-361-5541
Toll-free: 1-800-GRAVOL8
(1-800-472-8658)
Fax (Montréal): (514) 738-4124

Medical Information:

Tel.: (514) 731-3931
Toll-free: 1-800-361-5541
Fax: (514) 738-5509

Antiphlogistine Rub A-535
Antiphlogistine Rub A-535 Capsaicin
Antiphlogistine Rub A-535 Ice
Antiphlogistine Rub A-535 No Odour
Atasol® Preparations
Atasol®-8, -15, -30
Bionet®
Butisol® Sodium
Depen®
Diovol®
Diovol® Ex
Diovol Plus®
Diovol Plus® AF
Fermentol®
Gravergol®
Gravol® Preparations
Honvol®
Infantol®
Kemsol®
Maltlevol®/Maltlevol®-12
Maltlevol®-M
Ovol® Preparations
Peptol®
Procytox®
Soma®
Somnol®
Thyro-Block®
Univol®
Urasal®
Vivol®
VōSol®
VōSol® HC

CHARTON LABORATORIES

see "Technilab Inc."

CHATTEM (CANADA) INC.

2220 Argentia Rd.
Mississauga ON L5N 2K7
Tel.: (905) 821-4975
Fax: (905) 821-0544

Acnomel®
Acnomel® Acne Mask
Flexall®
Flexall® Stick
Pamprin®
Pamprin® Extra Strength
Pamprin® PMS

CIBA PHARMACEUTICALS

see "Novartis Pharmaceuticals Canada Inc."

CIBA SELF MEDICATION

see "Novartis Consumer Health Canada Inc."

CIBA VISION CANADA INC.

2150 Torquay Mews
Mississauga ON L5N 2M6
Tel.: (905) 821-4774
Fax: (905) 821-8106

Orders:

Toll-free: 1-888-366-2206

AquaSite™
Atropine
Atropisol®
Carbastat®
E-Pilo®
Gentacidin®
Genteal®
Hypotears®
Hypotears® Eye Ointment
ICAPS®
ICAPS Time Release™
Inflamase® Forte
Inflamase® Mild
Livostin™ Eye Drops
Miocarpine®
Miochol®-E
Ophtrivin-A®
Polycidin™ Eye/Ear Drops
Polycidin™ Ophthalmic Ointment
TearDrops®
Vasocidin®
Vasocon®
Vasocon-A®
Voltaren Ophtha®

CLINTEC

A Division of Baxter Corporation

4 Robert Speck Pkwy
Suite 700
Mississauga ON L4Z 3Y4
Tel.: (905) 270-1125
Toll-free: 1-800-387-8399
Fax: (905) 281-6560

Parenteral Nutrition

Primene®
Travasol®

CONNAUGHT LABORATORIES LIMITED

see "Pasteur Mérieux Connaught Canada"

CRYSTAAL CORPORATION

Subsidiary of Biovail Corporation International

2480 Dunwin Dr.
Mississauga ON L5L 1J9
Tel.: (905) 607-6555
Fax: (905) 607-3555

Ordering Center:

Toll-free (from 8:30 a.m.-7:30 p.m. EST): 1-888-214-6001
Fax (24 hrs a day): (905) 607-3555

Tiazac®

CYTEX PHARMACEUTICALS INC.

5545 Macara St.
Halifax NS B3K 1W1
Tel.: (902) 453-1230
Toll-free: 1-888-453-1230
Fax: (902) 453-5753
E-mail: cytex@netcom.ca

DERMIK LABORATORIES CANADA INC.

Head office:

6205 Airport Rd., Bldg. B
Suite 100
Mississauga ON L4V 1E1
Tel.: (905) 677-6399
Fax: (905) 677-6397

Distribution:

4707, rue Lévy
Ville St-Laurent QC H4R 2P9
Toll-free: 1-800-361-1141
Toll-free Fax: 1-800-267-0329

10 Benzagel® Acne Gel
Benzamycin®
Noritate®
Postacne®
Sulfacet-R®
Vitamin A Acid
Zetar® Preparations

DERMTEK PHARMACEUTICALS LTD.

1600 Trans-Canada Hwy
Dorval QC H9P 1H7
Tel.: (514) 685-3333
Toll-free: 1-800-465-8383
Fax: (514) 685-8828

Acnex®
Dilusol®
Pramox® HC
Reversa® AHA Preparations
Sebcur®
Sebcur/T®
Soluver®
Soluver® Plus

DESBERGERS LIMITED

Head Office & Plant:

8480 Saint-Laurent Blvd.
Montréal QC H2P 2M6
Tel.: (514) 381-5631
Toll-free: 1-800-361-3808
Fax: (514) 383-4493
E-mail: sylviet@rougier.com

Laboratories & Plant:

1000 Industriel Blvd.
Chambly QC J3L 3H9
Tel.: (514) 658-1704

Livingston Distribution Centres Inc.:

320 Edimburgh Dr.
Moncton NB E1C 8P2
Tel.: (506) 857-4960

7403 Progress Way
Delta BC V4G 1E7
Tel.: (604) 940-4116

4441-76th Ave. S.E.
Calgary AB T2C 2G8
Tel.: (403) 279-2700

10 Corinne Court
Vaughan ON L4K 4T7
Tel.: (905) 879-0114

Northwest Drug Co. Ltd
966 Powell St.
Winnipeg MB R3H 0H6
Tel.: (204) 633-9502

Ascofer®
Theophylline Solution

DIOPTIC LABORATORIES
Division of Akorn Pharmaceuticals Canada Ltd.

1405 Denison St.
Markham ON L3R 5V2
Tel.: (905) 513-6393
Toll-free: 1-800-465-3845
Fax: (905) 415-1440/(905) 415-0827

Orders:

Toll-free: 1-800-465-3845

Atropine
Diocaine
Diocarpine
Diochloram
Diodex
Diofluor® Injection
Diofluor Strips®
Diogent Ointment
Diogent Solution
Diomycin
Dionephrine
Diopentolate
Diophenyl-T
Diopred
Dioptimyd
Dioptrol
Diosulf
Diotrope
Fluoracaine™
Tears Encore®
Tim-AK

DISPENSAPHARM
Unit of Monsanto Canada Inc.

2233 Argentia Rd.
Mississauga ON L5N 2X7
Tel.: (905) 819-9666
Fax: (905) 819-9994

LaTour Digital
3333 Côte-Vertu, Suite 202
Ville St-Laurent QC H4R 2N1
Tel.: (514) 856-7470
Toll-free: 1-800-263-1705
Fax: (514) 745-2919

Orders:

Toronto & vicinity:
Tel.: (905) 819-9311
Toll-free: 1-800-263-1705
Fax: (905) 819-9344

Medical Inquiries:

Tel.: (905) 814-2421
Toll-free: 1-800-387-7942

Select™ 1/35

DORMER LABORATORIES INC.

91 Kelfield St., Unit 5
Rexdale ON M9W 5A3
Tel.: (416) 242-6167
Toll-free: 1-800-363-5040
Fax: (416) 242-9487

Cantharone®
Cantharone Plus®
X-Tar®
Z-Plus®

DRAXIS HEALTH INC.

6870 Goreway Dr.
Mississauga ON L4V 1P1
Tel.: (905) 677-5500
Fax: (905) 677-5502

Eldepryl®
Permax®

DUCHESNAY INC.

2925 Industrial Blvd.
Laval QC H7L 3W9
Tel.: (514) 668-5200
Toll-free: 1-888-666-0611
Fax: (514) 668-4173

Diclectin®

DUPONT PHARMA

2655 North Sheridan Way
Suite 180
Mississauga ON L5K 2P8
Tel.: (905) 855-4380
Fax: (905) 855-9278

Customer Service/Order Desk:

Toll-free: 1-800-268-5490
Fax: (905) 855-8876

Medical Information/Adverse Event Reporting:

Toll-free: 1-800-263-5901
Fax: (905) 855-8544

DuPont Pharma

Coumadin® *
Hycodan®
Hycomine®
Hycomine®-S
Intropin®
Narcan®
Nubain®
Numorphan®
Pentaspan®
Percocet®
Percocet®-Demi
Percodan®
Percodan®-Demi
ReVia®
Sinemet®
Sinemet® CR
Symmetrel® (Antiparkinson)
Symmetrel® (Antiviral)
Tridil®
Viaspan™

Endo

Endantadine®
Endocet®
Endodan®
Endo® Levodopa/Carbidopa

**Coumadin and the color and configuration of Coumadin tablets are trademarks of the DuPont Pharmaceutical Company. Any unlicensed use of these trademarks is expressly prohibited.*

ELI LILLY
see "Lilly"

ENDO CANADA INC.
see "DuPont Pharma"

FABRIGEN, INC.

PO Box 507
Pierrefonds QC H9H 4M6
Tel.: (514) 695-3165
Fax: (514) 695-5118

Distributor:

Technilab Inc.
17 800, rue Lapointe
Mirabel QC J7J 1P3
Tel.: (514) 433-7673
Fax: (514) 433-7434

Toll-free (Montréal): 1-800-361-6667;
(Toronto): 1-800-267-9999;
(Vancouver): 1-800-663-5611

Avirax™

FAULDING (CANADA) INC.

334 Aimé-Vincent
Vaudreuil QC J7V 5V5
Tel.: (514) 424-0490
Toll-Free: 1-800-567-2855
Fax: (514) 424-0489
E-mail: science@faulding.com

Customer Service only:

Fax: (514) 424-9247
Toll-free Fax: 1-800-471-9171
E-mail: customer@faulding.com

Acyclovir Sodium Injection
Atracurium Besylate Injection
Bleomycin Sulfate USP
Carboplatin Injection
Cisplatin Injection
Cytarabine Injection
Doxorubicin HCl For Injection USP
Leucovorin Calcium Injection
Methotrexate Sodium Injection USP
Methotrexate Tablets USP
Methylene Blue Injection USP
Methylprednisolone Sodium Succinate for Injection USP
Mitomycin For Injection, USP
Nitroglycerin Injection USP
Pacis™ *
Paraldehyde Injection BP
Pentamidine Isethionate For Injection BP
Pethidine Injection BP
Sodium Thiosulfate Injection USP
Thiamine HCl Injection USP
Trace Elements Solution
Vinblastine Sulfate Injection
Vincristine Sulfate Injection USP

**Manufactured by BioChem Vaccines Inc. Distributed by Faulding (Canada) Inc.*

Orders for controlled drugs must be addressed to:

Faulding (Canada) Inc.
a/s Livingston Pharmaceutical Distribution Ltd.
3015 Brabant-Marineau
Ville St-Laurent QC H4S 1R8
Tel.: (514) 956-1505
Fax: (514) 956-0325

Orders not addressed as above cannot be shipped.

Fentanyl Citrate Injection USP
Morphine Sulfate Injection BP (1 mg/mL and 2 mg/mL)
Morphine Sulfate Injection BP (50 mg/mL)

FERRING INC.

Head Office:

200 Yorkland Blvd., Suite 800
Toronto ON M2J 5C1
Tel.: (416) 490-0121
Toll-free: 1-800-263-4057
Fax: (416) 493-1692

Québec Office:

7333 Place des Roseraies
Suite 100
Anjou QC H1M 2X6
Tel.: (514) 354-3677
Fax: (514) 352-6090

Order Desk:

Metropolitan Toronto:
Tel.: (416) 661-7979
Fax: (905) 879-0123
Ontario:
Toll-Free: 1-800-268-4937
Fax: (905) 879-0123
Metropolitan Montréal:
Tel.: (514) 683-7717
Fax: (514) 683-9805
Quebec:
Toll-Free: 1-800-361-3362
Fax: (514) 683-9805
Atlantic Provinces:
Toll-free: 1-800-268-4937
Fax: (905) 879-0123
Western Canada:
Toll-free: 1-800-661-1237
Fax: (403) 236-9104
Calgary:
Tel.: (403) 236-1787
Fax: (403) 236-9104

Mail Orders:

Ferring Inc.
PO Box 4500
Concord ON L4K 1B6

Caltine®
Cervidil™
Cholecystokinin
DDAVP® Injection
DDAVP® Spray and Rhinyle Nasal Solutions
DDAVP® Tablets
Lutrepulse™
Octostim®
Pressyn®
Quintasa®
Rafton® Liquid
Rafton® Tablets
Secretin

FOURNIER PHARMA INC.

1010 Sherbrooke St. W.
PO Box 16, 19th floor
Montréal QC H3A 2R7
Tel.: (514) 287-1049
Fax: (514) 287-9798

Lipidil Micro®

FROSST

Division of Merck Frosst Canada Inc.

16711 Trans-Canada Hwy, Exit 52
Kirkland QC H9H 3L1

Mailing Address:

PO Box 1005
Pointe-Claire—Dorval QC H9R 4P8
Tel.: (514) 428-7920

Branches:

PO Box 1900
Mississauga ON L5M 2P1
Tel.: (905) 542-3010
Fax: (905) 542-9675

11131 Hammersmith Gate
Richmond BC V7A 5E6
Tel.: (604) 277-1433
Fax: (604) 277-0353

Customer Information Service:

Toll-free (Canada): 1-800-567-2594

Orders:

Toll-free (Canada): 1-800-463-7251

Blocadren®
Dolobid®
Flexeril®
Leritine® Injection
Leritine® Tablets
Ostoforte®
Papaverine HCl
Propyl-Thyracil®
Supres®
Timolide®
282® MEP®
292® Tablets
692® Tablets
Urecholine®
Vaseretic®
Vasotec®
Vasotec® I.V.
Warfilone®
Zocor®

FUJISAWA CANADA INC.

625 Cochrane Dr., Suite 800
Markham ON L3R 9R9
Tel.: (905) 470-7990
Toll-free: 1-800-668-8641
Fax: (905) 470-7799

Adenocard®
Prograf®

GALDERMA CANADA INC.

7300 Warden Ave.
Suite 210
Markham ON L3R 9Z6
Tel.: (905) 944-0717
Toll-free: 1-800-467-2081
Fax: (905) 944-0790
Web site: www.galderma.com

Benzac® AC 5
Benzac® AC 10
Benzac® W Wash 5
Benzac® W Wash 10
Benzac® W5
Benzac® W10
Calmurid®
Calmurid® HC
Desocort®
Differin®
Ionil®
Ionil-T®
Ionil-T® Plus
MetroCream™
MetroGel®
Psorigel®
Sans-Acne®

GEIGY PHARMACEUTICALS

see "Novartis Pharmaceuticals Canada Inc."

GENDERM CANADA INC.

see "Medicis Canada Ltd."

GENPHARM INC.

37 Advance Rd.
Etobicoke ON M8Z 2S6
Tel.: (416) 236-2631
Toll-free: 1-800-668-3174
Fax: (416) 236-2940

Dexiron™
Gen-Alprazolam
Gen-Amantadine (Antiparkinsonian)
Gen-Amantadine (Antiviral)
Gen-Atenolol
Gen-Azathioprine
Gen-Baclofen

Gen-Beclo Aq.
Gen-Bromazepam
Gen-Budesonide Aq.
Gen-Buspirone
Gen-Captopril
Gen-Cimetidine
Gen-Clobetasol
Gen-Clobetasol Scalp Application
Gen-Clomipramine
Gen-Clonazepam
Gen-Cromoglycate Nasal Solution
Gen-Cromoglycate Sterinebs®
Gen-Cycloprine
Gen-Diltiazem
Gen-Diltiazem SR
Gen-Famotidine
Gen-Fibro
Gen-Glybe
Gen-Indapamide
Gen-Medroxy
Gen-Metformin
Gen-Minocycline
Gen-Minoxidil
Gen-Nifedipine
Gen-Nortriptyline
Gen-Oxybutynin
Gen-Pindolol
Gen-Piroxicam
Gen-Ranitidine
Gen-Salbutamol Respirator Solution
Gen-Salbutamol Sterinebs™ P.F.
Gen-Selegiline
Gen-Sotalol
Gen-Tamoxifen
Gen-Temazepam
Gen-Timolol
Gen-Trazodone
Gen-Triazolam
Gen-Valproic
Gen-Verapamil SR

GERMIPHENE CORPORATION

1379 Colborne St. E.
PO Box 1748
Brantford ON N3T 5V7
Tel.: (519) 759-7100
Toll-free: 1-800-265-9931
Fax: (519) 759-1625

Orascan™
Oro-Clense

GLAXO WELLCOME INC.

Head Office:

7333 Mississauga Rd. N.
Mississauga ON L5N 6L4
Tel.: (905) 819-3000
Fax: (905) 819-3099

Bureau d'affaires du Québec:

771, rue Gougeon
Saint-Laurent QC H4T 2B4
Toll-free: 1-800-463-6314
Fax: (514) 738-9391

Customer Response Centre:

Toll-free: 1-800-268-0324
Fax: 1-800-367-9609

Medical Information/Adverse Event Reporting:

Toll-Free: 1-800-668-6051

Order Management/24 Hour Emergency Hospital Ordering Line:

Toll-free: 1-800-387-7374
Fax: 1-800-565-2935

Accounts Receivable Department:

Toll-free Fax: 1-888-224-1050

Alkeran®
Amerge®
Anectine®
Beclodisk®
Beclodisk® Diskhaler®
Becloforte®
Beclovent® Inhaler
Beclovent® Rotacaps®
Beclovent® Rotahaler®
Beconase Aq®
Bretylate®
Ceftin®
Ceptaz®
Cicatrin®
CoActifed® Preparations
Cortisporin®
Daraprim®
Dermovate®
Digibind®
Eltroxin®
Empracet®-30
Empracet®-60
Eumovate®
Exosurf® Neonatal
Flolan®
Flonase®
Flovent® Inhaler/Diskus
Fortaz®
Imitrex® Injection/Tablets
Imitrex® Nasal Spray
Imuran®
Kemadrin®
Lamictal®
Lanoxin®
Lanvis®
Leukeran®
Malarone®
Megral®
Mepron®
Mivacron®
Myleran®
Navelbine®
Neosporin® Preparations
Nimbex®
Nix® Dermal Cream
Nuromax®
Proloprim®
Purinethol®
Pylorid®
Quinidine Sulfate
Raxar™
Retrovir® (AZT™)
Septra®
Septra® DS
Septra® Injection
Serevent®
3TC®
Tracrium®
Ultiva®
Valtrex®
Vasoxyl®
Ventolin® Injection
Ventolin® Oral Liquid
Ventolin®, Ventodisk®, Ventodisk® Diskhaler®, Ventolin® Rotacaps®, Ventolin® Rotahaler®, Ventolin® Respirator Solution, Ventolin® Nebules P F
Viroptic®
Wellbutrin® SR
Wellferon®
Zantac®
Zantac® 75
Zinacef®
Zofran®
Zovirax® Cream
Zovirax® for Injection
Zovirax® Ointment
Zovirax® Oral
Zyloprim®

GLENWOOD LABORATORIES CANADA LTD.

2406 Speers Rd.
Oakville ON L6L 5M2
Tel.: (905) 825-8244
Fax: (905) 825-9543

Bichloracetic Acid®
Diodoquin®
Myotonachol®
Potaba®
Yocon®

HOECHST MARION ROUSSEL CANADA INC.

Head Office:

2150 St-Elzéar Blvd. W.
Laval QC H7L 4A8
Tel.: (514) 331-9220
Toll-free: 1-800-363-6364
Fax: (514) 334-8016

Customer Service and Medical Information:

Toll-free: 1-800-265-7927
Toll-free Fax: 1-800-268-3846

Actinac®
Alertonic®
Allegra™
Altace®
Anandron®
Anzemet™
AVC®
Bentylol®
Cardizem®
Cardizem® CD
Cardizem® SR
Cardizem® Injectable
Cidomycin®
Claforan®
Clomid®
Cophylac®
Diaβeta®
Eltor® 120
Fluotic®
Frisium®
Glucophage®
Lasix®
Lasix® Special
Loprox®
Maxeran®
Mercodol® with Decapryn®
Mersyndol® with Codeine
Nicoderm®
Nicorette®
Nicorette® Plus
Norpramin®
Novahistex® C
Novahistex® DH
Novahistex® DH Expectorant
Novahistex® DM
Novahistex® DM Decongestant
Novahistex® DM Decongestant Expectorant
Novahistine® DH
Novahistine® DM
Novahistine® DM Decongestant
Novahistine® DM Decongestant Expectorant
Orifer®.F
Panocaine®

Pentasa®
Proctosedyl®
Relefact® TRH
Renedil®
Rifadin®
Rifater™
Rythmodan®
Rythmodan®-LA
Sabril®
Seldane®
Sofracort®
Soframycin® Ointment
Soframycin® Ophthalmic
Sofra-Tulle®
Streptase®
Sulcrate®
Sulcrate® Suspension Plus
Supracaine®
Suprefact®
Suprefact® Depot
Surfak®
Surgam®
Surgam® SR
Tenuate®
Tenuate® Dospan®
Topicaine®
Topicort® Preparations
Trental®
Ultracaine® DS
Ultracaine® DS Forte

HOFFMANN-LA ROCHE LIMITED

Head Office:

2455 Meadowpine Blvd.
Mississauga ON L5N 6L7
Tel.: (905) 542-5555
Fax: (905) 542-7130

Customer Service:

Tel.: (905) 542-5500
Toll-Free: 1-800-268-0440

Medical Information:

Canada:
Tel.: (905) 542-5537
Fax: (905) 542-5610
Toll-free: 1-888-ROCHE88
E-mail: medinfo.canada@roche.com

Montréal:
Toll-free: 1-888-8ROCHE8
Fax: (514) 686-7697

Accutane™ Roche®
Activase® rt-PA
Anaprox®
Anaprox® DS
Anexate®
Bactrim™ Roche®
Bezalip®
Cardene®
CellCept®
Cytovene® Capsules
Cytovene® Injection
Dalmane®
Demadex®
Fansidar®
Fluorouracil Roche®
Hivid®
Inhibace®
Invirase™
Lariam®
Lectopam®
Librax®
Manerix®
Mobiflex®
Mogadon®
Naprosyn®
Nipride®
Nitoman®
Nutropin®
Nutropin® Aq
Ostac®
Prolopa®
Protropin®
Pulmozyme™
Redoxon®
Redoxon-B®
Redoxon-Cal®
Rhinalar®
Rivotril®
Rocaltrol®
Rocephin
Roferon®-A
Soriatane™
Synalar®
Tasmar™
Ticlid®
Toradol®
Toradol® IM
Valium® Roche® Injection
Valium® Roche® Oral
Versed®
Vesanoid™

IAF BIOVAC INC.

see "BioChem Vaccines"

ICN CANADA LTD.

1956 Bourdon St.
Montréal QC H4M 1V1
Tel.: (514) 744-6792
Toll-Free: 1-800-361-1448
Fax: (514) 744-1842
Web site: www.icncanada.com

Order Desk:

Toll-free: 1-800-361-4261
Toll-free Fax: 1-800-361-4266

Allerdryl®
Benuryl™
Bustab®
Carbolith™
C.E.S.®
Clonapam
Cortisone Acetate—ICN
Dexasone®
Duonalc®
Duonalc-E® Mild
Duonalc®-E Solution
Efudex®
Eldopaque™
Eldopaque™ Forte
Eldoquin™
Eldoquin™ Forte
Etibi®
Formulex®
Glycon
Hycort™
Isotamine®
Loperacap
Mestinon®
Mestinon®-SR
M.O.S.™
M.O.S.-SR™
M.O.S.-Sulfate
Multi-Tar® Plus
Nemasol Sodium®—ICN
Nitrazadon
Norventyl
Oxsoralen™
Oxsoralen-Ultra™
Oxybutyn
Oxyderm™ 5%
Oxyderm™ 10% and 20%
Phenazo™
Procyclid™
Propanthel™
Prostigmin® Preparations
Rofact™
Rylosol
S.A.S.™
Solaquin™
Solaquin™ Forte
Tebrazid™
Tensilon®
Trazorel
Trisoralen™
Tryptan™
Ulcidine®
Viquin Forte®
Virazole™ (lyophilized)
Winpred™

IMMUNO (CANADA) LTD.

see "Baxter Corporation "

JANSSEN-ORTHO INC.

19 Green Belt Dr.
Toronto ON M3C IL9
Tel.: (416) 449-9444
Toll-free: 1-800-567-5667
Fax: (416) 449-2658

Medical Information:

Toll-free: 1-800-567-3331

Pharmacovigilance:

Tel.: (416) 382-5105
Fax: (416) 449-5248

Alfenta®
Cyclen®
Duragesic®
Duralith®
Eprex®
Ergamisol®
Floxin™
Gyne-T® Intrauterine Copper Contraceptive
Gyne-T® 380 Slimline Intrauterine Copper Contraceptive
Haldol®
Haldol® LA
Imodium® Caplets, Capsules
Leustatin®
Levaquin®
Livostin® Nasal Spray
Micronor®
Motilium®
Nizoral® Cream
Nizoral® Tablets
Orap®
Ortho® 0.5/35
Ortho® 1/35
Ortho® 7/7/7
Ortho® 10/11
Ortho-Cept®
Orthoclone OKT® 3
Ortho® Dienestrol
Ortho-Novum® 1/50
Pancrease®
Pancrease® MT
Prepulsid®
Renova®
Retin-A®
Risperdal® Oral Solution
Risperdal® Tablets
Sporanox® Capsules
Sporanox® Oral Solution
Sufenta®
Sultrin®

Terazol®
Tolectin®
Topamax®
Tri-Cyclen®
Tylenol® with Codeine NO. 2
Tylenol® with Codeine NO. 3
Tylenol® with Codeine NO. 4
Tylenol® with Codeine Elixir
Vermox®

JANSSEN PHARMACEUTICA
see "Janssen-Ortho Inc."

JOHNSON & JOHNSON • MERCK CONSUMER PHARMACEUTICALS OF CANADA
890 Woodlawn Rd. W.
Guelph ON N1K 1A5
Tel.: (519) 826-6300
Toll-free: 1-888-730-4636
Fax: (519) 826-6301

Baciguent®
Entrophen®
Fleet Enema®
Fleet Enema® Mineral Oil
Fleet® Phospho®-Soda
Hismanal®
Kaopectate®
MSD® Enteric Coated ASA
Nicotrol®
Parafon Forte®
Parafon Forte® C8
Pepcid AC®
Periactin®
222® AF
222® Tablets

JOUVEINAL INC.
see "Axcan Pharma Inc."

KEY
Division of Schering Canada Inc.
3535 Trans-Canada Hwy
Pointe-Claire QC H9R 1B4
Tel.: (514) 426-7300; Telex: 05-821657
Fax: (514) 695-7641
Medical Information only:
Toll-free: 1-800-463-5442
Toll-free Fax: 1-800-369-3090
E-mail: med-afrs@schering.ca

K-Dur®
Nitro-Dur®

KNOLL PHARMA INC.
100 Allstate Pkwy, Suite 600
Markham ON L3R 6H3
Tel.: (905) 475-7070
Medical Information: Ext. 228/231
Fax: (905) 475-3064
All orders to Livingston Healthcare Services Inc.:
Atlantic Provinces:
320 Edimburgh Dr.
Moncton NB E1E 2L1
Mailing address:
PO Box 1010
Moncton NB E1C 8P2
Tel.: (506) 857-4960
Toll-Free: 1-800-561-3933
Fax: (506) 857-4970
Quebec:
Livingston Healthcare Services Inc.
3015 Brabant-Marineau
Saint-Laurent QC H4S 1R8
Tel. (Administration): (514) 956-1505;
(Order Desk): (514) 956-0768
Toll-free (Order Desk): 1-800-361-3362
Fax: (514) 956-0325
Ontario:
10 Corinne Court
Vaughan ON L4K 4T7
Tel.: (416) 661-7979
Inquiries: (905) 879-0114
Toll-Free: 1-800-268-4937
Fax: (905) 879-0123
Manitoba and the Lakehead:
989-A Keewatin St.
Winnipeg MB R2X 2X4
Tel.: (204) 633-2621
Toll-Free: 1-800-665-7315
Fax: (204) 694-2380
Alberta and Saskatchewan:
4441-76th Ave. S.E. West Building
Calgary AB T2C 2G8
Tel.: (403) 200-1707
Toll-Free: 1-800-661-1237
Fax: (403) 236-9104
British Columbia:
7403 Progress Way
Delta BC V4G 1E7
Tel.: (604) 940-4116
Toll-free: 1-800-661-1237
Fax: (604) 940-4102

Akineton®
Amatine®
Choloxin®
Chymodiactin®
Dilaudid®
Dilaudid-HP®
Dilaudid-HP-Plus®
Dilaudid-XP®
Dilaudid® Sterile Powder
Froben®
Froben SR®
Isoptin®
Isoptin® I.V.
Isoptin® SR
Kadian®
Mavik™
Rythmol®
Santyl®
SSD™
Synthroid®
Tarka®
Viprinex®

LABCATAL INC.
3750 East Cremazie Blvd.
Suite 408
Montréal QC H2A 1B6
Tel.: (514) 593-5504
Toll-free: 1-800-667-6544
Fax: (514) 593-1484
E-mail: labcatal@microtec.net

Oligosol®, Copper
Oligosol®, Copper-Gold-Silver
Oligosol®, Magnesium
Oligosol®, Manganese
Oligosol®, Manganese-Cobalt
Oligosol®, Manganese-Copper
Oligosol®, Zinc-Nickel-Cobalt

LEE-ADAMS LABORATORIES
Division of Pharmascience Inc.
8400 Darnley Rd.
Montréal QC H4T 1M4
Tel.: (514) 340-1114
Fax: (514) 342-7764
Service Office:
8521-132nd St.
Surrey BC V3W 4N8
Tel.: (604) 929-2521
Fax: (604) 929-0232

LEO PHARMA INC.
555 Kingston Rd. W.
Ajax ON L1S 6M1
Tel.: (905) 427-8828
Toll-free: 1-800-668-7234
Fax: (905) 427-8161
Medical Information:
Toll-free: 1-800-263-4218
Order Depots:
c/o Livingston Distribution Centres Inc.
10 Corinne Court
Vaughan ON L4K 4T7
Tel.: (905) 879-0114
Toll-free: 1-800-268-4937
Montréal QC
Tel.: (514) 683-9150
Toll-free: 1-800-361-3362/8/9
Calgary AB
Tel.: (403) 253-8216
Toll-free: 1-800-661-1237

Burinex®
Dovonex®
Fucidin® Cream
Fucidin® Intertulle
Fucidin® I.V.
Fucidin® Ointment
Fucidin® Suspension
Fucidin® Tablets
Heparin Leo®
Innohep®
One-Alpha®
Pondocillin®
Selexid®

LIGAND PHARMACEUTICALS (CANADA) INC.
10275 Science Center Dr.
San Diego, California
U.S.A. 92121
Tel.: (619) 535-3900
Fax: (619) 550-7707

Photofrin®
Proleukin®

ELI LILLY CANADA INC.
3650 Danforth Ave.
Scarborough ON M1N 2E8
Tel.: (416) 694-3221
Toll-free: 1-800-268-4446
Fax.: (416) 699-7274
Customer Service & Medical Information: (Hours of Operation: Monday to Friday, 8:00 a.m.-6:00 p.m EST)
Tel.: (416) 693-3510
Toll-free: 1-888-545-5972
Toll-free Fax: 1-888-898-2961

Amytal®
Aventyl®
Axid®
Brietal Sodium®

Ceclor®
Cesamet®
Darvon-N®
Dobutrex®
Eldisine® Injection
Ethyol®
Evista™
Gemzar®
Glucagon Injection
Hexalen®
Humalog™
Humatrope®
Humulin®
Iletin®
Iletin® II Pork
Ilosone®
Keflex®
Keflin®
Kefurox®
Kefzol®
Mandol®
Nalfon®
Nebcin®
Neutrexin®
Prozac®
Reopro™
Tapazole®
Tazidime®
Tes-Tape®
Vancocin®
Velbe®
Zyprexa®

LUNDBECK CANADA INC.

413 St-Jacques St. W.
Suite FB-230
Montréal QC H2Y 1N9
Tel.: (514) 844-8515
Fax: (514) 844-5495

Clopixol®
Clopixol-Acuphase®
Clopixol® Depot
Fluanxol® Depot Injection
Fluanxol® Tablets

MALLINCKRODT MEDICAL INC.

7500 Trans-Canada Hwy
Pointe-Claire QC H9R 5H8
Tel.: (514) 695-1220
Toll-Free: 1-800-361-7360
Fax: (514) 695-1889

7400 MacPherson Dr., Suite 100
Burnaby BC V5J 5B6
Tel.: (604) 435-3234
Fax: (604) 432-9289

Conray®-30
Conray®-43
Conray®-60
Cysto-Conray®
Cysto-Conray® II
Hexabrix® 200
Hexabrix® 320
MD-76®
Optiray®
Telebrix® 38 Oral

MAY & BAKER PHARMA

Head Office and Orders:

4707, rue Lévy
Ville St-Laurent QC H4R 2P9
Tel.: (514) 856-8300
Toll-free: 1-800-361-5870
Toll-free Fax: 1-800-267-0329

Oruvail®

McNEIL CONSUMER PRODUCTS COMPANY

890 Woodlawn Rd. W.
Guelph ON N1K 1A5
Tel.: (519) 836-6500
Toll-Free: 1-800-265-7323
Fax: (519) 826-6200

Imodium® Caplets, Oral Solution
Lactaid®
Micatin® *
Monistat® 7 Cream
Monistat® 7 Vaginal Suppositories
Monistat® 7 Dual-Pak® Package
Monistat® Derm Cream
Monistat® 3 Dual-Pak® Package
Monistat® 3 Vaginal Ovules
Motrin® (Children's)
Motrin ® IB
Nizoral® Shampoo
Tylenol®
Tylenol® Aches and Strains Medication
Tylenol® Allergy Sinus Medication
Tylenol® Cold Medications
Tylenol® Cough Medication
Tylenol® Decongestant
Tylenol® Flu Medication
Tylenol® Sinus Medication
Tylenol® with Codeine NO. 1
Tylenol® with Codeine NO. 1 Forte

**Registered trademark of Pharmacia & Upjohn Company*

McNEIL PHARMACEUTICAL

see "Janssen-Ortho Inc."

MEAD JOHNSON NUTRITIONALS™

Division of Bristol-Myers Squibb Canada Inc.

Executive Office:

333 Preston Ave.
Ottawa ON K1S 5N4
Tel.: (613) 567-3536
Toll-free: 1-800-263-7464
Fax: (613) 239-3996

Enfalac Lytren®
Enfalac Nutramigen®
Enfalac Pregestimil®
Enfalac ProSobee®
Fer-In-Sol®
Isocal®
Isocal® HN
Isocal® with Fibre
Lipisorb®
Lofenalac®
M.C.T.® Oil
Portagen®
Sustacal®
Tempra®

MEDIC LABORATORY LTD

2925 Industrial Blvd.
Laval QC H7L 3W9
Tel.: (514) 668-9750
Toll-free: 1-800-361-8559
Fax: (514) 668-3585

MEDICAN PHARMA INC.

1315 Bishop St. N., Suite 170
Cambridge ON N1R 6Z2
Tel.: (519) 740-6154
Toll-free: 1-800-727-2076
Fax: (519) 740-6941

Anthraforte®
Anthranol®
Anthrascalp®
Scabene®

MEDICIS CANADA LTD.

355 McCaffrey St.
St-Laurent QC H4T 1Z7
Tel.: (514) 738-1808
Toll-free: 1-800-661-DERM (3376)
Fax: (514) 738-5435

Lidemol®
Lidex®
Meted® Shampoo
Occlusal™
Occlusal™- HP
Pentrax®
Pramegel™
Salac™
Topsyn®
Zonalon
Zostrix®
Zostrix® H.P.

MEDISAN PHARMACEUTICALS AB

AR4, S-741 74 Uppsala
Sweden
Tel.: +46 18 34 99 00
Fax: +46 18 34 94 95

Hyskon® *
Rheomacrodex® *

**Distributed in Canada by Pharmacia & Upjohn Inc.*

MERCK SHARP & DOHME CANADA

Division of Merck Frosst Canada Inc.

16711 Trans-Canada Hwy, Exit 52
Kirkland QC H9H 3L1

Mailing Address:

PO Box 1005
Pointe-Claire—Dorval QC H9R 4P8
Tel.: (514) 428-7920

Branches:

PO Box 1900
Mississauga ON L5M 2P1
Tel.: (905) 542-3010
Fax: (905) 542-9675

11131 Hammersmith Gate
Richmond BC V7A 5E6
Tel.: (604) 277-1433
Fax: (604) 277-0353

Customer Information Service:

Toll-free (Canada): 1-800-567-2594

Orders:

Toll-free (Canada): 1-800-463-7251

Aldomet® Injection
Aldomet® Tablets
Aldoril®-15
Aldoril®-25
Aminohippurate Sodium
Antivenin (Latrodectus Mactans)
Benemid®
Cogentin®
Cortone® Suspension
Cortone® Tablets
Cosmegen®
Cozaar®
Crixivan®
Cuprimine®
Decadron® Phosphate Injection

Decadron® Tablets
Edecrin®/Sodium Edecrin®
Elavil®
Elavil Plus®
Fosamax®
HydroDIURIL®
Hydropres®-25
Hyzaar®
Indocid®
Indocid® SR
Indocid® P.D.A.
Lacrisert®
Mefoxin®
Mevacor®
Midamor®
Mintezol®
M-M-R® II
Moduret®
Mumpsvax®
Mustargen®
Noroxin®
Noroxin® Ophthalmic Solution
PedvaxHIB®
Pepcid®
Pepcid® I.V.
Pneumovax® 23
Primaxin®
Prinivil®
Prinzide®
Propecia®
Proscar®
Recombivax HB®
Singulair®
Timoptic®
Timoptic-XE®
Timpilo®
Triavil®
Triptil®
Trusopt®
Vaqta®

MILEX PRODUCTS, INC.

Head Office:

4311 N. Normandy
Chicago IL 60634-1403
Toll-free: 1-800-621-1278
Toll-free Fax: 1-800-972-0696
Web site: www.milexproducts.com

Amino-Cerv

NADEAU LABORATORY LIMITED

Head Office & Plant:

8480 Saint-Laurent Blvd.
Montréal QC H2P 2M6
Tel.: (514) 381-5631
Toll-Free: 1-800-361-3808
Fax: (514) 383-4493
E-mail: sylviet@rougier.com

Laboratories & Plant:

1000 Industriel Blvd.
Chambly QC J3L 3H9
Tel.: (514) 658-1704

Livingston Distribution Centres Inc.:

320 Edimburgh Dr.
Moncton NB E1C 8P2
Tel.: (506) 857-4960

7403 Progress Way
Delta BC V4G 1E7
Tel.: (604) 940-4116

4441-76th Ave. S.E.
Calgary AB T2C 2G8
Tel.: (403) 279-2700

10 Corinne Court
Vaughan ON L4K 4T7
Tel.: (905) 879-0114

Northwest Drug Co. Ltd
966 Powell St.
Winnipeg MB R3H 0H6
Tel.: (204) 633-9502

Creo-Rectal®
Glycerin Suppositories
Nadopen-V®
Nadostine® Preparations

NESTLÉ, CARNATION

25 Sheppard Ave. W.
North York ON M2N 6S8
Tel.: (416) 512-9000
Fax: (416) 218-2691

Alsoy™
Follow-Up®
Follow-Up Soy®
Good Start®

NEXSTAR PHARMACEUTICALS, INC.

Head Office:

5961 Hemingway Rd.
Mississauga ON L5M 5M1
Tel.: (905) 812-0743
Fax: (905) 812-0742

Manufacturing Site:

NeXstar Pharmaceuticals, Inc.
650 Cliffside Dr.
San Dimas, California 91773 U.S.A.

Customer Service and Order Department:

NeXstar Pharmaceuticals, Inc.
155 Orenda Rd., Unit 3
Brampton ON L6W 1W3
Tel.: (905) 451-5243
Toll-free: 1-888-756-1745
Fax: 1-800-786-1967

Orders received before 3:00 p.m. EST are picked up by carrier the same day. Orders not addressed as above cannot be shipped.

Medical Emergency:

For Medical Emergencies 24 hours a day, 7 days a week, including holidays, please call: 1-800-403-3945.

DaunoXome®

NOVARTIS CONSUMER HEALTH CANADA INC.

2233 Argentia Rd., Suite 205
Mississauga ON L5N 2X7
Tel.: (905) 812-4100
Fax: (905) 821-4936

Customer Service & Order Desk:

Tel.: 1-800-689-9916
Fax: 1-800-926-6693

Medical Information:

Tel.: 1-888-788-8181
Fax: (905) 812-4058

Habitrol® Toll-free Support Line:

Tel.: 1-888-227-5777
Web site: www.habitrol.com

Antibiotic Cold Sore Ointment
Aquasol® E
Aquasol® E TPGS
2.5 Benzagel® Acne Gel
5 Benzagel® Acne Gel
2.5 Benzagel® Acne Lotion
5 Benzagel® Acne Lotion
5 Benzagel® Acne Wash
Bradosol®
Bradosol® Extra-Strength
Calcium-Sandoz®
Calsan®
Delsym®
Desenex®
Doan's Backache Pills
Dycholium®
Eurax®
Ex-Lax® Chocolated Pieces
Ex-Lax® Sugar Coated Pills
Ex-Lax® Extra Strength Sugar Coated Pills
Ex-Lax® Stool Softener
Gas-X®
Gas-X® Extra Strength
Glysennid®
Gramcal®
Habitrol®
Lipactin®
Maalox®
Maalox® HRF
Maalox H2 Acid Controller™
Maalox® Plus
Maalox® Plus Extra Strength
Maalox® TC
NeoCitran Preparations
Nupercainal® Cream
Nupercainal® Ointment
Otrivin®
Phenergan® Expectorant with Codeine
Phenergan® Preparations
Prodiem® Plain
Prodiem® Plus
Pyribenzamine®
Saline from Otrivin®
Slow-Fe®
Slow-Fe Folic®
Tavist®
Tavist-D®
Triaminic® Cold and Allergy Syrup
Triaminic® Cold & Fever
Triaminic® Tablets
Triaminic® DM Daytime
Triaminic® DM Expectorant
Triaminic® DM Long Lasting for Children
Triaminic® DM Nighttime
Triaminic® Expectorant
Triaminic® Expectorant DH
Triaminic® Oral Pediatric Drops
Triaminicin®
Triaminicol® DM
Tussaminic® C Forte
Tussaminic® C Ped
Tussaminic® DH Forte
Tussaminic® DH Ped
Webber® Calcium Carbonate
Webber® Vitamin E Ointment

NOVARTIS NUTRITION CORPORATION

111 Consumers Dr.
Whitby ON L1N 5Z5
Toll-free: 1-800-265-6254
Fax: (905) 430-4272

Citrotein®
Compleat® Modified
Isosource®
Isosource® HN
Isosource® VHN
Meritene®
Novasource™ Renal

Nutrisource®
Nutrisource® HN
Resource®
Resource® Diabetic
Resource® Fruit Beverage
Resource® Just For Kids
Resource® Plus
Sandosource™ Peptide
Tolerex®
Vivonex® Pediatric
Vivonex® Plus
Vivonex® T.E.N.

NOVARTIS PHARMACEUTICALS CANADA INC.

Head Office:

PO Box 385
Dorval QC H9R 4P5
Tel.: (514) 631-6775
Fax: (514) 631-1867

Distribution, Customer Service and Order Desk:

111 Consumers Dr.
Whitby ON L1N 5Z5
Toll-free: 1-800-465-2244
Fax: 1-800-435-4423 or (905) 666-4711

Drug Information Centre:

Tel.: (514) 631-6775
Toll-free: 1-800-363-8883
Fax: (514) 633-7054

Clozaril Support and Assistance Network (CSAN):

Tel.: (514) 631-6775
Toll-free: 1-800-267-2726
Fax: 1-800-465-1312

Special Access Program (Dorval, Québec):

Tel.: (514) 631-6775
Toll-free: 1-800-263-6775
Fax: (514) 631-9303

Anafranil®
Anturan®
Apresoline®
Aredia®
Bellergal® Spacetabs®
Cafergot®
Cafergot-PB®
Clozaril®
Cytadren
Desferal®
Dihydroergotamine (DHE)
Diovan®
Estracomb®
Estraderm®
Femara®
Fiorinal®
Fiorinal®C 1/4, 1/2
Foradil®
Hydergine®
Hygroton®
Lamisil®
Lescol®
Lioresal®
Lioresal® Intrathecal
Locacorten® Vioform®
Locacorten® Vioform® Eardrops
Locasalen®
Lopresor®
Lotensin®
Ludiomil®
Mellaril®
Metandren®
Migranal®
Neoral®/Sandimmune® I.V.
Parlodel®
Phosphate-Novartis
Restoril®
Rimactane®
Ritalin®
Ritalin® SR
Rogitine®
Sandomigran®
Sandomigran DS®
Sandostatin®
Sanorex®
Sansert®
Ser-Ap-Es®
Serentil®
Serpasil®
Sintrom®
Slow-K®
Slow-Trasicor®
Synacthen® Depot
Tegretol®
Tofranil®
Transderm-Nitro®
Transderm-V®
Trasicor®
Vioform®
Vioform® Hydrocortisone
Viskazide®
Visken®
Vivelle®
Voltaren®
Voltaren® Rapide
Zaditen®

NOVO NORDISK CANADA INC.

2700 Matheson Blvd. E.
3rd Floor, West Tower
Mississauga ON L4W 4V9
Tel.: (905) 629-4222
Toll-Free (English): 1-800-465-4334; (French): 1-800-361-4191
Fax: (905) 629-8662

Human Insulin (Biosynthetic)

Novolin®ge Lente
Novolin®ge NPH
Novolin®ge NPH Penfill®
Novolin®ge 10/90 Penfill®
Novolin®ge 20/80 Penfill®
Novolin®ge 30/70
Novolin®ge 30/70 Penfill®
Novolin®ge 40/60 Penfill®
Novolin®ge 50/50 Penfill®
Novolin®ge Toronto
Novolin®ge Toronto Penfill®
Novolin®ge Ultralente

Injection Device

NovoFine® 28G
NovoFine® 30G
Novolin-Pen® 1.5
Novolin-Pen® 3

NOVOPHARM LIMITED

30 Novopharm Court
Toronto ON M1B 2K9
Tel.: (416) 291-8876; Telex: 065-25376
Toll-Free: 1-800-268-4127
Fax: (416) 291-1874

Branches:

4-3751 North Fraser Way
Burnaby BC V5J 5G4
Tel.: (604) 431-9300
Toll-Free: 1-800-663-1618
Fax: (604) 431-9199

Bay 7-6020 11th St., S.E.
Calgary AB T2H 2L7
Tel.: (403) 253-6020
Toll-Free: 1-800-661-8469
Fax: (403) 253-6656

7880 Trans-Canada Hwy
Ville St-Laurent QC H4T 1A5
Tel.: (514) 731-6451
Toll-Free: 1-800-361-9586
Fax: (514) 731-6286

21 Frazee Ave.
Dartmouth NS B3B 1Z4
Tel.: (902) 468-6686
Toll-Free: 1-800-565-1593
Fax: (902) 468-1016

133 Hamelin St.,
Winnipeg MB R3T 3Z1
Tel.: (204) 452-0432
Toll-Free: 1-800-665-6686
Fax: (204) 452-0497

Acyclovir Sodium For Injection
Azathioprine Sodium For Injection, USP
Carboplatin Injection
Cefazolin Sodium USP
Cefoxitin Sodium USP
Cytarabine For Injection USP
Daunorubicin Hydrochloride For Injection, USP
Diltiazem Hydrochloride Injection
Dobutamine Hydrochloride Injection
Doxorubicin Hydrochloride Injection
Droperidol Injection, USP
Etoposide Injection
Gentamicin Sulfate Injection USP
Leucovorin Calcium Injection USP
Methotrexate Sodium Injection USP
Mitomycin For Injection USP
Novamilor
Novamoxin®
Novasen
Novo-Acebutolol
Novo-Alprazol
Novo-Ampicillin
Novo-Atenol
Novo-Azt
Novo-Baclofen
Novo-Benzydamine
Novo-Bromazepam
Novo-Buspirone
Novo-Captoril
Novo-Carbamaz
Novo-Cholamine
Novo-Cholamine Light
Novo-Cimetine
Novo-Clobazam
Novo-Clobetasol
Novo-Clonidine
Novo-Clopamine
Novo-Clopate
Novo-Cloxin
Novo-Cromolyn
Novo-Cycloprine
Novo-Cyproterone
Novo-Desipramine
Novo-Difenac®
Novo-Difenac® SR
Novo-Diflunisal
Novo-Diltazem
Novo-Diltazem SR
Novo-Dipiradol
Novo-Domperidone
Novo-Doxepin
Novo-Doxylin
Novo-Famotidine
Novo-5-ASA

Novo-Fluoxetine
Novo-Flurprofen
Novo-Flutamide
Novo-Furantoin
Novo-Gemfibrozil
Novo-Gesic C8, C15, C30
Novo-Gliclazide
Novo-Glyburide
Novo-Hydroxyzin
Novo-Hylazin
Novo-Indapamide
Novo-Ipramide
Novo-Keto
Novo-Keto-EC
Novo-Ketorolac
Novo-Ketotifen
Novo-Levamisole
Novo-Levobunolol
Novo-Lexin®
Novo-Loperamide
Novo-Lorazem®
Novo-Maprotiline
Novo-Medopa®
Novo-Medrone
Novo-Meprazine
Novo-Metformin
Novo-Methacin
Novo-Metoprol
Novo-Mexiletine
Novo-Minocycline
Novo-Mucilax
Novo-Nadolol
Novo-Naprox
Novo-Naprox Sodium
Novo-Naprox Sodium DS
Novo-Nidazol
Novo-Nifedin
Novo-Nortriptyline
Novo-Oxybutynin
Novo-Pen-VK®
Novo-Peridol
Novo-Pindol
Novo-Pirocam®
Novo-Poxide
Novo-Prazin
Novo-Profen®
Novo-Ranidine
Novo-Rythro Encap
Novo-Salmol
Novo-Salmol Inhaler
Novo-Selegiline
Novo Sotalol
Novo-Spiroton
Novo-Spirozine
Novo-Sucralate
Novo-Sundac
Novo-Tamoxifen
Novo-Temazepam
Novo-Tenoxicam
Novo-Terazosin
Novo-Tetra
Novo-Theophyl SR
Novo-Tiaprofenic
Novo-Timol
Novo-Timol Ophthalmic Solution
Novo-Tolmetin
Novo-Trazodone
Novo-Triamzide
Novo-Trimel
Novo-Trimel D.S.
Novo-Tripramine
Novo-Valproic
Novo-Veramil
Novo-Veramil SR
Vincristine Sulfate Injection USP

NU-PHARM INC.

380 Elgin Mills Rd. E.
Richmond Hill ON L4C 5H2
Tel.: (905) 884-0470
Toll-free: 1-800-267-1438 (Canada); 1-800-661-8203 (AB, BC)
Fax: (905) 884-9876

Nu-Acebutolol
Nu-Acyclovir
Nu-Alpraz
Nu-Amilzide
Nu-Amoxi
Nu-Ampi
Nu-Atenol
Nu-Baclo
Nu-Bromazepam
Nu-Buspirone
Nu-Capto
Nu-Carbamazepine
Nu-Cefaclor
Nu-Cephalex
Nu-Cimet
Nu-Clonazepam
Nu-Clonidine
Nu-Cloxi
Nu-Cotrimox
Nu-Cromolyn
Nu-Cyclobenzaprine
Nu-Desipramine
Nu-Diclo
Nu-Diclo-SR
Nu-Diflunisal
Nu-Diltiaz
Nu-Domperidone
Nu-Doxycycline
Nu-Erythromycin-S
Nu-Famotidine
Nu-Fenofibrate
Nu-Fluoxetine
Nu-Flurbiprofen
Nu-Gemfibrozil
Nu-Glyburide
Nu-Hydral
Nu-Ibuprofen
Nu-Indapamide
Nu-Indo
Nu-Ipratropium
Nu-Ketoprofen
Nu-Ketoprofen-E
Nu-Ketoprofen-SR
Nu-Levocarb
Nu-Loraz
Nu-Loxapine
Nu-Medopa
Nu-Mefenamic
Nu-Megestrol
Nu-Metformin
Nu-Metoclopramide
Nu-Metop
Nu-Naprox
Nu-Nifed
Nu-Nifedipine-PA
Nu-Nortriptyline
Nu-Oxybutyn
Nu-Pentoxifylline-SR
Nu-Pen-VK
Nu-Pindol
Nu-Pirox
Nu-Prazo
Nu-Prochlor
Nu-Propranolol
Nu-Ranit
Nu-Salbutamol Solution
Nu-Salbutamol Tablets
Nu-Selegiline
Nu-Sotalol
Nu-Sucralfate
Nu-Sulfinpyrazone
Nu-Sulindac
Nu-Temazepam
Nu-Terazocin
Nu-Tetra
Nu-Tiaprofenic
Nu-Ticlopidine
Nu-Timolol
Nu-Trazodone
Nu-Trazodone-D
Nu-Triazide
Nu-Trimipramine
Nu-Verap
Nu-Zopiclone

NYCOMED AMERSHAM CANADA LIMITED

1166 South Service Rd. W.
Oakville ON L6L 5T7
Tel.: (905) 847-1166
Fax: (905) 847-7790

Hypaque® Parenteral
Omnipaque®
Omniscan®
Visipaque™

ODAN LABORATORIES LTD.

847 McCaffrey St.
St. Laurent QC H4T 1N3
Tel.: (514) 738-5567
Toll-free: 1-800-387-9342
Fax: (514) 738-7150
Toll-free Fax: 1-800-FAX-ODAN

Adasept® Preparations
Anodan™-HC
Biobase™
Biobase-G™
Bioderm®
Colchicine
Ferodan™ Infant Drops
Ferodan™ Syrup
Hexit™
Lidodan™ Endotracheal
Lidodan™ Ointment
Lidodan™ Viscous
Liquor Carbonis Detergens
Nu-Cal
Placebo
Proctodan™-HC
Selax®
Tardan
Targel Preparations
UriSec®
Yohimbine

OPHTAPHARMA CANADA INC.

1100 Crémazie E., Suite 708
Montréal QC H2P 2X2
Tel.: (514) 374-2556
Toll-free: 1-800-661-2556
Fax: (514) 374-4549

Biolon™
Eyestil
Fluorets™
Minims®

ORGANON CANADA LTD.

200 Consilium Place, Suite 700
Scarborough ON M1H 3E4
Tel.: (416) 290-6131
Toll-free: 1-800-387-1326
Fax: (416) 290-6133

E-mail:
organon@organon.srh.akzonobel.nl
Web site: www.organon.ca
Customer Service and Orders only:
All Canada except Quebec:
Toll-free: 1-800-465-7114
Quebec only:
Toll-free: 1-800-663-1326
Fax Orders only:
Fax: (416) 290-5050
Toll-free Fax: 1-888-974-5050
Marvelon Information Line:
Toll-free: 1-800-892-5201

Andriol
Cortrosyn®
Cotazym®
Deca-Durabolin®
Humegon®
Marvelon®
Norcuron®
Orgaran®
Pregnyl®
Puregon™
Zemuron™

ORGANON TEKNIKA INC.

30 North Wind Place
Scarborough ON M1S 3R5
Tel.: (416) 754-4344
Fax: (416) 754-4488
Orders:
Toll-free: 1-800-387-5348
Distribution Centres:
30 North Wind Place
Scarborough ON M1S 3R5
Tel.: (416) 754-4344
Fax: (416) 754-4488
13B-6125 12th St., S.E.
Calgary AB T2H 2K1
Tel.: (403) 253-9453
Fax: (403) 255-8994

Hepalean®
Hepalean®-Lok
Hexadrol® Phosphate Injection
OncoTICE™

ORTHO BIOTECH

see "Janssen-Ortho Inc."

ORTHO PHARMACEUTICAL

see "Janssen-Ortho Inc."

PARKE-DAVIS

Division of Warner-Lambert Canada Inc.

Head Office:
2200 Eglinton Ave. E.
Scarborough ON M1L 2N3
Tel.: (416) 288-2321
Fax: (416) 288-2180
Mailing Address:
PO Box 2200, Station A
Scarborough ON M1K 5C9
Medical Information:
Tel.: (416) 288-2402
Toll-free: 1-800-611-5889
Fax: (416) 701-3053
E-mail: medinfo@wl.com
Sales Offices:
3333 Côte-Vertu, Suite 810
St-Laurent QC H4R 2N1
Tel.: (514) 334-5045
Fax: (514) 334-5462
2200 Eglinton Ave. E.
Scarborough ON M1L 2N3
Tel.: (416) 288-2321
Fax: (416) 288-2180
Customer Service Centres:
PO Box 2200, Station A
Scarborough ON M1K 5C9
Tel. (Toronto local area): (416) 288-2321
Toll-Free: 1-800-387-6577
Fax: (416) 288-2283
Toll-free Fax: 1-800-563-2013
Laboratory:
2337 Parkdale Ave.
Brockville ON K6V 5W5
Tel.: (613) 342-4436
Fax: (613) 342-6584

Accupril™
Accuretic™
Adrenalin®
AMSA P-D™
Anugesic®-HC
Anusol®-HC
Beben®
Celontin®
Cerebyx®
Chloromycetin® Injection
Choledyl®
Choledyl® Expectorant
Choledyl® SA
Coly-Mycin® M Parenteral
Dilantin® Capsules
Dilantin® Infatabs
Dilantin®-30 Pediatric
Dilantin®-125
Ergodryl®
ERYC®
Humatin™
Ketalar®
Lipitor™
Loestrin™ 1.5/30
Lopid®
Mandelamine®
Minestrin™ 1/20
Nardil®
Neurontin™
Nitrostat™
Norlutate®
Ponstan®
Procan™ SR
Pyridium®
Thrombostat™
Thyroid Hormone
Zarontin®

PASTEUR MÉRIEUX CONNAUGHT CANADA

1755 Steeles Ave. W.
North York ON M2R 3T4
Web site: www.pmc-vacc.com
Product Orders:
Tel.: (416) 667-2611
Toll-free: 1-800-268-4171
Fax: (416) 667-2998
Vaccine Information Service:
Tel.: (416) 667-2779
Toll-free: 1-888-621-1146
Fax: (416) 667-2629

Act-HIB®
BCG Vaccine (Freeze-Dried)
Botulism Antitoxin Trivalent Types A, B and E (Equine)
Cholera Vaccine
Diphtheria and Tetanus Toxoids Adsorbed (DT Adsorbed)
Diphtheria and Tetanus Toxoids Adsorbed and Pertussis Vaccine (DPT Adsorbed)
Diphtheria and Tetanus Toxoids Adsorbed and Poliomyelitis Vaccine (DT Polio Adsorbed)
Diphtheria and Tetanus Toxoids Adsorbed and Pertussis Vaccine and Inactivated Poliomyelitis Vaccine (DPT Polio Adsorbed)
Diphtheria Antitoxin (Equine)
Diphtheria Toxoid
Fluzone®
ImmuCyst®
Imogam® Rabies Pasteurized
Inactivated Poliomyelitis Vaccine (Diploid Cell Origin)—IPV
Je-Vax™
Measles Virus Vaccine, Live Attenuated (Dried)
Meningococcal Polysaccharide Vaccine, Groups A, C, Y and W-135 combined, Menomune®
Multitest® CMI
Pentacel™
Pneumococcal Polysaccharide Vaccine Pneumo 23™
Poliovirus Vaccine Live Oral Trivalent
Purified Protein Derivative
Quadracel™
Rabies Vaccine Inactivated (Diploid Cell Origin), Dried
Td Polio Adsorbed (Tetanus and Diphtheria Toxoids and Inactivated Poliomyelitis Vaccine)
Tetanus and Diphtheria Toxoids Adsorbed (Td Adsorbed)
Tetanus Toxoid Adsorbed
Tuberculin Purified Protein Derivative (Mantoux)—Tubersol®
Typhim Vi™
Vaxigrip®
Yellow Fever Vaccine

PFIZER CANADA INC.

17300 Trans-Canada Hwy
Kirkland QC H9J 2M5
Mailing Address:
PO Box 800
Pointe-Claire—Dorval QC H9R 4V2
Tel.: (514) 695-0500
Fax: (514) 426-7423
Medical Information Pharmaceutical Group:
Tel.: 1-800-463-6001
Customer Service Pharmaceutical Group:
Tel.: (514) 426-7430
Toll-free: 1-800-387-4974
Toll-free Fax: 1-800-420-2019
Distribution Centres:
17300 Trans-Canada Hwy
Kirkland QC H9J 2M5
6404-6A St. S.W.
Calgary AB T2H 2B7

Plant:

Pfizer Canada Inc.
Box 3003
Arnprior ON K7S 3H7
Tel.: (613) 623-4221
Fax: (613) 623-1259

Antivert™
Aricept™
Atarax™
Bonamine™
Diabinese™
Diflucan™
Diflucan-150™
Diflucan™ Pediatrics
Feldene™
Lithane®
Minipress™
Navane™
Norvasc™
Sinequan™
Streptomycin Sulfate™
Vibra-Tabs™
Vibra-Tabs™ C-Pak™
Zithromax™
Zoloft™

PFIZER CANADA INC., CONSUMER HEALTH CARE DIVISION

17300 Trans-Canada Hwy
Kirkland QC H9J 2M5

Mailing Address:

PO Box 800
Pointe-Claire—Dorval QC H9R 4V2
Tel.: (514) 695-0500
Fax: (514) 426-6921

Branch:

6404–6A St., S.E.
Calgary AB T2H 2B7
Tel.: (403) 253-7235
Fax: (403) 255-9265

Plant:

Pfizer Canada Inc.
Box 3003
Arnprior ON K7S 3H7
Tel.: (613) 623-4221

Postal address:

PO Box 800
Pointe-Claire—Dorval QC H9R 4V2

Depot:

17300 Trans-Canada Hwy
Kirkland QC H9J 2M5

Combantrin®
GyneCure™
Reactine™
Trosyd™ AF
Trosyd™ J

PHARMACEUTICAL PARTNERS OF CANADA INC.

625 Cochrane Dr., Suite 800
Markham ON L3R 9R9
Tel.: (905) 513-7724
Toll-free: 1–877-821-7724
Fax: (905) 513-0029

Protamine Sulfate Injection
Vasopressin Injection

PHARMACIA & UPJOHN INC.

Head Office:

5100 Spectrum Way
Mississauga ON L4W 5J5
Tel.: (905) 212-8000
Toll-free: 1–800-563-5905
Fax: (905) 212-1212

Customer Service Orders:

Toll-free: 1–800-268-7879
Toll-free Fax: 1–800-361-6978
E-mail:
canada.customerservice@am.pnu.com

After hours (in case of product emergency):

Tel. (English): (416) 441-1504
Tel. (French): (514) 747-7329

Medical Information & Pharmacovigilance:

Toll-free: 1–800-268-7888
E-mail: micapu@am.pnu.com

Montréal Distribution Centre:

1157, ouest Autoroute Laval
Chomedy, Laval QC H3L 3W3
Tel.: (450) 967-2448
Fax: (450) 967-2445

Toronto Distribution Centre:

861 York Mills Rd.
Don Mills ON M3B 1Y2

Vancouver Distribution Centre:

8184 Winston St.
Burnaby BC V5A 2H5

Adriamycin®
Adrucil®
Ansaid®
Atgam®
Bacitracin
Camptosar™
Caverject™
Colestid®
Cortef®
Cyklokapron®
Cytosar®
Dalacin® C
Dalacin® C Flavored Granules
Dalacin® C Phosphate Sterile Solution
Dalacin® T Topical Solution
Dalacin® Vaginal Cream
Deltasone®
Depo-Medrol®
Depo-Medrol® with Lidocaine
Depo-Provera®
Depo-Testosterone Cypionate
Diazemuls®
Dipentum®
Emcyt®
Estring®
Fragmin®
Gelfilm®
Gelfoam®
Halcion®
Halotestin®
Healon®
Healon® GV
Idamycin®
Intralipid® 10%
Intralipid® 20%
Intralipid® 30%
Kabikinase®
Kaochlor®-10
Kaochlor®-20
Kaon®
Lincocin®
Loniten®
Medrol®
Medrol® Acne Lotion
Medrol® Veriderm® Cream
Microlax®
Motrin®
Mycifradin®
Myciguent®
Mycobutin®
Neo-Cortef® Preparations
Neo-Medrol® Acne Lotion
Neo-Medrol® Veriderm® Cream
Ogen®
Pharmorubicin®
Prepidil® Gel
Prostin® E_2
Prostin® E_2 Vaginal Gel
Prostin® VR
Provera®
Rogaine®
Salagen®
Salazopyrin®
Salazopyrin EN-Tabs®
Solu-Cortef®
Solu-Medrol®
Tamone®
Vamin® 18 Electrolyte-Free
Vamin® N
Xalatan™
Xanax®
Xanax® TS
Zanosar®
Zinecard™

PHARMASCIENCE INC.

8400 Darnley Rd.
Montréal QC H4T 1M4
Tel.: (514) 340-1114
Toll-free: 1–800-363-8805
Fax: (514) 342-7764

Medical Information:

Tel.: (514) 340-5073
Toll-free: 1–888-550-6060

Asaphen
Asaphen E.C.
Canthacur®
Canthacur®-PS
Cedocard® SR
Charcodote®
Charcodote®, Aqueous
Charcodate® TFS
Cromolyn Nasal Solution
Cromolyn Ophthalmic Solution
Dermazin™
Euglucon®
Fluor-A-Day®
Maglucate™
Pediatric Electrolyte
PegLyte™
Phosphates Solution
PMS-Atenolol
PMS-Baclofen
PMS-Benzydamine
PMS-Buspirone
PMS-Cefaclor
PMS-Cephalexin
PMS-Chloral Hydrate
PMS-Cholestyramine
PMS-Cimetidine
PMS-Clobetasol
PMS-Clonazepam
PMS-Desipramine
PMS-Dicitrate™
PMS-Diclofenac
PMS-Diclofenac SR
PMS-Diphenhydramine

PMS-Docusate Calcium
PMS-Docusate Sodium
PMS-Domperidone
PMS-Egozinc
PMS-Egozinc-HC
PMS-Erythromycin
PMS-Fluoxetine
PMS-Fluphenazine Decanoate
PMS-Flutamide
PMS-Gemfibrozil
PMS-Glyburide
PMS-Haloperidol LA
PMS-Hydromorphone
PMS-Hydroxyzine
PMS-Ipratropium
PMS-Isoniazid
PMS-Lactulose
PMS-Lindane
PMS-Lithium Carbonate
PMS-Lithium Citrate
PMS-Loxapine
PMS-Mefenamic Acid
PMS-Methotrimeprazine
PMS-Methylphenidate
PMS-Metoclopramide
PMS-Metoprolol-B
PMS-Metoprolol-L
PMS-Nifedipine
PMS-Notrtiptyline
PMS-Nystatin
PMS-Salbutamol Respirator Solution
PMS-Sennosides
PMS-Sodium Cromoglycate Nebulizer Solution
PMS-Sodium Polystyrene Sulfonate
PMS-Temazepam
PMS-Tiaprofenic
PMS-Timolol
PMS-Trazodone
PMS-Tryptophan
PMS-Valproic Acid
PMS-Valproic Acid E.C.
PMS-Yohimbine
Podofilm®
Rhinaris®
Ridaura®
Secaris®
SH-206
Soflax™
Soflax® Ex
Statex®
Urispas®
Vitinoin™
Wartec®

PROCTER & GAMBLE INC.

PO Box 355, Station A
Toronto ON M5W 1C5
Tel.: (416) 730-4711; Telex: 069-86195
Toll-free: 1-800-668-0152
Fax: (416) 733-0142

Metamucil® Preparations

PROCTER & GAMBLE PHARMACEUTICALS CANADA, INC.

Box 355, Station A
4711 Yonge St.
Toronto ON M5W 1C5
Tel.: (416) 730-4711
Toll-free: 1-800-565-0814
Fax: (416) 730-6049
Order Desk:
Tel.: (519) 622-3000 or
Toll-free: 1-800-265-8676
Medical Information:
Toll-free: 1-800-565-0814
After Hours Emergencies:
Toll-free: 1-800-565-0814

Asacol®
Dantrium® Capsules
Dantrium® Intravenous
Didrocal®
Didronel®
MacroBID®
Macrodantin®
Ultradol™

PRO DOC LIMITÉE

2925 Industrial Blvd.
Laval QC H7L 3W9
Tel.: (514) 668-9750
Toll-free: 1-800-361-8559
Fax: (514) 668-3585

PURDUE FREDERICK INC.

575 Granite Court
Pickering ON L1W 3W8
Tel.: (905) 420-6400
Toll-free: 1-800-387-5349
Fax: (905) 420-1075

Betadine® Topical Preparations
Betadine® Vaginal Preparations
Cardioquin®
Cerumenex®
Codeine Contin®
Entex® LA
Hydromorph Contin®
MS Contin®
MS•IR®
OxyContin®
Phyllocontin®
Phyllocontin®-350
Senokot® Preparations
Senokot®•S
Soropon®
Teejel®
Trilisate®
Uniphyl®
X-Prep®

R&D LABORATORIES, INC.

4640 Admiralty Way, Suite 710
Marina del Rey, California 90292 U.S.A.
Tel.: (310) 305-8053
Toll-free: 1-800-338-9066
Fax: (310) 305-8103

Dia-Vite® *

**Distributed in Canada by Schein Pharmaceutical Canada Inc.*

REED & CARNRICK

Division of Block Drug Company (Canada) Ltd.

7600 Danbro Cres.
Mississauga ON L5N 6L6
Tel.: (905) 542-7282
Fax: (905) 542-7785

Colpermin™
Colyte™
Cortifoam™
Kwellada-P™
Phazyme™ Preparations
Proctofoam™-HC
R & C™ Shampoo/Conditioner
R & C™ II Spray

RHODIAPHARM INC.

4707, rue Lévy
Ville St-Laurent QC H4R 2P9
Tel.: (514) 856-8300
Toll-free: 1-800-361-5870
Toll-free Fax: 1-800-267-0329
Orders/Customer Service:
Toll-free: 1-800-361-1141
Toll-free Fax: 1-800-267-0329

Rho®-Atenolol
Rhodacine®
Rhodiaprox®
Rhodis™
Rhodis-EC™
Rhodis SR™
Rho®-Fluphenazine Decanoate
Rho®-Haloperidol Decanoate
Rho®-Salbutamol
Rhotral
Rhotrimine®
Rhovane®

RHÔNE-POULENC RORER CANADA INC.

Head Office:
4707, rue Lévy
Ville St-Laurent QC H4R 2P9
Tel.: (514) 856-8300
Toll-free: 1-800-361-5870
Toll-free Fax: 1-800-267-0329
Orders/Customer Service:
Toll-free: 1-800-361-1141
Toll-free Fax: 1-800-267-0329
Medical Information:
Tel.: (514) 856-8301
Toll-free: 1-800-361-5870
Narcotic address:
Rhône-Poulenc Rorer Canada Inc.
4707, rue Lévy
Ville St-Laurent QC H4R 2P9
Toll-free: 1-800-361-1141
Toll-free Fax: 1-800-267-0329

Arlidin®
Arlidin® Forte
Azmacort®
Bacid®
Bonefos®
Calcimar®
Cerubidine®
Dagenan®
Duo-C.V.P.®
Ergomar®
Flagyl®
Flagystatin®
Flaxedil®
Gastrolyte®
Imovane® a
Intal® Inhaler/Intal® Syncroner®
Intal® Spincaps®/Intal® Nebulizer Solution
Ionamin®
Kidrolase®
Largactil®
Lovenox®
Majeptil®
M-Eslon®
Multipax®
M.V.I.®-12 (Multivitamin Infusion)
Myochrysine®
Nalcrom®
Nasacort™

Nasacort® Aq
Neuleptil®
Nitrol®
Nitrolingual Pumpspray
Nitrolingual® Spray
Nitrong® SR
Nozinan®
Omni-Tuss®
Oncaspar®
Orudis®
Orudis® E
Orudis® SR
Panectyl®
Parsitan®
Pediapred®
Pentacarinat®
Phenergan® Injectable
Piportil L4®
Rovamycine®
Sectral®
Slo-Bid®
Stemetil®
Suprax®
Surmontil®
Synvisc® [b]
Tamofen®
Taxotere®
Theo-SR®
Tilade®
Tussionex®
Vaponefrin®
Zaroxolyn®

[a]*Imovane 5 mg: Developed and manufactured by Rhône-Poulenc Rorer Canada Inc. Distributed by ICN Canada Ltd.*

[b]*Developed by Biomatrix Inc. and manufactured by Biomatrix Medical Canada Inc. Distributed by Rhône-Poulenc Rorer Canada Inc.*

RHO-PHARM INC.

4707, rue Lévy
Ville St-Laurent QC H4R 2P9
Tel.: (514) 856-8300
Toll-free: 1-800-361-5870
Toll-free Fax: 1-800-267-0329
Orders/Customer Service:
Toll-free: 1-800-361-1141
Toll-free Fax: 1-800-267-0329

Rhovail®

RHOXALPHARMA INC.

4707, rue Lévy
Ville St-Laurent QC H4R 2P9
Tel.: (514) 856-8300
Toll-free: 1-800-361-5870
Toll-free Fax: 1-800-267-0329
Orders/Customer Service:
Toll-free: 1-800-361-1141
Toll-free Fax: 1-800-267-0329

Rho®-Clonazepam
Rho®-Loperamide
Rho®-Metformin
Rho®-Nitrazepam
Rho®-Sotalol

LABORATOIRE RIVA INC.

660 Industriel Blvd.
Blainville QC J7C 3V4
Tel.: (514) 434-7482/(514) 389-6701
Toll-free: 1-800-363-7988
Fax: (514) 434-2500

Calcite 500
Calcite D-500
Dalmacol
Doxycin
Lomine
Minox
Rectogel
Rectogel HC
Rivanase Aq.
Riva-Senna
Rivasol
Rivasol HC
Suplevit
Theochron® SR
Vita 3B
Vita 3B+C

RIVEX OPHTHALMICS

3-305 Industrial Parkway South
Aurora ON L4G 6X7
Tel.: (905) 841-2300
Toll-free: 1-800-784-0975
Fax: (905) 841-2244
Toll-free Fax: 1-800-784-0976

Artificial Tears
Atropine Sulfate
Dexamethasone Sodium Phosphate
Erythromycin
Eye Drops
EyeWash
Gentamicin Sulfate
Levobunolol Hydrochloride
Pilocarpine Hydrochloride
Prednisolone Sodium Phosphate Forte
Red Away®
Tropicamide

RIVEX PHARMA INC.

3-305 Industrial Parkway South
Aurora ON L4G 6X7
Tel.: (905) 841-2300
Toll-free: 1-800-784-0975
Fax: (905) 841-2244
Toll-free Fax: 1-800-784-0976

Isoprinosine®
Klean-Prep®
Lactrase®
Levsin®
Normacol®
Pre-Pen®
Pro-Lax®
Revitalose-C-1000®

ROBERTS PHARMACEUTICAL CANADA INC.

400 Iroquois Shore Rd.
Oakville ON L6H 1M5
Tel.: (905) 337-3538
Toll-free: 1-800-268-2772
Fax: (905) 337-3539
Customer Enquiries:
Toll-free: 1-800-268-2772
Adverse Event Reporting:
Toll-free: 1-800-268-2772

Advantage 24™
Agrylin™
Alcojel®
Allenburys® Basic Soap
Amyl Nitrite
Ascorbic Acid
Bacitracin Zinc
Barriere™
Barriere-HC®
Betnesol® Preparations
Betnovate® Preparations
Cheracol®
Citrocarbonate®
Colace®
Dequadin® Preparations
Duvoid®
Eminase®
Entacyl®
Ephedrine HCl
Estrace®
Florinef®
Glaxal® Base
Grisovin® FP
K-Lyte®
K-Lyte®/Cl
Mucomyst®
Mycil®
Peri-Colace®
Prenavite®
Pro-Banthine®
Propaderm®
Replens®
Rimso®-50
Slow-Mag™
Stilbestrol
Trandate®

ROCHE

see "Hoffmann-La Roche Limited"

ROSS LABORATORIES

see "Abbott Laboratories Limited"

ROUGIER INC.

Distributor for:
Desbergers Ltd.
Nadeau Laboratory Ltd.
Rodeca Inc.
Welcker-Lyster Ltd.
Head Office & Plant:
8480 Saint-Laurent Blvd.
Montréal QC H2P 2M6
Tel.: (514) 381-5631
Toll-Free: 1-800-361-3808
Fax: (514) 383-4493
E-mail: sylviet@rougier.com
Laboratories & Plant:
1000 Industriel Blvd.
Chambly QC J3L 3H9
Tel.: (514) 658-1704
Livingston Distribution Centres Inc.:
320 Edimburgh Dr.
Moncton NB E1C 8P2
Tel.: (506) 857-4960
7403 Progress Way
Delta BC V4G 1E7
Tel.: (604) 940-4116
4441-76th Ave. S.E.
Calgary AB T2C 2G8
Tel.: (403) 279-2700
10 Corinne Court
Vaughan ON L4K 4T7
Tel.: (905) 879-0114
Northwest Drug Co. Ltd.
966 Powell St.
Winnipeg MB R3H OH6
Tel.: (204) 633-9502

Balminil® Camphorub
Balminil® Decongestant
Balminil® DM
Balminil® DM Children

Balminil® DM + Decongestant
Balminil® DM + Decongestant + Expectorant
Balminil® DM + Expectorant
Balminil® Expectorant
Citro-Mag®
Codeine Phosphate
Fermalac®
Fermalac® Vaginal
Glucodex®
Koffex® DM
Lanohex® Skin Cleanser
Magnesium-Rougier
Proviodine®
Quinate
Quinobarb®
Theo-Bronc
Yohimbine

SABEX INC.

145 Jules-Léger Rd.
Boucherville QC J4B 7K8
Tel.: (514) 596-0000
Toll-Free: 1-800-361-3062
Fax: (514) 596-1460

Climacteron®
Cortamed®
Cortrimyxin®
Haloperidol LA
Hydromorphone Hydrochloride
Infufer®
Morphine HP®
Nova Rectal®
Oligofer®
Optimyxin®
Optimyxin Plus®
Pentamycetin®
Pentamycetin®/HC
Penta-Thion®
Penta/3B®
Penta/3B® Plus
Penta/3B® + C
Protamine Sulfate Injection
Revitonus® C-1000
Supeudol®

SANDOZ CANADA INC.

see "Novartis Pharmaceuticals Canada Inc."

SANDOZ CANADA INC. CONSUMER HEALTH DIVISION

see "Novartis Consumer Health Canada Inc."

SANDOZ NUTRITION CORPORATION

see "Novartis Nutrition Corporation"

SANOFI CANADA INC.

Executive Offices:

90 Allstate Pkwy
Markham ON L3R 6H3
Tel.: (905) 513-4444

General Drug Inquiries:

Tel.: (905) 513-4495
Toll-free: 1-800-668-7401, Ext. 4495
Fax: (905) 513-4585

Medical Affairs:

Bonny Houghton
Suzanne Wighardt
Anson Tang

Customer Service:

Toll-Free:
Quebec and Atlantic Provinces: 1-800-263-2216;
Ontario: 1-800-263-2211;
Western Provinces: 1-800-263-2222

Aralen®
Avapro™ [a,b]
Betaxin®
Bronkaid® Mistometer®
Carbocaine®
Cyclomen®
Demerol®
Drisdol®
Fraxiparine™
Hytakerol®
Idarac®
Inocor®
Isuprel®
Kayexalate®
Levophed®
Marcaine®
Marinol®
NegGram®
Neo-Synephrine® Parenteral
Novocain®
pHisoHex®
Plaquenil®
Plavix™ [a]
Pontocaine®
Primacor®
Primaquine
Resonium Calcium
Talwin® Injection
Talwin® Tablets
Trinipatch® 0.2/Trinipatch® 0.4/ Trinipatch® 0.6
Zephiran®

[a] *Discovered by Sanofi Research. Distributed by Bristol-Myers Squibb/Sanofi Canada.*
[b] *Contact Bristol-Myers Squibb Canada Inc. for product information.*

SANOFI WINTHROP

see "Sanofi Canada Inc."

SCHEIN PHARMACEUTICAL CANADA INC.

77 Belfield Rd.
Etobicoke ON M9W 1G6
Tel.: (416) 248-3600
Fax: (416) 248-3605

Customer Service:

Toll-free: 1-800-329-2393

Cefuroxime Sodium USP, Sterile
Isoflurane, USP
Natavite™
Nifedipine PA 10
Nifedipine PA 20
Scheinpharm Artificial Tears
Scheinpharm Artificial Tears Plus
Scheinpharm Atenolol
Scheinpharm B12
Scheinpharm Cefaclor
Scheinpharm™ Clotrimazole
Scheinpharm Desonide
Scheinpharm Diphenhydramine
Scheinpharm™ Dobutamine
Scheinpharm™ Ferrous Fumarate
Scheinpharm Gentamicin
Scheinpharm Penicillin G Sodium
Scheinpharm Pilocarpine
Scheinpharm Testone-Cyp
Scheinpharm Tobramycin
Scheinpharm Triamcine-A

SCHERING CANADA INC.

3535 Trans-Canada Hwy
Pointe-Claire QC H9R 1B4
Tel.: (514) 426-7300
Fax: (514) 695-7641

Customer Service:

Montréal:
Tel. (French): (514) 426-7340; (English):(514) 426-7344

Province of Quebec:
Toll-free: 1-800-361-2431

Western Canada:
Toll-free: 1-800-661-3134

Ontario and Maritimes:
Toll-free: 1-800-361-6550

Medical Information Only:

Toll-free: 1-800-463-5442
Toll-free Fax: 1-800-369-3090
E-mail: med-afrs@schering.ca

Celestoderm®-V
Celestoderm®-V/2
Celestone®
Celestone® Soluspan®
Chlor-Tripolon®
Chlor-Tripolon® Decongestant Syrup
Chlor-Tripolon® Tablets
Chlor-Tripolon N.D.®
Claritin®
Claritin® Extra
Complex 15®
Coricidin® Cold Tablets
Coricidin "D"®
Coricidin® Non-Drowsy
Cortate® 0.5%
Cortate® 1%
Diprogen®
Diprolene™ Glycol
Diprosalic®
Diprosone®
Drixoral®, Drixtab®
Drixoral® Day/Night Cold Relief System
Drixoral® Nasal Solution
Drixoral® N.D.
Elocom
Estinyl®
Etrafon® Preparations
Euflex®
Fulvicin® P/G
Fulvicin® U/F
Garamycin® Ophthalmic/Otic Preparations
Garamycin® Parenteral
Garamycin® Topical Preparations
Garasone™ Ophthalmic/Otic Preparations
Hydrasense® Nasal Care
Hyperstat® I.V. Injection
Intron A®
Lotriderm®
Metimyd®
Metreton®
Netromycin®
Oculear®
Optimine®
Polaramine®
Proglycem®
Prometrium™
Schering® Base
Sodium Sulamyd®
Solganal®
Tinactin®
Tinactin® Jock Itch
Tinactin® Plus

Trilafon®
Trinalin®
Valisone® Scalp Lotion
Valisone-G®
Vancenase®
Vanceril®

SEARLE CANADA
Unit of Monsanto Canada Inc.
2233 Argentia Rd.
Mississauga ON L5N 2X7
Tel.: (905) 819-9666
Fax: (905) 819-9994
La Tour Digital
3333 Côte-Vertu, Suite 202
Ville St-Laurent QC H4R 2N1
Tel.: (514) 856-7470
Toll-free: 1-800-263-1705
Fax: (514) 745-2919
Orders:
Tel. (Toronto & vicinity):
(905) 819-9311
Toll-free: 1-800-263-1705
Fax: (905) 819-9344
Medical Inquiries:
Tel.: (905) 814-2421
Toll-Free: 1-800-387-7942

Aldactazide 25®
Aldactazide 50®
Aldactone®
Arthrotec®
Brevicon® 0.5/35
Brevicon® 1/35
Chronovera®
Cytotec®
Daypro™
Demulen® 30
Demulen® 50
Lomotil®
Norinyl® 1/50
Synarel® *
Synphasic®
**Distributed by Ferring Inc.*

SERONO CANADA INC.
1075 North Service Rd., Suite 100
Oakville ON L6M 2G2
Tel.: (905) 825-9200
Fax: (905) 825-9449

Fertinorm® HP
Gonal-F®
Pergonal®
Profasi® HP
Rebif™
Saizen®
Serophene®
Stilamin®

SERVIER CANADA INC.
235, boul. Armand-Frappier
Laval QC H7V 4A7
Tel.: (450) 978-9700
Orders:
Toll-free: 1-800-363-6093
Fax: (450) 978-0402
Medical Information:
Toll-free: 1-800-663-0839
Fax: (450) 978-0401

Coversyl®
Diamicron®
Lozide®
Vitathion®-A.T.P.

SHEPHERD PHARMACEUTICALS INC.
3332 Yonge St.
PO Box 94018
Toronto ON M4N 3R1
Tel.: (416) 488-7180
Fax: (416) 484-1875
Order Desk:
c/o Waymar Pharmaceuticals Inc.
330 Marwood Dr., Unit 4
Oshawa ON L1H 8B4
Tel.: (Oshawa) (905) 434-1814
Fax: (905) 434-1816

Trisulfaminic

SIGMA-TAU PHARMACEUTICALS, INC.
800 South Frederick Ave., Suite 300
Gaithersburg, MD 20877 U.S.A.
Tel.: (301) 948-1041
Toll-free: 1-800-447-0169
Fax: (Sales & Marketing):
(301) 948-3194;
(Scientific Affairs): (301) 948-3679;
(Regulatory Affairs): (301) 948-8627
E-mail: info@sigmatau.com

Carnitor®

SMITHKLINE BEECHAM CONSUMER HEALTHCARE
Division of SmithKline Beecham Inc.
2030 Bristol Circle
Oakville ON L6H 5V2
Tel.: (905) 829-2030
Fax: (905) 829-6071
Medical Information:
Tel. (Oakville): (905) 829-2030
Customer Service:
Tel. (Oakville): (905) 829-2030
Toll-free: 1-800-268-4600

Contac® Cold 12 Hour Relief Extra Strength
Contac® Cold 12 Hour Relief Non Drowsy
Contac® Cold 12 Hour Relief Regular Strength
Contac® Cough, Cold and Flu Day & Night™
Gaviscon® Heartburn Relief Formula

SMITHKLINE BEECHAM PHARMA
Division of SmithKline Beecham Inc.
2030 Bristol Circle
Oakville ON L6H 5V2
Tel.: (905) 829-2030
Fax: (905) 829-6064
Order Desk:
Toronto:
Tel.: (905) 829-2030
Ontario:
Toll-free: 1-800-565-5468
Quebec & Maritimes:
Toll-free: 1-800-663-1945
Western Provinces:
Toll-free: 1-800-565-9497
Medical Information & Clinical Drug Safety:
Tel. (Toronto): (905) 829-2030
Toll-free: 1-800-567-1550

Abenol®
Ancef®
Bactroban®
Cefizox®
Clavulin®
Coreg™
Dexedrine®
Dyazide®
Dyrenium®
Engerix®-B
Famvir™
Fastin®
Halfan™
Havrix™
Hycamtin™
K-10®
Kytril™
Mesasal™
Palafer®
Palafer® CF
Parnate®
Paxil®
Relafen™
Requip™
Stelabid® Preparations
Stelazine®
Tagamet®
Timentin®
Twinrix™

SMITH & NEPHEW INC.
2100, 52e Av.
Lachine QC H8T 2Y5
Tel.: (514) 636-0772; Telex: 05-822580
Fax: (514) 636-1684
Customer Action Centre:
Toll-free: 1-800-463-7439
Livingston Distribution Centre (Hospital Accounts Only):
7475 Flint Rd. S.E.
Calgary AB T2H 1G3
Tel.: (403) 253-8221
Fax: (403) 255-3386
Newfoundland Distribution Centre:
PO Box 13427
St. John's NF A1B 4B7
Tel.: (709) 744-3033
Fax: (709) 754-3014
Canadian Distribution Centre:
Smith & Nephew Inc.
185-A Courtneypark Dr.
Mississauga ON L5T 2T6

Ametop™
Aquaphor®
Bactigras®
Flamazine®
Flamazine® C

SOLVAY PHARMA INC.
50 Venture Dr.
Scarborough ON M1B 3L6
Tel.: (416) 284-7666
Medical Information and Pharmacovigilance:
Toll-free: 1-800-268-4276
Fax: (416) 284-6895

Cerumol®
Creon® 10
Creon® 25
Dicetel®
Duphalac®
Luvox®

Serc®
Sialor®

Solvay Pharma/Byk Canada

Pantoloc™

SPECTROPHARM DERMATOLOGY

Division of Draxis Health Inc.

6870 Goreway Dr.
Mississauga ON L4V 1P1
Tel.: (905) 677-5500
Fax: (905) 677-5502

Aquacort®
Spectro Derm®
Spectro Gluvs "19"®
Spectro Gram "2"™
Spectro Jel "609"®
Spectro Tar™ Antiseptic Shampoo
Spectro Tar Skin Wash™
Tiamol®
Ti-U-Lac® HC

SQUIBB CANADA INC.

see "Bristol-Myers Squibb Canada Inc."

STANLEY PHARMACEUTICALS LTD.

1353 Main St.
North Vancouver BC V7J 1C5

Head Office:

 # 117-260 West Esplanade
North Vancouver BC V7M 3G7
Tel.: (604) 987-3391
Toll-Free: 1-800-663-5903
Fax: (604) 984-8532

Plant and Laboratory:

1353 Main St.
North Vancouver BC V7J 1C5
Tel.: (604) 987-0445
Toll-free: 1-800-663-5903
Fax: (604) 980-4574

Branch Office:

Toronto ON
Tel.: (416) 289-7720
Toll-Free: 1-800-268-4130
Fax: (416) 289-7978

Acetaminophen
Acetaminophen, Caffeine and Codeine
Calcium Stanley
Niacin Sustained Release
Pedi-Dent™
Traveltabs

STIEFEL CANADA INC.

6635 Henri-Bourassa Blvd. W.
Montréal QC H4R 1E1
Tel.: (514) 332-3800
Toll-free: 1-800-363-2862
Fax: (514) 332-1961
Toll-free Fax: 1-800-561-1898
E-mail: stiefel.canada@sympatico.ca
Web site: www.stiefel.ca

Acetoxyl® 2.5% and 5%
Acetoxyl® 10%
Acne-Aid® Soap
Benoxyl® 5% Lotion
Benoxyl® 10% and 20% Lotion
Brasivol®
Cyclocort®
Dan-Gard®
Dan-Tar Plus®
Duofilm®
Duoforte® 27
Duoplant®
Epi-Lyt® AHA Medicated Lotion
Erysol®
Isotrex®
Lacticare® AHA
Nerisalic®
Nerisone®
Oilatum® Dermatological Shower and Bath Oil
Oilatum® Soap
Oxizole®
PanOxyl® Aquagel 2.5% and 5%, PanOxyl® Aquagel 10% and 20%
PanOxyl® 5% Wash, PanOxyl® 10% Wash
PanOxyl® 5%, PanOxyl 10%, 15% and 20%
Polytar® AF
Polytar® Preparations
Rejuva-A®
Retisol-A®
Sarna® HC
Sarna-P®
Sastid®
Solugel® 4
Solugel® 8
Stieva-A® Preparations
Stieva-A® Forte
Stievamycin®
Sulfoxyl®
Sulfur Soap
ZeaSORB®
ZeaSORB® AF
ZNP®

Glades Division, Stiefel Canada Inc.

Aristocort® Topicals
Aristocort® Parenteral
Aristocort® Tablets
Aristospan®
Capsaicin
Capsaicin HP

SUN PHARMACEUTICAL INDUSTRIES INC.

1111 Flint Rd., Unit 23
Downsview ON M3J 3C7
Tel.: (416) 665-4033
Fax: (905) 669-5299 or (416) 665-6923

Sun-Benz *

**Distributed by Kinsmor Pharmaceuticals Canada Inc. (1-800-454-6766).*

SWISS HERBAL REMEDIES LTD.

35 Leek Crescent
Richmond Hill ON L4B 4C2
Tel.: (905) 886-9500
Fax: (905) 886-5434

Regional Offices:

264 Benjamin-Hudon Rd.
St-Laurent QC H4N 1J4
Tel.: (514) 334-5740
Fax: (514) 334-7566

2439 Beta Ave., Unit 8
Burnaby BC V5C 5N1
Tel.: (604) 298-4114
Fax: (604) 298-4119

Cal-Mag
Children's Choice™ Super Multi-vitamins and Minerals
Echinacea Angustifolia
Evening Primrose Oil
Herbal Laxative
Herbal Nerve
Hi Potency B-Compound "50"
St.John's Wort
Swiss One
Timed Release Swiss One "50"
Timed Release Vitamin C 500 mg
Timed Release Vitamin C 1 000 mg
Vitamin C
Vitamin E

TANTA PHARMACEUTICALS INC.

1009 Burns St. E.
Whitby ON L1N 6A6
Tel.: (905) 430-8440
Toll-free: 1-800-668-2682
Fax: (905) 430-8449

DairyAid®
Tanta Orciprenaline
Yohimbine

TAP PHARMACEUTICALS

see "Abbott Laboratories Limited"

TARO PHARMACEUTICALS INC.

130 East Dr.
Bramalea ON L6T 1C3
Tel.: (905) 791-8276
Toll-Free: 1-800-268-1975
Fax: (905) 791-5008

Betaderm
Clotrimaderm
Cortoderm
Docusate Calcium
Docusate Sodium
Fluoderm
Hyderm
Lyderm
Micozole
Nyaderm
Oracort
Pitrex
Taro Gel
Taro-Carbamazepine CR
Taro-Sone
Testosterone Enanthate Injection, USP
Testosterone Propionate Injection, USP
Triaderm
Triamcinolone Diacetate Injectable Suspension, USP
Viaderm-K.C.
Vitamin B_{12}

TECHNILAB INC.

17 800 Lapointe St.
Mirabel QC J7J 1P3
Tel.: (514) 433-7673
Toll-free: 1-800-361-6667
Fax: (514) 433-7434
Web site: www.technilab.ca

Acetazone Forte
Acetazone Forte C8
Acilac®
Acti-B12®
Allernix
Anuzinc®
Asmavent®
Bisacodyl
Bismutal
Broncho-Grippol-DM
Buspirex
Caldomine®-DH
Calmydone®
Calmylin® Ace
Calmylin® Expectorant
Calmylin® Original with Codeine

Calmylin® with Codeine
Calmylin® Preparations
Captril
Chlorpromanyl
Codeine Phosphate
Coristex®-DH
Coristine®-DH
Cotridin
Cotridin Expectorant
Decongest
Deproic®
Dermasone® Preparations
Diclotec
Docusate Calcium
Docusate Sodium
Doxytec
Ectosone® Mild
Ectosone® Regular
Ectosone® Scalp Lotion
Electropeg
Emtec®-30
Fexicam
Flexitec
Garatec
Gentamicin Sulfate
Hemarexin®
Hemcort®-HC
Heracline®
Hormodausse®
Indotec®
Isoflurane
Laxilose®
Lenoltec No. 1, 2 & 3
Lenoltec No. 4
Levotec
Liotec
Lydonide
Methoxacet
Methoxacet-C
Methoxisal
Methoxisal-C
Monazole® 7
Morphitec®-1, -5, -10, -20
Motilidone
Neo-Laryngobis
Neotopic
Nilstat®
Orafen®
Orcipren®
Osmopak Plus
Oxycocet®
Oxycodan®
Para®
Pediatrix
Peridol®
Pilocarpine Hydrochloride
Polytopic Cream
Polytopic Ointment
Proctosone
Riphenidate
Salinex®
Salinol
Sopalamine/3B
Sopalamine/3B Plus C
Sotamol
Tecnal®
Tecnal® C1/4, C1/2
Tenolin®
Thalaris
Theophylline
Topilene®
Topisone
Triacomb®

THERAPEX
Division of E-Z-EM Canada, Inc.
11 100 Colbert Rd.
Ville d'Anjou QC H1J 2M9
Tel.: (514) 353-5820
Toll-free: 1-800-465-5820
Fax: (514) 351-3450

Lyteprep™
Trombovar®

3M PHARMACEUTICALS
Executive Office:
PO Box 5757
London ON N6A 4T1
Tel.: (519) 451-2500
Toll-free: 1-800-668-9295
Distribution Centre:
6611 Northwest Dr.
Mississauga ON L4V 1L1

Airomir™
Calcium Disodium Versenate™
Disalcid™
Disipal™
Hip-Rex™
Minitran™
Nidagel™
Norflex™
Norgesic™
Norgesic™ Forte
Tambocor™
Tantum™
Theolair™
Theolair™ Liquid
Theolair™-SR
Ulone™

TRANS CANADERM INC.
Subsidiary of Stiefel Canada Inc.
6635 Henri Bourassa Blvd. W.
Montréal QC H4R 1E1
Tel.: (514) 332-3800
Toll-free: 1-800-363-2862
Fax: (514) 332-1961
Toll-free Fax: 1-800-561-1898
E-mail: stiefel.canada@sympatico.ca
Web site: www.stiefel.ca

Buro-Sol®
Buro-Sol® Otic Solution
Cuplex®
Dehydral®
Doak™ Oil
Doak™ Oil Forte
Emo-Cort®
Prevex®
Prevex® B
Prevex® Baby Diaper Rash Cream
Prevex® HC
TersAc®
Tersaseptic®
Tersa-Tar®
Uremol® 10
Uremol® 20
Uremol®-HC
Versel®

TRIANON LABORATORIES INC.
660 Industriel Blvd.
Blainville QC J7C 3V4
Tel.: (514) 434-7482/(514) 389-6701
Toll-free: 1-800-363-7988
Fax: (514) 434-2500

Acetaminophen
Calcium 500
Calcium D 500
Codéine
Congest
Docusate Sodium
Trianal
Trianal C1/4, C1/2
Triatec-8
Triatec-8 Strong
Triatec-30

UCB PHARMA INC.
1950 Lake Park Dr.
Smyrna, Georgia 30080 U.S.A.
Tel.: (770) 437-5500
Fax: (770) 437-5511
Medical Affairs:
Suzan Leake

Zyrtec®

VITA HEALTH PRODUCTS INC.
150 Beghin Ave.
Winnipeg MB R2J 3W2
Tel.: (204) 661-8386
Fax: (204) 663-8386

VITA PHARM CANADA LTD.
2835 Kew Dr.
Windsor ON N8T 3B7
Tel.: (519) 944-7007
Fax: (519) 944-7796

WARNER-LAMBERT CONSUMER HEALTHCARE
Division of Warner-Lambert Canada Inc.
Head Office:
2200 Eglinton Ave. E.
Scarborough ON M1L 2N3
Tel.: (416) 288-2200
Fax: (416) 288-2588
Mailing Address:
PO Box 2200, Station A
Scarborough ON M1K 5C9
Medical Information:
Tel.: (416) 288-2402
Toll-free: 1-800-611-5889
Fax: (416) 701-3053
Consumer Helpline:
1-800-661-4659
Sales Offices:
3333 Côte-Vertu, Suite 810
St-Laurent QC H4R 2N1
Tel.: (514) 337-6186
Fax: (514) 337-6424
2200 Eglinton Ave. E.
Scarborough ON M1L 2N3
Tel.: (416) 288-2242
Fax: (416) 288-2588
Customer Service Centres:
PO Box 2200, Station A
Scarborough ON M1K 5C9
Tel.: (416) 288-2321
Toll-free: 1-800-387-6577
Fax: (416) 288-2283
Toll-free Fax: 1-800-563-2013
Laboratory:
2337 Parkdale Ave.
Brockville ON K6V 5W5
Tel.: (613) 342-4436
Fax: (613) 342-6584

Actifed®
Actifed™ Plus Extra Strength
Analgesic Balm
Anusol®
Anusol® Plus
Benadryl® Allergy/Sinus/Headache
Benadryl® Preparations
Benylin® Codeine 3.3 mg-D-E (OTC)
Benylin® DM
Benylin® DM 12 Hour
Benylin® DM For Children
Benylin® DM For Children 12 Hour
Benylin® DM-D (Adult)
Benylin® DM-D For Children
Benylin® DM-D-E
Benylin® DM-D-E Extra Strength
Benylin® DM-E
Benylin® DM-E Extra Strength
Benylin® E Extra Strength
Benylin® 4 Flu
Caladryl®
Gelusil®
Gelusil® Extra Strength
Glycerin Suppositories
Lidosporin® Cream
Lidosporin® Ear Drops
Mylanta™ Preparations
Nix® Cream Rinse
Polysporin® Antibiotic Burn Cream
Polysporin® Preparations
Sinutab®
Sinutab® Nightime
Sinutab® with Codeine
Sinutab® Non Drowsy
Sinutab® SA
Steri/Sol®
Sudafed® Cold & Cough Extra Strength
Sudafed® Cold & Flu
Sudafed® Decongestant
Sudafed® Decongestant Extra Strength
Sudafed® Decongestant 12 Hour
Sudafed® Head Cold and Sinus Extra Strength
Vanquin®
Zincofax®

WAYMAR PHARMACEUTICALS INC.

330 Marwood Dr., Unit 4
Oshawa ON L1H 8B4
Tel.: (905) 434-1814
Toll-free (Ontario and Quebec):
1-800-810-8065
Fax: (905) 434-1816
E-mail: kings@osha.igs.com

Roychlor®
Royflex®
Royvac®

WELCKER-LYSTER LTD.

Head Office & Plant:

8480 Saint-Laurent Blvd.
Montréal QC H2P 2M6
Tel.: (514) 381-5631
Toll-Free: 1-800-361-3808
Fax: (514) 383-4493
E-mail: sylviet@rougier.com

Laboratories & Plant:

1000 Industriel Blvd.
Chambly QC J3L 3H9
Tel.: (514) 658-1704

Livingston Distribution Centres Inc.:

320 Edimburgh Dr.
Moncton NB E1C 8P2
Tel.: (506) 857-4960

7403 Progress Way
Delta BC V4G 1E7
Tel.: (604) 940-4116

4441-76th Ave. S.E.
Calgary AB T2C 2G8
Tel.: (403) 279-2700

10 Corinne Court
Vaughan ON L4K 4T7
Tel.: (905) 879-0114

Northwest Drug Co. Ltd.
966 Powell St.
Winnipeg MB R3H 0H6
Tel.: (204) 633-9502

Colchicine
Rectocort
Yohimbine

WESTCAN PHARMACEUTICALS LTD.

Division of Vita Health Products Inc.

150 Beghin Ave.
Winnipeg MB R2J 3W2
Tel.: (204) 661-8386
Fax: (204) 663-8386

A.C.&C.
A.S.A.
A.S.A. Enteric Coated
Children's Acetaminophen Elixir Drops
Children's Acetaminophen Oral Solution
Children's Chewable Acetaminophen
Extra Strength Acetaminophen
Extra Strength Acetaminophen with Codeine
Regular Strength Acetaminophen
Regular Strength Acetaminophen with Codeine
Travel Tabs

WESTWOOD-SQUIBB

Division of Bristol-Myers Squibb Canada, Inc.

2365 Côte-de-Liesse St.
Montréal QC H4N 2M7

Order Desk:

Toll-free: 1-800-BMS-0005
Fax: (514) 333-6741

Executive Offices:

Toll-free: 1-800-333-0950
Fax: (716) 887-7735

Balnetar®
Candistatin®
Desquam-X® Preparations
Ecostatin® Preparations
Estar®
Halog® Preparations
Kenacomb® Preparations
Kenalog®
Kenalog® in Orabase
Kenalog®-10 Injection
Kenalog®-40 Injection
Keralyt®
Lac-Hydrin®
Moisturel®
Pernox®
PreSun® Sunblock 28
PreSun® Ultra 30 Preparations
Sebulex®
Sebulon®
Sebutone®
Staticin®
Trans-Plantar®
Trans•Ver•Sal®
T-Stat®
Ultravate™ Preparations
Westcort® Preparations

WHITEHALL-ROBINS INC.

5975 Whittle Rd.
Mississauga ON L4Z 3M6
Tel.: (905) 507-7000
Toll-free: 1-800-387-8647
Fax: (905) 507-7111

Distribution:

Quebec and Atlantic Provinces:
5950 Côte-de-Liesse St.
Montréal QC H4T 1E2

Ontario and Western Canada:
2360 Southfield Rd.
Mississauga ON L5N 3R6
Tel.: (905) 821-8820

Orders:

Tel.: (905) 507-7000
Toll-free: 1-800-387-8647

Advil®
Advil® Cold & Sinus
Anacin®
Anacin® Extra Strength
Anbesol® Preparations
Aquatain®
Auralgan®
Caltrate® 600
Caltrate 600 + D
Caltrate Plus
Centrum®
Centrum® Forte
Centrum® Junior Complete
Centrum® Junior Regular
Centrum® Protegra
Centrum® Select
Denorex®
Denorex® Extra Strength
Dimetane®
Dimetane® Expectorant
Dimetane® Expectorant-C
Dimetane® Expectorant-DC
Dimetapp®
Dimetapp®-A Sinus
Dimetapp®-C
Dimetapp® Chewables
Dimetapp® Clear
Dimetapp® Cough & Cold Liqui-Gels®
Dimetapp®-DM
Dimetapp® Liqui-Gels®
Dimetapp® Oral Infant Drops
Dimetapp® Quick Dissolve
Dristan®
Dristan® Extra Strength
Dristan® Long Lasting Nasal Mist/Spray
Dristan® Nasal Mist/Spray
Dristan® N.D.
Dristan® N.D. Extra Strength
Dristan Sinus
Preparation H® Cleansing Pads
Preparation H® Cooling Gel
Preparation H® Cream
Preparation H® Ointment
Preparation H® Suppositories
Riopan®
Riopan® Plus
Robaxacet®
Robaxacet® Extra Strength
Robaxacet®-8

Robaxin®
Robaxin®-750
Robaxisal®
Robaxisal® Extra Strength
Robaxisal®-C
Robitussin®
Robitussin® AC
Robitussin® Cough & Cold
Robitussin® Cough & Cold Liqui-Gels®
Robitussin® Cough, Cold & Flu Liqui-Gels®
Robitussin® DM
Robitussin® Extra Strength
Robitussin® Extra Strength Cough & Cold
Robitussin® Extra Strength DM
Robitussin® Pediatric
Robitussin® Pediatric Cough and Cold
Robitussin® with Codeine
Stresstabs®
Stresstabs® Plus
Stresstabs® with Iron
Stresstabs® with Zinc
Z-BEC®

WYETH-AYERST CANADA INC.

Head Office:

1025 Marcel Laurin Blvd.
St-Laurent QC H4R 1J6
Tel.: (514) 744-6771
Toll-free: 1-800-361-1336
Fax: (514) 744-4256

Commercial Office:

110 Sheppard Ave. E., 10th Floor
North York ON M2N 6R5
Tel.: (416) 225-7500
Toll-free: 1-800-268-1946
Fax: (416) 225-6111

Medical Information Requests:

Toll-free: 1-800-461-8844

Customer Service/Order Desk:

Tel.: (514) 744-3111
Toll-free: 1-800-665-2110;
1-800-361-6943
Fax: (514) 744-3208
Toll-free Fax: 1-888-233-9224

Distribution Centres:

Montréal:
1025 Marcel Laurin Blvd.
St-Laurent QC H4R 1J6
Tel.: (514) 748-3529
Fax: (514) 744-3208

Winnipeg:
975 Sherwin Rd.
Winnipeg MB R3H 0T8
Tel.: (204) 697-7634
Fax: (204) 694-0024

Acel-P™
Alesse™ 21
Alesse™ 28
Amicar®
Amoxil®
Antabuse®
Antivenin
A.P.L.®
Asendin®
Ativan®
Atromid-S®
Aureomycin®
Avlosulfon®
Beminal® with C Fortis Injectable
Bicillin® L-A
Bonamil®
Cefotan®
Colprone®
Cordarone®
Cordarone® I.V.
Declomycin®
Diamox®
Diban®
Donnagel®-PG Capsules
Donnagel®-PG Suspension
Donnatal®
Dopram®
Effexor®/Effexor® XR
Equanil®
Factrel®
Inderal®
Inderal®-LA
Inderide®
ISMO®
Isordil®
Ledercillin® VK
Lederle Leucovorin® Calcium
Loxapac®
Materna®
Methotrexate
Micro-K Extencaps®
Micro-K-10 Extencaps®
Minocin®
Min-Ovral® 21
Min-Ovral® 28
Monitan®
Myambutol®
Mysoline®
Neptazane®
Norplant®
Novantrone®
Nursoy®
Os-Cal®
Os-Cal® D
Ovral® 21
Ovral® 28
Paludrine®
Phenaphen® with Codeine
Phospholine Iodide®
Pipracil®
Pnu-Imune® 23
Premarin® Intravenous
Premarin® Tablets
Premarin® Vaginal Cream
Protopam® Chloride
Quinidex Extentabs®
Reglan®
Rheumatrex™
Robaxin® Injectable
Robidone®
Robinul®
Robinul® Forte
Robinul® Injectable
Serax®
SMA®, Preemie
SMA® Preparations
Sonacide®
Tazocin®
Thiotepa
Triphasil® 21
Triphasil® 28
Tuberculin, Old, Tine Test®
Verelan®
Wydase®

ZENECA PHARMA INC.

2505 Meadowvale Blvd.
Mississauga ON L5N 5R7
Tel.: (905) 821-8000
Toll-free: 1-800-268-3992

Medical Information:

Fax: (905) 821-8882
E-mail:
canada.medinfo@cams.zeneca.com

Order Desk:

Tel. (local): (905) 821-8156
Fax (local): (905) 821-4332
Toll-free (English): 1-800-387-8338
Toll-free (French): 1-800-668-6932
Toll-free Fax: 1-800-807-4242

Accolate®
Arimidex®
Brevibloc®
Casodex®
Diprivan®
Enlon®
Ethrane®
Forane®
Hibidil® 1:2 000
Hibitane® Skin Cleanser
Merrem®
Nolvadex®
Nolvadex®-D
Savlodil® 1:100
Savlon® Hospital Concentrate
Seroquel®
Suprane®
Tenoretic®
Tenormin®
Tomudex®
Zestoretic®
Zestril®
Zoladex®
Zoladex® LA

ZILA PHARMACEUTICALS INC.

1111 Flint Rd.
Downsview ON M3J 3C7
Tel.: (416) 665-2134
Fax: (416) 665-9251

Orders:

Toll-free: 1-800-433-5706

Medical Information:

Toll-free: 1-800-565-0814

Peridex®
5227 North 7th Street
Phoenix, Arizona 85014 U.S.A.
Tel.: (602) 266-6700
Fax: (602) 234-2264
Web site: www.zila.com

Zilactin®
Zilactin-B®
Zilactin-Baby®
Zilactin-L®
Zilactin-Lip®

CLIN-INFO

The Clin-Info section contains selected information for health care professionals based on clinical practice and a review of the literature. The editors have collaborated with the contributors to compile this information. Although the information is not intended to be all inclusive, the editors, contributors and publisher have tried to ensure its accuracy at the time of publication. Readers should be aware that the text may contain information different from that approved by the Health Protection Branch, Health Canada and that the pharmaceutical manufacturers' approval has not been sought for such information.

Drug therapy is constantly changing; consequently, it is the responsibility of the health care professional to seek additional and confirmatory information; to evaluate its appropriateness as it relates to the actual clinical situation; and to consider new developments.

CONTENTS

CONTENTS *(cont'd)*

POISON CONTROL CENTRES

The following list provides current contact information for Poison Control Centres across Canada. Poison treatment is available in the Emergency Departments of most active treatment hospitals.

Reviewed 1999 by the Canadian Association of Poison Control Centres (J. Courtemanche).

ALBERTA
Poison and Drug Information Service
Foothills Hospital
1403-29th St. N.W.
Calgary, AB
T2N 2T9
1-800-332-1414
(403) 670-1414
(403) 670-1472 fax

BRITISH COLUMBIA
B.C. Drug and Poison Information Centre
St. Paul's Hospital
1081 Burrard St.
Vancouver, BC
V0Z 1Y0
1-800-567-8911
(604) 682-5050
(604) 631-5262 fax

MANITOBA
Manitoba Poison Control Centre
Children's Hospital
840 Sherbrook St.
Winnipeg, MB
R3A 1S1
(204) 787-2591
(204) 787-1775 fax

NEW BRUNSWICK
Poison Information Centre
774 Main St., 6th floor
Moncton, NB
E1C 9Y3
Telephone calls will be automatically rerouted from each local hospital's emergency line.
(506) 867-3259 fax

NEWFOUNDLAND
Emergency Department
The Janeway Child Health Centre
710 Janeway Place
St. John's, NF
A1A 1R8
(709) 722-1110
(709) 726-0830 fax

NORTHWEST TERRITORIES
Emergency Department
Stanton Regional Hospital
P.O. Box 10
Yellowknife, NT
X1A 2N1
(867) 669-4100
(867) 669-4171 fax

NOVA SCOTIA
Poison Information Centre
The IWK Grace Health Centre
P.O. Box 3070
Halifax, NS
B3J 3G9
1-800-565-8161
(902) 428-8161
(902) 428-3213 fax

ONTARIO
Ottawa
Ontario Regional Poison Information Centre
Children's Hospital of Eastern Ontario
401 Smyth Rd.
Ottawa, ON
K1H 8L1
1-800-267-1373
(613) 737-1100
(613) 738-4862 fax

Toronto
Ontario Regional Poison Information Centre
The Hospital for Sick Children
555 University Ave.
Toronto, ON
M5G 1X8
1-800-268-9017
(416) 813-5900
(416) 813-7489 fax

PRINCE EDWARD ISLAND
See Nova Scotia listing for address.
1-800-565-8161

QUÉBEC
Centre anti-poison du Québec
2705, boul. Laurier
Sainte-Foy, QC
G1V 4G2
1-800-463-5060
(418) 656-8090
(418) 654-2747 fax

SASKATCHEWAN
Regina
Emergency Department
Regina General Hospital
1440-14th Ave.
Regina, SK
S4P 0W5
1-800-667-4545
(306) 766-4545
(306) 766-4357 fax

Saskatoon
Emergency Department
Royal University Hospital
Saskatoon, SK
S7N 0W8
1-800-363-7474
(306) 655-1010
(306) 655-1011 fax

YUKON TERRITORY
Emergency Department
Whitehorse General Hospital
5 Hospital Rd.
Whitehorse, YT
Y1A 3H7
(867) 667-8726
(867) 667-8762 fax

NARCOTIC AND CONTROLLED DRUGS

Table I summarizes the requirements for prescribing, dispensing and record keeping for narcotic and controlled drugs. This information is not intended to present a comprehensive review; the reader is therefore encouraged to seek additional and confirmatory information (e.g., Controlled Drugs and Substances Act, Narcotic Control Regulations, Food and Drugs Regulations).

Reviewed 1999 by the Bureau of Drug Surveillance, Health Canada.

Table I—Narcotic and Controlled Drugs Summary

Classification and Description	Legal Requirements
Narcotic Drugs[a] • 1 narcotic (e.g., cocaine, codeine, hydromorphone, morphine) • 1 narcotic + 1 active non-narcotic ingredient (e.g., Cophylac, Empracet-30, Penntuss, Tylenol No. 4) • All narcotics for parenteral use (e.g., fentanyl, pethidine) • All products containing diamorphine (hospitals only), hydrocodone, oxycodone, methadone or pentazocine • Dextropropoxyphene, propoxyphene (straight) (e.g., Darvon-N, 642)	• Written prescription required. • Verbal prescriptions not permitted. • Refills not permitted. • Written prescription may be prescribed to be dispensed in divided portions (part-fills). • For part-fills, copies of prescriptions should be made in reference to the original prescription. Indicate on the original prescription: the new prescription number, the date of the part-fill, the quantity dispensed and the pharmacist's initials. • Record and retain all drug sales and purchases in a manner that permits an audit. • Report the loss or theft of narcotic/controlled drugs as well as forged prescriptions within 10 days to your Regional Office, Drug Programme at the address indicated at the back of the Drug Forgery Report or the Drug Loss/Theft Report forms.
Narcotic Preparations[a] • Verbal prescription narcotics: 1 narcotic + 2 or more active non-narcotic ingredients (e.g., Cophylac Expectorant, Darvon-N Compound, Fiorinal with Codeine, 692, 282, 292, Tylenol No. 2 and No. 3) • Exempted codeine compounds: contain codeine up to 8 mg/solid dosage form or 20 mg/30 mL liquid + 2 or more active non-narcotic ingredients (e.g., Atasol-8, Robitussin with Codeine).	• Written or verbal prescriptions permitted. • Refills not permitted. • Written or verbal prescriptions may be prescribed to be dispensed in divided portions (part-fills). • For part-fills, copies of prescriptions should be made in reference to the original prescription. Indicate on the original prescription: the new prescription number, the date of the part-fill, the quantity dispensed and the pharmacist's initials. • Exempted codeine compounds when dispensed pursuant to a prescription follow the same regulations as for verbal prescription narcotics. • Record and retain all drug sales and purchases in a manner that permits an audit. • Report the loss or theft of narcotic/controlled drugs as well as forged prescriptions within 10 days to your Regional Office, Drug Programme at the address indicated at the back of the Drug Forgery Report or the Drug Loss/Theft Report forms.
Controlled Drugs[a] • Part I e.g., amphetamines (Dexedrine) methylphenidate (Ritalin) pentobarbital (Nembutal) secobarbital (Seconal, Tuinal) preparations: 1 controlled drug + 1 or more active noncontrolled drug(s) (Cafergot-PB)	• Written or verbal prescriptions permitted. • Refills not permitted for verbal prescriptions. • Refills permitted for written prescriptions if the prescriber has indicated in writing the number of refills and dates for, or intervals between, refills. • Written or verbal prescriptions may be prescribed to be dispensed in divided portions (part-fills). • For refills and part-fills, copies of prescriptions should be made in reference to the original prescription. Indicate on the original prescription: the new prescription number, the date of the repeat or part-fill, the quantity dispensed and the pharmacist's initials. • Record and retain all drug sales and purchases in a manner that permits an audit. • Report the loss or theft of narcotic/controlled drugs as well as forged prescriptions within 10 days to your Regional Office, Drug Programme at the address indicated at the back of the Drug Forgery Report or the Drug Loss/Theft Report forms.

Table I—Narcotic and Controlled Drugs Summary *(cont'd)*

Classification and Description	Legal Requirements
Controlled Drugs[a] *(cont'd)* • Part II e.g., barbiturates (amobarbital, phenobarbital) butorphanol (Stadol NS) diethylpropion (Tenuate) nalbuphine (Nubain) phentermine (Fastin, Ionamin) preparations: 1 controlled drug + 1 or more active noncontrolled ingredients (Fiorinal, Neo-Pause, Tecnal) • Part III e.g., anabolic steroids (methyltestosterone, nandrolone decanoate)	• Written or verbal prescriptions permitted. • Refills permitted for written or verbal prescriptions if the prescriber has authorized in writing or verbally (at the time of issuance) the number of refills and dates for, or intervals between, refills. • Written or verbal prescriptions may be prescribed to be dispensed in divided portions (part-fills). • For refills and part-fills, copies of prescriptions should be made in reference to the original prescription. Indicate on the original prescription: the new prescription number, the date of the repeat or part-fill, the quantity dispensed and the pharmacist's initials. • Record and retain all drug sales and purchases in a manner that permits an audit. • Report the loss or theft of narcotic/controlled drugs as well as forged prescriptions within 10 days to your Regional Office, Drug Programme at the address indicated at the back of the Drug Forgery Report or the Drug Loss/Theft Report forms.

[a] The products noted are examples only.

IMMUNIZATION SCHEDULES FOR INFANTS AND CHILDREN

The following is an overview on routine immunization schedules for infants and children. This information is not intended to present a comprehensive review; the reader is therefore encouraged to seek additional and confirmatory information.

Reviewed 1999 by V. Marchessault.

Few measures in preventive medicine are of such proven value and as easy to implement as routine immunization against infectious diseases. Immunizations carried out as recommended in the following schedules (Table I, II and III) will provide protection for most children against the diseases shown.

Both live and inactivated polio vaccines have been used in Canada with equal success in preventing the occurrence of paralytic poliomyelitis, but inactivated vaccine is now preferred.

Following a standard schedule ensures complete and adequate protection. However, modifications of the recommended schedule may be necessary because of missed appointments or illness. Interruption of a recommended series does not require starting the series over again, regardless of the interval elapsed.

Similar vaccines are now available from different manufacturers but they may not be identical. It is therefore essential for the user to read the appropriate chapter in the current *Canadian Immunization Guide*, as well as the manufacturer's package insert.

Table I—Routine Immunization Schedule for Infants and Children

Age/Time	DTaP[a]	IPV	Hib[b]	MMR	Td[c]	Hep B[d] (3 doses)
2 months old	X	X	X			Infancy
4 months old	X	X	X			
6 months old	X	X[e]	X			or
12 months old				X		
18 months old	X	X	X	X[f] or		
4–6 years old	X	X		X[f]		preadolescence
Grade 3–7						(9–13 yrs)
14–16 years old					X	

Legend: DTaP=diphtheria, tetanus and pertussis (acellular) vaccine, Hep B=recombinant hepatitis B vaccine series, Hib=Haemophilus influenzae b conjugate vaccine, IPV=inactivated polio vaccine, MMR=measles, mumps and rubella vaccine, Td=tetanus and diphtheria toxoid, "adult type".

Table II—Routine Immunization Schedule for Children <7 Years of Age Not Immunized in Early Infancy

Timing	DTaP[a]	IPV	Hib	MMR	Td[c]	Hep B[d] (3 doses)
1st visit	X	X	X	X[g]		
2 months after 1st visit	X	X	X[h]	X[f]		
2 months after 2nd visit	X	X[e]				
6–12 months after 3rd visit	X	X	X[h]			
4–6 years of age[i]	X	X				Preadolescence
14–16 years of age					X	(9–13 yrs)

Table III—Routine Immunization Schedule for Children ≥7 Years of Age Not Immunized in Early Infancy

Timing	Td[c]	IPV	MMR	Hep B[d] (3 doses)
1st visit	X	X	X	
2 months after 1st visit	X	X	X[f]	
6–12 months after 2nd visit	X	X		Preadolescence
10 years after 3rd visit	X			(9–13 yrs)

[a] DTaP (diphtheria, tetanus, acellular or component pertussis) vaccine is the preferred vaccine for all doses in the vaccination series, including completion of the series in children who have received ≥1 dose of DPT (whole cell) vaccine.

[b] Hib schedule shown is for PRP-T (e.g., Act-HIB) or HbOC (e.g., HibTITER) vaccine. If PRP-OMP (e.g., PedVax HIB), give at 2, 4 and 12 months of age.

[c] Td (tetanus and diphtheria toxoid), a combined adsorbed "adult type" preparation for use in persons ≥7 years of age, contains less diphtheria toxoid than preparations given to younger children and is less likely to cause reactions in older persons.

[d] Hepatitis B vaccine can be routinely given to infants or pre-adolescents, depending on the provincial/territorial policy; three doses at 0, 1 and 6 month intervals are preferred. The second dose should be administered at least 1 month after the first dose, and the third dose should be administered at least 4 months after the first dose, and at least 2 months after the second dose.

[e] This dose is not needed routinely, but can be included for convenience.

[f] A second dose of MMR is recommended, at least 1 month after the first dose given. For convenience, options include giving it with the next scheduled vaccination at 18 months of age or with school entry vaccinations at 4–6 years of age (depending on the provincial/territorial policy), or at any intervening age that is practicable.

[g] Delay until subsequent visit if child is <12 months of age.

[h] Recommended schedule and number of doses depend on the product used and the age of the child when vaccination is begun (see the current *Canadian Immunization Guide* or the product monograph for specific recommendations). Not required past age 5.

[i] Omit these doses if the previous doses of DTaP and polio were given after the 4th birthday.

Adapted from *Canadian Immunization Guide,* 5th edition, Health Canada, 1998, with permission of the Minister of Public Works and Government Services Canada, 1998.

Reference:

1. National Advisory Committee on Immunization. Canadian immunization guide, 5th ed. Ottawa, ON: Health Canada, 1998.

VACCINE-ASSOCIATED ADVERSE EVENTS: SURVEILLANCE AND REPORTING

The following is a description of the Vaccine-Associated Adverse Events (VAAE) Surveillance Program. This information is not intended to present a comprehensive review.

Reviewed 1999 by the Division of Immunization, Bureau of Infectious Diseases, Laboratory Centre for Disease Control, Health Canada (R. Pless).

Surveillance for adverse reactions to vaccines is done through a network that is linked to local, provincial and territorial public health authorities. The network is separate from that of the Adverse Drug Reaction Monitoring Program.

The following form is the national version of the Vaccine-Associated Adverse Event reporting form. The reader is encouraged to photocopy and use this form when needed. Provinces may have different versions or may use this form with their own logo and address. *Therefore, health care providers should consult their local public health unit for the specific reporting procedures in place in their jurisdiction, and for copies of reporting forms.*

Background

Reporting vaccine adverse events is of unique importance. Public confidence in vaccination programs depends on the safety and efficacy of vaccines. Surveillance of their safety is a joint responsibility between those who manufacture, those who license and those who administer vaccines. Practitioners provide the most valuable source of data to ensure the continued surveillance of vaccine safety by submitting case reports to public health authorities, who evaluate and forward them to the Division of Immunization and the Vaccine Products Division, Health Canada, for aggregation and analysis. With the case reports as the core, Canada has developed a unique program of safety monitoring that includes the following:

—an expert advisory committee, the Advisory Committee on Causality Assessment, that meets regularly to review selected cases and to assess emerging vaccine safety topics

—an active surveillance system, through the Canadian Paediatric Society, to monitor rare and serious adverse events seen at pediatric hospitals

—interaction with the National Advisory Committee on Immunization who reviews and updates the *Canadian Immunization Guide*

—interaction with the World Health Organization's International Drug Monitoring Program, that shares drug safety data among more than 50 participating countries which enhances our ability to detect concerns.

Reporting vaccine adverse events is a vital component of the informed consent process; especially since one of the criticisms raised is that adverse events to vaccines are grossly underreported, rendering any discussion of side effects “misleading”. By reporting adverse events health care professionals ensure a continuous feedback on the impact of immunizations. Opponents of immunization programs are few, but their messages are often well publicized. Therefore, the counselling of parents or patients about the safety of vaccination is becoming more difficult. Refer to the Selected Reading List at the end of this section for further information on vaccines, including a new book for parents—Your Child's Best Shot: a parents guide to vaccination. The current edition of the Canadian Immunization Guide incorporates a new chapter on consent issues and concerns regarding immunization, and the local public health unit can also be consulted for guidance.

Considerations When Reporting Adverse Events

Practitioners should be vigilant for, and are asked to report events that meet the following criteria:

- **Events which are "serious"** are those that require hospitalization or significant medical intervention, that cause congenital malformation, that result in persistent or significant disability or incapacity, that threaten life or that result in death. Assessing them for causality is vital for vaccine safety and patient counselling.
- **Events which are "unexpected",** implying that product literature did not describe the reaction and therefore patients could not have been adequately warned. Reporting these events is crucial to effect changes in the product literature or to counsel others on the expected likelihood and management of the event.
- **A change in frequency of expected events.** Reactions to vaccines are more predictable than those which occur with other drug products since there is a normal physiologic response to an immunization (e.g., a rash can occur 7 to 10 days following measles vaccine). Common and well-known events do not usually need to be reported. However, should common events (e.g., fever, redness and tenderness at the injection site) take place at unexpected frequencies, it may represent one of the following:
  —a more reactogenic or "bad lot" that resulted from a break in the "cold chain" during delivery from the manufacturer
  —some unexpected contamination during handling
  —very rarely, but vital to detect, is a problem with manufacturing and quality control.
- **Reactions to vaccines being used in special programs or to new vaccines on the market;** some vaccines may be the focus of attention from time to time (e.g., during a mass immunization campaign).
- **Adverse effects that pose a dilemma for subsequent vaccinations.** The *Canadian Immunization Guide* outlines the absolute contraindications and any precautions to vaccination. These recommendations are evidence-based and sometimes differ from what is listed in the product monograph. If there is hesitation from either the parent or the care provider regarding the provision of subsequent doses, public health authorities can assist with a recommendation. In addition, by reporting the clinical situation, information can be accumulated and incorporated into future vaccine information.

Selected Reading List

- National Advisory Committee on Immunization. Canadian immunization guide, 5th ed. Ottawa, ON. Health Canada, 1998. Available on the Internet at <www.hc-sc.gc.ca/hpb/lcdc/bid/di>.
- Canadian Paediatric Society. Your child's best shot: a parent's guide to vaccination. Ottawa, ON: Canadian Paediatric Society, 1997. Available by contacting 613-526-9397 or <www.cps.ca>.
- Grabenstein JD. ImmunoFacts:Vaccines and immunologic drugs. St. Louis, MO: Facts and Comparisons, 1995. Available by calling 314-878-2515 or by faxing 314-878-5563.
- Plotkin SA, Mortimer EA, eds. Vaccines, 2nd ed. Philadelphia, PA: WB Saunders, 1994.

References:

1. Division of Immunization. Vaccine-associated adverse events in Canada, 1992 report. Can Commun Dis Rep 1995; 21(13):117–28.
2. Duclos P, Pless R, et al. Adverse events temporally associated with immunizing agents. Can Fam Physician 1993; 39:1907–13.
3. Laboratory Centre for Disease Control. Proceedings of a workshop on post-marketing surveillance of vaccine-associated adverse events. Can Dis Wkly Rep 1991; 17S4:1–9.
4. Morris R, Halperin S, et al. IMPACT monitoring network: a better mousetrap. Can J Infect Dis 1993; 4(4):194–5.
5. Pless R, Duclos P, Advisory Committee on Causality Assessment. Reinforcing surveillance for vaccine-associated adverse events: the Advisory Committee on Causality Assessment. Can J Infect Dis 1996; 7(2):98–99.

Health Canada / Santé Canada

REPORT OF A VACCINE-ASSOCIATED ADVERSE EVENT

Protected when completed

In confidence to: Division of Immunization
L.C.D.C., Tunney's Pasture 0603E1
Ottawa, Ontario K1A 0L2
(613) 957-1340 1-800-363-6456 FAX (613) 998-6413

IDENTIFICATION

PATIENT IDENTIFIER	PROVINCE/TERRITORY	DATE OF BIRTH (YEAR / MONTH / DAY)	SEX: ☐ Male ☐ Female	DATE OF VACCINE ADMINISTRATION (YEAR / MONTH / DAY)

VACCINES

VACCINE(S) GIVEN	NUMBER IN SERIES	SITE	ROUTE	DOSAGE	MANUFACTURER	LOT NUMBER

ADVERSE EVENT(S)

Events marked with an asterisk (*) must be diagnosed by a physician. Report only events which cannot be attributed to co-existing conditions. Additional information for all events should be provided under SUPPLEMENTARY INFORMATION on reverse side. Record interval between vaccine administration and onset of each event in minutes, hours or days.

(Each event has a MIN. / HOURS / DAYS box.)

LOCAL REACTION AT INJECTION SITE

☐ **INFECTED ABSCESS** (tick one or both of the options below)
(i) positive gram stain or culture ☐
(ii) existence of purulent discharge with inflammatory signs ☐

☐ **STERILE ABSCESS/NODULE**
No evidence of acute microbiological infection

☐ **SEVERE PAIN AND/OR SEVERE SWELLING**
(tick one or both of the options below)
(i) lasting 4 days or more ☐
(ii) extending past nearest joint(s) ☐

☐ **SCREAMING EPISODE/PERSISTENT CRYING**
Inconsolable for 3 hours or more; OR quality of cry definitely abnormal for child and not previously heard by parents

☐ **FEVER**
Highest recorded temperature (Report only 39.0°C (102.2° F) or above)
Temperature: ________ °C (or ________ °F)
Site: rectal ☐ oral ☐ axilla ☐ skin ☐ tympanic ☐
Temperature believed to be high but not recorded ☐
Should be supported by the presence of other systemic symptoms

☐ **ADENOPATHY** (tick one or both of the options below)
(i) enlarged lymph node(s) ☐
(ii) drainage of lymph node(s) ☐
Site(s) ____________________

☐ **PAROTITIS**
Swelling with pain and/or tenderness of parotid gland(s)

*☐ **ANAPHYLAXIS OR SEVERE SHOCK**
Explosive, occurring within minutes after immunization, and evolving rapidly towards cardiovascular collapse AND requiring resuscitative therapy

☐ **OTHER ALLERGIC REACTIONS** (tick one or more of the options below)
(i) wheezing or shortness of breath due to bronchospasm ☐
(ii) swelling of mouth or throat ☐
(iii) skin manifestations (e.g., hives, eczema, pruritus) ☐
(iv) facial or generalized edema ☐

☐ **RASHES** (other than hives)
Lasting 4 days or more AND/OR requiring hospitalization
Generalized ☐ Localized (indicate site) ☐ ____________
Specify characteristics of rash ____________________

☐ **ARTHRALGIA/ARTHRITIS**
Joint pain/inflammation lasting at least 24 hours
If condition is an acute exacerbation of a pre-existing diagnosis, give details under **Supplementary Information**

☐ **SEVERE VOMITING AND/OR DIARRHEA**
Must be severe enough to interfere with daily routine

☐ **HYPOTONIC-HYPORESPONSIVE EPISODE** (in children < 2 yrs, only)
Characterised by all the features of: (i) generalized decrease/loss of muscle tone; AND (ii) pallor or cyanosis; AND (iii) decreased level of awareness or loss of consciousness
Should not be mistaken for fainting, a post-convulsion state, or anaphylaxis

☐ **CONVULSION/SEIZURE**
Febrile ☐ Afebrile ☐
Past history of: A) Febrile seizures Yes ☐ No ☐
B) Afebrile seizures Yes ☐ No ☐
Omit fainting, seizures occurring within 30 minutes of immunization, and seizures occurring as part of encephalopathy or meningitis/encephalitis

*☐ **ENCEPHALOPATHY**
Acute onset of major neurological illness characterized by any two or more of: (i) seizures; (ii) distinct change in level of consciousness or mental status (behaviour and/or personality) lasting 24 hours or more; (iii) focal neurological signs which persist for more than 24 hours

*☐ **MENINGITIS AND/OR ENCEPHALITIS**
Abnormal CSF findings AND an acute onset of: (i) fever with neck stiffness or positive meningeal signs; OR (ii) signs and symptoms of encephalopathy (see ENCEPHALOPATHY above)
Results of CSF examination should be provided under **Supplementary Information**

*☐ **ANAESTHESIA/PARAESTHESIA**
Lasting over 24 hours
Generalized ☐ Localized (indicate site) ☐ ____________

*☐ **GUILLAIN-BARRÉ SYNDROME**
Progressive subacute weakness of more than one limb (typically symmetrical) with **hyporeflexia/areflexia**

*☐ **PARALYSIS** (Do not code if Guillain-Barré Syndrome is coded)
Limb paralysis ☐ Facial or cranial paralysis ☐
Describe ____________________

*☐ **THROMBOCYTOPENIA**
Give lab results under **Supplementary Information**

☐ **OTHER SEVERE OR UNUSUAL EVENTS**
Include any adverse event believed to be related to immunization, that does not fit any of the categories listed above and for which no other cause is clearly established
Report events of clinical interest which require medical attention, and particularly events that are (i) fatal, (ii) life-threatening, (iii) require hospitalization, or (iv) result in residual disability

DESCRIPTION
____

REPORTER'S NAME	TELEPHONE NUMBER ( )	ADDRESS (Institution/No., Street, etc.)
PROFESSIONAL STATUS: MD ☐ RN ☐ OTHER ______		
SIGNATURE	DATE Year / Month / Day	City / Province / Postal Code

HC/SC 4229 (03-96) - 1

Canada

This reporting form has been formatted to conform to CPS page size. Reproduced with permission of the Minister of Public Works and Government Services Canada, 1998.

OUTCOME OF EVENT(S) AT TIME OF REPORT PLEASE FORWARD ANY FOLLOW UP INFORMATION	FULLY RECOVERED ☐	RESIDUAL EFFECTS (describe) ☐	FATAL ☐	LOST TO FOLLOW-UP ☐	PENDING ☐

SOUGHT MEDICAL ATTENTION (Emergency room, clinic, family physician etc.) NO ☐ YES ☐ (If yes, include relevant details of treatment under **Supplementary Information**)

HOSPITALIZED BECAUSE OF EVENT(S) NO ☐ YES ☐	**LENGTH OF STAY** (DAYS) ☐	**DATE ADMITTED** Year Month Day

CONCOMITANT MEDICATIONS (exclude those used to treat the adverse event)

DRUG(S) GIVEN

MEDICAL HISTORY Please provide information on relevant medical history or concurrent illness (See detailed instructions on reverse)

SUPPLEMENTARY INFORMATION

INSTRUCTIONS FOR COMPLETING REPORT OF A VACCINE-ASSOCIATED ADVERSE EVENT

1. Please use dark ink when completing form to improve legibility of copies.
2. Report only events which have a temporal association with a vaccine and which cannot be attributed to co-existing conditions. **A causal relationship does not need to be proven, and submitting a report does not imply causality.**
3. Events marked with an asterisk (*) must be diagnosed by a physician. Supply relevant details in the SUPPLEMENTARY INFORMATION box.
4. Record interval between vaccine administration and onset of each event in minutes, hours or days.
5. Provide relevant information, when appropriate, in the SUPPLEMENTARY INFORMATION box. Includes details of events diagnosed by physician (see 3 above), results of diagnostic or laboratory tests, hospital treatment, and discharge diagnoses where a vaccinee is hospitalised because of a vaccine-associated adverse event. If appropriate, and preferred, photocopies of original records may be submitted.
6. Provide details of medical history that are relevant to the adverse event(s) reported. Examples include a history of allergies in vaccinee, previous adverse event(s), and concurrent illnesses which may be associated with the current adverse event(s).

TO BE COMPLETED BY MEDICAL HEALTH OFFICER RECOMMENDATIONS FOR FURTHER IMMUNIZATION

NAME: ______________________ **PHONE:** ______________

SIGNATURE **DATE** Year Month Day

ADVERSE DRUG REACTIONS: SURVEILLANCE AND REPORTING

The following is a description of the Adverse Drug Reaction (ADR) Monitoring Program. This information is not intended to present a comprehensive review.

Reviewed 1999 by the Bureau of Drug Surveillance, Health Canada (H. Sutcliffe).

ADR Monitoring Program: Although drugs are carefully tested before licensing to ensure safety and efficacy, it is only after the drug is on the market, when sufficient numbers of patients are exposed, that rare adverse reactions are detected. Reports from health care professionals are crucial in detecting adverse reactions. The ADR Monitoring Program of Health Canada, in collecting adverse reaction reports from across the country, represents an important component of the continuous risk-benefit assessment of pharmaceutical products. The program generates drug safety information available to regulatory agencies for ongoing postmarketing surveillance. The key elements of this program consist of spontaneous adverse drug reaction (ADR) reporting, assessment of reactions and information dissemination.

Definition: The World Health Organization defines an ADR as a response to a drug which is noxious and unintended and which occurs at doses normally used or tested in humans for prophylaxis, diagnosis or therapy of disease or for the modification of physiologic function. This definition has been adopted by the Canadian program.

Recognition: In many cases, ADRs are not suspected because of clinical changes or events attributed to the patient's underlying disease. Often the clinical picture is so complex, particularly in the elderly or critically ill patients, that drug-related effects are not easily identified.

When a potential ADR is noticed, the following questions should be asked:

- Did the reaction follow a reasonable time sequence?
- Did the patient improve after stopping the drug (dechallenge)?
- Could the reaction be reasonably explained by the patient's clinical state?

Which ADRs to report: Health practitioners should report any undesirable patient effect suspected to be associated with drug use. These include the following:

- **all suspected** ADRs that are **unexpected**. An unexpected ADR is an undesirable patient effect that is not consistent with the product information or labeling.
- **all suspected** ADRs that are **serious**. A serious ADR is one that requires hospitalization or prolongation of existing hospitalization, that causes congenital malformation, that results in persistent or significant disability or incapacity, that threatens life or that results in death. ADRs that require significant medical intervention to prevent one of the other outcomes listed above are also considered to be serious.
- **all suspected** ADRs to **recently marketed drugs** (commercially available for less than 5 years) regardless of their nature or severity.

Reporting an ADR: *Reporting an ADR does not imply a causal link—it is sufficient that a temporal association or possible association exists.* To report an ADR, health practitioners should complete a copy of the form available in this section. The reporter and patient identities are kept strictly confidential.

For more information on the program, to obtain copies of the form or to submit a form or verbal report, physicians, pharmacists and other health practitioners are invited to contact (write, telephone or fax) one of the centres listed in Table I below.

Table I—Regional ADR Centres

British Columbia
BC Regional ADR Centre
c/o BC Drug and Poison Information Centre
1081 Burrard St.
Vancouver BC V6Z 1Y6
(604) 631-5625
Fax: (604) 631-5262
E-mail: adr@dpic.bc.ca

New Brunswick, Newfoundland, Nova Scotia and Prince Edward Island
Atlantic Regional ADR Centre
c/o Queen Elizabeth II Health Sciences Centre
Drug Information Centre
1796 Summer St., Rm 2421
Halifax NS B3H 3A7
(902) 473-7171
Fax: (902) 473-8612
E-mail: rxklsl@qe2-hsc.ns.ca

Ontario
Ontario Regional ADR Centre
LonDIS Drug Information Centre
London Health Sciences Centre
339 Windermere Rd.
London ON N6A 5A5
Fax: (519) 663-2968
E-mail: adr@lhsc.on.ca

Quebec
Quebec Regional ADR Centre
Drug Information Centre
Hôpital du Sacré-Coeur de Montréal
5400 boul. Gouin west
Montréal QC H4J 1C5
(514) 338-2961 or 1-888-265-7692
Fax: (514) 338-3670
E-mail: cip.hscm@sympatico.ca

Saskatchewan
Sask ADR Regional Centre
Dial Access Drug Information Service
College of Pharmacy and Nutrition
University of Saskatchewan
110 Science Pl.
Saskatoon SK S7N 5C9
(306) 966-6340 or 1-800-667-3425
Fax: (306) 966-6377

Other provinces and territories
National ADR Unit
Continuing Assessment Division
Bureau of Drug Surveillance
Therapeutic Products Programme
AL0201C2
Ottawa ON K1A 1B9
(613) 957-0337
Fax: (613) 957-0335
E-mail: cadrmp@hc-sc-gc.ca

Reference:
1. Drugs Directorate, Health Canada. Canadian adverse drug reaction newsletter. Can Med Assoc J 1996; 154(7): 1057–64.

Health Canada / Santé Canada

PROTECTED
PROTÉGÉ

Report of adverse reaction suspected due to drugs, cosmetics and biological products (Vaccines excluded)

Notification concernant un effet indésirable présumé dû à des médicaments, cosmétiques et produits biologiques (Vaccins exclus)

FOR H.P.B. USE ONLY
RÉSERVÉ À LA D.G.P.S.

Patient Data - Données relatives au patient

Initials - Initiales	Chart number - Numéro de dossier	Age - Âge	Sex - Sexe ☐ Male - Homme ☐ Female - Femme	Weight - Poids	Height - Taille	Ethnic origin - Origine éthnique

Allergies or previous adverse reactions / Allegies ou effets indésirables précédents ☐ No / Non ☐ Yes (Specify) / Oui (Préciser)

Relevant medical history - Histoire médicale pertinente

Adverse Reaction - Effet indésirable

ONSET - DÉBUT
☐ Gradual / Graduel ☐ Sudden (specify in min. and hrs.) / Soudain (préciser en min. et hres.) ☐ Other (Specify) / Autre (Préciser)

Date (D - M - Y) / (J - M - A)

Description of adverse reaction - Description de l'effet indésirable

Laboratory results - Résultats de laboratoire

Intensity of reaction / Intensité de l'effet ☐ Mild / Légère ☐ Moderate / Modérée ☐ Severe / Grave

Hospitalized because of reaction / Hospitalisé à cause de l'effet ☐ No / Non ☐ Yes / Oui

TREATMENT OF REACTION - TRAITEMENT DE L'EFFET
Suspected drug - Produit suspect
☐ Discontinued / Discontinué ☐ Dose reduced / Dose réduite ☐ Unchanged / Non changé ☐ Other (Specify) / Autre (Préciser)

Treatment drugs or therapy
Médicaments de traitement ou thérapie
☐ No / Non ☐ Yes (Specify) / Oui (Préciser)

OUTCOME OF REACTION - SUITES DE L'EFFET
☐ Recovered / Rétabli ☐ Recovered with residual effects / Rétabli avec séquelles ☐ Not yet recovered / Pas encore rétabli ☐ Unknown / Inconnues ☐ Fatal / Décès

Date (D - M - Y) (J - M - A) | Cause

Product Data - Données relatives au produit

Suspected drugs or products - Trade name / Chemicals / Lot number Médicaments ou produits suspects - Nom déposé / Produit chimique / No. de lot	Started (D-M-Y) Début (J-M-A)	Ended (D-M-Y) Fin (J-M-A)	Daily Dose / Dose quotidienne	Route / Voie d'administration	Reason for use / Raison de l'usage
Drugs taken concomitantly / Produits associés ☐ No / Non ☐ Yes (Specify) / Oui (Préciser)					Other comments / Autres commentaires

Reporter's name - Nom du déclarant	City - Ville	Province
Name of institution - Nom de l'établissement		Telephone number - Numéro de téléphone

HC 4016 (08-97)

Canada

SPECIAL ACCESS PROGRAMME

The following is a summary of Health Canada's Special Access Programme (formerly called the Emergency Drug Release Program). This information is not intended to present a comprehensive review.

Reviewed 1999 by the Special Access Programme, Health Canada (I. MacKay).

Mandate of the Program: The Special Access Programme (SAP) provides access to nonmarketed drugs for practitioners treating patients with serious or life-threatening conditions when conventional therapies have failed, are unsuitable, unavailable, or offer limited options. The SAP authorizes a manufacturer to sell a specific quantity of drug that cannot be otherwise sold or distributed in Canada. The SAP does not authorize the use or administration of a drug—this authority falls within the practice of medicine, which is regulated at the provincial level. Drugs considered for release by the SAP include pharmaceutical, biologic, and radiopharmaceutical products not approved for sale in Canada.

How to Request Special Access to an Emergency Drug: Practitioners may fax, phone or write to the SAP to request an emergency drug with the following information:

- practitioner's name and telephone number
- address of practitioner's office/clinic or hospital pharmacy where the drug is to be delivered
- drug name and dosage form (e.g., tablet, ointment)
- manufacturer's name and address
- total quantity of drug requested
- patient's initials, date of birth, gender
- medical indication for the use of the drug.

After consideration, an authorization may be granted. The manufacturer is then notified by telephone or fax or both. This initial authorization is followed by a Letter of Authorization, which is sent to the manufacturer and copied to the practitioner. The manufacturer has the final word on whether or not the drug will be supplied.

In seeking and receiving access to a drug through the SAP, the practitioner agrees to provide a report on the results of the use of the drug including information on adverse drug reactions and, on request, to account for all quantities of drug released.

Contact Information for emergency drug requests or current information on the SAP:

Special Access Programme
Therapeutic Products Programme
Finance Building, 2nd Floor
Tunney's Pasture
Ottawa, Ontario
K1A 1B6
Address Locator 0202C1

(613) 941-2108 (08:30–16:30 hours EST)
(613) 941-3061 (after hours)
(613) 941-3194 fax
Web site:
www.hc-sc.gc.ca/hpb-dgps/therapeut

HEALTH ORGANIZATIONS DIRECTORY

Table I provides a directory containing contact information for various health organizations. This information has been adapted with permission from *Pharmacy Practice* 1998; 14(7):19–24. Most of the organizations provide information suitable for public and professional services. The organizations are listed alphabetically by disease state or subject, where possible. This list is not exhaustive; the reader is therefore encouraged to seek other references.

Reviewed 1999

Table I—Health Organizations Directory

Acupuncture Foundation of Canada Institute
PO Box 93688
Postal Outlet, Shopper's World
3003 Danforth Ave.
Toronto ON M4C 5R5
Tel: (416) 752-3988
Fax: (416) 752-4398
E-mail: info@afcinstitute.com
Web site: www.afcinstitute.com

Addiction and Mental Health Services Corp.
Addiction Research Foundation Site
33 Russell St.
Toronto ON M5S 2S1
Tel: (416) 595-6014 or (416) 595-6552
Drug & Alcohol Information Line
1-800-INFO-ARF (Ontario)
Fax: (416) 595-6606
E-mail: ejanecek@arf.org
See also Concerns Canada; PRIDE Canada; and Substance Abuse, Canadian Centre on

AIDS Clearinghouse, National
c/o Canadian Public Health Association
400-1565 Carling Ave.
Ottawa ON K1Z 8R1
Tel: (613) 725-3434
Fax: (613) 725-1205
E-mail: aids/sida@cpha.ca
Web site: www.cpha.ca

AIDS Research, Canadian Foundation for
901-165 University Ave.
Toronto ON M5H 3B8
Tel: (416) 361-6281
1-800-563-CURE (English)
Fax: (416) 361-5736

AIDS Society, Canadian
400-100 Sparks St.
Ottawa ON K1P 5B7
Tel: (613) 230-3580
1-800-499-1986
Fax: (613) 563-4998
E-mail: cndaids@cyberus.ca
Web site: www.cdnaids.ca

Allergy/Asthma Information Association
750-30 Eglinton Ave. W.
Mississauga ON L5R 3E7
Tel: (905) 712-2242
Fax: (905) 712-2245

Allergy Foundation of Canada
PO Box 1904
Saskatoon SK S7K 3S5
Tel: (306) 373-7591
E-mail: sswoynarski@sk.sympatico.ca

Alzheimer Society of Canada
1200-20 Eglinton Ave. W.
Toronto ON M4R 1K8
Tel: (416) 488-8772
1-800-616-8816
Fax: (416) 488-3778
E-mail: info@alzheimer.ca
Web site: www.alzheimer.ca

Amyotrophic Lateral Sclerosis Society of Canada
(Lou Gehrig's Disease)
220-6 Adelaide St. E.
Toronto ON M5C 1H6
Tel: (416) 362-0269
1-800-267-4-ALS
Fax: (416) 362-0414
E-mail: alssoc@inforamp.net
Web site: www.als.ca

Apheresis Group, Canadian
206-435 St. Laurent Blvd.
Ottawa ON K1K 2Z8
Tel: (613) 748-9613
Fax: (613) 748-6392
E-mail: cag@magi.com

Aplastic Anemia Association of Canada
22 Aikenhead Rd.
Etobicoke ON M9R 2Z3
Tel: (416) 235-0468
1-888-840-0039 (English)
Fax: (416) 235-1756
E-mail: aplastic@enterprise.ca

The Arthritis Society
901-250 Bloor St. E.
Toronto ON M4W 3P2
Tel: (416) 967-1414
1-800-321-1433
Fax: (416) 967-7171
Web site: www.arthritis.ca

Asthma Society of Canada
425-130 Bridgeland Ave.
Toronto ON M6A 1Z4
Tel: (416) 787-4050
1-800-787-3880
Fax: (416) 787-5807
E-mail: asthma@myna.com
Web site: www.asthmasociety.com
See also Allergy/Asthma Information Association

Back Association of Canada
83 Cottingham St.
Toronto ON M4V 1B9
Tel: (416) 967-4670
Fax: (416) 967-0945

Back Institute, Canadian/ CBI Health
1200-330 Front St. W.
Toronto ON M5V 3B7
Tel: (416) 595-6185
1-800-463-2225
Fax: (416) 595-1658

Blind, Canadian Council of the
200-396 Cooper St.
Ottawa ON K2P 2H7
Tel: (613) 567-0311
Fax: (613) 567-2728

Blind, The Canadian National Institute for the
1929 Bayview Ave.
Toronto ON M4G 3E8
Tel: (416) 486-2500
Fax: (416) 480-7503
Web site: www.cnib.org

Breast Cancer Foundation, Canadian
1000-790 Bay St.
Toronto ON M5G 1N8
Tel: (416) 596-6773
1-800-387-9816 (Maritimes, Quebec and Ontario)
Fax: (416) 596-7857

Breastfeeding, drug exposure during: *See* Motherisk

British Institute of Homeopathy (Canada)
1960 Boake St.
Ottawa ON K4A 3K1
Tel: (613) 830-4759
1-800-579-4325
Fax: (613) 830-9174
Web site: www.homeopathy.com/index.html

Bulimia Anorexia Nervosa Association (BANA)
300 Cabana Rd. E.
Windsor ON N9G 1A3
Tel: (519) 969-2112
Fax: (519) 969-0227

Cancer Society, Canadian/National Cancer Institute of Canada
200-10 Alcorn Ave.
Toronto ON M4V 3B1
Tel: (416) 961-7223
1-888-939-3333
Fax: (416) 961-4189
E-mail: ccs@cancer.ca
Web site: www.cancer.ca

Table I—Health Organizations Directory *(cont'd)*

Cardiovascular Society, Canadian
1403-222 Queen St.
Ottawa ON K1P 5V9
Tel: (613) 569-3407
Fax: (613) 569-6574
E-mail: ccsinfo@ccs.ca
Web site: www.cc.ca

Celiac Association, Canadian
11-190 Britannia Rd.
Mississauga ON L4Z 1W6
Tel: (905) 507-6208
1-800-363-7296
Fax: (905) 507-4673

Child Health, Canadian Institute of
512-885 Meadowlands Dr. E.
Ottawa ON K2C 3N2
Tel: (613) 224-4144
Fax: (613) 224-4145
E-mail: cich@igs.net
Web site: www.cich.ca

Chronic fatigue syndrome
See M.E. Association of Canada

Chronic Pain Association of Canada
105-150 Central Park Dr.
Brampton ON L6T 2T9
Tel: (905) 793-5230
1-800-616-7246 (English)
Fax: (905) 793-8781
E-mail: nacpac@sympatico.ca
Web site: www3.sympatico.ca/nacpac

Concerns Canada
(Substance abuse prevention)
112-4500 Sheppard Ave. E.
Toronto ON M1S 3R6
Tel: (416) 293-3400
Fax: (416) 293-1142
E-mail: concerns@sympatico.ca
See also Addiction Research Foundation; PRIDE Canada; Substance Abuse, Canadian Centre on

Consumer Health Organization of Canada
412-1220 Sheppard Ave. E.
North York ON M2K 2S5
Tel: (416) 490-0986
Fax: (416) 490-9949
Web site: www.hookup.net/~cho

Crohn's and Colitis Foundation of Canada
301-21 St. Clair Ave. E.
Toronto ON M4T 1L9
Tel: (416) 920-5035
1-800-387-1479
Fax: (416) 929-0364
E-mail: ccfc@netcom.ca
Web site: www.ccfc.ca

Cystic Fibrosis Foundation, Canadian
601-2221 Yonge St.
Toronto ON M4S 2B4
Tel: (416) 485-9149
1-800-378-2233
Fax: (416) 485-0960
E-mail: info@ccff.ca
Web site: www.ccff.ca/~fwww/index.html

Deaf, Canadian Association of the
203-251 Bank St.
Ottawa ON K2P 1X3
Tel: (613) 565-2882
Fax: (613) 565-1207

Deafness: *See also* Hearing Society, Canadian; and Hard of Hearing Association, Canadian

Diabetes Association, Canadian
800-15 Toronto St.
Toronto ON M5C 2E3
Tel: (416) 363-3373
1-800-BANTING
Fax: (416) 363-3393
E-mail: info@diabetes.ca
Web site: www.diabetes.ca

Diabetes: *See also* Juvenile Diabetes Foundation Canada

Down Syndrome Society, Canadian
811-14th St. N.W.
Calgary AB T2N 2A4
Tel: (403) 270-8500
Fax: (403) 270-8291

Drug abuse: *See* Addiction Research Foundation; Concerns Canada; PRIDE Canada; and Substance Abuse, Canadian Centre on

Eating Disorder Information Centre, National
200 Elizabeth St.
College Wing, 1st Floor, Rm. 211
Toronto ON M5G 2C4
Tel: (416) 340-4156
Fax: (416) 340-4736
See also Bulimia Anorexia Nervosa Association; Nutrition, National Institute of

Endometriosis Association, International
8585 N. 76th Place
Milwaukee, WI 53223, USA
Tel: (414) 355-2200
1-800-426-2363 (Canada-wide)
Fax: (414) 355-6065
E-mail: endo@endometriosis.assn.org
Web site: www.endometriosis.assn.org

Epilepsy Canada
745-1470 Peel St.
Montreal QC H3A 1T1
Tel: (514) 845-7855
Fax: (514) 845-7866
E-mail: epilepsy@epilepsy.ca
Web site: www.epilepsy.ca

Freidereich's Ataxia, Canadian Association of
5620 C.A. Jobin St.
Montreal QC H1P 1H8
Tel: (514) 321-8684
1-800-222-3968
Fax: (514) 321-9257

Geriatrics: *See* Medication Use & the Elderly, Canadian Coalition on

Gerontology, Canadian Association on
500-1306 Wellington St.
Ottawa ON K1Y 3B2
Tel: (613) 728-9347
Fax: (613) 728-8913
E-mail: cagacg@magi.com
Web site: www.cadacg.ca

Hard of Hearing Association, Canadian
205-2435 Holly Lane
Ottawa ON K1V 7P2
Tel: (613) 526-1584
TTY: (613) 526-2692
1-800-263-8068
Fax: (613) 526-4718
E-mail: chhanational@cyberus.ca
See also Hearing Society, Canadian; and listings under "Deaf"

Hearing Impaired, Centre for
310 Elmgrove Ave.
Ottawa ON K1Z 6V1
Tel: (613) 729-1467
Fax: (613) 729-5167
E-mail: crchi@iosphere.net

Hearing Society, Canadian
271 Spadina Rd.
Toronto ON M5R 2V3
Tel: (416) 964-9595
TTY: (416) 964-0023
Fax: (416) 928-2525
Web site: www.chs.ca
See also Hard of Hearing Association, Canadian; and listings under "Deaf"

Heart and Stroke Foundation of Canada
1402-222 Queen St.
Ottawa ON K1P 5V9
Tel: (613) 569-4361
Fax: (613) 569-3278
Web site: www.hsf.ca

Hemochromatosis Society, Canadian
272-7000 Minoru Blvd.
Richmond BC V6Y 3Z5
Tel: (604) 279-7135
Fax: (604) 279-7138
E-mail: chcts@istar.ca
Web site: www.home.istar.ca/~chcts

Hemophilia Society, Canadian
1210-625 President Kennedy Ave.
Montreal QC H3A 1K2
Tel: (514) 848-0503
1-800-668-2686
Fax: (514) 848-9661
E-mail: chs@odyssee.net

Hemophilia, World Federation of
500-1310 Greene Ave.
Montreal QC H3Z 2B2
Tel: (514) 933-7944
Fax: (514) 933-8916
E-mail: wfh@wfh.org
Web site: www.wfh.org

Huntington Society of Canada
13 Water St. N., PO Box 1269
Cambridge ON N1R 7G6
Tel: (519) 622-1002
1-800-998-7398
Fax: (519) 622-7370

Table I—Health Organizations Directory *(cont'd)*

International Association for Medical Assistance to Travellers (IAMAT)
40 Regal Rd.
Guelph ON N1K 1B5
Tel: (519) 836-0102
Fax: (519) 836-3412
E-mail: iamat@sentex.net
Web site: www.sentex.net/~iamat

Interstitial Cystitis Society, Canadian
P.O. Box 28625, 406 S. Wellington Ave.
Burnaby BC V5C 6J4
Tel: (250) 758-3207
Fax: (250) 758-4894
Web site: www.ichelp.com

Juvenile Diabetes Foundation Canada
89 Granton Dr.
Richmond Hill ON L4B 2N5
Tel: (905) 889-4171
1-800-668-0274
Fax: (905) 889-4209
E-mail: general@jdfc.ca
Web site: www.jdfc.ca

Kidney Foundation of Canada
300-5165 Sherbrooke St. W.
Montreal QC H4A 1T6
Tel: (514) 369-4806
1-800-361-7494
Fax: (514) 369-2472
E-mail: kidney-f-c@vir.com
Web site: www.kidney.ca

Lactation, drug exposure during:
See Motherisk

Liver Foundation, Canadian
200-365 Bloor St. E.
Toronto ON M4W 3L4
Tel: (416) 964-1953
1-800-563-5483
Fax: (416) 964-0024
E-mail: clf@liver.ca
Web site: www.liver.ca

Lung Association, The Canadian
508-1900 City Park Dr.
Gloucester ON K1J 1A3
Tel: (613) 747-6776
Fax: (613) 747-7430
E-mail: info@lung.ca
Web site: www.lung.ca

Lupus Canada
PO 64034, 5512-4th Ave. N.W.
Calgary AB T2K 6J1
Tel: (403) 274-5599
(514) 849-0955 (French)
1-800-661-1468 (English)

Malignant Hyperthermia Association
127 Sheppard Ave. E.
Willowdale ON M2N 3A5
Tel: (416) 222-0150
Fax: (416) 224-0360

M.E. Association of Canada
(Myalgic Encephalomyelitis/ Chronic Fatigue Syndrome)
400-246 Queen St.
Ottawa ON K1P 5E4
Tel: (613) 563-1565
Fax: (613) 567-0614
E-mail: tharvey@netcom.ca

Medic-Alert Foundation, Canadian
301-250 Ferrand Dr.
Toronto ON M3C 2T9
Tel: (416) 696-0267
1-800-668-1507 (English)
1-800-668-6381 (French)
Fax: (416) 696-0156 or 1-800-392-8422
E-mail: medinfo@medicalalert.ca

Medication Use & the Elderly, Canadian Coalition on
1005-350 Sparks St.
Ottawa ON K1R 7S8
Tel: (613) 238-7624
Fax: (613) 235-4497
E-mail: iahale@ibm.net

Mental Health Association, Canadian
3rd Floor, 2160 Yonge St.
Toronto ON M4S 2Z3
Tel: (416) 484-7750
Fax: (416) 484-4617
E-mail: cmhanat@interlog.com
Web site: www.icomm.ca

Migraine Association of Canada
1912-365 Bloor St. E.
Toronto ON M4W 3L4
Tel: (416) 920-4916
1-800-663-3557 (English)
24-hour info line: (416) 920-4917
Fax: (416) 920-3677
E-mail: cindy@migraine.ca
Web site: www.migraine.ca

Motherisk
Division of Clinical Pharmacology
Hospital for Sick Children
555 University Ave.
Toronto ON M5G 1X8
Tel: (416) 813-6780
E-mail: momrisk@sickkids.on.ca
Web site: www.motherisk.org

Multiple Sclerosis Society of Canada
1000-250 Bloor St. E.
Toronto ON M4W 3P9
Tel: (416) 922-6065
1-800-268-7582
Fax: (416) 922-7538
Web site: www.mssoc.ca

Muscular Dystrophy Association of Canada
900-2345 Yonge St.
Toronto ON M4P 2E5
Tel: (416) 488-0030
1-800-567-2873
Fax: (416) 488-7523
Web site: www.mdac.ca

Nutrition, National Institute of
302-265 Carling Ave.
Ottawa ON K1S 2E1
Tel: (613) 235-3355
Fax: (613) 235-7032
E-mail: nin@nin.ca
Web site: www.nin.ca
See also Bulimia Anorexia Nervosa Association; Eating Disorder Information Centre, National

Occupational Health and Safety, Canadian Centre for
250 Main St. E.
Hamilton ON L8N 1H6
Tel: (905) 572-2981
1-800-263-8466
Fax: (905) 572-4500
E-mail: custserv@ccohs.ca
Web site: www.ccohs.ca

Osteoporosis Society of Canada
33 Laird Dr.
Toronto ON M4G 3S9
Tel: (416) 696-2663
1-800-463-6842 (English)
1-800-977-1778 (French)
Fax: (416) 696-2673

Paraplegic Association, Canadian
2nd Floor, 520 Sutherland Dr.
Toronto ON M4G 3V9
Tel: (416) 422-5644
Fax: (416) 422-5943
E-mail: cpaont@idirect.com

Parkinson Foundation of Canada
710-390 Bay St.
Toronto ON M5H 2Y2
Tel: (416) 366-0099
1-800-565-3000 (English)
1-800-720-1307 (French)
Fax: (416) 366-9190
Web site: www.parkinson.ca

Porphyria Foundation Inc., Canadian
PO Box 1206
Neepawa MB R0J 1H0
Tel: (204) 476-2800

PRIDE Canada (Parent Resources Institute for Drug Education)
College of Pharmacy and Nutrition
University of Saskatchewan
110 Science Place
Saskatoon SK S7N 5C9
Tel: (306) 975-3755
1-800-667-3747
Fax: (306) 975-0503
E-mail: pride@noinnovplace.saskatoon.sk.ca
See also Drug abuse listings

Pregnancy, drug exposure during:
See Motherisk

Psoriasis Foundation, Canadian
500A-1306 Wellington St.
Ottawa ON K1Y 3B2
Tel: (613) 728-4000
1-800-265-0926
Fax: (613) 728-8913

Table I—Health Organizations Directory *(cont'd)*

Psoriasis Society of Canada
PO Box 25015
Halifax NS B3M 4H4
Tel: (902) 443-8680
1-800-656-4494 (English)
Fax: (902) 457-1664

Schizophrenia Society of Canada
814-75 The Donway W.
Don Mills ON M3C 2E9
Tel: (416) 445-8204
1-800-809-HOPE
Fax: (416) 445-2270

Seniors: *See* Medication Use and the Elderly, Canadian Coalition on; Gerontology, Canadian Association on

Sleep/Wake Disorders Canada
5055-3080 Yonge St.
Toronto ON M4N 3N1
Tel: (416) 483-9654
1-800-387-9253 (English)
Fax: (416) 483-7081
E-mail: swdc@globalserve.net
Web site: www.geocities.com~sleepwake

Spina Bifida and Hydrocephalus Association of Canada
220-388 Donald St.
Winnipeg MB R3B 2J4
Tel: (204) 925-3650
1-800-565-9488
Fax: (204) 925-3654
E-mail: spinab@mts.net
Web site: www.sphac.ca

Sport, Canadian Centre for Ethics in
702-1600 James Naismith Dr.
Gloucester ON K1B 5N4
Tel: (613) 748-5755
Fax: (613) 748-5746
E-mail: info@cces.ca

Sport Medicine, Canadian Academy of
502-1600 James Naismith Dr.
Gloucester ON K1B 5N4
Tel: (613) 748-5851
Fax: (613) 748-5792
E-mail: jburke@globalserve.net

Sport Medicine & Science Council of Canada
1600 James Naismith Dr.
Gloucester ON K1B 5N4
Tel: (613) 748-5671
Fax: (613) 748-5729
E-mail: smscc@smscc.ca
Web site: www.smscc.ca

Stuttering Treatment & Research, Institute for
3rd Flr., 8220-114th St.
Edmonton AB T6G 2P4
Tel: (403) 492-2619
Fax: (403) 492-8457
E-mail: istar@gpu.srv.ualberta.ca

Substance Abuse, Canadian Centre on
300-75 Albert St.
Ottawa ON K1P 5E7
Tel: (613) 235-4048
Fax: (613) 235-8101
E-mail: webmaster@ccsa.ca
Web site: www.ccsa.ca
See also Addiction Research Foundation; PRIDE Canada; and Concerns Canada

Thyroid Foundation of Canada
C-1040 Gardiners Rd.
Kingston ON K7P 1R7
Tel: (613) 634-3426
1-800-267-8822
Fax: (613) 634-3483
E-mail: thyroid@limestone.kosone.com
Web site: home.ican.net/~thyroid/Canada.html

Tourette Syndrome Foundation of Canada
206-194 Jarvis St.
Toronto ON M5B 2B7
Tel: (416) 861-8398
1-800-361-3120
Fax: (416) 861-2472
E-mail: tsfc.org@sympatico.ca
Web site: www.tourette.ca

Travel: *See* International Association for Medical Assistance to Travellers (IAMAT)

Turner's Syndrome Society
814 Glencairn Ave.
North York ON M6B 2A3
Tel: (416) 781-2086
1-800-465-6744 (English)
Fax: (416) 781-7245
E-mail: tssincan@web.net

DRUG CONSIDERATIONS IN PORPHYRIA

The following is an overview of porphyria and general drug considerations. In particular, 3 porphyrias considered not rare in Canada are included: acute intermittent porphyria, porphyria cutanea tarda and erythropoietic protoporphyria. There are about 8 different porphyrias; however, the others are not included. This information is not intended to present a comprehensive review; therefore, the reader is encouraged to seek additional and confirmatory information.

Reviewed 1999 by G. Sweeney.

General

All porphyrias involve a defect in the synthesis of heme, which is the prosthetic group of cytochromes and hemoglobin. However, each porphyria is biochemically distinct involving a different enzyme or tissue. Figure I is a simplified outline of the sequence of this heme biosynthetic pathway.

Figure I—Heme Biosynthetic Pathway (simplified)

aminolevulinate (ALA) → porphobilinogen (PBG) → uroporphyrinogen → coproporphyrinogen → protoporphyrinogen → protoporphyrin → heme

Even the more common forms of porphyria are rare, consequently, there are no good clinical trials of therapy. All of the porphyrias are inherited conditions, but as penetrance is variable, a negative family history is not helpful in excluding the diagnosis.

- Acute Intermittent Porphyria (AIP) is a defect in PBG-deaminase which converts PBG to uroporphyrinogen. This results in ALA and PBG accumulation when this defect becomes rate-limiting. Acute porphyria attacks occur in AIP and in the rarer variegate porphyria and coproporphyria. It is likely that ALA accumulation is responsible for the clinical features of acute porphyria.
- Porphyria Cutanea Tarda (PCT) is seen mostly in dermatological practice and results from a block between uroporphyrinogen and coproporphyrinogen. However, a high degree of block affects only some cells in the liver. Synthetic estrogens (and certain hepatotoxins) may cause PCT, and 4-aminoquinolines (e.g., chloroquine) may cause a severe reaction in patients with PCT, but otherwise they respond normally to medications.
- Erythropoietic Protoporphyria (EPP) is usually seen in childhood as photosensitivity with an accelerated sunburn reaction. The affected enzyme is heme synthetase which incorporates iron into protoporphyrin. Drugs do not cause any special problems in subjects with EPP.

Clinical Features of Acute Intermittent Porphyria

Individuals with AIP and its 2 related conditions hereditary coproporphyria (HC) and variegate porphyria (VP) are all at risk of an acute porphyria attack. During the acute attack large amounts of ALA and PBG appear in the urine. Other symptoms seen during an attack are abdominal pain, vomiting, constipation, autonomic dysfunction, peripheral neuropathy (mostly motor) and a sodium-losing defect in salt and water handling by the kidney. There are many different defects possible in the PBG-deaminase gene, and the severity of the condition can vary greatly. At one extreme are women who, despite no exposure to drugs, experience frequent episodes of acute porphyria usually related to their menses. AIP is almost unknown in either sex before puberty and not all gene carriers for AIP will actually become ill. Treatment of acute attacks is effective in the short term, but this, particularly the use of panhematin, should be discussed with an expert.

Considerations for Drug Use

If a practitioner is confident that the type of porphyria has been correctly diagnosed (this is an important qualification), concern about adverse reactions to drugs in a person with porphyria is generally confined to AIP, HC and VP. Uncertainty remains regarding which drugs can be used safely in a person with AIP. Porphyrics are at risk of developing an acute attack if exposed to various precipitating factors, of which drugs are the most common factor. The following are 2 general considerations when deciding on drug use:

—avoid drugs that interact with the cytochrome P450 system in the liver if at all possible

—do not use drugs that induce the cytochrome P450 system since these are absolutely contraindicated. This induction increases flux through the heme biosynthetic pathway and causes the defect in PBG-deaminase to become critical.

Lists of drugs have been published categorizing drugs as "considered safe", "considered unsafe" and "uncertain". For example, some of the drugs considered contraindicated in the *CPS* product monographs and considered unsafe in the reference below are: barbiturates, carbamazepine, griseofulvin, meprobamate, progesterone and sulfonamides. However, setting aside those drugs that are clearly contraindicated, the approach is similar to using drugs in early pregnancy (i.e., avoid drug therapy if possible).

Reference:
1. Moore MR, Hift RJ. Drugs in the acute porphyrias-toxicogenetic diseases. Cell mol Biol 1997;43(1):89–94.

DRUGS USED IN CARDIAC RESUSCITATION

Tables I and II provide an overview on selected drugs used in adult and pediatric cardiac resuscitation. This information is not intended to present a comprehensive review; the reader is therefore encouraged to seek additional and confirmatory information.

Reviewed 1999 by the Drug information and pharmacy staff, London Health Sciences Centre, London, Ontario, and the Emergency Cardiac Care Subcommittee, Heart and Stroke Foundation of Canada (M. Ackerman).

Table I—Drugs Used in Adult Cardiac Resuscitation

Drug	Indications	Dose (i.v. unless otherwise specified)	Comments
Adenosine	Stable narrow-complex PSVT. May be used diagnostically (after lidocaine) for stable wide-complex tachycardia of uncertain type.	Initial dose is 6 mg rapid bolus over 1–3 s followed by 20 mL NS bolus. Repeat with 12 mg if no response in 1–2 min. A third dose of 12 mg may be given in 1–2 min.	Flushing, dyspnea and chest pain are usually transient. Transient asystole or bradycardia and ventricular ectopy may occur. PSVT may recur due to short half-life of <5 s. For recurrent PSVT, adenosine or a calcium channel blocker may be used. Theophylline and methylxanthines may block adenosine's effect. Dipyridamole potentiates the effect. Carbamazepine prolongs the effect.
Amiodarone	Refractory VT or VF despite lidocaine.	Initial dose: 150 mg over 10 min followed by 1 mg/min for 6 h. Maintenance infusion at 0.5 mg/min.	Monitor closely for hypotension. May be most effective drug for VF electrical storm.
ASA	Adjuvant therapy in acute MI.	Chew or swallow 160–325 mg p.o. as soon as possible.	Avoid in patients with allergy to ASA or active peptic ulcer. Use with caution in patients with asthma.
Atropine	Asystole (after epinephrine). Symptomatic bradycardia.	Asystole: 1 mg, repeat in 3–5 min if asystole persists, up to 3 mg or 0.04 mg/kg total. Bradycardia: 0.5–1 mg, repeat every 3–5 min, up to 3 mg or 0.04 mg/kg total. ET: 2–3 mg diluted in 10 mL NS.	Less than 0.5 mg can cause bradycardia. Use with caution in presence of acute myocardial ischemia or infarction.
Bretylium	Refractory or recurrent VF or VT despite epinephrine, lidocaine and/or defibrillation and for wide-complex tachycardias uncontrolled with lidocaine and adenosine. May be effective as first antiarrhythmic in hypothermic VF.	Cardiac arrest: 5 mg/kg i.v. push, may give 10 mg/kg in 5 min if needed. VT: 5–10 mg/kg in 50 mL D5W over 8–10 min. Max. total dose: 30–35 mg/kg. Maintenance infusion: 1 g in 250 mL D5W at 1–2 mg/min.	Frequent postural hypotension and possible nausea and vomiting. Sympathomimetic effects last for 20 min and are followed by adrenergic blockade.
Beta-blockers (see Metoprolol below)			
Calcium chloride	Calcium channel blocker overdose, hyperkalemia, profound hypocalcemia or prophylactic pretreatment before i.v. calcium channel blockers to prevent hypotension in patients with marginal blood pressure or left ventricular dysfunction.	Give 2–4 mg/kg (usually 2 mL of 10% solution) over 1–2 min for prophylactic pretreatment before i.v. calcium channel blockers. Give 8–16 mg/kg (usually 5–10 mL of 10% solution) for hyperkalemia and calcium channel blocker overdose.	Avoid mixing with sodium bicarbonate.
Diltiazem	Ventricular rate control in AF or refractory narrow-complex PSVT with adequate blood pressure.	Give 0.25 mg/kg over 2 min. May repeat in 15 min with 0.35 mg/kg over 2 min. Maintenance infusion: 5–15 mg/h.	Avoid in sick sinus syndrome or AV block. Monitor closely for hypotension, especially with concurrent administration of a beta-blocker.

Legend: AF = atrial fibrillation and flutter, AV = atrioventricular, ET = endotracheal, PSVT = paroxysmal supraventricular tachycardia, rt-PA = recombinant tissue plasminogen activator, TCA = tricyclic antidepressant, VF = ventricular fibrillation, VT = ventricular tachycardia.

Table I—Drugs Used in Adult Cardiac Resuscitation *(cont'd)*

Drug	Indications	Dose (i.v. unless otherwise specified)	Comments
Epinephrine	Asystole, VF, pulseless VT or pulseless electrical activity.	Give 1 mg i.v. push (10 mL of 1:10 000 solution) every 3–5 min during the arrest. ET: 2–2.5 mg diluted in 10 mL NS. High dose infusion (to replace boluses): 30 mg (use 30 mL of 1:1 000 solution) in 250 mL NS or D5W at 100 mL/h titrated to effect.	Intracardiac injection should be used only during open cardiac massage or when the other routes are unavailable. Avoid mixing with alkaline solutions.
	Symptomatic bradycardia.	Low dose infusion (inotropic and chronotropic drips): 1 mg in 250 mL NS and infuse at 30–150 mL/h (2–10 μg/min).	
Heparin	Adjunctive therapy with thrombolytic agents in acute MI.	With alteplase (rtPA), give 5 000 units i.v. bolus at same time as alteplase. Maintain at 1 000–1 200 units/h.	Check PTT in 6 and 12 h, then every 12 h. Keep PTT 1.5–2 times control for 48 h.
		With streptokinase (SK), the use of heparin remains unclear. For patients with high risk of thromboembolism, 7 500 units s.c. q12h has been used no earlier than 4 h after starting SK.	Monitor PTT at 4 h and maintain PTT 1.5–2 times control. If PTT is below range, change to i.v. heparin as for alteplase.
Isoproterenol	Refractory torsades de pointes and for temporary control of bradycardia in heart transplant patients.	Give 1 mg in 250 mL D5W at 2–10 μg/min titrated to heart rate and rhythm response.	Use only after atropine to maintain heart rate until a pacemaker is inserted. Transcutaneous pacing may be preferable to isoproterenol. Avoid mixing with alkaline solutions. In torsades de pointes titrate to increase heart rate until VT is suppressed.
Lidocaine	VF or pulseless VT not responsive to epinephrine and defibrillation. Stable VT, wide-complex tachycardias of uncertain type, wide-complex PSVT.	Cardiac arrest: Initial dose: 1–1.5 mg/kg bolus. May repeat once, in 3–5 min, before another antiarrhythmic is tried. Following resuscitation give maintenance infusion. ET: 2–4 mg/kg. Stable tachycardia: 1–1.5 mg/kg over 3–5 min. Repeat 0.5–0.75 mg/kg every 5–10 min, up to 3 mg/kg total. Maintenance infusion: 1 g in 250 mL D5W at 2–4 mg/min.	Toxic symptoms include slurred speech, altered consciousness, muscle twitching and seizures. Maintenance dose reduction may be required in elderly patients or those with hepatic impairment (do not reduce loading dose).
Magnesium sulfate	Hypomagnesemia, ensuing refractory VF/VT. Treatment of choice in torsades de pointes.	Cardiac arrest: 1–2 g (2–4 mL of 50% solution) i.v. push diluted in 10 mL D5W. Torsades de pointes: 1–2 g in 50–100 mL D5W over 5–60 min followed with 1–4 g/h titrated to effect.	Safeguard against clinically significant hypotension or asystole. Use cautiously in renal failure.
Metoprolol	Acute MI, refractory PSVT or AF.	Give 5 mg slow i.v. Repeat every 5–10 min for a total of 15 mg. After 15 min, if tolerated, 50 mg p.o. bid for 2 doses, then 100 mg p.o. bid.	Avoid in patients with HR <60, systolic BP <100, CHF, AV block or bronchospastic disease.
Morphine sulfate	Treats pain and reduces pulmonary edema.	Give 1–3 mg over 1–5 min; repeat every 5 min to response.	Respiratory depression and hypotension may occur.
Procainamide	Refractory VF/pulseless VT, refractory PSVT, recurrent VT not controlled by lidocaine, or stable wide-complex tachycardia of unknown origin.	Give 1 g in 250 mL D5W at 20–30 mg/min until effective or hypotension occurs or QRS widens by >50%, up to total of 17 mg/kg (1.2 g in 70 kg patient). Maintenance infusion: 1–4 mg/min.	It is a negative inotrope and vasodilator, therefore it can cause severe conduction delay and hypotension. Avoid in QT prolongation and torsades de pointes. Dosage should be reduced in renal failure.
Sodium bicarbonate	Hyperkalemia, TCA overdose, prolonged cardiac resuscitation with effective ventilation, or to alkalinize urine in drug overdoses.	Give 1 mmol/kg, then no more than 0.5 mmol/kg every 10 min.	Use only after confirmed interventions (adequate ventilation, compression, defibrillation and more than 1 trial of epinephrine) have been used. Use arterial blood gas analysis as a guide to therapy.

Table I—Drugs Used in Adult Cardiac Resuscitation *(cont'd)*

Drug	Indications	Dose (i.v. unless otherwise specified)	Comments
Thrombolytic agents (e.g., alteplase (rt-PA), streptokinase)	Acute MI ST segment elevation ≥1 mm in at least 2 contiguous leads.	Administer as quickly as possible after diagnosis of acute MI (within 30 min if possible). Streptokinase: 1.5 million IU in a 1-hour infusion. Alteplase: total dose based on weight, not to exceed 100 mg. Accelerated infusion: 15 mg bolus followed by 0.75 mg/kg over next 30 min (not to exceed 50 mg). Then 0.50 mg/kg over next 60 min (not to exceed 35 mg).	Search for exclusion criteria: bleeding, stroke, trauma, recent surgery, aortic dissection, uncontrolled hypertension, bleeding disorders, prolonged or traumatic CPR. Adjuvant therapy with ASA and heparin (see ASA and Heparin above). Use one i.v. line exclusively for thrombolytic administration.
Verapamil	Stable narrow-complex PSVT and adequate blood pressure.	Give 2.5–5 mg i.v. push over 1–2 min. Repeat doses of 5–10 mg every 15–30 min to max. of 30 mg may be used to produce therapeutic response. Administer more slowly in older patients.	Monitor closely for hypotension, sinus bradycardia and AV block (especially with concurrent administration of a beta-blocker or other antihypertensives).

Legend: AF = atrial fibrillation and flutter, AV = atrioventricular, ET = endotracheal, PSVT = paroxysmal supraventricular tachycardia, rt-PA = recombinant tissue plasminogen activator, TCA = tricyclic antidepressant, VF = ventricular fibrillation, VT = ventricular tachycardia.

References:
1. 1996 Handbook of emergency cardiac care for healthcare providers. Dallas, TX: American Heart Association, 1996.
2. Cummins RO, ed. Textbook of advanced cardiac life support. Dallas, TX: American Heart Association, 1997.
3. Handbook of ACLS algorithms, Heart and Stroke Foundation of Canada, 1994.
4. Kowey PR, Levine JH, et al. Randomized, double-blind comparison of intravenous amiodarone and bretylium in the treatment of patients with recurrent, hemodynamically destabilizing ventricular tachycardia or fibrillation. Circulation 1995; 92(11): 3255–63.

Table II—Drugs Used in Pediatric Cardiac Arrest and Resuscitation

Drug	Indication	Dose (i.v. or i.o. unless otherwise specified)	Dilution
Adenosine	Drug of choice for symptomatic PSVT in children <1 yr.	0.1 mg/kg rapid i.v. push over 1–3 s. Repeat at 0.2 mg/kg in 1–2 min if needed. Max. single dose: 12 mg. Note: very short half-life.	Undiluted. Follow with 2–3 mL NS flush (5–10 mL flush if via peripheral catheter).
Atropine	Symptomatic bradycardia unresponsive to oxygen, ventilation and epinephrine.	0.02 mg/kg (min. 0.1 mg). May double for second dose. Max. single dose 0.5 mg (child) and 1 mg (adolescent). Repeat every 5 min to max. total dose of 1 mg (child) and 2 mg (adolescent).	Undiluted; can be given ET.
Bretylium	Refractory VT/VF.	5 mg/kg rapid i.v. push. Repeat at 10 mg/kg if VT/VF persists.	Undiluted.
Calcium chloride	Hypocalcemia, hyperkalemia, hypermagnesemia, calcium channel blocker overdose.	0.2 mL (20 mg)/kg of 10% calcium chloride (5.4 mg/kg elemental calcium) slow i.v. push.	Undiluted.
Dobutamine	Support cardiac output.	2–20 μg/kg/min i.v. infusion.	6 x body wt (kg) = mg of drug added to i.v. solution to make a total volume of 100 mL. An infusion rate of 1 mL/h provides 1 μg/kg/min.
Dopamine	Support cardiac output.	2–20 μg/kg/min i.v. infusion.	
Epinephrine	Bradycardia.	0.01 mg/kg (1:10 000, 0.1 mL/kg). ET: 0.1 mg/kg (1:1 000, 0.1 mL/kg).	Infusion: 0.6 x body wt (kg) = mg of drug added to i.v. solution to make a total volume of 100 mL. An infusion rate of 1 mL/h provides 0.1 μg/kg/min.
	Asystole or pulseless arrest.	First dose: i.v./i.o.: 0.01 mg/kg (1:10 000, 0.1 mL/kg). ET: 0.1 mg/kg (1:1 000, 0.1 mL/kg). Second and repeat doses: i.v./i.o./ET: 0.1 mg/kg (1:1 000, 0.1 mL/kg) every 3–5 min. Doses up to 0.2 mg/kg (1:1 000, 0.2 mL/kg) may be effective. Neonates: 0.01–0.03 mg/kg (1:10 000, 0.1–0.3 mL/kg).	
	Support cardiac output.	0.1–1 μg/kg/min i.v. infusion.	
Glucose	Hypoglycemia.	0.5–1 g/kg i.v.	D25W (neonates: D10W).
Lidocaine	VF, pulseless VT not responsive to defibrillation and epinephrine.	1 mg/kg rapid bolus, followed by infusion of 20–50 μg/kg/min.	I.V. push: undiluted (a 2% solution = 20 mg/mL). Infusion: 60 x body wt (kg) = mg of drug added to i.v. solution to make a total volume of 100 mL. An infusion rate of 1 mL/h provides 10 μg/kg/min.
Naloxone	Opioid toxicity	0–5 yrs (≤ 20 kg): 0.1 mg/kg. ≥5 yrs (>20 kg): 2.0 mg. Repeat doses every 2–3 min as needed.	Undiluted; can be given ET.
		Infusion: 0.04–0.16 mg/kg/h.	Dilute to 4 μg/mL in D5W or NS.
Sodium bicarbonate	Use with caution only after confirmed interventions (adequate ventilation, compression, defibrillation, and epinephrine) have been used in prolonged arrest. Hyperkalemia or TCA toxicity.	1 mmol/kg. Infuse slowly and only if ventilation is adequate.	Undiluted 1 mmol/mL (child ≥2 yrs) *or* diluted to 0.5 mmol/mL with D5W (neonates and infants <2 yrs).

Legend: ET = endotracheal, i.o. = intraosseous, i.v. = intravenous, VT = ventricular tachycardia.

References:
1. 1996 Handbook of emergency cardiac care for healthcare providers. Dallas, TX: American Heart Association, 1996.
2. Handbook of ACLS algorithms, Heart and Stroke Foundation of Canada, 1994.
3. Phelps SJ, et al. Guidelines for administration of intravenous medications to pediatric patients, 5th ed. Bethesda, MD: American Society of Health-System Pharmacists, 1996.

CARDIAC ARREST ALGORITHMS

The following figures present adult and pediatric cardiac arrest algorithms consistent with those developed by the Emergency Cardiac Care Subcommittee of the Heart and Stroke Foundation of Canada. This information is not intended to present a comprehensive review; the reader is therefore encouraged to seek additional and confirmatory information.

Reviewed 1999 by the Emergency Cardiac Care Subcommittee, Heart and Stroke Foundation of Canada (M. Ackerman).

Adult Advanced Cardiac Life Support Algorithms (Figures I–VI)

Adult Figure I—Ventricular Fibrillation (VF)/ Pulseless Ventricular Tachycardia (VT)

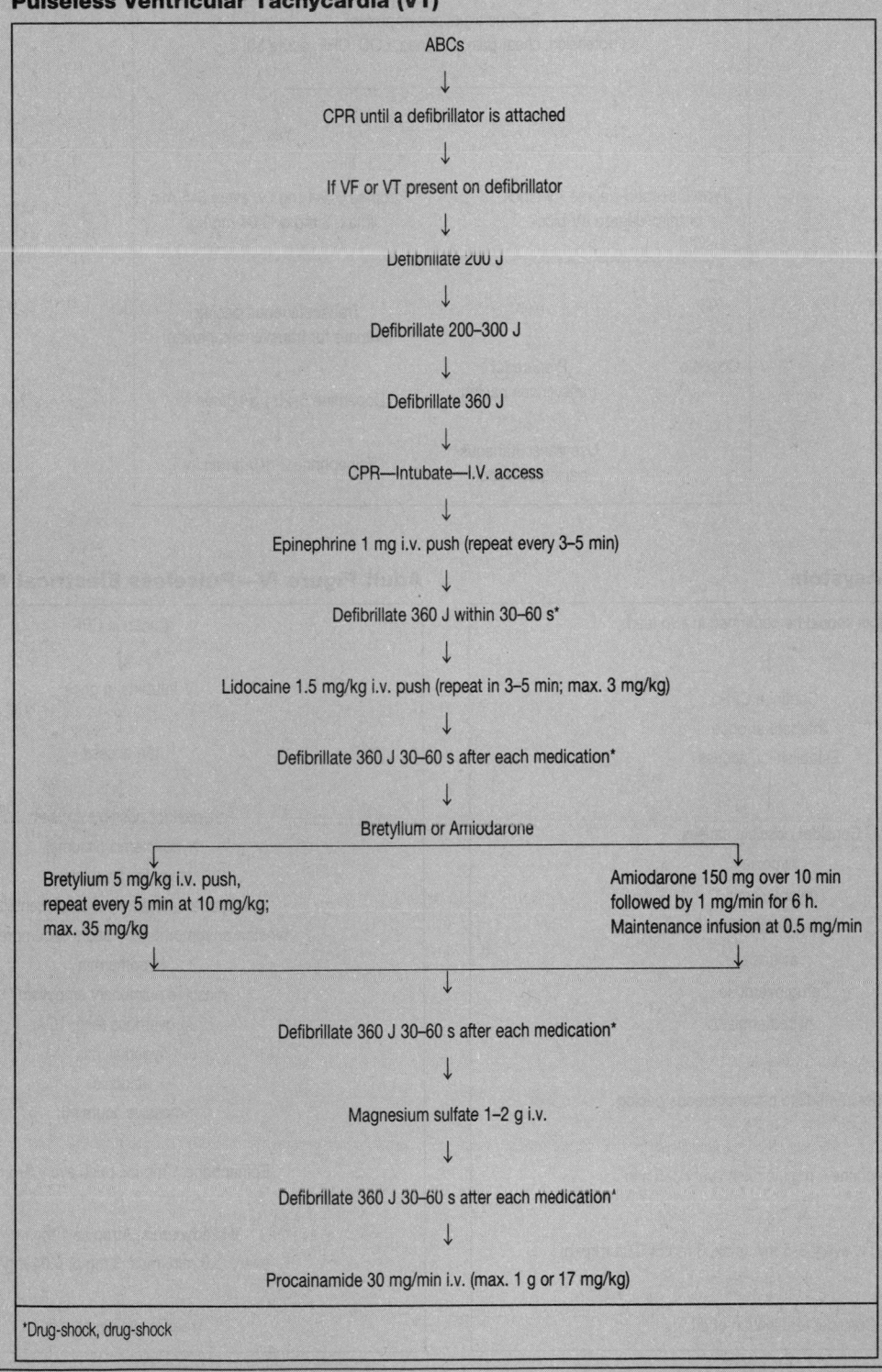

ABCs

↓

CPR until a defibrillator is attached

↓

If VF or VT present on defibrillator

↓

Defibrillate 200 J

↓

Defibrillate 200–300 J

↓

Defibrillate 360 J

↓

CPR—Intubate—I.V. access

↓

Epinephrine 1 mg i.v. push (repeat every 3–5 min)

↓

Defibrillate 360 J within 30–60 s*

↓

Lidocaine 1.5 mg/kg i.v. push (repeat in 3–5 min; max. 3 mg/kg)

↓

Defibrillate 360 J 30–60 s after each medication*

↓

Bretylium or Amiodarone

- Bretylium 5 mg/kg i.v. push, repeat every 5 min at 10 mg/kg; max. 35 mg/kg
- Amiodarone 150 mg over 10 min followed by 1 mg/min for 6 h. Maintenance infusion at 0.5 mg/min

↓

Defibrillate 360 J 30–60 s after each medication*

↓

Magnesium sulfate 1–2 g i.v.

↓

Defibrillate 360 J 30–60 s after each medication*

↓

Procainamide 30 mg/min i.v. (max. 1 g or 17 mg/kg)

*Drug-shock, drug-shock

Adult Advanced Cardiac Life Support Algorithms *(cont'd)*

Adult Figure II—Bradycardia (slow heart rate <60 beats/min)

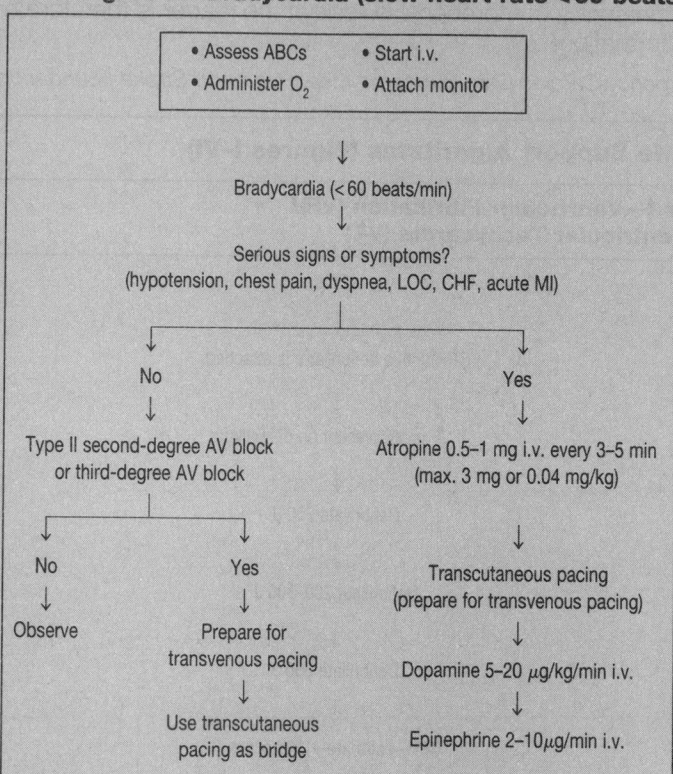

- Assess ABCs
- Start i.v.
- Administer O_2
- Attach monitor

↓

Bradycardia (<60 beats/min)

↓

Serious signs or symptoms?
(hypotension, chest pain, dyspnea, LOC, CHF, acute MI)

No ↓

Type II second-degree AV block or third-degree AV block

- No → Observe
- Yes → Prepare for transvenous pacing → Use transcutaneous pacing as bridge

Yes ↓

Atropine 0.5–1 mg i.v. every 3–5 min (max. 3 mg or 0.04 mg/kg)

↓

Transcutaneous pacing (prepare for transvenous pacing)

↓

Dopamine 5–20 μg/kg/min i.v.

↓

Epinephrine 2–10μg/min i.v.

Adult Figure III—Asystole

Asystole should be confirmed in two leads

↓

Continue CPR
Intubate at once
Establish i.v. access

↓

Consider possible causes:
hypoxia
hypokalemia
hyperkalemia
acidosis
drug overdose
hypothermia

↓

Consider immediate transcutaneous pacing

↓

Epinephrine 1 mg i.v. push every 3–5 min

↓

Atropine 1 mg i.v. every 3–5 min (max. 3 mg or 0.04 mg/kg)

↓

Consider termination of efforts

Adult Figure IV—Pulseless Electrical Activity (PEA)

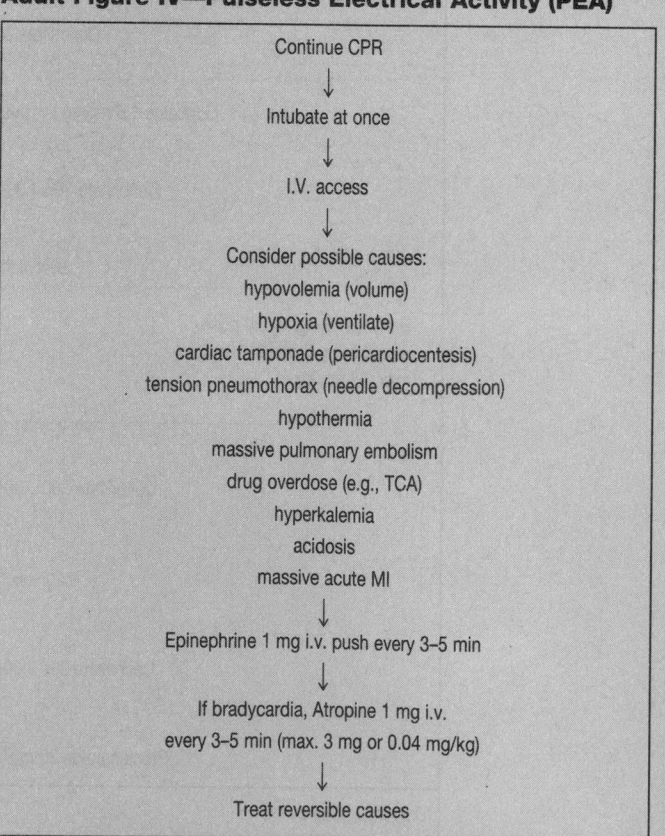

Continue CPR

↓

Intubate at once

↓

I.V. access

↓

Consider possible causes:
hypovolemia (volume)
hypoxia (ventilate)
cardiac tamponade (pericardiocentesis)
tension pneumothorax (needle decompression)
hypothermia
massive pulmonary embolism
drug overdose (e.g., TCA)
hyperkalemia
acidosis
massive acute MI

↓

Epinephrine 1 mg i.v. push every 3–5 min

↓

If bradycardia, Atropine 1 mg i.v. every 3–5 min (max. 3 mg or 0.04 mg/kg)

↓

Treat reversible causes

Adult Advanced Cardiac Life Support Algorithms *(cont'd)*

Adult Figure V—Wide Complex Tachycardia

- Assess ABCs
- Administer O_2
- Start i.v.
- Attach monitor
- Check O_2 saturation
- Assess vital signs
- History
- Physical exam
- ECG
- Chest x-ray

Unstable
(chest pain, dyspnea, LOC, hypotension, CHF, acute MI)

↓

Prepare for cardioversion. Premedicate with sedative (e.g., midazolam, diazepam) with or without analgesic (e.g., morphine, fentanyl, alfentanyl). Have flumazenil and naloxone available for oversedation.

↓

May give medication trial while awaiting cardioversion.

Stable

Wide complex tachycardia uncertain type
↓
Lidocaine
1–1.5 mg/kg i.v. over 3–5 min
↓
Lidocaine
0.5–0.75 mg/kg i.v. push every 5–10 min
(max. 3 mg/kg)
↓
Adenosine 6 mg i.v. push
↓
Adenosine 12 mg i.v. push → Procainamide or Amiodarone

V. tachycardia
↓
Lidocaine
1–1.5 mg/kg i.v. over 3–5 min
↓
Lidocaine 0.5–0.75 mg/kg i.v. push every 5–10 min
(max. 3 mg/kg)
↓
Procainamide or Amiodarone

Procainamide
20–30 mg/min i.v.
(max. 1 g or 17 mg/kg)

Amiodarone 150 mg over 10 min followed by 1 mg/min for 6 h, then 0.5 mg/min

↓

Bretylium 5–10 mg/kg i.v. over 8–10 min (max. 30 mg/kg over 24 hrs)

↓

Synchronized cardioversion

Adult Figure VI—Paroxysmal Supraventricular Tachycardia (PSVT)

- Assess ABCs
- Administer O_2
- Start i.v.
- Attach monitor
- Check O_2 saturation
- Assess vital signs
- History
- Physical exam
- ECG
- Chest x-ray

Unstable
(chest pain, dyspnea, LOC, hypotension, CHF, acute MI)

↓

Prepare for cardioversion. Premedicate with sedative (e.g., midazolam, diazepam) with or without analgesic (e.g., morphine, fentanyl, alfentanyl). Have flumazenil and naloxone available for oversedation.

Stable, narrow, complex SVT
↓
Vagal maneuvers
↓
Adenosine or Verapamil

Adenosine 6 mg i.v. rapid push
↓
Adenosine 12 mg i.v. rapid push
↓
Verapamil 2.5–5 mg i.v. (if BP normal)
↓
Verapamil 5–10 mg i.v.

Verapamil 2.5–5 mg i.v.
(if BP normal)
↓
Verapamil 5–10 mg i.v.

↓

Consider
Digoxin
ß-blockers
Diltiazem

↓

Synchronized cardioversion

Pediatric Advanced Cardiac Life Support Algorithms (Figures I–IV)

Pediatric Figure I—Asystole

Asystole should be confirmed in two leads

↓

Continue CPR
Secure airway
Hyperventilate with 100% O_2
Obtain i.v./i.o. access

↓

Epinephrine, first dose
i.v./i.o.: 0.01 mg/kg (1:10 000, 0.1 mL/kg)
ET: 0.1 mg/kg (1:1 000, 0.1 mL/kg)

↓

Epinephrine, second and repeat doses
i.v./i.o./ET: 0.1 mg/kg (1:1 000, 0.1 mL/kg)
Doses up to 0.2 mg/kg (1:1 000, 0.2 mL/kg) may be effective
Repeat every 3–5 min

Pediatric Figure II—Electromechanical Dissociation/ Pulseless Electrical Activity

Continue CPR
Secure airway
Hyperventilate with 100% O_2
Obtain i.v./i.o. access

↓

Identify and treat the cause:
severe hypoxia
severe acidosis
severe hypovolemia
cardiac tamponade
tension pneumothorax
severe hypothermia

↓

Continue CPR

↓

Protocol for asystole

Pediatric Figure III—Bradycardia

- Assess ABCs
- Secure airway
- Administer 100% O_2
- Start i.v. or i.o. access
- Assess vital signs

↓

Compressions are necessary,
if after oxygenation and ventilation, pulse <60/min,
and associated with poor systemic perfusion

↓

Epinephrine
i.v./i.o.: 0.01 mg/kg (1:10 000, 0.1 mL/kg)
ET: 0.1 mg/kg (1:1 000, 0.1 mL/kg)
Repeat the same dose every 3–5 min

↓

Atropine 0.02 mg/kg i.v.
Min. single dose: 0.1 mg
Max. single dose: 0.5 mg for child
Max. single dose: 1 mg for adolescent
Repeat the same dose if necessary

Pediatric Figure IV—Pulseless Ventricular Tachycardia/ Ventricular Fibrillation

Continue CPR
Secure airway
Hyperventilate with 100% O_2
Obtain i.v./i.o. access but
do not delay defibrillation

↓

Defibrillate 2 J/kg
Repeat if necessary 4 J/kg, 4 J/kg

↓

Epinephrine, first dose
i.v./i.o.: 0.01 mg/kg (1:10 000, 0.1 mL/kg)
ET: 0.1 mg/kg (1:1 000, 0.1 mL/kg)

↓

Defibrillate 4 J/kg 30–60 s after each medication

↓

Lidocaine 1 mg/kg i.v./i.o.

↓

Defibrillate 4 J/kg 30–60 s after each medication

↓

Epinephrine, second and repeat doses
i.v./i.o./ET: 0.1 mg/kg (1:1 000, 0.1 mL/kg)
Doses up to 0.2 mg/kg (1:1 000, 0.2 mL/kg) may be effective
Repeat every 3–5 min*

↓

Lidocaine 1 mg/kg i.v./i.o.*

↓

Consider Bretylium first dose 5 mg/kg i.v.,
second dose 10 mg/kg i.v.*

*Defibrillate 4 J/kg 30–60 s after each medication

Legend: ET=endotracheal, i.o.=intraosseous, i.v.=intravenous

References:
1. 1996 Handbook of emergency cardiac care for healthcare providers. Dallas, TX: American Heart Association, 1996.
2. Cummins RO, ed. Textbook of advanced cardiac life support. Dallas, TX: American Heart Association, 1997.
3. Handbook of ACLS algorithms, Heart and Stroke Foundation of Canada, 1994.
4. Kowey PR, Levine JH, et al. Randomized, double-blind comparison of intravenous amiodarone and bretylium in the treatment of patients with recurrent, hemodynamically destabilizing ventricular tachycardia or fibrillation. Circulation 1995; 92(11):3255–63.

NONPHARMACOLOGIC THERAPY FOR HYPERTENSION

Table I provides a summary of the recommendations on nonpharmacologic approaches for high blood pressure prevention and control that are consistent with those developed by the Canadian Working Group on Non-pharmacological Prevention and Control for Hypertension. This information is not intended to present a comprehensive review; the reader is therefore encouraged to seek additional and confirmatory information.

Reviewed 1999 by N. Campbell for the Canadian Coalition for High Blood Pressure Prevention and Control, Canadian Hypertension Society, Health Canada and the Heart and Stroke Foundation of Canada.

Table I—Nonpharmacologic Therapy for Hypertension

High Blood Pressure Considerations	Normotensive Individuals	Hypertensive Patients	Approaches for Health Care Professionals
Alcohol	Excessive intake of alcohol increases blood pressure. Reduce alcohol intake to 2 or fewer standard drinks/day (i.e., 4 oz wine, 1 oz liquor, 12 oz beer) with a consumption of not more than 14 drinks/week in men, 9 drinks/week in women.		Determine the alcohol consumption of patients. Advise on effects of excessive consumption and means of reduction; refer to appropriate community-based programs.
Weight	Weight gain increases blood pressure. Obesity is an important cause of hypertension. For overweight hypertensive patients, a weight loss of at least 4.5 kg is necessary for a significant decrease in blood pressure.		Determine body mass index (BMI) of patients and inform patient. For overweight patients advise a weight loss of at least 4.5 kg; refer for appropriate counselling/treatment. Ensure a blood pressure cuff of appropriate size is used.
Salt (sodium)	There is evidence that short-term sodium restriction does not significantly reduce blood pressure in normotensive persons, however this area is controversial. The diets of many Canadians contain large quantities of sodium which may be unsafe.	Sodium restriction reduces blood pressure in hypertensive patients. The recommended sodium intake target ranges are 90–130 mmol/d (2–3 g) of sodium or 5–7.5 g (1–1.5 tsp.) of sodium chloride.	Determine the sodium consumption of patients. Advise patients to choose low-salt foods, avoid salty foods, minimize adding salt at the table and in cooking. Advise patients to follow Canada's Food Guide to Healthy Eating.
Physical exercise	Regular low intensity (45–60% of maximal oxygen consumption) physical activity for 50–60 minutes, 3 or 4 times/week will lower blood pressure.		Encourage regular physical activity tailored to the patient, 3 or 4 times a week.
Calcium Magnesium Potassium	There is evidence that supplementation with calcium, magnesium or potassium will not reduce blood pressure. The diets of many Canadians are low in calcium and potassium.		Advise patients to follow Canada's Food Guide to Healthy Eating.
Relaxation and Stress management	There is inadequate evidence to determine the effect of stress management on blood pressure of normotensive persons.	Individualized cognitive behavioral interventions lower blood pressure of selected hypertensive patients.	Consider stress in hypertensive patients and refer those under high stress for psychological management where available.
Simultaneous nonpharmacologic measures	Simultaneous nonpharmacologic intervention can prevent the onset of hypertension in some high risk patients.	Simultaneous nonpharmacologic intervention can replace pharmacologic therapy in some patients with mild hypertension.	Individualize nonpharmacologic therapy for high risk and hypertensive patients. Weight control appears to be the most effective single nonpharmacologic intervention.

References:

1. Recommendations of the Canadian Working Group for Non-pharmacologic Prevention and Control of Hypertension. A satellite symposia to the 4th International Conference on Preventative Cardiology; 1997 Jul 4; Montreal.

DRUGS IN DENTISTRY

The following is a summary on the use of analgesics, anti-infectives, anesthetics as well as drugs for medical emergencies in dentistry. This information is not intended to present a comprehensive review; the reader is therefore encouraged to seek additional and confirmatory information.

Reviewed 1999 by W.C. Foong and D.A. Haas.

Analgesics

The following are considerations for the use of analgesics:

- Eliminate the source of pain.
- Individualize regimens.
- Optimize dose and frequency before switching.
- Maximize the nonopioid before adding the opioid.
- For nonsteroidal anti-inflammatory drugs (NSAIDs) consider a loading dose and/or a preoperative dose.
- Avoid chronic use of any analgesic.
- Reduce the dose in the elderly.
- Be aware of the following contraindications and cautions for ASA and NSAIDs:
  —allergic reaction to any NSAID including ASA
  —ASA-induced asthma and nasal polyps
  —gastric inflammatory or ulcerative disease
  —history of bleeding disorder or concurrent use of anticoagulants
  —concurrent use of antihypertensives (except calcium channel blockers) if NSAIDs are to be used for more than 5 days
  —concurrent use of antineoplastic doses of methotrexate
- Be aware of the following contraindications and cautions for opioids:
  —severe respiratory disease
  —severe inflammatory bowel disease
  —concurrent use of alcohol or other CNS depressants

Table I lists common analgesics and the recommended adult doses to treat orofacial pain.

Table I—Analgesics for Orofacial Pain

Drug	Recommended Adult Dose
Nonopioids (including NSAIDs)	
acetaminophen	325–1 000 mg q4–6h
ASA	325–1 000 mg q4–6h
diflunisal	500 mg q 12h
floctafenine	200–400 mg q6–8h
flurbiprofen	50 mg q4–6h
ibuprofen	400 mg q4–6h
ketoprofen	25–50 mg q6–8h
ketorolac	10 mg q4–6h
naproxen	250 mg q6–8h
Opioids (with a nonopioid)	
codeine	30–60 mg q4–6h
oxycodone	5–10 mg q4–6h

Antibiotics

Table II lists common antibiotics and the recommended adult doses for orofacial infections.

Table II—Antibiotic Dosage for Orofacial Infections

Drug	Recommended Adult Dose
amoxicillin	250–500 mg t.i.d.
amoxicillin/clavulanate	250–500 mg t.i.d.
cephalexin	250–500 mg q.i.d.
clarithromycin	250–500 mg b.i.d.
clindamycin	150–300 mg q.i.d.
cloxacillin	250–500 mg q.i.d.
doxycycline	100 mg once daily or b.i.d.
erythromycin	250–500 mg q.i.d.
metronidazole	250–500 mg t.i.d.
penicillin V	300–600 mg q.i.d.

Antibiotic Prophylaxis for Endocarditis

- Prophylactic antibiotic coverage **is recommended** for patients with the following conditions:
  Prosthetic heart valves
  Previous bacterial endocarditis
  Complex cyanotic congenital heart disease
  Surgically constructed systemic pulmonary shunts or conduits
  Rheumatic and other acquired valvular dysfunction
  Hypertrophic cardiomyopathy
  Mitral valve prolapse with regurgitation and/or thickened leaflets
  Most congenital cardiac malformations, other than those listed below.
- Prophylactic antibiotic coverage **is not recommended** for patients with the following conditions:
  Isolated secundum atrial septal defect
  Surgically repaired atrial septal defect, ventricular septal defect, or patent ductus arteriosus, without residua beyond 6 months
  Previous coronary artery bypass graft surgery
  Mitral valve prolapse without regurgitation
  Physiologic, functional, or innocent heart murmurs
  Previous Kawasaki disease without valvular dysfunction
  Previous rheumatic fever without valvular dysfunction
  Cardiac pacemakers and implanted defibrillators.
- Patients who have conditions which require prophylaxis, as listed above, should receive antibiotic coverage for the dental procedures listed in Table III:

Table III—Dental Procedures Requiring Antibiotic Prophylaxis

—Dental extractions
—Periodontal procedures including surgery, scaling, root planing, probing and recall maintenance
—Dental implant placement and reimplantation of avulsed teeth
—Endodontic instrumentation or surgery only beyond the apex
—Subgingival placement of antibiotic fibres or strips
—Initial placement of orthodontic bands but not brackets
—Intraligamentary local anesthetic injections
—Prophylactic cleaning of teeth or implants where bleeding is anticipated.

- Endocarditis prophylaxis **is not recommended** for the following dental procedures:
  Restorative dentistry (clinical judgement may indicate antibiotic use in selected circumstances that may create significant bleeding)
  Local anesthetic injections (nonintraligamentary)
  Intracanal endodontic treatment; post placement and buildup
  Placement of rubber dams
  Postoperative suture removal
  Placement of removable prosthodontic or orthodontic appliances
  Taking of oral impressions
  Fluoride treatments
  Taking of oral radiographs
  Orthodontic appliance adjustment
  Shedding of primary teeth.

The recommended antibiotic prophylaxis regimens for endocarditis are listed in Table IV. It is important that practitioners exercise their own judgement in determining the choice of antibiotics and number of doses that are to be administered in individual cases or special circumstances. Alternative regimens as recommended by the American Heart Association are also acceptable.

Table IV—Antibiotic Prophylaxis for Endocarditis[a]

A. Oral Regimen

Drug	Adult Dose	Pediatric Dose[b]
Standard regimen		
amoxicillin	2 g to be taken 1 h before procedure.	50 mg/kg to be taken 1 h before procedure.
Penicillin allergy		
clindamycin	600 mg to be taken 1 h before procedure.	20 mg/kg to be taken 1 h before procedure.
or azithromycin	500 mg to be taken 1 h before procedure.	15 mg/kg to be taken 1 h before procedure.
or clarithromycin	500 mg to be taken 1 h before procedure.	15 mg/kg to be taken 1 h before procedure.
or cephalexin[c]	2 g to be taken 1 h before procedure.	50 mg/kg to be taken 1 h before procedure.
or cefadroxil[c]	2 g to be taken 1 h before procedure.	50 mg/kg to be taken 1 h before procedure.

B. Regimen for Patients Unable to Take Oral Medications

Drug	Adult Dose	Pediatric Dose[b]
Standard regimen		
ampicillin	2 g i.m. or i.v. to be given within 30 min before procedure.	50 mg/kg i.m. or i.v. to be given within 30 min before procedure.
Penicillin allergy		
clindamycin	600 mg i.v. to be given within 30 min before procedure.	20 mg/kg i.v. to be given within 30 min before procedure.
or cefazolin[c]	1 g i.m. or i.v. to be given with 30 min before procedure.	25 mg/kg i.m. or i.v. to be given within 30 min before procedure.

[a] For a patient who is already taking an antibiotic normally used for endocarditis prophylaxis, the practitioner should consider selecting a drug from a different class. If possible, one could delay the procedure for at least 9 days after completion of the antibiotic, which would allow the use of the same drug.
[b] The total pediatric dose should not exceed the recommended adult dose.
[c] Cephalosporins should not be used in individuals with a history of immediate-type hypersensitivity reaction (urticaria, angioedema or anaphylaxis) to penicillins.

Antibiotic Prophylaxis for Dental Patients with Total Joint Replacements

- Antibiotic prophylaxis **is not indicated** for dental patients with pins, plates and screws, nor is it routinely indicated for most dental patients with total joint replacements.
- Antibiotic prophylaxis may be warranted for a small number of patients with total joint replacements who also have the following conditions:

—Immunocompromised/immunosuppressed patients:
  Inflammatory arthropathies; rheumatoid arthritis, systemic lupus erythematosus
  Disease-, drug- or radiation-induced immunosuppression
—Other patients:
  Insulin-dependent (Type 1) diabetes
  First two years following joint placement
  Previous prosthetic joint infections
  Malnourishment
  Hemophilia

Refer to Table III for the dental procedures requiring antibiotic prophylaxis and Table IV for the antibiotic regimens that may be used in these cases. Note that patients not allergic to penicillin may be given cephalexin 2 g orally, one hour before the procedure as the standard regimen instead of amoxicillin.

Table V—Antifungals for the Treatment of Oral Candidiasis

Drug	Adult Dose
Immunocompetent patients	
nystatin oral suspension	100 000–500 000 units q.i.d. × 10 days
Immunocompromised patients	
ketoconazole	200–400 mg once daily × 1–2 weeks
fluconazole	50–100 mg once daily × 1–2 weeks
itraconazole	200 mg once daily × 1–2 weeks

Local Anesthetics

Potential Interactions with Epinephrine or Levonordefrin

The addition of epinephrine or levonordefrin to the local anesthetic formulation improves the depth and duration of the local anesthetic block. However, caution must be exercised if a patient has a history of significant cardiovascular disease or is concomitantly taking any of the following drugs:

- nonselective β-blockers (e.g., nadolol, oxprenolol, pindolol, propranolol, sotalol, timolol) resulting in increased blood pressure
- tricyclic antidepressants (e.g., amitriptyline, doxepin, imipramine, nortriptyline, among others) possibly resulting in increased blood pressure and cardiac dysrhythmias
- phenothiazines, especially chlorpromazine, thioridazine and clozapine, resulting in hypotension.

In these cases, one should consider minimizing epinephrine and levonordefrin administration and limiting epinephrine to <40 μg and levonordefrin to <200 μg.

The vasoconstrictor dose per 1.8 mL dental cartridge is as follows:

—1 cartridge of 1:200 000 epinephrine = 9 μg
—1 cartridge of 1:100 000 epinephrine = 18 μg
—1 cartridge of 1:50 000 epinephrine = 36 μg
—1 cartridge of 1:20 000 levonordefrin = 90 μg.

The maximum recommended doses of local anesthetics are listed in Table VI and Table VII outlines their expected duration of action.

Table VI—Maximum Recommended Doses of Local Anesthetics

Drug	Maximum Adult Dose (mg/kg)	Maximum # of Cartridges*
articaine 4% with epinephrine 1:100 000 or 1:200 000	7	7
bupivacaine 0.5% with epinephrine 1:200 000	2	10
lidocaine 2% with epinephrine 1:50 000 or 1:100 000	7	13
mepivacaine 2% with levonordefrin 1:20 000	7	11
mepivacaine 3% plain	6	7
prilocaine 4% plain	8	8
prilocaine 4% with epinephrine 1:200 000	8	8

* 1.8 mL volume except articaine which may be 1.7 mL or 1.8 mL depending on the manufacturer.

Table VII—Expected Duration of Action (in minutes) of Local Anesthetics

Drug	Maxillary Infiltration		Inferior Alveolar Block	
	Tooth pulp	Soft tissue	Tooth pulp	Soft tissue
articaine 4% with epinephrine 1:100 000 or 1:200 000	60	170	90	220
bupivacaine 0.5% with epinephrine 1:200 000	40	340	240	440
lidocaine 2% with epinephrine 1:50 000 or 1:100 000	60	170	85	190
mepivacaine 2% with levonordefrin 1:20 000	50	130	75	185
mepivacaine 3% plain	25	90	40	165
prilocaine 4% plain	20	105	55	190
prilocaine 4% with epinephrine 1:200 000	40	140	60	220

Medical Emergencies

Treatment of a medical emergency in a dental office begins with assessment and, if necessary, treatment of airway, breathing and circulation (cardiopulmonary resuscitation). Most often, only after these basics are addressed should the use of the drugs listed in Table VIII be considered. They should, however, be readily available for such emergencies. Additional agents may be appropriate depending on the nature of the dental practice.

Table VIII—Drugs for Medical Emergencies

Drug	Indication	Recommended Adult Dose[a]	Pediatric Dose[b]
oxygen	Most medical emergencies.	100% inhalation	100% inhalation
epinephrine	Anaphylaxis. Asthmatic bronchospasm which is unresponsive to salbutamol. Cardiac arrest.	0.3 mg i.v. or 0.5 mg i.m. 0.3 mg i.v. or 0.5 mg i.m. 1 mg i.v. or i.m.	0.01 mg/kg i.v. or i.m.
nitroglycerin	Angina pectoris.	0.3 or 0.4 mg sublingual	
diphenhydramine or chlorpheniramine	Allergic reactions.	50 mg i.v. or i.m. 10 mg i.v. or i.m.	1 mg/kg i.v. or i.m.
salbutamol inhalation aerosol	Asthmatic bronchospasm.	2 puffs (100 μg/puff)	1 puff (100 μg)

[a] The dose suggested for the i.m. route is also appropriate for sublingual injections.
[b] The total pediatric dose should not exceed the recommended adult dose.

References:

1. American Dental Association; American Academy of Orthopaedic Surgeons. Advisory statement on antibiotic prophylaxis for dental patients with total joint replacements JADA 1997;128:1004–1008.
2. Becker DE. Drug interactions in dental practice: a summary of facts and controversies. Compend Contin Dent Educ 1994; 15:1228–43.
3. Coco JW, Pankey GA. The use of antimicrobials in dentistry. Compend Contin Dent Educ 1989; 10(12):664–72.
4. Dajani AS, Taubert KA, Wilson W, et al. Prevention of bacterial endocarditis. Recommendations of the American Heart Association. JAMA 1997; 277(22):1794–1801.
5. Dionne RA, Gordon SM. Nonsteroidal anti-inflammatory drugs for acute pain control. Den Clin North Am 1994; 38(4):645–67.
6. Haas DA. Current concepts in the use of analgesics in dentistry. Oral Health 1993; 82(2):7–12.
7. Haas DA. Pharmacologic considerations for the treatment of temporomandibular disorders. J Can Dent Assoc 1995; 61:105–14.
8. Jastak JT, Yagiela JA, Donaldson D, eds. Local anesthesia of the oral cavity. Philadelphia: Saunders, 1995.
9. Levine M, Lexchin J, Pellizzari R, eds. Drugs of choice: a formulary for general practice 2nd ed. Ottawa, ON: Canadian Medical Association, 1997:69.
10. Malamed SF. Handbook of local anesthesia. 4th ed. St. Louis: Mosby, 1997.
11. Malamed SF. Medical emergencies in the dental office. 4th ed. St. Louis: Mosby, 1993.
12. Pallasch TJ. Antibiotics for acute orofacial infections. California Dent Assoc J 1993; 21:34–44.
13. Pérusse R, Goulet JP, Turcotte JY. Contraindications to vasoconstrictors in dentistry. Oral Surg Oral Med Oral Pathol 1992; 74:679–97.
14. Peterson LJ. Principles of antibiotic therapy. In: Oral and Maxillofacial Infections, 3rd ed. Philadelphia: Saunders, 1994.
15. United States Pharmacopeial Drug Information Index, 1998.
16. Yagiela JA, Neidle EA, Dowd FJ, eds. Pharmacology and therapeutics for dentistry. 4th ed. St. Louis: Mosby, 1998.

PERIOPERATIVE MANAGEMENT OF MEDICATIONS

The following is an overview of the management of chronic drug use before anesthesia and surgery. The perioperative considerations noted in Table I represent a conservative approach to deal with most occurrences. Individual practices may vary. The information is not intended to present a comprehensive review; the reader is therefore encouraged to seek additional and confirmatory information.

Reviewed 1999 by M. Friedland, S. Otawa and N. Ramuscak.

In the context of the following discussion and table, "perioperative" refers to the times before, during and following surgery; "preoperative" refers to the time before surgery; and "intraoperative" refers to the time during surgery. Drugs that are medically essential to maintain physiologic homeostasis during the perioperative period require special consideration preoperatively.

Some basic principles for preoperative drug administration are listed below:

- decrease gastric load of nonessential medications.
- give essential medications required to maintain optimal homeostasis. Essential oral medications should be given up to 2 hours preoperatively to ensure some absorption and to decrease gastric contents. If the patient's regular administration time falls within the 0- to 2-hour preoperative period, then automatically adjust the administration time to 2 hours preoperatively.
- premedication drugs are used for their beneficial effects intraoperatively and may be given less than 2 hours preoperatively.

The anesthetist should be aware of prescription, over-the-counter, alcohol and illicit drug use to effectively manage intraoperative patient care. Table I outlines general recommendations for chronic drug therapy management before elective anesthesia and surgery. To optimize the risk-benefit ratio, modifications may be made based on the type of anesthesia, surgical technique and individual patient needs. Table II lists the half-lives of common cyclic antidepressants and NSAIDs. Table III outlines recommendations for perioperative corticosteroid coverage.

Table I—Perioperative Management of Medications

Drug(s)	Perioperative Considerations
Alzheimer's disease therapy	
Cholinesterase inhibitors (e.g., donepezil)	• May continue preoperatively. • Can exaggerate succinylcholine-type muscle relaxation during anesthesia.
Analgesics	
Nonsteroidal anti-inflammatory drugs (NSAIDs)	• Should be discontinued to allow for elimination of the drug, approximately 5 half-lives (see Table II). • Chronic preoperative use is associated with increased postoperative bleeding complications. May be used perioperatively for preemptive analgesia.
Opioids	• Continue chronic therapy preoperatively. • Be aware of preoperative doses and duration of use to avoid withdrawal.
Antacids	
Nonparticulate (e.g., citric acid and sodium citrate)	• Administer 15–30 minutes before induction of anesthesia. Recommended since no pulmonary damage is caused if aspirated.
Particulate (e.g., alumina-magnesia)	• Discontinue at least 4 hours preoperatively due to potential pulmonary damage if aspirated.
Antibacterials	• If used for chronic therapy (e.g., urinary tract infection), continue preoperatively.
Anticoagulants	• The management of anticoagulants preoperatively requires the consideration of several factors including: the medical indication for the use of the anticoagulant, the emergency nature of the surgery, the type of surgical procedure planned and the type of anesthetic planned. Weigh benefits versus risk.
Heparin	• Discontinue 4–6 hours preoperatively. • For urgent surgery, may be reversed with protamine 1mg/100 units of heparin estimated in circulation.
Low molecular weight heparins	• For prophylaxis, may be continued preoperatively. • For treatment, management depends on dosing regimen, i.e., for once daily, discontinue 24 hours preoperatively; or for twice daily, discontinue 12 hours preoperatively. • For urgent surgery, may be reversed with protamine 1 mg/kg to a maximum of 50 mg. • Risk vs. benefit should be carefully considered when spinal/epidural anesthesia is being considered.
Platelet aggregation inhibitors	
ASA	• Discontinue at least 7 days preoperatively. • Irreversibly inhibits platelet function for its life span (7–10 days). • Weigh risk of stroke vs. bleeding.

Table I—Perioperative Management of Medications *(cont'd)*

Drug(s)	Perioperative Considerations
Anticoagulants *(cont'd)*	
Platelet aggregation inhibitors *(cont'd)*	
ticlopidine	• Discontinue 14 days before surgery. • Irreversibly inhibits platelet function, has a broader spectrum of activity than ASA and markedly prolongs bleeding time. • Cannot be reversed with fresh frozen plasma.
Warfarin	• Usually discontinue 1–3 days preoperatively. • Patients may be admitted to hospital so that i.v. heparin can be temporarily instituted and discontinued 6 hours preoperatively. • Weigh risk of stroke vs. bleeding.
Anticonvulsants (e.g., carbamazepine, gabapentin, lamotrigine, phenytoin, topiramate, valproic acid, vigabatrin)	• Continue preoperatively.
Antidepressants	
Cyclic antidepressants	• May continue preoperatively. • Patients may be predisposed to intraoperative dysrhythmias. • In consultation with patient's psychiatrist, weigh risk of withdrawal vs. intraoperative risks. • If discontinued, allow at least 5 half-lives of drug (see Table II).
Monoamine oxidase inhibitors (MAOIs)	• Patients subject to autonomic instability due to inhibition of catecholamine breakdown. • May exhibit a greatly exaggerated hypertensive response to endogenous release of catecholamines as a result of endotracheal intubation or surgical manipulation. • Interaction with meperidine can lead to hyperpyrexia, cardiovascular instability and coma. May use morphine in reduced dosage. • Controversial, weigh risk of withdrawal vs. intraoperative risks.
moclobemide (reversible MAOI A)	• Discontinue at least 2 days preoperatively.
phenelzine (irreversible MAOI A & B)	• Discontinue at least 10–14 days preoperatively.
tranylcypromine (irreversible MAOI A & B)	• Discontinue 7 days preoperatively.
Selective serotonin reuptake inhibitors (SSRIs) (e.g., fluoxetine)	• May continue preoperatively.
Serotonin norepinephrine reuptake inhibitors (SNRI) (e.g., venlafaxine)	• No data available. • If to be discontinued, taper dosage gradually over 2 weeks preoperatively.
Antihistamines (e.g., astemizole, terfenadine)	• Continue perioperatively. • Patient may be more prone to arrhythmias.
Antineoplastics	• In consultation with patient's oncologist, may or may not be discontinued preoperatively.
Nonsteroidal aromatase inhibitors (e.g., anastrozole, letrozole)	• Continue preoperatively.*
Antiparkinsonian agents (e.g., anticholinergics, bromocriptine, levodopa, ropinirole, selegiline)	• Continue preoperatively. • Withdrawal of levodopa-carbidopa has been associated with a neuroleptic malignant-like syndrome.
Catechol-o-methyltransferase inhibitors (e.g., tolcapone)	• Continue preoperatively.
Antipsychotics (e.g., chlorpromazine, haloperidol, thioridazine)	• Continue preoperatively. • Sometimes given as premedication before anesthesia. • Patients may be more prone to hypotension.
Atypical antipsychotics (e.g., clozapine, olanzepine, quetiapine, risperidone)	• Continue preoperatively.*
Antituberculosis agents (e.g., ethambutol, isoniazid, rifampin)	• Continue preoperatively. • May affect the hepatic metabolism of some anesthetic agents.
Antitussives and Decongestants	• Discontinue preoperatively. • Patients with respiratory infections are usually not appropriate candidates for surgery.
Antivirals	
Nucleoside analogue reverse transcriptase inhibitors (e.g., didanosine, lamivudine, stavudine, zalcitabine, zidovudine)	• Continue preoperatively.*
Protease inhibitors (e.g., indinavir, ritonavir, saquinavir)	• Continue preoperatively.*

*Based on authors' clinical experience and assessment of drug pharmacology.

Table I—Perioperative Management of Medications *(cont'd)*

Drug(s)	Perioperative Considerations
Cardiovascular drugs alpha-adrenergic agonists antiarrhythmics beta-adrenergic blocking agents calcium channel blockers coronary vasodilators digoxin	• Continue preoperatively. • Administer approximately 2 hours preoperatively with sips of water. • If discontinued, beta-blockers and central alpha-adrenergic agonists should be gradually withdrawn due to withdrawal syndromes.
Angiotensin-converting enzyme (ACE) inhibitors (e.g., captopril, cilazapril, enalapril, lisinopril, quinapril) Angiotensin II receptor antagonists (e.g., losartan, valsartan)	• Normally continued preoperatively. May be discontinued for specific patients when even a brief period of hypotension is contraindicated (e.g., major cardiac or vascular surgery).
Corticosteroids, inhaled (e.g., beclomethasone, budesonide)	• Administer preoperatively. • Reduces pulmonary hyperreactivity caused by the insertion and removal of the endotracheal tube.
Corticosteroids, systemic (e.g., dexamethasone, prednisone)	• Patients with adrenal insufficiency (e.g., those on chronic steroid therapy) require replacement cortisol usually in the form of i.v. hydrocortisone immediately before, during and for 24–48 hours after major surgery (see Table III). The patient's usual oral steroid dose can then be restarted. • Administer the patient's usual oral steroid dose preoperatively before minor surgery.
Diabetes therapy Insulin	• Insulin requirements will need modification. • Insulin may be given as i.v. infusion or s.c. injection by sliding scale therapy depending on the severity of the diabetes, and the type and length of surgery.
Oral hypoglycemic agents	• Withhold oral agents on the morning of surgery since the patient is fasting; longer-acting agents (e.g., chlorpropamide) should be discontinued 1 day before surgery.
Diuretics Loop diuretics (e.g., furosemide) Potassium-sparing agents (e.g., spironolactone) Thiazides	• Withhold on the preoperative morning due to potential volume and electrolyte imbalances.
Drugs of Abuse Alcohol	• Chronic use can increase anesthetic requirements while acute intoxication will decrease anesthetic requirements. • Withdrawal symptoms (e.g., personality changes, tremor, agitation, confusion, restlessness, DTs, seizures) are a potential postoperative problem. • Treatment of DTs includes thiamine, electrolytes and benzodiazepines. • Consider prophylactic thiamine in patients at high risk.
Barbiturates — see Hypnotics and Sedatives	
Marijuana	• May cause cardiac depressant effects and affect temperature regulation.
Opioids — see Analgesics	
Stimulants (e.g., cocaine)	• May cause vasoconstriction, hypertension, tachyarrhythmias. • Chronic users require larger amounts of anesthetic; acutely intoxicated patients require less.
Gastrointestinal agents Histamine (H_2) receptor antagonists (e.g., cimetidine, ranitidine)	• Administer 2 hours preoperatively. • Often used as premedication to decrease gastric acidity.
Prokinetic agents Cisapride	• Risk vs. benefit needs to be assessed by physician. It is recommended to be discontinued preoperatively in patients with cardiac arrhythmic dysfunctions, ischemic heart disease and uncorrected electrolyte disorders (e.g., hypokalemia, hypomagnesemia).
Domperidone, metoclopramide	• Administer 2 hours preoperatively. • May be used as premedication to ensure gastric emptying, especially in diabetic patients.
Proton pump inhibitors (e.g., omeprazole)	• Administer 2 hours preoperatively.

Table I—Perioperative Management of Medications *(cont'd)*

Drug(s)	Perioperative Considerations
Gout therapy allopurinol	• Continue preoperatively.
Hypnotics and Sedatives Barbiturates	• Continue chronic therapy preoperatively. • Be aware of preoperative dosage and duration of therapy to avoid withdrawal.
Benzodiazepines	• May continue preoperatively (often used as a premedication). • Chronic therapy may cause delayed emergence from anesthesia. • If on chronic medication before admission, should be restarted postoperatively to prevent withdrawal.
Immunosuppressive agents (e.g., cyclosporine)	• Use is guided by consultation with patient's transplant surgeon.
Inflammatory bowel disease therapy (e.g., 5-aminosalicylic acid, olsalazine)	• Continue preoperatively.
Lipid lowering agents HMG-CoA reductase inhibitors (e.g., atorvastatin, fluvastatin, lovastatin, pravastatin, simvastatin)	• Discontinue 4–7 days before major surgery since the patient may be predisposed to rhabdomyolysis.
Mania therapy Lithium	• Continue preoperatively. • Sodium depletion due to fluid loss may enhance renal lithium reabsorption, leading to increased lithium levels.
Multivitamins and Iron	• Withhold on the morning of surgery, not medically essential.
Myasthenia gravis therapy (e.g., neostigmine, pyridostigmine)	• In consultation with patient's neurologist, usual dose may be continued preoperatively depending on patient needs. • If patient's symptoms are mild, drug may be withheld.
Ophthalmologicals	• Continue preoperatively, see below for systemic effects or anesthetic implications.
Beta-adrenergic blocking agents (e.g., betaxolol, timololl)	• May cause cardiac depression, possible increased airway resistance.
Cyclopentolate	• Anticholinergic effect may cause CNS toxicity: dysarthria, disorientation and psychosis.
Echothiophate	• Long-acting anticholinesterase miotic may prolong effects of succinylcholine.
Epinephrine and phenylephrine	• Cardiovascular effects include hypertension and tachycardia.
Respiratory system agents Beta-adrenergic agonists, inhaled (e.g., salbutamol)	• Administer preoperatively. • Additional dose may be given as premedication to maximize pulmonary function.
Leukotriene receptor antagonists (e.g., zafirlukast)	• Continue preoperatively.*
Theophyllines	• Continue preoperatively. • May increase arrhythmogenic potential. • General anesthesia decreases theophylline clearance.
Sex hormones Estrogens	• Withhold on the morning of surgery, although not implicated in thrombogenesis.
Oral contraceptives	• Discontinue 1 month preoperatively only if patient is undergoing major surgery with risk of thrombotic complications. • May continue until the evening before minor surgery.
Thyroid hormones	• Continue preoperatively.

*Based on authors' clinical experience and assessment of drug pharmacology.

Table II[a]—Half-lives of Cyclic Antidepressants and NSAIDs

Antidepressants	Half-life (hours)	NSAIDs[b]	Half-life (hours)
amitriptyline	10–50	diclofenac	2
amoxapine	8–30	diflunisal	8–12
clomipramine	35	etodolac	3–11
desipramine	12–30	fenoprofen	3
doxepin	8–24	floctafenine	8
imipramine	9–20	flurbiprofen	4
maprotiline	27–58	ibuprofen	2
nortriptyline	16–90	indomethacin	5
protriptyline	54–198	ketoprofen	2–4
trimipramine	7–40	ketorolac	4–9
		mefenamic acid	3–4
		nabumetone	23–30
		naproxen	13
		oxaprozin	50
		phenylbutazone	72
		piroxicam	50
		sulindac	8–16
		tenoxicam	32–110
		tiaprofenic acid	2
		tolmetin	1–3

[a] Half-lives may be increased in the elderly.
[b] Short-acting NSAIDs should be discontinued 4–7 days preoperatively and long-acting NSAIDs 7–10 days preoperatively. In surgery where even minor bleeding could be catastrophic (e.g., eye surgery) patients should be advised to discontinue their NSAIDs 2 weeks before the date of surgery.

Table III—Recommended Perioperative Corticosteroid Coverage for Adrenal Insufficiency

Degree of Surgical Stress	Equivalent Hydrocortisone Dose	Recommended Duration
Minor (e.g., inguinal hernia repair)	25 mg	Preoperatively
Moderate (e.g., open cholecystectomy)	50–75 mg/day	2 days
Severe (e.g., cardiac surgery with cardiopulmonary bypass)	100–150 mg/day	2–3 days

Selected References:

1. Barash PG, Cullen BF, Stoelting RK, eds. Clinical anesthesia. 3rd ed. Philadelphia: JB Lipincott Company, 1996.
2. Chung DC, Lam AM, eds. Essentials of anesthesiology. 3rd ed. Philadelphia: Saunders, 1996.
3. Connelly CS, Panush RS. Should nonsteroidal anti-inflammatory drugs be stopped before elective surgery? Arch Intern Med 1991; 151:1963–66.
4. Horlocker TT, Wedel DJ. Spinal and epidural blockade and perioperative low molecular weight heparin: smooth sailing on the Titanic. Anesth Analg 1998; 86:1153–56.
5. Longnecker DE, Murphy FL, eds. Introduction to anesthesia. 9th ed. Toronto: WB Saunders, 1997.
6. Matsuno A, Tsuchida H, Maeda T, et al. Perioperative hemodynamics in patients treated with angiotensin-converting enzyme inhibitors. Anesth Analg 1997; 84:s43.
7. McGoldrick KE. Ocular drugs and anesthesia. Int Anesth Clin 1990; 28:72–7.
8. McGough EK, Monroe MC, eds. Preoperative evalution, part II. Problems in Anesthesia 1992; 6:1–89.
9. Otawa SM, Ramuscak N. Pre- and postoperative care of surgical patients. Pharmacy Practice 1996; 12(2):(National CE program) 1–7.
10. Pennock JL. Perioperative management of drug therapy. Surg Clin North Am 1983; 63:1049–56.
11. Salem M, Tainsh RE, Bromberg J, et al. Perioperative glucocorticoid coverage. Ann Surg 1994; 219:416–25.
12. Smith MS, Muir H, Hall R. Perioperative management of drug therapy: clinical considerations. Drugs 1996; 51(2):238–59.
13. Stoelting RK. Pharmacology and physiology in anesthetic practice. 2nd ed. Philadelphia: Lippincott-Raven, 1991.

MALARIA PREVENTION

The following is a summary of the Canadian recommendations for malaria prevention that are consistent with those developed by the Committee to Advise on Tropical Medicine and Travel (CATMAT). This information is not intended to present a comprehensive review; the reader is therefore encouraged to seek additional and confirmatory information.

Reviewed 1999 by A. E. McCarthy and the Travel Medicine Program, Office of Special Health Initiatives, Health Canada (M. Bodie-Collins).

Malaria is caused by the genus Plasmodium (P.), of which 4 species infect humans: P. falciparum, P. vivax, P. ovale and P. malariae. All are transmitted by the bite of an infected female Anopheles mosquito. Rarely, transmission may occur by blood transfusion, by shared needle use or congenitally (from mother to fetus). The disease is characterized by fever and "flu-like" symptoms: myalgias, headaches, abdominal pain and malaise. Rigors and chills often occur. Severe malaria due to P. falciparum may cause seizures, coma, renal failure and respiratory failure, which may lead to death. It is important to note that malaria cannot be diagnosed with certainty without a blood film.

The widespread resistance of P. falciparum to chloroquine has complicated the prevention and treatment of malaria. Multiple drug-resistant strains of malaria are now common in several regions of the world. Zones have been established to indicate the geographic distribution of drug-resistant P. falciparum malaria. These zones need frequent updating as the malaria situation changes.

It is important to consult a traveller clinic for specific recommendations on individual needs. A listing of travel clinics in your area can be obtained through Health Canada's Travel Medicine Program at (613) 957-8739. The *1997 Canadian Recommendations for the Prevention and Treatment of Malaria Among International Travellers* can be obtained from the Canadian Medical Association (CMA) by contacting the Member Service Centre at (613) 731-8610 ext. 2307 or through the Laboratory Centre for Disease Control (LCDC) website (http://www.hc-sc.gc.ca) and through the fax retrieval system, FAXlink, by dialing (613) 941-3900 using the handset on your fax machine and following the instructions.

Risk of Acquiring Malaria

Malaria transmission occurs in most of sub-Saharan Africa and New Guinea; in large areas of Southern Asia, in parts of Southeast Asia, Oceania, Haiti, Central and South America, and in limited areas of Mexico, North Africa, the Dominican Republic and the Middle East. Transmission occurs between dusk and dawn, which corresponds to the biting habits of the female Anopheles mosquito. The risk of transmission is increased in rural areas and varies seasonally in many locations, being highest at the end of the rainy season. Risk is dependent upon the duration of an individual's exposure. Transmission decreases at altitudes above which the Anopheles mosquito does not breed (above 2 000 to 3 000 metres).

Advice for Travellers

There are two important components of malaria protection:

- Personal protection against mosquito bites: Travellers to malaria-endemic zones are advised to use personal insect-protective measures to reduce the risk of night-biting mosquitoes. The following measures will reduce exposure to the evening- and nighttime-feeding female Anopheles mosquito and thus will reduce the risk of acquiring malaria: remaining in well-screened or completely enclosed, air-conditioned areas; sleeping under insecticide-impregnated bed nets; and wearing clothing that reduces the amount of exposed skin.

  In addition, the use of insect repellent on exposed skin, particularly between dusk and dawn, is strongly recommended; N,N diethylmethyltoluamide (DEET) is the most effective. The concentration of DEET varies from product to product. The higher concentrations protect for longer periods of time (e.g., 35% DEET protects for 4 to 6 hours, whereas 95% DEET protects for 10 to 12 hours). In rare instances, application of insect repellents with concentrations of DEET >35% have been associated with seizures in young children. Therefore, in children DEET should be applied sparingly to exposed skin surfaces only and washed off after coming indoors. Formulations that contain a lower concentration (10 to 35%) of DEET and that protect for longer than 4 to 6 hours are available.

  Travellers at risk of acquiring malaria should be strongly encouraged to use insecticide-impregnated bed nets (permethrin or deltamethrin treated) unless their sleeping quarters are well-screened or otherwise protected from mosquitoes. Permethrin- or deltamethrin-impregnated nets are significantly more effective at preventing malaria than untreated bed nets and are safe for children and pregnant women. Impregnated bed nets are available in Canada and should be used in conjunction with the above measures.
- Chemosuppressive drugs (Table I): Travellers should be informed that although antimalarials decrease the risk of developing symptomatic malaria, **none** of these agents can guarantee complete protection against malaria. Symptoms due to malaria may occur as early as one week after first exposure, and as late as several years after leaving a malarial zone whether or not chemosuppression has been used.

  If travellers develop a febrile illness, particularly within the first three months after returning from a malaria-endemic area, they should seek **immediate** medical attention and request assessment to rule out malaria. This must include blood films to look for malaria.

Table I—Chemosuppressive Drugs for Malaria Prevention

Drug	Adult Dose[a]	Pediatric Dose[a]	Adverse Effects	Comments
Chloroquine phosphate	300 mg base once weekly	<4 mo: 25 mg base 4–11 mo: 50 mg base 1–2 yr: 75 mg base 3–4 yr: 100 mg base 5–7 yr: 125 mg base 8–10 yr: 200 mg base 11–13 yr: 250 mg base ≥14 yr: 300 mg base once weekly *or* 5 mg/kg base once weekly, up to 300 mg base once weekly.	**Common:** nonallergic pruritus (especially dark-skinned persons), nausea, headache. **Occasional:** skin eruptions, reversible corneal opacity, partial alopecia, blurred vision. **Rare:** nail and mucous membrane discoloration, nerve deafness, photophobia, myopathy, retinopathy with long-term high dose daily use, blood dyscrasia, psychosis and seizures.	Drug of choice in chloroquine-sensitive areas. May worsen psoriasis. Suitable for pregnant women and for all ages, but overdoses are frequently fatal. Reduce dose in renal failure.
Doxycycline	100 mg once daily	< 8 yrs: contraindicated ≥8 yrs: 1.5 mg/kg once daily, up to 100 mg daily.	**Common:** GI upset, vaginal candidiasis, photosensitivity. **Occasional:** azotemia in renal diseases. **Rare:** allergic reactions, blood dyscrasia.	Drug of choice in chloroquine- and mefloquine-resistant areas; also used in chloroquine-resistant areas by persons unable to take mefloquine. Should not be used in pregnancy, in lactation or in children under 8 yrs. Use a sunscreen that blocks UVA rays.
Mefloquine	250 mg once weekly[b]	< 5 kg: not recommended 5–20 kg: 62.5 mg[b] >20–30 kg: 125 mg[b] >30–45 kg: 187.5 mg[b] >45 kg: 250 mg[b] Given once weekly.	**Common:** dizziness, nausea, diarrhea, headache, insomnia, strange dreams, mood changes. **Rare:** psychosis, convulsions.	Drug of choice in chloroquine-resistant areas. Should not be used in persons with a seizure disorder or a history of serious psychiatric illness. Caution should be taken in pregnancy, especially in the 1st trimester; in children < 5 kg; in occupations or activities requiring fine coordination or where vertigo may be life threatening (e.g., pilots); in underlying cardiac conduction disturbances; and in concurrent use of chloroquine or quinine-like drugs including halofantrine. Severe neuropsychiatric reactions (psychosis, convulsions) are infrequent with prophylactic doses.
Proguanil	Chloroquine-resistant areas: 200 mg once daily plus weekly chloroquine.	<8 mo: 25 mg 8 mo–3 yrs: 50 mg 4–7 yrs: 75 mg 8–10 yrs: 100 mg 11–13 yrs: 150 mg ≥14 yrs: 200 mg	**Occasional:** anorexia, nausea, diarrhea, mouth ulcers. **Rare:** hematuria.	Use in combination with chloroquine in chloroquine-resistant areas when mefloquine or doxycycline can not be used. Chloroquine plus proguanil is less efficacious than mefloquine or doxycycline in chloroquine-resistant areas. Note that 100 mg/day of proguanil is no longer recommended in malaria-endemic areas.

[a] Begin all drugs 1 week before entering malarial area (except doxycycline and proguanil, which may be started 1 day before) and continue until 4 weeks after leaving malarial areas.

[b] A loading dose of mefloquine taken once daily for 3 days before travel followed by a once weekly dose (as above) may be used for travellers who will be at immediate high risk of drug-resistant falciparum malaria.

Reference:

1. Health Canada. 1997 Canadian recommendations for the prevention and treatment of malaria among international travellers. Can Commun Dis Rep (CCDR) 1997; 23S5 (Suppl).

WATER TREATMENT METHODS FOR TRAVELLERS

The following is an overview of water treatment principles and methods for travellers to foreign countries, as well as for travellers in Canada who may have to obtain their drinking water from lakes, rivers, streams or ponds. This information is not intended to present a comprehensive review; the reader is therefore encouraged to seek additional and confirmatory information.

Reviewed 1999 by D. Wong.

Many diseases of viral, bacterial or protozoal origin are contracted by drinking contaminated water. Hepatitis A, cholera, dysentery, typhoid fever, traveller's diarrhea, giardiasis and amebiasis are some of these diseases. The major bacterial and protozoal etiologic agents of traveller's diarrhea are enterotoxigenic Escherichia coli, Salmonella, Shigella, Campylobacter, Giardia lamblia (giardiasis), Entamoeba histolytica (amebiasis), Cyclospora and Cryptosporidium. Since adequate protection against the majority of these diseases cannot be obtained by vaccination, the traveller must take precautions to minimize the risk of infection.

Prevention Methods

Travellers should familiarize themselves with precautions regarding eating and drinking. Remember to *cook it, peel it* or *leave it*!

Water and Food Precautions

- Avoid brushing teeth with untreated tap water.
- Avoid ice, unless made with treated water.
- Avoid unpasteurized dairy products including milk, ice cream, and cheese.
- Avoid uncooked food especially shellfish, salads, raw or unpeeled fruit and vegetables. Fruit that the traveller can peel is usually safe.
- Eat food that has been well cooked and is still hot when served.
- Avoid food from street vendors.

The safest food source for infants less than 6 months of age is breast milk. Formula prepared from commercial powder and boiled water is the safest and most practical food for weaned infants.

Safe Beverages

When the safety of the water supply is in doubt, only the following beverages may be safe to drink:

- tea or coffee made with boiled water
- beer and wine
- canned or bottled carbonated water and soft drinks

Wet containers should be wiped clean and dry, especially the surfaces directly in contact with the mouth. Travellers should request that bottles and cans be opened in their presence to ensure a proper seal and they should drink directly from the bottle or can, rather than a questionable container. Bottled and canned beverages are generally available from hotels and restaurants. Those who travel away from the normal tourist routes are at greatest risk of contracting waterborne disease and should be strongly advised to select a reliable method of water treatment.

Water Treatment Methods

Cloudy water containing silt and algae should be strained through a clean cloth or filter before disinfection. The current recommended water treatment methods are outlined in Table I. Once water has been disinfected, it should be placed in a clean, covered container to reduce chances of recontamination.

- **Boiling** water is the most reliable and preferred method to make water pure for drinking. Previous recommendations on the length of time for boiling has decreased from 10 to 20 minutes to 1 to 3 minutes, thereby making this method much more practical.
- **Chemical disinfection** using iodine-based products (i.e., tincture of iodine 2%, saturated iodine solution or tetraglycine hydroperiodide tablets) is recommended if a heat source is not available. Chlorination is not as reliable as iodination nor is it recommended by the Centers for Disease Control (CDC). Chlorine treatment alone may not kill some enteric viruses, G. lamblia and E. histolytica cysts and Cryptosporidium species.
- Water treatment devices such as portable iodine-impregnated resin devices and filters or microfilters may be suggested by some travel clinics. The CDC makes no recommendation regarding the use of iodine-resins and microfilters because of a lack of published scientific literature. Filters or microfilters with sufficiently small pore size (0.2 micron) may remove protozoa, Giardia cysts and large bacteria, but will not remove viruses. Filtration alone is therefore inadequate to purify water.
- Water treatment devices (i.e., filters, iodine-resin devices) are available from camping stores and travel clinics. Table II lists selected water treatment devices. They are available as a cup for single person use or as pumps for treating larger volumes of water. Some may have prefilters which can be cleaned by backflushing or can be replaced at additional cost. Units are generally expensive and vary in size, weight, and in the maximum volume of water which can be treated. More information on a selected device may be obtained by contacting the manufacturer.
- As a last resort, if no means of water purification are available, it may be safer to utilize uncomfortably hot to touch tap water rather than cold tap water.

Table I—Recommended Water Treatment Methods

Method	Procedure	Efficacy	Advantages	Disadvantages	Comments
HEAT	Boil water vigorously for 1 min, then allow to cool to room temperature. At high altitudes (> 2 km), boil water for 3 min or chemical disinfection used adjunctively.	Most reliable and effective method of purifying water.	Destroys all organisms including Giardia cysts.	Reliable heat source may not be readily available.	"Flat" taste of water can be improved by adding a pinch of salt/L or by pouring water back and forth between 2 clean containers.
CHEMICAL **Iodination**					
Tincture of Iodine 2%[a]	Add 5 drops (0.25 mL)/L of clear water (10 drops if cloudy water). Mix thoroughly. Let stand for at least 30 min before drinking (longer if water is cold or cloudy). Treated water should have slight taste of iodine; if not, repeat procedure.	Method of choice when boiling is not feasible. Endorsed by the CDC. Efficacy decreases in cold water—contact time must be extended to ensure germicidal effects. May not be effective against Giardia cysts in cold water.	Readily available; inexpensive, portable.	Should avoid long-term use. Use with caution in pregnant women, infants, children, and travellers with thyroid disease. Stains. Imparts unpleasant taste to water. Inconvenient time to wait.	Palatability may be improved by adding a powdered soft drink mix after the required contact time has elapsed. Other iodine-based products should not be recommended e.g., povidone-iodine, Lugol's solution or stainless iodine.
Saturated Iodine Solution (Polar Pure®)[b]	Add 12.5 mL/L and let stand for 15–20 min (20 mL/L for at least 20 min if cold or cloudy water).	Same as for tincture of iodine.	Same as for tincture of iodine.	Same as for tincture of iodine.	Polar Pure® crystals to be reconstituted. Dosed by bottle capful and has adjustment guide based on temperature.
Tetraglycine hydroperiodide (Coghlan's Emergency Drinking Water Germicidal Tablets[c] or AquaXcell Tablets[d])	Use 1 tablet/L of room temperature water. Wait 15 min before use. Use 2 tablets/L of cold or turbid water. Wait 20 min.	Same as for tincture of iodine.	Same as for tincture of iodine.	Same as for tincture of iodine but non-staining.	Same as for tincture of iodine.

[a] Tincture of iodine 2% solution (e.g., from medicine chest or first aid kit). Available at most pharmacies.
[b] Polar Equipment, Saratoga, CA. Available through camping equipment stores.
[c] Coghlan's Ltd., Winnipeg, MB, (204) 284-9550. Available through drug wholesalers and sporting goods stores.
[d] AquaXcell—available through drug wholesalers, pharmacies or sporting goods stores. Canadian distributor: Aerokure International, Sherbrooke, QC (819) 821-2238.

Table II—Selected Water Treatment Devices

Device Type and Product Name	Manufacturer
Filters	
Katadyn Combi, Katadyn Mini, Katadyn Pocket	Katadyn. Distributed by Suunto Canada, 2151 Las Palmas Dr., Ste G. Carlsbad, CA 92009 1-800-776-7770
MSR MiniWorks Ceramic, MSR WaterWorks II	MSR Mountain Safety Research, Box 24547, Seattle, WA 98124 1-800-877-9677
PŪR Hiker, PŪR Pioneer	PŪR 9300 North 75th Ave, Minneapolis, MN 55428 1-800-787-5463
Sweetwater Guardian Microfilter, Sweetwater WalkAbout Microfilter	Sweetwater Cascade Designs Inc., 4000 First Ave., Seattle, WA 98134 1-800-531-9531
Sigg Microlite	Sigg AG. Distributed by Outbound Products, 8585 Fraser St., Vancouver, BC, V5X 3Y1 1-800-663-9262
Iodine-impregnated Resin Devices	
Watermate Travel Filter, Watermate Jug Filter System	Watermate. Distributed by World Famous Sales, 333 Confederation Pkwy., Concord, ON, L4K 4S1 1-905-738-4777

Table II—Selected Water Treatment Devices *(cont'd)*

Device Type and Product Name	Manufacturer
Combination Devices (filter & iodine-resin)	
Passport Adventure, Passport Travel Cup	Passport SMI Ltd., 181 Big Bay Point Rd., Barrie, ON, L4N 8M5 1-800-309-9977
PŪR Explorer, PŪR Scout, PŪR Voyageur	See PŪR above
Sweetwater Guardian, Sweetwater Global Water Express Kit	See Sweetwater Cascade Designs Inc. above
Travel Well Trekker, Travel Well Pocket	Travel Well. Distributed by Outbound Products, 8585 Fraser St., Vancouver, BC, V5X 3Y1 1-800-663-9262

References:

1. Backer H. Field water disinfection. JAMA 1988;259(21): 3185.
2. Harrison M., ed. Water treatment. Explore Gear Guide 1998:90–2.
3. Health Canada—Diarrhea associated with travel to the tropics. Health Protection Branch—Laboratory Centre for Disease Control. Ottawa, ON. <http://www.HC-SC.GC.CA/hpb/lcdc/osh/travel/diarre_e.html>. 13 Mar 1997.
4. Health and Welfare Canada, Environment Canada. Wilderness water—A guide to wilderness drinking water (Pamphlet). Ottawa, ON: Minister of Supply and Services, 1991.
5. Health Protection Branch. Water treatment devices—For microbiological purification of water. Issues 1991 Aug 15. Ottawa, ON: Health and Welfare Canada.
6. The Yellow Book: Health information for international travel 1996-97. Division of Quarantine, National Center for Infectious Diseases, Centers for Disease Control and Prevention. Atlanta, GA. <http://www.cdc.gov/travel/yellowbk/page182c.htm>. 10 Jul 1998.

DRUGS AND OLDER INDIVIDUALS

The following is an overview of drug use in older individuals. This information is not intended to present a comprehensive review; the reader is therefore encouraged to seek additional and confirmatory information.

Reviewed 1999 by R. Grymonpre and C. Patterson.

There is a greater consumption of medications by older individuals as they tend to have more illnesses and medical conditions than younger adults. The term "older individuals" rather than "elderly" best describes our elders as every individual ages in a unique way. While most individuals aged 70 to 80 years enjoy excellent health, many are suffering from the results of one or more chronic diseases such as vascular insufficiency, intellectual deterioration and degenerative processes. Blanket statements concerning drugs and older people are usually inappropriate. However, in general, it is true that the risks of adverse reactions associated with medications are greater in this population. This phenomenon has many causes, including the use of many medications, the increased prevalence of vascular, renal and neurological disorders together with the pharmacokinetic and pharmacodynamic consequences of aging. While most older individuals may be treated in a similar fashion to younger adults, certain changes should be appreciated and individuals at high risk for adverse drug reactions should be identified.

For information on Epilepsy in the Elderly, consult Antiepileptic Drug Therapy in the Clin-Info section.

Pharmacokinetic Changes

The pharmacokinetic consequences of aging include changes in absorption, distribution, metabolism and excretion of medications. Table I presents these pharmacokinetic changes, their consequences and examples of medications affected by these changes.

Pharmacodynamic Changes

Changes in the biochemical and physiological effects of drugs and their mechanisms of action (pharmacodynamics) are vitally important in older individuals. Response varies widely among individuals, yet the following generalizations can be made:

- The sedative potential of benzodiazepines is greater in older individuals.
- The hypotensive effects of vasodilators are exaggerated in older individuals.
- The analgesic and sedative properties of opioids tend to be greater in older individuals.
- The anticoagulant effects of warfarin are enhanced in older individuals.

Adverse Drug Reactions

General: Common adverse drug reactions (ADRs) include oversedation from sedatives, gastrointestinal (GI) irritation and constipation, fatigue, delirium and voiding problems. The risk of ADRs increases dramatically with the total number of medications consumed. Those at highest risk of ADRs include the very elderly (over 85 years of age), those with significant cardiac problems (present or previous congestive heart failure), those with reduced hepatic function (especially diffuse parenchymal disease), those with renal failure, those with malnutrition or those taking many medications. The presence of intellectual deterioration (dementing disorders, advanced Parkinson's disease or previous strokes) places individuals at particular risk for delirium. Those with any degree of postural instability have a greatly enhanced risk of falling and sustaining injury from sedative or antihypertensive agents. The risk of falls and the risk of motor vehicle crashes are greatly increased with the use of benzodiazepines, especially those that are long acting.

A nonspecific decline in physical, cognitive or affective state in a frail older person may be the principal manifestation of a wide spectrum of physical illnesses, progressive dementia or depression. Many medications cause nonspecific symptoms, making medication review imperative. For example, it is important to ensure that cholinesterase inhibitors used in Alzheimer's disease (e.g., donepezil) are not used simultaneously with anticholinergic agents as they can negate the effect of the cholinesterase inhibitor.

Table II presents some of the common adverse drug reactions in older individuals and examples of drugs that are likely to cause the ADR.

Prescribing Advice

The preceding information argues for a more cautious approach to prescribing in older individuals. Small initial doses and cautious dose escalation are advised when prescribing sedatives, antipsychotics, antidepressants, anticholinergic agents, antihypertensive agents and digoxin. The chronic use of benzodiazepines, digoxin, topical corticosteroids, antihypertensive agents, laxatives and anti-ulcer therapy should be carefully scrutinized periodically. Simple rules for rational prescribing include the following:

- establish a diagnosis before prescribing
- determine an endpoint
- select treatment; consider whether a nonpharmacologic approach is more appropriate
- review response in relation to the endpoint
- review medications and discontinue when possible
- keep total number of medications and number of daily doses to a minimum.

Adherence to Therapy

Factors such as increased prevalence of memory disorders, visual impairment, reduced hand function and complex drug regimens tend to exaggerate adherence difficulties in older individuals. Clear verbal instructions supplemented by clearly written information, current prescription drug label instructions, reduced dosing frequency (i.e., b.i.d. or daily), judicious use of nonchildproof containers and medication reminder systems can be helpful in improving adherence. Hoarding of medications and the use of medications prescribed for others should be discouraged.

Conclusion

While the approach to prescribing for older individuals must be more cautious, it is important not to deny effective treatment that can greatly enhance the quality of life and enable the individual to continue an independent lifestyle.

Table I—Pharmacokinetic Consequences of Aging

Pharmacokinetic Parameter	Representative Example*	Comments
Absorption	none significant	**Pharmacokinetic Change** • Moderate loss of small intestine absorptive function, slowed gastrointestinal transit and impaired mesenteric blood flow are common. **Consequence** • In general, changes in absorption seen with aging are the least clinically important. • Due to a reduced gastric acid secretion, there is a reduced absorption of drugs that require acid for absorption (e.g., ketoconazole, iron salts) or dissolution (e.g., calcium carbonate). • Absorption of sustained-release dosage forms may be highly erratic. This is due to a moderate loss of the absorptive function in the small intestine.
Distribution	**Lipid soluble** sedatives other psychotropic agents	**Pharmacokinetic Change** • Body composition changes with increasing age resulting in a reduced percentage of total body water and lean muscle mass relative to an increased fat content. **Consequence** • The changes in body composition partially explain the reason for prolonged duration of action of lipid-soluble drugs in older people. The volume of distribution for lipid-soluble drugs increases.
	Water soluble digoxin lithium	**Consequence** • Due to decreased total body water, the volume of distribution decreases for drugs primarily distributed in water; therefore, lower loading doses are required.
	Albumin bound oral hypoglycemics phenytoin warfarin **Alpha$_1$-acid glycoprotein bound** lidocaine propranolol	**Pharmacokinetic Change** • Decreased serum albumin due to advanced age, chronic disease or malnutrition. • Alpha$_1$-acid glycoprotein binds with mostly basic drugs and tends to rise with age and in acute illness (e.g., myocardial infarction, rheumatoid arthritis, cancer, surgery, chronic pain). **Consequence** • Caution is advised when interpreting serum drug concentrations that measure both free and bound fractions, especially for drugs that are highly protein bound.
Metabolism	**Liver metabolized** barbiturates benzodiazepines (e.g., chlordiazepoxide, diazepam, flurazepam) lidocaine nitrates propranolol theophylline verapamil	**Pharmacokinetic Change** • Decreased liver mass and blood flow in older people. • Oxidative metabolism may decline slightly with aging, especially in the frail malnourished elderly. • Conjugation and acetylation do not appear significantly altered by aging. **Consequence** • Reduced metabolism may lead to reduced drug clearance, resulting in higher steady-state serum levels and possibly toxic effects. • Increased bioavailability of drugs with significant first-pass metabolism (e.g., labetolol, morphine, nifedipine, propranolol).
Excretion	**Renal excreted** ACE inhibitors allopurinol amantadine aminoglycosides digoxin lithium NSAIDs procainamide	**Pharmacokinetic Change** • Many older individuals experience a decline in both concentrating ability and excretory renal function. However, many older individuals preserve stable renal function well into old age, making the measurement of renal function essential before the use of drugs excreted predominantly by the kidneys. Serum creatinine concentration may be a poor indicator of renal function, as levels may be normal in older people with decreased kidney function, due to a smaller muscle mass. The creatinine clearance can be estimated using the Cockroft and Gault formula (see Serum Drug Concentration Monitoring in the Clin-Info section). **Consequence** • Reduced clearance of drugs resulting in increased serum levels.

* The list of examples is not comprehensive. For further information refer to product monographs or specific geriatric references.

Table II—Adverse Drug Reactions in Older Individuals

Organ System and Effect	Representative Example*	Comments
Central nervous system		
Mental confusion (delirium)	acyclovir all sedative medications anticholinergic agents (e.g., antispasmodics, tricyclic antidepressants, some antiarrhythmics, antihistamines, antiparkinsonian agents) antiepileptic drugs antihypertensive agents (e.g., calcium channel blockers, beta-blockers) digoxin H_2-receptor blockers (e.g., cimetidine, ranitidine) NSAIDs (e.g., ASA, ibuprofen, indomethacin, naproxen) prednisone	• It is important to monitor older individuals closely for confusion and oversedation. Cumulative sedation is the most significant adverse drug reaction, resulting in impaired physical and mental performance. For the frail older individual this may be catastrophic as independence may be lost, falls may result in injury and premature consideration of institutional care may occur. • There is greater potential for mental confusion in those with intellectual impairment (e.g., Alzheimer's disease). • Delirium may result from the use of several agents together that, when used alone, may not cause the condition. • CNS toxicity from NSAIDs is most common with lipophilic NSAIDs as they readily cross the blood-brain barrier.
Cardiovascular		
Congestive heart failure (CHF)	negative inotropes (e.g., beta-blockers, calcium channel blockers, antiarrhythmic agents such as disopyramide and procainamide) NSAIDs (e.g., naproxen, diclofenac, ibuprofen, ketoprofen)	• Although beta-blockers and calcium entry blockers are valuable in diastolic dysfunction, and beta-blockers have a role in congestive cardiomyopathy, they should nonetheless be used with caution in older individuals at risk for left ventricular systolic failure. • NSAIDs, due to their potential to worsen fluid retention, should be used with extreme caution in patients with congestive heart failure.
Orthostatic hypotension	antihypertensive agents antiparkinsonian agents antipsychotic agents (e.g., chlorpromazine, thioridazine) diuretics nitrates tricyclic antidepressants	• The ability to regulate blood pressure is compromised in older individuals. • Reports of dizziness or falls should be evaluated by measuring the lying and standing blood pressures.
Gastrointestinal (GI)		
Ulcer, bleeding, perforation Esophagitis, strictures Bowel erosive disease	NSAIDs	• Bleeding, ulceration and perforation can occur at any time with or without warning symptoms during NSAID therapy. • Most reports of fatal GI events are in the aged population. To date no specific subset of patients is **not** at risk for peptic ulceration and bleeding. • Increased incidence of NSAID-induced complications has been associated with a previous history of any GI condition (e.g., peptic ulcer disease, GI bleeding), advanced age, long-term corticosteroid use, higher doses of NSAIDs, use of more than one NSAID, and the first 30 to 90 days after initiation or dosage increase of NSAID therapy. • Acetaminophen has been shown to be equally as effective as some NSAIDs in noninflammatory osteoarthritis. • Misoprostol may be used as a prophylactic GI protective agent, but its routine use in all older people taking NSAIDs is not justified. Omeprazole is indicated for the prevention or treatment of gastric or duodenal ulcers caused by NSAIDs. The use of H_2-receptor blockers and sucralfate as protective agents is not generally effective as prophylaxis.
Constipation	aluminum-containing antacids anticholinergic agents calcium channel blockers (e.g., diltiazem, nifedipine and especially verapamil) iron opioids (especially codeine)	• Nondrug management includes increased water and other fluid intake, increased exercise and increased fiber. • Use laxatives on a short-term basis and individualize depending on the patient's fluid status, activity level (e.g., hospitalized patients), concomitant medications and GI conditions. While bulk forming laxatives (e.g., bran, psyllium) are more physiological in most older people they are not recommended in cases of reduced GI motility (e.g., Parkinson's disease, opioid-induced constipation) where stool softeners ± stimulant laxatives (e.g., senna, bisacodyl) are the preferred agents.

Table II—Adverse Drug Reactions in Older Individuals *(cont'd)*

Organ System and Effect	Representative Example*	Comments
Renal and urinary		
Acute renal failure	ACE inhibitors aminoglycosides NSAIDs	• Before initiating drugs that may induce acute renal failure, renal function tests should be monitored at baseline and at regular intervals during therapy. • Acute renal failure associated with ACE inhibitors is most often seen in patients with bilateral renovascular disease or renal artery stenosis. • Renal function usually returns to baseline after discontinuing the NSAID or ACE inhibitor.
Fluid and electrolyte disturbance	ACE inhibitors antidepressants (tricyclics, SSRIs, MAOIs) calcium channel blockers (e.g., peripheral edema with nifedipine, felodipine) corticosteroids diuretics NSAIDs	• Diuretics are valuable agents in the treatment of hypertension, congestive heart failure and ascites. Their use in uncomplicated leg edema is inappropriate, due to the potential for adverse reactions such as volume depletion, orthostatic hypotension, incontinence and metabolic disturbances. Hyponatremia, hypokalemia, hyperglycemia, hypomagnesemia, hyperuricemia and metabolic alkalosis all occur with diuretic use. • Sodium retention and edema may result from the prostaglandin blocking effects of NSAIDs. • Hyponatremia may result from many drugs that cause Syndrome of Inappropriate ADH (SIADH), e.g., antidepressants, carbamazepine, chlorpropamide. Older people may be more susceptible to this effect. • Hyperkalemia is a recognized effect from use of NSAIDs, potassium-sparing diuretics and ACE inhibitors in the elderly. • Hypoglycemia from ACE inhibitors has been reported and may have severe consequences in older people with diabetes using insulin or sulfonylureas.
Involuntary loss of urine	diuretics (e.g., potent diuretics such as furosemide)	• Diuretics may lead to overflow incontinence especially in males with outflow obstruction due to prostatic hypertrophy. • Diuretics may aggravate other forms of incontinence due to the increased frequency and volume of urine output as well as increased bladder spasms.
Urinary retention	anticholinergic agents diuretics sympathomimetic agents (e.g., salbutamol, pseudoephedrine)	• Urinary retention is common, particularly in older men with prostatic hypertrophy.

* The list of examples is not comprehensive. For further information refer to product monographs or specific geriatric references.

References:

1. Delafuente JC, Stewart RB. Therapeutics in the elderly. 2nd ed. Cincinnati, Ohio: Harvey Whitney Books, 1995: 191–2, 364–5.
2. De Maagd GA. Review of the pharmacologic causes of delirium in the elderly. The Consult Pharm 1995; 10(5):461–74.
3. Girgis L, Brooks P. Nonsteroidal anti-inflammatory drugs: differential use in older patients. Drugs and Aging 1994; 4(2): 101–12.
4. Hemmelgarn B, Suissa S, et al. Benzodiazepine use and the risk of motor vehicle crash in the elderly. JAMA 1997; 278(1):27–31.
5. Iber FL, Murphy PA, et al. Age-related changes in the gastrointestinal system: effects on drug therapy. Drugs and Aging 1994; 5(1): 34–48.
6. Lederle FA. Epidemiology of constipation in elderly patients: drug utilisation and cost-containment strategies. Drugs and Aging 1995; 6(6): 465–79.
7. Morris AD, Boyle D, et al. ACE inhibitor use is associated with hospitalization for severe hypoglycemia in patients with diabetes. Diabetes Care 1997; 20(9):1363–67.
8. Ravid M, Ravid D. ACE inhibitors in elderly patients with hypertension: special considerations. Drugs and Aging 1996; 8(1):29–37.
9. Pitner JK, Wiley K, et al. Prevention of NSAID-induced gastropathy in the elderly. The Consult Pharm 1994; 9(5): 568–79.
10. Woodhouse K, Wynne H. Age-related changes in hepatic function: implications for drug therapy. Drugs and Aging 1992; 2(3): 243–55.

DRUG EXPOSURE DURING PREGNANCY

The following is an overview on drug use in pregnancy. This information is not intended to present a comprehensive review; the reader is therefore encouraged to seek additional and confirmatory information.

Reviewed 1999 by S. Ito and A. Massicotte.

Maternal medication consumption is rarely a sole contributing factor for adverse pregnancy outcomes. Nevertheless, caution should be exercised for some drugs. In addition, it is important to acknowledge that the risk-benefit ratio varies among individual patients. This section shows selected drugs that are commonly used, or known to significantly increase risks of adverse outcomes. The drugs have been selected based on the frequency of inquiries received by the Motherisk program at the Hospital for Sick Children in Toronto. Note the following when interpreting the information:

- a significantly increased fetal risk should not necessarily be interpreted as an indication for therapeutic abortion
- drugs are not included if their theoretical risks have not been substantiated
- abortifacient drugs, cancer chemotherapy agents and radioisotopes are not included
- final assessment of drug use in pregnancy should not be based solely on this section; it is not intended to be exhaustive in length and depth.

Amiodarone

Sporadic case reports suggest that exposure to amiodarone in utero may cause transient thyroid dysfunction (hypo- or hyperthyroidism). The exact incidence is unknown. As expected from its pharmacologic effects, transient bradycardia may also result. Reserve this drug for those who are unresponsive to other antiarrhythmic therapies.

Angiotensin-Converting Enzyme Inhibitors and Angiotensin II Receptor Antagonists

Angiotensin-converting enzyme (ACE) inhibitors, used especially during the second and third trimesters to control maternal hypertension during pregnancy, are associated with a risk of neonatal renal failure (anuria) and profound hypotension. The occurrence rate is unknown, but is probably very small. The drug-induced reduction of fetal renal blood flow may lead to oligohydramnios, potentially resulting in various fetal maldevelopments. Although the baseline rate of occurrence of neonatal anuria and hypotension in those born to hypertensive mothers receiving other antihypertensives is unknown, reserve the use of ACE inhibitors during pregnancy to women in whom alternative therapy is not available.

Fetal risk with the use of angiotensin II receptor antagonists (losartan) has not yet been assessed in humans. However, theoretically the same precautions as those for ACE inhibitors may apply.

Antiepileptics (also refer to Antiepileptic Drug Therapy in Clin-Info)

Women with idiopathic epilepsy (not an acquired type) have a higher chance of giving birth to newborns with malformations (about twice as high as the general baseline risk of 2 to 3%), even if they do not take antiepileptic medications.

Phenytoin poses a risk of fetal hydantoin (phenytoin) syndrome, which is primarily characterized by craniofacial changes, microcephaly, physical and mental growth retardation and nail hypoplasia. The risk of the full-blown syndrome is estimated to be 10% or less, and the risk of only minor abnormalities may be about 30%. A recent study suggests that cognitive function of infants exposed to the drug in utero is on average mildly lower than that of nonexposed controls. Interaction of phenytoin with vitamin K metabolism justifies vitamin K supplementation.

Vitamin K_1 (phytonadione) 10 mg/day should be given orally to women on antiepileptics (especially carbamazepine, phenobarbital and phenytoin) from 36 weeks of pregnancy onward to prevent hemorrhagic disease of the newborn. Tablets of vitamin K_1 are not available in Canada; therefore, the parenteral form can be added to juice and taken orally. Also give vitamin K_1 1 mg i.m. to the baby at birth.

Whether carbamazepine causes a typical fetal syndrome is still unclear, although a risk of open neural tube defects is estimated to be about 1% in those exposed to carbamazepine; the risk in the general population is about 0.1%. Note that the risk varies significantly among countries/provinces. A recent study showed that cognitive function of infants exposed to the drug in utero is not different from that of nonexposed controls. Folic acid supplementation is advised.

Valproic acid is associated with an increased risk of open neural tube defects of about 1 to 2%. Although some studies suggest an increased risk of minor malformations in infants exposed to the drug in utero, the causation is unclear. Folic acid supplementation is advised.

The critical period of neural tube formation is around 17 to 30 days postconception. Folic acid deficiency disturbs the neural tube formation, causing open neural tube defects. Therefore, folic acid supplementation (0.5 to 1 mg/day) is recommended for all women who are pregnant or planning a pregnancy to reduce the risk of open neural tube defects. Because antiepileptics, especially valproic acid and carbamazepine, are risk factors for the defect, prophylactic folic acid supplementation (4 to 5 mg/day) is necessary for women on antiepileptics beginning 4 weeks before conception and throughout pregnancy. Open neural tube defects can be detected by a combination of maternal blood screening followed by a level II ultrasound study and/or amniotic fluid analysis. Consultation with an experienced obstetrician is recommended.

Concerning the new antiepileptics gabapentin, lamotrigine, topiramate and vigabatrin, although animal teratology appears favorable, human pregnancy exposures are limited at this time and uncertainty about the teratogenicity of these antiepileptics still prevails.

Antihistamines

Antihistamines are often used in the treatment of allergy symptoms. A recent meta-analysis and a large cohort study have not linked the use of older sedative antihistamines during the first trimester to major congenital malformations. Most experience and reassuring data have been gathered with chlorpheniramine and tripelennamine. Also, results from small prospective, controlled observational studies of women who took astemizole, hydroxyzine or cetirizine during pregnancy did not support an increased risk of malformations. For allergic rhinitis, effective topical preparations should also be considered safe for use during pregnancy (sodium cromoglycate, nasal beclomethasone).

Antithyroid Drugs

Among the antithyroid medications, propylthiouracil (PTU) is the drug of choice for hyperthyroidism in pregnant women. However, goiter may develop in about 10 to 15% of fetuses exposed to the drug in utero. The PTU-induced goiters appear dose-independent and unpredictable. Nevertheless, the dose should be kept as low as possible (<400 mg/day). Methimazole and carbimazole (converted to methimazole in vivo) are not preferred agents because of a possible link (yet to be proven) between methimazole and aplasia cutis (scalp defects) in the exposed fetus.

Danazol

Limited data suggest that this synthetic androgen may cause virilization of the female fetus at an estimated occurrence of 20 to 30%. When the drug is discontinued before the 8th week of gestation (before androgen receptors become sensitive), the risk of female pseudohermaphroditism seems insignificant. No adverse effects in the male fetus have been associated with danazol.

Diuretics

Thiazide use during pregnancy does not seem to be associated with an increased risk of malformation. However, case reports of perinatal complications such as thrombocytopenia and electrolyte imbalance have been reported.

Information is scarce for amiloride and furosemide, though teratogenicity has not been strongly suggested so far.

Diuretics should be used with caution during pregnancy as diuresis may decrease maternal intravascular volume and therefore diminish uteroplacental perfusion and fetal oxygenation. This effect may be more pronounced with loop diuretics.

Ethanol

Drinking alcohol during pregnancy poses significant fetal risks. The incidence of fetal alcohol syndrome (FAS) is estimated to be about 30% in alcoholic pregnant women (alcohol consumption of ≥8 drinks/day or 2 g/kg/day of ethanol throughout pregnancy). FAS is characterized primarily by mental retardation, facial anomalies and general growth retardation. Fetal alcohol effects (FAE), characterized mainly by behavioral abnormalities and CNS dysfunction without typical morphological changes, are thought to occur more frequently than FAS. Whether binge drinking (intermittent heavy drinking) during sensitive periods causes FAS/FAE remains to be answered. Moderate use of alcohol can also increase the risk of spontaneous abortion. A safe level of maternal alcohol intake has not been established.

Hypoglycemics, Oral (Sulfonylureas)

Although some oral hypoglycemics have been shown to be teratogenic in animal studies, human teratogenicity remains unclear because of the inherently increased teratogenic potential of diabetes itself. A small-scale comparative study suggests that sulfonylurea increases chances of malformations, but it still is uncertain whether this is due to the drug or poor glycemic control. Other studies failed to show the possible link. Postnatal hypoglycemia has been reported in some cases. Clearly, this group of drugs is not a first choice during pregnancy as it does not provide good control of maternal blood glucose levels. Insulin is the preferred agent.

Iodine (Iodides)

The fetal thyroid gland starts functioning at about 10 to 12 weeks of gestation, before which iodine and antithyroid agents are not incorporated into the gland. From this period on, iodine accumulates in the fetal thyroid gland. Regular maternal use of iodides and iodine/iodide containing medications (e.g., expectorants, topical antiseptics and amiodarone) during pregnancy may cause iodide-induced goiter and/or hypothyroidism in the infant (see also amiodarone). While prolonged use of maternal iodine/iodides may cause fetal thyroid dysfunction (iodide goiter and/or hypothyroidism), short-term use such as a 10-day preparation course for maternal thyroid surgery does not appear to pose a risk.

Lithium

In one prospective cohort study comparing 148 pregnant women taking lithium during the first trimester with 148 control pregnant women, Ebstein's anomaly (downward displacement of the tricuspid valve into the right ventricle) was found in one fetus in the treatment group. Although the risk of this rare form of cardiac defect appears to be higher in women receiving lithium than in the general population (about 1 in 20 000), it is worth noting that the incidence may still be less than 1%. Other cardiovascular abnormalities and thyroid disorders have also been reported. If pregnant women need lithium, a level II ultrasound and fetal echocardiography may be justified as well as postnatal monitoring of general conditions and thyroid status.

Methotrexate

Antifolate metabolic effects of methotrexate relate directly to its mechanism of toxicity, which causes open neural tube defects and other CNS abnormalities, facial anomalies, growth retardation and so on (similar to those exposed to aminopterin, another folate antagonist). It also has abortifacient properties. In a small series of 8 women, a low-dose methotrexate regimen for rheumatoid arthritis (7.5 mg/week) resulted in 3 spontaneous abortions and 5 full-term normal babies. In another case report, a woman who was taking weekly low-dose methotrexate (12.5 mg/week) during the first 8 weeks of pregnancy, gave birth to a baby with multiple congenital anomalies. Due to possible retention of methotrexate in maternal tissues before conception, it is usually recommended that effective contraception be continued until 3 to 4 months after cessation of methotrexate. Daily supplementation of folic acid is strongly recommended for female patients of childbearing age. A level II ultrasound study at 16 to 18 weeks of gestation is also recommended to rule out major structural anomalies.

Misoprostol

Misoprostol is used as an anti-ulcer agent to protect gastric mucosa from NSAIDs. The drug also has a uterine contraction activity, for which it is tested to induce medical abortion in combination with methotrexate or mifepristone. Several case-series and a case-control study suggest a link between the use of misoprostol during the first trimester and a syndrome called Möbius sequence (e.g., congenital facial nerve palsy, limb defects). The incidence has not been established but may be less than 1%.

Nonsteroidal Anti-inflammatory Drugs

Although nonsteroidal anti-inflammatory drugs (NSAIDs) rarely pose risks in the first and second trimesters, their use in the last month of normal pregnancy may be of concern. Through their antiprostaglandin effects, NSAIDs can cause excessive uterine bleeding at delivery and prolong labor. They can also induce a constriction of the ductus arteriosus, which is mostly reversible upon discontinuation of the drug. Pulmonary hypertension of the newborn is a theoretical consequence of closure of the ductus, but the exact causal relation and the incidence have not been established. Cases of impaired renal function and oligohydramnios have also been reported. However, use of low-dose aspirin for pregnancy-induced hypertension may be justified.

When defervescence is intended, acetaminophen is the first choice for pregnant women, especially at term. It is difficult to make a blanket statement for pain relief during pregnancy because of the diversity of underlying conditions, but acetaminophen with or without opioids (see Opioids and Sedatives) may be tried first.

Opioids and Sedatives

Opioids and sedatives do not seem to increase the risk of major birth defects. However, prolonged maternal use of this class of drugs during pregnancy may cause neonatal withdrawal syndrome, the symptoms of which may last for several weeks after birth. Also, use of these drugs at delivery may result in neonatal sedation and cardiorespiratory depression.

Oral Contraceptives (Estrogens and Progestins)

Presently, oral contraceptives have not been associated with any major congenital malformation such as congenital heart defects and limb reduction defects. Several recent studies failed to show an increased risk for genital anomalies following in utero exposure to oral contraceptives and other progesterone compounds, though one recent report found an increased risk of congenital urinary tract anomalies. It is important to know that synthetic progestins at high doses may be associated with an increased risk of masculinization and pseudohermaphroditism in female infants.

Penicillamine

Although there are several case reports of malformations associated with penicillamine, the link has not been established beyond doubt. Theoretically, copper depletion as a result of penicillamine may inhibit collagen synthesis, thereby causing skin lesions such as cutis laxa (where the skin and subcutaneous tissues hypertrophy so that the skin hangs in folds). It should be noted that there are more than 100 known cases, in which penicillamine was used during pregnancy without abnormal fetal outcomes. During pregnancy, this drug should be reserved for those with Wilson's disease or other conditions, in which no alternative is available.

Retinoids, Oral (Acitretin, Etretinate, Isotretinoin)

Oral retinoids have been associated with a high incidence (≥25% for isotretinoin and etretinate) of major birth defects (craniofacial, CNS, skeletal) from first trimester exposure.

Effective contraception must be used for at least 1 month before starting oral retinoids. A reliable blood pregnancy test must be performed within 2 weeks before starting therapy and retinoids should be started on the second or third day of the next menstrual cycle only if the test is negative.

For isotretinoin, reliable contraceptive measures should be taken up to at least 1 month after discontinuation of the drug. Because of its relatively short elimination half-life (10 to 20 hours), more than 99% of the drug is eliminated from the body in a week.

For etretinate, its long elimination half-life (about 100 to 120 days) caused persistence of detectable serum levels of etretinate for more than 2 years after discontinuation of therapy. At present, it is unclear at what time after withdrawal of etretinate a woman can conceive safely.

For acitretin, it is recommended to carry reliable contraceptive measures up to at least 2 years after stopping the drug. Although acitretin has a shorter half-life (50 hours) than etretinate, some of it can be transformed into etretinate, especially in the presence of alcohol.

Retinoids, Topical (Tretinoin)

In a prospective cohort study, rates of malformations among fetuses exposed (94 cases) and nonexposed (133 controls) to topical tretinoin were compared. Pregnancy outcome did not differ between the two groups. There was no difference in the rates of live births, miscarriages and incidence of major malformations. A risk assessment model study supported that topical tretinoin is not a potential teratogen.

Sulfonamides

It is recommended to avoid sulfonamides late in pregnancy (1 or 2 weeks before the anticipated delivery date) because they may displace bilirubin from serum albumin, thereby increasing the risk of kernicterus in hyperbilirubinemic neonates. The sulfonamides themselves do not usually cause jaundice (except for G-6-PD deficiency patients with drug-induced hemolysis). Sulfonamides have not been identified as teratogens.

Tetracyclines

Discoloration (yellowish brown) of the deciduous teeth, which may be manifested in up to 50% of infants exposed to these drugs in utero after 14 to 16 weeks of gestation, has been the major concern of this class of antibiotics. Other antibiotics should be substituted for systemic tetracyclines during pregnancy, especially after the second trimester.

Warfarin

The fetal warfarin syndrome (FWS) is characterized by nasal hypoplasia, skeletal changes, and mental and physical growth retardation. The critical period of exposure appears to be between 6 to 9 weeks of gestation, with an incidence of embryopathy of about 25%. Exposures after the first trimester still carry a risk of CNS defects (5%) with long-term sequelae. If anticoagulation therapy is needed during pregnancy, subcutaneous heparin is the best choice until delivery. An alternative may be heparin in the first trimester followed by warfarin in the second and third trimesters with heparin again at term.

References:

1. Briggs GG, Freeman RK, Yaffe SJ. Drugs in pregnancy and lactation: a reference guide to fetal and neonatal risk. 4th ed. Baltimore, MD: Williams and Wilkins; 1994.
2. Bracken MB. Oral contraception and congenital malformations in offspring: a review and meta-analysis of the prospective studies. Obstet gynecol 1990; 76:552–7.
3. Buckley LM, Bullaboy CA, et al. Multiple congenital anomalies associated with weekly low-dose methotrexate treatment of the mother. Arthritis and Rheumatism 1997; 40:971–3.
4. Busser J, Rudolph S. Drug use in pregnancy. Pharmacy Practice 1994; (April): 28–36.
5. Castilla EE, Orioli IM. Teratogenicity of misoprostol: data from the Latin-American Collaborative Study of congenital malformations. Am J Med Genet 1994; 51:161–2.
6. Chan A, Hanna M, et al. Oral retinoids and pregnancy. Med J Aust 1996; 165:164–7.
7. Einarson A, Bailey B, et al. Prospective controlled study of hydroxyzine and cetirizine in pregnancy. Ann Allergy Asthma Immunol 1997; 78:183–6.
8. Hellmuth E, Damm P, Mølsted-Pedersen L. Congenital malformations in offspring of diabetic women treated with oral hypoglycemic agents during embryogenesis. Diabetic Medicine 1994; 11:471–4.
9. Johnson EM. A risk assessment of topical tretinoin as a potential human developmental toxin based on animal and comparative human data. J Am Acad Dermatol 1997; 36:S86–S90.
10. Knoben JE, Anderson PO. Handbook of clinical drug data. 7th ed. Hamilton: Drug Intelligence Publications; 1993.
11. Koren G. Maternal-fetal toxicology: a clinician's guide. 2nd ed. New York: Marcel Dekker Inc; 1994.
12. Kozlowski RD, Steinbrunner JV, et al. Outcome of first-trimester exposure to low-dose methotrexate in eight patients with rheumatic disease. Am J Med 1990; 88:589–92.
13. Li DK, Daling JR, et al. Oral contraceptive use after conception in relation to the risk of congenital urinary tract anomalies. Teratology 1995; 51:30–6.
14. Morrell MJ. The new antiepileptic drugs and women: efficacy, reproductive health, pregnancy, and fetal outcome. Epilepsia 1996; 37(Suppl 6): S34–S44.
15. Pastuszak A, Schick B, et al. The safety of astemizole in pregnancy. J Allergy Clin Immunol 1996; 98:748–750.
16. Raman-Wilms L, Tseng AL, et al. Fetal genital effects of first trimester sex hormone exposure: a meta-analysis. Obstet Gynecol 1995; 85:141–9.
17. Schatz M, Petitti D. Antihistamines and pregnancy. Ann Allergy Asthma Immunol 1997; 78:157–9.
18. Schatz M, Zeiger RS, et al. The safety of asthma and allergy medications during pregnancy. J Allergy Clin Immunol 1997; 100:301–6.
19. Seto A, Einarson T, Koren G. Pregnancy outcome following first trimester exposure to antihistamines: meta-analysis. Am J Perinatol 1997; 14:119–124.
20. Shapiro L, Pastuszak A, et al. Safety of first-trimester exposure to topical tretinoin: prospective cohort study. Lancet 1997; 350:1143–44.
21. Shepard TH. Möbius syndrome after misoprostol: a possible teratogenic mechanism. Lancet 1995; 346:780.
22. Stockton DL, Paller AS. Drug administration to the pregnant or lactating woman: a reference guide to dermatologists. J Am Acad Dermatol 1990; 23:87–103.
23. Towner D, Kjos SL, et al. Congenital malformations in pregnancies complicated by NIDDM. Diabetes Care 1995; 18:1446–51.

DRUG EXPOSURE DURING LACTATION

The following is an overview on drug use during lactation. This information is not intended to present a comprehensive review; the reader is therefore encouraged to seek additional and confirmatory information.

Reviewed 1999 by S. Ito.

The following general principles can be used by the clinician to manage cases where drug exposure in a breast-fed infant is questioned:

- Almost all drugs are excreted to some degree in breast milk.
- The concentration of the drug in breast milk usually does not exceed the maternal plasma concentration.
- Even when the breast milk:maternal plasma concentration ratio approaches or exceeds 1.0, the amount of drug ingested by the infant rarely attains therapeutic levels.
- A short exposure to a drug, as might be expected in the case of analgesics given to relieve postpartum pain, is usually of less concern than a drug given for long periods of time. The amount of drug ingested by the infant can, on occasion, be minimized by feeding the infant just before or at the time of maternal dosing.
- In the case of chronic drug therapy, the infant is usually exposed to lower concentrations of the drug while breast-feeding than while the fetus is in utero. Nevertheless, in most cases the long-term consequences of chronic exposure to subtherapeutic levels of medications is not known.
- Recommendations about breast-feeding where maternal medications are indicated depends on knowing if small amounts of the drug (subtherapeutic amounts) taken for even short periods of time may be associated with the following:
  —causing idiosyncratic reactions (e.g., chloramphenicol)
  —interfering with genetically abnormal metabolic pathways (e.g., nitrofurantoins in patients with G-6-PD deficiencies)
  —acting synergistically with drugs the infant receives therapeutically (e.g., theobromine in chocolate enhances an adverse response to theophylline).

This requires a reasonable knowledge of pharmacology and therapeutics in the newborn as well as a knowledge of the amount of drug excreted in the breast milk.

One can identify a number of review articles and book chapters about drug excretion in breast milk and recommendations for breast-feeding during maternal therapy. In fact, most of those reviewers have had to rely on data from isolated case reports of drug concentrations in breast milk, usually obtained from poorly controlled settings of maternal drug use. Many case reports are anecdotal and lack sufficient data to pharmacologically assess the dynamics of drug transfer into milk. Unfortunately, isolated single samples of plasma and milk may be misleading and multiple collections of milk over 24 hours rarely are attempted. The latter is unfortunate, since this is the only meaningful way in which the dose delivered to the nursing infant can be assessed with confidence.

The following brief paragraphs provide a rational basis from which individualized decisions for administering drugs during breast-feeding can be made. Of greatest importance in all these decisions is the assessment of the risk:benefit ratio for each therapeutic setting. The benefits of continuing breast-feeding are substantial. Therefore, one must always require a strong therapeutic benefit to the mother from the selected drug or a convincing reason to justify cessation of breast-feeding during the therapy.

Analgesics

In most peripartum and postpartum situations the need for analgesic medication is limited to a few hours or, at most, a few days. The amount of most narcotic analgesics excreted in breast milk is small and should be of no major concern. Similarly, nonsteroidal anti-inflammatory drugs are compatible with breast-feeding.

Anticholinergics

Documentation is lacking or conflicting about the excretion of anticholinergics (especially atropine) in breast milk and the reduction in milk production by these drugs. Although there is no documentation of problems in humans, it is advisable to closely monitor infants of nursing mothers for anticholinergic side effects.

Anticoagulants

Puerperal deep vein thrombophlebitis requires at least short-term and often long-term anticoagulation. A less common problem is a patient with a prosthetic heart valve who is being treated with long-term anticoagulation. Heparin, administered parenterally, for acute short-term therapy of thrombophlebitis, has not been shown to be excreted in breast milk. Moreover, heparin is not effective when taken orally. The oral anticoagulants are often used for long-term anticoagulation. They are more convenient for the patient, and have been contraindicated based on a single report where a nursing infant developed a hematoma at the site of an inguinal hernia repair. The infant's mother was anticoagulated with phenindione (not used in Canada). It was suspected that the infant had ingested a sufficient amount of drug in the breast milk to develop abnormal hemostasis.

More recent studies using warfarin showed that breast milk from mothers adequately anticoagulated contained no measurable drug and that the nursing infants showed no evidence of anticoagulation or other evidence of the drug in their plasmas. Warfarin appears to be compatible with breast-feeding.

Antiepileptics*

Most conventional antiepileptics (e.g., carbamazepine, phenytoin and valproic acid) result in the infant's exposure levels of less than 10% of those expected when the drug is given directly to an infant in a therapeutic dose. Despite sporadic case reports of adverse effects, these antiepileptics are believed to be compatible with breast-feeding.

On the other hand, phenobarbital, ethosuximide, and primidone may warrant more caution because the infant's exposure may reach therapeutic levels. The infant's exposure levels for phenobarbital, ethosuximide and primidone are estimated at 100%, 50% and >10%, respectively, of the levels expected when the drug is given directly to an infant in a therapeutic dose. These high-level exposures are mainly due to low clearance of phenobarbital and ethosuximide in the infant. However, whether this high-level exposure precludes breast-feeding or not depends on various factors in each individual case. In selected cases, regular monitoring of clinical signs (e.g., lethargy, poor feeding, sedation) and of drug concentrations in breast milk and in infant's plasma may guide breast-feeding.

Antihistamines*

Data are lacking on conventional H_1-antagonists such as diphenhydramine and dimenhydrinate. Terfenadine and loratadine result in infant's exposure levels of <1% of those expected when the drug is given directly to an infant in a therapeutic dose. Whether this low-level exposure causes symptoms awaits further studies. However, H_1-antagonists usually are not considered to be contraindicated during breast-feeding.

* The percentages expressing infant exposure levels are estimates based on values reported in the literature.

Antihypertensives*

All β-blockers appear to be compatible with breast-feeding. However, atenolol and sotalol (although the latter is not indicated as an antihypertensive agent) may cause relatively high exposure levels, 25% and 20% respectively, of those expected when the drug is given directly to an infant in a therapeutic dose. This may not be a problem in postneonatal infants. However, caution should be exercised in the early neonatal period because newborns may have low clearance of atenolol as a result of immature renal function (low GFR).

Diuretics and calcium channel blockers are safe to use during breast-feeding. Angiotensin-converting enzyme inhibitors such as captopril and enalapril are not excreted into breast milk in clinically significant amounts and are considered to be compatible with breast-feeding.

Antimicrobials

The most common use of antimicrobial therapy in postpartum infections is the relatively short course of antibiotics used to treat puerperal endometritis. The most commonly used drugs are penicillin or ampicillin combined with an aminoglycoside. Patients with a history of penicillin sensitivity are usually treated with a cephalosporin. Occasionally, anaerobic infections are suspected, in which case, clindamycin, chloramphenicol or metronidazole are considered. Urinary tract infections are frequent complications in the puerperium, the therapy of which can include ampicillin, sulfonamides, nitrofurantoins or one of the tetracyclines. Occasionally, long-term antibiotic therapy is necessary to prevent recurrent urinary tract infections. Vaginal infections such as Bacterial vaginosis and Trichomonas vaginitis respond to metronidazole therapy.

Most of the antimicrobial drugs studied have been found to be excreted in breast milk. The milk:plasma ratio for these drugs is usually less than one, but the data are often derived from only a few cases. For many of the drugs, the amounts ingested by a breast-fed infant will be below therapeutic levels (e.g., penicillin), but might be sufficient to result in idiosyncratic reactions (e.g., chloramphenicol) or cause anemia in a patient with G-6-PD deficiency (e.g., nitrofurantoins). Other potential problems that may arise in the breast-fed infant are modifications to the normal gastrointestinal flora leading to thrush and diarrhea, hypersensitivity response (e.g., penicillin) and interference with the interpretation of culture results if a fever work-up is required. However, clinical significance of these risks is usually not high enough to justify discontinuation of breast-feeding.

The aminoglycosides are excreted in breast milk when administered i.m. to the mother; because the drugs are poorly absorbed from the gastrointestinal tract, it is unlikely that renal toxicity or ototoxicity would occur in the infant.

Chloramphenicol is present in breast milk in sufficient amounts to cause concern for idiosyncratic bone marrow depression. This serious complication of chloramphenicol has never been reported in a breast-fed infant, but the theoretical danger warrants avoiding its use in a lactating patient.

Metronidazole has been cited as a drug contraindicated during lactation. This advice is based on reports that the drug is mutagenic in bacteria and carcinogenic in rodents when taken throughout their lives. Specific untoward effects in a nursing infant as a result of metronidazole ingestion have not been reported. Without more direct evidence of the harmful effects of short-term use in humans it seems overly conservative to withhold the drug or discontinue breast-feeding in patients with symptomatic parasitic infections (amebiasis, giardiasis or trichomoniasis) for which metronidazole may be the treatment of choice. This is particularly true if alternative forms of therapy have failed to cure the infection.

Quinolones (e.g., ciprofloxacin, norfloxacin) are excreted in breast milk in small amounts which do not result in significant serum drug concentrations in breast-fed infants. Also, there have been no adverse effects reported in breast-fed infants from maternal quinolone use. Quinolones are not absolute contraindications in the pediatric population. Some experts believe that quinolones are not compatible with breast-feeding. Alternative antibiotics should be sought first. However, quinolones are not considered absolute contraindications during breast-feeding.

The sulfonamides are excreted in breast milk, though the milk:plasma ratios for each individual drug have not been determined in humans. Nitrofurantoin is excreted in amounts that are difficult to detect in the breast milk of women. In each case there are concerns about these drugs causing anemia in an infant with G-6-PD deficiency. Consequently, alternative drugs should be used unless the infection (usually a urinary tract infection) is not responding to other therapy. If nitrofurantoins or sulfonamides become the drug of choice, the infant with G-6-PD deficiency should be observed closely for anemia.

Antithyroid Drugs*

Hyperthyroidism during pregnancy can be treated either by subtotal thyroidectomy or with antithyroid drugs, the latter being the more common choice in North America. Except for radioactive iodine, methimazole and propylthiouracil (PTU) are the two most commonly used antithyroid medications. Methimazole in small doses (e.g., ≤15 mg/day) may be used during breast-feeding if the infant's thyroid function is monitored at least biweekly. The amount of methimazole the infant would ingest through breast milk is estimated to be about 2 to 12% of the mother's dose on a weight basis. In contrast, the amount of propylthiouracil the infant would ingest is estimated to be less than 1% of the mother's dose on a weight basis, suggesting that PTU is the treatment of choice for hyperthyroid lactating women. Although this low-level exposure to PTU is unlikely to cause thyroid suppression in the infant, monitoring of TSH and T4 levels as well as clinical signs and symptoms may be justified until results from further extensive studies become available. For either drug, no adverse effect in breast-fed infants has been reported so far.

Methylxanthines

This group of compounds are often ingested as caffeine in coffee, tea or soft drinks; as theobromine in chocolate and cocoa; or theophylline as a prescribed drug for the treatment of asthma.

For caffeine, the milk:plasma ratio is 0.52. Hypothetically, a nursing infant ingesting 90 mL of milk 60 min and 120 min after a maternal dose of 150 mg of caffeine (1 to 2 cups of coffee), would ingest 170 µg or 0.11% of the maternal dose. This is probably an insignificant amount of the drug, but it must be remembered that the half-life of caffeine is 80 hours in the term newborn and 97.5 hours in a premature infant (20 to 30 times that of an adult). Consequently, repeated ingestion of caffeine might lead to accumulation of the drug during the first 2 weeks of postnatal life in the infant. This has yet to be studied.

Theophylline has been found to have a milk:plasma ratio of 0.6 to 0.73. The total amount of theophylline excreted in breast milk is estimated to be not more than 1% of the maternal dose. However, the prolonged half-life of theophylline in preterm infants (30.2 hours) and the fact that dietary caffeine and theobromine may act in additive fashion with theophylline must be kept in mind when the mother who desires to breast-feed her infant is being treated for asthma.

* The percentages expressing infant exposure levels are estimates based on values reported in the literature.

Psychotropics and Sedatives

If used occasionally as a sedative in the immediate peripartum period, benzodiazepines are not contraindicated during breast feeding.

Drugs taken over a longer period of time to treat chronic maternal conditions may be of greater concern. The most commonly used psychotropic drugs, the benzodiazepines and their metabolites, are excreted in breast milk, are poorly metabolized by the neonate, and have been associated with drowsiness in nursing infants. Lithium, the drug of choice for certain manic-depressive states, is excreted in breast milk, sometimes in quantities sufficient to reach exposure levels similar to those reached when the drug is given directly to an infant in a therapeutic dose. Consequently, the chronic use of either a benzodiazepine or lithium in breast-feeding mothers should be discouraged, unless drug concentrations in milk and the infant's condition are closely monitored.

The tricyclic antidepressants have not been systematically studied in lactating women. Although there is evidence of their excretion in breast milk, so far there are no reports of untoward effects of these drugs in breast-fed infants.

Recreational Drugs

Tobacco smoking and alcohol ingestion are the most common and socially acceptable sources of nonmedicinal drug exposure to breast-fed infants in Canada. Because they so often occur in the same individual, it is difficult to study their independent effects. Increasingly, these drugs are used together with other less fashionable and even illicit drugs such as marijuana and cocaine.

The effects of cigarette (tobacco) smoking on breast-fed infants are not well known. Small amounts of nicotine are known to be excreted in breast milk in women who smoke. Infant exposure to nicotine and smoke is largely through the inhalation of the products of tobacco combustion (i.e., second-hand smoke). Apart from the decreased suckling of infants that is associated with increased maternal smoking, no untoward effects attributable to maternal smoking are usually seen.

Maternal alcohol consumption is not compatible with breast-feeding. The milk:plasma ratio of ethanol is about 1.0 and the alcohol metabolizing capacity (alcohol and aldehyde dehydrogenases) is premature throughout the neonatal and infantile period. Overall, motor development is slightly slower in infants breast-fed by alcohol-drinking mothers. Also, short-term alcohol consumption by nursing mothers reportedly has an immediate effect on the odor characteristics of the milk and the feeding behavior of their infants resulting in less consumption of milk. Breast-feeding women should be aware of the potential effects of maternal alcohol consumption on their infants. Breast-feeding during and immediately after alcohol consumption should be avoided.

There are no systematic studies on drug or drug metabolite excretion in patients using other recreational or street drugs. However, drug withdrawal syndromes have been identified in infants of addicted mothers following weaning. This implies that over a long period of time, sufficient amounts of drug may be excreted in breast milk to cause physiological dependence in the infant. (An alternative explanation is that dependence occurred in utero and subsequent exposure to drugs in breast milk simply sustained the physiological dependence.)

Drugs Contraindicated During Breast-Feeding

The drugs considered compatible with breast-feeding far out number the drugs considered contraindicated during breast-feeding. Table I lists drugs considered contraindicated in breast-feeding that was originally published by the American Academy of Pediatrics.

Table I—Drugs Considered Contraindicated During Breast-Feeding

bromocriptine
cocaine
cyclophosphamide
cyclosporine
doxorubicin
ergotamine
lithium
methotrexate
phencyclidine (PCP)

Given the tremendous benefits of breast-feeding, drugs such as cyclosporine and lithium may be used during breast-feeding. This individualized approach becomes important especially when the mothers clearly understand the benefits and risks of breast-feeding during drug therapy and when close monitoring of the mother-infant pairs by experienced physicians is feasible.

Temporary cessation of breast-feeding is advised for a certain period of time for some radioactive compounds. The elected procedure may be performed after self-donation of breast milk in a quantity that can cover the period of interruption of breast-feeding. The period of cessation of breast-feeding depends on the particular radioactive compound used.

Checklist of Questions

There are several important questions that the clinician should consider whenever a lactating mother starts drug therapy:

- Is the drug absorbed orally?
- Is the drug ever given directly to infants for therapeutic reasons?
- Does the estimated dose delivered by milk approach a therapeutic quantity?
- Are the effects of the drug easily recognized in the infant?
- Are there idiosyncratic or allergic reactions to the drug that are not dose-related?
- Are there less toxic alternatives for maternal therapy?
- Is there a potential for drug accumulation during prolonged therapy?
- Could subtherapeutic doses of the drug mask early signs of medical conditions in the infant?
- Is the risk posed by the drug substantial enough to outweigh the significant proven benefits of breast-feeding?

References:

1. American Academy of Pediatrics, Committee on Drugs. The transfer of drugs and other chemicals into human milk. Pediatrics 1994; 93(1):137–50.
2. Briggs GG, Freeman RK, et al. Drugs in pregnancy and lactation. 4th ed. Baltimore, MD: Williams and Wilkins, 1994:349/e–350/e.
3. Little RE, Anderson KW, et al. Maternal alcohol use during breast-feeding and infant mental and motor development at one year. N Engl J Med 1989; 321(7):425–30.
4. Mennella JA, Beauchamp GK. The transfer of alcohol to human milk: effects on flavor and the infant's behavior. N Engl J Med 1991; 325(14):981–5.
5. Taddio A, Ito S. Drug use during lactation—a review. In: Koren G, ed. Maternal fetal toxicology: a clinician's guide. 2nd ed. New York: Marcel Dekker, 1994:133–219.

ANTIEPILEPTIC DRUG THERAPY

The following is a summary on drug use in epilepsy. This information is not intended to present a comprehensive review; the reader is therefore encouraged to seek additional and confirmatory information.

Reviewed 1999 by a committee of the Canadian League Against Epilepsy (C. Bayliff, J. Bruni, P. Camfield, S. Cowan, A. Guberman, M. Jones, S. Lovell, R.S. McLachlan, M. Sundaram and G.B. Young).

General Principles of Antiepileptic Drug Therapy

- If a patient requires an antiepileptic drug (AED), select a single, appropriate drug for that seizure type and give the drug an adequate trial. Do not abandon the drug until the following have been considered:
  —compliance has been confirmed, and
  —the drug dose has been increased until seizure control has been achieved or adverse effects occur.
- All drugs except phenytoin and ethosuximide should be introduced gradually to minimize dose-dependent adverse effects.
- Measurement of serum drug concentrations may be helpful if the patient has poor seizure control or if there is concern that the patient is experiencing toxic effects. However, the therapeutic range is only a guide to treatment and many patients achieve seizure control at serum concentrations below the standard therapeutic range. If the patient is free of adverse effects and the seizures are well controlled, the drug dose need not be adjusted if the serum concentration is below or even slightly above the therapeutic range. There is no established correlation between serum drug concentration and clinical efficacy for the newer AEDs (e.g., clobazam, gabapentin, lamotrigine, topiramate and vigabatrin). Therefore, determination of their serum concentration is not recommended for routine management.
- The free fraction (unbound portion) of the drug in serum is elevated in situations in which the drug is displaced from protein binding sites and the clearance or metabolism is reduced. This may happen when phenytoin and valproate are used together; valproate displaces phenytoin from the plasma proteins and slows its metabolism. Thus, the free fraction can become elevated to toxic values (therapeutic range 2.4 to 8 μmol/L) even though the total phenytoin concentration may be in the "therapeutic range" (40 to 80 μmol/L). Protein binding of phenytoin is also reduced in uremia, hypoalbuminemia and pregnancy; measurements of the free fraction can be helpful in making dosage adjustments.
- The routine monitoring of complete blood count, platelets and liver enzymes in patients receiving AEDs has never been demonstrated to be of value in predicting the serious adverse effects associated with these drugs. Routine laboratory monitoring may have a role in patients at high risk of a serious adverse drug effect, e.g., infants receiving valproic acid polytherapy. Patients should be informed of the early signs and symptoms of serious adverse effects before receiving the drug and should be advised to contact a physician immediately if they occur.
- Clinically significant drug interactions involving AEDs may occur. Consult the Drug Interactions table in the Clin-Info section and the Drug Interactions section of product monographs for further information. Phenytoin, phenobarbital, primidone and carbamazepine are potent enzyme inducers. Consequently, reduced activity or serum drug concentrations of some drugs (e.g., corticosteroids, cyclic antidepressants, cyclosporine, oral contraceptives, quinidine, theophylline, topiramate) may result when used concurrently with these AEDs. Increased activity or serum concentrations of some drugs (e.g., theophylline, warfarin) may result subsequent to the enzyme inducer being discontinued. The carbamazepine serum drug concentration is also decreased by the previously mentioned AEDs. In some cases, the clearance of drugs is inhibited and toxicity may occur, e.g., serum carbamazepine concentration may rise when carbamazepine is used with clarithromycin, erythromycin, verapamil or diltiazem; phenobarbital concentration may increase when phenobarbital is given with valproic acid (enzyme inhibitor). Reduced activity or serum concentrations of some drugs (e.g., digoxin, oral contraceptives) may result with concurrent topiramate use. Initial and maintenance doses of lamotrigine should be reduced when valproic acid is given concomitantly.

Starting Antiepileptic Drugs

Not every patient with one or more seizures needs to be placed on long-term antiepileptic drugs. Some patients with benign epilepsies can be managed without medication, such as benign Rolandic epilepsy of childhood where the convulsions are usually brief, nocturnal and daytime attacks are short and focal, and the child always "outgrows" the seizures.

After a single unprovoked seizure, the pooled risk of subsequent attacks is 35–50%. Most neurologists would not prescribe long-term drug therapy after a single seizure unless the subsequent risk for that patient was especially high (e.g., partial seizures with an abnormal neurological examination or imaging test and epileptiform activity on EEG) or if the risk of social or medical harm from another seizure was significant.

After two or three unprovoked seizures, the risk of subsequent episodes rises to about 75% over 4 years. Most recurrences occur within one year of the second or third seizure. The risk of a third seizure is higher in those individuals with a presumed cause for the epilepsy. The decision to treat patients with antiepileptic medication should be individualized, taking into account the risk of recurrence and the side effects of medication.

Stopping Antiepiletic Drugs

The decision regarding if and when to stop AED therapy depends on the estimated risk of seizures on and off treatment, the potential psychosocial and physical morbidity of recurrent seizures and the patients perception of the adverse (physical, psychological, convenience and cost) effects of drug therapy. The fear of losing their right to drive a motor vehicle, should seizures recur, may cause some adult patients to stay on therapy. The average relapse rate is 20–30% in children and 30–40% in adults after being tapered off AEDs following a seizure free interval of at least two years. Factors associated with a higher recurrence risk are:
—older age of onset (beyond childhood)
—poor initial control of seizures
—certain epileptic syndromes (e.g., juvenile myoclonic epilepsy)
—symptomatic epilepsy.

If EEGs show either generalized epileptiform activity or a worsening pattern during AED withdrawal, there is a greater likelihood of seizure recurrence.

When the decision is made to stop therapy, most AEDs should be withdrawn slowly, over at least 6 weeks. Benzodiazepines and barbiturates have a higher association with withdrawal seizures and are probably best withdrawn over several months. In patients on polypharmacy, the more sedating drugs (e.g., barbiturates, benzodiazepines and vigabatrin) are usually withdrawn first.

Management of Epilepsy in Pregnancy and Lactation

- The outcome of pregnancy is usually favorable in patients with epilepsy (risk of malformations is probably 4 to 6%); seizure control is usually achievable during pregnancy if the patient is followed closely with appropriate monitoring and, if needed, drug therapy is adjusted.
- It is desirable to prevent status epilepticus during pregnancy. Physicians need to weigh the risks of seizures against the risks of drugs in the first trimester. It is best to review this with the patient before conception.
- If AEDs are used, it is best to use one drug at the lowest effective dose if feasible. Consider giving the drug in multiple daily doses to avoid high peak serum concentrations.
- Give folic acid 5 mg/day beginning 4 weeks before conception and throughout pregnancy, especially during the first trimester. This is especially important when valproate and carbamazepine are used. Monitor serum and red blood cell folate during the first trimester.
- Vitamin K_1 (phytonadione) 10 mg/day should be given orally from 36 weeks of pregnancy onward to prevent hemorrhagic disease of the newborn. Tablets of vitamin K_1 are not available in Canada, therefore, the parenteral form can be added to juice and taken orally. Also give vitamin K_1 1 mg i.m. to the baby at birth.
- Perform ultrasound examination between 18 and 20 weeks to check for spina bifida and other neural tube defects, especially in women taking carbamazepine and valproate.
- Avoid valproate and carbamazepine, if possible, when there is a positive family history of neural tube defects.
- There are alterations in plasma protein binding of AEDs in pregnancy, especially phenytoin. For this reason, the serum concentration of the free fraction of phenytoin should be monitored throughout pregnancy in select cases. Dose adjustments may be necessary to maintain therapeutic concentrations especially in the third trimester.
- AEDs are present in breast milk. Breast-feeding is recommended providing the baby continues to gain weight and is not overly sedated.
- The pharmacokinetics of many AEDs are altered by pregnancy. If doses of AEDs were increased during pregnancy, they should be returned to baseline doses in the first month after delivery to avoid toxicity.
- Eclampsia is defined as the occurrence of one or more seizures in a patient with earlier pre-eclampsia. Pre-eclampsia is a multisystem disorder of pregnancy consisting primarily of recently elevated arterial blood pressure and proteinuria. Thrombocytopenia and elevation of serum aspartate transaminase are common accompaniments.

  Eclampsia is a special case of seizures and should be managed with magnesium sulfate. Severe pre-eclampsia also should be treated with this medication, as the likelihood of seizures is lessened. Magnesium sulfate should be used with caution in patients who are uremic, who have neuromuscular transmission defects, e.g., myasthenia gravis, or who are receiving neuromuscular blocking agents.

  Magnesium sulfate can be administered either by the i.m. or i.v. route. The latter may be advisable in emergency situations (e.g., active convulsions or severe hypertension) although one route is not superior to the other. Initially, give 4 g i.v. over 5 minutes followed by either 5 g i.m. into each buttock and a further 5 g i.m. into alternate buttocks every 4 hours for 24 hours, or continuous infusion of 1 g/h for 24 hours. Alternatively, give 10 g i.m. then 5 g i.m. every 4 hours in the same fashion. Patients should be monitored for magnesium toxicity to ensure that respirations are >12/min, urine output >100 mL every 4 hours and the knee jerk reflex is preserved. Magnesium intoxication is initially treated with 3.5 mmol (7 mEq) of i.v. calcium; additional doses may be necessary, depending on the response. (Note: 1 g calcium gluconate = 2.3 mmol Ca^{++} = 4.5 mEq Ca^{++} and 1 g calcium chloride = 6.8 mmol Ca^{++} = 13.5 mEq Ca^{++}).

Management of Febrile Seizures

- Febrile seizures are common convulsive events in children between the ages of 6 months and 5 years. The tendency is inherited and most seizures are brief and generalized. The vast majority of febrile seizures do no harm, although parents are usually terrified that their child is dying.
- Assessment must exclude meningitis. A lumbar puncture is mandatory if there is any question about the possibility of meningitis. Because the signs of meningitis are subtle in small children, a lumbar puncture should be strongly considered in most children less than 1 year of age presenting with a first febrile seizure. Other investigations should be directed to the cause of the fever. An EEG or CAT scan are of no benefit in the vast majority of cases and are usually not necessary. Treatment must emphasize reassurance.
- Following a first febrile seizure, the overall risk of recurrence is 40%. The risk is increased if the child's age is less than 1 year, if there is a low grade fever at the time of the seizure, if the illness is of more than a few hours' duration, if there is a family history of febrile seizures and possibly if the child attends a day care center. Absence of these factors is associated with a low risk of recurrence.
- Most patients do not need medications. Recurrent febrile seizures may be prevented by phenobarbital 4 mg/kg/day; however, behavioral, cognitive and adverse drug effects generally make daily medication unacceptable for this benign disorder. Carbamazepine and phenytoin are ineffective. Oral diazepam at the time of illness modestly reduces the risk of recurrence, but 40% of patients have significant adverse effects. Compulsive antipyretic treatment does not reduce recurrences, but increases "fever phobia".
- The parenteral preparation of diazepam given rectally (0.5 mg/kg) will often stop an ongoing seizure and can be used safely at home provided all caregivers are carefully instructed in the proper administrative technique. The following equipment is required for the rectal administration of diazepam:
  —1 ampul of diazepam (10 mg/2 mL)
  —18 gauge needle
  —3 mL syringe.

  The recommended procedure for administration is as follows:
  (a) Break open the ampul.
  (b) Place the needle on the end of the syringe.
  (c) Withdraw the required dosage.
  (d) Remove the needle from the syringe.
  (e) Gently insert the lubricated blunt end of the syringe up to its hub, into the rectum and instill the contents. Stay with the child for 20 minutes to monitor breathing.

  This approach minimizes medication exposure and reduces the risk of prolonged febrile seizures (>20 minutes). Rectal diazepam may be particularly effective in patients with a history of prolonged seizures, poor access to medical care or a high risk of recurrence of febrile seizures.
- Epilepsy develops in 2 to 4% of children with febrile seizures. The risk may approach 15% if there are two or more complicating features (e.g., focal in origin, prolonged (>15 minutes), multiple seizures in 24 hours, neurologic abnormality or family history of epilepsy). There is no evidence that prevention of febrile seizures alters this risk.

Status Epilepticus

Repetitive tonic-clonic seizures in which the patient does not recover consciousness between seizures is generalized convulsive status epilepticus. It represents a medical emergency that demands immediate therapy to prevent mortality and morbidity. To minimize the possibility of permanent neurologic sequelae, seizures should be controlled within 30 to 60 minutes of onset.

There are as many kinds of status epilepticus as there are seizure types (e.g., absence status epilepticus, complex partial status epilepticus, myoclonic status epilepticus). The following two sections outline the management of generalized convulsive status epilepticus in adults and children, respectively.

In the treatment of convulsive status epilepticus it is important to stop the seizure activity in the brain as well as the outward manifestations, as continuous seizure activity (except absence status) can be damaging to the brain.

Status Epilepticus in Adults: Management

1. General Measures: Assess cardiopulmonary function; clear the airway of vomitus and dentures. Place the patient in a semi-prone position; administer oxygen. Insert an oral airway if necessary for upper airway protection. Insert a large bore i.v. catheter and start a normal saline (NS) infusion.

   Obtain history from witnesses, friends or family and perform examination. Take blood for assessment of serum concentrations of AEDs, glucose, urea, electrolytes, calcium, magnesium and urine and/or blood for a drug screen when appropriate. Request serum concentration for theophylline if the patient has received this agent. Theophylline and other potentially convulsive drugs, including fluoroquinolones, should be avoided in the presence of ongoing seizures. An urgent EEG is advised, if patient remains obtunded after initial treatment measures, to check for nonconvulsive status epilepticus.

   Give 25 to 50 mL of 50% dextrose i.v. if hypoglycemia or if glucose measurement is not available.

   Give thiamine 100 mg i.v.

2. Drug Therapy and Monitoring: Infuse lorazepam 2 mg i.v. over 2 minutes and add 1 to 2 mg increments every 2 minutes, up to 8 mg if necessary to stop the seizure. Diazepam 5 to 10 mg i.v. at 2 mg/min may also be used, but lorazepam is preferred because of its longer duration of action. The protocol for lorazepam or diazepam can be repeated in 10 to 15 minutes if seizures recur or if seizure control is not achieved initially. Watch for respiratory depression. Give only when seizures are ongoing or recurring frequently.

   Simultaneously with the first dose of lorazepam or diazepam, start an infusion of phenytoin using a separate i.v. line with NS running (phenytoin precipitates in glucose solutions). Administer phenytoin 15 to 20 mg/kg, at ≤50 mg/min. Phenytoin should never be given i.m. Alternatively, fosphenytoin 15 to 20 mg phenytoin equivalents (PE)/kg can be administered i.m. or i.v. at 100 to 150 mg PE/min. Fosphenytoin may be given i.m. since it is more soluble and does not use a propylene glycol vehicle, however the therapeutic concentration may not be reached as quickly as with i.v., therefore the i.m. route should only be considered when i.v. access is not possible. Monitor blood pressure for hypotension and monitor the electrocardiogram for conduction defects. (Phenytoin is contraindicated in cardiac conduction defects and should be used only very cautiously in the presence of shock or hypotension.) A phenytoin oral maintenance dose can be started the next day.

   Another option includes phenobarbital i.v. at ≤100 mg/min until seizures stop or until a maximum of 20 mg/kg. Consider endotracheal intubation before administering barbiturates when benzodiazepines have been given earlier. Observe for cardiopulmonary depression. The patient may require assisted ventilation with high doses of phenobarbital if given after benzodiazepines.

   If these measures fail, consider the patient to have refractory status epilepticus. Summon an anesthetist for endotracheal intubation and assisted ventilation, and do continuous EEG monitoring if available. Either midazolam or propofol is suggested at this stage to induce anesthesia. Administer midazolam beginning with a loading dose of 200 μg/kg as a slow i.v. bolus, followed by 0.75 to 10 μg/kg/min by continuous infusion. Propofol is given as a 1 to 2 mg/kg i.v. bolus, followed by an infusion of 2 to 10 mg/kg/h. The dosage can be adjusted upwards or downwards, depending on the effect on EEG-recorded seizures. The EEG should be recorded either continuously or several times each hour until the seizures are controlled. A burst-suppression pattern or suppression of seizures or spikes is the end point. The administration of midazolam should be reviewed every hour and stopped when seizures are controlled.

   Alternatively, or if midazolam or propofol fails, pentobarbital is recommended, beginning with a loading dose of 5 mg/kg i.v. at ≤25 mg/min, followed by an infusion of 0.5 to 1 mg/kg/h, increasing if necessary up to 1 to 3 mg/kg/h. Boluses of 5 to 20 mg/kg i.v. may be repeated for breakthrough seizures. The EEG should be monitored continuously or several times each hour. A burst-suppression pattern is usually sufficient, but complete suppression may be necessary if seizures persist or if status epilepticus keeps recurring. **Note:** Isoflurane, paraldehyde and lidocaine have also been used for refractory cases.

Status Epilepticus in Children: Management

1. Assess cardiopulmonary function, establish an airway, administer oxygen and insert an i.v. line. Blood specimens should be obtained for visual evaluation of blood glucose (e.g., Dextrostix), measurement of AED serum concentrations, serum glucose, serum electrolytes, calcium, magnesium, liver enzymes, blood gases and complete blood count.
2. Check the visual blood glucose test immediately. If the result is less than 2.2 mmol/L, administer a bolus of i.v. dextrose (2.5 mL/kg of 10% dextrose in water for newborns; 1 mL/kg of 25% dextrose in water for older children), followed by an infusion of 10% dextrose solution.
3. Infuse i.v. diazepam or lorazepam. The i.v. diazepam dosage is 0.3 mg/kg (maximum 10 mg) over 2 minutes, and it may be repeated once after 10 minutes. The i.v. lorazepam dose is 0.05 to 0.1 mg/kg (maximum 4 mg) over 2 minutes; it may be repeated once after 10 minutes. If there is difficulty establishing an i.v. line, rectal diazepam is preferred because lorazepam administered by the rectal route is absorbed erratically. The rectal diazepam dosage is 0.5 mg/kg (maximum 10 mg/dose); the dose may be repeated once after 10 minutes.
4. Start phenytoin 18 mg/kg i.v. over 20 minutes (not to exceed 3 mg/kg/min) at the same time as the first dose of benzodiazepine. The blood pressure and heart rate should be monitored and the rate of infusion decreased if the patient becomes hypotensive. Further dilution of phenytoin with i.v. solutions is not recommended, especially those containing dextrose.
5. General anesthesia should be considered in patients who have had tonic-clonic seizures persisting for longer than 30 minutes and in whom the above treatment is not effective. Endotracheal intubation is recommended and general anesthesia should be achieved with either i.v. thiopental or pentobarbital. The thiopental dose is 3 to 5 mg/kg followed by 2 to 4 mg/kg/h administered by continuous i.v. infusion. The pentobarbital loading dose is 5 mg/kg followed by 1 to 3 mg/kg/h by continuous i.v. infusion. Both thiopental and pentobarbital should be titrated to maintain a burst suppression pattern on the EEG. The blood pressure must be monitored closely when either pentobarbital or thiopental is administered.

6. Other drugs that can be used in children with refractory status epilepticus include the following:
   —Phenobarbital administered i.v. at 10 to 20 mg/kg over 15 minutes; *or*
   —Paraldehyde administered rectally at a dose of 0.3 mL/kg up to a maximum of 5 mL using a 1 g/mL paraldehyde solution. The paraldehyde should be administered with an equal volume of mineral/vegetable oil; *or*
   —Lidocaine administered as an i.v. bolus of 2 to 3 mg/kg at a rate not exceeding 25 mg/min followed by a continuous i.v. infusion at 3 to 10 mg/kg/h. The maintenance dosage should be reduced gradually when the seizures have been controlled for 12 hours.
7. AED serum concentrations measured 1 hour after administration provide a guide to the time when maintenance antiepileptic drug therapy should be initiated and are useful if seizures recur. The maintenance dosages are as follows:
   —Phenytoin 5 to 10 mg/kg/day administered i.v./p.o. in three evenly divided doses. Children under 1 year of age often require a larger dose; *or*
   —Phenobarbital 3 to 5 mg/kg/day i.v./i.m./p.o. in two evenly divided doses.
8. An underlying cause for the status epilepticus should be investigated in previously normal patients. In particular, the possibility of bacterial meningitis or encephalitis should be considered in children with fever.

Epilepsy in the Elderly

The incidence of seizures increases after age 60 years and the prevalence of epilepsy may be as high as 140 per 100,000. Seizures are partial or focal in onset in 50 to 80% of elderly patients and the incidence varies with different types of practice. Specific etiologies (i.e., Alzheimer's disease, brain tumor, medication toxicity, metabolic encephalopathies, stroke and trauma) are identified in approximately two-thirds of patients whose seizures begin over age 60 years.

Seizures in the elderly are sometimes difficult to diagnose with certainty and need to be differentiated from cardiac or vascular events such as transient ischemic attacks and cardiogenic or orthostatic syncope, drop attacks, hypoglycemic reactions and vestibular disturbances. The consequences of seizures in the elderly are often serious (e.g., falls with broken bones or head injuries).

Antiepileptic drug therapy in the elderly is frequently complicated by polypharmacy with increased potential for drug interactions (see the subsection on General Principles of Antiepileptic Drug Therapy and the Drug Interactions table in Clin-Info). Furthermore, pharmacodynamic changes (e.g., increased drug sensitivities, especially to benzodiazepines and barbiturates) and pharmacokinetic changes (e.g., less efficient hepatic metabolism and renal excretion) may predispose the patient to toxicity.

In general, antiepileptic drugs (AEDs) should be started at smaller than usual adult doses and increased more slowly in the elderly than in middle-aged patients. The total daily dose is also lower in the elderly (e.g., phenytoin 200 mg/day). Determination of the free (unbound) fraction of AEDs that are usually highly protein bound (e.g., phenytoin and valproate) is often useful in the elderly, especially when drug toxicity is suspected.

Selected References:

Pregnancy and Lactation
1. Cornelissen M, Steegers-Theunissen R, et al. Supplementation of vitamin K in pregnant women receiving anticonvulsant therapy prevents neonatal vitamin K deficiency. Am J Obstet Gynecol 1993; 168:884–8.
2. Dansky LV, Andermann E, et al. Anticonvulsants, folate levels and pregnancy outcome: a prospective study. Ann Neurol 1987; 21:176–82.
3. Delgado-Escueta AV, Janz D, Beck-Mannagetta G. Pregnancy and teratogenesis in epilepsy. Neurology 1992; 42 Suppl 5:1–160.
4. Jones KL, Lacro RV et al. Pattern of malformations in the children of women taking carbamazepine during pregnancy. N Eng J Med 1989; 320:1661–66.
5. Lucas MJ, Levenko KJ, Cunningham FG. A comparison of magnesium sulfate with phenytoin for the prevention of eclampsia. N Eng J Med 1995; 333:201–5.
6. The Eclampsia Trial Collaborative Group. Which anticonvulsant for women with eclampsia? Evidence from the Collaborative Eclampsia Trial. Lancet 1995; 345:1455–63.

Status Epilepticus
1. Lowenstein DH, Alldredge BK. Status epilepticus. N Eng J Med 1998; 338:970–6.
2. Parent JM, Lowenstein DH. Treatment of refractory status epilepticus with continuous infusion of midazolam. Neurology 1994; 44:1837–40.
3. Shorvon S. Status epilepticus: its clinical features and treatment in children and adults. Cambridge: Cambridge University Press 1994.
4. Walsh GO, Delgado-Escueta AV. Status epilepticus. Neurologic Clinics 1993; 11(4):835–56.
5. Working Group on Status Epilepticus. Treatment of convulsive status epilepticus. Recommendation to the Epilepsy Foundation of America's Working Group on Status Epilepticus. JAMA 1993; 270(7):854–9.

Epilepsy in the Elderly
1. Sundaram M, Dostrow V. Epilepsy in the elderly. The Neurologist 1995; 1:232–9.
2. Thomas RJ. Seizures and epilepsy in the elderly. Arch Intern Med 1997; 157:605–17.
3. Wilmore LJ. Management of epilepsy in the elderly. Epilepsia 1996; 37 (Suppl 6):S23–S33.

Starting and Stopping Antiepileptic Drugs
1. Berg AT, Shinnar S. Relapse following discontinuation of antiepileptic drugs: a meta-analysis. Neurology 1994; 44:601–8.
2. Gilad R, Lampl Y, et al. Early treatment of a single generalized tonic-clonic seizure to prevent recurrence. Arch Neurol 1996; 53:1149–52.
3. Hauser WA, Rich SS, et al. Risk of recurrent seizures after two unprovoked seizures. N Eng J Med 1998; 338:429–34.
4. Overweg J. Withdrawal of antiepileptic drugs in seizure-free patients, risk factors for relapse with special attention for the EEG. Seizure 1995; 4:19–36.
5. Schmidt D, Gram L. A practical guide to when (and how) to withdraw antiepileptic drugs in seizure-free patients. Drugs 1996; 52(6):870–4.

ANTINEOPLASTIC DRUG THERAPY

The following provides an overview of the principles and practice of antineoplastic drug therapy, in particular cytotoxic agents. Other drugs used in systemic therapy, namely hormonal and biologic (biologic response modifier) agents are not included. This overview is not intended to present a comprehensive review; therefore the reader is encouraged to seek additional and confirmatory information.

Reviewed 1999 by M.P. Thirlwell.

Introduction

Since cancer is a common disease, health care professionals in all areas of practice are likely to have a patient who has cancer and is receiving antineoplastic therapy. The antineoplastic drug therapy is usually supervised by a medical oncologist; however, it is important to note that the optimal care of a patient with cancer is through a multidisciplinary team approach.

One essential point in the treatment of cancer is to decide on the goal of drug therapy. The goal must be balanced against the drug toxicities. The goal may be to cure the cancer or may be to provide palliative care by relieving the symptoms with or without prolongation of survival. To arrive at a treatment decision, the following must also be considered:

- the natural history of the cancer
- the extent of spread or stage of the malignancy
- the patient's performance status and general medical condition
- the efficacy of available drugs with their associated toxicities.

Natural History of the Cancer

The natural history of cancers is well covered in a number of oncology and general medical textbooks. Refer to the Selected Reading List at the end of this section.

Staging of Tumors

Staging for tumor burden at the time of diagnosis is extremely important for estimating the prognosis and planning the treatment. Only when the exact extent of the disease is established can the proper treatment regimen be devised. There is no absolute system of staging applicable to all cancers; however, the TNM system of classification was devised to standardize staging for solid tumors using basic principles applicable to all sites. The three aspects of the system are: T (0–4), indicating the extent of the primary tumor; N (0–3), describing the status of the regional lymph nodes; and M (0–1), denoting the absence or presence of distant metastases. The tumor stage is then based on groupings of TNM assignments which indicate increasing tumor burden.

A deficiency of TNM staging is that it does not take into account the biology or aggressiveness of a particular tumor and allow for the different prognostic factors to be identified. Prognostic characteristics are now often included to supplement staging information. Examples of prognostic characteristics of tumors are:

— the estrogen and progesterone receptors for breast cancer
— the level of serum tumor markers such as beta-HCG in choriocarcinoma
— histological grade in sarcoma
— the presence of genetic markers such as HER-2/*neu* oncogene in breast cancer.

In addition to the evaluation of the TNM components, it is also important to be aware of the point at which the patient is in the trajectory of the illness. For example, is the cancer newly diagnosed or in relapse and what was the type and extent of previous treatment, especially with radiation or chemotherapy?

Performance Status

The performance status (PS) is a measure of the level of activity of which the patient is capable. It is a value which reflects how much the cancer has affected the patient and a prognostic indicator of how well the patient is likely to do with treatment. Therefore, it is useful in determining whether chemotherapy will be clinically beneficial. Two commonly used PS scales are the Karnofsky scale and the Eastern Cooperative Oncology Group (ECOG) scale (see Table I). The Karnofsky scale has 11 levels of activity (100%–0) which allows for a high degree of discrimination but the ECOG with 5 levels of activity (0–4) is more popular and clinically useful because of its simplistic approach. In general, unless the cancer is highly responsive to chemotherapy (e.g., certain leukemias, lymphomas), a patient with a PS of 4 is unlikely to benefit from antineoplastic drug therapy.

PS is a component of various scales devised to assess the quality of life (QOL) of patients. Chemotherapy may improve or worsen the PS and QOL of patients.

Table I—ECOG Performance Status Scale

Grade	Level of Activity
0	Fully active; able to carry on all predisease performance without restriction.
1	Restricted in physically strenuous activity but ambulatory and able to carry out work of a light or sedentary nature.
2	Ambulatory and capable of all self-care but unable to carry out any work activities; up and about more than 50% of waking hours.
3	Capable of only limited self-care; confined to bed or chair more than 50% of waking hours.
4	Completely disabled; cannot carry on any self-care; totally confined to bed or chair.

Efficacy of Drugs

In the past, antineoplastic drugs were used in patients in whom cancer (e.g., breast) had recurred after failure of primary therapy (i.e., surgery and/or irradiation), or if the cancer was too advanced or not amenable to local or regional therapy (e.g., leukemia). However, antineoplastic chemotherapy is being increasingly applied in other settings. Its use as adjuvant therapy is designed to eradicate or suppress minimal residual disease or microscopic metastases after primary treatment. As a result, the rate of relapse of cancer and the duration of survival of the patient may be improved. This approach has been successful in childhood malignancies and in two common adult tumors; i.e., breast and colorectal cancer. In addition, cytotoxic drugs may be used as neoadjuvant or primary therapy to reduce the size and extent of the initial tumor (e.g., head and neck) before surgery or irradiation. As a result, there may be greater success in controlling the primary tumor as well as in preserving organ function.

The effectiveness of antineoplastic chemotherapy ranges from highly curative, as in choriocarcinoma in women, through to rarely if ever achieving even a transient response as in renal cell cancer. It is useful to have a perspective of the value of chemotherapy for various tumors. Table II presents one classification of the responsiveness of advanced cancers to antineoplastic drug therapy.

Table II—Effectiveness of Antineoplastic Chemotherapy

Classification	Response Rate	Examples
Curable	>70%	acute lymphocytic leukemia acute myelogenous leukemia childhood malignancies choriocarcinoma germ cell testicular tumors Hodgkin's disease non-Hodgkin's lymphoma (high grade)
Highly Responsive	>50–70%	bone sarcomas breast cancer chronic myelogenous leukemia multiple myeloma non-Hodgkin's lymphoma (low grade) ovarian cancer small cell lung cancer
Moderately Responsive	20–50%	adrenal cortical carcinoma bladder cancer carcinoid tumor cervical cancer colorectal cancer endometrial cancer esophageal cancer head and neck cancer insulinoma melanoma non-small cell lung cancer prostate cancer soft tissue sarcoma stomach cancer
Minimally Responsive	<20%	brain cancer (with some exceptions) hepatobiliary cancer pancreatic cancer renal cancer thyroid cancer

Responses to antineoplastic drug therapy based on change in tumor size are generally defined as follows:

- **Complete Remission (CR)** indicates that no clinically detectable cancer is found following treatment.
- **Partial Remission (PR)** indicates that measurable tumor (usually the sum of the products of two perpendicular diameters from all measurable lesions) is decreased by 50% following treatment, no new areas of cancer can be found, and no area of tumor shows progression.
- **Progression** refers to an increase of tumor mass by more than 25% or appearance of any new lesions.
- **Stable disease** is a change in tumor mass that does not meet the criteria for CR, PR or progression.

In general, CR may be associated with cure or prolonged survival, whereas PR may be associated with a relief of symptoms with or without prolonged survival. Although controversial, stable disease may be associated with relief of symptoms and improved survival in certain cases.

Classification of Cytotoxic Drugs

A classification of cytotoxic drugs is given under the heading "antineoplastics" in the Therapeutic Guide (pink section) and a detailed description of the drug may be found in the monographs (white section). Summarized descriptions of the dosage schedules and toxicities of various cytotoxic drugs and the types of cancer responsive to these agents are provided in tabular form in several sources (see Selected Reading List). Information on the dose modifications required depending on the patient's medical condition, in particular the renal and hepatic status, is also important to note. In deciding on the use of cytotoxic drug therapy, if cure is the goal, such as in Hodgkin's disease, it would be acceptable to have severe toxicities. For a cancer incurable with antineoplastic chemotherapy, such as advanced malignant melanoma, where the goal of treatment should be palliative, even moderately toxic antineoplastic chemotherapy may be hard to justify.

Combination Therapy

Cytotoxic drugs are generally used in combinations rather than alone. The choice of drugs that are used in combination is based on several principles including the following:

- only drugs known to be active by themselves should be used
- individual drugs should have different mechanisms of action
- the dose limiting toxicities should be different
- the drugs should be synergistic in anticancer effect.

The drug combinations that form an antineoplastic drug regimen are named using acronyms. For example, CMF for breast cancer refers to the use of Cyclophosphamide, Methotrexate and 5-Fluorouracil, and CHOP for non-Hodgkin's lymphoma refers to Cyclophosphamide, Hydroxydaunorubicin (doxorubicin) Oncovin (vincristine) and Prednisone. Combination regimens and their acronyms are listed in several oncology references (see Selected Reading List/References).

While most of the time anticancer drugs are given systemically, there are selected indications for local or regional infusion of cytotoxic drugs into the tumor site. Directed chemotherapy is based on the principle of achieving a higher concentration of the cytotoxic agents at the target tumor tissue while sparing normal tissue. Examples include the following:

—**intrathecal:** directly through a lumbar puncture needle or into an implanted Ommaya reservoir to treat meningeal leukemia and lymphoma
—**intrapleural:** through a needle or chest tube to control effusions
—**intraperitoneal:** using dialysis techniques as with the treatment of ovarian cancer
—**intravesical:** instillation of drug via cystoscopy
—**intraarterial:** such as hepatic or limb perfusion therapy to treat metastases selectively.

Dose Intensification

The use of very high marrow-ablating doses of cytotoxic drugs represents a new and rapidly developing area of antineoplastic therapy. The purpose of this approach is to achieve a cure in a number of malignancies such as leukemias and high risk non-Hodgkin's lymphoma in which allogenic or autologous bone marrow transplantation is possible. In addition, intense dose chemotherapy regimens with autologous bone marrow or peripheral blood progenitor cell rescue are being investigated in the high risk adjuvant or early relapse setting for patients with cancer of the breast or testis, among other cancers.

Drug Toxicity and Management

The type and extent of cytotoxic drug toxicity varies according to the agent. Toxicities that are related to the antiproliferative activity of these drugs include effects that manifest in normal tissues with the highest rate of cell turnover or proliferation, such as:

—in the bone marrow (resulting in myelosuppression)
—in the mucosa of the alimentary tract (resulting in mouth ulceration and diarrhea)
—in the hair follicle and skin (resulting in alopecia)
—in the gonads (resulting in impaired function).

Bone marrow depression is usually the most significant dose-limiting toxicity of cytotoxic chemotherapy. Autologous bone marrow or peripheral blood progenitor cell transplantation or rescue can reduce the myelosuppressive toxicity of chemotherapy; however, cost and toxicity limits its general use. Cytokine growth factors that stimulate erythroid proliferation (e.g., epoetin alfa) or myeloid proliferation (e.g., granulocyte colony stimulating factor [G-CSF] or granulocyte macrophage colony stimulating factor [GM-CSF]), are now used to ameliorate bone marrow toxicity. G-CSF and GM-CSF have been shown to shorten the duration of neutropenia following both standard and high-dose cytotoxic chemotherapy.

Thrombocytopenia remains a problem with high doses or prolonged exposure to cytotoxic drugs and may limit therapy. Several agents, including megakaryocyte growth factor (e.g., thrombopoietin) are under investigation. Spontaneous hemorrhage rarely occurs with platelet counts above 20 000/µL; however, below this level the risk of hemorrhage increases and platelet transfusions should be considered especially for levels below 10 000/µL.

Any patient with neutropenia, secondary to chemotherapy, who develops a fever should be regarded as having an infection until proven otherwise. This complication can have fatal consequences unless properly managed. Although the absolute criteria may vary, it is generally accepted that a patient with an absolute granulocyte count of 1 000/µL or less and a fever of 38.4°C (not otherwise attributable to a noninfectious cause) should have blood and appropriate cultures done and be started empirically on broad spectrum antibiotics.

Various drugs have specific organ toxicities such as:

- **bladder inflammation** is associated with cyclophosphamide or ifosfamide. Mesna, a cytoprotective agent, is used to prevent bladder toxicity of ifosfamide and high dose cyclophosphamide.
- **cardiomyopathy** is most commonly associated with anthracycline drugs (e.g., doxorubicin). Dexrazoxane (ICRF-187) is an agent used to protect against anthracycline-induced cardiomyopathy.
- **damage to local tissues** may result when drugs extravasate during intravenous injection, depending on whether they are vesicants (e.g., doxorubicin), irritants (e.g., etoposide), or non-toxic (e.g., methotrexate).
- **nausea and vomiting** acting via the gastrointestinal tract and central nervous system, may cause extreme physiological and psychological discomfort and may be reason enough for the patient to withdraw from therapy. Cytotoxic agents have been classed according to their emetic potential ranging from highly (e.g., cisplatin), moderately (e.g., doxorubicin), mildly (e.g., 5-fluorouracil) and minimally (e.g., vincristine) emetogenic. The problem of antineoplastic chemotherapy-induced nausea and vomiting has been reduced with the use of better antiemetic regimens that include serotonin type 3 (5-HT_3) antagonists such as ondansetron, granisetron and dolasetron.
- **nephrotoxicity** is associated with cisplatin. Amifostine is used to protect against cisplatin-induced nephrotoxicity.
- **peripheral neuropathy** such as with vinca alkaloids and cisplatin. Amifostine may protect against cisplatin-induced neuropathy.
- **pneumonitis** is associated with bleomycin.

The use of biochemical modulation to increase the therapeutic effect of antineoplastic chemotherapy may also result in increased toxicity to normal tissue. An example of this is the extreme diarrhea which may arise from the combination of leucovorin (i.e., folinic acid) followed by 5-fluorouracil.

Clinical Trials

Further research is needed for antineoplastic drug therapy. The use of new drugs or drug regimens in clinical trials is very common and important. These trials may be in one of three phases. The aim of *phase I* trials is to determine the optimal dose, frequency of administration and side effects of the treatment. The goal of *phase II* trials is to determine the types of cancer, if any, that respond to the treatment. *Phase III* trials compare a known effective treatment in *phase II* trials with either no therapy or another drug regimen. For clinical trials there are written protocols giving the background for the study and pertinent information, including drug doses and potential toxicities. These are available through cancer centers and through physicians involved in the trials.

Information concerning the treatment of cancers and specific clinical trials can be obtained through the U.S. National Cancer Institute, cancer information database "Physician Data Query" (PDQ) via the Internet, and through other online information sources such as CANCERLIT featured on Medline and OncoLink from the University of Pennsylvania Cancer Center.

Selected Reading List

General Oncology

- Bennett JC, Plum F, eds. Cecil textbook of medicine. 20th ed. Toronto: WB Saunders, 1996.
- DeVita VT, Hellman S, Rosenberg SA, eds. Cancer: principles and practice of oncology. 5th ed. Philadelphia: JB Lippincott, 1997.
- Peckham M, Pinedo J, Veronesi U, eds. Oxford textbook of oncology. Oxford: Oxford Press, 1995.
- Rakel RE, ed. Textbook of family practice. 5th ed. Toronto: WB Saunders, 1995.

Cytotoxic Drug Information

- Casciato DA, Lowitz BB, eds. Manual of clinical oncology. 3rd ed. Boston: Little, Brown and Co., 1995.
- Dorr RT, Van Hoff DD, eds. Cancer chemotherapy handbook. 2nd ed. Stamford: Appleton and Lange, 1994.
- Kirkwood JM, Lotze MT, Yasko JM, eds. Current cancer therapeutics. 3rd ed. Current Medicine, 1996.
- Perry M, ed. The chemotherapy source book. 2nd ed. London: Williams and Wilkins, 1996.
- Skeel RT, Lachant NA, eds. Handbook of cancer chemotherapy. 4th ed. Boston: Little Brown and Co., 1995.

Selected References:

1. Ellerby R, Ault S, et al. Quick reference handbook of oncology drugs. Toronto: WB Saunders, 1996.
2. Fleming ID, Cooper JS, et al, eds. AJCC cancer staging manual. 5th ed. Philadelphia: Lippincott-Raven, 1997.
3. Hancock B, ed. Cancer care in the hospital. New York; Radcliffe Medical Press, 1996.
4. Haskell C, ed. Cancer treatment. 4th ed. Toronto: WB Saunders, 1995.
5. Tierney LM, McPhee SJ, Papadakis MA, eds. Current medical diagnosis and treatment. 35th ed. Stamford: Appleton and Lange, 1996.
6. Williams CJ, ed. Cancer biology and management: an introduction. New York: John Wiley and Sons, 1990.
7. Young LY, Koda-Kimble MA, eds. Applied therapeutics: the clinical use of drugs. 6th ed. Vancouver, WA: Applied Therapeutics Inc., 1995.

SERUM DRUG CONCENTRATION MONITORING

The following is an overview on serum drug concentration monitoring. This information is not intended to present a comprehensive review; the reader is therefore encouraged to seek additional and confirmatory information. Specific patient management requires clinical judgement in the interpretation of the serum drug concentration. Therapeutic ranges vary widely according to drug assay methods and specific laboratory references.

Reviewed 1999 by M. Bédard and B. Hardy.

Serum drug concentration monitoring (SDCM), also known as therapeutic drug monitoring, pharmacokinetic monitoring or clinical pharmacokinetics, is the act of maximizing the information obtainable from serum drug concentration data and applying this knowledge in a rational manner, in light of the patient's clinical status, to optimize drug therapy.[1]

Information obtained can be used for the following:[2]

- determine or adjust a dosage regimen
- evaluate a drug response
- aid in the assessment of toxicity
- check compliance
- minimize the cost of hospitalization
- decrease the risk associated with medical-legal problems.

If the serum drug concentration is to be fully utilized, results must be interpreted in light of the complete clinical situation. The clinician must be aware of patient-specific factors that affect the drug's disposition. Patient's age, diet, smoking habits, concurrent drugs, metabolic/excretory ability and changing disease states are just some of the variables that need to be considered in association with the serum drug concentration.[1]

Which drugs are most appropriate for SDCM?

There are a number of characteristics common to drugs that are routinely monitored using serum concentrations:[1]

- narrow therapeutic index
- significant consequences associated with therapeutic failure or toxicity
- wide interpatient pharmacokinetic variability
- unpredictable dose-response relationship
- utility of SDCM as an intermediate endpoint to guide therapeutic decisions
- serum drug concentrations available to the prescriber within a reasonable time frame

When should drug concentrations be obtained?

Awareness of the sampling time relative to the last dose is critical for the proper interpretation of a drug level. In most cases, the serum sample should be obtained after the absorption and distribution phases are complete (e.g., trough level) and the drug has reached steady state (e.g., after administration of the same fixed dose for 4 to 5 half-lives). Levels obtained before a steady-state concentration exists may be erroneously low or high; adjusting the dosage based on such a result could produce toxic or subtherapeutic concentrations, respectively.[1–2] In cases where toxicity is a concern or is suspected, sampling can be undertaken at any time.[2]

Table I presents a commonly used formula to evaluate creatinine clearance (an estimate of a patient's renal function) using a stable serum creatinine level and patient demographics (e.g., age, gender).

Table II presents information on SDCM for selected drugs. Information is, for the most part, gathered from results in average individuals. The half-life may be prolonged in patients with renal or hepatic disease or may vary due to demographic differences (e.g., age, gender). Steady-state concentrations assume that the dosage has remained the same for 4 to 5 half-lives and that doses have not been changed or missed.

Collaboration of the hospital laboratory, physicians, nurses, i.v. technicians and pharmacists is essential for a successful SDCM service.

Table I—Creatinine Clearance Formula[a]

Males:

$$\text{Creatinine clearance (mL/s)}^{b} = \frac{(140 - \text{patient's age, years})\ (\text{TBW, kg})}{(50)\ (\text{serum creatinine, } \mu\text{mol/L})}$$

Females:
Multiply equation above by 0.85

Modification of creatinine clearance estimates may be required in some patients. The accuracy of using the serum creatinine value to predict creatinine clearance is influenced by diseases (e.g., cirrhosis), clinical conditions (e.g., malnutrition, obesity, spinal cord injuries) and dietary intake (e.g., high consumption of meat).

Legend: TBW = Total Body Weight
[a] Modified Cockcroft and Gault.[3]
[b] To convert from SI (mL/s) to (mL/min), multiply the (mL/s) value by 60.

References:
1. Hardy B. Therapeutic drug monitoring. In: Cornish P, Knowles S, eds. Focus on the literature. Metro Toronto Hospital Drug Information Service 1989; 88(3):1–6.
2. Mioduch HJ. Therapeutic drug monitoring. Hosp Pharm 1989; 24:614–8, 624–30, 632.
3. Cockcroft DW, Gault MH. Prediction of creatinine clearance from serum creatinine. Nephron 1976; 16:31–41.
4. Done AK. Salicylate intoxication. Pediatrics 1960; 26:805.
5. Evans WE, Schentag JJ, Jusko WJ, eds. Applied pharmacokinetics. Spokane, WA: Applied Therapeutics, Inc. 1992.

Table II—Recommendations for Serum Drug Concentration Monitoring

Drug	Route	Sampling Time	Drug Concentration	Monitoring Considerations
Acetaminophen	Oral	Overdose: at least 4 h after ingestion.	Refer to the Matthew-Rumack nomogram for acetaminophen poisoning in the Acetaminophen general monograph in the White Section for interpretation.	Half-life about 2–4 h.
Amikacin	I.V. intermittent infusion I.M.	Peak: 15 min after 1-h infusion; 30 min after 30-min infusion. Trough: within 5 min of the next dose. Peak: 1 h after administration. Trough: within 5 min of the next dose.	Peak: 20–30 mg/L. For serious gram-negative infections, peak of 25–30 mg/L desired. Trough: less than 8 mg/L.	Dosage should be stable for at least 3 doses. Usually obtain peak and trough levels. Half-life about 2–3 h in patients with normal renal function. Optimum levels have not yet been determined when using once-daily dosing regimen.
Amitriptyline	Oral	Trough: 12 h after the dose. For suspected toxicity, sample anytime.	430–900 nmol/L (parent drug + demethylated metabolite, nortriptyline).	Half-life 9–46 h. Routine monitoring as a therapeutic guideline is not warranted, but may be useful to assess noncompliance, nonresponders, suspected toxicity, drug interactions, elderly patients and children.
Carbamazepine	Oral	Trough: for periodic monitoring, sample just before the next dose. For suspected toxicity, sample anytime.	17–50 μmol/L.	Induces its own metabolism for up to 2–4 weeks. Half-life with chronic dosing 15–25 h.
Cyclosporine	Oral and I.V.	Trough: for periodic monitoring, sample just before the next dose. For suspected toxicity, sample anytime. Oral peak: within 2–4 h after the dose.	12-h trough values of 150–400 μg/L in whole blood (monoclonal specific RIA) or 50–125 μg/L in plasma (monoclonal specific RIA).	Half-life 10–27 h. Some institutions recommend a different therapeutic range for a specific transplant population. The ranges listed are intended for the early post-transplant period.
Desipramine	Oral	Trough: 12 h after the dose. For suspected toxicity, sample anytime.	430–675 nmol/L.	Half-life 12–28 h. Routine monitoring as a therapeutic guideline is not warranted but may be useful to assess noncompliance, nonresponders, suspected toxicity, drug interactions, elderly patients and children.
Digoxin	Oral and I.V.	Post-load: at least 6 h after last dose of loading regimen (i.v. or p.o.). For periodic monitoring, sample just before next dose. For suspected toxicity, sample anytime.	1–2.5 nmol/L.	Dosage should be stable for 5–7 days in patients with normal renal function. Half-life 35–40 h. Time to steady state prolonged in patients with decreased renal function.
Ethosuximide	Oral	Trough: For periodic monitoring, sample just before the next dose. For suspected toxicity, sample anytime.	280–710 μmol/L.	Dosage should be stable for 8 days in adults and 5 days in children. Half-life 40–60 h in adults and 26–36 h in children.
Gentamicin	I.V. intermittent infusion I.M.	Peak: 15 min after 1-h infusion; 30 min after 30-min infusion. Trough: within 5 min of the next dose. Peak: 1 h after administration. Trough: within 5 min of the next dose.	Peak: 5–10 mg/L. For serious gram-negative infections, 10–12 mg/L. Trough: Less than 2 mg/L.	Dosage should be stable for at least 3 doses. Usually obtain peak and trough levels. Half-life about 2 h in adults with normal renal function. Optimum levels have not yet been determined when using once-daily dosing regimen.
Imipramine	Oral	Trough: 12 h after the dose. For suspected toxicity, sample anytime.	550–1 015 nmol/L (parent drug + demethylated metabolite, desipramine).	Half-life 6–28 h. Routine monitoring as a therapeutic guideline is not warranted but may be useful to assess noncompliance, nonresponders, suspected toxicity, drug interactions, elderly patients and children.

Table II—Recommendations for Serum Drug Concentration Monitoring *(cont'd)*

Drug	Route	Sampling Time	Drug Concentration	Monitoring Considerations
Lithium	Oral	12 h after the last dose. For suspected toxicity, sample anytime.	0.8–1.2 mmol/L for acute therapy. 0.6–0.8 mmol/L for maintenance. 0.4–0.6 mmol/L for maintenance in the elderly.	Dosage stable for at least 3 days. Half-life 18–27 h, varies with renal function.
Netilmicin	I.V. intermittent infusion	Peak: 15 min after 1-h infusion; 30 min after 30-min infusion. Trough: within 5 min of the next dose.	Peak: 5–10 mg/L. For serious gram-negative infections, 10–12 mg/L. Trough: Less than 2 mg/L.	Dosage should be stable for at least 3 doses. Usually obtain peak and trough levels. Half-life about 2–3 h in patients with normal renal function. Optimum levels have not yet been determined when using once-daily dosing regimen.
	I.M.	Peak: 1 h after administration. Trough: within 5 min of the next dose.		
Nortriptyline	Oral	Trough: 12 h after the dose. For suspected toxicity, sample anytime.	170–495 nmol/L.	Half-life 18–56 h. Routine monitoring as a therapeutic guideline is not warranted but may be useful to assess noncompliance, nonresponders, suspected toxicity, drug interactions, elderly patients and children.
Phenobarbital	Oral and Parenteral	For periodic monitoring, sample just before the dose. For suspected toxicity, sample anytime.	65–170 μmol/L.	Time to steady state about 10–25 days in adults, 8–15 days in children. Half-life 75–126 h in adults, 37–73 h in children.
Phenytoin	Maintenance dose: Oral and I.V.	Trough: for periodic monitoring or suspected inadequate dose, sample just before the next dose. For suspected toxicity, sample anytime.	40–80 μmol/L (adults, children, infants >3 months). 25–55 μmol/L (preterm and term neonates 2 wks–3 months)	Time to steady state is highly variable, 1–5 weeks. Phenytoin kinetics are nonlinear and saturable, resulting in highly variable concentrations with even minor dosage changes. Free fraction (active) may increase in patients with renal or hepatic failure and/or hypoalbuminemia; lower dosages are usually necessary.
	I.V. loading dose	60 min after end of infusion.		
Primidone	Oral	Trough: for periodic monitoring, sample just before the next dose. For suspected toxicity, sample anytime.	23–55 μmol/L.	Time to steady state about 2 days. Half-life 6–18 h. Primidone is metabolized, in part, to phenobarbital.
Procainamide	Oral	Peak: 2.5 h after the dose. For periodic monitoring or suspected inadequate dose, sample just before the next dose. For suspected toxicity, sample anytime.	17–43 μmol/L. Limited data suggests that plasma concentrations as high as 43–85 μmol/L may be required.	Dosage should be stable for 1–2 days. Half-life 2.4–3.6 h in patients with normal renal function and increases to 6–13 h in patients with reduced renal function.
	Oral: Sustained release	Peak: 4 h after the dose. For periodic monitoring or suspected inadequate dose, sample just before the next dose. For suspected toxicity, sample anytime.		
	I.V. continuous infusion	2 h after the beginning of the maintenance infusion. For suspected toxicity, sample anytime.		

Table II—Recommendations for Serum Drug Concentration Monitoring *(cont'd)*

Drug	Route	Sampling Time	Drug Concentration	Monitoring Considerations
NAPA (n-acetyl-procainamide), active procainamide metabolite		For suspected toxicity, sample anytime.	< 115 µmol/L (procainamide + NAPA).	Half-life about 6–10 h in patients with normal renal function and increases to 10–40 h in patients with reduced renal function. Routine monitoring for therapeutic efficacy is not warranted; measure in patients with moderate to severe renal impairment to identify those at increased risk for toxicity.
Quinidine	Oral and Parenteral	Trough: for periodic monitoring, sample just before the next dose. For suspected toxicity, sample anytime.	6–15 µmol/L.	Dosage should be stable for 2 days. Half-life 6–9 h. Levels may be useful to assess compliance or toxicity.
Salicylate	Oral	Peak: 1–2 h after the dose. Trough: sample just before the next dose. Overdose: at least 6 h post-ingestion.	1.1–2.2 mmol/L therapeutic for anti-inflammatory effect. The Done nomogram may be used to assess toxicity in overdose.[5]	Half-life is dose-dependent: low doses (e.g., 325 mg ASA), 2–3 h; higher doses (10–20 g), 15–30 h. Time to steady state 5–7 days.
Theophylline	Oral: Sustained release	Peak: twice-daily products—about 4 h after the dose; once-daily products—about 10 h after the dose. Consult individual product monographs. Trough: sample just before the next dose. For suspected toxicity, sample anytime.	55–110 µmol/L. For neonatal apnea, 28–55 µmol/L. Higher levels may be tolerated.	Dosage should be stable for 48 h before sampling. Half-life varies greatly. Peak levels should be monitored to assess suspected toxicity. Trough levels may be monitored to assess efficacy at the end of the dosing interval.
	Liquid and Plain uncoated tablets	Peak: 2 h after the tablet dose. 1–2 h after the liquid dose. Trough: sample just before the next dose. For suspected toxicity, sample anytime.		
	I.V. loading dose	Sample 30 min after an i.v. loading dose.		
	Followed by I.V. continuous infusion	Sample 24–48 h after the start of the maintenance infusion. For suspected toxicity, sample anytime.		
Tobramycin	I.V. intermittent infusion	Peak: 15 min after 1-h infusion; 30 min after 30-min infusion. Trough: within 5 min of the next dose.	Peak: 5–10 mg/L. For serious gram-negative infections, 10–12 mg/L. Trough: Less than 2 mg/L.	Dosage should be stable for at least 3 doses. Usually obtain peak and trough levels. Half-life about 2–2.5 h in patients with normal renal function. Optimum levels have not yet been determined when using once-daily dosing regimen.
	I.M.	Peak: 1 h after administration. Trough: within 5 min of the next dose.		
Valproic Acid	Oral	Trough: for periodic monitoring, sample just before the next dose. Peak: 2–3 h after the dose. For suspected toxicity, sample anytime.	350–700 µmol/L.	Dosage should be stable for at least 2 days. Half-life 8–19 h. Free fraction (active) may increase in patients with renal or hepatic failure and/or hypoalbuminemia; lower doses are usually necessary.
Vancomycin	I.V. intermittent infusion	Peak: 15 min–1 h after 1-h infusion. Trough: within 5 min of the next dose.	Peak: 20–40 mg/L. Trough: Less than 10 mg/L.	Dosage should be stable for 20–30 h. Half-life about 6 h in patients with normal renal function. Usually obtain peak and trough levels. The association of peak and trough concentrations with efficacy and toxicity remains controversial.

BODY SURFACE AREA OF ADULTS

Reviewed 1999

Reprinted with permission from Lentner C, ed. Geigy scientific tables. 8th ed. vol. 1. Basle: Ciba-Geigy, 1981: 226–7.

Figure I—Nomogram for Adults

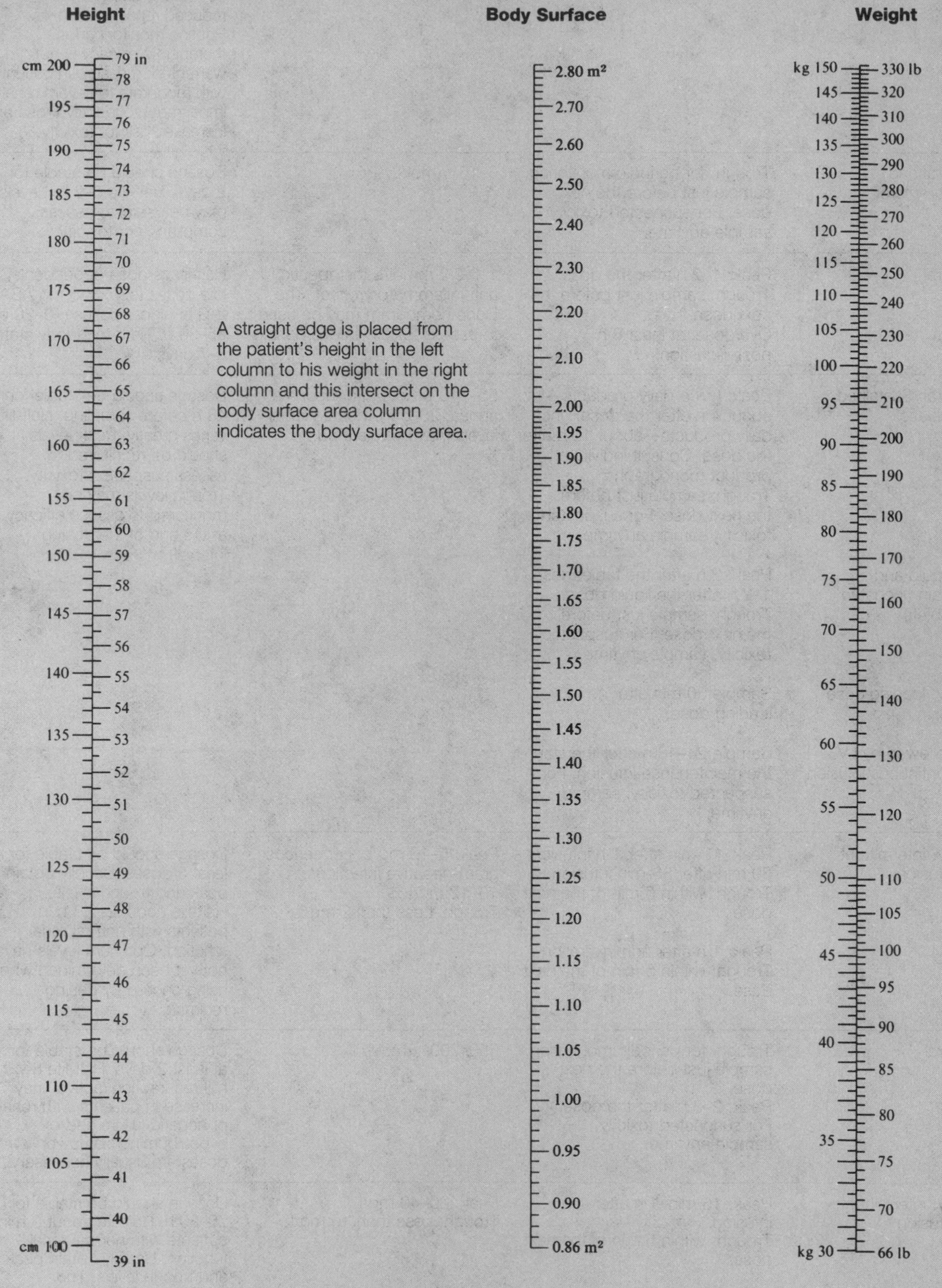

A straight edge is placed from the patient's height in the left column to his weight in the right column and this intersect on the body surface area column indicates the body surface area.

From the formula of DuBois and DuBois, Arch. Intern. Med., 17, 863 (1916): $S = M^{0.425} \times H^{0.725} \times 71.84$, or $\log S = \log M \times 0.425 + \log H \times 0.725 + 1.8564$ (S: body surface in cm^2, M: mass in kg, H: height in cm).

BODY SURFACE AREA OF CHILDREN

Reviewed 1999

Reprinted with permission from Lentner C, ed. Geigy scientific tables. 8th ed. vol. 1. Basle: Ciba-Geigy, 1981: 226–7.

Figure II—Nomogram for Children

Height **Body Surface** **Weight**

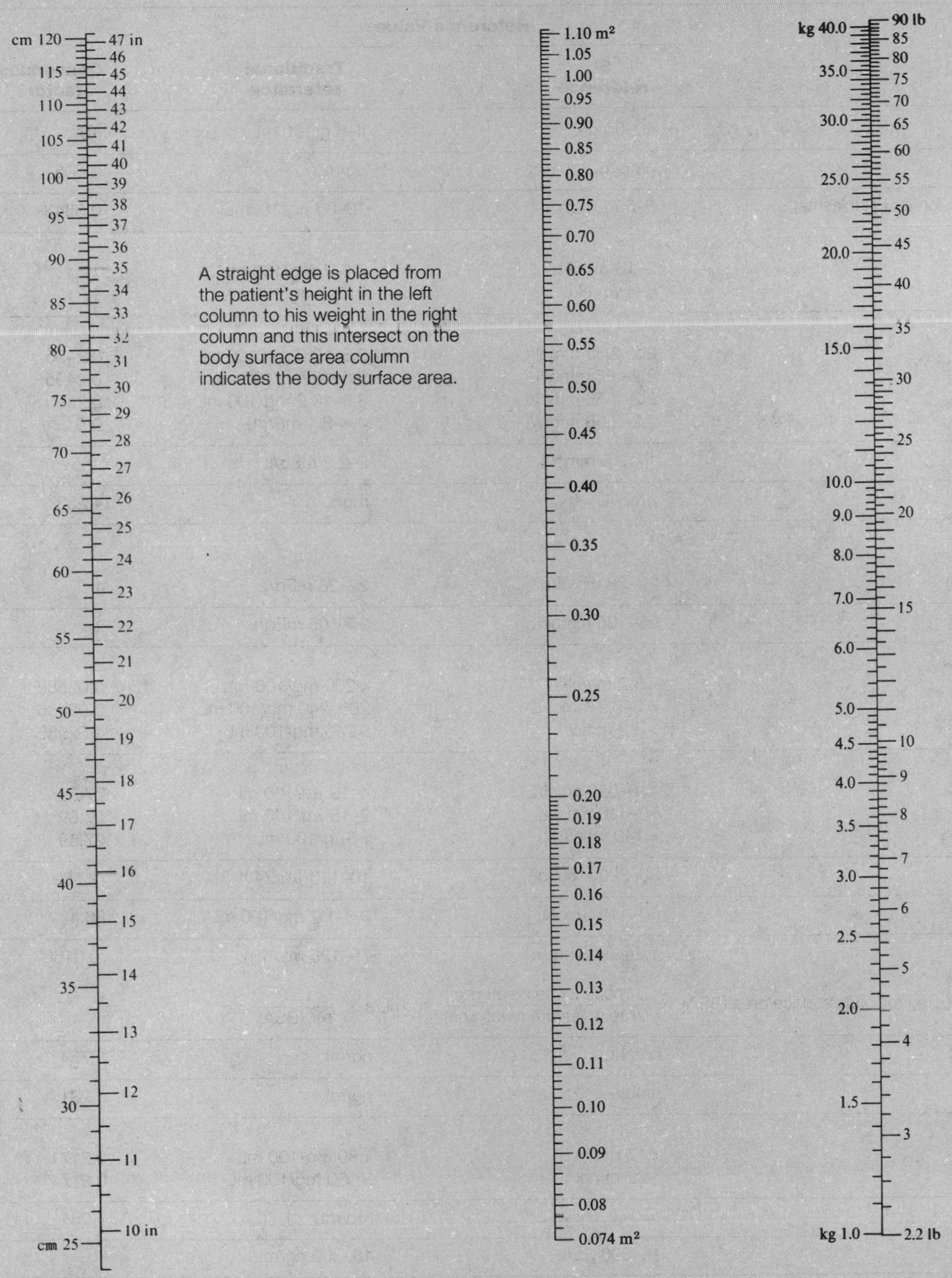

A straight edge is placed from the patient's height in the left column to his weight in the right column and this intersect on the body surface area column indicates the body surface area.

From the formula of DuBois and DuBois, Arch. Intern. Med., 17, 863 (1916): $S = M^{0.425} \times H^{0.725} \times 71.84$, or $\log S = \log M \times 0.425 + \log H \times 0.725 + 1.8564$ (S: body surface in cm^2, M: mass in kg, H: height in cm).

CLINICAL LABORATORY REFERENCE VALUES

Table I provides a summary of selected adult clinical laboratory reference values. This information is not intended to present a comprehensive review; the reader is therefore encouraged to seek additional and confirmatory information. Each laboratory establishes its own reference values.

Reviewed 1999 by M.J. McQueen.

Table I—Adult Laboratory Values

Laboratory Test	**Reference Values**		**Conversion factor**[a]
	SI reference	**Traditional reference**	
Albumin (serum)	40–60 g/L	4–6 g/100 mL	10
Amitriptyline[c]	nmol/L	ng/mL	3.605
Ammonia, as ammonium ion (NH_4^+) (plasma)	5–50 μmol/L	10–85 μg/100mL	0.5543
Bilirubin (serum)			
total	2–18 μmol/L	0.1–1 mg/100 mL	17.1
conjugated	0–4 μmol/L	0–0.2 mg/100 mL	17.1
Calcium (serum)			
male	2.2–2.58 mmol/L	8.8–10.3 mg/100 mL	0.2495
female < 50 years	2.2–2.5 mmol/L	8.8–10 mg/100 mL	0.2495
female > 50 years	2.2–2.56 mmol/L	8.8–10.2 mg/100 mL	0.2495
all populations	2.2–2.56 mmol/L	4.4–5.1 mEq/L	0.5
Calcium, ionized (serum)	1–1.15 mmol/L	2–2.3 mEq/L	0.5
Carbamazepine[c]	μmol/L	mg/L	4.233
Carbon dioxide (bicarbonate + CO_2) (blood, plasma, serum)	22–28 mmol/L	22–28 mEq/L	1
Chloride (serum)	95–105 mmol/L	95–105 mEq/L	1
Cholesterol, total (plasma)			
low risk	< 5.2 mmol/L	< 200 mg/100 mL	0.02586
moderate risk	5.2–6.2 mmol/L	200–240 mg/100 mL	0.02586
higher risk	> 6.2 mmol/L	> 240 mg/100 mL	0.02586
Cortisol (serum)			
0800 h	110–520 nmol/L	4–19 μg/100 mL	27.59
1600 h	50–410 nmol/L	2–15 μg/100 mL	27.59
2400 h	< 140 nmol/L	< 5μg/100 mL	27.59
Cortisol (urine)	30–300 nmol/day	10–110 μg/24 h	2.759
Creatinine (serum)	50–110 μmol/L	0.6–1.2 mg/100 mL	88.4
Creatinine clearance	1.24–2.08 mL/s	75–125 mL/min	0.01667
Creatinine clearance corrected for body surface area (BSA) = $\frac{\mu mol/L \text{ (urine creatinine)}}{\mu mol/L \text{ (serum creatinine)}} \times mL/s \times \frac{1.73}{m^2 \text{ (BSA)}}$			
Desipramine[c]	nmol/L	ng/mL	3.754
Digoxin[c]	nmol/L	ng/mL	1.281
Ethanol (plasma)			
legal limit (driving)[b]	< 17 mmol/L	< 80 mg/100 mL	0.2171
toxic	> 22 mmol/L	> 100 mg/100 mL	0.2171
Ethosuximide[c]	μmol/L	mg/mL	7.084
Ferritin (serum)	18–300 μg/L	18–300 ng/mL	1
Fibrinogen (plasma)	1.5–3.5 g/L	150–350 mg/100 mL	0.01
Folate, as folic acid, pteroylglutamic acid (serum)	4–22 nmol/L	2–10 ng/mL	2.266

Table I—Adult Laboratory Values *(cont'd)*

Laboratory Test	Reference Values: SI reference	Reference Values: Traditional reference	Conversion factor[a]
Gases (arterial blood)			
pO_2	10–13.3 kPa	75–100 mmHg	0.1333
pCO_2	4.7–6 kPa	35–45 mmHg	0.1333
Glucose, fasting (plasma)	3.9–6.1 mmol/L	70–110 mg/100 mL	0.05551
Glucose (CSF)	2.8–4.4 mmol/L	50–80 mg/100 mL	0.05551
Hemoglobin (blood)			
male	140–180 g/L	14–18 g/100 mL	10
female	115–155 g/L	11.5–15.5 g/100 mL	10
Imipramine[c]	nmol/L	ng/mL	3.566
Insulin, fasting (plasma, serum)	35–145 pmol/L	5–20 μU/mL	7.175
Iron (serum)			
male	14–32 μmol/L	80–180 μg/100 mL	0.1791
female	11–29 μmol/L	60–160 μg/100 mL	0.1791
Iron binding capacity (serum)	45–82 μmol/L	250–460 μg/100 mL	0.1791
Lithium[c]	mmol/L	mg/100 mL	1.441
Magnesium (serum)	0.8–1.2 mmol/L	1.8–3 μg/100 mL	0.4114
	0.8–1.2 mmol/L	1.6–2.4 mEq/L	0.5
Mean corpuscular volume (MCV) (blood)	76–110 fL	76–100 μm^3	1
Mean corpuscular hemoglobin concentration (MCHC) (blood)	330–370 g/L	33–37 g/100 mL	10
Mean corpuscular hemoglobin (MCH) (blood)	27–33 pg	27–33 pg	1
Methanol (plasma)	0 mmol/L	0 mg/100 mL	0.3121
Osmolality (plasma)	280–300 mmol/kg	280–300 mOsm/kg	1
Osmolality (urine)	50–1 200 mmol/kg	50–1 200 mOsm/kg	1
Nortriptyline[c]	nmol/L	ng/mL	3.797
Phenobarbital[c]	μmol/L	mg/100 mL	43.06
Phenytoin[c]	μmol/L	mg/L	3.964
Phosphate, as inorganic phosphorus (serum)	0.8–1.6 mmol/L	2.5–5 mg/100 mL	0.3229
Platelet count (blood)	130–400 x 10^9/L	130 000–400 000/mm^3	0.001
Potassium (serum)	3.5–5 mmol/L	3.5–5 mEq/L	1
Primidone[c]	μmol/L	mg/L	4.582
Procainamide[c]	μmol/L	mg/L	4.249
NAPA (n-acetylprocainamide)[c]	μmol/L	mg/L	3.606
Quinidine[c]	μmol/L	mg/L	3.082
Reticulocyte count (blood)	10–75 x 10^9/L	10 000–75 000/mm^3	0.001
Salicylate[c]	mmol/L	mg/100 mL	0.0724
Sodium (serum)	135–147 mmol/L	135–147 mEq/L	1
Theophylline[c]	μmol/L	mg/L	5.55

[a] To convert from traditional to SI units, multiply the traditional value by the conversion factor. To convert from SI to traditional units, divide the SI value by the conversion factor.

[b] Varies in different jurisdictions.

[c] Values vary depending on clinical condition. See Serum Drug Concentration Monitoring section in Clin-Info.

Table I—Adult Laboratory Values *(cont'd)*

Laboratory Test	Reference Values: SI reference	Reference Values: Traditional reference	Conversion factor[a]
Urea (serum)	3–6.5 mmol/L	8–18 mg/100 mL (BUN)	0.357
Valproic Acid[c]	µmol/L	mg/L	6.934
White cell count, WBC (blood)	3.2–9.8 x 10^9/L	3 200–9 800/mm^3	0.001
Zinc (serum)	11.5–18.5 µmol/L	75–120 µg/100 mL	0.153

[a] To convert from traditional to SI units, multiply the traditional value by the conversion factor. To convert from SI to traditional units, divide the SI value by the conversion factor.

[b] Varies in different jurisdictions.

[c] Values vary depending on clinical condition. See Serum Drug Concentration Monitoring section in Clin-Info.

References:

1. Health and Welfare Canada. SI manual in health care. 3rd rev. ed. Ottawa: 1986.
2. The SI conversion units for common laboratory tests. Ann Pharmacother 1993; 27:112–19.
3. Young LY, Smith GH. Interpretation of clinical laboratory tests. In: Koda-Kimble MA, Young LY, eds. Applied therapeutics: the clinical use of drugs. 5th ed. Vancouver, WA: Applied Therapeutics, Inc. 1992:3–14.

NONMEDICINAL INGREDIENTS

The following is an overview of nonmedicinal ingredients. This information is not intended to present a comprehensive review; the reader is therefore encouraged to seek additional and confirmatory information.

Reviewed 1999

In addition to the active drug, products may also contain nonmedicinal ingredients (NMIs) used as diluents, binders, lubricants, buffers, antioxidants, fillers, preservatives, flavors, coloring agents and sweeteners. Examples of NMIs are alcohol, gluten, lactose, sodium, sulfites and tartrazine. Some raw materials used in the manufacturing process are obtained from sources other than the pharmaceutical industry; therefore, the drug manufacturer may be unaware of unlabelled NMIs. For example, agents used to whiten powders may contain traces of sulfites, and dyes used to imprint names on capsules may contain traces of tartrazine or sulfites.

Canada Gazette, Part I for Schedule No. 743, February 14, 1994 reported that all NMIs would have to be listed alphabetically on the inner or outer label within a 2-year period, yet to be determined. In the last year, the Therapeutic Products Directorate has accepted the pharmaceutical industry's commitment to identify procedures which would supplement a product monograph-based system of NMI disclosure for prescription products, with the understanding that such a supplementary system should have an expectation of delivery within a reasonable timeframe, and that the expanded use of this information by third parties to facilitate patient access would not be hampered.

The availability of this voluntarily disclosed information for prescribed products will be monitored, and should access to this information to the patient be an issue, regulatory options would be reconsidered at that time.

A small percentage of individuals with the propensity to allergic reactions or particular sensitivities may experience adverse effects to some NMIs. Adverse effects may range from general discomfort to those which are life threatening.

Information on NMIs has been voluntarily provided to CPS editors and appears when available in the Supplied Section of the CPS product monograph. In addition, CPS editorial staff have compiled the following tables on selected NMIs:

- Table I—Alcohol-containing Pharmaceuticals
- Table II—Alcohol-free and Low-alcohol-content Pharmaceuticals
- Table III—Gluten-containing Pharmaceuticals
- Table IV—Gluten-free Drug Manufacturers
- Table V—Sulfite-containing Pharmaceuticals
- Table VI—Tartrazine-containing Pharmaceuticals
- Table VII—Tartrazine-free Drug Manufacturers

A statement on clinical relevance regarding these ingredients has been provided. The tables are not intended to be exhaustive. CPS users should refer to the CPS product monographs or contact the manufacturer directly regarding products not listed.

The clinical relevance of lactose as an NMI is worth noting. Many medications contain lactose as a filler, diluent, bulking agent and excipient. This may cause symptoms of lactose intolerance in patients who receive multiple medications containing lactose. Lactose sensitivity or intolerance occurs in persons with a deficiency of intestinal lactase and may lead to abdominal cramps, diarrhea, distension and flatulence. Drug-induced diarrhea due to lactose intolerance has been reported as a result of the lactose in pharmaceutical formulations.

Temporary or permanent lactose intolerance may also occur in persons when there has been intestinal problems such as intestinal infection, gastric surgery or the use of medications, particularly antibiotics or some of the anti-inflammatory agents.

The enzyme lactase can be used to increase the tolerance of lactose-intolerant individuals. It is available in drops or tablet form. For more information on this product, consult individual lactase product monographs within the CPS.

For information on specific drug products, consult the Supplied Section of the individual CPS product monographs for the lactose-content information or contact the manufacturer directly.

References:

1. Napke E. Excipients, adverse drug reactions and patients' rights. Can Med Assoc J 1994; 151(5):529–533.
2. Napke E. Additional Hidden Hazards in Drug Products. Can Pharm J 1995; 128(2):23–25.

ALCOHOL-CONTAINING PHARMACEUTICALS

Table I lists selected products that contain alcohol >1% (ethanol only) and is based on information provided by the manufacturers **for preparations included in the *CPS*.** It should not be assumed that products not listed are ethanol-free. This list is not exhaustive and should serve as an initial screening tool. For information on specific drug products, consult the Supplied Section of individual *CPS* product monographs or contact the manufacturer directly.

Reviewed 1999

Awareness of the alcohol (i.e., ethanol) content of pharmaceuticals will assist the health professional in providing appropriate advice on product selection for both prescription and over-the-counter medications. Alcohol is used as a preservative, flavoring agent and solvent in drugs.

Certain medications and conditions influence the need for awareness of the ethanol content of pharmaceuticals. For example, ethanol taken with disulfiram or calcium carbimide can provoke a potentially severe reaction. Similar unpleasant reactions may occur when ethanol is taken with metronidazole, chlorpropamide and some cephalosporins. Ethanol is a CNS depressant. When taken with drugs such as sedatives, hypnotics, antihistamines and antidepressants, the CNS depression may be enhanced. Ethanol should also be avoided in diabetic patients and children.

Table I—Alcohol-containing Pharmaceuticals

Product	Manufacturer	% Ethanol
Alertonic liquid	Hoechst Marion Roussel	15.0
Alkeran injection	Glaxo Wellcome	5.2
Allernix elixir	Technilab	11.2
Alti-Benzydamine oral liquid	Altimed	10.0
Anbesol gel	Whitehall-Robins	58.0
Anbesol liquid	Whitehall-Robins	60.0
Anbesol Maximum Strength liquid	Whitehall-Robins	58.0
Apo-Gain topical solution	Apotex	63.0
Baby's Own Gripe Water	Block Drug	3.2
Bactrim Roche injection	Roche	10.0
Beben gel	Parke-Davis	16.7
Benadryl elixir	Warner-Lambert Consumer Healthcare	15.0
Benylin 4 Flu syrup	Warner-Lambert Consumer Healthcare	5.0
Benylin Codeine 3.3 mg-D-E (OTC) syrup	Warner-Lambert Consumer Healthcare	5.0
Benylin DM-D-E Extra Strength syrup	Warner-Lambert Consumer Healthcare	5.0
Benylin DM-D-E syrup	Warner-Lambert Consumer Healthcare	5.0
Benylin DM-E Extra Strength syrup	Warner-Lambert Consumer Healthcare	5.0
Benylin DM-E syrup	Warner-Lambert Consumer Healthcare	5.0
Benylin E Extra Strength syrup	Warner-Lambert Consumer Healthcare	5.0
10 Benzagel Acne gel	Dermik	15.0
Benzamycin gel	Dermik	9.0
Betadine mouthwash	Purdue Frederick	8.0
BiCNU injection (when mixed)	Bristol	10.0
Biobase lotion	Odan	70.0
Biobase-G 6% topical solution	Odan	20.0
Biobase-G 8% topical solution	Odan	20.0
Brevibloc 250 mg/mL ampul	Zeneca	25.0
Bronkaid Mistometer inhaler	Sanofi	33.0
Caladryl lotion	Warner-Lambert Consumer Healthcare	2.0
Caldomine-DH Forte liquid	Technilab	3.0
Caldomine-DH Pediatric liquid	Technilab	3.0
Calmydone syrup	Technilab	3.9
Calmylin #3 syrup	Technilab	4.8
Calmylin #4 syrup	Technilab	2.8
Calmylin Ace syrup	Technilab	3.3
Calmylin Original with Codeine syrup	Technilab	2.8
Calmylin with Codeine syrup	Technilab	4.8
Cheracol syrup	Roberts	3.0
Children's Acetaminophen oral solution	WestCan	4.8
Chlor-Tripolon Decongestant syrup	Schering	7.0
Chlor-Tripolon syrup	Schering	7.0
Choledyl elixir	Parke-Davis	20.0
Choledyl Expectorant elixir	Parke-Davis	20.0
Coristex-DH liquid	Technilab	4.3
Coristine-DH liquid	Technilab	4.3
Crixivan 200 mg capsules	MSD	3.8
Crixivan 400 mg capsules	MSD	3.9
Dalacin T topical solution	Pharmacia & Upjohn	50.0
Dalmacol	Riva	5.0
Dequadin oral paint	Roberts	3.0
Dihydroergotamine (DHE) injection	Novartis Pharmaceuticals	4.7
Dilusol topical vehicle	Dermtek	38.7
Dimetane elixir	Whitehall-Robins	3.0
Dimetane Expectorant liquid	Whitehall-Robins	3.5
Dimetane Expectorant-C liquid	Whitehall-Robins	3.5
Dimetane Expectorant-DC liquid	Whitehall-Robins	3.5
Donnagel-PG suspension	Wyeth-Ayerst	5.0
Donnatal elixir	Wyeth-Ayerst	23.0
Duoforte 27 gel	Stiefel	45.0
Duonalc solution	ICN	70.0
Duonalc-E Mild Lotion	ICN	20.0
Duonalc-E Solution	ICN	47.5
Duragesic transdermal system	Janssen-Ortho	11-13
Erysol gel	Stiefel	74.9
Etoposide injection	BDH	2.4
Factrel injection (when mixed)	Wyeth-Ayerst	2.0
Fer-in-Sol drops	Mead Johnson	1.6
Fermentol liquid	Carter Horner	17.0
Gravol I.V. ampuls	Carter Horner	17.0
Heracline oral ampul	Technilab	17.9
Infantol liquid	Carter Horner	1.9
Ionil shampoo	Galderma	12.0
Ionil-T shampoo	Galderma	12.0
Isotrex gel	Stiefel	96.9
Isuprel Mistometer inhaler	Sanofi	35.7
Kaochlor-10 liquid	Pharmacia & Upjohn	5.0
Kaochlor-20 Concentrate liquid	Pharmacia & Upjohn	5.0
Kaon liquid	Pharmacia & Upjohn	5.0
Kemadrin elixir	Glaxo Wellcome	11.5
Lanoxin Adult injection	Glaxo Wellcome	11.0
Lanoxin Pediatric elixir	Glaxo Wellcome	11.5

Table I—Alcohol-containing Pharmaceuticals *(cont'd)*

Product	Manufacturer	% Ethanol
Lanoxin Pediatric injection	Glaxo Wellcome	10.5
Largactil drops	Rhône-Poulenc Rorer	17.5
Liquor Carbonis Detergens solution	Odan	80.0
Maltlevol liquid	Carter Horner	15.0
Maltlevol-12 liquid	Carter Horner	16.0
Mellaril solution	Novartis Pharmaceuticals	2.5
Mercodol with Decapryn syrup	Hoechst Marion Roussel	4.1
Minox topical solution	Riva	51.3
M.O.S. 1 mg/mL flavored syrup	ICN	5.0
M.O.S. 5 mg/mL flavored syrup	ICN	5.0
M.O.S. 10 mg/mL flavored syrup	ICN	5.0
Multi-Tar Plus shampoo	ICN	1.5
Naftin gel	Allergan	52.0
Nemasol Sodium–ICN tablet	ICN	5.0
Nembutal Sodium injection	Abbott	10.0
Neoral 10 mg capsules	Novartis Pharmaceuticals	9.5
Neoral 25 mg capsules	Novartis Pharmaceuticals	9.5
Neoral 50 mg capsules	Novartis Pharmaceuticals	9.5
Neoral 100 mg capsules	Novartis Pharmaceuticals	9.5
Neoral oral solution	Novartis Pharmaceuticals	9.5
Neuleptil drops	Rhône-Poulenc Rorer	12.0
Nimotop I.V. injection	Bayer	20.0
Nitrolingual Pumpspray	Rhône-Poulenc Rorer	20.0
Norvir capsules	Abbott	17.7
Norvir liquid	Abbott	43.0
Novo-Benzydamine oral rinse	Novopharm	8.0
Novo-Ketotifen syrup	Novopharm	1.9
Nozinan liquid	Rhône-Poulenc Rorer	2.0
Nozinan oral drops	Rhône-Poulenc Rorer	16.5
One-Alpha solution	Leo	10.0
Orascan solution	Germiphene	3.4
Oro-Clense	Germiphene	10.0
Paclitaxel Injection	Boehringer Ingelheim	49.7
Panoxyl gel	Stiefel	20.0
Periactin syrup	Johnson & Johnson • Merck	5.0
Peridex oral rinse	Zila Pharmaceuticals	11.6
Phenergan Expectorant with Codeine syrup	Novartis Consumer Health	7.5
Phenytoin Sodium injection	Abbott	10.0
PMS-Benzydamine liquid	Pharmascience	10.0
PMS-Diphenhydramine elixir	Pharmascience	14.0
PMS-Docusate Sodium 50 mg/mL syrup	Pharmascience	5.0
Postacne lotion	Dermik	20.0
Pramegel gel	Medicis	10.0
Procyclid elixir	ICN	10.0
Proglycem suspension	Schering	5.0
Prograf injection	Fujisawa	83.0
Prostin VR injection	Pharmacia & Upjohn	99.0
Psorigel gel	Galderma	33.0
R & C II spray	R & C	4.5
Retin-A gel	Janssen-Ortho	90.0
Revitonus C-1000 ampul	Sabex	1.1
Robidone liquid	Wyeth-Ayerst	3.2
Robitussin syrup	Whitehall-Robins	3.5
Robitussin AC syrup	Whitehall-Robins	3.5
Robitussin Cough & Cold syrup	Whitehall-Robins	4.8
Robitussin DM syrup	Whitehall-Robins	1.4
Robitussin with Codeine syrup	Whitehall-Robins	3.5
Rogaine topical solution	Pharmacia & Upjohn	63.0
Roychlor liquid	Waymar	5.0
Sandimmune I.V. concentrate	Novartis Pharmaceuticals	27.8
Sans-Acne topical solution	Galderma	44.0
Scabene aerosol	Medican	95.0
Sebcur/T shampoo	Dermtek	8.0
Senokot syrup	Purdue Frederick	6.0
Septra I.V. injection	Glaxo Wellcome	13.2
Spectro Derm cleanser	Spectropharm Dermatology	4.0
Spectro Jel "609" cleanser	Spectropharm Dermatology	5.0
Spectro Tar antiseptic shampoo	Spectropharm Dermatology	6.0
Spectro Tar skin wash	Spectropharm Dermatology	6.0
Steri/Sol liquid	Warner-Lambert Consumer Healthcare	9.0
Stieva-A gel	Stiefel	96.9
Stieva-A solution	Stiefel	95.0
Stievamycin gel	Stiefel	92.0
Sun-Benz liquid	Sun	10.0
Supracaine topical aerosol	Hoechst Marion Roussel	4.4
Tagamet liquid	SmithKline Beecham	2.9
Taxol injection	Bristol-Myers Squibb	49.7
Taxotere solution	Rhône-Poulenc Rorer	13.0
Teejel gel	Purdue Frederick	39.0
Theo-Bronc solution	Rougier	10.0
Theophylline elixir	Technilab	15.3
3TC oral solution	Glaxo Wellcome	6.0
Topicort gel	Hoechst Marion Roussel	23.6
Toradol I.M. injection	Roche	10.0
Triaminic DM Daytime syrup	Novartis Consumer Health	5.5
Triaminic-DM Expectorant liquid	Novartis Consumer Health	7.1
Triaminic Expectorant liquid	Novartis Consumer Health	7.8
Triaminic Expectorant DH elixir	Novartis Consumer Health	5.0
Tridil injection	DuPont Pharma	30.0
Tylenol with Codeine elixir	Janssen-Ortho	6.0
Valium Roche injection	Roche	8.0
Vepesid injection	Bristol	24.0
Vitamin A Acid gel	Dermik	3.5
Vumon Parenteral	Bristol	36.0
Wartec topical solution	Pharmascience	70.0
X-Prep liquid	Purdue Frederick	7.0
Zaditen syrup	Novartis Pharmaceuticals	2.0
Zantac oral solution	Glaxo Wellcome	7.5
Zarontin syrup	Parke-Davis	3.0
Zilactin gel	Zila Pharmaceuticals	73.0
Zilactin-B gel	Zila Pharmaceuticals	70.0
Zilactin-L liquid	Zila Pharmaceuticals	80.0

Reference:

1. Reynolds JEF, ed. Martindale: the extra pharmacopoeia. 31st ed. London: Royal Pharmaceutical Society, 1996.

ALCOHOL-FREE or LOW-ALCOHOL-CONTENT PHARMACEUTICALS

Table II lists selected products that contain low ethanol content (≤1%) or no ethanol. It is based on information provided by the manufacturers for **oral liquid preparations included in the *CPS***. It should not be assumed that products not listed contain more than 1% ethanol. This list is not exhaustive and should serve as an initial screening tool. For information on specific drug products, consult the Supplied Section of individual *CPS* product monographs or contact the manufacturer directly.

Reviewed 1999

Table II—Alcohol-free and Low-alcohol-content (≤1%) Pharmaceuticals

Product	Manufacturer
Acetaminophen Children's syrup	Stanley
Acetaminophen drops	Trianon
Acetaminophen oral solution	Trianon
Acilac solution	Technilab
Acti-B_{12} oral solution	Technilab
Actifed syrup	Warner-Lambert Consumer Healthcare
ADEK's Pediatric drops	Axcan Pharma
Alimentum liquid	Abbott
Alti-Orciprenaline syrup	AltiMed
Alti-Valproic syrup	Altimed
Alupent syrup	Boehringer Ingelheim
Amicar syrup	Wyeth-Ayerst
Amoxil suspension	Wyeth-Ayerst
Amphojel suspension	Axcan Pharma
Apo-Amoxi suspension	Apotex
Apo-Ampi suspension	Apotex
Apo-Cloxi oral suspension	Apotex
Apo-Fluoxetine syrup	Apotex
Apo-Haloperidol oral solution	Apotex
Apo-Ketotifen syrup	Apotex
Apo-Oxybutynin syrup	Apotex
Apo-Pen VK oral suspension	Apotex
Apo-Sulfatrim suspension	Apotex
Aquasol E drops	Novartis Consumer Health
Aquasol E TPGS liquid	Novartis Consumer Health
Aristospan suspension	Stiefel
Atarax syrup	Pfizer
Atasol drops	Carter Horner
Atasol oral solution	Carter Horner
Baby's Own Infant Drops	Block Drug
Bactrim Roche suspension	Roche
Balminil Decongestant syrup	Rougier
Balminil DM syrup	Rougier
Balminil DM Children liquid	Rougier
Balminil DM + Decongestant syrup	Rougier
Balminil DM + Decongestant + Expectorant syrup	Rougier
Balminil DM + Expectorant syrup	Rougier
Balminil DM Sucrose-Free solution	Rougier
Balminil Expectorant syrup	Rougier
Balminil Expectorant Sucrose-Free syrup	Rougier
Benadryl Children's liquid	Warner-Lambert Consumer Healthcare
Bentylol syrup	Hoechst Marion Roussel
Benylin DM syrup	Warner-Lambert Consumer Healthcare
Benylin DM 12 Hour syrup	Warner-Lambert Consumer Healthcare
Benylin DM for Children syrup	Warner-Lambert Consumer Healthcare
Benylin DM for Children 12 Hour syrup	Warner-Lambert Consumer Healthcare
Benylin DM-D (Adult) syrup	Warner-Lambert Consumer Healthcare
Benylin DM-D syrup, Children's	Warner-Lambert Consumer Healthcare
Biaxin pediatric granules for suspension	Abbott
Broncho-Grippol-DM liquid	Technilab
Calcium-Sandoz syrup	Novartis Consumer Health
Calcium Stanley liquid	Stanley
Calmylin #1 syrup	Technilab
Calmylin #2 syrup	Technilab
Calmylin Cough and Flu syrup	Technilab
Calmylin Expectorant syrup	Technilab
Calmylin Pediatric syrup	Technilab
Carnitor oral solution	Sigma-Tau Pharmaceuticals
Ceclor suspension	Lilly
Cefzil powder for oral solution	Bristol-Myers Squibb
Charcodote solution	Pharmascience
Charcodote Aqueous solution	Pharmascience
Charcodote TFS solution	Pharmascience
Children's Acetaminophen elixir drops	WestCan
Chlorpromanyl liquid	Technilab
Choledyl Pediatric syrup	Parke-Davis
Citro-Mag solution	Rougier
Citrotein liquid	Novartis Nutrition
Claritin syrup	Schering
Clavulin suspension	SmithKline Beecham
CoActifed syrup	Glaxo Wellcome
CoActifed Expectorant syrup	Glaxo Wellcome
Codeine Phosphate syrup	Rougier
Colace drops	Roberts
Colace syrup	Roberts
Combantrin suspension	Pfizer
Compleat Modified liquid	Novartis Nutrition
Cophylac solution	Hoechst Marion Roussel
Cophylac Expectorant solution	Hoechst Marion Roussel
Coptin oral suspension	Axcan Pharma
Cotridin liquid	Technilab
Cotridin Expectorant liquid	Technilab
Delsym suspension	Novartis Consumer Health
Depakene syrup	Abbott
Deproic syrup	Technilab
Dilantin suspension	Parke-Davis
Dilaudid liquid	Knoll
Dimetapp liquid	Whitehall-Robins
Dimetapp Clear liquid	Whitehall-Robins
Dimetapp Oral Infant Drops	Whitehall-Robins
Dimetapp-C syrup	Whitehall-Robins
Dimetapp-DM liquid	Whitehall-Robins
Diovol suspension	Carter Horner
Diovol Ex suspension	Carter Horner
Diovol Plus suspension	Carter Horner
Diovol Plus AF suspension	Carter Horner
Docusate Sodium drops	Technilab
Docusate Sodium syrup	Taro
Docusate Sodium syrup	Technilab
Drisdol solution	Sanofi
EES granules for suspension	Abbott
Elavil suspension	MSD
Entacyl suspension	Roberts
Erythrocin suspension	Abbott
Fer-In-Sol syrup	Mead Johnson
Ferodan Infant Drops	Odan
Ferodan Syrup	Odan
Fluor-A-Day drops	Pharmascience

Table II—Alcohol-free and Low-alcohol-content (≤1%) Pharmaceuticals *(cont'd)*

Product	Manufacturer	Product	Manufacturer
Fucidin suspension	Leo	Novo-Ampicillin suspension	Novopharm
Gaviscon HRF suspension	SmithKline Beecham Consumer	Novo-Lexin suspension	Novopharm
		Novo-Pen-VK suspension	Novopharm
Gelusil liquid	Warner-Lambert Consumer Healthcare	Novo-Tetra suspension	Novopharm
		Novo-Trimel suspension	Novopharm
Gelusil Extra Strength liquid	Warner-Lambert Consumer Healthcare	Nu-Amoxi suspension	Nu-Pharm
		Nu-Ampi suspension	Nu-Pharm
Glucodex liquid	Rougier	Nu-Cloxi liquid	Nu-Pharm
Gravol liquid	Carter Horner	Nu-Cotrimox suspension	Nu-Pharm
Hormodausse oral liquid	Technilab	Nutrisource liquid	Novartis Nutrition
Hycodan syrup	DuPont Pharma	Nutrisource HN liquid	Novartis Nutrition
Hycomine syrup	DuPont Pharma	Nyaderm suspension	Taro
Hycomine-S Pediatric syrup	DuPont Pharma	Oligosol, Copper	Labcatal
Ilosone liquid	Lilly	Oligosol, Copper-Gold-Silver	Labcatal
Infantol drops	Carter Horner	Oligosol, Magnesium	Labcatal
Isomil liquid	Abbott	Oligosol, Manganese	Labcatal
Isosource liquid	Novartis Nutrition	Oligosol, Manganese-Cobalt	Labcatal
Isosource HN liquid	Novartis Nutrition	Oligosol, Manganese-Copper	Labcatal
Isosource VHN liquid	Novartis Nutrition	Oligosol, Zinc-Nickel-Cobalt	Labcatal
Kaopectate Children's suspension	Johnson & Johnson • Merck	Omni-Tuss liquid	Rhône-Poulenc Rorer
		Orcipren syrup	Technilab
Kaopectate Extra Strength suspension	Johnson & Johnson • Merck	Ovol drops	Carter Horner
		Palafer suspension	SmithKline Beecham
Kaopectate Regular Strength suspension	Johnson & Johnson • Merck	Panectyl liquid	Rhône-Poulenc Rorer
		Pedialyte liquid	Abbott
Keflex suspension	Lilly	Pedialyte Freezer Pops	Abbott
Koffex DM syrup	Rougier	Pediasure liquid	Abbott
Koffex DM Sucrose-Free solution	Rougier	Pediatrix drops	Technilab
K-10 solution	SmithKline Beecham	Pediatrix oral solution	Technilab
Lactaid drops	McNeil Consumer Products	Pediazole granules for suspension	Abbott
		Pedi-Dent drops	Stanley
Largactil liquid	Rhône-Poulenc Rorer	Peglyte solution	Pharmascience
Lasix solution	Hoechst Marion Roussel	Peridol oral solution	Technilab
Lidodan Viscous liquid	Odan	Phosphates Solution	Pharmascience
Loxapac Oral Concentrate solution	Wyeth-Ayerst	PMS-Chloral Hydrate syrup	Pharmascience
Maalox suspension	Novartis Consumer Health	PMS-Dicitrate solution	Pharmascience
Maalox HRF suspension	Novartis Consumer Health	PMS-Docusate Sodium 10 mg/mL drops	Pharmascience
Maalox Plus suspension	Novartis Consumer Health	PMS-Hydromorphone syrup	Pharmascience
Maalox Plus Extra Strength suspension	Novartis Consumer Health	PMS-Hydroxyzine syrup	Pharmascience
Maalox TC suspension	Novartis Consumer Health	PMS-Isoniazid syrup	Pharmascience
Magnesium-Rougier solution	Rougier	PMS-Lactulose syrup	Pharmascience
Maxeran liquid	Hoechst Marion Roussel	PMS-Lithium Citrate syrup	Pharmascience
Mellaril suspension	Novartis Pharmaceuticals	PMS-Metoclopramide solution	Pharmascience
Meritene powder for oral liquid	Novartis Nutrition	PMS-Nystatin suspension	Pharmascience
Morphitec syrup	Technilab	PMS-Sodium Polystyrene Sulfonate oral suspension	Pharmascience
M.O.S. 1 mg/mL unflavored syrup	ICN		
M.O.S. 5 mg/mL unflavored syrup	ICN	Poliovirus Vaccine Live Oral Trivalent	Connaught
M.O.S. Concentrate 20 mg/mL syrup	ICN	Polycitra-K crystals for oral solution	Alza
M.O.S. Concentrate 50 mg/mL syrup	ICN	Polycitra-K oral solution	Alza
Motrin (Children's) suspension	McNeil Consumer Products	Pondocillin suspension	Leo
		Prepulsid suspension	Janssen-Ortho
Mucaine suspension	Axcan Pharma	Prozac liquid	Lilly
Mycifradin oral solution	Pharmacia & Upjohn	Rafton liquid	Ferring
Mycostatin oral suspension	Squibb	Reglan syrup	Wyeth-Ayerst
Mylanta Double Strength Plain suspension	Warner-Lambert Consumer Healthcare	Resource liquid	Novartis Nutrition
		Resource Diabetic liquid	Novartis Nutrition
Mylanta Extra Strength suspension	Warner-Lambert Consumer Healthcare	Resource Fruit Beverage liquid	Novartis Nutrition
		Resource Just For Kids liquid	Novartis Nutrition
Mylanta Regular Strength liquid	Warner-Lambert Consumer Healthcare	Resource Plus liquid	Novartis Nutrition
		Retrovir (AZT) syrup	Glaxo Wellcome
Nadopen-V oral solutions	Nadeau	Revitalose-C-1000 drinkable vials	Rivex Pharma
Nadostine oral suspension	Nadeau	Riopan suspension	Whitehall-Robins
Nadostine oral suspension (sucrose-free)	Nadeau	Risperdal Oral Solution	Janssen-Ortho
Naprosyn suspension	Roche	Robitussin Extra Strength syrup	Whitehall-Robins
Nilstat oral drops	Technilab	Robitussin Extra Strength Cough & Cold syrup	Whitehall-Robins
Novahistex C liquid	Hoechst Marion Roussel		
Novahistex DH liquid	Hoechst Marion Roussel	Robitussin Extra Strength DM syrup	Whitehall-Robins
Novahistex DH Expectorant liquid	Hoechst Marion Roussel	Robitussin Pediatric syrup	Whitehall-Robins
Novahistine DH liquid	Hoechst Marion Roussel	Robitussin Pediatric Cough & Cold syrup	Whitehall-Robins
Novamoxin suspension	Novopharm	Rocaltrol oral solution	Roche
NovaSource Renal liquid	Novartis Nutrition	Royvac solution	Waymar

Table II—Alcohol-free and Low-alcohol-content (≤1%) Pharmaceuticals *(cont'd)*

Product	Manufacturer
Sandosource Peptide liquid	Novartis Nutrition
Selax syrup	Odan
Seldane suspension	Hoechst Marion Roussel
Septra Pediatric suspension	Glaxo Wellcome
Similac LF liquid	Abbott
Sporanox Oral Solution	Janssen-Ortho
Statex drops	Pharmascience
Statex syrup	Pharmascience
Stemetil liquid	Rhône-Poulenc Rorer
Sulcrate Plus suspension	Hoechst Marion Roussel
Suprax suspension	Rhône-Poulenc Rorer
Symmetrel syrup	DuPont Pharma
Tanta Orciprenaline syrup	Tanta
Tegretol suspension	Novartis Pharmaceuticals
Telebrix 38 Oral solution	Mallinckrodt
Tempra drops	Mead Johnson
Tempra syrup	Mead Johnson
Tolerex powder for oral liquid	Novartis Nutrition
Triaminic Cold and Allergy syrup	Novartis Consumer Health
Triaminic Cold & Fever syrup	Novartis Consumer Health
Triaminic DM Long Lasting for Children suspension	Novartis Consumer Health
Triaminic DM Nighttime syrup	Novartis Consumer Health
Triaminic Oral Pediatric Drops	Novartis Consumer Health
Triaminicol DM syrup	Novartis Consumer Health
Trisulfaminic suspension	Shepherd
Tussaminic C Forte liquid	Novartis Consumer Health
Tussaminic C Ped liquid	Novartis Consumer Health
Tussaminic DH Forte liquid	Novartis Consumer Health
Tussaminic DH Ped liquid	Novartis Consumer Health
Tussionex suspension	Rhône-Poulenc Rorer
Tylenol drops	McNeil Consumer Products
Tylenol elixir	McNeil Consumer Products
Tylenol suspension	McNeil Consumer Products
Tylenol Cold Medication Children's suspension	McNeil Consumer Products
Tylenol Cough Medication suspension	McNeil Consumer Products
Univol suspension	Carter Horner
Vanquin suspension	Warner-Lambert Consumer Healthcare
Ventolin oral liquid	Glaxo Wellcome
Vivonex Pediatric powder for oral liquid	Novartis Nutrition
Vivonex Plus powder for oral liquid	Novartis Nutrition
Vivonex T.E.N. powder	Novartis Nutrition
Zofran oral solution	Glaxo Wellcome
Zovirax suspension	Glaxo Wellcome

GLUTEN-CONTAINING PHARMACEUTICALS

Gluten is a complex protein present in wheat and to a lesser extent in rye, barley and oats. A fraction of the gluten in these cereals, called prolamines, causes damage to the small intestine in sensitive individuals with celiac disease. The prolamines of corn and rice are not toxic. In the Supplied Section of the *CPS* product monographs, the statement "contains gluten" refers to the gluten derived from wheat, barley, oats and rye for only the nonmedicinal ingredients. This does not refer to gluten inherent in the active ingredient (e.g., psyllium).

Table III lists selected products that contain gluten and is based on information provided by the manufacturers for **preparations included in the *CPS***. In some cases, raw materials used in the manufacturing process are obtained from sources other than the pharmaceutical industry and may contain traces of gluten. It should not be assumed that products not listed are gluten-free. This list is not exhaustive and should serve as an initial screening tool. For information on specific drug products, consult the Supplied Section of individual CPS product monographs or contact the manufacturer directly.

Reviewed 1999

Table III—Gluten-containing Pharmaceuticals

Product	Manufacturer
A.C.&C. tablets	WestCan
A.S.A. Enteric Coated tablets	WestCan
A.S.A. tablets	WestCan
Contac Cough, Cold and Flu Day & Night caplets	SmithKline Beecham Consumer
Coptin tablets	Axcan Pharma
Dimetapp Extentabs	Whitehall-Robins
Diovol EX tablets	Carter Horner
Dyazide tablets	SmithKline Beecham
Dyrenium tablets	SmithKline Beecham
Gravol L/A capsules	Carter Horner
Honvol tablets	Carter Horner
Lactaid tablets	McNeil Consumer Products
Leukeran tablets	Glaxo Wellcome
Modulon tablets	Axcan Pharma
Nadostine tablets	Nadeau
Nadostine vaginal tablets	Nadeau
Parnate tablets	SmithKline Beecham
Trasicor 40 mg tablets	Novartis Pharmaceuticals
Ursofalk capsules	Axcan Pharma

Reference:
1. Reynolds JEF, ed. Martindale: the extra pharmacopoeia. 31st ed. London: Royal Pharmaceutical Society, 1996.

GLUTEN-FREE DRUG MANUFACTURERS

Table IV lists selected manufacturers that do not use gluten and is based on information provided by the manufacturers. Only manufacturers with **preparations in the *CPS*** have been included. In some cases, raw materials used in the manufacturing process are obtained from sources other than the pharmaceutical industry and may contain traces of gluten. It should not be assumed that manufacturers not listed use gluten. This list is not exhaustive and should serve as an initial screening tool. For information on specific drug products, consult the Supplied Section of individual *CPS* product monographs or contact the manufacturer directly.

Reviewed 1999

Table IV—Gluten-free Drug Manufacturers

Manufacturers
Abbott Laboratories Limited
Albert Pharma Inc.
Alcon Canada Inc.
Allerex Laboratory Ltd.
Allergan Inc.
AltiMed Pharmaceutical Company
Alza Canada
Amgen Canada Inc.
Apotex Inc.
Ashbury Biologicals, Inc.
Astra Pharma Inc.
Baxter Corporation
BDH Inc.
Berlex Canada Inc.
Berna Products, Corp.
BioChem Vaccines
Biomatrix Medical Canada Inc.
Block Drug Company (Canada) Ltd.
Boehringer Ingelheim (Canada) Ltd.
Bristol
Bristol-Myers Squibb Canada Inc.
Cangene Corporation
Chattem (Canada) Inc.
CIBA Vision Canada Inc.
Clintec Nutrition Company
Connaught Laboratories Limited
Crystaal Corporation
Dermik Laboratories Canada Inc.
Dermtek Pharmaceuticals Ltd.
Dioptic Laboratories
Dormer Laboratories Inc.
Draxis Health Inc.

Table IV—Gluten-free Drug Manufacturers *(cont'd)*

Manufacturers	Manufacturers
Duchesnay Inc.	Pfizer Canada Inc., Consumer Health Care Division
DuPont Pharma	Pharmacia & Upjohn Inc.
Endo Canada Inc.	Pharmascience Inc.
Fabrigen, Inc.	Procter & Gamble Inc.
Faulding (Canada) Inc.	Procter & Gamble Pharmaceuticals Canada, Inc.
Ferring Inc.	Purdue Frederick Inc.
Fournier Pharma Inc.	Reed & Carnrick
Frosst	Rhodiapharm Inc.
Fujisawa Canada Inc.	Rhône-Poulenc Rorer Canada Inc.
Galderma Canada Inc.	RHO-Pharm Inc.
Genpharm Inc.	Rhoxal Pharma Inc.
Glenwood Laboratories Canada Ltd.	Rivex Ophthalmics
Hoechst Marion Roussel Canada Inc.	Rivex Pharma Inc.
Hoffmann-La Roche Limited	Roberts Pharmaceutical Canada Inc.
ICN Canada Ltd.	Sanofi Canada Inc.
Janssen-Ortho Inc.	Schering Canada Inc.
Johnson & Johnson • Merck Consumer Pharmaceuticals	Serono Canada Inc.
Key	Servier Canada Inc.
Knoll Pharma Inc.	Shepherd Pharmaceuticals Inc.
Labcatal Inc.	Sigma-Tau Pharmaceuticals, Inc.
Laboratoire Riva Inc.	Smith & Nephew Inc.
Leo Laboratories Canada Ltd.	Solvay Pharma Inc.
Ligand Pharmaceuticals (Canada) Inc.	Spectropharm Dermatology
Lundbeck Canada Inc.	Squibb Canada
Mallinckrodt Medical Inc.	Stanley Pharmaceuticals Ltd.
May & Baker Pharma	Stiefel Canada Inc.
Medicis Canada Ltd.	Sun Pharmaceutical Industries Inc.
Merck Sharp & Dohme Canada	Swiss Herbal Remedies Ltd.
NeXstar Pharmaceuticals, Inc.	Tanta Pharmaceuticals Inc.
Novartis Consumer Health Canada Inc.	Taro Pharmaceuticals Inc.
Novartis Nutrition Corporation	Technilab Inc.
Novo Nordisk Canada Inc.	Trans CanaDerm Inc.
Novopharm Limited	Trianon Laboratories Inc.
Nu-Pharm Inc.	UCB Pharma Inc.
Nycomed Amersham Canada Limited	Waymar Pharmaceuticals Inc.
Odan Laboratories Ltd.	Westwood-Squibb
Ophtapharma Canada Inc.	Wyeth-Ayerst Canada Inc.
Organon Canada Ltd.	Zeneca Pharma Inc.
Organon Teknika Inc.	Zila Pharmaceuticals Inc.
Pfizer Canada Inc.	

SULFITE-CONTAINING PHARMACEUTICALS

Table V lists selected products which contain sulfites and is based on information supplied by the manufacturers for **preparations included in the *CPS*.** In some cases, raw materials used in the manufacturing process are obtained from sources other than the pharmaceutical industry and may contain traces of sulfite. Although reactions to these trace amounts are unlikely to be of clinical significance, it is recommended that first-dose monitoring be used as a precaution when any drug is administered to individuals sensitive to sulfites. It should not be assumed that products not listed are sulfite-free. The list is not exhaustive and should serve as an initial screening tool. For information on specific drug products consult the Supplied Section of the CPS product monographs or contact the manufacturer directly.

Reviewed 1999

The term sulfites includes sodium or potassium bisulfite, sodium or potassium metabisulfite, sodium sulfite and sulfur dioxide. Sulfiting agents are used as antioxidants in the preservation of foods and drugs.

Hypersensitivity reactions such as urticaria, nausea, diarrhea, wheezing and dyspnea have been reported most frequently after ingestion of restaurant foods treated with sulfites, but they also occur after exposure to drug products containing sulfites. The concentration of sulfites in pharmaceuticals is usually low but adverse reactions to sulfites are not always dose related. Adverse reactions to sulfites, particularly in asthmatics, may be life threatening. In asthmatics, sensitivity is more common to inhaled rather than ingested sulfites.

Many patients may have sulfite sensitivity rather than "food" or "drug allergy". Patients known to be sensitive to sulfites should carefully read the label of purchased food to verify if there are any sulfites in the product. Health professionals must be alert to the possible presence of sulfites contained in drug formulations.

Table V—Sulfite-containing Pharmaceuticals

Product	Manufacturer
Adrenalin aqueous solution	Parke-Davis
Aldomet injection	MSD
Alupent inhalation solution	Boehringer Ingelheim
Amikin injection	Bristol
Ana-Kit	Bayer
Anthranol cream	Medican Pharma
Anthrascalp lotion	Medican Pharma
Astracaine injection	Astra
Astracaine Forte injection	Astra
Atropine ophthalmic solution	Dioptic
Bactrim Roche injection	Roche
Betagan ophthalmic solution	Allergan
Cafergot-PB tablets	Novartis Pharmaceuticals
Chlorpromanyl-20 liquid	Technilab
Chlorpromanyl-40 liquid	Technilab
Citanest 4% Forte dental cartridges	Astra
Codeine Phosphate injection	Abbott
Codeine Phosphate syrup	Rougier
Codeine Phosphate tablets	Rougier
Cortisporin otic solution	Glaxo Wellcome
Decadron Phosphate injection	MSD
Dexamethasone Sodium Phosphate ophthalmic solution	Rivex Ophthalmics
Diophenyl-T ophthalmic solution	Dioptic
Diopred ophthalmic suspension	Dioptic
Dobutamine Hydrochloride injection	Abbott
Dobutrex injection	Lilly
Dopamine HCl and Dextrose injection	Abbott
Dopamine HCl and 5% Dextrose injection	Baxter
Enlon injection	Zeneca
Epinephrine injection	Abbott
Epipen injection	Allerex
Epipen Jr. injection	Allerex
Fer-in-Sol drops	Mead Johnson
Fer-in-Sol syrup	Mead Johnson
Ferodan solution	Odan
Flaxedil injection	Rhône-Poulenc Rorer
Fucidin suspension	Leo
Garamycin parenteral	Schering
Gentamicin Sulfate injection	Novopharm
Heparin Sodium in 5% Dextrose injection	Abbott
Innohep 20 000 anti-Xa IU/mL syringe	Leo
Innohep vials	Leo
Inocor injection	Sanofi
Intropin injection	DuPont Pharma
Isuprel inhalation solution	Sanofi
Isuprel injection	Sanofi
Largactil injection	Rhône-Poulenc Rorer
Leritine injection	Frosst
Leritine tablets	Frosst
Levobunolol Hydrochloride ophthalmic solution	Rivex Ophthalmics
Levophed injection	Sanofi
Lidocaine and Epinephrine injection	Abbott
Marcaine 0.25% with Epinephrine solution	Sanofi
Marcaine 0.5% with Epinephrine solution	Sanofi
Morphine Sulfate 1 and 2 mg/mL Rapiject injection	Faulding
Morphine Sulfate injection	Abbott
Mydfrin ophthalmic solution	Alcon
Nadostine oral suspension	Nadeau
Nadostine oral suspension (sucrose-free)	Nadeau
Nebcin injection	Lilly
Nebcin pharmacy bulk vials	Lilly
Neo-Synephrine parenteral	Sanofi
Nesacaine injection	Astra
Netromycin injection	Schering
Nizoral cream	Janssen-Ortho
Novocain injection	Sanofi
Nozinan injection	Rhône-Poulenc Rorer
Numorphan injection	DuPont Pharma
Nupercainal cream and ointment	Novartis Consumer Health
Ophtho-Bunolol ophthalmic solution	AltiMed
Ophtho-Tate ophthalmic suspension	AltiMed
Phenergan injection	Rhône-Poulenc Rorer
Polocaine 2% and Levonordefrin 1:20 000 dental cartridges	Astra
Postacne lotion	Dermik
Pred Forte 1% ophthalmic suspension	Allergan
Pred Mild 0.12% ophthalmic suspension	Allergan
Promazine Hydrochloride injection	Abbott
Pronestyl injection	Squibb
Quintasa enema	Ferring
Reversa HQ gel	Dermtek

Table V—Sulfite-containing Pharmaceuticals *(cont'd)*

Product	Manufacturer	Product	Manufacturer
Salofalk rectal suspension	Axcan Pharma	Travasol preparations (excluding Quick Mix products)	Clintec
Selexid tablets	Leo	Trilafon injection	Schering
Sensorcaine with Epinephrine (1:200 000) solution	Astra	Ultracaine DS dental cartridges	Hoechst Marion Roussel
Septra injection	Glaxo Wellcome	Ultracaine DS Forte dental cartridges	Hoechst Marion Roussel
Sodium Thiosulfate Injection USP	Faulding	Vaponefrin inhalation solution	Rhône-Poulenc Rorer
Stemetil injection	Rhône-Poulenc Rorer	Vasoxyl injection	Glaxo Wellcome
Streptomycin Sulfate injection	Pfizer	Xylocaine Dental Solutions	Astra
Sulfacet-R lotion	Dermik	Xylocaine Parenteral solutions with Epinephrine	Astra
Talwin tablets	Sanofi	Yutopar injection	Bristol
Tensilon injection	ICN		
Tersac gel	TCD		

References:
1. Yamamoto A, Wright D, Campbell J. We have a little list. Can Pharm J 1988; 121(10):642-7.
2. Parker WA, MacLachlan RA. Hypersensitivity to sodium bisulfite in Normosol-M with Dextrose. Can J Hosp Pharm 1987; 40(4):139-40, 152.
3. Miyata M, Schuster B, Schellenberg R. Sulfite-containing Canadian pharmaceutical products available in 1991. Can Med Assoc J 1992; 147(9):1333-1338.

TARTRAZINE-CONTAINING PHARMACEUTICALS

Tartrazine (FD&C Yellow No. 5) is a dye used to produce a yellow color (or, in combination with other dyes, red or green) in food, beverages and drugs. It is a member of the azo dye compounds which are most commonly implicated in dye-induced toxicity. The most common reactions to tartrazine are asthma or urticaria. Although the overall sensitivity to tartrazine is low, it is seen frequently in people with ASA hypersensitivity.

Table VI lists selected products that contain tartrazine and is based on information provided by the manufacturers for **preparations included in the *CPS*.** In some cases, raw materials used in the manufacturing process are obtained from sources other than the pharmaceutical industry and may contain traces of tartrazine. It should not be assumed that products not listed are tartrazine-free. This list is not exhaustive and should serve as an initial screening tool. For information on specific drug products, consult the Supplied Section of individual *CPS* product monographs or contact the manufacturer directly.

Reviewed 1999

Table VI—Tartrazine-containing Pharmaceuticals

Product	Manufacturer
Alti-Valproic 500 mg capsules	Altimed
Apresoline 10 mg tablets	Novartis Pharmaceuticals
Bellergal Spacetabs	Novartis Pharmaceuticals
Butisol Sodium 30 mg tablets	Carter Horner
Cafergot-PB tablets	Novartis Pharmaceuticals
Chlorpromanyl-20 liquid	Technilab
Chlorpromanyl-40 liquid	Technilab
Choloxin 2 mg tablets	Knoll
Citrotein powder	Novartis Nutrition
Depakene capsules	Abbott
Dexedrine Spansule capsules	SmithKline Beecham
Dexedrine tablets	SmithKline Beecham
Dulcolax tablets	Boehringer Ingelheim
Estrace 2 mg tablets	Roberts
Glysennid 12 mg tablets	Novartis Consumer Health
Halotestin tablets	Pharmacia & Upjohn
Kaochlor-10 liquid	Pharmacia & Upjohn
Lanohex Skin Cleanser	Rougier
Levotec 100 µg tablets	Technilab
Meritene powder	Novartis Nutrition
Morphitec syrup	Technilab
Mycostatin oral tablets	Squibb
Nadostine vaginal tablets	Nadeau
Nembutal Sodium capsules	Abbott
NeoCitran A (Allergies & Colds) pouch	Novartis Consumer Health
NeoCitran DM (Coughs & Colds) pouch	Novartis Consumer Health
One A Day Advance Fem tablets	Bayer Consumer
Orap 4 mg tablets	Janssen-Ortho
Oro-Clense liquid	Germiphene
Oxycodan tablets	Technilab
Penta-Thion granules	Sabex
Resource Fruit Beverage	Novartis Nutrition
Revitonus C-1000 ampuls	Sabex
Roychlor liquid	Waymar
Sandomigran tablets	Novartis Pharmaceuticals
Sanorex 2 mg tablets	Novartis Pharmaceuticals
Sansert tablets	Novartis Pharmaceuticals
Tes-Tape	Lilly
Vitathion-A.T.P. sachets	Servier

References:
1. Golightly LK, Smolinske SS, Bennett ML, et al. Pharmaceutical excipients: adverse effects associated with inactive ingredients in drug products (part I). Med Tox 1988; 3:128–165.
2. Smith JM, Dodd TRP. Adverse reactions to pharmaceutical excipients. Adv Drug Reac Ac Pois Rev 1982; 1:93–142.

TARTRAZINE-FREE DRUG MANUFACTURERS

Table VII lists selected manufacturers that do not use tartrazine and is based on information provided by the manufacturers. Only manufacturers with **preparations in the *CPS*** have been included. In some cases, raw materials used in the manufacturing process are obtained from sources other than the pharmaceutical industry and may contain traces of tartrazine. It should not be assumed that manufacturers not listed use tartrazine. This list is not exhaustive and should serve as an initial screening tool. For information on specific drug products, consult the Supplied Section of individual *CPS* product monographs or contact the manufacturer directly.

Reviewed 1999

Table VII—Tartrazine-free Drug Manufacturers

Manufacturers
Albert Pharma Inc.
Alcon Canada Inc.
Allerex Laboratory Ltd.
Allergan Inc.
Alza Canada
Amgen Canada Inc.
Apotex Inc.
Ashbury Biologicals, Inc.
Astra Pharma Inc.
Axcan Pharma Inc.
Baxter Corporation
BDH Inc.
Bencard Allergy Laboratories
Berlex Canada Inc.

Table VII—Tartrazine-free Drug Manufacturers *(cont'd)*

Manufacturers	Manufacturers
Berna Products, Corp.	Merck Sharp & Dohme Canada
BioChem Vaccines	NeXstar Pharmaceuticals, Inc.
Biomatrix Medical Canada Inc.	Novo Nordisk Canada Inc.
Block Drug Company (Canada) Ltd.	Novopharm Limited
Cangene Corporation	Nu-Pharm Inc.
Chattem (Canada) Inc.	Nycomed Amersham Canada Limited
CIBA Vision Canada Inc.	Odan Laboratories Ltd.
Clintec Nutrition Company	Ophtapharma Canada Inc.
Connaught Laboratories Limited	Organon Canada Ltd.
Crystaal Corporation	Organon Teknika Inc.
Dermik Laboratories Canada Inc.	Pfizer Canada Inc.
Dermtek Pharmaceuticals Ltd.	Pfizer Canada Inc., Consumer Health Care Division
Dioptic Laboratories	Procter & Gamble Inc.
Dispensapharm	Procter & Gamble Pharmaceuticals Canada, Inc.
Dormer Laboratories Inc.	Purdue Frederick Inc.
Draxis Health Inc.	Rhodiapharm Inc.
Duchesnay Inc.	Rhône-Poulenc Rorer Canada Inc.
DuPont Pharma	RHO-Pharm Inc.
Endo Canada Inc.	Rhoxal Pharma Inc.
Fabrigen, Inc.	Rivex Ophthalmics
Faulding (Canada) Inc.	Rivex Pharma Inc.
Ferring Inc.	Sanofi Canada Inc.
Fournier Pharma Inc.	Schering Canada Inc.
Frosst	Serono Canada Inc.
Fujisawa Canada Inc.	Shepherd Pharmaceuticals Inc.
Galderma Canada Inc.	Sigma-Tau Pharmaceuticals, Inc.
Genpharm Inc.	Smith & Nephew Inc.
Glaxo Wellcome Inc.	Solvay Pharma Inc.
Glenwood Laboratories Canada Ltd.	Stiefel Canada Inc.
Hoffmann-La Roche Limited	Sun Pharmaceutical Industries Inc.
ICN Canada Ltd.	Swiss Herbal Remedies Ltd.
Johnson & Johnson • Merck Consumer Pharmaceuticals	Tanta Pharmaceuticals Inc.
Key	Taro Pharmaceuticals Inc.
Labcatal Inc.	Trans CanaDerm Inc.
Laboratoire Riva Inc.	Trianon Laboratories Inc.
Leo Laboratories Canada Ltd.	UCB Pharma Inc.
Ligand Pharmaceuticals (Canada) Inc.	Westwood-Squibb
Lundbeck Canada Inc.	Whitehall-Robins Inc.
Mallinckrodt Medical Inc.	Wyeth-Ayerst Canada Inc.
May & Baker Pharma	Zeneca Pharma Inc.
McNeil Consumer Products Company	Zila Pharmaceuticals Inc.
Medicis Canada Ltd.	

DRUG INTERACTIONS

Table I provides an overview of some of the most clinically important drug-drug interactions. This information is not intended to present a comprehensive review; the reader is therefore encouraged to seek additional and confirmatory information.

Reviewed 1999

The purpose of the Drug-Drug Interactions Table (Table I) is to identify some of the most clinically important drug interactions and to outline the proposed mechanism and management options. Table I is updated annually using the manufacturer's product monograph and the references listed below.

The interactions were selected on the basis of the potential severity of their effects, estimated frequency of occurrence and the availability of adequate documentation. Drug interactions involving alcohol, food, smoking or drugs used primarily during surgery have not been included.

Some drugs are listed by drug group or class. Only the specific drugs implicated in the interaction have been listed under the drug group or class name. Use of other members of the class may be discussed in the comments column under Mechanism or Management.

Since few drug interactions are absolute contraindications, this should not be construed as a list of drugs that should never be used together. When no other alternatives are available, drugs with the potential to interact can sometimes be used concurrently with appropriate precautions (see Management). Problems are most likely to occur when there is a lack of awareness that an interaction is possible and when the appropriate precautions or countermeasures are not taken.

If a specific drug is not listed in the index, it may not have been included in this table or no information may be known about the interaction. To evaluate the potential for other interactions, you may consult comprehensive drug interaction references such as those listed below. The product monograph, usually in the Precautions section under Drug Interactions, may also be considered for more information.

Selected References:

1. Hansten PD, Horn JR, Koda-Kimble MA, Young LY, eds. Hansten and Horn's Drug Interactions Analysis and Management. Vancouver, WA: Applied Therapeutics, Inc., 1998.
2. Tatro DS, ed. Drug Interaction Facts. St. Louis, MO: Facts and Comparisons, 1998.
3. Zucchero FJ, Hogan MJ, Schultz CD, eds. Evaluations of Drug Interactions. St. Louis, MO: First Data Bank, 1997.

Table I—Drug-Drug Interactions

Drug	Interacting Drug	Mechanism	Management
Acebutolol, see antidiabetic agents, calcium channel blockers			
Acetylsalicylic acid (ASA), see anticoagulants (oral), methotrexate			
Acitretin, see contraceptives (oral)			
Allopurinol, see anticoagulants (oral), antimetabolites, theophyllines			
Amikacin, see aminoglycosides			
Amiloride, see potassium-sparing diuretics			
Aminoglutethimide, see anticoagulants (oral), corticosteroids, theophyllines			
Aminoglycosides amikacin gentamicin netilmicin streptomycin tobramycin	**Loop diuretics** ethacrynic acid	• Potent diuretics have been associated with 8th cranial nerve dysfunction. • Ototoxicity may be enhanced either by increasing the antibiotic concentration in serum and tissues or by a direct action on the auditory apparatus. • Impairment of 8th nerve function is most likely in patients with pre-existing renal damage especially if the drug is administered i.v.	• Concomitant use of ethacrynic acid with aminoglycosides should be avoided. • Patients on concurrent furosemide should be monitored, although evidence for enhanced toxicity is weak.
Aminophylline, see theophyllines			
Amiodarone, see anticoagulants (oral), cyclosporine, digitalis glycosides, phenytoin			
Amitriptyline, see antidepressants (cyclic), clonidine			
Amlodipine, see calcium channel blockers			
Amoxapine, see antidepressants (cyclic)			
Amphetamines, see sympathomimetics			
Androgens, see anticoagulants (oral), cyclosporine			
Angiotensin-converting enzyme (ACE) inhibitors, see lithium, potassium-sparing diuretics			
Angiotensin II receptor blockers, see lithium, potassium-sparing diuretics			
Antacids, see quinolones, tetracyclines			
Anticoagulants, oral warfarin	**Androgens** danazol fluoxymesterone methyltestosterone nandrolone oxymetholone testosterone	• A large increase in effect of the anticoagulant occurs, increasing bleeding risk. Severe bleeding has occurred. • The majority of hypoprothrombinemic effects occur within the first week of initiating the androgen. • Possible mechanisms include decrease in formation or increase in degradation of clotting factors, increased anticoagulant receptor-site affinity, inhibition of warfarin metabolism and increase in endogenous anticoagulants. • The fibrinolytic activity of the androgen possibly contributes to bleeding risk.	• Avoid the combination of anticoagulant and androgen if possible. • Monitor INR*. • Observe for signs and symptoms of bleeding. • Anticoagulant dose may need to be decreased when androgen is started, or increased when it is discontinued.
	Cephalosporins cefamandole cefoperazone cefotetan	• Cephalosporins with a methylthiotetrazole (MTT) ring appear to inhibit production of vitamin K-dependent clotting factors. • Hypoprothrombinemia and/or ↑ INR have also been reported with cefazolin, cefixime, cefotaxime, cefoxitin, ceftizoxime, ceftriaxone and cefaclor.	• Avoid concurrent use of warfarin with cephalosporins possessing a MTT ring (cefamandole, cefoperazone, cefotetan). • With other cephalosporins, monitor INR and ↓ warfarin dose as required.

Cholestyramine	• Reduced effect of warfarin occurs due to impaired absorption secondary to binding in the gastrointestinal tract. • Warfarin appears to undergo enterohepatic recirculation, and absorption may be impaired due to cholestyramine despite separation of doses by many hours. • Colestipol may have less effect than cholestyramine on the absorption of anticoagulants.	• Avoid the combination of anticoagulant and cholestyramine if possible; colestipol may be preferable, but caution is still recommended. • Monitor INR*. • Anticoagulant dose may need to be increased when cholestyramine is started, or decreased when it is discontinued. • Give anticoagulant at least 6 hours after cholestyramine; maintain a consistent number of hours between anticoagulant and cholestyramine dosing so effect on anticoagulant absorption will be relatively consistent.
Enzyme inducers aminoglutethimide barbiturates carbamazepine phenytoin primidone rifampin	• Reduced effect of anticoagulant occurs due to induction of hepatic microsomal enzymes, increasing the risk of thromboembolism. • If enzyme inducer is initiated in a patient on anticoagulant, maximum decrease in hypoprothrombinemic response varies from 5–10 days (with rifampin) to 2 weeks or more. If anticoagulant is started in a patient already receiving an enzyme inducer, effect on anticoagulant dosage requirements may be immediate. • Recovery of anticoagulant-induced hypoprothrombinemia may not be complete until several weeks after discontinuation of the enzyme inducer. • Phenytoin may transiently, during the first week, increase hypoprothrombinemic response in patients on an anticoagulant, by displacing the anticoagulant from plasma protein binding sites. This is followed by decreased hypoprothrombinemic response due to enzyme induction.	• Monitor INR*. • Anticoagulant dose may need to be increased when enzyme inducer is initiated, or decreased when it is discontinued. • Alternative hypnotics may be used instead of barbiturates.
Enzyme inhibitors allopurinol amiodarone chloramphenicol cimetidine ciprofloxacin disulfiram erythromycin fluconazole itraconazole ketoconazole metronidazole norfloxacin propafenone sulfamethoxazole-trimethoprim sulfinpyrazone zafirlukast	• Increased effect of anticoagulant is due to inhibition of hepatic microsomal enzymes, increasing the risk of bleeding. • If enzyme inhibitor is initiated in a patient on anticoagulant, maximum increase in hypoprothrombinemic response occurs in 10 days or more (potentially a month with amiodarone). If anticoagulant is started in a patient already receiving an enzyme inhibitor, effect on anticoagulant dosage requirements may be immediate. • New steady-state hypoprothrombinemia after discontinuation of the enzyme inhibitor tends to take 10 days or more, but may take several months after discontinuation of amiodarone. • Clarithromycin may inhibit hepatic metabolism and should be used with caution in patients receiving anticoagulants. *(cont'd)*	• Monitor INR*. • Anticoagulant dose may need to be decreased when enzyme inhibitor is initiated or increased when it is discontinued.

*INR=international normalized ratio.

Table I—Drug-Drug Interactions *(cont'd)*

Drug	Interacting Drug	Mechanism	Management
Anticoagulants, oral *(cont'd)*	**Enzyme inhibitors** *(cont'd)*	• Grepafloxacin, levofloxacin and ofloxacin are not known to interact with anticoagulants but should be used with caution. • Ranitidine, famotidine and possibly nizatidine are unlikely to affect the hypoprothrombinemic response to anticoagulants and should be used instead of cimetidine in patients receiving anticoagulants.	
	Lipid lowering agents **Fibrates** bezafibrate clofibrate fenofibrate gemfibrozil **HMG-CoA reductase inhibitors** lovastatin	• Increased effect of anticoagulant occurs, increasing bleeding risk. A fatal case of massive bleeding has been attributed to the interaction of clofibrate and anticoagulant. • Effect of clofibrate possibly occurs via enhancement of the anticoagulant's effect on synthesis of clotting factors and/or an effect on vitamin K turnover. • Hypoprothrombinemia begins within a few days after starting clofibrate and may continue to increase for up to 2 weeks or more. • Only one case of an interaction (nonfatal) has been reported with gemfibrozil, but caution is recommended. • Interaction is considered possible with all fibric acid derivatives. • Mechanism of interaction with HMG-CoA reductase inhibitors is not established. • Although atorvastatin, cerivastatin, fluvastatin and pravastatin may not interact and simvastatin only slightly increases anticoagulant response, caution should also be exercised with these drugs.	• Avoid the combination of anticoagulant and clofibrate. • Monitor INR*. • Anticoagulant dose may need to be decreased when lipid lowering agent is started or increased when it is discontinued.
	NSAIDs diclofenac diflunisal etodolac fenoprofen flurbiprofen ibuprofen indomethacin ketoprofen mefenamic acid naproxen oxaprozin phenylbutazone piroxicam sulindac tolmetin	• Phenylbutazone markedly increases hypoprothrombinemic response to warfarin by inhibition of its metabolism and may displace warfarin from plasma protein binding sites; severe bleeding has occurred. • Diflunisal, flurbiprofen, indomethacin, ketoprofen, mefenamic acid, piroxicam and sulindac are reported to increase hypoprothrombinemic response in some patients. • Diclofenac, ibuprofen, nabumetone, naproxen, tenoxicam and possibly tolmetin appear to be the least likely to affect hypoprothrombinemic response to anticoagulants. • NSAID-induced gastric erosions and inhibition of platelet function could theoretically increase the risk of bleeding in patients receiving anticoagulants. • All NSAIDs should be assumed capable of interacting with anticoagulants.	• Avoid phenylbutazone and select a NSAID which is least likely to affect the hypoprothrombinemic response to anticoagulants. • Monitor INR* more frequently for 1–2 weeks after initiating or withdrawing the NSAID. • Observe for signs and symptoms of bleeding.

	Salicylates ASA	• Even small doses of ASA inhibit platelet function and possibly produce gastric erosions, increasing the risk of bleeding. • Large doses of ASA (greater than 3 g/day) may increase the hypoprothrombinemic response to anticoagulants. • Nonacetylated salicylates (e.g., choline salicylate) have little effect on platelet function and theoretically are less likely to cause gastrointestinal bleeding	• Avoid concomitant use of ASA and ASA-containing products with an anticoagulant. • Monitor INR*; observe for signs and symptoms of bleeding. • Acetaminophen is preferable to ASA in these patients if a mild analgesic is needed.
	SSRIs paroxetine	• Paroxetine increases bleeding after several days of concurrent therapy via an unknown mechanism. • Fluvoxamine may increase warfarin concentrations by 65%, but the clinical significance is not established. • Sertraline slightly increases hypoprothrombinemic response to warfarin. • Fluoxetine has no effect on hypoprothrombinemic response but alone may increase bleeding.	• Avoid concurrent use with paroxetine. • Monitor INR* when starting, stopping or changing dosage of fluvoxamine or sertraline.
	Thyroid hormones levothyroxine liothyronine thyroid	• Increased hypoprothrombinemic response to anticoagulants occurs in patients started on thyroid hormones, possibly due to a reduction in serum albumin, the major plasma protein responsible for warfarin binding, as well as a reduction in its actual protein binding capacity, leading to increased risk of bleeding. • This effect is probably gradual over 2–3 weeks or more. • Hypothyroid patients may be somewhat resistant to warfarin, thus requiring higher doses; patients who are euthyroid, either naturally or from thyroid replacement therapy, have a normal hypoprothrombinemic response to warfarin. • Hyperthyroid patients have a greater response to anticoagulants than do euthyroid individuals. • Thyroid hormones may also increase catabolism of vitamin K-dependent clotting factors.	• Closely monitor (INR*, bleeding) patients stabilized on anticoagulant also requiring thyroid replacement therapy. • A decrease in the dose of anticoagulant usually becomes necessary within 1–4 weeks after starting therapy with a thyroid hormone. • Adding an anticoagulant to a clinically euthyroid patient on thyroid replacement is unlikely to be a problem; however, changes in the thyroid status of such a patient may cause changes in anticoagulant requirements.
Antidepressants, cyclic amitriptyline amoxapine clomipramine desipramine doxepin imipramine maprotiline nortriptyline protriptyline trimipramine	**Enzyme inducers** barbiturates carbamazepine	• Reduction in serum antidepressant concentration occurs due to induction of metabolism, possibly resulting in loss of therapeutic effect. • Interaction has not been reported with all cyclic antidepressants but is considered possible. • Interaction may theoretically be precipitated by primidone and phenytoin. • Effect on antidepressant effectiveness is gradual and may develop over several days to 1 week or more.	• Antidepressant dose may need to be increased when enzyme inducer is started or decreased when it is discontinued. • Benzodiazepines may provide an alternative to barbiturates. *(cont'd)*

*INR=international normalized ratio.

Table I—Drug-Drug Interactions *(cont'd)*

Drug	Interacting Drug	Mechanism	Management
Antidepressants, cyclic *(cont'd)*	**Enzyme inhibitors** cimetidine diltiazem fluoxetine neuroleptics propoxyphene quinidine verapamil	• Increased serum antidepressant concentration is probably due to inhibition of metabolism. • Interaction is well documented with cimetidine, fluoxetine and neuroleptics. • Interaction has not been reported with all cyclic antidepressants but is considered possible. • Antidepressant toxicity may not be noted for several days to a week or more after starting the enzyme inhibitor and includes dry mouth, blurred vision, urinary retention, postural hypotension, delirium. Seizures may result from combining fluoxetine and a cyclic antidepressant. • The effect of fluoxetine on antidepressant metabolism could theoretically require 2–4 weeks to dissipate after fluoxetine is discontinued. • Antidepressants may increase serum neuroleptic concentration, theoretically increasing neuroleptic therapeutic and toxic effects.	• Antidepressant dose may need to be decreased when enzyme inhibitor is started or increased when it is discontinued. • If fluoxetine is begun in a patient on an antidepressant, antidepressant dose may need to be decreased by as much as 75%. • If antidepressant is begun within several weeks of fluoxetine being discontinued, monitor for increased antidepressant side effects and start with a lower than usual antidepressant dose. A 5-week washout interval has been recommended when switching from fluoxetine to a cyclic antidepressant. • Monitor for increased neuroleptic side effects. • Ranitidine is unlikely to interact with antidepressants and may provide an alternative to cimetidine.
	MAOIs moclobemide phenelzine tranylcypromine	• Concurrent use of MAOIs and cyclic antidepressants may excessively increase CNS serotonin resulting in the "serotonin syndrome". • Deaths have been associated with combined use of clomipramine and a nonselective MAOI as well as with moclobemide. • Severe reactions have been reported with the combined use of MAOIs and imipramine. In most of the reported cases, the cyclic agent was given parenterally, or excessive drug doses were used, or other psychotropic drugs were also given. • Severe reactions have included excitation, hyperpyrexia mania and seizures. Disseminated intravascular coagulation has also been reported. • Interaction has not been reported with all cyclic antidepressants, but is considered more likely with inhibitors of serotonin reuptake, i.e., clomipramine, desipramine, imipramine, trazodone.	• Combined use of MAOIs with clomipramine or imipramine should be avoided. • If other cyclic antidepressants are used in combination with MAOIs: avoid large doses; give the drugs orally; monitor the patient closely for excitation, fever, mania or seizures.
Antidepressants (cyclic), see also clonidine			
Antidiabetic agents **Insulin** **Sulfonylureas** chlorpropamide gliclazide glyburide tolbutamide	**Beta-adrenergic blockers** **Cardioselective** acebutolol atenolol metoprolol **Noncardioselective** nadolol oxprenolol pindolol propranolol sotalol timolol	• Noncardioselective beta blockers may cause prolonged recovery from hypoglycemia, hypertension during hypoglycemia and inhibition of hypoglycemia-induced tachycardia. This is due to blockade of the hyperglycemic, vasodilatory and cardiac stimulatory effects of epinephrine which is released in response to hypoglycemia induced by insulin or sulfonylureas. • Cardioselective beta blockers are expected to have less effect than noncardioselective beta blockers on the response to hypoglycemia induced by insulin or sulfonylureas, but both will inhibit the tachycardiac response to hypoglycemia.	• In patients on insulin or a sulfonylurea, cardioselective beta blockers are preferred to noncardioselective beta blockers. Caution is still required. • Advise patient that usual tachycardiac response to hypoglycemia may be absent.

	Noncardioselective and alpha blocker carvedilol labetalol	• The combination of chlorpropamide or tolbutamide with propranolol has been reported to cause hyperglycemia.	
Antihistamines astemizole terfenadine	**Enzyme Inhibitors** clarithromycin erythromycin fluconazole fluoxetine fluvoxamine indinavir itraconazole ketoconazole ritonavir	• The metabolism of the antihistamine is inhibited, resulting in increased plasma levels. • Increased levels of the antihistamine are associated with QT prolongation and increased risk of ventricular tachyarrhythmias, such as torsades de pointes, ventricular tachycardia and ventricular fibrillation. • It is possible but unlikely that metronidazole also interacts. • Azithromycin does not appear to interact with these antihistamines. • The protease inhibitor, saquinavir, is only a weak inhibitor.	• Concurrent use of astemizole or terfenadine with these drugs should be avoided. • Other antihistamines (e.g., fexofenadine, loratadine, cetirizine) may be considered in place of astemizole or terfenadine.
Antimetabolites azathioprine mercaptopurine	**Allopurinol**	• Allopurinol impairs the conversion of mercaptopurine (6-MP) to inactive products by inhibiting xanthine oxidase, resulting in higher blood levels of 6-MP and increased risk of serious toxicity (e.g., bone marrow suppression, hepatotoxicity) even death. • Onset and offset (after discontinuation of allopurinol or the antimetabolite) of the adverse effects of this combination may take several weeks.	• Reduce initial dose of antimetabolite to as low as 25% of the recommended dosage when used with allopurinol. Then adjust based on clinical response and/or toxicity.
Astemizole, see antihistamines			
Atenolol, see antidiabetic agents, calcium channel blockers			
Azathioprine, see antimetabolites			
Barbiturates, see anticoagulants (oral), antidepressants (cyclic), contraceptives (oral), corticosteroids, methadone, phenobarbital, quinidine, theophyllines			
Benazepril, see lithium, potassium-sparing diuretics			
Benzodiazepines diazepam midazolam triazolam	**Enzyme inhibitors** clarithromycin fluconazole indinavir itraconazole ritonavir	• Metabolism of the benzodiazepine is inhibited, resulting in increased sedation and half-life. • Erythromycin also inhibits metabolism.	• Azithromycin does not appear to interact. • Temazepam, lorazepam and oxazepam are not expected to be affected. • Terbinafine does not appear to affect these benzodiazepines.

Table I—Drug-Drug Interactions *(cont'd)*

Drug	Interacting Drug	Mechanism	Management
Beta-adrenergic blockers nadolol oxprenolol pindolol propranolol sotalol timolol	**Sympathomimetics** epinephrine	• Hypertension, reflex bradycardia, decreased cardiac index may result when epinephrine is administered to a patient pretreated with a noncardioselective beta blocker, due to unopposed alpha effects (vasoconstriction) of epinephrine, while its usual beta effects (vasodilation, cardiac stimulation) are blocked. • Interaction occurs minimally with metoprolol and would theoretically also be minimal with other cardioselective beta blockers (e.g., acebutolol, atenolol) but data are lacking. • Combined alpha and beta blockers (e.g., labetalol) are unlikely to cause acute hypertensive reactions when given in combination with epinephrine. • Patients receiving propranolol who develop anaphylactic shock have been reported to respond poorly to epinephrine due to propranolol-induced inhibition of the pressor and bronchodilator response to epinephrine in anaphylaxis. • Whether cardioselective beta blockers or labetalol would antagonize the therapeutic effects of epinephrine in anaphylaxis is not known.	• Administer epinephrine cautiously to patients on a noncardioselective beta blocker; monitor vital signs. • Vigorous supportive care may be required for patients in anaphylaxis who have been receiving beta blocker therapy. • If epinephrine use is anticipated, discontinue beta blocker 3 days before exposure.
Beta-adrenergic blockers, see also antidiabetic agents, calcium channel blockers, theophyllines			
Betamethasone, see corticosteroids			
Bezafibrate, see anticoagulants (oral), HMG-CoA reductase inhibitors			
Bismuth, see tetracyclines			
Bupropion	**MAOIs** phenelzine tranylcypromine	• The acute toxicity of bupropion (agitation, seizures, headache) is enhanced by the MAOI.	• Avoid concurrent use. • At least 14 days should elapse between discontinuation of either drug and initiation of the other drug.
Buspirone	**MAOIs** phenelzine tranylcypromine	• Hypertension has been reported.	• Avoid concurrent use. • Do not use buspirone within 10 days of discontinuing the MAOI.
Calcium channel blockers amlodipine diltiazem felodipine nicardipine nifedipine nimodipine verapamil	**Beta-adrenergic blockers** acebutolol atenolol carvedilol labetalol metoprolol nadolol oxprenolol pindolol propranolol sotalol timolol	• The depressant effects on myocardial contractility, heart rate and AV conduction may be additive. • If used together, should be instituted gradually under careful supervision.	• Monitor patient's vital signs and clinical status if used; reassess need for therapy.

	Enzyme inducers carbamazepine rifampin	• Carbamazepine increases metabolism of most calcium channel blockers by inducing CYP3A4 Felodipine is most affected. • Rifampin reduces the bioavailability and protein binding of verapamil and induces the metabolism of diltiazem, nifedipine and verapamil. Effect is seen within 3–5 days.	• Monitor patients for a reduction in calcium channel blocker efficacy. • Avoid combination of carbamazepine with felodipine. Be aware that diltiazem and verapamil can produce carbamazepine toxicity. • Dose of calcium channel blocker may need to be increased when rifampin is started or decreased when it is discontinued.
Calcium channel blockers, see also antidepressants (cyclic), carbamazepine, cyclosporine, digitalis glycosides, theophyllines			
Captopril, see lithium, potassium-sparing diuretics			
Carbamazepine	**Enzyme inhibitors** cimetidine danazol diltiazem erythromycin fluoxetine isoniazid propoxyphene verapamil	• Increase in serum carbamazepine concentration occurs due to inhibition of metabolism, with increased risk of neurotoxicity (e.g., lethargy, ataxia, headache, nystagmus). • Toxic effects may appear as early as 2–3 days after initiation of the enzyme inhibitor. • The effect of the calcium channel blocker may be reduced by carbamazepine. • The effect of cimetidine on carbamazepine may dissipate after about 1 week of concurrent therapy.	• Watch for signs and symptoms of carbamazepine toxicity. • Monitor serum carbamazepine concentration. • Carbamazepine dose may need to be decreased when enzyme inhibitor is started or increased when it is discontinued. • Amlodipine, nicardipine and nifedipine do not affect carbamazepine clearance. • Ranitidine does not appear to interact with carbamazepine and could be used instead of cimetidine; famotidine and nizatidine are also considered unlikely to interact with carbamazepine. • Avoid concomitant use with propoxyphene. • Avoid concomitant use with fluoxetine. Fluvoxamine may also increase carbamazepine levels. No interaction noted with paroxetine or sertraline. • Avoid concomitant use with erythromycin. Clarithromycin may also interact. No interaction is seen with azithromycin.
Carbamazepine, see also anticoagulants (oral), antidepressants (cyclic), calcium channel blockers, contraceptives (oral), cyclosporine, methadone, theophyllines			
Carvedilol, see antidiabetic agents, calcium channel blockers			
Cefamandole, see anticoagulants (oral)			
Cefoperazone, see anticoagulants (oral)			
Cefotetan, see anticoagulants (oral)			
Cephalosporins, see anticoagulants (oral)			
Chloramphenicol, see anticoagulants (oral), phenytoin			
Chlorpropamide, see antidiabetic agents			
Cholestyramine, see anticoagulants (oral)			
Cilazapril, see lithium, potassium-sparing diuretics			
Cimetidine, see anticoagulants (oral), antidepressants (cyclic), carbamazepine, phenytoin, theophyllines			
Ciprofloxacin, see anticoagulants (oral), quinolones, theophyllines			

Table I—Drug-Drug Interactions *(cont'd)*

Drug	Interacting Drug	Mechanism	Management
Cisapride	**Enzyme inhibitors** clarithromycin erythromycin fluconazole indinavir itraconazole ketoconazole ritonavir	• The metabolism of cisapride is inhibited, resulting in increased plasma levels. • Increased cisapride levels are associated with QT prolongation and increased risk of ventricular tachyarrhythmias such as torsades de pointes, ventricular tachycardia and ventricular fibrillation.	• Concurrent use with these drugs should be avoided. • Azithromycin does not appear to interact with cisapride.
Clarithromycin, see antihistamines, benzodiazepines, cisapride, clozapine, cyclosporine, ergot alkaloids			
Clofibrate, see anticoagulants (oral), HMG-CoA reductase inhibitors			
Clomipramine, see antidepressants (cyclic)			
Clonidine	**Antidepressants, cyclic** amitriptyline desipramine imipramine	• Severely increased blood pressure due to inhibition of antihypertensive response to clonidine has been reported with desipramine and imipramine. • Effect on blood pressure usually takes a week or more after starting the antidepressant, but may occur within 1–2 days. • Interaction has not been reported with all cyclic antidepressants but is considered possible. • Maprotiline theoretically does not interact with clonidine, but this is unproven.	• Avoid combination if possible. • Monitor blood pressure if a cyclic antidepressant is added, discontinued or its dose changed in a patient receiving clonidine. • In a patient receiving a cyclic antidepressant and clonidine, clonidine withdrawal should be gradual; monitor patient closely.
Clozapine	**Enzyme inhibitors** clarithromycin erythromycin fluvoxamine ritonavir	• Increased levels of clozapine result from inhibition of its metabolism. • Seizures and markedly increased levels of clozapine have been reported. • ECG changes are possible.	• Avoid concurrent use. • Azithromycin is unlikely to interact. • Other SSRIs have little effect on cytochrome P4501A2, although increased levels of clozapine have also been reported with fluoxetine.
Contraceptives, oral	**Acitretin**	• Acitretin interferes with the contraceptive effect of progestin minipills (e.g., norethindrone) by an unknown mechanism.	• As acitretin is a known teratogen, reliable methods of contraception should be used to prevent pregnancy during acitretin therapy.
	Enzyme inducers barbiturates carbamazepine phenytoin primidone rifampin topiramate	• Reduced efficacy of contraceptives due to enhanced metabolism occurs resulting in unplanned pregnancies and menstrual irregularities.	• Use other methods of contraception instead of, or in addition to, oral contraceptives. • Continue additional protection for at least one cycle after discontinuation of rifampin and for several weeks after discontinuation of a barbiturate.
Contraceptives (oral), see also cyclosporine			
Corticosteroids betamethasone cortisone dexamethasone fludrocortisone hydrocortisone methylprednisolone	**Enzyme inducers** aminoglutethimide barbiturates phenytoin rifampin	• Reduced therapeutic effect of the corticosteroid (e.g., allograft failure, worsening of asthma symptoms, interference with dexamethasone suppression test) occurs due to induction of metabolism. • Dexamethasone has been reported both to increase and to decrease serum phenytoin concentration.	• Corticosteroid dose may need to be increased when enzyme inducer is started or decreased when it is discontinued. • Corticosteroid dose may need to be increased 2-fold or even more after addition of phenytoin or rifampin to corticosteroid therapy, or after addition of aminoglutethimide to dexamethasone therapy.

prednisolone prednisone triamcinolone		• Effect is gradual and may develop over several days to 1 week or more. • Interaction has not been reported with all corticosteroids but is considered possible.	• Monitor phenytoin concentration; adjust dose as required.
	Uterine-relaxing agents ritodrine	• Corticosteroids used concomitantly may lead to maternal pulmonary edema.	• Patient's state of hydration must be closely monitored. • Fluid overload must be avoided.
Cortisone, see corticosteroids			
Cyclosporine	**Enzyme inducers** carbamazepine phenytoin rifampin	• Marked reduction in cyclosporine concentration is due to induction of metabolism and/or increase in presystemic clearance, possibly resulting in loss of therapeutic effect (e.g., graft-versus-host disease or graft rejection). • Enzyme inducer discontinuation may be followed by cyclosporine-induced renal toxicity due to high cyclosporine concentration. • Reduction in cyclosporine effect may occur as early as 2 days after starting rifampin or phenytoin. • After rifampin or carbamazepine withdrawal, effect on cyclosporine has taken up to 3 weeks to dissipate.	• Cyclosporine dose may need to be increased substantially when enzyme inducer is begun (up to 5-fold with rifampin) or decreased when it is discontinued. • Monitor cyclosporine response, cyclosporine concentration and serum creatinine. • Successful use of cyclosporine with rifampin is possible if cyclosporine concentration is carefully monitored and cyclosporine dose is adjusted, but it is a difficult combination to manage. • Use of an immunosuppressive regimen not including cyclosporine could be considered for transplant recipients requiring rifampin. • Valproic acid has been substituted for carbamazepine with a satisfactory increase in cyclosporine concentration in a small number of patients receiving cyclosporine, and may provide an alternative in some cases.
	Enzyme inhibitors amiodarone androgens clarithromycin contraceptives, oral diltiazem erythromycin itraconazole ketoconazole nicardipine verapamil	• Increase in cyclosporine concentration occurs, possibly due to inhibition of metabolism, with increased risk of cyclosporine-induced renal toxicity when enzyme inhibitor is begun or possible loss of therapeutic effect (e.g., graft rejection) when it is discontinued. • The increase in cyclosporine concentration develops over 3–5 days, sooner with ketoconazole and over several weeks with oral contraceptives and androgens. • Interaction may occur with other enzyme inhibitors and high doses of fluconazole. • The addition of diltiazem, ketoconazole or verapamil to immunosuppressive regimens in organ transplantation has allowed a decrease in dose and cost of cyclosporine.	• Cyclosporine dose may need to be decreased by 50% or more when enzyme inhibitor is started or increased when it is discontinued. • Monitor cyclosporine concentration and serum creatinine; observe for cyclosporine toxicity.
Cyclosporine, see also HMG-CoA reductase inhibitors			
Danazol (Androgens), see anticoagulants (oral), carbamazepine, cyclosporine			
Demeclocycline, see tetracyclines			
Desipramine, see antidepressants (cyclic), clonidine			

Table I—Drug-Drug Interactions *(cont'd)*

Drug	Interacting Drug	Mechanism	Management
Dexamethasone, see corticosteroids			
Dextromethorphan	**MAOIs** moclobemide phenelzine selegiline tranylcypromine	• Dextromethorphan blocks serotonin uptake by neurons. • Accumulation of serotonin leads to serotonin syndrome. • Interaction with moclobemide and selegiline is theoretical.	• Avoid concurrent use.
Diazepam, see benzodiazepines			
Diclofenac, see anticoagulants (oral), lithium, methotrexate			
Didanosine, see quinolones			
Diflunisal, see anticoagulants (oral)			
Digitalis glycosides digitoxin digoxin	**Calcium channel blockers** diltiazem verapamil **Other cardiac drugs** amiodarone quinidine	• Increased serum digitalis glycoside concentration occurs with concurrent use of diltiazem and verapamil by reduction of renal clearance. • Verapamil and diltiazem in combination with digitalis glycosides have additive effects (i.e., slowed conduction) on atrioventricular node conduction. • Maximum effect of verapamil takes 5–7 days with digoxin, 3–5 weeks with digitoxin. • Amiodarone and quinidine reduce the renal and nonrenal clearance of digoxin, may increase its bioavailability and absorption, and displace it from tissue-binding sites. • Amiodarone's effect may not appear until after several days or even weeks of combined therapy with digoxin. Amiodarone and digoxin both depress the sinus node, possibly leading to bradycardia. • Quinidine may produce an increase in serum digoxin concentration beginning on the first day of concomitant therapy, reaching steady state within 3–6 days. • These interactions may lead to digoxin toxicity, bradycardia and worsening of heart failure.	• Monitor for evidence of increased serum digitalis concentration when these drugs are initiated. • Reduction of digoxin dose by 50% may be required on initiation of quinidine. • Procainamide, disopyramide and mexiletine do not interact with digoxin and could provide alternatives to quinidine in patients receiving digoxin.
Digitoxin, see digitalis glycosides			
Digoxin, see digitalis glycosides			
Dihydroergotamine, see ergot alkaloids, 5-HT_1 receptor agonists			
Diltiazem, see antidepressants (cyclic), calcium channel blockers, carbamazepine, cyclosporine, digitalis glycosides			
Disulfiram, see anticoagulants (oral), phenytoin, theophyllines			
Diuretics, see aminoglycosides, lithium, potassium-sparing diuretics			
Doxepin, see antidepressants (cyclic)			
Doxycycline, see tetracyclines			
Electrolytes, see potassium-sparing diuretics			

Enalapril, see lithium, potassium-sparing diuretics			
Ephedrine, see sympathomimetics			
Epinephrine, see beta-adrenergic blockers			
Ergot alkaloids dihydroergotamine ergotamine	**Enzyme inhibitors** clarithromycin erythromycin ritonavir	• Metabolism of ergotamine is inhibited which may result in ergotism including hypertension and ischemia.	• Azithromycin is unlikely to inhibit metabolism of ergot alkaloids.
Ergot alkaloids, see also 5-HT_1 receptor agonists			
Ergotamine, see ergot alkaloids, 5-HT_1 receptor agonists			
Erythromycin, see anticoagulants (oral), antihistamines, carbamazepine, cisapride, clozapine, cyclosporine, ergot alkaloids, HMG-CoA reductase inhibitors, theophyllines			
Ethacrynic acid, see aminoglycosides			
Etodolac, see anticoagulants (oral), lithium			
Felodipine, see calcium channel blockers			
Fenofibrate, see anticoagulants (oral), HMG Co-A reductase inhibitors			
Fenoprofen, see anticoagulants (oral)			
Fibrates, see anticoagulants (oral), HMG-CoA reductase inhibitors			
5-HT_1 receptor agonists naratriptan sumatriptan	**Ergot-containing drugs** dihydroergotamine ergotamine methysergide	• Ergot-containing drugs may cause prolonged vasospasm which may be additive with the 5-HT_1 receptor agonist.	• Avoid concurrent use of naratriptan and sumatriptan with ergot-containing drugs as well as use within 24 hours of each other.
	MAOIs moclobemide phenelzine tranylcypromine	• Sumatriptan is metabolized by monoamine oxidase A which is inhibited by moclobemide and nonselective MAOIs. Naratriptan does not affect MAO enzymes.	• Avoid concurrent use of sumatriptan with monoamine oxidase A inhibitors or within 2 weeks of discontinuing the MAOI.
Fluconazole, see anticoagulants (oral), antihistamines, benzodiazepines, cisapride, phenytoin			
Fludrocortisone, see corticosteroids			
Fluoxetine, see antidepressants (cyclic), antihistamines, carbamazepine, phenytoin, serotonin reuptake inhibitors			
Fluoxymesterone (Androgens), see anticoagulants (oral), cyclosporine			
Flurbiprofen, see anticoagulants (oral), methotrexate			
Fluvoxamine, see antihistamines, clozapine, serotonin reuptake inhibitors, theophylline			
Fosinopril, see lithium, potassium-sparing diuretics			
Gemfibrozil, see anticoagulants (oral), HMG Co-A reductase inhibitors			
Gentamicin, see aminoglycosides			
Gliclazide, see antidiabetic agents			
Glyburide, see antidiabetic agents			
Grepafloxacin, see anticoagulants (oral), quinolones, theophyllines			

Table I—Drug-Drug Interactions *(cont'd)*

Drug	Interacting Drug	Mechanism	Management
HMG-CoA reductase inhibitors lovastatin simvastatin	**Enzyme inhibitors** cyclosporine erythromycin itraconazole ketoconazole nefazodone **Fibrates** bezafibrate clofibrate fenofibrate gemfibrozil **Niacin**	• Increases in the concentration of the HMG-CoA reductase inhibitor occur. Rhabdomyolysis has been reported or is possible with each of the drugs. • Mechanism with fibric acid derivatives and niacin is not established but effects may be additive. • Interactions should be considered possible with atorvastatin, cerivastatin, fluvastatin and pravastatin. • Risk is less with lower doses of lovastatin (20 mg/day).	• Pravastatin may not be inhibited by itraconazole and ketoconazole to the same extent. • Nefazodone is one of the most potent CYP3A4 inhibitors among the antidepressants; selecting another agent is appropriate. • Terbinafine may have minimal effect on the metabolism of HMG-CoA reductase inhibitors. • If combined therapy is necessary, patients should be alert for symptoms of muscle pain, weakness or tenderness.
HMG-CoA reductase inhibitors, see also anticoagulants (oral)			
Hydrocortisone, see corticosteroids			
Ibuprofen, see anticoagulants (oral), lithium, methotrexate			
Imipramine, see antidepressants (cyclic), clonidine			
Indinavir, see antihistamines, benzodiazepines, cisapride, protease inhibitors			
Indomethacin, see anticoagulants (oral), lithium, methotrexate			
Insulin, see antidiabetic agents			
Irbesartan, see lithium, potassium-sparing diuretics			
Iron salts, see quinolones, tetracyclines			
Isoniazid, see carbamazepine, phenytoin			
Itraconazole	**Phenytoin**	• Phenytoin probably enhances metabolism of itraconazole by CYP3A4. • Itraconazole serum concentration is decreased by >90% resulting in probable therapeutic failure. • Ketoconazole is also likely to be affected.	• Fluconazole is unlikely to be affected by phenytoin but itself may inhibit phenytoin metabolism; monitor for increased effects of phenytoin.
Itraconazole, see also anticoagulants (oral), antihistamines, benzodiazepines, cisapride, cyclosporine, HMG-CoA reductase inhibitors			
Ketoconazole, see anticoagulants (oral), antihistamines, cisapride, cyclosporine, HMG-CoA reductase inhibitors			
Ketoprofen, see anticoagulants (oral), methotrexate			
Ketorolac, see lithium			
Labetalol, see antidiabetic agents, calcium channel blockers			
Levodopa	**MAOIs** phenelzine tranylcypromine	• Increased levels of dopamine at dopamine receptors occurs, resulting from inhibited peripheral degradation of levodopa-derived dopamine, and increased storage and release of norepinephrine, of which dopamine is a precursor. May result in a hypertensive response within 1 hour of levodopa administration or a worsening of akinesia and tremor. • Use with moclobemide, while not contraindicated, must be cautious. • This interaction does not occur with levodopa and selegiline.	• Combined use should be avoided. • The use of a decarboxylase inhibitor (e.g., carbidopa) with levodopa may blunt or prevent the hypertensive response.

Levofloxacin, see quinolones			
Levothyroxine, see anticoagulants (oral)			
Liothyronine, see anticoagulants (oral)			
Lisinopril, see lithium, potassium-sparing diuretics			
Lithium	**ACE inhibitors** benazepril captopril cilazapril enalapril fosinopril lisinopril perindopril quinapril ramipril trandolapril **Angiotensin II receptor blockers** irbesartan losartan valsartan	• Decreased renal lithium clearance is possibly due to ACE inhibitor-induced sodium depletion. • Lithium toxicity (tremor, ataxia, confusion, diarrhea, nausea, vomiting, anorexia, lethargy) may result. • Reaction tends to occur after 3–4 weeks of concomitant therapy. • Elderly patients may be especially at risk.	• Avoid concurrent use if possible. • If used together, monitor lithium levels and signs of toxicity carefully for the first month.
	NSAIDs diclofenac etodolac ibuprofen indomethacin ketorolac mefenamic acid nabumetone naproxen oxaprozin phenylbutazone piroxicam **Thiazide diuretics**	• Increased serum lithium concentration as a result of reduced renal excretion is probably due to NSAID-induced prostaglandin inhibition; increase in proximal tubule reabsorption of sodium by the diuretic results in increased lithium reabsorption, both leading to possible lithium toxicity. • Sulindac may have no effect or may temporarily decrease serum lithium concentration; ASA has little effect on lithium concentration. • Interaction has not been reported with all NSAIDs but is considered possible. • After a NSAID is begun in a patient receiving lithium, maximum increase in lithium concentrations takes 5–10 days; return to new steady-state lithium concentration usually occurs within 7 days after discontinuation of the NSAID.	• Monitor serum lithium concentration when NSAID therapy is initiated or discontinued and during co-therapy with a thiazide diuretic; observe for signs and symptoms of lithium toxicity (e.g., nausea, vomiting, diarrhea, tremor, confusion; in severe cases, seizures, cardiovascular collapse). • Lithium dose may need to be decreased when NSAID or thiazide diuretic is initiated or increased when discontinued. • Consider sulindac or ASA as NSAID in patients receiving lithium; monitoring is still required. • Furosemide appears to be less likely than thiazide diuretics to interact with lithium.
Losartan, see lithium, potassium-sparing diuretics			
Lovastatin, see anticoagulants (oral), HMG-CoA reductase inhibitors			
Maprotiline, see antidepressants (cyclic)			
Mefenamic acid, see anticoagulants (oral), lithium			
Meperidine	**Enzyme inhibitors** ritonavir	• Large increases in serum levels of meperidine are expected, increasing the risk of seizures, CNS side effects and arrhythmias.	• Avoid concurrent use.
	MAOIs moclobemide phenelzine selegiline tranylcypromine	• Meperidine appears to block neuronal serotonin uptake resulting in hypertension or hypotension, excitation, sweating, rigidity, hyperpyrexia, convulsions, coma. Respiratory depression, hypotension and coma possibly due to potentiation of the effects of the narcotic may also occur.	*(cont'd)*

Table I—Drug-Drug Interactions *(cont'd)*

Drug	Interacting Drug	Mechanism	Management
Meperidine *(cont'd)*	**MAOIs** *(cont'd)*	• The reaction is unpredictable and if it occurs, it is usually immediately after a dose of meperidine. • May occur weeks after withdrawal of the MAOI. • Deaths have resulted from this interaction. • Although a suspected case of morphine-MAOI interaction with hypotension and coma promptly reversed by naloxone has been reported, morphine is considered narcotic of choice with MAOIs. • A fatal case in which hypertension and hyperthermia were followed by treatment-resistant hypotension may have originated in, or been complicated by, the combination of tranylcypromine and fentanyl. • One case of a suspected severe reaction with concomitant use of selegiline and meperidine has been reported. • Concomitant use of moclobemide with meperidine may also be expected to produce a serious reaction, although no human cases have yet been reported.	• The combination of meperidine with these drugs should be avoided. • Use morphine or other narcotics cautiously and preferably at reduced doses.
Mercaptopurine, see antimetabolites			
Methadone	**Enzyme inducers** barbiturates carbamazepine phenytoin rifampin	• Metabolism of methadone is enhanced, causing decreased serum levels. • Methadone withdrawal may result.	• Avoid concurrent use. • If necessary to use together, monitor need to adjust dose of methadone.
Methotrexate	**NSAIDs** diclofenac flurbiprofen ibuprofen indomethacin ketoprofen naproxen phenylbutazone salicylates tolmetin	• Methotrexate concentration increased 30 to 70%, over several days, possibly by a renal mechanism, leading to increased toxicity (e.g., bone marrow suppression, nephrotoxicity) and even death. • Patients receiving low-dose oral or parenteral methotrexate for rheumatoid arthritis are less likely to be at risk for severe methotrexate toxicity. • It should be assumed that any NSAID may interact with methotrexate.	• Avoid concomitant use of NSAIDs with antineoplastic doses of methotrexate; use nonNSAID analgesic if possible. • NSAIDs may be used cautiously in patients receiving low-dose methotrexate for rheumatoid arthritis. • Dose of methotrexate may need to be decreased when a NSAID is started. • Observe for signs and symptoms of methotrexate toxicity (e.g., mucosal ulceration, renal dysfunction). • Consider longer duration of leucovorin rescue.
	Uricosuric agents probenecid	• Marked increase in serum methotrexate concentration occurs due to impaired renal excretion of methotrexate, with increased risk of methotrexate toxicity (e.g., bone marrow depression, hepatotoxicity, increased susceptibility to infection). • Methotrexate concentration may rise 2- to 4-fold after starting probenecid. • Interaction has been reported both with low-dose oral methotrexate used for rheumatoid arthritis and with antineoplastic doses.	• Avoid this combination if possible. • Need to decrease methotrexate dose should be expected when probenecid is begun; leucovorin rescue may need to be prolonged. • Monitor serum methotrexate concentration. • Monitor for methotrexate toxicity.

Methylphenidate, see sympathomimetics			
Methylprednisolone, see corticosteroids			
Methysergide, see 5-HT_1 receptor agonists			
Methyltestosterone (Androgens), see anticoagulants (oral), cyclosporine			
Metoprolol, see antidiabetic agents, calcium channel blockers			
Metronidazole, see anticoagulants (oral)			
Mexiletine, see theophyllines			
Midazolam, see benzodiazepines			
Minocycline, see tetracyclines			
Moclobemide, see antidepressants (cyclic), dextromethorphan, 5-HT_1 receptor agonists, meperidine, sympathomimetics			
Monoamine oxidase inhibitors (MAOIs), see antidepressants (cyclic), bupropion, buspirone, dextromethorphan, 5-HT_1 receptor agonists, levodopa, meperidine, nefazodone, serotonin reuptake inhibitors, sympathomimetics, venlafaxine			
Nabumetone, see lithium			
Nadolol, see antidiabetic agents, beta-adrenergic blockers, calcium channel blockers			
Nandrolone (Androgens), see anticoagulants (oral), cyclosporine			
Naproxen, see anticoagulants (oral), lithium, methotrexate			
Naratriptan, see 5-HT_1 receptor agonists			
Nefazodone	**MAOIs** phenelzine selegiline tranycypromine	• Excessive increases in CNS serotonin resulting in serotonin syndrome.	• Avoid concurrent use. • At least 14 days should elapse between discontinuation of either drug and initiation of the other drug.
Nefazodone, see also HMG-CoA reductase inhibitors			
Netilmicin, see aminoglycosides			
Neuroleptics, see antidepressants (cyclic)			
Niacin, see HMG-CoA reductase inhibitors			
Nicardipine, see calcium channel blockers, cyclosporine			
Nifedipine, see calcium channel blockers			
Nimodipine, see calcium channel blockers			
Nonsteroidal anti-inflammatory drugs (NSAIDs), see anticoagulants (oral), lithium, methotrexate			
Norethindrone, see contraceptives (oral)			
Norfloxacin, see anticoagulants (oral), quinolones			
Nortriptyline, see antidepressants (cyclic)			
Ofloxacin, see quinolones			
Omeprazole, see phenytoin			
Oxaprozin, see anticoagulants (oral), lithium			
Oxprenolol, see antidiabetic agents, beta-adrenergic blockers, calcium channel blockers			

Table I—Drug-Drug Interactions *(cont'd)*

Drug	Interacting Drug	Mechanism	Management
Oxtriphylline, see theophyllines			
Oxymetholone (Androgens), see anticoagulants (oral), cyclosporine			
Paroxetine, see anticoagulants (oral), serotonin reuptake inhibitors			
Perindopril, see lithium, potassium-sparing diuretics			
Phenelzine, see antidepressants (cyclic), bupropion, buspirone, dextromethorphan, 5-HT_1 receptor agonists, levodopa, meperidine, nefazodone, serotonin reuptake inhibitors, sympathomimetics, venlafaxine			
Phenobarbital	**Valproic acid**	• Increased serum phenobarbital concentration, due to inhibition of hepatic metabolism, with increased risk of toxicity (e.g., sedation).	• Phenobarbital dose may need to be decreased by up to 50% or more when valproic acid is begun or increased when it is discontinued. • Monitor serum phenobarbital concentration; observe for signs of toxicity.
Phenobarbital (Barbiturates), see also anticoagulants (oral), antidepressants (cyclic), contraceptives (oral), corticosteroids, methadone, quinidine, theophyllines			
Phenylbutazone, see anticoagulants (oral), lithium, methotrexate			
Phenylephrine, see sympathomimetics			
Phenylpropanolamine, see sympathomimetics			
Phenytoin	**Enzyme inhibitors** amiodarone chloramphenicol cimetidine disulfiram fluconazole fluoxetine isoniazid omeprazole	• Serum phenytoin concentration is increased by inhibition of its hepatic metabolism possibly resulting in toxicity. • After an enzyme inhibitor is started in a patient on phenytoin, toxicity may take several days to several weeks to appear. • Disulfiram administration may cause serum phenytoin concentration to rise within a few hours of the first disulfiram dose. • Serum amiodarone concentration may be decreased, due to phenytoin's effect on metabolism of amiodarone. • Phenytoin may cause an increase or decrease in serum chloramphenicol concentration. • Slow isoniazid acetylators may be at greater risk. • Caution is advised with all SSRIs until more data are available.	• Phenytoin dose may need to be decreased when enzyme inhibitor is started or increased when it is discontinued. • Watch for signs and symptoms of phenytoin toxicity (e.g., nystagmus, ataxia, mental impairment) when enzyme inhibitor is added and for decreased response when it is discontinued; monitor serum phenytoin concentration. • Avoid concomitant use of chloramphenicol and phenytoin. • Monitor serum amiodarone concentration and antiarrhythmic efficacy during concurrent therapy with phenytoin. • Lansoprazole, ranitidine and famotidine do not appear to interact significantly with phenytoin.
Phenytoin, see also anticoagulants (oral), contraceptives (oral), corticosteroids, cyclosporine, itraconazole, methadone, quinidine, theophyllines			
Pindolol, see antidiabetic agents, beta-adrenergic blockers, calcium channel blockers			
Piroxicam, see anticoagulants (oral), lithium			
Potassium, see potassium-sparing diuretics			
Potassium-sparing diuretics amiloride spironolactone	**ACE inhibitors** benazepril captopril cilazapril	• Increase in serum potassium concentration occurs potentially resulting in hyperkalemia, especially in predisposed patients, possibly due to additive potassium-retaining effects.	• Monitor serum potassium concentration. • Presence of a potassium-depleting diuretic such as furosemide does not necessarily protect against interaction.

triamterene	enalapril fosinopril lisinopril perindopril quinapril ramipril trandolapril **Angiotensin II receptor blockers** irbesartan losartan valsartan	• Predisposing factors include renal impairment, high potassium diet (including salt substitutes), concomitant use of potassium supplements, severe diabetes, old age and possibly other factors.	
	Electrolytes potassium	• Possible large increase in serum potassium concentration due to reduced renal potassium excretion caused by the diuretic, potentially results in hyperkalemia, especially in predisposed patients (causing weakness, ECG changes, bradycardia complete heart block, cardiac arrest). Deaths and severe disabilities have occurred. • Predisposing factors include renal impairment, high potassium diet (including salt substitutes), concomitant use of ACE inhibitors, severe diabetes, advanced age. • The increase in potassium concentration develops over several days.	• Do not use combination except in patients with documented symptomatic hypokalemia refractory to either agent alone. • If combination is used, monitor serum potassium concentration closely; restrict dietary potassium intake.
Prednisolone, see corticosteroids			
Prednisone, see corticosteroids			
Primidone, see anticoagulants (oral), contraceptives (oral), quinidine, theophyllines			
Probenecid, see methotrexate			
Propafenone, see anticoagulants (oral)			
Propoxyphene, see antidepressants (cyclic), carbamazepine			
Propranolol, see antidiabetic agents, beta-adrenergic blockers, calcium channel blockers			
Protease inhibitors (PI) indinavir ritonavir saquinavir	**Enzyme inducers** rifabutin rifampin	• The enzyme responsible for metabolism of the PI, CYP3A4, is induced, resulting in reduced serum concentration. Loss of efficacy and development of resistant organisms may result.	• Avoid concurrent use if possible. • If not possible, the dose of the PI may require a substantial increase.
Protease inhibitors, see also antihistamines, benzodiazepines, cisapride, clozapine, ergot alkaloids, meperidine			
Protriptyline, see antidepressants (cyclic)			
Pseudoephedrine, see sympathomimetics			
Quinapril, see lithium, potassium-sparing diuretics			

Table I—Drug-Drug Interactions *(cont'd)*

Drug	Interacting Drug	Mechanism	Management
Quinidine	**Enzyme inducers** barbiturates phenytoin primidone rifampin	• Reduction in serum concentration and half-life of quinidine due to induction of metabolism, possibly resulting in loss of arrhythmia control. • The decrease in quinidine concentration develops gradually over a week or more after starting the enzyme inducer. • Induction may persist for several days following discontinuation of rifampin. • Interaction may occur with other enzyme inducers. • Withdrawing the enzyme inducer may lead to dose-related quinidine toxicity.	• Quinidine dose may need to be increased when enzyme inducer started or decreased when it is discontinued. • Monitor serum quinidine concentration and ECG.
Quinidine, see also antidepressants (cyclic), digitalis glycosides			
Quinolones ciprofloxacin grepafloxacin levofloxacin norfloxacin ofloxacin	**Antacids** **Didanosine** **Iron salts, oral** **Sucralfate**	• Reduced serum quinolone concentration occurs due to decreased absorption caused by magnesium- and aluminum-containing antacids or the magnesium- and aluminum-containing buffers in didanosine (possibly by greater than 90%), calcium-containing antacids (up to 60%), sucralfate (up to 90%) or iron. May lead to antimicrobial therapeutic failure. • Interaction with oral iron salts and the buffers contained in didanosine has only been reported for ciprofloxacin but should be considered possible for all quinolones.	• Administer the quinolone 2–4 hours before or 6 hours after antacid. • Administer the quinolone several hours before sucralfate. • If adequate spacing of doses is not feasible, consider using an H_2-receptor antagonist (e.g., cimetidine) instead of an antacid or sucralfate, using a different antibiotic or administering the quinolone i.v. if merited by the severity of the infection. • Avoid concomitant use of quinolones and iron salts.
Quinolones, see also anticoagulants (oral), theophyllines			
Ramipril, see lithium, potassium-sparing diuretics			
Rifabutin, see protease inhibitors			
Rifampin, see anticoagulants (oral), calcium channel blockers, contraceptives (oral), corticosteroids, cyclosporine, methadone, protease inhibitors, quinidine, theophyllines			
Ritodrine, see corticosteroids			
Ritonavir, see antihistamines, benzodiazepines, cisapride, clozapine, ergot alkaloids, meperidine, protease inhibitors			
Salicylates, see anticoagulants (oral), methotrexate			
Saquinavir, see protease inhibitors			
Selegiline, see dextromethorphan, meperidine, nefazodone, serotonin reuptake inhibitors, venlafaxine			
Serotonin reuptake inhibitors (SSRIs) fluoxetine fluvoxamine paroxetine sertraline	**MAOIs** phenelzine selegiline tranylcypromine	• Concurrent use of MAOIs and SSRIs may excessively increase CNS serotonin resulting in the serotonin syndrome. • Severe or fatal serotonin syndrome has been reported when a MAOI was started in patients on fluoxetine or sertraline. • Severe reactions have included tremor, agitation, restlessness, hypomania and hypertension. • May occur following 1 to 2 doses of fluoxetine.	• Combined use should be avoided. • A waiting period of 2 weeks after stopping the MAOI or 5 weeks after stopping fluoxetine or 2 weeks after stopping the other shorter acting SSRIs is recommended before starting the other agent. • Large combined doses of the MAOI moclobemide and a SSRI should be avoided on theoretical grounds.

		• Serotonin syndrome has not been reported with concomitant use of the reversible inhibitor of monoamine oxidase A, moclobemide and the SSRIs, fluoxetine, fluvoxamine, paroxetine or sertraline. Three fatalities have been reported with combined overdose of moclobemide and the SSRI, citalopram (not available in Canada). • Mania, hypertension and pseudopheochromocytoma have been reported with combined use of fluoxetine and selegiline.	
Serotonin reuptake inhibitors (SSRIs), see also anticoagulants (oral), antidepressants (cyclic), carbamazepine, phenytoin, theophyllines			
Sertraline, see serotonin reuptake inhibitors			
Simvastatin, see HMG-CoA reductase inhibitors			
Sotalol, see antidiabetic agents, beta-adrenergic blockers, calcium channel blockers			
Spironolactone, see potassium-sparing diuretics			
Streptomycin, see aminoglycosides			
Sucralfate, see quinolones			
Sulfamethoxazole-trimethoprim, see anticoagulants (oral)			
Sulfinpyrazone, see anticoagulants (oral)			
Sulfonylureas, see antidiabetic agents			
Sulindac, see anticoagulants (oral)			
Sumatriptan, see 5-HT$_1$ receptor agonists			
Sympathomimetics amphetamines ephedrine methylphenidate phenylephrine phenylpropanolamine pseudoephedrine	**MAOIs** moclobemide phenelzine tranylcypromine	• Increased effects of sympathomimetics (amphetamines, pseudoephedrine) due to a MAOI-induced increase in the amount of norepinephrine available for release from storage sites occurs, leading to severe hypertension, hyperpyrexia, headache, cerebral hemorrhage. • Deaths have been attributed to this interaction. • May occur following 1 to 2 doses of the sympathomimetic. • May occur if an amphetamine is taken up to several weeks after discontinuing the MAOI. • As the actions of epinephrine and norepinephrine are not terminated mainly by monoamine oxidase, a significant interaction with them is unlikely. • Parenteral phenylephrine is less likely than oral phenylephrine to interact with MAOIs. • An interaction between selegiline, a MAO-B inhibitor, and sympathomimetics is theoretically possible. • Methylphenidate causes less severe reactions than amphetamines when used with MAOIs.	• Avoid using sympathomimetics concomitantly with MAOIs. Epinephrine, methylphenidate, norepinephrine or parenteral phenylephrine may be coadministered cautiously with MAOIs.
Sympathomimetics, see also beta-adrenergic blockers			

Table I—Drug-Drug Interactions *(cont'd)*

Drug	Interacting Drug	Mechanism	Management
Terfenadine, see antihistamines			
Testosterone (Androgens), see anticoagulants (oral), cyclosporine			
Tetracyclines demeclocycline doxycycline minocycline tetracycline	**Antacids (di- and trivalent)** **Bismuth** **Iron salts**	• Impaired absorption of tetracyclines through formation of insoluble chelates with di- and trivalent metallic ions (aluminum, magnesium, calcium) in the antacid or with iron or bismuth, occurs therefore reducing the serum concentration and anti-infective activity of the tetracycline. • Serum iron concentration is also decreased. • Even given parenterally, doxycycline which is recirculated enterohepatically may be bound by iron or aluminum ions. • Interaction has not been reported with each tetracycline but is theoretically possible.	• Tetracyclines should be administered at least 2 hours before or after the antacid. • Give ferrous salts 3 hours before or 2 hours after a tetracycline. • H_2-receptor antagonists or proton pump inhibitors could provide alternatives to antacids in patients receiving a tetracycline. • Avoid concurrent use with bismuth.
Theophyllines aminophylline oxtriphylline theophylline	**Enzyme inducers** aminoglutethimide barbiturates carbamazepine phenytoin primidone rifampin	• Decrease in serum theophylline concentration is due to an increase in its hepatic metabolism by induction of microsomal enzymes, possibly leading to loss of theophylline efficacy. • Serum theophylline concentration probably declines over 1–2 weeks in most patients after enzyme inducer is begun and over several weeks after aminoglutethimide is begun. • Serum phenytoin concentration may be decreased on coadministration with theophylline. • Interaction has not been reported with aminophylline or oxtriphylline but is theoretically possible.	• Monitor serum theophylline concentration. • Dose of theophylline may need to be increased when enzyme inducer is started or decreased when it is discontinued. • Monitor serum phenytoin concentration.
	Enzyme inhibitors allopurinol beta-adrenergic blockers cimetidine ciprofloxacin disulfiram erythromycin fluvoxamine grepafloxacin mexiletine ticlopidine verapamil	• Increase in serum theophylline concentration due to a decrease in its hepatic metabolism by inhibition of microsomal enzymes, possibly leading to theophylline toxicity (e.g., tachycardia, tremor, GI upset, seizures). • Symptoms of theophylline toxicity may develop within 2–3 days of starting the enzyme inhibitor. • Allopurinol doses <600 mg/day are unlikely to produce toxicity. • Beta-adrenergic blockers known to interact are propranolol and metoprolol. Atenolol and nadolol do not alter theophylline kinetics but may antagonize its pharmacologic effect. • Use of ranitidine, famotidine or nizatidine would minimize the potential for this interaction. • Concurrent use with levofloxacin, norfloxacin or ofloxacin does not cause theophylline toxicity. • Clarithromycin may increase theophylline concentration about 20% but does not usually require a dosage change. Azithromycin does not appear to interact.	• Monitor serum theophylline concentration. • Dose of theophylline may need to be decreased when enzyme inhibitor is started or increased when it is discontinued.

		• Serum erythromycin concentration may be decreased on co-administration with theophylline. • Other SSRIs such as fluoxetine, paroxetine and sertraline are less likely to interact than fluvoxamine.	
Thiazide diuretics, see lithium			
Thyroid, see anticoagulants (oral)			
Thyroid hormones, see anticoagulants (oral)			
Ticlopidine, see theophyllines			
Timolol, see antidiabetic agents, beta-adrenergic blockers, calcium channel blockers			
Tobramycin, see aminoglycosides			
Tolbutamide, see antidiabetic agents			
Tolmetin, see anticoagulants (oral), methotrexate			
Topiramate, see contraceptives (oral)			
Trandolapril, see lithium, potassium-sparing diuretics			
Tranylcypromine, see antidepressants (cyclic), bupropion, buspirone, dextromethorphan, 5-HT_1 receptor agonists, levodopa, meperidine, nefazodone, serotonin reuptake inhibitors, sympathomimetics, venlafaxine			
Triamcinolone, see corticosteroids			
Triamterene, see potassium-sparing diuretics			
Triazolam, see benzodiazepines			
Trimethoprim-sulfamethoxazole, see anticoagulants (oral)			
Trimipramine, see antidepressants (cyclic)			
Uricosuric agents, see methotrexate			
Uterine-relaxing agents, see corticosteroids			
Valproic acid, see phenobarbital			
Valsartan, see lithium, potassium-sparing diuretics			
Venlafaxine	**MAOIs** phenelzine selegiline tranylcypromine	• Serotonin syndrome has been reported.	• Avoid concurrent use. • At least 14 days should elapse between discontinuation of either drug and initiation of other drug.
Verapamil, see antidepressants (cyclic), calcium channel blockers, carbamazepine, cyclosporine, digitalis glycosides, theophyllines			
Warfarin, see anticoagulants (oral)			
Zafirlukast, see anticoagulants (oral)			

DIETARY CONSIDERATIONS

The following is an overview on vitamin and mineral supplementation, food sources (Table I and II) and recommended nutrient intake (Table III and IV). This information is not intended to present a comprehensive review; the reader is therefore encouraged to seek additional and confirmatory information.

Reviewed 1999 by the Nutrition Research Division, Health Canada (P.W.F. Fischer).

Dietary Supplementation

Nutrition experts generally recommend people obtain all their vitamin needs from food, but there are circumstances when supplementation is warranted.

Infants

- All newborn infants should routinely be given a single injection of vitamin K at birth.
- Breast-fed infants may also need supplementation of vitamin D.
- Vitamin B_{12} should be given to infants breast-fed from strict vegetarian mothers.

Pregnant and lactating mothers

- Supplements are often appropriate because of the increased recommended intake of vitamins.
- An iron supplement is recommended during the second and third trimesters on the assumption that pre-pregnant iron stores might be inadequate. With normal iron stores, a supplement is unnecessary because storage iron will be used to meet iron needs.
- In view of the role of folic acid in the prevention of neural tube defects, folic acid supplementation should be recommended for all women as early as possible when planning their pregnancy.

Strict vegetarians

- Those who avoid meat, milk and eggs need supplements of vitamin B_{12} and D.

Older individuals

- For those who eat less food than required and therefore have a lower intake of vitamins, a multivitamin supplement may be beneficial.

Smokers

- Vitamin C intake needed to maintain an adequate vitamin C status is up to 50% higher in heavy smokers.

Individuals with little or no exposure to sunlight

- For those who have little or no exposure to sunlight, a vitamin D supplement may be required.

Table I—Mineral Food Sources

Mineral	Food Sources
Calcium	Milk, cheese, sardines, dark green leafy vegetables, dried beans and nuts.
Chromium	Meat (e.g., liver), dairy products, whole grains and brewer's yeast.
Copper	Organ meat (e.g., liver), shellfish and seafood, nuts, whole grains, dried peas and dried beans.
Iodine	Dairy products, bread, seafood, iodized table salt.
Iron	Red meat, poultry, organ meats (e.g., liver), dark green leafy vegetables, dried fruit, whole grains, nuts, beans and fish. Iron from animal sources is better absorbed than from plant sources.
Magnesium	Green leafy vegetables, nuts, whole grains, beans and seafood.
Potassium	Green leafy vegetables, fruit (e.g., bananas, oranges), potatoes, lean meat, whole grains and milk.
Selenium	Meat, seafoods, whole grains, dairy products and eggs.
Zinc	Lean meat, seafood (e.g., oysters), whole grains and legumes.

References:
1. Berner MS, Rotenberg GN, eds. The Canadian Medical Association guide to prescription and over-the-counter drugs. Montreal: The Reader's Digest Association, 1990.
2. Hands ES. Food finder: food sources of vitamins and minerals. Salem, OR: ESHA Research, 1990.

Table II—Vitamin Food Sources

Vitamin	Food Sources
Fat Soluble	
Vitamin A	Yellow-orange vegetables, dark green leafy vegetables, liver, whole milk, fortified skim milk, fortified dairy products.
Beta-carotene	Deep yellow-orange and deep green fruits and vegetables (e.g., carrots, spinach, lettuce, broccoli, squash, sweet potatoes, papaya, apricots).
Vitamin D	Fortified dairy products, fish and fish liver oil, liver.
Vitamin E	Vegetable oil (e.g., corn, soybean, safflower, cottonseed), wheat germ, whole-grain cereals and breads, green leafy vegetables.
Vitamin K	Green leafy vegetables, dairy products, eggs.
Water Soluble	
Folic acid	Dark green leafy vegetables, whole-grain cereals and breads, organ meats.
Niacin (vitamin B_3)	Meat, milk and dairy products, whole-grain cereals.
Pantothenic acid (vitamin B_5)	Organ meats (e.g., liver), egg yolk, whole-grain cereals and breads.
Riboflavin (vitamin B_2)	Milk and dairy products, green leafy vegetables, organ meats (e.g., liver, kidney), whole-grain and enriched cereals and breads.
Thiamine (vitamin B_1)	Whole-grain and enriched cereals and breads, meat (especially pork), peas, beans, nuts.
Vitamin B_6 (pyridoxine)	Organ meats, bananas, legumes (e.g., lima beans), egg yolk, whole grains.
Vitamin B_{12} (cyanocobalamin)	Fish, egg yolk, fermented cheese, meat (e.g., beef and organ meats).
Vitamin C (ascorbic acid)	Citrus fruit (e.g., oranges, lemons, grapefruit), green vegetables (e.g., peppers, broccoli, cabbage), potatoes.

Reference:
1. US Pharmacopeial Convention, Inc. USP DI, Drug information for the health care professional. Rockville, MD: US Pharmacopeial, Inc., 1994.

Table III*—RNI[a] of Vitamins Expressed as Daily Rates

				Fat Soluble			Water Soluble					
Age	**Sex**	**Weight (kg)**	**Protein (g)**	**Vitamin A (RE[b])**	**Vitamin D (μg[c])**	**Vitamin E (mg)**	**Vitamin C (mg)**	**Folate (μg)**	**Thiamine (mg)**	**Riboflavin (mg)**	**Niacin (NE[d])**	**Vitamin B_{12} (μg)**
Months												
0–4	Both	6	12[e]	400	10	3	20	25	0.3	0.3	4	0.3
5–12	Both	9	12	400	10	3	20	40	0.4	0.5	7	0.4
Years												
1	Both	11	13	400	10	3	20	40	0.5	0.6	8	0.5
2–3	Both	14	16	400	5	4	20	50	0.6	0.7	9	0.6
4–6	Both	18	19	500	5	5	25	70	0.7	0.9	13	0.8
7–9	M	25	26	700	2.5	7	25	90	0.9	1.1	16	1
	F	25	26	700	2.5	6	25	90	0.8	1	14	1
10–12	M	34	34	800	2.5	8	25	120	1	1.3	18	1
	F	36	36	800	2.5	7	25	130	0.9	1.1	16	1
13–15	M	50	49	900	2.5	9	30[f]	175	1.1	1.4	20	1
	F	48	46	800	2.5	7	30[f]	170	0.9	1.1	16	1
16–18	M	62	58	1 000	2.5	10	40[f]	220	1.3	1.6	23	1
	F	53	47	800	2.5	7	30[f]	190	0.8	1.1	15	1
19–24	M	71	61	1 000	2.5	10	40[f]	220	1.2	1.5	22	1
	F	58	50	800	2.5	7	30[f]	180	0.8	1.1	15	1
25–49	M	74	64	1 000	2.5	9	40[f]	230	1.1	1.4	19	1
	F	59	51	800	2.5	6	30[f]	185	0.8[g]	1[g]	14[g]	1
50–74	M	73	63	1 000	5	7	40[f]	230	0.9	1.2	16	1
	F	63	54	800	5	6	30[f]	195	0.8[g]	1	14[g]	1
75+	M	69	59	1 000	5	6	40[f]	215	0.8	1	14	1
	F	64	55	800	5	5	30[f]	200	0.8[g]	1	14[g]	1
Pregnancy (additional)												
1st Trimester			5	0	2.5	2	0	200	0.1	0.1	1	0.2
2nd Trimester			15	0	2.5	2	10	200	0.1	0.3	2	0.2
3rd Trimester			24	0	2.5	2	10	200	0.1	0.3	2	0.2
Lactation (additional)			22	400	2.5	3	25	100	0.2	0.4	3	0.2

* The RNIs are currently under review by the Food and Nutrition Board to harmonize new dietary reference intakes for Canada and the USA.
[a] Recommended Nutrient Intake (RNI) is expressed on a daily basis but should be regarded as the average recommended intake over a period of time, such as a week.
[b] Retinol Equivalents: 1 RE=1 μg or 3.33 IU retinol. 1RE=6 μg or 10 IU beta-carotene.
[c] 1 μg vitamin D_2 (ergocalciferol) or vitamin D_3 (cholecalciferol)=40 IU.
[d] Niacin Equivalents: 1 NE=1 mg niacin or 60 mg tryptophan. About 3% of ingested tryptophan is oxidized to niacin.
[e] Protein source is assumed to be from breast milk and must be adjusted for infant formula.
[f] Smokers should increase vitamin C by 50%.
[g] Level below which intake should not fall.

Adapted from *Nutrition Recommendations—the Report of the Scientific Review Committee*, 1990, with permission of the Minister of Public Works and Government Services Canada, 1998.

Reference:

1. Health and Welfare Canada. Folic acid: the vitamin that helps protect against neural tube (birth) defects. Issues 1993; 1-5.

Table IV*—RNI[a] of Minerals Expressed as Daily Rates

Age	Sex	Weight (kg)	Protein (g)	Calcium[b] (mg)	Phosphorus (mg)	Magnesium (mg)	Iron (mg)	Iodine (μg)	Zinc (mg)
Months									
0–4	Both	6	12[c]	250[d]	150	20	0.3[e]	30	2[e]
5–12	Both	9	12	400	200	32	7	40	3
Years									
1	Both	11	13	500	300	40	6	55	4
2–3	Both	14	16	550	350	50	6	65	4
4–6	Both	18	19	600	400	65	8	85	5
7–9	M	25	26	700	500	100	8	110	7
	F	25	26	700	500	100	8	95	7
10–12	M	34	34	900	700	130	8	125	9
	F	36	36	1 100	800	135	8	110	9
13–15	M	50	49	1 100	900	185	10	160	12
	F	48	46	1 000	850	180	13	160	9
16–18	M	62	58	900	1 000	230	10	160	12
	F	53	47	700	850	200	12	160	9
19–24	M	71	61	800	1 000	240	9	160	12
	F	58	50	700	850	200	13	160	9
25–49	M	74	64	800	1 000	250	9	160	12
	F	59	51	700	850	200	13	160	9
50–74	M	73	63	800	1 000	250	9	160	12
	F	63	54	800	850	210	8	160	9
75+	M	69	59	800	1 000	230	9	160	12
	F	64	55	800	850	210	8	160	9
Pregnancy (additional)									
1st Trimester			5	500	200	15	0	25	6
2nd Trimester			15	500	200	45	5	25	6
3rd Trimester			24	500	200	45	10	25	6
Lactation (additional)			22	500	200	65	0	50	6

* The RNIs are currently under review by the Food and Nutrition Board to harmonize new dietary reference intakes for Canada and the USA.
[a] Recommended Nutrient Intake (RNI) is expressed on a daily basis, but should be regarded as the average recommended intake over a period of time, such as a week.
[b] Other RNI exist, such as the National Institutes of Health Consensus Development Conference Statement. Optimal Calcium Intake. Washington, DC June 6–8, 1994.
[c] Protein source is assumed to be from breast milk and must be adjusted for infant formula.
[d] A typical infant formula with high phosphorus should contain 375 mg calcium per 750 mL of formula.
[e] Breast milk is assumed to be the source of the mineral.

Adapted from *Nutrition Recommendations—the Report of the Scientific Review Committee*, 1990, with permission of the Minister of Public Works and Government Services Canada, 1998.

DRUG ADMINISTRATION AND FOOD

Table I provides an overview of current recommendations for administration of drugs with respect to food. This information is not intended to present a comprehensive review; the reader is therefore encouraged to seek additional and confirmatory information.

Reviewed 1999

Compliance with medication regimens may be encouraged by scheduling drug administration to coincide with routine activities such as meal times. Foods or beverages may interact with medications, affecting bioavailability, metabolism or excretion. While such interactions can influence the effectiveness of a drug by altering the anticipated therapeutic effect, the clinical significance of most food-drug interactions is not clear.

The recommendations for administration of drugs in relation to food are compiled from recognized sources including the information provided by the manufacturer for the *CPS* 1999. Whether medications should be chewed or crushed has also been noted. These recommendations are not absolute; clinical judgment must be used in their interpretation. More important is the consistency of drug administration to facilitate compliance and prevent fluctuations in the therapeutic effect of the drug.

The headings used in the table are described as follows:

- **Empty Stomach**—1 hour before or 2 hours after meals with a full glass of liquid, usually water.
- **Before Meals**—usually 15 to 30 minutes before meals.
- **Empty Stomach Preferably**—may be taken with food if gastric upset occurs.
- **With or After Meals.**
- **With or Without Food**—may be given without regard to meals.

Table I—Drug Administration and Food

Drug Name	Empty Stomach	Before Meals	Empty Stomach Preferably	With or After Meals	With or Without Food	Comments
acarbose				•		with first bite of meal
acebutolol					•	
acetaminophen					•	
acetazolamide					•	
acitretin				•		
acyclovir					•	
alendronate		•				at least 30 min before meals with a glass of water
alfacalcidol					•	
alginic acid					•	chew tablets
allopurinol				•		food decreases gastric irritation
alpha-D-galactosidase				•		
alprazolam					•	
altretamine				•		
aluminum and magnesium hydroxides					•	
amantadine					•	food decreases gastric irritation
amiloride					•	food decreases gastric irritation
aminoglutethimide					•	
aminophylline			•			with a glass of water
aminosalicylate sodium					•	
5-aminosalicylic acid		•				with a glass of water; do not crush or chew
amiodarone					•	food decreases gastric irritation
amitriptyline					•	
amlodipine					•	
amoxapine					•	
amoxicillin					•	
amoxicillin/clavulanic acid					•	food increases absorption
ampicillin	•					
anagrelide					•	
anastrozole					•	
anetholtrithione		•				
anileridine					•	
ASA—plain				•		
—EC				•		do not crush or chew
astemizole					•	

Table I—Drug Administration and Food *(cont'd)*

Drug Name	Empty Stomach	Before Meals	Empty Stomach Preferably	With or After Meals	With or Without Food	Comments
atenolol					•	food decreases gastric irritation
atorvastatin calcium					•	
atovaquone				•		
azatadine					•	
azathioprine					•	food decreases gastric irritation
azithromycin—capsules, suspension	•					
—tablets					•	
bacampicillin					•	with a glass of water
baclofen					•	food decreases gastric irritation
barbiturates					•	absorption faster on empty stomach
belladonna					•	
benazepril					•	
betahistine					•	
bethanechol	•					
bezafibrate—200 mg regular				•		with a glass of water
—400 mg SR				•		do not crush or chew
bicalutamide					•	do not crush or chew
biperiden				•		food decreases gastric irritation
bisacodyl	•					with a glass of water; do not take with milk; do not crush or chew
bismuth subsalicylate					•	
bromazepam					•	
bromocriptine				•		
budesonide		•				with a glass of water; do not crush or chew
bumetanide					•	
bupropion					•	
buspirone					•	
calcitriol					•	
calcium salts				•		food decreases gastric irritation; some foods decrease absorption
captopril			•			be consistent
carbamazepine—regular				•		
—CR				•		do not crush or chew
carisoprodol					•	food decreases gastric irritation
carvedilol				•		
cefaclor					•	
cefadroxil					•	food decreases gastric irritation
cefixime					•	
cefprozil					•	
cefuroxime axetil					•	do not crush or chew; food increases absorption
cephalexin					•	
cerivastatin					•	with the evening meal or at bedtime
cetirizine					•	
chlophedianol					•	
chloral hydrate					•	with a glass of water; do not crush or chew
chlorambucil					•	
chloramphenicol			•			food decreases gastric irritation
chlordiazepoxide					•	
chloroquine				•		
chlorpheniramine					•	
chlorpromazine					•	
chlorpropamide					•	long half-life; not necessary with meals
chlorthalidone				•		

Table I—Drug Administration and Food *(cont'd)*

Drug Name	Empty Stomach	Before Meals	Empty Stomach Preferably	With or After Meals	With or Without Food	Comments
chlorzoxazone				•		food decreases gastric irritation
cholecalciferol					•	
cholera vaccine	•					1 hour before a meal; with a glass of cold or lukewarm water only
cholestyramine				•		
choline salicylate				•		
cilazapril					•	be consistent
cimetidine					•	
ciprofloxacin					•	with a glass of water; food decreases gastric irritation
cisapride		•				
citric acid/sodium citrate				•		
clarithromycin					•	
clemastine		•				with a glass of water
clindamycin					•	with a glass of water
clobazam					•	
clodronate	•					with a glass of water; do not take with milk; do not crush or chew
clofibrate				•		
clomiphene					•	
clomipramine					•	food decreases gastric irritation
clonazepam					•	
clonidine					•	
clopidogrel					•	
clorazepate					•	
cloxacillin	•					
clozapine					•	
codeine					•	
colchicine					•	food decreases gastric irritation
colestipol—granules					•	
—tablets				•		with a glass of water; do not crush or chew
cortisone acetate				•		food decreases gastric irritation
cyclobenzaprine					•	
cyclophosphamide			•			food decreases gastric irritation
cycloserine					•	
cyclosporine					•	be consistent; do not crush or chew; do not take with grapefruit juice
cyproheptadine					•	
cyproterone				•		
danazol					•	
dantrolene					•	
dapsone				•		
dehydrocholic acid				•		
demeclocycline	•					do not take with milk
desipramine					•	
desmopressin acetate					•	
dexamethasone				•		
dexamphetamine					•	
dextromethorphan					•	
dextrothyroxine					•	
diazepam					•	
diazoxide					•	be consistent
diclofenac—regular				•		
—SR				•		do not crush or chew

Table I—Drug Administration and Food *(cont'd)*

Drug Name	Empty Stomach	Before Meals	Empty Stomach Preferably	With or After Meals	With or Without Food	Comments
dicyclomine					●	
didanosine	●					
diethylpropion	●					
diethylstilbestrol					●	
diflunisal				●		do not crush or chew
digoxin					●	
dihydrotachysterol					●	
diltiazem—regular		●				
—SR or CD					●	do not crush or chew
dimenhydrinate					●	
diphenhydramine					●	
diphenoxylate					●	
dipyridamole			●			food decreases gastric irritation
disopyramide					●	
disulfiram					●	
divalproex sodium				●		food decreases gastric irritation
docusate calcium/sodium					●	with a glass of water
dolasetron					●	
domperidone		●				
donepezil					●	
doxazosin					●	
doxepin					●	
doxycycline					●	with a glass of water; food or milk reduces absorption
doxylamine/pyridoxine					●	
dronabinol					●	
enalapril					●	
ergocalciferol					●	
ergoloid mesylates				●		
ergotamine				●		
erythromycin—base			●			if enteric coated, do not crush or chew
—estolate				●		food decreases gastric irritation
—ethylsuccinate			●			
—stearate			●			food decreases absorption
erythromycin/sulfisoxazole					●	
estramustine	●					with a glass of water; do not take with milk
estrogens					●	
ethacrynic acid				●		
ethambutol					●	food decreases gastric irritation
ethchlorvynol					●	
ethopropazine					●	
ethosuximide					●	food decreases gastric irritation
etidronate	●					with a glass of water; do not take with milk
etodolac				●		
famciclovir					●	do not crush or chew
famotidine					●	
felodipine					●	do not crush or chew
fenofibrate				●		
fenoprofen				●		
feverfew				●		with a glass of water
fexofenadine					●	
finasteride					●	
flavoxate				●		

Table I—Drug Administration and Food *(cont'd)*

Drug Name	Empty Stomach	Before Meals	Empty Stomach Preferably	With or After Meals	With or Without Food	Comments
flecainide					•	
floctafenine				•		with a glass of water
floxacillin	•					
fluconazole					•	food decreases gastric irritation
fludrocortisone				•		
flunarizine					•	
fluoxetine					•	
fluoxymesterone					•	
flupenthixol					•	
fluphenazine					•	
flurazepam					•	
flurbiprofen—regular				•		
—SR				•		do not crush or chew
flutamide					•	
fluvastatin					•	at bedtime
fluvoxamine					•	with a glass of water
folic acid					•	
fosinopril					•	food decreases absorption
furosemide					•	
fusidic acid				•		food decreases gastric irritation
gabapentin					•	
ganciclovir				•		
gemfibrozil		•				
gliclazide					•	long half-life; not necessary with food
glyburide					•	long half-life; not necessary with food
glycopyrrolate					•	
granisetron					•	
grepafloxacin					•	
griseofulvin					•	high fat meal increases absorption
guaifenesin					•	
guanethidine					•	
halofantrine	•					
haloperidol					•	
hydralazine					•	
hydrochlorothiazide					•	
hydrocodone				•		
hydrocortisone				•		
hydromorphone—regular					•	
—SR					•	do not crush or chew
hydroxychloroquine				•		
hydroxyurea					•	
hydroxyzine					•	
hyoscyamine					•	
ibuprofen				•		food decreases gastric irritation
imipramine					•	
indapamide					•	
indinavir			•			
indomethacin—regular				•		food decreases gastric irritation
—SR				•		do not crush or chew
inosiplex					•	
iodoquinol				•		
irbesartan					•	
iron salts			•			food decreases absorption

Table I—Drug Administration and Food *(cont'd)*

Drug Name	Empty Stomach	Before Meals	Empty Stomach Preferably	With or After Meals	With or Without Food	Comments
isoniazid			•			food decreases absorption
isosorbide dinitrate—regular	•					with a glass of water
—SR					•	do not crush or chew
isosorbide mononitrate					•	with a glass of water; do not crush or chew
isotretinoin				•		
itraconazole				•		
ketazolam					•	
ketoconazole				•		
ketoprofen—regular				•		food decreases gastric irritation
—EC or SR			•			do not crush or chew
ketorolac				•		food decreases gastric irritation
ketotifen				•		
labetalol				•		
lactase				•		immediately before meals
lactobacillus acidophilus				•		do not crush or chew
lactulose					•	with a glass of water
lamivudine					•	
lamotrigine					•	
lansoprazole		•				with a glass of water
letrozole					•	
levamisole					•	
levocarnitine					•	
levodopa/benserazide			•			be consistent
levodopa/carbidopa—regular			•			be consistent
—CR			•			do not crush or chew
levofloxacin					•	
levothyroxine	•					
lincomycin	•					
lisinopril					•	
lithium salts—regular					•	
—SR					•	do not crush or chew
lomustine	•					fasting decreases nausea and vomiting
loperamide					•	
loratadine	•					
lorazepam					•	
losartan					•	be consistent
lovastatin				•		with evening meal
loxapine					•	
magnesium salts					•	with a glass of water
maprotiline					•	
mazindol			•			
mebendazole					•	
meclizine					•	
meclizine/nicotinic acid		•				with meals if excessive flushing occurs
medroxyprogesterone					•	
mefenamic acid				•		
mefloquine				•		
megestrol					•	
melphalan					•	
meprobamate					•	
mercaptopurine					•	
mesoridazine					•	
metformin				•		food decreases gastric irritation

Table I—Drug Administration and Food *(cont'd)*

Drug Name	Empty Stomach	Before Meals	Empty Stomach Preferably	With or After Meals	With or Without Food	Comments
methazolamide					•	food decreases gastric irritation
methenamine				•		food decreases gastric irritation
methimazole					•	
methocarbamol					•	
methotrexate					•	food decreases gastric irritation
methotrimeprazine					•	
methoxsalen				•		
methsuximide					•	food decreases gastric irritation
methyldopa					•	
methylphenidate—regular			•			preferably 30–45 min before meals
—SR			•			do not crush or chew
methylprednisolone				•		
methyltestosterone					•	
methysergide				•		
metoclopramide		•				
metolazone					•	
metoprolol—regular					•	food increases absorption; be consistent
—SR					•	do not crush or chew
metronidazole					•	food decreases gastric irritation
mexiletine				•		with a glass of water
midodrine					•	
mineral oil	•					
minocycline					•	food or milk reduces absorption
minoxidil					•	with a glass of water
misoprostol				•		
moclobemide				•		
montelukast sodium					•	
morphine—regular					•	
—SR					•	do not crush or chew
multivitamins					•	
mycophenolate	•					be consistent; do not crush or chew
nabilone					•	
nabumetone				•		with a glass of water; do not crush or chew; food decreases gastric irritation
nadolol					•	
nalidixic acid				•		
naltrexone					•	
naproxen—regular				•		food decreases gastric irritation
—SR				•		do not crush or chew
naratriptan					•	
nefazodone					•	
neomycin					•	
niacin—regular				•		
—SR				•		do not crush or chew
nicardipine					•	
nicoumalone					•	be consistent
nifedipine—regular					•	
—XL					•	do not crush or chew
nilutamide		•				before breakfast
nimodipine					•	
nitrazepam					•	
nitrofurantoin				•		
nitroglycerin—regular	•					with a glass of water
—SR	•					do not crush or chew

Table I—Drug Administration and Food *(cont'd)*

Drug Name	Empty Stomach	Before Meals	Empty Stomach Preferably	With or After Meals	With or Without Food	Comments
nizatidine					•	
norfloxacin			•			
normethadone				•		
nortriptyline					•	
nylidrin					•	
nystatin					•	
ofloxacin					•	
olanzapine					•	
olsalazine				•		
omeprazole					•	
ondansetron					•	
orciprenaline					•	
orphenadrine					•	
oxaprozin				•		
oxazepam					•	
oxprenolol					•	
oxtriphylline—regular			•			with a glass of water
—SA			•			do not crush or chew
oxybutynin					•	
oxycodone					•	
pancreatic enzymes				•		with a glass of water; do not crush or chew
pantoprazole					•	with a glass of water; do not crush or chew
paraldehyde					•	in milk or fruit juice
paromomycin				•		
paroxetine					•	
PAS sodium				•		food decreases gastric irritation
pemoline					•	
penicillamine	•					push fluids; do not take with milk
penicillin G	•					
penicillin V					•	
pentaerythritol tetranitrate		•				
pentazocine				•		
pentosan polysulfate	•					with a glass of water
pentoxifylline				•		
peppermint oil	•					
pepsin				•		
pergolide					•	
pericyazine					•	
perindopril	•					
perphenazine					•	
pethidine					•	
phenazopyridine				•		
phenelzine					•	follow MAO inhibitor diet
phenoxymethyl penicillin	•					
phentermine		•				
phenylbutazone				•		
phenylpropanolamine					•	
phenytoin				•		food decreases gastric irritation
phosphates					•	with a glass of water
pilocarpine					•	do not crush or chew
pimozide					•	
pinaverium				•		with a glass of water
pindolol				•		

Table I—Drug Administration and Food *(cont'd)*

Drug Name	Empty Stomach	Before Meals	Empty Stomach Preferably	With or After Meals	With or Without Food	Comments
piroxicam				•		
pivampicillin					•	
pivmecillinam					•	
pizotifen					•	
potassium salts—regular				•		food decreases gastric irritation
—SR				•		do not crush or chew
pramipexole					•	
pravastatin					•	food decreases absorption
praziquantel				•		with a glass of water
prazosin					•	
prednisone				•		
primaquine				•		food decreases gastric irritation
primidone			•			
probenecid					•	food decreases gastric irritation
procainamide—regular					•	
—SR					•	do not crush or chew
procarbazine					•	
prochlorperazine					•	
procyclidine				•		
proguanil				•		
promethazine		•				
propafenone				•		
propantheline		•				
propoxyphene					•	
propranolol					•	food increases absorption; be consistent
propylthiouracil					•	
protriptyline					•	
pseudoephedrine					•	
psyllium					•	with a glass of water
pyrantel					•	
pyrazinamide					•	
pyridostigmine—regular					•	
—SR					•	do not crush or chew
pyridoxine					•	
pyrimethamine				•		
pyrvinium pamoate				•		
quetiapine					•	
quinapril					•	
quinidine					•	food decreases gastric irritation
quinine				•		
raloxifene					•	
ramipril					•	be consistent
ranitidine					•	
ranitidine bismuth citrate					•	
reserpine				•		
riboflavin					•	
rifabutin					•	food decreases gastric irritation
rifampin			•			
risperidone					•	
ritodrine					•	food decreases gastric irritation
ritonavir				•		
ropinirole					•	
salbutamol					•	

Table I—Drug Administration and Food *(cont'd)*

Drug Name	Empty Stomach	Before Meals	Empty Stomach Preferably	With or After Meals	With or Without Food	Comments
salsalate				•		
saquinavir				•		do not crush or chew
selegiline				•		follow MAO inhibitor diet
senna					•	with a glass of water
sertraline				•		
simethicone				•		
simvastatin					•	food increases absorption
sodium bicarbonate					•	
sodium chloride					•	
sodium cromoglycate		•				
sodium fluoride				•		
sotalol					•	
spiramycin					•	
spironolactone					•	food increases absorption
stavudine					•	
sterculia gum					•	with a glass of water; do not chew
sucralfate	•					with a glass of water
sulfadiazine	•					with a glass of water
sulfadiazine/trimethoprim				•		with a glass of water; food decreases gastric irritation
sulfadoxine/pyrimethamine				•		with a glass of water; food decreases gastric irritation
sulfamethoxazole/trimethoprim				•		with a glass of water; food decreases gastric irritation
sulfapyridine	•					with a glass of water
sulfasalazine—regular				•		
—EC				•		do not crush or chew
sulfinpyrazone				•		
sulfisoxazole	•					with a glass of water
sulindac				•		food decreases gastric irritation
sumatriptan					•	with a glass of water
tacrolimus					•	be consistent; do not crush or chew
tamoxifen					•	
tamsulosin				•		do not crush, chew or open capsules
temazepam					•	
tenoxicam				•		food decreases gastric irritation
terazosin					•	
terbinafine					•	food increases absorption
terbutaline					•	
terfenadine					•	
testosterone				•		
tetrabenazine					•	
tetracycline	•					with a glass of water; do not take with milk
theophylline—liquids			•			
—regular tablets			•			
—SR tablets,					•	be consistent; do not crush or chew
except Uniphyl				•		with evening meal; do not crush or chew
thiabendazole				•		
thiamine					•	
thioproperazine					•	
thioridazine					•	
thiothixene					•	
thyroid, dessicated					•	

Table I—Drug Administration and Food *(cont'd)*

Drug Name	Empty Stomach	Before Meals	Empty Stomach Preferably	With or After Meals	With or Without Food	Comments
tiaprofenic acid—regular				•		
—SR				•		do not crush or chew
ticlopidine				•		food decreases gastric irritation
timolol					•	
tocainide					•	
tolbutamide		•				short half-life; give before meals
tolcapone					•	
tolmetin				•		food decreases gastric irritation
topiramate					•	with a glass of water; do not crush or chew
torsemide					•	
trandolapril					•	
tranexamic acid					•	
tranylcypromine					•	follow MAO inhibitor diet
trazodone				•		food decreases gastric irritation
triamcinolone				•		
triamterene				•		
triamterene/hydrochlorothiazide				•		
triazolam					•	
trifluoperazine					•	
trihexyphenidyl					•	food decreases gastric irritation
trimebutine		•				
trimeprazine				•		
trimethoprim				•		
trimipramine					•	
trioxsalen				•		
tripelennamine					•	food decreases gastric irritation
l-tryptophan				•		food decreases gastric irritation
typhoid vaccine	•					with a cold or lukewarm drink; do not crush or chew
ursodiol				•		
valacyclovir					•	
valproic acid				•		food decreases gastric irritation
valsartan					•	
vancomycin					•	nonabsorbable
venlafaxine				•		
verapamil—regular				•		
—SR				•		do not crush or chew
vigabatrin					•	
vitamin A					•	
vitamin B_{12}					•	
vitamin C				•		with a glass of water
vitamin E					•	do not crush or chew
warfarin					•	avoid abrupt changes in diet to maintain constant vitamin K intake
yohimbine					•	
zafirlukast	•					
zalcitabine	•					
zidovudine	•					
zinc				•		
zopiclone					•	
zuclopenthixol					•	

References:

1. McCormack J (ed.). Drug Therapy Decision Making Guide. W.B. Saunders Company, Philadelphia, PA, 1996.
2. Olin BR (ed.). Facts and Comparisons. Facts and Comparisons, Inc., St. Louis, MO, 1996.

PATIENT INFORMATION

Information for the Patient sections are part of the Product Monograph as defined by Health Canada, but they are intended to be used separately as patient information. They contain information, in lay language, that is required by the patient for safe and effective use of the drug. Health care professionals may wish to supplement the advice given within these sections as necessary.

This section is provided for health care professionals to use in keeping their patients informed. Although the Canadian Pharmacists Association maintains copyright for this compiled work, we grant permission to photocopy the contents of these pages for the purpose of providing information to patients. Distribution of photocopies of this section in its entirety is not permitted.

References:

1. Health and Welfare Canada. Product Monographs. Ottawa, ON: Health and Welfare Canada, 1989.

PATIENT INFORMATION INDEX

PATIENT INFORMATION INDEX *(cont'd)*

PATIENT INFORMATION INDEX *(cont'd)*

* Information for the Patient on Oral Contraceptives is reproduced separately at the end of this section (p. B271–B275).

☐ ABENOL®

SmithKline Beecham

Acetaminophen

Analgesic—Antipyretic

Information for the Patient: This information is also intended to be used separately as a Consumer Insert.

Suppositories: Supplemental Information: **For rectal use only.**

Indications: Abenol suppositories are used to relieve mild to moderate pain, and to reduce fever.

Instructions:
- Wash hands with soap and water.
- Remove plastic wrapper.
- Moisten suppository with cool water.
- Lie on side with bottom leg straight and upper leg bent up towards chest. Gently push suppository as high as possible into rectum.
- Wash hands with soap and water.

Dosage: Adults: One suppository (650 mg) every 4 to 6 hours as necessary. Do not use immediately before bowel movement. Maximum daily dosage recommended is 6 suppositories.

Children: Under 2 years: As recommended by the physician. 2 to 4 years: One suppository (120 mg) every 4 hours. Maximum daily dosage recommended is 6 suppositories. 4 to 6 years: One suppository (325 mg) every 6 hours. Maximum daily dosage recommended is 4 suppositories. 6 to 12 years: One suppository (325 mg) every 4 hours. Maximum daily dosage recommended is 6 suppositories.

Drug Interaction: Concomitant use of acetaminophen and an anticoagulant may increase the time necessary for blood to coagulate.

A physician or pharmacist should be consulted prior to taking this medication in case of:
- allergy to acetaminophen, chronic alcoholism, kidney or liver disease; and
- intake of other medications containing acetaminophen and salicylates.

Adverse Effects: Rare instances of hypersensitivity to acetaminophen are usually manifested by a rash or urticaria.

Treatment of Overdosage: In the event of accidental ingestion of large quantities of suppositories, it is recommended to induce vomiting and to consult a physician.

Caution: Consult your physician if symptoms persist after more than 5 days treatment. Do not exceed recommended dosage unless advised by a physician, since excessive doses may cause liver damage.

Storage: Store at room temperature.

☐ ACCOLATE® ℞

Zeneca

Zafirlukast

Leukotriene Receptor Antagonist

Information for the Patient: Please read this leaflet carefully before you start to take your medicine. For further information or advice, ask your doctor or pharmacist.

Accolate tablets should be used only twice a day. Accolate is one of a group of medicines called leukotriene receptor antagonists. Accolate is used to prevent your asthma from getting worse, and control your asthma symptoms. Accolate's effect lasts up to 12 hours. That's why it is important to take Accolate twice a day, in the morning and evening. Regular use of Accolate will help to control your symptoms throughout the day and during the night.

Accolate should not be taken with meals. You should take your Accolate tablets on an empty stomach (at least 1 hour before or 2 hours after meals). This will ensure you absorb as much medicine as possible each time.

Accolate should not be used as relief medication. Accolate does not act quickly enough to be used as a relief medication. If you get a sudden attack of wheezing and breathlessness between doses of Accolate, you should take 1 or 2 puffs from a fast-acting relief medication (e.g., salbutamol) that your doctor has given you.

Remember, if you have an attack that does not get better when you take the relief medication you should see your doctor right away. You may need emergency treatment.

You should tell your doctor as soon as possible if you:
- are getting more attacks of wheezing, breathlessness or chest tightness,
- are using an increasing amount of fast-acting relief medication,
- start to wake up at night with chest tightness, wheezing or shortness of breath.

How Your Medicine Works: Accolate is a leukotriene receptor antagonist that blocks substances called leukotrienes. Leukotrienes cause narrowing and swelling of airways in your lungs. Blocking leukotrienes improves asthma symptoms and helps prevent asthma attacks.

Important Points to Note Before Taking Your Medicine: Have you ever had to stop taking another medication for your breathing problems because it caused problems or you were allergic to it? Have you ever been told that you have problems with your liver? If the answer is **yes** to either of these questions, make sure your doctor or pharmacist knows as soon as possible.

Make sure your doctor knows about **all** other medicines you are taking (**including nonprescription or over the counter products**), especially blood thinners (e.g., Coumadin), allergy medications (e.g., Seldane, Hismanal), ASA, antibiotics and theophylline.

Use of this Medication During Pregnancy or Breast-feeding: Do not take Accolate during pregnancy or while breast-feeding without discussing this with your doctor first. Similarly, let your doctor know about future pregnancies you are planning.

Taking your Medicine: Follow your doctor's instructions about when and how to take your tablets. Please **read the label** on the package. Ask your doctor or pharmacist if you are not sure. For patients 12 years of age and older: the usual treatment with Accolate is 20 mg twice daily.
- Swallow each tablet whole with a full glass of water.
- Do not take your tablet(s) with a meal (at least 1 hour before or 2 hours after meals).
- Try to take your medicine at the same times each day.

Regular use of Accolate is very important in controlling your asthma. Accolate is taken twice daily, in the morning and evening. To help you remember your schedule, your tablets are provided in convenient calendar packs labeled with the days of the week (2 spots/day, a.m. and p.m.). Before starting Accolate make sure you note the day of the week. Punch out and take the tablet labeled ''Start''. Your next tablet will be taken approximately 12 hours later. When it comes time for this dose, punch out the tablet corresponds with that day and time. Then, keep following the calendar system. This will help you remember whether you have taken 2 doses every day, in the morning and again in the evening. As you finish a tablet card, note the day and time of the last dose. Then, continue the next card approximately 12 hours later, at ''Start'', and follow the calendar system again. As you get to the end of your last card, call your pharmacist for a refill, preferably before using the last 4 tablets.

Remember: Do not stop taking your tablets even if you are feeling well, unless your doctor tells you.

Undesirable Effects that May be Experienced with Accolate: As with all medicines, undesirable effects are sometimes experienced. With Accolate these may include headache or gastrointestinal disturbances (indigestion or stomach upsets). These are usually mild and are unlikely to result in you needing to stop treatment. Allergic reactions including skin rash have been seen in a small number of patients given Accolate.

Tell your doctor or pharmacist if you think you have any of these or any other problems.

Occasionally Accolate may cause some changes to occur in your liver. In some people these changes could make you feel:
- sick or be sick,
- tired or lacking energy,
- like you have flu,
- itchy.

Other signs include:
- pain on the right side of your stomach, just below your ribs,
- a yellow coloring of your skin and eyes (jaundice).

If you think you have any of these **tell your doctor immediately.**

If you Take too Much: If you accidentally take a larger dose than recommended, tell your doctor as soon as possible.

For an excessive overdose tell your doctor immediately or contact your hospital emergency department.

If you Miss a Dose: If you forget to take a dose, do not worry. Take another tablet just as soon as you remember. **But** if it is near the time for the next dose, wait until this dose is due. Then go on as before. **Do not take a double dose.**

Storing your Medicine: Keep your medicine where children cannot reach it. Your medicine can harm them.

Accolate (cont'd)

You should store your tablets between 15 and 30°C (room temperature). Keep your tablets in the original package.

If your doctor decides to stop your treatment, return your tablets to the pharmacist for disposal.

Do not take your tablets after the expiry date on the package. Return the tablets to your pharmacist for disposal.

What's in your Accolate Tablet: Each Accolate tablet contains 20 mg of zafirlukast. Each tablet is film-coated and also contains the inactive ingredients: croscarmellose sodium, lactose, microcrystalline cellulose, polyvidone, magnesium stearate, methylhydroxypropylcellulose and titanium dioxide.

Remember: This medicine was prescribed only for **you.** Only a doctor knows who can use it safely. Never give it to someone else. It may harm them, even if their symptoms are the same as yours.

Further Information: If you go into hospital, let the medical staff know that you are taking Accolate.

If you have any questions or are not sure about anything to do with your medicine, then ask your doctor or pharmacist. You may need to read this leaflet again. **Please do not throw it away** until you have finished your medicine.

☐ ACCUTANE™ ROCHE® 🄿

Roche

Isotretinoin

Acne Therapy

Information for the Patient: Accutane is a medicine used to treat certain types of severe acne, difficult to treat by other methods. For your health, safety, and well being, it is **important** that you read the following information.

Accutane can cause deformed babies if it is taken by a female when she is pregnant. Your doctor has a line drawing of one of these deformed babies which you should ask to see.

Important Information for Female Patients:

- **Do not take Accutane if you are or may become pregnant during your Accutane treatment.**
- **You must avoid becoming pregnant while you are taking Accutane and for at least 1 month after you stop taking Accutane.**
- **You must discuss effective birth control with your doctor before beginning Accutane treatment, and you must use effective birth control: for at least 1 month before you start Accutane; while you are taking Accutane; and for at least 1 month after you stop taking Accutane; bearing in mind that any method of birth control can fail.**
- **It is recommended that you either abstain from sexual intercourse or use 2 reliable methods of birth control at the same time.**
- **Do not take Accutane until you are sure that you are not pregnant. You must have a serum or urine pregnancy test within the 2 weeks before you start Accutane. You must wait until the second or third day of your next normal menstrual period before you start Accutane.**
- **Contact your doctor immediately if you do become pregnant while taking Accutane or during the first month after treatment has stopped. You should discuss with your doctor the serious risk of your baby having severe birth deformities because you are taking or have taken Accutane. You should also discuss the desirability of continuing with your pregnancy.**
- **Do not breast-feed while taking Accutane.**

Important Information for All Patients: **Pregnancy must be avoided by any female taking Accutane as Accutane can cause deformed babies** (see Important Information for Female Patients).

- Be sure to return to your doctor as scheduled. It is important for your doctor to see you regularly, preferably every month, when you are taking Accutane. Blood tests and other tests allow your doctor to check your response to Accutane. Discuss your progress and any concerns with your doctor.
- Do not give Accutane to anyone else who has similar symptoms. Accutane has to be prescribed for each person by their own doctor because of possible side effects (see below). **Important: Accutane can cause deformed babies if taken by a female when she is pregnant.**
- Do not donate blood, while you are taking Accutane or for at least 1 month after you stop taking Accutane. This is because your blood should not be given to a pregnant female.

Things you should tell your doctor before starting Accutane:

- Tell your doctor if you or any members of your family have diabetes because Accutane may affect blood sugar levels. Your doctor may decide that blood sugar testing is important in your case.
- Tell your doctor if you or any member of your family have liver disease, heart disease or depression.
- Tell your doctor if you are sensitive to parabens. They are used in the Accutane gelatin capsule.

Treatment Progress:

- During the first few weeks of treatment, your acne may seem to get worse. Redness and itching of the affected skin are common initial effects. These should disappear as you continue to take Accutane. Most often, the first signs of healing occur after 2 to 3 weeks of treatment. It may take 1 to 2 months before beneficial effects are seen. Most patients with severe acne notice a marked improvement after 1 or 2 courses of treatment with Accutane.

Side Effects:

- Tell your doctor if any of your side effects do not clear up in a few weeks after you stop taking Accutane.
- As with other medications, unwanted effects may occur with Accutane. Some of the most common side effects are: dryness of the skin, lips, mouth, and lining of the nose. Some other reactions that may occur include: facial or body rash, flaking of the skin, itching, peeling of the palms and soles, increased sensitivity to the sun (see below), inflammation of the lips, mild nosebleed, bleeding and inflammation of the gums, aches and pains in joints (see below), easily injured skin and increased fatigue. You may experience some redness, dryness (see below), irritation of the eyes or decreased night vision (see below). These side effects are generally temporary and disappear when Accutane treatment is stopped. **Check with your doctor to see if any change in your medication is needed, especially if these effects become bothersome.**
- If you wear contact lenses, you may find them uncomfortable during treatment because Accutane may cause dry eyes. This may continue after treatment has stopped.
- In some patients thinning of hair has occurred. In rare cases this hair loss persisted after treatment was completed.

Special Precautions You Should Take:

- Do not use vitamin preparations or health food supplements that contain vitamin A. Accutane is related to vitamin A. The vitamin A in these products may add to the unwanted effects of Accutane. Check with your doctor or pharmacist if you are unsure about the vitamin A content of any product you are taking.
- Protect yourself from excessive exposure to the sun. Accutane may increase the sensitivity of your skin to the sun.
- A number of patients on Accutane have experienced decreased night vision. Onset can be sudden. Be careful when driving or operating any vehicle at night.

Special Symptoms You Should Tell Your Doctor About:

- Tell your doctor if you have aches or pains in bones or joints, or difficulty in moving. Bone changes have been detected by x-ray examination in patients taking Accutane. The extent of any harm from these changes is not presently known.
- **Tell your doctor as soon as possible, if you experience any of the following symptoms** because these side effects may possibly result in permanent effects. These symptoms may be early signs of rare, but more serious side effects which your doctor may want to check as soon as possible:
- Headaches, nausea, vomiting, blurred vision, other visual problems, changes in mood;
- Severe stomach pain, diarrhea, rectal bleeding;
- Persistent feeling of dry eyes, decrease in night vision;
- Yellowing of the skin or eyes and/or dark urine.
- **Tell your doctor about any unusual or severe symptoms that appear during treatment.**

General Guidelines When Taking Your Medication:

- **Call your doctor if you have any questions or have severe or troubling symptoms.**
- **Keep Accutane out of the reach of children.**
- **Read your prescription label carefully** and be sure to take the exact amount of medicine prescribed by your doctor. Your doctor may change your prescribed dose from time to time, therefore, it is important that you check the label each time you fill your Accutane prescription. If you have any questions call your doctor.

- **Take Accutane with food or just after a meal.** If you forget to take a dose of Accutane, it may be taken later the same day, but, do not take more Accutane in one day than your doctor has prescribed.
- **Protect Accutane capsules from light and heat.** Accutane does not need to be refrigerated.

This summary does not contain all known information about Accutane. Talk to your doctor if you have any questions.

□ ACTIFED®

Warner-Lambert Consumer Healthcare

Triprolidine HCl—Pseudoephedrine HCl

Antihistaminic—Decongestant

Information for the Patient: Warnings: May cause excitability especially in children. Do not give this product to children under 6 years except under the advice and supervision of a physician. May cause drowsiness. Do not exceed recommended doses because at higher doses nervousness, dizziness or sleeplessness may occur. If symptoms do not improve within 5 days or are accompanied by high fever, consult a physician before continuing use. Do not take this product if you have high blood pressure, heart disease, diabetes, thyroid disease, asthma, glaucoma or difficulty in urination due to enlargement of the prostate gland except under the advice and supervision of a physician. As with any drug, if you are pregnant or nursing a baby, seek the advice of a health professional before using this product.

Drug Interactions: Do not take this product if you are presently taking a prescription antihypertensive or antidepressant drug containing a MAO inhibitor except under the advice and supervision of a physician.

Caution: Keep this and all medicines out of children's reach. In case of accidental overdose, seek professional assistance or contact a Poison Control Centre immediately.

Occupational Hazards: May cause drowsiness. Do not drink alcoholic beverages, drive a motor vehicle or operate machinery requiring mental alertness.

□ ACTIFED™ PLUS EXTRA STRENGTH

Warner-Lambert Consumer Healthcare

Acetaminophen—Pseudoephedrine HCl—Triprolidine HCl

Analgesic—Antipyretic—Antihistamine—Decongestant

Information for the Patient: Caution: Do not exceed recommended dosage because at higher doses nervousness, dizziness, or sleepiness may occur. Consult a physician if: symptoms do not improve within 5 days or are accompanied by high fever; you are taking an antihypertensive or antidepressant; you have high blood pressure, liver, heart or thyroid disease, diabetes, chronic lung disease, glaucoma, difficulty in urinating due to enlargement of the prostate gland; you are elderly, pregnant, a nursing mother or taking other medication.

Warnings: May cause excitability, especially in children. May cause drowsiness. Do not drink alcoholic beverages, drive a motor vehicle or operate machinery requiring mental alertness. Keep out of children's reach. In case of accidental overdose, contact a physician or Poison Control Centre immediately.

□ ACTINAC® Ⓟ

Hoechst Marion Roussel

Chloramphenicol—Hydrocortisone Acetate—Butoxyethylnicotinate—Allantoin—Precipitated Sulfur

Acne Therapy

Information for the Patient: Actinac has been prescribed to you for the treatment of your skin condition. It is **important** that you use it **only** as directed by your physician, **only** for the disorder for which it was prescribed, and for no longer than the time period prescribed. This package insert has been prepared to help you to use Actinac in the correct way, so it is important that you follow the instructions carefully.

How to prepare the lotion: Empty the contents of 1 bottle of aqueous vehicle (white cap) into 1 bottle of powder (black cap), replace the cap securely and shake until the 2 ingredients are thoroughly mixed. The lotion is now ready for use and will remain active for 21 days. The lotion should be stored at room temperature. Any lotion remaining after 21 days should be discarded and a fresh supply prepared.

How to use Actinac: Before applying Actinac, the area to be treated should be washed thoroughly but gently with warm water and mild soap, rinsed well and patted dry. Shake the bottle of lotion before each application.

The lotion may then be applied with cotton wool or gauze. Apply before retiring and leave on for the night; reapply in the morning, washing the lotion off with soap and water before starting your daily activities. Continue this process for 4 days. After this 4-day period apply only at night.

In order to prevent recurrence, continue treatment for 3 nights after the spots have disappeared. Total duration of treatment should be 4 to 6 weeks. If your physician has given you different instructions, you should follow them.

What are the precautions to take while using Actinac? Actinac **must not** be used more often than prescribed by your doctor. Actinac contains hydrocortisone which may cause some side effects, especially when used in a way other than that prescribed by your doctor. In order to minimize that risk, the treated areas of the skin should not be bandaged or otherwise covered or wrapped as to be occlusive. Keep your medication in a safe place, out of the reach of children. Store at room temperature.

Actinac is for external use only. Avoid Actinac coming into contact with the eyes and mouth. If the medicine does get in the eyes, they must be washed out immediately but carefully, using large amounts of cool tap water. If the eyes continue to burn or remain painful, consult a physician. Do not use any other acne medication unless your doctor instructs you to do so.

What are the side effects of Actinac? Along with its beneficial effects, Actinac like any other medication, may sometimes cause undesirable effects. Early in the course of treatment, the skin to which Actinac is applied may become red and you may experience a feeling of warmth. This is a normal reaction and denotes an increased blood flow to the skin. However, in the unlikely event of a more severe reaction such as skin rash, itching, redness, other signs of irritation not present before using Actinac or any other unusual or unexpected effects, consult your physician before further use.

Chloramphenicol, one of the constituents of Actinac, has been implicated in the occurrence of a very severe and sometimes fatal blood adverse reaction namely aplastic anemia. This reaction, reported when chloramphenicol was used as an eye preparation or systemically (e.g., when taken by mouth or injected), was rare. Although this has not been reported with Actinac, such occurrences should be kept in mind when prescribing the product. Prolonged or irregular use of Actinac must be avoided. It is thus very important that you carefully follow your physician's instructions. Should sore throat, fever, fatigue and mouth sores develop while using the product or after the treatment, consult your doctor.

Actinac has been prescribed by your doctor for you: You must not allow other people to use it. If you require more information on Actinac, consult your doctor or pharmacist.

□ ACULAR® Ⓟ

Allergan

Ketorolac Tromethamine

Topical Anti-inflammatory

Information for the Patient: How to make Acular work best for you: Your doctor has decided that Acular (ketorolac tromethamine) ophthalmic solution is the best treatment for you. Remember that your chances of controlling your symptoms are greater if you cooperate fully with your doctor and try to become well informed about your condition.

This leaflet is not as thorough as the Official Product Monograph on Acular (which your doctor or pharmacist has available), and is meant to supplement what your doctor has told you. Your doctor knows and understands your personal condition; be sure to follow your doctor's instructions carefully and read any materials he or she gives you. If you have any questions after reading this information leaflet, be sure to ask your doctor.

What is Acular? Acular is the product name for ketorolac tromethamine, a medicine used for the prevention and relief of postoperative

Acular (cont'd)

eye inflammation. It belongs to a family of drugs known as nonsteroidal anti-inflammatory drugs (NSAIDs) or antiprostaglandin drugs.

What does Acular look like? Acular ophthalmic solution is supplied in a white opaque plastic bottle with a controlled dropper tip. Acular is also available as a preservative-free sterile solution in individual single use vials.

How does Acular work? Conditions like yours are usually associated with inflammation. Research shows that Acular works by reducing the production of certain substances (called prostaglandins) that the body normally produces to help control such functions as muscle contraction, inflammation, and numerous other body processes.

Clinical studies indicate that when prostaglandin levels are reduced, the intensity of pain, and inflammation is reduced as well.

Before using this medicine: To decide on the best treatment for your medical problem, your doctor should be told:

- If you have ever had any unusual or allergic reaction to Acular.
- If you are allergic to any substance. Most medicines contain more than their active ingredient. Your doctor, nurse, or pharmacist can help you avoid products that may cause a problem.
- If you are pregnant or if you may become pregnant. Acular is not recommended during pregnancy, labor or delivery.
- If you are breast-feeding. Acular is not recommended for treatment of nursing mothers.
- If you have any medical problems.
- If you are taking any other prescription or nonprescription (over-the-counter (OTC)) medicine.

How should you take Acular to make it work best for you? Use this medicine only as directed. Do not use more of it and do not use it more often than your doctor ordered. To do so may increase the chance of too much medicine being absorbed into the body and the chance of side effects.

To use:

- First, wash your hands. With the middle finger, apply pressure to the inside corner of the eye (and continue to apply pressure for 1 or 2 minutes after the medicine has been placed in the eye). Tilt the head back and with the index finger of the same hand, pull the lower eyelid away from the eye to form a pouch. Drop the medicine into the pouch and gently close the eyes. Do not blink. Keep the eyes closed for 1 or 2 minutes to allow the medicine to be absorbed.
- Immediately after applying the eye drops, wash your hands to remove any medicine that may be on them.
- To keep the medicine as germ-free as possible, do not touch the applicator tip to any surface (including the eye). Also, keep the container tightly closed.
- If you have received a 3 mL sample, make sure container is intact before use. To open, **completely twist off cap.** Do not reuse, discard unused portion. To avoid contamination, do not touch tip of container to any surface.
- Acular is available as a preservative-free sterile unit dose vial. The solution from one individual single use vial is to be used immediately after opening for administration to one or both eyes, and the remaining contents should be discarded immediately after administration. To avoid contamination do not touch unit dose tip to eye or any surface.

If you miss a dose of this medicine, apply it as soon as possible. However, if it is almost time for your next dose, skip the missed dose and go back to your regular dosing schedule. Do not double dose.

To store this medicine:

- Keep out of reach of children.
- Store containers at room temperature between 15 to 30°C. Protect from light.

Important! Your doctor may give you different instructions better suited to your specific needs. If you need more information about how to take Acular properly, double-check with your doctor or pharmacist.

Will the amount of Acular you take ever change? It might change. As time goes by, your doctor may decide that it is advisable to make adjustments in the dosage of Acular you are taking. He or she may suggest that you increase or decrease your medication according to how severe your symptoms are or how active you are.

Follow instructions; your doctor understands how to set the upper and lower dosage limits so that you get the greatest benefit from Acular.

Does Acular have side effects? Along with its needed effects, a medicine may cause some unwanted effects.

Most eye complaints reported in clinical studies could not be distinguished from side effects caused by the cataract surgery and the insertion of an intraocular lens. The most frequently reported complaints after Acular therapy include transient stinging and burning, redness, itching and/or swelling and visual blurring following instillation of the eye drops.

If you are allergic to ASA or to any of the other nonsteroidal anti-inflammatory drugs (e.g., diclofenac, diflunisal, fenoprofen, flurbiprofen, ibuprofen, indomethacin, ketoprofen, mefenamic acid, piroxicam, sulindac, tiaprofenic acid, tolmetin) used to treat arthritis or other muscle and joint conditions, do not take Acular. You may be allergic to it, too.

Are there any special do's and don't's about taking Acular? Do tell your doctor and pharmacist about any other medications you take, both prescription and nonprescription. This is important because some drugs can interact with each other and produce undesirable effects.

Do check with your doctor if:

—you are not getting relief

or

—you have any problems while taking Acular.

Do tell your physician if you are pregnant or are planning to become pregnant.

Don't take Acular if you are breast-feeding. Some drug does pass into the milk of nursing women.

Don't take Acular if you are allergic to it, or if you have had an allergic-type reaction to ASA or to any other drug used for pain relief or arthritis. **Do** check with your doctor.

Do cooperate with your doctor if he or she wants you to take certain lab tests to monitor the effectiveness of treatment or possible side effects.

☐ AIROMIR™ Ⓟ

3M Pharmaceuticals

Salbutamol Sulfate

Bronchodilator—β_2-adrenergic Stimulant

Information for the Patient: What you Should Know About Airomir Inhalation Aerosol: Please read this leaflet carefully before you start to take your medicine. For more information or advice, ask your doctor or your pharmacist.

About Your Medicine: The name of this product is Airomir Inhalation Aerosol. It contains salbutamol sulfate, a bronchodilator medicine that relieves the wheezing, breathlessness, and chest tightness caused by spasms or narrowing in the small air passages of the lungs. Each puff of aerosol from the can contains 100 micrograms of salbutamol.

Dosing information: Your doctor has decided on the best dose of Airomir Inhalation Aerosol for you to take and on how often you should take a dose. The label that the pharmacist puts on your inhaler indicates how many puffs to take and how often. If you do not understand the instructions on the label, check with your pharmacist or your doctor.

It is very important that you follow your doctor's instructions carefully so that you receive the maximum benefit from your medication.

Warnings: The action of Airomir Inhalation Aerosol should last up to 4 to 6 hours. Do not increase the number of puffs or do not take puffs more often than your doctor has told you. Unless your doctor has recommended otherwise, do not take more than 8 puffs in a day (24 hours). Unless the doctor has recommended otherwise, children should not take more than 4 puffs in a day. If you feel that the dose you are using does not help you, or if you feel that your breathing is becoming worse, follow the action plan which your doctor has given you and call your doctor right away. Your doctor may prescribe other medications for your condition, which may be used with Airomir. Do not take other medications, including over-the-counter medications, without consulting your doctor or your pharmacist. If you are pregnant or breast-feeding, ask your doctor about using Airomir.

Please Note: If you have any symptoms that you do not understand while using Airomir Inhalation Aerosol, be sure to talk to your doctor. People using this type of drug sometimes have palpitations, chest pain, rapid heart rate, tremor, or nervousness. These effects usually decrease or stop altogether after your body adjusts to the medication. If you find your side effects bothersome, do not discontinue your medicine. Instead, call your doctor or pharmacist to discuss your side effects with them. Never share your inhaler with anyone. This medication was prescribed for you by your doctor.

How to Use Airomir Inhalation Aerosol (see package insert for illustrations): Follow the instructions given below to use the inhaler. If you have any problems using the inhaler or if you do not understand the instructions below, ask your doctor or your pharmacist for help.

Airomir should only be used with the mouthpiece supplied with the product. You should test the mouthpiece and aerosol can before using them for the first time, or if you have not used your inhaler for more than 2 weeks. After shaking the inhaler well, test by spraying 4 test sprays into the air, away from your face. Avoid spraying into the eyes.

1. Shake the inhaler well right before each use. Then take the cap off of the mouthpiece. Check the mouthpiece for dirt or other objects before you use it. Make sure the aerosol can is pushed all the way into the actuator (the small vertical cylinder in the mouthpiece). It should fit tightly, without wobbling.
2. Breathe out as big a breath as you can through your mouth, pushing as much air out of your lungs as possible. Place the mouthpiece in your mouth between your teeth and close your lips around it. Make sure the inhaler stays straight up.
3. At the beginning of a deep, slow breath through your mouth, push all the way down on the top of the aerosol can.
4. Hold your breath for as long as you can. Before breathing out, take the inhaler out of your mouth and stop squeezing down on the aerosol can.
5. If your doctor has told you to take 2 puffs, wait 1 minute and shake the inhaler again. Repeat steps 2 through 4. Replace the cap after you are finished using the inhaler.
6. Keeping the plastic mouthpiece clean is very important to prevent the inhaler from becoming dirty and clogged. The mouthpiece should be washed, shaken to remove excess water, and air dried thoroughly at least once a week. The inhaler may stop spraying if not properly cleaned.

   Routine Cleaning Instructions: Step 1. To clean, remove the canister and mouthpiece cap. Wash the mouthpiece through the top and bottom with warm running water at least once per week. **Never put the metal can in water.** Step 2. To dry, shake off excess water as you can and let the mouthpiece air dry thoroughly, such as overnight. When the mouthpiece is dry, put the canister back in. Replace the cap. **If you use the inhaler before it is dry, you may cause it to clog.**

   If your inhaler has become blocked (little or no medication coming out of the mouthpiece), wash the mouthpiece as described in step 1 and air dry thoroughly as described in step 2.

   If you need to use your inhaler right after you have washed it, shake off excess water, put the canister back in and test spray it into the air twice, away from your face, to remove most of the water remaining in the mouthpiece. Then take your dose as prescribed. **After such use, re-wash and air dry thoroughly as described in steps 1 and 2.**
7. Airomir Inhalation Aerosol will deliver at least 200 sprays. However, after 200 sprays, the amount of drug delivered per spray may not be consistent. You should keep track of the number of sprays used from each canister of Airomir Inhalation Aerosol and discard the canister after 200 sprays.

Contents Under Pressure: The inhaler's contents are under pressure. Do not use the inhaler or keep the aerosol can near heat or open flame. Temperatures above 40°C may cause the aerosol can to burst. Never throw the aerosol can into a fire or an incinerator. Do not puncture the aerosol can, even when it seems to be empty. Keep the inhaler away from direct sunlight and protect it from freezing. Store between 15 and 30°C.

If your doctor changes your treatment and you no longer require Airomir Inhalation Aerosol, please return your inhaler to your pharmacy for disposal. Keep your inhaler away from children as children can hurt themselves with any medicine.

Further information: Please note that (CFC free) symbol shows that Airomir Inhalation Aerosol does not contain chlorofluorocarbons (CFCs) which damage upper stratospheric ozone. Instead, Airomir Inhalation Aerosol contains a hydrofluoroalkane (HFA-134a) which does not damage the ozone layer. You may notice a slightly different taste or spray force with Airomir Inhalation Aerosol compared to salbutamol aerosol inhalers that use CFC propellants.

□ ALBERT® DOCUSATE

Albert Pharma

Docusate Calcium

Stool Softener

Information for the Patient: Drink an increased amount of fluid. Do not use if abdominal pain, fever, nausea or vomiting is present. If a sudden change in bowel habits persists for 2 weeks or more, do not take any laxative without first seeking professional advice. Do not use any laxative for longer than 1 week unless so advised by your physician. If a laxative produces no effect after it has been used as recommended, or if rectal bleeding is observed, stop using the product and consult your doctor. Do not take docusate calcium at the same time as other drugs your doctor may have prescribed without first consulting the doctor. If you are pregnant, or if you are nursing an infant, do not take any drug, including docusate calcium without consulting a health professional. Do not administer concomitantly with mineral oil: increased absorption of the oil may result. Overuse or extended use may cause dependence for bowel function.

Keep medicines out of reach of children.

□ ALBERT® TIAFEN Ⓟ
□ ALBERT® TIAFEN SR Ⓟ

Albert Pharma

Tiaprofenic Acid

Anti-inflammatory—Analgesic

Information for the Patient: How to make Albert Tiafen/Albert Tiafen SR work best for you? Your doctor has decided that Albert Tiafen/Albert Tiafen SR (tiaprofenic acid) is the best treatment for you. As you take Albert Tiafen tablets or Albert Tiafen SR capsules, remember that your chances of controlling your symptoms are greater if you cooperate fully with your doctor and try to become well informed about your condition.

This leaflet is meant to supplement what your doctor or pharmacist has told you. Your doctor knows and understands your personal condition; be sure to follow your doctor's instructions carefully and read any materials he or she gives you. If you have any questions after reading this information leaflet, be sure to ask your doctor or pharmacist.

What is Albert Tiafen/Albert Tiafen SR and how does it work? Albert Tiafen/Albert Tiafen SR is the product name for tiaprofenic acid, a medicine used to relieve the pain and inflammation associated with certain types of arthritis. It belongs to a family of medicine known as nonsteroidal anti-inflammatory drugs (NSAIDs). It helps to relieve joint pain, swelling, stiffness and fever by reducing the production of certain substances (prostaglandins) and by helping to control inflammation. NSAIDs do not cure arthritis, but they promote suppression of the inflammation and the tissue damaging effects resulting from this inflammation. This medicine will help you only as long as you continue to take it.

What does Albert Tiafen/Albert Tiafen SR look like? Albert Tiafen is available as white round tablets. Albert Tiafen SR is available as a sustained release pink and maroon capsule containing off-white pellets. The tablets and capsules are clearly marked with the Roussel logo and the product name.

How should you take Albert Tiafen/Albert Tiafen SR to make it work best for you? Your doctor has chosen the strength (dose) that he or she thinks will be most effective in relieving your condition, based on experience with similar medical problems.

If you are taking Albert Tiafen: The usual dose of Albert Tiafen tablets is 600 mg daily taken as 1 tablet of 300 mg morning and night or 1 tablet of 200 mg 3 times daily.

If you are taking Albert Tiafen SR: Albert Tiafen SR capsules have been designed to provide a sustained release of the medicine and thus allow for a convenient once-a-day dosing. The usual dose of Albert Tiafen SR capsules is 2 capsules taken once daily. The off-white pellets contained in Albert Tiafen SR capsules must be swallowed whole (not crushed or chewed) for optimal results. For the most relief, take your Albert Tiafen SR at the same time each day.

You should take Albert Tiafen/Albert Tiafen SR only as directed by your doctor. Do not take more or less of it, do not take it more often and do not take it for a longer period of time than your doctor ordered.

Albert Tiafen (cont'd)

Taking too much of any of these medicines may increase the chance of unwanted effects, especially if you are an elderly patient.

Be sure to take Albert Tiafen/Albert Tiafen SR as prescribed. It is important to keep taking Albert Tiafen/Albert Tiafen SR even after you start to feel better. This helps to keep your pain, tenderness and stiffness under control. In some types of arthritis, up to 2 weeks may pass before you feel the full effects of this medicine. However, some people are able to feel improvement in their symptoms right away. If you are not getting adequate relief from your medicine, speak to your doctor before you stop taking it. During treatment, your doctor may decide to adjust the dosage according to your response to the medication.

Stomach upset is one of the common problems with NSAIDs: To lessen stomach upset, take this medicine immediately after a meal or with food or milk. Also, you should remain standing or sitting upright (i.e., do not lie down) for about 15 to 30 minutes after taking the medicine. This helps to prevent irritation that may lead to trouble swallowing. If stomach upset (indigestion, nausea, vomiting, stomach pain or diarrhea) occurs and continues, contact your doctor.

What to do if you miss a dose? If you miss a dose of Albert Tiafen tablets, take it as soon as possible. However, if it is almost time for your next dose, skip the missed dose and go back to your regular schedule.

If you miss a dose of Albert Tiafen SR capsules once-a-day and remember within 8 hours, take it right away and then resume your regular dosing schedule.

Never double dose.

Combining Albert Tiafen/Albert Tiafen SR with other medications? Do not take ASA (acetylsalicylic acid, Aspirin), ASA-containing compounds or other drugs used to relieve symptoms of arthritis while taking Albert Tiafen/Albert Tiafen SR unless directed to do so by your physician.

Does Albert Tiafen/Albert Tiafen SR have side effects? Along with its beneficial effects, Albert Tiafen/Albert Tiafen SR like all other NSAID drugs, may sometimes cause undesirable effects especially when used for a long time or in large doses. Relatively common unwanted side effects of NSAIDs are heartburn, stomach pain, indigestion, nausea, vomiting or diarrhea. If these side effects occur and continue, contact your doctor.

Elderly, frail or debilitated people often seem to experience more frequent or more severe side effects.

Although not all of the following side effects are common, when they do occur they may require medical attention.

Check with your doctor immediately if any of the following are noted:
- bloody or black tarry stools;
- shortness of breath, wheezing, any trouble in breathing or tightness in the chest;
- skin rash, swelling, hives or itching;
- persistent indigestion, nausea, vomiting, stomach or lower abdominal pain or diarrhea (particularly if you have a history of stomach upset or ulcers);
- yellow discoloration of the skin or eyes, with or without fatigue;
- any changes in the amount, frequency or colour of your urine (such as dark; red or brown);
- swelling of the feet or lower legs;
- malaise, fatigue, or loss of appetite;
- blurred vision or any visual disturbance;
- mental confusion, depression, dizziness, lightheadedness;
- hearing problems;
- any pain or difficulty experienced while urinating.

Other side effects not listed above may also occur in some patients. If you notice any other effects, check with your doctor.

If you are prescribed this medicine for use over a long period of time, your doctor will check your health during regular visits to assess your progress and to ensure that this medication is not causing unwanted effects.

What should you always remember? The risks of taking this medication must be weighed against the benefits it will have.

Before taking this medication tell your doctor and pharmacists if you:
- or a family member are allergic to or have had a reaction to Albert Tiafen/Albert Tiafen SR or other related medicines of the NSAID group (such as acetylsalicylic acid (Aspirin), diclofenac, diflunisal, fenoprofen, flurbiprofen, ibuprofen, indomethacin, ketoprofen, mefenamic acid, naproxen, piroxicam, sulindac, tolmetin, nabumetone or tenoxicam) manifesting itself by increased sinusitis, hives, the initiating or worsening of asthma or anaphylaxis (sudden collapse);
- or a family member has had asthma, nasal polyps, chronic sinusitis or chronic urticaria (hives);
- have a history of liver or kidney diseases;
- have a history of stomach upset or ulcers, since all NSAIDs may aggravate your problem and sometimes even cause bleeding or ulcers in your stomach or intestines;
- have blood or urine abnormalities;
- have high blood pressure;
- have diabetes;
- are on any special diet, such as a low-sodium or low-sugar diet.
- are pregnant or intend to become pregnant while taking this medication;
- are breast-feeding or intend to breast-feed while taking this medication;
- are taking any other medication (either prescription or nonprescription) such as other NSAIDs, high blood pressure medication, blood thinners, corticosteroids, methotrexate, cyclosporine, lithium, phenytoin. This is important because some medicines can interact with each other and cause some unwanted effects.
- have any other medical problem(s) such as alcohol abuse, bleeding problems, etc.

While taking this medication:
- tell any other doctor, dentist or pharmacist that you consult or see, that you are taking this medication;
- some NSAIDs may cause drowsiness or fatigue in some people taking them. Be cautious about driving or participating in activities that require alertness if you are drowsy, dizzy or lightheaded after taking this medication;
- check with your doctor if you are not getting any relief or if any problems develop;
- report any untoward reactions to your doctor. This is very important as it will aid in the early detection and prevention of potential complications.
- stomach problems may be more likely to occur if you drink alcoholic beverages. Therefore, do not drink alcoholic beverages while taking this medication;
- check with your doctor immediately if you experience unexpected weakness while taking this medication, or if you vomit any blood or have dark or bloody stools;
- some people may become more sensitive to sunlight than they are normally. Exposure to sunlight or sunlamps, even for brief periods of time, may cause sunburn, blisters on the skin, skin rash, redness, itching or discoloration; or vision changes. If you have a reaction from the sun, check with your doctor;
- check with your doctor immediately if chills, fever, muscle aches or pains, or other flu-like symptoms occur, especially if they occur shortly before, or together with, a skin rash. Very rarely, these effects may be the first signs of a serious reaction to this medication;
- **Your regular medical checkups are essential.**

How should you store Albert Tiafen/Albert Tiafen SR? Store Albert Tiafen/Albert Tiafen SR between 15 and 30°C. Protect from excessive heat, light and humidity.

The safety and efficacy of Albert Tiafen has not been established in children and its use in this age group is therefore not recommended.

Do not keep outdated medicine or medicine no longer needed.

This medication has been prescribed for your medical problem. Do not give it to anyone else.

Keep your medication out of children's reach.

If you require more information on this drug, consult your doctor or pharmacist.

☐ ALDACTAZIDE 25® Ⓟ
☐ ALDACTAZIDE 50® Ⓟ

Searle

Spironolactone—Hydrochlorothiazide

Aldosterone Antagonist—Diuretic

Information for the Patient: Avoid taking potassium supplements. Do not use salt substitutes which contain high levels of potassium, and avoid foods with high levels of potassium, especially in large quantities.

□ ALDACTONE® ℞
Searle

Spironolactone

Aldosterone Antagonist

Information for the Patient: Avoid taking potassium supplements. Do not use salt substitutes which contain high levels of potassium, and avoid foods with high levels of potassium, especially in large quantities.

□ ALKERAN® ℞
Glaxo Wellcome

Melphalan

Antineoplastic

Information for the Patient: Patients should be informed that the major acute toxicities of melphalan are related to bone marrow suppression, hypersensitivity reactions, gastrointestinal toxicity, and pulmonary toxicity. The major long-term toxicities are related to infertility and secondary malignancies. Patients should never be allowed to take the drug without close medical supervision and should be advised to consult their physicians if they experience skin rash, signs or symptoms of vasculitis, bleeding, fever, or persistent cough.

□ ALLEGRA™
Hoechst Marion Roussel

Fexofenadine HCl

Histamine H_1-Receptor Antagonist

Information for the Patient: Allegra (fexofenadine hydrochloride) 60 mg tablets: For fast relief from hayfever and seasonal allergy symptoms, such as runny nose, sneezing, itchy, watery eyes, and itchy palate or throat.

Directions: Adults and children 12 years of age and over: 1 tablet (60 mg) every 12 hours. Do not administer to children under 12 years of age. Do not exceed the recommended dosage. Avoid prolonged use unless advised by a physician.

Caution: Before using this product, consult your physician if you have kidney disease, as your dosage may need to be reduced. This product should not be used if you are pregnant or nursing, unless under the advice of a physician.

Do not take Allegra within 2 hours of taking an antacid that contains aluminum hydroxide or magnesium hydroxide, as these antacids may alter the effectiveness of Allegra.

Keep this and all medications safely out of reach of children.

Store between 15 and 30°C in a dry place.

Product Monograph available to physicians and pharmacists upon request.

Nonmedicinal Ingredients: Croscarmellose sodium, gelatin, hydroxypropyl methylcellulose, iron oxide, lactose, magnesium stearate, microcrystalline cellulose, povidone, polyethylene glycol, silicon dioxide, starch and titanium dioxide.

Availability: Allegra is available as a 60 mg tablet, packaged in individually sealed blister packs of 12, 24 and 36 tablets.

□ ALOMIDE® ℞
Alcon

Lodoxamide Tromethamine

Anti-allergy Agent

Information for the Patient: Indications: Your doctor has prescribed Alomide solution for you to treat the symptoms of allergy (itching, discomfort, tearing, etc.) in your eyes. Regular use of this product is essential to obtain relief from your allergic symptoms.

Precautions:
1. Remove your contact lenses before using Alomide solution.
2. Wait at least 15 minutes after using Alomide solution before inserting your lenses.
3. Do not touch the dropper tip to any surface to avoid contamination.

Instructions: Put 1 drop into each eye, 4 times per day at regular intervals (about every 4 hours) while awake. It is necessary to use Alomide solution regularly to obtain relief from your allergic eyes.

□ ALPHAGAN™ ℞
Allergan

Brimonidine Tartrate

Elevated Intraocular Pressure Therapy

Information for the Patient: You can help preserve your vision by taking your glaucoma eye drops exactly as your doctor tells you. But sometimes it is hard to remember when to take your drops. That's why your doctor has prescribed these drops. They have a special cap called the C Cap. It was designed to help you adhere to your eye drop schedule by making it easy to keep track of how many times you use your drops each day.

For Allergan's various glaucoma products there are several different versions of the C Cap. Your doctor has chosen the one that corresponds to the number of times you use your medicine each day.

How to use the C CAP?
1. The very first time you are ready to take your eye drops, and at the beginning of each day, look in the window of the cap to make sure the number "1" appears. If another number is showing, turn the cap clockwise until it is in the correct position. You will notice that the cap clicks as it changes positions.
2. Next, remove the C Cap and apply your eye drops as directed by your doctor. For Alphagan 0.2% this means that the eye drops are given 2 times daily 12 hours apart.
3. Replace the cap by turning clockwise until it is snug. Then, keep twisting the cap slowly until you hear the click. The number "2" will appear in the window.

   This means for Alphagan 0.2% that the next time you take your eye drops will be the second time for that day, 12 hours after the first time.
4. When it is time for your next eye drops, unscrew the cap and apply your drops.
5. Replace the cap and click it to the next position. For Alphagan 0.2% this will be number "1" again, as the next time you take the drops will be at the beginning of the next day.

Note: If you forget to apply your eye drops at your normal time, simply apply them as soon as you remember. Then go back to the original schedule as directed by your doctor. **Don't try to catch on missed drops by applying more than one dose at a time.**

Remember: Each time you replace the cap, you should keep turning until you hear the click.

Do not allow the dropper tip of the bottle to touch the eye or other surrounding structures, because this could contaminate the tip with common bacteria known to cause eye infections. Serious damage to the eye with subsequent loss of vision may result if you use eye drop solutions that have become contaminated. If you experience any type of eye condition or have surgery, immediately seek your doctor's advice concerning the continued use of the bottle you are using.

Patients Wearing Soft Contact Lenses: Lenses should be removed prior to application of Alphagan 0.2% and not re-inserted earlier than 15 minutes after use.

□ ALTACE® ℞
Hoechst Marion Roussel

Ramipril

Angiotensin Converting Enzyme Inhibitor

Information for the Patient: For patient with essential hypertension: What is hypertension? Hypertension is the medical term for high blood pressure. When blood flows through the blood vessels it pushes against their walls, almost like water pushing against the sides of a hose. Blood pressure is like that "push". When blood pressure is high (like the water pressure in a hose when the nozzle is partially shut), damage can occur to the heart and blood vessels.

Although you may not feel any symptoms for years, hypertension can lead to stroke, heart attack, kidney disease and other serious conditions.

Altace (cont'd)

What causes hypertension? In most cases, the exact cause of hypertension is not known. But we do know that several factors increase the risk of developing the disease.

Family history: Hypertension, like some other diseases, can run in families. If your parents have high blood pressure, your chances of developing it are greater.

Age: The risk of developing hypertension increases with age.

Race: In North America, there is a higher incidence of hypertension among blacks than among whites.

Diabetes: Diabetics are at higher risk of developing hypertension than nondiabetics.

Weight: The risk of high blood pressure is higher in people who are overweight.

Drinking: Heavy alcohol consumption increases risk of hypertension, as well as stroke and kidney disease.

Sedentary lifestyle: A physically inactive lifestyle can contribute to hypertension.

Smoking: While not a direct cause of hypertension, smoking a cigarette will temporarily increase blood pressure. Smoking also increases the risk of heart disease in people with high blood pressure.

Keeping your blood pressure controlled: Your doctor has prescribed Altace, a medication that helps to control blood pressure. Altace opens blood vessels to reduce blood pressure, like the way opening a hose reduces water pressure. It is not, however, a cure.

But it takes more than just medication to reduce blood pressure. Discuss the risk factors, and how they apply to your lifestyle, with your doctor. You may have to modify some of your daily habits to keep your blood pressure down.

Exercise: Exercise regularly. It will help to keep your weight down, make you feel more energetic and is a good way to deal with stress. If you are not exercising regularly, be sure to discuss a fitness plan with your doctor.

Most people with high blood pressure need to take only 1 Altace capsule per day. Remember, hypertension is a long-term disease without symptoms. Just because you feel fine does not mean you can stop taking your medication. If you stop, serious complications of the disease may occur. Therefore, you should continue to take it regularly, as prescribed by your doctor.

For patients following a recent heart attack: Your doctor has prescribed Altace to reduce the effort required by your heart to pump blood, to compensate for reduced pumping power that may have resulted from your heart attack.

Altace has been shown to improve survival and reduce hospitalizations in patients recovering from recent heart attacks.

If you have developed heart failure after a heart attack, you may have to limit your physical activities. Before you begin exercising, be sure to consult with your doctor.

When initiating therapy in patients with heart failure after a heart attack, Altace is usually given twice a day, in the morning and in the evening.

General: When to take your medication: It is important to take it at the same time every day as prescribed by your doctor.

Missed a dose? If you forget to take your Altace capsule, take it as soon as possible. However, if it is almost time for your next dose, skip the missed dose and go back to your regular dosing schedule. Do not double dose.

Managing your lifestyle: The ''lifestyle'' part of your treatment is as important as your medication. By working as a team with your doctor, you can help reduce the risk of complications to maintain the style of life you are accustomed to.

Alcohol: Avoid alcoholic beverages until you have discussed their use with your doctor. Alcohol consumption may alter your blood pressure and/or increase the possibility of dizziness or fainting.

Diet: Generally, avoid fatty foods and food that is high in salt or cholesterol.

Smoking: Avoid it completely.

Side effects: Along with its intended action, any medication, including Altace, may cause side effects. These include headache, dizziness, fatigue, nausea or coughing. These side effects will disappear once your system becomes used to the medication. If they persist, discuss this with your doctor. Your medication might have to be reduced or changed.

Dizziness or lightheadedness may occur after the first dose of this medicine. Make sure you know how you react to this medicine before you drive, operate machinery, or do anything requiring you to be alert.

If you are suffering from excessive sweating, vomiting or diarrhea, this may cause you to lose too much water and lead to problems with low blood pressure. See your doctor.

A rare, but potentially more serious, side effect is called angioedema—characterized by swollen mouth, lips, tongue, eyes, throat or difficulty in swallowing or breathing. **If you notice swelling or feel pain in these areas, inform your doctor immediately. You should also inform your doctor if you have an unexplained fever, rash or itching.**

Keep your doctor informed: Before taking Altace, it is important that you inform your doctor of the following:

- Are you currently taking any other medications, whether on prescription or otherwise? This is especially important if you are taking diuretics (water pills) or any other medication to reduce blood pressure which may add to the blood pressure lowering effect of Altace. You should not be taking salt substitutes, potassium supplements or potassium containing medicine without the advice of your doctor.
- Do you suffer from any other condition? The presence of other medical problems may affect the use of Altace. Make sure you tell your doctor if you have any other medical problems, especially if you have diabetes, liver disease, kidney disease, heart or blood vessel disease.

If you are being treated for other conditions by other doctors, keep them all informed of which medications you are taking. Some drugs may have negative effect on Altace or Altace may have a negative effect on other drugs. If you have to undergo any dental or other surgery, inform the dentist or physician in charge that you are taking this medicine.

- **Are you pregnant, breast-feeding or thinking of becoming pregnant?** Taking Altace during pregnancy can cause injury and even death to the fetus. It is not known if Altace passes into breast milk. You should not breast-feed while taking Altace.
- Are you possibly allergic to Altace (ramipril), including any of its nonmedicinal ingredients (pregelatinized starch NF, gelatin, titanium dioxide)?

After you have started taking Altace, it is important that you tell your doctor at once about any unexplained symptom you might experience. Examples of this are unexplained fever, rash, itching, any sign of infection, viral-like symptoms, flu-like symptoms, coughing, sore throat, abdominal pain, loss of appetite, sad mood, or jaundice.

Store in original container at room temperature, below 25°C and not beyond the date indicated on the container. Keep this medication out of the reach of children.

Remember: Use this drug as directed by your doctor. All drugs can have both helpful and harmful effects. Both depend on the person and his or her condition. This leaflet alerts you to some of the times you should call your doctor. Other situations which cannot be predicted can arise. Nothing in this leaflet should stop you from calling your doctor or pharmacist with any questions or concerns you have about Altace.

□ ALUPENT® Preparations Ⓟ

Boehringer Ingelheim

Orciprenaline Sulfate

Bronchodilator

Information for the Patient: Inhalation Aerosol: Important: DO NOT exceed the number of puffs prescribed by your physician. DO NOT inhale Alupent Metered Aerosol more often than directed by your physician. If difficulty in breathing persists, or if relief is not obtained with your usual dosage, consult your physician immediately; this is a sign of seriously worsening asthma that requires reassessment of treatment.

If you are using your Alupent inhaler on a regular daily basis, without using any other anti-asthma medication, consult your doctor for re-evaluation of your treatment.

Your doctor may prescribe this medication on a regular basis in association with other anti-asthma medication that control the airways inflammation.

Directions for Use:

1. Remove protective plastic cap from mouthpiece.
2. **Important**-Shake well each time before use.

3. Hold the apparatus so that the metal canister is upside down.
4. Breathe out as completely as possible and hold your breath.
5. Place the mouthpiece well into the mouth, closing your lips over it.
6. Breathe in deeply through the mouth, and at the same time firmly press the canister down into the mouthpiece. This releases the medication. (Repeat only as directed by your physician).
7. Hold your breath for a few seconds, then remove the mouthpiece and breath out slowly.

If troubled with sputum, try to clear your chest as completely as possible before inhalation of Alupent. This will facilitate the passage of Alupent more deeply into the lungs which in turn will allow more thorough clearing of mucus during subsequent coughing.

Dosage: 1 or 2 inhalations will usually provide control of an acute attack of bronchospasm, and offer protection against further attacks for up to 6 hours. As a general rule, one should not exceed a total of 12 inhalations in 24 hours.

Care of Mouthpiece: The mouthpiece must be kept clean. Remove the metal canister and rinse the mouthpiece in **warm** running water. Dry and replace.

Precautions: Persons with high blood pressure, heart disease, diabetes, glaucoma or thyroid disease should use Alupent only on the advice of a physician.

Availability: Alupent Metered Aerosol is supplied as a 15 mL metal canister (with free disposable mouthpiece) containing 300 individual doses.

Caution: Contents under pressure. **Do not incinerate.**

Alupent Syrup: When Alupent Syrup is taken as directed by your physician (see Directions for use), you will note easier breathing within 20 to 30 minutes, and this effect will persist for 3 to 6 hours. Taken regularly, Alupent often produces a reduction in frequency and severity of acute bronchospastic attacks, a corresponding relief of wheezing, chest congestion and shortness of breath. Alupent Syrup is useful in all patients who have difficulty in swallowing tablets, but it is particularly suitable for children and geriatric patients. Alupent Syrup has a pleasant taste.

Helpful Reminders for Patients with Chronic Bronchospastic Disorders: The following factors can sometimes significantly influence your ability to breathe efficiently. Your physician has, undoubtedly, discussed with you those points which are important in your case. It is essential that you follow his advice meticulously.

1. If your physician suggests breathing exercises or postural drainage, follow his directions carefully. Breathing exercises help increase the strength, coordination and efficiency of the muscles of respiration, and postural drainage helps to remove mucus from the lungs.
2. If your physician recommends a reducing diet, follow it closely since being overweight makes breathing more difficult.
3. Should you have allergies to certain foods, inhalants or drugs, avoidance of these factors may prove most beneficial.
4. Overwork, nervous tension and inadequate sleep all contribute to fatigue. Care should be taken to ensure an adequate amount of rest.
5. Coughs, colds and the ''flu'' frequently precipitate acute attacks of bronchospasm in the asthmatic or bronchitic patient. Considerable care should be taken to avoid contact with persons having cold or ''flu'' symptoms and should you develop a cold, consult your doctor as soon as possible.
6. The winter months can present additional problems for patients with bronchospasm. As much as possible, sudden temperature changes should be avoided. When venturing outside, the use of a scarf or handkerchief over the nose and mouth is advisable. It is also important that correct air humidification be maintained within your dwelling, particularly during the winter months.
7. Certain irritant inhalants cannot be avoided completely because of their seasonal or environmental presence, however, all measures should be taken to reduce exposure to these inhalants. The inhalation of tobacco smoke can and should be avoided. Dust control measures such as frequent household vacuuming and changing of furnace filters may prove helpful.

Directions for Use: For patient convenience, particularly during the night, Alupent Syrup comes equipped with its own calibrated measuring cap. Each 5 mL (1 capful equivalent to 1 teaspoonful) contains 10 mg of Alupent. For hygenic reasons, it is recommended that the measuring cap be washed after each use and replaced on the bottle.

Dosage: Ages 4 to 12: 10 mg (1 capful or 1 teaspoonful) 3 times daily; above 12: 20 mg (2 capsful or 2 teaspoonsful) 3 to 4 times daily.

Precautions: Persons with high blood pressure, heart disease, diabetes, glaucoma or thyroid disease should use Alupent only on the advice of a physician.

Availability: Alupent Syrup is available in amber colored bottles containing 250 mL of syrup. Each bottle is equipped with its own handy measuring cap.

□ AMERGE® Ⓟ

Glaxo Wellcome

Naratriptan HCl

Receptor Agonist—Migraine Therapy

Information for the Patient: Amerge (naratriptan hydrochloride) tablets.

Please read this leaflet carefully before you take Amerge tablets. This provides a summary of the information available on your medicine. Please do not throw away this leaflet until you have finished your medicine. You may need to read this leaflet again. This leaflet does not contain all the information on Amerge tablets. For further information or advice, ask your doctor or pharmacist.

Information About Your Medicine: The name of your medicine is Amerge tablets. It can be obtained only by prescription from your doctor. The decision to use Amerge tablets is one that you and your doctor should make jointly, taking into account your individual preferences and medical circumstances. The majority of patients who have taken Amerge have not experienced any significant side effects. However, drugs like Amerge have caused serious side effects in some patients, especially people with heart or blood vessel disease. If you have risk factors for heart disease (such as high blood pressure, high cholesterol, obesity, diabetes, smoking, strong family history of heart disease, or you are postmenopausal or a male over 40), you should tell your doctor, who should evaluate you for heart disease, in order to determine if Amerge is appropriate for you.

The Purpose of Your Medicine: Amerge tablets are intended to relieve your migraine headache and other associated symptoms of a migraine attack. Amerge tablets should not be used continuously to prevent or reduce the number of attacks you experience. Use Amerge tablets only to treat an actual migraine attack. Amerge should not be used to relieve pain other than that associated with migraine headache.

How Your Medicine Works: Migraine headache is believed to be caused by a widening of the blood vessels in the head. Amerge narrows these vessels and relieves the pain and other symptoms of migraine headache.

Important Questions to Consider Before Taking Amerge Tablets: If the answer to any of the following questions is **yes** or if you do not know the answer, then please discuss with your doctor before you use Amerge tablets.

- Are you pregnant? Do you think you might be pregnant? Are you trying to become pregnant? Are you using inadequate contraception? Are you breast-feeding?
- Do you ever suffer from any pain or tightness in the chest (which may or may not spread to your neck, jaw, or upper arm), heart or blood vessel disease, angina, shortness of breath, or irregular heartbeats? Have you had a heart attack or stroke?
- Do you have risk factors for heart disease (such as high blood pressure, high cholesterol, obesity, diabetes, smoking, strong family history of heart disease, or are you postmenopausal or a male over 40)?
- Have you ever had to stop taking this or any other medication because of an allergy or other problems?
- Have you had, or do you have, epilepsy or seizures?
- Are you taking any other migraine medications, including Imitrex (sumatriptan succinate/sumatriptan), ergotamine, dihydroergotamine, or methysergide?
- Are you taking any selective serotonin reuptake inhibitors (SSRIs) or other medications for depression?
- Have you ever experienced difficulty moving one side of your body when you have a headache?
- Have you had, or do you have, any disease of the kidney or liver?
- Is this headache different from your usual migraine attacks?

Remember, if you answered **yes** to any of the above questions, then discuss it with your doctor.

The Use of Amerge Tablets During Pregnancy: Do not use Amerge tablets if you are pregnant, think you might be pregnant, are trying to become pregnant, or are not using adequate contraception, unless you have discussed this with your doctor.

How to Use Amerge Tablets: For adults, the usual dose is a single 1 or 2.5 mg tablet (as recommended by your doctor) taken whole with

Amerge (cont'd)

fluids. The tablet should be taken as soon as your migraine appears, but it may be taken at anytime after the headache starts. A second tablet may be taken if your headache returns or if you need more relief, but not sooner than 4 hours following the first tablet. For an individual attack, if you have no response to the first tablet, do not take a second tablet without first talking to your doctor. Do not take more than a total of 5 mg in any 24-hour period. If you have kidney or liver disease, take as directed by your doctor.

If you taking any other migraine medications, check with your doctor first before taking Amerge.

Side Effects to Watch For: Although most patients who have taken Amerge have not experienced any significant side effects, some individuals have experienced problems.

- **Some patients experience sensations of pain, pressure or tightness in the chest, neck, throat, jaw or arms when using Amerge tablets. If this happens to you, then discuss it with your doctor before using any more Amerge tablets. If the chest pain is severe (may resemble an angina attack) or does not go away, call your doctor immediately.**
- Drowsiness may occur, therefore do not drive or operate machinery until you are sure that you are not drowsy.
- Rare cases of shortness of breath; wheeziness; swelling of eyelids, face, or lips; or a skin rash, skin lumps, or hives may happen. If it happens to you, then tell your doctor immediately. Do not take any more Amerge tablets unless your doctor tells you to do so.
- A few people may feel tingling, warmth, flushing (redness of face lasting a short time), heaviness or pressure, tiredness, or dizziness after treatment with Amerge tablets. Tell your doctor if you have any of these symptoms.
- If you have sudden and/or severe abdominal pain following Amerge tablets, call your doctor immediately.
- If you feel unwell in any other way or have any symptoms that you do not understand, you should contact your doctor immediately.

What to Do if an Overdose is Taken: If you have taken more medication than your doctor has instructed, contact either your doctor, hospital emergency department, or nearest poison control center immediately.

Storing Your Medicine: Keep your medicine in a safe place where children cannot reach it. It may be harmful to children.

Store your medication away from heat and light. Do not store at temperatures above 30°C.

If your medication has expired (the expiration date is printed on the treatment pack), throw it away.

If your doctor decides to stop your treatment, do not keep any leftover medicine unless your doctor tells you to.

What is in Your Medicine: Amerge tablets contain either 1 mg or 2.5 mg of naratriptan base, as the hydrochloride salt. The tablets also contain croscarmellose sodium, hydroxypropyl methylcellulose, indigo carmine aluminium lake (FD&C Blue No. 2) [2.5 mg tablet only], iron oxide yellow [2.5 mg tablet only], lactose, magnesium stearate, microcrystalline cellulose, titanium dioxide and triacetin.

Class of Medicine: This medicine is one of a group of antimigraine drugs.

Who Produces Your Medicine: Manufacturer: Glaxo Wellcome Inc. 7333 Mississauga Road North, Mississauga, Ontario L5N 6L4

Reminder: Remember: This medicine is for you. Only a doctor can prescribe it for you. Never give it to someone else. It may harm them even if their symptoms appear to be similar to yours.

□ ANA-KIT®

Bayer

Epinephrine—Chlorpheniramine Maleate

Allergy Therapy

Information for the Patient: Patient Directions for Use: Please read entire direction sheet before an emergency arises.

In the event of a life-threatening situation, follow these steps immediately to administer the epinephrine (see package insert for illustrations).

1. Remove (pull off) blue plastic needle cover. Hold syringe upright and push plunger to expel air and excess epinephrine (plunger will stop).
2. Rotate rectangular plunger ¼ turn to the right. Plunger will align with slot in barrel of syringe. Wipe injection site with alcohol swab.
3. Insert needle straight into arm or thigh.
4. Push plunger until it stops. Syringe will inject a 0.3 mL dose for adults and children over 12 years.

Children: Syringe barrel has 0.1 mL graduations so that smaller doses can be measured. Administer to infants to 2 years: 0.05 to 0.1 mL; 2 to 6 years: 0.15 mL; and 6 to 12 years: 0.2 mL.

Once the initial epinephrine injection has been administered, follow these additional steps.

1. **Contact physician, if possible.**
2. **Remove stinger** if stung by insect. (Use fingernails. **Do not** push, pinch or squeeze, or further imbed the stinger into the skin as this may cause further venom to be injected.)
3. **Apply tourniquet,** if stung on an arm or leg, between the sting and the body. (If the sting is elsewhere, on the neck, face, or body, for example, proceed immediately to step 5.) Do not obstruct arterial blood flow with the tourniquet.
4. **Tighten tourniquet.** To tighten, pull on the end of **one string.** Then, at least every 10 minutes, loosen the tourniquet by pulling on the small metal ring.
5. **Chew and swallow Chlo-Amine tablets.** For adults and children over 12 years, take 4 tablets; children 6 to 12 years take 2 tablets; children under 6 years take 1 tablet. These tablets are chewable antihistamine which is generally tolerated.
6. **Prepare syringe for a possible second injection.** Turn the rectangular plunger ¼ turn to the right to line up with rectangular slot in the syringe. (A slight wiggling may aid the turning and alignment of the plunger).
7. **The second injection.** If after 10 minutes from the first injection symptoms are not noticeably improved, a second injection is required. Cleanse skin area with alcohol swab and make second injection as in **Steps 3 and 4** for the first epinephrine injection. (A small amount of epinephrine will remain in syringe after the second dose and cannot be expelled). **Note: Dispose of syringe and remaining contents if second injection is not required.**
8. **Apply ice packs if available at site of the insect sting** (if applicable).
9. **Keep patient warm and avoid exertion.**

Precautions: Epinephrine: For s.c. or i.m. injection only. **Not intended for i.v. use.**

Epinephrine injection, USP, contains sodium bisulfite. Patients with a suspected sulfite sensitivity should consult their physician well in advance before the need to use this product becomes critical.

Epinephrine is light sensitive and should be stored in box provided. **Store at room temperature,** approximately 25°C. Protect from freezing. Any epinephrine solution in contact with the needle may cause rusting of the metal. **Do not try to force air out of the syringe until you are ready to use the epinephrine.** This may rupture the seal and allow the epinephrine solution to contact the metal promoting deterioration. **Never remove cover from needle until ready to use syringe** as this may cause needle and contents to become contaminated.

Parenteral drug products should be inspected visually for particulate matter and discoloration prior to administration, whenever solution and container permit. Do not use Epinephrine Injection, USP, if it has a pinkish or darker than slightly yellow color or contains a precipitate. Obtain replacement syringe from pharmacist. Periodically check expiration date on syringe. If expiration date is near, re-order new syringe and discard outdated syringe after new syringe has been received.

Chlo-Amine: As with any drug, if you are pregnant or nursing a baby, seek the advice of a health professional before using this product.

Patients should not drive or operate machinery after taking Chlo-Amine. Drowsiness, dizziness, blurred vision, dry mouth and gastrointestinal upsets may occur. Keep out of reach of children.

The asthmatic patient should take the chlorpheniramine maleate tablets with caution.

Limited Warranty: A number of factors beyond our control reduces the efficacy of this product or even results in an ill effect following its use. These include storage and handling of the product after it leaves our hands, diagnosis, dosage, method of administration and biological differences in individual patients. Because of these factors, it is important that this product be stored properly and that the directions be followed carefully during use.

The foregoing statement is made in lieu of any other warranty, express or implied, including any warranty of merchantability or fitness. Representatives of the Company are not authorized to vary the terms of this warranty or the contents of any printed labelling for this product except by printed notice from the Company's Spokane, WA office. The prescriber and user of this product must accept the terms hereof.

☐ ANANDRON® ℞

Hoechst Marion Roussel

Nilutamide

Nonsteroidal Antiandrogen

Information for the Patient: How to Make Anandron Work Best for You: Your doctor has decided that Anandron is the best treatment for you. Remember that the chances of controlling your illness are greater if you cooperate fully with your doctor and try to become well informed about your condition.

This leaflet is intended to provide you with only brief advice about Anandron tablets. It does not take the place of your doctor's advice or your pharmacist's advice. Your doctor knows and understands your personal condition; be sure to follow your doctor's instructions carefully and read any materials he gives you. If you have any questions after reading this information leaflet, be sure to ask your doctor or pharmacist. Please note that both your doctor and pharmacist have much more information about Anandron than the information contained in this brief leaflet.

Keep this leaflet with the medicine as you may need to use it again.

What is Anandron and How Does it Work? Anandron belongs to a group of medicines called "antiandrogens". It blocks the effect of hormones called androgens, which are naturally produced by your body. By blocking the effect of androgens, Anandron may help slow down the disease in your prostate gland. It will also help to reduce the symptoms you experience because of the disease.

What Does Anandron Contain? Anandron tablets contain the active ingredient nilutamide. Each tablet contains either 50 or 100 mg of nilutamide. Amongst nonactive ingredients is lactose (30 mg/tablet of Anandron 50 mg and 60 mg/tablet of Anandron 100 mg).

Anandron tablets are white to off-white in color. The word 'Anandron' is marked on one side of the tablet. The strength, either '50' or '100' is marked on the other side of the tablet.

How Should You Take Anandron to Make it Work Best for You? Anandron tablets are taken by mouth. The usual dose is 300 mg/day for the first 4 weeks of treatment and then 150 mg every day thereafter. Anandron is usually taken once per day, before breakfast. However, your doctor may recommend a different dose or a different schedule.

The number of tablets that you need to take each day will depend on whether your doctor has prescribed the 50 mg tablets or the 100 mg tablets. Please check with your doctor or pharmacist if you are unsure of the correct amount of tablets to take.

You should take Anandron only as directed by your doctor. Do not take more or less of it, do not take it more often, and do not take it for a longer period of time than your doctor ordered.

Your doctor will decide for how long you need to take Anandron. This will depend on your disease condition and on whether you experience side effects. Please discuss any concerns you have with your doctor.

What to do if You Miss a Dose? If you miss a dose, take it as soon as you remember and then resume your normal dosing schedule. However, you should not take more than 300 mg of Anandron in any one day during the first 4 weeks of treatment or more than 150 mg in any one day thereafter. Therefore, if it is almost time for your next dose when you remember that you have missed a dose, skip the dose you missed and take your next dose at the usual time (i.e., do not take a double dose). If you are concerned or if you have missed more than 1 dose, please speak to your doctor.

What to do if You Take too Many Tablets? If you take, by mistake, too many tablets on the same day, you may feel nauseous and dizzy, and you may vomit. These symptoms will normally go away after temporarily interrupting your treatment or reducing the dose, however these steps should only be taken on your doctor's advice. If you have taken more than 300 mg in 1 day, you should contact your doctor as soon as possible.

Does Anandron Have Side Effects? The various treatments of disease of the prostate, such as yours, can all cause hot flushes, decrease in sex drive, or impotence.

Anandron is usually well tolerated but like any other medicine, can cause side effects. Most side effects with Anandron occur early in the course of treatment and will usually lessen after 4 weeks when the dose is normally reduced to 150 mg daily.

The most common side effects affect the eyes. You may notice that your eyes require more time to adapt to darkness, especially when there is a sudden change in lighting (e.g., driving through a tunnel). When it occurs, this problem is almost always temporary and may be improved by wearing tinted glasses. However, until your eyes accommodate better to the dark, you should be very careful when driving or operating machinery.

Some patients may develop breathing problems or a worsening of a pre-existing breathing problem. Symptoms may include shortness of breath, coughing, chest pain and fever. It is important that you contact your doctor immediately if you have any breathing difficulties while taking Anandron.

In rare cases, Anandron may cause an increase in liver tests and, very rarely, hepatitis. Symptoms that may suggest a liver problem include: persistent lack of appetite, nausea (queasiness), vomiting, abdominal pain or tenderness, jaundice (yellow eyes and/or skin), dark urine, itching or unexplained flu-like symptoms. You should advise your doctor promptly if you develop any of these symptoms.

Anandron can also cause nausea and vomiting which are not related to liver problems. It can also cause dizziness. In most cases, these symptoms will improve following dosage reduction which normally occurs after 4 weeks of treatment. However, you should inform your doctor as soon as possible if you experience vomiting because it may be preferable to lower your dose earlier.

If you think that you are reacting badly to Anandron, please tell your doctor. This is especially important if you have any problem that is not mentioned in this leaflet.

Can I Take Anandron with Alcohol and Other Medicines? Some patients being treated with Anandron may have hot flushes or feel unwell after drinking alcohol. This is known as alcohol intolerance. If this happens to you, you should avoid alcohol completely. Please contact your doctor or pharmacist for advice.

Anandron may interfere or cause problems with other medicines that you are taking, so it is important that you tell your doctor and pharmacist about all of the medicines that you are taking, including those you have obtained without a prescription. This is especially important if you are taking any of the following medicines: warfarin [Coumadin] or nicoumalone [Sintrom] (to thin the blood), phenytoin [Dilantin and others] (for epilepsy), propranolol [Inderal and others] (for high blood pressure, angina, migraine or other conditions), chlordiazepoxide [Librium and others] or diazepam [Valium] (for anxiety), theophylline [Theodur and others](for asthma). Check the labels on your medicines for these names or ask your pharmacist for advice.

Your doctor will be able to advise you what to do if you are taking any of these medicines. In most cases, your doctor will reduce the dose of these medicines while you are taking Anandron. Your doctor may also perform some blood tests.

What Should I Remember? Before taking this medication tell your doctor and pharmacist if:

- You have previously been treated for your prostate condition with a hormone, and the treatment did not work;
- You have liver or breathing problems. You should not take Anandron if you have either a severe liver or severe breathing disorder. Please discuss this with your doctor if you believe that you have either of these conditions;
- You have lactose intolerance;
- You are taking any other medication;
- You have any other medical problem(s).

While Taking This Medication:

- Report any unusual reactions to your doctor without delay. This is important as it will aid in the early detection and prevention of potential complications;
- Anandron is intended for the treatment of prostate disease in men and therefore should not be taken under any circumstances by women or by children;
- Keep Anandron at room temperature below 25°C. Protect the tablets from excessive heat, light and humidity. As with all medicines, you should store the tablets in the original pharmacist container and out of the reach of children;
- If you require more information on this drug, consult your doctor or pharmacist.

What Else Do I Need to Know? Return any unused or expired Anandron tablets to your pharmacist for disposal.

☐ ANAPROX® Ⓟ
☐ ANAPROX® DS Ⓟ
Roche

Naproxen Sodium
Analgesic—Anti-inflammatory

Information for the Patient: How to make Anaprox or Anaprox DS work best for you: Your doctor has decided that Anaprox or Anaprox DS (naproxen sodium) is the best treatment for you. As you take your Anaprox or Anaprox DS tablets, remember that your chances of controlling your symptoms are greater if you cooperate fully with your doctor and try to become well informed about your condition.

This leaflet is not as thorough as the official Product Monograph on Anaprox and Anaprox DS (which your doctor or pharmacist has available), and is meant to supplement what your doctor has told you. Your doctor knows and understands your personal condition; be sure to follow your doctor's instructions carefully and read any materials he or she gives you. **If you have any questions after reading this information leaflet, be sure to ask you doctor.**

What is Anaprox/Anaprox DS? Anaprox and Anaprox DS are medicines used to relieve pain accompanied by inflammation in conditions such as musculoskeletal trauma and post-dental extraction. They are also indicated for the relief of pain associated with postpartum cramping and dysmenorrhea. They belong to a family of drugs known as nonsteroidal anti-inflammatory drugs (NSAIDs) or anti-prostaglandin drugs.

What do Anaprox and Anaprox DS look like? Anaprox (naproxen sodium) is only available as film coated 275 mg tablets which are of a Blue Oval design TM and have an NPS-275 engraved on one side. Anaprox DS (naproxen sodium) is also only available as film coated 550 mg tablets which are of a Blue Oval design™ and have an NPS 550 engraved on one side.

The Anaprox DS tablet is larger than the Anaprox tablet.

TM—The Blue Oval design of the tablets is Hoffmann-La Roche Limited's registered trade-mark for its naproxen sodium.

How do Anaprox and Anaprox DS work? Conditions like yours are usually associated with pain with or without inflammation. Research shows that Anaprox and Anaprox DS work by reducing the production of certain substances (called prostaglandins) that the body normally produces to help control such functions as muscle contraction, inflammation and numerous other body processes.

Clinical studies indicate that when prostaglandin levels are reduced, the intensity of pain and inflammation is reduced as well.

How should you take Anaprox or Anaprox DS to make it work best for you? Usually Anaprox is prescribed to be taken at a starting dose of two 275 mg tablets followed by one 275 mg tablet every 6 to 8 hours as required. The total daily dose should not exceed five 275 mg tablets. Alternatively, you may be prescribed Anaprox DS 550 mg tablet twice a day.

It's important to keep taking Anaprox or Anaprox DS even after you start to feel better. This helps to keep your pain and tenderness under control. You should take Anaprox or Anaprox DS with food or milk.

Important: Your doctor may give you different instructions better suited to your specific needs. If you need more information about how to take Anaprox or Anaprox DS properly, double-check with your doctor or pharmacist.

How long does it take before Anaprox or Anaprox DS begins to work? Anaprox and Anaprox DS are completely absorbed into your system usually within 1 hour. If Anaprox or Anaprox DS does not seem to be helping you, tell your doctor. You may need a different dosage, or your doctor may want to prescribe another treatment program for you.

Will the amount of Anaprox or Anaprox DS you take ever change? It might change. As time goes by, your doctor may decide that it is advisable to make adjustments in the dosage of Anaprox or Anaprox DS you are taking. He or she may suggest that you increase or decrease your medication according to how severe your symptoms are or how active you are.

Follow instructions; your doctor understands how to set the upper and lower dosage limits so that you get the greatest benefit from Anaprox or Anaprox DS.

Does Anaprox or Anaprox DS have side effects? Any medication can cause side effects; this is true for ASA and all of the nonsteroidal anti-inflammatory drugs that are used to treat conditions like yours. In most patients it has been well tolerated so the chances are that you will tolerate it well too. Side effects are significantly less than those occurring with ASA in doses used to treat arthritis. Do not take ASA, ASA-containing compounds or other drugs used to relieve symptoms of arthritis while taking Anaprox or Anaprox DS unless directed to do so by your physician.

Relatively common unwanted side effects of all nonsteroidal anti-inflammatory drugs are heartburn, pain in the gut, nausea, constipation and other gastrointestinal complaints. Remember to take Anaprox or Anaprox DS with meals or a glass of milk to reduce discomfort of this type.

If you have a history of stomach upset, or if you have an ulcer, tell your doctor. All nonsteroidal anti-inflammatory drugs may aggravate your problem and sometimes even cause bleeding, or ulcers in your stomach or intestines. These complications can sometimes be severe and occasional fatalities have been reported with all drugs of this class.

Contact your doctor immediately if you experience any of these symptoms:

- bloody or black tarry stools;
- shortness of breath, wheezing, any trouble in breathing or tightness in the chest;
- skin rash, swelling, hives or itching;
- indigestion, nausea, vomiting, stomach pain or diarrhea;
- yellow discoloration of the skin or eyes, with or without fatigue;
- any changes in the amount or color of your urine (such as dark; red or brown);
- swelling of the feet or lower legs;
- blurred vision or any visual disturbance.

Other effects that have been reported infrequently include headache, drowsiness, dizziness, depression and ringing in the ears. These reactions usually do not pose a serious problem, and most people can continue treatment. More rarely, visual or hearing disturbances and blood disorders have occurred. **Contact your doctor if you experience any problems.** Almost all of the side effects experienced with Anaprox or Anaprox DS stop when the medication is stopped.

If you are allergic to ASA or to any of the other nonsteroidal anti-inflammatory drugs (e.g. diclofenac, diflunisal, fenoprofen, flurbiprofen, ibuprofen, indomethacin, ketoprofen, mefenamic acid, piroxicam, sulindac, tiaprofenic acid, tolmetin) used to treat arthritis or other muscle and joint conditions, **do not take Anaprox or Anaprox DS.** You may be allergic to it too. **Also, you should not take Anaprox or Anaprox DS if you are already taking Naprosyn (naproxen), a related drug.**

Are there any special do's and don'ts about taking Anaprox or Anaprox DS? Do tell your doctor and pharmacist about any other medications you take, both prescription and nonprescription. This is important because some drugs can interact with each other and produce undesirable effects.

Do tell your doctor if you have an ulcer, liver disease, kidney disease, or history of any stomach problems.

Do be cautious about driving or participating in activities that require alertness if you are drowsy, dizzy, or light-headed after taking Anaprox or Anaprox DS (naproxen sodium).

Do check with your doctor if you are not getting relief or you have any problems while taking Anaprox or Anaprox DS.

Do tell your physician if you are pregnant or are planning to become pregnant.

Don't take Anaprox or Anaprox DS if you are breast-feeding. The drug does pass into the milk of nursing women.

Don't take Anaprox or Anaprox DS if you are allergic to it, or if you have had an allergic-type reaction to ASA or to any other drug used for pain relief or arthritis. Do check with your doctor.

Do cooperate with your doctor if he or she wants you to take certain lab tests to monitor the effectiveness of treatment or possible side effects.

☐ ANDRIOL ◈
Organon

Testosterone Undecanoate
Androgen

Information for the Patient: Andriol (testosterone undecanoate) which has been prescribed to you by your doctor, is a testosterone preparation. Testosterone is a male hormone, an androgen, which is naturally produced in the body and necessary for the normal sexual development of males. Androgens are used to replace the hormone when the body is unable to produce enough on its own or to stimulate the beginning of puberty in certain boys. In addition, some of these medicines may be used for other conditions as determined by your doctor.

There is no good medical evidence to support the belief that the use of androgens in athletes will increase muscle strength. When used for this purpose, it may be dangerous to health because of unwanted effects such as too much fluid in the body and liver disease; or swelling of breasts. You should take Andriol only as directed by your doctor. Do not take more of it, do not take it more often and do not take it for a longer period of time than your doctor ordered.

Before Using This Medicine: In order to decide on the best treatment for your medical problem, your doctor should be told:

- if you have ever had any unusual or allergic reaction to androgens or anabolic steroids.
- if you are on a low-salt, low-sugar, or any other special diet, or if you are allergic to any substance, such as foods, sulfites or other preservatives, or dyes. Most medicines contain more than their active ingredient. Your doctor, nurse, or pharmacist can help you avoid products that may cause a problem.
- if you are an adult male who plans to have children. High doses of androgens may cause infertility.
- if you have any of the following medical problems: breast cancer (in males), edema (swelling of face, hands, feet, or lower legs), enlarged prostate, kidney disease, diabetes mellitus (sugar diabetes), prostate cancer, liver disease, heart or blood vessel disease.
- if you are now taking **any** other prescription or nonprescription (OTC) medicine, especially anticoagulants (blood thinners).
- if you are bedridden.

How to Store this Medicine: Keep out of the reach of children.

Store between 15 and 25°C. Protect from light and moisture. Use within 90 days.

Do not keep outdated medicine or medicine no longer needed. Be sure that any discarded medicine is out of the reach of children.

Precautions While Using This Medicine: Your doctor should check your progress at regular visits in order to make sure this medicine does not cause unwanted effects. Any male adolescent patient receiving androgens for delayed puberty should have bone development checked every 6 months.

Diabetics: This medicine may affect blood sugar levels. If you notice a change in the results of your urine sugar test or if you have any questions about this, check with your doctor.

Side Effects of This Medicine: Discuss these possible effects with your doctor: Tumors of the liver, liver cancer, or peliosis hepatis, a form of liver disease, have occurred during long-term, high-dose therapy with androgens. Although these effects are rare, they can be very serious and may cause death.

When elderly male patients are treated with androgens, they may have an increased risk of enlarged prostate or cancer of the prostate.

Androgens may cause children to stop growing early or to develop too fast sexually. Radiographic examination of the hands and wrist should be performed every 6 months to determine the rate of bone maturation and to assess the effect of treatment on the epiphyseal centers.

Along with its needed effects, a medicine may cause some unwanted effects. Although not all of these side effects appear very often, when they do occur they may require medical attention.

Check with your doctor immediately if any of the following side effects occur:

- Yellow eyes or skin; flushing or redness of skin or any changes in skin color; skin rash or itching; hives;
- black, tarry, or light-colored stools; dark-colored urine;
- purple or red-colored spots on body or inside the mouth or nose;
- sore throat and/or fever;
- nausea or vomiting; vomiting of blood;
- abdominal or stomach pain (continuing); pain, tenderness, or swelling in the upper abdominal or stomach area;
- loss of appetite (continuing); unpleasant breath odor (continuing);
- confusion; dizziness; headache (frequent or continuing); mental depression;
- feeling of discomfort (continuing);
- shortness of breath;
- swelling of feet or lower legs;
- unusual bleeding; unusual tiredness;
- frequent or continuing erection; frequent urge to urinate;
- swelling of breasts or breast soreness.

For elderly males only:

- Difficult or frequent urination; unusual increase in sexual desire.

Other side effects may occur which usually do not require medical attention. These side effects may go away during treatment as your body adjusts to the medicine. However, check with your doctor if any of the following side effects continue or are bothersome: constipation; diarrhea; stomach pain; trouble in sleeping; unusual decrease or increase in sexual desire.

Other side effects not listed above may also occur in some patients. If you notice any other effects, check with your doctor.

□ ANSAID® Ⓟ

Pharmacia & Upjohn

Flurbiprofen

Anti-inflammatory—Analgesic

Information for the Patient: What is Ansaid: Ansaid is a product name for flurbiprofen, a medicine to relieve pain and reduce inflammation. Ansaid which has been prescribed to you by your doctor, is one of a large group of nonsteroidal anti-inflammatory drugs (NSAIDs), is not related to cortisone and does not contain acetylsalicylic acid (ASA).

Ansaid is used to treat certain types of arthritis (rheumatoid arthritis, osteoarthritis, ankylosing spondylitis); dysmenorrhea (menstrual pain); and mild to moderate pain accompanied by inflammation (bursitis, tendinitis, soft tissue trauma, pain following dental procedures).

Ansaid helps to relieve joint pain, swelling, stiffness and fever by reducing the production of certain substances (prostaglandins) and helping to control inflammation and other body reactions.

When to Take Ansaid: You should take Ansaid only as directed by your doctor. Do not take more of it, do not take it more often and do not take it for a longer period of time than your doctor ordered. Be sure to take Ansaid regularly as prescribed. In some types of arthritis, up to 2 weeks may pass before you feel the full effects of this medicine. During treatment, your doctor may decide to adjust the dosage according to your response to the medication.

Generally, patients are instructed to take Ansaid 2 to 4 times a day. Ansaid will work whether or not you take it with meals. However, if you take 3 doses, you may wish to take them with meals. First, this spaces the tablet throughout the day and makes it easier for you to remember to take your medication. Second, since some people may experience an upset stomach with products like Ansaid, taking the medication with meals can reduce or prevent stomach upset.

If your doctor prescribes 4 doses, the fourth dose is usually taken at bedtime. If Ansaid upsets your stomach, you may wish to take the bedtime dose with a snack.

The Best Dosage of Ansaid for You: Arthritis, as you know, is a condition that has its ups and downs, and the amount of pain and inflammation you experience can change from day to day and from week to week. After the initial period of treatment with Ansaid, your doctor may want to make adjustments to find the best dosage for you.

By accurately reporting how you feel, you can help your doctor decide whether the initial dosage should be increased or decreased. Ansaid comes in 2 tablet strengths—50 mg and 100 mg—so your doctor can easily lower or raise the dosage.

Increasing the Dosage: Sometimes higher doses of Ansaid may be needed because of the **success** of your treatment. The explanation is simple: as your ability to do things improves, you may find yourself automatically increasing your activities. This, in turn, may cause you to feel more pain. If this happens, your dosage of Ansaid may need to be increased to control the pain at this increased level of activity. If your symptoms get worse because of flare-up in your arthritis, your doctor may want you to increase your dosage of Ansaid until the symptoms are once again under control.

Upper and Lower Dosage Limits of Ansaid: When Ansaid is relieving the symptoms of your arthritis and you are accustomed to the medication, your doctor may set upper and lower dosage limits and tell you to adjust the dose within these limits, according to your pain and inflammation. It is important, however, not to go beyond the upper limits your doctor has set.

Specific Dosing Instructions: Rheumatoid Arthritis: Initially two 100 mg (blue) tablets per day to a maximum of six 50 mg (white) tablets or three 100 mg (blue) tablets per day.

Osteoarthritis: Initially two 100 mg (blue) tablets per day to a maximum of six 50 mg (white) tablets or three 100 mg (blue) tablets per day.

Ansaid (cont'd)

Ankylosing Spondylitis: Initially two 100 mg (blue) tablets per day to a maximum of six 50 mg (white) tablets or three 100 mg (blue) tablets per day.

Dysmenorrhea: One 50 mg (white) tablet 4 times per day.

Mild to Moderately Severe Pain: One 50 mg (white) tablet every 4 to 6 hours when needed for pain.

Do not take ASA (acetylsalicylic acid), ASA-containing compounds or other drugs used to relieve symptoms of arthritis while taking Ansaid unless directed to do so by your doctor or pharmacist.

If you are prescribed this medication for use over a long period of time, your doctor will check your health during regular visits to assess your progress to ensure that this medication is not causing unwanted effects.

Side Effects of Ansaid: Ansaid has been proven to be a relatively safe, trouble-free medication without serious side effects in most patients. **Any medication, even acetylsalicylic acid (ASA), may sometimes cause side effects, and the same is true of Ansaid.** If you know about these side effects, you may be able to prevent, reduce, or modify them if they occur. Your doctor may require certain tests to monitor the effectiveness of your treatment program and any possible side effects. Chances are excellent that you will be able to tolerate and experience the benefits of taking Ansaid.

The most frequent side effect of most medication, even acetylsalicylic acid (ASA), used to treat arthritis is some type of stomach upset. This side effect for Ansaid in clinical studies was much less than reported for acetylsalicylic acid (ASA), and can take the form of nausea, pain in the gut, heartburn, or a sense of fullness or bloating. Very often, as already mentioned, this discomfort can be controlled by taking Ansaid with meals or a glass of milk.

Elderly, frail or debilitated patients often seem to experience more frequent or more severe side effects. Although not all of these side effects are common, when they do occur they may require medical attention. Check with your doctor immediately if any of the following are noted:

—bloody or black tarry stools;
—shortness of breath, wheezing, any trouble in breathing or tightness in the chest;
—skin rash, swelling, hives or itching;
—indigestion, nausea, vomiting, stomach pain or diarrhea;
—yellow discoloration of the skin or eyes, with or without fatigue;
—any changes in the amount of color of your urine (such as dark red or brown);
—swelling of the feet or lower legs;
—blurred vision or any visual disturbance;
—mental confusion, depression, dizziness, lightheadedness, hearing problems.

Facts to Remember About Ansaid: Before taking this medication tell your doctor, pharmacist, or dentist if you:

—are allergic to Ansaid or other related medicines of the NSAID (non-steroidal anti-inflammatory drug) group such as acetylsalicylic acid (ASA), diclofenac, diflunisal, fenoprofen, flurbiprofen, ibuprofen, indomethacin, ketoprofen, mefenamic acid, piroxicam, sulindac, tiaprofenic acid or tolmetin;
—have a history of stomach upset, ulcers, or liver or kidney diseases;
—are pregnant or intend to become pregnant while taking this medication;
—are breast-feeding;
—are taking any other medication (either prescription or nonprescription);
—have any other medical problem(s).

While taking this medication:

—tell any other doctor, dentist or pharmacist that you consult or see, that you are taking this medication;
—be cautious about driving or particularly in activities that require alertness if you are drowsy, dizzy or lightheaded after taking this medication;
—check with your doctor if you are not getting any relief or if any problems develop;
—report any unusual reactions to your doctor. This is very important as it will aid in the early detection and prevention of potential complications;
—your regular medical checkups are essential;
—if you require more information on this drug, consult your doctor or pharmacist.

☐ ANZEMET™ Ⓟ

Hoechst Marion Roussel

Dolasetron Mesylate

Antiemetic

Information for the Patient: Please read this information leaflet carefully before you start to take your medicine, even if you have taken this drug before. Keep this leaflet handy in order to consult it while taking your medication. This leaflet is only a short summary of the information available. For further information or advice, ask your doctor or pharmacist.

What Is Anzemet?

- Anzemet (dolasetron mesylate) is a prescription medicine that belongs to a family of drugs called antiemetics.
- Anzemet is available in tablet form and as an i.v. injection. The i.v. injection is administered only by a doctor or nurse in a hospital or clinic setting.

How Does Anzemet Work?

- Anzemet is taken to prevent nausea (feeling of stomach sickness) and vomiting, which may occur in patients undergoing cancer chemotherapy. It is thought that chemotherapy treatments cause release of a naturally occurring substance in the body (serotonin), which can cause you to feel sick or vomit. Anzemet blocks the effect of serotonin, and may prevent you from feeling nauseous or vomiting.

What Do I Need to Do Before Taking Anzemet?
Tell Your Doctor:

- If you are allergic to any of the ingredients in Anzemet tablets (see list of ingredients at the end of this leaflet).

How Do I Take Anzemet Properly?

- The label on the container of your medicine should tell you how to take your medicine. It is important that you follow these instructions exactly. If you have any questions regarding these instructions, ask your doctor or pharmacist.
- **Do not take more tablets or take your tablets more often than prescribed.**
- Swallow your tablets whole with a little water. Anzemet tablets may be taken with or without food.
- If you vomit within 1 hour of taking your medicine, you should take the same amount of medicine again. If vomiting continues, consult your doctor.
- If you miss a dose and do not feel sick, take the next dose when it is scheduled. If you miss a dose and feel sick or vomit, take a tablet as soon as possible.

Can Anzemet Be Used During Pregnancy or Breast-Feeding?

- This medicine should not be taken if you are pregnant, if you are likely to become pregnant or if you are breast-feeding a baby.

What if I Have Problems While Taking Anzemet?

- If you experience wheezing and tightness of the chest, chest pain, heart throbbing, swelling of eyelids, face or lips, or develop a skin rash, skin lumps or hives, contact your doctor immediately. Do not take any more medicine unless your doctor tells you to do so.
- Most people have no problems after taking Anzemet tablets. However, a few people may have side effects such as headaches, diarrhea or dizziness. If you experience these effects, there is no need to stop taking this medicine, but you should tell your doctor about them at your next visit.
- Tell your doctor if your nausea or vomiting does not improve while taking Anzemet tablets.

What if I Take too Much Anzemet?

- If you accidentally take more tablets than prescribed, contact your doctor or hospital emergency department immediately.

Where Should I Store Anzemet?

- Leave your tablets in their original packaging and store at room temperature (15 to 30°C).
- Keep Anzemet out of the reach of children.
- If your doctor decides to stop treatment with this medicine, do not keep any left over medicine unless your doctor tells you to do so.

Who Do I Ask if I Have any Questions About Anzemet?

- Consult your doctor or pharmacist.

What Does Anzemet Contain?

- Anzemet Tablets contain either 50 mg or 100 mg of dolasetron mesylate. Each tablet also contains the following nonmedicinal ingredients: carnauba wax, croscarmellose sodium, hydroxypropyl methylcellulose, **lactose,** magnesium stearate, polyethylene glycol, polysorbate

80, pregelatinized starch, red iron oxide, titanium dioxide, and white wax.

Who Supplies Anzemet?

- Anzemet is supplied by:
  Hoechst Marion Roussel Canada Inc.
  2150 St. Elzear Blvd. W.
  Laval, Quebec
  H7L 4A8

Reminder:

- **Anzemet has been prescribed only for you. Do not give it to anybody else.**

☐ APO®-CROMOLYN ℞

Apotex

Sodium Cromoglycate

Seasonal Allergic Rhinitis Prophylaxis

Information for the Patient: Instructions for Use: The solution is intended to prevent your symptoms from occurring. It is important to continue your treatment even when you are free from symptoms.

Apo-Cromolyn nasal metered dose mist unit has a security clip around the neck of the pump. Remove the clip from the neck of the pump before use and **replace after each use to prevent accidental activation of the pump.**

Instructions:

1. Remove dust cap from pump. Remove the security clip from around the neck of the pump.
2. **Priming the Pump:** Press the bottle upwards, as indicated by the arrow, then release. Repeat until one full mist is delivered.
3. **Method of Use:** Holding the bottle upright, insert the tip into the nostril and press the bottle fully upwards with thumb then release. This represents one dose. Repeat procedure for other nostril.

To keep clean, wipe nose piece and replace the dust cap after use. **Replace the security clip to prevent accidental activation.**

Presentation: Apo-Cromolyn solution is a 2% aqueous solution of cromolyn sodium (sodium cromoglycate) containing benzalkonium chloride as an antimicrobial preservative, presented as a nasal metered dose mist.

Indications: Apo-Cromolyn is indicated for the prevention and relief of the nasal symptoms of seasonal allergic rhinitis, such as congestion (stuffy nose), sneezing and itchy, runny nose.

Directions for Use: Since Apo-Cromolyn therapy is essentially preventive, it is important to maintain regular dosage, as distinct from using the drug intermittently to relieve symptoms.

Dosage and Administration: Apo-Cromolyn therapy is a preventative measure, not a treatment.

It is recommended that treatment be instituted 1 week prior to the time at which the seasonal symptoms normally occur, since cromolyn sodium is more effective if started prior to exposure to the offending allergen.

Dosage for adults and children over 5 years of age: 1 metered-dose spray into each nostril 6 times daily (single dose 2.6 mg, total daily dose 15.6 mg cromolyn sodium).

Do not exceed recommended dose.

Maintenance Therapy: When adequate response has been obtained, the dosage should be reduced to 2 to 3 times/day (every 8 to 12 hours/day).

One dose delivers approximately 0.13 mL of the 2% w/v solution.

To help maintain relief, it is important to continue treatment throughout the allergy season even when you feel you are free of symptoms. Treatment should not be discontinued abruptly but dosage should be reduced gradually over a period of 1 week.

Due to the slow onset of action of this medication, other allergy medications may be used as required during **the first week** of therapy.

Warnings: If you do not obtain relief of your symptoms within 7 days of starting treatment, consult your doctor.

Patients with nasal polyps should not use this product except on the advice of a doctor.

If you are pregnant or nursing a baby, consult your doctor prior to use.

Store at room temperature (15 to 30°C).

Preserve in tight, light resistant containers.

☐ APO®-TICLOPIDINE ℞

Apotex

Ticlopidine HCl

Inhibitor of Platelet Function

Information for the Patient: Please read carefully. Apo-Ticlopidine (ticlopidine hydrochloride) is usually prescribed to patients who have had a previous stroke or who experienced one or more warning episodes indicating an increased risk of stroke, such as transient ischemic attacks, ischemic neurological changes or minor strokes. In clinical trials, ticlopidine has been shown to decrease both the stroke mortality and the occurrence of first or repeat stroke in such patients.

Apo-Ticlopidine contains ticlopidine hydrochloride, a drug that reduces the ability of blood platelets to stick to each other and to the walls of blood vessels. This action reduces the tendency of blood to clot in unwanted places such as in narrowed blood vessels.

Apo-Ticlopidine has been prescribed to you **to be used strictly as directed by your physician.** As certain adverse reactions may occur in some patients (see below), **you will be required to have a blood test** (to measure your blood count and some biochemical indices) **before you start taking Apo-Ticlopidine and then every 2 weeks for the first 3 months you are on Apo-Ticlopidine.** If you stop taking Apo-Ticlopidine for any reason within the first 3 months, you will still need to have your blood tested for an additional 2 weeks after you have stopped taking Apo-Ticlopidine. It is also very important that you report to your physician immediately if you have noticed the following:

- **any sign of infection** such as fever, chills, sore throat, ulcers in the mouth, etc.
- **abnormal bleeding and bruising.**
- signs of **jaundice** (yellow eyes or skin, dark urine or light-colored stool).
- **skin rash**
- persistent **diarrhea.**

If your doctor is not immediately available, discontinue the medication until he/she can be consulted with. In addition, **discuss with your physician any other medication** you may be required to take (ticlopidine is known to interfere with some other drugs).

If you are to have any surgery or dental extraction, **inform the surgeon or dentist that you are on Apo-Ticlopidine,** which may cause prolonged bleeding.

Adverse Reactions: About 20% of patients will experience some side effects caused by Apo-Ticlopidine. Most side effects develop during the first three months of treatment and they usually disappear within 1 to 2 weeks after ticlopidine hydrochloride is stopped. The potentially more serious adverse reactions are the following:

- Decreased white blood count occurs in about 2% of patients on ticlopidine treatment. This condition will cause reduced resistance to infection. Regular blood tests are necessary to detect this side effect early and stop the medication. In less than 1% of patients, the white blood count can drop to very low levels, but discontinuation of ticlopidine therapy will almost always result in complete recovery.
- Increased bleeding tendency manifested by prolonged bleeding from traumatic or surgical wounds, bruising, bleeding into the gastrointestinal tract (manifested by black stool), etc. occurs rarely, in less than 1% of patients, but has to be watched for if you have a history of bleeding disorders, gastroduodenal ulcers, etc. (discuss your medical history with your physician), or if you are about to have a surgical procedure (do not forget to inform the surgeon or dentist).
- Very rarely jaundice and/or liver failure, usually reversible upon withdrawal of ticlopidine, have been reported.

More common side effects are upset stomach - (to minimize this possibility, **always take Apo-Ticlopidine with meals**), diarrhea and skin rashes.

As with any drug, the possibility of an unexpected, previously unknown, potentially serious adverse reaction can never be ruled out.

If you do not understand this information or any part of it, ask your physician.

Warning: Use only as directed.

Keep out of reach of children.

☐ AREDIA® ℞

Novartis Pharmaceuticals

Pamidronate Disodium

Bone Metabolism Regulator

Information for the Patient: Please read this information carefully before starting treatment with Aredia (pamidronate disodium). If you have further questions, ask your doctor, pharmacist or nurse.

What is Aredia? Aredia contains an active ingredient called pamidronate disodium. It is available as a powder in vials. One vial contains 30 mg, 60 mg, or 90 mg of pamidronate disodium. Aredia is given as an infusion into a vein after appropriate dilution.

Aredia belongs to a group of medicines called bisphosphonates which strongly bind to the bone and slow down the rate of bone change. They are used to reduce the amount of calcium in the blood of some patients who have too much calcium in their blood circulation. Aredia can also be used in other conditions with increased bone change or pain.

What Does Aredia Do? Aredia is used to treat:

- the increased amount of calcium in the blood (hypercalcemia) in certain conditions
- bone tumors resulting from the spread of tumors at other sites and multiple myeloma
- Paget's disease of bone in patients with symptoms.

Before Starting Treatment with Aredia: Be sure that you have discussed Aredia treatment with your doctor. You may only be given Aredia after a full medical examination.

You should not be given Aredia if you have previously had an allergic reaction to Aredia or other bisphosphonates.

Before starting treatment with Aredia tell your doctor:

- if you have a heart or kidney problem
- if you suffer from calcium or vitamin D deficiency (for example owing to your diet or as a result of digestive problems).

Further Safety Measures: It is important that your doctor checks your progress at regular intervals. He or she may want to take repeated blood tests, especially after starting your treatment with Aredia.

Other Medicines or Substances That May Interfere With the Action of Aredia: Before starting Aredia treatment, talk to your doctor about any other medicines that you are using or intend to use. It is especially important that your doctor knows if you are being treated with another bisphosphonate, calcitonin, calcium tablets, or vitamin supplements.

Pregnancy or Breast-feeding: You should tell your doctor if you are pregnant, breast-feeding, or planning to become pregnant. Aredia should not be given during pregnancy except in special situations and only after a careful discussion with the doctor. Mothers treated with Aredia should not breast-feed their babies.

Use in Children and Elderly Patients: So far children have not been treated with Aredia. Until further experience is gained Aredia is only recommended for use in adult patients.

Elderly patients may be safely treated with Aredia, provided that they do not have a serious heart or kidney problem.

If You Drive a Vehicle or Use Machinery: Aredia may cause some patients to become sleepy or dizzy, especially immediately after the infusion. If this happens you should not drive or use machinery or perform other tasks that need full attention.

How to Take Aredia: Aredia can be given only by slow infusion into a vein. The dose will be decided by your doctor. This is usually 30 to 90 mg for patients with increased blood calcium and 90 mg every 3 to 4 weeks for patients with tumors which have spread to the bone or multiple myeloma. Patients with Paget's disease of bone usually receive between 30 to 60 mg in one infusion. An infusion may last 1 or more hours, depending on the dose given. Your doctor will decide how many infusions you need and how often you should receive them.

What Side Effects Can Aredia Have? Like all medicines, Aredia may have, in addition to its beneficial effects, some unwanted effects. The most common side effects are: short-lasting fever and flu-like condition with chills, sometimes together with a feeling of tiredness and general discomfort.

Less common side effects include: short-lasting muscle or joint pain, muscle cramps, pain, redness and swelling at the site of infusion, indigestion, nausea, vomiting, abdominal pain, constipation, diarrhea, loss of appetite, headache, dizziness, sleepiness, tiredness, confusion, agitation, skin rash, itching, eye irritation.

Other side effects not listed above may also occur in some patients. If you notice any other effects, tell your doctor immediately.

Further Information: Expiry Date: Aredia should not be used after the expiry date shown on the package label. Remember to take back any unused medicine to your pharmacist.

Storage Conditions: Protect vials from heat (store below 30°C).

Keep this medicine out of the reach of children.

Other Important Information: This medicine has been prescribed for your current medical problem only. Do not give it to other people.

☐ ARICEPT™ ℞

Pfizer

Donepezil HCl

Cholinesterase Inhibitor

Information for the Patient/Caregiver: Please read this leaflet carefully before you or the person you are caring for starts Aricept treatment. It contains a brief description and summary of information for the proper use of this medication. For further information or advice, contact your doctor or pharmacist.

Name of this Medicine: This medicine is called Aricept (also known as donepezil hydrochloride or E2020). Aricept can only be obtained with a prescription from a doctor.

Purpose of this Medicine: Aricept is intended for the symptomatic treatment of patients with mild to moderate Alzheimer's disease. In clinical studies with Aricept, most Alzheimer's patients' memory and other mental functions showed improvement, or no further decline, as compared with a placebo (a sugar tablet), for up to 6 months. However, Aricept may take as long as 12 weeks to begin working, and patient response to this medicine will vary. This medication should only be taken after proper diagnosis of your condition has been made by your doctor.

Class of Aricept: This medicine is one of a group of drugs called cholinesterase inhibitors which is used for the symptomatic treatment of patients with mild to moderate Alzheimer's disease.

How Aricept Works: There is a decrease in a neurotransmitter called acetylcholine in the brains of persons with Alzheimer's disease. Aricept acts by inhibiting an enzyme called acetylcholinesterase, leading to an increase in the level of acetylcholine in the brain. In order to obtain the best results from Aricept, it must be taken every day, exactly as prescribed by your doctor.

Important Point to Note Before Taking Aricept: You should tell the doctor if you are allergic to donepezil hydrochloride or piperidine derivatives such as Mycobutin (rifabutin), Ritalin (methylphenidate), Akineton (biperiden HCl), Artane, (trihexyphenidyl HCl), Bupivacaine HCl, and Paxil (paroxetine HCl). You should also tell your doctor if you have a condition affecting your heart or your lungs; if you have had seizures; if you have had fainting spells; and if you have a history of peptic ulcers or have an increased risk of developing ulcers (for example, if you are taking nonsteroidal anti-inflammatory drugs (NSAIDs) or high doses of acetylsalicylic acid [ASA (Aspirin)].

Use of this Medicine During Pregnancy and Breast-feeding: Aricept should not be used if you are pregnant or breast-feeding.

How to Take Aricept:

- Take Aricept only as prescribed by your doctor. Never change the dose yourself.
- Always take Aricept in the evening, just before going to bed.
- If you miss taking a dose of Aricept do not worry, just take the next dose when it is due. Do **not** take 2 doses at once.
- If you have problems remembering to take medications, it may be necessary to have someone manage this for you.
- Aricept may be taken with or without food.

While Taking Aricept: Along with its beneficial effect, Aricept may cause some undesirable reactions. The most common side effects include nausea, diarrhea, insomnia, vomiting, muscle cramps, fatigue and anorexia. In clinical studies, these effects were often mild, and generally went away with continued treatment. In clinical studies some patients treated with Aricept experienced fainting. If you feel unwell in any other way or have any symptoms that you do not understand, or find distressing, you should contact your doctor immediately.

What to Do if an Overdose is Taken: If more medication has been taken than what has been prescribed, contact either your doctor, hospital emergency department or the nearest Poison Control Centre immediately.

Storing Aricept:
- Keep this medicine in a safe place, **out of reach of children.**
- Keep this medicine in a cool dry place (15 to 30°C) and avoid exposure to moisture.
- If the doctor decides to stop Aricept treatment, return any leftover medicine to your pharmacist. Keep it only if the doctor tells you to do so.

What is in Aricept: Aricept tablets contain donepezil hydrochloride. The 5 mg tablets are **white** and the 10 mg tablets are **yellow.**

Who Produces Aricept: Pfizer Canada Inc., 17300 Trans-Canada Highway, Kirkland, Quebec H9J 2M5.

Reminder: This medicine has been prescribed only for you or for the person you are caring for. Never give it to anyone else.

Further Information: This leaflet is a brief description and summary of information about this medicine. If you have any questions about Aricept, ask your doctor or pharmacist.

□ ARIMIDEX® Ⓟ

Zeneca

Anastrozole

Nonsteroidal Aromatase Inhibitor

Information for the Patient: The information in this leaflet applies only to your medicine, Arimidex. Please read it carefully. It gives you important information but it can't tell you everything. If you have any questions, or are not sure about anything, ask your doctor or pharmacist.

What Is Your Medicine?
- Arimidex once-a-day tablets contain 1 milligram of anastrozole.
- Each tablet contains a number of inactive ingredients which allow it to be made. These are lactose, macrogol 300, magnesium stearate, sodium starch glycollate, methylhydroxypropylcellulose, polyvidone and titanium dioxide.
- Your medicine is made by Zeneca Pharmaceuticals.

Arimidex belongs to a group of medicines called aromatase inhibitors. It interferes with the actions of aromatase, an enzyme which affects the level of certain female sex hormones such as estrogens. Arimidex reduces the amount of estrogen in the body. This is helpful because estrogen may influence the growth of breast cancer cells.

What Is Your Medicine For?
- Arimidex is used to treat metastatic breast cancer in postmenopausal women with disease progression following tamoxifen therapy.

Before Using This Medicine: Before taking your medicine, you should tell your doctor if you:
- Are allergic to any medication, prescription or nonprescription (over the counter).
- Are taking any other medications (prescription or nonprescription).
- Have any other medical problems (e.g., liver or kidney problems).

When Should Arimidex Not Be Used?
- Before taking your medicine you should tell your doctor if you have previously taken Arimidex and experienced any allergic reaction.
- Arimidex must **not** be taken by premenopausal women or by women who are pregnant or breast-feeding.
- Arimidex must **not** be given to children.

What Precautions Should Be Taken With Arimidex?
- The tablets are **only** for you and must never be given to anyone else.
- If you go into a hospital let the medical staff know you are taking Arimidex.
- Your tablets contain lactose and titanium dioxide which may cause a problem in a small number of patients who are sensitive to them.
- Your tablets are unlikely to adversely affect your ability to drive a car or to operate machinery, however, some patients may occasionally feel weak or sleepy. If this happens ask your doctor for advice.

How Should I Take Arimidex?
- Follow your doctor's instructions about when and how to take your tablets. Please **read the label** on the container and ask your doctor or pharmacist if you are not sure.
- The usual adult dose is 1 tablet taken daily, with or without food.
- Swallow the tablet whole with a drink of water.
- Try to take your tablet at the same time each day.
- Take only as prescribed, however, if you miss a dose do not take an extra dose, just resume your usual schedule.
- If you take more than your normal dose, contact your doctor or nearest hospital.
- Do not stop taking your tablets even if you are feeling well, unless your doctor tells you.
- If you have any questions about your treatment you should talk to your doctor, pharmacist or nurse.

What Undesirable Events May Be Experienced With Arimidex? As with all medicines, undesirable events are sometimes experienced. With Arimidex these may include:
- Hot flushes (may be managed by taking Arimidex at bedtime; or, if night sweats interfere with sleep, by taking Arimidex in the morning)
- Nausea or vomiting or loss of appetite (may be relieved by taking Arimidex with food or right after a meal)
- Diarrhea
- Feeling weak or sleepy
- Thinning of the hair
- Vaginal dryness
- Headache
- Skin rash

Do not be alarmed by this list of possible events. You may not experience any of them. Tell your doctor, pharmacist or nurse if you think you have any of these or any other problems with your medicine.

How Should I Store Arimidex?
- Keep your tablets in the package they came in and store at room temperature.
- If your doctor decides to stop your treatment, dispose of your tablets in an appropriate way. (For example, return them to your pharmacy.)
- Do not take your tablets after the expiry date on the container. Dispose of them in an appropriate way.
- Keep your tablets in a safe place where children cannot see or reach them. Your tablets could harm them.

□ ARTHROTEC® Ⓟ

Searle

Diclofenac Sodium—Misoprostol

Anti-inflammatory—Analgesic—Mucosal Protective Agent

Information for the Patient: Arthrotec is a special medicine provided by your doctor to reduce the joint pain, swelling and stiffness that is often brought on by arthritis. Arthrotec is special because it contains 2 different medicines, a nonsteroidal anti-inflammatory drug (NSAID) called diclofenac and a drug that helps to protect the lining of your stomach called misoprostol (because NSAIDs can cause damage to your stomach). Arthrotec does not cure arthritis and will help you only as long as you continue to take it.

Be sure to take Arthrotec regularly as prescribed. In some types of arthritis, up to 2 weeks may pass before you feel the full effects of this medicine. During treatment, your doctor may decide to adjust the dosage according to your response to the medication.

What is an NSAID? If your joints become swollen and red, if they are painful and stiff, your doctor may prescribe one of many drugs called NSAIDs. This class of drugs is often the best choice your doctor can make to help you control your arthritis and lead a more normal life. NSAIDs are believed to help control arthritis by lowering a natural substance in your body called "prostaglandins".

How do NSAIDs cause stomach damage? Natural prostaglandins play an important role in protecting the stomach by working to keep a thick mucous layer on the inside surface of the stomach. If the lining of the stomach is not protected by a thick layer of mucus, it may be burned by natural stomach acids. NSAIDs lower natural prostaglandins both in the joints and in the stomach. This is good for the joints because it controls pain, swelling and stiffness. Unfortunately, lowering prostaglandins in the stomach can lead to burning stomach pain and the development of tiny holes in the lining of your stomach called "ulcers".

Oddly enough, some NSAID patients who do develop ulcers never feel any stomach pain. On the other hand, some patients who do feel stomach pain have nothing wrong with them. For this reason people must be very careful when taking NSAIDs.

To lessen stomach upset, take Arthrotec immediately after a meal or with food or milk. Also, do not lie down for about 15 to 30 minutes after taking the medicine. This helps to prevent irritation that may lead to trouble swallowing. If stomach upset (indigestion, nausea, vomiting, stomach pain or diarrhea) occurs and continues, contact your doctor.

Arthrotec (cont'd)

Do not take ASA (acetylsalicylic acid), ASA-containing compounds or other drugs used to relieve symptoms of arthritis while taking Arthrotec unless directed to do so by your physician.

If you are prescribed this medication for use over a long period of time, your doctor will check your health during regular visits to assess your progress and to ensure that this medicine is not causing unwanted effects.

How does misoprostol protect the stomach? Misoprostol is a synthetic form of a special kind of prostaglandin that is found in the stomach. Misoprostol replaces the prostaglandins that are lost when taking the NSAID medicine. It protects the thick mucous layer and reduces the acid in your stomach. This can help to protect your stomach from the NSAID.

Always Remember: The risk of taking this medication must be weighed against the benefits it will have.

Before taking this medication tell your doctor and pharmacist if you:

- or a family member are allergic to or have had a reaction to Arthrotec, misoprostol or anti-inflammatory drugs (such as acetylsalicylic acid (ASA), diclofenac, diflunisal, fenoprofen, flurbiprofen, ibuprofen, indomethacin, ketoprofen, mefenamic acid, piroxicam, tiaprofenic acid, tolmetin, nabumetone or tenoxicam) manifesting itself by increased sinusitis, hives, the initiating or worsening of asthma or anaphylaxis (sudden collapse);
- or a family member has had asthma, nasal polyps, chronic sinusitis or chronic urticaria (hives);
- have a history of stomach upset, ulcers, liver or kidney diseases;
- have blood or urine abnormalities;
- have high blood pressure;
- have diabetes;
- are on any special diet, such as a low-sodium or low-sugar diet;
- are pregnant or intend to become pregnant while taking this medication;
- are breast-feeding or intend to breast feed while taking this medication;
- are taking any other medication (either prescription or nonprescription) such as other NSAIDs, antihypertensives, anticoagulants, corticosteroids, methotrexate, cyclosporin, lithium, phenytoin;
- have any other medical problem(s) such as alcohol abuse, bleeding problems, etc.

While Taking This Medication:

- tell any other doctor, dentist or pharmacist that you consult or see, that you are taking this medication;
- some NSAIDs may cause drowsiness or fatigue in some people taking them. Be cautious about driving or participating in activities that require alertness if you are drowsy, dizzy or lightheaded after taking this medication;
- check with your doctor if you are not getting any relief of your arthritis or if any problems develop;
- report any untoward reactions to your doctor. This is very important as it will aid in the early detection and prevention of potential complications.
- stomach problems may be more likely to occur if you drink alcoholic beverages. Therefore, do not drink alcoholic beverages while taking this medication;
- some people may become more sensitive to sunlight than they are normally. Exposure to sunlight or sun lamps, even for brief periods of time, may cause sunburn, blisters on the skin, skin rash, redness, itching or discoloration; or vision changes. If you have a reaction from the sun, check with your doctor;
- check with your doctor immediately if chills, fever, muscle aches or pains, or other flu-like symptoms occur, especially if they occur shortly before, or together with a skin rash. Very rarely, these effects may be the first signs of a serious reaction to this medication;
- **Your regular medical checkups are essential.**

Special Note for Women of Childbearing Age: Arthrotec may cause a miscarriage and its effects on the fetus (developing baby) are not known. Therefore, if you are pregnant, you must not take this drug.

Miscarriages caused by Arthrotec are likely to be incomplete. An incomplete miscarriage may result in very serious medical complications, resulting in hospitalization, surgery and possible infertility.

If you think you are pregnant, do not take Arthrotec. You should avoid becoming pregnant while you are taking Arthrotec. This means using an effective form of birth control. Stop taking Arthrotec, and contact your doctor immediately if you do become pregnant during Arthrotec therapy.

What side effects does Arthrotec have? Along with its beneficial effects, Arthrotec like other NSAID drugs, may cause some undesirable reactions especially when used for a long time or in large doses.

Elderly, frail or debilitated patients often seem to experience more frequent or more severe side effects.

Although not all of these side effects are common, when they do occur they may require medical attention.

Check with your doctor immediately if any of the following are noted:

- bloody or black tarry stools;
- shortness of breath, wheezing, any trouble in breathing, or tightness in the chest;
- skin rash, hives or swelling, itching;
- vomiting or persistent indigestion, nausea, stomach pain or diarrhea;
- yellow discoloration of the skin or eyes;
- any change in the amount of or color of your urine (dark red or brown);
- any pain or difficulty experienced while urinating;
- swelling of the feet or lower legs;
- malaise, fatigue, loss of appetite;
- blurred vision or any visual disturbance;
- mental confusion, depression, dizziness, lightheadedness;
- hearing problems;
- diarrhea – because misoprostol increases mucus production some patients experience diarrhea. Keep taking your Arthrotec. It is just a sign that the drug is working. Usually the diarrhea goes away in 2 to 3 days. If it is not gone after a week, check with your doctor.
- stomach pain – while your body gets used to misoprostol you may feel a crampy pain in your stomach. Like the diarrhea it usually goes away in a few days. If it doesn't, check with your doctor.

Other side effects not listed above may also occur in some patients. If you notice any other effects, check with your doctor.

Dose: Arthrotec is recommended for short-term and long-term use in the relief of the signs and symptoms of rheumatoid arthritis and osteoarthritis.

The recommended oral dose of Arthrotec 50 is 1 tablet 2 or 3 times daily.

The recommended oral dose of Arthrotec 75 is 1 tablet twice daily. Arthrotec should be taken immediately after a meal or with food or milk.

Arthrotec should be swallowed whole.

What to do if you miss a dose: If you miss a dose of Arthrotec, take the next dose at the regular time. It is important that Arthrotec be taken as prescribed. Try to remember to take Arthrotec at the appropriate time. Having a regular routine associated with taking your medicine will help.

How should I take my Arthrotec? Do take your Arthrotec only as prescribed by your doctor.

Do take your Arthrotec with food. This may lessen the stomach upset and will help prevent loose stools and diarrhea, that may occur in the first few days of therapy.

Do take Arthrotec regularly as prescribed by your physician. This is particularly important with Arthrotec as the diarrhea and crampy stomach pain from starting misoprostol may reappear if you stop and then restart the drug.

Do not take ASA (acetylsalicylic acid), ASA-containing compounds, ibuprofen or other drugs to relieve the symptoms of arthritis while taking Arthrotec unless directed by your physician.

Do not take antacids that contain magnesium (because they can cause diarrhea) while you are taking Arthrotec. Ask your pharmacist to help you select a suitable brand.

Nonmedicinal Ingredients: Arthrotec 50: castor oil, cellulose, cellulose acetate phthalate, colloidal silicon dioxide, cornstarch, crospovidone, diethyl phthalate, hydroxypropyl methylcellulose, lactose, magnesium stearate, povidone.
Arthrotec 75: castor oil, cellulose, colloidal silicon dioxide, cornstarch, crospovidone, hydroxypropyl methylcellulose, lactose, magnesium stearate, methacrylic acid copolymer, povidone, sodium hydroxide, triethyl citrate.

Storage: Store at 15 to 25°C and protect from heat and humidity.

Arthrotec is not recommended for use in patients under 18 years of age since safety and effectiveness have not been established.

Do not keep outdated medicine or medicine no longer needed.

Keep out of the reach of children.

This medication has been prescribed for your medical problem, do not give it to anyone else.

If you require more information on this drug, consult your doctor or pharmacist.

□ ATROVENT® Inhalation Aerosol 🄿

Boehringer Ingelheim

Ipratropium Bromide

Bronchodilator

Information for the Patient: Before you use Atrovent Inhalation Aerosol, you should read the following information carefully.

Atrovent inhalation aerosol is an aerosol canister with a mouthpiece; it is used for the maintenance therapy of chronic bronchitis and asthma. It should not be used to decrease the symptoms of an acute asthmatic attack.

This information explains how to use the Atrovent inhalation aerosol and how to avoid problems while you are using it. If you have any questions, be sure to talk to your doctor or pharmacist.

Before You Use Atrovent Inhalation Aerosol: Be sure to tell your doctor:

- if you are pregnant or intend to become pregnant;
- if you are breast feeding;
- if you have any other health problems;
- if you have eye problems, such as glaucoma, or eye pain;
- if you are taking any other medications including eye drops or any medications you can buy without a prescription;
- if you have any allergies or reactions to foods, drugs or aerosols. This includes allergies to soya lecithin or related food products such as soybean and peanut.

How to Use Your Atrovent Inhalation Aerosol: Do not exceed the number of puffs prescribed by your doctor. Do not use the inhaler more often than your doctor recommends.

- The usual dose is 2 puffs taken up to 3 or 4 times daily. Some people may need up to 4 puffs at a time during early treatment. Do not use more than 8 puffs per day unless your doctor has told you to do so.
- If your symptoms get worse, contact your doctor immediately. While taking Atrovent inhalation aerosol, other inhaled medications should be used only as prescribed by your physician.
- If you are troubled with mucus try to clear your chest as completely as possible by coughing before you use Atrovent inhalation aerosol. This will allow the Atrovent inhalation aerosol to pass more deeply into your lungs.
- Before starting to use Atrovent inhalation aerosol, read the following instructions carefully; be sure that you know how to use the inhaler properly. If you use the inhaler incorrectly, you may not be getting all of the medication you need. If you have any questions about using the inhaler, check with your doctor.

Instructions:

1. Remove the protective cap from the inhaler.
2. Shake the unit well.
3. Breathe out as completely as possible: a) Place the mouthpiece into your mouth and close your lips around it. Keep your teeth apart and your tongue flat to allow free flow of the medication into your lungs. b) Press the canister down into the mouthpiece and breathe in deeply through your mouth at the same time.
4. Hold your breath for a few seconds, then breathe out slowly.
5. If your doctor has recommended a second puff, wait about one minute and then repeat steps 2, 3 and 4.
6. Replace the protective plastic cap.

Care of the Mouthpiece/Canister: The mouthpiece should be washed with warm water once a week. You must remove the mouthpiece from the canister before you begin to clean the mouthpiece. If you use soap or detergent, the mouthpiece should be well rinsed in clear water, and then allowed to air dry. The mouthpiece must be completely dry before you put the canister back into the mouthpiece.

Sometimes, the canister stem may also get dirty or blocked. Pull the canister out of the mouthpiece and check the small holes in the stem. If these two small holes seem blocked, rinse them with clear lukewarm water. When the canister is dry, put it back into the mouthpiece.

Please Remember:

1. Atrovent inhalation aerosol has been prescribed to treat **your** current condition. **Do not** give it to other people.
2. **Do not** take any other medication without your doctor's advice. Tell any **other** doctor, dentist, or pharmacist with whom you consult that you are using Atrovent inhalation aerosol.
3. **When using your Atrovent inhalation aerosol with the standard mouthpiece or with a spacer device, make sure you do not spray the aerosol into your eyes.**
4. Like any drug product, Atrovent inhalation aerosol may cause unwanted effects along with the good effects. If you do experience any unusual or unwanted effects while you are using Atrovent you should contact your doctor.
5. Consult your doctor immediately if you experience any of the following:
   - increased wheezing or tightness in the chest;
   - swelling of the tongue or lips;
   - difficulty in swallowing;
   - fast or irregular heartbeat;
   - blurred vision or pain in the eyes;
   - difficult or painful urination;
   - skin rash.
6. If you experience a dry mouth or bad taste, sucking on a sour candy or rinsing your mouth may help. Check with your doctor if the dry mouth or bad taste persist or if you experience constipation for a prolonged period of time.
7. **Keep this medication out of the reach of children.**
8. Keep from freezing.
9. Container may explode if heated. Contents under pressure. Do not place in hot water or near radiators, stoves, or other sources of heat. Do not puncture or incinerate container or store at temperatures over 30°C.

□ ATROVENT® Inhalation Solution 🄿

Boehringer Ingelheim

Ipratropium Bromide

Bronchodilator

Information for the Patient: Atrovent (Ipratropium Bromide) Solution (20 mL Bottle): Please read this information carefully and completely before you use Atrovent.

What is Atrovent Solution (20 mL Bottle): Atrovent solution is a bronchodilator which relieves the wheezing and shortness of breath caused by chronic bronchitis or by asthma. For the treatment of asthma, Atrovent solution must be used in conjunction with some other bronchodilating medication. Atrovent solution contains 250 μg/mL (0.025%) ipratropium bromide and the preservatives benzalkonium chloride and disodium ethylene diamine tetraacetic acid (EDTA-disodium). It is available only on prescription.

Before starting treatment with Atrovent solution, be certain that you are completely familiar with the use and proper care of your nebulizer.

What is COPD? COPD (Chronic Obstructive Pulmonary Disease) is a type of lung disease in which there is a permanent narrowing of the airways, leading to breathing difficulties. In many patients, this narrowing of the airways is a result of many years of cigarette smoking. Smoking cessation produces symptomatic benefits and will slow the progression of chronic bronchitis (which is a form of COPD). COPD can be helped by medication as well.

What is Asthma? Asthma is a disease in which the airways can become temporarily narrowed, leading to breathing difficulties. This narrowing of the airways is due to inflammation, which causes swelling and irritation of the airways and tightening of the muscles around the airways. The narrowed airway can be relieved with the help of medication.

It is important to know that the treatment of COPD and Asthma may be different for each patient. Your doctor will most likely discuss with you the best plan for the treatment of **your** particular condition. This plan may include taking other medication(s) in addition to Atrovent. It is necessary that you follow your doctor's directions for the treatment of your condition. If you have any questions about how you should treat your condition at home, you should consult your doctor.

What you should tell your doctor before you use Atrovent Solution? It is very important to tell your doctor the following:

- If you may be pregnant or wish to become pregnant;
- If you are breast-feeding;
- If you are taking any medications, including those you can buy without a prescription and including eye drops;
- If you have any other medical problems such as difficult urination or enlarged prostate;

Atrovent Inhalation Solution (cont'd)

- If you have eye problems, such as glaucoma or eye pain;
- If you have any special allergies to food or drugs.

20 mL Bottle (see package insert for illustrations): **Usage Instructions:** Your doctor or pharmacist will tell you how to prepare your Atrovent solution for inhalation. If you are told to dilute Atrovent solution, you must do so immediately before you plan to use the solution. In most cases, dilution of the dose with sterile preservative-free saline is not necessary. However, volumes of Atrovent solution less than 2 mL are not appropriate for nebulization and must be diluted with saline or another suitable nebulizer solution to make up for a total fill volume of 2 to 5 mL.

1) Immediately before you plan to use the nebulizer, using a syringe, withdraw the prescribed dose-usually ½ to 2 mL of Atrovent solution from the bottle and add to the nebulizer chamber. Do not store the prescribed dose in the syringe for later use.
2) If your doctor has instructed you to use another inhalation solution in combination with Atrovent solution, you should add the appropriate amount of that solution to the nebulizer chamber as well.
3) Add sodium chloride solution to the chamber, if you have been directed to do so by your physician or pharmacist.
4) Gently shake the nebulizer chamber and connect it to the mouthpiece or face mask. Then connect the nebulizer tube to the air or oxygen pump and begin therapy.
5) Breathe calmly and deeply through the mask or mouthpiece until no more mist is formed in the nebulizer chamber. This usually takes 10 to 15 minutes. **It is very important** to adjust the face mask, if required, to prevent the mist from getting in your eyes.
6) Store your re-capped bottle of Atrovent solution and sodium chloride solution in the refrigerator until the next treatment.
7) Follow the instructions provided by the nebulizer and air pump manufacturers for the proper care and maintenance of the equipment. Keep the nebulizer, nebulizer tube and face mask clean to minimize microbial contamination.

Please Remember:

- **Do not exceed the prescribed dose or frequency of treatments.**
- **Do not mix this medication with any other medications in the nebulizer unless instructed to do so by your doctor or pharmacist.**
- **This medication has been prescribed for you and should not be given to other people.**
- **Keep out of the reach of children.**
- **The solution is intended for inhalation only. Do not inject or drink it.**
- **Do not let the nebulized mist get into your eyes. Patients with glaucoma should use swimming goggles or a nebulizer with a mouthpiece to prevent nebulized solution getting into the eyes.**

As well as its desired effects, Atrovent solution, like any medication, may cause some unwanted effects.

If you experience a dry mouth or bad taste, sucking on a sour candy or rinsing your mouth may help.

Check with your doctor if the dry mouth or bad taste persist or if you experience constipation.

Consult your doctor immediately if you experience any of the following:

- **Increased wheezing or tightness in the chest;**
- **Swelling of the tongue or lips;**
- **Difficulty in swallowing;**
- **Fast or irregular heartbeat;**
- **Blurred vision or pain in the eyes;**
- **Difficult or painful urination;**
- **Skin rash.**

If you do not get the expected relief from your treatment, you should contact your doctor.

Remember to tell any other doctor, dentist or pharmacist you consult that you are taking this medication.

If you have any questions about Atrovent solution or your nebulizer, contact your doctor or pharmacist.

Atrovent (Ipratropium Bromide) Solution (UDV): Please read this information carefully and completely before you use Atrovent.

What is Atrovent Solution (UDV): Atrovent solution is a bronchodilator which relieves the wheezing and shortness of breath caused by chronic bronchitis or by asthma. For the treatment of asthma, Atrovent solution must be used in conjunction with some other bronchodilating medication. Atrovent solution UDV is available only on prescription.

Before starting treatment with Atrovent solution, be certain that you are completely familiar with the use and proper care of your nebulizer.

What is COPD? COPD (Chronic Obstructive Pulmonary Disease) is a type of lung disease in which there is a permanent narrowing of the airways, leading to breathing difficulties. In many patients, this narrowing of the airways is a result of many years of cigarette smoking. Smoking cessation produces symptomatic benefits and will slow the progression of chronic bronchitis (which is a form of COPD). COPD can be helped by medication as well.

What is Asthma? Asthma is a disease in which the airways can become temporarily narrowed, leading to breathing difficulties. This narrowing of the airways is due to inflammation, which causes swelling and irritation of the airways and tightening of the muscles around the airways. The narrowed airway can be relieved with the help of medication.

It is important to know that the treatment of COPD and Asthma may be different for each patient. Your doctor will most likely discuss with you the best plan for the treatment of **your** particular condition. This plan may include taking other medication(s) in addition to Atrovent. It is necessary that you follow your doctor's directions for the treatment of your condition. If you have any questions about how you should treat your condition at home, you should consult your doctor.

What you should tell your doctor before you use Atrovent Solution? It is very important to tell your doctor the following:

- If you may be pregnant or wish to become pregnant;
- If you are breast-feeding;
- If you are taking any medications, including those you can buy without a prescription and including eye drops;
- If you have any other medical problems such as difficult urination or enlarged prostate;
- If you have eye problems, such as glaucoma or eye pain;
- If you have any special allergies to foods or drugs.

2 mL Unit Dose Vial: 250 µg/mL: Each plastic vial contains 2 mL of Atrovent solution. Each millilitre (mL) of solution contains 250 µg (0.025%) ipratropium bromide in an isotonic solution.

125 µg/mL: Each plastic vial contains 2 mL of Atrovent solution. Each millilitre (mL) of solution contains 125 µg (0.0125%) ipratropium bromide in an isotonic solution.

1 mL Unit Dose Vial: 250 µg/mL: Each plastic vial contains 1 mL of Atrovent solution. Each millilitre (mL) of solution contains 250 µg (0.025%) ipratropium bromide in an isotonic solution.

Before starting treatment with Atrovent solution, be certain that you are completely familiar with the use and proper care of your nebulizer.

Usage Instructions (see package insert for illustrations): Your doctor or pharmacist will tell you how to prepare your Atrovent solution for inhalation. If you are told to dilute Atrovent solution, you must do so immediately before you plan to use the solution.

In most cases, dilution of the dose with sterile preservative-free saline is not necessary. However, volumes of Atrovent solution less than 2 mL are not appropriate for nebulization and must be diluted with saline or another suitable nebulizer solution to make up a total fill volume of 2 to 5 mL.

1) Detach one plastic vial by pulling it firmly from the strip.
2) Open the vial by twisting off the top. It is important that you use the contents of the vial **as soon as possible** after opening it.
3) Squeeze the contents of the plastic vial into your nebulizer chamber. If your doctor has instructed you to use less than one complete vial, use a syringe to withdraw the prescribed dose.
   Any solution left in the plastic vial must be thrown away.
4) If your doctor has instructed you to use another inhalation solution in combination with Atrovent solution, you should add the appropriate amount of that solution to the nebulizer chamber as well.
5) Using a syringe, add sodium chloride solution to the chamber if you have been directed to do so by your pharmacist or physician.
6) Gently shake the nebulizer chamber and connect it to the mouthpiece or face mask. Then connect the nebulizer tube to the air or oxygen pump and begin therapy.
7) Breathe calmly and deeply through the mask or mouthpiece until no more mist is formed in the nebulizer chamber. This usually takes 10 to 15 minutes. **It is very important** to adjust the face mask, if required, to prevent the mist from getting in your eyes.
8) Follow the instructions provided by the nebulizer and air pump manufacturers for the proper care and maintenance of the equipment. Keep the nebulizer, nebulizer tube and face mask clean to minimize microbial contamination.
9) The unit dose vials should be stored at room temperature. The vials should be protected from heat and light.

Please Remember:
- **Do not exceed the prescribed dose or frequency of treatments.**
- **Do not mix this medication with any other medications in the nebulizer unless instructed to do so by your doctor or pharmacist.**
- **This medication has been prescribed for you and should not be given to other people.**
- **Keep out of the reach of children.**
- **The solution is intended for inhalation only. Do not inject or drink it.**
- **Do not let the nebulized mist get into your eyes. Patients with glaucoma should use swimming goggles or a nebulizer with a mouthpiece to prevent nebulized solution getting into the eyes.**

As well as its desired effects, Atrovent solution, like any medication, may cause some unwanted effects.

If you experience a dry mouth or bad taste, sucking on a sour candy or rinsing your mouth may help.

Check with your doctor if the dry mouth or bad taste persist or if you experience constipation.

Consult your doctor immediately if you experience any of the following:
- **Increased wheezing or tightness in the chest;**
- **Swelling of the tongue or lips;**
- **Difficulty in swallowing;**
- **Fast or irregular heartbeat;**
- **Blurred vision or pain in the eyes;**
- **Difficult or painful urination;**
- **Skin rash.**

If you do not get the expected relief from your treatment, you should contact your doctor.

Remember to tell any other doctor, dentist or pharmacist you consult that you are taking this medication.

If you have any questions about Atrovent solution or your nebulizer, contact your doctor or pharmacist.

□ ATROVENT® Nasal Spray ℞

Boehringer Ingelheim

Ipratropium Bromide

Topical Anticholinergic

Information for the Patient: Atrovent (Ipratropium Bromide) Nasal Spray 0.03%: Read complete instructions carefully and use only as directed.

Atrovent Nasal Spray 0.03% is used to treat the runny nose associated with perennial allergic or nonallergic rhinitis. It works to stop the glands in your nose from producing excessive nasal secretions. Atrovent Nasal Spray must be prescribed by a doctor.

These instructions explain how to use Atrovent Nasal Spray and how to avoid problems while you are using the product. If you have any questions after reading these instructions, be sure to talk to your doctor or pharmacist.

Before You Start: Before you start to use Atrovent Nasal Spray, be sure to tell your doctor if:
- you are pregnant or intend to become pregnant;
- you are breast-feeding;
- you have any other health problems, now or in the past;
- you have eye problems, such as a predisposition to glaucoma;
- you have difficulty/trouble urinating or problems with your prostate;
- you are taking any other medications including eye drops or any medications you can buy without a prescription;
- you have any allergies or reactions to foods or drugs.

Remember to tell any other doctor, dentist or pharmacist whom you consult with that you are using Atrovent Nasal Spray.

How to Use Your Atrovent Nasal Spray: Do not exceed the number of sprays, or the length of use, prescribed by your doctor.

Atrovent Nasal Spray has been prescribed to treat your current condition. Do not give it to other people.

Do not take other medication without your doctor's advice.

Keep out of the reach of children.

1. Remove the clear plastic dust cap and the safety clip from the nasal spray pump. The safety clip prevents the accidental discharge of the spray in your pocket or purse.
2. The nasal spray pump must be primed before Atrovent Nasal Spray is used for the first time. To prime the pump, hold the bottle with your thumb at the base and your index and middle fingers on the white shoulder area. Make sure the bottle points upright and away from your eyes. Press your thumb firmly and quickly against the bottle 7 times. The pump is now primed and can be used. Your pump should not have to be reprimed unless you have not used the medication for more than 24 hours; repriming the pump will only require 1 or 2 sprays.
3. Before using Atrovent Nasal Spray, blow your nose gently to clear your nostrils if necessary.
4. Close one nostril by gently placing your finger against the side of your nose, tilt your head slightly forward and, keeping the bottle upright, insert the nasal tip into the other nostril. Point the tip toward the **back** and **outer** side of the nose.
5. Press firmly and quickly upwards with the thumb at the base while holding the white shoulder portion of the pump between your index and middle fingers. Following each spray, sniff deeply and breath out through your mouth.
6. After spraying the nostril and removing the unit, tilt your head backwards for a few seconds to let the spray spread over the back of the nose.
7. Repeat steps 4 through 6 in the other nostril.
8. Replace the clear plastic dust cap and safety clip.
9. When the amount of Atrovent Nasal Spray begins to run low, the amount of medication in each spray cannot be assured. Therefore, at some time before the medication is completely used up, you should consult your physician or pharmacist to determine whether a refill is needed. You should not take extra doses of Atrovent Nasal Spray without consulting your physician.

To Clean: If the nasal tip becomes clogged, remove the clear plastic dust cap and safety clip. Hold the nasal tip under running, warm tap water for about a minute. Dry the nasal tip, reprime the nasal spray pump (see step 2 above), and replace the plastic dust cap and safety clip.

Avoid spraying Atrovent Nasal Spray in or around your eyes. Should this occur, immediately flush your eyes with cool tap water for several minutes. If you accidentally spray Atrovent Nasal Spray in your eyes, you may experience a temporary blurring of vision and increased sensitivity to light, which may last a few hours.

Caution For Patients Using Atrovent Nasal Spray For Chronic Nasal Inflammation: Atrovent Nasal Spray is intended to relieve your rhinorrhea (runny nose) with regular use. It is therefore important that you use Atrovent Nasal Spray as prescribed by your physician. Some improvement in rhinorrhea is usually apparent during the first full day of treatment with Atrovent Nasal Spray. However, maximum benefit may not occur for up to several weeks after treatment has started.

Other Effects: Like any other drug product, Atrovent Nasal Spray may cause unwanted effects along with its good effects. If you do experience any of the unwanted effects listed below, you should contact your doctor. He/she may recommend that you lower your dose of Atrovent Nasal Spray.
- very dry nose
- dry mouth
- nasal irritation
- nose bleeds

If you experience any of the following unwanted effects, contact your doctor right away.
- blurred vision or pain in the eyes
- fast or irregular heartbeat
- difficult or painful urination
- skin rash
- increased wheezing or tightness in the chest
- swelling of the tongue or lips
- difficulty in swallowing

Nonmedicinal ingredients in Atrovent Nasal Spray 0.03% include: benzalkonium chloride, edetate disodium, hydrochloric acid, purified water, sodium chloride and sodium hydroxide.

Storage: Store tightly closed between 15 and 30°C. Avoid excessive heat or freezing. Keep out of reach of children.

Atrovent (Ipratropium Bromide) Nasal Spray 0.06%: Read complete instructions carefully and use only as directed.

Atrovent Nasal Spray 0.06% is used to treat the runny nose associated with the common cold. It works to stop the glands in your nose from producing excessive nasal secretions. Atrovent Nasal Spray must be prescribed by a doctor.

These instructions explain how to use Atrovent Nasal Spray and how to avoid problems while you are using the product. If you have any questions after reading these instructions, be sure to talk to your doctor or pharmacist.

Atrovent Nasal Spray (cont'd)

Before You Start: Before you start to use Atrovent Nasal Spray, be sure to tell your doctor if:
- you are pregnant or intend to become pregnant;
- you are breast-feeding;
- you have any other health problems, now or in the past;
- you have eye problems, such as a predisposition to glaucoma;
- you have difficulty/trouble urinating or problems with your prostate;
- you are taking any other medications including eye drops or any medications you can buy without a prescription;
- you have any allergies or reactions to foods or drugs.

Remember to tell any other doctor, dentist or pharmacist whom you consult with that you are using Atrovent Nasal Spray.

How to Use Your Atrovent Nasal Spray: Do not exceed the number of sprays, or the length of use, prescribed by your doctor.

Atrovent Nasal Spray has been prescribed to treat your current condition. Do not give it to other people.

Do not take other medication without your doctor's advice.

Keep out of the reach of children.

1. Remove the clear plastic dust cap and the safety clip from the nasal spray pump. The safety clip prevents the accidental discharge of the spray in your pocket or purse.
2. The nasal spray pump must be primed before Atrovent Nasal Spray is used for the first time. To prime the pump, hold the bottle with your thumb at the base and your index and middle fingers on the white shoulder area. Make sure the bottle points upright and away from your eyes. Press your thumb firmly and quickly against the bottle 7 times. The pump is now primed and can be used. Your pump should not have to be reprimed unless you have not used the medication for more than 24 hours; repriming the pump will only require 1 or 2 sprays.
3. Before using Atrovent Nasal Spray, blow your nose gently to clear your nostrils if necessary.
4. Close one nostril by gently placing your finger against the side of your nose, tilt your head slightly forward and, keeping the bottle upright, insert the nasal tip into the other nostril. Point the tip toward the **back** and **outer** side of the nose.
5. Press firmly and quickly upwards with the thumb at the base while holding the white shoulder portion of the pump between your index and middle fingers. Following each spray, sniff deeply and breath out through your mouth.
6. After spraying the nostril and removing the unit, tilt your head backwards for a few seconds to let the spray spread over the back of the nose.
7. Repeat steps 4 through 6 in the other nostril.
8. Replace the clear plastic dust cap and safety clip.
9. When the amount of Atrovent Nasal Spray begins to run low, the amount of medication in each spray cannot be assured. Therefore, at some time before the medication is completely used up, you should consult your physician or pharmacist to determine whether a refill is needed. You should not take extra doses of Atrovent Nasal Spray without consulting your physician.

To Clean: If the nasal tip becomes clogged, remove the clear plastic dust cap and safety clip. Hold the nasal tip under running, warm tap water for about a minute. Dry the nasal tip, reprime the nasal spray pump (see step 2 above), and replace the plastic dust cap and safety clip.

Avoid spraying Atrovent Nasal Spray in or around your eyes. Should this occur, immediately flush your eyes with cool tap water for several minutes. If you accidentally spray Atrovent Nasal Spray in your eyes, you may experience a temporary blurring of vision and increased sensitivity to light, which may last a few hours.

Caution For Patients Using Atrovent Nasal Spray For Chronic Nasal Inflammation: Atrovent Nasal Spray is intended to relieve your rhinorrhea (runny nose) with regular use. It is therefore important that you use Atrovent Nasal Spray as prescribed by your physician. Some improvement in rhinorrhea is usually apparent during the first full day of treatment with Atrovent Nasal Spray. However, maximum benefit may not occur for up to several weeks after treatment has started.

Other Effects: Like any other drug product, Atrovent Nasal Spray may cause unwanted effects along with its good effects. If you do experience any of the unwanted effects listed below, you should contact your doctor. He/she may recommend that you lower your dose of Atrovent Nasal Spray.
- very dry nose
- dry mouth
- nasal irritation
- nose bleeds

If you experience any of the following unwanted effects, contact your doctor right away.
- blurred vision or pain in the eyes
- fast or irregular heartbeat
- difficult or painful urination
- skin rash
- increased wheezing or tightness in the chest
- swelling of the tongue or lips
- difficulty in swallowing

Nonmedicinal ingredients in Atrovent Nasal Spray 0.06% include: benzalkonium chloride, edetate disodium, hydrochloric acid, purified water, sodium chloride and sodium hydroxide.

Storage: Store tightly closed between 15 and 30°C. Avoid excessive heat or freezing. Keep out of reach of children.

☐ AVIRAX™ Ⓟ

Fabrigen

Acyclovir

Antiviral

Information for the Patient: Herpes Zoster (shingles) and Genital Herpes: **Treatment:** If your physician has prescribed a course of Avirax for the treatment of a herpes, zoster (shingles) infection, it is important to understand that the drug must be taken as early as possible after the onset of the disease. This is because the herpes virus multiplies in and eventually destroys affected skin cells. Avirax stops the virus from multiplying and therefore from spreading to neighboring healthy cells. It cannot replace a cell which has been damaged by the multiplying virus, but it will facilitate the process of healing.

Suppression of Recurrences: If your physician suggested continuous use of Avirax to prevent frequent recurrences of genital herpes infections, you should follow dosing instructions carefully. The objective is to keep enough of the drug in the body at all times to prevent the herpes virus from multiplying. Your physician will try to prescribe the minimum dose required to do this in your case and may therefore increase or decrease your dose during the first few weeks. Follow your physician's instruction carefully to ensure that you get the best possible response to treatment.

Safety: Short-Term: The safety of Avirax in short-term use has been well studied. As with any widely prescribed medication, adverse events in association with its use are reported from time to time. The common ones are listed below; they have rarely been severe enough to make it necessary to stop taking the drug.

Headache, nausea, diarrhea, skin rash and upset stomach.

If you experience anything unusual while you are receiving treatment with Avirax, you should report it to your physician.

A complete listing of adverse events so far reported is contained in the Product Monograph supplied to your physician.

Long-Term: Your physician may periodically stop your drug therapy in order to reassess your need for continuous treatment. As with any new drug, the effect of long-term use in humans has not been fully assessed. Prudence is therefore suggested when choosing continuous, long-term therapy with Avirax. Suppression of recurrent genital herpes is therefore only recommended in those who are severely affected.

Pregnancy: You should consult your doctor if you become pregnant or intend to become pregnant or intend to breast-feed while taking Avirax.

Reproductive Toxicity: Although decreased sperm counts in animals treated with high doses, and breaks in chromosomes in high concentrations of acyclovir in the test tube, have been seen, these effects did not occur in humans given doses of 800 to 1 000 mg/day for at least 6 months.

General Information: Herpes infections cause painful blisters on the skin and mucous membranes. The fluid in these blisters contains the virus which causes the disease. The infection is easily spread either to yourself or to other people. If you touch your skin sores, wash your hands immediately and do not touch other parts of your body until you have done so. Especially avoid intimate contact with others when the disease is visible. Medication should not be shared with others. The prescribed dosage should not be exceeded. Avirax does not eliminate dormant viruses. Some patients experience increased severity of the first episode of genital herpes after stopping treatment.

For more information about Avirax and herpes infections, please consult your physician or pharmacist.

Chickenpox—Information for Parents: Common in childhood and contagious: Chickenpox is one of the most **common** infections in otherwise healthy children. It usually occurs in children before the age of 10, but anyone who has never had chickenpox can become infected—irrespective of age.

Chickenpox is caused by a virus called "varicella zoster" and it is **highly contagious.** Family members often give the disease to each other. For reasons that are not known, often the second or third child who catches it from a brother or sister will be sicker than the first child. Also, the disease tends to be more severe in teenagers than in younger children.

The disease can be mild with few pox or mild symptoms—alternatively, it could be severe with hundreds of pox. The pox can occur both outside and inside the body. There is **no way to predict the severity** of chickenpox.

Recognizing the Disease: The early symptoms of chickenpox may be vague and could include fever, itching, headache, aching joints and muscles, sore throat, general malaise: loss of appetite, restlessness and irritability. After that, itchy, small, red spots (the "pox") appear, and become blisters within a few hours. New spots and blisters continue to appear for about 5 days. The blisters start to dry up and within 6 or 7 days turn into scabs.

Incubation: Not all who are exposed come down with the disease. The incubation period may extend from 1 to 3 weeks after exposure. The virus is spread through the air when: (1) a person with chickenpox scratches the blisters, allowing the virus to become airborne; or (2) a person with chickenpox coughs or sneezes within close contact of others. The disease is most contagious shortly before the rash appears, through the early stages of the rash, until all the blisters have dried. A patient is **not** contagious once all the blisters have become scabs.

Early consultation with your physician: If you think your child has been exposed to chickenpox, be on the lookout for symptoms described above. **At the first sign of rash, call your physician**. There are more treatment options available when the infection is caught this early. Your physician may prescribe a medication which could offer the child less discomfort, and possibly a faster recovery.

Tips to bear in mind: It is important to follow the physician's orders with all medications prescribed—even if the patient seems to feel better. **Never use medications containing acetylsalicylic acid (ASA) in children with fever and chickenpox.** Acetaminophen may be given to reduce fever.

The rash can be soothed by coating with an anti-itch product such as calamine, or other medications that your physician recommends. The discomfort of itching can be relieved temporarily by baths and wet compresses. Bathing daily with soap and water can also help prevent infection. **Do not use antiseptics** on the sores; rather **consult your physician**, who might prescribe an antibiotic if necessary. Since infection or scarring can occur at scratch sites, it is important to discourage scratching and spreading of virus particles through the air. Keep the rash clean and dry. If possible keep the nails cut short, cover the hands and feet with cotton gloves, mitts or socks to discourage children scratching at sleep time.

Possible Complications: Complications are rare in the healthy child. The people who are at greatest risk of complications are: pregnant women, newborn babies, or people being treated for cancer, arthritis, asthma, or after organ transplants—where medicine is suppressing their immune systems. If anyone in your family falls within these groups **inform your physician** so that the preventive measures can be taken.

□ AZMACORT® Ⓟ

Rhône-Poulenc Rorer

Triamcinolone Acetonide

Corticosteroid

Information for the Patient: Your doctor has prescribed Azmacort (triamcinolone acetonide) to help control your asthma. Your Azmacort inhaler is one of the most efficient and easy to use devices available to help you take your prescribed medication. Used properly, it will effectively and reliably relieve your asthma symptoms.

To receive the maximum benefit, it is very important that you carefully read and follow all the instructions contained in this booklet for the daily use and care of your Azmacort inhaler.

Important Note: If you have used an inhaler before, you may expect the Azmacort inhaler to deliver a noticeable blast of medication into your mouth. Your Azmacort inhaler, however, is designed to provide a gentle mist, not a blast, when used. This gentle action makes it possible for your medication to be more effectively delivered into the passageways to your lungs, with very little left to linger in your mouth. In fact, you may not even feel the medication entering your mouth, but rest assured, that is how the Azmacort inhaler works.

Your Azmacort Special Delivery System:

Step 1: Prepare Your Azmacort Inhaler for Use:

1. Line up the arrows on the inhaler.
2. Gently pull the inhaler to its fully extended position. You will see the valve (small hole) where the medication will come out.
3. Adjust the inhaler into an L shape. It is hinged to swing in one direction only.
4. The ridge on the top part of the inhaler should fit into the notch on the bottom part.
5. Remove the mouthpiece cap. Your Azmacort inhaler is now ready for use.

Step 2: Using Your Azmacort Inhaler:

1. The metal Azmacort cartridge has already been inserted in the inhaler. Shake the inhaler well before each use. Important: You must shake the inhaler each and every time before inhaling the medication. If your doctor has instructed you to take more than one breath of medication at a time, you must shake the inhaler **each time** before each inhalation of medication, **not just once.**
2. Breathe out to empty your lungs completely before using the inhaler! This is important to make sure that you can breathe the medication deeply into your lungs.
3. Place mouthpiece into your mouth, and close your lips tightly around it.
4. Press down firmly and steadily on the metal cartridge while breathing in slowly and deeply **through your mouth only.** (If necessary, pinch your nose closed.) Remember, the Azmacort inhaler delivers a gentle mist of medication, so don't be surprised if you hardly feel it.

   Do not remove the inhaler from your mouth after breathing in the medication. Hold your breath for 10 seconds with the inhaler **still** in your mouth, **then** remove the inhaler and breathe out very slowly.
5. If your doctor has told you to take more than one breath of medication at a time, **wait at least 60 seconds** between each one, then start again at the first instruction in this section (Step 2).
6. After the prescribed number of inhalations, rinse out your mouth thoroughly with water. Note: If your mouth becomes sore or develops a rash, be sure to mention this to your physician, but do not stop using your inhaler unless he instructs you to do so. Do not stop or change dosage without consulting your doctor.

Step 3: Daily Care of Your Azmacort Inhaler: Your Azmacort Inhaler **must** be cleaned in lukewarm water only once each day to avoid buildup of medication particles in the inhaler that can block the spray of medication and interfere with proper operation. The use of soap, detergents or disinfectants is unnecessary.

1. Important: Remove metal cartridge from inhaler. Pull cartridge straight out from inhaler and place aside. Cartridge must be removed for proper cleaning of inhaler.
2. Pull apart remaining 2 plastic parts of inhaler, remove mouthpiece cap, and gently wash in lukewarm water. Dry thoroughly.
3. Snap the 2 plastic parts of the inhaler back together; push closed. Replace mouthpiece cap. Reinsert metal cartridge by gently turning while inserting. The cartridge should fit snugly without falling out.

Important Tips for Using Your Inhaler:

- Always use only as directed by your physician. Do not use it more often than instructed; do not skip doses.
- Follow all instructions in this booklet very closely and carefully for best results, especially those for use and cleaning.
- Store plastic inhaler and metal cartridge at room temperature.
- **Caution: Contents of cartridge under pressure.** Do not place in hot water or near radiators, stoves or other sources of heat. Even when empty do not puncture or incinerate containers or store at temperatures over 50°C.

Warning: Azmacort (triamcinolone acetonide) contains medication that is intended for treatment of your asthma. It does not contain medication intended to provide rapid relief of your breathing difficulties during an asthma attack.

It is very important that you use Azmacort regularly at the intervals recommended by your doctor, and not as an emergency measure. If ▶

Azmacort (cont'd)

you have an acute asthma attack you should use the medication which has been prescribed for this purpose and/or contact your doctor.

How to Check Contents of Your Cartridge: Shaking the cartridge will **not** give you a good estimate of how much Azmacort is left. A simple method is shown in the diagram of the package insert.

1. Float the cartridge in enough cold water to cover it when it is standing up, and note what position it takes. When empty, the cartridge will float horizontally on the surface (see diagram).
2. When the cartridge is almost empty, contact your physician or pharmacist for a refill.

□ BAYCOL® ℞

Bayer

Cerivastatin Sodium

Lipid Metabolism Regulator

Information for the Patient: Please read this information carefully. If you have any questions or concerns about Baycol, ask your doctor or pharmacist.

About Baycol Tablets: Your doctor has prescribed these pills to help lower your cholesterol. High cholesterol levels can cause heart disease by clogging the blood vessels that supply blood to your heart.

Ways to Lower Cholesterol: Taking medication is only part of your treatment for lowering your cholesterol. There are other things you can do, depending on your condition, to help lower your cholesterol.

- Change your diet to control your weight and lower cholesterol—being overweight is a risk factor for heart disease.
- Exercise on a regular basis—to help you control your weight and raise your levels of HDL (the good cholesterol).
- Quit smoking—smoking is a major risk factor for heart disease.
- Drink less alcohol or give it up completely.

Always follow your doctor's instructions and be sure to talk to him/her before changing your diet or starting any exercise program.

How Does Baycol Work? Baycol reduces the levels of LDL (the bad cholesterol) in your blood. It belongs to a group of drugs called HMG-CoA reductase inhibitors. It works by blocking your liver from using a substance it needs to create cholesterol. The cholesterol in your liver cells decreases and causes the cells to draw cholesterol from your bloodstream.

Baycol is the brand name for cerivastatin sodium and is manufactured by Bayer Inc. It is only available by prescription from your doctor.

Before You Start Baycol: Although Baycol is effective, there are some people who should not take it. Talk to your doctor if you:

- have liver disease
- are pregnant, planning to become pregnant or think you might be pregnant. If you become pregnant while taking Baycol, stop taking it and tell your doctor right away.
- are breast-feeding
- have already taken Baycol or any other similar drug and developed a reaction. These drugs include:
  - Lescol (fluvastatin)
  - Lipitor (atorvastatin)
  - Mevacor (lovastatin)
  - Pravachol (pravastatin)
  - Zocor (simvastatin)
- are taking any other medication such as:
  - corticosteroids
  - Sandimmune (cyclosporine)
  - Lopid (gemfibrozil)
  - Lipidil (fenofibrate)
  - lipid-lowering doses of niacin (nicotinic acid)
  - erythromycin or azole antifungal agents
  - Serzone (nefazadone)

How To Take Baycol: Always follow your doctor's instructions carefully and keep taking your medication even if you feel well. Sometimes it's easy to forget you have high cholesterol since you probably don't feel or look sick. Your doctor will monitor your cholesterol levels on a regular basis. These guidelines will help you use your medication properly:

- Take Baycol as one dose in the evening. You may take it with or without food.
- If you should miss taking one tablet, take it as soon as you remember. But if it is too close to the time of your next tablet, skip the missed one and just take the next dose. **Do not take a double dose.**
- Meet with your doctor on a regular basis to have your cholesterol levels checked. Use this opportunity to ask any questions you may have.
- Don't change the dose or stop taking the medication without first talking to your doctor.
- Tell your doctor if you have any muscle pain, tenderness, soreness or weakness.
- Keep your alcohol consumption to a minimum (less than 10 to 14 drinks per week). Talk to your doctor to find out exactly what this means for you.
- Tell your doctor about any illness you develop while you are taking Baycol.
- If you have to take any other medicine (prescription or nonprescription) while you are taking Baycol, be sure to tell your doctor or pharmacist first.
- Tell your doctor if you are going to have an operation.
- If for some reason you see a different doctor, inform him/her that you are taking Baycol.
- The safety of Baycol in teenagers and children has not been established.
- Talk to your doctor if you experience any of the following side effects (see below).

Side Effects and What You Should Do: Although most people do not have a problem with side effects when taking Baycol, all medications can cause unwanted side effects.

Some side effects may come and go, but you should mention them to your doctor as soon as possible if they become persistent or begin to bother you. These include:

- stomach pain or upset
- diarrhea
- headache
- dizziness
- skin rashes

Contact your doctor or pharmacist **right away** if you have any of the following:

- unexplained muscle pain
- muscle tenderness or soreness
- general weakness, especially if you do not feel well
- a fever

Some people may have other types of reactions. So, if you notice anything unusual, it's always best to check with your doctor or pharmacist.

Ingredients of Baycol: Each tablet of Baycol contains cerivastatin sodium. Baycol comes in two strengths: 0.2 mg (light yellow-brown) and 0.3 mg (yellow brown). The 0.2 mg tablet will be marked with 283 on one side and 200 MCG on the other. The 0.3 mg tablet will be marked with 284 on one side and 300 MCG on the other.

Other ingredients in Baycol tablets are: crospovidone, magnesium stearate, mannitol, povidone 25, sodium hydroxide, hydroxypropyl methylcellulose, polyethylene glycol 4000, titanium dioxide and ferric oxide.

Remember:

- This medicine is prescribed for you. Don't give it to other people.
- Keep all medicines out of the reach of children.
- Store Baycol at room temperature (15 to 25°C), away from heat and direct light. Do not store Baycol in warm or damp places such as the bathroom or kitchen.

If you need more information about Baycol, talk to your doctor or pharmacist.

□ BECLODISK® ℞
□ BECLODISK® DISKHALER®

Glaxo Wellcome

Beclomethasone Dipropionate

Corticosteroid for the Treatment of Bronchial Asthma

Information for the Patient: Your physician has prescribed a unique inhalation system for you called Beclodisk. Please follow the instructions carefully. It is important that you use the Beclodisk system properly to ensure you receive the maximum benefit from your medication.

Dosage: It is essential that you use Beclodisk as directed by your doctor. Do not stop or change dosage without consulting your doctor. Children should use Beclodisk under supervision of an adult and only as instructed by the doctor.

Total daily dose should not exceed: beclomethasone dipropionate 1 mg or 5 blisters of Beclodisk 200 μg or 10 blisters of Beclodisk 100 μg in adults or adolescents above 14 years of age; beclomethasone dipropionate 500 μg in children aged 6 years and above.

Caution: Beclodisk is not intended to give instant relief of your breathing difficulties but to correct the underlying disorder responsible for your attacks.

Many other inhalers contain bronchodilators to provide rapid relief and if your doctor prescribes one of these, you should use it according to the prescription order when you have an acute attack of asthma.

Diskhaler: Your Diskhaler device has the following components: a brown outer body which has a lift-up lid with a piercing plastic needle; a cleaning brush in the rear compartment underneath the device lid; a rotating white wheel which holds the Beclodisk Disk; a moveable white cartridge with mouthpiece; and a mouthpiece cover.

Step 1: Loading Your Diskhaler Device (see package insert for illustrations): Remove the dark brown cover and ensure the mouthpiece is clean. Grasp the white cartridge by the exposed corners and gently pull out until the ribbed sides of the cartridge are visible. Remove the cartridge by squeezing the ribbed sides and pulling the cartridge unit out from the Diskhaler device. Place the Beclodisk Disk on the wheel with the numbers face up, allowing the underside to fit into the holes of the wheel. Slide the cartridge back into the device body. Your Diskhaler device is now 'loaded'.

Step 2: Getting Ready for Your First Beclodisk Dose: Gently push in and pull out the loaded cartridge. Your device will mechanically rotate your Beclodisk Disk. Continue the rotation process until the number (8) appears in the side indicator window. By counting down from 8 (8, 7, 6, 5 etc.), the indicator window will display how many doses you have left in your Beclodisk Disk.

Step 3: Getting Ready for Inhalation: Hold the Diskhaler device firmly in a level position, lift the rear edge of the Diskhaler lid, and raise it as far as it will go until it is fully upright. The plastic needle on the lid will pierce the blister. By raising the lid as far as it will go, both upper and lower surfaces of the blister will be pierced. Once the blister is pierced, close the lid. Your device is now ready to use.

Warning: Do not lift the lid unless the cartridge is inside the Diskhaler body or the cartridge is completely removed. By following this warning, you will avoid breaking the needle which is essential in piercing the medication blister.

Step 4: Inhaling from the Diskhaler Device: Keep your device level. Breathe out fully. Raise the device to your mouth. Gently place the mouthpiece between your teeth and lips. Do not cover the air inlet holes on the sides of the mouthpiece. Breathe in through your mouth quickly and as deeply as you can. Hold your breath briefly as you remove the Diskhaler device from your mouth.

Step 5: Getting Ready for Your Next Inhalation: Pull the cartridge out once (see Step 2), push in once and the Beclodisk Disk will rotate to the next number in the indicator window. **Do not pierce your next blister until immediately before inhalation.** To inhale again, repeat Steps 3 and 4.

Step 6: Replacing a Beclodisk Disk: Each Disk has 8 blisters containing your medication. When the number 1 appears in the indicator window, you have one dose remaining. Replace the 8 Beclodisk Disk by repeating Step 1. **Remember: Do not throw the wheel away with the empty Beclodisk Disk.**

Cleaning: To clean any remaining powder away, a brush is provided in the rear compartment underneath the device lid. Remove the cartridge and wheel before using the brush.

Replace the Diskhaler device after 6 months' use.

□ BECLOFORTE® ℞

Glaxo Wellcome

Beclomethasone Dipropionate

Corticosteroid for the Treatment of Bronchial Asthma

Information for the Patient: What you should know about Becloforte Inhalation Aerosol: Please read this leaflet carefully before you start to take your medicine. For further information or advice, ask your doctor or pharmacist.

About Your Medicine: Beclomethasone dipropionate is sold by Glaxo Wellcome under the trademark Becloforte. Becloforte brand beclomethasone dipropionate is one of a group of medicines known as anti-inflammatory corticosteroids, frequently referred to simply as "steroids", and can only be obtained on the prescription of a doctor.

Becloforte is a medicine which your doctor has chosen to suit you and your condition. When taken every day in regularly spaced doses as ordered by your doctor it can help to ease your breathing problems by relieving swelling and irritation in the small air passages in the lungs.

Important Points to Note Before Taking Your Medicine: Have you ever had to stop taking other medicines for this illness because you were allergic to them or they caused problems? Are you having treatment, or have you recently received treatment for tuberculosis (TB)? Are you taking other "steroids" by mouth or by inhalation? If the answer is **yes** to any of these questions, tell your doctor or pharmacist as soon as possible if you have not already done so.

Use of This Medicine During Pregnancy and Breast-Feeding: Do not use this medication during pregnancy or breast-feeding without first discussing with your doctor.

Taking Your Medicine: Follow the instructions shown. If you have any problems, tell your doctor or pharmacist.

It is important that you take each dose as instructed by your doctor, nurse, or pharmacist. Your doctor will decide what dose you should take and how often.

The label provided by the pharmacist will usually tell you what dose to take and how often. If it doesn't, or you are not sure, ask your doctor or pharmacist.

For adults and adolescents above 16 years of age, the dose is one inhalation (250 μg) 2 to 4 times daily. Some patients may do well with 2 inhalations (500 μg) twice daily.

Do not take more doses or use your inhaler more often than your doctor advises.

Do not use this medicine to treat a sudden attack of breathlessness. You will probably need a different kind of medicine in a different color pack which your doctor may already have given you. If you have more than one medicine, be careful not to confuse them. **Do not stop** treatment—even if you feel better—unless told to do so by your doctor.

If you have to go into hospital for an operation, take your inhaler with you and tell the doctor what medicine(s) you are taking.

How to Use Your Becloforte Inhalation Aerosol Properly (see package insert for illustrations): Before using Becloforte Inhalation aerosol for the first time, or if your inhaler has not been used for a week or more, release 2 puffs into the air to ensure that it works properly.

1. Remove the cap from the mouthpiece; the strap on the cap will stay attached to the actuator. Check the mouthpiece inside and outside to ensure that it is clean.
2. Shake the inhaler vigorously.
3. Hold the inhaler upright between fingers and thumb with your thumb on the base, below the mouthpiece. Breathe out as far as is comfortable.
4. For the next step there are 2 alternatives (4.a and 4.b) depending on the technique preferred by your physician.
   4. a. Place the mouthpiece in your mouth between your teeth and close your lips around it, but do not bite it. Just after starting to breathe in through your mouth, press down on the top of the inhaler to release the drug while still breathing in steadily and deeply. **or**
   4. b. Place the inhaler 2 finger widths directly in front of your mouth. Begin a slow deep inward breath through your wide open mouth, at the same time pressing the canister down firmly into the inhaler. Be careful not to spray any of the drug into your eyes.
5. While holding your breath, take the inhaler from your mouth and take your finger from the top of the inhaler. Continue holding your breath for as long as is comfortable.
6. If you are to take further puffs, keep the inhaler upright and wait about half a minute before repeating steps 2 through 5.
7. After use, always snap the mouthpiece cover back into position to keep out dust and lint.
8. Rinse out your mouth with water after each dose. Do not swallow the water after rinsing.

Important: Do not rush steps 4 and 5. It is important that you start to breathe in as slowly as possible just before operating your inhaler. Practice in front of a mirror for the first few times. If you see "mist"

Becloforte (cont'd)

coming from the top of your inhaler or the sides of your mouth, you should start again from step 2.

If your doctor has given you different instructions for using your inhaler, please follow them carefully. Tell your doctor if you have any difficulties.

Cleaning: Your inhaler should be cleaned at least once per week.

1. Pull the metal canister out of the plastic casing of the inhaler and remove the mouthpiece cover.
2. Rinse the plastic casing and mouthpiece cover in warm water. A mild detergent may be added to the water. Then rinse thoroughly with clean water before drying. **Do not put the metal canister into water.**
3. Leave the casing and mouthpiece cover to dry in a warm place. Avoid excessive heat.
4. Replace the canister and mouthpiece cover.
5. After cleansing, release 1 puff into the air to make sure that the inhaler works.

After Using Your Becloforte Inhalation Aerosol: If you notice that your shortness of breath or wheeze is becoming worse, tell your doctor as soon as possible.

Very occasionally, some people find that their throat or tongue becomes sore after taking this medicine or that their voice becomes a little hoarse. In some people, an infection of the mouth and throat called candidiasis (thrush) may occur. Rinsing your mouth with water immediately after taking each dose may help. Tell your doctor but do not stop treatment unless told to do so.

If you feel unwell in any other way or have any symptoms that you do not understand, you should contact your doctor immediately.

If You Take Too Much Medicine: In the event of an overdose (more than the maximum recommended daily dose), tell your doctor without delay or contact your nearest hospital emergency department or poison centre.

If You Miss a Dose: It is **very important that you use Becloforte regularly;** however, if you miss a single dose, do not worry—just take the next dose when it is due.

What to Do if You Must Stop Taking Your Medicine: If your doctor decides to stop your treatment, do not keep any left over medicine unless your doctor tells you to.

Remember: This medicine is only for **you.** Only a doctor can prescribe it for you. Never give it to someone else. It may harm them even if their symptoms are the same as yours.

Storing Your Medicine: Keep your medicine in a safe place where children cannot reach it. Your medicine may harm them.

Protect from frost, direct sunlight and high temperatures. If the inhaler becomes very cold, remove the metal canister and warm **in your hand** for a few minutes. **Never** use other forms of heat.

Warning: The metal canister is pressurized. It may explode if heated. Do not place it in hot water or near radiators, stoves or other sources of heat. Do not puncture or burn the canister, even when apparently empty.

Further Information: If you have any questions or are not sure about anything, then you should ask your doctor or the pharmacist.

You may need to read this leaflet again. **Please do not throw it away** until you have finished your medicine.

TM: The appearance, namely the color, shape and size of the Becloforte inhalation device is a trademark of Glaxo Group Limited, Glaxo Wellcome Inc., licensed use.

☐ BECLOVENT® INHALER Ⓟ
☐ BECLOVENT® ROTACAPS® Ⓟ
☐ BECLOVENT® ROTAHALER®

Glaxo Wellcome

Beclomethasone Dipropionate

Corticosteroid for the Treatment of Bronchial Asthma

Information for the Patient: Inhaler: What you should know about Beclovent Inhalation Aerosol: Please read this leaflet carefully before you start to take your medicine. For further information or advice, ask your doctor or pharmacist.

About Your Medicine: The name of this medicine is Beclovent (beclomethasone dipropionate) Inhalation Aerosol. Beclovent is one of a group of medicines known as anti-inflammatory corticosteroids, frequently referred to simply as "steroids", and can only be obtained on the prescription of a doctor.

Beclovent is a medicine which your doctor has chosen to suit you and your condition. When taken every day at regularly spaced doses as ordered by your doctor it can help to ease your breathing problems by relieving the swelling and irritation in the small air passages in your lungs.

Do not use this medicine to treat a sudden attack of breathlessness. However, continue to take this medicine at the usual time, even if you use another medicine such as a bronchodilator to provide rapid relief of an acute asthma attack.

Do not stop taking this medicine or change dosage without your doctor's advice, even if your asthma seems better.

Important Points to Note Before Taking Your Medicine: Have you ever had to stop taking other medicines for this illness because you were allergic to them or they caused problems? Are you having treatment, or have you recently received treatment for tuberculosis (TB)? Are you taking other "steroids" by mouth or by inhalation? If the answer is **Yes** to any of these questions, tell your doctor or pharmacist as soon as possible if you have not already done so.

Pregnancy and Breast-Feeding: Do not use this medication during pregnancy or breast-feeding without first discussing with your doctor.

Taking Your Medicine: Follow the instructions shown. If you have any problems, tell your doctor or pharmacist.

It is important that you take each dose as instructed by your doctor, nurse, or pharmacist. Your doctor will decide what dose you should take and how often. The label provided by your pharmacist will usually tell you what dose to take and how often. If it doesn't, or you are not sure, ask your doctor or pharmacist.

Total daily dosage should not exceed 20 inhalations (1 000 μg beclomethasone dipropionate) in adults; 10 inhalations (500 μg beclomethasone dipropionate) in children aged 6 years and above; 3 inhalations (150 μg beclomethasone dipropionate) in children between 3 and 5 years of age.

Do not take more doses or use your inhaler more often than your doctor advises.

Do not use this medicine to treat a sudden attack of breathlessness. You will probably need a different kind of medicine in a different color pack which your doctor may already have given you. If you have more than one medicine, be careful not to confuse them. **Do not stop** treatment—even if you feel better—unless told to do so by your doctor.

If you have to go into hospital for an operation, take your inhaler with you and tell the doctor what medicine(s) you are taking.

How to Use Your Beclovent Inhalation Aerosol Properly (see package insert for illustrations):

Before using Beclovent Inhalation aerosol for the first time, or if your inhaler has not been used for a week or more, release 2 puffs into the air to ensure that it works properly.

1. Remove the cap from the mouthpiece; the strap on the cap will stay attached to the actuator. Check the mouthpiece inside and outside to ensure that it is clean.
2. Shake the inhaler vigorously.
3. Hold the inhaler upright between fingers and thumb with your thumb on the base, below the mouthpiece.
   Breathe out as far as is comfortable.
4. For the next step there are 2 alternatives (4.a or 4.b) depending on the technique preferred by your physician:
   - 4.a. Place the mouthpiece in your mouth between your teeth and close your lips around it, but do not bite it. Just after starting to breathe in through your mouth, press down on the top of the inhaler to release the drug while still breathing in steadily and deeply. **or**
   - 4.b. Place the inhaler 2 finger widths directly in front of your mouth as shown. Begin a slow deep inward breath through your wide open mouth, at the same time pressing the canister down firmly into the inhaler. Be careful not to spray any of the drug into your eyes.
5. While holding your breath, take the inhaler from your mouth and take your finger from the top of the inhaler. Continue holding your breath for as long as is comfortable.
6. If you are to take further puffs, keep the inhaler upright and wait about half a minute before repeating steps 2 through 5.

7. After use, always snap the mouthpiece cover back into position to keep out dust and lint.
8. Rinse out your mouth with water after each dose. Do not swallow the water after rinsing.

Important: Do not rush steps 4 and 5. It is important that you start to breathe in as slowly as possible just before operating your inhaler. Practice in front of a mirror for the first few times. If you see "mist" coming from the top of your inhaler or the sides of your mouth, you should start again from step 2.

If your doctor has given you different instructions for using your inhaler, please follow them carefully. Tell your doctor if you have any difficulties.

Children: Young children may need help and an adult may need to operate the inhaler for them. Encourage the child to breathe out and operate the inhaler just after the child starts to breathe in. Practice the technique together. Older children or people with weak hands should hold the inhaler with both hands. Put the two forefingers on top of the inhaler and both thumbs on the base below the mouthpiece.

Cleaning: Your inhaler should be cleaned at least once per week.

1. Pull the metal canister out of the plastic casing of the inhaler and remove the mouthpiece cover.
2. Rinse the plastic casing and mouthpiece cover in warm water. A mild detergent may be added to the water. Then rinse thoroughly with clean water before drying. **Do not put the metal canister into water.**
3. Leave the casing and mouthpiece cover to dry in a warm place. Avoid excessive heat.
4. Replace the canister and mouthpiece cover.
5. After cleaning, release one puff into the air to make sure that the inhaler works.

After Using Your Beclovent Inhalation Aerosol Inhaler: If you notice that your shortness of breath or wheeze is becoming worse, tell your doctor as soon as possible. Very occasionally, some people find that their throat or tongue becomes sore after taking this medicine or that their voice becomes a little hoarse. In some people, an infection of the mouth and throat called candidiasis (thrush) may occur. Rinsing your mouth with water immediately after taking each dose may help. Tell your doctor, but do not stop treatment unless you are told to do so.

If you feel unwell in any other way or have any symptoms that you do not understand, you should contact your doctor immediately.

If You Take Too Much Medicine: In the event of an excessive overdose (more than the maximum recommended daily dose), tell your doctor without delay or contact your nearest hospital emergency department or poison centre.

If You Miss a Dose: It is very important that you use Beclovent inhalation aerosol regularly; however, if you miss a single dose, do not worry—just take the next dose when it is due.

What to Do if You Must Stop Taking Your Medicine: If your doctor decides to stop your treatment, do not keep any left over medicine unless your doctor tells you to.

Remember: This medicine is only for **you**. Only a doctor can prescribe it for you. Never give it to someone else. It may harm them even if their symptoms are the same as yours.

Storing Your Medicine: Keep your medicine in a safe place where children cannot reach it. Your medicine may harm them.

Protect from frost, direct sunlight and high temperatures (30°C).

If the inhaler becomes very cold, remove the metal canister and warm **in your hand** for a few minutes. **Never** use other forms of heat.

Warning: The metal canister is pressurized. It may explode if heated. Do not place it in hot water or near radiators, stoves or other sources of heat. Do not puncture or burn the canister, even when apparently empty.

Further Information: If you have any questions or are not sure about anything, then you should ask your doctor or your pharmacist.

You may need to read this leaflet again. **Please do not throw it away** until you have finished your medicine.

Rotacaps/Rotahaler: Directions for the use of Beclovent Rotacaps in the Beclovent Rotahaler: Before using your Beclovent Rotacaps/Rotahaler, please read this insert carefully and follow these instructions.

Dosage: It is essential that you use Beclovent Rotacaps and Rotahaler daily at the intervals recommended by your doctor. Do not stop or change dosage without consulting your doctor.

Children should use the Beclovent Rotacaps/Rotahaler under the supervision of an adult who is aware of their proper use.

Total daily dosage should not exceed: five 200 μg capsules (5×200 μg of beclomethasone dipropionate) in adults; five 100 μg capsules (5×100 μg of beclomethasone dipropionate) in children aged 6 to 14 years of age; above 14 years of age, the adult dosage applies (i.e., total daily dosage should not exceed 1 000 μg of beclomethasone dipropionate).

Caution: Beclovent Rotacaps are not intended to give instant relief of your breathing difficulties but rather to correct the underlying disorder responsible for your attacks. Many other inhalers contain bronchodilators to provide rapid relief and if your doctor prescribed one of these, you should use it according to the prescription order when you have an acute attack of asthma.

Treatment with Beclovent Rotacaps should not be stopped abruptly, but tapered off gradually.

Care of the Rotahaler: At least every 2 weeks wash the 2 halves of your Rotahaler in warm water, making sure beforehand that the empty Rotacap shell is removed from the raised square hole.

Dry the Rotahaler thoroughly before reassembling it.

Avoid excessive heat.

Directions: Preparing the Rotahaler for use (see package insert for illustrations):

1. Remove the Rotahaler from its container.
2. Hold the Rotahaler by the mouthpiece and twist the barrel in either direction until it stops.
3. Take a Rotacap from its container. Holding the Rotahaler vertically, press the Rotacap firmly, clear end first, into the raised square hole making sure that the top of the Rotacap is level with the top of the hole. This will push the previously used Rotacap shell, if one is there, into the Rotahaler.
4. Hold the Rotahaler level (horizontal) with the white dot upper-most. Twist the barrel briskly in the opposite direction until it stops. This separates the 2 halves of the Rotacap. The Rotahaler is now ready for use.

Using the Rotahaler:

5. Breathe out slowly until no more air can be expelled from the lungs, then **immediately...**
6. Keeping the Rotahaler level raise it to your mouth. Place the mouthpiece over your tongue and well into your mouth. Close your lips around the mouthpiece and tilt your head slightly backwards.
7. Breathe in through your mouth as deeply and fully as you can.
8. Hold your breath and remove the Rotahaler from your mouth. Continue holding your breath as long as you comfortably can before breathing out.

After using the Rotahaler:

9. After use, pull the 2 halves of the Rotahaler apart and discard the empty Rotacap shells. There is no need to remove the shell that is still lodged in the square hole, except before cleaning.
10. Reassemble the Rotahaler.

If your doctor has instructed you to use a second Rotacap then repeat steps 2 to 10.

Beclovent Rotacap capsules are for inhalation use only, using a Beclovent Rotahaler inhaler.

Always keep the Rotahaler in its container to keep it clean. Remember to obtain a replacement Rotahaler after 6 months' use. Make a note of the date on which you received your current Rotahaler.

Precautions: Your doctor will tell you how frequently to use your Rotahaler. Do not exceed the dosage recommended by him/her.

Do not swallow the Rotacaps.

Follow all instructions carefully.

Only insert Rotacaps into the Rotahaler immediately prior to use.

When using Beclovent Rotacaps, rinse your mouth with water after each use.

□ BECONASE Aq® ℞

Glaxo Wellcome

Beclomethasone Dipropionate

Corticosteroid for Nasal Use

Information for the Patient: Before using your Beconase Aq nasal spray, please read this insert carefully and follow these instructions:

Directions (see package insert for illustrations):

1. Remove the dust cap and lock-ring from the nasal applicator. Shake the bottle.

Beconase Aq (cont'd)

2. The very first time the spray is used, prime the pump by pressing downwards on the white collar using your index and middle fingers while supporting the base of the bottle with your thumb. Press down until a fine spray appears. The spray is now ready for use. It should be necessary to prime the pump only when using the spray for the first time.
3. Gently blow your nose. Close one nostril. Tilt your head forward slightly and, keeping the bottle upright, carefully insert the nasal applicator into your other nostril.
4. For each spray your physician has instructed you to take, press firmly downwards once on the white collar using your index and middle fingers while supporting the base of the bottle with your thumb. Breathe gently inwards through the nostril, then breathe out through the mouth.
   Note: When Beconase Aq nasal spray is administered as 2 applications into each nostril, the first puff should be directed at the upper, and the second at the lower part of the nasal cavity to insure coverage of the entire nasal passage.
5. Repeat steps 3 and 4 for the other nostril.
6. Replace the lock-ring and the dust cap.

Dosage: It is essential that you use Beconase Aq nasal spray regularly at the intervals recommended by your doctor. Do not stop or change dosage without consulting your doctor. Children should use Beconase Aq nasal spray only under the supervision of an adult who is aware of its proper use.

The maximum daily dosage should not exceed 12 applications (600 µg beclomethasone dipropionate) in adults and 8 applications (400 µg beclomethasone dipropionate) in children. The safety and efficacy of Beconase Aq nasal spray in children under 6 years of age have not been established.

After Taking Your Medicine:
Check with your doctor if any of the following are observed:
- signs of infection of your nose, throat, or sinus occur;
- you do not detect any improvement in 3 weeks;
- repeated unusual bleeding occurs;
- your condition becomes worse;
- new medical problems develop;
- you start to take new medicines.

Caution: Beconase Aq nasal spray is not intended to give instant relief of your nasal congestion but to correct the underlying disorder responsible for your symptoms.

Cleaning: To clean the nasal applicator, remove the dust cap and the lock-ring, press gently upwards on the white collar and the nasal applicator will come free. Wash the applicator and the dust cap under cold water. Dry the applicator and replace the dust cap and lock-ring.

If the nasal applicator becomes blocked, remove the dust cap, unscrew the complete pump mechanism and soak it in warm water for a few minutes. Rinse with cold water, dry and refit to bottle.

Discard 3 months after first using the spray.

□ BENZAMYCIN® Ⓟ

Dermik Laboratories Canada

Erythromycin—Benzoyl Peroxide

Acne Therapy

Information for the Patient: Before you use **Benzamycin** (erythromycin and benzoyl peroxide topical gel, USP), please read this leaflet carefully. If you have **any** questions after reading this information, please talk to your doctor or pharmacist.

Benzamycin is available only on prescription. It has been prescribed by your doctor to treat your current condition. Do not give this medication to other people.

Benzamycin is a mixture of 2 acne medications, erythromycin and benzoyl peroxide. It is applied to the skin in a thin layer, and helps to treat acne.

Instructions for Use:
1. Prior to using Benzamycin, wash affected areas thoroughly with a nonmedicated soap, rinse with warm water, and then gently pat dry.
2. Apply Benzamycin to affected areas in a thin layer twice daily, morning and evening, or as directed by your doctor. Fair-skinned individuals should begin with once daily application. Wash hands after application. Do not apply more frequently than directed by your doctor.
3. Although improvement has been seen as early as 2 weeks, in certain cases 6 to 10 weeks of treatment may be required for best results. This product should be used as directed for the full duration prescribed by your doctor.

Things to remember:
- You should not use Benzamycin if you know you have an allergy to benzoyl peroxide or erythromycin.
- Store this medication in your refrigerator. Do not freeze.
- Benzamycin is for external use only. Avoid contact with the eyes, nose, lips, mouth and other mucous membranes. If contact occurs, rinse well with water. If soreness or redness develops contact your doctor.
- Do not use any other topical acne preparations unless directed to do so by your doctor.
- Slight stinging and/or redness may occur at the beginning of treatment. If excessive irritation or dryness occurs, discontinue your medication and consult your doctor.
- Benzamycin may bleach hair or colored fabric.
- Do not over-apply Benzamycin. Over-application will not speed up treatment, but may irritate your skin.
- Keep this medication out of the reach of children.
- If after 3 months from the time your prescription was filled you have not used up the Benzamycin, discard it and obtain a fresh supply.

□ BEROTEC® Inhalation Aerosol Ⓟ
□ BEROTEC® FORTE Inhalation Aerosol Ⓟ

Boehringer Ingelheim

Fenoterol HBr

Bronchodilator

Information for the Patient: Before you use Berotec 100 µg or Berotec forte Inhalation Aerosol, you should read the following information carefully.

Berotec 100 µg and Berotec forte Inhalation Aerosols are aerosol canisters with a mouthpiece; used to treat the wheezing or shortness of breath caused by asthma, chronic bronchitis, or emphysema.

The following information explains how to use the Berotec inhalation aerosols and how to avoid problems while you are using them. If you have any questions, be sure to talk to your doctor or pharmacist.

Before You Use Berotec 100 µg or Berotec forte Inhalation Aerosol: Be sure to tell your doctor: if you are pregnant or intend to become pregnant; if you are breast-feeding; if you have any other health problems; if you are taking any other medications, including those you can buy without a prescription; if you have any allergies or reactions to foods, drugs or aerosols.

How to Use Your Berotec 100 µg or Berotec forte Inhalation Aerosol: Do not exceed the number of puffs prescribed by your doctor. Do not use the inhaler more often than your doctor recommends.

If you are using your Berotec 100 µg or Berotec forte Inhaler on a regular daily basis, without using any other anti-asthma medication, consult your doctor for re-evaluation of your treatment.

The usual dose to relieve acute symptoms is one puff, which can be repeated 5 minutes later if necessary. If symptoms persist further puffs may be required and you should immediately consult your doctor or the nearest hospital.

Your doctor may prescribe this medication on a regular basis in association with other anti-asthma medication that control the airways inflammation: in this case the usual dose is 1 to 2 puffs up to 3 to 4 times/day, for Berotec 100 µg and 1 to 2 puffs up to 3 times/day for Berotec forte (200 µg).

If a previously effective dosage regimen fails to provide the usual relief or the effects of one dose last for less than 3 hours, you should see a doctor immediately; this is usually a sign of seriously worsening asthma that requires reassessment of treatment.

Before starting to use your inhalation aerosol, read the following instructions carefully; be sure that you know how to use the inhaler properly. If you use the inhaler incorrectly, you may not be getting all of the medication you need. If you have any questions about using the inhaler, check with your doctor.

Instructions:
1. Remove the protective cap from the inhaler.
2. **It is very important** to shake the unit well.

3. Your doctor will recommend a method of using the inhaler. Use whichever of the 2 methods below your doctor has suggested: a) Breathe out as completely as possible. Place the mouthpiece into your mouth and close your lips around it. Keep your teeth apart and your tongue flat to allow free flow of the medication into your lungs. Press the canister down into the mouthpiece and breathe in deeply through your mouth at the same time **or** b) Breathe out as completely as possible. Place the inhaler about 3 cm (1 inch) in front of your mouth. With your mouth wide open begin a slow, deep breath. At the same time, press the canister down into the mouthpiece, breathing the medication in deeply.
4. Hold your breath for a few seconds, then breathe out slowly.
5. If your doctor has recommended a second puff, wait about one minute and then repeat steps 2, 3 and 4.
6. Replace the protective plastic cap.

Care of the Mouthpiece/Canister: The mouthpiece should be washed with warm water once a week. You must remove the mouthpiece from the canister before you begin to clean the mouthpiece. If you use soap or detergent, the mouthpiece should be well rinsed in clear water, and then allowed to air dry. The mouthpiece must be completely dry before you put the canister back into the mouthpiece.

Sometimes, the canister stem may also get dirty or blocked. Pull the canister out of the mouthpiece and check the small holes in the stem. If these two small holes seem blocked, rinse them with clear lukewarm water. When the canister is dry, put it back into the mouthpiece.

When does the unit need to be replaced? If you are not sure how much inhalation aerosol is left in the canister, you can check by putting the canister in water. If the canister floats, you need to replace it.

Please remember:
- Berotec 100 μg or Berotec forte Inhalation Aerosol has been prescribed to treat **your** current condition. **Do not** give them to other people.
- **Do not** take any other medication without your doctor's advice. Tell any **other** doctor, dentist, or pharmacist with whom you consult that you are using Berotec 100 μg or Berotec forte inhalation aerosol.
- **Keep this medication out of the reach of children.**
- Keep from freezing.
- Container may explode if heated. Contents under pressure. Do not place in hot water or near radiators, stoves, or other sources of heat. Do not puncture or incinerate container or store at temperatures over 30°C.
- Like any drug product, Berotec 100 μg and Berotec forte may cause unwanted effects along with the good effects. If you do experience any unusual or unwanted effects while you are using your inhalation aerosol you should contact your doctor.

☐ BEROTEC® Inhalation Solution ℞

Boehringer Ingelheim

Fenoterol HBr

Bronchodilator

Information for the Patient: Berotec Solution: 20 mL Bottle: Before you use Berotec Solution you should read the following leaflet carefully.

Berotec solution is a bronchodilator which is to be used with a nebulizer to treat the wheezing or shortness of breath caused by asthma, chronic bronchitis or emphysema. Berotec solution is available only on prescription.

This information explains how to use Berotec solution and how to avoid problems while you are using it. If you have any questions be sure to talk to your doctor or pharmacist.

Before You Use Berotec Inhalation Solution: Be sure to tell your doctor:
- if you are pregnant or intend to become pregnant;
- if you are breast-feeding;
- if you have any other health problems;
- if you are taking any other medications, including those you can buy without a prescription;
- if you have any special allergies or reactions to foods or drugs.

How to Use Berotec Inhalation Solution (see package insert for illustrations): **Do not exceed the dose of Berotec solution prescribed by your doctor. Do not use your nebulizer more often than your doctor recommends.**

If you are using your Berotec Inhalation solution on a regular daily basis, without using any other anti-asthma medication, consult your doctor for re-evaluation of your treatment.

Your doctor may prescribe this medication on a regular basis in association with other anti-asthma medication that control the airways inflammation.

If a previously effective dosage regimen fails to provide the usual relief or the effects of one dose last for less than 3 hours, you should see a doctor immediately; this is usually a sign of seriously worsening asthma that requires reassessment of treatment.

Before you start your treatment with Berotec solution, be sure that you know how to use your nebulizer and how to properly maintain it.

In most cases, dilution of the dose with sterile preservative-free saline is not necessary. However, volumes of Berotec solution less than 2 mL are not appropriate for nebulization and must be diluted with saline or another suitable nebulizer solution to make-up a total fill volume of 2 to 5 mL.

1. Immediately before you plan to use the nebulizer, using a syringe, withdraw the dose of Berotec solution which your doctor has prescribed for you (usually 0.5 mL to 1.0 mL of solution). Add the solution to the nebulizing chamber.
   Do not store the prescribed dose in the syringe for later use.
2. Recap your bottle of Berotec solution and store it in a safe place until your next treatment. Once you have opened the Berotec solution bottle, the solution is good for 30 days. Be sure to make a note of the date that you first opened the bottle.
3. If you have been instructed to dilute the solution, using a syringe, add the amount of sterile preservative-free sodium chloride solution as per your doctor or pharmacist's instructions (usually 4 to 4.5 mL of sodium chloride solution).
4. Gently shake the nebulizer chamber and connect it to the mouthpiece or face mask. Connect the nebulizer tube to the air or oxygen pump and begin your treatment.
5. Adjust the face mask to keep the mist from getting in your eyes. Breathe calmly and deeply through the mask or mouthpiece until there is no more mist being formed in the nebulizer chamber. This usually takes 10-15 minutes.
6. Follow the instructions provided by the nebulizer and air pump manufacturers for the proper care and maintenance of the equipment.

Please Remember:
- **Berotec solution has been prescribed to treat your current condition. Do not give this medication to other people.**
- **Do not** take any other medication without your doctor's advice. Tell any **other** doctor, dentist, or pharmacist with whom you consult that you are using Berotec solution.
- **The solution is intended for inhalation only. Do not inject it or drink it.**
- **Keep this medication out of the reach of children.**
- Like any drug product, Berotec may cause unwanted effects along with the good effects. If you do experience any unusual or unwanted effects while you are using Berotec, you should contact your doctor.

Berotec UDV: 2 mL Unit Dose Vial: Berotec Inhalation Solution in Unit Dose Vials: Before you use Berotec solution, you should read the following information carefully.

Berotec solution is a bronchodilator which is to be used with a nebulizer to treat the wheezing and shortness of breath caused by asthma, chronic bronchitis or emphysema. Berotec solution is available only on prescription.

0.625 mg/mL: Each plastic vial contains 2 mL of Berotec solution. Each mL of solution contains 0.625 mg (0.0625%) fenoterol hydrobromide in an isotonic solution.

0.25 mg/mL: Each plastic vial contains 2 mL of Berotec solution. Each mL of solution contains 0.25 mg (0.025%) fenoterol hydrobromide in an isotonic solution.

This information explains how to use Berotec solution in Unit Dose Vials and how to avoid problems while you are using it. If you have any questions after reading this information be sure to talk to your doctor or pharmacist.

Before You Use Berotec Inhalation Solution: Be sure to tell your doctor:
- if you are pregnant or intend to become pregnant;
- if you are breast-feeding;
- if you have any other health problems;
- if you are taking any other medications, including those you can buy without a prescription;
- if you have any special allergies or reactions to foods or drugs.

Berotec Inhalation Solution (cont'd)

How To Use Berotec Inhalation Solution (see package insert for illustrations): **Do not exceed the dose of Berotec solution prescribed by your doctor. Do not use your nebulizer more often than your doctor recommends.**

If you are using your Berotec inhalation solution on a regular basis, without using any other anti-asthma medication, consult your doctor for re-evaluation of your treatment.

Your doctor may prescribe this medication on a regular basis in association with other anti-asthma medication that control the airways inflammation.

If a previously effective dosage regimen fails to provide the usual relief or the effects of one dose last for less than 3 hours, you should see a doctor immediately; this is usually a sign of seriously worsening asthma that requires reassessment of treatment.

Before you start your treatment with Berotec solution, be sure that you know how to use your nebulizer and how to properly maintain it.

In most cases, dilution of the dose with sterile preservative-free saline in not necessary. However, volumes of Berotec solution less than 2 mL are not appropriate for nebulization and must be diluted with saline or another suitable nebulizer solution to make-up a total fill volume of 2 to 5 mL.

Dilute your dose immediately before you plan to use the solution.

1. Detach one plastic vial by pulling it firmly from the strip.
2. Open the vial by twisting off the top. It is important that you use the contents of the vial **as soon as possible** after opening it.
3. Squeeze the contents of the plastic vial into your nebulizer chamber. If your doctor has instructed you to use less than one complete vial, use a syringe to withdraw the prescribed dose.
   Any solution left in the plastic vial must be thrown away.
4. If your doctor has instructed you to use another inhalation solution in combination with Berotec solution, you should add the appropriate amount of that solution to the nebulizer chamber as well.
5. Using a syringe, add sodium chloride to the chamber if you have been directed to do so by your pharmacist or physician.
6. Gently shake the nebulizer chamber and connect it to the mouthpiece or face mask. Then connect the nebulizer tube to the air or oxygen pump and begin therapy.
7. Adjust the mask to keep the mist from getting in your eyes. Breathe calmly and deeply through the mask or mouthpiece until no more mist is formed in the nebulizer chamber. This usually takes 10 to 15 minutes.
8. Follow the instructions provided by the nebulizer and air pump manufacturers for the proper care and maintenance of the equipment.
9. The unit dose vials should be stored at room temperature. The vials should be protected from heat and light.

Please Remember:

- Berotec solution has been prescribed to treat **your** current condition. Do not give this medication to other people.
- **Do not** take any other medication without your doctor's advice. Tell any **other** doctor, dentist, or pharmacist with whom you consult that you are using Berotec solution.
- **The solution is intended for inhalation only. Do not inject it or drink it.**
- **Keep this medication out of the reach of children.**
- Like any drug product, Berotec may cause unwanted effects along with the good effects. If you do experience any unusual or unwanted effects while you are using Berotec, you should contact your doctor.

□ BETASERON® 🄿

Berlex Canada

Interferon beta-1b

Immunomodulator

Information for the Patient: Betaseron (interferon beta-1b) is intended for use under the guidance and supervision of a physician. Your physician or his/her delegate should instruct you in the preparation and self-injection technique of Betaseron. Do not begin your Betaseron treatment without training.

Betaseron should be used as prescribed by your physician. However, if you miss a dose, take it as soon as you remember. While using Betaseron, please keep in mind the following facts:

- Betaseron must always be refrigerated. Do not freeze. Be sure to store Betaseron in a refrigerator before and after reconstitution.

  Before Reconstitution: If refrigeration is not possible, vials of Betaseron and diluent should be kept as cool as possible, below 30°C, away from heat and light, and **used within 7 days.**

  After Reconstitution: The vial or syringe containing the Betaseron solution must be kept in a refrigerator, and must be **used within 3 hours.**
- Keep syringes and needles away from children. Do not reuse needles or syringes. Discard used syringes and needles in a syringe disposal unit.
- **Women:** Betaseron should not be used during pregnancy or if you are trying to become pregnant. While using Betaseron women of childbearing age should use birth control measures. If you wish to become pregnant while using Betaseron, discuss the matter with your doctor. If you do become pregnant you should discontinue treatment and contact your doctor immediately.
- Injection site reactions are common. They include redness, pain, swelling, and discoloration. Less frequently, injection site necrosis (skin breakdown and tissue destruction) has been observed. To minimize the chances for a reaction, change injection areas every time you inject yourself and wait at least 1 week before reusing an area. Do not make an injection into skin that is tender, red, or hard. Do not use any areas where you feel lumps, depressions, pain or discoloration; talk to your doctor or nurse about anything you find. If you experience a break in the skin or drainage of fluid from the injection site, consult your doctor.
- Flu-like symptoms are also common. They include fever, chills, sweating, fatigue, and muscle aches. Taking Betaseron at night may help lessen the impact of flu-like symptoms.
- Depression, including suicide attempts, has been reported by patients. If you experience such symptoms, contact your doctor promptly.
- As with any prescription medication, side effects related to therapy can occur. Consult with your doctor if you have any problems, whether or not you think they may be related to Betaseron.

Self-Injection Procedure:

Step 1: Gathering All the Supplies: Collect all your equipment before you begin the process. **You'll need:** 1 vial of Diluent for Betaseron (Sodium Chloride 0.54%); 1 vial of Betaseron; 1 3-cc syringe with 21-gauge, 1-inch needle; 1 1-cc syringe with 27-gauge, ½ inch needle; At least 4 alcohol wipes; 1 disposal unit (an opaque, puncture-resistant, sealable container for used syringes/needles).

Step 2: Choosing an Injection Site: Betaseron should be injected into subcutaneous tissue (under the skin, between the fat layer and the muscles beneath). The best areas for injection are loose and soft, away from joints.

- **Choose an injection site from the following areas:**
- Abdomen, above the waistline (at least 5 cm on either side of the navel).
- Right thigh (at least 5 cm above the knee and 5 cm below the groin).
- Left thigh (at least 5 cm above the knee and 5 cm below the groin).
- Left buttock (upper, outer portion).
- Right buttock (upper, outer portion).
- Change injection areas every time you inject yourself. Give the site time to recover from the last injection. This will help prevent injection-site reactions.
- Wait at least 1 week before reusing an area.
- Do not use any areas where you feel lumps, depressions, pain or discoloration; talk to your doctor or nurse about anything you find.
- Keep a record of when and where you are giving yourself injections. Use the Betaseron diary in your training kit.

Step 3: Mixing the Solution: Only the vial of Diluent (liquid) that comes inside your prescription package should be used to dissolve the white cake of drug in the Betaseron vial.

1. Wash your hands thoroughly with soap and water.
2. Check the expiry date on both vials.
3. **Remove** the protective caps from both vials.
4. Use alcohol wipes to **clean** the tops of the vials—move in one direction and use one fresh wipe per vial.
5. Choose the Diluent vial.
6. Resting your forearms on a stable surface, **remove** the needle cover on the 3-cc syringe by pulling the cover straight off the needle.
7. **Pull back** the plunger to the 1.2-cc mark.

8. Holding the vial of Diluent for Betaseron on a stable surface, slowly **insert** the needle straight through the stopper. **Be sure** not to touch the needles or the stopper.
9. **Push in** the plunger all the way to gently inject air into the vial. Keep your thumb on the plunger. **Leave** the needle **in** the vial.
10. Turn the vial of Diluent **upside down.**
11. Resting your forearms on a stable surface, slowly **pull back** the plunger to the 1.2-cc mark. Make sure that the needle tip stays in the liquid.
12. Keeping the vial upside down, gently **tap** the syringe until air bubbles rise to the top of the syringe.
13. Carefully **push in** the plunger to eject the air out through the needle. Make sure that the syringe contains 1.2 cc of Diluent.
14. **Remove** the needle from the vial of Diluent.
15. Place the vial in the syringe disposal unit.
16. While you are holding the syringe, pick up the Betaseron vial with your other hand.
17. Hold the Betaseron vial on a stable surface. Slowly **insert** the needle of the syringe (which contains 1.2 cc of Diluent) all the way through the stopper.
18. **Push** the plunger down slowly, directing the needle toward the side of the vial.
19. **Remove** the needle from the Betaseron vial. If foaming occurs, wait until it disappears.
20. **Throw away** the 3-cc syringe into the disposal unit.
21. **Roll** the vial between your hands gently to completely dissolve the white cake of Betaseron **(Do not shake).**
22. **Look** closely at the solution. It should be clear and particle-free.

Step 4: Preparing the Injection:

1. **Remove** the needle cover of the 1-cc syringe and pull back the plunger to the 1-cc mark.
2. **Insert** the needle through the stopper of the Betaseron vial.
3. Gently **push** the plunger all the way down to inject air into the vial. Leave the needle in the vial.
4. Turn the vial of Betaseron solution **upside down.**
5. **Keep** the needle tip in the liquid and **pull back** the plunger to withdraw 1 cc of liquid.
6. Keeping the vial upside down, gently **tap** the syringe until air bubbles rise to the top of the syringe.
7. Carefully **push in** the plunger to eject **only the air** through the needle. Make sure that the syringe contains 1 cc of Betaseron.
8. **Remove** the needle from the vial.
9. **Recap** the needle.
10. Place the vial containing the remaining solution in the syringe disposal unit.

Step 5: Injecting Betaseron:

1. Use a fresh alcohol wipe to **clean** the skin at the injection site. Use a circular motion from the center of the injection site outward. Let the alcohol dry.
2. **Throw away** the wipe.
3. **Uncap** the needle.
4. Gently **pinch** the skin around the site to lift it up a bit.
5. **Stick** the needle straight into the skin at a 90° angle with a quick, firm motion.
6. **Inject** the drug by using a slow, steady push (push the plunger all the way in until the syringe is empty).
7. **Remove** the needle from the skin.
8. Gently **massage** the injection site with a fresh alcohol wipe.
9. Throw away the 1-cc syringe in the disposal unit.

☐ BEZALIP® ℞

Roche

Bezafibrate

Lipid Metabolism Regulator

Information for the Patient: Full prescribing information is available to doctors and pharmacists on request.

Bezalip is the registered trademark of Hoffmann-La Roche Ltd. for bezafibrate.

Bezalip reduces blood cholesterol, in particular cholesterol associated with low and very low density lipoproteins (LDL and VLDL-cholesterol). Bezalip also reduces high triglyceride levels.

Bezalip is only available on prescription. This medicine should only be used to supplement an appropriate diet recommended and followed up by your doctor for the long-term treatment of raised lipid levels: prescription of this medicine in no way replaces dietary treatment. In addition, depending on the situation, your doctor may recommend further physical exercise, weight loss or other measures.

Comply exactly to the terms of the prescription. Do not change the dose without your doctor's advice. Consult your doctor before stopping treatment since to do so may result in an increase in your blood lipid levels.

Before starting treatment with this medicine, your doctor must know:

- if you have taken Bezalip or any other drug in the fibrate class before and if it caused an allergy or was otherwise poorly tolerated,
- if you suffer from liver or kidney problems,
- if you are pregnant or intend to become pregnant, or are breast-feeding, or intend to breast-feed,
- if you are taking other medicines, in particular an oral anticoagulant such as warfarin (Warfilone) or cyclosporine (Sandimmune).

Proper Use of the Medicine: Bezalip 200 mg immediate release tablet: Standard dosage is one 200 mg tablet three (3) times daily. The 200 mg tablet should be swallowed without chewing and with sufficient fluid, with or after meals.

Bezalip 400 mg sustained release tablet: The dosage is one 400 mg sustained release tablet once (1) daily. The 400 mg sustained release tablet should be taken in the morning or evening with or after meals. The sustained release tablet should be swallowed without chewing with sufficient fluid.

- Your doctor will ask you to have regular medical check-ups and laboratory tests. It is important to respect the dates proposed: we strongly recommend that you keep faithfully these appointments.
- Inform your doctor of any health problem that occurs while taking Bezalip as well as any prescription or non-prescription medicine. If you need other medical treatment let the doctor know that you are taking Bezalip.
- If you are taking both Bezalip and a bile acid resin concurrently, an interval of 2 hours should be maintained between the two drugs.
- Tell your doctor if you are unwell while taking Bezalip (see Unwanted Effects).
- Safety in children and young adolescents has not been established with Bezalip.
- The effect of Bezalip in preventing heart attacks, artherosclerosis or heart disease is not known.
- Bezalip is contraindicated during pregnancy. In the event of pregnancy during treatment, Bezalip should be discontinued and the physician should be informed.
- Bezalip should not be taken while breast-feeding.

Unwanted Effects: In addition to its intended action any medicine may cause unwanted effects. Unwanted effects may occur in certain patients. They may appear and disappear without involving any particular risk but if any unwanted effects persist or become bothersome you must let your doctor know without delay. Such unwanted effects may consist of abdominal pains, constipation, diarrhea, nausea, headache, dizziness, skin reactions, muscular pain or cramps, fatigue.

This medicine is prescribed for a particular health problem and for your personal use. Do not give it to other persons.

Keep all medicines out of reach of children.

If you want further information, ask your doctor or pharmacist.

☐ BIAXIN® ℞

Abbott

Clarithromycin

Antibiotic

Information for the Patient: Biaxin (clarithromycin pediatric granules for suspension) can be taken with or without meals, can be taken with milk and should not be refrigerated.

H. pylori Eradication and Compliance: To ensure treatment success, patients receiving Triple or Dual therapy for the eradication of H. pylori should be advised to take all prescribed medication for the entire treatment duration.

Biaxin (cont'd)

If for some reason the patient cannot complete the treatment, his/her physician should be consulted.

□ BILTRICIDE® Ⓟ

Bayer

Praziquantel

Anthelmintic

Information for the Patient: Please read this leaflet carefully before you start to take your medicine. If you still have any questions after reading this, talk to your doctor or pharmacist.

Biltricide (praziquantel) can only be obtained with a prescription from your doctor. This drug has been prescribed by your doctor to treat the infection you have that is caused by worms and/or liver flukes. Do not give this medicine to other people.

Important Points to Note Before Taking Your Medicine:

1. You should not use Biltricide if you took it before and had an allergy to it.
2. You should not drive or operate machinery on the day of your treatment and during the next 24 hours as your reflexes may be impaired.
3. If any of the following apply to you, make sure you tell your doctor:
   (i) you are pregnant or think you may be
   (ii) you are breast-feeding
   (iii) you have impaired renal (kidney) function or uncompensated liver insufficiency.
4. The safety and effectiveness of Biltricide in children under 4 years of age has not been established.
5. Keep this medicine out of the reach of children.

How to Take Your Medicine:

1. The dose depends on your weight. You must take the medicine exactly as it is prescribed by your doctor. If you are not sure how many tablets to take or how often to take them, consult your doctor or pharmacist.
2. You should not change the dose prescribed by your doctor.
3. The tablets should be swallowed unchewed with some liquid, preferably during or after meals. Keeping the tablets (and pieces of the tablets) in your mouth may release a bitter taste which can cause you to gag or vomit.
4. With single daily doses, it is recommended to take the tablets in the evening. If multiple doses are prescribed by your doctor, the space between doses should be at least 4 hours and not more than 6 hours.
5. Biltricide is supplied as a 600 mg white, oblong tablet with three notches. It is marked BAYER on one side and LG on the other. When broken, each of the four pieces that result contains 150 mg of active ingredient (praziquantel). This allows your doctor to easily adjust the dose depending on your weight.
6. Pieces are broken off by pressing the notch with your thumbnails. If only one quarter of a tablet is required, this is best achieved by breaking the tablet from the outer end.

Side Effects: After taking your medicine you may experience some side effects. These vary according to the dose and duration of your treatment. They also depend on the type of infection you have, how long you have had the infection, and where in your body the infection is. The side effects, if there are any, are most often one or more of the following: abdominal pain, loss of appetite, nausea, vomiting, headache, weakness, dizziness, drowsiness, muscle pain or fever. Often it is hard to tell if the side effects are due to the medicine or the infection itself. If you are concerned about how you are feeling after you take the medicine, or if you feel noticeably worse, contact your doctor or pharmacist as soon as possible.

What to do if You Take an Overdose: It is important to follow exactly the dosage instructions on the label of your medicine. If you do take too much of the medicine, contact your doctor or the nearest hospital emergency department immediately.

Storing Your Medicine: Store this medicine at room temperature below 30°C. Keep this and all medicine in a safe place out of the reach of children. Do not store in a damp place and keep away from light.

Further Information: This leaflet is only a brief information summary about your medicine. If you still have any questions, you should ask your doctor or pharmacist.

□ BRICANYL® TURBUHALER® Ⓟ

Astra

Terbutaline Sulfate

Bronchodilator

Information for the Patient: Important information you should know about Bricanyl Turbuhaler: Before using Bricanyl Turbuhaler, read this leaflet carefully. It contains general points about Bricanyl Turbuhaler and should add to more specific advice from your doctor or pharmacist.

Please keep this leaflet to refer to until you have used up all medication in Bricanyl Turbuhaler.

What is Bricanyl Turbuhaler used for and how does it work (see package insert for illustrations):

Bricanyl is a brand name for a drug called terbutaline. It is used to treat asthma, chronic bronchitis or other disorders which lead to breathing difficulties. Terbutaline belongs to the class of drugs referred to as bronchodilators.

Turbuhaler is the brand name for a multiple dose, dry-powder inhaler. When you breathe in through the inhaler, your indrawn breath provides the necessary force to deliver the drug to your lungs.

Bricanyl Turbuhaler is used to improve your breathing during times such as an asthma attack. It opens up airways in people with asthma or other breathing problems. It relieves symptoms such as wheezing, cough and shortness of breath.

What is in Bricanyl Turbuhaler? Bricanyl Turbuhaler contains terbutaline sulfate as the active ingredient and comes in a concentration of 0.5 mg per inhalation. If you happen to shake the inhaler, the sound you hear is the drying agent built into the blue turning grip. This is not the medication and cannot be inhaled. Bricanyl Turbuhaler contains no other ingredients.

What Should I Tell My Doctor Before Taking Bricanyl Turbuhaler? Tell your doctor:

- about **all** health problems you have now or have had in the past, especially heart problems such as irregular heartbeat and high blood pressure;
- about other medicines you take, including ones you can buy without a prescription;
- if you have ever had a bad, unusual or allergic reaction to terbutaline;
- if you are pregnant, plan to become pregnant or are breast-feeding.

How Do I Take Bricanyl Turbuhaler Properly? Use Bricanyl Turbuhaler for relief of an asthma attack or when you feel a tightening of the airways. You usually get an effect within a few minutes. The effect lasts up to 7 hours. Treatment with Bricanyl Turbuhaler is effective even if you have an acute asthmatic attack.

Note: You may not taste or feel any medication when inhaling from Bricanyl Turbuhaler. This is common.

If you follow the instructions below, you will receive the medication (see package insert for illustrations):

1. Unscrew the cover and lift it off.
2. Load a dose by holding the inhaler upright. Turn the blue grip as far as it will go in one direction and turn it back to the original position. The ''click'' you heard means that the inhaler is ready to use.
3. Breathe out. Note: Never breathe out through the mouthpiece.
4. Put the mouthpiece between your teeth and close your lips around the mouthpiece. Do **not** chew or bite down hard on the mouthpiece. Inhale forcefully and deeply through your mouth.
5. Remove the inhaler from your mouth and try to hold your breath for 10 seconds.
6. Always replace the cover properly after use.

If you accidentally drop, shake or breathe out into Bricanyl Turbuhaler after it is loaded, you will lose your dose. If this happens, you should load a new dose and inhale it.

Cleaning: Clean the outside of the mouthpiece once a week with a **dry** tissue. **Never** use water or any other fluid. If fluid enters the inhaler it may not work properly.

How do I know when Bricanyl Turbuhaler is empty (see package insert for illustrations)?

Bricanyl Turbuhaler has a dose indicator. When a red mark first appears in the little window underneath the mouthpiece, there are approximately **20** doses left. Now is the time to obtain your next inhaler.

When the red mark reaches the bottom of the window, Bricanyl Turbuhaler is **empty.** If you shake the inhaler when it is empty, you will still be able to hear the sound of the drying agent. Bricanyl Turbuhaler cannot be re-filled with drug and should be discarded.

How Much Bricanyl Turbuhaler Should I Take? The dosage of Bricanyl Turbuhaler is individual.

Follow your doctor's directions carefully. They may differ from the information in this leaflet.

The usual dose for adults and children 6 years of age and older is 1 inhalation as required. If symptoms persist, further inhalations may be required and you should immediately consult your doctor or the nearest hospital. More than 6 inhalations (3.0 mg) should not be required in a 24 hour period.

You should see a doctor if:

- your usual dose does not provide relief;
- the effects of one dose last less than 3 hours;
- you are using Bricanyl Turbuhaler every day to relieve symptoms.

These may be signs that your asthma is getting worse. Your doctor may prescribe this medication in association with other antiasthma medication that controls airway inflammation.

Do not exceed the dose prescribed by your doctor.

What Should I Do in Case of Overdose? Telephone your doctor or go to your nearest hospital right away if you think that you or anyone else may have taken too much Bricanyl Turbuhaler.

Are There Any Side Effects? Like any medication, Bricanyl Turbuhaler may cause side effects in some people. The most common side effects are nervousness and shakiness. These side effects disappear in most cases over the first few days of treatment. Headache, increased heart rate, flushing, occasional muscle cramps, sleeplessness, stomach upset, weakness, dizziness and sweating have also been reported.

Medicines affect different people in different ways. Just because side effects have occurred in some patients, does not mean that you will get them. If any side effects bother you, please contact your doctor.

Where Should I Keep Bricanyl Turbuhaler? Remember to **keep Bricanyl Turbuhaler out of the reach of children** when you are not using it.

Always replace the cover after using Bricanyl Turbuhaler. Store the inhaler at room temperature in a dry place, away from moisture.

Do not keep or use Bricanyl Turbuhaler after the expiry date indicated on the label.

Important Note: This leaflet alerts you to some of the times you should contact your doctor. Other situations which cannot be predicted may arise. Nothing about this leaflet should stop you from calling your doctor or pharmacist with any questions or concerns you have about using Bricanyl Turbuhaler.

□ BRONALIDE® ℞

Boehringer Ingelheim

Flunisolide

Corticosteroid Aerosol

Information for the Patient: How to use your Bronalide (flunisolide aerosol) inhaler.

Before using Bronalide, it is important that you read the following simple instructions and familiarize yourself with the inhaler and its metal cartridge.

As your doctor has probably told you, Bronalide must be used for a few days before it begins working, and then should be used **regularly** to help reduce the frequency and severity of your asthma attacks. **It is not a bronchodilator and will not provide relief during an actual asthmatic attack,** but it can cut down the number of bad attacks if used regularly every day.

Note: Your Bronalide Inhalant System comes to you pre-assembled. To clean the assembly, see step 10.

1. Shake the inhalant system before each inhalation.
2. Remove cap from mouthpiece.
3. Breathe out as completely as possible.
4. Hold the inhalant system upright and put plastic mouthpiece in your mouth as shown, being sure to close your lips tightly around the mouthpiece.
5. Breathe in deeply and steadily through your mouth. At the same time, firmly press down on the metal cartridge with your index finger.
6. Hold your breath as long as you can.
7. While holding your breath, stop pressing on the cartridge and remove mouthpiece from your mouth.
8. If your doctor has prescribed two or more inhalations at each use, wait a minute to allow pressure to build up again in the metal canister, then repeat steps 2 through 8. Be sure to shake the inhalant system again **before each** inhalation.
9. After the prescribed number of inhalations, rinse out your mouth thoroughly with water.
10. Clean the inhalant system every few days. To do so, remove the metal cartridge, then rinse the plastic inhaler and cap with briskly running warm water. Dry thoroughly.
    Replace the cartridge and cap.

Note: If your mouth becomes sore or develops a rash, be sure to mention this to your doctor, but do not stop using your inhalant system unless he tells you to.

Warning: The contents of the metal cartridge are under pressure. Do not puncture. Do not use or store near heat or open flame. Exposure to temperature above 49°C may cause cartridge to explode. Never throw cartridge into fire or incinerator. Use by children should always be supervised by an adult.

□ CALTINE® ℞

Ferring

Synthetic Calcitonin Salmon (Salcatonin)

Paget's Disease Therapy—Hypercalcemia Treatment

Information for the Patient: Your doctor has selected Caltine brand of salmon calcitonin for your therapy. Caltine is supplied in single dose glass ampuls which contain either 50 IU in 0.5 mL, or 100 IU in 1.0 mL. Each ampul contains enough medication for 1 dose. Caltine has no added preservatives.

Caltine should be stored in the refrigerator between 2 to 8°C. Please check the expiry date which appears as month and year after the word "EXP" e.g. "EXP 10/96".

Please read the instructions below before injecting this medication (see package insert for illustrations).

1. Preparing the dose

- Wash your hands.
- Gather the following items: Caltine ampul, 1.0 mL disposable syringe (with 25 gauge, 0.5 inch needle), an alcohol swab, and the ampul breaker which has been supplied in each Caltine carton.
- Remove ampul from the tray.
- Hold bottom of ampul firmly between left thumb and index finger (Figure 1).
- Shake or tap ampul to empty the liquid from the tip and neck.
- Put the ampul breaker over the top of the ampul and hold between right thumb and index finger.
- Snap the top off the ampul with the right hand by forcing it downwards (Figure 2).
- Each ampul is scored at the narrow part of the neck which will assist in snapping the top off the ampul.
- Discard the ampul tip and set ampul down carefully.
- Retain the ampul breaker for future use.
- Remove outer wrapping from one syringe (Figure 3).
- Remove the protective cap from the needle (Figure 4).
- Insert the needle into the solution in the ampul and pull back the plunger slowly to draw all of the solution into the syringe. It may be necessary to tip the glass ampul to permit enough of the solution to be drawn into the syringe (Figure 5).
- Hold the syringe upright. Tap the side of the syringe to move the air bubbles to the top of the solution. Push the plunger slowly until all the air has been pushed out of the syringe and a clear drop of solution appears at the end of the needle (Figure 6).
- Advance the plunger slowly to either the 0.5 mL or 1.0 mL mark on the syringe, as per your doctor's dosing instructions.
- Lay syringe down, making sure the needle does not touch anything.

2. Injecting the dose

- Choose an injection site (choose a different spot each day).

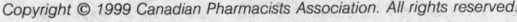

Caltine (cont'd)

- Cleanse the skin where the injection is to be made using the alcohol swab.
- With one hand stabilize the skin by spreading it or pinching up a large area of skin (Figure 7).
- Pick up the syringe with the other hand and hold it as you would a pencil. Insert needle straight into the skin. Be sure to insert the needle all the way. To inject the medication, push the plunger all the way down (Figure 8).
- Hold alcohol swab near the needle and pull the needle straight out of the skin. Press alcohol swab over the injection site for several seconds.
- Dispose of syringe and needle safely after use.

3. Precautions while using this medicine
- Your doctor should check your progress at regular visits to make sure that this medicine does not cause unwanted effects.
- If you are using this medicine for hypercalcemia, your doctor may want you to follow a low-calcium diet. If you have any questions about this, check with your doctor.

4. Side effects of this medicine
- Along with its needed effects, a medicine may cause some unwanted effects.
- Seek medical attention as soon as possible if any of the following side effects occur:

Rare:
- Trouble breathing, swelling of the tongue or throat
- Skin rash or hives
- Chills
- Dizziness
- Headache
- Pressure in chest
- Stuffy nose
- Tenderness or tingling of hands or feet
- Weakness

Other side effects may occur that usually do not require medical attention. These side effects may go away during treatment as your body adjusts to the medicine. However, check with your doctor if any of the following side effects continue or are bothersome:

More Common:
- Diarrhea
- Flushing or redness of face, ears, hands, or feet
- Loss of appetite
- Nausea or vomiting
- Pain, redness, soreness, or swelling at place of injection
- Stomach pain

Less Common:
- Increased frequency of urination.

□ CANESTEN® Topical

Bayer Consumer

Clotrimazole

Antifungal

Information for the Patient: For the treatment of athlete's foot, jock itch, ringworm and infections of the skin and mucous membranes.

1. **What is ''athlete's foot''?** ''Athlete's foot'' is an infection of the foot caused by a fungus. It usually starts between the 3rd, 4th and 5th toes and later can spread to the skin under the toes. There may be itching and burning of the infected areas, and liquid may ooze out. If the toes are spread apart, the skin is usually found to be white, swollen and torn. If the infection spreads beyond the spaces between the toes to the area under the toes and the bottom of the foot, blisters and broken skin are the most common symptoms.
2. **What is ''jock itch''?** ''Jock itch'' is an infection of the groin area caused by a fungus. It occurs more commonly in males. The first signs of the infection are scaling of the skin, irritation and itching in the groin area. The scaling or rash may affect the upper thighs and sometimes the scrotum. Red, raised lesions may also be found on the scrotum and may extend to the anus.
3. **What is ''ringworm''?** ''Ringworm'' is a fungal infection of the skin, which may or may not be accompanied by symptoms. If symptoms are present, they usually involve scaling of the skin, crusting and the formation of pink to red lesions with clear centres. The lesions may appear circular with a clear area in the middle. The infection may occur anywhere on the body.
4. **What is ''tinea versicolor''?** This is a common fungal infection in young adults. The most noticeable symptom is patches of skin which are different in color from the rest of the skin. These patches can be white, brown, or have no pigment. They are usually found on the chest, neck, abdomen, back and occasionally on the face. The skin in the affected areas may have scales, but these are not obvious unless the area is scratched. The condition is often noticed in the summer, because the white areas do not tan, but appear as white ''sun-spots'' of different sizes. Itching is uncommon and occurs only when the person is hot and sweating.
5. **What is ''candidiasis''?** ''Candidiasis'' is a yeast infection of the skin and mucous membranes. It often appears in the armpits, creases of the neck, the groin, between the toes or buttocks, and beneath large breasts. The usual symptoms are burning, itching, cracks and scaling of the skin with small, red lesions.
6. **How do I cure a fungal or yeast infection?** To cure an infection, it is necessary to kill the overgrowth of organisms that have caused the infection. Canesten Topical Cream or Topical Solution can cure most fungal or yeast infections such as athlete's foot, jock itch, ringworm, tinea versicolor and candidiasis. Even though the symptoms of your infection may be relieved in only a few days, you should use Canesten for the full treatment period. If your symptoms do not disappear or improve after 2 weeks of treatment (up to 4 weeks for athlete's foot), or if they get worse during treatment, discontinue treatment and contact your physician.
7. **How do I use Canesten Topical Cream or Topical Solution?** Thinly apply and gently massage sufficient Canesten Topical Solution or Topical Cream into the affected and surrounding skin areas twice daily, in the morning and evening. Do not cover the medication with a bandage unless advised to do so by your physician. For the treatment to be completely successful, Canesten Topical Solution and Topical Cream should be applied regularly and in sufficient quantities. If you miss a dose, do not apply twice as much medication at the next dosing. ''Athlete's foot'' should be treated for 4 weeks, while ''jock itch'', ''ringworm'', ''tinea versicolor'' and ''candidiasis'' usually require 2 weeks of treatment.
8. **How can I help prevent ''athlete's foot''?** Bathe your feet regularly with soap and water. Towel-dry your feet, paying special attention to the area between the toes. Let your feet air-dry for 5 to 10 minutes. Wear absorbent socks made of 100% cotton or wool and well-fitting shoes that allow air circulation. Change your socks and shoes frequently. Avoid walking in bare feet at health clubs, public pools and other wet areas.
9. **Important Warnings:** Do not use Canesten if you are pregnant, think you are, or are nursing, without first consulting your physician.

   If you experience a rash or new irritation while using Canesten, discontinue use and contact your physician.

   Canesten Topical Cream and Topical Solution are not suitable for treating fungal infections of the nail or scalp.

   Occlusive dressings should not be applied on top of Canesten Topical Cream or Topical Solution unless directed by a physician.

   Canesten Topical Cream and Topical Solution are for topical use only. If Canesten is accidentally swallowed, contact your local emergency room or Poison Control Centre immediately. Keep Canesten and all other medications out of the reach of children.

   Avoid contact with the eyes. If this happens, rinse thoroughly with water.

   Canesten should not be used by children less than 2 years of age.

   If you have any questions about Canesten or topical fungal infections, contact your physician or pharmacist.

Medicinal Ingredient: clotrimazole 1%.

Store at room temperature between 2 and 30°C.

□ CANESTEN® Vaginal

Bayer Consumer

Clotrimazole

Antifungal

Information for the Patient: For the treatment of vaginal yeast infections. Read this before using.

1. **What is a ''yeast infection''?** A ''yeast infection'' may occur any time there is an overgrowth of yeast organisms in the vagina. The

vagina normally has bacteria and yeast organisms present. Under some conditions, the number of yeast organisms rises, irritating the delicate tissues of the vagina and vaginal opening (the vulva). Conditions that make this more likely to occur are illness and the use of antibiotics (antibiotics do not affect the yeast organism). Changes in hormone levels may also increase the risk of a yeast infection. Changes that can occur during pregnancy, with the use of oral contraceptive pills, or just before a woman's period, may all increase the risk of a vaginal yeast infection. Some diseases, such as diabetes, can also make a person more susceptible. Even such things as hot humid weather, continuous use of panty liners, or tight, non-breathing clothing may increase a woman's chances of developing a yeast infection. These infections are not usually transmitted through sexual relations, even though a small percentage of male partners do have infections at the same time.

2. **How do I know if I have a "yeast infection?"** When a "yeast infection" occurs, the body responds with an increase in vaginal secretions. These secretions are generally thick and sticky, but odorless. These are often referred to as "cheesy" or "curd-like" because of their similarity to cottage cheese. These secretions are irritating to the tissues of the vagina and vulva, causing intense itching, redness, and swelling. Sometimes red spots or sores may develop, especially if the area has been scratched in response to the itching. Soreness in the vagina, discomfort when passing urine and pain during sexual relations is common.

   Yeast infections do not cause fever, chills, nausea, vomiting or diarrhea. If these symptoms are present, or if the vaginal discharge is foul-smelling, a more serious condition may be present and you should consult your physician immediately.

   Even if all of your symptoms point to a yeast infection, you should not attempt to treat yourself without consulting a physician if it is your first infection. If you have a second infection in less than 2 months, or experience frequent infections, contact your physician for evaluation and advice.

3. **How do I cure a "yeast infection"?** To cure a "yeast infection", it is necessary to kill the overgrowth of yeast organisms that cause the infection. Canesten can cure most vaginal yeast infections. Even though the symptoms of an infection may be relieved in only a few hours or days, you should use Canesten for a full 6 days, 3 days or 1 day depending on dosage form and strength chosen. This will decrease the chance of the infection returning. If your symptoms do not improve after 3 days or disappear within 7 days, or if they get worse, discontinue treatment and contact your physician.

4. **How do I use Canesten 1%, 2% and 10% vaginal creams?** Canesten 1%, 2% and 10% vaginal creams are used to treat vaginal yeast infections. Canesten 1% vaginal cream is inserted high into the vagina once a day (preferably at bedtime) for 6 consecutive days. Sufficient cream is provided for 6 intravaginal applications. Canesten 2% vaginal cream is inserted high into the vagina once a day (preferably at bedtime) for 3 consecutive days. Sufficient cream is provided for 3 intravaginal applications. Extra cream is supplied for use in relieving the external itching and burning sometimes associated with a vaginal yeast infection. Canesten 10% vaginal cream (prefilled applicator) is inserted high into the vagina once (preferably at bedtime). Canesten vaginal cream is only for use in the vagina and irritated vaginal area and should never be taken by mouth. The effectiveness of Canesten is not affected by menstruation. While you may have sexual relations during treatment with Canesten, most couples wait until treatment has finished. Canesten may reduce the effectiveness of some birth control methods, such as condoms, diaphragms, or vaginal spermicides. The effect is temporary and occurs only during treatment.

   Filling the Applicator: Canesten 1% and 2% vaginal creams: Remove the cap from the tube of Canesten and reverse it to puncture the safety seal over the end of the tube. To fill the applicator, screw the open end of the applicator on the end of the tube. Gently squeeze the tube. The plunger will rise as cream enters the applicator. When the plunger stops, the proper amount of Canesten has been pushed into the applicator and the applicator may be removed. Replace the cap and roll up the tube from the bottom so that the tube will be ready for the next use. Canesten 10% vaginal cream is in a ready-to-use prefilled applicator.

   Inserting the Medication: Canesten vaginal cream is inserted into the vagina in much the same way as a tampon. Stand, squat or lie on your back in a comfortable position. Insert the filled applicator into the vagina as far as it will comfortably go. Holding the barrel of the applicator steady, gently depress the plunger until it stops. This will release the medication high in the vagina where it will be most effective. Remove the applicator.

   Using the Cream Externally: A small amount of Canesten vaginal cream may be applied to the opening of the vagina to help provide extra relief of external symptoms. Squeeze a small amount of cream onto your finger and gently spread over the irritated vaginal area. Use the cream once or twice a day and only during the period when external symptoms are present, to a maximum of 7 days.

   Disposing of the Applicator: The Canesten vaginal applicator is recyclable where facilities exist.

   How do I use Canesten Combi-Pak 3-Day, 1-Day and 1-Day Cream Therapy? Canesten 200 mg and 500 mg vaginal inserts and 10% vaginal cream are used to treat the vaginal yeast infection while the Canesten 1% topical cream is used externally to relieve the itching associated with your vaginal yeast infection. The topical cream should be used only during the time when external symptoms are present and for no longer than 7 days.

   One Canesten 200 mg vaginal insert is placed high into the vagina once a day (preferably at bedtime) for 3 consecutive days. Canesten 500 mg vaginal insert is placed high into the vagina once (preferably at bedtime). Canesten 10% vaginal cream in a prefilled applicator is placed high in the vagina once (preferably at bedtime). Canesten vaginal inserts, vaginal cream and Canesten topical cream are only for use in the vagina and irritated vaginal area and should never be taken by mouth. The effectiveness of Canesten is not affected by menstruation. While you may have sexual relations during treatment with Canesten, most couples wait until treatment has finished. Canesten may reduce the effectiveness of some birth control methods, such as condoms, diaphragms or vaginal spermicides. This effect is temporary and occurs only during treatment.

   Using the Applicator: The applicator supplied with this package should be used to ensure proper placement of the vaginal insert high in the vagina, where it will provide the most benefit. To use the applicators supplied with the 3-day and 1-day therapies, first remove the Canesten vaginal insert from its protective foil wrapper. Next, pull the applicator's plunger outward until it stops. The vaginal insert is then placed into the end of the applicator and is ready for use. To use the applicators supplied with the 1-Day Cream Therapy, first remove the pre-filled applicator from its package. Insert the plunger into the barrel of the applicator. Detach red tip with twist motion.

   Inserting the Medication: Canesten vaginal inserts and 10% vaginal cream are placed into the vagina in much the same way as a tampon. Stand, squat or lie on your back in a comfortable position. Insert the loaded applicator into the vagina as far as it will comfortably go. Holding the barrel of the applicator steady, gently depress the plunger until it stops. This will release the medication high in the vagina where it will be most effective. Remove the applicator.

   Using the Cream: A small additional amount of Canesten cream may be applied to the opening of the vagina to help provide extra relief of external symptoms. Squeeze a small amount of cream onto your finger and gently spread over the irritated vaginal area. Use once or twice a day and only during the period when external symptoms are present, to a maximum of 7 days.

   The Canesten vaginal applicator is recyclable where facilities exist.

5. **Important Warnings:** If you are at increased risk for sexually transmitted diseases, have multiple sexual partners or change partners often, consult a doctor before starting each treatment.

   If this is your first yeast infection, it should be evaluated by your physician before you start any medication.

   Do not use Canesten if you have abdominal pain, fever or a foul-smelling vaginal discharge. If these symptoms are present, you could have a more serious condition and should consult your physician immediately.

   If there is no improvement in your symptoms in 3 days or if they have not disappeared within 7 days, you might not have a yeast infection. Consult your physician.

   If you have frequent vaginal infections, or if your yeast infection returns in less than 2 months, consult your physician prior to starting treatment.

   Do not use Canesten if you are pregnant, think you are, or are nursing, without first consulting your physician.

   If you experience a rash or new irritation while using the product, discontinue use and contact your physician.

   Canesten vaginal cream and inserts are for vaginal use only. Canesten topical cream is for external vaginal use only. If Canesten

Canesten Vaginal (cont'd)

is accidentally swallowed, contact your local emergency room or Poison Control Centre immediately. Keep Canesten and all other medications out of the reach of children.

Canesten topical cream should not be used for vaginal itching due to causes other than a yeast infection.

Canesten should not be used by girls less than 12 years of age unless advised by a physician.

If you have any questions about Canesten or vaginal infections, contact your pharmacist or physician.

Store at room temperature between 2 and 30°C.

☐ CARDURA-1™ Ⓟ
☐ CARDURA-2™ Ⓟ
☐ CARDURA-4™ Ⓟ

Astra

Doxazosin Mesylate

Antihypertensive Agent—Symptomatic Treatment of Benign Prostatic Hyperplasia (BPH)

Information for the Patient: Important information you should know about Cardura (doxazosin mesylate): Benign Prostatic Hyperplasia: Please read this leaflet before you start taking Cardura. Also read it each time you renew your prescription, in the event that something has changed. Remember that this leaflet does not replace careful discussions with your doctor.

Why Your Doctor has Prescribed Cardura: Your doctor has prescribed Cardura because you have a medical condition called benign prostatic hyperplasia or BPH. This condition occurs only in men. Cardura can also be used to treat high blood pressure (hypertension), but this leaflet describes Cardura only as a treatment for BPH.

What is BPH? BPH is an enlargement of the prostate gland. After age 50, most men develop enlarged prostates. The prostate is located below the bladder and surrounds the urethra which is a tube that drains urine from the bladder. The symptoms of BPH, however, can be caused by an increase in the tightness of muscles in the prostate. If the muscles inside the prostate tighten, they can squeeze the urethra and slow the flow of urine. This can lead to symptoms such as:

- weak or interrupted urinary stream
- sensation that you cannot completely empty your bladder
- sensation of delay or hesitation when you start to urinate
- need to urinate often, especially at night, or
- sensation that you must urinate immediately.

Treatment Options for BPH: There are 3 main treatment options for BPH:

1) **Monitoring Program or "Watchful Waiting":** If you have an enlarged prostate gland but suffer no symptoms or suffer from symptoms that are not bothersome, you and your doctor may decide to follow a monitoring program which includes regular check-ups instead of medication or surgery.
2) **Medication:** There are different kinds of medication used to treat BPH. Your doctor has prescribed Cardura for you. See "How does Cardura work?", below.
3) **Surgery:** Some patients may require surgery. Your doctor can prescribe several different surgical procedures for BPH. The procedure which is best for you depends on your symptoms and medical condition.

How Does Cardura Work? Cardura blocks smooth muscle receptors of the bladder neck and the prostate called alpha$_1$-adrenoceptors. This blockade causes the smooth muscles of the bladder neck and prostate to relax and decreases muscle tone. This can lead to a rapid improvement in urine flow and symptoms within a 1 to 2 week period. However, not all patients respond in the same way, and since each case of BPH is different, you should keep in mind the following:

- Prior to treatment with Cardura, you should have a thorough urological evaluation to determine the severity of your condition, and to exclude the need for immediate surgery or the possibility of carcinoma of the prostate.
- Even though taking Cardura has helped your condition, it is not known whether Cardura reduces the need for surgery.
- Cardura will not cure your benign prostatic hyperplasia (BPH). Cardura wil make your urine flow better and improve the symptoms of BPH. In some patients, bothersome adverse effects may occur as a result of the Cardura therapy.

What You Need to Know While Taking Cardura:

- You should see an effect on your symptoms in 1 to 2 weeks. While taking Cardura, you must have regular check-ups to evaluate your progress regarding your BPH and to monitor your blood pressure. Follow your doctor's advice about when to have these check-ups.
- Cardura can cause a sudden drop in blood pressure after the very first dose. You may feel dizzy, faint, or "light-headed", particularly after you get up from bed or from a chair. This is more likely to occur after you have taken the first few doses, but can occur at any time while you are taking the drug. It can also occur if you stop taking the drug and then restart treatment. If you feel very dizzy, faint or "light-headed" you should contact your doctor. Your doctor will discuss with you how often you need to visit and how often your blood pressure should be checked.
- You can take Cardura either in the morning or at bedtime and it will be equally effective. If you take Cardura at bedtime but need to get up from bed to go to the bathroom, get up slowly and cautiously until you are sure how the medication affects you. It is important to get up slowly from a chair or bed at any time until you learn how you react to Cardura. You should not drive or do any hazardous tasks until you are used to the effects of the medication. If you begin to feel dizzy, sit or lie down until you feel better.
- Other side effects you could have while taking Cardura include drowsiness, fatigue (tiredness), swelling of the feet and shortness of breath. Most side effects are mild. Discuss any unexpected effects you notice with your doctor.
- Extremely rarely, Cardura and similar medications have caused painful erection of the penis, sustained for hours and unrelieved by sexual intercourse or masturbation. This condition is serious, and if untreated it can be followed by permanent inability to have an erection. If you have a prolonged abnormal erection, call your doctor, or go to an emergency room as soon as possible.
- Your doctor has prescribed Cardura for symptomatic BPH and not for prostatic cancer. It is possible for men to have both BPH and prostate cancer at the same time. Doctors usually recommend that men be checked for prostate cancer once a year when they turn 50 (or 40 if a family member has had prostate cancer). These checks should continue while you are taking Cardura. Cardura is not a treatment for prostate cancer.
- About Prostate Specific Antigen (PSA). Your doctor may have done a blood test called PSA. Your doctor is aware that Cardura does not affect PSA levels. You may want to ask your doctor more about this if you have a PSA test done.

How to Take Cardura: Follow your doctor's instructions very carefully about how to take Cardura.

You will start with a 1 mg dose of Cardura once daily. Then the once daily dose will be increased as your body gets used to the effect of the medication. Follow your doctor's instructions about how to take Cardura. You must take it every day at the dose prescribed. Talk with your doctor if you don't take it for a few days for some reason; you may then need to restart the medication at a 1 mg dose, increase your dose gradually and again be cautious about possible dizziness. Do not share Cardura with anyone else; it was prescribed only for you.

Notify your doctor about any illness which may develop during your treatment with Cardura and about any new prescription or nonprescription medication you may take. If you require medical help for other reasons, inform the attending physician that you are taking Cardura.

This medicine is prescribed for your specific medical problem and for your own use. Use only as directed and do not give to other people.

Keep all medicines out of reach of children. For more information about Cardura and BPH, talk with your doctor or pharmacist.

Customer Inquiries: 1-800-668-6000.

☐ CASODEX® Ⓟ

Zeneca

Bicalutamide

Nonsteroidal Antiandrogen

Information for the Patient: The information in this leaflet applies only to your medicine, Casodex, please read it carefully. It gives you important information but it can't tell you everything. If you have any questions, or are not sure about anything, ask your doctor or pharmacist.

What Is Your Medicine?
- Casodex comes in tablets and each tablet contains 50 mg of bicalutamide.
- Each tablet contains a number of inactive ingredients which allow it to be made. These are lactose, sodium starch glycolate, polyvidone, magnesium stearate, methylhydroxypropylcellulose, polyethylene glycol 300 and titanium dioxide.
- Casodex comes in blister packs of 15 tablets, 30 tablets per package.
- Casodex belongs to a group of medicines called antiandrogens. This means that it interferes with some of the actions of androgens (male sex hormones) within the body.

Who Has Made Your Medicine? Your medicine is made by Zeneca Pharmaceuticals.

What Is Your Medicine For?
- Casodex is used to treat prostate cancer and is used together with other treatments such as drugs which reduce the levels of androgens in the body.

When Should Casodex Not Be Used?
- Before taking your medicine you should tell your doctor if you have previously taken Casodex and experienced an allergic reaction to it.
- Casodex must **not** be taken by women, including pregnant women or mothers who are breast-feeding their babies.
- Casodex must **not** be given to children.
- The tablets are only for you and must never be given to anyone else.

What Precautions Should Be Taken With Casodex? Before taking your medicine, tell your doctor if:
- You are suffering from any disorder or disease which affects your liver.
- You are taking any other medicines including those you have bought, in particular, if you are taking oral anticoagulants (to prevent blood clots).
- If you go to a hospital let the medical staff know you are taking Casodex.
- Your tablets contain lactose and titanium dioxide which may cause a problem in a small number of patients who are sensitive to them.
- Only stop taking your tablets if your doctor tells you.

Your tablets are unlikely to adversely affect your ability to drive a car or to operate machinery.

How Should I Take Casodex?
- Follow your doctor's instructions about when and how to take your tablets. Please **read the label** on the container. Ask your doctor or pharmacist if you are not sure.
- The usual adult dose is one tablet taken daily.
- Swallow the tablet whole with a drink of water.
- Try to take your tablet at the same time each day.
- You should take Casodex as prescribed. However, if you miss a dose do not take an extra dose, just resume your usual schedule.
- If you take more than your normal dose, contact your doctor or nearest hospital.
- Do not stop taking your tablets even if you are feeling well, unless your doctor tells you.

What Undesirable Events May Be Experienced With Casodex? As with all medicines, undesirable events are sometimes experienced. **Do not be alarmed by this list of possible events. You may not have any of them.** With Casodex these may include:
- Tender or enlarged breast tissue
- Hot flushes
- Nausea
- Vomiting
- Diarrhea
- Itching
- Dry skin
- Feeling weak
- Yellow skin and eyes (jaundice)

Occasionally Casodex may be associated with changes in your blood which may require your doctor to do certain blood tests.

Tell your doctor or pharmacist if you think you have any of these or any other problems with your tablets.

How Should I Store Casodex?
- Keep your tablets in the container they came in.
- If your doctor decides to stop your treatment, dispose of your tablets in an appropriate way.
- Do not take your tablets after the expiry date on the container. Dispose of them in an appropriate way.
- Keep your tablets in a safe place where children cannot see or reach them. Your tablets could harm them.

□ CAVERJECT™ ℞

Pharmacia & Upjohn

Alprostadil

Prostaglandin

Information for the Patient: Causes and Treatments of Impotence: There are several causes of impotence, a condition known medically as erectile dysfunction. These include: medications that you may be taking for other conditions, impaired blood circulation in the penis, nerve damage, emotional problems, excessive smoking or alcohol use, use of street drugs and hormonal imbalances. Often, impotence is due to more than 1 cause.

Treatments for impotence include: switching medications (if you are taking a medication that causes impotence), administration of hormones, penile injections, use of medical devices that produce an erection, surgical procedures to correct blood flow in the penis, penile implants, and psychological counselling. Your doctor has selected Caverject (alprostadil) for injection to treat your impotence. Your doctor can also discuss other available treatments. You should not stop taking any prescription medications, unless told to do so by your doctor.

About Caverject: Caverject is used to treat men who can not achieve and/or maintain an erection. Caverject Sterile Powder, which contains alprostadil (al-pros-ta-dil), is available by prescription only and should be used only as directed by your doctor. Your doctor may also use Caverject to help establish the cause of your impotency (or erectile dysfunction).

In response to visual or physical sexual stimulation, the nerves, arteries and veins in your penis act together to create an erection. The nerves cause the smooth muscle of the penis to relax and the blood vessels to expand. The blood becomes trapped in the penis and this allows your penis to become hard and erect.

When Caverject is injected into the blood-filled spaces on the penis (corpora cavernosa) it relaxes the smooth muscle of the penis. This allows more blood to flow into the penis and gives you an erection.

When to Use Caverject: You can use Caverject anytime before sexual intercourse. Caverject is injected into a specific area of the penis and should produce an erection in 5 to 20 minutes. Using the dose recommended by your doctor, you should have an erection lasting up to 1 hour. You may use Caverject for as long as your doctor decides is necessary. Do not use Caverject more than once a day, and not more than 3 times a week, with at least 24 hours between each use.

The Best Dose for You: Impotence can have a variety of causes that will be assessed by your doctor. The right dose of Caverject will depend on the nature of your impotence. Also, some people are more sensitive to the effects of Caverject than others. Your doctor must therefore find the best dose for you. To do this, your doctor will give you an initial injection, then slowly increase the dose for the next injections until the lowest dose for an effective erection is found. The maximum daily dose should not be greater than 60 μg.

Home Use of Caverject: After your doctor has assessed the correct dose, you will receive your first few injections in the doctor's office so you (or your partner) can receive training on how to inject yourself safely and hygienically. Once your doctor is assured that you (or your partner) are comfortable with the procedure (and can properly use sterile technique) home therapy can be started.

Caverject is supplied with everything you need, including complete instructions, plus diagrams, to help you.

During treatment, you may need your dose adjusted. **Never** increase or decrease the dose yourself without consulting your doctor. In fact, it is important to visit your doctor regularly, at least every 3 months during therapy, to ensure Caverject is working safely and effectively.

Who Should Not Use Caverject: Caverject should not be used if you have an allergy to any of its ingredients (lactose monohydrate, sodium citrate dihydrate, benzyl alcohol), or if you have a medical condition such as sickle cell anemia or trait, or certain cancers (e.g., multiple myeloma or leukemia) which might make you prone to painful and excessively long erections known as priapism.

Caverject should not be used by men who have been advised by their doctor to avoid sexual activity.

Do not use Caverject if you have a penile implant or a deformed penis (e.g., angulation, fibrosis, Peyronie's disease). Check with your doctor if you are not sure if you have or had any of these conditions.

Caverject is for use in **men** only, and should not be used in women or children. Caverject is only for use in treating impotence, do not use Caverject for other conditions.

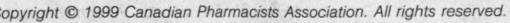

Caverject (cont'd)

Protect Yourself and Others: Always keep medications out of the reach of children. Do not save outdated medicine or medicine no longer needed. Do not use if solution is cloudy, colored or contains particles.

Caverject will **not** protect you from sexually transmitted diseases (including the human immunodeficiency virus, HIV). An injection of Caverject may cause a small amount of bleeding at the injection site. If you are infected with a blood-borne disease, even a little bleeding may increase the risk of passing blood-borne diseases to your partner(s). Take protective measures at all times.

What You Should Know Before Using Caverject: Substances like Caverject act on the blood vessels and may (when injected directly into the corpora cavernosa of the penis) lead to erections that last a long time and which may be painful and tender (priapism). An erection lasting longer than 3 hours is not a ''normal'' length of time for the penis to stay rigid. If this occurs, you have probably overdosed. Report this to your doctor immediately. Treat as a medical emergency.

If you are taking medication to prevent blood clotting, (such as warfarin or heparin) you may experience bruising at the injection site. To help prevent this, press down on the injection site with your thumb and hold for 5 minutes.

Discuss with your doctor the use of other medications (both prescription and nonprescription) while taking Caverject.

There is no apparent injectable treatment using multiple drug ingredients or ''cocktail'' for erectile dysfunction. In addition, there are no data on the efficacy and safety of these combinations.

What You Should Do if You Experience a Prolonged Erection: If you have an erection lasting longer than 2 hours, try to reduce the erection using methods suggested by your doctor. Do not wait, it is easier to reduce the erection if you treat it earlier rather than later. Erections that last more than 6 hours can cause serious and permanent damage.

If your penis is still hard after 3 hours see your doctor immediately or go to emergency. Write on a piece of paper the name of the drug, the dose and the time you took it and bring this with you to emergency.

Adverse Reactions from Using Caverject: The most common adverse effect is mild to moderate pain in the penis after injection or during an erection. About one-third of patients experience this effect. Other patients may experience a ''burning sensation'', ''discomfort'' or ''tension'' in the penis.

Occasionally you may have blood blisters (hematoma, ecchymosis) at the site of injection. These relate to improper injection technique rather than the effects of Caverject. If this occurs, ask your doctor to re-instruct you. Pressing down on the injection site will help avoid blood blisters.

Other local adverse effects include: fibrosis (formation of scar tissue in the penile tissues), irritation, sensitivity, penile rash and penile edema (fluid in the tissues).

Rarely occurring are: pain in the testicles or at the base of the penis, erythema (redness of the skin), penile lumps, tenderness, abnormal ejaculation, curved erections, balanitis (inflammation of the tip of the penis) and itching, swelling, inflammation or bleeding at the injection site, urethral bleeding and injuries resulting from poor injection technique.

Rare whole-body effects include: changes in blood pressure, irregular heartbeat, increased pulse rate, dizziness, headache, faintness.

Call your doctor if you notice any of the above or if you experience anything not listed here. Tell your doctor if you have a condition or are taking a medicine that interferes with blood clotting.

Guide to the Correct Use of Caverject: The information provided below only applies to the self-injection of Caverject. **Do not use these methods for taking any other medication.**

This guide does not replace the advice of your doctor. If you have any questions, please ask your doctor.

A case of Caverject has enough drug for 1 injection. The number of cases you need will depend on the length of your therapy.

Caverject Case Supplies (see package insert for illustrations): Each blue plastic case contains the following:

- **One vial of Caverject sterile powder in strengths of either 10 or 20 µg.** Ensure you have the correct strength Caverject vial for your dosage.
- **One prefilled syringe containing bacteriostatic water.** This is sterile water containing a preservative and is used to dissolve Caverject. This solution does not contain active drug. You will use this syringe after attaching the needle, to inject the drug into your penis.
- **A 27-gauge, 0.5-inch needle.** Keep the plastic cover on the needle until ready to inject.
- **Two alcohol swabs.** It is important to use the swabs to provide hygienic conditions and to prevent infection.

Storage and Handling:

1. You can store unused vials of Caverject Sterile Powder between 2 to 30°C. Do not freeze.
2. Do not use vials after the expiry date listed on the label.
3. Once dissolved, the Caverject solution must be used immediately. Do not freeze solution.
4. Use contents of each vial only once. Throw out unused solution. See ''Disposal of Used Materials'' at the end of this guide.

Important: Failure to comply with the following antiseptic measures may lead to infection.

5. To ensure sterile conditions, never contaminate the needle. The disposable needle and syringe require no sterilization steps if the package is intact.
6. **Do not** reuse needles or syringes. **Do not** give used needles or syringes to others.

Self-injection Method: Preparing the Medication:

1. Wash your hands thoroughly with soap and water.
2. Pull back on tabs of needle package to expose open end of needle. Do not let this end touch any surface.
3. Hold syringe tip upwards and remove rubber end cover. Continue to hold syringe upright in one hand. With free hand, pick up needle by covered end.
4. With needle cover still on, attach open end of needle to syringe tip by pushing down and twisting into place. Make sure the needle fits tightly.
5. Remove the plastic cap from the vial.
6. Wipe the rubber stopper of the vial, using one of the swabs provided. Discard the used swab (the second swab is needed later).
7. Handle the syringe by the barrel only. Remove needle cover carefully from the syringe. Do not allow needle to touch any surface.
8. Holding the syringe with needle pointing upward, push plunger to the 1-cc (mL) line marked on the syringe. (This will remove a slight amount of overfill in the syringe.)
9. Pierce needle through the centre portion of the vial's rubber cap. Push down plunger and inject entire contents of syringe (bacteriostatic water) into the vial.

   Carefully hold syringe and vial as a unit, and gently swirl the two (do not shake) until the powder dissolves completely. **Do not use** if the resulting solution is cloudy or colored, or if it contains particles.

Withdrawing the Medication:

1. To withdraw the medication, turn the vial (and syringe) upside down. Keep tip of needle below the level of the fluid. Then slowly withdraw syringe plunger until the amount of solution is level with the line recommended by your doctor.
2. If there are air bubbles in the syringe, tap syringe gently to remove them, or inject the solution back into the vial and slowly withdraw again.
3. Remove needle from bottle and carefully replace needle cover. **Do not** puncture the vial more than once, you could contaminate the solution.

Self-injecting the Medication (see package insert for illustrations): The medication must be injected into either of two areas of the corpora cavernosa (spongy tissue of penis). The corpora cavernosa run down both sides of the penis.

Follow these instructions carefully to ensure you inject the medication correctly:

1. Perform the self-injection while sitting in an upright reclining position and under good lighting.
2. Only use the injection areas described above. **Do not** inject the very top or underside of your penis. Change the injection site each time you use Caverject. (i.e., choose the right side for this injection, use the left side next time, and so on.) Within either area, the injection point should also be changed each time.
3. Grasp the head of your penis with your thumb and forefinger. Stretch your penis tautly and hold it firmly against your thigh so that it does not slip. In uncircumcised men, the foreskin must be pulled back to assure proper placement of the injection.
4. Clean the injection area thoroughly with a new alcohol swab. Put swab to one side; you will need to use it again.
5. Hold syringe between thumb and index finger. Do not put your thumb on the plunger. With syringe at a right angle (90°) to your penis, insert needle to penetrate the skin at the injection site. This is a

sensitive area, so expect a little discomfort. Avoid any area where veins are clearly visible.

Once the needle pierces the skin and resistance is felt, push needle firmly forward until a distinct ''give'' is felt and insert the needle all the way in with a steady, continuous motion.

6. Move your thumb or forefinger to the top of plunger and press down. Inject the entire contents of the syringe using a slow, steady motion.
7. Withdraw the needle from your penis and replace needle cover. Squeeze both sides of your penis immediately, and apply pressure with the alcohol swab to the injection site for about 3 minutes. If bleeding occurs, maintain pressure until the bleeding stops.

As long as you use your doctor's recommended dose, expect an erection to occur within 5 to 20 minutes after an injection.

A standard treatment goal is to produce an erection lasting up to an hour. If an erection is extremely painful (or persists after 3 hours) or if you have other adverse effects that concern you, consult your doctor immediately.

Disposal of Used Materials: Always safely dispose of the used syringe (needle), vial and swabs. To help you, the Caverject case is designed as a safe and convenient disposal unit that should be locked. (As another option, your pharmacist may supply a disposal box especially for syringes.)

1. Remove red plastic lock from its holder inside the case. Put this to the side.
2. Place used syringe, needle, vial and used swabs in the plastic case. Close firmly so the case snaps shut.
3. Remove centre part of Caverject label (perforated area) to show the keyhole.
4. To lock case, push the red lock through the hole in the case top. The case is now locked.

Note: Once locked, the Caverject container will be permanently closed.

You can now safely dispose of the case. Due to the contents, this is not a recyclable product, **do not** place in a recycle bin.

If you have any questions about the benefits and risks of using Caverject, ask your doctor.

□ CEFTIN® ℞

Glaxo Wellcome

Cefuroxime Axetil

Antibiotic

Information for the Patient: Patient Guidance Leaflet: What you should know about Ceftin tablets or Ceftin for Oral Suspension: Please read the leaflet carefully before you start to take your medicine.

This provides a summary of the information available on your medicine. For further information or advice, ask your doctor or pharmacist.

The Name of Your Medicine: The name of your medicine is Ceftin. It contains cefuroxime axetil. This medicine is similar to other medicines called cephalosporins, which are antibiotics.

How to Obtain Your Medicine: This medicine can only be obtained with a prescription from your doctor.

The Purpose of Your Medicine: Your doctor has prescribed Ceftin tablets or Ceftin suspension because you have an infection. Ceftin is used to kill the bacteria or 'germs' which cause infections. The infection can be cleared up if you take your medication in the proper way.

Important Points to Note Before Taking Your Medicine: You should not use Ceftin if you are allergic to cephalosporins. Tell your doctor also if you are allergic to or react badly to penicillins or other antibiotics.

If testing urine for sugar, false positive reactions may occur if using methods dependent on copper reduction such as Fehling's or Benedict's solution or with Clinitest tablets. For this reason enzyme-based tests such as Tes-Tape or Clinistix should be used.

The Use of This Medicine During Pregnancy and Breast-Feeding: Tell your doctor if you are pregnant or breast-feeding a baby. If you are pregnant or breast-feeding, your doctor may decide not to prescribe this medicine, although there may be circumstances when your doctor advises you differently.

How to Take Your Medicine: Tablets: You must take the medicine as prescribed by your doctor. If you are not sure how many tablets to take, or how often to take them, consult your doctor or pharmacist.

You should not increase or decrease the prescribed dose unless advised by your doctor.

The usual dose for adults is one 250 mg tablet twice a day.

Ceftin has a bitter taste, therefore, **do not chew or crush the tablets** but swallow each one whole with a drink of water.

Ceftin tablets are more effective if taken after food.

The usual length of treatment is 7 to 10 days, although your doctor may adjust the prescription to suit your treatment. During the course of treatment, all tablets must be taken to make sure that all germs have been killed. **Continue taking the tablets until they are finished, even if you begin to feel better.**

Suspension: The dose depends on the weight of the child. Your doctor or pharmacist will tell you exactly how many teaspoonful or 5 mL measures or how many sachets of the granules your child must take.

Bottles: Before removing the cap **you must shake the bottle** very well until the medicine can be heard moving in the bottle to make sure you get the right dose. Replace the cap securely after each opening. During treatment you should use a 5 mL spoon to take the medicine exactly as prescribed, taking care not to overfill the spoon. If desired, the dose may be added to one of the following cold beverages immediately prior to administration: milk (i.e. skim, 2% or homogenized), fruit juice (i.e. apple, orange or grape) or lemonade.

Sachets: Empty the granules into a glass and add at least 10 mL (2 teaspoons) of one of the following cold beverages: water, milk (i.e. skim, 2% or homogenized), juice (i.e. apple, orange, or grape) or lemonade. Stir well and drink it all immediately.

You should not increase or decrease the prescribed dose unless advised by your doctor.

Do not mix Ceftin for Oral Suspension with hot beverages before drinking.

Ceftin for Oral Suspension may be taken with or without food, although they are more effective if taken after food.

The usual length of treatment is 7 to 10 days, although your doctor may adjust the prescription to suit your treatment. During the course of treatment, all suspension must be taken to make sure that all germs have been killed. **Continue taking the suspension until it is finished, even if you begin to feel better.**

After Taking Your Medicine: If you experience wheeziness and tightness of chest, swelling of eyelids, face or lips, or develop skin lumps or hives, or a skin rash (red spots), tell your doctor immediately. Do not take any more medicine unless your doctor tells you to do so. He may decide to stop your treatment.

You may experience diarrhea, vomiting, or symptoms that you do not understand. There is no need to stop taking your tablets or suspension, but you should tell your doctor of any of these symptoms as soon as possible.

If you feel worse or you have taken all the tablets or all the suspension and do not feel better, **tell your doctor as soon as possible.**

What to Do if an Overdose is Taken: It is important to follow the dosage instructions on the label of your medicine. Taking more than this dose is unlikely to be dangerous unless a large quantity of tablets or suspension is taken all at once. In this case, contact your doctor or nearest hospital emergency department immediately.

Storing Your Medicine: Keep your tablets or suspension in a safe place where children cannot reach them.

The Tablets and Oral Suspension should be kept away from heat, which may spoil them. Store Ceftin Suspension preferably in a refrigerator.

What to Do if You Miss a Dose: If you forget to take a dose, take another as soon as possible. Then continue with the normal dose.

What to Do When You Stop Your Medicine: If your doctor decides to stop the treatment, do not keep any left over medicine unless your doctor tells you to. Please discard all unused Tablets or Oral Suspension.

What is In Your Medicine: Tablets: Ceftin Tablets are supplied in 2 strengths, containing 250 mg of cefuroxime (as cefuroxime axetil) or 500 mg of cefuroxime (as cefuroxime axetil). Your doctor will decide which strength you need.

Suspension: Each 5 mL of Ceftin for Oral Suspension contains 125 mg of cefuroxime (as cefuroxime axetil). Each sachet contains 250 mg of cefuroxime (as cefuroxime axetil).

Remember: This medicine is for you. Only a doctor can prescribe it for you. Never give it to someone else. It may harm them even if their symptoms are the same as yours.

Further Information: This leaflet does not contain the complete information about your medicine. If you have any questions you should ask your doctor or pharmacist.

Ceftin (cont'd)

You may need to read this leaflet again. Please do not throw it away until you have finished your medicine.

☐ CellCept®

Roche

Mycophenolate Mofetil

Immunosuppressant Agent

Information for the Patient: Your Doctor has prescribed a new drug CellCept. It is used after kidney transplantation to help prevent organ rejection.

Read this information carefully. It will help you learn about CellCept so you can make it work best for you.

This information leaflet is not as thorough as the official product monograph on CellCept (which your doctor or pharmacist has available), and is meant to supplement what your doctor or pharmacist has told you. Be sure to follow your doctor's instructions carefully. If you have any questions after reading this information leaflet, be sure to ask your doctor or pharmacist right away.

Important: Women must avoid pregnancy while taking CellCept as it may cause damage to the unborn baby.

What is CellCept? CellCept is the brand name for a drug called mycophenolate mofetil. It belongs to a family of drugs known as ''immunosuppressants''. These drugs work to ''suppress'' or reduce the body's immune response.

How Does CellCept Work? Your body's immune system works to protect you from infections and other foreign material. When you receive a transplant, your immune system recognizes the new organ as foreign, and will try to reject it. CellCept works to reduce this reaction, so that your body is more likely to accept the transplanted organ.

To work best for you, CellCept must be given with other drugs such as cyclosporine (Sandimmune) and corticosteroids (e.g., prednisone, prednisolone, methyl prednisolone, prenisolone acetate, methylprednisolone acetate) which also suppress your immune system. Together these drugs help prevent the rejection of your transplanted organ.

What Should I Tell My Doctor Before I Take CellCept? Before you take CellCept, be sure you have told your doctor:

- if you have had a bad, unusual or allergic reaction to CellCept (also known as mycophenolate mofetil) or mycophenolic acid;
- if you are pregnant, plan to become pregnant, or are breast-feeding a baby;
- about all other health conditions you have now, or have had in the past, especially problems with your stomach or bowel movements;
- about all other medicines or treatments you use, including any products you buy at a pharmacy, supermarket or health store.

How Should I Take CellCept To make It Work Best For Me?

- Your doctor has decided the dose you should take based on your medical condition and response to the drug. Do not take any more or any less of the drug than your doctor says.
- The initial dose of CellCept should be taken within 72 hours following transplantation. Always take the exact amount of CellCept your doctor tells you. If you are not sure of your dose, or when to take it, ask your doctor, pharmacist or nurse. A dose of 1 g taken twice a day (daily dose of 2 g) is recommended.
- Space your 2 doses of CellCept as evenly as you can throughout the day leaving about 12 hours between each dose.
- CellCept should be taken on an empty stomach.
- Try to take your doses at the same times each day. This will help keep a constant amount of drug in your body so it can continue to protect your transplanted organ. Taking your medicine at the same time each day will also help you remember each dose.
- Vomiting or diarrhea may prevent CellCept from being taken up into your body. **Always** call your doctor if you have either of these episodes.
- **Do not change the dose on your own, no matter how you are feeling.**

What Should I Do If I Miss A Dose of CellCept?

- It is important to take each of the doses your doctor prescribes to maximize the benefit from CellCept.
- If you have trouble remembering doses, or if you are uncertain about how to take them talk to your doctor, nurse or pharmacist and be sure to discuss any concerns you have about taking the drug as prescribed.
- Never allow your medication to run out between refills. **Plan to order your refills about one week ahead of time.** That way you will always have a supply in case the pharmacy is closed or out of the drug. Also be sure to take enough medication with you when you go on a holiday.
- If you ever do miss a dose of CellCept, do **not** catch up on your own; instead call your doctor or pharmacist right away for advice. It is also a good idea to ask your doctor ahead of time what to do about missed doses.

What Does CellCept Look Like? CellCept comes as a blue/brown hard gelatin **capsule** printed in black ink with CellCept 250 on the blue cap and ROCHE on the brown body. Each CellCept capsule contains 250 mg of mycophenolate mofetil. Ten capsules are contained in each blister pack.

CellCept also comes as a lavender-colored, caplet-shaped, film-coated tablet printed in black ink with ''CellCept 500'' on one side and ''ROCHE'' on the other. Each CellCept tablet contains 500 mg of mycophenolate mofetil. Ten tablets are contained in each blister pack.

How Do I Take CellCept? It is important to leave the capsules and tablets in the blister pack until you need a dose. When you are ready to take a dose, remove the number of capsules or tablets you need to make up the dose your doctor prescribed. Swallow the capsules or tablets whole.

Are There Any Special Do's and Don'ts About Taking CellCept?

- CellCept must be taken with other immunosuppressive medicines. Make sure you **do** know from your doctor, nurse or pharmacist if you are to stop, or to continue, the other immunosuppressant drugs you had been taking.
- **Do** tell all health professionals you see (doctor, dentist, nurses, pharmacists) that you are taking CellCept.
- **Do** not take any other drugs without asking your doctor or pharmacist first. This includes anything you can buy off the shelf such as over-the-counter medicines. Taking antacids at the same time as CellCept may affect the way CellCept works for you and therefore should not be taken simultaneously.
- Be sure to keep **all** appointments at your transplant clinic. During these visits, complete blood counts will need to be measured weekly in the first month, twice monthly for the second and third months of treatment, and then monthly for the remainder of the first year. Please note that your doctor sometimes may order additional blood tests.
- It is not known what effect CellCept has on the effectiveness of vaccinations and on the risk of getting an illness from vaccination with a live vaccine. **Do** discuss this with your doctor before you get any vaccinations or immunizations.
- **Do** tell your doctor immediately if you become pregnant while you are taking this drug. You will want to discuss the possible benefits and risks of continuing with this drug.
- **Do not stop taking CellCept on your own even if you have been taking it for several years.**

Special Note For Female Patients: CellCept may cause fetal abnormalities and malformations. For this reason it is recommended that you **do not** take CellCept if you are, or become pregnant. Before, during your treatment and for 6 weeks after stopping your treatment with CellCept, you must use 2 reliable methods of birth control. **Should you become pregnant during the time you are taking CellCept, you should inform your doctor at once.**

It is recommended that you **do not** breast-feed your baby if you are taking CellCept as it may pass into breast milk and may harm your baby.

Does CellCept Have Side Effects?

- Like all medicines, along with the beneficial effects of treatment, CellCept may cause side effects in people. In most patients CellCept has been well tolerated so the chances are that you will tolerate it well too.
- Because CellCept and the other medicines to be taken suppress your immune system, you are more likely to get infections. To help reduce complications from infections, tell your doctor about any cold or flu-like symptoms (such as fever or sore throat), any boils on your skin, or pain when you urinate (pass your water).
- The decreased function of your immune system may also increase your chances of developing cancer. Although cancers of the lymph glands and other types of cancer have occurred in people taking CellCept in combination with other immunosuppressive drugs, the chances of such cancers developing with CellCept are similar to the chances seen in patients taking other immunosuppressants.

- The following symptoms are some possible warning signs of cancer. To help detect any cancers as soon as possible, report any of these symptoms to your doctor right away:
  —A change in your bowel or bladder habits;
  —any sore that doesn't heal;
  —unusual bleeding or discharge;
  —the appearance of a lump or thickened areas in your breast or anywhere else on your body;
  —unexplained stomach upset or any trouble with swallowing;
  —an obvious change in a wart or a mole;
  —a nagging cough or hoarseness;
  —night sweats;
  —persistent and severe headaches.
- Other common symptoms which have been reported with CellCept, when used in combination with cyclosporine and corticosteroids, are listed here. Be sure to tell your doctor right away if you notice any of these symptoms, and especially if they continue, bother you in any way, or seem to increase in intensity: diarrhea, nausea, vomiting, constipation, heartburn; abdominal, chest or back pain; weakness; acne; involuntary trembling; fever; headache; increased cough, labored breathing; sleeplessness; dizziness; swelling of parts of your body; kidney problems, blood in the urine. Other symptoms that have been reported infrequently with CellCept include stomach pain and bloody or black tarry stools.
- Remember, only your doctor can tell if these symptoms might be from your treatment. If you think you are having side effects, talk to your doctor right away. Do not stop taking this drug on your own.

What Storage Conditions Are Necessary For CellCept?

- **Keep CellCept out of reach of children.** A child who accidentally takes the drug may be seriously harmed. A locked drawer or cupboard is best if you have small children in the house.
- CellCept capsules and tablets should be stored at room temperature. Remember to keep each capsule or tablet in its package until you need to take it.

If you have any further questions or concerns about your treatment with CellCept, please contact your doctor or pharmacist.

☐ CERUMENEX®

Purdue Frederick

Triethanolamine Polypeptide Oleate-condensate

Cerumenolytic

Information for the Patient: For removal of impacted ear wax. **Not** for routine wax removal or cleaning of the ear.

Directions: Fill ear canal with Cerumenex drops, insert cotton plug, allow to remain 15 to 20 minutes, then gently flush ear with warm water (avoid excessive pressure). **Do not leave Cerumenex drops in the ear for more than 20 minutes.** Avoid contacting skin areas around the ear; if contact occurs, wash with soap and water. If ear wax is not removed, consult your physician before re-using. If a skin reaction occurs, consult your physician.

Do not use if there is perforated eardrum, middle ear infection, atopic dermatitis or inflammation of the external ear, or a previous skin reaction to Cerumenex. **Use with extreme caution** in persons with a history of skin or other allergic reactions. If in doubt, consult your physician about use of a patch test. If you have or may have ear disease, consult your physician.

☐ CHOLOXIN® ℞

Knoll

Dextrothyroxine Sodium

Hypolipidemic Thyroactive Agent

Information for the Patient: In order to safely prescribe the best treatment, it is important for your doctor to know if you have any allergies, especially to dextrothyroxine or other thyroid medications; if you are on a special diet; if you are pregnant, may become pregnant or are breast-feeding; or if you are taking prescription or nonprescription medication. It is important for you to indicate to the doctor if you have any of the following medical problems: diabetes mellitus; heart or blood vessel disease; a past history of heart attack, heart failure or rheumatic heart disease; high blood pressure; kidney, liver or thyroid disease.

Before prescribing Choloxin, your doctor will probably try to control your elevated cholesterol level by a diet low in fats, sugars and/or cholesterol, and by exercise. If you are overweight, calorie restriction is also helpful.

It is important to take this medication exactly as directed without missing a dose. If you do, take the dose as soon as possible. If it is almost time for your next dose, skip the missed dose and go back to your regular schedule. Do not double dose.

While using this medicine, it is important that you see your doctor at regular intervals. Always inform your doctor or dentist of the medicines you are taking prior to any treatment.

Along with its described benefits, a medicine may cause unwanted side effects. If any of the following side effects occur, notify your doctor as soon as possible: chest pain; fast or irregular heartbeat or pulse; stomach pain (severe), nausea or vomiting; changes in menstrual periods; diarrhea; fever; hand tremor; headache; increased urination; irritability, nervousness or difficulty sleeping; leg cramps; shortness of breath; skin rash or itching; sweating; flushing or increased sensitivity to heat; weight loss or changes in appetite.

The above side effects are more likely to occur in the elderly (over 60 years of age) who are usually more sensitive to the effects of dextrothyroxine.

Keep all medicines out of the reach of children. Store away from heat, moisture and direct light.

☐ CLIMARA® ℞

Berlex Canada

Estradiol-17β

Estrogen

Information for the Patient: Uses of Estrogens: When a woman's menstrual periods cease (menopause) around the age of 50, the ovaries stop producing estrogens, the main female hormones. Sometimes the ovaries are removed by an operation causing "surgical menopause". Because estrogen deficiency is associated with a number of health risks, replacement of estrogens is recommended for the majority of menopausal women. In women with an intact uterus, estrogens are prescribed together with another female hormone called a progestin. This leaflet is designed to provide information about estrogen/progestin therapy.

When the amount of estrogen begins to decrease, some women develop very uncomfortable symptoms, such as feelings of warmth in the face, neck, and chest, or sudden intense episodes of heat and sweating ("hot flushes"). Hot flushes can cause frequent awakening at night, with sleep disturbance leading to fatigue, irritability and depression. The use of estrogen replacement can stop or greatly reduce the occurrence of menopausal flushes.

As a result of estrogen deficiency, changes occur in and around the vagina (causing itching, burning, dryness, painful intercourse) and urethra (causing difficulty or burning on urination and frequent voiding). These changes may be reversed by estrogen therapy.

Uses of Progestins: Progestins used in hormone replacement therapy have similar effects to the female sex hormone progesterone. During the child bearing years, progesterone is responsible for regulation of the menstrual cycle. The estradiol delivered by Climara not only relieves your menopausal symptoms, but, like estrogens produced by your body, may also stimulate growth of the inner lining of the uterus, the endometrium. In menopausal and postmenopausal women with an intact uterus, stimulation of growth of the endometrium may result in irregular bleeding. In some cases this may progress into a disorder of the uterus known as endometrial hyperplasia (overgrowth of the lining of the uterus). The development of estrogen-mediated disorders of the uterus can be reduced if a progestin is given regularly for a certain number of days with your estrogen replacement therapy. Each cycle of progestin administration should induce a periodic bleeding, whereby the inner lining of the uterus is regularly shed, thus protecting against endometrial hyperplasia

If your uterus has been surgically removed, endometrial hyperplasia cannot occur and cyclical administration of a progestin is not necessary.

When Estrogens Should Not Be Used: Since estrogens may stimulate the growth of certain cancers, you should not take estrogens if you have had cancer of the breast or endometrium (lining of the uterus). However, in certain situations, you and your doctor may decide that the benefits of the use of estrogen may outweigh the risks.

Climara (cont'd)

Dangers of Estrogens: Cancer of the Uterus: The risk of cancer of the lining of the uterus (endometrium) increases the longer estrogens are used without progestin and when larger doses of estrogens are taken. Therefore, it is important to take the lowest dose of estrogen that will control your symptoms. The addition of a progestin to estrogen replacement appears to eliminate totally the risk of developing estrogen-related uterine cancer. In a majority of women, the cyclic use of a progestin may lead to the occurrence of regular menstrual bleeding which is to be expected.

There is a higher risk of cancer of the lining of the uterus if you are overweight, diabetic, or have high blood pressure. If you have had your uterus removed (total hysterectomy), there is no danger of developing cancer of the uterus. Consequently, the addition of a progestin to estrogen replacement therapy is not required.

Cancer of the Breast: Some recent studies of the use of hormone replacement (estrogen with or without progestin) suggest an increased risk of breast cancer after long-term treatment. Other recent studies do not show this relationship. Adequate information is not available to assess differences among the various estrogens. The data presented in these epidemiological studies do not warrant a change in the current prescribing practice of hormone replacement therapy at this time, but the need for further investigation and ongoing surveillance must be emphasized.

Women with a family history of breast cancer, or with breast nodules, fibrocystic breast disease (lumps), or abnormal mammograms should consult with their doctor before starting hormone replacement therapy. The overall benefits and possible risks of hormone replacement therapy should be discussed with the physician. Regular breast examination by a health professional and monthly self-examination are recommended for all women.

Gallbladder Disease: Women who use estrogens after menopause are slightly more likely to develop gallbladder disease than women who do not use estrogens.

Restrictions on Use: Certain medical conditions may be aggravated by estrogens, therefore estrogens should either not be used at all or should be used with precaution under these conditions.

Estrogens Should Not Be Used During Pregnancy: Since pregnancy may be possible early in menopause while you are still having spontaneous periods, the use of nonhormonal birth control should be discussed with your doctor at this time. If you take estrogen during pregnancy, there is a small risk of your unborn child having birth defects.

Estrogens Should Not Be Used if you are Breast-feeding: You should not use Climara if you have had any unusual allergic reactions to estrogens or any other component of the patch.

Before using Climara, be sure to tell your doctor if you have any of the following medical problems. Climara should not be used under these conditions:

- cancer of the breast or uterus
- unexpected or unusual vaginal bleeding
- abnormal blood clotting
- migraine headaches
- stroke
- serious liver disease
- active phlebitis (inflamed varicose veins)

To help your doctor decide whether you should use Climara and what precautions should be taken during use, tell your doctor:

- what other prescription and nonprescription medicines, if any, you are taking. There are some medicines which interfere with the effects of estrogens.
- about any allergies or sensitivities to medicines or any other substances you may have.
- if you have ever had any of the following:
  —high blood pressure
  —heart, kidney, or liver disease
  —asthma
  —epilepsy or other neurological disorders
  —sugar diabetes
  —depression
  —abnormalities of the breast or uterus
  —endometriosis
  —breast disease, breast biopsies
  —uterine fibroids
  —phlebitis (inflamed varicose veins)
  —abnormal blood clotting

Monitoring Your Health While on Hormone Replacement Therapy: See your doctor regularly: While you are taking estrogen and progestin, it is important to visit your doctor at least once a year for a physical examination. Regular breast examinations by a health professional as well as by self-examination are recommended. A mammogram (breast X-ray) is suggested every year from the age of 50 onwards. If members of your family have had breast cancer or if you have ever had breast nodules or an abnormal mammogram, you may need to have more frequent breast examinations.

If you are taking estrogen without progestin, your doctor may take a sample of the lining of the uterus to make sure that it is normal. Any woman taking hormone replacement therapy who develops any irregular bleeding requires investigation.

Side Effects: The following side effects have been reported in women taking estrogens (these include estrogens used for birth control). Check with your doctor if these symptoms become troublesome:

- nausea
- retention of fluid
- migraine headaches
- localized darkening of the skin
- breast tenderness and excessive vaginal secretions (may be a sign that too much estrogen is taken)
- persistent upper abdominal pain, nausea, vomiting, tender abdomen (may be signs of gallbladder disease)
- easy bruising, excessive nose bleeds, excessive heavy periods (may be signs of abnormal blood clotting)
- lower abdominal pain or swelling, painful and/or heavy periods (may be signs of growth of fibroids in the uterus)
- yellowing of the eyes or skin (may be signs of jaundice)
- upper abdominal pain or swelling (may be signs of liver tumors)

Check with your doctor as soon as possible if any of the following occur:

- irregular vaginal bleeding
- intolerable breast tenderness
- breast enlargement
- pain and heaviness in the legs or chest
- shortness of breath
- severe headaches
- dizziness
- changes in vision
- persistent or severe skin irritation
- fluid retention or bloating persisting for more than 6 weeks

Check with your doctor immediately if you experience:

- narrowing of the throat
- shortness of breath
- tightness of the chest
- any other unusual symptom

In addition, Climara may produce some redness or irritation under or around the patch in some women.

How Climara Works: The Climara patch contains estradiol. When applied to the skin as directed below, Climara releases estradiol which passes through the skin into the bloodstream.

How and Where to Apply Climara? (see package insert for illustrations) Each Climara patch is individually sealed in a protective pouch. Tear open this pouch at the indentation (do not use scissors) and remove the patch.

A protective liner covers the adhesive side of the patch—the side that will be placed against your skin. This liner must be removed before applying the patch. Remove the protective liner and discard it. Try to avoid touching the adhesive.

Apply the adhesive side of the patch to a clean dry area of the skin on the trunk of your body or buttocks. **Do not apply Climara to your breasts.** Avoid the waistline, since tight clothing may rub and remove the patch. The sites of application must be rotated, with an interval of at least 1 week allowed between applications to a particular site. The area selected should not be oily, damaged, or irritated. Apply the patch immediately after opening the pouch and removing the protective liner. Press the patch firmly in place with the fingers for about 10 seconds, making sure there is good contact, especially around the edges.

Climara should be worn continuously for 1 week. You may wish to experiment with different locations when applying a new patch, to find ones that are most comfortable for you and where clothing will not rub on the patch.

When to Apply Climara: Climara should be changed once weekly.

When changing the patch, remove the used Climara patch and discard it. Throw it away, safely out of the reach of children or pets. Any adhesive that might remain on your skin can be easily rubbed off. Then place the new patch on a different skin site. (The same skin site should not be used again for at least 1 week after removal of the patch.)

Contact with water when you are bathing, swimming, or showering will not affect the patch. In the unlikely event that a patch should fall off, a new patch should be applied for the remainder of the 7-day dosing interval.

How Climara is Supplied: There are 2 strengths of the Climara patch. Your doctor has chosen the appropriate strength of the Climara patch for you. Each box contains 4 patches.

Do not store out of the pouch or above 30°C. Apply immediately upon removal from the protective pouch. Climara should be kept out of the reach of children and pets before and after use.

Helpful Hints: What to do if the Patch Falls Off: Should a patch fall off in a very hot bath or shower, shake the water off the patch. Dry your skin completely and reapply the patch (to a new area of skin) and continue your regular schedule. If it still does not stick, then apply a **new** patch and continue with your regular schedule.

If hot baths, saunas or whirlpools are something you enjoy and you find that the patch is falling off, you may consider removing the patch **temporarily** while you are in the water. If you do remove the patch temporarily, the adhesive side of the patch should be placed on the protective liner that was removed when originally applying the patch. Wax paper may be used as an alternative to the liner. This prevents the contents of the patch from emptying by evaporation while you are not wearing it.

In addition to exposure to very hot water, there are some other causes for the patch failing to stick. If you are having patches fall off regularly, this could be happening as a result of:

- using any type of bath oil
- using soaps with a high cream content
- using skin moisturizers before applying the patch

Patch adhesion may be improved if you avoid using these products, and by cleansing the site of application with rubbing alcohol before you apply the patch.

What to do if Your Skin Becomes Red or Irritated Under or Around the Patch? As with any product that covers the skin for a period of time (such as bandages), the Climara patch can produce some skin irritation in some women. This varies according to the sensitivity of each woman.

Usually this redness does not pose any health concern to you, but to reduce this problem, there are some things that you may do:

- choose the buttocks as the site of application
- change the site of application of the Climara patch every time a new patch is applied, usually once weekly.

If redness and/or itching continues, you should consult your doctor.

Always Remember: Your doctor has prescribed Climara for you after a careful review of your medical needs. Use it only as directed and do not give it to anyone else. Your doctor should re-examine you at least once a year.

If you have any questions, contact your doctor or pharmacist.

☐ CLOPIXOL® Ⓟ
☐ CLOPIXOL-ACUPHASE® Ⓟ
☐ CLOPIXOL® DEPOT Ⓟ

Lundbeck

Zuclopenthixol Dihydrochloride
Zuclopenthixol Acetate
Zuclopenthixol Decanoate

Antipsychotic

Information for the Patient: Please read this information leaflet carefully before you start your medicine, even if you have taken this drug before. Keep this leaflet handy in order to consult while taking your medication. For further information or advice, please contact your doctor or pharmacist.

What is Clopixol?

- Clopixol is a prescription medicine that belongs to a family of medicines used to treat schizophrenia.
- You may be given Clopixol in the form of tablets **or** by injection. Depending on the circumstances, your doctor will decide which form of Clopixol is right for you.
- Clopixol tablets need to be taken **every day** to be effective.
- If you receive Clopixol by injection, it will be administered by a doctor or nurse. There are actually 2 forms of Clopixol injection, one which is effective when administered every 2 to 3 days, and another which is effective when administered as infrequently as once every 2 to 4 weeks.

What Do I Need To Do Before Taking Clopixol?

Tell Your Doctor:

- About all your past and present medical conditions.
- If you have used Clopixol or any other treatment for schizophrenia before and if you had any problems.
- If you are taking any other prescription or nonprescription medicines.
- If you are pregnant or thinking of becoming pregnant, or if you are breast-feeding.
- If you regularly drink a lot of alcohol.
- If you have any liver problems, Parkinson's disease or have ever had seizures.
- If you have ever had any blood disorders.
- If you are allergic to any of the ingredients in Clopixol (see list of ingredients at the end of this leaflet).

How Do I Take Clopixol Properly?

Tablets:

- It is very important that you take Clopixol exactly as your doctor instructs you.
- Never increase or decrease the amount of Clopixol you are taking unless your doctor tells you to.
- If you miss a dose, take it as soon as you remember, as long as it is more than 6 hours before the next dose is due. If it is less than 6 hours before the next dose is due, just take your next regularly scheduled dose and try not to miss any more. Do not try to make up for a missed dose by doubling up on the next dose.
- Clopixol may be taken with or without food.

Injection:

- If you are prescribed Clopixol by injection it will be given by a doctor or nurse. It is very important to keep your scheduled appointments for the injections.
- If you miss an appointment, contact your doctor as soon as possible in order to schedule a new appointment.
- Consult your doctor before taking other medications, including over-the-counter medicines. Some drugs can produce additional side effects when they are used in combination with Clopixol.

What If I Have Problems While Taking Clopixol?

- At the beginning of treatment, Clopixol may make you feel drowsy or sleepy so you should not drive a car or operate machinery until you are sure Clopixol does not affect your mental alertness.
- Side effects that have been reported by patients taking Clopixol include: Muscle spasm, stiffness, shaking or uncontrolled body movements. These can happen in different parts of the body, such as the tongue, face, mouth, jaw, eyes, hands, arms and legs. Contact your doctor if this happens to you.

  Other possible side effects include dry mouth, dizziness, blurred or altered vision, constipation, excessive salivation or sweating, trouble passing urine. Decreases in blood pressure, increases in heart rate, weight changes, skin rash, decreased sexual interest or function, and changes in your monthly cycle (if you are female).

  Tell your doctor or pharmacist if you think you have any of these or other effects while taking Clopixol.
- Any fever (increased temperature) or soreness of the mouth, gums, or throat that happens while you are taking Clopixol should be reported to your doctor **immediately**.

What If I Take Too Much Clopixol?

- Contact your doctor or nearest hospital emergency department as soon as you realize you have taken too much Clopixol, even if you do not feel sick.

Where Should I Store Clopixol?

- Clopixol tablets should be kept in a safe place between 15 and 25°C.
- Keep Clopixol out of the reach of children.
- Safely discard any Clopixol that has passed the expiry date on the label.

Who Do I Ask If I Have Any Questions About Clopixol?

- Consult your doctor or pharmacist.

Clopixol (cont'd)

What Does Clopixol Contain?

- Each Clopixol tablet contains zuclopenthixol (zoo-clo-pen-thick-sol) dihydrochloride as the active medicinal ingredient, in three different strengths: 10 mg (light red-brown), 25 mg (red-brown) or 40 mg (dark red-brown). Nonmedicinal ingredients include castor oil, ferric oxide, glycerol, hydroxypropyl methylcellulose, lactose, Macrogol 6 000, magnesium stearate, microcrystalline cellulose, polyvidone acetate, potato starch, talc and titanium dioxide.
- Clopixol-Acuphase injection contains zuclopenthixol acetate as the active ingredient in fractionated coconut oil.
- Clopixol Depot injection contains zuclopenthixol decanoate as the active ingredient in fractionated coconut oil.

Who Supplies Clopixol?

- Clopixol is supplied by:
  Lundbeck Canada Inc.
  413 St-Jacques St. W.
  Suite FB-230
  Montreal, Quebec
  H2Y 1N9
- **Reminder: Clopixol has been prescribed only for you. Do not give it to anybody else.**

□ CLOZARIL® Ⓟ

Novartis

Clozapine

Antipsychotic Agent

Information for the Patient: What is Clozaril and what is it used for? Clozaril is a drug for the treatment of symptoms of schizophrenia in patients who do not respond to, or who experience serious side effects with other drugs used for the same purpose.

Clozaril can only be taken if prescribed by a doctor.

What should be borne in mind about Clozaril? Why is the testing of your blood by your doctor necessary? In rare instances (approximately 0.7% of cases), Clozaril can cause a suppression of white blood cells, necessary to help the body fight infection. Because this condition is potentially life-threatening, it is important to have regular blood testing done. To ensure that the required blood tests are performed, Clozaril is only available through a special program.

Blood testing must be done weekly during the first 26 weeks of treatment with Clozaril, because the risk for developing a deficiency of white blood cells is highest during this initial period. Thereafter, your doctor will evaluate with you the possibility of limiting blood checks to 2-week intervals, depending on your health condition. Regular blood testing must be done for as long as you are taking Clozaril.

In addition, you should consult your doctor immediately at the first signs of a cold, influenza, fever, sore throat, or any other signs of infection, as well as weakness or a general feeling of unwellness. The doctor may check your blood cell count and take further measures if necessary.

When should Clozaril not be used? You should not take Clozaril if you already have too few white blood cells, or if you have ever had a disease affecting blood cell formation. Clozaril should not be taken with other drugs known to affect blood cell formation. The same restrictions apply if you are suffering from severe liver, kidney, or heart disease, or uncontrolled epilepsy, or have ever had a bad, unusual or allergic reaction to Clozaril, or any of its components.

When taking Clozaril, what particular precautions are recommended? It is essential to inform your doctor if you suffer from enlargement of the prostate, history of seizures, glaucoma, allergy, or any other serious medical condition.

Due to the risk of convulsions during Clozaril treatment, you should avoid activities where a sudden loss of consciousness could cause risk to yourself or others (e.g., driving, using machines, swimming, climbing).

Clozaril may intensify the effects of alcohol, sleeping pills, tranquilizers and anti-allergy drugs. You should inform your doctor before taking any other medications (including the ones you may buy without a doctor's prescription).

Clozaril may lower your blood pressure, especially at the start of treatment. This may result in light-headedness or fainting.

Should Clozaril be taken during pregnancy or breast-feeding? Clozaril should only be taken during pregnancy if your doctor specifically prescribes it. Therefore, you should consult your doctor if you are or intend to become pregnant.

As Clozaril can pass into breast milk, mothers receiving Clozaril should not breast-feed.

How should Clozaril be taken? The dosage in each individual case is decided by the doctor according to the severity of the disease.

For the treatment to be successful, you must follow exactly your doctor's dosage instructions, and under no circumstances should you take more or less than the prescribed dose. If you think the dosage is too weak or too strong, you should discuss this matter with your doctor.

If you miss a dose of Clozaril, and remember within 2 hours, take the dose right away. Otherwise, skip the missed dose and continue with your regular dosing schedule. Do not take double doses. If you have stopped taking Clozaril for more than 2 days, do not restart taking the drug, but contact your doctor for dosing instructions.

What are the possible side effects of Clozaril? The most serious side effects of Clozaril are a possible fall in the white blood cell count, leading to an increased risk of infection, convulsions, fall in blood pressure, and fever.

The most frequent side effects are drowsiness, dizziness, increased or decreased production of saliva and rapid heartbeat.

Other side effects include: constipation, headache, tremor, fainting, sweating, weight gain, problems in passing or retaining urine, and abnormal movement behavior. In rare cases, Clozaril may cause confusion, restlessness, difficulties in swallowing or impairment of heart function. These side effects are not generally persistent.

What else should be borne in mind? Like all medicines, Clozaril should be kept out of the reach of children.

Further information can be obtained from your doctor or pharmacist.

What does Clozaril contain? The active ingredient of Clozaril is clozapine.

□ CODEINE CONTIN® Ⓝ

Purdue Frederick

Codeine Monohydrate—Codeine Sulfate Trihydrate

Opioid Analgesic

Information for the Patient: What is codeine? Codeine relieves pain and should help you live more comfortably and independently. It is effective and safe when used as directed by your doctor.

Your pain may increase or decrease from time to time and your doctor may need to change the amount of codeine you take daily (daily dosage).

Codeine Contin is a tablet that is made in such a way as to slowly release codeine over a 12-hour period, usually requiring a dose only every 12 hours to control your pain.

Codeine Contin tablets are available in 4 strengths: 50 mg (blue), 100 mg (yellow), 150 mg (red) and 200 mg (orange). It may be necessary for you to take more than one tablet strength (different colored tablets) at the same time in order to receive the total daily dosage prescribed by your doctor.

How to take your medication: Codeine Contin tablets must be taken regularly every 12 hours (with 4 to 6 oz. of water) to prevent pain all day and night. If your pain worsens, making you uncomfortable, contact your doctor immediately and she/he may decide that it is necessary to adjust your daily dosage of Codeine Contin.

Your starting dosage of Codeine Contin will be clearly labeled on the medication bottle. Be sure to follow these directions on the label exactly; this is very important. If your dosage is changed, be sure to write it down at the time your doctor calls you or sees you, and follow the new directions exactly.

Codeine Contin 50, 100, 150 and 200 mg tablets may be halved if directed by your doctor but should not be chewed or crushed.

Constipation: Codeine causes constipation. This is to be expected so your doctor may order a laxative and stool softener to help relieve your constipation while you are taking Codeine Contin. Tell your doctor about the problem if it arises.

Taking Other Medications: Your doctor should be made aware of any other medication you are taking including over-the-counter antihistamines or sleep-aids as they could affect the way you respond to codeine.

Driving: Driving or other tasks requiring full alertness should not be attempted for the first few days of taking Codeine Contin, since you may experience drowsiness or sedation.

Reordering Codeine Contin: A new written prescription is required from your doctor each time you need more Codeine Contin. Therefore, it is important that you contact your doctor at least 3 working days before your current supply runs out. It is very important that you do not miss any doses.

Should your pain increase, or any other complaint develop as a result of taking Codeine Contin, contact your doctor immediately.

□ COLESTID® ℞

Pharmacia & Upjohn

Colestipol HCl

Oral Antihypercholesterolemic

Information for the Patient: Colestid Granules and Colestid Orange Granules: The information in this insert is to be used for persons taking Colestid Granules or Colestid Orange Granules. The name Colestid refers to both these products.

What is Colestid used for? Colestid is the brand name for the drug colestipol hydrochloride.

Colestid helps to reduce the amount of cholesterol in the blood. Cholesterol is a fatty substance which is made and used by your body. Sometimes the cholesterol level in the blood becomes higher than it should. Over time, this can cause the arteries of the heart and other organs to thicken. When this happens, blood cannot reach these organs and they may become damaged.

How does Colestid work? Colestid works by preventing bile acids from being taken up in the blood.

Bile acids are formed when your body breaks down cholesterol. Colestid acts by trapping bile acids in the bowels. Bile acids trapped by Colestid pass out of your body instead of going into the blood. When there are less bile acids, your body is forced to break down more cholesterol, which will lower the cholesterol level in your blood.

What should I do before taking Colestid?

- Do not use Colestid Granules, if you have taken Colestid Orange Granules or Colestid Tablets before and had any allergic reactions.
- Do not use Colestid Orange Granules, if you have taken Colestid Granules or Colestid Tablets before and had any allergic reactions.
- Tell your doctor about any health problems you have now or have had in the past. Some conditions can affect your cholesterol level and should be treated before you take Colestid.
- Tell your doctor if you are pregnant, if you become pregnant or if you are breast-feeding your baby. Your doctor will tell you if he or she wants you to stop taking Colestid.
- Tell your doctor about all the medicine you are taking, even medicine you buy without a prescription.

Take other medication at least 1 hour before you take Colestid or wait 4 hours after you take Colestid before taking other medication.

When do I take Colestid? Take Colestid before, during, or after a meal. If you take Colestid more than once a day, take one dose at breakfast or lunch, and a second dose in the evening. For best results, your morning dose should be slightly smaller than your evening dose. Your doctor will advise you on how many packets or scoops of Colestid you should take.

If you are taking Colestid more than once a day, **do not miss the evening dose.** It is the most important dose to remember.

If you miss a dose of this medicine, take it as soon as possible. For the rest of the day continue on your regular schedule. But, if you miss a dose and it is almost time for the next dose, do not take the 2 doses together. Take only the dose you should be taking at this time.

Do not take a double dose of Colestid to make up for missed doses.

Your doctor will put you on a special diet to help lower your cholesterol. Follow the diet while you are taking Colestid. Taking Colestid **does not replace** the need to be on a special diet. It is important for your treatment that you do both.

How do I take Colestid? Never take this medicine in its dry form, as it can cause you to choke.

Always mix Colestid with liquids or foods.

- For liquids you may choose: water, milk, flavored drink, juice, pop or soda, or any other liquid of your choice.
- For foods you may choose: cereals (hot or cold), soups (avoid chunky soups), yogurt, pudding, cottage cheese or pulpy fruits (crushed pineapple, pears, peaches or fruit cocktail).

Step 1. Add the amount of your dose (packets or scoops) of Colestid to at least 100 mL (3 to 4 oz) of liquid or food. Note: a heavy or pulpy juice may reduce the "gritty" feel of the medicine.
Step 2. Stir the medicine until it is evenly mixed. In liquids, the medicine will not completely dissolve; you will still be able to see the granules.
Step 3. Drink or eat all of the mixture. When you are finished, rinse the glass or bowl with a small amount of liquid to make sure you take all the medicine.

What may I experience with Colestid? Since Colestid is not absorbed, it rarely causes any serious problems. At the start some people have constipation. In some cases this can be severe. Severe constipation may cause blood to appear in the feces. Stomach pain, nausea, gas, heartburn, ulcers, bloating or diarrhea may also occur. Call your doctor, if these effects continue or worsen. If you feel any other unusual effects not listed here, see your doctor.

What ingredients are in Colestid?

- Colestid Granules contain the active drug colestipol hydrochloride and a nonmedicinal ingredient silicon dioxide.
- Colestid Orange Granules contain the active drug colestipol hydrochloride. Nonmedicinal ingredients include mannitol, methylcellulose, citric acid, aspartame, maltol, beta carotene, glycerin, artificial and natural flavor. Also contains phenylalanine.

How do I store Colestid? Keep this medicine away from children. Store Colestid away from heat, direct sunlight and humid places like your bathroom. Colestid is best kept at room temperature in a dry place.

Talk to your doctor or pharmacist if you have more questions or need more information.

Colestid Tablets: What are Colestid Tablets used for? Colestid is the brand name for the drug colestipol hydrochloride.

Colestid Tablets help to reduce the amount of cholesterol in the blood. Cholesterol is a fatty substance which is made and used by your body. Sometimes the cholesterol level in the blood becomes higher than it should. Over time, this can cause the arteries of the heart and other organs to thicken. When this happens, blood cannot reach these organs and they may become damaged.

How do Colestid Tablets work? Colestid Tablets work by preventing bile acids from being taken up in the blood.

Bile acids are formed when your body breaks down cholesterol. The medicine in Colestid Tablets acts by trapping bile acids in the bowels. Bile acids trapped by Colestid Tablets pass out of your body instead of going into the blood. When there are less bile acids, your body is forced to break down more cholesterol, which will lower the cholesterol level in your blood.

What should I do before taking Colestid Tablets?

- Do not use Colestid Tablets if you have taken Colestid Granules or Colestid Orange Granules before and had any allergic reactions.
- Tell your doctor about any health problems you have now or have had in the past. Some conditions can affect your cholesterol level and should be treated before you take Colestid Tablets.
- Tell your doctor if you are pregnant, if you become pregnant or if you are breast-feeding your baby. Your doctor will tell you if he or she wants you to stop taking Colestid Tablets.
- Tell your doctor about all the medicine you are taking, even medicine you buy without a prescription.

Take other medication at least 1 hour before you take Colestid Tablets or wait 4 hours after you take Colestid Tablets before taking other medication.

When do I take Colestid Tablets? Take Colestid Tablets with your meals. If you take Colestid Tablets more than once a day, take one dose at breakfast or lunch, and a second dose in the evening. For best results, your morning dose should be slightly smaller than your evening dose. Your doctor will advise you on how many Colestid Tablets you should take.

If you are taking Colestid Tablets more than once a day, **do not miss the evening dose.** It is the most important dose to remember.

If you miss a dose of this medicine, take it as soon as possible. For the rest of the day continue on your regular schedule. But, if you miss a dose and it is almost time for the next dose, do not take the 2 doses together. Take only the dose you should be taking at this time.

Do not take a double dose of Colestid Tablets to make up for missed doses.

Your doctor will put you on a special diet to help lower your cholesterol. Follow the diet while you are taking Colestid Tablets. Taking

Colestid (cont'd)

Colestid Tablets **does not replace** the need to be on a special diet. It is important for your treatment that you do both.

How do I take Colestid Tablets? Do not cut, chew or crush the tablets. Swallow Colestid Tablets whole. Take them with a full glass of liquid. You may choose water, milk, flavored drink, juice, pop or soda, or any other liquid of your choice.

What may I experience with Colestid Tablets? Since the active drug in Colestid Tablets is not absorbed, it rarely causes any serious problems. At the start some people have constipation. In some cases this can be severe. Severe constipation may cause blood to appear in the feces. Stomach pain, nausea, gas, heartburn, ulcers, bloating or diarrhea may also occur. Call your doctor, if these effects continue or worsen. If you feel any other unusual effects not listed here, see your doctor.

What ingredients are in Colestid Tablets? Colestid Tablets contain the active drug colestipol hydrochloride. Nonmedicinal ingredients include povidone, colloidal silicon dioxide, magnesium stearate, cellulose acetate phthalate, triacetin, methyl-hydroxy-propyl-cellulose and carnauba wax.

How do I store Colestid Tablets? Keep this medicine away from children. Store Colestid Tablets away from heat, direct sunlight and humid places like your bathroom. Colestid Tablets are best kept at room temperature in a dry place.

Talk to your doctor or pharmacist if you have more questions or need more information.

□ COMBANTRIN®

Pfizer Consumer

Pyrantel Pamoate

Anthelmintic

Information for the Patient: Combantrin (pyrantel pamoate): For pinworms and roundworms: Warning: Combantrin pyrantel pamoate should not be used in pregnant women or in children under the age of one year.

How Worm Infection Occurs: Pinworm infection usually starts when children swallow worm eggs that have been picked up from sources such as shared play items, school toilet seats, and family pets. The egg then follows a cycle through the body that results in the mature worm working its way out through the anus during the night to deposit worm eggs on the skin, resulting in uncomfortable itching and scratching. And when scratching occurs, the eggs are immediately transferred by the child's hands to his mouth, starting the entire cycle off again. . . a cycle that is completed and ready to start again every 2 to 4 weeks.

How to Treat Worm Infection: For pinworms and roundworms, the **entire family** should take Combantrin as set out below: Combantrin gets rid of pinworms and roundworms with a single dose.

Treatment of Pinworm and Roundworm

Body Weight	Liquid	Tablets
11 kg or less (25 lb or less)	**2.5 mL** (½ teaspoon)	**1 tablet** 1 tablet
12–23 kg (26 to 50 lb)	**5 mL** (1 teaspoon)	**2 tablets** 2 tablets
24–45 kg (51 to 100 lb)	**10 mL** (2 teaspoons)	**4 tablets** 4 tablets
46–68 kg (101 to 150 lb)	**15 mL** (3 teaspoons)	**6 tablets** 6 tablets
69 kg and over (151 lb and over)	**20 mL** (4 teaspoons)	**8 tablets** 8 tablets

Shake liquid well before use. Do not exceed recommended dosage. On rare occasions a second dose has been found necessary.

How to Prevent Spreading and Re-infection: Even though Combantrin gets rid of pinworms and roundworms with a single dose, re-infection and the passing of the problem from one family member to another can occur if the eggs are not completely eradicated from all areas. So particular attention should be paid to personal hygiene and household cleanliness:

- Keep children's nails cut and scrubbed.
- Be sure children know that they should wash their hands regularly, particularly after toilet use.
- Wash all clothing, towels, and linen that have come into family contact since the problem was discovered.
- Pay particular attention to cleaning of bedrooms, bathrooms and laundry.

Prescribing information available to physicians and pharmacists on request.

□ COMBIVENT® Inhalation Aerosol Ⓟ

Boehringer Ingelheim

Ipratropium Bromide—Salbutamol Sulfate

Bronchodilator

Information for the Patient: Before you use Combivent Inhalation Aerosol, you should read this information leaflet carefully. If after reading this information you still have questions, please be sure to talk to your doctor or pharmacist.

What is Combivent Inhalation Aerosol? Combivent Inhalation Aerosol is an aerosol canister with a mouthpiece. Each puff delivers 20 μg ipratropium bromide and 120 μg salbutamol sulfate (equivalent to 100 μg salbutamol base).

Combivent is a combination of 2 bronchodilators (airways openers) in an aerosol that is inhaled using the standard mouthpiece or with a spacer device. You may already be familiar with one or both of these bronchodilators, since they are also available separately, with a prescription as Atrovent (ipratropium bromide) and Ventolin (salbutamol). Combivent can only be obtained with a prescription from your doctor.

Why has your doctor prescribed Combivent Inhalation Aerosol? Your doctor has prescribed Combivent to suit your condition. It is used to treat the wheezing or shortness of breath caused by COPD (chronic obstructive pulmonary disease which includes chronic bronchitis and emphysema). Combivent works by relaxing the muscle surrounding the bronchioles (airways to the lungs) and therefore helps to ease breathing problems.

What is COPD? COPD is a type of lung disease in which there is a permanent narrowing of the airways, leading to breathing difficulties. In many patients, this narrowing of the airways is a result of many years of cigarette smoking. In many patients that quit smoking, there are less symptoms and the course of the disease slows down or stops.

What you should tell your doctor before you use Combivent Inhalation Aerosol? You should tell your doctor the following before you use Combivent:

Before you use Combivent Inhalation Aerosol:

- if you are pregnant or intend to become pregnant;
- if you are breast feeding;
- if you have any other health problems, including a thyroid condition, difficulty in urination, enlarged prostate and diabetes mellitus, raised blood pressure or a heart problem;
- if you have eye problems, such as glaucoma, or eye pain;
- if you are taking any other medications including eye drops or any medications you can buy without a prescription;
- if you have any allergies or reactions to foods, drugs or aerosols.

When should you use Combivent Inhalation Aerosol? Your doctor will recommend when and how you should use Combivent (see ''How To Use Your Combivent Inhalation Aerosol''). You must follow any other direction that your doctor has given you for the treatment and/or monitoring of your condition.

Please Remember:

- Combivent Inhalation Aerosol has been prescribed to treat **your** current condition. **Do not** give it to other people.
- **Do not** take any other medication without your doctor's advice. Tell any other doctor, dentist, or pharmacist with whom you consult that you are using Combivent Inhalation Aerosol.
- **When using your Combivent Inhalation Aerosol with the standard mouthpiece or with a spacer device, make sure you do not spray the aerosol into your eyes.**

- Consult your doctor immediately if you experience any of the following:
  - -Increased wheezing or tightness in the chest;
  - -Swelling of the tongue or lips;
  - -Difficulty in swallowing;
  - -Fast or irregular heartbeat;
  - -Blurred vision or pain in the eyes;
  - -Difficult or painful urination;
  - -Skin rash.
- If you experience a dry mouth or bad taste, sucking on a sour candy or rinsing your mouth may help. Check with your doctor if the dry mouth or bad taste persist or if you experience constipation for a prolonged period of time.
- **Keep this medication out of the reach of children.**
- Container may explode if heated. Contents under pressure. Do not place in hot water or near radiators, stoves, or other sources of heat. Do not puncture or incinerate container or store at temperatures over 30°C.
- Like any drug product, Combivent may cause unwanted effects along with the good effects. If you do experience any unusual or unwanted effects while you are using your Inhalation Aerosol, you should contact your doctor.
- Combivent Inhalation Aerosol contains a beta-agonist, and taking additional doses in the form of other single agent, beta-agonists (fenoterol [Berotec], salbutamol [Ventolin] etc.) could cause deleterious cardiovascular effects. Therefore do not take additional bronchodilators by inhalation with Combivent Inhalation Aerosol unless instructed to do so by your doctor or pharmacist.

How To Use Your Combivent Inhalation Aerosol (see package insert for illustrations): **Do not exceed the number of puffs prescribed by your doctor. Do not use the inhaler more often than your doctor recommends.**

- The usual dose is 2 puffs taken 4 times daily. Do not use more than 12 puffs per day unless your doctor has told you to do so.
- If your symptoms get worse, contact your doctor immediately. While taking Combivent Inhalation Aerosol, other inhaled medications should be used only as prescribed by your physician.
- If you are troubled with mucous try to clear you chest as completely as possible by coughing before you use Combivent Inhalation Aerosol. This will allow the Combivent Inhalation Aerosol to pass more deeply into your lungs.
- Before starting to use Combivent Inhalation Aerosol, read the following instructions carefully; be sure that you know how to use the inhaler properly. If you use the inhaler incorrectly, you may not be getting all of the medication you need. If you have any questions about using the inhaler, check with your doctor.

1. Remove the protective cap from the inhaler.
2. **It is very important** to shake the unit well, as shown.
   It is recommended to test spray 3 times before using for the first time and in cases where the aerosol has not been in use for more than 24 hours. Make sure you do not spray the aerosol in your eyes.
3. Breathe out as completely as possible.
   a) Place the mouthpiece into your mouth and close your lips around it. Keep your teeth apart and your tongue flat to allow free flow of the medication into your lungs.
   b) Just after starting to breath in deeply through your mouth, press the canister down into the mouthpiece while still breathing in deeply and slowly.
4. Hold your breath for 10 seconds and then remove the mouthpiece from the mouth and breathe out slowly.
5. Wait approximately 2 minutes, shake the inhaler again and repeat second inhalation as outlined above.
6. Replace the protective plastic cap.
7. **Discard the canister after you have used the labeled number of inhalations.** The correct amount of medication in each inhalation cannot be assured after this point.

Care of the Mouthpiece/Canister: The mouthpiece should be washed with warm water once a week. You must remove the mouthpiece from the canister before you begin to clean the mouthpiece. If you use soap or detergent, the mouthpiece should be well rinsed in clear water, and then allowed to air dry. The mouthpiece must be completely dry before you put the canister back into the mouthpiece.

Sometimes, the canister stem may also get dirty or blocked. Pull the canister out of the mouthpiece and check the small holes in the stem. If these 2 small holes seem blocked, rinse them with clear lukewarm water. When the canister is dry, put it back into the mouthpiece.

□ COMBIVENT® Inhalation Solution Ⓟ

Boehringer Ingelheim

Ipratropium Bromide—Salbutamol Sulfate

Bronchodilator

Information for the Patient: Before you use Combivent inhalation solution, you should read this information leaflet carefully. If after reading this information you still have questions, please be sure to talk to your doctor or pharmacist.

What is Combivent Inhalation Solution? Combivent Inhalation Solution in unit dose vials (UDVs) is a combination of 2 bronchodilators ipratropium bromide monohydrate (0.5 mg) and salbutamol sulfate (equivalent to 2.5 mg salbutamol base) in a volume of 2.5 mL solution suitable for administration by inhalation by ventilator or compressor-driven nebulizer. If necessary, before use, doses may be diluted to a total nebulization volume of 3 to 5 mL with preservative free 0.9% sterile sodium chloride solution and used immediately. Discard any unused solution. Nebulize over 10 to 15 minutes at gas flow of 6 to 10 L/min. Repeat every 6 hours as necessary.

Combivent UDV should be used only in a properly functioning and regularly maintained nebulizer. Before starting treatment, be certain that you are completely familiar with the use and proper care of your nebulizer.

You may already be familiar with one or both of these bronchodilators, since they are also available separately, with a prescription as Atrovent (ipratropium bromide) and Ventolin (salbutamol).

Combivent can only be obtained with a prescription from your doctor.

Why has your doctor prescribed Combivent Inhalation Solution? Your doctor has prescribed Combivent to suit your condition. It is used to treat the wheezing or shortness of breath caused by COPD (chronic obstructive pulmonary disease which includes chronic bronchitis and emphysema). Combivent works by relaxing the muscle surrounding the bronchioles (airways to the lungs) and therefore helps to ease breathing problems.

What is COPD? COPD is a type of lung disease in which there is a permanent narrowing of the airways, leading to breathing difficulties. In many patients, this narrowing of the airways is a result of many years of cigarette smoking. In many patients that quit smoking, there are less symptoms and the course of the disease slows down or stops.

What you should tell your doctor before you use Combivent Inhalation Solution? You should tell your doctor the following before you use Combivent:

- if you are pregnant or intend to become pregnant;
- if you are breast-feeding;
- if you have any other health problems, including a thyroid condition, difficulty in urination, enlarged prostate and diabetes mellitus, raised blood pressure or a heart problem;
- if you have eye problems, such as glaucoma, or eye pain;
- if you are taking any other medications including eye drops or any medications you can buy without a prescription;
- if you have any allergies or reactions to foods or drugs.

When should you use Combivent Inhalation Solution? Your doctor will recommend when and how you should use Combivent (see Usage Instructions). You must follow any other direction that your doctor has given you for the treatment and/or monitoring of your condition.

Please Remember:

- Combivent Inhalation Solution has been prescribed to treat **your** current condition. **Do not** give it to other people.
- **Do not** take any other medication without your doctor's advice. Tell any **other** doctor, dentist, or pharmacist with whom you consult that you are using Combivent Inhalation Solution.
- **Do not let the nebulized mist get into your eyes. Patients with glaucoma should use swimming goggles or a nebulizer with a mouthpiece to prevent nebulized solution getting into the eyes.**
- The solution is intended for inhalation only. Do not inject or drink.
- **Keep out of the reach of children.**
- Consult your doctor immediately if you experience any of the following:
  - -Increased wheezing or tightness in the chest;
  - -Swelling of the tongue or lips;
  - -Difficulty in swallowing;

Combivent Inhalation Solution (cont'd)

- –Fast or irregular heartbeat;
- –Blurred vision or pain in the eyes;
- –Difficult or painful urination;
- –Skin rash
- If you experience a dry mouth or bad taste, sucking on a sour candy or rinsing your mouth may help. Check with your doctor if the dry mouth or bad taste persist or if you experience constipation for a prolonged period of time.
- Like any drug product, Combivent may cause unwanted effects along with the good effects. If you do experience any unusual or unwanted effects while you are using your Inhalation Solution, you should contact your doctor.
- Combivent Inhalation Solution contains a beta-agonist, and taking additional doses in the form of other single agent, beta-agonists (fenoterol [Berotec], salbutamol [Ventolin] etc.) could cause deleterious cardiovascular effects. Therefore, do not take additional bronchodilators by inhalation with Combivent Inhalation Solution unless instructed to do so by your doctor or pharmacist.

If you have any questions about Combivent Inhalation Solution or your nebulizer, contact your doctor or pharmacist.

Usage Instructions (see package insert for illustrations): Your doctor or pharmacist will tell you how to prepare your Combivent solution for inhalation. If you are told to dilute Combivent solution, you must do so immediately before you plan to use the solution. Your doctor or pharmacist might instruct you to use sterile sodium chloride solution (0.9%) to dilute the Combivent solution if necessary.

1) Detach one plastic vial by pulling it firmly from the strip.
2) Open the vial by twisting off the top. It is important that you use the contents of the vial **as soon as possible** after opening it.
3) Squeeze the contents of the plastic vial into your nebulizer chamber. If your doctor has instructed you to use less than one complete vial, use a syringe to withdraw the prescribed dose. Any solution left in the plastic vial must be thrown away.
4) Using a syringe, add sodium chloride solution to the chamber if you have been directed to do so by your pharmacist or physician.
5) Gently shake the nebulizer chamber and connect it to the mouthpiece or face mask. Then connect the nebulizer tube to the air or oxygen pump and begin therapy.
6) Breathe calmly and deeply through the mask or mouthpiece until no more mist is formed in the nebulizer chamber. This usually takes 10 to 15 minutes. **It is very important** to adjust the face mask, if required, to prevent the mist from getting in your eyes.
7) Follow the instructions provided by the nebulizer and air pump manufacturers for the proper care and maintenance of the equipment. Keep the nebulizer, nebulizer tube and face mask clean to minimize microbial contamination.
8) The unit dose vials should be stored at room temperature (15 to 25°C). The vials should be protected from heat and light.

☐ CONDYLINE™ ℞

Canderm Pharma

Podofilox

Antimitotic Agent

Information for the Patient: Notice: Treat only the warts indicated by the physician.

Contents: Condyline is a hydro-alcoholic solution containing 5 mg/mL podofilox, with a sodium lactate buffer that stabilizes the 1:10 aqueous solution with a pH between 2.5 and 4.

Indications: For the removal of external genital warts located on the penis and vulva.

Precautions: Condyline may not be able to prevent the reappearance of previously healed warts or the development of new warts at a location that was not previously treated.

Condyline is for external use only.

If Condyline is accidentally spilled on healthy skin, wipe off at once and wash vigorously with warm soapy water and rinse well. If spilled on mucous membranes or the eyes, flush repeatedly with a large amount of water for 15 minutes. See a physician **immediately.**

Keep this medication safely out of the reach of children.

Do not consume alcoholic beverages for several hours after treatment.

Do not permit Condyline to contact eyes, tongue or any mucosal tissue of the genital area including vagina, cervix, anus or perianus.

Do not use if growth or surrounding tissue is inflamed or irritated.

If you are a diabetic or have poor blood circulation, consult your physician before using this product.

Do not use on moles, birthmarks or unusual warts with hair growing from them.

Do not use on tissue which was recently exposed to laser surgery or cryosurgery.

Do not self-treat genital warts with surface areas greater than 10 cm^2 (approximately the size of a dollar coin).

Do not apply the solution to any other warts. Only apply the solution to the genital warts instructed. Always wash hands after using the solution.

Warnings: Condyline should be used only as directed by a physician. Keep out of the reach of children. Cap tightly and immediately after use. Extreme care should be taken to avoid all contact with the eyes.

Side Effects: Local discomfort is inevitable with the topical treatment of genital warts. Topical reactions are common and usually experienced on the second and third day of treatment in association with the beginning of necrosis of the warts. These reactions tend to be mild and well tolerated. However, a mild analgesic such as ASA with codeine or acetaminophen with codeine may be taken for pain management in some cases. Erythema (redness) with some pain and/or superficial ulceration of the skin in the treated area are to be expected.

Dosage and Administration: The first application of Condyline is to be administered by a physician. You will then apply the solution yourself, at home, and only on those warts pointed out by your doctor. Before applying the medication, gently wash the area to be treated with soap and water and gently pat dry. A skin protectant, such as petrolatum jelly, should be applied to the normal skin adjacent to the wart. Using one of the cotton-tipped applicators supplied, carefully apply only as much Condyline as is necessary to cover the warts while taking care to minimize contact with the surrounding healthy skin. **If you have multiple warts, you may need more solution to cover all the warts. In that case, you must take a fresh applicator. Never reuse an applicator or dip a used applicator into the bottle.** The use of a hand mirror may be helpful for proper application. If an area in the occluded prepuce (under the foreskin) is being treated, care should be taken to allow the solution to dry before letting the foreskin return to its normal position. Avoid contact with clothing until the solution has dried. Apply in the morning and evening for 3 consecutive days. **After each treatment, the used applicator should be properly and safely disposed of in a garbage can, out of the reach of children, and the hands should be properly washed.**

Do not use more than 2 times a day and not more than 3 days in a row.

This treatment procedure may be repeated at 1 week intervals with a 4 day time lapse between treatments, until a cure is obtained. **This should not exceed a 4 week treatment schedule.** If excessive burning or irritation occurs, discontinue treatment and consult a physician. Genital warts may be contagious and the patient should abstain from sexual intercourse. If this is not possible, a latex condom must be used by the male patient until the sexual partner receiving the treatment for genital warts is declared cured by a physician. When using a condom, avoid the simultaneous use of petrolatum or other lubricants because it may increase the risk of rupture of the condom during sexual intercourse.

☐ COREG™ ℞

SmithKline Beecham Pharma

Carvedilol

Congestive Heart Failure Agent

Information for the Patient: Please read this information before you start to take your medicine. Keep this leaflet until you have finished all your tablets as you may need to read it again. If you are helping someone take Coreg, read this leaflet before you give the first tablet. This leaflet does not contain all information about your medicine. **For further information or advice, please see your doctor or pharmacist.**

What you should know about Coreg:

- Coreg (carvedilol) belongs to a family of medicines used in the treatment of heart failure.
- Coreg has been prescribed to you by your doctor to help manage your symptoms of heart failure.

What you should tell your doctor before taking Coreg:
- all your medical conditions, including a history of heart, kidney or liver problems, asthma or breathing difficulties;
- if you suffer from diabetes, thyroid problems, Raynaud's phenomenon (coldness/spasm in the hands or feet) or cramping pains in the leg when exercising;
- if you suffer or have suffered from psoriasis (scaly red patches on the skin);
- any medications (prescription or nonprescription) which you are taking, especially antihypertensives, digoxin, insulin, hypoglycemics, stomach medication, tricyclic antidepressants, clonidine, and rifampin;
- tell the doctor if you change the amount of any other medicine you are taking;
- if you see another physician other than your heart doctor for another condition tell this physician that you are taking Coreg;
- if you are pregnant or thinking about becoming pregnant, or if you are breast-feeding.

How to take Coreg:
- **It is very important that you take Coreg exactly as your doctor has instructed.** The doctor will decide how many tablets you need to take each day, when and for how long. It may be necessary for the doctor to increase or decrease the dose.
- You should swallow the tablets whole with water. Do not chew or break your tablet.
- Take your tablets at the same time each day. You should take Coreg with food.
- If you forget to take a tablet, take it as soon as you remember. If possible take your next dose at the normal time, but do not take 2 doses within 6 hours of each other.
- If you miss more than 2 doses of Coreg contact your doctor for instructions. Do not restart Coreg until you have spoken to the doctor.
- Do **not** stop taking Coreg without first consulting with your doctor.

Remember: This medicine is for the person named by the doctor. Do not give it to anybody else.

When not to use Coreg:
- You should not take this medicine if you are pregnant or if you plan on being pregnant unless the doctor tells you to.
- Do not use Coreg if you are allergic to it or any of the components of its formulation (see list of components at the end of this section).

If you become unwell while taking Coreg tell your doctor at once.

Precautions when taking Coreg:
- Some people may have unwanted effects when taking Coreg. Dizziness, headache and tiredness are the most common and often occur when Coreg is started or the dose is changed. These symptoms generally go away. If they do not or appear to become more severe then tell your doctor.
- Other possible effects are: stomach complaints such as diarrhea, constipation, nausea and vomiting, allergic reactions such as rashes and hot or itching skin, pain in the side, passing water more or less frequently, breathing problems such as wheezing, breathlessness and stuffy nose, depressed mood, sleep disturbance, dry mouth, slowing of heart rate, dizziness when standing up, fainting, cold or painful hands and feet, general swelling of parts of the body, weight gain, impotence, blurred vision, cramping pain on exercise.
- If suffering from Raynaud's phenomenon (cold hands or feet with changes in color) an increase in symptoms of coldness/spasms in the hands may be seen.
- Psoriasis (scaly patches on the skin) may occur or, if you already have psoriasis, it may become worse.
- If you are diabetic you could become less aware of symptoms and hypoglycemia and you should monitor your blood sugar more carefully and tell your doctor if you see any appreciable changes.
- If you wear contact lenses you may suffer from dryness of the eyes while taking your tablets.
- If you develop any unusual discomfort, tell the doctor as soon as possible, especially if you have unusual dizziness, ankle swelling, tiredness or breathlessness when your dose is being increased.
- If you experience dizziness or fatigue while taking your tablets, do not drive or operate machinery.
- You should be especially careful when starting or changing the dose of Coreg.
- Coreg should not be taken with alcohol.

What to do in case of overdose:
- If you have taken more tablets than the recommended dose, tell your doctor or the nearest hospital emergency department immediately. Show the doctor your bottle of tablets and any other medications.

How to store Coreg:
- Store your tablets at room temperature (15 to 30°C) in a dry place. Protect from high humidity and light.
- Keep container tightly closed.
- The expiry date of Coreg is printed on the label. Do not use the medicine after this date.
- Keep out of reach of children.

What does Coreg contain:
- Coreg (carvedilol) is available as 3.125 mg, 6.25 mg, 12.5 mg and 25 mg white oval tablets. Carvedilol is the active ingredient. Non-medicinal ingredients include: sucrose, lactose, povidone, colloidal silicone dioxide, crospovidone, magnesium stearate, Opadry white, and Opadry clear. They do not contain tartrazine or any other azo dyes.

Who manufactures Coreg:
- Coreg tablets are manufactured by: SmithKline Beecham Pharma Inc. under License from: Hoffmann-La Roche Ltd.

□ COUMADIN® ℞

DuPont Pharma

Warfarin Sodium

Anticoagulant

Information for the Patient: The objective of anticoagulant therapy is to control the coagulation mechanism so that thrombosis is prevented, while avoiding spontaneous bleeding. Effective therapeutic levels with minimal complications are in part dependent upon cooperative and well-instructed patients who communicate effectively with their physicians. Patients should be advised of the following information:

1. Strict adherence to the prescribed dosage schedule is necessary,
2. Do not take or discontinue any other medication including salicylates (e.g., ASA and topical analgesics) and other over-the-counter medications, except on the advice of the physician,
3. Avoid excessive alcohol consumption,
4. Do not take Coumadin during pregnancy and do not become pregnant while taking it,
5. Avoid any activity or sport that may result in traumatic injury,
6. Prothrombin time tests and regular visits to physician or clinic are needed to monitor therapy. Carry identification stating that Coumadin is being taken,
7. If the prescribed dose of Coumadin is forgotten, notify the physician immediately. Take the dose as soon as possible on the same day but do not take a double dose of Coumadin the next day to make up for missed doses,
8. The amount of vitamin K in food may affect therapy with Coumadin. Eat a normal, balanced diet maintaining a consistent amount of vitamin K. Avoid drastic changes in dietary habits, such as eating large amounts of green leafy vegetables,
9. The patient should notify the physician:
   - If any illness such as diarrhea, infection or fever develops; or
   - If any unusual symptoms such as pain, swelling or discomfort appear; or
   - If prolonged bleeding from cuts, increased menstrual flow or vaginal bleeding, nosebleed or bleeding of gums from brushing, unusual bleeding or bruising, red or dark brown urine, red or tar black stools or diarrhea occurs,
10. If therapy with Coumadin is discontinued, patients should be cautioned that the anticoagulant effects of Coumadin may persist for about 2 to 5 days.

□ COZAAR® ℞

MSD

Losartan Potassium

Angiotensin II Receptor Antagonist

Information for the Patient: Cozaar Tablets: Please read this leaflet carefully before you start to take your medicine, even if you have just refilled your prescription. Some of the information in the previous leaflet may have changed.

Remember that your physician has prescribed this medicine only for you. Never give it to anyone else.

Cozaar (cont'd)

What is Cozaar? Cozaar (losartan potassium) is a green film-coated teardrop shaped tablet which contains either 25, 50 or 100 mg of losartan as the active ingredient.

In addition, Cozaar contains the following nonmedicinal ingredients: hydroxypropyl cellulose, hydroxypropyl methylcellulose, lactose, magnesium stearate, microcrystalline cellulose, cornstarch and coloring agents (D&C Yellow No. 10 aluminum lake, FD&C Blue No. 2 aluminum lake, and titanium dioxide).

Cozaar belongs to a class of drugs known as angiotensin II receptor antagonists. Its action is to lower blood pressure.

Why has my physician prescribed Cozaar? Your physician has prescribed Cozaar because you have a condition known as hypertension or high blood pressure.

- **What is blood pressure?** The pressure caused by your heart pumping blood to all parts of your body is called blood pressure. Your blood pressure changes during the day depending on activity, stress and excitement.

  Your blood pressure is made up of 2 numbers, for instance 120/80. The top number measures the force while your heart pumps. The bottom number measures the force at rest, between heartbeats.
- **What is high blood pressure (or hypertension)?** You have high blood pressure or hypertension if your blood pressure stays high even when you are calm and relaxed.
- **How do I know if I have high blood pressure?** There are usually no symptoms of high blood pressure. The only way of knowing that you have hypertension is to know your blood pressure. For that reason, you should have your blood pressure checked on a regular basis.
- **Why should high blood pressure be treated?** High blood pressure if left untreated can damage vital organs like the heart and the kidneys. You may feel fine and have no symptoms, but eventually hypertension can lead to strokes, heart attacks, heart failure, kidney failure or blindness.
- **How should high blood pressure be treated?** Once high blood pressure is diagnosed, some treatments other than drugs may be recommended. Your physician may recommend some changes in lifestyle. Your physician may decide that you also need medicine to control your blood pressure. Cozaar does not cure high blood pressure, but does help control it.

  Your physician can tell you what your individual blood pressure target should be. Keep this number in mind and follow your physician's advice on how to reach this target.
- **How does Cozaar treat high blood pressure?** Cozaar lowers blood pressure by specifically blocking a naturally-occurring substance called angiotensin II. Angiotensin II normally tightens your blood vessels. Treatment with Cozaar allows them to relax. Although your physician will be able to tell you that the medicine is working by measuring your blood pressure, you probably will feel no different while you are taking Cozaar.

What should I know before taking Cozaar?

- **Who should not take Cozaar?** Do not take Cozaar if you are allergic to any of its ingredients.
- **Use in pregnancy and breast-feeding:** It is not recommended to use Cozaar while you are pregnant or breast feeding. If you are pregnant or become pregnant while taking Cozaar, talk to your physician as soon as possible.
- **What should I tell my physician or pharmacist before taking Cozaar?** Tell your physician or pharmacist about any medical problems you have or have had, and about any allergies. Tell your physician if you have recently suffered from excess vomiting or diarrhea. It is particularly important to tell your physician if you have liver or kidney disease.
- **Use in children:** Cozaar should not be given to children.
- **Can I take Cozaar with other medicines?** As with most medicines, interaction with other drugs is possible. Therefore, do not take any other medicines unless you have discussed the matter with your physician or your pharmacist. Certain medicines tend to increase your blood pressure, for example, nonprescription preparations for appetite control, asthma, colds, coughs, hay fever and sinus problems.
- **Can I drive or operate machinery while using Cozaar?** Almost all patients can, but you should not perform tasks which may require special attention (for example, driving an automobile or operating dangerous machinery) until you know how you respond to your medicine.

How should I take Cozaar? Take Cozaar every day exactly as your physician has instructed. It is important to continue taking Cozaar for as long as your physician prescribes it in order to maintain smooth control of your blood pressure.

Cozaar may be taken with or without food, but it should be taken consistently with respect to food intake, at the same time every day.

What should I do if I miss a dose? Try to take Cozaar daily as prescribed. However, if you miss a dose, do not take an extra dose. Just resume your usual schedule.

What should I do in case of an overdose? In case of an overdose, contact your physician immediately so that medical attention may be given promptly.

What undesirable effects may Cozaar have? Any medicine may have unintended or undesirable effects, so-called side effects. Most patients do not have side effects from Cozaar; however, some patients may experience dizziness, lightheadedness or rash. Tell your physician or pharmacist promptly about these or any other unusual symptoms.

If you develop an allergic reaction involving swelling of the face, lips, and/or tongue, stop taking Cozaar and contact your physician immediately.

How can I learn more about Cozaar and high blood pressure? You may obtain further information from your physician or pharmacist, who have more detailed information about the product and high blood pressure.

How should I store Cozaar? Store Cozaar at room temperature (15 to 30°C). Keep container tightly closed. Protect from light.

Keep all medicines out of the reach of children.

☐ CRIXIVAN® ℞

MSD

Indinavir Sulfate

HIV Protease Inhibitor

Information for the Patient: Please read this leaflet carefully before you start to take your medicine, even if you have just refilled your prescription. Some of the information in the previous leaflet may have changed. Remember that your physician has prescribed this medicine only for you. Never give it to anyone else.

What is Crixivan? Crixivan is the brand name of Merck Frosst Canada Inc. for the substance, indinavir sulfate, available **only on prescription** from your physician.

Crixivan is a member of a class of drugs called protease inhibitors. It is active against the Human Immunodeficiency Virus (HIV) helping to reduce the amount of virus within the body.

Crixivan is available as white, semi-translucent capsules containing either 200 or 400 mg of indinavir as the active ingredient. Each capsule also contains the following nonmedicinal ingredients: ethanol, lactose and magnesium stearate; and gelatin, silicon dioxide, sodium lauryl sulfate and titanium dioxide (empty capsule shell).

Why has my physician prescribed Crixivan? Your physician has prescribed Crixivan for you because you have HIV infection.

HIV is a blood-borne disease spread by contact with blood or sexual contact with an infected individual.

What should I know before taking Crixivan? Who should not take Crixivan? Do not take Crixivan if you experience a severe allergic reaction to any component of the drug.

What should I tell my physician before I take Crixivan? Tell your physician about any past or present medical problems, including liver disease due to cirrhosis, or allergies.

You should always tell your physician about all drugs you are taking or plan to take, including those obtained without a prescription.

Tell your physician if you are pregnant or intend to become pregnant.

Pregnancy and Breast-feeding: You should not be breast-feeding if you are taking Crixivan. Consult your physician.

Children: The safety and effectiveness of Crixivan have not been established in children.

Can I take Crixivan with other medicines? Crixivan may be taken with a number of medications that are commonly used by people with HIV infection. These include zidovudine (AZT, Retrovir), didanosine (ddI, Videx), lamivudine (3TC), stavudine (d4T, Zerit), clarithromycin

(Biaxin), and trimethoprim/sulfamethoxazole (Bactrim, Roubac, Septra).

Some medications may be taken with Crixivan but require dosage adjustment of that medication or of Crixivan. These include rifabutin (Mycobutin) and ketoconazole (Nizoral).

Medications that may **not** be taken with Crixivan because it could result in serious or life-threatening events (such as problems with heart rhythm or excessive sleepiness) are triazolam (Halcion), astemizole (Hismanal), cisapride (Prepulsid), terfenadine (Seldane), and midazolam (Versed). In addition, you should not take Crixivan with rifampin (Rifater, Rifadin, Rimactane). Consult your physician before taking Crixivan with any other medication.

Can I drive or operate machinery while using Crixivan? Dizziness and blurred vision have been reported during treatment with Crixivan. If you experience these you should avoid driving or operating machinery.

How should I take Crixivan? Crixivan is in capsule form and must be taken orally. Take 800 mg (usually given as two 400 mg capsules) at regular 8-hour intervals. Crixivan must be taken at intervals of 8 hours for full effectiveness.

It is very important to take Crixivan exactly as prescribed to help ensure full effectiveness of the product.

Crixivan should be taken with water 1 hour before or 2 hours after a meal. If water is not preferred, Crixivan can be taken with skimmed or fat-free milk, juice, coffee, or tea; or a light meal such as dry toast and jam or fruit conserve, juice and coffee with skimmed or fat-free milk and sugar, or corn flakes, skimmed or fat free milk and sugar. At any other time you can follow your regular diet.

Taking Crixivan with a meal that is high in calories, fat, and protein reduces your body's ability to absorb the drug and in turn reduces its effectiveness.

It is important for you to drink at least 1.5 L (approximately 48 oz) of liquids during each day to ensure adequate hydration. This may help reduce the incidence of kidney stones (see What undesirable effects may Crixivan have?).

It is important that you take Crixivan exactly as your physician prescribes and that you do not stop taking it without first telling your physician.

What should I do if I miss a dose? Take Crixivan 3 times a day at regular 8-hour intervals. However, if you miss a dose by more than 2 hours, do not take it later in the day. Simply continue to follow your usual schedule.

What undesirable effects may Crixivan have? Any medicine may have unintended or undesirable effects, so-called side effects. Crixivan has been shown to be generally well tolerated. In clinical trials, approximately 4% of patients who received Crixivan alone or in combination with other antiretroviral agents have experienced kidney stones associated with severe back pain with or without blood in the urine. Other side effects include rapid breakdown of red blood cells (also called hemolytic anemia); weakness/fatigue; abdominal pain/swelling; liver problems; diarrhea; upset stomach; nausea; dizziness; headache; dry skin; change in skin color; hair loss; rash; allergic reactions; and taste perversion.

In some patients with hemophilia, increased bleeding has been reported.

There have been reports of diabetes and increased blood sugar (also called hyperglycemia) in patients treated with protease inhibitors. In some of these patients, this led to ketoacidosis, a serious condition resulting from poorly controlled blood sugar. Before starting protease inhibitors, some patients already had diabetes, others did not. Some patients required adjustments to their diabetes medication. Other patients needed new diabetes medication.

Your physician has a more complete list of side effects.

Tell your physician promptly about these or any other unusual symptoms. If the condition persists or worsens, seek medical attention.

In addition, tell your physician if you experience any symptoms that suggest an allergic reaction after taking Crixivan.

Other Considerations: You should know that Crixivan is not a cure for HIV infection and that you may continue to develop infections or other illnesses associated with HIV disease. You should, therefore, remain under the care of your physician while taking Crixivan.

The long-term effects of Crixivan are unknown at this time. Treatment with Crixivan has not been shown to reduce the risk of transmission of HIV to others through sexual contact or blood contamination. Studies evaluating the impact of Crixivan on HIV-1 disease progression (such as opportunistic infections and survival) are ongoing.

See your physician for more details.

How can I learn more about Crixivan? Not all the information about the drug is printed here. If you have any additional questions, ask your physician or pharmacist who have more detailed information about Crixivan and HIV infection.

How should I store Crixivan? Crixivan capsules are sensitive to moisture. Store in a tightly closed container at room temperature (15 to 30°C). Protect from moisture.

Keep all medicines out of the reach of children.

□ CYTOTEC® Ⓟ

Searle

Misoprostol

Mucosal Protective Agent

Information for the Patient: Keeping Track of Your Medicines: This chart will help you keep track of the medicines you take. Write down the names of the medicines you are taking and place an "x" in each box that shows the time a dose of medicine is to be taken. Extra boxes are provided for medicines that are taken at times other than breakfast, lunch, dinner or bedtime.

Medicine Record

Names of Medicines You Are Taking	Indicate the Time of Day You Have to Take Medicines						
	Breakfast		Lunch		Dinner		Bedtime
Cytotec							

What is Cytotec? Cytotec (also called misoprostol) is the only medicine approved in Canada to treat and help prevent gastroduodenal damage caused by arthritis medicines called NSAIDs. Gastroduodenal damage refers to damage in either the stomach or duodenum. The duodenum is the small portion of the intestine that is immediately adjacent to the stomach.

What is a NSAID? NSAID is an abbreviation for "nonsteroidal anti-inflammatory drug". "Nonsteroidal" means that this type of medicine does not contain steroids, such as cortisone or prednisone. "Anti-inflammatory" means that the medicine works by decreasing inflammation.

NSAID medicines are commonly prescribed to treat the pain and inflammation of arthritis and certain muscle conditions. While NSAIDs have many benefits, unfortunately they can cause stomach and gastrointestinal ulcers in some people. These ulcers often appear without any pain or warning symptoms.

Why Do NSAIDs Sometimes Cause Ulcers? Everyone's body contains a mucous layer on the inside of the stomach and intestine to protect it from stomach acids and digestive juices needed to digest food. The body produces natural substances called "prostaglandins" to keep this layer intact.

NSAIDs are believed to treat arthritis by lowering the amount of "prostaglandins". This has a good effect on the joints by helping to decrease the pain, redness and swelling of arthritis. Unfortunately, NSAIDs can also thin the protective mucous layer inside the stomach. The stomach can then become more prone to developing ulcers.

Who Is At Risk? You may be at higher risk of developing a NSAID-ulcer if you must continue taking the arthritis medicine and you:

- are older than 60 years of age.
- have had stomach upset in the past while taking NSAID medicines.
- have had a stomach ulcer(s).
- are taking high dosages of NSAIDs or multiple dosages of NSAIDs including taking over-the-counter NSAIDs such as ASA or ibuprofen.
- are taking certain other medicines such as corticosteroids or anticoagulants that are known to either damage the stomach or worsen the outcome of a damaged stomach.
- have other serious medical conditions or are in poor health.
- are severely disabled by an arthritic condition.

Cytotec (cont'd)

In addition, you may be at greater risk in the first 3 months after starting your NSAID.

How Does Cytotec Work? Cytotec is a manufactured prostaglandin similar to the prostaglandins found naturally in the body. Cytotec replaces the prostaglandins that the body is losing while you are taking the NSAID medicine. In doing this Cytotec helps protect your stomach and duodenum.

Cytotec helps protect the stomach and duodenum from NSAID ulcers in 2 ways:

- It protects the mucous layer on the inside of the stomach.
- It decreases the amount of acid that may irritate the lining of the stomach and duodenum.

Cytotec makes it possible for you to continue taking the NSAID medicine for your arthritis by protecting your stomach and duodenum.

Cytotec is also used to help heal duodenal ulcers.

How Do You Take Cytotec? Do: Take each dose of Cytotec after eating a meal or snack. This will help prevent loose stools, diarrhea and abdominal cramping that may occur in the first few days of therapy.

Do: Continue to take Cytotec if you develop these symptoms. Do not be alarmed. This is part of the effect of the medicine which your body is adjusting to. Keep taking Cytotec. These symptoms will usually disappear within a few days.

Do: Call your doctor if these symptoms become bothersome or do not go away within 1 week.

Don't: Do not take antacids that contain magnesium while you are taking Cytotec. Ask your doctor or pharmacist for help in selecting a suitable antacid.

Don't: Do not share Cytotec with anyone.

Do: Keep Cytotec and all other medicines out of the reach of children.

Special Note for Women of Childbearing Age: Cytotec may cause a miscarriage and its effects on the fetus (developing baby) are not known. Therefore, if you are pregnant, you must not take this drug.

Miscarriages caused by Cytotec are likely to be incomplete. An incomplete miscarriage may result in very serious medical complications, resulting in hospitalization, surgery and possible infertility.

If you think you are pregnant, you must not take Cytotec. You should avoid becoming pregnant while you are taking Cytotec. This means using an effective form of birth control. Stop taking Cytotec, and contact your doctor immediately if you do become pregnant during Cytotec therapy.

☐ CYTOVENE® Capsules Ⓟ
☐ CYTOVENE® Injection Ⓟ

Roche

Ganciclovir
Ganciclovir Sodium

Antiviral

Information for the Patient: All patients should be informed that the major toxicities of ganciclovir are granulocytopenia (neutropenia), anemia, and thrombocytopenia and that dose modifications may be required, including discontinuation. The importance of close monitoring of blood counts while on therapy should be emphasized.

Patients should be instructed to take Cytovene capsules with food to maximize bioavailability.

Patients should be advised that ganciclovir has caused decreased sperm production in animals and may cause infertility in humans. Women of childbearing potential should be advised that ganciclovir causes birth defects in animals and should not be used during pregnancy. Women of childbearing potential should be advised to use effective contraception during treatment with Cytovene (capsules and injection). Similarly, men should be advised to practise barrier contraception during and for at least 90 days following treatment with Cytovene (both formulations).

Patients should be advised that ganciclovir causes tumors in animals. Although there is no information from human studies, Cytovene (both formulations) should be considered a potential carcinogen.

Patients With AIDS and CMV Retinitis: Cytovene (both formulations) is not a cure for CMV retinitis, and immunocompromised patients may continue to experience progression of retinitis during or following treatment. Patients should be advised to have ophthalmologic followup examinations at a minimum of every 4 to 6 weeks while being treated with Cytovene (both formulations). Some patients will require more frequent followup. Patients with AIDS may be receiving zidovudine (ZDV; AZT); patients should be counseled that treatment with both ganciclovir and zidovudine simultaneously may not be tolerated by some patients and may result in severe granulocytopenia (neutropenia). Patients with AIDS may be receiving didanosine (ddI); patients should be counseled that concomitant treatment with both ganciclovir and didanosine can cause didanosine levels to be significantly increased.

Transplant Recipients: Transplant recipients should be counseled regarding the high frequency of impaired renal function in transplant recipients who received Cytovene for injection in controlled clinical trials, particularly in patients receiving concomitant administration of nephrotoxic agents such as cyclosporine and amphotericin B. Although the specific mechanism of this toxicity, which in most cases was reversible, has not been determined, the higher rate of renal impairment in patients receiving Cytovene (ganciclovir sodium for injection) compared with those who received placebo in the same trials may indicate that Cytovene injection played a significant role.

☐ DALACIN® T Topical Solution Ⓟ

Pharmacia & Upjohn

Clindamycin Phosphate

Antibiotic

Information for the Patient: Dalacin T Topical Solution (clindamycin phosphate) belongs to the family of antibiotics. When applied to the skin in a solution it helps to control acne (pimples commonly seen in teenagers and young adults). This medicine is available on a doctor's prescription only. With any questions concerning this medicine consult your doctor, or pharmacist.

Proper Use of this Medicine: Before applying this medicine, the area to be treated should be washed thoroughly but gently with warm water and bland soap, rinsed well and patted dry. Unless skin is oily, washing 2 or 3 times a day is enough. The face should not be washed for at least 2 hours after applying this medicine.

The medicine should be used for the full time of treatment recommended by your doctor even if the symptoms clear up after a few days. If the medicine is stopped too soon, the symptoms may return.

After shaving, it is best to wait 30 minutes before applying the medicine because the alcohol in it may irritate freshly shaven skin.

The medicine comes in a bottle with a separate applicator cap. To use the applicator: 1) remove cap from bottle and discard, 2) firmly press applicator into bottle, 3) seal firmly by tightening domed-cap.

The pharmacist may have assembled the bottle for you, in which case the applicator top will already be attached to the bottle. The applicator top may then be used to apply the medicine directly to the skin. The bottle should be tilted and pressed firmly against the skin using a dabing rather than a rolling motion. Reducing the pressure will decrease the flow.

A thin film of the medicine is to be applied to the whole area affected by acne, not just to the pimples themselves.

In order to prevent this medicine from getting in the eyes, nose, or mouth, it should be spread away from these areas on application. If the medicine does get in the eyes, they must be washed out immediately but carefully using large amounts of cool tap water. If the eyes still burn or are painful, a doctor should be consulted.

This medicine should not be used more often than prescribed by your doctor because it may cause dryness or irritation of the skin.

The bottle contains approximately a 4 week (30 mL size) or an 8 week supply (60 mL).

How to Store this Medicine: Keep out of the reach of children. Store away from heat and direct light. Keep medicine from freezing. Store in an upright fashion.

Precautions While Using this Medicine: This medicine may cause the skin to become unusually dry even with normal use. If this occurs check with your doctor.

If frequent diarrhea occurs it should not be treated without first checking with your doctor.

Side Effects of this Medicine: check with your doctor **immediately** if any of the following very rare effects occur: abdominal or stomach cramps, pain or bloating is severe; diarrhea (watery and severe) which may also be bloody; nausea or vomiting.

Also check with your doctor as soon as possible if any of the following side effects occur: skin rash, itching, redness or other signs of irritation not present before using this medicine.

Other side effects that do not normally require medical attention may occur. These include the following: dry or scaly skin, peeling of skin, stinging or burning feeling.

If any other unusual or unexpected effects occur, check with your doctor.

□ DALACIN® Vaginal Cream ℗

Pharmacia & Upjohn

Clindamycin Phosphate

Antibacterial

Information for the Patient: Read this flyer carefully. It has been prepared by Pharmacia & Upjohn to help you get the most benefit from this medicine. It contains general points about this medicine and should add to more specific advice from your doctor or pharmacist.

This flyer should not replace your doctor's or pharmacist's advice. Because of your health condition, they may have given you different instructions. If so, be sure to follow their advice. Also, if you have any questions or concerns after reading this flyer, talk to your doctor or pharmacist.

What is Dalacin Vaginal Cream? This medicine is an antibiotic. Antibiotics kill bacteria (germs) that cause infections. This infection is called "bacterial vaginosis". This medicine kills the bacteria that causes bacterial vaginosis.

What is Bacterial Vaginosis? This is an infection of the vagina that is caused by a high growth of bacteria. You may notice a milky discharge from your vagina. There may also be a fishy odor. Almost one-third of all women with vaginal infections have bacterial vaginosis. It is as common as yeast infections.

What is in Dalacin Vaginal Cream? This medicine contains an active drug called clindamycin phosphate. It also contains nonmedicinal ingredients like sorbitan monostearate, polysorbate 60, propylene glycol, stearic acid, cetostearyl alcohol, cetyl palmitate, mineral oil, benzyl alcohol and purified water.

If you know you have an allergy or sensitivity to any of these ingredients, call your doctor before using this medicine.

What Should I Know Before I take Dalacin Vaginal Cream? Do not use condoms or vaginal contraceptive diaphragms for 3 days after you use this medicine. The mineral oil in this medicine can weaken latex or rubber products. This might make condoms and diaphragms less effective and you will not be fully protected.

Do not start using this medicine if you have your period (menstruating). Wait until your period is finished before using this medicine.

Do not use this medicine if you are pregnant or breast-feeding unless your doctor has told you to.

Call Your Doctor If:

- You notice worsening of, or new vaginal symptoms (vaginal discharge, itchiness, odor).
- You experience nausea, vomiting or diarrhea. It is very unlikely that this will happen to you, however if it does, call your doctor.
- You experience any other unusual or unexpected effects.

How and When Should I Take Dalacin Vaginal Cream? Take this medicine each day, even when you feel well. This drug works best when there is a constant amount in your body. If the medicine is stopped too soon, your symptoms may return. Do not miss doses, or take extra doses, unless your doctor tells you.

Take this medicine each night before you go to bed. Use 1 full applicator of cream.

There are 7 plastic applicators in the package. The applicator consists of both a plunger and a barrel. The tube of cream contains enough medicine to last for 7 days.

Use the plastic applicator to permit proper placement of the cream in the vagina.

Note: This cream is inserted into the vagina in much the same way as a tampon.

Follow these steps to load the applicator:

1. Remove the cap from the tube of cream.
2. Screw the open end of the applicator on the threaded end of the tube.
3. Gently squeeze the other end of the tube. This will push the cream into the barrel of the applicator. As the cream enters the barrel, the plunger will be forced outward. The applicator is full when the plunger stops.
4. Unscrew the applicator from the tube when the barrel is full.
5. Replace the cap on the tube of cream. Roll the tube from the bottom.

Follow these steps to insert the vaginal cream:

1. Stand, squat or lie on your back in a comfortable position.
2. Insert the loaded applicator gently into the vagina as far as it will comfortably go.
3. Hold the barrel of the applicator steady. Slowly press the plunger until it stops. This will deposit the cream in the vagina.
4. Remove the applicator and throw out. Remember to use a new applicator each and every time you insert this cream.

Special Precautions:

- Keep out of reach of children.
- Store at room temperature, away from heat and direct light.
- Do not store in the fridge or freezer.
- Do not store in the bathroom as moisture and heat can cause damage.

Remember this medicine is for you. Only a doctor can prescribe it for you. Never give it to someone else even if their symptoms are the same as yours.

□ DALMANE® ℗

Roche

Flurazepam HCl

Hypnotic

Information for the Patient: Introduction: Dalmane (flurazepam hydrochloride) is intended to help you sleep. It is one of several benzodiazepine sleeping pills that have generally similar properties.

If you are prescribed one of these medications, you should consider both their benefits and risks. Important risks and limitations include the following:

- you may become dependent on the medication.
- the medication may affect your mental alertness or memory, particularly when not taken as prescribed.

In order to guide you in the safe use of the product, this leaflet will inform you about this class of medication in general and about Dalmane in particular.

But this leaflet should not replace a discussion between you and your doctor about the risks and benefits of Dalmane.

Safe Use of Dalmane Sleeping Pills:

- Dalmane is a prescription medication, intended to help you sleep. Follow your doctor's advice about how to take Dalmane, when to take it, and how long to take it. **Do not take** Dalmane if it is not prescribed for you.
- **Do not take** Dalmane for more than 7 to 10 days without first consulting your doctor.
- **Do not take** Dalmane when a full night's sleep is not possible before you would again need to be active and functional; e.g., an overnight flight of less than 8 hours. Memory lapses may occur in such situations. Your body needs time to eliminate the medication from your system.
- **Do not take** Dalmane at any time during pregnancy. Tell your doctor if you are planning to become pregnant, if you are pregnant, or if you become pregnant while taking this medication.
- Tell your doctor about any alcohol consumption (present or past) or any medicine you are taking now, including drugs you can buy without a prescription. **Do not consume alcohol while taking** Dalmane.
- **Do not increase the prescribed dose.**
- **Do not drive a car** or operate potentially dangerous machinery until you experience how this drug will affect you.
- If you develop any unusual disturbing thoughts or behavior while using Dalmane, discuss the matter immediately with your doctor.
- You may experience an increase in sleep difficulties (rebound insomnia) and/or increased daytime anxiety (rebound anxiety) for 1 or 2 days after discontinuing Dalmane.

Effectiveness of Benzodiazepine Sleeping Pills: Benzodiazepine sleeping pills are effective medications and are relatively free of serious problems when used for the short-term management of insomnia. Symptoms of insomnia may vary: you may have difficulty in falling asleep, or awaken often during the night, or awaken early in the morning, or you may have all three symptoms.

Dalmane (cont'd)

Insomnia may last only for a short time and may respond to brief treatment. The risks and benefits of prolonged use should be discussed with your doctor.

Side Effects: Common Side Effects: Benzodiazepine sleeping pills may cause drowsiness, dizziness, lightheadedness, and difficulty with coordination. Users must be cautious about engaging in hazardous activities requiring complete mental alertness, e.g., operating machinery or driving a motor vehicle.

Avoid alcohol while using Dalmane. **Do not use** benzodiazepine sleeping pills along with other medications without first discussing this with your doctor.

How sleepy you are the day after you use one of these sleeping pills depends on your individual response and on how quickly your body gets rid of the medication. The larger the dose, the more likely that you will experience drowsiness, etc., the next day. For this reason, it is important that you use the lowest effective dose. Benzodiazepines, which are eliminated rapidly, tend to cause less drowsiness the next day, but may cause withdrawal problems the day after use.

Special Concerns: Memory Problems: All benzodiazepine sleeping pills can cause a special type of memory loss (amnesia); you may not recall events that occurred during some period of time, usually several hours, after taking the drug. This lapse is usually not a problem, because the person taking the sleeping pill intends to be asleep during this critical period of time. But it can be a problem if you take the medication to induce sleep while travelling, such as during an airplane flight, because you may wake up before the effect of the drug is gone. This has been called "traveller's amnesia".

Tolerance/Withdrawal Symptoms: After nightly use for more than a few weeks benzodiazepines may lose some of their effectiveness. You may also develop a degree of dependence.

"Withdrawal" effects can occur when patients stop taking benzodiazepine sleeping pills. The effects may occur following use for only a week or two but may be more common and severe after long periods of continuous use. One type of withdrawal symptom is known as "rebound insomnia", i.e., on the first few nights after stopping the medication, insomnia may be worse than before the sleeping pill was given.

Other withdrawal symptoms following abrupt stopping of sleeping pills may range from unpleasant feelings to a major withdrawal syndrome that may include abdominal and muscle cramps, vomiting, sweating, tremor, and rarely, convulsions. The severe symptoms are uncommon.

Dependence/Abuse: All benzodiazepine sleeping pills can cause dependence (addiction) especially when used regularly for more than a few weeks, or at higher doses. Some people develop a need to continue taking these drugs, either at the prescribed dose or at higher doses—not only for continued therapeutic effect, but also to avoid withdrawal symptoms or to achieve nontherapeutic effects.

Individuals who depend, or have depended at any time in the past, on alcohol or other drugs may be at particular risk of becoming dependent on drugs of this class. But **all people are at some risk.** Consider this matter before you take these medications beyond a few weeks.

Mental and Behavioral Changes: A variety of abnormal thinking and behavior changes may occur when you use benzodiazepine sleeping pills. Some of these changes include aggressiveness and extroversion which seem out of character. Other changes, although rare, can be more unusual and extreme such as confusion, strange behavior, restlessness, illusions, hallucinations, feeling like you are not yourself, and worsening depression, including suicidal thinking.

It is rarely clear whether such symptoms are caused by the medication, or by an underlying illness, or are simply spontaneous happenings. In fact, worsened insomnia may in some cases be associated with illnesses that were present before the medication was used.

Important Note: Regardless of the cause, if you take medications, report any mental or behavioral changes promptly to your doctor.

Effects on Pregnancy: Certain benzodiazepine sleeping pills have been linked to birth defects when taken during the early months of pregnancy. In addition, benzodiazepine sleeping pills taken during the last weeks of pregnancy have been known to sedate the baby. Therefore, **avoid using this medication during pregnancy.**

☐ DAUNOXOME® ℞

NeXstar

Liposomal Daunorubicin

Antineoplastic

Information for the Patient: DaunoXome (liposomal daunorubicin) is used for the treatment of advanced HIV-related Kaposi's sarcoma.

The common adverse events associated with the use of DaunoXome include nausea, vomiting, poor appetite, sores in the mouth, back pain, facial flushing, chest tightness, mild hair loss and diarrhea. An important side effect is bone marrow suppression. The bone marrow is a factory which serves as the site of production of blood cells; this factory may be damaged by DaunoXome. A reduced white blood cell count may make the patient more susceptible to infection, and may require treatment with antibiotics. The first sign of an infection may be a fever and patients should contact their physician if this should occur. Anemia (a reduction of the red blood cells) may require treatment with red blood cell transfusions. A reduced platelet count (another type of blood cell) may result in increased bleeding and transfusion of platelets may be necessary. Although not all of these side effects are common, when they do occur they may require medical attention. Patients should contact their physician to report any side effect.

☐ DAYPRO™ ℞

Searle

Oxaprozin

Anti-inflammatory—Analgesic

Information for the Patient: Your doctor is your primary source of information about your health and the medicine you take. Consult with your doctor if you have questions about your health, any medication you take, or the information given here.

Daypro (oxaprozin) which has been prescribed to you by your doctor, is one of a large group of nonsteroidal anti-inflammatory drugs (also called NSAIDs) and is used to treat the symptoms of certain types of arthritis. It helps to relieve joint pain, swelling, stiffness and fever by reducing the production of certain substances (prostaglandins) and helping to control inflammation and other body reactions. However, this medicine does not cure arthritis and will help you only as long as you continue to take it.

You should take Daypro only as directed by your doctor. Do not take more of it, do not take it more often and do not take it for a longer period of time than your doctor ordered. Taking too much of any of these medicines may increase the chance of unwanted effects, especially in elderly patients.

Be sure to take Daypro regularly as prescribed. In some types of arthritis, up to 2 weeks may pass before you feel the full effects of this medicine. During treatment, your doctor may decide to adjust the dosage according to your response to the medication.

Stomach upset is one of the common problems with NSAIDs: To lessen stomach upset, take this medicine immediately after a meal or with food or milk. Also, do not lie down for about 15 to 30 minutes after taking the medicine. This helps to prevent irritation that may lead to trouble swallowing. If stomach upset (indigestion, nausea, vomiting, stomach pain or diarrhea) occurs and continues, contact your doctor.

Daypro is usually taken once a day, after breakfast or with some food or milk. Some people are told by their doctor to take it twice a day. The first dose is taken in the morning and the second in the evening, after a meal or with some food or milk. When Daypro is taken twice a day, the morning dose may be larger than the evening dose.

Do not take ASA (acetylsalicylic acid), ASA-containing compounds, or other drugs used to relieve symptoms of arthritis while taking Daypro unless directed to do so by your doctor.

If you are prescribed this medication for use over a long period of time, your doctor will check your health during regular visits to assess your progress and to ensure that this medicine is not causing unwanted effects.

Always Remember: The risks of taking this medication must be weighed against the benefits it will have.

Before taking this medication tell your doctor and pharmacists if you:

- or a family member are allergic to or have had a reaction to Daypro or other anti-inflammatory drugs (such as acetylsalicylic acid (ASA), diclofenac, diflunisal, fenoprofen, flurbiprofen, ibuprofen, indometh-

acin, ketoprofen, mefenamic acid, naproxen, piroxicam, sulindac, tiaprofenic acid, tolmetin, nabumetone or tenoxicam) manifesting itself by increased sinusitis, hives, the initiating or worsening of asthma or anaphylaxis (sudden collapse);
- or a family member has had asthma, nasal polyps, chronic sinusitis or chronic urticaria (hives);
- have a history of stomach upset, ulcers, or liver or kidney diseases;
- have blood or urine abnormalities;
- have high blood pressure;
- have diabetes;
- are on any special diet, such as a low-sodium or low-sugar diet;
- are pregnant or intend to become pregnant while taking this medication;
- are breast-feeding or intend to breast-feed while taking this medication;
- are taking any other medication (either prescription or non-prescription) such as other NSAIDs, antihypertensives, anticoagulants, antimalarials, corticosteroids, methotrexate, cyclosporine, lithium, phenytoin, gold therapy;
- have any other medical problem(s) such as alcohol abuse, bleeding problems, etc.

While Taking This Medication:
- tell any other doctor, dentist or pharmacist that you consult or see, that you are taking this medication;
- some NSAIDs may cause drowsiness or fatigue in some people taking them. Be cautious about driving or participating in activities that require alertness if you are drowsy, dizzy or lightheaded after taking this medication;
- check with your doctor if you are not getting any relief of your arthritis or if any problems develop;
- report any untoward reactions to your doctor. This is very important as it will aid in the early detection and prevention of potential complications;
- stomach problems may be more likely to occur if you drink alcoholic beverages. Therefore, do not drink alcoholic beverages while taking this medication;
- some people may become more sensitive to sunlight than they are normally. Exposure to sunlight or sunlamps, even for brief periods of time, may cause sunburn, blisters on the skin, skin rash, redness, itching or discoloration, or vision changes. If you have a reaction from the sun, check with your doctor;
- check with your doctor immediately if chills, fever, muscle aches or pains, or other flu-like symptoms occur, especially if they occur shortly before, or together with, a skin rash. Very rarely, these effects may be the first signs of a serious reaction to this medication;
- **Your regular medical checkups are essential.**

Side Effects of This Medication: Along with its beneficial effects, Daypro like other NSAIDs, may cause some undesirable reactions especially when used for a long time or in large doses.

Elderly, frail, or debilitated patients often seem to experience more frequent or more severe side effects.

Although not all of these side effects are common, when they do occur they may require medical attention.

Check with your doctor immediately if any of the following are noted:
- bloody or black tarry stools;
- shortness of breath, wheezing, any trouble in breathing or tightness in the chest;
- skin rash, hives or swelling, itching;
- vomiting or persistent indigestion, nausea, stomach pain or diarrhea;
- yellow discoloration of the skin or eyes;
- any change in the amount of or color of your urine (dark red or brown);
- any pain or difficulty experienced while urinating;
- swelling of the feet or lower legs;
- malaise, fatigue, loss of appetite;
- blurred vision or any visual disturbance;
- mental confusion, depression, dizziness, lightheadedness;
- hearing problems.

Other side effects not listed above may also occur in some patients. If you notice any other effects, check with your doctor.

Dosing: Usual Adult Dose: Rheumatoid Arthritis: Initially 1 200 mg once daily. Dose may be decreased or increased depending on patient's response. Maximum daily dose: 1 800 mg (1 200 mg in the morning and 600 mg in the evening).

Osteoarthritis: Initially 1 200 mg once daily. Decrease to 600 mg once daily according to patient's response.

Product monograph available upon request.

What to do if you Miss a Dose: Skip the missed dose and take the next dose at the scheduled time.

Storage: Store at room temperature, at or below 25°C. Protect from light.

Daypro is not recommended for patients under 18 years of age since safety and effectiveness have not been established.

Do not keep outdated medicine or medicine no longer needed.

Keep out of the reach of children.

This medicine has been prescribed for your medical problem. Do not give it to anyone else.

If you require more information on this drug, consult your doctor or pharmacist.

Nonmedicinal ingredients present in oxaprozin caplets include cornstarch, cellulose, hydroxypropyl methylcellulose, magnesium stearate, methylcellulose, polacrilin potassium, polyethylene glycol, titanium dioxide.

□ DDAVP® Spray and Rhinyle Nasal Solutions ℞

Ferring

Desmopressin Acetate

Antidiuretic

Information for the Patient: DDAVP Rhinyle Nasal Solution: Instructions for Use (see package insert for illustrations):

1. Pull plastic tag on neck of bottle and tear off security seal.
2. Remove plastic cap and **retain for reclosure.**
3. Twist-off the inner seal at the tip of the plastic teat and **retain for reclosure.**
4. Take the arrowmarked end of the tube in one hand and place the finger and thumb of the other hand around the plastic teat. Insert the tip of the plastic teat in a downward position into the arrowmarked end of the tube and gently squeeze the teat until the solution has reached the desired graduation mark.
   N.B.: In order to prevent air bubbles forming in the tube, maintain steady pressure on the plastic teat. If difficulty filling the tube is experienced, a diabetic or tuberculin syringe may be used to draw up the dose and load the tube.
5. Hold the tube with the tips of finger and thumb 1½ to 2 cm from the arrowmarked end and insert it into a nostril until the finger tips touch the nostril.
6. Place the other end of the tube in the mouth. Hold the breath, tilt back the head and then blow with a short strong puff through tube so that the solution reaches the right place in the nasal cavity. Through this procedure, medication is limited to the nasal cavity and the solution does not pass down into the pharynx.
7. After use, close the bottle using both the inner plastic tip seal and the outer plastic cap. **The use of both seals prevents wasteful loss by evaporation during refrigeration storage.** Rinse the tube under running water and shake thoroughly until no more water is left. The tube can then be used for the next application.

Caution: Headache, nausea or mild abdominal cramps may be symptoms of overdosing. Consult your doctor for advice and dose adjustment if required. Careful restriction of fluid intake is recommended with use in the elderly and children under 12 years of age because of increased risk of water retention.

Note: 0.05 mL solution contains 5 μg; 0.1 mL solution contains 10 μg; 0.2 mL solution contains 20 μg.

DDAVP Spray: Instructions for Use (see package insert for illustrations):

1. **Gently blow your nose.**
2. Remove the protective cap.
3. **The very first time** the spray is used, prime the pump by pressing downwards on the white collar using your index and middle fingers while supporting the base of the bottle with your thumb. Press down 4 times or until an even spray appears. The spray is now ready for use.
4. In a standing or sitting position, **hold the bottle in a way which places the dip tube in the liquid solution.** Tilt your head backward slightly and carefully insert the nasal applicator into one nostril.
5. For each spray your physician has instructed you to take, press firmly downwards once on the white collar using your index and

DDAVP Spray and Rhinyle Nasal Solutions (cont'd)

middle fingers while supporting the base of the bottle with your thumb. Hold your breath as you administer the dose.
6. If more than 1 spray is prescribed by your physician, repeat steps 4 and 5 for the other nostril. **Alternate nostrils for each additional spray.**
7. Replace the protective cap on the bottle.
8. Store at room temperature, 15 to 30°C. **Do not freeze.**

Important: The end of the tube inside the bottle must always be submerged in the liquid when administering the spray. Always keep the bottle upright and store in an upright position.

If the spray has not been used during the last 7 days, it is necessary to prime it again. Press downwards on the white collar a couple of times until an even spray appears before placing the nasal applicator in the nostril.

Caution: Headache, nausea, mild abdominal cramps may be symptoms of overdosing. Consult your physician for advice and dose adjustment if required. Careful restriction of fluid intake after suppertime is recommended with use in the elderly and children under 12 years of age because of increased risk of water retention.

DDAVP Spray available in 2 sizes: 25 mL (25 sprays) and 50 mL (50 sprays).

☐ DEMADEX® Ⓟ

Roche

Torsemide

Diuretic—Antihypertensive

Information for the Patient: Please read this leaflet carefully before you start to take your medicine. This provides a summary of the information available on your medicine. For further information or advice, ask your doctor or pharmacist.

The Name of Your Medicine: The name of your medicine is Demadex (torsemide). Demadex can only be obtained with a prescription from your doctor.

The Purpose of Your Medicine: Demadex is a diuretic and antihypertensive agent. It is used to lower blood pressure (hypertension) and to treat edema, an excessive fluid build up in your body.

How Your Medicine Works: Demadex acts on your kidneys to increase urination therefore reducing a fluid build-up in your body (edema). This in turn has a direct effect on lowering your blood pressure.

What is in Your Medicine: Demadex tablets contain either 5, 10, 20, or 100 mg of the active ingredient torsemide. The tablets also contain lactose, in addition to other nonmedicinal ingredients.

Important Points to Note Before Taking Your Medicine: There are important things to consider before taking Demadex.

Do not take this medication if you are pregnant, intend to become pregnant; or are breast-feeding, unless you have discussed this with your doctor.

The safety of this medication in children has not been studied and is therefore unknown.

If the answer to any of the following questions is yes, do not take Demadex until you have discussed the situation with your doctor:

- Have you ever had to stop taking Demadex or another medication for your condition because you were allergic to it or it caused problems?
- Are you taking other medications, including high doses of salicylates (Asprin) or indomethacin?
- Are you taking a medicine called cholestyramine?
- Are you taking a medicine called probenecid?
- Are you taking medicines for depression (lithium)?
- Are you taking antibiotics or other diuretics?

If any of the above applies to you, your doctor may decide that you should not take Demadex.

How to Take Your Medicine: The label on the container of your medicine should tell you the strength of Demadex tablets which you are taking, either 5 mg, 10 mg, 20 mg or 100 mg. The amount of daily medication as prescribed to you by your doctor should be taken **once daily.** This medication may be taken at anytime in relation to your meals.

If you are not sure about the instructions you are to follow, ask your doctor or pharmacist. **Do not** take more tablets, or take you medicine more often than you are told.

The success of treatment with Demadex depends very much on how carefully and consistently you follow the doctor's instructions about taking this medication and any other advice your doctor has given you.

While You are Taking Your Medicine: Your regular medical checkups are essential.

It is very important not to miss any of the tests which your doctor orders, including blood and urine tests.

Based on the blood and urine test results, your doctor might make changes in the amount of Demadex you must take. **Never make dose changes on your own.**

Never allow your medication to run out. If you plan a holiday, please remember to take enough supplies to cover your needs. **Do not** stop this medication unless instructed to do so by your doctor.

If you forget to take a scheduled dose, most doctors will suggest that you take it at the time you remember and then go on with your normal schedule. (Check with your doctor to see if this procedure is acceptable).

Tell any other doctor, dentist or pharmacist that you consult or see, that you are taking this medication.

Unwanted Effects: In addition to its intended action, any medicine may cause unwanted effects. Inform your doctor of any unusual health problem that occurs while taking this medication. This may include dizziness, headache, nausea/vomiting, weakness, excessive thirst, drowsiness, stomach cramps, muscle cramps, muscular fatigue, chest pain, diarrhea, rectal bleeding, excessive urination, tinnitus, hearing loss and syncope. Your doctor will decide whether you can continue your medicine.

Storing Your Medicine: Keep your tablets in a safe place where children cannot reach them. Your medicine may harm them.

Store your tablets at room temperature.

If your doctor decides to stop your treatment, do not keep any leftover medicine unless your doctor tells you to. Return your tablets to your Pharmacy for disposal.

Remember: This medicine is only for you. Only a doctor can prescribe it for you. Never give it to someone else. It may harm them even if their symptoms appear to be similar to yours.

Further Information: This leaflet does not contain the complete information about your medicine. If you have any questions or concerns about the medication, then you should ask your doctor or pharmacist.

☐ DEPO-PROVERA® Ⓟ

Pharmacia & Upjohn

Medroxyprogesterone Acetate

Progestogen

Information for the Patient: A. Information for women considering the use of Depo-Provera as a contraceptive: Read this pamphlet very carefully. It has been prepared to help you make an informed decision on whether or not to choose Depo-Provera as your method of conception control (contraception), and help you get the best results from this medicine. Even if you have already decided to use Depo-Provera, read this pamphlet very carefully. It contains general information and directions about this medicine and should add to the advice from your health practitioner.

This pamphlet should not replace your health practitioner's advice. They may have given you different directions. If so, follow their advice. Also, if you have any questions or concerns after reading this pamphlet, talk to your health practitioner.

Please contact your health practitioner if any of the following apply:

- If you do not understand any parts of this pamphlet
- If you want further information on other contraceptive methods
- If you are concerned that you should not use Depo-Provera

Important: Depo-Provera is one of the most effective ways to prevent pregnancy other than sterilization.

Depo-Provera does not protect you against HIV infection (AIDS) and other sexually transmitted diseases. Latex or polyurethane condoms are recommended for this purpose.

You are required to have 4 injections a year with this method of contraception.

There is some risk associated with the use of any medication. Depo-Provera is no exception. If you are thinking about using

Depo-Provera as a contraceptive, it is important that you understand the risks. Some of these risks may continue after you have stopped using Depo-Provera. Discuss these risks with your health practitioner before taking Depo-Provera, only you can decide whether Depo-Provera is the best contraceptive choice for you.

Your health practitioner is the best person to discuss the risks and benefits of Depo-Provera. This pamphlet, however, will help you understand the most important information. **It will also explain how you can help your health practitioner prescribe Depo-Provera as safely as possible by providing your complete medical history, and by being alert for the earliest signs of any possible problems.**

Make your decision to use Depo-Provera for contraception carefully. Think about the long-term action of Depo-Provera; once you get an injection of Depo-Provera, you must wait 3 months or more for the effects to wear off. Consider other methods of contraception if you wish to become pregnant shortly, or if you think that irregular or the complete lack of menstrual periods would upset you.

What is Depo-Provera? Depo-Provera is an injectable conception control agent (contraceptive) that is given as 150 mg of the hormone medroxyprogesterone acetate. Medroxyprogesterone acetate is a chemical similar to (but not the same as) the natural hormone progesterone that is produced by your ovaries during the second half of your menstrual cycle. Depo-Provera does not contain the hormone estrogen. One injection of Depo-Provera provides protection against pregnancy for 3 months. Therefore you must have one injection every 3 months (up to 13 weeks).

How Does Depo-Provera Work? During the 3 months following an injection, Depo-Provera stops the ripening of eggs in the ovaries; that is, it stops ovulation (the monthly release of an egg by the ovaries). When there is no ripe egg to be fertilized by the sperm, pregnancy cannot occur.

Depo-Provera changes the lining of the uterus (the endometrium) so that it does not easily receive a fertilized egg. It also causes thickening of the secretions (mucus) in the cervix, making it more difficult for the sperm to enter the uterus.

How Effective is Depo-Provera? Depo-Provera is more than 99.7% effective for conception control. This means less than 1 pregnancy for every 100 women who use Depo-Provera for 1 year (exactly as directed). Depo-Provera has been used as a conception control method by more than 30 million women in over 100 countries.

Depo-Provera and oral contraceptives ("the pill") are theoretically equally effective at preventing pregnancy. But in actual use, Depo-Provera is more effective because women sometimes forget to take their "pills".

Depo-Provera is more effective than IUDs, condoms (sometimes called rubber sheaths or prophylactics), diaphragms, or other contraceptive methods as shown in Table I below.

Other Ways to Prevent Pregnancy: Other methods of contraception are available to you. Other than Depo-Provera, sterilization, Norplant, and IUDs, how well other methods of contraception work depends in part on how reliably they are used. Faithful users may achieve pregnancy rates in the lower ranges, others may expect pregnancy rates more in the middle of the ranges, of those shown in Table I below.

Table I shows the reported pregnancy rates for various forms of birth control, including no birth control. The reported rates represent the number of women out of 100 who would become pregnant during the first year of use.

Who Should Not Use Depo-Provera? Depo-Provera should not be used by certain women. Tell your health practitioner if you have any of the following conditions, only your health practitioner can determine if you should not use Depo-Provera.

1. If you are pregnant, or think that you may be pregnant.
2. If you want to become pregnant shortly **(see following information on Return of Fertility).**
3. Unusual or unexplained vaginal bleeding that your health practitioner does not know about.
4. Lumps, swelling or tenderness of the breast that your health practitioner does not know about.
5. Problems with your liver or liver disease (e.g., hepatitis).
6. If you are currently taking anticoagulant (blood-thinning) medication (e.g., warfarin).
7. If you are allergic to medroxyprogesterone acetate, or any of the other ingredients found in Depo-Provera (polyethylene glycol, polysorbate 80, sodium chloride, methylparaben, propylparaben, water for injection).

Table I

Reported Pregnancies per 100 Women per Year

Method	Lowest expected	Typical
Depo-Provera	**0.3**	**0.3**
Norplant (6 capsules—s.c. implants)	0.2	0.2
Female sterilization	0.2	0.4
Male sterilization	0.1	0.15
Oral Contraceptives (the pill)	0.1-0.5	3
IUD		
Copper T 380A	0.8	3
Progestasert	2	3
Condom	2	12
Diaphragm	6	18
Sponge		
women who have not had any children	6	18
women who have had children	9	28
Cap	6	18
Withdrawal	4	18
Periodic abstinence	1-9	20
Spermicides	3	21
Chance (no birth control)	85	85

What Should Your Health Practitioner Know? Tell your health practitioner if you or any immediate family member has ever had any of the following. Women with these conditions may need to be checked more often by their health practitioner if they choose Depo-Provera.

- Breast cancer, abnormal breast exam or x-ray (mammogram)
- Diabetes
- Seizures, convulsions, epilepsy
- Migraine (headaches)
- Asthma
- Problems with heart, heart attack
- Stroke, blood clots (coagulation disorder)
- Problems with kidneys
- High blood pressure
- Mental depression
- Scanty or irregular menstrual periods

Tell your health practitioner if you are taking, or begin taking, any other medicines, even medicines you buy without a prescription. Some medicines may interfere with each other in your body.

The Risks of Using Depo-Provera:

1. **Formation of Tumors:** A long-term examination of women using Depo-Provera shows no overall increased risk of ovarian, liver, or cervical cancer. The same examination showed a prolonged, protective effect of reducing the risk of endometrial cancer in the population of users.

   Women who had ever used Depo-Provera showed no increased risk of breast cancer. And overall, there was no increase in risk of breast cancer with increasing duration of use of Depo-Provera. However, in a certain set of women, those who first took the drug within the previous 4 years and who were under 35 years of age showed a slight increase of breast cancer associated with use of Depo-Provera.
2. **Use in Pregnancy: Do not use Depo-Provera if you are pregnant, or think that you may be pregnant.** It will not prevent the pregnancy from continuing, but may interfere with the normal development of your baby.

   To reduce the risk of using Depo-Provera while you are pregnant, get your injection: **only** within the first 5 days of the beginning of your normal (menstrual) period, or **only** within the first 5 days after giving birth if you are **not** breast-feeding.
3. **Use While Breast-feeding:** Before using Depo-Provera while breast-feeding, discuss with your health practitioner. Depo-Provera does not affect the amount or quality of your milk. Children, whose mothers used Depo-Provera while breast-feeding for about 6 months, show no harmful effects up to 14 to 16 years of age. There is no further information on these children beyond 16 years old.

   A very small amount of the medicine in Depo-Provera is transferred to the milk of nursing mothers. Discuss with your health practitioner, he/she can help you decide what is best in your situation.
4. **Development of Osteoporosis:** Depo-Provera may be a risk factor for osteoporosis, similar to race, family history, low weight/height ratio, sedentary lifestyle and smoking. If you are considering using Depo-Provera, discuss with your health practitioner if you have any

Depo-Provera (cont'd)

two of the following: slim build, do not do any exercise, your bones are brittle (weak), or you smoke.

The Risks of Depo-Provera Compared to the Risks of Other Contraceptive Methods: The risks of various methods of contraception have been analyzed to estimate the risk of death associated with each. This analysis has 2 parts: (a) the risk of the method itself, and (b) the risk of death due to pregnancy in the event that the method fails.

A risk of death due to the method of contraception is associated with IUDs and oral contraceptives. However, this risk is low—less than the risk of death from childbirth. The exception is women over 35 years of age who use "the pill" and smoke, where the risk of death is greater than that from childbirth. The estimated mortality rate for Depo-Provera is lower than that for IUDs, oral contraceptives or childbirth.

What Can You Expect from Depo-Provera? Some women have side effects from this medicine. Remember, medicines affect different people in different ways. Just because side effects have occurred in other women, this does not mean you will get them. The side effect that occurs most often are changes in menstrual patterns (during treatment).

1. **Changes in Menstrual Patterns:** Depo-Provera slowly and continuously releases a hormone into your body for about 3 months. Because of this, you are not likely to have regular periods. For the first 3 to 6 months, most women have irregular, unpredictable or even continuous bleeding. The bleeding may be as heavy as a typical period or it may be lighter. This unpredictable bleeding pattern may be inconvenient, but it is normal due to the change Depo-Provera causes in the lining of your uterus. The lining no longer thickens each month and therefore, does not need to be lost as menstrual flow.

   As you continue to use Depo-Provera, bleeding generally decreases until most women no longer have monthly periods by the end of the first year of use. The lack of bleeding is **not** a sign of pregnancy.

   After you stop using Depo-Provera, the uterine lining will start to thicken again. Periods will start again as soon as the effects of Depo-Provera completely wear off. The time this takes varies from woman to woman.

   Very heavy bleeding that persists for several days is not a normal effect of Depo-Provera. If this happens, call your health practitioner immediately.

2. **Return of Fertility:** Depo-Provera will not make you infertile. Because Depo-Provera is a long-acting method of contraception, it takes some time after the last injection for its effect to wear off. This varies from woman to woman. Most women, however, must wait from 6 to 8 months after the last injection to start ovulating, have regular periods, and be able to become pregnant.

   If you stop using Depo-Provera and you do **not** want to become pregnant, start using another method of contraception 3 months after your last injection of Depo-Provera.

   If you want to become pregnant, tell your health practitioner. Fifty-four percent of women who wish to become pregnant do so within 6 months after their last injection of Depo-Provera. Seventy-six percent of all women become pregnant within 1 year, and 92% became pregnant within 2 years. The average time to pregnancy is 9 months after the last injection.

   Table II shows the percent of women that become pregnant after stopping the use of Depo-Provera, Oral contraceptives, and IUDs.

Table II

The percent of women that become pregnant after stopping the use of Depo-Provera, oral contraceptives ("the pill"), and intrauterine devices (IUDs)

Months since stopping contraception	Depo-Provera Users	"The Pill" Users	IUD Users
6	54%	75%	60%
12	76%	85%	76%
24	92%	95%	93%

In rare cases, it can take 2 years or longer for ovulation and regular periods to return, and for you to be able to become pregnant. This delay in return of fertility (after stopping Depo-Provera injections) is not related to how long Depo-Provera has been used. In very rare cases, women have not become pregnant after stopping injections of Depo-Provera. The reason is not known. There are many reasons why women are unable to become pregnant, including increased age and the start of menopause. In the general population, 7 out of every 100 women are unable to get pregnant.

3. **Weight Gain:** Some women gain weight due to an increased appetite while using Depo-Provera. If you notice a large increase in your weight (more than 15 lbs or 7 kg) in a short period of time that is not easily explained, tell your health practitioner.

4. **Mental Depression:** Women who have a history of depression may find that Depo-Provera will worsen this condition. If this happens to you, or if you become depressed, tell your health practitioner.

5. **Other Side Effects:** Just as some women notice bodily changes before their period, you may notice some of the same changes after an injection of Depo-Provera. Although reported less often than changes in bleeding patterns, the following side effects have been reported in rare cases by some women. Tell your health practitioner right away if any of the following continue, bother you, or are not easily explained: headaches, weight gain, nausea, vomiting, nervousness, stomach cramps, backache, bloating in the stomach, breast discharge and breast tenderness, spotty darkening of the skin, skin rashes, depressed feeling, tiredness, dizziness, loss of hair from your head, increase in growth of body hair, vaginal dryness during sexual intercourse, increase or decrease in sex drive, increase or decrease in blood pressure.

   The injection itself may cause slight pain and a slight lump may appear under the skin. The lump will usually disappear in a few days.

   Other side effects which cannot be predicted may happen in rare cases. If you have any bothersome or unusual effects while using Depo-Provera check with your health practitioner right away.

How and When Should You Use Depo-Provera? After you have discussed the use of Depo-Provera with your health practitioner and have decided to use Depo-Provera:

1. **Injections Every 3 Months:** Depo-Provera is injected into muscle—for example, into the fleshy part of the hip (buttocks) or upper arm. For Depo-Provera to prevent you from getting pregnant, you must get an injection every 3 months (up to 13 weeks). This means you will have to schedule 4 injections a year.

2. **The First Injection:** If your bleeding pattern is unusual, have a pregnancy test before you receive your first injection.

   Do not use Depo-Provera if you are pregnant, or think that you may be pregnant. It will not prevent the pregnancy from continuing, but may interfere with the normal development of your baby. For this reason, get your first injection: **only** within the first 5 days from the beginning of your (menstrual) period, or **only** within the first 5 days after giving birth if you are **not** breast-feeding. Before using Depo-Provera while breast-feeding, discuss with your health practitioner. When this procedure is followed, Depo-Provera will be effective from the day of injection.

   If Depo-Provera is given after the first 5 days of the beginning of your (menstrual) period, it may not prevent you from getting pregnant for the first 3 to 4 weeks after the injection. Use another nonhormonal contraceptive method (e.g., condom, diaphragm, sponge, cervical cap, abstinence) during these 3 to 4 weeks.

3. **Repeat Injections:** See your health practitioner a week or two early if you know that it will be difficult to get your next injection 3 months after the last one. This contraceptive method does require you to plan ahead. If scheduling injections every 3 months would be difficult, then Depo-Provera is probably not the best contraceptive method for you.

4. **If You Miss Your Injection of Depo-Provera:** You can get your injection up to 13 weeks, or as early as 10 weeks, after your last injection. If you have not had your injection by the 13th week, you should have a pregnancy test done before any further injections.

5. **Duration of Use:** At the present time, no known reason exists to limit the length of time you can use Depo-Provera for conception control. No known medical reason exists for stopping its use periodically. If you continue to use Depo-Provera until you approach the usual age of menopause, ask your health practitioner when to stop using Depo-Provera.

6. **Steps After Childbirth, Miscarriage or Therapeutic Abortion:** If you plan to use Depo-Provera following childbirth, get your injection during the first 5 days after giving birth if you are **not** breast-feeding. If you choose to breast-feed, discuss with your health practitioner the possibility of getting pregnant, other possible contraceptives, and when you may start using Depo-Provera. **(See previous informa-**

tion on Use While Breast-feeding.)

After miscarriage or therapeutic abortion, talk to your health practitioner about when you may start using Depo-Provera.

7. **If You See a Different Health Practitioner:** If you see a different health practitioner, tell him/her that you are using Depo-Provera.
8. **If You Take Other Medications:** Tell your health practitioner if you are taking, or begin taking, any other medicines, even medicines you buy without a prescription. Some medicines may interfere with each other in your body. Remind him/her that you are taking Depo-Provera.

B. Information for Women Using Depo-Provera for Contraception: Read this pamphlet carefully. It has been prepared to help you get the best results from this medicine. It contains general information and directions about this medicine and should add to the advice from your health practitioner.

This pamphlet should not replace your health practitioner's advice. Because of your health condition, they may have given you different directions. If so, follow their advice. Also, if you have any questions or concerns after reading this pamphlet, talk to your health practitioner.

If you are considering the use of Depo-Provera as a contraceptive, read Information for Women Considering the Use of Depo-Provera as a Contraceptive. Read it carefully before receiving your first injection. It describes the benefits and risks of using Depo-Provera.

Important: Depo-Provera is one of the most effective ways to prevent pregnancy other than sterilization.

Depo-Provera does not protect you against HIV infection (AIDS) and other sexually transmitted diseases. Latex or polyurethane condoms are recommended for this purpose.

You are required to have 4 injections a year with this method of contraception.

What is Depo-Provera and How Does it Work? Depo-Provera is an injectable conception control agent (contraceptive) that is given as 150 mg of the hormone medroxyprogesterone acetate. Medroxyprogesterone acetate is a chemical similar to (but not the same as) the natural hormone progesterone that is produced by your ovaries during the second half of your menstrual cycle. Depo-Provera does not contain the hormone estrogen. One injection of Depo-Provera provides protection against pregnancy for 3 months. Therefore you must have one injection every 3 months (up to 13 weeks).

During the 3 months following an injection, Depo-Provera stops the ripening of eggs in the ovaries; that is, it stops ovulation (the monthly release of an egg by the ovaries). When there is no ripe egg to be fertilized by the sperm, pregnancy cannot occur.

Depo-Provera changes the lining of the uterus (the endometrium) so that it does not easily receive a fertilized egg. It also causes thickening of the secretions (mucus) in the cervix, making it more difficult for the sperm to enter the uterus.

Who Should Not Use Depo-Provera? Depo-Provera should not be used by certain women. Tell your health practitioner if you have any of the following conditions, only your health practitioner can determine if you should not use Depo-Provera.

1. If you are pregnant, or think that you may be pregnant.
2. If you want to become pregnant shortly. **(See following information on Return of Fertility.)**
3. Unusual or unexplained vaginal bleeding that your health practitioner does not know about.
4. Lumps, swelling or tenderness of the breast that your health practitioner does not know about.
5. Problems with your liver or liver disease (e.g., hepatitis).
6. If you are currently taking anticoagulant (blood-thinning) medication (e.g., warfarin).
7. If you are allergic to medroxyprogesterone acetate, or any of the other ingredients found in Depo-Provera (polyethylene glycol, polysorbate 80, sodium chloride, methylparaben, propylparaben, water for injection).

What Should Your Health Practitioner Know? Tell your health practitioner if you or any immediate family member has ever had any of the following. Women with these conditions may need to be checked more often by their health practitioner if they use Depo-Provera.

- Breast cancer, abnormal breast exam or x-ray (mammogram)
- Diabetes
- Seizures, convulsions, epilepsy
- Migraine (headaches)
- Asthma
- Problems with heart, heart attack
- Stroke, blood clots (coagulation disorder)
- Problems with kidneys
- High blood pressure
- Mental depression
- Scanty or irregular menstrual periods

Tell your health practitioner if you are taking, or begin taking, any other medicines, even medicines you buy without a prescription. Some medicines may interfere with each other in your body.

What Can You Expect from Depo-Provera? Some women have side effects from this medicine. Remember, medicines affect different people in different ways. Just because side effects have occurred in other women, this does not mean you will get them. The side effect that occurs most often are changes in menstrual patterns (during treatment).

1. **Changes in Menstrual Patterns:** Depo-Provera slowly and continuously releases a hormone into your body for about 3 months. Because of this, you are not likely to have regular periods. For the first 3 to 6 months, most women have irregular, unpredictable or even continuous bleeding. The bleeding may be as heavy as a typical period or it may be lighter. This unpredictable bleeding pattern may be inconvenient, but it is normal due to the change Depo-Provera causes in the lining of your uterus. The lining no longer thickens each month and therefore, does not need to be lost as menstrual flow.

   As you continue to use Depo-Provera, bleeding generally decreases until most women no longer have monthly periods by the end of the first year of use. The lack of bleeding is **not** a sign of pregnancy.

   After you stop using Depo-Provera, the uterine lining will start to thicken again. Periods will start again as soon as the effects of Depo-Provera completely wear off. The time this takes varies from woman to woman.

Very heavy bleeding that persists for several days is not a normal effect of Depo-Provera. If this happens, call your health practitioner immediately.

2. **Return of Fertility:** Depo-Provera will not make you infertile. Because Depo-Provera is a long-acting method of contraception, it takes some time after the last injection for its effect to wear off. This varies from woman to woman. Most women, however, must wait from 6 to 8 months after the last injection to start ovulating, have regular periods, and be able to become pregnant.

   If you stop using Depo-Provera and you do **not** want to become pregnant, start using another method of contraception 3 months after your last injection of Depo-Provera.

   If you want to become pregnant, tell your health practitioner. Fifty-four percent of women who wish to become pregnant do so within 6 months after their last injection of Depo-Provera. Seventy-six percent of all women become pregnant within 1 year, and 92% became pregnant within 2 years. The average time to pregnancy is 9 months after the last injection.

   Table III shows the percent of women that become pregnant after stopping the use of Depo-Provera, Oral contraceptives, and IUD's.

Table III

The percent of women that become pregnant after stopping the use of Depo-Provera, oral contraceptives ("the pill"), and intrauterine devices (IUDs)

Months since stopping contraception	Depo-Provera Users	"The Pill" Users	IUD Users
6	54%	75%	60%
12	76%	85%	76%
24	92%	95%	93%

   In rare cases, it can take 2 years or longer for ovulation and regular periods to return, and for you to be able to become pregnant. This delay in return of fertility (after stopping Depo-Provera injections) is not related to how long Depo-Provera has been used. In very rare cases, women have not become pregnant after stopping injections of Depo-Provera. The reason is not known. There are many reasons why women are unable to become pregnant, including increased age and the start of menopause. In the general population, 7 out of every 100 women are unable to get pregnant.

3. **Weight Gain:** Some women gain weight due to an increased appetite while using Depo-Provera. If you notice a large increase in your weight (more than 15 lbs or 7 kg) in a short period of time that is not easily explained, tell your health practitioner.

Depo-Provera (cont'd)

4. **Mental Depression:** Women who have a history of depression may find that Depo-Provera will worsen this condition. If this happens to you, or if you become depressed, tell your health practitioner.
5. **Other Side Effects:** Just as some women notice bodily changes before their period, you may notice some of the same changes after an injection of Depo-Provera. Although reported less often than changes in bleeding patterns, the following side effects have been reported in rare cases by some women. Tell your health practitioner right away if any of the following continue, bother you, or are not easily explained: headaches, weight gain, nausea, vomiting, nervousness, stomach cramps, backache, bloating in the stomach, breast discharge and breast tenderness, spotty darkening of the skin, skin rashes, depressed feeling, tiredness, dizziness, loss of hair from your head, increase in growth of body hair, vaginal dryness during sexual intercourse, increase or decrease in sex drive, increase or decrease in blood pressure.

   The injection itself may cause slight pain and a slight lump may appear under the skin. The lump will usually disappear in a few days.

   Other side effects which cannot be predicted may happen in rare cases. If you have any bothersome or unusual effects while using Depo-Provera check with your health practitioner right away.

How and When Should You Use Depo-Provera? After you have discussed the use of Depo-Provera with your health practitioner and have decided to use Depo-Provera:

1. **Injections Every 3 Months:** Depo-Provera is injected into muscle—for example, into the fleshy part of the hip (buttocks) or upper arm. For Depo-Provera to prevent you from getting pregnant, you must get an injection every 3 months (up to 13 weeks). This means you will have to schedule 4 injections a year.
2. **The First Injection:** If your bleeding pattern is unusual, have a pregnancy test before you receive your first injection.

   Do not use Depo-Provera if you are pregnant, or think that you may be pregnant. It will not prevent the pregnancy from continuing, but may interfere with the normal development of your baby. For this reason, get your first injection: **only** within the first 5 days from the beginning of your (menstrual) period, or **only** within the first 5 days after giving birth if you are **not** breast-feeding. Before using Depo-Provera while breast-feeding, discuss with your health practitioner. When this procedure is followed, Depo-Provera will be effective from the day of injection.

   If Depo-Provera is given after the first 5 days of the beginning of your (menstrual) period, it may not prevent you from getting pregnant for the first 3 to 4 weeks after the injection. Use another non-hormonal contraceptive method (e.g., condom, diaphragm, sponge, cervical cap, abstinence) during these 3 to 4 weeks.
3. **Repeat Injections:** See your health practitioner a week or two early if you know that it will be difficult to get your next injection 3 months after the last one. This contraceptive method does require you to plan ahead. If scheduling injections every 3 months would be difficult, then Depo-Provera is probably not the best contraceptive method for you.
4. **If You Miss Your Injection of Depo-Provera:** You can get your injection up to 13 weeks, or as early as 10 weeks, after your last injection. If you have not had your injection by the 13th week, you should have a pregnancy test done before any further injections.
5. **Duration of Use:** At the present time, no known reason exists to limit the length of time you can use Depo-Provera for conception control. No known medical reason exists for stopping its use periodically. If you continue to use Depo-Provera until you approach the usual age of menopause, ask your health practitioner when to stop using Depo-Provera.
6. **Steps After Childbirth, Miscarriage or Therapeutic Abortion:** If you plan to use Depo-Provera following childbirth, get your injection during the first 5 days after giving birth if you are **not** breast-feeding. If you choose to breast-feed, discuss with your health practitioner the possibility of getting pregnant, other possible contraceptives, and when you may start using Depo-Provera. **(See previous information on Use While Breast-feeding.)**

   After miscarriage or therapeutic abortion, talk to your health practitioner about when you may start using Depo-Provera.
7. **If You See a Different Health Practitioner:** If you see a different health practitioner, tell him/her that you are using Depo-Provera.
8. **If You Take Other Medications:** Tell your health practitioner if you are taking, or begin taking, any other medicines, even medicines you buy without a prescription. Some medicines may interfere with each other in your body. Remind him/her that you are taking Depo-Provera.

□ DIANE®-35 Ⓟ

Berlex Canada

Cyproterone Acetate—Ethinyl Estradiol

Acne Therapy

Information for the Patient: Composition: Diane-35 is a preparation which contains 2 sex hormones, cyproterone acetate and ethinyl estradiol, in a specific ratio. Each tablet contains 2 mg cyproterone acetate and 0.035 mg ethinyl estradiol.

> Diane-35 has many properties in common with estrogen/progestogen-combination oral contraceptives ("The Pill") and the same Contraindications, Warnings and Precautions applicable to this class of drugs should be considered. Your doctor should be consulted in this regard.
>
> Oral contraceptives should not be taken during treatment with Diane-35.

Properties and Indications: The cyproterone acetate contained in Diane-35 inhibits the influence of the androgens (male hormones) which are also naturally produced by women. It can be used to treat conditions that are caused by either an increased production of androgens or an increased sensitivity to these hormones. Examples of androgen-dependent conditions in women are pronounced forms of acne, especially those which are accompanied by seborrhea, inflammation or formation of nodes, and mild forms of hirsutism (excess hair on the face, chest, abdomen or legs).

The cyproterone acetate in Diane-35 reduces the activity of the sebaceous gland which plays an important role in the development of acne and seborrhea. This leads, usually within 3 to 6 months of therapy, to the healing or improvement of existing acne. The excessive greasiness of the hair and skin generally disappears earlier. The loss of hair which frequently accompanies seborrhea likewise diminishes.

Apart from the described antiandrogen effect, cyproterone acetate has also a pronounced progestational action. If cyproterone acetate were administered alone it would cause menstrual cycle disturbances. This effect is avoided by its combination with ethinyl estradiol (a female hormone) in Diane-35. The menstrual cycles remain regular as long as medication is taken cyclically according to instructions.

During treatment with Diane-35, ovulation will not take place if the medication is taken as prescribed (see section "How to Take DIANE-35"). Therefore, the simultaneous use of hormonal contraceptives is not advisable.

You should know that, as with other medications, this product should not be used by certain women. In a small number of others, potentially serious adverse effects may occur. Your doctor is in the best position to decide whether or not any conditions are present that pose a risk to you.

Who Should Not Take Estrogen/Progestogen Combinations: There are several groups of women who should not use estrogen/progestogen-combination pills. You should not use this type of medication if you have or have had any of the following conditions:

- Unusual vaginal bleeding that has not yet been diagnosed.
- Blood clots in the legs, lungs, eyes or elsewhere.
- A stroke, heart attack, or chest pain (angina pectoris).
- Known or suspected cancer of the breast or sex organs.
- Liver tumor associated with the use of the pill or other estrogen-containing products.
- Jaundice or liver disease if still present.

This class of medication should not be taken if you are pregnant or if pregnancy is suspected.

> You should know that cigarette smoking increases the risk of serious adverse effects on the heart and blood vessels from estrogen/progestogen-combination use. This risk increases with age and heavy smoking (15 or more cigarettes a day) and is more marked in women over 35 years of age. Women who use estrogen/progestogen combinations should not smoke.

When You Are Taking Estrogen/Progestogen Combinations: If you and your doctor have elected for you to use Diane-35, you should be aware that periodic medical supervision is necessary.

1. Take Diane-35 only on the advice of your doctor and carefully follow all directions given to you. It is important to take the tablets exactly as prescribed; otherwise, you may become pregnant.
2. After the age of 35 years, it is generally inadvisable to use estrogen/progestogen combinations. Your doctor should be consulted in this regard.
3. Contact your doctor regularly after the initial visit.
4. **You should be alert for signs of serious adverse effects and call your doctor immediately if they occur:**
   - Sharp pain in the chest, coughing blood, or sudden shortness of breath (indicating a possible blood clot in the lung).
   - Pain in the calf (indicating a possible blood clot in the leg).
   - Crushing chest pain or heaviness (indicating possible heart attack).
   - Sudden severe headache or vomiting, dizziness or fainting, disturbance of vision or speech, or weakness or numbness in an arm or leg (indicating a possible stroke).
   - Sudden partial or complete loss of vision (indicating a possible blood clot in the eye).
   - Severe pain or lump in the abdomen (indicating a possible tumor of the liver).
   - Severe depression.
   - Yellowing of the skin (jaundice).
   - Unusual swelling of the extremities.
   - Breast lumps (you should ask your doctor for advice and instructions on how to examine your own breasts regularly).
5. Estrogen/progestogen combinations should never be taken if you think you are pregnant. They will not prevent the pregnancy from continuing and may interfere with the normal development of the baby.
6. If you wish to become pregnant, your doctor may recommend that you discontinue the use of Diane-35 and delay pregnancy until at least 1 spontaneous menstrual cycle has occurred. Contact your doctor for advice on this and for recommendations on appropriate methods of contraception that may be used during this time.
7. Consult your doctor before resuming the use of estrogen/progestogen combinations after childbirth, miscarriage, or therapeutic abortion. Hormones in estrogen/progestogen combinations are known to appear in the milk and may decrease its flow.
8. If for any reason you should require elective surgery, the surgeon should be informed that you are using an estrogen/progestogen so that you can be correctly advised about discontinuing their use one month before surgery and substituting another contraceptive method.
9. If you have occasion to see a different physician, be sure to inform him or her that you are taking estrogen/progestogen-combination pills.
10. It is important to inform your doctor if you are taking or if you start to take any other medication (prescription or nonprescription drugs) because this may alter the effectiveness and/or cycle control of the medication.

How to Take Diane-35:

1. If instructed to do so by your doctor, a nonhormonal method of contraception should be employed while taking Diane-35.
2. For your first pack of Diane-35, begin taking tablets on the first day of menstrual bleeding.
3. Take your first tablet from the pack out of the section marked with the corresponding day of the week (for example "MO" for Monday), press it through the aluminum foil, and swallow it whole with some liquid. You should take your tablet at the same time each day.
4. Take 1 tablet each day, following the directions of the arrows.
5. When you have taken all 21 tablets in this pack, wait 7 days and then start a new pack of Diane-35. During the 7 days that you are not taking any tablets, you should have your period, usually 2 to 4 days after you have taken your last tablet.
6. The first tablet in every subsequent pack will always be taken on the same day of the week that you first began taking Diane-35 tablets regardless of whether your bleeding has already ceased (which it usually has) or is still continuing.

Please Note: Irregular tablet-taking, vomiting or intestinal affections with diarrhea, some very rare individual metabolic disturbances or prolonged simultaneous use of certain medical preparations can affect the efficacy of Diane-35.

Missed Tablets, Vomiting or Diarrhea: If you forget to take your tablet at the usual time, you must take it within the next 12 hours at the latest. If more than 12 hours have passed from the time that you normally take your tablet, you must discard the missed tablet and continue to take the remaining tablets in the pack at the usual time to prevent premature bleeding.

Also in case of vomiting or diarrhea you must continue to take the remaining tablets. However, a supplementary nonhormonal method of contraception must be used for the remainder of the cycle of use to prevent pregnancy.

Missed Period: If bleeding fails to occur during the 7 days that you are not taking any tablets, do not start a new pack and contact your doctor to rule out pregnancy.

Unscheduled Period: If an "unscheduled" period occurs during the 3 weeks in which Diane-35 tablets are being taken, continue taking the tablets. Slight bleeding will usually stop spontaneously. However, if the bleeding is heavy, similar to menstrual bleeding, you should consult your doctor.

Presentation: Package of 21 tablets.

☐ DICLECTIN® Ⓟ

Duchesnay

Doxylamine Succinate—Pyridoxine HCl

Antinauseant against Nausea and Vomiting of Pregnancy

Information for the Patient: Summary: Diclectin is indicated for the treatment of nausea and vomiting that could occur during the first weeks of pregnancy. Take Diclectin only when prescribed and on the directions of your doctor. Diclectin could cause drowsiness, so before you know how it will affect you, be cautious while driving a car or operating any machine.

More information on Diclectin is found in this insert. Read it and keep it for further reference. Nausea and vomiting at the beginning of pregnancy are frequent. They are usually not signs of disease and they diminish or disappear after a few weeks, without treatment. Diclectin contains 2 pharmaceutical ingredients: an antihistamine (doxylamine) and vitamin B_6.

How to Use Diclectin: Take Diclectin strictly in accordance with your doctor's instructions. Diclectin takes several hours to reach its optimal effect and as nausea and vomiting of pregnancy generally occur in the morning, your doctor will normally recommend you take 2 tablets at bedtime so that the medication will be effective in the morning. If symptoms persist during the day, your doctor may recommend another tablet in the morning or one in mid-afternoon. Your doctor may change the dosage, depending on when your symptoms occur and their severity. If you forget to take a dose of Diclectin, take it as soon as you remember. Take the remaining doses as indicated. Do not take 2 doses at the same time, unless prescribed by your doctor.

Pregnancy and Congenital Abnormalities: Out of 100 newborns, 2 or 3 have a serious congenital abnormality. This risk can be increased if the mother takes certain drugs or other substances like alcohol during pregnancy.

Many studies have been performed in women taking this medication during pregnancy. The overall conclusion from these studies indicates that there is no evidence that Diclectin increases the risk of congenital malformations.

Nursing mothers should be aware that a small quantity of the drug could be ingested by the infant. It is not known whether undesirable effects could be produced in the baby.

General Precautions: Diclectin may cause drowsiness. As long as you do not know how you are reacting to the medication, be cautious while driving a car or operating a machine. Deeper drowsiness could be produced if Diclectin is taken in combination with alcohol or other drugs such as drugs for cough or colds, antidepressants, analgesics or tranquilizers.

Diclectin (cont'd)

If you have had a severe reaction to an antihistamine or to Diclectin in the past, advise your doctor. These reactions are severe drowsiness, insomnia, gastric pain. If you experience some of these secondary effects or any other effects, consult your doctor.

Adverse Effects: In addition to drowsiness, Diclectin can produce vertigo, headache, confusion, irritability, insomnia and gastric pain. If you experience some of these adverse effects or any other effects, consult your doctor.

Other Information: For Diclectin to be effective, it must be taken as recommended by your doctor and as indicated on the label. This drug is specifically prescribed for you and your actual state of health. Do not give it to others, even if they have the same symptoms, and you yourself must not use it for any other condition than the one for which it was prescribed.

If you think that you or someone else has taken an overdose, immediately call a Poison Control Centre, your doctor, your pharmacist or the emergency service of the nearest hospital. **Keep this drug and all other drugs out of reach of children.**

If you want more information on Diclectin, consult your doctor or your pharmacist. They have available a more technical document (product monograph) that you could read.

☐ DICLOTEC ℞

Technilab

Diclofenac Sodium

Anti-inflammatory—Analgesic

Information for the Patient: Diclotec (diclofenac sodium), which has been prescribed to you by your physician, is one of a large group of nonsteroidal anti-inflammatory drugs (also called NSAIDs) and is used to treat the symptoms of certain types of arthritis. It helps to relieve joint pain, swelling, stiffness and fever by reducing the production of certain substances (prostaglandins) and by helping to control inflammation. NSAIDs do not cure arthritis, but they promote suppression of the inflammation and the tissue-damaging effects resulting from this inflammation. This medicine will help you only as long as you continue to take it.

You should take Diclotec only as directed by your physician. Do not take more of it, do not take it more often and do not take it for a longer period of time than your physician ordered. Taking too much of any of these medicines may increase the chance of unwanted effects, especially if you are an elderly patient.

Be sure to take Diclotec regularly as prescribed. In some types of arthritis, up to two weeks may pass before you feel the full effects of this medicine. During treatment, your physician may decide to adjust the dosage according to your response to the medication.

Stomach upset is one of the common problems with NSAIDs. To lessen stomach upset, diclofenac tablets should be taken immediately after a meal or with food or milk. Also, you should remain standing or sitting upright (i.e., do not lie down) for about 15 to 30 minutes after taking the medicine. This helps to prevent irritation that may lead to trouble swallowing. If stomach upset (indigestion, nausea, vomiting, stomach pain or diarrhea) occurs and continues, contact your physician.

Do not take ASA (acetylsalicylic acid), ASA-containing compounds or other drugs used to relieve symptoms of arthritis while taking Diclotec unless directed to do so by your physician.

If you are prescribed this medication for use over a long period of time, your physician will check your health during regular visits to assess your progress and to ensure that this medicine is not causing unwanted effects.

Use whole suppositories. Do not split or use portions of suppositories. The maximum daily dose of diclofenac sodium is 150 mg.

Always Remember: The risks of taking this medication must be weighed against the benefits it will have.

Before taking this medication tell your physician and pharmacist if you:

- or a family member are allergic to or have had a reaction to diclofenac sodium or other anti-inflammatory drugs (such as acetylsalicylic acid (ASA), diflunisal, fenoprofen, fluriprofen, ibuprofen, indomethacin, ketoprofen, mefenamic acid, piroxicam, tiaprofenic acid, tolmetin, nabumetone or tenoxicam) manifesting itself by increased sinusitis, hives, the initiating or worsening of asthma or anaphylaxis (sudden collapse);
- or a family member has had asthma, nasal polyps, chronic sinusitis or chronic urticaria (hives);
- have a history of stomach upset, ulcers, liver or kidney diseases;
- have blood or urine abnormalities;
- have high blood pressure;
- have diabetes;
- are on any special diet, such as a low-sodium or low-sugar diet;
- are pregnant or intend to become pregnant while taking this medication;
- are breast-feeding or intend to breast-feed while taking this medication;
- are taking any other medication (either prescription or nonprescription) such as other NSAIDs, high blood pressure medication, blood thinners, corticosteroids, methotrexate, cyclosporin, lithium, phenytoin;
- have any other medical problem(s) such as alcohol abuse, bleeding problems, etc.;
- had any side effects from other medicine that you have taken in the past for arthritis, rheumatism or sore joints.

While taking this medication:

- tell any other physician, dentist or pharmacist that you consult or see, that you are taking this medication;
- some NSAIDs may cause drowsiness or fatigue in some people taking them. Be cautious about driving or participating in activities that require alertness if you are drowsy, dizzy or lightheaded after taking this medication;
- check with your physician if you are not getting any relief of your arthritis or if any problems develop;
- report any untoward reactions to your physician. This is very important as it will aid in the early detection and prevention of potential complications;
- stomach problems may be more likely to occur if you drink alcoholic beverages. Therefore, do not drink alcoholic beverages while taking this medication;
- check with your physician immediately if you experience unexpected weakness while taking this medication, or if you vomit any blood or have dark or bloody stools;
- some people may become more sensitive to sunlight than they are normally. Exposure to sunlight or sunlamps, even for brief periods of time, may cause sunburn, blisters on the skin, skin rash, redness, itching or discoloration; or vision changes. If you have a reaction from the sun, check with your physician;
- check with your physician immediately if chills, fever, muscle aches or pains, or other flu-like symptoms occur, especially if they occur shortly before, or together with, a skin rash. Very rarely, these effects may be the first signs of a serious reaction to this medication;
- **Your regular medical checkups are essential.**

Side effects of this medication: Along with its beneficial effects, diclofenac sodium, like other NSAID drugs, may cause some undesirable reactions especially when used for a long time or in large doses.

Elderly, frail or debilitated patients often seem to experience more frequent or more severe side effects.

Although not all of these side effects are common, when they do occur they may require medical attention.

Check with your physician immediately if any of the following are noted:

- bloody or black tarry stools;
- shortness of breath, wheezing, any trouble in breathing or tightness in the chest;
- skin rash, hives, swelling or itching;
- vomiting or persistent indigestion, nausea, stomach pain or diarrhea;
- yellow discoloration of the skin or eyes;
- any changes in the amount or color of your urine (dark red or brown);
- any pain or difficulty experienced while urinating;
- swelling of the feet or lower legs;
- headache, malaise, fatigue, loss of appetite;
- blurred vision or any visual disturbance;
- mental confusion, depression, dizziness, lightheadedness;
- hearing problems;
- tenderness just under your ribs on your right side;
- ''flu-like'' symptoms;
- rectal itching or bleeding.

Other side effects not listed above may also occur in some patients. If you notice any other effects, check with your physician.

Dosing: Diclotec suppositories 50 mg and 100 mg: 50 or 100 mg may be given as substitute for the last of the 3 oral daily doses, to a maximum dose of 150 mg per day.

Use whole suppositories. Do not split or use portions of suppositories. Make sure that the wrapping is fully removed before inserting the suppository into the rectum. Do not take suppositories by mouth.

Not recommended for use in patients under 16 years of age.

Storage: Diclotec 50 and 100 mg suppositories are torpedo-shaped with a smooth surface, and yellowish-white color. Boxes of 30 suppositories. Suppositories should be protected from light and elevated humidity. Keep away from excessive heat. Store between 15 to 30°C.

Diclotec is not recommended for use in patients under 16 years of age since safety and effectiveness have not been established.

Do not keep outdated medicine or medicine no longer needed.

Keep this product and all medicine out of the reach of children.

This medication has been prescribed for your medical problem. Do not give it to anyone else.

If you require more information on this drug, consult your physician or pharmacist.

☐ DIDROCAL® Ⓟ

Procter & Gamble Pharmaceuticals

Etidronate Disodium
Calcium Carbonate

Bone Metabolism Regulator

Information for the Patient: How to take Didrocal: Very important information on Bone Metabolism Regulator. Read before taking the medicine. Keep this leaflet for future reference.

Inside Package: first card–white tablets; 3 cards–blue tablets; refill reminder card; last card–blue tablets.

Didrocal Therapy: Your doctor has prescribed the Didrocal therapy for your postmenopausal osteoporosis. While this booklet contains important information about the Didrocal therapy, it does not contain all information about this product.

If you have any questions on the use of the Didrocal therapy, you should ask your doctor or pharmacist.

How to Take the Didrocal Therapy (this Didrocal package provides 90 days of therapy):

1. Start the therapy with the first card (white tablets).
   1) Begin in the top row on Monday.
   2) Take 1 tablet with plenty of water at bedtime each day for 14 days. Take at least 2 hours before or after eating.
   3) Finish all white tablets before taking any blue tablets.

Do not take the white tablet within 2 hours of taking the foods or medicines below. They will stop the white tablet from working properly.

- Food, especially food high in calcium, such as milk or milk products
- Antacids
- Vitamins with mineral supplements such as iron
- Calcium supplements
- Laxatives containing magnesium

2. Then, start the next card (blue tablets).
   1) Begin in the top row on Monday. If the tablet is hard to swallow, crush or chew it.
   2) Take 1 tablet with plenty of water at bedtime each day, with or without food. (A few people have low stomach acid. If you do, you should take the blue tablet with food. Ask your doctor or pharmacist for more information.)
   3) Finish all blue tablets on each card before going to the next card.

3. Read the refill reminder card. Ask you doctor or pharmacist about ordering your refill.

4. Finish with the last card (blue tablets). If you follow the directions above, you will finish this package on a Saturday. Start your refill on Monday.

5. Get your refill from your pharmacist.

What is Osteoporosis? Osteoporosis is a bone thinning disease that causes your bones to become weak and more likely to break. As the bones weaken, people with osteoporosis can experience:

- Broken bones
- Pain
- Loss of height
- Humped back

At first, osteoporosis works ''silently'', with no symptoms you can feel. Over time, however, it produces a harmful level of bone loss—as much as 30 to 40%. When this occurs, your bones become weak. They can break (fracture) during normal activities or from minor falls.

Broken bones in the back (spinal fractures) from osteoporosis are very common. Spinal fractures often cause back pain, loss of height, and a humped back. Your body cannot restore spinal fractures to normal.

Osteoporosis can also lead to fractures of the hip or wrist. A hip fracture can cause you to be hospitalized. Later you may need help with daily activities.

The good news is that you and your doctor can help stop bone loss in your spine, from osteoporosis, with the Didrocal therapy.

How Your Bones Become Weak: To understand how the Didrocal therapy works, it is important to understand how your body lost bone mass.

Bone is living tissue that your body constantly renews. In this normal process, your body breaks down old bone tissue and replaces it with new bone. After menopause, your body goes through many changes. One change is that your body may remove more bone than it forms. The resulting bone loss can make your bones weak and likely to break. This is **osteoporosis.**

How the Didrocal Therapy Can Help You: To treat your osteoporosis, your doctor has prescribed the Didrocal therapy. The Didrocal therapy is the first nonhormonal osteoporosis treatment that increases spinal bone mass.

Proven Successful: Doctors tested the Didrocal therapy in long-term studies in women with osteoporosis. The therapy successfully **increased** bone mass in the spine. Without therapy, women past menopause may **lose** bone mass every year. This loss weakens bones and makes them more likely to break.

Your Role: To increase your spinal bone mass, your doctor has prescribed the Didrocal therapy. Follow the instructions in this booklet. For the therapy to work properly, you must take it for as long as your doctor prescribes. Remember, it took many years for your bones to become thin and weak. Remember to refill your prescription as directed.

The Didrocal therapy consists of two different tablets. You must take them in the right order for the treatment to work properly.

The white tablets help stop the destructive process that weakens your bones after menopause.

The blue tablets contain calcium that your body needs to harden new bone.

Questions about Osteoporosis and the Didrocal Therapy:

Q Does the Didrocal therapy have any side effects?

A With any medication, there is some chance of side effects. In research studies, the most commonly reported side effects are stomach problems, such as nausea and diarrhea. Some Didrocal patients have reported other, less common, side effects. **If you have any symptoms that you think are not normal, let your doctor know right away.**

Q What if I made a mistake and drank milk or any other dairy products when I took a white tablet?

A You should not expect any problem from taking them together. The calcium in milk keeps your body from absorbing the medication. Thus, the medication cannot work properly. Next time, please take it with water.

Q Does either the white or blue tablet contain lactose?

A No. Neither tablet contains any lactose.

Q Why must I take the white and blue tablets separately?

A The Didrocal therapy stops **bone** loss with the white tablets and hardens new bone with the blue tablets. The blue tablets will stop the white tablets from working if you take them together. Please follow the directions carefully.

Q Can't I just take calcium tablets to treat my osteoporosis?

A Calcium tablets alone have not been proven as effective in the treatment of osteoporosis as the Didrocal therapy. The Didrocal therapy has been shown to stop bone loss **and** increase spinal bone mass.

Q Why should I start the therapy on a Monday?

A The tablet cards start on Monday. This will help you remember to take your tablet each day. If you start on a day other than Monday, take the tablet labelled for that day. Take 1 tablet each day. Finish all the tablets on a card before starting the next card.

Didrocal (cont'd)

Q What if I miss a day (or more) of the treatment?

A Do not take 2 tablets the same day. Take 1 tablet on the day you remember and continue with the therapy. Be sure to finish all the tablets on a card before you begin the tablets on the next card.

Q Will the Didrocal therapy relieve my pain?

A The Didrocal therapy is not a pain reliever. It can stop bone loss and increase your spinal bone mass. You should tell your doctor if you have back pain. He or she can advise you of what to take for relief.

Q If I already have a humped back, will I be able to stand up straight after taking the Didrocal therapy?

A The Didrocal therapy cannot help you stand up straight. No medicine can undo spinal fractures. However, if you stay on this therapy, as your doctor has prescribed, you can stop further bone loss from osteoporosis.

Q How long should I stay on the Didrocal therapy?

A Your doctor will determine how long you should stay on the therapy. Be sure to refill your prescription just before you finish each package. Stay on the therapy for as long as your doctor prescribes.

While this booklet contains important information about the Didrocal therapy, it does not contain all information about this product.

If you have any questions on the use of the Didrocal therapy, you should ask your doctor or pharmacist.

☐ DIFFERIN® Ⓟ

Galderma

Adapalene

Acne Therapy

Information for the Patient: What is Differin? Differin (adapalene) is a cream or gel that contains a drug used to treat acne.

What is acne? Acne is a disease of the oil glands that are found on your face, back and chest. So, your acne can occur on any or all these areas. Acne begins when a plug made of skin and oil forms in the pore of one of these oil glands. The plug appears as a blackhead or whitehead on your skin. These plugs are not due to dirt or lack of washing. Too much washing and scrubbing with strong cleansers will not stop these plugs from forming and in fact may make your acne worse. Any area with acne should be washed with a gentle cleanser. After the plug forms, the oil from the gland cannot get out of the pore and bacteria can grow in the plugged gland. This can lead to redness and swelling of the skin around the gland forming a pimple. Your doctor can explain more to you about your acne if you wish.

How does Differin work? Differin cream or gel works by unplugging your blocked oil glands and by preventing these plugs from forming in the first place. Your acne should improve in 4 to 8 weeks and you should see more improvement as you continue to use Differin.

How should I use Differin? Use Differin once a day at night before you go to bed. You should first wash your face with a gentle cleanser and blot it dry with a soft towel — do not rub your face. Then apply a thin film of Differin to the areas where you have acne. Keep Differin away from your eyes, lips and the corners of your nose. Use only the amount of Differin your doctor recommends. Using more Differin will not make it work better or faster.

Are there any special instructions for using Differin? Yes, you should know some other things.

- **If you are a female of child-bearing years, you should only use Differin after consulting your doctor about contraceptive counselling. If you are pregnant, you should discontinue use of Differin.**
- Do not use Differin if you have eczema or severely irritated skin (e.g., seborrheic dermatitis).
- Do not be discouraged if Differin causes some redness, burning or peeling when you first start to use it (2 to 4 weeks). This happens when your skin is adjusting to Differin's action of unplugging clogged pores. If these problems continue to happen or if they are getting worse, talk to your doctor.
- Before you go out in the sun, use a good sunscreen (SPF of 15 or higher) that is designed not to clog pores (noncomedogenic).
- Avoid using oily makeup or creams, products that make your skin dry or peel, and any products with alcohol. These may make your acne worse.
- Do not use any other acne medicines with Differin unless your doctor recommends them.
- **Your doctor has given you Differin for your use only. Do not allow anyone else to use it.**

☐ DIFLUCAN-150™ Ⓟ

Pfizer

Fluconazole

Antifungal Agent

Information for the Patient: Indication: Your doctor has prescribed Diflucan-150 (fluconazole) for a vaginal yeast (fungal) infection.

Diflucan 150 is used for the treatment of vaginal yeast infection and is taken orally. Diflucan is convenient because one capsule taken by mouth provides a full course of therapy.

How to Take Diflucan-150: Diflucan-150 may be taken anytime day or night, with or without meals so you should take the one capsule of Diflucan-150 **by mouth immediately** to ensure the earliest possible relief from the infection and its symptoms.

When to Expect Relief of Symptoms: Clearing a yeast infection does take time. Although Diflucan-150 is taken only once, Diflucan-150 remains active in your body for several days.

Most patients can expect to see symptom relief begin within 24 hours after taking the capsule. As Diflucan-150 works to cure the infection, symptoms will lessen and eventually disappear. If your symptoms have not improved within 3 to 5 days, contact your doctor.

Possible Side Effects of this Medication: In clinical studies of Diflucan-150, the most common side effects were headache, nausea, abdominal pain, and diarrhea. Most reported side effects were mild to moderate in nature.

Very infrequently, some patients develop skin eruptions or allergy symptoms such as hives after they take this drug. Rarely, severe allergic reactions have occurred.

Cautions: You should not take Diflucan-150 if you ever had an allergic reaction to it or to other antifungal drugs of the same family. If you are in doubt, talk to your doctor or pharmacist.

If you are pregnant, or think you may be pregnant, or if you are nursing do not take this medication except on the advice of a physician.

If you could become pregnant while taking Diflucan-150, you should consider using a reliable means of contraception, because the possible effects of this medication on a developing fetus are not known. This is true of many medications.

If you take drugs containing antihistaminic preparations such as terfenadine (Seldane) or astemizole (Hismanal), consult your doctor before taking Diflucan-150.

Also inform your doctor if you take oral medicine for diabetes, epilepsy or if you take blood-thinning medication.

Nonmedicinal ingredients: Diflucan-150 capsule contains the following nonmedicinal ingredients: colloidal silicon dioxide, lactose, magnesium stearate, maize starch and sodium lauryl sulfate; the capsule shell contains gelatin and titanium dioxide.

Storage: Store between 15 to 30°C.

If you have any questions, or for more information about Diflucan-150 and the treatment of vaginal yeast infections, ask your doctor or pharmacist.

☐ DIOVAN® Ⓟ

Novartis Pharmaceuticals

Valsartan

Angiotensin II AT_1 Receptor Blocker

Information for the Patient: Before you use Diovan (valsartan), please read this leaflet carefully because it contains important information about this medicine. If you have further questions or special concerns, ask your doctor or pharmacist.

What is Diovan? Diovan capsules contain the active substance valsartan. Diovan also contains the following nonmedicinal ingredients: microcrystalline cellulose, polyvidone, sodium lauryl sulfate, crospovidone and magnesium stearate. The capsule shell contains: gelatin, black iron oxide, red iron oxide and titanium dioxide. If you are on a special diet, or if you are allergic to any substance, ask your doctor or pharmacist whether any of these ingredients may cause a problem.

Diovan belongs to a new class of medicines known as angiotensin II AT_1 receptor blocker, which help to control high blood pressure. Angiotensin II is a natural hormone produced in the body, and is part of your body's system that usually keeps blood pressure at normal levels. One function of angiotensin II is to increase blood pressure, usually when it becomes too low. Diovan works by blocking the effect of angiotensin II. As a result, blood pressure is lowered.

Do I really need to treat my high blood pressure? I feel fine! High blood pressure increases the workload of the heart and arteries. If this condition continues for a long time, damage to the blood vessels of the brain, heart, and kidneys can occur, and may eventually result in a stroke, heart failure or kidney failure. High blood pressure also increases the risk of heart attacks. Reducing your blood pressure decreases your risk of developing these illnesses.

Patients who have high blood pressure often do not notice any signs or symptoms of this condition. Indeed, many may feel quite normal for a long time. So even though you are feeling well, your health may be getting worse. This makes it all the more important for you to continue your treatment program and to keep your appointments with your doctor.

Remember that this medicine does not cure your high blood pressure; it only may help to control it. Therefore, if you want to lower your blood pressure and keep it down, you must continue to take Diovan as directed.

Using Diovan Safely: You should not take Diovan if:
- you have ever had an unusual or allergic reaction to valsartan or to any other component of this product,
- you are pregnant (see below).

Diovan is not recommended for children.

What does your doctor need to know about you? To be sure that you can use Diovan safely your doctor must know whether you have certain medical conditions. Before taking Diovan make sure your doctor knows if you:
- have a serious kidney or liver disease,
- are suffering from vomiting or diarrhea.

Before taking Diovan make sure your doctor knows about all the medications you are taking. It may be necessary to change the dose, take other precautions, or perhaps stop one of the medicines. This applies to both prescription and nonprescription medicines, especially:
- medicines used to lower blood pressure, including diuretics (water pills),
- potassium-sparing medicines, potassium supplements or salt substitutes containing potassium,
- lithium therapy.

Are you pregnant or breast-feeding? Do not take Diovan if you are pregnant. Similar medicines were associated with serious harm to fetuses when they were taken after the first 3 months of pregnancy. (It is not known if they are harmful during the first 3 months). It is therefore important to tell your doctor immediately if you think you may have become pregnant, or planning to become pregnant.

Although it is not known whether Diovan can pass into human breast milk, this does happen in animals. Therefore do not breast-feed during treatment. Tell your doctor if you are breast-feeding, so that other treatment options can be tried.

What if you drive a vehicle or use machinery? Like many other medicines used to treat high blood pressure, Diovan may rarely cause dizziness and affect your concentration. So before you drive a vehicle, use machinery, or do other things that need concentration, make sure you know how you react to the effects of Diovan.

How to Take Diovan: Usual Dosage: The usual dosage is one 80 mg capsule once a day. In some cases, your doctor may prescribe a higher dose (e.g., the 160 mg capsule) or prescribe it together with another medicine (e.g., a diuretic).

You can take Diovan with or without food, but it should be taken the same way each day.

What happens if a dose is missed? Try to take your dose at the same time each day, preferably in the morning. However, if you have completely forgotten to take your dose during the day, carry on with the next one at the usual time. Do not double doses.

What to do in case of overdose? If you experience severe dizziness and/or fainting, contact your doctor immediately so that medical attention may be given promptly.

Side Effects: Like all medicines, Diovan may cause unwanted reactions, so-called side effects. Most patients do not experience side effects from Diovan, however, some patients may experience dizziness, lightheadedness or rash including hives. Tell your physician or pharmacist promptly about these or any unusual symptoms.

If you develop an allergic reaction involving swelling of the face, lips, and/or tongue, stop taking Diovan and contact your physician immediately.

Expiry Date: Do not take Diovan past the expiry date shown on the pack.

How to Store Diovan: Store your Diovan capsules in a dry place at room temperature and avoid temperatures above 30°C.

Always Remember: This medicine has been prescribed to you for your current medical problem only. Do not give it to other people.

It is very important that you take this medicine exactly as your doctor tells you in order to get the best results and reduce the chance of side effects.

Keep this medicine out of the reach of children.

□ DOLOBID® ℞

Frosst

Diflunisal

Analgesic—Anti-inflammatory

Information for the Patient: Dolobid is the brand name of Frosst for diflunisal.

Purpose of this Medicine: Dolobid, which has been prescribed to you by your physician, is one of a large group of nonsteroidal anti-inflammatory drugs (NSAIDs) and is used to treat the symptoms of certain types of arthritis, or relief of mild to moderate pain accompanied by inflammation. It helps to relieve joint pain, swelling, stiffness and fever by reducing the production of certain substances (prostaglandins) and helping to control inflammation and other body reactions.

Important Notice: Advise your physician before you take Dolobid: If you ever had an allergic reaction (especially difficulty breathing, a runny nose, skin rashes or hives) to Dolobid, to acetylsalicylic acid (ASA) (ASA is the active ingredient of many pain and fever preparations that can be sold without prescription), or to any other anti-inflammatory medication used in the treatment of arthritis such as diclofenac, fenoprofen, flurbiprofen, ibuprofen, indomethacin, ketoprofen, mefenamic acid, piroxicam, sulindac, tiaprofenic acid or tolmetin.

A previous allergic reaction to one of these could increase the risk of an allergic reaction to Dolobid.
- If you ever had an ulcer, with or without bleeding, of the stomach, duodenum, or any part of the digestive tract, liver or kidney diseases or any other medical problems.
- If you are taking other medications (prescription or nonprescription drugs) your physician will advise you on the appropriate course of action.

Note also that Dolobid is not recommended for use during pregnancy and that breast-feeding should not be undertaken while on Dolobid.

Availability: Dolobid is available for oral administration as tablets containing 500 mg (oranged colored) of the active ingredient, diflunisal and the following nonmedicinal ingredients: cellulose, FD & C Yellow #6 aluminum lake, hydroxypropyl cellulose, hydroxypropyl methylcellulose, magnesium stearate, starch, talc and titanium dioxide.

How to use this medicine:
- Tablets should be swallowed in whole, not crushed or chewed. To lessen stomach upset, take this medicine immediately after a meal or with food or milk. If stomach upset (indigestion, nausea, vomiting, stomach pain or diarrhea) occurs and continues, contact your physician.
- **Please adhere to the dosage and administration instructions which your physician has given you.**
- Do not take more of it, do not take it more often, and do not take it for a longer period of time than your physician prescribed.
- If you are taking Dolobid to relieve arthritis, you must take it regularly as prescribed by your physician. In some types of arthritis, up to 2 weeks may pass before you begin to feel better and up to 1 month may pass before you feel the full effects of this medicine. During treatment, your physician may decide to adjust the dosage according to your response to this medication.

If you miss a dose: If you miss a dose of Dolobid and remember within an hour or so, take it right away. Then go back to your regular dosing schedule.

Dolobid (cont'd)

But if you do not remember until later, do not take the missed dose at all and do not double the next one. Instead, go back to your regular dosing schedule.

Do not take ASA (acetylsalicylic acid), ASA-containing compounds or other drugs used to relieve symptoms of arthritis while taking Dolobid unless directed to do so by your physician.

If you are prescribed this medication for use over a long period of time, your physician will check your health during regular visits to assess your progress and to ensure that this medication is not causing unwanted effects.

Along with its beneficial effects, Dolobid like other NSAID drugs, may cause some undesirable reactions. Elderly, frail or debilitated patients often seem to experience more frequent or more severe side effects. Although not all of these side effects are common, when they do occur they may require medical attention. **Check with your physician immediately if any of the following are noted:** bloody or black tarry stools; shortness of breath, wheezing, any trouble in breathing or tightness in the chest; skin rash, swelling, hives or itching; indigestion, nausea, vomiting, stomach pain or diarrhea; yellow discoloration of the skin or eyes, with or without fatigue; any changes in the amount or color of your urine (such as dark; red or brown); swelling of the feet or lower legs; blurred vision or any visual disturbance; mental confusion, depression, dizziness, lightheadedness; hearing problems.

While taking this medication:

- tell any other physician, dentist or pharmacist that you consult or see, that you are taking this medication;
- be cautious about driving or participating in activities that require alertness if you are drowsy, dizzy or lightheaded after taking this medication;
- check with your physician if you are not getting any relief or if any problems develop;
- report any untoward reactions to your physician. This is very important as it will aid in the early detection and prevention of potential complications;
- your regular medical checkups are essential;
- if you require more information on this drug, consult your physician or pharmacist.

Keep this medication, and all others, out of the reach of children.

☐ DOVONEX®

Leo

Calcipotriol

Topical Nonsteroidal Antipsoriatic

Information for the Patient: This leaflet is intended to give you some important information about using Dovonex in the treatment of your psoriasis. If you have any questions please talk to your doctor or pharmacist.

What is Dovonex? Dovonex contains calcipotriol (50 μg/g or 50 μg/mL). Calcipotriol is designed to control the excessive production of skin cells in areas affected by psoriasis and has proven benefits in the treatment of this condition.

Dovonex cream and ointment have been developed as smooth preparations making them easy to use. Dovonex scalp solution is a colorless, slightly viscous solution.

Before Using your Cream, Ointment or Scalp Solution: Tell your doctor:

- If you are pregnant or breast-feeding or if you become pregnant during your treatment.

Using your Cream, Ointment or Scalp Solution: How Should I Use Dovonex?

- **Cream or Ointment:** Remove the cap and check that the aluminum seal is intact before first use. To break the seal, reverse the cap and pierce. Dovonex should be applied to the areas of your skin affected by psoriasis and gently rubbed in.
  Scalp Solution: Remove the cap and place the nozzle through the hair next to the scalp. Squeeze the bottle gently and apply a few drops on to the affected area. Rub in gently with your fingertips. One or two drops should cover the area of a postage stamp.
- Wash your hands after using Dovonex to avoid inadvertent transfer to your face from other body parts. Your usual clothes may then be worn as Dovonex need not be specially covered. Do not worry if you accidentally get some Dovonex on the surrounding normal skin, but wash it off if it spreads too far.
- Dovonex should not be used on the face. If it accidentally gets on your face, wash it off. If you get the scalp solution in your eye, bathe the eye with water.
- After washing your hair, dry it thoroughly before using the scalp solution. Do not wash your hair just after using Dovonex scalp solution or it will wash out.
- Infants: Dovonex ointment and cream are not recommended for use in infants under 2 years of age. Use beneath diapers has not been investigated and should be avoided as diapers may be occlusive.
- You must not use more than the recommended weekly amount of Dovonex:

Age (years)	Dose (g/week)
2-5	25
6-10	50
11-14	75
Adults (over 14)	100

The maximum weekly dose of Donovex cream and/or ointment for children is based on the adult dose of 100 g/week adjusted for body surface area (maximum 50 g/week/m²). The dosage regimen is based on the following expected body surface area: 2 to 5 years: 0.5 m² (25% of adult); 6 to 10 years: 1.0 m² (50% of adult); 11 to 14 years: 1.5 m² (75% of adult).

When cream, ointment or scalp solution are used together, the total dose of calcipotriol should not exceed the recommended weekly amount for each age group (i.e., 2 to 5 years: 1.25 mg; 6 to 10 years: 2.5 mg; 11 to 14 years: 3.75 mg; adults: 5 mg in any week). As an example, adults should not use more than one 30 mL bottle of scalp solution plus one 60 g tube of ointment or cream.

- Administration to children should be supervised by a responsible individual to ensure proper administration and dosage.
- Dovonex is usually used twice a day (morning and night). Most patients will begin to see an improvement within 2 weeks. Follow your doctor's instructions carefully.

What should I do if I forget to use my Dovonex?

- If you forget to use your Dovonex at the right time, use it as soon as you remember. Then go on as before.

After using your Dovonex:

- Dovonex may cause irritation of your skin for a short while after you have applied it. Try not to scratch the area.
- See your doctor if the irritation persists, if you get a facial rash or if Dovonex upsets you in any other way.

Storing your Dovonex:

- Keep Dovonex in a safe place where children cannot reach it.
- Store at room temperature (cream: between 15 and 30°C; ointment: between 15 and 25°C); scalp solution: below 25°C.
- Dovonex has an expiry date marked on the bottom of each tube or bottle. Please do not use the contents after this date.

☐ DPE™

Alcon

Dipivefrin HCl

Glaucoma Therapy

Information for the Patient: To avoid contamination, do not touch tip of container to the eye, eyelid, or any surface.

☐ DUOVENT® UDV

Boehringer Ingelheim

Ipratropium Bromide—Fenoterol Hydrobromide

Bronchodilator

Information for the Patient: Please read this leaflet carefully before you use Duovent UDV. It provides a summary of the information that you should know about Duovent UDV, and how it should be used. If after reading this information you still have questions, please be sure to talk to your doctor or pharmacist.

What is Duovent UDV? Duovent UDV Inhalation solution: Each plastic unit dose vial (UDV) contains a total of 0.5 mg of ipratropium bromide and 1.25 mg fenoterol hydrobromide in four millilitres (4 mL) of sodium chloride solution.

Duovent UDV is a combination of 2 bronchodilators (airway openers) in a solution that is inhaled using a nebulizer. You may already be familiar with one or both of these bronchodilators, since they are also available separately, with a prescription, as Atrovent (ipratropium bromide) and Berotec (fenoterol hydrobromide). Duovent UDV can only be obtained with a prescription from your doctor.

Why has your doctor prescribed Duovent UDV? Your doctor has prescribed Duovent UDV to suit you and your condition. It can relieve wheezing, coughing, chest tightness and/or shortness of breath if you have an acute attack of asthma or COPD (Chronic Obstructive Pulmonary Disease which includes chronic bronchitis and emphysema). Duovent works by relaxing the muscle surrounding the bronchioles (airways in the lungs) and therefore helps to ease breathing problems.

What is Asthma? Asthma is a disease in which the airways can become temporarily narrowed, leading to breathing difficulties. This narrowing of the airways is due to inflammation, which causes swelling and irritation of the airways and tightening of the muscles around the airways. The narrowed airways can be relieved with the help of medication.

What is COPD? COPD is a type of lung disease in which there is a permanent narrowing of the airways, leading to breathing difficulties. In many patients, this narrowing of the airways is a result of many years of cigarette smoking. In many patients that quit smoking, there are less symptoms and the course of the disease slows down or stops.

It is important to know that the treatment of asthma and COPD may be different for each patient. Your doctor will most likely discuss with you the best plan for the treatment of your particular condition. This plan may include taking other medication(s) in addition to Duovent UDV. It is necessary that you follow your doctor's directions for the treatment of your condition. If you have any questions about how you should treat your condition at home, you should consult your doctor.

What should you tell your doctor before you use Duovent UDV? You should tell your doctor if any of the following apply to you, **before** you use Duovent UDV.

- you are pregnant or intend to become pregnant
- you are breast-feeding
- you have eye problems such as glaucoma or eye pain
- you are taking other medications, including those you can buy without a prescription and including eye drops
- you have special allergies or reactions to foods or drugs
- you have other health problems such as difficult urination, enlarged prostate, heart or blood vessel disease, high blood pressure, diabetes mellitus

When should you use Duovent UDV? Your doctor will recommend when and how often you should use Duovent UDV (see "Why has your doctor prescribed Duovent UDV?" and "How to use Duovent UDV"). You must also follow any other directions that your doctor has given you for the treatment and/or monitoring of your condition. This **may** include taking other medication(s) in addition to Duovent UDV.

If you have asthma and you find that you are needing to use Duovent UDV on a regular, daily basis, but you are not taking other medication(s) that control the inflammation of the airways (anti-inflammatory medication), you should contact your doctor so that your treatment can be re-evaluated.

If Duovent UDV does not relieve your symptoms within 10 minutes after the nebulization is finished, if the dosage of medication(s) recommended by your doctor does not provide relief for longer than 3 hours, or if you experience a change of your symptoms, for example, more coughing, chest tightness, waking up at night, or increased usage of other relief medication (e.g., Ventolin), you should contact your doctor or go to the nearest hospital. These are signs that your condition may be worsening, and that you need to be reassessed by a doctor.

If you have COPD and Duovent UDV does not relieve your symptoms within 10 minutes after the nebulization is finished, or if the dosage of medication(s) recommended by your doctor does not provide relief for longer than 3 hours, you should contact your doctor or go to the nearest hospital. These are signs that your condition may be worsening, and that you need to be reassessed by a doctor.

Please remember:

- **Do not use a higher dose of Duovent UDV than your doctor has recommended;**
- **Do not use your nebulizer more often than your doctor has recommended.;**
- **Contact your doctor if you feel that you need more medication than he/she has recommended;**
- **Duovent UDV contains a beta agonist, and the taking of additional doses in the form of other single agent, beta agonists (fenoterol [Berotec], salbutamol [Ventolin] etc.) could lead to deleterious cardiovascular effects. If concomitant use is necessary, this should take place only under strict supervision.**

How to use Duovent UDV (see package insert for illustrations):

1) Separate one plastic vial from the strip by pulling it firmly.
2) Open the vial by twisting off the top. It is important that you use the contents of the vial **as soon as possible** after opening it.
3) Squeeze the plastic vial to empty its contents into your nebulizer chamber. If your doctor has instructed you to use less than the contents of one complete vial, use a syringe to transfer the necessary amount from the vial to the nebulizer chamber.
   Any solution left in the plastic vial must be thrown away.
4) Using a syringe, add sterile, preservative-free 0.9% sodium chloride solution to the chamber if you have been directed to do so by your pharmacist or doctor (sodium chloride solution may be added to fill your nebulizer chamber to a maximum of 5 mL).
5) Gently swirl the nebulizer chamber to mix the liquid, and connect it to the mouthpiece or face mask. Then connnect the nebulizer tube to the air pump or oxygen supply and begin therapy.
6) Breathe calmly and deeply through the mask or mouthpiece until no more mist is formed in the nebulizer chamber. This usually takes 10 to 15 minutes. **It is very important** to adjust the face mask, if required, to prevent the mist from getting in your eyes.
7) Follow the instructions provided by the nebulizer and air pump manufacturers for the proper care, maintenance and cleaning of the equipment. Keep the nebulizer, nebulizer tube and face mask clean to minimize microbial contamination.
8) The unit dose vials should be stored at room temperature (15 to 25°C) and protect from light and heat.

You must remember:

- Duovent UDV has been prescribed to treat **your** current condition. Do not give this medication to other people.
- **Do not** take any other medication without your doctor's advice. Tell any **other** doctor, dentist, or pharmacist with whom you consult that you are using Duovent UDV.
- **The solution is to be administered only using a nebulizer. DO NOT inject it or drink it.**
- **Do not let the nebulized mist get into your eyes. Patients with glaucoma should use swimming goggles to prevent nebulizer solution getting into the eyes.**
- **Keep this medication out of the reach of children.**
- Consult your doctor immediately if you experience any of the following:
  - Increased wheezing or tightness in the chest
  - Swelling of the tongue or lips
  - Difficulty in swallowing
  - Fast or irregular heartbeat
  - Blurred vision or pain in the eyes
  - Difficult or painful urination
  - Skin rash
- If you experience a dry mouth or bad taste, sucking a sour candy or rinsing your mouth may help. Check with your doctor if the dry mouth or bad taste persist, or if you experience constipation.
- Like any medication, Duovent UDV may cause unwanted effects along with the good effects. The most common side effects of Duovent UDV are tremor (shakiness), dry mouth/throat and a feeling that your heart is beating fast. If you experience any unusual or unwanted effects while you are using Duovent UDV, you should contact your doctor.
- Duovent UDV is a combination of 2 bronchodilators. Excessive use of bronchodilators may cause unwanted side effects (increased heart rate, low blood pressure and/or irregular heartbeat). Therefore do not take additional bronchodilators by inhalation with Duovent UDV unless instructed to do so by your doctor or pharmacist.

□ DUPHALAC®

Solvay Pharma

Lactulose Crystals

Laxative

Information for the Patient: Read this information carefully. It has been prepared by the makers of Duphalac to help you get the most

Duphalac (cont'd)

benefit from this product. It also contains general information about the proper use of laxatives and how to manage constipation with diet and lifestyle measures.

You can buy Duphalac without a prescription. But sometimes a doctor will ''prescribe'' this product and give you different instructions than are written here. If so, be sure to follow his or her advice—it is designed for **your** specific health condition. If you have **any** questions after reading this leaflet, be sure to talk to your pharmacist or doctor.

What is Duphalac? Duphalac is the brand name for a drug called ''lactulose'' (pronounced lack-two-lows). It belongs to the ''laxative'' group of drugs and is used to help relieve constipation. Duphalac is the crystal powder form of lactulose. It comes in small paper packets that fit into most pockets and purses. Each packet has a ''pre-measured'' amount of Duphalac, so you don't need to measure it yourself.

What is in a Duphalac packet? Each packet of Duphalac has about one level tablespoonful (15 mL) of crystal powder. Most of this is lactulose (10 g). The rest is small amounts of galactose (less than 2.2 g), lactose (less than 1.2 g), and other sugars (less than 1 g in total). Energy: approximately 2 kcal/packet.

How does Duphalac work? Duphalac works gradually, in several ways, to help relieve constipation.

At least 98 percent of the Duphalac you swallow reaches your colon (large bowel) unchanged. Once it's there, natural bacteria in your colon ''split'' lactulose into its ''active'' parts. These active parts help to increase the action of your bowel and keep water in your bowel so that your stools are moved through your bowels and are softer and easier to pass.

These actions happen gradually—most people find Duphalac starts to relieve constipation in about 24 to 48 hours.

Before you use Duphalac: Duphalac is safe for most people, most of the time. But there are a few times Duphalac **should not be used** without a doctor's advice. Check with your doctor before taking Duphalac if you:

- are on a ''low galactose'' diet—although less than two (2) percent of Duphalac goes into the rest of your body, it does contain galactose.
- have sugar diabetes (diabetes mellitus)—Duphalac contains a small amount of digestible sugars [galactose (less than 2.2 g), lactose (less than 1.2 g) and other sugars (less than 1 g in total)], and your doctor can tell you if this amount will affect control of your diabetes.
- are pregnant, or plan to become pregnant—no problems have been reported with this product, but as with any medicine, always check with your doctor before using a laxative.

Note: Be sure to also read the section ''Using Laxatives Wisely.'' It tells you about other times to check with a doctor before using **any** laxative.

How do I take Duphalac? There are two different ways to take Duphalac. You can either:

- Swallow the crystals dry, then drink a glass of liquid such as water or juice. Many people empty the packet directly into their mouth, but if you prefer to use a spoon, make sure you use an oversized spoon to avoid spilling any of the crystals.

  or
- Sprinkle the crystals on some food (such as cereal or yogurt) or mix the crystals with a glass of liquid (such as water or juice). Then eat or drink all of the food or liquid.

Different people need different amounts of Duphalac. To find the amount you need, start with 1 or 2 packets a day for at least 2 days. (Remember, Duphalac needs 24 to 48 hours to start working.) If you're not getting the relief you need after this time, you may increase your dose up to 3 or 4 packets a day, for another 2 or 3 days.

The most Duphalac you should take without your doctor's advice is 4 packets in a 24 hour period.

Regardless of the number of packets you use, you should take Duphalac once a day. For example, if you are using 2 packets a day, take both at the same time. You will not get faster or better relief by spreading your dose out over the day. For best results, you should take your dose at about the same time each day, for example with breakfast.

Are there any side effects or precautions I should know?

- Most people have few or no side effects from Duphalac. Bowel gas or cramping may occur with the first one or two doses, or when you increase the number of packets that you are using. This side effect usually lasts only a short while and should go away on its own.
- Diarrhea or very loose stools may be a sign you are using too much Duphalac for your system. If this happens, reduce the number of packets you're taking (for example, from 4 packets back to 2 packets) or stop taking it altogether. Be sure to ask your doctor or pharmacist if you have any questions about this—he or she can help you find the ''right'' amount of Duphalac for your needs.
- A few people have reported nausea while taking Duphalac. Nausea can also come with constipation, but let your doctor or pharmacist know if it continues or if it bothers you.
- Unless your doctor tells you to, it's best not to use other laxatives while taking Duphalac. Otherwise you won't be able to tell which laxative is helping, or which one is causing possible side effects.

Where should I keep Duphalac?

- Keep Duphalac at room temperature (between 10 and 25°C) until you are ready to use it. For example, don't keep it in the fridge or on top of a hot radiator.
- Keep Duphalac well out of sight and reach of children. As with all medicines, a locked location is best, especially since children may not think of a ''sprinkle powder'' as a medicine.

Using Laxatives Wisely: For most people, constipation is a short-term problem that's easy to correct with lifestyle measures, and perhaps an occasional laxative. But laxatives are not for everyone, and in some cases constipation may be a sign of some other health problem. Here are a few ''rules'' about how long to use laxatives in general and when to see a doctor about your symptoms.

- As with all laxatives, using too much, or using a laxative too often can create bowel dependency. No laxative should be used for more than one week unless your doctor tells you to. Even if the laxative is helping, stop the product to see if your bowel habits have returned to normal. And if you haven't had results after one week, see your doctor so he or she can examine possible causes for your constipation.
- Some types of constipation should always be checked by a doctor. For example, see your doctor if you have a sudden change in bowel habits that lasts more than two weeks, or that keeps coming back. It may not be serious, but it's best to have a doctor look for other possible causes before it becomes a problem.
- Other symptoms or health problems may affect which, if any, laxative is best to use. Do not use any type of laxative on your own if you have:
  - signs of possible appendicitis or an inflamed bowel (for example, pain in your stomach, side or bowel area, nausea, vomiting, severe cramping). Instead, check with your doctor as soon as you can.
  - bleeding from your rectum, or any blood in your stools. A doctor should be told about these symptoms right away.
  - had recent bowel surgery, or have any other bowel conditions such as ulcerative colitis or Crohn's disease. In these cases, a doctor should be the one to decide how to manage your constipation symptoms.

Note: This is not a complete list. Always tell your doctor about all symptoms you are experiencing and about all other medical conditions you have. Some laxatives may lead to other problems when certain conditions are present.

- Always tell your doctor, pharmacist and nurse about any laxative you are using. Some laxatives can interfere with the way other medicines work. Knowing what laxatives you're using also gives your doctor a better idea of what to do about symptoms you're having.
- Remember, **healthy** lifestyle habits are an important way to prevent and relieve constipation. Even if you are using a laxative, it's important to also have eating and bathroom habits that help encourage bowel movements.

Lifestyle Hints For Managing Constipation: Constipation can be caused by a number of things. Some of the more usual causes are:

1. Low fibre diet
2. Resisting the urge to have a bowel movement
3. Little physical activity
4. Stress
5. Pregnancy
6. Some types of medicine
7. Long-term laxative use

Fibre provides the bulk, or roughage, that helps the large intestines carry away body waste. Fibre also absorbs water, which keeps the stools soft and easier to move. Low fibre diets often result in less frequent movements and harder stools.

A full feeling and urge to contract the rectal muscles signal the need to pass stools. Resisting this urge often because it is the wrong time or place can cause the bowel reflexes to stop working reliably. As a result, stools may stay in the intestines too long, becoming hard and difficult to move.

Strong stomach and intestinal muscles assist in effective bowel movements. Since inactive lifestyles and inadequate exercise don't keep these muscles toned, natural bowel movements can be more difficult.

Stress can also affect bowel movements. Tension often causes people to tighten their muscles, which makes the natural contractions of a bowel movement more difficult.

Pregnancy is similar to an inactive lifestyle because it often results in reduced muscle tone in the abdominal muscles. While relaxation helps a bowel movement, too much relaxation or lack of muscle tone reduces the muscles' normal ability to move stools through the intestine.

Your intestines have a normal bacterial environment that helps form stools and creates the urges to move those stools. Some medications cause changes in the intestinal environment that result in reduced muscle action or hard stools. Your doctor or pharmacist can usually advise you of a drug's potential side effects.

What You Can Do To Avoid Constipation:

Develop a regular routine. ''Regularity'' can be achieved by setting aside the same time each day to relax for a bowel movement. Your body will become accustomed to this pattern of relaxation in time. If you can't have a movement, don't worry and don't strain.

Respond to your urges. Don't wait—by listening to your body right away, your bowel reflexes are more likely to become normal and reliable.

□ DURAGESIC® Ⓝ

Janssen-Ortho

Fentanyl

Opioid Analgesic

Information for the Patient: Duragesic (fentanyl transdermal system): Your doctor has prescribed Duragesic to help control the chronic (long-lasting) pain you are experiencing. This leaflet provides you with information about Duragesic and its use. Please read it carefully. If you have any questions or want more information, ask your doctor.

What is Duragesic? Duragesic is a thin, adhesive, rectangular patch that is placed on your skin. Duragesic delivers a medicine called fentanyl continuously through the skin and into the bloodstream to control your pain around-the-clock.

When Not to Use Duragesic: Do not use Duragesic if you know you are hypersensitive to the product.

Before Using Duragesic: Be sure to tell your doctor if you have any other medical conditions (such as diseases of the heart, lung, brain, liver and kidney), are pregnant or plan to become pregnant, are breast-feeding, and if you are taking any other medications. This will help your doctor decide whether you should use Duragesic and what extra care should be taken during its use.

Duragesic is not suited for the relief of pain following surgery. Duragesic is not for children unless your doctor has decided otherwise.

Possible Unwanted Effects: Like all medications, Duragesic may cause unwanted effects. Most unwanted effects appear during the first month of treatment. These effects may be more pronounced if you have a fever.

The most frequently reported unwanted effects are nausea, vomiting, tiredness, constipation, sweating, dry mouth, confusion and irritation at the application site.

Slowed breathing has been reported by a small number of patients using Duragesic. If this occurs, contact your doctor immediately.

Do not drive a car or operate machinery until you are sure that using the patch does not make you drowsy.

Avoid alcohol when you are using Duragesic since their combined effect may cause drowsiness. Drowsiness can also occur if Duragesic is taken with certain other medications (e.g., tranquilizers, sleeping pills). Be sure to inform your doctor when taking other medications.

Overdose: The most important sign of overdose is suppressed breathing. If a person is breathing abnormally slowly or weakly, remove the patch and call the doctor immediately. Meanwhile, keep the person awake by talking or by shaking him/her every now and then.

Where to Apply Duragesic: Select a **dry,** nonhairy area on your chest, back, flank or upper arm. If the area you choose has body hair, clip (do not shave) the hair close to the skin with scissors.

Do **not** put the patch on skin that is excessively oily, burned, broken out, cut, irritated or damaged in any way. If you need to clean the skin where the patch will be applied, use only clear water. Soaps, oils, lotions, alcohol or other products may irritate the skin under the patch.

How to Apply Duragesic (see package insert for illustrations):

Step 1. Each patch is sealed in its own protective pouch. Do not remove the patch from the pouch until you are ready to use it. When you are ready, tear open the pouch along one of the edges or at one of the ends.

Step 2. A stiff protective liner covers the sticky side of the patch—the side that will be put on your skin. Hold the liner at the edge and pull the patch from the liner. Try not to touch the sticky side of the patch. Throw away the liner.

Step 3. Immediately after you have removed the liner, apply the sticky side of the patch to a dry area of your chest, back, flank or upper arm. Press the patch firmly on your skin with the palm of your hand for about 30 seconds. Make sure the patch sticks well to your skin, especially around the edges.

Not all adhesive products stick to all patients. If the patch does not stick well, or loosens after application, tape the edges down with first aid tape. In the event that the patch falls off, discard it and put a new one on at a different skin site (see ''Disposing of Duragesic'')

Step 4. Wash your hands when you have finished applying the patch.

Step 5. Special labels are provided to help you remember when you last put on your patch. After putting on the patch, write the date and time on a label, then stick the label on the patch.

Step 6. After wearing the patch for 3 days, or as directed by your doctor, remove it (see Disposing of Duragesic). Then choose a **different** place on your skin to apply a new patch and repeat steps 1 to 5 in order.

What to Expect from Duragesic: Because the medicine in Duragesic is gradually released from the patch and slowly absorbed through the skin, do **not** expect immediate pain relief after you apply your **first** patch. During this initial period, your doctor may ask you to take additional pain medication until you experience the full benefits of Duragesic.

While most patients obtain adequate pain relief with Duragesic, your pain may vary and occasionally break through. This is not unusual. If this occurs, your doctor may prescribe additional pain medication.

It is important to let your doctor know whether or not your pain is under control. If you frequently need additional short-acting pain medication, or if pain is waking you at night, you may need a change in your Duragesic dose. **If you continue to have pain, call your doctor.**

Always follow your doctor's instructions carefully and ask advice before **changing** or **stopping** your Duragesic treatment.

Tolerance: Duragesic may lead to tolerance in the long run. It is therefore possible that your doctor will prescribe a higher dose of Duragesic after some time to produce the same result.

Water and Duragesic: You can bathe, swim or shower while you are wearing Duragesic. If the patch falls off, apply a new one, making sure the **new** skin area you choose is dry.

Heat and Duragesic: While wearing Duragesic you should **not** expose the patch area to sources of heat such as heating pads, electric blankets, heated waterbeds, heat lamps, saunas and hot tubs, intensive sunbathing, etc., as this may increase the drug's ability to go through the skin. This may also occur if you develop a fever.

Disposing of Duragesic: Before putting on a new Duragesic, remove the patch you have been wearing. Fold the used patch in half so the sticky side sticks to itself, and flush down the toilet immediately.

Dispose of any patches that are left over from your prescription as soon as they are no longer needed. Remove the left-over patches from their protective pouches and remove the protective liners. Fold the patches in half and flush down the toilet. Do **not** flush the pouch or protective liner.

Safety and Handling: Duragesic is sealed to keep the gel from getting on your hands or body. If the gel from the drug reservoir accidentally touches the skin, wash the area with large amounts of water. Do not use soap, alcohol, or other solvents to remove the gel because they may increase the drug's ability to go through the skin.

Do not cut or damage Duragesic. Duragesic will not work properly, or may not be safe, if it is damaged in any way.

Do not let anyone else use your Duragesic. If your patch dislodges and accidently sticks to the skin of another person, take the patch off immediately and call a doctor.

Do not exceed the dose recommended by your doctor.

Storage: Keep Duragesic out of the reach of children.

Keep Duragesic in its protective pouch until you are ready to use it. Store Duragesic between 15 and 25°C. Remember, the inside of your car can reach temperatures much higher than 25°C on a sunny day.

☐ EFFEXOR® Ⓟ
☐ EFFEXOR® XR Ⓟ

Wyeth-Ayerst

Venlafaxine HCl

Antidepressant

Information for the Patient: Please read this information carefully before you start to take your medicine, even if you have taken this drug before. Do not throw away this leaflet until you have finished your medicine as you may need to read it again. For further information or advice, please see your doctor or pharmacist.

What should you know about Effexor/Effexor XR?

- Effexor/Effexor XR (venlafaxine hydrochloride) belongs to the family of medicines called antidepressants.
- Effexor/Effexor XR has been prescribed to you by your doctor to relieve your symptoms of depression.

Before Taking Effexor/Effexor XR Your Doctor Has To Know:

- all your medical conditions, including a history of seizures, liver disease, heart or blood pressure problems;
- any medications (prescription or nonprescription) which you are taking, especially other antidepressants, sleeping pills or antianxiety drugs;
- if you are pregnant or thinking about becoming pregnant, or if you are breast-feeding;
- your habits of alcohol consumption.

How To Take Effexor/Effexor XR:

- It is very important that you take Effexor/Effexor XR exactly as your doctor has instructed.
- Never increase the amount of Effexor/Effexor XR you are taking unless your doctor tells you to.
- As with all antidepressants improvement with Effexor/Effexor XR is gradual. You may not have noticeable effect in the first few days of treatment. Some symptoms may begin to improve within about 2 weeks but significant improvement can take several weeks.
- Effexor/Effexor XR should be taken with food.

When Not To Use Effexor/Effexor XR:

- Do not use Effexor/Effexor XR if you are allergic to it or to any of the components of its formulation (see list of components at the end of this section). Stop taking the drug and contact your doctor immediately if you experience an allergic reaction or any severe or unusual side effects.

Precautions When Taking Effexor/Effexor XR:

- You may experience some side effects such as headache, nausea, dry mouth, constipation, sleepiness, dizziness, insomnia, sexual problems, weakness, sweating, nervousness. Consult your doctor if you experience these or other side effects, as the dose may have to be adjusted.
- If you happen to miss a dose, do not try to make up for it by doubling up on the dose next time. Just take your next regularly scheduled dose and try not to miss any more.
- Refrain from potentially hazardous tasks, such as driving a car or operating dangerous machines, until you are sure that this medication does not affect your mental alertness or physical coordination.

What To Do In Case Of Overdose:

- Contact your doctor or the nearest hospital emergency department, even though you may not feel sick.

How To Store Effexor/Effexor XR:

- Store **tablets** at room temperature (15 to 30°C), in a dry place. Store **capsules** at room temperature (15 to 30°C), in a dry place.
- Keep container tightly closed.
- Keep out of reach of children.

What Does Effexor Contain:

Effexor Tablets

- Effexor is available in tablets containing 37.5 and 75 mg venlafaxine as the active ingredient. Nonmedicinal ingredients include: microcrystalline cellulose NF, lactose NF hydrous, cosmetic brown iron oxide, ferric oxide NF yellow, sodium starch glycolate NF and magnesium stearate NF.

Effexor XR Capsules

- Effexor XR is available in capsules containing 37.5, 75 and 150 mg venlafaxine as the active ingredient. Nonmedicinal ingredients include: microcrystalline cellulose NF, hydroxypropyl methylcellulose USP, ethylcellulose NF, gelatin NF, red iron oxide*, yellow iron oxide*, titanium dioxide*, sicomet-85 black iron oxide**, White ink TekPrint SB-0007P***, Opacode Red ink S-1-15034****, talc.

*Present (in capsule) in all strengths.

**Present (in capsule) in 37.5 mg strength only.

***150 mg strength.

****37.5 and 75 mg strengths.

Who Manufactures Effexor/Effexor XR: Effexor tablets and Effexor XR capsules are manufactured by: Wyeth-Ayerst Canada Inc., 1025 Marcel Laurin Blvd., Saint Laurent, Quebec H4R 1J6 (514) 744-6771, (416) 225-7500.

Reminder: This medicine has been prescribed only for you. Do not give it to anybody else. If you have any further questions, please ask your doctor or pharmacist.

☐ EMLA® Cream/Patch

Astra

Lidocaine—Prilocaine

Topical Anesthetic for Dermal Analgesia

Information for the Patient: Important Information you Should Know About EMLA Cream: Before using EMLA cream, read this leaflet carefully. It contains general points about EMLA cream and should add to more specific advice from your doctor or pharmacist.

Please keep this leaflet to refer to until you have used up all your EMLA cream.

What is EMLA Cream Used for and How Does it Work? EMLA is the brand name for a topical anesthetic that contains the drugs lidocaine and prilocaine. Topical anesthetics are used to cause a temporary loss of sensation or numbness on the area where they are applied.

EMLA is used on healthy, unbroken skin prior to minor skin surgery, or when getting a needle or having blood taken. It may also be used on the genital mucosa and leg ulcers. The anesthetic effect of EMLA is optimal approximately 1 to 2 hours after it is applied to skin and within 5 to 10 minutes after it is applied to genital mucosa, and approximately 30 minutes after it is applied to a leg ulcer.

You may still experience sensations such as pressure and touch in the area where EMLA is applied.

What is in EMLA Cream? EMLA cream contains lidocaine and prilocaine as the active ingredients. It also contains carboxypolymethylene, polyoxyethylene hydrogenated castor oil, and sodium hydroxide.

Check with your doctor if you think you might be sensitive to any of the above ingredients.

What Should I Tell my Doctor or Pharmacist Before Using EMLA Cream? Tell your doctor or pharmacist:

- about all health problems you have now or have had in the past;
- about all other medicines you take, including ones you can buy without a prescription;
- if you have ever had a bad, unusual or allergic reaction to lidocaine or prilocaine, also available under the brand names Xylocaine (lidocaine) and Citanest (prilocaine);
- if you think you may be sensitive or allergic to other ingredients of the cream (see above);
- if you think you may be sensitive or allergic to ingredients in adhesive dressings;
- if you are suffering from methemoglobinemia;
- if there is an infection, skin rash, cut, or wound at or near the area you want to apply EMLA;
- if you have dermatitis or any other skin problems or diseases;
- if you have severe kidney or liver disease;
- if you are pregnant, plan to become pregnant or are breast-feeding.

How Do I Use EMLA Cream Properly? If this medicine is recommended by your doctor, be sure to follow the directions for use that have been given. If you are treating yourself, follow the directions below.

EMLA is for use on healthy, unbroken skin, with the exception of leg ulcers. It may also be used on genital mucosa. **Do not apply on open wounds.**

Do not put EMLA cream near the eyes, as it may cause some irritation. If you accidentally get EMLA in the eyes, rinse them well with lukewarm water.

EMLA cream should not be applied inside the ear.

Instructions for Application of EMLA Cream on Intact Skin (see package insert for illustrations): EMLA cream is available in 5 and 30 gram (g) tubes. 2.5 g is half of a 5 g tube and 10 g is either two of the 5 g tubes or one-third of a 30 g tube.

1. Apply cream in a thick layer at the site of the procedure as follows:

Adults and children over 1 year: For minor procedures on skin such as surgical treatment of lesions, or when getting a needle or having blood taken, apply approximately half of a 5 g tube (2.5 g). Leave EMLA on for at least 1 hour. EMLA should not be left on the skin for more than 5 hours.

For dermal procedures on larger areas such as split-skin grafting, apply approximately 1.5 to 2 g/10 cm^2. (A 10 cm^2 area is 2 cm x 5 cm or a circle with a diameter of 3.5 cm.) When applied to larger areas, EMLA should be left on for at least 2 hours.

Infants between 6 and 12 months: Apply no more than 2 g of cream on a total skin area not larger than 16 cm^2 (4 cm×4 cm or a circle with a diameter of 4.5 cm). Leave the cream on for at least 1 hour. EMLA should not be left on the skin for more than 4 hours in this age group.

EMLA cream should not be used in infants under 6 months of age.

2. Cover treated area with an airtight dressing such as Tegaderm or plastic wrap. Tegaderm is provided with the 5 g tubes only. If using plastic wrap, adhesive or medical tape can be used to hold the dressing in place and to secure it airtight.

If using Tegaderm, remove the centre cut-out piece. Peel the paper liner from the paper-framed dressing.

3. Carefully cover the EMLA cream so that you are left with a thick layer of cream underneath the dressing. Do not spread out the cream. Smooth down the dressing edges carefully and ensure it is secure to avoid leakage. This is especially important when the patient is a child.
4. If using Tegaderm, remove the paper frame. The time of application can easily be marked directly on the Tegaderm with a ballpoint pen. If using plastic wrap, the time of application can be marked on the medical tape that is holding the dressing in place.
5. Remove the dressing when the application time is up, which for most procedures, is after 1 hour. Wipe off the EMLA cream, and clean the entire area with alcohol. If you are travelling to the doctor's office, you should leave the dressing on and have it removed by your doctor before the procedure.

Dosage of EMLA Cream on Genital Mucosa: Adults: For needle insertion, half of a 5 g tube (2.5 g) is applied at the selected site for 5 to 10 minutes.

For the surgical treatment of small lesions, such as the removal of genital warts or when having a biopsy, approximately 2.5 g per lesion is applied for 5 to 10 minutes.

An airtight dressing is not required when using EMLA on the genital mucosa. Your doctor will begin the surgical procedure immediately after the removal of the cream.

EMLA cream should not be applied to the genital mucosa in children.

Dosage of EMLA Cream on Leg Ulcers: For topical anesthesia prior to cleansing/debridement of leg ulcers, a thick layer of EMLA cream, approximately 1 to 2 g per 10 cm^2 is applied over the leg ulcer(s) and covered with an occlusive dressing, i.e., plastic wrap. A maximum of 10 g may be applied.

EMLA should be applied to the ulcer for at least 30 minutes, however, an application time of 60 minutes may improve the anesthesia further. The cleansing/debridement should begin within 10 minutes after removal of the cream.

Are There Any Side Effects? Like any medication, EMLA cream may cause side effects in some people.

Mild side effects that are common with use of EMLA are whitening or redness of the skin, slight puffiness, and initial burning or itching on the area on which EMLA is applied. These are normal reactions caused by the active ingredients and will disappear without any treatment.

Allergic reactions to the active ingredients have been seen but are rare.

EMLA can cause serious side effects if too much is applied. These include drowsiness, numbness of the tongue, light-headedness, sight or hearing problems, vomiting, dizziness, unusually slow heartbeat, fainting, nervousness, unusual sweating, trembling or seizures.

EMLA, in extremely rare cases, can affect the level of oxygen that the blood carries, resulting in an increase in the methemoglobin level in your blood. This condition, known as methemoglobinemia, will cause the color of the skin to become brownish or greyish.

Medicines affect different people in different ways. Just because side effects have occurred in some patients, does not mean that you will get them. If any side effects bother you, or if you experience any unusual effects while you are using EMLA, stop using it and check with your doctor or pharmacist as soon as possible.

What Should I Do in Case of Overdose? In case of EMLA overdose or if you think you or anyone else is experiencing any of the above signs or methemoglobinemia, telephone your doctor or go to the nearest hospital right away.

Where Should I Keep EMLA Cream? Remember to keep EMLA cream well out of the reach of children when you are not using it.

Store EMLA cream at room temperature. Protect from freezing.

Important Note: This leaflet alerts you to some of the times you should call your doctor. Other situations that cannot be predicted may arise. Nothing about this leaflet should stop you from calling your doctor or pharmacist with any questions or concerns you have about using EMLA cream.

Important Information You Should Know About EMLA Patch: Before using EMLA patch, read this leaflet carefully. It contains general points about EMLA patch and should add to more specific advice from your doctor or pharmacist.

Please keep this leaflet to refer to until you have used up all your EMLA patches.

What is EMLA Patch Used for and how Does it Work? EMLA is the brand name for a topical anesthetic that contains the drugs lidocaine and prilocaine. Topical anesthetics are used to cause a temporary loss of sensation or numbness on the area where they are applied.

EMLA patch is used on healthy, unbroken skin prior to getting a needle or having blood taken. The anesthetic effect of EMLA is optimal approximately 1 to 2 hours after it is applied. You may still experience sensations such as pressure and touch on the area where EMLA patch is applied.

What is in EMLA Patch? EMLA patch is composed of a skin-colored adhesive tape with a round white pad in the centre that contains EMLA. The adhesive tape is protected with a peel-off backing which is removed before the patch is applied.

EMLA patch contains lidocaine and prilocaine as the active ingredients. It also contains carboxypolymethylene, polyoxyethylene hydrogenated castor oil, and sodium hydroxide. The patch adhesive is made from acrylate. The patch does not contain latex.

Check with your doctor if you think you might be sensitive to any of the above ingredients.

What Should I Tell my Doctor or Pharmacist Before Using EMLA Patch? Tell your doctor or pharmacist:

- about all health problems you have now or have had in the past;
- about all other medicines you take, including ones you can buy without a prescription;
- if you have ever had a bad, unusual or allergic reaction to lidocaine or prilocaine, also available under the brand names Xylocaine (lidocaine) and Citanest (prilocaine);
- if you think you may be sensitive or allergic to other ingredients of the patch (see above);
- if you are suffering from methemoglobinemia;
- if there is an infection, skin rash, cut, or wound at or near the area you want to apply EMLA;
- if you have dermatitis or any other skin problems or diseases;
- if you have severe kidney or liver disease;
- if you are pregnant, plan to become pregnant or are breast-feeding.

How Do I Use EMLA Patch Properly? If this medicine is recommended by your doctor, be sure to follow the directions for use that have been given. If you are treating yourself, follow the directions below.

EMLA is for use on healthy, unbroken skin. **Do not apply on open wounds.**

Do not put EMLA patch near the eyes, as it may cause some irritation. If you accidentally get EMLA in the eyes, rinse them well with lukewarm water.

Adults and children over 1 year: EMLA patch must be applied for at least 1 hour before the procedure. The patch should not be left on for longer than 5 hours.

Infants between 6 and 12 months: No more than 2 EMLA patches should be applied at the same time. Application time is at least 1 hour but no more than 4 hours.

EMLA patch is not recommended for use in children under 6 months of age.

Do not reuse the EMLA patch.

Instructions for Application of EMLA Patch (see package insert for illustrations):

EMLA Cream/Patch (cont'd)

1. Make sure that the area of skin to be treated is clean and dry. Take hold of the aluminum flap at the corner of the patch and bend it back.
2. Take hold of the corner of the skin-colored patch layer. Pull the 2 layers apart separating the adhesive surface from the aluminum paper backing. Make sure that you do not touch the white, round pad which contains EMLA.
3. Apply EMLA patch so that the white, round pad containing EMLA covers the area to be treated (if necessary shave the area prior to application). Press **firmly** only around the **edges** of the patch to ensure a good adhesion to the skin. Press **gently** on the **centre** of the patch to ensure that EMLA comes into contact with the skin.
4. The time of application can be easily marked directly on the patch with a ballpoint pen. EMLA patch must be applied for at least 1 hour before the start of the procedure. Care should be taken that the patch does not become detached (especially in young children) during the 60-minute wait.
5. Remove EMLA patch and clean the entire area with alcohol. If you are travelling to the doctor's office, you should leave the patch on and have it removed by your doctor before the procedure.

Are There Any Side Effects? Like any medication, EMLA patch may cause side effects in some people.

Mild side effects that are common with use of EMLA are whitening or redness of the skin, slight puffiness, and initial burning or itching on the area on which EMLA is applied. These are normal reactions caused by the active ingredients and will disappear without any treatment.

Allergic reactions to the active ingredients have been seen but are rare.

EMLA can cause serious side effects if too much is applied. These include drowsiness, numbness of the tongue, light-headedness, sight or hearing problems, vomiting, dizziness, unusually slow heartbeat, fainting, nervousness, unusual sweating, trembling or seizures.

EMLA, in extremely rare cases, can affect the level of oxygen that the blood carries, resulting in an increase in the methemoglobin level in your blood. This condition, known as methemoglobinemia, will cause the color of the skin to become brownish or greyish.

Medicines affect different people in different ways. Just because side effects have occurred in some patients, does not mean that you will get them. If any side effects bother you, or if you experience any unusual effects while you are using EMLA, stop using it and check with your doctor or pharmacist as soon as possible.

What Should I Do in Case of Overdose? In case of EMLA overdose or if you think you or anyone else is experiencing any of the above signs or methemoglobinemia, telephone your doctor or go to the nearest hospital right away.

Where Should I Keep EMLA Patch? Remember to keep EMLA patch well out of the reach of children. The patches are for single use and should not be reused.

Store EMLA patch at room temperature. Protect from freezing.

Important Note: This leaflet alerts you to some of the times you should call your doctor. Other situations that cannot be predicted may arise. Nothing about this leaflet should stop you from calling your doctor or pharmacist with any questions or concerns you have about using EMLA patch.

□ ENTOCORT® Capsules 🄿

Astra

Budesonide

Glucocorticosteroid for the Treatment of Crohn's Disease Affecting the Ileum and/or Ascending Colon

Information for the Patient: Important Information You Should Know About Entocort Capsules (Budesonide): Read this leaflet carefully. It has been prepared by the makers of Entocort Capsules to help you get the most benefit from this medicine. It contains general points about Entocort Capsules and should add to more specific advice from your doctor or pharmacist.

This Leaflet Should Not Replace Your Doctor's or Pharmacist's Advice. Because of your health condition, they may have given you different instructions. If so, be sure to follow their advice. Also, if you have any questions or concerns after reading this leaflet, talk to your doctor or pharmacist.

What is Entocort? Entocort is a brand name for a drug called budesonide. It is an anti-inflammatory drug which belongs to the steroid family of drugs.

What is In Entocort Capsules? Entocort Capsules are filled with a large number of small grains and contain 3 mg of the medicine budesonide. When swallowed, the medicine passes through the stomach intact, and is gradually released in the small bowel.

Most medicines contain more than just the active drug. These are needed to keep medicines in a form you can use. Check with your doctor if you think you might be allergic to any of these items: ethylcellulose, acetyltributyl citrate, methacrylic acid copolymer, triethylcitrate, dimethicone, polysorbate 80, talc, sucrose, gelatin, sodium lauryl sulphate, titanium dioxide and iron oxide.

How do Entocort Capsules Work? Entocort Capsules are used for Crohn's disease, which is an inflammatory bowel disease causing symptoms like stomach pain, diarrhea and fever. Entocort Capsules reduce inflammation in the small bowel and also in the first part of the large bowel.

What Should I do Before Starting Entocort Capsules? Be sure you've told your doctor:

- about **all** health problems you have now or have had in the past, especially tuberculosis and any other recent infection, liver disease, brittle bones (osteoporosis), stomach ulcer, high blood pressure, eye disease, diabetes or a family history of diabetes or glaucoma;
- about **all** other medicines you take, including ones you can buy without a prescription;
- if you take, or have taken steroid medicines within the past several months;
- if you are pregnant, plan to become pregnant or are breast-feeding;
- if you have ever had an allergic, bad or unusual reaction to Entocort Capsules or the medicine budesonide;
- if you are allergic to ''nonmedicinal'' substances like food products, preservatives, or dyes, which may be present in Entocort Capsules (see 'What is in Entocort Capsules').

How do I Take Entocort Capsules Properly? Take all doses of Entocort Capsules, as recommended by your doctor, even if you feel better. The full effect of Entocort Capsules is usually achieved within 2 to 4 weeks. Do not miss doses, or take extra doses, unless your doctor tells you. If you miss a dose, just take the next dose on time. Never take a double dose of Entocort capsules to make up for missed doses.

Entocort Capsules should be swallowed whole with water. The capsules must not be broken or chewed. Entocort Capsules should be taken before meals.

Acute Treatment: The usual dose for treatment of acute symptoms is 9 mg/day, for up to 8 weeks. The dose can be given once daily as three 3 mg capsules in the morning.

Long-Term Treatment: The usual starting dose for long-term treatment is 6 mg/day. Take two 3 mg capsules in the morning, before breakfast. Your doctor may want to change the dose, depending on the activity of your disease.

Continue taking Entocort Capsules until your doctor tells you to stop. Your doctor may want to slowly reduce the dose.

Overdose: Telephone your doctor or go to your nearest hospital immediately if you think that you or anyone else may have taken too many Entocort Capsules even if there are no signs of discomfort or poisoning.

Are There Any Side Effects? Entocort Capsules, like any medication, may cause side effects in some people. These may not be caused by Entocort Capsules in your case, but only a doctor can assess this.

Side effects that do occur are usually mild. However, be sure to tell your doctor if any of the following side effects bother you: swelling of the face; indigestion; menstrual problems; nervousness; muscle cramps; trembling; rapid heart beats; blurred vision and skin rash.

Other unwanted effects which cannot be predicted may occur in rare cases. If you have any bothersome or unusual effects while using Entocort Capsules, check with your doctor or pharmacist right away.

Medicines affect different people in different ways. Just because side effects have occurred in other patients does not mean you will get them.

Do not stop taking Entocort Capsules on your own. Your doctor may want to slowly reduce your dose, especially if you have been using Entocort Capsules for a long time. Although rare, symptoms of steroid withdrawal i.e., fatigue, muscle or joint aches may occur if Entocort Capsules are stopped too quickly.

Where Should I Keep Entocort Capsules? Remember to **keep Entocort Capsules well out of the reach of children.**

Entocort Capsules come in a container with a drying agent in the top. Always keep Entocort Capsules in the container. If you don't, moisture from the air may damage the capsules.

Store Entocort Capsules at room temperature and in a dry place. Do not keep them in the bathroom medicine cabinet or other warm, moist places.

Do not use Entocort Capsules after the expiry date marked on the package.

Important Note: This leaflet alerts you to some of the times you should call your doctor. Other situations which cannot be predicted may arise. Nothing about this leaflet should stop you from calling your doctor or pharmacist with any questions or concerns you have about using Entocort Capsules.

□ ENTOCORT® Enema 🅿

Astra

Budesonide

Glucocorticosteroid

Information for the Patient: About Entocort Retention Enema: Before using Entocort retention enema, please read this instruction leaflet. Before using this, or any other enema with rigid tubing, colostomy and ileostomy patients should consult with their doctor. The budesonide enema should be administered in the evening before going to bed. The budesonide enema (0.02 mg/mL) consists of a dispersible tablet (I) and solution (II).

I. 1 dispersible tablet contains: budesonide 2.3 mg, lactose, color (riboflavin-5-phosphate sodium) and constituents.
II. 1 mL solution contains: sodium chloride, preservatives (methyl- and propylparahydroxybenzoate) and up to 1 mL purified water.

How to Prepare the Enema (see package insert for illustrations):

1. Remove the nozzle, with the protective cap on, from the bottle.
2. Take a tablet from the aluminum foil pack and put it into the bottle. **Do not swallow the tablet.**
3. Put the nozzle back on the bottle and make sure that the protective cap is firmly on. Shake the bottle vigorously for at least 10 seconds or until the tablet has dissolved and a slightly yellowish liquid has been formed.

   A plastic bag has been enclosed which you may use to protect your hand when you administer the enema.
4. Lie down on your left side. Shake the bottle again before removing the protective cap. Empty the contents into the rectum.
5. Roll over on your stomach. Stay in this position for 5 minutes.
6. Choose a suitable position to sleep in. Try to retain the enema as long as possible, preferably for the whole night.

Note: After preparation, the budesonide enema is intended for immediate use.

1. Put your hand inside the plastic bag and grip the bottle.
2. Empty the contents into the rectum.
3. After use, remove the plastic bag from your hand by pulling it over the bottle.

□ ENTROPHEN®

Johnson & Johnson • Merck

ASA

Nonsteroidal Anti-inflammatory—Analgesic—Platelet Aggregation Inhibitor

Information for the Patient: What Entrophen Contains: Entrophen Coated Tablets and Caplets contain acetylsalicylic acid, also known as ASA.

What Entrophen Does: Entrophen Coated Tablets and Caplets have the following characteristics:

Action: Entrophen Coated Tablets and Caplets contain ASA. Clinical practice has established the suitability of ASA in relieving pain associated with conditions such as minor body aches, muscle, back and joint pain.

Special, enteric coating to help prevent stomach upset: The special enteric coating of Entrophen enables the tablet or caplet to pass, undissolved, through the acidic stomach and enter the upper portion of the small intestine, a less acidic environment. It is then that the tablet or caplet is dissolved, thus it is less likely to cause stomach irritation that is sometimes associated with plain or buffered ASA.

Onset of Action: Because Entrophen Coated Tablets and Caplets are specially coated to reduce the risk of stomach upset, the ASA is not absorbed by the stomach and the onset of action will be somewhat delayed.

When To Take Entrophen: Entrophen is indicated for the relief of minor aches and pains including the pain of inflammation associated with arthritis and rheumatism. Entrophen may be used for backache, bursitis pain, knee pain, joint pain, muscle aches, lower back pain and tennis elbow. It is also useful in relieving pain and aches associated with colds.

How To Take Entrophen: Adults: The tablets and caplets must be swallowed whole, with a large glass of water (250 mL); do not crush or break up. It is hazardous to exceed the maximum recommended dose (650 mg per single dose or 4 g daily) unless advised by your physician. Consult your physician if your condition does not improve after 5 days of continued product use.

Precautions: If you are taking other medication, carefully read the labels to ensure that they do not also contain acetylsalicylic acid which could result in an overdose. If in doubt, consult your physician or pharmacist.

If you expect to undergo surgery, including dental surgery within 5 to 7 days of taking ASA or Entrophen Coated Tablets or Caplets, consult your physician or pharmacist.

Consult a physician before taking this drug during the last three months of pregnancy or when breast-feeding.

Do not administer Entrophen to children and teenagers who have chickenpox or flu symptoms before a physician or a pharmacist is consulted about Reye's Syndrome, a rare and serious illness.

There is enough drug in each package to seriously harm a child. Keep this medicine out of the reach of children.

When to Consult Your Physician or Pharmacist about Entrophen: A physician or pharmacist should be consulted prior to taking this medication in case of:

- allergy to salicylates or asthma;
- during pregnancy or when breast-feeding;
- if you have stomach problems, peptic ulcer, severe liver disease or gout;
- a history of blood coagulation defects, or when receiving anticoagulant drugs;
- ASA is not recommended 5 to 7 days prior to surgery or in the presence of severe anemia;
- intake of other medications containing salicylates or acetaminophen, anti-inflammatory drugs, anticonvulsants, antidiabetic or gout medicine.

Possible Side Effects: Entrophen Coated Tablets and Caplets occasionally may produce some unwanted effects. A physician should be contacted if any of the following reactions develop during treatment:

- bleeding or irritation of stomach (nausea, vomiting, pain);
- any loss of hearing, including ringing or buzzing in the ears;
- skin rashes, hives or itching;
- breathing difficulties.

What To Do In Case Of Overdose: In case of accidental or suspected overdose, contact at once a physician, a Poison Control Centre, or the Emergency Department of a hospital immediately, even if there are no symptoms.

The signs and symptoms of an overdose usually occur within a few hours after ingestion. They may include: stomach upset, convulsions (seizures), hearing loss, mental confusion, ringing or buzzing in the ears, severe drowsiness or tiredness, severe excitement or nervousness and unusually fast or deep breathing, hallucinations or changes in behavior (especially in children).

Entrophen (cont'd)

Description: Enteric-coated tablets or caplets printed in black with product name and potency declared in mg per tablet or caplet.

Regular Strength Entrophen	Extra Strength Entrophen	Super Extra Strength Entrophen 10
325 mg tablets and caplets	**500 mg tablets**	**650 mg tablets and caplets**
Usual dosage	Usual dosage	Usual dosage
1-2 tablets or caplets every 4 hours	1-2 tablets every 4 hours	1 tablet or caplet every 4 hours
Maximum daily dose (4 000 mg a day) 12 tablets/caplets	Maximum daily dose (4 000 mg a day) 8 tablets	Maximum daily dose (4 000 mg a day) 6 tablets/caplets
• For low dose ASA therapy. For relief of mild aches and pains due to muscle and joint strain.	• For relief of moderate aches and pains due to backache, muscle and/or joint pain.	• For relief of moderate joint pain caused by arthritis and athletic injuries.

Product Monograph available to pharmacists and physicians upon request.

☐ EPIVAL®

Abbott

Divalproex Sodium

Anticonvulsant

Information for the Patient: Please read the following information carefully before you start to take Epival, even if you have taken this drug before.

What Is Epival: Epival, the brand name for divalproex sodium, has been prescribed to you to control your epilepsy. Please follow your doctor's recommendations carefully.

Before Taking Epival: Please inform your Doctor:

- If you have a history of, or suffer from a liver disease, such as jaundice (yellowing of skin and eyes).
- If you ever had an unusual or allergic reaction to Epival.
- If you are allergic to any component of Epival tablets.
- If you are pregnant or are planning to become pregnant.
- If you are breast-feeding (nursing); Epival is excreted in breast milk.
- If you are taking any other prescription or over-the-counter medicine.
- If you have liver or kidney disease, or other medical conditions.
- If you consume alcohol on a regular basis.

How To Take Epival:

- It is very important that you take Epival exactly as your doctor instructed.
- Your doctor may increase or decrease your medication according to your specific needs; carefully follow the instructions you were given. Do not change the dose yourself.
- Do not stop taking your medicine abruptly, because your seizures may increase.
- If you happen to miss a dose, do not try to make up for it by doubling up on the dose next time. Just take your next regularly scheduled dose and try not to miss any more. Epival may be taken with or without food.
- Consult your doctor before taking any other medication, including over-the-counter medicines. Some drugs can produce various side effects when they are used in combination with Epival.
- It is important to keep your appointments for medical checkups.

Precautions While Taking Epival: If you develop malaise, weakness, lethargy, facial edema, anorexia and vomiting, particularly in the first weeks of therapy, contact your doctor immediately. If you are a parent whose child is taking Epival, report to your doctor immediately if your child develops any of these symptoms.

- Your doctor will monitor your response to Epival on a regular basis. However, if your seizures get worse, tell your doctor immediately. (The onset of pregnancy should be reported promptly).
- Different side effects have been reported by patients taking Epival. The most commonly reported adverse reactions are nausea, vomiting and indigestion. However, this does not mean that you will experience such effects, because people can react in different ways to the same medicine.
- Since Epival may cause poor coordination and/or drowsiness, do not engage in hazardous activities, such as driving and operating machinery, until you know that you don't become drowsy from the drug. Consult your doctor.
- If you notice any bothersome or unusual effects while taking Epival check with your doctor or pharmacist right away.
- Do not stop taking your medication unless directed by your doctor. Always check that you have an adequate supply of Epival. Remember that this medicine was prescribed only for you; never give it to anyone else.

What To Do In Case Of An Overdose: If you accidentally take an overdose of Epival, contact your doctor or nearest hospital emergency, even though you may not feel sick.

How To Store Epival: Store your Epival tablets at room temperature (15 to 30°C). Cap the bottle tightly immediately after use. **Keep out of reach of children.**

What Do Epival Tablets Contain: Epival tablets contain divalproex sodium and the following nonmedicinal ingredients: cellulosic polymers, silica gel, diacetylated monoglycerides, povidone, pregelatinized starch (contains cornstarch), talc, titanium dioxide and vanillin.

In addition, individual tablets contain: 125 mg tablets: FD&C Blue No.1 and FD&C Red No.40; 250 mg tablets: FD&C Yellow No.6 and iron oxide; 500 mg tablets: D&C Red No.30, FD&C Blue No.2, and iron oxide.

☐ EPREX®

Janssen-Ortho

Epoetin Alfa

Erythropoiesis Regulating Hormone

Information for the Patient: Information for Self-administration: Introduction: Please read this carefully before you start to take your medicine. This is only a summary of the information available to your doctor. If you have any questions about this medicine ask your doctor or pharmacist.

What Does Eprex (epoetin alfa) Contain? Eprex Sterile Solution is a clear, colorless solution containing epoetin alfa as the active ingredient. Inactive ingredients contained in Eprex Sterile Solution are albumin (human), sodium chloride, water for injection, and either, sodium citrate and citric acid, or sodium phosphate. Single-use vials and single-use, prefilled syringes do not contain preservatives. The 20 000 IU/mL multi-use vial contains benzyl alcohol as a preservative.

What is Eprex? Eprex is a protein made in the laboratory which acts like a substance naturally made in the human body called erythropoietin. Erythropoietin controls the production of red blood cells in the body.

What is Eprex Used for? Eprex is used to increase the production of red blood cells. It may be used in adults with kidney disease; adults who have HIV-infection and are receiving a drug called zidovudine; adult cancer patients; and adults scheduled to undergo major, elective surgery.

Before Taking Eprex...

- Tell your doctor about any medical problems and about any allergies you have or have had in the past.
- You should not use Eprex if you are allergic to any of the ingredients in the product.
- Tell your doctor if you have or have had high blood pressure, seizures, blood clots, liver disease, porphyria, or gout.
- While you are treated with Eprex your doctor will need to check your blood pressure. Your blood pressure will be monitored carefully and any changes outside of the guidelines that your doctor has given you must be reported. If your blood pressure increases, you may need medication to lower it. If you already take blood pressure medication, your doctor may increase the amount.
- Your doctor will also measure your serum iron levels, red blood cell levels and other factors in your blood, prior to starting and during treatment with Eprex, as deemed appropriate.
- If you are on dialysis, your dialysis prescription may need to be changed while you are being treated with Eprex. Your doctor will take blood tests to determine if any change is needed. Your doctor may also need to adjust any medication you receive to prevent blood clotting.

- Tell your doctor if you are pregnant, if you think you might be pregnant, or if you are trying to become pregnant.
- Tell your doctor if you are breast-feeding.
- In many women with severe kidney failure, the monthly period may stop. When these women take Eprex they may restart their monthly cycle. If you are a woman with kidney disease you should discuss contraception with your doctor.
- In patients with kidney disease, due to the possibility of an increase in blood pressure there is a small chance of having a seizure when therapy starts. During the initial phase of treatment your doctor may advise you to avoid driving, using machines or doing anything else that could be dangerous if you are not alert.
- Tell your doctor about all medications you are using, including those obtained without a prescription and any other remedies or dietary supplements. It is especially important that your doctor know if you are taking high blood pressure medication.
- If you are a home dialysis patient, you should continue to check your access, as your doctor or nurse has shown you, to make sure it is working. Be sure to let your health care professional know right away if there is a problem.

How Should I Use Eprex? Follow your doctor's instructions about when and how to take this medication.

Eprex is injected under the skin (subcutaneously) into the arms, legs or abdomen.

While you are receiving Eprex your doctor will measure your red blood cells. Your doctor will use this information to adjust the dose to the amount right for you.

Do not shake Eprex. The solution in the vial or prefilled syringe should always be clear and colorless. Do not use Eprex if the contents of the vial or prefilled syringe appear discolored or cloudy, if the vial or prefilled syringe appears to contain lumps, flakes, or particles. If the vial or prefilled syringe has been shaken vigorously, the solution may appear to be frothy and should not be used.

Single-use vials and prefilled syringes of Eprex do not contain preservatives and therefore are to be used once and discarded. Any unused portion of a vial or prefilled syringe should not be used. Multi-use vials contain benzyl alcohol as a preservative and may be re-entered. Multi-use vials should be discarded 30 days after first entry.

If you accidentally take too much Eprex, obtain immediate medical advice.

If you miss a dose, contact your doctor for instructions.

Preparing the Dose (see package insert for illustrations): **Important: To help avoid contamination and possible infection, follow these instructions exactly.**

Single-Use and Multi-Use Vials: Use the Correct Syringe: Your doctor has instructed you on how to give yourself the correct dosage of Eprex. This dosage will usually be measured in units per millilitre or ccs. It is important to use a syringe that is marked in tenths of millilitres (for example, 0.1, 0.2, etc., mL or cc). Failure to use the proper syringe can lead to a mistake in dosage, and you may receive too much or too little Eprex. Only use disposable syringes and needles as they do not require sterilization; they should be used once and disposed of as instructed by your doctor.

1. Check the date on the Eprex vial to be sure that the drug has not expired. If using a multi-use vial, record the date of first entry for each vial on the inside flap of the box.
2. Remove the vial of Eprex from the refrigerator and allow it to reach room temperature. Do not use any methods to warm the vial other than holding it in your hand. Single-use vials of Eprex are designed to be used only once; do not re-enter the single-use vial. The multi-use vial may be re-entered and should therefore be refrigerated following each injection. **Do not shake Eprex.** Shaking may damage the product. Assemble the other supplies you will need for your injection.
3. Wash hands thoroughly with soap and water before preparing the medication.
4. Cleanse the skin with an antiseptic swab where the injection is to be made.
5. Flip off the protective cap but do not remove the rubber stopper. Wipe the top of the rubber stopper with an antiseptic swab.
6. Carefully remove the needle cover. Put the needle through the rubber stopper of the Eprex vial.
7. Turn the vial and syringe upside down in one hand. Be sure the tip of the needle is in the Eprex solution. Your other hand will be free to move the plunger. Draw back on the plunger slowly to draw the correct dose of Eprex into the syringe.
8. Check for air bubbles. The air is harmless, but too large an air bubble will reduce the Eprex dose. To remove air bubbles, gently tap the syringe to move the air bubbles to the top of the syringe. Move the tip of the needle above the level of the solution in the vial and use the plunger to push the air back into the vial. Then re-measure your correct dose of Eprex.
9. Double-check your dose. Remove the needle from the vial. Do not lay the syringe down or allow the needle to touch anything.

Single Use Prefilled Syringe (see package insert for illustrations):

1. Check the dose on the Eprex prefilled syringe. Make sure you are using the dose that has been prescribed by your doctor.
2. Check the date on the Eprex prefilled syringe to be sure that the drug has not expired.
3. Remove the Eprex prefilled syringe from the refrigerator and allow it to reach room temperature. Do not use any methods to warm the syringe other than holding it in your hand. The prefilled syringe is for single use only. **Do not shake Eprex.** Shaking may damage the product. Assemble the other supplies you will need for your injection.
4. Wash hands with soap and water before injecting.
5. Cleanse the skin with an antiseptic swab where the injection is to be made.
6. Locate on the syringe the dose of Eprex to be injected. Units of Eprex are written on the syringe with a corresponding colored line from each dose.
7. Remove rubber cap from needle. **Do not bend needle while removing rubber cap.**
8. Hold syringe upright with needle at the top. Air bubbles should rise to the top of the syringe. If not, then gently tap the syringe to move air bubbles to the top of the syringe.
9. Double-check your dose of Eprex and gently push plunger so that the **rim** of the rubber stopper lines up with the dose to be injected. **This will remove the air bubbles from the syringe.**
10. Do not lay the syringe down or allow the needle to touch anything.

Injecting the Dose (see package insert for illustrations):

1. With one hand, stabilize the previously cleansed skin by spreading it or by pinching up a large area with your free hand.
2. Hold the syringe with the other hand, as you would a pencil. Double-check that the correct amount of Eprex is in the syringe. Insert the needle to ensure injection into the subcutaneous layer. Pull the plunger back slightly. If blood comes into the syringe, do not inject Eprex, as the needle has entered a blood vessel. Take the needle out, put the syringe in the disposal container and start again with another syringe. Inject the Eprex by pushing the plunger all the way down.
3. After injection hold an antiseptic swab near the needle and pull the needle straight out of the skin. Press the antiseptic swab over the injection site for several seconds.
4. **Use the disposable syringe only once.** Dispose of syringes and needles as directed by your doctor (see **Disposal of Syringes**).
5. Always change the site for each injection as directed. Occasionally a problem may develop at the injection site. If you notice a lump, swelling, or bruising that doesn't go away, contact your doctor. You may wish to record the site just used so that you can keep track.

Disposal of Syringes:

1. Place all used needles and syringes in a hard plastic container with a screw-on-cap, or a metal container with a plastic lid, such as a coffee can properly labeled as to content. If a metal container is used, cut a small hole in the plastic lid and tape the lid to the metal container. If a hard-plastic container is used, always screw the cap on tightly after each use. When the container is full, tape around the cap or lid, and dispose of according to your doctor's instructions.
2. Do not use glass or clear plastic containers (or any container) that will be recycled or returned to a store.
3. Always store the container out of the reach of children.
4. Please check with your doctor, nurse, or pharmacist for other suggestions.

What Undesirable Effects May Eprex Have? Any medicine may have unwanted effects. The side effects you might experience may vary depending on the reason you are taking Eprex. Tell your doctor or pharmacist about any unusual sign or symptom whether listed or not. The most often reported side effects in all patients receiving Eprex are:

- flu-like symptoms such as dizziness, drowsiness, fever, headache, muscle and joint pain and weakness
- redness, burning and pain at the site Eprex is given
- gastrointestinal disturbances (nausea, vomiting, diarrhea)

Eprex (cont'd)

Additional side effects which have been reported more often in chronic renal failure patients than in other patients include:
- increases in blood pressure
- clotting of hemodialysis equipment
- changes in blood tests
- blood clots
- seizures

Be sure to tell your doctor if you have an increase in headaches or develop unusual headaches as this may be a sign of increased blood pressure.

There is a possible association of a worsening of increased blood pressure if red blood cell production occurs too rapidly. Your doctor may need to reduce your dose of Eprex and initiate or increase blood pressure medication. Tell your doctor if you are experiencing any of the following: chest pain, shortness of breath, an increase in headaches or unusual headaches, lightheadedness.

If you develop signs of allergy such as difficulty breathing, hives, itching, rash, or swelling of the throat, face, eyelids, mouth or tongue, discontinue the use of Eprex and contact your doctor or obtain medical help immediately.

How Should I Store Eprex?
- Store in a refrigerator. Do not freeze. Protect from light.
- Do not use this product after the expiry date written on the package.
- Keep this and all medicines in a safe place away from children.
- The multi-use vial may be re-entered and therefore should be stored in the refrigerator following each injection.
- Discard the multi-use vial 30 days after the date of first entry into the vial, which you recorded on the inside flap of the box.

Eprex is available only by prescription. Further information may be obtained from your doctor or pharmacist.

☐ ERGOMAR®

Rhône-Poulenc Rorer

Ergotamine Tartrate

Migraine Therapy

Information for the Patient: Indications: Acute migraine and related types of vascular headache.

Pharmacology: The mode of action of ergotamine in aborting attacks of migraine and other vascular headache may be due to its direct vasoconstrictive action on the cranial vessels with resultant reduction in the amplitude of their pulsations.

Contraindications: Ergomar is contraindicated in peripheral vascular disease (thromboangiitis obliterans, luetic arteritis, severe arteriosclerosis, thrombophlebitis, Raynaud's disease), coronary heart disease, hypertension, angina pectoris, cardiac arrhythmias, heart blocks, impaired hepatic or renal function, severe pruritus, sepsis, peptic ulcer, infectious states, malnutrition. It is also contraindicated in patients who are hypersensitive to any of its components. Ergomar is contraindicated in women who are pregnant, who may become pregnant or who are breast-feeding.

Warnings: Undesirable reactions to Ergomar may best be prevented by avoidance of excessive dosage and careful supervision of the patient so that they will not use the drug in larger dosage, more frequently, or for a longer time than prescribed by the physician.

Because of the possible cumulative effects of ergotamine tartrate, the dosage of Ergomar must not exceed 3 tablets in any 24-hour period; and, not more than 5 tablets in 1 week. Patients should be cautioned to use the minimal effective dose to control their symptoms.

Individual sensitivity to the vascular effects of ergotamine varies considerably and symptoms of arterial insufficiency have been reported after as little as 2 mg taken orally. This is a rare occurrence, but if such symptoms develop the use of ergotamine should be discontinued. Failure to recognize the early symptoms of arterial insufficiency has on rare occasions led to irreversible vascular change with therapeutic doses of ergotamine.

Precautions: Ergomar is not recommended as a prophylactic agent in migraine. Prolonged use should be avoided because of risk of potential serious adverse effects.

Patients who have prolonged specific neurological phenomena (visual, sensory, motor) require great caution and careful follow up.

Like all drugs, ergotamine should be kept out of reach of children.

Children: The safety and efficacy of Ergomar in children has not been established. It is not recommended for use in children.

Pregnancy: Ergotamine may cause fetal harm when administered to a pregnant woman by virtue of its powerful uterine stimulant actions. It is contraindicated in women who are, or may become pregnant.

Lactation: Ergotamine is secreted into human milk. It can reach the breast-fed infant and exert pharmacologic effects, therefore ergotamine is contraindicated in nursing women.

Drug Dependence: Patients who take ergotamine for extended periods of time may become dependent upon it and require progressively increasing doses for relief of vascular headaches or to prevent the increasing dysphoric effects which may follow withdrawal of the drug.

Drug Interactions: The concomitant use of ergotamine alkaloids and beta-blocking agents increases the risks of peripheral vasoconstriction. Among patients treated concomitantly with ergotamine and propranolol a few cases of vasospastic reactions have been reported.

There is some evidence that the concomitant use of triacetyloleandomycin (TAO/Troleandomycin), erythromycin or josamycin and ergotamine can result in an elevated concentration of ergotamine in the plasma, thereby increasing the risk of adverse effects.

Adverse Effects: Undesirable reactions to ergotamine tartrate may be best prevented by avoidance of excessive dosage, nevertheless the following adverse reactions have been reported after therapeutic doses: nausea, vomiting, diarrhea, polydipsia, tingling of the hands and feet, muscle pains and cramps, thrombophlebitis, vascular spasm, transient tachycardia or bradycardia. Rare cases of gangrene, sleepiness, exhaustion, ECG changes, precordial pain, angina and myocardial infarction have also been reported.

Dosage: Adults: Initiate therapy as soon as possible after the first symptoms of the attack are noted, since success is proportional to rapidity of treatment, and lower dosages will be effective. At the first sign of an attack, or to relieve the symptoms of the full-blown attack, place 1 tablet beneath the tongue. An additional tablet may be taken at half-hour intervals thereafter, if necessary, but dosage must not exceed 6 mg (3 tablets) in any 24-hour period. Limit dosage to not more than 10 mg (5 tablets) in any one week.

☐ ERYSOL®

Stiefel

Erythromycin—Ethyl Alcohol

Topical Acne Therapy

Information for the Patient: Your physician has prescribed Erysol (erythromycin and ethyl alcohol) Topical Gel with sunscreens to treat your acne. It is important to read and follow these Directions for Use of your medication.
1. First wash the affected areas with a mild soap (not medicated), rinse well and pat dry.
2. Apply Erysol to the areas affected by acne with your fingertips, carefully avoiding the eyes, mouth, nostrils and other mucous membranes.
3. Wash your hands thoroughly after using the medication.
4. Apply the medication only as often as your physician directs.

Precautions:
1. Keep your medication in a safe place, out of the reach of children.
2. Erysol is for external use only.
3. Keep Erysol away from your eyes, nostrils, mouth and other mucous membranes.
4. Avoid contact with eyes. If contact occurs, flush eyes with copious amounts of water for at least 5 minutes. If discomfort persists, consult your physician.
5. Do not use any other acne medications unless your physician instructs you to do so.
6. Keep Erysol away from open flame during application.

If you have a problem:
1. If you experience excessive peeling, redness, tenderness, drying, itching or irritation consult your physician for advice.
2. Do not expect to see immediate improvement of your acne, but be patient and apply your medication as your physician has directed.

Remember: Erysol has been prescribed by your physician for you; do not allow other people to use it.

Erysol contains sunscreens (SPF15).

☐ ESTRACOMB®

Novartis Pharmaceuticals

Estradiol-17β—Norethindrone Acetate—Estradiol-17β

Estrogen—Progestin

Information for the Patient: Estracomb and How To Use It (See package insert for illustrations):

Introduction: Estracomb contains two types of transdermal therapeutic systems (patches) that are used in sequence. The round patch is called Estraderm 50 (Estraderm) and the twin patch is called Estragest 250/50 (Estragest). (See How to Administer Estracomb). Estraderm contains the natural estrogen hormone, estradiol, while Estragest contains estradiol as well as a progestin, norethindrone acetate (NETA). Estracomb can alleviate menopausal symptoms and/or prevent osteoporosis.

This information describes the uses of estrogens and progestins, precautions to take when using these hormones and how to use Estracomb. Please read it carefully. **If you want to know more or have any questions, please ask your doctor or pharmacist.**

Decisions regarding hormone replacement therapy and the length of time that a woman takes estrogen must be individualized and are made between each woman and her doctor.

Uses of Estrogens:

1. To reduce moderate or severe menopausal symptoms: Your body normally makes estrogens and progestins (female hormones) mainly in the ovaries. Between ages 45 and 55, the ovaries gradually stop making estrogens. This leads to a decrease in body estrogen levels and a natural menopause (the end of monthly menstrual periods). If both ovaries are removed during an operation before natural menopause takes place, the sudden decrease in estrogen levels causes "surgical menopause".

   Menopause is not a disease—it is a natural life event and different women experience menopause and its symptoms differently. Not all women suffer obvious symptoms of estrogen deficiency. When the estrogen levels begin decreasing, some women develop very uncomfortable symptoms, such as feelings of warmth in the face, neck, and chest, or sudden intense episodes of heat and sweating ("hot flashes" or "hot flushes"). Using estrogen drugs can help the body adjust to lower estrogen levels and reduce these symptoms.
2. To treat vulval and vaginal atrophy: Some women may also develop vulval or vaginal atrophy (itching, burning or dryness in or around the vagina, difficulty or burning on urination) in association with menopause. These changes may be improved by estrogen therapy.
3. To prevent osteoporosis: Osteoporosis is a thinning of the bones that makes them weaker and allows them to break more easily. In osteoporosis, the bones of the spine, wrists and hips break most often. The bones of both men and women start to thin after about age 40, but women lose bone faster after menopause. Using estrogens after menopause slows down bone thinning and may prevent bones from breaking. Lifelong adequate calcium intake, either in the diet (such as dairy products) or by taking calcium supplements (to reach a total daily intake of 1 000 to 1 500 mg/day), and certain types of exercise may help to prevent osteoporosis. Before you change your calcium intake or exercise habits, it is important to discuss these lifestyle changes with your doctor to find out if they are safe for you.

   Some women are more likely to develop osteoporosis after menopause than others. Women who are underweight, heavy users of tobacco and/or alcohol, caucasian or oriental, have an inactive lifestyle, have a family history of osteoporosis (e.g., mother, sister or aunt) or have had a surgical or spontaneous menopause at a young age may be more likely to develop osteoporosis than other women.

Uses of Progestins: Progestins used in hormone replacement therapy have similar effects to the female sex hormone progesterone. During the childbearing years, progesterone is responsible for regulation of the menstrual cycle. The estradiol delivered by Estracomb not only relieves your menopausal symptoms, but, like estrogens produced by your body, may also stimulate growth of the inner lining of the uterus, the endometrium. In menopausal and postmenopausal women with an intact uterus, stimulation of growth of the endometrium may result in irregular bleeding. In some cases this may progress into a disorder of the uterus known as endometrial hyperplasia (overgrowth of the lining of the uterus). The development of estrogen-mediated disorders of the uterus can be reduced if a progestin, such as norethindrone acetate, is given regularly for a certain number of days with your estrogen replacement therapy. Each cycle of progestin administration should induce a periodic bleeding, whereby the inner lining of the uterus is regularly shed, thus protecting against endometrial hyperplasia.

If your uterus has been surgically removed, endometrial hyperplasia cannot occur and cyclical administration of a progestin is not necessary.

Precautions: Although estrogens and progestins provide health benefits, certain precautions should be taken before their use and in some situations their use may not be appropriate.

The use of estrogens has been reported to increase the risk of cancer of the lining of the uterus (endometrial cancer) in women after the menopause. **This risk is significantly reduced when estrogen is used along with a progestin.** If you have had your uterus removed by a hysterectomy, uterine cancer would not be a risk for you and cyclical administration of a progestin is not necessary. Therefore, Estracomb should not be used in this situation.

Some scientific studies have documented an association between a modest increase in the risk of developing breast cancer and the use of hormone replacement therapy in menopause for periods exceeding 5 years. Therefore, women with a family history of breast cancer, or with breast nodules, fibrocystic breast disease (lumps), or abnormal mammograms should consult with their doctor before starting hormone replacement therapy. The overall benefits and possible risks of hormone replacement therapy should be discussed with the physician. Regular breast examinations by a health professional and monthly self-examination are recommended for all women.

The use of oral estrogens after menopause has been reported to increase the risk of gallbladder disease requiring surgery.

Restrictions on Use: Certain medical conditions may be aggravated by estrogens and progestins, therefore these hormones should either not be used at all or should be used with precaution under these conditions.

Estrogens and progestins should not be used during pregnancy. Since pregnancy may be possible early in menopause while you are still having spontaneous periods, the use of nonhormonal birth control should be discussed with your physician at this time. If you take estrogen during pregnancy, there is a small risk of your unborn child having birth defects.

Estrogens and progestins should not be used if you are breastfeeding. You should not use Estracomb if you have had any unusual allergic reaction to estrogens or any other component of the patch (see What Does Estracomb Contain?).

Before using Estracomb, be sure to tell your doctor if you have ever had any of the following medical problems. Estracomb should not be used under these conditions:

- cancer of the breast or uterus
- unexpected or unusual vaginal bleeding
- abnormal blood clotting
- migraine headaches
- stroke
- serious liver disease
- active phlebitis (inflamed varicose veins)
- porphyria

To help your doctor decide whether you should use Estracomb and what precautions should be taken during use, tell your doctor:

- what other prescription and nonprescription medicines, if any, you are taking. There are some medicines which interfere with the effects of estrogens.
- about any allergies or sensitivities to medicines or any other substances you may have.
- if you are undergoing surgery or need long bed rest.
- if you have ever had any of the following:
  - —high blood pressure
  - —heart, kidney or liver disease
  - —asthma
  - —epilepsy or other neurological disorders
  - —sugar diabetes
  - —depression
  - abnormalities of the breast or uterus
  - —endometriosis
  - —breast disease, breast biopsies
  - —uterine fibroids
  - —phlebitis (inflamed varicose veins)
  - —abnormal blood clotting
  - —high levels of lipids in your blood
  - —jaundice or itching related to estrogen use or during pregnancy

Estracomb (cont'd)

Side Effects: The following effects have been reported in women taking estrogens (these include estrogens used for birth control). Check with your doctor if these symptoms become troublesome:
- nausea
- retention of fluid
- migraine headaches
- localized darkening of the skin
- breast tenderness and excessive vaginal secretions (may be a sign that too much estrogen is taken)
- persistent upper abdominal pain, nausea, vomiting, tender abdomen (may be signs of gallbladder disease)
- easy bruising, excessive nose bleeds, excessive heavy periods (may be signs of abnormal blood clotting)
- lower abdominal pain or swelling, painful and/or heavy periods (may be signs of growth of fibroids in the uterus)
- yellowing of the eyes or skin (may be signs of jaundice)
- upper abdominal pain or swelling (may be signs of liver tumors)

Progestins may produce side effects such as breast tenderness, mood swings and weight changes.

Check with your doctor as soon as possible if any of the following occur:
- irregular vaginal bleeding
- intolerable breast tenderness
- breast enlargement or lumps
- severe headaches
- changes in vision
- persistent or severe skin irritation
- fluid retention or bloating persisting for more than 6 weeks.

Check with your doctor immediately if you experience:
- trouble breathing or tightness of the chest
- tender or painful inflammation of the veins
- pain or heaviness in the legs or chest
- sudden shortness of breath
- coughing blood
- rapid pulse or dizziness
- any other unusual symptom

In addition, Estracomb may produce some redness or irritation under or around the patch in some women (see Helpful Hints).

How to Administer Estracomb: Each Estracomb pack contains 4 Estraderm and 4 Estragest patches. The round Estraderm patch provides the estrogen, estradiol. The twin Estragest patch provides estradiol and the progestin, norethindrone acetate (NETA). **All 8 patches are to be used in a 28-day treatment cycle.**

Therapy is started with the Estraderm patches which are used for the first 2 weeks followed by the Estragest patches for the next 2 weeks. The Estraderm and Estragest patches are applied twice weekly on the same days of each week. Each patch should be worn continuously for 3 to 4 days.

Regular cyclical bleeding usually starts towards the end of the Estragest application phase (i.e., while you are wearing the 4th Estragest patch of that cycle). The duration of bleeding is around 6 days. Bleeding is of light intensity or spotting for 60 to 70% of this time.

As therapy with Estracomb is continuous, the next treatment cycle is again started with Estraderm immediately after removal of the last Estragest patch, and regardless of whether there is still bleeding (i.e., you will have a patch on at all times).

It is important that you take your medication as your physician has prescribed. Do not discontinue or change your therapy without consulting your physician first.

How Estracomb Works: Treatment with Estracomb offers relief from menopausal symptoms for women with uteruses. With Estracomb, you receive estradiol throughout the entire 28-day cycle, and norethindrone acetate (NETA), a progestin, during the last 2 weeks of the 28-day cycle. The progestin provides important protection for your uterus. (See Uses of Progestins).

The main estrogen produced by your ovaries prior to menopause is estradiol, and this is the same estrogen that is in Estraderm and Estragest. When applied to the skin, the Estraderm patch continually releases small, controlled quantities of estradiol, which pass through your skin and into your bloodstream. The amount of estrogen prescribed depends on your body's needs.

By providing estradiol, Estracomb offers relief from menopausal symptoms, slows down bone loss and may prevent bones from breaking.

How and Where to Apply Estracomb: It is recommended that you change the site of application each time the patch is applied. However, each time you apply a patch you should always apply it to the same area of your body (i.e., if the patch is applied to the buttocks, move the patch from right side to left side, twice a week or more if there is any redness under the patch).

1. **Preparing the Skin:** In order for the patch to stick, the skin should be clean, dry and free of creams, lotions or oils. If you wish, you may use body lotion **after** the patch has been properly applied to the skin. The skin should not be irritated or broken, since this may alter the amount of hormone you get. Contact with water (bath, pool, or shower) won't affect the patch, although very hot water or steam may loosen it and therefore should be avoided **(see Helpful Hints).**
2. **Where to Apply the Estraderm or Estragest Patches:** The buttock is the preferred place to apply the patches. Other suitable application sites are the side, lower back or lower abdomen. Change the site of application each time you put a patch on. You can use the same spot more than once but **not twice in a row.**

   Avoid areas of the skin where clothing may rub the patch off or areas where the skin is very hairy or folded. Also avoid areas where the patch is likely to be exposed to the sun since this may affect how the patch works.

   Do not apply the patches to your breast, since this may cause unwanted effects and discomfort.
3. **Opening the Pouch:** Each Estraderm or Estragest patch is individually sealed in a protective pouch. **Tear** open this pouch at the indented notch and remove the patch. Do not use scissors, as you may accidentally cut and destroy the patch. There may or may not be bubbles in the patch, but this is normal. Do not cut the twin Estragest patch in half.
4. **Removing the Liner:** One side of the patch has the adhesive that attaches to your skin. The adhesive is covered by a protective liner that must be removed.

   To separate the patch from the liner, hold the patch with your thumb on the smooth liner, your other fingers on the patch. Press your thumb against your other fingers by using the motion of snapping your fingers slowly.

   This will allow you to easily separate the patch and liner. Holding the **edge** of the patch you can now peel away the liner. Avoid touching the adhesive.

   Don't worry if the patch buckles slightly because you can flatten it out after the liner has been removed. Apply the patch soon after opening the pouch and removing the liner.
5. **Applying the Estraderm and Estragest Patches:** Apply the adhesive side to the spot you have chosen. Press it firmly in place with the palm of your hand for about 10 seconds, then run your finger around the edge, making sure there is good contact with the skin.
6. **When and How to Remove the Patch:** The Estraderm and Estragest patches should be changed twice weekly. Always change it on the same 2 days of the week. If you forget to change it at the scheduled time, there is no cause for alarm. Just change it as soon as possible and **continue** to follow your usual schedule.

   After you remove the patch fold it in half with adhesive sides inwards. **Throw it away, safely out of the reach of children or pets.**

   Any adhesive left on your skin should rub off easily. Apply a new Estraderm or Estragest patch on a different spot of clean, dry skin.

Storage: Estraderm and Estragest should be stored at room temperature (below 25°C). Do not freeze. **Do not store the patches out of the pouch.** Estraderm and Estragest patches should be kept out of the reach of children and pets before and after use.

What Does Estracomb Contain? Like most medicines, Estracomb contains other substances in addition to estrogen and progestin. The other substances are cellulose compounds, ethanol, ethylene-vinyl acetate copolymer, light mineral oil, polyester and polyisobutylene.

Helpful Hints for using Estraderm and Estragest: What to do if the patch falls off: Should a patch fall off in a very hot bath or shower, shake the water off the patch. Dry your skin completely and reapply the patch (to a new area of skin) and continue your regular schedule. If it still does not stick, then apply a **new** patch and continue with your regular schedule.

If hot baths, saunas or whirlpools are something you enjoy and you find that the patch is falling off, you may consider removing the patch **temporarily** while you are in the water. If you do remove the patch temporarily, the adhesive side of the patch should be placed on the protective liner that was removed when originally applying the patch. Wax paper may be used as an alternate to the liner. This prevents the contents of the patch from emptying by evaporation while you are not wearing it.

In addition to exposure to very hot water, there are some other causes for the patch failing to stick. If you are having patches fall off regularly, this could be happening as a result of: using any type of bath oil, using soaps with a high cream content, using skin moisturizers before applying the patch.

Patch adhesion may be improved if you avoid using these products, and by cleansing the site of application with rubbing alcohol before you apply the patch.

What to do if your skin becomes red or irritated under or around the patch: As with any product that covers the skin for a period of time (such as bandages), the Estraderm or Estragest patch can produce some skin irritation in some women. This varies according to the sensitivity of each woman.

Usually this redness does not pose any health concern to you but to reduce this problem, there are some things that you may do: choose the buttock as the site of application, change the site of application of the Estraderm or Estragest patch every time a new patch is applied, usually twice weekly.

Experience with Estraderm has shown that if you allow the patch to be exposed to the air for approximately 10 seconds after the protective liner has been removed, skin redness may not occur.

If redness and/or itching continues, you should consult your physician.

Always Remember: Your doctor has prescribed Estracomb for you after a careful review of your medical needs. Use it only as directed and do not give it to anyone else. Your doctor should re-examine you at least once a year.

If you have any questions, contact your doctor or pharmacist.

□ ESTRADERM® Ⓟ

Novartis Pharmaceuticals

Estradiol 17-β

Estrogen

Information for the Patient: Introduction: Estraderm is a transdermal therapeutic system (patch) which contains the natural estrogen hormone, estradiol. Estraderm can alleviate menopausal symptoms and/or prevent osteoporosis. In women with osteoporosis, treatment with Estraderm may retard further bone loss.

This leaflet describes the uses of estrogens and progestins, precautions to take when using these hormones and how to use Estraderm. Please read it carefully. **If you want to know more or have any questions, please ask your doctor or pharmacist.**

Decisions regarding hormone replacement therapy and the length of time that a woman takes estrogen must be individualized and are made between each woman and her doctor.

Uses of Estrogens:

1. To reduce moderate or severe menopausal symptoms: Your body normally makes estrogens and progestins (female hormones) mainly in the ovaries. Between ages 45 and 55, the ovaries gradually stop making estrogens. This leads to a decrease in body estrogen levels and a natural menopause (the end of monthly menstrual periods). If both ovaries are removed during an operation before natural menopause takes place, the sudden decrease in estrogen levels causes "surgical menopause".

   Menopause is not a disease; it is a natural life event and different women experience menopause and its symptoms differently. Not all women suffer obvious symptoms of estrogen deficiency. When the estrogen levels begin decreasing, some women develop very uncomfortable symptoms, such as feelings of warmth in the face, neck, and chest, or sudden intense episodes of heat and sweating ("hot flashes" or "hot flushes"). Using estrogen drugs can help the body adjust to lower estrogen levels and reduce these symptoms.
2. To treat vulval and vaginal atrophy: Some women may also develop vulval or vaginal atrophy (itching, burning or dryness in or around the vagina, difficulty or burning on urination) in association with menopause. These changes may be improved by estrogen therapy.
3. To prevent osteoporosis: Osteoporosis is a thinning of the bones that makes them weaker and allows them to break more easily. In osteoporosis, the bones of the spine, wrists and hips break most often. The bones of both men and women start to thin after about age 40, but women lose bone faster after menopause. Using estrogens after menopause slows down bone thinning and may prevent bones from breaking. Lifelong adequate calcium intake, either in the diet (such as dairy products) or by taking calcium supplements (to reach a total daily intake of 1 000-1 500 mg/day), and certain types of exercise may help to prevent osteoporosis. Before you change your calcium intake or exercise habits, it is important to discuss these lifestyle changes with your doctor to find out if they are safe for you.

   Some women are more likely to develop osteoporosis after menopause than others. Women who are underweight, heavy users of tobacco and/or alcohol, caucasian or oriental, have an inactive lifestyle, have a family history of osteoporosis (e.g., mother, sister or aunt) or have had a surgical or spontaneous menopause at a young age may be more likely to develop osteoporosis than other women.

Uses of Progestins: Progestins used in hormone replacement therapy have similar effects to the female sex hormone progesterone. During the childbearing years, progesterone is responsible for regulation of the menstrual cycle. The estradiol delivered by Estraderm not only relieves your menopausal symptoms, but, like estrogens produced by your body, may also stimulate growth of the inner lining of the uterus, the endometrium. In menopausal and postmenopausal women with an intact uterus, stimulation of growth of the endometrium may result in irregular bleeding. In some cases this may progress into a disorder of the uterus known as endometrial hyperplasia (overgrowth of the lining of the uterus). The development of estrogen-mediated disorders of the uterus can be reduced if a progestin is given regularly for a certain number of days with your estrogen replacement therapy. Each cycle of progestin administration should induce a periodic bleeding, whereby the inner lining of the uterus is regularly shed, thus protecting against endometrial hyperplasia.

If your uterus has been surgically removed, endometrial hyperplasia cannot occur and cyclical administration of a progestin is not necessary.

Precautions: Although estrogens provide health benefits, certain precautions should be taken before their use and in some situations their use may not be appropriate.

The use of estrogens has been reported to increase the risk of cancer of the lining of the uterus (endometrial cancer) in women after the menopause. **This risk is significantly reduced when estrogen is used along with a progestin.** If you have had your uterus removed by a hysterectomy, uterine cancer would not be a risk for you and cyclical administration of a progestin is not necessary.

Some scientific studies have documented an association between a modest increase in the risk of developing breast cancer and the use of hormone replacement therapy in menopause for periods exceeding 5 years. Therefore, women with a family history of breast cancer, or with breast nodules, fibrocystic breast disease (lumps), or abnormal mammograms should consult with their doctor before starting hormone replacement therapy. The overall benefits and possible risks of hormone replacement therapy should be discussed with the physician. Regular breast examinations by a health professional and monthly self-examination are recommended for all women.

The use of oral estrogens after menopause has been reported to increase the risk of gallbladder disease requiring surgery.

Restrictions on Use: Certain medical conditions may be aggravated by estrogens, therefore estrogens should either not be used at all or should be used with precaution under these conditions.

Estrogens should not be used during pregnancy. Since pregnancy may be possible early in menopause while you are still having spontaneous periods, the use of nonhormonal birth control should be discussed with your physician at this time. If you take estrogen during pregnancy, there is a small risk of your unborn child having birth defects.

Estrogens should not be used if you are breast-feeding.

You should not use Estraderm if you have had any unusual allergic reaction to estrogens or any other component of the patch **(see What Does Estraderm Contain?).**

Before using Estraderm, be sure to tell your doctor if you have any of the following medical problems. Estraderm should not be used under these conditions:

- cancer of the breast or uterus
- unexpected or unusual vaginal bleeding
- abnormal blood clotting
- migraine headaches
- stroke

Estraderm (cont'd)

- serious liver disease
- active phlebitis (inflamed varicose veins)
- porphyria

To help your doctor decide whether you should use Estraderm and what precautions should be taken during use, tell your doctor:

- what other prescription and nonprescription medicines, if any, you are taking. There are some medicines which interfere with the effects of estrogens.
- about any allergies or sensitivities to medicines or any other substances you may have.
- if you are undergoing surgery or need long bed rest.
- if you have ever had any of the following:
  —high blood pressure
  —heart, kidney, or liver disease
  —asthma
  —epilepsy or other neurological disorders
  —sugar diabetes
  —depression
  —abnormalities of the breast or uterus
  —endometriosis
  —breast disease, breast biopsies
  —uterine fibroids
  —phlebitis (inflamed varicose veins)
  —abnormal blood clotting
  —high levels of lipid in your blood
  —jaundice or itching related to estrogen use or during pregnancy

Side Effects: The following effects have been reported in women taking estrogens (these include estrogens used for birth control). Check with your doctor if these symptoms become troublesome.

- nausea
- retention of fluid
- migraine headaches
- localized darkening of the skin
- breast tenderness and excessive vaginal secretions (may be a sign that too much estrogen is taken)
- persistent upper abdominal pain, nausea, vomiting, tender abdomen (may be signs of gallbladder disease)
- easy bruising, excessive nose bleeds, excessive heavy periods (may be signs of abnormal blood clotting)
- lower abdominal pain or swelling, painful and/or heavy periods (may be signs of growth of fibroids in the uterus)
- yellowing of the eyes or skin (may be signs of jaundice)
- upper abdominal pain or swelling (may be signs of liver tumors).

Check with your doctor as soon as possible if any of the following occur:

- irregular vaginal bleeding
- intolerable breast tenderness
- breast enlargement or lumps
- severe headaches
- changes in vision
- persistent or severe skin irritation
- fluid retention or bloating persisting for more than 6 weeks

Check with your doctor immediately if you experience:

- trouble breathing or tightness of the chest
- tender or painful inflammation of the veins
- pain or heaviness in the legs or chest
- sudden shortness of breath
- coughing blood
- rapid pulse or dizziness
- any other unusual symptom

In addition, Estraderm may produce some redness or irritation under or around the patch in some women (see **Helpful Hints**).

How to Administer Estraderm: Your doctor will explain when to start using Estraderm. The Estraderm patches are applied twice weekly on the same days of each week. Each patch should be worn continuously for 3 to 4 days.

Estrogen is usually taken in a cyclic fashion (although your physician's instructions may be different depending upon your personal situation). This means that you would take estrogen on the first 21 or 25 days of the cycle, followed by 5 to 7 days without. Your next cycle starts with the next patch application.

Each box contains 8 Estraderm patches. If your treatment is for less than 28 days of estrogen (cyclical therapy), you will have 1 or 2 patches left over which can be used for the next month.

It is important that you take your medication as your physician has prescribed. Do not discontinue or change your therapy without consulting your physician first.

How Estraderm Works: The main estrogen produced by your ovaries prior to menopause is estradiol, and this is the same estrogen that is in Estraderm. When applied to the skin, the Estraderm patch continually releases small, controlled quantities of estradiol, which pass through your skin and into your bloodstream. The amount of estrogen prescribed depends on your body's needs. Your doctor may adjust the amount you get by prescribing another (different) patch size.

By providing estradiol, Estraderm offers relief from menopausal symptoms, slows down bone loss and may prevent bones from breaking.

How and Where to Apply Estraderm (see package insert for illustrations): It is recommended that you change the site of application each time the patch is applied. However, each time you apply a patch you should always apply it to the same area of your body (i.e., if the patch is applied to the buttocks, move the patch from right side to left side, twice a week or more if there is any redness under the patch).

1. **Preparing the Skin:** In order for the patch to stick, the skin should be clean, dry and free of creams, lotions or oils. If you wish, you may use body lotion after the patch has been properly applied to the skin. The skin should not be irritated or broken, since this may alter the amount of hormone you get. Contact with water (bath, pool, or shower) won't affect the patch, although very hot water or steam may loosen it and therefore should be avoided (see **Helpful Hints**).
2. **Where to Apply the Estraderm Patch:** The buttock is the preferred place to apply the patch. Other suitable application sites are the sides, hip, lower back or lower abdomen. Change the site of application each time you put a patch on. You can use the same spot more than once but **not twice in a row.**

   Avoid areas of the skin where clothing may rub the patch off or areas where the skin is very hairy or folded. Also avoid areas where the patch is likely to be exposed to the sun since this may affect how the patch works.

   Do not apply Estraderm to your breast, since this may cause unwanted effects and discomfort.
3. **Opening the Pouch:** Each Estraderm patch is individually sealed in a protective pouch. **Tear** open this pouch at the indented notch and remove the patch. Do not use scissors, as you may accidentally cut and destroy the patch. There may or may not be bubbles in the patch, but this is normal.
4. **Removing the Liner:** One side of the patch has the adhesive that attaches to your skin. The adhesive is covered by a protective liner that must be removed.

   To separate the patch from the liner, hold the patch with your thumb on the smooth liner, your other fingers on the patch. Press your thumb against your other fingers by using the motion of snapping your fingers slowly.

   This will allow you to easily separate the patch and liner. Holding the **edge** of the patch you can now peel away the liner. Avoid touching the adhesive.

   Don't worry if the patch buckles slightly because you can flatten it out after the liner has been removed. Apply the patch soon after opening the pouch and removing the liner.
5. **Applying the Estraderm Patch:** Apply the adhesive side to the spot you have chosen. Press it firmly in place with the palm of your hand for about 10 seconds, then run your finger around the edge, making sure there is good contact with the skin.
6. **When and How to Remove the Patch:** The Estraderm patch should be changed twice weekly. Always change it on the same 2 days of the week. If you forget to change it at the scheduled time, there is no cause for alarm. Just change it as soon as possible and **continue** to follow your usual schedule.

   After you remove the patch fold it in half with the adhesive sides inwards. **Throw it away, safely out of the reach of children or pets.**

   Any adhesive left on your skin will rub off easily. Apply a new Estraderm patch on a different spot of clean, dry skin.

Storage: Estraderm should be stored at room temperature (below 25°C). Do not freeze. **Do not store it out of the pouch.** Estraderm patches should be kept out of the reach of children and pets before and after use.

What Does Estraderm Contain? Like most medicines, Estraderm contains other substances in addition to estrogen. The other substances are cellulose compounds, ethanol, ethylene-vinyl acetate copolymer, light mineral oil, polyester and polyisobutylene.

Helpful Hints for Using Estraderm: What to do if the patch falls off: Should a patch fall off in a very hot bath or shower, shake the water off the patch. Dry your skin completely and reapply the patch (to a new area of skin) and continue your regular schedule. If it still does not stick, then apply a **new** patch and continue with your regular schedule.

If hot baths, saunas or whirlpools are something you enjoy and you find that the patch is falling off, you may consider removing the patch **temporarily** while you are in the water. If you do remove the patch temporarily, the adhesive side of the patch should be placed on the protective liner that was removed when originally applying the patch. Wax paper may be used as an alternate to the liner. This prevents the contents of the patch from emptying by evaporation while you are not wearing it.

In addition to exposure to very hot water, there are some other causes for the patch failing to stick. If you are having patches fall off regularly, this could be happening as a result of:

- using any type of bath oil
- using soaps with a high cream content
- using skin moisturizers before applying the patch

Patch adhesion may be improved if you avoid using these products, and by cleansing the site of application with rubbing alcohol before you apply the patch.

What to do if your skin becomes red or irritated under or around the patch: As with any product that covers the skin for a period of time (such as bandages), the Estraderm patch can produce some skin irritation in some women. This varies according to the sensitivity of each woman.

Usually this redness does not pose any health concern to you but to reduce this problem, there are some things that you may do:

- Choose the buttock as the site of application.
- Change the site of application of the Estraderm patch every time a new patch is applied, usually twice weekly.

Experience with Estraderm has shown that if you allow the patch to be exposed to the air for approximately 10 seconds after the protective liner has been removed, skin redness may not occur.

If redness and/or itching continues, you should consult your physician.

Always Remember: Your doctor has prescribed Estraderm for you after a careful review of your medical needs. Use it only as directed and do not give it to anyone else. Your doctor should re-examine you at least once a year.

If you have any questions, contact your doctor or pharmacist.

□ ESTRING® ℞

Pharmacia & Upjohn

Estradiol

Estrogen

Information for the Patient: Introduction: This leaflet describes when and how to use Estring (estradiol vaginal ring), and the risks and benefits of estrogen treatment. Please read this information carefully before starting treatment.

Estrogens have important benefits but also some risks. You must decide, with your doctor, whether the risks to you of estrogen use are acceptable because of their benefits. If you use estrogens, check with your doctor to be sure you are using the dose that is appropriate for you, and that you don't use them longer than necessary. How long you need to use estrogens should be decided by you and your doctor.

1. **Estrogens increase the risk of cancer of the uterus in women who have had their menopause (''change of life'').**
   If you use any estrogen-containing drug, it is important to visit your doctor regularly and report any unusual vaginal bleeding right away. Your doctor should evaluate any unusual vaginal bleeding to find out the cause.
2. **Estrogens should not be used during pregnancy.** Estrogens do not prevent miscarriage (spontaneous abortion) and are not needed in the days following childbirth. If you take estrogens during pregnancy, your unborn child has a greater than usual chance of having birth defects. The risk of developing these defects is small, but clearly larger than the risk in children whose mothers did not take estrogens during pregnancy. These birth defects may affect the baby's urinary system and sex organs. Daughters born to mothers who took DES (an estrogen drug) have a higher than usual chance of developing cancer of the vagina or cervix when they become teenagers or young adults. Sons may have a higher than usual chance of developing cancer of the testicles when they become teenagers or young adults.

Uses of Estrogen: Estrogens are hormones made by the ovaries of women during their reproductive years. Between ages 45 and 55, the ovaries normally stop making estrogens. This leads to a drop in body estrogen levels which causes the ''change of life'' or menopause (the end of monthly menstrual periods). If both ovaries are removed during an operation before natural menopause takes place, the sudden drop in estrogen levels results in what is known as ''surgically induced menopause''.

When the estrogen levels begin dropping, some women develop very uncomfortable symptoms, such as feelings of warmth in the face, neck, and chest, or sudden intense episodes of heat and sweating (''hot flashes'' or ''hot flushes''). Using estrogen drugs can help the body adjust to lower estrogen levels and reduce these symptoms. Estring **does not provide enough estrogen to reduce these symptoms.**

The declining estrogen levels associated with advancing age after menopause may also result in thinning and drying of the tissue in the urinary tract and vagina (urogenital atrophy). Vaginal symptoms of this condition include dryness in the vagina (atrophic vaginitis), genital itching and burning, and pain with intercourse. Urinary symptoms may include urinary urgency and pain on urination. Small amounts of estrogen delivered directly to the local tissue can be used to help reduce these symptoms.

Use of Estring: Estring is a local estrogen therapy designed to relieve vaginal and urinary symptoms of postmenopausal estrogen deficiency for a full 90 days. Estring exerts its effect locally in the lower urogenital tract and has not been shown to have significant effects in other estrogen-sensitive organs or tissues of the body. Consequently, **Estring provides relief of local symptoms of menopause only.**

Description: Estring contains a drug reservoir of 2 mg of the estrogen, estradiol, in its core. Estring releases estradiol into the vagina in a consistent, stable manner for 90 days. The soft, flexible ring is placed in the upper third of the vagina (by the physician or the patient) and worn continuously for 90 days, then removed and replaced if continuation of therapy is indicated.

Who Should not Use Estring: Estring should not be used:

1. **During pregnancy.** Women who are definitely postmenopausal cannot become pregnant. Women who believe they are postmenopausal because their menstrual cycles have recently stopped should confirm that they are not pregnant before using any form of estrogen-containing drug. Using estrogens while pregnant may cause the unborn child to have birth defects. Estrogens do not prevent miscarriage.
2. **In the presence of unusual vaginal bleeding which has not been evaluated by a doctor.** Unusual vaginal bleeding after menopause can be a warning sign of cancer of the uterus. Estrogens may increase the risk of cancer of the uterus in women who have had their menopause (''change of life''). If you use any estrogen-containing drug, it is important to visit your doctor regularly and report any unusual vaginal bleeding right away. Your doctor should evaluate any unusual vaginal bleeding to find out the cause.
3. **If there is a history of certain types of cancer.** Estrogens may increase the risk of certain types of cancer. In general, Estring should not be used in women who have ever had cancer of the breast or uterus.
4. **During treatment for vaginal infection with vaginal antimicrobial therapy.** It is recommended that Estring be discontinued while other vaginal medications are being used to treat a vaginal infection. Use of Estring can be resumed after termination of the other vaginal medication, and after first consulting with a physician.
5. **After childbirth or when breast-feeding a baby.** Estring should not be used to try to stop the breasts from filling with milk after a baby is born. Women who are breast-feeding should avoid using any drugs because many drugs pass through to the baby in the milk. While nursing a baby, drugs should only be taken on the advice of your healthcare giver.

Possible Risks From Treatment with Estrogens: The following risk factors apply to estrogens in general:

1. **Cancer of the uterus.** Estrogens increase the risk of developing a condition (endometrial hyperplasia) that may lead to cancer of the lining of the uterus (endometrial cancer). The risk of endometrial cancer is greater in estrogen users than nonusers. Studies have

Estring (cont'd)

shown that this increased risk depends on estrogen dose, duration of treatment, and treatment regimen. If the uterus has been removed (total hysterectomy), there is no danger of developing cancer of the uterus.

2. **Cancer of the breast.** Most studies have not shown a higher risk of breast cancer in women who have ever used estrogens. However, some studies have reported that breast cancer developed more often (up to twice the usual rate) in women who used estrogens for long periods of time (especially more than 10 years), or who used higher doses for shorter time periods. Regular breast examinations by a health professional and monthly self-examination are recommended for all women.
3. **Gallbladder disease and abnormal blood clotting.** Gallbladder disease and abnormal blood clotting are risk factors associated with medium to high doses of estrogen. Most studies of low dose estrogen usage by women do not show an increased risk of these complications, and to date have not been seen with Estring treatment.

Side Effects: Like all medications, Estring may cause side effects. The most frequently reported side effect is increased vaginal secretions. Many of these vaginal secretions are like those that occur normally prior to menopause and indicate that Estring is working. Vaginal secretions that are associated with a bad odor, vaginal itching, or other signs of vaginal infection are **not** normal and may indicate a risk or a cause for concern. Other side effects may include vaginal discomfort, abdominal pain, or genital itching.

Estrogens in General: In addition to the risks listed above, the following side effects have been reported with estrogen use: Nausea and vomiting. Breast tenderness or enlargement. Enlargement of benign tumors (''fibroids'') of the uterus. Retention of excess fluid. This may worsen some conditions, such as asthma, epilepsy, migraine, heart disease, or kidney disease. Spotty darkening of the skin, particularly on the face.

Reducing Risk of Estrogen Use: If you use estrogens, you may reduce your risks by doing these things: See your doctor regularly. While you are using estrogens, it is important to visit your doctor at least once a year for a check-up. If you develop vaginal bleeding while taking estrogens, call your doctor—you may need further evaluation. If members of your family have had breast cancer or if you have ever had breast lumps or an abnormal mammogram (breast x-ray), you may need to have more frequent breast examinations.

Reassess your need for estrogens. You and your doctor should reevaluate whether or not you still need estrogens at least every 6 months.

Be alert for warning signs. If any of these warning signals (or any other unusual symptoms) happen while you are using estrogens, call your doctor immediately: Abnormal bleeding from the vagina (possible uterine cancer). Pains in the calves or chest, sudden shortness of breath, or coughing blood (possible clot in the legs, heart, or lungs). Severe headache or vomiting, dizziness, faintness, changes in vision or speech, weakness or numbness of an arm or leg (possible clot in the brain or eye). Breast lumps (possible breast cancer; ask your doctor or health professional to show you how to examine your breasts monthly). Yellowing of skin or eyes (possible liver problem). Pain, swelling, or tenderness in the abdomen (possible gallbladder problem).

Other Information:

1. Estrogens increase the risk of developing a condition (endometrial hyperplasia) that may lead to cancer of the lining of the uterus. Progestin, another hormone drug, is usually prescribed with higher-dose estrogen preparations to lower the risk of developing endometrial hyperplasia. Progestins are not usually needed for women using Estring alone.
2. Some women have experienced moving or sliding of Estring within the vagina. If this happens, Estring can be gently pushed back into position with a clean finger. Instances of Estring slipping out of the vagina have been infrequent and were usually associated with moving the bowels, straining, or constipation within the first few weeks of treatment. If this occurs, Estring can be washed with lukewarm (**not** hot) water and reinserted. If this happens repeatedly, you should consult with your doctor or healthcare giver and determine whether continued treatment is appropriate for you.
3. Estring may not be suitable for women with narrow, short, or stenosed (constricted) vaginas. A narrow vagina, vaginal stenosis (constriction), significant prolapse, and vaginal infections are conditions that make the vagina more susceptible to irritation or ulceration caused by Estring. Women with signs or symptoms of vaginal irritation should alert their doctor or healthcare giver.
4. Vaginal infection is generally more common in postmenopausal women. Vaginal infections should be treated with appropriate antimicrobial therapy before initiation of Estring. If a vaginal infection develops during use of Estring, then Estring should be removed and reinserted only after the infection has been appropriately treated. See your doctor or healthcare giver if you have vaginal discomfort or suspect you have a vaginal infection.
5. Your doctor has prescribed this drug for you and you alone. Do not give the drug to anyone else.
6. Keep this and all drugs out of the reach of children.
7. This leaflet provides a summary of important information about Estring. If you want more information, ask your doctor or pharmacist.

How Supplied: Each Estring is individually packaged in a heat-sealed rectangular pouch. The pouch is provided with a tear-off notch on one side.

Estring 2 mg available in single units.

Storage: Store at controlled room temperature 15 to 30°C.

Estring is available upon prescription only.

A Patient Guide to Estring 2 mg Insertion and Removal (see package insert for illustrations):

Estring Insertion: Estring can be inserted and removed by you or your doctor. To insert Estring yourself, choose the position that is most comfortable for you: standing with one leg up, squatting, or lying down.

1. After washing and drying your hands, remove Estring from its pouch using the tear-off notch on the side. (Since the ring becomes slippery when wet, be sure your hands are dry before handling it.)
2. Hold Estring between your thumb and index finger and press the opposite sides of the ring together as shown.
3. Gently push the compressed ring into your vagina as far as you can.

Estring Placement: The exact position of Estring is not critical, as long as it is placed in the upper third of the vagina.

When Estring is in place, you should not feel anything. If you feel uncomfortable, Estring is probably not far enough inside. Use your finger to gently push Estring further into your vagina. There is no danger of Estring being pushed too far up in the vagina or getting lost. Estring can only be inserted as far as the end of the vagina, where the cervix (the narrow, lower end of the uterus) will block Estring from going any further (see diagram of Female Anatomy).

Estring Use: Once inserted, Estring should remain in place in the vagina for 90 days. Most women and their partners experience no discomfort with Estring in place during intercourse, so it is **not** necessary that the ring be removed. If Estring should cause you or your partner any discomfort, you may remove it prior to intercourse (see Estring Removal, below). Be sure to reinsert Estring as soon as possible afterwards. Estring may slide down into the lower part of the vagina as a result of the abdominal pressure or straining that sometimes accompanies constipation. If this should happen, gently guide Estring back into place with your finger. There have been rare reports of Estring falling out in some women following intense straining or coughing. If this should occur, simply wash Estring with lukewarm (**not** hot) water and reinsert it.

Estring Drug Delivery: Once in the vagina, Estring begins to release estradiol immediately. Estring will continue to release a low, continuous dose of estradiol for the full 90 days it remains in place.

It will take about 2 to 3 weeks to restore the tissue of the vagina and urinary tract to a healthier condition and to feel the full effect of Estring in relieving vaginal and urinary symptoms. If your symptoms persist for more than a few weeks after beginning Estring therapy, contact your doctor.

One of the most frequently reported effects associated with the use of Estring is an increase in vaginal secretions. These secretions are like those that occur normally prior to menopause and indicate that Estring is working. However, if the secretions are associated with a bad odor or vaginal itching or discomfort, be sure to contact your doctor.

Estring Removal: After 90 days there will no longer be enough estradiol in the ring to maintain its full effect in relieving your vaginal or urinary symptoms. Estring should be removed at that time and replaced with a new Estring, if your doctor determines that you need to continue your therapy.

To remove Estring:

1. Wash and dry your hands thoroughly.

2. Assume a comfortable position, either standing with one leg up, squatting, or lying down.
3. Loop your finger through the ring and gently pull it out.
4. Discard the used ring in a waste receptacle. (Do not flush Estring).

If you have any additional questions about removing Estring, contact your doctor or healthcare giver.

☐ FAMVIR™ ℞

SmithKline Beecham

Famciclovir

Antiviral Agent

Information for the Patient: Herpes Zoster: What is in your tablets?
- Famvir tablets are white, oval, marked FAMVIR on one side and 500 on the other side. Check with your doctor or pharmacist if your tablets look different from this.
- Each Famvir tablet contains 500 mg of famciclovir.
- The tablets also contain some inactive ingredients to make up the bulk of each tablet: hydroxypropyl cellulose, hydroxypropyl methylcellulose, lactose, magnesium stearate, polyethylene glycols, sodium starch glycolate and titanium dioxide.
- If you know you are allergic to any of these substances tell your doctor before you start taking these tablets.
- The tablets are gluten-free.
- The tablets do not contain sucrose, tartrazine or any other azo dyes.
- Famvir is an antiviral medicine.

Who makes Famvir? Famvir is made by SmithKline Beecham Pharma Inc., Oakville, Ontario L6H 5V2.

What is Famvir for? Famvir treats infections caused by a virus called varicella zoster which causes shingles. Your doctor has decided that Famvir is the right treatment for your illness.

Famvir stops the virus spreading. This cuts down blistering and pain of the rash.

Before you take Famvir:
- Are you pregnant?
- Might you be pregnant soon?
- Are you allergic to Famvir?
- If you took Famvir before, did you have unwanted effects (side effects)?
- Will you be breast-feeding your baby while you are taking the tablets?
- Have you got kidney trouble?

If you answer **yes** to any questions, **do not** take this medicine. Go back to your doctor and ask what to do.

Can you take Famvir while taking other medicines? Always tell your doctor about other medical conditions you have or any medicines you are taking. This means medicines you bought for yourself as well as medicines on prescription. Your doctor or pharmacist will know if it is safe to take Famvir as well.

How to take your tablets: The usual dose is one Famvir tablet three times a day. Follow your doctor's instructions about how and when to take your tablets. Start taking them as soon as you can for the best effect. Most people take one tablet when they get up in the morning, one in the middle of the afternoon and one before going to bed at night.

People with kidney trouble may not have to take these tablets as often.
- Famvir will work whether or not you take it with food.
- Swallow each tablet whole with water. Do not chew it.
- Finish all the tablets you have been given even if you start to feel better. The treatment lasts for 7 days.

What if you miss a dose? If you miss taking a Famvir tablet, don't worry. Take it as soon as you remember. Take your next tablet at the normal time. Carry on as normal until you have finished all the tablets. It is important that you finish all the tablets you have been given.

What if you take too many tablets? All tablets are risky if you take too many. If you take too many Famvir tablets at once, tell your doctor or hospital Emergency Department as soon as possible. Show them your tablets.

Does Famvir cause side effects? Any medicine can cause side effects. With Famvir, side effects are usually mild and you usually don't have to stop taking your tablets. Some people may feel sick or get a mild headache. Other side effects include diarrhea, tiredness, dizziness, abdominal pain, itching, sleepiness, constipation or fever. If you get these or any other problems while you are taking Famvir, tell your doctor or pharmacist.

Look after your tablets.
- Keep Famvir in the bottle or package provided by the pharmacist.
- Store at room temperature.
- Keep out of the reach of children.
- Don't take your tablets if they are past their expiry date.
- Never let anyone else take your tablets, even if they have shingles as well.
- Finish all the tablets in the way you have been told.

More information about shingles. What is shingles like?
- At first you might feel burning and tingling where the rash is coming. You may get pain for a few days before you see the rash.
- Most people with shingles get a blistery rash down one side of their body or face. This can be painful.
- New blisters will keep coming for about 5 days. After this, the blisters will dry to form scabs.
- You may feel weak and tired.
- The rash usually lasts for 2 to 3 weeks. Afterwards, people can have pain where the rash was, sometimes for several months.

Who gets shingles? People of any age can get shingles. Most people who get it are middle-aged or older. You can only get shingles if you have had chickenpox. Fifty percent of people have had shingles by the age of 85.

What causes shingles?
- Shingles is caused by the same virus that causes chickenpox.
- After you have had chickenpox, the inactive virus stays in your body.
- Many years later the virus can start to work again. This may happen when you are run down or tired.

How is shingles treated? Tablets for shingles, such as Famvir, stop the virus spreading. They cut down blistering and pain of the rash. They help you get better quicker if you take them early in your illness.

What else can you do?
- to stop the rash itching, have cool baths—do not use perfumed soap or bath oils. You can also put ice cubes wrapped in a washcloth on the rash, or cover it with a soothing lotion like calamine for the first three days.
- Keep the rash clean and dry.
- Wear loose clothes.
- Do not scratch the rash. It could get infected and take longer to get better.
- Rest when you feel tired.
- Try to eat well and drink plenty of fluids.
- Tell your doctor right away if you start to have trouble with your eyes. Shingles can sometimes cause eye problems which can be treated.

Can other people catch your shingles? Shingles is caused by the same virus that causes chickenpox. Most doctors agree that people do not catch shingles from each other. When you have shingles, you can give chickenpox to someone who has never had chickenpox before—but this is unlikely.

Recurrent Genital Herpes: What is Genital Herpes? Genital herpes is a viral infection of the genital (sex organ) area which is caused by the herpes simplex virus. You might suspect the onset of this infection if you see the appearance of sores or blisters or feel a burning sensation in your genital region.

Type II herpes simplex virus is the main cause of the sores and blisters that develop in your genital area, but you can also catch genital herpes from herpes simplex type I which can be the cause of cold sores which occur around your mouth.

Genital herpes can occur as a first-episode attack or recurrent infection. Unlike many other viruses, recovery from the first attack does not leave you with lifelong protection from reinfection. The virus is able to remain hidden in the nerves after the initial infection and stays there until reactivated.

Since your body still carries the highly infectious virus, you can easily infect someone else, even if you feel fine and you have no symptoms of genital herpes. This explains why genital herpes is one of the most common sexually transmitted diseases (STD).

The risk is higher for people who are more sexually active and have more sexual partners. It is therefore recommended that you avoid sexual activity if you or your partner have any symptoms of herpes, even if you have started your treatment.

What you should know about Famvir? Famvir (famciclovir) is an antiviral medication. It has been prescribed for you by your doctor to treat the viral infection which causes genital herpes. Famvir does not stop you from spreading herpes to another person. It is important to understand that the drug must be taken as early as possible as soon as you know that an attack is starting.

Famvir (cont'd)

Identify your medication:
- 125 mg tablet—round, white tablet with a raised hexagonal shaped area and marked with FAMVIR on one side and 125 on the other side.
- 250 mg tablet—round, white tablet with a raised hexagonal shaped area and marked with FAMVIR on one side and 250 on the other side.

Check with your doctor or pharmacist if the identifying markings or color of your tablets are not the same as this.

The tablets also contain some inactive ingredients to make up the bulk of each tablet. These inactive ingredients include the color agent titanium dioxide, polyethylene glycol and lactose. They do not contain sucrose, tartrazine or any other azo dyes.

Before using Famvir: Here are some things to mention to your doctor so that your doctor can determine if Famvir is suitable for you.
- Allergy (including itching) when previously taking Famvir.
- Past history of (or current) kidney disease.
- Pregnancy or intention to become pregnant while using Famvir.
- Infant breast-feeding.
- Unwanted effects (side effects) when previously taking Famvir.
- Other medical conditions.
- Taking any other medications for other medical conditions. It is important to tell your doctor, dentist or pharmacist if you are taking other medication, as combining drugs can sometimes result in a change from the expected drug effects, or cause harmful effects.

How to take your medication: You should take Famvir only as directed by your doctor. Do not take more of it, do not take it more often and do not take it for a longer period of time than your doctor ordered.

Be sure to take Famvir regularly as prescribed. Try to take your tablets at the same time each day. You should continue to take your medicine even if you do not feel better, as it may take a few days for your medicine to work.

If your kidneys are not working very well, your doctor will probably have you take this medicine less often, check with your doctor if you have kidney problems.

Famvir will work whether or not you take it with food. You should swallow the tablets whole, with water. Do not chew them.

Treating an outbreak of recurrent genital herpes: If you have had herpes infections of the genitals before (called recurrent genital herpes), your doctor may decide to treat the outbreak. You will likely be told to take one 125 mg tablet twice a day for 5 days. Most people with recurrent genital herpes take one tablet when waking, and one tablet just before going to bed. Famvir should be taken as soon as possible after the early symptoms (pain, burning, blisters) begin to appear.

Preventing outbreaks of recurrent genital herpes: If you have had herpes infections of the genitals before (called recurrent genital herpes), then your doctor may decide to prevent future outbreaks. Your doctor will likely tell you that you should continually take one 250 mg tablet twice a day. Most people with recurrent genital herpes take one tablet when waking, and one tablet before going to bed.

If you miss a dose: If you forget to take your tablet, take it as soon as you remember. Take your next dose at the normal time, then carry on as before. It is important that you finish all the tablets you have been given, unless your doctor tells you to stop taking them.

If you take too many tablets: If you take too many Famvir tablets at once, tell your doctor or Poison Control Centre immediately. Bring your pack of tablets with you. Taking too much of any type of medicine is risky.

Important: Your doctor may give you different instructions better suited to your specific needs. If you need more information on how to take Famvir properly, double-check with your doctor or pharmacist.

Side Effects: Any medication can cause side effects. Most people tolerate the medicine well. The most common adverse effects associated with Famvir are listed below; they have rarely been severe enough to make it necessary to stop taking the drug: headache, upset stomach, dizziness, fever, itching, tiredness, sleepiness, stomach pain, constipation, diarrhea.

If you experience anything unusual, while you are receiving treatment with Famvir, you should report it to your physician. A more complete listing of side effects reported to date, is contained in the product monograph supplied to your physician.

Note that Famvir should not interfere with your ability to drive or operate machinery.

While taking this medication:

—remember that your infection is contagious.

—tell any other doctor, pharmacist or dentist you see, that you are taking Famvir.

—contact your doctor if you develop any unusual discomfort.

—you should not take Famvir when pregnant or breast-feeding unless your doctor tells you to.

—do not give Famvir to others because it may not be suitable for them.

—store your tablets in a dry place at room temperature in the original container provided by the pharmacy.

—keep this medication out of reach of children.

—read your prescription label carefully; consult your doctor or pharmacist if you have any questions or require further information.

□ FANSIDAR® Ⓟ

Roche

Sulfadoxine—Pyrimethamine

Antimalarial

Information for the Patient: What is Malaria? Malaria is an infectious disease caused by microscopic parasites called plasmodia. These are transmitted to human blood from the bite of infected mosquitoes. There are 4 species of these blood parasites which commonly infect humans. P. falciparum is the most dangerous of these species. If left untreated, the malaria caused by P. falciparum can result in death.

Malaria is widespread in tropical and subtropical areas of Africa, Latin America, Asia and the Pacific. Several different types of malaria may exist within one area, each type requiring its own protective medication.

The most common symptoms of a malaria attack are chills followed by fever and sweating. These symptoms may recur at intervals of 48 hours or less and may be associated with headache, diarrhea, abdominal and muscle pain. These latter symptoms, which may initially be mistaken for flu, occur as the microscopic parasites enter and destroy red blood cells. This follows an incubation period of one or more weeks during which the parasites reproduce within the liver. Due to the complex life cycle of the malaria parasite in humans, malaria symptoms can occur in individuals not taking antimalarial medication after departure from a malarious area. If left untreated, falciparum malaria can rapidly result in anemia, damage to internal organs such as the liver and spleen, coma and death.

What is Fansidar: Fansidar is the trade name for an antimalarial product containing the 2 drugs sulfadoxine and pyrimethamine.

It may be used to treat or, in some cases, prevent the symptoms of a malaria attack caused by P. falciparum in the areas where this organism is no longer affected by chloroquine, the drug which is used most commonly against malaria.

Fansidar does not prevent the mosquito from infecting humans nor does it prevent the first stage of malaria which involves parasite reproduction within the liver. Fansidar suppresses the symptoms associated with the second phase of malaria, that which occurs within human blood.

Proper Use of Fansidar: To Prevent a Malaria Attack: The recommended adult prophylactic dose is 1 tablet once a week. Your doctor will reduce this dose for your children according to their weight.

Fansidar should not be given to children less than 2 months of age.

Fansidar should be taken:
- for 2 weeks before arrival at a malarious area,
- throughout your stay and,
- for 6 weeks after leaving the area.

The reason for taking the drug before reaching the danger zone is to allow your doctor, when possible, to test your tolerance to the medication and for you to get into the routine of taking the tablets. The reason for taking the tablets for 6 weeks after leaving the area infected by malarious mosquitoes relates to the initial liver phase of the parasite life cycle. This period may not be associated with any symptoms. It is important, therefore, that you keep taking Fansidar on the same day of the week for the full time recommended by your doctor. If you miss taking a dose, take it as soon as the oversight is detected and then take subsequent doses at weekly intervals, counting from the day that you took the missed dose. **Do not take more than 1 tablet in any 1 week.**

Fansidar should be taken with plenty of water and with meals, if possible, in order to minimize the possibility of experiencing unwanted side effects, such as upset stomach. Do not chew the tablets. After returning from your trip, be sure to return to your doctor when scheduled. If you will be taking Fansidar for several months, it is important that a qualified physician perform blood and urine tests regularly in order to assess your tolerance to the drug.

To Treat a Malaria Attack: If you suspect that you have contracted malaria, immediately contact a doctor. Self-treatment of malaria should only be attempted if there is no doctor available within 12 to 24 hours of the symptoms described above. Be sure to contact a qualified physician as soon as possible after self-treatment with Fansidar.

The appropriate amount of Fansidar for the treatment of malaria in an adult is a single dose of 3 tablets taken together. Children receive a lower dose based upon their weight (2 tablets for 30 to 45 kg; 1 tablet for 11 to 29 kg; ½ tablet for 5 to 10 kg).

Fansidar should not be given to children less than 2 months of age. If you choose to take children younger than 2 months of age to a malarious area, you should discuss with your physician the action to take if they contract malaria.

General Precautions: Fansidar has been prescribed for the prevention or treatment of a very specific infection. **Use Fansidar only for the trip for which it was prescribed.** Your doctor has decided that Fansidar is suitable protection against a form of malaria found in the regions to which you are traveling. However, it may not provide protection against other forms of malaria found in that same area or elsewhere.

Do not give Fansidar to anyone else. Your doctor has decided that Fansidar is suitable protection for you. If given to someone for whom Fansidar is unsuitable, that person may not receive appropriate antimalarial protection in the area of destination and in addition, may be at risk of experiencing severe reactions. Keep Fansidar out of the reach of children. It is best to avoid alcoholic drinks during treatment with Fansidar. **During treatment with Fansidar excessive exposure to the sun or artificial ultraviolet rays must be strictly avoided.**

You should not take other medications that contain sulfonamides, pyrimethamine or trimethoprim. Trimethoprim-sulfamethoxazole combinations, for example, are common anti-infectives sometimes used in traveller's diarrhea. Taking these or certain other drugs with Fansidar may add to the unwanted effects of Fansidar. Unless you are sure that the other medications which you are taking will not interact with Fansidar, consult with your doctor.

Special Precautions: Fansidar should not be used by: nursing mothers; persons with a known sensitivity to sulfonamides or to pyrimethamine; persons suffering from severe kidney, liver or blood disease, porphyria, or certain types of anemia; infants under 2 months of age; women who are or may become pregnant.

Adverse Events: Fansidar is usually well tolerated by most patients. Minor intolerances often include gastrointestinal discomfort, nausea, headache and increased skin sensitivity to sunlight.

The drug, however, has been associated with very serious adverse reactions in a small proportion of patients. The most serious relate to allergic reactions which are characterized by: soreness, stinging and swelling of the tongue, severe skin rashes, itchiness, fever, sore throat, paleness of the skin, and/or aching joints.

Persons with severe allergies or asthma may be at greater risk of experiencing severe drug side effects. The following symptoms which may not be related to allergic phenomena have also been observed: unexplained bruising, dark urine, yellowing of the skin and whites of the eyes, severe bacterial or fungal infections.

If you experience any of these effects, stop taking Fansidar and consult a doctor immediately.

After taking Fansidar to treat a malaria attack you may become faint. Bed rest should help to alleviate this effect.

Pregnancy: If you are pregnant, it may be unwise to travel in malarious areas. You should avoid becoming pregnant while in such areas. During pregnancy, a malarial infection is dangerous for both the mother-to-be and the unborn child. If a trip into a malarious area is unavoidable, be sure to discuss all of your travel plans with your doctor. He will advise you as to which form of protection against malaria is best for you.

You should avoid becoming pregnant while you are taking Fansidar. Fansidar has caused birth defects in the offspring of pregnant laboratory animals. The first 3 months of pregnancy are of particular concern in fetal development. Fansidar taken at the end of pregnancy may produce liver damage in your baby which is associated with severe nervous system symptoms.

Consult a doctor if you are planning to become pregnant or if you do become pregnant while using Fansidar, so that he may advise you about the risks involved in continuing, stopping or changing antimalarial medication.

How Can You Further Protect Yourself Against Malaria? The best way to minimize the possibility of contracting malaria is to reduce your contact with mosquitoes, which are more prevalent from dusk to dawn. This includes the wearing of light colored clothes which cover most of the body, applying mosquito repellent to uncovered areas of the skin, sleeping under mosquito netting and spraying insecticides in sleeping quarters. For your best protection, consult your doctor or local travel clinic on these subjects.

□ FELDENE™ Ⓟ

Pfizer

Piroxicam

Anti-inflammatory—Analgesic

Information for the Patient: Feldene (piroxicam) which has been prescribed to you by your doctor, is one of a large group of nonsteroidal anti-inflammatory drugs (NSAIDs) and is used to treat the symptoms of certain types of arthritis. It helps to relieve joint pain, swelling, stiffness and fever by reducing the production of certain substances (prostaglandins) and helping to control inflammation and other body reaction.

You should take Feldene only as directed by your doctor. Do not take more of it, do not take it more often and do not take it for a longer period of time than your doctor ordered.

Be sure to take Feldene regularly as prescribed. In some types of arthritis, up to 2 weeks may pass before you feel the full effects of this medicine. During treatment, your doctor may decide to adjust the dosage according to your response to the medication.

To lessen stomach upset, take this medication immediately after a meal or with food or milk. If stomach upset (indigestion, nausea, vomiting, stomach pain or diarrhea) occurs and continues, contact your doctor.

If you take Feldene once a day and if you miss a dose of this medicine and remember within 8 hours of the missed dose, take it right away. If you take the drug twice a day and if you miss a dose and remember within 2 hours of the missed dose, take it right away. Then go back to your regular dosing schedule. If you have any questions about this, check with your doctor or pharmacist.

Do not take ASA (acetylsalicylic acid), ASA-containing compounds or other drugs to relieve symptoms of arthritis while taking Feldene unless directed to do so by your physician.

If you are prescribed this medication for use over a long period of time, your doctor will check your health during regular visits to assess your progress and to ensure that this medication is not causing unwanted effects.

Along with its beneficial effect, Feldene like other NSAID drugs, may cause some undesirable reactions. Elderly, frail or debilitated patients often seem to experience more frequent or more severe side effects. Although not all of these side effects are common, when they do occur they may require medical attention. Check with your doctor immediately if any of the following are noted:

—bloody or black tarry stools;
—shortness of breath, wheezing, any trouble in breathing, or tightness in the chest;
—skin rash, hives or swelling, itching;
—indigestion, nausea, vomiting, stomach pain or diarrhea;
—yellow discoloration of the skin or eyes, with or without fatigue;
—any change in the amount or color of your urine (such as dark; red or brown);
—swelling of the feet or lower legs;
—blurred vision, or any visual disturbance;
—mental confusion, depression, dizziness, lightheadedness; hearing problems.

Always Remember: Before taking this medication tell your doctor and pharmacists if you:

—are allergic to Feldene or other related medicines of the NSAID group such as ASA, diclofenac, diflucinal, fenoprofen, flurbiprofen, ibuprofen, indomethacin, ketoprofen, mefenamic acid, sulindac, tiaprofenic acid or tolmetin;
—have a history of stomach upset, ulcers, or liver or kidney diseases;
—are pregnant or intend to become pregnant while taking this medication;
—are breast feeding;
—are taking any other medication (either prescription or nonprescription);

Feldene (cont'd)

—have any other medical problem(s).

While Taking This Medication:

—tell any other doctor, dentist or pharmacist that you consult or see, that you are taking this medication;

—be cautious about driving or participating in activities that require alertness if you are drowsy, dizzy or lightheaded after taking this medication;

—check with your doctor if you are not getting any relief or if any problems develop.

—Report any untoward reactions to your doctor. This is very important as it will aid in the early detection and prevention of potential complications.

—Your regular medical checkups are essential.

—If you require more information on this drug, consult your doctor or pharmacist.

□ FEMARA® Ⓟ

Novartis

Letrozole

Nonsteroidal Aromatase Inhibitor—Inhibitor of Estrogen Biosynthesis—Antitumor Agent

Information for the Patient: Before using Femara (letrozole), please read this leaflet carefully since it contains important information about this medicine. If you have further questions or further concerns, ask your doctor or pharmacist.

What is Femara? Femara tablets contain the active substance letrozole. Femara also contains the following nonmedicinal ingredients needed to make the tablets: cellulose compounds, cornstarch, iron oxide, lactose, magnesium stearate, polyethylene glycol, sodium starch glycolate, silicon dioxide, talc and titanium dioxide. If you are on a special diet, or if you are allergic to any substance, ask your doctor or pharmacist whether any of these ingredients may cause a problem.

What does Femara do? Femara is an aromatase inhibitor used to treat breast cancer in women who have passed menopause and who have been treated previously with antiestrogens (e.g., tamoxifen, which blocks the effects of estrogen). This applies to patients whose menopause was artificially induced, as well as to those who have been through a natural menopause. Femara is known as an aromatase inhibitor. It acts by reducing the effects of the sex hormone, estrogen, in your body. Estrogens may stimulate the growth of certain types of breast cancer.

Before you take Femara: It is important to tell your doctor if you have other medical problems or if you are taking other medicines.

Make sure your doctor knows:

- if you have ever had an unusual or allergic reaction to letrozole or any other ingredient in Femara
- if you still have menstrual periods
- if you are pregnant or breast-feeding

If the answer to any of these questions is **yes,** Femara is not suitable for you.

Femara should not be used in children.

Before using Femara please inform your doctor if you:

- have a serious kidney disease
- are taking hormone replacement therapy
- are taking other medication to treat your cancer

Driving a vehicle or using machinery: Femara may make you feel dizzy or drowsy. If this happens, do not drive, use machinery or perform any other activities which may become dangerous if you are not alert.

How to take Femara: The usual dosage is one 2.5 mg tablet once daily by mouth. The tablet should be swallowed with a small glass of water. You can take Femara with or without food. It is best to take Femara at about the same time every day. Your doctor will decide for how long you should be treated with Femara.

What if you miss a dose? If you forget to take a dose of Femara, don't worry, take the missed dose as soon as you remember. However, if it is almost time for the next dose, skip the missed dose and go back to your regular dosage schedule. Do not double doses.

Medicines or substances that may interfere with the action of Femara: So far there have been no reports of unwanted effects when Femara was taken together with some other medications. Nevertheless, you should ask your doctor or pharmacist before you start using any other prescription or over-the-counter medicines during your treatment with Femara.

What if you are pregnant or breast-feeding? Femara must not be used during pregnancy or while you are breast-feeding.

Overdose: Femara is well tolerated even at doses higher than the one prescribed for you. However, if overdosage is known or suspected, contact your doctor or the nearest Poison Control Centre immediately.

What Side Effects can Femara have? Like all medicines, Femara may cause some unwanted effects (side effects). Most of the unwanted effects that have been observed were mild to moderate and rarely severe enough to stop the treatment with Femara. Many unwanted effects may be caused by your disease or by the consequences of stopping hormone production in your body (such as hot flushes, hair thinning).

Although not all of the unwanted effects may occur, if they do occur they may need medical attention. Check with your doctor if the unwanted effects do not go away during treatment or are bothersome.

Side effects which may occur are: headache; swelling or puffiness due to retained body fluid, weight increase; fatigue; nausea, vomiting, indigestion, increase or loss of appetite, constipation; hot flushes; hair thinning; skin rash; pain in muscles, pain in bones (e.g., arms, legs, back); vaginal bleeding, vaginal discharge; dizziness; increased sweating.

If you notice any other effects not listed above, check with your doctor, nurse, or pharmacist.

Expiry date: Do not take Femara after the expiry date shown on the pack. Remember to take any unused medication back to your pharmacist.

How to store Femara: Store your tablets in a dry place at room temperature. Avoid places where the temperature may rise above 30°C.

Keep this medicine out of the reach of children.

Always remember: This medicine has been prescribed to you for your current medical condition only. Do not give it to other people. Do not use it yourself for other problems.

□ FEXICAM Ⓟ

Technilab

Piroxicam

Nonsteroidal Anti-inflammatory—Analgesic—Antipyretic

Information for the Patient: Fexicam (piroxicam), which has been prescribed to you by your physician, is one of a large group of nonsteroidal anti-inflammatory drugs (also called NSAIDs) and is used to treat the symptoms of certain types of arthritis. Fexicam helps to relieve joint pain, swelling, stiffness and fever by reducing the production of certain substances (prostaglandins) and by helping to control inflammation. NSAIDs do not cure arthritis, but they promote suppression of the inflammation and the tissue-damaging effects resulting from this inflammation. This medicine will help you only as long as you continue to take it.

You should take Fexicam only as directed by your physician. Do not take more of it, do not take it more often and do not take it for a longer period of time than your physician ordered. Taking too much of any of these medicines may increase the chance of unwanted effects, especially if you are an elderly patient.

Be sure to take Fexicam regularly as prescribed. In some types of arthritis, up to 2 weeks may pass before you feel the full effects of this medicine. During treatment, your physician may decide to adjust the dosage according to your response to the medication.

Do not take ASA (acetylsalicylic acid), ASA-containing compounds or other drugs to relieve symptoms of arthritis while taking Fexicam (piroxicam) unless directed to do so by your physician.

If you are prescribed this medication for use over a long period of time, your physician will check your health during regular visits to assess your progress and to ensure that this medication is not causing unwanted effects.

Always Remember: The risks of taking this medication must be weighed against the benefits it will have.

Before taking this medication tell your physician and pharmacists if you:

- or a family member are allergic to or have had a reaction to piroxicam or other anti-inflammatory drugs [such as acetylsalicylic acid (ASA), diclofenac, diflunisal, fenoprofen, flurbiprofen, ibuprofen, indomethacin, mefenamic acid, ketoprofen, tiaprofenic acid, tolmetin, nabumetone or tenoxicam] manifesting itself by increased sinusitis, hives, the initiating or worsening of asthma or anaphylaxis (sudden collapse);
- or a family member has had asthma, nasal polyps, chronic sinusitis or chronic urticaria (hives);
- have a history of stomach upset, ulcers, liver or kidney diseases;
- have blood or urine abnormalities;
- have high blood pressure;
- have diabetes;
- are on any special diet, such as a low-sodium or low-sugar diet;
- are pregnant or intend to become pregnant while taking this medication;
- are breast-feeding or intend to breast-feed while taking this medication;
- are taking any other medication (either prescription or nonprescription) such as other NSAIDs, high blood pressure medication, blood thinners, corticosteroids, methotrexate, cyclosporin, lithium, phenytoin;
- have any other medical problem(s) such as alcohol abuse, bleeding problems, etc.

While Taking This Medication:
- Tell any other physician, dentist or pharmacist that you consult or see, that you are taking this medication.
- Some NSAIDs may cause drowsiness or fatigue in some people taking them. Be cautious about driving or participating in activities that require alertness if you are drowsy, dizzy or lightheaded after taking this medication.
- Check with your physician if you are not getting any relief of your arthritis or if any problems develop.
- Report any untoward reactions to your physician. This is very important as it will aid in the early detection and prevention of potential complications.
- Stomach problems may be more likely to occur if you drink alcoholic beverages. Therefore, do not drink alcoholic beverages while taking this medication.
- Check with your physician immediately if you experience unexpected weakness while taking this medication, or if you vomit any blood or have dark or bloody stools.
- Some people may become more sensitive to sunlight than they are normally. Exposure to sunlight or sunlamps, even for brief periods of time, may cause sunburn, blisters on the skin, skin rash, redness, itching or discoloration; or vision changes. If you have a reaction from the sun, check with your physician.
- Check with your physician immediately if chills, fever, muscle aches or pains, or other flu-like symptoms occur, especially if they occur shortly before, or together with, a skin rash. Very rarely, these effects may be the first signs of a serious reaction to this medication.
- **Your regular medical checkups are essential.**

Side Effects Of This Medication: Along with its beneficial effects, piroxicam, like other NSAID drugs, may cause some undesirable reactions especially when used for a long time or in large doses.

Elderly, frail or debilitated patients often seem to experience more frequent or more severe side effects.

Although not all of these side effects are common, when they do occur, they may require medical attention. **Check with your physician immediately if any of the following are noted:**
- bloody or black tarry stools;
- shortness of breath, wheezing, any trouble in breathing or tightness in the chest;
- skin rash, hives or swelling, itching;
- vomiting or persistent indigestion, nausea, stomach pain or diarrhea;
- yellow discoloration of the skin or eyes;
- any changes in the amount or color of your urine (dark red or brown);
- any pain or difficulty experienced while urinating;
- swelling of the feet or lower legs;
- malaise, fatigue, loss of appetite;
- blurred vision or any visual disturbance;
- mental confusion, depression, dizziness, lightheadedness;
- hearing problems.

Other side effects not listed above may also occur in some patients. If you notice any other effects, check with your physician.

Dosing: Adults: **Oral:** In rheumatoid arthritis and ankylosing spondylitis it is recommended that therapy with piroxicam capsules be initiated as a single daily dose of 20 mg. If desired, this dose may be given as 10 mg b.i.d. Most patients will be maintained on 20 mg daily. A relatively small number of patients may be maintained on 10 mg daily.

In osteoarthritis the recommended starting dosage of piroxicam is 20 mg once daily. If desired, this dose may be given as 10 mg b.i.d. The usual maintenance dose is 10 to 20 mg daily.

Piroxicam should not be given in doses greater than 20 mg daily owing to an increased incidence of gastrointestinal side effects.

Geriatrics and Debilitated: As elderly patients appear to be at higher risk from a variety of adverse reactions from nonsteroidal anti-inflammatory drugs and as elderly, frail or debilitated patients tolerate gastrointestinal side effects less well, consideration should be given to a starting dose that is lower than usual and to an increase of the dose only if symptoms remain uncontrolled. Such patients must be very carefully supervised.

In primary dysmenorrhea the treatment is initiated at the earliest onset of symptoms with a recommended starting dose of 40 mg given as a single daily dose on the first day. For the remainder of the treatment period (usually 2 to 4 days), the dose should be reduced to 20 mg daily.

Rectal: For each indication, the dosage of Fexicam (piroxicam) suppositories, when used alone, is identical with the dosage of piroxicam capsules.

Fexicam suppositories offer an alternative route of administration for those physicians who may wish to prescribe them in certain patients, or for those patients who prefer them.

Combined Administration: The total daily dose of piroxicam administered as capsule and/or suppositories should not exceed 20 mg per day.

Fexicam is available only as a 20 mg suppository.

What to Do If You Miss a Dose: If you take Fexicam (piroxicam) once a day and if you miss a dose of this medicine and remember within 8 hours of the missed dose, take it right away. Then go back to your regular dosing schedule. **Use whole suppositories. Do not split or use portions of suppositories.** If you have any questions about this, check with your physician or pharmacist.

Storage: Store between 15 and 30°C.

Fexicam suppositories are not recommended for use in patients under 16 years of age since safety and effectiveness have not been established.

Do not keep outdated medicine or medicine no longer needed.

Keep out of the reach of children.

This medication has been prescribed to your medical problem. Do not give it to anyone else.

If you require more information on this drug, consult your physician or pharmacist.

☐ FLOLAN® ℞

Glaxo Wellcome

Epoprostenol Sodium

Vasodilator

Information for the Patient: Primary Pulmonary Hypertension (PPH) is defined as pulmonary hypertension (high blood pressure in the pulmonary artery) with no known cause. The pulmonary artery carries the blood from the right ventricle to the lungs where it picks up oxygen. This oxygenated blood then flows to the left side of the heart. The left ventricle then pumps out this blood to the rest of the body. The normal pulmonary artery pressure is in the range of 14 mm Hg. In the patient with PPH, the mean pulmonary artery pressure will be above 30 mm Hg. Changes occur in the small blood vessels in the lungs which results in an increased resistance to blood flow through the vessels. This causes the right ventricle to work much harder in order to push sufficient quantities of blood through the lungs.

Incidence: PPH is a rare disorder with about 60 new cases recognized each year in Canada. The disease usually affects women between the ages of 20 to 40, although cases have been reported in infants and people over the age of 60. There may be a genetic predisposition to this disease.

Cause: There is no known cause. It is a diagnosis that is arrived at by exclusion. When all recognized causes of pulmonary hypertension such as congenital heart disease, valvular heart disease, primary myocardial disease, obstructing lung disease, hypoxemia, collagen vascular disease, liver disease and pulmonary emboli have been eliminated, then the diagnosis of PPH can be made. PPH is a rare disease that can result in death.

Flolan (cont'd)

Signs and Symptoms: Patients usually complain of shortness of breath with effort (dyspnea), chest pain, fatigue and think "they are out of shape". Some people experience difficulty in breathing even at rest, dizziness and fainting. PPH patients also notice swelling of the feet and ankles and palpitations. Unfortunately, some patients will not be diagnosed until the advanced stage.

About Your Medicine: Not all patients respond the same way to medications. Your physician will decide the best therapy for you. Flolan is a very potent vasodilator and on continuous i.v. infusions it has been shown to be effective in treating patients with PPH.

Flolan must be reconstituted only with specific sterile diluent for Flolan.

Flolan is a very complicated medication to administer. The drug must be prepared daily under rigorous conditions. You will need to learn about the drug, the delivery system (the central venous catheter) and the pump. You will need to have a significant other who is willing to learn along with you and to be available in case of need. Your doctor or nurse will teach you and your "significant other" how to prepare the medication and use the pump for administering the medication.

Flolan has to be administered by a continuous i.v. infusion. The dosage may have to be increased gradually. **It must never be stopped abruptly.**

Because it requires administration by continuous controlled infusion, a central venous catheter will be inserted into a vein in the chest. Flolan will be delivered via a computer-operated portable pump (e.g,. CADD1-Pump). This pump will deliver a prescribed amount of the drug through the catheter directly to the heart.

Flolan should improve the way you feel. You (the patient) and your "significant other" will learn about Flolan and be able to recognize the side effects that are associated with this drug. Some of the expected reactions are: flushing, headache, lightheadedness, restlessness, nausea, abdominal pain, diarrhea, dizziness and jaw discomfort. Some of these effects are more noticeable at the onset of therapy.

I. Procedures for Reconstituting Flolan (epoprostenol sodium) Injection: The purpose of this section is to help you better understand the proper procedures to be used for reconstituting Flolan (epoprostenol sodium) for Injection. **It should supplement instructions given to you by your doctor or nurse.**

Flolan should only be reconstituted with specific sterile diluent for Flolan. Reconstituted Flolan solution should not be mixed with other solutions/medicines.

Your doctor will tell you how much Flolan and sterile diluent you will need to use when making up your daily supply. The general procedure for reconstituting Flolan solution is described below.

1. First clean your worksite and gather your supplies. Wash your hands thoroughly and then open all the packages. Remove the vial caps from the vial containing specific **sterile diluent** for Flolan and clean the tops of the vials with alcohol swabs.
2. Once you finish cleaning the tops of your vials and opening your supplies, attach a needle to the syringe. Now break the syringe seal by gently pulling the plunger out slightly and then pushing it back. Draw air into the syringe; the amount of air that you draw into the syringe should be equal to the amount of sterile diluent you've been instructed to withdraw from the vial. Insert the needle through the rubber seal of the vial and press the plunger down to inject the air into the vial. Once all the air has been injected, pull the plunger gently back up to withdraw the prescribed amount of diluent. Without withdrawing the needle, invert the vial and syringe and tap the syringe gently so that any air bubbles trapped in the syringe rise towards the top. If necessary, depress the plunger gently to force the air bubbles out and then withdraw sufficient additional diluent to restore the required volume in the syringe. Once the required volume has been drawn into the syringe, withdraw the needle.
3. Now insert the needle through the rubber seal of the Flolan vial and inject the sterile diluent gently onto the side of the vial. Always direct the flow of sterile diluent towards the side of the vial and inject it gently so the Flolan doesn't foam. Allow the pressure to equalize and withdraw the needle from the vial. Now, mix the Flolan by gently swirling the vial. Turn the vial upside down to catch any undissolved powder near the top. **Never shake the vials.** If you need to mix more than one vial of Flolan, simply repeat this process.
4. Your doctor or nurse will advise you on the amount of reconstituted Flolan to be withdrawn. First, by gently pulling the plunger back, fill the syringe with the amount of air that is equal to the amount of Flolan to be withdrawn. Remember to wipe the tops of the vials with an alcohol swab. Now, insert the needle through the seal of the Flolan vial and inject the air. Then pull the plunger gently back to withdraw the reconstituted Flolan into the syringe. Remove any air that may be trapped in the syringe as described in step 2 above. Withdraw the needle and place the cap back on the syringe.
5. You are now ready to inject the Flolan into your cassette. Remove the end cap from the cassette tubing; then carefully remove the needle from the syringe, discard in an appropriate manner and attach the syringe to the cassette tubing. Now, while holding the cassette in one hand, you can use the tabletop as a third hand while you push down on the syringe to inject the solution into the cassette. Once the syringe is empty, clamp the cassette tubing near the syringe, disconnect the syringe and cap the tubing with the red cap.
6. Now you will withdraw the contents of the sterile diluent vials and inject them into the cassette. Using a 60 cc syringe, attach a new needle to the syringe, break the seal on the syringe by pulling the plunger out and pushing it back in. Next fill the syringe with the amount of air that is equal to the amount of sterile diluent you will remove from the first vial. Remember to wipe the top of the sterile diluent vial with an alcohol swab before you insert the needle. Once it is dry, insert the needle through the rubber seal, inject some of the air into the vial and allow the fluid to flow into the syringe. With the larger syringe, it may be easier to hold it in the vertical position. Push more air in as needed until you have withdrawn all of the contents of the vial. Remove any air that may be in the syringe as described in step 2 above. Once the vial is emptied, allow the pressure to equalize before you pull the needle out. If you don't you may lose fluid from the syringe or the vial and you would need to start the whole process over again. Withdraw the needle and place the cap back on the syringe.
7. Now you are ready to inject the first syringe full of sterile diluent into the cassette. To do this, first uncap the cassette tubing. Then carefully remove the needle from the syringe, discard in an appropriate manner and attach the syringe to the cassette tubing. Unclamp the cassette tubing and then carefully inject the solution into the cassette. When the syringe is empty, clamp the cassette tubing near the syringe, disconnect the syringe and cap the cassette tubing. You will repeat this same process to transfer the contents of the required sterile diluent vial as specified by your doctor into the cassette.
8. After you have completed the transfer of all the required diluent, leave the syringe attached to the cassette tubing while you mix the solution. Gently invert the cassette at least 10 times, thoroughly mixing the Flolan. Now you need to remove all of the air from the cassette.
9. In order to remove the air inside the cassette first you have to collect the air bubbles. Simply rotate the cassette around until all of the small bubbles join to form one big air pocket. Then tilt the cassette carefully so that the air pocket is in the corner where the tubing connects to the bag. To remove the air from the cassette, unclamp the tubing and pull back the plunger of the syringe until you see fluid fill the tubing. Then clamp the tubing near the connector, disconnect it and cap it with the red cap. To avoid any confusion, label the cassette with the date and time you made up the Flolan. That's it, you're done.

Now put the cassette into the refrigerator until it is time to use it. Store it on the top shelf to avoid spilling any food or drink onto your cassette. Each day, you will make up a new cassette and use the cassette you refrigerated the day before. That way, you will always have a back-up.

II. Administration of Flolan Injection by a Continuous Infusion Pump: You will use a pump to receive medication by continuous delivery. The instructions for use may vary depending on the particular make and model of the pump you are using. **Your doctor or nurse will give detailed instructions on how to use and care for the specific pump and accessories that you will use for administering your medicine (including changing the pump battery, cassette and tubing).**

Remember: Change the gel packs every 12 hours or every 8 hours if the ambient temperature approaches 30°C.

III. Central Venous Catheter and Its Care: Description: The catheter is a thin soft flexible tube that has been placed into one of the large veins in your upper chest. These veins are sometimes called central veins, and the catheter may be referred to as central venous line. The tip of the catheter lies in a vein that leads to the entrance to your heart.

The catheter is inserted under a local anesthetic in the operating room. Sterile conditions are maintained during this procedure to avoid the risk of infection. You will not feel it inside your body. The catheter has been tunneled into place inside your chest. The catheter has a Dacron fibre cuff which is under the skin. This will hold the catheter in place and avoid infection. The catheter may also be sutured into position.

Your doctor will decide which type of catheter is best suited for you.

Your nurse will teach you how to care for the catheter, how to keep the skin around the catheter exit site clean and free from infection. You will learn how to change the dressing and to protect your skin. Your physician and nurse will make sure that you are comfortable in caring for the catheter site.

Should you develop sudden fever, contact your doctor as soon as possible.

Catheter Exit Site: Change dressing 1 to 2 times per week or more frequently if needed.

Equipment: Dressing set, 2 sterile containers, Proviodine swabs, 70% alcohol, Betadine ointment, Sterile Q Tips, Adhesive tape (nonallergenic), transparent dressing (such as Op Site or Tegaderm) 10 cm× 12 cm, or 6 cm× 7 cm.

Steps: Maintain sterile technique at all times. If you suspect that you have contaminated anything, discard equipment and begin again.

1. Assemble equipment.
2. Stabilize catheter while removing old transparent dressing.
3. Open sterile dressing kit.
4. Pour alcohol into sterile container.
5. Pour Proviodine into sterile container.
6. Pour Betadine ointment into sterile field.
7. Open transparent dressings onto sterile field.
8. Remove old transparent dressing.
9. Clean the catheter exit site with Proviodine-soaked 5×5 cm swabs, starting at the catheter exit site. Work outward in a circular extending motion, extending to an 8 cm radius.
10. Repeat step 9, 3 times.
11. **Never return to the catheter exit site using the same swab.**
12. Repeat steps 9 and 10 using alcohol-soaked 5×5 cm swab.
13. Apply Betadine ointment to catheter exit site with sterile Q Tip.
14. Apply new sterile transparent dressing.
15. Tape catheter to skin using "stress loop".

□ FLOMAX® ℞

Boehringer Ingelheim

Tamsulosin HCl

Selective Antagonist of Alpha$_{1A}$-adrenoceptor Subtype in the Prostate

Information for the Patient: Flomax is for use by men only.

Please read this leaflet before you start taking Flomax. Also, read it each time you renew your prescription, just in case new information has been added. Remember, this leaflet does not take the place of careful discussions with your doctor. You and your doctor should discuss Flomax when you start taking your medication and at regular checkups.

Why your doctor has prescribed Flomax? Your doctor has prescribed Flomax because you have a medical condition called benign prostatic hyperplasia or BPH. This occurs only in men.

What is BPH? BPH is an enlargement of the prostate gland. After age 50, most men develop enlarged prostates. The prostate is located below the bladder. As the prostate enlarges, it may slowly restrict the flow of urine. This can lead to symptoms such as:

- a weak or interrupted urinary stream;
- a feeling that you cannot empty your bladder completely;
- a feeling of delay or hesitation when you start to urinate;
- a feeling that you must urinate right away;
- painful urination;
- frequent sleep interruption caused by a need to urinate.

What Flomax does? Flomax acts by relaxing muscles in the prostate and bladder neck at the site of the obstruction, resulting in improved urine flow, and reduced BPH symptoms.

What you need to know while taking Flomax?

- **You must see your doctor regularly.** While taking Flomax, you must have regular checkups. Follow your doctor's advice about when to have these checkups.
- **About side effects.** Like all prescription drugs, Flomax may cause side effects. Side effects due to Flomax may include dizziness, insomnia, runny nose, or ejaculatory problems. In some cases side effects may decrease or disappear while the patient continues to take Flomax.

  Some men may experience dizziness or fainting caused by a decrease in blood pressure after taking Flomax. Although these symptoms are unlikely, you should avoid driving or hazardous tasks for 12 hours after the initial dose or after your doctor recommends an increase in dose. If you interrupt your treatment for several days or more, resume treatment at 1 capsule/day, after consulting with your physician.

  You should discuss side effects with your doctor before taking Flomax and anytime you think you are having a side effect.

How to take Flomax? Follow your doctor's advice about how to take Flomax. You should take it approximately 30 minutes following the same meal every day.

Do not share Flomax with anyone else; it was prescribed only for you.

Do not crush, chew, or open capsules of Flomax sustained-release formulation. These capsules are specially formulated to control the delivery of tamsulosin HCl to the blood stream.

Each capsule of Flomax sustained-release formulation to be taken orally contains tamsulosin HCl 0.4 mg, and the following inactive ingredients: calcium stearate, Eudragit L30D-55*, FD&C Blue No. 2, ferric oxide (red and yellow), gelatin, microcrystalline cellulose, talc, titanium dioxide and triacetin. (*Contains methacrylic acid copolymer, polysorbate 80, and sodium lauryl sulfate.) Printing ink contains: black iron oxide, dimethylpolysiloxane, 2-ethoxyethanol, industrial methylated spirit, purified water, shellac, soya lecithin.

Keep Flomax and all medicines out of reach of children.

For more information about Flomax and BPH, talk with your doctor. In addition, talk to your pharmacist or other health care provider.

□ FLONASE® ℞

Glaxo Wellcome

Fluticasone Propionate

Corticosteroid for Nasal Use

Information for the Patient: Please read this leaflet carefully before you start to take your medicine. For further information or advice, ask your doctor or pharmacist.

Name of Your Medicine: The name of your medicine is Flonase (fluticasone propionate aqueous nasal spray). This is one of a group of medicines called corticosteroids.

Flonase can only be obtained on the prescription of a doctor.

Instructions for Use of Your Flonase Nasal Spray (see package insert for illustrations):

Before Using:

A. Shake the bottle gently, then remove the dust cover by gently squeezing the ribs between your finger and thumb and lifting off.
B. Hold the spray as shown with your forefinger and middle finger on either side of the nozzle and your thumb underneath the bottle.
C. If using Flonase for the first time or if you have not used it for a week or more test the spray as follows: with the nozzle pointing away from you, press down several times as shown until a fine mist comes out of the nozzle.

Using the Spray:

D. Blow your nose gently.
E. Close one nostril as shown in the diagram and put the nozzle in the other nostril. Tilt your head forward slightly and keep the spray upright.
F. Start to breathe in through your nose and **while breathing in** press down with your fingers **once** to release one spray.
G. Breathe out through your mouth. If a second spray in that nostril is required repeat steps F and G.
H. Repeat E, F, and G for the other nostril.

After Use:

I. Wipe the nozzle with a tissue or handkerchief and replace the cover.

Cleaning:

J. Gently pull off the nozzle. Wash it in warm water.
K. Shake off excess water and allow to dry in a warm place but avoid excessive heat.
L. Gently push the nozzle back on top of the brown bottle. Replace the dust cover.
M. If the nozzle becomes blocked it can be removed as above and left to soak in warm water. Rinse under a cold tap, allow to dry and

Flonase (cont'd)

refit. Do not try to unblock the nozzle by inserting a pin or other sharp objects.

Important Points to Remember: Follow the **instructions for use** described above. If you have any problems tell your doctor or pharmacist.

- Have you ever had to stop taking other medicines for this illness because you were allergic to it or it caused problems? If the answer is **Yes,** tell your doctor or pharmacist as soon as possible, if you have not already done so.
- Tell your doctor if you notice that any discharge from your nose is yellow or green, if you have not already done so.
- It is important that you inhale each dose through the nose as instructed by your doctor or nurse. The label will usually tell you how many doses to take and how often. If it does not, or if you are not sure, ask your doctor of pharmacist.

Adults: The usual dose is 2 sprays (2×50 micrograms) into each nostril, once a day, in the morning. Your doctor may advise you to increase this to 2 sprays (2×50 micrograms) into each nostril, twice a day.

Children Aged 4 to 11 Years: The usual dose is one spray (50 micrograms) into each nostril, once a day in the morning. Your doctor may advise you to increase this to 2 sprays (2×50 micrograms) into each nostril, once a day.

- **Do not** inhale more doses or use your nasal spray more often than your doctor advises.
- It takes a few days for this medicine to work. **It is very important that you use it regularly. Do not stop** treatment even if you feel better unless told to do so by your doctor.
- If your symptoms have not improved after 3 weeks of treatment with Flonase, tell your doctor.
- If you also have itchy, watery eyes you should tell your doctor. He may give you an additional medicine to treat your eyes. Be careful not to confuse them, particularly if the additional medicine is eye drops.

About Your Medicine: Flonase is used to treat seasonal allergic rhinitis (including hay fever) and perennial rhinitis. Symptoms of these conditions include itching, a blocked up feeling in the nose and excessive sneezing. Flonase reduces the irritation and inflammation in the lining of the nose and nasal passages and so it relieves the blocked up feeling in the nose, the runny nose, itching and sneezing.

Use of This Medicine During Pregnancy and Breast-Feeding: Please tell your doctor if you are pregnant, likely to become pregnant or if you are breast feeding a baby. Your doctor may decide not to prescribe this medicine in these circumstances.

Adverse Reactions:

- Occasionally you may sneeze a little after using this spray but this soon stops. You may experience an unpleasant taste or smell.
- If your nose or throat becomes painful or if you have a severe nose bleed after using the nasal spray tell your doctor as soon as possible.
- If you feel unwell or have any other problems tell your doctor and follow the advice given.

What To Do If An Overdose Is Taken: Tell your doctor if you use more than you were told.

What To Do If You Miss A Dose: If you miss a dose do not worry; take a dose when you remember and take the next dose when it is due.

What To Do If You Stop Your Medicine: If your doctor decides to stop your treatment, do not keep any left over medicine unless your doctor tells you to.

Storage of Your Medicine:

- Keep your nasal spray in a safe place where children cannot reach it. Your medicine may harm them.
- Keep your nasal spray below 30°C.

A Reminder: Remember this medicine is for **you.** Only a doctor can prescribe it for you. Never give it to others. It may harm them even if their symptoms are the same as yours.

Further Information: If you have questions or are not sure about anything, then you should ask your doctor or the pharmacist.

You may want to read this leaflet again. Please **do not throw it away** until you have finished your medicine.

□ FLOVENT® Ⓟ

Glaxo Wellcome

Fluticasone Propionate

Corticosteroid

Information for the Patient: What you should know about Flovent Inhalation Aerosol and Diskus: Please read this leaflet carefully before you start to take your medicine. For further information or advice, ask your doctor or pharmacist.

About your medicine: The name of this medicine is Flovent (fluticasone propionate). Flovent is one of a group of medicines known as corticosteroids, frequently referred to simply as ''steroids'', and can only be obtained on the prescription of a doctor.

Flovent is a medicine which your doctor will have chosen to suit you and your condition. When taken every day at the regularly spaced doses as ordered by your doctor, it can help to ease your breathing problems by relieving the swelling and irritation in the small air passages in the lungs.

Flovent Inhalers are available in four strengths: 25 µg fluticasone propionate in each puff; 50 µg fluticasone propionate in each puff; 125 µg fluticasone propionate in each puff; 250 µg fluticasone propionate in each puff.

Flovent Diskus is available in 4 strengths: 50 µg fluticasone propionate in each blister; 100 µg fluticasone propionate in each blister; 250 µg fluticasone propionate in each blister; 500 µg fluticasone propionate in each blister.

Your doctor will decide which strength you need.

Important points to note before taking your medicine: Have you ever had to stop taking other medicines for this illness because you were allergic to them or they caused problems? Are you having treatment, or have you recently received treatment for tuberculosis (TB)? Are you taking other ''steroids'' by mouth or inhalation?

If the answer is **yes** to any of these questions, tell your doctor or pharmacist as soon as possible if you have not already done so.

Use of this medicine during pregnancy and breast-feeding: Do not use this medication during pregnancy or breast-feeding without first discussing with your doctor.

Taking your medicine: Follow the instructions shown. If you have any problems, tell your doctor or pharmacist.

It is important that you take each dose as instructed by your doctor, nurse or pharmacist. Your doctor will decide what dose you should take and how often. Your doctor will also decide which strength you should use.

The label will usually tell you what dose to take and how often. If it doesn't, or you are not sure, ask your doctor or pharmacist.

For adults, and adolescents above 16 years of age, the usual dose is 100 to 500 µg twice daily. Patients with very severe asthma requiring higher doses of corticosteroids, such as those patients currently requiring oral steroids, may use doses up to 1 000 µg twice daily.

The usual children's dose is 50 to 100 µg twice daily.

Inhalation Aerosol: Each prescribed dose should be given by a minimum of 2 inhalations.

Diskus: When using Flovent Diskus, the usual prescribed dose is 1 blister (inhalation) twice a day.

Do not take more doses or use your Inhalation Aerosol or Diskus more often than your doctor advises.

Remember this medicine must not be swallowed but should only be inhaled. If you have any difficulties or do not understand the leaflet that comes with it, ask your doctor or pharmacist.

It may take up to a week for this medicine to work and it is **very important that you use it regularly.** If your shortness of breath or wheeze does not get better after 7 days, tell your doctor. **Do not stop** treatment—even if you feel better—unless told to do so by your doctor.

Do not use this medicine to treat a sudden attack of breathlessness. You will probably need a different kind of medicine in a different color pack which your doctor may already have given you. If you have more than one medicine, be careful not to confuse them.

If you have to go into hospital for an operation, take your Inhalation Aerosol or Diskus with you and tell the doctor what medicine(s) you are taking.

How to use your Flovent Inhaler properly (see package insert for illustrations): Before you use your Flovent Inhaler for the first time, or if your inhaler has not been used for a week or more, release 4 puffs into the air to ensure that it works properly.

1. Remove the cap from the mouthpiece; the strap on the cap will stay attached to the actuator. Check the mouthpiece inside and outside to ensure that it is clean.
2. Shake the inhaler vigorously.
3. Hold the inhaler upright between fingers and thumb with your thumb on the base, below the mouthpiece. Breathe out as far as comfortable.
4. For the next step there are 2 alternatives (4a or 4b) depending on the technique preferred by your doctor.

4a. Place the mouthpiece in your mouth between your teeth and close your lips around it, but do not bite it. Just after starting to breathe in through your mouth, press down on the top of the inhaler to release the drug while still breathing in steadily and deeply, **or**

4b. Place the mouthpiece 2 finger widths directly in front of your mouth. Begin a slow, deep inward breath through your wide open mouth, at the same time pressing the canister down firmly into the inhaler.

5. While holding your breath, take the inhaler from your mouth and take your finger from the top of the inhaler. Continue holding your breath for as long as is comfortable.
6. If you are to take further puffs, keep the inhaler upright and wait about half a minute before repeating steps 2 through 5.
7. After use, always snap the mouthpiece cover back into position to keep out dust and lint.
8. Rinse out your mouth with water after each dose. Do not swallow the water after rinsing.

Important: Do not rush steps 4 and 5. It is important that you start to breathe in as slowly as possible just before operating your inhaler. Practice in front of a mirror for the first few times. If you see "mist" coming from the top of your inhaler or the sides of your mouth, you should start again from step 2.

If your doctor has given you different instructions for using your inhaler, please follow them carefully. Tell your doctor if you have any difficulties.

Children: Young children may need help and an adult may need to operate the inhaler for them. Encourage the child to breathe out and operate the inhaler just after the child starts to breathe in. Practice the technique together. Older children or people with weak hands should hold the inhaler with both hands. Put the 2 forefingers on top of the inhaler and both thumbs on the base below the mouthpiece.

Cleaning: Your inhaler should be cleaned at least once per week.
1. Pull the metal canister out of the plastic casing of the inhaler and remove the mouthpiece cover.
2. Rinse the plastic casing and mouthpiece cover in warm water. A mild detergent may be added to the water. Then rinse thoroughly with clean water before drying. **Do not put the metal canister into water.**
3. Leave the casing and mouthpiece cover to dry in a warm place. Avoid excessive heat.
4. Replace the canister and mouthpiece cover.
5. After cleaning, release 1 puff into the air to make sure that the inhaler works.

How to use your Flovent Diskus properly: About your Flovent Diskus: Flovent Diskus is a plastic inhaler device containing a foil strip with 28 or 60 blisters. Each blister contains 50, 100, 250 or 500 µg of the active ingredient fluticasone propionate and lactose, which acts as a 'carrier'. The blisters protect the powder for inhalation from the effects of the atmosphere. The device has a dose counter which tells you the number of doses remaining. It counts down from 28 or 60 to 1. To show when the last 5 doses have been reached, the numbers appear in red.

When you take your Flovent Diskus out of its box, it will be in the **closed position**.

A new Diskus contains 28 or 60 individually protected doses of your medicine, in powder form. The dose indicator tells you how many doses are left.

Each dose is accurately measured and hygienically protected. It requires no maintenance, and no refilling. Numbers 5 to 0 will appear in **red** to warn you when there are only a few doses left.

How your Diskus works: The Diskus is easy to use. When you need a dose, just follow the 4 simple steps illustrated (see package insert for illustrations): 1. Open. 2. Slide. 3. Inhale. 4. Close.

Sliding the lever of your Diskus opens a small hole in the mouthpiece and unwraps a dose ready for you to inhale it. When you close the Diskus, the lever automatically moves back to its original position ready for your next dose when you need it. The outer case protects your Diskus when it is not in use.

1. **Open:** To open your Diskus hold the outer case in one hand and put the thumb of your other hand on the thumb grip. Push your thumb away from you as far as it will go.
2. **Slide:** Hold your Diskus with the mouthpiece towards you. Slide the lever away from you as far as it will go—until it clicks. Your Diskus is now ready to use. Every time the lever is pushed back, a dose is made available for inhaling. This is shown by the dose counter. Do not play with the lever as this releases doses which will be wasted.
3. **Inhale:** Before you start to inhale the dose, read through this section carefully.

- Hold the Diskus away from your mouth. Breathe out as far as is comfortable. Remember—never breathe into your Diskus.
- Put the mouthpiece to your lips. Breathe in steadily and deeply—through the Diskus, not through your nose.
- Remove the Diskus from your mouth.
- Hold your breath for about 10 seconds or for as long as is comfortable.
- Breathe out slowly.

4. **Close:** To close your Diskus, put your thumb in the thumb grip, and slide the thumb grip back towards you, as far as it will go.

When you close the Diskus, it clicks shut.
The lever automatically returns to its original position and is reset.

Your Diskus is now ready for you to use again.

If you have been instructed to take 2 inhalations you must close the Diskus and repeat stages 1 to 4.

Remember: Keep your Diskus dry. Keep it closed when not in use. Never breathe into your Diskus. Only slide the lever when you are ready to take a dose.

After using your Flovent Inhalation Aerosol or Diskus: If you notice that your shortness of breath or wheeze is becoming worse, tell your doctor as soon as possible.

Very occasionally, some people find that their throat or tongue becomes sore after taking this medicine or that their voice becomes a little hoarse. In some people, an infection of the mouth and throat called candidiasis (thrush) may occur. Rinsing your mouth with water immediately after taking each dose may help. Do not swallow the water after rinsing. Tell your doctor but do not stop treatment unless told to do so.

If you feel unwell in any other way or have any symptoms that you do not understand, you should contact your doctor immediately.

If you take too much medicine: In the event of an excessive overdose (more than the maximum recommended daily dose), tell your doctor without delay or contact your nearest hospital emergency department or poison centre.

If you miss a dose: It is **very important that you use Flovent regularly;** however, if you miss a single dose, do not worry—just take the next dose when it is due.

What to do if you must stop taking your medicine: If your doctor decides to stop your treatment, do not keep any leftover medicine unless your doctor tells you to.

Remember: This medicine is only for **you.** Only a doctor can prescribe it for you. Never give it to someone else. It may harm them even if their symptoms are the same as yours.

Storing your medicine: Keep your medicine in a safe place where children cannot reach it. Your medicine may harm them.

Inhalation Aerosol: Store between 2 and 30°C. Protect from frost, direct sunlight and high temperatures (30°C).

If the inhaler becomes very cold, remove the metal canister and warm **in your hand** for a few minutes. **Never** use other forms of heat.

Warning: The metal canister is pressurized. Do not puncture it or burn it, even when apparently empty.

Diskus: Store between 2 and 30°C.

Keep Flovent Diskus away from direct frost, heat or sunlight and protect it from high temperatures (above 30°C). Do not store in a damp environment such as a bathroom.

Further information: If you have any questions or are not sure about anything, then you should ask your doctor or the pharmacist.

You may need to read this leaflet again. **Please do not throw it away** until you have finished your medicine.

Flovent is a registered trade mark of Glaxo Group Ltd., Glaxo Wellcome Inc. is a licensed user.

☐ FORADIL® ℞

Novartis Pharmaceuticals

Formoterol Fumarate

Bronchodilator

Information for the Patient: Before using Foradil, please read these instructions carefully. It contains information about Foradil which may add to the specific advice from your doctor and pharmacist. If, after reading this material, you have further questions, ask your doctor or pharmacist.

What is Foradil and how does it work? Foradil is the brand name for a medication called formoterol fumarate. Foradil is a new type of drug known as a **long-acting bronchodilator.** Foradil is used for the treatment of breathing problems in asthma. It makes breathing easier by opening the small air passages in the lungs, and helps them remain opened and relaxed for about 12 hours.

Your doctor will have explained that you are to take this drug twice daily regularly, **as well as** the drug which reduces the **inflammation** of the lungs due to your asthma (also known as a preventive medication). You will also have a **short-acting** bronchodilator (also known as a quick reliever) to use when you are aware of the shortness of breath, tightness, coughing and wheezing of your asthma.

Follow your doctor's directions carefully. They may differ from the information outlined here.

What is in Foradil? Foradil comes as gelatin capsules containing a dry powder. The dry powder is **inhaled** into the lungs using the inhaler provided. Each capsule contains 12 μg of formoterol fumarate. The capsules also contain lactose. Foradil comes in blister packs containing 60 capsules.

What should I tell my doctor before taking Foradil? Tell your doctor:

- about all the health problems you have now or have had in the past — especially heart disease, diabetes, overactive thyroid.
- about other medications you take including ones you can buy without a prescription especially medications used to treat depression or sad mood (monoamine oxidase inhibitors and tricylic antidepressants), sympathomimetic agents, antihistamines, water pills (diuretics), β-blockers for high blood pressure and certain eye drops for the treatment of glaucoma, drugs containing quinidine, disopyramide, procainamide, phenothiazine or xanthine derivatives (theophylline or aminophylline).
- if you are severely allergic to milk or have ever had any unusual or allergic reaction to Foradil.
- if you are pregnant, plan to become pregnant, or are breast-feeding.

What if you are pregnant, plan to become pregnant or are breast-feeding? You should tell your doctor if you are pregnant, plan to become pregnant or are breast-feeding. Avoid using Foradil during pregnancy. Mothers who are breast-feeding should not use Foradil.

Can my adolescent child take foradil? Foradil inhalation powder is suitable for adolescent children aged 12 years or more. The severity of asthma changes with age. Your child should therefore be periodically re-examined by a physician. It is important to make sure that your child also understands and properly follows the asthma therapies prescribed to him/her. These will include in addition to Foradil, a drug which reduces the inflammation in the lung due to asthma (also known as a preventive medication) and a short-acting bronchodilator (also known as a quick reliever).

How do I take Foradil properly? Foradil should not be taken more than twice daily. If you have difficulty breathing, tightness, wheezing or coughing and need relief, use the short-acting bronchodilator medication your doctor has prescribed for that purpose.

You must continue to regularly take the anti-inflammatory medications (e.g., inhaled steroids) your doctor has prescribed. Your anti-inflammatory medications and Foradil are designed to act together to best treat your condition. Even though you feel better, **do not stop** or reduce your doses of Foradil or your anti-inflammatory medications.

It is important that you take Foradil correctly. The exact instructions for using Foradil capsules with the inhaler are outlined in detail in this insert.

If you have any questions or problems, ask your doctor or pharmacist.

Each capsule contains 1 puff of medication. The regular dose for adults, including elderly patients, is 1 or 2 capsules twice a day, once in the morning and again in the evening. The recommended dose for children aged 12 years or more is 1 capsule twice a day (morning and evening).

The capsules are not to be swallowed; like most asthma medications, Foradil is inhaled. Exact directions for using the inhaler are in this insert. Once your doctor and or your pharmacist has shown you how to use Foradil, the diagrams and directions in this insert will serve as a reminder of the technique. It is suggested that you display it wherever you usually administer Foradil.

Where should I keep Foradil? Keep this medication **at room temperature, in a dry place.** Your car or the bathroom are not good choices.

The capsules should be removed from the blister pack just before use.

Keep this medicine out of the reach of children because it may harm them.

Do not use Foradil after the expiry date marked on the carton.

Are there any side effects? Like any medication, Foradil may cause unwanted side effects in some people. The side effects that do occur are usually mild and go away a short time after starting Foradil.

Foradil may occasionally cause mild side effects such as tremor, fast and irregular heartbeat, headache, dizziness or irritation of the mouth or throat. Rarely, more serious side effects, such as muscle cramps and pain, agitation, feeling nervous or tired, difficulties in sleeping, and, very rarely, bronchospasm (an attack of asthma) can occur. In isolated cases allergic reactions with severe drop of blood pressure and swelling of the face, eyelids, lips have been reported. You should check with your doctor if:

- the mild side effects persist,
- the more serious ones occur,
- you notice any other effects not listed here.

Important notes: It is very important that you take Foradil exactly as your doctor tells you. If the relief of your asthma is not as good as usual or does not last as long as usual, **tell your doctor right away.** A change from ''usual'' includes more wheezing, coughing, tightness or shortness of breath.

If you are using more of your short-acting bronchodilating medication or if you feel that it is less effective **tell your doctor right away.** Your doctor may adjust your treatment.

If your symptoms are waking you up at night **tell your doctor right away.** Your doctor may adjust your treatment.

If you have taken all your medication and an hour at rest has not relieved your symptoms, **you may need emergency treatment.**

Nothing in this material should stop you from calling your doctor or pharmacist with any questions or concerns you may have about using Foradil.

Information for the consumer about administering Foradil inhalation powder capsules: Before using Foradil, please read these instructions carefully (see package insert for illustrations). They contain information about Foradil which may add to the specific advice from your doctor and pharmacist. If, after reading this material, you have further questions, ask your doctor or pharmacist.

Your doctor will have explained that you are to take this drug regularly, as well as the drug which reduces the inflammation of the lungs due to your asthma. You will also probably have a short-acting bronchodilator to use when you are aware of the tightening, coughing and wheezing of your asthma.

How do I use the Foradil inhaler and capsules?

1. Pull off cap.
2. To open, hold base of the inhaler firmly and turn the mouthpiece in the direction of the arrow.
3. Remove the capsule from the blister pack. It is important to keep the capsule in the blister pack until you are ready to use it. Place the capsule in the capsule shaped compartment in the base of the inhaler.
4. Return the mouthpiece to the closed position.
5. Keeping the inhaler upright, firmly squeeze the two blue buttons fully **only once.** This will pierce the capsule. Release the buttons. Although the capsule is now pierced, the powder will not be released until you inhale it.

   Please note that the capsule might splinter at this step and small fragments of gelatin might reach your mouth and throat. This gelatin is edible and is therefore not harmful. You can minimize the tendency of the capsule splintering by:
   - piercing the capsule only once,
   - keeping the capsules stored in a dry place at room temperature,
   - keeping the capsule in the blister pack until you are ready to use it.
6. Breathe out fully.
7. Place the mouthpiece in your mouth and tilt your head slightly backward. Close your lips around the mouthpiece and breathe in steadily

as deeply as you can. As you breathe in, you will inhale the medication into your lungs.

You should hear a whirring noise as you breathe in because inhalation causes the capsule to spin around in the inhaler. **Please note** if you do not hear the whirring noise, the capsule may be stuck in the capsule-shaped compartment. If this occurs, re-open the inhaler carefully and pry the capsule out. You cannot loosen the capsule by repeatedly pressing the buttons.

8. If you have heard the whirring noise, **hold your breath** for as long as you comfortably can while removing the inhaler from your mouth. Then breathe out.
9. After use, open the inhaler. Check that the capsule is empty. If it is not close the inhaler and re-inhale following steps 6, 7 and 8. Remove the empty capsule. Close the mouthpiece. Replace the cap.

What if I miss a dose? Foradil should not be used more often than twice a day. If you forget to take a dose, take it as soon as possible. However, if it is almost time for your next dose, do not take the missed one, just go back to your regular dosing schedule. Never take a double dose.

How do I clean the inhaler? To remove any powder residues, wipe the mouthpiece and capsule compartment with a dry cloth or a small, soft, clean brush.

□ FOSAMAX® Ⓟ

MSD

Alendronate Sodium

Bone Metabolism Regulator

Information for the Patient: Osteoporosis: Please read this insert carefully before starting Fosamax and every time your prescription is renewed.

How should I take Fosamax? These are the important things you must do to help make sure you will benefit from Fosamax:

1. **After getting up for the day, swallow your Fosamax tablet with a full glass (200 to 250 mL) of plain water** only: not mineral water, not coffee or tea, not juice.

   Although it has not been tested, because of high mineral content, "hard water" may decrease absorption of Fosamax. If your normal drinking water is classified as "hard water", you should consider taking this medication with distilled water (i.e., not mineral water).
2. **After swallowing your Fosamax tablet do not lie down—stay fully upright (sitting or standing) for at least 30 minutes and until after your first food of the day. Do not chew or suck on a tablet of Fosamax.**
3. **Do not take Fosamax at bedtime or before getting up for the day.**

   The above actions will help the Fosamax tablet reach your stomach quickly and help avoid irritation of your esophagus (the tube that connects your mouth with your stomach).
4. **After swallowing your Fosamax tablet, wait at least 30 minutes before taking your first food, beverage, or other medication of the day,** including antacids, calcium supplements and vitamins. Fosamax is effective only if taken when your stomach is empty.
5. **If you develop difficulty or pain upon swallowing, chest pain, or new or worsening heartburn, stop taking Fosamax immediately and call your doctor.**
6. Take Fosamax once a day, every day.
7. It is important that you continue taking Fosamax for as long as your doctor prescribes it. Fosamax can treat your osteoporosis or help prevent you from developing osteoporosis only if you continue to take it.

   You should always tell your physician about all drugs you are taking or plan to take, including those obtained without a prescription.

Fosamax is the brand name of Merck Frosst Canada Inc. for the substance alendronate sodium available **only on prescription** from your physician. Alendronate sodium is a member of a class of nonhormonal drugs called aminobisphosphonates.

Fosamax is available as a 5 mg tablet for prevention of osteoporosis and 10 mg tablet for treatment of osteoporosis.

Your physician has prescribed Fosamax because you have a disease, known as osteoporosis or to prevent you from developing the disease. This will help prevent you from developing fractures.

How is normal bone maintained? Bone undergoes a normal process of rebuilding that occurs continuously throughout your skeleton. First, old bone is removed (resorbed), then new bone is laid down (formed). This balanced process of resorbing and forming bone keeps your skeleton healthy and strong.

What is osteoporosis and why should it be treated or prevented? Osteoporosis is a thinning and weakening of the bones that is common in postmenopausal women. The menopause occurs when the ovaries stop producing the female hormone, estrogen, or are removed (which may occur, for example, at the time of a hysterectomy). After the menopause, bone is removed faster than it is formed, so bone loss occurs and bones become weaker. The earlier a woman reaches the menopause, the greater the risk of osteoporosis. Maintaining bone mass and preventing further bone loss are important to keep your skeleton healthy.

Early on, osteoporosis usually has no symptoms. If left untreated, however, it can result in fractures (broken bones). Although fractures usually cause pain, fractures of the bones of the spine may go unnoticed until they cause height loss. Fractures may occur during normal, everyday activity, such as lifting, or from minor injury that would not ordinarily fracture normal bone. Fractures usually occur at the hip, spine, or wrist and can lead not only to pain, but also to considerable deformity and disability (such as stooped posture from curvature of the spine, and loss of mobility).

How can osteoporosis be treated or prevented? Your physician has prescribed Fosamax to treat your osteoporosis or to help prevent you from developing osteoporosis. Fosamax not only prevents the loss of bone but actually helps to rebuild bone you may have lost and makes bone less likely to fracture. Thus, Fosamax prevents or reverses the progression of osteoporosis.

In addition, your physician may recommend one or more of the following lifestyle changes:

Stop smoking. Smoking appears to increase the rate at which you lose bone and, therefore, may increase your risk of fracture.

Exercise. Like muscles, bones need exercise to stay strong and healthy. Consult your physician before you begin any exercise program.

Eat a balanced diet. Your physician can advise you whether to modify your diet or to take any dietary supplements.

Why is it important to continue to take Fosamax? It is important to take Fosamax over the long term to continue to prevent loss of bone and to help rebuild bone you may have lost. It is, therefore, important to follow your physician's instructions for taking Fosamax without skipping doses or varying from your prescribed treatment schedule. It is also important to continue to follow your physician's advice on lifestyle changes.

What should I know before taking Fosamax? Who should not take Fosamax? Do not take Fosamax if you:

- Have certain disorders of the esophagus (the tube that connects your mouth with your stomach)
- Are unable to stand or sit upright for at least 30 minutes
- Are allergic to any of its ingredients
- Have been told by doctor that you currently have low blood calcium.

Do not take Fosamax if you have severe kidney disease. If you have any doubts if this applies to you, speak to your physician.

What should I tell my physician or pharmacist before taking Fosamax? Tell your physician or pharmacist about any medical problems you have or have had, including known kidney disease, and about any allergies. If you have any swallowing or digestive problems, discuss them with your physician before taking Fosamax.

Pregnancy and Breast-feeding: Do not take Fosamax if you are pregnant or breast-feeding.

Children: Fosamax is not indicated for anyone under 18 years of age and should not be given to them.

Elderly: Fosamax works equally well in and is equally well tolerated by patients older and younger than 65 years of age.

Can I take Fosamax with other medicines? See "How should I take Fosamax?"

Can I drive or operate machinery while using Fosamax? Fosamax should not affect your ability to drive or operate machinery.

Remember to keep Fosamax and all medications safely away from children.

What should I do in case of an overdose? If you take too many tablets, drink a full glass of milk and contact your physician immediately. Do not induce vomiting. Do not lie down.

What should I do if I miss a dose? Take Fosamax once daily as prescribed. However, if you miss a dose, do not take an extra dose. Just resume your usual schedule of 1 tablet once a day.

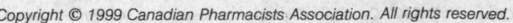

Fosamax (cont'd)

What undesirable effects may Fosamax have? Most patients do not have side effects from Fosamax; however, as with any medicine, Fosamax may have unintended or undesirable effects. Side effects usually have been mild. Some patients may experience digestive disturbances such as nausea or vomiting. Some digestive disturbances may be severe including irritation or ulceration of the esophagus (the tube that connects your mouth with your stomach) which can cause chest pain, heartburn or difficulty or pain upon swallowing. These reactions may occur especially if patients do not drink a full glass of water with Fosamax and/or if they lie down in less than 30 minutes **and** before their first food of the day. Esophageal reactions may worsen if patients continue to take Fosamax after developing symptoms suggesting irritation of the esophagus.

Some patients may experience bone, muscle or joint pain or, rarely, a rash. Allergic reactions such as hives, or rarely, swelling of the face, lips, tongue and/or throat which may cause difficulty in breathing or swallowing may occur. Rarely stomach or other peptic ulcers (some severe) have occurred, but it is not known whether these were caused by treatment with Fosamax. Mouth ulcers have occurred when the tablet was chewed or dissolved in the mouth.

Your physician or pharmacist has a more complete list. Tell your physician or pharmacist promptly about these or any other unusual symptoms.

How can I learn more about Fosamax and osteoporosis? You may obtain further information from your physician or pharmacist, who have more detailed information about Fosamax and osteoporosis.

How long should I keep my medicine? Do not use this medicine after the month and year shown by the 4 numbers following EX (or EXP) on the container. The first two numbers indicate the month; the last two numbers indicate the year.

How should I store Fosamax? Store Fosamax at room temperature (15 to 30°C).

Ingredients: Active ingredients: Each white, round, 5 mg or 10 mg tablet of Fosamax contains alendronate. Nonmedicinal ingredients: anhydrous lactose, croscarmellose sodium, magnesium stearate, microcrystalline cellulose.

Paget's Disease of Bone: Please read this insert carefully before starting Fosamax and every time your prescription is renewed.

How should I take Fosamax? These are the important things you must do to help make sure you will benefit from Fosamax:

1. **After getting up for the day, swallow your Fosamax tablet with a full glass (200 to 250 mL)** of **plain water** only: not mineral water, not coffee or tea, not juice.

   Although it has not been tested, because of high mineral content, "hard water" may decrease absorption of Fosamax. If your normal drinking water is classified as "hard water", you should consider taking this medication with distilled water (i.e., not mineral water).
2. **After swallowing your Fosamax tablet do not lie down—stay fully upright (sitting or standing) for at least 30 minutes and until after your first food of the day. Do not chew or suck on a tablet of Fosamax.**
3. **Do not take Fosamax at bedtime or before getting up for the day.**

   The above actions will help the Fosamax tablet reach your stomach quickly and help avoid irritation of your esophagus (the tube that connects your mouth with your stomach).
4. **After swallowing your Fosamax tablet, wait at least 30 minutes before taking your first food, beverage, or other medication of the day,** including antacids, calcium supplements and vitamins. Fosamax is effective only if taken when your stomach is empty.
5. **If you develop difficulty or pain upon swallowing, chest pain, or new or worsening heartburn, stop taking Fosamax immediately and call your doctor.**
6. Take Fosamax once a day, every day.
7. It is important that you continue taking Fosamax for as long as your doctor prescribes it.

   You should always tell your physician about all drugs you are taking or plan to take, including those obtained without a prescription.

Fosamax is the brand name of Merck Frosst Canada Inc. for the substance alendronate sodium available **only on prescription** from your physician. Alendronate sodium is a member of a class of nonhormonal drugs called aminobisphosphonates.

Your physician has prescribed Fosamax because you have a disease known as Paget's disease of bone.

How is normal bone maintained? Bone undergoes a normal process of rebuilding that occurs continuously throughout your skeleton. First, old bone is removed (resorbed), then new bone is laid down (formed). This balanced process of resorbing and forming bone keeps your skeleton healthy and strong.

What is Paget's disease? In Paget's disease, bone resorption and formation are abnormally increased resulting in weakened bone. This may lead to pain, deformity, and/or fracture.

How can Paget's disease be treated? Your physician has prescribed Fosamax to treat this disease. Fosamax slows down bone resorption, which allows the bone-forming cells time to rebuild normal bone.

What should I know before taking Fosamax? Who should not take Fosamax? Do not take Fosamax if you:

- Have certain disorders of the esophagus (the tube that connects your mouth with your stomach)
- Are unable to stand or sit upright for at least 30 minutes
- Are allergic to any of its ingredients
- Have been told by your doctor that you currently have low blood calcium.

Do not take Fosamax if you have severe kidney disease. If you have any doubts if this applies to you, speak to your physician.

What should I tell my physician or pharmacist before taking Fosamax? Tell your physician or pharmacist about any medical problems you have or have had, including known kidney disease, and about any allergies. If you have any swallowing or digestive problems, discuss them with your physician before taking Fosamax.

Pregnancy and Breast-feeding: Do not take Fosamax if you are pregnant or breast-feeding.

Children: Fosamax is not indicated for anyone under 18 years of age and should not be given to them.

Elderly: Fosamax works equally well in and is equally well tolerated by patients older and younger than 65 years of age.

Can I take Fosamax with other medicines? The use of acetylsalicylic acid (ASA) with 40 mg of Fosamax may increase the chance of stomach upset. You should speak to your physician if you take ASA.

See "How should I take Fosamax?"

Can I drive or operate machinery while using Fosamax? Fosamax should not affect your ability to drive or operate machinery.

Remember to keep Fosamax and all medications safely away from children.

What should I do in case of an overdose? If you take too many tablets, drink a full glass of milk and contact your physician immediately. Do not induce vomiting. Do not lie down.

What should I do if I miss a dose? Take Fosamax once daily as prescribed. However, if you miss a dose, do not take an extra dose. Just resume your usual schedule of 1 tablet once a day.

What undesirable effects may Fosamax have? Most patients do not have side effects from Fosamax; however, as with any medicine, Fosamax may have unintended or undesirable effects. Side effects usually have been mild. Some patients may experience digestive disturbances such as nausea or vomiting. Some digestive disturbances may be severe including irritation or ulceration of the esophagus (the tube that connects your mouth with your stomach) which can cause chest pain, heartburn or difficulty or pain upon swallowing. These reactions may occur especially if patients do not drink a full glass of water with Fosamax and/or if they lie down in less than 30 minutes **and** before their first food of the day. Esophageal reactions may worsen if patients continue to take Fosamax after developing symptoms suggesting irritation of the esophagus.

Some patients may experience bone, muscle or joint pain or, rarely, a rash. Allergic reactions such as hives, or rarely, swelling of the face, lips, tongue and/or throat which may cause difficulty in breathing or swallowing may occur. Rarely stomach or other peptic ulcers (some severe) have occurred, but it is not known whether these were caused by treatment with Fosamax. Mouth ulcers have occurred when the tablet was chewed or dissolved in the mouth.

Your physician or pharmacist has a more complete list. Tell your physician or pharmacist promptly about these or any other unusual symptoms.

How can I learn more about Fosamax and Paget's disease of bone? You may obtain further information from your physician or pharmacist, who have more detailed information about Fosamax and Paget's disease of bone.

How long should I keep my medicine? Do not use this medicine after the month and year shown by the 4 numbers following EX (or EXP) on the container. The first two numbers indicate the month; the last two numbers indicate the year.

How should I store Fosamax? Store Fosamax at room temperature (15 to 30°C).

Ingredients: Active ingredients: Each white, triangular-shaped 40 mg tablet of Fosamax contains alendronate. Nonmedicinal ingredients: anhydrous lactose, croscarmellose sodium, magnesium stearate, microcrystalline cellulose.

□ FRAGMIN® Ⓟ

Pharmacia & Upjohn

Dalteparin Sodium

Anticoagulant—Antithrombotic

Information for the Patient: Prefilled Syringes for Injection: Indications and Actions: Fragmin is used to prevent blood clotting (coagulation) whenever surgery is performed, to treat the acute formation of blood clots in deep veins, and to prevent clotting in blood dialysis and filtration equipment in connection with acute kidney failure or kidney disease.

Precautions to Be Taken Before Treatment: It is necessary that you advise your doctor of any serious medical problems you have had or currently have, as these conditions could affect the action of Fragmin.

If you have had or currently suffer from any of the disorders listed below, it is necessary that you inform your doctor before starting treatment:

—Allergy to Fragmin
—Bleeding due to acute gastroduodenal ulcer
—Severe liver and renal insufficiencies
—A history of cerebral hemorrhage (bleeding of the brain)
—A severe blood clotting disorder (hemorrhagic diathesis)
—Bacterial infection of the heart (septic endocarditis)
—Injuries to and/or operations on the central nervous system, eyes, ears
—A history of thrombocytopenia (decrease in the number of platelets)
—High blood pressure
—Disorders of the retina of the eye due to diabetes or bleeding
—Any other diseases that could involve an increased risk of bleeding

Certain medications may intensify the anticoagulant effect of Fragmin. Therefore, it is important for you to advise your doctor of all drugs you are presently taking.

If you are pregnant or breast-feeding, you should tell your doctor so that the possible risks to you and your child can be assessed.

Instructions for Use: Fragmin is obtained on prescription only. You must use Fragmin as instructed by your doctor. Fragmin is administered as an injection underneath the surface of the skin (subcutaneous).

In Hospital: General Surgery: Your doctor or nurse will give you your first injection of Fragmin subcutaneously 1 to 2 hours before the operation to prevent problems with blood clotting. After the operation, you will receive a subcutaneous injection each morning until you become mobile, in general 5 to 7 days or longer.

General Surgery Associated With Other Risk Factors and Elective Surgery: Your doctor or nurse will give you your first injection of Fragmin subcutaneously the evening before the operation to prevent blood clotting problems. After the operation, you will receive a subcutaneous injection that night and an injection each successive night thereafter until you become mobile. As an alternative, your doctor or nurse may divide the initial dose and give you your first subcutaneous injection of Fragmin 1 to 2 hours before the operation followed by another injection 8 to 12 hours later. Each day thereafter, an injection would be received until you become mobile.

At Home: It may be necessary for you to continue your treatment with Fragmin for a few days at home.

Before your release from the hospital, your doctor or nurse will show you how to give yourself the injections of Fragmin. It is very important that you follow the instructions exactly. If there is anything you don't understand or would like clarified, make sure to ask your doctor or nurse for more information so that when you go home, you are comfortable self-administering Fragmin.

Fragmin is available in ready-to-use, prefilled syringes. Each syringe contains the required amount of Fragmin for one injection. Avoid pressing on the syringe plunger so as not to lose any of the syringe content.

Instructions for Injection at Home: With your thumb and forefinger, create a fold of skin in the lower right or left region of your abdomen. This fold must be maintained throughout the injection.

While maintaining this skin fold with your thumb and forefinger, insert the needle into the skin fold vertically, as far as it will go. You then press on the plunger and withdraw the needle when you have injected all the content of the syringe.

Dispose of the used syringe and needle in a safe manner and **ensure that it is kept out of the reach of children.**

Note: Fragmin can also be injected into the side of the thigh. As for the injection in the abdomen, it is important that the needle is inserted into a skin fold created with the thumb and forefinger which is maintained throughout the injection.

Important: Fragmin is a powerful medication and it is necessary that you follow the instructions of your doctor or nurse carefully. Only give yourself the injections prescribed for the entire time period specified by your doctor.

Do not take any drugs other than those prescribed by your doctor while you are taking Fragmin.

If you need to consult with another doctor or see your dentist, be absolutely sure to tell them that you are being treated with Fragmin.

Adverse Events: Fragmin causes very few side effects.

If you notice any of the following effects while you are in hospital or at home, contact your doctor immediately:

—Bleeding at the injection site and/or from surgical sites
—Other bleeding: nosebleed, blood in the urine; bleeding from the mouth, vagina, anus
—Easy bruising or bruising without apparent cause
—Allergic reactions

Treatment of Overdose: Overdose of Fragmin can result in very heavy bleeding. If you feel you have accidentally taken too much Fragmin, you must call your doctor immediately, whether or not you notice any of the events listed above. Your doctor will arrange to have you admitted to the hospital for observation and treatment if necessary.

□ FRAXIPARINE™ Ⓟ

Sanofi

Nadroparin Calcium

Anticoagulant—Antithrombotic

Information for the Patient: What is Fraxiparine Used for? Fraxiparine is used to prevent the blood from clotting after having surgery, during hemodialysis and also to treat existing blood clots that are blocking blood vessels.

How Does Fraxiparine Work? Fraxiparine works by delaying the action by which blood clots. This results in the blood remaining thin and prevents formation of clots which may become lodged in blood vessels.

When Should Fraxiparine Not Be Used ? Before giving you Fraxiparine, your doctor will have checked if:

1. You are pregnant or breast-feeding.
   You should inform your doctor at once if you are pregnant or if you are breast-feeding, so that he/she can evaluate the possible risks to you and the infant.
2. You have had a previous allergy to the drug.
3. You suffer from liver or kidney problems.
4. You have a history of thrombocytopenia—a low blood platelet count.
5. You have a history of peptic ulceration.

Your doctor should also know what drugs you are currently taking regularly, for example, medication for arthritis, blood thinners, ASA etc. You must tell your doctor if you are taking any other medicines, including those that you buy without a prescription, as these medicines may affect the way that Fraxiparine works. While you are taking Fraxiparine, it is important that you do not take any medicine other than that prescribed by your doctor. If you should see another doctor or a dentist while you are taking Fraxiparine, you should inform them that you are taking Fraxiparine.

How Fraxiparine is Given (see package insert for illustrations): Fraxiparine is a prescription drug and must be used as directed. It is administered as a subcutaneous (s.c.) injection, which means the injection is made just under the surface of the skin. While you are in the hospital, your doctor or nurse will give your first injection of Fraxiparine within 24 hours of your operation.

Fraxiparine (cont'd)

It is possible that after you go home, you may need to continue your injections of Fraxiparine for a few days.

Instructions for Self-injection of Fraxiparine: Your doctor may want you to continue your Fraxiparine injections at home. If so, a health professional will show you how to administer your Fraxiparine injections before you are released from hospital. It is essential that you follow these instructions exactly. If you have questions, be sure you ask your doctor or nurse to provide the explanations you require.

Removal of Packaging: To avoid damaging the syringe presentation it is recommended that the following steps are followed.
- To separate the packaged syringes, carefully fold the twin pack several times so that the syringes are back to back, then slowly, using even pressure, separate the two packaged syringes starting from the plunger end of the pack.
- To remove the syringe from its plastic packaging, gently tear the top backing paper completely from the plastic tray (starting at the plunger end), then allow the syringe to roll onto the palm of your other hand.

Preparation of the Syringe for Subcutaneous Injection: Removal of the cap from the syringe needle:
- Hold the syringe vertically (grey cap uppermost).
- Hold the grey cap by its collar, and the syringe barrel in your other hand, then slowly rotate the syringe barrel, gently pulling downwards at the same time, until the needle is fully withdrawn from the cap.
- Do not pull the cap upwards from the syringe as this could bend the needle.

Fraxiparine 0.2 mL, 0.3 mL and 0.4 mL prefilled syringes are intended for administration of unit dosages only. There may be a small air bubble in the syringe but this does not have to be removed.

Fraxiparine 0.6 mL, 0.8 mL and 1.0 mL prefilled graduated syringes may be used to administer adjusted dosages.

Hold the syringes vertically with the needle uppermost and ensure the air bubble is at the top of the syringe.

Advance the plunger to the volume/dosage required, expelling air and any excess.

Pay special attention to the instructions for the product you are using. Always ask your doctor's advice.

Injection Technique:
- Lie down on your back and grab a pinched-up fold of skin between your thumb and forefinger, from the right or left side of your abdomen, near your waist.
- Insert the entire length of the needle vertically (never at an angle), to its full depth into the skin fold. Depress the plunger injecting the Fraxiparine (over 10 to 15 seconds).
- Still holding the pinched-up skin until the injection is finished, withdraw the needle vertically.
- You should then safely dispose of the syringe and needle, so they remain out of reach of children. Any unused portion of Fraxiparine should be discarded.
- Do not rub the site of injection as this increases the incidence of bruising.
- You should alternate your daily injections between the right and left side of your abdomen.

Remember, Fraxiparine is a potent medicine and it is important that you follow your doctor's instructions carefully. The dose of Fraxiparine you will need will depend on why you are being treated with Fraxiparine and also on your body weight. Administer only the dose and number of injections prescribed per day and continue to administer the injections for exactly the number of days specified.

Unwanted Effects: Fraxiparine helps most people in the treatment or prevention of blood clots, however, it may have unwanted effects in some people. You should alert your doctor immediately if you notice any of the following symptoms:
- Bleeding from the surgical wound.
- Other bleeding episodes, e.g., nosebleeds, blood in the urine, or if you throw up blood.
- Signs of an allergic reaction.
- Purplish or reddish discoloration of the skin around the injection site.
- Pain and bruising around the injection site.
- Unexpected bruising, bleeding of gums when brushing teeth.

Overdosage and Treatment: Accidental overdosage may result in hemorrhaging (internal or external bleeding), which cannot be treated at home. Therefore, if you suspect that you have used too much Fraxiparine, call your doctor immediately even if you do not yet observe any unusual symptoms. Your doctor can then make arrangements to admit you to hospital for observation and/or treatment.

Storage Conditions: Fraxiparine should be stored between 15 and 30°C. Do not refrigerate as cold injections may be painful. Do not freeze.

☐ FROBEN® ℞
☐ FROBEN SR® ℞
Knoll

Flurbiprofen

Anti-inflammatory—Analgesic

Information for the Patient: Froben (flurbiprofen) which has been prescribed to you by your doctor, is one of a large group of nonsteroidal anti-inflammatory drugs (NSAIDs) and is used to treat the symptoms of certain types of arthritis, ankylosing spondylitis and for the relief of pain associated with dysmenorrhea. It helps to relieve joint pain, swelling, stiffness and fever by reducing the production of certain substances (prostaglandins) and helping to control inflammation and other body reactions.

How to take your medication: You should take Froben only as directed by your doctor. Do not take more of it, do not take it more often and do not take it for a longer period of time than your doctor ordered.

Be sure to take Froben regularly as prescribed. In some types of arthritis, up to 2 weeks may pass before you feel the full effects of this medicine. During treatment, your doctor may decide to adjust the dosage according to your response to the medication.

To lessen stomach upset, take this medicine immediately after a meal or with food or milk. If stomach upset (indigestion, nausea, vomiting, stomach pain or diarrhea) occurs and continues, contact your doctor.

Dosage and Administration: **Adults: Froben Tablets:** Rheumatoid Arthritis: The usual recommended initial dose is 150 to 200 mg/day given in 3 or 4 divided doses. Some patients may initially require 250 to 300 mg/day. The dose may be adjusted by your doctor until the minimum effective maintenance dose is established. During the course of treatment, your doctor may increase the daily dose to a maximum of 300 mg as a temporary measure to treat severe symptoms.

Osteoarthritis: The usual recommended initial dose is 100 to 150 mg/day given in 2 or 3 divided doses. Some patients may initially require 200 to 300 mg/day. The dose may be adjusted by your doctor until the minimum effective maintenance dose is established. During the course of treatment, your doctor may increase the daily dose to a maximum of 300 mg as a temporary measure to treat severe symptoms.

Ankylosing Spondylitis: The usual recommended initial dose is 200 mg/day given in 4 divided doses. Some patients may initially require 250 to 300 mg/day. The dose may be adjusted by your doctor until the minimum effective maintenance dose is established. During the course of treatment, your doctor may increase the daily dose to a maximum of 300 mg as a temporary measure to treat severe symptoms.

Dysmenorrhea: The usual recommended dosage is 50 mg given 4 times daily, beginning with the onset of dysmenorrhea and ending with the cessation of pain.

Froben SR: The recommended daily dose of Froben SR is one 200 mg capsule, taken in the evening after food. The capsule should be swallowed whole.

If you have not taken your dose of Froben SR at the prescribed time you may take it right away, but you should wait at least 12 hours before taking the next dose. You may then continue taking your dose at the prescribed time thereafter. **Never double doses.**

Important: Do not take ASA, ASA-containing compounds or other drugs used to relieve symptoms of arthritis while taking Froben unless directed to do so by your physician. If you are prescribed this medication for use over a long period of time, your doctor will check your health during regular visits to assess your progress and to ensure that this medication is not causing unwanted effects.

Along with its beneficial effects, Froben like other NSAID drugs, may cause some undesirable reactions. Elderly, frail or debilitated patients often seem to experience more frequent or more severe side effects. Although not all of these side effects are common, when they do occur they may require medical attention. Check with your doctor immediately if any of the following are noted: bloody or black tarry stool; shortness of breath, wheezing, any trouble in breathing or tightness in the chest; skin rash, swelling, hives or itching; indigestion, nausea, vomiting, stomach pain or diarrhea; yellow discoloration of the skin or eyes; with or without fatigue; any changes in the amount or color of your urine (such as dark; red or brown); swelling of the feet or lower legs; blurred vision or any visual disturbance; mental confusion, depression, dizziness, lightheadedness; hearing problems.

Always Remember: Before taking this medication tell your doctor or pharmacist if you: are allergic to Froben or other related medicines of the NSAID group such as ASA, diclofenac, diflusinal, fenoprofen, flurbiprofen, ibuprofen, indomethacin, ketoprofen, mefenamic acid, piroxicam, sulindac, tiaprofenic acid or tolmetin; have a history of stomach upset, ulcers, or liver or kidney diseases; are pregnant or intend to become pregnant while taking this medication; are breast feeding; are taking any medication (either prescription or nonprescription); have any other medical problem(s).

While taking this medicine: tell any other doctor, dentist or pharmacist that you consult or see, that you are taking this medication; be cautious about driving or participating in activities that require alertness if you are drowsy, dizzy or lightheaded after taking this medication; check with your doctor if you are not getting any relief or if any problems develop. Report any untoward reactions to your doctor. This is very important as it will aid in the early detection and prevention of potential complications. Your regular medical checkups are essential. If you require more information on this drug, consult your doctor or pharmacist.

Children: The safety and efficacy of Froben has not been established in children and therefore its use in this group is not recommended.

□ GLUCAGON INJECTION

Lilly

Glucagon HCl

Hyperglycemic Agent

Information for the Patient: Notice: Do not use Glucagon For Injection after date stamped on the green-striped (No. 2) bottle label. Glucagon should be used immediately after mixing with diluent.

Directions for Use:

1. Glucagon is an emergency drug to be used only under the direction of a physician. **Become familiar with the following instructions before the emergency arises.**
2. In case of insulin coma or severe insulin reactions, administer glucagon and call a physician promptly.
3. Act quickly. Prolonged unconsciousness may be very harmful.
4. Inject glucagon in the same way that insulin is injected (see following directions). Turn the patient on his/her side.
5. The patient usually awakens within 15 minutes. Feed the patient as soon as he/she awakens and is able to swallow.
6. There is no danger of overdosage.
7. If recommended by physician, give ½ of the mixed dose of glucagon to small children.

Indications: Glucagon is indicated for the treatment of hypoglycemia (low blood glucose). Symptoms of low blood glucose include:

- sweating
- dizziness
- drowsiness
- sleep disturbances
- palpitation
- tremor
- hunger
- restlessness
- tingling in the hands, feet, lips, or tongue
- lightheadedness
- inability to concentrate
- headache
- anxiety
- blurred vision
- slurred speech
- depressive mood
- irritability
- abnormal behavior
- unsteady movement
- personality changes

If not treated, the patient may progress to severe hypoglycemia which can include:

- disorientation
- unconsciousness
- seizures
- death

The occurrence of early symptoms calls for prompt and, if necessary, repeated administration of some form of carbohydrate, for example, candy, orange juice, corn syrup, honey or a lump of sugar.

If improvement does not occur or if administration of carbohydrate is impossible, glucagon should be given. Glucagon, a naturally occurring substance produced by the pancreas, is helpful because it enables the patient to produce his/her own blood glucose to correct the hypoglycemic state. The patient can then take carbohydrate by mouth. In this way, severe hypoglycemic reactions can be avoided, and diabetic control will be easier to accomplish. Patients who are unable to take sugar orally, or who are unconscious, require an injection of glucagon or should be treated with intravenous administration of glucose at a medical facility. **The physician should always be notified promptly whenever severe hypoglycemic reactions occur.**

Note: The patient with diabetes may also be in coma from diabetic acidosis (hyperglycemia) rather than from hypoglycemia and in such cases will not respond to glucagon. These patients require immediate medical attention for the treatment of the diabetic acidosis. Contact the physician immediately.

To Prepare Glucagon Injection: Note: Glucagon should not be prepared for injection until the emergency arises

1. Remove the flip-off seals on bottles Nos. 1 and 2.
2. Wipe the rubber stoppers on both bottles with an alcohol swab.
3. Use a sterile U-100 or insulin syringe and needle. Remove the needle protector from the syringe.
4. Draw the plunger of the syringe back to the 50-unit mark on a U-100 syringe. The syringe now contains ½ mL of air.
5. Pick up the smaller, white-labeled bottle (No. 1) containing the diluting solution. Pierce the center of the stopper with the needle attached to the syringe containing ½ mL of air.
6. Turn the bottle upside down and slowly inject air from the syringe into the bottle. It will now be possible to remove the diluting solution more easily.
7. Keep the tip of the needle in the diluting solution and withdraw all of the solution into the syringe.
8. Remove syringe from bottle No. 1 and insert same needle into the bottle with green-striped label (No. 2) containing the glucagon. Inject all of the diluting solution from the syringe into bottle No. 2.
9. Remove syringe. Shake bottle gently until glucagon dissolves and the solution becomes clear. **Glucagon should not be used unless the solution is clear and of a water-like consistency.**

To Administer Glucagon: Use Same Technique as for Injecting Insulin:

1. Using the same syringe, withdraw all of the solution from bottle No. 2.
2. Cleanse injection site on buttock, arm, or thigh with alcohol swab.
3. Insert the needle into the loose tissue under the cleansed injection site and inject the glucagon solution. Apply light pressure at the injection site and withdraw the needle.
4. If recommended by physician, give ½ of the mixed dose of glucagon to small children.

Feed the patient as soon as he/she awakens and is able to swallow. If the patient does not awaken within about 15 minutes, give another dose of glucagon and **call a physician immediately.**

Caution: Low blood glucose may cause convulsions. When an unconscious patient awakens, he/she may vomit. To prevent the patient from choking on vomit, turn the patient on his/her side.

□ GONAL-F® Ⓟ

Serono

Follitropin alpha (rDNA origin)

Gonadotropin

Information for the Patient: First, a few words about Gonal-F. Gonal-F (follitropin alpha for injection, rDNA origin) is the most recent treatment available to help couples achieve pregnancy. It is a highly purified hormone for the treatment of infertility, and should be taken under close supervision of your doctor.

Gonal-F (cont'd)

Before you begin treatment, it is important that you understand what Gonal-F is, how it can help you conceive and what you can expect from it. Please read this information carefully and discuss any questions or concerns you may have with your doctor.

What is Gonal-F?: Gonal-F is a gonadotropin hormone produced by recombinant DNA technology. It consists of highly purified FSH (follicle stimulating hormone), and contains no LH (lutenizing hormone).

Gonal-F provides you with FSH that is necessary for the recruitment, growth, and maturation of the ovarian follicles which contains eggs known as ova. This occurs at the beginning of the cycle. After Gonal-F is given to help develop the ovarian follicle, another hormone, hCG (human chorionic gonadotropin), is given mid-cycle to mature the egg and induce ovulation.

Why Have I Been Prescribed Gonal-F? Your doctor has probably prescribed Gonal-F because your pituitary gland does not release FSH or it releases FSH and LH in an improper balance. This imbalance means the follicles are unable to mature, so ovulation cannot take place. Gonal-F helps to provide the required amount of FSH to the ovaries thereby allowing the ovarian follicles to develop.

My Doctor has Told me Gonal-F is a New Product. How is it Different From Other Treatments? Over the years, the gonadotropin drugs used in the treatment of infertility have undergone significant changes and improvement. Previous gonadotropin products contain FSH and varying amounts of LH and urinary proteins.

Gonal-F is produced through rDNA technology and consists of highly purified FSH with neither urinary proteins nor LH.

How is Gonal-F Administered? Gonal-F cannot be taken orally because it would be digested in the stomach and for this reason, it must be taken by injection. Due to its high level of purity, Gonal-F is approved for subcutaneous injection, which makes it easier and less painful than intramuscular injections. In fact, with professional guidance, you can learn to inject yourself, in the comfort and privacy of your own home.

How Long Will my Treatment Last? This depends on your response to therapy. Every treatment is individualized and your doctor will need to carefully evaluate how you respond. If you fail to achieve pregnancy with Gonal-F your doctor will discuss further treatment or other options.

Are There any Side Effects with Gonal-F? All drugs have the potential to cause side effects and Gonal-F is no exception. The greatest concern your doctor will have is Ovarian Hyperstimulation Syndrome (OHSS). To avoid the development of OHSS, your doctor will carefully monitor your response to Gonal-F. Ovarian enlargement, sometimes accompanied by abdominal bloating and pain, may occur in about 20% of women taking gonadotropins. This is generally reversed with cessation of treatment and severe life-threatening cases are rare.

Other adverse reactions may include allergic sensitivity such as a rash and local swelling at the injection site. If you experience any unusual symptoms or side effects, you should report them to your doctor immediately. It is also wise to discuss the possibility of side effects with your doctor before you begin treatment.

Will Gonal-F put me at the Risk of Multiple Birth? The incidence of multiple births with Gonal-F is no different from any other gonadotropin and is dependent upon the protocol used by the clinic. The majority of births—about 80%—are single babies. Of those women who do have multiple births, the majority of these are twins. Only very few women conceive and deliver 3 or more babies. Your doctor will monitor you closely to help minimize the possibility of multiple gestations. Even so, neither single nor multiple births can be totally guaranteed.

How to Inject Gonal-F: A Step by Step Guide: Before you Start: It is important that you read this information. It will help familiarize you with the correct procedure for injecting Gonal-F and clarify any concerns you may have. This information relates only to the use of Gonal-F. If you have been prescribed any fertility treatment other than Gonal-F, consult your physician.

Understandably, you may be a little apprehensive at first about injecting yourself directly. That is why this booklet had been produced. Refer to it as necessary and follow each instruction step by step. If you have any questions or concerns that are not addressed here, please consult your clinic office.

Every treatment is individualized. Yours has been carefully designed for you by your doctor according to your own specific needs. It is very important that you keep your appointments and follow your doctor's instructions, particularly with regard to the amount and frequency of the medication you are taking. For your convenience, we have provided a diary for you to record and monitor your therapy. If you forget or miss an injection, do not panic, but you should call your doctor or nurse for advice.

Your Gonal-F Patient Kit contains the following:

- 3cc syringes with 1½ inch, 21 or 22 gauge needles (for mixing);
- 25 or 27½ gauge needles (for injection);
- alcohol swabs;
- patient diary;
- needle disposal container (all used needles and ampuls should be discarded into this container);
- patient question and answer booklet.

Always follow the basic principles of self injection:

- maintain sterile conditions;
- check medication—be sure it is clear, colorless and free of lumps;
- check dosage and instructions for mixing;
- alternate injection sites each day;
- be on safety alert.

Important Points to Remember:

- Gonal-F ampuls may be stored in the refrigerator, or at room temperature (3 to 25°C) away from light and direct heat or severe cold.
- Always check expiry date before use—never use expired Gonal-F.
- Only make up the Gonal-F solution when you are ready to use it. **Do not use if cloudy, lumpy or discolored. Be sure to use the correct number of Gonal-F ampuls, correct strength, and correct amount of diluent.**
- Check site of previous injection.
- Record injection sites in patient diary each time you inject.
- It is recommended that you inject Gonal-F at around the same time each day.
- Discard any unused solution.

If you are unsure about the mixing of the solution, or have difficulty with the injections, call your clinic office immediately.

Eleven Steps for Self Injection (see product monograph for illustrations):

1. **Cleanse:** Before you start, wash your hands well with soap and water. It is important that your hands and the items you use be as clean as possible. Needles should not touch any surface except inside the ampuls and alcohol-cleaned skin; keep them capped prior to use. Make sure you use a new needle each time you inject to avoid contamination. Dispose of all used needles and glass in the disposal container provided.

2. **Assemble Everything you Need:** On a clean work surface, lay out everything you will need:
   - one alcohol wipe;
   - one mixing syringe with long needle;
   - one 25 or 27½ gauge needle;
   - Gonal-F and diluent ampuls.

   If you use your kitchen to prepare the injection, ensure that all medicines and needles are kept well away from food. As for the injection itself, it can be given in any room where you feel comfortable.

3. **Prepare the Mixing Syringe:** Remove the 3 cc mixing syringe from its packaging, being careful to keep the protective needle cover in place. Hold onto the collar of the needle and loosen the cover, but do not remove it yet. Carefully set aside on your work surface.

4. **Open the Ampul(s):** You should have 1 ampul containing clear liquid (diluent) and a set number of ampuls, as prescribed by your doctor, containing Gonal-F (white powder). On the head of the diluent ampul, you will see a small colored dot. Directly below this is where the neck of the ampul has been treated to make it easier to break open.

   Gently flick the top section of the ampul so that any fluid or powder in the neck of the ampul drop into the bottom chamber.

   Wrap the alcohol wipe (still in the package) firmly around the top of the ampul. Break the ampul **away** from the colored dot. Carefully place the open ampul on the work surface and discard the top into the disposal container. Continue to open all ampuls in this manner.

5. **Draw up Diluent:** Pick up the mixing syringe and carefully uncover the needle, taking care not to let the needle touch any surface. With the syringe in one hand, pick up the open ampul of diluent with the other hand. Insert the needle and draw up the required amount of diluent. Discard the empty ampul into the disposal container.

   Reconstitution Volumes: Volumes used for reconstitution should be between 0.5 and 1 mL; up to 3 ampuls of Gonal-F may be dissolved in 1 mL of Sterile Water for Injection, USP. Reconstituted ampuls should be used immediately, and any unused solution should be discarded.

6. **Prepare Injection Solution:** Slowly inject the required amount of diluent into the ampul. If you have been prescribed more that 1 ampul of Gonal-F, gently draw the solution back into the syringe and reinject the solution into another ampul until you have the prescribed number of powder ampuls dissolved in the solution. The powder will dissolve instantly without the need to shake or mix. **Do not use if solution appears cloudy, lumpy or discolored.**
7. **Draw up the Solution:** Draw up the entire contents of the ampul (or the last of multiple ampuls) into the syringe, being careful not to pull the plunger out of the syringe. It may help to slowly tip the ampul. Discard empty ampuls in the disposal container.
8. **Change Needle:** Hold the syringe with the needle pointing upwards and gently flick the syringe if there are any visible air bubbles. The air bubbles will collect at the top of the syringe. If there are no air bubbles, or if there is no air space at the top of the syringe, pull the plunger back to allow an air space of 0.1 mL.

   Recap the needle and twist to remove; replace with the 25 or 27 gauge needle with cap. Lay syringe down on the clean surface. Do not worry if you are unable to remove very tiny bubbles; they will do no harm. When you invert the syringe, the air space will be next to the plunger. This space will ensure that all of the medication has been injected. The air will remain in the needle.
9. **Prepare the Injection Site:** Select the site of injection (e.g., top of thigh, tummy). Refer to the injection site diagram on your patient diary and record the chosen site of your injection with an "X". Wipe the chosen area with an alcohol swab, cleansing an area of approximately 2″×2″. Lay the used side of the swab next to your working surface or on the alcohol swab wrapper.
10. **Injecting the Solution:** Pick up the syringe and remove the cap from the needle. Invert the needle and hold as if "throwing a dart". With your other hand, gently squeeze the skin together to make a little elevation at the injection site. Using a "dart like motion", insert the needle at a 90 degree angle. (You need very little force but quick action.) Once the needle is inserted into the tissue all the way, inject the solution by pushing gently on the plunger with your thumb of the hand holding the syringe. Take as much time as you need to inject all the solution. Immediately withdraw the needle and clean the site with the clean side of the alcohol swab using a circular motion. If there is minor oozing you may need to apply a small amount of pressure for a minute.
11. **Dispose of all Used Items:** Once you have finished your injection, immediately discard the needles and syringe (without recapping the needle) into the disposal container.

Possible Side Effects:
- Local skin reactions (pain, swelling, irritation, redness) are unlikely to occur if you vary the injection site. If they do occur, they will disappear within a few days. Bruises may also occasionally occur at the injection site even when the injection is given correctly. These will disappear.
- Dermatological symptoms (dry skin, body rash, hair loss, hives).
- Mild to moderate ovarian enlargement occurs in 20% of patients and will regress in 2 to 3 weeks after discontinuing Gonal-F.
- Gastrointestinal symptoms (nausea, vomiting, diarrhea, abdominal cramping, bloating).
- Headache.
- Abdominal pain.
- Multiple pregnancy.
- Breast tenderness.
- Ovarian cysts.
- Hemoperitoneum.
- Adnexal torsion.
- Pulmonary and vascular complications.
- Possible allergic reactions (fever, chills, joint pains, headache and fatigue).
- Ovarian cancer (a **causal** relationship between use of this drug and ovarian cancer has not been established. There has been a very small number of infertile women that have reported ovarian cancer after treatment with fertility drugs).
- Ovarian Hyperstimulation Syndrome (OHSS) may occur **after** treatment has been completed and reaches its maximum on the seventh to tenth day after hCG administration (incidence is low). Symptoms may progress rapidly: early warning signs are severe pelvic pain, nausea, vomiting, weight gain, and may progress to abdominal distention, nausea, vomiting, diarrhea, severe ovarian enlargement, shortness of breath, decreased urine output. Patients with any of these symptoms should call the clinic office right away.

□ GYNECURE™
Pfizer Consumer

Tioconazole

Antifungal Agent

Information for the Patient: Gynecure Ointment Tandempak: Indication: For the relief of vaginal itching, burning and discharge associated with vaginal yeast infection. Cures **most** vaginal yeast infections.

Your doctor has just told you that you have a vaginal yeast infection and recommended Gynecure. You are not alone. It is estimated that over 1.5 million Canadian women per year are affected by vaginal yeast infections. About 75% of women will suffer from an episode at least once in their lifetime, with almost a third of these women experiencing a recurrence of the infection.

Here are answers to some common questions women have about Gynecure and vaginal yeast infections.

How does Gynecure work? Gynecure Vaginal Ointment is a unique formula that provides you with an effective therapy, in just one dose, to cure your vaginal yeast infection. It is premeasured and prefilled, making it convenient and easy to use: simply apply Gynecure once at bedtime and throw away the applicator.

It is important to remember that Gynecure's intensive 1-day therapy **does not** mean a 1-day cure! It's a different way of delivering the medication to ensure you benefit from the full therapy. Although some women may feel better within the first 24 hours, most women experience symptom relief anywhere from **24 to 72 hours** after application. And Gynecure continues to work for you even after your symptoms have disappeared, to help completely cure your infection.

The Vulvar Cream included in this Tandempak will give you relief from the itching, burning and irritation you are experiencing on your external genitals (vulva). It helps you get through the day to bedtime when Gynecure's Vaginal Ointment goes to work curing your infection.

How can I be sure I have a vaginal yeast infection? There are 3 common types of vaginal infections: yeast, bacterial and trichomonas. Symptoms of each include (respectively):

Yeast (Candida): burning, itching, redness/irritation vulva, pain vulva/vagina. Discharge: whitish-(or white), odorless, curd-like (clumpy).

Bacterial: May have no symptoms. Discharge: fishy odor.

Trichomonas: vaginal/vulvar irritation, vaginal itching, abdominal pain. Discharge: excessive/foul odor.

Symptoms of yeast infections occur in 2 locations: your vagina and vulva (external genitals). They are caused by a fungus called **Candida**, which starts to grow when the normal conditions in your vagina change.

If you have never had a vaginal yeast infection before and suspect you have one now, or if you are not entirely sure that your symptoms are that of a yeast infection, you must see your doctor for confirmation. Not all vaginal infections are caused by yeast. Gynecure is only for the treatment of a yeast infection and should not be used for other purposes.

How did I get this infection? In its normal state, your vaginal secretions are acidic (a low pH level) which provides a healthy, protective environment. Increased pH reduces the vagina's natural resistance to infection.

There are several medical factors that can contribute to changing your vagina's natural state, creating an environment where **Candida** will flourish:
- Hormonal influences: pregnancy, menstrual cycle, oral contraceptives (with high estrogen), estrogen therapy (during menopause)
- Antibiotics
- Uncontrolled diabetes (mellitus)
- Weakened immune system: HIV infection, corticosteroid therapy, chemotherapy

Your doctor will have ruled out any underlying diseases that may be contributing to your recurring vaginal yeast infections.

Why does it keep recurring? For some women, vaginal yeast infections are a recurring problem. There is not much you can do about the contributing medical factors mentioned above, such as taking antibiotics. However, a common reason that an infection may keep coming back is because it wasn't completely cured the first time you had it.

Curing your infection is a two-step process. The first step is when your symptoms go away (your doctor may refer to this as the clinical cure) and the second step is when the infection itself goes away (this is known as the mycological cure). Many women stop taking their

Gynecure (cont'd)

medication after their symptoms of burning and itching have disappeared because they feel better. But often the infection itself is still there and stopping treatment before you have finished your medication allows the infection to take hold again and the symptoms return. So if you don't use all your medication, for whatever length of therapy you have chosen, the infection will keep coming back.

This is also the case with home remedies such as douches, yogurt and baking soda. These preparations may relieve the symptoms temporarily but they don't treat the infection. There is a very high rate of recurrence in women who use home remedies for vaginal yeast infections.

Gynecure was specially formulated to work with only 1 application, to help women treat their vaginal yeast infections quickly, easily and effectively. You don't have to remember to keep taking your medication because 1 dose of Gynecure may be all you need to relieve your symptoms and cure the infection.

Can I help prevent a recurrence? There are steps you can take to keep recurrences of a vaginal yeast infection to a minimum.

- Avoid using chemical irritants such as feminine hygiene sprays, douches and perfumed toilet paper. Chlorine in pools can also contribute to changes in your vagina's natural pH level.
- General hygienic measures such as wearing loose fitting cotton underwear and changing it daily, drying the vaginal area well after bathing, avoiding damp clothing (e.g., bathing suits), feminine hygiene sprays and perfumed tampons, and cleansing the vaginal area from front to back after using the toilet, are important to the successful treatment of vaginal infections and help prevent reinfection.
- Reduce your sugar intake as high sugar diets can be a contributing factor to a vaginal yeast infection.

Can I have sexual intercourse while using Gynecure? Sexual intercourse could lessen the effectiveness of Gynecure, increasing your chances of a recurrence of the infection, so it's a good idea to abstain for about 7 days. Also, please keep in mind that Gynecure may be incompatible with the rubber in both contraceptive condoms and diaphragms. Gynecure is not a contraceptive and does not prevent pregnancy.

Who can I call for more information? If we haven't answered all your questions about vaginal yeast infections and Gynecure, please don't hesitate to bring this insert to your pharmacist or doctor for further discussion. Or please feel free to call Pfizer at 1-800-260-8988. A nurse will be available to answer your call.

Directions and Instructions (see package insert for illustrations): **Vaginal Ointment:** Apply Gynecure at bedtime, only after reading all the instructions and warnings on this information sheet. The prefilled applicator provided in this package is specifically designed to permit proper placement of a measured dose of vaginal ointment. **The applicator consists of a cap, a plunger and a barrel.**

1. Insert the plunger into the barrel of the applicator, and **remove the white cap from the end of the applicator prior to insertion.**
2. While lying on your back, hold the prefilled applicator by the barrel and gently insert **the ointment end** of the applicator into the vagina **as deep as it will go comfortably.**
3. Holding the applicator in place, depress the plunger slowly and **completely to deposit the measured dose** of ointment into the vagina.
4. Withdraw the applicator and dispose of it.

Directions: Vulvar Cream:

- Apply a small amount of cream with your finger and gently rub onto the irritated area, moving from front to back only, from the vulva to the anal region. Use 1 or 2 times a day for up to 7 days as needed.
- The cream should not be used for vulvar itching due to other causes than yeast infection.
- For external use only.

Warnings:

1. Use only if you have already had a vaginal yeast infection diagnosed by a physician and you have the same symptoms now; otherwise consult your physician. These symptoms include itching and burning of the vagina and, sometimes, a white discharge.
2. Consult a physician if there is no improvement in 3 days, as not all vaginal infections are caused by yeast.
3. Consult a physician if you have abdominal pain, fever or foul-smelling vaginal discharge before or during use of this medication.
4. If symptoms recur within 2 months consult a physician.
5. If you are pregnant, or think you may be pregnant, or if you are nursing do not use except on the advice of a physician.
6. Do not use in children under 12 years of age except on the advice of a physician.
7. If skin rash or new irritation occurs, discontinue use and consult a physician.
8. If you are at increased risk for sexually transmitted diseases, have multiple partners or change partners often, consult a physician before starting each treatment.
9. Do not use 72 hours prior to a vaginal examination by a doctor.
10. Vulvar cream should not be used in patients who have a history of sensitization to tioconazole or to any of the nonmedicinal ingredients or to other imidazole antifungal agents.
11. Vulvar cream is not for ophthalmic use.

Cautions:

- Constituents of the Gynecure vaginal ointment and vulvar cream may be incompatible with the rubber in both contraceptive condoms and diaphragms; do not use in the presence of these.
- Open applicator pouch just prior to use to prevent contamination.
- Keep this and all medications out of the reach of children.
- In case of accidental ingestion, seek professional assistance or contact a Poison Control Centre immediately.
- Avoid contact with eyes; if this happens, rinse thoroughly with water.

Nonmedicinal Ingredients: Vaginal Ointment: aluminum magnesium silicate, butylated hydroxyanisole and white soft paraffin. **Vulvar Cream:** benzyl alcohol, ethoxylated cetostearyl alcohol, mineral oil, white petrolatum, propylene glycol, stearic acid, stearyl alcohol, water.

Store at 15 to 30°C (room temperature); avoid freezing.

Product monograph available to physicians and pharmacists on request.

Gynecure Ovule Tandempak: Indication: For the relief of vaginal itching, burning and discharge associated with vaginal yeast infection. Cures **most** vaginal yeast infections.

Your doctor has just told you that you have a vaginal yeast infection and recommended Gynecure. You are not alone. It is estimated that over 1.5 million Canadian women per year are affected by vaginal yeast infections. About 75% of women will suffer from an episode at least once in their lifetime, with almost a third of these women experiencing a recurrence of the infection.

Here are answers to some common questions women have about Gynecure and vaginal yeast infections.

How does Gynecure work? Gynecure Vaginal Ovule is a unique formula that provides you with an effective therapy easy-to-use in just one dose, to cure your vaginal yeast infection. It is a convenient and easy to use ovule: simply apply Gynecure once at bedtime and throw away the applicator.

It is important to remember that Gynecure's intensive 1-day therapy **does not** mean a 1-day cure! It's a different way of delivering the medication to ensure you benefit from the full therapy. Although some women may feel better within the first 24 hours, most women experience symptom relief anywhere from **24 to 72 hours** after application. And Gynecure continues to work for you even after your symptoms have disappeared, to help completely cure your infection.

The Vulvar Cream included in this Tandempak will give you relief from the itching, burning and irritation you are experiencing on your external genitals (vulva). It helps you get through the day to bedtime when Gynecure's Vaginal Ovule goes to work curing your infection.

How can I be sure I have a vaginal yeast infection? There are 3 common types of vaginal infections: yeast, bacterial and trichomonas. Symptoms of each include (respectively):
Yeast (Candida): burning, itching, redness/irritation vulva, pain vulva/vagina. Discharge: whitish-(or white), odorless, curd-like (clumpy).
Bacterial: May have no symptoms. Discharge: fishy odor.
Trichomonas: vaginal/vulvar irritation, vaginal itching, abdominal pain. Discharge: excessive/foul odor.

Symptoms of yeast infections occur in 2 locations: your vagina and vulva (external genitals). They are caused by a fungus called **Candida**, which starts to grow when the normal conditions in your vagina change.

If you have never had a vaginal yeast infection before and suspect you have one now, or if you are not entirely sure that your symptoms are that of a yeast infection, you must see your doctor for confirmation. Not all vaginal infections are caused by yeast. Gynecure is only for the treatment of a yeast infection and should not be used for other purposes.

How did I get this infection? In its normal state, your vaginal secretions are acidic (a low pH level) which provides a healthy, protective environment. Increased pH reduces the vagina's natural resistance to infection.

There are several medical factors that can contribute to changing your vagina's natural state, creating an environment where **Candida** will flourish:

- Hormonal influences: pregnancy, menstrual cycle, oral contraceptives (with high estrogen), estrogen therapy (during menopause)
- Antibiotics
- Uncontrolled diabetes (mellitus)
- Weakened immune system: HIV infection, corticosteroid therapy, chemotherapy

Your doctor will have ruled out any underlying diseases that may be contributing to your recurring vaginal yeast infections.

Why does it keep recurring? For some women, vaginal yeast infections are a recurring problem. There is not much you can do about the contributing medical factors mentioned above, such as taking antibiotics. However, a common reason that an infection may keep coming back is because it wasn't completely cured the first time you had it.

Curing your infection is a two-step process. The first step is when your symptoms go away (your doctor may refer to this as the clinical cure) and the second step is when the infection itself goes away (this is known as the mycological cure). Many women stop taking their medication after their symptoms of burning and itching have disappeared because they feel better. But often the infection itself is still there and stopping treatment before you have finished your medication allows the infection to take hold again and the symptoms return. So if you don't use all your medication, for whatever length of therapy you have chosen, the infection will keep coming back.

This is also the case with home remedies such as douches, yogurt and baking soda. These preparations may relieve the symptoms temporarily but they don't treat the infection. There is a very high rate of recurrence in women who use home remedies for vaginal yeast infections.

Gynecure was specially formulated to work with only 1 application, to help women treat their vaginal yeast infections quickly, easily and effectively. You don't have to remember to keep taking your medication because 1 dose of Gynecure may be all you need to relieve your symptoms and cure the infection.

Can I help prevent a recurrence? There are steps you can take to keep recurrences of a vaginal yeast infection to a minimum.

- Avoid using chemical irritants such as feminine hygiene sprays, douches and perfumed toilet paper. Chlorine in pools can also contribute to changes in your vagina's natural pH level.
- General hygienic measures such as wearing loose fitting cotton underwear and changing it daily, drying the vaginal area well after bathing, avoiding damp clothing (e.g., bathing suits), feminine hygiene sprays and perfumed tampons, and cleansing the vaginal area from front to back after using the toilet, are important to the successful treatment of vaginal infections and help prevent reinfection.
- Reduce your sugar intake as high sugar diets can be a contributing factor to a vaginal yeast infection.

Can I have sexual intercourse while using Gynecure? Sexual intercourse could lessen the effectiveness of Gynecure, increasing your chances of a recurrence of the infection, so it's a good idea to abstain for about 7 days. Also, please keep in mind that Gynecure may be incompatible with the rubber in both contraceptive condoms and diaphragms. Gynecure is not a contraceptive and does not prevent pregnancy.

Who can I call for more information? If we haven't answered all your questions about vaginal yeast infections and Gynecure, please don't hesitate to bring this insert to your pharmacist or doctor for further discussion. Or please feel free to call Pfizer at 1-800-260-8988. A nurse will be available to answer your call.

Directions and Instructions (see package insert for illustrations): **Vaginal Ovule:** Apply Gynecure at bedtime, only after reading all the instructions and warnings on this information sheet. The applicator provided in this package is specifically designed to permit proper placement of the unit-dose ovule. **The applicator consists of a plunger and a receptacle.**

1. Remove the ovule from the foil package and place it in the receptacle of the applicator.
2. While lying on your back, hold the filled applicator by the barrel and gently insert **the end** of the applicator into the vagina **as deep as it will go comfortably.**
3. Holding the applicator in place, depress the plunger to deposit the ovule into the vagina.
4. Withdraw the applicator and dispose of it.

Directions: Vulvar Cream:

- Apply a small amount of cream with your finger and gently rub onto the irritated area, moving from front to back only, from the vulva to the anal region. Use 1 or 2 times a day for up to 7 days as needed.
- The cream should not be used for vulvar itching due to other causes than yeast infection.
- For external use only.

Warnings:

1. Use only if you have already had a vaginal yeast infection diagnosed by a physician and you have the same symptoms now; otherwise consult your physician. These symptoms include itching and burning of the vagina and, sometimes, a white discharge.
2. Consult a physician if there is no improvement in 3 days, as not all vaginal infections are caused by yeast.
3. Consult a physician if you have abdominal pain, fever or foul-smelling vaginal discharge before or during use of this medication.
4. If symptoms recur within 2 months consult a physician.
5. If you are pregnant, or think you may be pregnant, or if you are nursing do not use except on the advice of a physician.
6. Do not use in children under 12 years of age except on the advice of a physician.
7. If skin rash or new irritation occurs, discontinue use and consult a physician.
8. If you are at increased risk for sexually transmitted diseases, have multiple partners or change partners often, consult a physician before starting each treatment.
9. Do not use 72 hours prior to a vaginal examination by a doctor.
10. Vulvar cream should not be used in patients who have a history of sensitization to tioconazole or to any of the nonmedicinal ingredients or to other imidazole antifungal agents.
11. Vulvar cream is not for ophthalmic use.

Cautions:

- Constituents of the Gynecure vaginal ointment and vulvar cream may be incompatible with the rubber in both contraceptive condoms and diaphragms; do not use in the presence of these.
- Open applicator pouch just prior to use to prevent contamination.
- Keep this and all medications out of the reach of children.
- In case of accidental ingestion, seek professional assistance or contact a Poison Control Centre immediately.
- Avoid contact with eyes; if this happens, rinse thoroughly with water.

Nonmedicinal Ingredients: Vaginal Ovule: beeswax, gelatin, glycerin, glycine, hydrogenated vegetable fat, lecithin, liquid paraffin, polysorbate, potassium sorbate, titanium dioxide, water. **Vulvar Cream:** benzyl alcohol, ethoxylated cetostearyl alcohol, mineral oil, white petrolatum, propylene glycol, stearic acid, stearyl alcohol, water.

Store at 15 to 30°C (room temperature); avoid freezing.

Product monograph available to physicians and pharmacists on request.

□ HABITROL®

Novartis Consumer Health

S(-)-Nicotine

Smoking Cessation Aid

Information for the Patient: Important safety information: Keep new or used patches out of the reach of children and pets. The active ingredient in Habitrol is nicotine. It can be very toxic, and small amounts can cause serious illness in children. Even used patches contain enough nicotine to poison children and pets. Follow the directions given under 'How to Apply a Habitrol Patch', when disposing of used patches, and be sure to dispose of them out of the reach of children and pets. If, in any way, a child comes in contact with a patch that is not in the pouch, take the patch away, and **contact a poison control centre or doctor immediately**. If the child has touched the sticky (active) side of a patch, you may flush the area **with water only**, and dry it. **Do not use soap**, as this will increase the absorption of nicotine.

Introduction: You have chosen Habitrol to relieve the symptoms of nicotine withdrawal. The patch, while it is an effective aid, is only one part of your smoking cessation program. Before attempting to stop, it is important that you are firmly committed to quitting. It is also important that you prepare a behavioral plan to help you stop smoking. The Habitrol Support Guide (the booklet included in this package of Habitrol) provides you with advice on all the things you should be doing, in addition to using Habitrol, that will increase the chances that you will stop smoking. In addition, the Habitrol Toll-Free Support Information

Habitrol (cont'd)

Line is available to answer your questions about Habitrol and smoking cessation.

It is important that your doctor knows you are using Habitrol if you are taking other medications or have other medical conditions. You should stop smoking completely while you are using Habitrol. Do not use Habitrol if you are an occasional smoker.

This leaflet provides you with information on how the patch works, and how to use it safely. **Please read all of it carefully**, especially the section marked Precautions, before you start using the patches. If you have any questions about Habitrol after reading this leaflet, or any other time while you are using Habitrol, call our Toll-Free Support Information Line.

Nicotine Addiction and Smoking: In addition to many other chemicals, cigarette smoke contains nicotine. Although toxic, it does not play an important role in most diseases associated with smoking, such as lung disease and various cancers. It is the nicotine to which smokers are addicted. As you may have experienced when you first started smoking, nicotine produces effects such as: stimulation (especially in a boring situation), calming (during stressful periods), relaxation, enhancement of memory and concentration. In time, dependence develops, so that if nicotine is not made available to the brain, withdrawal symptoms such as irritability, frustration, anger, anxiety, difficulty in concentration, and restlessness appear.

Nicotine addiction may be a product of either a desire to obtain the pleasant effects and/or to avoid the withdrawal symptoms. Habitrol is designed to relieve these symptoms. Unfortunately, nicotine addiction is one of the most difficult drug addictions to break.

Information about Habitrol Patches: How Habitrol Works: Habitrol is designed to temporarily replace some of the nicotine that cigarettes would normally supply. While it is worn, controlled quantities of nicotine pass from the patch into your skin, and then into your bloodstream. Because some nicotine is left in your skin when you take the patch off, the nicotine will continue to pass into your bloodstream for several hours after patch removal.

Which patch size should I use? Habitrol comes in 3 patch sizes, which give doses of 21 mg/day (Step 1), 14 mg/day (Step 2) and 7 mg/day (Step 3). Typically, a pack-a-day smoker would wear each size for 3 to 4 weeks, gradually reducing nicotine delivery by going from Step 1 to Step 2 to Step 3.

Starting sizes: If you smoke 20 or more cigarettes per day:
- Start with Step 1 (21 mg), wearing one 21 mg patch daily for 3 to 4 weeks before moving on to Step 2.
- Next, wear Step 2 (14 mg) for an additional 3 to 4 weeks before moving on to Step 3.
- Finish by wearing Step 3 (7 mg) for 3 to 4 weeks.

If you smoke less than 20 cigarettes per day:
- Start at Step 2 (14 mg), wearing one 14 mg patch daily for 6 to 8 weeks before moving on to Step 3.
- Finish by wearing Step 3 (7 mg) for 3 to 4 weeks.

You may have to switch sizes during the first week or two of therapy in order to determine the correct size for you. If you still have withdrawal symptoms or cigarette cravings with 14 mg/day, try 21 mg/day. If you are experiencing side effects, use the next lower dose.

Weaning down: As you move from step to step, you will end up using the smallest patch last (Step 3, 7 mg), and after a while, stop using patches completely. The entire process should not go beyond 12 weeks. However, your stop smoking program does not end when you stop using the patches. If you are to remain successful in quitting, you must continue with all other aspects of your program. Remember, the Habitrol Support Guide and the Habitrol Toll-Free Support Information Line will provide you with advice on all the things you should be doing, in addition to using Habitrol, that will increase the chances that you will stop smoking.

Never wear more than 1 patch at a time as overdosage may occur.

Precautions: There are immediate beneficial effects on your health when you stop smoking. However, when using Habitrol to assist you, certain precautions must be taken to ensure safe use of the patches.

Do you have any other medical conditions? In certain medical conditions, Habitrol should not be used at all. **Do not** use Habitrol if you have had:
- a recent heart attack (myocardial infarction)
- heart disease
  unstable or worsening angina (chest pain)
  severely irregular heart beat (arrhythmia)
- recent stroke
- skin diseases
- known allergy to the patches or to nicotine
- if you are pregnant or breast-feeding.

Medical conditions other than the above require a doctor's judgment to know if Habitrol can be used safely.

Do not use Habitrol if you are under 18 years of age.

Experience with Habitrol in the elderly is limited.

Consult your doctor first if you have ever had any of the following:
- irregular heart beat (arrhythmia)
- angina (heart pain)
- high blood pressure
- heart failure
- overactive thyroid (hyperthyroidism)
- stomach ulcers
- kidney or liver disease
- diabetes requiring insulin
- treatment for poor circulation
- stroke, or treatment for circulation disorders of the brain (cerebral ischemia)
- allergies to drugs
- rashes from adhesive tape or bandages

Are you taking other medicines? It is important that your doctor knows you are using Habitrol if you are taking other medicines. Smoking may alter the effects of some medicines. Once you have quit, it may be necessary for your doctor to adjust the doses. This is especially important if you are a diabetic, taking medicine for high blood pressure or heart disease, antidepressants, tranquilizers or sleeping pills.

May I use Habitrol if I am pregnant or breast-feeding? No.

Nicotine, whether it comes from cigarettes or Habitrol, may be harmful to an unborn baby if used during pregnancy. It can also pass into breast milk, and harm a nursing infant. Therefore, if you are pregnant or breast-feeding, do not use Habitrol and do not smoke. If you are already using Habitrol and you think (or know) you have become pregnant, tell your doctor. Stop using Habitrol and do not smoke.

Are there side effects? You may experience headache, insomnia, dizziness, anxiety, irritability, fatigue, stomach upset, diarrhea, and constipation. Some of these effects may be nicotine withdrawal symptoms or may be caused by nicotine. Therefore, your dose may need to be adjusted. Be sure to tell your doctor if you have any or all of the symptoms listed above.

Remove the nicotine patch and consult your doctor if you experience irregular heart beat, chest pain, palpitations or leg pain occurs or if severe persistent stomach upset (indigestion, heartburn) develops.

If you continue to smoke while using Habitrol, you may be absorbing more nicotine than your body is used to, and this excess could make you feel ill. Therefore, **do not continue to smoke, chew nicotine gum or use any other form of tobacco product while using the patch**. Signs and symptoms of nicotine overdose include severe headaches, dizziness, upset stomach, drooling, vomiting, diarrhea, cold sweats, blurred vision, difficulty in hearing, mental confusion, weakness, and fainting. If you experience any of these symptoms, tell your doctor immediately.

What if my skin reacts to the patch? It is normal to experience mild itching, burning or tingling when you first apply a patch, but this should disappear within an hour. After you remove a patch, the skin underneath may be somewhat red, but it should not stay that way for more than 2 days. If the skin under the patch becomes swollen or very red, or if you develop a rash, remove the patch and call your doctor. Do not put on a new patch. It is possible that you may be allergic to one of the components of the patch.

If you become allergic to the nicotine in the patch, you may experience very unpleasant side effects if later you use cigarettes or other nicotine-containing products.

Other Important Information: The Habitrol patch should be removed 2 hours before engaging in prolonged strenuous exercise.

How to Apply a Habitrol Patch:
1. Choose an area of skin on your upper body or the upper outer part of your arm. **To ensure that the patch will stick on well, make sure the skin is non-hairy, clean (not oily), dry, and free of creams, lotions, oils or powder. Hair will interfere with the application of Habitrol, and should be clipped away. Do not shave the area as this may irritate the skin**. Do not put a Habitrol patch on skin that is inflamed, burned, has broken out, or is irritated in any way, because these conditions may alter the amount of drug absorbed.

Women should not apply the patch to their breasts. Be sure to apply the patch to a different area each day. The same area should not be used again for at least one week.

2. Do not remove the Habitrol patch from the pouch until you are ready to apply it. Using scissors, carefully cut open the pouch along the edge. Save the pouch as you will need it when you dispose of the used patch.
3. Peel the patch you are replacing off your skin, and fold it in half, with the adhesive (sticky) side inward. Place it in the opened foil pouch and **dispose of the pouch (with the folded old patch inside) in the garbage, out of the reach of children and pets**. Any adhesive left on your skin may be removed with rubbing alcohol.
4. A square, shiny protective liner covers the adhesive side of the patch (the side that you will stick onto your skin). Note that there is a pre-cut slit along the length of the liner. It is designed to help you remove the patch from the liner.
   To remove the patch from the liner, start by removing the strip of liner formed by the pre-cut slit. To do this, hold the liner with the patch facing you, and the slit along the top. Hold a bottom corner of the liner. Now, starting from one edge, pull away the strip from along the top and discard it. To remove the main part of the liner, hold the Habitrol patch at the free edge, (touching the sticky side as little as possible), and peel the liner off of the patch. Discard the liner.
5. Immediately apply the sticky side of the patch to your skin and firmly press it on with the palm of your hand. Continue pressing firmly for 10 to 20 seconds. Make sure that it is sticking well, especially around the edges, but do not test the patch by pulling at it once you have stuck it on.
6. When you have finished applying the patch, wash your hands with water only. Any nicotine on your hands could get into your eyes or nose, and cause stinging, redness or other more serious problems.

When to Apply a Habitrol Patch: The patch should be worn for approximately 24 hours and then removed, and discarded as described in 'How to Apply a Habitrol Patch'. Do not leave it on for more than 24 hours because it may irritate your skin, and because it loses strength after that time. You should always replace your patch at the same time each day. This will help you to remember to change it.

Helpful Hints for Using Habitrol: What If The Patch Gets Wet? Water will not usually affect the patch if it is applied correctly. You may bathe, swim, shower, or exercise while wearing the patch. The Habitrol patch should be removed 2 hours before engaging in prolonged strenuous exercise.

What If The Patch Falls Off? If a patch does fall off, dispose of it as described in 'How To Apply a Habitrol Patch' and put on a new patch as soon as possible. **Be sure the area is non-hairy, clean (not oily), dry, and free of creams, lotions, oils or powder.** You should remove this replacement patch at the time you regularly change the patch (the time you would have replaced the other patch if it had not fallen off).

How To Store Habitrol: Store your patches at room temperature (below 25°C) away from direct heat and light. Remember that the inside of your car can reach temperatures much higher than this in the summer. Do not store patches outside the pouch. Keep them out of the reach of children and pets.

Always Remember: Use Habitrol only as directed. Dispose of used patches only in the manner described in this leaflet, out of the reach of children and pets. If you have any questions, call the Habitrol Toll-Free Support Information Line, or ask your doctor or your pharmacist. If you suspect you are experiencing any side effects, remove the patch and call your doctor immediately.

Note: You cannot adjust your dose by cutting a patch, even though the smallest patch contains half the nicotine contained in the next size up. Cutting a patch will cause the nicotine to evaporate rapidly, making all the pieces useless.

Questions? Contact Habitrol Toll-Free Support Information 1-888-227-5777. Internet address: www.habitrol.com.

□ HALCION® Ⓟ

Pharmacia & Upjohn

Triazolam

Hypnotic

Information for the Patient: Halcion is intended to help you sleep. It is one of several benzodiazepine sleeping pills that have generally similar properties.

If you are prescribed one of these medications, you should consider both their benefits and risks. Important risks and limitations include the following:

- the longer you use the medication, the less effective it may become,
- you may become dependent on the medication,
- the medication may affect your mental alertness or memory, particularly when not taken as prescribed.

In order to guide you in the safe use of the product, this leaflet will inform you about this class of medication in general, and about Halcion in particular.

But this leaflet should not replace a discussion between you and your doctor about the risks and benefits of Halcion.

Safe use of Halcion sleeping pills:

- Halcion is a prescription medication, intended to help you sleep. Follow you doctor's advice about how to take Halcion, when to take it, and how long to take it. **Do not take Halcion** if it is not prescribed for you.
- **Do not take Halcion** for more than 7 to 10 days without first consulting your doctor.
- **Do not take Halcion** when a full night's sleep is not possible before you would again need to be active and functional; e.g., an overnight flight of less than 8 hours. Memory lapses may occur in such situations. Your body needs time to eliminate the medication from your system.
- **Do not take Halcion** at any time during pregnancy. Tell your doctor if you are planning to become pregnant, if you are pregnant, or if you become pregnant while taking this medication.
- Tell your doctor about any alcohol consumption (present or past) or any medicine you are taking now, including drugs you can buy without a prescription. **Do not consume alcohol while taking Halcion.**
- **Do not increase the prescribed dose.**
- **Do not drive a car** or operate potentially dangerous machinery until you experience how this drug will affect you.
- If you develop any unusual disturbing thoughts or behavior while using Halcion, discuss the matter immediately with your doctor.
- You may experience an increase in sleep difficulties (rebound insomnia) and/or increased daytime anxiety (rebound anxiety) for 1 or 2 days after discontinuing Halcion.

Effectiveness of benzodiazepine sleeping pills: Benzodiazepine sleeping pills are effective medications and are relatively free of serious problems when used for the short-term management of insomnia. Symptoms of insomnia may vary: you may have difficulty in falling asleep, or awaken often during the night, or awaken early in the morning, or you may have all three symptoms.

Insomnia may last only for a short time and may respond to brief treatment. The risks and benefits of prolonged use should be discussed with your doctor.

Side Effects: Common Side Effects: Benzodiazepine sleeping pills may cause drowsiness, dizziness, lightheadedness, and difficulty with coordination. Users must be cautious about engaging in hazardous activities requiring complete mental alertness, e.g., operating machinery or driving a motor vehicle.

Avoid alcohol while using Halcion. **Do not use** benzodiazepine sleeping pills along with other medications without first discussing this with your doctor.

How sleepy you are the day after you use one of these sleeping pills depends on your individual response and on how quickly your body gets rid of the medication. The larger the dose, the more likely that you will experience drowsiness, etc., the next day. For this reason, it is important that you use the lowest effective dose. Benzodiazepines, which are eliminated rapidly (like Halcion), tend to cause less drowsiness the next day, but may cause withdrawal problems the day after use (see Tolerance/Withdrawal Symptoms).

Special Concerns: Memory Problems: All benzodiazepine sleeping pills can cause a special type of memory loss (amnesia); you may not recall events that occurred during some period of time, usually several hours, after taking the drug. This lapse is usually not a problem, because the person taking the sleeping pill intends to be asleep during this critical period of time. But it can be a problem if you take the medication to induce sleep while travelling, such as during an airplane flight, because you may wake up before the effect of the drug is gone. This has been called "traveller's amnesia". Halcion is more likely than other benzodiazepine sleeping pills to cause this problem.

Tolerance/Withdrawal Symptoms: After nightly use for more than a few weeks these drugs may lose some of their effectiveness. You may also develop a degree of dependence.

Halcion (cont'd)

For benzodiazepine sleeping pills that the body eliminates quickly, there may be a deficiency of the drug in the body at some point between each night's use. This can lead to (1) being awake during the last third of the night, and (2) increased daytime anxiety or nervousness. These side effects have been reported in particular with Halcion.

More severe "withdrawal" effects can occur when patients stop taking benzodiazepine sleeping pills. The effects may occur following use for only a week or two but may be more common and severe after long periods of continuous use. One type of withdrawal symptom is known as "rebound insomnia", i.e., on the first few nights after stopping the medication, insomnia may be worse than before the sleeping pill was given.

Other withdrawal symptoms following abrupt stopping of sleeping pills may range from unpleasant feelings to a major withdrawal syndrome that may include abdominal and muscle cramps, vomiting, sweating, tremor, and rarely, convulsions. The severe symptoms are uncommon.

Dependence/Abuse: All benzodiazepine sleeping pills can cause dependence (addiction) especially when used regularly for more than a few weeks, or at higher doses. Some people develop a need to continue taking these drugs, either at the prescribed dose or at higher doses—not for continued therapeutic effect, but to avoid withdrawal symptoms or to achieve nontherapeutic effects.

Individuals who depend on alcohol or other drugs may be at particular risk of becoming dependent on drugs of this class. But **all people are at some risk.** Consider this matter before you take these medications beyond a few weeks.

Mental and Behavioral Changes: A variety of abnormal thinking and behavior changes may occur when you use benzodiazepine sleeping pills. Some of these changes include aggressiveness and extroversion which seem out of character. Other changes, however, can be more unusual and extreme such as confusion, strange behavior, restlessness, hallucinations, feeling like you are not yourself, and worsening depression, including suicidal thinking.

It is rarely clear whether such symptoms are caused by the medication, or by an underlying illness, or are simply spontaneous happenings. In fact, worsened insomnia may in some cases be associated with illnesses that were present before the medication was used.

Important Note: Regardless of the cause, if you take these medications, report any mental or behavioral changes promptly to your doctor.

Effects on Pregnancy: Certain benzodiazepine sleeping pills have been linked to birth defects when taken during the early months of pregnancy. In addition, benzodiazepine sleeping pills taken during the last weeks of pregnancy have been known to sedate the baby. Therefore, **avoid using this medication during pregnancy.**

☐ HALFAN™ ℞

SmithKline Beecham Pharma

Halofantrine HCl

Antimalarial

Information for the Patient: What is Malaria? Malaria is an infectious disease caused by microscopic parasites called plasmodia. These are transmitted to human blood from the bite of infected mosquitoes. There are 4 species of these blood parasites which commonly infect humans. P. falciparum is the most dangerous of these species. If left untreated, the malaria caused by P. falciparum can result in death.

The most common symptoms of a malaria attack are chills followed by fever and sweating. These symptoms may recur at intervals of 48 hours or less and may be associated with headache, diarrhea, abdominal and muscle pain. These latter symptoms, which may initially be mistaken for flu, occur as the microscopic parasites enter and destroy red blood cells. This follows an incubation period of 1 or more weeks during which the parasites reproduce within the liver. Due to the complex life cycle of the malaria parasite in humans, malaria can develop while a person is in the malarious area or after departure from it. Malaria can also occur in a person who is receiving preventative medication, if the parasite is resistant to the drug or if the person is not properly following the dosing instructions. If left untreated, falciparum malaria can rapidly result in anemia, damage to internal organs such as the liver and spleen, and also coma and death.

What is Halfan: Halfan is a medicine used to treat malaria. It contains the drug halofantrine hydrochloride and is available as 250 mg tablets.

Proper Use of Halfan: Special Precautions: Halfan should not be used in patients with a history of certain types of heart disease/condition. Discuss this with your doctor if you are not sure or if you have ever experienced fainting or heart palpitations. Halfan should not be taken by pregnant or nursing mothers unless the doctor tells you to do so (see section on Pregnancy and Breast-feeding).

Halfan must **not** be taken with food. It is important that Halfan be taken on an empty stomach, not less than 1 hour before or 3 hours after meals. The tablets must be swallowed whole and **not** chewed. Do not take more than 2 tablets at once. Consult a doctor immediately if you take more tablets than prescribed. If you forget to take your tablets, take them as soon as you remember and wait at least 8 hours before taking the next dose.

Halfan Should not be Used to Prevent a Malaria Attack: Many antimalarials are used to prevent malaria. These antimalarials are taken in advance of a trip into an endemic area and guard against malarial infection. Halfan should not be used this way. Halfan should only be used for the treatment of malaria.

Pregnancy and Breast-feeding: Halfan is not recommended for use in pregnancy or while breast-feeding. Be sure to tell your doctor if you are or may become pregnant while travelling in malarious areas or while using Halfan, or if you intend to breast-feed while taking Halfan, so that he may advise you about the risks/benefits of antimalarial therapies.

Use of Other Medicines: Some medicines may cause unwanted effects if they are taken before or at the same time as Halfan. Tell the doctor if you have taken recently, or are taking, any other medicines particularly any drug which may affect the way your heart works. Tell the doctor if you are taking or plan to take any other drugs for protection against malaria or treatment of malaria.

Do not Give Halfan to Anyone Else: Your doctor has decided that Halfan is suitable treatment for you. If given to someone for whom Halfan is unsuitable, that person may be at risk of experiencing adverse reactions which may be serious.

Adverse Events: Side effects with Halfan are generally mild but may occasionally be serious (see below). A few people may have some unwanted effects. These have included feeling sick (nausea), stomach pain, diarrhea (several loose bowel movements a day), itching and skin rashes. If these symptoms continue or become severe, tell the doctor.

Halfan should not be used by patients who have specific heart conditions. Very rarely, Halfan may be associated with additional serious heart problems symptoms of which may include palpitations and fainting. These symptoms are more likely to occur if you have a heart condition, or if you are taking medicines which can affect your heart. It is very important to tell your doctor of any heart conditions you may have, or heart medications you may be using when seeking advice about antimalarial medications (see also Special Precautions).

If you develop any unusual discomfort while you are taking your medicine, tell your doctor as soon as possible.

How To Keep Your Medicine? The expiry date of this medicine is printed on the label. Do not use the medicine after this date. Keep your tablets in their original pack in a dry place, at room temperature (below 30°C). Store all medicines out of the reach of children.

How Can You Further Protect Yourself Against Malaria? The best way to minimize the possibility of contracting malaria is to reduce your contact with mosquitoes, which are more prevalent from dusk to dawn. This includes the wearing of light-colored clothes that cover most of the body, applying mosquito repellent to uncovered areas of the skin, sleeping under mosquito netting and spraying insecticides in sleeping quarters. For your best protection consult your doctor or local travel clinic on these subjects.

☐ HIVID® ℞

Roche

Zalcitabine

Antiretroviral Agent

Information for the Patient: Other names: zalcitabine, ddC.

Hivid interferes with the ability of the Human Immunodeficiency Virus (HIV) to make more of itself (replicate). This has been shown in laboratory studies. Hivid slows the disease by slowing down viral replication. It is not a cure. Hivid does not prevent secondary infections associated with HIV, so the medications prescribed to treat or prevent secondary infections should be continued unless your doctor tells you otherwise. It is very important to keep appointments with your doctor and report any changes in your health.

HIV is usually spread by sexual contact or by contaminated needles. This risk still exists during Hivid therapy; thus continue practicing safe sex and do not share needles.

What You Should Tell Your Doctor Before Starting Therapy: Before you start your therapy with Hivid, you should tell your doctor if you have or have had any of the following diseases or symptoms as this may affect your treatment with Hivid.

1. Allergy to lactose.
2. Numbness, tingling, burning sensation or pain of the hands and/or legs and feet.
3. High cholesterol or high triglycerides.
4. Pancreatitis.
5. Excessive alcohol intake.
6. Pre-existing liver disease.
7. Diabetes.
8. Pregnancy.

Tell your doctor about all the medications, vitamins and alternative therapies you are currently taking.

Side Effects: The most common side effect of Hivid therapy is peripheral neuropathy. This is a nerve abnormality in the feet, legs and hands which causes numbness, tingling, burning sensations upon contact, sharp shooting pains, and severe continuous burning pains. A serious side effect of Hivid therapy is pancreatitis usually noticed by severe abdominal pain. Any of these symptoms should be immediately reported to your doctor.

Other side effects experienced by patients treated with Hivid include: mouth sores, headache, rash, fatigue, nausea, muscle pain, itching, dizziness, abdominal pain, sore throat and vomiting. These symptoms generally resolve after 1 to 2 weeks even with continued treatment. Many of these side effects can be treated.

Special Symptoms You Should Tell Your Doctor About:

- Tell your doctor as soon as possible, if you experience any of the following symptoms because these side effects may possibly result in permanent effects. These symptoms may be early signs of rare, but more serious side effects which your doctor may want to check as soon as possible.
- Severe nausea, vomiting, severe abdominal pain (stomach pain), bloating or indigestion.
- Numbness, tingling or burning sensation in the hands, legs or feet.
- Yellowing of the skin or eyes and/or dark orange urine.
- Tell your doctor about any unusual or severe symptoms that appear during treatment.

General Information About Your Medication:

- Call your doctor if you have any questions or troubling symptoms.
- Keep Hivid out of reach of children.
- Store at room temperature in a dry location. Hivid does not require refrigeration.
- Read your prescription label carefully and take the exact amount of Hivid in the schedule prescribed by your doctor.
- Hivid has been prescribed for you by your doctor and should not be given to any one else.
- Females of childbearing potential should use effective contraception.
- If you forget a dose, do not take a double dose, take the next dose at your usual time.

This summary does not contain all known information about Hivid. Talk to your doctor if you have any questions.

□ HUMALOG™

Lilly

Insulin Lispro

Antidiabetic Agent

Information for the Patient: Warnings: This Lilly human insulin analogue differs from other insulins because it has a unique structure, a very quick onset of action and a short duration of activity. Humalog (insulin lispro injection) should be given within 15 minutes of a meal.

Any change of insulin should be made cautiously and only under medical supervision. Changes in purity, strength, brand (manufacturer), type (regular, NPH, lente, etc), species (beef, pork, beef-pork, human), and/or method of manufacture (recombinant DNA versus animal-source insulin) may result in the need for a change in dosage.

Mixing of Humalog with either animal insulins or insulin preparations produced by other manufacturers is not recommended.

Patients taking Humalog may require a change in dosage from that used with other insulins. If an adjustment is needed, it may occur with the first dose or over a period of several weeks.

Insulin and Diabetes: Insulin is a hormone produced by the pancreas, a large gland that lies near the stomach. This hormone is necessary for the body's correct use of food, especially sugar. Diabetes occurs when the pancreas does not make enough insulin to meet your body's needs.

To control your diabetes, your doctor has prescribed injections of insulin, insulin lispro injection, or both, to keep your blood glucose at a near-normal level. Proper control is important. Uncontrolled diabetes (hyperglycemia) over a long period of time can result in a number of serious problems such as blindness, kidney failure, poor circulation/heart attacks, strokes and/or nerve damage. These problems can be prevented or reduced by good diabetes management. This will require close and constant cooperation with your diabetes healthcare team including: yourself, your doctor and your diabetes educators (nurses, dietitians, social workers, pharmacists and other health care professionals). Thus, you can lead an active, healthy and productive life by eating a balanced daily diet, exercising regularly, and taking your insulin injections as prescribed.

You have been instructed to test your blood and/or your urine regularly for glucose. If your blood tests consistently show above-or below-normal glucose levels or your urine tests consistently show the presence of glucose, your diabetes is not properly controlled and you must let your doctor know.

Always keep an extra supply of Humalog as well as a spare syringe and needle on hand. Always wear diabetic identification so that appropriate treatment can be given if complications occur away from home.

Humalog: Insulin lispro injection vials or cartridges, manufactured by Eli Lilly and Company, have the trademark Humalog.

Cartridges of Humalog, 1.5 or 3 mL, are available in boxes of 5. Humalog cartridges are designed for use with B-D pen cartridge systems or future Lilly injector systems. The cartridge containing Humalog is not designed to allow any other insulin to be mixed in the cartridge or for the cartridge to be reused.

Humalog is a recombinant DNA sourced human insulin analogue. Humalog consists of zinc-insulin lispro crystals dissolved in a clear fluid. It takes effect more rapidly and has a shorter duration of activity as compared to regular insulin. The rapid onset of activity requires Humalog to be given closer to a meal. The time course of action of any insulin may vary to some extent in different individuals or at different times in the same individual. As with all insulin preparations, the duration of action of Humalog is dependent on dose, site of injection, blood supply, temperature, and physical activity.

Your doctor has prescribed the type of insulin that he/she believes is best for you, depending on your metabolic requirements and your lifestyle.

Do not use any other insulin except on your doctor's advice and direction.

Dosage: Your doctor has told you which insulin to use, how much, and when and how often to inject it. Because each patient's case of diabetes is different, this schedule has been individualized for you.

Your usual Humalog dose may be affected by changes in your food, activity, or work schedule. Carefully follow your doctor's instructions to allow for these changes. Other things that may affect your Humalog dose are:

Illness: Illness, especially with nausea and vomiting, may cause your insulin requirements to change. Even if you are not eating, you will still require insulin. You and your doctor should establish a sick day plan for you to use in case of illness. When you are sick, test your blood/urine frequently and call your doctor as instructed.

Pregnancy: Good control of diabetes is especially important for you and your unborn baby. Pregnancy may make managing your diabetes more difficult. If you are planning to have a baby, are pregnant, or are nursing a baby, consult your doctor.

Medication: Insulin requirements may be increased if you are taking other drugs with hyperglycemic activity, such as oral contraceptives, corticosteroids, or thyroid replacement therapy. Insulin requirements may be reduced in the presence of drugs with hypoglycemic activity, such as oral hypoglycemics, salicylates, sulfa antibiotics, and certain antidepressants. Always discuss any medications you are taking with your doctor.

Humalog (cont'd)

Exercise: Exercise may lower your body's need for Humalog during and for some time after the activity. Exercise may also speed up the effect of a Humalog dose, especially if the exercise involves the area of injection site. Discuss with your doctor how you should adjust your regimen to accommodate exercise.

Travel: Persons travelling across more than 2 time zones should consult their doctor concerning adjustments in their insulin schedule.

Insulin Reaction and Shock: Cause: Hypoglycemia (too little glucose in the blood) is one of the most frequent adverse events experienced by insulin users. It can be brought about by:

1. Missing or delaying meals
2. Taking too much insulin
3. Exercising or working more than usual
4. An infection or illness (especially with diarrhea or vomiting)
5. A change in the body's need for insulin
6. Diseases of the adrenal, pituitary, or thyroid gland, or progression of kidney or liver disease
7. Interactions with other drugs that lower blood glucose, such as oral hypoglycemics, salicylates, sulfa antibiotics, and certain antidepressants
8. Consumption of alcoholic beverages

Dietary Implications: If a usual meal cannot be obtained at the appropriate time, then to avoid hypoglycemia, you should take the amount of carbohydrate prescribed for this meal in the form of orange juice, syrup, candy, or bread and milk, without changing your insulin dosage. If it becomes necessary to omit a meal on account of nausea and vomiting, you should test your blood sugar level and notify your doctor.

Symptoms and Treatment: Symptoms of mild to moderate hypoglycemia may occur suddenly and can include:

- sweating
- dizziness
- palpitation
- tremor
- hunger
- restlessness
- tingling in the hands, feet, lips, or tongue
- lightheadedness
- inability to concentrate
- headache
- drowsiness
- sleep disturbances
- anxiety
- blurred vision
- slurred speech
- depressive mood
- irritability
- abnormal behavior
- unsteady movement
- personality changes

Signs of severe hypoglycemia can include:

- disorientation
- unconsciousness
- seizures
- death

Therefore, it is important that assistance be obtained immediately.

Early warning symptoms of hypoglycemia may be different or less pronounced under certain conditions, such as long duration of diabetes, diabetic nerve disease, medications such as beta-blockers, change in insulin preparations, or intensified control (3 or more injections/day) of diabetes. A few patients who have experienced hypoglycemic reactions after transfer from animal-source insulin to human insulin have reported that the early warning symptoms of hypoglycemia were less pronounced or different from those experienced with their previous insulin.

Without recognition of early warning symptoms, you may not be able to take steps to avoid more serious hypoglycemia. Be alert for all of the various types of symptoms that may indicate hypoglycemia. Patients who experience hypoglycemia without early warning symptoms should monitor their blood glucose frequently, especially prior to activities such as driving. If the blood glucose is below your normal fasting glucose, you should consider eating or drinking sugar-containing foods to treat your hypoglycemia.

Mild to moderate hypoglycemia may be treated by eating foods or drinks that contain sugar. Patients should always carry a quick source of sugar, such as candy mints or glucose tablets. More severe hypoglycemia may require the assistance of another person. Patients who are unable to take sugar orally or who are unconscious should be treated with intravenous administration of glucose at a medical facility or should be given an injection of glucagon (either intramuscular or subcutaneous). The patient should be given oral carbohydrates as soon as consciousness is recovered.

You should learn to recognize your own symptoms of hypoglycemia. If you are uncertain about these symptoms, you should monitor your blood glucose frequently to help you learn to recognize the symptoms that you experience with hypoglycemia.

If you have frequent episodes of hypoglycemia or experience difficulty in recognizing the symptoms, you should consult your doctor to discuss possible changes in therapy, meal plans, and/or exercise programs to help you avoid hypoglycemia.

Diabetic Acidosis and Coma: Hyperglycemia (too much glucose in the blood) may develop if your body has too little insulin.

Hyperglycemia can be brought about by any of the following:

1. Omitting your insulin or taking less than the doctor has prescribed
2. Eating significantly more than your meal plan suggests
3. Developing a fever, infection, or other significant stressful situation

In patients with insulin-dependent diabetes, prolonged hyperglycemia can result in diabetic acidosis. The first symptoms of diabetic acidosis usually come on gradually, over a period of hours or days, and include a drowsy feeling, flushed face, thirst, loss of appetite, and fruity odor on the breath. With acidosis, urine tests show large amounts of glucose and acetone. Heavy breathing and a rapid pulse are more severe symptoms. If uncorrected, prolonged hyperglycemia or diabetic acidosis can lead to nausea, vomiting, dehydration, loss of consciousness, or death. Therefore, it is important that you obtain medical assistance immediately.

Lipodystrophy: Rarely, administration of insulin subcutaneously can result in lipoatrophy (depression in the skin) or lipohypertrophy (enlargement or thickening of tissue). If you notice either of these conditions, consult your doctor. A change in your injection technique may help alleviate the problem.

Allergy to Insulin: Local Allergy: Patients occasionally experience redness, swelling, and itching at the site of injection. This condition, called local allergy, usually clears up in a few days to a few weeks. In some instances, this condition may be related to factors other than insulin, such as irritants in the skin cleansing agent or poor injection technique. If you have local reactions, contact your doctor.

Systemic Allergy: Less common, but potentially more serious, is generalized allergy to insulin, which may cause rash over the whole body, shortness of breath, wheezing, reduction in blood pressure, fast pulse, or sweating. Severe cases of generalized allergy may be life threatening. If you think you are having a generalized allergic reaction, notify a doctor immediately.

Instructions for Use: Humalog is a sterile solution. Humalog preparations should be given by subcutaneous injection. The concentration of Humalog in 10 mL vials, 1.5 or 3 mL cartridges is 100 units/mL (U-100).

Humalog is a clear and colorless liquid with a water-like appearance and consistency. Do not use if it appears cloudy, thickened, or slightly colored or if solid particles are visible. Always check the appearance of your vial or cartridge of Humalog before using, and if you note anything unusual in its appearance or notice your insulin requirements changing markedly, consult your doctor.

Storage: Vials: Humalog vials should be stored in a refrigerator but not in the freezer. If refrigeration is not possible, the vial of Humalog that you are currently using can be kept unrefrigerated, up to 28 days, as long as it is kept as cool as possible (below 30°C) and away from direct heat and light. Do not use Humalog if it has been frozen. Do not use a vial of Humalog after the expiration date stamped on the label.

Cartridges: Humalog cartridges should be stored in a refrigerator but not in the freezer. The pen and cartridge of Humalog that you are currently using should not be refrigerated but should be kept as cool as possible (below 30°C) and away from direct heat and light. Do not use Humalog if it has been frozen. Unrefrigerated cartridges should be discarded after 28 days, even if they still contain Humalog. Do not use a cartridge of Humalog after the expiration date stamped on the label.

Injection Procedures: Vials: Correct Syringe: Doses of insulin are measured in units. Humalog is available in 100 units/mL (U-100). It is important that you understand the markings on your syringe, because the volume of Humalog you inject depends on the strength, that is, the number of units/mL. For this reason, you should always use a syringe marked for U-100 insulin preparations. Failure to use the proper syringe can lead to a mistake in dosage, causing serious problems for you, such as a blood glucose level that is too low or too high.

Syringe Use: To help avoid contamination and possible infection, follow these instructions exactly.

Disposable plastic syringes and needles should be used only once and then discarded. **Needles and syringes must not be shared.**

Reusable glass syringes and needles must be sterilized before each injection. **Follow the package directions supplied with your syringe.**

Preparing the Dose:

1. Wash your hands.
2. Inspect the Humalog in the vial. It should look clear and colorless. Do not use Humalog if it appears cloudy, thickened, or slightly colored or if solid particles are visible.
3. If using a new vial, flip off the plastic protective cap, but do not remove the stopper.
4. Wipe the top of the vial with an alcohol swab.
5. If you are mixing insulins, refer to the instructions for mixing that follow.
6. Remove the cover from the needle. Draw air into the syringe equal to your Humalog dose. Put the needle through rubber top of the Humalog vial and inject the air into the vial.
7. Turn the vial and syringe upside down. Hold the vial and syringe firmly in one hand.
8. Making sure the tip of the needle is in the Humalog, withdraw the correct dose into the syringe.
9. Before removing the needle from the vial, check your syringe for air bubbles, which reduce the amount of Humalog. If bubbles are present, hold the syringe straight up and tap its side until the bubbles float to the top. Push them out with the plunger and withdraw the correct dose.
10. Remove the needle from the vial and lay the syringe down so that the needle does not touch anything.

Mixing Humalog with Longer-Acting Insulin Formulations: Mixing Humalog with either animal insulins or insulin preparations produced by other manufacturers is not recommended.

1. Humalog should be mixed with longer-acting Humulin insulins only on the advice of your doctor.
2. Draw air into your syringe equal to the amount of longer-acting Humulin insulin you are taking. Insert the needle into the longer-acting insulin vial and inject the air, taking care not to come in contact with the insulin in the vial. Withdraw the needle.
3. Now inject air into your Humalog vial in the same manner, but do not withdraw the needle.
4. Turn the vial and syringe upside down.
5. Making sure the tip of the needle is in the Humalog, withdraw the correct dose of Humalog into the syringe.
6. Before removing the needle from the vial of Humalog, check your syringe for air bubbles, which reduce the amount of Humalog in it. If bubbles are present, hold the syringe straight up and tap its side until the bubbles float to the top. Push them out with the plunger and withdraw the correct dose. Gently roll or shake the long-acting Humulin vial until the insulin is mixed.
7. Remove the needle from the vial of Humalog and insert it into the vial of the longer-acting Humulin insulin. Turn the vial and syringe upside down. Making sure the tip of the needle is in the insulin, withdraw your dose of longer-acting Humulin insulin.
8. Remove the needle and lay the syringe down so that the needle does not touch anything.

Follow your doctor's instructions on mixing your insulin just before giving your injection. Humalog should be injected immediately after mixing. It is important to be consistent in your method.

Syringes from different manufacturers may vary in the amount of space between the bottom line and the needle. Because of this, do not change the sequence of mixing, or the model and brand of syringe or needle that the doctor has prescribed.

Injection: Cleanse the skin with alcohol where the injection is to be made. Stabilize the skin by spreading it or pinching up a large area. Insert the needle as instructed by your doctor. Push the plunger in as far as it will go. Pull the needle out and apply gentle pressure over the injection site for several seconds. Do not rub the area. To avoid tissue damage, give the next injection at a site at least 1 cm (0.5 inches) from the previous injection site.

Cartridges: Preparing a Cartridge of Humalog for Insertion in a Pen:

1. Wash your hands.
2. Before inserting the Humalog cartridge into the pen, inspect it to make sure the contents look clear and colorless. Do not use the Humalog cartridge if it appears cloudy, thickened, or slightly colored or if solid particles are visible.
3. Follow the pen manufacturer's directions carefully for loading the cartridge into the pen.

Injecting the Dose:

1. Wash your hands.
2. Use an alcohol swab to wipe the exposed rubber surface on the metal cap end of the cartridge.
3. Inspect the Humalog in the cartridge. It should look clear and colorless. Do not use Humalog if it appears cloudy, thickened, or slightly colored or if solid particles are visible.
4. Follow pen manufacturer's directions for attaching needle.
5. Hold the pen with needle pointing straight up. If there are large bubbles, tap the side of the pen until they float to the top. Remove the bubbles and the air in the needle by setting the pen to a 2-unit dose and depressing the plunger. Repeat this step if necessary until a drop of Humalog appears at the end of the needle.
6. To avoid tissue damage, injection sites can be rotated so that the same site is not used more than approximately once a month.
7. Cleanse the skin with alcohol where the injection is to be made.
8. With one hand, stabilize the skin by spreading it or pinching up a large area.
9. Insert the needle as instructed by your doctor.
10. To inject Humalog, follow the pen manufacturer's instructions.
11. Pull the needle out and apply gentle pressure over the injection site for several seconds. Do not rub the area.
12. Immediately after an injection, remove the needle from the pen. This will ensure sterility and prevent leakage, reentry of air, and potential needle clogs. Dispose of the needle in a responsible manner. Do not reuse needle. **Needles, cartridges, and pens must not be shared.**
13. Once the 1.5 mL cartridge is in use, do not continue to use it if the leading edge of the plunger is into or beyond the colored band on the cartridge. Use the gauge on the side of the cartridge to help you judge how much Humalog remains. The distance between each mark is approximately 10 units for 1.5 mL cartridges.

If using a 3 mL cartridge, there is no corresponding colored band on the cartridge. Use the gauge on the side of the cartridge to help you judge how much Humalog remains. The distance between each mark is approximately 20 units for 3 mL cartridges. When the leading edge of the plunger reaches the last mark on the gauge there is approximately 20 units of Humalog remaining in the cartridge.

□ HUMULIN®

Lilly

Insulin, Human Biosynthetic

Antidiabetic Agent

Information for the Patient: e.g. Humulin 40/60 (insulin, human biosynthetic) vials and cartridges:

Warnings: This Lilly human insulin product differs from animal-source insulins, because it is structurally identical to the insulin produced by your body's pancreas and because of its unique manufacturing process.

Any change of insulin should be made cautiously and only under medical supervision. Changes in refinement, purity, strength, brand (manufacturer), type (Regular, NPH, Lente, etc.), species (pork, beef-pork, human), and/or method of manufacture (recombinant DNA versus animal-source insulin) may result in the need for a change in dosage.

Some patients taking Humulin will require a change in dosage from that used with animal-source insulins. If an adjustment is needed, it may be made with the first dose or over a period of several weeks.

Insulin and Diabetes: Your doctor has explained that you have diabetes. You have learned that the treatment of your diabetes requires injections of insulin.

Insulin is a hormone produced by the pancreas, a large gland that lies near the stomach. This hormone is necessary for the body's correct use of food, especially sugar. Diabetes occurs when the pancreas does not make enough insulin to meet your body's needs.

To control your diabetes, your doctor has prescribed injections of insulin to keep your blood sugar at a nearly normal level and to keep your urine as free of sugar as possible. Each case of diabetes is different. Your doctor has told you which insulin to use, how much, and

Humulin (cont'd)

when and how often to inject it. This schedule has been individualized for you. Proper control of your diabetes requires close and constant co-operation with your doctor.

In spite of diabetes, you can lead an active, healthy, and useful life if you eat a balanced diet daily, exercise regularly, and take your insulin injections exactly as prescribed by your doctor.

You have been instructed to test your blood and/or your urine regularly for sugar. If your blood tests consistently show above or below normal sugar levels or your urine tests consistently show the presence of sugar, your diabetes is not properly controlled and you must let your doctor know.

If you become ill from any cause, especially with nausea and vomiting, your insulin requirements may change. Test your blood and/or urine and notify your doctor at once.

Always keep an extra supply of insulin. Always wear diabetic identification so that appropriate treatment can be given if complications occur away from home.

Use the Proper Type of Insulin: This insulin, manufactured by Eli Lilly and Company, has the trademark Humulin, insulin, human biosynthetic (rDNA Origin)—Lilly, and is available in several formulations.

These products can be identified by the large letter(s) or numbers that appear on the carton and vial or cartridge label following the name Humulin: i.e., Humulin R (Regular), Humulin N (NPH), Humulin L (Lente), Humulin U (Ultralente), Humulin 10/90 (10% Regular/90% NPH), Humulin 20/80 (20% Regular/80% NPH), Humulin 30/70 (30% Regular/70% NPH), Humulin 40/60 (40% Regular/60% NPH), and Humulin 50/50 (50% Regular/50% NPH).

These types of insulin differ mainly in the time they require to take effect and in the length of time their action lasts. Your doctor has prescribed the type of insulin that he/she believes is best for you. **Do not use any other insulin except on your doctor's advice and direction.**

When you receive your insulin from the pharmacy, always check to see that:

1. The name Humulin appears on the carton and vial or cartridge label and is followed by the proper letter designation and name for the insulin formulation: R-Regular; N-NPH; L-Lente; U-Ultralente; 10/90-10% Regular/90% NPH; 20/80-20% Regular/80% NPH; 30/70-30% Regular/70% NPH; 40/60-40% Regular/60% NPH; 50/50-50% Regular/50% NPH.
2. The carton and the vial or cartridge label is correct for your type of insulin.
3. The human insulin is of rDNA origin.
4. The insulin strength is U-100.
5. The expiration date on the package will allow you to use the insulin before that date.

40/60, Insulin, Human Biosynthetic: Humulin has been produced by recombinant DNA processes. Humulin 40/60 is a fixed mixture of 40% Humulin R (insulin injection, human biosynthetic) and 60% Humulin N (insulin isophane, human biosynthetic). It is an intermediate-acting insulin with a more rapid onset of action than NPH insulin alone. The duration of activity may last up to 24 hours following injection.

Humulin 40/60 is for s.c. use only.

Warnings: (see additional Warnings above): Humulin 40/60 should be used only if your doctor has prescribed insulins mixed in a ratio of 40% Regular and 60% NPH. You should not attempt to change the ratio of this product by adding additional NPH or Regular insulin to this bottle. If Humulin N and Humulin R mixtures are prescribed in a different proportion, the individual insulins should be mixed as instructed in the amounts recommended by your doctor or purchased as mixtures in the ratio recommended if available.

Usage in Pregnancy: Control of the blood sugar is vital to assure the birth of a healthy child. Normalization of the blood sugar should have occurred before conception and should continue throughout the pregnancy. Since pregnancy may make diabetes worse and because of the importance of good diabetic control, patients who contemplate pregnancy or who are pregnant should seek expert medical advice.

Diabetic patients who are nursing may require adjustments in insulin dose and/or diet.

Insulin Reaction and Shock: Cause: Insulin reaction (too little sugar in the blood, also called ''hypoglycemia'') can be brought about by:

1. Taking too much insulin
2. Missing or delaying meals
3. Exercising or working too hard just before a meal
4. An infection or illness (especially with diarrhea or vomiting)
5. A change in the body's need for insulin

Dietary Implications: If a usual meal cannot be obtained at the appropriate time, then to avoid hypoglycemia, you should take the amount of carbohydrate prescribed for this meal in the form of orange juice, syrup, candy, or bread and milk, without changing your insulin dosage. If it becomes necessary to omit a meal on account of nausea and vomiting, you should test your blood sugar level and notify your doctor.

Symptoms and Treatment: The first symptoms of insulin reaction usually come on suddenly and may include vague symptoms of fatigue, nervousness or shakiness , rapid heartbeat, nausea, and a cold sweat. It is of utmost importance that you understand that these symptoms demand immediate attention.

A few patients who experienced hypoglycemic reactions after being transferred to Humulin have reported that these early warning symptoms were less pronounced than they were with animal-source insulin.

Eating sugar or a sugar-sweetened product will often correct the condition and prevent more serious symptoms. Artificial sweeteners are not useful for the treatment of hypoglycemia.

If a diabetic becomes delirious or mentally confused, or suffers from loss of memory or delusions, corn syrup diluted or orange juice with sugar should be administered by mouth. In severe reactions, it may be desirable for your doctor to administer i.v. from 15 to 20 g of dextrose (d-glucose) in sterile solution. In the event of a hypoglycemic reaction, whether mild or severe, you should notify your doctor promptly so that any desirable change in diet or dosage can be determined.

Diabetic Acidosis and Coma: Diabetic acidosis may develop if your body has too little insulin. (This is the opposite of insulin reaction, which is the result of too much insulin in the blood). Diabetic acidosis may be brought on if you omit your insulin or take less than the doctor has prescribed, eat significantly more than your diet calls for, or develop a fever or infection. With acidosis, urine tests show a large amount of sugar and acetone.

The first symptoms of diabetic acidosis usually come on gradually, over a period of hours or days, and include a drowsy feeling, flushed face, thirst, and loss of appetite. Heavy breathing and a rapid pulse are more severe symptoms.

If uncorrected, loss of consciousness, coma, or death can result. Therefore, it is important that you obtain medical assistance immediately.

Allergy to Insulin: Patients occasionally experience redness, swelling, and itching at the site of injection of insulin. This condition, called local allergy, usually clears up in a few days to a few weeks. If you have local reactions, contact your doctor, who may recommend a change in the type or species of insulin.

Less common, but potentially more serious, is generalized allergy to insulin, which may cause rash over the whole body, shortness of breath, wheezing, reduction in blood pressure, fast pulse, or sweating. Severe cases of generalized allergy may be life threatening. If you think you are having a generalized allergic reaction to insulin, notify a doctor immediately. Your doctor may recommend skin testing, that is, injecting small doses of other insulins into the skin, in order to select the best insulin for you to use. Patients who have had severe generalized allergic reactions to insulin should be skin tested with each new preparation to be used before treatment with that preparation is started.

Important Notes:

1. Never change from the insulin that has been prescribed for you to another insulin without instructions from your doctor. Changing the type, strength, source, or manufacturer of insulin can cause problems with your diabetes.
2. Your doctor will tell you what to do if you miss a dose of insulin or miss a meal because of illness. Always keep on hand an extra supply of insulin, as well as a spare needle. If you miss a meal, as a substitute use sugar, sugar-sweetened candy, fruit juice, or sugar-sweetened beverage according to your doctor's instructions. If a shortage of insulin appears inevitable, a temporary reduction in the size of dose may be made, accompanied by limitation of food to two-thirds its usual quantity and a liberal increase in fluids of little or no food value, such as water, tea, coffee, broths, or clear soups.
3. If you become ill from any cause, especially with nausea and vomiting, your insulin requirements may change. Test your urine and/or blood and notify your doctor at once.
4. Consult your doctor if you notice anything unusual or have doubts about your condition or your use of insulin.
5. Consult your doctor concerning adjustments in your insulin schedule if you travel across more than 2 time zones.
6. Always wear diabetic identification so that appropriate treatment can be given if complications occur away from home.

7. Understand how to manage your diabetes so that your life can be active and healthy.

Instructions for Use for Vials (see package insert for illustrations): Humulin 40/60 should be used only if it has been prescribed by your doctor. Humulin 40/60 is for s.c. use only. Do not inject into a vein.
Vial (Bottle) Inspection: **Do not use after expiry date. Do not use a bottle of Humulin 40/60 if after resuspending there are clumps floating in the insulin or if solid white particles stick to the bottom or wall of the bottle giving it a frosted appearance. (Resuspend the insulin by following instruction 2 under Preparing the Dose). A bottle that appears frosted or contains clumps should be returned to the place of purchase for exchange.**

If you notice anything unusual in the appearance or effect of your insulin, consult your doctor.

Storage: Your unused Humulin bottles should be stored in the refrigerator (2 to 10°C). **Do not freeze.** The bottle of insulin currently in use does not have to be refrigerated but should be kept at a temperature below 25°C, away from direct heat and sunlight and protected from freezing. Bottles in use or not refrigerated should be discarded after 28 days even if they contain insulin.

Injection Procedures for Vials: Correct Syringe: Doses of insulin are measured in units. U-100 insulin contains 100 units/mL. It is important to use a syringe that is marked for U-100 insulin preparations. Failure to use the proper syringe can lead to a mistake in dosage, causing serious problems for you, such as a blood glucose level that is too low or too high.

Syringe Use. To help avoid contamination and possible infection, follow these instructions exactly.

Disposable syringes and needles should be used only once and then discarded. **Needles and syringes must not be shared.** Reusable syringes and needles must be sterilized before each injection. **Follow the package directions supplied with your syringe.**

Preparing The Dose:
1. Wash your hands.
2. Carefully shake or rotate the insulin bottle several times to completely mix the insulin.
3. Inspect the insulin. Humulin 40/60 should look uniformly cloudy or milky. Do not use it if you notice anything unusual in the appearance.
4. If using a new bottle, flip off the plastic protective cap, but do not remove the stopper. Wipe the top of the bottle with an alcohol swab.
5. Draw air into the syringe equal to your insulin dose. Put the needle through the rubber top of the insulin bottle and inject the air into the bottle.
6. Turn the bottle and syringe upside down. Hold the bottle and syringe firmly in 1 hand.
7. Making sure the tip of the needle is in the insulin, withdraw the correct dose of insulin into the syringe.
8. Before removing the needle from the bottle, check your syringe for air bubbles which reduce the amount of insulin in it. If bubbles are present, hold the syringe needle up and tap its side until the bubbles float to the top. Push them out with the plunger and withdraw the correct dose.
9. Remove the needle from the bottle and lay the syringe down so that the needle **does not touch anything.**

Injecting The Dose: Cleanse the skin with alcohol where the injection is to be made. Stabilize the skin by spreading it or pinching up a large area. Insert the needle as instructed by your doctor. Push the plunger in as far as it will go. Pull the needle out and apply gentle pressure over the injection site for several seconds. **Do not rub the area.** To avoid tissue damage, give the next injection at a site at least 1.5 cm from the previous site.

Instructions for Use for Cartridges: Humulin cartridges are designed for use with the B-D Pen, the B-D Pen Ultra cartridge system, or future Lilly injector systems.

Humulin cartridges are not designed to allow any other insulin to be mixed in the cartridge. Humulin cartridges **must not** be refilled and are not designed for use with a traditional syringe. However, it is recommended that you carry a syringe in the pen case, so that in the event of an emergency, i.e., pen does not work, you can withdraw insulin from the cartridge for a single use. This cartridge should not be reused.

Humulin 40/60 should be used only if it has been prescribed by your doctor. Humulin 40/60 cartridges are for s.c. use only. Do not inject into a vein.

Cartridge Inspection: **Do not use after expiry date. Do not use a cartridge of Humulin 40/60 if after resuspending there are clumps floating in the insulin or if solid white particles stick to the bottom or wall of the cartridge giving it a frosted appearance. (Resuspend the insulin by following instruction 2 under Preparing the Dose). A cartridge that appears frosted or contains clumps should be returned to the place of purchase for exchange.**

If you notice anything unusual in the appearance or effect of your insulin, consult your doctor.

Storage: Your unused Humulin cartridges should be stored in the refrigerator (2 to 10°C). **Do not freeze.** The cartridge of insulin currently in use should be left in the pen and may be carried with you. The pen and cartridge do not have to be refrigerated but should be kept at a temperature below 25°C, away from direct heat and sunlight and protected from freezing. Cartridges in use or not refrigerated should be discarded after 28 days even if they contain insulin.

Preparing The Dose (see package insert for illustrations):
1. Wash your hands.
2. Always examine the cartridge of Humulin 40/60 after removing from the box. Resuspend the insulin by rolling the cartridge between the palms 10 times and inverting it 180° 10 times. Inspect the cartridge for uniform resuspension; if the Humulin 40/60 does not look uniformly cloudy or milky, repeat the resuspension procedure as often as necessary. **Do not use** if the white insulin particles stick to the bottom or sides of the cartridge or if there are clumps floating in the insulin.
3. Carefully load the cartridge into the pen following the manufacturers directions.
4. Wipe the exposed rubber membrane on the metal cap end of the cartridge with an alcohol swab and attach the needle.
5. Carefully resuspend the Humulin 40/60 by rolling the cartridge and pen in your hands 10 times and inverting it 180° 10 times. This must be performed each time before you give yourself an injection even after just loading the pen.
6. Prime the pen as directed by the manufacturer. If air bubbles are present, hold the pen with the needle pointing up and tap the side of the pen until the bubbles float to the top. With the pen still vertical, purge the needle with a 2 unit dose setting of the pen. Repeat until an insulin drop appears at the end of the needle. There may be small bubbles left; the air is harmless but too large an air bubble will affect the accuracy of the insulin dose administered.
7. Set the dose as instructed by your doctor. A gauge has been provided on the side of the cartridge to help you judge the amount of insulin remaining. The distance between each mark represents approximately 10 units for 1.5 mL cartridges and 20 units for 3.0 mL cartridges.

Injecting The Dose:
1. Cleanse the skin with alcohol where the injection is to be made. To avoid tissue damage, always change the site for each injection by at least 1.5 cm from the previous site, rotating sites on the body.
2. With one hand stabilize the skin by pinching up a large area.
3. Insert the needle as instructed by your doctor or nurse.
4. To inject the insulin, follow the instructions of the pen's manufacturer.
5. Pull the needle out and apply gentle pressure over the injection site for several seconds. **Do not rub the area.**
6. Immediately after injection, remove the needle from the pen. This will ensure sterility and prevent leakage, re-entry of air and potential needle clogs.

□ HYDROMORPH CONTIN® Ⓝ

Purdue Frederick

Hydromorphone HCl

Opioid Analgesic

Information for the Patient: What is hydromorphone? Hydromorphone relieves pain and should help you to live more comfortably and independently. It is effective and safe when used as directed by your doctor.

Your pain may increase or decrease from time to time and your doctor may need to change the amount of hydromorphone you take (daily dosage).

What is Hydromorph Contin? Hydromorph Contin is a capsule that is made in such a way as to slowly release hydromorphone over a 12-hour period, usually requiring a dose only every 12 hours to control your pain.

Hydromorph Contin capsules are available in 5 strengths: 3 mg (green), 6 mg (pink), 12 mg (orange), 24 mg (grey) and 30 mg (red). It may be necessary for you to take more than one capsule strength

Hydromorph Contin (cont'd)

(different colored capsules) at the same time in order to receive the total daily dosage prescribed by your doctor.

Hydromorph Contin capsules should be swallowed intact. If directed by your physician the contents may be sprinkled on soft food, but neither the capsules nor the beads should be crushed or chewed.

How to take your medication: Hydromorph Contin capsules must be taken regularly every 12 hours (with 120 to 180 mL of water) to prevent pain all day and night. If your pain worsens, making you uncomfortable, contact your doctor immediately and she/he may decide that it is necessary to adjust your daily dosage of Hydromorph Contin.

Your starting dosage of Hydromorph Contin will be clearly labelled on the medication bottle. Be sure to follow these directions on the label exactly; this is very important. If your dosage is changed, be sure to write it down at the time your doctor calls you or sees you. And follow the new directions exactly.

Constipation: Hydromorphone causes constipation. This is to be expected so your doctor may order a laxative and stool softener to help relieve your constipation while you are taking Hydromorph Contin. Tell your doctor about the problem if it arises.

Taking other medications: Your doctor should be made aware of any other medication you are taking including over-the-counter antihistamines or sleep-aids as they could affect the way you respond to hydromorphone.

Driving: Driving or other tasks requiring full alertness should not be attempted for the first few days of taking Hydromorph Contin, since you may experience drowsiness or sedation.

Reordering Hydromorph Contin: A new written prescription is required from your doctor each time you need more Hydromorph Contin. Therefore, it is important to contact your doctor at least 3 working days before your current supply runs out. It is very important that you do not miss any doses. Should your pain increase, or any other complaint develop as a result of taking Hydromorph Contin, contact your doctor immediately.

☐ HYTRIN® Ⓟ

Abbott

Terazosin HCl

Antihypertensive—Symptomatic Treatment of Benign Prostatic Hyperplasia

Information for the Patient: Benign prostatic hyperplasia: Please read this leaflet before you start taking Hytrin. Also read it each time you renew your prescription, in the event that something has changed. Remember that this leaflet does not replace careful discussions with your doctor.

Why your doctor has prescribed Hytrin? Your doctor has prescribed Hytrin because you have a medical condition called benign prostatic hyperplasia or BPH. This condition occurs only in men. Hytrin is also used to treat high blood pressure (hypertension), but this leaflet describes Hytrin only as a treatment for BPH.

What is BPH? BPH is an enlargement of the prostate gland. After age 50, most men develop enlarged prostates. The prostate is located below the bladder and surrounds the urethra which is a tube that drains urine from the bladder. The symptoms of BPH, however, can be caused by an increase in the tightness of muscles in the prostate. If the muscles inside the prostate tighten, they can squeeze the urethra and slow the flow of urine. This can lead to symptoms such as:

- weak or interrupted urinary stream
- sensation that you cannot completely empty your bladder
- sensation of delay or hesitation when you start to urinate
- need to urinate often, especially at night, or
- sensation that you must urinate immediately

Treatment options for BPH: There are 3 main treatment options for BPH:

1. **Monitoring Program or "Watchful Waiting":** If you have an enlarged prostate gland but suffer no symptoms or suffer from symptoms that are not bothersome, you and your doctor may decide to follow a monitoring program which includes regular check-ups instead of medication or surgery.
2. **Medication:** There are different kinds of medication used to treat BPH. Your doctor has prescribed Hytrin for you. See "How does Hytrin work?", below.
3. **Surgery:** Some patients may require surgery. Your doctor can prescribe several different surgical procedures for BPH. The procedure that is best for you, depends on your symptoms and medical condition.

How does Hytrin work? Hytrin blocks smooth muscle receptors of the bladder neck and the prostate called alpha$_1$-adrenoceptors. This blockade causes the smooth muscles of the bladder neck and prostate to relax and decreases muscle tone. This can lead to a rapid improvement in urine flow and symptoms within a 2-week period. However, not all patients respond in the same way, and since each case of BPH is different, your should keep in mind the following:

- Prior to treatment with Hytrin, you should have a thorough urological evaluation to determine the severity of your condition, and to exclude the need for immediate surgery or the possibility of carcinoma of the prostate.
- Even though taking Hytrin has helped your condition, it is not known whether Hytrin reduces the need for surgery.
- Terazosin will not cure your benign prostatic hyperplasia (BPH). Terazosin will make your urine flow better and improve the symptoms of BPH. In some patients, bothersome adverse effects will occur as a result of the terazosin therapy.

What you need to know while taking Hytrin:

- You should see an effect on your symptoms in 2 to 4 weeks. While taking Hytrin, you must have regular check-ups to evaluate your progress regarding your BPH and to monitor your blood pressure. Follow your doctor's advice about when to have these check-ups.
- Hytrin can cause a sudden drop in blood pressure after the very first dose. You may feel dizzy, faint, or "light-headed", particularly after you get up from bed or from a chair. This is more likely to occur after you have taken the first few doses, but can occur at any time while you are taking the drug. It can also occur if you stop taking the drug and then restart treatment.

  Because of this effect, your doctor may have told you to take Hytrin at bedtime. If you take Hytrin at bedtime but need to get up from bed to go to the bathroom, get up slowly and cautiously until you are sure how the medicine affects you. It is also important to get up slowly from a chair or bed at anytime until you learn how you react to Hytrin. You should not drive, operate heavy machinery, or do any hazardous task, until you are used to the effects of the medication. You should also avoid situations where injury could result should syncope occur during initiation of terazosin therapy. If you begin to feel dizzy, sit or lie down until you feel better.
- Other side effects you could have while taking Hytrin include drowsiness or somnolence, blurred or hazy vision, nausea, or "puffiness" of the feet or hands. Discuss any unexpected effects you notice with your doctor.
- Your doctor has prescribed Hytrin for symptomatic BPH and not for prostatic cancer. It is possible for men to have both BPH and prostate cancer at the same time. Doctors usually recommend that men be checked for prostate cancer once a year when they turn 50 (or 40 if a family member has had prostate cancer). These checks should continue while you are taking Hytrin. Hytrin is not a treatment for prostate cancer.
- About Prostate Specific Antigen (PSA). Your doctor may have done a blood test called PSA. Your doctor is aware that Hytrin does not affect PSA levels. You may want to ask your doctor more about this if you have a PSA test done.

How to take Hytrin: Follow your doctor's instructions very carefully about how to take Hytrin. The starting dose is 1 mg at bedtime. The 1 mg dose should be maintained during the first week of treatment, and should be taken every day as prescribed by your doctor. Your doctor will then gradually increase the strength of your prescription to 2, 5 and 10 mg depending on how well you respond. Talk to your doctor if you do not take Hytrin for a few days. You may have to restart at the 1 mg dose. Be cautious about possible dizziness.

If your doctor prescribed the Starter Pack, it is important to complete the Starter Pack as indicated before starting your Hytrin prescription.

Do not share Hytrin with anyone else. It was prescribed for you only.

Notify your doctor about any illness which may develop during your treatment with Hytrin and about any new prescription or nonprescription medication you may take. If you require medical help for other reasons, inform the attending physician that you are taking Hytrin.

This medicine is prescribed for your specific medical problem and for your own use. Use only as directed and do not give to other people.

Keep all medicines out of reach of children. For more information about Hytrin and BPH, talk with your doctor or pharmacist.

☐ HYZAAR® ℞

MSD

Losartan Potassium—Hydrochlorothiazide

Angiotensin II Receptor Antagonist—Diuretic

Information for the Patient: Please read this leaflet carefully before you start to take your medicine, even if you have just refilled your prescription. Some of the information in the previous leaflet may have changed.

Remember that your physician has prescribed this medicine only for you. Never give it to anyone else.

What is Hyzaar? Hyzaar (losartan potassium and hydrochlorothiazide) is a yellow, teardrop-shaped, film-coated tablet which contains 50 mg of losartan potassium and 12.5 mg of hydrochlorothiazide as the active ingredients.

In addition, Hyzaar contains the following nonmedicinal ingredients: hydroxypropyl cellulose, hydroxypropyl methylcellulose, lactose hydrous, magnesium stearate, microcrystalline cellulose, pregelatinized starch, and coloring agents (D&C yellow No. 10 aluminum lake, and titanium dioxide). Hyzaar also contains 4.24 mg (0.108 mEq) of potassium.

Although Hyzaar contains a very small amount of potassium, it cannot replace potassium supplements. If your physician has prescribed potassium supplements, continue to follow his advice.

Hyzaar is a combination of an angiotensin II receptor antagonist (losartan) and a diuretic (hydrochlorothiazide). Losartan and hydrochlorothiazide work together to lower high blood pressure.

Why has my physician prescribed Hyzaar? Your physician has prescribed Hyzaar because you have a condition known as hypertension or high blood pressure.

- **What is blood pressure?** The pressure caused by your heart pumping blood to all parts of your body is called blood pressure. Your blood pressure changes during the day depending on activity, stress and excitement.

  Your blood pressure is made up of 2 numbers, for instance 120/80. The top number measures the force while your heart pumps. The bottom number measures the force at rest, between heartbeats.
- **What is high blood pressure (or hypertension)?** You have high blood pressure or hypertension if your blood pressure stays high even when you are calm and relaxed.
- **How do I know if I have high blood pressure?** There are usually no symptoms of high blood pressure. The only way of knowing that you have hypertension is to know your blood pressure. For that reason, you should have your blood pressure checked on a regular basis.
- **Why should high blood pressure be treated?** High blood pressure if left untreated can damage vital organs like the heart and the kidneys. You may feel fine and have no symptoms, but eventually hypertension can lead to strokes, heart attacks, heart failure, kidney failure or blindness.
- **How should high blood pressure be treated?** Once high blood pressure is diagnosed, some treatments other than drugs may be recommended. Your physician may recommend some changes in lifestyle. Your physician may decide that you also need medicine to control your blood pressure. Hyzaar does not cure high blood pressure, but does help control it.

  Your physician can tell you what your individual blood pressure target should be. Keep these numbers in mind and follow your physician's advice on how to reach this target.
- **How does Hyzaar treat high blood pressure?** The losartan ingredient of Hyzaar lowers blood pressure by specifically blocking a naturally occurring substance called angiotensin II. Angiotensin II normally tightens your blood vessels. The losartan ingredient of Hyzaar allows them to relax. The hydrochlorothiazide ingredient of Hyzaar works by making your kidneys pass more water and salt. Together, losartan and hydrochlorothiazide lower high blood pressure. Although your physician will be able to tell you that the medicine is working by measuring your blood pressure, you probably will feel no different while you are taking Hyzaar.

What should I know before taking Hyzaar?

- **Who should not take Hyzaar?** Do not take Hyzaar:
  - — if you are allergic to any of its ingredients (see **What is Hyzaar?**);
  - — if you are allergic to any sulfonamide-derived drugs (ask your physician or pharmacist if you are not sure what sulfonamide-derived drugs are);
  - — if you are not passing urine.

If you are not sure whether you should start taking Hyzaar, contact your physician or your pharmacist.

- **Pregnancy and Breast-feeding:** It is not recommended to use Hyzaar while you are pregnant or breast-feeding. If you are pregnant or become pregnant while taking Hyzaar, talk to your physician as soon as possible.
- **What should I tell my physician or pharmacist before taking Hyzaar?** Tell your physician or pharmacist about any medical problems you have or have had, and about any allergies. Tell your physician if you have recently suffered from excess vomiting or diarrhea.

  It is particularly important to tell your physician if you have liver or kidney disease, gout, diabetes, lupus erythematosus, or if you are being treated with other diuretics (water tablets). In these cases, your physician may need to adjust the dose of your medications.

  Before surgery and general anesthesia (even at the dentist's office), tell the physician or dentist that you are taking Hyzaar, as there may be a sudden fall in blood pressure associated with general anesthesia.
- **Children:** Hyzaar should not be given to children.
- **Can I take Hyzaar with other medicines?** As with most medicines, interaction with other drugs is possible. Therefore, do not take any other medicines unless you have discussed the matter with your physician or your pharmacist. Certain medicines tend to increase your blood pressure, for example, nonprescription preparations for appetite control, asthma, colds, coughs, hay fever and sinus problems.

  It is especially important for your physician and your pharmacist to know if you are taking other drugs to reduce blood pressure, other diuretics (water tablets), resins which reduce high cholesterol, medications to treat diabetes including insulin, muscle relaxants, pressor amines such as epinephrine, steroids, certain pain and arthritis medicines, or lithium (a drug used to treat a certain kind of depression). Sedatives, tranquilizers, narcotics, alcohol and analgesics may increase the blood pressure-lowering effect of Hyzaar, so tell your physician or your pharmacist if you take any of these.
- **Can I drive or operate machinery while using Hyzaar?** Almost all patients can, but you should not perform tasks which may require special attention (for example, driving an automobile or operating dangerous machinery) until you know how you tolerate your medicine.

How should I take Hyzaar? Take Hyzaar every day exactly as your physician has instructed. It is important to continue taking Hyzaar for as long as your physician prescribes it in order to maintain smooth control of your blood pressure.

Hyzaar may be taken with or without food, but it should be taken consistently with respect to food intake, at the same time every day.

What should I do if I miss a dose? Try to take Hyzaar daily as prescribed. However, if you miss a dose, do not take an extra dose. Just resume your usual schedule.

What should I do in case of an overdose? In case of an overdose, contact your physician immediately so that medical attention may be given promptly.

What undesirable effects may Hyzaar have? Any medicine may have unintended or undesirable effects, so-called side effects. In most patients, Hyzaar is well tolerated. Side effects may include dizziness. Your physician or pharmacist has a more complete list. Tell your physician or pharmacist promptly about these or any other unusual symptoms.

How can I learn more about Hyzaar and high blood pressure? You may obtain further information from your physician or pharmacist, who have more detailed information about the product and high blood pressure.

How should I store Hyzaar? Store Hyzaar at room temperature (15 to 30°C). Keep container tightly closed.

Keep all medicines out of the reach of children.

☐ IDARAC® ℞
Sanofi

Floctafenine

Anti-inflammatory—Analgesic

Information for the Patient: What is Idarac? Idarac tablets contain floctafenine, a member of the class of drugs called nonsteroidal antiinflammatory drugs (NSAID's). Idarac tablets are used to relieve mild to moderate acute pain, in conditions such as muscle or joint strains or damage, or after a tooth extraction.

Idarac tablets help to relieve pain and swelling by reducing the production of certain substances (prostaglandins) and by helping to control inflammation.

How should Idarac be taken? You should take Idarac tablets only as directed by your doctor. Do not take more Idarac; do not take it more often and do not take it for a longer period of time than your doctor or dentist has ordered.

The usual adult dose of Idarac is one 200 or 400 mg tablet every 6 to 8 hours as required. You should not take more than 1 200 mg in a day unless directed by your doctor or dentist. The tablets should be taken with a glass of water.

Who should not use Idarac? Do not use this product if you have a peptic ulcer or any active inflammatory disease of the gastrointestinal tract, or if you are sensitive (allergic) to floctafenine.

Idarac should not be used by women of childbearing potential or by nursing women unless the possible risk is discussed with the doctor.

Idarac should not be used by children, except as recommended by a doctor.

Long-term use of Idarac is not recommended.

What precautions should be followed when using Idarac? If you have kidney disease, heart disease, peptic ulcers or other serious disease, are pregnant or nursing, or are taking anticoagulant medication (blood thinners), beta-blockers or other prescription or over-the-counter medicine consult with your doctor before taking this drug.

Take Idarac only as directed by your doctor or dentist. Do not take more of it, do not take it more often, and do not take it for a longer period of time than ordered by your doctor or dentist. Along with its needed effects, Idarac may cause some unwanted effects. Although these side effects do not appear very often, when they do they may require medical attention. Check with your doctor immediately if any of the following occur: shortness of breath, trouble breathing , wheezing or tightness in chest; bloody or black tarry stools; skin rash, hives or itching; blurred vision; ringing in your ears; drowsiness, dizziness, headache, insomnia, nervousness, irritability; nausea, diarrhea, abdominal pain or discomfort, heartburn, constipation, abnormal liver function; any changes in the amount or color of your urine or painful and/or strong smelling urine; abnormalities of taste, dry mouth, stomach cramps, gas, hot flushes and sweating, rapid heartbeat, weakness and tiredness.

Always remember:

Before taking this medication tell your doctor, dentist or pharmacist if you:

- Are allergic to Idarac tablets or other related medicines of the nonsteroidal antiinflammatory drug group such as acetylsalicylic acid, diclofenac, diflunisal, fenoprofen, flurbiprofen, ibuprofen, indomethacin, ketoprofen, ketorolac, mefenamic acid, naproxen, naproxen sodium, oxyphenbutazone, phenylbutazone, piroxicam, sulindac, tenoxicam, tiaprofenic acid or tolmetin.
- Have a history of stomach upset, ulcers, liver, heart or kidney diseases.
- Are pregnant or intend to become pregnant while taking this medicine.
- Are breast-feeding.
- Are taking any other medicine (either prescription or nonprescription).
- Have any other medical problem(s).

While taking this medication:

- Tell any other doctor, dentist or pharmacist that you consult or see, that you are taking this medication.
- Be cautious about driving, using machinery or participating in activities that require alertness if you are drowsy, dizzy or lightheaded after taking this medication.
- Check with your doctor if you are not getting any relief or if any problems develop.
- Report any untoward reaction to your doctor. This is very important as it will aid in the early detection and prevention of potential complications.
- Your regular medical checkups are essential.
- If you require more information on this drug, consult your doctor or pharmacist.

☐ IMDUR®
Astra

Isosorbide-5-Mononitrate

Antianginal

Information for the Patient: Important information you should know about Imdur: Read this leaflet carefully. It has been prepared by the makers of Imdur to help you get the most benefit from this drug. It contains general points about Imdur and should add to more specific advice from your doctor or pharmacist.

This leaflet should not replace your doctor's or pharmacist's advice. Because of your health condition, they may have given you additional instructions. If so, be sure to follow their advice. Also, if you have any questions or concerns after reading this leaflet, talk to your doctor or pharmacist. **Do not decide on your own to stop taking Imdur.**

What is Imdur? Imdur is the brand name for the drug isosorbide-5-mononitrate. It is a tablet to be taken once a day.

What should I tell my doctor before starting Imdur? Be sure you've told your doctor:

- about all health problems you have now, and have had in the past.
- about all other medicines you take, including any you take for high blood pressure, and ones you can buy without a prescription.
- if you are pregnant, plan to become pregnant, or are breast-feeding.
- if you have ever had an allergic, bad or unusual reaction to nitrates or to any medicine for heart problems.
- if you are allergic to nonmedicinal substances like food products, preservatives, or dyes, which may be present in Imdur (see What does Imdur contain?).

What does Imdur contain? Most medicines contain more than their ''active'' ingredient. These other ingredients are needed to keep medicines in a form you can use. For people with certain allergies, the following is a list of all ingredients in Imdur. Check with your doctor if you think you might be sensitive to any of these items.

The active ingredient in Imdur is isosorbide-5-mononitrate. Nonmedicinal ingredients are: aluminum silicate, colloidal silicon dioxide, hydroxypropylcellulose, hydroxypropylmethylcellulose, iron oxide yellow, magnesium stearate, paraffin, polyethylene glycol and titanium dioxide.

How do I use the Imdur Compliance Pack? This unique 30-day package is designed to make it easy to keep track of your medication.

Twenty-eight of the tablets are labelled with a day of the week. To start, take a tablet in the first row that matches the day you begin this pack. Then take a tablet on each of the following days to complete the 28 labelled tablets. The 2 extra nonlabelled tablets should be taken after all other tablets are gone.

Remember to get a new prescription from your doctor or a refill from your pharmacy a few days before all 30 tablets are taken.

How do I take Imdur? Take Imdur exactly as your doctor tells you. Usually, this is 1 tablet in the morning. If your doctor tells you to take 2 tablets each day, they must be taken together in the morning. Check with your doctor or pharmacist if you have any questions about your directions.

Imdur tablets should be swallowed whole, with half a glass of water or other liquid e.g., fruit juice or milk. **Do not chew or crush the tablets.**

If needed, the tablets may be broken in half along the scored line.

Do not take extra doses of Imdur, unless your doctor tells you. Using more can increase the chance of unwanted effects.

What do I do if I miss a dose? It is important to take Imdur at about the same time every day.

If you miss a dose of Imdur and remember within 6 hours, take your usual dose as soon as possible. Then go back to your regular schedule. But if it is more than 6 hours when you remember, do not take the missed dose. Just take the next dose on time.

Never take a double dose of Imdur to make up for missed tablets. If you are still unsure, check with your doctor or pharmacist to see what you should do.

What are the side effects of Imdur? Imdur, like any medication, may produce side effects.

The most common side effect is headache. It often occurs at the beginning of the treatment, but usually goes away after a few days. If you get a bad headache, and it becomes a problem, be sure to tell your doctor.

If too much Imdur is taken, a pulsing headache might occur. You may feel lightheaded, dizzy, excited, flushed, have cold sweats, nausea (feeling sick) and vomiting. If any of these symptoms occur, lie down with your feet raised and get someone to call your doctor right away.

Some people feel Imdur makes them dizzy, faint, or tired. This is more likely when Imdur is first started. If you have any of these effects, please tell your doctor.

Do not stop taking Imdur until your doctor tells you. He or she may want to reduce your dose slowly.

Remember, medicines affect different people in different ways. Just because other people have had side effects does not mean you will get them. Discuss how you feel on Imdur with your doctor or pharmacist.

Other side effects which cannot be predicted may occur in rare cases. If you have any bothersome or unusual effects while using Imdur, check with your doctor of pharmacist right away.

Are there any special precautions? Unused medicines which you know you will no longer need should be carefully discarded. Small quantities may be disposed of in the toilet or you may wish to seek advice from your pharmacist.

The Compliance Pack protects each tablet. When you first open the pack, if you find any damage to the plastic seal or foil which exposes the tablet, ask your pharmacist to check the package.

How do I store Imdur? Although Imdur tablets are protected in this Compliance Pack, it is best to keep it at normal room temperature and in a dry place. Do not keep Imdur in the bathroom. Do not keep or use Imdur after the expiry date marked on the Compliance Pack.

Do not transfer Imdur to other containers. To protect your Imdur tablets, keep them in the original Compliance Pack.

Keep Imdur out of the reach of children. Never take medicine in front of small children as they may want to copy you.

General Information: Imdur is for your current condition only. Do not use it for other problems unless your doctor tells you. Never give it to other people to use.

Be sure to tell your doctors, dentists and pharmacists that you take Imdur.

All drugs can have both helpful and harmful effects. Both depend on the person and his or her health condition. This leaflet alerts you to some of the times you should call your doctor. Other situations which cannot be predicted may arise. Nothing about this leaflet should stop you from calling your doctor with any questions or concerns you have about Imdur.

☐ IMITREX® Injection/Tablets 🄿

☐ IMITREX® Nasal Spray 🄿

Glaxo Wellcome

Sumatriptan Succinate
Sumatriptan

Migraine Therapy

Information for the Patient: Please read this leaflet carefully before you take Imitrex Tablets/Injection/Nasal Spray. This provides a summary of the information available on your medicine. Please do not throw away this leaflet until you have finished your medicine. You may need to read it again. This leaflet does not contain all the information on Imitrex Tablets/Injection/Nasal Spray. For further information or advice, ask your doctor or pharmacist.

Information About Your Medicine:
The name of your medicine is Imitrex (sumatriptan succinate) Tablets/Injection or Imitrex (sumatriptan) Nasal Spray (for Nasal Spray only). It can be obtained only by prescription from your doctor. The decision to use Imitrex is one that you and your doctor should make jointly, taking into account your individual preferences and medical circumstances. If you have risk factors for heart disease (such as high blood pressure, high cholesterol, obesity, diabetes, smoking, strong family history of heart disease, or you are postmenopausal or a male over 40), you should tell your doctor, who should evaluate you for heart disease in order to determine if Imitrex is appropriate for you.

1. **The Purpose of Your Medicine:** Imitrex is intended to relieve your migraine headache and other associated symptoms of a migraine attack. Imitrex should not be used continuously to prevent or reduce the number of attacks you experience. Use Imitrex only to treat an actual migraine headache attack.
2. **How Your Medicine Works:** Migraine headache is believed to be caused by a widening of the blood vessels in the head. Imitrex narrows these vessels and relieves the symptoms of migraine headache.
3. **Important Questions to Consider Before Taking Imitrex:** If the answer to any of the following questions is **yes** or if you do not know the answer, then please discuss with your doctor before you use Imitrex.
   - Are you pregnant? Do you think you might be pregnant? Are you trying to become pregnant? Are you using inadequate contraception? Are you breast-feeding?
   - Do you have any chest pain, heart disease, shortness of breath, or irregular heartbeats? Have you had a heart attack? Do you have angina?
   - Do you have risk factors for heart disease (such as high blood pressure, high cholesterol, obesity, diabetes, smoking, strong family history of heart disease, or are you postmenopausal or a male over 40)?
   - Do you have high blood pressure?
   - Have you ever had to stop taking this or any other medication because of an allergy or other problems? Are you allergic to sulfa-containing drugs?
   - Are you taking any medications, including migraine medications containing ergotamine or dihydroergotamine?
   - Have you ever experienced difficulty moving one side of your body when you have a headache?
   - Have you ever had a stroke?
   - Are you over 65 years of age?
   - Are you taking any medication for depression (lithium, monoamine oxidase inhibitors or selective serotonin reuptake inhibitors [SSRIs])?
   - Have you had, or do you have, any disease of the liver or kidney?
   - Have you had, or do you have, epilepsy or seizures?
   - Is this headache different from your usual migraine attacks?

   Remember, if you answered **yes** to any of the above questions, then discuss it with your doctor.
4. **The Use of Imitrex During Pregnancy:** Do not use Imitrex if you are pregnant, think you might be pregnant, are trying to become pregnant, or are not using adequate contraception, unless you have discussed this with your doctor.
5. **How to Use Imitrex:** The label on the container of your medicine or the leaflet inside should tell you how often to take a dose and the amount you should take in each dose. If it does not or you are not sure, ask your doctor or pharmacist. **Do not** take more tablets, injections, or nasal sprays, or take your medicine more often than you are told.

   Do not take any ergotamine-containing preparation or ergot derivatives (such as dihydroergotamine) within 6 hours after using Imitrex. Conversely, Imitrex should not be taken until 24 hours have elapsed after ergotamine administration.

   Imitrex can be taken at any time during your migraine headache.

   Tablets: Adults: The usual dose is a single 100 mg tablet, although your doctor may prescribe a lower dose if you have liver disease or do not tolerate the 100 mg dose. If the first tablet does not relieve your headache, do not take further doses of sumatriptan for the same attack. You may take pain medication other than ergotamine-containing preparations for further pain relief. Sumatriptan may be taken for subsequent attacks.

   A second tablet may be taken if your symptoms come back. Do not take more than 300 mg in any 24-hour period.

   Imitrex may be taken with or without food. The tablet should be swallowed whole with water. It should not be crushed, chewed or split.

   Autoinjector: Before using the autoinjector, see the enclosed instruction booklet for information on loading your autoinjector and discarding the empty syringes.
   Adults: Inject 6 mg (single injection), into the tissues just below the skin (on the outside of the thigh).

   If the first injection does not relieve your headache, do not take further doses of sumatriptan for the same attack. However, you may take pain medication other than ergotamine-containing preparations

Imitrex (cont'd)

for further pain relief. Sumatriptan may be taken for subsequent attacks.

A second injection (6 mg) can be taken if your symptoms come back provided 1 hour has passed since your last dose. Do not take more than 2 injections (2x6 mg) in any 24-hour period.

Nasal Spray: Do not test the spray before using. Unlike other nasal sprays you may have used, Imitrex Nasal Spray comes ready to use.

Adults: Use 1 spray in 1 nostril **only** as directed by your doctor. If the first nasal spray does not relieve your headache do not take a further dose of sumatriptan for the same attack. However, you may take pain medication other than ergotamine-containing preparations for further pain relief. Sumatriptan may be taken for subsequent attacks.

A second nasal spray can be taken if your symptoms come back provided 2 hours have passed since the last dose. Do not take more than 40 mg in any 24-hour period.

6. **Side Effects to Watch for:** Although the vast majority of those who have taken Imitrex have not experienced any significant side effects, some individuals have experienced problems.
   - Some patients experience pain or tightness in the chest or throat when using Imitrex. If this happens to you, then discuss it with your doctor before using any more Imitrex. If the chest pain is severe or does not go away, call your doctor immediately.
   - Shortness of breath; wheeziness; heart throbbing; swelling of eyelids, face, or lips; or a skin rash, skin lumps, or hives happens rarely. If it happens to you, then tell your doctor immediately. Do not take any more Imitrex unless your doctor tells you to do so.
   - Some people may have feelings of tingling, heat, flushing (redness of face lasting a short time), heaviness or pressure after treatment with Imitrex. A few people may feel drowsy, dizzy, tired, or sick. You may have irritation or burning in the throat or nasal bleeding (Nasal Spray only). Tell your doctor of these symptoms at your next visit.
   - You may experience pain or redness at the site of Injection, but this usually lasts less than an hour.
   - Drowsiness may occur as a result of Imitrex. Do not drive or operate machinery until you are sure that you are not drowsy.
   - You may notice a slight taste after using your nasal spray. This is normal and will soon pass (Nasal Spray only).
   - If you feel unwell in any other way or have any symptoms that you do not understand or find distressing, you should contact your doctor immediately.
7. **What to Do If an Overdose Is Taken:** If you have taken more medication than you have been told, contact either your doctor, hospital emergency department, or nearest Poison Control Centre immediately.
8. **Storing Your Medicine:** Keep your medicine in a safe place where children cannot reach it. It may be harmful to children.

   Keep your tablets in a cool, dry place (2 to 30°C). Keep your syringes and nasal spray device away from heat and light which may spoil them. Always keep your injection in the case and your nasal spray device in the carton provided and store at 2 to 30°C.

   If your medication has expired (the expiration date is printed on the treatment pack), throw it away as instructed. Do not throw away your autoinjector.

   If your doctor decides to stop your treatment, do not keep any leftover medicine unless your doctor tells you to. Throw away your medicine as instructed.
9. **What is in Your Medicine:** Imitrex Tablets contain 50 or 100 mg of sumatriptan base, as the succinate salt. The tablets also contain croscarmellose sodium, lactose, magnesium stearate and microcrystalline cellulose. The tablets are coated with Opadry Pink (100 mg)/ Opadry White (50 mg) containing methylhydroxypropyl cellulose, titanium dioxide, triacetin and iron oxide red (100 mg only).

   Imitrex syringe for use in the autoinjector, contains 6 mg of sumatriptan base, as the succinate salt, in 0.5 mL of solution. It also contains sodium chloride and water for injection.

   Imitrex Nasal Spray contains 5 or 20 mg of sumatriptan base as a hemisulfate salt, in a solution. It also contains anhydrous dibasic sodium phosphate, monobasic potassium phosphate, purified water, sodium hydroxide and sulfuric acid.
10. **Class of Medicine:** This medicine is one of a group of antimigraine drugs.
11. **Who Produces Your Medicine:** Manufacturer: Glaxo Wellcome Inc., 7333 Mississauga Road North, Mississauga, Ontario L5N 6L4.
12. **Reminder: Remember:** This medicine is for you. Only a doctor can prescribe it for you. Never give it to someone else. It may harm them even if their symptoms appear to be similar to yours.

Instructions for Use of Your Imitrex Nasal Spray (see package insert for illustrations):

The Nasal Spray Pack:

- Your Imitrex Nasal Spray is packed in a box containing the nasal spray devices individually sealed in blisters. Each device contains one dose of Imitrex.
- **Do not open a blister until you are ready to use your medication.** Each nasal spray device is sealed in a blister to help keep it clean and safe. If you carry a nasal spray device around out of the blister, or in an open blister, it may not work properly when you need it.
- **Keep your Imitrex Nasal Spray in the box to help protect it from light and damage.** If you want to carry only one nasal spray device around with you, you may split the blister pack in two.
- **Keep this information leaflet in a safe place.** This leaflet tells you how to use your nasal spray device and provides other useful information about your medicine.

The Imitrex Nasal Spray device consists of the following parts:

The Nozzle: This is the part that you put into your nostril. The spray comes out of a tiny hole in the top.

The Finger-Grip: This is the part that you hold when you use the device.

The Blue Plunger: When you press the plunger the entire dose sprays into your nostril. The Plunger only works once so **do not press it until you have inserted the nozzle into your nostril or you will waste the dose.**

How to use Imitrex Nasal Spray: Do not remove the nasal spray device from the blister packaging until you are ready to use it.

- Blow your nose if it feels blocked.
- Peel open a blister pack and take out a nasal spray device.
- Hold the nasal spray device gently with your fingers and thumb as shown in the picture.
- **Do not press the blue plunger yet.**
- Block one nostril by pressing a finger firmly on the side of your nose, and breathe out gently through your mouth.
- Put the nozzle of the nasal spray device into your other nostril, as far as it feels comfortable.
- Now tilt your head back **slightly,** as shown in the picture and close your mouth.
- Start to breathe in gently through your nose and at the same time press the blue plunger firmly with your thumb. This will spray the entire dose into your nostril. **Note:** The plunger may feel a bit stiff and you may hear it click.
- **Keep your head tilted back and breathe gently through your mouth for 10 to 20 seconds.** This helps the medicine stay in your nose. You can remove the device and your finger from the other side of your nose while you do this.
- Your nose may feel wet inside and you may notice a slight taste after using the spray—this is normal and will soon pass.
- Your nasal spray device is now empty. It should be disposed of safely and hygienically.

☐ IMOVANE® Ⓟ

Rhône-Poulenc Rorer

Zopiclone

Hypnotic

Information for the Patient: Facts on Imovane (zopiclone).

Introduction: Imovane is intended to help you sleep. It is one of several prescription sleeping pills that have generally similar properties.

If you are prescribed one of these medications, you should consider both their benefits and risks. Important risks and limitations include the following:

- the medication may cause dependence.
- the medication may affect your mental alertness or memory, particularly when not taken as prescribed.

In order to guide you in the safe use of the product, this leaflet will inform you about this class of medication in general, and about Imovane in particular.

But this leaflet should not replace a discussion between you and your doctor about the risks and benefits of Imovane.

Safe use of Imovane:

- Imovane is a prescription medication, intended to help you sleep. Follow your doctor's advice about how to take Imovane, when to take it, and how long to take it. **Do not take Imovane** if it is not prescribed for you.
- **Do not take Imovane** for more than 7 to 10 days without first consulting your doctor.
- **Do not take Imovane** when a full night's sleep is not possible before you would again need to be active and functional; e.g., an overnight flight of less than 8 hours. Memory lapses may occur in such situations. Your body needs time to eliminate the medication from your system.
- **Do not take Imovane** at any time during pregnancy. Tell your doctor if you are planning to become pregnant, if you are pregnant, or if you become pregnant while taking this medication.
- Tell your doctor about any alcohol consumption (present or past) or any medicine you are taking now, including drugs you can buy without a prescription. **Do not consume alcohol while taking Imovane.**
- **Do not increase the prescribed dose.**
- **Do not drive a car** or operate potentially dangerous machinery until you experience how this drug will affect you the next day.
- If you develop any unusual disturbing thoughts or behavior while using Imovane, discuss the matter immediately with your doctor.
- You may experience an increase in sleep difficulties (rebound insomnia) and/or "increased daytime anxiety" (rebound anxiety) for 1 or 2 days after discontinuing Imovane.

Effectiveness of Imovane: Imovane is an effective medication and is relatively free of serious problems when used for the short-term management of insomnia. Symptoms of insomnia may vary: you may have difficulty in falling asleep, or awaken often during the night, or awaken early in the morning, or you may have all 3 symptoms.

Insomnia may last only for a short time and may respond to brief treatment. The risks and benefits of prolonged use should be discussed with your doctor.

Side Effects: Common Side Effects: Imovane may cause drowsiness, dizziness, lightheadedness, and difficulty with coordination. Users must be cautious about engaging in hazardous activities requiring complete mental alertness, e.g., operating machinery or driving a motor vehicle.

Avoid alcohol while using Imovane. **Do not use Imovane** along with other medications without first discussing this with your doctor.

How sleepy you are the day after you use one of these sleeping pills depends on your individual response and on how quickly your body gets rid of the medication. The larger the dose, the more likely that you will experience drowsiness, etc., the next day. It is important that you comply with the dose your physician has prescribed. Prescription sleeping pills which are eliminated rapidly, tend to cause less drowsiness the next day, but may cause withdrawal problems the day after use (see below).

Special Concerns: Memory Problems: Imovane may cause a special type of memory loss (amnesia); you may not recall events that occurred during some period of time, usually several hours, after taking the drug. This lapse is usually not a problem, because the person taking the sleeping pill intends to be asleep during this critical period of time. But it can be a problem if you take the medication to induce sleep while travelling, such as during an airplane flight, because you may wake up before the effect of the drug is gone. This has been called "traveller's amnesia".

Tolerance/Withdrawal Symptoms: After nightly use, sleeping pills may lose some of their effectiveness and you may also develop a degree of dependence.

When taking Imovane, you may awake during the last third of the night or feel anxious or nervous during the day. If this occurs, tell your doctor.

You may also experience "withdrawal effects" when you stop the medication after taking it for only 1 week or 2. But usually, these withdrawal effects are more common and severe after long periods of continuous use. For instance, on the first few nights after stopping the medication, you may find that insomnia is worse than before taking the sleeping pills. This type of withdrawal symptom is known as "rebound insomnia".

Other withdrawal effects following abrupt stopping of sleeping pills may range from unpleasant feelings to a major withdrawal syndrome that may include abdominal and muscle cramps, vomiting, sweating, tremor, and rarely, convulsions. The severe symptoms are uncommon. If you have been taking sleeping pills for a long time, discuss with your physician when and how it would be best for you to stop.

Dependence/Abuse: All prescription sleeping pills can cause dependence (addiction) especially when used regularly for more than a few weeks, or at higher doses. Some people develop a need to continue taking these drugs, not only for continued therapeutic effect, but also to avoid withdrawal symptoms or to achieve nontherapeutic effects.

Individuals who depend, or have depended at any time in the past, on alcohol or other drugs may be at particular risk of becoming dependent on drugs of this class. But **all people are at some risk.** Consider this matter before you take these medications beyond a few weeks.

Mental and Behavioral Changes: a variety of abnormal thinking and behavioral changes may occur when you use prescription sleeping pills. Some of these changes include aggressiveness and extroversion which seem out of character. Other changes, although rare, can be more unusual and extreme. These include confusion, strange behavior, restlessness, illusions, hallucinations, feeling like you are not yourself, and feeling more depressed, which may lead to suicidal thinking.

It is rarely clear whether such symptoms are caused by the medication, or by an underlying illness, or are simply spontaneous happenings. In fact, worsened insomnia may in some cases be associated with illnesses that were present before the medication was used.

Important Note: Regardless of the cause, if you take these medications, report any mental or behavioral changes promptly to your doctor.

Effects on Pregnancy: Certain benzodiazepine sleeping pills have been linked to birth defects when taken during the early months of pregnancy. It is not yet known if Imovane could cause similar effects. In addition, sleeping pills taken during the last weeks of pregnancy have been known to sedate the baby. Therefore, **avoid using this medication during pregnancy.**

☐ INDOCID® Ⓟ
☐ INDOCID® SR Ⓟ

MSD

Indomethacin

Nonsteroidal Anti-inflammatory

Information for the Patient: Name: Indocid is the proprietary name of Merck Sharp & Dohme for indomethacin.

Purpose of this medicine: Indocid which has been prescribed to you by your physician, is one of a large group of nonsteroidal anti-inflammatory drugs (NSAIDs) and is used to treat the symptoms of certain types of arthritis, including gout. It helps to relieve joint pain, swelling, stiffness and fever by reducing the production of certain substances (prostaglandins) and helping to control inflammation and other body reactions.

Remember: This medicine is prescribed for the particular condition that you have. **Do not give this medicine to other people, nor use it for any other condition.**

Do not use outdated medicine.

Read the following information carefully. **If you need any explanations, or further information, ask your physician or pharmacist.**

Before taking this medicine: Tell your physician about any medical conditions you have or have had including: allergies; ulcers or other stomach or intestinal problems; mental disturbance; convulsions; heart, kidney, or liver problems; infections; diabetes; bleeding tendency; high blood pressure, and Parkinson's disease.

Do not take Indocid if you:

- Are allergic to indomethacin or any of its ingredients.
- Have experienced asthma attacks, hives, itching, or runny nose after taking acetylsalicylic acid or other nonsteroidal anti-inflammatory medicines such as diclofenac, diflunisal, fenoprofen, flurbiprofen, ibuprofen, ketoprofen, mefenamic acid, piroxicam, sulindac, tiaprofenic acid or tolmetin.
- If you have an active peptic ulcer or have had peptic ulcers more than once.
- **If you are taking other medications (nonprescription or prescription drugs),** particularly medications to thin the blood (anticoagulants) or medications to lower the level of sugar in the blood (hypoglycemic agents).
- Have had an inflamed rectum or recent rectal bleeding (for Indocid suppositories).

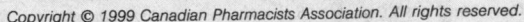

Who should not take Indocid: Should women who are pregnant or breast-feeding take Indocid? Indocid is not recommended for use

Indocid (cont'd)

during pregnancy. If you are pregnant or may become pregnant tell your physician, who will help you weigh the benefits of the drug against possible hazards.

Use of Indocid while breast-feeding is not recommended. Since Indocid passes into human milk, there is a possibility of harm to the infant. If you are breast-feeding or intend to breast-feed, tell your physician.

Should children take Indocid? Indocid is not recommended for use in children.

Proper use of this medicine: To lessen stomach upset, take this medicine with food or an antacid. If stomach upset (indigestion, nausea, vomiting, stomach pain or diarrhea) occurs and continues, contact your physician.

Please adhere to the dosage and administration instructions which your physician has given you.

- Do not take more of it, do not take it more often, and do not take it for a longer period of time than your physician prescribed.
- If you are taking Indocid to relieve arthritis, you must take it regularly as prescribed by your physician. In some types of arthritis, up to 2 weeks may pass before you begin to feel better and up to 1 month may pass before you feel the full effects of this medicine.

If you miss a dose...

If you miss a dose of Indocid and remember within an hour or so, take it right away. Then go back to your regular dosing schedule.

But if you do not remember until later, do not take the missed dose at all and do not double the next one. Instead, go back to your regular dosing schedule.

May I take Indocid with other medicines? Your physician has a more complete list of medicines to avoid while taking Indocid. Tell your physician about all medicines you are taking or plan to take, including those obtained without prescription.

If you are prescribed this medication for use over a long period of time, your physician will check your health during regular visits to assess your progress and to ensure that this medication is not causing unwanted effects.

Side effects of this medicine – and what you should do: Along with its beneficial effects, Indocid like other NSAIDs, may cause some undesirable reactions. Elderly, frail or debilitated patients often seem to experience more frequent or more severe side effects. Although not all of these side effects are common, when they do occur they may require medical attention. **Check with your physician immediately if any of the following are noted:**

- bloody or black tarry stools;
- shortness of breath, wheezing, any trouble in breathing or tightness in the chest;
- skin rash, swelling, hives or itching;
- indigestion, nausea, vomiting, loss of appetite, stomach pain, constipation or diarrhea;
- yellow discoloration of the skin or eyes, with or without fatigue;
- any changes in the amount or color of your urine (such as dark, red or brown);
- swelling of the feet or lower legs;
- blurred vision or any visual disturbance;
- headache, mental confusion, depression, dizziness, vertigo, lightheadedness, fatigue, hearing problems;
- ulcers or bleeding of the esophagus, stomach, duodenum or intestines may also occur;
- rectal bleeding or discomfort and straining at stool is sometimes associated with the use of Indocid Suppositories.

While taking this medication:

- tell any other physician, dentist or pharmacist that you consult or see, that you are taking this medication;
- be cautious about driving or participating in activities that require alertness if you are drowsy, dizzy or lightheaded after taking this medication;
- check with your physician if you are not getting any relief or if any problems develop;
- report any untoward reactions to your physician. This is very important as it will aid in the early detection and prevention of potential complications.
- your regular medical checkups are essential;
- if you require more information on this drug, consult your physician or pharmacist.

Storage: Capsules: Store at room temperature (15 to 30°C).
Suppositories: Store below 25°C.

Availability: Capsules: Indocid SR capsules for extended-release oral administration contain 75 mg of indomethacin and the following nonmedicinal ingredients: allura red, black iron oxide, confectioner's sugar, cornstarch, gelatin, hydroxypropyl methylcellulose, indigotine, magnesium stearate, microcrystalline cellulose, polyvinyl acetate-crotonic acid copolymer, quinoline yellow, sunset yellow, and titanium dioxide. The product conforms to the requirements of the USP Drug Release Test No. 1.

Suppositories: Indocid suppositories for rectal use contain either 50 mg or 100 mg of indomethacin and the following nonmedicinal ingredients: butylated hydroxyanisole, butylated hydroxytoluene, edetic acid, glycerin, polyethylene glycol 3350, polyethylene glycol 8000 and sodium chloride for 50 mg only.

□ INDOTEC® Ⓟ

Technilab

Indomethacin

Nonsteroidal Anti-inflammatory—Analgesic

Information for the Patient: Indotec (indomethacin), which has been prescribed to you by your physician, is one of a large group of nonsteroidal anti-inflammatory drugs (also called NSAIDs) and is used to treat the symptoms of certain types of arthritis such as rheumatoid arthritis, ankylosing spondylitis, gout and selected cases of osteoarthritis, including degenerative disease of the hip. It helps to relieve joint pain, swelling, stiffness and fever by reducing the production of certain substances (prostaglandins) and by helping to control inflammation. NSAIDs do not cure arthritis, but they promote suppression of the inflammation and the tissue damaging effects resulting from this inflammation. This medicine will help you only as long as you continue to take it.

You should take Indotec only as directed by your physician. Do not take more of it, do not take it more often and do not take it for a longer period of time than your physician ordered. Taking too much of any of these medicines may increase the chance of unwanted effects, especially if you are an elderly patient.

Be sure to take Indotec regularly as prescribed. In some types of arthritis, up to 2 weeks may pass before you feel the full effects of this medicine. During treatment, your physician may decide to adjust the dosage according to your response to the medication.

Stomach Upset Is One of the Common Problems With NSAIDs: To lessen stomach upset, take this medicine immediately after a meal or with food or milk. Also, you should remain standing or sitting upright (i.e., do not lie down) for about 15 to 30 minutes after taking the medicine. This helps to prevent irritation that may lead to trouble swallowing. If stomach upset (indigestion, nausea, vomiting, stomach pain or diarrhea) occurs and continues, contact your physician.

Do not take ASA (acetylsalicylic acid), ASA-containing compounds or other drugs used to relieve symptoms of arthritis while taking Indotec unless directed to do so by your physician.

If you are prescribed this medication for use over a long period of time, your physician will check your health during regular visits to assess your progress and to ensure that this medicine is not causing unwanted effects.

Always Remember: The risks of taking this medication must be weighed against the benefits it will have.

Before taking this medication tell your physician and pharmacists if you:

- or a family member are allergic to or have had a reaction to indomethacin or other anti-inflammatory drugs (such as acetylsalicylic acid (ASA), diclofenac, diflunisal, fenoprofen, flurbiprofen, ibuprofen, ketoprofen, mefenamic acid, piroxicam, tiaprofenic acid, tolmetin, nabumetone or tenoxicam) manifesting itself by increased sinusitis, hives, the initiating or worsening of asthma or anaphylaxis (sudden collapse);
- or a family member has had asthma, nasal polyps, chronic sinusitis or chronic urticaria (hives);
- have a history of stomach upset, ulcers, liver or kidney diseases;
- have blood or urine abnormalities;
- have high blood pressure;
- have diabetes;

- are on any special diet, such as a low-sodium or low-sugar diet;
- are pregnant or intend to become pregnant while taking this medication;
- are breast-feeding or intend to breast-feed while taking this medication;
- are taking any other medication (either prescription or nonprescription) such as other NSAIDs, high blood pressure medication, blood thinners, corticosteroids, methotrexate, cyclosporine, lithium, phenytoin and probenecid;
- have any other medical problem(s) such as alcohol abuse, bleeding problems, etc.;
- have had an inflamed rectum or recent rectal bleeding (for Indotec suppositories).

While Taking This Medication:

- tell any other physician, dentist or pharmacist that you consult or see, that you are taking this medication;
- some NSAIDs may cause drowsiness or fatigue in some people taking them. Be cautious about driving or participating in activities that require alertness if you are drowsy, dizzy or lightheaded after taking this medication;
- check with your physician if you are not getting any relief of your arthritis or if any problems develop;
- report any untoward reactions to your physician. This is very important as it will aid in the early detection and prevention of potential complications;
- stomach problems may be more likely to occur if you drink alcoholic beverages. Therefore, do not drink alcoholic beverages while taking this medication;
- check with your physician immediately if you experience unexpected weakness while taking this medication, or if you vomit any blood or have dark or bloody stools;
- some people may become more sensitive to sunlight than they are normally. Exposure to sunlight or sunlamps, even for brief periods of time, may cause sunburn, blisters on the skin, skin rash, redness, itching or discoloration; or vision changes. If you have a reaction from the sun, check with your physician;
- check with your physician immediately if chills, fever, muscle aches or pains, or other flu-like symptoms occur, especially if they occur shortly before, or together with, a skin rash. Very rarely, these effects may be the first signs of a serious reaction to this medication;
- **Your regular medical check-ups are essential.**

Side Effects of This Medication: Along with its beneficial effects, indomethacin like other NSAID drugs, may cause some undesirable reactions especially when used for a long time or in large doses.

Elderly, frail or debilitated patients often seem to experience more frequent or more severe side effects.

Although not all of these side effects are common, when they do occur they may require medical attention.

Check With Your Physician Immediately if Any of the Following Are Noted:

- bloody or black tarry stools;
- shortness of breath, wheezing, any trouble in breathing or tightness in the chest;
- skin rash, hives, swelling or itching;
- vomiting or persistent indigestion, nausea, stomach pain or diarrhea;
- yellow discoloration of the skin or eyes;
- any changes in the amount or color of your urine (dark red or brown);
- any pain or difficulty experienced while urinating;
- swelling of the feet or lower legs;
- malaise, fatigue, loss of appetite;
- blurred vision or any visual disturbance;
- mental confusion, depression, dizziness, lightheadedness;
- hearing problems;
- constipation, headache, vertigo;
- ulcers or bleeding of the esophagus, stomach, duodenum or intestines may also occur;
- rectal bleeding or discomfort is sometimes associated with the use of Indotec suppositories.

Other side effects not listed above may also occur in some patients. If you notice any other effects, check with your physician.

Dosing: In chronic disorders, treatment should be started with a dosage of 25 mg 2 or 3 times a day. By starting therapy with low dosage, increased gradually when necessary, maximum benefit will be produced with fewer adverse reactions.

Always give indomethacin with food, immediately after meals, or with antacids to reduce gastric irritation.

As with all drugs, the lowest possible effective dose should be utilized for each individual patient.

The drug should not be prescribed for children because safe conditions for use have not been established.

Since advancing years appear to increase the possibility of adverse reactions, indomethacin should be used with greater care in the elderly.

Adult Dosage Recommendations: Rheumatoid arthritis and ankylosing (rheumatoid) spondylitis: Initial dosage: 25 mg 2 or 3 times a day. If the response is not adequate, increase the daily dosage by 25 mg at about weekly intervals until a satisfactory response is obtained or a dosage of 150 to 200 mg/day is reached. If a satisfactory response is not obtained with 200 mg a day, larger doses probably will not be effective.

If adverse reactions develop as the dosage is increased, reduce the dosage to a tolerated level and maintain this for 3 to 4 weeks. If an adequate response has not been obtained, gradually increase the daily dosage by 25 mg at about weekly intervals to 150 to 200 mg daily.

For patients with acute rheumatoid arthritis or with acute flares of chronic rheumatoid arthritis, increase the dosage daily by 25 mg until a satisfactory response is obtained or a total daily dosage of 150 to 200 mg is reached. If adverse effects develop as the dosage is increased, the dosage should be reduced to a tolerated level for 2 or 3 days, and then, gradually increased by 25 mg every few days as tolerated. After the acute phase is under control, it is often possible to reduce the daily dosage gradually to 75 to 100 mg.

Reduction of steroid dosage: Use of indomethacin often will permit a gradual reduction of steroid dosage by 25 to 50%. In some patients, steroids can be slowly discontinued over a period of several weeks or months. The usual precautions should be observed in withdrawing steroids.

Severe osteoarthritis and degenerative joint disease of the hip: Initial dosage: 25 mg 2 or 3 times a day. If the response is not adequate, increase the daily dosage by 25 mg at about weekly intervals until a satisfactory response is obtained or a dosage of 150 to 200 mg a day is reached. If a satisfactory response is not obtained with 200 mg a day, larger doses will probably not be effective.

If adverse reactions develop as the dosage is increased, reduce the dosage to a tolerated level and maintain this for 3 to 4 weeks. If an adequate response has not then been obtained, gradually increase the daily dosage by 25 mg at about weekly intervals to 150 to 200 mg daily.

Gout: To control acute attacks: 50 mg 3 times a day until all signs and symptoms subside. Definite relief of pain has been reported within 2 to 4 hours. Tenderness and heat usually subside in 24 to 36 hours, and swelling gradually disappears in 3 to 5 days.

Use of Alternate Dosage Forms: Indotec suppositories: The recommended dosage of Indotec suppositories is 100 to 200 mg daily and should be individually adjusted to the patient's response and tolerance. Daily dose of 100 mg can be given as 50 mg twice daily or as 100 mg at night. Doses higher than 100 mg must be given on a twice daily schedule.

Combined Administration: One 50 mg or 100 mg suppository at bedtime, supplemented the following day by 25 mg capsules as needed up to a total of 150 mg to 200 mg of indomethacin. The total daily dose of Indotec (capsules and suppositories) should not exceed 200 mg.

Children: Indotec should not be prescribed for children because safe conditions for use have not been established (See Warnings).

What You Should Do if You Miss a Dose: If you miss a dose of Indotec and remember within an hour or so, take it right away. Then go back to your regular dosing schedule.

But if you do not remember until later, do not take the missed dose at all and do not double the next one. Instead, go back to your regular dosing schedule.

Storage: Indotec 50 and 100 mg suppositories should be stored below 30°C. Protect from light and elevated humidity. Keep away from excessive heat. Preserve in well-closed containers, at controlled room temperature.

Indotec 25 and 50 mg capsules should be stored between 15 and 30°C. Protect from light and moisture. Store in a tight container.

Indotec is not recommended for use in children since safety and effectiveness have not been established.

Do not keep outdated medicine or medicine no longer needed.

Indotec (cont'd)

Keep this product and all medicine out of the reach of children. This medication has been prescribed for your medical problem. Do not give it to anyone else.

If you require more information on this drug, consult your physician or pharmacist.

☐ INNOHEP® 🄿

Leo

Tinzaparin Sodium

Anticoagulant—Antithrombotic

Information for the Patient: Innohep (tinzaparin sodium): Prefilled unit dose syringes (nonpreserved, no sodium metabisulfite) containing: 3 500 anti-Xa IU/syringe or 4 500 anti-Xa IU/syringe; unit dose syringes (nonpreserved, contains sodium metabisulfite) containing: 10 000 anti-Xa IU/syringe, 14 000 anti-Xa IU/syringe or 18 000 anti-Xa IU/syringe; multidose vials (preserved, contains sodium metabisulfite) containing: 10 000 anti-Xa IU/mL or 20 000 anti-Xa IU/mL.

The following is important information about using Innohep for the prevention or treatment of deep vein thrombosis. If you have any questions please talk to your doctor or pharmacist.

What is Innohep? Innohep is a low molecular weight heparin used for the prevention and/or treatment of deep venous thrombosis (complications due to blood clots).

Before using Innohep: It is important for you to advise your doctor of all drugs you are presently taking. Innohep should be used with caution in conjunction with other drugs that affect blood coagulation (e.g., ASA or salicylates, vitamin K antagonists, or dextran).

You must also inform your doctor if you have active bleeding from a local lesion such as an acute gastrointestinal ulcer or if you develop allergy or hypersensitivity to Innohep.

Tell your doctor if you are pregnant or breast-feeding so that the doctor will be aware of your status during management.

Dosage and Administration: Innohep must be used as instructed by your doctor. Innohep is administered as a s.c. injection (beneath the surface of the skin).

In Hospital: Prevention of postoperative venous thromboembolism: **General Surgery:** Innohep 3 500 anti-Xa IU (available in a prefilled syringe) s.c. 2 hours before surgery, followed by 3 500 anti-Xa IU once daily for 7 to 10 days.

Orthopedic Surgery: Hip Surgery: Innohep 50 anti-Xa IU/kg body weight given by s.c. injection 2 hours before surgery followed by 50 anti-Xa IU/kg once daily for 7 to 10 days; **or** Innohep 75 anti-Xa IU/kg body weight given postoperatively by s.c. injection once daily for 7 to 10 days.

Knee Surgery: Innohep 75 anti-Xa IU/kg body weight given postoperatively by s.c. injection once daily for 7 to 10 days.

For convenience, the following prefilled syringes are available for dosing by body weight:

	Preoperative 50 anti-Xa IU/kg	Postoperative 75 anti-Xa IU/kg
Doses per syringe	**Body weight**	**Body weight**
3 500 anti-Xa IU	60-80 kg	35-55 kg
4 500 anti-Xa IU	80-100 kg	50-70 kg

Patients outside of these weight ranges should be dosed on an individual basis.

Treatment of deep vein thrombosis: Innohep 175 anti-Xa IU/kg body weight once daily. Innohep is available in unit dose graduated syringes (10 000 anti-Xa IU/0.5 mL, 14 000 anti-Xa IU/0.7 mL and 18 000 anti-Xa IU/0.9 mL) and multidose vials containing 20 000 anti-Xa IU/mL.

At Home: It may be necessary for you to continue treatment with Innohep at home. Before you are released from the hospital, your doctor will instruct you on how much Innohep to administer and show you how to give yourself s.c. injections. It is very important that you follow the instructions exactly. If there is anything you don't understand or would like clarified, be sure to ask your doctor for more information.

Instructions for Injection at Home: Innohep is available in ready-to-use, prefilled syringes. **Important:** When using Innohep unit dose graduated syringes, the volume should be adjusted prior to administration to the amount prescribed by your doctor. Once the volume has been adjusted to the amount prescribed for you, the entire volume should be administered according to the injection technique described in the next section.

When using Innohep in multidose vials (10 000 or 20 000 anti-Xa IU/mL), administer Innohep using a 1 mL syringe and a small (25 gauge, ½ inch) needle. Withdraw the appropriate volume of Innohep into a syringe and needle assembly held vertically with the needle upward. Tap the syringe with your finger to dislodge air bubbles and depress the syringe plunger to remove any air from the assembly.

Injection Technique: See package insert for illustrations. Proper subcutaneous administration of Innohep is essential to prevent pain and bruising at the site of injection.

1. The recommended site for injection is into the fat tissue of the lower abdomen. Alternatively, Innohep can be injected into the side of the thigh, provided care is taken not to inject Innohep into muscle tissue.
2. Cleanse (do not rub) the skin with an alcohol swab. Select a different site of the abdomen for each injection. With your thumb and forefinger, gather a fold of skin on your lower abdomen. This fold must be maintained throughout the injection.
3. Then holding the needle like a dart, insert the needle perpendicularly into the skin fold between your thumb and finger as far as it will go. Once the needle has been inserted, the needle tip should not be moved and the plunger should not be pulled back. Push the plunger in to inject the Innohep.
4. Remove the needle perpendicularly and apply brief compressing pressure with an alcohol swab. This action will help to minimize any oozing of Innohep or bleeding. Do not rub the injection site. Dispose of the used syringe and needle in a safe manner.

Important: It is essential that you follow the instructions of your doctor carefully. Administer Innohep for the entire period prescribed by your doctor.

Do not take any drugs other than those prescribed by your doctor while you are taking Innohep.

If you see another doctor or your dentist, be sure to tell them that you are being treated with Innohep.

If you notice any of the following effects while you are being treated with Innohep, contact your doctor:

- bleeding at the injection site and/or from surgical sites and/or other bleeding
- easy bruising or bruising without apparent cause
- allergic reactions

Treatment of Overdosage: Overdose of Innohep can result in excessive bleeding. If you think you have accidentally taken too much Innohep, call your doctor immediately. Your doctor will determine the appropriate corrective measures to be taken.

Storage of Innohep: Store at 15 to 25°C. Protect from light.

Keep Innohep and your syringes and needles in a safe place where children cannot reach them.

☐ INTAL® INHALER 🄿
☐ INTAL® SYNCRONER® 🄿

Rhône-Poulenc Rorer

Sodium Cromoglycate

Asthma Prophylaxis

Information for the Patient: Intal Inhaler: Preventive Medication: Sodium cromoglycate works to prevent asthmatic attacks. **To get the full benefit from sodium cromoglycate it should be used regularly according to your doctor's instructions.** During the time you are following the regimen, keep a record of the incidence and severity of any asthmatic attacks or symptoms—loss of sleep, wheezing, coughing, etc. Your doctor may have provided you with a diary in which to do this. At the end of the month, or other period of time your doctor has designated, this diary can be invaluable in evaluating your sodium cromoglycate regimen. Your doctor will want to know as much as he can about the effect of sodium cromoglycate on the patient's symptoms. You will want to know, too, **if you or your child is one of the individuals this medicine helps. It can bring a big change for the better in your life. Take the medicine for at least 1 full month to receive the best results and it will have to be taken month after month for as long as your doctor feels is necessary.**

Sodium cromoglycate is a preventive medication. It doesn't work immediately so you should continue taking your other medications until your doctor advises otherwise. Do not discontinue use or miss taking the recommended doses without your doctor's approval.

Instructions for Use: To obtain maximum benefit, you must use Intal Inhaler correctly to allow the medication to reach deeply into the lungs. Before using your Intal Inhaler, please read this leaflet, and follow the instructions carefully.

Usual Dosage: Adults and Children over 6 years—2 inhalations 4 times daily (e.g., 2 inhalations on rising; 2 at noon; 2 at 6:00 p.m.; and 2 at bedtime). The number of inhalations and the frequency of use of the inhaler will be determined by your physician. For protection against bronchospasm induced by exercise INTAL should be taken 15 to 30 minutes beforehand.

Important: Do not stop usage or change dosage without consulting your physician. Wash the unit regularly to keep the plastic outlet in the mouthpiece free from powder build-up.

Caution: The canister is pressurized. Do not attempt to puncture it, or dispose of it by burning, even when empty.

Storage: Store at room temperature in a dry location. Keep the cap on when not in use.

Important: How to Get the Best Out of Your Inhaler: Follow instructions. Keep the unit clean. Wash the unit twice a week.

1. Shake the unit well. Remove the **blue cover** from the mouthpiece. Ensure that the canister is properly inserted into the inhaler unit.
2. Holding the inhaler well away from your mouth, breathe out gently (but not fully). To avoid condensation and blockage of the device, **do not** breathe out through the mouthpiece.
3. Place the mouthpiece in your mouth over your tongue and close your lips around it. Tilt your head well back. Breathe in slowly and deeply through the mouthpiece and, at the same time, press the top of the metal canister down firmly to deliver the Intal. Note: It is essential that the canister is pressed **while you are breathing in** so that you will get the correct amount of the drug.
4. Remove the inhaler from your mouth. **Important: Hold your breath for as long as is comfortable (several seconds) to allow the medication to spread through your lungs.**
5. **Wait 1 minute. Repeat steps 2, 3 and 4.** After use replace the cover on the mouthpiece.

Cleaning: Important: Keep the plastic body clean to prevent build-up of spare powder. **Remove the metal canister** and wash the **plastic body** in warm water at least twice a week. Leave to dry in a warm place overnight. No harm will come from washing the mouthpiece every day.

Note: Check your technique in front of a mirror from time to time. If you see the white mist escaping into the air, you may not have your lips properly closed around the mouthpiece. Alternatively, you may not be breathing in as you press the canister.

Helpful Hints: Before using the inhaler for the first time—or if it hasn't been used for a while—give the inhaler one press to test it. For parents: Children may need some help to use the Intal Inhaler correctly. You can help by practising pressing the canister just after the child has started to breathe in.

Each metered inhalation contains sodium cromoglycate micronized 1 mg.

Living a Full Life With Asthma: This information sheet will tell you more about asthma and how to deal with it.

What is asthma? You already know from experience some of the important things about asthma. When you or your child has an attack, breathing becomes very difficult. You also know that, between attacks, you or your child has no problem breathing. So, you know the real problem in having asthma is the "attack". To live more comfortably, you must reduce the number of attacks, stop the attack in progress or reduce the severity of the attack.

What happens during an asthma attack? An asthma attack does two things to the breathing system. First, it constricts the muscles that control the air passages. These muscles which are wrapped around the outside of the air passages go into spasm which tightens and narrows the air passages. This makes it difficult for air to get in and even more difficult for it to be expelled.

The inside of air passages also is affected by an asthma attack. The inside swells and secretes more mucus than normally, and this mucus interferes with breathing.

What Causes Theses Attacks?

1. Allergy producing substances (ragweed, pollen, dust, some foods and medicines, etc.);
2. Respiratory infections (colds, flu, etc.);
3. Strenuous exercise;
4. Sudden changes in temperature and/or humidity, (e.g. exposure to cold air);
5. Irritants (chlorine, perfume, etc.);
6. Emotional stress (difficult situations at home, school, work).

Relief Measures: Since there is no medicine a patient can take that will cure asthma (that is, end the asthmatic condition forever), relief must concentrate on the prevention of attacks and lessening their severity if they do occur.

Prevention is the key and can be accomplished partially by avoiding the specific triggers of the attack in the individual cases. Try to identify the substances that may cause the attacks you are concerned about—substances such as foods, dust, animal dander, etc. Some measures in this area may be very difficult for children. It may be necessary to find a new home for a family pet or remove a favorite stuffed toy. Even though such steps are unpleasant they may be important and necessary. Pay particular attention to the asthmatic's bedroom: no feather pillows, mattresses or quilts. If a specific food seems to cause problems, eliminate it from the diet. Air conditioning the home reduces the amount of airborne irritants and electrostatic filters, or the newer micropore (HEPA) filters, if practical, may help too. Be careful of certain medicines. Aspirin produces asthmatic reactions in some people and should be avoided if this occurs.

Other Do's and Don'ts: Anyone subject to asthmatic attacks should follow a sensible health promoting lifestyle that includes good nutrition, adequate rest, exercise and these do's and don'ts:

1. Don't smoke. Avoid being in the same room with smokers.
2. Avoid fresh paint.
3. Avoid sudden changes in temperature. Don't go in and out of extremely cool air-conditioned buildings during hot weather.
4. Stay home in extremely cold weather, if possible.
5. Stay away from people with colds and flu.
6. Try not to become involved in emotionally upsetting situations.
7. Get plenty of liquid in your daily diet—6 to 8 glasses.
8. Don't overdo it—but do plan regular exercise, especially the kind that helps develop lung capacity.
9. Don't take any medicine without telling your doctor.
10. Do take all the medication prescribed by your doctor exactly according to his directions.
11. Avoid sleeping pills or sedatives, even if asthma keeps you awake. Prop yourself up with extra pillows until your asthma medication takes effect.
12. Avoid inhaling insecticides, deodorants, cleaning fluids, chlorine vapor etc.

Intal Syncroner: Each metered inhalation contains: sodium cromoglycate micronized 1 mg.

This is a **preventive** treatment and it must be used every day as directed by your physician. It will not provide **immediate** relief of symptoms, but when correctly used should help to significantly reduce the frequency and intensity of attacks. **To obtain maximum benefit, you must use Intal Syncroner correctly to allow the medication to reach deeply into the lungs.**

Before using your Intal Syncroner, please read this leaflet carefully, and follow these instructions.

Usual Dosage: Adults and Children over 6 years—2 inhalations 4 times daily. (e.g., 2 inhalations on rising, 2 at mid-day, 2 at 6:00 p.m. and 2 before retiring). The number of inhalations and the frequency of use of the inhaler will be determined by your physician. For protection against bronchospasm induced by exercise INTAL should be taken 15 to 30 minutes beforehand.

Important: Do not stop or change dosage without consulting your physician.

Cleaning: Keep the unit closed and the cap on when not in use. The inhaler may be cleaned by removing the canister and rinsing the plastic mouthpiece in warm water. Dry thoroughly before replacing the canister.

Caution: The canister is pressurized. Do not attempt to puncture it or to dispose of it, even when empty, by burning.

Storage: Store at room temperature.

How to Use Your Intal Syncroner: The Syncroner is a training device which will enable you to see whether you are using the inhaler correctly. The dose delivered from the inhaler can be seen as a fine white mist. If you are **not** using the device correctly, a cloud of white mist will swirl up in front of your face. To correct this, check that you are breathing in at the right time, as defined in step 6. Follow the instructions below and check your technique in front of a mirror.

Intal Inhaler (cont'd)

1. Shake the Syncroner well. Remove the blue cover from the mouthpiece. Ensure that the canister is properly inserted into the inhaler unit.
2. Open the inhaler unit to its fullest extent and lock into position.
3. Hold the unit firmly between your thumb and forefinger, using the thumb grip the base of the unit.
4. Breathe out slowly until you cannot expel any more air from your lungs.
5. Put the mouthpiece into your mouth, close your lips around it and tilt your head well back.
6. Breathe in slowly and deeply through the mouthpiece **and at the same time** press the top of the metal canister down firmly to deliver the Intal inhalant.
7. **This is most important:** Hold your breath for as long as it is comfortable (several seconds) to allow the Intal inhalant to spread through your lungs, then take the inhaler out of your mouth and breathe out.
8. Repeat the inhalation (steps 4 to 7), close the unit and replace the mouthpiece cover.

Note: It is essential that the canister is pressed as you start to breathe in, so that you will get the correct amount of the drug.

☐ INTAL® SPINCAPS® Ⓟ
☐ INTAL® NEBULIZER SOLUTION Ⓟ

Rhône-Poulenc Rorer

Sodium Cromoglycate

Asthma Prophylaxis

Information for the Patient: How to Use Intal and the Spinhaler: What is Intal? Intal is a white powder for inhalation into the lungs. It is used in the treatment of bronchial asthma to prevent attacks before they start. It will only work if used regularly and with the correct technique of using the special Spinhaler explained in this leaflet.

How Often Should Intal be Taken? Unless your doctor has told you otherwise, inhale 4 Intal Spincaps every day, for example one first thing in the morning, one at lunchtime, one at dinner and one last thing at night. You should only stop or reduce the dose when told to do so by your doctor.

When using Intal, some of the powder may be left in your mouth. To inhale as much as possible, it is important to use the Spinhaler correctly.

How is Intal Taken? Intal must be inhaled (or sucked) into your lungs using the Spinhaler. Intal does not work in asthma when swallowed.

How to Load the Spinhaler: First, make sure your hands are clean and dry. Tear open the sachet and press out a Spincap through the foil. Load the Spinhaler as follows:

1. Hold it upright with the mouthpiece pointing downwards; then unscrew the body.
2. Check that the propeller is on its spindle, then firmly push a Spincap (colored end downwards) into the cup of the propeller. Make sure that the propeller spins easily and then screw the body tightly back onto the mouthpiece.
3. Still holding the Spinhaler upright, slide the grey outer sleeve down as far as it will go and then back up again. This pierces the Spincap and makes the Spinhaler ready for use.

How to Inhale Intal:

1. Make sure the mouthpiece and the body of the Spinhaler are still tightly screwed together.
2. Breathe out, put the mouthpiece in your mouth and close your lips around it so that they are right up against the lip of the Spinhaler.
3. Tilt your head well back and breathe in as deeply as you can.
4. Hold your breath for as long as comfortable, then take the Spinhaler right out of your mouth and breathe out.
5. Keep repeating this process until the Spincap is empty. Two or three attempts should be enough and it does not matter if a little powder is left.
6. If you have a little irritation in your throat afterwards have a drink of water.

Remember: Time and patience spent taking Intal correctly can save you from countless attacks of asthma and the upheaval they cause.

Parents: Your doctor or pharmacist can get you a whistle to put on the end of the Spinhaler. This could make taking Intal more fun for your child and may help him or her to learn to take it properly.

How to Look After Your Spinhaler and Spincaps: Always keep your Spinhaler in its container. This will make sure no dirt can get into it.

For best results, the parts of the Spinhaler must be kept free from any powder remains. At least once a week, it is important that you brush off any powder left sticking to the propeller and wash all parts of the Spinhaler in warm water. Make certain everything is quite **dry** before reassembling.

What is Asthma? Asthma is a condition characterized by periodic attacks of shortness of breath, wheeziness (audible noise when breathing) and occasionally cough. It thus may interfere with everyday activities such as sleep, meals, work and play. The effect on an individual may be variable.

What Happens During an Asthma Attack? During an attack, the muscles surrounding the outside of the air passages go into spasm, as a result of the release of certain substances, causing tightening of the air passages and this interferes with normal breathing.

What Causes These Attacks: Asthma can be caused by a number of factors:

1. Allergy-producing substances (ragweed, pollen, dust, some foods and medicines).
2. Respiratory infections (cold, flu).
3. Emotional stress (difficult situations at home, school, work).
4. Strenuous exercise.
5. Irritant chemicals (chlorine, perfume, etc.).
6. Sudden changes in temperatures and/or humidity.

Relief Measures: There is no medication a patient can take that will "cure" asthma (that is, end the asthmatic condition forever). Relief must concentrate on the prevention of attacks and lessening their severity if they do occur. Partial prevention of an attack may be achieved if a definite cause for the attack can be established—such as an allergy to certain animals, dust, foods or medications—and that cause is avoided.

Why Intal? Your doctor has prescribed Intal as an integral part of your prevention program. Intal has a unique method of action to help asthma sufferers. Intal works to prevent the release of substances that cause the asthma attacks.

Intal is preventive medicine that requires regular usage for full benefit. By taking Intal regularly even when you feel well, asthma can be controlled and most attacks prevented, resulting in a more normal healthy lifestyle.

Intal Halermatic: Intal Halermatic is a device for inhaling the contents of Intal Spincaps cartridges into the lungs. Read instructions through before using; all instruction must be carried out correctly to receive the proper dose.

How to Load the Halermatic: Cartridges should only be inserted immediately prior to use.

1. Remove the mouthpiece cover and then pull off the mouthpiece.
2. Push an Intal Spincaps cartridge firmly down to the bottom of the slot.
3. Slide the mouthpiece back on to the body, pushing down slowly as far as it will go. This action pierces the cartridge and lifts it into the rotation chamber—the inhaler is now ready to use.

Note: Step 3 must not be repeated as the cartridge must be pierced once only.

How to Use the Intal Halermatic:

1. Breathe out as far as possible holding the device away from the mouth.
2. Tilt the head back and breathe in quickly and steadily through the mouthpiece, keeping the lips closed around it. Be sure not to obstruct the flow of Intal into the lungs as long as possible.
3. Hold your breath to keep the Intal in the lungs as long as possible, remove the device from your mouth and then breathe out.
4. Repeat steps 1 to 3 until all the Intal powder has been inhaled.
5. If the throat becomes dry or irritated, drink a little water before and after inhalation.
6. If there is any difficulty, be sure: the device is clean; the air inlets are not obstructed when breathing in, (e.g., by your fingers); the cartridge is free to rotate. Do not place the cartridge back in the slot if it is already pierced; the cartridge has been pierced. If not, begin again by pushing the cartridge back into the slot.

Cleaning the Intal Halermatic:

1. Brush away powder deposits daily with the brush provided.
2. When powder deposits build up, wipe away with a lightly dampened cloth.
3. The mouthpiece may be washed separately if necessary.

Do not wet the blue-based body of the Intal Halermatic and be sure the mouthpiece grid is dry before reassembling the device.

Replace the Intal Halermatic every 6 months.

Always handle Intal Spincaps cartridges with clean, dry hands and keep the Intal Halermatic in a dry place at room temperature.

Intal Nebulizer Solution: Directions for use: For inhalation only.

Method of Administration: Intal Nebulizer solution should be administered from a power-operated nebulizer having an adequate flow rate, equipped with a suitable face mask.

The doctor will advise on the choice of a suitable nebulizer and how it should be used. Do not use any other appliance without consulting the doctor.

Dosage: Nebulization should be carried out 4 times a day using the contents of a fresh ampul each time, or as directed by the doctor. Nebulization for 5 to 10 minutes is the clinically effective nebulization period. Any solution remaining in the nebulizer should be discarded.

Inhalation: Assemble and use the device according to the instructions provided by the manufacturer or your doctor.

Precautions: Other medications for nebulization should not be mixed with Intal Nebulizer Solution. Use a fresh ampul for each dose.

Contraindications: There are no specific contraindications, other than hypersensitivity to sodium cromoglycate. It is an accepted medical principle to be cautious of using any medication during the first 3 months of pregnancy.

Cleaning Instructions for Home Use: It is very important that your nebulizer is kept thoroughly clean. Follow the instructions given by the manufacturer.

Storage: Intal Nebulizer Solution should be stored at room temperature. Protect open box from direct sunlight.

If further information on Intal Nebulizer Solution or nebulization is required, consult the doctor.

Availability: Packs containing 48 × 2 mL ampuls.

Ampul Emptying Instructions: (see package insert for illustrations):
Important: To prevent particles from entering the solution: Break the ampul well away from the nebulizer unit. Break off the lower end each time. Ensure hands are clean.
Note: Before use read the directions. The ampul is an "easy-break" ampul. The glass is weakened at each end so that the ends of the ampul can easily be broken off using the enclosed opener.

1. Hold the opener **firmly closed.** Insert the **lower end** of the ampul up to the yellow line and break off. No solution will come out.
2. Discard the glass tip from the ampul opener by releasing the hinge. Turn the ampul so that the broken end faces upwards.
3. Place forefinger carefully over the open end of the ampul. Keeping the finger firmly in place and with the opener again firmly closed break off the lower end, in the same way as instruction 1.
4. Then hold the ampul over the solution container and release forefinger. The solution will now flow out.

☐ INTRON A® Ⓟ

Schering

Interferon alfa-2b

Biological Response Modifier

Information for the Patient: Before using your Intron A (interferon alfa-2b), you should read the following information and carefully follow the instructions.

If you are using the Intron A Premix Solution see the Subcutaneous Injection section.

To Prepare Intron A Solution:

1. With pencil or pen, mark the date you add the diluent in the space provided on the Intron A vial.
2. Wash your hands thoroughly with soap and water, rinse, and towel dry.
3. Remove the protective plastic cap from the top of both the diluent and Intron A vial, leaving the rubber stopper and aluminum ring in place.
4. Clean the rubber stopper on the top of each vial with an alcohol swab.
   Your physician will tell you what size syringe and needle to use for mixing and how much diluent to add to the Intron A vial.
5. Remove the protective cap from the syringe needle and fill with air by pulling the plunger to the volume of diluent to be added.
6. Hold the diluent upright without touching the top of the cleaned vial with your hands.
7. Insert the needle into the vial containing the diluent and inject the air into the vial.
8. Invert the vial and make sure that the top of the needle is in the liquid.
9. Withdraw the diluent to be added to the Intron A vial by pulling the plunger to the exact amount your physician has told you. The marks on the side of the syringe indicate the amount of diluent withdrawn. Withdraw the needle from the vial.

To prepare the Intron A solution insert the needle through the rubber top of the Intron A vial and gently place the needle top against the glass wall of the vial.

Slowly inject the diluent, aiming the stream of liquid at the glass wall of the vial in order to avoid production of air bubbles.

Do not aim the stream at the white powder at the bottom of the vial.

Remove needle, replace needle cap on needle and place syringe on a flat surface.

To dissolve the white contents, swirl the vial of Intron A with a gentle rotatory motion until the contents are completely dissolved. **Do not shake vial.**

If air bubbles do form, wait until the solution has settled and all bubbles have risen to the top of the solution and disappeared before injecting the dose.

Stability and Storage: Before reconstitution*, Intron A should be stored in the refrigerator at 2 to 8°C. After reconstitution with Sterile Water for Injection, the solution is stable for 24 hours at 2 to 30°C. However, storage at 2 to 8°C is recommended.

After reconstitution with Bacteriostatic Water for Injection containing 0.9% benzyl alcohol, the solution is clear and colorless to light yellow in color. The reconstitution solution is stable for at least 30 days when stored between 2 to 8°C, for 2 weeks when stored at room temperature (15 to 30°C), and for 1 day when stored at 35°C. The reconstituted solution may be kept in the freezer up to 30 days, and during this period it may be thawed and refrozen up to 2 times.

When Intron A powder is reconstituted with Bacteriostatic Water for Injection, the resulting solution can be stored in polypropylene syringes at 2 to 8°C for 30 days.

Frozen storage of the filled syringes is not recommended.

Subcutaneous Injection (see package insert for illustrations):

- Find a comfortable, well-lit place and assemble supplies (vial, syringe, swabs and disposable container). Leave vial at room temperature for 10 minutes. Do not shake.

Step 1: Selecting an Injection Site:

- Do not inject in area that is red or sore.
- Use the same site only once every 6 or 7 weeks.

Injection Sites: Thighs, outer surface of upper arms, abdomen—except navel or below waistline.

Step 2: Filling the Syringe with Intron A:

- Check solution for change in color, cloudiness, and expiry date.
- Wash hands with soap. Dry with clean towel.
- Remove cap from vial and discard.
- Wipe top with an alcohol swab.
- If syringe is cracked, or needle is bent, put into disposable bottle.
- Pull needle cap straight off. With vial on flat surface, push needle through rubber stopper of Intron A vial.
- With needle in vial, turn vial upside down making sure needle is in solution.
- Pull back plunger and slowly withdraw prescribed amount of solution into syringe. Check dose again.
- Remove needle from vial. Keep needle end up. Do not touch needle. Gently tap syringe to clear air bubbles. Gently push plunger to get rid of air from end of syringe.
- Replace the cover on the needle and put the syringe on a clean flat surface.

Step 3: Preparing to Inject:

- Using a circular motion, clean site with an alcohol swab (approximately for 10 seconds). Allow area to dry.
- Remove the needle cap.
- Hold syringe between thumb and forefinger—like holding a pencil.
- With other hand grab skin where injection will be made.
- Hold needle at a 45 to 90 degree angle to the skin about 5 cm above the skin surface, insert the needle with a quick jab as if throwing a dart. The entire needle or at least 3/4 of it should go into the skin.
- Pull back on plunger 0.8 cm. If you see blood in the syringe, do not inject. Withdraw and discard the syringe, prepare a new syringe and inject at a new site. If you do not see blood in the syringe, slowly push the plunger to inject the Intron A.
- After injecting solution, pull out needle. Put alcohol swab over site for a few seconds. Do not press down.
- If needed, put on bandaid.

Step 4: Cleaning Up:

- Do not put cover back on needle.

Intron A (cont'd)

- Place empty syringe with needle in disposal bottle. Check with your nurse or pharmacist for proper disposal.

Intramuscular Injection:

- If preferred, you may administer i.m. providing you are taught by your doctor to administer by this route.

* Reconstituting means adding a liquid (diluent) to a dry powder.

☐ INVIRASE™ 🄿

Roche

Saquinavir Mesylate

HIV Protease Inhibitor—Antiretroviral Agent

Information for the Patient You have been prescribed Invirase (saquinavir mesylate) by your doctor. Invirase is the first of a new class of drugs used to fight the human immunodeficiency virus (HIV). Invirase contains the active ingredient saquinavir, which fights the spread of HIV through your body. Please read this information carefully, as it will help you learn about Invirase and how to make this drug work best for you. If you have any questions or concerns after reading this information, speak with your doctor or pharmacist.

What is HIV Infection? HIV is the virus that causes AIDS. As you may know, the immune system is the body's main defense against infection. The immune system includes special cells that recognize and destroy harmful bacteria and viruses. As HIV grows, it destroys these cells–leaving fewer immune cells, and a greater risk of infection.

Over time, HIV disease usually ''progresses''– it gets more severe. With fewer immune cells, it is easier for you to get sick. Your doctor will watch you carefully to tell how you are doing. Your doctor may also do blood tests to measure the number of immune cells in your body (CD4 cell counts) and to measure how much virus is in your blood. All of this information can be used to help you and your doctor decide how best to manage your HIV disease.

What is Invirase? Invirase is the brand name for saquinavir capsules. Saquinavir belongs to a new class of drugs called protease inhibitors (pronounced PRO-tee-ase). It interferes with a different step in virus reproduction than other drugs previously available to fight HIV.

Each Invirase capsule contains 200 mg of the active ingredient (saquinavir). The capsules also contain additional (nonmedicinal) ingredients, these are: lactose, microcrystalline cellulose, povidone, sodium starch glycolate, talc and magnesium stearate. The capsule shells are made from gelatin, titanium dioxide, iron oxide and indigotine. **If you know you have an allergy or have had a serious reaction to any of the ingredients, you must not use Invirase.**

How does Invirase work? Invirase interferes with an important step in virus reproduction in cells. Before Invirase, all of the prescription drugs for the treatment of HIV disease worked at the same place. These drugs, called nucleoside analogues, include Retrovir [AZT], Hivid [ddC], Videx [ddI], and 3TC [lamivudine]. Now however, with the addition of Invirase, we can fight the growth of HIV at different places in its life cycle.

Invirase is not a cure for HIV and/or AIDS, though it may help to slow the progression of HIV disease in your body. While taking Invirase however, you may continue to acquire illnesses associated with advanced HIV infection (i.e., opportunistic infections).

It is important to remember that there is **no** evidence which suggests that Invirase can prevent the transmission of HIV. Invirase is **not** therefore a substitute for other measures which have been proven effective in this regard. To avoid transmission of HIV, you should not donate blood, share needles, or engage in unprotected sexual activity (i.e., without a condom).

How should Invirase be taken? Your doctor has prescribed Invirase after carefully studying your case, because he/she believes that you may benefit from this medication. This may not be true for other patients with HIV infection, even those who exhibit symptoms similar to yours. **As with any prescription drug, Invirase should only be taken on the advice of a physician. Do not give your Invirase to any other person.**

The recommended dose of Invirase is 3 capsules every 8 hours (for a total of 9 capsules each day), taken anytime within 2 hours of having eaten a meal or a substantial snack. For example, if you've eaten lunch at 1:00 PM, you can take your mid-day dose with that meal, or anytime between 1:00 and 3:00 PM. **The effectiveness of Invirase may depend on taking it with food.** Capsules should be swallowed unchewed, with water or some other nonalcoholic drink. You should avoid excessive consumption of alcohol during your treatment with Invirase. Your doctor may prescribe Invirase in combination with other drugs which are used to control HIV infection. Your physician may adjust the recommended dose to suit your particular needs. **Follow the advice of your doctor.**

What if you miss a dose of Invirase? The missed dose should be taken as soon as you remember, then just carry on with your regular dosing schedule. However, do not take 2 doses (6 capsules) at the same time. If you are unsure what to do, consult your doctor or pharmacist.

What should you tell your doctor before taking Invirase? Before beginning treatment with Invirase, make sure your doctor knows if:

- you have ever had a bad reaction to saquinavir (Invirase) or any component of the capsules;
- you have a problem with your liver or kidneys;
- you have any other illnesses besides HIV infection;
- you are taking **any** other drugs (including those not prescribed by your doctor); or
- you are pregnant, plan on becoming pregnant, or are breast-feeding a child.

This information will help you and your physician decide if the potential benefits of treating your condition with Invirase outweigh the possible risks.

What are the possible unwanted effects of Invirase? As with any drug, the beneficial effects of Invirase may be accompanied by unwanted effects (also known as side effects or adverse events). It is often difficult to determine whether these adverse events are the result of taking Invirase, an effect of your HIV-infection, or a side effect from other drugs being used to treat the HIV-infection. **It is very important however, to inform your physician of any change in your condition.**

Most side effects reported with Invirase are mild. Those reported most often in two clinical studies when Invirase was used in combination with other drugs used to treat HIV, were: fatigue (5% of patients), diarrhea (3% of patients), abdominal discomfort (2% of patients), headache, muscle pain, nausea, abdominal pain (each in 1% of patients), upset stomach and dizziness (both in less than 1% of patients).

Other rare side effects which may affect your physical and/or psychological well-being have also been reported by patients taking Invirase. Further information on such events is available from your doctor or pharmacist.

Regular blood testing to detect any abnormalities with your liver, pancreas or blood is a recommended part of your Invirase therapy. These abnormalities do not always cause side effects that you can detect yourself, so it is very important to adhere to the blood testing schedule recommended by your doctor.

In hemophiliacs, there have been reports of increased bleeding epidoses among patients treated with Invirase or other drugs of this class (protease inhibitors). If you suffer from hemophilia, remember to report all bleeding episodes to your doctor.

Side effects known to be associated with other drugs used to treat HIV may still occur when Invirase is used in combination with these medicines. However, Invirase does not appear to increase the frequency or severity of the unwanted effects. These side effects (associated with drugs such as ddC and AZT) include skin rash, inflammation or sores in the mouth and disturbances of the nerves (especially in the hands and feet). These disturbances may take the form of numbness, pins and needles, or shooting/burning pain in the hands and feet. If you are concerned about these or any other unexpected effects experienced while taking Invirase, talk to your doctor or pharmacist.

How should Invirase be stored? Always keep your Invirase in its original package at room temperature. **Keep this and any other drugs out of sight and out of reach of children.** Do not use this medicine after the expiry date (''EXP'') shown on the outside of the package.

Important notes to remember about your Invirase therapy:

- Your dosage of Invirase: 3 capsules, 3 times a day;
- Invirase should be taken with food (anytime within 2 hours after eating a full meal);
- It is very important that you follow all your doctor's instructions when taking Invirase;
- Contact your doctor if you are having trouble adjusting to your medication, or if you are experiencing any unexpected or bothersome symptoms.

This brochure does not contain all known information about Invirase. If you have any further questions or concerns about your treatment with Invirase, please contact your doctor or pharmacist.

☐ ISOTREX® ℞

Stiefel

Isotretinoin

Acne Therapy

Information for the Patient: Indication: Isotrex (isotretinoin 0.5%) Gel has been prescribed for the treatment of acne.

How to Use Isotrex Gel: Your physician may advise you to allow the effects of previously used peeling agents to subside prior to starting the use of Isotrex Gel.

Apply Isotrex Gel as directed by your physician. The skin being treated should be thoroughly cleansed with a mild soap such as Acne-Aid soap or other cleansing agents and dried. Apply Isotrex Gel thinly with a gentle rubbing motion.

You may notice a feeling of warmth or a stinging sensation which disappears rapidly.

Local irritation and peeling of the skin may occur within 2 to 3 weeks at the site of application. This is one of the ways in which Isotrex Gel improves the acne. However, if it makes you feel uncomfortable, consult your physician; you may be advised to use less medication, use the medication less frequently or discontinue its use temporarily.

Oil-free cosmetics may be used; the area of skin to be treated should be thoroughly cleansed and dried before Isotrex Gel application.

How Soon Can You Expect Results When Applying Isotrex Gel? The best results may not be achieved until after 8 to 10 weeks of treatment. Although improvement can be noticed after 2 to 3 weeks, some acne blemishes may appear worse at this time. Once the acne has responded satisfactorily, it may be possible to maintain the improved state with less frequent applications.

Take the Following Precautions While You Are Using Isotrex Gel.

1. Do not apply Isotrex Gel to areas of skin where you have other problems, such as eczema.
2. Do not apply to eyelids or to the skin at the corners of eyes and mouth; also avoid the angles of nose, the lips and the inside of the mouth.
3. No advantages will be obtained by using more than the recommended amounts, since marked redness, peeling and discomfort may occur.
4. Do not use other acne preparations while using this product without the advice of your physician.
5. Exposure to sunlight or sunlamps should be minimized during the use because they may lead to more intense action by the drug. If sunburn does occur, it is advisable to stop using Isotrex Gel and call your physician for advice.
6. Use of sunscreen products over treated areas may be prudent when exposure cannot be avoided.
7. Isotrex Gel has been prescribed for your use only, do not allow other people to use it.
8. If you are a female of childbearing age, you should only use Isotrex Gel after consulting your physician and seeking his/her advice for contraceptive counselling. If you are pregnant, you should discontinue the use of Isotrex and consult your physician.

☐ KADIAN® Ⓝ

Knoll

Morphine Sulfate

Opioid Analgesic

Information for the Patient: About Your Kadian Capsules: This provides a summary of the information available on your medicine. If you have any questions or are not sure about anything, ask your doctor or pharmacist.

What is the name of my medicine? The name of your medicine is Kadian.

What is Kadian? Kadian capsules contain 20 mg, 50 mg or 100 mg morphine sulfate.

As well as the active ingredient, morphine sulfate, Kadian also contains a number of inactive ingredients: sucrose, hypromellose, ethylcellulose, maize starch, methacrylic acid copolymer, polyethylene glycol, diethyl phthalate, talc, gelatin and a black ink containing: shellac, propylene glycol, ammonium hydroxide, potassium hydroxide and the coloring agent E172. Kadian capsules are gluten-free.

The 20 mg capsules are marked "K20" with 2 black bands, the 50 mg capsules are marked "K50" with 3 black bands and the 100 mg capsules are marked "K100" with 4 black bands.

Morphine sulfate is one of a group of medicines called the opioid analgesics.

What is Kadian used for? Your doctor has prescribed Kadian capsules to allow for long lasting pain relief.

Before you take your medicine. Kadian should **not** normally be used if:

- you are pregnant or breast-feeding.
- you have taken preparations containing morphine before and suffered with severe side effects, particularly allergic reactions, (e.g., rash, itching, swelling of the face or other areas, fainting or breathing problems), or you are allergic/sensitive to any of the other ingredients of Kadian (see What is Kadian?). You are reminded that Kadian contains sucrose and propylene glycol.
- you are suffering with acute or severe bronchial asthma, or other severe breathing difficulty, biliary colic (which causes painful abdominal spasms) or gastrointestinal obstruction.
- you are being treated with a medicine classed as a monoamine oxidase inhibitor (MAO inhibitor), or you have taken such a medicine within the last 14 days.
- It is important to tell your doctor if any of the above conditions apply to you, before you start to take Kadian. The doctor may wish to prescribe alternative medication.
- Doctors need to be cautious about using Kadian in patients with any of the following: head or brain injury, hypotension (low blood pressure), kidney or liver problems, Addison's disease, hypothyroidism (underactive thyroid), urinary or prostate problems, depression or nervous disorders, alcoholism or convulsive disorders (epilepsy). If your doctor is not fully aware that any of these conditions apply to you, it is important that you inform him/her. The doctor may wish to change the dose or prescribe alternative medication.
- Tell your doctor or pharmacist about any other medicines you are currently taking, whether they were prescribed for you by a doctor, or bought without a prescription from a pharmacy or elsewhere. In particular tell your doctor or pharmacist if you are taking any of the following medicines, (ask your doctor or pharmacist if you are not sure): MAO inhibitors (e.g., phenelzine, tranylcypromine, isocarboxazid or moclobemide), antihistamines, sedatives, sleeping tablets, tranquilizers or antidepressants, muscle relaxants, (e.g., diazepam, dantrolene or baclofen), diuretics (water tablets), strong pain killers (those obtained with a doctor's prescription) or cimetidine (remedy for excess stomach acid).

While taking Kadian, do not take any other medicines unless they are recommended by a doctor or pharmacist. Remember to tell the doctor or pharmacist that you are taking Kadian.

- If you suffer from diarrhea while taking Kadian, tell your doctor or pharmacist, as diarrhea may reduce the effectiveness of Kadian therapy.
- Morphine may cause daytime drowsiness. Driving or operating machinery or other tasks requiring full mental alertness should not be attempted during the first few days of taking Kadian, or thereafter if you are experiencing drowsiness or sedation. When combined with alcohol or certain medicines such as sleeping tablets or tranquilizers, troublesome drowsiness may occur. Alcohol should be avoided while taking Kadian.

How do I take Kadian capsules? Use your Kadian as your doctor has told you. The label should tell you how much Kadian to use and how often to take it. Kadian must be taken regularly to prevent pain. Ask your doctor or pharmacist if you are unsure.

Do not take more capsules than your doctor tells you to.

The amount of Kadian needed to give good pain relief varies in each patient. The doctor will take into account your age, weight, level of pain and medical history when choosing the correct dose.

It is important to note that Kadian is designed to be taken regularly, **not** as needed to relieve pain. Taking Kadian at regular times means that the next dose will already have been taken before the pain returns.

If pain occurs between doses (known as breakthrough pain), **do not** take extra doses of Kadian. Tell your doctor as soon as possible. Taking more than the dose prescribed by your doctor can be dangerous.

If the pain lessens, tell your doctor. **Do not** stop taking Kadian unless your doctor tells you to.

Kadian can be taken with or without food but it should be taken at about the same time each day, either before or after a meal. This way you will remember to take every dose.

Kadian capsules should normally be swallowed whole with plenty of fluid; however, for patients who have difficulty swallowing, the capsules ▶

Kadian (cont'd)

may be opened and the pellets sprinkled onto a small amount of soft food (such as yogurt or jam). This should be taken within 30 minutes of sprinkling. The mouth should be rinsed to ensure that all the pellets have been swallowed.

The pellets in Kadian capsules should not be chewed or crushed.

What do I do if my Kadian capsules do not have the usual effect? If you have done what your doctor says, but the pain gets worse, tell your doctor.

What do I do if I take too many Kadian capsules? The symptoms of overdose with Kadian are the same as for morphine overdose, these being difficult breathing, extreme drowsiness (possible unconsciousness), and cold and clammy skin. In the event of an overdosage urgently seek the advice of your doctor or your nearest hospital emergency department.

What do I do if I miss a dose of Kadian? If you forget to take a dose of Kadian, contact your doctor or pharmacist for advice.

Is Kadian addictive? People who have taken Kadian for several weeks may develop physical dependence, but this is not the same as addiction. Your doctor can advise you how to manage this. See the section entitled What side effects does Kadian have?

Do not stop taking Kadian unless your doctor tells you to.

What side effects does Kadian have? Along with their intended effects, medicines may cause some unwanted effects (side effects). This applies to Kadian. Some side effects will not be serious, but some may require medical attention.

- **Common side effects:** constipation, nausea, vomiting, sweating, lightheadedness, dizziness, drowsiness, and convulsion.

  Although this list may worry you, it is rare for treatment to be stopped because of these side effects. Normally they ease with time or the doctor is able to prescribe a suitable treatment. If you develop any of these side effects, particularly if they start or get worse just after your doctor has changed the way you take your Kadian (how much you take or how often you take it), tell your doctor or pharmacist.
- **Less common side effects:** weakness, insomnia, dry mouth, colic, difficulty in urinating, reduced sex drive, blurred vision, rash and swelling.

  Please consult your doctor or pharmacist if you experience any of these side effects.
- **Important:** Please check with your doctor or pharmacist immediately if any of the following side effects occur: difficulty in breathing such as tight chest or wheezing, fainting, rapid heartbeat (palpitations).
- **Withdrawal effects:** Long-term use of Kadian may lead to physical dependence, whereby symptoms such as nervousness, trembling, sweating, colic, diarrhea and nausea, may occur if Kadian is suddenly withdrawn. These effects are minimized when Kadian is withdrawn gradually over several weeks under the doctor's supervision.

Ask your doctor or pharmacist if you do not understand any of the side effects described above.

Other side effects, not listed above, may occur in some patients. Also, as with any medicine, there may be some side effects which are not yet known. If you notice any other effects, tell your doctor or pharmacist.

Your doctor or pharmacist can tell you more about the safety of Kadian.

Where should I store my Kadian capsules? Keep your Kadian capsules in a safe place where children cannot reach them. Your medicines could harm a child.

Keep your Kadian capsules away from strong heat and light. Keep your Kadian capsules in a cool, dry place (below 25°C).

Further Information: If your doctor decides to stop treatment, return any leftover medicine to the pharmacist. Only keep it if the doctor tells you to.

Remember this medicine is for you. Only a doctor can prescribe it for you. Never give it to others. It may harm them.

This information only applies to Kadian capsules 20 mg, 50 mg, and 100 mg.

Reordering Kadian: A new written prescription is required from your doctor each time you need more Kadian. Therefore it is important to contact your doctor at least 3 working days before your current supply runs out. It is very important that you do not miss any doses.

Should your pain increase, or any other complaints develop as a result of taking Kadian, contact your doctor immediately.

☐ KWELLADA-P™

R & C

Permethrin

Topical Scabicide

Information for the Patient: Single treatment kills scabies mites and eggs in most cases. **For external use only. Keep out of reach of children.**

This leaflet is a guide with some important facts about the product. If you have any questions, please consult your doctor or pharmacist.

What does Kwellada-P Lotion contain? 5% permethrin as the active ingredient.

When should you use Kwellada-P Lotion? Kwellada-P Lotion is indicated for the treatment of scabies (Sarcoptes scabiei). It kills scabies mites and eggs.

When should you not use Kwellada-P Lotion? It is not to be used on individuals with known sensitivities or reactions to permethrin, any synthetic pyrethroid or pyrethrin or to chrysanthemums.

Pregnancy: If you are pregnant, consult your physician before using Kwellada-P Lotion.

Nursing Mothers: If you are nursing, consult your physician before using Kwellada-P Lotion.

Children: For children 2 years and up. Use as directed. Consult a doctor before using on children under 2 years of age. Long sleeve shirts, pants, mittens and socks should be worn on young children to prevent any contact of the treated skin with the mouth.

What precautions should you take? This product may irritate your eyes. In case of contact, rinse with plenty of water. If swallowed contact your doctor or Poison Control Centre. If a reaction occurs, discontinue use and consult your doctor.

How should you use Kwellada-P Lotion? Directions: Shake well.

1. Before applying Kwellada-P lotion, ensure that the skin is clean, dry and cool. Do not take a hot bath before treatment.
2. Thoroughly massage a sufficient quantity of the lotion into the skin to cover the entire area from the neck to the soles of the feet, paying particular attention to the areas between the fingers and toes, under the fingernails and toenails, wrists, armpits, genital area and buttocks.
3. Put on clean clothes.
4. Leave on for 12 to 14 hours. During the treatment period, if hands are washed, the lotion should be reapplied after washing.
5. Wash the entire body (shower or bath).
6. Change into clean clothes.
7. A second application may be given 7 to 10 days after the first treatment if live scabies mites are present or new skin lesions appear.
8. All clothing, towels, bedding, etc. should be washed in very hot water and by using the hot cycle in the dryer for at least 20 minutes. Dry cleaning should suffice for blankets, jackets and other non-washables. Mattresses which have been used by an infested person should not be used for 48 hours. Toilet seats, combs, etc. should be disinfected, being careful to rinse thoroughly.

Note: Itching may last for several weeks following treatment with the drug. Retreatment is only necessary if live mites appear or new lesions develop.

The nature of Kwellada-P lotion is such that it disappears when rubbed gently into the skin. Therefore, it is not necessary to apply the lotion until it remains detectable on the surface.

Some itching may still persist for up to 2 weeks after treatment. This is due to the eggs and fecal pellets left behind by the mites in your skin. The itching will subside with the natural loss of the upper layer of skin.

A single application is usually sufficient but the procedure may be repeated 7 to 10 days later if new lesions develop.

Check all household members and treat them if necessary to prevent re-infestations.

How should you store Kwellada-P Lotion? Store the product between 15 and 30°C.

What is scabies? Scabies is a contagious infestation. The itching is the allergic response of the body to the mite. Just visible to the naked eye, the female mite burrows through the epidermal (upper) layer of the skin, leaving eggs and fecal pellets in the burrow behind her. It is proteins in the fecal material seeping into the tissue around the burrow which causes the body's reaction. The burrows can sometimes be detected, but are often scarce and difficult to find.

Like any allergy, it takes some time to become sensitized to the allergen and most people do not have any symptoms at all for 4 to 6 weeks after catching the infection. This means that there is plenty of time to pass the disease on to others unknowingly!

Who suffers from scabies? Getting scabies is not as bad as you think; anyone can catch it. It is not a sign of uncleanliness, or poor health habits. The mite does not discriminate against age, sex, wealth, profession or race. So it is wise to learn how to recognize a scabies infection, and how to treat it successfully. Anyone with whom there is skin to skin contact could be a donor.

How does someone get scabies? Scabies is transmitted by skin to skin contact when the mites pass from person to person. This happens most frequently during that commonest of contacts—holding hands.

What signs should I look for? In people with normal immune systems (i.e., the majority of the general population) scabies produces classical symptoms. The most common is a widespread itchy rash which is particularly severe at night, or when the body is warm, e.g., after exercise or a warm bath. The classical scabies rash is widespread and can affect almost any part of the body. In adults it is absent from the centre of the chest and back and the head, but in infants the rash may be found in these places. In addition, you may also find skin lesions—wavy, threadlike, very small slightly elevated lesions between the fingers, on the elbows, hands and wrists. Other common sites of infestation are the stomach, thighs, genital area and buttocks.

Should other household members be treated? Yes. These infestations are spread by contact; all household members and sexual partners should be carefully examined and treatment instituted where necessary to prevent the spread of infestation.

☐ KYTRIL™ Ⓟ

SmithKline Beecham

Granisetron HCl

Antiemetic

Information for the Patient: What you should know about Kytril Tablets: Please read this leaflet carefully before you begin to take this medicine. This leaflet provides a summary of the information available on your medicine. For further information or advice, please speak to your doctor or pharmacist.

The Name of Your Medicine: Kytril (granisetron hydrochloride) Tablets is the name of your medicine. This medicine is one of a group called antiemetics and it can only be obtained with a prescription from your doctor.

What is In Your Medicine: Kytril Tablets are supplied in one strength: 1 mg tablets. Each tablet contains 1 mg of granisetron, the active ingredient, and the following inactive ingredients: hydroxypropyl methylcellulose, lactose, magnesium stearate, microcrystalline cellulose, polyethylene glycol, polysorbate 80, sodium starch glycolate and titanium dioxide.

The Purpose of Your Medicine: Kytril Tablets are intended to prevent nausea (feeling sick) and vomiting which may occur after you receive chemotherapy for cancer.

Cancer chemotherapies are thought to cause the release of serotonin, a natural substance in the body. Serotonin can cause you to feel sick and to vomit. Granisetron, the active ingredient in Kytril Tablets, will stop the action of serotonin and help prevent you from feeling sick and vomiting.

How to Take Your Medicine: Follow your doctor's instructions about how often you should take your medicine and how many tablets you should take. This information is also on the label of the container of your medicine and if not, or if you have any questions, you should consult your doctor or pharmacist.

Do not take more tablets or take your tablets more often than your doctor prescribes.

Do not take this medicine if you are allergic to granisetron.

After Taking Your Medicine: If you experience an allergic reaction (e.g., shortness of breath, drop in blood pressure, skin lumps or hives) **contact your doctor immediately. Do not take any more medicine unless instructed to do so by your doctor.**

You may experience headaches, constipation, weakness, diarrhea or abdominal pain while taking Kytril Tablets. There is no need to stop the medicine but you should tell your doctor about these symptoms at your next visit.

If you have any symptoms that you do not understand, you should contact your doctor immediately.

What to Do If You Miss A Dose: If you forget to take a tablet at the time it should have been taken, take the tablet as soon as you remember it was missed.

What to Do If An Overdose Is Taken: Problems of overdosage are unlikely with this medicine. In the event that you accidentally take more tablets than your doctor prescribes, immediately contact your doctor, hospital emergency department, or the nearest Poison Control Centre, even if you do not feel ill.

The Use of This Medicine During Pregnancy and Breast-feeding: As a normal precaution, this medicine should not be taken if you are pregnant, if you are likely to become pregnant or if you are breast-feeding, unless your doctor advises you otherwise.

Storing Your Medicine: Kytril Tablets should be kept at room temperature in their original pack.

The expiry date of this medicine is printed on the label. Do not use the medicine after this date.

Keep your medicine in a safe place out of the reach of children.

A Reminder: This medicine is only for you, the person for whom the prescription was written. Do not give this medication to others.

This leaflet does not contain all the information about your medicine. If you have any questions, or if you require more information about your medicine, please ask your doctor.

Since you may want to read this leaflet again, please do not destroy it until you have finished your medicine.

☐ LAMICTAL® Ⓟ

Glaxo Wellcome

Lamotrigine

Antiepileptic

Information for the Patient: Please read the following information carefully before you start to take Lamictal, even if you have taken this drug before. Please do not discard this leaflet; you may need to read it again.

What is Lamictal: Lamictal, the brand name for lamotrigine, has been prescribed to you to control your epilepsy. Please follow your doctor's recommendations carefully.

Before taking Lamictal: Please inform your doctor:

- If you ever had an unusual or allergic reaction to Lamictal.
- If you are allergic to any component of Lamictal tablets.
- If you are pregnant or are planning to become pregnant.
- If you are breast-feeding (nursing).
- If you are taking any other prescription or over-the-counter medicine.
- If you have liver or kidney disease, or other medical conditions.
- If you consume alcohol on a regular basis.

How to take Lamictal:

- It is very important that you take Lamictal exactly as your doctor instructed.
- You doctor may increase or decrease your medication according to your specific needs. Carefully follow the instructions you were given. Do not change the dose yourself.
- Do not stop taking your medicine abruptly, because your seizures may increase.
- If you happen to miss a dose, do not try to make up for it by doubling up on the dose next time. Just take your next regularly scheduled dose and try not to miss any more.
- Lamictal may be taken with or without food.
- Consult your doctor before taking any other medication, including over-the-counter medicines. Some drugs can produce various side-effects when they are used in combination with Lamictal.
- It is important to keep your appointments for medical checkups.

Precautions while taking Lamictal:

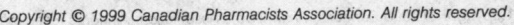

- If you develop **fever, rash, swollen lymph nodes, hives, sore mouth, sore eyes or swelling of lips or tongue,** particularly in the first 6 weeks of therapy, contact your doctor immediately.
- Your doctor will monitor your response to Lamictal on a regular basis. However, if **your seizures get worse,** tell your doctor immediately.
- Different side effects have been reported by patients taking Lamictal. These effects were generally mild and included **dizziness, headaches, double vision (diplopia), poor coordination (ataxia), nausea,**

Lamictal (cont'd)

blurred vision, sleepiness/drowsiness (somnolence), nasal congestion (rhinitis), and rash. However, this does not mean that you will experience such effects, because people can react in different ways to the same medicine.

- If you experience **dizziness, blurred vision, poor coordination, headaches, drowsiness, or similar effects, it is very important that you do not perform any hazardous tasks such as driving or operating machinery.** Consult your doctor.
- If you notice any bothersome or unusal effects while taking Lamictal check with your doctor or pharmacist right away.
- Do not stop taking your medication unless directed by your doctor. Always check that you have an adequate supply of Lamictal. Remember that this medicine was prescribed only for you; never give it to anyone else.

What to do in case of an overdose: If you accidentally take an overdose of Lamictal, contact your doctor or the nearest hospital emergency, even though you may not feel sick.

How to store Lamictal: Store your Lamictal tablets at room temperature (15 to 30°C) in a dry place and protected from light. Cap the bottle tightly immediately after use. **Keep out of reach of children.**

What do Lamictal tablets contain: Lamictal tablets contain lamotrigine and the following nonmedicinal ingredients: cellulose, lactose, magnesium stearate, povidone, sodium starch glycolate and the following coloring agents: 25 mg (white tablets)–none; 100 mg (peach tablets)–sunset yellow FCF lake; 150 mg (cream tablets)–ferric oxide (yellow).

Who produces Lamictal: Lamictal is a patented medicine of: Glaxo Wellcome Inc., Mississauga, Ontario, Canada L5N 6L4.

If you have any other questions, please ask your pharmacist or doctor.

☐ LAMISIL® Tablets ℞

Novartis

Terbinafine HCl

Antifungal

Information for the Patient: Lamisil (Tablets): Take once daily, preferably at the same time each day.

About Your Medicine: Lamisil is used to treat fungal infections of the skin, fingernails and toenails. The treatment should **only be taken as prescribed by your doctor.** Some evidence of infection may still be present at the end of treatment. This will gradually diminish.

If any of the information in this leaflet causes you special concern or if you want additional information about your medicine and its use, contact your doctor or pharmacist. Remember, keep this and all other medicines out of the reach of children and never share your medicines with others.

Before Using This Medicine: Discuss with your doctor the possible side effets that may be caused by this medicine.

Tell your doctor if you:

- are allergic to any medicines, either prescription or nonprescription (OTC), or foods;
- are pregnant or intend to become pregnant while using this medicine;
- are breast-feeding; Lamisil is excreted in breast milk;
- are taking any other medicine, prescription or nonprescription (OTC), especially cimetidine or rifampicin;
- have a history of other medical problems, especially liver diseases such as jaundice (yellowness to skin and/or eyes), kidney disease, alcohol abuse, serious skin reactions, or blood diseases such as anemia.

Proper Use of This Medicine: To help clear up your infection completely, it is very important that you keep taking this medicine for the prescribed treatment period, even if your symptoms begin to clear up or you begin to feel better after a few days. Since fungal infections may be very slow to clear up, stopping your medication too soon can cause the symptoms and the fungal infection to flare up again. Try not to miss any doses. If you do miss a dose, take it as soon as possible. However, if it is almost time for your next dose, skip the missed dose and go back to your regular schedule. Do not double the doses and never make dose changes on your own. Take as prescribed by your doctor.

- Keep your regular appointments with your doctor.
- If you think you have taken an overdose of this medicine, check with your doctor.
- Store at temperatures between 15 and 30°C. Protect tablets from light.

Precautions While Using Lamisil: Some individuals may be either very sensitive to Lamisil or may have had some liver disease in the past. These individuals are at risk of developing abnormal liver function. Stop taking Lamisil and consult your doctor immediately should you develop jaundice (yellowness to skin and/or eyes).

Very occasionally some patients have developed blood abnormalities while being treated with Lamisil. These reactions usually resolve on their own after stopping Lamisil treatment.

If you have any questions about this, check with your doctor.

Always remember to follow your doctor's instructions and have any medical tests done that your doctor may request. Keep your appointments for follow-up visits.

Possible Side Effects of Lamisil: Tell your doctor if you notice any of these possible side effects:

Side Effects

	Signs/Symptoms	Course of Action
Common	Gastrointestinal discomfort (diarrhea, cramps, nausea, vomiting, feeling of fullness or bloating).	These possible side effects may go away during treatment; however, if they continue or are bothersome, contact your doctor.
Less Common	Dry mouth, taste disturbance, tiredness, lack of concentration, nonserious skin disorders (red, itchy skin), headache, pain (back, knee, legs, feet, kidney).	These side effects should be reported to your doctor **as soon as possible.**
Rare and Serious	Severe skin rash, hives. * Sore throat and fever, jaundice (yellowness to skin and/or eyes), unusual fatigue, lack of appetite, dark urine, pale stools.	Stop taking Lamisil and notify your doctor **immediately.** Your doctor will decide whether or not you should continue your Lamisil treatment.

* These signs may indicate blood or liver disorders.

Other side effects not listed above may also occur in some patients. If you notice any other effects, check with your doctor.

Ask your doctor if you do not understand these instructions or want more information.

☐ LARIAM® ℞

Roche

Mefloquine HCl

Antimalarial Agent

Information for the Patient: What is malaria? Malaria is an infectious disease caused by very tiny parasites called plasmodia. These enter human blood from the bite of infected mosquitoes. There are 4 species of these blood parasites which commonly infect humans. Plasmodium falciparum is the most dangerous of these species.

If left untreated, the malaria caused by Plasmodium falciparum can result in death.

Malaria is widespread in tropical and subtropical areas of Africa, Latin America, Asia and the Pacific. Several different types of malaria may exist within one area, each type requiring its own protective medication.

The most common symptoms of a malaria attack are chills followed by fever and sweating. These symptoms may recur at intervals of 48 hours or less and may be associated with headache, diarrhea, abdominal and muscle pain. These last 4 symptoms, which may initially be mistaken for flu, occur as the tiny parasites enter and destroy red blood cells. This follows a period of 1 or more weeks during which the parasites reproduce within the liver. Due to the complex life cycle of the malaria parasite in humans, malaria symptoms can occur in people who are not taking antimalarial medication after they have left a malaria zone. If left untreated, falciparum malaria can rapidly result in anemia (inadequate red blood cells), damage to internal organs such as the liver and spleen, coma and death.

What is Lariam? Lariam is the trade name for an antimalarial product containing the drug mefloquine.

Each Lariam 250 mg tablet contains 250 mg of mefloquine (base) present as mefloquine hydrochloride. The nonmedicinal ingredients are microcrystalline cellulose, lactose, crospovidone, cornstarch, ammonium-calcium alginate, talc, magnesium stearate and poloxamer.

The tablets should be stored at 15 to 30°C. The tablets are sensitive to moisture and should remain in their blister until consumed.

Lariam may be used to prevent or treat the symptoms of a malaria attack caused by Plasmodium falciparum in the areas where this parasite is no longer affected by chloroquine, the drug which is used most commonly against malaria. Lariam may also be used to prevent or treat the symptoms of malaria caused by Plasmodium vivax.

Lariam does not prevent the mosquito from biting and infecting humans nor does it prevent the first stage of malaria which involves parasite reproduction within the liver. Lariam destroys the parasite after its release from the liver into the blood.

Proper Use of Lariam: To Prevent a Malaria Attack: The recommended adult "prophylactic" (preventative) dose is 1 tablet once a week. Your doctor will reduce this dose for your children according to their weight.

Lariam should not be given to children less than 3 months old or weighing less than 5 kg.

Lariam should be taken:

- For 1 week before arrival in a malaria zone (if this is not possible, your doctor may prescribe a so-called loading dose),
- throughout your stay and,
- for 4 weeks after leaving the area.

The reason for taking the drug before reaching the danger zone is to allow blood levels of mefloquine to reach effective levels. It also allows your doctor, when possible, to test your tolerance to the medication and for you to get into the routine of taking the tablets. The reason for taking the tablets for 4 weeks after leaving the area where malaria is found relates to the initial phase where the parasite reproduces in the liver. This period may not be associated with any symptoms. It is important, therefore, that you keep taking Lariam according to the dosage schedule for the full time recommended by your doctor. If you miss taking a dose, take it as soon as you realize you have forgotten and then take each remaining dose according to the dosage schedule, counting from the day that you took the missed dose. **Do not take more than 1 tablet in any 1 week except for initial loading dose option.**

Lariam should be taken with food and with plenty of water, if possible, in order to minimize the possibility of experiencing unwanted side effects, such as upset stomach. Do not chew the tablets. If unable to swallow the tablets whole or if administering them to a child, the tablets may be crushed and suspended in a small amount of water, milk or other beverage. After returning from your trip, be sure to return to your doctor when scheduled. If you will be taking Lariam for a prolonged period, it is advisable to consult with your doctor prior to your departure as to what medical follow up may be necessary while you are on Lariam prophylaxis.

To Treat a Malaria Attack: If you suspect that you have contracted malaria, immediately contact a doctor. Your physician may recommend specific self-treatment in certain instances where a physician may not be available within 12 to 24 hours of onset of symptoms. Be sure to contact a qualified physician as soon as possible after self-treatment.

Mefloquine should not be given to children less than 3 months old or weighing less than 5 kg. If you choose to take children less than 3 months old or weighing less than 5 kg to a malaria zone, you should discuss with your physician the action to take if they contract malaria.

General Precautions with Lariam: Lariam has been prescribed for the prevention or treatment of a very specific infection. **Use Lariam only for the trip for which it was prescribed.** Your doctor has decided that Lariam is suitable protection against a form of malaria found in the regions to which you are travelling. However, it may not provide protection against other forms of malaria found in that same area or elsewhere.

Do not give Lariam to anyone else. Your doctor has decided that Lariam is suitable protection for you. If given to someone for whom Lariam is unsuitable, that person may not receive appropriate antimalarial protection in the area of destination and in addition, may be at risk of experiencing adverse reactions. Keep Lariam out of the reach of children.

You should inform your doctor of all medications which you are currently taking. In particular, medications that contain quinine, quinidine, or chloroquine; other antimalarial drugs (halofantrine); anticonvulsants (valproic acid, carbamazepine, phenobarbital, phenytoin); and medications which may affect the heart such as certain heart and high blood pressure medications (beta-blockers, calcium channel blockers), antihistamines, and certain antidepressants (tricyclic antidepressants). Taking these or certain other drugs with Lariam may add to the unwanted effects of Lariam. Unless you are sure that the other medications which you are taking will not interact with Lariam, consult with your doctor.

Special Precautions with Lariam: Lariam should not be used by:

1. Persons with a known sensitivity to mefloquine or related compounds. (Check with your doctor).
2. Persons with a history of psychiatric disturbances.
3. Persons with a history of convulsions.
4. Persons suffering from severe liver or cardiac disease.
5. Women who are or may become pregnant.
6. Nursing mothers.
7. Children less than 3 months old or weighing less than 5 kg since the tablet cannot be accurately subdivided into less than ¼ tablet.

What are the possible unwanted effects of Lariam: The following unwanted effects have been reported to occur with Lariam: nausea, vomiting, dizziness, lightheadedness or loss of balance, headache, sleepiness, inability to sleep, abnormal dreams, loose stools or diarrhea, and abdominal pain. In rare cases, loss of appetite, abnormal heartbeat, itching of the skin or skin rash, hair loss, eyesight problems, muscle pains, convulsions, and disturbances of mood (depressed mood, mental confusion, anxiety states) may occur. Because many of these symptoms accompany malaria, it is often difficult to tell whether the symptoms are due to malaria or are unwanted effects of Lariam.

When Lariam is used as **malaria prevention,** these events usually subside within a short period of time after drug administration. If these adverse events are not severe in nature and are tolerable, it is in your best interest to continue Lariam prophylaxis since the consequences of contracting malaria are cause for greater concern.

It is best to avoid alcoholic drinks during treatment with Lariam.

You should not operate vehicles or other hazardous machinery or engage in any other activity requiring your full attention until you know how you react to this medicine.

If you experience unexplained anxiety, depression, restlessness or irritability, or confusion, stop taking Lariam and consult a doctor immediately.

Pregnancy and Nursing: If you are pregnant, it may be unwise to travel in a malaria zone. You should avoid becoming pregnant while in such areas. During pregnancy, a malarial infection is dangerous for both the mother-to-be and the unborn child. If a trip into a malaria zone area is unavoidable, be sure to discuss all of your travel plans with your doctor. He will advise you as to which form of protection against malaria is best for you.

You should avoid becoming pregnant while you are taking Lariam and for 3 months after the last dose. Lariam has caused birth defects in the offspring of pregnant laboratory animals. The first 3 months of pregnancy are of particular concern in fetal development.

Consult a doctor if you are planning to become pregnant or if you do become pregnant while using Lariam, so that he may advise you about the risks involved in continuing, stopping or changing antimalarial medication.

Lariam passes into breast milk in small amounts which are insufficient to protect your baby against malaria.

How Can You Further Protect Yourself Against Malaria? The best way to minimize the possibility of contracting malaria is to reduce your contact with mosquitoes, which are more prevalent from dusk to dawn. This includes avoiding the outdoors in the evenings, the wearing of light-colored clothes which cover most of the body, applying mosquito repellent to uncovered areas of skin, sleeping under mosquito netting and spraying insecticides in sleeping quarters. For your best protection, consult your doctor or local travel clinic on these subjects.

☐ LESCOL® 🅿
Novartis Pharmaceuticals
Fluvastatin Sodium
Lipid Metabolism Regulator

Information for the Patient: Full prescribing information is available to the physician and pharmacist.

Lescol is the proprietary name of Novartis Pharmaceuticals Canada Inc. for fluvastatin sodium.

Lescol lowers the level of cholesterol, particularly low density lipoprotein (LDL) cholesterol, in the blood. Lescol reduces cholesterol production by the liver and induces some changes of cholesterol transport and disposition in the blood and tissues.

Lescol is available only with your physician's prescription. It is to be used as an adjunct to a medically recommended and carefully supervised diet for the long-term treatment of hypercholesterolemia and is not a substitute for such a diet. In addition, depending on your condition, your physician may recommend an appropriate regimen of exercise, weight control and other measures. If you suffer from coronary heart disease, your physician may also prescribe Lescol to slow the progression of coronary atherosclerosis.

Use only as specifically directed. Do not alter the dosage unless ordered to do so by your physician. Check with your physician before discontinuing medication since this may result in an increase of your blood lipids.

Before using this medication, you should have told your physician if:
- you have already taken Lescol or any other lipid-lowering agent of the same class such as lovastatin (Mevacor), simvastatin (Zocor), atorvastatin (Lipitor) or pravastatin (Pravachol) and have developed an allergy or intolerance to any of them,
- you suffer from liver disease,
- you are pregnant, intend to become pregnant or are breast-feeding, or intend to breast-feed,
- you are taking any other medication, particularly corticosteroids, cyclosporine (Neoral), gemfibrozil (Lopid), anticoagulant (e.g., warfarin (Warfilone), phenytoin, oral hypoglycemics, NSAIDs, erythromycin, lipid lowering doses of niacin (nicotinic acid) and nefazodone (Serzone).

Proper Use of this Medicine:
- Lescol administered as a single dose should be taken with or after the evening meal or at bedtime. Lescol administered in 2 divided doses should be taken in the morning and in the evening, with or after meals. Take only the amount directed by your physician.
- Your physician will monitor your clinical condition and your blood tests at regular intervals. It is important to have these check-ups done on schedule. Please keep your appointments accurately.
- Avoid excessive alcohol intake.
- Notify your physician about any illness which may develop during your treatment with Lescol and about any new prescription or nonprescription medication you may take. If you require medical help for other reasons, inform the attending physician that you are taking Lescol.
- Notify your physician if you are going to have major surgery or have sustained a severe injury.
- Notify your physician of any muscle pain, tenderness or weakness developing during treatment with Lescol (see Side Effects).
- The safety of Lescol in adolescents and children has not been established.
- You should be aware that the effects of Lescol in the prevention of heart attacks, arteriosclerosis or heart disease are not yet known.
- Lescol is contraindicated during pregnancy since its use in the event of pregnancy may harm the unborn. Only female patients who are highly unlikely to conceive can be candidates for Lescol treatment. In the event of pregnancy during treatment, Lescol should be discontinued and the physician should be informed.

Side Effects: Along with its intended action, any medication may cause unwanted effects.

Check with your physician **as soon as possible** if any of the following side effects occurs: aching muscles, muscle cramping, tiredness or weakness, fever.

Other side effects may occasionally occur which usually do not require stopping treatment. They may come and go during treatment without any particular danger, but you should mention them to your physician, without undue delay, if they become persistent or bothersome. Such adverse experiences include abdominal pain/indigestion, constipation, diarrhea, nausea, headache, insomnia, dizziness and skin rashes.

This medicine is prescribed for your specific medical problem and for your own use only. Do not give to other people.

Keep all medicines out of the reach of children.

If you need any further information, ask your physician or your pharmacist.

☐ LEVOTEC 🅿
Technilab
Levothyroxine Sodium
Hypothyroidism Therapy

Information for the Patient: Levotec (levothyroxine sodium tablets USP): 25, 50, 75, 100, 112, 125, 150, 175, 200 and 300 μg tablets.

Patients on thyroid preparations and parents of children on thyroid therapy should be informed that replacement therapy is to be taken essentially for life, with the exception of cases of transient hypothyroidism, usually associated with thyroiditis, and in those patients receiving a therapeutic trial of the drug.

Patients should immediately report to the physician experiences during the course of therapy of any signs or symptoms of thyroid hormone toxicity, e.g., chest pain, increased pulse rate, palpitations, excessive sweating, heat intolerance, nervousness, or any other unusual event.

Patients with concurrent diabetes mellitus or who are on concurrent oral anticoagulant therapy should be warned of the need for close monitoring and possible dosage adjustments.

Parents should be warned that partial loss of hair may be experienced by children in the first few months of thyroid therapy, but this is usually a transient phenomenon and later recovery is normally the rule.

☐ LIORESAL® Intrathecal 🅿
Novartis Pharmaceuticals
Baclofen
Muscle Relaxant—Antispastic

Information for the Patient: Introduction: Lioresal Intrathecal belongs to a group of medicines called muscle relaxants. It is used to reduce and relieve the excessive tension in your muscles (spasms) occurring in various illnesses such as, for example, multiple sclerosis, diseases or injuries of the spinal cord, and certain brain disorders.

This leaflet provides you and those caring for you with important information about Lioresal Intrathecal and the risks of this mode of treatment. Please read it carefully. If you want to know more or have any questions, please ask your doctor.

What is Lioresal Intrathecal? Lioresal Intrathecal contains an active substance called baclofen. It is available as a solution which is contained in an ampul (glass vial).

The solution is injected or infused into the fluid space around the spinal cord by use of a special pump which is implanted under the skin. From the pump a constant amount of the solution is delivered into the fluid space around the spinal cord through a tiny tube.

Due to the beneficial effect on muscle contractions and the consequent relief from pain, Lioresal Intrathecal improves your mobility, makes it easier for you to manage your daily activities without aid, and facilitates physiotherapy.

Before Treatment with Lioresal Intrathecal: Lioresal Intrathecal is suitable for many patients with muscle spasms, but not for all. Therefore, tell your doctor if you:
- have had any unusual sensitivity (rash or other possible signs of allergy) to previous baclofen (e.g., Lioresal tablets) use
- have any kind of infection
- have certain mental illnesses accompanied by confusion
- suffer from epilepsy (seizures)
- have or have had disorders of the heart or kidneys, breathing problems, or acute pain in your stomach

Some medicines may interfere with the action of Lioresal Intrathecal. Tell your doctor what other prescription and nonprescription (over the counter) medicines, if any, you are taking. Your doctor may change the dosage or sometimes stop one of the medicines.

Do not drink alcohol during treatment with Lioresal Intrathecal.

Lioresal Intrathecal may make you feel sleepy or dizzy. So be careful when driving a car or using a machine or doing other things that need your careful attention.

Women should tell their doctor if they are pregnant, plan to become pregnant or are breast-feeding. The doctor will decide if you may receive Lioresal Intrathecal in these special situations. Only very small quantities of Lioresal pass into the breast milk. As long as your doctor agrees in your individual case, and your baby is closely watched for side effects, you may breast-feed.

Overdose: Signs of overdose may appear suddenly or insidiously e.g., by a malfunctioning of the pump. It is very important that you and those caring for you recognize signs of overdosage. If you experience any one or a combination of the following symptoms, tell your doctor without delay as the amount of drug you receive may be too high:

- excessive muscular weakness
- sleepiness
- lightheadedness/dizziness
- excessive salivation
- feeling sick and/or vomiting
- difficulties in breathing, seizures or loss of consciousness

What Side Effects Can Lioresal Intrathecal Have? Like all medicines, Lioresal Intrathecal, along with its desired effects, may also cause some unwanted effects. These occur more often early in treatment when you are in hospital, but may also occur later and should be checked with your doctor.

More common: drowsiness, weakness in the legs, dizziness, headache, sleepiness, feeling sick and/or vomiting, tingling in hands and feet, slurred speech, blurred vision.

Less common: unusually slow heartbeat, constipation.

Rare: swelling of the ankles, feet, or lower legs, loss of muscle coordination, insomnia, memory loss, confusion, feeling of anxiety, feeling of depression, mood or mental changes, hallucinations, difficulty in swallowing, decreased appetite, dry mouth, itching, continuous uncontrollable eye movements, diarrhea, urinary incontinence.

Tell your doctor if you notice any other effect.

How to Use Lioresal Intrathecal: Lioresal Intrathecal can be administered only by experienced doctors by direct injection or infusion into the fluid space around the spinal cord, for which special medical equipment is needed. For this reason hospitalization will be necessary, at least at the beginning of therapy.

At a first stage the doctor will find out if Lioresal improves your muscular spasm. If this is the case a special pump will be implanted under your skin, which permits continuous delivery of small quantities of drug.

It may take several days to find out the optimal dose of the drug needed for your individual situation, and close checks by your doctor are essential. Once the optimum treatment is established, it is very important that your doctor checks your progress and functioning of the pump at regular visits.

It is of utmost importance that appointments to refill the pump are kept, otherwise spasm may recur.

Should you experience a gradual or sudden reappearance of spasms, contact your doctor immediately.

Please consult the pump manufacturer's literature for information regarding proper home care of the pump and the insertion site.

☐ LIPIDIL MICRO® ℞

Fournier

Fenofibrate (Micronized)

Lipid Metabolism Regulator

Information for the Patient: Full prescribing information is available to doctors and pharmacists on request.

Lipidil Micro is the registered trademark of Laboratoires Fournier S.C.A. for micronized fenofibrate.

Lipidil Micro reduces blood cholesterol, in particular cholesterol associated with low and very low density lipoproteins (LDL and VLDL-cholesterol). Lipidil Micro also reduces high triglyceride levels associated with hypercholesterolemia. Blood uric acid levels are also reduced by Lipidil Micro treatment. The mechanism of action of Lipidil Micro is not fully established.

Lipidil Micro is only available on prescription. This medicine should only be used to supplement an appropriate diet recommended and followed up by your doctor for the long-term treatment of raised lipid levels; prescription of this medicine in no way replaces dietary treatment. In addition, depending on the situation, your doctor may recommend further physical exercise, weight loss or other measures.

Comply exactly to the terms of the prescription. Do not change the dose without your doctor's advice. Consult your doctor before stopping treatment since to do so may result in an increase in your blood lipid levels.

Before starting treatment with this medicine, your doctor must know:

—if you have taken Lipidil Micro before and if it caused an allergy or was otherwise poorly tolerated,
—if you suffer from liver or kidney problems,
—if you have gallbladder or gallstone problems,
—if you are pregnant, or intend to become pregnant, or are breast-feeding, or intend to breast-feed,
—if you are taking other medicines, in particular an oral anticoagulant such as warfarin (Warfilone).

Proper Use of the Medicine:

- Lipidil Micro should be taken as a once-a-day dose with one of the main meals.
  It is particularly important to follow this advice because Lipidil Micro is less well absorbed and hence less effective when not taken with food.

—Your doctor will ask you to have regular medical check-ups and laboratory tests. It is important to respect the dates proposed: we strongly recommend that you faithfully keep these appointments.
—Inform your doctor of any health problem that occurs while you are taking Lipidil Micro as well as any prescription or nonprescription medicine. If you need other medical treatment let the doctor know that you are taking Lipidil Micro.
—Tell your doctor if you feel in any way unwell while taking Lipidil Micro (see Unwanted Effects).
—Safety of use in children and young adolescents has not been established with Lipidil Micro.
—The effect of Lipidil Micro in preventing heart attacks, atherosclerosis or heart disease is not known.
—Lipidil Micro is contraindicated during pregnancy. In the event of pregnancy during treatment, Lipidil Micro should be discontinued and the physician should be informed.
—It is not recommended to take Lipidil Micro while breast-feeding.

Unwanted Effects: In addition to its intended action, any medicine may cause unwanted effects.

Unwanted effects may occur in certain patients. They may appear and disappear without involving any particular risk but if any unwanted effects persist or become bothersome, you must let your doctor know without delay. Such unwanted effects may consist of abdominal pain, constipation, diarrhea, nausea, headache, dizziness, skin reactions, muscular pain or cramps, fatigue.

This medicine is prescribed for a particular health problem and for your personal use. Do not give it to other persons.

Keep all medicines out of the reach of children.

If you want further information, ask your doctor or pharmacist.

☐ LIPITOR™ ℞

Parke-Davis

Atorvastatin Calcium

Lipid Metabolism Regulator

Information for the Patient: Lipitor Tablets: Please read this information carefully. If you have questions, talk to your doctor or pharmacist.

About Lipitor tablets: Your doctor has prescribed these pills to help lower your cholesterol. High cholesterol levels can cause heart disease by clogging the blood vessels that feed blood and oxygen to your heart.

Lipitor is just part of the treatment your doctor will plan with you to help keep you healthy. Depending on your health and your lifestyle, your doctor may recommend:

- a change in your diet to control your weight and reduce your cholesterol;
- exercise that is right for you;
- quitting smoking or avoiding smoky places;
- giving up alcohol or drinking less.

Follow your doctor's instructions carefully.

Lipitor belongs to the class of medicines known as HMG-CoA reductase inhibitors. It is effective in reducing low density lipoprotein cholesterol (LDL-C) in the blood. You can only get Lipitor by prescription after seeing your doctor. It is made with the drug atorvastatin. Lipitor

Lipitor (cont'd)

is the brand name of atorvastatin and is manufactured by Parke-Davis, a Division of Warner-Lambert Canada Inc.

Before you use this medicine: Some people should not take Lipitor. Talk to your doctor if:
- You have liver disease.
- You are pregnant, planning to get pregnant, or think you might be pregnant. This medicine should not be used during pregnancy. If you get pregnant during treatment, you should stop taking this medicine and tell your doctor immediately.
- You are breast-feeding your baby. This medicine may be included in your breast milk.
- You have taken any of the following medicines before, and you had a reaction:
  - Lipitor (atorvastatin)
  - Zocor (simvastatin)
  - Mevacor (lovastatin)
  - Pravachol (pravastatin)
  - Lescol (fluvastatin)
  - Baycol (cerivastatin)
- You are taking any other medicines, prescription or nonprescription, especially:
  - corticosteroids (cortisone-like medicines)
  - cyclosporine (Sandimmune)
  - gemfibrozil (Lopid)
  - fenofibrate (Lipidil Micro) or bezafibrate (Bezalip)
  - lipid-lowering doses of niacin (nicotinic acid)
  - erythromycin or azole antifungal agents (ketoconazole or itraconazole)
  - nefazodone (Serzone)
  - terfenadine
- Please note that there is little experience with this medicine in adolescents (teenagers) and children.

How to use this medicine: We often cannot see or feel the problems that high cholesterol causes until a lot of time has passed. That's why it is important to take these pills just as your doctor tells you to. You and your doctor will be watching your cholesterol levels to get them down to a safe range. Here are some important tips.
- Keep your medicine at room temperature (15 to 25°C), away from warm or damp places like the bathroom or kitchen.
- Follow the plan that you and your doctor make for diet, exercise and weight control.
- Take your Lipitor as a single dose. It does not matter if you take it with food or without food. Your doctor will usually tell you to take it in the evenings.
- If you miss taking a pill, take it as soon as you can. But if it is almost time for your next dose, skip the missed dose and just take the next dose. **Don't take a double dose.**
- Never change the dose unless your doctor tells you to.
- Don't drink too much alcohol while you are taking Lipitor. Talk to your doctor about how much is too much for you.
- If you get sick, have an operation, or need medical treatment while you are taking Lipitor, inform your doctor or pharmacist that you are taking Lipitor.
- If you have to take any other medicine—prescription or nonprescription—while you are taking Lipitor, talk to your doctor or pharmacist first.
- If you have to see a different doctor for any reason, be sure to inform them that you are taking Lipitor.
- Tell your doctor if you have any muscle pain, tenderness, soreness or weakness during treatment with Lipitor (see Side Effects).
- Talk to your doctor right away if you feel any side effects (see below).

Side effects and what you should do: Most people do not have any problems with side effects when taking this medicine. However, all medicines can cause unwanted side effects. Check with your doctor or pharmacist promptly if any of the following persist or become troublesome:
- stomach pain or upset
- gas
- constipation
- diarrhea
- vomiting or throwing up
- headache
- skin rash

Talk to your doctor **right away** if you have:
- muscle pain that you can't explain
- muscle tenderness or soreness
- weakness and not feeling well
- fever

Some people may have other side effects. If you notice anything unusual, talk to your doctor or pharmacist.

Ingredients: The active ingredient in your Lipitor tablets is atorvastatin. The tablets are available in 3 strengths: 10, 20 and 40 mg. The other commonly used ingredients in your Lipitor tablets are:
— calcium carbonate
— croscarmellose sodium
— lactose monohydrate
— microcrystalline cellulose
— polyethylene glycol
— titanium dioxide
— simethicone emulsion
— candelilla wax
— hydroxypropyl cellulose
— magnesium stearate
— hydroxypropyl methylcellulose
— talc
— polysorbate 80

Important: Your doctor prescribed this medicine for you only.
Don't give your pills to anyone else.
Always keep medicine well out of the reach of children.
Keep your medicine at room temperature (15 to 25°C), away from warm and damp places like the bathroom or kitchen.

Do you need more information? Please talk to your doctor or your pharmacist.

☐ LOCACORTEN® VIOFORM® Ⓟ

Novartis Pharmaceuticals

Flumethasone Pivalate—Clioquinol

Topical Corticosteroid—Antibacterial—Antifungal

Information for the Patient: Please read this information carefully before starting Locacorten Vioform treatment.

What is Locacorten Vioform? The active ingredients of Locacorten Vioform are flumethasone pivalate and clioquinol. Flumethasone pivalate belongs to a group of medicines called corticosteroids. Clioquinol is an anti-infective agent.

What is Locacorten Vioform for? In infected, inflammatory skin diseases, Locacorten Vioform relieves symptoms such as itching and redness. It also stops the growth of bacteria and fungi that cause certain types of skin infections.

Before starting treatment with Locacorten Vioform: Be sure to tell your doctor:
- if you have kidney or liver disease,
- if you have ever had any unusual or allergic reactions to corticosteroids, iodine or iodine-containing preparations, clioquinol or hydroxyquinolines, or any other substances, including foods and dyes,
- if you are pregnant or intend to become pregnant while using Locacorten Vioform, or if you are breast-feeding.

In these cases your doctor will decide whether you may apply Locacorten Vioform to your skin.

How to use Locacorten Vioform: Locacorten Vioform must be used as directed by your doctor. Do not use more of it, do not use it more often, and do not use it for a longer period of time than your doctor has specified.

Apply Locacorten Vioform as directed in a thin layer to the affected areas only. Do not wrap or bandage the areas treated unless otherwise instructed by your doctor.

Locacorten Vioform is for **external use only.** Do not take by mouth.

What side effects can Locacorten Vioform have? Like all medicines, Locacorten Vioform may cause some unwanted effects in addition to its desired effects. If redness, burning, itching or other signs not present before using Locacorten Vioform occur during treatment, consult your doctor or pharmacist.

If there is no improvement or if your skin condition becomes worse after you have used Locacorten Vioform for 1 week, see your doctor.

Remember that Locacorten Vioform has been prescribed for your present medical problem only. Do not use it to treat other skin conditions without checking with your doctor first.

Other Precautions: Do not use Locacorten Vioform in the eyes and be very cautious when using it near the eyes. If it gets in the eyes accidentally, flush them at once with plenty of water.

Locacorten Vioform may turn yellow when exposed to the air. Locacorten Vioform may stain hair, fabric, skin or nails.

Locacorten Vioform is not recommended in children under 2 years of age.

Storage: Protect from heat (store between 15 and 30°C) and freezing. Keep out of reach of children.

□ LOCACORTEN® VIOFORM® Eardrops

Novartis Pharmaceuticals

Flumethasone Pivalate—Clioquinol

Topical Aural Corticosteroid—Antibacterial—Antifungal

Information for the Patient: Please read this information carefully before starting Locacorten Vioform Eardrops treatment.

What are Locacorten Vioform Eardrops? Locacorten Vioform Eardrops contain flumethasone pivalate, which belongs to a group of medicines called corticosteroids, and clioquinol, an anti-infective agent.

What do Locacorten Vioform Eardrops do? Locacorten Vioform Eardrops relieve the symptoms of ear infections, such as itching and redness. They also stop the growth of bacteria and fungi that cause ear infections.

Before using Locacorten Vioform Eardrops: Be sure to tell your doctor:

- if you have ever had any unusual or allergic reactions to corticosteroids, iodine or iodine-containing preparations, clioquinol or hydroxyquinolines, or any other substances, including foods and dyes.
- if you have any problems with your ear, including a punctured eardrum.
- if you are pregnant or intend to become pregnant while using Locacorten Vioform Eardrops, or if you are breast-feeding.

In these cases, your doctor will decide if you may use Locacorten Vioform Eardrops.

How to use Locacorten Vioform Eardrops: Locacorten Vioform Eardrops must be used as directed by your doctor. Do not use more of it, do not use it more often, and do not use it for a longer period of time than your doctor has specified.

Some ear infections cause a discharge. As your ear must be clean for Locacorten Vioform to effectively combat the infection, your doctor or pharmacist may show you how to clean your ears before instilling the drops. You may warm the ear drops to body temperature (but not warmer) before applying them to the ear by holding the bottle in your hands.

To instill the ear drops:

1) Lie down with the infected ear up and pull down gently on the ear lobe.
2) Instill the prescribed number of drops in the ear canal.
3) Gently push on the ear until the drops are evenly spread in the ear before sitting up.

To avoid contamination of the ear drops, do not let the dropper touch any surface (including the ear).

Keep the container tightly closed after use.

Locacorten Vioform Eardrops are for **external use only.** Do not take by mouth.

What side effects can Locacorten Vioform Eardrops have? Like all medicines, Locacorten Vioform Eardrops may cause some unwanted effects, in addition to their desired ones. If redness, burning, itching or other signs not present before using Locacorten Vioform Eardrops occur, stop treatment, and consult your doctor or pharmacist.

If there is no improvement or if your ear infection becomes worse after you have used Locacorten Vioform Eardrops for 1 week, see your doctor.

Other Precautions: Remember that Locacorten Vioform Eardrops have been prescribed for your present medical problem only. Do not use it to treat other ear conditions without checking with your doctor first.

Do not use Locacorten Vioform Eardrops in the eyes. If it gets in the eyes accidentally, flush them at once with plenty of water.

Locacorten Vioform Eardrops may stain hair, skin, nails and fabric yellow.

Locacorten Vioform Eardrops are not suitable for children under 2 years of age.

Storage: Protect from heat (store between 15 and 30°C) and light. Locacorten Vioform Eardrops may turn yellow when exposed to air and may cause staining of the skin, nails, hair or fabrics.

Keep out of the reach of children.

□ LONITEN®

Pharmacia & Upjohn

Minoxidil

Antihypertensive

Information for the Patient: Loniten tablets contain minoxidil, a powerful medicine for the treatment of high blood pressure. Loniten is used for the treatment of severe hypertension that is difficult to control. It is taken with other medicines.

Be sure to take all of your medicines for high blood pressure according to your doctor's instructions. Your doctor will need to see you regularly while you are taking Loniten. Be sure to keep all your appointments or to arrange for new ones if you must miss one. Do not stop taking Loniten unless your doctor tells you to. Do not give any of your medication to other people.

What is Loniten? Loniten tablets contain minoxidil which is a powerful drug for lowering the blood pressure. It works by relaxing and enlarging certain small blood vessels so that blood flows through them more easily.

Who Should Take Loniten? There are many people with high blood pressure, but most of them do not need Loniten. Loniten is used **only** when your doctor decides that:

1. Your high blood pressure is severe;
2. Your high blood pressure is causing symptoms or damage of vital organs and
3. Other medicines did not work well enough or had very disturbing side effects.

Loniten should be taken only when a doctor prescribes it. Never give any of your Loniten tablets, or any other high blood pressure medicine, to a friend or a relative.

Pregnancy: In some cases, doctors may prescribe Loniten for women who are pregnant or who are planning to have children. However, its safe use in pregnancy has not been established. If you are pregnant or are planning to become pregnant, be sure to tell your doctor.

How to Take Loniten? Usually, your doctor will prescribe two other medicines along with Loniten. These will help lower blood pressure and will help prevent undesired effects of Loniten.

Often, when a medicine like Loniten lowers blood pressure, your body tries to return the blood pressure to the original, higher level. It does this by retaining the water and salt (so there will be more fluid to pump) and by making your heart beat faster.

To prevent this, your doctor will usually prescribe a water tablet to remove the extra salt and water from your body and another medicine to slow your heartbeat.

You must follow your doctor's instructions exactly, taking all the prescribed medicines, in the right amounts, each day. These medicines will decrease the side effects you might otherwise have and will also help keep your blood pressure down.

You may take Loniten with water or with other liquids, either with or between meals. Loniten tablets come in two strengths (2½ mg and 10 mg) that are marked on each tablet. Pay close attention to the tablet markings to be sure you are taking the correct strength. Your doctor may prescribe half a tablet; the tablets are scored (partly cut on one side) so that you can easily break them.

When you first start taking Loniten, your doctor may need to see you often in order to adjust your dosage. Take all your medicine according to the schedule prescribed by your doctor. Do not skip any doses. If you should forget a dose of Loniten, wait until it is time for your next dose, then continue with your regular schedule. Remember, do not stop taking Loniten, or any of your other high blood pressure medicines, without checking with your doctor. Make sure that any doctor treating or examining you knows that you are taking high blood pressure medicines, including Loniten.

Warning Signals: Even if you take all your medicines correctly, you may have side effects. If any of the following warning signals occur, you must call your doctor immediately as your treatment may have to be adjusted.

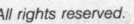

1. Increase in heart rate: You should measure your heart rate by counting your pulse rate while you are resting. If you have an

Loniten (cont'd)

increase of 20 beats or more per minute over your normal pulse, contact your doctor. Ask your doctor how often to check your pulse.
2. Weight Gain: You should weigh yourself daily. If you quickly gain 5 or more pounds (2 or more kg), or if there is any swelling or puffiness in the face, hands, ankles, or stomach area, this could be a sign that you are retaining body fluids and you should call your doctor. A smaller weight gain (2 or 3 pounds or 1 to 1.5 kg) often occurs when treatment is started. You may lose this extra weight with continued treatment.
3. Also call your physician if you notice:
   a) increased difficulty in breathing, especially when lying down,
   b) new or worsening of pain in the chest, arm or shoulder or signs of severe indigestion and
   c) dizziness, lightheadedness or fainting.

Hair Growth: About 8 out of 10 patients who have taken Loniten noticed that fine body hair grew darker or longer on certain parts of the body. This happened about 3 to 6 weeks after beginning treatment. The hair may first be noticed on the forehead and temples, between the eyebrows, or on the upper part of the cheeks. Later, hair may grow on the back, arms, legs, or scalp. Although hair growth may not be noticeable to some patients, it often is bothersome in women and children. Unwanted hair can be controlled with a hair remover or by shaving. The extra hair is not permanent, it disappears within 1 to 6 months of stopping Loniten. Nevertheless, you should not stop taking Loniten without first talking to your doctor.

A few patients have developed a rash or breast tenderness while taking Loniten tablets, but this is unusual.

☐ LOSEC® P

Astra

Omeprazole Magnesium

H+, K+-ATPase Inhibitor

Information for the Patient: Read this leaflet carefully. It contains general points about Losec and should add to more specific advice from your doctor or pharmacist.

What is Losec used for and how does it work? Losec is the brand name for a drug called omeprazole.

The most common uses of Losec are:

- for stomach ulcers or for duodenal ulcers, including ulcers caused by infection with a bacterium called Helicobacter pylori;
- for ulcers caused by your medicine for pain and joint problems (NSAID-associated gastric and duodenal ulcers);
- for reflux esophagitis (tissue damage caused by stomach contents flowing back up the food pipe);
- and for symptoms of reflux disease such as heartburn and regurgitation.

Losec may also be used in rare conditions like "Zollinger-Ellison syndrome," where the stomach produces large amounts of acid. Losec works by reducing the amount of acid made in your stomach. This helps in treating acid-related and bacteria-related stomach problems.

Your doctor will have explained why you are being treated with Losec and will have told you what dose to take. Follow those directions carefully. They may differ from the information contained in this leaflet.

What is in Losec? Each Losec tablet contains omeprazole magnesium as the active ingredient. In addition, it contains the following nonmedicinal ingredients (listed in alphabetical order): hydroxypropyl methylcellulose, iron oxide, mannitol, methacrylic acid copolymer, microcrystalline cellulose, paraffin, polyethylene glycol, sodium starch glycolate, sodium stearyl fumarate, talc and titanium dioxide.

Check with your doctor if you think you might be allergic to any of the above ingredients.

What should I tell my doctor before taking Losec? Tell your doctor:

- about **all** health problems you have now or have had in the past;
- about other medicines you take, including ones you can buy without a prescription;
- if you are allergic to "nonmedicinal" substances which may be present in Losec (See "What is in Losec?");
- if you are pregnant, plan to become pregnant or are breast-feeding.

How do I take Losec properly? Take all doses of Losec, as recommended by your doctor, even when you feel well. Daily doses are needed to help damaged areas heal. The recommended dose for treating acute disease is 10 to 40 mg once a day for 2 to 8 weeks. Your doctor may recommend that you continue taking Losec 10 to 40 mg to control symptoms of reflux disease, or to prevent severe cases of reflux esophagitis from coming back, or Losec 20 mg to prevent ulcers from returning while you continue to take your medicine for pain and joint problems.

Losec may be used in combinations which include clarithromycin, amoxicillin and/or metronidazole (antibiotic drugs) for 1 week to get rid of ulcers caused by Helicobacter pylori if you have had ulcers. If your ulcer is bothering you, your doctor may recommend further treatment with Losec to make sure that your ulcer is healed.

If you are given Losec in combination with antibiotic drugs, it is important that you take all medications at the correct time of day and for the entire treatment period, to ensure they will work properly. Studies have shown that patients, who take their medications as prescribed, have better ulcer healing rates and greater success getting rid of their H. pylori infection.

Take Losec until your doctor tells you to stop. Even if you start to feel better in a few days, your symptoms may return if Losec is stopped too soon. Losec needs to be taken for the full duration of treatment to help correct acid problems.

If you miss a dose of Losec and remember within 12 hours, take it as soon as possible. Then go back to your regular schedule. However, if more than 12 hours have passed when you remember, do not take the missed tablet. Just take your next dose on time.

Losec may be taken with food or on an empty stomach.

How do I use the Losec compliance pack? Losec comes in a 14-day or 28-day pack which contains 1 or 2 blister strips of 14 days each. The blister strips are labelled with the days of the week.

To start, take a tablet in the first row that matches the day you begin the pack. Then take a tablet on each of the following days until you complete the blister strip.

To treat ulcers caused by Helicobacter pylori, take one 20 mg tablet from each row (2 tablets per day) that match the day you begin the pack.

Are there any side effects? Like any medication, Losec may cause side effects in some people. Side effects that do occur are usually mild and go away a short time after starting Losec. Tell your doctor if any of the following are severe or bother you for more than 1 or 2 days: nausea, stomach upset, diarrhea, constipation, headache, or skin rash. These may not be caused by Losec in your case, but only a doctor can assess this.

Other unwanted effects which cannot be predicted may occur in rare cases. If you experience any bothersome or unusual effects while using Losec, check with your doctor or pharmacist.

What should I do in case of overdose? Call your doctor or pharmacist right away in case of an overdose. However, no severe symptoms have been seen in patients who have taken doses up to 400 mg.

Where should I keep Losec? Keep all tablets sealed in the blister strips until it is time for a dose. If you do not, moisture from the air may damage the tablets.

Remember to keep Losec well out of reach of children. Keep the compliance pack at room temperature (15 to 30°C). Do not keep Losec in the bathroom medicine cabinet or other warm, moist places.

Do not use Losec after the expiry date marked on the pack.

Important Note: This leaflet alerts you to some of the times you should call your doctor. Other situations which cannot be predicted may arise. Nothing in this leaflet should stop you from calling your doctor or pharmacist with any questions or concerns you have about using Losec.

For additional information on acid-related diseases, please call 1-800-668-6000.

☐ LOTENSIN® P

Novartis Pharmaceuticals

Benazepril HCl

Angiotensin Converting Enzyme Inhibitor

Information for the Patient: Your doctor has decided to use Lotensin (benazepril HCl) to treat your high blood pressure. Here are some things to know about Lotensin in order to use it safely, and get the most benefit.

Patients who have high blood pressure are often unaware of any signs of this problem. In fact, many feel quite normal. Yet, if high blood pressure is not treated, it can cause serious problems such as heart disease, blood vessel disease, stroke or kidney disease. Some patients have to take medicine to control high blood pressure for the rest of their lives. It is very important that you take your medicine exactly as directed and keep regular appointments with your doctor even if you feel well.

Lotensin belongs to a class of drugs known as **A**ngiotensin **C**onverting **E**nzyme (ACE) inhibitors. Lotensin helps to control high blood pressure by preventing your body from producing a substance (angiotensin) that increases blood pressure.

Using Lotensin safely: What does your doctor need to know about you? To decide whether you can take Lotensin safely, your doctor must know whether you have certain medical conditions. Before taking Lotensin, make sure your doctor knows if you have:
— allergic reactions to drugs
— kidney disease
— previously taken medications, especially diuretics (''water pills'')
— other medical problems.

Are you pregnant or breast-feeding? You should not take Lotensin if you are pregnant since it can cause injury or even death to a developing fetus. If you become pregnant, you should report to your doctor immediately. Also, since Lotensin can pass into breast milk, it is not recommended that you take Lotensin while breast-feeding.

What about taking other drugs at the same time? Please give your doctor precise information on any other drugs you may be taking, especially other drugs that lower blood pressure, drugs serving to remove fluids (diuretics, ''water pills'') or potassium supplements (e.g., Slow K).

Salt substitute preparations: You should not take any salt substitutes containing potassium while using Lotensin. Read the label of these products to see if they contain potassium.

What are the side effects? Along with its intended action, any medication, including Lotensin, may cause side effects. Most people do not have any problems with side effects, but if they do occur they may require medical attention.

During the first few days of Lotensin therapy, some patients may experience lightheadedness or dizziness. If this happens to you it should be reported to your doctor. If your dizziness is severe and causes fainting, stop taking Lotensin and contact your doctor. Dizziness or lightheadedness may also occur during your Lotensin therapy if you experience an extreme loss of body water due to excessive sweating, inadequate fluid intake, vomiting or diarrhea.

In rare instances, patients who have been given an ACE inhibitor drug have developed swelling of the face, lips, tongue, ankles, wrists, or difficulty swallowing or breathing. In the event that you develop any of these symptoms, you should stop taking Lotensin and contact your doctor immediately.

The following reactions may also occur at the start of treatment with Lotensin: tiredness, drowsiness, nervousness, difficulty sleeping, feelings of anxiety, headache, stomach upset, palpitations, hot flushes and noises in the ears. These reactions often go away within 1 to 2 weeks of treatment. However, if these or any other problems appear and do not go away during treatment, you should report them to your doctor.

Please tell your doctor if any of the following happens:
— a sign of infection (e.g., sore throat, fever)
— ''viral-like'' symptoms (e.g., fever, a feeling of illness, muscle pain, rash, enlargement of glands), abdominal pain, nausea, vomiting, loss of appetite, jaundice (yellowing of skin and/or eyes), itching or any other unexplained symptoms that occur in the first weeks to months of therapy
— coughing, sore throat, sinusitis
— sad mood (depression)
— pain in the chest.

Sometimes drugs for the treatment of high blood pressure may adversely affect your powers of concentration. Make sure you know how you react to Lotensin before you drive, use machines or do other tasks that require you to be alert.

How to take Lotensin: Always take your dose of Lotensin as directed by your doctor. Never change the dose unless told to do so. You can take your Lotensin before, during or after a meal since food will not decrease its effectiveness.

Lotensin will not cure high blood pressure, but it does help to control it. You must continue to take Lotensin as directed if you expect to lower your blood pressure and keep it down. It is important that your doctor check your progress at regular visits to make sure that this medicine is working the way it should.

To help you to remember to take your medicine, try to take it at the same time each day. If you miss a dose, try to take the missed dose as soon as possible. If it is less than 10 hours until your next dose anyway, skip the missed dose and then go back to your regular dosing schedule. Do not take two doses at the same time.

Storage: Protect your tablets from heat (store at 15 to 30°C) and humidity.

Always remember: Your doctor has prescribed Lotensin for you after a careful review of your medical condition. Use it only as directed and do not give it to anyone else. If you require more information, consult your doctor or pharmacist. Keep this and all medication out of the reach of children. If you suspect you are experiencing side effects, stop taking the tablets and notify your doctor.

□ LOVENOX® Ⓟ

Rhône-Poulenc Rorer

Enoxaparin

Anticoagulant—Antithrombotic

Information for the Patient: Indications/Actions: Lovenox is used to prevent the formation of deep vein thromboses (blood clots), which can occur as a complication of orthopedic surgery, such as hip or knee surgery, or of intra-abdominal surgeries; to treat the deep vein thrombosis with or without pulmonary embolism; to treat the unstable angina and non-Q-wave myocardial infarction, concurrently with ASA.

Precautions to Take Prior to Treatment: It is important that you provide your doctor with an accurate history of any serious illnesses you may have had in the past or any current medical conditions, as these may influence the action of Lovenox.

Therefore, tell your doctor if you have had or currently have any of the following conditions:
• stroke (cerebrovascular accident),
• a known allergy to Lovenox or any of its constituents,
• a major clotting disorder,
• thrombocytopenia (a severe decrease in the number of platelets in the blood),
• gastric or duodenal ulcer,
• hypertension (high blood pressure),
• liver dysfunction,
• severe inflammation of the retina due to diabetes or hemorrhage,
• bacterial endocarditis.

You should also inform your doctor at once if you are pregnant or if you are breast-feeding, so he can evaluate the possible risks to you and the infant.

Your doctor should also know what drugs you are currently taking regularly, for example, medication for arthritis, heart trouble, diabetes, etc.

Instructions and Administration Techniques: Lovenox is a prescription drug and must be used as directed. It is administered as a s.c. injection, which means the injection is made just under the surface of the skin.
Hip or Knee Replacement Surgery: While you are in the hospital, your doctor or a nurse will give your first injection within 24 hours after your operation, so as to prevent blood clots from forming. After that, your doctor or a nurse will give you 2 injections every day (every 12 hours) while you are in hospital.
Abdominal or Colorectal Surgery: While you are in the hospital, your doctor or a nurse will give your first injection 2 hours prior to surgery. After that, your doctor or a nurse will give you 1 injection once a day while you are in hospital.
Treatment of Deep Vein Thrombosis with or without Embolism: While you are in the hospital, your doctor or a nurse will give you 1 injection once or twice daily for about 10 days.
Treatment of Unstable Angina and Non-Q-Wave Myocardial Infarction: While you are in the hospital, your doctor or a nurse will give you 2 injections every day (every 12 hours) along with oral ASA (100 to 325 mg once daily) for a minimum of 2 days.

It is possible that after you go home, you may need to continue your injections of Lovenox for a few days.
Instructions for self-injection of Lovenox: Your doctor may want you to continue your Lovenox injections at home for a few days. **If so, he or a nurse will show you how to administer your Lovenox injections before you are released from hospital. It is essential that you follow these instructions exactly. If you have questions, be sure you ask your doctor or nurse to provide the explanations you require.**

Lovenox (cont'd)

When at home, there is nothing for you to prepare. The syringe is prefilled with the exact amount of drug required. Do not press on the plunger prior to injection.

Lie down on your back and grasp a fold of skin from your right or left flank between your thumb and forefinger. Then introduce the entire length of the needle vertically into the skin fold. Depress the plunger, then withdraw the needle. You should alternate your daily injections between the right and left side.

You should then safely dispose of the syringe and needle so they remain out of reach of children.

Remember, Lovenox is a potent medication and it is important that you follow your doctor's instructions carefully. Give only the number of injections prescribed per day and continue giving the injections for exactly the number of days specified.

Important: While you are using Lovenox, it is important that you do not take any medication other than that prescribed by your doctor.

If you should see another doctor or a dentist while you are using Lovenox, you should inform them that you are using this medication.

Adverse Effects: Adverse effects occur very rarely with Lovenox administration.

During your hospital stay or when using Lovenox at home, it is important that you notify your doctor immediately if you notice any of the following symptoms:

- bleeding or oozing from the surgical wound,
- any other bleeding episodes, for example, at the site of the injection, nosebleeds, blood in the urine or if you cough or throw up blood,
- spontaneous bruising (a bruise not caused by a blow or any apparent reason),
- pain or swelling in any part of your leg, foot or hip,
- dizziness,
- rapid or unusual heartbeat,
- chest pain or shortness of breath,
- vomiting,
- confusion.

Overdosage and Treatment: Accidental overdosage may result in hemorrhaging, which cannot be treated at home. Therefore, if you suspect that you have used too much Lovenox, call your doctor immediately even if you do not yet observe any unusual symptoms. Your doctor can then make arrangements to bring you to hospital for observation and/or treatment.

☐ LUPRON® Ⓟ
☐ LUPRON DEPOT® 3.75 mg/7.5 mg Ⓟ

Abbott/Tap Pharmaceuticals

Leuprolide Acetate

Gonadotropin-releasing Hormone Analog for Management of Central Precocious Puberty in Children

Information for the Patient: What is Precocious Puberty? Precocious puberty occurs when girls under the age of 8 or boys under the age of 9 begin to develop signs of sexual maturity. This happens to about one child in every 5 000 to 10 000.

Signs and Symptoms:

- Girls develop breasts and may have monthly periods.
- In boys, the penis and testicles grow larger.
- Behavior may change; children may become aggressive or moody.
- Pubic hair grows in both sexes.
- Children may have oily skin and/or acne.
- Your child may be the tallest in the class; there is a sudden growth spurt like that usually seen in teenagers.

Why does it happen? In most cases, there is no special reason for your child's early development. It is not caused by anything we do and is not necessarily passed on from parents to children. However, there may be some physical problem, like a tumor, causing precocious puberty; this would require other treatment. Your physician will perform tests to rule out some possible physical causes.

How will Lupron Depot help? Lupron Depot is a hormone-like agent. It is given by injection **once a month** to adjust your child's body clock (daily injections are also available).

- Your child will stop making some hormones at adult levels.
- Pubertal changes (pubic hair, girl's period, breasts, etc.) should stop and may even become less obvious.
- Growth rate becomes more normal.
- When it's right for your child, your physician will stop administering the shots and puberty will begin again.

Proper use of Lupron for daily injection (subcutaneous use):

1. Your child needs **one injection a day,** as prescribed by your physician.
2. It is very important that your physician check your child's progress at regular medical visits.
3. Only a small amount of Lupron is needed once a day. Use the recommended ½ cc presterilized disposable syringe (see "Instructions for Use" leaflet). Syringes are provided in the Patient Administration Kit.
4. Occasionally, a local skin reaction may occur: itching, redness, burning and/or swelling at the injection site. These reactions usually are mild and disappear after a few days. If they do not or get worse, tell your physician.
5. Change the site of injection as instructed by the physician. As a guide, the usual sites of injection are indicated in the package insert.
6. Store Lupron vials or kits in the refrigerator (2 to 8°C) and protect from light (keep in carton until use).

As with other medications, **keep out of reach of children.**

Proper use of Lupron Depot (intramuscular use):

1. Your child only needs **one injection a month,** as prescribed by your doctor.
2. It is very important that your physician check your child's progress at regular medical visits.
3. Occasionally, a local skin reaction may occur: itching, redness, burning, and/or swelling at the injection site. These reactions usually are mild and disappear after a few days. If they persist or worsen, tell your physician.

Regular injections are important! Adherence to 4-week drug administration schedules must be accepted if therapy is to be successful. For best results, your child should have the right amount of Lupron Depot in his or her body at all times. If you miss a shot or are a week late, your child's pubertal development could begin again.

Stay on schedule! Keep your appointments; this is absolutely necessary for success. Irregular dosing could restart the maturation process.

When to call your physician: The following items are not necessarily problems, but your doctor will want to know about them. Call your physician if:

- There is redness or puffiness of the skin around where the shot was given.
- Pubertal changes continue.
- Your daughter has a period, especially after the first months of treatment with Lupron.
- You have problems keeping the monthly injection schedule.
- Your child needs to take other medication, including nonprescription drugs (for colds, nausea, etc.)
- Anything else happens that causes you concern.

Things to mention at your next appointment: If your child has substantial mood swings (write down the date this happens). Any behavioral changes (boys may become aggressive; girls may become moody).

☐ LUPRON® Ⓟ
☐ LUPRON DEPOT® 7.5 mg/22.5 mg Ⓟ

Abbott

Leuprolide Acetate
Leuprolide Acetate for Depot Suspension

Gonadotropin-releasing Hormone Analog

Information for the Patient: Applies to Lupron for daily s.c. use only: Lupron is a drug which contains 5 mg of leuprolide acetate per millilitre.

Your physician is in the best position to decide whether or not any conditions are present that pose a risk to you. Carefully follow the instructions given by your physician, and always contact him/her if you experience any difficulties.

Proper Use of Lupron:

1. You need 1 injection a day, as prescribed by your physician.

2. It is very important that your physician check your progress at regular medical visits.
3. Only a small amount of Lupron is needed once a day. Use the recommended ½ cc presterilized disposable syringe (see "Instructions for Use" leaflet). Syringes are provided in the Patient Administration Kit.
4. Occasionally, a local skin reaction may occur: itching, redness, burning and/or swelling at the injection site. These reactions usually are mild and disappear after a few days. If they persist or worsen, tell your physician.
5. You may get hot flashes when treated with Lupron. If they continue and make you feel uncomfortable, consult your physician.
6. Contact your physician immediately if you develop: severe bone pain, severe hot flashes, heavy sweating, severe pain in the chest or abdomen, abnormal swelling or numbness of limbs, persistent nausea or vomiting, rapid heartbeat, nervousness or persistent difficulty in urinating.
7. Change the site of injection as instructed by your physician. As a guide, the usual sites of injection are indicated in the package insert.
8. Store Lupron vials or kits in the refrigerator (2 to 8°C) and protect from light (keep in carton until use).

As with other medications, **keep out of reach of children.**

Always Remember:
1. Check with your physician or pharmacist before taking any other drugs, including nonprescription drugs (for colds, nausea).
2. If you forget to take Lupron at the usual time, take it as soon as you remember.
3. Do not stop your daily injections because you feel better. You need 1 injection a day to make sure Lupron keeps working for you.
4. If you need more information, ask your physician.

Applies to Lupron Depot for i.m. use only: Lupron Depot 7.5 mg (1-month slow release) contains 7.5 mg of leuprolide acetate as sustained-release microspheres and must be reconstituted with a special diluent prior to **i.m. administration once a month.**

Lupron Depot 22.5 mg (3-month slow release) contains 22.5 mg leuprolide acetate as sustained-release microspheres and must be reconstituted with the appropriate diluent prior to **i.m. injection once every 3 months.**

Your physician is in the best position to decide whether or not any conditions are present that pose a risk to you. Carefully follow the instructions given by your physician, and always contact him/her if you experience any difficulties.

Proper Use of Lupron Depot:
1. You only need **1 injection a month of Lupron Depot 7.5 mg (1-month slow release) or 1 injection every 3 months of Lupron Depot 22.5 mg (3-month slow release),** as prescribed by your physician.
2. It is very important that your physician check your progress at regular medical visits.
3. Occasionally, a local skin reaction may occur: itching, redness, burning and/or swelling at the injection site. These reactions usually are mild and disappear after a few days. If they persist or worsen, tell your physician.
4. You may get hot flashes when treated with Lupron Depot. If they continue and make you feel uncomfortable, consult your physician.
5. Contact your physician immediately if you develop: severe bone pain, severe hot flashes, heavy sweating, severe pain in the chest or abdomen, abnormal swelling or numbness of limbs, persistent nausea or vomiting, rapid heartbeat, nervousness or persistent difficulty in urinating.

Always Remember:
1. Check with your physician or pharmacist before taking any other drugs, including nonprescription drugs (for colds, nausea).
2. If you are taking Lupron Depot 7.5 mg (1-month slow release) report to your physician **once every month** for your injection. If you are taking Lupron Depot 22.5 mg (3-month slow release), report to your physician **once every 3 months** for your injection.
3. Do not stop your injections because you feel better. You need **1 injection a month** to make sure Lupron Depot 7.5 mg (1-month slow release) keeps working for you or **one injection once every 3-months** to make sure Lupron Depot 22.5 mg (3-month slow release) keeps working for you.
4. If you need more information, ask your physician.

□ LUPRON® DEPOT® 3.75 mg Ⓟ

Abbott

Leuprolide Acetate

Gonadotropin-releasing Hormone Analog

Information for the Patient: Lupron Depot (leuprolide acetate for depot suspension) contains 3.75 mg of leuprolide acetate as sustained-release microspheres and must be reconstituted with a special diluent prior to **i.m. administration once a month.**

Proper Use of Lupron Depot:
1. You only need **one injection a month** for 6 months, as prescribed by your physician.
2. It is very important that your physician check your progress at regular medical visits.
3. Occasionally, a local skin reaction may occur: itching, redness, burning and/or swelling at the injection site. These reactions usually are mild and disappear after a few days. If they persist or worsen, tell your physician.
4. You may get hot flashes when treated with Lupron Depot. If they continue and make you feel uncomfortable, consult your physician.
5. Contact your doctor immediately if you develop: severe bone pain, severe hot flashes, heavy sweating, severe pain in the chest or abdomen, abnormal swelling or numbness of limbs, persistent nausea or vomiting, rapid heartbeat or nervousness.
6. Contact your physician immediately if you suspect that you are pregnant.

Always Remember:
1. Check with your physician or pharmacist before taking any other drugs, including nonprescription drugs (for colds, nausea).
2. Report to your physician **once every month** for your injection.
3. Do not stop your monthly injections because you feel better. You need one injection **a month** to make sure Lupron Depot keeps working for you.
4. If you need more information, ask your physician.

□ LUVOX® Ⓟ

Solvay Pharma

Fluvoxamine Maleate

Antidepressant—Antiobsessional Agent

Information for the Patient: Your doctor has chosen Luvox as the best medication to help you with your condition. This summary provides basic information about using Luvox and is intended only to supplement the advice of your doctor. Be sure to follow your doctor's advice as he or she best understands your medical condition.

What is Luvox? Luvox is a prescription medication containing the active ingredient, fluvoxamine maleate. Luvox is intended for the relief of symptoms of depression, or the reduction of symptoms associated with obsessive-compulsive disorder (OCD).

How does it work? Luvox is believed to work by enhancing the availability of serotonin, one of the chemical transmitters in the brain. Depression and OCD have been associated with a decrease in the flow of serotonin between certain brain cells.

Before taking Luvox your doctor needs to know:
- Any other medical condition that you may have including a history of seizures, heart or liver disease;
- How much alcohol you consume;
- Whether you are planning to get pregnant, are currently pregnant or are nursing an infant;
- Any other prescription or over-the-counter medication that you are currently taking. Of particular importance are monoamine oxidase (MAO) inhibitors, other antidepressants, neuroleptics, warfarin, propranolol, phenytoin, theophylline, lithium and tryptophan.

When not to use Luvox:
- Stop taking the drug and contact your doctor immediately if you experience any severe or unusual side effects, or if you experience an allergic reaction.

How to take Luvox:
- It is very important that you take Luvox exactly as your doctor has instructed. Luvox should be taken at bedtime. Swallow the tablet(s) with water and without chewing.

Luvox (cont'd)

- Establishing an effective dosage level will vary from one person to another. For this reason, your doctor may increase your dosage gradually during treatment.
- Never change the amount of Luvox you are taking unless instructed to do so by your doctor.
- Never double up on your next dose to make up for a missed dose.

What to expect with Luvox:
- As with all antidepressants, improvement with Luvox is gradual.
- You may experience some side effects such as nausea (sometimes with vomiting), constipation, diarrhea, loss of appetite, upset stomach, sleepiness, sleeplessness, dry mouth, tremor, dizziness, or headache. Some side effects may be temporary. Consult your doctor if you experience these or other side effects, as the dose may have to be adjusted.
- Refrain from potentially hazardous tasks, such as driving a car or operating dangerous machines, until you are certain that this medication does not affect your mental alertness or physical coordination.

What to do in case of an overdose: Contact your doctor or nearest hospital emergency department even though you may not feel sick.

What does Luvox contain? The 50 mg tablets contain 50 mg fluvoxamine maleate and the following nonmedicinal ingredients: colloidal anhydrous silica, maize starch, mannitol, methylhydroxypropyl cellulose, polyethylene glycol 6000, pregelatinized starch, sodium stearyl fumarate, talc and titanium dioxide.

The 100 mg tablets contain 100 mg fluvoxamine maleate and the following nonmedicinal ingredients: colloidal anhydrous silica, maize starch, mannitol, methylhydroxypropyl cellulose, polyethylene glycol 6000, pregelatinized starch, sodium stearyl fumarate, talc and titanium dioxide.

What does Luvox look like? The 50 mg tablets are round, white, biconvex and scored in the middle. The tablet is stamped with the number "291" (twice) on one side and a stylized "S" on the other. The 100 mg tablets are oval, white, biconvex and scored in the middle. The tablet is stamped with the number "313" (twice) on one side and a stylized "S" on the other.

How to store Luvox: Keep your Luvox in a tightly closed container, in a dry place, at temperatures between 0°C (freezing) and 30°C. **Keep Luvox out of reach of children.**

Reminder: This medicine has been prescribed only for you. Do not give it to anybody else. If you have any further questions, please ask your doctor or pharmacist.

Keep this summary handy for future reference.

☐ MACROBID® 🄿

Procter & Gamble Pharmaceuticals

Nitrofurantoin Monohydrate—Nitrofurantoin Macrocrystals

Urinary Tract Antibacterial

Information for the Patient:
1. Take MacroBID with food (ideally breakfast and dinner) to enhance tolerance and improve drug absorption.
2. Complete the full course of therapy and contact your physician if any unusual symptoms occur during therapy.
3. Do not use antacid preparations containing magnesium trisilicate while taking MacroBID.
4. With some glucose test tablets, a false positive result may be noted when taking MacroBID.

☐ MANERIX® 🄿

Roche

Moclobemide

Antidepressant

Information for the Patient: Manerix (moclobemide) is a drug used to treat symptoms of depression. Depression is not the same as simply feeling sad for a day or two. Major depression includes feeling depressed nearly every day, or no longer being interested in or enjoying activities. The symptoms can include sleeping or eating difficulties, low sex drive, poor concentration, trouble with self-esteem and a sense of hopelessness. The good news is that it is a treatable illness. With treatment, most people recover completely and return to their normal activities and lifestyle.

One of the treatment methods for depression is the use of medication called antidepressants. One group of antidepressants is called RIMA (Reversible Inhibitor of Monoamine Oxidase-type A). Manerix belongs to the RIMA groups of antidepressants. The antidepressants act by changing levels of certain chemicals in the brain. They are not "uppers" or "downers". **The drugs take from a few days to several weeks to be really effective, so patience is needed to give the drug a chance to work.** Even though they may take a while to work there is a high likelihood of success. **It is very important that the program is not discontinued, interrupted or changed in any way without consulting your doctor.** If any change in medication or alteration in dose is required, this should be done at the discretion of the doctor.

Remember the Following Do's and Don'ts of Depression:
- Do follow treatment instructions, especially dosages and length of use of your medication.
- Do tell your doctor if you are feeling worse after you have begun treatment.
- Don't ignore early symptoms, especially if you have had a previous episode of depression. The earlier depression is treated, the better the treatment results will be.
- Don't use alcohol or nonprescription medications to try and cope with any symptoms of depression. Alcohol can make a depression worse.
- Don't stop taking Manerix as soon as you feel better. Discuss how long drug treatment should continue, especially if you have had more than one episode of depression.

Before you Start your Medicine: Please tell your doctor at once if you are pregnant, have high blood pressure, suffer from a liver complaint or are taking any other medication (particularly cimetidine, meperidine, clomipramine or anesthetics). You should always consult your doctor or pharmacist before using other medications while on Manerix.

Conditions which should be reported to your doctor and/or pharmacist if they occur while taking this medicine include:
- finding out you are pregnant
- deciding you are going to breast-feed your baby
- return of depressive symptoms or shifts in mood or behavior.

Contact your doctor or pharmacist immediately if a combination of the following symptoms occur:
- severe throbbing headache which starts at the back of the head and radiates forward
- neck stiffness
- heart fluttering, fast or slow heartbeat.

Side Effects: Generally, Manerix is well tolerated. However, as with any medication, in some people unwanted side effects may develop. In many cases, these lessen as therapy is continued. Occasionally the dose may be reduced by your doctor. Side effects may sometimes occur before beneficial effects are noticed. Although side effects are annoying, it is important that you do not stop your medication without first checking with your doctor.

Some of the most bothersome side effects which may occur are insomnia, dizziness, nausea and headaches. You should talk to your doctor or pharmacist if these or any other unusual side effects become unpleasant or do not go away. Take your medication immediately after meals to minimize the potential of side effects.

Remember:
1. No special dietary restrictions are necessary. Examples of amounts of foods that can be safely eaten are: up to 7.5 times the normal serving of aged or overripe cheese, up to 1 kg (2.2 lb) to 2 kg (4.4 lb) of mild cheese, up to 200 g (7 oz) of strong cheese, up to 70 g (2.5 oz) of Marmite yeast extract.
2. Take your medication immediately after your meals.
3. Talk to your doctor or pharmacist before taking any other medications including nonprescription medications.
4. Store your medication in a clean, dry area at room temperature. Keep this, and all medication out of the reach of children.
5. Inform all health professionals involved in your care that you are on this type of medication.
6. You should avoid consumption of **excessive** alcohol.

If you have any questions, do not hesitate to contact your doctor or pharmacist. This leaflet does not provide full information concerning Manerix.

☐ MAVIK™ ℞

Knoll

Trandolapril

Angiotensin Converting Enzyme Inhibitor

Information for the Patient: For Patients Taking Mavik for the Treatment of Hypertension: What is Hypertension? Hypertension is the medical term for high blood pressure. When blood flows through the blood vessels it pushes against their walls, almost like water pushing against the sides of a hose. Blood pressure is like that "push". When blood pressure is high (like the water pressure in a hose when the nozzle is partially shut), damage can occur to the heart and blood vessels.

Although you may not feel any symptoms for years, hypertension can lead to stroke, heart attack, kidney disease and other serious conditions.

What Causes Hypertension? In most cases, the exact cause of hypertension is not known. But we do know that several factors increase the risk of developing the disease.

Family History: Hypertension, like some other diseases, can run in families. If your parents have high blood pressure, your chances of developing it are greater.

Age: The risk of developing hypertension increases with age.

Race: In North America, there is a higher incidence of hypertension among blacks than among whites.

Diabetes: Diabetics are at higher risk of developing hypertension than nondiabetics.

Weight: The risk of high blood pressure is higher in people who are overweight.

Drinking: Heavy alcohol consumption increases risk of hypertension, as well as stroke and kidney disease.

Sedentary Lifestyle: A physically inactive lifestyle can contribute to hypertension.

Smoking: While not a direct cause of hypertension, smoking a cigarette will temporarily increase blood pressure. Smoking also increases the risk of heart disease in people with high blood pressure.

Keeping Your Blood Pressure Controlled: Your doctor has prescribed Mavik (trandolapril), a medication that helps to control blood pressure. Mavik opens blood vessels to reduce blood pressure, like the way opening a hose reduces water pressure. It is not, however, a cure.

But it takes more than just medication to reduce blood pressure. Discuss the risk factors, and how they apply to your lifestyle, with your doctor. You may have to modify some of your daily habits to keep your blood pressure down.

When to Take Your Medication: You can take your medication with a meal, or if you prefer, on an empty stomach. It is important to take it at the same time every day as prescribed by your doctor. Most people with high blood pressure need to take only 1 Mavik capsule/day.

Remember, hypertension is a long-term disease without short-term symptoms. Just because you feel fine does not mean you can stop taking your medication. If you stop, serious complications of the disease may occur. Therefore, you should continue to take it regularly, as prescribed by your doctor.

Missed a Dose? If you forget to take your Mavik capsule, simply wait until it is time for your next dose. Do not take 2 doses at once.

Managing Your Lifestyle: The "lifestyle" part of your treatment is as important as your medication. By working as a team with your doctor, you can help reduce the risk of hypertension complications to maintain the style of life you are accustomed to.

Together, you and your physician can determine how each of the following applies to you:

Alcohol: Avoid alcoholic beverages until you have discussed their use with your doctor. Alcohol consumption may alter your blood pressure and/or increase the possibility of dizziness or fainting.

Diet: Generally, avoid fatty foods and food that is high in salt or cholesterol.

Exercise: Exercise regularly. It will help to keep your weight down, make you feel more energetic and is a good way to deal with stress. If you are not exercising regularly, be sure to discuss a fitness plan with your doctor.

Smoking: Avoid it completely.

Side Effects: Along with its intended action, any medication, including Mavik, may cause side effects. These include headache, dizziness, fatigue, nausea or coughing. With your first dose of Mavik your blood pressure may drop too low and you may experience a sensation of lightheadedness. Chances are that some of these side effects will disappear once your system becomes used to the medication. If they persist, discuss this with your doctor. Your medication might have to have the dose reduced or be changed.

If you are suffering from excessive sweating, vomiting or diarrhea, your blood pressure may drop too low. See your doctor.

A rare, but potentially more serious, side effect is called angioedema—characterized by swollen mouth, lips, tongue, eyes, throat or difficulty in swallowing or breathing. **If you notice swelling or feel pain in these areas, stop taking Mavik and inform your doctor immediately. You should also inform your doctor if you have an unexplained fever, rash or itching.**

Keep Your Doctor Informed: Before taking Mavik, it is important that you inform your doctor of the following:

- Are you currently taking any other medications? This is especially important if you are taking diuretics (water pills) which may add to the blood pressure lowering effect of Mavik. You should not be taking salt substitutes without the advice of your doctor.
- Do you suffer from any conditions other than hypertension? The presence of other medical problems may affect the use of Mavik. Make sure you tell your doctor if you have any other medical problems, especially if you have diabetes, liver disease, kidney disease, heart or blood vessel disease.
- **Are you pregnant, breast-feeding or thinking of becoming pregnant? If you do become pregnant while taking Mavik, discontinue use and consult your doctor.** Taking Mavik during pregnancy can cause injury and even death to the fetus. It is not known if Mavik passes into breast milk. You should not breast-feed if taking Mavik.
- Are you possibly allergic to Mavik, including any of its nonmedicinal ingredients (cornstarch NF, lactose, povidone, gelatin, sodium stearyl fumarate or titanium dioxide)?

After you have started taking Mavik, it is important that you tell your doctor at once about any unexplained symptom you might experience. Examples of this are unexplained fever, rash, itching, any sign of infection, viral-like symptoms, flu-like symptoms, coughing, sore throat, abdominal pain, loss of appetite, sad mood or jaundice.

If you are being treated for other conditions by other doctors, keep them all informed of which medications you are taking. Some drugs may reduce the effectiveness of Mavik or conversely Mavik may reduce the effectiveness of other drugs. If you have to undergo any dental or other surgery, inform the dentist or physician in charge that you are taking this medication.

Remember: Follow your doctor's instructions and keep him/her informed about any concerns you may have. Use this drug as directed by your doctor. If you have side effects, tell your doctor.

Keep this drug out of the reach of children.

Storage Conditions: Store Mavik in the original container at room temperature, below 25°C and not beyond the date indicated on the container.

☐ M-ESLON® Ⓝ

Rhône-Poulenc Rorer

Morphine Sulfate

Opioid Analgesic

Information for the Patient: What is morphine? Morphine relieves pain and should help you to live more comfortably and independently. It is effective and safe when used as directed by your doctor.

Your pain may increase or decrease from time to time and your doctor may need to change the amount of morphine you take (daily dosage).

What is M-Eslon? M-Eslon is a capsule that is made in such a way as to slowly release morphine over a 12-hour period, usually requiring a dose only every 12 hours to control your pain. However, when more convenient, your doctor may ask you to take your medication every 8 hours.

M-Eslon is available in 6 capsule strengths: 10 mg (#4 capsule printed with the logo , "M-ESLON" and "10" in black; opaque white cap and body), 15 mg (#4 capsule printed with the logo , "M-ESLON" and "15" in black; opaque yellow cap and transparent natural body), 30 mg (#4 capsule printed with the logo , "M-ESLON" and "30" in black; opaque pink cap and transparent natural body), 60 mg (#3 capsule printed with the logo ,

M-Eslon (cont'd)

"M-ESLON" and "60" in black; opaque orange cap and transparent natural body), 100 mg (#2 capsule printed with the logo , "M-ESLON" and "100" in black; opaque white cap and transparent natural body) or 200 mg (#0 capsule printed with the logo , "M-ESLON" and "200" in black; transparent natural cap and body). It may be necessary for you to take more than one capsule strength at the same time in order to receive the total daily dosage prescribed by your doctor.

Available in cartons containing blister packs of 20. Also available in white, opaque polypropylene bottles of 50 capsules, with tamper-evident polyethylene caps.

M-Eslon 10, 15, 30, 60, 100 and 200 mg capsules may be swallowed whole, or the capsules may be opened and the contents sprinkled on your food.

How to take your medication: M-Eslon must be taken regularly every 12 hours (with 120 to 180 mL of water) to prevent pain all day and night. If your pain worsens, making you uncomfortable, contact your doctor immediately and she/he may decide that it is necessary to adjust your daily dosage of M-Eslon.

Your starting dosage of M-Eslon will be clearly labeled on the medication bottle. Be sure to follow these directions on the label exactly; this is very important. If your dosage is changed, be sure to write it down at the time your doctor calls you or sees you, and follow the new directions exactly.

Constipation: Morphine causes constipation. This is to be expected so your doctor may order a laxative and stool softener to help relieve your constipation while you are taking M-Eslon. Tell your doctor about the problem if it arises.

Concomitant Medications: Your doctor should be made aware of any other medication you are taking including over-the-counter antihistamines or sleep aids as they could affect the way you respond to morphine.

Driving: Driving or other tasks requiring full alertness should not be attempted for the first few days of taking M-Eslon, since you may experience drowsiness or sedation.

Reordering M-Eslon: A new written prescription is required from your doctor each time you need more M-Eslon. Therefore, it is important to contact your doctor at least 3 working days before your current supply runs out. It is very important that you do not miss any doses. Should your pain increase, or any other complaint develop as a result of taking M-Eslon, contact your doctor immediately.

□ METHOTREXATE TABLETS USP

Faulding

Antimetabolite

Information for the Patient: Methotrexate tablets 2.5 mg supplied by Faulding are small, round, yellow uncoated tablets engraved with M 2.5/F. These tablets contain 2.5 mg of methotrexate, a potent medication which has been prescribed by your doctor and dispensed by your pharmacist.

It is possible that you have previously taken a different brand of Methotrexate Tablets 2.5 mg, which looked slightly different and which were packaged differently. Whatever the source, Methotrexate Tablets 2.5 mg are expected to be very effective in treating your rheumatoid arthritis. If you have any questions about this, you should ask your pharmacist or doctor for further information.

Before Using This Medication: Pre-existing Medical Conditions: Tell your doctor if you have the following medical conditions: liver disease, peptic ulcer, ulcerative colitis, nausea and vomiting (which may have resulted in dehydration), lung disease, blood disorders such as anemia, kidney disease, any current infection, recent immunization, alcoholism.

Drug Interactions: It is essential that your doctor and pharmacist are informed of all drugs that you are taking before you start Methotrexate (see Precautions While Using This Medication).

Tell your doctor if you have previously taken Methotrexate; this is particularly important if you have suffered severe side effects, allergies or intolerance to Methotrexate.

Pregnancy, Conception and Breast-feeding: Tell your doctor if you are pregnant or breast-feeding, or if you plan to conceive (both men and women) or breast-feed. (see Precautions While Using This Medication).

Proper Use of This Medication: Dose: Your doctor or pharmacist will know the correct dose for you, from the results of your blood tests and other tests which may have been done.

A common dosage is 7.5 mg (or 3 tablets) taken each week, either all at once or in a divided dose schedule, which your doctor will describe to you.

However, your doctor may choose to start with a different dose. Your doctor may alter your dosage if you suffer side effects from Methotrexate. Side effects may be discovered after repeating your blood tests. You may also be asked to have a liver biopsy to check for side effects to your liver (see Side Effects).

The safe and effective use of this medication depends upon full co-operation with your doctor's instructions for dosage, and in having the tests which may be necessary from time to time throughout your treatment.

It is important to remember that Methotrexate Tablets 2.5 mg are given on a weekly basis, **not** daily. This intermittent or "pulse" dosage has been found to produce fewer side effects.

Because the strength of the medication is based on a weekly dosage, accidently taking the medication daily can produce very serious side effects, which may be fatal (see What To Do in Case of Overdose).

Missed Dose: Tell your doctor or pharmacist if you miss a dose of Methotrexate Tablets. Do **not** double doses without consulting your doctor or pharmacist.

What to do in Case of Overdose: In a case of accidental overdose or if a child takes this medication accidentally, an antidote must be given as soon as possible. **Obtain emergency treatment immediately.** Take the remaining Methotrexate Tablets to the emergency clinic with you, and show them to the attending doctor.

Precautions While Using This Medication: Reproductive Effects: Methotrexate has caused fetal death and birth defects, and should **not** be used by pregnant women or by women who wish to become pregnant. In men and women of fertile age, steps should be taken to avoid conception during treatment with Methotrexate Tablets. The risk of genetic (birth) defects may persist after discontinuing treatment. Thus it is recommended that both men and women avoid intercourse leading to conception for at least 8 weeks after completing treatment.

Tell your doctor immediately if you do become pregnant while taking Methotrexate.

Drug Interactions: Several drugs, such as antibiotics, may increase the risk of side effects if taken at the same time as Methotrexate Tablets. ASA and the so-called "NSAID" drugs may be given concurrently with Methotrexate for rheumatoid arthritis by your doctor; however, do not start these drugs without your doctor's knowledge.

Do not begin to take any other medications (**not** even vitamins), while taking Methotrexate Tablets, without asking your doctor.

Alcohol should be avoided, since it may increase the risk of liver disturbances.

Signs and symptoms requiring immediate medical attention: mouth ulceration; black tarry stools; bloody diarrhea or vomit; stomach pain; unusual bleeding or bruising; fever, chills, or sore throat; cough (dry and nonproductive), shortness of breath, or pneumonia-like symptoms; swelling of feet or lower legs; dark urine, yellowish eyes and skin; infections.

Signs and symptoms requiring medical attention only if they are bothersome or persistent: loss of appetite; nausea or vomiting; skin rash, itching.

Side Effects: Side effects of potent medications are sometimes unavoidable, and may indicate that the medication is working. Side effects may occur at any time during your treatment with Methotrexate Tablets.

Common side effects include nausea which may be accompanied by vomiting, anorexia (loss of appetite), diarrhea, stomatitis (sores in the mouth).

Less common side effects include liver malfunction, kidney malfunction, blood disorders, decreased resistance to infection.

Rare side effects include pulmonary toxicity (lung complications), hepatic fibrosis (liver scarring).

Arthritic "flare" or a worsening of arthritic symptoms may occur within 3 to 6 weeks after discontinuing Methotrexate treatment.

Proper Storage of This Medication: Methotrexate Tablets may be stored at normal room temperature. Make sure that this and other medications are not subject to extreme heat and direct light, and are not stored in high humidity areas such as in some bathrooms.

Discard outdated medications and medications that are no longer needed.

Keep this and all medications out of reach of children.

Do not share this or any other medication with another person.

☐ MEVACOR® ℞

MSD

Lovastatin

Lipid Metabolism Regulator

Information for the Patient: Full prescribing information is available to the physician and pharmacist.

Mevacor is the brandname of Merck Frosst Canada Inc. for the substance lovastatin **available only on prescription from your physician.** Lovastatin is one of a class of medicines known as **Lipid Metabolism Regulators.** They **inhibit,** in other words block, an enzyme that is necessary for the body to make cholesterol. In this way, less cholesterol is produced in the liver.

When it is necessary to lower cholesterol, physicians usually try to control the condition, known as hypercholesterolemia, with a carefully supervised diet. Also your physician may recommend other measures such as exercise and weight control. Medicines like this one are prescribed **along with,** and **not as a substitute for,** a special diet and other measures. Lovastatin is used to lower the levels of cholesterol (particularly Low Density Lipoprotein (LDL) cholesterol) and other fats in the blood. This may help prevent heart disease if caused by cholesterol clogging the blood vessels or slow the progression of atherosclerosis (hardening) of the arteries that nourish your heart, so-called coronary heart disease (CHD).

Remember: This medicine is prescribed for the particular condition that you have. **Do not give this medicine to other people, nor use it for any other condition.**

Do not use outdated medicine.

Store your tablets in a tightly closed container (at 15 to 30°C), away from heat and direct light. Keep all medicines out of the reach of children.

Read the following information carefully. **If you need any explanations, or further information, ask your physician or pharmacist.**

Before Taking This Medicine: This medicine may not be suitable for certain people. So, tell your physician if you think **any** of the following applies to you:

- You have previously taken lovastatin or any other medication in the same class—example, simvastatin (Zocor), pravastatin (Pravachol) or fluvastatin (Lescol)—and were allergic, or had reacted badly to it.
- **You are pregnant or intend to become pregnant.** This medicine should **not** be used during pregnancy.
- You are breast-feeding or intend to breast-feed.
- You have liver disease.

Your physician also needs to know if you are taking any other medication, whether on prescription or otherwise. It is particularly important to inform your physician if you are taking:

- cyclosporine (Sandimmune), gemfibrozil (Lopid), lipid-lowering doses of niacin (nicotinic acid), corticosteroids, or an anticoagulant (e.g., warfarin [Warfilone]), digoxin or erythromycin.

The safety of this medicine has not been established in adolescents and children.

Proper Use of This Medicine:

- Take this medicine **exactly** as your physician ordered. It is usually recommended as a single dose with the evening meal or in two divided doses with the morning and evening meals.
- If you miss taking a tablet at its usual time, take it as soon as possible. But, if it is too close to the time of your next dose: take only the prescribed dose at the appointed time. **Do not take a double dose.**
- Carefully follow any measures that your physician has recommended for diet, exercise or weight control.
- It is important to continue taking the tablets as instructed. Do not alter the dosage or stop taking the medicine without consulting your physician.
- Keep your appointments regularly with your physician so that your blood can be tested and your progress checked at proper intervals. Your physician may also arrange for periodic eye examination by an ophthalmologist.
- Avoid drinking large quantities of alcohol.
- **Do not start taking any other medicines** unless you have discussed the matter with your physician.
- Let your physician know if you suffer a severe injury, or severe infection.
- If you have to undergo any dental or other surgery, tell your physician about the planned surgery; and also inform the dentist or the physician in charge that you are taking this or any other medicine.

Side Effects of This Medicine—And What You Should Do: Along with its intended action, any medication may cause unwanted effects. Most people do not have any problem when taking this medicine; but if you notice any of the following reactions, **check with your physician as soon as possible:** aching muscles, muscle cramps, tiredness or weakness; fever; blurred vision.

Some other side effects that may occur, generally do not require medical attention, and may come and go during treatment. But if any of the following persist or become troublesome, **do check with your physician or pharmacist:** constipation, diarrhea, gas, stomach upset, nausea; pain in the abdomen; headache, dizziness; skin rash.

Some people may have other reactions. If you notice **any unusual effect,** check with your physician or pharmacist.

Ingredients: Active ingredient: Each tablet of Mevacor contains lovastatin. It comes in two strengths: 20 mg (light blue), and 40 mg (green).

Nonmedicinal ingredients: butylated hydroxyanisole, microcrystalline cellulose, lactose, magnesium stearate, pregelatinized starch. Tablets Mevacor 20 mg also contain indigotine on alumina. Tablets Mevacor 40 mg contain indigotine, quinoline yellow, both on alumina substratum.

☐ MIGRANAL® ℞

Novartis Pharmaceuticals

Dihydroergotamine Mesylate

Migraine Therapy

Information for the Patient: Keep this information handy. Read this now, but prepare the sprayer only when you have a migraine attack. Contains medication to treat 1 migraine. (4 sprays as instructed ensures optimal efficacy and lasting relief.) Before using Migranal for the first time, please read this information carefully.

Purpose of your medication: Migranal is indicated for the treatment of the acute attack of migraine headaches. **As with other acute migraine medications, Migranal should not be used on a daily basis, as an attempt to prevent or to reduce the number of attacks you experience.**

Do not use Migranal if you:

- are pregnant or breast-feeding;
- have any disease affecting your heart, arteries or circulation.

Important questions to consider before using Migranal: Please answer the following questions before you use Migranal. **If you answer yes to any of these questions, or are unsure of the answer, you should talk to your doctor before using Migranal.**

- Do you have high blood pressure?
- Do you have chest pain, shortness of breath, heart disease, or have you had any surgery on your heart arteries?
- Do you have any problems with blood circulation in your arms or legs, fingers or toes?
- Are you sexually active and not using birth control?
- Have you ever had to stop taking this or any other medication because of an allergy or bad reaction?
- Are you taking any other migraine medications containing sumatriptan or ergotamine, erythromycin or other macrolide antibiotics, or medications for blood pressure prescribed by your doctor, or any other medicines obtained from your drugstore without a doctor's prescription?
- Have you had, or do you have, any disease of the liver?
- Have you ever experienced difficulty moving one side of your body when you have a headache?

Remember to tell your doctor if you have answered yes to any of these questions.

How to get your Migranal ready for use (see package insert for illustrations): It is best to use Migranal at the beginning of a migraine attack. However, it may be used at any stage of an attack.

Your Migranal package contains: (A) a bottle containing medication to treat 1 migraine, (B) the sprayer, (C) a blue plastic protective cap, and (D) a transparent plastic protective cover.

Migranal (cont'd)

Only start to prepare the sprayer when you have a migraine attack. Slowly lift and bend back the lip of the blue seal to show the rubber stopper. Try not to break the blue seal.

Completely remove the seal and metal collar in one piece, if possible. If the two should break apart, carefully continue removing the metal collar. **The edge of the collar is sharp—please handle with care.**

Gently pull the rubber stopper out of the bottle being careful not to spill the contents.

Gently remove the transparent plastic protective cover from the bottom of the sprayer. Insert the sprayer into the bottle and tighten firmly onto the bottle in a clockwise direction.

Holding the bottle upright, gently remove the blue plastic protective cap from the top of the sprayer.

Holding the bottle upright, pump firmly 4 times (not in your nostrils). Some medication will spray out; this is normal and prepares the sprayer for accurate delivery of the medication.

Hold your head straight.

- Insert the sprayer into one of your nostrils and pump the sprayer once to release the medication.
- Repeat in the other nostril (a total of 2 sprays).
- Don't blow your nose.
- Wait about 15 minutes. If you have not already experienced sufficient relief, or to obtain optimal and long lasting relief, repeat spraying once in each nostril.

Spraying 4 times as shown ensures optimal efficacy and lasting relief. Discard the bottle and sprayer after use.

One complete dose of Migranal is 1 bottle, which is 4 sprays, after priming.

- Do not use more than 2 bottles of Migranal (8 sprays) in a 24-hour period.
- Do not use more than 6 bottles (24 sprays) in 1 week.

Important Notes:

- The return of pain within 24 hours (migraine recurrence) following the administration of one bottle of Migranal is low.
- Throw away the sprayer and bottle after use.

Possible Side Effects: In clinical trials, most migraine patients have used Migranal without serious side effects. You may experience nasal irritation, nasal congestion, excessive sneezing, runny nose, taste disturbance, application site reactions, nausea and vomiting after using Migranal. These side effects are temporary and usually do not require you to stop using Migranal. Although the following reactions rarely occur, they can be serious and should be reported to your physician immediately:

- Numbness or tingling in your fingers and toes;
- Pain, tightness or discomfort in your chest;
- Weakness in your legs;
- Temporary speeding or slowing of your heart rate;
- Swelling or itching.

What to do in case of an overdose: If you have used more medication than you have been instructed, contact your doctor, hospital emergency department, or nearest Poison Control Centre immediately.

Storing Migranal: Keep medication in a safe place away from children. Keep Migranal away from heat.

- Store Migranal at room temperature (15 to 25°C).
- Never freeze Migranal.

Do not keep an opened Migranal bottle for more than 8 hours.

Check the expiration date printed on the bottle containing medication. If the date has passed, do not use it.

Answers to patients' questions about Migranal: How quickly does Migranal work? You should start to feel relief in less than 30 minutes and your migraine and associated symptoms should continue to improve.

Can I prepare the sprayer so it is ready before I need to use it? No. The bottle containing your medication must remain sealed until you are ready to use it.

Why do I have to prime the sprayer before using? Am I wasting the medication? You have to prime the sprayer (pump 4 times) to make sure that you get the proper amount of medication when you use it. Although you will see some medication spray out, there is still enough medication in each bottle to allow you to prepare your applicator properly and still receive a full dose of Migranal (4 sprays).

Can I reuse my Migranal Sprayer? No. After completing the full dose (4 sprays), you must throw the sprayer and bottle out.

Can I use Migranal if I have a stuffy nose, cold or allergies? Yes. You can use Migranal if you have a stuffy nose, cold or allergies. However, if you are taking any medications for your cold or allergies, even those you can buy without a doctor's prescription, speak with your doctor or pharmacist before using Migranal.

Do I need to sniff the medication when I spray it in my nose? No, you should not sniff, because Migranal is absorbed through the lining of the nose.

What does Migranal contain? Each Migranal bottle contains a solution containing dihydroergotamine mesylate. It also contains caffeine, dextrose, carbon dioxide and water.

What if I need help in using Migranal? If you have any questions or if you need help in preparing, or using Migranal, speak to your doctor or pharmacist.

This medicine is prescribed for your specific medical problem and for your own use only. Do not give to other people.

Keep all medicines out of the reach of children.

This leaflet does not contain all the information on Migranal. If you need any further information, ask your doctor or pharmacist.

□ MINITRAN™

3M Pharmaceuticals

Nitroglycerin

Antianginal

Information for the Patient: Minitran, the long-acting form of nitroglycerin which your doctor has prescribed for you, is a transdermal nitroglycerin system which is applied to the skin. Unlike oral medications, which have to be taken frequently, or messy ointments, Minitran provides nitroglycerin in a convenient once-a-day dosage form. You can't see the nitroglycerin in Minitran because it is mixed in with the adhesive on the patch. When you apply Minitran to your skin, the nitroglycerin is slowly absorbed through your skin and into your bloodstream. The nitroglycerin in Minitran enters your body in a controlled way, a little at a time. Minitran helps prevent angina (heart pain) attacks and reduces the need for under-the-tongue nitroglycerin tablets.

Possible Side Effects: As with all nitroglycerin products, you may develop a headache at the start of Minitran treatment. Such headaches are usually mild and often disappear as treatment is continued or dosage is adjusted. Headache may be treated with mild pain medications such as aspirin. Although uncommon, dizziness, faintness or flushing may occur, especially when you move suddenly from a lying down to sitting up position. Be sure to inform your doctor if these symptoms occur.

Skin irritation may occur. It can usually be avoided if you change the place you wear your patch every day and you make sure the area is thoroughly dry before applying. If irritation persists, ask your doctor about it.

Important: Minitran is to be used for preventing attacks of angina. It is not meant to be used like under-the-tongue nitroglycerin tablets for stopping an attack that has already started.

If your angina attacks become more severe, last longer or occur more frequently, tell your doctor immediately.

Additional Information: Minitran sticks well to the skin and remains in place during bathing, swimming and showering. In the unlikely event that the patch becomes loose, discard it and put a new one on a different skin site.

Do not apply Minitran immediately after showering or bathing—wait until you are sure that the skin is completely dry.

Do not reuse a Minitran patch once it has been removed from the skin.

Allow Minitran to stay in place for 12 to 14 hours unless otherwise instructed by your physician.

Apply Minitran at the same time every day.

Where to Apply Minitran: You can apply Minitran to the chest, shoulders, upper arm or back. Do not apply Minitran to the lower arm or lower leg. You should apply the patch to a nonhairy area so that hair will not prevent direct contact of the patch with the skin. If hair is likely to interfere with adhesion of the patch, the area may be lightly shaved. The skin area should be clean, dry and free of irritation or cuts. Use a different skin site each time you use a new Minitran patch.

Patient Instructions (see package insert for illustrations):

1. Start at notched corner. Tear pouch along dotted line. Remove patch from pouch.

2. Bend patch so that the dotted liner notch pops up; remove tab and discard dotted liner.
3. Apply sticky side of patch to upper arm or chest. Remove and discard dotted liner.
4. Press patch firmly in place.
5. Carefully remove the other piece of plastic liner and discard.
6. Press patch firmly in place.

Store at controlled room temperature, 15 to 30°C.

Warning: Store and discard systems in a manner that prevents accidental application or ingestion by children or others.

□ MIRAPEX® ℞

Boehringer Ingelheim

Pramipexole Dihydrochloride

Antiparkinsonian Agent—Dopamine Agonist

Information for the Patient: Before you start taking Mirapex, please read the following information carefully.

Mirapex is used to treat early and late stage Parkinson's disease. In late stage Parkinson's disease, Mirapex will be used in combination with levodopa. It is important that your doctor increases your dosage of Mirapex **gradually** to avoid side effects and to achieve the best therapeutic effect. Your dose will probably change each week until your doctor and you decide what is the best dose for you. Your doctor may decide to lower your dose of levodopa to prevent excessive side effects and to make sure that you are getting the best results from both drugs. Pay close attention to your doctor's instructions and never change the dose of either drug yourself.

This information leaflet explains how to use Mirapex and how to avoid problems while you are taking this medication. This leaflet does not contain all the information about the drug. **For further information or advice please see your doctor or pharmacist.**

Before you Take Mirapex: Be sure to tell your doctor:

- if you have any health problems, especially problems with your kidneys;
- if you have any unusual conditions related to your eyes or eyesight;
- if you have previously taken Mirapex and became unwell, or you are allergic to Mirapex, or any of the nonmedicinal ingredients of the product (for complete list see "What does Mirapex contain" section), tell the doctor before taking these tablets;
- if you have any allergies or reactions to foods or drugs;
- if you are pregnant or intend to become pregnant;
- if you are breast-feeding;
- if you are taking any other medications, including any drugs you can buy without a prescription.

How to Take Mirapex:

- During the first several weeks that you are taking Mirapex, your doctor will be changing your dose on a weekly basis. Make sure that you only use the tablet strength that your doctor has prescribed.
- You may take Mirapex with food if you find that you feel sick to your stomach while taking the tablet.
- If you forget to take a dose, take it as soon as you remember, then carry on as before. Do not take more than 1 dose at a time.
- If you accidentally take too many tablets, you should get medical help immediately, either by calling your doctor or by going to the nearest hospital (do not drive yourself). Always take the labelled medicine container with you whether or not there are any Mirapex tablets left.
- You should not change the dose or discontinue treatment with Mirapex without the recommendation of your doctor.

Side Effects when Taking Mirapex:

- Mirapex may cause hallucinations, or unwanted fidgety movements (dyskinesia). Tell your doctor right away if you have any of these symptoms.
- Mirapex can lower blood pressure in some patients when they are sitting or standing. This means that if you sit or stand up after lying down, you may feel dizzy, lightheaded, sick, faint, or you may sweat. These effects happen most often at the start of treatment. Be sure to tell your doctor if you feel like this.
- Mirapex may also cause other unwanted effects such as nausea. If you do experience any unusual or unwanted effects while you are taking Mirapex, be sure to tell your doctor. It is important that he/she knows of any unwanted effects to determine the best dose of Mirapex for you.
- Until you know how Mirapex will affect you, you should not drive a car, or operate machinery that may be dangerous. This is because you may feel dizzy or sleepy while taking Mirapex, especially during the first few weeks of treatment.

How to Store Mirapex:

- Keep this drug away from light. Mirapex may change color when exposed to light.
- Mirapex should be stored at room temperature (15 to 30°C).
- The expiry date of this medicine is printed on the label. Do not use the medicine after this date.
- Keep this drug out of the reach of children.

What Does Mirapex Contain: Mirapex (pramipexole dihydrochloride) Tablets are available in bottles of 90 tablets.

0.25 mg: white, oval, scored tablet with "U" twice on one side and "4" twice on the reverse side containing 0.25 mg pramipexole dihydrochloride as pramipexole dihydrochloride monohydrate.

1.0 mg: white, round scored tablet with "U" twice on one side and "6" twice on the reverse side containing 1.0 mg pramipexole dihydrochloride as pramipexole dihydrochloride monohydrate.

1.5 mg: white, round scored tablet with "U" twice on one side and "37" twice on the reverse side containing 1.5 mg pramipexole dihydrochloride as pramipexole dihydrochloride monohydrate.

Nonmedicinal Ingredients: colloidal silicon dioxide, corn starch, magnesium stearate, mannitol and povidone.

Please Remember:

- Mirapex has been prescribed for you. Do not give these tablets to anyone else, even if you think they have the same condition as you.
- Do not take any other medication unless your doctor tells you to. Tell any other doctor, dentist or pharmacist that you talk to that you are taking Mirapex.

□ MIREZE® ℞

Allergan

Nedocromil Sodium

Antiallergic—Anti-inflammatory

Information for the Patient: Please read carefully before starting Mireze (nedocromil sodium) and every time your prescription is renewed.

Mireze (nedocromil sodium 2%) ophthalmic solution relieves and treats the symptoms of itchy watery red eyes caused by allergies.

About Mireze and Allergies: Mireze is a 2% solution of nedocromil sodium in water and contains benzalkonium chloride and disodium edetate as preservatives. It is useful for the relief and treatment of symptoms caused by allergy in the eye, known as allergic conjunctivitis.

Allergic conjunctivitis results in inflammation of the conjunctiva, the thin, outer, transparent membranes under the eyelids and over the external part of the eyes. This disorder is usually preceded by exposure to allergy-provoking substances in the environment (e.g., tree, grass or weed pollens, mould spores, animal dander and dust). Allergic conjunctivitis is common in the hay fever season.

The symptoms of allergic conjunctivitis are irritation, itchiness, grittiness, soreness, and excessive watering of the eyes. These symptoms are generally accompanied by a stuffy, runny nose (acute allergic rhinitis) commonly known as hay fever.

Important: Mireze must be used regularly to ensure optimum control of symptoms. You should start using Mireze as closely as possible to the start of your symptoms.

- **Soft contact lenses must not be worn** during the treatment period with Mireze. Benzalkonium chloride, a constituent of the formulation, may accumulate in soft contact lenses. This preservative, when slowly released, could possibly irritate the cornea.

  In patients who continue to wear hard or gas permeable contact lenses during Mireze treatment, the lenses should be taken out of the eye prior to instillation of the drops. They should be inserted again not earlier than 5 minutes after administration, in order to allow an even conjunctival distribution of the solution.
- To avoid contamination of the contents, do not touch any surface with the tip of the container.
- Discard any remaining contents 28 days after opening the bottle.
- Store between 4 and 25°C. Protect from direct sunlight.

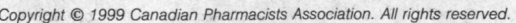

Mireze (cont'd)

Always Remember: Before taking this medication tell your doctor and pharmacist if you:
- are allergic to or have had a reaction to nedocromil sodium, or any of its components, in the past;
- are, or intend to become, pregnant;
- are, or intend to, breast-feed;
- are taking any other medications, either prescription or nonprescription (over the counter);
- have any other medical problems.

While taking this medication:
- Tell any other doctor, dentist or pharmacist, that you consult or see, that you are taking this medication.
- Check with your doctor if you are not getting any relief of your symptoms.
- Report any untoward reaction to your doctor. This is very important as it will aid in the early detection and prevention of potential complications.
- **Your regular medical checkups are essential.**

Precautions: Very little nedocromil sodium is absorbed into the body when using Mireze as directed in the eye.

Along with its benefits, Mireze, like other drugs, may cause some undesirable reactions. Although not all these side effects may occur, if they do occur they may need medical attention. Local side effects in the eye are generally mild and tend to disappear promptly if treatment is stopped.

Check with your doctor if any of the following side effects occur:
- eye irritation (burning or stinging sensation of the eyes);
- headache;
- blurred vision;
- unpleasant taste.

Other side effects not listed may also occur in some patients. If you notice any other effects, check with your doctor.

Dosing: The dose of Mireze may be different for different people.

Adults and Children Over 6 Years of Age: The usual dosage is one drop into each eye, twice daily. When necessary, your doctor may adjust the dose to 1 drop 4 times daily.

Directions for Use:
1. Sit down in front of a mirror so that you can see what you are doing.
2. Pull the lower eyelid down gently and then carefully place 1 drop into the gap between the eye and lower eyelid taking care not to touch the eye with the tip of the bottle.
3. Release the lower eyelid and blink a few times to ensure the whole eye is covered by the liquid.
4. Repeat the process for the other eye.

Missed Dose: Try to take the drops at regular times, to help you remember to take them. If you miss a dose, take it as soon as you realize the omission; then proceed as normal.

Clinical experience with pregnant women or children under 6 years of age is limited.

Do not keep outdated medicine or medicine no longer needed. Keep out of the reach of children.

This medicine has been prescribed for your medical problem. Do not give it to anyone else.

If you require more information on this drug, consult your doctor or pharmacist.

□ MOBIFLEX® Ⓟ

Roche

Tenoxicam

Anti-inflammatory—Analgesic

Information for the Patient: Important information you should know about Mobiflex (tenoxicam): Mobiflex (tenoxicam) is a nonsteroidal, anti-inflammatory agent. It has been prescribed by your doctor to relieve symptoms such as inflammation, swelling, fever, stiffness, and joint pain, often caused by certain types of arthritis.

Mobiflex has been prescribed to you. It should not be given to other people or used for other problems unless specified by your doctor.

Mobiflex should be taken only as directed by your doctor. Do not take more of it, do not take it more often or do not take if for a longer period of time than prescribed by your doctor.

Mobiflex's effect is evident in early treatment, however, in certain types of arthritis, up to 2 weeks may pass before the full benefit may be felt by you.

Before Using Mobiflex: Things You Should Tell Your Doctor:
- If you have a history of stomach upset, ulcer, liver or kidney disease.
- If you are pregnant or if you intend to become pregnant.
- If you are breast-feeding.
- If you are taking any medication for other unrelated medical problems, such as anticoagulants and/or antidiabetics.
- If you have had any unusual or allergic reactions with other nonsteroidal anti-inflammatory agents or ASA (acetylsalicylic acid) related products.
- If you are presently taking medications to relieve your symptoms of arthritis.

Side Effects: As with other medications, some unwanted effects may occur with Mobiflex. The most common adverse reactions encountered are gastrointestinal, such as abdominal distress or discomfort, nausea, and heartburn.

Other side effects do not appear very often, however, they may require medical attention. Consult your doctor if the following occur:
—tightness in chest, shortness of breath, or troubled breathing
—bloody or black tarry stool
—blurred vision
—hearing problems
—skin rash, itching or hives
—swelling of face, feet or lower legs
—mental confusion or depression
—indigestion, nausea, vomiting, stomach pain or diarrhea.

Note: Elderly people should report adverse reactions, immediately.

How to Use Mobiflex:
- Take Mobiflex **as directed** by your doctor.
- Take this medicine immediately after a meal or with food to lessen the chance of stomach upset.

Note: If stomach upset (nausea, vomiting, stomach pain, diarrhea, or indigestion) occurs and persists, check with your doctor.

Tablet color may change slightly between prescriptions. This is normal and is due to natural coloring agents.

Remember:
—Tell your doctor, dentist or pharmacist that you consult or see, that you are taking this medication.
—If you are drowsy, dizzy or lightheaded after taking this medication, be cautious about driving or participating in activities that require alertness.
—Call your doctor, if you have any questions or troubling symptoms.
—Keep this medicine out of the reach of children.
—Read your prescription label carefully; ask you pharmacist if you have any questions.
—Take your medication as directed by your doctor.
—Check with your doctor, if you are not getting relief or if any problems develop.

□ MOGADON® Ⓟ

Roche

Nitrazepam

Hypnotic—Anticonvulsant

Information for the Patient: Facts on Mogadon (nitrazepam):

Introduction: Mogadon is intended to help you sleep. It is one of several benzodiazepine sleeping pills that have generally similar properties.

If you are prescribed one of these medications, you should consider both their benefits and risks. Important risks and limitations include the following:
- the longer you use the medication, the less effective it may become,
- you may become dependent on the medication,
- the medication may affect your mental alertness or memory, particularly when not taken as prescribed.

In order to guide you in the safe use of the product, this leaflet will inform you about this class of medication in general, and about Mogadon in particular.

But this leaflet should not replace a discussion between you and your doctor about the risks and benefits of Mogadon.

Safe Use of Mogadon Sleeping Pills:
- Mogadon is a prescription medication, intended to help you sleep. Follow your doctor's advice about how to take Mogadon, when to take it, and how long to take it. **Do not take** Mogadon if it is not prescribed for you.

- **Do not take** Mogadon for more than 7 to 10 days without first consulting your doctor.
- **Do not take** Mogadon when a full night's sleep is not possible before you would again need to be active and functional; e.g., an overnight flight of less than 8 hours. Memory lapses may occur in such situations. Your body needs time to eliminate the medication from your system.
- **Do not take** Mogadon at any time during pregnancy. Tell your doctor if you are planning to become pregnant, if you are pregnant, or if you become pregnant while taking this medication.
- Tell your doctor about any alcohol consumption (present or past) or any medicine you are taking now, including drugs you can buy without a prescription. **Do not consume alcohol while taking Mogadon.**
- **Do not increase the prescribed dose.**
- **Do not drive a car** or operate potentially dangerous machinery until you experience how this drug will affect you.
- If you develop any unusual disturbing thoughts or behavior while using Mogadon, discuss the matter immediately with your doctor.
- You may experience an increase in sleep difficulties (rebound insomnia) and/or increased anxiety (rebound anxiety) for one or two days after discontinuing Mogadon.

Effectiveness of Benzodiazepine Sleeping Pills: Benzodiazepine sleeping pills are effective medications and are relatively free of serious problems when used for the short-term management of insomnia. Symptoms of insomnia may vary: you may have difficulty in falling asleep, or awaken often during the night, or awaken early in the morning, or you may have all three symptoms.

Insomnia may last only for a short time and may respond to brief treatment. The risks and benefits of prolonged use should be discussed with your doctor.

Side Effects: Common Side Effects: Benzodiazepine sleeping pills may cause drowsiness, dizziness, lightheadedness, and difficulty with coordination. Users must be cautious about engaging in hazardous activities requiring complete mental alertness, e.g., operating machinery or driving a motor vehicle.

Avoid alcohol while using Mogadon. **Do not use** benzodiazepine sleeping pills along with other medications without first discussing this with your doctor.

How sleepy you are the day after you use one of these sleeping pills depends on your individual response and on how quickly your body gets rid of the medication. The larger the dose, the more likely that you will experience drowsiness, etc., the next day. For this reason, it is important that you use the lowest effective dose. Benzodiazepines, which are eliminated rapidly, tend to cause less drowsiness the next day, but may cause withdrawal problems the day after use.

Special Concerns: Memory Problems: All benzodiazepine sleeping pills can cause a special type of memory loss (amnesia); you may not recall events that occurred during some period of time, usually several hours, after taking the drug. This lapse is usually not a problem, because the person taking the sleeping pill intends to be asleep during this critical period of time. But it can be a problem if you take the medication to induce sleep while travelling, such as during an airplane flight, because you may wake up before the effect of the drug is gone. This has been called ''traveller's amnesia''.

Tolerance/Withdrawal Symptoms: After nightly use for more than a few weeks benzodiazepines may lose some of their effectiveness. You may also develop a degree of dependence.

''Withdrawal'' effects can occur when patients stop taking benzodiazepine sleeping pills. The effects may occur following use for only a week or two but may be more common and severe after long periods of continuous use. One type of withdrawal symptom is known as ''rebound insomnia'', i.e., on the first few nights after stopping the medication, insomnia may be worse than before the sleeping pill was given.

Other withdrawal symptoms following abrupt stopping of sleeping pills may range from unpleasant feelings to a major withdrawal syndrome that may include abdominal and muscle cramps, vomiting, sweating, tremor, and rarely, convulsions. The severe symptoms are uncommon.

Dependence/Abuse: All benzodiazepine sleeping pills can cause dependence (addiction) especially when used regularly for more than a few weeks, or at higher doses. Some people develop a need to continue taking these drugs, either at the prescribed dose or at higher doses—not only for continued therapeutic effect, but also to avoid withdrawal symptoms or to achieve nontherapeutic effects.

Individuals who depend, or have depended at any time in the past, on alcohol or other drugs may be at particular risk of becoming dependent on drugs of this class. But **all people are at some risk.** Consider this matter before you take these medications beyond a few weeks.

Mental and Behavioral Changes: A variety of abnormal thinking and behavior changes may occur when you use benzodiazepine sleeping pills. Some of these changes include aggressiveness and extroversion which seem out of character. Other changes, although rare, can be more unusual and extreme such as confusion, strange behavior, restlessness, illusions, hallucinations, feeling like you are not yourself, and worsening depression, including suicidal thinking.

It is rarely clear whether such symptoms are caused by the medication, or by an underlying illness, or are simply spontaneous happenings. In fact, worsened insomnia may in some cases be associated with illnesses that were present before the medication was used.

Excessive Salivation: On rare occasions in infants and young children, as well as elderly, bedridden patients, there may be excessive secretion of saliva and fluid in the lungs which may lead to chest infections.

Important Note: Regardless of the cause, if you take these medications, report any mental or behavioral changes promptly to your doctor.

Effects on Pregnancy: Certain benzodiazepine sleeping pills have been linked to birth defects when taken during the early months of pregnancy. In addition, benzodiazepine sleeping pills taken during the last weeks of pregnancy have been known to sedate the baby. Therefore, **avoid using this medication during pregnancy.**

□ MOTRIN® Ⓟ

Pharmacia & Upjohn

Ibuprofen

Anti-inflammatory—Analgesic

Information for the Patient: What is Motrin? Motrin tablets contain ibuprofen, a member of the class of drugs called nonsteroidal anti-inflammatory drugs (NSAIDs). Motrin is used to treat the symptoms of certain types of arthritis by helping to relieve joint pain, swelling, stiffness and inflammation. Motrin may also be used to relieve mild to moderate pain, accompanied by inflammation, in conditions such as muscle or joint strains or damage, or after a tooth extraction procedure. It may also be used for the relief of menstrual pain.

Motrin helps to relieve joint pain, swelling, stiffness and fever by reducing the production of certain substances (prostaglandins) and helping to control inflammation and other body reactions.

How should Motrin be taken? You should take Motrin only as directed by your doctor. Do not take more of it, do not take it more often and do not take it for a longer period of time than your doctor or dentist ordered.

Be sure to take Motrin regularly as prescribed. In some types of arthritis, up to 2 weeks may pass before you feel the full effects of this medicine. During treatment, your doctor may decide to adjust the dosage according to your response to the medication.

To lessen stomach upset, take this medicine immediately after a meal or with food or milk. If stomach upset (indigestion, nausea, vomiting, stomach pain or diarrhea) occurs and continues, contact your doctor.

For the treatment of rheumatoid arthritis and osteoarthritis, the initial adult dosage is 1 200 mg divided into 3 or 4 equal doses.

For the treatment of mild to moderate pain with inflammation, in conditions such as muscle or joint strains or damage, after a tooth extraction procedure or for the relief of menstrual pain, you should take one 400 mg tablet every 4 to 6 hours as required. You should not take more than 2 400 mg in a day unless directed by your doctor or dentist.

Who should not use Motrin? Do not use this product if you are sensitive (allergic) to ibuprofen or products containing acetylsalicylic acid (ASA), other salicylates or other anti-inflammatory drugs unless directed to do so by your doctor.

Motrin should not be used by children under 12 years of age, except as recommended by a doctor.

What precautions should be followed when using Motrin? Consult your doctor before taking this drug if you have peptic ulcers, high blood pressure, heart failure, kidney or liver disease, any other serious disease, are pregnant or nursing, or are taking any other prescription or over-the-counter medicine.

Motrin (cont'd)

Take Motrin only as directed by your doctor, or dentist. Do not take more of it, do not take it more often, and do not take it for a longer period of time than ordered by your doctor or dentist.

If you will be taking this medicine for a long time, your doctor should check your progress at regular visits in order to make sure that this medicine is not causing unwanted effects.

Along with its needed effects, Motrin may cause some unwanted effects. Elderly, frail and debilitated patients appear to be at higher risk of more frequent or severe side effects. Although not all of these side effects appear very often, when they do occur they may require medical attention. Check with your doctor immediately if any of the following occur: bloody or black tarry stools; skin rash, hives or itching; blurred vision; swelling of feet or lower legs; hearing problems; mental confusion or depression; shortness of breath, troubled breathing, wheezing, or tightness in the chest; indigestion, nausea, vomiting, stomach pain or diarrhea; yellow discoloration of the skin or eyes, with or without fatigue; any changes in the amount or color of your urine (such as dark, red or brown).

Always Remember: Before taking this medication tell your doctor, dentist or pharmacist if you:

- are allergic to Motrin tablets or other related medicines of the NSAID group such as ASA, diclofenac, diflusinal, fenoprofen, flurbiprofen, ibuprofen, indomethacin, ketoprofen, mefenamic acid, piroxicam, sulindac, tiaprofenic acid or tolmetin;
- have a history of stomach upset, ulcers, or liver or kidney diseases;
- are pregnant or intend to become pregnant while taking this medicine;
- are breast-feeding;
- are taking any other medicine (either prescription or non-prescription);
- have any other medical problem(s).

While taking this medication:

- Tell any other doctor, dentist or pharmacist that you consult or see, that you are taking this medicine.
- Be cautious about driving or participating in activities that require alertness if you are drowsy, dizzy or lightheaded after taking this medication.
- Check with your doctor if you are not getting any relief or if any problems develop.
- Report any untoward reaction to your doctor. This is very important as it will aid in the early detection and prevention of potential complications.
- Your regular medical check-ups are essential.
- If you require more information on this drug, consult your doctor or pharmacist.

□ MS CONTIN® Ⓝ

Purdue Frederick

Morphine Sulfate

Opioid Analgesic

Information for the Patient: What is morphine? Morphine relieves pain and should help you to live more comfortably and independently. It is effective and safe when used as directed by your doctor.

Your pain may increase or decrease from time to time and your doctor may need to change the amount of morphine you take (daily dosage).

What is MS Contin? MS Contin is an oral tablet or a rectal suppository that is made in such a way as to slowly release morphine over a 12-hour period, usually requiring a dose only every 12 hours to control your pain. However, where more convenient, your doctor may ask you to take medication every 8 hours.

MS Contin tablets are available in five strengths: 15 mg (green), 30 mg (violet), 60 mg (orange), 100 mg (grey) and 200 mg (red). MS Contin suppositories are available in 30, 60, 100 and 200 mg strengths. It may be necessary for you to take more than one tablet strength (different colored tablets) or use more than one suppository strength at the same time, in order to receive the total daily dosage prescribed by your doctor.

MS Contin **15, 30, 60 and 100 mg** tablets must be swallowed intact, not chewed or crushed. The **200 mg** tablet may be broken in half along the indentation on the tablet; do not crush or chew the whole or half tablets.

How to Use Your Medication: Your starting dosage of MS Contin will be clearly labelled on the medication bottle or package. Be sure to follow the directions on the label exactly; this is very important. If your dosage is changed, be sure to write it down at the time your doctor calls you or sees you. And follow the new directions exactly.

MS Contin Tablets: MS Contin tablets must be taken regularly every 12 hours (with 4 to 6 oz. of water) or as directed by your doctor to prevent pain all day and night. If your pain worsens, making you uncomfortable, contact your doctor immediately and she/he may decide that it is necessary to adjust your daily dosage of MS Contin tablets.

MS Contin Suppositories: MS Contin suppository administration is achieved by finger length insertion into the rectum (after removing the plastic and foil packaging), while lying on your back. If you have the urge for a bowel movement, it is better to insert the suppository after the bowel movement. If you have a bowel movement after insertion of the suppository, do not insert another MS Contin suppository until the next scheduled dose.

MS Contin suppositories must be inserted regularly every 12 hours, or as directed by your doctor, to prevent pain all day or night. If your pain worsens, making you uncomfortable, contact your doctor immediately to ascertain if it is necessary to adjust your daily dosage of MS Contin suppositories.

Constipation: Morphine causes constipation. This is to be expected so your doctor may order a laxative and stool softener to help relieve your constipation while you are using MS Contin. Tell your doctor about the problem if it arises.

Taking Other Medications: Your doctor should be made aware of any other medication you are taking including over-the-counter antihistamines or sleep-aids as they could affect the way you respond to morphine.

Driving: Driving or other tasks requiring full alertness should not be attempted for the first few days of using MS Contin, since you may experience drowsiness or sedation.

Reordering MS Contin: A new written prescription is required from your doctor each time you need more MS Contin. Therefore, it is important to contact your doctor at least 3 working days before your current supply runs out. It is very important that you do not miss any doses.

Should your pain increase, or any other complaint develop as a result of taking MS Contin, contact your doctor immediately.

□ MSD® ENTERIC COATED ASA

Johnson & Johnson • Merck

ASA

Nonsteroidal Anti-inflammatory—Analgesic—Platelet Aggregation Inhibitor

Information for the Patient: What MSD Enteric Coated ASA Contains: MSD Enteric Coated ASA tablets contain acetylsalicylic acid, also known as ASA.

What MSD Enteric Coated ASA Does: MSD Enteric Coated ASA tablets have the following characteristics: **Action:** MSD Enteric Coated ASA tablets contain ASA. Clinical practice has established the suitability of ASA in relieving pain associated with conditions such as minor body aches, muscle, back and joint pain.

Special Enteric Coating to Help Prevent Stomach Upset: The special enteric coating of MSD Enteric Coated ASA enables the tablet to pass, undissolved, through the acidic stomach and enter the upper portion of the small intestine, a less acidic environment. It is then that the tablet is dissolved, thus it is less likely to cause stomach irritation that is sometimes associated with plain or buffered ASA.

Onset of Action: Because MSD Enteric Coated ASA tablets are specially coated to reduce the risk of stomach upset, the ASA is not absorbed by the stomach and the onset of action will be somewhat delayed.

When to Take MSD Enteric Coated ASA: MSD Enteric Coated ASA is indicated for the relief of minor aches and pains, such as backache, bursitis pain, knee pain, joint pain, muscle aches, lower back pain, tennis elbow, and muscular aches associated with arthritic and rheumatic pain. It is also useful in relieving pain and aches associated with colds.

How to Take MSD Enteric Coated ASA: Adults: The tablets must be swallowed whole, with a large glass of water (250 mL); do not crush or break up. It is hazardous to exceed the maximum recommended dose (650 mg per single dose or 4 g daily) unless advised by your physician. Consult your physican if your condition does not improve after 5 days of continued product use.

Precautions: If you are taking other medication, carefully read the labels to ensure that they do not also contain acetylsalicylic acid which could result in an overdose. If in doubt, consult your physician or pharmacist.

If you expect to undergo surgery, including dental surgery within 5 to 7 days of taking ASA or MSD Enteric Coated ASA tablets, consult your physician or pharmacist.

Consult a physician before taking this drug during the last 3 months of pregnancy or when breast-feeding.

Do not administer MSD Enteric Coated ASA tablets to children and teenagers who have chickenpox or flu symptoms before a physician or a pharmacist is consulted about Reye's Syndrome, a rare and serious illness.

There is enough drug in each package to seriously harm a child. Keep this medicine out of the reach of children.

When to Consult Your Physician or Pharmacist About MSD Enteric Coated ASA: A physician or pharmacist should be consulted prior to taking this medication in case of:

- allergy to salicylates or asthma
- during pregnancy or when breast-feeding
- if you have stomach problems, peptic ulcer, severe liver disease or gout
- a history of blood coagulation defects, or when receiving anticoagulant drugs
- ASA is not recommended 5 to 7 days prior to surgery or in the presence of severe anemia
- intake of other medications containing salicylates or acetaminophen, anti-inflammatory drugs, anticonvulsants, antidiabetic or gout medicine.

Possible Side Effects: MSD Enteric Coated ASA tablets occasionally may produce some unwanted effects. A physician should be contacted if any of the following reactions develop during treatment.

- bleeding or irritation of stomach (nausea, vomiting, pain)
- any loss of hearing, including ringing or buzzing in the ears
- skin rashes, hives or itching
- breathing difficulties.

What to Do in Case of Overdose: In case of accidental or suspected overdose, contact at once a physician, a Poison Control Centre, or the Emergency Department of a hospital immediately, even if there are no symptoms.

If emergency help is not available, vomiting should be induced at once (within 30 minutes) by syrup of ipecac; **vomiting should never be induced in unconscious individuals or in children younger than 1 year old without medical help.**

The signs and symptoms of an overdose usually occur within a few hours after ingestion. They may include: stomach upset, convulsions (seizures), hearing loss, mental confusion, ringing or buzzing in the ears, severe drowsiness or tiredness, severe excitement or nervousness and unusually fast or deep breathing, hallucinations or changes in behavior (especially in children).

Description of MSD Enteric Coated ASA Unprinted Tablets

Product Number	**490**	**491X**
Strength (mg)	**325**	**650**
Shape/Color	**round/brown**	**oval/orange**
Nonmedicinal Ingredients		
Cellulose acetate phthalate	x	x
Cornstarch	x	x
Diethyl phthalate	x	x
Guar gum	x	x
Hydrogenated vegetable oil	x	x
Hydroxypropyl cellulose	x	x
Hydroxypropyl methylcellulose	x	x
Microcrystalline cellulose	x	x
Polyvinyl acetate phthalate	x	—
Sodium lauryl sulfate	x	x
Sucrose	x	—
Coloring Agents		
Red ferric oxide	x	—
Sunset yellow aluminum lake	—	x
Titanium dioxide	—	x

Prescribing information available to pharmacists and physicians upon request.

☐ MYLERAN®

Glaxo Wellcome

Busulfan

Antileukemic

Information for the Patient: Patients beginning therapy with busulfan should be informed of the importance of having periodic blood counts and to immediately report any unusual fever or bleeding. Aside from the major toxicity of myelosuppression, patients should be instructed to report any difficulty in breathing, persistent cough or congestion. They should be told that diffuse pulmonary fibrosis is an infrequent but serious and potentially life-threatening complication of long-term busulfan therapy. Patients should be alerted to report any signs of abrupt weakness, unusual fatigue, anorexia, weight loss, nausea and vomiting, and melanoderma that could be associated with a syndrome resembling adrenal insufficiency. Patients should never be allowed to take the drug without medical supervision and they should be informed that other encountered toxicities to busulfan include infertility, amenorrhea, skin hyperpigmentation, drug hypersensitivity, dryness of the mucous membranes and rarely cataract formation. Women of childbearing potential should be advised to avoid becoming pregnant. The increased risk of a secondary malignancy should be explained to the patient.

☐ NAPROSYN®

Roche

Naproxen

Anti-inflammatory—Analgesic

Information for the Patient: How to make Naprosyn work best for you: Your doctor has decided that Naprosyn (naproxen) is the best treatment for you. As you take your Naprosyn tablets, remember that your chances of controlling your symptoms are greater if you cooperate fully with your doctor and try to become well informed about your condition.

This leaflet is not as thorough as the official Product Monograph on Naprosyn (which your doctor or pharmacist has available), and is meant to supplement what your doctor has told you. Your doctor knows and understands your personal condition; be sure to follow your doctor's instructions carefully and read any materials he or she gives you. **If you have any questions after reading this information leaflet, be sure to ask your doctor.**

What is Naprosyn? Naprosyn is the product name for naproxen, a medicine used to relieve the pain and inflammation associated with arthritis. It belongs to a family of drugs known as nonsteroidal anti-inflammatory drugs (NSAIDs) or anti-prostaglandin drugs.

What does Naprosyn look like? Naprosyn is available in easy to swallow, tablets, enteric-coated tablets and as a sustained release tablet which allows once daily dosing. A liquid form (a suspension), which has an orange-pineapple flavor, and a rectal suppository are also available.

Your doctor has chosen the strength (dose) that he or she thinks will be most effective in relieving your condition, based on experience with similar medical problems.

How does Naprosyn work? Conditions like yours are usually associated with three symptoms: pain, inflammation, and/or stiffness. Research shows that Naprosyn works by reducing the production of certain substances (called prostaglandins) that the body normally produces to help control such functions as muscle contraction, inflammation, and numerous other body processes.

Clinical studies indicate that when prostaglandin levels are reduced, the intensity of pain, stiffness, and inflammation is reduced as well.

How should you take Naprosyn to make it work best for you? Usually Naprosyn tablets or suspension is prescribed to be taken twice a day. It doesn't need to be taken more often than that. You don't have to carry your medication with you everywhere—just take 1 dose in the morning and 1 dose in the evening. The sustained release Naprosyn SR tablets have been designed for convenient once daily dosing in the morning or evening. The maximum daily dose of Naprosyn SR must not be exceeded and should be swallowed whole. For the most relief, take your Naprosyn at the same time each day.

If Naprosyn Suppositories have been prescribed, your doctor or pharmacist will explain how to use them.

Naprosyn (cont'd)

It's important to keep taking Naprosyn even after you start to feel better. This helps to keep your pain, tenderness, and stiffness under control. You should take Naprosyn with food or milk.

Important: Your doctor may give you different instructions better suited to your specific needs. If you need more information about how to take Naprosyn properly, double-check with your doctor or pharmacist.

How long does it take before Naprosyn begins to work? Naprosyn is completely absorbed into your system usually within 2 to 4 hours. Some people are able to feel improvement in their symptoms right away; for others, improvement may take up to 2 weeks. By the end of 2 weeks, if Naprosyn does not seem to be helping you, tell your doctor. You may need a different dosage, or your doctor may want to prescribe another treatment program for you.

Will the amount of Naprosyn you take ever change? It might change. Your condition, as your doctor may have explained to you, has its ups and downs. The amount of pain, stiffness, and inflammation in your joints may vary from week to week. As time goes by, your doctor may decide that it is advisable to make adjustments in the dosage of Naprosyn you are taking. He or she may suggest that you increase or decrease your medication according to how severe your symptoms are or how active you are.

Follow instructions; your doctor understands how to set the upper and lower dosage limits so that you get the greatest benefit from Naprosyn.

Does Naprosyn have side effects? Any medication can cause side effects; this is true for ASA and all of the nonsteroidal anti-inflammatory drugs that are used to treat conditions like yours. Naprosyn has been prescribed for over 10 000 000 people worldwide in the last 10 years. In most patients it has been well tolerated so the chances are that you will tolerate it well too. Side effects are significantly less than those occurring with acetylsalicylic acid (ASA) in doses used to treat arthritis.

Do not take ASA, ASA-containing compounds or other drugs used to relieve symptoms of arthritis while taking Naprosyn unless directed to do so by your physician.

Relatively common unwanted side effects of all nonsteroidal anti-inflammatory drugs are heartburn, pain in the gut, nausea constipation, and so forth. Remember to take Naprosyn with meals or with a glass of milk to reduce discomfort of this type.

If you have a history of stomach upset, or if you have an ulcer, tell your doctor. All nonsteroidal anti-inflammatory drugs may aggravate your problem and sometimes even cause bleeding, or ulcers in your stomach or intestines. These complications can sometimes be severe and occasional fatalities have been reported with all drugs of this class.

Contact your doctor immediately if you experience any of these symptoms: bloody or black tarry stools; shortness of breath, wheezing, any trouble in breathing or tightness in chest; skin rash, swelling, hives or itching; indigestion, nausea, vomiting, stomach pain or diarrhea; yellow discoloration of the skin or eyes, with or without fatigue; any changes in the amount or color of your urine (such as dark; red or brown); swelling of the feet or lower legs; blurred vision or any visual disturbance.

Other effects that have been reported infrequently include headache, drowsiness, dizziness, depression and ringing in the ears. These reactions usually do not pose a serious problem, and most people can continue treatment. More rarely, visual or hearing disturbances and blood disorders have occurred. **Contact your doctor if you experience any problems.** Almost all of the side effects experienced with Naprosyn stop when the medication is stopped.

The use of rectal suppositories has in some patients, caused a burning sensation in the rectum and rarely rectal bleeding.

If you are allergic to ASA or to any of the other nonsteroidal anti-inflammatory drugs (e.g. diclofenac, diflunisal, fenoprofen, flurbiprofen, ibuprofen, indomethacin, ketoprofen, ketorolac, mefenamic acid, piroxicam, sulindac, tiaprofenic acid, tolmetin) used to treat arthritis or other muscle and joint conditions, **do not take Naprosyn.** You may be allergic to it too. **Also, you should not take Naprosyn if you are already taking Anaprox (naproxen sodium), a related drug.**

Are there any special do's and don'ts about taking Naprosyn? Do tell your doctor and pharmacist about any other medications you take, both prescription and nonprescription. This is important because some drugs can interact with each other and produce undesirable effects.

Do tell your doctor if you have an ulcer, liver disease, kidney disease, or history of any stomach problems.

Do be cautious about driving or participating in activities that require alertness if you are drowsy, dizzy, or light-headed after taking Naprosyn (naproxen).

Do check with your doctor if: you are not getting relief or you have any problems while taking Naprosyn.

Do tell your physician if you are pregnant or are planning to become pregnant.

Don't take Naprosyn if you are breast-feeding. The drug does pass into the milk of nursing women.

Don't take Naprosyn if you are allergic to it, or if you have had an allergic-type reaction to ASA or to any other drug used for pain relief or arthritis. Do check with your doctor.

Do cooperate with your doctor if he or she wants you to take certain lab tests to monitor the effectiveness of treatment or possible side effects.

□ NASACORT™ Ⓟ

Rhône-Poulenc Rorer

Triamcinolone Acetonide

Corticosteroid

Information for the Patient:

—Use regularly as directed by your physician.
—Do not exceed the prescribed dose.
—Nasacort is not intended to give immediate relief of your nasal symptoms and it may take a few days (and up to 2 weeks) before you notice any improvement.

Contact your physician if:

- no improvement occurs after 3 weeks
- nasal irritation occurs
- colored (yellow or green) nasal secretions appear
- repeated nasal bleeding occurs

Before **each use** of your Nasacort nasal inhaler, gently blow your nose, making sure your nostrils are clear. Then follow these steps (see package insert for illustrations):

Step 1. Remove the white protective cap from the nasal inhaler.
Step 2. Shake the canister well.
Step 3. Hold the inhaler between your thumb and forefinger.
Step 4. Tilt your head back slightly and insert the end of the inhaler into one nostril, pointing it slightly toward the outside nostril wall, while holding your other nostril closed with one finger.
Step 5. Press down on the canister to release 1 dose and, at the same time, inhale gently.
Step 6. Hold your breath for a few seconds, then breathe out slowly through your mouth.
Step 7. Withdraw the nasal inhaler from your nostril.
Step 8. **Repeat the process in your other nostril.**
Note: When the physician prescribes more than 1 puff per nostril, for each puff repeat steps 4 through 8.
Step 9. Replace the white protective inhaler cap on the nasal inhaler.
Note: Avoid blowing your nose for the next 15 minutes.

Your Nasacort inhaler should be cleaned weekly. Clean the nasal adapter **thoroughly** in luke warm water. Allow the adapter to **dry completely** before inserting canister for the next use.

Contents under pressure. Do not place in hot water or near radiators, stoves, or other sources of heat. Even when empty do not puncture or incinerate containers or store at temperatures over 50°C.

□ NASACORT® AQ Ⓟ

Rhône-Poulenc Rorer

Triamcinolone Acetonide

Corticosteroid

Information for the Patient: Nasacort AQ (Triamcinolone Acetonide Aqueous Nasal Spray): Please read this leaflet carefully before you start to take your medication. For further information or advice, ask your doctor or pharmacist.

The Name of Your Medicine: The name of your medicine is Nasacort AQ (triamcinolone acetonide aqueous nasal spray). This is one of a group of medicines called corticosteroids.

Nasacort AQ can only be obtained on the prescription of a doctor.

About Your Medicine: Nasacort AQ is used to treat seasonal allergic rhinitis (including hayfever) and perennial rhinitis. Symptoms of these conditions include itching, a blocked up feeling in the nose and excessive sneezing. Nasacort AQ reduces the irritation and inflammation in the lining of the nose and nasal passages and so it relieves the blocked up feeling in the nose, the runny nose, itching and sneezing.

Before Using This Medication: Tell your doctor or pharmacist (if you have not already done so) any of the following before you start taking the medication:
- If you have already taken Nasacort AQ or any other corticosteroids and developed an allergy or intolerance to any of them;
- If you are allergic to any other substances, such as food, preservatives or dyes;
- If you are pregnant or breast-feeding, or likely to become pregnant or breast-feed. Your doctor may decide not to prescribe this medication in these circumstances;
- If you are taking any other prescription or nonprescription (over-the-counter) medicines;
- If you suffer from any other medical problems or if you have had a recent injury or surgery to your nose.

Proper Use of This Medication: Follow the **Instructions for Use** described below. If you have any problems tell your doctor or pharmacist.
- It is important that you inhale each dose through the nose as instructed. The label will usually tell you how many doses to take. If it does not, ask your doctor or pharmacist.
- **Do not** inhale more doses or use your nasal spray more often than your doctor advises.
- It takes a few days for this medicine to work. **It is very important that you use it regularly. Do not stop** treatment even if you feel better, unless told to do so by your doctor.
- If your symptoms have not improved after 3 weeks of treatment with Nasacort AQ, tell your doctor.
- Adults and children 12 years of age and older: The usual dose is 2 sprays into each nostril once daily (220 μg).
- Children 4 to 12 years of age: The recommended dose is 110 μg/day given as 1 spray in each nostril once a day.
- Nasacort AQ is not recommended for children under 4 years of age.

Instructions for Use (see package insert for illustrations): It is important to shake the bottle well before each use. Also, the bottle should be discarded after 120 sprays. Do not transfer any remaining suspension to another bottle.

Before each use of your Nasacort AQ nasal spray, gently blow your nose, making sure your nostrils are clear. Then follow these steps.

Prior to Use:
1. Pull the cover and the clip off the spray pump unit. Do not attempt to enlarge the tiny hole in the spray tip. If the actuator has come off the pump stem, re-insert stem in actuator.
2. Shake the spray pump unit.

Preparing for Use:
3. To prepare for use, the spray pump unit must be primed prior to the first use. To prime, put 2 fingers on the ''shoulders'' of the bottle. Push bottle with thumb **firmly** and **quickly** for a full-stroke actuation until a fine spray appears (5 pumps). Now your spray pump unit is primed and ready for use.
4. A fine mist can only be produced by a rapid and firm pumping action.
5. Repriming is only necessary when the spray pump unit has not been used for more than 14 days. To reprime, shake the bottle and pump only once. Now the spray pump unit is reprimed.

To Use:
6. Gently blow nose to clean nostrils, if needed.
7. Pull the cover and the clip off the spray pump unit, and shake pump unit.
8. Hold spray pump unit firmly as shown with the index and middle finger on either side of the spray tip and thumb on bottom of the bottle. Rest back of index finger against upper lip. **Be careful so fingers will not slip off spray pump unit as you spray.**
9. Put the spray tip into one nostril (tip should not reach far into the nose). **Bend head forward** so spray will aim toward the back of the nose.
10. Point tip straight back into nose. Close the other nostril with finger. Pump spray unit by pushing the bottle with thumb **firmly** and **quickly** for a full-stroke actuation and sniff gently at the same time. Repeat procedure for the other nostril.
11. Repeat steps 8, 9, 10 if instructed to use more than 1 spray per nostril.
12. Avoid blowing nose for 15 minutes following dosing.
13. Keep the cover and the clip on the spray pump unit when not in use.

We have included a convenient check-off chart to assist you in keeping track of medication sprays used. This will help assure that you receive the 120 ''Full Sprays'' of medication present. Please note that the bottle has been filled with extra solution to accommodate the initial priming activity.

What to Do if You Miss a Dose: If you miss a dose do not worry; take a dose if you remember within an hour or so. However, if you do not remember until later, skip the missed dose and go back to your regular dosing schedule. Do not double doses.

What to Do if an Overdose is Taken: Tell your doctor if you use more than you were told.

What to Do if You Stop Your Medicine: If your doctor decides to stop your treatment, do not keep any left over medicine unless your doctor tells you to.

Storage of Your Medicine: Keep out of the reach of children.

Store at controlled room temperature (15 to 30°C).

Side Effects of this Medication: Along with its needed effects, a medicine may cause some unwanted effects. Contact your physician as soon as possible if any of the following occur:
- If you notice that any discharge from your nose is yellow or green;
- If you experience an unpleasant taste or smell;
- If your nose or throat becomes painful or if you have a severe nose bleed after using the nasal spray;
- If you feel unwell or have any other problems.

Other side effects may occur that usually do not need medical attention. They may go away as your body adjusts to the medicine. However, check with your doctor if any of the following side effects continue or are bothersome:
- Sneezing;
- Headaches;
- Burning, dryness or other irritation inside the nose (lasting only a short time after applying the medication).

Other side effects not listed above may also occur in some patients. If you notice any other effects, check with your doctor.

A Reminder: Remember this medicine is for **you.** Only a doctor can prescribe it for you. Never give it to others. It may harm them even if their symptoms are the same as yours.

Keep all medicines out of the reach of children.

If you have questions or are not sure about anything, then you should ask your doctor or pharmacist.

You may want to read this leaflet again. Please **do not throw it away** until you have finished your medicine.

☐ NEORAL® Ⓟ

Novartis Pharmaceuticals

Cyclosporine
Immunosuppressant

Information for the Patient: Your doctor has prescribed a powerful drug Neoral. It is used after organ transplants to help prevent organ rejection, or to treat autoimmune conditions such as psoriasis, rheumatoid arthritis and nephrotic syndrome.

Read this information carefully, even if you have already been taking Neoral or Sandimmune. It will help you learn about this drug so you can benefit from its use.

This information should not replace your doctor's or pharmacist's advice. Because of your specific condition, these people may have given you different or additional instructions. If any information in this text concerns you, talk to your doctor or pharmacist right away.

What is Neoral? Neoral is the brand name for a drug called ''cyclosporine''. It belongs to a family of drugs known as ''immunosuppressants''. These drugs work to ''suppress'' or reduce the body's immune response.

You may have been taking a drug called Sandimmune, which is another form of cyclosporine.

Neoral is like Sandimmune, except that it is in a ''microemulsion'' form. This form allows more reliable absorption of cyclosporine from your stomach. This means almost the same amount will go into your body each time you take the drug, and that food will have less of an effect on the amount of cyclosporine that gets absorbed.

Neoral (cont'd)

What does Neoral do? Your body's immune system normally works to protect you from infections and other foreign material. When you receive a transplant, this system does not recognize the new organ, and will try to reject it. Neoral works to reduce this response, so your body is more likely to accept the new organ.

Neoral does not completely suppress the immune system, so your body will still have some infection-fighting ability.

Neoral may be given alone, but is often given with other drugs which also suppress your immune system. Together these help prolong the life of an organ transplant.

There is also increasing evidence that the immune system is involved in causing a variety of conditions considered to be of autoimmune origin, such as psoriasis, rheumatoid arthritis and nephrotic syndrome, and your doctor has prescribed Neoral to suppress certain functions of your immune system to treat your condition.

What should I Do Before I Take Neoral? Before you take Neoral, be sure you have told your doctor:

- about all other health conditions you have now, or have had in the past;
- about all other medicines or treatments you use, including any products you buy at a pharmacy, supermarket or health food store;
- if you have ever had a bad, unusual or allergic reaction to cyclosporine, Sandimmune or Neoral.
- if you are pregnant, plan to become pregnant, or are breast-feeding a baby.

How Much Neoral Should I Take?

- Always take the exact amount of Neoral your doctor tells you. If you are not sure of your dose, or when to take it, ask your doctor, pharmacist or nurse.
- Different people will need different amounts of this drug. Your doctor has decided your specific dose based on your weight, medical conditions, and response to this drug. Do not take any more, or any less, of this drug than your doctor says.
- Blood tests are one of the ways your doctor tells how much Neoral you need. Based on these tests, and on your response to this drug, your doctor may change your dose from time to time. Do not change the dose on your own, no matter how you are feeling.

When Should I Take Neoral?

- Space your doses of Neoral as evenly as you can throughout the day. For example, if you take the drug 2 times a day, leave about 12 hours between each dose. If you take it more than 2 times a day, ask your doctor how many hours you should have between each dose.
- Try to take your dose(s) at the same time(s) each day. This will help keep a constant amount of drug in your body. Taking your medicine at the same time(s) each day will also help you remember each dose.
- Neoral may be taken with or without food. But it is best to be consistent: once you decide when you are going to take it in relation to food, do it the same way each time.
- Never take Neoral **with grapefruit juice.** This drink may increase the amount of cyclosporine that goes into your body. Other kinds of drinks do not cause this problem.
- Vomiting or diarrhea may stop Neoral from being absorbed (going) into your body. **Always** call your doctor if you have either of these symptoms. A different dose or another form of this drug may be needed.
- **For Patients Switching From Sandimmune Oral Formulations:** If you are switching from Sandimmune to Neoral, you may need a different dose. Your response will also need to be checked. Be sure to go to all your check-ups while you are changing to this product.

What Happens If I Miss A Dose of Neoral?

- For transplant patients, missing even a few doses of Neoral may lead to rejection of your transplanted organ. That is why it is so important to take each of the doses your doctor prescribes.
- Talk to your doctor, nurse or pharmacist if you have trouble remembering doses, or if you are uncertain about how to take them. Also be sure to discuss any concerns you have about taking this drug as prescribed. These people can often suggest ways to overcome problems you have taking your medication.
- Never allow your medication to run out between refills. Plan to order your refills about 1 week ahead of time—that way you will always have a supply in case the pharmacy is closed or out of the drug. Also be sure to take enough medication with you when you go on a holiday.
- If you ever do miss a dose of Neoral, do not try to catch up on your own. Instead, call your doctor or pharmacist right away for advice. It is also a good idea to ask your doctor ahead of time what to do about missed doses.

How Do I Take Neoral? Neoral comes in 2 forms: a soft gelatin **capsule** and an **oral solution.** The following points tell you how to take the form you have been given.

Capsules:

- Neoral capsules come with 10 mg, 25 mg, 50 mg or 100 mg of cyclosporine. Each capsule is contained in a foil strip.
- Leave the capsules in the foil until you need a dose. When you are ready to take a dose remove the number of capsules you need to make up the dose your doctor prescribed.
- Swallow the capsules whole. You may use any kind of drink except grapefruit juice.

Solution: Neoral solution comes in 50 millilitre bottles. Each dose must be measured accurately and taken exactly as described below.

To open the bottle for the first time:

1. Flip off plastic cap and bend right back.
2. Tear off whole of cap and sealing ring.
3. Remove black stopper and throw away.
4. Push tube until firmly into neck of bottle.
5. Insert syringe into white stopper.
6. Draw up prescribed volume of solution.
7. Expel any **large** bubbles by depressing and withdrawing plunger a few times before removing syringe containing prescribed dose from bottle. The presence of a few tiny bubbles is of no importance and will not affect the dose in any way.

Turn the syringe so the tip is pointing down. Place it over a cup about half-full of the drink you will be using.* Put your dose into the cup by pressing down on the syringe plunger. **Do not let the syringe touch the liquid in the cup.** Stir the solution well and **drink it right away.**

*Have the drink at room temperature. **Do not use grapefruit juice as the drink.** Most other drinks may be used—for example, apple juice, orange juice or a soft drink. Once you have chosen a drink, use the same one each time.

8. When you are finished, wipe only the outside of the syringe with a dry tissue. Put it back in the case and close the bottle with the cap. The white stopper and tube should remain in the bottle. Do not rinse the syringe with water, alcohol or any other liquid.

Once the bottle is opened the first time, you can start at point number 5 above for your next dose.

- Be sure to ask your doctor, nurse or pharmacist if you have any questions about how to measure the solution.
- If you accidentally take too much of your medicine (i.e., more than twice the prescribed dose), tell your doctor right away, or call your nearest emergency room or Poison Control Centre.

What Precautions Should I Follow With Neoral?

- Neoral is often given with other medicines. Make sure you know if you are to stop, or to continue, other immunosuppressant drugs you had been taking.
- Tell **all** health professionals you see (doctor, dentists, nurses, pharmacists) that you are taking Neoral. It is also a good idea to wear a medic-alert bracelet.
- Do **not** take any other drugs without asking your doctor or pharmacist first. This includes anything you can buy off the shelf such as over-the-counter medicines (including aspirin-like medicines) and herbal or home remedies. These may affect the way Neoral works for you.
- Neoral may make vaccinations less effective or increase your risk of getting an illness from a live vaccine. Always discuss this possibility with your doctor before you get any vaccinations or immunizations.
- Be sure to keep **all** appointments at your clinic. Some of these visits will be used to check the level of cyclosporine in your blood. For transplant patients, levels that are too low can cause transplant rejection, while levels that are too high may cause damage to other organs. It is therefore very important not to miss any tests or check-ups your doctor orders.
- Tell your doctor at once if you become pregnant while you are taking this drug. You will want to discuss the possible benefits and risks of continuing with this drug.
- Like all medicines, Neoral causes side effects in some people. It does, however, affect different people in different ways. Just because side effects have occurred in other people does not mean you will get them. Be sure to talk to your doctor if you have any concerns

about this. He or she may be able to suggest ways to help prevent or reduce any problems you might have.

- **Do not stop taking Neoral on your own even if you have been taking it for several years. Transplant patients: Although you may not notice any symptoms of rejection for several weeks, missing even a few doses of Neoral may lead to rejection of your transplanted organ.**
- Neoral may cause tender or swollen gums. This effect can be reduced with good dental care. Brush your teeth carefully and often with a soft toothbrush, and use dental floss daily. It may also help to massage your gums daily with a soft toothbrush. Have regular dental check-ups and if your gums do become tender, swollen or red, tell your doctor or dentist right away.
- Increased growth of fine hairs on the body can also occur. This may be reduced by shaving or by using ''depilatory'' cream (a cream that removes hair). Be sure to ask your doctor or pharmacist if you have any questions about these products.
- Because Neoral reduces the function of your immune system, you are more likely to get bacterial, fungal or viral infections. To help reduce complications from these infections, tell your doctor **right away** about any cold or flu-like symptoms (such as a fever or sore throat), any boils on your skin, or pain when you urinate (pass your water).
- The decreased function of your immune system may also increase your chances of developing cancer. Although very rare, cancers of the white blood cells (lymphomas) and other types of cancer have occurred in people taking cyclosporine.

The following are some possible warning signs of cancer. To help detect any cancers as soon as possible, report any of these symptoms to your doctor right away: a change in your bowel or bladder habits; any sore that doesn't heal; unusual bleeding or discharge; the appearance of a lump or thickened areas in your breast or anywhere else on your body; unexplained stomach upset or any trouble with swallowing; an obvious change in a wart or a mole; a nagging cough or hoarseness; night sweats.

- Other side effects which have been reported with Neoral are listed here. Be sure to tell your doctor right away if you notice any of these symptoms, and especially if they continue, bother you in any way, or seem to increase in intensity: loss of appetite, nausea, vomiting or diarrhea; acne or oily skin; slight trembling of the hands (this often goes away on its own); tingling in the fingers, toes or mouth; muscle or joint pains or cramping; weakness, anxiety, blurred vision or headache; night sweats; hearing loss; swelling of the face; high blood pressure; increased cholesterol levels; kidney or liver problems; increased potassium in the body (your doctor may instruct you to avoid high dietary potassium intake); ulcers (rare); convulsions (quite rare).
- Remember, only a doctor can tell if these symptoms might be from Neoral. If you think you are having side effects, talk to your doctor right away. Do not stop taking this drug on your own.
- **Special Note for Female Patients:** There is an increased risk of difficult pregnancies (up to 25% of pregnancies) in patients who have taken cyclosporine during pregnancy. These difficult pregnancies have resulted in an increased risk to the babies during and immediately after birth. As well, some babies have been born with abnormalities. Most of the experience of the effect of cyclosporine on pregnancy has been with patients who have taken cyclosporine (often with other powerful drugs) for transplants, so we do not know to what extent these difficulties in pregnancies are due to other conditions or to cyclosporine. For these reasons it is recommended that you do not take Neoral if you are, or become pregnant. During your treatment with Neoral and for 2 months after stopping your Neoral treatment, you must use a reliable method of birth control. Should you become pregnant during the time you are taking your Neoral you should inform your doctor at once.

Do not breast-feed your baby if you are taking Neoral as it passes into breast milk and may harm your baby.

Where Should I Keep Neoral?

- **Keep Neoral out of the reach of children.** A child who accidentally takes this drug may be seriously harmed. A locked drawer or cupboard is best if you have small children in the house.
- Neoral **capsules** should be kept in a dry place, at a temperature between 15 and 25°C. Remember to leave each capsule in its foil pack until you need to take it.
- Neoral oral solution should be kept at room temperature (15 to 30°C), preferably not below 20°C for prolonged periods. Do not put it in the fridge, and do not let it freeze. Once the bottle has been opened, the contents must be used within 2 months. Be sure to keep the solution in the original bottle.
- A jelly-like formation may occur if the **oral solution** goes below 20°C. This should go away when the solution is warmed to 30°C. Little flakes (or a slight sediment) may still be seen. Having this happen does not change the effectiveness or safety of the product, and dosing by means of the syringe remains accurate.

☐ NEOSPORIN® Preparations ℞

Glaxo Wellcome

Polymyxin B—Neomycin Compound

Antibiotic

Information for the Patient: General: If redness, irritation, swelling or pain persists or increases, discontinue use and notify physician.
Eye and Ear Solution: Avoid contaminating the dropper with material from the eye, ear, fingers or other source. This caution is necessary if the sterility of the solution is to be preserved.
Ophthalmic Ointment: Avoid contaminating the applicator tip with material from the eye, fingers or other source. This caution is necessary if the sterility of the preparation is to be preserved.

☐ NEURONTIN™ ℞

Parke-Davis

Gabapentin

Antiepileptic

Information for the Patient: Please read this information carefully before you start to take your medicine, even if you have taken this drug before. Do not throw away this leaflet until you have finished your medicine as you may need to read it again. For further information or advice, please ask your doctor or pharmacist.

What is Neurontin:

- Neurontin (gabapentin) belongs to the family of medicines called antiepileptic drugs for treating epilepsy.
- Neurontin has been prescribed for you by your doctor to reduce your number of seizures.

Important Points You Must Tell Your Doctor Before Taking Neurontin:

- Tell about all your medical conditions, especially if you have any kidney disease.
- If you are pregnant or thinking about becoming pregnant, or if you are breast-feeding.
- Any other medicines (prescription and nonprescription) you are taking.
- Inform your doctor of your usual alcohol consumption.

How to Take Neurontin:

- It is very important that you take Neurontin exactly as your doctor has instructed.
- Never increase or decrease the amount of Neurontin you are taking unless your doctor tells you to.
- Do not stop taking it abruptly because your seizures may increase.
- If you miss a dose, take it as soon as possible. However, if it is within 4 hours of your next dose do not take the missed dose and return to your regular dosing schedule.
- Neurontin may be taken with or without food.

When Not to Use Neurontin:

- Do not use Neurontin if you are allergic to it or any of the components in the formulation (see list of components at the end of this leaflet).

Precautions When Taking Neurontin:

- Call your doctor immediately if your seizures get worse.
- Contact your doctor immediately if you experience any severe, unusual or allergic reactions.
- When you first begin taking Neurontin you may experience some side effects such as drowsiness, dizziness, and fatigue. Consult your doctor if you experience any of these, as the dose may have to be adjusted.
- If your epilepsy is not controlled, it is very important not to perform any potentially hazardous tasks, such as driving a car or operating dangerous machines. If your epilepsy is controlled, it is important to refrain from potentially dangerous tasks until you are sure this medication does not affect your mental alertness or physical coordination.
- Avoid alcoholic drinks while taking Neurontin.

Neurontin (cont'd)

What to Do in Case of Overdose:
- Contact your doctor or nearest hospital emergency department, even though you may not feel sick.

How to Store Neurontin:
- Store at room temperature (15 to 30°C).
- Keep out of reach of children.

What Does Neurontin Contain:
- Neurontin is available in capsules containing 100 mg, 300 mg or 400 mg of gabapentin as the active medicinal ingredient. Nonmedicinal ingredients include lactose, cornstarch, talc, gelatin, titanium dioxide, silicon dioxide, sodium lauryl sulfate, FD&C Blue No. 2, and yellow iron oxide or red iron oxide.

Who Manufactures Neurontin:
- Neurontin capsules are manufactured by: Parke-Davis Division, Warner-Lambert Canada Inc., Scarborough, Ontario M1L 2N3.

Reminder: This medicine has been prescribed only for you. Do not give it to anybody else.

If you require any further information or advice, please consult your doctor or pharmacist.

☐ NICODERM®

Hoechst Marion Roussel

Nicotine

Smoking Cessation Aid

Information for the Patient: Nicoderm User's Guide: Important: Read these instructions carefully before using Nicoderm. Do not throw away the carton or User's Guide. They contain important information that you may need to read again.

Keys to Success:
1. You must really want to quit smoking for Nicoderm to help you.
2. Apply a new patch every day.
3. You should follow your Nicoderm program for its full duration.
4. Nicoderm works best when used together with a stop smoking support program.
5. If you have trouble using Nicoderm or understanding the Nicoderm program, ask your doctor or pharmacist.

Congratulations! You have taken an important first step towards becoming a nonsmoker. **Starting now, you must give up smoking completely.** Your strength and willpower, combined with the proper use of Nicoderm, will help you wean yourself off nicotine gradually, while reducing nicotine withdrawal symptoms.

Quitting Smoking is Hard: If you've tried to quit before and haven't succeeded, don't be discouraged. Quitting isn't easy. It takes time, and most people try a few times before they are successful. The important thing is to try again until you succeed. This User's Guide will give you support as you become a nonsmoker. It answers common questions about Nicoderm and gives tips to help you stop smoking, and should be referred to often.

Where to Get Help: You are more likely to stop smoking by using Nicoderm with a support program that helps you break your smoking habit. Your doctor or pharmacist may be able to recommend stop smoking support groups in your area. For additional information on Nicoderm you can call us any time at 1-800-265-7927.

Understanding Your Habit: Many of the cigarettes you smoke are **''habit''** cigarettes, you've gotten into the habit of having them at certain times, like:
- after meals
- while talking on the phone
- when you're under stress
- with morning coffee
- while driving your car
- while having a drink with friends

The other cigarettes you smoke are cigarettes your body feels it **''needs''**. Nicotine is a chemical your body has come to like and depend on. When you smoke, nicotine is released into your bloodstream, topping up its supply. After a while, your blood levels of nicotine decrease until you feel a craving telling you to top up again.

How Nicoderm Patches Work: Nicoderm provides a lower level of nicotine to your blood than cigarettes, and allows you to gradually do away with your body's need for nicotine. It works as a temporary aid to help you quit smoking by reducing nicotine cravings and nicotine withdrawal symptoms such as irritability, frustration, anxiety, difficulty concentrating and restlessness. Without these powerful urges for the cigarettes you ''need'', getting rid of the ''habit'' cigarettes becomes much easier.

Nicoderm is the only patch that has a rate-controlling membrane, to give your body a steady supply of nicotine to help protect you against cravings. This unique feature offers 24-hour-a-day protection, even against the early morning cravings many people find the most difficult.

The Nicoderm Program:
1. **First, check that you bought the right starting dose.** Most smokers should start with **Step 1** (21 mg/day). However, you should start with **Step 2** (14 mg/day), if **one or more** of the following conditions apply to you:
- smoke less than 10 cigarettes a day;
- weigh less than 45 kg (100 lbs);
- have heart disease and your doctor recommended Nicoderm.

2. **Next, choose your Quit Day:** Pick a Quit Day. This is the day you will quit smoking cigarettes and begin using Nicoderm to reduce your cravings for nicotine.
3. **Follow the Nicoderm 10 Week Program that is right for you.** If you:
- smoke less than 10 cigarettes a day, or
- weigh less than 45 kg (100 lbs), or
- have heart disease, and your doctor recommended Nicoderm

then **Read and Follow** the 10 Week Program in **Section 3A**.

If none of these conditions apply to you, Read and Follow the 10 Week Program in **Section 3B**.

A. Nicoderm 10 Week Program for smokers who:
- smoke less than 10 cigarettes a day, or
- weigh less than 45 kgs (100 lbs), or
- have heart disease and their doctor recommended Nicoderm.

Step 1: Go directly to Step 2.
Step 2: Initial Treatment Period: For the first 6 weeks, you'll use the **Step 2** (14 mg/day) Nicoderm patch. Be sure to follow the directions under the section **''How to Use Nicoderm Patches''**.
Step 3: Step-Down Treatment Period: For weeks 7 and 8, you'll use the **Step 3** (7 mg/day) Nicoderm patch. This step reduces your nicotine intake, and prepares you to stop using Nicoderm all together. If you need to, use the **Step 3** (7 mg/day) Nicoderm patch for an additional two weeks (weeks 9 and 10).

B. Nicoderm 10 Week Program for those smokers not covered under Section 3A:
Step 1: Initial Treatment Period: For the first 6 weeks you'll use the highest strength **Step 1** (21 mg/day) Nicoderm patch, because at first your body's cravings will be strongest. Be sure to follow the directions under the section **''How to Use Nicoderm Patches''**.
Step 2: First Step-Down Treatment Period: For weeks 7 and 8, you'll use the **Step 2** (14 mg/day) Nicoderm patch. Switching to Step 2 after 6 weeks begins to gradually reduce your nicotine usage.
Step 3: Final Step-Down Treatment Period: For weeks 9 and 10, you'll use the **Step 3** (7 mg/day) Nicoderm patch. This last step further reduces your nicotine intake, and prepares you to stop using Nicoderm all together.

C. Important For All Smokers Using Nicoderm: Stop using Nicoderm at the end of week 10. If after this 10 week program, you still feel the need to smoke or have restarted smoking and wish to repeat the program, talk with your doctor or pharmacist to determine when the next best time to try again would be. **Do not use Nicoderm continuously for more than 3 months.**

Completing the full step-down program is important. The step-down treatment period allows you to gradually reduce the amount of nicotine you get, rather than stopping suddenly, and will increase your chances of quitting successfully.

How to Use Nicoderm Patches: Read all of the following instructions before using Nicoderm patches. Refer to them often to make sure you're using Nicoderm correctly.

Important:
- **Stop smoking completely before you start using Nicoderm.**
- **Do not use more than one patch at a time, as this may cause nicotine overdose.**
- **Remove the Nicoderm patch 2 hours before engaging in prolonged, strenuous exercise, as this may increase nicotine absorption through the skin and cause symptoms of nicotine overdose.**

How to Apply Nicoderm Patches:
1. Do not remove the Nicoderm patch from its sealed protective pouch until you are ready to use it. Nicoderm patches will lose nicotine to

the air if you store them out of the pouch. Before putting on the patch, tear open the pouch. Do not use scissors to open the pouch because you might accidentally cut the patch.

2. Choose a non-hairy, clean, dry area of your front or back above the waist or the upper outer area of your arm. Do not put Nicoderm patches on skin that is burned, broken out, cut, or irritated in any way. Make sure your skin is free of lotion and soap before applying a patch.
3. A clear protective liner covers the sticky silver side of the Nicoderm patch, which is the side that will be put on your skin. The liner has a slit down the middle to help you remove it from the patch. With the silver side facing you, pull one half of the liner away from the Nicoderm patch starting at the middle slit. Hold the Nicoderm patch at one of the outside edges (touch the silver side as little as possible), and pull off the other half of the protective liner. Throw away this liner.
4. Immediately apply the sticky side of the Nicoderm patch to your skin. Press the patch firmly on your skin with the heel of your hand for at least 10 seconds. Make sure it sticks well to your skin, especially around the edges.
5. Rinse your hands with water when you have finished applying the Nicoderm patch. Do not use soap as it may increase the absorption of nicotine by your skin. Nicotine on your hands could get into your eyes and nose, and cause stinging, redness or more serious problems.
6. After 24 hours, remove the Nicoderm patch you have been wearing (see section on Disposing of Nicoderm patches). Choose a **different** place on your skin to apply the next patch and repeat steps 1 to 5. Do not return to a previously used skin site for at least one week. Do not leave the patch on for more than 24 hours, as it may irritate your skin and because it loses strength after 24 hours.

When You Apply Nicoderm Patches: Applying the Nicoderm patch at about the same time each day (first thing in the morning, for example) will help you to remember when to put on a new patch. If you want to change the time when you put on your patch, you can do so. At the new time, just remove the Nicoderm patch you are wearing and put on a new one. After that, apply the Nicoderm patch at the new time each day.

If Your Nicoderm Patch Gets Wet While Wearing: Water will not harm the Nicoderm patch you are wearing. You can bathe, shower, swim or use a hot tub for short periods while you are wearing the Nicoderm patch.

If Your Nicoderm Patch Comes Off During Wearing: Nicoderm patches generally stick well to most people's skin. However, if your patch falls off, put on a new one, making sure you select a non-hairy, non-irritated area of skin that is clean and dry. Remove the Nicoderm patch at your regular time to keep your schedule the same, or 24 hours after applying the replacement patch if you wish to change the time each day that you apply a new patch.

If the soap you use has lanolin or moisturizers, the patch may not stick well. Using a different soap may help. Body creams, lotions and sunscreens can also cause problems with keeping your patch on. Do not apply creams or lotions to the place on your skin where you will put the patch. If your skin is oily, or if you have trouble getting the patch to stick, try cleaning your skin with rubbing alcohol first.

If you have followed the directions and the patch still does not stick to you, try using medical adhesive tape over the patch.

Disposing of Nicoderm Patches: Fold the used Nicoderm patch in half with the sticky sides together. After you put on a new Nicoderm patch, take the opened pouch from the new patch and place the used folded Nicoderm patch inside it. Throw the pouch in the trash away from children. Even used patches have enough nicotine to poison children and pets. Wash your hands with water (do not use soap).

You May Experience Side Effects: Common side effects of quitting smoking may include: irritability, trouble sleeping, increased appetite and headaches. However, these should disappear after the first few days.

Nicoderm patches can cause: minor skin irritation, headache, lightheadedness, insomnia, stomach upset and vivid dreams. These side effects may be eliminated by stepping down to a lower strength Nicoderm patch.

If your skin reacts to the Nicoderm patch: When you first put on a Nicoderm patch, mild itching, burning or tingling is normal and should go away within an hour. After you remove a Nicoderm patch, the skin under the patch might be somewhat red. Your skin should not stay red for more than one day. If you get a skin rash after using a Nicoderm patch, or if the skin under the patch becomes swollen or very red, remove the patch, wash the area with water (do not use soap) and call your doctor. Do not put on a new patch. You may be allergic to one of the components of the Nicoderm patch.

Who Should Not Use Nicoderm Patches: You should not use Nicoderm patches if you:

- Continue to smoke, chew tobacco, use snuff, nicotine chewing gum or other nicotine-containing products.
- Are an occasional or nonsmoker
- Are under 18 years of age
- Are pregnant or nursing
- Have a generalized skin condition (e.g., hives, rash)
- Have ever had an allergic reaction to Nicoderm or nicotine

Check with your doctor before using Nicoderm patches if you have or have had any of the following:

- a heart attack (myocardial infarction)
- irregular heart beat (arrhythmia)
- stroke
- diabetes requiring insulin
- kidney or liver disease
- rashes from adhesive tape or bandages
- allergies to drugs
- heart pain (angina)
- high blood pressure
- circulation problems
- stomach ulcers
- overactive thyroid
- skin diseases

Smoking may alter the effects of some medicines. Once you quit, it may be necessary for your doctor to adjust the doses of the medicines you may be using. Therefore, it is important to tell your doctor about all the medicines you are taking. If you are unsure about something, ask your doctor or pharmacist.

Some Important Precautions: Nicoderm patches are only for those who want to stop smoking. If you smoke, chew tobacco, use snuff, nicotine chewing gum or other nicotine-containing products while using Nicoderm patches, you may get a nicotine overdose. Signs of an overdose include bad headaches, dizziness, nausea, abdominal pain, drooling, vomiting, diarrhea, cold sweat, blurred vision, difficulty with hearing, mental confusion, weakness and fainting, rapid heartbeat and difficulty breathing.

In the case of an overdose, or if a child applies or swallows a Nicoderm patch, consult your physician or poison control center at once. Remove the patch from the skin and flush the area with water (do not use soap). Young children are especially sensitive to the effects of even small doses of nicotine. Nicotine can be lethal to children.

Stop Using Nicoderm and Consult Your Doctor If:

- You have chest pain, irregular heartbeat or palpitations, or leg pain
- Your skin swells or you get a rash
- You have skin redness caused by the patch that does not go away after four days
- You think you are pregnant. Avoid becoming pregnant while using Nicoderm. Nicotine in any form may cause harm to your unborn baby.
- You have symptoms of nicotine overdose, as described above under Some Important Precautions.

Consult your doctor if you have difficulty stopping the use of Nicoderm patches at the end of your Nicoderm program.

How to Store Nicoderm Patches: Store each Nicoderm patch in its protective pouch until you are ready to use it, because the patch will lose nicotine into the air if it is outside the pouch. Store Nicoderm patches at room temperature (between 15 and 30°C).

Nicoderm patches are medicine and must be kept out of the reach of children. Nicoderm can be extremely poisonous to children or pets if applied to the skin or swallowed.

Staying Smoke Free: Take up an activity that might have been difficult —if not impossible — to do while you smoked. Join a health club, or start exercising at home. It can make you feel doubly good about yourself for quitting. Some other helpful tips:

- Try to avoid alcohol, coffee and other beverages you associate with smoking.
- Keep your hands occupied by playing with a pencil, paper clip, marble, etc.
- Instead of smoking after meals, try brushing your teeth, or going for a walk.
- Try to avoid people or situations you associated with smoking — at least for a while.

Nicoderm (cont'd)

- Each month, on the anniversary of your Quit Day, plan a special celebration.
- Get extra help if you need it. Your doctor or pharmacist will be able to recommend a support program or self-help group in your area.

Coping with Relapse: If you do relapse, don't feel embarrassed or ashamed. Most people who successfully quit smoking do so after several attempts. Most relapses occur within the first week or within the first three months after quitting, especially during situations you used to associate with smoking, like stress or when drinking alcohol. Knowing that these situations can be difficult can help you prepare for them or, better yet, avoid them in the first place. It's important to have the support of friends and family.

Reward Yourself Regularly: Successfully quitting smoking is a major accomplishment, so you deserve to feel proud. A little reward now and then to congratulate yourself for your success is a reminder that you are doing something good for your well being, and will encourage you to continue the good work.

□ NICORETTE®

Hoechst Marion Roussel

Nicotine Polacrilex

Smoking Cessation Aid

Information for the Patient: Important: Read these instructions carefully before using Nicorette. Do not throw away the carton or User's Guide. They contain important information that you may need to read again.

Keys to Success: 1) You must really want to quit smoking for Nicorette to help you. 2) You can greatly increase your chances for success by using the recommended number of pieces every day (see Dosage Chart). 3) Continue to use Nicorette for the full 3 months (see Dosage Chart). 4) Nicorette works best when used together with a support program. 5) If you have trouble using Nicorette or have any questions, ask your doctor or pharmacist.

Congratulations: You have taken an important first step towards becoming a nonsmoker. **Starting now, you must give up smoking completely.** Your strength and willpower, combined with the proper use of Nicorette, will help you wean yourself off nicotine gradually, while reducing nicotine withdrawal symptoms.

Quitting Smoking Is Hard! If you've tried to quit before and haven't succeeded, don't be discouraged. The important thing is to try again until you succeed. This User's Guide will give you support as you become a nonsmoker. It answers common questions about Nicorette and gives tips to help you stop smoking, and should be referred to often.

Where to Get Help: You are more likely to stop smoking by using Nicorette with a support program that helps you break your smoking habit. Your doctor or pharmacist may be able to recommend support groups in your area. For additional information on Nicorette you can also call us anytime at 1-800-265-7927.

If you start smoking again after using Nicorette, remember breaking this addiction doesn't happen overnight. You may want to talk to a health care professional who can help you improve your chances of quitting the next time you try Nicorette.

Understanding Your Smoking Habit: Many of the cigarettes you smoke are little more than **"habit"** cigarettes; you've gotten into the habit of having them at certain times, like after meals, with morning coffee, while talking on the phone, while driving your car, when you're under stress, or while having a drink with friends.

The other cigarettes you smoke are cigarettes your body feels it **"needs"**. Nicotine is a chemical your body has come to like and depend on. When you smoke, nicotine is released into your bloodstream, "topping up" its supply. After a while, your blood levels decrease until you feel a craving telling you to "top up" again.

How Nicorette Gum Works: Nicorette sugar-free chewing pieces provide a lower level of nicotine to your blood than cigarettes, and allow you to gradually do away with your body's need for nicotine. They work as a temporary aid to help you quit smoking by reducing nicotine withdrawal symptoms, such as irritability, frustration, anxiety, difficulty in concentration and restlessness. Without these powerful cravings for the **cigarettes you "need"**, getting rid of the **"habit" cigarettes** becomes much easier.

Set a Quit Day: Your chances of quitting smoking increase dramatically when you set a **Quit Day** for yourself. Your **Quit Day** shouldn't be too far in the future. Before your **Quit Day**, go over in your mind all the reasons for wanting to quit, and try and imagine yourself without cigarettes.

Choosing The Proper Strength of Nicorette Gum For You: Nicorette gum is available in 2 strengths. Nicorette (2 mg) contains 2 mg of nicotine per piece of gum, and should be used by less heavily addicted smokers, such as those smoking up to 25 cigarettes a day. Nicorette Plus (4 mg) contains 4 mg of nicotine per piece of gum and should be used by more heavily addicted smokers, such as those smoking more than 25 cigarettes per day.

To find out which strength you should use, complete the following questionnaire (note that not all questions have an answer in Column C). If your score is 6 or less, you should use Nicorette (2 mg). If your score is 7 or greater, Nicorette Plus (4 mg) is recommended for you.

Table I—Nicorette

Nicorette Strength Selection Quiz

	A=0 points	B=1 point	C=2 points	Score
How soon after you wake do you smoke your first cigarette?	After 30 minutes	Within 30 minutes		
How many cigarettes a day do you smoke?	1-15	16-25	more than 26	
Does the brand you smoke have a low, medium or high nicotine content?	Low, less than 0.4 mg	Medium, between 0.5 and 0.8 mg	High, greater than 0.9 mg	
Which of all the cigarettes you smoke a day is the most satisfying one?	Any other than the first one in the morning	The first one in the morning		
Do you smoke more during the morning than during the rest of the day?	No	Yes		
Do you smoke when you are so ill that you are in bed most of the day?	No	Yes		
Do you find it difficult to refrain from smoking in places where it is forbidden, such as the library, theatre, doctor's office?	No	Yes		
How often do you inhale smoke from your cigarette?	Never	Sometimes	Always	
			Score	

*The Fagerström Nicotine Tolerence Scale.

How to Use Nicorette Gum: It is very important that you use Nicorette properly. Nicorette is medicine, not ordinary chewing gum, and it can make you feel lightheaded, nauseous, or give you the hiccups if you chew it improperly. Go slowly. Bite it once or twice, then "park it" between your cheek and gum. Wait a minute, and repeat. **Bite. Bite. Park. Bite. Bite. Park**. Slow down if you start feeling uncomfortable. After about 30 minutes, you will have released all the medication. Discard the gum out of the reach of children, and start a new piece as soon as you get an urge for a cigarette.

Do not chew more than one piece of Nicorette gum at a time.

Avoid drinking acidic beverages such as coffee, tea, soft drinks, alcohol or citrus juices when chewing Nicorette. They can prevent it from working properly.

How Long Should You Use Nicorette Gum? You should use a piece of Nicorette whenever you have the desire to smoke. Use the following Dosage Chart as a guide. **Do not exceed 20 pieces per day.**

Table II—Dosage Chart

	Month 1		Month 2	Month 3	Month 4-6
Number of Cigarettes	**First 2 Weeks**	**Second 2 Weeks**			
Smoked Per Day	**Pieces/ Day**	**Pieces/ Day**	**Pieces/ Day**	**Pieces/ Day**	**Pieces/ Day**
20+ (1 pack)	20	15	10	5	Chew 1 piece of Nicorette if the urge to smoke returns.
15-19 (¾ pack)	16	12	6	3	
11-14 (½ pack)	12	9	5	3	
10 or less	10	8	4	2	

As your Nicorette therapy begins to work and your urge to smoke decreases, you can gradually decrease the number of pieces you use. Finally, when you are down to 1 or 2 pieces of Nicorette a day, you will be ready to give up Nicorette altogether. Do not rush it. For most people, treatment will take about 3 months, although some people may require up to 6 months.

Do not use for more than 6 months without consulting a physician.

Carry Nicorette with you at all times for up to 3 months after you stop smoking in case you feel the urge to smoke again. One cigarette is enough to start smoking again.

You May Experience Side Effects: Common side effects of quitting smoking may include: irritability, trouble sleeping, increased appetite and headaches. **However, these should disappear after the first few days.**

Nicorette can cause: headache, lightheadedness, hiccups, upset stomach and other stomach problems, especially if chewed too quickly or not chewed correctly. Other common side effects include mouth or throat soreness.

Because Nicorette is a gum-based product, chewing it can cause dental fillings to loosen and aggravate other mouth, tooth and jaw problems. It may also stick to dental work.

Because Nicorette has been designed to release nicotine only when chewed, no harmful effects will occur should you accidentally swallow a piece of gum.

In the case of overdose or if a child chews or swallows 1 or more pieces of Nicorette, contact your doctor or local Poison Control Centre at once. Young children are especially sensitive to the effects of even small doses of nicotine. Nicotine can be lethal to children and pets.

Who Should Not Use Nicorette? You should not use Nicorette if you:
- Continue to smoke, chew tobacco, use snuff or use a nicotine patch or other nicotine containing products
- Are an occasional or nonsmoker
- Are pregnant or nursing
- Are under 18 years of age
- Have a jaw disorder, such as temporomandibular joint disorder

Check with your doctor before using Nicorette if you:
- Have or have had heart, thyroid, circulation, stomach, throat or mouth problems, angina, coronary artery disease, peripheral vascular disease, irregular heartbeat, or high blood pressure
- Are taking insulin or any prescription medication. The dose of your prescription medicine may need to be adjusted.

Some Important Precautions: Stop using Nicorette and consult your doctor if:
- Irregular heartbeat, chest pain or leg pain occurs or if severe or persistent stomach upset (indigestion, heartburn) develops
- You think you are pregnant. Avoid becoming pregnant while using Nicorette. Nicotine in any form can cause harm to your unborn baby.
- You develop symptoms of overdose such as nausea, abdominal pain, vomiting, cold sweat, dizziness, confusion, weakness, rapid heartbeat or difficulty breathing.

Consult your dentist or doctor if injury or irritation to the mouth, teeth or dental work occurs.

Consult your doctor if you have difficulty in reducing the quantity of pieces used within 3 months.

How to Store Nicorette: Store Nicorette in its original packaging at room temperature between 15 and 30°C, and protect from light.

Nicorette is a drug and must be kept out of the reach of children.

Staying Smoke-free: Take up an activity that might have been difficult—if not impossible—to do while you smoked. Join a health club, or start exercising at home. It can make you feel doubly good about yourself for quitting. Some other helpful tips:
- Try to avoid alcohol, coffee and other beverages you associate with smoking.
- Keep your hands occupied by playing with a pencil, paper clip, marble, etc.
- Instead of smoking after meals, try brushing your teeth, or going for a walk.
- Try to avoid people or situations you associated with smoking—at least for a little while.
- Each month, on the anniversary of your **Quit Day**, plan a special celebration.
- You may also need additional help. This is nothing to be ashamed of, and your doctor or pharmacist will be able to recommend a self-help group or support program in your area.

Coping With Relapse: If you do relapse, don't feel embarrassed or ashamed. Most people who successfully quit smoking do so after several attempts.

Most relapses occur within the first week or within the first 3 months after quitting, especially during situations you used to associate with smoking, like stress or when drinking alcohol. Knowing that these situations can be difficult can help you prepare for them or, better yet, avoid them in the first place. It's important to have the support from friends and family.

Reward Yourself Regularly: Quitting smoking is a very difficult thing to do and you deserve to feel proud. A little reward now and then to congratulate yourself for your success is a reminder that you are doing something good for your well-being and will encourage you to continue the good work.

☐ NICORETTE® PLUS

Hoechst Marion Roussel

Nicotine Polacrilex

Smoking Cessation Aid

Information for the Patient: Important: Read these instructions carefully before using Nicorette Plus. Do not throw away the carton or User's Guide. They contain important information that you may need to read again.

Keys to Success: 1) You must really want to quit smoking for Nicorette Plus to help you. 2) You can greatly increase your chances for success by using the recommended number of pieces every day (see Dosage Chart). 3) Continue to use Nicorette Plus for the full 3 months (see Dosage Chart). 4) Nicorette Plus works best when used together with a support program. 5) If you have trouble using Nicorette Plus or have any questions, ask your doctor or pharmacist.

Congratulations: You have taken an important first step towards becoming a nonsmoker. **Starting now, you must give up smoking completely.** Your strength and willpower, combined with the proper use of Nicorette, will help you wean yourself off nicotine gradually, while reducing nicotine withdrawal symptoms.

Quitting Smoking Is Hard! If you've tried to quit before and haven't succeeded, don't be discouraged. The important thing is to try again until you succeed. This User's Guide will give you support as you become a nonsmoker. It answers common questions about Nicorette Plus and gives tips to help you stop smoking, and should be referred to often.

Where to Get Help: You are more likely to stop smoking by using Nicorette Plus with a support program that helps you break your smoking habit. Your doctor or pharmacist may be able to recommend support groups in your area. For additional information on Nicorette you can also call us anytime at 1-800-265-7927.

If you start smoking again after using Nicorette Plus, remember breaking this addiction doesn't happen overnight. You may want to talk to a health care professional who can help you improve your chances of quitting the next time you try Nicorette Plus.

Nicorette Plus (cont'd)

Understanding Your Smoking Habit: Many of the cigarettes you smoke are little more than **"habit"** cigarettes; you've gotten into the habit of having them at certain times, like after meals, with morning coffee, while talking on the phone, while driving your car, when you're under stress, or while having a drink with friends.

The other cigarettes you smoke are cigarettes your body feels it **"needs"**. Nicotine is a chemical your body has come to like and depend on. When you smoke, nicotine is released into your bloodstream, "topping up" its supply. After a while, your blood levels decrease until you feel a craving telling you to "top up" again.

How Nicorette Plus Gum Works: Nicorette Plus sugar-free chewing pieces provide a lower level of nicotine to your blood than cigarettes, and allow you to gradually do away with your body's need for nicotine. They work as a temporary aid to help you quit smoking by reducing nicotine withdrawal symptoms, such as irritability, frustration, anxiety, difficulty in concentration and restlessness. Without these powerful cravings for the **cigarettes you "need"**, getting rid of the **"habit" cigarettes** becomes much easier.

Set a Quit Day: Your chances of quitting smoking increase dramatically when you set a **Quit Day** for yourself. Your **Quit Day** shouldn't be too far in the future. Before your **Quit Day**, go over in your mind all the reasons for wanting to quit, and try and imagine yourself without cigarettes.

Choosing The Proper Strength of Nicorette Plus Gum For You: Nicorette gum is available in 2 strengths. Nicorette (2 mg) contains 2 mg of nicotine per piece of gum, and should be used by less heavily addicted smokers, such as those smoking up to 25 cigarettes a day. Nicorette Plus (4 mg) contains 4 mg of nicotine per piece of gum and should be used by more heavily addicted smokers, such as those smoking more than 25 cigarettes per day.

To find out which strength you should use, complete the following questionnaire (note that not all questions have an answer in Column C). If your score is 6 or less, you should use Nicorette (2 mg). If your score is 7 or greater, Nicorette Plus (4 mg) is recommended for you.

How to Use Nicorette Plus Gum: It is very important that you use Nicorette Plus properly. Nicorette Plus is medicine, not ordinary chewing gum, and it can make you feel lightheaded, nauseous, or give you the hiccups if you chew it improperly. Go slowly. Bite it once or twice, then "park it" between your cheek and gum. Wait a minute, and repeat. **Bite. Bite. Park. Bite. Bite. Park.** Slow down if you start feeling uncomfortable. After about 30 minutes, you will have released all the medication. Discard the gum out of the reach of children, and start a new piece as soon as you get an urge for a cigarette.

Do not chew more than one piece of Nicorette Plus gum at a time.

Avoid drinking acidic beverages such as coffee, tea, soft drinks, alcohol or citrus juices when chewing Nicorette Plus. They can prevent it from working properly.

How Long Should You Use Nicorette Plus Gum? You should use a piece of Nicorette Plus whenever you have the desire to smoke. Use the following Dosage Chart as a guide. **Do not exceed 20 pieces per day.**

As your Nicorette Plus therapy begins to work and your urge to smoke decreases, you can gradually decrease the number of pieces you use. Finally, when you are down to 1 or 2 pieces of Nicorette Plus a day, you will be ready to give up Nicorette Plus altogether. Do not rush it. For most people, treatment will take about 3 months, although some people may require up to 6 months.

Do not use for more than 6 months without consulting a physician.

Carry Nicorette Plus with you at all times for up to 3 months after you stop smoking in case you feel the urge to smoke again. One cigarette is enough to start smoking again.

You May Experience Side Effects: Common side effects of quitting smoking may include: irritability, trouble sleeping, increased appetite and headaches. **However, these should disappear after the first few days.**

Nicorette Plus can cause: headache, lightheadedness, hiccups, upset stomach and other stomach problems, especially if chewed too quickly or not chewed correctly. Other common side effects include mouth or throat soreness.

Because Nicorette Plus is a gum-based product, chewing it can cause dental fillings to loosen and aggravate other mouth, tooth and jaw problems. It may also stick to dental work.

Nicorette Strength Selection Quiz*

	A=0 points	B=1 point	C=2 points	Score
How soon after you wake do you smoke your first cigarette?	After 30 minutes	Within 30 minutes		
How many cigarettes a day do you smoke?	1–15	16–25	more than 26	
Does the brand you smoke have a low, medium or high nicotine content?	Low, less than 0.4 mg	Medium, between 0.5 and 0.8 mg	High, greater than 0.9 mg	
Which of all the cigarettes you smoke a day is the most satisfying one?	Any other than the first one in the morning	The first one in the morning		
Do you smoke more during the morning than during the rest of the day?	No	Yes		
Do you smoke when you are so ill that you are in bed most of the day?	No	Yes		
Do you find it difficult to refrain from smoking in places where it is forbidden, such as the library, theatre, doctor's office?	No	Yes		
How often do you inhale smoke from your cigarette?	Never	Sometimes	Always	
			Score	

*The Fagerström Nicotine Tolerance Scale.

Dosage Chart

Number of Cigarettes Smoked Per Day	Month 1 First 2 Weeks Pieces/Day	Month 1 Second 2 Weeks Pieces/Day	Month 2 Pieces/Day	Month 3 Pieces/Day	Month 4-6 Pieces/Day
20+ (1 pack)	20	15	10	5	Chew 1 piece of Nicorette Plus if the urge to smoke returns.
15-19 (3/4 pack)	16	12	6	3	
11-14 (1/2 pack)	12	9	5	3	
10 or less	10	8	4	2	

Because Nicorette Plus has been designed to release nicotine only when chewed, no harmful effects will occur should you accidentally swallow a piece of gum.

In the case of overdose or if a child chews or swallows 1 or more pieces of Nicorette Plus, contact your doctor or local Poison Control Centre at once. Young children are especially sensitive to the effects of even small doses of nicotine. Nicotine can be lethal to children and pets.

Who Should Not Use Nicorette Plus? You should not use Nicorette Plus if you:

- Continue to smoke, chew tobacco, use snuff or use a nicotine patch or other nicotine containing products
- Are an occasional or nonsmoker
- Are pregnant or nursing
- Are under 18 years of age
- Have a jaw disorder, such as temporomandibular joint disorder

Check with your doctor before using Nicorette Plus if you:

- Have or have had heart, thyroid, circulation, stomach, throat or mouth problems, angina, coronary artery disease, peripheral vascular disease, irregular heartbeat, or high blood pressure
- Are taking insulin or any prescription medication. The dose of your prescription medicine may need to be adjusted.

Some Important Precautions: Stop using Nicorette Plus and consult your doctor if:

- Irregular heartbeat, chest pain or leg pain occurs or if severe or persistent stomach upset (indigestion, heartburn) develops
- You think you are pregnant. Avoid becoming pregnant while using Nicorette Plus. Nicotine in any form can cause harm to your unborn baby.
- You develop symptoms of overdose such as nausea, abdominal pain, vomiting, cold sweat, dizziness, confusion, weakness, rapid heartbeat or difficulty breathing.

Consult your dentist or doctor if injury or irritation to the mouth, teeth or dental work occurs.

Consult your doctor if you have difficulty in reducing the quantity of pieces used within 3 months.

How to Store Nicorette Plus: Store Nicorette Plus in its original packaging at room temperature between 15 and 30°C, and protect from light.

Nicorette Plus is a drug and must be kept out of the reach of children.

Staying Smoke-free: Take up an activity that might have been difficult—if not impossible—to do while you smoked. Join a health club, or start exercising at home. It can make you feel doubly good about yourself for quitting. Some other helpful tips:

- Try to avoid alcohol, coffee and other beverages you associate with smoking.
- Keep your hands occupied by playing with a pencil, paper clip, marble, etc.
- Instead of smoking after meals, try brushing your teeth, or going for a walk.
- Try to avoid people or situations you associated with smoking—at least for a little while.
- Each month, on the anniversary of your **Quit Day**, plan a special celebration.
- You may also need additional help. This is nothing to be ashamed of, and your doctor or pharmacist will be able to recommend a self-help group or support program in your area.

Coping With Relapse: If you do relapse, don't feel embarrassed or ashamed. Most people who successfully quit smoking do so after several attempts.

Most relapses occur within the first week or within the first 3 months after quitting, especially during situations you used to associate with smoking, like stress or when drinking alcohol. Knowing that these situations can be difficult can help you prepare for them or, better yet, avoid them in the first place. It's important to have the support from friends and family.

Reward Yourself Regularly: Quitting smoking is a very difficult thing to do and you deserve to feel proud. A little reward now and then to congratulate yourself for your success is a reminder that you are doing something good for your well-being and will encourage you to continue the good work.

□ NICOTROL®

Johnson & Johnson • Merck

Nicotine

Smoking Cessation Aid

Information for the Patient: Introduction: This leaflet provides general information about nicotine and specific information about Nicotrol treatment. Please read all of it carefully, especially the section marked "Important Cautions", before you start using the patches. If you have any questions or want more information, be sure to ask your doctor or pharmacist or call 1-888-730-INFO.

How to succeed: Nicotrol can help you stop smoking cigarettes. Although it may be an effective aid, it is only one part of your stop smoking program. Your own chances of quitting smoking depend on how much you want to quit, how strongly you are addicted to nicotine, and how closely you follow a stop smoking program, like the **Stop Smoking Now!** Program that is available with the Nicotrol patch. For information on the **Stop Smoking Now!** Program designed by professionals at the Ottawa Heart Institute, and enrolment in a personal counselling program, call 1-888-730-INFO. **Your success in this program is directly related to your commitment to stop smoking.**

Important Cautions: There are immediate beneficial effects on your health when you stop smoking. However, when using Nicotrol certain precautions must be taken for their safe use.

Can you smoke or use other nicotine-containing products while using Nicotrol?

You must **not** smoke, chew nicotine gum or tobacco, or use snuff while using a Nicotrol patch because you may overdose on nicotine. Signs of a nicotine overdose include bad headaches, dizziness, upset stomach, drooling, vomiting, diarrhea, cold sweat, blurred vision, difficulty with hearing, mental confusion, weakness and fainting. If you experience any of these symptoms, consult your doctor, or local poison control center, immediately.

Do You Have Any Medical Conditions? In certain medical conditions, Nicotrol should not be used. Be sure to tell your doctor or pharmacist before trying Nicotrol if you have had any of the following:

- a heart attack (myocardial infarction) or stroke
- irregular heartbeat (arrhythmia)
- severe or worsening heart pain (angina)
- heart disease
- stomach problems or ulcers
- allergies to drugs
- allergic reaction from adhesive tape or bandages
- skin diseases
- high blood pressure
- overactive thyroid
- diabetes requiring insulin
- kidney or liver disease
- treatment for poor circulation
- treatment of circulation disorders of the brain

Are you taking other medicines? Smoking may alter the effects of some medicines. Once you have quit, it may be necessary for your doctor to adjust the doses of medicines you may be using. Therefore, it is important to tell your doctor or pharmacist about **all** medicines you are taking and consult them before you use Nicotrol.

Are you pregnant or nursing? Nicotine in any form may cause harm to your unborn baby if you use nicotine while you are pregnant. Do not use Nicotrol patches if you are pregnant or nursing. Be careful not to become pregnant while using Nicotrol patches. If you think you might be pregnant, do not use Nicotrol patches until you have talked to your doctor.

How the Nicotrol Patch Works: Nicotrol is a skin patch containing nicotine designed to help you quit smoking cigarettes. When you put a Nicotrol patch on your skin, nicotine passes from the patch through the skin and into your blood. It is the nicotine in cigarettes that causes addiction to smoking. The Nicotrol patch replaces some of the nicotine you crave when you stop smoking, and helps to relieve symptoms of nicotine withdrawal such as irritability, frustration, anger, anxiety, difficulty in concentration and restlessness.

A Nicotrol patch is applied when you wake up each day and worn during your waking hours for 16 hours. The patch is removed at bedtime, thus allowing a patch-free period while you sleep.

The Nicotrol Program: There are 3 steps in the Nicotrol Program.

Step 1: Establish your quit date and stop smoking completely before you begin using Nicotrol. You will begin treatment with the 15 mg Nicotrol patch. Use one patch daily for 6 weeks. After that you may stop or, if you prefer you can slowly reduce the amount of Nicotrol you use until you stop using the patches completely.

Step 2: Begin your weaning phase by using the 10 mg patch for 2 weeks.

Step 3: Complete your weaning phase by using the 5 mg patch for 2 weeks.

Do not use Nicotrol for more than 10 consecutive weeks without consulting a doctor.

How to Apply Nicotrol Patches?

1) When you wake up each day, put a new Nicotrol patch on a healthy nonhairy, clean, dry area of the upper part of your arm or on the hip. Do not shave the area, as this may be irritating to the skin, when the patch is applied. Do not put the Nicotrol patch on skin that is very oily, inflamed, swollen, red, burned, broken out, cut, or

Nicotrol (cont'd)

irritated in any way, since these conditions may alter the amount of drug absorbed.

2) Do not remove the Nicotrol patch from its sealed protective pouch until you are ready to use it because it will lose strength if stored out of the pouch. Using scissors, cut along the dotted line to open the pouch. Save the pouch, because you will use it when throwing away the Nicotrol patch at bedtime (see 6).
3) A clear protective release liner covers the sticky side of the Nicotrol patch — the side that will be put on your skin. The liner has a partial cut in it to help you remove it from the patch. With the sticky side facing you, pull the liner away from the Nicotrol patch. Try not to touch the adhesive surface with your hands.
4) Immediately apply the sticky side of the Nicotrol patch to your skin. Press the Nicotrol patch on your skin with the palm of your hand for about 10 to 20 seconds. Make sure it sticks well to your skin, especially around the edges.
5) Rinse your hands with water (**Do not use soap**, soap increases the absorption of nicotine) when you have finished applying the Nicotrol patch. Nicotine on your hands could get into your eyes and nose and could cause stinging, redness, or more serious problems.
6) Remove the patch before you go to bed, thus allowing for a patch-free period during sleep. Fold the used patch in half with the sticky side together. Place it in its pouch (kept from the morning application) or place it in a piece of aluminum foil. Dispose of the used patch out of the reach of children and pets.
7) Choose a different place on your skin to apply a new Nicotrol patch the next day and repeat 1 to 6. The same area should not be used again for at least 1 week.

When to Apply and Remove the Nicotrol Patch? You should put on a new Nicotrol patch each day at about the same time after you wake up so that you don't forget. The patch should be removed at bedtime to provide a patch-free (nicotine-free) period. Do not wear it for more than 16 hours each day. The patch should be removed 2 hours before engaging in **prolonged strenuous exercise**. Fold the used patch in half with the sticky side together. Place it in its pouch or in a piece of aluminum foil. Dispose of the used patch out of the reach of children and pets. Reapply a new patch after exercising.

What If the Nicotrol Patch Gets Wet? The Nicotrol patch adheres very firmly to the skin. You may keep it on while using a hot tub, bathing, or taking a shower.

What If the Nicotrol Patch Comes Off? If the Nicotrol patch falls off, put a new one on a different skin area that is clean and dry. Remove the new patch, as usual, at bedtime.

What If Your Skin Reacts To the Patch? When you first put on a Nicotrol patch, mild itching, burning, or tingling is common and should go away within an hour. After you remove the patch, the skin under the patch might be somewhat red, but it should not stay red for more than a day. If you get a skin rash after using a Nicotrol patch or if the skin under the patch becomes swollen or very red, remove the patch and call your doctor. Do not put on a new patch. It is possible you may be allergic to one of the components of the patch.

If you do become allergic to Nicotrol patches, you could get sick from using cigarettes or other nicotine-containing products.

How to Store Nicotrol Patches? Keep each Nicotrol patch in its protective pouch until you are ready to use it because the patch will lose nicotine into the air if it is stored outside the pouch.

Store at room temperature below 30°C because the patches are sensitive to heat. Remember, the inside of your car can reach temperatures much higher than this in the summer.

Important Safety Information: Nicotrol can be poisonous and extremely dangerous to children or pets if applied to the skin or swallowed. Keep new or used Nicotrol patches out of the reach of children and pets.

Do not smoke even when you are not wearing the patch. The nicotine in your skin will still be entering your bloodstream for several hours after you take the patch off.

Remove the nicotine patch and consult your doctor if you experience irregular heartbeat, chest pain, palpitations or leg pain or if severe stomach upset (indigestion, heartburn) develops.

☐ NIDAGEL™ Ⓟ

3M Pharmaceuticals

Metronidazole

Antibacterial

Information for the Patient: Directions for Use (see package insert for illustrations):

Box contents: tube containing 70 g of NidaGel and 5 plastic vaginal applicators.

1. Filling the Applicator:

- Remove cap and puncture metal seal on tube with the pointed tip of cap.
- Screw end of applicator onto tube.
- Slowly squeeze gel out of tube and into applicator. Plunger will stop when the applicator is full.
- Unscrew applicator and replace cap on tube.

2. Inserting the Applicator:

- The applicator may be inserted while lying on your back with your knees bent or in any comfortable position.
- Hold filled applicator by barrel, and gently insert into vagina as far as it will comfortably go.
- Slowly press the plunger until it stops to deposit gel into vagina and then withdraw the applicator.

3. Care of the Applicator (if prescribed twice daily):

- After use, pull the plunger out of the barrel.
- Wash both plunger and barrel in warm soapy water and rinse thoroughly.
- To reassemble applicator, gently push plunger back into barrel.

Important: Insert 1 applicator full (approximately 5 g) of NidaGel (metronidazole) 0.75% vaginal gel into the vagina once daily at bedtime for 5 days, or twice daily at morning and bedtime for 5 days as directed by your physician.

Precautions:

- NidaGel should not be used during the first trimester (first 3 months) of pregnancy **and should only be used under the supervison of a physician during the second and third trimesters (last 6 months) of pregnancy.**
- If significant irritation develops from the use of this medication, discontinue use and consult your physician.
- For vaginal use only.
- Alcohol should be avoided during use of NidaGel and for 1 day following use.
- It is advisable to abstain from intercourse during use of NidaGel.
- Use of NidaGel during menses is not recommended.
- Keep this and all medications out of reach of children.
- Store between 15 and 25°C. Avoid exposure to extreme heat or cold. See end of carton and bottom of tube for lot number and expiration date.

☐ NITOMAN® Ⓟ

Roche

Tetrabenazine

Monoamine Depleting Agent

Information for the Patient: This leaflet is meant to supplement what your pharmacist and doctor have told you about Nitoman. Your pharmacist and doctor know and best understand your personal condition. Be sure to follow your doctor's and pharmacist's instructions carefully and read any materials given to you. If you have any questions after reading this information leaflet, be sure to ask your doctor and pharmacist.

What is Nitoman used for? Nitoman is known chemically as tetrabenazine. Nitoman is given to people who suffer from medical conditions that lead to unwanted movements of different parts of their body, such as their arms, legs, mouth and tongue. The types of medical conditions for which Nitoman is used are: Huntington's Chorea, hemiballismus, senile chorea, tic and Gilles de la Tourette syndrome or tardive dyskinesia.

Nitoman **is not** to be used to improve movement in people who are taking certain kinds of drugs for parkinsonism (levodopa/carbidopa, e.g., Sinemet, Sinemet CR or levodopa/benserazide, e.g., Prolopa).

Do's and Dont's of taking Nitoman:

- **Do** inform your doctor immediately if you are feeling sad, down or blue (depressed), or if there is a worsening of your condition while taking the medication.
- **Do** inform your doctor if you are planning on becoming pregnant, or are pregnant, while taking Nitoman.
- **Do** inform any doctor or dentist you may see that you are taking Nitoman.
- **Do not** drive a vehicle or operate dangerous machinery until you know how you react to this medication.

What side effects may you see while taking Nitoman? Generally, Nitoman is well tolerated. However, as with any medication, in some people side effects may develop. You should let your doctor know if any side effect is bothersome.

Below is a list of side effects that can occur with Nitoman in the order of most common to least common. This list is not a complete list. Your doctor and pharmacist can advise you of any other information important to you.

- Feeling down, sad, blue (depressed)
- Tremors, rigidity, or noticeably decreased mobility
- Drowsiness, tiredness, weakness
- Anxiousness, nervousness
- Insomnia
- Restlessness
- Drooling
- Feeling irritable or agitated
- Nausea, vomiting, stomach pain
- Feeling confused or disoriented
- Low blood pressure
- Feeling faint because of dizziness

How to take Nitoman? Your doctor will start you with a small dose of Nitoman. This will be increased until the dose that helps you is reached. Your doctor will give you a schedule of how many tablets and how often to take your medication. It is important to follow the schedule your doctor gives you. Remember to take your medication with a full glass of water. You can take Nitoman on a full or empty stomach.

What to do if you miss a dose? If you miss a dose, take that dose as soon as you remember, except if the missed dose is close to the time of the next dose. **Do not double your next dose**, just continue with your regular schedule. If you are unsure what to do, call your pharmacist or doctor.

This leaflet does not contain all information on Nitoman. Your doctor or pharmacist have more information on Nitoman.

Nitoman® trademark of Hoffmann-La Roche Limited.
Prolopa® is a registered trademark of Hoffmann-La Roche Limited.
Sinemet®, Sinemet CR® is a registered trademark of Dupont.

☐ NITRO-DUR®

Key

Nitroglycerin

Antianginal

Information for the Patient: This leaflet provides information about the Nitro-Dur patch and its use. Please read this instruction sheet carefully before using Nitro-Dur.

Nitro-Dur Nitroglycerin Transdermal System: Summary: Nitroglycerin is a medication your doctor has prescribed for you to help reduce the frequency and severity of angina attacks (chest pain).

How your Nitro-Dur Nitroglycerin Transdermal System works: Nitro-Dur is applied directly to the skin. The nitroglycerin passes from the adhesive surface through the skin - allowing medication to be absorbed directly into the bloodstream. Nitroglycerin causes the blood vessels to relax and increases the supply of blood and oxygen to the heart. This helps prevent attacks of anginal pain (chest pain) from occurring. Because nitroglycerin is released slowly from Nitro-Dur, **it will not relieve an attack that has already started.**

The amount of Nitro-Dur you need will depend upon your body's needs. Observe the dosing instructions given to you by your doctor and report to him/her if chest pain attacks continue to occur.

Instructions for Use: Placement Area: Select a reasonably hair-free application site. **Avoid extremities below the knee or elbow, skin folds, scar tissure, burned or irritated areas.**

Application: Wash hands before applying. Hold the unit with brown lines facing you, in an up and down position. Bend the sides of the unit away from you, then toward you until you hear the **snap.** Twist the patch gently to lift the plastic backing. Peel off **one** side of the plastic backing. Using the other half of the backing as a handle, apply the sticky side of the patch to the skin. Press the sticky side on the skin, and smooth down. Fold back the remaining side of the patch. Gently push the plastic applicator parallel to the skin until the whole patch is in place. Smooth down with your finger. Wash hands to remove any drug.

Removal: Press down on the center of the system to raise its outer edge away from the skin. Grasp the edge gently, and slowly peel the patch away from the skin. Wash skin area with soap and water. Towel dry. Wash hands. You should use a different application site every day.

Skin Care:

1. After you remove Nitro-Dur, your skin may feel warm and appear red. This is normal. The redness will disappear in a short time. If the area feels dry, you may apply a soothing lotion.
2. Any redness or rash that does not disappear within a few hours should be called to your physician's attention.

Things to be Aware of: There are certain things you and your doctor should be aware of before you use Nitro-Dur.

Before using Nitro-Dur be sure to tell your doctor if you have ever had any unusual or allergic reactions to nitrates or nitrites, or have had a recent heart attack, or other serious heart disease, stroke, or head injury, severe anemia or narrowing of the heart valves. Tell your doctor if you are breast-feeding or pregnant or intend to become pregnant while using this medicine. This will help the doctor decide whether you should use Nitro-Dur and what extra care should be taken during its use. There are some medicines which may affect how Nitro-Dur works. Tell your doctor what other medicines or remedies, if any, your are using.

Check with your doctor as soon as possible if any of the following occur: angina (chest pain), particularly while patch is off; dizziness or fainting; feeling of pressure in the head; shortness of breath; unusual tiredness or weakness; weak or unusually fast heartbeat.

Possible Unwanted Effects: Like all medicines, along with its helpful effects, Nitro-Dur may cause unwanted effects. You should know about them so that if they do occur, you can report them to your doctor right away.

When you start using Nitro-Dur, you may get a headache. This is a common effect. If you need to, you may take a mild pain reliever for this. If it continues or becomes severe, check with your doctor. Flushing of the face may also occur. Nitro-Dur may also lower the blood pressure and cause dizziness, lightheadedness, or a fainting feeling, especially when you get up quickly from lying or sitting. Getting up slowly may help. If you feel dizzy, sit or lie down. You may be more likely to experience headaches, dizziness, or lightheadedness if you drink alcohol, stand for a long time, or if the weather is hot. While using Nitro-Dur, be careful about the amount of alcohol you drink. Also use extra care when exercising, standing for a long time, driving, or during hot weather.

Other Information:

1. Allow Nitro-Dur to stay in place as directed by your physician.
2. Showering is permitted with Nitro-Dur in place.
3. Nitro-Dur should be kept out of reach of children and pets.
4. Store at controlled room temperature 15 to 30°C. Do not refrigerate.
5. Nitro-Dur is packaged so that you have a 30-day supply. Be sure to check your supply periodically. Before it runs low, you should visit your pharmacist for a refill or ask your physician to renew your Nitro-Dur prescription.
6. It is important that you do not miss a day of your Nitro-Dur therapy. If your schedule needs to be changed, your physician will give you specific instructions.
7. Nitro-Dur has been prescribed for you. Do not give your medication to anyone else.
8. Nitro-Dur is for the prevention of angina; not for treatment of an acute angina attack.
9. Notify your physician if angina attacks change for the worse.
10. Do not cut or use part patches.
11. Do not reuse patch. Discard after first use.

If you have any questions about Nitro-Dur, ask your physician or pharmacist.

□ NITROLINGUAL® PUMPSPRAY

Rhône-Poulenc Rorer

Nitroglycerin

Antianginal

Information for the Patient: Before using your Nitrolingual Pumpspray, read this leaflet carefully and follow instructions.

Nitrolingual Pumpspray is a metered dose spray containing nitroglycerin. Each metered dose provides 0.4 mg nitroglycerin per spray emission.

How To Use Nitrolingual Pumpspray:

1. Holding container in upright position, remove the plastic cover. **Do not shake.**
2. The container must be primed prior to the first use. To prime, point away from face, press the button firmly with the forefinger to release one spray. Repeat this until you have released a total of 3 sprays. Now your container is primed and ready for use.

   Repriming is only necessary when the container has not been used for more than 14 days. To reprime, release 1 spray as directed previously. There is no need to reprime the container between more frequent usage.
3. Hold the container upright with forefinger on top of the grooved button. There is no need to shake the container.
4. Open your mouth and bring the container as close to it as possible.
5. Press the button firmly with the forefinger to release the spray onto or under the tongue. **Do not inhale the spray.**
6. Release button and close mouth.
7. If you require a second dose, repeat steps 4, 5 and 6.
8. Replace the plastic cover.

When using this product for the first time, familiarize yourself with how to use it by testing the spray into the air (away from yourself and others). Get the feel of the finger resting on the groove button so that you can use the spray in the dark.

Dosage: During an anginal attack, 1 or 2 doses should be sprayed onto or under the tongue, **without inhaling.** A dose may be repeated twice at 5 to 10 minute intervals. Your doctor can help you to discover the exact dose which will be best for you. If the pain persists, notify your physician.

Make sure that you have a spare Pumpspray readily available (to prevent running out when needed).

Adverse Effects: Headache, sometimes severe and persistent is the most common side effect of nitroglycerin. Transient episodes of dizziness and weakness, flushing, palpitation and occasionally nausea and vomiting may follow the use of Nitrolingual Pumpspray. If these adverse effects occur, you should discuss them with your physician.

Special Caution: Contains alcohol. Do not open container forcefully or burn after use. Do not spray toward flames.

Keep in a safe place and out of the reach of children. Store at room temperature.

□ NIX® Creme Rinse

Warner-Lambert Consumer Healthcare

Permethrin

Topical Pediculicide—Ovicide

Information for the Patient: Indications: Nix Creme Rinse is indicated for the treatment of infestation with head lice and their nits (eggs). This unique creme rinse leaves the hair manageable and easy to comb.

What Are Head Lice? Head lice are small insects that live and feed on the human scalp causing itching and irritation. They range in color from beige to black. Lice lay eggs, called nits, on the hair shaft close to the scalp. The nits are tiny, oval shaped and shiny, and range in color from creamy white to brown. Nits normally hatch in 7 to 10 days. The adult lice cannot survive away from the head for much more than 24 hours.

How Does a Lice Infestation Spread? Head lice spread easily, primarily by close head to head contact with persons who have lice and occasionally by sharing personal articles such as clothing, hats, combs, hair accessories, towels and bed linen.

What to Do if You or a Member of Your Family Has Head Lice: Head lice affect millions of people each year, especially school aged children. They **do not** transmit or cause disease and are **not** a sign of poor personal hygiene. A head lice infestation can be effectively treated with a topical pediculicide and ovicide treatment (a treatment effective at destroying lice and their eggs) such as Nix Creme Rinse.

Directions for Use of Nix Creme Rinse:

1. Wash the hair with **conditioner-free shampoo.** Do not use a conditioner. Rinse with water and towel dry thoroughly.
2. Shake Nix bottle well. Apply a sufficient amount of Nix (½ to 1 bottle) to thoroughly saturate the hair and scalp especially behind the ears and at the base of the neck.
3. Leave Nix on the hair for **10 minutes.**
4. Rinse Nix off hair with water.
5. Towel dry hair.
6. Comb hair with regular comb to remove tangles.
7. Remove nits: Part hair into sections; starting as close to the scalp as possible, remove the nits using a fine toothed (nit) comb or fingers. Be sure to comb to the end of the hair shaft. The nit comb should be disinfected by soaking in hot water after each use. Inspect full head of hair thoroughly for any stray nits. The nit removal procedure should be repeated daily for the 7 days following treatment.

A single application is usually sufficient to eliminate a head lice infestation. The active ingredient in Nix persists on the hair for 10 days, even after subsequent washing with a conditioner-free shampoo. If you see live lice or nits after the first application, the residual effect should kill these. If you still see live lice or nits on the 7th day (or after) following the first application, Nix Creme Rinse should be applied a second time, as described above.

How to Help Prevent Reinfestation: Cleaning of personal articles is also an important part of head lice management and may help prevent reinfestation. Personal belongings including recently worn clothing, towels and bed linens should be machine washed in hot water and dried using the hot cycle of the dryer for at least 20 minutes. Personal articles of clothing or bedding that cannot be washed may be dry cleaned or sealed in a plastic bag for a period of two weeks. Combs and brushes should be disinfected by soaking in hot water (above 54°C) for 5 to 10 minutes.

Children should be advised not to use any borrowed combs or brushes, nor wear anyone else's clothes, especially hats.

Inspect all family members from time to time for any new lice infestation. If a new infestation is found treat with Nix Creme Rinse.

Precautions: General: Head lice infestation is often accompanied by itching, redness, and swelling. Treatment with Nix may temporarily worsen these conditions. Do not use if allergic to any of its ingredients, synthetic pyrethroids or pyrethrin, or chrysanthemums. Discontinue use if reaction occurs.

Eye Irritation: Nix is not irritating to eyes; however if it should get into them, rinse eyes immediately with water.

In Case of Swallowing: Consult your physician or Poison Control Centre immediately.

Pregnant or Nursing Women: There are no adequate or well-controlled studies in pregnant or nursing women. Consult a physician before using this drug.

Children: Nix is safe and effective in children two years of age or older. Safety and effectiveness in children less than two years of age have not been established. Consult your physician.

Keep out of reach of children. To prevent accidental ingestion by children, the remaining contents of Nix should be discarded after use.

Adverse Reactions: In clinical studies, occasional itching has been known to occur. This is usually a consequence of head lice infestation itself, but may be temporarily worsened following treatment with Nix. Other reactions which are less frequent include: stinging/burning, tingling, numbness or discomfort, redness, and swelling or rash of the scalp. All these reactions were mild and temporary.

Ingredients: Permethrin is the active ingredient in Nix Creme rinse; it is present at a concentration of 1%. In addition, Nix Creme Rinse also contains the following nonactive components: balsam Canada, cetyl alcohol, citric acid, FD&C Yellow No. 6, hydrolyzed animal protein, hydroxyethylcellulose, isopropyl alcohol, methylparaben, perfume, polyoxyethylene 10 cetyl ether, propylene glycol, propylparaben, and stearalkonium chloride.

☐ NIX® Dermal Cream

Glaxo Wellcome

Permethrin

Topical Scabicide

Information for the Patient: Indications: Nix dermal cream (permethrin) 5% is indicated for the treatment of infestation with Sarcoptes scabiei (scabies).

Directions for Use:

1. Clean and dry skin.
2. Apply sufficient amounts of Nix dermal cream (30 g) and thoroughly massage cream from the head to the soles of the feet, paying special attention to creases in the skin, hands, feet, between fingers and toes, underarms and groin. Put on clean clothes. Long-sleeved shirts, pants and mittens should be worn by young children to avoid contact with mouth.
3. Leave Nix dermal cream on skin for 12 to 14 hours.
4. Wash off by taking a shower or a bath.
5. Change into clean clothes.
6. Scabies will be killed, but itching may persist. This is normal and should not be interpreted as treatment failure.
7. **One single application is effective** in most cases. If necessary, a second application may be given 7 to 10 days after the first, but only if live mites can be demonstrated or new lesions appear.
8. To reduce the risk of transmission or eliminate reinfestation, it is recommended that family members and close contacts, including sexual partners, be treated with Nix dermal cream.
9. All clothing, bed linens, and towels used within the 2 days prior to treatment should be machine-washed in hot water and dried on dryer hot cycle for at least 20 minutes, or dry cleaned following treatment. Mattresses which have been used by an infested person should not be used for 24 hours. Toilet seats should be disinfected.
10. Discontinue use of other topical medications and cosmetics during treatment.

Note: Do not take a hot bath before treatment.

Precautions: General: Scabies infestation is often accompanied by itching, redness and swelling. Treatment with Nix dermal cream may temporarily worsen these symptoms. Do not use this product if you are allergic to any of its ingredients, to synthetic pyrethroids or pyrethrin, or to chrysanthemums. Discontinue use if a reaction occurs. Pruritus (itching) caused by an acquired sensitivity to mites and their products frequently persists for one to several weeks following treatment with the drug. This reaction does not indicate treatment failure. Retreatment is only necessary if live mites appear or new lesions develop.

Eye Irritation: Nix dermal cream is not irritating to eyes, however, if it should get into eyes, rinse them immediately with water.

In Case of Swallowing: Consult your physician or a Poison Control Centre.

Pregnancy: Studies have been performed in rats and rabbits and have revealed no evidence of reduced fertility or harm to the fetus due to permethrin. There are, however, no adequate or well-controlled studies in pregnant women. Because animal reproduction studies are not always predictive of human response, this drug should be used during pregnancy only after consulting your physician.

Lactation: It is not known whether this drug is excreted in human milk. Because many drugs are excreted in human milk, and because of the evidence for tumorigenic potential of permethrin in some animal species, consideration should be given to discontinuing nursing temporarily or not using the drug while nursing.

Children: Nix dermal cream is safe and effective in children 2 years of age and older. Before using in children under 2 years of age, consult your physician.

Keep out of the reach of children. In order to prevent accidental ingestion by children, the remaining contents of Nix should be discarded after use.

Adverse Reactions: In clinical studies, occasional itching has occurred. This is usually a consequence of the scabies infestation itself, but may be temporarily worsened following treatment with Nix. Other reactions which are less frequent include: mild, temporary stinging/burning, tingling, numbness or skin discomfort, redness, and swelling or rash of the skin.

☐ NOLVADEX® Ⓟ
☐ NOLVADEX®-D Ⓟ

Zeneca

Tamoxifen Citrate

Antineoplastic

Information for the Patient: Description: Nolvadex (tamoxifen citrate) is a medicine that blocks the effects of the hormone estrogen in the body. It is used to treat breast cancer.

The exact way that tamoxifen works against cancer is not known, but it may be related to the way it blocks the effects of estrogen on the body.

Nolvadex is available only with your doctor's prescription.

Before Using This Medication: In deciding to use a medicine, the risks of taking the medicine must be weighed against the good it will do. This is a decision you and your doctor will make.

Before taking Nolvadex, tell your doctor if any of the following apply to you:

- If you have ever had any unusual or allergic reaction to tamoxifen.
- If you are pregnant or if you intend to become pregnant. It is best to use some kind of birth control while you are taking Nolvadex and for about 2 months after you stop taking it. Please see your doctor for advice on what contraceptive precautions you should take, as some may be affected by Nolvadex. Tell your doctor right away if you think you have become pregnant while taking tamoxifen or within 2 months of having stopped it.
- It is important that you tell your doctor immediately if you have any unusual vaginal bleeding or other gynecological symptoms (such as pelvic pain or pressure) when you are taking Nolvadex or anytime afterwards. This is because a number of changes to the lining of the womb (the endometrium) may occur, some of which may be serious and could include cancer.
- If you are breast-feeding or intend to breast-feed.
- If you are taking any other prescription or over-the-counter medicine.
- If you have any other medical problems, especially cataracts (or other eye problems) or low blood cell counts.
- If you go into the hospital, let medical staff know you are taking Nolvadex.

Proper Use of This Medication: Use this medication only as directed by your doctor. Do not use more or less of it and do not use it more often than your doctor ordered. Taking too much may increase the chance of side effects, while taking too little may not improve your condition.

Nolvadex sometimes causes nausea and vomiting. However, it may have to be taken for several weeks or months to be effective. Even if you begin to feel ill, **do not stop using this medicine without first checking with your doctor.** Ask your health care professional for ways to lessen these effects.

Missed dose—If you miss a dose, take the dose as soon as you remember. Do not take 2 doses at the same time.

To store this medicine:

- **Keep out of the reach of children.**
- **Store away from heat and direct light.**
- **Do not store in damp places. Heat or moisture may cause the medicine to break down.**
- **Do not keep outdated medicine or medicine no longer needed.**

Precautions While Using This Medicine: It is important to use some type of birth control while you are taking Nolvadex. Please see your doctor for advice on what contraceptive precautions you should take, as some may be affected by Nolvadex. Tell your doctor right away if you think you have become pregnant while taking this medicine or within 2 months of stopping it.

Side Effects of This Medicine: Along with its needed effects, a medicine may cause some unwanted effects. Some side effects will have signs or symptoms that you can see or feel. Your doctor will watch for others by doing certain tests.

Also, because of the way this medicine acts on the body, there is a chance that it might cause other unwanted effects that may not occur until months or years after the medicine is used.

Nolvadex has been reported to increase the chance of cancer of the uterus (womb) as well as fibroids (noncancerous tumors) in the uterus in some women taking it. It may also cause a drop in some of your blood cell counts. In addition, Nolvadex has been reported to cause cataracts and other eye problems. Discuss these possible effects with your doctor.

Nolvadex (cont'd)

Check with your doctor or pharmacist as soon as possible if any of the following undesirable events occur:

Do not be alarmed by this list of possible events. You may not have any of them.
- Hot flushes
- Menstrual disturbances
- Effects on the endometrium (lining of the womb), which may also be seen as vaginal bleeding
- Fibroids (causes enlargement of the womb), which may also be seen as discomfort in the pelvis or as vaginal bleeding
- Itching around the vagina
- Vaginal discharge
- Stomach upsets (including nausea and vomiting)
- Lightheadedness
- Fluid retention (possibly seen as swollen ankles)
- Bruising more easily (thrombocytopenia)
- Skin rash
- Hair loss
- Certain liver problems such as jaundice (yellow eyes)
- Disturbances of vision
- Difficulties in seeing properly due to cataracts, changes to the cornea or disease of the retina
- Ovarian cysts (fluid sacs on ovaries) in premenopausal women
- Increased risk of blood clots
- At the beginning of treatment, a worsening of the symptoms of your breast cancer such as an increase in pain and/or an increase in the size of the affected tissue may occur. In addition if you experience excessive nausea, vomiting and thirst, you should tell your doctor. This may indicate possible changes in the amount of calcium in your blood and your doctor may have to do certain blood tests.

Other side effects not listed above may also occur in some patients. If you notice any other effects, check with your doctor.

If you need any further information ask your doctor or pharmacist.

□ NOROXIN® Ⓟ
MSD

Norfloxacin
Antibacterial Agent

Information for the Patient: Noroxin Tablets: Noroxin is the brand name of Merck Frosst Canada Inc. for the substance norfloxacin, available **only on prescription** from your physician. Norfloxacin is one of a group of medicines known as antibacterials. Antibacterials are used to treat infections caused by bacteria or germs; norfloxacin works against a large variety of species of bacteria, killing them or preventing them from developing.

Norfloxacin has been prescribed by your physician to treat an infection of the urogenital tract.

Remember: This medicine is prescribed for the particular infection you have at this time. **Do not give to other people, nor use this for other infections.**

Keep all medicines out of the reach of children.

Read the following information carefully. If you need any explanations, or further information, ask your physician or pharmacist.

Before Taking this Medicine: This medicine may not be suitable for certain people. So, tell your physician if you think any of the following applies to you:
- You have previously taken norfloxacin or any related medicines, example, ciprofloxacin (Cipro) or nalidixic acid (NegGram), and were allergic, or had reacted badly to it.
- You suffer from kidney disease.
- You have ever suffered from convulsions.
- You are pregnant or intend to become pregnant or are breast-feeding or intend to breast-feed.
- Inform your physician if you are taking any of the following medications: probenecid, nitrofurantoin, theophylline, cyclosporine, blood-thinning medicines, multivitamins or products containing iron, zinc, caffeine.
- Also inform your physician if you are taking any other medications (prescription or nonprescription drugs).

This medicine is not recommended for children before puberty.

Proper Use of this Medicine:
- Take this medicine exactly as your physician ordered for the specified number of days. **Do not stop even if you feel better. Stopping too soon might bring on your symptoms again.**
- It is best to take the tablet 1 hour **before**, or 2 hours **after** meal or milk ingestion, with a **full glass of water.** It is good to drink plenty of liquids—water or juice—every day, unless your physician has told you otherwise. Noroxin should not be taken within 2 hours of taking iron, zinc supplements or multivitamins containing them.
- Sucralfate (Sulcrate) and antacids (such as Diovol, Maalox or Amphojel) may interact with this medicine. If you have to take these medications, take them at least 2 to 3 hours before or after you take norfloxacin.
- If you forget to take a dose, take the recommended dose next time, as scheduled. **Do not double the dose to make up.** If you happen to take too many tablets by accident, contact your physician or pharmacist as **soon** as possible.
- If you develop any new medical problem while using this medicine, or you wish to begin using any other medicine, on prescription or not, check with your physician or pharmacist.
- Store your tablets at 15 to 30°C in a tightly closed container, away from heat and direct light, and out of damp places such as the bathroom or kitchen.

Side Effects of this Medicine—and What You Should Do: Along with its intended action, any medication, including norfloxacin, may cause side effects. Most people do not have any problem when taking this medicine; but if you notice any of the following effects, check with your physician or pharmacist as soon as possible.
- Dizziness, headache.
- If you experience any of the above effects, or visual problems, avoid driving and any other activity, or job that requires alertness, coordination or good vision.

Other possible effects which occur less commonly are: confusion, convulsions (seizures), swollen or inflamed joints, abdominal or stomach pain with: indigestion, gas, nausea, vomiting, diarrhea or loss of appetite; heartburn, rash; drowsiness and trouble sleeping.

Stop taking Noroxin and contact your doctor immediately in any of the following cases:

If you develop allergic reactions such as swelling of the face, lips and/or throat (with difficulty in breathing or swallowing), or hives;

If you develop skin reactions, including severe reaction to sunlight, such as rash, redness or increased sensitivity of skin or eyes to sunlight, swelling or blistering. **Stay out of direct sunlight,** wear protective clothing and use a sunblock preparation.

If you develop pain in your tendons (tendinitis, tendon rupture);

If you experience any worsening of your myasthenia gravis symptoms;

If you develop any signs of mental disturbances, including mood changes such as anxiety or depression.

Some people may have other reactions. If you notice any unusual effect, check with your physician or pharmacist.

Ingredients: Active Ingredient: Each tablet of Noroxin contains 400 mg of norfloxacin.

Nonmedicinal Ingredients: carnauba wax, croscarmellose sodium, hydroxypropyl cellulose, hydroxypropyl methylcellulose, magnesium stearate, microcrystalline cellulose, titanium dioxide.

□ NORPLANT® Ⓟ
Wyeth-Ayerst

Levonorgestrel
Contraceptive Implant

Information for the Patient: This product is intended to prevent pregnancy. It does not protect against HIV infection (AIDS) and other sexually transmitted diseases.

What you should know about Norplant before you decide to use it.

You need to read and understand this brochure before you decide to use the Norplant. The brochure contains information vital to your health. It tells you about the benefits and risks of Norplant. Discuss it with your doctor or nurse. Ask them to explain anything you do not understand.

There is a more technical brochure about Norplant that was written for doctors and nurses. If you would like to read that brochure too, ask your doctor or nurse for a copy. You may need their help to understand some of the information.

There is also a videotape that provides more information about Norplant. If you would like to watch it, ask your doctor or nurse.

Before you decide to use Norplant or any other birth control method, compare it to other birth control methods. If you want to learn more about other methods, ask your doctor or nurse. One of these other methods may be better for you than Norplant.

Norplant is different from other methods of birth control. The capsules are made of Silastic, a solid state silicone elastomer. It must be inserted in your arm during a minor surgical procedure. The procedure can be performed by a doctor or nurse in the office. You should know that some doctors and nurses have more experience than others in inserting Norplant. Be sure to discuss with your doctor or nurse whether he/she has received instruction in how to insert Norplant and remove it and his/her level of confidence in insertion and removal procedures.

You can decide to have Norplant removed at any time. You should know that removing Norplant may be more difficult than inserting it. It may take longer and involve more pain. It may leave scars. This risk does not exist with most other birth control methods.

Some women should not use Norplant. To find out whether you are one of those women, talk to your doctor or nurse and read below the sections entitled "Who Should Not Use Norplant" and "Other Considerations Before Choosing Norplant."

Some women who use Norplant will experience side effects. You should know the danger signs. To learn about them, talk to your doctor or nurse and read below the sections entitled "Risks of Using Norplant," "Warning Signals," "Precautions" and "Side Effects of Norplant."

What I Know About Norplant: I have read this brochure and have discussed it with my doctor or nurse. They have answered all my questions. I understand that there are risks as well as benefits from using Norplant. I understand that there are other forms of contraception that do not have the risks of Norplant, but may have different risks.

I also understand that this form is important. It demonstrates that I am making an informed and carefully considered decision to use Norplant. I have checked below those statements that I agree with:

- I have been told how Norplant works to keep women from getting pregnant.
- I have been told that the risk of getting pregnant while using Norplant is 1% (This means that about 1 woman out of every 100 who use Norplant may get pregnant each year).
- I have been told that I can have Norplant taken out at any time and for any reason. I have also been told that, if I have trouble finding a doctor or nurse to remove it, I can call (tel. no.) for help.
- I understand that the Norplant capsules are made of Silastic, a solid state silicone elastomer.
- I have been told that the Norplant capsules are implanted under the skin of my arm during an in-office surgical procedure.
- I have been told that the Norplant capsules must be removed at the end of the 5 years. The removal procedure is also an in-office surgical procedure and may cause more discomfort and scarring than the insertion procedure.
- I have been told about the side effects of Norplant, including that most women have changes in their menstrual bleeding. I have been told that the side effects may vary in severity from one woman to another.
- I have been told about the Norplant warning signs and know that I should seek medical attention if any warning signs appear.
- I have been told that I need to receive a medical check-up yearly or any time I am having problems.
- I have been told that Norplant does not protect me from AIDS or any other sexually transmitted disease.

I have considered all the information in this brochure and voluntarily choose to have Norplant inserted by:

(Name of Healthcare Provider)

(Patient Signature) (Date)

Witnessed By:
The patient above has signed this brochure in my presence after I counselled her and answered her questions.

(Healthcare Provider) (Date)
Signature

Introduction: Each woman who considers using Norplant contraceptive implants should understand the benefits and risks of this form of family planning as compared with other contraceptive methods. This leaflet will give you much of the information you will need to make this decision, but it is not a replacement for a careful discussion with your healthcare provider. You should discuss the information provided in this leaflet with him or her, both when choosing whether to use Norplant and during revisits. You should also follow your healthcare provider's advice with regard to regular check-ups while using Norplant.

Norplant consists of 6 thin, flexible capsules, made of Silastic, that are inserted just under the skin on the inside of your upper arm in a minor, out-patient surgical procedure. The capsules contain a synthetic hormone, levonorgestrel, that is also used as one of the active ingredients in many oral contraceptives. Immediately after insertion of Norplant, a low continuous dose of the hormone is released into your body. Pregnancy is prevented through a combination of mechanisms. The most important ways are by inhibiting ovulation, so eggs will not be released regularly, and thickening the cervical mucus, making it more difficult for the sperm to reach the egg. There may also be other mechanisms that contribute to these contraceptive effects. When Norplant is removed, you will return to your previous level of fertility.

Effectiveness of Norplant: Norplant is one of the most effective reversible contraceptive methods. No contraceptive is 100% effective. The average pregnancy rate over a 5-year period for Norplant is less than 1%—less than 1 pregnancy for every 100 women during the first year of use. In comparison, pregnancy rates that have been experienced with other methods of family planning during the first year of use are as follows:

Reported Pregnancies per 100 Women per Year

Norplant	less than 1
Combination pill	less than 1 to 2
Intrauterine Device (IUD)	less than 1 to 6
Condom with spermicidal foam or gel	1 to 6
Mini-pill	3 to 6
Condom	2 to 12
Diaphragm with spermicidal foam or gel	3 to 18
Spermicide	3 to 21
Sponge with spermicide	3 to 28
Cervical cap with spermicide	5 to 18
Periodic abstinence (rhythm), all types	2 to 20
No birth control	60 to 85

Except for Norplant, sterilization and the IUD, the efficacy of these methods depends in part on how reliably they are used.

Norplant provides 5 years of protection but can be removed at any time. At the end of the fifth year, the implants will be less effective and must be removed; a new set may be inserted at the time of removal for continued protection.

Who Should Not Use Norplant: Some women should not use Norplant. For example, you should not have the implants inserted if you are pregnant or think you may be pregnant. You should not use Norplant if you have:

- Acute liver disease; non-cancerous or cancerous liver tumors;
- Unexplained vaginal bleeding (until a diagnosis is reached by your healthcare provider);
- Breast cancer;
- Blood clots in the legs (thrombophlebitis), lungs (pulmonary embolism), eyes or elsewhere. Women who have had previous blood clots should consult with their healthcare provider whether to use Norplant;
- History of idiopathic intracranial hypertension (pseudotumor cerebri, benign intracranial hypertension);
- Hypersensitivity to levonorgestrel or any of the other components of Norplant.

Other Considerations Before Choosing Norplant: Tell your healthcare provider if you or any family member has ever had:

- Breast nodules, fibrocystic disease of the breast, an abnormal breast x-ray or mammogram;
- Diabetes;
- Elevated cholesterol or triglycerides;
- High blood pressure;
- Headaches;
- Gallbladder, heart, or kidney disease;
- History of scanty or irregular menstrual periods;
- History of blood clots, heart attack or stroke;
- Depression;
- Migraine;
- Ectopic pregnancy.

Women with these conditions may need to be checked more often by their healthcare provider if they choose Norplant.

Be sure to inform your healthcare provider if you smoke or are on any medications.

Norplant (cont'd)

The Risks of Using Norplant:

1. **Irregular Menstrual Bleeding:** Most women experience some change in their usual monthly pattern. These menstrual irregularities vary from woman to woman and include:
   - Prolonged bleeding (more days than you usually experience) commonly during the first months of use;
   - Untimely bleeding or spotting between periods;
   - No bleeding at all for several months; or
   - A combination of these patterns.

   Although there is increased frequency of bleeding in some women, the monthly blood loss is usually less than normal menses.

   It cannot be predicted what kind of change you may experience. If increased frequency of bleeding occurs, the quantity of blood loss is rarely enough to cause anemia, but there have been a few cases that required treatment. The irregularities frequently diminish gradually with continuing use.
2. **Delayed Disappearance of Ovarian Follicles/Ovarian Cysts.** If follicles (eggs and their surrounding cells) in the ovary develop while using Norplant, disintegration or disappearance of the follicles is sometimes delayed and the follicles may continue to grow beyond the size they would normally reach. These enlarged follicles, which are sometimes called ovarian cysts, may produce discomfort in some women, although most users would not be aware of them unless they were found incidentally on a physical exam. In the majority of women, enlarged follicles will disappear on their own and should not require surgery. Rarely, they may twist or rupture so that surgery is required. You should discuss this with your healthcare provider.
3. **Ectopic Pregnancies:** Clinical studies have shown that ectopic pregnancies (development of the fertilized egg outside of the uterus, sometimes called a tubal pregnancy) have occurred among Norplant users, at similar rates to those experienced by users of no method or of IUDs. Symptoms of an ectopic pregnancy include spotting and cramping pain, which usually begin shortly after the first missed period. Contact your healthcare provider should you miss a period or experience abdominal pain.
4. **Diseases of the Heart and Blood Vessels:** As with oral contraceptives, there have been reports of blood clots and blockage of blood vessels in Norplant users. Blood clots and blockage of blood vessels can be serious. In particular, a clot in the veins of the legs can cause inflammation and risk of further clots, and a clot that travels to the lungs can cause a sudden blocking of the vessel carrying blood to the lungs, resulting in respiratory collapse and even death. Rarely, clots occur in the blood vessels of the eye and may cause double vision, impaired vision, or even blindness. There have also been reports of heart attacks and strokes while Norplant has been in place. Any of these conditions can cause serious disability or death. Patients who develop blood clots in the legs, arms, lungs, or eyes should have Norplant removed. In addition, patients restricted to bed rest or who have limited movement for a prolonged period due to surgery or other illness may be at increased risk of developing blood clots. Norplant may need to be removed in such patients.
5. **Risks Based on Experience With Combination Oral Contraceptives:** Combination pills contain a progestin such as levonorgestrel and an estrogen, another type of hormone. Some rare but serious side effects have been associated with use of the combination pill. It is unknown whether the risks associated with combined oral contraceptive use may also be risks with progestin-only contraceptives like Norplant.
6. **Idiopathic Intracranial Hypertension (pseudotumor cerebri, benign intracranial hypertension):** An increase in intracranial pressure has been reported in Norplant users. Symptoms may include headache (associated with change in frequency, pattern, severity, or persistence; of particular importance are those headaches that do not stop) and visual disturbances. Contact your physician or healthcare provider if you experience these symptoms, particularly if you are obese or have had a recent weight gain. Your healthcare provider may recommend that the Norplant be removed.

Warning Signals: If any of these adverse effects occur following insertion of Norplant (subdermal levonorgestrel), call your healthcare provider immediately:

- Sharp chest pain, coughing of blood, or sudden shortness of breath (indicating a possible clot in the lung)
- Pain in the calf (indicating a possible clot in the leg)
- Crushing chest pain or heaviness in the chest (indicating a possible heart attack)
- Sudden severe or persistent headache or vomiting, dizziness or fainting, disturbances of vision or speech, weakness, or numbness in an arm or leg (indicating a possible stroke or other neurologic problem)
- Persistent headaches, particularly if obese or recent weight gain (indicating possible idiopathic intracranial hypertension)
- Sudden partial or complete loss of vision (indicating a possible clot in the eye)
- Breast lumps (indicating possible breast cancer or fibrocystic disease of the breast; ask your doctor or healthcare provider to show you how to examine your breasts)
- Severe pain or tenderness in the stomach area or lower abdominal area (indicating an ectopic pregnancy, a ruptured or twisted ovarian follicle, or possibly a ruptured liver tumor)
- Difficulty in sleeping, weakness, lack of energy, fatigue, or change in mood (possibly indicating severe depression)
- Jaundice or a yellowing of the skin or eyeballs, accompanied frequently by fever, fatigue, loss of appetite, dark-colored urine, or light-colored bowel movements (indicating possible liver problems)
- Heavy vaginal bleeding
- Delayed menstrual cycles after a long interval of regular cycles
- Arm pain
- Pus or bleeding at implant site
- Expulsion of an implant.

Side Effects of Norplant: The most frequently reported side effects are menstrual cycle irregularities. Such changes vary from woman to woman and may include:

- Prolonged menstrual bleeding (more days than you would usually experience) commonly during the first months of use;
- Untimely bleeding or spotting between periods;
- Frequent onset of bleeding;
- Scanty bleeding;
- No bleeding at all for several months; or
- A combination of these patterns.

It cannot be predicted before insertion of Norplant what kind of bleeding pattern you will have. Many women can expect an altered bleeding pattern to become more regular after 9 to 12 months. Despite the increased frequency of bleeding in some women, the monthly blood loss is usually less than normal menses. In fact, in some studies, patient blood counts have improved.

Contact your healthcare provider if you experience heavy bleeding. If you have normal cyclic periods and then miss a period, a pregnancy test should be obtained. If you are pregnant, Norplant must be removed.

There have been rare reports of birth defects in offspring of women who were using Norplant unintentionally during early pregnancy. Though the association has been neither confirmed nor refuted, you should check with your healthcare provider about the risks to your unborn child of any medication taken during pregnancy.

In clinical studies, women using Norplant have complained about the following conditions, which are possibly related to Norplant:

- Headache
- Nervousness/anxiety
- Nausea/vomiting
- Dizziness
- Enlargement of the ovaries and/or fallopian tubes
- Dermatitis (inflammation of the skin)/rash
- Acne
- Change in appetite
- Weight gain
- Mastalgia (breast tenderness)
- Hirsutism (excessive growth of body or facial hair) or alopecia (hair loss)
- Discoloration of the skin over the site of implantation (usually reversible).

Pre-existing conditions of acne or excessive growth of body or facial hair could also be worsened. Occasionally, an infection may occur at the implant site, or there may be a brief incidence of pain or itching. Removals may be more difficult than insertions in some cases.

An enlargement of ovarian follicles, (sometimes called ovarian cysts) may occur in Norplant users. These would be detectable during a physical examination. The enlarged follicles usually disappear on their own without surgical intervention, but in rare instances they may twist or rupture so that surgery is required.

There are a number of other complaints reported by Norplant users or discovered by healthcare providers but an association with Norplant has been neither confirmed nor refuted. They include:

- Breast discharge
- Cervicitis (inflammation of the cervix, detected by physician)
- Muscle and skeletal pain
- Abdominal discomfort
- Leukorrhea (whitish discharge from the vagina and uterine cavity)
- Vaginitis (inflammation of the vagina)
- Idiopathic intracranial hypertension (pseudotumor cerebri)
- Mood swings
- Birth defects
- Thrombotic thrombocytopenic purpura (TTP)
- Blood clots
- Heart attack
- Stroke
- Pruritus (itching)
- Urticaria (hives)
- Dysmenorrhea (pain during menstruation)
- Arm pain
- Migraine
- Numbness
- Tingling
- Fatigue/weakness
- Depression

General Precautions:

1. **Missed Periods:** There may be times when you may not menstruate regularly while using Norplant. However, if you think you may be pregnant contact your healthcare provider.
2. **While Breast-feeding:** Women who are breast-feeding or intend to breast-feed should discuss this with their healthcare provider when considering the use of Norplant. Studies have shown no significant effects on the growth or health of infants whose mothers used Norplant beginning 5 to 7 weeks after childbirth. There is no experience to support the use of Norplant earlier than this after childbirth.
3. **Infections:** Infection at the Norplant implant site does not commonly occur. Norplant should be inserted by a healthcare provider who is familiar with the appropriate insertion and removal techniques. This will reduce the possibility of an infection. If infection does occur, contact your healthcare provider for treatment. Norplant may need to be removed in the event that infection continues.
4. **Laboratory Tests:** If you are scheduled for any laboratory tests tell your healthcare provider that you are using Norplant. Certain blood tests are affected by synthetic hormones.
5. **Drug Interactions:** Certain drugs may interact with the hormone delivered by Norplant to make the implants less effective in preventing pregnancy. Such drugs include drugs used for epilepsy such as phenytoin (Dilantin is one brand) and carbamazepine (Tegretol is one brand). Certain other drugs may also make the Norplant less effective. You may need to use additional contraception when you take drugs that can make Norplant less effective. Discuss this with your healthcare provider.
6. **Sexually Transmitted Diseases:** Norplant does not protect against sexually transmitted diseases (STDs) including HIV/AIDS. For protection against STDs, it is advisable to use latex condoms along with Norplant.
7. **Autoimmune Diseases:** No definitive evidence exists to support or rule out the link between the development of autoimmune diseases and the use of silicone-containing devices, but studies have raised the possibility of developing antibodies against silicone.
8. **Carbohydrate and Lipid Metabolism:** Blood sugar levels may be increased by progestin-only contraceptives such as Norplant. Diabetic and prediabetic patients should be observed carefully while using Norplant.

   Some progestins may increase lipid (e.g., cholesterol, triglycerides) levels. Patients being treated for increased lipid levels should be followed closely while using Norplant.
9. **Liver Function:** Norplant may need to be removed if yellowing of the skin or whites of the eyes occurs. Hormones may be poorly metabolized in patients with liver diseases.
10. **Emotional Disorders:** Norplant may need to be removed if you become severely depressed.
11. **Capsule Expulsion and Displacement (Movement):** Expulsion of Norplant capsules (i.e., when a capsule unintentionally comes out of the insertion site/skin) does not commonly occur. However, expulsion may occur if the capsules are placed too close to the skin, too close to the incision or if infection is present. If expulsion of a capsule occurs, your healthcare provider should replace it with a new capsule that has not been previously used. If infection is present, it should be treated and cured before capsule(s) is (are) replaced. To avoid pregnancy, a back-up method of contraception should be used if less than 6 capsules are in place.

    After Norplant capsules are inserted, they sometimes move from the original position. Infrequently, movement of a few to several inches has been reported. Some Norplant users have reported movement accompanied by pain and discomfort. Contact your healthcare provider in the event that capsule movement accompanied by pain and/or discomfort occurs.

Insertion of Norplant: Insertion and removal of Norplant should be performed by a healthcare provider knowledgeable of the procedures.

Prior to insertion of Norplant, your healthcare provider will inquire about your medical history and perform a physical examination. To make sure you are not already pregnant, Norplant should be inserted within 7 days after the onset of menstrual bleeding or immediately following an abortion. If Norplant capsules are inserted at any other time during the cycle, pregnancy must be excluded, and a nonhormonal contraceptive method (such as condoms, spermicides, or diaphragms) must be used for the remainder of that cycle following insertion.

Norplant implants are inserted under the skin on the inner surface of your upper arm during a minor, out-patient surgical procedure under sterile conditions. A local anesthetic is used to numb a small area in the upper arm, after which a small incision, about 2 mm long, is made in the same area. The 6 implants/capsules are placed one at a time with a special instrument just under the skin in a fan shape. The insertion process should take no longer than 10 to 15 minutes. The incision is covered with a small adhesive bandage and protective gauze.

Because a local anesthetic is used, there should be little or no discomfort during insertion. When the anesthetic wears off, there may be some tenderness in the area of the implants for a day or two. Some discoloration, bruising, and swelling may also be present for a few days after the procedure. This should not interfere with your usual activities. Other skin reactions that have been reported include blistering, sloughing, and ulceration.

Following insertion, you can resume work and other activities. Be careful, however, not to bump the site or get the incision wet for at least 3 days. Also avoid heavy lifting for 2 to 3 days. The protective gauze should remain in place for 24 hours and a small adhesive bandage for 3 days.

If the implants are inserted during menses, you may resume sexual relations as soon as you wish. If the capsules are inserted more than 7 days after the onset of menses, then a nonhormonal contraceptive method must be used for the remainder of that cycle following insertion.

Be sure to have periodic check-ups as advised by your healthcare provider while the implants are in place.

Removal of Norplant: The implants must be removed at the end of 5 years when the method starts to become less effective. They can be removed at any time before then, however, if you want to stop using the method for any reason.

Just as for insertion, your healthcare provider will apply a local anesthetic. Under sterile conditions, a small (4 mm) incision will be made, through which all the implants will be removed. The removal process usually takes from 15 to 20 minutes, but may take longer. If some of the capsules are more difficult to remove, an additional visit and incision may be required. A nonhormonal method of contraception (such as condoms, spermicides, or diaphragms) should be used if less than 6 capsules are in place.

As after insertion, avoid bumping the incision site for a few days. The area should be kept clean, dry and bandaged until healed (3 to 5 days), to avoid infection. Bruising may occur at the implant site following removal.

If you want to continue using Norplant, you may receive a new implant at the same time the old set is removed. The second Norplant can be placed in the same arm, and frequently through the incision from which the earlier set was removed, or in the other arm. If you do not want to continue with Norplant and do not want to become pregnant, make sure your healthcare provider recommends another contraceptive method.

Insertion and removal of Norplant should be performed by a healthcare provider knowledgeable of the procedures.

There have been reports of arm pain, numbness, tingling and scarring following these procedures.

Once the implants are removed, the contraceptive effects cease quickly and a woman can become pregnant as rapidly as women who

Norplant (cont'd)

have not used the method. If you would like more information about Norplant, consult your healthcare provider.

☐ NORVIR® Ⓟ

Abbott

Ritonavir

Human Immunodeficiency Virus (HIV) Protease Inhibitor

Information for the Patient: Patients should be informed that Norvir (ritonavir) is not a cure for HIV infection and that they may continue to acquire illnesses associated with advanced HIV infection, including opportunistic infections.

Patients should be told that the long-term effects of ritonavir are unknown at this time. They should be informed that ritonavir therapy has not been shown to reduce the risk of transmitting HIV to others through sexual contact or blood contamination.

Patients should be advised to take ritonavir with food, if possible.

Patients should be informed to take ritonavir every day as prescribed. Patients should not alter the dose or discontinue ritonavir without consulting their doctor. If a dose is missed, patients should take the next dose as soon as possible. However, if a dose is skipped, the patient should not double the next dose.

Since ritonavir interacts with a number of drugs when taken together, patients should be advised to report to their doctor the use of any other medications, including prescription and nonprescription drugs.

Patients should be advised of the likelihood of experiencing muscle weakness, nausea, diarrhea, vomiting, abdominal pain, loss of appetite, numbness and tingling, and/or taste perversion while taking ritonavir.

The ritonavir oral solution dosage cup should be cleaned immediately with hot water and dish soap after use. When cleaned immediately, drug residue is removed. The dosage cup must be dry prior to use.

☐ NOVO-DIFENAC® Ⓟ
☐ NOVO-DIFENAC® SR Ⓟ

Novopharm

Diclofenac Sodium

Anti-inflammatory—Analgesic

Information for the Patient: Diclofenac sodium, which has been prescribed to you by your doctor, is one of a large group of nonsteroidal anti-inflammatory drugs (NSAIDs) and is used to treat the symptoms of certain types of arthritis (rheumatism). It helps to relieve joint pain, swelling, stiffness and fever by reducing the production of certain substances (prostaglandins) and helping to control inflammation and other body reactions.

You should take diclofenac sodium only as directed by your doctor. Do not take more of it, do not take it more often and do not take it for a longer period of time than your doctor ordered. The maximum daily dose of diclofenac sodium in any form is 150 mg.

Be sure to take diclofenac sodium regularly as prescribed. In some types of arthritis, up to 2 weeks may pass before you feel the full effects of this medicine. During treatment, your doctor may decide to adjust the dosage according to your response to the medication.

To lessen stomach upset, take this medicine immediately after a meal or with food or milk. If stomach upset (indigestion, nausea, vomiting, stomach pain or diarrhea) occurs and continues, contact your doctor.

This medicine is available only with your doctor's prescription. Remember: This medicine has been prescribed for your current medical problem only. It must not be given to other people or used for other problems unless you are otherwise directed by your doctor.

Proper Use of This Medicine: Taking Slow Release tablets once a day: If you are taking Novo-Difenac SR 75 mg or 100 mg tablets once a day, it is best to take it at the same time each day unless your doctor has told you differently. If you have not taken this tablet at the prescribed or your regular time you may take it right away, but you should wait at least 12 hours before taking the next dose. You may then continue taking your tablet at the prescribed or your regular time thereafter.

Taking Slow Release tablets twice a day: **Slow Release 100 mg** tablets may **not** be taken more than once a day. If you are taking Novo-Difenac SR 75 mg tablets twice a day, it is best to take this tablet morning and evening, unless your doctor has told you differently. If you have not taken this tablet at the prescribed or your regular time you may take it right away. If a second dose on the same day is necessary, you should wait preferably 12 hours and no less than 6 hours before taking the next dose. You may then continue taking your tablet at the prescribed or your regular time the next day.

Novo-Difenac SR tablets should be swallowed whole with liquid, preferably at mealtime.

If you are taking Novo-Difenac (50 and 100 mg) suppositories: Novo-Difenac suppositories are wrapped in foil. Make sure that the foil wrapping is fully removed before inserting the suppository rectally. Suppositories are not to be taken by mouth.

Whether you have been prescribed oral tablets and/or rectal suppositories make sure that you do not take more than a total of 150 mg per day.

Do not take ASA (acetylsalicylic acid), ASA-containing compounds or other drugs used to relieve symptoms of arthritis while taking diclofenac sodium unless directed to do so by your physician.

If you are prescribed this medication for use over a long period of time, your doctor will check your health during regular visits to assess your progress and to ensure that this medication is not causing unwanted effects.

Side Effects of This Medicine: Along with its beneficial effects, diclofenac sodium, like other NSAID drugs, may cause some undesirable reactions. Elderly, frail or debilitated patients often seem to experience more frequent or more severe side effects. Although not all of these side effects are common, when they do occur they may require medical attention. Check with your doctor immediately if any of the following are noted:

- Bloody or black tarry stools.
- Shortness of breath, wheezing, any trouble in breathing or tightness in the chest.
- Skin rash, swelling, hives or itching.
- Indigestion, nausea, vomiting, stomach pain or diarrhea.
- Yellow discoloration of the skin or eyes, with or without fatigue.
- Any changes in the amount or color of your urine (such as dark; red or brown).
- Swelling of the feet or lower legs.
- Blurred vision or any visual disturbance.
- Mental confusion, depression, dizziness, lightheadedness.
- Hearing problems.

Always Remember: Before taking this medication tell your doctor and pharmacist if you:

- are allergic to diclofenac sodium or other related medicines of the NSAID group such as acetylsalicylic acid, diflunisal, fenoprofen, flurbiprofen, ibuprofen, indomethacin, ketoprofen, mefenamic acid, piroxicam, sulindac, tiaprofenic acid or tolmetin.
- have a history of stomach upset, ulcers, or liver or kidney diseases.
- are pregnant or intend to become pregnant while taking this medication.
- are breast-feeding.
- are taking any other medication (either prescription or nonprescription).
- have any other medical problem(s).

While taking this medication:

- Tell any other doctor, dentist or pharmacist that you consult or see, that you are taking this medication.
- Be cautious about driving or participating in activities that require alertness if you are drowsy, dizzy or lightheaded after taking this medication.
- Check with your doctor if you are not getting any relief or if any problems develop.
- Report any untoward reactions to your doctor. This is very important as it will aid in the early detection and prevention of potential complications.
- Your regular medical checkups are essential.

Storage: Store between 15 and 30°C and protect from humidity.

- If you want more information about this medicine, ask your doctor or pharmacist.

☐ **NUTROPIN®** ℞
☐ **NUTROPIN® AQ** ℞

Roche

Somatropin

Growth Hormone

Information for the Patient/Parent: Nutropin (somatropin for injection, lyophilized powder). See package insert for illustrations: **Do not mix (reconstitute) the drug or inject it, until your physician or nurse has thoroughly trained you in the proper techniques.**

Reconstituting means adding a liquid (diluent) to a dry powder. In this case, Nutropin **must** be mixed with Bacteriostatic Water for Injection, USP (benzyl alcohol preserved), the sterile diluent provided, before it can be injected.

Use the sterile technique as instructed by your physician or nurse. Dispose of syringes and needles properly after each use, out of the reach of children. See item 6 ''Giving the Medication'' for instructions on the proper disposal of used needles and syringes.

Reconstituting a Nutropin Vial: Reconstitute the Nutropin vials **only** with Bacteriostatic Water for Injection, USP, **preserved with benzyl alcohol** provided in the carton. Do not use other solutions for reconstitution unless instructed to do so by your physician. Unused contents of a reconstituted Nutropin vial should not be used to reconstitute a new Nutropin vial.

Your physician or nurse will tell you what size syringe and needle to use for mixing and how much diluent to add to the Nutropin vial. See package insert for illustrations.

1. Wash your hands thoroughly with soap and water before preparing the medication. This helps prevent infection.
2. Remove the protective plastic cap from the top of both the diluent and Nutropin vials. Clean the rubber stopper on the top of each vial with an alcohol swab. After cleaning, do not touch the top of the vials.
3. Fill the syringe with air by pulling the plunger to the level indicated by your physician.
4. Remove the plastic needle guard and set it aside. Insert the needle into the diluent vial and inject the air into the vial.
5. Turn the diluent vial upside down with the syringe needle still in it and hold the vial in one hand. Make sure the tip of the needle is in the diluent. Withdraw the diluent to be added to the Nutropin vial by pulling the plunger to the exact amount your physician has told you. Check to make sure you have the correct amount of diluent in the syringe. Withdraw the needle from the diluent vial and replace the plastic needle guard.
6. Before adding the diluent to the Nutropin vial, check to make sure you have withdrawn the correct amount. To prepare the Nutropin solution, remove the plastic needle guard and insert the needle into the cleaned vial top of the Nutropin vial. Gently place the needle tip against the glass wall of the vial. Slowly inject the diluent, aiming the stream of water at the glass wall of the vial. **Do not aim the stream at the white powder** at the bottom of the vial. Withdraw the needle and replace the plastic needle guard. See item 6 ''Giving The Medication'' for instructions on the proper disposal of used needles and syringes.
7. Swirl the Nutropin vial with a gentle rotary motion until the contents are completely dissolved. Never shake the Nutropin vial after it has been reconstituted. Because Nutropin growth hormone is a protein, shaking can result in a cloudy solution. Immediately after reconstitution, the solution should be clear and should not have any solid particles floating on the surface. If you notice lumps of powder that float or stick to the sides of the vial, continue to gently swirl the solution until all of the powder has dissolved. If air bubbles form, wait until they have risen to the top of the solution and have disappeared before proceeding further. Do not inject the Nutropin solution if it is cloudy or hazy, but return the Nutropin vial to your pharmacist or prescribing physician.
8. Write the date on both the diluent vial and the reconstituted Nutropin vial. This way you will know the date you first opened and used the diluent vial, and when the Nutropin vial was reconstituted. A diluent vial that you have opened and removed diluent from can be used for 14 days. The reconstituted vial of Nutropin cannot be used after 14 days and should be returned to the physician or pharmacist. Store all vials in a clean, safe place in the refrigerator. **Do not freeze.**

Note: Unopened diluent and Nutropin can be used until the expiration date (EXP.) printed on the vial labels.

Measuring the Dose: Before each use, check the expiration date printed on the vial label, the date of reconstitution, and ensure that the Nutropin solution is clear. Occasionally, after refrigeration, you may notice that small colorless particles of protein are present in the Nutropin solution. This is not unusual for solutions containing proteins like Nutropin and does not indicate any decrease in potency of this product. Allow the vial to come to room temperature and gently swirl. If the solution is cloudy or hazy, do not inject it, but return the vial of Nutropin to your pharmacist or prescribing physician.

1. Wash your hands thoroughly with soap and water before preparing the dose. This helps prevent infection.
2. Check the date you wrote on the reconstituted Nutropin vial to be sure it is not more than 14 days old.
3. Wipe the rubber stopper located on top of the Nutropin vial with an alcohol swab. Fingers and hands should not touch the top of the vial.
4. Draw air into the syringe by pulling back on the plunger. The amount of air should be equal to the Nutropin dose. Place your fingers on the tip of the plunger.
5. Remove and save the plastic needle guard. Slowly insert the needle straight through the center of the rubber stopper of the vial containing the Nutropin solution.
6. Gently push the plunger to discharge the air into the vial.
7. Turn the vial upside down with the syringe needle still in it and hold the vial in one hand. Be sure the tip of the needle is in the Nutropin solution. Using your other hand, slowly pull back on the plunger in a continuous motion until the correct amount of Nutropin solution is in the syringe.
8. Remove the needle from the Nutropin vial and replace the plastic needle guard until time of administration or injection. Be careful not to touch the needle with your fingers. The injection should be given as soon after filling the syringe as possible; do not store Nutropin in the syringe.

Selecting the Injection Site: Your child's physician or nurse will teach you how to locate appropriate injection sites. It is very important that you rotate the site of an injection each time you give the medication. Even if your child develops a preference for one site—as many children do—you still should rotate the injection site.

The injection sites most often recommended for children are:

- upper arm
- abdomen
- thigh

Giving the Medication: Your physician or nurse will provide you with hands-on training on how to give an injection. Needles and syringes should be used only once to ensure sterility of both the needle and the syringe. The following is a review of the steps involved in giving the medication:

1. Cleanse the injection site with an alcohol-saturated cotton ball or cotton swab.
2. Double check that the correct amount of Nutropin solution is in the syringe. Remove the needle guard from the syringe filled with the proper dose of solution and hold the syringe the way you would hold a pencil.
3. Squeeze the skin between your thumb and index finger before and during the injection. Insert the needle into the skin at a 45 to 90° angle with a quick, firm motion. This hurts less than pushing the needle in slowly. Your physician or nurse will tell you the correct angle to use for your child.
4. Slowly (within a few seconds) inject the solution by gently pushing the plunger until the syringe is empty.
5. Withdraw the needle quickly, pulling it straight out, and apply pressure over the injection site with a dry gauze pad or cotton ball. A drop of blood may appear. Put an adhesive bandage on the injection site if desired.
6. To prevent injury, safely dispose of all used needles and syringes after a single use as instructed by your physician or nurse by following these simple steps:
   - Place all used needles and syringes in a hard, plastic container with a screw-on cap, or a metal container with a plastic lid, such as a coffee can properly labeled as to content. If a metal container is used, cut a small hole in the plastic lid and tape the lid to the metal container. When the metal container is full, cover the hole with tape and throw it away. If a hard, plastic container is used, always screw the cap on tightly after each use. When the plastic container is full, tape around the cap and throw it away.
   - Do not use glass or clear, plastic containers, or any container that will be recycled or returned to a store.
   - Always store the container out of the reach of children.

Nutropin (cont'd)

- Please check with your physician, nurse or pharmacist for other suggestions. There may be special provincial and local laws that they will discuss with you.

7. Occasionally a problem may develop at the injection site. If you notice any of the following signs or symptoms, contact your physician or nurse:
   - a lump or swelling that doesn't go away
   - bruising that doesn't go away
   - any signs of infection or inflammation at an injection site (pus, persistent redness surrounding skin that is hot to the touch, persistent pain after the injection).

Storage: Nutropin **must** be refrigerated before reconstitution (powder form) and after reconstitution (liquid form).

Reconstituted Nutropin cannot be used after 14 days and should be returned to your physician or pharmacist.

The unopened and opened vials of Bacteriostatic Water for Injection, USP (benzyl alcohol preserved) should also be refrigerated. The opened vials can only be used for 14 days.

Refrigerate at 2 to 8°C.

The Nutropin vial, after reconstitution, and the vial of Bacteriostatic Water for Injection, USP (benzyl alcohol preserved) must not be frozen.

If you have any questions, contact your physician, nurse or pharmacist.

Information for the Patient/Parent: Nutropin AQ (somatropin injection) See package insert for illustrations: **Do not inject the drug until your physician or nurse has thoroughly trained you in the proper techniques.**

Your physician or nurse will tell you what size syringe and needle to use for giving the medication.

Use the sterile technique as instructed by your physician or nurse. Dispose of syringes and needles properly after each use, out of the reach of children.

Preparing the Dose:

1. Wash your hands thoroughly with soap and water before preparing the medication. This helps prevent infection.
2. Write the date on the Nutropin AQ vial. This way you will know the date you first opened and used the Nutropin AQ vial. The vial of Nutropin AQ cannot be used 28 days after first use and should be discarded. Store all vials in a clean, safe place in the refrigerator. **Do not freeze.**
3. Remove the protective plastic cap from the top of the Nutropin AQ vial. Clean the rubber stopper on the top of the vial with an alcohol swab. After cleaning, do not touch the top of the vial.

Measuring the Dose: Before each use, check the expiration date printed on the vial label, the date the vial was first used, and ensure that the Nutropin AQ solution is clear. Occasionally, after refrigeration, you may notice that small colorless particles of protein are present in the Nutropin AQ solution. This is not unusual for solutions containing proteins like Nutropin AQ and does not indicate any decrease in potency of this product. Allow the vial to come to room temperature and gently swirl. If the solution is cloudy or hazy, do not inject it, but return the vial of Nutropin AQ to your pharmacist or prescribing physician.

1. Wash your hands thoroughly with soap and water before preparing the dose. This helps prevent infection.
2. Check the date you wrote on the Nutropin AQ vial to be sure it is not more than 28 days old.
3. Wipe the rubber stopper located on top of the Nutropin AQ vial with an alcohol swab. Fingers and hands should not touch the top of the vial.
4. Draw air into the syringe by pulling back on the plunger. The amount of air should be equal to the Nutropin AQ dose. Place your fingers on the tip of the plunger.
5. Remove and save the plastic needle guard. Slowly insert the needle straight through the center of the rubber stopper of the vial containing the Nutropin AQ solution.
6. Gently push the plunger to discharge the air into the vial.
7. Turn the vial upside down with the syringe needle still in it and hold the vial in one hand. Be sure the tip of the needle is in the Nutropin AQ solution. Using your other hand, slowly pull back on the plunger in a continuous motion until the correct amount of Nutropin AQ solution is in the syringe.
8. Remove the needle from the Nutropin AQ vial and replace the plastic needle guard until time of administration or injection. Be careful not to touch the needle with your fingers. The injection should be given as soon after filling the syringe as possible; do not store Nutropin AQ in the syringe.

Selecting the Injection Site: Your child's physician or nurse will teach you how to locate appropriate injection sites. It is very important that you rotate the site of an injection each time you give the medication. Even if your child develops a preference for one site—as many children do—you still should rotate the injection site.

The injection sites most often recommended for children are:

- upper arm
- abdomen
- thigh

Giving the Medication: Your physician or nurse will provide you with hands-on training on how to give an injection. Needles and syringes should be used only once to ensure sterility of both the needle and the syringe. The following is a review of the steps involved in giving the medication:

1. Cleanse the injection site with an alcohol-saturated cotton ball or cotton swab.
2. Double check that the correct amount of Nutropin AQ solution is in the syringe. Remove the needle guard from the syringe filled with the proper dose of solution and hold the syringe the way you would hold a pencil.
3. Squeeze the skin between your thumb and index finger before and during the injection. Insert the needle into the skin at a 45 to 90° angle with a quick, firm motion. This hurts less than pushing the needle in slowly. Your physician or nurse will tell you the correct angle to use for your child.
4. Slowly (within a few seconds) inject the solution by gently pushing the plunger until the syringe is empty.
5. Withdraw the needle quickly, pulling it straight out, and apply pressure over the injection site with a dry gauze pad or cotton ball. A drop of blood may appear. Put an adhesive bandage on the injection site if desired.
6. To prevent injury, safely dispose of all used needles and syringes after a single use as instructed by your physician or nurse by following these simple steps:
   - Place all used needles and syringes in a hard, plastic container with a screw-on cap, or a metal container with a plastic lid, such as a coffee can properly labeled as to content. If a metal container is used, cut a small hole in the plastic lid and tape the lid to the metal container. When the metal container is full, cover the hole with tape and throw it away. If a hard, plastic container is used, always screw the cap on tightly after each use. When the plastic container is full, tape around the cap and throw it away.
   - Do not use glass or clear, plastic containers, or any container that will be recycled or returned to a store.
   - Always store the container out of the reach of children.
   - Please check with your physician, nurse or pharmacist for other suggestions. There may be special provincial and local laws that they will discuss with you.
7. Occasionally a problem may develop at the injection site. If you notice any of the following signs or symptoms, contact your physician or nurse:
   - a lump or swelling that doesn't go away
   - bruising that doesn't go away
   - any signs of infection or inflammation at an injection site (pus, persistent redness surrounding skin that is hot to the touch, persistent pain after the injection).

Storage: Nutropin AQ **must** be refrigerated and cannot be used 28 days after first use and should be discarded.

Refrigerate at 2 to 8°C.

The Nutropin AQ vial must not be frozen.

If you have any questions, contact your physician, nurse or pharmacist.

☐ NYTOL™
☐ NYTOL™ Extra Strength

Block Drug

Diphenhydramine HCl

Sleep Aid

Information for the Patient: Use: Nytol tablets are intended for the relief of occasional nighttime sleeplessness when difficulty in falling asleep due to fatigue or over-work is particularly bothersome. It should not be taken for more than a few consecutive nights.

It should be borne in mind that normal function is quite compatible with variable periods of nighttime sleep. In addition, sleep requirements are normally reduced with advancing age, thus wakefulness often does not justify or require the use of sleep aids.

However, insomnia may be a symptom of serious illness. Therefore, if it persists for more than 2 weeks it is recommended that you consult your physician. If pain or other causes interfere with sleep, such conditions should be treated and sleep-aids are not indicated.

Precautions: Nytol should not be taken if alcohol is being consumed.

If you are presently taking a prescription drug or other medication, do not take Nytol without consulting your physician or pharmacist.

Do not take this product if you are pregnant or nursing a baby.

Nytol should not be used by elderly patients who experience confusion at nighttime. It is contraindicated in patients suffering from asthmatic attacks, narrow angle glaucoma or difficulty in urination due to enlargement of the prostate gland. These drugs may produce excitation rather than sedation in the elderly, therefore, they should be avoided in this age group.

Dosage: The usual adult dose of Regular Strength Nytol taken before retiring is 50 mg (two 25 mg white tablets). In some persons excessive drowsiness may be experienced with the 50 mg dose, in which case the medication should be subsequently continued with only 1 white 25 mg Nytol tablet.

The usual adult dose of Extra Strength Nytol taken before retiring is 50 mg (one 50 mg blue tablet or one 50 mg blue caplet). In some persons excessive drowsiness may be experienced with the 50 mg dose, in which case the medication should be subsequently continued with only 1 white 25 mg Nytol tablet.

For occasional use only.

Keep out of reach of children.

□ NYTOL™ NATURAL SOURCE

Block Drug

Valerian Root

Sleep Aid

Information for the Patient: Use: Nytol Natural Source is a nonsynthetic mild herbal sleep aid approved in Canada for the relief of insomnia (restlessness, difficulty in falling asleep) due to overwork, tiredness or fatigue.

The product is formulated from a powdered extract of the dried roots of the valerian plant (Valeriana officinalis L.) native to Europe and Asia. Popular as a medicine in ancient Greece, Rome, India and China, valerian has established a reputation in the West since the 17th century.

Nytol Natural Source is intended for relief of occasional nighttime sleeplessness when difficulty in falling asleep is particularly bothersome. Insomnia may be a symptom of serious medical illness. Therefore, if sleeplessness persists for more than 2 weeks, it is recommended that you consult your physician.

□ OCUFLOX™ Ⓟ

Allergan

Ofloxacin

Antibacterial Agent

Information for the Patient: Systemic quinolones, including ofloxacin, have been associated with hypersensitivity reactions, even following a single dose. Discontinue use immediately and contact your physician at the first sign of a rash or allergic reaction.

Patients should be advised to avoid contamination of the dropper tip.

Use While Wearing Contact Lenses: The use of ofloxacin ophthalmic solution while wearing contact lenses has not been studied. Therefore, its use is not recommended while the lens is on the eye.

□ ONCOTICE™

Organon Teknika

Bacillus Calmette-Guérin (BCG), strain TICE

Antineoplastic

Information for the Patient: OncoTICE, [Bacillus Calmette-Guérin (BCG), strain TICE], is retained in the bladder 2 hours and then voided. Patients should void while seated for safety reasons following instillation of suspension. Within 6 hours after treatment, urine voided should be disinfected for 15 minutes with an equal volume of household bleach before flushing. Patients should be instructed to increase fluid intake to "flush" the bladder in the hours following BCG treatment. Patients may experience a burning sensation with the first void after treatment. Patients should be attentive to side effects, such as fever, chills, malaise, flu-like symptoms, or increased fatigue. If the patient experiences severe urinary side effects, such as burning or pain on urination, urgency, frequency of urination, blood in urine, joint pain, cough, or skin rash, the physician should be notified.

□ OPTICROM®

Allergan

Sodium Cromoglycate

Antiallergic

Information for the Patient: Opticrom: Sterile sodium cromoglycate ophthalmic solution 2% w/v. Helps prevent and relieve the symptoms of red, itchy, watery eyes due to allergies.

What are allergies? Most allergic reactions are caused by exposure to substances in the environment. These include pollens, mold spores, house dust and animal dander.

Allergy symptoms include irritation, grittiness, redness and excessive watering of the eyes.

Your allergy symptoms may only occur at certain times of the year in reaction to a particular pollen. These are seasonal allergies.

Why do they occur? Special (mast) cells which are present in the mucus membranes of your nose and eyes react to allergens such as pollen or dust by releasing histamine. This release of histamine then sets off the whole cycle of allergic symptoms.

How can you tell if you have allergies? If this is the **first time** you have had the symptoms, you should confirm the diagnosis with your doctor. It is likely that your symptoms are due to allergies if:

- both eyes are affected
- you have a runny or congested nose as well
- your sight is not affected

But if:

- only one eye is affected
- you have no nose symptoms
- your sight is affected
- you feel pain in your eye(s)

you cannot be sure your symptoms are due to allergies and should consult your doctor before you use Opticrom.

How does Opticrom work? Opticrom works by blocking the release of histamine from the mast cells. This helps **prevent** the allergic response from taking place and so helps prevent the symptoms of red, itchy, watery eyes. Opticrom use should be started prior to your usual allergy season to gain maximum preventative effect. In the case of unexpected exposure, begin treatment immediately at the first onset of symptoms. To maintain the symptom-free effect, it should be taken continuously throughout the season even when you feel you are free from your symptoms.

How to use Opticrom: Adults and children over 5 years: 2 drops into each eye 4 times daily. Do not exceed recommended dosage.

Opticrom are easily applied to the eye. First, you should tilt your head back and gently pull your lower lid down. Then carefully squeeze out two drops into each eye while looking up toward your forehead. Close your eyes gently for a few moments.

Opticrom should be used continually throughout your usual allergy season, even when you feel you are free from symptoms. Continued use will help **ensure** you remain symptom-free.

To maintain sterility, prevent touching the tip of the dropper with the eye or other surfaces. Discard the opened bottle after four weeks. Keep out of reach of children.

Caution: Those people who are sensitive may experience mild irritation of the eye, during the first few days of use. These effects are infrequent, minimal and reversible.

Opticrom should not be used with any other eye treatment except on the advice of a doctor.

Warning: Opticrom should only be used for allergic conditions of the eye. In some instances irritation or redness may be due to serious eye conditions such as infection, foreign body in the eye, or other mechanical or chemical corneal injury requiring the attention of a

Opticrom (cont'd)

doctor. If you experience eye pain, changes in vision, pain on exposure to light, acute redness of the eye, excessive or milky (nonclear) discharge, abnormal pupils, if condition worsens or if relief is not obtained with 72 hours consult your doctor immediately.

Soft contact lenses should not be worn during treatment with Opticrom.

Pregnancy and Lactation: As with any drug, if you are pregnant or nursing a baby, seek a doctor's advice before using this product.

Contains: Sodium cromoglycate 2%, edetate disodium and benzalkonium chloride 0.01% as a preservative.

Store at 15 to 30°C and protect from direct sunlight.

Product Monograph is available to physician and pharmacists on request.

☐ ORAFEN® ℞

Technilab

Ketoprofen

Nonsteroidal Anti-inflammatory—Analgesic

Information for the Patient: Orafen (ketoprofen), which has been prescribed to you by your physician, is one of a large group of nonsteroidal anti-inflammatory drugs (also called NSAIDs) and is used to treat the symptoms of certain types of arthritis. Orafen may also be used for treating mild to moderate acute pain, including menstrual cramps. It helps to relieve joint pain, swelling, stiffness and fever by reducing the production of certain substances (prostaglandins) and by helping to control inflammation. NSAIDs do not cure arthritis, but they promote suppression of the inflammation and the tissue damaging effects resulting from this inflammation. This medicine will help you only as long as you continue to take it.

You should take Orafen only as directed by your physician. Do not take more of it, do not take it more often and do not take it for a longer period of time than your physician ordered. Taking too much of any of these medicines may increase the chance of unwanted effects, especially if you are an elderly patient.

Be sure to take Orafen regularly as prescribed. In some types of arthritis, up to 2 weeks may pass before you feel the full effects of this medicine. During treatment, your physician may decide to adjust the dosage according to your response to the medication.

Stomach Upset Is One of the Common Problems With NSAIDs: To lessen stomach upset, ketoprofen tablets should be taken immediately after a meal or with food or milk. Also, you should remain standing or sitting upright (i.e., do not lie down) about 15 to 30 minutes after an oral dose of this medicine. This helps to prevent irritation that may lead to trouble swallowing. If stomach upset (indigestion, nausea, vomiting, stomach pain or diarrhea) occurs and continues, contact your physician.

Use whole suppositories. Do not split or use portions of suppositories. Make sure that the wrapping is fully removed before inserting the suppository into the rectum. Do not take suppositories by mouth.

Do not take ASA (acetylsalicylic acid), ASA-containing compounds or others used to relieve symptoms of arthritis while taking Orafen unless directed to do so by your physician.

If you are prescribed this medication for use over a long period of time, your physician will check your health during regular visits to assess your progress and to ensure that this medicine is not causing unwanted effects.

Always Remember: The risks of taking this medication must be weighed against the benefits it will have.

Before taking this medication tell your physician and pharmacist if you:

- or a family member are allergic to or have had a reaction to ketoprofen or other anti-inflammatory drugs (such as acetylsalicylic acid (ASA), diclofenac, diflunisal, fenoprofen, flurbiprofen, ibuprofen, indomethacin, mefenamic acid, piroxicam, tiaprofenic acid, tolmetin, nabumetone or tenoxicam) manifesting itself by increased sinusitis, hives, the initiating or worsening of asthma or anaphylaxis (sudden collapse);
- or a family member has had asthma, nasal polyps, chronic sinusitis or chronic urticaria (hives);
- have a history of stomach upset, ulcers, liver or kidney diseases;
- have blood or urine abnormalities;
- have high blood pressure;
- have diabetes;
- are on any special diet, such as a low-sodium or low-sugar diet;
- are pregnant or intend to become pregnant while taking this medication;
- are breast-feeding or intend to breast-feed while taking this medication;
- are taking any other medication (either prescription or nonprescription) such as other NSAIDs, high blood pressure medication, blood thinners, corticosteroids, methotrexate, cyclosporine, lithium, phenytoin, probenecid, etc.;
- have any other medical problem(s) such as alcohol abuse, bleeding problems, etc.

While Taking This Medication:

- tell any other physician, dentist or pharmacist that you consult or see, that you are taking this medication;
- some NSAIDs may cause drowsiness or fatigue in some people taking them. Be cautious about driving or participating in activities that require alertness if you are drowsy, dizzy or lightheaded after taking this medication;
- check with your physician if you are not getting any relief of your arthritis or if any problems develop;
- report any untoward reactions to your physician. This is very important as it will aid in the early detection and prevention of potential complications;
- stomach problems may be more likely to occur if you drink alcoholic beverages. Therefore, do not drink alcoholic beverages while taking this medication;
- check with your physician immediately if you experience unexpected weakness while taking this medication, or if you vomit any blood or have dark or bloody stools;
- some people may become more sensitive to sunlight than they are normally. Exposure to sunlight or sunlamps, even for brief periods of time, may cause sunburn, blisters on the skin, skin rash, redness, itching or discoloration; or vision changes. If you have a reaction from the sun, check with your physician;
- check with your physician immediately if chills, fever, muscle aches or pains, or other flu-like symptoms occur, especially if they occur shortly before, or together with, a skin rash. Very rarely, these effects may be the first signs of a serious reaction to this medication;
- **your regular medical check-ups are essential.**

Side Effects of This Medication: Along with its beneficial effects, Orafen like other NSAID drugs, may cause some undesirable reactions especially when used for a long time or in large doses.

Elderly, frail or debilitated patients often seem to experience more frequent or more severe side effects.

Although not all of these side effects are common, when they do occur they may require medical attention.

Check with your physician immediately if any of the following are noted:

- bloody or black tarry stools;
- shortness of breath, wheezing, any trouble in breathing or tightness in the chest;
- skin rash, hives, swelling or itching;
- vomiting or persistent indigestion, nausea, stomach pain or diarrhea;
- yellow discoloration of the skin or eyes;
- any changes in the amount or color of your urine (dark red or brown);
- any pain or difficulty experienced while urinating;
- swelling of the feet or lower legs;
- malaise, fatigue, loss of appetite;
- blurred vision or any visual disturbance;
- mental confusion, depression, dizziness, lightheadedness;
- hearing problems.

Other side effects not listed above may also occur in some patients. If you notice any other effects, check with your physician.

Dosing: Adults: Rheumatoid Arthritis and Osteoarthritis: Oral: The usual dosage for ketoprofen capsules or enteric-coated tablets is 150 to 200 mg/day in 3 or 4 divided doses.

Once the maintenance dosage has been established, patients may be tried on a twice daily dosing regimen. Clinical trials, however, show that some rheumatoid arthritis patients respond better to more frequent dosing. The usual maintenance dose is 100 mg twice daily.

Rectal: Orafen suppositories offer an alternative route of administration for those patients who prefer it. Administer one suppository morning and evening or one suppository at bedtime supplemented as needed by divided oral doses.

Use whole suppositories. Do not split or use portions of suppositories. Make sure that the wrapping is fully removed before inserting the suppository into the rectum. Do not take suppositories by mouth.

The total daily dose of ketoprofen capsules, tablets and suppositories should not exceed 200 mg/day. When the patient's response warrants it, the dose may be decreased to the minimum effective level.

In severe cases, during flare-up of rheumatic activity or if a satisfactory response cannot be obtained with the lower dose, a daily dosage in excess of 200 mg may be used. However, a dose of 300 mg/day should not be exceeded.

Primary Dysmenorrhea and Mild to Moderate Pain: Oral: The usual dose for ketoprofen is 25 to 50 mg 3 or 4 times daily as necessary.

A larger dose may be tried if the patient's response to a previous dose was less than satisfactory, but individual doses above 50 mg have not been shown to give added analgesia. The total daily dose should not exceed 300 mg. In most types of acute pain, a course of 3 to 7 days has been shown to be sufficient.

Elderly and debilitated patients: Initial dosage should be reduced by ½ to ⅓ in patients with impaired renal function and the elderly.

Children: Orafen is not indicated in children under 12 years of age because clinical experience in this group of patients is insufficient.

What You Do if You Miss a Dose: If you miss a dose of Orafen suppositories, take it as soon as possible. However, if it is almost time for your next dose, skip the missed dose and go back to your regular schedule. **Never double doses.**

Storage: Orafen 100 mg suppository is an off-white, smooth, torpedo-shaped suppository. They are packaged in a plastic mold. This plastic material must be completely removed before inserting into the rectum. Lubricate the tapered end of the suppository for ease of insertion. The suppository should be inserted as high as possible into the rectum. If it is felt that the bowels require to be emptied, this should be done before insertion of the suppository.

Boxes of 30 suppositories. Keep away from excessive heat, elevated humidity and light. Store below 30°C.

Orafen is not recommended for use in patients under 12 years of age since safety and effectiveness have not been established.

Do not keep outdated medicine or medicine no longer needed.

Keep this product and all medicine out of the reach of children.

This medication has been prescribed to your medical problem. Do not give it to anyone else.

If you require more information on this drug, consult your physician or pharmacist.

☐ ORAMORPH SR™ Ⓝ

Boehringer Ingelheim

Morphine Sulfate

Narcotic Analgesic

Information for the Patient: What is morphine? Morphine relieves pain and should help you to live more comfortably and independently. It is effective and safe when used as directed by your doctor.

Your pain may increase or decrease from time to time and your doctor may need to change the amount of morphine you take (daily dosage).

What is Oramorph SR? Oramorph SR is a tablet that is made in such a way as to slowly release morphine over a 12 hour period, usually requiring a dose only every 12 hours to control your pain. However, where more convenient, your doctor may ask you to take medication every 8 hours.

Oramorph SR is available in 3 strengths: 30 mg, 60 mg, and 100 mg white tablets. It may be necessary for you to take more than one tablet strength at the same time in order to receive the total daily dosage prescribed by your doctor.

Oramorph SR tablets must be swallowed whole in order to work effectively. **Do not break, crush or chew the tablets.**

How to take your medication: Oramorph SR should be taken as directed by your doctor, usually every 12 hours with 120 to 180 mL (4 to 6 oz) of water to prevent pain all day and night. If your pain worsens, making you uncomfortable, contact your doctor immediately and she/he may decide that it is necessary to adjust your daily dosage of Oramorph SR. Your starting dosage of Oramorph SR will be clearly indicated on the medication label. Be sure to follow these directions on the label exactly; this is very important. If your dosage is changed, be sure to write it down at the time your doctor calls you or sees you, and follow the new directions exactly. Do not change your dosage without consulting your doctor.

It is important not to take any liquid containing alcohol while taking Oramorph SR.

Remember to keep this and all other medication out of the reach of children.

Constipation: Morphine causes constipation. This is to be expected, so your doctor may order a laxative and stool softener to help relieve your constipation while you are taking Oramorph SR. Tell your doctor about the problem if it arises.

Concomitant medications: Your doctor should be made aware of any other prescription medication you are taking including over-the-counter antihistamines and sleep-aids as they could affect the way you respond to morphine.

Driving and Operating Machinery: Driving or other tasks requiring full alertness should not be attempted for the first few days of taking Oramorph SR, since you may experience drowsiness or sedation.

Reordering Oramorph SR: A new written prescription is required from your doctor each time you need more Oramorph SR. Therefore, it is important to contact your doctor at least 3 working days before your current supply runs out. It is very important that you do not miss any doses.

Should your pain increase, or any unwanted effects develop as a result of taking Oramorph SR, contact your doctor immediately.

☐ ORUDIS® Ⓟ
☐ ORUDIS® E Ⓟ
☐ ORUDIS® SR Ⓟ

Rhône-Poulenc Rorer

Ketoprofen

Anti-inflammatory—Analgesic

Information for the Patient: Name and Indications: Orudis which has been prescribed to you by your doctor, is one of a large group of nonsteroidal anti-inflammatory drugs (NSAIDs) and is used to treat the symptoms of certain types of arthritis. It helps to relieve joint pain, swelling, stiffness and fever by reducing the production of certain substances (prostaglandins) and helping to control inflammation. NSAIDs do not cure arthritis, but they promote suppression of the inflammation and the tissue damaging effects resulting from this inflammation. This medicine will help you only as long as you continue to take it.

Orudis may also be used for treating mild to moderate acute pain, including menstrual cramps.

How to Use this Medicine: You should take Orudis only as directed by your doctor. Do not take more of it, do not take it more often and do not take it for a longer period of time than your doctor ordered. Taking too much of any of these medicines may increase the chance of unwanted effects, especially if you are an elderly patient.

Be sure to take Orudis regularly as prescribed. In some types of arthritis, up to 2 weeks may pass before you feel the full effects of this medicine. During treatment, your doctor may decide to adjust the dosage according to your response to the medication.

If you are taking Orudis enteric-coated tablets (Orudis E) or Orudis sustained-release tablets (Orudis SR), take them preferably 1 to 2 hours before meals or at least 2 hours after meals. Swallow your tablets whole. Do not break, crush or chew.

If you are taking Orudis capsules, take them immediately after a meal or with food to lessen stomach upset. Swallow your capsules whole. Also, you should remain standing or sitting upright (i.e., do not lie down) for about 15 to 30 minutes after taking the medicine. If stomach upset (indigestion, nausea, vomiting, stomach pain or diarrhea) occurs and continues, contact your doctor.

If you miss a dose: If you miss a dose of Orudis capsules or enteric-coated tablets, take it as soon as possible. However if it is almost time for your next dose, skip the missed dose and go back to your regular schedule.

If you take Orudis SR tablets once a day and if you miss a dose and remember within 8 hours, take it right away and then resume your regular dosing schedule.

Never double doses.

Orudis is not recommended for use in patients under 12 years of age since safety and effectiveness have not been established.

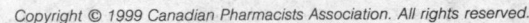

Do not keep outdated medicine or medicine no longer needed. ▶

Orudis (cont'd)

Keep out of the reach of children.

Important Notice: Do not take ASA (acetylsalicylic acid), ASA-containing compounds or other drugs used to relieve symptoms of arthritis while taking Orudis unless directed to do so by your physician.

If you are prescribed this medication for use over a long period of time, your doctor will check your health during regular visits to assess your progress and to ensure that this medication is not causing unwanted effects.

Side Effects: Along with its beneficial effects, Orudis like other NSAIDs may cause some undesirable reactions, especially when used for a long time or in large doses. Elderly frail or debilitated patients often seem to experience more frequent or more severe side effects. Although not all of these side effects are common, when they do occur they may require medical attention. Check with your doctor immediately if any of the following are noted:

- bloody or black tarry stools;
- shortness of breath, wheezing, any trouble in breathing or tightness in the chest;
- skin rash, swelling, hives or itching;
- persistent indigestion, nausea, vomiting, stomach pain or diarrhea;
- yellow discoloration of the skin or eyes, with or without fatigue;
- any changes in the amount or color of your urine (such as dark, red or brown);
- any pain or difficulty experienced while urinating;
- swelling of the feet or lower legs;
- blurred vision or any visual disturbance;
- mental confusion, depression, dizziness, lightheadedness, hearing problems.

Always Remember: Before taking this medication tell your doctor and pharmacists if you:

- or a family member are allergic to or have had a reaction to Orudis or other related medicines of the NSAID group such as acetylsalicylic acid, diclofenac, diflunisal, fenoprofen, flurbiprofen, ibuprofen, indomethacin, mefenamic acid, nabumetone, piroxicam, tenoxicam, sulindac, tiaprofenic acid or tolmetin manifesting itself by increased sinusitis, hives, the initiating or worsening of asthma or anaphylaxis (sudden collapse);
- or a family member has had asthma, nasal polyps, chronic sinusitis or chronic urticaria (hives);
- have a history of stomach upset, ulcers, or liver or kidney diseases;
- have blood or urine abnormalities;
- have high blood pressure;
- have diabetes;
- are on any special diet, such as a low-sodium or low sugar diet;
- are pregnant or intend to become pregnant while taking this medication;
- are breast-feeding;
- are taking any other medication (either prescription or nonprescription) such as other NSAIDs, high blood pressure medication, blood thinners, corticosteroids, cyclosporine, methotrexate, lithium, phenytoin;
- have any other medical problem(s) such as alcohol abuse, bleeding problems, etc.

While Taking This Medication:

- tell any other doctor, dentist or pharmacist that you consult or see, that you are taking this medication;
- some NSAIDs may cause drowsiness or fatigue in some people taking them—be cautious about driving or participating in activities that require alertness if you are drowsy, dizzy or lightheaded after taking this medication;
- check with your doctor if you are not getting any relief or if any problems develop;
- report any untoward reactions to your doctor. This is very important as it will aid in the early detection and prevention of potential complications;
- stomach problems may be more likely to occur if you drink alcoholic beverages. Therefore, do not drink alcoholic beverages while taking this medication;
- check with your doctor immediately if you experience unexpected weakness while taking this medication, or if you vomit any blood or have dark and bloody stools;
- some people may become more sensitive to sunlight than they are normally. Exposure to sunlight or sunlamps, even for brief periods of time, may cause sunburn, blisters on the skin, skin rash, redness, itching or discoloration, or vision changes. If you have a reaction from the sun, check with your doctor;
- check with your doctor immediately if chills, fever, muscle aches or pains, or other flu-like symptoms occur, especially if they occur shortly before, or together with, a skin rash. Very rarely, these effects may be the first signs of a serious reaction to this medication.

Your regular medical check-ups are essential.

If you require more information on this drug, consult your doctor or pharmacist.

This medication has been prescribed for your medical condition. Do not give it to anyone else. Keep this and all medication out of the reach of children.

☐ ORUVAIL® Ⓟ

May & Baker Pharma

Ketoprofen

Anti-inflammatory—Analgesic

Information for the Patient: Name and Indications: Oruvail which has been prescribed to you by your doctor, is one of a large group of nonsteroidal anti-inflammatory drugs (NSAIDs) and is used to treat the symptoms of certain types of arthritis. It helps to relieve joint pain, swelling, stiffness and fever by reducing the production of certain substances (prostaglandins) and helping to control inflammation and other body reactions. NSAIDs do not cure arthritis, but they promote suppression of the inflammation and the tissue damaging effects resulting from this inflammation. This medicine will help you only as long as you continue to take it.

How to Use This Medicine: You should take Oruvail only as directed by your doctor. Do not take more of it, do not take it more often and do not take it for a longer period of time than your doctor ordered. Taking too much of any of these medicines may increase the chance of unwanted effects, especially if you are an elderly patient.

Be sure to take Oruvail regularly as prescribed. In some types of arthritis, up to 2 weeks may pass before you feel the full effects of this medicine. During treatment, your doctor may decide to adjust the dosage according to your response to the medication.

If you are taking Oruvail capsules, take them immediately after a meal or with food, early in the morning or late at night. Swallow your capsules whole. Also, you should remain standing or sitting upright (i.e., do not lie down) for about 15 to 30 minutes after taking the medicine. If stomach upset (indigestion, nausea, vomiting, stomach pain or diarrhea) occurs and continues, contact your doctor.

If You Miss a Dose: You will be taking Oruvail capsules once a day, and if you miss a dose and remember within 8 hours, take it right away and then resume your regular dosing schedule.

Never double doses.

Oruvail is not recommended for use in patients under 12 years of age since safety and effectiveness have not been established.

Do not keep outdated medicine or medicine no longer needed.

Keep out of the reach of children.

Important Notice: Do not take ASA (acetylsalicylic acid), ASA-containing compounds or other drugs used to relieve symptoms of arthritis while taking Oruvail unless directed to do so by your physician.

If you are prescribed this medication for use over a long period of time, your doctor will check your health during regular visits to assess your progress and to ensure that this medication is not causing unwanted effects.

Side Effects: Along with its beneficial effects, Oruvail like other NSAID drugs, may cause some undesirable reactions, especially when used for a long time or in large doses. Elderly, frail or debilitated patients often seem to experience more frequent or more severe side effects. Although not all of these side effects are common, when they do occur they may require medical attention. Check with your doctor immediately if any of the following are noted:

- bloody or black tarry stools;
- shortness of breath, wheezing, any trouble in breathing or tightness in the chest;
- skin rash, swelling, hives or itching;
- persistent indigestion, nausea, vomiting, stomach pain or diarrhea;
- yellow discoloration of the skin or eyes, with or without fatigue;
- any changes in the amount or color of your urine (such as dark; red or brown);
- any pain or difficulty experienced while urinating;

- swelling of the feet or lower legs;
- blurred vision or any visual disturbance;
- mental confusion, depression, dizziness, lightheadedness, hearing problems.

Always Remember: Before taking this medication tell your doctor and pharmacists if you:

- or a family member are allergic to or have had a reaction to Oruvail or other related medicines of the NSAID group such as acetylsalicylic acid, diclofenac, diflunisal, fenoprofen, flurbiprofen, ibuprofen, indomethacin, mefenamic acid, nabumetone, piroxicam, tenoxicam, sulindac, tiaprofenic acid or tolmetin manifesting itself by increased sinusitis, hives, the initiating or worsening of asthma or anaphylaxis (sudden collapse);
- or a family member has had asthma, nasal polyps, chronic sinusitis or chronic urticaria (hives);
- have a history of stomach upset, ulcers, or liver or kidney diseases;
- have blood or urine abnormalities;
- have high blood pressure;
- have diabetes;
- are on any special diet, such as a low-sodium or low sugar diet;
- are pregnant or intend to become pregnant while taking this medication;
- are breast-feeding;
- are taking any other medication (either prescription or nonprescription) such as other NSAIDs, high blood pressure medication, blood thinners, corticosteroids, cyclosporine, methotrexate, lithium, phenytoin;
- have any other medical problem(s) such as alcohol abuse, bleeding problems, etc.

While Taking this Medication:

- tell any other doctor, dentist or pharmacist that you consult or see, that you are taking this medication;
- Some NSAIDs may cause drowsiness or fatigue in some people taking them–Be cautious about driving or participating in activities that require alertness if you are drowsy, dizzy or lightheaded after taking this medication;
- check with your doctor if you are not getting any relief or if any problems develop.
- report any untoward reactions to your doctor. This is very important as it will aid in the early detection and prevention of potential complications.
- stomach problems may be more likely to occur if you drink alcoholic beverages. Therefore, do not drink alcoholic beverages while taking this medication;
- check with your doctor immediately if you experience unexpected weakness while taking this medication, or if you vomit any blood or have dark and bloody stools;
- some people may become more sensitive to sunlight than they are normally. Exposure to sunlight or sunlamps, even for brief periods of time, may cause sunburn, blisters on the skin, skin rash, redness, itching or discoloration, or vision changes. If you have a reaction from the sun, check with your doctor;
- check with your doctor immediately if chills, fever, muscle aches or pains, or other flu-like symptoms occur, expecially if they occur shortly before, or together with, a skin rash. Very rarely, these effects may be the first signs of a serious reaction to this medication.

Your regular medical check-ups are essential.

If you require more information on this drug, consult your doctor or pharmacist.

This medication has been prescribed for your medical condition. Do not give it to anyone else.

Keep this and all medication out of the reach of children.

□ OSTAC® ℞

Roche

Clodronate Disodium

Bone Metabolism Regulator

Information for the Patient: What You Should Know About Ostac: This leaflet provides brief information on your medicine. Please read it carefully. If you have any questions or are not sure about anything, ask your doctor or pharmacist.

Things to Remember About Ostac:

1. Take your medicine as advised by your doctor and carefully read the label.
2. Please **do not** take this medicine with milk.
3. This medicine has been prescribed for your current medical problem. Do not give it to other people.
4. Keep your medicine out of the reach of children.

Before Taking Your Medicine:

—Do you have any kidney problems?
—Are you pregnant or breast-feeding?
—Do you have stomach pain or a bowel disturbance?
—Have you been allergic to similar medicines before?

If the answer is **yes** to any of these questions, do not take this medicine until you have talked to your doctor about it.

Some Guidelines For Using Ostac: The name of this medicine is Ostac. It contains the active ingredient clodronate disodium.

What is Ostac: Ostac belongs to a class of compounds known as bisphosphonates which act to reduce the rate of removal and replacement of bone tissue. In certain cancers, there is a greater breakdown of bone than there is new production which is called osteolysis. This can be accompanied by an increased release of calcium into the blood which is called hypercalcemia. Ostac attaches specifically to bone and effectively prevents osteolysis. In cases where there is bone breakdown and an increased release of calcium into the blood, Ostac effectively reduces high calcium blood levels hence preventing or delaying some of the consequences of hypercalcemia. Although effective in the treatment of osteolysis and hypercalcemia of malignancy, the use of Ostac will not provide a cure for cancer.

What is the dose of Ostac? Your doctor will tell you how much Ostac to take each day. The dosage is prescribed to suit your particular needs. The doctor will also tell you how to divide your dosage through the day. For example, he or she might prescribe a total dosage of 1 600 mg per day, to be taken as one or two equally divided doses. Therefore, you must take the exact amount which has been prescribed for you.

The success of treatment with Ostac depends very much on how **carefully** and consistently you follow the doctor's instructions about taking Ostac.

Follow instructions exactly and ask your doctor or hospital pharmacist if you are unsure. It is very important not to miss any of the tests which your doctor orders, including blood tests and tests to determine the function of your kidneys.

Based on blood tests and other tests, your doctor might make changes in the amount of Ostac you must take. **Never make dose changes on your own.**

Always take your medication on time and never allow your medication to run out. If you plan a holiday, please remember to take enough supplies to cover your needs.

How is Ostac taken? When in hospital, you may have received this medication intravenously. These instructions are for taking the Ostac 400 mg white gelatin capsules and should be followed exactly, because the success of your treatment depends very much on how carefully and consistently you follow your doctor's instructions.

White gelatin capsules: The white gelatin form is supplied in 400 mg capsules. Packs of 120 capsules contain 12 full aluminum blister strips of 10 capsules each. Your dose of Ostac capsules, to be taken once or twice daily, simply consists of removing the number of capsules that are required to make up the dose that your physician has prescribed for you. Swallow the capsules whole, with liquid (except milk). Do not take the capsules with food or within 1 hour before or after food or milk. Please take the capsules even if you are not eating at present.

Please **do not** take the capsules with milk. If Ostac is taken with drinks containing milk, it is more difficult for the medicine to enter the blood and so it is not as effective. For the same reason, **do not** take Ostac with antacid indigestion tablets or mineral supplements as these may also make the medicine less effective.

Other medicines or substances that may interfere with the action of Ostac: Before starting treatment with Ostac, talk to your doctor about any other medicines that you are using or intending to use. It is especially important that your doctor knows that you are being treated with another bisphosphonate, calcitonin, calcium tablets or vitamin supplements.

What side effects can Ostac have? Like all medicines, Ostac may have, in addition to its beneficial effects, some unwanted effects.

The most common side effects are associated with the digestive system and include nausea and diarrhea.

Drug related allergies such as skin rashes have been reported less commonly.

Other side effects not listed above may also occur in some patients. If you notice any other effects, tell your doctor immediately.

Ostac (cont'd)

Storage conditions: Ostac capsules should be stored at room temperature (15 to 30°C) and should be protected from high humidity.

Important points to remember: Your doctor or nurse will help you to plan how to divide your dosage through the day.

Pay close attention to the amount of drug you are taking. Make sure it is the amount your doctor has prescribed for you.

If you forget to take a scheduled dose, most doctors will suggest that you take it at the time you remember and then go on with your normal schedule. (Check with your doctor to see if this procedure is acceptable.)

☐ OXEZE® TURBUHALER® ℞

Astra

Formoterol Fumarate Dihydrate

Bronchodilator

Information for the Patient: Important information you should know about Oxeze Turbuhaler (formoterol fumarate dihydrate): **Before using Oxeze Turbuhaler, read this leaflet carefully.** It contains general points about Oxeze Turbuhaler and should add to more specific advice from your doctor or pharmacist.

Please keep this leaflet to refer to until you have used up all medication in Oxeze Turbuhaler.

What Is Oxeze Turbuhaler Used for and How Does It Work? (See package insert for illustrations.) Oxeze Turbuhaler contains an inhalation powder. The powder is a mixture of the medicine formoterol and lactose. (It is unlikely that the very small amount of lactose in the powder would cause any problems to patients who are intolerant to lactose.) Formoterol widens the airways enabling you to breathe more easily.

Turbuhaler is the brand name for a multiple dose, dry powder inhaler. When you breathe in through the mouthpiece, your breath provides the necessary force to deliver the drug to your lungs.

Oxeze Turbuhaler gives long-lasting (up to 12 hours) relief or prevention of symptoms such as shortness of breath in patients with asthma and other similar conditions. Oxeze Turbuhaler should be taken together with an anti-inflammatory medication, such as a corticosteroid. A short-acting bronchodilator should be used in case you feel symptoms during the day or night.

What Should You Tell Your Doctor Before Taking Oxeze Turbuhaler? Tell your doctor:

- about all health problems you have now or have had in the past, especially if you have a heart disorder, diabetes, or a disturbed thyroid function (thyrotoxicosis).
- about all medicines you take, including those you have bought without a prescription. Certain types of medicines for example beta-blockers (some heart medicines or eye drops) may reduce or block the effect of Oxeze Turbuhaler when taken at the same time.
- If you have ever had a bad, unusual or allergic reaction to formoterol or lactose or to other medicines for breathing problems.
- If you are pregnant, plan to become pregnant or are breast-feeding.

How Do You Take Oxeze Turbuhaler Properly? Before you start using Oxeze Turbuhaler for the first time it is important that you read the instructions below and follow them carefully.

Turbuhaler is a multidose inhaler from which very small amounts of powder are administered. When you breathe in through Turbuhaler the powder is delivered to the lungs. It is therefore important that you inhale forcefully and deeply through the mouthpiece.

Oxeze Turbuhaler is very easy to use.

If you follow the instructions (see package insert for illustrations), **you will receive the medication.**

1. Unscrew the cover and lift it off.
2. Load a dose by holding the inhaler upright. Turn the greenish-blue grip as far as it will go in one direction and then turn it back to the original position. The "click" you heard means that the inhaler is ready to use.
3. Breathe out.
   Note: Never breathe out through the mouthpiece.
4. Put the mouthpiece between your teeth and close your lips around the mouthpiece. Do **not** chew or bite down hard on the mouthpiece. Inhale forcefully and deeply through your mouth.
5. Remove the inhaler from your mouth. If more than 1 dose has been prescribed, repeat Steps 2 to 5.
6. Always replace the cover properly after use.

If you accidentally drop, shake or breathe out into Oxeze Turbuhaler after it is loaded, you will lose your dose. If this happens, you should load a new dose and inhale it.

Cleaning: Clean the outside of the mouthpiece once a week with a **dry** tissue. **Never** use water or any other fluid. If fluid enters the inhaler it may not work properly.

As the amount of powder dispensed is very small, you may not be able to taste it after inhalation. However, you can still be confident that the dose has been inhaled if you have followed the instructions.

How Do You Know When Oxeze Turbuhaler Is Empty?

Oxeze Turbuhaler has a dose indicator. A new Turbuhaler provides 60 doses for inhalation. When a red mark first appears in the little window underneath the mouthpiece, there are approximately **20** doses left. Now is the time to obtain your next inhaler.

When the red mark reaches the bottom of the window, Oxeze Turbuhaler is **empty**. If you shake the inhaler when it is empty, you will still be able to hear the sound of the drying agent. Oxeze Turbuhaler cannot be refilled with drug and should be discarded.

How Much Oxeze Turbuhaler Should You Take? The dosage of Oxeze Turbuhaler is individual. Follow your doctor's instructions carefully. They may differ from the information contained in this leaflet.

Adults: The usual dose is 6 or 12 μg, twice daily, at 12-hour intervals. Some adults may need 24 μg, twice daily. The maximum daily dosage for adults, 48 μg, should not be exceeded.

Adolescent Children (12 to 16 years): The usual dose is 6 μg, twice daily, at 12-hour intervals. Some children may need 12 μg, twice daily. The maximum daily dosage for adolescent children, 24 μg, should not be exceeded.

You usually get an effect of Oxeze Turbuhaler within 1 to 3 minutes. The effect of Oxeze Turbuhaler lasts up to 12 hours.

You should see your doctor if:

- your usual dose does not provide relief;
- the effects of 1 dose last less than 12 hours.

These may be signs that your asthma is getting worse.

Do not exceed the dose prescribed by your doctor.

What Do I Do if I Miss a Dose? If you miss a dose of Oxeze Turbuhaler and remember within 6 hours, you should take your usual dose as soon as possible. Then go back to your regular schedule. If it is more than 6 hours when you remember, do not take the missed dose. Just take the next dose on time.

Never take a double dose of Oxeze Turbuhaler to make up for missed doses. If you are still unsure, check with your doctor or pharmacist to see what you should do.

What Should You Do in Case of Overdose? There is no clinical experience on the management of overdose. The most common signs and symptoms that may occur after overdosage are trembling, headache and rapid heartbeat. **Contact your doctor or go to the nearest hospital immediately if any of these symptoms bother you, or if you think you have taken too much Oxeze Turbuhaler.**

Are There Any Side Effects? Usually you do not feel any side effects when you use Oxeze Turbuhaler. However, like any medication, Oxeze Turbuhaler may cause side effects in some people. The most common side effects are trembling, rapid heartbeat and headache. Rare or uncommon side effects are muscle cramps, skin rash, agitation, chest pain, restlessness and sleep disturbances and in extreme cases, drugs for inhalation may cause bronchospasm (cramp in the airways).

Side effects that do occur are usually mild and disappear by themselves within 1 or 2 weeks of treatment, however, be sure to tell your doctor if any of the side effects bother you or if they continue. Also contact your doctor if any other unusual effects bother you while you are using Oxeze Turbuhaler.

Where Should You Store Oxeze Turbuhaler? Remember to **keep Oxeze Turbuhaler out of the reach of children.**

Always replace the cover after using Oxeze Turbuhaler. Store the inhaler at room temperature (15 to 30°C) **away from moisture.**

How Do You Use Oxeze Turbuhaler With Other Asthma Drugs? Oxeze Turbuhaler should not be used more often than twice a day.

Oxeze is taken twice daily, regularly in the morning and in the evening. It should provide relief of symptoms such as shortness of breath within 1 to 3 minutes and this relief generally lasts for up to 12 hours. It is very important that you take Oxeze Turbuhaler exactly as your doctor tells you. Do **not** exceed the number of inhalations prescribed by your doctor and do **not** use more often than twice a day.

Oxeze Turbuhaler should not be used as relief medication. Oxeze Turbuhaler is taken only twice daily and should **not** be used for immediate relief of asthma symptoms that may occur during the day or night. A short-acting bronchodilator (e.g., terbutaline or salbutamol) should be used to provide relief of asthma symptoms such as shortness of breath, tightness, coughing and wheezing that may occur between the 2 daily doses of Oxeze Turbuhaler.

Oxeze Turbuhaler should be taken together with an anti-inflammatory medication, such as a corticosteroid, to reduce inflammation of the lungs due to asthma. You must continue to regularly take the anti-inflammatory medications your doctor has prescribed. Your anti-inflammatory medications and Oxeze Turbuhaler are designed to act together to best treat your condition. Even though you feel better, **do not stop** or reduce your doses of anti-inflammatory medications or Oxeze Turbuhaler without first consulting your doctor.

How Do You Identify Your Different Asthma Medications? You may be prescribed the following Astra medications to help control your asthma (see Table I). It is important that you understand how to tell them apart and when to use each medication.

Table I—Oxeze Turbuhaler

Identification of Astra Asthma Medications

Medication	Strength	Identification
Oxeze Turbuhaler (formoterol)	6 μg/dose	Turning grip is light greenish-blue. A braille code is embossed on the turning grip.
Oxeze Turbuhaler (formoterol)	12 μg/dose	Turning grip is dark greenish-blue. A braille code is embossed on the turning grip.
Pulmicort Turbuhaler (budesonide)	100 μg/dose	Turning grip is light brown. Budesonide 100 is embossed on the turning grip.
Pulmicort Turbuhaler (budesonide)	200 μg/dose	Turning grip is brown. Budesonide 200 is embossed on the turning grip.
Pulmicort Turbuhaler (budesonide)	400 μg/dose	Turning grip is dark brown. Budesonide 400 is embossed on the turning grip.
Bricanyl Turbuhaler (terbutaline)	0.5 mg/dose	Turning grip is blue. Terbutaline sulfate 0.5 mg/dose is embossed on the turning grip.

Specific information on product identification is provided on the drug product label. Ask your doctor or pharmacist for clarification if you are having difficulty understanding when or how often your medications should be taken.

Important Information on When to Call Your Doctor: If the relief of your asthma is not as good as usual or does not last as long as usual, **tell your doctor right away.** A change from usual includes more wheezing, coughing, tightness or shortness of breath.

If you experience bronchospasm, stop taking Oxeze Turbuhaler and contact your doctor immediately.

If you are using more of your short-acting bronchodilating medication or if you feel that it is less effective **tell your doctor right away.** Your doctor may adjust your treatment.

If your symptoms are waking you up at night, **tell your doctor right away.** Your doctor may adjust your treatment.

If you have taken all your medication as instructed by your doctor and an hour at rest has not relieved your symptoms, **you may need emergency treatment.**

Important Note: This leaflet alerts you to some of the times you should call your doctor. Other situations which cannot be predicted may arise. Nothing about this leaflet should stop you from calling your doctor or pharmacist with any questions or concerns you have about using Oxeze Turbuhaler.

□ OXIZOLE® Ⓟ

Stiefel

Oxiconazole Nitrate

Topical Antifungal Agent

Information for the Patient: Oxizole cream or lotion is a medication indicated for the treatment of athlete's foot (tinea pedis). The active ingredient of Oxizole is oxiconazole nitrate which is a broad-spectrum antifungal agent.

Instructions for Use:

1. Before applying Oxizole cream or lotion, the affected areas should be cleansed with a mild soap (such as Oilatum Soap) and water and gently dried.
2. Apply Oxizole cream or lotion to cover affected and surrounding areas twice daily in the morning and the evening. Gently massage medication into the skin. If used for the treatment of athlete's foot, pay special attention to spaces between the toes and wear well-fitted, ventilated shoes and cotton socks. When using Oxizole lotion, remember to shake the bottle well before using.
3. The hands should be washed after application.
4. For the treatment of athlete's foot, Oxizole cream or lotion should be used for 1 month.
5. Use Oxizole cream or lotion for the full treatment period even though symptoms may have subsided. This will assure healing and decrease the possibility of recurrence.
6. When treating athlete's foot, if no effects or improvement of your condition is seen after 4 weeks, consult your physician to have the diagnosis reviewed.

Precautions:

1. Oxizole cream or lotion should be used up to a maximum of 4 consecutive weeks of treatment.
2. If irritation or sensitivity develops with the use of Oxizole cream or lotion, treatment should be discontinued and your physician should be consulted.
3. Notify your physician if the area of application reveals signs of increased irritation (redness, itching, burning, swelling or oozing).
4. Avoid the use of bandages or wrappings over the area of the body on which Oxizole cream or lotion is applied, unless otherwise directed by your physician.
5. Oxizole cream or lotion should be kept away from the eyes, nose, mouth and other mucous membranes. If contact with the eyes occurs, rinse thoroughly with water.
6. Do not use Oxizole cream or lotion for infection of the scalp or nails.

Use in Pregnancy: Oxizole preparations should not be used during pregnancy except on the advice of a doctor.

Use in Nursing Mothers: Oxizole preparations should not be used by a nursing mother except on the advice of a doctor.

Pediatric Use: Oxizole preparations should not be used on children under the age of 12 except on the advice of a doctor.

Note: Store Oxizole Cream at 15 to 30°C. Store Oxizole Lotion at 15 to 30°C. **Protect from light.**

Warning: Oxizole cream or lotion is for external use only—not for ophthalmic or intravaginal use.

□ OXYCONTIN® Ⓝ

Purdue Frederick

Oxycodone HCl

Opioid Analgesic

Information for the Patient: What is Oxycodone? Oxycodone relieves pain and should help you live more comfortably and independently. It is effective and safe when used as directed by your doctor. Your pain may increase or decrease from time to time and your doctor may need to change the amount of oxycodone you take daily (daily dosage).

What is OxyContin? OxyContin is a tablet that is made in such a way as to slowly release oxycodone over a 12 hour period, requiring a dose only every 12 hours to control your pain.

OxyContin tablets are available in 4 strengths: 10 mg (white), 20 mg (pink), 40 mg (yellow) and 80 mg (green). It may be necessary for you to take more than one tablet strength (different colored tablets) at the same time in order to receive the total daily dosage prescribed by your doctor.

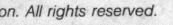

OxyContin (cont'd)

How to Take Your Medication: OxyContin tablets must be taken regularly every 12 hours (with 4 to 6 oz. of water) to prevent pain all day and night. If your pain worsens, making you uncomfortable, contact your doctor immediately and she/he may decide that it is necessary to adjust your daily dosage of OxyContin.

Your dose of OxyContin will be clearly labeled on the medication bottle. Be sure to follow these directions on the label exactly; this is very important. If your dosage is changed, be sure to write it down at the time your doctor calls you or sees you and follow the new directions exactly.

OxyContin tablets should not be broken, chewed or crushed.

Constipation: Oxycodone causes constipation. This is to be expected so your doctor may order a laxative and stool softener to help relieve your constipation while you are taking OxyContin. Tell your doctor about the problem if it arises.

Concomitant Medications: Your doctor should be made aware of any other medication you are taking including over-the-counter antihistamines or sleep-aids as they could affect the way you respond to oxycodone.

Driving: Driving or other tasks requiring full alertness should not be attempted for the first few days of taking OxyContin, since you may experience drowsiness or sedation.

Reordering OxyContin: A new written prescription is required from your doctor each time you need more OxyContin. Therefore, it is important that you contact your doctor at least 3 working days before your current supply runs out. It is very important that you do not miss any doses.

Should your pain increase, or any other complaint develop as a result of taking OxyContin, contact your doctor immediately.

□ PANTOLOC™ Ⓟ

Solvay Pharma/Byk Canada

Pantoprazole

H⁺, K⁺-ATPase Inhibitor

Information for the Patient: Please read the following information carefully.

This (booklet/leaflet/sheet) contains general information about Pantoloc. If you need more specific information, ask your doctor or pharmacist. It is important for you to follow carefully your doctor's instructions regarding how and when to take Pantoloc.

What is Pantoloc used for and how does it work? Pantoloc is the brand name for the medication, pantoprazole.

Pantoloc is used to treat acid-related stomach problems such as stomach ulcers (also known as gastric ulcers), duodenal ulcers, and reflux esophagitis (a severe form of heartburn). Pantoloc works by reducing the amount of acid made in your stomach.

What is in Pantoloc? Each Pantoloc tablet contains pantoprazole as the active ingredient. Other nonmedicinal ingredients are: crospovidone, methylhydroxypropyl cellulose, yellow iron oxide, mannitol, poly(ethylacrylate, methacrylic acid) 1:1, propylene glycol, anhydrous sodium carbonate, polyvidone K90, calcium stearate, triethyl citrate, polyvidone K25, polysorbate 80, sodium lauryl sulfate and titanium dioxide.

Check with your doctor whether you might be allergic to any of the above ingredients.

What should I tell my doctor before taking Pantoloc? Tell your doctor:
- about all health problems you have now or have had in the past;
- about all other medicines you take, including ones you can get without a prescription;
- if you are allergic to "nonmedicinal" substances which may be present in "Pantoloc" (see "What is in Pantoloc?");
- if you are pregnant, plan to become pregnant or are breast-feeding.

How do I take Pantoloc properly? Your doctor has recommended you take Pantoloc tablets for a specific number of weeks. Keep taking Pantoloc until you have finished all your tablets, as recommended by your doctor. Do not stop even when you start to feel better. If you stop taking Pantoloc too soon, your symptoms may return.

If you forget to take one dose of Pantoloc, take a tablet as soon as you remember, unless it is almost time for your next dose. If it is, do not take the missed tablet at all. Never double-up on a dose to make up for the one you have missed, just go back to your regular schedule.

Pantoloc may be taken in the morning, with or without food. Swallow the tablet(s) whole, with water. Do not crush or chew the tablet(s).

Are there any side effects? Like any medication, Pantoloc may cause side effects in some people. When side effects have been reported, they have been generally mild and did not last a long time. Headache and diarrhea are the most common side effects; less often rash, itchiness and dizziness can occur. If any of these become troublesome, consult your doctor. If you experience any unusual or unexpected symptoms while using Pantoloc, consult your doctor.

What should I do in case of overdose? If you or someone you know takes a lot more than the recommended dose (an overdose), you should contact a doctor or pharmacist immediately. No severe symptoms have been seen up to now in cases of overdose. Doses up to 240 mg of an injectable solution of pantoprazole have been administered and were well tolerated.

Where should I keep Pantoloc? Keep your tablets at room temperature (15 to 30°C) and in a safe place, where children cannot reach them.

Important Note: This information is intended to alert you to some of the times when you should call your doctor. Other situations which cannot be predicted may arise while you are taking medicines. Nothing should stop you from calling your doctor with any questions or concerns you have about using Pantoloc.

□ PAXIL® Ⓟ

SmithKline Beecham

Paroxetine HCl

Antidepressant—Antiobsessional—Antipanic Agent

Information for the Patient: Please read this information before you start to take your medicine. Keep this leaflet until you have finished all your tablets as you may need to read it again. **For further information or advice, please see your doctor or pharmacist.**

What you should know about Paxil:
- Paxil (paroxetine hydrochloride) belongs to the family of medicines used in the treatment of depression, obsessive-compulsive disorder and panic disorder.
- Paxil has been prescribed to you by your doctor to relieve your symptoms of depression, obsessions and compulsions, or panic disorder.

What you should tell your doctor before taking Paxil:
- all your medical conditions, including a history of seizures, liver or kidney disease, or heart problems;
- any medications (prescription or nonprescription) which you are taking, especially monoamine oxidase inhibitor antidepressants (e.g., phenelzine sulfate, moclobemide) or any other antidepressants, drugs used to prevent fits (anticonvulsants), drugs for Parkinson's disease, drugs used to thin the blood (anticoagulants) or drugs containing tryptophan;
- If you are pregnant or thinking about becoming pregnant, or if you are breast-feeding;
- your habits of alcohol consumption.

How to take Paxil:
- It is very important that you take Paxil exactly as your doctor has instructed. Generally most people take between 20 and 40 mg of Paxil/day for depression, obsessive-compulsive disorder and panic disorder although your doctor may start you at 10 mg/day for panic disorder. Your doctor may increase the dose.
- Never increase the amount of Paxil you are taking unless your doctor tells you to.
- You should continue to take your medicine even if you do not feel better, as it may take a number of weeks for your medicine to work.
- Take your tablets in the morning, preferably with food. You should swallow the tablets whole with water. Do not chew them.
- Keep taking your tablets until the doctor tells you to stop. The doctor may tell you to continue to take your medicine for several months. Continue to follow the doctor's instructions.
- If you forget to take your tablet in the morning, take it as soon as you remember. Take your next dose at the normal time the next morning, then carry on as before.

Remember: This medicine has been prescribed only for you. Do not give it to anybody else.

When not to use Paxil:

- Do not use Paxil if you are allergic to it or to any of the components of its formulation (see list of components at the end of this section). Stop taking the drug and contact your doctor immediately if you experience an allergic reaction or any severe or unusual side effects.

Precautions when taking Paxil:

- You may experience some side effects such as nausea, dry mouth, drowsiness, weakness, dizziness, sweating, nervousness, sleep disturbances and sexual problems. Other effects may include loss of appetite, constipation, and diarrhea. Consult your doctor if you experience these or other side effects, as the dose may have to be adjusted.
- Paxil does not usually affect people's normal activities. However, some people feel sleepy while taking it, in which case they should not drive or operate machinery.
- Avoid alcoholic drinks while taking Paxil.

What to do in case of overdose:

- If you have taken a large number of tablets all at once, contact your doctor or the nearest hospital emergency department immediately, even though you may not feel sick. Show the doctor your pack of tablets.

How to store Paxil:

- Store at room temperature (15 to 30°C) in a dry place.
- Keep container tightly closed.
- Keep out of reach of children.

What Paxil contains: Paxil (paroxetine hydrochloride) is available as 10 mg (yellow tablets), 20 mg (pink tablets) and 30 mg (blue tablets). Paroxetine is the active ingredient. Nonmedicinal ingredients include: dibasic calcium phosphate dihydrate USP, sodium starch glycolate NF, hydroxypropyl methyl cellulose USP, magnesium stearate NF, opadry yellow (10 mg), opadry pink (20 mg), blue (30 mg), and clear (all strengths). They do **not** contain sucrose, tartrazine or any other azo dyes.

Who manufactures Paxil:

- Paxil tablets are manufactured by: SmithKline Beecham Pharma Inc.

☐ PEDIAPRED® 🄿

Rhône-Poulenc Rorer

Prednisolone Sodium Phosphate

Glucocorticoid—Anti-inflammatory

Information for the Patient: Full prescribing information is available to the physician and pharmacist.

Description of Medication: Pediapred is the proprietary name of Rhône-Poulenc Rorer for prednisolone sodium phosphate, USP.

Pediapred is an adrenocorticoid, which belongs to the general family of medicines called steroids. There are many uses for this type of product: it may help replace those normally produced by your body, or it may be useful to provide relief from inflammation or allergic reactions which accompany a large number of different diseases such as skin problems, asthma or arthritis. It may also be given to you by your doctor as part of a treatment for your particular problem.

Pediapred is available only with your physician's prescription.

Before Using this Medication: You should inform your physician if any of the following apply to you:

- You have already taken Pediapred or any other adrenocorticoid or corticotropin and developed an allergy or intolerance to any of them. Also, tell your physician if you are allergic to any other substances, such as foods, preservatives or dyes.
- You are pregnant, intend to become pregnant or are breast-feeding, or intend to breast-feed.
- You are taking other medication, especially antacids, barbiturates, carbamazepine (e.g., Tegretol), phenytoin (e.g., Dilantin), antidiabetics (oral or insulin), digitalis, diuretics or medicine containing potassium or sodium.
- You suffer from other medical problems especially AIDS, systemic or local infections, stomach or intestine problems, bone disease, diabetes, heart disease, high blood pressure, kidney disease or kidney stones, myasthenia gravis, recent surgery or serious injury or if you are going to have skin test injections.

While you are being treated with this medication, and even after you have stopped taking it, do not have any immunizations without your doctor's approval. Also, other people living in your home should not receive oral polio vaccine, since there is a chance they could pass the polio virus on to you.

Proper Use of this Medication: Pediapred is a potent medicine and it is very important that you follow your doctor's directions on how to use it. Do not use more or less than you are supposed to. Do not take it more or less often than you are supposed to, and do not continue to use it for longer periods than you are supposed to.

Do not stop using Pediapred without your doctor's approval. In many cases, Pediapred must be gradually reduced before stopping completely, or serious side effects can occur.

Stomach problems may be more likely to occur if you drink alcoholic beverages while being treated with this medication.

Your physician will monitor your clinical condition and may ask for blood tests at regular intervals. It is important to attend these visits because your doctor may want to change the dosage and ensure there are no unwanted effects occurring.

Notify your physician about any illness which may develop during your treatment with Pediapred and about any new prescription or nonprescription medication you make take. If you require medical help for other reasons, inform the attending physician that you are taking Pediapred.

For patients taking this medicine by mouth, take this medicine with food to help prevent stomach upset. If stomach upset, burning, or pain continues, check with your doctor.

Missed Doses: If you miss a dose of this medicine and your suggested dosing schedule is:

One dose every other day—Take the missed dose as soon as possible if you remember it the same morning, then go back to your regular dosing schedule. If you do not remember the missed dose until later, wait and take it the following morning. Then skip a day and start your regular dosing schedule again.

One dose a day—Take the missed dose as soon as possible, then go back to your regular dosing schedule. If you do not remember until the next day, skip the missed dose and do not double the next one.

Several doses a day—Take the missed dose as soon as possible, then go back to your regular dosing schedule. If you do not remember until your next dose is due, double the next dose.

If you have any questions about this, check with your physician or pharmacist.

Notify your physician if you suffer any side effects (see next section).

Storage Information: Store at 15 to 30°C. Do not refrigerate. Keep bottle tightly closed.

This medicine is prescribed for your specific medical problem and for your own use only. **Do not give it to other people.**

Keep all medicines out of the reach of children.

Side Effects of this Medication: Pediapred may cause some unwanted side effects. Usually these do not occur if you are taking the medication for a short period; however, if you do experience one of the following after a short period of time of using Pediapred, contact your doctor: decreased or blurred vision, frequent urination, increased thirst, skin rash.

If you are taking Pediapred for a long time, consult your doctor if any of the following occur: acne or other skin problems, back or rib pain, bloody or black tarry stools, filling or rounding of the face, irregular heartbeats, menstrual problems, depression, mood or mental changes, muscle cramps or pains or weakness, nausea or vomiting, if you see halos around lights, sore throat and fever, continued stomach pain or burning, swelling of feet or lower legs, unusual tiredness or weakness, wounds that will not heal.

Other side effects may occur which usually go away during treatment: indigestion, increased appetite, nervousness or restlessness, trouble sleeping or weight gain. If these symptoms persist, contact your doctor.

After you stop taking Pediapred, especially if you have been taking it or similar medication to it for a long time, your body may need time to adjust. During this time, you should contact your doctor if you experience any of the following symptoms: pain in the abdomen, stomach or back, dizziness or fainting, fever, loss of appetite, muscle or joint pain, nausea or vomiting, shortness of breath, unusual tiredness or weakness, unusual weight loss.

Other side effects not listed above may also occur in some patients. If you notice any other effects, check with your doctor.

If you need any further information, ask your physician or pharmacist.

☐ PENTACARINAT® ℞

Rhône-Poulenc Rorer

Pentamidine Isethionate

Antiparasitic Agent

Information for the Patient: Pentacarinat (pentamidine isethionate) belongs to the family of medicines called antiprotozoals. This medicine is given by inhalation into the lungs to try to prevent Pneumocystis carinii pneumonia (PCP), a very serious and common form of pneumonia in immunocompromised individuals. Inhaled pentamidine does not prevent illness in other parts of the body outside the lungs.

Before using this Medication: To decide on the best treatment for your medical problem, your doctor should be told: if you have ever had any unusual or allergic reaction to pentamidine; if you are allergic to other substances such as foods, preservatives or dyes; if you are **pregnant** or if you may become pregnant. Studies on birth defects have not been done in humans. If you are **breast-feeding.** It is not known whether pentamidine passes into breast milk. However, pentamidine has not been shown to cause problems in nursing babies. If you suffer from asthma.

Proper Use of this Medication: To help prevent the development or return of Pneumocystis pneumonia, you must receive pentamidine inhalation on a regular basis, even if you are feeling well.

If you miss a dose of this medicine by more than a few days, return to your physician to discuss the rescheduling of your treatment.

Precautions while using this Medication: If you are also using the inhalation form of a bronchodilator (medicine used to help relieve breathing problems), allow 5 to 10 minutes to pass between using the bronchodilator and the pentamidine inhalation, unless otherwise directed by your doctor. This will help to reduce the possibility of side effects. Do not mix pentamidine with any other medication in the nebulizer.

A bitter or metallic taste may occur during use of this medicine. Sucking on a hard candy after each treatment can help reduce this problem.

Cigarette smoking can increase the chance of coughing and difficulty in breathing during pentamidine inhalation therapy.

Side Effects of this Medication: Along with its needed effects, a medicine may cause some unwanted effects. Although not all of these side effects may occur, if they do occur, they may need medical attention.

Check with your doctor or nurse immediately if any of the following side effects occur: More common: burning pain, dryness, or sensation of lump in throat; chest pain or congestion; coughing; difficulty in breathing; difficulty in swallowing; skin rash; wheezing. Rare, with daily treatment doses only: anxiety, chills, cold sweats, cool pale skin, decreased urination, headache, increased hunger, loss of appetite, nausea and vomiting, nervousness, shakiness, stomach pain, unusual tiredness.

Other side effects not listed above may also occur in some patients. If you notice any other effects, check with your doctor.

☐ PEPCID AC®

Johnson & Johnson • Merck

Famotidine

Histamine H_2 Receptor Antagonist

Information for the Patient: What Is Pepcid AC? Pepcid AC **Acid Controller** tablets are clinically proven to provide fast and effective relief from heartburn and acid indigestion. Pepcid AC contains the ingredient famotidine which has previously been available only with a prescription. Pepcid AC works by actually reducing the flow of excess stomach acid which can lead to heartburn pain, unlike antacids which neutralize existing stomach acid. One (1) Pepcid AC tablet controls stomach acid for up to 9 hours. Pepcid AC is available in small easy-to-swallow film-coated tablets and in chewable mint-flavored tablets.

For What Conditions Should Pepcid AC Be Taken? Pepcid AC offers fast and effective relief from heartburn, acid indigestion and upset or sour stomach due to excess stomach acid. Pepcid AC also prevents these symptoms brought on by consuming food and/or beverage.

How Should Pepcid AC Be Taken? Adults and children 12 years of age or older: For relief of symptoms, take one (1) tablet. For prevention of acid-related symptoms brought on by consuming food and/or beverage, take one (1) tablet 1 hour before eating. If symptoms return, you may take another tablet. Do not take more than 2 tablets during a 24-hour period. If symptoms persist for more than 2 consecutive weeks, consult your physician.

When Should a Physician or Pharmacist Be Consulted? This medicine may not be suitable for some people. Consult with your physician or pharmacist before using if:

- You are allergic to any component of this product.
- You are pregnant or breast-feeding.
- You have difficulty swallowing, or persistent abdominal discomfort.
- You have severe kidney disease or any other severe illnesses.
- You are over 40 and you are experiencing new or recently changed symptoms of acid indigestion or heartburn.
- You are taking nonsteroidal anti-inflammatory drugs [NSAIDs] (because these medicines may be causing your symptoms).
- You have a previous history of ulcer disease complications.
- You are experiencing unintended weight loss in association with your symptoms of acid indigestion or heartburn.

Pepcid AC is generally well tolerated. Should any unusual symptoms occur, a physician should be consulted.

What Else Can Be Done to Help Avoid Symptoms:

- Do not lie down soon after eating.
- If you are overweight, lose weight.
- If you smoke, stop or cut down.
- Avoid or limit foods such as caffeine, chocolate, fatty foods and alcohol.
- Do not eat just before bedtime.

Description: Film-coated Tablets: Each regular pink, rounded, square-edged tablet has Pepcid AC embossed on one side and is film-coated to ease swallowing.

Chewable Tablets: Each pink, round, mint-flavored chewable tablet has Pepcid AC embossed on one side.

Ingredients: Active ingredient: Each film-coated and chewable tablet of Pepcid AC contains 10 mg of famotidine, respectively.

Nonmedicinal Ingredients: Film-coated Tablets: hydroxypropyl cellulose, hydroxypropyl methylcellulose, magnesium stearate, microcrystalline cellulose, red ferric oxide, starch, talc and titanium dioxide.

Chewable Tablets: aspartame, cellulose acetate, citric acid (flavors), hydroxypropyl cellulose, hydroxypropyl methylcellulose, lactose, magnesium stearate, maltodextrin, mannitol, microcrystalline cellulose, modified food starch, red ferric oxide and starch.

How Should Pepcid AC Be Stored?

- Store these tablets at room temperature (15 to 30°C) and protect from moisture.
- It is advisable to keep blisters in carton until all tablets are used.
- Keep this and all medicines out of the reach of children.

Consult your physician or pharmacist if you need further information.

If you have questions or comments, please call 1-800-4PEPCID.

☐ PEPCID® Tablets ℞

MSD

Famotidine

Histamine H_2 Receptor Antagonist

Information for the Patient: Full prescribing information is available to the physician and pharmacist.

Pepcid is the brandname of Merck Frosst Canada Inc. for the medication famotidine available **only on prescription** from your physician. Famotidine belongs to a class of medicines known as histamine H_2 receptor antagonists. It reduces the amount of acid produced by the stomach. For this reason it is used in the treatment of certain ulcers of the stomach or duodenum, and other conditions, for example the treatment of gastroesophageal reflux disease or Zollinger-Ellison syndrome, in which the stomach produces too much acid.

Remember—This medicine is prescribed for the particular condition that you have. **Do not give this medicine to other people, nor use it for any other condition.**

Do not use outdated medicine.

Keep all medicines out of the reach of children.

Read the following information carefully. **If you need any explanations, or further information, ask your physician or pharmacist.**

Before Taking this Medicine: This medicine may not be suitable for some patients. So, tell your physician if you think **any** of the following applies to you:

- You have previously taken Pepcid or any other medication in the same class (Histamine H_2 receptor antagonists) and developed an allergy or reacted badly to it.
- You are pregnant or intend to become pregnant.
- You are breast-feeding or intend to breast-feed.
- You have confirmed kidney or liver ailment.

Your physician also needs to know if you are taking any other medication (example, a prescription or over the counter drugs).

Proper Use of this Medicine:

- Take this medicine **exactly** as directed by your physician. For the treatment of ulcers, it is often recommended as a single dose at bedtime; but some conditions may require different dosing. In any case, follow the instructions provided by your physician and your pharmacist.
- If necessary, your physician may also recommend an antacid.
- If you miss the usual time for a tablet, take it as soon as possible. But, if it is too close to the time of your next dose, take only the prescribed dose at the appointed time. **Do not take a double dose.**
- **The safety of Pepcid in children has not been established.**
- Carefully follow any dietary measures that your physician has recommended. Certain foods and drinks and certain medicines, such as aspirin, may irritate the stomach and worsen your condition.
- Take this medicine for the full duration of treatment, even if you begin to feel better. The pain usually subsides before complete healing is obtained. **Do not alter the dosage or stop taking the medicine without consulting your physician.**
- Pepcid does not usually interfere with other medicines that you may be taking. It is important, however, to tell your physician about all the drugs that you are taking, including those obtained without a prescription.
- Store at 15 to 30°C in a tightly closed container. Protect from light.

Side Effects of this Medicine—and What you Should Do: Along with its intended action, any medication may cause unwanted effects. Most people do not have any problem when taking this medicine.

Check with your physician as soon as possible if any of the following side effects occur: headache, dizziness, constipation and diarrhea.

Other effects not listed above may also occur in some patients. If you notice these side effects or any other unusual symptoms, check with your physician.

Ingredients: Active ingredient: Each tablet of Pepcid contains famotidine. It comes in two strengths: 20 mg (beige), and 40 mg (light brownish-orange).

Nonmedicinal ingredients: hydroxypropyl cellulose, hydroxypropyl methylcellulose, magnesium stearate, microcrystalline cellulose, red ferric oxide, starch pregelatinized, talc, titanium dioxide and yellow ferric oxide.

☐ PERIDEX® Ⓟ

Zila Pharmaceuticals

Chlorhexidine Gluconate

Antigingivitis

Information for the Patient: What to Expect when Using Peridex: Your dentist has prescribed Peridex Oral Rinse to treat your gingivitis—to help reduce the redness and swelling of your gums, and also to help you control any gum bleeding. Use Peridex regularly, as directed by your dentist, in addition to daily brushing and flossing. Do not swallow Peridex.

Peridex may cause some tooth discoloration or increases in tartar (calculus) formation, particularly in areas where plaque is more difficult to remove with normal brushing alone. It is important to do a thorough job of cleaning your teeth and to see your dentist at least every 6 months, or more frequently if your dentist advises.

- Both stain and tartar can be removed by your dentist or hygienist. Peridex may cause permanent discoloration of some front-tooth fillings. To minimize discoloration, you should brush and floss daily, emphasizing areas which begin to discolor. In some cases discoloration may be permanent.
- Peridex should not be used by persons who have a sensitivity to chlorhexidine gluconate.
- Peridex may taste bitter to some patients and may affect the taste of foods and beverages. This will become less noticeable in most cases with continued use of Peridex. To avoid taste interference, rinse with Peridex **after** meals. Do not rinse with water or other mouthrinses immediately after rinsing with Peridex.
- For maximum effectiveness avoid rinsing your mouth, brushing your teeth, eating or drinking for about 30 minutes after using Peridex.

If you have any questions or comments about Peridex, contact your dentist or pharmacist.

☐ PETHIDINE INJECTION BP Ⓝ

Faulding

Meperidine HCl

Opioid Analgesic

Information for the Patient: Directions for use of Rapiject prefilled syringe:

1. Remove protective caps from vial and injector.
2. Insert vial into injector.
3. Rotate vial 3 turns in a clockwise direction until some resistance occurs. Then rotate the vial another turn or 2. The needle will then be in contact with the meperidine solution.
4. Remove the needle cap and expel air.
5. The Rapiject is now ready for use.

☐ PHOTOFRIN®

Ligand

Porfimer Sodium

Antineoplastic Photosensitizing Agent

Information for the Patient: Photodynamic therapy is a cancer treatment that uses a photosensitive drug called Photofrin, in combination with a laser light delivery system. When injected i.v., Photofrin tends to be retained for a longer period of time by cancer cells than by most other tissues, thus minimizing any effect to normal tissue. Exposing the drug to light causes a chemical reaction which results in the destruction of cancer cells containing the drug.

In addition to retention by cancer cells, Photofrin is retained by the skin for a period of time, normally 4 to 6 weeks. Due to this retention by the skin, the major side effect of Photofrin is skin photosensitivity. Exposure of unprotected skin to sunlight or focused indoor lighting may result in erythema or blistering. Ocular discomfort, commonly described as sensitivity to sun, bright lights, or car headlights, has also been reported in patients who received Photofrin. Therefore, following the injection of Photofrin, patients must be advised to take precautions to protect the eyes and skin from exposure to direct or indirect sunlight or bright focused indoor light for a period of 30 days. The duration of photosensitivity may vary from patient to patient. It is important that each patient determine their individual photosensitivity reaction to the drug through a careful test program which should be explained by their physician: after 30 days, patients may expose a small area of skin (finger or dorsum of hand) to the sun for 5 minutes to test for residual photosensitivity. If significant erythema or blistering results, the patients should continue precautions against sun and bright light exposure for another 2 weeks before retesting the effects of limited sun exposure. UV sunscreens are of no value, because photoactivation is caused by visible light. While photosensitivity precautions must be considered, patients should also be advised to avoid total darkness. Exposure to normal ambient lighting is important to aid in the clearance of Photofrin from the skin through the process of photobleaching.

Patients should be instructed to raise any additional questions regarding this treatment with their physician.

☐ PHYLLOCONTIN® Ⓟ
☐ PHYLLOCONTIN®-350 Ⓟ

Purdue Frederick

Aminophylline

Bronchodilator

Information for the Patient: Phyllocontin and Phyllocontin-350 tablets are designed to help you breathe more easily. The tablets release their medication gradually and are intended for regular use. They are **not to be used** to quickly help you breathe better in an emergency.

Take the tablets:

1) either whole or broken in half but **do not crush or chew the tablets;**

Phyllocontin (cont'd)

2) with a full glass of water while sitting upright or standing;
3) regularly and only at the times and in the exact quantity directed by your doctor. (**Do not** take a double dose to make up for one you forgot.)

Inform your doctor:
a) about all medications you are currently taking;
b) as soon as you start or stop taking any medication;
c) if you are breast-feeding, pregnant or want to become pregnant;
d) immediately if breathing problems worsen;
e) immediately if you get a headache, nausea, vomiting or other side effects;
f) immediately if you get a fever or viral infection (e.g. flu);
g) if you start or stop smoking.

In these situations, your dosage may need to be adjusted.
Store tablets at room temperature (below 30°C).

□ PLAVIX™

Sanofi/Bristol-Myers Squibb

Clopidogrel Bisulfate

Platelet Aggregation Inhibitor

Information for the Patient: Please read this leaflet carefully. It contains important information about your prescribed medicine and your medical condition. If you have any questions after reading this leaflet, please talk to your doctor or pharmacist.

What do Plavix tablets contain? Each Plavix tablet contains 75 mg of a drug called clopidogrel.

What else do Plavix tablets contain? As well as the active ingredient in Plavix (clopidogrel), the tablets contain a number of other nonmedicinal ingredients. Some people may be sensitive or allergic to one or more of these ingredients, which are: anhydrous lactose, microcrystalline cellulose, pregelatinized starch, polyethylene glycol 6000, and hydrogenated castor oil. The pink film coating contains hydroxypropyl methylcellulose 2910, titanium dioxide, polyethylene glycol 6000 and ferric oxide (red). The tablets are polished with carnauba wax.

What do Plavix tablets look like? Plavix tablets are round, pink and engraved on one side with the number 75. They are supplied in cartons containing a blister card of 28 tablets.

What type of medicine is Plavix? Clopidogrel, the active ingredient in Plavix tablets, belongs to a group of medicines called antiplatelet drugs. Platelets are very small structures in blood, smaller than red or white blood cells, which clump together during blood clotting. By preventing this clumping, antiplatelet drugs reduce the chances of blood clots forming (a process called thrombosis).

What is Plavix used for? You have been prescribed Plavix because you have experienced symptoms of a condition known as hardening of the arteries (atherosclerosis). Atherosclerosis results in a narrowing of the blood vessels (arteries) and an increased risk of unwanted blood clots (thrombi). These blood clots can lead to symptoms which present in different manners, such as strokes, heart attacks, or peripheral vascular disease (leg pain on walking or at rest). Since you have already had one of these events, Plavix is taken to prevent further blood clots from forming in hardened arteries. This reduces the risk of having a second stroke or heart attack.

This product has been prescribed for you personally and you should not pass it on to others.

Who should not take Plavix? You should not take Plavix:
- If you have had a bad reaction (allergy) in the past to any of the substances contained in the tablets. Please make sure you read "What do Plavix tablets contain?" and "What else do Plavix tablets contain?" above.
- If you have a medical condition that is causing bleeding such as a stomach ulcer.

If you think you may have any of these problems, or if you are in any doubt at all, consult your doctor before taking Plavix.

What needs to be considered before taking Plavix? If any of the following situations apply to you, you should tell your doctor at once:
- You have had a recent serious injury
- You have recently undergone surgery (including dental surgery)
- You have a blood disorder that makes you prone to internal bleeding (bleeding inside any tissues, organs or joints of your body) or tend to bleed longer than 10 minutes without taking any drugs
- You have a medical condition that puts you at risk of internal bleeding (such as stomach ulcer)
- You will be having surgery (including dental surgery) in the next 2 weeks
- You are taking another type of medication. This includes **all** medications, even those which you have purchased yourself at a pharmacy or a supermarket
- You have liver disease or damage.

What if you experience prolonged bleeding when taking Plavix? If you cut or injure yourself, it may take slightly longer than usual for bleeding to stop. This is linked to the way your medicine works. For minor cuts and injuries e.g., cutting yourself shaving, this is of no concern. However, if you are in any doubt at all, you should contact your doctor immediately.

What if you are pregnant or breast-feeding? If you are pregnant or if you are breast-feeding a baby, you should tell your doctor before taking Plavix. If you become pregnant while taking Plavix, inform your doctor immediately.

Will Plavix have any effects on your ability to drive or operate machinery? Your ability to drive or operate complicated machinery should not be affected by Plavix.

What if you take other medicines while you are taking Plavix? Some other medicines, whether prescribed by your doctor or bought over the pharmacy counter, may interact with the actions of Plavix to have unwanted effects. If you are in doubt about whether you should take another medicine while taking Plavix, please ask your doctor or pharmacist.

Medicines that are not recommended while taking Plavix:
- ASA (acetylsalicylic acid), when taken for prolonged periods, except when it has been specifically recommended by your doctor. An occasional dose of ASA (no more than 1 000 mg in any 24-hour period) should not cause a problem.
- Other drugs used to reduce blood clotting such as warfarin and heparin.
- Nonsteroidal Anti-Inflammatory Drugs (drugs used to treat painful and/or inflammatory conditions of muscles or joints) when taken for prolonged periods.

How should Plavix be taken? Adults (including the elderly): You should take one 75 mg tablet of Plavix per day, by mouth. Plavix can be taken with or without food. You should take your medicine regularly and at the same time each day.

Children and adolescents: Plavix is not recommended for children or adolescents below 18 years of age.

How long should you continue to take Plavix? You should take Plavix for as long as your doctor continues to prescribe it.

What if you take too many Plavix tablets at once? If you take an overdose of tablets inform your doctor at once or go to the nearest hospital emergency department. A large dose of tablets could put you at risk of serious bleeding, requiring emergency treatment.

What if you miss a dose of Plavix? If you forget to take a dose of Plavix, but remember within 12 hours of your usual time, take your tablet immediately and then take your next tablet at the normal time. If you forget for more than 12 hours simply take the next single dose at the usual time. Do not take a double dose to make up for the one you missed. You can check the day on which you last took a tablet of Plavix by referring to the calendar printed on the blister strip.

What undesirable effects may Plavix cause? Occasional side effects reported with Plavix are:
- Rashes and/or itching
- Diarrhea
- Abdominal pain
- Indigestion or heartburn
- Constipation
- Bleeding in the stomach, bowels or into the eye

Bleeding from blood vessels inside the head has been reported in a very small number of cases.

If you notice any undesirable effects, including any not mentioned above, tell your doctor or pharmacist.

How long should you keep Plavix tablets? Do not use your tablets after the expiry date stated on the carton and blister pack.

How should your Plavix tablets be stored? Plavix tablets should be stored in a safe place and be kept out of the reach of children. Do not leave them near a radiator, on a window sill or in a humid place. Do not remove tablets from the blister pack until you are ready to take them.

□ PLENDIL® Ⓟ

Astra

Felodipine

Antihypertensive Agent

Information for the Patient: Important information you should know about Plendil (felodipine extended release tablets): Plendil is a brand name for the drug felodipine (said as, fell-o'-di-peen). It belongs to the group of drugs called "calcium channel blockers" or "calcium antagonists".

Plendil is used to treat hypertension (high blood pressure). Its main action is to relax the arteries, letting the blood flow more freely; thereby lowering the blood pressure.

Read this leaflet carefully. It does not replace your doctor's or pharmacist's advice. They may have given you different instructions for your particular health condition. Be sure to follow their advice. If you have any questions, talk to your doctor or pharmacist. **Do not decide on your own how to take Plendil.**

Before You Start Plendil: Be sure you have told your doctor:
- **If you are pregnant or plan to become pregnant.**
- **If you are breast-feeding.**
- About all health problems you have or have had in the past.
- About all medicines you take, including ones you can buy without a prescription.
- If you visit more than one doctor make sure that each knows about all the medicines you are taking.
- If you are allergic to "non-medicinal" substances like food products, preservatives, or dyes, which may be present in Plendil tablets (see Plendil ingredients).
- If you have ever had a bad, unusual or allergic reaction to "felodipine".

Plendil Ingredients: Most medicines contain more ingredients than just the active drug. These ingredients are needed to keep medicines in a form that you can swallow. Check with your doctor if you think you might be allergic to any of these items (listed in alphabetical order): aluminum silicate, carnauba wax, castor oil, felodipine, hydrogen peroxide, hydroxypropyl cellulose, hydroxypropyl methylcellulose, iron oxide, lactose, microcrystalline cellulose, polyethylene glycol, propyl gallate, sodium stearyl fumarate, titanium dioxide.

How to Use The Plendil Compliance Pack: This unique 30-day package is designed to make it easy to keep track of your medication.

Twenty-eight of the tablets are labelled with a day of the week. To start, take a tablet in the first row that matches the day you begin the pack. Then, take a tablet on each of the following days to complete the 28 labelled tablets. The 2 extra nonlabelled tablets should be taken after all other tablets are gone.

Remember to get a new prescription from your doctor or a refill from your pharmacy a few days before all 30 tablets are taken.

How to Take Plendil:
- Take Plendil exactly as your doctor tells you. Do not miss doses or take extra doses, unless your doctor tells you. If you are not clear about the directions, ask your doctor or pharmacist.
- Plendil is taken once a day. Even if your doctor has prescribed 2 tablets a day, both should be taken at the same time, unless otherwise indicated.
- Try to take Plendil with something you do regularly each day; for example, upon waking or at breakfast. This will help you remember each dose.
- Plendil may be taken with food or on an empty stomach.
- **Grapefruit juice increases the amount of Plendil in your body and should be avoided.**
- Swallow Plendil whole with a glass of water. Do not crush, chew, break or suck on the tablets.
- Do not transfer Plendil to other pill containers. To protect your Plendil tablets, keep them in the original Compliance Pack.

If You Miss A Dose: If you miss a dose of Plendil and remember within 12 hours, you should take your usual dose as soon as possible. Then go back to your regular schedule. But if it is more than 12 hours when you remember, do not take the missed dose. Just take the next dose on time.

Never take a double dose of Plendil to make up for missed tablets. If you are still unsure, check with your doctor or pharmacist to see what you should do.

Side Effects To Be Aware Of: Along with its effects on controlling blood pressure, Plendil, like any medication, may include side effects.

Some side effects may occur when Plendil is first started or when the dose is increased. These side effects are usually mild and should go away as your body gets used to Plendil.

It is important that you keep your doctor informed of all side effects, especially if you experience any of the following for more than a week:
- swelling of the ankles;
- flushing or a feeling of warmth;
- dizziness;
- a racing heartbeat;
- headache;
- unusual tiredness.

Medicines affect different people in different ways. Just because side effects have occurred in other patients does not mean you will get them. Discuss how you feel on Plendil with your doctor and pharmacist. **Do not stop taking Plendil on your own.**

A few patients report mild tenderness or swelling of their gums while taking Plendil. This effect can be prevented with good dental care. Brush your teeth carefully and often with a soft toothbrush, and use dental floss daily.

Massaging your gums regularly with a soft toothbrush will also help. If your gums do become tender, red or swollen, be sure to tell your doctor or dentist.

Other side effects have been reported in a few cases. These include tingling in the hands, arms, feet or legs, stomach upset and diarrhea. Again, if any of these effects bother you, be sure to tell your doctor.

You should be certain to contact your doctor immediately if you experience anything unusual.

Some Precautions You Should Take: Keep Plendil out of sight and out of the reach of children. Never take medicine in front of small children as they will want to copy you.

Unused medicines which you know you will no longer need should be carefully discarded. Small quantities may be disposed of in the toilet or you may wish to seek advice from your pharmacist.

The Compliance Pack protects each tablet. When you first open the package, if you find any damage to the plastic seal or foil which exposes the tablet, ask your pharmacist to check the package.

Check with your doctor if you want to drink alcohol (including wine with your meals) while you are taking Plendil. Drinking alcohol while on Plendil may make you feel dizzier than usual. Alcohol may also cause an uncomfortable drop in blood pressure.

Remember, you may not notice any signs of high blood pressure. **Therefore it is important to take Plendil even when you feel well.** A constant amount of drug is needed in your body to control your blood pressure. **Do not stop taking Plendil on your own.**

How To Store Plendil: Although the Plendil tablets are protected in this Compliance Pack, it is best to keep the package at normal room temperature and in a dry place. Do not keep Plendil in the bathroom. **Keep Plendil out of the reach of children.** Do not keep or use Plendil after the expiry date indicated on the Compliance Pack.

General Information: All drugs can have both helpful and harmful effects. Both depend on the person and his or her health condition. This leaflet alerts you to some of the times you should call your doctor. Other situations which cannot be predicted may arise. Nothing in this leaflet should stop you from calling your doctor or pharmacist with any questions or concerns you have about Plendil.

☐ POLIOVIRUS VACCINE LIVE ORAL TRIVALENT

Connaught

Poliovirus Types 1, 2 and 3

Active Immunizing Agent

Information for the Patient: Parents should be fully informed of the benefits and risks of immunization with Poliovirus Vaccine Live Oral Trivalent such as the possibility of vaccine-associated paralysis.

The importance of hand washing immediately after diapering the infant, particularly during the 6 to 8 week period of fecal viral excretion following vaccine administration should be emphasized.

☐ POTABA®

Glenwood

Aminobenzoate Potassium

Antifibrotic

Information for the Patient: What is Potaba? Potaba is part of the Vitamin B complex. It is a naturally occurring substance that participates in many biologically important processes.

Why is Potaba prescribed? Potaba is prescribed for conditions such as scleroderma, dermatomyositis, morphea and linear scleroderma, and Peyronie's disease. It is believed to produce a skin/plaque softening in patients when given in adequate dosage over sufficient time.

How does it work? Understanding of drug mechanisms at the cellular level is incomplete in the case of many medications. It is thought that Potaba has an antifibrotic effect due to increased oxygen uptake at the tissue level.

How is it administered? Orally, according to the following schedule:

Potaba Capsules (0.5 g): Take 6 capsules with a glass of water after meals and at bedtime with a snack.

Potaba Powder Envules (2 g/pack): Add 1½ envules to a glass of chilled water or juice; stir to dissolve, and drink after eating.

Potaba Tablets (0.5 g): Crush 6 tablets and add to a glass of chilled water or juice; stir thoroughly and drink after eating.

If you are unable to eat, omit dosage until you resume eating again.

Medication burnout is a term used to describe a situation in which the patient stops taking medication. In consequence, the desired results of therapy will not be seen. Changing dosage form may prevent medication burnout.

What is the advantage of taking Potaba? Therapy with Potaba is a nontoxic, low-risk treatment for conditions that are usually long-term. This regimen represents a good possibility of softening hardened tissue. As there is a very low incidence of drug interactions, many other medications may be continued while you are taking Potaba. It is highly soluble in water and therefore readily absorbed.

Where can I get Potaba? Potaba requires a physician's prescription. It can be obtained from your local pharmacy.

Are there any contraindications to Potaba? Your doctor should know if you are taking antimicrobial sulfonamides as Potaba may nullify the antibacterial effect.

Potaba should be administered with caution in the following medical conditions:

- diabetes mellitus (sugar diabetes);
- hypoglycemia (chronic low blood sugar);
- allergy to Potaba or PABA; and
- kidney disease.

How long should I take Potaba? How soon will I see results? Length of therapy varies considerably with disease state and from person to person. It may be 2 to 3 months before results are noticeable.

Are there foods, drink, or activities I should avoid while taking Potaba? Potaba therapy is most acceptable when taken in conjunction with meals or snacks. There are no specific foods or drinks to avoid, but it is good to keep a normal dietary intake to prevent stomach upset or low blood sugar. The doctor should know if you are on a special diet. Usual activities can be encouraged. If you are pregnant, planning to become pregnant, or nursing an infant, your doctor should be notified so this can be taken into consideration when prescribing Potaba or any prescription medication.

Are there any side effects? Anorexia, nausea, fever and rash have occurred rarely.

What should I do if these symptoms occur? Notify the doctor, stop taking the medication until symptoms subside. The doctor may then write a schedule to accomplish densensitization* and to resume therapy.

Are there any other considerations before beginning Potaba therapy? With **any** prescription drug it is wise to consider the following:

- the prescription is for the specific condition and for the use of the patient only;
- keep medicine out of the reach of children; and
- if you have any questions about the information presented here, ask your doctor, pharmacist, or nurse.

*Desensitization schedules are available from Glenwood Laboratories.

☐ PRANDASE®

Bayer

Acarbose

Oral Antidiabetic Agent—Alpha-glucosidase Inhibitor

Information for the Patient: Why Have I Been Prescribed Prandase? Your doctor has told you that you have non-insulin dependent diabetes mellitus (NIDDM), also called Type 2 diabetes. The most important part of treating your diabetes is to follow the diabetic diet prescribed by your healthcare professional. Prandase (acarbose) has been prescribed by your doctor in combination with your diet or in combination with your diet and a sulfonylurea (an oral antidiabetic drug) to manage your blood sugar (glucose) levels. Prandase will slow the absorption of glucose from your gut to reduce the high blood glucose levels that occur after each meal.

When and How Do I Take Prandase? Take the tablets as prescribed by your doctor. Tablets should be taken orally with the first bite of a main meal. Do not take Prandase between meals. It is important that you closely follow your prescribed diabetic diet and exercise regimen while you are taking Prandase.

When Should I Monitor My Blood Glucose Levels? You should continue to monitor your blood glucose levels according to the instructions given to you by your healthcare professional.

Are There Any Side Effects? You may experience some side effects while taking Prandase. The most common are gastrointestinal in nature, such as flatulence (gas) and abdominal discomfort. It is also possible that you may pass softer stools or even experience diarrhea, particularly after a meal containing foods with sucrose (ordinary sugar). Normally, these symptoms will diminish with continued treatment. Do not take antacid preparations for treating these symptoms, as they are unlikely to have any beneficial effects. If your symptoms persist, or if you have any other undesirable effects, consult your doctor.

Due to its action, Prandase should not cause hypoglycemia. However, since sulfonylureas (oral antidiabetic drugs) may cause hypoglycemia, the combination of a sulfonylurea and Prandase may also cause hypoglycemia. If you do experience hypoglycemia while you are taking Prandase, do not treat it with ordinary sugar (sucrose); instead, take glucose tablets (also known as dextrose).

Do You Have Any Other Medical Conditions? If you have certain medical conditions, you should not take Prandase. Be sure to inform your doctor if you have any of the following conditions.

–inflammation or ulceration of the bowel (e.g., ulcerative colitis or Crohn's disease)

–partial obstruction of your bowel or a predisposition to obstruction of your bowel

–a disease that affects your digestion or absorption of food from your intestine

–a kidney disorder or a large hernia

–other medical problems.

Do not take Prandase if you have previously had an allergic reaction to any of its ingredients. If you are unsure about this, ask your doctor.

Do not take Prandase if you are pregnant or breast-feeding. If you are taking Prandase and think that you may be pregnant or if you are planning a family, consult your doctor.

How Should I Store My Prandase Tablets? It is best if you keep your tablets in their original carton. The tablets should be kept in a dry place at a temperature between 15 and 25°C.

Keep out of the reach of children.

Do not use the tablets beyond the expiry date.

Remember: Your doctor has prescribed Prandase for you after a careful review of your medical condition. Use it only as directed, and do not give it to anyone else. If you require more information consult your healthcare professional.

☐ PRAVACHOL®

Squibb

Pravastatin Sodium

Lipid Metabolism Regulator

Information for the Patient: Full prescribing information is available to the physician and pharmacist.

Pravachol is the proprietary name of Squibb Canada, division of Bristol-Myers Squibb Canada Inc. for pravastatin sodium.

Pravachol lowers the level of cholesterol, particularly low density lipoprotein (LDL) cholesterol, in the blood. Pravachol reduces cholesterol production by the liver and induces some changes of cholesterol transport and disposition in the blood and tissues.

Pravachol is available only with your physician's prescription. It is to be used as an adjunct to a medically recommended and carefully supervised diet for the long-term treatment of hypercholesterolemia and is not a substitute for such a diet. This may help prevent heart disease if caused by cholesterol clogging the blood vessels or slow the progression of atherosclerosis (hardening) of the arteries that nourish your heart, so-called coronary heart disease (CHD). In addition, depending on your condition, your physician may recommend an appropriate regimen of exercise, weight control and other measures.

Use only as specifically directed. Do not alter the dosage unless ordered to do so by your physician. Check with your physician before discontinuing medication since this may result in an increase of your blood lipids.

Before using this medication, you should have told your physician if:

—you have already taken Pravachol or any other lipid lowering agent of the same class and have developed an allergy or intolerance to any of them,

—you suffer from liver disease,

—you are pregnant, intend to become pregnant or are breast-feeding, or intend to breast-feed,

—you are taking any other medication, particularly corticosteroids, cyclosporine (Sandimmune), gemfibrozil (Lopid), an anticoagulant [e.g., warfarin (Warfilone)], erythromycin, or digoxin.

Proper use of this medicine:

—Pravachol should be taken as a single dose at bedtime, as prescribed by your physician.

—Your physician will monitor your clinical condition and your blood tests at regular intervals including periodic eye examinations. It is important to have these check-ups done on schedule. Please keep your appointments accurately.

—Avoid excessive alcohol intake.

—Notify your physician about any illness which may develop during your treatment with Pravachol and about any new prescription or nonprescription medication you may take. If you require medical help for other reasons, inform the attending physician that you are taking Pravachol.

—Notify your physician if you are going to have major surgery or have sustained a severe injury.

—Notify your physician of any muscle pain, tenderness or weakness developing during treatment with Pravachol (see Side Effects).

—The safety of Pravachol in adolescents and children has not been established.

—Pravachol is contraindicated during pregnancy since its use in the event of pregnancy may harm the unborn. Only female patients who are highly unlikely to conceive can be candidates for Pravachol treatment. In the event of pregnancy during treatment, Pravachol should be discontinued and the physician should be informed.

Side Effects: Along with its intended action, any medication may cause unwanted effects.

Check with your physician as soon as possible if any of the following side effects occurs: aching muscles, muscle cramping, tiredness or weakness, fever and blurred vision.

Other side effects may occasionally occur which usually do not require stopping treatment. They may come and go during treatment without any particular danger, but you should mention them to your physician, without undue delay, if they become persistent or bothersome. Such adverse experiences include abdominal pain, constipation, diarrhea, nausea, headache, dizziness and skin rashes.

This medicine is prescribed for your specific medical problem and for your own use only. Do not give to other people.

Keep all medicines out of the reach of children.

If you need any further information, ask your physician or your pharmacist.

☐ PREMARIN® TABLETS

Wyeth-Ayerst

Conjugated Estrogens

Estrogenic Hormones

Information for the Patient: Using Premarin: Premarin (conjugated estrogens) contains a mixture of estrogens obtained exclusively from natural sources. This leaflet describes when and how to use estrogens and the risks of estrogen treatment. Please read it carefully. **If you want to know more or have any questions, please ask your doctor or pharmacist.**

Estrogen Drugs: Estrogens have several important uses but also some risks. You must decide, with your doctor, if the benefits of estrogen outweigh any risks. If you decide to start taking estrogens, check with your doctor to make sure you are using the lowest possible effective dose. The length of treatment with estrogens will depend upon the reason for use. This should also be discussed with your doctor.

Uses of Estrogen:

1. **To reduce menopausal symptoms:** Estrogens are hormones produced by the ovaries. The decrease in the amount of estrogen that occurs in all women, usually between the ages 45 and 55, marks the beginning of the menopause. Sometimes the ovaries are removed by an operation, causing ''surgical menopause''. When the amount of estrogen begins to decrease, some women develop very uncomfortable symptoms, such as feelings of warmth in the face, neck, and chest or sudden intense episodes of heat and sweating (''hot flashes'').

In some women the symptoms are mild; in others they can be severe. These symptoms may last only a few months or longer. Taking Premarin can alleviate these symptoms. If you are not taking estrogen for other reasons, such as the prevention of osteoporosis, you should take Premarin only as long as you need it for relief from your menopausal symptoms.

2. **To Prevent Osteoporosis (Brittle Bones):** After age 40, and especially after menopause, some women develop osteoporosis. This is a thinning of the bones that makes them weaker and more likely to break, often leading to fractures of vertebrae, hip, and wrist bones. Taking estrogens after the menopause slows down bone loss and may prevent bones from breaking. Eating foods that are high in calcium (such as milk products) or taking calcium supplements (1 000 to 1 500 mg/day) and certain types of exercise may also help prevent osteoporosis. Since estrogen use is associated with some risk, its use in the prevention of osteoporosis should be confined to women who appear to be susceptible to this condition. The following characteristics are often present in women who are likely to develop osteoporosis: white and Asian races, slim, family history of osteoporosis, physical inactivity, excessive caffeine intake, cigarette smoking, alcohol abuse, below average calcium intake, early menopause.

Women who had their menopause by the surgical removal of their ovaries at a relatively young age are good candidates for estrogen replacement therapy to prevent osteoporosis.

3. **To treat certain types of abnormal uterine bleeding due to hormonal imbalance when your doctor has found no serious cause of the bleeding.**

4. **To treat atrophic vaginitis (itching, burning, dryness in or around the vagina).**

5. **To treat vulvar atrophy.**

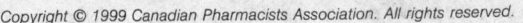

Uses of Progestins: Progestins used in hormone replacement therapy have similar effects to the female sex hormone progesterone. During

Premarin Tablets (cont'd)

the childbearing years, progesterone is responsible for regulation of the menstrual cycle. Premarin not only relieves your menopausal symptoms, but, like estrogens produced by your body, may also stimulate growth of the inner lining of the uterus, the endometrium. In menopausal and postmenopausal women with an intact uterus, stimulation of growth of the endometrium may result in irregular bleeding. In some cases this may progress into a disorder of the uterus known as endometrial hyperplasia (overgrowth of the lining of the uterus). The development of estrogen-mediated disorders of the uterus can be reduced if a progestin is given regularly for a certain number of days with your estrogen replacement therapy.

Precautions: Although estrogens provide health benefits, certain precautions should be taken before their use and in some situations their use may not be appropriate.

The use of estrogens has been reported to increase the risk of cancer of the lining of the uterus (endometrial cancer) in women after the menopause. **This risk is significantly reduced when estrogen is used along with a progestin.** If you have had your uterus removed by a hysterectomy, uterine cancer is not a risk for you and administration of a progestin is not necessary.

Most studies have not shown a higher risk of breast cancer in women who have ever used estrogens. However, some published epidemiologic studies have documented an association between a modest increase in the risk of developing breast cancer and the use of hormone replacement therapy in menopause when given for periods exceeding 10 years. Therefore, women with a family history of breast cancer, or with breast nodules, fibrocystic breast disease (lumps), or abnormal mammograms should consult with their doctor before starting hormone replacement therapy. Regular breast examinations by a physician and self-examinations are recommended for all women.

The use of oral estrogens after menopause has been reported to increase the risk of gallbladder disease requiring surgery.

Women on estrogen replacement therapy, taken alone or in combination with a progestin, have been reported in some studies to have an increased risk of thrombophlebitis, and/or thromboembolic disease. You should alert the physician if any of the following symptoms occur: changes in vision, tightness in chest, shortness of breath, severe pain in one or both legs, numbness affecting one side or one part of the body, and first migraine.

Restrictions On Use: Certain medical conditions may be aggravated by estrogens, therefore estrogens should either not be used at all or should be used with precaution under these conditions.

Estrogens should not be used during pregnancy. Since pregnancy may be possible early in the premenopause while you are still having spontaneous periods, the use of nonhormonal birth control should be discussed with your physician at this time. If you accidentally take estrogen during pregnancy, there is a small risk of your unborn child having birth defects.

Estrogens should not be used if you are breast-feeding.

You should not use Premarin if you have had any unusual allergic reaction to its ingredients.

Before using Premarin, be sure to tell your doctor if you have any of the following medical problems.

Premarin should not be used under these conditions:
- cancer of the breast or uterus
- unexpected or unusual vaginal bleeding
- stroke
- serious liver disease
- active phlebitis

To help your doctor decide whether you should use Premarin and what precautions should be taken during use, tell your doctor:
- what other prescription and nonprescription medicines, if any, you are taking. There are some medicines which interfere with the effects of estrogens;
- about your allergies or sensitivities to medicines or any other substances you may have;
- if you have ever had any of the following:
  - –high blood pressure
  - –heart, kidney, or liver disease
  - –asthma
  - –epilepsy or other neurological disorders
  - –sugar diabetes
  - –depression
  - –abnormalities of the breast or uterus including cancer
  - –breast disease, breast biopsies
  - –uterine fibroids
  - –phlebitis (inflamed veins)
  - –stroke, heart attack or blood clot
  - –migraine headache
  - –high triglyceride levels.

Side Effects: The following effects have been reported in women taking estrogens (these include estrogens used for birth control). Check with your doctor if these symptoms become troublesome.
- nausea
- retention of fluid
- migraine headaches
- localized darkening of the skin
- breast tenderness and excessive vaginal secretions (may be a sign that too much estrogen is being taken)
- persistent upper abdominal pain, nausea, vomiting, tender abdomen (may be signs of gallbladder disease)
- easy bruising, excessive nose bleeds, excessive heavy periods (may be signs of abnormal blood clotting)
- lower abdominal pain or swelling, painful and/or heavy periods (may be signs of growth of fibroids in the uterus)
- yellowing of the eyes or skin (may be signs of jaundice)
- upper abdominal pain or swelling (may be signs of liver tumors).

Check with your doctor as soon as possible if any of the following occur:
- irregular vaginal bleeding
- intolerable breast tenderness
- breast enlargement or lumps
- pain or heaviness in the legs or chest
- severe headaches
- dizziness
- changes in vision
- persistent or severe skin irritation
- fluid retention or bloating persisting for more than 6 weeks
- inflammation of the pancreas

Check with your doctor immediately if you experience:
- shortness of breath
- tightness of the chest
- severe pain in one or both legs or very marked numbness suddenly affecting one side or one part of the body
- sudden change in vision
- first migraine
- any other unusual symptom

How Supplied: Premarin tablets for oral administration are available as follows: Tablets: 0.3 mg (green), 0.625 mg (maroon), 0.9 mg (pink), 1.25 mg (yellow).

☐ PREVACID® ℞

Abbott

Lansoprazole

H⁺, K⁺-ATPase Inhibitor

Information for the Patient: Prevacid (lansoprazole) Delayed-Release Capsules should be taken before breakfast. Patients should be cautioned that Prevacid should not be opened, chewed or crushed. Capsules should be swallowed whole with sufficient water before breakfast.

H. pylori Eradication and Compliance: To ensure treatment success, when receiving Triple or Dual therapy for the eradication of H. pylori, make sure you take all prescribed medication for the entire treatment duration. Daily doses should be taken before meals.

If for some reason you cannot complete the treatment, consult your physician.

☐ PRINIVIL® ℞

MSD

Lisinopril

Angiotensin Converting Enzyme Inhibitor

Information for the Patient: Prinivil is the brandname of Merck Frosst Canada Inc. for the substance—lisinopril, available **only on prescription** from your physician. Lisinopril is one of a class of medicines known as angiotensin converting enzyme (ACE) inhibitors. They are usually prescribed to reduce **high blood pressure.**

When blood pressure is high, the workload of the heart and arteries increases so that over time, these organs may not function as they should. As a consequence, this could lead to the damage of the "vital organs": brain—heart—kidneys, resulting in stroke, heart failure, heart attack, blood vessel disease or kidney disease.

Prinivil may also be used to treat patients with **heart failure.** This is a condition where the heart cannot pump adequate amounts of blood to satisfy the needs of the body.

Remember—This medicine is prescribed for the particular condition that you have. **Do not give this medicine to other people, nor use it for any other condition.**

Do not use outdated medicine.

Keep all medicines out of the reach of children.

Read the following information carefully. **If you need any explanations, or further information, ask your physician or pharmacist.**

Before Taking this Medicine: This medicine may not be suitable for certain people. Tell your physician if you think **any** of the following applies to you:

- You have previously taken lisinopril or other medication of the same type—Angiotensin Converting Enzyme (ACE) inhibitors with the names usually ending with 'pril' such as lisinopril, enalapril, captopril, etc., and you were allergic or reacted badly to it, particularly if you experienced swelling of the face, lips, tongue, or throat, or had sudden difficulty breathing or swallowing.
- **You are pregnant or intend to become pregnant.** This medicine should **not be used during pregnancy,** because of possible risks to the fetus.
- You are breast-feeding or intend to breast-feed.
- You have any of these conditions:
  —diabetes
  —heart or blood vessel disease
  —liver disease
  —kidney disease

Your physician also needs to know if you are taking any other medication, whether on prescription or otherwise. It is particularly important to inform your physician if you are taking:

- Diuretics or "water pills"; any other medicines to reduce blood pressure; potassium-containing medicines, potassium supplements, or salt substitutes that contain potassium.

You should also inform your physician if you are vomiting or have severe diarrhea.

This medicine is not recommended for children.

Proper Use of this Medicine:

- Take this medicine exactly as your physician ordered.
- The absorption of this medicine is not affected by food; so it can be taken with or without a meal.
- Try to take your medicine every day at the same time. This way it becomes easy to remember your doses.
- If you miss a dose of this medicine, take it as soon as possible. However, if no more than 6 hours have elapsed since the missed dose, you may take that day's dose of medication and then go back to your regular dosing schedule. **Do not take a double dose.**
- In case of an overdose, contact your doctor immediately so that medical attention may be given promptly. The most likely symptom would be a feeling of lightheadedness or dizziness due to a sudden or excessive drop in blood pressure.
- Store your tablets at 15 to 30°C, in a tightly closed container, away from heat and direct light, and out of damp places, such as the bathroom or kitchen.
- If your physician has recommended a particular diet, for instance—less salt—follow the diet carefully. Your physician may also recommend weight loss. Do follow these suggestions.
- This medicine does not cure high blood pressure, nor congestive heart failure, **but does help control these conditions.** It is important to continue taking the tablets regularly. You may have to take high blood pressure medicine for life.
- Keep your regular appointments with your physician, even if you feel well. High blood pressure may not be easily recognized by you because you may not feel any symptoms; but your physician can measure very easily and check how the medicine is helping to control it.
- **Do not take any other medicines** unless you have discussed the matter with your physician. Certain medications tend to increase your pressure, for example, non-prescription preparations for appetite control, asthma, colds, coughs, hay fever and sinus problems. Other medicines may also react badly with Prinivil.
- If you have to undergo any dental or other surgery, inform the dentist or the physician in charge that you are taking this medicine.

Side Effects of This Medicine—and what you should do: Along with its intended action, any medication, including lisinopril, may cause side effects. Most people do not experience any problem when taking this medicine; but if you notice any of the following, medical attention may be needed:

- Sudden difficulty in breathing or swallowing
- Swelling of the face, eyes, lips, tongue and/or throat, hands or feet
- Dizziness, lightheadedness or fainting following exercise, and/or when it is hot and you have lost a lot of water by sweating
- Flu-like symptoms such as fever, malaise, muscle pain, rash, itching, abdominal pain, nausea, vomiting, diarrhea, jaundice, loss of appetite

Stop taking the medication and contact your physician or pharmacist at once. You may require immediate care. If condition worsens, seek medical attention.

- Initial dose may cause a greater fall in blood pressure than will occur following continued treatment. You may notice this as faintness or dizziness and it may help to lie down. If concerned, please consult your physician.
- If any fainting occurs, **stop** taking the medicine.
- If dizzy, **avoid** driving or any activity/job requiring alertness.
- **Use extra care** during exercise or hot weather.
- Dry cough, sore throat
- Unusual tiredness and/or weakness
- Headache
- Less or no urine being produced

If you notice any of the above or have other side effects, contact your physician or pharmacist. If the condition persists or worsens, seek medical attention.

Ingredients: Active Ingredient: Each tablet of Prinivil contains lisinopril. There are three different strengths: 5 mg (white), 10 mg (yellow) and 20 mg (peach).

Nonmedicinal ingredients: calcium phosphate, cornstarch, magnesium stearate and mannitol. The 10 mg and 20 mg also contain iron oxides.

□ PRINZIDE® Ⓟ

MSD

Lisinopril—Hydrochlorothiazide

Angiotensin Converting Enzyme Inhibitor—Diuretic

Information for the Patient: Prinzide is the brandname of Merck Frosst Canada Inc. for the combination of the substances—lisinopril and hydrochlorothiazide. Lisinopril is one of a class of medicines known as angiotensin converting enzyme inhibitors and hydrochlorothiazide is a thiazide diuretic, often termed a "water pill". This combination is available **only on prescription** from your physician. It is usually prescribed to reduce **high blood pressure.**

When blood pressure is high, the workload of the heart and arteries increases so that over time, these may not function as they should. In turn, this could lead to damage of the "vital organs": brain – heart – kidneys, and result in stroke, heart failure, heart attack, blood vessel disease or kidney disease.

Remember: This medicine is prescribed for the particular condition that you have. **Do not give this medicine to other people, nor use it for any other condition.**

Do not use outdated medicine.

Keep all medicines out of the reach of children.

Read the following information carefully. **If you need any explanations, or further information, ask your physician or pharmacist.**

Before Taking this Medicine: This medicine may not be suitable for certain people. So, tell your physician if you think any of the following applies to you:

- You have previously taken **any** of the following and were allergic or reacted badly to it: hydrochlorothiazide or any other diuretic or "water pill"; sulfonamides (sulfa medicine); lisinopril or any other medication of the same type—Angiotensin Converting Enzyme (ACE) inhibitors with the names usually ending with 'pril' such as lisinopril, enalapril, captopril, particularly if you experienced swelling of the face, lips, tongue, or throat, or had sudden difficulty breathing or swallowing.
- **You are pregnant or intend to become pregnant.** This medicine should **not be used during pregnancy,** because of possible risks to the fetus.

Prinzide (cont'd)

- You are breast-feeding or intend to breast-feed.
- You have any of these conditions:
  - –diabetes
  - –heart or blood vessel disease
  - –liver disease
  - –kidney disease, or difficulty in producing urine
  - –bronchial asthma
  - –lupus erythematosus or a history of this condition
  - –gout or history of gout

Your physician also needs to know if you are taking any other medication, whether they be prescription medications or over-the-counter products. It is particularly important to inform your physician if you are taking:

- diuretics or "water pills"; any other medicines to reduce blood pressure; potassium-containing medicines, potassium supplements, or salt substitutes that contain potassium; insulin for diabetes; lithium (a drug used to treat a certain kind of depression) or anti-inflammatory medicines used in arthritis.

You should also inform your physician if you are vomiting or have severe diarrhea.

This medicine is not recommended for children.

Proper Use of this Medicine:

- Take this medicine exactly as your physician ordered.
- The absorption of this medicine is not affected by food; so it can be taken with or without a meal.
- Try to take your medicine every day at the same time. This way it becomes easy to remember your doses.
- If you miss a dose of this medicine, take it as soon as possible. However, if no more than 6 hours have elapsed since the missed dose, you may take that day's dose of medication and then go back to your regular dosing schedule. **Do not take a double dose.**
- In case of an overdose, contact your doctor immediately so that medical attention may be given promptly. The most likely symptom would be a feeling of lightheadedness or dizziness due to a sudden or excessive drop in blood pressure.
- If your physician has recommended a particular diet, for instance less salt, follow the diet carefully. This could help your medicine to control your blood pressure. Your physician may also recommend weight loss. Do follow these suggestions.
- This medicine does not cure high blood pressure, **but does help control it.** So, it is important to continue taking the tablets regularly to keep your blood pressure down. You may have to take high blood pressure medicine for life.
- Keep your regular appointments with your physician, even if you feel well. High blood pressure may not be easily recognized by you, because you may not "feel any symptoms"; but your physician can measure your pressure very easily, and check how the medicine is controlling it.
- **Do not take any other medicines** unless you have discussed the matter with your physician. Certain medications tend to increase your pressure, for example, non-prescription preparations for appetite control, asthma, colds, coughs, hay fever and sinus problems.
- If you have to undergo any dental or other surgery, inform the dentist or the physician in charge that you are taking this medicine.
- Store your tablets at 15 to 30°C in a tightly closed container, away from heat and direct light, and out of damp places, such as the bathroom or kitchen.

Side Effects of this Medicine – and What you Should Do: Along with its intended action, any medication, including lisinopril with hydrochlorothiazide, may cause side effects. Most people do not experience any problem when taking this medicine; but if you notice any of the following, medical attention may be needed.

- Sudden difficulty in breathing or swallowing
- Swelling of face, eyes, lips, tongue and/or throat, hands or feet
- Dizziness, lightheadedness or fainting following exercise, and/or when it is hot and you have lost a lot of water by sweating
- Flu-like symptoms such as fever, malaise, muscle pain, rash, itching, abdominal pain, nausea, vomiting, diarrhea, jaundice, loss of appetite

Stop taking the medication and contact your physician or pharmacist at once. You may require immediate care. If condition worsens seek medical attention.

If any fainting occurs, stop taking the medicine. If dizzy, avoid driving or any activity/jobs requiring alertness. Use extra care during exercise or hot weather.

You may experience increased skin sensitivity to sunlight. Avoid too much sunlight and do not use a sunlamp.

- Dry cough, sore throat
- Unusual tiredness and/or weakness
- Chest pain
- Impotence
- Headache
- Palpitations
- Tingling of the skin
- Less or no urine being produced

If you notice any of the above or have other side effects, contact your physician or your pharmacist. If the condition persists or worsens, seek medical attention.

Ingredients: Active ingredients: Each blue tablet Prinzide 10/12.5 contains 10 mg of lisinopril and 12.5 mg of hydrochlorothiazide. Each yellow tablet of Prinzide 20/12.5 contains 20 mg of lisinopril and 12.5 mg of hydrochlorothiazide. Each orange tablet of Prinzide 20/25 mg contains 20 mg of lisinopril and 25 mg of hydrochlorothiazide.

Nonmedicinal ingredients: calcium phosphate, cornstarch, magnesium stearate and mannitol. Prinzide 10 mg/12.5 mg tablets contain indigotine on aluminum substrate. Prinzide 20 mg/12.5 mg tablets and Prinzide 20 mg/25 mg tablets contain iron oxide.

☐ PROBETA® Pr

Allergan

Levobunolol HCl—Dipivefrin HCl

Glaucoma Therapy

Information for the Patient: C Cap—A Simple Reminder: You can help preserve your vision by taking your glaucoma medications exactly as you doctor tells you. But sometimes it is hard to remember when to take your eye drops. That's why your doctor has prescribed this medicine. It has a special cap called the C Cap. It was designed to help you adhere to your medication schedule by making it easy to keep track of how many times you use your medicine each day.

For Allergan's various glaucoma products there are several different versions of the C Cap. Your doctor has chosen the one that corresponds to the number of times you use your medicine each day.

Here's How to Use the C CAP:

1. The very first time you are ready to take your medicine and at the beginning of each day, look in the window of the cap to make sure the number "1" appears. If another number is showing, turn the cap clockwise until it's in the correct position. You will notice that the cap "clicks" as it changes stations.
2. Next, remove the C Cap and apply your medication as directed by your doctor.
3. Replace the cap by turning clockwise until it is snug. Then keep twisting slowly until you hear the "click". The number "2" will appear in the window. This means: You are supposed to take your drops more than once a day. The number "2" reminds you that the next time you take your drops will be the second time for that day.
4. When it is time for your next drop, unscrew the cap and apply your medication.
5. Replace the cap and click to the next station.

Note: If you forget to apply your medication at your normal time, simply apply it when you remember. **Don't try to catch on missed drops by applying more than one dose at a time.**

Remember: Each time you replace the cap, you should keep turning until you hear the click.

☐ PROCAN™ SR Pr

Parke-Davis

Procainamide HCl

Antiarrhythmic Agent

Information for the Patient: Practitioners should give the following information and instructions to patients receiving Procan SR:

1. Do not crush or chew these tablets. Swallow them whole.
2. Take this medicine exactly as directed by your doctor. Do not stop taking this medicine without first checking with your doctor.
3. If you miss a dose and remember within 1 hour or so, take it as soon as possible. Then go back to your regular dosing schedule. Do

not take double doses. If you have any questions about this, check with your doctor.

4. Report to your doctor any flu-type symptoms such as malaise and aches, as well as any soreness of the mouth, throat or gums, unexplained fever, skin rash, unusual bleeding or bruising, symptoms that resemble arthritis or symptoms of an upper respiratory tract infection.
5. Do not be concerned if you occasionally notice in your stool something that looks like a tablet. In Procan SR tablets, the drug is held in a wax core that has been especially designed to slowly release the drug for your body to absorb. When this process is completed, the empty, non-absorbable wax core which looks nearly unchanged is eliminated from your body.
6. Keep container tightly closed and store in a cool, dry place.

☐ PROGRAF® ℞

Fujisawa

Tacrolimus

Immunosuppressant

Information for the Patient: You have received a prescription for Prograf capsules from your doctor. As you know, you need special medication, every day, to help keep your transplanted organ healthy and functioning. Prograf is a drug that is used to help your body accept your transplanted organ.

It is very important that you read the following information carefully. Your doctor, nurse, and pharmacist have explained Prograf to you, and this information will answer some of the questions you may have about your new medication. The success of treatment with this drug depends on how carefully you follow your doctor's instructions. As you review this information, write down any questions that you may have. Then, talk with your doctor, nurse or pharmacist. This information should not replace your doctor's or pharmacist's advice.

Pregnancy should be avoided while taking Prograf because its effect on pregnancy or on an unborn baby is not known. Breast-feeding is not recommended while taking Prograf. It is important to notify your doctor right away if you become pregnant or father a child while taking Prograf.

What is Prograf? Prograf is the brand name for tacrolimus. You may have also heard it called FK506. Prograf is an immunosuppressant that is used concomitantly with adrenal corticosteroids to prevent or treat rejection of your transplanted organ.

How Does Prograf Work? Your body's immune system is your defence system. Immunity is the way your body protects itself from infections and other foreign material. When you receive a transplant, your immune system recognizes the transplanted organ as foreign and will try to reject it. Prograf is an anti-rejection drug that helps your body accept your transplanted organ(s).

What Should I Tell My Doctor Before I Take Prograf? Before you take Prograf, be sure you have told your doctor the following:

- If you have taken Prograf, FK506 or tacrolimus before and had a bad, unusual or allergic reaction;
- If you are pregnant, plan to become pregnant, or are breast-feeding a baby;
- About all other medicines or treatments you use, including any products you buy off the shelf such as over-the-counter drugs and herbal or home remedies;
- About all other health conditions you have now, or have had in the past.

What Does Prograf Look Like? Prograf is available in 1 milligram capsules and 5 milligram capsules. The 1 milligram capsules are white and oblong, with "1 mg" written on the capsule top. The 5 milligram capsules are grayish/red, oblong, and have "5 mg" written on the capsule top.

How Much Prograf Should I Take? Your doctor will give you specific instructions about how much Prograf you should take each day. Your doctor has decided the dose you should take based on your medical condition and response to the drug. **It is very important to take the exact amount of Prograf that your doctor has told you.** Blood tests are one of the ways your doctor decides how much Prograf you need. Based on these tests and your response to Prograf, your doctor may change your dose from time to time. **Do not change your dose on your own.**

Are There Any Special Concerns For Women? Prograf may cause fetal abnormalities and malformations. For this reason it is recommended that you do not take Prograf if you are, or become pregnant. You must use a reliable method of birth control before, during your treatment and for 6 weeks after stopping your treatment with Prograf. **Should you become pregnant during the time you are taking Prograf, you should inform your doctor at once.** However, never stop taking Prograf without first consulting your doctor.

When and How Do I Take Prograf? Your doctor will tell you when and how many times a day to take Prograf.

- Try to take your doses at the same time every day. This will help keep the same amount of Prograf in your body so it can continue to protect your transplanted organ.
- Space your doses of Prograf as evenly as you can throughout the day. For example, if you take Prograf twice a day, doses should be 12 hours apart. Ask your transplant nurse or pharmacist about a dosing schedule that best fits your lifestyle.
- Prograf may be taken with or without food. But it is best to be consistent. Once you decide when you are going to take it in relation to food, do it the same way each time.
- Swallow the capsules whole. Do not cut, crush, or chew the Prograf capsule.

What Happens if I Miss a Dose of Prograf? Missing even a few doses of Prograf may cause your body to reject your transplanted organ. That is why it is very important to take each dose as your doctor prescribed. If you have trouble remembering doses, or if you are uncertain about how to take them, talk to your doctor, nurse or pharmacist and be sure to discuss any concerns you have about taking Prograf as prescribed.

If you miss a dose of Prograf do not try to catch up on your own; instead call your doctor or pharmacist right away for advice. It is also a good idea to ask your doctor ahead of time what to do about missed doses.

Never allow your medication to run out between refills and be sure to take enough medication with you when you will be away from home for any extended period of time.

Are There Any Special Do's and Don'ts About Taking Prograf?

- Prograf is often given with other medications. Make sure you know if you are to stop, or continue, other immunosuppressive drugs you had been taking.
- Be sure to keep all appointments at your transplant clinic. This is very important to help ensure that you receive the maximum benefit from your medications.
- It is not known what effect Prograf has on the effectiveness of vaccinations and on the risk of getting an illness from vaccination with a live vaccine. Do discuss this with your doctor before you get any vaccinations or immunizations.
- Be sure that you are taking the correct dose of Prograf prescribed by your doctor.
- Tell all health professionals you see that you are taking Prograf. It is also a good idea to wear a Medic-Alert bracelet.
- Prograf should not be taken with grapefruit or grapefruit juice.

What are the Side Effects of Prograf? Like other medicines, Prograf may cause side effects in some people. If you think that you are having side effects, talk to your doctor right away. **DO NOT stop taking Prograf on your own.**

- Because Prograf decreases the function of your immune system you may be more likely to get an infection. Tell your doctor right away about any cold or flu-like symptoms (such as fever or sore throat), any mouth sores or burning discomfort with urination.
- Be sure to tell your doctor right away if you notice any of these symptoms, and especially if they continue, bother you in any way, or seem to increase in intensity: diarrhea, nausea, constipation, vomiting, loss of appetite, stomach pain; headache, tremors, convulsions, tiredness or fatigue, difficulty sleeping, nightmares; urinary tract infection, increased potassium in your body; decreased or increased urine volumes, kidney or liver problems; diabetes/increased blood sugar, swelling or tingling in your hands and feet; heart dysfunction, abnormal heart rhythms, chest pain, high blood pressure; fever, back pain; changes in mood or emotions; difficulty in breathing.
- Immunosuppressive drugs including Prograf may also increase your chances of developing certain types of cancer. The following are possible warning signs of cancer and should be reported to your doctor as soon as possible.
  –any sore that does not heal;
  –unusual bleeding or discharge;

Prograf (cont'd)

–the appearance of a lump or thickened areas in your breast or anywhere else on your body;
–unexplained stomach upset or any trouble with swallowing;
–any noticeable change in a wart or a mole;
–a nagging cough or hoarseness;
–night sweats;
–persistent and severe headaches;
–swollen lymph nodes;
–a change in your bowel or bladder habits.

It is important to regularly tell your doctor how you are feeling and if you have developed any new symptoms while taking Prograf.

How Should I Store or Keep Prograf?

- Keep Prograf out of reach and away from children. A child who accidentally takes Prograf may be seriously harmed. All drugs should be kept in a locked drawer or cupboard if there are children who may accidentally take your drugs. Should anyone accidentally or mistakenly take Prograf, contact your physician immediately.
- Always store Prograf at room temperature (15 to 30°C) in the container or package that was dispensed by your pharmacist.

What Other Medications Can I Take With Prograf? Tell your doctor, dentist, nurse, and pharmacist about all the drugs that you are taking. Other drugs may affect the way Prograf works for you and it is important that your doctor and pharmacist know all the medications you are taking. Do not take any other drugs without asking your doctor first. This includes anything you can buy off the shelf such as over-the-counter drugs and herbal or home remedies.

Who Can I Call With Questions About Prograf? If you have additional questions or would like to talk with someone to explain something you are worried about, ask your doctor, nurse, pharmacist, or other members of the Transplant Team. They are your best resource for guidance and information.

□ PROMETRIUM™ Ⓟ

Schering

Progesterone

Progestin

Information for the Patient: Before you start to use Prometrium, please read this page carefully. If you have any questions or concerns, consult your doctor or pharmacist.

What's in Prometrium: Active substance: progesterone; 100 mg per capsule. Other substances: arachis (peanut) oil, gelatin, glycerin, lecithin. The coloring agent is titanium dioxide.

General Information about Prometrium and How It Works: The active substance in Prometrium capsules is progesterone, a natural female hormone. In healthy women of childbearing age, progesterone is produced by the ovaries each month during the second part of the menstrual cycle. Progesterone plays a role in the monthly shedding of the inner lining of the uterus (endometrium) and the menstrual bleeding that follows.

Progesterone has a strong influence on the inner lining of the uterus and is used with estrogen therapy during and after menopause. The purpose of using progesterone is to protect the inner lining of your uterus from overgrowth caused by estrogen therapy.

How and When to Take Prometrium: Take Prometrium only as directed by your doctor or pharmacist.

Hormone Replacement Therapy for Menopause: The recommended dose is 2 capsules (200 mg) of Prometrium per day for the last 14 days of estrogen treatment each cycle **or** 3 capsules per day (300 mg) for the last 12 to 14 days of estrogen treatment each cycle. If you are being treated with 2 capsules (200 mg) a day you should take them both at bedtime. If you are being treated with 3 capules (300 mg) a day, you should split the daily dose in two parts by taking 1 capsule in the morning and 2 at bedtime.

A few days after completing a Prometrium course of 3 capsules daily, the inner lining of the uterus will usually shed. This is accompanied by a vaginal bleeding (resembling a normal monthly period). With a dosage of 2 capsules daily, many women will **not** have such vaginal bleeding, although the uterus **will** also be protected against overgrowth.

What to Do if You Miss a Dose: If you are being treated with 2 capsules a day (total dose at bedtime) and you forget to take this dose, you should take 1 capsule the following morning and continue taking the rest of the capsules as prescribed. If you are being treated with 3 capsules a day and you forget to take a morning or evening dose, you should not take the missed dose.

When Not to Use Prometrium: Do not use Prometrium if:

- you have a severe liver disease such as jaundice (yellowing of the eyes or skin), inflammation of the liver (hepatitis), tumors of the liver, Rotor syndrome or Dubin-Johnson syndrome (or if the liver has not recovered yet from such a disease);
- you have unexpected vaginal bleeding;
- you have ever had one of the following disorders during pregnancy or previous use of hormones: severe itching, jaundice, skin rash (herpes gestationis), porphyria (a metabolic disease of the liver), or deterioration of hearing (otosclerosis);
- you have cerebral apoplexy or thrombophlebitis;
- you suspect you have an undiagnosed breast disease or tumor;
- **you are allergic to peanuts.**

Precautions and Possible Problems: Extra supervision by your doctor may be necessary in some cases. Therefore, tell your doctor if you have ever had:

- liver disease, such as jaundice;
- chloasma (brown, blotchy spots on exposed skin often appearing during pregnancy);
- heart or blood vessel disease (excluding varicose veins), although there are no indications of increased risk with Prometrium;
- breast disease, abnormal mammogram of previous breast surgery.

Ask your doctor to teach you how to correctly do self-examination of your breasts. Regular breast examination by a health professional and monthly self-examination is recommended for all women.

If you are pregnant or breast-feeding, or think you may be pregnant: do not use Prometrium.

Prometrium may cause some people to feel dizzy or sleepy, 1 to 4 hours after ingestion of the capsules. Therefore, be careful with driving and other jobs that require alertness.

What to Do if Someone Accidentally Takes too Much Prometrium: If someone has taken several capsules at once, you should consult a doctor. Symptoms that may arise are nausea, vomiting, sleepiness and dizziness.

Side Effects Prometrium May Have: Depending on the dosage of Prometrium and the sensitivity of the patient, the following side effects are possible: vaginal bleeding or spotting (minor vaginal bleeding) in between the normal periods (mainly during the first 2 months); irregular periods; breast pain; nausea; dizziness; sleepiness; fatigue; headaches (migraine).

Side effects which have been observed with progesterone-like substances and which may possibly occur during Prometrium treatment are: gastrointestinal disturbances (other than nausea); brown, blotchy spots on exposed skin (chloasma); skin rash, itching; jaundice (yellowing of the eyes or skin); depressive mood; increase or decrease in sexual desire.

You should consult your doctor if you feel any side effects to be serious or troublesome, or if they continue to bother you.

During your first 2 to 4 months of hormone replacement therapy, you may experience minor unscheduled vaginal bleeding (at times other than when you would expect a normal period). This is a normal response of your body as it adjusts to the return of estrogen and progesterone to the levels that were seen before menopause. Should unscheduled vaginal bleeding persist, you should consult your doctor.

How to Store This Medicine: Keep the capsules in the original box out of the reach of children. The storage conditions are given on the box. The date the capsules should be used by is printed on the strip after the term "Exp." (expiry date).

General Things to Remember:

1. This medication has been prescribed only for your current medical condition. Do not use it for other medical conditions.
2. Do not allow other people to use your medications and do not use medications meant for other people.
3. Tell any doctor treating you what medications you are taking. Always carry a medical information card stating which medications you are using. This can be very important in case you are involved in an accident.
4. Return unused medications to the pharmacy for disposal.
5. Make sure that other people you live with or who look after you read this information.

☐ PROPECIA® 🄿

MSD

Finasteride

Type II 5 Alpha-reductase Inhibitor

Information for the Patient: Propecia is for use by men only.

What is Propecia? Propecia is a tan-colored, 8-sided, film-coated tablet. It contains 1 mg of finasteride as the active ingredient.

Propecia blocks an important enzyme (Type II 5-alpha reductase) involved in the regulation of the hair follicle.

Please read this leaflet before you start taking Propecia. Also, read it each time you renew your prescription, just in case anything has changed. Remember, this leaflet does not take the place of careful discussions with your physician. You and your physician should discuss Propecia when you start taking your medication.

Why has your physician prescribed Propecia? Your physician has prescribed Propecia because you have male pattern hair loss (also known as androgenetic alopecia).

Note: Propecia is **not** for use by women or children.

How does scalp hair grow? On average, your hair grows about 1 cm each month. Hairs grow from hair follicles, which are located beneath the skin.

A single scalp hair grows continuously for 2 to 4 years (growth phase) and then stops growing for 2 to 4 months (rest phase). After that time the hair falls out. In its place a new healthy hair begins to grow, and the cycle is repeated. The hairs on your scalp are always in different stages of this cycle so it is normal to lose scalp hair every day.

What is male pattern hair loss? Male pattern hair loss is a common condition in which men experience thinning of the hair on the scalp. Often, this results in a receding hairline and/or balding on the top of the head. This condition is thought to be caused by a combination of heredity and a particular hormone, DHT (dihydrotestosterone).

DHT contributes to shortening of the growth phase and thinning of the hair. This process leads to male pattern hair loss. These changes typically start to occur in some men in their 20s and become more common with age. Once hair loss has occurred over a long period of time, the hair may be permanently lost.

How does Propecia work? Propecia lowers the levels of DHT in the scalp, a major cause of male pattern hair loss.

What should I know before taking Propecia: In whom is Propecia expected to work? Men with mild to moderate, but not complete, hair loss can expect to benefit from the use of Propecia.

In most men, Propecia prevented further hair loss during 2 years of use. Moreover, for the majority of men, Propecia increased the number of scalp hairs, helping to fill in thin or balding areas of the scalp. Although results will vary, in general, you will not be able to grow back all of the hair you have lost.

Who should not take Propecia? Propecia should not be taken by women or children.

Women who are or may potentially be pregnant must not use Propecia (see Pregnancy).

Do not take Propecia if you think you are allergic to any of its ingredients.

What should I tell my physician before taking Propecia? Tell your physician about any medical problems you have or have had and about any allergies.

Pregnancy: Propecia is for the treatment of male pattern hair loss in men only. Women who are or may potentially be pregnant must not use Propecia. They should also not handle crushed or broken tablets of Propecia. If the active ingredient in Propecia is absorbed after oral use or through the skin by a woman who is pregnant with a male baby, it may cause the male baby to be born with abnormalities of the sex organs. If a woman who is pregnant comes into contact with the active ingredient in Propecia, a physician should be consulted. Propecia tablets are coated and will prevent contact with the active ingredient during normal handling, provided that the tablets are not broken or crushed.

If you have questions, ask your physician.

Can I take Propecia with other medications? Propecia usually does not interfere with other medicines. However, you should always tell your physician about all medicines you are taking or plan to take, including those obtained without prescription.

Can I continue my current hair care routine? There should be no need to change your current hair care routine (for example, shampooing or haircuts).

Can I drive or operate machinery while using Propecia? Propecia should not affect your ability to drive or operate machinery.

How should I take Propecia? Take 1 tablet of Propecia every day, with or without food. Follow your physician's advice.

- **Can I use Propecia more than once a day?** Propecia will not work faster or better if you take it more than once a day. You should only take one tablet of Propecia each day.
- **How long do I need to use Propecia?** It is important to take Propecia for as long as your physician prescribes it. Propecia can only work over the long term if you continue taking it.
- **When can I expect to see results from using Propecia?** Male pattern hair loss is a condition that develops over a long period of time. On average, healthy hair grows only about 1 cm each month. Therefore, it will take time to see any effect. In general, daily use for three months or more may be necessary before you notice that hair growth is increased or further hair loss is prevented.
- **What happens if I stop using Propecia?** Continued use of Propecia is recommended to obtain maximum benefit. If you stop taking Propecia, you will likely lose the hair you have gained within 12 months of stopping treatment.

What should I do in case of an overdose? If you take too many tablets, contact your physician promptly.

What should I do if I miss a dose? Try to take Propecia as your physician has prescribed. However, if you miss a dose, do not take an extra one. Just take the next tablet as usual.

What undesirable effects may Propecia have? Like any medicine, Propecia may have unintended or undesirable effects, so-called side effects. These are uncommon and do not affect most men.

Only a small number of men may experience less desire to have sex and/or difficulty in achieving an erection. An even smaller number may have a decrease in the amount of semen released during sex (this does not appear to interfere with normal sexual function). In clinical studies, these side effects disappeared in men who stopped taking Propecia and in most men (58%) who continued treatment.

Tell your physician or pharmacist promptly about these or any other unusual symptoms.

Propecia can affect a blood test called PSA (prostate-specific antigen) used for the screening of prostate cancer. If you have a PSA test done, you should tell your physician that you are taking Propecia.

- **Does the use of Propecia affect the hair on other parts of my body?** In clinical studies, Propecia did not affect hair on other parts of the body.

How can I learn more about Propecia and male pattern hair loss? If after reading this leaflet you still have any questions or are not sure about anything, ask your physician or pharmacist, who have more detailed information about Propecia and male pattern hair loss.

This medicine is prescribed for your specific medical condition and for your own use. Use only as specifically directed and do not give to other people.

Keep all medicines out of the reach of children.

Store Propecia in a dry place at room temperature (15 to 30°C) and protect from moisture. Keep blister in the outer carton until all tablets are used.

Nonmedicinal ingredients: docusate sodium, hydroxypropylcellulose, lactose monohydrate, magnesium stearate, methylhydroxypropylcellulose, microcrystalline cellulose, pregelatinized starch, sodium starch glycolate, talc, titanium dioxide, red ferric oxide and yellow ferric oxide.

☐ PROSCAR® 🄿

MSD

Finasteride

5 Alpha-reductase Inhibitor

Information for the Patient: Proscar is for use by men only.

Full prescribing information is available to the physician and pharmacist.

Each tablet of Proscar contains 5 mg of finasteride. It is available only with your physician's prescription for the treatment of benign prostatic hyperplasia.

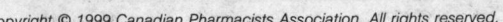

Please read this leaflet before you start taking Proscar. Also, read it each time you renew your prescription, just in case anything has changed. Remember, this leaflet does not take the place of careful

Proscar (cont'd)

discussions with your doctor. You and your doctor should discuss Proscar when you start taking your medication and at regular checkups.

Why your doctor has prescribed Proscar? Your doctor has prescribed Proscar because you have a medical condition called benign prostatic hyperplasia or BPH. This occurs only in men.

What is BPH? BPH is an enlargement of the prostate gland. After age 50, most men develop enlarged prostates. The prostate is located below the bladder. As the prostate enlarges, it may slowly restrict the flow of urine. This can lead to symptoms such as:

- weak or interrupted urinary stream
- feeling that you cannot empty your bladder completely
- feeling of delay or hesitation when you start to urinate
- need to urinate often, especially at night
- feeling that you must urinate right away

Treatment Options for BPH: There are 3 main treatment options for BPH:

- **Program of monitoring or "Watchful Waiting".** If a man has an enlarged prostate gland and no symptoms or if his symptoms do not bother him, he and his doctor may decide on a program of monitoring which would include regular checkups, instead of medication or surgery.
- **Medication.** Your doctor may prescribe Proscar for BPH. See "What Proscar does" below.
- **Surgery.** Some patients may need surgery. Your doctor can describe several different surgical procedures for BPH. Which procedure is best depends on your symptoms and medical condition.

What Proscar Does: Proscar lowers levels of a key hormone called DHT (dihydrotestosterone), which is a major cause of prostate growth. Lowering leads to shrinkage of the enlarged prostate gland in most men. This can lead to gradual improvement in urine flow and symptoms over the next several months. However, not all patients respond and since each case of BPH is different, you should know that:

- Prior to treatment with Proscar, you should have a thorough urological evaluation to determine the severity of your condition, and to exclude the need for immediate surgery or the possibility of carcinoma of the prostate.
- Even though the prostate shrinks, you may **not** see an improvement in urine flow or symptoms.
- You may need to take Proscar for 6 months or more to see whether it helps you. However, 85 to 90% of those patients who do respond to Proscar, do so during the first 12 months of treatment. Your physician will help you decide how long you should remain on this medication.
- Even though you take Proscar and it may help you, it is not known whether Proscar reduces the need for surgery.

What you Need to Know While Taking Proscar:

- **You must see your doctor regularly.** While taking Proscar, you must have regular checkups. Follow your doctor's advice about when to have these checkups.
- **About side effects.** Like all prescription drugs, Proscar may cause side effects. Side effects due to Proscar may include impotence (or inability to have an erection) and less desire for sex. Each of these side effects occurred in less than 4% of patients in clinical studies. In some cases side effects went away while the patient continued to take Proscar.
- Some men taking Proscar may have a decrease in the amount of semen released during sex. This decrease does not appear to interfere with normal sexual function.
- Rarely, some men have reported swelling and/or tenderness or allergic reactions such as lip swelling and rash.
- You should discuss side effects with your doctor before taking Proscar and anytime you think you are having a side effect.
- **Checking for prostate cancer.** Your doctor has prescribed Proscar for symptomatic BPH and not for cancer—but a man can have BPH and prostate cancer at the same time. Doctors usually recommend that men be checked for prostate cancer once a year when they turn 50 (or 40 if a family member has had prostate cancer). These checks should continue while you take Proscar. Proscar is not a treatment for prostate cancer.
- **About Prostate Specific Antigen (PSA).** Your doctor may have done a blood test called PSA. Proscar can alter PSA values. For more information, talk to your doctor.

A Warning about Proscar and Pregnancy: Proscar is for use by **men** only.

Proscar is generally well tolerated in men.

Women must not use Proscar, nor handle broken tablets of Proscar, when they are pregnant or could potentially become pregnant. If the active ingredient in Proscar is absorbed after oral use or through the skin by a woman who is pregnant with a male baby, it may cause the male baby to be born with abnormalities of the genitalia. Whole tablets are coated to prevent contact with the active ingredient during normal handling. If this coating is broken, the tablets should not be handled by women who are pregnant or who could become pregnant.

If a woman who is pregnant comes into contact with the active ingredient in Proscar, a doctor should be consulted.

How to Take Proscar: Follow your doctor's advice about how to take Proscar. You must take it every day. You may take it with or between meals. To avoid forgetting to take Proscar, it may be helpful to take it at the same time every day.

Do not share Proscar with anyone else; it was prescribed only for you.

Notify your physician about any illness which may develop during your treatment with Proscar and about any new prescription or nonprescription medication you may take. If you require medical help for other reasons, inform the attending physician that you are taking Proscar.

This medicine is prescribed for your specific medical problem and for your own use. Use only as specifically directed and do not give to other people.

Keep all medicines out of the reach of children. For more information about Proscar and BPH, talk with your physician or your pharmacist.

Store at room temperature (15 to 30°C) and protect from light.

Nonmedicinal ingredients: cellulose and cellulose derivatives, docusate sodium, FD&C Blue 2/aluminum lake, lactose, magnesium stearate, sodium starch glycolate, starch, talc, titanium dioxide and yellow ferric oxide.

□ PROTROPIN® Ⓟ

Roche

Somatrem

Growth Hormone

Information for the Patient: Do not mix (reconstitute) the drug, or inject it, until your physician or nurse has thoroughly trained you in the proper techniques.

Reconstituting means adding a liquid (diluent) to a dry powder. In this case, Protropin **must** be mixed with Bacteriostatic Water for Injection, USP (benzyl alcohol preserved), the sterile diluent provided, before it can be injected.

Use the sterile technique as instructed by your physician or nurse. Dispose of syringes and needles properly after each use, out of the reach of children. See item 6 of the "Giving the Medication" instructions below for instructions on the proper disposal of used needles and syringes.

Reconstituting Protropin Vial (see package insert for illustrations): Reconstitute the Protropin vials **only** with Bacteriostatic Water for Injection, USP, **preserved with benzyl alcohol** provided in the carton. Do not use other solutions for reconstitution unless instructed to do so by your physician. Unused contents of a reconstituted Protropin vial should **not** be used to reconstitute a new Protropin vial.

Your physician or nurse will tell you what size syringe and needle to use for mixing and how much diluent to add to the Protropin vial.

1. Wash your hands thoroughly with soap and water before preparing the medication. This helps prevent infection.
2. Remove the protective plastic cap from the top of both the diluent and Protropin vials. Clean the rubber stopper on the top of each vial with an alcohol swab. After cleaning, do not touch the top of the vials.
3. Fill the syringe with air by pulling the plunger to the level indicated by your physician.
4. Remove the plastic needle guard and set it aside. Insert the needle into the diluent vial and inject the air into the vial.
5. Turn the diluent vial upside down with the syringe needle still in it and hold the vial in one hand. Make sure the tip of the needle is in the diluent. Withdraw the diluent to be added to the Protropin vial by pulling the plunger to the exact amount your physician has told you. Check to make sure you have the correct amount of diluent in the syringe. Withdraw the needle from the diluent vial and replace the plastic needle guard.

6. Before adding the diluent to the Protropin vial, check to make sure you have withdrawn the correct amount. To prepare the Protropin solution, remove the plastic needle guard and insert the needle into the cleaned vial top of the Protropin vial. Gently place the needle tip against the glass wall of the vial. Slowly inject the diluent, aiming the stream of water at the glass wall of the vial. **Do not aim the stream at the white powder** at the bottom of the vial. Withdraw the needle and replace the plastic needle guard. See item 6 of the ''Giving The Medication'' instructions below for instructions on the proper disposal of used needles and syringes.
7. Swirl the Protropin vial with a gentle rotary motion until the contents are completely dissolved. Never shake the Protropin vial after it has been reconstituted. Because Protropin growth hormone is a protein, shaking can result in a cloudy solution. Immediately after reconstitution, the solution should be clear and should not have any solid particles floating on the surface. If you notice lumps of powder that float or stick to the sides of the vial, continue to gently swirl the solution until all of the powder has dissolved. If air bubbles form, wait until they have risen to the top of the solution and have disappeared before proceeding further. Do not inject the Protropin solution if it is cloudy or hazy, but return the Protropin vial to your pharmacist or prescribing physician.
8. Write the date on both the diluent vial and the reconstituted Protropin vial. This way you will know the date you first opened and used the diluent vial, and when the Protropin vial was reconstituted. A diluent vial that you have opened and removed diluent from can be used for 14 days. The reconstituted vial of Protropin cannot be used after 14 days and should be returned to your physician or pharmacist. Store all vials in a clean, safe place in the refrigerator. **Do not freeze.**

Note: Unopened diluent and Protropin can be used until the expiration date (EXP.) printed on the vial labels.

Measuring the Dose: Before each use, check the expiration date printed on the vial label, the date of reconstitution, and ensure that the Protropin solution is clear. Occasionally, after refrigeration, you may notice that small colorless particles of protein are present in the Protropin solution. This not unusual for solutions containing proteins like Protropin and does not indicate any decrease in potency of this product. Allow the vial to come to room temperature and gently swirl. If the solution is cloudy or hazy, do not inject it, but return the vial of Protropin to your pharmacist or prescribing physician.

1. Wash your hands thoroughly with soap and water before preparing the dose. This helps prevent infection.
2. Check the date you wrote on the reconstituted Protropin vial to be sure it is not more than 14 days old.
3. Wipe the rubber stopper located on top of the Protropin vial with an alcohol swab. Fingers and hands should not touch the top of the vial.
4. Draw air into the syringe by pulling back on the plunger. The amount of air should be equal to the Protropin dose. Place your fingers on the tip of the plunger.
5. Remove and save the plastic needle guard. Slowly insert the needle straight through the center of the rubber stopper of the vial containing the Protropin solution.
6. Gently push the plunger to discharge the air into the vial.
7. Turn the vial upside down with the syringe needle still in it and hold the vial in one hand. Be sure the tip of the needle is in the Protropin solution. Using your other hand, slowly pull back on the plunger in a continuous motion until the correct amount of Protropin solution is in the syringe.
8. Remove the needle from the Protropin vial and replace the plastic needle guard until time of administration or injection. Be careful not to touch the needle with your fingers. The injection should be given as soon after filling the syringe as possible; do not store Protropin in the syringe.

Selecting the Injection Site: Your child's physician or nurse will teach you how to locate appropriate injection sites. It is very important that you rotate the site of an injection each time you give the medication. Even if your child develops a preference for one site—as many children do—you still should rotate the injection site.

The injection sites most often recommended for children are the upper arm, abdomen and thigh (see package insert for illustrations).

Giving the Medication (see package insert for illustrations): Your physician or nurse will provide you with hands-on training on how to give an injection. Needles and syringes should be used only once to ensure sterility of both the needle and the syringe. The following is a review of the steps involved in giving the medication:

1. Cleanse the injection site with an alcohol-saturated cotton ball or cotton swab.
2. Double check that the correct amount of Protropin solution is in the syringe. Remove the needle guard from the syringe filled with the proper dose of solution and hold the syringe the way you would hold a pencil.
3. Squeeze the skin between your thumb and index finger before and during the injection. Insert the needle into the skin at a 45 to 90° angle with a quick, firm motion. This hurts less than pushing the needle in slowly. Your physician or nurse will tell you the correct angle to use for your child.
4. Slowly (within a few seconds) inject the solution by gently pushing the plunger until the syringe is empty.
5. Withdraw the needle quickly, pulling it straight out, and apply pressure over the injection site with a dry gauze pad or cotton ball. A drop of blood may appear. Put a Band-Aid on the injection site if desired.
6. To prevent injury, safely dispose of all used needles and syringes after a single use as instructed by your physician or nurse by following these simple steps:
   - Place all used needles and syringes in a hard, plastic container with a screw-on cap, or a metal container with a plastic lid, such as a coffee can properly labeled as to content. If a metal container is used, cut a small hole in the plastic lid and tape the lid to the metal container. When the metal container is full, cover the hole with tape and throw it away. If a hard, plastic container is used, always screw the cap on tightly after each use. When the plastic container is full, tape around the cap and throw it away.
   - Do not use glass or clear, plastic containers, or any container that will be recycled or returned to a store.
   - Always store the container out of the reach of children.
   - Please check with your physician, nurse or pharmacist for other suggestions. There may be special provincial and local laws that they will discuss with you.
7. Occasionally a problem may develop at the injection site. If you notice any of the following signs or symptoms, contact your physician or nurse:
   - A lump or swelling that doesn't go away.
   - Bruising that doesn't go away.
   - Any signs of infection or inflammation at an injection site (pus, persistent redness surrounding skin that is hot to the touch, persistent pain after the injection).

Storage: Protropin **must** be refrigerated before reconstitution (powder form) and after reconstitution (liquid form).

Reconstituted Protropin cannot be used after 14 days and should be returned to your physician or pharmacist.

The unopened and opened vials of Bacteriostatic Water for Injection, USP (benzyl alcohol preserved) should also be refrigerated. The opened vials can only be used for 14 days.

Refrigerate at 2 to 8°C.

The Protropin vial, after reconstitution, and the vial of Bacteriostatic Water for Injection, USP (benzyl alcohol preserved) must not be frozen.

If you have any questions, contact your physician, nurse or pharmacist.

□ PULMICORT® NEBUAMP® 🄿

Astra

Budesonide

Glucocorticosteroid—Asthma Therapy

Information for the Patient: Important information you should know about Pulmicort Nebuamp (budesonide): Before using Pulmicort Nebuamp, read this leaflet carefully. It contains general points about Pulmicort Nebuamp and should add to more specific advice from your doctor or pharmacist.

Please keep this leaflet to refer to until you have used up all Pulmicort Nebuamp units in this package.

What is Pulmicort Nebuamp used for and how does it work? Pulmicort is the brand name for an inhaled drug called budesonide. It belongs to a group of medicines called corticosteroids which are used to reduce inflammation. Asthma is caused by inflammation in the airways. Pulmicort Nebuamp reduces and prevents this inflammation. In some cases,

Pulmicort Nebuamp (cont'd)

several weeks of regular use may be needed before the full effect is seen.

Pulmicort Nebuamp will not relieve an asthma attack that has already started. Many inhalers contain bronchodilators to provide rapid relief. If your doctor prescribed one of these, you should follow his or her directions when you have an acute attack of asthma.

What is in Pulmicort Nebuamp? Pulmicort Nebuamp contains budesonide as the active ingredient and comes in concentrations of either 0.125 mg/mL, 0.25 mg/mL or 0.5 mg/mL. Each unit contains 2 mL. This means that one unit of the 0.125 mg/mL strength contains 0.25 mg of active drug. One unit of the 0.25 mg/mL strength contains 0.5 mg of active drug. One unit of the 0.5 mg/mL strength contains 1.0 mg of active drug.

Most medicines contain more ingredients than just the active drug. Check with your doctor if you think you might be allergic to any of these items (listed in alphabetical order): budesonide, citric acid, disodium edetate, polysorbate 80, sodium chloride, sodium citrate.

What should I tell my doctor before taking Pulmicort Nebuamp? Tell your doctor:

- about **all** health problems you have now or have had in the past, especially if you have had lung tuberculosis or any other recent infection;
- about other medicines you take, including ones you can buy without a prescription;
- if you take, or have taken steroid medicines within the past several months;
- if you are pregnant, plan to become pregnant or are breast-feeding;
- if you are allergic to "nonmedicinal" substances like food products, preservatives, or dyes, which may be present in Pulmicort Nebuamp (see What Is In Pulmicort Nebuamp?).
- if you have ever had a bad, unusual or allergic reaction to any medicine containing "budesonide".

How do I take Pulmicort Nebuamp Properly? Pulmicort Nebuamp is for use in a nebulizer or respirator. **Do not use in an ultrasonic nebulizer.** Be sure you know how to use your nebulizer or respirator before you start this drug.

Nebulization should take place using a gas flow (oxygen or compressed air) of 6 to 10 L/minute. A suitable volume fill for most nebulizers is 2 to 4 mL.

It is important that you use Pulmicort Nebuamp daily as recommended by your doctor, even when you feel well. Do not take more doses than prescribed by your doctor. Using more can increase the chance of unwanted effects. **Contact your doctor right away if your asthma seems worse.**

Before use, check to make sure the strength on the label matches the strength your doctor prescribed.

Follow these directions for each dose of Pulmicort Nebuamp (see package insert for illustrations):

1. Remove 1 Pulmicort Nebuamp from a sheet of 5 units. Return the other units to the envelope.
2. Gently shake the unit.
3. Open by holding the unit upright and twisting off the top "wing".
4. Slowly squeeze the contents of the unit into the nebulizer cup. If you only need to use half the contents of a unit, add sterile saline to the cup as instructed by your doctor or pharmacist. Before you use the rest of the unit for the next dose, swirl it gently.
5. Connect one end of the cup to the face mask or mouthpiece, and the other end to the air pump.
6. Just before you start treatment, gently shake the contents of the cup again. Then start the treatment.
7. Breathe calmly and evenly until no more mist comes out (about 10 to 15 minutes).
8. Rinse your mouth and spit out as soon as you are done.
9. If you use a face mask, wash your face after treatment.

Cleaning: When you have finished, you have to clean the nebulizer. Wash the cup and the mouth piece or mask in warm water, using a mild detergent. Rinse well. Dry by connecting the nebulizer cup to the compressor or to the air inlet. See the manufacturer's instructions for complete details.

How much Pulmicort Nebuamp should I take? The dosage of Pulmicort Nebuamp is individual. Follow your doctor's directions carefully. They may differ from the information in this leaflet.

Suggested Doses Are:

Initially: Children (3 months to 12 years): 0.25 to 0.5 mg twice daily. Adults: Usually 1 to 2 mg twice daily.

Maintenance: After the desired effect has been obtained, your doctor can reduce your dose to the smallest amount necessary to control your asthma symptoms.

Dosage Table

	Volume of Pulmicort Nebuamp		
Dose (mg)	**0.125 mg/mL**	**0.25 mg/mL**	**0.5 mg/mL**
0.125 mg	1 mL* (½ unit)	—	—
0.25 mg	2 mL (1 unit)	1 mL* (½ unit)	—
0.5 mg	4 mL (2 units)	2 mL (1 unit)	—
0.75 mg		3 mL (1½ units)	—
1 mg			2 mL (1 unit)
1.5 mg	—	—	3 mL (1½ units)
2 mg	—	—	4 mL (2 units)

*This should be mixed with 0.9% saline to a volume of 2 mL.

What do I do if I miss a dose? If you miss a dose of Pulmicort Nebuamp, take it as soon as possible. Then go back to your regular schedule. If it is almost time for your next dose, skip the missed dose and take the next dose on time.

Never take a double dose of Pulmicort Nebuamp to make up for ones you missed. If you are still unsure, check with your doctor or pharmacist to see what you should do.

Do not stop treatment with Pulmicort Nebuamp abruptly. Treatment should be tapered off gradually.

What should I do in case of overdose? Telephone your doctor or go to your nearest hospital right away if you think that you or anyone else may have taken too much Pulmicort Nebuamp.

Are there any side effects? Like any medication, Pulmicort Nebuamp may cause side effects in some people.

The most common side effects are cough, throat irritation, and hoarseness. Other side effects that may occur are bad taste, headache, nausea, dryness of the throat, tiredness, thirst, and diarrhea. Skin irritation on the face has been reported in a few cases when a nebulizer with face mask has been used. This can be prevented by washing the face after use of the face mask, or applying a thin layer of vaseline on the face, before using the mask.

In rare cases skin reactions like rash, nervousness, restlessness, depression, behavioral disturbances and feeling of tightness of the airways may occur.

Medicines affect different people in different ways. Just because side effects have occurred in other patients does not mean you will get them. If any side effects bother you, please contact your doctor.

Do not stop taking Pulmicort Nebuamp on your own. Your doctor may want to slowly reduce your dose, especially if you have been using Pulmicort Nebuamp for a long time. Although rare, symptoms of steroid withdrawal (i.e., fatigue, muscle or joint aches) may occur if Pulmicort Nebuamp is stopped too quickly.

Where should I keep Pulmicort Nebuamp? Remember to **keep Pulmicort Nebuamp well out of the reach of children** when you are not using it.

Always keep unopened units in the foil envelope so they are well protected from light.

Do not use Pulmicort Nebuamp after the expiry date marked on the foil envelope and the outer carton.

- Record the date when the foil envelope is first opened. Do not use units from a foil envelope that has been opened for 3 months or more.
- If you are only required to use half the contents of a unit, the remainder must be used within 12 hours after the unit has been opened. If you do not use a full unit for each dose, protect the rest from light.

Store Pulmicort Nebuamp between 5 and 30°C, protected from light.

Important Note: This leaflet alerts you to some of the times you should call your doctor. Other situations which cannot be predicted may arise. Nothing about this leaflet should stop you from calling your doctor or pharmacist with any questions or concerns you have about using Pulmicort Nebuamp.

□ PULMICORT® TURBUHALER® ℞

Astra

Budesonide

Glucocorticosteroid for the Treatment of Bronchial Asthma

Information for the Patient: Important Information You Should Know About Pulmicort Turbuhaler: Before Using Pulmicort Turbuhaler, read this leaflet carefully. It contains general points about Pulmicort Turbuhaler and should add to more specific advice from your doctor or pharmacist.

Please keep this leaflet to refer to until you have used up all medication in Pulmicort Turbuhaler.

What is Pulmicort Turbuhaler Used For and How Does it Work? (See package insert for illustrations). Pulmicort is a brand name for a drug called budesonide. Pulmicort is an inhaled form of the drug budesonide. It belongs to a group of medicines called corticosteroids which are used to reduce inflammation. Asthma is caused by inflammation in the airways. Pulmicort Turbuhaler reduces and prevents this inflammation. In some cases, several weeks of regular use may be needed before the full effect is seen.

Turbuhaler is the brand name for a multiple dose, dry-powder inhaler. When you breathe in through the inhaler, your indrawn breath provides the necessary force to deliver the drug to your lungs.

Pulmicort Turbuhaler is not meant to relieve an asthma attack that has already started. Many inhalers contain bronchodilators to provide rapid relief. If your doctor prescribed one of these, you should follow his or her directions when you have an acute attack of asthma.

What is in Pulmicort Turbuhaler? Pulmicort Turbuhaler contains budesonide as the active ingredient and comes in concentrations of either 100 μg, 200 μg, or 400 μg per inhalation.

If you happen to shake the inhaler, the sound you hear is the drying agent built into the brown turning grip. This is not the medication and cannot be inhaled. Pulmicort Turbuhaler contains no other ingredients.

What Should I Tell my Doctor Before Taking Pulmicort Turbuhaler? Tell your doctor:

- about **all** health problems you have now or have had in the past, especially if you have had lung tuberculosis or any other recent infection;
- about other medicines you take, including ones you can buy without a prescription;
- if you take, or have taken steroid medicines within the past several months;
- if you have ever had a bad, unusual or allergic reaction to "budesonide";
- if you are pregnant, plan to become pregnant or are breast-feeding.

How Do I Take Pulmicort Turbuhaler Properly? It is important that you use Pulmicort Turbuhaler daily at the intervals recommended by your doctor. Do not stop or change dosage without asking your doctor.

Note: You may not taste or feel any medication when inhaling from Pulmicort Turbuhaler. This is common.

If you follow the instructions below, you will receive the medication (see package insert for illustrations):

1. Unscrew the cover and lift it off.
2. Load a dose by holding the inhaler upright. Turn the brown grip as far as it will go in one direction and then turn it back to the original position. The "click" you heard means that the inhaler is ready to use.
3. Breathe out. Note: Never breathe out through the mouthpiece.
4. Put the mouthpiece between your teeth and close your lips around the mouthpiece. Do **not** chew or bite down hard on the mouthpiece. Inhale forcefully and deeply through your mouth.
5. Remove the inhaler from your mouth and try to hold your breath for 10 seconds.
6. Always replace the cover properly after use.
7. Rinse your mouth out with water.

If you accidentally drop, shake or breathe out into Pulmicort Turbuhaler after it is loaded, you will lose your dose. If this happens, you should load a new dose and inhale it.

Cleaning: Clean the outside of the mouthpiece once a week with a **dry** tissue. **Never** use water or any other fluid. If fluid enters the inhaler it may not work properly.

How Do I Know When Pulmicort Turbuhaler is Empty? (See package insert for illustrations). Pulmicort Turbuhaler has a dose indicator. When a red mark first appears in the little window underneath the mouthpiece, there are approximately **20** doses left. Now is the time to obtain your next inhaler.

When the red mark reaches the bottom of the window, Pulmicort Turbuhaler is **empty.** If you shake the inhaler when it is empty, you will still be able to hear the sound of the drying agent. Pulmicort Turbuhaler cannot be re-filled with drug and should be discarded.

How Much Pulmicort Turbuhaler Should I Take? The dosage of Pulmicort Turbuhaler is individual.

Follow your doctor's directions carefully. They may differ from the information in this leaflet.

Important: Do not exceed the dose prescribed by your doctor. If difficulty in breathing persists, contact your doctor.

Do not stop taking Pulmicort Turbuhaler on your own. Your doctor may want to slowly reduce your dose, especially if you have been using Pulmicort Turbuhaler for a long time.

Suggested **starting doses** are:

Adults and Children 12 years of age and older: 400 to 2 400 μg daily, divided into 2 to 4 administrations.

Children 6 to 12 years old: 200 to 400 μg daily, divided into 2 administrations.

Maintenance Dose: Use the lowest dose necessary to control symptoms.

Adults and Children 12 years of age and older: 200 to 400 μg daily, divided into 2 administrations.

Children 6 to 12 years old: Use the lowest dose necessary to control symptoms.

In adults who require 400 μg daily, Pulmicort Turbuhaler may be taken once daily, either in the morning or evening.

What Do I Do if I Miss a Dose? If you miss a dose of Pulmicort Turbuhaler and remember within 6 hours, you should take your usual dose as soon as possible. Then go back to your regular schedule. If it is more than 6 hours when you remember, do not take the missed dose. Just take the next dose on time.

Never take a double dose of Pulmicort Turbuhaler to make up for missed doses. If you are still unsure, check with your doctor or pharmacist to see what you should do.

You may notice that your symptoms improve after the first dose of Pulmicort Turbuhaler. However, several weeks may pass before the full effect is achieved. Don't forget to take it even when you feel well.

Treatment with Pulmicort Turbuhaler should not be stopped abruptly, but tapered off gradually. Follow your doctor's directions.

If you have been prescribed Pulmicort Turbuhaler and are still using "cortisone" tablets, your doctor may gradually (over a period of weeks or months) reduce your dose of tablets. You may even be able to eventually stop using the tablets.

Note: If your medication is changed from "cortisone" tablets to Pulmicort Turbuhaler, you may temporarily regain symptoms which may have bothered you earlier, e.g., runny nose, rash, pain in muscle and joints. If any of these symptoms bother you, or if you get symptoms such as headache, tiredness, nausea or vomiting, please contact your doctor.

What Should I Do in Case of Overdose? Telephone your doctor or go to your nearest hospital right away if you think that you or anyone else may have taken too much Pulmicort Turbuhaler.

Are There Any Side Effects? Like any medication, Pulmicort Turbuhaler may cause side effects in some people.

The most common side effects are cough, throat irritation, and hoarseness. Other side effects include bad taste, headache, nausea, and dryness of the throat. There have been occasional reports of tiredness, thirst, and diarrhea.

Occasionally, throat or mouth infections may occur. Rare side effects include skin reactions like rash, and increase in chest tightness, nervousness, restlessness, depression, and behavioral disturbances in children. These may not be caused by Pulmicort Turbuhaler in your case, but only a doctor can tell this.

Medicines affect different people in different ways. Just because side effects have occurred in other patients does not mean you will get them. If any side effects bother you, please contact your doctor.

Where Should I Keep Pulmicort Turbuhaler? Remember to **keep Pulmicort Turbuhaler out of the reach of children** when you are not using it.

Always replace the cover after using Pulmicort Turbuhaler. Store the inhaler at room temperature (15 to 30°C) in a dry place, away from moisture.

Pulmicort Turbuhaler (cont'd)

Important Note: This leaflet alerts you to some of the times you should call your doctor. Other situations which cannot be predicted may arise. Nothing about this leaflet should stop you from calling your doctor or pharmacist with any questions or concerns you have about using Pulmicort Turbuhaler.

□ PUREGON™ ℞

Organon

Follitropin Beta

Gonadotropin

Information for the Patient: What You Should Know about Puregon: Before administration of this medicine, please read this information carefully. If you have any questions, ask your physician.

Your Medicine: The name of your medicine is Puregon. It contains follicle-stimulating hormone (FSH), corresponding to 50 or 100 international units (IU) per ampul. Puregon is produced by mammalian cells, which by recombinant DNA technology were changed to carry the genes for human FSH.

It is very similar to the natural human FSH, which is normally secreted by a small gland at the base of the brain, the pituitary. Together with luteinizing hormone (LH), FSH controls the action of the sexual glands (ovaries in women and testes in men).

In women FSH is important for the monthly ripening of the follicle, a tiny cyst in the ovary in which the egg cell develops. If the body does not produce enough FSH, infertility may be the result. In these cases Puregon can be used to make up for the shortage. To determine the right dosage, a daily check may be necessary. Follicle ripening is determined by means of ultrasound, and the amount of estrogens (female hormones) in blood or urine can be measured. When the follicle is big enough, a hormone preparation with a strong LH activity is given (human chorionic gonadotropin, hCG). This causes ovulation (release of the egg).

In spite of careful monitoring, often more than one egg cell is released. This increases the chance of having more than one baby.

Poor production of FSH is not the only reason for infertility. In these cases medically assisted reproduction programs can sometimes be used, for instance in-vitro ('test tube') fertilization. For this technique several egg cells are needed and Puregon can then be used to cause a number of egg cells to develop.

Puregon only works if it is injected. It is presented as a dry powder, which should be dissolved with the solvent provided in a separate ampul.

Next to FSH, the powder contains sucrose, sodium citrate, and polysorbate 20; the solvent contains sodium chloride and water for injections.

Puregon belongs to a group of medicines called 'gonadotropins'.

Before using Puregon: Do not use Puregon if you have a tumor of the ovaries, breasts, uterus, or pituitary gland.

Close supervision of patients by a doctor is very important. Usually ultrasound scans of the ovaries are performed, and blood or urine samples are taken at least every other day. The results of these tests allow the doctor to choose the proper dose from day to day. This is very important since too high a dose may lead to unwanted overstimulation of the ovaries. This may be noticed as pain in the abdomen, weight gain, trouble breathing, nausea, diarrhea. If you are troubled with these discomforts, contact your doctor without delay.

Pregnancy. In pregnancies occurring after treatment with gonadotropic preparations, there is an increased risk of having twins or multiple births.

Ability to drive or operate machinery. As far as is known, Puregon has no effect on alertness and concentration.

Using This Medicine Properly: How much? The dose is chosen by the doctor. For ovulation induction, treatment is usually started with 75 IU FSH daily. Women participating in assisted reproduction programs are usually started on a daily dose of 150 to 225 IU Puregon.

Injections are given for about 10 days to approximately 4 weeks.

How the injections are given. The powder should be dissolved with the solvent provided. The injections are given slowly into a muscle (for instance in the buttock, upper leg or upper arm) or under the skin (for instance in the abdominal wall).

By whom? The injections into a muscle should only be given by a doctor or a nurse. In some instances, you or your partner may give the injections yourselves. In that case, Puregon should be injected under the skin. Your doctor will tell you when and how to do this.

Side Effects Puregon May Have: Treatment with gonadotropic preparations may lead to unwanted overstimulation of the ovaries. The first symptoms of ovarian stimulation may be noticed as pain in the abdomen, feeling sick or diarrhea. More severe cases may have accumulation of fluid in the abdomen and/or chest, weight gain and the occurrence of blood clots. Contact your doctor without delay if you are experiencing any of these symptoms during treatment or within a few days after the last injection.

Looking after Your Medicine:

- This medicine has been prescribed only for your current medical problem. It should not be used for other medical conditions or by other people.
- Keep Puregon in the original box in a safe place out of the reach of children.
- The storage conditions are given on the box.
- The expiry date is printed on the label after "exp." Do not use after this date.

General Things to Remember about Medicines:

1. Tell any doctor treating you what medicines you are taking. Always carry a medical information card stating which medicines you are using. This can be very important in case you are involved in an accident.
2. Return unused medicines to the pharmacy for disposal.
3. Make sure that other people you live with or who look after you read this information.

□ PYLORID® ℞

Glaxo Wellcome

Ranitidine Bismuth Citrate

Histamine H_2-receptor Antagonist with H. pylori Suppressive Activity

Information for the Patient: What you should know about Pylorid Tablets. Please read this leaflet carefully before you start to take your medicine. This provides a summary of the information available on your medicine. For more information or advice, ask your doctor or pharmacist.

The Name of Your Medicine: The name of your medicine is Pylorid Tablets. Its active ingredient is ranitidine bismuth citrate.

Pylorid can only be obtained with a prescription from your doctor.

The Purpose of Your Medicine: Pylorid tablets belong to a new class of medicine that combines H_2-antagonist properties, action against the bacteria Helicobacter pylori, and protection of the stomach lining.

The H_2-antagonist activity in your medicine reduces the amount of acid produced by your stomach. The bacteria Helicobacter pylori can make your ulcers return. Your medicine works against this bacteria in your stomach, and stops the ulcers from coming back.

The use of this Medicine During Pregnancy and Breast-feeding: As a normal precaution, this medicine should not be taken if you are pregnant, if you are likely to become pregnant or if you are breast-feeding. However, there may be circumstances when your doctor advises you to use this medicine during pregnancy.

Before Taking Your Medicine: If you answer yes to any of the following questions, tell your doctor before taking your medicine.

- Have you been told you are allergic to Pylorid tablets, ranitidine bismuth citrate, or any of the ingredients in Pylorid tablets?
- Are you pregnant, or trying to become pregnant, or breast-feeding?
- Do you have kidney or liver problems?
- Do you suffer from a rare condition called porphyria?
- Do you have any other illnesses, or are you taking any other medicines, including those you have bought yourself?
- Have you recently completed a course of these tablets?

How to Take Your Medicine: Take your medicine as your doctor has told you. The label on the container of your medicine should tell you how often to take your medicine and how many tablets you should take each time. If not, or if you are not sure, ask your doctor or pharmacist.

The adult dose is 1 Pylorid tablet in the morning and 1 in the evening. Swallow each tablet with a drink of water. Your doctor will also give you an antibiotic to take as well as your Pylorid tablets for 2 weeks to treat your ulcer caused by Helicobacter pylori. Your doctor may recommend further treatment with Pylorid to make sure that your ulcer is healed.

After Taking Your Medicine: Most people taking this medicine find that it causes no problems. As with all medicines, a few people may find that it causes side effects. Some people can be allergic to medicines. If you experience any of the following symptoms soon after taking your medicine, **stop** taking the tablets and tell your doctor immediately.
—lumpy skin rash (hives) anywhere on the body;
—swelling of eyelids, face or lips;
—sudden wheeziness and chest pain or tightening.

Tell your doctor as soon as possible if you experience skin rash (red spots) or itching.

Tell your doctor at your next visit if you notice any of the following side effects:
—diarrhea, indigestion, gas, stomach cramps or tarry black bowel movement;
—headache.

These tablets often make bowel movements darker. Your doctor may wish to check whether this is related only to your medicine. You may also notice that your tongue gets darker. This common and harmless side effect will disappear when your treatment is finished.

Your medicine may upset the results of certain blood tests including blood counts.

Pylorid tablets contain ranitidine bismuth citrate. The side effects below have been reported with other forms of ranitidine. They may or may not have occurred with your medicine.

Tell your doctor as soon as possible if you experience any of the following.
—nausea and loss of appetite, which are worse than normal and/or jaundice (yellow coloring of the skin or the whites of the eyes);
—slow or irregular heartbeat, dizziness, tiredness or fainting;
—feeling of depression, confusion or hallucinations;
—severe stomach pain or a change in the type of pain;
—unusual tiredness, shortness of breath, or tendency to infections or bruising which can be caused by upsets to blood counts.

Tell your doctor at your next visit if you experience joint or muscle pains, or if you are a man, breast tenderness and/or breast enlargement.

If you are unwell, or have any unusual discomfort you do not understand, please talk to your doctor or pharmacist.

What to do if you Miss a Dose: If you forget to take a tablet, don't worry, take another as soon as you remember. Then continue as before, taking the dose in the morning and evening for the rest of the treatment course.

What to do if an Overdosage is Taken: In the event you accidentally take more tablets than prescribed, immediately contact your doctor or hospital emergency department or nearest poison control centre.

Storing Your Medicine: Keep your medicine in a safe place out of the reach of children. Your medicine may harm them.

Keep your tablets away from heat which could spoil them.

What is in Your Medicine: Pylorid tablets contain 400 mg of ranitidine bismuth citrate. Each tablet also contains indigo carmine aluminum lake, magnesium stearate, methylhydroxypropylcellulose, microcrystalline cellulose, Polyvidone K30, sodium carbonate (anhydrous), titanium dioxide and triacetin.

Remember: This medicine is for you. Only a doctor can prescribe it for you. Never give it to someone else. It may harm them even if their symptoms are the same as yours.

Further Information: This leaflet does not contain the complete information about your medicine. If any questions remain unanswered or you are not sure about something, you should ask your doctor or pharmacist.

You may want to read this leaflet again. **Please do not throw it away** until you have finished your medicine.

☐ QUINTASA® Ⓟ

Ferring

5-Aminosalicylic Acid

Lower Gastrointestinal Anti-inflammatory

Information for the Patient: Quintasa Enema: How to Use the Enema (see package insert for illustrations): Best results are achieved if the bowel is emptied immediately before the enema is given. Unless otherwise directed, 1 enema should be used at bedtime. Retain the enema overnight for best results.

1. Removing the Bottle: Remove the bottle from the protective foil pouch by using scissors. Be careful not to puncture the bottle inside.

2. Preparing the Medication for Use:

a) Immediately after removing the bottle from the foil, shake the bottle well until the suspension is evenly distributed.
b) Twist off the small top section of the bottle and discard.
c) Lubricate tip with petroleum jelly.
d) For sanitary purposes, a plastic bag is provided which can be used to cover your hand, while administering the enema.

3. Assuming the Correct Body Position:

a) Best results are obtained by lying on the left side with the left leg extended and the right leg flexed forward for balance.
b) An alternative position is the ''knee-chest'' position.

4. Administering the Enema: Gently insert the entire lubricated applicator into the rectum. Point slightly toward the navel. Maintain steady hand pressure while slowly dispensing the entire contents of the enema.

5. Withdrawing the Applicator Tip:

a) Withdraw the applicator tip with the container still compressed.
b) Pull up the plastic and wrap around the tip of the applicator.
c) Remain in the administration position for 5 to 10 minutes or until the urge to pass the enema has disappeared.
d) Discard the empty container.

Quintasa Suppository: Suppositories are not be be taken by mouth.

1. We recommend that the bowel be emptied, if possible, prior to the suppository being administered.
2. Unwrap the suppository from the foil pouch and discard the used packaging material.
3. Using a rubber finger protector on your index finger, insert the suppository, pointed side first, into the rectum. Note: The inserting of the suppository can be done while in a standing position or lying down with one leg bent. The suppository should be placed as far into the rectum as possible.
4. For best results, retain the suppository as long as possible. Note: If the suppository is discharged within the first 10 minutes, a new one can be inserted.
5. Discard the rubber finger protector.

☐ RAXAR™ Ⓟ

Glaxo Wellcome

Grepafloxacin HCl

Antibacterial

Information for the Patient: What you should know about Raxar (grepafloxacin hydrochloride). **Please read this leaflet carefully before you start to take your medicine.** For further information or advice ask your doctor or pharmacist.

The Name of Your Medicine: The name of your medicine is Raxar. It contains grepafloxacin hydrochloride. This medicine is similar to other medicines called quinolones, which are antibiotics.

How to Obtain your Medicine: Raxar can only be obtained with a prescription from your doctor.

The Purpose of Your Medicine: Your doctor has prescribed Raxar because you have an infection. Raxar is used to kill the bacteria or ''germs'' which cause infections. The infection can be cleared up if you take your medication in the proper way.

Important Points to Note Before Taking your Medicine: You should not use Raxar if you are allergic to quinolones.

You should not take terfenadine during treatment with Raxar.

You should not use Raxar if you are on certain other medications—check with your doctor or pharmacist to ensure that any medication you are currently taking would not have potential to interfere with the effects of Raxar.

Raxar should not be taken by patients with certain heart diseases or conditions. Please advise your doctor of any heart conditions you may be aware of.

You should not take Raxar if you suffer from liver disease.

Advise your doctor if you are taking theophylline.

You should not take multivitamins containing iron or zinc, antacids containing magnesium, calcium, or aluminum or sucralfate within 4 hours before or 4 hours after taking Raxar.

Raxar (cont'd)

You should drink lots of fluids while taking Raxar.

Raxar may increase the effects of caffeine. You should limit intake of coffee, tea, chocolate.

Raxar may cause dizziness, and headaches. If you experience any of these side effects, avoid driving and any other activity, or job that requires alertness or coordination.

You should avoid excessive sunlight or artificial ultraviolet light while taking Raxar and to discontinue therapy if phototoxicity (e.g., sunburn-like reaction or skin eruptions) occurs.

The Use of This Medicine During Pregnancy and Breast-feeding: If you are pregnant or breast-feeding, your doctor may decide not to prescribe this medicine, although there may be circumstances when your doctor advises you differently.

How to Take Your Medicine: You must take the medicine exactly as prescribed by your doctor. If you are not sure how many tablets to take, or how often to take them, consult your doctor or your pharmacist. **You should not increase the prescribed dose unless advised by your doctor.**

Raxar may be taken with or without food.

The usual dose for adults is two 200 mg tablets or three 200 mg tablets once a day.

Raxar has a bitter taste, therefore, do not chew or crush the tablets but swallow each one whole with a drink of water.

The usual length of treatment is 7 to 10 days, although your doctor may adjust the prescription to suit your treatment. During the course of treatment, all the tablets must be taken to make sure that all the bacteria have been killed. Continue taking the tablets until they are finished, even if you begin to feel better.

After Taking your Medicine: Discontinue your medicine and contact your doctor at the first sign of sunburn like reaction, rash, hives or skin eruptions, a rapid heartbeat, difficulty in breathing or swallowing or any other symptom of an allergic reaction. Do not take any more medicine unless your doctor tells you to do so. Your doctor may decide to stop your treatment.

At the first sign of tendon pain or joint pain, contact your doctor immediately and refrain from exercise.

Other possible effects which may occur are diarrhea, vomiting and nausea. Some people may have other reactions. If you notice any unusual effects, check with your doctor or pharmacist.

If you feel worse or have taken all the tablets and do not feel better tell your doctor as soon as possible.

What to Do if an Overdose is Taken: It is important to follow the dosage instructions on the label of your medicine. If you take more than the recommended dose, contact your doctor or nearest hospital emergency department immediately.

Storing your Medicine: Keep your tablets in a safe place where children cannot reach them.

Raxar should be stored at room temperature (15 to 30°C) in a tightly closed container away from heat and direct light.

What to Do if You Miss a Dose: If you forget to take a dose, take another as soon as possible. Then continue with the normal dose the next day. Do not take 2 doses in one day.

What to Do When You Stop Your Medicine: If your doctor decides to stop the treatment, do not keep any leftover medicine unless your doctor tells you to. Please discard all unused Raxar tablets.

What is in Your Medicine: Each Raxar tablet contains 200 mg of grepafloxacin hydrochloride. It also contains grey printing ink, hydroxypropyl cellulose, hydroxypropyl methylcellulose, low-substituted hydroxypropyl cellulose, magnesium stearate, microcrystalline cellulose, talc and titanium dioxide.

Remember: This medicine is for you. Only a doctor can prescribe it for you. Never give it to someone else. It may harm them even if their symptoms are the same as yours.

Further Information: This leaflet does not contain the complete information about your medicine. If you have any questions you should ask your doctor or pharmacist.

You may need to read this leaflet again. Please do not throw it away until you have finished your medicine.

□ REACTINE™

Pfizer Consumer

Cetirizine HCl

Histamine H_1-Receptor Antagonist

Information for the Patient: Use: Reactine is a direct-action metabolite* indicated for fast and long lasting relief of itchy, watery eyes, sneezing and runny nose caused by seasonal and year round allergies (hayfever, trees, grass, dust, pets, molds).

Reactine also relieves allergic skin reactions such as hives.

Directions: Adults and children 12 years of age and over: 1 to 2 (5 mg) or 1 (10 mg) tablet depending on the severity of symptoms, taken every 24 hours. Do not exceed recommended dosage. Prolonged use only as directed by a physician.

Adults 65 years of age and over: take one 5 mg tablet or half (5 mg) of a 10 mg tablet or consult a physician if unsure about dosage.

Caution: This product should not be taken if you are pregnant or nursing a baby, or if you have liver or kidney disease, unless under the advice of a physician. If drowsiness ocurs, do not drive or operate machinery. Keep this and all medications safely out of reach of children.

- Store below 30°C.
- Product monograph available to physicians and pharmacists upon request.

*A direct-action metabolite does not require biotransformation to become active.

Nonmedicinal Ingredients: cornstarch, hydroxypropyl methylcellulose, lactose, magnesium stearate, polyethylene glycol, povidone, titanium dioxide.

Availability: Reactine is available as a 5 or 10 mg scored tablet packaged in individually sealed blisters in 14 and 21 tablets for the 5 mg and in 6, 12, 18 and 30 tablet packages for the 10 mg.

□ REBIF™ Ⓟ

Serono

Interferon beta-1a

Immunomodulator

Information for the Patient: Administration Information for the Rebif Patient: Your doctor has prescribed Rebif treatment for relapsing-remitting Multiple Sclerosis. As with any prescription medication, there are things you need to know about your treatment and what you can expect from it. The following is important patient information about how to administer Rebif, and how to get more information should you have questions.

This information relates only to the use of Rebif in the treatment of relapsing/remitting Multiple Sclerosis. If you have been prescribed any MS treatment other than Rebif, or if you have been prescribed Rebif for the treatment of any other condition, these instructions will not apply.

Note: Rebif is available in two formats:

1. ready to inject, pre-filled syringes; and

2. lyophilized powder in vials for reconstitution prior to injection.

Be sure to follow the instructions for the Rebif format prescribed for you.

When using Rebif always follow the basic principles of injection:

- Maintain sterile conditions
- Check medication
- Check expiry date
- Check dosage and instructions
- Be on ''safety alert''
- Rotate injection sites

Six Steps of Rebif Subcutaneous Injection of Prefilled Syringes: Important: Store all injection materials and your Rebif out of the reach of children at all times.

Step 1: Cleanse: Before you start, wash your hands well with soap and water. It is important that your hands and the items you use be as clean as possible. Needles should not touch any surface except alcohol-cleaned skin; keep them capped prior to use. Make sure you use a new syringe each time you inject to avoid contamination. Dispose of all syringes in a disposal container specifically designed for used injection equipment.

Step 2: Assembly of Injection Materials: Find a clean area and lay out everything you will need (alcohol swabs, prefilled syringe, disposal container). The injection can be given in any room where you feel comfortable. If you use your kitchen, ensure that all medicines and needles are kept well away from food.

Step 3: Preparing the Rebif Injection: Remove the cap from the needle and set it on your work surface (you will need to use the needle cap again—do not throw away yet).

If you see any air bubbles in the syringe, hold the syringe with the needle pointing straight up. Gently tap the syringe until all the air collects at the top. Carefully push the plunger in until the air bubbles are gone. Do not worry if small bubbles remain in the solution, because injecting them subcutaneously (that is, just under the surface of the skin) will do no harm. Put the needle cap back on to keep it sterile while you prepare the injection site.

Step 4: Selecting the Injection Site: Rebif is injected just under the skin, in the layer of subcutaneous tissue. For your own comfort, you should avoid injecting into the same area too often. There are many possible injection sites on your body (e.g., arms, thighs, buttocks, abdomen)—refer to the package insert for the diagram. It is difficult to self-inject into the back of the arm; you will likely require assistance if you choose this site. It is a good idea to plan an injection site rotation schedule and note it in a diary.

Note: Do not inject in any area in which you feel lumps, firm knots or pain. Consult your doctor or health care professional about any such abnormalities you find.

Optional: Autoinjector: If you have been given an autoinjector, you should follow the detailed instructions that are supplied with the unit.

Step 5: Preparing the Injection Site and Injecting Rebif subcutaneously: Your doctor or nurse will have already advised you where to inject (e.g., abdomen, front of thigh, back of arm, buttock). Refer to the injection sites diagram from the package insert (keeping a diary of injection sites as they are used is recommended). Follow the detailed instructions below each time you inject Rebif prefilled syringes. If you have questions about injecting Rebif, contact your health care professional or call Multiple Support at 1-888-MS-REBIF (1-888-677-3243).

Note: Your first Rebif injection should be done under the supervision of your doctor or an appropriately qualified health care professional.

- Use an alcohol swab to clean the skin at the selected injection site. Let the skin dry completely (15 to 20 seconds) to avoid possible burning, then discard the alcohol swab.
- Pick up the syringe and uncap the needle. Hold the syringe like a pencil or dart.
- With your other hand, gently pinch the skin around the injection site to lift it up a bit.
- Resting your wrist on the skin near the site, use a quick, firm motion to insert the needle straight into the skin at a 90° angle.
- Inject Rebif by gently pushing the plunger all the way down. Take as much time as you need to inject all of the solution.
- Remove the needle from the skin and gently massage the injection site with a dry cotton ball or gauze.
- Discard the used syringe, needle cap and alcohol swab in the disposal unit.

Step 6: Disposal of Used Items: Once you have finished your injection, immediately discard the needle in the disposal container provided. When the disposal container is full, consult your clinic for the safe disposal of its contents. They should not be disposed of in household garbage.

Six Steps of Rebif Subcutaneous Injection of Lyophilized Powder for Reconstitution and Injection: Important: Store all injection materials and your Rebif out of the reach of children at all times.

Note: We strongly recommend that your first Rebif injection be done with the supervision of your doctor or an appropriately qualified health care professional.

Step 1: Cleanse: Before you start, wash your hands well with soap and water. It is important that your hands and the items you use be as clean as possible. Needles should not touch any surface except alcohol-cleaned skin; keep them capped prior to use. Make sure you use a new syringe each time you inject to avoid contamination. Dispose of all syringes in a disposal container specifically designed for used injection equipment.

Step 2: Assembly of Injection Materials: Assemble everything you need for your Rebif injection: clear a clean area (counter top or table) and lay your injection materials out. For each Rebif injection, you will need:

- alcohol swabs;
- one ampul of diluent;
- one vial of Rebif;
- one 3 cc syringe with needle used for mixing;
- one 27 gauge subcutaneous injection needle; and
- your syringe and needle disposal unit (e.g., Vacutainer, Sharps container).

Step 3: Reconstituting Rebif and Preparing the Injection: Opening the ampul of diluent: On the neck of the ampul, you will see a small colored dot. Directly below this dot, the glass has been treated to make it easier to break. Gently tap the tip of the ampul to make sure all the liquid is in the bottom. Then, holding the ampul in one hand, place the thumb of your other hand on the ampul neck, just above the colored dot, and with your second or third finger on the opposite side of the neck (away from the colored dot), press firmly to snap the ampul top off, away from the colored dot. Carefully place the open ampul upright on your work surface. Discard the ampul top in the disposal container.

Drawing up the diluent: Unwrap the 3 cc syringe. Remove the needle cap and discard. With the syringe in one hand, pick up the open ampul, insert the syringe needle into the ampul and draw the required amount of diluent (see Table I) into the syringe by pulling back the syringe plunger. Carefully set the filled syringe down on the work surface, taking care not to touch the needle or let the needle touch the work surface. Discard the empty glass ampul in the disposal container.

Table I—Rebif

Reconstitution Table

Strength	Volume of Diluent to be Added to Vial	Approximate Available Volume	Nominal Concentration/mL
11 µg (3 MIU)	0.5 mL	0.5 mL	22 µg (6 MIU)
44 µg (12 MIU)	0.5 mL	0.5 mL	88 µg (24 MIU)

Reconstituting Rebif: Remove the protective aluminum cap from the vial of Rebif powder. Pick up the syringe of diluent. Hold the Rebif vial firmly on the work surface and slowly insert the needle of the syringe containing the diluent straight through the vial's rubber stopper. Slowly push the syringe plunger all the way down so that all of the diluent is emptied into the Rebif vial. Keeping the needle in the vial, wait until the powder is completely dissolved in the diluent (1 minute should be sufficient). You may pick the vial up and swirl it gently—**do not shake.** When completely dissolved, the Rebif solution may be yellowish in color: this is normal.

Turn the vial of Rebif solution upside down (with the syringe still in place). Making sure the needle tip stays in the Rebif solution, pull the plunger back to draw the Rebif solution into the syringe. Pull the needle back out of the vial. Discard the empty Rebif vial in the disposal container. Unscrew the mixing needle from the syringe and discard the needle in the disposal container. Set the syringe down on the work surface.

Preparing the Rebif subcutaneous injection. Unwrap the 27 gauge subcutaneous injection needle and screw it onto the syringe. Remove the cap from the needle and set it on the work surface (you will need to use the needle cap again—do not throw it away yet). If you see any air bubbles in the syringe, hold the syringe with the needle pointing straight up. Gently tap the syringe until the air collects at the top. Carefully push the plunger in until the air bubbles are gone. Do not worry if small bubbles remain in the solution, because injecting them subcutaneously (that is, just under the surface of the skin) will do no harm. Put the needle cap back on to keep it sterile while you prepare the injection site.

Step 4: Selecting the Injection Site: Rebif is injected just under the skin, in the layer of subcutaneous tissue. For your own comfort, you should avoid injecting into the same area too often. There are many possible injection sites on your body (e.g., arms, thighs, buttocks, abdomen)—refer to the package insert for the diagram. It is difficult to self-inject into the back of the arm; you will likely require assistance if you choose this site. It is a good idea to plan an injection site rotation schedule and note it in a diary.

Note: Do not use any areas in which you feel lumps, firm knots, or pain; talk to your doctor or health care professional about any such abnormalities you find.

Optional: Autoinjector: If you have been given an autoinjector, you should follow the detailed instructions that are supplied with the unit.

Step 5: Preparing the Injection Site and Injecting Rebif Subcutaneously: Your doctor or nurse will have already advised you where to inject (e.g., abdomen, front of thigh, back of arm, buttock). Refer to the package insert for injection sites diagram (keeping a diary of injection sites as they are used is recommended). Follow the detailed instructions below each time you inject Rebif. If you have questions about injecting Rebif, contact your health care professional or call Multiple Support at 1-888-MS-Rebif (1-888-677-3243).

Rebif (cont'd)

Note: Your first Rebif injection should be done under the supervision of your doctor or an appropriately qualified health care professional.

- Use an alcohol swab to clean the skin at the selected injection site. Let the skin dry completely (15 to 20 seconds) to avoid possible burning, then discard the alcohol swab.
- Pick up the syringe and uncap the needle. Hold the syringe like a pencil or dart.
- With your other hand, gently pinch the skin around the injection site to lift it up a bit.
- Resting your wrist on the skin near the site, use a quick, firm motion to insert the needle straight into the skin at a 90° angle.
- Inject Rebif by gently pushing the plunger all the way down. Take as much time as you need to inject all of the solution.
- Remove the needle from the skin and gently massage the injection site with a dry cotton ball or gauze.
- Discard the used syringe, needle cap and alcohol swab in the disposal unit.

Step 6: Disposal of Used Items: Once you have finished your injection, immediately discard the needle in the disposal container provided. When the disposal container is full, consult your clinic for the safe disposal of its contents. They should not be disposed of in household garbage.

Possible Sites for Injecting Rebif: Refer to package insert for diagram.

Some additional advice... It is important that you are familiar with the correct injection technique as outlined in these instructions before beginning your treatment with Rebif.

If the injection site bleeds afterwards, firmly press a cotton ball or gauze over the injection site immediately after removing the needle. This usually stops any further bleeding.

Local skin reactions are less likely to occur if you vary the injection site. If they do occur, they usually will disappear within a few days. In the meantime, icing the area may help reduce irritation. Swelling and irritation at the injection site may also be reduced by gently massaging the area for five minutes after the injection has been given. If a generalized rash develops, you should always report it to your doctor or nurse. Bruises may also occasionally occur at the injection site—even when the injection has been given correctly—but they will disappear.

Finally, remember that every treatment is individualized. Yours has been carefully designed for you by your doctor according to your own specific needs. It is very important that you keep your appointments and follow your doctor's instructions, particularly with regard to the amount and frequency of the medication you are taking. If you forget or miss an injection, do not panic, but you should consult your doctor or nurse for advice.

Rebif should be stored in the refrigerator (2 to 8°C), out of the reach of children at all times.

☐ REJUVA-A® ℞

Stiefel

Tretinoin

Agent for the Treatment of Photodamaged Skin

Information for the Patient: Rejuva-A (tretinoin cream USP 0.025%): What it is, what it does and how it works: Rejuva-A is a tretinoin cream containing moisturizers. Rejuva-A improves skin damaged by the sun (photodamaged). Sun damaged skin loses elasticity. Rejuva-A has been shown to increase the thickness and collagen level of the skin.

The tretinoin in Rejuva-A moisturizing cream, also has an exfoliative effect which means that the skin's outer layers may peel off to leave a smoother, healthier looking surface and skin tone.

It is important to understand that your doctor has given you a prescription specially suited to your particular needs and skin type. **Do not allow others to use it.** Also, over-application of Rejuva-A may irritate your skin and is unlikely to speed up treatment.

Following your doctor's directions carefully will minimize common reactions such as mild burning sensations and redness. During the first 3 weeks of treatment, your doctor may recommend application of Rejuva-A on every second day to allow your skin to adjust to the medication.

Dermatologists usually advise patients that, with regular use of topical tretinoin, clinical benefits will be obtained after 6 months to 1 year of therapy, so be patient.

Your doctor may recommend a daytime moisturizer if your skin is particularly dry.

If you are a female of childbearing age, you should only use Rejuva-A after consulting your doctor and seeking his/her advice about contraceptive counseling. If you are pregnant, you should discontinue the use of Rejuva-A and consult your doctor.

Instructions for use:

1. Wash the affected area with a mild soap and warm water and gently pat dry with a soft towel.
2. Rejuva-A should be applied to the affected area once a day just before bedtime.
3. Your doctor will probably recommend to start the therapy by applying one pea-size amount to the forehead and spreading it evenly over the entire face. After tolerance to the medication is established, the dose may be doubled by applying a pea-size amount to each temple.
4. Use your fingertips to spread the medication over your entire face and smooth it in with a gentle rubbing motion.
5. Special care should be taken when treating wrinkles around the eyes (Crow's feet) and mouth to minimize contact with the eyes, lips and mucous-producing areas. Avoid areas of the skin where you have other problems such as eczema.
6. If you intend to treat thin-skinned, sensitive areas such as the neck region, it is recommended to develop gradually the tolerance to Rejuva-A by applying the medication every third night in the beginning and then every other night.
7. In the morning, wash your face using a mild soap.
8. At the beginning, you may experience redness, a burning sensation and peeling while your skin adjusts to the medication. To minimize these reactions, your doctor may ask you, for the first few weeks of therapy, to apply the medication every other night or every third night.

Precautions:

1. Do not apply Rejuva-A to areas of the skin where you have problems such as eczema, severely inflamed skin or other open lesions.
2. Avoid sensitive and mucus-producing areas such as eyes, mouth, lips and angles of the nose.
3. Do not over-apply Rejuva-A. Doing so will not speed up treatment but only irritate your skin.
4. While using Rejuva-A, do not use other skin medications without the advice of your physician.
5. Prolonged exposure to sunlight, sunlamps, wind and cold should be avoided during treatment. If exposure to sun is unavoidable, use a sunscreen with a minimum SPF 15 as well as protective clothing. The sunscreen should be reapplied each time you have been swimming.
6. If sunburn occurs, stop using Rejuva-A and call your doctor for advice.
7. Rejuva-A has been prescribed for your use only. Do not allow others to use it.

☐ RELAFEN™ ℞

SmithKline Beecham

Nabumetone

Nonsteroidal Anti-inflammatory Agent

Information for the Patient: Relafen (nabumetone) is a nonsteroidal anti-inflammatory drug (NSAID). It has been prescribed for you by your doctor to treat arthritic symptoms such as swelling, stiffness and joint pain.

Identify your medication: 500 mg tablet—white, pillow-shaped, with RELAFEN on one side and 500 on the other side. 750 mg tablet—beige, pillow-shaped, with RELAFEN on one side and 750 on the other side. Check with your doctor or pharmacist if the identifying markings or color of your tablets appear different.

Before using Relafen: It is important that you tell your doctor about any of the following items so that your doctor may determine if Relafen is suitable for you.

- Allergy (including rash or asthma) when previously taking Relafen or related anti-inflammatory medicines (e.g. ASA [acetylsalicylic acid], diclofenac, diflunisal, fenoprofen, flurbiprofen, ibuprofen, indomethacin, ketoprofen, mefenamic acid, naproxen, piroxicam, tiaprofenic acid and tolmetin).
- Past history of (or current) stomach upset, ulcer, or liver, kidney or heart disease.
- Pregnancy or intention to become pregnant while using Relafen.

- Infant breast-feeding.
- Other medical conditions.
- Taking any other medications for arthritis or other medical conditions. It is important to tell your doctor, dentist and pharmacist if you are taking other medication, as combining drugs can sometimes result in a change from the expected drug effects, or cause harmful effects.

How to take your medication: You should take Relafen only as directed by your doctor. Do not take more of it, do not take it more often and do not take it for a longer period of time than your doctor ordered.

Be sure to take Relafen regularly as prescribed. Try to take your tablets at the same time each day. Relafen's effect is evident early in treatment, however, in some types of arthritis, up to 1 week may pass before you feel the full relief from this medicine. It is important to keep taking Relafen even after you start to feel better.

Generally, patients are instructed to take 2 Relafen tablets (1 000 mg) once a day. During treatment, your doctor may decide to increase the dosage up to 4 tablets (2 000 mg) each day, according to your response to the medication. In that case it may be divided in 2 doses per day. If you forget to take a tablet, leave out that dose completely. Take your next dose at the normal time it is due.

Relafen will work whether or not you take it with food or milk. You should swallow the tablets whole, with water or milk. Do not chew them.

Important: Your doctor may give you different instructions better suited to your specific needs. If you need more information on how to take Relafen properly, double-check with your doctor or pharmacist.

Side Effects: Any medication can cause side effects. Most people tolerate the medicine well. The most common adverse effects associated with Relafen are gastrointestinal, such as diarrhea, indigestion, abdominal pain, nausea, constipation and flatulence. Other complaints such as headaches, tiredness, dizziness, drowsiness, insomnia have also been observed.

Consult your doctor if these symptoms become troublesome or if the following occur:

- shortness of breath, wheezing, troubled breathing or tightness in chest
- black or bloody stools
- blurred vision or ringing in the ears
- skin rash, hives, swelling or itching
- swelling of face, feet or lower legs

If you develop a skin rash or asthma while you are taking Relafen, do not take any more tablets and contact your doctor at once.

While taking this medication:

- tell any other doctor, pharmacist or dentist you see, that you are taking Relafen.
- there is a risk of dizziness after taking Relafen. If this occurs, do not drive or operate machinery.
- contact your doctor if you develop any unusual discomfort.
- you should not take Relafen when pregnant or breast-feeding unless your doctor tells you to.
- do not take ASA (acetylsalicylic acid) or other drugs to relieve your arthritis unless directed by your doctor.
- do not give Relafen to others because it may not be suitable for them.
- store your tablets in a dry place at room temperature in the original container provided by the pharmacy.
- keep this medication out of reach of children.
- read your prescription label carefully; consult your doctor or pharmacist if you have any questions or require further information.

□ RENEDIL® Ⓟ

Hoechst Marion Roussel

Felodipine

Antihypertensive Agent

Information for the Patient: Important Information You Should Know About Renedil (Felodipine Extended Release Tablets): Renedil is a brand name for the drug felodipine (said as, fell-o'-di-peen). It belongs to the group of drugs called "calcium channel blockers" or "calcium antagonists".

Renedil is used to treat hypertension (high blood pressure). Its main action is to relax the arteries, letting the blood flow more freely; thereby lowering the blood pressure.

Read this leaflet carefully. It does not replace your doctor's or pharmacist's advice. They may have given you different instructions for your particular health condition. Be sure to follow their advice. If you have any questions, talk to your doctor or pharmacist. **Do not decide on your own how to take Renedil.**

Before you Start Renedil: Be sure you have told your doctor:

- **If you are pregnant or plan to become pregnant.**
- **If you are breast-feeding.**
- About all health problems you have or have had in the past.
- About all medicines you take, including ones you can buy without a prescription.
- If you visit more than one doctor make sure that each knows about all the medicines you are taking.
- If you are allergic to "nonmedicinal" substances like food products, preservatives, or dyes, which may be present in RENEDIL tablets (see Renedil Ingredients).
- If you have ever had a bad, unusual or allergic reaction to "felodipine".

Renedil Ingredients: Most medicines contain more ingredients than just the active drug. These ingredients are needed to keep medicines in a form that you can swallow. Check with your doctor if you think you might be allergic to any of these items (listed in alphabetical order): aluminum silicate, carnauba wax, castor oil, felodipine, hydrogen peroxide, hydroxypropyl cellulose, hydroxypropyl methylcellulose, iron oxide, lactose, microcrystalline cellulose, polyethylene glycol, propyl gallate, sodium stearyl fumarate and titanium dioxide.

How to use the Renedil Compliance Pack: This unique 30-day package is designed to make it easy to keep track of your medication.

Twenty-eight of the tablets are labelled with a day of the week. To start, take a tablet in the first row that matches the day you begin the pack. Then, take a tablet on each of the following days to complete the 28 labelled tablets. The 2 extra nonlabelled tablets should be taken after all other tablets are gone.

Remember to get a new prescription from your doctor or a refill from your pharmacy a few days before all 30 tablets are taken.

How to Take Renedil:

- Take Renedil exactly as your doctor tells you. Do not miss doses or take extra doses, unless your doctor tells you. If you are not clear about the directions, ask your doctor or pharmacist.
- Renedil is taken once a day. Even if your doctor has prescribed 2 tablets a day, both should be taken at the same time, unless otherwise indicated.
- Try to take Renedil with something you do regularly each day; for example, upon waking or at breakfast. This will help you remember each dose.
- Renedil may be taken with food or on an empty stomach.
- **Grapefruit juice increases the amount of Renedil in your body and should be avoided.**
- Swallow Renedil whole with a glass of water. Do not crush, chew, break or suck on the tablets.
- Do not transfer Renedil to other pill containers. To protect your Renedil tablets, keep them in the initial Compliance Pack.

If you Miss a Dose: If you miss a dose of Renedil and remember within 12 hours, you should take your usual dose as soon as possible. Then go back to your regular schedule. But if it is more than 12 hours when you remember, do not take the missed dose. Just take the next dose on time.

Never take a double dose of Renedil to make up for missed tablets. If you are still unsure, check with your doctor or pharmacist to see what you should do.

Side Effects to be Aware of: Along with its effects on controlling blood pressure, Renedil, like any medication, may include side effects.

Some side effects may occur when Renedil is first started or when the dose is increased. These side effects are usually mild and should go away as your body gets used to Renedil.

It is important that you keep your doctor informed of all side effects, especially if you experience any of the following for more than a week:

- swelling of the ankles;
- flushing or a feeling of warmth;
- dizziness;
- a racing heartbeat;
- headache;
- unusual tiredness.

Medicines affect different people in different ways. Just because side effects have occurred in other patients does not mean you will get them. Discuss how you feel on Renedil with your doctor and pharmacist. **Do not stop taking Renedil on your own.**

A few patients report mild tenderness or swelling of their gums while taking Renedil. This effect can be prevented with good dental care.

Renedil (cont'd)

Brush your teeth carefully and often with a soft toothbrush, and use dental floss daily.

Massaging your gums regularly with a soft toothbrush will also help. If your gums become tender, red or swollen be sure to tell your doctor or dentist.

Other side effects have been reported in a few cases. These include tingling in the hands, arms, feet or legs, stomach upset and diarrhea. Again, if any of these effects bother you, be sure to tell your doctor.

You should be certain to contact your doctor immediately if you experience anything unusual.

Some Precautions You Should Take: Keep Renedil out of sight and out of the reach of children. Never take medicine in front of small children as they will want to copy you.

Unused medicines which you know you will no longer need should be carefully discarded. Small quantities may be disposed of in the toilet or you may wish to seek advice from your pharmacist.

The Compliance Pack protects each tablet. When you first open the package, if you find any damage to the plastic seal or foil which exposes the tablet, ask your pharmacist to check the package.

Check with your doctor if you want to drink alcohol (including wine with your meals) while you are taking Renedil. Drinking alcohol while on Renedil may make you feel dizzier than usual. Alcohol may also cause an uncomfortable drop in blood pressure.

Remember, you may not notice any signs of high blood pressure. **Therefore it is important to take Renedil even when you feel well.** A constant amount of drug is needed in your body to control your blood pressure. **Do not stop taking Renedil on your own.**

How to Store Renedil: Although the Renedil tablets are protected in this Compliance Pack, it is best to keep the package at normal room temperature and in a dry place. Do not keep Renedil in the bathroom. **Keep Renedil out of the reach of children.** Do not keep or use Renedil after the expiry date indicated on the Compliance Pack.

General Information: All drugs can have both helpful and harmful effects. Both depend on the person and his or her health condition. This leaflet alerts you to some of the times you should call your doctor. Other situations which cannot be predicted may arise. Nothing in this leaflet should stop you from calling your doctor or pharmacist with any questions or concerns you have about Renedil.

Customer Inquiries: 1-800-265-7927.

☐ RENOVA® ℞

Janssen-Ortho

Tretinoin

Agent for the Treatment of Photodamaged Skin

Information for the Patient: Renova emollient cream is a yellow cream with a light, pleasant fragrance. It contains 0.05% tretinoin and is available in 20 gram tubes.

Renova emollient cream 0.05% improves fine wrinkling, spotty pigmentation, and roughness sometimes seen in skin which has been chronically overexposed to the sun. Your doctor has prescribed Renova emollient cream 0.05% for you because your skin exhibits some or all of these signs.

Renova emollient cream 0.05% is available only with your physician's prescription. It should be used under medical supervision as part of a comprehensive skin protection program, including the use of sunscreen products and protective clothing.

Use only as specifically directed. Do not alter the dosage or frequency of application unless ordered to do so by your physician.

If you are a female of childbearing age, you should only use Renova emollient cream 0.05% after consulting your doctor about contraceptive counselling. If you are pregnant you should discontinue use of Renova emollient cream 0.05%.

Do Not Use This Medication If:

- you have already used any products containing tretinoin and have developed an allergy or intolerance to it.

Proper Use of This Medicine: Renova emollient cream 0.05% should be applied in the evening before bedtime, as follows:

- Gently wash your face using a mild soap containing no medications. Pat your face dry with a towel. Do **not** rub. Rubbing is abrasive to the skin.
- Allow for up to 20 to 30 minutes for your face to dry before applying Renova emollient cream 0.05%. This may help decrease the likelihood of developing skin irritation.
- Squeeze a ''pea-size'' amount of Renova emollient cream 0.05% on your fingertip.
- Gently smooth Renova emollient cream 0.05% on your entire face until it vanishes. Do not over-apply Renova emollient cream 0.05%. The ''pea-size'' amount is sufficient for the treatment of sun-damaged skin. Use of larger quantities of Renova emollient cream 0.05% may increase your chances of developing skin irritation and will not necessarily speed up the improvement process.
- Do not place Renova emollient cream 0.05% in your eyes, mouth, angles of the nose or mucous membranes. If you get Renova emollient cream 0.05% in your eyes by mistake, rinse your eyes several times with lukewarm water. If the irritation continues, contact your physician.
- Do not spot treat.
- Do not wash your face after applying Renova emollient cream 0.05%. Allow the areas treated with Renova emollient cream 0.05% to remain undisturbed overnight.
- Upon wakening the next morning, you may wash your face with a mild soap containing no medications.
- Avoid or minimize exposure to the sun because Renova emollient cream 0.05% heightens the susceptibility of your skin to the adverse effects of the sun.
- When you are exposed to the sunlight while using Renova emollient cream 0.05%, your physician, as part of a skin protection program, will advise you to use an effective sunscreen with a minimum SPF of 15 as well as protective clothing when exposure to the sun cannot be avoided. The sunscreen should be reapplied each time after you have been swimming.
- During the course of therapy with Renova emollient cream 0.05%, avoid using preparations having an abrasive, drying or peeling effect, including soaps, shampoos, cosmetics, perfumes and astringents (especially those containing alcohol, lime or spices).
- Three to 6 months of treatment may be necessary before beneficial effects are seen.

Side Effects: Along with its intended action, any medication may cause unwanted effects. The following side effects may occur: dry or peeling skin, burning, stinging, redness or itching.

These side effects, with the exception of dry or peeling skin, usually occur early in the course of treatment. They are usually well tolerated and generally decrease over time.

The use of a non-alcohol containing moisturizer may reduce the chance of side effects.

This medicine was prescribed to treat your specific medical problem and is for your use only. Do not share it with others.

Keep all medicines out of the reach of children.

If you need any further information, ask your physician or your pharmacist.

☐ REQUIP™ ℞

SmithKline Beecham

Ropinirole HCl

Antiparkinsonian Agent—Dopamine Agonist

Information for the Patient: Please read this information before you start to take your medicine. Keep this leaflet until you have finished all your tablets as you may need to read it again. If you are helping someone else to take Requip, read this leaflet before you give the first tablet. This leaflet does not contain all the information about this medicine. **For further information or advice please see your doctor or pharmacist.**

What You Should Know About Requip:

- Requip, also known as ropinirole, is used to treat Parkinson's disease.
- You may receive Requip on its own but it may also be given with another drug used to treat Parkinson's disease (levodopa) to make that drug work better.

What You Should Tell Your Doctor Before Taking Requip:

- If you have previously taken Requip and became unwell, or you are allergic to Requip, or any of the nonmedicinal ingredients of the product (for complete list see ''What does Requip contain'' section), tell the doctor before taking these tablets.

- If you have a heart, liver or kidney complaint, tell the doctor before you take your tablets.
- If you have recently taken, or are taking, any other medicines, tell the doctor before you start taking the tablets. Requip may be affected by some other medicines. If you are taking a drug used to help with breathing difficulties called theophylline, or an antibiotic called ciprofloxacin or hormone replacement therapy (HRT), tell the doctor if you change the amount that you are taking of these medicines or if you stop taking them.
- Tell the doctor that you are taking Requip if he/she is going to prescribe you any other medicine.
- If you are pregnant or think you may be pregnant, or if you are breast-feeding, it is important to tell your doctor. You should not be taking Requip if you are pregnant or breast-feeding.

How to Take Requip:

- Follow the doctor's instructions about how and when you should take your tablets. Your doctor will decide how many tablets you need to take each day and you should always follow his/her instructions. When you first start taking Requip, the amount you take will be increased gradually.
- Your doctor may increase or decrease the amount that you are taking to give you the maximum benefit from the medicine. You will usually be told to take Requip 3 times a day.
- If you are taking other medicines for Parkinson's disease, the doctor may decrease the dose of these medicines while you are taking Requip.
- You should swallow the tablets whole with water. Do not chew. Requip should preferably be taken with food.
- You should continue to take your medicine even if you do not feel better, as it may take a number of weeks for the medicine to work.

Remember: This medicine is for the person named by the doctor. Do not give it to anybody else.

Side Effects when Taking Requip:

- Requip may cause hallucinations, unwanted, fidgety movements (dyskinesia) or confusion. If you feel any of these symptoms, tell your doctor immediately.
- Requip may cause dizziness or lightheadedness which may indicate a fall in your blood pressure, especially at the start of treatment.
- Side effects with Requip are generally mild and may become less after you have taken the medicine for a short time. Some people may feel or be sick or they may get stomach ache. The medicine may make you feel drowsy.
- This medicine does not usually affect people's normal activities. However, some people feel sleepy or dizzy while taking it, especially at the start of treatment. You should not drive or operate machinery until you are reasonably certain that Requip does not affect your ability to carry out these activities.
- If these symptoms become troublesome tell the doctor. If you develop any unusual discomfort tell the doctor as soon as possible.

What To Do in Case of Overdose:

- If you have taken a large number of tablets all at once, contact a doctor immediately. Show the doctor your pack of tablets.

How to Store Requip:

- The expiry date of this medicine is printed on the label. Do not use the medicine after this date.
- Keep your tablets in their original pack in a dry place away from light. They should be kept at room temperature (between 15 and 30°C).
- Keep out of reach of children.

What Does Requip Contain:

- Requip (ropinirole as ropinirole hydrochloride) is available as 0.25 mg (white), 0.5 mg (pale yellow), 1 mg (pale green), 2 mg (pale pink) and 5 mg (pale blue) tablets. Ropinirole hydrochloride is the active ingredient. Nonmedicinal ingredients include: hydrous lactose, microcrystalline cellulose, croscarmellose sodium, magnesium stearate, hydroxypropyl methylcellulose, polyethylene glycol, titanium dioxide, iron oxide yellow (1 and 2 mg tablets), iron oxide red (2 mg tablets), FD&C Blue No.2 aluminium lake (1 and 5 mg tablets), polysorbate 80 (0.25 mg tablets), talc (5 mg tablets). They do not contain sucrose, tartrazine or any other azo dyes.

Who Manufactures Requip:

- Requip tablets are manufactured by: SmithKline Beecham Pharma.

☐ RESTORIL® Ⓟ

Novartis Pharmaceuticals

Temazepam

Hypnotic

Information for the Patient: Facts on Restoril (temazepam): Introduction: Restoril (temazepam) is intended to help you sleep. It is one of several benzodiazepine sleeping pills that have generally similar properties.

If you are prescribed one of these medications, you should consider both their benefits and risks. Important risks and limitations include the following:

- **The longer you use the medication, the less effective it may become.**
- **You may become dependent on the medication.**
- **The medication may affect your mental alertness or memory, particularly when not taken as prescribed.**

In order to guide you in the safe use of the product, this leaflet will inform you about this class of medication in general, and about temazepam in particular.

But this leaflet should not replace a discussion between you and your doctor about the risks and benefits of Restoril.

Safe Use of Restoril Sleeping Pills: Restoril is a prescription medication, intended to help you sleep. Follow your doctor's advice about how to take Restoril, when to take it, and how long to take it. **Do not take Restoril** if it is not prescribed for you.

Do not take Restoril for more than 7 to 10 days without first consulting your doctor.

Do not take Restoril when a full night's sleep is not possible before you would again need to be active and functional; e.g., an overnight flight of less than 8 hours. Memory lapses may occur in such situations. Your body needs time to eliminate the medication from your system.

Do not take Restoril at any time during pregnancy. Tell your doctor if you are planning to become pregnant, if you are pregnant, or if you become pregnant while taking this medication.

Tell your doctor about any alcohol consumption (present or past) or any medicine you are taking now, including drugs you can buy without a prescription. **Do not consume alcohol while taking Restoril.**

Do not increase the prescribed dose.

Do not drive a car or operate potentially dangerous machinery until you experience how this drug will affect you.

If you develop any unusual disturbing thoughts or behavior while using Restoril discuss the matter immediately with your doctor.

You may experience an increase in sleep difficulties (rebound insomnia) and/or increased daytime anxiety (rebound anxiety) for 1 or 2 days after discontinuing Restoril.

Effectiveness of Benzodiazepine Sleeping Pills: Benzodiazepine sleeping pills are effective medications and are relatively free of serious problems when used for the short-term management of insomnia. Symptoms of insomnia may vary: you may have difficulty in falling asleep, or awaken often during the night, or awaken early in the morning, or you may have all three symptoms.

Insomnia may last only for a short time and may respond to brief treatment. The risk and benefits of prolonged use should be discussed with your doctor.

Side Effects: Common Side Effects: Benzodiazepine sleeping pills may cause drowsiness, dizziness, lightheadedness, and difficulty with coordination. Users must be cautious about engaging in hazardous activities requiring complete mental alertness, e.g., operating machinery or driving a motor vehicle.

Avoid alcohol while using Restoril. Do not use benzodiazepine sleeping pills along with other medications without first discussing this with your doctor.

How sleepy you are the day after you use one of these sleeping pills depends on your individual response and on how quickly your body gets rid of the medication.

The larger the dose, the more likely that you will experience drowsiness, etc., the next day. For this reason, it is important that you use the lowest effective dose.

Benzodiazepines, which are eliminated rapidly, tend to cause less drowsiness the next day, but may cause withdrawal problems the day after use (see below).

Special Concerns: Memory problems: All benzodiazepine sleeping pills can cause a special type of memory loss (amnesia); you may not recall

Restoril (cont'd)

events that occurred during some period of time, usually several hours, after taking the drug. This lapse is usually not a problem, because the person taking the sleeping pill intends to be asleep during this critical period of time. But it can be a problem if you take the medication to induce sleep while travelling, such as during an airplane flight, because you may wake up before the effect of the drug is gone. This has been called "traveller's amnesia".

Tolerance/Withdrawal Symptoms: After nightly use for more than a few weeks these drugs may lose some of their effectiveness. You may also develop a degree of dependence.

For benzodiazepine sleeping pills that the body eliminates quickly, there may be a deficiency of the drug in the body at some point between each night's use. This "withdrawal" can lead to (1) being awake during the last third of the night, and (2) increased daytime anxiety or nervousness.

Withdrawal effects can occur when patients stop taking benzodiazepine sleeping pills. The effects may occur following use for only a week or two but may be more common and severe after long periods of continuous use. One type of withdrawal symptom is known as "rebound insomnia", i.e., on the first few nights after stopping the medication, insomnia may be worse than before the sleeping pill was given.

Other withdrawal symptoms following abrupt stopping of sleeping pills may range from unpleasant feelings to a major withdrawal syndrome that may include abdominal and muscle cramps, vomiting, sweating, tremor, and rarely, convulsions. The severe symptoms are uncommon.

Dependence/Abuse: All benzodiazepine sleeping pills can cause dependence (addiction) especially when used regularly for more than a few weeks, or at higher doses. Some people develop a need to continue taking these drugs, either at the prescribed dose or at higher doses—not only for continued therapeutic effect, but also to avoid withdrawal symptoms or to achieve nontherapeutic effects.

Individuals who depend, or have depended at any time in the past, on alcohol or other drugs may be at particular risk of becoming dependent on drugs of this class. But **all people are at some risk.** Consider this matter before you take these medications beyond a few weeks.

Mental and Behavioral Changes: A variety of abnormal thinking and behavior changes may occur when you use benzodiazepine sleeping pills. Some of these changes include aggressiveness and extroversion which seem out of character. Other changes, although rare, can be more unusual and extreme such as confusion, strange behavior, restlessness, illusions, hallucinations, feeling like you are not yourself, and worsening depression, including suicidal thinking.

It is rarely clear whether such symptoms are caused by the medication, or by an underlying illness, or are simply spontaneous happenings.

In fact, worsened insomnia may in some cases be associated with illnesses that were present before the medication was used.

Important: Regardless of the cause, if you take these medications, report any mental or behavioral changes to your doctor.

Effect on Pregnancy: Certain benzodiazepine sleeping pills have been linked to birth defects when taken during the early months of pregnancy. In addition, benzodiazepine sleeping pills taken during the last weeks of pregnancy have been known to sedate the baby. Therefore, **avoid using this medication during pregnancy.**

☐ RETIN-A® ℞

Janssen-Ortho

Tretinoin

Comedolytic Agent

Information for the Patient: What is acne? Acne vulgaris is a common disease. It affects 90% of the population to some degree at some point in their lifetime. Acne is not just a teenage disease. In some people it may start for the first time in the twenties or even later. In some it lasts through the adult years. However, in most people, acne clears with time.

Acne is a disease of the oil gland. The face, chest and back have the largest number of oil glands and thus acne may involve any or all of these areas.

Acne begins with the formation of a plug in the oil gland. The plug is made up of surface skin, oil and bacteria. It is not due to dirt or lack of washing. The plug is seen in the skin as a blackhead or whitehead.

After formation of the plug, some of the oil in the gland escapes into the surrounding skin. It causes inflammation which is seen in the skin as a red swelling, namely papules, pustules, or cysts.

What Causes Acne? Acne is due to many different factors.

Heredity is most important. Although your parents may or may not have had acne, you still can inherit oil glands which are susceptible to acne.

Acne is not due to an imbalance of **hormones.** Your normal hormones stimulate the oil glands and contribute to acne.

Bacteria are also important. Acne is not an infection. However, bacteria in the oil glands produce substances which in turn cause the inflammation of acne.

Further information about the causes of acne may be obtained from your doctor.

How to Help Yourself: Diet: Most dermatologists agree that acne is not due to diet. However, it is wise to avoid iodides (excess salt, kelp, seaweed) which can aggravate acne.

Cosmetics: Oil-based cosmetic creams, moisturizing creams, suntan oils, and makeup should be avoided. They all can make acne worse. Use oil-free, water based liquid makeup or powder.

Washing: Avoid excess washing or harsh scrubbing which can make acne worse. Wash gently and frequently enough to keep the skin dry but not irritated.

Hands Off: Avoid picking or touching affected areas as this makes acne worse.

Facts About Retin-A Cream and Gel: What is it? Retin-A Cream or Gel contains vitamin A acid. Retin-A Cream or Gel is effective against blackheads, whiteheads, and minor inflammatory lesions of acne such as papules and pustules.

Adverse Effects: Peeling, burning, itching, stinging, redness and eye irritation may occur with some people during the first 1 or 2 weeks of therapy. These reactions can easily be minimized by following the instructions carefully. Should the effects become excessively troublesome, discontinue use and consult your doctor.

Safety:

1. **Topical tretinoin should be used by women of childbearing years only after contraceptive counselling. Pregnant women should discontinue use of topical tretinoin.**
2. Retin-A Cream or Gel has been prescribed by your physician for your use only. Do not allow other people to use it.
3. Retin-A Cream or Gel is for topical use only.
4. Do not apply Retin-A Cream or Gel to areas of skin where you have other problems such as eczema, severely inflamed skin or open lesions.
5. Retin-A Cream or Gel can make your skin more sensitive and increase the possibility of sunburn. Minimize exposure of areas treated with Retin-A Cream or Gel to sunlight or sunlamps during treatment. Wear protective clothing whenever you have to go out in the sun, even on hazy days. Also use a sunscreen on areas treated with Retin-A Cream or Gel.
6. Avoid excessive exposure to wind or cold as skin treated with Retin-A Cream or Gel may be more vulnerable to these extremes.
7. Use other acne medication only on your physician's advice and follow the physician's instructions carefully.
8. Try to avoid using topical products with a high concentration of alcohol, spices, or lime as they cause needless stinging and burning on treated skin.
9. Excessive medication will not produce better results, and marked redness, peeling and discomfort may occur. It is recommended that you apply a moisturizer or a moisturizer with sunscreen that will not aggravate your acne (noncomedogenic) every morning after you wash.
10. **Gels are flammable.** Note: Keep away from heat and flame. Keep tube tightly closed.

How to Use:

1. Wash with a mild soap and dry skin gently.
2. Wait 20 minutes before applying medication so that your skin is completely dry.
3. Apply Retin-A Cream or Gel once daily before bedtime (or as directed by your doctor).
4. Squeeze a small amount (about the size of a pea) on your fingertip. Spread on the skin where acne lesions appear, using enough to cover the entire affected area lightly.

5. Keep the medication away from the corners of the nose, mouth, eyes and mucous membranes or other areas where treatment is not intended. Spread away from these areas when applying.
6. Keep container closed when not in use.
7. The medication should become invisible almost immediately. If it is still visible or if dry flaking occurs within a minute or so, you are using too much.
8. If your doctor has prescribed another topical acne treatment (i.e., benzoyl peroxide or topical antibiotic), do not apply Retin-A Cream or Gel at the same time of day as the other products.
9. After 3 to 6 weeks of therapy some patients notice new blemishes. At this stage it is very important to continue using Retin-A Cream or Gel. Do not expect an overnight cure. With the use of Retin-A Cream or Gel, you will notice a gradual improvement over 8 to 12 weeks.

☐ RETISOL-A® ℞

Stiefel

Tretinoin

Acne Therapy

Information for the Patient: Retisol-A (tretinoin): What it is, what it does, and how it works: Retisol-A (tretinoin) is a cream containing a drug dermatologists have long prescribed in the treatment of acne. Retisol-A creams have a moisturizing base plus sunscreens with an SPF 15.

It works by penetrating deeply into the skin to unplug pores, and then aiding the natural flow and elimination of excess oils from the sebaceous glands.

In addition, Retisol-A has an exfoliative effect, which means the skin's outer layers may peel off to leave a smoother, healthier-looking surface and skin tone.

After many years of experience, with tretinoin, dermatologists usually advise patients that with regular use of Retisol-A, visible improvement should be seen in 6 to 8 weeks, so be patient.

It is important to understand that your physician has given you a prescription specially suited to your particular needs and skin type. **Do not allow others to use it.** Also, over-application of Retisol-A may irritate your skin and is unlikely to speed up treatment.

Following your physician's directions carefully will minimize common reactions such as mild burning sensations and redness.

During the first 3 weeks of treatment, your physician may recommend application of Retisol-A on every second day to allow your skin to adjust to the medication.

Use of any other acne or skin medication should be discontinued when using Retisol-A unless your physician advises otherwise. It is best to use only water-based cosmetics and avoid alcohol-based lotions. Your physician may recommend an additional daytime moisturizer if your skin is particularly dry.

Instructions for use:

1. Wash affected area with a mild soap and warm water and gently dry. Wait 20 to 30 minutes for the face to fully dry.
2. Apply Retisol-A sparingly and evenly, once daily. Use your finger-tip to apply enough to cover the required area, and smooth in. Retisol-A with moisturizing base plus sunscreen may be applied in the morning.
3. Avoid sensitive areas such as eyes, lips and mucous-producing areas. Also avoid areas of the skin where you have other problems, such as eczema.
4. At the beginning, you may experience redness, a burning sensation, and peeling while your skin adjusts to the medication which flushes existing oil and debris out of your pores.
5. To minimize these reactions, your physician may start you on the mildest strength of Retisol-A 0.01% and go up gradually until you reach the strength that your physician feels is most suitable for your skin type.
6. Since Retisol-A works from beneath the skin's surface, it takes several weeks of regular use before you can expect noticeable improvement.

Precautions:

1. Do not apply Retisol-A to areas of skin where you have problems such as eczema, severely inflamed skin or other open lesions.
2. Avoid sensitive and mucous-producing areas such as eyes, mouth, lips, angles of nose, and corners of eyes and mouth.
3. Do not over-apply Retisol-A. Doing so will not speed up treatment, but only irritate your skin.
4. While using Retisol-A, do not use other acne or skin medications without the advice of your physician.
5. Prolonged exposure to sunlight, sunlamps, wind and cold should be avoided during treatment.
6. If sunburn occurs, stop using Retisol-A and call your physician for advice.
7. Retisol-A has been prescribed for your use only. Do not allow others to use it.
8. If you are a female of childbearing age, you should only use Retisol-A after consulting your physician and seeking his/her advice for contraceptive counselling. If you are pregnant, you should discontinue the use of Retisol-A and consult your physician.

☐ RETROVIR® (AZT™) ℞

Glaxo Wellcome

Zidovudine

Antiretroviral Agent

Information for the Patient: The patient should be counselled about the use of Retrovir (AZT). The following text is a guideline.

Retrovir (AZT) is prescribed to slow down the effects of the HIV virus; it is not a cure. Illnesses associated with HIV infection, including other infections, may still happen. Therefore, it is very important to keep appointments with your doctor and to report any change in your health as it occurs.

Retrovir (AZT) has been extensively studied in humans for limited periods of time. Studies have shown that treatment will benefit your health. However, the effectiveness and overall safety of Retrovir (AZT) is unknown beyond the length of time for which it has been studied.

The effectiveness and overall safety of Retrovir (AZT) in women, i.v. drug users, and ethnic minorities are not different than that observed in white males.

An important but reversible side-effect of Retrovir (AZT), particularly in patients with more severe disease, can be a fall in the number of red blood cells (which carry oxygen) and a reduction in the number of white blood cells (which fight infection). Since a reduction in these cells can directly affect your health, it is important to have your blood tested as often as your doctor requests it. In some cases, it may be necessary to adjust the dose of the drug, temporarily discontinue the drug, give a blood transfusion, or stop the drug altogether.

It is important to understand that although these blood effects can occur at any stage, they are more common in more advanced disease and in patients who start Retrovir (AZT) therapy late in their illness.

Other side-effects of Retrovir (AZT) include nausea and vomiting. Contact your doctor if you experience muscle weakness, shortness of breath, symptoms of hepatitis or pancreatitis (which your physician can explain to you) or any other unexpected adverse events while being treated with Retrovir (AZT).

An additional precaution is that some other drugs may change the usefulness and safety of Retrovir (AZT). It is therefore very important that you tell your doctor about all the drugs you are taking. Ask your doctor before you decide to take any new drugs, even if these are available without a prescription.

It is also important to take Retrovir (AZT) exactly as prescribed. Altering the dose without the direct advice of your physician is unwise, as is sharing your medication with others.

For pregnant women who are considering the use of Retrovir (AZT) during pregnancy for the prevention of HIV-transmission to their infants, it is important to understand that transmission may still occur in some cases (about 8%) despite using Retrovir (AZT). The long-term safety in treated fetuses, neonates, or infants has not been established. HIV-infected women should not breast-feed in order to prevent transmission of HIV to a child who may not yet be infected.

HIV is usually spread by sexual contact or by contaminated needles. This risk still exists during Retrovir (AZT) therapy; thus, the practice of 'safe sex' and avoidance of sharing needles is imperative.

For patients receiving combination therapy with Retrovir (AZT) and zalcitabine, it is important to understand that the major toxicity of zalcitabine is peripheral neuropathy. Pancreatitis is another serious and potentially life-threatening toxicity that has been reported in less than 1% of patients treated with zalcitabine alone. Symptoms of peripheral neuropathy include tingling, burning, pain, or numbness in the hands or feet. Symptoms of pancreatitis include abdominal pain, and nausea and vomiting. These symptoms should be promptly reported to your

Retrovir (AZT) (cont'd)

physician. Since the development of peripheral neuropathy seems to be dose-related to zalcitabine, you should follow your physician's instructions regarding the prescribed dose. The long-term effects of zalcitabine in combination with Retrovir (AZT) are presently unknown. If you are a female of child-bearing age, you should use effective contraception while using zalcitabine.

☐ REVIA® ℞

DuPont Pharma

Naltrexone HCl

Opioid Antagonist

Information for the Patient: Please read this leaflet carefully before you start to take ReVia. If you have any questions or are not sure about anything just ask your doctor or pharmacist.

Use: Revia is used together with your other forms of treatment such as counselling to help you to remain free from your dependence on alcohol, heroin, methadone or other similar opiate drugs of addiction.

How It Works: Opiate drugs affect certain parts of the brain known as opiate receptors, producing euphoria (or "a high") and other effects. ReVia is an opiate receptor blocker. ReVia locks onto these receptor sites and blocks the effects of opiate drugs as well as the body's own opioids. The body's own opioids which occur naturally in the brain may be involved in alcoholism. While it is not completely understood how ReVia works, in the treatment of alcoholism, in patients who have stopped drinking, ReVia may help to prevent a return to heavy alcohol use. ReVia will not make you sick as a result of drinking alcohol. It is not addictive.

How to Take It: For the treatment of alcoholism, the recommended daily dose is 50 mg.

If you are being treated for narcotic dependence, you must have stopped taking opiate drugs for at least 7 to 10 days. Your physician will carry out a test which will show that you are free from these drugs before starting treatment. You will be given a starting dose of 25 mg and then 1 tablet (50 mg) daily, or it may be more convenient to take 2 tablets (100 mg) on Monday and Wednesday, and 3 tablets (150 mg) on Friday. Your doctor will decide which is best for you.

What Happens if You Miss a Dose: It is important to continue taking ReVia as it only remains effective against alcohol and opiate drugs as long as you continue to take the tablets.

If you forget 1 dose it would have no long-term consequences as the effect of ReVia lasts for up to 2 days, but take the tablet as soon as possible. However, do not double-up on your dose. Do not take more than your prescribed dose.

If you stop taking ReVia and restart the use of opiate drugs or alcohol, there is a danger that you will relapse and become dependent on these drugs or alcohol again.

If you have restarted opiate drugs you must not take ReVia until you have seen your doctor, who will make sure you are opiate-free.

If you take ReVia right after taking an opiate you will suffer withdrawal symptoms (cold turkey) (such as nausea, vomiting, shakiness, sweating and anxiety) which may be severe.

Duration of Treatment: You should continue to take ReVia for as long as it is prescribed by your doctor. This could be for 3 months or longer. ReVia does not produce "a high" and you cannot become addicted to it.

What Happens if You Drink Alcohol While Taking ReVia: You should not experience any unpleasant reaction if you drink alcohol while taking ReVia. However, your blood alcohol level will still increase and you will become physically and mentally impaired if you do drink alcohol while taking ReVia.

Warnings: If you take large amounts of an opiate in an attempt to overcome the blocking effects of ReVia, then you could be in trouble. Large doses of opiate can lead to difficulty in breathing and even to death. **Do not give your tablets to other people** particularly those who are known to be dependent on opiate drugs because a withdrawal syndrome "cold turkey" may be precipitated. Signs and symptoms (such as nausea, vomiting, shakiness, sweating and anxiety) which may be severe, may develop within 5 minutes. If this happens call a doctor.

You should not take ReVia if you are allergic to this product, or if you have acute hepatitis or liver failure. However, your doctor will advise you on these matters when the possibility of ReVia treatment is first discussed.

Your doctor will request that a blood sample is taken before you start treatment and at various times during treatment. This is necessary because ReVia is processed by the liver and these tests indicate if your liver is working well.

Do not drink alcohol during the time you are taking ReVia as this could cause damage to your liver. If you develop abdominal pain lasting more than a few days, white bowel movements, dark urine, or yellowing of your eyes, you should stop taking ReVia immediately and see your doctor as soon as possible.

Tell your doctor if you are pregnant or breast-feeding as the effects of ReVia on the baby are not known.

If you experience any unusual sensations or feel unwell after starting ReVia tell your doctor.

Some medicines may contain opiates, for example certain cough medicines, antidiarrheals (such as kaolin with morphine) and analgesics (pain killers). Revia may block the effects of these medicines. If you are ill and require treatment you must tell the doctor or pharmacists that you are taking ReVia. They can then recommend a medicine which will be effective.

Overdose: In the event of an accidental overdosage go to your nearest hospital emergency department or tell your doctor immediately, even though you may not feel sick.

Storing Your Medicine: Keep your tablets in a safe place where children cannot reach them. These tablets could harm them.

If your doctor decides to stop the treatment, return any leftover tablets to the pharmacist.

☐ RHEUMATREX™ ℞

Wyeth-Ayerst

Methotrexate Sodium

Antirheumatic Agent

Information for the Patient: Full prescribing information is available from your physician or pharmacist.

Rheumatrex is a proprietary name of Wyeth-Ayerst Canada Inc. for methotrexate 2.5 mg.

Rheumatrex, which has been prescribed by your doctor, is a potent medicine which can be very effective in treating severe rheumatoid arthritis. It usually shows some benefit in 3 to 6 weeks.

However, it can cause side effects, which occasionally can be serious. Most side effects can be detected **before** they become serious and for that reason your physician will keep you under close supervision, arranging for regular visits and periodic laboratory tests. For the safe treatment of your rheumatoid arthritis it is important that you carry out your physician's instructions faithfully and promptly report any side effects or symptoms you may develop.

Before taking this medication, you should inform your physician whether:

—You have already taken Rheumatrex and have developed an allergy or intolerance to it.
—You suffer from liver disease.
—You are pregnant, intend to become pregnant, are breast-feeding or intend to breast-feed.
—You are taking any other medicine, especially ASA, ASA-like drugs, or other 'arthritis drugs' (the so-called NSAIDs) or antibiotics.
—You have a peptic ulcer.
—You suffer from severe pulmonary disease.
—You are being treated for or were ever treated for any blood disease such as anemia.

How to take Rheumatrex:

—Rheumatrex is given weekly rather than daily; this is different than most medications. The importance of this **weekly** schedule cannot be overstated. The weekly dose is taken either singly or in divided doses. The weekly dosage you receive will depend on the results of your blood tests. After a blood test, check with your doctor's office **before** your next dose. It is important to follow the instructions on the prescription label.
—Taking Rheumatrex incorrectly can result in serious side effects. If doses are taken too often, notify your physician **at once**. If an acci-

dental overdose occurs, an antidote is necessary, and must be given as early as possible.

—Notify your physician **at once** if you develop fever, cough, and/or shortness of breath.

—Unrelated medical conditions especially dehydration (excess loss of body fluid), can also increase the risk of Rheumatrex toxicity. Abdominal upset, especially when accompanied by significant vomiting, diarrhea and/or decreased fluid intake can lead to dehydration. Excessive thirst may be a symptom of dehydration. Notify your physician immediately if these symptoms develop.

—Other medicines you are taking may result in an increase in side effects or a decrease in the effectiveness of Rheumatrex. Tell your physician **all** the medicines you are taking, whether they are prescription or nonprescription medicines. **Do not begin or change the dosage of any** medicine without first checking with your physician. This is **especially** true of ASA, ASA-like drugs or other 'arthritis drugs' (the so-called NSAIDs) or antibiotics.

—Alcoholic beverages (including beer and wine) may increase some of the side effects, including the chance of liver damage, and should be severely restricted or preferably avoided altogether.

Information about Side Effects: Side effects can occur at **any time** during your treatment. Periodic laboratory tests and sometimes other types of tests arranged by your physician are necessary for the safe use of Rheumatrex. Your cooperation is essential.

The most common side effects of Rheumatrex are loss of appetite, nausea (but rarely vomiting), diarrhea, abnormal liver tests (the periodic blood tests will check for this) or sores or ulcers in the mouth. If these or other problems trouble you, or should you develop any signs of infection or unusual bleeding, notify your doctor **at once**. These side effects are usually temporary, but frequently require dose changes.

Skin rash and other skin disorders are an infrequent side effect of Rheumatrex therapy. Should you develop any unusual skin rash, contact your physician **at once**.

Rheumatrex is known to cause birth defects and may cause miscarriage or stillbirth, especially in the first 3 months of pregnancy. Pregnant women **must not** take Rheumatrex and women of childbearing age **must not** become pregnant during or shortly after taking Rheumatrex. Adequate contraceptive measures are essential. Both men and women should take appropriate steps to avoid conception during and for several months after stopping Rheumatrex.

A rare side effect of long-term therapy may be the development of scarring (fibrosis) in the liver. Sometimes the removal of a small specimen of liver tissue with a needle (liver biopsy) is necessary to determine if scarring is present. If and when to do a liver biopsy is a matter of discussion between you and your physician.

Also, rarely, Rheumatrex can cause a lung reaction similar to pneumonia. The symptoms are usually fever, cough (often dry and hacking) and shortness of breath (which can become quite severe). Should you develop such symptoms notify your physician promptly.

In very rare cases, a tumor of the lymph nodes has been reported in patients receiving weekly doses of methotrexate. In the event of such a case, treatment options should be discussed with your doctor.

Always Remember:

1. Follow your physician's instructions **faithfully.**
2. Take your Rheumatrex **weekly** not daily.
3. Notify your physician **at once** if an accidental overdose is suspected.
4. Notify your physician **at once** if you develop fever, cough, and/or shortness of breath.
5. Notify your physician **at once** if you develop an unusual skin rash.
6. Notify your physician **at once** if you think you are getting an infection.
7. Notify your physician should any side effects or symptoms of dehydration occur **before** the next dose of Rheumatrex.
8. Do not begin or change any medicines without first checking with your physician.
9. Avoid alcoholic beverages.
10. Obtain the tests ordered by your physician.
11. Avoid pregnancy during and for a time after Rheumatrex.

Keep this medicine out of the reach of children and remember it has been prescribed for your current medical problem. It must not be given to other people.

□ RHINOCORT® AQUA ℞

Astra

Budesonide

Glucocorticosteroid

Information for the Patient: Important information you should know about Rhinocort Aqua (Budesonide). Before using Rhinocort Aqua, read this leaflet carefully. It contains general points about Rhinocort Aqua and should add to more specific advice from your doctor or pharmacist.

Please keep this leaflet to refer to until you have used up all medication in Rhinocort Aqua.

What is Rhinocort Aqua Used for and How Does it Work? Rhinocort is a brand name for a drug called budesonide. Rhinocort is an inhaled form of the drug budesonide. It belongs to a group of medicines called corticosteroids which are used to reduce inflammation. Rhinocort Aqua reduces and prevents the inflammation.

You should use Rhinocort Aqua when you experience symptoms such as congestion (blocked nose), runny nose, sneezing and nasal itching. These symptoms may be felt when you are exposed to pollen such as ragweed or grass (hayfever) or dust in your house.

Rhinocort Aqua can also be used to treat nasal polyps. It can prevent new polyps from appearing as well as get rid of ones you already have.

What is in Rhinocort Aqua? Rhinocort Aqua contains budesonide as the active ingredient and comes in a concentration of 64 μg per spray.

Most medicines contain more ingredients than just the active drug. Check with your doctor if you think you might be allergic to any of these items: budesonide, carboxymethylcellulose sodium, disodium edetate, glucose anhydrous, hydrochloric acid, microcrystalline cellulose, polysorbate 80, potassium sorbate and purified water.

What Should I Tell My Doctor Before Taking Rhinocort Aqua? Tell your doctor:

- about **all** health problems you have now or have had in the past, especially if you have had lung tuberculosis or any other recent infection;
- about other medicines you take, including ones you can buy without a prescription;
- if you take, or have taken steroid medicines within the past several months;
- if you have ever had a bad, unusual or allergic reaction to budesonide;
- if you are pregnant, plan to become pregnant or are breast-feeding.

How Do I Take Rhinocort Aqua Properly? It is important that you use Rhinocort Aqua daily at the intervals recommended by your doctor. Do not stop or change dosage without asking your doctor.

If you follow the instructions below, you will receive the medication (see package insert for illustrations).

1. Before use, turn the bottle upside-down 3 to 4 times. Remove the protective cap from the nose piece.
2. When using the spray for the first time, you must load the pump by pressing downwards on the collar. Use your index and middle fingers while supporting the base of the bottle with your thumb. Press down 5 to 10 times until a fine mist spray appears. The spray is now ready for use. If not used daily the pump must be loaded again. This time it is sufficient to pump just once into the air.
3. Gently blow your nose. Hold the bottle as shown. Tilt your head forward slightly, close one nostril with a finger and **gently** insert the tip of the nose piece into the other nostril.
4. For each spray your doctor has instructed you to take, press firmly downwards once on the collar. Breathe gently inwards through the nostril, then breathe out through the mouth.
5. Repeat the procedure for the other nostril.
6. Replace the protective cap on the nose piece. Keep the bottle in an upright position. Store between 15 and 30°C.

Cleaning: Clean the nose piece and protective cap regularly. To clean the nose piece, remove the protective cap, press upwards on the collar and the nose piece will come off. Wash the nose piece and protective cap under lukewarm water. Air dry and replace the nose piece and the protective cap back on the bottle and reload as in Instruction #2.

How Much Rhinocort Aqua Should I Take? The dosage of Rhinocort Aqua is individual. Follow your doctor's directions carefully. They may differ from the information in this leaflet.

Caution: Rhinocort Aqua does not give immediate relief of your nasal symptoms. It may take a few days (and up to 2 weeks) before you notice any improvement. Contact your doctor if:

Rhinocort Aqua (cont'd)

- no improvement occurs after 3 weeks,
- the inside of your nose becomes sore (nasal irritation),
- colored (yellow or green) nasal secretions appear,
- repeated bleeding from the nose occurs.

Adults and children over 6 years: **Rhinitis:** Suggested **starting doses** are: Total daily dose 4 sprays (256 µg). In children, do not exceed this dose. Rhinocort Aqua can be taken once or twice daily.
Once daily: 2 sprays (128 µg) into each nostril, once in the morning.
Twice daily: 1 spray (64 µg) into each nostril, morning and evening.
Maintenance dose: Use lowest effective dose.
Nasal Polyps: 1 spray (64 µg) into each nostril, morning and evening (total daily dose 256 µg).

Important: Use regularly as directed by your doctor. **Do not exceed the dose prescribed by your doctor.**

What Do I Do if I Miss a Dose? If you miss a dose of Rhinocort Aqua, take it as soon as possible. Then go back to your regular schedule. If it is almost time to take your next dose, skip the missed dose and take the next dose on time.

Never take a double dose of Rhinocort Aqua to make up for ones you missed. If you are still unsure, check with your doctor or pharmacist to see what you should do.

You may notice that your symptoms improve after the first dose of Rhinocort Aqua. However, several weeks may pass before the full effect is achieved. Don't forget to take Rhinocort Aqua even when you feel well.

Treatment with Rhinocort Aqua should not be stopped abruptly, but tapered off gradually.

What Should I do in Case of Overdose? Telephone your doctor or go to your nearest hospital right away if you think that you or anyone else may have taken too much Rhinocort Aqua.

Are There Any Side Effects? Like any medication, Rhinocort Aqua may result in side effects in some people.

The most common side effects are nasal and throat irritation, nasal bleeding, crusting and dryness. Other side effects include sneezing (at the start of treatment), itching throat, sore throat, cough, fatigue, nausea/dizziness and headache.

In rare cases, allergic conditions such as asthma or a skin rash may occur. These may not be caused by Rhinocort Aqua in your case, but only a doctor can tell this. A very few people who have used steroids in the nose have found small holes or ulcers in the skin inside the nose. It is very unlikely this will happen to you. If you notice anything unusual about the skin inside your nose, talk to your doctor.

Medicines affect different people in different ways. Just because side effects have occurred in other patients does not mean you will get them. If any side effects bother you, please contact your doctor.

Do not stop taking Rhinocort Aqua on your own. Your doctor may want to slowly reduce your dose, especially if you have been using Rhinocort Aqua for a long time. Although rare, symptoms of steroid withdrawal (i.e., fatigue, muscle or joint aches) may occur if Rhinocort Aqua is stopped too quickly.

Where Should I Keep Rhinocort Aqua? Remember to **keep Rhinocort Aqua out of the reach of children** when you are not using it.

Store the bottle at room temperature (15 to 30°C) in a dry place, away from moisture.

Do not keep or use Rhinocort Aqua after the expiry date indicated on the label.

Important Note: This leaflet alerts you to some of the times you should call your doctor. Other situations which cannot be predicted may arise. Nothing about this leaflet should stop you from calling your doctor or pharmacist with any questions or concerns you have about using Rhinocort Aqua.

☐ RHINOCORT® TURBUHALER® ℞

Astra

Budesonide

Glucocorticosteroid

Information for the Patient: Important information you should know about Rhinocort Turbuhaler (budesonide). Before using Rhinocort Turbuhaler, please read this leaflet carefully. It contains general points about Rhinocort Turbuhaler and should add to more specific advice from your doctor or pharmacist.

Please keep this leaflet to refer to until you have used up all medication in Rhinocort Turbuhaler.

What is Rhinocort Turbuhaler Used for and How Does it Work? Rhinocort is a brand name for a drug called budesonide. Rhinocort is an inhaled form of the drug budesonide. It belongs to a group of medicines called corticosteroids which are used to reduce inflammation. Rhinitis is caused by inflammation of the nasal mucosa. Rhinocort Turbuhaler reduces and prevents this inflammation. In some cases, several weeks of regular use may be needed before the full effect is seen.

Turbuhaler is the brand name for a multiple-dose, dry-powder inhaler. When you breathe in through the inhaler, your indrawn breath provides the necessary force to deliver the drug to your nasal passages.

What is in Rhinocort Turbuhaler? Rhinocort Turbuhaler contains budesonide as the active ingredient and comes in one strength: 100 µg per inhalation.

If you happen to shake the inhaler, the sound you hear is the drying agent built into the turning grip. This is not the medication and cannot be inhaled. Rhinocort Turbuhaler contains no other ingredients.

What Should I Tell My Doctor Before Taking Rhinocort Turbuhaler? Tell your doctor:

- about **all** health problems you have now or have had in the past, especially if you have had lung tuberculosis or any other recent infection;
- about other medicines you take, including ones you can buy without a prescription;
- if you take, or have taken steroid medicines within the past several months;
- if you have ever had a bad, unusual or allergic reaction to "budesonide";
- if you are pregnant, plan to become pregnant or are breast-feeding.

How Do I Take Rhinocort Turbuhaler Properly? It is important that you use Rhinocort Turbuhaler daily at the intervals recommended by your doctor. Do not stop or change dosage without asking your doctor.

Note: You may not taste or feel any medication when inhaling from Rhinocort Turbuhaler. This is common.

If you follow the instructions below, you will receive the medication (see package insert for illustrations).

1. Blow your nose. Unscrew the cover and lift it off.
2. Load a dose by holding Rhinocort Turbuhaler upright. Turn the grey grip as far as it will go in one direction and then turn it back to the original position. The "click" you heard means that Rhinocort Turbuhaler is ready to use.
3. Breathe out. Note: Never breathe out through the nasal adapter.
4. Place the nasal adapter so the nostril fits tightly around the adapter and block the opposite nostril with a finger. Sniff quickly (0.5 second) and forcefully.
5. Remove Rhinocort Turbuhaler from your nose before breathing out.
6. Repeat Steps 2 to 4 for the other nostril.
7. Replace the cover and screw it shut.

If you accidentally drop, shake or breathe out into Rhinocort Turbuhaler after it is loaded, you will lose your dose. If this happens, you should load a new dose and inhale it.

Cleaning: Clean the outside of the nasal adapter once a week with a **dry** tissue. **Never** use water or any other fluid for cleaning the nasal adapter. If fluid enters Rhinocort Turbuhaler it may not work properly.

How Do I Know When Rhinocort Turbuhaler Is Empty? (See package insert for illustrations.) Rhinocort Turbuhaler has a dose indicator. When a red mark first appears in the little window underneath the mouthpiece, there are approximately **20** doses left. Now is the time to obtain your next inhaler.

When the red mark reaches the bottom of the window, Rhinocort Turbuhaler is **empty**. If you shake the inhaler when it is empty, you will still be able to hear the sound of the drying agent. Rhinocort Turbuhaler cannot be refilled with drug and should be discarded.

How Much Rhinocort Turbuhaler Should I Take? The dosage of Rhinocort Turbuhaler is individual.

Follow your doctor's directions carefully. They may differ from the information in this leaflet.

Important: Do not exceed the dose prescribed by your doctor.

It is important that you use Rhinocort Turbuhaler daily at the intervals recommended by your doctor. Do not stop or change dosage without asking your doctor.

Rhinitis: Initial Dose: Adults: 2 applications into each nostril in the morning (total daily dose: 400 μg). **Children** (6 years and older): 2 applications into each nostril in the morning (total daily dose: 400 μg). This dose should not be exceeded in children.

Maintenance Dose: Adults and Children (6 years and older): Use the lowest effective dose necessary to control symptoms.

Nasal Polyps: 1 application (100 μg) into each nostril, morning and evening (total daily dose: 400 μg).

Caution: Rhinocort Turbuhaler is not intended to give immediate relief of your nasal symptoms and it may take a few days (and up to 2 weeks) before you notice any improvement. Contact your doctor if:

- no improvement occurs after 3 weeks,
- nasal irritation occurs,
- colored (yellow or green) nasal secretions appear,
- repeated nasal bleeding occurs.

What Do I Do If I Miss A Dose? Rhinitis: If you miss a dose of Rhinocort Turbuhaler and remember within 12 hours, you should take your usual dose as soon as possible. Then go back to your regular schedule. If it is more than 12 hours when you remember, do not take the missed dose. Just take the next dose on time.

Nasal Polyps: If you miss a dose of Rhinocort Turbuhaler and remember within 6 hours, you should take your usual dose as soon as possible. Then go back to your regular schedule. If it is more than 6 hours when you remember, do not take the missed dose. Just take the next dose on time.

Never take a double dose of Rhinocort Turbuhaler to make up for a missed dose. If you are still unsure, check with your doctor or pharmacist to see what you should do.

You may notice that your symptoms improve after the first dose of Rhinocort Turbuhaler. However, several weeks may pass before the full effect is achieved. Don't forget to take it even when you feel well.

Treatment with Rhinocort Turbuhaler should not be stopped abruptly, but tapered off gradually. Follow your doctor's directions.

If you have been prescribed Rhinocort Turbuhaler and are still using ''cortisone'' tablets, your doctor may gradually (over a period of weeks or months) reduce your dose of tablets. You may even be able to eventually stop using the tablets.

Note: If your medication is changed from ''cortisone'' tablets to Rhinocort Turbuhaler, you may temporarily regain symptoms which may have bothered you earlier, e.g., runny nose, rash, pain in muscle and joints. If any of these symptoms bothers you, or if you get symptoms such as headache, tiredness, nausea or vomiting, contact your doctor.

What Should I Do in Case of Overdose? Telephone your doctor or go to your nearest hospital right away if you think that you or anyone else may have taken too much Rhinocort Turbuhaler.

Are There Any Side Effects? Like any medication, Rhinocort Turbuhaler may cause side effects in some people.

The most commonly reported side effects include: nasal and throat irritation, nasal bleeding, crusting and dryness. Other side effects include sneezing (at initiation of therapy), itching throat, sore throat, cough, fatigue, nausea/dizziness and headache.

In rare cases, skin reactions like rash may occur in association with local corticosteroid therapy. A very few people who have used steroids in the nose have found small holes or ulcers in the skin, inside the nose. It is very unlikely this will happen to you. If you notice anything unusual about the skin inside your nose, talk to your doctor.

Medicines affect different people in different ways. Just because side effects have occurred in other patients does not mean you will get them. If any side effects bother you, contact your doctor.

Where Should I Keep Rhinocort Turbuhaler? Remember to **keep Rhinocort Turbuhaler out of the reach of children.**

Always replace the cover after using Rhinocort Turbuhaler. Store the inhaler at room temperature (15 to 30°C) in a dry place, away from moisture.

Do not keep or use Rhinocort Turbuhaler after the expiry date indicated on the label.

Important Note: This leaflet alerts you to some of the times you should call your doctor. Other situations which cannot be predicted may arise. Nothing about this leaflet should stop you from calling your doctor or pharmacist with any questions or concerns you have about using Rhinocort Turbuhaler.

□ RIDAURA® ℞

Pharmascience

Auranofin

Antirheumatic Agent

Information for the Patient: Educational information for patients beginning Ridaura therapy is available from the manufacturer upon request. The information provided is as follows: ''Understanding Rheumatoid Arthritis and Psoriatic Arthritis''.

Your doctor has prescribed Ridaura (oral gold) as part of your treatment program. Because you and your family may wish to know more about the disease and its treatment, SmithKline Beecham has developed this informative booklet and a companion cassette tape to supplement the information your doctor has given you. These are provided at no additional charge with your first month's supply of Ridaura capsules.

Your doctor has decided that Ridaura is a proper medication for you; it may not be appropriate for others. **Do NOT give any Ridaura capsules to other family members or friends who may appear to have a condition similar to yours.** Advise them to consult their doctor for proper diagnosis and treatment.

Rheumatoid arthritis is a disease affecting primarily the joints, causing joint swelling, pain and stiffness.

It is a fairly common ailment, affecting about 1% of the population. The disease occurs most frequently in adults (ages 20 to 60), but it may develop at any age. Rheumatoid arthritis is 3 times more common in women than in men.

Psoriatic arthritis is a disease affecting primarily the joints, causing joint swelling, pain and stiffness and is also associated with skin or nail lesions of psoriasis.

In the general populations, 1 to 2% are affected by psoriatic arthritis. The disease occurs most frequently in adults ages 30 to 50 years. Psoriasis precedes the onset of arthritis in approximately 75% of the patients, and occurs simultaneously in about 15%. In a small number of patients, arthritis precedes the appearance of skin lesions.

In order to understand the nature of the disease, it is helpful to review the joint's normal structure.

The Normal Joint: A joint is an area where 2 bones meet end-to-end. Joints can be thought of as hinges that enable us to walk, lift objects, bend, turn, and sit down. Muscles and ligaments support the joint, and keep the bones aligned within the joint capsule, permitting movement and providing protection from injury.

The ends of the opposing bones are covered by tough elastic sheaths of **cartilage** and separated by a pocket of fluid—**synovial fluid**—which is produced by the **synovium** (the inner lining of the joint capsule). Synovial fluid has 2 main functions: 1) to lubricate the cartilage, reducing the mechanical stress caused by movement, and 2) to supply nutrients that maintain the health of surrounding tissues. Disorders such as rheumatoid arthritis that adversely affect the synovium or synovial fluid will alter the joint's delicate architecture, possibly impairing joint function and movement.

The Arthritic Joint: The causes of rheumatoid and psoriatic arthritis are unknown. Whatever the cause, the result is joint inflammation and its accompanying symptoms and, later, joint damage. Inflammation attracts blood components that release enzymes capable of attacking the synovium. Once irritated and inflamed, the synovium produces excess fluid, which puts painful pressure on surrounding tissues. Cellular debris from the inflammatory process, called **pannus**, accumulates on the cartilage surfaces and releases enzymes that can destroy the joint tissues and, eventually, the bone. Such damage is irreversible, eventually limiting joint motion.

Disease Symptoms and Diagnosis: The first symptom of rheumatoid arthritis is usually general fatigue, accompanied by overall muscle soreness, stiffness, aches and pain. Joint inflammation is marked by pain, swelling, warmth and tenderness of one or more joints in the hands or feet. It can also affect the wrist, shoulders, elbows, hips and knees.

Once rheumatoid arthritis develops, it may progress over many months and years. Symptoms and discomfort can vary greatly from day to day or month to month. There may be repeated and prolonged periods when symptoms disappear and discomfort is greatly reduced (apparent remissions), as well as episodes when symptoms intensify (exacerbations), increasing discomfort.

A diagnosis of rheumatoid arthritis is based on the patient's history of symptoms and an examination of joint involvement. The results of x-rays and blood tests for inflammation and rheumatoid arthritis markers may also contribute to the diagnosis.

Ridaura (cont'd)

A diagnosis of psoriatic arthritis is based on the presence of symptoms of inflammatory arthritis coupled with typical skin or nail lesions of psoriasis.

Rheumatoid and Psoriatic Arthritis Treatment Programs: Although there is presently no known cure for rheumatoid or psoriatic arthritis, much can be done to relieve pain, improve function and, in some cases, delay further joint damage. Given the unpredictable nature of rheumatoid arthritis, the best treatment usually requires several therapeutic measures in a total management program. Such programs include rest, limited physical exercise and medication.

Lifestyle: Your doctor may recommend altering your daily routine to include periods of rest and exercise. With the support of physician, family and friends, this will help you feel better and maintain an active lifestyle.

Because rheumatoid arthritis causes fatigue, adequate rest is an integral part of therapy. Your doctor will probably recommend that you take short rest periods during the day and get a full night's sleep. Bed rest is usually required only during severe flare-ups. Too much rest can actually make you stiffer and weaker.

It is important not to overwork any part of your body that is affected by the disease. In some cases, it may be necessary to change your routine at home or work to prevent excessive fatigue.

Your doctor may recommend specific exercises. These regular but limited exercises are intended to prevent joint stiffness and reduced motion. The doctor may also recommend whirlpool baths, the use of supports or splints, or the application of warm or cold compresses.

A healthy lifestyle should also include a well-balanced diet (**not** fad diets).

Although these measures can be effective, they are usually accompanied by drug therapy used to relieve symptoms. In some severe cases, programs incorporate certain drugs that can influence the course of the disease.

Drug Therapy: In most psoriatic arthritis patients, psoriasis is successfully treated with creams or ointments; in some patients, the psoriasis requires no therapy at all. Adequate control of skin disease may lead to improvement of the joint disease in an occasional patient.

Some patients with psoriatic arthritis will have more progressive joint disease and should be treated similarly to those with progressive rheumatoid arthritis.

Because rheumatoid arthritis and psoriatic arthritis are chronic diseases, drug therapy is long-term. The goals of drug therapy are to relieve pain and, if possible, slow the progression of the disease. Drugs used in the management of rheumatoid arthritis and mild to moderate psoriatic arthritis can be divided into 2 groups.

First, there are drugs such as acetylsalicylic acid (ASA, e.g., Aspirin) and other nonsteroidal anti-inflammatory drugs (NSAIDs) that combat inflammation and provide relief of pain and other symptoms of rheumatoid arthritis. You have been taking one of these drugs. However, because of insufficient response to this drug and the nature of your disease, your doctor has decided that other drug measures, which may modify the progress of the disease, may be beneficial.

These other drugs are intended to slow the progress of rheumatoid arthritis. Such drugs include injectable gold, Ridaura, penicillamine, and certain drugs that suppress the immune system. Although effective, these drugs do not provide immediate relief from pain or stiffness, and are normally given with ASA or other NSAIDs.

All these drugs have some potentially serious side effects and you must keep your appointments with your doctor who will monitor your condition carefully.

Facts About Ridaura: As part of your overall treatment program, your doctor has prescribed Ridaura—oral gold. The recommended dose for initial therapy is 2 capsules per day.

Clinical experience has demonstrated that Ridaura is effective in the long-term management of rheumatoid and psoriatic arthritis—relieving pain, morning stiffness and fatigue, reducing the number of tender or swollen joints, and improving daily activity. Ridaura may also modify the progression of the disease. However, the precise mechanism of action of Ridaura is still unknown.

The beneficial effects of Ridaura take time to become apparent. A response may be seen after 3 to 4 months, but it may take up to 6 months. Your doctor will instruct you to continue taking ASA or NSAIDs to relieve more immediate symptoms of rheumatoid arthritis.

Because your disease is chronic and took many months or even years to develop, it is important that you do not become discouraged if you do not feel significant improvement immediately with this regimen. Patience is the key. You should continue taking Ridaura and other medications as your doctor instructs, even if you have no pain. Your doctor will be monitoring therapy with frequent laboratory tests and office visits and will make any necessary adjustments in your therapy.

Side effects may occur with Ridaura. The most frequent adverse reaction to Ridaura has been a change in stool pattern—loose stools or diarrhea. Stomach pain, nausea, skin rashes, itching, eye inflammation (conjunctivitis), and inflammation of the tissues of the mouth (stomatitis) have also been reported during therapy with Ridaura. These events generally occur early in the treatment program and can usually be relieved without discontinuing Ridaura therapy, but sometimes discontinuation is necessary.

Rarely, more severe reactions occur which include changes in blood cells or kidneys. These can be reversed if discovered early. If you notice any unusual or troublesome symptoms including fever, sore throat, lesions in the mouth, spontaneous bruising, black or tarry stools, skin reactions, or persistent or severe indigestion while taking Ridaura contact your doctor **immediately**.

In Summary: Millions of people are coping with rheumatoid arthritis and psoriatic arthritis. And like you, they have had to modify their lifestyle by changing their daily routines.

The treatment program that your doctor has recommended is designed to keep you active and feeling good. Pay careful attention to your doctor's instructions regarding regular rest periods, specific exercises, and medications.

Be sure to take Ridaura and other medications exactly as directed and contact your doctor if you notice any unusual or troublesome symptoms.

Finally, if you have any questions concerning rheumatoid arthritis or Ridaura, note these on the following pages and discuss them with your doctor during your next appointment. You may also wish to fill out the diary to follow your treatment instructions.

An abbreviated information leaflet accompanies all prescriptions (see Supplied). The text follows:

Your doctor has prescribed Ridaura (oral gold) as part of your treatment program for arthritis. To provide you and your family with helpful information about this disease and its treatment, SmithKline Beecham has developed a valuable patient education program especially for new patients starting treatment with Ridaura.

This program consists of an educational booklet, ''Understanding Rheumatoid Arthritis and Psoriatic Arthritis'', and an accompanying cassette tape. These are available upon request from SmithKline Beecham Pharma Inc.: Ridaura Patient Education Program, c/o Medical Department, SmithKline Beecham Pharma Inc., 2030 Bristol Circle, Oakville, Ontario, L6H 5V2. When you receive the cassette tape and booklet, be sure to complete the booklet's treatment diary so that you can follow your treatment program from month to month.

Ridaura is an oral preparation containing gold. Gold in the form of an injection has been used in treatment of severe rheumatoid arthritis for a number of years. Clinical experience has shown that Ridaura is helpful in the management of rheumatoid arthritis which is not satisfactorily controlled by such drugs as acetylsalicylic acid (ASA, e.g. Aspirin) or other nonsteroidal anti-inflammatory drugs. Be sure to take Ridaura and other medications exactly as directed. **Do NOT increase dosage** unless instructed to do so by your doctor.

Side effects may occur with Ridaura. The most frequent adverse reaction to Ridaura has been a change in stool pattern—loose stools or diarrhea. Stomach pain, nausea, skin rashes, itching, eye inflammation (conjunctivitis), and inflammation of the tissues of the mouth (stomatitis) have also been reported during therapy with Ridaura. These events generally occur early in the treatment program and can usually be relieved without discontinuing Ridaura therapy, but sometimes discontinuation is necessary.

Rarely, more severe reactions occur which include changes in blood cells or kidneys. These can be reversed if discovered early. Therefore, your doctor will be monitoring therapy with frequent laboratory tests and office visits and will make any necessary adjustments in your therapy. If you notice any unusual or troublesome symptoms including fever, sore throat, lesions in the mouth, spontaneous bruising, black or tarry stools, skin reactions, or persistent or severe indigestion while taking Ridaura, contact your doctor **immediately**.

Although your doctor has decided that Ridaura is the proper medication for you, it may not be appropriate for others. **Do NOT give any Ridaura capsules to family members or friends** who may appear to have a condition similar to yours. Advise them to consult their doctor for proper diagnosis and treatment.

The treatment program that your doctor has recommended is designed to keep you active and feeling good. Pay careful attention to your doctor's instructions regarding regular rest periods, specific exercises, and medications.

□ RISPERDAL® Oral Solution

Janssen-Ortho

Risperidone Tartrate

Antipsychotic Agent

Information for the Patient: Oral Solution 1 mg/mL: Directions for Opening the Bottle and Using the Pipette (see package insert for illustrations):

1. Push the plastic screw cap down while turning counter clockwise. Remove the unscrewed cap.
2. Firmly pull the dispensing-pipette out of its plastic storage case and insert the pipette into the bottle.
3. While holding the outer barrel of the pipette, pull the plunger up to the level (see markings on side) that equals the dosage prescribed by your physician.
4. Holding the outer barrel of the pipette, remove the entire pipette from the bottle, being careful not to depress the plunger prematurely.
5. Empty the entire contents of the pipette into 100 mL of any nonalcoholic beverage (see list below), by pushing the plunger down inside the pipette barrel. Stir the mixture thoroughly before consuming. Tests indicate that Risperdal oral solution is compatible with the following beverages: water, coffee, orange juice and low-fat milk; however, it is **not** compatible with cola or tea.
6. Rinse the empty dispensing-pipette with water, and place it back into the plastic storage case; replace the plastic cap on the bottle.

Dosage: Take as directed by your physician.

Storage: Store bottle at controlled room temperature (15 to 30°C) away from children; avoid freezing and protect from light.

□ RITALIN®
□ RITALIN® SR

Novartis Pharmaceuticals

Methylphenidate HCl

CNS Stimulant

Information for the Patient: Introduction: Ritalin is used in two different medical conditions: 1) Attention-Deficit Hyperactivity Disorder (ADHD) and 2) Narcolepsy. Information on the use of Ritalin in each of these conditions is given in separate sections of this leaflet. Please refer to either ''Ritalin in Attention-Deficit Hyperactivity Disorder—Information for the Parents'' or ''Ritalin in Narcolepsy—Information for the Patient'' for information suited to your needs.

Ritalin in Attention-Deficit Hyperactivity Disorders—Information for the Parents: The doctor has prescribed Ritalin for your child's behavioral condition known as Attention-Deficit Hyperactivity Disorder. The following information will tell you about Attention-Deficit Hyperactivity Disorder and the use of Ritalin in this condition. If you want to know more or have any questions, please ask the doctor or pharmacist.

About Attention-Deficit Hyperactivity Disorder: Attention-Deficit Hyperactivity Disorder is a behavioral disorder in children and adolescents. It has been called by many other names including: Attention Deficit Disorder, Hyperkinetic Child Syndrome, Minimal Brain Damage, Minimal Cerebral Dysfunction and Minor Cerebral Dysfunction.

Children who suffer from Attention-Deficit Hyperactivity Disorder show behavioral problems such as difficulty concentrating, impulsiveness and restlessness. They may fail at school although they may have adequate intelligence. Such children may be unpopular among children of the same age because of their clumsiness, intrusive behavior and failure to follow the rules of games. Many prefer to be friends with younger children. Parents often feel that these children need more coaching and supervising than their brothers and sisters in most daily activities. Discipline usually cannot change such children's behavior. Teachers complain about their disruptiveness and constant need for attention. Most children with Attention-Deficit Hyperactivity Disorder do not complain of any problems; therefore, these children may not receive medical help unless the teacher(s) or parent(s) are aware of the nature of the problem. Medical exams, psychological and educational tests are all necessary in diagnosing Attention-Deficit Hyperactivity Disorder.

About the Use of Ritalin in Attention-Deficit Hyperactivity Disorder: Ritalin belongs to a group of medicines called central nervous system stimulants. When used in Attention-Deficit Hyperactivity Disorder, Ritalin improves behavior by reducing restlessness and increasing attention. Ritalin, however, will not cure Attention-Deficit Hyperactivity Disorder. Treatment with Ritalin or other stimulants should always be combined with other treatment measures, such as psychological counseling and educational tutoring by skilled and experienced therapists.

There is no evidence that children with ADHD become addicted to Ritalin, or that they tend to abuse drugs later in life. Central nervous stimulants, including Ritalin should only be given under close medical supervision to patients whose condition has been properly diagnosed.

How Ritalin Should be Taken: Ritalin comes in tablets to be taken by mouth. The doctor determines how much and how often your child should take Ritalin according to your child's individual needs. In order for your child to receive the most benefits from Ritalin, it is important that Ritalin be taken only as directed by the doctor. Take only the amount of medication at the time intervals and for the time period that the doctor has prescribed. Your child should not take more than 60 mg of Ritalin per day. If Ritalin SR (extended-release) tablets have been prescribed for your child, these tablets must be swallowed whole and never be crushed or chewed.

What You Should Be Aware Of: Use of Ritalin may be unsuitable or require special attention under certain medical conditions. You should let the doctor know if your child has conditions such as a previous allergy to Ritalin or any of its components, high blood pressure, heart disorders, thyroid disorders, glaucoma (increased eye pressure), epilepsy, agitation, tension, motor tics or family history or diagnosis of Tourette's syndrome, depression, or a history of severe depression, psychosis, anxiety, drug or alcohol abuse, or other medical problems. Alcohol should be avoided. Ritalin may increase seizures in some patients with a history of seizures.

Ritalin should not be used in children under 6 years of age.

It is important to tell the doctor and pharmacist if your child takes other medications besides Ritalin since combining drugs can sometimes result in changing the expected drug effects or cause harmful effects.

Get medical help immediately in cases of overdose.

Possible Unwanted Effects: Contact the doctor if your child experiences any of the following unwanted effects: fast heartbeat, breathing difficulties, chest pain, sweating, vomiting, bruising, muscle twitching or tics, sore throat and fever, confusion, hallucination and convulsions. Other side effects not listed above may occur in some patients. If you notice any other effects, tell your doctor immediately.

Your child may experience stomach discomforts, nausea and/or loss of appetite with Ritalin. These problems may go away with time.

Taking Ritalin with food may reduce stomach discomforts.

Ritalin may reduce weight gain or growth in children. To help restrict this problem to a minimum, the doctor may want to withhold Ritalin over weekends and during vacations.

Ritalin may cause sleeplessness if taken too close to bedtime.

How Ritalin Should be Stored: Protect Ritalin from moisture and heat. Keep out of reach of children.

Further Information: Expiry Date: Ritalin tablets should not be used after the expiry date shown on the package label. Remember to take back unused medicine to your pharmacist.

Other Important Information: Use this medicine only as directed by your doctor. Do not take more of it, do not take it more often, and do not take it for a longer time than your doctor ordered.

Ritalin SR tablets must be swallowed whole and never broken before taking them.

Ritalin in Narcolepsy—Information for the Patient: The doctor has prescribed Ritalin for your medical condition known as narcolepsy. The following information will tell you about narcolepsy and the use of Ritalin in this condition. If you want to know more or have any questions, please ask the doctor or pharmacist.

About Narcolepsy: Persons who suffer from narcolepsy experience attacks of sleepiness during the day although they may have enough sleep at night. These attacks usually occur in unusual situations such as standing, eating or the middle of a conversation. Some people find their head falling forward, jaw dropping, knees buckling or even falling to the ground while they are conscious. These attacks may be brought on by emotional situations such as hearty laughter, excitement, sadness or anger.

About the Use of Ritalin in Narcolepsy: Ritalin belongs to a group of medicines called central nervous system stimulants. When used in

Ritalin (cont'd)

narcolepsy, Ritalin may relieve the inappropriate daytime sleepiness; however, many people suffering from narcolepsy need additional treatment aimed at other aspects of this condition.

How Ritalin Should Be Taken: Ritalin comes in tablets to be taken by mouth. Your doctor determines how much and how often you should take Ritalin according to your individual needs. In order for you to receive the most benefits from Ritalin, it is important that Ritalin be taken only as directed by your doctor. Take only the amount of medication at the time intervals and for the time period that the doctor has prescribed. If Ritalin SR (extended-release) tablets have been prescribed for you, these tablets should never be crushed or chewed.

What You Should Be Aware Of: Ritalin should not be used to relieve normal tiredness.

Use of Ritalin may be unsuitable or require special attention under certain medical conditions. You should let the doctor know if you have conditions such as a previous allergy to Ritalin or any of its components, high blood pressure, heart disorders, thyroid disorders, glaucoma (increased eye pressure), epilepsy, agitation, tension, motor tics or family history or diagnosis of Tourette's syndrome, depression, or a history of severe depression, psychosis, anxiety, drug or alcohol abuse, or other medical problems. Alcohol should be avoided. Ritalin may increase seizures in some patients with a history of seizures.

Tell your doctor if you are pregnant or breast-feeding.

Ritalin should not be used during pregnancy. Mothers taking Ritalin should not breast-feed their babies.

It is important to tell the doctor and pharmacist if you take other medications besides Ritalin since combining drugs can sometimes result in changing the expected drug effects or cause harmful effects. Alcohol should be avoided.

Ritalin may affect your ability to drive or operate machinery.

Get medical help immediately in cases of overdose.

Possible Unwanted Effects: You may experience stomach discomforts, nausea and/or loss of appetite with Ritalin. These problems may go away with time. Taking Ritalin with food may reduce stomach discomfort.

Weight loss may occur when Ritalin is taken over a long period of time.

Ritalin may cause sleeplessness if taken too close to bedtime.

Contact your doctor immediately if you experience any of the following unwanted effects: fast heartbeat, breathing difficulties, chest pain, sweating, vomiting, bruising, muscle twitching or tics, sore throat and fever, confusion, hallucination and convulsions. Other side effects not listed above may occur in some patients. If you notice any other effects, tell your doctor immediately.

How Ritalin Should Be Stored: Protect Ritalin from moisture and heat. Keep out of reach of children.

Further Information: Expiry Date: Ritalin tablets should not be used after the expiry date shown on the package label. Remember to take back unused medicine to your pharmacist.

Other Important Information: Use this medicine only as directed by your doctor. Do not take more of it, do not take it more often, and do not take it for a longer time than your doctor ordered.

Ritalin SR tablets must be swallowed whole and never broken before taking them.

☐ ROFERON®-A 🄿

Roche

Interferon alfa-2a

Biological Response Modifier

Information for the Patient (see package insert for illustrations): **Instructions for self-administration:** Roferon-A is injected into the tissue just under the skin. This is known as s.c. injection. Usually Roferon-A is administered 3 times a week. You should inject approximately the same time every day. The most suitable places for injection are the top of the thighs and the abdomen, except for the belly button area.

Rotate injection site to avoid the risk of soreness at any one site.

1. Before preparing the syringe

- Do not use Roferon-A after the expiry date shown on the prefilled syringe label.
- Check the dose that you have been prescribed.
- Check the liquid has no discoloration, cloudiness or particles.
- Let the syringe stand for 30 minutes at room temperature.
- Wash you hands thoroughly.
- Place everything you need within easy reach; syringe, needle and alcohol wipes.

2. How to prepare the syringe

- Take the sealed needle in both hands and snap the orange cup backwards. Remove the orange cap. **Do not** remove the plastic needle shield (steps 1 and 2).
- Remove the rubber tip from the syringe (step 3).
- Attach the needle with the plastic shield firmly to the syringe (step 4).
- Remove the plastic cover from the needle while holding the orange fitting hub. Avoid pushing the plunger stopper (step 5).

The syringe is now ready to use.

3. How to inject Roferon-A

- Disinfect the skin using an alcohol wipe and pinch the skin between the thumb and forefinger, without squeezing.
- Insert the needle fully into the skin at an angle of approximately 45°. Pull slightly on the plunger to check that a blood vessel has not been punctured. If you see blood in the syringe, remove the needle and insert it in another place.
- Inject the liquid slowly and continuously, keeping the skin pinched.
- After injecting remove the needle and release the skin. Disinfect the skin with a clean alcohol wipe.

Remember: Most people can learn to give themselves a s.c. injection, but if you experience difficulty, please do not be afraid to ask for help and advice from your doctor, nurse or pharmacist.

4. How to dispose of used syringes

Never put used syringes into your normal household waste bin. **Consult your doctor or pharmacist** for the proper disposal of Roferon-A syringes.

☐ ROGAINE® 🄿

Pharmacia & Upjohn

Minoxidil

Hair Growth Stimulant

Information for the Patient: What is Rogaine? Rogaine solution contains minoxidil, a special formulation that has been shown to grow hair on the scalp of men who are bald or balding. Rogaine is a clear, colorless-to-slightly yellow solution. The color will not alter the effectiveness of the product.

Who may use Rogaine? Rogaine Solution may only be used by males, ages 18 to 65, for the treatment of male-pattern baldness.

Who should not use Rogaine? Do not use this product if you are sensitive (allergic) to minoxidil, propylene glycol or alcohol. If you think you have, or have had any heart problems or heart disease, consult your doctor before using Rogaine.

Cautions:

1) Discontinue Rogaine use and contact your doctor if you have any of the following reactions.
   —Rapid heart rate or palpitations
   —Unexplained rapid weight gain of 2.5 kg or more
   —Swelling or puffiness of hands, face, ankles, or stomach
   —Dizziness, lightheadedness, or fainting
   —Blurred vision
   —New or worsening pain in the chest, arm, or shoulder
   —Signs of severe indigestion
   —Severe scalp irritation
2) **Avoid contact with eyes and any irritated skin areas.** If either happens, wash the area thoroughly with cool water. If any reaction (local) persists, contact your doctor.
3) **Use this product only as directed by your doctor.**
   (a) **Don't use** it more often than directed.
   (b) **Don't apply** it over large surface areas of your body.
   (c) **Don't use** greater quantities than prescribed.
   All these could lead to possible side effects.
4) **Don't ingest (swallow) this solution.**
   Rogaine is for External use only. If anyone ingests the solution, contact your doctor immediately.
5) **Keep this (and all medications) out of the reach of children.**

How to use Rogaine:

1) Wash your hair daily, using a mild shampoo.

2) Apply 1 mL of Rogaine twice per day at 12-hour intervals, to the centre of the bald area and spread to cover entire affected area. Do not exceed a total dose of 2 mL, unless directed by your doctor. Do not apply Rogaine to any other areas of the body.

Avoid contact with eyes or other sensitive areas.

Wash your hands thoroughly after applying Rogaine.

3) Apply Rogaine when the hair and scalp are thoroughly dry. (Do not use a hair dryer to speed the drying of Rogaine Solution on the scalp. Blowing air on the scalp may decrease Rogaine's effectiveness.)
4) Don't apply other medications to your scalp while using Rogaine.

Application Methods: The method of application depends on the type of (disposable) applicator you use.
Pump-Spray Applicator: Works best for applying Rogaine to large areas.
Extended-Spray-Tip Applicator: Works best for applying Rogaine to small areas of the scalp, or under hair.
Rub-On Applicator: Works best for applying Rogaine to small areas of the scalp.

To avoid spillage and/or loss of solution continue to use the applicator, which you have selected, until the bottle is empty.

Pump-Spray applicator (see package insert for illustrations): Works best for applying Rogaine to large areas.
1) Remove large outer cap and keep it.
2) Remove small inner cap and discard it.
3) Insert the pump spray applicator into bottle and screw on firmly.
4) After aiming the pump toward the centre of the bald area of the scalp, press the pump once and spread Rogaine Solution with fingertips to cover all the bald area. Repeat for a total of 6 times, to apply a dose of 1 mL.

Avoid breathing spray mist.

5) Replace large outer cap over the pump spray applicator when not in use.

Extended-Spray-Tip Applicator (see package insert for illustrations): Works best for applying Rogaine to small areas of the scalp, or under hair.
1) Remove large outer cap and discard it.
2) Remove small inner cap and discard it.
3) Insert the pump spray applicator into bottle and screw on firmly.
4) Remove small spray head from top of pump spray applicator.
5) Fit the extended spray tip applicator onto the spray shaft and push down firmly.
6) Remove the small cap on the end of the extended tip and keep it.
7) After aiming the applicator toward the centre of the bald area of the scalp, press the pump once and spread Rogaine Solution with fingertips to cover all the bald area. Repeat for a total of 6 times to apply a dose of 1 mL.

Avoid breathing spray mist.

8) If desired, replace the small cap onto the end of the extended tip when not in use.

Rub-On applicator (see package insert for illustrations): Works best for applying Rogaine to small areas of the scalp.
1) Remove large outer cap and keep it.
2) Remove small inner cap and discard it.
3) Insert the rub-on applicator into bottle and screw on firmly.
4) Hold the bottle upright and squeeze it once to fill the upper chamber to the black line. The chamber now contains one full dose (1 mL).
5) Hold the bottle upside down then rub applicator on your scalp to apply Rogaine over the entire bald area—until the chamber is completely empty.
6) Replace large outer cap over the rub-on applicator when not in use.

When to look for results: Four or more months of continuous use may be necessary before hair growth takes place. The degree of hair growth varies from one person to another.

Reports indicate that the regrown hair may disappear 3 to 4 months after stopping Rogaine application and balding process will continue.

□ SABRIL® ℞

Hoechst Marion Roussel

Vigabatrin

Antiepileptic

Information for the Patient: Information for the Consumer or Caregiver: Please read this leaflet carefully before you start to take your medicine, even if you have taken this medicine before. It contains a brief description and summary of information needed for the proper use of Sabril. If you have any questions or are not sure about anything, ask your doctor or pharmacist. Please do not throw this leaflet away until you have finished all the medication prescribed by your doctor. You may need to read it again.

1. **The Name of Your Medicine:** Your medicine is called Sabril (vigabatrin). Sabril can only be obtained with a prescription from your doctor.
2. **The Purpose of Your Medicine:** Sabril was prescribed to you to reduce the frequency of epileptic seizures.
3. **How Your Medicine Works:** It is thought that a shortage of a naturally occurring brain chemical may be involved in epilepsy. Treatment with Sabril causes a rise in the levels of this chemical in the brain.
4. **Important Points to Note Before Taking Your Medicine:** Eye examinations are recommended before beginning Sabril treatment and at regular intervals (approximately every 3 months) thereafter. Advise your doctor immediately of any change in your eyesight such as narrowing of your field of vision or blurred vision.

   You should tell your doctor if you have had any nervous or mental illnesses in the past.

   If you currently have, or have ever had any kidney problems, make sure your doctor knows.

   In some patients, Sabril may cause side effects. You can find more information in this leaflet (see Item 7).
5. **The Use of This Medicine During Pregnancy and Breast-Feeding:** Sabril should not be used if you are pregnant or breast-feeding. Before you use this medicine, tell your doctor if you are pregnant, are likely to become pregnant, or are planning to become pregnant.

   Tell your doctor immediately if you become pregnant, or suspect that you may be pregnant, during your treatment.
6. **How to Take Your Medicine:** It is important to follow your doctor's instructions exactly. Never change the dose yourself.

   Do not stop taking your medicine abruptly. Discontinuation of your medicine should be done gradually over a few weeks and only in consultation with your doctor. Always check that you have enough medicine and do not run out.

   If you forget to take a dose, take it as soon as you remember, and then go on as usual. However, if it is almost time for your next dose, skip the dose you forgot, and go on as usual.

   Sabril tablets may be taken with or without food.

   If you are using sachets, dissolve the entire contents of the sachet(s) in a glass of cold or room temperature water, juice or milk immediately before taking your medicine.

   To give Sabril to your baby, dissolve the whole sachet in a 10 mL volume of either water, fruit juice, milk or infant formula. Use an oral syringe to measure the 10 mL volume. Give your baby the appropriate amount of this made up medicine, using an oral syringe to measure the exact volume. Your doctor will have told you how much medicine to give to your child. Each dose should be made up just before you give the medicine to your child.
7. **After Taking Your Medicine:** This medicine may cause side effects. Your doctor will be monitoring your response to Sabril on a regular basis; however, if you develop any of the following side effects tell your doctor immediately:
   - vision disorders
   - confusion
   - drowsiness
   - tiredness
   - headache
   - stomach upset
   - dizziness

   Your doctor will ensure that you receive appropriate attention and treatment.

   If your epilepsy is uncontrolled, it is very important that you do not perform any hazardous tasks such as driving or operating machinery. If, however, your epilepsy is controlled by medication it is very important that you refrain from any hazardous tasks until you are sure the medication does not cause drowsiness or impair your ability to drive or operate machinery.

   If you feel unwell in any other way or have any symptoms that you don't understand, tell your doctor immediately.
8. **What to Do if an Overdose is Taken:** If you accidentally take an overdose of your medicine, tell your doctor immediately or if necessary, go to the nearest hospital.
9. **Storing Your Medicine:** Leave your tablets in their original packaging and keep them in a safe place out of the reach of children.

   Keep your medicine in a cool dry place (15 to 30°C).

Sabril (cont'd)

If your doctor decides to stop your treatment, return any leftover medicine to your pharmacist. Only keep it if your doctor tells you to do so.

10. **What is in Your Medicine: Tablets:** Sabril tablets are white to off-white oval tablets and each one contains 500 mg of vigabatrin. **Sachets:** Sabril sachets are available in strengths of 0.5 g, 1 g, 2 g and 3 g of vigabatrin, as a white to off-white granular powder. Both the tablets and sachets are lactose-free.
11. **The Class of Your Medicine:** This medicine is one of a group of drugs called antiepileptics.
12. **Who Produces Your Medicine:** Manufacturer: Hoechst Marion Roussel Canada Inc. Laval, Quebec H7L 4A8.
13. **A Reminder: Remember** this medicine has been prescribed only for you. Never give it to anyone else.
14. **Further Information:** This leaflet is a brief description and summary of information about your medicine. If you are unsure about anything, ask your doctor or pharmacist.

□ SALAGEN® Ⓟ

Pharmacia & Upjohn

Pilocarpine HCl

Cholinomimetic Agent

Information for the Patient: Read this leaflet carefully. It has been prepared to help you get the best results from this medicine. It contains general information and directions about this medicine and should add to the advice from your doctor or pharmacist.

This leaflet should not replace your doctor's or pharmacist's advice. Because of your health condition, they may have given you different directions. If so, follow their advice. Also, if you have any questions or concerns after reading this leaflet, talk to you doctor or pharmacist.

What is Salagen? Salagen tablets contain the drug called pilocarpine which is a natural substance obtained from the leaves of a South American plant. Salagen tablets also contain the inactive ingredients: stearic acid and cellulose.

How do Salagen Tablets Work? Depending on your condition, your doctor has prescribed Salagen tablets to restore comfort to your dry mouth and/or your dry eyes. Salagen tablets cause your salivary glands and your tear glands to make more of your natural saliva and tears. If you have a dry mouth, Salagen tablets will make your mouth will feel less dry, you will have less pain in your mouth, it will be easier to talk, chew, swallow, and wear dentures, and you will not need to drink as much water or other liquids that help to keep your mouth wet. If you have dry eyes, Salagen tablets will make your eyes feel less dry, you will have less burning, itching, and redness, and you will not need to use as much artificial tears or other liquids that help keep your eyes moist.

Why do you Need Saliva? Saliva is not water. Most of your saliva is produced by 3 major pairs of salivary glands, all located in and around your mouth. Saliva contains many important ingredients such as proteins, enzymes and minerals which protect your teeth, gums and mouth. Each person needs adequate amounts of saliva to:

- control the growth of bacteria, viruses, and fungi which lead to infections and tooth decay
- clean the mouth of food
- continually rinse the teeth with minerals to keep them strong and prevent cavities
- lubricate the mouth and throat to make speaking, chewing, and swallowing easier
- dissolve foods and let you taste them better
- provide enzymes that help you digest your food

Why do you Need Tears? Like saliva, tears are not water. Most of your tears are produced by your major tear glands located in the inside upper part of your eyelids. Tears contain many important ingredients such as proteins and enzymes which protect your eye and the surrounding soft tissues. Each person needs adequate amounts of tears to:

- prevent and control the growth of bacteria, viruses, and fungi which lead to infections
- lubricate and protect the surface of the eye
- rinse and clean the eye of foreign objects

What Should Your Doctor Know Before you Start Taking Salagen?

- If you have ever had any problem with:
  - asthma
  - allergy to pilocarpine
  - heart (e.g., abnormal heartbeat, heart failure)
  - blood pressure (e.g., high blood pressure, low blood pressure)
  - lungs (e.g., difficulty breathing, bronchitis, emphysema)
  - liver (e.g., hepatitis, liver disease)
  - eyes or vision (e.g., blurred vision, difficulty seeing at night, glaucoma, iritis)
  - stomach (e.g., frequent heartburn or indigestion, ulcers)
  - kidneys (e.g., difficulty urinating, kidney failure, kidney stones)
  - gallbladder (e.g., gall stones)
  - nervous system (e.g., confusion, tremors, psychiatric illness)

  Some medical problems may get worse while you are taking Salagen tablets. Your doctor will tell you if he or she wants you to take Salagen tablets.
- if you are pregnant, if you become pregnant, or if you are breast-feeding your baby. Your doctor will tell you if he or she wants you to take Salagen tablets.
- if you are taking, or if you begin taking, any other medicines, even medicines you buy without a prescription. Some medicines may interfere with each other in your body.

How and When Should you Take Salagen Tablets? Take Salagen tablets exactly as your doctor tells you.

Most people take Salagen 3 or 4 times a day. Salagen tablets can be taken with or without food. Usually, you would take 1 tablet about the same time every day with something you do regularly—for example 1 tablet around breakfast, another around lunch, and another around your evening meal or at bedtime. This will help you remember each dose.

Do not chew or bite on the tablet.

Do not take more than 2 tablets at a time or more than 6 tablets/day unless your doctor tells you.

What if you Forget to Take a Dose of Salagen Tablets? If you miss a dose of Salagen, just take the next dose when you normally would.

How Long Will it Take for Salagen Tablets to Work? How well and how quickly Salagen works varies from person to person. It depends on your individual condition, and how long you have had a dry mouth and/or dry eyes. You may start to feel relief of your dry mouth and/or dry eyes within a week of starting Salagen tablets, or it could take 3 months or longer.

For best results, you should do the following:

- help your doctor find the right dose for you;
- give it enough time to work.

If your dry mouth and/or dry eyes do not start to feel better after 1 week, do not stop taking your tablets, tell your doctor. Your doctor may decide to adjust your dose. Take Salagen tablets exactly as your doctor tells you. Ask your doctor when he or she wants to see you for a check-up. If at that time your dry mouth and/or dry eyes is still not starting to feel better, tell your doctor. He or she may decide to adjust your dose again.

How Long Will you Have to Take Salagen Tablets? This depends on your condition. You may need to take Salagen tablets for a long period of time to keep from having a dry mouth and/or dry eyes.

What Precautions Should you Take? Some people have unwanted effects from this medicine. Remember, medicines affect different people in different ways. Just because side effects have occurred in other people does not mean you will get them.

Some people find Salagen tablets affects their vision. Make sure you know how this medicine affects you before you do dangerous activities at night or in low light (example: drive a car or use machines).

Tell your doctor right away if you notice any of the following. These may not be caused by Salagen tablets in your case, but only a doctor can tell.

- you feel weak and have to lie down
- you feel confused, agitated, or very depressed
- you get very red, swollen or painful eyes
- you get chest pain, a rapid heartbeat, or your pulse races
- you have difficulty breathing
- you get a skin rash
- you get severe pain in your stomach or abdomen
- you collapse
- if any of the following continue, bother you, or are not easily explained: mild to moderate sweating, chills, nausea (feeling sick) and vomiting, diarrhea, passing urine more often, constipation, prob-

lems with digestion, vision abnormalities, dizziness, runny eyes, runny nose, headache, flushing (redness in face).

Check with your doctor or pharmacist right away if you have **any** bothersome or unusual effects while taking Salagen tablets.

How Should You Store Salagen Tablets? Keep Salagen tablets out of the reach of children.

Store at room temperature (15 to 30°C).

Do not store in the bathroom where heat and moisture may damage this medicine.

Remember this medicine is for you. Only a doctor can prescribe it for you. Never give it to someone else even if their symptoms are the same as yours.

☐ SALAZOPYRIN® Ⓟ
☐ SALAZOPYRIN EN-TABS® Ⓟ

Pharmacia & Upjohn

Sulfasalazine

Anti-inflammatory

Information for the Patient: All dosage forms. Read the bold information first. Then go back and read the rest. If you do not recognize the names of medical conditions or medicines included in this information, check with your doctor, nurse, or pharmacist. Brand names for the generic drug names listed can also be found in the index. It is a good idea for you to learn both the generic and brand names of your medicines and to write them down for future use.

Sulfasalazine, a sulfonamide or sulfa medicine, belongs to the general family of medicines called anti-infectives. It is taken by mouth to help control active rheumatic arthritis and inflammatory bowel disease such as enteritis or colitis.

Sulfasalazine is available only with your doctor's prescription.

Remember:

- This medicine has been prescribed for your present medical problem only. Even though other people may have the same symptoms as you, they may have a different kind of problem. Your medicine may not work for them and may even cause them harm. **Therefore, your medicine must not be given to other people or used for other problems** unless you are otherwise directed by your doctor.
- In order for this medicine to work, it must be taken as directed.
- Keep all medicines out of the reach of children.
- If you want more information about this medicine, ask your doctor, nurse or pharmacist.
- If any of the following information causes you special concern, do not decide against taking this medicine without first checking with your doctor.

Before using this medicine: In order to decide on the best treatment for your medical problem, your doctor should be told:

- If you have ever had any unusual or allergic reactions to any of the sulfonamides, furosemide or thiazide diuretics (water pills), dapsone, sulfoxone, oral hypoglycemics (diabetes medicine you take by mouth), glaucoma medicine you take by mouth (for example, acetazolamide, dichlorphenamide, methazolamide) or salicylates (for example, aspirin).
- If you are pregnant or if you intend to become pregnant while taking this medicine, although sulfasalazine has not been shown to cause birth defects and other problems do not usually occur.
- If you are breast-feeding an infant. Sulfonamides pass into the breast milk in small amounts and may cause unwanted effects in infants with glucose-6-phosphate dehydrogenase (G6PD) deficiency.
- If you intend to father a child (oligospermia).
- If you have any of the following medical problems: blockage of stomach, intestines, or urinary tract; blood problems; glucose-6-phosphate dehydrogenase (G6PD) deficiency; kidney disease; liver disease or porphyria.
- If you are now taking any of the following medicines or types of medicine: anthralin; antibiotics; anticoagulants, coumarin- or indandione-type (blood thinners); antidiabetic agents, oral (diabetes medicine you take by mouth); coal tar; dapsone; digitalis glycosides (heart medicine); dipyrone; diuretics (water pills or high blood pressure medicine); ethotoin; folic acid; furazolidone; mephenytoin; methenamine; methotrexate; methoxsalen; nalidixic acid; nitrofurantoin; other sulfonamides; oxyphenbutazone; phenothiazines (tranquilizers); phenylbutazone; phenytoin; primaquine; probenecid; sulfinpyrazone; sulfoxone; tetracyclines; trioxsalen; vitamin K.

Proper use of this medicine: Salazopyrin tablets (sulfasalazine) is best taken after meals or with food to lessen stomach upset. If stomach upset continues or is bothersome, check with your doctor.

Each dose of sulfasalazine should also be taken with a full glass (240 mL) of water. Several additional glasses of water should be taken every day, unless otherwise directed by your doctor. Drinking extra water will help to prevent unwanted side effects of the sulfonamide.

For patients taking the enteric-coated tablet form of this medicine: Swallow tablets whole, do not break or crush. Contact your doctor if you notice any undisintegrated tablets in your stools.

Keep taking this medicine for the full time of treatment even if you begin to feel better after a few days; do not miss any doses.

If you do miss a dose of this medicine, take it as soon as possible. However, if it is almost time for your next dose, do not take the missed dose or double your next dose. Instead, go back to your regular dosing schedule.

Do not give sulfasalazine to infants under 2 years of age unless directed to by your doctor.

How to store this medicine: Store away from heat and direct light, out of the reach of children. Do not store in the bathroom medicine cabinet because the heat or moisture may cause the medicine to break down. Do not keep outdated medicine or medicine no longer needed. Flush it down the toilet.

Precautions While Using the Medicine: If your symptoms (including diarrhea) do not improve within a month or 2 or if they become worse, check with your doctor.

It is important that your doctor check your progress at regular visits.

Before having any kind of surgery (including dental surgery) with a general anesthetic, tell the physician or dentist in charge that you are taking a sulfonamide.

Some people who take sulfonamides may become more sensitive to sunlight than they are normally. When you begin to take this medicine, avoid too much sun or too much use of a sunlamp until you see how you react, especially if you tend to burn easily. You may still be more sensitive to sunlight or sunlamps for many months after you stop taking this medicine. If you have a severe reaction, check with your doctor.

Side Effects of this Medicine: Along with its needed effects, a medicine may cause some unwanted effects. Although not all of these side effects appear very often, when they do occur they may require medical attention. **Stop taking this medicine and check with your doctor immediately** if any of the following side effects occur:

More common: headache (continuing), itching, skin rash.

Less common: aching of joints and muscles; difficulty in swallowing; fever; pale skin; redness, blistering, peeling, or loosening of skin; sore throat; unusual bleeding or bruising; unusual tiredness or weakness; yellowing of eyes or skin.

Rare: blood in urine, lower back pain, pain or burning while urinating, swelling of front part of neck.

Also, check with your doctor as soon as possible if the following side effect occurs:

More common: increased sensitivity of skin to sunlight.

Other side effects may occur which usually do not require medical attention. These side effects may go away during treatment as your body adjusts to the medicine. However, check with your doctor if any of the following side effects continue or are bothersome:

More common: diarrhea, dizziness, loss of appetite, nausea or vomiting.

In some patients this medicine may also cause the urine to become orange-yellow. This side effect does not require medical attention.

Other side effects not listed above may also occur in some patients. If you notice any other effects, check with your doctor.

☐ SALBUTAMOL NEBUAMP® Ⓟ

Astra

Salbutamol Sulfate

Bronchodilator

Information for the Patient: Important information you should know about Salbutamol Nebuamp (salbutamol sulfate).

Each Salbutamol Nebuamp is prediluted in normal saline (0.9% sodium chloride).

Before using Salbutamol Nebuamp, read this leaflet carefully. It contains general points about Salbutamol Nebuamp and should add to more specific advice from your doctor or pharmacist.

Salbutamol Nebuamp (cont'd)

Please keep this leaflet to refer to until you have used up all Salbutamol Nebuamp units in this package.

What is Salbutamol Nebuamp Used For and How Does it Work? Salbutamol Nebuamp is a bronchodilator medicine. It is used to treat bronchospasm associated with bronchial asthma, chronic bronchitis or other disorders which lead to breathing difficulties. It opens up airways in people with asthma or other breathing problems. It relieves symptoms such as wheezing, cough and shortness of breath. Salbutamol Nebuamp works by relieving spasm in the small air passages in the lungs and so helps to ease breathing problems.

What is in Salbutamol Nebuamp? Each Salbutamol Nebuamp is made with salbutamol sulfate and contains salbutamol base as the active ingredient. It comes in concentrations of either 0.5 mg/mL, 1 mg/mL or 2 mg/mL. Each ampul contains 2.5 mL. That means one ampul of 0.5 mg/mL strength contains 1.25 mg of active drug. One ampul of 1 mg/mL strength contains 2.5 mg of active drug, and one ampul of 2 mg/mL strength contains 5 mg of active drug.

Most medicines contain more ingredients than just the active drug. Check with your doctor if you think you might be allergic to any of these items (listed in alphabetical order): salbutamol sulfate, sodium chloride, sodium hydroxide, sulfuric acid.

What Should I Tell my Doctor Before Taking Salbutamol Nebuamp? Tell your doctor:

- about all health problems you have now or have had in the past;
- if you are being treated for a thyroid condition;
- if you are being treated for high blood pressure or a heart problem;
- about other medicines you take, including ones you can buy without a prescription;
- if you are pregnant, plan to become pregnant or are breastfeeding. Your doctor may decide not to prescribe this medication during the first 3 months of pregnancy, nor if you are breastfeeding a baby. However, there may be circumstances when your doctor advises you differently;
- if you have ever had a bad, unusual or allergic reaction to salbutamol sulfate.

How Do I Take Salbutamol Nebuamp Properly? Salbutamol Nebuamp is for use in a power-operated nebulizer with a face-mask. Be sure you know how to use your nebulizer properly before you start this drug.

Nebulization should take place using a gas flow (oxygen or compressed air) of 6 to 10 L/min. A suitable volume fill for most nebulizers is 2 to 5 mL. Discard any solution remaining in the nebulizer.

Do not take more doses than prescribed by your doctor.

Before use, check to make sure the strength on the label matches the strength your doctor prescribed.

Follow These Directions for Each Dose of Salbutamol Nebuamp:

1. Remove 1 Salbutamol Nebuamp from a sheet of 10 units. Return the other units to the carton.
2. Gently shake the unit.
3. Open by holding the unit upright and twisting off the top.
4. Slowly squeeze the contents into the nebulizer cup.
5. Connect one end of the cup to the face mask or mouthpiece, and the other end to the air pump.
6. Just before you start, gently shake the contents of the cup. Then start the treatment.
7. Breathe calmly and evenly until no more mist comes out (5 to 10 minutes).
8. Wash your face after treatment.

Cleaning: When you have finished, you have to clean the nebulizer. Wash the cup and the mouthpiece or mask in warm water, using a mild detergent. Rinse well. Dry by connecting the nebulizer cup to the compressor or to the air inlet. See the manufacturer's instructions for complete details.

How Much Salbutamol Nebuamp Should I Take? Your doctor will have explained why you are being treated with Salbutamol Nebuamp and told you what dose to take. Follow those directions carefully. They may differ from the information contained in this leaflet.

An effective treatment with Salbutamol Nebuamp may last up to 6 hours and should last at least 4 hours. **Call your doctor immediately if the effect of your usual dose lasts for less than 3 hours or if you notice a sudden worsening of your shortness of breath and you wheeze after using your Salbutamol Nebuamp. If you regularly use Salbutamol Nebuamp 2 or more times per day, and take no other asthma medication, you should talk to your doctor who may want to reassess your treatment plan. If you do not get relief from 3 or 4 treatments during a day, contact your doctor.** Do not increase the dose or how often you take your medicine without informing your doctor. If symptoms get worse, tell your doctor as soon as possible.

Suggested doses are: Adults: Patients requiring doses of 2.5 to 5.0 mg salbutamol may be administered the contents of a single Salbutamol Nebuamp unit (0.1% or 0.2% solution, respectively). Treatment may be repeated 4 times a day if necessary.

Children: Salbutamol Nebuamp should be used under the supervision of an adult who understands the proper use of the nebulizer, and only as prescribed by the doctor.

Children (5 to 12 years) requiring doses of 1.25 to 2.5 mg salbutamol may be administered the contents of a single Salbutamol Nebuamp unit (0.05% or 0.1% solution, respectively). More refractory cases may be administered a single unit of 5 mg salbutamol (0.2% solution).

Dosage

Dose of Salbutamol Base in mg	Volume of Salbutamol Nebuamp 0.05% (0.5 mg/mL)	0.1% (1.0 mg/mL)	0.2% (2.0 mg/mL)
1.25	2.5 mL (1 unit)	—	—
2.5	5.0 mL (2 units)	2.5 mL (1 unit)	—
5.0	—	5.0 mL (2 units)	2.5 mL (1 unit)

What Should I Do if I Miss a Dose? If you miss a dose of Salbutamol Nebuamp, take it as soon as possible. Then go back to your regular schedule. If it is almost time to take your next dose, skip the missed dose and take the next dose on time.

Never take a double dose of Salbutamol Nebuamp to make up for ones you missed. If you are still unsure, check with your doctor or pharmacist to see what you should do.

What Should I Do in Case of Overdose? If you accidentally take a **larger dose than prescribed** you may notice that your heart is beating faster than usual and that you feel shaky. These effects usually wear off within a few hours but you should tell your doctor as soon as possible.

Telephone your doctor or pharmacist without delay, or go to your nearest hospital or poison control centre right away if you think you or anyone else may have taken too much Salbutamol Nebuamp.

Are There any Side Effects? Like any medication, Salbutamol Nebuamp may cause side effects in some people.

Occasionally some people feel a little shaky or have a headache after using Salbutamol Nebuamp. Muscle cramps can occur although these are quite rare.

These effects usually wear off with continued treatment. Tell your doctor but do not stop using the medicine unless told to do so. These may not be caused by Salbutamol Nebuamp in your case, but only a doctor can assess this.

Medicines affect different people in different ways. Just because side effects have occurred in other patients does not mean you will get them. If any side effects bother you, please contact your doctor.

After taking your medicine if you notice a sudden worsening of your shortness of breath and wheeze shortly after taking your medicine, tell your doctor as soon as possible. If the relief of wheezing or chest tightness is not as good as usual, tell your doctor as soon as possible. It may be that your chest condition is worsening and you may need to add another type of medicine to your treatment.

If you have any bothersome or unusual effects while taking Salbutamol Nebuamp, check with your doctor or pharmacist.

Where Should I Keep Salbutamol Nebuamp? Remember to keep Salbutamol Nebuamp well out of the reach of children when you are not using it.

Keep all units in the carton until it is time for a dose. If you don't, light may damage the solution.

Do not use Salbutamol Nebuamp after the expiry date marked on the pack.

Keep the pack at room temperature (15 to 25°C). Do not use the solution if it contains particles.

Without preservative.

Important Note: This leaflet alerts you to some of the times you should call your doctor. Other situations which cannot be predicted may arise. Nothing in this leaflet should stop you from calling your doctor or pharmacist with any questions or concerns you have about using Salbutamol Nebuamp.

☐ SALOFALK® ℞

Axcan Pharma

5-Aminosalicylic Acid

Lower Gastrointestinal Anti-inflammatory

Information for the Patient: Best results are achieved with Salofalk rectal suspension if the bowel is emptied immediately before the enema is given. Salofalk rectal suspension contains sodium benzoate as a microbial preservative and potassium metabisulfite as an antioxidant.

1. **Preparing the Enema:**
   a) Shake the bottle well to make sure that the suspension is homogeneous.
   b) Remove the protective sheath from the applicator tip. Hold the bottle at the neck so as not to cause any of the medication to be discharged.
2. **Assuming the Correct Body Position:**
   a) Best results are obtained by lying on the left side with left leg extended and right leg flexed forward for balance.
   b) An alternative to lying on the left side is the ''knee-chest'' position.
3. **Administering the Rectal Suspension:**
   a) Gently insert lubricated applicator tip into the rectum, pointed slightly toward the navel.
   b) Grasp the bottle firmly, then tilt slightly so that the nozzle is aimed toward the back, and squeeze slowly to instill the medication. Steady hand pressure will discharge most of the solution. After administering, withdraw and discard the used unit.
   c) Remain in position for at least 30 minutes to allow thorough distribution of the medication internally. Retain the rectal suspension all night, if possible.

☐ SANDOSTATIN® ℞

Novartis Pharmaceuticals

Octreotide Acetate

Synthetic Octapeptide Analogue of Somatostatin

Information for the Patient: The information that follows is intended as a guide for patients who must self-administer Sandostatin for the control of symptoms associated with carcinoid tumors, VIPomas or acromegaly.

What is a Gastroenteropancreatic (GEP) Endocrine Tumor? GEP endocrine tumors are growths that have developed from endocrine cells in the gastrointestinal tract (the stomach, intestines, appendix) or the pancreas.

GEP endocrine tumors grow very slowly and are often silent—not letting you know that they are there. Sometimes, however, they produce symptoms that are very noticeable. Some of these symptoms come about because GEP endocrine tumors produce and secrete chemical substances called peptides, i.e., small proteins.

These same peptides are normally produced in your body—but in very small amounts. In other words, enough to do the jobs they are meant to do. The peptides don't build up; they don't enter the body's circulatory system; they simply do their job, degrade, and pass out of the body causing no symptoms, causing no harm.

The problem is that when GEP endocrine tumors produce and secrete these very same peptides, they often do it to excess—overloading the system. When that happens, the body cannot handle the extra amounts of peptide in a normal way. The oversupply of peptide gets into the circulatory system, travels through the body, and causes a variety of abnormal reactions, including diarrhea and flushing. The particular peptide that is released by the tumor, as well as the location of the tumor, determine the reactions or symptoms you will experience.

Carcinoid Tumors: Carcinoid tumors are the most common type of GEP endocrine tumor. These growths can occur in the esophagus, stomach, intestines, appendix, as well as the lungs.

Most carcinoid tumors produce only a small amount of peptide, which generally goes unnoticed. In some cases, however, carcinoid cells from the tumor spread through the bloodstream to the liver, where they form new tumors. When this occurs, the peptide they produce and secrete has easy access to the body's circulatory system through the liver. As the excess peptide travels through the body, it may cause a number of reactions or symptoms. This group of symptoms is referred to as the carcinoid syndrome.

The most common symptoms of the carcinoid syndrome are diarrhea and flushing. Other symptoms of carcinoid syndrome include: wheezing or other asthma-like symptoms; and symptoms of heart disease, such as breathlessness.

VIPomas: VIPomas are GEP endocrine tumors that secrete vasoactive intestinal peptide (VIP). They almost always occur in the pancreas—a large gland behind the stomach that produces insulin and other secretions used in digestion.

Normal secretion of VIP helps to moisten the stool so that it can pass through the bowel more easily. VIPomas, however, produce excessive amounts of VIP—allowing too much fluid to enter the intestines. The flooding of the intestines causes very watery diarrhea—producing as many as 15 or more bowel movements a day.

The body cannot tolerate diarrhea of this volume for very long. The loss of so much fluid causes **dehydration,** with the body losing not only a significant part of its water supply but important chemicals (**electrolytes**), such as sodium and potassium, as well.

It is very important to stop the diarrhea and to replace the loss of water and electrolytes as quickly as possible.

What is Acromegaly? Acromegaly is a life-time, uncommon, debilitating disease characterized by changes in facial bone structure and specific hormonal abnormalities.

Signs and symptoms of acromegaly due to excessive hormonal secretion include oily skin acne, excessive sweating, headache, depression, visual disturbances, joint pain, changes in facial bone structure, muscle weakness, menstrual disorders. Acromegalic patients may also experience increased activity of the thyroid, diabetes, respiratory problems and daytime somnolence.

It is frequently associated with arthritis and cardiac and neurologic problems.

Acromegaly is the result of an overproduction of growth hormone by the pituitary gland. This in turn results in overproduction of somatomedin C (IGF-I) by the liver.

Approximately 20 to 30% of acromegalic patients also demonstrate high blood pressure.

What Does Sandostatin (octreotide acetate) Do? GEP Endocrine Tumors: Somatostatin is another peptide hormone that occurs naturally in the body. It acts as a modulator, helping to keep many of the body's peptides—including the GEP endocrine peptides, the growth hormone and the IGF-I (somatomedin C)—at their appropriate levels. Sandostatin (octreotide acetate) is a synthetic peptide that was created to mimic the natural modulating effects of somatostatin. The advantage of Sandostatin is that it is stronger and has a much longer duration of action than somatostatin, which makes it more useful in therapy. In fact, injection of Sandostatin 2 or 3 times a day—which a patient can easily learn to do—offers round-the-clock symptom control for people with GEP endocrine tumors and acromegaly.

Sandostatin helps slow down the release of the peptides that cause the diarrhea and flushing. It stimulates fluid and electrolyte absorption, and it prolongs the transit time through the small intestine. These activities combine to dramatically curb diarrhea and the threat of dehydration. Bowel movements may decrease from 10 or 20 a day to 2 or 3.

For many people, flushing episodes disappear completely. For others, the number and severity of episodes decrease substantially; and the duration of the attacks decreases from hours to minutes a day.

Acromegaly: Sandostatin has been shown to lower the growth hormone and Somatomedin C levels in the blood.

As these hormones are principally responsible for the clinical signs and symptoms of acromegaly, normalization of hormone levels improves the symptoms of headache, soft tissue swelling, joint pain, excessive perspiration, depression, fatigue, cystic acne and somnolence.

Some Guidelines for Using Sandostatin: What is the Dose of Sandostatin? Your doctor will tell you how much Sandostatin to take each day. The dosage is prescribed to suit your particular needs. The doctor will also tell you how to divide your dosage through the day. For example, he or she might prescribe a total dosage of 450 μg/day, to be taken in 3 equal injections of 150 μg each. Very often patients start at a low dose for the first few days of treatment and then increase slowly to a higher dose.

How is Sandostatin Taken? Currently, Sandostatin is given by subcutaneous injection. That means that the drug is injected just under the skin. This is the same kind of injection procedure used by people who have diabetes and need insulin. It is easy to learn. It is easy to do. And preparing and taking the injections (usually 2 or 3 a day) will take very little time—probably only a total of 15 minutes a day.

Sandostatin (cont'd)

How to Prepare Your Injection of Sandostatin? You will receive your supply of Sandostatin either in ampuls or in multidose vials.

Ampuls:

1. Before breaking open the ampul, tap the neck portion so that any medication that may be trapped will flow down into the bottom portion of the ampul.
2. Once the ampul is opened, insert the needle and pull back the plunger to fill the syringe with the desired amount of drug. (Your doctor or nurse will tell you how to read the markings on your syringe so that you can fill it with the right amount of drug for your dose.) Discard any unused medication.
3. Check to see if there are any air bubbles in the syringe. If bubbles do appear, hold the syringe upright (with the needle pointed up) and lightly tap the barrel. This should make the bubbles rise to the top of the syringe. Then gently press the plunger to push the bubbles out.

Multidose Vials:

1. Peel off the aluminum seal.
2. Wipe the top of the vial with an alcohol swab.
3. Remove the cap from the needle and insert the needle into the vial through the rubber stopper.
4. Leave the needle in the bottle.
5. Turn the vial and the syringe upside down. Keep the needle tip within the liquid. Pull the plunger and carefully withdraw the prescribed amount of Sandostatin (your doctor or nurse will tell you how to read the markings on the syringe so that you fill it with the correct amount of drug for your dose).
6. Turn the bottle and syringe back upright.
7. Withdraw the needle from the vial.
8. Check to see if there are any air bubbles in the syringe. If bubbles do appear, hold the syringe upright (with the needle pointed up) and lightly tap the barrel. This should make the bubbles rise to the top of the syringe. Then gently press the plunger to push the bubbles out.

How to Inject Your Dose of Sandostatin?

1. Choose the area of your hip, thigh, or abdomen where you want to make your injection.
2. Clean the site with a fresh alcohol wipe, and keep it nearby.
3. Hold the syringe like a pencil, and remove the needle cap.
4. Use the thumb and forefinger of your other hand to gently pinch up a fold of skin at the place you want to inject. This will lift the subcutaneous tissue away from the muscle underneath.
5. Hold the syringe at a 45° angle, and insert the entire length of the needle into the fold of skin in one quick motion.
6. Once the needle is inserted, let go of the skin.
7. Using your free hand, pull back on the plunger slightly to check whether you have placed the needle in a blood vessel. (You don't want to.) If any blood appears in the syringe, this is not a proper site for your injection. You will have to remove and discard the syringe and needle and start over.
8. Once the needle is inserted properly, slowly inject all of the medication.
9. When you are finished injecting the medicine, place your alcohol wipe where the needle enters the skin. Press lightly.
10. Withdraw the needle at the same angle it is inserted.
11. Gently hold the wipe on your skin for about 5 seconds.
12. Put the cap back on the needle and dispose of the syringe and needle safely. Do not reuse the syringe and needle. Single-use syringes and needles are used to reduce the chance of infection. Collect your used needles and syringes in a metal container, such as a coffee can, and then dispose of them in a covered garbage can. This will keep others (especially children) from injuring themselves.

Important Points to Remember: Pay close attention to the amount of drug you are taking into the syringe for injection. Make sure it is the amount your doctor has prescribed for you.

If you forget to take a scheduled injection, most doctors will suggest that you take it at the time you remember and then go on with your normal schedule. (Check with your doctor to see if this procedure is acceptable.) You will not be harmed by forgetting a dose; however, you may get some temporary breakthrough of the symptom (e.g., diarrhea or flushing) that you are treating. This will then correct itself as you proceed with your normal schedule.

A Possible Side Effect—Burning at the Injection Site: Some patients say that they experience a burning sensation at the site where they are injecting the drug. Others do not experience this sensation at all. It depends, in part, on the size of the dose they are taking. The reason for the burning is due to the formulation of the drug. For most people, the burning lasts only a few moments. They inject and then rub the spot gently and, in a few seconds, the stinging is gone.

For those who find it uncomfortable and want to alleviate the burning sensation, you may want to try injecting the drug at room temperature rather than cold from the refrigerator. In other words, you can take the medication out of the refrigerator for 20 minutes before you intend to use it and let it warm a bit. But don't forget, Sandostatin ampuls **must be refrigerated,** they cannot be heated without destroying the medication.

When to Take Your Injection of Sandostatin? Your doctor or nurse will help you plan how to divide your dosage through the day. Symptom control is best achieved when the doses are evenly distributed over a 24-hour period.

Storage: For prolonged storage, Sandostatin must be refrigerated at 2 to 8°C—typical refrigerator temperatures. However, you may leave your daily dose of Sandostatin **ampuls** out at a room temperature of up to 30°C for up to 2 weeks. If the drug is left out at room temperature for longer than 2 weeks, the medication may break down and become ineffective. The ampuls should be opened just prior to administration and any unused portion discarded.

The **multidose vial** may be kept at room temperature for up to 2 weeks even after you start using it. If the drug is left out at room temperature for more than 2 weeks the medication can break down and become ineffective.

A supply of Sandostatin can be kept refrigerated for up to 3 years without deteriorating. However, the drug should never be frozen. Because peptides are very delicate, freezing and thawing the drug can damage it and impair its effectiveness. Sandostatin should be protected from light.

□ SER-AP-ES® ℞

Novartis Pharmaceuticals

Reserpine—Hydralazine HCl—Hydrochlorothiazide

Antihypertensive

Information for the Patient: Before you use Ser-Ap-Es please read these instructions carefully because they contain important information. If you have further questions, ask your doctor or pharmacist.

What is Ser-Ap-Es? Ser-Ap-Es is a medicine that combines 3 medicinal ingredients for lowering high blood pressure: reserpine, hydralazine hydrochloride, and hydrochlorothiazide. It is available as a tablet containing 0.1 mg reserpine, 25 mg hydralazine, and 15 mg hydrochlorothiazide.

Like most medicines, Ser-Ap-Es contains other nonmedicinal ingredients in addition to its medicinal ingredients. If you are on a special diet, or if you have an allergy, your doctor or pharmacist will advise you on which other nonmedicinal ingredients may cause a problem. The other nonmedicinal ingredients include acacia, cornstarch, Erythrosine Lake, FD&C Green #3, lactose, polyethylene glycol, stearic acid, sugar and Sunset Yellow Lake.

Hydralazine belongs to a group of medicines which widen the blood vessels and so lower high blood pressure. Reserpine also lowers blood pressure, but by a different mechanism. It also counteracts the unwanted increase in heart rate that may be produced by hydralazine. Hydrochlorothiazide is a diuretic which reduces the amount of salt and water in the body by increasing the flow of urine. With longer use this helps to reduce and control blood pressure. Hydrochlorothiazide also counteracts the unwanted accumulation of fluid in the body that may be caused by hydralazine.

What does Ser-Ap-Es do? Ser-Ap-Es is used to lower high blood pressure. High blood pressure increases the workload of the heart and arteries. If this continues for a long time, it can damage the blood vessels of the brain, heart, and kidneys, resulting in a stroke, heart failure, or kidney failure. High blood pressure increases the risk of heart attacks. These problems are less likely to occur if Ser-Ap-Es is used to control blood pressure.

Ser-Ap-Es works by 3 different, but complementary, mechanisms (see above). In this way it lowers blood pressure.

Before you take Ser-Ap-Es: You may only take Ser-Ap-Es after a medical examination. Ser-Ap-Es is not suitable for all patients.

You should not take Ser-Ap-Es:

- If you have had any unusual or allergic reaction to hydralazine, reserpine, hydrochlorothiazide or related substances;

- If you have:—serious heart disease, especially any disease involving the valves of the heart;
- depression (or a history of depression), or recent treatment with antidepressants;
- Parkinson's disease or epilepsy;
- stomach ulcers, a serious liver or kidney disease;
- fever, skin rash and joint pain, which may be signs of systemic lupus erythematosus;
- gout (or a history of gout);
- if you are pregnant, or breast-feeding.

Tell your doctor before taking Ser-Ap-Es if you have any of the following:

- liver or kidney disease;
- a circulatory disorder;
- a history of gastrointestinal disorders (e.g., ulcers, gastritis);
- diabetes;
- high levels of cholesterol in your blood;

Also tell your doctor if you are already taking medicine of any kind (see below).

Medicines or substances that may interfere with the action of Ser-Ap-Es: Before taking any medicine at the same time as Ser-Ap-Es talk to your doctor or pharmacist. It may be necessary to change the dose or in some cases for you to stop taking one of the medicines. This applies to both prescription and nonprescription (over-the-counter) medicines, especially:

- medicines used to lower blood pressure;
- medicines for treating depression, especially monoamine oxidase inhibitors;
- medicines for treating mental disorders (neuroleptics);
- medicines for treating heart failure or heart rhythm disorders;
- medicines containing epinephrine or similar substances, e.g. eye drops, nasal drops, and cough or common cold medicines;
- lithium, a medicine used to treat some psychological conditions;
- medicines used to relieve pain or inflammation, especially nonsteroidal anti-inflammatory agents;
- cortisone-like medicines, steroids;
- digoxin (a heart medicine);
- insulin or antidiabetic medicines taken by mouth;
- cholestyramine and colestipol, resins used mainly to treat high levels of lipids in the blood.

Avoid alcohol until you have talked to your doctor. Alcohol may make blood pressure fall more and/or increase the possibility of dizziness or fainting.

Further safety measures: What if you are pregnant or breast-feeding? Do not take Ser-Ap-Es if you are pregnant or breast-feeding. Ser-Ap-Es passes into the breast milk. It is therefore important to tell your doctor if you are pregnant, breast-feeding, or planning to become pregnant.

What about children and elderly patients? Ser-Ap-Es should not be used in children. If you are 65 years or older you may be more sensitive to the effects of Ser-Ap-Es.

What if you drive a vehicle or use machinery? Like many other medicines used to treat high blood pressure, Ser-Ap-Es may cause dizziness and affect your concentration. So before you drive a vehicle, use machinery, or do other things that need quick reactions, make sure you know how Ser-Ap-Es affects you.

How should you take Ser-Ap-Es? Patients who have high blood pressure often do not notice any signs of this problem. Many may feel quite normal. This makes it all the more important to take your medicine as directed by the doctor and to keep your appointments with the doctor even if you are feeling well. Remember that this medicine will not cure your high blood pressure, although it may help to control it. You must therefore continue to take it as directed if you want to lower your blood pressure and keep it down.

What is the usual dosage? Treatment is started with the smallest dose and the dosage is then increased gradually. For most people 1 to 2 tablets daily are enough, and you should not take more than this. You should normally take the tablets once or twice daily at mealtimes with liquid. Some patients have to take medicine to control high blood pressure for the rest of their lives. Help yourself remember to take your medicine by trying to get into the habit of taking it at the same time each day.

What if you have missed a dose? If you miss a dose of this medicine, take the missed dose as soon as possible. If it is almost time for your next dose, skip the missed dose and then take the next one at the usual time.

What if you have taken an overdose? The following symptoms may occur in cases of overdose:

- severe dizziness, fainting, coma, or collapse;
- fits;
- shortness of breath;
- irregular heartbeat and chest pain;
- unusual tiredness, weakness, or muscle cramps.

What should you be aware of while taking Ser-Ap-Es? It is important for your doctor to check your progress at regular visits to make sure that this medicine is working properly.

It may be necessary from time to time to measure the amount of potassium or other minerals in your blood, especially if you are over 65 years old, have certain heart, liver, or kidney diseases, or are taking potassium supplements. Your doctor will advise you about this.

What side effects can Ser-Ap-Es have? Like all medicines, Ser-Ap-Es may cause unwanted reactions in addition to its good effects. Although not all of these unwanted effects are common, if they do occur they may require medical attention.

Check with your doctor as soon as possible if any of the following side effects occur: Occasional: depression or inability to concentrate, irregular or slow heartbeat.

Rare/Isolated: sore throat, fever, or chills (sign of a blood disorder); yellow eyes or skin (jaundice); abdominal pain with nausea, vomiting, or fever, (sign of pancreatitis or a liver disorder or inflammation); numbness or tingling in the hands, feet or lips; skin rash or itching; pain in the chest; bloody vomit or black stools; shortness of breath; trembling and shaking of hands and fingers; painful or difficult urination; blood in the urine with or without kidney pain (sign of glomerulonephritis); unusual bleeding or bruising (sign of thrombocytopenia); fever, skin rash and joint pains (sign of Systemic Lupus Erythematosus-like syndrome); swelling or enlargement of the breasts, milk secretion; blurred vision; hearing problems; breathing problems (signs of pneumonitis and pulmonary edema); bloatedness with breathing problems (signs of paralytic ileus).

Many side effects will clear up without you having to stop the treatment.

Check with your doctor if any of the following persist or are distressing: Frequent: headache, fast heartbeat.

Occasional: dizziness or lightheadness when getting up from a lying or sitting position: nausea, vomiting, diarrhea, stomach upset; dry mouth; heartburn or stomach pain (sign of ulcer); unusual tiredness or weakness (sometimes a sign of potassium loss), vivid dreams or nightmares; stuffy nose; loss of appetite or weight gain; blurred vision; watering or irritated eyes; swelling of the hands and feet; trembling; increased sensitivity of the skin to sunlight; difficulty in achieving erection or loss of interest in sex.

Rare: nervousness; anxiety; flushing; sleep problems; increased appetite or weight loss; muscle pain; nosebleed; reddening of the skin (purpura).

If you notice any other effects not listed above, check with your doctor.

Further Information: Expiry date: Do not use Ser-Ap-Es after the expiry date shown on the pack.

How to store Ser-Ap-Es: Store below 30°C (2 to 30°C), away from direct sunlight and moisture.

Keep this medicine out of the reach of children because it may harm them.

Other Important Information: This medicine has been prescribed for your current medical problem only. Do not give it to other people. Do not use it yourself for other problems unless your doctor tells you to do so.

It is very important that you take this medicine exactly as your doctor tells you in order to get the best results and reduce the risk of side effects.

☐ SEREVENT® ℞

Glaxo Wellcome

Salmeterol Xinafoate

Bronchodilator—β_2-Adrenergic Stimulant

Information for the Patient: Serevent Inhalation Aerosol, Diskhaler Disk and Diskus: Please read this leaflet carefully before you start

Serevent (cont'd)

to take your medicine. For further information or advice, ask your doctor or pharmacist.

Serevent should be used only twice a day.

Serevent is one of a group of medicines called bronchodilators. The effect of Serevent lasts 12 hours—therefore, it is very important that you use Serevent not more than twice a day, in the morning and again in the evening. This will help protect you against breakthrough symptoms throughout the day and during the night.

Serevent should not be used as relief medication.

Serevent does not act quickly enough to be used as a relief medication. Serevent should not be used to provide relief for a sudden attack or breathlessness. If you get a sudden attack of wheezing and breathlessness between your doses of Serevent, you should take 1 or 2 puffs from a fast-acting relief medication (e.g., Ventolin) which your doctor has given you.

If you take more than 1 inhaled medicine, make sure you know which is which and when you should use them. Remember, if you have an attack which does not get better when you take the relief medication you should see your doctor right away. You may need emergency treatment.

You should tell your doctor as soon as possible if you feel you are getting more attacks of wheezing, breathlessness or chest tightness, or if you are using an increasing amount of your fast-acting relief medication. Also, if you start waking up at night with chest tightness, wheezing or shortness of breath you should tell your doctor as soon as possible.

Use in Adolescent Children: Serevent is suitable for adolescent children 12 years of age and older. The severity of asthma changes with age. Your adolescent child should therefore be periodically re-examined by a physician. It is important to make sure that he/she understands and properly follows the asthma therapies that have been prescribed. These will include in addition to Serevent, a drug which reduces the inflammation in the lung due to asthma (also known as a preventative medication), and a short-acting bronchodilator (also known as a quick reliever).

How Your Medicine Works: Serevent works by relieving spasm or narrowing in the small air passages in the lung causing chest tightness and wheezing. However it cannot be used as a relief medication in case of an asthma attack, because it does not act quickly enough. Serevent does not replace your fast-acting relief medication (e.g., Ventolin) or inhaled anti-inflammatory therapy (e.g., Beclovent, Becloforte). Its overuse can be serious.

Important Points to Note Before Taking Your Medicine: Have you ever had to stop taking another medication for your breathing problems because you were allergic to it or it caused problems?

Are you having treatment for a thyroid condition, diabetes, raised blood pressure, or heart problem?

If the answer is **yes** to any of these questions, tell your doctor or pharmacist as soon as possible if you have not already done so.

Make sure that your doctor knows what other medicines you are taking (such as those for allergies, nervousness, depression, migraine, etc.).

Use of This Medicine During Pregnancy and Breast-Feeding: Don't take this medication during pregnancy or breast-feeding, without first discussing this with your doctor.

Taking Your Medicine: Follow the instructions shown. It is important that you inhale each dose as instructed by your doctor. If you have any problems taking this medicine, tell your doctor or pharmacist. Patients 12 years of age or older: **Inhaler:** The usual dose is 2 puffs (2×25 μg) twice daily (2 puffs in the morning and 2 puffs in the evening). **Disks:** The usual dose is 1 blister (1×50 μg), twice daily (1 blister in the morning and 1 blister in the evening). **Diskus:** The usual dose is 1 blister (1 x 50 μg), twice daily (1 blister in the morning and 1 blister in the evening).

Remember the medicine in Serevent disk blisters should only be inhaled using a special kind of inhaler called a Diskhaler inhalation device. Make sure that you have one and can use it properly. If you have any difficulties or do not understand the package insert that comes with it, ask your doctor or pharmacist.

Serevent should not be used more than twice daily.

If you are breathless or wheezy between doses of Serevent you may need a fast-acting relief medication (e.g., Ventolin) which your doctor may already have given you.

After you have started taking Serevent it is likely that you will not need to use the fast-acting relief medication as often. If you have more than one medicine be careful not to confuse them.

You must continue to take your anti-inflammatory medicines (e.g., inhaled corticosteroids) regularly to treat your chest condition. These act together with Serevent to give the best treatment to control or prevent your getting breathless or wheezy. It is important that you continue taking these regularly and do not stop or reduce the dose unless your doctor tells you, even if you feel much better.

How to Use Your Serevent Inhaler Properly (see package insert for illustrations): Before you use your new Serevent inhaler for the first time release the first 2 puffs into the air.

1. Remove the cap from the mouthpiece, the strap on the cap will stay attached to the actuator. Check the mouthpiece inside and outside to see that it is clean.
2. Shake the inhaler well.
3. Hold the inhaler upright between fingers and thumb with your thumb on the base, below the mouthpiece. Breathe out as far as comfortable.
4. For the next step there are two alternatives (4a or 4b) depending on the technique preferred by your physician.

4a. Place the mouthpiece in your mouth between your teeth and close your lips around it, but do not bite it. Just after starting to breathe in through your mouth, press down on the top of the inhaler to release the drug while still breathing in steadily and deeply.

4b. Place the inhaler two finger widths directly in front of the mouth. Begin a slow deep inward breath through the wide open mouth, at the same time pressing the canister down firmly into the inhaler.

5. While holding your breath, take the inhaler from your mouth and take your finger from the top of the inhaler. Continue holding your breath for as long as is comfortable.
6. If you are to take a further puff keep the inhaler upright and wait about half a minute before repeating steps 2 through 5.
7. After use, always replace the mouthpiece cover to keep out dust and lint.

Important: Do not rush steps 4 and 5. It is important that you start to breathe in as slowly as possible just before operating your inhaler. Practice in front of a mirror for the first few times. If you see "mist" coming from the top of your inhaler or the sides of your mouth you should start again from step 2 (applicable to step 4a only).

If your doctor has given you different instructions for using your inhaler, please follow them carefully. Tell your doctor if you have any difficulties.

Cleaning: Your inhaler should be cleaned at least once a week.

1. Pull the metal canister out of the plastic casing of the inhaler.
2. Rinse the plastic casing and mouthpiece cover in warm water. A mild detergent may be added to the water (your pharmacist will advise you). Then rinse thoroughly with clean water before drying. **Do not put the metal canister into water.**
3. Leave the casing and mouthpiece cover to dry in a warm place. Avoid excessive heat.
4. Replace the canister and mouthpiece cover.
5. After cleaning release one puff into the air to make sure it works.

How to Use Your Serevent Diskhaler Properly (see package insert for illustrations): The Serevent Diskhaler device is used together with a Serevent diskhaler disk for inhaling medication.

The Diskhaler device consists of:

- an outer colored body with a hinged lid and piercing needle
- a cleaning brush contained at the rear of the body
- a colored mouthpiece cover
- a white sliding tray with mouthpiece
- a white wheel to support the disk

The Serevent disk consists of 4 blisters. Each blister contains a measured dose of dry powder medication.

Warning: Do not puncture any disk blister until loaded into the Diskhaler device.

To Load the Serevent Disk Into the Diskhaler Device:

1. Remove the mouthpiece cover and check inside and outside to ensure that the mouthpiece is clean.
2. Hold the corners of the white tray and pull out gently until you can see all the plastic ridges on the sides of the tray.
3. Put your finger and thumb on the ridges, squeeze inwards and gently pull the tray out of the Diskhaler body.
4. Place the disk on the wheel with the numbers uppermost. Then slide the tray back fully into the Diskhaler body.

To Rotate the Diskhaler to the First Dose:

5. Hold the corners of the tray and rotate the disk by gently pulling the tray out and pushing it in until the number '4' appears in the indicator hole. The Diskhaler is now ready for use.

The indicator hole always shows the number of doses remaining in the Diskhaler.

To Pierce the Blister in the Serevent Disk:

6. Raise the lid as far as it will go into the fully upright position. Both surfaces of the blister must be pierced. Some resistance will be felt as the upper, and especially the lower surfaces of the blister, are pierced. Then close the lid.

Warning: Do not try to lift the lid unless the tray is positioned fully within the body of the Diskhaler device or is completely removed, e.g., when cleaning the Diskhaler device.

To Inhale From the Diskhaler:

7. Breathe out as far as is comfortable. Keeping the Diskhaler device level, raise it to your mouth and gently place the mouthpiece between your teeth and lips but do not bite the mouthpiece. Do not cover the air inlets on either side of the mouthpiece. Breathe in through your mouth steadily and as deeply as you can. Hold your breath and remove the Diskhaler device from your mouth. Continue to hold your breath for as long as is comfortable.

To Prepare for the Next Inhalation:

8. Rotate the Diskhaler disk to the next blister by gently pulling the tray out once and in again. Do not pierce the blister until immediately before inhalation.
9. Always replace the mouthpiece cover after use.

To Replace the Serevent Disk

10. Each disk consists of 4 blisters containing medication. When the number '4' reappears in the indicator hole, the disk is empty and should be replaced with a new disk by repeating steps 2 to 5.

Warning: Do not throw the wheel away with the empty disk.

Care of the Diskhaler: A brush is provided at the rear of the Diskhaler body to clean any remaining powder from the Diskhaler device. This should be done with the tray and wheel removed from the Diskhaler body before inserting a new disk.

You may need to replace your Diskhaler device after about 6 months of use.

How to Use Your Serevent Diskus Properly (see package insert for illustrations): **About your Diskus:** Serevent Diskus is a plastic inhaler device containing a foil strip with 60 blisters. Each blister contains 50 µg of the active ingredient salmeterol (as the xinafoate salt) and lactose which acts as the "carrier". The blisters protect the powder for inhalation from effects of atmosphere. The device has a dose counter which tells you the number of dose remaining. It counts down from 60 to 1. **To show when the last 5 doses have been reached the numbers appear in red.**

When you take your Diskus out of its box, it will be in the **closed position.**

A new Diskus contains 60 individually protected doses of your medicine, in powder form. The dose indicator tells you how many doses are left.

Each dose is accurately measured and hygienically protected. It requires no maintenance, and no refilling. Numbers 5 to 0 will appear in **red** to warn you when there are only a few doses left.

How your Diskus works: The Diskus is easy to use. When you need a dose, just follow the four simple steps below:

1. Open
2. Slide
3. Inhale
4. Close

Sliding the lever of your Diskus opens a small hole in the mouthpiece and unwraps a dose ready for you to inhale it. When you close the Diskus, the lever automatically moves back to its original position ready for your next dose when you need it. The outer case protects your Diskus when it is not in use.

1. Open: To open your Diskus, hold the outer case in one hand and put the thumb of your other hand on the thumb grip. Push your thumb away from you as far as it will go.

2. Slide: Hold your Diskus with the mouthpiece towards you. Slide the lever away from you as far as it will go—until it clicks. Your Diskus is now ready to use. Every time the lever is pushed back a dose is made available for inhaling. This is shown by the dose counter. Do not play with the lever as this releases doses which will be wasted.

3. Inhale: Before you start to inhale the dose, read through this section carefully.

- Hold the Diskus away from your mouth. Breathe out as far as is comfortable. Remember—never breathe into your Diskus.
- Put the mouthpiece to your lips. Breathe in steadily and deeply—through the Diskus, not through your nose.
- Remove the Diskus from your mouth.
- Hold your breath for about 10 seconds or for as long as is comfortable.
- Breathe out slowly.

4. Close: To close your Diskus, put your thumb in the thumb grip, and slide the thumb grip back towards you, as far as it will go.

When you close the Diskus, it clicks shut. The lever automatically returns to its original position and is reset. Your Diskus is now ready for you to use again.

After Taking Your Serevent Inhaler, Diskhaler or Diskus: If you notice a sudden worsening of your shortness of breath and wheeze shortly after using your device, tell your doctor as soon as possible.

If the relief of wheezing or chest tightness is not as good as usual or does not last for as long as usual after taking your Serevent device, tell your doctor as soon as possible. A change from "usual" includes more wheezing, coughing, chest tightness or increased use of fast-acting relief medication (e.g., Ventolin). If these symptoms wake you up at night, call your doctor as soon as possible. Your chest condition may be getting worse and perhaps your doctor may add another type of medicine to your treatment.

Even if you feel much better after starting to use Serevent, you must continue to use your other asthma medication(s) according to your doctor's instructions.

Very occasionally some people feel a little shaky or have a headache or notice that their heart is beating faster than usual. These effects usually wear off with continued treatment. Tell your doctor but do not stop using the medicine unless told to do so.

If you feel unwell or have any symptoms that you do not understand, you should contact your doctor immediately.

If You Take Too Much: If you accidentally take a **larger dose than recommended,** you may notice that your heart is beating faster than usual, that you have a headache and that you feel shaky. Tell your doctor as soon as possible.

In the event of an excessive overdose, tell your doctor without delay or contact your hospital emergency department or nearest Poison Control Centre.

If You Miss a Dose: If you forget to inhale a dose do not worry, inhale another as soon as you remember **but** if it is near to the time for the next dose, wait until this is due. Do not take a double dose. Then go on as before.

What to Do if You Stop Your Medicine: If your doctor decides to stop the treatment, do not keep any leftover medicine unless your doctor tells you to.

Storing Your Medicine: Keep your medicine in a safe place where children cannot reach it. Your medicine may harm them.

Inhaler: Protect from frost, direct sunlight and high temperatures (above 30°C).

If your aerosol inhaler becomes very cold, remove the metal canister and warm **in your hand** for a few minutes before use. **Never** use other forms of heat.

Warning: The metal canister is pressurized. Do not puncture it or burn even when empty.

Disks: Keep away from direct heat or sunlight and protect them from high temperatures (above 25°C) Keep them in a dry place.

Diskus: Keep below 30°C and in a dry place.

What's in Your Inhaler: Serevent inhalation aerosol contains 25 µg salmeterol in each puff. It also contains lecithin, dichlorodifluoromethane and trichlorofluoromethane. Each canister contains 60 or 120 puffs.

What's in Your Serevent Diskhaler Disk: Serevent Diskhaler Disks are circular foil disks each having 4 blisters around the edge. Each blister represents one dose and contains salmeterol (50 µg) and lactose, in the form of a very fine powder which you inhale using a Serevent Diskhaler device.

What's In Your Serevent Diskus: Serevent Diskus is a plastic inhaler device containing a foil strip with 60 blisters. Each blister contains 50 µg of the active ingredient salmeterol (as the xinafoate salt) and lactose which acts as the "carrier".

Serevent (cont'd)

Remember: This medicine is for **you.** Only a doctor can prescribe it for you. Never give it to someone else. It may harm them even if their symptoms are the same as yours.

Further Information: If you have any questions or are not sure about anything to do with your medicine, then you should ask your doctor or pharmacist.

You may need to read this package insert again. **Please do not throw it away** until you have finished your medicine.

□ SEROPHENE® Ⓟ

Serono

Clomiphene Citrate

Ovulatory Agent

Information for the Patient: Consider advising the patient on the following:

Before Using this Medication: Possibility of multiple pregnancy. **See Precautions.**

Proper Use of this Medication: Compliance with therapy; clarification of schedule; taking at the same time every day to aid in remembering each dose. Missed dose: Taking as soon as possible; doubling dose if not remembered until time of next dose; checking with physician if more than one dose missed.

Precautions While Using this Medication: Importance of not taking medication while pregnant; importance of close monitoring by physician. Importance of following physician's instructions for recording of temperature and timing of intercourse. Caution when driving or doing jobs requiring alertness because of visual disturbances, dizziness or light-headedness.

□ SEROQUEL® Ⓟ

Zeneca

Quetiapine Fumarate

Antipsychotic

Information for the Patient: What is Seroquel? Seroquel (quetiapine fumarate) (pronounced SER-O-KWELL) is a medication that can help you achieve a normal life. It has been proven to be effective in the treatment of the symptoms of schizophrenia.

Seroquel belongs to a new class of medicines called atypical antipsychotics.

With these medications you're less likely to experience the side effects that older medications can cause. Fewer side effects make it easier to stick with your treatment. And the longer you can stick with your treatment, the better you'll feel.

How does Seroquel Work? Schizophrenia, bipolar disorder and schizo-affective disorder may be due to certain chemicals in the brain being out of balance. This is what causes many of the symptoms you may be experiencing.

Seroquel is thought to work by regulating the chemicals in the brain. It can't cure your condition but it can help you manage your symptoms better. The more control you have over your symptoms, the more control you have over your life.

It's important that Seroquel be taken regularly and continuously, even after you begin to feel better.

How Should I be Taking Seroquel? If you're not sure where to begin, just read on.

Seroquel comes in tablet form and is taken orally. In order to get its full benefit you must take Seroquel every day as prescribed. No matter how you're feeling, don't stop taking Seroquel without talking to your doctor first.

Relief from your symptoms will take some time. In the meanwhile the best thing you can do is stick to your dosing schedule. Your symptoms will gradually improve over the first few weeks, and eventually Seroquel will help keep them from returning.

What if I Miss a Dose? Timing is everything. If you miss a dose, take it as soon as possible. But if it is time for your next dose skip the missed pill and return to your regular dosing schedule. Never take 2 doses at once.

Some tips on how to remember to take your medication:

- Take your doses at the same time every day.
- Choose a daily event which will help you remember to take your medication, e.g., mealtime or bedtime.
- Use a pill container that separates your medication by the days of the week.
- Use a calendar to note the day and time of your dosing.
- Put a written reminder to take your Seroquel where it can be easily seen, e.g., on a mirror or on the refrigerator.
- Have a family member or friend remind you to take your medication.

Do I Have to Take Seroquel with Food? If you are hungry then by all means eat. The effects of Seroquel aren't influenced by food.

What are Possible Side Effects with Seroquel? Everyone has different experiences when it comes to medication. Some people who take Seroquel will experience side effects while others may not.

The most common side effects of Seroquel are headache, dizziness, drowsiness and lightheadedness caused by standing up too quickly. The dizziness and drowsiness are usually mild and will go away with treatment.

Even if you find that Seroquel works well for you, don't hesitate to call your doctor, health care professional or case manager with any questions or concerns.

What are Some Important Things I Should Know About my Treatment with Seroquel?

- During the first 3 to 5 days of therapy with Seroquel or after an increase in dosage, you may experience lightheadedness or dizziness, especially when standing too quickly or getting out of bed. So take your time getting up.
- During the first 3 to 5 days after you begin taking Seroquel or when you have an increase in dosage, you may experience drowsiness. So use caution if you have to drive, operate machinery, or do anything else that requires alertness.
- You shouldn't drink alcohol while taking Seroquel.
- Avoid becoming overheated or dehydrated while you're taking Seroquel.

What Important Issues Should I Talk to my Doctor About?

- Keep your doctor informed on how you are feeling. Feel free to call anytime with questions or concerns.
- Discuss any side effects or symptoms you are experiencing regarding your treatment with Seroquel.
- Talk to your doctor or pharmacist about any other medications you're taking, in case there's a conflict.
- Notify your doctor if you are pregnant or planning to become pregnant while taking Seroquel.
- Notify your doctor if you are planning to breast-feed because you shouldn't do this while taking Seroquel.

Remember to take your Seroquel every day as directed and don't stop without talking to your doctor first.

Seroquel when taken as directed, is as good to the body as it is to the mind.

People are There to Help. There's always someone to reach out to. In addition to family and friends remember that physicians, nurses, pharmacists, social workers, and other health care providers are there to help if you have any questions or problems. The Schizophrenia Society of Canada and the Canadian Mental Health Association (CMHA) are national organizations that work with local chapters to provide support for individuals and families living with mental illnesses. They are always there to lend a hand:

Schizophrenia Society of Canada: 75 The Donway West, Suite 814, Don Mills, Ontario M3C 2B9, Telephone: (416) 445-8204, Fax: (416) 445-2270.

Canadian Mental Health Association: 2160 Yonge St. 3rd Floor, Toronto, Ontario M4S 2Z3, Telephone: (416) 484-7750, Fax: (416) 484-4617.

□ SERZONE® Ⓟ

Bristol-Myers Squibb

Nefazodone HCl

Antidepressant

Information for the Patient: What Is Serzone?

- Serzone (nefazodone hydrochloride) belongs to the family of medicines called antidepressants.
- Serzone has been prescribed to you by your doctor to relieve your symptoms of depression.

Important Points: You Must Tell Your Doctor Before Taking Serzone:
- all your medical conditions, including a history of seizures, liver disease, or heart or blood pressure disorders;
- any medications (prescription or nonprescription) which you are taking, especially monoamine oxidase inhibitor antidepressants, such as Nardil (phenelzine), Parnate (tranylcypromine), or Manerix (moclobemide) or certain benzodiazepines, such as the sleeping pill, Halcion (triazolam), or such as the anti-anxiety drug, Xanax (alprazolam), or gastrointestinal agents such as Prepulsid (cisapride), or antihistamines, such as Hismanal (astemizole), or Seldane (terfenadine); or cholesterol-lowering drugs such as: Mevacor (lovastatin), Zocor (simvastatin), Lipitor (atorvastatin) or Baycol (cerivastatin);
- if you are pregnant or thinking about becoming pregnant, or if you are breast-feeding;
- your habits concerning alcohol consumption.

How to Take Serzone:
- It is very important that you take Serzone exactly as your doctor has instructed.
- Never increase the amount of Serzone you are taking unless your doctor tells you to.
- The antidepressant effects of Serzone may be delayed for 4 weeks or longer.
- Serzone may be taken with or without food.

When Not to Use Serzone:
- Do not use Serzone if you are allergic to it or to any of the components of its formulation (see list of components at the end of this section). Stop taking the drug and contact your doctor immediately if you experience an allergic reaction or any severe or unusual side effects.

Precautions When Taking Serzone:
- You may experience some side effects such as dry mouth, nausea, drowsiness, dizziness, constipation, weakness, lightheadedness, or blurred vision. Consult your doctor if you experience these or other side effects, as the dose may have to be adjusted.
- Refrain from potentially hazardous tasks, such as driving a car or operating dangerous machines, until you are sure that this medication does not affect your mental alertness or physical coordination.
- Avoid alcoholic drinks while taking Serzone.
- Male patients with prolonged or inappropriate erections should immediately discontinue Serzone and consult their doctors. If the condition persists for more than 24 hours, a urologist should be consulted.
- When taking Serzone check with your doctor before taking any other drugs, (prescription or over-the-counter), as there is potential for drug interactions.

What to Do in Case of Overdose:
- Contact your doctor or the nearest hospital emergency department, even though you may not feel sick.

How to Store Serzone:
- Store at room temperature (15 to 30°C).
- Keep container tightly closed.
- Keep out of reach of children.

What Does Serzone Contain?
- Serzone is available in tablets containing 50, 100, 150 or 200 mg of nefazodone hydrochloride as the active ingredient. Nonmedicinal ingredients include microcrystalline cellulose, povidone, sodium starch glycolate, colloidal silicon dioxide, magnesium stearate, red ferric oxide (50 and 150 mg tablets) and yellow ferric oxide (150 and 200 mg tablets).

Reminder: This medicine has been prescribed only for you. Do not give it to anybody else. If you have any further questions, please ask your doctor or pharmacist.

☐ SH-206
Pharmascience

Acetic Acid—Camphor—Lemon Extract Oil—Sodium Lauryl Ether Sulfate
Pediculicide

Information for the Patient: In order to avoid reinfestation, it is important that the consumers understand that the treatment of lice infestation should not be limited to the elimination of the lice found on the infested person. Other household members should be treated if there is any evidence of further infestation.

Head lice live on hair and lay small whitish eggs (nits) near the scalp. Lice and nits are observed more easily at the back of the neck or behind the ears. All headgear, scarves, coats and linen should be disinfected by washing in a machine (hot water) and by drying, using the hottest cycle of a dryer for at least 20 minutes. All personal linen and bedding items that cannot be **washed** can be dry cleaned or sealed in a plastic bag for about 2 weeks. Combs and brushes can be disinfected by soaking in hot water (temperature higher than 55°C) for 10 minutes. A good vacuuming of the patient's room is recommended.

☐ SINGULAIR® Ⓟ
MSD

Montelukast Sodium
Leukotriene Receptor Antagonist

Information for the Patient: Please read this leaflet carefully before you or your child starts to take this medicine, even if you have just refilled your prescription. Some of the information in the previous leaflet may have changed.

Remember that your physician has prescribed this medicine only for you or your child. Never give it to anyone else.

What is Singulair? Singulair is a leukotriene receptor antagonist that blocks substances called leukotrienes. Leukotrienes cause narrowing and swelling of airways in your lungs. Blocking leukotrienes improves asthma symptoms and helps prevent asthma attacks.

Why has my physician prescribed Singulair? Your physician has prescribed Singulair to treat your asthma or your child's asthma, including preventing your asthma symptoms during the day and night. When taken as prescribed, Singulair also prevents the narrowing of airways triggered by exercise.

What is asthma? Asthma is a chronic lung disease. It cannot be cured—only controlled.

Characteristics of Asthma Include: Narrowed airways causing breathing to become difficult. This narrowing worsens and improves in response to various conditions. Inflamed airways; that is, the lining of airways become swollen. Sensitive airways that react to many things, such as cigarette smoke, pollen, or cold air.

Symptoms of Asthma Include: Coughing, wheezing, and chest tightness. Not all people with asthma wheeze. For some, coughing may be the only symptom of asthma. Symptoms often occur during the night or after exercise.

How do I know if I have asthma? Your physician will determine if you have asthma based on your symptoms and/or on how well you are able to move air out of your lungs. Your physician may use a device called a peak flow meter or a spirometer to test your lung function.

Treatment can control asthma. It is important to treat even mild symptoms of asthma so that you can prevent them from getting worse.

How should asthma be treated? To help prevent asthma symptoms and improve your breathing you will have to work closely with your physician to: Plan ways to avoid or reduce contact with conditions that may trigger an asthma episode (e.g., smoking including second-hand smoke, house dust mites, cockroaches, molds, pollen, animal dander, changes in weather and temperature, and infections in the upper airway, such as colds). Develop a treatment plan that best controls your asthma.

How does Singulair treat asthma? Singulair blocks substances in your lungs called leukotrienes that cause narrowing and inflammation of airways.

Why is compliance (taking my medicine as prescribed) important? Taking your medicine as your physician or health care provider instructs may help reduce the severity of your asthma and the frequency of your asthma attacks.

What should I know before and while taking Singulair? It is important that you or your child **continue taking Singulair daily as prescribed by your physician, even when you or your child has no symptoms or if you or your child has an asthma attack.**

If your or your child's asthma symptoms get worse, you should contact your physician immediately.

Oral tablets of Singulair are not for the treatment of acute asthma attacks. If an attack occurs, you or your child should follow the instructions your physician has given you for that situation.

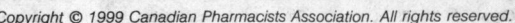

Singulair (cont'd)

When should Singulair not be taken? Do not take Singulair if you or your child are allergic to any of its components.

What should I tell my physician (or health care provider) before using Singulair? Tell your physician (or health care provider) about any medical problems or allergies you or your child has now or has had.

Use in Children: Singulair chewable tablet is for children 6 to 14 years old. Safety and effectiveness of Singulair in children less than 6 years old have not yet been established.

Phenylketonurics: Singulair chewable tablets contain 0.842 mg phenylalanine.

Use in Pregnancy: Women who are pregnant or intend to become pregnant should consult their physician before taking Singulair.

Use in Breast-feeding: It is not known if Singulair appears in breast milk. You should consult your physician before taking Singulair if you are breast-feeding or intend to breast-feed.

Can I take Singulair with other medicines? In general, Singulair does not interfere with other medicines that you or your child may be taking. It is important, however, to tell your physician about all drugs that you or your child is using or plan to use, including those obtained without a prescription.

Can I drive or operate machinery while using Singulair? Singulair is not expected to affect your ability to drive a car or operate machinery.

How should I take Singulair? Take Singulair once a day at bedtime with or without food, as your physician has prescribed. The dose for adults and adolescents 15 years and older is one 10 mg tablet daily. The dose for children 6 to 14 years old is one 5 mg chewable tablet daily.

It is important to continue taking Singulair for as long as your physician prescribes it in order to maintain control of your or your child's asthma. Singulair can treat your or your child's asthma only if you or your child continues to take it.

What should I do in case of an overdose? Contact your physician immediately.

What should I do if I or my child misses a dose? Try to take Singulair as prescribed. However, if you or your child misses a dose, just resume the usual schedule of one tablet once daily.

What undesirable effects may Singulair have? Any medicine may have unintended or undesirable effects, so-called side effects. Singulair is generally well tolerated. In studies, the most common side effects reported were abdominal pain and headache. These were usually mild and occurred as often in patients treated with Singulair or placebo (a pill containing no medication). Tell your physician or pharmacist if you or your child develops any unusual symptom, or if any known symptom continues or worsens.

How can I learn more about Singulair and the condition for which it was prescribed? You may obtain further information from your physician or pharmacist, who have more detailed information about Singulair and your condition.

How long should I keep my medicine? Do not use this medicine after the date shown by the four numbers following EX (or EXP) on the container. The first 2 numbers indicate the month; the last two numbers indicate the year.

How should I store Singulair? Store at room temperature (15 to 30°C) in a dry place. **Keep all medicines safely away from children.**

Ingredients: Singulair (montelukast sodium) contains montelukast sodium as the active ingredient. It is available either as a 10 mg tablet for adults and adolescents 15 years and older **or** a 5 mg chewable tablet for children 6 to 14 years old.

Each 10 mg film-coated tablet contains the following nonmedicinal ingredients: croscarmellose sodium, hydroxypropyl cellulose, lactose monohydrate, magnesium stearate and microcrystalline cellulose. The film-coating consists of: carnauba wax, hydroxypropyl methylcellulose, hydroxypropyl cellulose, red iron oxide, titanium dioxide, and yellow iron oxide.

Each 5 mg chewable tablet contains the following nonmedicinal ingredients: aspartame, croscarmellose sodium, hydroxypropyl cellulose, magnesium stearate, mannitol, and microcrystalline cellulose, red ferric oxide and cherry flavor.

□ 692® Tablets Ⓝ

Frosst

ASA—Caffeine—Propoxyphene HCl

Analgesic

Information for the Patient: 692 Tablets: This drug contains 2 pain relievers—propoxyphene and acetylsalicylic acid. It is used to relieve pain and is available only with your physician's prescription.

Proper Use of this Medicine: Take this medication only as directed by your physician. Do not take more of it, do not take it more often, and do not take it for a longer period of time than your physician ordered. If taken for a too prolonged period of time, it may become habit-forming (causing mental or physical dependence) or lead to medical problems. This medication was prescribed specifically for you. Do not give it to anyone else even if his or her condition seems to be the same as yours.

If a dose is missed, do not double the next dose. Instead, go back to your regular schedule.

Keep this medication out of reach of children since overdose is very dangerous in young children. Propoxyphene is not recommended for children under 12 years of age.

Precautions while using this medication: This medication will add to the effects of alcohol and other medications that slow down the nervous system (Central Nervous System depressants). CNS depressants include antihistamines or medication for hay fever, other allergies, or colds; sedatives, tranquilizers, or sleeping medication; prescription pain medication or narcotics; barbiturates; medication for seizures; antidepressants; anesthetics, including some dental anesthetics. **Check with your physician before taking any of these while you are using this medication. Before having any kind of surgery, tell your physician or dentist that you are using propoxyphene.**

Important Notice: Refrain from any alcohol while taking propoxyphene. Heavy use of alcohol with propoxyphene is hazardous and may lead to overdosage symptoms.

Do not take this medication during pregnancy unless your physician knows you are pregnant and prescribes its use. If you intend to become pregnant, inform your physician.

Do not take any dosage form of propoxyphene if you have had an allergic reaction to any dosage form of it.

If you have allergies, hay fever or asthma **or** if you have ever been allergic to acetylsalicylic acid or propoxyphene, tell your physician before you take this drug.

This medication may cause some people to become drowsy, dizzy, or lightheaded, or to feel a false sense of well-being. **Make sure you know how you react to this medication before you drive, use machines, or do other jobs that require you to be alert and clearheaded.**

Other side effects which could occur are nausea and vomiting. Less common side effects include constipation, abdominal pain, itching, skin rashes, lightheadedness, headache, weakness, minor visual disturbances, feelings of elation or discomfort, (difficulty in breathing, swelling of the eyelids or face, ringing or buzzing in the ears, loss of hearing).

If any one or more of these side effects occur, contact your physician.

Overdosage: If you think you may have taken an overdose, get emergency help right away. Taking an overdose of propoxyphene or taking alcohol or CNS depressants with propoxyphene may lead to signs of overdose, including unconsciousness or death. Signs of overdose include convulsions, mental confusion, severe nervousness or restlessness, seizures, severe dizziness, severe drowsiness, shortness of breath or troubled breathing, and severe weakness. In **any** suspected overdosage situation, **get emergency help immediately.**

Always Remember: Tell your physician and pharmacist what other drugs you are taking. Some drugs if used with propoxyphene and ASA can cause **increased unwanted effects.** If you need more information, ask your physician or pharmacist.

□ SLO-BID® Ⓟ

Rhône-Poulenc Rorer

Theophylline

Bronchodilator

Information for the Patient: Your doctor has prescribed Slo-Bid capsules which contain the drug theophylline incorporated in a sustained-release system. Theophylline opens the airway in your lungs so that you may breathe more easily, and Slo-Bid's sustained-release mechanism gradually releases theophylline so that most patients need to take Slo-Bid only twice per day.

Many medicines interact with theophylline, therefore it is important that your doctor knows all the medications which you are taking.

It is important that you take your Slo-Bid regularly, at the time and in the exact quantity that your doctor has directed. Missed doses can cause your symptoms of asthma or bronchitis to reappear and taking more Slo-Bid than prescribed can lead to side effects such as headache, nausea, or vomiting. If these side effects occur at any time during Slo-Bid therapy, you should contact your doctor before taking any additional doses. If your symptoms become more severe and you have been taking your medication regularly, you should also contact your doctor. However, do **not** increase your Slo-Bid dose unless specifically directed to do so by your doctor.

To swallow Slo-Bid more easily, and to ensure that the capsules promptly reach your stomach, each dose should be taken with a glass (120 mL to 180 mL) of water while you are standing or sitting upright. Do not crush or chew the capsules as this will affect the sustained-release mechanism. Unless directed otherwise by your doctor, Slo-Bid should be taken either with food, or shortly after a meal.

Sprinkle Technique Method of Administration: Administration of Slo-Bid by the sprinkle technique does not alter the rate or extent of absorption of Slo-Bid. This is particularly useful if you are unable to swallow whole capsules.

Instructions for Use by the Sprinkle Technique:

1. Hold the capsule horizontally above a spoonful of cool soft food that is easy to swallow such as apple sauce, pudding, fruit puree or ice cream.
2. Rotate the capsule ends slightly in opposite directions to loosen them and gently pull apart, sprinkling the beads onto the food.
3. Do not chew the drug/food mixture, but swallow immediately.
4. Do not save or reuse any medicine that has already been sprinkled on food.
5. If the beads are spilled while sprinkling, start over to make sure you get the proper dose.

If you find that you have missed a dose and less than 3 hours have elapsed since your scheduled dosing time, take your regular dose immediately. If more than 3 hours have elapsed since your missed dose, wait for your next scheduled dosing time and then resume your regular dosage regimen.

Slo-Bid capsules, a sustained-release formulation, are not appropriate for use in an emergency where rapid relief of bronchospasm is required.

During a viral infection your dosage of Slo-Bid may need to be adjusted. If you develop side effects during such an infection, do not take your next dose of Slo-Bid; instead, call your doctor.

If you have any other problems, call your doctor.

□ SOLGANAL® 🄿

Schering

Aurothioglucose

Antiarthritic

Information for the Patient: Rheumatoid arthritis is a chronic inflammatory disease which is systemic in nature. That is, inflammation can occur in various organs and tissues in the body. However, rheumatoid arthritis is usually characterized by joint inflammation which may result in joint damage and deformity.

Gold has been used in the treatment of medical disorders since 1890, and in the treatment of rheumatoid arthritis since 1935. Its usefulness has been repeatedly confirmed in clinical studies. Although not all patients benefit, injectable gold can gradually reduce disease activity and, in some patients, produce a remission.

At the beginning of a course, gold is given by i.m. injection on a weekly basis. Three to 4 months may be required before a measurable improvement occurs. Once your arthritis has improved the dosage schedule can be adjusted so that you may continue to receive injections every 2 to 4 weeks. Careful initial assessment and follow up are necessary to detect and avoid unwanted side effects.

Side effects occur in 30% to 50% of patients. They usually occur during the first 6 months of treatment but they can develop at any time. At regular visits your doctor will inquire about side effects which can include itchy skin or skin rash, sores in the mouth or on the tongue, temporary increase in joint pain associated with gold injections, and vaginal burning or ulceration. The rash may vary in appearance and may occur almost anywhere on the body; it is best to report any skin changes to your doctor. Most side effects are not serious but it may be necessary to modify or discontinue treatment because of side effects.

Before treatment begins, and regularly during therapy, blood tests and urine tests will be done to detect other side effects which are uncommon. These can include a decrease in white blood cells or platelets, and loss of protein in the urine. A fall in platelets (blood cells which aid in clotting) is rare but can occur suddenly, resulting in bruising and bleeding. Any abnormal bleeding should be reported to your doctor.

□ SORIATANE™ 🄿

Roche

Acitretin

Keratinization Disorder Therapy

Information for the Patient: (Male and Female): Soriatane is a medicine used to treat certain severe types of skin disorders. For your own health, safety and well-being, it is **important** that you read the following information carefully.

Soriatane can cause deformed babies if it is taken by a female before or during pregnancy. Your doctor has a line drawing of one of these deformed babies which you should ask to see.

Important Information for Female Patients of Childbearing Potential:

- **Do not take Soriatane if you are or may become pregnant during treatment or for an undetermined period of time of at least 2 years' duration after treatment has stopped. (Discuss this with your doctor.)**
- **You must avoid becoming pregnant while you are are taking Soriatane and for an undetermined period of time of at least 2 years' duration after you stop taking Soriatane. (Discuss this with your doctor.)**
- **You must discuss effective birth control with your doctor before beginning treatment and you must use effective birth control:**
  - **For at least 1 month before you start Soriatane;**
  - **While you are taking Soriatane; and**
  - **For an undetermined period of time of at least 2 years' duration after you stop taking Soriatane. (Discuss this with your doctor.)**

Bearing in mind that any method of birth control can fail.

- **It is recommended that you either abstain from sexual intercourse or use 2 reliable methods of birth control at the same time.**
- **Do not take Soriatane until you are sure that you are not pregnant.**
  - **You must have a serum or urine pregnancy test within 2 weeks before you start Soriatane.**
  - **You must wait until the second or third day of your next normal menstrual period before you start Soriatane.**

- **Contact your doctor immediately if you do become pregnant while taking Soriatane or after treatment has stopped. You should discuss with your doctor the serious risk of your baby having severe birth deformities** because you are taking or have taken Soriatane. You should also discuss the desirability of continuing with your pregnancy.

- **Do not breast-feed while taking Soriatane or for an undetermined period of time of at least 2 years' duration after treatment has stopped. (Discuss this with your doctor.)**

Important Information for All Patients (Male and Female): Pregnancy must be avoided by any female taking Soriatane as Soriatane can cause deformed babies (see Important Information for Female Patients of Childbearing Potential).

- Females: Do not drink alcohol while taking acitretin and for 2 months after you have stopped treatment.

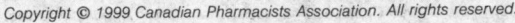

Soriatane (cont'd)

- Males: Avoid or limit consumption of alcohol while taking acitretin and for 2 months after you have stopped treatment.
- **Be sure to return to your doctor as scheduled.** It is important for your doctor to see you regularly, preferably every month, when you are taking Soriatane. Blood tests and other tests allow your doctor to check your response to Soriatane. Discuss your progress and any concerns with your doctor.
- **Do not give Soriatane to anyone else who may have similar symptoms.** Soriatane has to be prescribed for each person by their own doctor because of possible side effects (see below) **Important: Soriatane can cause deformed babies if taken by a female before or during pregnancy.**
- **Do not donate blood while taking Soriatane** or for an undetermined period of time of at least 2 years' duration after treatment has stopped. This is because your blood should not be given to pregnant females.

Please Continue Reading

Other Information for All Patients (Male and Female): Things you should tell your doctor before starting Soriatane:

- **Tell your doctor if you or any members of your family have diabetes, liver disease, heart disease, depression, alcoholism or obesity.**

Treatment Progress:

- A temporary worsening of your skin condition may occur during the first month of treatment with Soriatane. Occasionally, there will be more redness or itching at first, but this will normally fade as treatment continues. It may take 2 to 3 months before the full benefit of Soriatane is seen.
- **Contact your doctor if you notice a worsening of your skin condition.** This may happen within a few months after stopping Soriatane. Another course of treatment will usually produce the same response as the first course.

Side Effects:

- In the first few weeks, perhaps before you see any healing, **you may begin to have some side effects. Some of the most common are:** chapped lips; peeling of fingertips, palms, and soles; loss of hair (see below); itching, sticky skin; or runny or dry nose. **Check with your doctor to see if any change in your medication is needed, especially if these effects become bothersome.**
- Most patients experience some degree of hair loss, but the condition varies among patients. The extent of hair loss that you may experience and whether or not all your hair will return to normal after treatment cannot be predicted.
- If you wear contact lenses, you may find them uncomfortable during and after treatment because Soriatane may cause dry eyes.
- **Tell your doctor if any of your side effects do not clear up in a few weeks after you stop taking Soriatane.**

Special Precautions You Should Take:

- **Do not use vitamin preparations or health food supplements that contain vitamin A.** Soriatane is related to vitamin A. The vitamin A in these products may add to the unwanted effects of Soriatane. Check with your doctor or pharmacist if you are unsure about the vitamin A content of any product you are taking.
- **Protect yourself from excessive exposure to the sun.** Soriatane may increase the sensitivity of your skin to the sun.
- A few patients on Soriatane have experienced decreased night vision. Since the onset can be sudden, you should be particularly careful when driving or operating any vehicle at night. If you experience any visual difficulties, stop taking Soriatane and consult your doctor.

Special Symptoms You Should Tell Your Doctor About:

- **Tell your doctor if you have aches or pains in bones or joints, or difficulty in moving.** Bone changes have been detected by x-ray examination in patients taking Soriatane. The extent of any harm from these changes is not presently known.
- **Tell your doctor as soon as possible, if you experience any of the following symptoms because these side effects may possibly result in permanent effects. These symptoms may be early signs of rare, but more serious side effects which your doctor may want to check as soon as possible.**
  - **headaches, nausea, vomiting, blurred vision, other visual problems, changes in mood.**
  - **persistent feeling of dry eyes, decrease in night vision.**
  - **aches or pains in bones or joints, or difficulty in moving.**
  - **yellowing of the skin or eyes and/or dark urine, flu-like symptoms.**
  - **Tell your doctor about any unusual or severe symptoms that appear during treatment.**

General Guidelines When Taking Your Medication...

- **Call your doctor if you have any questions or have any severe or troubling symptoms.**
- **Keep Soriatane out of the reach of children.**
- **Read your prescription label carefully** and be sure to take the exact amount of medicine prescribed by your doctor. Your doctor may change your prescribed dose from time to time, therefore, it is important that you check the label after each refill. If you have any questions call your doctor.
- **Take Soriatane with food or just after a meal.** If you forget to take a dose of Soriatane, it may be taken later the same day, but, do not take more Soriatane in 1 day than your doctor has prescribed.
- **Protect Soriatane capsules from sunlight and heat.** Soriatane does not need to be refrigerated.

This summary does not contain all known information about Soriatane. Talk to your doctor if you have any questions.

□ STADOL NS™ ⟐

Bristol-Myers Squibb

Butorphanol Tartrate

Analgesic

Information for the Patient: Please read this information carefully before you start to take your medicine, even if you have taken this drug before. Do not throw away this leaflet until you have finished your medicine as you may need to read it again. For further information or advice, please ask your doctor or pharmacist.

What Is Stadol NS?

- Stadol NS (butorphanol tartrate) belongs to the family of medicines called analgesics.
- Stadol NS has been prescribed to you by your doctor to relieve your symptoms of pain.

Important Points: You Must Tell Your Doctor Before Taking Stadol NS:

- all your medical conditions, including a history of drug dependency, head injuries, central nervous system diseases, respiratory impairment, liver disease, kidney disease, heart or blood pressure disorders.
- any medications (prescription or nonprescription) which you are taking, especially central nervous system depressants, such as alcohol, barbiturates, tranquilizers and antihistamines; medications that affect the ability of the liver to metabolize drugs, such as erythromycin and theophylline, or monoamine oxidase antidepressants, such as phenelzine, trancyclopromine or moclobemide.
- if you are pregnant or thinking about becoming pregnant, or if you are breast-feeding.
- your habits concerning alcohol consumption.

How to Use Stadol NS: Take the medication as directed by your physician. For proper use of the nasal spray bottle, read the following instructions carefully.

Instructions (see package insert for illustrations):

1. Blow your nose.
2. Pull the clear cover off pump unit. Remove protective clip.
3. Prior to initial use, prime the unit by pumping sprayer **firmly** and **quickly** until a fine spray appears.
4. Insert the spray tip approximately 1 cm into **one nostril,** close the other nostril with your forefinger and pump the spray unit once firmly and quickly.
5. Your doctor will tell you whether a 2-spray dose is needed. If needed, administer a second spray in the other nostril.

Usual dose is 1 spray: Spray only once into 1 nostril only. Do not spray into both nostrils unless directed by your doctor. Do not repeat sooner than directed by your doctor.

If not used for 48 hours or longer, the unit must be primed with 1 or 2 strokes.

Note: Each priming reduces the number of effective doses per bottle.

Stadol NS should not be used by anyone other than the person for whom it was prescribed. To prevent this, and to reduce the chance of children taking the drug, it is important to dispose of any excess Stadol NS as soon as it is no longer needed.

The best way to safely dispose of the unit is to unscrew the cap, rinse the bottle and spray assembly under the water faucet, and dispose of the parts in a waste can where children cannot easily get to them.

When Not to Use Stadol NS:

- Do not use Stadol NS if you are allergic to it or to any of the components of its formulation (see list of components at the end of this section). Stop taking the drug and contact your doctor immediately if you experience an allergic reaction or any severe or unusual side effects.

Precautions When Taking Stadol NS:

- You may experience some side effects such as drowsiness, dizziness, somnolence and nausea. Consult your doctor if you experience these or other side effects.
- Refrain from potentially hazardous tasks, such as driving a car or operating dangerous machines until you are sure that this medication does not affect your mental alertness or physical coordination.
- Avoid alcoholic drinks and other central nervous system depressants such as barbiturates, tranquilizers and antihistamines while taking Stadol NS.

What to Do in Case of Overdose:

- Contact your doctor or the nearest hospital emergency department.

How to Store Stadol NS:

- Store at room temperature (15 to 30°C).
- Store spray unit in the child-resistant container.
- Keep out of reach of children.

What Does Stadol NS Contain?

- Stadol NS is available as an aqueous solution containing 10 mg/mL of butorphanol tartrate as the active ingredient. Nonmedicinal ingredients include sodium chloride, citric acid, 0.2 mg/mL benzethonium chloride as a preservative, purified water with sodium hydroxide and/or hydrochloric acid added to adjust the pH.

Reminder: This medicine has been prescribed only for you. Do not give it to anybody else. If you have any further questions, please ask your doctor or pharmacist.

Stadol NS is a drug that must be used carefully and appropriately to relieve your pain. Use Stadol NS only as directed. If you feel that you are using Stadol NS more often than prescribed, consult your doctor immediately.

☐ STIEVAMYCIN® Preparations 🄿

Stiefel

Erythromycin—Tretinoin

Topical Acne Therapy

Information for the Patient: Stievamycin (tretinoin and erythromycin) topical gels: what they are, what they do, and how they work.

Stievamycin topical gels are a combination of erythromycin with tretinoin which dermatologists have long prescribed in the treatment of acne.

It works by penetrating deeply into the skin to unplug pores, and thereby aiding the natural flow and elimination of excess oils from the sebaceous glands.

In addition, Stievamycin topical gels have an exfoliative effect, which means the skin's outer layers may peel off to leave a smoother, healthier-looking surface and skin tone.

The erythromycin component results in a more rapid reduction of the inflammatory lesions of your acne and reduces the burning sensation which may be felt when using tretinoin alone.

Your physician usually advises that with regular use of Stievamycin topical gels visible improvement should be seen in 6 to 8 weeks, so be patient.

It is important to understand that your physician has given you a prescription specially suited to your particular needs and skin type. **Do not allow others to use it.** Also, over-application of Stievamycin topical gels may irritate your skin and is unlikely to speed up treatment.

Following your physician's directions carefully will minimize common reactions such as mild burning sensations and redness. During the first 3 weeks of treatment, your physician may recommend application of Stievamycin topical gels on every second day to allow your skin to adjust to the medication.

The use of any other acne or skin medications should be discontinued when using Stievamycin topical gels unless your physician advises otherwise. It is best to use only water-based cosmetics and avoid alcohol-based lotions. Your physician may recommend a daytime moisturizer if your skin is particularly dry.

If your are a female of childbearing age, you should only use Stievamycin gel after consulting your physician and seeking his/her advice for contraceptive counselling. If your are pregnant, you should discontinue the use of Stievamycin gel and consult your physician.

Instructions for use:

1. Wash affected area with a mild soap and warm water and gently dry. Wait 20 to 30 minutes for the face to fully dry.
2. Apply Stievamycin topical gels sparingly and evenly once daily, preferably before bedtime. Use your finger-tip to apply enough to cover the required area, and smooth in. Wash your hands thoroughly **before** and **after** applying Stievamycin topical gels.
3. Avoid sensitive areas such as eyes, lips and mucous-producing areas. Also avoid areas of skin where you have other problems, such as eczema.
4. In the morning, wash your face using a mild soap.
5. At the beginning, you may experience redness, a burning sensation, and peeling while your skin adjusts to the medication which flushes existing oil and debris out of your pores.
6. To minimize these reactions, your physician may start you on the mildest strength of Stievamycin gel and go up gradually until you reach the strength that your doctor feels is most suitable for your skin type. Your physician may advise you to apply the Stievamycin gel less frequently than every day.
7. Since Stievamycin topical gels work from beneath the skin's surface, it takes several weeks of regular use before you can expect noticeable improvement.

Precautions:

1. Do not apply Stievamycin topical gels to areas of skin where you have problems such as eczema, severely inflamed skin or other open lesions.
2. Avoid sensitive and mucous-producing areas such as eyes, mouth, lips, angles of nose, and corners of eyes and mouth.
3. Do not over-apply Stievamycin topical gels. Doing so will not speed up treatment, but only irritate your skin.
4. While using Stievamycin topical gels, do not use other acne or skin medications without the advice of your physician.
5. Prolonged exposure to sunlight, sunlamps, wind and cold should be avoided during treatment. If exposure to sun is unavoidable, use a sunscreen with a minimum SPF 15.
6. If sunburn occurs, stop using Stievamycin gel and call your physician for advice.
7. Stievamycin gel has been prescribed for your use only. Do not allow others to use it.
8. **Caution: Keep away from open flame.**
9. **Call your physician if you have any unusual reaction to Stievamycin gel.**

☐ SUPREFACT® 🄿
☐ SUPREFACT® DEPOT 🄿

Hoechst Marion Roussel

Buserelin Acetate

Luteinizing Hormone-Releasing Hormone (LH-RH) Analog

Information for the Patient: Keep medicines out of reach of children: Suprefact (buserelin acetate injection and nasal solution) or Suprefact Depot (buserelin acetate implant) has been prescribed for you by your doctor and the information provided below is intended to assist you in the safe and effective use of this treatment. This information is not intended to supersede the instructions you have received from your doctor: they should be carefully followed. Any difficulties you encounter should be discussed with your doctor, or pharmacist.

Suprefact Injection: This product should be kept at room temperature, below 25°C. Do not permit the product to freeze and do not expose it to sources of heat. Do not use Suprefact beyond the expiry date printed on the label.

It is important that you follow-up your doctor's instructions carefully and it is also important that your treatment be assessed by your doctor on a regular basis.

Suprefact treatment results in suppression of your sex hormones. Consequently, the complaints you may experience may be related to this hormone-suppressing action of the drug. Your complaints may

Suprefact (cont'd)

include hot flushes and loss of sex drive. In rare instances, you may experience an increase in your disease process such as pain, or increased pain, or increased difficulty in urinating. Should you experience events such as these, contact your doctor without delay. Occasionally, reddening, itching or swelling may occur at the Suprefact injection site. These occurrences can be minimized by rotating the site of injection. In the event of persisting problems of this nature consult your doctor. Do not make any changes in your treatment programme without first discussing the intended change with your doctor.

Administration: The Suprefact vial is supplied with a plastic cap which can be removed by pressing upwards with the thumb. This cap serves to ensure that the vial has not been previously entered. After removal (the cap can be discarded) the rubber diaphragm of the vial is exposed. Proceed:

1. Wash your hands, with soap and water, and dry on a clean towel.
2. Clean the rubber diaphragm of the Suprefact vial with a cotton swab previously dipped in alcohol. Leave to dry.
3. Select an appropriate sterile, disposable syringe and needle assembly (your doctor or pharmacist will help you select a syringe of appropriate bore and cylinder graduations) and remove it from its sterile packaging.
4. Draw the syringe piston as far back as the volume (see syringe cylinder graduation) of solution you wish to withdraw from the vial.
5. Remove the needle sheath (protector).
6. Without touching the needle with your fingers, push the needle through the centre of the rubber diaphragm of the vial.
7. Push on the syringe plunger so that the selected air volume is expelled into the vial.
8. Keeping the needle in the vial, invert the vial into the vertical position adjusting the needle tip to a position below the surface of the solution in the vial.
9. Draw the required solution from the vial by withdrawing the syringe piston.
10. Carefully withdraw the needle and syringe assembly from the vial.
11. Choose your injection site (vary the site for each injection as discussed with your doctor or pharmacist) and clean the skin with an alcohol impregnated swab.
12. Pinch the site, if you wish, between index finger and thumb and, with the needle at an angle introduce the needle quickly under the skin as far as possible.
13. Withdraw the syringe piston a little and, if no blood is withdrawn into the syringe, then push on the piston steadily to inject the solution.
14. Upon completion of the injection, and resting the alcohol-impregnated swab over the needle entry site, remove the needle in a reverse fashion of the entry motion. Hold swab to injection site for a few seconds, then remove.
15. Discard needle and syringe assembly along with the swab in a safe manner. Return the Suprefact vial to its storage area.

If you are taking Suprefact by injection 3 times each day, try and space the injections 8 hours apart. If you are taking Suprefact injection once daily administer it at the same time of day every day. Should you forget to take a dose, administer it as soon as you remember.

Suprefact Nasal Solution: This product should be kept at room temperature, below 25°C. Do not permit the product to freeze and do not expose it to sources of heat. Do not use Suprefact beyond the expiry date printed on the label.

It is important that you follow your doctor's instructions carefully and it is also important that your treatment be assessed by your doctor on a regular basis.

Suprefact treatment results in suppression of your sex hormones. Consequently, the complaints you may experience may be related to this hormone-suppressing action of the drug. Your complaints may include hot flushes, and loss of sex drive. In rare instances, you may experience an increase in your disease process such as pain, or increased pain, or increased difficulty urinating. Should you experience events such as these, contact your doctor without delay. Occasionally headaches may be troublesome and nasal irritation or dryness may appear. In the event of persisting problems consult your doctor. Do not make any changes in your treatment program without first discussing the intended change with your doctor.

Premenopausal Women: Suppression of your sex hormones can also result in a small loss of mineral from bone, some of which may not be reversible. During one 6-month treatment period, this small loss of mineral from bone should not be important.

There are certain conditions that may increase the possibility of the thinning of your bones when you take a drug such as Suprefact. They are:

- family history of severe osteoporosis (thinnning of bones with fractures);
- taking other medications that can cause thinning of the bones.

You should discuss the possibility of osteoporosis or thinning of the bones with your physician before starting Suprefact. You should also be aware that repeat treatments are not recommended since they may put you at greater risk of bone thinning particularly if you have the above conditions.

During treatment with Suprefact, menstruation stops. If regular menstruation persists contact your doctor. Breakthrough menstrual bleeding may occur if treatment with Suprefact is interrupted.

You must not use Suprefact if you are pregnant, breast-feeding or have undiagnosed abnormal vaginal bleeding. Oral contraceptives must be discontinued before starting treatment with Suprefact. Therefore pregnancy must be avoided by the use of nonhormonal methods of contraception. Should pregnancy occur, discontinue treatment with Suprefact immediately and contact your doctor.

Administration (see package insert for illustrations): The Suprefact bottle is supplied in a carton complete with the required administration device, a metered-dose pump (nebulizer) which has a mechanical (spring-loaded) action. The pump contains no chemical propellants. To administer Suprefact using this pump proceed as follows, bearing in mind that these instructions are not intended to supersede instructions you may have received from your doctor:

1. Wash your hands with soap and water and dry on a clean towel.
2. Remove the dose pump from the enclosed transparent plastic container; pull off both protective caps on top and bottom carefully
3. Remove Suprefact bottle from the container. Unscrew cap and discard it. Securely screw dose pump into glass bottle. The interior of the bottle is tapered towards the bottom. That feature, along with the concaved end to the pump tube, means that the pump can still usefully operate even though small quantities of solution (drug) remain. Do not tilt bottle when using the pump.
4. Before first application, hold bottle with pump in a vertical position and pump several times until a uniform mist is released.
   This pump-priming may be necessary again after the pump has been stored between use.
5. Keeping the pump and bottle in a vertical position, place the pump aperture or nozzle into the nostril (if necessary, clean the nose prior to Suprefact administration) and operate as before, once. Gentle sniffing aids the distribution of Suprefact over the nasal passages from where it is absorbed. Nasal congestion will not prevent Suprefact absorption/use.
6. After use, the pump remains in the bottle with its protective cap in position. Store bottle in an upright position at room temperature (below 25°C) avoiding exposure to sources of heat.
7. Follow your doctor's instructions closely. Do not make any changes in the treatment pattern unless you have first discussed the subject with the doctor.

Suprefact Depot (implant): This product should be kept between 15 and 30°C in the original container. Do not permit the product to freeze and do not expose it to sources of heat. Do not use Suprefact Depot beyond the expiry date printed on the label.

Suprefact Depot is administered to you by your doctor once every 8 weeks. It is important that you follow-up your doctor's instructions carefully and it is also important that your treatment be assessed by your doctor on a regular basis.

Suprefact Depot is a drug containing 6.3 mg of buserelin in a white-cream coloured cylindrical rod-shaped implants. Suprefact Depot treatment results in suppression of your sex hormones. Consequently, any complaints you may experience may be related to this hormone-suppressing action of the drug. Your complaints may include hot flushes and loss of sex drive. In rare instances, you may experience an increase in your disease process such as pain, or increased pain, or increased difficulty urinating. Should you experience events such as these, contact your doctor without delay. Occasionally, a local skin reaction may occur at the injection site such as itching, redness, burning and swelling. These reactions are mild and disappear after a few days. In the event of persisting problems of this nature, consult your doctor.

Do not make any changes in your treatment program without first discussing the intended change with your doctor. If you forget to have Suprefact Depot administered by your doctor on the specified day, once every 8 weeks, have it administered as soon as you can. If you need more information, ask your doctor.

☐ SURFAK®

Hoechst Marion Roussel

Docusate Calcium

Stool Softener

Information for the Patient: Do not use if abdominal pain, nausea or vomiting is present. If a sudden change in bowel habits persist for 2 weeks or more, do not take any laxative without first seeking professional advice. Do not use any laxative for longer than 1 week unless so advised by your physician. If a laxative produces no effect after it has been used as recommended for 1 week, or if rectal bleeding is observed, stop using the product and consult your doctor. Do not take docusate calcium at the same time as other drugs your doctor may have prescribed without first consulting the doctor.

Pregnancy and Lactation: If you are pregnant, or if you are nursing an infant, do not take any drug, including docusate calcium, without consulting a health professional. Do not administer concomitantly with mineral oil: increased absorption of the oil may result.

Storage: Capsules should be stored in the container in which they were purchased. Do not expose container or contents to humidity or to sources of heat. Store the container at controlled room temperature, below 25°C. Do not use the product after the expiration date printed on the container.

☐ SURGAM® ℞

☐ SURGAM® SR ℞

Hoechst Marion Roussel

Tiaprofenic Acid

Anti-inflammatory—Analgesic

Information for the Patient: How to make Surgam/Surgam SR work best for you? Your doctor has decided that Surgam/Surgam SR (tiaprofenic acid) is the best treatment for you. As you take Surgam tablets or Surgam SR capsules, remember that your chances of controlling your symptoms are greater if you cooperate fully with your doctor and try to become well informed about your condition.

This leaflet is meant to supplement what your doctor or pharmacist has told you. Your doctor knows and understands your personal condition; be sure to follow your doctor's instructions carefully and read any materials he or she gives you. If you have any questions after reading this information leaflet, be sure to ask your doctor or pharmacist.

What is Surgam/Surgam SR and how does it work? Surgam/Surgam SR is the product name for tiaprofenic acid, a medicine used to relieve the pain and inflammation associated with certain types of arthritis. It belongs to a family of medicine known as nonsteroidal anti-inflammatory drugs (NSAIDs). It helps to relieve joint pain, swelling, stiffness and fever by reducing the production of certain substances (prostaglandins) and by helping to control inflammation. NSAIDs do not cure arthritis, but they promote suppression of the inflammation and the tissue damaging effects resulting from this inflammation. This medicine will help you only as long as you continue to take it.

What does Surgam/Surgam SR look like? Surgam is available as white round tablets. Surgam SR is available as a sustained release pink and maroon capsule containing off-white pellets. The tablets and capsules are clearly marked with the Roussel logo and the product name.

How should you take Surgam/Surgam SR to make it work best for you? Your doctor has chosen the strength (dose) that he or she thinks will be most effective in relieving your condition, based on experience with similar medical problems.

If you are taking Surgam: The usual dose of Surgam tablets is 600 mg daily taken as 1 tablet of 300 mg morning and night or 1 tablet of 200 mg 3 times daily.

If you are taking Surgam SR: Surgam SR capsules have been designed to provide a sustained release of the medicine and thus allow for a convenient once-a-day dosing. The usual dose of Surgam SR capsules is 2 capsules taken once daily. The off-white pellets contained in Surgam SR capsules must be swallowed whole (not crushed or chewed) for optimal results. For the most relief, take your Surgam SR at the same time each day.

You should take Surgam/Surgam SR only as directed by your doctor. Do not take more or less of it, do not take it more often and do not take it for a longer period of time than your doctor ordered. Taking too much of any of these medicines may increase the chance of unwanted effects, especially if you are an elderly patient.

Be sure to take Surgam/Surgam SR as prescribed. It is important to keep taking Surgam/Surgam SR even after you start to feel better. This helps to keep your pain, tenderness and stiffness under control. In some types of arthritis, up to 2 weeks may pass before you feel the full effects of this medicine. However, some people are able to feel improvement in their symptoms right away. If you are not getting adequate relief from your medicine, speak to your doctor before you stop taking it. During treatment, your doctor may decide to adjust the dosage according to your response to the medication.

Stomach upset is one of the common problems with NSAIDs: To lessen stomach upset, take this medicine immediately after a meal or with food or milk. Also, you should remain standing or sitting upright (i.e., do not lie down) for about 15 to 30 minutes after taking the medicine. This helps to prevent irritation that may lead to trouble swallowing. If stomach upset (indigestion, nausea, vomiting, stomach pain or diarrhea) occurs and continues, contact your doctor.

What to do if you miss a dose? If you miss a dose of Surgam tablets, take it as soon as possible. However, if it is almost time for your next dose, skip the missed dose and go back to your regular schedule.

If you miss a dose of Surgam SR capsules once-a-day and remember within 8 hours, take it right away and then resume your regular dosing schedule.

Never double dose.

Combining Surgam/Surgam SR with other medications? Do not take ASA (acetylsalicylic acid, Aspirin), ASA-containing compounds or other drugs used to relieve symptoms of arthritis while taking Surgam/Surgam SR unless directed to do so by your physician.

Does Surgam/Surgam SR have side effects? Along with its beneficial effects, Surgam/Surgam SR like all other NSAID drugs, may sometimes cause undesirable effects especially when used for a long time or in large doses. Relatively common unwanted side effects of NSAIDs are heartburn, stomach pain, indigestion, nausea, vomiting or diarrhea. If these side effects occur and continue, contact your doctor.

Elderly, frail or debilitated people often seem to experience more frequent or more severe side effects.

Although not all of the following side effects are common, when they do occur they may require medical attention.

Check with your doctor immediately if any of the following are noted:

- bloody or black tarry stools;
- shortness of breath, wheezing, any trouble in breathing or tightness in the chest;
- skin rash, swelling, hives or itching;
- persistent indigestion, nausea, vomiting, stomach or lower abdominal pain or diarrhea (particularly if you have a history of stomach upset or ulcers);
- yellow discoloration of the skin or eyes, with or without fatigue;
- any changes in the amount, frequency or colour of your urine (such as dark; red or brown);
- swelling of the feet or lower legs;
- malaise, fatigue, or loss of appetite;
- blurred vision or any visual disturbance;
- mental confusion, depression, dizziness, lightheadedness;
- hearing problems;
- any pain or difficulty experienced while urinating.

Other side effects not listed above may also occur in some patients. If you notice any other effects, check with your doctor.

If you are prescribed this medicine for use over a long period of time, your doctor will check your health during regular visits to assess your progress and to ensure that this medication is not causing unwanted effects.

What should you always remember? The risks of taking this medication must be weighed against the benefits it will have.

Before taking this medication tell your doctor and pharmacists if you:

- or a family member are allergic to or have had a reaction to Surgam/Surgam SR or other related medicines of the NSAID group (such as acetylsalicylic acid (Aspirin), diclofenac, diflunisal, fenoprofen, flurbiprofen, ibuprofen, indomethacin, ketoprofen, mefenamic acid, naproxen, piroxicam, sulindac, tolmetin, nabumetone or tenoxicam) manifesting itself by increased sinusitis, hives, the initiating or worsening of asthma or anaphylaxis (sudden collapse);

Surgam (cont'd)

- or a family member has had asthma, nasal polyps, chronic sinusitis or chronic urticaria (hives);
- have a history of liver or kidney diseases;
- have a history of stomach upset or ulcers, since all NSAIDs may aggravate your problem and sometimes even cause bleeding or ulcers in your stomach or intestines;
- have blood or urine abnormalities;
- have high blood pressure;
- have diabetes;
- are on any special diet, such as a low-sodium or low-sugar diet.
- are pregnant or intend to become pregnant while taking this medication;
- are breast-feeding or intend to breast-feed while taking this medication;
- are taking any other medication (either prescription or nonprescription) such as other NSAIDs, high blood pressure medication, blood thinners, corticosteroids, methotrexate, cyclosporine, lithium, phenytoin. This is important because some medicines can interact with each other and cause some unwanted effects.
- have any other medical problem(s) such as alcohol abuse, bleeding problems, etc.

While taking this medication:

- tell any other doctor, dentist or pharmacist that you consult or see, that you are taking this medication;
- some NSAIDs may cause drowsiness or fatigue in some people taking them. Be cautious about driving or participating in activities that require alertness if you are drowsy, dizzy or lightheaded after taking this medication;
- check with your doctor if you are not getting any relief or if any problems develop;
- report any untoward reactions to your doctor. This is very important as it will aid in the early detection and prevention of potential complications.
- stomach problems may be more likely to occur if you drink alcoholic beverages. Therefore, do not drink alcoholic beverages while taking this medication;
- check with your doctor immediately if you experience unexpected weakness while taking this medication, or if you vomit any blood or have dark or bloody stools;
- some people may become more sensitive to sunlight than they are normally. Exposure to sunlight or sunlamps, even for brief periods of time, may cause sunburn, blisters on the skin, skin rash, redness, itching or discoloration; or vision changes. If you have a reaction from the sun, check with your doctor;
- check with your doctor immediately if chills, fever, muscle aches or pains, or other flu-like symptoms occur, especially if they occur shortly before, or together with, a skin rash. Very rarely, these effects may be the first signs of a serious reaction to this medication;
- **Your regular medical checkups are essential.**

How should you store Surgam/Surgam SR? Store Surgam/Surgam SR between 15 and 30°C. Protect from excessive heat, light and humidity.

The safety and efficacy of Surgam has not been established in children and its use in this age group is therefore not recommended.

Do not keep outdated medicine or medicine no longer needed.

This medication has been prescribed for your medical problem. Do not give it to anyone else.

Keep your medication out of children's reach.

If you require more information on this drug, consult your doctor or pharmacist.

☐ SYNAREL® Ⓟ

Searle

Nafarelin Acetate

Gonadotropin Releasing Hormone (GnRH) Analogue

Information for the Patient: Your doctor has prescribed Synarel Nasal Solution to treat your symptoms of endometriosis. This pamphlet has 2 purposes: 1) to review information your doctor has given you about Synarel; and 2) to give you information about how to use Synarel properly.

Please read this pamphlet carefully. If you still have questions after reading it or if you have questions at any time during your treatment with Synarel, be sure to check with your doctor.

Synarel is used to relieve the symptoms of endometriosis. The lining of the uterus is called the endometrium, and part of it is shed during menses. In endometriosis, endometrial tissue is also found outside the uterus and, like normal endometrial tissue, can bleed during a menstrual cycle. It is, in part, this monthly activity that causes you to have symptoms during your cycle. Most often, this out-of-place endometrial tissue is found around the uterus, ovaries, the intestine or other organs in the pelvis. Altough some women with endometriosis have no symptoms, many have problems such as severe menstrual cramps, pain during sexual intercourse, low back pain, and painful bowel movements.

Endometrial tissue is affected by the body's hormones, especially estrogen which is made by the ovaries. When estrogen levels are low, endometrial tissue shrinks (perhaps even disappears), and symptoms of endometriosis ease. Synarel temporarily reduces estrogen in the body and temporarily relieves the symptoms of endometriosis.

Important Information About Synarel:

1. You should **not** use Synarel if:
   - you are pregnant;
   - you are breast-feeding;
   - you have abnormal vaginal bleeding that has not been evaluated by your doctor;
   - you are allergic to any of the ingredients of Synarel (nafarelin base, benzalkonium chloride, acetic acid, sodium hydroxide, hydrochloric acid, sorbitol, purified water).
2. Synarel is a prescription medicine that should be used according to your doctor's directions. Synarel comes as a special nasal spray that gives a measured amount of medicine. To be effective, Synarel must be used every day, twice a day, for the whole treatment period.
3. It is important to use a non-hormonal method of contraception (such as diaphragm with contraceptive jelly, IUD, condoms) while taking Synarel. **You should not use birth control pills while taking Synarel.** If you miss successive doses of Synarel and have not been using contraception as described above, release of an egg from the ovary (ovulation) may occur, with the possibility of pregnancy if you are sexually active. Under these circumstances you must see your physician to make sure you are not pregnant. There is no experience in administering Synarel to pregnant women.
4. During the first 2 months of Synarel use, vaginal bleeding (often called breakthrough bleeding) may occur. This may also occur if you miss one or more doses of Synarel.
5. Because Synarel works by temporarily reducing the body's production of estrogen, you may have some of the same changes that normally occur at the time of menopause when the body's production of estrogen naturally decreases. Estrogen is a female hormone that is produced in the ovaries. Initially, you can expect a decrease in menstrual flow, and later on your periods will stop altogether. If regular menstruation persists after 2 months of treatment, inform your doctor. Other changes due to decreased estrogen level include hot flashes, vaginal dryness, headaches, mood changes, and decreased interest in sex. Some patients may also experience acne, muscle pain, reduced breast size, and irritation of the tissues inside the nose. These symptoms should disappear after you stop taking the drug.
6. In about 0.2% of adult patients treated with Synarel symptoms suggestive of drug sensitivity such as shortness of breath, chest pain, urticaria, rash and pruritus may occur. If you should experience any of these symptoms, discontinue the use of Synarel and inform your doctor immediately.
7. When you take Synarel, your estrogen levels will be low. Low estrogen levels can result in a small loss of mineral from bone, some of which may not be reversible. During one 6-month treatment period, this small loss of mineral from bone should not be important.

   There are certain conditions that may increase the possibility of the thinning of your bones when you take a drug such as Synarel. They are:
   - family history of severe osteoporosis (thinning of the bones with fractures);
   - taking other medications that can cause thinning of the bones.

   You should discuss the possibility of osteoporosis or thinning of the bones with your physician before starting Synarel. You should also be aware that repeat treatments are not recommended since they may put you at greater risk of bone thinning particularly if you have the above conditions.

8. During clinical studies with Synarel, menstruation usually resumed within 2 to 3 months of stopping treatment with Synarel.
   The distribution of patients, treated with 400 μg/day, by symptom severity at admission, end of treatment and 6 months after treatment was as follows:

		Symptom Severity Score			
	N	0 None	1–2 Mild	3–5 Moderate	6–9 Severe
At Admission	73	6 (8%)	26 (36%)	28 (38%)	13 (18%)
End of treatment	73	44 (60%)	23 (32%)	5 (7%)	1 (1%)
6 months after treatment	73	37 (51%)	24 (33%)	12 (16%)	— —

9. The safety of retreatment with Synarel has not yet been established.
10. You may use a nasal decongestant spray while you are being treated with Synarel if you follow these simple rules. Use Synarel first. Wait at least 30 minutes after using Synarel before you use the decongestant spray.

Proper Use of Synarel:
1. When you start to use Synarel, the first dose should be taken between the second and fourth day after the beginning of your menstrual bleeding. You should continue taking Synarel every day as prescribed. **Do not miss a single dose.**
2. Unless your doctor has given you special instructions, follow the steps for using Synarel **twice each day**, about 12 hours between doses:
   - once in the morning in one nostril (for example, 7 a.m.);
   - once in the evening in the other nostril (for example, 7 p.m.).
   The length of treatment is usually about 6 months, unless your doctor has given you special instructions.
3. Because it is so important that you do not miss a single dose of Synarel here are some suggestions to help you remember:
   - Keep your Synarel in a place where you will be reminded to use it each morning and each evening—next to your toothbrush is one possibility.
   - Keep track of each dose on a calendar.
   - Make a note on your calendar on the day you start a new bottle of Synarel. You can also mark the date you started right on the bottle. Be sure to refill your prescription before you finish the bottle so you will have a new bottle on hand.
4. A bottle of Synarel should not be used for longer than stated on the container. The 10 mL bottle contains enough solution for 60 sprays, enough to last 30 days using 12 sprays/day. The 6.5 mL bottle contains enough solution for 30 sprays enough to last 15 days. After the stated number of sprays have been delivered, a small amount of liquid will be left in the bottle. Do not try to use up that leftover amount because you might get too low a dose, which could interfere with the effectiveness of your treatment. Dispose of the bottle and do not reuse.
5. If your doctor increases your daily dose of Synarel, then your bottle will not last the standard 15 or 30 days. Please discuss this with your doctor to be sure that you have an adequate supply for uninterrupted treatment with Synarel to complete the recommended treatment period.

How to Use Your Synarel Nasal Spray Unit: To Prime the Pump: **Caution:** Avoid breathing in the spray during priming. Before you use a bottle of Synarel nasal spray for the first time, you have to prime the spray pump. Follow these steps: 1. Remove the plastic wrap from the spray bottle.
2. Remove the safety clip and the plastic dust cover from the spray bottle.
3. Put 2 fingers on the "shoulders" of the spray bottle and put your thumb on the bottom of the bottle.
4. Point the tip of the bottle away from you and push the bottle—quickly and firmly 7 to 10 times—with your thumb, until a fine spray appears. Usually the spray will appear after about 7 pumps.
5. The pump is now primed. Priming only needs to be done once, when you start using a new bottle of Synarel. You will waste medication if you prime the pump before each use and will not have enough drug for the number of sprays stated on the bottle.

Important Tips about Using Synarel:
1. Your pump should produce a fine mist, which can only be produced by a quick and firm pumping action. If Synarel comes out of the pump as a thin stream of liquid rather than as a fine mist, it may not be as effective and you should see your pharmacist.
2. **Do not try to enlarge the tiny hole in the sprayer.** If the hole is enlarged, the pump will deliver an improper dose of Synarel.
3. The pump is made to deliver only a set amount of medicine, no matter how hard you squeeze it.

To Use Synarel:
1. Gently blow your nose to clear both nostrils before you use Synarel nasal spray.
2. Remove the safety clip and plastic dust cover from the spray bottle.
3. Bend your head forward a little and put the spray tip into one nostril. (The tip should not reach too far into your nose.) Aim the tip toward the **back** and **outer side** of your nose.
4. Close the other nostril with your finger.
5. Applying pressure **evenly** to the "shoulders", **quickly and firmly** pump the sprayer **one time,** at the same time as you sniff in gently.
6. Remove the sprayer from your nose and tilt your head backwards for a few seconds. This lets the spray spread over the back of your nose.
7. Do not spray in the other nostril unless your doctor has specifically instructed you to do so.
8. Wipe tip of pump with a soft cloth or tissue after each use. Replace the safety clip and plastic dust cover on the spray bottle.

To clean: 1. Be sure to clean the spray tip after every use. Failure to do so may result in a clogged tip that could cause improper dose delivery.
2. Hold bottle in horizontal position. Rinse spray tip with **warm** water while wiping tip with finger or soft cloth for 15 seconds.
3. Wipe spray tip with a soft cloth or tissue to dry. Replace the safety clip and plastic dust cover on the spray bottle.
4. **Do not attempt to clean spray tip using a pointed object. Do not attempt to disassemble pump.**

Important Reminder: Treatment with Synarel must be uninterrupted—with no missed doses—to be effective. Make sure you use Synarel once each morning and once each evening. Also, make sure to note the date you start each bottle so that you can have your prescription refilled in time to have a new bottle on hand. That way, your treatment will go smoothly without any missed doses.

Storage Instructions: Store the bottle upright at room temperature. Avoid storing it at temperatures above 30°C. Protect bottle from light. Do not freeze.

□ SYNTHROID® ℞

Knoll

Levothyroxine Sodium

Thyroid Hormone

Information for the Patient:
1. Synthroid is intended to replace a hormone that is normally produced by your thyroid gland. It is generally taken for life, except in cases of temporary hypothyroidism associated with an inflammation of the thyroid gland.
2. Before or at any time while using Synthroid you should tell your doctor if you are allergic to any foods or medicines, are pregnant or intend to become pregnant, are breast-feeding, are taking or start taking any other prescription or nonprescription (OTC) medications, or have any other medical problems (especially hardening of the arteries, heart disease, high blood pressure, or history of thyroid, adrenal or pituitary gland problems).
3. Use Synthroid only as prescribed by your doctor. Do not discontinue Synthroid or change the amount you take or how often you take it, except as directed by your doctor.
4. Synthroid, like all medicines obtained from your doctor, must be used only by you and for the condition determined appropriate by your doctor.
5. It may take a few weeks for Synthroid to begin working. Until it begins working, you may not notice any change in your symptoms.
6. You should notify your doctor if you experience any of the following symptoms, or if you experience any other unusual medical event: chest pain, shortness of breath, hives or skin rash, rapid or irregular heartbeat, headache, irritability, nervousness, sleeplessness, diarrhea, excessive sweating, heat intolerance, changes in appetite, vomiting, weight gain or loss, changes in menstrual periods, fever, hand tremors, leg cramps.
7. You should inform your doctor or dentist that you are taking Synthroid before having any kind of surgery.

Synthroid (cont'd)

8. You should notify your doctor if you become pregnant while taking Synthroid. Your dose of this medicine will likely have to be increased while you are pregnant.
9. If you have diabetes, your dose of insulin or oral antidiabetic agent may need to be changed after starting Synthroid. You should monitor your blood or urinary glucose levels as directed by your doctor and report any changes to your doctor immediately.
10. If you are taking an oral anticoagulant drug such as warfarin, your dose may need to be changed after starting Synthroid. Your coagulation status should be checked often to determine if a change in dose is required.
11. Partial hair loss may occur rarely during the first few months of Synthroid therapy, but it is usually temporary.
12. Synthroid is the trade name for tablets containing the thyroid hormone levothyroxine sodium, manufactured by Knoll Pharma Inc. Other manufacturers also make tablets containing levothyroxine. Neither you or your pharmacist should change to another manufacturer's product without discussing that change with your doctor first. Repeat blood tests and a change in the amount of levothyroxine you take may be required.
13. Keep Synthroid out of the reach of children. Store Synthroid away from heat, light and moisture.

☐ TAMOFEN® Ⓟ

Rhône-Poulenc Rorer

Tamoxifen Citrate

Antineoplastic

Information for the Patient: Description: Tamoxifen is a medicine that blocks the effects of the hormone estrogen in the body. It is used to treat breast cancer.

The exact way that tamoxifen works against cancer is not known, but it may be related to the way it blocks the effects of estrogen on the body.

Tamoxifen is available only with your doctor's prescription.

Before Using this Medication: In deciding to use a medicine, the risks of taking the medicine must be weighed against the good it will do. This is a decision you and your doctor will make.

Before taking tamoxifen, tell your doctor if any of the following apply to you:

- If you have ever had any unusual or allergic reaction to tamoxifen.
- If you are pregnant or if you intend to become pregnant. It is best to use some kind of birth control while you are taking tamoxifen and for about 2 months after you stop taking it. Please see your doctor for advice on what contraceptive precautions you should take, as some may be affected by tamoxifen. Tell your doctor right away if you think you have become pregnant while taking tamoxifen or within 2 months of having stopped it.
- It is important that you tell your doctor immediately if you have any unusual vaginal bleeding when you are taking tamoxifen or anytime afterwards. This is because a number of changes to the lining of the womb (the endometrium) may occur, some of which may be serious and could include cancer.
- If you are breast-feeding or intend to breast-feed.
- If you are taking any other prescription or over-the-counter medicine.
- If you have any other medical problems, especially cataracts (or other eye problems) or low blood cell counts.
- If you go into the hospital, let medical staff know you are taking tamoxifen.

Proper Use of This Medication: Use this medication as directed by your doctor. Do not use more or less of it and do not use it more often than your doctor ordered. Taking too much may increase the chance of side effects, while taking too little may not improve your condition.

Tamoxifen sometimes causes nausea and vomiting. However, it may have to be taken for several weeks or months to be effective. Even if you begin to feel ill, **do not stop using this medicine without first checking with your doctor.** Ask your health care professional for ways to lessen these effects.

Missed dose: If you miss a dose, take the dose as soon as you remember. Do not take 2 doses at the same time.

To Store this Medicine:

- **Keep out of the reach of children.**
- Store away from heat and direct light.
- Do not store in damp places. Heat or moisture may cause the medicine to break down.
- Do not keep outdated medicine or medicine no longer needed.

Precautions While Using This Medicine: It is important to use some type of birth control while you are taking tamoxifen. Please see your doctor for advice on what contraceptive precautions you should take, as some may be affected by tamoxifen. Tell your doctor right away if you think you have become pregnant while taking this medicine or within 2 months of stopping it.

Side Effects of This Medicine: Along with its needed effects, a medicine may cause some unwanted effects. Some side effects will have signs or symptoms that you can see or feel. Your doctor will watch for others by doing certain tests.

Also, because of the way this medicine acts on the body, there is a chance that it might cause other unwanted effects that may not occur until months or years after the medicine is used. Tamoxifen has been reported to increase the chance of cancer of the uterus (womb) as well as fibroids (noncancerous tumors) in the uterus in some women taking it. It may also cause a drop in some of your blood cell counts. In addition, tamoxifen has been reported to cause cataracts and other eye problems. Discuss these possible effects with your doctor.

Check with your doctor or pharmacist as soon as possible if any of the following undesirable events occur. **Do not be alarmed by this list of possible events. You may not have any of them.**

- Hot flushes
- Menstrual disturbances
- Effects on the endometrium (lining of the womb), which may also be seen as vaginal bleeding
- Fibroids (causes enlargement of the womb), which may also be seen as discomfort in the pelvis or as vaginal bleeding
- Itching around the vagina
- Vaginal discharge
- Stomach upsets (including nausea and vomiting)
- Lightheadedness
- Fluid retention (possibly seen as swollen ankles)
- Bruising more easily (thrombocytopenia)
- Skin rash
- Hair loss
- Certain liver problems such as jaundice (yellow eyes)
- Disturbances of vision
- Difficulties in seeing properly possibly due to cataracts, changes to the cornea or disease of the retina
- Ovarian cysts (fluid sacs on ovaries) in premenopausal women
- Increased risk of blood clots

At the beginning of treatment, a worsening of the symptoms of your breast cancer such as an increase in pain and/or an increase in the size of the affected tissue may occur. In addition, if you experience excessive nausea, vomiting and thirst, you should tell your doctor. This may indicate possible changes in the amount of calcium in your blood and your doctor may have to do certain blood tests.

Other side effects not listed above may also occur in some patients. If you notice any other effects, check with your doctor.

If you need further information ask your doctor or pharmacist.

☐ TASMAR™ Ⓟ

Roche

Tolcapone

Antiparkinsonian—COMT-inhibitor

Information for the Patient: The information presented in this leaflet is not complete. Complete information is available from your doctor or pharmacist. This leaflet is meant to supplement what your doctor and pharmacist have told you about Tasmar. Be sure to follow your doctor's and pharmacist's instructions and read materials given to you. If you have any questions after reading this information leaflet, be sure to ask your doctor or pharmacist.

What is Tasmar used for? Tasmar, also known as tolcapone, is used together with levodopa/carbidopa (Sinemet) or levodopa/benserazide (Prolopa) to treat Parkinson's disease.

Do's and Don't's of taking Tasmar:

- **Do** take Tasmar and any other medication as prescribed by your doctor.
- **Do** tell your doctor if you are pregnant or plan to become pregnant. **You should not be taking Tasmar if you are pregnant.** Animal studies

have shown that Tasmar increases the incidence of malformations caused by levodopa.

- **Do** tell your doctor before starting Tasmar if you:
  have a liver condition
  have any other illness
  have any allergies to medicines, foods or dyes
  are taking any medications, including those you can buy without a prescription
- **Do** tell your doctor about all other medicines you are taking, especially antidepressants, alpha-methyldopa, apomorphine, dobutamine, adrenaline and isoprenaline. **When you are taking Tasmar with the blood thinner, warfarin, your doctor may do regular blood tests.**
- **Do** go for any blood or laboratory tests your doctor orders.
- **Do** tell any new doctor you may see or your dentist that you are taking Tasmar.
- **Do not** take Tasmar if you have an allergy to tolcapone or to any of the nonmedicinal ingredients of the product (for complete list see ''What does Tasmar contain'' section).
- **Do not** take Tasmar if you are also taking one of the following drugs: phenelzine or tranylcypromine for the treatment of depression.
- **Do not** suddenly stop or reduce Tasmar unless recommended by your doctor.
- **Do not** breast-feed while taking Tasmar. The effects of Tasmar have not been studied in infants.

How to take Tasmar? Your doctor will decide the dose of Tasmar you need to start with. This dose may change during your therapy. The dose of levodopa (Sinemet or Prolopa) may also change once you start taking Tasmar.

The recommended dose of Tasmar is 100 mg or 200 mg 3 times a day. The first dose of Tasmar is to be taken with the first levodopa (Sinemet, Sinemet CR or Prolopa) dose of the day. The next tablet is to be taken about 6 hours later and the third tablet after a further 6 hours.

It is important to follow your doctor's instructions. If you have any concerns about the schedule for taking your medication talk to your doctor or pharmacist to help you sort it out.

Tasmar should be swallowed with a full glass of water. It does not need to be taken with food. Do not break or crush tablets and do not take any tablets that are damaged.

What to expect when you start taking Tasmar? Soon after beginning and during your treatment with Tasmar, you may see an increase in uncontrolled movements (dyskinesia) and nausea. This is because Tasmar increases the availability of levodopa (Sinemet or Prolopa) and enhances both its effectiveness and adverse events. This is also why your doctor may suggest a decrease in your daily dose of levodopa (Sinemet or Prolopa). You should not drive a car or operate machinery until you are reasonably certain that Tasmar does not affect your ability to carry out these activities.

Do tell your doctor if you do not feel well after starting Tasmar.

What to do if you missed a dose? If you forget to take your Tasmar at any time, take it as soon as you remember, then continue to take it at the usual times. If you have missed several doses, please inform your doctor immediately and follow the advice given to you.

Do not change the dose of your Tasmar unless instructed by your doctor.

Adverse Events of Tasmar: Along with its desired effects, Tasmar may cause adverse events. Tell your doctor or a pharmacist as soon as possible if you do not feel well while you are taking Tasmar.

The adverse events of Tasmar include: involuntary movement (dyskinesia), hallucinations, nausea, sleeping problems, decreased appetite, and dizziness. These adverse events are most likely to occur when you begin treatment with Tasmar. Diarrhea may occur after about 1 to 3 months of treatment and it may be severe. **Please inform your doctor immediately if diarrhea occurs.**

Tasmar may also cause postural (orthostatic) hypotension. You should not rise rapidly after having been sitting or lying for prolonged periods, especially when you start taking Tasmar.

Tasmar may also cause other adverse events. If you have any questions or concerns about these effects you should talk to your doctor or pharmacist.

Tasmar may turn your urine yellow. This is due to the color of Tasmar and is not harmful to you.

Do you need to be tested while taking Tasmar? Your doctor may ask you to have regular blood tests to monitor how your liver is working. Treatment with Tasmar may sometimes lead to an increase in the level of liver enzymes.

What will happen if you suddenly reduce or stop Tasmar? Very rarely, after suddenly reducing the dose or stopping Tasmar or other antiparkinsonian drugs, you may experience severe symptoms of muscle stiffness, fever or altered consciousness. If this happens you should call your doctor immediately. **Do not suddenly stop or reduce Tasmar unless recommended by your doctor.**

What does Tasmar look like? Tasmar comes in tablets of 2 strengths, a 100 mg tablet and a 200 mg tablet.

The 100 mg tablet is a pale to light yellow, six-sided, rounded film-coated tablet with ''Roche'' and ''100'' engraved on one side.

The 200 mg tablet is a brown to orange yellow, six-sided, rounded film-coated tablet with ''Roche'' and ''200'' engraved on one side.

Remember: This medicine is prescribed for you. Do not give it to anybody else.

What does Tasmar contain? Tasmar 100 mg and 200 mg film-coated tablets contain 100 mg and 200 mg of tolcapone, respectively. The nonmedicinal ingredients are (in alphabetical order): calcium hydrogen phosphate, ethylcellulose, hydroxypropyl methylcellulose, iron oxide, lactose, magnesium stearate, microcrystalline cellulose, povidone K30, sodium lauryl sulfate, sodium starch glycolate, talc, titanium dioxide, and triacetin.

This medication should be stored in a cool, dry place and kept out of reach from children.

☐ TAXOTERE®

Rhône-Poulenc Rorer

Docetaxel

Antineoplastic

Information for the Patient: What is Taxotere and How Does it Work? Taxotere is a medication used to treat people with some types of cancer. Like all cancer medications, Taxotere works by attacking cancer cells in your body. Different medications attack cancer cells in different ways.

Here is how Taxotere works: Every cell in your body contains a supporting structure (almost like a ''skeleton''). If this ''skeleton'' is changed or damaged, the cell can't grow or reproduce.

Taxotere makes the ''skeleton'' in cancer cells unnaturally stiff. The cells then can no longer grow or reproduce.

How Often Will I Get Treated with Taxotere? Taxotere is usually given in a 1-hour intravenous (i.v.) dose every 21 days. Every patient is different; your physician will determine what dose of Taxotere is right for you... and how often you should receive it.

What Do I Need to Do Before Each Taxotere Treatment? The administration of Taxotere requires you to take medication before each treatment begins. Every time you receive Taxotere, your physician will require you to take some premedication; the purpose of this premedication is to help lessen the fluid retention you may experience during treatment. Usually, the premedication consists of corticosteroid pills that are taken orally 1 day before each Taxotere treatment, on the same day as each treatment, and for 3 consecutive days after each treatment. Your physician or nurse will tell you exactly what premedication you need to take, and for how long.

If you forget to take your premedication as directed, make sure to tell your physician or nurse before you get your Taxotere treatment.

Will I Experience Side Effects During Taxotere Treatment? Most of the side effects that occur with Taxotere are manageable. Occasionally it is necessary for a patient's Taxotere treatment to be stopped because of side effects. And remember: If you **do** experience side effects, your physician and nurse can give you a number of medications and explain techniques to help make you more comfortable.

What Are the Side Effects I May Experience? Low White Blood Cell Count: Your white blood cells protect your body against infection. There are 3 types of white blood cells; the most important in preventing infections are cells called neutrophils. Many cancer medications, including Taxotere, cause a temporary drop in neutrophils (a condition known as neutropenia); however, most people receiving Taxotere don't develop infections, even when they have neutropenia. Your doctor will be checking routinely your white blood count and will alert you if your white count is low.

Fever: Fever is one of the most common signs of infection. So if you have a fever, make sure to tell your physician or nurse immediately.

Taxotere (cont'd)

Hair Loss: Loss of hair (including eyebrows, eyelashes, pubic hair, underarm hair and the hair on your head), which is known as alopecia, occurs in most patients taking Taxotere. Hair loss may happen shortly after treatment has begun. However, your hair should grow back once you've finished treatment. In the meantime, your physician or nurse can probably refer you to a special store that carries turbans and wigs specifically for patients with cancer.

Weakness: Many patients receiving Taxotere experience a feeling of weakness during their treatment. If weakness is accompanied by joint or muscle pain, make sure to tell your physician or nurse; your physician can prescribe pain medication to help make you feel more comfortable.

Rash: Patients on Taxotere may develop a rash. This usually occurs on the feet and hands, but may also appear on the arms, face or body. The rash generally appears within a week after each Taxotere treatment, and disappears again before the next treatment. The rash is rarely serious, and it is rare for a patient to discontinue Taxotere therapy because of rash or other skin problems.

Nerve Pain: Patients receiving Taxotere may experience nerve pain; some people feel this pain as numbness, tingling, or burning in their hands and feet. This nerve pain is rarely severe and usually goes away after treatment is completed. However, if you are bothered by nerve pain, make sure to tell your physician or nurse; your physician can prescribe pain medication to help make you feel more comfortable.

Fluid Retention: Fluid retention can occur in patients receiving Taxotere. It may begin as swelling on the legs. Your doctor will prescribe medication which is important for you to take to reduce the likelihood that the fluid retention will be serious or cause your treatment to be discontinued.

Other Possible Side Effects: The side effects listed above are the most common in patients receiving Taxotere, but they are not the only ones that may occur. Other possible side effects include: upset stomach, sores in the mouth, irregular or rapid heartbeat, dizziness or faintness, redness and dryness of the skin, nail changes and swelling at the site of injection. Rarely are these side effects severe enough to discontinue your Taxotere treatment. Make sure to report any unusual symptoms you experience to your physician or nurse.

When will I not be administered Taxotere? Taxotere will not be used if:

- you experienced in the past a severe allergic reaction to it or to polysorbate 80 which is contained in the product;
- the number of white cells is low;
- you have a severe liver disease;
- you are pregnant or breast-feeding.

May Taxotere be taken together with other medicines? It is not advisable to use any medical treatment, without telling your doctor as there may be interactions between Taxotere and other medicines.

Tell your doctor if you are taking any medicine which has been prescribed for you or which you bought without a prescription.

What If I Have Other Questions? Your physician and nurse are always your best source of information about your condition and treatment. If you have additional questions or concerns, be sure to ask them.

□ TAZORAC™ Ⓟ

Allergan

Tazarotene

Antipsoriasis—Antiacne

Information for the Patient: Psoriasis: If you are a female of childbearing age, you should only use Tazorac (tazarotene) gel after consulting your doctor about contraceptive counselling. If you are pregnant you should discontinue use of Tazorac.

Before you Use this Medicine: Tell your doctor:

1. If you are pregnant or are considering becoming pregnant. You should contact the doctor if you become pregnant while using this drug.
2. If you are breast-feeding.
3. If you are allergic to any ingredients in this medicine. Ingredients include benzyl alcohol, ascorbic acid, butylated hydroxyanisole, butylated hydroxytoluene, Carbomer 934P, edetate disodium, hexylene glycol, purified water, poloxamer 407, polyethylene glycol 400, polysorbate 40 and tromethamine.
4. If you are already using other products that make your skin dry.
5. If you have a skin condition called eczema. Tazorac may cause severe irritation if applied to eczematous skin.

How to Use this Product: Your doctor may have told you to use Tazorac in a different way to that recommended in this leaflet. If so, follow your doctor's instructions about when and how to use the gel. Read the directions on your prescription label carefully. Ask your doctor or pharmacist to explain anything that you do not understand.

If you use a cream or lotion to lubricate your skin, apply it to your skin before applying Tazorac.

Remove the cap and check that the seal is not broken before you first use the gel. To break the seal, use the back of the cap.

After applying Tazorac, some people notice a feeling of itching, burning or stinging. This feeling may occur less often as your skin gets used to the medication. Contact your doctor if this irritation becomes troublesome.

Avoid excessive exposure to sun or ultraviolet light. Use sunscreen and protective clothing when exposed to sunlight.

Do not cover treatment areas with dressings or bandages.

Excessive use of Tazorac will not provide faster or better results, and severe irritation or discomfort could occur.

Wash your hands after applying the medication unless you are treating your hands for psoriasis. If the gel accidentally gets on areas you do not need to treat, wash it off.

If Tazorac comes in contact with your eyes, wash your eye with large amounts of cool water, and contact a doctor if eye irritation persists.

Missed Doses: If you forget a dose of Tazorac, do not try to "make it up". Return to your normal application schedule as soon as you can.

Directions for Use: If you bathe or shower, be sure the skin is dry before applying Tazorac. Apply a thin film of the gel to your psoriasis lesions once a day before going to bed.

Avoid application to normal skin. Tazorac is sometimes more irritating to normal skin.

If you need to treat your hands, avoid contact with your eyes.

Usually, you will notice an improvement in your psoriasis after about 1 week. Continue to use Tazorac as directed by your doctor. Contact your doctor if your psoriasis becomes worse.

Special Notes: If Tazorac is swallowed, contact your doctor or Poison Control Centre.

Do not use Tazorac after the expiration date found on the crimp of the tube.

This medicine was prescribed to treat your specific medical problem and is for your use only. Do not share it with others. It may harm them even if their skin problem appears to be the same as yours.

Keep the tube tightly closed when not in use. Store it in a safe place where children cannot reach it.

Acne: If you are a female of childbearing age, you should only use Tazorac (tazarotene) gel after consulting your doctor about contraceptive counselling. If you are pregnant you should discontinue use of Tazorac.

Before you Use this Medicine: Tell your doctor:

1. If you are pregnant or are considering becoming pregnant. You should contact the doctor if you become pregnant while using this drug.
2. If you are breast-feeding.
3. If you are allergic to any ingredients in this medicine. Ingredients include benzyl alcohol, ascorbic acid, butylated hydroxyanisole, butylated hydroxytoluene, Carbomer 934P, edetate disodium, hexylene glycol, purified water, poloxamer 407, polyethylene glycol 400, polysorbate 40 and tromethamine.
4. If you are already using other products that make your skin dry.
5. If you have a skin condition called eczema. Tazorac may cause severe irritation if applied to eczematous skin.

How to Use this Product: Your doctor may have told you to use Tazorac in a different way to that recommended in this leaflet. If so, follow your doctor's instructions about when and how to use the gel.

Read the directions on your prescription label carefully. Ask your doctor or pharmacist to explain anything that you do not understand.

If you use a cream or lotion to lubricate your skin, apply it to your skin before applying Tazorac.

Remove the cap and check that the seal is not broken before you first use the gel. To break the seal, use the back of the cap.

After applying Tazorac, some people notice a feeling of itching, burning or stinging. This feeling may occur less often as your skin gets used to the medication. Contact your doctor if this irritation becomes troublesome.

Avoid excessive exposure to sun or ultraviolet light. Use sunscreen and protective clothing when exposed to sunlight.

Do not cover treatment areas with dressings or bandages.

Excessive use of Tazorac will not provide faster or better results, and severe irritation or discomfort could occur.

Wash your hands after applying the medication unless you are treating your hands for psoriasis. If the gel accidentally gets on areas you do not need to treat, wash it off.

If Tazorac comes in contact with your eyes, wash your eye with large amounts of cool water, and contact a doctor if eye irritation persists.

Missed Doses: If you forget a dose of Tazorac, do not try to ''make it up''. Return to your normal application schedule as soon as you can.

Directions for Use: Clean your skin gently. After it is dry, apply Tazorac once a day, before going to bed, to the areas where you have acne lesions. Use enough gel to cover the entire affected area with a **thin film.**

Follow your doctor's directions for other routine skin care and the use of make-up. Talk to your doctor about the use of cosmetics, especially those that dry your skin.

Usually, your acne will begin to improve in about 4 weeks. Continue to use Tazorac as directed by you doctor.

Contact your doctor if your acne becomes worse.

Special Notes: If Tazorac is swallowed, contact your doctor or Poison Control Centre.

Do not use Tazorac after the expiration date found on the crimp of the tube.

This medicine was prescribed to treat your specific medical problem and is for your use only. Do not share it with others. It may harm them even if their skin problem appears to be the same as yours.

Keep the tube tightly closed when not in use. Store it in a safe place where children cannot reach it.

How Supplied: Tazorac (tazarotene) gel is available in concentrations of 0.1 and 0.05%. It comes in collapsible aluminum tubes with tamper evident tube openings and screw caps, in 10, 30 and 100 g sizes. A 3.5 g physician's sample size is also available.

☐ TEGRETOL® Ⓟ

Novartis Pharmaceuticals

Carbamazepine

Anticonvulsant—Trigeminal Neuralgia Therapy—Antimanic

Information for the Patient: Please read this information carefully before you start to take your medicine, even if you have taken this drug before. Do not throw away this leaflet until you have finished your medicine as you may need to read it again. For further information or advice, please ask your doctor or pharmacist.

What is Tegretol:

- Tegretol (carbamazepine) belongs to the family of medicines called anticonvulsants for treating epilepsy. Tegretol is also used for treating the pain of trigeminal neuralgia and for treating mania.
- Tegretol has been prescribed for you by your doctor to reduce your number of seizures; to relieve the pain of trigeminal neuralgia; or to treat your acute mania or bipolar disorder.

Important Points you must tell your doctor before taking Tegretol:

- Tell about your medical conditions, especially if you have any liver disease, heart disease or blood disorders.
- If you are pregnant or thinking about becoming pregnant, or if you are breast-feeding.
- Any other medicines (prescription and nonprescription) you are taking.
- Inform your doctor of your usual alcohol consumption.
- Inform your doctor of any allergies you may have.

How to take Tegretol:

- It is very important that you take Tegretol exactly as your doctor instructed.
- Never increase or decrease the amount of Tegretol you are taking unless your doctor tells you to.
- Do not stop taking it abruptly, because your symptoms may increase.
- If you miss a dose, take your Tegretol as soon as possible. However, if the time is close to the next dose, do not take the missed dose and return to your regular dosing schedule.
- Tegretol tablets, Chewtabs and suspension should be taken in 2 to 4 divided doses daily, with meals whenever possible. Tegretol CR tablets should be swallowed unchewed with a little liquid during or after a meal.
- Shake Tegretol suspension well before you take it or else you may not receive the correct dose.

When not to use Tegretol:

- Do not use Tegretol if you are allergic to it or any of the components in the tablets or suspension (see list of components at the end of this leaflet).

Precautions when taking Tegretol:

- Call your doctor immediately if your seizures get worse.
- Contact your doctor immediately if you experience any severe, unusual or allergic reactions.
- If you experience any side effects such as drowsiness, headache, unsteadiness on the feet, double vision, dizziness, nausea or vomiting, consult your doctor.
- Do not drive a car or operate dangerous machinery until you are sure that Tegretol does not affect your alertness.
- Avoid alcoholic drinks when taking Tegretol.

What to do in case of overdose:

- Contact your doctor or nearest hospital emergency ward, even though you may not feel sick.

How to store Tegretol:

- Store at room temperature (below 30°C). Protect from humidity, such as in bathrooms where you shower often.
- Protect Tegretol Chewtabs and suspension from light.
- Keep out of reach of children.

What does Tegretol contain:

- Tegretol 200 mg tablets: cellulose compounds, magnesium stearate, silicon dioxide.
- Tegretol 100 and 200 mg Chewtabs: cherry-mint flavor, cornstarch, erythrosine, gelatin, glycerin, magnesium stearate, silicon dioxide, sodium starch glycolate, stearic acid, sugar.
- Tegretol CR 200 and 400 mg: acrylic esters, castor oil derivative, cellulose compounds, iron oxides, magnesium stearate, silicon dioxide, talc, titanium dioxide.
- Tegretol 100 mg/tsp (5 mL) suspension: citric acid, citrus-vanilla flavor, FD&C Yellow No. 6, pluronic polyol, potassium sorbate, propylene glycol, sucrose, sorbitol, water and xanthan gum.

Who manufactures Tegretol:

- Tegretol tablets, Chewtabs, Tegretol CR and Tegretol suspension are manufactured by: Geigy Pharmaceuticals, Ciba-Geigy Canada Ltd., Mississauga, Ontario L5N 2W5 or Dorval, Quebec H9S 1B1.

Reminder: This medicine has been prescribed only for you. Do not give it to anybody else!

If you require any further information or advice, please consult your doctor or pharmacist.

☐ TERAZOL® Ⓟ

Janssen-Ortho

Terconazole

Antifungal

Information for the Patient: Terazol 3 Dual-Pak Package: Terazol 3 Dual-Pak Package contains 3 Terazol 3 Vaginal Ovules (80 mg terconazole) and a 9 g tube of Terazol 3 Cream (0.8% terconazole).

Terazol 3 Dual-Pak Package has been prescribed to you for the local treatment of vulvovaginal candidiasis (moniliasis) and should only be used under medical supervision.

Do not use this medication if you have already taken any products containing terconazole and have developed an allergy or intolerance to it.

This medication should not be used in the first trimester of pregnancy. If you are pregnant or think you are pregnant, consult your physician before using this medication.

Proper Use of This Medicine: Use only as specifically directed. Do not alter the dosage or frequency of application unless ordered to do so by your physician.

This medicine was prescribed to treat your specific medical problem and is for your use only. Do not share it with others.

Complete the prescribed course of treatment to reduce the chance of reinfection.

Avoid tight-fitting undergarments, pants, pantyhose, etc.

Keep all medicines out of reach of children.

Terazol (cont'd)

Please Note: Terazol 3 Vaginal Ovules affect natural rubber and must not be used with products such as condoms or diaphragms.

Dosage and Directions for Use (see package insert for illustrations): **Both the ovules and cream should be used once daily at bedtime for 3 consecutive days.**

Insertion of Ovule:
- Remove one ovule from the package. Place ovule in the receptacle of applicator as shown. The unit is now ready for insertion.
- Hold the filled applicator by the cylinder and gently insert it into vagina as far as it will go comfortably. Press plunger and deposit ovule. While keeping plunger depressed, remove the applicator from vagina.

Following Insertion of the Ovule:
- Rub a thin layer of cream directly onto the vulva for 3 consecutive days.

Care of Applicator:
- After each use, clean the applicator by holding the cylinder of the applicator with one hand and remove the plunger with the other hand by pulling in the opposite direction. Wash with soap and warm water. To reassemble, gently push plunger back into cylinder as far as it will go.

Side Effects: Along with its intended action, any medication may cause unwanted effects. Some of the side effects that have been reported include: headache, burning, pain, itching and irritation.

Should you experience these or any other side effects contact your doctor.

If you need any further information, ask your physician or your pharmacist.

□ TES-TAPE®

Lilly

Glucose Enzymatic Test Strip

Diagnostic Aid

Information for the Patient: Directions (see package insert for illustrations): You will find Tes-Tape the most convenient urine sugar test available. It indicates whether or not glucose is present in the urine. The test is specific for glucose (the type of sugar present in positive tests in diabetes); other sugars will not react with the tape. When Tes-Tape strip is matched with the color chart, the reading indicates positive or negative.

1. **Lift top lid** of dispenser and withdraw approximately 4 cm (1½ inches) of tape.
2. **While keeping a slight tension on the tape, close lid and hold. Tear tape by pulling straight out.**
3. **Dip 1 cm (¼ inch) of the tape into the urine specimen; remove immediately.** The strip should be moistened uniformly, but the end of the tape held between the fingers should be kept dry. Do not place the tape on the sink or on paper or allow moistened portion to contact fingers.
4. **Wait 2 minutes.** Color development in the moistened tape is finished in 2 minutes.
5. **Then immediately compare the darkest area on the test strip while holding tape beside the white area above color chart.** Yellow color indicates urine is free of sugar (glucose) and should be recorded as negative. If tape matches any area of the positive color bar, the urine contains sugar and should be recorded as positive.

Important: The reliability of a roll of Tes-Tape may easily be checked by dipping a piece in a properly prepared glucose solution.* The tape should be removed immediately, as one would when testing a urine specimen. After 2 minutes have elapsed, the reading obtained when the tape is compared with the color chart should be positive. If such a reading is not obtained, the tape has apparently deteriorated and should not be used.

Precautions:
1. **Do not use tape if it has turned dark yellow or brown.**
2. **Protect from direct light, excessive moisture and heat. Do not store in a hot or humid room, such as a kitchen or bathroom.**
3. **The activity of Tes-Tape must be checked periodically, especially if it is in use over a prolonged period of time. If the urine tests are consistently negative, or if a reduction in insulin dosage based on negative readings of Tes-Tape is instructed by the physician. The Coca-Cola test described below should be used to confirm the activity of Tes-Tape.**

What To Do If Tape Breaks (see package insert for illustrations):
1. Open lid. Insert tip of blade under ridge next to black dot on direction label.
2. Tilt blade handle upward to loosen tape holder from case; slide out like a drawer.
3. Place loose end of tape **over** raised platform on holder. Slide holder back into case.

* If a properly prepared glucose solution is not available, Coca-Cola from a freshly opened bottle is satisfactory. Coca-Cola is a well-controlled, carefully standardized product that can be relied upon to give the same reaction as a properly prepared glucose solution.

For chart on patient's record of urine sugar tests with Tes-Tape, contact the manufacturer.

□ THEO-DUR® Ⓟ

Astra

Theophylline

Bronchodilator

Information for the Patient: Important information you should know about Theo-Dur (theophylline anhydrous tablets): Theo-Dur is our brand name for a drug called theophylline. It is used to treat breathing conditions such as asthma, bronchitis, and emphysema. Theo-Dur works to open up air passages in the lungs and helps prevent wheezing and shortness of breath.

Theo-Dur is a sustained-release form of theophylline. This means its effects last longer than some other forms of this drug. Other brands of sustained-release theophylline are available. In general, these work in a similar way to Theo-Dur and have the same side effects.

Read this leaflet carefully. It has been prepared by the manufacturer to help you become more informed about Theo-Dur. It contains general information about this drug and is intended to add to more specific advice provided by your doctor or pharmacist.

This leaflet should not take the place of information given by your doctor or pharmacist. Because of **your** specific health condition, these professionals may have given you different or additional information. If so, be sure to follow their advice. If you have any questions or concerns after reading this leaflet, or if any of the information seems different, talk to your doctor or pharmacist as soon as you can. **Do not stop taking your Theo-Dur without the advice of your doctor.**

Before you start Theo-Dur: Before you start Theo-Dur, be sure you have told your doctor:
- about all other health problems you have now, or have had in the past;
- about all other medicines you take, including ones you can buy without a prescription;
- about any allergies or bad reactions you have or have had in the past, to foods or drugs;
- if you are pregnant or plan to become pregnant;
- if you are breast-feeding;
- if you are on any kind of diet;
- if you smoke, or have smoked regularly within the past 2 years.

How to take Theo-Dur:
- **Take Theo-Dur exactly as prescribed by your doctor.** Do not miss doses and do not take extra tablets without your doctor's advice. If you are not clear about the directions, ask your doctor or pharmacist.
- **It is important to take all doses of Theo-Dur, even when you feel well.** This keeps a constant amount of Theo-Dur in your body so it can help prevent breathing problems.
- Take Theo-Dur at evenly spaced times through the day. For example, if you are to take 2 tablets a day, take each one about 12 hours apart. You should also get into the habit of taking each dose around the same time(s) every day.
- It is a good idea to ask your doctor or pharmacist ahead of time what to do about missed doses. In general, if you remember a missed dose within several hours, take it as soon as possible; then go back to your regular schedule. However, if it is almost time for your next dose, do not take the missed dose. Just take your next dose on

schedule. **Never take a double dose of Theo-Dur to make up for missed tablets.**

- Theo-Dur tablets must **not** be crushed, chewed or broken into small pieces. If you are having trouble swallowing Theo-Dur, your pharmacist can show you how to break them in half.
- **Theo-Dur should not be used to relieve sudden breathing attacks** because it would take too long to start working.

Special Precautions:

- Theo-Dur has been prescribed for **your current condition only.** Do not use it for any other problem unless your doctor tells you. Do **not** give it to other people to use.
- Do not change brands or dosage forms of Theo-Dur without your doctor's advice. Check the bottle label for the name Theo-Dur and if a refill of your medicine looks different, check with your pharmacist.
- Do not take any other medicine(s) without the advice of a doctor or pharmacist. Some medicines **may** affect the way Theo-Dur works for you. This includes vaccines (e.g., for flu), and medicines you can buy without a prescription.
- Your dose of Theo-Dur may need to be changed under certain conditions. Check with your doctor at once if:
  - you develop diarrhea, chest infection, fever or flu (influenza);
  - you plan to become pregnant;
  - you start or stop smoking;
  - you eat large amounts of charcoal broiled foods;
  - you wish to go on a high protein, low carbohydrate diet or low protein, high carbohydrate diet.
- **Keep Theo-Dur out of the reach of children.** As heat and moisture may cause the medicine to break down, do not keep your bottle in the bathroom medicine cabinet or other such places.

Possible Side Effects: Theo-Dur is very effective for breathing problems. But like all medicines, it may cause side effects in some people. These can occur with any theophylline medicine.

Theophylline affects different people in different ways. Just because other people have reported these effects, it does not mean you will get them.

The following may be early warning signs of too much theophylline for your body. Tell your doctor right away if you notice any of these symptoms. Theo-Dur may **not** have caused these problems in your case, but only a doctor can assess this. Remember, if any of this information concerns you, **do not stop taking Theo-Dur on your own.** Instead, discuss your concerns with your doctor as soon as you can:

- unexplained digestive or stomach problems, such as: nausea, vomiting, heartburn;
- loss of appetite, stomach pains, diarrhea, black stools (bowel movements) or blood in your stools;
- unexplained changes in general well-being, such as: mood change (restlessness, nervousness, irritability, difficulty sleeping), confusion, memory problems;
- dizziness, unusual tiredness or weakness, trembling or muscle twitching;
- convulsions (seizures);
- any of the following unless easily explained by something else: hearing changes (e.g., ringing or buzzing in the ears), vision changes (e.g., seeing flashes of light), unusually fast breathing, unusually fast, pounding or irregular heartbeat, headache;
- fever, flushing, extreme flushing, extreme thirst, or an unusual increase or decrease in urination (''passing water'').

Other side effects which cannot be predicted may occur in some people. If you notice any bothersome or unusual effects while taking Theo-Dur, check with a doctor (or pharmacist) right away.

General Information: Remember, this leaflet is not a substitute for talking with your doctor. All drugs can have both helpful and harmful effects. Both depend on the individual person and his or her particular health condition. Your doctor has decided that the benefits outweigh the risks in your case. This leaflet alerts you to many of the times you should call your doctor, but other situations which cannot be predicted may arise. Nothing about this leaflet should prevent you from talking with your doctor about any questions or concerns you have regarding Theo-Dur.

More detailed information about Theo-Dur has been written for health professionals. This information may be obtained through your doctor or pharmacist.

☐ THEO-SR®

Rhône-Poulenc Rorer

Theophylline

Bronchodilator

Information for the Patient: Your doctor has prescribed Theo-SR, a sustained-release preparation of theophylline.

Properties of the sustained-release product: Theo-SR contains theophylline, a bronchodilator, in a controlled-release formulation. It is designed to release the medication in your blood slowly and maintain its effect over a prolonged period. Theo-SR produces maximum blood concentrations between 4 and 6 hours after you have taken your pills and, in most patients, therapeutic blood levels persist for 12 hours.

Theo-SR is intended for maintenance therapy only. **Do not use in emergency situations where rapid relief of bronchospasm is required.**

What does theophylline do? Theophylline is taken by mouth to treat the symptoms of bronchial asthma, asthmatic bronchitis, and other respiratory (lung) conditions. This medicine relieves cough, wheezing, shortness of breath, and troubled breathing. It works by opening up the bronchial tubes or air passages of the lungs and increasing the flow of air through them.

Many medications interact with theophylline, therefore it is important that your doctor know all the medications which you are taking.

How should you take Theo-SR? Unless your doctor indicates otherwise, you will take your Theo-SR every 12 hours. Take your medication with a glass of water preferably on an empty stomach (either 30 minutes or 1 hour before meals or 2 hours after meals).

In some cases, your doctor may want you to take this medicine with meals or right after meals to lessen stomach upset.

Whether you take Theo-SR with or without food, do it consistently: always with your meals or outside of meal hours.

Importance of dosage and regular intake: In order for this medicine to help your medical problem, it must be taken every day in regularly spaced doses as recommended. This is necessary to keep a constant amount of this medicine in the blood.

To help keep this amount constant, do not miss any doses.

What to do when a dose is missed? If you do miss a dose of this medicine, take it as soon as possible. However, if it is almost time for your next dose, skip the missed dose and go back to your regular dosing schedule. Do not double doses.

Consequences of excess doses: **Take Theo-SR only as directed.** Do not take more of it or do not take it more often than recommended by your doctor. To do so may increase the chance of serious side effects.

With excess doses, the most common side effects are gastric irritation, nausea, vomiting, stomach pain and tremor. These side effects may go away during treatment as your body adjusts to the medicine. However, check with your doctor if any of these symptoms continue or get worse.

Caution: Theo-SR tablets may be halved and still retain their sustained-release properties. However, **do not chew or crush** before swallowing.

During a viral infection, your dosage of Theo-SR may need to be adjusted. If you develop side effects during such an infection, do not take your next dose and call your doctor.

If you have any other problems, call your doctor.

☐ 3TC®

Glaxo Wellcome

Lamivudine

Antiretroviral Agent

Information for the Patient: Please read this leaflet carefully before you start to take your medicine. For further information or advice, ask your doctor or pharmacist.

3TC (lamivudine) is intended for use in combination with zidovudine. Please read the information given with zidovudine before you take lamivudine.

About Your Medicine: The name of your medicine is 3TC (lamivudine). Lamivudine can only be obtained with a prescription from your doctor.

How Your Medicine Works: The human immunodeficiency virus (HIV) is a retrovirus. Infection with HIV damages the immune system and can lead to Acquired Immune Deficiency Syndrome (AIDS) and other related illnesses (e.g., AIDS-Related Complex or ARC).

3TC (cont'd)

3TC (lamivudine) is an antiretroviral medication. It is used together with zidovudine (AZT) to delay the progression of HIV infection. Lamivudine does not cure AIDS or kill the HIV virus, but helps to prevent further damage to the immune system by slowing down production of new viruses.

Important Points to Note Before Taking Your Medicine:
- Have you ever had to stop taking this or another medication for this illness because you were allergic to them or they caused problems?
- Have you had, or do you have, any diseases of the kidney?
- Have you had, or do you have, any diseases of the liver, particularly hepatitis B infection?

If the answer is **yes** to any of these questions, tell your doctor or pharmacist as soon as possible, if you have not already done so.

It is important that your doctor knows about all your medicines so that you get the best possible treatment. Tell your doctor about all your medicines, including vitamin supplements, herbal remedies or homeopathic remedies, including those you have bought yourself.

Remember that treatment with 3TC (lamivudine) does not reduce the risk of passing the infection on to others. You will still be able to pass HIV by sexual contact or by blood transfer and you should use appropriate precautions.

While taking 3TC (lamivudine) or any other therapy for HIV disease, you may continue to develop other infections and other complications of HIV infection. Therefore, you should keep in regular contact with the doctor who is treating your condition.

Because your medicine helps to control your condition but does not cure it, you will need to take it every day. Do not stop taking your medicine without first talking to your doctor.

It is important that your doctor knows about all your symptoms even if you think they are not related to HIV infection. Your doctor may need to change the dose of your medicine.

3TC (lamivudine) oral solution contains a small quantity of alcohol, which is unlikely to have any effect. If you are a diabetic, please note that each adult dose (150 mg=15 mL) of lamivudine oral solution contains 3 g of sugar. Due to this sugar content, lamivudine oral solution users should clean their teeth regularly to reduce the risk of tooth decay.

Use of This Medicine During Pregnancy and Breast-Feeding: If you are pregnant, or likely to become pregnant soon, or if you are breast-feeding, please inform your doctor before taking any drugs, including 3TC (lamivudine).

Taking Your Medicine: Take your medicine as your doctor has advised you. The label on it will usually tell you the amount to take, and how frequently. If it does not, or you are not sure, ask your doctor or pharmacist.

Adults and Adolescents (at least 12 years old): As a general guide, swallow 1 tablet (150 mg) or 3 teaspoonfuls (15 mL) of oral solution twice a day. The usual dose of zidovudine is 600 mg a day, taken in 3 divided doses.

If you have a kidney problem, your dose may be altered. Please follow the instructions of your doctor.

Children (at least 3 months of age): If you are giving 3TC (lamivudine) to a child, carefully follow the instructions of your doctor.

After Taking Your Medicine: Some people can be allergic to medicines. If you have any of the following symptoms soon after taking 3TC (lamivudine) you must **stop** taking the medicine and tell your doctor **immediately.**
- sudden wheeziness and chest pain or tightening
- swelling of eyelids, face or lips
- skin rash or 'hives' anywhere on the body
- very severe stomach cramps, which may be due to a condition called pancreatitis

Consult your doctor **at your next visit** if any of the following undesirable events occur: headaches, nausea, vomiting, diarrhea, fever, rash, fatigue, a general feeling of being unwell, or a numbness, tingling sensation, or sensation of weakness in your limbs.

3TC (lamivudine) may also cause a decrease in certain types of blood counts (including red blood cells, white blood cells and platelets) and increase in certain liver enzymes.

Always tell your doctor or pharmacist about any undesirable effects, even those not mentioned in this leaflet.

If you feel unwell in any other way or have any symptoms that you do not understand, you should contact your doctor immediately.

If You Take Too Much: Accidentally taking too much of your medicine is unlikely to cause any serious problems. However, you should **immediately** contact either your doctor, your hospital emergency department or the nearest Poison Control Centre.

If You Miss a Dose: If you forget to take your medicine, take it as soon as you remember. Then continue as before.

Storing Your Medicine: Store 3TC (lamivudine) tablets between 2 and 30°C and lamivudine oral solution between 2 and 25°C.

As with all medicines, keep 3TC (lamivudine) out of the reach of children.

Do not take your medicine after the expiry date shown on the bottle and the carton.

What's In Your Medicine: Each 3TC (lamivudine) tablet contains 150 mg of lamivudine. It also contains microcrystalline cellulose, sodium starch glycolate, magnesium stearate, hydroxypropyl methylcellulose, titanium dioxide, polyethylene glycol and polysorbate. Each bottle contains 60 tablets.

3TC (lamivudine) oral solution contains 50 mg of lamivudine in each teaspoon (10 mg in each mL). It also contains alcohol (ethanol 6% v/v), artificial strawberry and banana flavors, citric acid (anhydrous), edetate disodium, methylparaben, propylparaben, propylene glycol, and sucrose. Each bottle contains 240 mL of lamivudine oral solution.

Remember: This medicine is for you. Never give it to someone else. It may harm them even if their symptoms are the same as yours.

Further Information: This leaflet does not tell you everything about your medicine. If you have any questions or are not sure about anything, then ask your doctor or pharmacist. You may need to read this leaflet again. Please do not throw it away until you are no longer taking 3TC (lamivudine).

□ TIAZAC® Ⓟ

Crystaal

Diltiazem HCl

Antihypertensive—Antianginal

Information for the Patient: Important information you should know about Tiazac (diltiazem hydrochloride) capsules. Tiazac is a brand name for once daily extended-release capsules for the drug diltiazem. It belongs to the group of drugs called "calcium channel blockers" or "calcium antagonists". Your doctor may have prescribed Tiazac, a medication that helps control high blood pressure and/or symptoms of effort-associated angina. Tiazac relaxes the arteries, thereby lowering blood pressure.

Read this leaflet carefully. It does not replace your doctor's or pharmacist's advice. They may have given you different instructions for your particular health condition. Be sure to follow their advice. If you have any questions, talk to your doctor or pharmacist.

Before you take Tiazac you should tell your doctor the following:
- If you are pregnant or plan to become pregnant.
- If you are breast-feeding.
- About all health problems you have or have had in the past.
- About all medicines you take including ones you can buy without a prescription.
- If you visit more than one doctor, make sure each knows about all the medicines you are taking.
- If you are allergic to nonmedicinal substances like food products, preservatives or dyes, which may be present in Tiazac capsules (see Tiazac ingredients).
- If you have ever had a bad, unusual or allergic reaction to any drug containing diltiazem in the past.

Tiazac Ingredients: diltiazem, microcrystalline cellulose, sucrose stearate, polyacrylate dispersion (30%), povidone, talc, magnesium stearate, hydroxypropylmethylcellulose, titanium dioxide, polysorbate, simethicone, gelatin, FD&C Blue #1, FD&C Red #40, D&C Red #28, FD&C Green #3, black iron oxide.

How to take Tiazac: Take Tiazac **exactly** as your doctor tells you. Do not miss doses or take extra doses, unless your doctor tells you. If you are not clear about the direction, ask your doctor or pharmacist.
- Tiazac is taken once daily.
- It is important to take Tiazac at about the same time every day.
- If you miss a dose, check with your doctor or pharmacist to see what you should do.
- Capsules are not to be chewed or crushed.

Side Effects: Tiazac like any medication, may have some side effects. It is important that you keep your doctor informed of all side effects especially if you experience one of the following for more than a week. The most common side effects are: headache, dizziness, peripheral edema (swelling of the ankles), nausea (feeling like vomiting), flushing or feeling unusually warm, a racing heartbeat and unusual tiredness.

Discuss how you feel on Tiazac with your doctor or pharmacist. **Do not stop or restart Tiazac on your own.**

Some precautions you should take:

- Keep Tiazac out of sight and reach of children.
- Do not give Tiazac to other patients because it may not be suitable for them.
- Store your capsules in a dry place at room temperature.
- Read your prescription label carefully. Consult your doctor or pharmacist if you have any questions.

☐ TICLID® ℞

Roche

Ticlopidine HCl

Inhibitor of Platelet Function

Information for the Patient: Ticlid is usually prescribed to patients who have had a previous stroke or who experienced one or more warning episodes indicating an increased risk of stroke, such as transient ischemic attacks, ischemic neurological changes or minor strokes. In clinical trials, Ticlid has been shown to decrease both the stroke mortality and the occurrence of first or repeat stroke in such patients.

Ticlid contains ticlopidine, a drug that reduces the ability of blood platelets to stick to each other and to the walls of blood vessels. This action reduces the tendency of blood to clot in unwanted places such as in narrowed blood vessels.

Ticlid has been prescribed to you **to be used strictly as directed by your physician.** As certain adverse reactions may occur in some patients (see below), **you will be required to have a blood test** (to measure your blood count and some biochemical indices) **before you start taking Ticlid and then every 2 weeks for the first 3 months you are on Ticlid.** If you stop taking Ticlid for any reason within the first 3 months, you will still need to have your blood tested for an additional 2 weeks after you have stopped taking Ticlid. It is also very important that you report to your physician immediately if you have noticed the following:

- **any sign of infection** such as fever, chills, sore throat, ulcers in the mouth, etc.
- **abnormal bleeding and bruising.**
- signs of **jaundice** (yellow eyes or skin, dark urine or light colored stool).
- **skin rash.**
- persistent **diarrhea.**

If your physician is not immediately available, discontinue the medication until he/she can be consulted.

In addition, **discuss with your physician any other medication** you may be required to take (Ticlid is known to interfere with some other drugs).

If you are to have any surgery or dental extraction, **inform the surgeon or dentist that you are on Ticlid,** which may cause prolonged bleeding.

Adverse Effects: About 20% of patients will experience some side effects caused by Ticlid. Most side effects develop during the first 3 months of treatment and they usually disappear within 1 to 2 weeks after Ticlid is stopped. The potentially more serious adverse reactions are the following:

- Decreased white blood count occurs in about 2% of patients on Ticlid treatment. This condition will cause reduced resistance to infection. Regular blood tests are necessary to detect this side effect early and stop the medication. In less than 1% of patients, the white blood count can drop to very low levels, but discontinuation of Ticlid therapy will almost always result in complete recovery.
- Increased bleeding tendency manifested by prolonged bleeding from traumatic or surgical wounds, bruising, bleeding into gastrointestinal tract (manifested by black stool), etc. occurs rarely, in less than 1% of patients, but has to be watched for if you have a history of bleeding disorders, gastroduodenal ulcers, etc. (discuss your medical history with your physician), or if you are about to have a surgical procedure (do not forget to inform the surgeon or dentist).
- Very rarely jaundice and/or liver failure, usually reversible upon withdrawal of Ticlid, have been reported.

More common side effects are upset stomach—(to minimize this possibility, **always take Ticlid with meals),** diarrhea, and skin rashes.

As with any drug, the possibility of an unexpected, previously unknown, potentially serious adverse reaction can never be ruled out.

If you do not understand this information or any part of it, ask your physician.

Warning: Use only as directed. Keep out of reach of children.

☐ TILADE® ℞

Rhône-Poulenc Rorer

Nedocromil Sodium

Bronchial Anti-inflammatory Agent

Information for the Patient: Please read this insert carefully before starting Tilade (nedocromil sodium) and every time your prescription is renewed.

About Your Medical Problem: Asthma is a condition characterized by periodic attacks of shortness of breath, wheezing (audible noise when breathing) and occasionally cough. When you have an attack, breathing becomes very difficult. Asthma may interfere with your everyday activities, such as work, sleep, meals and sports activities. The effect on an individual may be variable.

During an asthma attack, the muscles surrounding the outside of the air passages go into spasm, as a result of the release of certain substances, causing tightening and narrowing of the air passages. This makes it difficult for air to get in and even more difficult for it to be expelled.

The inside of air passages is also affected by an asthma attack. The inside swells and secretes more mucus than normal, and this mucus interferes with breathing.

Bronchospasm and Asthma Attacks Can Be Caused by:

1. allergy producing substances (ragweed, pollen, dust, some foods and medicines);
2. respiratory infections (cold, flu);
3. strenuous exercise;
4. sudden changes in temperature and/or humidity;
5. irritant chemicals (chlorine, perfume).

About Your Medication: This medicine is available only with your doctor's prescription.

Tilade is a medicine for inhalation into the lungs. Tilade is the brand name for a drug called nedocromil sodium. Nedocromil sodium is an anti-inflammatory agent. Tilade is inhaled directly into the lungs where it works by acting on certain inflammatory cells to prevent them from releasing substances that cause asthma symptoms or bronchospasm (wheezing or difficulty in breathing). Tilade is used to treat the inflammation of asthma and prevent the symptoms of asthma. When used regularly, Tilade will diminish the number and decrease the severity of asthma attacks because it reduces the inflammation in the lungs.

Tilade can also be used on an occasional basis to prevent bronchospasm (wheezing or difficulty in breathing) provoked by stimulants, such as: allergy producing substances, cold air, atmospheric pollutants and exercise.

Tilade may be used alone or in combination with other asthma medicines.

Tilade should not be used for the relief of an acute attack of asthma or bronchospasm that has already started. Tilade will not provide immediate relief of the symptoms.

Taking This Medication: You should take Tilade only as directed by your doctor. Do not take more or less of it and do not take it more or less often. Taking too much may increase the chances of unwanted effects.

Up to 1 week or more may pass before you start to feel the desired effect of the medication.

Always Remember: Before taking this medication tell your doctor and pharmacist if you:

- are allergic to or have had a reaction to Tilade (nedocromil sodium), or to any of its components, in the past;
- are, or intend to become, pregnant;
- are, or intend to breast-feed;
- are taking any other medications, either prescription or nonprescription (over the counter);
- have any other medical problems.

Tilade (cont'd)

While Taking This Medication:
- Tell any other doctor, dentist or pharmacist, that you consult or see, that you are taking this medication.
- You should insure that your technique for using Tilade is correct. This can be done by asking your doctor or pharmacist to watch you while you take your medication. If you are experiencing difficulties using the inhaler, your doctor may suggest the use of Tilade Syncroner (which is used as a spacer and training device) to assist you.
- Even if your asthma seems better, you should **not** stop taking any other asthma medication you were previously taking without asking your doctor first.
- You should gargle or rinse your mouth after each dose of Tilade to help relieve or prevent throat irritation and unpleasant taste.
- Check with your doctor if you are not getting any relief of your symptoms.
- Report any untoward reaction to your doctor. This is very important as it will aid in the early detection and prevention of potential complications.
- **Your regular medical check-ups are essential.**

Use in Children: The effective use of Tilade (nedocromil sodium) depends on the ability of each individual child to learn the proper use of the device. During inhalation, children should be assisted or supervised by an adult who knows the proper use of the Tilade inhaler.

Side Effects of Your Medication: Along with its benefits, Tilade, like other drugs, may cause some undesirable reactions. Although not all these side effects may occur, if they do occur they may need medical attention.

Check with your doctor if any of the following side effects occur:
- unpleasant taste;
- headache;
- nausea;
- vomiting;
- dyspepsia;
- abdominal pain.

Tilade may also produce cough or bronchospasm in certain individuals.

Other side effects not listed may also occur in some patients. If you notice any other effects, check with your doctor.

Dosing: The dose of Tilade will be different for different patients. Follow your doctor's instructions. In general the following are the usual doses:

Adults and children over 6 years of age: 2 sprays 4 times daily. According to your response, your doctor may adjust this dose.

Tilade in a single dose of 2 sprays up to 30 minutes before exposure, may provide protection against bronchospasm provoked by stimulants, such as, cold air, exercise, atmospheric pollutants or any other substance that may cause an attack.

Missed Dose: If you are using Tilade regularly and you miss a dose of this medicine, take it as soon as possible. Then take any remaining doses for that day at regularly spaced times.

How to Tell if Your Canister is Empty: The Tilade (nedocromil sodium) canister provides about 112 inhalations. You should keep a record of the number of inhalations you use so you will know when the canister is almost empty. **This canister, unlike other aerosol canisters, cannot be floated in water to test its fullness.**

Directions for Use - Tilade: If the aerosol has not been used for some time, test it by giving the canister one press before inhalation. Be sure the canister is properly inserted into the inhaler.

To ensure the correct dose of Tilade reaches your lungs it is very important that these instructions are followed (see package insert for illustrations):
1. Shake the inhaler well.
2. Pull the dustcap off the inhaler.
3. Holding the inhaler well away from your mouth, breathe out gently (but not fully). To avoid condensation and blocking of the spray, **do not breathe out through the inhaler.**
4. **Tilt your head back** and, holding the inhaler, place it in your mouth and close your lips around it.
5. At the same time that you start breathing in slowly and deeply through your mouth, press the metal canister firmly and continue to breathe in deeply.
6. Remove the inhaler from your mouth and hold your breath for 10 seconds, or for as long as is comfortable, before breathing out slowly.

Repeat steps 3, 4, 5 and 6. After use, replace the dustcap on the inhaler.

Note: Check your technique in front of a mirror from time to time. If you see a mist escaping from your mouth during the inhalation, you must improve your technique. (You may not have your lips properly closed around the mouthpiece, or you may not be breathing in and deeply as you press the canister.)

7. **Cleaning Instructions: It is very important to keep the plastic mouthpiece clean** to prevent the build-up of excess powder. Remove the metal canister and dustcap.

   Wash the plastic mouthpiece thoroughly **by hand hot water** at least twice a week. Shake off excess water and **leave to dry** in a warm place overnight, before replacing the metal canister and dustcap.

   The mouthpiece can be washed every day.

   Note: Do not remove the plastic cover from the metal canister.
   - Wash through the top.
   - Wash through the bottom.
   - Do not remove the plastic cover.

Storage:
- Store away from heat and direct sunlight.
- Keep this medicine from freezing.
- Do not puncture, break, or burn the aerosol container, even if it is empty.
- Always keep the dust cover on the mouthpiece when the inhaler is not in use.

Do not keep outdated medicine or medicine no longer needed. Keep out of the reach of children.

This medicine has been prescribed for your medical problem. Do not give it to anyone else.

If you require more information on this drug, consult your doctor or pharmacist.

☐ TIMPILO® 🄿

MSD

Timolol Maleate—Pilocarpine HCl

Elevated Intraocular Pressure Therapy

Information for the Patient: Instructions for Use: To activate the solution for administration (see package insert for illustrations):
1. Remove the clear plastic protective sleeve from the entire vial by pulling the tab near the top of the cap. Remove the white bottom cap to expose the bottom chamber containing the solution. **Do not** unscrew the top cap at this time.
2. Against a hard surface (e.g., a table), push the vial toward the surface. A slight ''popping'' sound can usually be heard as the plug, separating the 2 solutions, is displaced. The contents are now ready for mixing.
3. Invert the container several times to mix the contents.
4. Unscrew the top cap.
5. Hold the container in an inverted position and gently depress the bottom of the vial to expel and discard 2 drops. The solution is now ready for use.
6. Instill as directed by physician in affected eye(s).
7. Replace the bottom and top caps after use.

There is no need to repeat steps 1 through 5 each time Timpilo is used: The contents of the bottle do not have to be mixed again.

☐ TOLECTIN® 🄿

Janssen-Ortho

Tolmetin Sodium

Anti-inflammatory—Analgesic—Antipyretic

Information for the Patient: Tolectin (tolmetin sodium), which has been prescribed for you by your doctor, is one of a large group of nonsteroidal anti-inflammatory drugs (NSAIDs) and is used to treat the symptoms of certain types of arthritis or spondylitis. It helps to relieve joint pain, swelling, stiffness and fever by reducing the production of certain substances (prostaglandins) and helping to control inflammation and other body reactions.

You should take Tolectin only as directed by your doctor. Do not take more of it, do not take it more often and do not take it for a longer period of time than your doctor ordered.

Be sure to take Tolectin regularly as prescribed. In some types of arthritis, up to 2 weeks may pass before you feel the full effects of this medicine. During treatment, your doctor may decide to adjust the dosage according to your response to the medication.

To lessen stomach upset, take this medicine immediately after a meal or with food or milk. If stomach upset (indigestion, nausea, vomiting, stomach pain or diarrhea) occurs and continues, contact your doctor.

Do not take ASA, ASA-containing compounds or other drugs used to relieve symptoms of arthritis while taking tolmetin unless directed to do so by your physician.

If you are prescribed this medication for use over a long period of time, your doctor will check your health during regular visits to assess your progress and to ensure that this medication is not causing unwanted effects. Along with its beneficial effects, tolmetin, like other NSAID drugs, may cause some undesirable reactions. Elderly, frail or debilitated patients often seem to experience more frequent or more severe side effects with this group of drugs. Although not all of these side effects are common, when they do occur they may require medical attention. Check with your doctor immediately if any of the following are noted:

- bloody or black tarry stools;
- shortness of breath, wheezing, any trouble in breathing or tightness in the chest;
- skin rash, swelling, hives or itching;
- indigestion, nausea, vomiting, stomach pain or diarrhea;
- yellow discoloration of the skin or eyes, with or without fatigue;
- any changes in the amount or color of your urine (such as dark red or brown);
- swelling of the feet or lower legs;
- blurred vision or any visual disturbance;
- mental confusion, depression, dizziness, lightheadedness; hearing problems.

Always Remember: Before taking this medication tell your doctor and pharmacist if you:

—are allergic to tolmetin or other related medicines of the NSAID group such as ASA, diclofenac, diflunisal, fenoprofen, flurbiprofen, ibuprofen, indomethacin, ketoprofen, mefenamic acid, piroxicam, sulindac or tiaprofenic acid;
—have a history of stomach upset, ulcers, or liver or kidney diseases;
—are pregnant or intend to become pregnant while taking this medication;
—are breast-feeding;
—are taking any other medication (either prescription or non-prescription);
—have any other medical problem(s).

While taking this medication:

—tell any other doctor, dentist or pharmacist that you consult or see, that you are taking this medication;
—be cautious about driving or participating in activities that require alertness if you are drowsy, dizzy, or lightheaded after taking this medication;
—check with your doctor if you are not getting any relief or if any problems develop;
—report any untoward reactions to your doctor. This is very important as it will aid in the early detection and prevention of potential complications.
—Your regular medical checkups are essential.

If you require more information on this drug, consult your doctor or pharmacist.

☐ TOPAMAX® Ⓟ

Janssen-Ortho

Topiramate

Antiepileptic

Information for the Patient: Please read this carefully before you start to take Topamax (topiramate), even if you have taken this drug before. Please do not discard this leaflet; you may need to read it again. If you have any questions about this medicine ask your doctor or pharmacist.

What is Topamax? Topamax, the brand name for topiramate, has been prescribed to you to control your epilepsy. Please follow your doctor's recommendations carefully.

Before Taking Topamax: Tell your doctor about any medical problems and about any allergies you have or have had in the past.

You should not use Topamax if you are allergic to any of the ingredients in the product (see What does Topamax contain?).

Tell your doctor if you have or have had kidney stones or kidney disease. Your doctor may want you to increase the amount of fluids you drink while you are taking this medicine.

Tell your doctor if you are pregnant, or if you are planning to become pregnant.

Tell your doctor if you are breast-feeding (nursing).

Topamax may cause some people to be less alert than normal. Make sure you know how you are affected by this medicine before you drive, use machines or do anything else that could be dangerous if you are not alert.

Tell your doctor about all medications (prescription and nonprescription) and dietary supplements you are using. It is especially important that your doctor know if you are taking digoxin, oral contraceptives or any other antiepileptic drugs, such as phenytoin or carbamazepine. Inform your doctor of your usual alcohol consumption or if taking medicines that slow down the nervous system (CNS depressants).

How should I use Topamax? Follow your doctor's instructions about when and how to take this medicine.

The usual dose is 200 to 400 mg/day. Topamax is usually taken twice a day, however, your doctor may tell you to use it once a day or at a higher or lower dose.

Your doctor will start with a low dose and slowly increase the dose to the lowest amount needed to control your epilepsy.

Always swallow the tablets with plenty of water. You can take the tablets with or without food.

If you miss a dose, take it as soon as you remember. But, if it is almost time for the next dose, do not take the missed dose. Instead, take the next scheduled dose.

Do not suddenly stop taking this medicine without first checking with your doctor.

Always check that you have enough tablets and do not run out.

What undesirable effects may Topamax have? Any medicine may have unwanted effects. Tell your doctor or pharmacist about any unusual sign or symptom whether listed or not.

Those reported most often were: coordination problems, changes in thinking, including difficulty concentrating, slow thinking, confusion and forgetfulness, dizziness, tiredness, tingling and drowsiness. Less frequently reported side effects are: agitation, decrease in appetite, speech disorders, depression, vision disorders, mood swings, nausea, taste changes, weight loss, kidney stones that may be present as blood in the urine or pain in the lower back or genital area.

What to do in case of an overdose? If you accidentally take an overdose of Topamax, contact your doctor or the nearest hospital emergency, even though you may not feel sick.

How should I store Topamax? Do not use this product after the expiry date written on the package. Store in a cool, dry place. Keep this and all medicines in a safe place away from children.

What does Topamax contain? Topamax contains topiramate as the active ingredient and the following inactive ingredients: lactose monohydrate, pregelatinized starch, pregelatinized starch (modified), purified water, carnauba wax, microcrystalline cellulose, sodium starch glycolate and magnesium stearate. Depending upon the color, Topamax may also contain: hydroxypropyl methylcellulose, titanium dioxide, polyethylene glycol, synthetic iron oxide and polysorbate 80.

☐ TORADOL® Ⓟ
☐ TORADOL® IM Ⓟ

Roche

Ketorolac Tromethamine

NSAID Analgesic

Information for the Patient: Toradol Tablets: How To Make Toradol Work Best For You: Your doctor has decided that Toradol (ketorolac tromethamine) is the best treatment for you. As you take your Toradol tablets, remember that your chances of controlling your symptoms are greater if you cooperate fully with your doctor and try to become well informed about your condition.

This leaflet is not as thorough as the official Product Monograph on Toradol (which your doctor or pharmacist has available) and is meant to supplement what your doctor has told you. Your doctor knows and

Toradol (cont'd)

understands your personal condition. Be sure to follow your doctor's instructions carefully and read any materials he or she gives you. **If you have any questions after reading this information leaflet, be sure to ask your doctor.**

What Is Toradol?

- Toradol tablets contain ketorolac tromethamine, a member of the class of drugs called nonsteroidal anti-inflammatory drugs (NSAIDs).
- Toradol tablets are used for the **short-term** relief of pain including pain that occurs following surgery (such as general, orthopedic and dental surgery), and postpartum uterine cramping pain. It is also used for pain relief following injuries.

How Does Toradol Work? Toradol helps to relieve pain by reducing the production of certain pain-causing substances called prostaglandins. Clinical studies indicate that when prostaglandin levels are reduced, the intensity of pain is reduced as well.

How Should Toradol Be Taken? You should take Toradol tablets only as directed by your doctor. Do not take more of them, do not take them more often and do not take them for a longer period of time than your doctor or dentist ordered.

The usual oral dose of Toradol in adults is 10 mg (1 tablet) every 4 to 6 hours for pain as required. Doses exceeding 40 mg per day (4 tablets) are not recommended.

Toradol may be taken after a meal or with food or milk if desired. However, the presence of food in the stomach may delay the onset of pain relief. If stomach upset occurs (indigestion, nausea, vomiting, stomach pain or diarrhea) contact your doctor.

Toradol tablets are recommended for short-term use only (not to exceed 5 days following surgery or 7 days for patients with pain from muscular strains, sprains and injuries).

Important! Your doctor may give you different instructions better suited to your specific needs. If you need more information about how to take Toradol properly, double-check with your doctor or pharmacist.

How Long Does It Take Before Toradol Begins To Work? Some people are able to feel improvement in their symptoms right away; for others, improvement may take up to 1 day. By the end of 1 day, if Toradol does not seem to be helping you, tell your doctor. You may need a different dosage or your doctor may want to prescribe another treatment program for you.

Who should not use Toradol?

- Do not use Toradol if you are sensitive or allergic to ketorolac (Toradol) or products containing acetysalicylic acid (ASA), or other salicylates or other nonsteroidal anti-inflammatory drugs (NSAIDs). Allergic reactions may include runny nose, difficulty breathing with wheezing, swelling, skin rashes or hives. NSAIDs include products such as diclofenac, diflunisal, fenoprofen, floctafenine, flurbiprofen, ibuprofen, indomethacin, ketoprofen, mefenamic acid, nabumetone, naproxen, naproxen sodium, oxyphenbutazone, phenylbutazone, piroxicam, sulindac, tenoxicam, tiaprofenic acid or tolmetin.

  Please consult your doctor or pharmacist if you are unsure what your product contains.

  A partial list of brand name products which contain ASA, NSAIDs or ibuprofen is included at the end of this leaflet.
- Do not use Toradol if you have an ulcer or active inflammatory disease of the stomach or intestines. If you have a history of stomach upset, tell your doctor. All NSAIDs may aggravate your problem and sometimes even cause bleeding or ulcers in your stomach or intestines. These complications can sometimes be severe and occasional fatalities have been reported with all drugs of this class.
- Toradol should not be used by children under 16 years of age, except as recommended by a doctor or dentist.
- Do not use Toradol if you intend to become pregnant, are pregnant or breast-feeding.
- Do not use Toradol if you are taking ASA, products containing ASA or other NSAIDs, e.g., drugs to relieve symptoms of arthritis.

Consult your doctor before taking Toradol if you:

- are allergic (see definition above) to Toradol tablets or other related medicines of the NSAID group such as ASA, diclofenac, diflunisal, fenoprofen, floctafenine, flurbiprofen, ibuprofen, indomethacin, ketoprofen, mefenamic acid, nabumetone, naproxen, naproxen sodium, oxyphenbutazone, phenylbutazone, piroxicam, sulindac, tiaprofenic acid, tenoxicam or tolmetin;
- have a history of stomach upset, ulcers, or liver or kidney diseases;
- have high blood pressure or heart failure;
- are pregnant or intend to become pregnant while taking this medicine;
- are breast-feeding;
- are taking any other medicine (either prescription or nonprescription);
- have any other medical problem.

Does Toradol Have Any Side Effects? Any medication can cause side effects; this is true for acetylsalicylic acid (ASA) and all of the nonsteroidal anti-inflammatory drugs. Elderly (generally over 65) patients may be more sensitive to the effects of all NSAIDs including Toradol.

Relatively common unwanted side effects of all nonsteroidal anti-inflammatory drugs are heartburn, abdominal pain, nausea, diarrhea, constipation and so forth. You may take Toradol with meals or a snack to reduce discomfort of this type but this may delay the beginning of pain relief.

All NSAIDs may aggravate gastrointestinal problems and sometimes even cause bleeding or ulcers in your stomach or intestines. These complications can sometimes be severe and occasional fatalities have been reported with all drugs of this class.

Contact your doctor immediately if you experience any of these symptoms:

- bloody or black tarry stools;
- shortness of breath, wheezing, and trouble in breathing or tightness in the chest;
- skin rash, swelling, hives or itching;
- indigestion, nausea, vomiting, stomach pain or diarrhea;
- yellow discoloration of the skin or eyes, with or without fatigue;
- any changes in the amount or color of your urine (as dark red or brown);
- swelling of the feet or lower legs;
- blurred vision or any visual disturbance.

Other effects that have been reported infrequently include headache, drowsiness, dizziness, depression, and ringing in the ears. These reactions usually do not pose a serious problem, and most people can continue treatment. More rarely, visual or hearing disturbances and blood disorders have occurred. **Contact your doctor if you experience any problems.** Almost all of the side effects experienced with Toradol stop when the medication is stopped.

Are There Any Special Do's And Don'ts About Taking Toradol?

Do's: Do tell your doctor and pharmacist about any other medications you take, both prescription and nonprescription. This is important because some drugs can interact with each other and produce undesirable effects.

Do tell your doctor if you have an ulcer, liver disease, kidney disease or history of any stomach problems.

Do be cautious about driving or participating in activities that require alertness if you are drowsy, dizzy or light-headed after taking Toradol.

Do check with your doctor if: you are not getting relief or you have any problems while taking Toradol.

Do tell your physician if you are pregnant or are planning to become pregnant.

Don'ts: Don't take Toradol if you are breast-feeding. The drug does pass into the milk of nursing women.

Don't take ASA (acetylsalicylic acid), ASA-containing products or other NSAIDs, e.g., drugs to relieve symptoms of arthritis, while taking Toradol unless specifically directed to do so by a physician. Consult your doctor or pharmacist if you are unsure what your product contains. A partial list of brand name products containing ASA, NSAIDs and Ibuprofen is included in the following table.

ASA-Containing OTC Brands	NSAID-Containing Brands	Ibuprofen-Containing Brands
Anacin, Bufferin, Aspirin, Alka-Seltzer, C2, Entrophen, 222, Midol, Robaxisal, Coricidin D, Dristan Tablets	Voltaren, Arthrotec, Dolobid, Nalfon, Froben, Ansaid, Indocid, Orudis, Ponstan, Naprosyn, Feldene, Clinoril, Mobiflex, Surgam, Tolectin, Idarac, Motrin, Anaprox, Relafen	Advil, Actiprofen, Nuprin, Medipren, Motrin IB

Don't take Toradol if you are allergic to it, or if you have had an allergic-type reaction to ASA or to any other drug used for pain relief or arthritis.

Don't take Toradol if you have a stomach ulcer, or active inflammatory disease of the intestine.

□ TRANSDERM-NITRO®

Novartis Pharmaceuticals

Nitroglycerin

Transdermal Antianginal

Information for the Patient: Transderm-Nitro and How To Use It: Introduction: Your doctor has prescribed Transderm-Nitro to help reduce the frequency and severity of attacks of anginal pain (chest pain). Your package leaflet provides you with information about the Transderm-Nitro patch and its use. **Please read it carefully.**

How Transderm-Nitro Works: When Transderm-Nitro is applied to the skin, it releases small amounts of nitroglycerin at a steady rate. This passes through the skin, into your bloodstream. It relaxes and widens the blood vessels and increases the supply of blood and oxygen to the heart. This helps prevent attacks of anginal pain (chest pain) from occurring. Because nitroglycerin is released slowly from Transderm-Nitro, it **will not relieve an attack that has already started.** In such cases you may need faster-acting nitrates (sublingual tablets or spray) as recommended by your doctor.

The amount of Transderm-Nitro you need will depend upon your body's needs. Observe the dosing instructions given to you by your doctor and report to him/her if chest pain attacks continue to occur.

Transderm-Nitro is designed as a complete unit. Do not cut the patch.

Things To Be Aware Of: There are certain things you and your doctor should be aware of before you use Transderm-Nitro.

Be sure to tell your doctor if you have ever had any of the following medical problems:

- any unusual or allergic reactions to nitrates, nitrites, or other substances;
- poor circulation with very low blood pressure;
- increased intracranial pressure (a condition that your doctor can tell you about);
- a recent heart attack, or other serious heart disease, stroke, or head injury;
- narrowing of heart valves;
- blood vessel disorder other than angina;
- severe anemia;
- lung disease.

To help the doctor decide whether you should use Transderm-Nitro and what extra care should be taken during its use, tell your doctor:

- if you are breast-feeding or pregnant or intend to become pregnant while using this medicine.
- what other medicines or remedies, if any, you are using. There are some medicines which may affect how Transderm-Nitro works.

Check with your doctor **as soon as possible** if any of the following occur:

- angina (chest pain), particularly while patch is off;
- greyish-blue colored lips, fingernails or palms of hands;
- dizziness or fainting;
- feeling of pressure in the head;
- shortness of breath;
- unusual tiredness or weakness;
- weak or unusually fast heartbeat.

Possible Side Effects: Like all medicines, along with its helpful effects, Transderm-Nitro may cause unwanted side effects. The elderly may be more sensitive to the effects of nitrates. You should know about them so that if they do occur, you can report them to your doctor right away.

When you start using Transderm-Nitro, you may get a headache. This is a common effect. If you need to, you may take a mild pain reliever for this. If it continues or becomes severe, check with your doctor. Flushing of the face may also occur. Transderm-Nitro may also lower the blood pressure and cause dizziness, lightheadedness, or a fainting feeling, especially when you get up quickly from lying or sitting. Getting up slowly may help. If you feel dizzy, sit or lie down. You may be more likely to experience headaches, dizziness, or lightheadedness if you drink alcohol, stand for a long time, or if the weather is hot. While using Transderm-Nitro, be careful about the amount of alcohol you drink. Also use extra care when exercising, standing for a long time, driving or doing other things that need your attention, or during hot weather.

In certain cases Transderm-Nitro may cause mild itching under the patch and reddening of the skin after it has been removed. The reddening usually goes away within a few hours. A mild skin cream may be used if needed. It is also important to apply each patch to a different area of skin. If any redness or rash continues, you should consult your doctor.

How to Use Transderm-Nitro (see package insert for illustrations):

1. **Deciding Where to Apply the Patch:** Choose any area of skin which is most comfortable for you, but **not** past the knees or elbows. Many patients prefer the chest. It is best if the area is hairless. Avoid skin folds. The skin should not be scarred, burned, irritated or broken, since this may alter the amount of medicine you get. You should use a different area of skin each day, and wait several days before using the same area again. To help you remember to change the site of patch application regularly, you may wish to use the same area of skin on a particular day of the week.
2. **Preparing the Skin:** In order for the patch to stick, the skin must be clean and dry without any creams, lotions, oil or powder. If hair is likely to interfere with the patch sticking or its removal, it can be clipped but not shaved since this may irritate the skin.
3. **Opening the Pouch:** Each Transderm-Nitro patch is individually sealed in a protective pouch. Tear open this pouch at the indentation and remove the patch. Do not use scissors, since you may accidentally cut the patch (see package insert, Figures 2 and 3).
4. **Recognizing the Patch and Removing the Liner: The patch itself is tan-coloured.** A plastic liner covers the adhesive (sticky) side of the patch during storage, and must be removed and discarded before patch use. **The plastic liner will be either white on both sides or clear,** depending on the size of the patch.

   Pick up the patch lengthwise with the tab up, and the plastic liner facing you (see package insert, Figure 4). If you are left-handed it might be easier to start with the tab down and the tan-colored side facing you. Firmly bend the tab forward with the thumb. With both thumbs, carefully remove the plastic protective liner from the patch starting at the tab (see package insert, Figure 5). Continue to peel back the plastic liner along the length of the patch, allowing the patch to rest on the outside of your fingers. (see package insert, Figure 6).

   By removing the plastic liner you have exposed the adhesive side. The adhesive side of the patch appears to have a silver-colored edge. From this side you should also be able to see the white cream containing nitroglycerin within the patch.

   Avoid touching the adhesive. If another person applies the patch for you, he/she must be careful not to touch the surface which will be applied to the skin. Apply the tan-colored patch immediately after opening the pouch and removing the plastic liner. Discard the plastic liner.
5. **Applying the Patch:** Remember the skin should be clean and dry without creams, lotions, oil or powder. Place the exposed adhesive side of the patch (i.e., the silver-edged side) on the area you have chosen as explained above. Press it **firmly** in place with the palm of your hand for 10 to 20 seconds (see package insert, Figure 7). Circle the outside edge of the patch with one or two fingers. Once the patch is in place, do not test the adhesion by pulling on it. When applied correctly, the tan-colored side will be seen when looking at the patch on the skin.
6. **When and How to Remove the Patch:** The Transderm-Nitro patch should be changed according to the schedule prescribed by your doctor. It is important to respect the patch-off period recommended by your doctor. If you forget to remove it at the scheduled time just remove it as soon as possible and continue to follow your original schedule. Remove the patch by pulling on the tab. Each patch can only be applied once. After use, fold the patch in half with the adhesive side inwards. Throw it away safely out of the reach of children. Any adhesive left on the skin can be removed with rubbing alcohol or light mineral oil.
7. **What to Do if Transderm-Nitro Falls Off:** Contact with water (as in bathing, swimming, showering) or physical activity will not affect the patch. It is unlikely that the patch will fall off. If the patch does fall off, discard it and put a new patch on a different area of skin. Continue to follow your original schedule.

Storage: Transderm-Nitro should be stored at temperatures below 25°C. Do not freeze. Do not store it out of the individually sealed pouch. Transderm-Nitro should be kept out of the reach of children and pets both before and when disposing of used patches. If your

Transderm-Nitro (cont'd)

patch becomes stuck to a child or another person, remove the patch at once and contact a doctor.

Always Remember: Your doctor has prescribed Transderm-Nitro for you after a careful review of your medical needs. Use it only as directed and do not give it to anyone else since their needs may be different from yours. If you have any questions, contact your doctor or pharmacist.

□ TRANSDERM-V®

Novartis Pharmaceuticals

Scopolamine

Anti-Motion Sickness Agent

Information for the Patient: Transderm-V (scopolamine) and How To Use It: Transdermal Therapeutic System: **Introduction:** This leaflet is intended to help you understand what Transderm-V is and how it helps to prevent nausea and vomiting associated with motion sickness in adults. **Please read it carefully.** If you want to know more or have any questions, please ask your doctor or pharmacist.

How Transderm-V Prevents Motion Sickness: In some people, motion of ships, airplanes, trains, automobiles and buses increases activity of the nerve fibres of the inner ear, which are part of the body's balance mechanism. The result is motion sickness, which is characterized by dizziness, nausea and vomiting. A person suffering from motion sickness may experience one, all or any combination of these symptoms. Scopolamine is an effective medication for the prevention of nausea and vomiting because it reduces the activity of the nerve fibres in the inner ear and acts on the motion sickness centres in the brain.

Transderm-V is a small, flexible adhesive disc. When placed behind the ear, it delivers scopolamine to the skin surface from where it is absorbed into the bloodstream over a prolonged period of up to 3 days.

Things To Be Aware of: Although Transderm-V provides health benefits, certain precautions should be taken before their use and in some situations their use may not be appropriate.

Restrictions on Use: Do not use Transderm-V if you are allergic to scopolamine or have glaucoma.

Transderm-V should not be used in children. The safety of its use in children has not been determined. Children are particularly sensitive to the effects of scopolamine.

Precautions: Before using Transderm-V, seek your doctor's advice if you:

- are breast-feeding or pregnant or plan to become pregnant while using this medicine
- have any obstructions of the stomach or intestines
- have trouble urinating due to prostate enlargement or any bladder obstruction
- have (or have had) any metabolic, liver or kidney disease
- have suffered in the past or are now suffering from pain in the eyes, blurred vision or rainbow-colored halos around lights
- have a history of skin allergy or hypersensitivity to any other substance
- have had epileptic seizures in the past or are now suffering from epilepsy
- taking any other medicines or remedies, as there are some medicines which may affect how Transderm-V works.

Any of these conditions could make Transderm-V unsuitable for you.

Elderly patients should also consult their doctor before using Transderm-V as they may be particularly sensitive to the effects of scopolamine.

Avoid drinking alcohol while using Transderm-V.

Be careful about driving or operating any machinery while using the system because the drug might make you drowsy.

Possible Side Effects: Like all medicines, along with its helpful effects, Transderm-V may cause unwanted side effects. It is wise to be aware of them so that if they do occur you can report them to your doctor:

- temporary dryness of the mouth
- drowsiness
- difficulty in urinating
- localized skin irritation; in isolated cases generalized skin rash
- slight decrease in blood pressure
- impairment of memory or concentration, restlessness, giddiness, dizziness, disorientation, confusion, hallucinations

Should you find such effects troublesome, remove the Transderm-V disc at once and notify your doctor.

Eye Effects: Temporary blurring of vision and dilation (widening) of the pupils may occur, especially if traces of the drug are on your fingers or hands and come in contact with your eyes. Dry, itchy or reddened whites of the eye and eye pain have been reported infrequently. In the unlikely event that you experience pain in the eye and reddened whites of the eye, which may be accompanied by widening of the pupil and blurred vision, remove the disc and consult your doctor promptly. Widening of the pupils and blurred vision without pain or reddened whites of the eye is usually temporary and not serious.

Possible Effects After Removing the Disc: There have been complaints of transient dizziness, nausea, vomiting, headache and disturbances of balance following discontinuation of Transderm-V. If this happens, please consult a doctor.

Dosage: Only 1 Transderm-V disc can be used at any one time. Each disc may be worn for a maximum period of 3 days. Treatment with Transderm-V must not exceed 6 days, i.e., 1 disc worn for 3 days followed by a new disc worn for a second 3 days.

Apply 1 Transderm-V disc on the hairless area behind 1 ear approximately 12 hours before the drug's antinausea and antivomiting effect is needed. The disc may be worn for up to 3 days, and then it should be removed. If the disc is only needed for a shorter time, it should be removed at the end of the journey.

If you wish to control nausea for longer than 3 days, a second disc should be placed on a different skin site behind the other ear. The second disc may be worn for up to 3 days if needed.

Discontinue using Transderm-V once the second disc has been worn for 3 days.

How To Use Transderm-V:

1. Select a non-hairy area of skin on the head behind the ear, taking care to avoid a site containing any cuts or irritations. Wipe the area with a clean, dry tissue.
2. Each Transderm-V disc is individually sealed in a protective foil pouch. Before removing the disc from its pouch, be sure to wash your hands with soap and water.
3. Peel the foil pouch open and remove the tan-colored disc complete with its clear plastic 6 sided protective liner (see leaflet for Figure 1).
4. Holding the disc only by its edge—and taking care not to touch the adhesive surface (metallic side) with your hands—peel off the clear plastic protective liner (see leaflet for Figure 2).
5. Firmly apply the adhesive surface (metallic side) of the disc to the dry area of skin behind the ear so that the tan-colored side is showing (see leaflet Figure 3). Press firmly to make good contact especially around the edge. Once you have placed the disc behind your ear, do not touch it for the duration of desired use.
6. **Important: Be sure to wash your hands thoroughly with soap and water immediately after handling the disc, so that any drug that might get on your hands will not come into contact with your eyes (see Possible Side Effects).**
7. Remove the disc after 3 days and carefully dispose of it. (You may remove it sooner if you are no longer concerned about motion sickness).
   After removing the disc, be sure to wash your hands and the application site.
8. If you wish to control nausea for longer than 3 days, remove the first disc after 3 days and place a new disc on a different skin site behind the other ear. Use the same procedures and precautions described above. Discontinue using Transderm-V once the second disc has been worn for a maximum of 3 days.
9. Limited contact with water, as in bathing or swimming, will not affect the functioning of the disc. It is preferable, however, to keep the disc dry to prevent it from falling off. In the unlikely event that the disc falls off, carefully discard it and put a new one behind the other ear.

Storage: Transderm-V should be stored at temperatures below 25°C. Do not freeze. Do not store it out of the individually sealed pouch.

Transderm-V should be kept out of the reach of children and pets both before and after use. If your disc becomes stuck to a child or another person, remove the disc at once and contact a doctor.

☐ TRILISATE® ℞
Purdue Frederick

Choline Magnesium Trisalicylate
Anti-inflammatory—Analgesic

Information for the Patient: Trilisate, which has been prescribed to you by your doctor, is one of a large group of nonsteroidal anti-inflammatory drugs (NSAIDs) and is used to treat the symptoms of certain types of arthritis. It helps to relieve joint pain, swelling, stiffness and fever by reducing the production of certain substances (prostaglandins) and helping to control inflammation and other body reactions.

You should take Trilisate only as directed by your doctor. Do not take more of it, do not take it more often and do not take it for a longer period of time than your doctor ordered.

Be sure to take Trilisate regularly as prescribed. In some types of arthritis, up to 2 weeks may pass before you feel the full effects of this medicine. During treatment, your doctor may decide to adjust the dosage according to your response to the medication.

To lessen stomach upset, take this medicine immediately after a meal or with food or milk. If stomach upset (indigestion, nausea, vomiting, stomach pain or diarrhea) occurs and continues, contact your doctor.

For adults, the usual dosing range for Trilisate is from 1 to 2 tablets 3 times/day or 2 to 3 tablets twice daily. You should not change your dose without consulting your doctor and should not take more than 6 tablets per day unless advised to do so by your doctor. Trilisate should not be taken when pregnant or while nursing, unless recommended by your physician. Trisilate is not recommended for patients less than 12 years of age and children older than 12 should not take it when they have chickenpox or flu symptoms unless they have first consulted their doctor concerning Reye's syndrome, a rare but serious illness.

This medicine should be kept out of the reach of children. In the event of overdose, consult your physician, hospital or poison control centre at once. The following signs of overdose usually occur within a few hours of ingestion: stomach upset, ringing or buzzing in ears, hearing loss, mental confusion, hallucinations or changes in behavior (especially in children), severe excitement or nervousness, unusually fast or deep breathing, severe drowsiness, convulsions (seizures). If emergency help is not available right away, induce vomiting at once, (within 30 minutes) by syrup of ipecac, but never do so in an unconscious person or in children younger than one year old without medical help.

Do not take ASA, ASA-containing compounds or other drugs used to relieve symptoms of arthritis while taking Trilisate unless directed to do so by your physician.

If you are prescribed this medication for use over a long period of time, your doctor will check your health during regular visits to assess your progress and to ensure that this medication is not causing unwanted effects.

Along with it beneficial effects, Trilisate like other NSAID medications, may cause some undesirable reactions. Elderly, frail or debilitated patients often seem to experience more frequent or more severe side effects. Although not all of these side effects are common, when they do occur they may require medical attention.

Check with your doctor immediately if any of the following are noted:
- bloody or black tarry stools;
- shortness of breath, wheezing, any trouble in breathing or tightness in the chest;
- skin rash, swelling, hives or itching;
- indigestion, nausea, vomiting, stomach pain or diarrhea;
- yellow discoloration of the skin or eyes;
- any changes in the amount or color of your urine (such as dark; red or brown);
- swelling of the feet or lower legs;
- blurred vision or any visual disturbances;
- mental confusion, depression, dizziness, lightheadedness; hearing problems (including ringing or buzzing in the ear).

Always Remember: Before taking this medication tell your doctor and pharmacists if you:
- are allergic to Trilisate or other related medicines of the NSAID group such as ASA, diclofenac, diflusinal, fenoprofen, flurbiprofen, floctafenine, ibuprofen, indomethacin, ketoprofen, mefenamic acid, naproxen, piroxicam, sulindac, tiaprofenic acid or tolmetin;
- have a history of stomach upset, ulcers, or liver or kidney disease;
- are pregnant or intend to become pregnant while taking this medication;
- are breast feeding;
- are taking any other medication (either prescription or non-prescription);
- have any other medical problem(s).

While taking this medication:
- tell any other doctor, dentist or pharmacist that you consult or see, that you are taking this medication;
- be cautious about driving or participating in activities that require alertness if your are drowsy, dizzy or lightheaded after taking this medication;
- check with your doctor if you are not getting any relief or if any problems develop;
- report any untoward reactions to your doctor. This is very important as it will aid in the early detection and prevention of potential complications;
- your regular medical checkups are essential;
- if you require more information on this drug, consult your doctor or pharmacist.

☐ TRINIPATCH® 0.2
☐ TRINIPATCH® 0.4
☐ TRINIPATCH® 0.6
Sanofi

Nitroglycerin Transdermal Delivery System
Antianginal

Information for the Patient: How to use the Trinipatch (Nitroglycerin Transdermal Delivery System) for the prevention of angina: Introduction: Your doctor has prescribed Trinipatch to help reduce the frequency and severity of attacks of anginal pain (chest pain). This leaflet provides you with information about the Trinipatch patch and its use. **Please read it carefully.**

How Trinipatch Works: When Trinipatch is applied to the skin, it releases small amounts of nitroglycerin at a steady rate. This passes through the skin, into your bloodstream. It relaxes and widens the blood vessels and increases the supply of blood and oxygen to the heart. This helps prevent attacks of anginal pain (chest pain) from occurring. Because nitroglycerin is released slowly from Trinipatch, it **will not relieve an attack that has already started.**

The amount of Trinipatch you need will depend upon your body's needs. Observe the dosing instructions given to you by your doctor and report to him/her if chest pain attacks continue to occur.

Trinipatch is designed as a complete unit. **Do not cut the patch.**

Things to be Aware of: There are certain things you and your doctor should be aware of before you use Trinipatch.

Before using Trinipatch be sure to tell your doctor if you have ever had any unusual or allergic reactions to nitrates or nitrites, or have had a recent heart attack, or other serious heart disease, stroke, or head injury; severe anemia or narrowing of the heart valves. Tell your doctor if you are breast-feeding or pregnant or intend to become pregnant while using this medicine. This will help the doctor decide whether you should use Trinipatch and what extra care should be taken during its use. There are some medicines which may affect how Trinipatch works. Tell your doctor what other medicines or remedies, if any, you are using.

Check with your doctor as soon as possible if any of the following occur: angina (chest pain), particularly while patch is off; dizziness or fainting; feeling of pressure in the head; shortness of breath; unusual tiredness or weakness; weak or unusually fast heartbeat.

Possible Unwanted Effects: Like all medicines, along with its helpful effects, Trinipatch may cause unwanted effects. You should know about them so that if they do occur, you can report them to your doctor right away.

When you start using Trinipatch, you may get a headache. This is a common effect. If you need to, you may take a mild pain reliever for this. If it continues or becomes severe, check with your doctor. Flushing of the face may also occur. Trinipatch may also lower the blood pressure and cause dizziness, lightheadedness, or a fainting feeling, especially when you get up quickly from lying or sitting. Getting up slowly may help. If you feel dizzy, sit or lie down. You may be more likely to experience headaches, dizziness, or lightheadedness if you drink alcohol, stand for a long time, or if the weather is hot. While using Trinipatch, be careful about the amount of alcohol you drink. Also use

Trinipatch (cont'd)

extra care when exercising, standing for a long time, driving; or during hot weather.

In certain cases Trinipatch may cause mild itching under the patch and reddening of the skin after it has been removed. The reddening usually goes away within a few hours. A mild skin cream may be used if needed. It is also important to apply each patch to a different area of skin.

How to Use Trinipatch: The Trinipatch Nitroglycerin Transdermal Delivery System is easy to use, it has a clear plastic backing and a special adhesive that keeps the system firmly in place. The active nitroglycerin is contained in the adhesive which is directly in contact with your skin.

1. **Where to apply the patch:** Select any area of skin on the body, **except** the extremities below the knee or elbow. The chest is the preferred site. The area should be clean, dry and hairless. If hair is likely to interfere with system adhesion or removal, it can be clipped but not shaved. Take care to avoid areas with cuts or irritations. Do **not** apply the system immediately after showering or bathing. It is best to wait until you are certain the skin is completely dry.
2. **How to apply** (see package insert for illustrations): a) Open the package by tearing at the small notch or cut in the side of the pouch. Carefully pick up the system with the overlapping split film facing you. b) Remove one side of the overlapping film, exposing the adhesive layer on one side of the system. c) Apply the side of the system with the adhesive exposed to the application site which you have selected. d) Gently fold the system in half and roll the patch across the intended application site to apply the other half of the system. The overlapping films may be discarded. e) Firmly press the entire surface of the patch to insure good adherence to your skin.
3. **When and how to remove patch:** At the time recommended by your physician, remove the patch. Removal may be accomplished by peeling up one edge and then pulling off the patch. The application area may be gently wiped with a dry tissue. Do not wash the application site or apply lotions or creams until the skin has a chance to return to normal, about 2 to 3 hours. Used patches should be discarded away from children or pets.
4. **What to do if Trinipatch falls off:** Contact with water, as in bathing, swimming, or showering will not affect the system. In the unlikely event that a system falls off, discard it and put a new one on a different skin site.

Storage: Trinipatch should be stored under controlled room temperature (between 15 and 30°C). Do not store it out of the individually sealed pouch.

Trinipatch should be kept **out of the reach of children** both before and after use.

Always Remember: Your doctor has prescribed Trinipatch for you after a careful review of your medical needs. Use it only as directed and do not give it to anyone else as their needs may be different from yours. If you have any questions, contact your doctor or pharmacist.

☐ TROSYD™ AF
☐ TROSYD™ J

Pfizer Consumer

Tioconazole

Antifungal Agent

Information for the Patient: Indication: Trosyd AF and Trosyd J (tioconazole cream 1% w/w) are indicated as an antifungal agent for the topical treatment of patients with athlete's foot (tinea pedis), jock itch (tinea cruris) and ringworm (tinea corporis). For effective relief of itching, scaling, burning, cracking, redness and soreness of athlete's foot, jock itch or ringworm.

Dosage and Administration: Dosage: Trosyd AF and Trosyd J cream 1% w/w contain 10 mg/g of tioconazole in a vanishing cream base.

Directions: Cleanse skin with soap and water and dry thoroughly. Apply a thin layer over affected area morning and night for a full treatment period of 2 weeks for jock itch and 4 weeks for athlete's foot and ringworm. In athlete's foot pay special attention to spaces between toes and wear well-fitting, ventilated shoes and cotton socks.

Warnings:

1. For external use only.
2. If you are pregnant, or think you may be pregnant, of if you are nursing do not use except on the advise of a physician.
3. Do not use in children under 2 years of age, except under advise and supervision of a doctor.
4. Avoid contact with eyes; if this happens, rinse thoroughly with water.
5. If new irritation occurs or if there is no improvement within the full treatment of 2 weeks for jock itch and 4 weeks for athlete's foot and ringworm, discontinue use and consult a doctor.
6. Children under 12 years of age should be supervised when using these products.
7. These products should not be used on patients who have a history of sensitization to tioconazole or other imidazole antifungal agents.
8. These products should not be used for infections of the scalp or nails.

Cautions: Keep this and all medication out of the reach of children. In case of accidental ingestion seek professional assistance immediately.

Store at 15 to 30°C; avoid freezing.

Product monograph available to physicians and pharmacists on request.

Nonmedicinal Ingredients: benzyl alcohol, ethoxylated cetostearyl alcohol, mineral oil, white petrolatum, propylene glycol, stearic acid, stearyl alcohol, water.

Availability: Trosyd AF and Trosyd J (tioconazole) cream 1% w/w are available as a white homogeneous cream in 5, 15 and 30 g tubes.

☐ TRUSOPT® ℞

MSD

Dorzolamide HCl

Elevated Intraocular Pressure Therapy—Topical Carbonic Anhydrase Inhibitor

Information for the Patient: Trusopt (dorzolamide hydrochloride) Sterile Ophthalmic Solution 2%: Trusopt is the brandname of Merck Frosst Canada Inc. for the medication dorzolamide hydrochloride available **only on prescription** through your physician. Trusopt is an ophthalmic carbonic anhydrase inhibitor. Trusopt is prescribed to lower the raised pressure in your eye(s) because you have increased pressure in your eye(s) or glaucoma.

Remember: This medicine is prescribed for the particular condition that you have.

-Do not give this medicine to other people, nor use it for any other condition.
-Do not use outdated medicine.
-Do not use Trusopt if you are allergic to any of its components.
-Do not use Trusopt if you currently have severe kidney problems.
-Do not use Trusopt if you are currently taking oral carbonic anhydrase inhibitors.

Keep all medicines out of the reach of children.

Read the following information carefully. **If you need any explanations, or further information, ask your physician or pharmacist.**

Before Applying Trusopt: This medicine may not be suitable for some patients. So, tell your physician if you think **any** of the following applies to you:

- If you have any medical problems now or have had any in the past;
- If you have any allergies to any medications;
- If you wear contact lenses, you should consult your physician before using Trusopt;
- If you are pregnant or intend to become pregnant;
- If you are breast-feeding or intend to breast-feed;
- If you have now or have had in the past kidney or liver problems.

Your physician also needs to know about drugs (including eye drops) that you are using or plan to use, including drugs obtained without a prescription, in particular, large doses of ASA.

Trusopt is not recommended for children.

Proper Use of this Medicine:

- It is important to apply Trusopt as prescribed by your physician. If you miss a dose, apply it as soon as possible. However, if it is almost time for the next dose, skip the missed dose and go back to your regular dosing schedule.
- Do not start taking any other medicines unless you have discussed the matter with your physician.

- If you suspect that Trusopt is causing an allergic reaction (for example, skin rash or itching) stop its use and contact your physician as soon as possible.
- If you develop any eye irritation or any new eye problems such as redness of the eye or swelling of the eyelids, contact your physician immediately.
- The appropriate dosage and duration of treatment will be established by your physician.
- When Trusopt is used alone, the dose is 1 drop in the affected eye(s) in the morning, in the afternoon and in the evening.
- If your physician has recommended you use Trusopt with a beta-blocker eye drop to lower eye pressure, then the dose is 1 drop of Trusopt in the affected eye(s) in the morning and in the evening.
- Do not change the dosage of the drug without consulting your physician. If you must stop treatment, contact your physician immediately.

Instructions for Use:

1. First, wash your hands. Remove the cap and place it in a clean location. To avoid possible contamination, keep the tip of the container away from contact with any surface.
2. Tilt your head back and look towards the ceiling. With your index finger, gently pull the lower eyelid away from the eye to form a pouch.

   Apply 1 drop of Trusopt into the pouch but do not allow the tip of the container to touch the eye or areas around the eye.
3. Apply pressure with your index finger to the inside corner of the eye for 1 to 2 minutes. This will prevent the eyedrop from dripping down through the tear duct.

   Repeat with the other eye, if prescribed by your physician.

   If you are using Trusopt with another eyedrop, the drops should be instilled at least 10 minutes apart.
4. Wash your hands again to remove any medication.

Side Effects of This Medicine—and What You Should Do:

- Any medicine may have unintended or undesirable effects, so-called side effects.
- You may experience eye symptoms such as burning and stinging, blurred vision, itching, tearing, redness of the eye (s) or swelling of the eyelids. You may sense a bitter taste after putting in your eyedrops.
- Other side effects may include headache, nausea, tiredness and rarely, rash.
- Your physician or pharmacist has a complete list of the possible side effects from this medication. Please tell your physician or pharmacist promptly about any unusual symptom.
- Possible side effects such as visual disturbances may affect the ability to drive and use machines.
- If the contents of the bottle are swallowed, you should contact your physician immediately.

  The contents of Trusopt should not be used for more than 28 days after the date on which the container is first opened.

  Store at 15 to 25°C. Protect from light.

  Keep all medicines safely away from children.

Ingredients: Active Ingredients: Trusopt (dorzolamide hydrochloride) ophthalmic solution 2% is a sterile eyedrop. It contains 2% dorzolamide present as the hydrochloride salt, a sulfonamide-related compound.
Nonmedicinal Ingredients: hydroxyethyl cellulose, mannitol, sodium citrate dihydrate, sodium hydroxide and water for injection. Benzalkonium chloride is added as a preservative.

□ T-STAT® Ⓟ

Westwood-Squibb

Erythromycin—Ethyl Alcohol

Topical Anti-acne Therapy

Information for the Patient: Your physician has prescribed T-Stat (erythromycin: ethyl alcohol) topical lotion to treat your acne. It is important to read and follow these Directions for Use of your medication.

1. First wash the affected areas with a mild soap (not medicated), rinse well and pat dry.
2. Apply T-Stat topical lotion to the areas affected by acne with the applicator, fingertips or as your physician directs, carefully avoiding the eyes, mouth, nose and other mucous membranes.

   If using pre-moistened pads, apply T-Stat to acne and surrounding area, using the sweeping motion you would with a cleansing pad.
3. Wash your hands thoroughly after using the medication.
4. Apply the medication only as often as your physician directs.

To Install Applicator:

1. Remove and discard the temporary shipping cap.
2. Push applicator firmly into the bottle using the cap as holder.
3. Screw the cap down to seat the applicator.

Precautions:

1. Keep your medication in a safe place, out of the reach of children.
2. T-Stat topical lotion is for external use only.
3. Keep T-Stat topical lotion away from your eyes, nostrils, mouth and other mucous membranes.
4. Avoid contact with eyes. If contact occurs, flush eyes with copious amounts of water for at least 5 minutes. If discomfort persists, consult your doctor.
5. Do not use any other acne medications unless your doctor instructs you to do so.
6. Keep T-Stat topical lotion away from open flame.
7. Store the bottle or jar, tightly closed, in a cool dry place.
8. To avoid leakage, store bottle or jar in an upright position.

If you have a problem:

1. If you experience excessive peeling, redness, tenderness, drying, itching or irritation consult your doctor for advice.
2. When you first apply T-Stat, you may notice an 'oily' feeling. This will disappear after a few minutes and will not make your skin more oily.
3. Do not expect to see immediate improvement of your acne, but be patient and apply your medication as your doctor has directed.

Remember: T-Stat topical lotion has been prescribed by your doctor for you; do not allow other people to use it.

□ 222® TABLETS Ⓝ

Johnson & Johnson • Merck

ASA—Caffeine—Codeine Phosphate

Analgesic—Antipyretic

Information for the Patient: Description: 222 tablets contain 375 mg acetylsalicylic acid also known as ASA, 15 mg caffeine (equivalent to 30 mg of caffeine citrate) and 8 mg codeine phosphate, and the following nonmedicinal ingredients: cornstarch, disodium edetate, ethylcellulose, hydrogenated vegetable oil, microcrystalline cellulose, sodium carboxymethylcellulose and sodium lauryl sulfate.

Indications: 222 tablets are used for the symptomatic relief of mild to moderate pain, fever and inflammation such as headaches, pain due to cold symptoms, toothache, pain of menstrual cramps, arthritic pain and the pain caused by muscle strains and sprains.

Recommended Dosage and Administration: Adults: 1 or 2 tablet(s), 1 to 3 times daily (every 4 to 8 hours), as required. **Do not exceed** 4 g ASA (10 tablets) a day. **Not recommended for use in children.**

Children: Warning: Do not administer to children or teenagers who have chickenpox or flu symptoms before a physician or pharmacist is consulted about Reye's Syndrome, a rare and serious illness. 222 tablets should not be given to children, unless recommended by a physician or dentist.

Children's Dosage, when recommended by a physician or dentist: 10 to 14 years, 1 tablet 1 to 3 times daily (every 4 to 8 hours); 5 to 10 years, one-half tablet 1 to 3 times daily (every 4 to 8 hours).

Precautions: If you are taking other medication, read all labels to ensure that they do not also contain acetylsalicylic acid which could result in an overdose. If in doubt, consult your pharmacist or physician.

If you expect to undergo surgery, including dental surgery, consult your pharmacist or physician.

Keep this medicine out of reach of children as it contains enough drug to seriously harm a child.

Significant Incompatibilities and Drug Interactions: It is hazardous to exceed the maximum recommended dose, unless advised by a physician.

Consult your physician or pharmacist before taking this medication in case of:

—allergy to salicylates, codeine, caffeine;
—asthma;
—kidney disease, stomach problems, peptic ulcers, severe liver disease, or gout;
—severe anemia or blood coagulation defects;

222 Tablets (cont'd)

—and if you are taking anticoagulants (blood thinners), medication for diabetes, anti-inflammatory drugs, anticonvulsants, or medication for gout.

Consult a physician if the underlying condition requires continued use for more than 5 days.

Consult a physician before taking this product during the last 3 months of pregnancy or during breast-feeding.

Side Effects: Along with its needed effects, a drug may cause some unwanted effects. Check with your physician or pharmacist if any of the following occur: nausea, vomiting, abdominal pain and constipation, bleeding or irritation of stomach, any loss of hearing including ringing or buzzing in the ears, skin rashes, hives or itching, shortness of breath, tightness in chest, wheezing, and dizziness.

As this medicine contains codeine, it will add to the effects of alcohol and other medicines that slow down the nervous system, for example: medicine for hay fever (antihistamines), tranquilizers, sedatives, narcotics, medicine for depression, barbiturates, muscle relaxants or anesthetics.

This medicine may cause drowsiness in some patients. Exercise caution when driving a motor vehicle, operating machinery or when doing other jobs requiring mental alertness. Avoid alcoholic beverages.

Overdosage: Caution: Store 222s in a safe place, out of the reach of children. It is hazardous to exceed the maximum recommended dose unless advised by a physician.

Management: In case of accidental or suspected overdose, even if there are no symptoms, contact immediately a physician, a Poison Control Centre, or the Emergency Department of a hospital.

Prompt medical attention is critical, even in the absence of symptoms.

☐ ULTRADOL™ Ⓟ

Procter & Gamble Pharmaceuticals

Etodolac

Nonsteroidal Anti-inflammatory—Analgesic

Information for the Patient: Ultradol, which has been prescribed to you by your physician, is one of a large group of nonsteroidal anti-inflammatory drugs (also called NSAIDs). It is used to treat mild to moderate pain as well as the symptoms of certain types of arthritis. It helps to relieve pain, swelling, stiffness and fever by reducing the production of certain substances (prostaglandins) and helping to control inflammation. NSAIDs do not cure arthritis, but they promote suppression of the inflammation and the tissue damaging effects resulting from this inflammation. This medicine will help you only as long as you continue to take it.

You should take Ultradol only as directed by your physician. Do not take more of it, do not take it more often and do not take it for a longer period of time than your physician ordered. Taking too much of any of these medicines may increase the chance of unwanted effects, especially if you are an elderly patient.

Be sure to take Ultradol regularly as prescribed. In some types of arthritis, up to 2 weeks may pass before you feel the full effects of this medicine. During treatment, your physician may decide to adjust the dosage according to your response to the medication.

Stomach upset is one of the common problems with NSAIDs: To lessen stomach upset, take this medicine immediately after a meal or with food or milk. Also, you should remain standing or sitting upright (i.e., do not lie down) for about 15 to 30 minutes after taking the medicine. This helps to prevent irritation that may lead to trouble swallowing. If stomach upset (indigestion, nausea, vomiting, stomach pain or diarrhea) occurs and continues, contact your physician.

Do not take ASA (acetylsalicylic acid), ASA-containing compounds or other drugs used to relieve symptoms of arthritis while taking Ultradol unless directed to do so by your physician.

If you are prescribed this medication for use over a long period of time, yor doctor will check your health during regular visits to assess your progress and to ensure that this medication is not causing unwanted effects.

Always Remember: The risks of taking this medication must be weighed against the benefits it will have.

Before taking this medication, tell your doctor and pharmacist if you:

- or a family member are allergic to or have had a reaction to Ultradol or other anti-inflammatory drugs (such as acetylsalicylic acid, diclofenac, diflusinal, fenoprofen, flurbiprofen, ibuprofen, indomethacin, ketoprofen, mefenemic acid, piroxicam, sulindac, tiaprofenic acid, tolmetin, ketorolac tromethamine, tenoxicam, naproxen, choline magnesium trisalicylate, floctafenine, nabumetone, salsalate or phenylbutazone) manifesting itself by increased sinusitis, hives, the initiating or worsening of asthma or anaphylaxis (sudden collapse);
- or a family member has had asthma, nasal polyps, chronic sinusitis or chronic urticaria (hives);
- have a history of stomach upset, ulcers, liver or kidney disease;
- have blood or urine abnormalities;
- have high blood pressure;
- have diabetes;
- are on any special diet, such as a low-sodium or low-sugar diet;
- are pregnant or intend to become pregnant while taking this medication;
- are breast-feeding or intend to breast-feed while taking this medication;
- are taking any other medication (either prescription or nonprescription) such as other NSAIDs, high blood pressure medication, blood thinners, corticosteroids, methotrexate, cyclosporine, lithium, phenytoin;
- have any other medical problem(s) such as alcohol abuse, bleeding problems, etc.

While Taking This Medication:

- tell any other doctor, dentist or pharmacist that you consult or see, that you are taking this medication;
- some NSAIDs may cause drowsiness or fatigue in some people taking them. Be cautious about driving or participating in activities that require alertness if you are drowsy, dizzy or lightheaded after taking this medication;
- check with your doctor if you are not getting any relief or if any problems develop;
- report any untoward reactions to your doctor. This is very important as it will aid in the early detection and prevention of potential complications;
- stomach problems may be more likely to occur if you drink alcoholic beverages. Therefore, do not drink alcoholic beverages while taking this medication;
- check with your doctor immediately if you experience unexpected weakness while taking this medication, or if you vomit any blood or have dark or bloody stools;
- some people may become more sensitive to sunlight than they are normally. Exposure to sunlight or sunlamps, even for brief periods of time, may cause sunburn, blisters on the skin, skin rash, redness, itching or discoloration; or vision changes. If you have a reaction from the sun, check with your doctor;
- check with your doctor immediately if chills, fever, muscle aches or pains, or other flu-like symptoms occur, especially if they occur shortly before, or together with, a skin rash. Very rarely, these effects may be the first signs of a serious reaction to this medication;
- **Your regular medical checkups are essential.**

Side Effects of this Medication: Along with its beneficial effects, Ultradol like other NSAID drugs, may cause some undesirable reactions especially when used for a long time or in large doses.

Elderly, frail or debilitated patients often seem to experience more frequent or more severe side effects.

Although not all of these side effects are common, when they do occur they may require medical attention.

Check with your doctor immediately if any of the following are noted:

- bloody or black tarry stools;
- shortness of breath, wheezing, any trouble in breathing or tightness in the chest;
- skin rash, hives or swelling, itching;
- vomiting or persistent indigestion, nausea, stomach pain or diarrhea;
- yellow discoloration of the skin or eyes;
- any changes in the amount or color of your urine (such as dark red or brown);
- any pain or difficulty experienced while urinating;
- swelling of the feet or lower legs;
- malaise, fatigue, loss of appetite;
- blurred vision or any visual disturbance;
- mental confusion, depression, dizziness, lightheadedness;
- hearing problems.

Other side effects not listed above may also occur in some patients. If you notice any other effects, check with your doctor.

Dosing: Take Ultradol with food or water.

Arthritis: If you have any questions about the amount of Ultradol you should take or when you should take it, talk to your doctor or pharmacist. Most adults will take 1 capsule twice a day. Some people will take 2 capsules in the evening.

Pain: Take 1 or 2 of the 200 mg capsules every 6 to 8 hours. For some people, pain will go away when taking the capsules only every 12 hours. Take Ultradol for no more than 7 days. If you are still experiencing painful symptoms talk to your doctor.

All Patients: Do not take more than 1 000 mg**/day** without discussing with your doctor or pharmacist.

Storage: Store at room temperature (25°C) and protect from moisture.

Ultradol is not recommended for use in children since safety and effectiveness have not been established.

Do not keep outdated medicine or medicine no longer needed.

Keep out of the reach of children.

This medication has been prescribed for your medical problem. Do not give it to anyone else.

If you require more information on this drug, consult your doctor or pharmacist.

□ ULTRAVATE™ Preparations

Westwood-Squibb

Halobetasol Propionate

Topical Corticosteroid

Information for the Patient:

1. This medication is to be used as directed by the physician and should not be used longer than the prescribed time period. It is for external use only. Avoid contact with eyes.
2. This medication should not be used for any disorder than that for which it is prescribed.
3. The treated skin should not be bandaged or otherwise covered or wrapped so as to be occulsive.
4. Any signs of local adverse reaction should be reported to your physician.

□ UNIPHYL®

Purdue Frederick

Theophylline

Bronchodilator

Information for the Patient: Your doctor has prescribed Uniphyl tablets, which contain the drug theophylline incorporated into a sustained release system. Theophylline opens the airways in your lungs so that you may breathe more easily, and Uniphyl's sustained release mechanism gradually releases theophylline so that most patients need to take Uniphyl only once per day.

Many medications interact with theophylline, therefore it is important that your doctor knows all the medications which you are taking and if you stop taking them. You should also inform your doctor if you start or stop smoking or if you are breast-feeding, pregnant or want to become pregnant. In these situations, your dosage may need to be adjusted.

It is important that you take your Uniphyl regularly, at the time and in the exact quantity that your doctor has directed. Missed doses can cause your symptoms of asthma or bronchitis to reappear and taking more Uniphyl than prescribed can lead to side effects such as headache, nausea or vomiting. If these side effects occur at any time during Uniphyl therapy, you should contact your doctor before taking any additional doses. If your symptoms become more severe and you have been taking your medication regularly, you should also contact your doctor. **However, do NOT increase your Uniphyl dose unless specifically directed to do so by your doctor.**

To swallow Uniphyl more easily, and to ensure that the tablets promptly reach your stomach, each dose should be taken with a glass (120 to 180 mL) of water while you are standing or sitting upright. Your tablets should be taken whole or halved (if a dosage containing halved tablets was directed by your doctor) but **do not crush or chew** the tablets as this will affect the sustained release mechanism. Unless directed otherwise by your doctor, **Uniphyl should be taken either with food, or shortly after a meal.**

If you find that you have missed a dose, and less than 6 hours has elapsed since your scheduled dosing time, take your regular dose immediately. If between 6 and 18 hours has elapsed, take ½ your regular dose immediately then resume taking your full regular dose at your next scheduled dosing time. If more than 18 hours has elapsed since your missed dose, wait for your next scheduled dosing time and then resume your regular dosage regimen.

Uniphyl tablets, a sustained release formulation, are not appropriate for use in an emergency where rapid relief of bronchospasm is required.

During a viral infection your dosage of Uniphyl may need to be adjusted. If you develop side effects during such an infection, do not take your next dose of Uniphyl and call your doctor.

If you have any other problems, call your doctor.

□ URSOFALK®

Axcan Pharma

Ursodiol

Litholytic Agent—Cholestatic Liver Diseases

Information for the Patient: Full prescribing information is available to doctors and pharmacists on request.

- You have been prescribed, by your physician, Ursofalk for the treatment of your problem.
- Ursofalk is used in patients who have refused gallbladder surgery or in whom surgery is best avoided because of other medical problems. It is also used for the management of cholestatic liver diseases, such as primary biliary cirrhosis.
- Ursofalk is only available on prescription.

Please read the following instructions carefully in order to get the full benefit of this medication.

- This medication should only be used as instructed by your doctor. Comply with the term of the prescription. Do not change the dose or stop the treatment without your doctor's advice. Your doctor will ask you to have regular medical checkups, it is important to respect the dates proposed.
- Before you begin using any new medicine (prescription or nonprescription) or if you develop any new medical problem while using this medicine, check with your doctor.
- Before starting treatment with this medicine (Ursofalk), your doctor must know:
  —if you have taken Ursofalk before and if it was not well tolerated or caused an allergy,
  —if you are pregnant, or intend to become pregnant, or are breast-feeding or intend to breast-feed,
  —if you are taking other prescription and nonprescription medicines.
- Proper use of the medication. Ursofalk should be taken in 2 divided doses, normally in the morning with breakfast and before bedtime with food, as described on the label.
- Take Ursofalk for the full time of treatment, even if you begin to feel better.
- In the case of patients with gallstones, it is thought that body weight and kind of diet the patient follows may affect how fast the stones dissolve and whether new stones will form. However, check with your doctor before going on any diet.
- If you need other medical treatment by another doctor, let him or her know that you are taking Ursofalk.
- Inform your doctor if you feel in any way unwell while taking Ursofalk (see Unwanted Effects).
- Safety of Ursofalk in children has not been established.
- The use of Ursofalk during pregnancy must be decided by your doctor. In the event of pregnancy during treatment with Ursofalk, your doctor may decide to discontinue the use of Ursofalk.
- Therapy with Ursofalk is not recommended while breast-feeding because of lack of information available.

Unwanted Effects: In addition to its intended action, any medication may cause unwanted effects.

These effects may appear in certain patients. They may appear and disappear without involving any particular risk but if any unwanted effect persists or becomes bothersome, you must let your doctor know about it without delay. These effects may consist of diarrhea, dyspepsia, stomach cramps and hair loss.

Ursofalk (cont'd)

This medication is prescribed for a particular health problem and for your personal use only. Do not give it to other person.

Keep this and all other medication out of the reach of children.

If you want further information, ask your doctor or pharmacist.

☐ VALTREX® Ⓟ

Glaxo Wellcome

Valacyclovir HCl

Antiviral Agent

Information for the Patient: Shingles: What you should know about Valtrex caplets for the treatment of shingles. Please read this leaflet carefully before you start to take your medicine. For further information or advice, ask your doctor or pharmacist.

About Your Medicine: The name of your medicine is Valtrex. It contains valacyclovir HCl. This is the active ingredient. Valtrex can only be obtained with a prescription from your doctor.

How Your Medicine Works: Valtrex is an antiviral medicine. It is used to treat shingles (herpes zoster) infections. Shingles is caused by the varicella-zoster virus which damages nerves and skin. Valtrex stops the virus from multiplying, therefore reducing the damage.

Important Points to Note Before Taking Your Medicine: You should not use Valtrex if you are allergic to or react badly to valacyclovir or acyclovir. Tell your doctor if you have ever had an allergic reaction to any of these ingredients.

Use of This Medicine During Pregnancy and Breast-feeding: If you are pregnant, or likely to become pregnant soon, or if you are breast-feeding, please inform your doctor before taking any drugs, including Valtrex. If you are pregnant or breast-feeding, your doctor may decide not to prescribe this medicine, although, there may be circumstances when your doctor advises you differently.

How to Take your Medicine: You must take Valtrex as prescribed by your doctor. If you are not sure how many caplets to take, or how often to take them, consult your doctor or pharmacist.

For the best effect, start taking your Valtrex caplets as soon as you can.

You should not increase or decrease the prescribed dose unless advised by your doctor.

The usual dose is two Valtrex caplets 3 times a day. Most people take 1 dose when they get up in the morning, 1 dose mid-afternoon and 1 dose before they go to bed at night. Spreading the doses evenly throughout the day will help to shorten your rash and discomfort. The treatment lasts for 7 days.

After Taking Your Medicine: Valtrex does not often have side effects. Some people may feel sick or have a mild headache. Tell your pharmacist or doctor if you notice any other side effects from your medicine which are not mentioned here.

If you feel worse or you have taken all the caplets and do not feel better **tell your doctor as soon as possible.**

What to Do if an Overdose is Taken: It is important to follow the dosage instructions on the label of your medicine. In the event of an overdose, you should **immediately** contact either your doctor, the nearest hospital emergency department or Poison Control Centre.

What to Do if You Miss a Dose: If you forget to take a dose, take another as soon as possible. Then continue with the next dose at the right time.

Storing Your Medicine: Store Valtrex caplets between 15 and 25°C. Keep them away from direct heat and sunlight. Keep your Valtrex caplets in a safe place where children cannot reach them. Do not take any caplets after the expiry date shown on the pack.

What to Do When You Stop Your Medicine: If your doctor decides to stop the treatment, do not keep any left over medicine unless your doctor tells you to. Please discard all unused Valtrex caplets.

What is in Your Medicine: Each Valtrex caplet contains 500 mg valacyclovir (as valacyclovir HCl). In addition it contains carnauba wax, cellulose, crospovidone, hydroxypropyl methylcellulose, Indigotine Aluminum Lake, magnesium stearate, polyethylene glycol, polysorbate 80, povidone, silicon dioxide, and titanium dioxide.

Remember: This medicine is for you. Only a doctor can prescribe it for you. Never give it to someone else. It may harm them even if their symptoms are the same as yours.

Further Information: This leaflet does not contain the complete information about your medicine. If you have any questions you should ask your doctor or pharmacist. You may need to read this leaflet again. Please do not throw it away until you have finished your medicine.

What you should know about Valtrex caplets for the treatment of recurrent genital herpes. About Your Medicine: The brand name of your medicine is Valtrex. Your Valtrex caplets contain the active ingredient valacyclovir hydrochloride. Valtrex caplets can only be obtained with a prescription from your doctor.

How Your Medicine Works: Valtrex is an antiviral medicine. It is used to treat genital herpes which is caused by the herpes simplex virus (HSV).

HSV causes small, fluid-filled blisters which break down into ulcers/sores which may be itchy or painful. The blisters contain many infectious HSV particles. Valtrex stops HSV from multiplying which helps to shorten the time that the virus is released from the skin and mucous membranes. It reduces the number of painful blisters and also helps them to heal more quickly. If you start taking Valtrex as soon as you feel an infection starting, you may actually prevent the blisters from developing.

Important Points to Note Before Taking Your Medicine: You should not use Valtrex if you are allergic to or react badly to valacyclovir or acyclovir. Tell your doctor if you have ever had an allergic reaction to any of these ingredients.

Use of This Medicine During Pregnancy and Breast-feeding: If you are pregnant, or likely to become pregnant soon, or if you are breast-feeding, please inform your doctor before taking any drugs, including Valtrex. If you are pregnant or breast-feeding, your doctor may decide not to prescribe this medicine, although, there may be circumstances when your doctor advises you differently.

How to Take your Medicine: You must take Valtrex as prescribed by your doctor. If you are not sure how many caplets to take, or how often to take them, consult your doctor or pharmacist.

You should not increase or decrease the prescribed dose unless advised by your doctor.

The usual dose is one Valtrex caplet twice a day for 5 days. Take 1 caplet in the morning and 1 in the evening.

After Taking Your Medicine: Valtrex does not often have side effects. Some people may feel sick or have a mild headache. Tell your pharmacist or doctor if you notice any other side effects from your medicine which are not mentioned here.

If you feel worse or you have taken all the caplets and do not feel better **tell your doctor as soon as possible.**

What to Do if an Overdose is Taken: It is important to follow the dosage instructions on the label of your medicine. In the event of an overdose, you should **immediately** contact either your doctor, the nearest hospital emergency department or Poison Control Centre.

What to Do if You Miss a Dose: If you forget to take a dose, take another as soon as possible. Then continue with the next dose at the right time.

Storing Your Medicine: Store Valtrex caplets between 15 and 25°C. Keep caplets away from direct heat and sunlight.

Keep your Valtrex caplets in a safe place where children cannot reach them.

Do not take any caplets after the expiry date shown on the package.

What to Do When You Stop Your Medicine: If your doctor decides to stop the treatment, do not keep any left over medicine unless your doctor tells you to. Please discard all unused Valtrex caplets.

What is in Your Medicine: Each Valtrex caplet contains 500 mg valacyclovir (as valacyclovir hydrochloride). In addition, it contains carnauba wax, cellulose, crospovidone, hydroxypropyl methylcellulose, Indigotine Aluminum Lake, magnesium stearate, polyethylene glycol, polysorbate 80, povidone, silicon dioxide, and titanium dioxide.

Remember: This medicine is for you. Only a doctor can prescribe it for you. Never give it to someone else. It may harm them even if their symptoms are the same as yours.

Genital Herpes: What is genital herpes? Genital herpes is a sexually transmitted disease caused by herpes simplex virus, the same family of viruses that causes cold sores or fever blisters. You can get genital herpes by having sex (skin-to skin contact including genital, anal and/or oral contact) with a person who has herpes. Genital herpes does not always occur on the genitals. It may occur on the buttocks or on the thighs.

Are there any warning signs of a genital herpes attack? Lots of people have genital herpes and don't even know it. Here are some of the signs that may signal a genital herpes outbreak:

- Swelling, pain, itching, or burning in your genital area
- Redness, tiny blisters, or sores
- Burning feeling when urinating
- Genital discharge
- Muscle aches, tiredness, or headaches

It is a feature of all herpes viruses that once in the body, they stay there throughout life, and sometimes become active again. No one is really sure why an infection recurs. Some people know what triggers their genital herpes infection to become active again, others do not. Some factors that may trigger the virus into activity are lack of sleep, poor diet, stress and menstruation.

Try to notice if these factors cause your infection to return, as you may be able to avoid some of them. Taking your Valtrex caplets as soon as you get the warning signs may actually prevent the blisters from developing.

How did I get genital herpes? Genital herpes is passed from one person to another through direct intimate contact. It is often transmitted sexually, usually by direct contact with the blisters or sores. These blisters contain many infectious virus particles. Small cuts or scratches in the skin or mucous membranes allow the virus to gain entry into the body more easily. These may not be visible to the naked eye. Some people may spread genital herpes without even knowing. This may be because they have such a mild infection that there are no signs or symptoms.

Genital herpes cannot be spread via handshakes, toilet seats, swimming pools, saunas or water slides.

Can I spread genital herpes to other people? Yes. It is important to remember herpes virus particles may occasionally be released when you do not have blisters or sores. For this reason, it is safest to believe that you can spread the infection to your partner even when sores are not present. This is more common in the first year after getting the infection, and in people with frequent outbreaks.

How can I reduce the risk of spreading genital herpes to other parts of my body or to other people? You do not have to stop having sex if you have genital herpes infection. However, in order to reduce the risk of transmission:

- Avoid sexual contact when your genital herpes infection is active.
- Use condoms with spermicide, each time you engage in sexual intercourse even when there are no signs of infection.
- Avoid touching or breaking the blisters or sores and do not pick the scabs when they form.
- Always wash your hands if you touch the blisters, sores, or scabs.
- If you or your partner has an active genital herpes infection (or even the warning signs), avoid close skin contact with the blisters or sores.
- Discuss with your doctor, what is best for both you and your partner.

What about genital herpes and pregnancy? There is no evidence that having genital herpes affects fertility in men or women and is unlikely to complicate a pregnancy. The measures described above will also help to reduce the risk of transmitting genital herpes during pregnancy. Special precautions should be taken during pregnancy to avoid transmission to a pregnant woman if her partner has herpes. Care is needed at the time of birth if there is an active infection present. Discuss the options available with your doctor.

Further Information: This leaflet does not contain the complete information about your medicine. If you have any questions, you should ask your doctor or pharmacist. You may need to read this leaflet again. Please do not throw it away until you have finished your medicine.

Information on genital herpes can also be obtained by calling the National Patient Support Network (1-888-426-9555). The National Patient Support Network was developed with leading Canadian genital herpes experts and provides:

- Toll free, 24 hour service
- Connection to an interactive telephone system
- Confidential and anonymous support
- Information updated regularly

□ VASERETIC® ℞

Frosst

Enalapril Maleate—Hydrochlorothiazide

Angiotensin Converting Enzyme Inhibitor—Diuretic

Information for the Patient: Vaseretic is the brandname of Merck Frosst Canada Inc. for the combination of the substances—enalapril maleate and hydrochlorothiazide. Enalapril is one of a class of medicines known as angiotensin converting enzyme inhibitors and hydrochlorothiazide is a thiazide diuretic, often termed a ''water pill''. This combination is available **only on prescription** from your physician. It is usually prescribed to reduce **high blood pressure.**

When blood pressure is high, the workload of the heart and arteries increases so that over time, these may not function as they should. In turn, this could lead to damage of the ''vital organs'': brain - heart - kidneys, and result in stroke, heart failure, heart attack, blood vessel disease or kidney disease.

Remember: This medicine is prescribed for the particular condition that you have. **Do not give this medicine to other people, nor use it for any other condition.**

Do not use outdated medicine.

Keep all medicines out of the reach of children.

Read the following information carefully. **If you need any explanations, or further information, ask your physician or pharmacist.**

Before Taking This Medicine: This medicine may not be suitable for certain people. So, tell your physician if you think any of the following applies to you:

- You have previously taken **any** of the following and were allergic or reacted badly to it: hydrochlorothiazide or any other diuretic or ''water pill''; sulfonamides (sulfa medicine); enalapril or any other medication of the same type—Angiotensin Converting Enzyme (ACE) inhibitors with the names usually ending with 'pril' such as enalapril, lisinopril, captopril, particularly if you experienced swelling of the face, lips, tongue, or throat, or had sudden difficulty breathing or swallowing.
- **You are pregnant or intend to become pregnant.** This medicine should **not be used during pregnancy,** because of possible risks to the fetus.
- You are breast-feeding or intend to breast-feed.
- You have any of these conditions:
  - —diabetes
  - —heart or blood vessel disease
  - —liver disease
  - —kidney disease, or difficulty in producing urine
  - —bronchial asthma
  - —lupus erythematosus or a history of this condition
  - —gout or history of gout

  Your physician also needs to know if you are taking any other medication, whether they be prescription medications or over-the-counter products. It is particularly important to inform your physician if you are taking:
- Diuretics or ''water pills''; any other medicines to reduce blood pressure; potassium containing medicines, potassium supplements, or salt substitutes that contain potassium; insulin for diabetes; lithium (a drug used to treat a certain kind of depression); or anti-inflammatory medicines used in arthritis.

You should also inform your physician if you are vomiting or have severe diarrhea.

This medicine is not recommended for children.

Proper use of this Medicine:

- Take this medicine exactly as your physician ordered.
- The absorption of this medicine is not affected by food; so it can be taken with or without a meal.
- Try to take your medicine every day at the same time. This way it becomes easy to remember your doses.
- If you miss a dose of this medicine, take it as soon as possible. However, if no more than 6 hours have elapsed since the missed dose, you may take that day's dose of medication and then go back to your regular dosing schedule. **Do not take a double dose.**
- In case of an overdose, contact your doctor immediately so that medical attention may be given promptly. The most likely symptom would be a feeling of lightheadedness or dizziness due to a sudden or excessive drop in blood pressure.
- If your physician has recommended a particular diet, for instance less salt, follow the diet carefully. This could help your medicine to control your blood pressure. Your physician may also recommend weight loss. Do follow these suggestions.

Vaseretic (cont'd)

- This medicine does not cure high blood pressure, **but does help control it.** So, it is important to continue taking the tablets regularly to keep your blood pressure down. You may have to take high blood pressure medicine for life.
- Keep your regular appointments with your physician, even if you feel well. High blood pressure may not be easily recognized by you, because you may not ''feel any symptoms''; but your physician can measure your pressure very easily, and check how the medicine is controlling it.
- **Do not take any other medicines** unless you have discussed the matter with your physician. Certain medications tend to increase your pressure, for example, non-prescription preparations for appetite control, asthma, colds, coughs, hay fever and sinus problems.
- If you have to undergo any dental or other surgery, inform the dentist or the physician in charge that you are taking this medicine.
- Store your tablets at 15 to 30°C in a tightly closed container, away from heat and direct light, and out of damp places, such as the bathroom or kitchen.

Side Effects Of This Medicine—And What You Should Do: Along with its intended action, any medication, including enalapril with hydrochlorothiazide, may cause side effects. Most people do not experience any problem when taking this medicine; but if you notice any of the following, medical attention may be needed.

- Sudden difficulty in breathing or swallowing
- Swelling of face, eyes, lips, tongue and/or throat, hands or feet
- Dizziness, lightheadedness or fainting following exercise, and/or when it is hot and you have lost a lot of water by sweating
- Flu-like symptoms such as fever, malaise, muscle pain, rash, itching, abdominal pain, nausea, vomiting, diarrhea, jaundice, loss of appetite

Stop taking the medication and contact your physician or pharmacist at once. You may require immediate care. If condition worsens seek medical attention.

If any fainting occurs, stop taking the medicine. If dizzy, avoid driving or any activity/jobs requiring alertness. Use extra care during exercise or hot weather.

- You may experience increased skin sensitivity to sunlight. Avoid too much sunlight and do not use a sunlamp.
- Dry cough, sore throat
- Unusual tiredness and/or weakness
- Chest pain
- Impotence
- Headache
- Palpitations
- Tingling of the skin

If you notice any of the above or have other side effects, contact your physician or your pharmacist. If the condition persists or worsens, seek medical attention.

Ingredients: Active ingredient: Each red tablet of Vaseretic 10/25 contains 10 mg of enalapril maleate and 25 mg of hydrochlorothiazide.
Nonmedicinal ingredients: cornstarch, lactose, magnesium stearate, red ferric oxide, sodium bicarbonate.

☐ VASOTEC® ℞

Frosst

Enalapril Maleate

Angiotensin Converting Enzyme Inhibitor

Information for the Patient: Vasotec Tablets: Vasotec is the brandname of Merck Frosst Canada Inc. for the substance—enalapril, available **only on prescription** from your physician. Enalapril is one of a class of medicines known as angiotensin-converting enzyme inhibitors. They are usually prescribed to reduce **high blood pressure.**

When blood pressure is high, the workload of the heart and arteries increases so that over time, these organs may not function as they should. In turn, this could lead to damage of the ''vital organs'': brain - heart - kidneys, and result in stroke, heart failure, heart attack, blood vessel disease or kidney disease.

Enalapril may also be used to treat patients with **heart failure.** This is a condition where the heart cannot pump adequate amounts of blood to satisfy the needs of the body.

Remember: This medicine is prescribed for the particular condition that you have. **Do not give this medicine to other people, nor use it for any other condition.**

Do not use outdated medicine.

Keep all medicines out of the reach of children.

Read the following information carefully. **If you need any explanations, or further information, ask your physician or pharmacist.**

Before Taking This Medicine: This medicine may not be suitable for certain people. So, tell your physician if you think **any** of the following applies to you:

- You have previously taken enalapril or other medication of the same type—Angiotensin-Converting Enzyme (ACE) inhibitors with the names usually ending with 'pril' such as enalapril, lisinopril, captopril, and you were allergic or reacted badly to it, particularly if you experienced swelling of the face, lips, tongue, or throat, or had sudden difficulty breathing or swallowing.
- **You are pregnant or intend to become pregnant.** This medicine should **not be used during pregnancy,** because of possible risks to the fetus.
- You are breast-feeding or intend to breast-feed.
- You have any of these conditions:
  —diabetes
  —heart or blood vessel disease
  —liver disease
  —kidney disease

  Your physician also needs to know if you are taking any other medication, whether on prescription or otherwise. It is particularly important to inform your physician if you are taking:
- Diuretics or ''water pills''; any other medicines to reduce blood pressure; potassium-containing medicines, potassium supplements, or salt substitutes that contain potassium.

  You should also inform your physician if you are vomiting or have severe diarrhea.

  This medicine is not recommended for children.

Proper Use of this Medicine:

- Take this medicine exactly as your physician ordered.
- The absorption of this medicine is not affected by food; so it can be taken with or without a meal.
- Try to take your medicine every day at the same time. This way it becomes easy to remember your doses.
- If you miss a dose of this medicine, take it as soon as possible. However, if no more than 6 hours have elapsed since the missed dose, you may take that day's dose of medication and then go back to your regular dosing schedule. **Do not take a double dose.**
- In case of an overdose, contact your doctor immediately so that medical attention may be given promptly. The most likely symptom would be a feeling of lightheadedness or dizziness due to a sudden or excessive drop in blood pressure.
- Store your tablets between 15 and 30°C, in a tightly closed container, away from heat and direct light, and out of damp places, such as the bathroom or kitchen.

For patients with high blood pressure:

- If your physician has recommended a particular diet, for instance - less salt - follow the diet carefully. This could help your medicine to better control your blood pressure. Your physician may also recommend weight loss. Do follow these suggestions.
- This medicine does not cure high blood pressure, **but does help control it.** So, it is important to continue taking the tablets regularly to keep your blood pressure down. You may have to take high blood pressure medicine for life.
- Keep your regular appointments with your physician, even if you feel well. High blood pressure may not be easily recognized by you, because you may not ''feel any symptoms''; but your physician can measure your pressure very easily, and check how the medicine is controlling it.

For all patients, please note:

- **Do not take any other medicines** unless you have discussed the matter with your physician. Certain medications tend to increase your pressure, for example, nonprescription preparations for appetite control, asthma, colds, coughs, hay fever and sinus problems, or may also react badly with Vasotec.
- If you have to undergo any dental or other surgery, inform the dentist or the physician in charge that you are taking this medicine.

Side Effects of this Medicine—And What You Should Do: Along with its intended action, any medication, including enalapril, may cause side effects. Most people do not experience any problem when taking this medicine; but if you notice any of the following, medical attention may be needed:

- Sudden difficulty in breathing or swallowing
- Swelling of face, eyes, lips, tongue and/or throat, hands or feet
- Dizziness, lightheadedness or fainting following exercise, and/or when it is hot and you have lost a lot of water by sweating
- Flu-like symptoms such as fever, malaise, muscle pain, rash, itching, abdominal pain, nausea, vomiting, diarrhea, jaundice, loss of appetite

Stop taking the medication and contact your physician or pharmacist at once. You may require immediate care. If condition worsens seek medical attention.

If any fainting occurs, stop taking the medicine. If dizzy, avoid driving or any activity/jobs requiring alertness. Use extra care during exercise or hot weather.

- Dry cough, sore throat
- Unusual tiredness and/or weakness
- Headache

If you notice any of the above or have other side effects, contact your physician or pharmacist. If the condition persists or worsens, seek medical attention.

Ingredients: Active ingredient: Each tablet of Vasotec contains enalapril maleate. There are 4 different strengths: 2.5 mg (yellow), 5 mg (white), 10 mg (rust-red) and 20 mg (peach).

Nonmedicinal ingredients: cornstarch, lactose, magnesium stearate, pregelatinized starch, sodium bicarbonate. Tablets 2.5, 10 and 20 mg contain red and/or yellow iron oxides.

□ VEXOL™ ℞

Alcon

Rimexolone

Corticosteroid

Information for the Patient: Shake well before using. Do not touch dropper tip to any surface, as this may contaminate the suspension.

□ VIOFORM®

Novartis Pharmaceuticals

Clioquinol

Antibacterial—Antifungal

Information for the Patient: Please read this information carefully before starting Vioform treatment.

What is Vioform? The active ingredient of Vioform is clioquinol, an anti-infective agent. Clioquinol stops the growth of bacteria and fungi that cause certain types of skin infections.

Before starting treatment with Vioform: Be sure to tell your doctor:

- if you have kidney or liver problems,
- if you have ever had any unusual or allergic reactions to iodine or iodine-containing preparations, clioquinol or hydroxyquinolines,
- if you are allergic to any other substances including foods and dyes,
- if you are pregnant or breast-feeding.

In these cases, your doctor will decide if you may use Vioform.

How to use Vioform: Vioform should be applied to the affected skin area in a thin layer 2 to 3 times daily or as directed by your doctor.

Do not wrap or bandage the areas treated unless instructed to do so by your doctor.

Vioform is for **external use only.** Do not take by mouth.

What side effects can Vioform have? Like all medicines, Vioform may cause some unwanted effects in addition to the desired effects. Therefore, if redness, burning, itching or other signs appear or worsen while using Vioform, check with your doctor or pharmacist.

If there is no improvement after you have used Vioform for 1 week or if your skin condition becomes worse, see your doctor.

Other Precautions: Do not use Vioform in the eyes and be very cautious when using it around the eyes. If accidental contact with the eyes occurs, flush them at once with plenty of water.

Vioform may turn yellow when exposed to air. Vioform may stain hair, fabric, skin or nails.

During breast-feeding, avoid any contact of the infant with the treated skin area.

Vioform is not suitable for treating large areas of skin. Do not apply Vioform to relatively large open skin lesions.

Vioform should not be used in children under 2 years of age.

Storage: Protect from heat (store between 15 to 30°C). Vioform may turn yellow when exposed to air and may cause staining of the skin, nails, hair or fabrics.

Keep out of the reach of children.

□ VIOFORM® HYDROCORTISONE ℞

Novartis Pharmaceuticals

Clioquinol—Hydrocortisone

Antibacterial—Antifungal—Topical Corticosteroid

Information for the Patient: Please read this information carefully before starting Vioform Hydrocortisone treatment.

What is Vioform Hydrocortisone? The active ingredients of Vioform Hydrocortisone are clioquinol and hydrocortisone. Clioquinol is an anti-infective agent. Hydrocortisone belongs to a group of medicines called corticosteroids.

What does Vioform Hydrocortisone do? In infected inflammatory skin diseases, Vioform Hydrocortisone relieves symptoms such as itching and redness when applied to the skin. It also stops the growth of bacteria and fungi that cause certain types of skin infections.

Before starting treatment with Vioform Hydrocortisone: Be sure to tell your doctor:

- if you have kidney or liver disease,
- if you have ever had any unusual or allergic reactions to corticosteroids, iodine or iodine-containing preparations, clioquinol or hydroxyquinolines, or any other substances, including foods and dyes,
- if you are pregnant or intend to become pregnant while using Vioform Hydrocortisone, or if you are breast-feeding.

In these cases, your doctor will decide whether you may apply Vioform Hydrocortisone to your skin.

How to use Vioform Hydrocortisone: Vioform Hydrocortisone must be used as directed by your doctor. Do not use more of it, do not use it more often, and do not use it for a longer period of time than your doctor has specified.

Apply Vioform Hydrocortisone as directed in a thin layer to the affected areas only. Do not wrap or bandage the areas treated unless instructed to do so by your doctor.

Vioform Hydrocortisone is for **external use only.** Do not take by mouth.

Vioform Hydrocortisone is not recommended in children under 2 years of age.

What side effects can Vioform Hydrocortisone have? Like all medicines, Vioform Hydrocortisone may cause some unwanted effects in addition to the desired ones. Therefore, if redness, burning, itching or other signs not present before using Vioform Hydrocortisone occur, stop treatment and consult your doctor or pharmacist.

Other Precautions: If there is no improvement, or if your skin condition becomes worse after you have used Vioform Hydrocortisone for 1 week, see your doctor.

Remember that Vioform Hydrocortisone has been prescribed for your present medical problem only. Do not use it to treat other skin conditions without checking with your doctor first.

Do not use Vioform Hydrocortisone in the eyes and be very cautious when using it near the eyes. If it gets in the eyes accidentally, flush them at once with plenty of water.

Storage: Protect from heat (store between 15 and 30°C) and freezing. Vioform Hydrocortisone may turn yellow when exposed to air and may cause staining of the skin, nails, hair or fabrics.

Keep out of reach of children.

□ VITAMIN A ACID ℞

Dermik Laboratories Canada

Tretinoin

Acne Therapy

Information for the Patient: What You Should Expect: Your doctor has recommended Vitamin A acid Gel or Cream for topical application in the treatment of acne.

Vitamin A acid is a highly effective medication, but it is important to recognize that it is not a quick cure. It is valuable to view the treatment as a 6 to 12 week program that will take time before the best results are seen.

Vitamin A Acid (cont'd)

Since Vitamin A acid works from beneath the skin surface, clearing usually takes from 6 to 12 weeks.

For most patients excellent results are achieved. During the early weeks, the primary objective is to allow your skin to slowly build up a tolerance to this medication as it is potentially irritating. Later your skin will adapt and clearing will occur. Keeping a long-term perspective, following your doctor's instruction, and maintaining your commitment over a 6 to 12 week time period will help you to get the most from your treatment program.

- **If you are a female of childbearing years, you should use Vitamin A acid only after consulting your doctor and seeking his advice for contraceptive counseling. If you are pregnant, you should discontinue use of Vitamin A acid.**
- **Your doctor has given you Vitamin A acid for your use only. Do not allow anyone else to use it.**

Please Review the Usage Guidelines:

1. Getting Started: Before starting therapy with Vitamin A Acid products, it is advisable to discontinue previous topical acne medications, unless otherwise specified by your doctor. It is also advisable to discontinue medicated or abrasive soaps and cleaners, soaps that have a strong drying effect and products with a high concentration of alcohol or astringents, such as shaving lotions during Vitamin A acid therapy.
2. Application: The affected area should be washed with lukewarm water and patted dry. **Wait at least 20 minutes before applying medication.** Apply Vitamin A acid **sparingly** with the fingertips to the affected area once daily just prior to bedtime. Smooth in lightly with the fingertips and avoid ''rubbing'' into the skin. Care must be taken not to apply near the eyes, lips, nostrils or open sores, as these are most sensitive to irritation.
3. Caution: If medication is applied excessively, more rapid or better results will not be obtained, and marked redness, peeling or discomfort may occur. It is better to start out with a light application, building this up rather than vice versa. A light, even application will bring positive results over time.
4. Sensitivity: As your skin may be more sensitive to the sun rays, wind and cold, avoid direct or prolonged exposure to the sun rays and use of sunlamps. If exposure to sun rays is unavoidable, use a protective sunscreening agent.
5. Considerations: Some redness, burning or peeling may occur during the first few weeks of use until your skin adapts to the medication. Your acne condition may also appear to worsen after a week or two as Vitamin A acid works to unseat previously unseen acne lesions. This is expected and indicates that the medication is working. Inform your doctor of these changes.

Should the redness, burning or peeling worsen or persist, reduce the frequency of application as advised by your doctor.

The use of the product should be discontinued if any unusual reaction occurs; keep your doctor informed.

After noticeable improvement occurs, Vitamin A acid can be used on a reduced schedule with your doctor's approval, to prevent new acne blemishes from developing.

☐ VIVELLE™ Ⓟ

Novartis Pharmaceuticals

Estradiol-17β

Estrogen

Information for the Patient: Vivelle And How to Use It: Introduction: Vivelle is a transdermal therapeutic system (patch) which contains the natural estrogen hormone, estradiol. Vivelle can alleviate menopausal symptoms.

This leaflet describes the uses of estrogens and progestins, precautions to take when using these hormones and how to use Vivelle. Please read it carefully. **If you want to know more or have any questions, please ask your doctor or pharmacist.**

Decisions regarding hormone replacement therapy and the length of time that a woman takes estrogen must be individualized and are made between each woman and her doctor.

Uses of Estrogens:

1. To reduce moderate or severe menopausal symptoms: Your body normally makes estrogens and progestins (female hormones) mainly in the ovaries. Between ages 45 and 55, the ovaries gradually stop making estrogens. This leads to a decrease in body estrogen levels and a natural menopause (the end of monthly menstrual periods). If both ovaries are removed during an operation before natural menopause takes place, the sudden decrease in estrogen levels causes ''surgical menopause''.

   Menopause is not a disease; it is a natural life event and different women experience menopause and its symptoms differently. Not all women suffer obvious symptoms of estrogen deficiency. When the estrogen levels begin decreasing, some women develop very uncomfortable symptoms, such as feelings of warmth in the face, neck, and chest, or sudden intense episodes of heat and sweating (''hot flashes'' or ''hot flushes''). Using estrogen drugs can help the body adjust to lower estrogen levels and reduce these symptoms.
2. To treat vulval and vaginal atrophy: Some women may also develop vulval or vaginal atrophy (itching, burning or dryness in or around the vagina, difficulty or burning on urination) in association with menopause. These changes may be improved by estrogen therapy.

Uses of Progestins: Progestins used in hormone replacement therapy have similar effects to the female sex hormone progesterone. During the childbearing years, progesterone is responsible for regulation of the menstrual cycle. The estradiol delivered by Vivelle not only relieves your menopausal symptoms, but, like estrogens produced by your body, may also stimulate growth of the inner lining of the uterus, the endometrium. In menopausal and postmenopausal women with an intact uterus, stimulation of growth of the endometrium may result in irregular bleeding. In some cases this may progress into a disorder of the uterus known as endometrial hyperplasia (overgrowth of the lining of the uterus). The development of estrogen-mediated disorders of the uterus can be reduced if a progestin is given regularly for a certain number of days with your estrogen replacement therapy. Each cycle of progestin administration should induce a periodic bleeding, whereby the inner lining of the uterus is regularly shed, thus protecting against endometrial hyperplasia.

If your uterus has been surgically removed, endometrial hyperplasia cannot occur and cyclical administration of a progestin is not necessary.

Precautions: Although estrogens provide health benefits, certain precautions should be taken before their use and in some situations their use may not be appropriate.

The use of estrogens has been reported to increase the risk of cancer of the lining of the uterus (endometrial cancer) in women after the menopause. **This risk is significantly reduced when estrogen is used along with a progestin.** If you have had your uterus removed by a hysterectomy, uterine cancer would not be a risk for you and cyclical administration of a progestin is not necessary.

Some scientific studies have documented an association between a modest increase in the risk of developing breast cancer and the use of hormone replacement therapy in menopause for periods exceeding 5 years. Therefore, women with a family history of breast cancer, or with breast nodules, fibrocystic breast disease (lumps), or abnormal mammograms should consult with their doctor before starting hormone replacement therapy. The overall benefits and possible risks of hormone replacement therapy should be discussed with the physician. Regular breast examinations by a health professional and monthly self-examination are recommended for all women.

The use of oral estrogens after menopause has been reported to increase the risk of gallbladder disease requiring surgery.

Restrictions on Use: Certain medical conditions may be aggravated by estrogens, therefore estrogens should either not be used at all or should be used with precaution under these conditions.

Estrogens should not be used during pregnancy: Since pregnancy may be possible early in menopause while you are still having spontaneous periods, the use of nonhormonal birth control should be discussed with your physician at this time. If you take estrogen during pregnancy, there is a small risk of your unborn child having birth defects.

Estrogens should not be used if you are breast-feeding.

You should not use Vivelle if you have had any unusual allergic reaction to estrogens or any other component of the patch (see What Does Vivelle Contain?).

Before using Vivelle, be sure to tell your doctor if you have ever had any of the following medical problems. Vivelle should not be used under these conditions:

- cancer of the breast or uterus;
- unexpected or unusual vaginal bleeding;

- abnormal blood clotting;
- migraine headaches;
- stroke;
- serious liver disease;
- active phlebitis (inflamed varicose veins);
- porphyria.

To help your doctor decide whether you should use Vivelle and what precautions should be taken during use, tell your doctor:

- what other prescription and nonprescription medicines, if any, you are taking. There are some medicines which interfere with the effects of estrogens.
- about any allergies or sensitivities to medicines or any other substances you may have.
- if you are undergoing surgery or need long bed rest.
- if you have ever had any of the following:
  - —high blood pressure;
  - —heart, kidney, or liver disease;
  - —asthma;
  - —epilepsy or other neurological disorders;
  - —sugar diabetes;
  - —depression;
  - —abnormalities of the breast or uterus;
  - —endometriosis;
  - —breast disease, breast biopsies;
  - —uterine fibroids;
  - —phlebitis (inflamed varicose veins);
  - —abnormal blood clotting;
  - —high levels of lipids in your blood;
  - —jaundice or itching related to estrogen use or during pregnancy.

Side Effects: The following effects have been reported in women taking estrogens (these include estrogens used for birth control). Check with your doctor if these symptoms become troublesome.

- nausea;
- retention of fluid;
- migraine headaches;
- localized darkening of the skin;
- breast tenderness and excessive vaginal secretions (may be a sign that too much estrogen is taken);
- persistent upper abdominal pain, nausea, vomiting, tender abdomen (may be signs of gallbladder disease);
- easy bruising, excessive nose bleeds, excessive heavy periods (may be signs of abnormal blood clotting);
- lower abdominal pain or swelling, painful and/or heavy periods (may be signs of growth of fibroids in the uterus);
- yellowing of the eyes or skin (may be signs of jaundice);
- upper abdominal pain or swelling (may be signs of liver tumors).

Check with your doctor as soon as possible if any of the following occur:

- irregular vaginal bleeding;
- intolerable breast tenderness;
- breast enlargement or lumps;
- severe headaches;
- changes in vision;
- persistent or severe skin irritation;
- fluid retention or bloating persisting for more than 6 weeks.

Check with your doctor immediately if you experience:

- trouble breathing or tightness of the chest;
- tender or painful inflammation of the veins;
- pain or heaviness in the legs or chest;
- sudden shortness of breath;
- coughing blood;
- rapid pulse or dizziness;
- any other unusual symptom.

In addition, Vivelle may produce some redness or irritation under or around the patch in some women (see Helpful Hints).

How to Administer Vivelle: Your doctor will explain when to start using Vivelle. The Vivelle patches are applied twice weekly on the same days of each week. Each patch should be worn continuously for 3 to 4 days.

Estrogen is usually taken in a cyclic fashion (although your physician's instructions may be different depending upon your personal situation). This means that you would take estrogen on the first 21 or 25 days of the cycle, followed by 5 to 7 days without. Your next cycle starts with the next patch application.

Each box contains 8 Vivelle patches. If your treatment is for less than 28 days of estrogen (cyclical therapy), you will have 1 or 2 patches left over which can be used for the next month.

It is important that you take your medication as your physician has prescribed. Do not discontinue or change your therapy without consulting your physician first.

How Vivelle Works: The main estrogen produced by your ovaries prior to menopause is estradiol, and this is the same estrogen that is in Vivelle. When applied to the skin, the Vivelle patch continually releases small, controlled quantities of estradiol, which pass through your skin and into your bloodstream. The amount of estrogen prescribed depends on your body's needs. Your doctor may adjust the amount you get by prescribing another (different) patch size.

By providing estradiol, Vivelle offers relief from menopausal symptoms.

How and Where to Apply Vivelle: It is recommended that you change the site of application each time the patch is applied. However, each time you apply a patch you should always apply it to the same area of your body (i.e., if the patch is applied to the buttocks, move the patch from right side to left side, twice a week or more if there is any redness under the patch).

1. **Preparing the Skin:** In order for the patch to stick, the skin should be clean, dry and free of creams, lotions or oils. If you wish, you may use body lotion after the patch has been properly applied to the skin. The skin should not be irritated or broken, since this may alter the amount of hormone you get. Contact with water (bath, pool, or shower) won't affect the patch, although very hot water or steam may loosen it and therefore should be avoided (see Helpful Hints).
2. **Where to Apply the Vivelle Patch** (see package insert for illustrations): The buttock is the preferred place to apply the patch. Other suitable application sites are the sides, hip, lower back or lower abdomen. Change the site of application each time you put a patch on. You can use the same spot more than once but **not twice in a row.**

   Avoid areas of the skin where clothing may rub the patch off or areas where the skin is very hairy or folded. Also avoid areas where the patch is likely to be exposed to the sun since this may affect how the patch works.

   Do not apply Vivelle to your breast, since this may cause unwanted effects and discomfort.
3. **Opening the Pouch** (see package insert for illustrations): Each Vivelle patch is individually sealed in a protective pouch. **Tear** open this pouch at the indented notch and remove the patch. Do not use scissors, as you may accidentally cut and destroy the patch.
4. **Removing the Liner** (see package insert for illustrations): One side of the patch has the adhesive that attaches to your skin. The adhesive is covered by a protective liner that must be removed.

   To separate the patch from the liner, hold the patch with the protective liner facing you. Peel off one side of the protective liner and discard it. Try to avoid touching the sticky side of the patch with your fingers.

   Using the other half of the liner as a handle, apply the sticky side of the system to a dry area of intact skin on the trunk of the body. Press the sticky side on the skin and smooth down.

   Fold back the remaining side of the edge of the protective liner and pull it across the skin. Avoid touching the adhesive.

   Don't worry if the patch buckles slightly because you can flatten it out after the liner has been removed. Apply the patch soon after opening the pouch and removing the liner.
5. **Applying the Vivelle Patch:** Apply the adhesive side to the spot you have chosen. Press it firmly in place with the palm of your hand for about 10 seconds, then run your finger around the edge, making sure there is good contact with the skin.
6. **When and How to Remove the Patch:** The Vivelle patch should be changed twice weekly. Always change it on the same 2 days of the week. If you forget to change it at the scheduled time, there is no cause for alarm. Just change it as soon as possible and **continue** to follow your usual schedule.

   After you remove the patch fold it in half with the adhesive sides inwards. **Throw it away, safely out of the reach of children or pets.**

   Any adhesive left on your skin will rub off easily. Apply a new Vivelle patch on a different spot of clean, dry skin.

Storage: Vivelle should be stored at room temperature (below 25°C). Do not freeze. **Do not store it out of the pouch.** Vivelle patches should be kept out of the reach of children and pets before and after use.

What Does Vivelle Contain? Like most medicines, Vivelle contains other substances in addition to estrogen. The other substances are

Vivelle (cont'd)

acrylic copolymers, bentonite, butylene, dipropylene and propylene glycols, ethylene-vinyl alcohol copolymer, mineral oil, oleic acid, phosphatidylcholine, polyester, polysiobutylene, polyurethane and synthetic rubber, vinyl acetate resin.

Helpful Hints: What to do if the Patch Falls off: Should a patch fall off in a very hot bath or shower, shake the water off the patch. Dry your skin completely and reapply the patch (to a new area of skin) and continue your regular schedule. If it still does not stick, then apply a **new** patch and continue with your regular schedule.

If hot baths, saunas or whirlpools are something you enjoy and you find that the patch is falling off, you may consider removing the patch **temporarily** while you are in the water. If you do remove the patch temporarily, the adhesive side of the patch should be placed on the protective liner that was removed when originally applying the patch. Wax paper may be used as an alternate to the liner. This prevents the contents of the patch from emptying by evaporation while you are not wearing it.

In addition to exposure to very hot water, there are some other causes for the patch failing to stick. If you are having patches fall off regularly, this could be happening as a result of:

- using any type of bath oil;
- using soaps with a high cream content;
- using skin moisturizers before applying the patch.

Patch adhesion may be improved if you avoid using these products, and by cleansing the site of application with rubbing alcohol before you apply the patch.

What to do if Your Skin Becomes Red or Irritated Under or Around the Patch: As with any product that covers the skin for a period of time (such as bandages), the Vivelle patch can produce some skin irritation in some women. This varies according to the sensitivity of each woman.

Usually this redness does not pose any health concern to you, but to reduce this problem, there are some things that you may do:

- choose the buttock as the site of application;
- change the site of application of the Vivelle patch every time a new patch is applied, usually twice weekly.

Experience with Vivelle has shown that if you allow the patch to be exposed to the air for approximately 10 seconds after the protective liner has been removed, skin redness may not occur.

If redness and/or itching continues, you should consult your physician.

Always Remember: Your doctor has prescribed Vivelle for you after a careful review of your medical needs. Use it only as directed and do not give it to anyone else. Your doctor should re-examine you at least once a year.

If you have any questions, contact your doctor or pharmacist.

□ VOLTAREN® Ⓟ

Novartis Pharmaceuticals

Diclofenac Sodium

Anti-inflammatory—Analgesic

Information for the Patient: Your doctor has decided to use Voltaren (diclofenac sodium) to treat your problem. Here are some things to know about Voltaren in order to use it safely, and get the most benefit.

Voltaren belongs to a class of drugs known as nonsteroidal anti-inflammatory drugs (NSAIDs). NSAIDs are used to treat arthritic (inflammatory) symptoms such as joint pain, swelling, stiffness, relieve pain, inflammation and fever.

You have received one of the following dosage forms: enteric-coated tablet, slow release tablet or suppository.

Identify your medication: Voltaren 25 mg (enteric-coated): yellow, round, 25 on one side and VOLTAREN on the other.
Voltaren 50 mg (enteric-coated): light brown, round, 50 on one side and VOLTAREN on the other.
Voltaren Slow Release 75 mg: light pink, triangular, VOLTAREN on one side and SR/75 on the other.
Voltaren Slow Release 100 mg: pink, round, VOLTAREN SR on one side and 100 on the other.
Voltaren suppositories 50 mg and 100 mg: torpedo-shaped with smooth surface, yellowish-white color.

Check with your pharmacist if the identifying markings or color appear different.

Using Voltaren safely: Whether you have been prescribed oral tablets and/or rectal suppositories make sure that you do not take more than a total of 150 mg/day.

What does your doctor, pharmacist and dentist need to know about you? To decide whether you can take Voltaren safely, your doctor must know whether you have certain medical conditions. Before taking Voltaren, make sure your doctor knows if you have:

- an allergy to Voltaren (diclofenac sodium), aspirin (ASA or acetylsalicylic acid), ibuprofen, other pain relievers, or anti-inflammatory medicines (NSAIDs).
- had any side effects from medicines that you have taken in the past for arthritis, rheumatism or sore joints,
- a history of stomach upset, or ulcer,
- liver disease,
- kidney disease,
- other medical problems.

If you see another doctor, or a dentist while taking Voltaren, be sure they know you are taking it.

Are you pregnant or breast-feeding? If you are pregnant, or intend to become pregnant, tell your doctor. Voltaren is generally not recommended during pregnancy, especially during the final 3 months. Similarly, since Voltaren can pass into breast milk, it is not recommended that it be taken while breast-feeding. However, your doctor will decide the most appropriate use of Voltaren should you need it.

What about taking other drugs at the same time? It is important to tell your doctor, dentist and pharmacist if you are taking other medication, as combining drugs can sometimes result in changing expected drug effects or cause harmful effects.

While taking Voltaren, do not take aspirin (ASA or acetylsalicylic acid), ASA containing compounds, ibuprofen, Voltaren Rapide, or other drugs that are used to relieve pain, arthritis or inflammation symptoms, unless your doctor directs otherwise.

What are the side effects? Like any other medication, Voltaren can produce side effects. It is wise to be aware of them, especially if you are getting on in years. The most common side effects with all NSAIDs, including Voltaren, are stomach problems. Taking your tablets with food can minimize these problems. Be aware that Voltaren can make some people feel drowsy, dizzy, or lightheaded. Should you experience these symptoms, avoid driving and other activities that require alertness and do not take any sedating medication such as tranquilizers, sleeping pills and certain antihistamines unless approved by your doctor.

There are some side effects that cause only mild discomfort, but are important for your doctor to know about, should you have any of them. Tell your doctor as soon as possible if any one of the following occurs:

- bloody or black, tarry stools,
- stomach pain, nausea, vomiting, indigestion, diarrhea, rectal itching or bleeding,
- yellow discoloration of skin or eyes,
- ''flu-like'' symptoms,
- tenderness just under your ribs on your right side,
- itching, rash, hives, swelling,
- shortness of breath, wheezing, troubled breathing, or tightness in chest,
- swelling of feet or lower legs,
- blurred vision or any visual disturbance or hearing problem,
- changes in the amount or color of your urine (such as dark red or brown),
- mental confusion, depression, headache, dizziness, lightheadedness,
- any other unusual effect.

The above is a **partial** list of unwanted effects that can occur while taking Voltaren or other NSAID medications. A more detailed list is provided in the Product Monograph, available on request.

Visits to your doctor: Anyone who takes Voltaren for more than 2 to 3 weeks should routinely contact their doctor to make sure that no unnoticed unwanted effects are occurring.

How to take your medication: In order to receive optimum benefits from Voltaren it is essential that you take Voltaren regularly as directed by your doctor. Take only the amount of medication at the time intervals and for as long as your doctor has prescribed. The **maximum** daily dosage for any form or combination of Voltaren is 150 mg. A lower daily dosage may have been prescribed for you. Harmful effects or a lack of benefit can result if you do not follow instructions carefully.

If you are not getting adequate relief from your medication, speak to your doctor before you stop taking it, as you may need up to 2 weeks to feel adequate relief.

To help reduce the possibility of stomach upset you should take a Voltaren tablet with a meal or food.

Taking Slow Release Tablets Once a Day: If you are taking Voltaren Slow Release 100 mg tablet or Voltaren Slow Release 75 mg tablet **once** a day, it is best to take this tablet at the same time each day unless your doctor has told you differently. If you have not taken this tablet at the prescribed or your regular time you may take it right away, but you should wait at least 12 hours before taking the next dose. You may then continue taking your tablet at the prescribed or your regular time thereafter.

Taking Slow Release Tablets Twice a Day: Voltaren Slow Release 100 mg tablet may **not** be taken more than once a day. If you are taking a Voltaren Slow Release 75 mg tablet **twice** a day, it is best to take this tablet morning and evening, unless your doctor has told you differently. If you have not taken this tablet at the prescribed or your regular time you may take it right away. If a second dose on the same day is necessary, you should wait preferably 12 hours and no less than 6 hours before taking the next dose. You may then continue taking your tablet at the prescribed or your regular time the next day.

Voltaren Slow Release tablets should be swallowed whole with liquid, preferably at mealtime.

Voltaren suppositories (50 and 100 mg) are wrapped in foil. Make sure that the foil wrapping is fully removed before inserting the suppository into the rectum. Do not take suppositories by mouth.

Storage: Protect tablets from heat (i.e., store at temperatures below 30°C) and humidity. Protect suppositories from heat (i.e., store at temperatures below 30°C). Keep this and all medication out of the reach of children.

Always remember: Your doctor has prescribed Voltaren for you after a careful review of your medical condition. Use it only as directed and do not give it to anyone else. If you require more information, consult your doctor or pharmacist. If you suspect you are experiencing side effects, stop taking Voltaren, and notify your doctor right away.

□ VOLTAREN OPHTHA® Ⓟ

CIBA Vision

Diclofenac Sodium

Anti-inflammatory—Analgesic

Information for the Patient: Your doctor has prescribed Voltaren Ophtha for you, which is a nonsteroidal anti-inflammatory drug (NSAID), used to treat symptoms of inflammation of the eye. Voltaren Ophtha eye drops reduce pain and inflammation by reducing the production of certain substances called prostaglandins.

You should use Voltaren Ophtha eye drops only as directed by your doctor.

How to Use Your Medication: In order to receive the optimum benefits from Voltaren Ophtha, it is essential to use the eye drops regularly (usually 3 to 5 times a day) as directed by your physician.

Single-Dose Unit: Cut pouch along dotted line and remove the strip of single-use units. Tear off one single-dose unit from the strip. Hold it by the tab with the nozzle pointing downwards and tap the unit gently until all the air bubbles are above the solution. Twist the tab off the single-dose unit. Make sure that the tip of the unit does not touch anything. Hold the single-dose unit in one hand between the thumb and forefinger. With your head tilted back, use the forefinger of your other hand to pull down the lower lid of your eye. Place the single-dose unit tip close to your eye, but without touching your eye or lid, and gently squeeze the unit to allow one drop to be applied. Close your eyelid and gently press the inner corner of your eye with your forefinger for one minute. Discard the single-dose unit and the remaining solution.

Occasionally you may experience a mild to moderate burning sensation when Voltaren Ophtha is instilled in the eye. This symptom usually disappears rapidly, but if it or any other side effects persist, check with your doctor.

If you experience any blurring of vision, you should refrain from driving or operating any machinery.

Always Remember: Before taking this medication, tell your doctor and pharmacist if you:
- are allergic to Voltaren Ophtha or other medications of the NSAID group such as ASA, diflusinal, ibuprofen, flurbiprofen, ketoprofen, fenoprofen, indomethacin, mefenamic acid, piroxicam, sulindac, tiaprofenic acid or tolmetin:
- are pregnant or intend to become pregnant while taking this medication;
- are breast-feeding;
- are taking any other drug (either prescription or nonprescription);
- have any other medical problem(s).

While taking this medication:
- tell any other doctor, dentist or pharmacist that you consult that you are taking Voltaren Ophtha Ophthalmic Drops;
- check with your doctor if you are not getting any relief or if any problems develop;
- report any untoward reactions to your doctor. This is very important, as it will aid in the early detection and prevention of potential complications.

Your regular medical checkups are essential.

Storage: Store preserved multi-dose bottles at room temperature and protect from light. Store single-dose units in a cool place (8 to 15°C).

Keep bottle tightly closed when not in use. Keep this and all medication out of the reach of children.

If you require more information about this drug, consult with your doctor or pharmacist.

□ VOLTAREN RAPIDE® Ⓟ

Novartis Pharmaceuticals

Diclofenac Potassium

Anti-inflammatory—Analgesic

Information for the Patient: Your doctor has decided to use Voltaren Rapide (diclofenac potassium) to treat your problem. Here are some things to know about Voltaren Rapide in order to use it safely and get the most benefit.

Voltaren Rapide belongs to a class of drugs known as nonsteroidal anti-inflammatory drugs (NSAIDs). Other NSAIDs include aspirin (ASA) and ibuprofen. NSAIDs relieve pain, inflammation and fever. Voltaren Rapide acts rapidly to relieve pain and swelling in conditions such as: ankle sprains, tooth extraction and painful menstrual periods (dysmenorrhea).

Using Voltaren Rapide safely: What does your doctor, pharmacist and dentist need to know about you? To decide whether you can take Voltaren Rapide safely, your doctor must know whether you have certain medical conditions. Before taking Voltaren Rapide, make sure your doctor knows if you have:

—an allergy to aspirin (ASA or acetylsalicylic acid), ibuprofen or other pain relievers,
—had any side effects from medicines for arthritis, rheumatism or sore joints that you have taken in the past,
—a history of stomach upset, or ulcer,
—liver disease,
—kidney disease,
—other medical problems.

If you see another doctor or a dentist while taking Voltaren Rapide, be sure they know you are taking it.

Are you pregnant or breast-feeding? If you are pregnant, or intend to become pregnant, tell your doctor. Voltaren Rapide is generally not recommended in pregnancy, especially during the final 3 months. Similarly, since Voltaren Rapide can pass into breast milk, it is not recommended that it be taken while breast-feeding. However, your doctor will decide the most appropriate use of Voltaren Rapide should you need it.

What are the side effects? Like any other medication, Voltaren Rapide can produce side effects. It is wise to be aware of them, especially if you are getting on in years. The most common side effects with all NSAIDs, including Voltaren Rapide, are stomach problems. Taking your tablets with food can minimize these problems. Be aware that Voltaren Rapide can make some people feel drowsy, dizzy or lightheaded. Should you experience these symptoms, avoid driving and other activities that require alertness.

There are some side effects that cause only mild discomfort, but are important for your doctor to know about, should you have any of them. Tell your doctor as soon as possible if any one of the following occurs:

—bloody or black, tarry stools,
—stomach pain, nausea, vomiting, indigestion, diarrhea, rectal itching or bleeding,
—yellow discoloration of skin or eyes,

Voltaren Rapide (cont'd)

—"flu-like" symptoms,
—tenderness just under your ribs on your right side,
—itching, rash, hives, swelling,
—shortness of breath, wheezing, troubled breathing or tightness in chest,
—swelling of feet or lower legs,
—blurred vision or any visual disturbance or hearing problem,
—changes in the amount or color of your urine (such as dark, red or brown),
—mental confusion, depression, headache, dizziness, lightheadedness,
—any other unusual effect.

What about taking other drugs at the same time? Aspirin (ASA), ASA-containing compounds, or other drugs such as ibuprofen that are used to relieve pain or swelling must not be taken while you are taking Voltaren Rapide, unless your doctor directs otherwise. Make sure your doctor is aware of all other drugs you are taking.

Have you been given the correct tablets? Voltaren Rapide 50 mg are reddish-brown, round, biconvex, sugar-coated tablets. VOLTAREN is printed in white on one side, and RAPIDE 50 on the other.

How to take Voltaren Rapide: The usual dose is 1 tablet 2 or 3 times daily, taken with food. The total daily dose should not exceed 3 tablets. However, for painful menstrual cramps your doctor may prescribe 2 tablets for the first dose. If so, you may take 4 tablets the first day. Always take the correct amount each time, and don't take your medicine more often than was prescribed.

Storage: Protect your tablets from heat (store at temperatures below 30°C) and humidity.

Always remember: Your doctor has prescribed Voltaren Rapide for you after a careful review of your medical condition. Use it only as directed and do not give it to anyone else. If you require more information, consult your doctor or pharmacist. Keep this and all medication out of the reach of children. If you suspect you are experiencing side effects, stop taking the tablets, and notify your doctor right away.

☐ WELLBUTRIN® SR 🄿

Glaxo Wellcome

Bupropion HCl

Antidepressant

Information for the Patient: Please read this information carefully before you take Wellbutrin SR (bupropion hydrochloride) tablets. Do not throw away this leaflet until you have finished your medicine because you may need to read it again. This provides only a summary of the information available on Wellbutrin SR. For further information or advice, ask your doctor or pharmacist.

Information About Your Medicine: The name of your medicine is Wellbutrin SR Tablets. It is one of a group of drugs called antidepressants. The decision to use Wellbutrin SR tablets is one that you and your doctor should make jointly, taking into account your individual preferences and medical circumstances. This medication can be obtained only by prescription from your doctor. **Remember,** this prescription is for you alone. Never give it to someone else. It may harm them even if their symptoms appear to be similar to yours.

Important Warning: Wellbutrin SR tablets should not be used if you are taking Zyban or any other medications containing bupropion hydrochloride, because this will increase the likelihood of you experiencing a seizure.

At the maximum recommended dose of 300 mg each day, there is a chance that approximately 1 out of every 1 000 people taking bupropion, the active ingredient in Wellbutrin SR, will have a seizure. The chance of this happening increases if you:
- have a seizure disorder (for example, epilepsy)
- have or have had an eating disorder (for example, bulimia or anorexia nervosa)
- take more than the recommended amount of Wellbutrin SR

Alcohol consumption may also alter your seizure threshold. Therefore, consumption of alcohol should be minimized, and, if possible, avoided completely.

Important Questions To Consider Before Taking Wellbutrin SR Tablets: If the answer to any of the following questions is **yes**, or if you do not know the answer, please discuss this with your doctor **before** you use Wellbutrin SR tablets.
- Are you pregnant? Do you think you might be pregnant? Are you trying to become pregnant? Are you breast-feeding?
- Are you taking any prescription or over-the-counter medications? Are you planning on taking any prescription or over-the-counter medications during your therapy?
- Do you have any other medical conditions? Do you have a history of seizures or of an eating disorder? Are you allergic to any of the ingredients in the tablets (see "What is in your medicine:" at the end of this section)?

How To Take Your Wellbutrin SR Tablets: Wellbutrin SR tablets are specially designed to release drug gradually into your system over a period of several hours. In order for the medicine to work properly it is important that you do not chew, divide or crush tablets. Please swallow Wellbutrin SR tablets whole, with fluids, so that the release rate is not altered.

Take only the recommended dose prescribed by your doctor. The effects of your medication may not be noticeable in the first few days of treatment, and significant improvement may take several weeks. This is common with antidepressant medicines. If you are concerned that your medicine is not working, discuss this with your doctor. Never increase the dose of your medicine unless your doctor tells you to. If you forget to take a dose, do not take an extra tablet to "catch up". Wait and take your next tablet at the regular time.

Side Effects To Watch For: The most common side effects of Wellbutrin SR are: loss of appetite, dry mouth, skin rash, sweating, ringing in the ears, and shakiness. The side effects of Wellbutrin SR are generally mild and often disappear after a few weeks. If you have nausea, you may want to take your medicine with food. If you have difficulty sleeping, avoid taking your medicine too close to bedtime. Contact your doctor or health care professional if you develop a skin rash or other troublesome side effects.

Wellbutrin SR may impair your ability to perform tasks requiring judgment or motor and cognitive skills. Consequently, until you are reasonably certain that Wellbutrin SR does not adversely affect your performance you should refrain from driving an automobile or operating complex, hazardous machinery.

What To Do If An Overdose Is Taken: If you have taken more medication than your doctor has instructed, contact either your doctor, hospital emergency department, or nearest poison control centre immediately.

Storing Your Medicine: Store your medication at room temperature, out of direct sunlight. Keep it in a tightly closed container in a safe place where children cannot reach it. It may be harmful to children. If your doctor decides to stop your treatment, do not keep any leftover medicine unless your doctor tells you to.

What Is In Your Medicine: Wellbutrin SR tablets are supplied for oral administration as 100 mg (blue) and 150 mg (purple), film-coated, sustained release tablets. Each tablet contains the labeled amount of bupropion hydrochloride and the inactive ingredients: carnauba wax, cysteine hydrochloride, hydroxypropyl methylcellulose, magnesium stearate, microcrystalline cellulose, polyethylene glycol, and titanium dioxide and is printed with edible black ink. In addition, the 100 mg tablet contains FD&C Blue No. 1 Lake and polysorbate 80, and the 150 mg tablet contains FD&C Blue No. 2 Lake, FD&C Red No. 40 Lake, and polysorbate 80.

Wellbutrin SR tablets have a slight odor. If present, this odor is normal.

Who Makes Your Medication: Glaxo Wellcome Inc. 7333 Mississauga Road North, Mississauga, Ontario L5N 6L4

☐ WELLFERON® 🄿

Glaxo Wellcome

Interferon alpha-n1 (Ins)

Biological Response Modifier

Information for the Patient: Please read this carefully before you start to use your medication.

This leaflet contains important information about your treatment. If you have any doubts or questions or you are not sure about anything ask your doctor or pharmacist.

What's in your medication: The name of your medicine is Wellferon (containing human alpha-interferon). Interferon is used to help maintain your body's defence mechanism against certain diseases.

Wellferon comes in vials containing 3, 5 and 10 megaunits of human alpha-lymphoblastoid interferon in tris-glycine buffered saline. Wellferon also contains Albumin Solution (Human).

Keep your medication and administration equipment out of reach of children.

Before using your medication: Ask these questions before using Wellferon.

- Have you previously experienced an allergic or bad reaction to Wellferon or another interferon?
- Have you recently taken, are you currently taking or are you likely to be taking **any** other medicines whilst you are using Wellferon?
- Are you asthmatic?
- Are you pregnant, trying to become pregnant or breast-feeding?
- Do you suffer from heart, kidney, liver or central nervous system disease (e.g., epilepsy)?
- Do you suffer from, or have you ever suffered from mental disturbance?
- Do you suffer from any blood disorder?

If the answer is **yes** to any of these questions, and if you have not already discussed them with your doctor, tell him before you use your medication.

Using your medication:

- It is important to use your medication at the right times. You must use it as directed by your doctor. The label will tell you how much to use and how often. If it doesn't or you are not sure, ask your doctor.
- The dosage is very variable and it may be changed from time to time by your doctor. If you are unsure or if the dosage on the label has changed for no apparent reason, consult your doctor. The length of time you stay on treatment will also vary.
- During your course of treatment your doctor will want you to have a blood test from time to time to check the blood cell count and to adjust the dosage if necessary.
- Do not drive or operate machinery while using this medication.
- Your doctor or nurse will have shown you how to inject your medication. If you are unsure of the procedure, check with your doctor or somebody at the clinic.
- The injection is given into the layer just below the surface of the skin. Injections can be given in the abdomen, upper arms, thighs or buttocks.
- Visible blood vessels should be avoided.
- Use a different site daily or for each injection.
- Make sure you keep a record of the site you have used, the Wellferon batch number and the date.

After taking your medication: This medication may cause side effects; if any problems arise contact your doctor or somebody at the hospital.

Some of the side effects that might be expected, and what can be done to help them, are shown below:

Common side effects:

- Flu-like symptoms e.g.: chills, fever, malaise, muscle aches and headache.
- In order to minimize these symptoms inject your medication in the evening and your doctor may advise you take paracetamol tablets. Drinking plenty of fluids also helps. Cold or lukewarm baths or showers may help if you have a very high temperature. It is also a good idea to plan fewer activities and allow for a rest period on the day of your injection. Ask for help from family and friends, limit visitors and avoid stressful situations.
- Poor appetite—avoid foods that upset your stomach, select food you enjoy eating and make sure you eat at least 3 times a day.
- Weight loss.
- Increased need for sleep.
- Psychological effects e.g.: irritability, anxiety and mild depression.
- Hair loss.

Uncommon side effects:

- Anemia—leading to tiredness.
- Low white blood cell count leading to increased risk of infection. If you develop a sore throat or a lot of mouth ulcers then contact your doctor.
- Low blood platelet leading to increased risk of bruising and bleeding e.g.: nose bleeds.

In order to detect any of the above at an early stage your blood counts will be regularly checked at the clinic. These effects are fully reversible when Wellferon therapy is stopped.

- Dizziness, feeling faint, racing heart (palpitations)
- Diarrhea
- Unexplained swelling of hands, feet and/or face
- Blood in the urine or passing water less frequently
- Coldness of the fingers or toes

If any of these or any other unusual effects occur, or if you begin to feel more unwell while taking Wellferon, contact your doctor.

Storing your medication: Keep your Wellferon in the refrigerator (2 to 8°C). Check the expiry date on your vial; if the Wellferon is past the expiry date, do not use it and consult your pharmacist.

Take the vials out half an hour before your injection to bring the solution to room temperature.

Who produces your medicine: Manufacturer: The Wellcome Foundation Ltd., London.

Distributor: Glaxo Wellcome Inc. 7333 Mississauga Road North, Mississauga, Ontario L5N 6L4

Remember: This medication is for **you**. Only a doctor can prescribe it for you. Never give it to others. It may harm them even if their symptoms are the same as yours.

□ XALATAN™ Ⓟ

Pharmacia & Upjohn

Latanoprost

Prostaglandin $F_{2}\alpha$ Analogue

Information for the Patient: Please read this carefully before using Xalatan. It provides useful information about this medication and effects you may experience. If you have any questions or need explanations, please ask your doctor or pharmacist. Remember: This medication is prescribed for the particular condition that you have. Never give this medication to others. Do not use it for any other condition.

What Kind of Medication is Xalatan and how Does it Work? Xalatan is a solution for use only in the eyes. The active ingredient in Xalatan is one of a group of medications known as prostaglandins. It helps to lower the pressure within the eye by increasing the natural outflow of fluid from inside the eye. Xalatan has been shown to work by itself to lower pressure in the eye.

What is Xalatan for? Xalatan is used to treat a type of glaucoma called open angle glaucoma, and a condition known as ocular hypertension. Both these conditions are caused by an increase in pressure within the eye and eventually they may affect your eyesight.

What is Xalatan made up of? Active Ingredients: Each milliliter (mL) contains 50 micrograms of latanoprost. **Other Ingredients:** Benzalkonium chloride, sodium chloride, sodium dihydrogen phosphate monohydrate, disodium phosphate anhydrous, water for injection.

Each bottle contains 2.5 mL of solution, approximately 80 drops.

Before using Xalatan you should tell your doctor if:

- You are allergic to any of the ingredients in Xalatan.
- You are using any other eye drops or taking any other medication.
- You are pregnant, think you might be pregnant or you are planning a pregnancy.
- You are breast-feeding.

Xalatan contains a preservative that may be absorbed by contact lenses and stains them a brown color. Contact lenses can be reinserted 15 minutes after applying the eye drops. If you are using more than 1 type of eye drop medication, wait at least 5 minutes between each different eye drop.

How to use Xalatan? One drop of Xalatan should be dropped into the affected eye(s) **once daily**. The best time to do this is **in the evening.**

Do not allow the dropper tip of the bottle to touch the eye or other surrounding structures, because this could contaminate the tip with common bacteria known to cause eye infections. Serious damage to the eye with subsequent loss of vision may result if you use eye drop solutions that have become contaminated. If you experience any type of eye condition or have surgery, immediately seek your doctor's advice concerning the continued use of the bottle you are using.

If you forget to use your eye drops at the usual time, wait until it is time for your next dose. If you put too many drops in your eye(s), you may feel some slight irritation.

Xalatan is not recommended for use in children.

Follow these steps to help you use Xalatan properly:

1. Wash your hands and sit or stand comfortably. If you wear contact lenses, remove them before using your eye drops.

Xalatan (cont'd)

2. Once the bottle is opened, hold it in one hand and steady your thumb against your brow or the bridge of your nose.
3. Use your index finger to gently pull down the lower eyelid of the affected eye(s) to create a pocket for the drop.
4. Gently press, or lightly tap, the side of the bottle to allow only a single drop to fall into the pocket. Do not let the tip of the bottle touch your eye.
5. Close your eye for 2 to 3 minutes.
6. If your doctor has told you to use drops in both eyes, repeat the process for the other eye. Xalatan should be used until your doctor tells you to stop.

What Might Happen While you are Using Xalatan: In some patients, Xalatan may cause a gradual change in eye color by increasing the amount of brown pigment in the iris (the colored part of the eye). This change may not be noticeable for several months to years. This effect may be more noticeable in patients with eye colors that are mixtures of green and brown, blue/gray and brown, or yellow and brown. The brown pigment may gradually spread outward toward the outside edge of the iris. However, the entire iris or parts of it may become more brownish in appearance. This change may be more noticeable if you are only treating one eye. Your doctor will examine you regularly to make sure that your medication is working and look for changes in eye color. If you should experience any changes in eye color, your doctor can stop treatment. However, any color change that has already occurred may be permanent, even after the medication is stopped.

Xalatan may also cause your eye lashes to darken, appear thicker and longer than they usually do. A very small number of people may notice their eye lids look darker after using Xalatan for some time. These changes may be more noticeable if you are only treating one eye.

When using Xalatan, you might feel as if there is something in your eye(s). Your eye(s) might water and become red. As with other eye drops, if your vision is blurred when you first put your drops in, wait until this wears off before you drive or operate machinery. A few people using Xalatan have developed a skin rash.

A few people may experience changes in their vision, sometimes in combination with a red and sore/painful eye. These changes do not always occur right after administering the drops, and if they occur, you may find that reading and seeing fine details more difficult. Although unlikely, if you experience any of these changes, stop using Xalatan and contact your doctor immediately.

Be sure to tell your doctor (or pharmacist) if you notice any other unwanted side effects.

Be sure to tell your doctor (or pharmacist) if you notice any other unwanted side effects.

How to Store Xalatan. Before Xalatan is first opened, keep it in a fridge (between 2 and 8°C), out of direct light. Once the bottle has been opened, Xalatan must be kept in a cool place (refrigerate if possible). Xalatan must be used within 6 weeks after opening the bottle. Discard the bottle and/or unused contents after 6 weeks. Xalatan should not be used after the expiry date on the bottle.

Keep all medicines in a safe place, out of the reach of children.

□ XANAX® Ⓟ

Pharmacia & Upjohn

Alprazolam

Anxiolytic—Antipanic

Information for the Patient: What Are Panic Attacks? Most of us at different times experience tension, anxiety or fear. A panic attack is much different in quality and in intensity from these common experiences.

It occurs out of the blue. The patient, for no apparent reason, suddenly feels a sense of severe discomfort along with physical symptoms.

The physical symptoms can be:

- Shortness of breath or a smothering sensation
- Dizziness or faintness
- Accelerated heart rate
- Trembling or shaking
- Sweating
- Choking
- Nausea or abdominal distress
- Chest discomfort or pain
- Numbness or tingling sensations
- Hot flashes or chills

Symptoms such as difficulty breathing, chest pain or dizziness can mimic symptoms of asthma, heart disease or a neurological condition. In addition to the severe discomfort, fear or panic, and physical symptoms, there are often feelings of detachment or unreality and a fear of dying, going crazy, or losing control.

A panic attack usually lasts a few minutes but can last for hours. It can occur at varying frequencies such as several times a month, a week or even several times a day.

What is Panic Disorder? The difference between a **panic attack** and **panic disorder** lies with the frequency of attacks. A person who suffers four or more panic attacks in any 4-week period (or has less than four attacks, followed by a month of repeated fear of having another attack) is considered to have **panic disorder.**

What is Phobic Avoidance? Typically, people who suffer from **panic disorder** remember everything about their first panic attack, including not knowing why they would experience intense fear out of the blue. When future attacks occur, also for no apparent reason, victims begin to seek causes and ways to prevent attacks.

A common effect of recurring attacks: victims begin to avoid situations they associate with past attacks. For instance, one woman suffered her first panic attack in a department store. She then became a catalogue shopper because she feared that being in a store caused her attacks.

Avoiding situations out of the fear of experiencing a panic attack in the situation is called **phobic avoidance.** This unexplained fear of ordinary places and activities can greatly restrict a person's ability to lead a normal, full life.

What is Fearing the Fear? Repeated severe attacks tend to create a reaction called **anticipatory anxiety,** which is simply the ongoing fear or worry of having another attack. This anticipatory anxiety can produce phobic avoidance in much the same way as an actual attack.

What is Agoraphobia? Agoraphobia is the term commonly used for any phobic avoidance. This is not only the fear of leaving home. It is the fear of being in any situation where escape would be difficult if a panic attack occurred. It can be the result of untreated panic disorder.

What Causes Panic Disorder? The attacks are not the result of mental weakness or personal failure.

The exact causes of panic disorder are not known. Scientific evidence suggests that biological and/or psychological factors play a role in the cause or maintenance of panic disorder and agoraphobia.

Whatever its causes (biological and/or psychological), panic disorder can be associated with such serious complications as depression, alcohol or drug abuse, and even suicide attempts.

Men and Women are both affected: Panic disorder affects both women and men. The best research to date suggests that women suffer panic disorder with agoraphobia about twice as often as men. But some experts suspect panic attacks in men may go unreported.

Large medical studies reveal that 1 to 2% of all adults will suffer panic disorder during their lives, while another 4 to 5% of adults report having panic attacks and agoraphobic symptoms, but don't qualify for a full diagnosis of panic disorder.

The twenties and thirties are high-risk age ranges for the onset of panic disorder. But it can occur in adolescence or advanced age. In general, the treatments now available reduce or completely prevent panic disorder symptoms, so that people can lead more normal or completely normal lives.

Where Can I Get Help? Organized groups of fellow sufferers can provide support to sufferers by educating both patients and their families about panic disorder and agoraphobia. These groups exist across Canada. You may find one by checking your local telephone book under "panic", "agoraphobia", "fear", "freedom from fear" or "phobia". However, it is important that the support obtained from organized groups adequately complements psychological and/or medication treatment.

Can Panic Disorder Be Treated? Yes. The following methods alone or in combination have been successful.

Cognitive therapy involves different learning techniques which help patients identify attitudes and perceptions that could lead to a panic attack and improve coping with panic attacks.

Behavioral therapy involves techniques that slowly expose patients (alone, accompanied by a therapist or other support person) to situations they fear, in a series of gradual, preplanned steps. This slow exposure helps patients better handle the feared situation and the feelings it provokes.

Medications can be used in the treatment of panic disorder. Xanax is the first and only medication approved in Canada for treating panic disorder.

Other medications have also shown efficacy. They include antianxiety agents, like Xanax, and antidepressants.

Because medications offer specific advantages, treatment should be customized to suit each patient.

What is Xanax? Xanax is an antianxiety and antipanic medication. Your doctor will slowly adjust dosage to your exact needs. Panic attacks can be prevented in most people who suffer panic disorder with doses between 2 and 6 mg/day. They notice a marked reduction in anticipatory anxiety and phobic avoidance behavior. Lower doses may be sufficient but higher doses may be necessary, as every person differs in the way their body absorbs, reacts to and eliminates medication.

Do not increase, decrease or stop the dose without consulting your doctor.

How Long will I Stay on Xanax? Your doctor will assess length of treatment. A course of treatment up to eight months along with other therapy is often recommended.

Take your medication as prescribed. Drug treatment alone may not completely relieve your condition. Follow all treatments prescribed by your doctor. After a while of being free of panic attacks, your doctor will consider a **very slow reduction in dose.** This slow reduction should be no more than 10% of the initial dose every 2 to 3 weeks.

Panic disorder may reappear. In this case, your doctor will decide on the most appropriate treatment.

What Side Effects May I Experience? The most common side effects of Xanax involve drowsiness, loss of balance and of coordination. They are generally observed during the first few days of treatment and thereafter decrease and may even disappear.

In rare instances, adverse behavioral effects such as stimulation, agitation, sleep disturbance and increased muscle spasticity may occur. Should you experience such effects, consult your doctor immediately.

What Precautions Should I Take?

- Take your medication regularly at the dose and time schedule prescribed by your doctor.
- Do not stop your treatment suddenly—as you may worsen your condition or even suffer a seizure. **Treatment with Xanax should be slowly tapered off,** and only under your doctor's close supervision.
- It is best to avoid drinking alcohol with Xanax. The combined effect of alcohol and Xanax will make you sleepier than either agent alone.
- **Do not take any over-the-counter drugs** (from your drug store) with Xanax—without checking with your pharmacist or doctor; the combination of drugs may harm you.
- Tell any other doctor, pharmacist or dentist that you are taking Xanax.
- Do not drive a car or operate machinery until you see how this medication affects you.
- Do not share this drug with anyone, including family or friends.
- Do not take Xanax if it is not prescribed for you.
- If you are pregnant (or think you may be pregnant), consult your doctor before taking Xanax or any other medication.

□ XYLOCAINE® JELLY 2%

Astra

Lidocaine HCl

Topical Anesthetic

Information for the Patient: Important information you should know about Xylocaine Jelly 2%: Before using Xylocaine Jelly, read this leaflet carefully. It contains general points about Xylocaine Jelly and should add to more specific advice from your doctor or pharmacist.

Please keep this leaflet to refer to until you have used up all your Xylocaine Jelly.

What is Xylocaine Jelly used for and how does it work? Xylocaine Jelly is the brand name for a topical anesthetic that contains the drug lidocaine. Topical anesthetics are used to produce a temporary loss of sensation or numbness on the area where they are applied.

Xylocaine Jelly produces a temporary loss of feeling in a part of your body before certain types of examinations done by your doctor. It may also be used to help relieve the pain from inflammation of the urinary bladder and the urethra. Xylocaine Jelly should start to work within 5 to 15 minutes after you apply it. The effect usually lasts 20 to 30 minutes.

What is in Xylocaine Jelly? Xylocaine Jelly contains lidocaine hydrochloride as the active ingredient. It also contains hydroxypropyl methylcellulose, and sodium hydroxide and/or hydrochloric acid.

Xylocaine Jelly in tubes also contains methylparaben and propylparaben.

Check with your doctor if you think you may be sensitive to any of the above ingredients.

What should I tell my doctor or pharmacist before using Xylocaine Jelly? Tell your doctor or pharmacist:

- about all health problems you have now and have had in the past;
- about other medicines you take, including ones you can buy without a prescription;
- if you have ever had a bad, unusual or allergic reaction to Xylocaine Jelly or any other medicines ending with ''caine'';
- if you think you may be allergic or sensitive to any ingredients in Xylocaine Jelly (see above);
- if there is an infection, skin rash, cut, or wound at or near the area you want to apply Xylocaine Jelly;
- if you have a skin condition that is severe or that covers a large area;
- if you have a severe heart, kidney or liver disease;
- if you are pregnant, plan to become pregnant or are breast-feeding.

How do I use Xylocaine Jelly properly? If this medicine is recommended by your doctor, be sure to follow the directions for use that have been given. If you are treating yourself, follow the directions below. Check with your doctor or pharmacist if you have any questions about your directions.

Xylocaine Jelly comes in a tube size of 30 mL with a special protective seal on the tube opening. If this seal is broken when you buy Xylocaine Jelly, exchange it at the pharmacy for a new tube. To break the protective seal the first time you use Xylocaine Jelly, firmly press the pointed end of the white cap into the seal.

The following are general guidelines for the maximum amount of Xylocaine Jelly that should be used without a doctor's advice. These guidelines apply only to otherwise healthy people. If you have a special skin or other condition that requires a doctor's supervision, ask your doctor about the maximum amount of jelly that you should use.

- If possible, clean the affected area well, before each application of jelly.
- Use the smallest amount of jelly needed to control your symptoms.

Dose for Adults: The dose of the jelly depends on the application site. For oral use of Xylocaine Jelly a dose of 20 mL (⅔ tube) is usually safe. For use in the urethra (i.e., before insertion of urinary catheters or urinary procedures), 5 to 20 mL (about ⅔ of a tube) is usually enough. A safe dose for use in the urethra and bladder is 40 mL (1⅓ tubes). No more than 4 doses should be given during a 24-hour period.

Dose for Children (under 12 years of age): The dose depends on the child's weight. No more than 3 mL of jelly per 10 kg of the child's weight should be used per dose. No more than 4 doses should be given during a 24-hour period.

- If you have any questions about how to measure the above amounts, be sure to ask your pharmacist.
- If you are treating yourself and your condition does not seem to improve within 3 to 5 days, check with your doctor about continuing to use Xylocaine Jelly.

Do not use Xylocaine Jelly more often or for a longer period of time than your doctor ordered, or than these package directions suggest.

Are there any side effects? Like any medication, Xylocaine Jelly may cause side effects in some people. The following symptoms may mean that you are extra sensitive to Xylocaine Jelly: redness, itching or swelling of your skin, hives, burning, stinging, or any other skin problems, swelling of the neck area, or any difficulty with breathing, not present before using this medicine.

Xylocaine Jelly can cause serious side effects if too much is applied. These include: drowsiness, numbness of your tongue, lightheadedness, ringing in your ears, blurred vision, vomiting, dizziness, unusually slow heartbeat, fainting, nervousness, unusual sweating, trembling or seizures.

The above are extremely rare and usually require large amounts of Xylocaine Jelly over a long period of time.

Be careful when Xylocaine Jelly is used in the mouth or throat since numbness in these areas may also interfere with swallowing. Numbness of the tongue or gum may also increase the danger of injury due to biting.

Medicines affect different people in different ways. Just because side effects have occurred in some patients, does not mean that you will

Xylocaine Jelly 2% (cont'd)

get them. If any side effects bother you, or if you experience any unusual effects while you are using Xylocaine Jelly, stop using it and check with your doctor or pharmacist as soon as possible.

What should I do in case of overdose? In case of Xylocaine Jelly overdose, or if you think you or anyone else is experiencing any of the above signs, telephone your doctor or go to the nearest hospital right away.

Where should I keep Xylocaine Jelly? Remember to **keep Xylocaine Jelly well out of the reach of children** when you are not using it.

Keep Xylocaine Jelly at room temperature. Protect from freezing. Do not keep Xylocaine Jelly in the bathroom medicine cabinet or other warm, moist places.

Do not use Xylocaine Jelly after the expiry date marked on the package.

Important Note: This leaflet alerts you to some of the times you should call your doctor. Other situations which cannot be predicted may arise. Nothing about this leaflet should stop you from calling your doctor with any questions or concerns you have about using Xylocaine Jelly.

☐ XYLOCAINE® OINTMENT 5%

Astra

Lidocaine

Topical Anesthetic

Information for the Patient: Important information you should know about Xylocaine Ointment 5%: Before using Xylocaine Ointment, read this leaflet carefully. It contains general points about Xylocaine Ointment and should add to more specific advice from your doctor or pharmacist.

Please keep this leaflet to refer to until you have used up all your Xylocaine Ointment.

What is Xylocaine Ointment used for and how does it work? Xylocaine Ointment is the brand name for a topical anesthetic that contains the drug lidocaine. Topical anesthetics are used to produce a temporary loss of sensation or numbness on the area where they are applied. Xylocaine Ointment is used to produce a temporary loss of feeling in a part of your body before certain types of examinations done by your doctor. It may also be used to help relieve the pain from skin abrasions, sunburn or other minor burns, sore nipples, insect bites and hemorrhoids.

Xylocaine Ointment should start to work within 5 minutes after you apply it.

What is in Xylocaine Ointment? Xylocaine Ointment contains lidocaine as the active ingredient. It also contains polyethylene glycol and propylene glycol.

Check with your doctor if you think you may be sensitive to any of the above ingredients.

What should I tell my doctor or pharmacist before using Xylocaine Ointment? Tell your doctor or pharmacist:

- about all health problems you have now or have had in the past;
- about other medicines you take, including ones you can buy without a prescription;
- if you have ever had a bad, unusual or allergic reaction to Xylocaine Ointment or any other medicines ending with ''caine'';
- if you think you may be allergic or sensitive to any ingredients in Xylocaine Ointment (see above);
- if you have bleeding hemorrhoids and wish to use the ointment in that area;
- if there is an infection, skin rash, cut or wound at or near the area you want to apply Xylocaine Ointment;
- if you have a skin condition that is severe or that covers a large area;
- if you have a severe heart, kidney or liver disease;
- if you are pregnant, plan to become pregnant or are breast-feeding.

How do I use Xylocaine Ointment properly? If this medicine is recommended by your doctor, be sure to follow the directions for use that have been given. If you are treating yourself, follow the directions below. Check with your doctor or pharmacist if you have any questions about your directions.

Xylocaine Ointment comes in tube sizes of 15 or 30 g with a special protective seal on the tube opening. If this seal is broken when you buy Xylocaine Ointment, exchange it at the pharmacy for a new tube. To break the protective seal the first time you use Xylocaine Ointment, firmly press the pointed end of the white cap into the seal.

The following are general guidelines for the maximum amount of Xylocaine Ointment that should be used without a doctor's advice. These guidelines apply only to otherwise healthy people. If you have a special skin or other condition that requires a doctor's supervision ask your doctor about the maximum amount of ointment that you should use.

- If possible, clean the affected area well, before each application of ointment.
- Use the smallest amount of ointment needed to control your symptoms.
- Apply a thin layer, using only enough to cover the affected area, and reapply it only when you need it.
- For broken or burned skin: To avoid touching the affected area with your hands, apply the ointment to a sterile gauze pad. Then secure the gauze pad in place over the affected area.
- If used on sore nipples it is essential that you clean the nipple area completely before each feeding. This will ensure that the baby does not take in any of this medicine.

Dose for Adults: Apply no more than 20 g of the ointment in a 24-hour period.

Dose for Children (under 12 years of age): The dose depends on the child's weight. No more than 1 g of ointment per 10 kg of the child's weight. No more than three doses should be given during a 24-hour period.

- If you have any questions about how to measure the above amounts, be sure to ask your pharmacist.
- If you are treating yourself and your condition does not seem to improve within 3 to 5 days, check with your doctor about continuing to use Xylocaine Ointment.

Do not use Xylocaine Ointment more often or for a longer period of time than your doctor ordered, or than these package directions suggest.

Are there any side effects? Like any medication, Xylocaine Ointment may cause side effects in some people. The following symptoms may mean that you are extra sensitive to Xylocaine Ointment: redness, itching or swelling of your skin, hives, burning, stinging, or any other skin problems, swelling of the neck area or any difficulty with breathing, not present before using this medicine.

Xylocaine Ointment can cause serious side effects if too much is applied. These include: drowsiness, numbness of your tongue, lightheadedness, ringing in your ears, blurred vision, vomiting, dizziness, unusually slow heartbeat, fainting, nervousness, unusual sweating, trembling or seizures.

The above are extremely rare and usually require large amounts of Xylocaine Ointment applied over a long period of time.

Be careful when Xylocaine Ointment is used in the mouth or throat since numbness in these areas may interfere with swallowing. Numbness of the tongue or gum may also increase the danger of injury due to biting.

Medicines affect different people in different ways. Just because side effects have occurred in some patients, does not mean that you will get them. If any side effects bother you, or if you experience any unusual effects while you are using Xylocaine Ointment, stop using it and check with your doctor or pharmacist as soon as possible.

What should I do in case of overdose? In case of Xylocaine Ointment overdose, or if you think you or anyone else is experiencing any of the above signs, telephone your doctor or go to the nearest hospital right away.

Where should I keep Xylocaine Ointment? Remember to **keep Xylocaine Ointment well out of the reach of children** when you are not using it.

Keep Xylocaine Ointment at room temperature. Protect from freezing. Do not keep Xylocaine Ointment in the bathroom medicine cabinet or other warm, moist places.

Do not use Xylocaine Ointment after the expiry date marked on the package.

Important Note: This leaflet alerts you to some of the times you should call your doctor. Other situations that cannot be predicted may arise. Nothing about this leaflet should stop you from calling your doctor with any questions or concerns you have about using Xylocaine Ointment.

□ XYLOCAINE® VISCOUS 2%

Astra

Lidocaine HCl

Topical Anesthetic

Information for the Patient: Important Information you should know about Xylocaine Viscous 2%: Before using Xylocaine Viscous, read this leaflet carefully. It contains general points about Xylocaine Viscous and should add to more specific advice from your doctor or pharmacist.

Please keep this leaflet to refer to until you have used up all your Xylocaine Viscous.

What is Xylocaine Viscous used for and how does it work? Xylocaine Viscous is the brand name for a topical anesthetic that contains the drug lidocaine. Topical anesthetics are used to produce a temporary loss of sensation or numbness on the area where they are applied. Xylocaine Viscous is used to produce a temporary loss of feeling in a part of your body before certain types of examinations done by your doctor.

Xylocaine Viscous could also:

- relieve the pain and discomfort of a sore throat, such as after the tonsils are removed;
- provide relief in other painful conditions of the mouth, throat or esophagus;
- cause a loss of feeling in the throat area, before certain types of examinations are performed by your doctor.

Xylocaine Viscous should start to work within 5 minutes after you apply it. The effect usually lasts 20 to 30 minutes.

What is in Xylocaine Viscous? Xylocaine Viscous contains lidocaine hydrochloride as the active ingredient. It also contains sodium carboxymethylcellulose, methylparaben, propylparaben, amaranth, and sodium hydroxide and/or hydrochloric acid.

Check with your doctor if you think you may be sensitive to any of the above ingredients.

What should I tell my doctor or pharmacist before using Xylocaine Viscous? Tell your doctor or pharmacist:

- about all health problems you have now or have had in the past;
- about other medicines you take, including ones you can buy without a prescription;
- if you have ever had a bad, unusual or allergic reaction to Xylocaine Viscous or any other medicines ending with "caine";
- if you think you may be allergic or sensitive to any ingredients in Xylocaine Viscous (see above);
- if there is an infection, skin rash, cut or wound at or near the area you want to apply Xylocaine Viscous;
- if you have a skin condition that is severe or that covers a large area;
- if you have a severe heart, kidney or liver disease;
- if you are pregnant, plan to become pregnant or are breast-feeding.

How Do I use Xylocaine Viscous properly? If this medicine is recommended by your doctor, be sure to follow the directions for use that have been given. If you are treating yourself, follow the directions below. Check with your doctor or pharmacist if you have any questions about your directions.

Xylocaine Viscous comes in bottles of 50 or 100 mL.

The following are general guidelines for the maximum amount of Xylocaine Viscous that should be used without a doctor's advice. These guidelines apply only to otherwise healthy people. If you have a special skin or other condition that requires a doctor's supervision, ask your doctor about the maximum amount of Xylocaine Viscous that you should use.

Shake the bottle well before using this medicine, so that you get an even dose each time you use it.

- Use the smallest amount needed to control your symptoms.
- When used in the mouth or throat try to increase the length of time Xylocaine Viscous is in contact with the affected area. For example, if you are treating mouth sores, swish the liquid around in your mouth and then spit it out. For a sore throat, roll the liquid around at the back of your throat or gargle, and then swallow the liquid.
- Do not drink water or other liquids right after you use Xylocaine Viscous, as this will decrease the amount of relief you get from the medicine.

Dose for Adults: The usual effective dose for adults is 5 to 10 mL at a time. Do not use this amount more than 6 times in a 24-hour period. An oral dose of 15 mL Xylocaine Viscous is usually safe.

Dose for Children (under 12 years of age): The dose depends on the child's weight. No more than 1 mL per 5 kg of the child's weight should be used per dose. Excess solution should be spat out. No more than 4 doses should be given during a 12- to 24-hour period.

Dose for Children (under 3 years of age): There may be special considerations for children under 3 years of age. **Do not** use Xylocaine Viscous for children in this age group without a doctor's supervision. The solution should be applied to the affected area with a cotton tip applicator. No more than 4 doses should be given during a 12- to 24-hour period.

- If you have any questions about how to measure the above amounts, be sure to ask your pharmacist.
- If you are treating yourself and your condition does not seem to improve within 3 to 5 days, check with your doctor about continuing to use Xylocaine Viscous.

Do not use Xylocaine Viscous more often or for a longer period of time than your doctor ordered, or than these package directions suggest.

Are there any side effects? Like any medication, Xylocaine Viscous may cause side effects in some people. The following symptoms may mean that you are extra sensitive to Xylocaine Viscous: redness, itching or swelling of your skin, hives, burning, stinging, or any other skin problems, swelling of the neck area or any difficulty with breathing, not present before using this medicine.

Xylocaine Viscous can cause serious side effects if too much is used. These include: drowsiness, numbness of your tongue, lightheadedness, ringing in your ears, blurred vision, vomiting, dizziness, unusually slow heartbeat, fainting, nervousness, unusual sweating, trembling or seizures.

The above are extremely rare and usually require large amounts of Xylocaine Viscous over a long period of time.

Be careful when Xylocaine Viscous is used in the mouth or throat since numbness in these areas may interfere with swallowing. Numbness of the tongue or gum may also increase the danger of injury due to biting.

Medicines affect different people in different ways. Just because side effects have occurred in some patients, does not mean that you will get them. If any side effects bother you, or if you experience any unusual effects while you are using Xylocaine Viscous, stop using it and check with your doctor or pharmacist as soon as possible.

What should I do in case of Overdose? In case of Xylocaine Viscous overdose, or if you think you or anyone else is experiencing any of the above signs, telephone your doctor or go to the nearest hospital right away.

Where should I keep Xylocaine Viscous? Remember to **keep Xylocaine Viscous well out of the reach of children** when you are not using it.

Keep Xylocaine Viscous at room temperature. Protect from freezing. Do not keep Xylocaine Viscous in the bathroom medicine cabinet or other warm, moist places.

Do not use Xylocaine Viscous after the expiry date marked on the package.

Important Note: This leaflet alerts you to some of the times you should call your doctor. Other situations that cannot be predicted may arise. Nothing about this leaflet should stop you from calling your doctor with any questions or concerns you have about using Xylocaine Viscous.

□ ZADITEN® Ⓟ

Novartis Pharmaceuticals

Ketotifen Fumarate

Pediatric Asthma Prophylactic—Antiallergic Agent

Information for the Patient/Parents: Zaditen is a new type of asthma medication which, when taken every day by mouth, may reduce the frequency, severity and duration of asthma symptoms or attacks in children.

Your physician will have prescribed Zaditen if your child's asthma is not well controlled, or to allow a reduction in your child's daily use of other antiasthma medications.

Zaditen is taken orally twice a day. **Zaditen does not provide relief for an acute attack,** so that inhaled bronchodilator medication will still be required for rapid relief of symptoms when a severe attack occurs.

Remember:

- In case of deterioration, you should contact your doctor immediately.

Zaditen (cont'd)

- This medication has been prescribed for your child's current medical problem only. It must not be given to other people or used for other problems unless otherwise directed by your doctor.
- Like all medicines, Zaditen should be kept out of reach of small children.
- Do not discontinue using this medicine without first consulting with your doctor, and if you would like more information about this medicine, ask your doctor, nurse, or pharmacist.

Before Using this Medicine: In order to decide on the best treatment, your doctor should be told if your child:
- has had any unusual or allergic reaction to Zaditen, benzoates or any of the product constituents (see Product Ingredients).
- is taking any oral antidiabetic medication.

Zaditen should not be used by anyone who is pregnant or breast-feeding a baby.

Proper Use of this Medicine: Since Zaditen interferes gradually with the chain of events leading to an asthma attack, at least 10 weeks of **continuous use** may be required before you and your physician can establish that it is effectively reducing your child's asthma symptoms.

Since Zaditen works continuously to prevent asthma attacks, you should find that in time your child's symptoms become less severe and inhaled bronchodilators are needed less frequently. As your child's asthma improves, it is necessary to keep taking Zaditen, and to consult your physician if and when you feel other asthma medications can be reduced.

Side Effects of this Medicine: Along with its beneficial effect, Zaditen may occasionally cause some unwanted effects. Side effects which may occur usually do not require medical attention; these include sedation, weight gain, rash, dryness of the mouth, dizziness, nausea and headaches. If any side effect becomes bothersome, consult with your physician.

The drowsiness which occurs in some patients at the start of treatment with Zaditen is usually temporary and disappears as your child adjusts to the medication. The drowsiness may be worse if Zaditen is taken with sedatives, hypnotics, antihistamines or alcohol. If drowsiness occurs, children may have trouble with activities requiring mental alertness, and older children should not drive a car or operate dangerous machinery.

Product Ingredients: Tablets: calcium hydrogen phosphate, ketotifen hydrogen fumarate, magnesium stearate and maize starch.

Syrup: alcohol, citric acid, ketotifen hydrogen fumarate, methyl p-hydroxybenzoate, propyl-p-hydroxybenzoate, sodium phosphate, sorbitol solution, sucrose, strawberry flavor and water.

□ ZANTAC® 75

Glaxo Wellcome

Ranitidine HCl

Histamine H_2-receptor Antagonist

Information for the Patient: What is Zantac 75? Zantac 75 is a new product which contains the nonprescription strength of ranitidine.

Zantac 75 relieves and treats the burning and discomfort of heartburn, acid indigestion and upset and sour stomach, providing fast and effective relief. Zantac 75 reduces and controls stomach acid for up to 12 hours, day or night.

Zantac 75 can also effectively prevent symptoms of heartburn and acid indigestion when taken 30 to 60 minutes before eating and drinking.

Zantac 75 works by reducing the production of excess stomach acid, which causes the burning and discomfort of heartburn and acid indigestion. This is what makes Zantac 75 different from antacids which only neutralize the acid in your stomach. Antacids do not reduce the production of excess stomach acid.

What symptoms does Zantac 75 relieve, treat, and prevent? Zantac 75 provides fast relief, treatment and prevention, day or night, of the following symptoms:
- heartburn
- acid indigestion
- upset or sour stomach

Should you take Zantac 75? Please consult your doctor or pharmacist before taking Zantac 75:
- if you are allergic to ranitidine or any of the ingredients in Zantac 75 tablets;
- if you have a stomach or duodenal ulcer;
- if you have difficulty swallowing or persistent abdominal discomfort;
- if you are taking nonsteroidal anti-inflammatory drugs (NSAIDs), because these medicines may be causing your symptoms;
- if you are pregnant or breast-feeding;
- if you have kidney problems;
- if you suffer from porphyria (a rare blood disorder);
- if you experience unintended weight loss associated with acid indigestion;
- if you are over 40 years of age and are experiencing new or recently changed symptoms of heartburn or acid indigestion;
- if you have any other illness, are taking any prescription medicines, are seeing a doctor regularly;
- if you are under 16 years of age.

How should you take Zantac 75 tablets? Adults and children 16 years and older: take 1 tablet as needed. If symptoms return, take another tablet. Do not take more than 2 tablets during a 24-hour period. If symptoms persist for more than 2 consecutive weeks, consult your doctor.

For prevention of symptoms brought on by consuming food and beverages, take 1 tablet 30 to 60 minutes before eating a meal that you expect to cause symptoms.

Zantac 75 and prescription doses of antacids should be taken 1 hour apart.

What can you do to help avoid symptoms?
- do not lie down soon after eating;
- if you are overweight, lose weight;
- if you smoke, stop or cut down;
- avoid or limit foods such as: caffeine (coffee, tea, or cola drinks), chocolate, spicy or fatty fried foods and alcohol.

How should you keep Zantac 75? Keep in a safe place out of the reach of children.

Store between 2 and 30°C.

What ingredients are in Zantac 75? Each tablet contains 75 mg of ranitidine, as ranitidine hydrochloride. Nonmedicinal ingredients: microcrystalline cellulose, magnesium stearate, hydroxypropyl methylcellulose, titanium dioxide, iron oxide and triacetin. Zantac 75 is sodium- and sugar-free.

Questions? Speak to your pharmacist, doctor, or call if you have any questions about Zantac 75: 1-800-661-4659.

□ ZESTRIL® Ⓟ

Zeneca

Lisinopril

Angiotensin Converting Enzyme Inhibitor

Information for the Patient: Zestril (active ingredient lisinopril) (pronounced Lie-sin-o-pril) belongs to a class of medicines called angiotensin converting enzyme inhibitors (ACE inhibitors for short).

Zestril is used to treat high blood pressure, heart failure and patients who have suffered a heart attack. This medicine and dosage was prescribed for your particular condition.

Zestril affects angiotensin II in your body, and relaxes your blood vessels so that blood can flow much more easily. As a result, less work is placed on the heart and less pressure is exerted on the blood vessels. This is especially important in the patients who are being treated for heart attack and heart failure.

It is important to treat high blood pressure because, if left untreated, it can damage organs such as the heart, kidneys, eyes and brain. Zestril is also used to treat heart failure; a condition when the heart cannot pump efficiently to meet all the demands of the body. Patients who have recently had a heart attack can benefit from Zestril as well because it has been shown to reduce complications associated with heart attack.

You cannot feel high blood pressure, so it is important to take Zestril regularly, exactly as your physician has prescribed. Remember that treatment of blood pressure is a long term process and only regular treatment along with lifestyle changes can benefit you.

Before You Start Taking Zestril: Your physician would have considered many things before prescribing Zestril for you. If any of the following apply to you, it is important that your physician and pharmacist knows. Tell your physician and pharmacist if you:

- or a family member have ever had an allergic reaction to any medication (prescription or non prescription)
- have ever had an allergic reaction to Zestril or any of its ingredients or to any other ACE inhibitors—even someone in your family
- you are pregnant, breast-feeding or even planning to become pregnant. All ACE inhibitors can harm the baby, so it is important that your physician knows
- have had heart problems (for example aortic stenosis or hypertrophic cardiomyopathy (HOCM))
- are taking other drugs for blood pressure or any other conditions - even the ones that don't need a prescription. This is important because some medicines may react with Zestril and lessen the benefit you achieve
- have low blood pressure. You would notice this as faintness or dizziness
- are taking salt substitutes
- have had kidney problems (for example renal artery stenosis)
- once you start taking Zestril, let your doctor or dentist know before surgery. Always keep your pharmacist informed of the medications you are taking

How should I take Zestril? Zestril has a long duration of action, so it is taken once daily. It is important to take Zestril at approximately the same time of day. It may be easier for you to remember if you take it with a specific meal. Take the required dose with a glass of water.

If you miss a dose—take it as soon as you remember. However, if it is near the time for your next dose, skip the missed pill and go back to your regular schedule. **Do not double your doses.**

Do not stop taking the medicine unless your physician asks you to. Zestril **is not intended for children**—it can harm them. Keep all medicines safely out of reach of children.

How should I store Zestril? Store Zestril in a dry area at room temperature. Kitchens and bathrooms are **not** good places to store medicines in general. Keep Zestril and all other medicines safely out of reach of children. **There is enough medicine in each tablet to harm a child.**

What side effects can I expect? As with all medicines, you may experience some undesirable effects. It is important for you to be informed as to what you may expect. You may not even experience any of these, nevertheless it is important for you to pay attention to your body and be informed.

Some effects are common and mild - usually go away with continued treatment with Zestril:

- the first dose may cause a greater fall in blood pressure than will occur with continued treatment. You may notice this as faintness or dizziness, especially after standing up quickly or climbing stairs too quickly
- headache
- diarrhea
- in some people, Zestril may cause drowsiness or tiredness. **Do not operate a vehicle or machinery until you know how you react to Zestril**
- nausea
- cough

If any of these become especially bothersome, then tell your physician. There are options available to lessen these effects.

Other possible, but less frequent effects may include:

- a feeling of weakness
- vomiting
- rash
- feeling more tired than usual during the day or difficulty going to sleep at night
- numbness or tingling in the fingers and toes
- vertigo—meaning that you feel as though you or your surroundings are spinning around

Some rare effects may be noticed. These effects usually take a long time to develop. Tell your physician immediately if you notice any of the following:

- jaundice (yellow eyes or skin)
- severe abdominal pain
- less urine production than usual or no urine at all
- indigestion
- flu like symptoms (muscle aches, pains, sore throat, fever, general unwellness) that persist for long periods of time

Rarely, some patients cannot tolerate ACE inhibitors in general even though your physician has carefully considered many factors. Stop taking Zestril immediately and seek medical attention if:

- you experience swelling of the face, hands, feet, ankles, tongue or throat
- you develop difficulty in breathing **with or without** swelling of the face, hands, feet, ankles, tongue or throat
- severe rash with raised lumps

What are the ingredients in the Zestril tablets? Each tablet of Zestril contains lisinopril (active ingredient) and various inactive ingredients. These are: calcium hydrogen phosphate, cornstarch, magnesium stearate, mannitol, pregelatinized cornstarch and red iron oxide.

Who makes your medicine? Your medicine is made by Zeneca Pharmaceuticals, 2505 Meadowvale Blvd., Mississauga, Ont., L5N 5R7.

The information in this leaflet applies only to your medicine, Zestril. It gives you important information but it can't tell you everything. **If you have questions, or are not sure about anything, ask your pharmacist or doctor.**

☐ ZOCOR® Ⓟ

Frosst

Simvastatin

Lipid Metabolism Regulator

Information for the Patient: The product monograph is available on request to the physician and pharmacist only.

Zocor is the brand name of Merck Frosst Canada Inc. for the substance—simvastatin, available **only on prescription** from your physician. Simvastatin is one of a class of medicines known as HMG-CoA reductase **inhibitors**. They **inhibit**, in other words block, an enzyme that is necessary for the body to make cholesterol. In this way, less cholesterol is produced in the liver.

When it is necessary to lower cholesterol, physicians usually try to control the condition, known as hypercholesterolemia, with a carefully supervised diet. Also your physician may recommend other measures such as exercise and weight control. Medicines like this one are prescribed **along with**, and **not as a substitute for**, a special diet and other measures. Simvastatin is used to lower the levels of cholesterol (particularly Low Density Lipoprotein (LDL) cholesterol) in the blood.

Elevated cholesterol can cause coronary heart disease (CHD) by clogging the blood vessels which carry oxygen and nutrients to the heart. If you have coronary heart disease (CHD) and elevated cholesterol levels, your physician has prescribed Zocor to help prolong your life, to lessen the risk of a heart attack, and to decrease the risk of needing a surgical procedure to increase the blood flow to your heart. Although, you should be aware that the exact effects of Zocor in the prevention of heart attacks, blood vessel disease, or heart disease **in patients who have never experienced these conditions,** are not yet known. However studies and investigation are proceeding.

Remember: This medicine is prescribed for the particular condition that you have. **Do not give this medicine to other people, nor use it for any other condition.**

Do not use outdated medicine.

Store your tablets in a tightly closed container away from heat and direct light. Keep all medicines out of the reach of children.

Read the following information carefully. **If you need any explanations, or further information, ask your physician or pharmacist.**

Before Taking This Medicine: This medicine may not be suitable for certain people. So, tell your physician if you think **any** of the following applies to you:

- You have previously taken simvastatin or any other medication in the same class—example, fluvastatin (Lescol), lovastatin (Mevacor) or pravastatin (Pravachol)—and were allergic, or reacted badly to it.
- **You are pregnant or intend to become pregnant.** This medicine should **not** be used during pregnancy.
- You are breast-feeding or intend to breast-feed.
- You have liver disease.

Your physician also needs to know if you are taking any other medication, whether on prescription or otherwise. It is particularly important to inform your physician if you are taking:

- cyclosporine (Sandimmune), gemfibrozil (Lopid), lipid-lowering doses of niacin (nicotinic acid), corticosteroids, an anticoagulant (drugs that prevent blood clots, such as warfarin [Warfilone]), digoxin, erythromycin, antifungal agents (itraconazole) or nefazodone (Serzone).

The safety of this medicine has not been established in adolescents and children.

Zocor (cont'd)

Proper Use Of This Medicine:
- Take this medicine **exactly** as your physician ordered. It is usually recommended as a single dose with the evening meal.
- If you miss taking a tablet at its usual time, take it as soon as possible. But, if it is too close to the time of your next dose: take only the prescribed dose at the appointed time. **Do not take a double dose.**
- Carefully follow any measures that your physician has recommended for diet, exercise or weight control.
- It is important to continue taking the tablets as instructed. **Do not alter the dosage or stop taking the medicine without consulting your physician.**
- Keep your appointments regularly with your physician so that your blood can be tested and your progress checked at proper intervals.
- Avoid drinking large quantities of alcohol.
- **Do not start taking any other medicines** unless you have discussed the matter with your physician.
- Let your physician know if you suffer a severe injury, or severe infection.
- If you have to undergo any kind of surgery, tell your physician about the planned surgery; and also inform the physician in charge that you are taking this medicine.
- Store your tablets at room temperature (15 to 30°C), in a tightly closed container, away from heat and direct light, and out of damp places, such as the bathroom or kitchen.

Side Effects Of This Medicine—And What You Should Do: Along with its intended action, any medication may cause unwanted effects. Most people do not have any problem when taking this medicine; but if you notice any of the following reactions, **check with your physician as soon as possible:** aching muscles, muscle cramps, tiredness or weakness; fever; blurred vision.

Some other side effects that may occur, generally do not require medical attention, and may come and go during treatment. But if any of the following persist or become troublesome, **do check with your physician or pharmacist:** constipation, diarrhea, gas, stomach upset, nausea; pain in the abdomen; headache; skin rash.

Some people may have other reactions. If you notice **any unusual effect** check with your physician or pharmacist.

Ingredients: Active ingredients: Each tablet of Zocor contains simvastatin. It comes in 4 strengths: 5 mg (buff), 10 mg (peach), 20 mg (tan) and 40 mg (brick red).

Nonmedicinal ingredients: ascorbic acid, butylated hydroxyanisole, citric acid, hydroxypropyl cellulose, lactose, magnesium stearate, methylcellulose, microcrystalline cellulose, pregelatinized starch, red ferric oxide (10, 20 and 40 mg only), talc, titanium dioxide and yellow ferric oxide (5, 10 and 20 mg only).

□ ZOFRAN® Ⓟ

Glaxo Wellcome

Ondansetron HCl Dihydrate

Antiemetic

Information for the Patient: What you should know about Zofran Tablets and Oral Solution: Please read this leaflet carefully before you start to take your medicine.

This provides a summary of the information available on your medicine. For further information or advice, ask your doctor or pharmacist.

The Name of Your Medicine: The name of your medicine is Zofran (ondansetron hydrochloride dihydrate). This medicine is one of a group called antiemetics.

Zofran can only be obtained with a prescription from your doctor.

The Purpose of Your Medicine: Zofran is intended to prevent the nausea (feeling of sickness) and vomiting, which can occur while undergoing cancer chemotherapy and radiotherapy, or after receiving general anaesthesia during an operation.

These treatments are thought to cause the release of a natural substance (serotonin), which can cause you to feel sick and to vomit. Zofran stops this from happening and help prevent you from vomiting or feeling sick.

The Use of this Medicine During Pregnancy and Breast-feeding: As a normal precaution, this medicine should not be taken if you are pregnant, if you are likely to become pregnant or if you are breast feeding a baby. However, there may be circumstances when your doctor advises you to use this medicine during pregnancy.

How to Take Your Medicine: The label on the container of your medicine should tell you how often to take your medicine and how many tablets or teaspoons you should take each time. If not, or if you are not sure, consult your doctor or pharmacist.

Do not take more tablets or oral solution, or take your medicine more often than your doctor prescribes. If, however you vomit within 1 hour of taking your medicine, you should take the same amount of medicine again. If vomiting persists, consult your doctor.

After Taking Your Medicine: If you experience wheezing and tightness of the chest, heart throbbing, swelling of eyelids, face or lips, or develop a skin rash, skin lumps or hives, **contact your doctor immediately. Do not take any more medicine unless your doctor tells you to do so.**

You may experience headaches, a feeling of warmness in the head and stomach, flushing or constipation, while taking Zofran. There is no need to stop taking your medicine, but you should tell your doctor about these symptoms at your next visit.

If your nausea (feeling of sickness) or vomiting do not improve while taking Zofran, consult your doctor for further advice.

If you feel unwell or have any symptoms that you do not understand, you should contact your doctor immediately.

What to Do if an Overdosage is Taken: In the event you accidentally take more tablets or teaspoons than prescribed, immediately contact your doctor or hospital emergency department or nearest poison control centre.

Storing Your Medicine: Keep your medicine in a safe place where children cannot reach it. Your medicine may harm them.

Your Zofran tablets should be kept at room temperature in a well closed container and protected from light. Do not refrigerate or freeze.

Your Zofran oral solution should be kept in its bottle, standing up at room temperature. Do not refrigerate or freeze. Do not lay the bottle on its side.

What to Do if You Miss a Dose: If you miss a dose and do not feel sick, take the next dose when it is due.

If you forget to take your medicine and feel sick or vomit, take a dose as soon as possible.

What to Do if You Stop Your Medicine: If your doctor decides to stop the treatment, do not keep any left over medicine unless your doctor tells you to.

What is in Your Medicine: Tablets: The tablets are supplied in 2 strengths, one contains 4 mg of ondansetron and the other contains 8 mg of ondansetron. Your doctor will decide which strength you need. These tablets also contain lactose, microcrystalline cellulose, pregelatinized starch, magnesium stearate, methyl hydroxypropyl cellulose and a small amount of a coloring agent called Opaspray or Opadry yellow.

Oral Solution: The oral solution is supplied in one strength, 4 mg of ondansetron per teaspoon, in bottles. Your doctor will decide how many teaspoons you need. The oral solution also contains citric acid, sodium benzoate, sodium citrate dihydrate and strawberry flavor. Zofran oral solution is sugar-free and is sweetened with sorbitol.

A Reminder: Remember: This medicine is for you. Only a doctor can prescribe it for you. Never give it to someone else. It may harm them even if their symptoms are the same as yours.

Further Information: This leaflet does not contain the complete information about your medicine. If any questions remain unanswered or you are not sure about something, you should ask your doctor or pharmacist.

You may want to read this leaflet again. **Please do not throw it away** until you have finished your medicine.

□ ZOLADEX® Ⓟ

Zeneca

Goserelin Acetate

LHRH Analog

Information for the Patient: Keep medications out of the reach of children.

Zoladex (goserelin acetate) is a drug containing 3.6 mg of goserelin in a hard, cream-colored, rod-shaped depot. Your doctor has prescribed Zoladex for you and the information provided below is intended to assist you in the effective use of this treatment. This information is not intended to supersede the instructions given by your doctor, since each case is unique; therefore, follow his or her instructions carefully. If you experience any difficulties, contact your doctor or pharmacist.

Zoladex treatment, given once every 28 days, results in suppression of your sex hormones. Any complaints you experience may be related to this hormone-suppressing action of Zoladex. These complaints may include hot flushes and reduction in sex drive. If these continue to make you feel uncomfortable, consult your doctor.

Suppression of your sex hormones can also result in a small loss of mineral from bone, some of which may not be reversible. For the treatment of endometriosis, this small loss of mineral from bone should not be important.

There are certain conditions that may increase the possibility of the thinning of your bones when you take a drug such as Zoladex. They are:

- family history of severe osteoporosis (thinning of the bones with fractures);
- taking other medications that can cause thinning of the bones.

You should discuss the possibility of osteoporosis or thinning of the bones with your physician before starting Zoladex. You should also be aware that repeat treatments are not recommended since they may put you at greater risk of bone thinning particularly if you have the above conditions.

Occasionally, a local skin reaction may occur at the injection site such as itching, redness, burning and swelling. These reactions generally are mild and disappear after a few days. If they get worse or do not go away, tell your doctor.

Premenopausal Women: Menstruation stops with the monthly depot of Zoladex. If regular menstruation persists, notify your doctor. If a monthly Zoladex depot is missed, breakthrough menstrual bleeding may occur.

You should not use Zoladex if you have ever had an allergic reaction to Zoladex, if you are pregnant, breast-feeding or have undiagnosed abnormal vaginal bleeding. Contraception is not ensured during treatment with Zoladex. Therefore, pregnancy must be avoided by the use of nonhormonal methods of contraception. Following the last Zoladex depot, nonhormonal contraception must be continued until the return of menses or for at least 12 weeks (see Contraindications).

Cancer Patients: Contact your doctor immediately if you develop: severe increased pain, numbness or weakness of the limbs, or persistent difficulty in urinating (prostate cancer).

Always Remember:

1. Check with your doctor or pharmacist before taking any other drugs, including nonprescription drugs (for colds, nausea, etc.).
2. If you forget to have Zoladex administered on the specified day, generally once every 28 days, have it administered as soon as you can.
3. It is very important your doctor checks your progress at regular medical visits. Don't stop your Zoladex treatment if you feel better; consult your doctor before you decide to change your treatment.
4. If you need more information, ask your doctor.

☐ ZOLADEX® LA 🄿

Zeneca

Goserelin Acetate

Luteinizing Hormone-Releasing Hormone Analog

Information for the Patient: Keep medications out of the reach of children.

Zoladex LA (goserelin acetate) is a drug containing 10.8 mg of goserelin in a hard, cream-colored, rod-shaped depot. Your doctor has prescribed Zoladex LA for you and the information provided below is intended to assist you in the effective use of this treatment. This information is not intended to supersede the instructions given by your doctor, since each case is unique; therefore, follow his or her instructions carefully. If you experience any difficulties, contact your doctor or pharmacist.

Zoladex LA treatment, given once every 12 weeks, results in suppression of your sex hormones. Any complaints you experience may be related to this hormone-suppressing action of Zoladex LA. These complaints may include hot flushes, swollen or tender breasts and reduction in sex drive.

As with all medicines, other undesirable events are sometimes experienced. With Zoladex LA these may include:

- Skin rashes
- Pains in your joints

When you first start receiving Zoladex LA you may feel some pain in your bones. If this happens tell your doctor and you may be given something for this. Very occasionally you may have trouble passing urine or experience lower back pain. If this happens, tell your doctor and you may be given something for this.

If these continue to make you feel uncomfortable, consult your doctor.

Occasionally, a local skin reaction may occur at the injection site such as itching, redness, burning and swelling. These reactions generally are mild and disappear after a few days. If they get worse or do not go away, tell your doctor.

Contact your doctor immediately if you develop: severe increased pain, numbness or weakness of the limbs, or persistent difficulty in urinating.

Always remember:

1. Check with your doctor or pharmacist before taking any other drugs, including nonprescription drugs (for colds, nausea, etc.).
2. If you forget to have Zoladex LA administered on the specified day, once every 12 weeks, have it administered as soon as you can.
3. It is very important your doctor checks your progress at regular medical visits. Don't stop your Zoladex LA treatment if you feel better, consult your doctor before you decide to change your treatment.
4. If you need more information, ask your doctor.

☐ ZOLOFT™ 🄿

Pfizer

Sertraline HCl

Antidepressant—Antipanic—Antiobsessional Agent

Information for the Patient: Please read this information before you start to take your medicine, even if you have taken this drug before.

What you should know about Zoloft: Zoloft (sertraline hydrochloride) belongs to a family of medicines called SSRIs; **S**elective **S**erotonin **R**euptake **I**nhibitors.

Zoloft has been prescribed to you by your doctor to relieve your symptoms of depression, panic disorder or obsessive-compulsive disorder.

What you should tell your doctor before taking Zoloft: All your medical conditions, including a history of seizures, liver or kidney disease; Any medications (prescription or nonprescription) which you are taking especially monoamine oxidase inhibitor antidepressants (e.g., phenelzine sulfate, tranylcypromine sulfate or moclobemide) or any other antidepressants, drugs used to treat diabetes, drugs used to thin the blood (anticoagulants) or drugs containing tryptophan; If you are pregnant or thinking about becoming pregnant, or if you are breast-feeding; Your habits concerning alcohol consumption.

How to take Zoloft: It is very important for you to take Zoloft exactly as your doctor has instructed. The usual starting dose is 50 mg of Zoloft/day for depression and obsessive-compulsive disorder. If you are taking Zoloft for panic disorder, your doctor may start you at 25 mg/day. Your doctor may decide to increase the dose up to 200 mg/day.

Never increase the amount of Zoloft you are taking unless your doctor tells you to. You should continue to take your medicine even if you do not feel better, as it may take approximately 4 weeks for your medicine to work.

Zoloft should be taken with food; either in the morning or evening. You should swallow the capsule whole; do not chew it.

Keep taking Zoloft until your doctor tells you to stop. Your doctor may tell you to continue to take your medicine for several months. Continue to follow your doctor's instructions.

If you miss taking a dose of Zoloft, do not worry, just take the next dose when you normally do. Do not take 2 doses at once. It is important to discuss with your doctor what you should do if you miss several doses of Zoloft.

When not to use Zoloft: Do not use Zoloft if you are allergic to it or to any of the components of its formulation (see list of components at the end of this section). Stop taking the drug and contact your doctor immediately if you experience an allergic reaction or any severe or unusual side effect.

Precautions when taking Zoloft: You may experience some side effects such as nausea, headache, dry mouth, diarrhea, sleep disturbance and loss of appetite. Other effects may include drowsiness, sexual prob-

Zoloft (cont'd)

lems, nervousness and tremor. Consult your doctor if you experience these or other side effects, as the dose may have to be adjusted.

Zoloft does not usually affect people's normal activities. However, some people feel sleepy while taking it, in which case they should not drive or operate machinery. Avoid alcoholic drinks while taking Zoloft.

What to do in case of overdose: If you have taken a large number of capsules all at once, contact either your doctor, hospital emergency department or nearest Poison Control Centre immediately, even though you may not feel sick.

How to store Zoloft: Store at room temperature (15 to 30°C) in a dry place. Keep the container tightly closed. Keep out of reach of children. If your doctor decides to stop Zoloft treatment, return any leftover medicine to your pharmacist to safely dispose of it. Keep it only if your doctor tells you to do so.

What Zoloft contains: Zoloft is available as 25 mg (yellow capsule), 50 mg (white and yellow capsule) and 100 mg (orange capsule). Sertraline is the active ingredient. Nonmedicinal ingredients include: cornstarch; lactose (anhydrous); magnesium stearate; sodium lauryl sulfate. Capsule shells contain gelatin, titanium dioxide and dye D&C Yellow No. 10. Capsules 25 and 50 mg also contain dye FD&C Yellow No. 6 and capsules 100 mg also contain dye FD&C No. 40. The capsules do not contain tartrazine or gluten.

Who manufactures Zoloft: Zoloft capsules are manufactured by: Pfizer Canada Inc.

Reminder: This medicine has been prescribed only for you. Do not give it to anybody else. If you have any further questions, please ask your doctor or pharmacist.

☐ ZOVIRAX® Oral ℞

Glaxo Wellcome

Acyclovir

Antiviral Agent

Information for the Patient: Herpes Zoster (shingles) and Genital Herpes: Treatment: If your physician has prescribed a course of Zovirax for the treatment of a herpes, zoster (shingles) infection, it is important to understand that the drug must be taken as early as possible after the onset of the disease. This is because the herpes virus multiplies in and eventually destroys affected skin cells. Zovirax stops the virus multiplying and therefore from spreading to neighbouring healthy cells. It cannot replace a cell which has been damaged by the multiplying virus, but it will facilitate the process of healing.

Suppression of Recurrences: If your physician suggested continuous use of Zovirax to prevent frequent recurrences of genital herpes infections, you should follow dosing instructions carefully. The objective is to keep enough of the drug in the body at all times to prevent the herpes virus from multiplying. Your physician will try to prescribe the minimum dose required to do this in your case and may therefore increase or decrease your dose during the first few weeks. Follow your physician's instruction carefully to ensure that you get the best possible response to treatment.

Safety: Short-Term: The safety of Zovirax in short-term use has been well studied. As with any widely prescribed medication, adverse events in association with its use are reported from time to time. The common ones are listed below; they have rarely been severe enough to make it necessary to stop taking the drug.

Headache, nausea, diarrhea, skin rash and upset stomach.

If you experience anything unusual, while you are receiving treatment with Zovirax, you should report it to your physician.

A complete listing of adverse events so far reported is contained in the Product Monograph supplied to your physician.

Long-Term: Your physician may periodically stop your drug therapy in order to reassess your need for continuous treatment. As with any new drug, the effect of long-term use in humans has not been fully assessed. Prudence is therefore suggested when choosing continuous, long-term therapy with Zovirax. Suppression of recurrent genital herpes is therefore only recommended in those who are severely affected.

Pregnancy: You should consult your doctor if you become pregnant or intend to become pregnant or intend to breast-feed while taking Zovirax.

Reproductive Toxicity: Although decreased sperm counts in animals treated with high doses, and breaks in chromosomes in high concentrations of acyclovir in the test tube, have been seen, these effects did not occur in humans given doses of 800 to 1 000 mg/day for at least 6 months.

General Information: Herpes infections cause painful blisters on the skin and mucous membranes. The fluid in these blisters contains the virus which causes the disease. The infection is easily spread either to yourself or other people. If you touch your skin sores, wash your hands immediately and do not touch other parts of your body until you have done so. Especially avoid intimate contact with others when the disease is visible. Medication should not be shared with others. The prescribed dosage should not be exceeded. Zovirax does not eliminate dormant viruses. Some patients experience increased severity of the first episode of genital herpes after stopping treatment.

For more information about Zovirax and herpes infections, please consult your physician or pharmacist.

Chickenpox—Information for Parents: Common in childhood and contagious: Chickenpox is one of the most **common** infections in otherwise healthy children. It usually occurs in children before the age of 10, but anyone who has never had chickenpox can become infected—irrespective of age.

Chickenpox is caused by a virus called ''varicella zoster'' and it is **highly contagious.** Family members often give the disease to each other. For reasons that are not known, often the second or third child who catches it from a brother or sister will be sicker than the first child. Also, the disease tends to be more severe in teenagers than in younger children.

The disease can be mild with few pox or mild symptoms—alternatively, it could be severe with hundreds of pox. The pox can occur both outside and inside the body. There is **no way to predict the severity** of chickenpox.

Recognizing the Disease: The early symptoms of chickenpox may be vague and could include fever, itching, headache, aching joints and muscles, sore throat, general malaise: loss of appetite, listlessness and irritability. After that, itchy, small, red spots (the ''pox'') appears, and become blisters within a few hours. New spots and blisters continue to appear for about 5 days. The blisters start to dry up and within 6 or 7 days turn into scabs.

Incubation: Not all who are exposed come down with the disease. The incubation period may extend from 1 to 3 weeks after exposure. The virus is spread through the air when: (1) a person with chickenpox scratches the blisters, allowing the virus to become airborne: or (2) a person with chickenpox coughs or sneezes within close contact of others. The disease is most contagious shortly before the rash appears, through the early stages of the rash, until all the blisters have dried. A patient is **not** contagious once all the blisters have become scabs.

Early Consultation With Your Physician: If you think your child has been exposed to chickenpox, be on the lookout for symptoms described above. **At the first sign of rash, call your physician**. There are more treatment options available when the infection is caught this early. Your physician may prescribe a medication which could offer the child less discomfort, and possibly a faster recovery.

Tips to Bear in Mind: It is important to follow the physician's orders with all medications prescribed—even if the patient seems to feel better. **Never use medications containing acetylsalicylic acid (ASA) in children with fever and chickenpox.** Acetaminophen may be given to reduce fever.

The rash can be soothed by coating with an anti-itch product such as calamine, or other medications that your physician recommends. The discomfort of itching can be relieved temporarily by baths and wet compresses. Bathing daily with soap and water can also help prevent infection. **Do not use antiseptics** on the sores; rather **consult your physician**, who might prescribe an antibiotic if necessary. Since infection or scarring can occur at scratch sites, it is important to discourage scratching and spreading of virus particles through the air. Keep the rash clean and dry. If possible keep the nails cut short, cover the hands and feet with cotton gloves, mitts or socks to discourage children scratching at sleep time.

Possible Complications: Complications are rare in the healthy child. The people who are at greatest risk of complications are: pregnant women, newborn babies, or people being treated for cancer, arthritis, asthma, or after organ transplants—where medicine is suppressing their immune systems. If anyone in your family falls within these groups **inform your physician** so that the preventive measures can be taken.

☐ ZYPREXA® ℞

Lilly

Olanzapine

Antipsychotic

Information for the Patient: Why Zyprexa? The name of your medicine is Zyprexa and your doctor has prescribed it to help relieve the symptoms that are bothering you. Zyprexa can help to control your symptoms and reduce the risk of relapse. Although Zyprexa cannot cure your symptoms, it can help you keep them under control as you continue your treatment.

This information should answer some of the questions you may have and help you understand how to take Zyprexa to get the best results. If you have any concerns about taking this medicine, talk to your doctor or pharmacist.

Keep this information with your medicine in case you need to read it again.

What is Zyprexa? Zyprexa contains the active ingredient called olanzapine. Zyprexa belongs to a group of medicines called antipsychotics. Zyprexa is used to treat symptoms of schizophrenia and related psychotic disorders. Schizophrenia may cause symptoms such as hallucinations (e.g., hearing, seeing, or sensing things which are not there), delusions, unusual suspiciousness, and emotional withdrawal. People with schizophrenia may also feel depressed, anxious or tense.

Your doctor may have prescribed Zyprexa for another reason. Ask your doctor if you have any questions about why Zyprexa has been prescribed for you.

What should I do before starting Zyprexa? Before starting Zyprexa and to get the best possible treatment, be sure to tell your doctor if you:

- are pregnant or breast-feeding
- have had an allergic reaction to any medicine which you have taken previously to treat your current condition
- are a smoker
- suffer from lactose intolerance because Zyprexa tablets contain lactose
- have ever had blackouts or seizures
- are taking any other medicines (prescriptions or over-the-counter medicines)
- drink alcoholic beverages or use drugs
- exercise vigorously or work in hot or sunny places
- have a history of liver problems, hepatitis, or jaundice
- have prostate problems
- have intestinal congestion (paralytic ileus)
- have raised pressure within the eye (glaucoma).

It is important for your doctor to have this information before prescribing your treatment and dosage.

How should I take Zyprexa? The most important thing about taking Zyprexa is to take it the way your doctor has prescribed—the right dose, every day. Your doctor has decided on the best dosage for you based on your individual situation and needs. Your doctor may increase or decrease your dose depending on your response.

Although Zyprexa cannot cure your condition, it can help relieve your symptoms. If your symptoms improve or disappear, it is probably because your treatment is working. Studies have shown that, after coming off medication, a relapse of symptoms occurs in about 2 out of 3 patients and is more than double that of patients staying on their medication. That is why it is so important to keep taking Zyprexa, even after your symptoms have improved or disappeared. Zyprexa should be taken for as long as you and your doctor believe it is helping you.

Do not take Zyprexa if you have had an allergic reaction to Zyprexa or any of the ingredients listed at the end of this information. Signs of allergic reaction may include a skin rash, itching, shortness of breath or swelling of the face, lips or tongue.

Zyprexa tablets should be swallowed whole with a glass of water. Zyprexa tablets can be taken with or without food.

Take your prescribed dose at the same time each day. If you miss a dose of Zyprexa by a few hours, take the dose when you remember. If most of the day has passed, wait until your next scheduled dose and try not to miss any more. **Do not take 2 doses at once.** If you take too much, immediately contact your doctor or go to your nearest hospital emergency department. Show the doctor your bottle of tablets. Do this even if there are no signs of discomfort or poisoning. The most common signs if you have taken too much Zyprexa are drowsiness and slurred speech.

Can I take other medicines with Zyprexa? Tell all doctors, dentists and pharmacists who are treating you that you are taking Zyprexa.

Tell your doctor or pharmacist that you are taking Zyprexa before you start taking any new medicines.

A combination of Zyprexa with the following medicines might make you feel drowsy:

- medicines taken for anxiety or to help you sleep
- medicines taken for depression

The effects of alcohol could be made worse while taking Zyprexa. It is recommended that you **do not** drink alcohol while taking Zyprexa.

Do not give Zyprexa to anyone else. Your doctor has prescribed it for you and your condition.

Does Zyprexa cause side effects? Like other medicines, Zyprexa can cause some side effects. These side effects are most likely to be minor and temporary. However, some may be serious and need medical attention. Many of the side effects are dose related, so it is important not to exceed your prescribed dose. The most common side effects of Zyprexa are:

- drowsiness
- weight gain
- dizziness
- increased appetite
- fluid retention
- constipation
- dry mouth
- a feeling of restlessness (akathisia)

Tell your doctor immediately if you experience muscle twitching or abnormal movements of the face or tongue. You should also tell your doctor if you notice any symptoms that worry you, even if you think the problems are not connected with the medicine or are not listed here.

Because some people experience drowsiness, you should avoid driving a car or operating machinery until you know how Zyprexa affects you. Some people may feel dizzy in the early stages of treatment, especially when getting up from a lying or sitting position. This side effect usually passes after taking Zyprexa for a few days.

After prolonged use in women, medicines of this type can cause milk secretion or changes in the regularity of their monthly period. On rare occasions, after prolonged use in men, medicines of this type have been associated with breast enlargement. As well, abnormal liver function tests have been reported on occasion.

Do not be alarmed by this list of possible side effects. You may not experience any of them. If any of these side effects are experienced, they are usually mild and temporary.

How should I store Zyprexa? All medicines should be kept out of the reach of children. Zyprexa should be stored in its original package at room temperature, in a dry place and out of direct light. The expiry date of this medicine is printed on the package label. Do not use the medicine after this date. If your doctor tells you to stop taking Zyprexa or you find that they have passed their expiry date, please return any left over medicine to your pharmacist.

What does Zyprexa contain? Each Zyprexa tablet contains olanzapine as the active ingredient. Zyprexa tablets also contain the following inactive ingredients: carnauba wax, color mixture white (hydroxypropyl methylcellulose, titanium dioxide, polyethylene glycol, and polysorbate 80) crospovidone, FD&C Blue No. 2 Aluminum Lake, hydroxypropyl cellulose, hydroxypropyl methylcellulose, lactose, magnesium stearate, and microcrystalline cellulose.

☐ ZYRTEC®

UCB Pharma

Cetirizine HCl

Histamine H_1-Receptor Antagonist

Information for the Patient: Use: Zyrtec is a direct-action metabolite* indicated for fast and long lasting relief of itchy, watery eyes, sneezing and runny nose caused by seasonal and year-round allergies (hayfever, trees, grass, dust, pets, mold). Zyrtec also relieves allergic skin reactions such as hives.

Directions: Adults and children 12 years of age and over: 1 tablet (10 mg) every 24 hours. Do not administer to children under 12 years of age. Do not exceed recommended dosage. Prolonged use only as directed by a physician.

Elderly patients: take one half of 1 tablet (5 mg) or consult a physician if unsure about dosage.

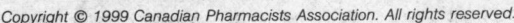

Zyrtec (cont'd)

Caution: This product should not be taken if you are pregnant or nursing a baby, or if you have liver or kidney disease, unless under the advice of a physician. Due caution should be exercised when driving or operating a vehicle or potentially dangerous machinery. Keep this and all medications safely out of the reach of children.

- Store below 30°C.
- Product monograph available to physicians and pharmacists upon request.

*A direct-action metabolite does not require biotransformation to become active.

Nonmedicinal Ingredients: cornstarch, hydroxypropyl methylcellulose, lactose, magnesium stearate, polyethylene glycol, povidone and titanium dioxide.

Availability: Zyrtec is available as a 10 mg scored tablet packaged in individually sealed blisters in 6, 12 and 18 tablet packages.

ORAL CONTRACEPTIVES*

Classification of Oral Contraceptives According to Their Pharmacological Category (Monophasic, Biphasic, Triphasic)

Category/Product	Content: Estrogen	Content: Progestin
Monophasic:		
50 μg estrogen		
Demulen® 50	50 μgEE	1 mgEDA
Norinyl® 1/50	50 μgM	1 mgNE
Ortho-Novum® 1/50	50 μgM	1 mgNE
Ovral®	50 μgEE	0.5 mgNG
<50 μg estrogen		
Alesse™	20 μgEE	0.1 mgLNG
Brevicon® 0.5/35	35 μgEE	0.5 mgNE
Brevicon® 1/35	35 μgEE	1 mgNE
Cyclen®	35 μgEE	0.25 mgNGS
Demulen® 30	30 μgEE	2 mgEDA
Loestrin™ 1.5/30	30 μgEE	1.5 mgNEA
Marvelon®	30 μgEE	0.15 mgD
Minestrin™ 1/20	20 μgEE	1 mgNEA
Min-Ovral®	30 μgEE	0.15 mgLNG
Ortho® 0.5/35	35 μgEE	0.5 mgNE
Ortho® 1/35	35 μgEE	1 mgNE
Ortho-Cept™	30 μgEE	0.15 mgD
Select™ 1/35	35 μgEE	1 mgNE
No estrogen		
Micronor®		0.35 mgNE
Biphasic:		
Ortho® 10/11	35 μgEE ×21d	0.5 mgNE × 10d 1 mgNE × 11d

Category/Product	Content: Estrogen	Content: Progestin
Triphasic:		
Ortho® 7/7/7	35 μgEE × 21d	0.5 mgNE × 7d 0.75 mgNE × 7d 1 mgNE × 7d
Synphasic®	35 μgEE × 21d	0.5 mgNE × 7d 1 mgNE × 9d 0.5 mgNE × 5d
Tri-Cyclen™	35 μgEE × 21d	0.18 mgNGS × 7d 0.215 mgNGS × 7d 0.25 mgNGS × 7d
Triphasil®	30 μgEE × 6d 40 μgEE × 5d 30 μgEE × 10d	0.05 mgLNG × 6d 0.075 mgLNG × 5d 0.125 mgLNG × 10d
Triquilar®	30 μgEE × 6d 40 μgEE × 5d 30 μgEE ×10d	0.05 mgLNG × 6d 0.075 mgLNG × 5d 0.125 mgLNG × 10d

Abbreviations:
D: Desogestrel
EDA: Ethynodiol diacetate
EE: Ethinyl estradiol
LNG: Levonorgestrel
M: Mestranol
NE: Norethindrone
NEA: Norethindrone acetate
NG: Norgestrel
NGS: Norgestimate

*Directions for use of estrogen-progestin combination oral contraceptives (OCs), Health Canada, Ottawa, ON, 1994.

SUPPLEMENTARY INFORMATION BOOKLET FOR PATIENTS CONSIDERING THE USE OF ORAL CONTRACEPTIVES (BIRTH CONTROL PILLS)

Introduction

This booklet will give you information to make an informed choice on the use of oral contraceptives. Oral contraceptives are also known as birth control pills or "the pill".

You should read this booklet if you are thinking about any method of birth control. If you have decided to take birth control pills, this booklet will help you understand both the risks and the benefits. It also will give you information on how to use birth control pills.

When taken as directed, birth control pills are a very effective way to prevent pregnancy. Only sterilization is more effective. The pill is convenient and has many benefits other than birth control. Most women do not develop serious and unpleasant side effects from using birth control pills.

The pill has important advantages over other methods of birth control. It also has certain risks that no other method has. Your doctor is the best person to explain the consequences of any possible risks.

You can help your doctor prescribe birth control pills as safely as possible. Tell your doctor about yourself, and be alert for the earliest signs of possible trouble.

> Read this booklet carefully and discuss its contents with your doctor.

Types of Birth Control Pills

There are two types of birth control pills:

1. The "combination pill" is the most common type. It contains two female sex hormones—an estrogen and a progestin. The amounts and types of estrogen and progestin differ from one preparation to another. The amount of estrogen is more important. The effectiveness and some dangers of birth control pills are related mainly to the amount of estrogen.
2. The "mini-pill" is the second type. It contains only one female sex hormone—a progestin.

How Birth Control Pills Work

Birth control pills work in two ways:

1. They inhibit the monthly release of an egg by the ovaries.
2. They change the mucus produced by the cervix. This slows the movement of the sperm through the mucus and through the uterus (womb).

Effectiveness of Birth Control Pills

Combination birth control pills are more than 99% effective in preventing pregnancy when

- the pill is **taken as directed,** and
- the amount of estrogen is 20 μg or more.

A 99% effectiveness rate means that if 100 women used birth control pills for 1 year, one woman in the group would get pregnant.

The mini-pill (progestin only) is slightly less effective than combination birth control pills.

Other Ways to Prevent Pregnancy

Other methods of birth control are available to you. They are usually less effective than birth control pills. Used properly, however, other methods of birth control are effective enough for many women.

Table I gives reported pregnancy rates for various forms of birth control, including no birth control. The reported rates represent the number of women out of 100 who would become pregnant in 1 year.

Table I—Supplementary Information Booklet

Reported Pregnancies per 100 Women per Year	
Combination pill	less than 1 to 2
Intrauterine device (IUD)	less than 1 to 6
Condom with spermicidal foam or gel	1 to 6
Mini-pill	3 to 6
Condom	2 to 12
Diaphragm with spermicidal foam or gel	3 to 18
Spermicide	3 to 21
Sponge with spermicide	3 to 28
Cervical cap with spermicide	5 to 18
Periodic abstinence (rhythm), all types	2 to 20
No birth control	60 to 85

Pregnancy rates vary widely because people differ in how carefully and regularly they use each method. (This does not apply to IUDs since they are implanted in the uterus.) Regular users may achieve pregnancy rates in the lower ranges. Others may expect pregnancy rates more in the middle ranges.

The effective use of birth control methods other than birth control pills and IUDs requires more effort than taking a single pill every day. It is an effort that many couples undertake successfully.

Who Should Not Use Birth Control Pills

You should not use birth control pills if you have or have had any of the following conditions:

- unusual vaginal bleeding that has not yet been diagnosed;
- blood clots in the legs, lungs, eyes, or elsewhere;
- a stroke, heart attack or chest pain (angina pectoris);
- known or suspected cancer of the breast or sex organs;
- liver tumor associated with the use of birth control pills or other estrogen-containing products and/or
- jaundice or liver disease if still present.

The pill should not be taken if you are pregnant or if pregnancy is suspected.

There are also conditions that your doctor will want to watch closely or that might cause your doctor to recommend a method of contraception other than birth control pills:

- breast conditions:
  — a strong family history of breast cancer
  — breast disorders including pain, discharge from the nipples, thickenings or lumps. In some circumstances, benefit may be derived from taking the pill; in other cases, adverse effects may follow.
- diabetes
- high blood pressure
- abnormal levels of fats in the bloodstream (high cholesterol or triglycerides)
- cigarette smoking
- migraine headaches
- heart or kidney disease
- epilepsy
- depression
- fibroid tumors of the uterus
- gallbladder or pancreatic disease
- plans for forthcoming surgery
- history of jaundice or other liver disease

You also should inform your doctor about a family history of blood clots, heart attacks or strokes.

The Risks of Birth Control Pills

1. Circulatory disorders (including blood clots in legs, lungs, heart, eyes or brain)

Blood clots are the most common serious side effect of birth control pills. Clots can occur in many areas of the body.

- In the brain, a clot can result in a stroke.
- In a blood vessel of the heart, a clot can result in a heart attack.
- In the legs and pelvis, a clot can break off and travel to the lung resulting in a pulmonary embolus.
- In a blood vessel leading to an arm or leg, a clot can result in damage to or loss of a limb.

Any of these conditions can cause death or disability. Clots also occur rarely in the blood vessels of the eye, resulting in blindness or impaired vision.

Women who use birth control pills have a higher incidence of blood clots. The risk of clotting seems to increase with higher estrogen doses. **It is important, therefore, to use as low a dosage of estrogen as possible.**

Cigarette smoking increases the risk of serious adverse effects on the heart and blood vessels. This risk increases with age and becomes significant in birth control pill users over 35 years of age. Women should not smoke.

2. Breast cancer

The most significant risk factors for breast cancer are increasing age and a strong history of breast cancer in the family (mother or sister). Other established risk factors include obesity, never having children and having your first full-term pregnancy at a late age.

Some women who use birth control pills may be at increased risk of developing breast cancer before menopause, which occurs around age 50. These women may be long-term users of birth control pills (more than 8 years) or women who start using birth control pills at an early age. In a few women, the use of birth control pills may accelerate the growth of an existing but undiagnosed breast cancer. Early diagnosis, however, can reduce the effect of breast cancer on a woman's life expectancy. The potential risks related to birth control pills seem to be small, however.

Women with the following conditions should be examined yearly by their doctors no matter what method of contraception they use:

- a strong history of breast cancer in the family;
- breast nodules or thickenings; and/or
- discharge from the nipple.

3. Dangers to developing child if birth control pills are used during pregnancy

Birth control pills should not be taken by pregnant women. There is no evidence, however, that the pill can damage a developing child.

There is also no evidence that the use of birth control pills immediately before a pregnancy will adversely affect a baby's development. When a woman stops taking birth control pills to become pregnant, however, her doctor may recommend a different method of contraception until she has a period on her own. In this way, the pregnancy can be more accurately dated.

4. Gallbladder disease and liver tumors

Users of birth control pills have a greater risk of developing gallbladder disease requiring surgery within the first year of use. The risk may double after 4 or 5 years of use.

The short- and long-term use of birth control pills also has been linked with the growth of liver tumors. Such tumors are **extremely** rare.

5. Other side effects of birth control pills

Some users of birth control pills have unpleasant side effects. These side effects are temporary and are not hazardous to health.

There may be tenderness of the breasts, nausea and vomiting. Some users will experience weight gain or loss. Many of these side effects occurred with high-dose combination birth control pills. These side effects are less common with the low-dose pills prescribed today.

Unexpected vaginal bleeding or spotting and changes in the usual menstrual period also may occur. These side effects usually disappear after the first few cycles. They are **not** an indication to stop taking birth control pills. Unless more significant complications occur, a decision to stop using the pill or to change the brand of pill should be made only after 3 consecutive months of use. Occasionally, users develop high blood pressure that may require stopping the use of birth control pills.

Other side effects may include:

- growth of pre-existing fibroid tumors of the uterus;
- depression;
- liver problems with jaundice (yellowing of the skin);
- an increase or decrease in hair growth, sex drive and appetite;
- skin pigmentation;
- headaches;
- rash; and/or
- vaginal infections.

Infrequently, there is a need to change contact lens prescription or an inability to use contact lenses.

A woman's menstrual period may be delayed after stopping birth control pills. There is no evidence that the use of the pill leads to a decrease in fertility. As mentioned, it is wise to delay starting a pregnancy for one menstrual period after stopping birth control pills.

Non-contraceptive Benefits of Birth Control Pills

Several health advantages have been linked to the use of birth control pills.

- Combination estrogen and progestin birth control pills reduce the incidence of cancer of the uterus and ovaries.
- Birth control pills reduce the likelihood of developing benign (non-cancerous) breast disease and ovarian cysts.
- Users of birth control pills lose less menstrual blood and have more regular cycles. The risk of developing iron-deficiency anemia is thus reduced.
- There may be a decrease in painful menstruation and in premenstrual syndrome (PMS).
- Acne, excessive hair growth and male hormone-related disorders also may be improved.

Birth control pills **do not protect** against sexually transmitted diseases (STDs), including HIV/AIDS. For protection against STDs, it is advisable to use latex condoms **in combination with** birth control pills.

Periodic Examination

A complete medical and family history is necessary before birth control pills are prescribed. A physical examination should include measuring blood pressure and examining the breasts, abdomen, pelvic organs and limbs.

A second visit to your doctor should take place 3 months or sooner after starting birth control pills. During this visit, any side effects should be evaluated and your blood pressure checked again. Afterward, an annual examination similar to the first visit is recommended. A Pap smear is usually taken before starting birth control pills and then at intervals recommended by your doctor.

If You Decide to Take Birth Control Pills

If you and your doctor decide that, for you, the benefits of birth control pills outweigh the risks, you should be aware of the following:

1. Cigarette smoking increases the risk of serious adverse effects on the heart and blood vessels. This risk increases with age and becomes significant in birth control pill users older than 35 years of age. Women should not smoke.
2. Take the pills only on the advice of your doctor and carefully follow all directions given to you. You must take the pills exactly as prescribed. Otherwise, you may become pregnant.
3. Visit your doctor 3 months or sooner after the initial examination. Afterward, visit your doctor at least once a year.
4. Be alert for the following symptoms and signs of serious adverse effects. Call your doctor immediately if they occur:
   - sharp pain in the chest, coughing blood, or sudden shortness of breath. These symptoms could indicate a possible blood clot in the lung;
   - pain in the calf. This symptom could indicate a possible blood clot in the leg;
   - crushing chest pain or heaviness. This symptom could indicate a possible heart attack;
   - sudden severe or worsening headache or vomiting, dizziness or fainting, disturbance of vision or speech, or weakness or numbness in an arm or leg. These symptoms could indicate a possible stroke;
   - sudden partial or complete loss of vision. This symptom could indicate a possible blood clot in the eye;
   - severe pain or lump in the abdomen. These symptoms could indicate a possible tumor of the liver;
   - severe depression;
   - yellowing of the skin (jaundice);
   - unusual swelling of the extremities; and/or
   - breast lumps. **Ask your doctor for advice and instruction on regular self-examination of your breasts.**
5. Birth control pills should never be taken if you think you are pregnant. They will not prevent the pregnancy from continuing.
6. You will have a menstrual period when you stop taking birth control pills. You should delay pregnancy until another menstrual period occurs within 4 to 6 weeks. Contact your doctor for recommendations on alternate methods of contraception during this time.
7. Your doctor will advise you of the appropriate time to start the use of birth control pills after childbirth, miscarriage or therapeutic abortion.
8. The hormones in birth control pills are known to appear in breast milk. These hormones may decrease the flow of breast milk. If birth control pills are not resumed until nursing is established, however, the quantity and quality of breast milk does not seem to be affected. There is no evidence that birth control pills are harmful to the nursing infant.

9. Should you require **major** surgery, inform your surgeon that you are using birth control pills.
10. **If you see a different doctor, inform him or her that you are taking birth control pills.** Tell the doctor that your birth control pills are *(Product Name).*
11. **Inform your doctor if you are taking or if you start to take other medications.** This applies to both prescription and nonprescription drugs. These medications may change the effectiveness and/or cycle control of your birth control pills. **You may need to use a back-up method of birth control.**
12. **There is no need to stop taking birth control pills for a rest period.**

13. Birth control pills **do not protect** against sexually transmitted diseases (STDs), including HIV/AIDS. For protection against STDs, it is advisable to use latex condoms **in combination with** birth control pills.

HOW TO TAKE BIRTH CONTROL PILLS

1. **Read these directions:**
   - before you start taking your pills, and
   - any time you are not sure what to do.
2. **Look at your pill pack** to see if it has 21 or 28 pills:
   - **21-Pill Pack:** 21 active pills (with hormones) taken daily for 3 weeks, and then no pills taken for 1 week,

   or
   - **28-Pill Pack:** 21 active pills (with hormones) taken daily for 3 weeks, and then 7 "reminder" pills (no hormones) taken daily for 1 week.

   Also check: *There is a picture of pill pack here, showing: 1) where to start, 2) direction to take pills in, and 3) week numbers.*
3. You may wish to use a second method of birth control (e.g., latex condoms and spermicidal foam or gel) for the first 7 days of the first cycle of pill use. This will provide a back-up in case pills are forgotten while you are getting used to taking them.
4. **When receiving any medical treatment, be sure to tell your doctor that you are using birth control pills.**
5. **Many women have spotting or light bleeding, or may feel sick to their stomach during the first 3 months on the pill.** If you do feel sick, do not stop taking the pill. The problem will usually go away. If it does not go away, check with your doctor or clinic.
6. **Missing pills also can cause some spotting or light bleeding,** even if you make up the missed pills. You also could feel a little sick to your stomach on the days you take 2 pills to make up for missed pills.
7. **If you miss pills at any time, you could get pregnant. The greatest risks for pregnancy are:**
   - when you start a pack late, or
   - when you miss pills at the beginning or at the very end of the pack.
8. **Always be sure you have ready:**
   - **another kind of birth control** (such as latex condoms and spermicidal foam or gel) to use as a back-up in case you miss pills, and
   - **an extra, full pack of pills.**
9. **If you experience vomiting or diarrhea, or if you take some medicines,** such as antibiotics, your pills may not work as well. Use a back-up method, such as latex condoms and spermicidal foam or gel, until you can check with your doctor or clinic.
10. **If you forget more than 1 pill 2 months in a row,** talk to your doctor or clinic about how to make pill-taking easier or about using another method of birth control.
11. **If your questions are not answered here, call your doctor or clinic.**

WHEN TO START THE FIRST PACK OF PILLS

Be sure to read these instructions (see package insert for illustrations):
- before you start taking your pills, and
- any time you are not sure what to do.

Decide with your doctor or clinic what is the best day for you to start taking your first pack of pills. Your pills may be either a 21-day or a 28-day type.

A. 21-Day Combination

With this type of birth control pill, you are on pills for 21 days and off pills for 7 days. You must not be off the pills for more than 7 days in a row.

1. **The first day of your menstrual period (bleeding) is Day 1 of your cycle.** Your doctor may advise you to start taking the pills on Day 1, on Day 5, or on the first Sunday after your period begins. If your period starts on Sunday, start that same day.
2. Take 1 pill at approximately the same time every day for 21 days; **then take no pills for 7 days.** Start a new pack on the eighth day. You will probably have a period during the 7 days off the pill. (This bleeding may be lighter and shorter than your usual period.)

B. 28-Day Combination

With this type of birth control pill, you take 21 pills that contain hormones and 7 pills that contain no hormones.

1. **The first day of your menstrual period (bleeding) is Day 1 of your cycle.** Your doctor may advise you to start taking the pills on Day 1, on Day 5, or on the first Sunday after your period begins. If your period starts on Sunday, start that same day.
2. Take 1 pill at approximately the same time every day for 28 days. Begin a new pack the next day, **not missing any days.** Your period should occur during the last 7 days of using that pill pack.

WHAT TO DO DURING THE MONTH

1. **Take a pill at approximately the same time every day until the pack is empty.**
   - Try to associate taking your pill with some regular activity such as eating a meal or going to bed.
   - Do not skip pills even if you have bleeding between monthly periods or feel sick to your stomach (nausea).
   - Do not skip pills even if you do not have sex very often.
2. **When you finish a pack:**
   - **21 Pills**

     Wait 7 days to start the next pack. You will have your period during that week.
   - **28 Pills**

     Start the next pack **on the next day.** Take 1 pill every day. Do not wait any days between packs.

WHAT TO DO IF YOU MISS PILLS

Table II outlines the actions you should take if you miss 1 or more of your birth control pills. Match the number of pills missed with the appropriate starting time for your type of pill pack.

Table II—Supplementary Information Booklet

Sunday Start	Other Than Sunday Start
Miss 1 pill	**Miss 1 pill**
Take it as soon as you remember and take the next pill at the usual time. This means that you might take 2 pills in one day.	Take it as soon as you remember and take the next pill at the usual time. This means that you might take 2 pills in one day.
Miss 2 pills in a row	**Miss 2 pills in a row**
First 2 Weeks 1. Take 2 pills the day you remember and 2 pills the next day. 2. Then take 1 pill a day until you finish the pack. 3. Use a back-up method of birth control if you have sex in the 7 days after you miss the pills. **Third Week** 1. Keep taking 1 pill a day until Sunday. 2. On Sunday, safely discard the rest of the pack and start a new pack that day. 3. Use a back-up method of birth control if you have sex in the 7 days after you miss the pills. 4. You may not have a period this month. **If you miss 2 periods in a row, call your doctor or clinic.**	**First 2 Weeks** 1. Take 2 pills the day you remember and 2 pills the next day. 2. Then take 1 pill a day until you finish the pack. 3. Use a back-up method of birth control if you have sex in the 7 days after you miss the pills. **Third Week** 1. Safely dispose of the rest of the pill pack and start a new pack that same day. 2. Use a back-up method of birth control if you have sex in the 7 days after you miss the pills. 3. You may not have a period this month. **If you miss 2 periods in a row, call your doctor or clinic.**
Miss 3 or more pills in a row	**Miss 3 or more pills in a row**
Anytime in the Cycle 1. Keep taking 1 pill a day until Sunday. 2. On Sunday, safely discard the rest of the pack and start a new pack that day. 3. Use a back-up method of birth control if you have sex in the 7 days after you miss the pills. 4. You may not have a period this month. **If you miss 2 periods in a row, call your doctor or clinic.**	**Anytime in the Cycle** 1. Safely dispose of the rest of the pill pack and start a new pack that same day. 2. Use a back-up method of birth control if you have sex in the 7 days after you miss the pills. 3. You may not have a period this month. **If you miss 2 periods in a row, call your doctor or clinic.**

Note: 28-Day Pack: If you forget any of the 7 "reminder" pills (without hormones) in Week 4, just safely dispose of the pills you missed. Then keep taking 1 pill each day until the pack is empty. You do not need to use a back-up method.

Always be sure you have on hand:

- a back-up method of birth control (such as latex condoms and spermicidal foam or gel) in case you miss pills, and
- an extra, full pack of pills.

If you forget more than 1 pill 2 months in a row, talk to your doctor or clinic about ways to make pill-taking easier or about using another method of birth control.

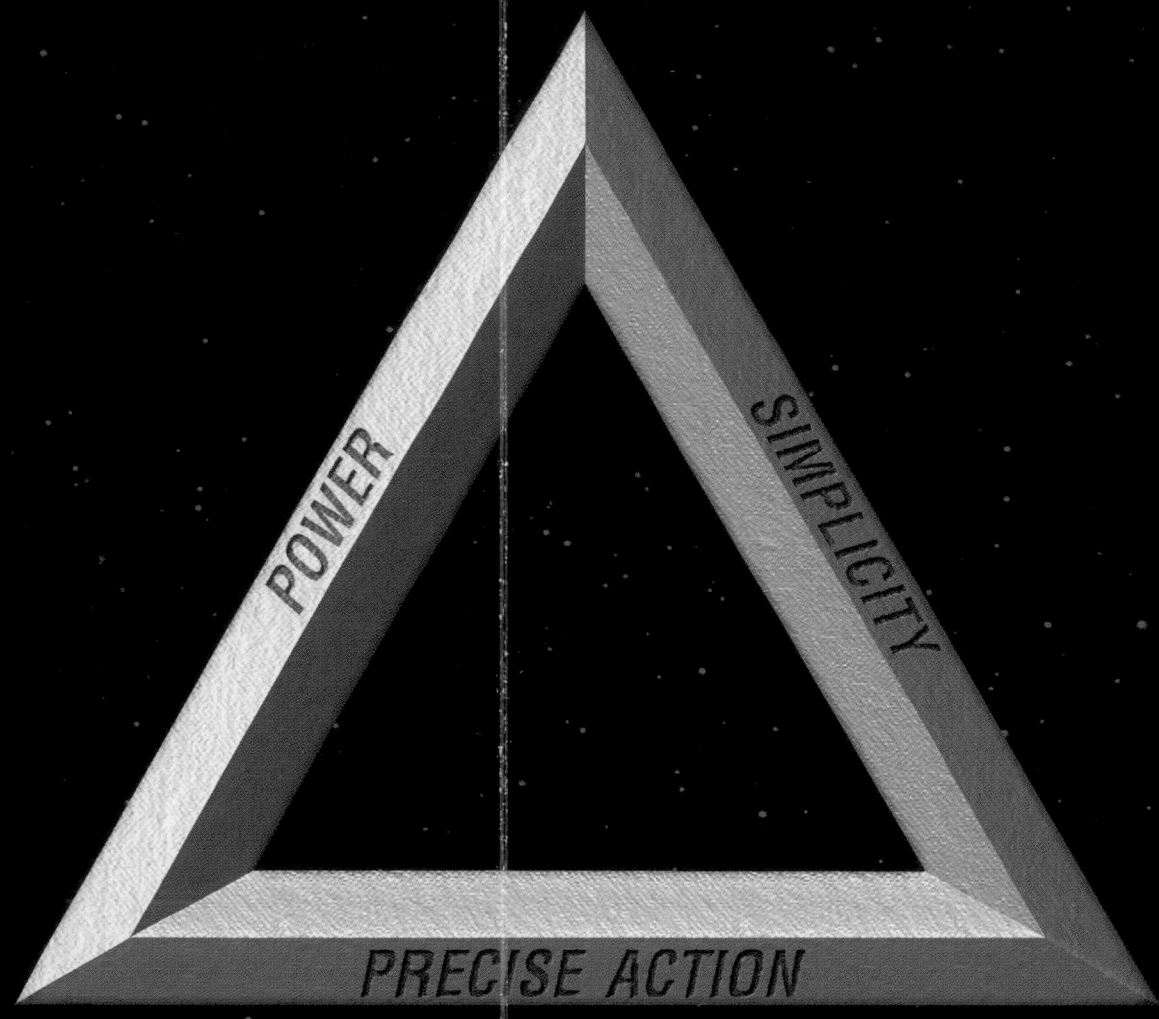

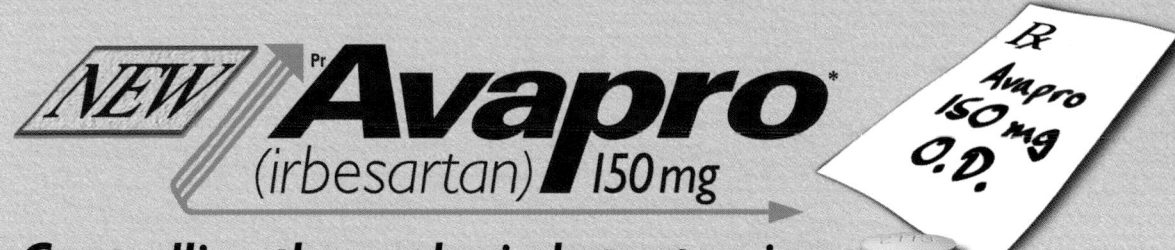

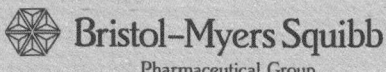

MONOGRAPHS OF PHARMACEUTICALS AND SPECIALTIES

GENERAL MONOGRAPHS

Canadian Pharmacists Association (CPhA)

The following is a list of general monographs which appear in the white pages of the *CPS*. The monographs have been compiled by CPhA editorial staff and reviewed by the *CPS* Editorial Advisory Panel, and they are lightly shaded to distinguish them from the manufacturers' product monographs. Readers should be aware that the text may contain information different from that approved by Therapeutic Products Programme, Health Canada and that the pharmaceutical manufacturers' approval has not been requested.

A

ACE Inhibitors ℞
Acetaminophen
Acetohexamide ℞—see Sulfonylureas
Acetylsalicylic Acid—see ASA
Allopurinol ℞
Alprazolam ℞—see Benzodiazepines
Amcinonide ℞—
see Corticosteroids: Topical
Aminophylline ℞—
see Theophylline and its Salts
Aminosalicylate Sodium ℞—
see PAS Sodium
Amitriptyline ℞
Amobarbital ⊕—see Barbiturates
Amoxicillin ℞
Anileridine Ⓝ—see Opioid Analgesics
ASA
Ascorbic Acid—see Vitamin C

B

Barbiturates ⊕
Beclomethasone ℞—
see Corticosteroids: Eye Ear Nose
see Corticosteroids: Inhaled
Benazepril ℞—see ACE Inhibitors
Benzodiazepines ℞
Benztropine Mesylate ℞
Betamethasone ℞—
see Corticosteroids: Eye Ear Nose
see Corticosteroids: Systemic
see Corticosteroids: Topical
Bromazepam ℞—see Benzodiazepines
Budesonide ℞—
see Corticosteroids: Eye Ear Nose
see Corticosteroids: Inhaled
Butabarbital ⊕—see Barbiturates
Butorphanol Ⓝ—
see Opioid Analgesics

C

Calcium Salts: Oral
Calcium Salts: Parenteral
Captopril ℞—see ACE Inhibitors
Carbachol ℞
Chloral Hydrate ℞
Chloramphenicol ℞
Chlordiazepoxide ℞—
see Benzodiazepines
Chlorpromazine ℞
Chlorpropamide ℞—see Sulfonylureas
Chlortetracycline ℞—see Tetracyclines
Cholecalciferol—see Vitamin D
Cilazapril ℞—see ACE Inhibitors
Clobazam ℞—see Benzodiazepines
Clobetasol ℞—
see Corticosteroids: Topical
Clobetasone ℞—
see Corticosteroids: Topical
Clonazepam ℞—see Benzodiazepines
Clorazepate ℞—see Benzodiazepines
Codeine Ⓝ—see Opioid Analgesics
Colchicine (Oral)
Corticosteroids: Eye Ear Nose ℞
Corticosteroids: Inhaled ℞
Corticosteroids: Systemic ℞
Corticosteroids: Topical ℞
Cortisone ℞—
see Corticosteroids: Systemic
Cyanocobalamin—see Vitamin B_{12}
Cyclopentolate HCl ℞

D

Dalteparin ℞—
see Heparins: Low Molecular Weight
Demeclocycline ℞—see Tetracyclines
Desonide ℞—
see Corticosteroids: Topical
Desoximetasone ℞—
see Corticosteroids: Topical
Dexamethasone ℞—
see Corticosteroids: Eye Ear Nose
see Corticosteroids: Systemic
Diamorphine Ⓝ—
see Opioid Analgesics
Diazepam ℞—see Benzodiazepines
Diflucortolone ℞—
see Corticosteroids: Topical
Diphenylhydantoin ℞—see Phenytoin
Doxycycline ℞—see Tetracyclines

E

Enalapril ℞—see ACE Inhibitors
Enalaprilat ℞—see ACE Inhibitors
Enoxaparin ℞—
see Heparins: Low Molecular Weight
Ergocalciferol—see Vitamin D
Ergometrine ℞—
see Ergonovine Maleate
Ergonovine Maleate ℞
Erythromycin ℞
Ethambutol HCl ℞

F

Fentanyl Ⓝ—see Opioid Analgesics
Fludrocortisone ℞—
see Corticosteroids: Systemic
Flumethasone ℞—
see Corticosteroids: Topical
Flunisolide ℞—
see Corticosteroids: Eye Ear Nose
see Corticosteroids: Inhaled
Fluocinolone ℞—
see Corticosteroids: Topical
Fluocinonide ℞—
see Corticosteroids: Topical
Fluorometholone ℞—
see Corticosteroids: Eye Ear Nose
Fluoxetine ℞—
see Selective Serotonin Reuptake Inhibitors
Fluphenazine ℞
Flurandrenolide ℞—
see Corticosteroids: Topical
Flurazepam ℞—see Benzodiazepines
Fluticasone ℞—
see Corticosteroids: Eye Ear Nose
see Corticosteroids: Inhaled
Fluvoxamine ℞—
see Selective Serotonin Reuptake Inhibitors
Folic Acid ℞
Fosinopril ℞—see ACE Inhibitors

G

Gliclazide ℞—see Sulfonylureas
Glyburide ℞—see Sulfonylureas
Guaifenesin

H

Halcinonide ℞—
see Corticosteroids: Topical
Heparins: Low Molecular Weight ℞
Heparin: Unfractionated
Homatropine
Hydrochlorothiazide ℞
Hydrocodone Ⓝ—
see Opioid Analgesics
Hydrocortisone ℞—
see Corticosteroids: Eye Ear Nose
see Corticosteroids: Systemic
see Corticosteroids: Topical

GENERAL MONOGRAPHS *(cont'd)*

Hydromorphone Ⓝ—
 see Opioid Analgesics
Hydroxocobalamin—see Vitamin B_{12}
Hyoscine—see Scopolamine

I

Ipecac Syrup
Iron Salts
Isoniazid Pr

L

Lisinopril—see ACE Inhibitors
Lithium Pr
Lorazepam Pr—see Benzodiazepines

M

Meperidine Ⓝ—
 see Opioid Analgesics
Methadone Ⓝ—
 see Opioid Analgesics
Methylprednisolone Pr—
 see Corticosteroids: Systemic
 see Corticosteroids: Topical
Metronidazole Pr
Midazolam Pr—see Benzodiazepines
Minocycline Pr—see Tetracyclines
Mometasone Pr—
 see Corticosteroids: Eye Ear Nose
 see Corticosteroids: Topical
Morphine Ⓝ—see Opioid Analgesics

N

Nalbuphine Ⓝ—
 see Opioid Analgesics
Narcotic Analgesics Ⓝ—
 see Opioid Analgesics
Niacin/Niacinamide
Nicotinamide—
 see Niacin/Niacinamide
Nicotinic Acid—
 see Niacin/Niacinamide
Nitrazepam Pr—see Benzodiazepines
Nitroglycerin

O

Opioid Analgesics Ⓝ
Oxazepam Pr—see Benzodiazepines
Oxtriphylline Pr—
 see Theophylline and its Salts
Oxycodone Ⓝ—
 see Opioid Analgesics
Oxymorphone Ⓝ—
 see Opioid Analgesics

P

Pantothenic Acid
Paroxetine Pr—
 see Selective Serotonin Reuptake Inhibitors
PAS Sodium Pr
Penicillin G Pr**/Penicillin V** Pr
Pentazocine Ⓝ—see Opioid Analgesics
Pentobarbital Ⓒ—see Barbiturates
Perindopril Pr—see ACE Inhibitors
Pethidine Ⓝ—see Opioid Analgesics
Phenobarbital Ⓒ—see Barbiturates
Phenytoin Pr
Phytonadione Pr—see Vitamin K
Potassium Salts
Prednisolone Pr—
 see Corticosteroids: Eye Ear Nose
 see Corticosteroids: Systemic
Prednisone Pr—
 see Corticosteroids: Systemic
Propoxyphene Ⓝ—
 see Opioid Analgesics
Pyridoxine—see Vitamin B_6

Q

Quinapril Pr—see ACE Inhibitors
Quinidine
Quinine Sulfate

R

Ramipril Pr—see ACE Inhibitors
Riboflavin—see Vitamin B_2
Rifampin Pr

S

Scopolamine
Secobarbital Ⓒ—see Barbiturates
Sodium Bicarbonate
Selective Serotonin Reuptake Inhibitors
Sertraline Pr—
 see Selective Serotonin Reuptake Inhibitors
Streptomycin Pr
Sulfapyridine Pr
Sulfonylureas Pr

T

Temazepam Pr—see Benzodiazepines
Tetanus Immune Globulin (Human)
Tetracyclines Pr
Theophylline and its Salts Pr
Thiamine—see Vitamin B_1
Tinzaparin Pr—
 see Heparins: Low Molecular Weight
Tolbutamide Pr—see Sulfonylureas
Triamcinolone Pr—
 see Corticosteroids: Eye Ear Nose
 see Corticosteroids: Inhaled
 see Corticosteroids: Systemic
 see Corticosteroids: Topical
Triazolam Pr—see Benzodiazepines
Trihexyphenidyl HCl Pr

V

Vitamin A
Vitamin B_1
Vitamin B_2
Vitamin B_3—see Niacin/Niacinamide
Vitamin B_5—see Pantothenic Acid
Vitamin B_6
Vitamin B_{12}
Vitamin C
Vitamin D
Vitamin E
Vitamin K Pr

CPS NOMENCLATURE FOR MICROORGANISMS

Nomenclature: In order to develop a standard nomenclature for microorganisms, the following terminology will apply in the *CPS* monographs, unless otherwise specified.

Full Name	Abbreviated Name
Bacteria:	
Acinetobacter calcoaceticus	A. calcoaceticus
Actinomyces bovis	A. bovis
Actinomyces israelii	A. israelii
Aerobacter aerogenes—see Enterobacter aerogenes	
Alcaligenes faecalis	A. faecalis
Bacillus anthracis	B. anthracis
Bacillus subtilis	B. subtilis
Bacteroides bivius—see Prevotella bivia	
Bacteroides distasonis	B. distasonis
Bacteroides fragilis	B. fragilis
Bacteroides funduliformis—see Fusobacterium necrophorum	
Bacteroides melaninogenicus	B. melaninogenicus
Bacteroides ovatus	B. ovatus
Bacteroides thetaiotaomicron	B. thetaiotaomicron
Bacteroides uniformis	B. uniformis
Bacteroides ureolyticus	B. ureolyticus
Bacteroides vulgatus	B. vulgatus
Bartonella bacilliformis	B. bacilliformis
Bordetella pertussis	B. pertussis
Borrelia burgdorferi	B. burgdorferi
Borrelia recurrentis	B. recurrentis
Branhamella catarrhalis—see Moraxella catarrhalis	
Calymmatobacterium granulomatis	C. granulomatis
Campylobacter fetus	C. fetus
Campylobacter jejuni	C. jejuni
Chlamydia pneumoniae	C. pneumoniae
Chlamydia psittaci	C. psittaci
Chlamydia trachomatis	C. trachomatis
Citrobacter diversus	C. diversus
Citrobacter freundii	C. freundii
Clostridium difficile	C. difficile
Clostridium perfringens	C. perfringens
Clostridium tetani	C. tetani
Corynebacterium acnes—see Propionibacterium acnes	
Corynebacterium diphtheriae	C. diphtheriae
Diplococcus pneumoniae—see Streptococcus pneumoniae	
Enterobacter aerogenes	E. aerogenes
Enterobacter cloacae	E. cloacae
Enterococcus faecalis	E. faecalis
Escherichia coli	E. coli
Eubacterium lentum	E. lentum
Francisella tularensis	F. tularensis
Fusobacterium necrophorum	F. necrophorum
Gardnerella vaginalis	G. vaginalis
Haemophilus aegyptius	H. aegyptius
Haemophilus ducreyi	H. ducreyi
Haemophilus influenzae	H. influenzae
Haemophilus parainfluenzae	H. parainfluenzae
Helicobacter pylori	H. pylori
Klebsiella oxytoca	K. oxytoca
Klebsiella pneumoniae	K. pneumoniae
Legionella pneumophila	L. pneumophila
Leptospira canicola	L. canicola
Leptospira interrogans	L. interrogans
Listeria monocytogenes	L. monocytogenes
Moraxella catarrhalis	M. catarrhalis
Moraxella lacunata	M. lacunata
Morganella morganii	M. morganii
Mycobacterium avium-intracellulare	M. avium-intracellulare
Mycobacterium bovis	M. bovis
Mycobacterium genavense	M. genavense
Mycobacterium intracellulare	M. intracellulare
Mycobacterium kansasii	M. kansasii
Mycobacterium leprae	M. leprae
Mycobacterium marinum	M. marinum
Mycobacterium tuberculosis	M. tuberculosis
Mycobacterium xenopi	M. xenopi
Mycoplasma pneumoniae	M. pneumoniae
Neisseria catarrhalis—see Moraxella catarrhalis	
Neisseria gonorrhoeae	N. gonorrhoeae
Neisseria meningitidis	N. meningitidis
Nocardia asteroides	N. asteroides
Pasteurella pestis—see Yersinia pestis	
Pneumococcus—see Streptococcus pneumoniae	
Prevotella bivia	P. bivia
Prevotella disiens	P. disiens
Prevotella intermedia	P. intermedia
Propionibacterium acnes	P. acnes
Proteus mirabilis	P. mirabilis
Proteus vulgaris	P. vulgaris
Providencia rettgeri	P. rettgeri
Providencia stuartii	P. stuartii
Pseudomonas aeruginosa	P. aeruginosa
Salmonella choleraesuis	S. choleraesuis
Salmonella enteritidis	S. enteritidis
Salmonella paratyphi	S. paratyphi
Salmonella typhi	S. typhi
Serratia marcescens	S. marcescens
Shigella boydii	S. boydii
Shigella dysenteriae	S. dysenteriae
Shigella flexneri	S. flexneri
Shigella sonnei	S. sonnei
Spirillum minor	S. minor
Staphylococcus aureus	S. aureus
Staphylococcus epidermidis	S. epidermidis
Staphylococcus saprophyticus	S. saprophyticus
Streptobacillus moniliformis	S. moniliformis
Streptococcus agalactiae	S. agalactiae
Streptococcus bovis	S. bovis
Streptococcus faecalis—see Enterococcus faecalis	
Streptococcus milleri	S. milleri
Streptococcus mitior	S. mitior
Streptococcus mutans	S. mutans
Streptococcus pneumoniae	S. pneumoniae
Streptococcus pyogenes	S. pyogenes
Streptococcus sanguis	S. sanguis
Streptococcus viridans	S. viridans
Streptomyces tsukubaensis	S. tsukubaensis
Treponema pallidum	T. pallidum
Treponema pertenue	T. pertenue
Ureaplasma urealyticum	U. urealyticum
Vibrio cholerae	V. cholerae
Xanthomonas maltophilia	X. maltophilia
Yersinia enterocolitica	Y. enterocolitica
Yersinia pestis	Y. pestis
Yersinia pseudotuberculosis	Y. pseudotuberculosis
Blood Parasites:	
Plasmodium falciparum	P. falciparum
Plasmodium malariae	P. malariae
Plasmodium ovale	P. ovale
Plasmodium vivax	P. vivax

CPS NOMENCLATURE FOR MICROORGANISMS *(cont'd)*

Full Name	Abbreviated Name
Fungi:	
Aspergillus fumigatus	A. fumigatus
Aspergillus niger	A. niger
Aspergillus terreus	A. terreus
Blastomyces dermatitidis	B. dermatitidis
Candida albicans	C. albicans
Candida krusei	C. krusei
Coccidioides immitis	C. immitis
Cryptococcus neoformans	C. neoformans
Epidermophyton floccosum	E. floccosum
Histoplasma capsulatum	H. capsulatum
Malassezia furfur	M. furfur
Microsporum audouini	M. audouini
Microsporum canis	M. canis
Microsporum gypseum	M. gypseum
Paracoccidioides brasiliensis	P. brasiliensis
Trichophyton crateriform	T. crateriform
Trichophyton gallinae	T. gallinae
Trichophyton interdigitale	T. interdigitale
Trichophyton megninii	T. megninii
Trichophyton mentagrophytes	T. mentagrophytes
Trichophyton rubrum	T. rubrum
Trichophyton schoenleinii	T. schoenleinii
Trichophyton sulfureum	T. sulfureum
Trichophyton tonsurans	T. tonsurans
Trichophyton verrucosum	T. verrucosum
Trichophyton violaceum	T. violaceum
Protozoa/Parasites:	
Clonorchis sinensis	C. sinensis
Entamoeba histolytica	E. histolytica
Giardia lamblia	G. lamblia
Opisthorchis viverrini	O. viverrini
Pneumocystis carinii	P. carinii
Schistosoma haematobium	S. haematobium
Schistosoma japonicum	S. japonicum
Schistosoma mansoni	S. mansoni
Schistosoma mekongi	S. mekongi
Toxoplasma gondii	T. gondii
Trichomonas vaginalis	T. vaginalis
Viruses:	
Cytomegalovirus	CMV
Epstein-Barr virus	EBV
Hepatitis Type A virus	HAV
Hepatitis Type B virus	HBV
Herpes Simplex virus Type 1	HSV-1
Herpes Simplex virus Type 2	HSV-2
Human Immunodeficiency virus	HIV
Human T cell Lymphotrophic retrovirus	HTLV-1
Human Papillomavirus	HPV
Respiratory Syncytial virus	RSV

CPS ABBREVIATIONS, MEDICAL AND PHARMACEUTICAL

ACE—angiotensin converting enzyme
ACTH—adrenocorticotropic hormone
ADH—antidiuretic hormone
AHA—American Heart Association
AIDS—acquired immunodeficiency syndrome
ALT—alanine transferase (SGPT)
ANC—absolute neutrophil count
APTT—activated partial thromboplastin time
ASA—acetylsalicylic acid
AST—aspartate transferase (SGOT)
AUC—area under the concentration curve
AV—atrioventricular
b.i.d.—twice daily
BMI—body mass index
BMR—basal metabolic rate
BP—British Pharmacopoeia; blood pressure
BPP—biophysical profiling
BSA—body surface area
BSP—Bromsulphalein
BUN—blood urea nitrogen
BWFI—bacteriostatic water for injection
°C—degrees Celsius
^{14}C—radioactive carbon isotope of atomic weight 14
Ⓒ—controlled drug
cc—cubic centimetre
CHF—congestive heart failure
CK—creatine kinase
cm—centimetre
CNS—central nervous system
CPK—creatine phosphokinase
CPR—cardiopulmonary resuscitation
CPS—Compendium of Pharmaceuticals and Specialties
cp—centipoise
CP—cisplatin
CSD—Canadian Standard Drug
CSF—cerebrospinal fluid
CST—contraction stress testing
CT—computed tomography
CVA—cerebrovascular accident
DIC—disseminated intravascular coagulation
DNA—deoxyribonucleic acid
DSA—digital subtraction angiography
ECG—electrocardiogram
ECT—electroconvulsive therapy
EEG—electroencephalogram
EENT—ear, eye, nose and throat
ESR—erythrocyte sedimentation rate
ET—endotracheal
FBS—fasting blood sugar
FSH—follicle-stimulating hormone
g—gram
GFR—glomerular filtration rate
GGT—gamma-glutamyl transpeptidase, γ glutamyltransferase
G-6-PD—glucose-6-phosphate dehydrogenase
GU—genitourinary
GVHD—graft-versus-host disease
h—hours
hCG—human chorionic gonadotropin
HIV—human immunodeficiency virus
hs—bedtime
^{131}I—radioactive iodine isotope of atomic weight 131
I.M. or i.m.—intramuscular
INR—international normalized ratio
IOP—intraocular pressure
IU—international unit
IUD—intrauterine contraceptive device
I.V. or i.v.—intravenous
J—joule
kg—kilogram
L—litre
lb—pound
LE—lupus erythematosus
LGL—Lown-Ganong-Levine
LH—luteinizing hormone
μ—micron
μg—microgram
μL—microlitre
μm—micrometer
μmol—micromole
M—molar
MAO—monoamine oxidase
MAOI—monoamine oxidase inhibitor
mEq—milliequivalent
mg—milligram
MI—myocardial infarction
min—minim; minute
mIU—milli international unit
MJ—megajoule
mL—millilitre
mmol—millimole
mOsm—milliosmole
MRI—magnetic resonance imaging
ms—millisecond
MS—multiple sclerosis
N—Normal
Ⓝ—narcotic
NF—National Formulary
NMS—neuroleptic malignant syndrome
NPN—nonprotein nitrogen
NSAID—nonsteroidal anti-inflammatory drug
NST—nonstress test
od—once daily
OHSS—ovarian hyperstimulation syndrome
oz—ounce
PABA—para-aminobenzoic acid
PBI—protein bound iodine
PBP—penicillin binding protein
pg—picogram (10^{-12})
pH—the logarithm, on the base 10, of the reciprocal of the hydrogen-ion concentration
pmol—picomole (10^{-12})
po—orally
ppm—parts per million
Ⓟ—prescription required
PRA—plasma renin activity
prn—when needed
PSP—phenolsulfonphthalein
PSVT—paroxysmal supraventricular tachycardia

CPS ABBREVIATIONS, MEDICAL AND PHARMACEUTICAL *(cont'd)*

PT—prothrombin time
PTCA—percutaneous transluminal coronary angioplasty
q.i.d.—4 times daily
®—registered trademark
RAI—radioactive iodine
r-hFSH—recombinant human follicle-stimulating hormone
RIA—radioimmunoassay
RNI—recommended nutrient intake
s—second
SA—sinoatrial
S.C. or s.c.—subcutaneous
SGOT—serum glutamic oxaloacetic transaminase (AST)
SGPT—serum glutamic pyruvic transaminase (ALT)
SMA—sequential multiple analysis
SSPE—subacute sclerosing panencephalitis
SSRI—selective serotonin reuptake inhibitor
t.i.d.—3 times daily
TM—trade mark
TSH—thyroid stimulating hormone
TT—thrombin time
USP—United States Pharmacopeia
v/v—volume in volume
WBC—white blood cell
WPW—Wolff-Parkinson-White
w/v—weight in volume
w/w—weight in weight

A

ABBOKINASE® Ⓟ
Abbott
Urokinase
Fibrinolytic

Pharmacology: Urokinase acts on the endogenous fibrinolytic system. It converts plasminogen to the enzyme plasmin. Plasmin degrades fibrin clots as well as fibrinogen.

I.V. infusion of urokinase in doses recommended for lysis of pulmonary embolism is followed by increased fibrinolytic activity. This effect disappears within a few hours after discontinuation, but a decrease in plasma levels of fibrinogen and plasminogen and an increase in the amount of circulating fibrinogen degradation products may persist for 12 to 24 hours. There is a lack of correlation between clot lysis and changes in coagulation and fibrinolytic assay results.

Information is incomplete about the pharmacokinetic properties in man. Urokinase administered by i.v. infusion is cleared rapidly by the liver. The serum half-life in man is 20 minutes or less. Patients with impaired liver function (e.g., cirrhosis) would be expected to show a prolongation in half-life. Small fractions of an administered dose are excreted in bile and urine.

Indications: Pulmonary Embolism: Urokinase is indicated in adults for the lysis of acute massive pulmonary emboli, defined as obstruction of blood flow to a lobe or multiple segments, and for the lysis of pulmonary emboli accompanied by unstable hemodynamics, i.e., failure to maintain blood pressure without supportive measures.

The diagnosis should be confirmed by objective means, such as pulmonary angiography via an upper extremity vein, or noninvasive procedures such as lung scanning.

Angiographic and hemodynamic measurements demonstrate a more rapid improvement with lytic therapy than with heparin therapy.

Urokinase treatment should be instituted as soon as possible after onset of pulmonary embolism, preferably no later than 7 days after onset. Any delay in instituting lytic therapy to evaluate the effect of heparin decreases the potential for optimal efficacy.

Coronary Artery Thrombosis: Urokinase has been reported to lyse acute thrombi obstructing coronary arteries, associated with evolving transmural myocardial infarction. The majority of patients who received urokinase by intracoronary infusion within 6 hours following onset of symptoms showed recanalization of the involved vessel.

It has not been established that intracoronary administration of urokinase during evolving transmural myocardial infarction results in salvage of myocardial tissue, nor that it reduces mortality. The patients who might benefit from this therapy cannot be defined.

When urokinase is used for the treatment of coronary artery thrombosis associated with evolving transmural myocardial infarction, therapy should be instituted within 6 hours of symptom onset.

Peripheral Arterial and Graft Thromboembolic Occlusion: Urokinase has been shown to be effective in lysing occlusive thromboemboli in peripheral arteries and grafts, resulting in revascularization of the ischemic limb. The use of urokinase to lyse arterial emboli originating from the left side of the heart (e.g., in mitral stenosis accompanied by atrial fibrillation) should be avoided due to the danger of new embolic phenomena, including those to cerebral vessels (see Warnings).

When urokinase is used for the treatment of peripheral arterial thromboembolic occlusion, therapy should be instituted as soon as possible after the diagnosis has been established.

I.V. Catheter Clearance: Urokinase is indicated for the restoration of patency to i.v. catheters, including central venous catheters, obstructed by clotted blood or fibrin. A product called Abbokinase Open-Cath is also available for this purpose in Dil-U-Vial containing 5 000 IU/vial.

Contraindications: Because thrombolytic therapy increases the risk of bleeding, urokinase is contraindicated in the following situations (see Warnings): active internal bleeding, history of cerebrovascular accident, recent (within 2 months) intracranial or intraspinal surgery, recent trauma including cardiopulmonary resuscitation, intracranial neoplasm, arteriovenous malformation or aneurysm, known bleeding diathesis, severe uncontrolled arterial hypertension, aortic dissection. The drug is also contraindicated in patients with a history of hypersensitivity to urokinase.

Urokinase alone or in combination with anticoagulants may cause bleeding complications. Therefore careful monitoring is advised.

Rapid lysis of coronary thrombi, resulting in reperfusion, has been reported occasionally to cause atrial or ventricular dysrhythmias requiring immediate treatment.

Thrombolytic revascularization should not be attempted in any patient whose ischemia has been of sufficient severity and/or duration to cause both motor and sensory paresis.

Warnings: Bleeding: The aim of urokinase treatment is the production of sufficient amounts of plasmin for lysis of intravascular deposits of fibrin; however, fibrin deposits which provide hemostatis, for example, at sites of needle puncture, will also lyse, and bleeding from such sites may occur. Therefore, urokinase therapy requires careful attention to an increased frequency of bleeding complications in patients with predisposing hemostatic defects, to potential bleeding sites e.g., catheter entry sites, arterial puncture sites, and prosthetic Dacron and Gore-Tex grafts.

I.M. injections and nonessential handling of the patient must be avoided during treatment with urokinase. Venipunctures should be performed carefully and as infrequently as possible.

Should an arterial puncture be necessary (except for intracoronary administration), upper extremity vessels are preferable. Pressure should be applied for at least 30 minutes, a pressure dressing applied, and the puncture site checked frequently for evidence of bleeding.

Should serious spontaneous bleeding (not controllable by local pressure) occur, the infusion of urokinase should be terminated immediately, and treatment instituted as described in the Adverse Effects.

In the following conditions, the risks of therapy may be increased and should be weighed against the anticipated benefits: recent (within 10 days) major surgery, obstetrical delivery, organ biopsy, previous puncture of non-compressible vessels; recent (within 10 days) serious gastrointestinal bleeding; recent trauma including cardiopulmonary resuscitation; severe uncontrolled arterial hypertension; high likelihood of a left heart thrombus, e.g., mitral stenosis with atrial fibrillation; subacute bacterial endocarditis; hemostatic defects including those secondary to severe hepatic or renal disease; pregnancy; cerebrovascular disease; diabetic hemorrhagic retinopathy; any other condition in which bleeding might constitute a significant hazard or be particularly difficult to manage because of its location.

Fibrinogen levels should be kept greater than 100 mg/100 mL.

Complications in Ischemia: During treatment of peripheral arterial and graft thromboembolic occlusion in patients who have had prolonged and/or severe ischemia, systemic complications including adult respiratory distress syndrome (ARDS) and acute tubular necrosis (ATN) have occurred following revascularization. Hypotension, hyperkalemia, lactic acidosis, ATN, congestive heart failure/ARDS, disseminated intravascular coagulation and death have been reported following the use of urokinase to revascularize a nonviable limb.

Distal embolization of the lysing clot with an associated increase in ischemic severity has been reported during intra-arterial treatment of peripheral arterial and graft thromboembolic occlusions. This condition usually responds to continued urokinase infusion at the site of the distally migrated clot (see Dosage).

Use of Anticoagulants: Concurrent use of anticoagulants with i.v. administration of urokinase is not recommended. However, concurrent use of heparin should be used during intracoronary or intra-arterial administration of urokinase.

Clinical studies with concurrent use of heparin and urokinase during intracoronary and intra-arterial administration have demonstrated no tendency toward increased bleeding that would not be attributable to the procedure or urokinase alone. Nevertheless, careful monitoring for excessive bleeding is advised.

Arrhythmias: Coronary thrombolysis may result in arrhythmias associated with reperfusion. These arrhythmias (such as bradycardia, accelerated idioventricular rhythm, ventricular premature depolarization, ventricular tachycardia) are not different from those often seen in the ordinary course of acute myocardial infarction and may be managed with standard antiarrhythmic measures. It is recommended that antiarrhythmic therapy for bradycardia and/or ventricular irritability be available in patients who receive urokinase.

Cholesterol Embolization Syndrome: Cholesterol embolization has been reported in the literature following the i.v. administration of thrombolytic agents.

I.V. Catheter Clearance: Excessive pressure should be avoided when urokinase is injected into the catheter. Such force could cause rupture of the catheter or expulsion of the clot into the circulation.

During attempts to determine catheter occlusion, vigorous suction should not be applied due to possible damage to the vascular wall or collapse of soft-wall catheters.

Catheters may be occluded by substances other than fibrin clots, such as drug precipitates. Urokinase is not effective in such cases and there is the possibility that the substances may be forced into the vascular system.

Precautions: Urokinase should be used in hospitals where the recommended diagnosis and monitoring techniques are available.

Thrombolytic therapy should be considered in all situations where the benefits to be achieved outweigh the risk of potentially serious hemorrhage. When internal bleeding does occur, it may be more difficult to manage than that which occurs with conventional anticoagulant therapy.

Pregnancy: Reproduction studies have been performed in mice and rats at doses up to 1 000 times the human dose and have revealed no evidence of impaired fertility or harm to the fetus due to urokinase. There are, however, no adequate and well-controlled studies in pregnant women. Because animal reproduction studies are not always predictive of human response, this drug should be used during pregnancy only if clearly needed.

Lactation: It is not known whether this drug is excreted in human milk. Because many drugs are excreted in human milk, caution should be exercised when urokinase is administered to a nursing woman.

Children: Safety and effectiveness in children have not been established.

Drug Interactions: The interaction of urokinase with other drugs has not been studied. Drugs that alter platelet function should not be used. Common examples are: ASA, indomethacin and phenylbutazone.

Although a bolus dose of heparin is recommended in conjunction with intracoronary or intra-arterial use of urokinase, oral anticoagulants or heparin should not be given concurrently with large doses of urokinase such as those used for pulmonary embolism. Concomitant use of i.v. urokinase and oral anticoagulants or heparin may increase the risk of hemorrhage (see Warnings).

Laboratory Tests: Before commencing thrombolytic therapy, obtain a hematocrit, platelet count, and a thrombin time (TT), activated partial thromboplastin time (APTT), or prothrombin time (PT).

If heparin has been given, it should be discontinued during the i.v. administration of urokinase for pulmonary embolism. Heparin should be used in conjunction with urokinase for intracoronary or intra-arterial administration.

During the infusion, coagulation tests and/or measures of fibrinolytic activity may be performed if desired. Results do not, however, reliably predict either efficacy or a risk of bleeding. The clinical response should be observed frequently, and vital signs, i.e., pulse, temperature, respiratory rate and blood pressure should be checked at least every 4 hours. The blood pressure should not be taken in the lower extremities to avoid dislodgment of possible deep vein thrombi.

Following the i.v. infusion of urokinase for pulmonary embolism, before reinstituting heparin, the TT or APTT should be less than twice the normal control value.

Following intracoronary infusion of urokinase, blood coagulation parameters should be determined and heparin therapy continued as appropriate.

Following intra-arterial infusion of urokinase, the administration of heparin is discontinued. The infusion catheter is

Abbokinase (cont'd)

removed 1 hour after cessation of heparin and urokinase infusion. Protamine sulfate (30 mg i.v.) is usually given a few minutes before the removal of the catheter.

Adverse Effects: The following adverse reactions have been associated with i.v. therapy but may also occur with intra-arterial infusion.

Bleeding: The type of bleeding associated with thrombolytic therapy can be placed into two broad categories: a) superficial or surface bleeding, observed mainly at invaded or disturbed sites (e.g., venous cutdowns, arterial punctures, sites of recent surgical intervention, etc.), and b) internal bleeding, involving e.g., the gastrointestinal tract, genitourinary tract, vagina, or i.m., retroperitoneal, or intracerebral sites. Bleeding through Gore-Tex grafts has been reported.

Several fatalities due to intracranial or retroperitoneal hemorrhage have occurred during thrombolytic therapy.

Should serious bleeding occur, urokinase infusion should be discontinued, and if necessary, blood loss and reversal of the bleeding tendency can be effectively managed with whole blood (fresh blood preferable), packed red blood cells and cryoprecipitate or fresh frozen plasma. Dextran should not be used. Although the use of aminocaproic acid (ACA, Amicar) in humans as an antidote for urokinase has not been documented, it may be considered in an emergency situation.

Allergic Reactions: In vitro tests with urokinase, as well as intradermal tests in humans, gave no evidence of induced antibody formation. Relatively mild allergic type reactions, e.g., bronchospasm and skin rash, have been reported rarely. When such reactions occur, they usually respond to conventional therapy. In addition, rare cases of anaphylaxis have been reported.

Miscellaneous: Fever and chills, including shaking chills (rigors), nausea and/or vomiting, transient hypotension or hypertension, dyspnea, tachycardia, cyanosis, back pain, hypoxemia, and acidosis have been reported together and separately. Rare cases of myocardial infarction have also been reported. A cause and effect relationship has not been established.

Febrile episodes have occurred in approximately 2 to 3% of treated patients. Symptomatic treatment of fever with acetaminophen is usually sufficient to alleviate discomfort. The use of acetaminophen rather than ASA is recommended.

Overdose: Symptoms and Treatment: Therapy should be discontinued if there is bleeding and fresh whole blood or fresh-frozen plasma should be administered; if these fail to control bleeding, the use of aminocaproic acid (ACA) is suggested although there is no documented evidence for this use in humans.

Mild external bleeding is usually controlled by the application of local pressure.

Local reaction involving development of a compartment syndrome and systemic effects including ARDS, ATN, DIC, lactic acidosis, hyperkalemia and hypotension have been observed as revascularization complications.

Dosage: Urokinase is intended for intravascular and intra-coronary infusion only after reconstitution according to the recommendations described under "Reconstituted Solutions".

Pulmonary Embolism: Heparin should be discontinued during the i.v. administration of urokinase for pulmonary embolism.

Reconstituted urokinase (see Reconstituted Solutions) should be diluted with either 0.9% Sodium Chloride Injection USP or 5% Dextrose Injection USP prior to i.v. infusion (see Parenteral Products, Dilution Before Use and Table I).

Administer urokinase by means of a constant infusion pump that is capable of delivering a total volume of 195 mL.

A priming dose of 4 400 IU/kg of urokinase is given as urokinase 0.9% Sodium Chloride Injection or 5% Dextrose Injection admixture at a rate of 90 mL/hour over a period of 10 minutes. This is followed by a continuous infusion of 4 400 IU/kg/hour of urokinase at a rate of 15 mL/hour for 12 hours.

Since some urokinase admixture will remain in the tubing at the end of an infusion pump delivery cycle, the following flush procedure should be performed to insure that the total dose of urokinase is administered. A solution of 0.9% Sodium Chloride Injection, USP or 5% Dextrose Injection USP approximately equal in amount to the volume of the tubing in the infusion set should be administered via the pump to flush the urokinase admixture from the entire length of the infusion set. The pump should be set to administer the flush solution at the continuous infusion rate of 15 mL/hour.

Anticoagulation After Terminating Urokinase Treatment: At the end of urokinase therapy, treatment with heparin by continuous i.v. infusion is recommended to prevent recurrent thrombosis. Heparin treatment, without a loading dose, should not begin until the thrombin time has decreased to less than twice the normal control value (approximately 3 to 4 hours after completion of the infusion). See manufacturer's prescribing information for proper use of heparin. This should then be followed by oral anticoagulants in the conventional manner.

Lysis of Coronary Artery Thrombi: Intracoronary administration: Reconstituted urokinase (see Reconstituted Solutions) should be diluted with 5% Dextrose Injection USP to give a concentration of approximately 1 500 IU/mL prior to intracoronary administration (see Parenteral Products, Dilution Before Use for Lysis of Coronary Artery Thrombi). No other medication should be added to the solution.

Before the infusion of urokinase, a bolus dose of heparin ranging from 2 500 to 10 000 units should be administered i.v. to maintain an increase in coagulation test parameters of 1.5 to 2 times the normal. Prior heparin administration should be considered when calculating the heparin dose for this procedure. Following the bolus dose of heparin, the prepared urokinase solution should be infused into the occluded artery at a rate of 4 mL/minute (6 000 IU/minute) for periods up to 2 hours to a maximal dose of 720 000 IU. In a clinical study, the average total dose of urokinase utilized for lysis of coronary artery thrombi was 500 000 IU.

To determine response to urokinase therapy, periodic angiography during the infusion is recommended. It is suggested that the angiography be repeated at approximately 15-minute intervals.

Urokinase therapy should be continued until the artery is maximally opened, usually 15 to 30 minutes after the initial opening. Following the infusion, coagulation parameters should be determined. It is advisable to continue heparin therapy after the artery is opened by urokinase.

When urokinase was administered selectively into thrombosed coronary arteries via coronary catheter within 6 hours following onset of symptoms of acute transmural myocardial infarction, 60% of the occlusions were opened.

Thrombolytic therapy may be used in conjunction with other therapeutic modalities (anticoagulation, surgery or percutaneous transluminal angioplasty).

Peripheral Arterial and Graft Thromboembolic Occlusion: Reconstituted urokinase (see Reconstituted Solutions) should be diluted with 0.9% Sodium Chloride Injection USP to give a concentration of approximately 2 500 IU/mL prior to administration (see Parenteral Products, Dilution Before Use; Peripheral Arterial and Graft Thromboembolic Occlusion).

Mechanical disruption of the clot with guide-wire or catheter seems to improve the fibinolytic process. The ability of the guide-wire to penetrate the clot appears to be one of the best predictors of probable success.

Advance a catheter to the site of occlusion. Infuse urokinase directly onto the clot at a rate ranging from 60 000 IU/hour to 240 000 IU/hour, with the higher doses used initially until antegrade blood flow is reestablished and/or in the presence of significant ischemia or when the catheter cannot be placed in contact with the clot. In a clinical study antegrade blood flow was reestablished in 73% of the patients at a rate of 4 000 IU/min for a mean infusion time of 3.3 hours.

I.V. heparin therapy should be administered concurrently to maintain an increase in coagulation test parameters of 3 to 4 times the normal values around the infusion catheter until reestablishment of antegrade blood flow. During the infusion, monitor thrombolytic progress by arteriography minimally every 500 000 IU increments (2 hours at an initial rate of 4 000 IU/min or 8 hours at a rate of 1 000 IU/min).

Create a thin channel with the guide-wire in the remaining distal clot and advance the catheter tip into the clot as lysis progresses. Following reestablishment of antegrade blood flow, reposition the catheter tip just proximal to the remaining clot and continue the infusion until all the remaining clot has been lysed or until no further progress can be documented between arteriograms (<10% reduction in clot length after a 500 000 IU increment).

Complete thrombus lysis was achieved in 83% (70/84) of the completed urokinase infusions with a mean infusion time of 18±15 hours.

In 83% of the patients who completed infusion, complete clot lysis was observed with a mean infusion time of 18 hours. Following reestablishment of antegrade blood flow using high doses of urokinase, the dose may be reduced to 1 000 IU/min to lyse all of the remaining clot. In the event of distal migration of the lysing clot, advance the catheter either into the migrated clot or the vessel it is occluding and continue the urokinase infusion at high doses until complete clot lysis has occurred.

A low incidence (1%) of rethrombosis, after thrombolytic therapy, was observed in patients who received concomitant heparin (to maintain the PTT at 3 to 4 times normal) and percutaneous transluminal angioplasty (PTA) immediately after complete clot lysis (residual stenoses ≥50%). Surgery may be necessary in patients who do not respond to PTA.

I.V. Catheter Clearance: Reconstitute urokinase (see Reconstituted Solutions) and add 1 mL of the reconstituted drug to 9 mL Sterile Water for Injection USP to make a final dilution equivalent to 5 000 IU/mL. One mL of this preparation is to be utilized for each catheter clearing procedure.

When the following procedure is used to clear a central venous catheter, the patient should be instructed to exhale and hold his breath any time the catheter is not connected to i.v. tubing or a syringe. This is to prevent air from entering the open catheter.

Aseptically disconnect the i.v. tubing connection at the catheter hub and attach a 10 mL syringe. Determine occlusion of the catheter by gently attempting to aspirate blood from the catheter with the 10 mL syringe. If aspiration is not possible, remove the 10 mL syringe and attach a 1 mL tuberculin syringe filled with prepared urokinase to the catheter. Slowly and gently inject an amount of urokinase equal to the volume of the catheter.

Aseptically remove the tuberculin syringe and connect an empty syringe (e.g., 5 mL) to the catheter. Wait at least 5 minutes before attempting to aspirate the drug and residual clot with the empty syringe. Repeat aspiration attempts every 5 minutes. If the catheter is not open within 30 minutes, the catheter may be capped allowing urokinase to remain in the catheter for 30 to 60 minutes before again attempting to aspirate. A second injection of urokinase may be necessary in resistant cases.

When patency is restored, aspirate 4 to 5 mL of blood to assure removal of all drug and clot residual. Remove the blood-filled syringe and replace it with a 10 mL syringe filled with 0.9% Sodium Chloride Injection USP. The catheter should then be gently irrigated with this solution to assure patency of the catheter. After the catheter has been irrigated, remove the 10 mL syringe and aseptically reconnect sterile i.v. tubing to the catheter hub.

Reconstituted Solutions: Reconstitute Abbokinase vials by aseptically adding 5 mL of Sterile Water for Injection USP to each vial of 250 000 IU. After reconstitution each mL contains 50 000 IU.

Abbokinase should be reconstituted only with Sterile Water for Injection USP without preservatives. Bacteriostatic Water for Injection should not be used.

The solution may be terminally filtered, e.g., through a 0.45 micron or smaller cellulose membrane filter. No other medication should be added to this solution.

Because Abbokinase contains no preservative, it should not be reconstituted until immediately before using. Any unused portion of the reconstituted material should be discarded.

To minimize formation of filaments, avoid shaking the vial during reconstitution. Roll and tilt the vial to enhance reconstitution.

Each vial should be visually inspected for discoloration (practically colorless solution) and for the presence of particulate material. Highly colored solution should not be used.

Parenteral Products, Dilution Before Use: Reconstituted urokinase should be diluted with either 0.9% Sodium Chloride Injection USP or 5% Dextrose Injection USP prior to infusion (see dilution for use for each indication).

No other medication should be added to this solution. The solution may be terminally filtered, e.g., through a 0.45 micron or smaller cellulose membrane filter.

The admixture should be administered immediately as described earlier.

Note: Adsorption of drug from dilute protein solutions to various materials has been reported in the literature. Therefore, the directions for Preparation and Administration must be followed to assure that significant drug loss does not occur.

Because Abbokinase contains no preservatives, it should not be prepared until immediately before using. Any solution remaining after administration should be discarded.

Pulmonary Embolism: Reconstitute the appropriate number of vials for the weight of the patient and add contents of the reconstituted urokinase vials to 0.9% Sodium Chloride Injection USP, or 5% Dextrose Injection USP as indicated in Table I.

Table I—Abbokinase

Dose Preparation—Pulmonary Embolism

Weight (kg)	Total Dose[a] Urokinase (IU)	Number of Vials of Abbokinase[a]	Volume of Abbokinase[a] after reconstitution (mL)[b]	Volume of I.V. Diluent (mL)	Final Volume (mL)
36–40	2 250 000	9	45	150	195
41–45	2 500 000	10	50	145	195
46–50	2 750 000	11	55	140	195
51–55	3 000 000	12	60	135	195
56–59	3 250 000	13	65	130	195
60–64	3 500 000	14	70	125	195
65–68	3 750 000	15	75	120	195
69–73	4 000 000	16	80	115	195
74–77	4 250 000	17	85	110	195
78–82	4 500 000	18	90	105	195
83–86	4 750 000	19	95	100	195
87–91	5 000 000	20	100	95	195
92–95	5 250 000	21	105	90	195
96–100	5 500 000	22	110	85	195
101–105	5 750 000	23	115	80	195
106–109	6 000 000	24	120	75	195
110–114	6 250 000	25	125	70	195

Infusion Rate:	Priming Dose	Dose for 12-Hour Period
	15 mL/10 min[c]	15 mL/hr for 12 hours

[a]Priming dose + dose administered during 12-hour period.
[b]After addition of 5 mL of Sterile Water for Injection USP per vial (see Reconstituted Solutions).
[c]Pump rate=90 mL/hr.

Lysis of Coronary Artery Thrombi: Intracoronary infusion: Add the contents of 3 reconstituted Abbokinase vials to 500 mL of 5% Dextrose Injection USP to give a concentration of approximately 1 500 IU/mL. No other medication should be added to this solution.

Peripheral Arterial and Graft Thromboembolic Occlusion: Add the contents of 2 reconstituted Abbokinase vials to 190 mL of 0.9% Sodium Chloride Injection USP. The resulting solution admixture will have a concentration of approximately 2 500 IU/mL (500 000 IU/200 mL).

Stability of Solutions: The admixture should be administered immediately. Any solution remaining after administration should be discarded.

Supplied: Each 5 mL vial of sterile lyophilized powder contains: urokinase activity 250 000 IU, mannitol, albumin (human) and sodium chloride. Sodium hydroxide and/or hydrochloric acid have been added prior to lyophilization for pH adjustment. Store powder at 2 to 30°C.

ABBOKINASE® OPEN-CATH® ℞

Abbott

Urokinase

Fibrinolytic

Pharmacology: Urokinase acts on the endogenous fibrinolytic system. It converts plasminogen to the enzyme plasmin. Plasmin degrades fibrin clots as well as fibrinogen.

When used as directed for i.v. catheter clearance only small amounts of urokinase may reach the circulation; therefore, therapeutic serum levels are not expected to be achieved. Nevertheless, one should be aware of the clinical pharmacology of urokinase.

I.V. infusion of urokinase in doses recommended for lysis of pulmonary embolism is followed by increased fibrinolytic activity. This effect disappears within a few hours after discontinuation, but a decrease in plasma levels of fibrinogen and plasminogen and an increase in the amount of circulating fibrin (ogen) degradation products may persist for 12 to 24 hours. There is a lack of correlation between clot embolysis and changes in coagulation and fibrinolytic assay results.

Information is incomplete about the pharmacokinetic properties in man. Urokinase administered by i.v. infusion is cleared rapidly by the liver. The serum half-life in man is 20 minutes or less. Patients with impaired liver function (e.g., cirrhosis) would be expected to show a prolongation in half-life. Small fractions of an administered dose are excreted in bile and urine.

Indications: For the restoration of patency to i.v. catheters, including central venous catheters, obstructed by clotted blood or fibrin.

Contraindications: This drug is contraindicated in individuals with a history of hypersensitivity to urokinase.

Because thrombolytic therapy increases the risk of bleeding, urokinase is contraindicated in the following situations: active internal bleeding, history of cerebrovascular accident, recent (within 2 months), intracranial or intraspinal surgery, recent trauma including cardiopulmonary resuscitation, intracranial neoplasm, arteriovenous malformation, or aneurysm, known bleeding diathesis, severe uncontrolled arterial hypertension and aortic dissection.

There have been no reports however, which would suggest a contraindication for the use of urokinase for i.v. catheter clearance.

Warnings: Excessive pressure should be avoided when urokinase is injected into the catheter. Such force could cause rupture of the catheter or expulsion of the clot into the circulation. During attempts to determine catheter occlusion, vigorous suction should not be applied due to possible damage to the vascular wall or collapse of soft-wall catheters.

Catheters may be occluded by substances other than fibrin clots, such as precipitates. Urokinase is not effective in such cases and there is the possibility that the substances may be forced into the vascular system.

Precautions: *Pregnancy:* Reproduction studies have been performed in mice and rats at doses up to 1 000 times the human dose and have revealed no evidence of impaired fertility or harm to the fetus due to urokinase.

There are, however, no adequate and well-controlled studies in pregnant women. Because animal reproduction studies are not always predictive of human response, this drug should be used during pregnancy only if clearly needed.

Lactation: It is not known whether this drug is excreted in human milk. Because many drugs are excreted in human milk, caution should be exercised when urokinase is administered to a nursing woman.

Children: Safety and effectiveness in children have been established.

Adverse Effects: The potential exists for adverse reactions to occur as a result of using urokinase for the removal of clot obstruction for i.v. catheters.

The following adverse reactions have been associated with i.v. therapy: Bleeding: The type of bleeding associated with thrombolytic therapy can be placed into 2 broad categories: a) superficial or surface bleeding, observed mainly at invaded or disturbed sites (e.g., venous cutdowns, arterial punctures, sites of recent surgical intervention, etc.), and b) internal bleeding, involving e.g., the gastrointestinal tract, genitourinary tract, vagina, or i.m. retroperitoneal, or intracerebral sites. Bleeding through Gore-Tex grafts has been reported.

Several fatalities due to intracranial or retroperitoneal hemorrhage have occurred during thrombolytic therapy.

Should serious bleeding occur, urokinase infusion should be discontinued and, if necessary, blood loss and reversal of the bleeding tendency can be effectively managed with whole blood (fresh blood preferable), packed red blood cells and cryoprecipitate or fresh frozen plasma.

Dextran should not be used. Although the use of epsilon aminocaproic acid in humans as an antidote for urokinase has not been documented, it may be considered in an emergency situation.

Allergic Reactions: In vitro tests with urokinase, as well as intradermal tests in humans, gave no evidence of induced antibody formation. Relatively mild allergic type reactions, e.g., bronchospasm and skin rash, have been reported rarely. When such reactions occur, they usually respond to conventional therapy. In addition, rare cases of anaphylaxis have been reported.

Miscellaneous: Fever and chills, including shaking chills (rigors), nausea and/or vomiting, transient hypotension or hypertension, dyspnea, tachycardia, cyanosis, back pain, hypoxemia, and acidosis have been reported together and separately. Rare cases of myocardial infarction have also been reported. A cause and effect relationship has not been established.

Febrile episodes have occurred in approximately 2 to 3% of treated patients. Symptomatic treatment of fever with acetaminophen is usually sufficient to alleviate discomfort. The use of acetaminophen rather than ASA is recommended.

Overdose: Symptoms and Treatment: Urokinase therapy should be discontinued if there is bleeding and fresh whole blood or fresh-frozen plasma should be administered; if these fail to control bleeding, the use of epsilon aminocaproic acid (EACA) is suggested although there is not documented evidence for this use in humans.

Mild external bleeding is usually controlled by the application of local pressure.

Dosage: Reconstitute according to the recommendations described under Preparation of Solution. One mL or 1.8 mL of this preparation is to be utilized for each catheter clearing procedure. **Because Abbokinase contains no preservatives, any unused portion should be discarded.**

Administration: **When the following procedure is used to clear a central venous catheter, the patient should be instructed to exhale and hold his breath any time the catheter is not connected to i.v. tubing or a syringe. This is to prevent air from entering the open catheter. As an added precaution, any central venous catheter not connected to i.v. tubing or a syringe should be clamped or connected to a closed stopcock.**

Aseptically disconnect the i.v. tubing connection at the catheter hub and attach an empty 10 mL syringe. Determine occlusion of the catheter by gently attempting to aspirate blood from the catheter with the 10 mL syringe.

If aspiration is not possible, remove the 10 mL syringe and attach a tuberculin syringe filled with prepared urokinase equal to the internal volume of the catheter. Slowly and gently inject the solution into the catheter. Care must be taken to avoid rupture of the catheter or expulsion of the intact clot into the circulation. Aseptically remove the tuberculin syringe and connect an empty syringe (e.g., 5 mL) to the catheter. Wait at least 5 minutes before attempting to aspirate the solution and residual clot with the empty syringe. Repeat aspiration attempts every 5 minutes. If the catheter is not open within 30 minutes, the catheter may be capped allowing urokinase to remain in the catheter for 30 to 60 minutes before again attempting to aspirate. A second injection of urokinase into the catheter may be necessary in resistant cases.

When patency is restored, aspirate 4 to 5 mL of blood to assure removal of all urokinase solution and clot residue. Remove the blood-filled syringe and replace it with a 10 mL syringe filled with 0.9% Sodium Chloride Injection USP. The catheter should then be gently irrigated with this solution to assure patency of the catheter. After the catheter has been irrigated, remove the 10 mL syringe and aseptically reconnect sterile i.v. tubing to the catheter hub.

Preparation of Solution: Dil-U-Vial:
1. Remove protective cap. Turn plunger-stopper a quarter turn and press to force diluent into lower chamber.
2. Roll and tilt to effect solution. **Do not shake.** Use only a clear, colorless solution.
3. Sterilize top of stopper with a suitable germicide.
4. Insert needle through the centre of stopper until tip is barely visible. Withdraw dose. **No further dilution is required.**

It is recommended that vigorous shaking be avoided during reconstitution; roll and tilt to enhance reconstitution. Parenteral drug products should be inspected visually for particulate matter and discoloration prior to administration, whenever solution and container permit.

Supplied: Each vial of sterile lyophilized powder contains: urokinase activity 5 000 IU/mL. Nonmedicinal ingredients: gelatin, mannitol, monobasic sodium phosphate anhydrous and sodium chloride. Sodium hydroxide and/or hydrochloric acid have been added prior to lyophilization for pH adjustment. Vials of 1 mL. Store powder below 25°C. Avoid freezing.

Reviewed 1998

ABENOL®

SmithKline Beecham

Acetaminophen

Analgesic—Antipyretic

Pharmacology: Acetaminophen is the major metabolite of phenacetin and acetanilide. Animal and clinical studies have shown acetaminophen to have antipyretic and analgesic activity equal to that of ASA. Acetaminophen lacks anti-inflammatory effects.

Unlike the salicylates, acetaminophen does not interfere with tubular secretion of uric acid nor does it affect acid-base balance if taken in therapeutic doses. Acetaminophen does not interfere with hemostasis and, in particular does not inhibit platelet aggregation. Allergic reactions are rare and thus the drug is useful in patients who cannot tolerate salicylates and those with an allergic diathesis, including bronchial asthmatics. The rate of acetaminophen absorption from the gastrointestinal tract following oral administration is a function of stomach emptying rate and is generally rapid and complete

Abenol (cont'd)

with peak plasma concentrations of free drug being achieved in 0.5 to 1 hour following administration. The plasma half-life of unchanged drug is about 2 hours with approximately 85% of a 1 g oral dose being recovered in the urine in 24 hours. Approximately 3% is excreted unchanged with the balance being eliminated principally as the glucuronide and sulfate conjugates.

A small portion of the administered acetaminophen is converted by hepatic microsomal enzymes to a reactive metabolite. At therapeutic doses this minor metabolite is rapidly inactivated by conjugation with glutathione and eliminated by renal excretion. However, where hepatic glutathione has been depleted, covalent binding of the reactive metabolite to liver-cell macromolecules occurs and hepatic cell necrosis ensues. It has been shown that glutathione precursors such as N-acetylcysteine, cysteine, cysteamine and methionine can decrease experimental acetaminophen-induced hepatic necrosis when administered promptly after a toxic dose of acetaminophen. Rectal absorption of acetaminophen, as with most rectally administered drugs, is more erratic than absorption following oral administration. Absorption rate is generally slower. Peak blood levels of free acetaminophen are not reached until 1.5 to 3 hours following rectal administration and the peak concentration in the blood is approximately 50% of that observed following an equivalent oral dose. The percentage of a rectal dose of acetaminophen absorbed also varies giving wide variances in bioavailability. In view of these observations higher rectal doses or more frequent administration may be required to achieve and/or maintain blood concentrations of acetaminophen comparable to those obtained following oral administration.

Indications: For the treatment of mild to moderate pain and the reduction of fever.

Contraindications: Hypersensitivity to acetaminophen or to its nonmedicinal ingredients.

Warnings: Acetaminophen poisoning can result in severe hepatic damage.

Precautions and Adverse Effects: When used as directed, acetaminophen is virtually free of severe toxicity or side effects. The incidence of gastrointestinal upset is less than after salicylate administration. If a rare sensitivity reaction occurs, discontinue the drug.

Hypersensitivity to acetaminophen is usually manifested by a rash or urticaria.

Regular use of acetaminophen has been shown to produce a slight increase in prothrombin time in patients receiving oral anticoagulants but the clinical significance of this effect is not clear.

Overdose: Symptoms: In adults hepatotoxicity may occur after ingestion of a single dose of 10 to 15 g (200 to 250 mg/kg) of acetaminophen; a dose of 25 g or more is potentially fatal. In adults, nonfatal overdoses (ranging from 12.5 to 31.5 g) have been reported and 1 death after 30 g of acetaminophen had been ingested. A 13 year old child is reported to have died after ingesting 15 g.

Symptoms during the first 2 days of acute poisoning by acetaminophen do not reflect the potential seriousness of the intoxication. Nausea, vomiting, anorexia and abdominal pain occur during the initial 24 hours and may persist for a week of more. Liver injury may become manifest the second day, initially by elevation of serum transaminase and lactic dehydrogenase activity, increased serum bilirubin concentration and prolongation of prothrombin time. Alkaline phosphatase activity and serum albumin concentration may remain normal. The hepatotoxicity may progress to encephalopathy, coma and death. Liver biopsy reveals centrilobular necrosis with sparing of the periportal area. In nonfatal cases, the hepatic lesions are reversible over a period of weeks or months. Transient azotemia is apparent in most patients and acute renal failure occurs in some. Hypoglycemia may occur, but glycosuria and impaired glucose tolerance have also been reported. Both metabolic acidosis and metabolic alkalosis have been noted, cerebral edema and nonspecific myocardial depression have also occurred. Since acetaminophen is metabolized primarily by the liver, in cases of acute poisoning, prolongation of the plasma half-life beyond 3 hours may be indicative of liver injury. Hepatic necrosis should be anticipated if the half-life exceeds 4 hours, and hepatic coma is likely if the half-life is greater than 12 hours. A single determination of serum acetaminophen concentration is a less reliable predictor of hepatic injury. However, only minimal liver damage has developed when the serum concentration was below 120 μg/mL at 4 hours or less than 50 μg/mL at 12 hours after ingestion of the drug. Encephalopathy should also be anticipated if serum bilirubin concentration exceeds 4 mg/100 mL during the first 5 days.

Treatment: Early diagnosis is vital. Vigorous supportive therapy is essential when intoxication is severe. Procedures to limit continuing absorption of the drug must be initiated promptly. When the oral route of administration is used induction of vomiting or gastric lavage should be performed and should be followed by oral administration of activated charcoal (50 g). Hemodialysis, if it can be initiated within the first 12 hours, has been advocated for all patients with a plasma concentration of acetaminophen greater than 120 μg/mL 4 hours after drug ingestion. If administered within the first few hours after ingestion of acetaminophen, sulfhydryl compounds, which replete glutathione, have been shown to effectively prevent or reduce the hepatotoxic effects of acetaminophen. N-acetylcysteine, available commercially as a sterile 20% solution (Mucomyst), has been shown to be particularly effective and well tolerated when given orally as a 5% solution diluted with cola, fruit juice, or water. The accepted treatment regimen is a loading dose of 140 mg/kg followed by 70 mg/kg every 4 hours for 17 doses or until plasma concentrations of acetaminophen are indicative of a low risk of hepatotoxicity.

Dosage: Adults: 650 mg every 4 to 6 hours as necessary. Maximum daily dosage recommended is 6 suppositories.

Children: Under 2 years: As recommended by the physician. 2 to 4 years: 120 mg every 4 hours. Maximum daily dosage recommended is 6 suppositories. 4 to 6 years: 325 mg every 6 hours. Maximum daily dosage recommended is 4 suppositories. 6 to 12 years: 325 mg every 4 hours. Maximum daily dosage recommended is 6 suppositories.

A physician should be consulted for treatment regimens lasting longer than 5 days. Inherent in the rectal route of administration is the possibility of erratic absorption, lower blood concentrations and lower bioavailability in some patients relative to the oral route. Therefore, more frequent rectal administration is acceptable when deemed necessary by the prescriber.

Information for the Patient: See Blue Section—Information for the Patient "Abenol".

Supplied: Each suppository contains: acetaminophen 120, 325 or 650 mg. Nonmedicinal ingredients: Novata. Suppositories are individually sealed in plastic moulds. Boxes of 4 and 12. Store at room temperature.

Reviewed 1999

A.C.&C. Ⓝ

WestCan

ASA—Caffeine—Codeine

Analgesic—Antipyretic—Anti-inflammatory

Supplied: Each tablet contains: ASA 325 mg, caffeine 15 mg and codeine phosphate 8 mg. Bottles of 40, 50 and 100 with child resistant caps. Bottles of 200 without child resistant cap.

ACCOLATE® Ⓟ

Zeneca

Zafirlukast

Leukotriene Receptor Antagonist

Pharmacology: Zafirlukast is a selective and competitive receptor antagonist of leukotriene D_4 and E_4 (LTD_4 and LTE_4), components of slow-reacting substance of anaphylaxis (SRSA). Cysteinyl leukotriene production and receptor occupation have been correlated with the pathophysiology of asthma, including airway edema, smooth muscle constriction, and altered cellular activity associated with the inflammatory process, which contribute to the signs and symptoms of asthma. Patients with asthma were found in 1 study to be 25 to 100 times more sensitive to the bronchoconstricting activity of inhaled LTD_4 than nonasthmatic subjects.

In vitro studies demonstrated that zafirlukast antagonized the contractile activity of 3 leukotrienes (LTC_4, LTD_4 and LTE_4) in conducting airway smooth muscle from laboratory animals and humans. Zafirlukast prevented intradermal LTD_4-induced increases in cutaneous vascular permeability and inhibited inhaled LTD_4-induced influx of eosinophils into animal lungs. Inhalational challenge studies in sensitized sheep showed that zafirlukast suppressed the airway responses to antigen; this included both the early- and late-phase response and the nonspecific hyperresponsiveness.

In humans, zafirlukast inhibited bronchoconstriction caused by several kinds of inhalational challenges. Pretreatment with single oral doses of zafirlukast inhibited the bronchoconstriction caused by sulfur dioxide and cold air in patients with asthma. Pretreatment with single doses of zafirlukast attenuated the early- and late-phase reaction caused by inhalation of various antigens such as grass, cat dander, ragweed, and mixed antigens in patients with asthma. Zafirlukast also attenuated the increase in bronchial hyperresponsiveness to inhaled histamine that followed inhaled allergen challenge.

Clinical Studies: Three double-blind, randomized, placebo-controlled, 13-week clinical trials in 1 380 patients with mild to moderate asthma demonstrated that zafirlukast improved daytime asthma symptoms, nighttime awakenings, mornings with asthma symptoms, rescue β_2-agonist use, FEV_1, and morning peak expiratory flow rate. In these studies, the patients had a mean baseline FEV_1 of approximately 75% of predicted normal and a mean baseline β-agonist requirement of approximately 4 to 5 puffs of salbutamol/day. The results of the largest of the trials are shown in Table I.

Table I—Accolate

Mean Change from Baseline at Study Endpoint

Parameter		Accolate 20 mg twice daily N=514	Placebo N=248
Daytime Asthma Symptom Score	(0-3 scale)	-0.44*	-0.25
Nighttime Awakenings	(number/week)	-1.27*	-0.43
Mornings with Asthma Symptoms	(days/week)	-1.32*	-0.75
Rescue β_2-agonist use	(puffs/day)	-1.15*	-0.24
FEV_1	(L)	+0.15*	+0.05
Morning PEFR	(L/min)	+22.06*	+7.63
Evening PEFR	(L/min)	+13.12	+10.14

* $p<0.05$, compared to placebo.

In a second and smaller study, the effect of zafirlukast on most efficacy parameters was comparable to the active control (inhaled sodium cromoglycate 1 600 μg 4 times/day) and superior to placebo at endpoint for decreasing rescue β-agonist use.

In these trials, improvement in asthma symptoms occurred within 1 week of initiating treatment with zafirlukast. The role of zafirlukast in the management of patients with more severe asthma, patients receiving antiasthma therapy other than as needed, inhaled β_2-agonists, or as an oral or inhaled corticosteroid-sparing agent remains to be fully characterized.

Pharmacokinetics: Absorption: Zafirlukast is rapidly absorbed following oral administration. The absolute bioavailability of zafirlukast is unknown. Peak plasma concentrations are achieved 3 hours after dosing. In 2 separate studies, one using a high fat and the other a high protein meal, administration of zafirlukast with food reduced the mean bioavailability by approximately 40%.

Plasma Kinetics and Disposition: The mean terminal elimination half-life of zafirlukast is approximately 10 hours in both normal subjects and patients with asthma. Steady-state plasma concentrations of zafirlukast are proportional to the dose and predictable from single dose pharmacokinetic data. In the concentration range of 0.25 to 10 μg/mL, zafirlukast is >99% bound to plasma proteins, predominantly albumin.

Biotransformation: Zafirlukast is extensively metabolized. Following oral administration of a radiolabeled dose, urinary excretion accounts for approximately 10% of the dose and the remainder is excreted in feces. Unmetabolized zafirlukast is not detected in urine. In vitro studies using human liver microsomes showed that the hydroxylated metabolites of zafirlukast are formed through the cytochrome P450 2C9 (CYP2C9) enzyme pathway. Additional in vitro studies utilizing human liver microsomes show that zafirlukast inhibits the cytochrome P450 CYP3A4 and CYP2C9 isoenzymes at concentrations close to the clinically achieved plasma concentrations. The metabolites of zafirlukast found in plasma are at least 90 times less potent as LTD_4 receptor antagonists than zafirlukast in a standard in vitro test of activity.

Special Populations: Geriatrics: Cross-study comparisons in patients ranging from 7 years to greater than 65 years of age show that mean dose (mg/kg) normalized AUC and C_{max} increase and plasma clearance (Cl) decreases with increasing age. In patients above 65 years of age, there is an approximately 2- to 3-fold greater C_{max} and AUC compared to young adult patients.

Hepatic Impairment: In a study of patients with hepatic impairment (biopsy-proven cirrhosis), there was a 50 to 60% greater C_{max} and AUC compared to normal subjects.

Renal Impairment: Based on a cross-study comparison, there are no apparent differences in the pharmacokinetics of zafirlukast between renally impaired patients and normal subjects.

Indications: For the prophylaxis and chronic treatment of asthma in adults and children 12 years of age and older.

Contraindications: In patients who have previously experienced hypersensitivity to the product or any of its ingredients.

Warnings: Zafirlukast is not indicated for use in the reversal of bronchospasm in acute asthma attacks, including status asthmaticus.

Warfarin Interaction: Warfarin coadministration with zafirlukast produces clinically significant increases in prothrombin time (PT). Patients on oral warfarin anticoagulant therapy and zafirlukast should have their prothrombin times monitored closely and anticoagulant dose adjusted accordingly (see Precautions, Drug Interactions).

Hepatic Effects: Rarely, elevations of one or more liver enzymes have occurred in patients receiving zafirlukast in controlled clinical trials. Most of these cases have been observed in asymptomatic patients at doses 4 times higher than the recommended dose, and return to the normal range after a variable period of time upon discontinuation of zafirlukast therapy. Liver function test abnormalities could represent early evidence of hepatotoxicity that may occur with prolonged administration. This risk appears to be greater in women. Rare cases of symptomatic hepatitis and hyperbilirubinemia, without other attributable causes, have occurred in patients who have received the recommended doses of zafirlukast (40 mg/day). In these patients, the liver enzymes returned to normal or near normal after stopping zafirlukast. If clinical signs or symptoms of liver dysfunction (e.g., right upper quadrant abdominal pain, nausea, fatigue, lethargy, pruritus, jaundice, and "flu-like" symptoms) are noted, it is reasonable to recommend that standard liver tests be obtained and the patient managed accordingly. A decision to discontinue zafirlukast should be individualized to the patient's condition, weighing the risk of hepatic dysfunction against the clinical benefit of zafirlukast to the patient.

Precautions: General: Zafirlukast should be taken regularly as prescribed, even during symptom-free periods. Zafirlukast therapy can be continued during acute exacerbations of asthma.

Zafirlukast is not a bronchodilator and should not be used to treat acute episodes of asthma.

Patients receiving zafirlukast should be instructed not to decrease the dose or stop taking any other antiasthma medications unless instructed by a physician.

Eosinophilic Conditions: When oral steroid reduction is considered, caution is required. Reduction of the oral steroid dose, in some asthma patients on zafirlukast therapy, has been followed, in rare cases, by the occurrence of eosinophilia, vasculitic rash, worsening pulmonary symptoms, cardiac complications, and/or neuropathy, sometimes presenting as Churg-Strauss syndrome, a systemic eosinophilic vasculitis. A causal relationship with zafirlukast has not been established.

Hepatic Effects: See Warnings.

Children: The efficacy and safety of zafirlukast in children under 12 years has not been established.

Carcinogenesis and Mutagenicity: In 2-year oral carcinogenicity studies, zafirlukast was administered at daily doses of 10 to 300 mg/kg to mice and 40 to 2 000 mg/kg to rats. At 300 mg/kg/day male mice had an increased incidence of hepatocellular adenomas and female mice showed a greater incidence of whole body histocytic sarcomas. The plasma concentrations at these tumorigenic doses were approximately 220 times maximum recommended human daily oral dose. Male and female rats given 2 000 mg/kg/day had an increased incidence of urinary bladder transitional cell papillomas. The plasma concentrations at these tumorigenic doses were approximately 200 times the plasma concentrations in humans at the maximum recommended human daily oral dose. The clinical significance of these findings for the long-term use of zafirlukast is unknown.

No mutagenic potential was evident in point mutation assays or chromosomal aberrations clastogenic assays.

Reproduction and Fertility: Reproduction and fertility studies in rats showed no effect on fertility due to zafirlukast at doses up to 2 000 mg/kg (approximately 400 times the maximum recommended human daily oral dose on mg/m² basis). In the 1-year toxicity studies in dogs, zafirlukast produced an increase in absolute and relative uterine and ovarian weights at an oral dose of 150 mg/kg, resulting in approximately 85 times the systemic exposure (AUC_{0-12h}) in humans at the maximum recommended human oral daily dose.

Pregnancy: The safety of zafirlukast in human pregnancy has not been established. The potential risks should be weighed against the benefits of continuing therapy during pregnancy; zafirlukast should be used only if clearly needed.

No teratogenicity was observed in the following species for the given oral doses (the approximate equivalence to the maximum recommended human daily oral dose on a mg/m² basis is given in brackets): mice 1 600 mg/kg/day (160 times); rats 2 000 mg/kg/day (400 times); cynomolgus monkeys 2 000 mg/kg/day (800 times).

At these doses, maternal toxicity was manifested in rats (as deaths and increased incidence of early fetal resorption), and cynomolgus monkeys (as spontaneous abortions). There are no adequate and well-controlled trials in pregnant women. Because animal reproduction studies are not always predictive of human response, zafirlukast should be used during pregnancy only if clearly needed.

Lactation: Zafirlukast is excreted in human breast milk. Following repeated 40 mg twice-a-day dosing in healthy women, average steady-state concentrations of zafirlukast in breast milk were 50 ng/mL compared to 255 ng/mL in plasma. Because of the potential for tumorigenicity shown for zafirlukast in mouse and rat studies and the enhanced sensitivity of neonatal rats and dogs to the adverse effects of zafirlukast, it should not be administered to mothers who are breast-feeding.

Drug Interactions: Zafirlukast may be administered with other therapies routinely used in the management of asthma and allergy. Examples of agents which have been coadministered with zafirlukast without adverse interaction include inhaled steroids, inhaled and oral bronchodilator therapy, antihistamines and antibiotics.

Coadministration with: 1) erythromycin will result in decreased plasma levels of zafirlukast. In a drug interaction study in 11 asthmatic patients, coadministration of a single dose of zafirlukast (40 mg) with erythromycin (500 mg 3 times daily for 5 days) to steady-state resulted in decreased mean plasma levels of zafirlukast by approximately 40% due to a decrease in zafirlukast bioavailability. 2) ASA may result in increased plasma levels of zafirlukast. Coadministration of zafirlukast (40 mg/day) with ASA (650 mg 4 times daily) resulted in mean increased plasma levels of zafirlukast by approximately 45%. 3) Theophylline may result in decreased plasma levels of zafirlukast, without effect on plasma theophylline levels. Coadministration of zafirlukast (80 mg/day) at steady-state with a single dose of a liquid theophylline preparation (6 mg/kg) in 13 asthmatic patients resulted in decreased mean plasma levels of zafirlukast by approximately 30%, but no effect on plasma theophylline levels was observed. 4) Terfenadine decreases zafirlukast AUC, but has no effect on plasma terfenadine levels. In a drug interaction study in 16 healthy male volunteers, coadministration of zafirlukast (320 mg/day), with terfenadine (60 mg twice daily) to steady-state resulted in a decrease in the mean C_{max} (-66%) and AUC (-54%) of zafirlukast. No effect of zafirlukast on terfenadine plasma concentrations or ECG parameters (i.e., QTc interval) was seen. No formal drug-drug interaction studies between zafirlukast and other drugs known to be metabolized by the P450 3A4 (CYP 3A4) isoenzymes have been conducted (see Cytochrome P450 Enzyme Inhibition). 5) Warfarin increases in prothrombin time by approximately 35%. In a drug interaction study in 16 healthy male volunteers, coadministration of multiple doses of zafirlukast (160 mg/day) to steady-state with a single 25 mg dose of warfarin resulted in a significant increase in the mean AUC (+63%) and half-life (+36%) of S-warfarin. The mean prothrombin time (PT) increased by approximately 35%. This interaction is probably due to an inhibition by zafirlukast of the cytochrome P450 2C9 isoenzyme system. Patients on oral warfarin anticoagulant therapy and zafirlukast should have their prothrombin times monitored closely and anticoagulant dose adjusted accordingly (see Warnings).

Oral contraceptives may be administered with zafirlukast without adverse interaction. In a single-blind, parallel-group, 3-week study in 39 healthy female subjects taking oral contraceptives, 40 mg twice daily of zafirlukast had no significant effect on ethinyl estradiol plasma concentrations or contraceptive efficacy.

Cytochrome P450 Enzyme Inhibition: Aside from warfarin and terfenadine, no formal zafirlukast drug-drug interaction studies have been conducted with other drugs known to be metabolized by cytochrome P450 isoenzymes. However, care should be exercised when zafirlukast is coadministered with metabolised drugs such as: tolbutamide, phenytoin, carbamazepine (isozyme 2C9); dihydropyridine calcium channel blockers, cyclosporin, cisapride, astemizole (isozyme CYP 3A4).

Food Interaction: Zafirlukast bioavailability may be altered when taken with a meal (see Pharmacology, Pharmacokinetics).

Adverse Effects: The safety database for zafirlukast consists of more than 4 000 healthy volunteers and patients who received zafirlukast, of which 1 723 were asthmatics enrolled in trials of 13-weeks duration or longer. A total of 671 patients received zafirlukast for 1 year or longer. The majority of the patients were 18 years of age or older; however 222 patients between the age of 12 and 18 years received zafirlukast.

A comparison of adverse events reported by ≥ 1% of zafirlukast-treated patients, and at rates numerically greater than in placebo-treated patients, is shown for all trials in Table II.

Table II—Accolate

Comparison of Adverse Events Reported by ≥ 1% of Zafirlukast-treated Patients vs Placebo-treated Patients

Number of Patients Adverse Event	Accolate 4 058 (%)	Placebo 2 032 (%)
Headache	12.9	11.7
Infection	3.5	3.4
Nausea	3.1	2.0
Diarrhea	2.8	2.1
Pain (Generalized)	1.9	1.7
Asthenia	1.8	1.6
Abdominal Pain	1.8	1.1
Accidental Injury	1.6	1.5
Dizziness	1.6	1.5
Myalgia	1.6	1.5
Fever	1.6	1.1
Back Pain	1.5	1.2
Vomiting	1.5	1.1
ALT Elevation	1.5	1.1
Dyspepsia	1.3	1.2

Liver Enzymes: Rarely, elevations of one or more liver enzymes have occurred in patients receiving zafirlukast in controlled clinical trials. Most of these have been observed in asymptomatic patients at doses 4 times higher than the recommended dose and returned to the normal range after a variable period of time upon discontinuation of zafirlukast therapy. Rare cases of symptomatic hepatitis and hyperbilirubinemia, without other attributable cause, have occurred in patients who had received the recommended doses of zafirlukast (40 mg/day). In these patients, the liver enzymes returned to normal or near normal after stopping zafirlukast (See Warnings and Precautions).

Infections and Age: In clinical trials, an increased proportion of zafirlukast patients over the age of 55 years reported infections as compared to placebo-treated patients. A similar finding was not observed in other age groups studied. These infections were mostly mild or moderate in intensity and predominantly affected the respiratory tract. Infections occurred equally in both sexes, were dose proportional to total mg of zafirlukast exposure, and were associated with coadministration of inhaled corticosteroids. The clinical significance of this finding is unknown.

Eosinophilic Conditions: The reduction of the oral steroid dose, in some patients on zafirlukast therapy has been followed in rare cases by the occurrence of eosinophilia, vasculitic rash, worsening pulmonary symptoms, cardiac complications, and/or neuropathy sometimes presenting as Churg-Strauss syndrome, a systemic eosinophilic vasculitis. A causal relationship with zafirlukast has not been established (See Precautions).

Hypersensitivity reactions, including urticaria angioedema and rashes, with or without blistering, have been reported in association with zafirlukast therapy.

Overdose: Symptoms and Treatment: No deaths occurred at oral zafirlukast doses of 2 000 mg/kg in mice (approximately 200 times the maximum recommended human daily oral dose on a mg/m² basis), 2 000 mg/kg in rats (approximately 400 times the maximum recommended human daily oral dose on a mg/m² basis), and 500 mg/kg in dogs (approximately 330 times the maximum recommended human daily oral dose on a mg/m² basis).

There is no experience to date with zafirlukast overdose in humans. It is reasonable to employ the usual supportive measures in the event of an overdose; e.g., remove unabsorbed material from the gastrointestinal tract, employ clinical monitoring, and institute supportive therapy, if required.

Dosage: Zafirlukast is indicated for the chronic treatment of asthma and should be taken regularly as prescribed, even during symptom-free periods.

Accolate (cont'd)

Zafirlukast is not a bronchodilator, and should not be used to treat acute episodes of asthma.

Patients receiving zafirlukast should be instructed not to decrease the dose or stop taking any other antiasthma medications unless instructed by a physician.

Adults and Children Aged 12 Years and Over: The recommended dose is 20 mg, twice daily for a total daily dose of 40 mg.

Since food reduces the bioavailability of zafirlukast, the drug should be taken at least 1 hour before or 2 hours after meals.

Geriatrics: The clearance of zafirlukast is reduced in elderly patients (>65 years old), such that C_{max} and AUC are approximately twice those of younger adults. However, accumulation of zafirlukast is not evident in elderly patients. In clinical trials, a dose of 20 mg b.i.d. was not associated with an increase in the incidence of adverse events or withdrawals because of adverse events in elderly patients.

Children: The safety and efficacy in children under 12 years has not been established.

Renal Impairment: Dosage adjustment is not required in patients with renal impairment.

Hepatic Impairment: Zafirlukast is not recommended for patients with hepatic impairment, including hepatic cirrhosis.

The clearance of zafirlukast is reduced in patients with stable alcoholic cirrhosis such that C_{max} and AUC are approximately 50 to 60% greater than those of normal adults.

Information for the Patient: See Blue Section—Information for the Patient "Accolate".

Supplied: Each white, round, biconvex, film-coated, intagliated tablet contains: zafirlukast 20 mg. Nonmedicinal ingredients: croscarmellose sodium, lactose, magnesium stearate, methylhydroxypropylcellulose, microcrystalline cellulose, polyvidone and titanium dioxide. Calendar packs of 60. Store between 15 and 30°C.

(Shown in Product Recognition Section)

New Product 1998

ACCUPRIL™ ℞

Parke-Davis

Quinapril HCl

Angiotensin Converting Enzyme Inhibitor

Pharmacology: Quinapril is a nonpeptide, nonsulphydryl inhibitor of angiotensin converting enzyme (ACE), which is used in the treatment of hypertension.

Angiotensin converting enzyme (ACE) is a peptidyl dipeptidase that catalyzes the conversion of angiotensin I to the vasoconstrictor angiotensin II. After absorption, quinapril is rapidly de-esterified to quinaprilat (quinapril diacid), its principal active metabolite. Its primary mode of action is to inhibit circulating and tissue ACE, thereby decreasing vasopressor activity and aldosterone secretion. Although the decrease in aldosterone is small, it results in a small increase in serum K^+ (see Precautions). Removal of angiotensin II negative feedback on renin secretion leads to increased plasma renin activity. Although quinapril had antihypertensive activity in all races studied, black hypertensive patients (usually a low-renin hypertensive population) had a smaller average response to ACE inhibitor monotherapy than nonblack patients.

ACE is identical to kininase II. Thus, quinapril may interfere with the degradation of bradykinin, a potent peptide vasodilator. However, it is not known whether this system contributes to the therapeutic effects of quinapril.

The antihypertensive effect of quinapril outlasts its inhibitory effect on circulating ACE in animal studies. Tissue ACE inhibition more closely correlates with the duration of antihypertensive effects and this may be related to enzyme binding characteristics as shown for quinapril on purified ACE from human kidney and heart.

Pharmacokinetics: Following oral administration of quinapril, peak plasma concentrations of quinapril occur within 1 hour. Based on the recovery of quinapril and its metabolites in urine, the extent of absorption is at least 60%. Following absorption, quinapril is de-esterified to its major active metabolite, quinaprilat (quinapril diacid) a potent ACE inhibitor, and to minor inactive metabolites. Quinapril has an apparent half-life in plasma of approximately 1 hour. Peak plasma quinaprilat concentrations occur approximately 2 hours after an oral dose of quinapril. Quinaprilat is eliminated primarily by renal excretion and has an effective accumulation half-life of approximately 3 hours. Quinaprilat has an elimination half-life in plasma of approximately 2 hours with a prolonged terminal phase of 25 hours. Approximately 97% of either quinapril or quinaprilat circulating in plasma is bound to proteins.

Pharmacokinetic studies in patients with end-stage renal disease on chronic hemodialysis or continuous ambulatory peritoneal dialysis indicate that dialysis has little effect on the elimination of quinapril and quinaprilat.

The disposition of quinapril and quinaprilat in patients with renal insufficiency is similar to that in patients with normal renal function until creatinine clearance is 60 mL/minute or less. With creatinine clearance less than 60 mL/minute, peak and trough quinaprilat concentrations increase, apparent half-life increases, and time to steady state may be delayed. The elimination of quinaprilat may be reduced in elderly patients (>65 years) and in those with heart failure; this reduction is attributable to decrease in renal function (see Dosage). Quinaprilat concentrations are reduced in patients with alcoholic cirrhosis due to impaired de-esterification of quinapril.

The rate and extent of quinapril absorption are diminished moderately (approximately 25 to 30%) when quinapril tablets are administered during a high-fat meal. However, no effect on quinapril absorption occurs when taken during a regular meal.

Studies in rats indicate that quinapril and its metabolites do not cross the blood-brain barrier.

Pharmacodynamics: Administration of 10 to 40 mg of quinapril to patients with essential hypertension results in a reduction of both sitting and standing blood pressure with minimal effect on heart rate. Antihypertensive activity commences within 1 hour with peak effects usually achieved by 2 to 4 hours after dosing. Achievement of maximum blood pressure lowering effects may require 2 weeks of therapy in some patients. At the recommended doses, antihypertensive effects are maintained throughout the 24-hour dosing interval in most patients. While the dose response relationship is relatively flat, a dose of 40 mg was somewhat more effective at trough than 10 to 20 mg, and twice daily dosing tended to give a somewhat lower blood pressure than once daily dosing with the same total daily dose. The antihypertensive effect of quinapril was maintained during long-term therapy with no evidence of loss of effectiveness.

Hemodynamic assessments in patients with essential hypertension indicate that blood pressure reduction produced by quinapril is accompanied by a reduction in total peripheral resistance and renal vascular resistance with little or no change in heart rate and cardiac index. There was an increase in renal blood flow which was not significant. Little or no change in glomerular filtration rate or filtration fraction was observed.

When quinapril is given together with thiazide-type diuretics, the antihypertensive effects are approximately additive.

Administration of quinapril to patients with congestive heart failure (CHF) reduces peripheral vascular resistance, systolic and diastolic blood pressure, pulmonary capillary wedge pressure, and increases cardiac output. The onset of effects was observed within 1 hour and maximal effects occurred at 1.25 to 4 hours after administration of quinapril. Peak hemodynamic effects correlated well with peak plasma levels of quinaprilat (1 to 4 hours after administration).

Exercise tolerance was improved with quinapril therapy.

The effect of quinapril on survival in patients with heart failure has not been evaluated.

Therapeutic effects appear to be the same for elderly (>65 years of age) and younger adult patients given the same daily dosages, with no increase in adverse events in elderly patients.

The antihypertensive effect of ACE inhibitors is generally lower in black patients than in non-blacks.

Indications: Hypertension: In the treatment of essential hypertension. It is usually administered in association with other drugs, particularly thiazide diuretics.

In using quinapril consideration should be given to the risk of angioedema (see Warnings).

Quinapril should normally be used in those patients in whom treatment with a diuretic or a beta-blocker was found ineffective or has been associated with unacceptable adverse effects. Quinapril can also be tried as an initial agent in those patients in whom use of diuretics and/or beta-blockers is contraindicated or in patients with medical conditions in which these drugs frequently cause serious adverse effects.

The safety and efficacy of quinapril in renovascular hypertension have not been established; therefore, use in this condition is not recommended.

Congestive Heart Failure: In the treatment of congestive heart failure as adjunctive therapy when added to diuretics and/or digitalis glycosides.

Treatment with quinapril should be initiated under close medical supervision.

When used in pregnancy during the second and third trimesters, ACE inhibitors can cause injury or even death of the developing fetus. When pregnancy is detected quinapril should be discontinued as soon as possible (see Warnings, Pregnancy and Information for the Patient).

Contraindications: Patients who are hypersensitive to this product, and patients with a history of angioedema related to previous treatment with an ACE inhibitor.

Warnings: Angioedema: Angioedema has been reported in patients treated with quinapril. Angioedema associated with laryngeal involvement may be fatal. If laryngeal stridor or angioedema of the face, tongue, or glottis occurs, quinapril should be discontinued immediately, the patient treated appropriately in accordance with accepted medical care, and carefully observed until the swelling disappears. In instances where swelling is confined to the face and lips, the condition generally resolves without treatment, although antihistamines may be useful in relieving symptoms. Where there is involvement of the tongue, glottis or larynx, likely to cause airway obstruction, appropriate therapy (including but not limited to 0.3 to 0.5 mL of s.c. epinephrine solution 1:1 000) should be administered promptly (see Adverse Effects).

The incidence of angioedema during ACE inhibitor therapy has been reported to be higher in black than in non-black patients.

Patients with a history of angioedema unrelated to ACE inhibitor therapy may be at increased risk of angioedema while receiving an ACE inhibitor (see Contraindications).

Hypotension: Symptomatic hypotension has occurred after administration of quinapril, usually after the first or second dose or when the dose was increased. It is more likely to occur in patients who are volume depleted by diuretic therapy, dietary salt restriction, dialysis, diarrhea or vomiting. In patients with ischemic heart or cerebrovascular disease, an excessive fall in blood pressure could result in a myocardial infarction or cerebrovascular accident (see Adverse Effects). Because of the potential fall in blood pressure in these patients, therapy with quinapril should be started under close medical supervision. Such patients should be followed closely for the first weeks of treatment and whenever the dose is increased. In patients with severe congestive heart failure, with or without associated renal insufficiency, excessive hypotension has been observed and may be associated with oliguria and/or progressive azotemia, and rarely with acute renal failure and/or death.

If hypotension occurs, the patient should be placed in supine position and, if necessary, receive an i.v. infusion of 0.9% sodium chloride. A transient hypotensive response is not a contraindication to further doses which usually can be given without difficulty once the blood pressure has increased after volume expansion. However, lower doses of quinapril and/or reduced concomitant diuretic therapy should be considered.

Neutropenia/Agranulocytosis: Agranulocytosis and bone marrow depression have been caused by ACE inhibitors. Agranulocytosis did occur during quinapril treatment in 1 patient with a history of neutropenia during previous captopril therapy. Periodic monitoring of white blood cell counts should be considered, especially in patients with collagen vascular disease and/or renal disease.

Pregnancy: ACE inhibitors can cause fetal and neonatal morbidity and mortality when administered to pregnant women. Several dozen cases have been reported in the world literature. When pregnancy is detected, quinapril should be discontinued as soon as possible.

In rare cases (probably <0.1% of pregnancies) in which no alternative to ACE inhibitor therapy will be found, the mothers should be apprised of the potential hazards to their fetuses. Serial ultrasound examinations should be performed to assess fetal development and well-being and the volume of amniotic fluid.

If oligohydramnios is observed, quinapril should be discontinued unless it is considered life-saving for the mother. A nonstress test (NST), and/or a biophysical profiling (BPP) may be appropriate, depending upon the week of pregnancy. If concerns regarding fetal well-being still persist, a contraction stress testing (CST) should be considered. Patients and physicians should be aware, however, the oligohydramnios may not appear until after the fetus has sustained irreversible injury.

Infants with a history of in utero exposure to ACE inhibitors should be closely observed for hypotension, oliguria and hyperkalemia. If oliguria occurs, attention should be directed toward support of blood pressure and renal perfusion. Exchange transfusion or dialysis may be required as a means of reversing hypotension and/or substituting for impaired renal function; however, limited experience with those procedures has not been associated with significant clinical benefit. Hemodialysis and peritoneal dialysis have little effect on the elimination of quinapril and quinaprilat.

Human Data: It is not known whether exposure limited to the first trimester of pregnancy can adversely affect fetal outcome. The use of ACE inhibitors during the second and third trimesters of pregnancy has been associated with fetal and neonatal injury including hypotension, neonatal skull hypoplasia, anuria, reversible or irreversible renal failure, and death. Oligohydramnios has also been reported, presumably resulting from decreased fetal renal function; oligohydramnios in this setting has been associated with fetal limb contractures, craniofacial deformation and hypoplastic lung development. Prematurity, intrauterine growth retardation and patent ductus arteriosus have also been reported, although it is not clear whether these occurrences were due to the ACE inhibitor exposure.

Animal Data: No fetotoxic or teratogenic effects were observed in rats at doses as high as 300 mg/kg/day (180 times the maximum daily human dose), despite maternal toxicity at 150 mg/kg/day. Offspring body weights were reduced in rats treated late in gestation and during lactation with doses of 25 mg/kg/day or more. Quinapril was not teratogenic in rabbits; however, maternal and embryo toxicity were seen in some rabbits at 1 mg/kg/day.

No adverse effects on fertility or reproduction were observed in rats at dose levels up to 100 mg/kg/day (60 times the maximum daily human dose).

Precautions: Renal Impairment: As a consequence of inhibiting the renin-angiotensin-aldosterone system, changes in renal function have been seen in susceptible individuals. In patients whose renal function may depend on the activity of the renin-angiotensin-aldosterone system, such as patients with bilateral renal artery stenosis, unilateral renal artery stenosis to a solitary kidney, or severe congestive heart failure, treatment with agents that inhibit this system has been associated with oliguria, progressive azotemia, and rarely, acute renal failure and/or death. In susceptible patients, concomitant diuretic use may further increase risk.

Use of quinapril should include appropriate assessment of renal function.

Anaphylactoid Reactions during Membrane Exposure: Anaphylactoid reactions have been reported in patients dialyzed with high-flux membranes (e.g.: polyacrylonitrile [PAN]) and treated concomitantly with an ACE inhibitor. Dialysis should be stopped immediately if symptoms such as nausea, abdominal cramps, burning, angioedema, shortness of breath and severe hypotension occur. Symptoms are not relieved by antihistamines. In these patients consideration should be given to using a different type of dialysis membrane or a different class of antihypertensive agents.

Anaphylactoid Reactions during LDL Apheresis: Rarely, patients receiving ACE inhibitors during low density lipoprotein apheresis with dextran sulfate have experienced life-threatening anaphylactoid reactions. These reactions were avoided by temporarily withholding the ACE inhibitor therapy prior to each apheresis.

Anaphylactoid Reactions during Desensitization: There have been isolated reports of patients experiencing sustained life-threatening anaphylactoid reactions while receiving ACE inhibitors during desensitizing treatment with hymenoptera (bees, wasps) venom. In the same patients, these reactions have been avoided when ACE inhibitors were temporarily withheld for at least 24 hours, but they have reappeared upon inadvertent rechallenge to an ACE inhibitor.

Hyperkalemia and Potassium-Sparing Diuretics: Elevated serum potassium (>5.7 mEq/L) was observed in approximately 2% of patients receiving quinapril. In most cases these were isolated values which resolved despite continued therapy. Hyperkalemia was a cause of discontinuation of therapy in less than 0.1% of hypertensive patients. Risk factors for the development of hyperkalemia may include renal insufficiency, diabetes mellitus, and the concomitant use of agents to treat hypokalemia (see Drug Interactions and Adverse Effects).

Valvular Stenosis: There is concern on theoretical grounds that patients with aortic stenosis might be at particular risk of decreased coronary perfusion when treated with vasodilators because they do not develop as much afterload reduction.

Surgery/Anesthesia: In patients undergoing major surgery or during anesthesia with agents that produce hypotension, quinapril will block angiotensin II formation secondary to compensatory renin release. If hypotension occurs and is considered to be due to this mechanism, it can be corrected by volume expansion.

Patients with Impaired Liver Function: Hepatitis (hepatocellular and/or cholestatic), elevations of liver enzymes and/or serum bilirubin have occurred during therapy with other ACE inhibitors in patients with or without pre-existing liver abnormalities. In most cases the changes were reversed on discontinuation of the drug.

Elevations of liver enzymes and/or serum bilirubin have been reported for quinapril (see Adverse Effects). Should the patient receiving quinapril experience any unexplained symptoms particularly during the first weeks or months of treatment, it is recommended that a full set of liver function tests and any other necessary investigation be carried out. Discontinuation of quinapril should be considered when appropriate.

There are no adequate studies in patients with cirrhosis and/or liver dysfunction. Quinapril should be used with particular caution in patients with pre-existing liver abnormalities. In such patients baseline liver function tests should be obtained before administration of the drug and close monitoring of response and metabolic effects should apply.

Cough: A dry, persistent cough, which usually disappears only after withdrawal or lowering of the dose of quinapril has been reported. Such possibility should be considered as part of the differential diagnosis of the cough.

Lactation: Quinapril is secreted to a limited extent in milk of lactating rats (5% or less of the plasma drug concentration was found in rat milk). It is not known whether quinapril or its metabolites are secreted in human milk. Because many drugs are secreted in human milk, caution should be exercised when quinapril is given to a nursing mother, and in general, nursing should be interrupted.

Children: The safety and effectiveness of quinapril in children have not been established; therefore, use in this age group is not recommended.

Drug Interactions: Concomitant Diuretic Therapy: Patients concomitantly taking ACE inhibitors and diuretics, and especially those in whom diuretic therapy was recently instituted, may occasionally experience an excessive reduction of blood pressure after initiation of therapy. The possibility of hypotensive effects after the first dose of quinapril can be minimized by either discontinuing the diuretic or increasing the salt intake (except in patients with heart failure), prior to initiation of treatment with quinapril. If it is not possible to discontinue the diuretic, the starting dose of quinapril should be reduced and the patient should be closely observed for several hours following initial dose and until blood pressure has stabilized (see Warnings and Dosage).

Agents Increasing Serum Potassium: Since quinapril decreases aldosterone production, elevation of serum potassium may occur. Potassium sparing diuretics such as spironolactone, triamterene or amiloride, or potassium supplements should be given only for documented hypokalemia and with caution and frequent monitoring of serum potassium, since they may lead to a significant increase in serum potassium. Salt substitutes which contain potassium should also be used with caution.

Agents Causing Renin Release: The antihypertensive effect of quinapril is augmented by antihypertensive agents that cause renin release (e.g., diuretics).

Agents Affecting Sympathetic Activity: Agents affecting sympathetic activity (e.g., ganglionic blocking agents or adrenergic neuron blocking agents) may be used with caution. Beta-adrenergic blocking drugs add some further antihypertensive effect to quinapril.

Tetracycline: Concomitant administration of tetracycline with quinapril reduced the absorption of tetracycline in healthy volunteers (by 28 to 37%) due to the presence of magnesium carbonate as an excipient in the formulation. This interaction should be considered with concomitant use of quinapril and tetracycline or other drugs which interact with magnesium.

Lithium: As with other drugs which eliminate sodium, the lithium elimination may be reduced. Therefore, the serum lithium levels should be monitored carefully if lithium salts are to be administered.

Other Agents: In single dose pharmacokinetic studies, no important changes in pharmacokinetic parameters were observed when quinapril was used concomitantly with propranolol, hydrochlorothiazide, digoxin or cimetidine. No change in prothrombin time occurred when quinapril and warfarin were given together.

Information for the Patient: **Note:** As with many other drugs, certain advice to patients being treated with quinapril is warranted. This information is intended to aid in the safe and effective use of this medication. It is not a disclosure of all possible adverse or intended effects.

Angioedema: Angioedema, including laryngeal edema, may occur especially following the first dose of quinapril. Patients should be so advised and told to report immediately any signs or symptoms suggesting angioedema, such as swelling of face, extremities, eyes, lips, tongue, difficulty in swallowing or breathing. They should immediately stop taking quinapril and consult with their physician.

Hypotension: Patients should be cautioned to report light-headedness, especially during the first few days of quinapril therapy. If actual syncope occurs, the patients should be told to discontinue the drug and consult with their physician.

All patients should be cautioned that excessive perspiration and dehydration may lead to an excessive fall in blood pressure because of reduction in fluid volume. Other causes of volume depletion such as vomiting or diarrhea may also lead to a fall in blood pressure; patients should be advised to consult with their physician.

Agranulocytosis/Neutropenia: Patients should be told to report promptly to their physician any indication of infection (e.g., sore throat, fever), as this may be a sign of neutropenia.

Impaired Liver Function: Patients should be advised to return to the physician if he/she experiences any symptoms possibly related to liver dysfunction. This would include "viral-like symptoms" in the first weeks to months of therapy (such as fever, malaise, muscle pain, rash or adenopathy which are possible indicators of hypersensitivity reactions), or if abdominal pain, nausea or vomiting, loss of appetite, jaundice, itching or any other unexplained symptoms occur during therapy.

Hyperkalemia: Patients should be told not to use salt substitutes containing potassium without consulting their physician.

Surgery: Patients planning to undergo surgery and/or anesthesia should be told to inform their physician that they are taking an ACE inhibitor.

Pregnancy: Since the use of ACE inhibitors during pregnancy can cause injury and even death of the developing fetus, patients should be advised to report promptly to their physician if they become pregnant.

Adverse Effects: Hypertension: Quinapril monotherapy has been evaluated for safety in 2 005 hypertensive patients enrolled in placebo-controlled clinical trials. These trials included 313 elderly patients. There was no increase in the incidence of adverse events in elderly patients given the same daily dosages. Quinapril has been evaluated for long-term safety in over 1 100 patients treated for 1 year or more. Adverse events were usually mild and transient in nature.

The most serious adverse event was angioedema (0.1%). Renal insufficiency (1 case), agranulocytosis (1 case) and mild azotemia (2 cases in CHF patients) have been reported. Myocardial infarction and cerebrovascular accident occurred, possibly secondary to excessive hypotension in high risk patients (see Warnings).

The most frequent adverse events in controlled clinical trials were headache (8.1%), dizziness (4.1%), cough (3.2%), fatigue (3.2%), rhinitis (3.2%), nausea and/or vomiting (2.3%), and abdominal pain (2.0%).

Discontinuation of therapy because of adverse events was required in 4.7% of patients treated with quinapril in placebo controlled trials.

Congestive Heart Failure: At least 1 adverse event was experienced by 605 (55%) of the 1 108 patients with congestive heart failure. Five hundred twenty five of these patients were evaluated for safety in controlled clinical trials. The frequencies of adverse events were similar for both sexes as for younger (<65 years) and older (≥65 years) patients.

The most serious nonfatal adverse events/reactions were angioedema (0.1%), chest pain of unknown origin (0.8%), angina pectoris (0.4%), hypotension (0.1%), and impaired renal function. Myocardial infarct and cerebrovascular accident occurred (see Warnings).

The most frequent adverse events in controlled clinical trials were dizziness (11.2%), cough (7.6%), chest pain (6.5%), dyspnea (5.5%), fatigue (5.1%), and nausea/vomiting (5.0%).

Accupril (cont'd)

Discontinuation due to adverse events in controlled clinical trials was required for 41 (8.0%) of patients. Hypotension (0.8%) and cough (0.8%) were the most common reasons for withdrawal.

Adverse events occurring in ≥0.5% of 2 005 hypertensive patients treated with quinapril monotherapy and in 525 patients with congestive heart failure treated with quinapril as adjunctive therapy, in controlled clinical trials, are presented in Table I.

Table I—Accupril

Adverse Events in Patients (≥0.5%) with Hypertension and Congestive Heart Failure in Controlled Clinical Trials (Irrespective of Causal Relationship)

	Hypertension[a] % Patients (n=2 005)	Congestive Heart Failure[b] % Patients (n=525)
Body as a Whole		
Chest Pain	1.2	6.5
Fatigue	3.2	5.1
Headache	8.1	3.2
Back Pain	1.3	1.7
Asthenia	1.0	1.7
Peripheral Edema	0.9	1.5
Generalized Edema	0.7	0.2
Cardiovascular		
Hypotension	1.0	3.4
Angina Pectoris	0.2	2.3
Palpitation	0.4	1.3
Tachycardia	0.2	1.1
Myocardial Infarct		0.6
Arrhythmia	0.1	0.6
Digestive		
Nausea and/or vomiting	2.3	5.0
Abdominal pain	2.0	2.5
Diarrhea	1.9	3.4
Dyspepsia	1.9	1.5
Dry mouth or throat	0.4	0.8
Musculoskeletal		
Myalgia	1.7	2.9
Nervous		
Dizziness	4.1	11.2
Insomnia	1.3	1.1
Paresthesia	1.0	1.3
Nervousness	1.0	0.2
Somnolence	0.9	0.6
Syncope	0.3	0.6
Vertigo	0.4	0.8
Depression	0.6	1.0
Respiratory		
Cough	3.2	7.6
Dyspnea	0.9	5.5
Hemoptysis	—	0.6
Rhinitis	3.2	2.5
Skin and Appendages		
Rash	0.6	1.9
Sweating increased	0.8	1.1
Pruritus	0.6	0.4
Urogenital		
Impotence	0.5	0.2
Special Senses		
Amblyopia	0.3	1.3
Unusual Taste	0.1	0.8
Abnormal Vision	0.1	0.6
Taste Loss	0.2	0.6

[a]Accupril monotherapy.
[b]Accupril as adjunctive therapy to diuretic and/or digitalis.

Adverse events occurring in <0.5% of patients with hypertension or congestive heart failure include: Body as a whole: allergy, face edema, chill, weight increase, dehydration.

Cardiovascular: vasodilatation, cerebrovascular accident, heart failure, ventricular tachycardia, atrial flutter.

Digestive: constipation, tongue edema, gastrointestinal hemorrhage, flatulence, anorexia, bloody stools.

Hemic and Lymphatic: anemia, including hemolytic anemia, thrombocytopenia, agranulocytosis.

Nervous: confusion, amnesia, anxiety.

Musculoskeletal: arthritis.

Respiratory: asthma, hoarseness.

Skin and Appendages: dermatitis, photosensitivity reaction, urticaria, eczema, pemphigus, exfoliative dermatitis, Stevens-Johnson syndrome.

Urogenital: dysuria, polyuria, impaired renal function.

Special Senses: tinnitus.

Laboratory Deviations: hematuria, WBC decreased, elevated BUN, hyperglycemia, azotemia.

Clinical Laboratory Test Findings: Hematology: See Warnings.

Hyperkalemia: See Precautions.

Creatinine and Blood Urea Nitrogen: Increases (>1.25 times the upper limit of normal) in serum creatinine and blood urea nitrogen were observed in 2% and 2%, respectively, of patients treated with quinapril alone. Increases are more likely to occur in patients receiving concomitant diuretic therapy than in those on quinapril alone. These increases often reversed on continued therapy. In controlled studies of heart failure, increases in blood urea nitrogen and serum creatinine were observed in 11% and 8%, respectively, of patients treated with quinapril. Most often these patients were receiving diuretics with or without digitalis.

Hepatic: Elevations of liver enzymes and/or serum bilirubin have occurred (see Precautions).

Overdose: Symptoms and Treatment: No data are available regarding overdosage of quinapril in humans. The most likely clinical manifestation would be symptoms attributable to severe hypotension, which should be normally treated by i.v. volume expansion with 0.9% sodium chloride. Hemodialysis and peritoneal dialysis have little effect on the elimination of quinapril and quinaprilat.

Dosage: Dosage must be individualized.

Hypertension: Initiation of therapy requires consideration of recent antihypertensive drug treatment, the extent of blood pressure elevation and salt restriction. The dosage of other antihypertensive agents being used with quinapril may need to be adjusted.

Monotherapy: The recommended initial dose of quinapril in patients not on diuretics is 10 mg once daily. An initial dose of 20 mg once daily can be considered for patients without advanced age, renal impairment, or concomitant heart failure and who are not volume depleted (see Precautions, Hypotension). Dosage should be adjusted according to blood pressure response, generally at intervals of 2 to 4 weeks. A dose of 40 mg daily should not be exceeded.

In some patients treated once daily, the antihypertensive effect may diminish towards the end of the dosing interval. This can be evaluated by measuring blood pressure just prior to dosing to determine whether satisfactory control is being maintained for 24 hours. If it is not, either twice daily administration with the same total daily dose, or an increase in dose should be considered. If blood pressure is not controlled with quinapril alone, a diuretic may be added. After the addition of a diuretic, it may be possible to reduce the dose of quinapril.

Concomitant Diuretic Therapy: Symptomatic hypotension occasionally may occur following the initial dose of quinapril and is more likely in patients who are currently being treated with a diuretic. The diuretic should, if possible, be discontinued for 2 to 3 days before beginning therapy with quinapril to reduce the likelihood of hypotension (see Warnings). If the diuretic cannot be discontinued, an initial dose of 5 mg quinapril should be used with careful medical supervision for several hours and until blood pressure has stabilized. The dosage should subsequently be titrated (as described above) to the optimal response.

Dosing Adjustment in Renal Impairment: See Precautions for use in hemodialysis patients.

Starting doses should be reduced according to the guidelines in Table II.

Table II—Accupril

Dosing Guidelines in Renal Impairment

Creatinine Clearance (mL/min)	Maximum Recommended Initial Dose (mg)
>60	10
30–60	5
10–30	2.5
<10	Insufficient data for dosage recommendation

Patients should subsequently have dosage titrated (as described above) to the optimal response.

Dosage in the Elderly (over 65 years): The recommended initial dosage is 10 mg once daily (depending on renal function), followed by titration (as described above) to the optimal response.

Congestive Heart Failure: Indicated as adjunctive therapy to diuretics, and/or cardiac glycosides. Therapy should be initiated under close medical supervision. Blood pressure and renal function should be monitored, both before and during treatment with quinapril because severe hypotension and, more rarely, consequent renal failure have been reported (see Warnings and Precautions).

Initiation of therapy requires consideration of recent diuretic therapy and the possibility of severe salt/volume depletion. If possible, the dose of diuretic should be reduced before beginning treatment, to reduce the likelihood of hypotension. Serum potassium should also be monitored (see Precautions, Drug Interactions).

The recommended starting dose is 5 mg once daily to be administered under close medical supervision to determine the initial effect on blood pressure. After the initial dose, the patient should be observed for at least 2 hours, or until the pressure has stabilized for at least an additional hour (see Warnings, Hypotension). This dose may improve symptoms of heart failure, but increases in exercise duration have generally required higher doses. Therefore, if the initial dosage of quinapril is well tolerated or after effective management of symptomatic hypotension following initiation of therapy, the dose should be increased gradually to 10 mg once daily, then 20 mg once daily, and to 40 mg per day given in 2 equally divided doses, depending on the patient's response. The maximum daily dose is 40 mg.

The dose titration may be done at weekly intervals, as indicated by the presence of residual signs or symptoms of heart failure.

Renal Impairment or Hyponatremia: Kinetic data indicate that quinapril elimination is dependent on the level of renal function. The recommended initial dose is 5 mg in patients with a creatinine clearance of 30 to 60 mL/minute and 2.5 mg in patients with a creatinine clearance of 10 to 30 mL/minute. There is insufficient data for dosage recommendation in patients with a creatinine clearance less than 10 mL/minute. If the initial dose is well tolerated, quinapril may be administered the following day as a twice daily regimen. In the absence of excessive hypotension or significant deterioration of renal function, the dose may be increased at weekly intervals based on clinical and hemodynamic response.

Supplied: 5 mg: Each brown, film-coated, elliptical tablet, embossed ''PD/527'' on one side and ''5'' on the other, contains: quinapril 5 mg. Nonmedicinal ingredients: candelilla wax, crospovidone, gelatin, hydroxypropylcellulose, hydroxypropylmethylcellulose, lactose, magnesium carbonate, magnesium stearate, polyethylene glycol, synthetic red iron oxide and titanium dioxide. Bottles of 90.

10 mg: Each brown, film-coated, triangular tablet, embossed ''PD/530'' on one side and ''10'' on the other, contains: quinapril 10 mg. Nonmedicinal ingredients: candelilla wax, crospovidone, gelatin, hydroxypropylcellulose, hydroxypropylmethylcellulose, lactose, magnesium carbonate, magnesium stearate, polyethylene glycol, synthetic red iron oxide and titanium dioxide. Bottles of 90.

20 mg: Each brown, film-coated, round tablet, embossed ''PD/532'' on one side and ''20'' on the other, contains: quinapril 20 mg. Nonmedicinal ingredients: candelilla wax, crospovidone, gelatin, hydroxypropylcellulose, hydroxypropylmethylcellulose, lactose, magnesium carbonate, magnesium stearate, polyethylene glycol, synthetic red iron oxide and titanium dioxide. Bottles of 90.

40 mg: Each brown, film-coated, elliptical tablet, embossed ''PD/535'' on one side and ''40'' on the other, contains: quinapril 40 mg. Nonmedicinal ingredients: candelilla wax, crospovidone, gelatin, hydroxypropylcellulose, hydroxypropylmethylcellulose, lactose, magnesium carbonate, magnesium stearate, polyethylene glycol, synthetic red iron oxide and titanium dioxide. Bottles of 90.

All strengths are gluten-, paraben-, sodium-, sulfite- and tartrazine-free. Store at controlled room temperature, 15 to 30°C. Protect from moisture. Dispense in well-closed containers.

(Shown in Product Recognition Section)

Reviewed 1999

Did you know that the *CPS* provides information on certain drugs or drug classes in the shaded monographs in the WHITE SECTION? Check out the index at the beginning of the section.

ACCURETIC™ ℞

Parke-Davis

Quinapril HCl—Hydrochlorothiazide

Angiotensin-Converting Enzyme Inhibitor—Diuretic

Pharmacology: Accuretic is a fixed-combination tablet which combines the antihypertensive actions of an angiotensin-converting enzyme (ACE) inhibitor, quinapril HCl, and a diuretic, hydrochlorothiazide. In clinical studies, administration of this combination produced greater reductions in blood pressure than the single agents given alone.

Pharmacokinetics and Metabolism: Quinapril: Following oral administration of quinapril, peak plasma concentrations of quinapril occur within 1 hour. Based on the recovery of quinapril and its metabolites in urine, the extent of absorption is at least 60%. Following absorption, quinapril is de-esterified to its major active metabolite, quinaprilat (quinapril diacid), a potent ACE inhibitor, and to minor inactive metabolites. Quinapril has an apparent half-life in plasma of approximately 1 hour. Peak plasma quinaprilat concentrations occur approximately 2 hours after an oral dose of quinapril. Quinaprilat is eliminated primarily by renal excretion and has an effective accumulation half-life of approximately 3 hours. Quinaprilat has an elimination half-life in plasma of approximately 2 hours with a prolonged terminal phase of 25 hours. Approximately 97% of either quinapril or quinaprilat circulating in plasma is bound to proteins.

Pharmacokinetic studies in patients with end-stage renal disease or chronic hemodialysis or continuous ambulatory peritoneal dialysis indicate that dialysis has little effect on the elimination of quinapril and quinaprilat.

The disposition of quinapril and quinaprilat in patients with renal insufficiency is similar to that in patients with normal renal function until creatinine clearance is 60 mL/min or less. With creatinine clearance less than 60 mL/min, peak and trough quinaprilat concentrations increase, apparent half-life increases, and time to steady-state may be delayed. The elimination of quinaprilat may be reduced in elderly patients (>65 years) and in those with heart failure; this reduction is attributable to decrease in renal function (See Dosage). Quinaprilat concentrations are reduced in patients with alcoholic cirrhosis due to impaired de-esterification of quinapril.

The rate and extent of quinapril absorption are diminished moderately (approximately 25 to 30%) when administered during a high-fat meal. However, no effect on quinapril absorption occurs when taken during a regular meal.

Studies in rats indicate that quinapril and its metabolites do not cross the blood-brain barrier.

Hydrochlorothiazide: After oral administration of hydrochlorothiazide, diuresis begins within 2 hours, peaks in about 4 hours, and lasts about 6 to 12 hours; the extent of absorption is approximately 50 to 80%. Hydrochlorothiazide is excreted unchanged by the kidney. When plasma levels have been followed for at least 24 hours, the plasma half-life has been observed to vary between 4 to 15 hours. At least 61% of the oral dose is eliminated unchanged within 24 hours. Hydrochlorothiazide crosses the placental but not the blood-brain barrier.

Quinapril/Hydrochlorothiazide: Concomitant administration of quinapril and hydrochlorothiazide has little or no effect on the bioavailability or the pharmacokinetics of either drug.

Pharmacodynamics: Quinapril: Quinapril is a nonpeptide, nonsulphydryl ACE inhibitor. ACE is a peptidyl dipeptidase that catalyzes the conversion of angiotensin I to the vasoconstrictor angiotensin II. After absorption, quinapril is rapidly de-esterified to quinaprilat (quinapril diacid), its principal active metabolite. Its primary mode of action is to inhibit circulating and tissue ACE, thereby decreasing vasopressor activity and aldosterone secretion. Although the decrease in aldosterone is small, it results in a small increase in serum K^+ (see Precautions). Removal of angiotensin II negative feedback on renin secretion leads to increased plasma renin activity.

ACE is identical to kininase II. Thus, quinapril may interfere with the degradation of bradykinin, a potent peptide vasodilator. However, it is not known whether this system contributes to the therapeutic effects of quinapril.

The antihypertensive effect of quinapril outlasts its inhibitory effect on circulating ACE in animal studies. Tissue ACE inhibition more closely correlates with the duration of antihypertensive effects and this may be related to enzyme-binding characteristics as shown for quinapril on purified tissue ACE from human kidney and heart.

Administration of 10 to 40 mg of quinapril to patients with essential hypertension results in a reduction of both sitting and standing blood pressure with minimal effect on heart rate. Antihypertensive activity commences within 1 hour with peak effects usually achieved by 2 to 4 hours after dosing. Achievement of maximum blood pressure lowering effects may require 2 to 4 weeks of therapy in some patients. At the recommended doses, antihypertensive effects are maintained throughout the 24-hour dosing interval in most patients. While the dose response relationship is relatively flat, a dose of 40 mg was somewhat more effective at trough than 10 to 20 mg, and twice daily dosing tended to give a somewhat lower blood pressure than once daily dosing with the same total daily dose. The antihypertensive effect of quinapril was maintained during long-term therapy with no evidence of loss of effectiveness.

Hemodynamic assessments in patients with essential hypertension indicate that blood pressure reduction produced by quinapril is accompanied by a reduction in total peripheral resistance and renal vascular resistance with little or no change in heart rate and cardiac index. There was an increase in renal blood flow that was not significant. Little or no change in glomerular filtration rate or filtration fraction was observed.

Therapeutic effects appear to be the same for elderly (>65 years of age) and younger adult patients given the same daily dosages, with no increase in adverse events in elderly patients.

The antihypertensive effect of angiotensin-converting enzyme inhibitors is generally lower in black patients than in non-blacks.

Hydrochlorothiazide: Hydrochlorothiazide acts directly on the kidney to increase excretion of sodium and chloride and an accompanying volume of water. Hydrochlorothiazide also increases the excretion of potassium and bicarbonate and decreases calcium excretion.

As a result of its diuretic effect, hydrochlorothiazide increases plasma renin activity, increases aldosterone secretion, decreases serum potassium and increases urinary potassium loss. Administration of quinapril inhibits the renin-angiotensin-aldosterone axis and tends to attenuate the potassium decrease associated with hydrochlorothiazide.

The mechanism underlying the antihypertensive activity of diuretics is unknown. During chronic administration, peripheral vascular resistance is reduced; however, this may be secondary to changes in sodium balance.

Quinapril/Hydrochlorothiazide: When quinapril and hydrochlorothiazide are given together, the antihypertensive effects are approximately additive.

Indications: For the treatment of essential hypertension in patients for whom combination therapy is appropriate.

In using Accuretic, consideration should be given to the risk of angioedema (see Warnings, Angioedema).

Quinapril should normally be used in those patients in whom treatment with a diuretic or a beta-blocker was found ineffective or has been associated with unacceptable adverse effects. Quinapril can also be tried as an initial agent in those patients in whom use of diuretics and/or beta-blockers is contraindicated or in patients with medical conditions in which these drugs frequently cause serious adverse effects.

Accuretic is not indicated for initial therapy. Patients in whom quinapril and hydrochlorothiazide are initiated simultaneously can develop symptomatic hypotension (see Warnings, Hypotension and Precautions, Drug Interactions).

Patients should be titrated on the individual drugs. If the fixed combination represents the dosage determined by this titration, the use of Accuretic may be more convenient in the management of patients. If during maintenance therapy dosage adjustment is necessary, it is advisable to use individual drugs.

When used in pregnancy during the second and third trimesters, ACE inhibitors can cause injury or even death of the developing fetus. When pregnancy is detected, Accuretic should be discontinued as soon as possible (see Warnings, Pregnancy and Information for the Patient).

Contraindications: Patients who are hypersensitive to any component of this product (see Supplied) and patients with a history of angioedema related to previous treatment with an ACE inhibitor.

Because of the hydrochlorothiazide component, this product is contraindicated in patients with anuria or hypersensitivity to other sulfonamide-derived drugs.

Warnings: Angioedema: Angioedema has been reported in patients treated with ACE inhibitors, including quinapril. Angioedema associated with laryngeal involvement may be fatal. If laryngeal stridor or angioedema of the face, tongue, or glottis occurs, treatment with Accuretic should be discontinued immediately, the patient treated appropriately in accordance with accepted medical care and carefully observed until the swelling disappears. In instances where swelling is confined to the face and lips, the condition generally resolves without treatment, although antihistamines may be useful in relieving symptoms. Where there is involvement of the tongue, glottis or larynx likely to cause airway obstruction, appropriate therapy (including but not limited to 0.3 to 0.5 mL of s.c. epinephrine solution 1:1 000) should be administered promptly (see Adverse Effects).

The incidence of angioedema during ACE inhibitor therapy has been reported to be higher in black than in non-black patients.

Patients with a history of angioedema unrelated to ACE inhibitor therapy may be at increased risk of angioedema while receiving an ACE inhibitor (see Contraindications).

Hypotension: Symptomatic hypotension has occurred after administration of quinapril, usually after the first or second dose or when the dose was increased. It is more likely to occur in patients who are volume-depleted by diuretic therapy, dietary salt restriction, dialysis, diarrhea, or vomiting. In patients with ischemic heart or cerebrovascular disease, an excessive fall in blood pressure could result in a myocardial infarction or cerebrovascular accident (see Adverse Effects). Because of the potential fall in blood pressure in these patients, therapy with Accuretic should be started under close medical supervision. Such patients should be followed closely for the first weeks of treatment and whenever the dose of Accuretic is increased. In patients with severe congestive heart failure, with or without associated renal insufficiency, excessive hypotension has been observed and may be associated with oliguria and/or progressive azotemia and rarely with acute renal failure and/or death.

If hypotension occurs, the patient should be placed in supine position and, if necessary, receive an i.v. infusion of 0.9% sodium chloride. A transient hypotensive response is not a contraindication to further doses which usually can be given without difficulty once the blood pressure has increased after volume expansion. If symptoms persist, the dosage should be reduced or the drug discontinued.

Neutropenia/Agranulocytosis: Agranulocytosis and bone marrow depression have been caused by ACE inhibitors. Agranulocytosis did occur during quinapril treatment in one patient with a history of neutropenia during previous captopril therapy. Periodic monitoring of white blood cell counts should be considered, especially in patients with collagen vascular disease and/or renal disease.

Azotemia: Azotemia may be precipitated or increased by hydrochlorothiazide. Cumulative effects of the drug may develop in patients with impaired renal function. If increasing azotemia and oliguria occur, Accuretic should be discontinued.

Impairment of Liver Function: Hepatitis (hepatocellular and/or cholestatic), elevations of liver enzymes and/or serum bilirubin have occurred during therapy with other ACE inhibitors in patients with or without pre-existing liver abnormalities. In most cases the changes were reversed on discontinuation of the drug.

Elevations of liver enzymes and/or serum bilirubin have been reported for Accuretic (see Adverse Effects). Should the patient receiving Accuretic experience any unexplained symptoms particularly during the first weeks or months of treatment, it is recommended that a full set of liver function tests and any other necessary investigation be carried out. Discontinuation of Accuretic should be considered when appropriate.

There are no adequate studies in patients with cirrhosis and/or liver dysfunction. Accuretic should be used with particular caution in patients with pre-existing liver abnormalities. In such patients baseline liver function tests should be obtained before administration of the drug and close monitoring of response and metabolic effects should apply.

Hypersensitivity to Hydrochlorothiazide: Sensitivity reactions to hydrochlorothiazide may occur in patients with or without a history of allergy or bronchial asthma. Exacerbation or activation of systemic lupus erythematosus has been reported in patients treated with hydrochlorothiazide.

Pregnancy: ACE inhibitors can cause fetal and neonatal morbidity and mortality when administered to pregnant women. Several dozen cases have been reported in the world literature. When pregnancy is detected, Accuretic should be discontinued as soon as possible.

In rare cases (probably less than 0.1% of pregnancies) in which no alternative to ACE inhibitor therapy will be found, the mothers should be apprised of the potential hazards to their fetuses. Serial ultrasound examinations should be performed to assess fetal development and well-being and the volume of amniotic fluid.

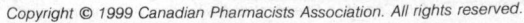

If oligohydramnios is observed, quinapril should be discontinued unless it is considered life-saving to the mother. A nonstress test (NST) and/or a biophysical profiling (BPP) may be appropriate, depending on the week of pregnancy. If concerns regarding fetal well-being still persist, a contraction stress test

Accuretic (cont'd)

(CST) should be considered. Patients and physicians should be aware, however, that oligohydramnios may not appear until after the fetus has sustained irreversible injury.

Infants with a history of in utero exposure to ACE inhibitors should be closely observed for hypotension, oliguria and hyperkalemia. If oliguria occurs, attention should be directed toward support of blood pressure and renal perfusion. Exchange transfusion or dialysis may be required as a means of reversing hypotension and/or substituting for impaired renal function; however, limited experience with those procedures has not been associated with significant clinical benefit. Hemodialysis and peritoneal dialysis have little effect on the elimination of quinapril and quinaprilat.

Human Data: It is not known whether quinapril exposure limited to the first trimester of pregnancy can adversely affect fetal outcome. The use of ACE inhibitors during the second and third trimesters of pregnancy has been associated with fetal and neonatal injury including hypotension, neonatal skull hypoplasia, anuria, reversible or irreversible renal failure and death. Oligohydramnios has also been reported, presumably resulting from decreased fetal renal function; oligohydramnios in this setting has been associated with fetal limb contractures, craniofacial deformation and hypoplastic lung development. Prematurity, intrauterine growth retardation and patent ductus arteriosus have also been reported, although is not clear whether these occurrences were due to the ACE-inhibitor exposure.

Thiazides cross the placental barrier and appear in cord blood. Although studies in humans have not been done, effects to the fetus may include fetal or neonatal jaundice, thrombocytopenia and possibly other adverse reactions which have occurred in the adult.

Animal Data: No fetotoxic or teratogenic effects were observed in rats at quinapril doses as high as 300 mg/kg/day (180 times the maximum daily human dose) despite maternal toxicity at 150 mg/kg/day. Offspring body weights were reduced in rats treated late in gestation and during lactation with doses of 25 mg/kg/day or more. Quinapril hydrochloride was not teratogenic in rabbits; however, maternal and embryo toxicity were seen in some rabbits at doses as low as 0.5 mg/kg/day and 1 mg/kg/day, respectively.

No adverse effects on fertility or reproduction were observed in rats at quinapril dose levels up to 100 mg/kg/day (60 times the maximum daily human dose).

Precautions: Renal Impairment: As a consequence of inhibiting the renin-angiotensin-aldosterone system, changes in renal function have been seen in susceptible individuals. In patients whose renal function may depend on the activity of the renin-angiotensin-aldosterone system, such as patients with bilateral renal artery stenosis, unilateral renal artery stenosis to a solitary kidney, or severe congestive heart failure, treatment with agents that inhibit this system has been associated with oliguria, progressive azotemia and, rarely, acute renal failure and/or death. In susceptible patients, concomitant diuretic use may further increase risk.

Use of Accuretic should include appropriate assessment of renal function.

Thiazides may not be appropriate diuretics for use in patients with renal impairment and are ineffective at creatinine clearance values of 30 mL/min or below (i.e., moderate or severe renal insufficiency).

Hyperkalemia: Elevated serum potassium (greater than 5.7 mEq/L) was observed in approximately 2% of patients receiving quinapril. In most cases these were isolated values which resolved despite continued therapy. Hyperkalemia was a cause of discontinuation of therapy in less than 0.1% of hypertensive patients. Risk factors for the development of hyperkalemia may include renal insufficiency, diabetes mellitus, and the concomitant use of agents to treat hypokalemia (See Precautions, Drug Interactions: Agents Increasing Serum Potassium, and Adverse Effects). The addition of a potassium-sparing diuretic to Accuretic, which contains a diuretic, is not recommended.

Patients with Impaired Liver Function: Accuretic should be used with caution in patients with impaired hepatic function or progressive liver disease, since minor alterations of fluid and electrolyte balance may precipitate hepatic coma. Also, since the metabolism of quinapril to quinaprilat is normally dependent upon hepatic esterase, patients with impaired liver function could develop markedly elevated plasma levels of quinapril.

Valvular Stenosis: There is concern on theoretical grounds that patients with aortic stenosis might be at particular risk of decreased coronary perfusion when treated with vasodilators because they do not develop as much afterload reduction.

Metabolism: Hyperuricemia may occur, or acute gout may be precipitated, in certain patients receiving thiazide therapy.

Thiazides may decrease serum PBI levels without signs of thyroid disturbance.

Increase in cholesterol, triglyceride and glucose levels may be associated with thiazide diuretic therapy. Overt diabetes may be precipitated in susceptible individuals.

Initial and periodic determination of serum electrolytes should be performed at appropriate intervals to detect possible electrolyte imbalance.

As with other ACE inhibitors, patients on quinapril alone may have increased serum potassium levels (see Precautions, Hyperkalemia). Conversely, treatment with thiazide diuretics has been associated with hyperkalemia. The opposite effects of hydrochlorothiazide and quinapril on serum potassium may approximately balance each other in many patients so that no net effect will be seen. In other patients, one or the other effect may be dominant.

In addition to hypokalemia, treatment with thiazide diuretics has also been associated with hyponatremia and hypochloremic alkalosis. These disturbances have sometimes been manifest as one or more of the following: dryness of mouth, thirst, weakness, lethargy, drowsiness, restlessness, muscle pain or cramps, muscular fatigue, hypotension, oliguria, tachycardia, nausea, confusion, seizures and vomiting. Hypokalemia can also sensitize or exaggerate the response of the heart to the toxic effects of digitalis. The risk of hypokalemia is greatest in patients with cirrhosis of the liver, in patients experiencing a brisk diuresis, in patients who are receiving inadequate oral intake of electrolytes, and in patients receiving concomitant therapy with corticosteroids or ACTH. Chloride deficits secondary to thiazide therapy are generally mild and require specific treatment only under extraordinary circumstances (e.g., in liver disease or renal disease). Dilutional hyponatremia may occur in edematous patients, especially in hot weather; appropriate therapy is water restriction rather than administration of salt, except when the hyponatremia is life-threatening. In actual salt depletion, replacement of salt is the therapy of choice.

Thiazides may decrease calcium excretion. Thiazides may cause intermittent and slight elevation of serum calcium in the absence of known disorders of calcium metabolism. Marked hypercalcemia may be evidence of hidden hypoparathyroidism. In a few patients on prolonged thiazide therapy, pathological changes in the parathyroid gland have been observed with hypercalcemia and hypophosphatemia. More serious complications of hyperparathyroidism (renal lithiasis, bone resorption and peptic ulceration) have not been seen. Thiazides should be discontinued before performing tests for parathyroid function.

Thiazides increase the urinary excretion of magnesium and hypomagnesemia may result.

Surgery/Anesthesia: In patients undergoing major surgery or during anesthesia with agents that produce hypotension, ACE inhibitors will block angiotensin II formation secondary to compensatory renin release. If hypotension occurs and is considered to be due to this mechanism, it can be corrected by volume expansion.

Systemic Lupus Erythematosus: Thiazide diuretics have been reported to cause exacerbation or activation of systemic lupus erythematosus.

Cough: A dry, persistent cough, which usually disappears only after withdrawal or lowering of the dose of quinapril, has been reported. Such possibility should be considered as part of the differential diagnosis of the cough.

Lactation: Quinapril and quinaprilat are secreted in trace amounts in human milk. Thiazides appear in human milk. Caution should be exercised when Accuretic is given to a nursing mother and, in general, nursing should be interrupted.

Children: The safety and effectiveness of Accuretic in children have not been established; therefore, use in this age group is not recommended.

Anaphylactoid Reactions during Membrane Exposure: Anaphylactoid reactions have been reported in patients dialysed with high-flux membranes (e.g., polyacrylonitrile [PAN]) and treated concomitantly with an ACE inhibitor. Dialysis should be stopped immediately if symptoms such as nausea, abdominal cramps, burning, angioedema, shortness of breath and severe hypotension occur. Symptoms are not relieved by antihistamines. In these patients consideration should be given to using a different type of dialysis membrane or a different class of antihypertensive agent.

Anaphylactoid Reactions during LDL Apheresis: Rarely, patients receiving ACE inhibitors during low density lipoprotein apheresis with dextran sulfate have experienced life-threatening anaphylactoid reactions. These reactions were avoided by temporarily withholding the ACE inhibitor therapy prior to each apheresis.

Anaphylactoid Reactions during Desensitization: There have been isolated reports of patients experiencing sustained life-threatening anaphylactoid reactions while receiving ACE inhibitors during desensitizing treatment with hymenoptera (bees, wasps) venom. In the same patients, these reactions have been avoided when ACE inhibitors were temporarily withheld for at least 24 hours, but they have reappeared upon inadvertent rechallenge to an ACE inhibitor.

Drug Interactions: Concomitant Diuretic Therapy: Patients concomitantly taking ACE inhibitors and diuretics, and especially those in whom diuretic therapy was recently instituted, may occasionally experience an excessive reduction of blood pressure after initiation of therapy. The possibility of hypotensive effects after the first dose of quinapril can be minimized by either discontinuing the diuretic or increasing the salt intake (except in patients with heart failure) prior to initiation of treatment with quinapril. If it is not possible to discontinue the diuretic, the starting dose of quinapril should be reduced and the patient should be closely observed for several hours following initial dose and until blood pressure has stabilized (see Warnings and Dosage).

Agents Increasing Serum Potassium: Since quinapril decreases aldosterone production, elevation of serum potassium may occur. Potassium-sparing diuretics, such as spironolactone, triamterene or amiloride, or potassium supplements, should be given only for documented hypokalemia and with caution and frequent monitoring of serum potassium since they may lead to a significant increase in serum potassium. Salt substitutes which contain potassium should also be used with caution.

Agents Affecting Sympathetic Activity: Agents affecting sympathetic activity (e.g., ganglionic blocking agents or adrenergic neuron blocking agents) may be used with caution. Beta-adrenergic blocking drugs add some further antihypertensive effect to quinapril.

Tetracycline: Concomitant administration of tetracycline with quinapril reduced the absorption of tetracycline in healthy volunteers (by 28 to 37%) due to the presence of magnesium carbonate as an excipient in the formulation. This interaction should be considered with concomitant use of Accuretic and tetracycline or other drugs which interact with magnesium.

Lithium: In general, lithium should not be given with diuretics or ACE inhibitors. Diuretic agents and ACE inhibitors reduce the renal clearance of lithium and add a high risk of lithium toxicity.

Cardiac Glycosides: Thiazide diuretics may enhance digitalis toxicity associated with hypokalemia or hypomagnesemia.

Alcohol, Barbiturates, or Narcotics: Potentiation of orthostatic hypotension may occur in the presence of hydrochlorothiazide.

Antidiabetic Drugs: Dosage adjustment of oral hypoglycemic agents and insulin may be required.

Other Antihypertensive Agents: Additive effects may occur.

Corticosteroids, ACTH: Intensified electrolyte depletion, particularly hypokalemia, may occur when administered with hydrochlorothiazide.

Pressor Amines, (e.g., norepinephrine): Possible decreased response to pressor amines may occur in the presence of a thiazide diuretic, but is not sufficient to preclude their use.

Nondepolarizing Neuromuscular Blocking Agents (e.g., d-tubocurarine): Hydrochlorothiazide may increase responsiveness to these drugs.

Nonsteroidal Anti-inflammatory Drugs: In some patients, the administration of a nonsteroidal anti-inflammatory agent can reduce the diuretic, natriuretic and antihypertensive effects of loop, potassium-sparing and thiazide diuretics. Therefore, when Accuretic and nonsteroidal anti-inflammatory agents are used concomitantly, the patient should be observed closely to determine if the desired effect of Accuretic is obtained.

Anion Exchange Resins: Absorption of hydrochlorothiazide is impaired in the presence of anion exchange resins, such as cholestyramine and colestipol. Single doses of the resins bind the hydrochlorothiazide and reduce its absorption from the gastrointestinal tract by up to 85% and 43%, respectively.

Information to be Provided to the Patient: Note: As with many other drugs, certain advice to patients being treated with Accuretic is warranted. This information is intended to aid in the safe and effective use of this medication. It is not a disclosure of all possible adverse or intended effects.

Angioedema: Angioedema, including laryngeal edema, may occur with ACE inhibitors, especially following the first dose. Patients should be so advised and told to report immediately any signs or symptoms suggesting angioedema, such as swelling of face, extremities, eyes, lips, tongue, difficulty in swallowing or breathing. They should immediately stop taking Accuretic and consult with their physician.

Pregnancy: Since the use of quinapril during pregnancy can cause injury and even death of the developing fetus, patients should be advised to report promptly to their physician if they become pregnant.

Hypotension: Patients should be cautioned to report light-headedness, especially during the first few days of Accuretic therapy. If actual syncope occurs, patients should be told to discontinue the drug and consult with their physician.

All patients should be cautioned that excessive perspiration and dehydration may lead to an excessive fall in blood pressure because of reduction in fluid volume. Other causes of volume depletion such as vomiting or diarrhea may also lead to a fall in blood pressure; patients should be advised to consult with their physician.

Agranulocytosis/Neutropenia: Patients should be told to report promptly to their physician any indication of infection (e.g., sore throat, fever) as this may be a sign of neutropenia.

Impaired Liver Function: Patients should be advised to return to their physician if they experience any symptoms possibly related to liver dysfunction. This would include "viral-like symptoms" in the first weeks to months of therapy (such as fever, malaise, muscle pain, rash or adenopathy which are possible indicators of hypersensitivity reactions) or if abdominal pain, nausea or vomiting, loss of appetite, jaundice, itching or any other unexplained symptoms occur during therapy.

Hyperkalemia: Patients should be told not to use salt substitutes containing potassium without consulting their physician.

Surgery: Patients planning to undergo surgery and/or anesthesia should be told to inform their physician that they are taking an ACE inhibitor.

Adverse Effects: Accuretic has been evaluated for safety in 1 571 patients with essential hypertension, including 943 patients in controlled studies (see Table I), 345 patients in placebo-controlled trials and 517 patients who were treated with Accuretic for at least 1 year. Adverse reactions have been limited to those reported previously with quinapril or hydrochlorothiazide when used separately for the treatment of hypertension.

Serious or clinically significant adverse reactions observed in less than 0.2% of patients treated with quinapril and hydrochlorothiazide were: hematemesis, gout, syncope and angioedema. Therapy was discontinued in 2.1% of patients due to an adverse event. Headache (0.5%) and dizziness (0.3%) were the most frequent reasons for withdrawal.

The most frequent adverse experiences in controlled trials were headache (6.7%), dizziness (4.8%), cough (3.2%) and fatigue (2.9%). The cough is characteristically nonproductive, persistent and resolves after discontinuation of therapy (see Warnings, Angioedema and Hypotension).

Clinical adverse events, regardless of relationship to therapy, occurring in >0.5% to <1% of patients treated with quinapril plus hydrochlorothiazide in controlled and uncontrolled trials and less frequent clinically significant events seen in clinical trials or in postmarketing experience included:

Cardiovascular: tachycardia, hypotension, palpitations.

Gastrointestinal: flatulence, dry mouth or throat, pancreatitis.

Respiratory: dyspnea, sinusitis.

Integumentary: erythema multiforme, exfoliative dermatitis, alopecia, pemphigus, pruritus, rash.

Nervous/Psychiatric: paresthesia, nervousness.

Urogenital: impotence, urinary tract infection.

Other: arthralgia, peripheral edema, hemolytic anemia.

Rare adverse events, not listed above, which have been reported with either hydrochlorothiazide, quinapril, or the combination, include: Cardiovascular: cerebrovascular accident, heart failure, atrial flutter, vasodilation, necrotizing angiitis, myocardial ischemia, heart arrest, transient ischemic attack. Orthostatic hypotension may occur, especially in elderly patients with reduced plasma volume, and may be potentiated by alcohol, barbiturates, or narcotics.

Gastrointestinal: anorexia, gastric irritation, cramping, constipation, jaundice (intrahepatic cholestatic), pancreatitis, sialadenitis, gastrointestinal hemorrhage, bloody stools.

Respiratory: respiratory distress including pneumonitis, asthma, hoarseness.

Integumentary: photosensitivity, rash, urticaria, Stevens-Johnson syndrome, eczema.

Nervous System: paresthesias, xanthopsia, confusion, amnesia, anxiety, facial paralysis, polyneuritis.

Hematological: leukopenia, thrombocytopenia, agranulocytosis, aplastic anemia, hemolytic anemia, purpura.

Urogenital: dysuria, polyuria, impaired renal function, hematuria, glycosuria.

Table I—Accuretic

Adverse Events in ≥1% of Quinapril/Hydrochlorothiazide Patients in Controlled Clinical Studies

Adverse Events	Quinapril/HCTZ N=943 (% Patients)	Quinapril N=799 (% Patients)
Body as a Whole		
Asthenia	1.1	1.2
Fatigue	2.9	2.0
Headache	6.7	4.8
Back pain	1.5	0.7
Chest pain	1.0	1.2
Viral infection	1.9	2.0
Cardiovascular		
Vasodilation	1.0	0.4
Digestive		
Dyspepsia	1.2	1.9
Nausea and/or vomiting	1.8	2.0
Diarrhea	1.4	1.7
Abdominal pain	1.7	1.6
Musculoskeletal		
Myalgia	2.4	0.9
Nervous System		
Dizziness	4.8	2.7
Insomnia	1.2	1.5
Somnolence	1.2	0.9
Vertigo	1.0	0.3
Respiratory		
Pharyngitis	1.1	1.4
Rhinitis	2.0	3.0
Bronchitis	1.2	1.3
Coughing	3.2	2.7
Upper respiratory infection	1.3	1.1

Special Senses: tinnitus, transient blurred vision, taste disturbance.

Other: muscle spasm, weakness, restlessness, chill, weight increase, dehydration, arthritis, allergy, face edema, fever, anaphylactic reactions, fracture.

Laboratory Deviations: WBC decreased, hyperglycemia, azotemia, hyperglycemia, transient hyperlipidemia, hyperuricemia.

Clinical Laboratory Test Findings: Creatinine, Blood Nitrogen: Increases (>1.25 times the upper limit of normal) in serum creatinine and blood urea nitrogen were observed in 3% and 4% respectively of patients treated with Accuretic (see Precautions).

Hepatic: Elevations of liver enzymes and/or serum bilirubin have occurred (see Precautions).

Glucose: Elevations in glucose values have occurred (see Precautions).

Triglyceride: Elevations in triglyceride values have occurred (see Precautions).

Serum Uric Acid: Elevations in serum uric acid values have occurred (see Precautions).

Hematology: Possibly clinically important increases and decreases in hematology parameters have occurred (see Warnings).

Other laboratory test values with clinically important deviations during controlled and uncontrolled trials included: magnesium, cholesterol, PBI, parathyroid function tests and calcium (see Precautions); hematology (see Warnings).

Overdose: Symptoms and Treatment: No data are available regarding overdosage of Accuretic or quinapril in humans. The most likely clinical manifestation would be symptoms attributable to severe hypotension, which should be normally treated by i.v. volume expansion with 0.9% sodium chloride.

Hemodialysis and peritoneal dialysis have little effect on the elimination of quinapril and quinaprilat.

The most common signs and symptoms observed for hydrochlorothiazide monotherapy overdosage are those caused by electrolyte depletion (hypokalemia, hypochloremia, hyponatremia) and dehydration resulting from excessive diuresis. If digitalis has also been administered, hypokalemia may accentuate cardiac arrhythmias.

Dosage: Dosage must be individualized. The fixed combination is not for initial therapy. The dose of Accuretic should be determined by titration of the individual components.

Once the patient has been successfully titrated with the individual components as described below, Accuretic may be substituted if the titrated doses and dosing schedule can be achieved by the fixed combination (see Indications and Warnings). In some patients, a twice daily administration may be required.

Patients do not generally require hydrochlorothiazide in excess of 50 mg daily, particularly when combined with other antihypertensive agents.

Monotherapy: The recommended initial dose of quinapril in patients not on diuretics is 10 mg once daily. An initial dose of 20 mg once daily can be considered for patients without advanced age, renal impairment, or concomitant heart failure and who are not volume-depleted (see Precautions, Hypotension). Dosage should be adjusted according to blood pressure response, generally at intervals of 2 to 4 weeks. A dose of 40 mg daily should not be exceeded.

In some patients treated once daily, the antihypertensive effect may diminish towards the end of the dosing interval. This can be evaluated by measuring blood pressure just prior to dosing to determine whether satisfactory control is being maintained for 24 hours. If it is not, either twice daily administration with the same total daily dose, or an increase in dose should be considered. If blood pressure is not controlled with quinapril alone, a diuretic may be added. After the addition of a diuretic, it may be possible to reduce the dose of quinapril.

Concomitant Diuretic Therapy: Symptomatic hypotension occasionally may occur following the initial dose of quinapril and is more likely in patients who are currently being treated with a diuretic. The diuretic should, if possible, be discontinued for two to three days before beginning therapy with quinapril to reduce the likelihood of hypotension (see Warnings). If the diuretic cannot be discontinued, an initial dose of 5 mg of quinapril should be used with careful medical supervision for several hours and until blood pressure has stabilized. The dosage of quinapril should subsequently be titrated (as described above) to the optimal response.

Dosage Adjustment in Renal Impairment: For use in hemodialysis patients, see Precautions, Anaphylactoid Reactions during Membrane Exposure. Quinapril should be administered on days when dialysis is not performed.

Starting doses should be reduced according to the guidelines in Table II.

Table II—Accuretic

Dosage Adjustment in Renal Impairment

Creatinine Clearance (mL/min)	Maximum Recommended Initial Dose (mg)
>60	10
30-60	5
10-30	2.5
<10	Insufficient data for dosage recommendation

Patients should subsequently have dosage titrated (as described above) to the optimal response as described under Monotherapy.

When concomitant diuretic therapy is required in patients with severe renal impairment, a loop diuretic rather than a thiazide is preferred for use with quinapril. Therefore, for patients with severe renal dysfunction, Accuretic is not recommended.

Geriatrics: The recommended initial dosage of quinapril is 10 mg once daily (depending on renal function) followed by titration to the optimal response as described above under Monotherapy.

Supplied: 10/12.5: Each pink, scored, elliptical, biconvex, film-coated tablet contains: quinapril 10 mg and hydrochlorothiazide 12.5 mg. Nonmedicinal ingredients: candelilla wax, crospovidone, lactose, magnesium carbonate, magnesium stearate, povidone, synthetic red iron oxide, synthetic yellow iron oxide and titanium dioxide. Blisters of 28.

20/12.5: Each pink, scored, triangular, biconvex, film-coated tablet contains: quinapril 20 mg and hydrochlorothiazide 12.5 mg. Nonmedicinal ingredients: candelilla wax, crospovidone, lactose, magnesium carbonate, magnesium stearate, povidone, synthetic red iron oxide, synthetic yellow iron oxide and titanium dioxide. Blisters of 28.

Store at controlled room temperature 15 to 30°C. Dispense in well-closed containers.

(Shown in Product Recognition Section)

New Product 1998

New drugs require close post-marketing surveillance. Report suspected adverse reactions and interactions to the Health Protection Branch using the form provided in the CLIN-INFO SECTION.

ACCUTANE™ ROCHE®

Roche

Isotretinoin

Acne Therapy

Pharmacology: The mechanism of action of isotretinoin is unknown. Vitamin A is important for functional integrity of the skin and is known to affect the keratinization process. In acne patients, improvement occurs in association with a reduction in sebum secretion. The decrease in sebum secretion is temporary and is related to either the dose or duration of isotretinoin administration and reflects a reduction in sebaceous gland size and an inhibition of sebaceous gland differentiation.

Following oral administration of 80 mg, peak plasma concentrations ranged from 167 to 459 ng/mL with a mean time to peak of 3.2 hours in volunteers, while in acne patients peak plasma concentrations ranged from 98 to 535 ng/mL (mean 262 ng/mL) with a mean time to peak of 2.9 hours. Isotretinoin is 99.9% protein bound in human plasma, almost exclusively to albumin. The mean terminal elimination half-life of isotretinoin in volunteers and patients ranged from 9 to 22 hours. Following oral administration of ^{14}C-isotretinoin, ^{14}C activity in blood declined with a mean half-life of 90 hours. Approximately equal amounts of radioactivity were recovered in the urine and feces, with 65 to 83% of the dose recovered.

The major metabolite identified in blood and urine was 4-oxo-isotretinoin. Tretinoin and 4-oxo-tretinoin were also observed. The apparent half-life for elimination of the 4-oxo-isotretinoin ranged from 11 to 50 hours with a mean of 28 hours. Following 80 mg of isotretinoin administered orally, maximum plasma concentrations of the 4-oxo-isotretinoin was 87 to 399 ng/mL and maxima were observed between 6 and 20 hours. The blood concentration of the major metabolite generally exceeded that of isotretinoin after 6 hours. The data suggest that both isotretinoin and the major metabolite are excreted in the bile and reabsorbed.

The mean minimum steady state blood concentrations of isotretinoin were 160 ng/mL in 10 patients receiving 40 mg twice daily. After single and multiple doses, the mean ratio of areas under the curves of 4-oxo-isotretinoin to isotretinoin was between 3 and 3.5.

Indications: The treatment of severe nodular and/or inflammatory acne, acne conglobata and recalcitrant acne.

Because of significant side effects associated with its use, isotretinoin should be reserved for patients where the conditions listed above are unresponsive to conventional therapy, including systemic antibiotics. Isotretinoin should only be prescribed by physicians knowledgeable in the use of retinoids systemically. It is recommended that each isotretinoin prescription be limited to preferably a 1 month supply in order to encourage patients to return for their regular appointments.

Contraindications: *Pregnancy:* Isotretinoin is contraindicated in pregnancy. Females must not become pregnant while taking isotretinoin or for at least 1 month after its discontinuation. Isotretinoin causes severe birth defects in a very high percentage of infants born to women who take this drug even for a short period of time during pregnancy (see Warnings: Pregnancy, Pregnancy Testing and Contraception).

Isotretinoin is contraindicated in females of childbearing potential unless **all** of the following conditions apply:

1. The patient has severe disfiguring nodular and/or inflammatory acne, acne conglobata or recalcitrant acne that has not responded to standard therapy, including systemic antibiotics.
2. The patient is reliable in understanding and carrying out instructions.
3. The patient is able to comply with the mandatory contraceptive measures.
4. The patient has received, and acknowledged understanding of, a careful oral and printed explanation of the hazards of fetal exposure to isotretinoin, and the risk of possible contraception failure. This explanation may include showing a line drawing to the patient of an infant with the characteristic external deformities resulting from isotretinoin exposure during pregnancy.
5. The patient has had a serum or urine pregnancy test with a sensitivity of at least 50 mIU/mL with a negative result, performed in a licensed laboratory, within 2 weeks prior to initiating therapy. The patient has had 2 or 3 days of the next normal menstrual period before isotretinoin therapy is initiated.

Note: Re: items 2 to 5 see Warnings: Pregnancy, Pregnancy Testing and Contraception.

Isotretinoin is also contraindicated in patients who are sensitive to parabens or to those with known hypersensitivity to retinoids.

Warnings: *Pregnancy*: Pregnancy, Pregnancy Testing and Contraception: There is an extremely high risk (25% or greater) that major human fetal abnormalities will occur if pregnancy occurs during treatment with isotretinoin or up to 1 month following its discontinuation. Potentially any exposed fetus can be affected. These abnormalities, associated with isotretinoin administration during pregnancy, have been reported and include: CNS (hydrocephalus, hydranencephaly, microcephaly, posterior fossa abnormalities, cranial nerve dysfunction, cerebellar malformation); craniofacial (anotia, microtia, low set ears, small or absent canals, microphthalmia, facial dysmorphia, cleft palate); cardiac (septal defects, aortic arch abnormalities, tetralogy of Fallot); thymus gland abnormalities; and parathyroid hormone deficiency.

Female patients of childbearing potential must not be given isotretinoin until pregnancy is excluded. A pregnancy test must be performed within 2 weeks prior to starting treatment. Isotretinoin treatment should start on the second or third day of the next normal menstrual period following this negative pregnancy test. Effective contraception must be used for at least 1 month before starting isotretinoin treatment, during treatment and for at least 1 month following the discontinuation of treatment. It is recommended that 2 reliable forms of contraception be used simultaneously unless abstinence is the chosen method. Pregnancy occurring during treatment with isotretinoin and for 1 month after its discontinuation, carries the risk of fetal malformation (see Warnings above). Females should be fully counselled on the serious risk to the fetus should they become pregnant while undergoing treatment. If pregnancy does occur during this time the physician and patient should discuss the desirability of continuing the pregnancy.

It is strongly recommended that all female patients of childbearing potential treated with isotretinoin have regular monthly pregnancy tests during treatment and 1 month after the discontinuation of treatment. These pregnancy tests will: serve primarily to reinforce to the patient the necessity of avoiding pregnancy and in the event of accidental pregnancy, provide the physician and patient an immediate opportunity to discuss the serious risk to the fetus from this exposure to isotretinoin and the desirability of continuing the pregnancy in view of the potential teratogenic effect of isotretinoin (see Warnings above).

Lactation: It is not known whether isotretinoin is excreted in human milk. Because of the potential for adverse effects, women should not breast-feed if they are receiving isotretinoin.

Hyperostosis: In clinical trials of disorders of keratinization, with a mean dose of 2.24 mg/kg/day, a high prevalence of skeletal hyperostosis was noted. Two children showed x-ray findings suggestive of premature closure of the epiphysis. Additionally, skeletal hyperostosis was noted in 6 of 8 patients in a prospective study of disorders of keratinization. Minimal skeletal hyperostosis has also been observed by x-rays in prospective studies of cystic acne patients treated with a single course of therapy at recommended doses.

Hepatotoxicity: Liver function tests should be monitored before treatment and at regular intervals during treatment. Several cases of clinical hepatitis have been noted which are considered to be possibly or probably related to isotretinoin therapy. Additionally, mild to moderate elevations of liver enzymes have been observed in approximately 15% of individuals treated during clinical trials, some of which normalized with dosage reduction or continued administration of the drug. If normalization does not readily occur, or if hepatitis is suspected during treatment with isotretinoin, the drug should be discontinued and the etiology further investigated.

Precautions: Benign Intracranial Hypertension (pseudotumor cerebri): Isotretinoin has been associated with a number of cases of benign intracranial hypertension. Early signs and symptoms of this disorder usually include headache, visual disturbances, nausea and vomiting. Patients with these symptoms should be examined for papilledema. If present, isotretinoin should be discontinued immediately and the patient referred to a neurologist for diagnosis and care.

Decreased Night Vision: A number of cases of decreased night vision have occurred during isotretinoin therapy. Because the onset in some patients was sudden, patients should be advised of this potential problem and warned to be cautious when driving or operating any vehicle at night. Visual problems should be carefully monitored.

Corneal Opacities: Corneal opacities have occurred in patients receiving isotretinoin for acne and more frequently when higher drug dosages were used in patients with disorders of keratinization. All isotretinoin patients experiencing visual difficulties should discontinue the drug and have an ophthalmological examination. The corneal opacities that have been observed in patients treated with isotretinoin have either completely resolved or were resolving at follow-up 6 to 7 weeks after discontinuation of the drug (see Adverse Effects).

Inflammatory Bowel Disease: Isotretinoin has been temporally associated with inflammatory bowel disease (including regional ileitis) in patients without a prior history of intestinal disorders. Patients experiencing abdominal pain, rectal bleeding or severe diarrhea should discontinue isotretinoin immediately.

Lipids: Blood lipid determinations should be performed before isotretinoin is given and then at intervals until the lipid response to isotretinoin is established, which usually occurs within 4 weeks.

Approximately 25% of patients receiving isotretinoin experienced an elevation in plasma triglycerides. Approximately 15% developed a decrease in high density lipoproteins and about 7% showed an increase in cholesterol levels. These effects on triglycerides, HDL and cholesterol were reversible upon cessation of isotretinoin therapy.

Patients with increased tendency to develop hypertriglyceridemia include those with diabetes mellitus, obesity, increased alcohol intake and familial history.

The cardiovascular consequences of hypertriglyceridemia are not well understood, but may increase the patient's risk status. In addition, elevation of serum triglycerides in excess of 800 mg/dL has been associated with acute pancreatitis. Therefore, every attempt should be made to control significant triglyceride elevation. Some patients have been able to reverse triglyceride elevation by reduction in weight, restriction of dietary fat and alcohol, and reduction in dose while continuing isotretinoin. An obese male patient with Darier's disease developed elevated triglycerides and subsequent eruptive xanthomas.

Diabetes: Patients with diabetes or a family history of diabetes may experience problems with the control of their blood sugar during isotretinoin therapy. Therefore, known or suspected diabetics should have periodic blood sugar determinations.

Vitamin A: Because of the relationship of isotretinoin to vitamin A, patients should be advised against taking vitamin supplements containing vitamin A, to avoid additive toxic effects.

Children: The long-term safety of isotretinoin in prepubertal children has not been established.

Blood Donation: It is recommended that blood donation for transfusion purposes be deferred during therapy with isotretinoin and for 1 month after discontinuation of treatment. Theoretically, blood from such donors could present a small risk to the fetus if transfused to a pregnant mother during the first trimester of pregnancy.

Adverse Effects: Many of the side effects and adverse reactions seen or expected in patients receiving isotretinoin are similar to those described in patients taking high doses of vitamin A.

Clinical Adverse Experiences: The most common side effects are mucocutaneous or dermatologic. The common side effects include: cheilitis (96%), facial dermatitis (55%), dry nose (51%), desquamation (50%), pruritus (30%), dry skin (22%), conjunctivitis (19%), alopecia (13%), irritation of the eyes (11%), rash (<10%). Dryness of the nasal mucosa may be associated with mild epistaxis. Mild-to-moderate conjunctivitis may be alleviated by use of an ophthalmic ointment. In rare cases, hair loss persisted after treatment was completed.

Approximately 13% of patients experience joint pain during treatment.

Peeling of palms and soles, skin infections, increased susceptibility to sunburn, nonspecific urogenital symptoms, nonspecific gastrointestinal symptoms, headache, fatigue occur in approximately 5% of patients.

Skeletal hyperostosis has been observed on x-rays of patients treated with isotretinoin (see Warnings, Hyperostosis).

Isotretinoin has been associated with a number of cases of pseudotumor cerebri, some of which involved concomitant use of tetracyclines (see Precautions, Benign Intracranial Hypertension).

Of 72 patients who had normal pretreatment ophthalmological examinations, 5 developed corneal opacities while on isotretinoin (all 5 patients had a disorder of keratinization). Corneal opacities have also been reported in nodular and/or inflammatory acne patients treated with isotretinoin (see Precautions, Corneal Opacities). Decrease in night vision has been reported and in rare instances has persisted (see Precautions, Decreased Night Vision). Cataracts and visual disturbances have also been reported.

Isotretinoin has been temporally associated with inflammatory bowel disease, including regional ileitis (see Precautions, Inflammatory Bowel Disease).

Other adverse reactions which have been reported infrequently and may bear no relationship to therapy include:
Mucocutaneous and Dermatologic: flushing, changes in skin pigment, urticaria, bruising, disseminated herpes simplex, hair problems (other than thinning), hirsutism, erythema nodosum, paronychia, nail dystrophy, pyogenic granuloma, bleeding and inflammation of the gums, acne fulminans.
CNS: seizures, emotional instability, dizziness, nervousness, drowsiness, malaise, weakness, insomnia, lethargy, paresthesia.
Ophthalmologic: optic neuritis, photophobia, eye lid inflammation.
Gastrointestinal: mild gastrointestinal bleeding, rectal bleeding, pancreatitis.
Cardiovascular: edema, transient pain in the chest, palpitations, tachycardia.
Respiratory: respiratory infections.
Urogenital: abnormal menses.
Other: weight loss, arthritis, anemia, lymphadenopathy, vasculitis including Wegener's granulomatosis.

Depression has been reported during and after therapy. In some of these patients, depression has subsided with discontinuation of therapy and recurred when isotretinoin therapy was reintroduced.

Dry eyes and/or decreased tolerance to contact lenses have also been reported during therapy. In some instances these conditions have persisted after cessation of therapy.

Laboratory Abnormalities: Isotretinoin therapy induces changes in serum lipids in a significant number of treated subjects. These changes consisted of: elevation of serum triglycerides, (25% of patients) mild to moderate decreases in serum high density lipoprotein (HDL) (16% of patients), and minimal elevations of serum cholesterol (7% of patients). Abnormalities of serum triglycerides, HDL and cholesterol were reversible upon cessation of therapy.

A rise in serum levels of liver enzymes may occur, especially with higher dosages. Although the changes have usually been within the normal range and may return to baseline levels despite continued treatment, significant increases have occurred in a few cases, necessitating dosage reduction or discontinuation of isotretinoin (see Warnings, Hepatotoxicity). An elevated erythrocyte sedimentation rate may also occur (40% of patients).

Other less commonly reported laboratory abnormalities were: decreases in red blood cell parameters and white blood cell counts, elevated platelet counts, white cells in the urine, proteinuria, red blood cells in the urine, elevated fasting blood sugar, elevated creatinine phosphokinase (CPK) or hyperuricemia.

Dose-relationship and duration: Cheilitis and hypertriglyceridemia are usually dose related.

Adverse reactions were generally reversible when therapy was discontinued; however, some have persisted after cessation of therapy.

Overdose: Symptoms and Treatment: In the event of acute overdose, evacuation of the stomach should be considered during the first few hours after this overdose. Signs and symptoms of acute overdose have been associated with headache, vomiting, facial flushing, cheilitis, abdominal pain, dizziness and ataxia. To date, all symptoms quickly resolved without apparent residual effects and usually without treatment. Elevated intracranial pressure has been reported with patients receiving therapeutic doses of isotretinoin. Patients with an isotretinoin overdose should be monitored closely for signs of increased intracranial pressure.

Limited data exist on the pharmacokinetic characteristics of isotretinoin in an overdose situation. Following the oral administration of single 80, 160, 240 and 340 mg doses to 12 healthy male subjects C_{max} was 366, 820, 1 056 and 981 ng/mL, and $t_{1/2}$ was 13.6, 14.1, 14.4 and 16.5 hours for isotretinoin, respectively. Twenty-three compromised cancer patients received weekly oral doses of 200 (3 patients); 400 (7 patients); 660 (2 patients); 1 000 (3 patients); 1 400 (6 patients) and 1 800 (1 patient) mg/m². Normal body surface area for healthy subjects is 1.73 m². After the first dose, C_{max} was 1.5, 3.8, 3.5, 2.5, 2.7 and 4.6 µg/mL, and $t_{1/2}$ was 45, 9.1, 14.5, 57, 13.1 and 6.1 hours for isotretinoin, respectively. The absorption of isotretinoin appears to be a saturable process.

Since it is difficult to extrapolate from the results of these studies to the overdose situation, the following precautions should be taken with all female patients of childbearing potential who have taken an overdose of isotretinoin.

1. At the time of the overdose, a pregnancy test must be performed and a blood sample collected for the determination of isotretinoin and metabolite concentrations.
2. One complete menstrual cycle after the overdose, a second pregnancy test must be performed and a second blood sample collected for the determination of isotretinoin and metabolite concentrations.
3. Effective contraception must be used for at least one complete menstrual cycle after the overdose and continued longer if necessary until isotretinoin and its metabolites are no longer measurable in the blood.

Patients who present with a positive pregnancy test at the time of the overdose, one complete menstrual cycle after the overdose, or while isotretinoin or metabolite blood concentrations are measurable, should be fully counselled on the serious risk to the fetus from this exposure to isotretinoin and the physician and patient should discuss the desirability of continuing the pregnancy (see Contraindications and Warnings).

Canadian Regional Poison Information Centres have been advised on the proper collection and handling of isotretinoin blood samples and also on the laboratory(s) equipped to assay these samples.

Dosage: The therapeutic response to isotretinoin is dose-related and varies between patients. This necessitates individual adjustments of dosage according to the response of the condition and the patient's tolerance of the drug. In most cases complete or near-complete suppression of acne is achieved with a single 12- to 16-week course of therapy. If a second course of therapy is needed, it can be initiated 8 or more weeks after completion of the first course, since experience has shown that patients may continue to improve while off the drug.

Initial Therapy: The initial dose should be individualized according to the patient's weight and severity of the disease.

In general patients initially should receive isotretinoin 0.5 mg/kg body weight daily for a period of 2 to 4 weeks, when their responsiveness to the drug will usually be apparent. It should be noted that transient exacerbation of acne is occasionally seen during this initial period.

The daily dosage should be taken with food in the nearest number of whole capsules, either as a single dose or in 2 divided doses during the day, whichever is more convenient.

Maintenance Therapy: Maintenance dose should be adjusted between 0.1 and 1 mg/kg body weight daily and, in exceptional instances, up to 2 mg/kg body weight daily, depending upon individual patient response and tolerance to the drug.

A complete course of therapy consists of 12 to 16 weeks of isotretinoin administration.

Patients may show additional improvement for up to several months after a course of isotretinoin has been completed. With effective treatment, appearance of new lesions will not normally be evident for a period of at least 3 to 6 months.

Information for the Patient: See Blue Section—Information for the Patient "Accutane Roche".

Supplied: 10 mg: Each opaque, oval-shaped, soft gelatin capsule contains: isotretinoin 10 mg (purple, imprinted ROA/10). Nonmedicinal ingredients: beeswax, canthaxanthin 10%, gelatin, glycerin, hydrogenated palm oil, Karion 83, soybean and hydrogenated soybean oil and titanium dioxide. Energy: 6.4 kJ (1.5 kcal).

40 mg: Each opaque, oval-shaped, soft gelatin capsule contains: isotretinoin 40 mg (yellow, imprinted ROA/40). Nonmedicinal ingredients: beeswax, gelatin, glycerin, methylparaben, hydrogenated palm oil, propylparaben, quinoline yellow WS, soybean and hydrogenated soybean oil, sunset yellow FCF and titanium dioxide. Energy: 11.7 kJ (2.8 kcal).

Alcohol-, gluten-, lactose-, sodium-, sulfite- and tartrazine-free. Blister packs of 30. Protect from light at all times. Store at 15 to 30°C. Dispense with information for the consumer.

(Shown in Product Recognition Section)

ACE INHIBITORS

General Monograph, CPhA

Benazepril
Captopril
Cilazapril
Enalapril
Enalaprilat
Fosinopril
Lisinopril
Perindopril
Quinapril
Ramipril
Trandolapril

Angiotensin Converting Enzyme Inhibitor

This monograph has been compiled by CPhA. It may contain information different from that approved by Therapeutic Products Programme, Health Canada, and the pharmaceutical manufacturers' approval has not been requested.

Pharmacology: The renin angiotensin system is a complex neuroendocrine system involved in the regulation of hemodynamics and water and electrolyte balance. When released from the kidney in response to a decrease in blood volume, renal perfusion pressure or plasma sodium concentration, renin acts on its substrate, angiotensinogen, to form angiotensin I. Angiotensin converting enzyme (ACE) catalyzes the conversion of angiotensin I to angiotensin II. Inhibitors of ACE suppress the production of angiotensin II, which is the most vasoactive product of the renin-angiotensin system.

Patients with lower levels of renin, e.g., blacks, may experience a lesser antihypertensive response to monotherapy with ACE inhibitors.

Angiotensin II exerts many varied physiologic effects, including stimulation of aldosterone secretion, a direct systemic and coronary vasoconstrictive action as well as a positive inotropic effect, both directly and indirectly, through enhanced sympathetic outflow. Inhibition of ACE leads to decreased systemic arteriolar resistance and mean diastolic and systolic blood pressure. In patients with CHF, inhibition of ACE results in decreased afterload and heart rate as well as increased cardiac output, stroke volume and stroke work.

ACE inhibitors have many clinical applications, including the treatment of hypertension, CHF, left ventricular dysfunction and diabetic nephropathy. While large scale studies have not been conducted with every agent for every indication, evidence to date suggests that the clinical and adverse effects of ACE inhibitors tend to apply to these drugs as a class rather than to individual agents.

When ACE inhibitors are combined with thiazide diuretics, the antihypertensive effect is approximately additive.

ACE is known to be the same enzyme as kininase II, which catalyzes other physiologic reactions including the breakdown of the vasodilating autocoid, bradykinin. The extent to which potentiation of bradykinin is responsible for the beneficial or adverse clinical effects of ACE inhibitors is not clearly known.

The action of ACE inhibitors may not completely block the production of angiotensin II. Alternative pathways such as tissue-based chymases may facilitate the formation of angiotensin II from its precursors, independently of ACE.

Pharmacokinetics: With the exception of enalaprilat, which is given i.v., ACE inhibitors are absorbed to varying degrees from the gastrointestinal tract after oral administration. The rate and/or extent of absorption of certain agents may be decreased in the presence of food, although it is not clear whether this is clinically important in every case.

Some ACE inhibitors are converted in the liver and/or gastrointestinal mucosa to active metabolites; elimination of unchanged drug or metabolites may be renal or fecal. Table I (on following page) contains various comparative pharmacokinetic parameters.

Indications: The pharmacologic effects of ACE inhibitors are thought to be of a class rather than individual nature (see Pharmacology). However, the labeled indications for specific agents may differ. At present, all of the ACE inhibitors available in Canada are marketed as antihypertensives for the treatment of mild to moderate essential hypertension, either alone or in combination with other drugs, particularly thiazide

ACE Inhibitors (cont'd)

Table I—ACE Inhibitors

Pharmacokinetics

ACE Inhibitor	Effect of Food on Absorption: Decreased Rate of Absorption	Effect of Food on Absorption: Decreased Extent of Absorption	Active Metabolite	Time to Peak Effect (hours)	Duration of Action (hours)	Elimination	Effective Accumulation Half-life (hours)
Benazepril	Yes	No	Benazeprilat	2 to 4	24	Renal[a]: 88% Biliary: 12%	10 to 11
Captopril	Yes	Yes	NA[b]	1 to 1.5	6 to 12[c]	Renal[a]	<3
Cilazapril	Yes	Yes	Cilazaprilat	2 to 4	24	Renal[a]	8.9
Enalapril	No	No	Enalaprilat	Oral: 4 to 6 I.V.: 1 to 4	Oral: 24 I.V.: 6	Renal[a]	11
Fosinopril	Yes	No	Fosinoprilat	2 to 6	24	Renal: 50% Fecal: 50%	11.5
Lisinopril	No	No	NA[b]	6	24	Renal[a]	12
Perindopril	No	No[d]	Perindoprilat	6	24	Renal[a]	3 to 10
Quinapril	Yes[e]	No	Quinaprilat	2 to 24	24[c]	Renal[a]: 60% Fecal: 40%	3
Ramipril	Yes	No	Ramiprilat	4 to 6.5	24	Renal[a]: 60% Fecal: 40%	13 to 17
Trandolapril	Yes	No	Trandolaprilat	2 to 4	24	Renal: 33% Fecal: 67%	16 to 24

[a]Dosage adjustment recommended in patients with renal failure.
[b]Not applicable.
[c]Dose related.
[d]The extent of biotransformation to perindoprilat may be decreased in the presence of food, resulting in slightly decreased pharmacodynamic effect.
[e]Especially high fat meals.

diuretics. Several agents (captopril, cilazapril, enalapril, fosinopril, lisinopril and quinapril) include an indication for the treatment of CHF, in combination with other agents such as thiazide diuretics or digoxin. Three agents, captopril, enalapril and ramipril, are indicated in the treatment of left ventricular dysfunction, to prevent symptomatic heart failure and reduce the frequency of hospitalization (see Table II). Captopril includes an indication for the treatment of diabetic nephropathy in patients with proteinuria.

The i.v. formulation of enalaprilat is indicated for the treatment of hypertension when the oral route is not practical.

Table II lists the labeled indications of the various ACE inhibitors.

Contraindications: In patients with known hypersensitivity to a particular ACE inhibitor, the specific agent in question is contraindicated. All ACE inhibitors are contraindicated in patients with a history of angioedema related to previous use of any member of this class. Products containing a fixed combination of an ACE inhibitor and a thiazide diuretic are also contraindicated in anuric patients and those with hypersensitivity to thiazides or other sulfonamide-derived drugs.

Warnings: *Pregnancy* (see Precautions, Pregnancy): **When used in pregnancy during the second and third trimesters, ACE inhibitors may cause significant fetal morbidity or mortality and should be discontinued as soon as possible if pregnancy is detected.**

Angioedema: Angioedema has been reported with the use of ACE inhibitors. Involvement of the larynx may be fatal. If swelling is limited to the face and lips, discontinuation of the ACE inhibitor is usually the only corrective measure required. However, if there is involvement of the tongue, glottis or larynx, appropriate therapy (e.g., epinephrine) should be instituted as life-threatening airway obstruction may occur. Patients should be advised that swelling in the mouth or facial area or difficulty breathing or swallowing may be signs of angioedema and that they should discontinue the ACE inhibitor and contact their physician immediately if any of these symptoms occur.

Hypotension: Severe hypotension may occur with the use of ACE inhibitors, particularly in patients who are volume depleted, hyponatremic, receiving concomitant diuretics or on dialysis. ACE inhibitors should be used with caution in patients with cerebrovascular disease or ischemic heart disease, as severe hypotension could have serious consequences in these patients. In patients with severe heart failure with or without pre-existing renal insufficiency, ACE inhibitors may cause excessive hypotension with oliguria, azotemia and potentially fatal renal failure. In these patient groups, ACE inhibitors should be initiated under close medical supervision and monitored closely for the first few weeks of therapy and whenever the dose is increased.

Patients taking ACE inhibitors should be advised that vomiting, diarrhea, excessive perspiration or dehydration due to low fluid intake may cause an exaggerated decrease in blood pressure and that they should inform their physician if any of these conditions occur.

Neutropenia/Agranulocytosis: Neutropenia and bone marrow depression have occurred during therapy with ACE inhibitors. Periodic monitoring of white blood cell count is suggested, especially in patients with risk factors such as collagen vascular disease, renal failure or drug therapy that may cause immunosuppression. ACE inhibitors should be used with caution in these patients.

Patients should be advised to report any symptoms of infection, such as sore throat or fever, to their physician.

Precautions: Impaired Renal Function: Renal function should be evaluated prior to the initiation of ACE inhibitor therapy. Patients with impaired renal function, particularly those with bilateral or unilateral renal artery stenosis, may experience further deterioration of renal function, including acute renal failure, while taking ACE inhibitors. Patients with CHF or those receiving concomitant diuretic therapy may also be at increased risk. Reduction of ACE inhibitor dosage or discontinuation of diuretic therapy may be sufficient to restore adequate renal perfusion.

Although ACE inhibitors have been found to slow the progression of diabetic nephropathy in type I diabetic patients with documented proteinuria, some patients with pre-existing renal disease may be at increased risk of developing proteinuria while on ACE inhibitor therapy.

Hypersensitivity: Sudden, life-threatening anaphylactoid reactions have occurred during therapy with ACE inhibitors in patients undergoing hemodialysis with polyacrylonitrile (PAN) high-flux membranes and in patients being desensitized to hymenoptera venom (e.g., bees, wasps). Dialysis should be stopped immediately if symptoms such as nausea, abdominal cramps, burning, angioedema or shortness of breath occur, and appropriate treatment initiated. Antihistamines do not appear to provide symptomatic relief in these situations.

Hyperkalemia: Increases in serum potassium can occur during therapy with ACE inhibitors. Significant hyperkalemia usually occurs only in patients who are not on a concomitant thiazide diuretic, patients with impaired renal function, CHF or diabetes, or those who are taking other drugs which may raise serum potassium such as potassium-sparing diuretics, potassium supplements or potassium-containing salt substitutes.

Impaired Liver Function: Increases in liver enzymes and/or bilirubin, cholestatic jaundice and cases of hepatocellular injury with or without cholestasis have occurred during ACE inhibitor therapy, even in patients with no pre-existing liver disease. In most cases, these changes were reversible upon discontinuation of the drug. Patients reporting symptoms such as abdominal pain, muscle aches, vomiting, loss of appetite, etc., should be investigated for possible hepatic adverse effects. Patients with pre-existing liver disease should have baseline liver function tests prior to initiation of treatment. ACE inhibitors should be used with caution in these patients.

Cough: A persistent, dry cough has been reported with the use of ACE inhibitors, and a possible association must be considered in the differential diagnosis of patients presenting with cough. Accumulation of kinins in the respiratory tract, secondary to inhibition of kininase II, is thought to be a possible cause for the cough. A decrease in the ACE inhibitor dose may alleviate the cough and obviate the need for discontinuation. Cough has been associated with all ACE inhibitors; therefore, switching to a different agent may not result in improvement.

Pregnancy (see Warnings): ACE inhibitors should not be taken during pregnancy. Hypotension, reversible or irreversible renal failure, anuria, skull hypoplasia and/or death have occurred in neonates exposed to ACE inhibitors during the second and third trimesters of pregnancy. Oligohydramnios, which may be associated with contractures of the limbs, craniofacial deformities, lung hypoplasia and intrauterine growth retardation, has also occurred. These effects do not appear to result from exposure during the first trimester; however, ACE inhibitor therapy should be discontinued as soon as possible if pregnancy is detected. In extremely rare cases where a therapeutic alternative is not found, the patient should be informed of the potential harm to the fetus and serial ultrasound examinations should be performed to monitor fetal development and intra-amniotic fluid status. If oligohydramnios occurs, the ACE inhibitor should be discontinued unless it is considered life-saving for the mother.

Lactation: Detectible levels of various ACE inhibitors have been found in breast milk. Although the respective manufacturers generally advise not to breast feed while taking ACE inhibitors, there is no evidence to date of harmful effects in infants.

Children: Although there is limited experience with the use of captopril in infants and children, safety and efficacy of ACE inhibitors in the pediatric population have not been established. There appear to be specific risks associated with their use in neonates and infants, such as oliguria and neurologic abnormalities, possibly caused by decreased renal and cerebral perfusion due to prolonged, excessive hypotension. Most manufacturers advise against the use of their product in children. The manufacturer of captopril recommends its use only

Table II—ACE Inhibitors

Labeled Indications

ACE Inhibitor	Hypertension	CHF	Left Ventricular Dysfunction	Diabetic Nephropathy
Benazepril	Yes	–	–	–
Captopril	Yes	Yes	Yes[a]	Yes
Cilazapril	Yes	Yes	–	–
Enalapril	Yes	Yes	Yes	–
Enalaprilat	Yes	–	–	–
Fosinopril	Yes	Yes	–	–
Lisinopril[b]	Yes	Yes	–[b]	–
Perindopril	Yes	–	–	–
Quinapril	Yes	Yes	–	–
Ramipril	Yes	–	Yes[a]	–
Trandolapril	Yes	–	Yes[a]	–

[a]Following acute MI.
[b]Lisinopril is approved for use in hemodynamically stable patients within 24 hours of acute MI, to improve survival.

when other measures for controlling blood pressure have not been successful.

Geriatrics: ACE inhibitors are presumed to be more effective in the treatment of hypertensive patients with high or normal plasma renin activity. Although renin activity may decrease with advancing age, an age-related decline in renal function may result in a higher area under the concentration-time curve for ACE inhibitors. The net effect is that no significant differences in blood pressure response or adverse effects have been reported in elderly patients taking ACE inhibitors, compared to the general population. However, the possibility of increased sensitivity to the hypotensive effects of these drugs in some elderly patients should be borne in mind.

Drug Interactions: Agents Causing Renin Release: The antihypertensive effect of ACE inhibitors is augmented by antihypertensive agents which cause renin release, such as thiazide diuretics.

Agents Increasing Serum Potassium: ACE inhibitors cause decreased aldosterone production which may lead to increased potassium retention by the kidney. When combined with agents such as potassium-sparing diuretics, potassium supplements or potassium-containing salt substitutes, severe hyperkalemia may occur. Patients with diabetes, impaired renal function or CHF may be at increased risk. Frequent monitoring of serum potassium is recommended in patients when these agents are used concomitantly with an ACE inhibitor.

Allopurinol: Although a causal relationship has not been proven, it is possible that ACE inhibitor therapy has predisposed patients to hypersensitivity reactions to allopurinol including Stevens-Johnson syndrome and anaphylaxis. Due to the seriousness of the reaction, it is recommended that this combination be avoided until further study establishes the cause.

Alpha-blocking Agents: Patients taking ACE inhibitors may experience an exaggerated hypotensive response to the first dose of an alpha-blocker (e.g., doxazosin, prazosin, terazosin).

These drugs should be introduced at a lower initial dosage, with caution.

Diuretics: Patients on severe dietary salt restriction or those on diuretic therapy, especially if the diuretic was recently instituted, may experience excessive hypotension when ACE inhibitor therapy is initiated. This effect may be minimized by increasing salt intake or discontinuing the diuretic 2 to 7 days prior to introduction of the ACE inhibitor. If this is not feasible, the initial dose of the ACE inhibitor should be reduced and the patient's blood pressure carefully monitored following the dose. If hypotension occurs, the patient should be in a supine position, and i.v. normal saline may be given if necessary. Hypotension should subside once volume expansion occurs and is a not a contraindication to further ACE inhibitor therapy, once blood pressure has stabilized.

Iron: ACE inhibitor therapy may augment the systemic adverse effects of i.v. iron, such as fever, arthralgia and hypotension, possibly by decreasing the metabolism of kinins. This does not seem to be the case with oral iron salts. Concomitant ACE inhibitor and i.v. iron therapy should be avoided whenever possible.

Lithium: Lithium toxicity, including CNS symptoms, ECG changes and renal failure, has occurred in patients taking ACE inhibitors. Proposed mechanisms include decreased renal elimination of lithium due to decreased aldosterone secretion or decreased renal function. Frequent monitoring of lithium levels is recommended in patients taking these agents concurrently.

NSAIDs: There is some evidence that the antihypertensive effect of ACE inhibitors may be antagonized by NSAIDs. Patients taking these agents concurrently should be monitored for signs of worsening heart failure or renal function.

Tetracyclines: The absorption of tetracyclines may be reduced when taken concurrently with quinapril, due to the presence of magnesium carbonate as an excipient in its pharmaceutical formulation.

Vasodilators: Although data on the combined effect of ACE inhibitors and other vasodilating drugs are not yet available, some manufacturers recommend that when possible, drugs such as nitrates should be discontinued prior to initiation of ACE inhibitor therapy. They should be given with caution at a lower dosage if subsequently resumed during ACE inhibitor treatment.

Adverse Effects: Cardiovascular: Hypotension may occur in patients taking ACE inhibitors, particularly during initial therapy and in patients with other risk factors (see Warnings). Rarely, other cardiovascular effects symptoms such as chest pain, tachycardia, palpitations, angina and MI have occurred.

Dermatologic: A maculopapular rash has occurred, more frequently in patients with renal impairment. It usually appears within the first month of therapy and may disappear on its own, with a dosage reduction or discontinuation of the ACE inhibitor, or with oral antihistamine therapy. It has been postulated that this rash is mediated by kinins.

Photosensitivity and pemphigoid lesions have also occurred in patients taking ACE inhibitors.

Hematologic: Neutropenia, agranulocytosis and other blood dyscrasias have occurred during therapy with ACE inhibitors, especially in patients with additional risk factors (see Warnings). Patients should be advised to report symptoms such as sore throat or fever to their physician.

Hypersensitivity: Angioedema (see Warnings), serum sickness and bronchospasm have been reported. Anaphylactoid reactions have occurred in patients undergoing hemodialysis with PAN membranes or desensitization to hymenoptera venom (see Precautions).

Renal: Deterioration of renal function has occurred during therapy with ACE inhibitors, particularly in patients with predisposing conditions (see Precautions). Proteinuria, potentially progressing to nephrotic syndrome, has also been reported.

Respiratory: A persistent dry cough has been associated with the use of ACE inhibitors (see Precautions).

Taste Disturbances: Although more commonly reported with the use of captopril, all ACE inhibitors may cause a decrease in taste acuity or altered taste perception (e.g., metallic or salty taste). Taste disturbance usually occurs during the first 3 months of therapy and is usually reversible over 2 to 3 months, even if the ACE inhibitor is continued. Weight loss may accompany loss of taste.

Overdose: Symptoms and Treatment: There are few reports of ACE inhibitor overdose in the literature. The most likely manifestations are hypotension, which may be severe, hyperkalemia, hyponatremia and renal impairment with metabolic acidosis. Treatment should be mainly symptomatic and supportive, with volume expansion using normal saline to correct hypotension and improve renal function, and gastric lavage followed by activated charcoal and a cathartic to prevent further absorption of the drug. Captopril, enalapril, lisinopril and perindopril are known to be removable by hemodialysis.

Dosage: Oral: The initial dosage of ACE inhibitor therapy must be individualized, mainly due to the risk of hypotension, taking into consideration factors such as renal and/or hepatic failure, CHF, diuretic therapy, volume depletion or hyponatremia. Patients at increased risk should receive lower initial doses, with the first dose given under close medical supervision. Observation of patient should continue for at least 2 hours following administration, or until blood pressure has been stable for 1 hour.

Ideally, diuretic therapy should be discontinued 2 to 7 days prior to the introduction of an ACE inhibitor, and if necessary, resumed with caution once ACE inhibitor therapy is established. When discontinuation of diuretic prior to initiation of ACE inhibitor therapy is not possible, a reduced diuretic dosage should be considered.

Once therapy has been initiated, ACE inhibitor dosage should be gradually titrated to achieve the desired effect, depending on the indication for use. Table III lists dosage recommendations for ACE inhibitors in the treatment of hypertension, including initial, maintenance and maximum dosages. More detailed information may be found within individual product monographs, including specific dosage recommendations for different indications, titration guidelines and dosage adjustment in renal or hepatic failure.

I.V.: When the oral route is not feasible, the usual initial dosage of enalaprilat in the treatment of hypertension is 1.25 mg every 6 hours, administered i.v., either undiluted or mixed with up to 50 mL compatible diluent, over a period of at least 5 minutes (see product monograph). When converting from i.v. enalaprilat to oral enalapril, the initial dose should be 5 mg once daily, with subsequent adjustments as necessary.

Patients on diuretic therapy should receive a lower initial i.v. enalaprilat dosage of 0.625 mg over 5 minutes, with a second dose after 1 hour if an inadequate response is seen. Additional doses may be repeated at 6-hour intervals.

Reviewed 1999

Table III—ACE Inhibitors

Oral Dosage

Drug	Usual Initial Dosage[a]	Usual Maintenance Dosage[a]	Recommended Maximum Daily Dose
Benazepril[b]	10 mg once daily	20 mg once daily[c]	40 mg
Captopril[b]	25 mg 2 to 3 times daily[d]	50 mg 2 to 3 times daily	450 mg
Cilazapril[b]	2.5 mg once daily	2.5 to 5 mg once daily[c]	10 mg
Enalapril[b]	5 mg once daily	10 to 40 mg daily in one single or two divided doses	40 mg
Fosinopril[e]	10 mg once daily	20 mg once daily[c]	40 mg
Lisinopril[b]	10 mg once daily	10 to 40 mg once daily[c]	80 mg
Perindopril[b]	4 mg once daily	4 to 8 mg once daily[c]	8 mg
Quinapril[b]	10 mg once daily	10 to 20 mg once daily[c]	40 mg
Ramipril[b]	2.5 mg once daily	2.5 to 10 mg once daily[c]	20 mg
Trandolapril[f]	1 mg once daily	1 to 2 mg once daily[c]	4 mg

[a] As monotherapy in the treatment of hypertension, in patients with no additional risk factors such as renal failure, CHF or concomitant diuretic therapy (see Warnings and Precautions).

[b] Dosage and/or interval require adjustment in renal failure (see individual product monographs).

[c] Some patients may experience diminished antihypertensive effect toward the end of a 24-hour dosing interval. Splitting the same dose into two equal 12-hourly doses or increasing the once daily dose may be considered (see individual product monographs).

[d] The manufacturer of captopril recommends that doses be taken 1 hour before meals.

[e] No dosage adjustment necessary in patients with renal failure and normal hepatic function, and vice versa.

[f] Dosage adjustment required in renal or hepatic failure.

ACEL-P™

Wyeth-Ayerst

Acellular Pertussis Vaccine Adsorbed

Active Immunizing Agent

Pharmacology: Pertussis disease (whooping cough) is caused by a gram-negative coccobacillus, B. pertussis. Acellular pertussis vaccine adsorbed is an acellular pertussis vaccine indicated for primary immunization against disease caused by B. pertussis.

Pertussis (whooping cough) has 3 typical stages (catarrhal, paroxysmal, and convalescent). The second phase is characterized by severe paroxysmal coughing that persists for weeks. The disease primarily affects infants and young children, and morbidity and mortality rates generally are inversely related to age. Infants do not acquire adequate maternal immunity, so they are highly susceptible to infection. Transmission and atypical respiratory infections are known to occur in adults who were immunized as children.

The infection appears to be localized to the cilia of the respiratory tract and the epithelial surfaces of the bronchial tree. The cause of the paroxysmal coughing (the whoop) is uncertain. It may be a result of the tenacious nature of the secretions and the loss of ciliary action.

In the 1940s, a vaccine consisting of whole B. pertussis cells killed by heat or formalin treatment was developed. Based on clinical experience of almost 50 years, the benefits of the whole-cell pertussis vaccines are well established and the vaccine has been shown to be useful in the control of pertussis. However, many children experience discomfort or adverse local reactions from the immunization.

Recently, public acceptance of the whole cell vaccine decreased considerably and, in the late 1970s, the incidence of pertussis disease increased with the decline in use of the whole-cell vaccines. Today, pertussis disease remains a significant contributor to infant mortality in developing countries causing approximately 600 000 deaths annually.

Acellular pertussis vaccines have been used in Japan since 1981, mostly in 2-year-old children. The vaccine used has been of 2 general types: the Takeda (T-type) vaccine and the

Acel-P (cont'd)

Biken-type (B-type) vaccine. The Takeda acellular pertussis (T-type) vaccine accounts for 80% of the Japanese market.

Evidence for the efficacy of acellular pertussis vaccines, as a group, is demonstrated by the decline in pertussis disease with their routine use in that country. In addition, a review of epidemiological studies of the Japanese acellular pertussis vaccines estimated that these vaccines, as a group, were 88% efficacious in protecting against clinical pertussis on household exposure, with a 95% confidence interval of 79 to 93%. In 3 Japanese household contact studies which employed retrospective case ascertainment and nonstandard case definitions, the vaccine-specific efficacy of the Takeda vaccine ranged between 89 and 94%, but confidence intervals were wide due to the small number of children in each study. Although there were differences in study methods, these estimates of efficacy are quite comparable to that for whole-cell pertussis vaccine in the United States.

Immunogenicity of the monovalent acellular pertussis vaccine was studied in 249 German children 15 months to 6 years of age who had previously been immunized against diphtheria and tetanus, but had been unvaccinated against pertussis. A 3-dose primary series was administered at 6- to 10-week intervals, and antibody responses against the vaccine antigens were investigated. The antibody responses were pronounced, with 93 to 100% of vaccinees demonstrating at least a 4-fold titer rise above the pre-immunization level after the third dose. In addition, local and systemic reactions were minimal in frequency and severity, and overall reactogenicity was lower than that seen in children of similar ages vaccinated with the same acellular pertussis component in combination with diphtheria and tetanus toxoid as a booster dose. These findings indicated that acellular pertussis vaccine was immunogenic with low reactogenicity, and was therefore appropriate for catch-up immunization in older children who had not previously received pertussis vaccination.

The efficacy of an APDT vaccine containing the Takeda acellular pertussis vaccine component was examined, in particular in a non-blinded household contact study in Japan, conducted by Lederle Laboratories, that included both retrospective and prospective case evaluation. As a consequence of the immunization schedule in Japan at the time of study, none of the vaccinated contacts were less than 2 years of age while some of the unvaccinated contacts were less than 2 years of age. When analysis of results was limited to vaccinated and unvaccinated household contacts 2 years of age and over, efficacy was estimated to be 79% (95% confidence interval, 60 to 89%) for physician-diagnosed pertussis disease. This included respiratory illnesses that may have been mild pertussis. When cases were restricted to disease diagnosed as typical pertussis, omitting mild suspect cases, efficacy was estimated to be 97% (95% confidence interval, 82 to 99%).

When unvaccinated household contacts under 2 years of age are also included in the analysis, efficacy was estimated to be 81% (95% confidence interval, 64 to 90%) against pertussis disease (including mild suspect cases) and 98% (95% confidence interval 84 to 99%) against typical pertussis. While there is some uncertainty with regard to the absolute magnitude of these estimates, the data as a whole demonstrate the efficacy of the Takeda Pertussis Vaccine.

Immunogenicity of an acellular DPT vaccine containing the acellular pertussis vaccine component (Acel-Imune) compared with whole-cell DPT was studied in approximately 1 000 U.S. children receiving these vaccines as a fourth or fifth dose at 17 to 24 months or 4 to 6 years of age. Antibody response following Acel-Imune was similar to whole-cell DPT for LPF, 69kd protein, and agglutinins, and higher than DPT for FHA (the DPT used in these comparative studies was manufactured by Lederle Laboratories). All children achieved protective antibody levels to diphtheria and tetanus toxoids. A serologic correlate to protection against pertussis disease has not been established. Acel-Imune was less reactogenic than the whole-cell DPT vaccine (manufactured by Lederle Laboratories) in these studies with regard to local reactions, including less pain/tenderness, erythema, induration and warmth at the injection site. In addition, there was less drowsiness, fretfulness, fever and antipyretic use following Acel-Imune as compared with DPT. The relative frequency of rare events that may be associated with immunization can only be determined in large post-marketing surveillance studies.

While whole cell pertussis vaccines contain the antigenic components necessary to elicit protective immunity, they may also contain substances irrelevant to protection and possibly related to undesirable side effects of the vaccine. Progress has been made in characterizing the various components of the B. pertussis organism thought to play a role in protective immunity including filamentous hemagglutonin (FHA), lymphocytosis promoting factor (LPF) also known as pertussis toxin (PT), a 69 kilodalton (69Kd) outer membrane protein, and fimbriae (pertussis-specific agglutinogens).

The Takeda acellular pertussis vaccine component used in Acel-P contains inactivated PT, FHA, 69kd outer membrane protein and type 2 fimbriae (pertussis-specific agglutinogen), with minimal endotoxin compared to that in whole-cell pertussis vaccine. The pertussis component induces immunity against pertussis (whooping cough).

Indications: For primary immunization of children of 15 months to 6 years of age against disease caused by B. pertussis (whooping cough).

For booster immunization as a 4th dose (completion of the primary immunization) for children older than 15 months who previously received their primary immunization (3 doses) of a whole cell pertussis vaccine.

Contraindications: Hypersensitivity to any component of the vaccine, including thimerosal, a mercury derivative, is a contraindication.

Patients exposed to pertussis and likely to become ill with pertussis.

Immunization should be deferred during the course of any febrile illness or acute infection. A minor illness such as mild upper respiratory infection is usually not a reason to defer immunization.

The following recommendations are based on the experience with whole cell vaccines. They should be followed with acellular pertussis vaccine until a wider base of experience is available: Children with progressive neurological illness who manifest frequent convulsions should not be vaccinated. These illnesses are not an absolute contraindication against immunization with pertussis vaccine. However, an increase of the severity of the illness or the occurrence of convulsions might be attributed to the vaccine. On the other hand, with the incidence of pertussis being very high, these patients especially might be at risk. Therefore, the immunizing physician should make a careful assessment of the risks involved. A family history of febrile convulsions and convulsions is not a contraindication.

As fever can trigger a convulsive episode, antipyretics should be used freely in children predisposed to convulsions.

The decision to administer a pertussis-containing vaccine to such children must be made by the physician on an individual basis, with consideration of all relevant factors and assessment of potential risks and benefits for that individual. The physician should review the full text of NACI, ACIP and AAP guidelines prior to considering vaccination for such children. The parent or guardian should be advised of the potential increased risk involved.

If any of the following events occur in temporal relation to receipt of a pertussis vaccine, the decision to give subsequent doses of vaccine containing the pertussis component should be carefully considered: **contraindications and precautions to further pertussis vaccination:** Contraindication: An immediate anaphylactic reaction.

Precautions: 1. Temperature of $\geq$40.5°C within 48 hours not due to another identifiable cause. 2. Collapse or shock-like state (hypotonic—hyporesponsive episode) within 48 hours. 3. Convulsions with or without fever occurring within 3 days.

Although these events were considered absolute contraindications in previous NACI or ACIP recommendations, there may be circumstances, such as a high incidence of pertussis, in which the potential benefits outweigh possible risks particularly because these events are not associated with permanent sequelae.

Warnings: Not recommended for use in children below the age of 15 months as the efficacy of the vaccine in children younger than 15 months has not been fully determined.

If the vaccine is used in persons deficient in producing antibody, whether due to genetic defect or immunosuppressive illness or therapy, the expected immune response may not be obtained.

This product is not recommended for immunizing persons on or after their 7th birthday.

As with any vaccine, acellular pertussis vaccine may not protect 100% of individuals receiving the vaccine.

Precautions: If applicable, immunization can be done simultaneously with DT given contra laterally.

Acellular pertussis vaccine is for i.m. use only. The vaccine should not be given intradermally or i.v. since the safety and immunogenicity of these routes have not been evaluated.

Prior to administration of any dose of acellular pertussis vaccine, the parent or guardian should be asked about the personal history, family history and recent health status. The health care provider should ascertain previous immunization history, current health status and occurrence of any symptoms and/or signs of an adverse event after previous immunizations in the child to be immunized to determine the existence of any contraindication to immunization with acellular pertussis vaccine and to allow an assessment of benefits and risks.

Before the injection of any biological, the health care provider should take all precautions known for the prevention of allergic or any other side reactions. This should include: a review of the patient's history regarding possible sensitivity; the ready availability of epinephrine 1:1 000 and other appropriate agents used for control of immediate allergic reactions; and a knowledge of the recent literature pertaining to use of the biological concerned, including the nature of side effects and adverse reactions that may follow its use.

Children with impaired immune responsiveness, whether due to the use of immunosuppressive therapy (including irradiation, corticosteroids, antimetabolites, alkylating agents, and cytotoxic agents), a genetic defect, human immunodeficiency virus (HIV) infection, or other causes, may have reduced antibody response to active immunization procedures. Deferral of administration of vaccine may be considered in individuals receiving immunosuppressive therapy. Other groups should receive this vaccine according to the usual recommended schedule (see Drug Interactions).

This product is not contraindicated for use in individuals with HIV.

Since this product is a suspension containing an adjuvant, shake vigorously to obtain a uniform suspension prior to withdrawing each dose.

A separate sterile syringe and needle or a sterile disposable unit should be used for each individual patient to prevent transmission of hepatitis or other infectious agents from one person to another. Needles should be disposed of properly and should not be recapped.

Special care should be taken to prevent injection into a blood vessel.

As with other aluminum-containing vaccines, a nodule may occasionally be palpable at the injection site for several weeks. Although not seen in studies with acellular pertussis vaccine, sterile abscess formation or s.c. atrophy at the injection site may also occur.

Children: **This product is not recommended for use in children below the age of 15 months.**

Pregnancy and *Lactation:* Not applicable (outside the indication).

Carcinogenesis, Mutagenesis, Impairment of Fertility: Acellular pertussis vaccine has not been evaluated for its carcinogenic, mutagenic potentials or impairment of fertility.

Drug Interactions: Simultaneous immunization is possible with attenuated live vaccines, inactivated vaccines and immunoglobulins if the application is given at separate sites.

Children receiving immunosuppressive therapy may have a reduced response to active immunization procedures.

As with other i.m. injections, acellular pertussis vaccine should be given with caution to children on anticoagulant therapy.

Information to be Provided to the Patient: Prior to administration of this vaccine, health care personnel should inform the parent, guardian, or other responsible adult of the recommended immunization schedule for protection against pertussis and the benefits and risks to the child receiving a vaccine containing an acellular pertussis component. Guidance should be provided on measures to be taken should adverse events occur, such as antipyretic measures for elevated temperatures and the need to report adverse events to the health care provider.

Adverse Effects: Adverse reactions associated with acellular pertussis vaccine have been evaluated in 249 children 15 months to 6 years receiving this vaccine as the 3-dose primary series. The percent of local and systemic reactions occurring at any time within 72 hours following immunization is summarized in Table I.

Table I—Acel-P

Local and Systemic Reactions within the First 72 Hours after 743 Immunizations

	Total %	Mild/Moderate %*
Local Reactions		
Pain	18	17/1
Erythema	16	15/1
Induration	13	12/1
Swelling	1	1/0
Site temperature (warm)	9	9/0
Systemic Reactions		
Rectal temperature (≥38°C)	12	11/1
Drowsiness	6	6/0
Irritability	5	5/0

*"Mild" was defined as: occurrence of a symptom that is easily tolerable: "moderate" was defined as: complaints interfering with normal activities (normal condition/normal reactions). No reaction was considered to be severe, i.e., that makes normal activities impossible.

Adverse reactions associated with acellular pertussis vaccine have occasionally been noted as transient local reactions (e.g., redness, induration and warmth at the injection site).

Occasionally can be seen: fever, sleepiness, fussiness, loss of appetite and vomiting.

Convulsions, unusual sleepiness, rash at the injection site, hypotonic—hyporesponsive episodes and inconsolable crying can occur in particular cases. Neuralgia can occur as with all injections.

As with any injection of biological material, anaphylactic reactions should be expected.

Overdose: Symptoms and Treatment: In case of anaphylactic reactions, the usual procedures for shock therapy apply.

Dosage: Primary immunization with acellular pertussis vaccine of children not previously immunized against pertussis consists of 3 doses of 0.5 mL each, given at an interval of at least 6 weeks(but not more than 10 weeks) between doses. The dose of 0.5 mL is to be given i.m. only.

The 4th or booster dose of acellular pertussis vaccine given after previous immunization with whole cell pertussis vaccine or as completion of primary immunization with acellular pertussis vaccine, consists of a single dose of 0.5 mL approximately 1 year after the 3rd primary immunization dose.

Administration: Simultaneous administration of live and inactivated vaccines is possible if given at separate sites.

Shake vigorously to obtain a uniform suspension prior to withdrawing each dose from the multiple-dose vial. The vaccine should not be used if it cannot be resuspended.

Parenteral drug products should be inspected visually for particulate matter and discoloration prior to administration whenever solution and container permit.

The vaccine should be injected i.m. Do not inject s.c. or i.v. (Vaccine applied mistakenly i.v. can result in anaphylactic reactions, including shock.)

The preferred sites are the anterolateral aspect of the thigh or the deltoid muscle of the upper arm. The vaccine should not be injected in the gluteal area or areas where there may be a major nerve trunk. Before injection, the skin at the injection site should be cleansed and prepared with a suitable germicide. After insertion of the needle, aspirate to help avoid inadvertent injection into a blood vessel.

Do not use the vaccine past the expiration date.

Supplied: Each dose (0.5 mL) of white to off-white, cloudy, aqueous suspension contains: adsorbed acellular pertussis vaccine 300 hemagglutinating units (HAU). The pertussis component contains approximately 41 µg (but not more than 60 µg) pertussis antigens per 0.5 mL dose, including: filamentous hemagglutonin (FHA) approximately 35.9 µg (86%), pertussis toxoid (PT) approximately 2.9 µg (8%), 69 kilodalton (69kd) outer membrane protein approximately 1.6 µg (4%), fimbriae type 2 (pertussis-specific agglutinogen) approximately 0.7 µg (2%).

Purification of the acellular pertussis vaccine component is accomplished by ammonium sulfate fractionation steps and a final sucrose density gradient centrifugation. The acellular pertussis vaccine component is detoxified with formaldehyde and thimerosal (mercury derivative) is added as a preservative. Nonmedicinal Ingredients: aluminum gel (aluminum phosphate, aluminum hydroxide), 2-(ethylmercurithio) benzoic acid, sodium salt (thimerosal) and phosphate buffered saline. Thimerosal (mercury derivative) is present in a final concentration of 1:10 000. The final product may also contain gelatin and polysorbate 80 which are used in early stages of the process.

Vials of 0.5 mL (1 dose), packages of 1. **Do not freeze.** Store refrigerated away from freezer compartment at 2 to 8°C. Product which has been exposed to freezing should not be used. Do not use this vaccine past the expiration date.

New Product 1998

ACETAMINOPHEN

General Monograph, CPhA

Paracetamol

Analgesic—Antipyretic

This monograph has been compiled by CPhA. It may contain information different from that approved by Therapeutic Products Programme, Health Canada, and the pharmaceutical manufacturers' approval has not been requested.

Pharmacology: Acetaminophen is a synthetic derivative of p-aminophenol. Animal and clinical studies have shown acetaminophen to have antipyretic and analgesic activity equal to that of ASA. However, acetaminophen does not possess anti-inflammatory activity equal to that of ASA.

Unlike salicylates, acetaminophen does not interfere with tubular secretion of uric acid, nor does it affect acid-base balance in normal therapeutic doses. Acetaminophen does not interfere with hemostasis and does not inhibit platelet aggregation.

Pharmacokinetics: Acetaminophen is rapidly and completely absorbed from the gastrointestinal tract. Peak plasma concentrations of the free and conjugated drug are achieved ½ to 1 hour after administration. Approximately 85% of a 1 g dose is recovered from the urine in 24 hours. About 3% is excreted unchanged, the balance being conjugated principally to the glucuronide or sulfate. The plasma half-life is 1.25 to 3 hours. The half-life may be prolonged in acute overdose or severe liver disease.

Small amounts of acetaminophen are normally converted to a highly reactive metabolite by hepatic microsomal enzymes. At therapeutic doses, the small amounts of the active metabolite so formed are rapidly inactivated by hepatic glutathione and removed by renal excretion. However, where hepatic glutathione has been rapidly depleted by a large dose of acetaminophen, covalent binding of the metabolite to liver-cell macromolecules occurs and is presumed to be responsible for hepatic cell necrosis. Prompt administration of acetylcysteine is indicated to prevent acetaminophen-induced hepatic necrosis (see Overdose).

Indications: The treatment of mild to moderate pain and the reduction of fever.

Contraindications: Hypersensitivity to acetaminophen.

Precautions: Chronic excessive alcohol consumption may increase the risk of acetaminophen-induced hepatotoxicity, even with the use of therapeutic doses of acetaminophen.

Drug Interactions: Chronic, high-dose administration of acetaminophen may potentiate the anticoagulant effect of warfarin. Patients stabilized on oral anticoagulants should be advised to limit their intake of acetaminophen to not more than 2 g daily for no more than a few days at a time. ASA should not be used as an alternative.

Barbiturates and other enzyme inducers such as carbamazepine, phenytoin or rifampin, may enhance the metabolism of acetaminophen. The combination of enzyme inducers with excessive doses of acetaminophen may accelerate the production of hepatotoxic metabolites of acetaminophen.

Cholestyramine reduces the absorption of acetaminophen. Oral doses of cholestyramine and acetaminophen should be given at least 1 hour apart.

Concurrent long-term use of analgesic-antipyretic agents with ASA may be associated with analgesic nephropathy (papillary necrosis and tabulointerstitial inflammation).

Lactation: Acetaminophen passes into breast milk but is not likely to have an adverse effect on the infant at therapeutic doses. Peak concentrations in the milk occur 1 to 2 hours after a dose.

Pregnancy: Acetaminophen crosses the placenta and is apparently safe for short-term use when therapeutic doses are used.

Adverse Effects: In therapeutic doses, acetaminophen is relatively non-toxic. Chronic use of large doses of acetaminophen may produce more significant toxicity.

Hepatic: Hepatic toxicity has been associated with acetaminophen in overdose. Chronic use of high doses, e.g., ≥5 g daily for several weeks in adults or 150 mg/kg/day for 2 to 4 days in children, has also been associated with hepatotoxicity. Alcoholics, patients with liver disease, the malnourished and patients taking drugs that induce hepatic microsomal enzymes, may be at increased risk for hepatic toxicity.

Renal: Nephropathy, including papillary renal failure has been reported following consumption of large amounts of acetaminophen. Renal tubular necrosis has been associated occasionally with hepatic injury produced by acetaminophen overdose.

Hematologic: Neutropenia and thrombocytopenia purpura have been reported and rarely agranulocytosis.

Hypersensitivity: Laryngeal edema, angioedema and anaphylactoid reactions may occur rarely.

Overdose: In adults, hepatotoxicity may occur after ingestion of a single dose of more than 7.5 g (adults) or 150 mg/kg (children) of acetaminophen; a dose of 10 g or more is potentially fatal. However, reports have indicated hepatic necrosis with a single dose of 6 g and death occurring with a single dose of 13 g. Non fatal overdoses of 12.5 to 31.5 g have also been reported.

Symptoms: Early symptoms (nausea, vomiting, weakness, diaphoresis) usually occur after acute ingestion of an acetaminophen overdose large enough to cause hepatic toxicity. However, since some patients may exhibit few or none of these early signs, in cases of suspected acetaminophen overdose, antidotal therapy should begin as soon as possible. A latent period of 24 to 36 hours exists between ingestion and the onset of symptoms of hepatic injury. Laboratory evidence usually appears within 24 to 48 hours if severe hepatotoxicity is to occur. In mild cases, clinical evidence of hepatotoxicity may be delayed for as long as 5 days. Consequently, overdose patients should be monitored by liver function tests for several days following the overdose. Following the latent period, vomiting, pain in the upper right quadrant and manifestations of hepatic failure, including the onset of coma, may ensue. Maximum hepatic necrosis appears 2 to 5 days following overdose. The predominant changes in serum chemistries are a gross elevation of hepatic enzymes ALT, AST, an elevation of serum bilirubin, a prolongation of prothrombin time and hypoglycemia.

In addition to hepatic damage, clotting defects, and myocardial damage with ST segment abnormalities, T wave flattening and pericarditis have been reported.

Treatment: Treatment of acute acetaminophen overdose includes supportive measures, such as control of respiration and fluid and electrolyte balance, as well as decontamination of the gastrointestinal tract and prompt administration of acetylcysteine as an antidote. Laboratory determinations include plasma acetaminophen levels, AST, ALT, prothrombin time, bilirubin, creatinine, urea, blood glucose and electrolyte concentrations.

Gastric lavage or emesis can be used if the drug has been recently ingested. Persistent vomiting induced by ipecac may interfere with acetylcysteine administration. If activated charcoal has been administered prior to initiation of acetylcysteine therapy, gastric lavage should be performed before the first dose of oral acetylcysteine is given, as charcoal may interfere with acetylcysteine absorption and reduces its effectiveness.

Properly timed plasma acetaminophen levels are key prognosticators in determining a patient's risk of hepatotoxicity. The first level should be drawn at least 4 hours postingestion as peak concentrations may not be reached before this time. The Matthew-Rumack Nomogram for Acetaminophen Poisoning (see Figure I) should be used to determine probability of hepatotoxicity and need for acetylcysteine therapy. When serum levels are above 990 µmol/L at 4 hours, above 460 µmol/L at 8 hours or above 260 µmol/L at 12 hours postingestion, acetylcysteine therapy should be instituted to minimize hepatic toxicity.

Even in the absence of acetaminophen serum level determinations, therapy with acetylcysteine should be promptly instituted if a massive acetaminophen overdose is suspected (i.e., >7.5 g in adults or >150 mg/kg in children) and 24 hours or less have elapsed since ingestion. Maintenance doses may be discontinued if the **initial** acetaminophen serum level is nontoxic. Subsequent levels are not predictive of toxicity and should not be used as criteria for acetylcysteine discontinuation. Antidotal therapy with acetylcysteine is most effective if initiated within 10 hours following acetaminophen overdose.

Acetylcysteine Dosing in Acetaminophen Overdose: Oral: Loading dose: 140 mg/kg. Maintenance dose: 70 mg/kg every 4 hours for a total of 17 doses. Each oral dose should be diluted to a final concentration of 5% acetylcysteine (i.e., 3 mL of soft drinks, fruit juice or water added for each mL of 20% acetylcysteine solution) and consumed within 1 hour of preparation. If vomiting occurs within 1 hour following any oral dose, the entire dose should be repeated.

Acetaminophen (cont'd)

I.V.: Acetylcysteine may be given by the i.v. route if necessary. Loading dose: 150 mg/kg in 5% dextrose over 15 minutes. Maintenance infusion: 12.5 mg/kg/hour for 4 hours, followed by 6.25 mg/kg/hour for 16 hours (consult manufacturer's product monograph for details pertaining to dilution and infusion).

Figure I—Acetaminophen

Matthew-Rumack Nomogram for Acetaminophen Poisoning

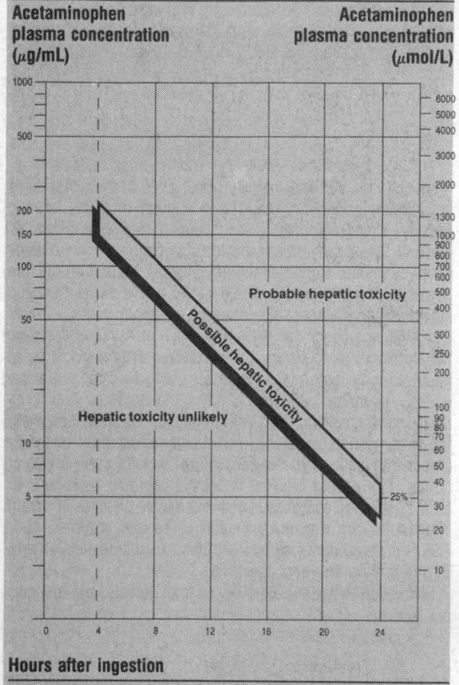

Conditions for the use of this chart:
1) The time coordinates refer to the time of ingestion.
2) Serum levels drawn before 4 hours may not represent peak levels.
3) The graph should be used only in relation to a single acute ingestion.
4) The lower solid line 25% below the standard nomogram is included to allow for possible errors in acetaminophen plasma assays and estimated time from ingestion of an overdose.

Adapted with permission from: Pediatrics 1975; 55: 871-6 (Copyright 1975, American Academy of Pediatrics) and Arch Intern Med 1981; 141: 380-5 (Copyright 1981, American Medical Association).

Dosage: Adults (oral or rectal): 325 to 650 mg every 4 to 6 hours, not to exceed 4 000 mg/24 hours.

Children (oral or rectal): 10 to 15 mg/kg every 4 to 6 hours, not to exceed 65 mg/kg/24 hours. Alternatively, see Table I.

Table I—Acetaminophen

Pediatric Dosing

Age	Single Dose (mg)	Maximum Daily Dose (mg)
0 to under 4 months	40	200
4 to under 12 months	80	400
12 to under 24 months	120	600
2 to under 4 years	160	800
4 to under 6 years	240	1 200
6 to under 9 years	320	1 600
9 to under 11 years	400	2 000
11 to under 12 years	480	2 400

Dosing for children must not exceed 5 doses in 24 hours unless under the advice of a physician, because of the risk of toxicity.

Acetaminophen should not be used in adults or children for self-medication of marked fever (greater than 39.5°C), fever persisting longer than 3 days, or recurrent fever, unless directed by a physician, since such fevers may indicate serious illness requiring prompt medical attention.

Acetaminophen should not be used for self-medication of pain for longer than 10 days in adults or 5 days in children, unless directed by a physician, since pain of such intensity and duration may indicate a pathological condition requiring medical evaluation.

Note: Acetaminophen drops tend to be approximately 2.5 to 5 times more concentrated than the elixir or syrup formulations. Care must be taken to ensure that this is taken into account when doses are expressed in mL.

ACETAMINOPHEN
Stanley

Analgesic—Antipyretic

Supplied: Children: Syrup: Each 5 mL of clear, red, viscous, fruit-flavored liquid with berry odor contains: acetaminophen USP 160 mg. Nonmedicinal ingredients: citric acid, FD&C Red No. 2, flavor, glycerin, polyethylene glycol, propylene glycol, sodium benzoate, sodium cyclamate, sorbitol and water. Alcohol-, gluten-, starch-, sugar- and tartrazine-free. Natural polyethylene round bottles of 100 mL with Clic-Loc II caps and plastic dosing cups.

Tablets: Each pink, mottled, bisected, flat, beveled-edge, compressed tablet contains: microencapsulated acetaminophen 80 mg. Nonmedicinal ingredients: aspartame, citric acid, colloidal silicon dioxide, D&C Red No. 27, FD&C Red No. 40, flavor, magnesium stearate, mannitol, microcrystalline cellulose, sorbitol and starch. Gluten-, sugar- and tartrazine-free. White polyethylene oblong bottles of 24 with snap caps.

Infants: Drops: Each mL of clear, red, viscous fruit-flavored liquid with berry odor contains: acetaminophen USP 80 mg. Nonmedicinal ingredients: aspartame, citric acid, FD&C Red No. 2, flavor, polyethylene glycol, propylene glycol, sodium benzoate, sodium cyclamate and water. Alcohol-, gluten-, starch-, sugar- and tartrazine-free. Natural high-density polyethylene round bottles of 24 mL with Clic-Loc II caps and bulb droppers.

Store in tightly-closed containers. Keep out of reach of children.

ACETAMINOPHEN
Trianon

Analgesic—Antipyretic

Supplied: Tablets: 325 mg: Each white tablet (round, caplet or "blazon" shape) contains: acetaminophen USP 325 mg. Nonmedicinal ingredients: polyvinylpyrrolidone, starch and stearic acid. Gluten-, lactose- and tartrazine-free. Bottles of 24, 30, 36, 60 and 120.

500 mg: Each white tablet (round, caplet or "blazon" shape) contains: acetaminophen USP 500 mg. Nonmedicinal ingredients: polyvinylpyrrolidone, starch and stearic acid. Gluten-, lactose- and tartrazine-free. Bottles of 24, 30, 60 and 120.

Chewable Tablets: 80 mg: Each purple children's tablet contains: acetaminophen USP 80 mg. Nonmedicinal ingredients: aspartame, cellulose, citric acid, compressible sugar, FD&C Blue, FD&C Red, flavoring, magnesium stearate and mannitol. Gluten- and tartrazine-free. Bottles of 24.

160 mg: Each purple children's tablet contains: acetaminophen USP 160 mg. Nonmedicinal ingredients: aspartame, cellulose, citric acid, compressible sugar, FD&C Blue, FD&C Red, flavoring, magnesium stearate and mannitol. Gluten- and tartrazine-free. Bottles of 20.

Drops: Each mL of children's oral solution contains: acetaminophen USP 80 mg. Nonmedicinal ingredients: Citric acid, FD&C Red #2, flavoring, glycerin, polyethylene glycol, propylene glycol, sodium cyclamate, sodium benzoate, sodium phosphate and sorbitol. Gluten-, lactose- and tartrazine-free. Bottles of 15 and 24 mL.

Oral Solution: 80 mg/5 mL: Each 5 mL of children's oral solution contains: acetaminophen USP 80 mg. Gluten-, lactose- and tartrazine-free. Bottles of 100 mL.

160 mg/5 mL: Each 5 mL of children's solution contains: acetaminophen USP 160 mg. Gluten-, lactose- and tartrazine-free. Bottles of 100 mL.

ACETAMINOPHEN, CAFFEINE and CODEINE Ⓝ
Stanley

Analgesic—Antipyretic

Supplied: Caplets: Each white, capsule-shaped, bisected tablet (caplet) contains: acetaminophen with povidone D/C granules 300 mg, caffeine anhydrous USP 15 mg and codeine phosphate BP 8 mg. Nonmedicinal ingredients: microcrystalline cellulose, povidone, starch, stearic acid and talc. Gluten-, sugar- and tartrazine-free. White polyethylene oblong bottles of 30, 100 and 200.

Tablets: Each white, bisected tablet contains: acetaminophen with povidone D/C granules 300 mg, caffeine anhydrous USP 15 mg and codeine phosphate BP 8 mg. Nonmedicinal ingredients: microcrystalline cellulose, povidone, starch, stearic acid and talc. Gluten-, sugar- and tartrazine-free. White polyethylene oblong bottles of 30, 100 and 200.

Store in tightly-closed, light-resistant containers at room temperature. Keep out of reach of children.

ACETAZONE FORTE
ACETAZONE FORTE C8 Ⓝ
Technilab

Chlorzoxazone—Acetaminophen

Chlorzoxazone—Acetaminophen—Codeine Phosphate

Muscle Relaxant—Analgesic

Supplied: Acetazone Forte: Each round, hard, uncoated, green tablet, imprinted with a horizontal line on one side and "TEC" on the reverse, contains: chlorzoxazone USP 250 mg and acetaminophen USP 300 mg. Nonmedicinal ingredients: cornstarch, crospovidone, D&C yellow #10 aluminum lake, FD&C blue #1 aluminum lake, magnesium stearate, microcrystalline cellulose, povidone, pregelatinized starch, sodium benzoate, sodium docusate, sodium croscarmellose and stearic acid. Bottles of 100. Blister packs of 20.

Acetazone Forte C8: Each round, hard, uncoated, pink tablet, imprinted with a horizontal line on one side and "TEC" on the reverse, contains: chlorzoxazone USP 250 mg, acetaminophen USP 300 mg and codeine phosphate USP 8 mg. Nonmedicinal ingredients: artificial coloring, cornstarch, crospovidone, magnesium stearate, microcrystalline cellulose, povidone, pregelatinized starch, sodium benzoate, sodium docusate, sodium croscarmellose and stearic acid. Blister packs of 20.

Keep the bottle tightly closed. Store at room temperature. Protect from light.

ACETOHEXAMIDE Ⓟ
General Monograph, CPhA

see SULFONYLUREAS

ACETOXYL® 2.5% and 5%
ACETOXYL® 10% Ⓟ
Stiefel

Benzoyl Peroxide

Acne Vulgaris Therapy

Supplied: Each plastic tube contains: benzoyl peroxide 2.5% (Acetoxyl 2.5), 5% (Acetoxyl 5) or 10% (Acetoxyl 10) in an acetone gel base. Nonmedicinal ingredients: acetone, carbomer 940 NF, propylene glycol, purified water USP, sodium lauryl sulfate solution and trolamine. Tubes of 60 g. Store at room temperature.

ACETYLSALICYLIC ACID
General Monograph, CPhA

see ASA

ACILAC®
Technilab

Lactulose

Portal-systemic Encephalopathy Therapy—Laxative

Supplied: Each mL of solution contains: lactulose 667 mg. Nonmedicinal ingredients: FD&C yellow #6 and purified water. Bottles of 500 mL and 1 L.

ACNE-AID® SOAP
Stiefel

Acne Therapy

Supplied: Each g consists of a hypoallergenic blend of neutral soap and surfactant. Nonmedicinal ingredients: butylated hydroxytoluene, purified water USP, quaternium-15, soap chips and trisodium HEDTA. Bars of 75 g.

ACNEX®
Dermtek

Salicylic Acid Wash

Acne Therapy

Supplied: Each bottle contains: salicylic acid 2% as well as a built in antibacterial in a lathering lotion form. Plastic bottles of 170 mL.

ACNOMEL®
Chattem

Resorcinol—Sulfur Compound

Acne Therapy

Indications: Treatment of acne: basic topical medication for acne. The tinted cream may be used by patients who desire a medicated preparation to mask lesions.

Contraindications: Should not be applied to diffuse, acutely inflamed areas. Keep out of eyes and off eyelids.

Precautions: Moderate erythema and scaling are normal and expected results of therapy. However, should these reactions become excessive, the patient should apply the product less frequently or discontinue until they subside.

Pregnancy and *Lactation:* As with any drug, the use of this product is not recommended during pregnancy, or when nursing, unless the physician is convinced that the potential benefits outweigh the possible risk to mother and child.

Pharmaceutical Compatibility: Should not be diluted or compounded with other drugs. Dispense in the original container.

Overdose: Involves the skin primarily.

Symptoms: Moderate erythema and scaling are normal and expected results of therapy. Overdosage is marked by excessive drying and erythema or by burning and itching.

Treatment: In severe cases, discontinue medication and apply a bland ointment or cold cream.

Accidental Ingestion: In case of accidental ingestion by children, the amount which the child succeeds in swallowing would be expected to be small, and symptoms would generally consist merely of mild gastrointestinal disturbance. Treatment consists of general measures such as inducing emesis; gastric lavage; catharsis; and forcing fluids.

Dosage: Before application, wash affected areas with soap and water, then dry.

Cream: Apply a thin coating with fingertips. Stroke on lightly; do not rub in. One or two applications daily are usually adequate. Patients with oily skin may apply more frequently.

Supplied: Skin Tone Cream: Each g of skin tone cream contains: resorcinol 2%, sulfur 8% and isopropyl alcohol 11% (w/w) in a stable, greaseless, flesh tinted base. Tubes of 25 and 40 g.

Vanishing Cream: Each g of vanishing cream contains: resorcinol 2% and sulfur 8% in a water-washable, greaseless, vanishing cream base. Tubes of 25 g.

ACNOMEL® Acne Mask
Chattem

Salicylic Acid

Acne Therapy

Indications: For treatment of acne.

Precautions: Avoid contact with eyes.

Dosage: Splash face with warm water. Apply the acne mask over entire face, avoiding eyes. Leave on as a mask for 10 minutes. Rinse off with warm water. Use once or twice weekly.

Supplied: Each mL contains: salicylic acid 1.5% in cream base with 100% natural clays. Tubes of 70 mL.

Act-HIB®
Connaught

Haemophilus b Conjugate Vaccine (Tetanus Protein—Conjugate)

Active Immunizing Agent

Pharmacology: Clinical Data (PRP-T): Haemophilus b Conjugate Vaccine has been administered during clinical trials to over 110 000 infants and children in Canada, the U.S., Finland, France, Chile, Israel, and the United Kingdom using local immunization schedules, and has been used widely in immunization programmes.

In clinical trials where 921 infants were given the vaccine at 2, 4 and 6 months, a titer of at least 0.15 μg/mL was achieved after dose 3 in 99% and a titre of at least 1 μg/mL in 93%. The weighted GMT achieved was 7 μg/mL (95% confidence limits are 3.4 to 14.2 μg/mL). Protective levels of anti-PRP developed after the second dose in 92.8% of these infants.

Two clinical trials supported by the U.S. National Institutes of Health (NIH) compared the anti-PRP response of 4 Hib conjugate vaccines in a racially mixed population of infants. In these studies, infants were immunized with Hib conjugate vaccines at 2, 4 and 6 months of age (see Tables I and II). Connaught Laboratories, Inc.'s DPT vaccine was given concomitantly, at a separate site.

Multicenter trials in the U.S. have evaluated a single dose of Act-HIB in 12 to 15, 18, and 17 to 24 month-old children. In this age group, a single dose of Act-HIB produced an anti-PRP response which was comparable to that seen after 3 doses were administered in infants.

Following 3 doses of Act-HIB at 6 weeks, 4 and 6 months of age, 81% of native Alaskan infants showed an anti-PRP titre of ≥1 μg/mL with a GMT of 4.17 μg/mL.

In clinical trials conducted in England and France, infants received 3 doses of Act-HIB at one month intervals. Anti-PRP responses were comparable to those trials where 2-month intervals were used.

Clinical Data—Act-HIB Reconstituted with DPT Adsorbed: In a clinical trial conducted in Canada, 424 infants received 3 doses of either Act-HIB reconstituted with Connaught's DPT Adsorbed or the same vaccines administered simultaneously at separate sites. Anti-PRP responses were comparable after either vaccination regimen (see Table III on following page).

Protective antitoxin levels (≥0.01 IU/mL) against diphtheria and tetanus toxoids were achieved in 100% of recipients.

Pertussis agglutinins were detected in 99.6% of participants. Over 96% had titers ≥1:64. The combination of Act-HIB with DPT Adsorbed resulted in lower titers to pertussis when compared to administration at separate sites; GMT's differed by 11.5% to 32%. However, 95% of recipients receiving the vaccine at the same site still had titers ≥1:64.

Three hundred and fifty-eight of these infants were available for follow-up and received one dose of either Act-HIB reconstituted with Connaught's DPT Adsorbed (n=180) or the same vaccines administered at separate sites (n=178) at age 18 months. Anti-PRP levels were ≥1 μg/mL in 100%. This demonstrates T-cell dependent (memory) responses for anti-PRP.

Clinical Data—Act-HIB Reconstituted with DPT Polio Adsorbed: In a clinical trial conducted in Canada, 427 infants received 3 doses of either Act-HIB reconstituted with Connaught's DPT Polio Adsorbed or the same vaccines administered simultaneously at separate sites. Anti-PRP responses following the third dose did not differ significantly between groups (see Table III on following page).

Pertussis agglutinins were detected in all but 2 subjects and 92.4% had titers ≥1:64. The responses in terms of distribution of titers and GMT's were similar in the combined and separate groups.

There was no difference in diphtheria antitoxin response after combined and separate vaccine, with 99.1% of infants developing a minimum protective antitoxin level (≥0.01 IU/mL) after the third dose of combined vaccines.

Protective levels of tetanus antitoxin (≥0.01 IU/mL) developed in 99.5% of infants after the third dose of combined vaccines, and 100% of infants after separate vaccines. However, the geometric mean antitoxin concentrations were significantly lower after combined (0.50 μg/mL) than after separate vaccine (0.76 μg/mL).

There were no significant differences in the polio neutralizing antibody in response to separate or combined vaccine. The proportions of infants with titers of ≥8 after 3 doses of combined vaccines were 98.6% to type 1, 98.1% to type 2, and 100% to type 3.

Clinical Data—Act-HIB Reconstituted with Quadracel: In clinical trials conducted in Canada, 215 infants received 3 doses of either Act-HIB reconstituted with Quadracel or the same vaccines administered simultaneously at separate sites at 2, 4 and 6 months of age. An additional 186 18-month old children received a single dose of either Act-HIB reconstituted with Quadracel or the same vaccines administered simultaneously at separate sites. With the exception of tetanus, no differences were found in immunogenicity between the 2 methods of immunization. Tetanus antitoxin levels were lower in the combined vaccine groups, but all children had protective levels

Table I—Act-HIB

Anti-PRP Antibody Responses in 2-month-old Infants NIH Trial in Tennessee

		Geometric Mean Titer (GMT) (μg/mL)			Post Third Immunization
Vaccine	N[a]	Preimmunization	Post Second Immunization	Post Third Immunization	%>1 μg/mL
PRP-T[b]	65	0.10	0.30	3.64	83%
PRP-D[c]	62	0.07	0.08	0.28	29%
PRP-OMP[d]	64	0.11	0.84	1.14	55%
HbOC[e]	61	0.07	0.13	3.08	75%

Table II—Act-HIB

Anti-PRP Antibody Responses in 2-month-old Infants NIH Trial in Minnesota and Texas

		Geometric Mean Titer (GMT) (μg/mL)			Post Third Immunization
Vaccine	N[a]	Preimmunization	Post Second Immunization	Post Third Immunization	%>1 μg/mL
PRP-T[b]	106	0.23	1.14[f]	6.64	98%
PRP-OMP[d]	103	0.17	4.69[g]	6.48	88%
HbOC[e]	99	0.16	0.46	6.83	93%

[a] N=Number of children.
[b] Haemophilus b Conjugate Vaccine (Tetanus Protein-Conjugate).
[c] Haemophilus b Conjugate Vaccine (Diphtheria Toxoid-Conjugate).
[d] Haemophilus b Conjugate Vaccine (Meningococcal Protein Conjugate).
[e] Haemophilus b Conjugate Vaccine (Diphtheria CRM_{197} Protein Conjugate).
[f] P=0.0001 for PRP-T vs HbOC.
[g] P=0.0001 for PRP-OMP vs PRP-T, and for PRP-OMP vs HbOC.

Act-HIB (cont'd)

Table III—Act-HIB

Summary of Anti-PRP Responses with Various Diluents

		Anti-PRP (Post 3rd Dose)		
	n	**≥0.15 μg/mL**	**≥1 μg/mL**	**GMT μg/mL**
Act-HIB+DPT combined	209	97.6%	88.1%	4.44
Act-HIB+DPT separate	213	98.6%	87.9%	4.06
Act-HIB+DPT Polio combined	211	93.8%	71.6%	2.04
Act-HIB+DPT Polio separate	211	98.1%	78.7%	2.76
Act-HIB+Diluent (saline)	65	99.0%	83.0%	3.64
Act-HIB+Quadracel combined	107	99.1%	84.9%	5.04
Act-HIB+Quadracel separate	108	100%	88.9%	3.83

(≥0.01 EU/mL). Following the 18-month dose, all children had tetanus antitoxin levels ≥0.10 EU/mL and all but one had diphtheria antitoxin levels ≥0.10 EU/mL. Anti-PRP responses were comparable. All children were protected against polio. Pertussis responses were not affected by method of administration.

Indications: Routine: For the routine immunization of all children between **2 and 59 months** of age. In infants, 3 injections are to be given i.m. at **2, 4, and 6 months** of age, followed by a booster at **18* months** of age.

Infants starting their primary immunization series between the age of **3 and 6 months** should receive 3 doses at 2 month intervals with a booster dose at **18* months** of age. (While an interval of 2 months between doses is recommended, an interval as short as 1 month is acceptable.)

For infants between the age of **7 and 11 months,** 2 doses should be given at an interval of 2 months, followed by a booster at **18* months** of age.

Children between **12 and 14 months** of age who have not previously received any Haemophilus b vaccine should receive one dose of the vaccine followed by a booster at or after **18 months*** of age.

Unvaccinated children between **15 and 59 months** of age should receive a single dose of vaccine.

*The booster dose may be given as early as 15 months of age provided that at least 2 months have elapsed since the previous dose.

Older children or adults with chronic conditions associated with increased risk of invasive Hib disease such as persons with splenic dysfunction (e.g., sickle cell disease, asplenia), antibody deficiency, HIV infection or certain malignancies may be immunized with a single dose of the vaccine.

Connaught's DPT Adsorbed may be used for the reconstitution of lyophilized Act-HIB in place of the saline diluent. This provides an efficient means of administering routine immunization against diphtheria, tetanus, pertussis and H. influenzae type b in a single injection at a single visit.

Connaught's DPT Polio Adsorbed may be used for the reconstitution of lyophilized Act-HIB in place of the saline diluent. This provides an efficient means of administering routine immunization against diphtheria, tetanus, pertussis, poliomyelitis and H. influenzae type b in a single injection at a single visit.

Connaught's Quadracel may be used for the reconstitution of lyophilized Act-HIB in place of the saline diluent. This provides an efficient means of administering routine immunization against diphtheria, tetanus, pertussis, poliomyelitis and H. influenzae type b in a single injection at a single visit.

Act-HIB may be administered simultaneously with DPT, DT, DPT Polio, IPV, Quadracel, or Tripacel at separate sites with separate syringes and OPV.

Act-HIB may also be given simultaneously with MMR at separate sites with separate syringes. This is based on data for MMR and Act-HIB alone. Because simultaneous administration of common childhood vaccines is not known to affect the efficacy or safety of any of the routine recommended childhood vaccines, if return of a vaccine recipient for further immunization is doubtful, simultaneous administration of all vaccines appropriate for age and previous vaccination status (including MMR, other H. influenzae type b conjugate vaccines, hepatitis B vaccine) at separate sites with separate syringes is indicated.

Data on whether vaccination prevents acquisition and carriage of Hib are still limited. Thus, rifampin or other appropriate chemoprophylaxis should be used, in accordance with the usual recommendations, for families and people in daycare centres in which a case of invasive Hib disease has occurred and in which there are one or more contacts less than 48 months of age who have not been fully vaccinated against Hib.

At the present time, Haemophilus b conjugate vaccines are not recommended for infants younger than 2 months of age.

Contraindications: General: Immunization with Act-HIB should be deferred in the presence of any acute illness, including febrile illness. A minor afebrile illness such as mild upper respiratory infection is not usually reason to defer immunization.

Allergy to any component of Haemophilus b Conjugate Vaccine including tetanus protein, or an allergic or anaphylactic reaction to a previous dose of Act-HIB are contraindications to vaccination. When Act-HIB is reconstituted with Connaught's DPT Adsorbed, DPT Polio Adsorbed or Quadracel the contraindications for DPT Adsorbed, DPT Polio Adsorbed or Quadracel must also be considered.

Elective immunization of individuals over 6 months of age should be deferred during an outbreak of poliomyelitis.

Warnings: I.M. injections should be given with care in patients suffering from coagulation disorders because of the risk of hemorrhage.

If Haemophilus b Conjugate Vaccine is used in persons with malignancies, receiving immunosuppressive therapies, including irradiation, antimetabolites, alkylating agents, cytotoxic drugs, or who are otherwise immunocompromised (including HIV infected individuals), the expected immune response may not be obtained.

Corticosteroid therapy can result in immunosuppression although the exact dose and duration of therapy required to suppress the immune system is not well defined. Persons treated with high doses of systemic steroids, e.g., ≥2 mg/kg/day of prednisone orally for more than 2 weeks, should be considered to have a compromised immune system.

As with any vaccine, immunization with Haemophilus b Conjugate Vaccine may not protect 100% of susceptible individuals.

Capsular polysaccharide antigen can be detected in the urine of vaccinees for up to 2 weeks following immunization with conjugate vaccines. This phenomenon should not be confused with invasive Hib infections.

Precautions: General: Care is to be taken by the health-care provider for the safe and effective use of Haemophilus b Conjugate Vaccine.

The possibility of allergic reactions in individuals sensitive to components of the vaccine should be evaluated. Epinephrine (1:1 000) and other appropriate agents should be available for immediate use in case an anaphylactic or acute hypersensitivity reaction occurs. When Act-HIB is reconstituted with Connaught's DPT Adsorbed or DPT Polio Adsorbed or Quadracel, the possibility of allergic reactions to the components of these vaccines must also be evaluated. Health care providers should be familiar with current recommendations for the initial management of anaphylaxis in non-hospital settings.

Before an injection of any vaccine, all appropriate precautions should be taken to prevent adverse reactions. This includes a review of the patient's history with respect to possible hypersensitivity to the vaccine or similar vaccine, determination of previous immunization history, and the presence of any contraindications to immunization, current health status, and a current knowledge of the literature concerning the use of the vaccine under consideration.

Special care should be taken to ensure that the product is not injected into a blood vessel.

A separate, sterile needle and syringe or a sterile disposable unit must be used for each individual patient to prevent the transmission of infectious agents. There have been case reports of transmission of HIV and hepatitis by failure to scrupulously observe sterile technique.

Needles should not be recapped and should be disposed of properly.

Before administration of Act-HIB, health-care personnel should inform the parent or guardian of the patient of the benefits and risks of immunization, and also inquire about the recent health status of the patient to be injected.

Act-HIB may be of benefit in preventing the occurrence of secondary cases. However, epidemiological studies have not been done and rifampin or other appropriate prophylaxis is still recommended. Because the vaccine will not protect against non-typeable strains of H. influenzae which cause recurrent upper respiratory disease, otitis media and sinusitis, the vaccine is not recommended for these conditions.

Although some immune response to the tetanus protein component may occur, immunization with this vaccine does not substitute for routine tetanus immunization. Individuals who have received multiple doses of products containing tetanus toxoid show no differences in reaction rates when immunized with this vaccine.

Pregnancy: Animal reproduction studies have not been conducted with Act-HIB. It is also not known whether Act-HIB can cause fetal harm when administered to a pregnant woman or can affect reproduction capacity. Act-HIB is not recommended for use in pregnant women.

Children with Symptomatic HIV Infection: Available data suggest that routine childhood immunizations are not hazardous to HIV-infected children. Furthermore, there is no evidence that immunization with routine vaccines leads to deterioration of the clinical condition of HIV-infected persons. Immunization with DPT (Diphtheria, Pertussis and Tetanus), IPV (Inactivated Poliomyelitis Vaccine) and Act-HIB is recommended, although immunization may be less effective than it would be for immunocompetent children.

Adverse Effects: Physicians, nurses and pharmacists should report any occurrences temporally related to the administration of the product in accordance with local requirements and to the Medical Director, Connaught Laboratories Limited, 1755 Steeles Avenue West, Toronto, Ontario, Canada, M2R 3T4.

Local Reactions: Pain, redness, swelling or induration are seen in 5 to 30% of vaccinees. It is generally early, transient, and of moderate intensity. There have been rare cases of edematous reactions of the lower extremities reported. These consist of oedema with cyanosis or transient purpura which appears within soon after immunization and resolves rapidly and spontaneously. There has been no accompanying cardiorespiratory signs or symptoms. These reactions have been reported mainly when Haemophilus b Conjugate Vaccine is administered concurrently with another vaccine.

Systemic Reactions: Systemic reactions including fever, irritability, drowsiness, prolonged or abnormal crying, anorexia and vomiting have occurred after immunization with Act-HIB in conjunction with DPT. The rates of reactions observed were generally comparable to those usually reported following DPT with the exception that there were slightly more febrile reactions reported among PRP-T recipients within 6 to 24 hours of vaccination. Table IV (on following page) shows systemic reactions reported in a controlled clinical trial.

Act-HIB reconstituted with DPT Adsorbed: In a clinical trial conducted in Canada, 442 infants received at least one dose of Act-HIB reconstituted with Connaught's DPT Adsorbed or the same vaccines administered simultaneously at separate sites.

Local adverse reactions to Act-HIB when administered alone were infrequent and mild. No increase was seen with successive doses. Mixed Act-HIB and DPT vaccines did not cause local redness or swelling more often than did DPT vaccine alone but tenderness increased from 18.1% with DPT alone to 26.2% with the combination ($p<0.001$). No increase in systemic adverse effects was seen following the mixed vaccines. However, events were rated as moderate/severe slightly more often after mixed vaccines (12.4%) than after separate vaccinations (8.8%, $p<0.05$).

In the Canadian study, one hypotensive-hyporesponsive episode occurred after the administration of Act-HIB reconstituted with DPT Adsorbed. This child recovered fully with no sequelae. No other serious adverse reactions were reported.

Act-HIB reconstituted with DPT Polio Adsorbed: In a clinical trial in Canada, 427 infants received 3 doses of Act-HIB reconstituted with DPT Polio Adsorbed or the same vaccine administered simultaneously at separate sites. Local adverse reactions to Act-HIB alone were infrequent and mild. A slight increase was seen with successive doses. Although local redness, swelling and tenderness were significantly more common after vaccines containing DPT Polio Adsorbed compared to Act-HIB alone, reaction rates were lower after the combined vaccines than after DPT Polio Adsorbed alone.

No significant differences in systemic adverse events was seen following Act-HIB and DPT Polio Adsorbed administered at separate sites or combined.

Table IV—Act-HIB

Systemic Reactions (%) within 24 Hours of Vaccination

Group	First Dose PRP-T and DPT[a]	First Dose DPT	Second Dose PRP-T and DPT[a]	Second Dose DPT	Third Dose PRP-T and DPT[a]	Third Dose DPT
Any Systemic Reactions	77.8	81.8	87.7	75.0	76.5	68.8
Fever						
38°C–38.9°C	27.7	17.5	27.1[b]	6.5[b]	16.4	12.1
>39°C	4.1	0.0	2.9	1.6	1.5	3.0
Irritability	51.8	57.1	47.7	51.9	41.7	41.6
Drowsiness	43.2	41.6	44.4	28.6	33.3	26.0
Loss of Appetite	8.6	15.6	13.6	15.6	21.2	11.7
Vomiting	3.7	3.9	0.0	0.0	3.7	3.9
Diarrhea	0.0	1.3	2.5	6.5	6.2	6.5

[a]PRP-T Vaccine and DPT Vaccine administered at 2 different sites.
[b]P>0.001.

Three severe adverse events temporally associated with vaccination resulted in hospitalization. These included one infant who developed supraventricular tachycardia 48 hours after dose 1 (combined), one infant who woke 3 hours after dose 1 (separate) with cough, respiratory distress and cyanosis whose diagnosis was suspected aspiration or gastroesophageal reflux, and one infant with an episode of screaming and apnea 4 hours after dose 1 (separate). All three infants recovered completely. No causal relationship between the adverse events and vaccination was demonstrated.

Act-HIB reconstituted with Quadracel: In clinical trials conducted in Canada, 215 infants received 3 doses of either Act-HIB reconstituted with Quadracel or the same vaccines administered simultaneously at separate sites at 2, 4 and 6 months of age. An additional 186 18-month old children received a single dose of either Act-HIB reconstituted with Quadracel or the same vaccines administered simultaneously at separate sites. The rates of local and systemic reactions for the combination of Act-HIB and Quadracel were consistently lower than for the combination of Act-HIB and DPT-Polio Adsorbed (PENTA 1). The incidence of local reactions at the Quadracel site was lower when the vaccines are given separately, but severe local reactions are uncommon (<.0% for any dose). Systemic reactions were comparable between the 2 groups. No hypotonic-hyporesponsive episodes following Quadracel and Act-HIB administration were reported during these trials. There were 3 reports of febrile seizures (6 days to 1 month following immunization with Quadracel and Act-HIB), all attributed to intercurrent febrile illness.

Rare cases of allergic reactions including urticaria, pruritus, and facial and laryngeal edema have been reported.

Physicians should be aware that recipients of Haemophilus b vaccine are not protected against Hib disease in the week after vaccination, prior to the onset of the protective effects of the vaccine.

As with any vaccine, there is the possibility that broad use of the vaccine could reveal rare adverse reactions not observed in clinical trials. A temporal association of neurological disorders has been reported following the parenteral injection of other biological products and should always be carefully considered when an immunization is indicated.

Dosage: Parenteral biological products should be inspected visually for extraneous particulate matter and/or discoloration before administration whenever solution and container permit. If these conditions exist, the product should not be administered.

This vaccine is indicated for routine immunization against invasive disease caused by H. influenzae type b in infants and children starting at 2 months of age (see Indications). Each dose is a single injection of 0.5 mL given i.m.

Reconstitution of Freeze-Dried Vaccine: Reconstitute the vaccine using only the diluent supplied, Connaught's DPT Adsorbed, DPT Polio Adsorbed, or Quadracel. The use of any other vaccine to reconstitute Haemophilus b Conjugate Vaccine is not recommended.

Do not remove the rubber stopper from the vial.

Apply a **sterile** piece of cotton moistened with a suitable antiseptic to the surface of the rubber stopper of the vial of vaccine. Withdraw the diluent into a syringe. Holding the plunger of the syringe containing the diluent steady, pierce the centre of the rubber stopper in the vial and **slowly** inject the 0.5 mL of diluent into the freeze-dried vaccine. Shake the vial gently until a clear, colorless solution results. **Avoid foaming** since this will prevent withdrawal of the proper dose. Withdraw the entire contents of the reconstituted vaccine into the syringe and inject the total volume (about 0.5 mL).

When Connaught's DPT Adsorbed, DPT Polio Adsorbed or Quadracel is used for the reconstitution of Act-HIB, **shake the single dose ampul or vial well** to uniformly distribute the suspension before withdrawing entire contents (about 0.5 mL). Before withdrawing the contents from an ampul, tap the container first to ensure that all the vaccine is in the lower portion. Once the ampul has been opened, any of its contents not used immediately should be discarded. Before withdrawing the contents from a rubber-stoppered vial, do not remove either the rubber stopper or the metal seal holding it in place. Inject all the DPT Adsorbed, DPT Polio Adsorbed or Quadracel into the vial of Act-HIB vaccine. Swirl the vial until a cloudy, uniform suspension results. Avoid foaming since this will prevent withdrawal of the proper dose. Use a sterile needle and syringe to withdraw the entire contents for 1 dose.

Before injection, the skin over the site to be injected should be cleansed with a suitable germicide.

Administer the vaccine **i.m.** The preferred site is into the anterolateral aspect of the mid-thigh (vastus lateralis muscle) or into the deltoid muscle.

In children >1 year of age, the deltoid is the preferred site since use of the anterolateral thigh results in frequent complaints of limping due to muscle pain.

After insertion of the needle, aspirate to ensure that the needle has not entered a blood vessel.

Do not inject i.v.

Each person who is immunized should be given a permanent personal immunization record. In addition, it is essential that the physician or nurse record the immunization history in the permanent medical record of each patient. This permanent office record should contain the name of the vaccine, date given, dose, manufacturer and lot number.

Supplied: Act-HIB—Haemophilus b Conjugate Vaccine (Tetanus Protein-Conjugate) (PRP-T) is a lyophilized vaccine of purified polyribose ribitol phosphate capsular polysaccharide (PRP) of H. influenzae type b, covalently bound to tetanus protein. Each single dose of 0.5 mL after reconstitution contains 10 µg of purified capsular polysaccharide covalently bound to 20 µg of tetanus protein.

Act-HIB reconstituted with Diluent: The diluent for reconstitution is a 0.4% saline solution. After reconstitution the vaccine appears clear and colourless and does not contain a preservative.

Act-HIB reconstituted with Connaught's DPT Adsorbed: After reconstitution, the vaccine appears cloudy and uniform and the solution contains thimerosal 0.01% used in DPT Adsorbed as a preservative.

Act-HIB reconstituted with Connaught's DPT Polio Adsorbed: After reconstitution, the vaccine appears cloudy and uniform. From the DPT Polio Adsorbed, the solution contains 2-phenoxyethanol 0.5% as preservative and trace amounts of polymyxin B and neomycin may be present from the cell growth medium.

Act-HIB reconstituted with Connaught's Quadracel: After reconstitution, the vaccine appears cloudy and uniform. From the Quadracel, the solution contains 0.6%±0.1% 2-phenoxyethanol as preservative and trace amounts of polymyxin B and neomycin may be present from the cell growth medium.

Packages containing 5 single dose vials of Act-HIB and 5×0.5 mL (single dose) ampuls of Connaught's diluent, 0.4% Saline for reconstitution of Haemophilus b Conjugate Vaccine. Packages containing 5 single dose vials of Act-HIB and 5×0.5 mL (single dose) ampuls of Connaught's DPT Adsorbed for reconstitution in place of the diluent. Packages containing 5 single dose vials of Act-HIB and 5×0.5 mL (single dose) ampuls of Connaught's DPT Polio Adsorbed for reconstitution in place of the diluent. Packages containing 5 single dose vials of Act-HIB and 5×0.5 mL (single dose) ampuls of Connaught's Quadracel to be used for reconstitution in place of the diluent and sold under the trade name Pentalel.

Store between 2 and 8°C. **Do not freeze.** The vaccine should be used immediately after reconstitution. Do not use after the expiration date.

Reviewed 1999

ACTI-B$_{12}$®
Technilab

Hydroxocobalamin

Hematopoietic

Supplied: Each 10 mL vial of oral solution contains: hydroxocobalamin 500 µg and certain amino acids. Boxes of 10.

ACTIFED®
Warner-Lambert Consumer Healthcare

Triprolidine HCl—Pseudoephedrine HCl

Antihistaminic—Decongestant

Indications: The prophylaxis and treatment of symptoms associated with the common cold, acute and subacute sinusitis, acute eustachian salpingitis, serous otitis media with eustachian tube congestion, aerotitis media and croup; in allergic conditions which respond to antihistamines, including hay fever, pollenosis, allergic and vasomotor rhinitis.

Contraindications: Hypersensitivity to triprolidine or pseudoephedrine. Should not be administered to patients receiving MAO inhibitors or who have taken them within preceding 2 weeks. Patients with severe hypertension or severe coronary artery disease.

Precautions: Occupational Hazards: Patients should be cautioned not to operate vehicles or hazardous machinery until their response to the drug has been determined.

Since the depressant effects of antihistamines are additive to those of other drugs affecting the CNS, patients should be cautioned against drinking alcoholic beverages or taking hypnotics, sedatives, psychotherapeutic agents or other drugs with CNS depressant effects during antihistaminic therapy.

Hypertension and unconsciousness following the ingestion of 60 mg pseudoephedrine by a normotensive individual has been reported and should be regarded as an extremely rare example of pseudoephedrine intolerance.

The antibacterial agent, furazolidone, is known to cause a dose-related inhibition of MAO. Although there are no reports of a hypertensive crisis caused by the concurrent administration of pseudoephedrine and furazolidone, they should not be taken together.

As with other sympathomimetic agents and decongestants, this product should be used with caution in patients with prostatic enlargement or bladder dysfunction. In severe hepatic or renal dysfunction, this product should be given at less than the usual recommended dose and the patient's response used as a guide to the dosage requirement for further administration.

Pregnancy and *Lactation:* Use with caution. Pseudoephedrine and triprolidine have been reported to be excreted into breast milk of lactating women.

Drug Interactions: Concomitant use of this product with sympathomimetic agents such as decongestants, appetite suppressants, and amphetamine-like psychostimulants or with monoamine oxidase inhibitors may occasionally cause a rise in blood pressure.

Because of its pseudoephedrine component, this product may partially reverse the hypotensive action of drugs which interfere with sympathetic activity including bretylium, bethanidine, guanethidine, debrisoquine, methyldopa, beta and/or alpha adrenergic blocking agents.

Adverse Effects: Some patients may exhibit mild sedation or mild stimulation. Sleep disturbance and rarely hallucinations have been reported.

Urinary retention may occasionally occur in male subjects where prostatic enlargement is present. Fixed drug eruption due to pseudoephedrine and lichenoid skin eruption due to triprolidine have been reported but both these reactions should be regarded as rare events.

Overdose: Symptoms: Insomnia, tremors, tachycardia, difficulty in micturition, irritability, drowsiness, lethargy, dizziness, ataxia, weakness, hypotonicity, respiratory depression, dryness of the skin and mucous membranes, hypertension, hyperpyrexia, hyperactivity, convulsions.

Actifed (cont'd)

Treatment: There is no specific antidote for triprolidine or pseudoephedrine. General measures to eliminate the drug and reduce its absorption should be undertaken. Gastric lavage should be performed up to 3 hours after ingestion if indicated. If desired the elimination of pseudoephedrine can be accelerated by urine acidification. If respiratory depression is severe, intubation and artificial respiration should be used. Convulsions should be treated with diazepam. Maintain blood pressure through fluid replacement and supportive measures. Catheterization of the bladder may be necessary. Hypertension may be controlled with alpha-adrenoceptor blocking drugs and tachycardia with beta-adrenoceptor blocking drugs.

Dosage: To be given every 4 to 6 hours. Do not exceed 4 doses in 24 hours. Adults and children 12 years of age and over: 1 tablet. Children 6 to 11 years of age: ½ tablet.

Persons over 65 or under 6 years, use as directed by a physician.

Information for the Patient: See Blue Section—Information for the Patient "Actifed".

Supplied: Each white, biconvex tablet, with code number ACTIFED M2A on same side as score mark, contains: triprolidine HCl 2.5 mg and pseudoephedrine HCl 60 mg. Nonmedicinal ingredients: gelatin, lactose, magnesium stearate and starches. Packages of 12 and 24. Bottles of 100. Store at 15 to 25°C and protect from light.

(Shown in Product Recognition Section)

ACTIFED™ PLUS EXTRA STRENGTH

Warner-Lambert Consumer Healthcare

Acetaminophen—Pseudoephedrine HCl—Triprolidine HCl

Analgesic—Antipyretic—Antihistamine—Decongestant

Indications: The prophylaxis and treatment of symptoms associated with the common cold, acute and subacute sinusitis; in allergic conditions which respond to antihistamines, including hay fever, pollenosis, allergic and vasomotor rhinitis. Relieves nasal congestion, runny nose, sneezing, sinus pain, headache and fever.

Contraindications: Hypersensitivity to triprolidine, pseudoephedrine or acetaminophen. Should not be administered to patients receiving MAO inhibitors or who have taken them within preceding 2 weeks. Patients with severe hypertension or severe coronary artery disease.

Precautions: Occupational Hazards: Patients should be cautious not to operate vehicles or hazardous machinery until their response to the drug has been determined.

Since the depressant effects of antihistamines are addictive to those of other drugs affecting the CNS, patients should be cautious against drinking alcoholic beverages or taking hypnotics, sedatives, psychotherapeutic agents or other drugs with CNS depressant antihistaminic therapy.

Hypertension and unconsciousness following the ingestion of 60 mg pseudoephedrine by a normotensive individual has been reported and should be regarded as an extremely rare example of pseudoephedrine intolerance. The antibacterial agent, furazolidone, is known to cause a dose-related inhibition of MAO. Although there are no reports of a hypertensive crisis caused by the concurrent administration of pseudoephedrine and furazolidone, they should not be taken together.

As with other sympathomimetic agents and decongestants, this product should be used with caution in patients with prostatic enlargement or bladder dysfunction. In severe hepatic or renal dysfunction, this product should be given at less than the usual recommended dose and the patient's response used as a guide to the dosage requirement for further administration.

Pregnancy and *Lactation:* Use with caution. Pseudoephedrine and triprolidine have been reported to be excreted into breast milk of lactating women.

Drug Interactions: Concomitant use of this product with sympathomimetic agents such as decongestants, appetite suppressants, and amphetamine-like psychostimulants or with MAO inhibitors may occasionally cause a rise in blood pressure.

Because of its pseudoephedrine component, this product may partially reverse the hypotensive action of drugs which interfere with sympathetic activity including bretylium, bethanidine, guanethidine, debrisoquine, methyldopa, beta and/or alpha adrenergic blocking agents.

Adverse Effects: Some patients may exhibit mild sedation or mild stimulation. Sleep disturbances and rarely hallucinations have been reported.

Urinary retention may occasionally occur in male subjects where prostatic enlargement is present. Fixed drug eruption due to pseudoephedrine and lichenoid skin eruption due to triprolidine have been reported but both these reactions should be regarded as rare events.

Dosage: Adults and children 12 years and over: 1 caplet every 4 to 6 hours. Do not exceed 4 doses in 24 hours. Children 12 years and under: use only as directed by a physician. Geriatrics: Persons over 65: use only as directed by a physician.

Information for the Patient: See Blue Section—Information for the Patient "Actifed Plus Extra Strength".

Supplied: Each white caplet, engraved F2F, contains: triprolidine HCl 2.5 mg, pseudoephedrine HCl 60 mg and acetaminophen 500 mg. Nonmedicinal ingredients: cellulose, magnesium stearate and povidone. Packages of 12 and 24. Store between 15 and 25°C. Protect from light and keep dry.

(Shown in Product Recognition Section)

ACTINAC® Ⓟ

Hoechst Marion Roussel

Chloramphenicol—Hydrocortisone Acetate—Butoxyethylnicotinate—Allantoin—Precipitated Sulfur

Acne Therapy

Pharmacology: The roles of the individual ingredients in Actinac and their collective mechanisms of action in the topical treatment of acne have not been elucidated. Hydrocortisone, chloramphenicol and precipitated sulfur are however, widely recognized for their respective anti-inflammatory, antibacterial and desquamating properties.

Chloramphenicol is usually bacteriostatic in action, but may be bactericidal in high concentrations or against highly susceptible organisms. Chloramphenicol acts by inhibiting the protein synthesis in susceptible organisms by binding reversibly to the 50S ribosomal subunits, thus preventing successful attachment of complete transfer RNA to the ribosome and consequently disrupting peptide bound formation and protein synthesis.

Following topical application, corticosteroids produce anti-inflammatory, antipruritic and vasoconstrictor actions. The activity of the drugs is thought to result at least in part from binding with a steroid receptor. Corticosteroids decrease inflammation by stabilizing leukocyte lysosomal membranes, preventing release of destructive acid hydrolases from leukocytes; inhibiting macrophage accumulation in inflamed areas; reducing leukocyte adhesion to capillary endothelium; reducing capillary wall permeability and edema formation; decreasing complement components; antagonizing histamine activity and release of kinine from substrates; reducing fibroblast proliferation, collagen deposition, and subsequent scar tissue formation; and possibly by other mechanisms as yet unknown.

At a concentration greater than 5%, as contained in Actinac, sulfur exerts a keratolytic effect. Although the mechanism of sulfur's keratolytic action has not been determined, it may depend on formation of hydrogen sulfide when the drug comes in contact with skin. Topically applied sulfur has mild antifungal and antibacterial activity. It has been suggested that when applied topically to the skin, sulfur forms hydrogen sulfide and/or polythionic acid, which may exert germicidal activity. In vitro sulfur has also been shown to have some antibacterial activity. The exact mechanism(s) of action of sulfur in the treatment of acne is not fully understood but is presumed to involve the drug's keratolytic and antibacterial effects.

Allantoin assists in the healing of damaged epithelium, by fibrinolysis of damaged tissue, stimulation of cell granulation and keratolytic activity.

Butoxyethylnicotinate, an ester of nicotinic acid, produces a rapid vasodilatation of moderate intensity and duration and increases local blood flow allowing the active ingredients to diffuse into the affected tissue.

Indications: For the topical treatment of acne vulgaris where treatment with chloramphenicol and a steroid is considered appropriate. The use of Actinac has been associated with a reduction in papules, pustules and the accompanying inflammation and erythema. Its efficacy in treating the comedone and cyst components of acne has not been established. Actinac should be restricted to conditions where safer agents are considered inappropriate.

Cases of significant blood dyscrasias or aplastic anemia have been reported with the oral, parenteral and ophthalmic use of chloramphenicol. Although this has not been reported following the topical use of Actinac, the possibility of such serious adverse reactions should always be considered when prescribing Actinac. Hematological parameters should be monitored when possible. Excessively prolonged or irregular applications should be avoided.

Contraindications: Patients who have demonstrated sensitivity to any one of its constituents. It is also contraindicated in the presence of tuberculosis of the skin, viral infections including herpes simplex, vaccinia or varicella and superficial fungal or yeast infections. Actinac should not be used in patients with a history of, or presenting with, hematological abnormalities or disorders.

Warnings: Bone marrow hypoplasia, including agranulocytosis and aplastic anemia have been reported following the use of chloramphenicol. Chloramphenicol-related agranulocytosis and aplastic anemia have been associated in the vast majority of cases with oral, and rarely with parenteral and ophthalmic administrations. Topicals applied to intact skin have not been implicated. Irreversible bone marrow depression leading to aplastic anemia is not considered dose-related. Aplastic anemia with associated pancytopenia is reported to develop in the first 1 or 2 weeks of therapy but in some patients, aplasia reportedly becomes evident weeks to months after chloramphenicol therapy. The incidence of this adverse reaction was initially estimated to be 1/25 000 to 1/40 000 courses of oral therapy which was said to be approximately 13 times the background incidence in the general population. These figures are considered by some to significantly overestimate risk. The precise mechanism of aplastic anemia is unknown, but toxic chloramphenicol metabolites have been suspected of local marrow suppression in enzyme deficient individuals. Though very little chloramphenicol is absorbed through skin after topical Actinac applications in acne, compared to the use of oral, parenteral and ophthalmic preparations, the possibility of serious adverse reactions should always be considered in patients receiving any form of chloramphenicol, including topicals. Excessively prolonged or irregular applications should be avoided.

Pharmacokinetic studies conducted in healthy volunteers and in patients with acne lesions have shown minimal absorption of chloramphenicol (total absorbed is less than 1% of total dose on average) following repeated applications of Actinac. However, the possibility that the keratolytic agents and the vasodilating effects of butoxyethylnicotinate in this preparation may promote the systemic absorption of chloramphenicol and hydrocortisone, should be considered.

Precautions: Keep away from the eyes and mouth. Discontinue use temporarily if excessive drying, irritation, or scaling occurs. Sensitization and irritation to chloramphenicol and corticosteroids may result from topical application of the drugs. If these occur, the preparation should be discontinued. Application of corticosteroids to extensive areas, too frequent application, or application under occlusive dressings may result in systemic absorption with symptoms of adrenal suppression, or in localized epidermal and dermal atrophy. If secondary bacterial infection exists, other appropriate means of antibacterial therapy may also be initiated. However, if overgrowth develops, medication with Actinac should be discontinued.

Interim assessments of the patient's progress should be made at not less than 2-week intervals. It is recommended that treatment should be discontinued after maximum benefit has been obtained and reinstituted only when the patient's condition starts to reoccur. Should no significant improvement in the patient's condition be seen within 4 to 6 weeks, treatment should be discontinued.

Children: Prolonged percutaneous absorption of the corticosteroid can produce systemic effects such as adrenal suppression, moon facies and suppression of growth in children. Actinac is, however, not intended for pediatric use.

Pregnancy: Safety for use of Actinac in pregnancy has not been established. Topical corticosteroids and chloramphenicol should be used during pregnancy only if therapeutic benefit outweighs the risk to the fetus. Studies in animals have shown that topical corticosteroids are systemically absorbed and may cause teratogenic effects especially when used in large amounts, for prolonged periods of time or if the more potent agents are used. Chloramphenicol readily crosses the placenta.

Lactation: Safety for use of Actinac in lactation has not been established. The use of Actinac is not recommended in nursing mothers. It is not known whether topical corticosteroids are distributed into milk; however, systemically administered corticosteroids are excreted in breast milk. Chloramphenicol is excreted in breast milk.

Patients with Special Diseases and Conditions: Topical corticosteroids should not be used in patients with markedly impaired circulation since skin ulceration has occurred in these patients following use of the drug.

Corticosteroid-containing preparations should be used with caution in patients with impaired T cell function or in those receiving other immunosuppressive therapy. The immunosuppressive effects of corticosteroids may be associated with impairment of the normal function of T cells and macrophages; such impairment may result in activation of latent infection or exacerbations of intercurrent infections.

As for other products containing chloramphenicol, Actinac should not be utilized in patients with abnormal hematology or history of hematopoietic disorders. Actinac should not be administered concomitantly with drugs or chemicals capable of inducing hematopoietic abnormalities (see Contraindications).

Chloramphenicol is metabolized by the liver and excreted largely by the kidney, and therefore ought only be administered with caution to patients with liver or renal impairment, or to patients taking drugs dependent upon liver for their metabolism. The potential for additive and synergistic effects should be kept in mind.

Information for the Patient: Patients should be instructed to use Actinac only as directed by the physician, only for the disorder for which it was prescribed, and for no longer than the time period prescribed. They should also be instructed how to recognize signs of bone marrow depression (unusual fever, fatigue, sore throat and mouth sores) and to immediately report these to their physician. Patients should be instructed that the treated areas of skin should not be bandaged or otherwise covered or wrapped as to be occlusive.

Adverse Effects: Reported adverse reactions to Actinac lotion include: excessive drying of the skin, erythema, contact dermatitis, eye irritation, a burning sensation and facial flushing. Drying of the skin and erythema have also been noted following use of a vehicle control from which hydrocortisone and chloramphenicol were omitted.

Following topical administration of chloramphenicol preparations, signs of local irritation with subjective symptoms of itching or burning, angioneurotic edema, urticaria, vesicular and maculopapular dermatitis have been reported in patients sensitive to chloramphenicol and are cause for discontinuing the medication (see Warnings).

Chloramphenicol has been reported to cause two forms of hematopoietic failure following oral, parenteral and ophthalmic administrations. This has however not been reported following topical use of Actinac for acne, where only comparatively minimal absorption of chloramphenicol occurs, or with other topicals containing the antibiotic when administered to non-traumatized skin. Agranulocytosis is considered to be dose-related (>25 µg/mL plasma concentration), generally reversible and rarely lethal. Aplastic anemia is considered idiosyncratic, non dose-related and possibly caused by toxic chloramphenicol metabolites in enzyme deficient subjects. It may occur weeks to months after completion of therapy, and can be progressive and very often lethal.

Potential interactions with chloramphenicol include drugs that rely upon the liver for their metabolism as well as drugs, chemicals, diseases or procedures that inhibit hematopoiesis.

Topical corticosteroids may cause atrophy of the epidermis, s.c. tissue, and dermal collagen, and drying and cracking or tightening of the skin. Epidermal thinning, telangiectasia, increased fragility of cutaneous blood vessels, purpura, and atrophic striae may also occur. Other adverse dermatologic effects of topical corticosteroids include acneiform eruption, vesiculation, irritation, pruritus, hypertrichosis, rosacea-like eruptions of the face, erythema, hyperesthesia, perioral dermatitis, burning or stinging sensation, folliculitis and hypopigmentation. Adverse dermatologic effects of topical corticosteroids usually improve when the drug is discontinued but may persist for long periods. Atrophic striae may be permanent. The anti-inflammatory activity of corticosteroids can also mask the manifestations of infections. Predictable adverse reactions to topical corticosteroids are directly related to prolonged use, application on highly absorptive areas (such as face and neck), skin condition and use of occlusive dressings. The frequency of their occurrence is however less with hydrocortisone than with the fluorinated steroids and has not been reported with Actinac.

Topically applied sulfur may cause local irritation of the skin, eyes or respiratory tract. Allergic reactions to sulfur occur rarely. Repeated applications may cause dermatitis.

Systemic toxicity (e.g., headache, vomiting, muscle cramps, dizziness, collapse) has reportedly occurred following topical application of precipitated sulfur to patients with eczema but symptoms resolved within several hours.

Overdose: Symptoms and Treatment: In case of accidental ingestion of Actinac lotion, the amount swallowed would be expected to be small. The chloramphenicol content of a whole bottle is 200 mg. Oral chloramphenicol is usually administered as 50 mg/kg/day in divided doses. Hence, in the case of accidental ingestion of Actinac lotion, the chloramphenicol content ingested is well below the minimum content of the usual oral therapeutic dose. Symptoms would probably consist of mild gastrointestinal disturbances. In the event of a severe reaction, emergency treatment consists of general measures such as induction of emesis, gastric lavage, catharsis and forcing of fluids.

Dosage: Should be applied twice daily in the morning and at bedtime, for the first 4 days and once daily at bedtime thereafter, to the areas affected by acne. Before application these areas should be washed with mild soap, well rinsed and dried. The reconstituted Actinac lotion should be applied with cotton wool or gauze. Duration of treatment: for 4 to 6 weeks or as instructed by treating physician.

Information for the Patient: See Blue Section—Information for the Patient "Actinac".

Supplied: Each g of powder contains: chloramphenicol BP 40 mg, hydrocortisone acetate BP 40 mg, 2-butoxyethylnicotinate 24 mg, allantoin 24 mg and precipitated sulfur BPC 320 mg. Nonmedicinal ingredients: myrj 53, powdered tragacanth, purified td talc, syloid 244 and titanium dioxide. The vehicle is composed by lavender water soluble and, as a preservative, benzoic acid BP 0.1%, in purified water BP. Concentrations of the active ingredients in the reconstituted suspension are chloramphenicol 0.97%, hydrocortisone acetate 0.97%, 2-butoxyethylnicotinate 0.58%, allantoin 0.58%, sulfur 7.78%. Single pack of 2 bottles each containing 5 g of powder and 2 bottles each containing 16 mL of aqueous vehicle. Store at room temperature, below 25°C. Excessive heat should be avoided.

The lotion is prepared by emptying the contents of 1 bottle of aqueous vehicle (white cap) into 1 bottle of powder (black cap). The cap should then be replaced securely and the bottle shaken until the 2 ingredients are thoroughly mixed. The lotion remains stable at room temperature for 21 days.

Reviewed 1997

ACTIPROFEN™

Bayer Consumer

Ibuprofen

Analgesic—Antipyretic

Supplied: Each white, oblong, film-coated caplet, imprinted with pink "A 200", contains: ibuprofen USP 200 mg. Nonmedicinal ingredients: cornstarch, croscarmellose sodium, FD&C Red #3, hydroxypropyl methylcellulose, lactose, magnesium stearate, microcrystalline cellulose, silicon dioxide and triacetin. Sucrose-, sulfite- and tartrazine-free. Blister packages of 24. Bottles of 50 and 100.

(Shown in Product Recognition Section)

ACTIVASE® rt-PA

Roche

Alteplase

Fibrinolytic Agent

Pharmacology: Alteplase is a serine protease which has the property of fibrin-enhanced conversion of plasminogen to plasmin. It produces minimal conversion of plasminogen in the absence of fibrin; and when introduced into the systemic circulation, alteplase binds to fibrin in a thrombus and converts the entrapped plasminogen to plasmin. This initiates local fibrinolysis with minimal systemic effects. Following administration of alteplase there is a decrease (20 to 30%) in circulating fibrinogen. Decreases in plasminogen and α_2-antiplasmin are also evident.

Alteplase is cleared rapidly from circulating plasma with an initial half-life of less than 5 minutes. There is no difference in the dominant initial plasma half-life between the 3-hour and accelerated regimens for acute myocardial infarction (AMI). The plasma clearance of alteplase is approximately 500 mL/min. The clearance is mediated primarily by the liver.

An occlusive thrombus is present in the infarct-related coronary artery in approximately 80% of patients experiencing a transmural myocardial infarction evaluated within 4 hours of onset of symptoms.

Acute Myocardial Infarction Patients: Two alteplase dose regimens have been studied in patients experiencing AMI: accelerated infusion, and 3-hour infusion. The comparative efficacy of these 2 regimens has not been evaluated.

90-Minute Accelerated Infusion in Patients with Acute Myocardial Infarction: Accelerated infusion of alteplase was studied in an international, multicentre trial (GUSTO) where 41 021 patients with acute myocardial infarction were randomized to 4 thrombolytic regimens: accelerated infusion of alteplase (<100 mg over 90 minutes) plus i.v. heparin; streptokinase (1.5×10^6 units over 60 minutes) plus i.v. heparin; streptokinase (1.5×10^6 units over 60 minutes) plus s.c. heparin; or combined alteplase (1.0 mg/kg over 60 minutes) plus streptokinase (1.0×10^6 units over 60 minutes). ASA was administered daily. The results are shown in Table I (on following page). The 30-day mortality for the accelerated infusion of alteplase was 1% lower (14% relative risk reduction) than for streptokinase (i.v. or s.c. heparin). In addition, the combined incidence of 30-day mortality or nonfatal stroke for accelerated alteplase was 1% lower (12% relative risk reduction) than for streptokinase (i.v. heparin) and 0.8% lower (10% relative risk reduction) than for streptokinase (s.c. heparin). Once a year follow-up data suggest a sustained mortality benefit.

Subgroup analysis of patients by age, infarct location, and time from symptom onset to thrombolytic treatment showed consistently lower 30-day mortality for the group receiving the accelerated infusion of alteplase. For patients who were over 75 years of age, a predefined subgroup consisting of 12% of patients enrolled, the incidence of stroke was 4.0% for the group receiving the accelerated infusion of alteplase, 2.8% for streptokinase (i.v. heparin), and 3.2% for streptokinase (s.c. heparin); the incidence of combined 30-day mortality or nonfatal stroke was 20.6% for accelerated infusion of alteplase, 21.5% for streptokinase (i.v. heparin), and 22.0% for streptokinase (s.c. heparin).

In-hospital events in the overall patient population, as well as events in patients who survived beyond 30 days are shown in Table II (on following page).

An angiographic substudy of the GUSTO trial provided data on infarct-related artery patency. Results are shown in Table III (on following page). Reocclusion rates were similar for all 3 treatment regimens.

3-Hour Infusion in Patients with Acute Myocardial Infarction: In patients studied with coronary angiography prior to and following infusion of alteplase, the use of alteplase resulted in reperfusion of documented obstructed vessels within 90 minutes after the commencement of thrombolytic therapy in approximately 70% of patients. In 2 studies involving 145 patients, alteplase produced reperfusion in 73% of patients who received 70 to 100 mg (40.6 to 58×10^6 IU) over 90 minutes. In 2 double blind randomized controlled trials in patients with AMI, the patients infused with 80 to 100 mg of alteplase experienced improved ventricular function and reduced incidence of clinical congestive heart failure compared to those treated with placebo.

In a double-blind study involving 5 013 patients (ASSET Study) where patients were infused with either alteplase or placebo within 5 hours of onset of symptoms of AMI, improved 30-day survival was shown in patients receiving alteplase compared to placebo. At 1 month, the overall mortality rates were 7.2% for the alteplase-treated group and 9.8% for the placebo-treated group (p=0.001). This benefit was maintained at 6 months (10.4% and 13.1% for alteplase and placebo-treated patients respectively, p=0.008).

In the LATE study involving 5 711 patients where patients were infused with either alteplase (100 mg over 3 hours) or placebo within 6 to 24 hours of onset of AMI symptoms, the 35-day mortality rates were 8.9% for Activase rt-PA treated patients and 10.3% for placebo-treated patients (p=not significant). Prespecified survival analysis according to treatment within 12 hours of symptom onset showed a significant reduction in mortality for the alteplase treated patients, 8.9% versus 12.0% for the placebo treated patients (p=0.0229).

Indications: For i.v. use in adults for: the lysis of suspected occlusive coronary artery thrombi associated with evolving transmural myocardial infarction; and the reduction of mortality associated with AMI, the improvement of ventricular function following AMI and the reduction in the incidence of congestive heart failure.

Activase rt-PA (cont'd)

Table I—Activase rt-PA

Accelerated Infusion in Patients with Myocardial Infarction

Event	Accelerated Activase rt-PA (i.v. heparin)	Streptokinase (i.v. heparin)	p-value*	Streptokinase (s.c. heparin)	p-value*
30-Day Mortality	6.3%	7.3%	0.003	7.3%	0.007
30-Day Mortality or Nonfatal Stroke	7.2%	8.2%	0.006	8.0%	0.036
24-Hour Mortality	2.4%	2.9%	0.009	2.8%	0.029

* Two-tailed p-value is for comparison of accelerated infusion of alteplase to the respective streptokinase control arm.

Table II—Activase rt-PA

In-Hospital Clinical Events/Procedures[a]

	Overall			30-Day Survivors[b]		
	SK (pooled) %		Activase %	SK (pooled) %		Activase %
Reinfarction	3.9		4.1	3.4		3.6
Cardiogenic Shock	6.5	***	5.0	3.2	***	2.3
CABG	8.3		9.0	8.6		9.2
PTCA (IRA)[c]	14.3		14.6	14.8		15.2
CHF or Pulmonary Edema	16.7	***	15.0	14.3	**	13.1
Recurrent Ischemia	20.3		19.7	20.1		19.6
Sustained Hypotension	12.8	***	10.0	9.4	***	7.0
2° or 3° Atrioventricular Block	8.9	***	7.3	7.6	***	6.2
Ventricular Tachycardia	6.5	*	5.7	4.8		4.4
Ventricular Fibrillation	6.9	*	6.2	5.0		4.6
Asystole	6.0	**	5.1	1.9		1.7
Atrial Fibrillation/Flutter	9.9	**	8.7	9.1	**	8.0
Acute Mitral Regurgitation	1.5		1.3	1.3		1.1
Swan-Ganz Catheter	12.6	**	11.5	11.5		10.7
Cardioversion	9.8	**	8.6	7.4	*	6.7
Angiography	55.0	*	56.5	57.4	*	58.9

[a] Events other than death, stroke and bleeding.
[b] Patients alive at 30-day timepoint.
[c] IRA=Infarct-Related Artery.
*$p<0.05$, **$p<0.01$, ***$p<0.001$.

Table III—Activase rt-PA

Data on Infarct-Related Artery Patency

	Accelerated Activase rt-PA			Streptokinase (i.v. heparin)			Streptokinase (s.c. heparin)		
Patency	TIMI 2 or 3	TIMI 3	(N)	TIMI 2 or 3	TIMI 3	(N)	TIMI 2 or 3	TIMI 3	(N)
90-Minute	81.3%*	54.8%	(272)	59.0%	30.7%	(261)	53.5%	27.3%	(260)
180-Minute	76.3%	41.3%	(80)	72.4%	38.2%	(76)	71.6%	34.7%	(95)
24 Hours	88.9%	39.5%	(81)	87.5%	47.2%	(72)	82.1%	56.7%	(67)
5-7 Day	83.3%	63.9%	(72)	90.9%	67.5%	(77)	78.7%	58.7%	(75)

* $p<0.001$ compared to streptokinase with i.v. heparin and s.c. heparin. No other treatment groups were significantly different.

Treatment should be initiated as soon as possible after the onset of acute myocardial symptoms. Greater benefit appears to be associated with earlier treatment of alteplase, following the onset of symptoms.

Alteplase is effective in patients in whom therapy is initiated within 6 hours of onset of symptoms for the accelerated infusion regimen or up to 12 hours after onset of symptoms for the 3-hour infusion regimen. The GUSTO study was designed to enrol patients within a 6-hour period following the onset of myocardial infarct symptoms. The data available from this trial are insufficient to support a recommendation for use of the accelerated infusion regimen in patients presenting more than 6 hours after the onset of symptoms.

Contraindications: Because thrombolytic therapy increases the risk of bleeding, alteplase is contraindicated in the following situations: active internal bleeding; history of stroke; patients receiving other i.v. thrombolytic agents; recent (within 2 months) intracranial, or intraspinal surgery or trauma (see Warnings); intracranial neoplasm, arteriovenous malformation, or aneurysm; known bleeding diathesis; severe uncontrolled hypertension, i.e., diastolic BP$\geq$110 mm Hg and/or systolic BP$\geq$180 mm Hg; recent traumatic cardiopulmonary resuscitation; recent severe trauma.

Warnings: Bleeding: The most common complication encountered during therapy with alteplase is bleeding. The type of bleeding associated with thrombolytic therapy can be divided into 2 broad categories: internal bleeding involving the gastrointestinal tract, genitourinary tract, respiratory tract, retroperitoneal or intracranial sites; superficial or surface bleeding, observed mainly at invaded or disturbed sites (e.g., venous cutdowns, arterial punctures, sites of recent surgical intervention).

The concomitant use of heparin anticoagulation contributes to the risk of bleeding.

Fibrin will be lysed during the infusion of alteplase and bleeding from recent puncture sites may occur. Therefore, therapy with alteplase, as with other thrombolytic agents, requires careful attention to all potential bleeding sites (including catheter insertion sites, arterial and venous puncture sites, cutdown sites and needle punctures sites).

I.M. injections and nonessential handling of the patient should be avoided during and immediately following treatment with alteplase. Venipunctures should be performed carefully and only as required.

Should an arterial puncture be necessary during an infusion of alteplase, it is preferable to use an upper extremity vessel that is accessible to manual compression. Pressure should be applied for at least 30 minutes, a pressure dressing applied and the puncture site checked frequently for evidence of bleeding.

Should serious bleeding in a critical location (not controllable by local pressure) occur, the infusion of alteplase and any other concomitant anticoagulant should be discontinued immediately and treatment initiated (see Overdose: Symptoms and Treatment).

In the following conditions, the risks of alteplase therapy may be increased and should be weighed against the anticipated benefits: recent (within 10 days) major surgery, e.g., coronary artery bypass graft, obstetrical delivery, organ biopsy, previous puncture of noncompressible vessels; clinical evidence or history of transient ischemic attacks; recent gastrointestinal or genitourinary bleeding (with 10 days); recent trauma (within 10 days); a history or clinical evidence of hypertensive disease in a patient over 70 years old; advanced age, e.g., over 75 years old; high likelihood or known presence of left heart thrombus, e.g., mitral stenosis with atrial fibrillation; apical MI, with thrombus; acute pericarditis; subacute bacterial endocarditis; hemostatic defects including those secondary to severe hepatic or renal disease; significant liver dysfunction, e.g., prolonged prothrombin time; pregnancy; diabetic hemorrhagic retinopathy, or other hemorrhagic ophthalmic conditions; septic thrombophlebitis or occluded AV cannula at seriously infected site; patients currently receiving oral anticoagulants, e.g., warfarin sodium; any other condition in which bleeding constitutes a significant hazard or would be particularly difficult to manage because of its location.

Cholesterol Embolization: Cholesterol embolization has been reported rarely in patients treated with all types of thrombolytic agents; the true incidence is unknown. This serious condition, which can be lethal, is also associated with invasive vascular procedures (e.g., cardiac catheterization, angiography, vascular surgery) and/or anticoagulant therapy. Clinical features of cholesterol embolism include livedo reticularis, "purple toe" syndrome, acute renal failure, gangrenous digits, hypertension, pancreatitis, myocardial infarction, cerebral infarction, spinal cord infarction, retinal artery occlusion, bowel infarction, and rhabdomyolysis.

Arrhythmias: Coronary thrombolysis may result in arrhythmias associated with reperfusion. These arrhythmias (such as sinus bradycardia, accelerated idioventricular rhythm, ventricular premature depolarizations, ventricular tachycardia) are not different from those often seen in the ordinary course of AMI and may be managed with standard antiarrhythmic measures. It is recommended that antiarrhythmic therapy for bradycardia and/or ventricular irritability be available when infusions of alteplase are administered.

Use of Antithrombotics: ASA and heparin may be administered concomitantly with and following infusions of alteplase. Because either heparin, ASA or alteplase alone may cause bleeding complications, careful monitoring for bleeding is advised, especially at arterial puncture sites.

Precautions: General: Alteplase should be administered in a hospital setting where the appropriate diagnostic and monitoring techniques are readily available.

Routine management of myocardial infarction should not be deferred after evidence of successful thrombolysis is seen. Evaluation and management of underlying atherosclerotic heart disease should be carried out as clinically indicated.

Noncompressible arterial puncture must be avoided. Arterial and venous punctures should be minimized. In the event of serious bleeding, alteplase and heparin should be discontinued immediately. Heparin effects can be reversed by protamine.

Drug Interactions: The interaction of alteplase with other drugs has not been studied. In addition to bleeding associated with heparin and warfarin, drugs that alter platelet function (such as ASA) may increase the risk of bleeding if administered prior to, during or after alteplase infusion.

Laboratory Tests: During alteplase infusion, coagulation tests and/or measures of fibrinolytic activity may be performed if desired. However, routine measurements of fibrinogen as well as fibrinogen degradation products are unreliable, and should not be undertaken unless specific precautions are taken to prevent in vitro artifacts. Alteplase is a serine protease that when present in blood in pharmacologic concentrations remains active under in vitro conditions. This can lead to degradation of fibrinogen in a blood sample removed for analysis. Collection of blood samples on aprotinin (150 to 200 units/mL) can to some extent mitigate this phenomenon.

Geriatrics: The risks of therapy may be increased in the elderly (see Pharmacology, Warnings and Adverse Effects).

Children: Safety and effectiveness of alteplase in children has not been established. Therefore treatment of such patients is not recommended.

Pregnancy: Reproduction studies have not been conducted with alteplase. It is also not known whether alteplase can cause fetal harm when administered to a pregnant woman. Alteplase should be given to a pregnant woman only if clearly needed.

Lactation: It is not known whether alteplase is excreted in human milk. Because many drugs are excreted in human milk, caution should be exercised when alteplase is administered to a nursing woman.

Readministration: There has been little documentation of readministration of alteplase. Readministration should be undertaken with caution. Less than 0.5% of patients receiving single courses of alteplase therapy have experienced transient antibody formation. Nevertheless, if an anaphylactoid reaction

Table IV—Activase rt-PA

Incidence of Stroke and Intracranial Hemorrhage

	rt-PA	SK (i.v.)		SK (s.c.)	
	%	%	p-value	%	p-value
Stroke	1.6%	1.4%	0.32	1.2%	0.03
Intracranial hemorrhage	0.7%	0.6%	0.22	0.5%	0.02
Stroke in >75 yrs	4.0%	2.8%	0.09	3.2%	0.27
Intracranial hemorrhage >75 yrs	2.0%	1.1%	0.06	1.3%	0.17

p-value is for pairwise comparison to rt-PA.

occurs, the infusion should be discontinued immediately and appropriate therapy initiated.

Adverse Effects: Bleeding: The most frequent adverse reaction associated with alteplase is bleeding. The type of bleeding associated with thrombolytic therapy can be divided into 2 broad categories: internal bleeding, involving the gastrointestinal tract, genitourinary tract, respiratory tract, retroperitoneal or intracranial sites; superficial or surface bleeding, observed mainly at invaded or disturbed sites (e.g., venous cutdowns, arterial punctures, sites of recent surgical intervention).

The incidence of all strokes for the accelerated alteplase regimen in the GUSTO trial was 1.6%, while the incidence of nonfatal stroke was 0.9%. The incidence of hemorrhagic stroke was 0.7%, not all of which were fatal. Data from previous trials utilizing a 3-hour infusion indicates that the incidence of total stroke in 6 randomized double-blind placebo controlled trials was 1.2% (37/3 161) in alteplase-treated patients (≤100 mg) compared with 0.9% (27/3 092) in placebo-treated patients.

Although the incidence of all strokes, as well as that for hemorrhagic stroke, increased with increasing age, treatment with accelerated regimen of alteplase was still shown to reduce mortality in older patients. For patients who were over 75 years of age, a predefined subgroup consisting of 12% of patients enrolled, the incidence of stroke was 4.0% for the accelerated regimen of alteplase group, 2.8% for streptokinase (i.v. heparin), and 3.2% for streptokinase (s.c. heparin) (see Table IV). However, combined 30-day mortality or non fatal stroke was 20.6% for accelerated regimen of alteplase, 21.5% for streptokinase (i.v. heparin) and 22.0% for streptokinase (s.c. heparin) in the GUSTO study.

The following incidence of significant internal bleeding (estimated as ≥250 mL blood loss) has been reported in studies involving over 1 300 patients treated at all doses of alteplase, administered as a 3-hour infusion regimen: gastrointestinal 5%, genitourinary 4%.

The following incidence of moderate or severe bleeding was reported when ≤100 mg alteplase was administered by accelerated infusion to >10 000 patients [GUSTO study]: gastrointestinal 1.5%, genitourinary 0.5%.

Incidence of ≤1% of ecchymosis, retroperitoneal bleeding, epistaxis and gingival bleeding has been reported in clinical studies involving alteplase.

The incidence of intracranial bleeding in patients treated with up to 120 mg alteplase (3-hour infusion) has been 0.4%. At doses in excess of 120 mg (120 to 180 mg) the incidence of intracranial bleeding increased to 1.3%. The incidence of intracranial bleeding in patients treated ≤100 mg alteplase (accelerated infusion, weight adjusted) was 0.7%. The maximum total dose of alteplase should not exceed 100 mg.

Death and permanent disability have been reported in patients who have experienced stroke and other serious bleeding episodes.

Allergic Reactions: Allergic-type reactions, e.g., anaphylactoid reaction, laryngeal edema, rash and urticaria have been reported very rarely (<0.02%). A cause and effect relationship to alteplase therapy has not been established.

Other Adverse Reactions: Patients with myocardial infarction can experience disease-related events such as cardiogenic shock, arrhythmias, pulmonary edema, heart failure, cardiac arrest, recurrent ischemia, reinfarction, myocardial rupture, mitral regurgitation, pericardial effusion, pericarditis, cardiac tamponade, venous thrombosis and embolism, and electromechanical dissociation. These events may lead to death. Other adverse reactions have been reported, principally nausea and/or vomiting, hypotension, and fever. These reactions are frequent sequelae of myocardial infarction and may or may not be attributable to alteplase therapy.

Overdose: Symptoms and Treatment: Overdosage could lead to serious bleeding. Should serious bleeding occur in a critical location, the infusion of alteplase and any other concomitant anticoagulant should be discontinued immediately. If necessary, blood loss and reversal of the bleeding tendency can be managed with whole blood or packed red cells. In the event of clinically significant fibrinogen depletion, fresh frozen plasma or cryoprecipitate can be infused.

Dosage: Alteplase is intended for i.v. use only. It should be given via a dedicated i.v. line with an infusion pump. Extravasation of alteplase infusion can cause ecchymosis and/or inflammation. Management consists of terminating the infusion at the i.v. site and application of local therapy.

Acute Myocardial Infarction: Administer alteplase as soon as possible after the onset of symptoms.

There are 2 dose regimens for alteplase for use in the management of AMI. The comparative efficacy of these 2 regimens has not been evaluated.

90-Minute Accelerated Infusion. See Table V. The recommended total dose is based upon patient weight, not to exceed 100 mg. For patients weighing >67 kg, the recommended dose is 100 mg, administered as a 15 mg i.v. bolus, followed by 50 mg infused over 30 minutes and then 35 mg infused over the next 60 minutes.

For patients weighing <67 kg, the recommended dose is 15 mg administered as an i.v. bolus, followed by 0.75 mg/kg to a maximum of 50 mg, infused over the next 30 minutes, and then 0.50 mg/kg to a maximum of 35 mg infused over the next 60 minutes.

Preparation and Administration: The alteplase dose administered by accelerated infusion may be prepared and administered as follows: A. The bolus dose may be prepared in one of the following ways: 1. By removing 15 mL from the vial of reconstituted (1 mg/mL) alteplase using a syringe and needle. For 50 mg vials, the syringe should not be primed with air and the needle should be inserted into the alteplase vial stopper. If the 100 mg vial is used, the needle should be inserted away from the puncture mark made by the transfer device. 2. By removing 15 mL from a port (second injection site) on the infusion line after the infusion set is primed. 3. By programming an infusion pump to deliver a 15 mL (1 mg/mL) bolus at the initiation of the infusion. B. The remainder of the alteplase dose may be administered as follows: **50 mg vials:** Administer using either a polyvinyl chloride bag or glass vial and infusion set. **100 mg vials:** Insert the spike end of an infusion set through the same puncture site created by the transfer device in the stopper of the vial of reconstituted alteplase. Hang the vial of alteplase from the plastic molded capping attached to the bottom of the vial.

3-Hour Infusion: The recommended dose is 100 mg administered as 60 mg (34.8×10⁶ IU) in the first hour, of which 6 to 7 mg is administered as a bolus over the first 1 to 2 minutes and the remainder is administered by continuous infusion, 20 mg (11.6×10⁶ IU) by continuous infusion during the second hour, and 20 mg (11.6×10⁶ IU) by continuous infusion over the following 1 to 4 hours. For smaller patients (<65 kg), a dose of 1.25 mg/kg may be warranted. The alteplase dose administered by 3-hour infusion may be prepared and administered as follows: A. The bolus dose may be prepared in one of the following ways: 1. By removing 6 to 10 mL from the vial of reconstituted (1 mg/mL) alteplase using a syringe and needle. For 50 mg vials, the syringe should not be primed with air and the needle should be inserted into the alteplase vial stopper. If the 100 mg vial is used, the needle should be inserted away from the puncture mark made by the transfer device. 2. By removing 6 to 10 mL from a port (second injection site) on the infusion line after the infusion set is primed. 3. By programming an infusion pump to deliver a 6 to 10 mL (1 mg/mL) bolus at the initiation of the infusion. B. The remainder of the alteplase dose may be administered as follows: **50 mg vials:** Administer using either a polyvinyl chloride bag or glass vial and infusion set. **100 mg vials:** Insert the spike end of an infusion set through the same puncture site created by the transfer device in the stopper of the vial of reconstituted alteplase. Hang the vial of alteplase from the plastic molded capping attached to the bottom of the vial.

Anticoagulation During and After Treatment with Alteplase: To date, heparin has been administered concomitantly in more than 90% of patients given alteplase. Adjunctive i.v. heparin administration is recommended to obtain a therapeutic partial thromboplastin time (PTT). The infusion of heparin should be initiated prior to the termination of the infusion of alteplase.

Reconstitution and Dilution: Alteplase should be reconstituted by aseptically adding to the vial, the appropriate volume of Sterile Water for Injection, USP (50 mL for 50 mg vials, 100 mL for 100 mg vials). It is important that alteplase be reconstituted only with Sterile Water for Injection, USP, without preservatives. Do not use Bacteriostatic Water for Injection. The reconstituted preparation results in a colorless to pale yellow transparent solution containing alteplase 1 mg/mL at a pH of 7.3. The osmolality of this solution is approximately 215 mOsm/kg.

Before further dilution or administration, parenteral drug products should be visually inspected for particulate matter and discoloration prior to administration whenever solution and container permit. Because alteplase contains no preservatives, it should be reconstituted immediately before use (see Stability and Storage).

The reconstituted solution may be diluted further immediately before administration to yield concentrations as low as 0.5 mg/mL in 0.9% Sodium Chloride for Injection, USP or 5% Dextrose for Injection, USP. Excessive agitation during dilution should be avoided; mixing should be accomplished with gentle swirling and/or slow inversion. Do not use other infusion solutions e.g., Sterile Water for Injection, USP, or preservative containing solutions for further dilution.

Table V—Activase rt-PA

Accelerated Regimen: Infusion Chart

Patient Weight		Bolus	Volume of tPA Added to Empty PVC Bag or Glass Vial	0.75 mg/kg over 30 Minutes		0.50 mg/kg over 60 Minutes			tPA Total Dose (mg) (bolus + main-tenance) (maximum dose = 100 mg)
(lb)	(kg)	15 mg* (15 mL) over 2 Minutes	(mL)	Infusion Dose (mg) (max dose = 50 mg)	Infusion Rate (mL/h)	Volume to be Infused (mL)	Infusion Dose (mg) (max dose = 35 mg)	Infusion Rate (mL/h)	Volume to be Infused (mL)	
90-94	41-42	15	52	31	62	31	21	21	21	67
95-97	43-44	15	54	32	64	32	22	22	22	69
98-104	45-47	15	57	34	68	34	23	23	23	72
105-109	48-49	15	60	36	72	36	24	24	24	75
110-114	50-51	15	63	38	75	38	25	25	25	78
115-119	52-54	15	65	39	78	39	26	26	26	80
120-124	55-56	15	68	41	82	41	27	27	27	83
125-129	57-58	15	71	43	86	43	28	28	28	86
130-134	59-60	15	73	44	88	44	29	29	29	88
135-139	61-63	15	76	46	92	46	30	30	30	91
140-144	64-65	15	80	48	96	48	32	32	32	95
145-149	66-67	15	83	50	100	50	33	33	33	98
>149	>67	15	85	50	100	50	35	35	35	100

*1 mg = 1 mL.

Activase rt-PA (cont'd)

No other medication should be added to alteplase solution. Solutions should be administered as described above. Unused infusion solution should be immediately discarded.

50 mg vials: Using a large bore needle (e.g., 18 gauge), **and the accompanying 50 mL Sterile Water for Injection, USP,** direct the stream of Sterile Water for Injection, USP into the lyophilized cake. **Do not use if vacuum is not present.** Slight foaming upon reconstitution is not unusual; standing undisturbed for several minutes is usually sufficient to allow dissipation of any large bubbles. Excessive or vigorous shaking should be avoided.

100 mg vials: Using the transfer device provided, the contents of the accompanying 100 mL vial of Sterile Water for Injection, USP should be added to the contents of the 100 mg vial of alteplase powder. Slight foaming upon reconstitution is not unusual; standing undisturbed for several minutes is usually sufficient to allow dissipation of any large bubbles. **No vacuum is present in 100 mg vials.** Please refer to the accompanying instructions for Reconstitution and Administration of the 100 mg vials:

1. Use aseptic technique throughout.
2. Remove the protection flip-caps from 1 vial of alteplase and 1 vial of Sterile Water for Injection, USP.
3. Open the package containing the transfer device by peeling the paper label off the package.
4. Remove the protective cap from one end of the transfer device and keeping the vial of Sterile Water for Injection upright, insert the piercing pin vertically into the centre of the stopper of the vial of Sterile Water for Injection.
5. Remove the protective cap from the other end of the transfer device. **Do not invert the vial of Sterile Water for Injection.**
6. Holding the vial of alteplase upside-down, position it so that the centre of the stopper is directly over the exposed piercing pin of the transfer device.
7. Push the vial of alteplase down so that the piercing pin is inserted through the centre of the alteplase stopper.
8. Invert the 2 vials so that the vial of alteplase is on the bottom (upright) and the vial of Sterile Water for Injection is upside-down, allowing the Sterile Water for Injection to flow down through the transfer device. Allow the entire contents of the vial of Sterile Water for Injection to flow into the alteplase vial (approximately 0.5 mL of Sterile Water for Injection will remain in the diluent vial). Approximately 2 minutes are required for this procedure.
9. Remove the transfer device and the empty Sterile Water for Injection vial from the alteplase vial. Safely discard both the transfer device and the empty diluent vial according to institutional procedures.
10. Swirl gently to dissolve the alteplase powder. **Do not shake.**

Stability and Storage: Lyophilized alteplase is stable up to the expiration date stamped on the vial when stored at controlled temperatures between 2 and 30°C. Protect the lyophilized material during extended storage from excessive exposure to light.

Unused reconstituted alteplase (in the vial) may be stored at 2 to 30°C for up to 8 hours. After that time, any unused portion of the reconstituted material should be discarded. During the period of reconstitution and infusion, protection from light is not necessary.

Supplied: 50 mg: Each vial of sterile, lyophilized powder contains: alteplase 50 mg. Nonmedicinal ingredients: L-arginine, phosphoric acid, polysorbate 80. Phosphoric acid and/or sodium hydroxide may be used prior to lyophilization for pH adjustment. Vials of 50 mg with vacuum present. Boxes of 1 vial of Activase rt-PA 50 mg (29×10^6 IU), and 1 vial of Sterile Water for Injection, USP 50 mL, for preparing a sterile solution of Activase rt-PA.

100 mg: Each vial of sterile, lyophilized powder contains: alteplase 100 mg. Nonmedicinal ingredients: L-arginine, phosphoric acid, polysorbate 80. Phosphoric acid and/or sodium hydroxide may be used prior to lyophilization for pH adjustment. Vials of 100 mg with no vacuum present. Boxes of 1 vial of Activase rt-PA 100 mg (58×10^6 IU) and 1 vial of Sterile Water for Injection, USP 100 mL, and 1 transfer device for preparing a sterile solution of Activase rt-PA.

Biological potency is determined by an in vitro clot lysis assay and is expressed in International Units (58×10^4 IU/mg alteplase).

Reviewed 1997

ACULAR® ℞
Allergan

Ketorolac Tromethamine

Topical Anti-inflammatory

Pharmacology: Ketorolac is a nonsteroidal, anti-inflammatory agent demonstrating analgesic and anti-inflammatory activity. At concentrations of 0.02 to 0.5%, ketorolac solution did not irritate the eyes of rats, dogs and monkeys. Up to 4% concentrations were nonirritating in albino rabbits.

Ketorolac has demonstrated anti-inflammatory activity when applied topically in several animal models of ocular inflammation. The compound significantly inhibited the inflammatory response to silver nitrate-induced cauterization of the corneas of rat eyes at concentrations of 0.25 and 0.5%. Concentrations of ketorolac ranging from 0.02 to 0.5% blocked vascular permeability changes caused by endotoxin-induced uveitis in the eyes of rabbits. Using the same model, ketorolac also blocked endotoxin-induced elevation of aqueous humor PGE2. It prevented the development of increased intraocular pressure induced in rabbits with topically applied arachidonic acid. Ketorolac did not inhibit rabbit lens aldose reductase in vitro.

Applications of a 0.5% ketorolac solution did not delay the healing of experimental corneal wounds in rabbits. This solution did not enhance the spread of experimental ocular infections induced in rabbits with C. albicans, Herpes simplex virus type one, or P. aeruginosa.

Two drops (0.1 mL) of 0.5% ketorolac ophthalmic solution, instilled into the eyes of patients 12 hours and 1 hour prior to cataract extraction, achieved measurable levels in 8 of 9 patients' eyes. The mean ketorolac concentration was 95 ng/mL in the aqueous humor and the range was 40 to 170 ng/mL. The mean concentration of PGE2 was 80 pg/mL in the aqueous humor of eyes receiving vehicle and 28 pg/mL in the eyes receiving 0.5% ketorolac ophthalmic solution.

One drop (0.05 mL) of 0.5% ketorolac ophthalmic solution was instilled into one eye and 1 drop of the vehicle into the other eye t.i.d. for 21 days in 26 healthy subjects. Only 5 of 26 subjects had detectable amounts of ketorolac in their plasma (range 10.7 and 22.5 ng/mL) when tested 15 minutes after the morning dose on day 10.

When ketorolac is given systemically to relieve pain, the average plasma level following chronic systemic treatment was approximately 850 ng/mL.

The recommended daily dose for ophthalmic use topically is from 1/20th to 1/50th of the recommended oral daily dose used to relieve pain.

Ketorolac given systemically does not cause pupil constriction. Results from clinical studies indicate that Acular ophthalmic solution has no significant effect upon intraocular pressure.

Indications: For the prophylaxis and the relief of postoperative ocular inflammation in patients undergoing cataract extraction with or without implantation of an intraocular lens.

Contraindications: In patients who have previously exhibited hypersensitivity to any of the ingredients in the formulation.

The potential for cross-sensitivity to ASA and other nonsteroidal anti-inflammatory drugs exists although it has not been reported. Ketorolac ophthalmic solution therefore should not be used in patients who have previously exhibited sensitivities to these drugs.

Warnings: *Pregnancy:* Ketorolac is not recommended during pregnancy, labor or delivery.

Lactation: Ketorolac is not recommended for treatment of nursing mothers. Secretion of ketorolac in human milk after systemic administration is limited. The milk-to-plasma ratio of ketorolac concentrations ranged between 0.015 and 0.037 in a study of 10 women.

Precautions: General: It is recommended that ketorolac ophthalmic solution be used with caution in patients with known bleeding tendencies or who are receiving other medications which may prolong bleeding time.

Children: Safety and efficacy in children have not been established.

Drug Interactions: There have been no reports in the controlled trials of interactions of ketorolac ophthalmic solution with topical or injectable drugs used pre-, intra-, or postoperatively including antibiotics (e.g., gentamicin, tobramycin, neomycin, polymyxin), sedatives (e.g., diazepam, hydroxyzine, lorazepam, promethazine HCl), miotics, mydriatics, cycloplegics (e.g., acetylcholine, atropine, epinephrine, physostigmine, phenylephrine, timolol maleate), hyaluronidase, local anesthetics (e.g., bupivacaine HCl, cyclopentolate HCl, lidocaine HCl, tetracaine) or corticosteroids.

Carcinogenesis, Mutagenesis and Impairment of Fertility: Long-term studies in mice and rats have shown no evidence of carcinogenicity, teratogenicity or impairment of fertility, with ketorolac. No mutagenic potential of ketorolac was found in the Ames bacterial or the micronucleus test for mutagenicity.

Infection: In common with other anti-inflammatory drugs, ketorolac may mask the usual signs of infection.

Ophthalmology: Blurred and/or diminished vision has been reported with the use of ketorolac and other nonsteroidal anti-inflammatory drugs. If such symptoms develop this drug should be discontinued and an ophthalmologic examination performed. Ophthalmic examination should be carried out at periodic intervals in any patient receiving this drug for an extended period of time.

Adverse Effects: Since other nonsteroidal anti-inflammatory drugs have been known to irritate the eye upon topical application, ketorolac was studied for its ocular irritation potential in animals and man.

In 2 multidose studies in healthy volunteers, 1 drop of 0.5% ketorolac ophthalmic solution was applied 3 times daily for 21 days. Mild to moderate transient ocular burning/stinging was reported.

Most ocular complaints reported in clinical studies could not be distinguished from adverse events caused by the trauma of cataract surgery and the insertion of an intraocular lens.

The most frequent adverse reactions were conjunctivitis (redness, scratchiness, foreign body sensation, 10%) eye pain (pain, ache and burn, 6%), ptosis (5%) and keratitis (corneal edema, 3%). Iritis, corneal lesion, eye disorder, photophobia pupillary disorder, blepharitis and glaucoma were each reported with a prevalence of 2%.

Up to 2 drops (0.1 mL or 0.5 mg) of 0.5% ketorolac ophthalmic solution per eye every 6 to 8 hours have been administered postsurgically.

None of the typical adverse reactions reported with the systemic nonsteroidal anti-inflammatory agents or ketorolac have been observed at the doses used in topical ophthalmic therapy.

Overdose: Symptoms and Treatment: The absence of experience with acute overdosage systemically or topically precludes characterization of sequelae and assessment of antidotal efficacy at this time. If ingested accidentally, drink fluids to dilute.

Dosage: The recommended dose is 1 to 2 drops (0.25 to 0.5 mg) every 6 to 8 hours beginning 24 hours before surgery and continuing for 3 to 4 weeks for prophylaxis and relief of postoperative ocular inflammation.

Information for the Patient: See Blue Section—Information for the Patient "Acular".

Supplied: Multidose Bottles: Each mL contains: ketorolac tromethamine 5 mg. Nonmedicinal ingredients: benzalkonium chloride, edetate disodium, octoxynol 40, purified water, sodium chloride and sodium hydroxide and/or hydrochloric acid to adjust to pH 7.4. White opaque plastic multidose bottles of 5 and 10 mL with a controlled dropper tip.

Unit Dose Vials: Each mL contains: ketorolac tromethamine 5 mg. Nonmedicinal ingredients: purified water, sodium chloride, sodium hydroxide and/or hydrochloric acid to adjust to pH 7.4. Preservative-free. Unit dose vials of 0.4 mL, boxes of 24.

When stored at room temperature (15 to 30°C), has a 24-month expiry date with protection from light.

Reviewed 1998

ACYCLOVIR SODIUM FOR INJECTION ℞
Abbott

Antiviral

Supplied: 500 mg: Each vial of sterile powder contains: acyclovir sodium equivalent to acyclovir 500 mg. Nonmedicinal ingredients: sodium hydroxide (as pH adjuster). Single dose vials of 10 mL, cartons of 5.

1 g: Each vial of sterile powder contains: acyclovir sodium equivalent to acyclovir 1 g. Nonmedicinal ingredients: sodium hydroxide (as pH adjuster). Single dose vials of 20 mL, cartons of 5.

Store between 15 and 25°C.

New Product 1998

ACYCLOVIR SODIUM FOR INJECTION ℞

Novopharm

Antiviral

Pharmacology: Acyclovir, a synthetic acyclic purine nucleoside analog, is a substrate with a high degree of specificity for herpes simplex and varicella-zoster-specified thymidine kinase. Acyclovir is a poor substrate for host cell-specified thymidine kinase. Herpes simplex and varicella-zoster-specified thymidine kinase transform acyclovir to its monophosphate which is then transformed by a number of cellular enzymes to acyclovir diphosphate and acyclovir triphosphate. Acyclovir triphosphate is both an inhibitor of, and a substrate for, herpes virus-specified DNA polymerase. Although the cellular α-DNA polymerase in infected cells may also be inhibited by acyclovir triphosphate, this occurs only at concentrations of acyclovir triphosphate which are higher than those which inhibit the herpes virus-specified DNA polymerase. Acyclovir is selectively converted to its active form in herpes virus-infected cells and is thus preferentially taken up by these cells. Acyclovir has demonstrated a very much lower toxic potential in vitro for normal uninfected cells because: 1) less is taken up; 2) less is converted to the active form; 3) cellular α-DNA polymerase has a lower sensitivity to the action of the active form of the drug. A combination of the thymidine kinase specificity, inhibition of DNA polymerase and premature termination of DNA synthesis results in inhibition of herpesvirus replication. No effect on latent non-replicating virus has been demonstrated. Inhibition of the virus reduces the period of viral shedding, limits the degree of spread and level of pathology, and thereby facilitates healing. During suppression there is no evidence that acyclovir prevents neural migration of the virus. It aborts episodes of recurrent herpes due to inhibition of viral replication following reactivation.

Pharmacokinetics: The pharmacokinetics of acyclovir has been evaluated in 95 patients (9 studies). Results were obtained in adult patients with normal renal function during Phase I/II studies after single doses ranging from 0.5 to 15 mg/kg and after multiple doses ranging from 2.5 to 15 mg/kg every 8 hours. Pharmacokinetics was also determined in pediatric patients with normal renal function ranging in age from 1 to 17 years at doses of 250 mg/m² or 500 mg/m² every 8 hours. In these studies, dose-independent pharmacokinetics is observed in the range of 0.5 to 15 mg/kg. Proportionality between dose and plasma levels is seen after single doses or at steady state after multiple dosing.

Renal excretion of unchanged drug by glomerular filtration and tubular secretion is the major route of acyclovir elimination, accounting for 62 to 91% of the dose administered. The half-life and total body clearance of acyclovir in pediatric patients over 1 year of age is similar to those in adults with normal renal function.

Indications: For the treatment of initial and recurrent mucosal and cutaneous herpes simplex (HSV-1 and HSV-2) infections and varicella zoster (shingles) infections in immunocompromised adults and children. It is also indicated for severe initial episodes of herpes simplex infections in patients who may not be immunocompromised. Use in other herpes group infections is the subject of ongoing study.

The indications are based on the results of a number of double-blind, placebo-controlled studies which examined changes in virus excretion, total healing of lesions, and relief of pain. Because of the wide biological variations inherent in herpes simplex infections, the following summary is presented merely to illustrate the spectrum of responses observed to date. As in the treatment of any infectious disease, the best response may be expected when the therapy is begun at the earliest possible moment.

Herpes Simplex Infections in Immunocompromised Patients: A multicenter trial of acyclovir sodium sterile powder at a dose of 250 mg/m² (acyclovir) every 8 hours infused over 1 hour (750 mg/m²/day) for 7 days was conducted in 98 immunocompromised patients with orofacial, esophageal, genital and other localized infections (52 treated with acyclovir and 46 with placebo). Acyclovir significantly decreased virus excretion, reduced pain, and promoted scabbing and rapid healing of lesions.

Initial Episodes of Herpes Genitalis: A controlled trial was conducted in 28 patients with initial severe episodes of herpes genitalis with an acyclovir dosage of 5 mg/kg, infused over 1 hour, every 8 hours for 5 days (12 patients with acyclovir and 16 with placebo). Significant treatment effects were seen in elimination of virus from lesions and in reduction of healing times.

In a similar study, 15 patients with initial episodes of genital herpes were treated with acyclovir 5 mg/kg, infused over 1 hour, every 8 hours for 5 days and 15 with placebo. Acyclovir decreased the duration of viral excretion, new lesion formation, duration of vesicles and promoted more rapid healing of all lesions.

Varicella Zoster Infections in Immunocompromised Patients: A multicenter trial of acyclovir for injection at a dose of 500 mg/m² every 8 hours for 7 days was conducted in immunocompromised patients with zoster infections (shingles). Ninety-four patients were evaluated (52 patients were treated with acyclovir and 42 with placebo). Acyclovir halted progression of infection as determined by significant reductions in cutaneous dissemination, visceral dissemination, or the proportion of patients deemed treatment failures.

A comparative trial of acyclovir and vidarabine was conducted in 22 severely immunocompromised patients with zoster infections. Acyclovir was shown to be superior to vidarabine as demonstrated by significant differences in the time of new lesion formation, the time to pain reduction, the time to lesion crusting, the time to complete healing, the incidence of fever and the duration of positive viral cultures.

In addition, cutaneous dissemination occurred in none of the 10 acyclovir recipients compared to 5 of the 10 vidarabine recipients who presented with localized dermatomal disease.

Healing Process: Because complete re-epithelialization of herpes-disrupted integument necessitates recruitment of several complex repair mechanisms, the physician should be aware that the disappearance of visible lesions is somewhat variable and will occur later than the cessation of virus excretion.

Diagnosis: Whereas cutaneous lesions associated with herpes simplex and varicella zoster infections are often pathognomonic, Tzanck smears prepared from lesion exudate or scrapings may assist in diagnosis. Positive cultures for herpes simplex virus offer the only absolute means for confirmation of the diagnosis. Appropriate examinations should be performed to rule out other sexually transmitted diseases. The Tzanck smear does not distinguish varicella-zoster from herpes simplex infections.

Contraindications: For patients who have hypersensitivity to the drug.

Warnings: Acyclovir sodium for injection is for slow i.v. infusion only. I.V. infusions must be given over a period of at least 1 hour to reduce the risk of renal tubular damage (see Precautions and Dosage).

In severely immunocompromised patients, the physician should be aware that prolonged or repeated courses of acyclovir may result in selection of resistant viruses associated with infections which may not respond to continued acyclovir therapy. This, however, remains to be clearly established and should be considered as a factor when undertaking therapy. The effect of the use of acyclovir on the natural history of herpes simplex or varicella zoster infection is unknown.

Precautions: Precipitation of acyclovir crystals in renal tubules can occur if maximum solubility (2.5 mg/mL at 37°C in water) is exceeded. This phenomenon is reflected by a rise in serum creatinine and blood urea nitrogen and a decrease in creatinine clearance. With sufficient renal tubular compromise, urine output decreases.

Acute increases in serum creatinine and decreased creatinine clearance have been observed in humans receiving acyclovir sodium for injection who were pooly hydrated; or receiving concomitant nephrotoxic drugs (e.g., amphotericin B and aminoglycoside antibiotics); or had pre-existing renal compromise or damage; or had the dose administered by rapid i.v. injection (less than 10 minutes). Observed alterations in renal function have been transient, in some instances resolving spontaneously without change in acyclovir dosing regimen. In other instances, renal function improved following increased hydration, dosage adjustment, or discontinuation of acyclovir therapy.

Administration of acyclovir by i.v. infusion must be accompanied by adequate hydration. Since maximum urine concentration occurs within the first 2 hours following infusion, particular attention should be given to establishing sufficient urine flow during that period in order to prevent precipitation in renal tubules. Recommended urine output is ≥500 mL/g of drug infused.

When dosage adjustments are required they should be based on estimated creatinine clearance (see Dosage).

Approximately 1% of patients receiving i.v. acyclovir have manifested encephalopathic changes characterized by either lethargy, obtundation, tremors, confusion, hallucinations, agitation, seizures or coma. Acyclovir should be used with caution in those patients who have underlying neurologic abnormalities and those with serious renal, hepatic, or electrolyte abnormalities or significant hypoxia. It should also be used with caution in patients who have manifested prior neurologic reactions to cytotoxic drugs or those receiving concomitant intrathecal methotrexate or interferon.

Lactation: Acyclovir is excreted in human milk. Caution should therefore be exercised when acyclovir is administered to a nursing mother.

Pregnancy: Teratology studies carried out to date in animals have been negative in general. However, in a non-standard test in rats, there were fetal abnormalities such as head and tail anomalies, and maternal toxicity; since such studies are not always predictive of human response, acyclovir should not be used during pregnancy unless the physician feels the potential benefit justifies the risk of possible harm to the fetus. The potential for high concentrations of acyclovir to cause chromosome breaks in vitro should be taken into consideration in making this decision.

No data exist at this time that demonstrate that the use of acyclovir will prevent transmission of herpes simplex infection to other persons.

Consideration should be given to an alternative treatment regimen if after 5 days of treatment there is no expected clinical improvement in the signs and symptoms of the infection.

Strains of herpes simplex virus which are less susceptible to acyclovir have been isolated from herpes lesions and have also emerged during i.v. treatment with acyclovir.

Drug Interactions: Co-administration of probenecid with i.v. acyclovir has been shown to increase the mean half-life and the area under the concentration-time curve. Urinary excretion and renal clearance were correspondingly reduced.

Please refer to the product monographs of zidovudine, cyclosporine, methotrexate sodium, diltiazem HCl, and netilmycin sulfate for other potential drug interactions.

Adverse Effects: The adverse reactions listed below have been observed in controlled and uncontrolled clinical trials in approximately 700 patients who received acyclovir at ~5 mg/kg (250 mg/m²) and approximately 200 patients who received ~10 mg/kg (500 mg/m²).

The most frequent adverse reactions reported during acyclovir administration were inflammation or phlebitis at the injection site in approximately 9% of the patients, and transient elevations of serum creatinine or BUN in 5 to 10% [the higher incidence occurred usually following rapid (less than 10 minutes) i.v. infusion]. Nausea and/or vomiting occurred in approximately 7% of the patients (the majority occurring in nonhospitalized patients who received 10 mg/kg). Itching, rash or hives occurred in approximately 2% of patients. Elevation of transaminases occurred in 1 to 2% of patients.

Approximately 1% of patients receiving i.v. acyclovir have manifested encephalopathic changes characterized by either lethargy, obtundation, tremors, confusion, hallucinations, agitation, seizures or coma (see Precautions).

Adverse reactions which occurred at a frequency of less than 1% and which were probably or possibly related to i.v. acyclovir administration were: anemia, anuria, hematuria, hypotension, edema, anorexia, lightheadedness, thirst, headache, diaphoresis, fever, neutropenia, thrombocytopenia, abnormal urinalysis (characterized by an increase in formed elements in urine sediment) and pain on urination.

Other reactions have been reported with a frequency of less than 1% in patients receiving acyclovir, but a causal relationship between acyclovir and the reaction could not be determined. These include pulmonary edema with cardiac tamponade, abdominal pain, chest pain, thrombocytosis, leukocytosis, neutrophilia, ischemia of digits, hypokalemia, purpura fulminans, pressure on urination, hemoglobinemia and rigors.

Overdose: Symptoms and Treatment: Overdose has been reported following administration of bolus injections, or inappropriately high doses, and in patients whose fluid and electrolyte balance was not properly monitored. This has resulted in elevations in BUN, serum creatinine and subsequent renal failure. Lethargy, convulsions and coma have been reported rarely. Precipitation of acyclovir in renal tubules may occur when the solubility (2.5 mg/mL) in the intratubular fluid is exceeded (see Precautions).

A 6-hour hemodialysis results in a 60% decrease in plasma acyclovir concentration. Data concerning peritoneal dialysis are incomplete but indicate that this method may be significantly less efficient in removing acyclovir from the blood. In the event of acute renal failure and anuria, the patient may benefit from hemodialysis until renal function is restored (see Dosage).

Dosage: Caution: Acyclovir sodium for injection for slow i.v. infusion only, over a period of at least 1 hour.

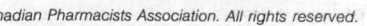

Acyclovir Sodium for Injection (cont'd)

Herpes Simplex Infections: Mucosal and Cutaneous Herpes Simplex (HSV-1 and HSV-2) in Immunocompromised Patients: Adults: 5 mg/kg infused at a constant rate over at least 1 hour, every 8 hours for 7 days in adult patients with normal renal function.

Children: In children under 12 years of age, equivalent plasma concentrations are attained by infusing 250 mg/m² at a constant rate over at least 1 hour, every 8 hours for 7 days.

Severe Initial Clinical Episodes of Herpes Genitalis in Immunocompetent Patients: The same dose given above–administered for 5 days.

Varicella Zoster Infections: Zoster in Immunocompromised Patients: Adults: 10 mg/kg infused at a constant rate over at least 1 hour, every 8 hours for 7 days in adult patients with normal renal function.

Children: In children under 12 years of age, equivalent plasma concentrations are attained by infusing 500 mg/m² at a constant rate over at least 1 hour, every 8 hours for 7 days.

Obese patients should be dosed at 10 mg/kg (Ideal Body Weight).

A maximum dose equivalent to 500 mg/m² every 8 hours should not be exceeded for any patient.

Patients with Acute or Chronic Renal Impairment: Use the recommended doses and method of administration; and adjust the dosing interval as indicated in Table I.

Table I—Acyclovir Sodium for Injection

Dosing Interval

Creatinine Clearance (mL/min/1.73 m²)	Percent of Recommended Dose	Dosing Interval (hours)
>50	100	8
25-50	100	12
10-25*	100	24
0-10*	50	24-48

* Hemodialysis: For patients who require hemodialysis, the mean plasma half-life of acyclovir during dialysis is approximately 5 hours, which results in a 60% decrease in plasma concentrations following a 6-hour dialysis period. Recommended doses should be administered every 24 to 48 hours, and after hemodialysis.

Reconstituted Solutions: The reconstituted and diluted solution should be inspected visually for discoloration, haziness, particulate matter and leakage prior to administration. Discard unused portion.

Solutions for Reconstitution: Sterile Water for Injection. Do not use Bacteriostatic Water for Injection which contains benzyl alcohol or parabens. See Table II.

Table II—Acyclovir Sodium for Injection

Reconstitution Table

Vial Size	Volume to be Added to Vial	Approximate Available Volume	Approximate Average Concentration
500 mg	10 mL	10 mL	50 mg/mL
1 g	20 mL	20 mL	50 mg/mL

Shake well until dissolved. Assure complete dissolution before measuring and transferring dose. For i.v. infusion only. Must be diluted before use. Unused portions of the reconstituted solution should be discarded.

Diluted Solutions for I.V. Infusion: The calculated dose of the reconstituted solution should be removed and added to an appropriate i.v. solution listed below at a volume selected for administration during each 1-hour infusion. **Infusion concentrations exceeding 10 mg/mL are not recommended.**

Since the vials do not contain any preservatives, any unused portion of the reconstituted solution should be discarded.

Solutions for I.V. Infusion: 5% Dextrose Injection, 5% Dextrose and 0.9% Sodium Chloride Injection, 5% Dextrose and 0.2% Sodium Chloride Injection, Ringer's Injection, Normal Saline Injection and Lactated Ringer's Injection.

Stability and Storage of Solution: Reconstituted solutions at a concentration of 50 mg/mL should be used within 24 hours if kept at room temperature. Refrigeration may result in the formation of a precipitate which will redissolve at room temperature.

Once diluted, the admixtures are to be administered within 24 hours of the initial preparation. The admixtures are not to be refrigerated. Unused portions of the diluted solution should be discarded.

Incompatibility: Acyclovir should not be added to biologic or colloidal fluids (e.g., blood products, protein hydrolysates or amino acids, fat emulsions).

Supplied: 500 mg: Each vial contains: acyclovir sodium equivalent to acyclovir 500 mg. Nonmedicinal ingredients: sodium hydroxide to adjust pH. Single use vials of 10 mL, boxes of 5.

1 g: Each vial contains: acyclovir sodium equivalent to acyclovir 1 g. Nonmedicinal ingredients: sodium hydroxide to adjust pH. Single use vials of 20 mL, boxes of 5.

The pH of freshly reconstituted solution is approximately 11. Store between 15 and 25°C.

New Product 1998

ACYCLOVIR SODIUM INJECTION ℞

Faulding

Antiviral

Pharmacology: Acyclovir, a synthetic acyclic purine nucleoside analog, is a substrate with a high degree of specificity for herpes simplex and varicella-zoster-specified thymidine kinase. Acyclovir is a poor substrate for host cell-specified thymidine kinase. Herpes simplex and varicella-zoster-specified thymidine kinase transform acyclovir to its monophosphate which is then transformed by number of cellular enzymes to acyclovir diphosphate and acyclovir triphosphate. Acyclovir triphosphate is both an inhibitor of, and a substrate for, herpes virus-specified DNA polymerase. Although the cellular α-DNA polymerase in infected cells may also be inhibited by acyclovir triphosphate, this occurs only at concentrations of acyclovir triphosphate which are higher than those which inhibit the herpes virus-specified DNA polymerase. Acyclovir is selectively converted to its active form in herpes virus-infected cells and is thus preferentially taken up by these cells. Acyclovir has demonstrated a very much lower toxic potential in vitro for normal uninfected cells because: 1) less is taken up; 2) less is converted to the active form; 3) cellular α-DNA polymerase has a lower sensitivity to the action of the active form of the drug. A combination of the thymidine kinase specificity, inhibition of DNA polymerase and premature termination of DNA synthesis results in inhibition of herpes virus replication. No effect on latent nonreplicating virus has been demonstrated. Inhibition of the virus reduces the period of viral shedding, limits the degree of spread and level of pathology, and thereby facilitates healing. During suppression there is no evidence that acyclovir prevents neural migration of the virus. It aborts episodes of recurrent herpes due to inhibition of viral replication following reactivation.

Pharmacokinetics: The pharmacokinetics of acyclovir has been evaluated in 95 patients (9 studies). Results were obtained in adult patients with normal renal function during Phase I/II studies after single doses ranging from 0.5 to 15 mg/kg and after multiple doses ranging from 2.5 to 15 mg/kg every 8 hours. Pharmacokinetics was also determined in pediatric patients with normal renal function ranging in age from 1 to 17 years at doses of 250 mg/m² or 500 mg/m² every 8 hours. In these studies, dose-independent pharmacokinetics is observed in the range of 0.5 to 15 mg/kg. Proportionality between dose and plasma levels is seen after single doses or at steady state after multiple dosing.

Renal excretion of unchanged drug by glomerular filtration and tubular secretion is the major route of acyclovir elimination, accounting for 62 to 91% of the dose administered. The half-life and total body clearance of acyclovir in pediatric patients over 1 year of age is similar to those in adults with normal renal function.

Indications: For the treatment of initial and recurrent mucosal and cutaneous herpes simplex (HSV-1 and HSV-2) infections and varicella-zoster (shingles) infections in immunocompromised adults and children. It is also indicated for severe initial episodes of herpes simplex infections in patients who may not be immunocompromised. Use in other herpes group infections is the subject of ongoing study.

The indications are based on the results of a number of double-blind, placebo-controlled studies which examined changes in virus excretion, total healing of lesions, and relief of pain. Because of the wide biological variations inherent in herpes simplex infections, the following summary is presented merely to illustrate the spectrum of responses observed to date. As in the treatment of any infectious disease, the best response may be expected when the therapy is begun at the earliest possible moment.

Herpes Simplex Infections in Immunocompromised Patients: A multicentre trial of acyclovir at a dose of 250 mg/m² every 8 hours infused over 1 hour (750 mg/m²/day) for 7 days was conducted in 98 immunocompromised patients with oro-facial, esophageal, genital and other localized infections (52 treated with acyclovir and 46 with placebo). Acyclovir significantly decreased virus excretion, reduced pain, and promoted scabbing and rapid healing of lesions.

Initial Episodes of Herpes Genitalis: A controlled trial was conducted in 28 patients with initial severe episodes of herpes genitalis with an acyclovir dosage of 5 mg/kg, infused over 1 hour, every 8 hours for 5 days (12 patients with acyclovir and 16 with placebo). Significant treatment effects were seen in elimination of virus from lesions and in reduction of healing times.

In a similar study, 15 patients with initial episodes of genital herpes were treated with acyclovir 5 mg/kg, infused over 1 hour, every 8 hours for 5 days and 15 with placebo. Acyclovir decreased the duration of viral excretion, new lesion formation, duration of vesicles and promoted more rapid healing of all lesions.

Varicella-zoster Infections in Immunocompromised Patients: A multicentre trial of acyclovir for injection at a dose of 500 mg/m² every 8 hours for 7 days was conducted in immunocompromised patients with zoster infections (shingles). Ninety-four patients were evaluated (52 patients were treated with acyclovir and 42 with placebo). Acyclovir halted progression of infection as determined by significant reductions in cutaneous dissemination, visceral dissemination, or the proportion of patients deemed treatment failures.

A comparative trial of acyclovir and vidarabine was conducted in 22 severely immunocompromised patients with zoster infections. Acyclovir was shown to be superior to vidarabine as demonstrated by significant differences in the time of new lesion formation, the time to pain reduction, the time to lesion crusting, the time to complete healing, the incidence of fever and the duration of positive viral cultures. In addition, cutaneous dissemination occurred in none of the 10 acyclovir recipients compared to 5 of the 10 vidarabine recipients who presented with localized dermatomal disease.

Healing Process: Because complete re-epithelialization of herpes-disrupted integument necessitates recruitment of several complex repair mechanisms, the physician should be aware that the disappearance of visible lesions is somewhat variable and will occur later than the cessation of virus excretion.

Diagnosis: Whereas cutaneous lesions associated with herpes simplex and varicella-zoster infections are often pathognomonic, Tzanck smears prepared from lesion exudate or scrapings may assist in diagnosis. Positive cultures for herpes simplex virus offer the only absolute means for confirmation of the diagnosis. Appropriate examinations should be performed to rule out other sexually transmitted diseases. The Tzanck smear does not distinguish varicella-zoster from herpes simplex infections.

Contraindications: Patients who have hypersensitivity to the drug.

Warnings: Acyclovir for injection is for slow i.v. infusion only. I.V. infusions must be given over a period of at least 1 hour to reduce the risk of renal tubular damage (see Precautions and Dosage).

In severely immunocompromised patients, the physician should be aware that prolonged or repeated courses of acyclovir may result in selection of resistant viruses associated with infections which may not respond to continued acyclovir therapy. This, however, remains to be clearly established and should be considered as a factor when undertaking therapy. The effect of the use of acyclovir on the natural history of herpes simplex or varicella-zoster infection is unknown.

Precautions: Precipitation of acyclovir crystals in renal tubules can occur if maximum solubility (2.5 mg/mL at 37°C in water) is exceeded. This phenomenon is reflected by a rise in serum creatinine and blood urea nitrogen and a decrease in creatinine clearance. With sufficient renal tubular compromise, urine output decreases.

Acute increases in serum creatinine and decreased creatinine clearance have been observed in humans receiving acyclovir for injection who were poorly hydrated; or receiving concomitant nephrotoxic drugs (e.g., amphotericin B and aminoglycoside antibiotics); or had pre-existing renal compromise or damage; or had the dose administered by rapid i.v. injection (less than 10 minutes). Observed alterations in renal function have been transient, in some instances resolving spontaneously without change in acyclovir dosing regimen. In other instances, renal function improved following increased hydration, dosage adjustment, or discontinuation of acyclovir therapy.

Administration of acyclovir by i.v. infusion must be accompanied by adequate hydration. Since maximum urine concentration occurs within the first 2 hours following infusion, particular attention should be given to establishing sufficient urine flow during that period in order to prevent precipitation in renal tubules. Recommended urine output is ≥500 mL/g of drug infused.

When dosage adjustments are required they should be based on estimated creatinine clearance (see Dosage).

Approximately 1% of patients receiving i.v. acyclovir have manifested encephalopathic changes characterized by either lethargy, obtundation, tremors, confusion, hallucinations, agitation, seizures or coma. Acyclovir should be used with caution in those patients who have underlying neurologic abnormalities and those with serious renal, hepatic, or electrolyte abnormalities or significant hypoxia. It should also be used with caution in patients who have manifested prior neurologic reactions to cytotoxic drugs or those receiving concomitant intrathecal methotrexate or interferon.

Lactation: Acyclovir is excreted in human milk. Caution should therefore be exercised when acyclovir is administered to a nursing mother.

Pregnancy: Teratology studies carried out to date in animals have been negative in general. However, in a nonstandard test in rats, there were fetal abnormalities such as head and tail anomalies, and maternal toxicity; since such studies are not always predictive of human response, acyclovir should not be used during pregnancy unless the physician feels the potential benefit justifies the risk of possible harm to the fetus. The potential for high concentrations of acyclovir to cause chromosome breaks in vitro should be taken into consideration in making this decision.

No data exist at this time that demonstrate that the use of acyclovir will prevent transmission of herpes simplex infection to other persons.

Consideration should be given to an alternative treatment regimen if after 5 days of treatment there is no expected clinical improvement in the signs and symptoms of the infection.

Strains of herpes simplex virus which are less susceptible to acyclovir have been isolated from herpes lesions and have also emerged during i.v. treatment with acyclovir.

Drug Interactions: Coadministration of probenecid with i.v. acyclovir has been shown to increase the mean half-life and the area under the concentration-time curve. Urinary excretion and renal clearance were correspondingly reduced.

Adverse Effects: The adverse reactions listed below have been observed in controlled and uncontrolled clinical trials in approximately 700 patients who received acyclovir at approximately 5 mg/kg (250 mg/m²) and approximately 200 patients who received approximately 10 mg/kg (500 mg/m²).

The most frequent adverse reactions reported during acyclovir administration were inflammation or phlebitis at the injection site in approximately 9% of the patients, and transient elevations of serum creatinine or BUN in 5% to 10% [the higher incidence occurred usually following rapid (less than 10 minutes) i.v. infusion]. Nausea and/or vomiting occurred in approximately 7% of the patients (the majority occurring in nonhospitalized patients who received 10 mg/kg). Itching, rash or hives occurred in approximately 2% of patients. Elevation of transaminases occurred in 1 to 2% of patients.

Approximately 1% of patients receiving i.v. acyclovir have manifested encephalopathic changes characterized by either lethargy, obtundation, tremors, confusion, hallucinations, agitation, seizures or coma (see Precautions).

Adverse reactions which occurred at a frequency of less than 1% and which were probably or possibly related to i.v. acyclovir administration were: anemia, anuria, hematuria, hypotension, edema, anorexia, lightheadedness, thirst, headache, diaphoresis, fever, neutropenia, thrombocytopenia, abnormal urinalysis (characterized by an increase in formed elements in urine sediment) and pain on urination.

Other reactions have been reported with a frequency of less than 1% in patients receiving acyclovir, but a causal relationship between acyclovir and the reaction could not be determined. These include pulmonary edema with cardiac tamponade, abdominal pain, chest pain, thrombocytosis, leukocytosis, neutrophilia, ischemia of digits, hypokalemia, purpura fulminans, pressure on urination, hemoglobinemia and rigors.

Overdose: Symptoms: Overdose has been reported following administration of bolus injections, or inappropriately high doses, and in patients whose fluid and electrolyte balance was not properly monitored. This has resulted in elevations in BUN, serum creatinine and subsequent renal failure. Lethargy, convulsions and coma have been reported rarely. Precipitation of acyclovir in renal tubules may occur when the solubility (2.5 mg/mL) in the intratubular fluid is exceeded (see Precautions).

Treatment: A 6-hour hemodialysis results in a 60% decrease in plasma acyclovir concentration. Data concerning peritoneal dialysis are incomplete but indicate that this method may be significantly less efficient in removing acyclovir from the blood. In the event of acute renal failure and anuria, the patient may benefit from hemodialysis until renal function is restored (see Dosage).

Dosage: Caution: Acyclovir for injection is for slow i.v. infusion only, over a period of at least 1 hour.

Herpes Simplex Infections: Mucosal and Cutaneous Herpes Simplex (HSV-1 and HSV-2) in Immunocompromised Patients: Adults: 5 mg/kg infused at a constant rate over at least 1 hour, every 8 hours for 7 days in adult patients with normal renal function.

Children: In children under 12 years of age, equivalent plasma concentrations are attained by infusing 250 mg/m² at a constant rate over at least 1 hour, every 8 hours for 7 days.

Severe Initial Clinical Episodes of Herpes Genitalis in Immunocompetent Patients: The same dose given above, administered for 5 days.

Varicella-zoster Infections: Zoster in Immunocompromised Patients: Adults: 10 mg/kg infused at a constant rate over at least 1 hour, every 8 hours for 7 days in adult patients with normal renal function.

Children: In children under 12 years of age, equivalent plasma concentrations are attained by infusion 500 mg/m² at a constant rate over at least 1 hour, every 8 hours for 7 days.

Obese patients should be dosed at 10 mg/kg (Ideal Body Weight).

A maximum dose equivalent to 500 mg/m² every 8 hours should not be exceeded for any patient.

Patients with Acute or Chronic Renal Impairment: Use the recommended doses and method of administration, and adjust the dosing interval as indicated in Table I.

Table I—Acyclovir Sodium Injection

Dosing in Function of the Creatinine Clearance

Creatinine Clearance (mL/min/1.73 m²)	Percent of Recommended Dose	Dosing Interval (hours)
>50	100	8
25-50	100	12
10-25*	100	24
0-10*	50	24-48

*Hemodialysis: For patients who require hemodialysis, the mean plasma half-life of acyclovir during dialysis is approximately 5 hours, which results in a 60% decrease in plasma concentrations following a 6-hour dialysis period. Recommended doses should be administered every 24 to 48 hours, and after hemodialysis.

Diluted Solutions for I.V. Infusion: The calculated dose of the solution should be removed and added to an appropriate i.v. solution listed below at a volume selected for administration during each 1-hour infusion. **Infusion concentrations exceeding 10 mg/mL are not recommended.**

Since the vials do not contain any preservatives, any unused portion of the solution should be discarded.

The diluted solution should be inspected visually for discoloration, haziness, particulate matter and leakage prior to administration.

Solutions for I.V. Infusion: 5% Dextrose Injection, 5% Dextrose and 0.9% Sodium Chloride Injection, 5% Dextrose and 0.2% Sodium Chloride Injection, Ringer's Injection, Normal Saline Injection, Lactated Ringer's Injection.

Stability and Storage of Solution: Once diluted, the admixtures are to be administered within 24 hours of the initial preparation. The admixtures are not to be refrigerated.

Unused portions of the diluted solution should be discarded.

Incompatibility: Acyclovir should not be added to biologic or colloidal fluids (e.g., blood products, protein hydrolysates or amino acids, fat emulsions).

Supplied: 500 mg: Each vial of sterile, white crystalline powder contains: acyclovir sodium equivalent to acyclovir 500 mg. Nonmedicinal ingredients: hydrochloric acid or sodium hydroxide to adjust pH. Single use vials of 20 mL, boxes of 1.

1 g: Each vial of sterile, white crystalline powder contains: acyclovir sodium equivalent to acyclovir 1 g. Nonmedicinal ingredients: hydrochloric acid or sodium hydroxide to adjust pH. Single use vials of 40 mL, boxes of 1.

Store between 15 and 25°C. Protect from light.

New Product 1998

ADALAT®

Bayer

Nifedipine

Antianginal

Pharmacology: Nifedipine is a calcium ion influx inhibitor (calcium entry blocker or calcium ion antagonist). The antianginal effect of this group of drugs is believed to be related to its specific cellular action of selectively inhibiting transmembrane influx of calcium ions into cardiac muscle and vascular smooth muscle. The contractile processes of these tissues are dependent upon the movement of extracellular calcium into the cells through specific ion channels. Nifedipine blocks the transmembrane influx of calcium through the slow channel without affecting to any significant degree the transmembrane influx of sodium through the fast channel. This results in a reduction of free calcium ions available within cells of the above tissues. Nifedipine does not alter total serum calcium.

The specific mechanism by which nifedipine relieves angina has not been fully determined, but it is believed to be brought about largely by its vasodilatory action.

Nifedipine dilates the main coronary arteries and coronary arterioles both in normal and ischemic regions and is a potent inhibitor of coronary artery spasm. This property increases myocardial oxygen delivery and is responsible for the effectiveness of nifedipine in vasospastic angina.

Nifedipine, by its vasodilatory action on peripheral arterioles, reduces the total peripheral vascular resistance. This reduces the workload of the heart and thus reduces the myocardial energy consumption and oxygen requirements and probably accounts for the effectiveness of nifedipine in chronic stable angina.

The negative inotropic effect of nifedipine is usually not of major clinical significance because at therapeutic doses, nifedipine's vasodilatory property evokes a baroreceptor mediated reflex tachycardia which tends to counterbalance this negative inotropic effect.

Although nifedipine causes a slight depression of sinoatrial node function and AV conduction in isolated myocardial preparations, such effects have not been seen in studies in intact animals or in man. In formal electrophysiologic studies, predominantly in patients with normal conduction systems, nifedipine has had no tendency to prolong AV conduction or sinus node recovery time, or to slow sinus rate.

Pharmacokinetics: In man, oral administration of 10 mg ^{14}C-nifedipine resulted in more than 90% absorption of the drug. Radioactivity was detectable in the serum 20 minutes after oral ingestion and peak serum levels were reached in 1 to 2 hours. 70 to 80% of the activity was eliminated via the kidneys and the remainder via the feces.

The bi-exponential analysis of the disappearance of nifedipine in the plasma yields an initial fast half-life ($T_{1/2}\alpha$) of 2.5 to 3 hours and a terminal slow half-life ($Tt_{1/2\beta}$) of 5 hours.

Studies in man, dog, and rat showed that nifedipine is almost completely metabolized in the body. It is transformed into 2 pharmacologically inactive metabolites. The main metabolite is the hydroxycarboxylic acid derivative which represents about 95%. The other is the corresponding lactone, which represents 5%. The acid form is mainly excreted in the urine. Protein binding of circulating nifedipine exceeds 90%.

Nifedipine is metabolized by the cytochrome P450 enzyme system, predominantly via CYP3A4, but also by CYP1A2 and CYP2A6 isoenzymes.

Pharmacokinetic studies in patients with hepatic cirrhosis showed a clinically significant alteration in the kinetics of nifedipine (prolonged elimination half-life and decreased total clearance). In these patients, there is a considerable risk of accumulation (see Precautions).

Compounds found in grapefruit juice inhibit the cytochrome P450 system, especially isoenzyme CYP3A4. In a grapefruit juice-nifedipine interaction study in healthy male volunteers pharmacokinetics of nifedipine showed significant alteration. Following administration of a single dose of nifedipine 10 mg with 250 mL of grapefruit juice, the mean value of nifedipine AUC increased by 34% and the T_{max} increased from 0.8 to 1.2 hours, as compared to water (see Precautions, Interaction With Grapefruit Juice).

Adalat (cont'd)

Indications: For the management of angina resulting from coronary artery spasm.

For the management of chronic stable angina (effort-associated angina) without evidence of vasospasm in patients who remain symptomatic despite adequate doses of beta-blockers and/or organic nitrates, or who cannot tolerate those agents.

Nifedipine may be used in combination with beta-blocking drugs in patients with chronic stable angina. However, information is not sufficient to predict with confidence the effects of concurrent treatment, especially in patients with compromised left ventricular function or cardiac condition abnormalities. When introducing such concomitant therapy, care must be taken to monitor blood pressure closely, since severe hypotension can occur from the combined effects of the drugs (see Warnings).

Contraindications: *Pregnancy* and *Lactation:* In pregnancy, during lactation and in women of childbearing potential. Fetal malformations and adverse effects on pregnancy have been reported in animals.

An increase in the number of fetal mortalities and resorptions occurred after the administration of 30 and 100 mg/kg nifedipine to pregnant mice, rats and rabbits. Fetal malformations occurred after the administration of 30 and 100 mg/kg of nifedipine to pregnant mice and 100 mg/kg to pregnant rats.

In patients with acute myocardial infarction (See Warnings, Patients With Myocardial Infarction).

In patients with cardiovascular shock.

In patients with hypersensitivity to nifedipine.

In patients with severe hypotension.

Warnings: Nifedipine should be used with care in the following conditions:

Excessive Hypotension: Since nifedipine lowers peripheral vascular resistance and blood pressure, it should be used cautiously in patients who are prone to develop hypotension. Occasional patients have had excessive and poorly tolerated hypotension. Syncope has been reported (see Adverse Effects). These responses have usually occurred during initial titration or at the time of subsequent upward dosage adjustment, and may be more likely in patients on concomitant beta-blockers. If excessive hypotension occurs, dosage should be lowered or the drug should be discontinued (see Contraindications).

Severe hypotension and/or increased fluid volume requirements have been reported in patients receiving nifedipine together with a beta-blocking agent who underwent coronary artery bypass surgery using high dose fentanyl anesthesia. The interaction with high dose fentanyl appears to be due to the combination of nifedipine and a beta-blocker, but with the possibility that it may occur with nifedipine alone, with low doses of fentanyl, in other surgical procedures, or with other narcotic analgesics cannot be ruled out. In nifedipine treated patients where surgery using high dose fentanyl anesthesia is contemplated, the physician should be aware of these potential problems and, if the patient's condition permits, sufficient time (at least 36 hours) should be allowed for nifedipine to be washed out of the body prior to surgery.

Patients With Myocardial Infarction: Immediate-release nifedipine should not be used within 1 week after myocardial infarction and not before the patient has stabilized. Randomized, placebo-controlled clinical trials have indicated that nifedipine may increase the risk of reinfarction and worsen survival in patients treated early after myocardial infarction.

Patients With Unstable Angina: Some clinical trials have shown that treatment with immediate-release nifedipine in this setting increases the risk of myocardial infarction and recurrent ischemia.

Hypertension: Immediate-release nifedipine should not be used for the management of essential hypertension.

Acute Reduction of Blood Pressure: Immediate-release nifedipine should not be used for acute reduction of blood pressure. Strokes have occurred when nifedipine was used in this setting.

Increased Angina and/or Myocardial Infarction: Rarely, patients, particularly those who have severe obstructive coronary artery disease, have developed well-documented increased frequency, duration and/or severity of angina or acute myocardial infarction on starting nifedipine or at the time of dosage increase. The mechanism of this effect is not established.

Beta-Blocker Withdrawal: Patients recently withdrawn from beta-blockers may develop a withdrawal syndrome with increased angina, probably related to increased sensitivity to catecholamines. Initiation of nifedipine treatment will not prevent this occurrence and might be expected to exacerbate it by provoking reflex catecholamine release. There have been occasional reports of increased angina in a setting of beta-blocker withdrawal and nifedipine initiation. It is important to taper beta-blockers if possible, rather than stopping them abruptly before beginning nifedipine.

Patients With Heart Failure: There have been isolated reports of severe hypotension and lowering of cardiac output following administration of nifedipine to patients with severe heart failure. Rarely, patients, usually receiving a beta-blocker, have developed heart failure after beginning nifedipine therapy.

In patients with severe aortic stenosis, nifedipine will not produce its usual afterload reducing effects and there is a possibility that an unopposed negative inotropic action of the drug may produce heart failure if the end diastolic pressure is raised.

Caution should therefore be exercised when using nifedipine in patients with these conditions.

Precautions: Hypotension: Because nifedipine is an arterial and arteriolar vasodilator, hypotension, and a compensatory increase in heart rate may occur. Thus, blood pressure and heart rate should be monitored carefully during nifedipine therapy. Close observation is especially recommended for patients who are prone to develop hypotension, those with a history of cerebrovascular insufficiency, and those who are taking medications that are known to lower blood pressure (see Warnings).

Peripheral Edema: Mild to moderate peripheral edema, typically associated with arterial vasodilation and not due to left ventricular dysfunction, has been reported to occur in patients treated with nifedipine (see Adverse Effects). This edema occurs primarily in the lower extremities and usually responds to diuretic therapy. With patients whose angina is complicated by congestive heart failure, care should be taken to differentiate this peripheral edema from the effects of increasing left ventricular dysfunction.

Geriatrics: Nifedipine should be administered cautiously to elderly patients, especially to those with a history of hypotension or cerebral vascular insufficiency (see Dosage).

Diabetic Patients: The use of nifedipine in diabetic patients may require adjustment of their control.

Patients With Impaired Liver Function: Use with caution in patients with impaired liver function (see Pharmacology). A dose reduction, particularly in severe cases, may be required. Close monitoring of response and metabolic effect should apply.

Interaction With Grapefruit Juice: Published data indicate that through inhibition of cytochrome P450, flavonoids present in the grapefruit juice can increase plasma levels and augment pharmacodynamic effects of some dihydropyridine calcium channel blockers, including nifedipine (see Pharmacology, Pharmacokinetics). Therefore, consumption of grapefruit juice prior to or during treatment with nifedipine should be avoided.

Drug Interactions: As with all drugs, care should be exercised when treating patients with multiple medications. Dihydropyridine calcium channel blockers undergo biotransformation by the cytochrome P450 system, mainly via the CYP3A4 isoenzyme. Coadministration of nifedipine with other drugs which follow the same route of biotransformation may result in altered bioavailability. Dosages of similarly metabolized drugs, particularly those of low therapeutic ratio, and especially in patients with renal and/or hepatic impairment, may require adjustment when starting or stopping concomitantly administered nifedipine to maintain optimum therapeutic blood levels.

Drugs known to be inhibitors of the cytochrome P450 system include: azole antifungals, cimetidine, cyclosporine, erythromycin, quinidine, terfenadine and warfarin.

Drugs known to be inducers of the cytochrome P450 system include: phenobarbital, phenytoin and rifampin.

Drugs known to be biotransformed via P450 include: benzodiazepines, flecainide, theophylline, imipramine and propafenone.

The antihypertensive effect of beta-blockers may be augmented by nifedipine's reduction of peripheral vascular resistance. The concomitant administration of nifedipine with beta-adrenergic blocking drugs warrants caution and careful monitoring of the blood pressure and pulmonary signs and symptoms of congestive failure (see Warnings).

Long-acting Nitrates: Nifedipine may be safely coadministered with nitrates but there have been no controlled studies to evaluate the antianginal effectiveness of this combination.

Antihypertensives: Nifedipine may potentiate the effects of hypotensive agents.

Concomitant use of nifedipine with short-acting nitrates, furosemide and anticoagulants has shown no interaction or unusual toxic effects.

Administration of nifedipine with digoxin may lead to reduced digoxin clearance, and therefore, an increase in the plasma digoxin level. It is recommended that digoxin levels be monitored when initiating, adjusting and discontinuing nifedipine to avoid possible under- or over-dosing with digitalis.

The addition of nifedipine to a stable quinidine regimen may reduce the quinidine concentration by 50%; an enhanced response to nifedipine may also occur. The addition of quinidine to a stable nifedipine regimen may result in elevated nifedipine concentrations and a reduced response to quinidine. Some patients have experienced elevated quinidine levels when nifedipine was discontinued. Therefore, patients receiving concomitant therapy of nifedipine and quinidine, or those who had their nifedipine discontinued while still receiving quinidine, should be closely monitored, including determination of plasma levels of quinidine. Consideration should be given to dosage adjustment.

Pharmacokinetic studies have shown that concurrent administration of cimetidine or ranitidine with nifedipine results in significant increases in nifedipine plasma levels (approximately 80% with cimetidine and 70% with ranitidine). Patients receiving either of these drugs concomitantly with nifedipine should be monitored carefully for the possible exacerbation of effects of nifedipine, such as hypotension. Adjustment of nifedipine dosage may be necessary.

Adverse Effects: A safety analysis from the world literature (controlled and open studies) was carried out in a heterogeneous group of 7 146 patients who were treated with nifedipine. Adverse effects were reported in 27.9% of patients and required discontinuation of treatment in 5.5% of patients.

The most common adverse effects, which generally result from nifedipine's vasodilating effects, were: headache (7.2%); dizziness, lightheadedness and giddiness (6.7%); nausea, vomiting and gastrointestinal distress (6.7%); flushing and heat sensation (5.8%); peripheral edema (3.7%) and hypotension (2.0%).

As a part of the above analysis, a more comprehensive safety evaluation (controlled and open studies) was carried out in 3 074 patients, some of whom were severely ill and were receiving a variety of concomitant drugs, such as beta-blockers, nitrates, antiarrhythmics, cardiac glycosides, diuretics and antiplatelet drugs, etc.

The following adverse effects divided by systems were reported in these 3 074 patients:

Cardiovascular: peripheral edema, fluid retention, swelling (8.3%); flushing, heat sensation (7.4%); hypotension (3.5%); palpitation and increased heart rate (2.6%); syncope (0.4%).

Rarely, and possibly due to tachycardia, nifedipine has been reported to have precipitated an angina pectoris attack.

In addition, more serious events were occasionally observed, not readily distinguishable from the natural history of the disease in these patients. It remains possible, however, that some or many of these events were drug related. These events included myocardial infarction, congestive heart failure or pulmonary edema, and ventricular arrhythmias or conduction disturbances.

CNS: dizziness, lightheadedness, giddiness (11.9%); headache (7.8%); general weakness (6.3%); shakiness, nervousness and jitteriness (1.9%); sleep disturbances (1.1%); blurred vision (0.9%); depression (0.6%).

Gastrointestinal: nausea and vomiting (6.4%); abdominal discomfort and heartburn (2.0%); diarrhea (0.9%); constipation (0.6%).

Musculoskeletal: joint stiffness, muscle pain and cramps (4.3%).

Respiratory Tract: shortness of breath, dyspnea (1.3%); nasal congestion (0.5%).

Others: pruritus, dermatitis, urticaria and rash (1.9%); fever, sweating and chills (1.4%).

Isolated cases of angioedema have been reported. Angioedema may be accompanied by breathing difficulty.

One case of anaphylactic reaction has been reported.

Two cases of hypersensitivity have been reported resulting in an allergic hepatitis which resolved when the drug was discontinued. In 1 case, recurrence was observed on rechallenge.

Nifedipine has been reported to cause, in a small number of patients, gingival hyperplasia similar to that caused by diphenylhydantoin. The lesions usually regressed on discontinuation of nifedipine. However, on occasion, gingivectomy was necessary.

Gynecomastia has been observed rarely in older men on long-term therapy, but has so far always regressed completely on discontinuation of the drug.

Laboratory Tests: Rarely, mild to moderate transient elevations of enzymes, such as alkaline phosphatase, CPK, LDH, AST and ALT have been noted after treatment with nifedipine. These laboratory abnormalities have rarely been associated with clinical symptoms, however, cholestasis with or without jaundice has been reported. Infrequent reversible elevations in BUN and serum creatinine have been reported in patients with pre-existing chronic renal Insufficiency taking nifedipine.

Overdose: Symptoms: There are several well documented cases of nifedipine overdosage. The following symptoms are observed in cases of severe nifedipine intoxication: disturbance of consciousness to the point of coma, a drop in blood pressure, tachycardia/bradycardia, hyperglycemia, metabolic acidosis, hypoxia, cardiogenic shock with pulmonary edema.

Treatment: As far as treatment is concerned, elimination of the active substance and the restoration of stable cardiovascular conditions have priority. After oral ingestion, thorough gastric lavage is indicated, if necessary in combination with irrigation of the small intestine. Hemodialysis serves no purpose, as nifedipine is not dialyzable, but plasmapheresis is advisable (high plasma protein binding, relatively low volume of distribution).

Clinically significant hypotension calls for active cardiovascular support including monitoring of cardiac and respiratory function including elevation of extremities and attention to circulating fluid volume and urine output.

Hypotension as a result of arterial vasodilation can also be treated with calcium (10 mL of 10% calcium gluconate solution administered slowly via i.v. route and repeated if necessary). As a result, the serum calcium can reach the upper normal range to slightly elevated levels. If an insufficient increase in blood pressure is achieved with calcium, vasoconstricting sympathomimetics such as dopamine or norepinephrine are additionally administered as a last resort only in patients without cardiac arrhythmia or ischemic heart disease and when other safer measures have failed. The dosage of these drugs is determined solely by the effect obtained. Additional liquid or volume must be administered with caution because of the danger of overloading the heart.

Bradycardia and/or bradyarrhythmias have been observed in some cases of nifedipine overdosage. Appropriate clinical measures, according to the nature and severity of the symptoms, should be applied.

Dosage: In all cases, dosage should be adjusted to individual patient requirements.

The starting dose is one 10 mg capsule, swallowed whole, 3 times/day. The usual effective dose range is 10 to 20 mg 3 times daily. Some patients, especially those with evidence of coronary artery spasm, respond only to higher doses, more frequent administration, or both. In such patients, doses of 20 to 30 mg 3 or 4 times daily may be effective. A maximum daily dose of 120 mg may be used.

In general, there should be an interval of at least 3 days between increases in dose in order to adequately assess the response to a particular dose level. In hospitalized patients under close observation, the titration phase may proceed more rapidly.

Nifedipine should be administered cautiously to elderly patients and the dosage should be carefully and gradually adjusted depending on patient tolerance and response (see Precautions).

Adalat 5 mg capsules provide for greater flexibility of dose titration, e.g., in elderly patients.

Supplied: 5 mg: Each gelatin capsule contains: nifedipine 5 mg. Nonmedicinal ingredients: gelatin, glycerol, iron oxide yellow, peppermint oil, polyethylene glycol, purified water and titanium dioxide. Bottles of 100.

10 mg: Each gelatin capsule contains: nifedipine 10 mg. Nonmedicinal ingredients: gelatin, glycerol, iron oxide yellow, peppermint oil, polyethylene glycol, purified water and titanium dioxide. Bottles of 500. Blister packs of 120 (12×10 capsules).

Store below 30°C and avoid freezing. Protect from light.

(Shown in Product Recognition Section)

Reviewed 1999

ADALAT® PA 10
ADALAT® PA 20

Bayer

Nifedipine

Antihypertensive

Pharmacology: Nifedipine is a calcium ion influx inhibitor (calcium channel blocker or calcium ion antagonist).

The antihypertensive action of this group of drugs is believed to be related to its specific cellular action of selectively inhibiting transmembrane influx of calcium ions into vascular smooth muscles. The contractile processes of vascular smooth muscle are dependent upon the movement of extracellular calcium into the cells through specific ion channels. Nifedipine selectively inhibits the transmembrane influx of calcium through the slow channel without affecting to any significant degree the transmembrane influx of sodium through the fast channel. This results in a reduction of free calcium ions available within the muscle cells and an inhibition of the contractile processes. Nifedipine does not alter total serum calcium.

The specific mechanisms by which nifedipine reduces blood pressure have not been fully determined but are believed to be brought about largely by its vasodilatory action on peripheral blood vessels, which thereby reduces peripheral vascular resistance.

The negative inotropic effect is usually not of major clinical significance because at therapeutic doses, nifedipine's vasodilatory property evokes a baroreceptor mediated reflex tachycardia which tends to counterbalance this negative inotropic effect. Continued administration of nifedipine to hypertensive patients has shown no significant increase in heart rate.

Although nifedipine causes a slight depression of sinoatrial node function and AV conduction in isolated myocardial preparations, such effects have not been seen in studies in intact animals or in man. In formal electrophysiologic studies, predominantly in patients with normal conduction systems, nifedipine has had no tendency to prolong AV conduction or sinus node recovery time, or to slow sinus rate.

Pharmacokinetics: In man, after oral administration of a single tablet of Adalat PA 20, nifedipine was detected in plasma after about 30 minutes and peak plasma concentrations (approximately 26 ng/mL) were reached in about 4 hours. The subsequent decline in concentrations was slow, with a terminal (absorption) half-life of 10 hours, such that concentrations of 10 to 15 ng/mL were still present after 12 hours. The absorption and disposition data were not dose dependent nor did the pharmacokinetic character of the tablet vary after prolonged administration (2 tablets daily for 7 days).

The absolute bioavailability of nifedipine from Adalat PA 10 or 20 is between 50 and 70%. Administration of Adalat PA with food increases the rate of drug absorption and the extent of drug bioavailability possibly due to an increase in hepatic blood flow as a result of the meal.

Nifedipine is transformed into 2 pharmacologically inactive metabolites. The main metabolite (95%) is the hydroxycarboxylic acid derivative which is mainly excreted in the urine; the other (5%) is the corresponding lactone. Protein binding of circulating nifedipine exceeds 90%.

Nifedipine is metabolized by the cytochrome P450 enzyme system, predominantly via CYP3A4, but also by CYP1A2 and CYP2A6 isoenzymes.

Pharmacokinetic studies in patients with hepatic cirrhosis showed a clinically significant alteration in the kinetics of nifedipine (prolonged elimination half-life and decreased total clearance). In these patients, there is a considerable risk of accumulation (see Precautions).

Compounds found in grapefruit juice inhibit the cytochrome P450 system, especially isoenzyme CYP3A4. In a grapefruit juice-nifedipine interaction study in healthy male volunteers, pharmacokinetics of nifedipine showed significant alteration. Following administration of a single dose of nifedipine 10 mg with 250 mL grapefruit juice, the mean value of nifedipine AUC increased by 34% and the T_{max} increased from 0.8 to 1.2 hours as compared to water (see Precautions, Interaction With Grapefruit Juice).

Indications: In the treatment of essential hypertension. Nifedipine should normally be used in those patients in whom treatment with diuretics or beta-blockers has been ineffective, or has been associated with unacceptable adverse effects.

Nifedipine can be tried as an initial agent in those patients in whom the use of diuretics and/or beta-blockers is contraindicated, or in patients with medical conditions in which these drugs frequently cause serious adverse effects.

Combination of nifedipine with a diuretic or beta-blocker has been found to be compatible, and has shown added antihypertensive effect (see Precautions).

Contraindications: *Pregnancy* and *Lactation:* In pregnancy, during lactation, and in women of childbearing potential. Fetal malformations and adverse effects on pregnancy have been reported in animals.

An increase in the number of fetal mortalities and resorptions occurred after the administration of 30 and 100 mg/kg of nifedipine to pregnant mice, rats and rabbits. Fetal malformations occurred after the administration of 30 and 100 mg/kg nifedipine to pregnant mice and 100 mg/kg to pregnant rats.

Adalat PA 10 or 20 is contraindicated in patients with hypersensitivity to nifedipine.

Nifedipine is contraindicated in patients with cardiovascular shock.

Warnings: Increased Angina and/or Myocardial Infarction: Rarely, patients, particularly those who have severe obstructive coronary artery disease have developed well-documented increased frequency, duration and/or severity of angina or acute myocardial infarction on starting nifedipine or at the time of dosage increase. The mechanism of this effect is not established.

Since there has not been a study of Adalat PA in acute myocardial infarction reported, similar effects of Adalat PA to that of immediate-release nifedipine cannot be excluded. Immediate-release nifedipine is contraindicated in acute myocardial infarction.

Beta-blocker Withdrawal: Patients with angina recently withdrawn from beta-blockers may develop a withdrawal syndrome with increased angina, probably related to increased sensitivity to catecholamines. Initiation of nifedipine treatment will not prevent this occurrence and might be expected to exacerbate it by provoking reflex catecholamine release. There have been occasional reports of increased angina in a setting of beta-blocker withdrawal and initiation of nifedipine. If a beta-blocker has to be discontinued, it must be tapered off gradually rather than stopped abruptly.

Patients with Heart Failure: There have been isolated reports of severe hypotension and a lowering of cardiac output following administration of nifedipine to patients with severe heart failure. Rarely, patients, usually receiving a beta-blocker, have developed heart failure after beginning nifedipine therapy.

In patients with severe aortic stenosis, nifedipine will not produce its usual afterload reducing effects and there is a possibility that an unopposed negative inotropic action of the drug may produce heart failure if the end-diastolic pressure is raised.

Caution should therefore be exercised when using nifedipine in patients with these conditions.

Precautions: Heart Rate: Because nifedipine is an arterial and arteriolar vasodilator, a compensatory increase in heart rate may occur in some patients. Thus, heart rate should be monitored carefully during nifedipine therapy.

Peripheral Edema: Mild to moderate peripheral edema, typically associated with arterial vasodilation and not due to left ventricular dysfunction, has been reported to occur in patients treated with nifedipine (see Adverse Effects). This edema occurs primarily in the lower extremities and usually responds to diuretic therapy. With patients whose hypertension is complicated by congestive heart failure, care should be taken to differentiate this peripheral edema from the effects of increasing left ventricular dysfunction.

Hypotension: Symptomatic hypotension may occasionally occur in hypertensive patients treated with nifedipine. Careful monitoring of blood pressure during the initial administration and titration of the drug is recommended, especially in patients with a history of cerebrovascular insufficiency, and those who are taking medications known to lower blood pressure.

Geriatrics: Nifedipine should be administered cautiously to the elderly since the incidence of adverse reactions reported in these patients is approximately 10% higher than in patients below 65 years of age. The adverse reactions occurring more frequently in this group include syncope, peripheral edema and palpitations (see Dosage).

Diabetic Patients: The use of nifedipine in diabetic patients may require adjustment of their control.

Patients With Impaired Liver Function: Nifedipine should be used with caution in patients with impaired liver function (see Pharmacology). A dose reduction, particularly in severe cases, may be required. Close monitoring of response and metabolic effect should apply.

Interaction With Grapefruit Juice: Published data indicate that through inhibition of cytochrome P450, flavonoids present in the grapefruit juice can increase plasma levels and augment pharmacodynamic effects of some dihydropyridine calcium channel blockers, including nifedipine (see Pharmacology, Pharmacokinetics). Therefore, consumption of grapefruit juice prior to or during treatment with nifedipine should be avoided.

Drug Interactions: As with all drugs, care should be exercised when treating patients with multiple medications. Dihydropyridine calcium channel blockers undergo biotransformation by the cytochrome P450 system, mainly via the CYP3A4 isoenzyme. Coadministration of nifedipine with other drugs which follow the same route of biotransformation may result in

Adalat PA (cont'd)

altered bioavailability. Dosages of similarly metabolized drugs, particularly those of low therapeutic ratio, and especially in patients with renal and/or hepatic impairment, may require adjustment when starting or stopping concomitantly administered nifedipine to maintain optimum therapeutic blood levels.

Drugs known to be inhibitors of the cytochrome P450 system include: azole antifungals, cimetidine, cyclosporine, erythromycin, quinidine, terfenadine and warfarin.

Drugs known to be inducers of the cytochrome P450 system include: phenobarbital, phenytoin and rifampin.

Drugs known to be biotransformed via cytochrome P450 include: benzodiazepines, flecainide, theophylline, imipramine and propafenone.

Nifedipine may potentiate the effects of other agents having antihypertensive activity. The concomitant administration of nifedipine with beta-blockers warrants caution and careful monitoring of blood pressure and pulmonary signs and symptoms of congestive failure (see Warnings).

Concomitant use of nifedipine with short-acting nitrates, furosemide and anticoagulants has shown no interaction or unusual toxic effects. There have been no controlled studies to evaluate the concurrent use of long-acting nitrates and nifedipine.

Administration of nifedipine with digoxin may lead to reduced digoxin clearance, and therefore, an increase in the plasma digoxin level. It is recommended that digoxin levels be monitored when initiating, adjusting and discontinuing nifedipine to avoid possible under- or over-dosing with digitalis.

The addition of nifedipine to a stable quinidine regimen may reduce the quinidine concentration by 50%; an enhanced response to nifedipine may also occur. The addition of quinidine to a stable nifedipine regimen may result in elevated nifedipine concentrations and a reduced response to quinidine. Some patients have experienced elevated quinidine levels when nifedipine was discontinued. Therefore patients receiving concomitant therapy of nifedipine and quinidine, or those who had their nifedipine discontinued while still receiving quinidine, should be closely monitored, including determination of plasma levels of quinidine. Consideration should be given to dosage adjustment.

Pharmacokinetic studies have shown that concurrent administration of cimetidine or ranitidine with nifedipine results in significant increases in nifedipine plasma levels (approximately 80% with cimetidine, and 70% with ranitidine). Patients receiving either of these drugs concomitantly with nifedipine should be monitored carefully for the possible exacerbation of effects of nifedipine, such as hypotension. Adjustment of nifedipine dosage may be necessary.

Adverse Effects: Safety evaluations of controlled and open studies have been carried out for Adalat PA 20.

In 814 hypertensive patients treated with Adalat PA 20, either alone or in combination with other antihypertensive agents, adverse effects were reported in 32.3% of patients and required discontinuation of therapy in 3.8% of patients. The most common adverse effects were: flushing and heat sensation (13.9%), headache (7.9%), peripheral edema (4.7%), tiredness/weakness (4.7%) and dizziness/lightheadedness (4.5%).

The following percentage of adverse effects, divided by system, were reported.

Cardiovascular: flushing, heat sensation or reddening of skin (13.9%); peripheral edema, fluid retention or swelling (4.7%); palpitation or tachycardia (1.2%); hypotension (0.5%); syncope (0.2%).

In patients with angina, rarely, and possibly due to tachycardia, nifedipine has been reported to have precipitated an angina pectoris attack. In addition, more serious events were occasionally observed, not readily distinguishable from the natural history of the disease in these patients. It remains possible, however, that some or many of these events were drug related. These events include myocardial infarction, congestive heart failure or pulmonary edema, and ventricular arrhythmias or conduction disturbances.

CNS: headache (7.9%); tiredness or weakness (4.7%); dizziness, lightheadedness or giddiness (4.5%); shakiness, nervousness or jitteriness (0.6%).

Gastrointestinal: nausea or vomiting (2.2%), abdominal discomfort or heartburn (3.3%), constipation (0.6%).

Musculoskeletal: joint stiffness, muscle pain or cramps (2.2%).

Others: pruritus, dermatitis, urticaria or rash (1.4%); polyuria (1.6%).

The following additional adverse effects have occurred in an incidence of less than 0.5% in clinical trials: insomnia, hypokalemia, numbness/tingling, paresthesia, dry mouth, dyspnea on effort, extrasystole, chest pain, vision disturbance, nightmares, neuralgia, diminished concentration, impotence and decreased libido.

Isolated cases of angioedema have been reported. Angioedema may be accompanied by breathing difficulty.

One case of anaphylactic reaction has been reported.

Two cases of hypersensitivity have been reported following nifedipine administration, resulting in allergic hepatitis, which resolved when the drug was discontinued. In 1 case, recurrence was observed on rechallenge.

In a small number of patients nifedipine has been reported to cause gingival hyperplasia similar to that caused by diphenylhydantoin. The lesions usually regressed on discontinuation of the drug. However, on occasion, gingivectomy was necessary.

Gynecomastia has been observed rarely in older men on long-term therapy, but has so far always regressed completely on discontinuation of the drug.

Laboratory Tests: Rarely, mild to moderate transient elevations of enzymes such as alkaline phosphatase, CPK, LDH, AST and ALT have been noted after treatment with nifedipine. These laboratory abnormalities have rarely been associated with clinical symptoms, however, cholestasis with or without jaundice has been reported. Infrequent reversible elevations in BUN and serum creatinine have been reported in patients with pre-existing chronic renal insufficiency taking nifedipine.

Overdose: Symptoms: There are several well documented cases of nifedipine overdosage. The following symptoms are observed in cases of severe nifedipine intoxication: disturbance of consciousness to the point of coma, a drop in blood pressure, tachycardia/bradycardia, hyperglycemia, metabolic acidosis, hypoxia, cardiogenic shock with pulmonary edema.

Treatment: As far as treatment is concerned, elimination of the active substance and the restoration of stable cardiovascular conditions have priority. After oral ingestion, thorough gastric lavage is indicated, if necessary in combination with irrigation of the small intestine. Particularly in cases of intoxication with slow-release products like Adalat PA, elimination must be as complete as possible, including the small intestine, to prevent the otherwise inevitable subsequent absorption of the active substance. Hemodialysis serves no purpose, as nifedipine is not dialyzable, but plasmapheresis is advisable (high plasma protein binding, relatively low volume of distribution).

Clinically significant hypotension calls for active cardiovascular support including monitoring of cardiac and respiratory function including elevation of extremities and attention to circulating fluid volume and urine output.

Hypotension as a result of arterial vasodilation can also be treated with calcium (10 mL of 10% calcium gluconate solution administered slowly via i.v. route and repeated if necessary). As a result, the serum calcium can reach the upper normal range to slightly elevated levels. If an insufficient increase in blood pressure is achieved with calcium, vasoconstricting sympathomimetics such as dopamine or norepinephrine are additionally administered as a last resort only in patients without cardiac arrhythmia or ischemic heart disease and when other safer measures have failed. The dosage of these drugs is determined solely by the effect obtained. Additional liquid or volume must be administered with caution because of the danger of overloading the heart.

Bradycardia and/or bradyarrhythmias have been observed in some cases of nifedipine overdosage. Appropriate clinical measures, according to the nature and severity of the symptoms, should be applied.

Dosage: Dosage should be individualized depending on patient's tolerance and responsiveness to nifedipine and to concurrent antihypertensive medications (see Indications and Precautions).

The recommended initial dose is 10 to 20 mg twice daily. The usual adult dose is 20 mg twice daily. If required, the dose may be increased to 40 mg twice daily. A maximum daily dose of 80 mg should not be exceeded.

At a given dosage regimen, the full reduction in blood pressure may take at least 3 weeks. Therefore, in order to assess adequately the response to a particular dose level, there should be an interval of at least 3 weeks between increases in dose.

Supplied: 10 mg: Each dusty-rose, round biconvex tablet, marked 10 on one side, contains: nifedipine 10 mg. Nonmedicinal ingredients: hydroxypropyl methylcellulose, polyethylene glycol, iron oxide red, lactose, magnesium stearate, microcrystalline cellulose, polysorbate, starch and titanium dioxide. Blister packs in units of 6 strips of 10.

20 mg: Each dusty-rose, round, biconvex tablet, marked 20 on one side, contains: nifedipine 20 mg. Nonmedicinal ingredients: hydroxypropyl methylcellulose, polyethylene glycol, iron oxide red, lactose, magnesium stearate, microcrystalline cellulose, polysorbate, starch and titanium dioxide. Blister packs in units of 6 strips of 10.

Store below 30°C. Avoid freezing. Protect from light. Broken tablets should not be used.

(Shown in Product Recognition Section)

Reviewed 1999

ADALAT® XL® Ⓟ

Bayer

Nifedipine

Antianginal—Antihypertensive

System Components and Performance: Adalat XL extended release tablets, while similar in appearance to a conventional tablet, nonetheless consist of a semipermeable membrane surrounding an osmotically active drug core. The core itself is divided into 2 layers: an "active" layer containing the drug, and a "push" layer containing pharmacologically inert, but osmotically active components. As water from the gastrointestinal tract enters the tablet, pressure increases in the osmotic layer and "pushes" against the drug layer, forcing drug through the orifice in the active layer.

Drug delivery is essentially constant as long as the osmotic gradient remains constant, and then gradually falls to zero as drug is exhausted from the tablet. Upon swallowing, the biologically inert components of the tablet remain intact during gastrointestinal transit and are eliminated in the feces as an insoluble shell.

Pharmacology: Nifedipine is a calcium ion influx inhibitor (calcium channel blocker or calcium ion antagonist).

The antianginal and antihypertensive actions of nifedipine are believed to be related to a specific cellular action of selectively inhibiting transmembrane influx of calcium ions into cardiac muscle and vascular smooth muscle. The contractile processes of these tissues are dependent upon the movement of extracellular calcium into the cells through specific ion channels. Nifedipine selectively inhibits the transmembrane influx of calcium through the slow channel without affecting, to any significant degree, the transmembrane influx of sodium through the fast channel. This results in a reduction of free calcium ions available within the muscle cells and an inhibition of the contractile processes. Nifedipine does not alter total serum calcium.

The specific mechanisms by which nifedipine relieves angina and reduces blood pressure have not been fully determined but are believed to be brought about largely by its vasodilatory action.

Nifedipine dilates the main coronary arteries and coronary arterioles both in normal and ischemic regions resulting in an increase in blood flow and hence in myocardial oxygen delivery.

Nifedipine by its vasodilatory action on peripheral arterioles, reduces the total peripheral vascular resistance. This reduces the workload of the heart and thus reduces myocardial energy consumption and oxygen requirements which probably accounts for the effectiveness of nifedipine in chronic stable angina.

The mechanism by which nifedipine reduces arterial blood pressure involves peripheral arterial vasodilation and subsequent reduction in peripheral vascular resistance. The increased peripheral vascular resistance that is an underlying cause of hypertension results from an increase in active tension in the vascular smooth muscle. Studies have demonstrated that the increase in active tension reflects an increase in cytosolic free calcium.

The negative inotropic effect of nifedipine is usually not of major clinical significance because at therapeutic doses, nifedipine's vasodilatory property evokes a baroreceptor mediated reflex tachycardia which tends to counterbalance this negative inotropic effect. Continued administration of nifedipine to hypertensive patients has shown no significant increase in heart rate.

Although nifedipine causes a slight depression of sinoatrial node function and AV conduction in isolated myocardial preparations, such effects have not been seen in studies in intact animals or in man. In formal electrophysiologic studies, predominantly in patients with normal conduction systems, nifedipine has had no tendency to prolong AV conduction or sinus node recovery time, or to slow sinus rate.

Pharmacokinetics: Nifedipine is completely absorbed after oral administration. Plasma drug concentrations rise at a gradual, controlled rate exhibiting zero-order absorption kinetics after nifedipine administration and reach a plateau at approximately 6 hours after the first dose. For subsequent doses, relatively constant plasma concentrations at this plateau are maintained with minimal fluctuations over the 24-hour dosing interval. About a 4-fold higher fluctuation index (ratio of peak to trough plasma concentration) was observed with the conventional immediate release Adalat capsule at t.i.d. dosing than with once daily Adalat XL tablets. At steady state the bioavailability of the Adalat XL tablet is 86% relative to Adalat capsules. Administration of the Adalat XL tablet in the presence of food slightly alters the early rate of drug absorption, but does not influence the extent of drug bioavailability. Markedly reduced gastrointestinal retention time over prolonged periods (i.e., short bowel syndrome), however, may influence the pharmacokinetic profile of the drug which could potentially result in lower plasma concentrations. Pharmacokinetics of Adalat XL tablets are linear over the dose range of 30 to 180 mg in that plasma drug concentrations are proportional to dose administered. There was no evidence of dose dumping either in the presence or absence of food.

Nifedipine is extensively metabolized to highly water-soluble, inactive metabolites accounting for 60 to 80% of the dose excreted in the urine. The remainder is excreted in the feces in metabolized form, most likely as a result of biliary excretion. The main metabolite (95%) is the hydroxycarbolic acid derivative, the remaining 5% is the corresponding lactone. Only traces (less that 0.1% of the dose) of unchanged nifedipine can be detected in the urine. Thus, the pharmacokinetics of nifedipine are not significantly influenced by the degree of renal impairment. Patients in hemodialysis or chronic ambulatory peritoneal dialysis have not reported significantly altered pharmacokinetics of nifedipine.

Since hepatic biotransformation is the predominant route for the disposition of nifedipine, the pharmacokinetics may be altered in patients with chronic liver disease. Pharmacokinetic studies in patients with hepatic cirrhosis showed a clinically significant prolongation of elimination half-life and a decrease in total clearance of nifedipine. The degree of serum protein binding of nifedipine is high (92 to 98%). Protein binding may be greatly reduced in patients with renal or hepatic impairment (see Precautions).

Nifedipine is metabolized by the cytochrome P450 enzyme system, predominantly via CYP3A4, but also by CYP1A2 and CYP2A6 isoenzymes.

Compounds found in grapefruit juice inhibit the cytochrome P450 system, especially CYP3A4. In a grapefruit juice-nifedipine interaction study in healthy male volunteers pharmacokinetics of nifedipine showed significant alteration. Following administration of a single dose of nifedipine 10 mg with 250 mL of grapefruit juice, the mean value of nifedipine AUC increased by 34% and the t_{max} increased from 0.8 to 1.2 hours, as compared to water (see Precautions, Interaction With Grapefruit Juice).

Indications: Chronic Stable Angina: In the management of chronic stable angina (effort-associated angina) without evidence of vasospasm in patients who remain symptomatic despite adequate doses of beta-blockers and/or nitrates, or who cannot tolerate these agents.

May be used in combination with beta-blocking drugs in patients with chronic stable angina. However, available information is not sufficient to predict with confidence the effects of concurrent treatment, especially in patients with compromised left ventricular function or cardiac conduction abnormalities. When introducing such concomitant therapy, care must be taken to monitor blood pressure closely, since severe hypotension can occur from the combined effects of the drugs (see Warnings).

Hypertension: In the management of mild to moderate essential hypertension. Should normally be used in those patients in whom treatment with diuretics or beta-blockers has been ineffective, or has been associated with unacceptable adverse effects.

It can be tried as an initial agent in those patients in whom the use of diuretics and/or beta-blockers is contraindicated, or in patients with medical conditions in which these drugs frequently cause serious adverse effects.

Combination of Adalat XL with a diuretic has been found compatible and has shown added antihypertensive effect.

Safety of concurrent use of Adalat XL with other antihypertensive agents has not been established.

Contraindications: *Pregnancy* and *Lactation:* Nifedipine is contraindicated in pregnancy, during lactation, and in women of childbearing potential. Fetal malformations and adverse effects on pregnancy have been reported in animals.

An increase in the number of fetal mortalities and resorptions occurred after the administration of 30 and 100 mg/kg of nifedipine to pregnant mice, rats and rabbits. Fetal malformations occurred after the administration of 30 and 100 mg/kg nifedipine to pregnant mice and 100 mg/kg to pregnant rats.

In patients with hypersensitivity to nifedipine.

In patients with severe hypotension.

Warnings: Excessive Hypotension in Patients with Angina: Since nifedipine lowers peripheral vascular resistance and blood pressure, it should be used cautiously in patients with angina who are prone to develop hypotension and those with a history of cerebrovascular insufficiency. Occasional patients have had excessive and poorly tolerated hypotension. Syncope has been reported (see Adverse Effects). These responses have usually occurred during initial titration or at the time of subsequent upward dosage adjustment, and may be more likely in patients on concomitant beta-blockers. If excessive hypotension occurs, dosage should be lowered or the drug should be discontinued (see Contraindications).

Severe hypotension and/or increased fluid volume requirements have been reported in patients receiving nifedipine, with a beta-blocker, who underwent coronary artery bypass surgery using high dose fentanyl anesthesia. The interaction with high dose fentanyl appears to be due to the combination of nifedipine and a beta-blocker, but the possibility that it may occur with nifedipine alone, with low doses of fentanyl in other surgical procedures, or with other narcotic analgesics cannot be ruled out. In nifedipine-treated patients where surgery using high dose fentanyl anesthesia is contemplated, the physician should be aware of these potential problems and if the patient's condition permits, sufficient time (at least 36 hours), should be allowed for nifedipine to be washed out of the body prior to surgery.

The following information should be taken into account in those patients who are being treated for hypertension as well as angina.

Increased Angina and/or Myocardial Infarction: Rarely, patients, particularly those who have severe obstructive coronary artery disease have developed well-documented increased frequency, duration and/or severity of angina or acute myocardial infarction on starting nifedipine or at the time of dosage increase. The mechanism of the response is not established.

Since there has not been a study of Adalat XL in acute myocardial infarction reported, similar effects of Adalat XL to that of immediate-release nifedipine cannot be excluded. Immediate-release nifedipine is contraindicated in acute myocardial infarction.

Beta-blocker Withdrawal: Patients with angina recently withdrawn from beta-blockers may develop a withdrawal syndrome with increased angina, probably related to increased sensitivity to catecholamines. Initiation of treatment with nifedipine will not prevent this occurrence and might be expected to exacerbate it by provoking reflex catecholamine release. There have been occasional reports of increased angina in a setting of beta-blocker withdrawal and initiation of nifedipine. It is important to taper beta-blockers if possible, rather than stopping them abruptly before beginning nifedipine.

Patients with Heart Failure: There have been isolated reports of severe hypotension and lowering of cardiac output following administration of nifedipine to patients with severe heart failure. Thus, nifedipine should be used cautiously in patients with severe heart failure. Rarely, patients usually receiving a beta-blocker, have developed heart failure after beginning nifedipine therapy.

In patients with severe aortic stenosis, nifedipine will not produce its usual afterload reducing effects and there is a possibility that an unopposed negative inotropic action of the drug may produce heart failure if the end-diastolic pressure is raised. Caution should therefore be exercised when using nifedipine in patients with these conditions.

Patients with Pre-existing Gastrointestinal Narrowing: Since the Adalat XL delivery system contains a nondeformable material, caution should be used when administering it in patients with pre-existing severe gastrointestinal narrowing (pathologic or iatrogenic). There have been rare reports of obstructive symptoms in patients with known strictures in association with the ingestion of Adalat XL tablets.

Precautions: Hypotension/Heart Rate: Because nifedipine is an arterial and arteriolar vasodilator, hypotension and a compensatory increase in heart rate may occur. Thus, blood pressure and heart rate should be monitored carefully during nifedipine therapy. Close monitoring is especially recommended for patients who are prone to develop hypotension, those with a history of cerebrovascular insufficiency, and those who are taking medications that are known to lower blood pressure (see Warnings).

Peripheral Edema: Mild to moderate peripheral edema, typically associated with arterial vasodilation and not due to left ventricular dysfunction, has been reported to occur in patients treated with nifedipine (see Adverse Effects). This edema occurs primarily in the lower extremities and may respond to diuretic therapy. With patients whose angina or hypertension is complicated by congestive heart failure, care should be taken to differentiate this peripheral edema from the effects of increasing left ventricular dysfunction.

Geriatrics: Nifedipine should be administered cautiously to elderly patients, especially to those with a history of hypotension or cerebral vascular insufficiency.

Diabetic Patients: The use of nifedipine in diabetic patients may require adjustment for their control.

Patients With Impaired Liver Function: Nifedipine should be used with caution in patients with impaired liver function (see Pharmacology). A dose reduction, particularly in severe cases, may be required. Close monitoring of response and metabolic effect should apply.

Interaction With Grapefruit Juice: Published data indicate that through inhibition of cytochrome P450, flavonoids present in the grapefruit juice can increase plasma levels and augment pharmacodynamic effects of some dihydropyridine calcium channel blockers, including nifedipine (see Pharmacology). Therefore, the administration of nifedipine with grapefruit juice should be avoided.

Drug Interactions: As with all drugs, care should be exercised when treating patients with multiple medications. Dihydropyridine calcium channel blockers undergo biotransformation by the cytochrome P450 system, mainly via the CYP3A4 isoenzyme. Coadministration of nifedipine with other drugs which follow the same route of biotransformation may result in alter bioavailability. Dosages of similarly metabolized drugs, particularly those of low therapeutic ratio, and especially in patients with renal and/or hepatic impairment, may require adjustment when starting or stopping concomitantly administered nifedipine to maintain optimum therapeutic blood levels.

Drugs known to be inhibitors of the cytochrome P450 system include: azole antifungals, cimetidine, cyclosporine, erythromycin, quinidine, terfenadine and warfarin.

Drugs known to be inducers of the cytochrome P450 system include: phenobarbital, phenytoin and rifampin.

Drugs known to be biotransformed via cytochrome P450 include: benzodiazepines, flecainide, theophylline, imipramine and propafenone.

Beta Adrenergic Blocking Agents: Concomitant administration of nifedipine and beta-blocking agents is usually well tolerated but there have been occasional literature reports suggesting that the combination may increase the likelihood of congestive heart failure, severe hypotension, or exacerbation of angina. Therefore, caution and careful monitoring of patients on concomitant therapy is recommended (see Indications and Warnings).

Long-acting Nitrates: Nifedipine may be safely coadministered with nitrates, but there have been no controlled studies to evaluate the antianginal effectiveness of this combination.

Digoxin: Administration of nifedipine with digoxin may lead to reduced digoxin clearance, and therefore, an increase in the plasma digoxin level. It is recommended that digoxin levels be monitored when initiating, adjusting and discontinuing nifedipine to avoid possible "under-" or "over-" dosing with digitalis.

Coumarin Anticoagulants: There have been rare reports of increased prothrombin time in patients taking coumarin anticoagulants to whom nifedipine was administered. However, the relationship to nifedipine therapy is uncertain.

Quinidine: The addition of nifedipine to a stable quinidine regimen may reduce the quinidine by 50%, an enhanced response to nifedipine may also occur. The addition of quinidine to a stable nifedipine regimen may result in elevated nifedipine concentrations and a reduced response to quinidine. Some patients have experienced elevated quinidine levels when nifedipine was discontinued. Therefore, patients receiving concomitant therapy of nifedipine and quinidine, or those who had their nifedipine discontinued while still receiving quinidine, should be closely monitored, including determination of plasma levels of quinidine. Consideration should be given to dosage adjustment.

Cimetidine and Ranitidine: Pharmacokinetic studies have shown that concurrent administration of cimetidine or ranitidine with nifedipine results in significant increases in nifedipine plasma levels (ca. 80% with cimetidine, and 70% with

Adalat XL (cont'd)

ranitidine). Patients receiving either of these drugs concomitantly with nifedipine should be monitored carefully for the possible exacerbation of effects of nifedipine, such as hypotension. Adjustment of nifedipine dosage may be necessary.
Information for Patients: Adalat XL tablets must be swallowed whole. Patients should be advised to not chew, divide or crush the tablet as this can result in a massive immediate release of the drug. In Adalat XL, the medication is packed within a nonabsorbable shell that has been specially designed to slowly release the drug so the body can absorb it. When this is completed, the empty tablet is eliminated in the stool.

Adverse Effects: Angina: In 257 chronic stable angina patients treated in controlled and long-term open studies, adverse effects were reported in 30% of patients and required discontinuation of therapy in 8.5% of patients.

The most common adverse effects were: edema (10.1%), headache (3.1%) and angina pectoris (3.1%).

The following adverse effects were also reported. Incidences greater than 1% are given in parenthesis: Cardiovascular: palpitation (2.3%), tachycardia, myocardial infarction, ventricular arrhythmia, extrasystoles, dyspnea, chest pain.

In patients with angina, rarely, and possibly due to tachycardia, nifedipine has been reported to have precipitated an angina pectoris attack. In addition, more serious events were occasionally observed, not readily distinguishable from the natural history of the disease in these patients. It remains possible, however, that some or many of these events were drug related. These events include myocardial infarction, congestive heart failure or pulmonary edema, and ventricular arrhythmias or conduction disturbances.
CNS: dizziness (2.3%), hypoesthesia (1.2%), confusion, insomnia, somnolence, nervousness, asthenia, hyperkinesia.
Gastrointestinal: constipation (1.9%), dyspepsia (1.2%), abdominal pain (1.2%), diarrhea, nausea, melena.
Genitourinary: impotence, hematuria, polyuria, dysuria.
Musculoskeletal: leg cramps, paresthesia, myalgia, arthralgia.
Dermatologic: rash, pruritus.
Other: fatigue (1.2%), pain, periorbital edema.
Hypertension: In 661 hypertensive patients treated in controlled trials with nifedipine, adverse effects were reported in 54% of patients and required discontinuation of therapy in 11.9% of patients. The majority of adverse effects reported occurred within the first 3 months of therapy.

The most common adverse effects reported were edema, which was dose related and ranged in frequency from approximately 10 to 30% in the 30 to 120 mg dose range, headache (16.6%), fatigue (6.2%), dizziness (4.4%), constipation (3.5%) and nausea (3.5%).

The following adverse effects were also reported. Incidences greater than 1% are given in parenthesis: Cardiovascular: flushing (2.4%), palpitation (2.3%), tachycardia (1.2%), chest pain (1.1%), ventricular arrhythmia, hypotension, syncope.
CNS: insomnia (1.8%), nervousness (1.8%), somnolence (1.5%), depression, tremor, decreased libido, migraine, vertigo, amnesia, anxiety, impaired concentration, twitching, ataxia, hypertonia, paresthesia, hypoesthesia.
Gastrointestinal: dyspepsia (1.5%), flatulence (1.5%), abdominal pain (1.4%), dry mouth (1.1%), diarrhea, vomiting, thirst, melena, eructation, weight increase.
Genitourinary: impotence (1.5%), polyuria (1.5%), dysuria, nocturia, oliguria, urinary incontinence, urinary frequency, menstrual disorder.
Musculoskeletal: arthralgia, back pain, myalgia.
Special Senses: abnormal vision, abnormal lacrimation, taste disturbance, conjunctivitis, tinnitus.
Dermatologic: rash (2.3%), pruritus (1.1%), erythematous rash, alopecia.
Respiratory: dyspnea (1.7%), bronchospasm, pharyngitis, upper respiratory tract infection, epistaxis.
Other: leg cramps (2.7%), pain (2.7%), asthenia (2.0%), face edema, gout, allergy, fever, breast pain.

An open, nonrandomized postmarketing surveillance study (EXACT), involving 1 700 mild to moderate hypertensive patients, was conducted in the offices of general practitioners across Canada. Patients were enrolled in the study if they had been previously treated with either single or dual antihypertensive therapy and the physician considered Adalat XL an appropriate monotherapy. Patients were to be started on Adalat XL 30 mg. If after 3 or 6 weeks of therapy with Adalat XL 30 mg, blood pressure was uncontrolled (i.e., sitting diastolic blood pressure was >95 mm Hg), then the patient was given 60 mg Adalat XL at the physician's discretion. Twelve patients were started immediately on Adalat XL 60 mg. Patients were followed for 20 weeks. Adverse events were reported in 605/1 700 patients (35.6%). These adverse events were typical of those seen with the dihydropyridine class of calcium channel blockers (edema, headache, dizziness) and are related to the vasodilatory properties of this class of compounds.

The following is a summary of adverse effects which occurred with a frequency of ≥1% during this 20-week study. See Table I.

Table I—Adalat XL

Adverse Effects

Adverse Effect	All Patients (n=1 700) %	(n)
Patients with ≥1 Adverse Effect	35.6	(605)
Headache	12.2	(207)
Peripheral Edema	8.1	(137)
Dizziness	2.9	(50)
Asthenia	2.8	(48)
Vasodilatation	2.5	(43)
Constipation	2.4	(40)
Palpitations	1.7	(29)
Nausea	1.5	(26)
Anxiety	1.2	(20)
Dyspepsia	1.1	(18)
Insomnia	1.1	(18)
Tachycardia	1.0	(17)

Table II illustrates the time period during which the adverse effects in the preceding table occurred. The majority of the adverse effects occurred during the first 3 weeks that the patients received Adalat XL. The incidence rate of adverse effects continued to diminish as the length of exposure to Adalat XL increased.

Table II—Adalat XL

Adverse Effects Occurring During Each Time Period

Adverse Events	Unknown n	(%)	0-3 Weeks n	(%)	3-6 Weeks n	(%)	6-12 Weeks n	(%)	12-20 Weeks n	(%)
Headache	7	(0.7)	148	(13.8)	41	(3.8)	22	(2.1)	6	(0.6)
Peripheral Edema	2	(0.2)	56	(5.2)	42	(3.9)	33	(3.1)	18	(1.7)
Dizziness	2	(0.2)	27	(2.5)	11	(1.0)	7	(0.7)	4	(0.4)
Asthenia	2	(0.2)	23	(2.1)	15	(1.4)	9	(0.8)	0	(0)
Vasodilatation	2	(0.2)	27	(2.5)	5	(0.5)	4	(0.4)	6	(0.6)
Constipation	0	(0)	25	(2.3)	8	(0.7)	5	(0.5)	3	(0.3)
Palpitations	1	(0.1)	17	(1.6)	6	(0.6)	2	(0.2)	4	(0.4)
Nausea	0	(0)	21	(2.0)	4	(0.4)	2	(0.2)	0	(0)
Anxiety	2	(0.2)	5	(0.5)	6	(0.6)	2	(0.2)	6	(0.6)
Dyspepsia	1	(0.1)	5	(0.5)	5	(0.5)	5	(0.5)	2	(0.2)
Insomnia	1	(0.1)	6	(0.6)	3	(0.3)	3	(0.3)	6	(0.6)
Tachycardia	1	(0.1)	5	(0.5)	3	(0.3)	6	(0.6)	3	(0.3)

The following adverse events have been reported with nifedipine rarely.

Rare instances of allergic hepatitis, cholestasis with, or without jaundice have been reported in patients treated with nifedipine.

Gingival hyperplasia similar to that caused by phenytoin has been reported in patients treated with nifedipine. The lesions usually regressed on discontinuation of the drug. However on occasion, gingivectomy was necessary.

Gynecomastia has been observed rarely in older men on long-term therapy, but has so far always regressed completely on discontinuation of the drug.

Isolated cases of angioedema have been reported. Angioedema may be accompanied by breathing difficulty. Anaphylaxis has been reported rarely.

In postmarketing experience, there have been rare reports of exfoliative dermatitis and Stevens-Johnson syndrome. Gastrointestinal irritation and gastrointestinal bleeding were also reported; however, the causal relationship is uncertain.
Laboratory Tests: Rare, usually transient, but occasionally significant elevations of enzymes such as CPK, AST and ALT have been noted. The relationship to drug therapy is uncertain in most cases, but probable in some. These laboratory abnormalities have rarely been associated with clinical symptoms, however, cholestasis with or without jaundice has been reported.

An increase (5.4%) in mean alkaline phosphatase was noted in patients treated with nifedipine. This was an isolated finding not associated with clinical symptoms and rarely resulted in values which exceeded the upper limit of the normal range.

Serum potassium was unchanged in patients receiving nifedipine in the absence of concomitant diuretic therapy, and slightly decreased in patients receiving concomitant diuretics.

Nifedipine decreases platelet aggregation in vitro. Limited clinical studies have demonstrated a moderate but statistically significant decrease in platelet aggregation and increase in bleeding time in some nifedipine treated patients. This is thought to be a function of inhibition of calcium transport across the platelet membrane. No clinical significance for these findings has been demonstrated.

Positive direct Coombs' tests, with or without associated hemolytic anemia, have been reported but a causal relationship between nifedipine administration and positivity of this laboratory test, including hemolysis, could not be determined.

Rare reversible elevations in BUN and serum creatinine have been reported in patients with pre-existing chronic renal insufficiency. The relationship to therapy with nifedipine is uncertain in most cases, but probable in some.

Overdose: Symptoms: There are several well documented cases of nifedipine overdosage. The following symptoms are observed in cases of severe nifedipine intoxication: disturbance of consciousness to the point of coma, a drop in blood pressure, tachycardia/bradycardia, hyperglycemia, metabolic acidosis, hypoxia, cardiogenic shock with pulmonary edema.

Treatment: As far as treatment is concerned, elimination of the active substance and the restoration of stable cardiovascular conditions have priority. After oral ingestion, thorough gastric lavage is indicated, if necessary in combination with irrigation of the small intestine. Particularly in cases of intoxication with slow-release products like Adalat XL, elimination must be as complete as possible including the small intestine to prevent the otherwise inevitable subsequent absorption of the active substance. Hemodialysis serves no purpose, as nifedipine is not dialyzable, but plasmapheresis is advisable (high plasma protein binding, relatively low volume of distribution).

Clinically significant hypotension calls for active cardiovascular support including monitoring of cardiac and respiratory function including elevation of extremities and attention to circulating fluid volume and urine output.

Hypotension as a result of arterial vasodilation can also be treated with calcium (10 mL of 10% calcium gluconate solution administered slowly via i.v. route and repeated if necessary). As a result, the serum calcium can reach the upper normal range to slightly elevated levels. If an insufficient increase in blood pressure is achieved with calcium, vasoconstricting sympathomimetics such as dopamine or norepinephrine are additionally administered as a last resort only in patients without cardiac arrhythmia or ischemic heart disease and when other safer measures have failed. The dosage of these drugs is determined solely by the effect obtained. Additional liquid or volume must be administered with caution because of the danger of overloading the heart.

Bradycardia and/or bradyarrhythmias have been observed in some cases of nifedipine overdosage. Appropriate clinical measures, according to the nature and severity of the symptoms, should be applied.

Dosage: Dosage should be individualized depending on patient tolerance and response.

Adalat XL tablets must be swallowed whole and should not be bitten or divided.

In general, titration steps should proceed over a 7 to 14 day period so that the physician can assess the response to each dose level before proceeding to higher doses. Since steady-state plasma levels are achieved on the second day of dosing, if symptoms so warrant, titration may proceed more rapidly provided that the patient is closely monitored.
Angina: Therapy should normally be initiated with 30 mg once daily. Experience with doses greater than 90 mg daily in patients with angina is limited; therefore, doses greater than 90 mg daily are not recommended.

Angina patients controlled on Adalat capsules alone or in combination with beta-blockers may be safely switched to

Adalat XL tablets at the nearest equivalent daily dose. Subsequent titration to higher or lower doses may be necessary and should be initiated as clinically warranted.
Hypertension: Therapy should normally be initiated with 30 mg once daily. Some patients, such as the elderly, may benefit from initiation of therapy at 20 mg once daily. The usual maintenance dose is 30 to 60 mg once daily. Doses greater than 90 mg are not recommended.

Patients switched from Adalat PA 10 or 20 to Adalat XL therapy should receive an initial dosage of Adalat XL no higher than 30 mg once daily, based on previously prescribed dosing regimen. If clinically warranted, the dosage of Adalat XL should be increased to 60 mg once daily. Blood pressure and patient symptoms should be monitored closely following the switch from Adalat PA to Adalat XL.

No "rebound effect" has been observed upon discontinuation of Adalat XL. However, if discontinuation of nifedipine is necessary, sound clinical practice suggests that the dosage should be decreased gradually under close physician supervision.

Supplied: 20 mg: Each dusty rose, extended-release tablet, imprinted with "ADALAT 20" on one side, contains: nifedipine 20 mg. Nonmedicinal ingredients: cellulose acetate, hydroxypropylcellulose, hydroxypropyl methylcellulose, magnesium stearate, Opadry OY-S-24914, polyethylene glycol, polyethylene oxide, red ferric oxide, sodium chloride and titanium dioxide. Bottles of 100 and 500.

30 mg: Each dusty rose, extended-release tablet, imprinted with "ADALAT 30" on one side, contains: nifedipine 30 mg. Nonmedicinal ingredients: cellulose acetate, hydroxypropylcellulose, hydroxypropyl methylcellulose, magnesium stearate, pharmaceutical shellac, polyethylene glycol, polyethylene oxide, red ferric oxide, sodium chloride, synthetic black iron oxide and titanium dioxide. Lactose-free. Bottles of 100 and 500.

60 mg: Each dusty rose, extended-release tablet, imprinted with "ADALAT 60" on one side, contains: nifedipine 60 mg. Nonmedicinal ingredients: cellulose acetate, hydroxypropylcellulose, hydroxypropyl methylcellulose, magnesium stearate, pharmaceutical shellac, polyethylene glycol, polyethylene oxide, red ferric oxide, sodium chloride, synthetic black iron oxide and titanium dioxide. Lactose-free. Bottles of 100.

Store between 15 and 30°C. Protect from light, humidity and moisture.

(Shown in Product Recognition Section)

Reviewed 1999

ADASEPT® Preparations
Odan

Triclosan Compound
Acne Therapy

Supplied: Acne Gel: Each bottle contains: triclosan 0.5%, salicyclic acid 2% and sodium thiosulfate 8% in a colorless gel base. Plastic applicator bottles of 50 mL.

Shampoo: Each bottle of dermatological shampoo for oily hair contains: alkyl alcohol sulfate, betaine amphoteric and coconut alkanolamide. Plastic applicator bottles of 250 and 500 mL. Acid pH.

Skin Cleanser: Each bottle contains: triclosan 0.5% in a blend of amphoteric and anionic surfactants and lactic acid. Nonmedicinal ingredients: brilliant green, cocoamide diethanolamine, disodium cococamphodiacetate, Germaben II, PEG methylglucose dioleate, perfume, propylene glycol, purified water and sodium lauryl ether sulfate. Acid pH. Plastic bottles of 250 and 500 mL with dispensing pump applicator.

ADEKs® Pediatric Drops 🅿
ADEKs® Tablets 🅿
Axcan Pharma

Multiple Vitamins—Zinc Sulfate
Multiple Vitamins—Zinc Oxide
Multiple Vitamin—Mineral Supplement

Pharmacology: Deficiencies of one or more of the fat-soluble vitamins may occur in the presence of steatorrhea or other malabsorption, hepatic dysfunction, protein malnutrition, zinc deficiency, and very low fat diets. As with all vitamins, adequate levels are essential to good health and proper growth. Early nutritional intervention in disease such as cystic fibrosis appears crucial to growth and long-term outcome of these patients. Deficiencies lead to a wide variety of pathologies.

Vitamin A is essential for growth and bone development, vision, reproduction and maintenance of the integrity of mucosal and epithelial surfaces. Vitamin A deficiencies may lead to xerophthalmia, epithelial metaplasia of mucous membranes, decreased resistance to infection (characteristic change in epithelium of eye), night blindness and hyperkeratosis of the skin.

Vitamin D is essential for the absorption and utilization of calcium and phosphate and aids in the mobilization of bone calcium and maintenance of serum calcium concentrations.

Vitamin E is considered an essential element of human nutrition. Many of its actions are related to its antioxidant properties. Vitamin E deficiency rarely causes clinical symptoms in adults. In premature neonates, irritability, edema, thrombosis, and hemolytic anemia may be caused by vitamin E deficiency.

Vitamin K is necessary for synthesis in the liver of factor II (prothrombin), factor VII (proconvertin), factor IX (thromboplastin), and factor X. Deficiency of vitamin K or disturbances of liver function lead to deficiencies of these factors, with either latent or manifest hemorrhage. Vitamin K deficiency may occur in patients with biliary obstruction or other conditions limiting absorption of vitamin K such as celiac disease, ulcerative colitis, sprue, regional enteritis, cystic fibrosis, and intestinal resection and in patients receiving drugs that may affect liver function or intestinal flora.

Indications: To provide nutritional supplementation in individuals with malabsorptive conditions. ADEKs uses water-miscible forms of the fat-soluble vitamins to improve absorption in these individuals. It also provides vitamin C, B complex vitamins, and other vitamins plus zinc to supplement dietary intake.

For nutritional supplementation in individuals with deficient diets or difficulty in absorbing fat-soluble vitamins such as may occur in cystic fibrosis. For use solely under medical supervision.

Contraindications: None known.

Precautions: General: Do not exceed recommended dose. Pernicious anemia should be excluded before using this product since folic acid in doses above 0.1 mg daily may mask symptoms.

Pregnancy: Excessive amounts of vitamin A may be hazardous to the embryo or fetus when taken during pregnancy. Women of childbearing potential should consult their physicians regarding total vitamin A intake.

Anticoagulant Therapy: Vitamin K interferes with actions of anticoagulant drugs. Patients taking anticoagulants should consult their physicians before taking ADEKs.

Dosage: Pediatric Drops: 0 months to 1 year: 1 mL daily; 1 to 3 years: 2 mL daily, or as directed by physician. Intended for use solely under medical supervision. Shake well before each use.

Tablets: 4 to 10 years: 1 tablet daily; over 10 years: 2 tablets daily, or as directed by physician.

Tablets must be chewed or crushed thoroughly. Tablets may also be crushed and given with soft foods for children unable to chew tablets.

Supplied: Pediatric Drops: Each mL contains: vitamin A (palmitate) 1 500 IU, vitamin D (cholecalciferol) 400 IU, vitamin E (δ-α-tocopheryl) (vitamin E in water-miscible form as δ-α-tocopheryl polyethylene glycol-1 000 succinate) 40 IU, vitamin K (phytonadione) 0.1 mg, vitamin C (ascorbic acid) 45 mg, thiamine (vitamin B_1) 0.5 mg, riboflavin (vitamin B_2) 0.6 mg, niacinamide 6 mg, vitamin B_6 (pyridoxine HCl) 0.6 mg, vitamin B_{12} (cyanocobalamin) 4 μg, biotin 15 μg, pantothenic acid (δ-pantothenol) 3 mg, zinc (as sulfate) 5 mg and beta carotene (source of vitamin A) 1 mg. Nonmedicinal ingredients: glycerin, natural and artificial flavors, propylene glycol, simethicone emulsion, sodium hydroxide, sodium saccharin and water. Bottles of 60 mL. **Do not use if seal on cap is broken or missing. Keep out of reach of children.** Store in a cool place away from direct light.

Tablets: Each tan tablet contains: vitamin A (palmitate) 4 000 IU, beta carotene (source of vitamin A) 3 mg, vitamin D (cholecalciferol) 400 IU, vitamin E (succinate) 150 IU, vitamin K (phytonadione) 0.15 mg, vitamin C (ascorbic acid) 60 mg, folic acid 0.2 mg, thiamine (vitamin B_1) 1.2 mg, riboflavin (vitamin B_2) 1.3 mg, niacin 10 mg, vitamin B_6 (pyridoxine) 1.5 mg, vitamin B_{12} (cyanocobalamin) 12 μg, biotin 50 μg, pantothenic acid 10 mg and zinc (oxide) 7.5 mg. Nonmedicinal ingredients: dextrose with corn syrup solids, flavor, fructose, glycirrhizic acid, magnesium stearate, silicon dioxide and stearic acid. Contains no dyes or artificial sweeteners. Bottles of 60. Dispense in tight, light-resistant containers.

(Shown in Product Recognition Section)

Reviewed 1997

ADENOCARD® 🅿
Fujisawa

Adenosine
Antiarrhythmic

Pharmacology: Adenosine is an endogenous nucleoside occurring in all cells of the body. When injected i.v. adenosine slows atrioventricular (AV) nodal conduction, can interrupt the reentry pathways through the AV node and can restore normal sinus rhythm in patients with paroxysmal supraventricular tachycardia (PSVT), including PSVT associated with Wolff-Parkinson-White syndrome.

Adenosine is antagonized competitively by methylxanthines such as caffeine and theophylline and potentiated by blockers of nucleoside transport such as dipyridamole. Adenosine is not blocked by atropine.

In controlled clinical trials, cumulative 60% and 92% of patients converted to normal sinus rhythm within 1 minute after 6 mg and 12 mg bolus doses of adenosine, respectively. In other controlled clinical trials with bolus doses of 3, 6, 9 and 12 mg some patients with paroxysmal supraventricular tachycardia converted to normal sinus rhythm on 3 mg of adenosine.

Adenosine is not effective in converting rhythms other than PSVT, such as atrial flutter, atrial fibrillation, or ventricular tachycardia to normal sinus rhythm.

Hemodynamics: Adenosine is a potent vasodilator in most vascular beds, except in renal afferent arterioles and hepatic veins where it produces vasoconstriction. The usual i.v. bolus dose of 6 or 12 mg adenosine has no systemic hemodynamic effects. When larger doses are given by infusion, adenosine decreases blood pressure by decreasing peripheral resistance.

Pharmacokinetics: I.V. administered adenosine is rapidly cleared from the circulation through cellular uptake, mainly by erythrocytes and vascular endothelial cells, with a half-life of less than 10 seconds. Intracellular adenosine is rapidly metabolized either via phosphorylation to adenosine monophosphate by adenosine kinase, or via deamination to inosine by adenosine deaminase in the cytosol. Adenosine monophosphate formed by phosphorylation of adenosine is incorporated into the high-energy phosphate pool. Inosine formed by deamination of adenosine can leave the cell intact or can be metabolized to hypoxanthine, xanthine and ultimately uric acid.

Since neither the kidney nor the liver are required for the metabolism or elimination of adenosine, the activity of adenosine should be unaffected by hepatic or renal insufficiency.

Indications: For the conversion to sinus rhythm of paroxysmal supraventricular tachycardia (PSVT), including that associated with accessory bypass tracts (Wolff-Parkinson-White Syndrome). When clinically advisable, appropriate vagal maneuvers (e.g. Valsalva maneuver) should be attempted prior to adenosine administration.

Adenosine is indicated to aid in the diagnosis of broad or narrow complex supraventricular tachycardia. Although adenosine is not effective in converting atrial flutter, atrial fibrillation or ventricular tachycardia to sinus rhythm, the transient atrioventricular nodal block produced helps diagnosis of atrial activity.

It is essential to ascertain that adenosine actually reaches the systemic circulation (see Dosage).

Adenosine **does not** convert atrial flutter, atrial fibrillation or ventricular tachycardia to normal sinus rhythm.

Adenosine should only be used with appropriate cardiac monitoring.

Contraindications: Second- or third-degree AV block (except in patients with a functioning artificial pacemaker). Sick sinus syndrome (except in patients with a functioning artificial pacemaker). Symptomatic bradycardia (except in patients with a functioning artificial pacemaker). Known hypersensitivity to adenosine.

Warnings: Heart Block: Adenosine exerts its effect by decreasing conduction through the AV node and may produce a short lasting first-, second- or third-degree heart block. In extreme cases, transient asystole may result (one case has been reported in a patient with atrial flutter who was receiving carbamazepine). Appropriate therapy should be instituted as needed. Patients who develop high level block on one dose of adenosine should not be given additional doses. Because of

Adenocard (cont'd)

the very short half-life of adenosine (<10 seconds), these effects are generally self-limiting.

Rarely, ventricular fibrillation/flutter has been reported following adenosine administration, including both resuscitated and fatal events. In most instances, these cases were associated with the concomitant use of digoxin **and, less frequently with digoxin and verapamil.** Adenosine should be used with caution in patients receiving digoxin **or digoxin and verapamil in combination.** Appropriate resuscitative measures should be available.

Patients with atrial fibrillation/flutter and an accessory bypass tract may develop increased conduction down the anomalous pathway.

Arrhythmias at Time of Conversion: At the time of conversion to normal sinus rhythm, a variety of new rhythms may appear on the ECG. They generally last only a few seconds without intervention, and may take the form of premature ventricular contractions, atrial premature contractions, sinus bradycardia, sinus tachycardia, skipped beats, and varying degrees of AV nodal block. These arrhythmias and conduction disturbances were observed in about 55% of patients.

Bronchoconstriction: Adenosine has been administered to a limited number of patients with asthma and serious exacerbation of their symptoms has been reported in some patients. Respiratory compromise has occurred during adenosine infusion in patients with chronic obstructive pulmonary disease (COPD). Therefore, the use of adenosine should be avoided in patients with COPD or asthma.

Adenosine therapy should be discontinued in any patient who develops severe respiratory difficulties.

Precautions: *Pregnancy:* Adenosine is a substance naturally present in the body and therefore no fetal effects would be anticipated. However, since it is not known whether adenosine can cause fetal harm when administered to pregnant women, it should not be used during pregnancy unless potential benefits outweigh the potential risks to the fetus.

Children: The safety and efficacy of adenosine in children have not been established.

Drug Interactions: Cardioactive Drugs: Adenosine has been effectively administered in the presence of other cardioactive drugs, such as quinidine, beta-adrenergic blocking agents, calcium channel blocking agents and angiotensin converting enzyme inhibitors, without any change in the adverse reaction profile. **Digoxin and verapamil use may be rarely associated with ventricular fibrillation when combined with adenosine (see Warnings).** Because of the synergistic depressant effects on the SA and AV nodes, adenosine should be used with caution in the presence of these agents.

Methylxanthines: The effects of adenosine are antagonized by methylxanthines (such as caffeine and theophylline). In the presence of methylxanthines, larger doses of adenosine may be required or adenosine may not be effective.

Dipyridamole: Adenosine effects are potentiated by dipyridamole. Thus, smaller doses of adenosine may be effective in the presence of dipyridamole.

Carbamazepine: Carbamazepine has been reported to increase the degree of heart block produced by other agents. Since the primary effect of adenosine is to decrease conduction through the AV node, higher degrees of heart block may be produced in the presence of carbamazepine.

Adverse Effects: In controlled clinical trials 268 patients received adenosine. One hundred and two patients (38%) experienced one or more adverse events. These adverse events appeared immediately after administration of adenosine and usually lasted less than 1 minute. The most common adverse reactions were: facial flushing (18%), dyspnea (12%), chest pressure (7%) and nausea (3%).

Cardiovascular: facial flushing (18%), headache (2%), sweating, palpitations, chest pain, hypotension (less than 1%). A variety of arrhythmias and conduction disturbances were observed in about 55% of patients at the time of conversion to normal sinus rhythm (see Warnings).

Respiratory: shortness of breath/dyspnea (12%), chest pressure (7%), hyperventilation, head pressure (less than 1%).

CNS: lightheadedness (2%), dizziness, tingling in arms, numbness (1%), apprehension, blurred vision, burning sensation, heaviness in arms, neck and back pain (less than 1%).

Gastrointestinal: nausea (3%), metallic taste, tightness in throat, pressure in groin (less than 1%).

Overdose: Symptoms and Treatment: No cases of overdosage associated with the use of adenosine have been reported. It is unlikely that the true overdosage will occur because adenosine has a short half-life (<10 seconds) and is dosed by a rapid bolus injection. If prolonged adverse events associated with the use of adenosine occur, treatment should be individualized and directed toward the specific event. To date, no patient has required administration of adenosine antagonists such as aminophylline to counteract adverse events associated with the use of adenosine.

In clinical studies on the use of adenosine as a diagnostic agent in imaging, less than 0.1% of the patients exposed to adenosine were described as having severe, prolonged, adverse events. These prolonged adverse events were treated with aminophylline after discontinuation of the adenosine infusion. The usual concentration of aminophylline used was 1.25 mg/mL (125 mg in 100 mL) administered i.v. over 5 to 6 minutes. An additional 1.25 mg/mL (125 mg in 100 mL) can be administered, but clinical experience has demonstrated that this is rarely required.

Dosage: Adenosine should only be used with appropriate cardiac monitoring.

Adenosine should be given as a rapid bolus i.v. injection. To be certain the solution reaches the systemic circulation, it should be administered either directly into a peripheral vein or, if given into an i.v. line, it should be given as close to the patient as possible and followed by a rapid saline flush.

The recommended i.v. doses for adults are as follows: Initial dose: 6 mg administered as a rapid i.v. bolus given over a 1- to 2-second time period.

Additional Doses: If the initial dose does not terminate supraventricular tachycardia within 1 to 2 minutes, 12 mg dose should be given as a rapid i.v. bolus. This 12 mg dose may be repeated a second time if required. Single bolus injections greater than 12 mg are not recommended.

Note: Adenosine injection should be inspected visually for particulate matter and discoloration prior to administration.

The injection should not be refrigerated as crystallization may occur. If crystallization has occurred, dissolve crystals by warming to room temperature. The solution must be clear at the time of use.

Supplied: Each mL of sterile solution for rapid bolus i.v. injection contains: adenosine 3 mg and sodium chloride 9 mg in water for injection. The pH of the solution is between 5.5 and 7.5. Additive-, color- and preservative-free. Single-dose flip-top vials of 2 mL. Prefilled sterile syringes of 2 and 4 mL (with a 22G needle). Any portion of the vial or syringe not used at once should be discarded.

Store at controlled room temperature 15 to 30°C. **Do not refrigerate** as crystallization may occur. If crystallization has occurred, dissolve crystals by warming to room temperature. The solution must be clear at the time of use.

Reviewed 1998

ADRENALIN®
Parke-Davis

Epinephrine HCl
Sympathomimetic

Supplied: Parenteral: Ampuls: Each mL of aqueous solution 1:1 000 contains: epinephrine HCl 1 mg dissolved in isotonic chloride solution. Nonmedicinal ingredients: hydrochloric acid, sodium bisulfite and sodium chloride. Ampuls of 1 mL, boxes of 10.

Vials: Each mL of aqueous solution 1:1 000 contains: epinephrine HCl 1 mg dissolved in isotonic chloride solution. Nonmedicinal ingredients: chlorobutanol, hydrochloric acid, sodium bisulfite and sodium chloride. Vials of 30 mL.

Topical: Each mL of aqueous solution 1:1 000 contains: epinephrine HCl 1 mg dissolved in isotonic chloride solution. Nonmedicinal ingredients: chlorobutanol, hydrochloric acid, sodium bisulfite and sodium chloride. Screw-capped bottles of 30 mL for topical use.

ADRIAMYCIN® Ⓟ
Pharmacia & Upjohn

Doxorubicin HCl
Antineoplastic Agent

Pharmacology: Though not completely elucidated, the mechanism of action of doxorubicin is related to its ability to bind to DNA and inhibit nucleic acid synthesis. Cell culture studies have demonstrated rapid cell penetration and perinucleolar chromatin binding, rapid inhibition of mitotic activity and nucleic acid synthesis, mutagenesis and chromosomal aberrations. Animal studies have shown activity in a wide spectrum of experimental tumors, immunosuppression, carcinogenic properties in rodents, induction of a variety of toxic effects, including delayed and progressive cardiac toxicity, myelosuppression in all species and atrophy of testes in rats and dogs.

Pharmacokinetics: The i.v. administration of normal or radiolabeled doxorubicin for injection is followed by rapid plasma clearance and significant tissue binding. Urinary excretion, as determined by fluorimetric methods, accounts for approximately 4 to 5% of the administered dose in 5 days. Biliary excretion represents the major excretion route, 40 to 50% of the administered dose being recovered in the bile or feces in 7 days. Impairment of liver function results in slower excretion and, consequently, increases retention and accumulation in plasma and tissues. Doxorubicin does not cross the blood brain barrier.

Indications: Doxorubicin has been used successfully both as a single agent and also in combination with other approved cancer chemotherapeutic agents to produce regression in neoplastic conditions such as acute lymphoblastic leukemia, acute myeloblastic leukemia, Wilms' tumor, neuroblastomas, soft tissue sarcomas, bone sarcomas, breast carcinomas, gynecologic carcinomas, testicular carcinomas, bronchogenic carcinoma, Hodgkin's disease, non-Hodgkin's lymphoma, thyroid carcinoma, bladder carcinomas, squamous cell carcinoma of the head and neck, and gastric carcinoma.

Doxorubicin has also been used by instillation into the bladder for the topical treatment of superficial bladder tumors.

A number of other solid tumors have also shown some responsiveness to doxorubicin alone or in combination with other drugs (see Dosage). Studies to date have shown malignant melanoma, kidney carcinoma, large bowel carcinomas, brain tumors and metastases to the CNS not to be significantly responsive to doxorubicin therapy.

Contraindications: Doxorubicin therapy should not be started in patients who have marked myelosuppression induced by previous treatment with other antineoplastic agents or by radiotherapy. Conclusive data are not available on pre-existing heart disease as a cofactor of increased risk of doxorubicin-induced cardiac toxicity. Preliminary data suggest that in such cases cardiac toxicity may occur at doses lower than the recommended cumulative limit. It is therefore not recommended that doxorubicin be started in such cases. Doxorubicin treatment is contraindicated in patients who received previous treatment with complete cumulative doses of doxorubicin and/or other anthracyclines and anthracenes.

Warnings: Doxorubicin is a potent drug and should be used only by physicians experienced with cancer chemotherapeutic drugs (see Precautions). Blood counts and hepatic function tests should be performed regularly. Because of the experience with cardiac toxicity, a total dose of doxorubicin exceeding 550 mg/m² with the 21 day regimen and 700 mg/m² with the weekly regimen is not recommended. Cardiac monitoring is advised in those patients who have received mediastinal radiotherapy, other anthracycline or anthracene therapy, with pre-existing cardiac disease, or who have received prior doxorubicin cumulative doses exceeding 400 mg/m² with the 21 day regimen and 550 mg/m² utilizing the weekly regimen.

Cardiac Toxicity: Special attention must be given to the cardiac toxicity exhibited by doxorubicin. Although uncommon, acute left ventricular failure has occurred, particularly in patients who have received a total dosage of the drug exceeding the currently recommended limit of 550 mg/m² for the 21 day regimen or a higher dose limit on the order of 700 mg/m² for the weekly regimen. This limit appears to be lower (400 mg/m² and 550 mg/m², respectively) in patients who received radiotherapy to the mediastinal area or concomitant therapy with other potentially cardiotoxic agents such as cyclophosphamide. Congestive heart failure and/or cardiomyopathy may occur several weeks after discontinuation of doxorubicin therapy. Children appear to be at particular risk for development of delayed doxorubicin cardiotoxicity in that doxorubicin impairs myocardial growth as they mature, leading to subsequent possible development of congestive heart failure during early adulthood.

Available evidence appears to indicate that cardiotoxicity is cumulative across members of the anthracycline and anthracene class of drugs. Patients who have previously received other anthracyclines and anthracenes are at particular risk for possible cardiotoxic effects of doxorubicin at a lower total dose than previously untreated patients and therefore, should be carefully monitored.

Cardiac failure is often not favorably affected by presently known medical or physical therapy for cardiac support. Early clinical diagnosis of drug induced heart failure appears to be essential for successful treatment with digitalis, diuretics, low salt diet, and bed rest. Reduction of afterload with vasodilating agents appears to be beneficial in refractory doxorubicin induced heart failure. Severe cardiac toxicity may occur precipitously without antecedent ECG changes. Transient ECG changes consisting of T wave flattening, ST depression, and arrhythmias lasting for up to 2 weeks after a dose or course of doxorubicin are presently not considered indications for suspension of doxorubicin therapy. Doxorubicin cardiomyopathy has been reported to be associated with a persistent reduction in the voltage of the QRS wave, a prolongation of the systolic time interval and a reduction of the left ventricular ejection fraction as determined by echocardiography or radionuclide angiography. None of these tests have yet been confirmed to consistently identify those individual patients that are approaching their maximally tolerated cumulative dose of doxorubicin. If test results indicate change in cardiac function associated with doxorubicin, the benefit of continued therapy must be carefully evaluated against the risk of producing irreversible cardiac damage.

Because of the experience with cardiac toxicity, a total dose of doxorubicin exceeding 550 mg/m² with the 21 day regimen and 700 mg/m² with the weekly regimen, is not recommended.

Acute life-threatening arrhythmias have been reported to occur during or within a few hours after doxorubicin administration.

There is a high incidence of bone marrow suppression, primarily of leukocytes, requiring careful hematologic monitoring. With the recommended dosage schedule, leukopenia is usually transient, reaching its nadir 10 to 14 days after treatment with recovery usually occurring by the 21st day. WBC counts as low as 1 000/mm³ are to be expected during treatment with appropriate doses of doxorubicin. Red blood cell and platelet levels should also be monitored since they may also be suppressed. Hematologic toxicity may require dose reduction or suspension or delay of doxorubicin therapy. Persistent severe myelosuppression may result in superinfection or hemorrhage.

Doxorubicin may potentiate the toxicity of other anticancer therapies. Exacerbation of cyclophosphamide induced hemorrhagic cystitis and enhancement of the hepatotoxicity of 6-mercaptopurine have been reported. Radiation induced toxicity to the myocardium, mucosae, skin and liver has been reported to be increased by the administration of doxorubicin.

Toxicity to recommended doses of doxorubicin is enhanced by hepatic impairment, therefore, prior to the individual dosing, evaluation of hepatic function is recommended using conventional clinical laboratory tests such as AST, ALT, alkaline phosphatase and bilirubin (see Dosage).

Necrotizing colitis manifested by typhlitis (cecal inflammation), bloody stools and severe and sometimes fatal infections have been associated with a combination of doxorubicin given by i.v. push daily for 3 days and cytarabine given by continuous infusion daily for 7 or more days.

On i.v. administration of doxorubicin, extravasation may occur with or without accompanying stinging or burning sensation, and even if blood returns well on aspiration of the infusion needle (see Dosage). If any signs or symptoms of extravasation have occurred, the injection or infusion should be immediately terminated and restarted in another vein.

Doxorubicin and related compounds have also been shown to have mutagenic and carcinogenic properties when tested in experimental models.

Doxorubicin may impart a red coloration to the urine for 1 to 2 days after administration and patients should be advised to expect this during active therapy.

Pregnancy: There is no conclusive information about doxorubicin adversely affecting human fertility, or causing teratogenesis; however, doxorubicin is embryotoxic and teratogenic in rats and embryotoxic and abortifacient in rabbits. Therefore, women of childbearing potential should be advised to avoid pregnancy.

If doxorubicin is to be used during pregnancy, or if the patient becomes pregnant during therapy, the patient should be informed of the potential hazard to the fetus.

Lactation: Mothers should be advised not to breast-feed while undergoing chemotherapy with doxorubicin.

Precautions: Initial treatment with doxorubicin requires close observation of the patient and extensive laboratory monitoring. Like other cytotoxic drugs, doxorubicin may induce hyperuricemia secondary to rapid lysis of neoplastic cells, particularly in patients with leukemia. The clinician should monitor the patient's serum chemistry and blood uric acid level and be prepared to use such supportive and pharmacologic measures as might be necessary to control this problem.

Doxorubicin is not an antimicrobial agent.

Adverse Effects: Dose limiting toxicities of therapy are myelosuppression and cardiotoxicity (see Warnings). Other reactions reported are: Cutaneous: Reversible complete alopecia occurs in most cases. Hyperpigmentation of nailbeds and dermal creases, primarily in children, have been reported in a few cases. Recall of skin reaction due to prior radiotherapy has occurred with doxorubicin administration.

Gastrointestinal: Acute nausea and vomiting occurs frequently and may be severe. This may be alleviated by antiemetic therapy. Mucositis (stomatitis and esophagitis) may occur 5 to 10 days after administration. The effect may be severe leading to ulceration and represents a site of origin for severe infections. The dose regimen consisting of administration of doxorubicin on 3 successive days results in the greater incidence and severity of mucositis. Ulceration and necrosis of the colon, especially the cecum, may occur leading to bleeding or severe infections which can be fatal. This reaction has been reported in patients with acute non-lymphocytic leukemia treated with a 3 day course of doxorubicin combined with cytarabine. Anorexia and diarrhea have been occasionally reported.

Vascular: Phlebosclerosis has been reported especially when small veins are used or a single vein is used for repeated administration. Facial flushing may occur if the injection is given too rapidly.

Local: Severe cellulitis, vesication and tissue necrosis will occur if doxorubicin is extravasated during administration. Erythematous streaking along the vein proximal to the site of the injection has been reported (see Dosage).

Bladder, local: Instillation of doxorubicin into the bladder may cause pain, hemorrhage and occasionally decreased bladder capacity.

Hypersensitivity: Fever, chills and urticaria have been reported occasionally. Anaphylaxis may occur. A case of apparent cross sensitivity to lincomycin has been reported.

Hematological: The occurrence of secondary acute myeloid leukemia with or without a preleukemic phase has been reported rarely in patients concurrently treated with doxorubicin in association with DNA-damaging antineoplastic agents. Such cases could have a short (1 to 3 years) latency period.

Other: Conjunctivitis and lacrimation occur rarely.

Overdose: Symptoms: Acute overdosage enhances the toxic effects of mucositis, leukopenia, and thrombocytopenia.

Treatment: Treatment of acute overdosage consists of treatment of the severely myelosuppressed patient with hospitalization, antibiotics, platelet and granulocyte transfusions and symptomatic treatment of mucositis.

Chronic overdosage with cumulative doses exceeding 550 mg/m² increases the risk of cardiomyopathy and resultant congestive heart failure. Treatment consists of vigorous management of congestive heart failure with digitalis preparations and diuretics. The use of peripheral vasodilators has been recommended.

Dosage: Refer to Guidelines for safe preparation and handling. A variety of dose schedules has been used. The following recommendations are for use as a single agent only.

The most commonly used dosage schedule is 60 to 75 mg/m² as a single i.v. injection administered at 21 day intervals. The lower dose should be given to patients with inadequate marrow reserves due to old age, or prior therapy, or neoplastic marrow infiltration. An alternative dose schedule is weekly doses of 20 mg/m² which has been reported to produce a lower incidence of congestive heart failure. Also, 30 mg/m² on each of 3 successive days repeated every 4 weeks has been used. Doxorubicin dosage must be reduced if the bilirubin is elevated as follows: serum bilirubin 1.2 to 3 mg/dL: give half of normal dose; >3 mg/dL: give a fourth of normal dose.

When doxorubicin is instilled intravesically for the treatment of superficial bladder carcinomas, the usual dose employed ranges from 50 to 80 mg in a total volume of 50 to 100 mL of 0.9% sodium chloride injection with a contact time of 1 to 2 hours. Care should be taken to ensure that the tip of the catheter is in the bladder cavity before instilling the doxorubicin solution. Instillation is repeated weekly for 4 weeks and subsequently at monthly intervals. Therapy may continue for 1 year or longer as no significant systematic toxicity has been reported. Care should be exercised in the handling and disposal of the voided urine (see Guidelines for safe preparation and handling). PVC gloves should be worn and the urine should be inactivated by decolorizing it with 10 mL or more of sodium hypochlorite solution (household bleach).

Other methods of administration have been investigated including intra-arterial administration and also continuous or long-term i.v. infusion utilizing appropriate infusion pumps.

Clinical studies support the efficacy of doxorubicin used concurrently with other chemotherapeutic agents. Listed below are tumor types and drugs used concurrently with doxorubicin:

Acute Lymphocytic Leukemia in Adults: doxorubicin with vincristine and prednisone or with cytosine arabinoside, vincristine and prednisone.

Acute Lymphocytic Leukemia in Children: doxorubicin with L-asparaginase, vincristine and prednisone.

Acute Non-lymphocytic Leukemia: doxorubicin with cytosine arabinoside or with cytosine arabinoside, vincristine and prednisone.

Carcinoma of the Breast: doxorubicin with 5-fluorouracil and/or cyclophosphamide or with vincristine with or without cyclophosphamide.

Bronchogenic Carcinoma, Non-small Cell: doxorubicin with cyclophosphamide, methotrexate and procarbazine or with cyclophosphamide and cisplatin.

Bronchogenic carcinoma, small cell: doxorubicin with vincristine or etoposide (VP-16) and cyclophosphamide.

Hodgkin's Disease: doxorubicin with bleomycin, vincristine and dacarbazine.

Non-Hodgkin's Lymphoma: doxorubicin with cyclophosphamide, vincristine and prednisone, or bleomycin, cyclophosphamide, vincristine and prednisone.

Carcinoma of the Ovary: doxorubicin with cisplatin.

Soft tissue sarcoma: doxorubicin with dacarbazine, or with dacarbazine, cyclophosphamide and vincristine.

Carcinoma of the Bladder: doxorubicin with methotrexate, vinblastine and cisplatinum or cisplatinum and cyclophosphamide or with 5-fluorouracil.

Carcinoma of the Stomach: doxorubicin with 5-fluorouracil and mitomycin-C.

Administration: Care in the administration of doxorubicin will reduce the chance of perivenous infiltration. It may also decrease the chance of local reactions such as urticaria and erythematous streaking. On i.v. administration of doxorubicin, extravasation may occur with or without an accompanying stinging or burning sensation and even if blood returns well on aspiration of the infusion needle. If any signs or symptoms of extravasation have occurred, the injection or infusion should be immediately terminated and restarted in another vein.

If it is known or suspected that s.c. extravasation has occurred, the following steps are recommended: attempt aspiration of the infiltrated doxorubicin solution; local intermittent application of ice for up to 3 days; elevation of the affected limb; close observation of the lesion; consultation with a plastic surgeon familiar with drug extravasations if local pain persists or skin changes progress after 3 to 4 days. If ulceration begins, early wide excision of the involved area should be considered.

Adriamycin RDF 10 mg, 50 mg and 150 mg vials should be reconstituted with 5 mL, 25 mL and 75 mL respectively of 0.9% Sodium Chloride Injection to give a final concentration of 2 mg/mL of doxorubicin. Bacteriostatic diluents are not recommended.

After adding the diluent, the vial should be shaken until the contents are dissolved. A slight suspension may form which will completely dissolve on further shaking. The vials are under negative pressure and care should be taken to avoid a pressure build-up. The reconstituted solution is stable for 24 hours at room temperature and 48 hours under refrigeration at 2 to 8°C. The solution should be protected from exposure to direct light. For single dose vials, any unused solution should be discarded.

Doxorubicin should be slowly administered into the tubing of a freely running i.v. infusion of 0.9% Sodium Chloride Injection or 5% Dextrose Injection. The tubing should be attached to a Butterfly needle or other suitable device and inserted preferably into a large vein. If possible, avoid veins over joints or in extremities with compromised venous or lymphatic drainage. The rate of administration is dependent on the size of the vein and the dosage, however, the dosage should be administered in not less than 3 to 5 minutes. Local erythematous streaking along the vein as well as facial flushing may be indicative of too rapid administration.

Unless specific compatibility data are available, the mixing of doxorubicin solutions with other drugs is not recommended. Precipitation occurs with 5-fluorouracil and heparin.

Guidelines for Safe Preparation and Handling: 1. Preparation and Handling: Preparation of antineoplastic solutions should be done in a vertical laminar flow hood (Biological Safety Cabinet—Class II). 2. Personnel preparing doxorubicin solutions should wear PVC gloves, safety glasses and protective clothing such as disposable gowns and masks. If doxorubicin contacts the skin or mucosa, the area should be washed with

Adriamycin (cont'd)

soap and water immediately. 3. Personnel regularly involved in the preparation and handling of antineoplastics should have blood examinations on a regular basis.

Directions for Dispensing from Pharmacy Bulk Vials: The use of pharmacy bulk vials is restricted to hospitals with a recognized i.v. admixture program. The pharmacy bulk vial is intended for single puncture, multiple dispensing and for i.v. use only.

Entry into the vial must be made with a sterile dispensing device such as the Econ-O-Set Sterile Transfer System. Multiple use of a syringe with needle is not recommended since it may cause leakage as well as it may increase the potential for microbial and particulate matter contamination.

Swab the vial stopper with an antiseptic solution. Following carefully the manufacturer's instructions, insert the device into the vial. Withdraw contents of vial into syringes, using aseptic technique. Discard any unused portion within 8 hours of initial entry.

Disposal: 1. Avoid contact with skin and inhalation of airborne particles by use of PVC gloves and disposable gowns and masks.

2. All needles, syringes, vials and other materials which have come in contact with doxorubicin should be segregated in plastic bags, sealed and marked as hazardous waste. Incinerate at 1 000°C or higher. Sealed containers may explode if a tight seal exists.

3. If incineration is not available, doxorubicin may be detoxified by adding sodium hypochlorite solution (household bleach) to the vial, in sufficient quantity to decolorize the doxorubicin, care being taken to vent the vial to avoid a pressure build-up of the chlorine gas which is generated. Dispose of detoxified vials in a safe manner.

Needles, Syringes, Disposable and Nondisposable Equipment: Rinse equipment with an appropriate quantity of sodium hypochlorite solution. Discard the solution in the sewer system with running water and discard disposable equipment in a safe manner. Thoroughly wash nondisposable equipment in soap and water.

Spillage/Contamination: Wear gloves, mask, protective clothing. Treat spilled powder or liquid with sodium hypochlorite solution. Carefully absorb solution with gauze pads or towels, wash area with water and absorb with gauze or towels again and place in polyethylene bag; seal, double bag and mark as hazardous waste. Dispose of waste by incineration or by other methods approved for hazardous materials. Personnel involved in cleanup should wash with soap and water.

Supplied: Adriamycin RDF: Vials: 10 mg: Each vial contains: doxorubicin HCl USP 10 mg as a sterile red-orange lyophilized powder. Also contains lactose and methylparaben (added to enhance dissolution). Cartons of 10. Protect from light. Store powder at 15 to 30°C.

50 mg: Each vial contains: doxorubicin HCl USP 50 mg as a sterile red-orange lyophilized powder. Also contains lactose and methylparaben (added to enhance dissolution). Cartons of a single vial. Protect from light. Store powder at 15 to 30°C.

Pharmacy Bulk Vials (150 mg): Each vial contains: doxorubicin HCl USP 150 mg as a sterile red-orange lyophilized powder. Also contains lactose and methylparaben (added to enhance dissolution). Cartons of a single vial. Protect from light. Store powder at 15 to 30°C.

Adriamycin PFS: Vials: 10 mg: Each vial of sterile, isotonic, nonpreserved solution contains: doxorubicin HCl USP 10 mg, sodium chloride USP 45 mg, water for injection USP and hydrochloric acid USP for pH adjustment. Vials of 5 mL, cartons of 10. Store under refrigeration (2 to 8°C), protect from light and retain in carton until time of use. Discard unused solution.

50 mg: Each vial of sterile, isotonic, nonpreserved solution contains: doxorubicin HCl USP 50 mg, sodium chloride USP 225 mg, water for injection USP and hydrochloric acid USP for pH adjustment. Vials of 25 mL, cartons of 4. Store under refrigeration (2 to 8°C), protect from light and retain in carton until time of use. Discard unused solution.

Pharmacy Bulk Vials (200 mg): Each vial of sterile, isotonic, nonpreserved solution contains: doxorubicin HCl USP 200 mg, sodium chloride USP 900 mg, water for injection and hydrochloric acid USP for pH adjustment. Vials of 100 mL, cartons of a single vial. Store under refrigeration (2 to 8°C), protect from light and retain in carton until time of use. Discard unused solution.

Reviewed 1998

ADRUCIL® Ⓟ

Pharmacia & Upjohn

Fluorouracil

Antineoplastic

Pharmacology: The mechanism of action of fluorouracil is mainly related to competitive inhibition of thymidylate synthetase, the enzyme catalyzing the methylation of deoxyuridylic acid to thymidylic acid. The consequent thymidine deficiency results in inhibition of deoxyribonucleic acid (DNA) synthesis, thus inducing cell death. Also, moderate inhibition of ribonucleic acid (RNA) and incorporation of fluorouracil into RNA have been observed. The predominant mechanism of antitumor action appears to be dependent, at least in part, on individual tumor intracellular metabolism.

The effects of DNA and RNA deprivation are most marked on those cells which grow rapidly and which take up fluorouracil at a more rapid pace. Inactive degradation products (e.g., CO_2, urea, α-fluoro-β-alanine) result from the extensive catabolic metabolism of fluorouracil. Following i.v. injection, no intact drug can be detected in the plasma after 3 hours and 60 to 80% of the dose is excreted as respiratory CO_2 in 8 to 12 hours. Within 6 hours approximately 15% of the total drug administered is excreted unchanged in the urine with over 90% of this excretion occurring in the first hour.

Indications: Used alone, is effective in the palliative management of carcinoma of the colon, rectum, breast, stomach and pancreas. Clinical studies support the efficacy of fluorouracil used with other chemotherapeutic agents in patients with carcinoma of the breast, stomach and pancreas. Listed below are tumor types and drugs used concurrently with fluorouracil.

Carcinoma of the Breast: Fluorouracil with cyclophosphamide and doxorubicin; fluorouracil with cyclophosphamide and epirubicin; fluorouracil with cyclophosphamide and doxorubicin, vincristine and prednisone.

Carcinoma of the Stomach: Fluorouracil with doxorubicin and mitomycin-C or fluorouracil with epirubicin.

Carcinoma of the Pancreas: Fluorouracil with doxorubicin and mitomycin-C; fluorouracil with mitomycin-C and streptozotocin.

A number of other solid tumors have also shown some responsiveness to fluorouracil alone or in combination with other drugs. These include the following:

Cancer of the Urinary Bladder: fluorouracil alone; fluorouracil with doxorubicin; fluorouracil with doxorubicin and cisplatin; fluorouracil with doxorubicin and cyclophosphamide; fluorouracil with methotrexate, cyclophosphamide and vincristine.

Cancer of the Prostate: fluorouracil alone; fluorouracil with doxorubicin and cyclophosphamide.

Cancer of the Head and Neck: fluorouracil with cisplatin.

Cancer of the Ovary: fluorouracil with hexamethylmelamine, cyclophosphamide and doxorubicin.

No studies performed to date have shown malignant melanoma, kidney carcinoma, the leukemias and lymphomas, soft tissue and bone sarcomas, bronchogenic carcinoma, brain tumors and metastases to the CNS to be significantly responsive to fluorouracil therapy.

Contraindications: Should not be started in patients in a poor nutritional state, with depressed bone marrow function, or with potentially serious infections.

Warnings: Use fluorouracil with extreme caution in poor risk patients with a history of high dose pelvic irradiation, previous use of alkylating agents, or who have widespread involvement of bone marrow by metastatic tumors, or impaired renal or hepatic function. Although severe toxicity and fatalities are more likely to occur in poor risk patients, these effects have occasionally been encountered in patients in relatively good condition. Severe hematologic toxicity, gastrointestinal hemorrhage, and even death may result from the use of fluorouracil despite meticulous selection of patients and careful dosage adjustment.

Pregnancy: Fluorouracil's safe use has not been established with respect to adverse effects on fetal development. Therefore, the drug should not be used during pregnancy, particularly in the first trimester, unless in the judgment of the physician, the potential benefits to the patient outweigh the hazards.

Because the risk of mutagenesis has not been evaluated, such possible effects on males and females must be considered.

Precautions: Fluorouracil is a highly toxic drug with a narrow margin of safety and thus, special attention must be given to its toxicity. Patients should be advised of expected toxic effects especially oral manifestations. White blood counts with differential and platelet counts are recommended before each dose. Knowledge of WBC nadir is necessary for eventual subsequent dosage adjustments.

Discontinue fluorouracil administration promptly if any of the following signs of toxicity appear: stomatitis or esophagopharyngitis (at first visible sign); leukopenia (WBC $<3\,500/mm^3$) or rapidly falling WBC count; intractable vomiting; diarrhea (frequent bowel movements or watery stools); gastrointestinal ulceration and bleeding; thrombocytopenia (platelets $<100\,000/mm^3$); hemorrhage from any site.

Fluorouracil should be resumed only when the patient has recovered from the above signs.

Drug Interactions: Fluorouracil with leucovorin, the latter usually given 24 hours after sequential administration of methotrexate and fluorouracil may result in increased potency and toxicity.

Fluorouracil causes a change in the spectrophotometric spectrum of cytarabine, possibly reducing its effectiveness. Fluorouracil mixed with methotrexate alters the spectra of both agents. Fluorouracil is physically incompatible with doxorubicin, epirubicin and with diazepam; a precipitate forms when fluorouracil is mixed with these drugs. It is recommended that complete i.v. line flushing take place between injections of fluorouracil and cytarabine, methotrexate, doxorubicin, epirubicin or diazepam.

Adverse Effects: Stomatitis and esophagopharyngitis (which may lead to sloughing and ulceration), diarrhea, anorexia and emesis are common.

Myelosuppression almost uniformly accompanies a course of adequate therapy with fluorouracil. Low WBC counts are usually first observed between the 9th and 14th day after the first course of treatment with the nadir occurring during the third week, although at times delayed for as long as 25 days. By the 30th day the count is usually within the normal range. Thrombocytopenia also may occur.

Alopecia and dermatitis are seen in a substantial number of cases and patients should be advised of this consequence of treatment. The alopecia is reversible. The dermatitis is often a pruritic maculopapular rash generally appearing on the extremities and less frequently on the trunk. It is usually reversible and responsive to symptomatic treatment. Palmar-plantar erythrodysesthesia has been reported in association with the continuous infusion of fluorouracil. Dry skin and fissuring have also been noted.

Photosensitivity, as manifested by erythema or increased skin pigmentation, may occasionally occur.

Also reported were photophobia, lacrimation, epistaxis, euphoria, acute cerebellar syndrome (which may persist following discontinuation of treatment), nail changes including banding or loss of nails and vein discoloration proximal to injection sites. Myocardial ischemia has also been reported.

Overdose: Symptoms and Treatment: Signs and symptoms of overdosage include stomatitis, diarrhea, fever, infection and petechiae with bleeding. No antidotes are available; management of overdosage consists of supportive therapy including fluid replacement, antibiotics and platelet transfusions.

Dosage: The recommended route of administration is by i.v. injection, using care to avoid extravasation. No dilution of Adrucil is required. Although fluorouracil can be used orally, the product is not formulated for this clinical application.

It is recommended that all dosages be based on the patient's actual weight. However, if the patient is obese or if there has been a spurious weight gain due to edema, ascites, or other forms of abnormal fluid retention, then the estimated lean body mass (dry weight) should be used.

Prior to treatment, it is recommended that each patient be carefully evaluated to accurately estimate the optimum initial fluorouracil dosage.

Initial Therapy: See Contraindications, Warnings and Precautions before prescribing. Patients should be hospitalized during the first course of therapy. Daily dosage generally should not exceed 800 mg. In good risk patients a dose of 12 mg/kg (500 mg/m²) is given daily for 5 days and repeated every 28 days. In poor risk patients a dose of 6 to 10 mg/kg (250 to 400 mg/m²) is given daily for 5 days and repeated every 28 days. When used in combination with other chemotherapeutic agents various schedules may be used including a single dose per course, a dose on day 1 and day 8 and daily for 4 or 5 days. The dose given varies, depending on the regimen used.

A sequence of 1 to 5 injections constitutes a "course of therapy". Therapy should be discontinued promptly when any of the signs of toxicity listed under Precautions appear.

Maintenance Therapy: When toxicity has not been a problem, or after the toxic signs from the initial course of therapy have subsided, therapy should be continued using either of the following schedules:

A. Repeat dosage of the first course, beginning 28 days after the first day of the previous course of treatment.
B. Administer a maintenance dosage of 10 to 15 mg/kg/week. Reduced doses should be used for poor risk patients.

The dosage of drug to be used should take into account the patient's reaction to the previous course of therapy and be adjusted accordingly. Some patients have received from 9 to 45 courses of treatment during periods which ranged from 12 to 60 months.

Adrucil should not be mixed with i.v. additives or other chemotherapeutic agents.

Guidelines for Safe Handling and Disposal: Handling: Personnel involved in handling fluorouracil solutions or in the clean-up of spillage and disposal operations should wear protective clothing, gloves, and glasses. If the solution contacts the skin, the area should be washed with soap and water immediately. If the solution accidentally contacts the eyes, irrigate immediately with water or saline. Personnel regularly involved in the preparation and handling of antineoplastics should have blood examinations on a regular basis.

Disposal: All needles, syringes, vials and other materials which have come in contact with fluorouracil should be segregated in plastic bags, sealed and marked as hazardous waste. Incinerate at 1 000°C or higher. Sealed containers may explode if a tight seal exists. If incineration is not available, fluorouracil may be detoxified by adding sodium hypochlorite solution (household bleach). Dispose of detoxified fluorouracil solution in a safe manner. Nondisposable equipment should be rinsed in sodium hypochlorite solution and then washed in soap and water.

Spillage: Deactivate with sodium hypochlorite solution and rinse well with water.

Note: The use of pharmacy bulk vials is restricted to hospitals with a recognized i.v. admixture program. The pharmacy bulk vial is intended for single puncture, multiple dispensing and for i.v. use only.

Entry into the vial must be made with a suitable, sterile transfer or dispensing device. Multiple use of a syringe with needle is not recommended since it may cause leakage as well as it may increase the potential for microbial and particulate matter contamination.

In a suitable work area such as a laminar flow hood, swab the vial stopper with an antiseptic solution. Insert the device into the vial.

Withdraw contents of the vial into sterile syringes using strict aseptic techniques. Dispensing from the pharmacy bulk vial should be completed within 8 hours of **the initial entry** because of the potential for microbial contamination. Discard any unused portion. The contents of the syringes filled from the pharmacy bulk vial should be used within 24 hours at room temperature **from the time of the initial entry into the pharmacy bulk vial.**

Supplied: Each mL of colorless to faint yellow aqueous solution, buffered with sodium hydroxide to pH 8.6 to 9.4, contains: fluorouracil 50 mg. Glass vials of 10 mL, cartons of 10. Pharmacy bulk vials of 50 mL, cartons of 1. Store at controlled temperature (15 to 30°C). Protect from freezing.

Note: Adrucil solution may turn a very pale yellowish color during storage. A highly colored solution is evidence of degradation and its use is not recommended. If a precipitate occurs due to exposure to low temperatures, resolubilize by heating to 60°C with vigorous shaking; allow to cool to body temperature before using.

ADVANTAGE 24™
Roberts

Nonoxynol-9

Vaginal Contraceptive Gel

Pharmacology: Nonoxynol-9 (paranonyl-phenoxypolyethoxyethanol) is a commonly used spermicidal agent. Nonoxynol-9 is responsible for cell membrane breakage; it decreases surface tension and kills epithelial cells.

The vaginal contraceptive gel is a new gel designed to provide a steady release of nonoxynol-9 after a single vaginal application. Commonly available spermicidal formulations must be used close to the time of intercourse if they are not in a steady release preparation. The vaginal contraceptive gel utilizes a bioadhesive polymer delivery system to achieve its steady release profile. The delivery system has been shown to remain on epithelial surfaces for extended periods of time following application. The nonoxynol-9 is present at a concentration of 3.5% in the bioadhesive delivery system which attaches to the vaginal epithelial surface. Once attached, the vaginal contraceptive gel allows the release of nonoxynol-9 to occur at a slow, steady rate over a period of 24 hours. Available clinical data show that the gel provides effective contraceptive protection for up to 24 hours following initial application prior to a single act of intercourse.

Indications: For the prevention of conception. Provides contraceptive protection for up to 24 hours prior to a single act of intercourse.

The contraceptive gel will not harm latex condoms.

Contraindications: Known sensitivity to nonoxynol-9 or other constituents of the product.

Precautions: If pregnancy is medically contraindicated, the patient's contraceptive program should be prescribed by a physician or family planning clinic.

The vaginal contraceptive gel provides an effective and convenient method of contraception. However, no product, even with regular use, can provide an absolute guarantee against becoming pregnant.

Keep out of reach of children.

Adverse Effects: Occasional burning and irritation of the vagina or penis can occur. If this happens, discontinue use and/or consult your physician.

Dosage: One applicatorful of the vaginal contraceptive gel should be inserted into the vagina prior to each act of intercourse. An additional applicatorful is required prior to each time intercourse is repeated.

The vaginal contraceptive gel offers the advantage of a lower dose of nonoxynol-9 without compromising the efficacy in pregnancy protection due to its patented bioadhesive technology. Each dose contains 3.5% (52.5 mg) nonoxynol-9. This lower dose of nonoxynol-9 enhances product tolerability.

Supplied: Each dose of the nongreasy, nonstaining gel contains: 3.5% (52.5 mg) nonoxynol-9. Each applicator delivers 1.5 g of gel. Nonmedicinal ingredients: carbomer 934P, glycerin, hydrogenated palm oil glyceride, methylparaben, mineral oil, polycarbophil, purified water, sorbic acid and sodium hydroxide added to adjust pH. Fragrance-free. Boxes of 3 individually wrapped, disposable, prefilled applicators.

(Shown in Product Recognition Section)

Reviewed 1997

ADVIL®
Whitehall-Robins

Ibuprofen

Analgesic—Antipyretic

Indications: Adults and Children over 12: For fast and effective relief of headaches, toothache and menstrual pain, and for minor aches and pain associated with arthritis, muscles, joints and backache, and for reduction of fever.

Children 12 and under: For fever and pain due to colds, sore throat, immunizatin and earache.

Contraindications: Hypersensitivity to ibuprofen. Patients with active peptic ulcers or gastrointestinal bleeding, or patients with the angioedema syndrome, nasal polyps or bronchospastic reactivity to ASA or other nonsteroidal anti-inflammatory agents.

Pregnancy and *Lactation:* Safety in pregnancy or in nursing mothers has not been established.

Aseptic meningitis, fever and rash have been reported in connection with ibuprofen therapy in patients with systemic lupus erythematosus. It should not be used by patients with systemic lupus erythematosus except under a physician's supervision.

Warnings: Anaphylactoid reactions have occurred in patients with known ASA hypersensitivity. Peptic ulcerations and gastrointestinal bleeding, sometimes severe, have been reported in patients receiving prescription doses of ibuprofen. Like other nonsteroidal anti-inflammatory agents, ibuprofen can inhibit platelet aggregation, therefore should be avoided by persons with intrinsic coagulation defects and those on anticoagulant therapy. However, compared to ASA, the effect is quantitatively less, or shorter duration, and is reversible upon discontinuation of ibuprofen.

Precautions: Conditions associated with dehydration appear to increase the risk of renal toxicity. Ibuprofen should not be given to children who are dehydrated due to vomiting, diarrhea or lack of fluid intake. Ibuprofen should therefore be used with caution in patients with diminished renal function, liver disease, congestive heart disease or hypertension being treated with diuretics.

Adverse Effects: The following adverse reactions have been noted in patients treated with prescription regimens of ibuprofen:

Gastrointestinal: The adverse reactions most frequently seen with prescribed ibuprofen therapy involve the gastrointestinal system: nausea, epigastric pain, heartburn, diarrhea, abdominal distress, vomiting, indigestion, constipation, abdominal cramps, fullness of the gastrointestinal tract (bloating or flatulence).

CNS: dizziness, headache, nervousness.

Dermatologic: rash (including maculopapular type), pruritus.

Special Senses: tinnitus.

Metabolic: decreased appetite, edema, fluid retention. Fluid retention generally responds promptly to drug discontinuation

Overdose: Symptoms: Nausea, heartburn or stomach pain, dizziness, headache, nervousness, rapid eye movement, lack of response to moderate pain, respiratory distress, flushing or bluish coloration of skin or mucous membranes, rapid weak heartbeats or palpitations.

Treatment: Acute ibuprofen overdose does not normally result in significant morbidity or mortality, although serious toxicity has been reported following very large overdoses. Deaths have been rare. Treatment is directed towards specific clinical signs and symptoms, and is generally supportive.

Adverse effects associated with ibuprofen overdose usually depend on the amount of drug ingested and the time elapsed; however, because each individual response may vary, each occurrence of overdose has to be evaluated individually. In general, ingestion of up to 200 mg/kg usually does not cause symptoms of toxicity, and observation at home is recommended. If symptoms are to appear, they usually occur within 4 hours of poisoning, and the patient should be taken to a medical facility. For overdoses greater than 200 mg/kg, the patient should be referred to a medical facility and gastrointestinal decontamination using activated charcoal (1 g/kg) should be instituted. Little drug is likely to be captured if the time elapsed after ingestion is greater than 1 hour. Because seizures can occur in children with ibuprofen overdose, emesis should not be induced at this level of overdose. The onset of symptoms is usually within 4 hours of ingestion so the patient should be observed for at least this period of time.

For overdoses greater than 400 mg/kg, in-hospital observation is indicated. Initial laboratory tests should include arterial blood gases, electrolyte levels, blood urea nitrogen (BUN), creatinine and liver function studies.

Dosage: Adults and Children over 12 years: Recommend 1 or 2 tablets, caplets or gel caplets every 4 hours as needed. Do not exceed 6 units in 24 hours unless deemed necessary by the physician.

Note: Children's suspension may be administered to adults who have difficulty in swallowing tablets, 200 to 400 mg every 4 hours as needed. Do not exceed 1 200 mg in 24 hours, unless directed by a physician.

Children 12 and under: Administer children's suspension according to dosage table below (see Table I). For children over 2 the dose is 10 mg/kg, children under 2 should be given 5 mg/kg. Dose may be repeated every 6 to 8 hours while symptoms persist, up to 3 doses a day. Shake well before using.

Table I—Advil

Dosage—Children's Suspension

Age (yr)	Weight (kg)	Dose	
Under 2	Under 10.8	5 mg/kg (0.25 mL of suspension/kg)	To be calculated
2-3	10.9-15.9	10 mg/kg	6.0 mL=1¼ teaspoons
4-5	16.0-21.3	10 mg/kg	10.0 mL=2 teaspoons
6-8	21.4-26.7	10 mg/kg	12.5 mL=2½ teaspoons
9-10	26.8-32.5	10 mg/kg	15.0 mL=3 teaspoons
11-12	32.6-43.0	10 mg/kg	19.0 mL=3¾ teaspoons

Supplied: Caplets (Gel): Each oval-shaped, gelatin-coated tablet contains: ibuprofen 200 mg. Nonmedicinal ingredients, cellulose, cornstarch, croscarmellose sodium, FD&C Red No. 40, FD&C Yellow No. 6, gelatin, glycerin, iron oxides, lecithin, pharmaceutical glaze, pregelatinized starch, propylgallate, silicon dioxide, simethicone, sodium lauryl sulfate, stearic acid, titanium dioxide and triacetin. Bottles of 16, 32 and 72.

Children's Suspension: Each 5 mL of fruit-flavored or grape-flavored suspension contains: ibuprofen 100 mg. Nonmedicinal ingredients: cellulose gum, citric acid, disodium EDTA, FD&C Blue No. 1 (grape-flavored only), FD&C Red No. 40, flavors, glycerin, microcrystalline cellulose, polysorbate 80,

Advil (cont'd)

sodium benzoate, sorbitol, sucrose, water and xanthan gum. Bottles of 100 mL.

Tablets/Caplets (Sugar-coated): Each brown, sugar-coated tablet/caplet contains: ibuprofen 200 mg. Nonmedicinal ingredients: acetylated monoglyceride, beeswax, carnauba wax, cellulose, cornstarch, croscarmellose sodium, ethoxyethanol, iron oxides, lecithin, parabens, pharmaceutical glaze, pharmaceutical shellac, povidone, pregelatinized starch, silicon dioxide, simethicone, sodium benzoate, sodium lauryl sulfate, stearic acid, sucrose and titanium dioxide. Blister packs of 8 tablets. Bottles of 24, 50 and 100 tablets or caplets. Easy-to-open bottles of 150 tablets.

Store at room temperature (15 to 30°C).

Reviewed 1999

ADVIL® COLD & SINUS

Whitehall-Robins

Ibuprofen—Pseudoephedrine HCl

Analgesic—Antipyretic—Decongestant

Pharmacology: Ibuprofen has exhibited analgesic and antipyretic activity in animal studies designed to specifically demonstrate these effects. Ibuprofen has been shown to have no glucocorticoid-like activity.

Pseudoephedrine is an orally effective nasal decongestant when administered in doses of 60 mg/dose, up to 240 mg/day. In order to comply with the flexible dosing schedule approved for nonprescription ibuprofen, clinical studies were conducted to demonstrate the efficacy of 30 mg pseudoephedrine when administered in the combination product and evidence of dose response between the 30 and 60 mg doses.

A 3-way bioavailability study of ibuprofen, pseudoephedrine and a combination of ibuprofen/pseudoephedrine indicated that the absorption and the disposition of the 2 drugs were **not** different, i.e., there was no pharmacokinetic interaction when the 2 drugs were combined.

In another 3-way bioequivalence comparison of ibuprofen, pseudoephedrine and a combination of the 2 drugs, **no** statistically significant differences were noted among the 3 treatments for any pharmacokinetic variables for ibuprofen or pseudoephedrine.

Indications: For the temporary relief of symptoms associated with the common cold, sinusitis or flu including nasal congestion, headache, fever, body aches and pains.

Contraindications: In patients who have previously exhibited hypersensitivity to it, or to its components (ibuprofen, pseudoephedrine), or in individuals with the angioedema syndrome, nasal polyps or bronchospastic reactivity to ASA or other nonsteroidal anti-inflammatory agents (see Warnings).

In patients with hypertension, coronary artery disease and in patients on MAO inhibitor therapy (see Drug Interactions).

Pregnancy, Lactation and Children: Advil Cold & Sinus should not be used during pregnancy, in nursing mothers or in pediatric patients because its safety under these conditions has not been established.

Aseptic meningitis, fever and rash have been reported in connection with ibuprofen therapy in patients with systemic lupus erythematosus.

Advil Cold & Sinus should not be used by patients with systemic lupus erythematosus except under a physician's supervision.

Advil Cold & Sinus should not be taken by patients with active peptic ulcer disease or gastrointestinal bleeding unless directed by a physician.

Warnings: Anaphylactoid reactions have occurred in patients with known ASA hypersensitivity (see Contraindications).

Peptic ulcerations and gastrointestinal bleeding, sometimes severe, have been reported in patients receiving prescription doses of ibuprofen. Peptic ulcerations, perforation or severe gastrointestinal bleeding can have a fatal outcome, and although few such reports have been received with ibuprofen, a cause and effect relationship has not been established. Patients with a history of upper gastrointestinal tract disease should take Advil Cold & Sinus under the supervision of a physician.

Like other nonsteroidal anti-inflammatory agents, ibuprofen can inhibit platelet aggregation. However, compared to ASA, the effect is quantitatively less, of shorter duration, and reversible upon discontinuation of ibuprofen. Bleeding time has also been prolonged by ibuprofen though within the normal range in normal subjects. Because this effect on bleeding time may be exaggerated in patients with underlying hemostatic defects, Advil Cold & Sinus should be avoided by persons with intrinsic coagulation defects and those on anticoagulant therapy.

Patients with high blood pressure, heart disease, diabetes, narrow-angle glaucoma, thyroid disease or difficulty in urination due to enlargement of the prostate gland should take Advil Cold & Sinus only under the advice and supervision of a physician.

Precautions: Conditions associated with dehydration appear to increase the risk of renal toxicity. Advil Cold & Sinus should therefore be used with caution in patients with chronic renal failure, congestive heart failure or hypertension being treated chronically with diuretics. Caution should be observed in elderly patients, due to increased susceptibility to effects of sympathomimetic amines and increased risk of toxicity with ibuprofen, and patients with diminished renal function.

Patients on Advil Cold & Sinus should be cautioned to report to their physician any signs or symptoms of gastrointestinal ulceration or bleeding, blurred vision or other eye symptoms, skin rash, weight gain, edema, tinnitus, dizziness or respiratory difficulties.

If Advil Cold & Sinus is taken in conjunction with prolonged corticosteroid therapy and it is decided to discontinue the latter therapy, as under other circumstances, the corticosteroid dosage should be tapered slowly to avoid exacerbation of disease or adrenal insufficiency.

There is a possibility of insomnia if this medicine is taken before bedtime.

If the symptoms do not improve or are accompanied by a high fever, the patient should be advised to report to the physician.

<u>*Drug Interactions:*</u> Coumarin-Type Anticoagulants: Several short-term controlled studies failed to show that ibuprofen significantly affected prothrombin time for a variety of other clotting factors when administered to individuals on coumarin-type anticoagulants. The physician should be cautious when administering Advil Cold & Sinus to patients on anticoagulants.

ASA: Animal studies show that ASA given with nonsteroidal anti-inflammatory agents including ibuprofen yields a net decrease in anti-inflammatory activity with lowered blood levels of the non-ASA drug. Single dose bioavailability studies in normal volunteers have failed to show an effect of ASA on ibuprofen blood levels. Correlative clinical studies have not been conducted.

Other Anti-inflammatory Agents (NSAIDs): The addition of Advil Cold & Sinus to a pre-existent prescribed NSAID regimen in patients with a condition such as rheumatoid arthritis may result in increased risk of adverse effects.

Diuretics: Because of its fluid retention properties, high doses of ibuprofen can decrease the diuretic and antihypertensive effects of diuretics, and increased diuretic dosage may be required. Patients with impaired renal function who are taking potassium-sparing diuretics should not take Advil Cold & Sinus.

Hypoglycemic Agents: Ibuprofen may increase hypoglycemic effects of oral antidiabetic agents and insulin.

Acetaminophen: Although interactions have not been reported, concurrent use with Advil Cold & Sinus is not advisable, as it may increase the risk of adverse renal effect.

Other Drugs: Although ibuprofen binds extensively to plasma proteins, interactions with other protein-bound drugs occur rarely. Nevertheless, caution should be observed when other drugs, also having a high affinity for protein binding sites, are used concurrently. Some observations have suggested a potential for ibuprofen to interact with furosemide, pindolol, digoxin, phenytoin and lithium salts. However, the mechanisms and clinical significance of these observations are presently not known. No interactions have been reported when ibuprofen has been used in conjunction with hypoglycemic agents, probenecid, digitalis, thyroxine, steroids, antibiotics or benzodiazepines.

Adverse Effects: Ibuprofen: The following adverse reactions have been noted in patients treated with prescription regimens of ibuprofen.

Gastrointestinal: The adverse reactions most frequently seen with prescribed ibuprofen therapy involve the gastrointestinal system: nausea, epigastric pain, heartburn, diarrhea, abdominal distress, vomiting, indigestion, constipation, abdominal cramps, fullness of the gastrointestinal tract (bloating or flatulence).

CNS: dizziness, headache, nervousness.

Dermatologic: rash (including maculopapular type), pruritus.

Special Senses: tinnitus.

Metabolic: decreased appetite, edema, fluid retention. Fluid retention generally responds promptly to drug discontinuation.

Pseudoephedrine: Pseudoephedrine may cause mild CNS stimulation, especially in patients who are hypersensitive to the effects of sympathomimetic drugs. Nervousness, excitability, restlessness, dizziness, weakness and insomnia may occur. Headache and drowsiness have also been reported. Large doses may cause lightheadedness, nausea and/or vomiting. In addition, the possibility of other adverse effects associated with sympathomimetic drugs, including fear, anxiety, tenseness, tremor, hallucinations, seizures, pallor, respiratory difficulty, dysuria and cardiovascular collapse should be considered.

Although oral administration of usual doses of pseudoephedrine to normotensive patients usually produced negligible pressor effects, the drug should be used with caution in hypertensive patients. Pseudoephedrine may increase the irritability of the heart muscle and may alter the rhythmic function of the ventricles, especially in large doses or when administered to patients who are hypersensitive to the myocardial effects of sympathomimetic drugs. Tachycardia or palpitation may occur.

Overdose: Symptoms and Treatment: Due to the rapid absorption of pseudoephedrine and ibuprofen from the gut, emetics and gastric lavage must be instituted within 4 hours of overdosage to be effective. Charcoal is useful only if given within 1 hour. Cardiac status should be monitored and the serum electrolytes measured. If there are signs of cardiac toxicity, propranolol may be administered i.v. A slow infusion of a dilute solution of potassium chloride should be initiated in the event of a drop in the serum potassium levels. Despite hypokalemia, the patient is unlikely to be potassium-depleted; therefore, overload must be avoided. Monitoring of the serum potassium is advisable for several hours after administration of the salt. For delirium or convulsions, i.v. administration of diazepam is indicated.

Dosage: Adults and children over 12 years: Take 1 or 2 caplets every 4 hours as needed. Do not exceed 6 caplets in 24 hours, unless directed by a physician.

Do not give to children under 12 years of age, except under the advice and supervision of a physician.

Supplied: Each caplet contains: ibuprofen 200 mg and pseudoephedrine HCl 30 mg. Nonmedicinal ingredients: acetylated monoglyceride, carnauba wax, cellulose, cornstarch, croscarmellose sodium, ethoxyethanol, iron oxides, lecithin, parabens, pharmaceutical glaze, pharmaceutical shellac, povidone, pregelatinized starch, silicon dioxide, simethicone, sodium benzoate, sodium lauryl sulfate, stearic acid, sucrose and titanium dioxide. Blister packages of 10 and 20. Bottles of 40. Store at room temperature (15 to 30°C).

AGRYLIN™ Ⓟ

Roberts

Anagrelide HCl

Platelet-reducing Agent

Pharmacology: The mechanism by which anagrelide reduces blood platelet count is still under investigation. Studies in patients support a hypothesis of dose-related reduction in platelet production resulting from a decrease in megakaryocyte hypermaturation. In blood withdrawn from normal volunteers treated with anagrelide, a disruption was found in the postmitotic phase of megakaryocyte development and a reduction in megakaryocyte size and ploidy. At therapeutic doses anagrelide does not produce significant changes in white cell counts or coagulation parameters, and may have a small, but clinically insignificant effect on red cell parameters. Platelet aggregation is inhibited in humans at doses higher than those required to reduce platelet count. Anagrelide inhibits cyclic AMP phosphodiesterase, as well as ADP- and collagen-induced platelet aggregation.

Following oral administration of ^{14}C-anagrelide in humans, more than 70% of the radioactivity was recovered in urine. Based on limited data, there appears to be a trend toward dose linearity between doses of 0.5 and 2 mg. At fasting and at a dose of 0.5 mg of anagrelide, the plasma half-life is 1.3 hours. The available plasma concentration time data at steady-state in patients showed that anagrelide does not accumulate in plasma after repeated administration. The drug is extensively metabolized; less than 1% is recovered in the urine as anagrelide.

When a 0.5 mg dose of anagrelide was taken after food, its bioavailability (based on AUC values) was modestly reduced by an average of 13.8% and its plasma half-life slightly increased (to 1.8 hours), when compared with drug administered to the same subjects in the fasted state. The peak plasma level was lowered by an average of 45% and delayed by 2 hours.

Indications: For the treatment of patients with essential thrombocythemia (ET) to reduce the elevated platelet count and the risk of thrombosis and to ameliorate associated symptoms.

Anagrelide is intended for chronic usage and has not been evaluated for treatment of the acute life-threatening complications of thrombocytosis.

Warnings: Cardiovascular: Anagrelide should be used with caution in patients with known or suspected heart disease, and only if the potential benefits of therapy outweigh the potential risks. Because of the positive inotropic effects and side effects of anagrelide, a pre-treatment cardiovascular examination is recommended along with careful monitoring during treatment. In humans, therapeutic doses of anagrelide may cause cardiovascular effects, including vasodilation, tachycardia, palpitations, and congestive heart failure.

Renal: It is recommended that patients with renal insufficiency (creatinine ≥ 2 mg/dL) receive anagrelide when, in the physician's judgment, the potential benefits of therapy outweigh the potential risks. These patients should be monitored closely for signs of renal toxicity while receiving anagrelide (see Adverse Effects, Urogenital).

Hepatic: It is recommended that patients with evidence of hepatic dysfunction (bilirubin, AST, or measures of liver function >1.5 times the upper limit of normal) receive anagrelide when, in the physician's judgment, the potential benefits of therapy outweigh the potential risks. These patients should be monitored closely for signs of hepatic toxicity while receiving anagrelide (see Adverse Effects, Hepatic).

Children: The safety and efficacy of anagrelide in patients under the age of 16 years have not been established.

Pregnancy: There are no adequate and well-controlled studies in pregnant women. Anagrelide should be used during pregnancy only if the potential benefit justifies the potential risk to the fetus.

Anagrelide is not recommended in women who are or may become pregnant. If this drug is used during pregnancy, or if the patient becomes pregnant while taking this drug, the patient should be apprised of the potential harm to the fetus. Women of childbearing potential should be instructed that they must not be pregnant and that they should use contraception while taking anagrelide. Anagrelide may cause fetal harm when administered to a pregnant woman.

Lactation: It is not known whether this drug is excreted in human milk. Because many drugs are excreted in human milk and because of the potential for serious adverse reaction in nursing infants from anagrelide, a decision should be made whether to discontinue nursing or to discontinue the drug, taking into account the importance of the drug to the mother.

Precautions: The decision to treat asymptomatic young adults with essential thrombocythemia should be individualized.

Sudden discontinuation or interruption of anagrelide treatment is followed by an increase in platelet count. Following discontinuation, an increase in platelet count can be observed within 4 days.

Drug Interactions: Bioavailability studies evaluating possible interactions between anagrelide and other drugs have not been conducted. The most common medications used concomitantly with anagrelide have been ASA, acetaminophen, furosemide, iron, ranitidine, hydroxyurea, and allopurinol. The most frequently used concomitant cardiac medication has been digoxin. Although drug-to-drug interaction studies have not been conducted, there is no clinical evidence to suggest that anagrelide interacts with any of these compounds.

There is a single case report which suggests that sucralfate may interfere with anagrelide absorption.

Food has no clinically significant effect on the bioavailability of anagrelide.

Monitoring: Anagrelide therapy requires close clinical supervision of the patient. To monitor the effect of anagrelide and prevent the occurrence of thrombocytopenia, platelet counts should be performed every 2 days during the first week of treatment and at least weekly thereafter, until the maintenance dosage is reached. Typically, platelet count begins to respond within 7 to 14 days at the proper dosage. Most patients will experience an adequate response at a dose of 1.5 to 3 mg/day. In case of overdose, close clinical supervision of the patient is required, including monitoring of the platelet count for thrombocytopenia. Dosage should be decreased or stopped as appropriate, until platelet count returns to within the normal range. However, in patients with hepatic insufficiency or renal insufficiency, liver function and kidney function tests should be performed at least once/month or when deemed necessary in the physician's judgment.

Adverse Effects: While most reported adverse events during anagrelide therapy have been mild in intensity and have decreased in frequency with continued therapy, serious adverse events reported in patients with ET and/or in patients with thrombocythemias of other etiologies include: congestive heart failure, myocardial infarction, cardiomyopathy, cardiomegaly, complete heart block, atrial fibrillation, cerebrovascular accident, pericarditis, pulmonary infiltrates, pulmonary fibrosis, pulmonary hypertension, pancreatitis, gastric/duodenal ulceration, and seizure. Of the 551 ET patients treated with anagrelide for a mean duration of 65 weeks, 82 (15%) were discontinued from the study because of adverse events or abnormal laboratory test results. The most common adverse events for treatment discontinuation were headache, diarrhea, edema, palpitation, and abdominal pain. Overall, the occurrence rate of all adverse events was 17.9 per 1 000 treatment days. The occurrence rate of adverse events increased at higher dosages of anagrelide.

The most frequently reported adverse reactions to anagrelide in 5% or greater of 551 patients with essential thrombocythemia in clinical trials were: headache 44.5%; palpitations 27.2%; diarrhea 24.3%; asthenia 22.1%; edema, other 19.8%; abdominal pain 17.4%; nausea 15.1%; pain, other 14.7%; dizziness 14.5%; dyspnea 10.5%; flatulence 10.5%; chest pain 7.8%; rash, including urticaria 7.8%; vomiting 7.4%; paresthesia 7.3%; tachycardia 7.3%; peripheral edema 7.1%; dyspepsia 6.4%; back pain 6.4%; anorexia 5.8% and malaise 5.8%.

Adverse events with an incidence of 1% to $<5\%$ included the following:

Body as a Whole: fever, flu symptoms, chills, neck pain, photosensitivity.

Cardiovascular: arrhythmia, hemorrhage, cardiovascular disease, angina pectoris, heart failure, postural hypotension, vasodilation, migraine, syncope.

Digestive: constipation, gastrointestinal distress, gastrointestinal hemorrhage, gastritis, melena, aphthous stomatitis, eructation, nausea and vomiting.

Hemic and Lymphatic: anemia, thrombocytopenia, ecchymosis, lymphadenoma.

Platelet counts below 100 000/μL occurred in 35 patients and reduction below 50 000/μL occurred in 7 of the 551 ET patients while on anagrelide therapy. Thrombocytopenia promptly recovered upon discontinuation of anagrelide.

Hepatic: Elevated liver enzymes were observed in 2 of 551 patients during anagrelide therapy.

Musculoskeletal: arthralgia, myalgia, leg cramps.

Nervous System: depression, somnolence, confusion, insomnia, hypertension, nervousness, amnesia.

Nutritional Disorders: dehydration.

Respiratory: rhinitis, epistaxis, respiratory disease, sinusitis, pneumonia, bronchitis, asthma.

Skin and Appendages: pruritus, skin disease, alopecia.

Special Senses: amblyopia, abnormal vision, tinnitus, visual field abnormality, diplopia.

Urogenital: dysuria, hematuria.

Of the 551 ET patients, 10 were found to have renal abnormalities. Six of the 10 experienced renal failure (approximately 1%) while on anagrelide treatment; in 2, the renal failure was considered to be possibly related to anagrelide treatment. The remaining 4 were found to have pre-existing renal impairment and were successfully treated with anagrelide. Doses ranged from 1.5 to 6 mg/day, with exposure periods of 2 to 12 months. Serum creatinines remained within normal limits, and no dose adjustment was required because of renal insufficiency.

The adverse event profile for patients in clinical trials on anagrelide therapy is shown in Table I which compares the percentage of each adverse event reported in patients with essential thrombocythemia (ET) to those found in patients with thrombocytosis of other etiologies.

Table I—Agrylin

Adverse Events

	ET Subjects (N=551) %	All Other Subjects with Thrombocythemia of Various Etiologies (N=391) %
Body as a Whole		
Asthenia	22.1	24.55
Fever	4.7	14.83
Headache	44.5	42.46
Malaise	5.8	7.16
Pain	14.7	15.35
Pain (abdominal)	17.4	15.09
Pain (back)	6.4	5.37
Pain (chest)	7.8	8.18
Cardiovascular		
Palpitations	27.2	24.55
Tachycardia	7.3	7.93
Gastrointestinal		
Anorexia	5.8	10.49
Diarrhea	24.3	27.62
Dyspepsia	6.4	3.58
Flatulence	10.5	9.72
Nausea	15.1	19.95
Vomiting	7.4	10.70
Hemic		
Anemia	4.9	2.30
Metabolic		
Edema	19.8	21.74
Edema (per)	7.1	10.49
Nervous		
Dizziness	14.5	16.62
Paresthesia	7.3	4.09
Respiratory		
Cough	5.4	7.42
Dyspnea	10.5	13.81
Pharyngitis	6.0	7.93
Skin and Appendages		
Pruritus	3.8	7.93
Rash	7.8	8.95

Overdose: Symptoms: There are no reports of overdosage with anagrelide. Platelet reduction from anagrelide therapy is dose related; therefore, thrombocytopenia, which can potentially cause bleeding, is expected from overdosage. Should overdosage occur, cardiac and CNS toxicity can also be expected.

Treatment: In case of overdosage, close clinical supervision of the patient is required; this especially includes monitoring of the platelet count for thrombocytopenia. Dosage should be decreased or stopped, as appropriate, until the platelet count returns to within the normal range.

Dosage: Treatment should be initiated under close medical supervision. The decision to treat asymptomatic young adults with essential thrombocythemia should be individualized. The recommended starting dose is 0.5 mg q.i.d. or 1 mg b.i.d., which should be maintained for at least 1 week. Dosage should then be adjusted to the lowest effective dosage required to reduce and maintain platelet count below 600 000/μL, and ideally to the normal range. The dosage should be increased by not more than 0.5 mg/day in any 1 week. Dosage should not exceed 10 mg/day or 2.5 mg in a single dose (see Precautions).

To monitor the effect of anagrelide and prevent the occurrence of thrombocytopenia, platelet counts should be performed every 2 days during the first week of treatment and at least weekly thereafter until the maintenance dosage is reached.

Typically, platelet count begins to respond within 7 to 14 days at the proper dosage. Most patients will experience an adequate response at a dose of 1.5 to 3 mg/day. Patients with known or suspected heart disease, renal insufficiency, or hepatic dysfunction should be monitored closely.

Supplied: Each white, opaque capsule, imprinted with "ROBERTS 063" in black ink, contains: anagrelide base 0.5 mg (as anagrelide HCl). Nonmedicinal ingredients: black iron oxide, crospovidone, gelatin, lactose, magnesium stearate, microcrystalline cellulose, povidone, silicon dioxide, sodium lauryl

Agrylin (cont'd)

sulfate and titanium oxide. Bottles of 100. Store from 15 to 25°C in a light-resistant container.

(Shown in Product Recognition Section)

Reviewed 1998

A-HYDROCORT ℞
Abbott

Hydrocortisone Sodium Succinate
Glucocorticoid

Supplied: 100 mg Dil-U-Vial: Each 2 mL (when mixed) contains: hydrocortisone sodium succinate equivalent to hydrocortisone 100 mg. Also contains monobasic sodium phosphate anhydrous 0.8 mg, dibasic sodium phosphate anhydrous 8.73 mg and benzyl alcohol 18 mg. Boxes of 10.

250 mg Dil-U-Vial: Each 2 mL (when mixed) contains: hydrocortisone sodium succinate equivalent to hydrocortisone 250 mg. Also contains monobasic sodium phosphate anhydrous 2 mg, dibasic sodium phosphate anhydrous 21.8 mg and benzyl alcohol 18 mg. Boxes of 10.

500 mg Dil-U-Vial: Each 4 mL (when mixed) contains: hydrocortisone sodium succinate equivalent to hydrocortisone 500 mg. Also contains monobasic sodium phosphate anhydrous 4 mg, dibasic sodium phosphate anhydrous 44 mg and benzyl alcohol 36 mg. Boxes of 5.

1 000 mg Dil-U-Vial: Each 8 mL (when mixed) contains: hydrocortisone sodium succinate equivalent to hydrocortisone 1 000 mg. Also contains monobasic sodium phosphate anhydrous 8 mg, dibasic sodium phosphate anhydrous 88 mg and benzyl alcohol 72 mg. Boxes of 5.

The pH of each formula was adjusted with sodium hydroxide and/or hydrochloric acid. When reconstituted as directed, the pH of the solutions ranges from 7 to 8 and the tonicities are, for the 100 mg/2 mL solution, 0.36 Osm; for the 250 mg/2 mL, 500 mg/4 mL, and 1 000 mg/8 mL solutions, 0.57 Osm. [Isotonic saline (0.9 Sodium Chloride Injection, USP) = 0.28 Osm].

AIROMIR™ ℞
3M Pharmaceuticals

Salbutamol Sulfate
Bronchodilator—β_2-adrenergic Stimulant

Pharmacology: Salbutamol produces bronchodilation through stimulation of β_2-adrenergic receptors in bronchial smooth muscle, thereby causing relaxation of bronchial muscle fibers. This action results in improved pulmonary function as demonstrated by spirometric measurements. At therapeutic doses, salbutamol has little action on the β_1-adrenergic receptors in cardiac muscle.

Clinical experience has shown that inhaled salbutamol, like other β-adrenergic agonists, can produce significant cardiovascular effects in some patients, as measured by pulse rate, blood pressure and/or ECG changes. Other effects common to this class of drugs and probably mediated by β-adrenoreceptors are tremor and hypokalemia.

The time to onset of a 15% increase in FEV_1 is 5 to 15 minutes after inhalation of salbutamol and the time to peak effect occurs within 60 to 90 minutes. The mean duration of effect as measured by a 15% increase in FEV_1 is about 3 hours. In some patients, duration of effect is as long as 6 hours.

Indications: For the symptomatic relief and prevention of bronchospasm due to bronchial asthma, chronic bronchitis and other chronic bronchopulmonary disorders in patients in whom reversible bronchospasm is a complicating factor. In addition, salbutamol inhalation aerosol is indicated for the prevention of exercise-induced asthma.

Contraindications: In patients hypersensitive to salbutamol or any of the components in the Airomir Inhalation Aerosol. (see Supplied).

Warnings: Use of Anti-inflammatory Agents: In accordance with the present practice for asthma treatment, concomitant anti-inflammatory therapy (e.g., corticosteroids) should be part of the regimen if inhaled salbutamol needs to be used on a regular daily basis (see Dosage). It is essential that the physician instruct the patient in the need for further evaluation if the patient's asthma becomes worse.

Cardiovascular Effects: In individual patients, any β_2-adrenergic agonist, including salbutamol, may have a clinically significant cardiac effect. Care should be taken with patients suffering from cardiovascular disorders, especially coronary insufficiency, cardiac arrhythmias, and hypertension. Special care and supervision are required in patients with idiopathic hypertrophic subvalvular aortic stenosis, in whom an increase in the pressure gradient between the left ventricle and the aorta may occur, causing increased strain on the left ventricle.

Paradoxical Bronchospasm: With repeated excessive use of sympathomimetic inhalation preparations, some patients have been reported to have developed severe paradoxical bronchospasm, occasionally leading to death. The cause of either the refractory state or death is unknown. However, it is suspected in the fatal episodes that cardiac arrest occurred following the unexpected development of a severe acute asthmatic crisis and subsequent hypoxia.

Do Not Exceed the Recommended Dose: Fatalities have been reported in association with excessive use of inhaled sympathomimetic drugs. The exact cause of death is unknown, but cardiac arrest following the unexpected development of a severe acute asthmatic crisis and subsequent hypoxia is suspected.

Immediate Hypersensitivity Reactions: Immediate hypersensitivity reactions may occur after administration of salbutamol inhalation aerosol, as demonstrated by rare cases of urticaria, angioedema, rash, bronchospasm, anaphylaxis, and oropharyngeal edema.

Patients with Special Diseases and Conditions: Care should be taken in patients with convulsive disorders, hyperthyroidism, or in patients who are unusually responsive to sympathomimetic amines.

Precautions: General: If salbutamol therapy does not produce a significant improvement or if the patient's condition worsens, medical advice must be sought to determine a new plan of treatment. In the case of acute or rapidly worsening dyspnea, a physician should be consulted immediately.

Failure to respond for at least 3 hours to a previously effective dose of salbutamol indicates a deterioration of the condition and the physician should be contacted promptly. Patients should be warned not to exceed the recommended dose. Increasing use of β_2-agonists to control symptoms is usually a sign of worsening asthma. In worsening asthma it is inadequate to increase β_2-agonist use only, especially over an extended period of time. Instead, a reassessment of the patient's therapy plan is required and concomitant anti-inflammatory therapy should be considered (see Dosage).

Geriatrics: As with other β_2-agonists, special caution should be observed when using salbutamol in elderly patients who have concomitant cardiovascular disease that could be adversely affected by this class of drug.

Children: Safety and effectiveness in children below the age of 6 years have not been established.

Pregnancy: Salbutamol has been in widespread use for many years in human beings without apparent ill consequence. However, there are no adequate or well-controlled studies in pregnant women, and there is little published evidence of its safety in the early stages of human pregnancy. Administration of any drug to pregnant women should only be considered if the anticipated benefits to the expectant woman are greater than any possible risks to the fetus.

A reproduction study in rats was performed with salbutamol inhalation aerosol and no teratogenic effects were observed. Studies of propellant HFA-134a in pregnant rats or rabbits have not shown any specific hazard.

Labor and Delivery: Although there have been no reports concerning the use of salbutamol inhalation aerosol during labor and delivery, it has been reported that high doses of salbutamol administered i.v. inhibit uterine contractions. Although this effect is extremely unlikely as a consequence of aerosol use, it should be kept in mind.

Lactation: Since salbutamol is likely excreted in breast milk, and because of the potential for tumorigenicity shown for salbutamol in animal studies, a decision should be made whether to discontinue nursing or to discontinue the drug, taking into account the importance of the drug to the mother. It is not known whether salbutamol in breast milk has a harmful effect on the neonate.

Patients with Special Diseases and Conditions: Large doses of i.v. salbutamol have been reported to aggravate pre-existing diabetes and ketoacidosis. Additionally, β-agonists, including salbutamol given i.v. may cause a decrease in serum potassium possibly through intracellular shunting. The relevance of this observation to the use of salbutamol inhalation aerosol given at the recommended daily dosing is unknown, since the aerosol dose is much lower than doses given i.v.

<u>*Drug Interactions:*</u> MAO Inhibitors or Tricyclic Antidepressants: Salbutamol should be administered with extreme caution to patients being treated with MAO inhibitors or tricyclic antidepressants, or within 2 weeks of discontinuation of such agents, because the action of salbutamol on the cardiovascular system may be potentiated.

Other Inhaled Sympathomimetics/Epinephrine: Other inhaled sympathomimetic bronchodilators or epinephrine should not be used concomitantly with salbutamol. If additional adrenergic drugs are to be administered by any route to the patient using inhaled salbutamol, the adrenergic drugs should be used with caution to avoid deleterious cardiovascular effects. Such concomitant use must be individualized and not given on a routine basis. If regular coadministration is required then alternative therapy must be considered.

β-Blockers: β-adrenergic receptor blocking agents, especially the noncardioselective ones, may effectively antagonize the action of salbutamol, and therefore salbutamol and nonselective β-blocking drugs, such as propranolol, should not usually be prescribed together.

Diuretics: The ECG changes and/or hypokalemia which may result from the administration of non-potassium sparing diuretics (such as loop or thiazide diuretics) can be acutely worsened by β-agonists, especially when the recommended dose of the β-agonist is exceeded. Although the clinical significance of these effects is not known, caution is advised in the coadministration of β-agonists with non-potassium sparing diuretics.

Digoxin: Mean decreases of 16 and 22% in serum digoxin levels were demonstrated after single dose i.v. and oral administration of salbutamol, respectively, to normal volunteers who had received digoxin for 10 days. The clinical significance of these findings for patients with obstructive airway disease who are receiving salbutamol and digoxin on a chronic basis is unclear; however, careful evaluation of serum digoxin levels is recommended in patients who are currently receiving digoxin and salbutamol.

Information to be Provided to the Patient: Patients should be advised to always carry their salbutamol inhalation aerosol to use immediately if an episode of asthma is experienced.

See the illustrated Information for the consumer insert that is dispensed with the product.

It is important that patients be instructed on how to use salbutamol inhalation aerosol correctly and how it should be used in relation to other medication they are taking. Patients should be given the following information: The action of salbutamol inhalation aerosol should last for 4 to 6 hours. Salbutamol inhalation aerosol should not be used more frequently than recommended. Do not increase the number of puffs or the frequency of doses of salbutamol inhalation aerosol without consulting your physician. If you find that treatment becomes less effective for symptomatic relief, your symptoms become worse, and/or you need to use the product more frequently than usual, seek medical attention immediately. While you are taking salbutamol inhalation aerosol, other inhaled drugs should be taken only as directed by your physician. If you are pregnant or nursing, contact your physician about the use of salbutamol inhalation aerosol. You may notice a different taste or spray force with Airomir compared to salbutamol aerosol inhalers that contain CFC propellants.

Common adverse effects of your treatment with inhaled salbutamol include palpitations, chest pain, rapid heart rate, tremor, or nervousness.

Adverse Effects: A 12-week double-blind study compared Airomir Inhalation Aerosol, Ventolin inhaler (U.S. source), and HFA-134a placebo in 565 asthmatic patients. Table I (on following page) lists the incidence of all adverse events (whether considered drug related or not related to drug by the investigator) from this study which occurred at a rate of at least 3% in the Airomir Inhalation Aerosol group. Only those adverse events which occurred more frequently in either the Airomir Inhalation Aerosol treatment group or the Ventolin treatment group than the placebo group are listed.

Adverse events reported by less than 3% of the patients receiving Airomir, and by a greater proportion of Airomir Inhalation Aerosol patients than placebo patients, which have the potential to be related to Airomir Inhalation Aerosol include: dysphonia, contact dermatitis, increased sweating, dry mouth, chest pain, edema, rigors, ataxia, leg cramps, hyperkinesia, eructation, flatulence, tinnitus, diabetes mellitus, anxiety, depression, somnolence and rash.

In a small cumulative dose study, tremor, nervousness, and headache appeared to be dose-related. Palpitation has also been observed with Airomir.

Table I—Airomir

Adverse Experience Incidences (% of patients) in a Large 12-Week Clinical Trial*

Body System/Adverse Event (Preferred Term)	Airomir Inhalation Aerosol N=193	Ventolin (U.S.)-I Inhaler N=186	HFA-134a Placebo Inhaler N=186
Application Site Disorders			
Inhalation Site Sensation	6	9	2
Inhalation Taste Sensation	4	3	3
Body As A Whole			
Allergic Symptoms	6	4	<1
Back Pain	4	2	3
Fever	6	2	5
Central and Peripheral Nervous System			
Dizziness	5	8	6
Tremor	7	8	2
Gastrointestinal System			
Nausea	10	9	5
Vomiting	7	2	3
Heart Rate and Rhythm Disorder			
Tachycardia	7	2	<1
Psychiatric Disorders			
Nervousness	7	9	3
Respiratory System Disorders			
Respiratory Disorder	6	4	5
Rhinitis	16	22	14
Upper Respiratory Tract Infection	21	20	18
Urinary System Disorder			
Urinary Tract Infection	3	4	2

*This table includes all adverse events (whether considered drug related or not related to drug) which occurred at an incidence rate of at least 3% in the Airomir Inhalation Aerosol group and more frequently in the Airomir Inhalation Aerosol group than in the HFA-134a placebo inhaler group.

Rare cases of urticaria, angioedema, rash, bronchospasm and oropharyngeal edema have been reported after the use of inhaled salbutamol. In addition, salbutamol, like other sympathomimetic agents, can cause adverse reactions such as hypertension, angina, vomiting, vertigo, CNS stimulation, insomnia, headache, unusual taste and drying or irritation of the oropharynx.

Overdose: Symptoms and Treatment: Manifestations of overdosage may include anginal pain, hypertension, hypokalemia, tremor and tachycardia and exaggeration of other pharmacological effects as listed in Adverse Effects.

As with all sympathomimetic aerosol medications, cardiac arrest and even death may be associated with abuse.

The oral LD_{50} in male and female rats and mice was greater than 2 000 mg/kg. The aerosol LD_{50} could not be determined.

In the event of overdose, supportive therapy should be instituted. Dialysis is not appropriate treatment for overdosage of salbutamol inhalation aerosol. The judicious use of a cardioselective β-receptor blocker is suggested, bearing in mind the danger of inducing an asthmatic attack.

Dosage: Dosage should be individualized, and the patient's response should be monitored by the prescribing physician on an ongoing basis.

In accordance with the present practice for asthma treatment, if salbutamol is required for relief of symptoms more than twice a day on a regular daily basis or for an extended period of time, anti-inflammatory therapy (e.g., corticosteroids) should be part of the regimen.

Increasing demand for salbutamol preparations in bronchial asthma is usually a sign of worsening asthma and indicates that the treatment plan should be reviewed.

If a previously effective dose fails to provide the usual relief, or the effects of a dose last for less than 3 hours, patients should seek prompt medical advice since this is usually a sign of worsening asthma.

As there may be adverse effects associated with excessive dosing, the dosage or frequency of administration should only be increased on medical advice. However, if a more severe attack has not been relieved by the usual dose, additional doses may be required. In these cases, patients should immediately consult their doctors or the nearest hospital.

Acute Symptoms: Patients 12 years and older: 1 to 2 inhalations (100 to 200 μg). Children (6 to 11 years): 1 inhalation (100 μg).

If a more severe attack has not been relieved by the usual dose (1 to 2 inhalations), further inhalations may be required. In these cases, patients should immediately consult their doctors or the nearest hospital.

Intermittent and Long-term Treatment: If despite appropriate maintenance therapy, regular daily use of the inhalation aerosol remains necessary for the control of bronchospasm, the recommended dose is: Patients 12 years and older: 1 to 2 inhalations (100 to 200 μg) 3 to 4 times daily, not exceeding 8 inhalations (800 μg/day. Children (6 to 11 years): 1 inhalation (100 μg), not exceeding 4 inhalations (400 μg/day.

Prevention of Exercise-induced Asthma: Patients 12 years and older: 2 inhalations (200 μg) 30 minutes before exertion. The effectiveness of Airomir in preventing exercise-induced asthma in children younger than 12 years of age has not been established.

Total Daily Dose Should Not Exceed: Patients 12 years and older: 8 inhalations (800 μg). Patients 6 to 11 years: 4 inhalations (400 μg).

Information for the Patient: See Blue Section—Information for the Patient "Airomir".

Supplied: Each pressurized inhalation aerosol delivers salbutamol sulfate, USP equivalent to 120 ex-valve μg into the mouthpiece of the adapter. Nonmedicinal ingredients: ethanol, oleic acid and propellant HFA-134a. The inhalation aerosol does not contain chlorofluorocarbons (CFCs).

Ethanol has been previously used in inhaled medication, as a cosolvent. The small amounts used in inhalers are not known to cause safety problems in asthmatics. A metered dose from Airomir Inhalation Aerosol delivers 0.0054 mL of ethanol per puff which is subject to evaporation as the aerosol expands and is diluted in body fluids as it expands.

Individual packages of 100- or 200-dose inhalers. The 200-dose product contains a minimum net content weight of 6.7 g and will provide a minimum of 200 inhalations. The 100-dose product (hospital pack) contains a minimum net content weight of 3.7 g and will provide a minimum of 100 inhalations.

Store between 15 and 30°C. Protect from direct sunlight and frost. **Prime the inhaler when new and after 2 or more weeks of non-use by discharging a minimum of 4 sprays to the atmosphere.** Shake well before using. As the vial is pressurized no attempt should be made to puncture it or dispose of it by burning.

New Product 1998

AKINETON® Ⓟ

Knoll

Biperiden HCl

Anticholinergic—Antiparkinson Agent

Pharmacology: Biperiden is an anticholinergic agent which acts primarily on the CNS. Parkinsonism is thought to result from an imbalance between the excitatory (cholinergic) and inhibitory (dopaminergic) systems. Accordingly, the mechanism of action of centrally active anticholinergic drugs, such as biperiden, is considered to relate to competitive antagonism of acetylcholine at the cholinergic receptors in the corpus striatum, which restores the balance. Similarly, biperiden has been shown to antagonize the Parkinson-like effects of agents with central cholinergic properties.

The peripheral anticholinergic effects of biperiden are small in comparison with atropine; giving rise to a lower incidence of antisecretory and mydriatic effects.

Biperiden binds competitively to peripheral and central muscarinic receptors. In vitro, it has a higher affinity for the M1 receptor compared to the M2 muscarinic receptor subtype. Although the clinical significance of this selectivity has not been established, it may account for lower peripheral side effects in those tissues where M2 receptors predominate.

Pharmacokinetics: After oral administration of a single dose of 4 mg to young healthy subjects, absorption, after a mean lag time of 27 minutes to the appearance of detectable concentrations in the plasma, was rapid, a mean C_{max} of 5.1 ng/mL being reached after 1.5 hours.

In comparative repeat dose studies (4 mg on day 1, followed by 2 mg b.i.d. from day 8 to 14) in young healthy subjects, (19 to 28 years) and older Parkinson patients (72 to 82 years), the following mean C_{max} and T_{max} were found (see Table I).

Table I—Akineton

Comparative Repeat Dose Studies

	Young healthy subjects		Older Parkinson patients	
	C_{max} (ng/mL)	T_{max} (hours)	C_{max} (ng/mL)	T_{max} (hours)
Day 1	4.3±2.6	0.9±0.4	7.2±4.4	1.6±0.7
Day 15	2.5±1.4	0.8±0.3	4.2±2.2	1.6±0.3

Thereafter, the concentration curves exhibited an initially rapid, biphasic decline (see Table II).

Table II—Akineton

Elimination Half-lives

Terminal plasma elimination t½ lives:	Young healthy subject	Older Parkinson patients
Single dose elimination	14.2±3.2	30.2±6.4
Steady state elimination	24.5±8.8	38.5±12.2

Systemic bioavailability is only 33±5%, due to intensive metabolism. The main metabolite is produced by hydroxylation at the bicyclus with some hydroxylation of the piperidine ring structure. No unchanged biperiden was found in the urine. Binding to plasma proteins was found to be 94% in women and 93% in men.

Indications: As an adjunct in the therapy of all forms of Parkinsonism (postencephalitic, arteriosclerotic, idiopathic), especially in cases where akinesia muscular rigidity and to a lesser extent tremor are the major presenting symptoms. Biperiden is also useful in the control of extrapyramidal disorders due to neuroleptic agents.

Parkinson's Disease: In treating Parkinsonism, improvement of symptoms (primarily of rigidity) occasionally may occur as early as the second day at a dose of 1 to 2 mg 3 times daily. Usually, the maximum effect does not appear until after the first 3 to 4 days of treatment.

There are wide individual variations in the response of Parkinson's disease to biperiden. Although excellent therapeutic results have been obtained, as well as satisfactory or moderate responses, the overall effect is at times inadequate. In view of this, the addition of drugs administered concomitantly is well accepted in the treatment of Parkinson's disease. Nevertheless, it is advisable to start treatment with biperiden alone and not to institute additional therapy until is has been established that the effect of biperiden alone, at adequate dose, is unsatisfactory.

Drug-Induced Extrapyramidal Reactions: For drug-induced extrapyramidal reactions the effect of oral biperiden, depending on the nature and severity of the symptomatology, appears within a few hours to a few days. The duration of actions is dependent on the nature, severity and duration of extrapyramidal symptomatology, the type and dose of the psychotropic drug, the route of administration, whether and when administration of the psychoactive drug was discontinued, and on the dosage of biperiden.

Contraindications: Hypersensitivity to biperiden; untreated narrow angle glaucoma; stenosis in the gastrointestinal tract; megacolon.

Warnings: The use of biperiden is **not** recommended in patients with prostate adenoma, or with diseases which could lead to perilous tachycardia.

Akineton (cont'd)

Isolated instances of mental confusion, euphoria, agitation and disturbed behavior have been reported following biperiden administration.

Precautions: Dependence Liability: Biperiden abuse has been observed, which may be related to a mood-lifting effect which has been occasionally observed.

Pregnancy: The safe use of biperiden in pregnancy has not been established and therefore it should not be used during pregnancy unless in the opinion of the prescribing physician the anticipated benefits outweigh the potential risks to the fetus.

Lactation: Although no data exists with regard to biperiden, anticholinergics in general may inhibit lactation. Biperiden has been found to pass into mother's milk and can reach the same concentrations as those found in the mother's plasma. Since the type and extent of metabolism in neonates are not known and since pharmacological and toxicological effects cannot be excluded, ablactation is generally recommended.

Children: Safety and effectiveness in children have not been adequately established.

Geriatrics: Elderly patients, particularly those with cerebral lesions of a vascular or degenerative nature, may exhibit increased sensitivity to biperiden (see Dosage).

Glaucoma: Caution should be observed in patients with manifest glaucoma, though no prohibitive rise in intraocular pressure has been noted following oral or parenteral administration of biperiden.

General: Patients with prostatism, epilepsy or cardiac arrhythmias should be given biperiden with caution.

Occupational Hazards: Occasionally drowsiness may occur following biperiden administration, and patients who drive a car or operate potentially dangerous machinery should be warned of this possibility.

As with other drugs affecting the CNS, the consumption of alcohol should be avoided during therapy with biperiden.

Side effects (see Adverse Effects) may occur in the early stages of treatment and particularly if the dose is increased too rapidly (see Dosage).

Except in the case of medical emergency, abrupt discontinuation of the drug is to be avoided, due to the risk of rebound imbalance between the cholinergic and dopaminergic regulatory systems.

The change from another antiparkinson drug to biperiden is best carried out gradually, i.e., biperiden is started at a low dose and gradually increased and the other drug is gradually decreased and discontinued. If L-Dopa is the other drug, it should be continued unless unacceptable toxicity occurs.

Drug Interactions: The central and peripheral side effects of biperiden may be potentiated when administered concomitantly with other anticholinergic drugs, or with drugs which have secondary anticholinergic activity, e.g. certain narcotic analgesics such as meperidine, the phenothiazines and other antipsychotics, tricyclic antidepressants, certain antiarrhythmics such as the quinidine salts, certain antihistamines and antispasmodics. The effect of metoclopramide is antagonized by biperiden.

The concurrent administration of biperiden with levodopa may potentiate dyskinesia. Tardive dyskinesia induced by neuroleptics may be intensified by biperiden. However, in cases where there is already tardive dyskinesia, occasionally the Parkinsonian symptoms may be so severe that continuation of biperiden therapy is justified.

Adverse Effects: The common side effects which occur with biperiden administration in therapeutic doses, are dry mouth and blurred vision. These effects can be decreased or eliminated by reduction in oral dosage. Gastric irritation after oral biperiden may be avoided by administering the drug during or shortly after meals. A decrease in urinary flow has been noted in a few patients. Some patients may exhibit short periods of euphoria or disorientation.

In patients in the early stage of treatment in whom the dosage has been increased too rapidly, or in elderly patients with cerebral lesions of a vascular or degenerative nature, increased sensitivity to the recommended therapeutic doses may occur. In such cases, central side effects may take the form of fatigue, dizziness, euphoria or disorientation, at higher doses restlessness and confusion, occasionally impairment of memory and in rare cases, hallucinations. Peripheral side effects include dry mouth, blurred vision, hypohidrosis, constipation, urinary retention, and increase in heart rate, very rarely a decrease in heart rate.

Allergic skin rashes and dyskinesia have also been observed occasionally.

Overdose: Symptoms: Overdosage with biperiden produces both the central and peripheral symptoms typical of atropine toxicity.

Correct diagnosis depends upon recognition of the peripheral signs of parasympathetic blockade including: dilated and sluggish pupils; warm, dry skin; facial flushing; decreased secretions of the mouth, pharynx, nose and bronchi; foul-smelling breath; elevated temperature; tachycardia; cardiac arrhythmias; decreased bowel sounds; urinary retention.

Neuropsychiatric signs such a delirium, disorientation, anxiety, hallucinations, illusions, confusion, incoherence, agitation, hyperactivity, ataxia, loss of memory, paranoia, combativeness and seizures may be present.

The condition can progress to stupor, coma, paralysis, cardiac and respiratory arrest and death.

Treatment: Treatment of acute overdosage revolves around symptomatic and supportive therapy. Gastric lavage or other measures to limit absorption should be initiated. A small dose of diazepam or a short-acting barbiturate may be administered if CNS excitation is observed. **Phenothiazines are contraindicated** due to their antimuscarinic activity, which may intensify toxicity, causing coma.

Respiratory support, artificial respiration or the use of a vasopressor agent may be necessary. Hyperpyrexia must be reversed, fluid volume replaced and acid-base balance maintained. Urinary catheterization may be necessary.

The routine use of parenteral acetylcholine esterase inhibition, physostigmine is controversial. Delirium, hallucinations, coma and supraventricular tachycardia (but not ventricular tachycardia, nor conduction defects) seem to respond well to physostigmine 0.5 to 1.0 mg i.m. or by slow i.v. infusion. If there is no response within 20 minutes, an additional 1 mg dose may be given; this may be repeated until a total of 4 mg has been administered, a reversal of toxic effects is observed, or excessive cholinergic signs are seen. Frequent monitoring of clinical signs should be done. Since physostigmine is rapidly destroyed, additional injections may be required every 1 or 2 hours to maintain control. The relapse intervals tend to lengthen as the toxic anticholinergic agent is metabolized, so the patient should be carefully observed for 8 to 12 hours following the last relapse.

Dosage: General: Treatment with biperiden should be initiated with small doses, progressing gradually to optimum amounts. The dosage depending on the therapeutic effect and the side effects. The total daily oral dose should be distributed evenly throughout the day, and taken with or after food.

In older patients, especially those with cerebro-organic symptoms, conservative dosing is called for.

Experience with the use of biperiden in children is limited and arises mostly from short-term use in drug-induced dystonia (induced by neuroleptics, metoclopramide, or similar compounds).

Parkinson's Disease: Treatment may be initiated with an oral dose of 1 mg twice daily. The dose can then be increased by 2 mg/day, up to a maximum of 16 mg/day. The average dose is 2 mg 3 to 4 times a day.

Drug-induced Extrapyramidal Reactions: The intensity of the extrapyramidal reaction, not the dosage of the drug inducing the reaction, is the decisive factor in determining the dosage of biperiden necessary for control. Size and weight of the patient and previous response to other antiparkinson drugs are also important in determining dosage.

A dose of 2 mg 1 to 3 times daily has proved to be of benefit for the prophylaxis and treatment of drug-induced extrapyramidal symptoms.

Supplied: Each white, uncoated tablet, imprinted with the number 11 on one side and the Knoll triangle imprinted on the other side, contains: biperiden HCl USP 2 mg. Nonmedicinal ingredients: lactose anhydrous and magnesium stearate. Bottles of 100.

(Shown in Product Recognition Section)

ALBALON®-A LIQUIFILM®

Allergan

Antazoline Phosphate—Naphazoline HCl

Antihistamine—Decongestant

Supplied: Each mL contains: antazoline phosphate 0.5% and naphazoline HCl 0.05%. Nonmedicinal ingredients: benzalkonium chloride 0.004%, disodium edetate, polyvinyl alcohol (Liquifilm), povidone, sodium acetate and sodium chloride. Plastic dropper bottles of 15 mL. Protect from light.

ALBERT® DOCUSATE

Albert Pharma

Docusate Calcium

Stool Softener

Indications: For short-term use in the relief of occasional constipation caused by hard, dry stools. Stool softening generally occurs within 24 to 48 hours postdosing.

Dosage: Adults: 1 capsule daily. The capsules are to be swallowed whole. Do not exceed the recommended dose.

Information for the Patient: See Blue Section—Information for the Patient "Albert Docusate".

Supplied: Each soft, red, gelatin capsule contains: docusate calcium USP 240 mg. Sodium- and tartrazine-free. Plastic bottles of 1 000. Store in the container in which they were purchased. Do not expose container or contents to humidity or to sources of heat. Store the container at room temperature, below 25°C. Do not use the product after the expiration date printed on the container.

Reviewed 1998

ALBERT® GLYBURIDE Ⓟ

Albert Pharma

Glyburide

Oral Hypoglycemic

Pharmacology: The principal action of glyburide results in an increased insulin release from the beta cells of the pancreas. Other mechanisms leading to a reduction of blood glucose are also believed to be influenced by glyburide. The insertion of an alkylene chain on the benzene nucleus results in a product of very high potency.

Schulz and Schmidt indicated that the presence of a sulfonamide (sulfaphenazole) decreased the distribution volume of glyburide without influence on the half-life of the oral hypoglycemic agent. As a result, insulin and serum concentrations of glyburide were higher and hypoglycemic attacks could be expected.

Hirn and Konigstein have observed hypoglycemia when phenylbutazone and oxyphenbutazone were added to glyburide. Schulz and Schmidt confirmed that phenylbutazone has an enhancing effect on the blood sugar lowering effect of glyburide and found higher insulin levels. The plasma half-life of glyburide did not change with phenylbutazone administration. However, a significant decrease in the renal excretion of the main metabolite of glyburide was observed, suggesting that the elimination in the bile may compensate for the amount not excreted in the urine.

Glyburide micronized powder is well absorbed from the intestinal tract. Glyburide is highly bound to plasma proteins after absorption from the gastrointestinal tract. It is completely metabolized by hydroxylation of the cyclohexyl ring into 3-cis and 4-trans derivatives in the liver, and the kidneys play only a minor role in their biotransformation and elimination from plasma. The metabolites have no essential hypoglycemic effect and they are not stored in the body, but they are eliminated via the bile, and in approximately the same amounts in the urine conjugated to glucuronic acid and in the feces.

Maximal plasma levels of insulin, after an oral dose of 5 mg glyburide in normal subjects were reached 90 minutes after dosing.

Minimal blood levels of glucose, after an oral dose of 5 mg glyburide in normal subjects, were reached 120 minutes after dosing corresponding to a reduction of about 35%.

Raptis et al. found that the effect of an i.v. injection of 1 mg of glyburide on blood glucose and serum insulin levels of healthy subjects was slower in onset and lasted longer than that of 1 g of tolbutamide. Furthermore, when a second injection of glyburide was given 1 hour later, the effects were undiminished. When glyburide was injected at 4-hour intervals in patients with adult-onset diabetes, the effects of glyburide were not diminished.

Indications: To control hyperglycemia in glyburide-responsive diabetes mellitus of stable, mild, nonketosis-prone, maturity-onset or adult-type which cannot be controlled solely by proper dietary management, exercise and weight reduction or when insulin therapy is not appropriate.

Contraindications: Patients with known hypersensitivity or allergy to the active ingredient or any other component of the formulation. Glyburide should not be given to patients with:

unstable and/or insulin-dependent diabetes mellitus; ketoacidosis; diabetic precoma; coma; in the presence of pre-existing complications peculiar to diabetes; during stress conditions such as severe infections, trauma or surgery; in the presence of liver disease or renal impairment; or frank jaundice.

Pregnancy: During pregnancy, no oral antidiabetic agent should be given.

Lactation: Due to the possible excretion in human milk, the patient should discontinue nursing or discontinue taking the drug depending on the importance of the drug to the mother. If glyburide is discontinued, the patient should be transferred to insulin therapy.

Warnings: The use of glyburide will not prevent the development of complications peculiar to diabetes mellitus.

The use of glyburide must be considered as treatment in addition to a proper dietary regimen and not as a substitute for diet.

Over a period of time, patients may become progressively less responsive to therapy with oral hypoglycemic agents because of deterioration of their diabetic state. If a loss of adequate blood glucose lowering response to glyburide is detected, the drug should be discontinued.

Precautions: Patient Selection and Followup: Careful selection of patients is important. It is imperative that there be rigid attention to diet, adherence to regular exercise, reduction of body weight in obese patients, careful adjustment of dosage, instruction of the patient on hypoglycemic reactions and their control as well as regular, thorough followup examinations.

Since the effects of oral hypoglycemic agents on the vascular changes and other long-term sequelae of diabetes mellitus are not fully known, patients receiving such drugs must be closely observed for both short and long-term complications.

Periodic assessment of cardiovascular, ophthalmic, hematologic, renal and hepatic status is advisable.

In patients stabilized on glyburide therapy, loss of blood sugar control may occur in cases of acute intercurrent disease or in stressful situations such as trauma or surgery. Under these conditions, discontinuation of glyburide and administration of insulin should be considered.

Oral hypoglycemic agents should be administered with caution to patients with Addison's disease.

Pregnancy: The use of glyburide is not recommended for women planning a pregnancy (see Contraindications); these patients should be changed over to insulin therapy.

Hypoglycemic Reactions: Severe hypoglycemia can be induced by all sulfonylurea drugs. Particularly susceptible are elderly subjects, patients with impaired hepatic and renal function, those who are debilitated or malnourished, and patients with primary or secondary adrenal insufficiency. Hypoglycemia is more likely to occur when the caloric intake is inadequate or after strenuous or prolonged exercise.

Drug Interactions: Patients who receive or discontinue certain medications while undergoing treatment with glyburide may experience changes in blood glucose control.

Hypoglycemia may be potentiated when a sulfonylurea is used concurrently with agents such as: insulin and other oral antidiabetics, anabolic steroids and androgens, azapropazone, chloramphenicol, clofibrate, coumarin derivatives, cyclophosphamide, disopyramide, fenfluramine, fibrates, fluoxetine, ifosfamide, miconazole, MAO inhibitors, oxyphenbutazone, para-aminosalicylic acid, phenylbutazone, probenecid, propranolol, quinolones, salicylates, sulfinpyrazone, sulfonamides, sympatholytic agents (e.g., beta-blockers, guanethidine) tetracyclines, tuberculostatics.

Certain drugs tend to produce hyperglycemia and may lead to loss of blood sugar control; these include: acetazolamide, barbiturates, corticosteroids, diazoxide, diuretics (thiazides, furosemide), glucagon, laxatives (after protracted use), nicotinic acid (in pharmacologic doses), oral contraceptives (estrogen plus progestogen), phenothiazines, phenytoin, rifampin, sympathomimetic agents (e.g., epinephrine) and thyroid hormones.

Under the influence of sympatholytic drugs such as beta-blockers, clonidine, guanethidine, and reserpine, the signs of adrenergic counter-regulation to hypoglycemia may be reduced or absent.

Concurrent use of H_2-receptor antagonists, clonidine or reserpine with glyburide may lead to either a potentiation or an attenuation of the blood-glucose-lowering effect.

Both acute and chronic alcohol intake may potentiate or weaken the blood-glucose-lowering action of glyburide in an unpredictable fashion. Intolerance to alcohol (disulfiram-like reaction: flushing, sensation of warmth, giddiness, nausea, and occasionally tachycardia) may occur in patients treated with oral hypoglycemic drugs. These reactions can be prevented by avoiding the use of alcohol.

Barbiturates should be used cautiously in patients receiving an oral hypoglycemic agent since their action may be prolonged.

Glyburide may potentiate or weaken the effects of coumarin derivatives.

Occupational Hazards: Until optimal control has been achieved, when changing the antidiabetic preparation, or when the tablets have not been taken regularly, alertness and reaction time may be altered to such an extent that the patient cannot safely cope with road traffic or operate machinery.

Adverse Effects: Hypoglycemia (see Precautions): Severe hypoglycemia, which may be prolonged and has occasionally been life-threatening, may occur and mimics acute CNS disorders (see Overdose: Symptoms and Treatment). Hepatic and/or renal disease, malnutrition and/or irregular meals, exercise without adequate caloric supplementation, debility, advanced age, patient noncompliance, alcoholism, certain disorders of thyroid function, adrenal or pituitary insufficiency, excessive glyburide dosage, treatment with glyburide in the absence of indication or concurrent use with other agents may be predisposing factors.

Gastrointestinal: Nausea, epigastric fullness and heartburn are common reactions. Vomiting, diarrhea, and abdominal pain have also been reported. These tend to be dose-related and may disappear when dosage is reduced.

Dermatologic and Sensitivity Reactions: Allergic and pseudoallergic skin reactions such as pruritus, erythema, urticaria, morbilliform, or maculopapular eruptions have been reported in a number of patients. These may subside on continued use of glyburide, but if they persist the drug should be discontinued. Mild reactions such as urticaria may very rarely develop into serious and life-threatening reactions including dyspnea, hypotension or shock. Porphyria cutanea tarda and photosensitivity reactions have been associated with the use of oral hypoglycemic drugs. Allergic vasculitis have been observed very rarely in patients receiving glyburide and in some circumstances may be life-threatening.

Cross-sensitivity to sulfonamides or their derivatives may occur in patients treated with oral sulfonylurea hypoglycemic agents.

Hematologic: Rare cases of mild to severe thrombocytopenia which can manifest itself as purpura have been reported. Leukopenia, agranulocytosis, pancytopenia (which may be due to myelosuppression), erythrocytopenia, granulocytopenia, hemolytic anemia and aplastic anemia have been observed very rarely with glyburide therapy. These reactions may be reversible following discontinuation of the sulfonylurea antidiabetic agent.

Metabolic: Hepatic porphyria and disulfiram-like reactions have been observed in patients treated with oral hypoglycemic drugs. Elevation of liver enzyme levels has been reported very rarely in patients treated with glyburide. In isolated cases, impairment of liver function (e.g., cholestasis and jaundice) and hepatitis have been observed which can regress after withdrawal of the drug or may lead to life-threatening liver failure.

Endocrine: Reduced radioactive iodine uptake by the thyroid gland has been reported with oral hypoglycemic therapy.

Other: Transient visual disturbances may occur at the commencement of treatment due to fluctuations in blood glucose levels.

In isolated cases, reduction of serum sodium concentrations has been observed in patients receiving glyburide.

Overdose: Symptoms: Overdosage with sulfonylureas may result in hypoglycemia, but it should be noted that the dosage which causes hypoglycemia varies widely, and may be within the accepted therapeutic range in sensitive individuals.

The manifestations of hypoglycemia include: flushing or pallor, chilliness, excessive hunger, trembling, headache, dizziness, nausea, vomiting, restlessness, aggressiveness, depression, speech disorders, sensory and/or visual disturbances, helplessness, lassitude, shallow respiration or bradycardia. In more severe cases, the clinical symptoms of a stroke or coma appear. However, symptoms of hypoglycemia are not necessarily as typical as described above and sulfonylureas may cause insidious development of symptoms mimicking cerebrovascular insufficiency (e.g., disordered sleep, somnolence, impaired alertness and reactions, confusion, delirium, cerebral convulsions, paralytic symptoms or loss of consciousness).

Signs of adrenergic counter-regulation to hypoglycemia include: sweating, damp skin, anxiety, tachycardia, hypertension, palpitations, angina pectoris and cardiac arrhythmias. However, these symptoms may be milder or absent in patients who develop hypoglycemia gradually, patients with autonomic neuropathy, or patients who receive concurrent treatment with sympatholytic agents (e.g., beta-blockers, clonidine, reserpine, guanethidine).

Treatment: Discontinue medication and treat hypoglycemia by giving dextrose promptly and in sufficient quantity.

The symptoms of hypoglycemia nearly always subside when blood glucose control is attained. However, some sulfonylurea-induced hypoglycemias may be refractory to treatment and susceptible to relapse, especially in elderly or malnourished patients. Continuous dextrose infusions for hours to days have been necessary.

Dosage: In diabetic subjects, there is no fixed dosage regimen for management of blood glucose levels. Individual determination of the minimum dose that will lower the blood glucose adequately should be made.

If the maximal recommended dose fails to lower blood glucose adequately in patients on initial trial, glyburide should be discontinued. During the course of therapy a loss of effectiveness may occur. It is advisable to ascertain the contribution of the drug in the control of blood glucose by discontinuing the medication semi-annually or at least annually with careful monitoring of the patient. If the need for the drug is not evident, the drug should not be resumed. In some diabetic subjects, short-term administration of the drug may be sufficient during periods of transient loss of blood sugar control.

Adjustment of glyburide dosage should be considered whenever factors predisposing the patient to the development of hypo- or hyperglycemia, such as weight or life-style changes, are present (see Contraindications, Warnings, Precautions and Adverse Effects).

Newly-Diagnosed Diabetics: The initial dose is 5 mg daily (2.5 mg in patients over 60 years of age) and it should be continued for 5 to 7 days. Depending on the response, the dosage should then be either increased or decreased by steps of 2.5 mg. The maximum daily dose of glyburide is 20 mg (because higher doses normally have no additional effect on control of metabolic state). Occasionally, control is maintained with 2.5 mg daily. The majority of cases can be controlled by 5 to 10 mg (1 to 2 tablets) daily given as a single dose during or immediately after breakfast. Patients who eat only a light breakfast should defer the first dose of the day until lunchtime. If more than 10 mg (2 tablets) daily is required, the excess should be taken with the evening meal.

Changeover From Other Oral Hypoglycemic Agents: There is no exact dosage relationship between glyburide and other oral antidiabetic agents. Discontinue previous oral medication and start glyburide 5 mg daily (2.5 mg in patients over 60 years of age). This also applies to patients changed over from the maximum dose of other oral antidiabetic medication. Determine maintenance dosage as in newly diagnosed diabetics.

Consideration must be given to the potency and duration of action of the previous antidiabetic agent. A break from medication may be required to avoid any summation of effects entailing a risk of hypoglycemia.

Changeover From Insulin: If a change from insulin to glyburide is contemplated in a patient with stable, mild, maturity-onset diabetes, treatment with insulin should be discontinued for a period of 2 or 3 days to determine whether any therapy other than dietary regulation and exercise is needed. During this insulin-free interval, the patient's urine should be tested at least 3 times daily for glucose and ketone-bodies, and the results monitored carefully by a physician. The appearance of significant ketonuria accompanied by glucosuria within 12 to 24 hours after the withdrawal of insulin strongly suggests that the patient is ketosis-prone and precludes the change from insulin to glyburide.

Supplied: 2.5 mg: Each white, round, uncoated, beveled tablet, with score-break and code letters GLY (imprinted both above and below the score-break) on obverse and Albert logo trademark on reverse, contains: glyburide 2.5 mg. Nonmedicinal ingredients: colloidal silicon dioxide, cornstarch, lactose hydrous, magnesium stearate, purified water and talc. Tartrazine-free. Cartons of 30 (3×10) and 300 (10×30) in blister packs. Plastic bottles of 300.

5 mg: Each white, oblong, uncoated, beveled tablet, with score-break, number 5 and Albert logo trademark on obverse, contains: glyburide 5 mg. Nonmedicinal ingredients: colloidal silicon dioxide, cornstarch, lactose hydrous, magnesium stearate, purified water and talc. Tartrazine-free. Cartons of 30 (3×10) and 300 (10×30) in blister packs. Plastic bottles of 300.

Store at room temperature, below 25°C, and not beyond the expiry date indicated on the package.

Reviewed 1998

ALBERT® OXYBUTYNIN Ⓟ

Albert Pharma

Oxybutynin Chloride

Anticholinergic—Antispasmodic Agent

Pharmacology: Oxybutynin is a tertiary amine anticholinergic agent which exerts antimuscarinic as well as direct antispasmodic action on smooth muscle. In vitro studies have shown that its anticholinergic effects are weaker than those of atropine, but it possesses greater antispasmodic activity. No blocking effects occur at skeletal neuromuscular junctions or in autonomic ganglia (no antinicotinic effects).

In addition to its smooth muscle relaxing effects, oxybutynin exerts an analgesic and a local anesthetic effect. In animal studies the CNS and cardiovascular actions of oxybutynin were shown to be similar to but weaker than those of atropine.

Oxybutynin relaxes bladder smooth muscle. In patients with uninhibited neurogenic and reflex neurogenic bladder, cystometric studies have demonstrated that oxybutynin increases bladder (vesical) capacity, diminishes the frequency of uninhibited contractions of the detrusor muscle, and delays the initial desire to void. Oxybutynin thus decreases urgency and the frequency of both incontinent episodes and voluntary urination. These effects are more consistently improved in patients with uninhibited neurogenic bladder.

Oxybutynin is readily absorbed from the gastrointestinal tract. The onset of action is approximately 1 hour after an oral dose and its duration 6 to 10 hours.

Indications: For the relief of symptoms associated with voiding in patients with uninhibited neurogenic bladder and reflex neurogenic bladder (i.e., urgency, frequency, urinary leakage, urge incontinence, dysuria).

Contraindications: In patients with glaucoma, partial or complete obstruction of the gastrointestinal tract, paralytic ileus, intestinal atony of the elderly or debilitated patient, megacolon, toxic megacolon complicating ulcerative colitis, severe colitis, myasthenia gravis, obstructive uropathy, and when the patient has an unstable cardiovascular status in acute hemorrhage. Oxybutynin is contraindicated in patients who have demonstrated hypersensitivity to the product.

Warnings: Oxybutynin, when administered in the presence of high environmental temperature, can cause heat prostration (fever and heat stroke due to decreased sweating).

Diarrhea may be an early symptom of incomplete intestinal obstruction, especially in patients with ileostomy or colostomy. In such cases, treatment with oxybutynin would be inappropriate and possibly harmful.

Occupational Hazards: Oxybutynin may produce drowsiness or blurred vision. The patient should be cautioned regarding activities requiring mental alertness, such as operating a motor vehicle or other machinery or performing hazardous work while taking this drug. Alcohol or other sedative drugs may enhance the drowsiness caused by oxybutynin.

Pretreatment examinations should include cystometry, and other appropriate diagnostic procedures. Cystometry should be repeated at appropriate date intervals to evaluate response to therapy. The appropriate antibiotic therapy should be instituted in the presence of infection.

Precautions: Oxybutynin should be used with caution in the elderly and in patients with autonomic neuropathy, hepatic or renal disease. Administration of oxybutynin in large doses to patients with ulcerative colitis may suppress intestinal motility to the point of producing a paralytic ileus and precipitate or aggravate toxic megacolon, a serious complication of the disease.

The symptoms of hyperthyroidism, coronary heart disease, congestive heart failure, cardiac arrhythmias, tachycardia, hypertension and prostatic hypertrophy may be aggravated following administration of oxybutynin. Oxybutynin should be administered with caution to patients with hiatal hernia associated with reflux esophagitis, since anticholinergic drugs may aggravate this condition.

Pregnancy: The safety of oxybutynin in pregnancy has not been established. Therefore, oxybutynin should not be used in women of childbearing potential, unless, in the opinion of the physician, the expected benefit to the patient outweighs the possible risk to the fetus.

Children: Because the safety of oxybutynin in children under the age of 5 has not been established, use of the drug in this age group is not recommended.

Lactation: It is not known whether this drug is excreted in human milk. Because many drugs are excreted in human milk, caution should be exercised when oxybutynin is administered to a nursing woman.

Adverse Effects: The following adverse reactions have been reported with oxybutynin administration: dry mouth and throat, difficulty swallowing, decreased sweating, urinary hesitance and retention, blurred vision, dilation of the pupil, cycloplegia, increased ocular tension, palpitations, tachycardia, chest pain, syncope, flushing, nose bleed, drowsiness, weakness, dizziness, headache, insomnia, mood changes, nausea, vomiting, anorexia, metallic taste, constipation, bloated feeling, edema, impotence, suppression of lactation, interference with normal heat regulation, severe allergic reactions or drug idiosyncrasies including urticaria and other dermal manifestations.

Overdose: Symptoms: The symptoms of overdosage with oxybutynin may be any of those seen with other anticholinergic agents. Symptoms may include signs of CNS excitation (e.g., restlessness, tremor, irritability, delirium, hallucinations), flushing, fever, nausea, vomiting, tachycardia, hypotension or hypertension, respiratory failure, paralysis and coma.

Treatment: In the event of an overdose or exaggerated response, treatment should be symptomatic and supportive. Induce emesis or perform gastric lavage (emesis is contraindicated in precomatose, convulsive, or psychotic state) and maintain respiration. Activated charcoal may be administered as well as magnesium sulfate. Physostigmine may be considered to reverse symptoms of anticholinergic intoxication. Hyperpyrexia may be treated symptomatically with ice bags or other cold applications and alcohol sponges.

Dosage: Oxybutynin tablets are for oral administration.

Adults: The usual dose is one 5 mg tablet 2 or 3 times a day. The maximum recommended dose is one 5 mg tablet 4 times a day. In elderly and debilitated patients, it is advisable to initiate treatment at the lowest recommended dosage and to increase the dosage carefully according to tolerance and response.

Children over 5 years of age: The usual dose is one 5 mg tablet 2 times a day. The maximum recommended dose is one 5 mg tablet 3 times a day.

Supplied: Each scored biconvex, blue tablet, marked BRL on the unscored side and 47 and 77 above and below the score mark on the scored side, contains: oxybutynin chloride 5 mg. Nonmedicinal ingredients: calcium stearate, FD&C Blue #1 lake, lactose and microcrystalline cellulose. Bottles of 100 and 500. Store at 15 to 30°C in tight, light-resistant containers.

Reviewed 1998

ALBERT® PENTOXIFYLLINE Ⓟ

Albert Pharma

Pentoxifylline

Vasoactive Agent

Pharmacology: Pentoxifylline is a xanthine derivative. It belongs to a group of vasoactive drugs which improve peripheral blood flow and thus enhance peripheral tissue oxygenation. The mechanism by which pentoxifylline achieves this effect has not been determined, but it is likely that the following factors are involved: Pentoxifylline, as other xanthine derivatives, relaxes certain smooth muscles including those of the peripheral vessels, thus causing vasodilatation or preventing spasm. This action, however, may have a limited role in patients with chronic obstructive arterial disease when peripheral vessels are already maximally dilated.

Pentoxifylline improves flexibility of red blood cells. This increase in the flexibility of red blood cells probably contributes to the improvement of the ability of blood to flow through peripheral vessels (hemorheologic action). This property was seen during in vitro and in vivo experiments with pentoxifylline but the correlation between it and the clinical improvement of patients with peripheral vascular diseases has not been determined.

Pentoxifylline promotes platelet deaggregation.

Improvement of red blood cell flexibility and platelet deaggregation contribute to the decrease in blood viscosity.

Pentoxifylline is almost completely absorbed after oral administration. The pentoxifylline 400 mg sustained-release tablet showed an initial peak plasma pentoxifylline concentration 2 to 3 hours postadministration. The drug is extensively metabolized. Biotransformation products are almost exclusively eliminated by the kidneys.

Food intake before the administration of pentoxifylline delayed the absorption but did not decrease it.

Indications: For the symptomatic treatment of patients with chronic occlusive peripheral vascular disorders of the extremities. In such patients pentoxifylline may give relief of signs and symptoms of impaired blood flow, such as intermittent claudication or trophic ulcers.

Contraindications: In patients with acute myocardial infarction, patients with severe coronary artery disease when, in the physician's judgement, myocardial stimulation might prove harmful, patients with hemorrhage, patients who have previously exhibited intolerance to pentoxifylline or other xanthines such as caffeine, theophylline and theobromine and in patients with peptic ulcers or recent history thereof.

Warnings: Since pentoxifylline is extensively metabolized in the liver and eliminated through the kidneys, the use of this drug is not recommended in patients with marked impairment of kidney or liver function. Patients with less severe impairment of the liver and patients with impaired renal function (creatine clearance below 30 mL/min) should be closely monitored during pentoxifylline therapy and they may require lower doses.

The administration of pentoxifylline has been associated with bleeding and/or prolonged prothrombin time (see Precautions, Drug Interactions). The risk of bleeding may be increased by combined treatment with anticoagulant agents. Therefore, in patients on anticoagulant therapy, pentoxifylline should be used with caution and only when in the physician's judgment the potential benefit outweighs the risk.

Children: The use of pentoxifylline in patients below the age of 18 years is not recommended as safety and effectiveness have not been established in this age group.

Precautions: Low, Labile Blood Pressure: Caution should be exercised when administering pentoxifylline to patients with low or labile blood pressure. In such patients any dose increase should be done gradually.

Geriatrics: Pentoxifylline should be used with caution in elderly patients as peak plasma levels of pentoxifylline and its metabolites are moderately higher in this age group. Elderly patients had a slight increase in the incidence of some adverse effects. Careful dose adjustment is therefore recommended.

Pregnancy: Reproduction studies have been performed in rats, mice and rabbits at doses up to 23, 2 and 11 times the maximum recommended daily human dose and have revealed no evidence of impaired fertility or harm to the fetus due to pentoxifylline. The drug has been shown to cross the blood-placenta barrier in mice. There is no adequate experience in pregnant women. Therefore, pentoxifylline is not recommended for women who are, or may become, pregnant unless the expected benefits for the mother outweigh the potential risk to the fetus.

Lactation: Pentoxifylline and its major metabolites are excreted in human milk, following a 400 mg single oral dose of pentoxifylline. The patient should be advised to discontinue nursing or to discontinue taking the drug depending on the importance of the drug to the mother.

Drug Interactions: Antihypertensive Agents: Pentoxifylline may potentiate the action of antihypertensive agents. Patients receiving these agents require blood pressure monitoring and possibly a dose reduction of the antihypertensive agents.

Sympathomimetics: Combined use with other xanthines or with sympathomimetics may cause excessive CNS stimulation.

Theophylline: Although causality has not been established, concurrent use of pentoxifylline with theophylline has resulted in elevated theophylline plasma levels, which may enhance the possibility of adverse effects.

Erythromycin: No data are available on the possible interaction of pentoxifylline and erythromycin. However concurrent administration of erythromycin and theophylline has resulted in significant elevation of serum theophylline levels with toxic reactions.

Hypoglycemic Agents: In patients treated with hypoglycemic agents, a moderate adjustment in the dose of these agents may be required when pentoxifylline is prescribed.

Anticoagulants: There have been reports of bleeding and/or prolonged prothrombin time in patients treated with pentoxifylline with and without anticoagulants or platelet aggregation inhibitors. Patients on warfarin should have more frequent monitoring of prothrombin time, while patients with other risk factors complicated by hemorrhage (e.g., recent surgery) should have periodic examinations for signs of bleeding, including hematocrit and hemoglobin.

Antacids: In patients with digestive side effects, antacids may be administered with pentoxifylline. In a comparative bioavailability study, no interference with absorption of pentoxifylline by antacids was observed.

Cimetidine: During concurrent use of cimetidine and pentoxifylline, cimetidine has been shown to significantly increase the steady-state plasma concentration of pentoxifylline, which may enhance the possibility of adverse effects.

Adverse Effects: The most frequent adverse effect reported with pentoxifylline is nausea (14%). Individual signs/symptoms not marked with an asterisk occurred at an incidence below 1% (* = incidence between 1 and 3%).
Cardiovascular: flushing*, chest pain, arrhythmia, hypertension, dyspnea, edema, hypotension, angina, tachycardia.
CNS: dizziness/lightheadedness (9.4%), headache (4.9%), drowsiness/sleepiness, tremor, agitation, anxiety, confusion, insomnia, restlessness.
Gastrointestinal: nausea (14%), vomiting (3.4%), abdominal discomfort*, bloating*, diarrhea*, dyspepsia*, abdominal burning, abdominal pain, anorexia, flatus, constipation, hemorrhage, heartburn, salivation, dry mouth/throat, hepatitis, jaundice, increased liver enzymes.
Hemic and Lymphatic: decreased serum fibrinogen, pancytopenia, purpura, thrombocytopenia, leukopenia, anemia, aplastic anemia.
Hypersensitivity: pruritus, rash, urticaria, angioedema.
Organs of Special Sense: blurred vision, scotoma, lacrimation, epistaxis.
Miscellaneous: malaise*, muscle aches/spasms, weight change, backache, bad taste in mouth, leg cramps, fever, weakness, sweating.

Overdose: Overdosage with pentoxifylline has been reported in children and adults.

Symptoms: Symptoms appear to be dose related and usually occurred 4 to 5 hours after ingestion and lasted about 12 hours. The highest amount ingested was 80 mg/kg; flushing, hypotension, convulsions, somnolence, loss of consciousness, fever, and agitation occurred. All patients recovered.

Treatment: In addition to symptomatic treatment and gastric lavage, special attention must be given to supporting respiration, maintaining systemic blood pressure, and controlling convulsions with i.v. diazepam. Activated charcoal has been used to adsorb pentoxifylline in patients who have overdosed.

Dosage: The recommended starting dosage of pentoxifylline is 400 mg twice daily after meals. The usual maintenance dose is 400 mg 2 or 3 times daily. A maximum dose of 400 mg 3 times daily should not be exceeded.

It may take up to 2 months to obtain full results.

Tablets must be swallowed whole.

Supplied: Each pink, oblong, film-coated, sustained-release tablet contains: pentoxifylline 400 mg. Nonmedicinal ingredients: FD&C Red No. 3, hydroxyethyl cellulose, hydroxypropyl methylcellulose, magnesium stearate, polyethylene glycol, povidone, talc and titanium dioxide. Unit pack boxes of 60 (6×10 blister-packed). Plastic bottles of 500 and 100. Store between 15 and 30°C.

Reviewed 1998

ALBERT® TIAFEN Pr
ALBERT® TIAFEN SR Pr

Albert Pharma

Tiaprofenic Acid

Anti-inflammatory—Analgesic

Pharmacology: Tiaprofenic acid, a propionic acid derivative, is a nonsteroidal anti-inflammatory agent with analgesic and antipyretic properties. Its mechanism of action, as with other nonsteroidal anti-inflammatory agents, is not yet completely known. Tiaprofenic acid is an inhibitor of prostaglandin synthetase enzymes which are known to be associated with inflammation and pain. The therapeutic effect of tiaprofenic acid does not result from pituitary-adrenal stimulation.

In vitro and ex vivo studies in different experimental models with cartilage and cultures of human chondrocytes obtained from biopsy specimens have shown that exposure to tiaprofenic acid did not depress the biosynthesis of proteoglycans nor alter the differentiation of proteoglycans secreted. The degradation of proteoglycan aggregates was inhibited. In vivo data in osteoarthritis patients showed a significant reduction in stromelysin (proteoglycanase) activity further to pretreatment with tiaprofenic acid. These results support tiaprofenic acid as an effective inhibitor of stromelysin and also suggest a positive effect on the joint cartilage under experimental conditions in patients receiving therapeutic doses. The clinical significance of these findings is under further investigation.

Pharmacokinetics: Tiaprofenic acid given orally is rapidly absorbed at the gastric and duodenal levels. Peak serum levels are achieved in 30 to 90 minutes. It is extensively plasma protein bound (98%). Following a single dose of 200 mg the plasma half-life is approximately 1.7 hours. Food delays the absorption and the time to reach peak plasma concentrations by 10%.

Tiaprofenic acid is largely eliminated in the urine as unaltered tiaprofenic acid with its 2 metabolites (II and III) accounting for less than 10%; these metabolites have almost no activity.

Chronic administration of tiaprofenic acid at the dosage of 200 mg t.i.d. confirmed rapid elimination and absence of accumulation. Steady state was reached after 1 day's treatment and plasma levels approached 0 within 24 hours of the last dose.

In 2 groups of arthritic patients treated with tiaprofenic acid 200 mg t.i.d. and 300 mg b.i.d. receiving the drug for 7 days or more, the times to each mean peak serum levels were respectively 78 and 50 minutes; in synovial fluid, the mean time to peak levels was approximately 4 hours for both dosages. Following a 200 mg dose, peak serum and synovial fluid levels reached 26 μg/mL and 5.3 μg/mL respectively and 50 μg/mL and 7.7 μg/mL after a 300 mg dose. At 8 hours serum blood levels were lower than those of synovial fluids, but by 11 hours these levels were approximately the same.

In another study, rheumatoid arthritis patients were given tiaprofenic acid 200 mg t.i.d. for 7 days. After the first dose, a fall in the synovial PGE_2 level occurred inversely to a rise in drug level. The level of PGE_2 remained low after 1 week's continuous medication. These results indicate that tiaprofenic acid reaches its target organ and is retained within the joint. It also suggests that reduction in PGE_2 production is one of the ways in which tiaprofenic acid acts. The clinical significance of the relative serum and synovial fluid levels has, however, not been elucidated.

The results of a 3-month study in elderly osteoarthritis patients receiving tiaprofenic acid 300 mg b.i.d. showed no significant differences for all pharmacokinetic parameters (C_{max}, T_{max}, C_9, AUC_{0-9h}, $t_{1/2}$) measured at weeks 0, 4, 8 and 12, thus suggesting a lack of accumulation.

Fecal blood loss at usual clinical dose was less than with usual clinical doses of ASA.

Following repeated administration of 2 capsules of tiaprofenic acid sustained release 300 mg once daily, C_{max} was reached 4 to 8 hours later, with a significantly higher concentration at 6 hours than that obtained with the regular tablets. Steady state was reached 12 hours after the first dose. There were no significant differences in C_{max}, C_{min} and AUC_{0-24h} between the regular and the sustained release formulations.

In patients with rheumatoid arthritis treated with repeated doses of tiaprofenic acid sustained release 600 mg once daily, the time to synovial fluid C_{max} was 8 hours and the synovial fluid AUC_{0-24h} was approximately 36% of the plasma AUC_{0-24h}. Twenty-four hours after the last dose, the tiaprofenic acid concentration was higher in the synovial fluid than in the plasma. The elimination half-life from synovial fluid (median: 8.6 hours) was at least twice that from plasma (median: 4.2 hours).

In a pharmacokinetics study in elderly patients, no accumulation of tiaprofenic acid was found following repeated once daily administration of sustained-release capsules. The mean half-life was 4.4 hours.

The effect of food on the bioavailability of sustained-release tiaprofenic acid capsules is not known as no studies have been carried out.

Indications: For the relief of signs and symptoms of rheumatoid arthritis and osteoarthritis (degenerative joint disease).

Contraindications: Active peptic ulcer, a history of recurrent ulceration or active inflammatory disease of the gastrointestinal system.

Known or suspected hypersensitivity to the drug or other nonsteroidal anti-inflammatory drugs (NSAIDs). The potential for cross-reactivity between different NSAIDs must be kept in mind.

Tiaprofenic acid is contraindicated in patients with a history of asthma, whether or not induced by ASA or NSAIDs.

Tiaprofenic acid should not be used in patients with the complete or partial syndrome of nasal polyps, or in whom asthma, anaphylaxis, urticaria, rhinitis or other allergic manifestations are precipitated by ASA or other NSAIDs. Fatal anaphylactoid reactions have occurred in such individuals. As well, individuals with the above medical problems are at risk of a severe reaction even if they have taken NSAIDs in the past without any adverse effects.

Significant hepatic impairment or active liver disease.

Severely impaired or deteriorating renal function (creatinine clearance <30 mL/minute). Individuals with lesser degrees of renal impairment are at risk of deterioration of their renal function when prescribed NSAIDs and must be monitored.

Tiaprofenic acid is not recommended for use with other NSAIDs because of the absence of any evidence demonstrating synergistic benefits and the potential for additive side effects.

Pregnancy (See Warnings).

Warnings: Gastrointestinal System: Serious gastrointestinal toxicity, such as peptic ulceration, perforation and gastrointestinal bleeding, **sometimes severe and occasionally fatal** can occur at any time, with or without symptoms in patients treated with NSAIDs including tiaprofenic acid.

Minor upper gastrointestinal problems, such as dyspepsia, are common, usually developing early in therapy. Physicians should remain alert for ulceration and bleeding in patients treated with NSAIDs, even in the absence of previous gastrointestinal tract symptoms.

In patients observed in clinical trials of such agents, symptomatic upper gastrointestinal ulcers, gross bleeding, or perforation appear to occur in approximately 1% of patients treated for 3 to 6 months and in about 2 to 4% of patients treated for 1 year. The risk continues beyond 1 year and possibly increases.

The incidence of these complications increases with increasing dose.

Tiaprofenic acid should be given under close medical supervision to patients prone to gastrointestinal tract irritation particularly those with a history of peptic ulcer, diverticulosis or other inflammatory disease of the gastrointestinal tract such as ulcerative colitis and Crohn's disease. In these cases the physician must weigh the benefits of treatment against the possible hazards.

Physicians should inform patients about the signs and/or symptoms of serious gastrointestinal toxicity and instruct them to contact a physician immediately if they experience persistent dyspepsia or other symptoms or signs suggestive of gastrointestinal ulceration or bleeding.

Because serious gastrointestinal tract ulceration and bleeding can occur without warning symptoms, physicians should follow chronically treated patients by checking their hemoglobin periodically and by being vigilant for the signs and symptoms of ulceration and bleeding and should inform the patients of the importance of this follow-up.

If ulceration is suspected or confirmed, or if gastrointestinal bleeding occurs, tiaprofenic acid should be discontinued immediately, appropriate treatment instituted and the patient monitored closely.

No studies, to date, have identified any group of patients **not** at risk of developing ulceration and bleeding. A prior history of serious gastrointestinal events and other factors such as excess alcohol intake, smoking, age, female gender and concomitant oral steroid and anticoagulant use have been associated with increased risk.

Studies to date show that all NSAIDs can cause gastrointestinal tract adverse events. Although existing data does not clearly identify differences in risk between various NSAIDs, this may be shown in the future.

Genitourinary Tract: Some NSAIDs are known to cause persistent urinary symptoms (bladder pain, dysuria, urinary frequency), hematuria or cystitis. The onset of these symptoms may occur at any time after the initiation of therapy with a NSAID. Some cases have become severe on continued treatment. Tiaprofenic acid appears to have a greater propensity than other NSAIDS to generate reports of cystitis. Although the reaction is generally reversible, nonrecognition has led to extensive investigations and even surgical intervention, in some patients. Should urinary symptoms occur, treatment with tiaprofenic acid **must be stopped immediately** to obtain recovery. This should be done before any urological investigations or treatments are carried out. Before starting treatment with tiaprofenic acid, the patient should be asked to inform his/her physician of any urinary symptoms, even if the patient is familiar with these symptoms from the patient's medical history.

Geriatrics: Patients older than 65 years and frail or debilitated patients are most susceptible to a variety of adverse reactions from NSAIDs: the incidence of these adverse reactions increases with dose and duration of treatment. In addition, these patients are less tolerant to ulceration and bleeding. Most reports of fatal gastrointestinal events are in this population. Older patients are also at risk of lower esophageal ulceration and bleeding.

For such patients, consideration should be given to a starting dose lower than the one usually recommended, with individual adjustment when necessary and under close supervision (see Precautions for further advice).

Albert Tiafen (cont'd)

Cross-sensitivity: Patients sensitive to any of the NSAIDs may be sensitive to any one of the other NSAIDs also. There is a risk of cross-sensitivity among ASA and NSAIDs, including the group to which tiaprofenic acid belongs. These pseudoallergic reactions may include symptoms such as rash, urticaria, angioedema or more potentially severe manifestations (e.g., laryngeal edema, bronchoconstriction, shock). The risk of pseudoallergic reactions is greater in patients with recurrent rhino sinusitis, nasal polyposis or chronic urticaria. Asthmatic patients are particularly at risk of dangerous reactions. Therefore, tiaprofenic acid must not be administered to patients with asthma.

Aseptic Meningitis: In occasional cases, with some NSAIDs, the symptoms of aseptic meningitis (stiff neck, severe headaches, nausea and vomiting, fever or clouding of consciousness) have been observed. Patients with autoimmune disorders (systemic lupus erythematosus, mixed connective tissues diseases, etc.) seem to be predisposed. Therefore, in such patients, the physician must be vigilant to the development of this complication.

Pregnancy and *Lactation:* The safe use of tiaprofenic acid in pregnancy and lactation has not been established. Although no teratogenic effects were seen in animal studies, parturition was delayed and prolonged, and there was an increase in the number of stillbirths. There is also the possible risk of premature closure of the ductus arteriosus, and development of a bleeding tendency or renal risk in the neonate. Tiaprofenic acid crosses the placental barrier and is secreted in breast milk. The use of this drug is not, therefore, recommended during pregnancy and lactation.

Children: The safety and efficacy of tiaprofenic acid has not been established in children and its use in this age group is therefore not recommended.

Infection: In common with other anti-inflammatory drugs, tiaprofenic acid may mask the usual signs of infection. If tiaprofenic acid is used against symptoms of inflammation accompanying infectious disorders, effective anti-infective therapy is mandatory.

Fluid Balance: Tiaprofenic acid may cause sodium and water retention with edema. At the start of therapy, urine volume and renal function should be carefully monitored in patients with cardiac insufficiency, liver cirrhosis, or nephrotic syndrome and in patients on diuretics (see also Precautions).

Precautions: Gastrointestinal: There is no definitive evidence that the concomitant administration of histamine H_2-receptor antagonists and/or antacids will either prevent the occurrence of gastrointestinal side effects or allow the continuation of tiaprofenic acid therapy when and if these adverse reactions appear.

Renal Function: Long-term administration of NSAIDs to animals has resulted in renal papillary necrosis and other abnormal renal pathology. In humans, there have been reports of acute interstitial nephritis with hematuria, proteinuria, and occasionally nephrotic syndrome.

A second form of renal toxicity has been seen in patients with prerenal conditions leading to the reduction in renal blood flow or blood volume, where the renal prostaglandins have a supportive role in the maintenance of renal perfusion. In these patients, administration of a NSAID may cause a dose-dependent reduction in prostaglandin formation and may precipitate overt renal decompensation. Patients at greatest risk of this reaction are those with impaired renal function, heart failure, liver dysfunction, those taking diuretics, and the elderly. Discontinuation of nonsteroidal anti-inflammatory therapy is usually followed by recovery to the pretreatment state.

Tiaprofenic acid and its metabolites are eliminated primarily by the kidneys, therefore the drug should be used with great caution in patients with impaired renal function. In these cases utilization of lower doses of tiaprofenic acid should be considered and patients carefully monitored.

During long-term therapy kidney function should be monitored periodically.

Hepatic Function: As with other NSAIDs, borderline elevations of one or more liver function tests may occur. Though these have been seen in up to 15% of patients treated with other NSAIDs, they have been reported in less than 1% of patients treated with tiaprofenic acid during clinical trials (see Adverse Effects). These abnormalities may progress, may remain essentially unchanged, or may be transient with continued therapy. A patient with symptoms and/or signs suggesting liver dysfunction, or in whom an abnormal liver test has occurred, should be evaluated for evidence of the development of more severe hepatic reaction while on therapy with this drug. Severe hepatic reactions including jaundice and cases of fatal hepatitis have been reported with NSAIDs.

Although such reactions are rare, if abnormal liver tests persist or worsen, if clinical signs and symptoms consistent with liver disease develop, or if systemic manifestations occur (e.g., eosinophilia, rash, etc.), this drug should be discontinued.

During long-term therapy, liver function tests should be monitored periodically. If there is a need to prescribe this drug in the presence of impaired liver function, it must be done under strict observation.

Fluid and Electrolyte Balance: Fluid retention and edema have been observed in patients treated with tiaprofenic acid. Therefore, as with many other NSAIDs, the possibility of precipitating congestive heart failure in elderly patients or those with compromised cardiac function should be borne in mind. Tiaprofenic acid should be used with caution in patients with heart failure, hypertension or other conditions predisposing to fluid retention.

With NSAID treatment, there is a potential risk of hyperkalemia particularly in patients with conditions such as diabetes mellitus or renal failure; elderly patients; or in patients receiving concomitant therapy with beta-adrenergic blockers, angiotensin-converting-enzyme inhibitors or some diuretics. Serum electrolytes should be monitored periodically during long-term therapy, especially in those patients who are at risk.

Hematology: Drugs inhibiting prostaglandin biosynthesis do interfere with platelet function to varying degrees; therefore, patients who may be adversely affected by such an action should be carefully observed when tiaprofenic acid is administered.

Blood dyscrasias (such as neutropenia, leukopenia, thrombocytopenia, aplastic anemia and agranulocytosis) associated with the use of NSAIDs are rare, but could occur with severe consequences.

Ophthalmology: Blurred and/or diminished vision has been reported with the use of tiaprofenic acid and other NSAIDs. If such symptoms develop this drug should be discontinued and an ophthalmologic examination performed; ophthalmologic examination should be carried out at periodic intervals in any patient receiving this drug for an extended period of time.

CNS: Some patients may experience drowsiness, dizziness, vertigo, insomnia or depression with the use of tiaprofenic acid. If patients experience these side effects, they should exercise caution in carrying out activities that require alertness.

Geriatrics: Tiaprofenic acid should be used with caution in the elderly, and the dosage adjusted individually.

Drug interactions: ASA or other NSAIDs: The use of tiaprofenic acid in addition to any other NSAID, including those over-the-counter ones (such as ASA and ibuprofen) is not recommended due to the possibility of additive side effects.

Concomitant administration of ASA results in decreased peak serum concentrations of tiaprofenic acid and slight increases in both clearance and apparent half-life. The clinical significance of these changes is unknown.

Drugs Affecting Blood Formation and Coagulation: Numerous studies have shown that the concomitant use of NSAIDs and anticoagulants increases the risk of gastrointestinal adverse events such as ulceration and bleeding.

Because prostaglandins play an important role in hemostasis, and NSAIDs affect platelet function, concurrent therapy of tiaprofenic acid with warfarin requires close monitoring to be certain that no change in anticoagulant dosage is necessary.

Tiaprofenic acid is not recommended for coadministration with vitamin K antagonists, ticlopidine, and heparin due to increased risk of hemorrhage. The possibility of interaction with thrombolytics must be taken into account.

Diuretics: Tiaprofenic acid may reduce the activity of diuretics (i.e., both their diuretic and antihypertensive effects).

Antihypertensives: NSAIDs can reduce the antihypertensive effect of propranolol and other beta-blockers as well as other antihypertensive agents. Coadministration of NSAIDs and ACE-inhibitors can promote impairment of renal function and/or hyperkalemia.

Glucocorticoids: Numerous studies have shown that the concomitant use of NSAIDs and oral glucocorticoids increases the risk of GI side effects such as ulceration and bleeding. This is especially the case in older (>65 years of age) individuals.

In patients receiving concomitant steroid therapy, any reduction in steroid dosage should be gradual to avoid the possible complications of sudden steroid withdrawal.

Lithium: Tiaprofenic acid can reduce the renal excretion of lithium.

Methothrexate: Tiaprofenic acid can interfere with the plasma protein binding and renal clearance of methothrexate.

Other Drug Interactions: Tiaprofenic acid is extensively bound to serum albumin (98%). This may lead to interaction with sulfonylurea, hypoglycemic agents, sulfonamides, phenytoin. Therefore, caution should be observed when these drugs are used concurrently.

Laboratory and Diagnostic Tests: No interference known.

Adverse Effects: The most common adverse reactions encountered with NSAIDs are gastrointestinal, of which peptic ulcer, with or without bleeding, is the most severe. Fatalities have occurred, particularly in the elderly.

In clinical trials with tiaprofenic acid encompassing 1 361 patients, the detailed breakdown of side effects is shown in Table I.

Table I—Albert Tiafen

Clinical Tolerance

Adverse Effects	Percentage of Incidence Short-term (up to 8 wks)	Long-term (3 to 36 mths)
Gastrointestinal (16%)		
Indigestion	3.1	13.5
Nausea	5.8	8.2
Heartburn	3.3	6.0
Epigastric pain	2.5	5.3
Vomiting	1.1	4.1
Abdominal pain	2.4	3.1
Constipation	2.9	2.7
Flatulence	1.5	2.2
Diarrhea	2.9	2.2
Less than 1%		
Enterocolitis	0.4	0.2
Melena	0.4	0.0
Although not seen in this series there have been rare incidents of gastric or duodenal ulceration.		
CNS (6.2%)		
Dizziness	2.4	3.9
Drowsiness	0.4	3.1
Headache	2.9	3.4
Depression	0.8	1.9
Less than 1% (range 0.2 to 0.7%)		
Disorientation, tinnitus, insomnia, anxiety, tiredness/weakness		
Cutaneous (2.1%)		
Rash, erythema, pruritus	1.7	7.2
Less than 1% (range 0.2 to 0.8%)		
Dry skin, onycholysis		
Cardiovascular (1.1%)		
Hot flushes	1.0	1.4
Less than 1% (range 0.3 to 0.5%)		
Chest pain, angina, bruising		
Renal (1.1%)		
Edema	1.2	1.9
Less than 1% (range 0.1 to 0.5%)		
Incontinence, polyuria, oliguria		
Hepatic (less than 1%) (see Laboratory and Biochemical Tolerance)		
Miscellaneous (2.2%)		
Dry mouth/tongue, stomatitis	1.1	2.4
Nosebleeds	0.1	1.4
Less than 1% (range 0.1 to 0.5%)		
Eye itching/conjunctivitis/red eyes, minor eye ulcers, blurred vision, anorexia, weight gain, cramps, dyspnea, intermenstrual bleeding/vaginal spotting, paresthesia of fingers, sneezing, sweating		

Laboratory and Biochemical Tolerance: Combined decrease of hematocrit and hemoglobin: 2.8% of patients. Decrease of hemoglobin: 2.8% of patients. Increased white blood cell count 0.6%; decreased count 0.3%.

Increased GGT and AST: less than 1%. Increased alkaline phosphatase from previously normal levels: less than 1%. In patients with initially high alkaline phosphatase the levels remained high or increased.

Increase in blood urea nitrogen (BUN): 2.5% of total patients (11.8% in the elderly). Increase in BUN and creatinine: 0.4% of patients.

Hyperkalemia: 2.4% of patients.

In addition, the following side effects have been reported in clinical and postmarket use of tiaprofenic acid: Gastrointestinal: disorders of intestinal transit, ulcer, perforation, overt or occult gastrointestinal hemorrhage resulting in anemia.

Muco-cutaneous: purpura, urticaria, very rarely erythema multiforme and bulbous eruptions (Stevens-Johnson syndrome or exceptionally toxic epidermal necrolysis); very rarely photosensitivity reactions.

Hypersensitivity Reactions: asthmatic attacks, especially in subjects allergic to ASA and other NSAIDs, angioedema, anaphylactic shock.

Hematological: thrombocytopenia, prolongation of bleeding time.

Urinary: Urinary symptoms (bladder pain, dysuria, and frequency), hematuria or cystitis may occur. When treatment with tiaprofenic acid has been continued for months after onset of the urinary symptoms, inflammatory changes to the urinary tract, sometimes severe, have been observed and a few patients have undergone surgical procedures. Therefore, should any urinary symptom occur, treatment with tiaprofenic acid must be discontinued immediately. Complete recovery after discontinuation is the rule (see Warnings).

Nervous System: vertigo, tinnitus, tremor.

Renal: sodium and water retention (see Warnings). As with other NSAIDs, isolated cases of acute interstitial nephritis have been reported with tiaprofenic acid.

Hepatic: liver test abnormalities.

Other: palpebral edema, palpitations.

Overdose: Symptoms and Treatment: There have been no reports of overdosage. No specific antidote is known, therefore, treatment should by symptomatic and supportive. Early gastric lavage is indicated.

Dosage: Sustained-Release Capsules: Rheumatoid Arthritis or Osteoarthritis: The initial and maintenance dose is 2 sustained release capsules of 300 mg once daily. Capsules should be swallowed whole.

Tablets: Rheumatoid Arthritis: The usual initial and maintenance dose is 600 mg daily in 3 divided doses. Some patients may do well on 300 mg twice daily. The maximum daily dose is 600 mg.

Osteoarthritis: The usual initial and maintenance dose is 600 mg daily in 2 or 3 divided doses. In rare instances patients may be maintained on 300 mg daily in divided doses. The maximum maintenance daily dose is 600 mg.

Information for the Patient: See Blue Section—Information for the Patient "Albert Tiafen/Albert Tiafen SR".

Supplied: Capsules: Each hard gelatin, sustained-release capsule, with a transparent pink body and opaque maroon cap printed with "Albert Tiafen SR" on one side and the Roussel logo on the other, each containing off-white spheroidal pellets, contains: tiaprofenic acid 300 mg. Nonmedicinal ingredients: glyceryl monostearate, microcrystalline cellulose and talc. Shell: gelatin. Cap: erythrosine, indigo carmine, titanium dioxide. Body: erythrosine, indigo carmine. White opaque polyethylene bottles of 60 and 500.

Tablets: 200 mg: Each white, biconvex tablet, marked with the Roussel logo on one side, the reverse side with a break-line, one half embossed "ALBERT TIAFEN" and the other half "200", contains: tiaprofenic acid 200 mg. Nonmedicinal ingredients: magnesium stearate, maize starch, Pluronic F68 and talc. Amber glass bottles of 100.

300 mg: Each white, biconvex tablet, marked with the Roussel logo on one side, the reverse side with a break-line, one half embossed "ALBERT TIAFEN" and the other half "300", contains: tiaprofenic acid 300 mg. Nonmedicinal ingredients: magnesium stearate, maize starch, Pluronic F68 and talc. Amber glass bottles of 100 and 500.

Store between 15 and 30°C. Protect from excessive heat, light and humidity.

Reviewed 1999

...The GREEN SECTION lists the brand and generic names of products available in Canada.

ALCAINE®
Alcon

Proparacaine HCl

Ophthalmic Anesthetic

Supplied: Each Drop-Tainer dispenser contains: proparacaine HCl 0.5%, preserved with benzalkonium chloride. Nonmedicinal ingredients: glycerin, hydrochloric acid, purified water and sodium hydroxide. Drop-Tainer dispensers of 15 mL. Refrigerate after opening.

ALCOJEL®
Roberts

Isopropanol

Antiseptic—Emollient

Supplied: Each bottle contains: jellied isopropanol (70%). Plastic squeeze bottles of 175 and 350 mL with flip top spout.

ALCOMICIN® Ⓟ
Alcon

Gentamicin Sulfate

Ophthalmic Antibiotic

Supplied: Each mL of ophthalmic solution contains: gentamicin sulfate 5 mg (equivalent to 3 mg gentamicin base). Benzalkonium Cl 0.01%. Nonmedicinal ingredients: purified water, sodium chloride and sodium phosphates. Store at room temperature. Drop-Tainer dispensers of 5 mL with dropper tip.

ALDACTAZIDE 25® Ⓟ
ALDACTAZIDE 50® Ⓟ
Searle

Spironolactone—Hydrochlorothiazide

Aldosterone Antagonist—Diuretic

Pharmacology: A combination of two diuretic agents with different but complementary mechanisms and sites of action. Spironolactone component helps to minimize the potassium loss which may be induced by the thiazide component. Spironolactone is a specific pharmacologic antagonist of the adrenal mineralocorticoid, aldosterone, acting primarily through competitive binding with receptors at the aldosterone-dependent sodium/potassium exchange site in the distal convoluted renal tubule. Hydrochlorothiazide promotes excretion of sodium and water primarily by inhibiting their reabsorption by the cortical diluting segment of the renal tubule, in contrast to spironolactone which exerts its effect more distally. Both spironolactone and hydrochlorothiazide reduce exchangeable sodium and plasma volume.

The effects of hydrochlorothiazide will be observed on the day of administration, but the spironolactone component does not attain its maximal effect until the third day.

Spironolactone is rapidly and extensively metabolized. Sulfur-containing products are the predominant metabolites and are thought to be primarily responsible for the therapeutic effects of the drug. Approximately 25 to 30% of the dose administered is converted to canrenone, which attains peak serum levels 2 to 4 hours after single oral administration of spironolactone. In the dose range of 25 to 200 mg, an approximately linear relationship exists between a single dose of spironolactone and plasma levels of canrenone.

Plasma concentrations of canrenone decline in 2 distinct phases, the first phase lasting from 3 to 12 hours, being more rapid than the second phase lasting from 12 to 96 hours. Canrenone clearance data, following multiple doses of spironolactone, indicate that accumulation of canrenone in the body with 100 mg once a day would be lower than with 25 mg 4 times a day. Both spironolactone and canrenone are more than 90% bound to plasma proteins. The metabolites of spironolactone are excreted both in the urine (32 to 53%), and through biliary excretion in the feces (14 to 36%).

Hydrochlorothiazide is rapidly absorbed following oral administration, with onset of action occurring within 1 hour, and the duration of action is 6 to 12 hours. Plasma concentration attains a peak at 1 to 2 hours and declines with a half-life of 4 to 5 hours. Hydrochlorothiazide undergoes only slight metabolic alteration and is excreted in the urine. It is distributed throughout the extracellular space, with essentially no tissue accumulation except in the kidney. Hydrochlorothiazide is eliminated rapidly by the kidney.

Indications: Fixed dose combination drugs are not indicated for initial therapy. Patients should be titrated on the individual drugs. If the fixed combination represents the dosage so determined, its use may be more convenient in patient management. If during maintenance therapy dosage adjustment is necessary, it is advisable to use the individual drugs.

Edematous conditions for patients with the following: Congestive heart failure: Management of edema and sodium retention when the patient is only partially responsive to, or is intolerant of, other therapeutic measures. The treatment of diuretic induced hypokalemia in patients with congestive heart failure when other measures are considered inappropriate. The treatment of patients with congestive heart failure taking digitalis when other therapies are considered inadequate or inappropriate.

Cirrhosis of the liver accompanied by edema and/or ascites: Aldosterone levels may be exceptionally high in this condition. Aldactazide is indicated for maintenance therapy, together with bed rest and the restriction of fluid and sodium.

Nephrotic syndrome: In nephrotic patients who are not responsive to glucocorticoid therapy and who do not respond to other diuretics. However, Aldactazide has not been shown to affect the basic pathological process.

Essential hypertension: In patients with essential hypertension in whom other measures are considered inadequate or inappropriate. In hypertensive patients for the treatment of a diuretic induced hypokalemia when other measures are considered inappropriate.

Contraindications: Anuria, acute renal insufficiency, significant impairment of renal function, hyperkalemia, sensitivity to spironolactone and sensitivity to thiazides or other sulfonamide-derived drugs. Aldactazide may be contraindicated in patients with severe or progressive liver disease.

Warnings: Potassium Supplementation: Do not give potassium supplementation (including dietary potassium) in conjunction with Aldactazide therapy.

Excessive potassium intake may cause hyperkalemia in patients receiving Aldactazide. Do not administer concurrently with other potassium-sparing diuretics.

Tumorigenicity: Spironolactone, in chronic toxicity studies, has been shown to be a tumorigen in rats.

Use Aldactazide only for conditions described under Indications.

Precautions: Electrolyte Balance: Because of the diuretic action of Aldactazide, patients should be carefully evaluated for possible disturbance of fluid and electrolyte balance.

Hyperkalemia: Hyperkalemia may occur in patients treated with Aldactazide. This can cause cardiac irregularities, some of which may be fatal. Hyperkalemia may also occur in the absence of excessive potassium intake, particulary in patients with impaired renal function, elderly patients, or patients with diabetes.

Consequently, no potassium supplement should ordinarily be given with Aldactazide. Hyperkalemia can be treated promptly by rapid i.v. administration of glucose (20 to 50%) and regular insulin, using 0.25 to 0.5 units of insulin per gram of glucose. This is a temporary measure to be repeated if required. Aldactazide should be discontinued and potassium intake (including dietary potassium) restricted.

Hypokalemia: Hypokalemia may develop, especially with brisk diuresis, in severe cirrhosis or during concomitant use of loop diuretics, glucocorticoids, or ACTH. Digitalis therapy may exaggerate the metabolic effects of hypokalemia especially with reference to myocardial activity. If hypokalemia occurs, Aldactazide should be discontinued and consideration given to one of the following therapeutic regimens: use of hydrochlorothiazide alone with potassium supplementation as needed, or use of spironolactone alone.

Hyponatremia: During the administration of Aldactazide, patients suffering from sodium depletion must be attentively monitored and signs of electrolyte imbalance must be carefully checked.

Aldactazide may, if administered concomitantly with other diuretics, cause or aggravate hyponatremia, as manifested by dryness of the mouth, thirst, lethargy and drowsiness. A true low-salt syndrome may develop with drug therapy and may be manifested by increasing mental confusion similar to that observed with hepatic coma. This syndrome was differentiated from dilutional hyponatremia in that it does not occur with obvious fluid retention. Its treatment requires that diuretic therapy be discontinued and sodium administered.

Aldactazide (cont'd)

Metabolic Effects: Hyperchloremic metabolic acidosis: Reversible hyperchloremic metabolic acidosis, usually in association with hyperkalemia, has been reported in decompensated hepatic cirrhosis, even in the presence of normal renal function.

Hypochloremic Alkalosis: Hypochloremic alkalosis occurs infrequently and is rarely severe. Unduly restricted dietary sodium may complicate therapy. A chloride deficit may be corrected by using ammonium chloride (except in renal or hepatic disease) and is largely prevented by a near-normal sodium/chloride intake.

Drug Interactions: Diuretics and Antihypertensives: Although Aldactazide may be administered concomitantly with diuretics and antihypertensives, the effect is additive. Thus, it is advisable to reduce the dose of these drugs. In particular, the dose of ganglionic blocking agents should be reduced by at least 50% when Aldactazide is included in the regimen.

Hyperkalemia has been associated with the use of angiotensin converting enzyme (ACE) inhibitors in combination with potassium-sparing diuretics.

Norepinephrine and Tubocurarine: Since hydrochlorothiazide and spironolactone each reduce vascular responsiveness to norepinephrine, caution should be exercised in the management of patients subjected to regional or general anesthesia. Thiazides may also increase responsiveness to tubocurarine. Consideration should be given to discontinuation of Aldactazide therapy prior to elective surgery.

Digoxin: Spironolactone has been shown to increase the half-life of digoxin. This may result in increased serum digoxin levels and subsequent digitalis toxicity. It may be necessary to reduce the maintenance dose of digoxin when Aldactazide is administered, and the patient should be carefully monitored to avoid over- or under-digitalization.

Carbenoxolone: Carbenoxolone may cause sodium retention and thus decrease the effectiveness of spironolactone. Concurrent use of the 2 agents should be avoided.

Nonsteroidal Anti-inflammatory Drugs: It has been reported that ASA, mefenamic acid and indomethacin may interfere with the diuretic action of spironolactone. The mechanism may be due to the inhibition of intrarenal synthesis of prostaglandins. However, it has been shown that ASA does not alter the effect of spironolactone on blood pressure, serum electrolytes, urea nitrogen, or plasma renin activity in hypertensive patients.

Hyperkalemia has been associated with the use of indomethacin in combination with potassium-sparing diuretics.

Insulin: Insulin requirements in diabetics may be increased, decreased or unchanged. Hyperglycemia and glycosuria may be manifested in latent diabetics.

Gynecomastia: Gynecomastia may develop with the use of spironolactone and physicians should be advised of its possible occurrence. The development of gynecomastia appears to be related to both dosage and duration of therapy, and is normally reversible when Aldactazide is discontinued. If gynecomastia develops, discontinue the drug. In rare instances, some breast enlargement may persist.

Pregnancy: Spironolactone or its metabolites may, and thiazides do cross the placental barrier and appear in cord blood. When hydrochlorothiazide is used in women of child-bearing age, the potential benefits of the drug should be weighed against the possible hazards to the fetus. These hazards include fetal or neonatal jaundice, thrombocytopenia, and possibly other adverse reactions which have occurred in the adult. In rats, feminization of the male fetus has been reported at high doses.

Lactation: Certain adverse reactions to thiazide therapy (e.g. hyperbilirubinemia, thrombocytopenia, altered carbohydrate metabolism) can occur in the newborn since thiazides have been demonstrated to appear in breast milk. Canrenone, a metabolite of spironolactone, also appears in breast milk. If use of these drugs is deemed essential, an alternative method of infant feeding should be instituted.

Laboratory Tests: General: Aldactazide therapy may result in a transient elevation of BUN, especially when azotemia exists at the beginning of treatment. This appears to represent a concentration phenomenon rather than renal toxicity, since the BUN returns to normal after Aldactazide is discontinued. Progressive elevation of BUN is suggestive of the presence of pre-existing renal impairment.

Several reports of possible interference with digoxin radioimmunoassays by spironolactone or its metabolites have appeared in the literature. Neither the extent nor the potential clinical significance of this interference (which may be assay-specific) has been fully established. Discontinue spironolactone for at least 4, and preferably 7 days prior to plasma cortisol determinations, **if they are to be done by the method of Mattingly,** that is, by fluorometric assay. No interference has been demonstrated with the competitive protein binding technique or radioimmunoassay technique.

Thiazides may decrease serum PBI levels without evidence of alteration of thyroid function.

Adrenal Vein Catheterization and Plasma Renin Activity: Discontinue spironolactone several days prior to adrenal vein catheterization for measurement of aldosterone concentrations and measurements of plasma renin activity.

Impaired Hepatic Function: Aldactazide should be used with caution in patients with impaired hepatic function, because minor alterations in electrolyte balance may precipitate hepatic coma. In the treatment of the edema/ascites of cirrhosis, when high doses are required, it is recommended that the drug dosage be decreased before diuresis is complete, in order to avoid dehydration. If mental confusion occurs, Aldactazide should be temporarily discontinued.

Miscellaneous: Orthostatic hypotension may occur and may be potentiated by alcohol, barbiturates or narcotics.

Pathological changes in the parathyroid gland, with resultant hypercalcemia and hypophosphatemia, have been observed in a few patients on prolonged thiazide therapy.

Exacerbation or activation of systemic lupus erythematosus has been reported for sulfonamide derivatives, including thiazides.

Caution is necessary in patients with hyperuricemia or a history of gout, because gout may be precipitated by thiazides.

Adverse Effects: Spironolactone: The adverse reactions encountered most frequently with spironolactone are gynecomastia and gastrointestinal symptoms.

Gastrointestinal: nausea, cramping and diarrhea, vomiting, gastric bleeding, gastritis and ulceration.

CNS: drowsiness, dizziness, headache, mental confusion, ataxia, lethargy.

Dermatologic: maculopapular or erythematous cutaneous eruptions, urticaria.

Endocrinologic: gynecomastia, impotence, inability to achieve or maintain erection, abnormal semen (decreased motility and sperm count), irregular menses or amenorrhea and postmenopausal bleeding. Carcinoma of the breast has been reported in patients taking spironolactone, but a cause and effect relationship has not been established.

Miscellaneous: drug fever. A few cases of agranulocytosis have been reported in patients taking spironolactone.

Hydrochlorothiazide: Gastrointestinal: anorexia, gastric irritation, nausea, vomiting, cramps, diarrhea, constipation, jaundice (intrahepatic cholestatic), acute pancreatitis.

CNS: dizziness, vertigo, paresthesia, headache, xanthopsia.

Dermatologic: hypersensitivity, purpura, photosensitivity, rash, urticaria, necrotizing angiitis, pruritus and erythema multiforme.

Hematologic: leukopenia, thrombocytopenic purpura, agranulocytosis, aplastic anemia.

Cardiovascular: orthostatic hypotension may occur and may be potentiated by alcohol, barbiturates or narcotics.

Miscellaneous: muscle spasm, weakness, nitrogen retention, hypokalemia, hyperglycemia, glycosuria and hyperuricemia.

Adverse reactions due to Aldactazide are usually reversible upon discontinuation of Aldactazide. In rare instances, some gynecomastia may persist.

Overdose: Symptoms: There have been no reports of fatal overdose in man (except indirectly through hyperkalemia). Nausea and vomiting occurs, and (much more rarely) drowsiness, mental confusion, diarrhea or a maculopapular or erythematous rash. These manifestations disappear promptly on discontinuation of medication. Hyperkalemia may be exacerbated. Thrombocytopenic purpura and granulocytopenia have occurred with thiazide therapy.

Treatment: No specific antidote. No persistent toxicity has occurred or is expected. Appearance of effects described above requires only discontinuation of drug. Induce vomiting and evacuate the stomach by lavage. For hyperkalemia, discontinue Aldactazide, reduce potassium intake, consider administration of potassium-excreting diuretics, i.v. glucose with regular insulin (see Precautions), ion-exchange resins, or dialysis. Treat fluid depletion and electrolyte imbalances appropriately if present.

Dosage: Optimal dosage should be established by individual titration of the components.

Treatment should be continued for 2 weeks before optimal effectiveness can be assessed.

Adults: Edema (congestive heart failure, hepatic cirrhosis, nephrotic syndrome): Daily dosage of 2 to 4 tablets Aldactazide 25 or 1 to 2 tablets Aldactazide 50 in single or divided doses should be adequate for most patients, but may range from 2 to 8 tablets Aldactazide 25 daily or 1 to 4 tablets Aldactazide 50.

Children: Edema: The usual daily maintenance dose of Aldactazide should be that which provides 1.65 to 3.3 mg of spironolactone/kg of body weight.

Essential hypertension: In essential hypertension, a daily dosage of 2 to 4 Aldactazide 25 tablets or 1 to 2 Aldactazide 50 tablets in single or divided doses, will be adequate for most patients, but may range from 2 to 8 tablets of Aldactazide 25 or 1 to 4 tablets of Aldactazide 50.

Since Aldactazide increases the action of other antihypertensive drugs, especially the ganglionic blocking agents, the dosage of such drugs should be reduced by at least 50% when Aldactazide is added to the regimen.

Information for the Patient: See Blue Section—Information for the Patient "Aldactazide 25/Aldactazide 50".

Supplied: Aldactazide 25: Each white to off-white round, standard biconvex, compressed tablet, 9.5 mm in diameter, impressed "201/SEARLE" on one side, plain on the other, contains: spironolactone 25 mg and hydrochlorothiazide 25 mg. Nonmedicinal ingredients: calcium sulfate, cornstarch, magnesium stearate, peppermint flavoring and povidone. Bottles of 250. Store below 30°C.

Aldactazide 50: Each white to off-white round, standard biconvex, compressed tablet, 11.1 mm in diameter, impressed "244/SEARLE" on one side, plain on the other, contains: spironolactone 50 mg and hydrochlorothiazide 50 mg. Nonmedicinal ingredients: calcium sulfate, cornstarch, magnesium stearate, peppermint flavoring and povidone. Bottles of 250. Store below 30°C.

(Shown in Product Recognition Section)

Reviewed 1998

ALDACTONE® 🅿

Searle

Spironolactone

Aldosterone Antagonist

Pharmacology: Spironolactone is a specific pharmacologic antagonist of aldosterone, acting primarily through competitive binding of receptors at the aldosterone-dependent, sodium-potassium exchange site in the distal convoluted renal tubule. Spironolactone causes increased amounts of sodium and water to be excreted, while potassium loss is minimized. Spironolactone acts both as a diuretic and as an antihypertensive drug by this mechanism. It may be given alone or with other diuretic agents which act more proximally in the renal tubule.

Increased levels of the mineralocorticoid, aldosterone, are present in primary and secondary hyperaldosteronism. Edematous states in which secondary aldosteronism is usually involved include congestive heart failure, hepatic cirrhosis, and nephrotic syndrome. By competing with aldosterone for receptor sites, spironolactone provides effective therapy for the edema and ascites in those conditions. Spironolactone counteracts secondary aldosteronism induced by the volume depletion and associated sodium loss caused by diuretic therapy.

Spironolactone is effective in lowering the systolic and diastolic blood pressure in patients with primary hyperaldosteronism. It is also effective in most cases of essential hypertension, despite the fact that aldosterone secretion may be within normal limits in benign essential hypertension.

Through its action in antagonizing the effect of aldosterone, spironolactone inhibits the exchange of sodium for potassium in the distal renal tubule and helps to prevent potassium loss.

Spironolactone has not been demonstrated to elevate serum uric acid, to precipitate gout, or to alter carbohydrate metabolism.

Spironolactone is rapidly and extensively metabolized. Sulfur-containing products are the predominant metabolites and are thought to be primarily responsible for the therapeutic effects of the drug. Approximately 25 to 30% of the dose administered is converted to canrenone, which attains peak serum levels 2 to 4 hours after single oral administration of spironolactone. In the dose range of 25 to 200 mg, an approximately linear relationship exists between a single dose of spironolactone and plasma levels of canrenone.

Plasma concentrations of canrenone decline in 2 distinct phases, the first phase lasting from 3 to 12 hours, being more rapid than the second phase lasting from 12 to 96 hours. Canrenone clearance data, following multiple doses of spironolactone, indicate that accumulation of canrenone in the body with 100 mg once a day would be lower than with 25 mg 4 times a day. Both spironolactone and canrenone are more than 90% bound to plasma proteins. The metabolites of spironolactone are excreted both in the urine (32 to 53%), and through biliary excretion in the feces (14 to 36%).

Indications: Primary Hyperaldosteronism: A useful agent in the diagnosis of primary hyperaldosteronism. In the presence of hypokalemic alkalosis and hypertension, a diagnosis of primary hyperaldosteronism should be considered if both blood pressure and serum electrolytes return to normal following treatment with spironolactone.

Spironolactone is useful in the preoperative treatment of patients with primary hyperaldosteronism and for the maintenance therapy of such patients who decline surgery, or who are unsuitable for surgery.

Edematous Conditions: Congestive Heart Failure (CHF): Spironolactone is useful in the management of edema and sodium retention in CHF when the patient is only partially responsive to, or intolerant of, other therapeutic measures. Spironolactone may be used alone or with thiazides. It is indicated in patients with CHF taking digitalis when other therapies are considered inappropriate.

Cirrhosis of the Liver Accompanied by Edema and/or Ascites: Aldosterone levels may be exceptionally high in this condition. Spironolactone is indicated for maintenance therapy, in combination with bed rest and the restriction of fluid and sodium.

Nephrotic Syndrome: Spironolactone is useful for inducing a diuresis in patients not responsive to glucocorticoid therapy (for the nephrotic syndrome), and not responding to other diuretics. However, spironolactone has not been shown to affect the basic pathological process.

Essential Hypertension: Spironolactone is indicated, usually in combination with other drugs, for patients who cannot be treated adequately with other agents or for whom other agents are considered inappropriate. Spironolactone alone has mild to moderate antihypertensive activity.

Hypokalemia: Spironolactone is indicated for treatment of hypokalemia when other measures are considered inappropriate or inadequate. It is also indicated for the prophylaxis of hypokalemia in digitalis therapy when other measures are inadequate or inappropriate.

Contraindications: Anuria, acute renal insufficiency, significant impairment of renal function, hyperkalemia, and sensitivity to spironolactone.

Warnings: Potassium (K^+) Supplementation: Do not give potassium supplementation (including dietary potassium) in conjunction with spironolactone therapy. Excessive potassium intake may cause hyperkalemia in patients receiving spironolactone. Do not administer spironolactone concurrently with other potassium sparing diuretics.

Turmorigenicity: Spironolactone, in chronic toxicity studies, has been shown to be a tumorigen in rats.

Use spironolactone only for conditions described under Indications.

Precautions: Electrolyte Balance: Because of the diuretic action of spironolactone, patients should be carefully evaluated for possible disturbance of fluid and electrolyte balance.

Hyperkalemia: Hyperkalemia may occur in patients treated with spironolactone if the potassium intake is excessive. This can cause cardiac irregularities, some of which may be fatal. Hyperkalemia may also occur even in the absence of potassium supplementation, particularly in patients with impaired renal function, elderly patients, or patients with diabetes. Consequently, no potassium supplementation should ordinarily be given with spironolactone. Hyperkalemia can be treated promptly by rapid i.v. administration of glucose (20 to 50%) and regular insulin, using 0.25 to 0.5 units of insulin/g of glucose. This is a temporary measure to be repeated if required. Spironolactone should be discontinued and potassium intake (including dietary potassium) restricted.

Hyponatremia: During the administration of spironolactone, patients suffering from sodium depletion must be attentively monitored and signs of electrolyte imbalance must be carefully checked.

Spironolactone may, if administered concomitantly with other diuretics, cause or aggravate hyponatremia, as manifested by dryness of the mouth, thirst, lethargy, and drowsiness.

Metabolic Effects: Hyperchloremic metabolic acidosis: Spironolactone may induce or worsen hyperchloremic metabolic acidosis.

Acidosis and Renal Function: Rare reports of acidosis have been reported with spironolactone.

Drug Interactions: Diuretics and Antihypertensives: Although spironolactone may be administered concomitantly with diuretics and antihypertensives, the effect of spironolactone is additive. Thus, it is advisable to reduce the dose of these drugs. In particular, the dose of ganglionic blocking agents should be reduced by at least 50% when spironolactone is added to the regimen.

Hyperkalemia has been associated with the use of angiotensin converting enzyme (ACE) inhibitors in combination with potassium-sparing diuretics.

Norepinephrine: Spironolactone reduces the vascular responsiveness to norepinephrine. Caution should be exercised in the management of patients subjected to regional or general anesthesia.

Digoxin: Spironolactone has been shown to increase the half-life of digoxin. This may result in increased serum digoxin levels and subsequent digitalis toxicity. It may be necessary to reduce the maintenance dose of digoxin when spironolactone is administered, and the patient should be carefully monitored to avoid over- or underdigitalization.

Carbenoxolone: Carbenoxolone may cause sodium retention and thus decrease the effectiveness of spironolactone. Concurrent use of the two agents should be avoided.

Nonsteroidal Anti-Inflammatory Drugs: Although it has been reported that ASA, mefenamic acid, and indomethacin may interfere with the diuretic action of spironolactone, due to inhibition of intrarenal synthesis of prostaglandins, it has been shown that ASA does not alter the effect of spironolactone on blood pressure, serum electrolytes, urea nitrogen, or plasma renin activity in hypertensive patients.

Hyperkalemia has been associated with the use of indomethacin in combination with potassium-sparing diuretics.

Gynecomastia: Gynecomastia may develop with the use of spironolactone and physicians should be advised of its possible occurrence. The development of gynecomastia appears to be related to both dosage and duration of therapy and is normally reversible when the drug is discontinued. If gynecomastia develops, discontinue the drug. In rare instances some breast enlargement may persist.

Management of Cirrhosis: Although high doses of spironolactone are required to treat edema and ascites in patients with cirrhosis, the drug dosage may be decreased before diuresis is complete to avoid the possibility of dehydration.

Pregnancy and *Lactation:* Spironolactone and its metabolites may cross the placental barrier. Therefore, the use of spironolactone requires that the potential benefits be weighed against the possible hazard to the mother and fetus. In rats, feminization of the fetus has been reported at high doses. Canrenone, a metabolite of spironolactone, appears in breast milk. If use of the drug is deemed essential, an alternative method of infant feeding should be instituted.

Laboratory Tests: General: Spironolactone therapy may cause transient elevation of BUN, especially in patients with preexisting renal impairment.

Several reports of possible interference with digoxin radioimmunoassays by spironolactone or its metabolites have appeared in the literature. Neither the extent nor the potential clinical significance of this interference (which may be assay-specific) has been fully established.

Discontinue spironolactone for at least 4, and preferably 7 days prior to plasma cortisol determinations, **if they are to be done by the method of Mattingly,** that is, by fluorometric assay. No interference has been demonstrated with the competitive protein binding technique or radioimmunoassay technique.

Adrenal Vein Catheterization and Plasma Renin Activity: Discontinue spironolactone several days prior to adrenal vein catheterization for measurement of aldosterone concentrations and measurements of plasma renin activity.

Adverse Effects: Gynecomastia is observed not infrequently. In rare instances, gynecomastia may persist. Other adverse effects that have been reported in association with spironolactone are: gastrointestinal symptoms (including nausea, vomiting, cramping, diarrhea, gastric bleeding, gastritis and ulceration), drowsiness, lethargy, headache, maculopapular or erythematous cutaneous eruptions, urticaria, mental confusion, drug fever, ataxia, inability to achieve or maintain erection, impotence, abnormal semen (decreased motility and sperm count), irregular menses or amenorrhea and postmenopausal bleeding. Carcinoma of the breast has been reported in patients taking spironolactone, but a cause and effect relationship has not been established. A few cases of agranulocytosis have been reported in patients taking spironolactone.

Adverse reactions are usually reversible upon discontinuation of the drug.

Overdose: Symptoms: There have been no reports of fatal overdose in man (except indirectly through hyperkalemia). Nausea and vomiting occur and (much more rarely) drowsiness, mental confusion, diarrhea, or a maculopapular or erythematous rash. These manifestations disappear promptly on discontinuation of medication. Hyperkalemia may be exacerbated.

Treatment: No specific antidote. No persistent toxicity has occurred or is expected. Appearance of effects described above require only discontinuance of the drug. Induce vomiting and evacuate the stomach by lavage. For hyperkalemia, discontinue spironolactone, reduce potassium intake, consider administration of potassium excreting diuretics, i.v. glucose with regular insulin (see Precautions), ion exchange resins, or dialysis. Treat fluid depletion and electrolyte imbalances appropriately if present.

Dosage: Diagnosis and Treatment of Primary Hyperaldosteronism: As an initial diagnostic measure to provide presumptive evidence of primary hyperaldosteronism while patients are on normal diets.

Long Test: Administer 400 mg/day for 3 to 4 weeks. Correction of hypokalemia and hypertension provides presumptive evidence for the diagnosis of primary hyperaldosteronism.

Short Test: Administer 400 mg/day for 4 days. If serum potassium increases or urinary potassium decreases during spironolactone administration, but reverts when spironolactone is discontinued, a presumptive diagnosis of primary hyperaldosteronism should be considered.

After the diagnosis of primary hyperaldosteronism has been established by more definitive testing procedures, spironolactone may be administered in doses of 75 to 400 mg/day in preparation for surgery. For those unsuitable for surgery, spironolactone may be employed for long-term maintenance therapy at the lowest effective dosage determined for the individual.

Edematous Disorders Associated with Congestive Heart Failure, Cirrhosis and the Nephrotic Syndrome: When given as the sole agent for diuresis, continue administration for at least 5 days. If an adequate response has been achieved within 5 days, continue dosage at the same level (or in selected patients, at a reduced dosage) in either single or divided daily doses. Some may respond adequately to a dosage of only 75 mg daily. If adequate diuresis is not obtained within 5 days, a second diuretic also should be given for additive effect. Occasionally for severe, resistant edema, one may add a potent glucocorticoid to this combined therapy. Normally, an initial daily dosage of 100 mg (but may range from 25 to 200 mg/day) of spironolactone administered in either single or divided doses is recommended.

Children: The initial daily dosage should provide approximately 3 mg/kg of body weight administered in either single or divided doses. This dose should be reduced to 1 to 2 mg/kg for maintenance therapy or combination use with other diuretics.

Essential Hypertension: Usually in combination with other drugs, spironolactone is indicated for patients who cannot be treated adequately with other agents or for whom other agents are considered inappropriate. Spironolactone has mild to moderate antihypertensive activity.

Adults: Initial daily dosage: 50 to 100 mg/day (in either single or divided doses) of spironolactone is recommended. Spironolactone may also be given with diuretics that act more proximally in the renal tubule or with other antihypertensive agents. Since a stabilized response may not occur before 2 weeks, continue treatment in either single or divided daily doses for ▶

Aldactone (cont'd)

that duration of time. Subsequently, adjust dosage in response to patient's needs. Most patients will respond to doses not exceeding 200 mg/day.

Hypokalemia: Ranging from 25 to 100 mg/day is useful in treating a diuretic-induced hypokalemia, when oral potassium supplements or other potassium-sparing regimens are inappropriate.

See Table I for summary of dosage recommendations.

Table I—Aldactone

Dosage Recommendations*

Condition	Type of Test	In Single or Divided Daily Doses: Initial Dosage	Maximum Dosage
Primary Hyperaldosteronism:			
	Long Test	400 mg/day x 3–4 weeks	—
	Short Test	400 mg/day x 4 days	—
In Preparation for Surgery:		100–400 mg/day	400 mg/day
Edematous Disorders:			
Congestive Heart Failure	—	100 mg/day	200 mg/day
Cirrhosis	Urinary: Na^+/K^+ ratio > 1	100 mg/day	100 mg/day
	Na^+/K^+ ratio < 1	200–400 mg/day	400 mg/day
Nephrotic Syndrome	—	100 mg/day	200 mg/day
Essential Hypertension	—	50–100 mg/day	200 mg/day
Hypokalemia	—	25–100 mg/day	100 mg/day

*Maintenance dosage should be individually determined and may be lower than the recommended initial dose.

Information for the Patient: See Blue Section—Information for the Patient "Aldactone".

Supplied: 25 mg: Each white to off-white, round, standard, biconvex tablet, 8.7 mm diameter impressed SEARLE 205 on one side, the other side plain and with peppermint aroma, contains: spironolactone 25 mg. Nonmedicinal ingredients: calcium sulfate, cornstarch, magnesium stearate, peppermint flavoring and povidone. Bottles of 250. Store below 30°C.

100 mg: Each white to off-white, round, standard, biconvex tablet, 11.1 mm diameter impressed SEARLE 210 on one side, the other side plain and with peppermint aroma, contains: spironolactone 100 mg. Nonmedicinal ingredients: calcium sulfate, cornstarch, magnesium stearate, peppermint flavoring and povidone. Bottles of 100. Store below 30°C.

(Shown in Product Recognition Section)

Reviewed 1998

ALDOMET® Injection ℞
ALDOMET® Tablets ℞
MSD
Methyldopa HCl
Methyldopa
Antihypertensive

Indications: The treatment of arterial hypertension. May be employed in a general treatment program in conjunction with a diuretic and/or other antihypertensive drugs as needed for proper response in patients with hypertension of various severity.

May be employed as the initial agent in the treatment of hypertension in those patients for which treatment should not be started with a diuretic.

The treatment of hypertensive crises may be initiated with methyldopa injection.

Contraindications: Active hepatic disease, such as acute hepatitis and active cirrhosis. If previous methyldopa therapy has been associated with liver disorders or hemolytic anemia (see Precautions). Hypersensitivity to methyldopa.

Precautions: With prolonged methyldopa therapy, 10 to 20% of patients develop a positive direct Coombs' test which usually occurs between 6 and 12 months of methyldopa therapy. Lowest incidence is at a daily dosage of 1 g or less. This on rare occasions may be associated with hemolytic anemia, which could lead to potentially fatal complications. One cannot predict which patients with a positive direct Coombs' test may develop hemolytic anemia.

Prior existence or development of a positive direct Coombs' test is not in itself a contraindication to use of methyldopa. If a positive Coombs' test develops during methyldopa therapy, the physician should determine whether hemolytic anemia exists and whether the positive Coombs' test may be a problem. For example, in addition to a positive direct Coombs' test there is less often a positive indirect Coombs' test which may interfere with cross matching of blood.

At the start of methyldopa therapy, it is desirable to do a blood count (hematocrit, hemoglobin, or red cell count) for a baseline or to establish whether there is anemia. Periodic blood counts should be done during therapy to detect hemolytic anemia. It may be useful to do a direct Coombs' test before therapy and at 6 and 12 months after the start of therapy.

If Coombs' positive hemolytic anemia occurs, the cause may be methyldopa and the drug should be discontinued. Usually the anemia remits promptly. If not, corticosteroids may be given and other causes of anemia should be considered. If hemolytic anemia occurs, the drug should not be reinstituted.

When methyldopa causes Coombs' positivity alone or with hemolytic anemia, the red cell is usually coated with gamma globulin of the IgG (gamma G) class only. The positive Coombs' test may not revert to normal until weeks to months after methyldopa is stopped.

Should the need for transfusion arise in a patient receiving methyldopa, both a direct and an indirect Coombs' test should be performed on his blood. In the absence of hemolytic anemia, usually only the direct Coombs' test will be positive. A positive direct Coombs' test alone will not interfere with typing or cross matching. If the indirect Coombs' test is also positive, problems may arise in the major cross match and the assistance of a hematologist or transfusion expert will be needed.

Occasionally, fever has occurred within the first 3 weeks of methyldopa therapy, associated in some cases with eosinophilia or abnormalities in one or more liver function tests, such as serum alkaline phosphatase, serum transaminases (AST, ALT), bilirubin, cephalin cholesterol flocculation, prothrombin time and bromsulphalein retention. Jaundice, with or without fever, may occur with onset usually within the first 2 to 3 months of therapy. In some patients the findings are consistent with those of cholestasis.

Rarely, fatal hepatic necrosis has been reported after use of methyldopa. These hepatic changes may represent hypersensitivity reactions. Periodic determination of hepatic function should be done particularly during the first 6 to 12 weeks of therapy or whenever an unexplained fever occurs. If fever, abnormalities in liver function tests, or jaundice appear, stop therapy with methyldopa. If caused by methyldopa, the temperature and abnormalities in liver function characteristically have reverted to normal when the drug was discontinued. Methyldopa should not be reinstituted in such patients. Methyldopa should be used with caution in patients with a history of previous liver disease or dysfunction.

Rarely, a reversible reduction of the white blood cell count with a primary effect on the granulocytes has been seen. The granulocyte count returned promptly to normal on discontinuance of the drug. Rare cases of granulocytopenia have been reported. In each instance, upon stopping the drug, the white cell count returned to normal. Reversible thrombocytopenia has occurred rarely.

When methyldopa is used with other antihypertensive drugs, potentiation of antihypertensive effect may occur. Patients should be followed carefully to detect adverse effects or unusual manifestations of drug idiosyncrasy. A paradoxical pressor response has been reported with i.v. methyldopate HCl.

When methyldopa and lithium are given concomitantly, the patient should be carefully observed for symptoms of lithium toxicity.

Pregnancy and *Lactation:* Methyldopa has been used for treatment of hypertension during pregnancy. Such use requires close medical and obstetrical supervision. No unusual adverse reactions have been reported in association with the use of methyldopa during pregnancy. Although no obvious teratogenic effects have been reported, the possibility of fetal injury cannot be excluded and the use of the drug in women who are or may become pregnant or who are nursing their newborn infant requires that anticipated benefits be weighed against possible risks.

Methyldopa does cross the placental barrier and appears in cord blood and breast milk.

Methyldopa should be used with caution in patients with a history of previous liver disease or dysfunction.

Methyldopa may interfere with measurement of urinary uric acid by the phosphotungstate method, serum creatinine by the alkaline picrate method, and AST by colorimetric methods. Interference with spectrophotometric methods for AST analysis has not been reported.

Since methyldopa causes fluorescence in urine samples at the same wave lengths as catecholamines, falsely high concentrations of urinary catecholamines may be reported. This will interfere with the diagnosis of pheochromocytoma. It is important to recognize this phenomenon before a patient with a possible pheochromocytoma is subjected to surgery. Methyldopa does not interfere with measurement of VMA (vanillylmandelic acid), a test for pheochromocytoma, by those methods which convert VMA to vanillin. Methyldopa is not recommended for the treatment of patients with pheochromocytoma. Rarely, when urine is exposed to air after voiding, it may darken because of breakdown of methyldopa or its metabolites.

Rarely, involuntary choreoathetotic movements have been observed during therapy with methyldopa in patients with severe bilateral cerebrovascular disease. Should these movements occur, stop therapy.

Methyldopa is largely excreted by the kidney and patients with impaired renal function may respond to smaller doses. Syncope in older patients may be related to an increased sensitivity and advanced arteriosclerotic vascular disease. This may be avoided by lower doses.

Patients may require reduced doses of anesthetics when on methyldopa. If hypotension does occur during anesthesia, it usually can be controlled by vasopressors. The adrenergic receptors remain sensitive during treatment with methyldopa.

Hypertension has recurred occasionally after dialysis in patients given methyldopa because the drug is removed by this procedure.

Sulfites have been reported to cause severe allergic reactions in certain susceptible individuals, particularly patients with asthma. Aldomet injection contains sodium bisulfite. Aldomet tablets contain no sulfites.

Adverse Effects: Sedation, usually transient, may occur during the initial period of therapy or whenever the dose is increased. Headache, asthenia, or weakness may be noted as early and transient symptoms.

CNS: sedation, headache, asthenia or weakness, dizziness, lightheadedness, symptoms of cerebrovascular insufficiency (may be due to lowering of blood pressure), paresthesias, parkinsonism, Bell's palsy, decreased mental acuity, involuntary choreoathetotic movements. Psychic disturbances including nightmares and reversible mild psychoses or depression. Toxic encephalopathy.

Cardiovascular: bradycardia, prolonged carotid sinus hypersensitivity, aggravation of angina pectoris. Orthostatic hypotension (decrease daily dosage). Edema (and weight gain) usually relieved by use of a diuretic. (Discontinue methyldopa if edema progresses or signs of heart failure appear.)

Gastrointestinal: nausea, vomiting, distention, constipation, flatus, diarrhea, colitis, mild dryness of mouth, sore or "black" tongue, pancreatitis, sialadenitis.

Hepatic: abnormal liver function tests, jaundice, hepatocellular damage.

Hematologic: positive Coombs' test, hemolytic anemia, bone marrow depression, leukopenia, granulocytopenia, thrombocytopenia. Positive tests for antinuclear antibody, LE cells and rheumatoid factor.

Allergic: drug related fever, myocarditis, pericarditis, lupus like syndrome.

Dermatologic: rash as in eczema or lichenoid eruption; toxic epidermal necrolysis.

Other: nasal stuffiness, rise in BUN, breast enlargement, gynecomastia, lactation, hyperprolactinemia, amenorrhea, impotence, decreased libido, dermatologic reactions including eczema and lichenoid eruptions, mild arthralgia, with or without joint swelling, myalgia.

Overdose: Symptoms: Acute overdosage may produce acute hypotension with other major responses attributable to brain and gastrointestinal malfunction (excessive sedation, weakness, bradycardia, dizziness, lightheadedness, constipation, distention, flatus, diarrhea, nausea, vomiting).

Potentiation of antihypertensive action may occur in combination therapy with other antihypertensives.

Chronic overdosage may produce hypotension and syncope, especially in the presence of advanced arteriosclerosis.

Treatment: Discontinue the drug. If ingestion is recent, gastric lavage or emesis may reduce absorption; when ingestion has been earlier, infusions may be helpful to promote urinary excretion. Otherwise, management includes symptomatic treatment with special attention to cardiac rate and output, blood volume, electrolyte balance, paralytic ileus, urinary function, and cerebral activity. Administration of sympathomimetic drugs may be indicated.

Dosage: Oral: Adults: The usual starting dosage is 250 mg 2 or 3 times a day in the first 48 hours. The daily dosage then may be increased or decreased, preferably at intervals of not less than 2 days, until an adequate response is achieved. To minimize the sedation, start dosage increases in the evening. By adjustment of dosage, morning hypotension may be prevented without sacrificing control of afternoon blood pressure.

The usual daily maintenance dosage of methyldopa is 500 mg to 2 g in 2 to 4 doses. Although occasional patients have responded to higher doses, the maximum recommended daily dosage is 3 g.

The 125 mg tablet is valuable when small increments of methyldopa are required for adjustment of antihypertensive response. This dosage form is not designed for use as initial therapy in previously untreated hypertensive patients.

When methyldopa is given to patients on other antihypertensives, the dose of these agents may need to be adjusted to effect a smooth transition. When methyldopa is added to a thiazide, the dosage of thiazide usually need not be changed. A thiazide may be added at any time during methyldopa therapy and is recommended if therapy has not been started with a thiazide or if effective control of blood pressure cannot be maintained on 2 g of methyldopa daily. When methyldopa is given with antihypertensives other than thiazides, its initial dosage should be limited to 500 mg daily in divided doses.

Studies suggest that once optimum dosage is ascertained, the antihypertensive effect can be maintained by giving the same total daily dose once every 24 hours.

Occasionally, tolerance may occur, usually between the second and third month of therapy. Adding a diuretic or increasing the dosage of methyldopa frequently will restore effective control of blood pressure.

Smaller doses may be needed in patients with impaired renal function or in older patients with an increased sensitivity or an advanced arteriosclerotic vascular disease (see Precautions).

Children: Initial dosage is based on 10 mg/kg daily in 2 to 4 doses. The daily dosage then is increased or decreased until an adequate response is achieved. The maximum dosage is 65 mg/kg or 3 g daily, whichever is less.

Parenteral: Adults: This preparation has been given i.v. in single doses of 100 mg to 3 g. The usual adult dosage is 250 to 500 mg i.v. at 6 hour intervals as required; doses up to 1 g may be used in severe cases if necessary to obtain a beneficial effect, but at the present time the maximum recommended dose is 1 g every 6 hours. If renal function is impaired, the dose required for effective lowering of the blood pressure may be less than that for patients with little renal dysfunction.

The desired dose should be added to 100 mL of 5% Dextrose Injection USP. This i.v. infusion should be given slowly over a period of 30 to 60 minutes.

Methyldopa, when administered i.v. in effective doses, will produce a decline in blood pressure that may begin in 4 to 6 hours and extend 10 to 16 hours after injection.

When control has been obtained, oral therapy may be substituted for i.v. therapy, starting with the same dosage schedule being used for the parenteral route.

Supplied: Ampuls: Each mL of clear, colorless solution contains: methyldopate HCl 50 mg, citric acid anhydrous 5 mg, sodium bisulfite 3.2 mg, disodium edetate 500 µg, monothioglycerol 2 mg, sodium hydroxide to adjust pH, with methylparaben 1.5 mg and propylparaben 200 µg and water for injection. Ampuls of 5 mL.

Tablets: Each yellow, film-coated, biconvex shaped tablet, engraved Aldomet on one side and MSD 401 on the other side, contains: methyldopa 250 mg. Gluten-, lactose-, sulfite- and tartrazine-free. Bottles of 100 and 500.

(Shown in Product Recognition Section)

ALDORIL®-15 Ⓟ
ALDORIL®-25 Ⓟ
MSD
Methyldopa—Hydrochlorothiazide
Antihypertensive

Pharmacology: In Aldoril, 2 antihypertensive agents with complementary properties are combined for the treatment of hypertension.

Methyldopa: Methyldopa, an antihypertensive agent, is an aromatic-amino-acid decarboxylase inhibitor in animals and in man. Although the mechanism of action has yet to be conclusively demonstrated, the antihypertensive effect of methyldopa probably is due to its metabolism to alpha-methylnorepinephrine, which then lowers arterial pressure by stimulation of central inhibitory alpha-adrenergic receptors, false neurotransmission, and/or reduction of plasma renin activity. Methyldopa has been shown to cause a net reduction in the tissue concentration of serotonin, dopamine, norepinephrine and epinephrine.

Hydrochlorothiazide: Hydrochlorothiazide, when given orally, is an effective diuretic and antihypertensive. Hydrochlorothiazide interferes with the renal tubular mechanism of electrolyte reabsorption. It increases excretion of sodium and chloride in approximately equivalent amounts. Natriuresis causes a secondary loss of potassium and bicarbonate.

Aldoril: The concomitant use of methyldopa and hydrochlorothiazide, as provided in Aldoril, frequently produces a more pronounced antihypertensive response than when either compound is the sole therapeutic agent. In those cases of hypertensive vascular disease where sodium and water retention is a problem, the hydrochlorothiazide component of Aldoril will help control the fluid imbalance.

Indications: Fixed-dose combination drugs are not indicated for initial therapy. Patients should be titrated on the individual drugs. If the fixed combination represents the dosage so determined, its use may be more convenient in patient management. If during maintenance therapy dosage adjustment is necessary it is advisable to use the individual drugs.

Aldoril is recommended for maintenance therapy of patients with essential hypertension.

Contraindications: Active hepatic disease, such as acute hepatitis and active cirrhosis, is a contraindication for use of methyldopa.

Because of the diuretic action of hydrochlorothiazide, Aldoril is contraindicated in anuria. See also Warnings, Pregnancy and Lactation.

This product is also contraindicated in the presence of hypersensitivity to any component of the produce (see Supplied), including hepatic disorders or hemolytic anemia associated with previous methyldopa therapy or sulfonamide-derived drugs.

Warnings: Methyldopa: It is important to recognize that a positive Coombs' test, hemolytic anemia, and liver disorders may occur with methyldopa therapy. The rare occurrences of hemolytic anemia or liver disorders could lead to potentially fatal complications unless properly recognized and managed. Read this section carefully to understand these reactions. With prolonged methyldopa therapy, 10 to 20 % of patients develop a positive direct Coombs' test which usually occurs between 6 and 12 months of methyldopa therapy. Lowest incidence is at a daily dosage of 1 g or less. This on rare occasions may be associated with hemolytic anemia, which could lead to potentially fatal complications. One cannot predict which patients with a positive direct Coombs' test may develop hemolytic anemia.

Prior existence or development of a positive direct Coombs' test is not in itself a contraindication to use of methyldopa. If a positive Coombs' test develops during methyldopa therapy, the physician should determine whether hemolytic anemia exists and whether the positive Coombs' test may be a problem. For example, in addition to a positive direct Coombs' test there is less often a positive indirect Coombs' test which may interfere with cross matching of blood.

At the start of methyldopa therapy, it is desirable to do a blood count (hematocrit, hemoglobin, or red cell count) for a baseline or to establish whether there is anemia. Periodic blood counts should be done during therapy to detect hemolytic anemia. It may be useful to do a direct Coombs' test before therapy and at 6 and 12 months after the start of therapy.

If Coombs' positive hemolytic anemia occurs, the cause may be methyldopa and the drug should be discontinued. Usually the anemia remits promptly. If not, corticosteroids may be given and other causes of anemia should be considered. If hemolytic anemia occurs the drug should not be reinstituted.

When methyldopa causes Coombs' positivity alone or with hemolytic anemia, the red cell is usually coated with gamma globulin of the IgG (gamma G) class only. The positive Coombs' test may not revert to normal until weeks to months after methyldopa is stopped.

Should the need for transfusion arise in a patient receiving methyldopa, both a direct and an indirect Coombs' test should be performed on his blood. In the absence of hemolytic anemia, usually only the direct Coombs' test will be positive. A positive direct Coombs' test alone will not interfere with typing or cross matching. If the indirect Coombs' test is also positive, problems may arise in the major cross match and the assistance of a hematologist or transfusion expert will be needed.

Occasionally, fever has occurred within the first 3 weeks of methyldopa therapy, associated in some cases with eosinophilia or abnormalities in one or more liver function tests. Jaundice, with or without fever, may occur with onset usually within the first 2 to 3 months of therapy. In some patients the findings are consistent with those of cholestasis.

Rarely fatal hepatic necrosis has been reported after use of methyldopa. Liver biopsy, performed in several patients with liver dysfunction, showed a microscopic focal necrosis compatible with drug hypersensitivity. Periodic determination of hepatic function should be done particularly during the first 6 to 12 weeks of therapy or whenever an unexplained fever occurs. If fever, abnormalities in liver function tests, or jaundice appear, stop therapy with methyldopa. If caused by methyldopa, the temperature and abnormalities in liver function characteristically have reverted to normal when the drug was discontinued. Methyldopa should not be reinstituted in such patients. Methyldopa should be used with caution in patients with a history of previous liver disease or dysfunction.

Rarely, a reversible reduction of the white blood cell count with a primary effect on the granulocytes has been seen. The granulocyte count returned promptly to normal on discontinuance of the drug. Rare cases of granulocytopenia have been reported. In each instance, upon stopping the drug, the white cell count returned to normal. Reversible thrombocytopenia has occurred rarely.

Hydrochlorothiazide: Azotemia may be precipitated or increased by hydrochlorothiazide. Cumulative effects of the drug may develop in patients with impaired renal function. If increasing azotemia and oliguria occur during treatment of severe progressive renal disease, the diuretic should be discontinued.

Thiazides should be used with caution in patients with impaired hepatic function or progressive liver disease, since minor alterations of fluid and electrolyte balance may precipitate hepatic coma.

Sensitivity reactions may occur in patients with or without a history of allergy or bronchial asthma.

Hydrochlorothiazide adds to or potentiates the action of other antihypertensive drugs. Therefore, the dosage of these agents, especially ganglionic or peripheral adrenergic blocking drugs, must be reduced by at least 50% as soon as hydrochlorothiazide is added to the regimen.

The possibility of exacerbation or activation of systemic lupus erythematosus has been reported for sulfonamide derivatives, including thiazides.

Pregnancy and *Lactation:* The routine use of diuretics in otherwise healthy pregnant women with or without mild edema is not indicated and exposes mother and fetus to unnecessary hazard. Diuretics do not prevent development of toxemia of pregnancy and there is no satisfactory evidence that they are useful in the treatment of toxemia.

Use of any drug in women who are or may become pregnant requires that anticipated benefits be weighed against possible risks. Methyldopa and thiazides cross the placental barrier and appear in cord blood. These hazards include fetal or neonatal jaundice, thrombocytopenia, and possibly other adverse reactions which have occurred in the adult.

Lactation: Methyldopa and thiazides appear in breast milk. If use of Aldoril is deemed essential, the patient should stop nursing.

Precautions: Methyldopa: Methyldopa should be used with caution in patients with a history of previous liver disease or dysfunction (see Warnings).

Methyldopa may interfere with measurement of: urinary uric acid by the phosphotungstate method, serum creatinine by the alkaline picrate method, and AST by colorimetric methods. Interference with spectrophotometric methods for AST analysis has not been reported.

Since methyldopa causes fluorescence in urine samples at the same wave lengths as catecholamines, falsely high levels of urinary catecholamines may be reported. This will interfere with the diagnosis of pheochromocytoma. It is important to recognize this phenomenon before a patient with a possible pheochromocytoma is subjected to surgery. Methyldopa does not interfere with measurement of VMA (vanillylmandelic acid), a test for pheochromocytoma, by those methods which convert VMA to vanillin. Methyldopa is not recommended for the treatment of patients with pheochromocytoma. Rarely, when urine is exposed to air after voiding, it may darken because of breakdown of methyldopa or its metabolites.

Aldoril (cont'd)

Rarely involuntary choreoathetotic movements have been observed during therapy with methyldopa in patients with severe bilateral cerebrovascular disease. Should these movements occur, stop therapy.

Methyldopa is largely excreted by the kidney and patients with impaired renal function may respond to smaller doses. Syncope in older patients may be related to an increased sensitivity and advanced arteriosclerotic vascular disease. This may be avoided by lower doses.

Hypertension has recurred occasionally after dialysis in patients given methyldopa because the drug is removed by this procedure.

Drug Interactions: When methyldopa is used with other antihypertensive drugs, potentiation of antihypertensive effect may occur. Patients should be followed carefully to detect side effects or unusual manifestations of drug idiosyncrasy. A paradoxical pressor response has been reported with i.v. methyldopate HCl.

The adrenergic receptors remain sensitive during treatment with methyldopa. Dialysis removes methyldopa; therefore, hypertension may recur after this procedure.

Patients may require reduced doses of anesthetics when on methyldopa. If hypotension does occur during anesthesia, usually it can be controlled by vasopressors. The adrenergic receptors remain sensitive during treatment with methyldopa.

Hydrochlorothiazide: When creatinine clearance falls below 30 mL/min, thiazide diuretics are ineffective.

Azotemia may be precipitated or increased by hydrochlorothiazide. Cumulative effects of the drug may develop in patients with impaired renal function. If increasing azotemia and oliguria occur during treatment of renal disease, the diuretic should be discontinued.

Careful check should be kept for signs of fluid electrolyte imbalance, namely, hyponatremia, hypochloremic alkalosis, hypokalemia and hypomagnesemia. Serum and urine electrolyte determinations are particularly important when the patient is vomiting excessively or receiving parenteral fluids. Warning signs, irrespective of cause, are: dryness of mouth, thirst, weakness, lethargy, drowsiness, restlessness, seizures, muscle pains or cramps, muscular fatigue, hypotension, oliguria, tachycardia, and gastrointestinal disturbances such as nausea and vomiting.

Hypokalemia may develop with hydrochlorothiazide as with any other potent diuretic, especially with brisk diuresis, after prolonged therapy or when severe cirrhosis is present. Hypokalemia can sensitize or exaggerate the response of the heart to the toxic effects of digitalis (e.g., increased ventricular irritability).

Hepatic Disease: Thiazides should be used with caution in patients with impaired hepatic function or progressive liver disease, since minor alterations of fluid and electrolyte balance may precipitate hepatic coma.

Hypokalemia may be avoided or treated by use of potassium chloride or giving foods with a high potassium content. Any chloride deficit is generally mild and usually does not require specific treatment except under extraordinary circumstances (as in liver disease or renal disease).

Diuretic induced hyponatremia is usually mild and asymptomatic. In a few patients hyponatremia may become severe and symptomatic. Such patients require immediate attention and appropriate treatment.

Thiazides may decrease urinary calcium excretion. Thiazides may cause intermittent and slight elevation of serum calcium in the absence of known disorders of calcium metabolism.

Pathological changes in the parathyroid glands with hypercalcemia and hypophosphatemia have been observed in a few patients on prolonged thiazide therapy. The common complications of hyperparathyroidism such as renal lithiasis, bone resorption, and peptic ulceration have not been seen.

Hyperuricemia may occur or gout may be precipitated in certain patients receiving thiazide therapy.

Thiazide therapy may impair glucose tolerance.

The possibility of exacerbation or activation of systemic lupus erythematosus has been reported.

Increases in cholesterol and triglyceride levels may be associated with thiazide therapy.

Drug Interactions: When given concurrently the following drugs may interact with thiazide diuretics.

Alcohol, Barbiturates, or Narcotics: Potentiation of orthostatic hypotension may occur.

Antidiabetic Drugs (oral agents and insulin): Dosage adjustment of the antidiabetic drug may be required.

Other Antihypertensive Drugs: additive effect. Diuretic theapy should be discontinued for 2 to 3 days prior to initiation of therapy with an ACE-inhibitor to reduce the likelihood of first dose hypotension.

Corticosteroids, ACTH: intensified electrolyte depletin, particularly hypokalemia.

Pressor Amines (e.g., epinephrine): possible decreased response to pressor amines but not sufficient to preclude their use.

Skeletal Muscle Relaxants, Nondepolarizing (e.g., tubocurarine): possible increased responsiveness to the muscle relaxant.

Lithium: generally should not be given with diuretics. Diuretic agents reduce the renal clearance of lithium and add a high risk of lithium toxicity.

Nonsteroidal Anti-inflammatory Drugs: In some patients, the administration of a nonsteroidal anti-inflammatory agent can reduce the diuretic, natriuretic, and antihypertensive effects of diuretics.

Drug/Laboratory Test Interactions: Because of their effects on calcium metabolism, thiazides may interfere with tests for parathyroid function (see Precautions).

Adverse Effects: Methyldopa: Sedation, usually transient, may occur during the initial period of therapy or whenever the dose is increased. Headache, asthenia, or weakness may be noted as early and transient symptoms. CNS: sedation, headache, asthenia or weakness, dizziness, lightheadedness, symptoms of cerebrovascular insufficiency, paresthesias, parkinsonism, Bell's palsy, decreased mental acuity, involuntary choreoathetotic movements. Psychic disturbances including nightmares and reversible mild psychoses or depression. Toxic encephalopathy.

Cardiovascular: bradycardia, prolonged carotid sinus hypersensitivity , aggravation of angina pectoris. Orthostatic hypotension (decrease daily dosage). Edema (and weight gain) usually relieved by use of a diuretic. (Discontinue methyldopa if edema progresses or signs of heart failure appear.)

Gastrointestinal: nausea, vomiting, distention, constipation, flatus, diarrhea, colitis, mild dryness of mouth, sore or "black" tongue, pancreatitis, sialadenitis.

Hepatic: liver disorders including hepatitis, abnormal liver function tests, jaundice.

Hematologic: positive Coombs' test, hemolytic anemia, bone marrow depression, leukopenia, granulocytopenia, thrombocytopenia. Positive tests for antinuclear antibody, LE cells, and rheumatoid factor.

Allergic: drug-related fever and lupus-like syndrome, myocarditis, pericarditis.

Dermatologic: rash as in eczema or lichenoid eruption, toxic epidermal necrolysis.

Others: nasal stuffiness, rise in BUN, breast enlargement, gynecomastia, lactation, hyperprolactinemia, amenorrhea, impotence, decreased libido, mild arthralgia, with or without joint swelling, myalgia.

Hydrochlorothiazide: Gastrointestinal: anorexia, gastric irritation, nausea, vomiting, cramping, diarrhea, constipation, jaundice (intrahepatic cholestatic jaundice), pancreatitis, sialadenitis.

CNS: dizziness, vertigo, paresthesias, headache, xanthopsia.

Hematologic: leukopenia, agranulocytosis, thrombocytopenia, aplastic anemia, hemolytic anemia.

Cardiovascular: orthostatic hypotension (may be aggravated by alcohol, barbiturates or narcotics).

Hypersensitivity: purpura, photosensitivity, rash, urticaria, necrotizing angiitis (vasculitis, cutaneous vasculitis), fever, respiratory distress including pneumonitis and pulmonary edema, anaphylactic reactions.

Metabolic: hyperglycemia, glycosuria, hyperuricemia, electrolyte imbalance.

Renal: renal dysfunction, interstitial nephritis, renal failure.

Others: muscle spasm, weakness, restlessness, transient blurred vision.

Overdose: Symptoms and Treatment: The most common signs and symptoms observed are those caused by electrolyte depletion (hypokalemia, hypochloremia, hyponatremia) and dehydration resulting from excessive diuresis. If digitalis has also been administered, hypokalemia may accentuate cardiac arrhythmias.

In the event of overdosage, symptomatic and supportive measures should be employed. If ingestion is recent, emesis should be induced or gastric lavage performed. Dehydration, electrolyte imbalance, hepatic coma and hypotension should be corrected by established procedures. If required, give oxygen or artificial respiration for respiratory impairment.

Dosage: Dosage must be determined for individual patients by titration of each component separately. Where the fixed combination in Aldoril provides the dosage so determined Aldoril may be used for maintenance therapy. If during maintenance therapy dosage adjustment is necessary, it is advisable to use the individual drugs.

The usual maintenance dose is 1 to 4 tablets twice daily.

Although occasional patients have responded to higher doses, the maximal recommended daily dose is 3 g of methyldopa and 100 to 200 mg of hydrochlorothiazide. Where maximum dosage has provided inadequate blood pressure control, it is suggested that additional methyldopa be given as the single drug to obtain the maximal blood pressure response.

When necessary, another antihypertensive agent may be added gradually, beginning with 50% of the usual recommended starting dose to avoid excessive reduction in blood pressure.

Patients with impaired kidney function may respond to smaller doses of the drug since methyldopa is excreted primarily by the kidney. Lower doses may also be required in elderly patients.

Tolerance may occur occasionally as either an early or late event in treatment, but it is more likely to occur between the second and third month after initiation of therapy. Patients may require titration on individual drugs to restore effective blood pressure control.

Supplied: Aldoril-15: Each biconvex-shaped, salmon-colored, film-coated tablet, engraved MSD 423 on one side and Aldoril on the other, contains: methyldopa 250 mg and hydrochlorothiazide 15 mg. Nonmedicinal ingredients: carnauba wax, citric acid, colloidal silicon dioxide, dibasic calcium phosphate, edetate calcium disodium, ethylcellulose, guar gum, hydroxypropyl methylcellulose, magnesium stearate, powdered cellulose, propylene glycol, red ferric oxide, talc and titanium dioxide. Bottles of 100.

Aldoril-25: Each biconvex-shaped, white, film-coated tablet, engraved MSD 456 on one side and Aldoril on the other, contains: methyldopa 250 mg and hydrochlorothiazide 25 mg. Nonmedicinal ingredients: carnauba wax, citric acid, colloidal silicon dioxide, dibasic calcium phosphate, edetate calcium disodium, ethylcellulose, guar gum, hydroxypropyl methylcellulose, magnesium stearate, powdered cellulose, propylene glycol, talc and titanium dioxide. Bottles of 100.

Store at 15 to 30°C. Protect from light.

(Shown in Product Recognition Section)

ALERTONIC® Ⓟ

Hoechst Marion Roussel

Pipradrol—Vitamin Compound

Indications: Short-term use in cases of vitamin B deficiencies accompanied by functional fatigue.

Contraindications: As with other drugs with CNS stimulating action, pipradrol is contraindicated in hyperactive, agitated, or anxious patients and depressive illness, chorea, or obsessive compulsive states.

Precautions: *Pregnancy:* Although animal reproductive studies have not indicated adverse effects, this drug should not be used during the first trimester of pregnancy unless in the opinion of the prescribing physician, the potential benefits outweigh the potential risks.

Dependence Potential: As with other CNS stimulant with dependence potential, pipradrol should not be administered for long periods, or given to patients who are prone to drug dependence.

Adverse Effects: CNS stimulation reported as agitation, insomnia, excitement, and irritability; allergic reactions usually related to the skin such as urticaria, rash, itching, and erythema; gastrointestinal disturbances manifested by gastritis, vomiting, nausea, abdominal distress, diarrhea, and constipation.

Excessive overdosing has occurred in a few instances with severe reactions related to CNS stimulation and gastrointestinal disturbances.

Dosage: Adults, 15 mL 3 times daily 30 minutes before meals for limited periods only.

Supplied: Each 45 mL of red liquid contains: alcohol 15%, pipradrol HCl 2 mg, thiamine HCl 10 mg, riboflavin 5 mg, pyridoxine HCl 1.9 mg, niacinamide 50 mg, choline 100 mg, inositol 100 mg. Nonmedicinal ingredients: alcohol, artificial date flavor, butylparaben, caramel flavor, cherry flavor, dextrose, FD&C Blue #1, FD&C Red #2, fructose, hydrochloric acid, sodium hydroxide and sorbitol. Energy: 32 kJ (7.7 kcal)/15 mL. Sodium: <1 mmol (1.2 mg)/15 mL. Bottles of 500 mL and 2 L.

ALESSE™ 21 ℞
ALESSE™ 28 ℞
Wyeth-Ayerst

Levonorgestrel—Ethinyl Estradiol

Oral Contraceptive

Pharmacology: Although the primary mechanism of action is inhibition of ovulation, the effectiveness of Alesse may also result from other mechanisms of action, such as hostility of the cervical mucus to sperm penetration and migration.

Indications: For conception control.

Contraindications: History of or actual thrombophlebitis or thromboembolic disorders. History of or actual cerebrovascular disorders. History of or actual myocardial infarction or coronary arterial disease. Active liver disease or history of or actual benign or malignant liver tumors. Known or suspected carcinoma of the breast. Known or suspected estrogen-dependent neoplasia. Undiagnosed abnormal vaginal bleeding. Any ocular lesion arising from ophthalmic vascular disease, such as partial or complete loss of vision or defect in visual fields. When pregnancy is suspected or diagnosed.

Warnings: Predisposing Factors for Coronary Artery Disease: Cigarette smoking increases the risk of serious cardiovascular side effects and mortality. Birth control pills increase this risk, especially with increasing age. Convincing data are available to support an upper age limit of 35 years for oral contraceptive use in women who smoke.

Other women who are independently at high risk for cardiovascular disease include those with diabetes, hypertension, abnormal lipid profile, obesity or a family history of these. Whether oral contraceptives accentuate this risk is unclear.

In low risk, nonsmoking women of any age, the benefits of oral contraceptive use outweigh the possible cardiovascular risks associated with low dose formulations. Consequently, oral contraceptives may be prescribed for these women up to the age of menopause.

> Cigarette smoking increases the risk of serious adverse effects on the heart and blood vessels. This risk increases with age and becomes significant in oral contraceptive users older than 35 years of age. Women should be counselled not to smoke.

Discontinue Medication at the Earliest Manifestation of the Following:

A. Thromboembolic and cardiovascular disorders such as thrombophlebitis, pulmonary embolism, cerebrovascular disorders, myocardial ischemia, mesenteric thrombosis, and retinal thrombosis.

B. Conditions that predispose to venous stasis and to vascular thrombosis (e.g., immobilization after accidents or confinement to bed during long-term illness). Other nonhormonal methods of contraception should be used until regular activities are resumed. For use of oral contraceptives when surgery is contemplated, see Precautions.

C. Visual defects, partial or complete.

D. Papilledema or ophthalmic vascular lesions.

E. Severe headache of unknown etiology or worsening of preexisting migraine headache.

A meta-analysis from 54 epidemiological studies reported that there is a slightly increased relative risk (RR=1.24) of having breast cancer diagnosed in women who are currently using combined oral contraceptives. The increased risk gradually disappears during the course of the 10 years after cessation of combined oral contraceptive use. Because breast cancer is rare in women under 40 years of age, the excess number of breast cancer diagnoses in current and recent combined oral contraceptive users is small in relation to the lifetime risk of breast cancer. These studies do not provide evidence for causation. The observed pattern of increased risk maybe due to an earlier diagnosis of breast cancer in combined oral contraceptive users, the biological effects of combined oral contraceptives or a combination of both. The breast cancers diagnosed in ever-users tend to be less advanced clinically than the cancers diagnosed in never-users.

Precautions: Physical Examination and Followup: Before oral contraceptives are used, a thorough history and physical examination should be performed, including a blood pressure determination. Breasts, liver, extremities and pelvic organs should be examined and a Papanicolaou smear should be taken if the patient has been sexually active.

The first followup visit should be 3 months after oral contraceptives are prescribed. Thereafter, examinations should be performed at least once a year or more frequently if indicated. At each annual visit, examination should include those procedures that were done at the initial visit as outlined above or per recommendations of the Canadian Workshop on Screening for Cancer of the Cervix. Their suggestion was that, for women who had two consecutive negative Pap smears, screening could be continued every 3 years to the age of 69.

Pregnancy: Oral contraceptives should not be taken by pregnant women. However, if conception accidentally occurs while taking the pill, there is no conclusive evidence that the estrogen and progestin contained in the oral contraceptive will damage the developing child.

Lactation: In breast-feeding women, the use of oral contraceptives results in the hormonal components being excreted in breast milk and may reduce its quantity and quality. If the use of oral contraceptives is initiated after the establishment of lactation, there does not appear to be any effect on the quantity and quality of the milk. There is no evidence that low-dose oral contraceptives are harmful to the nursing infant.

Hepatic Function: Patients who have had jaundice, including a history of cholestatic jaundice during pregnancy, should be given oral contraceptives with great care and under close observation.

The development of severe generalized pruritus or icterus requires that the medication be withdrawn until the problem is resolved.

If a patient develops jaundice that proves to be cholestatic in type, the use of oral contraceptives should not be resumed. In patients taking oral contraceptives, changes in the composition of the bile may occur and an increased incidence of gallstones has been reported.

Hepatic nodules (adenoma and focal nodular hyperplasia) have been reported, particularly in long-term users of oral contraceptives. Although these lesions are extremely rare, they have caused fatal intra-abdominal hemorrhage and should be considered in women with an abdominal mass, acute abdominal pain, or evidence of intra-abdominal bleeding.

Hypertension: Patients with essential hypertension whose blood pressure is well controlled may be given oral contraceptives but only under close supervision. If a significant elevation of blood pressure in previously normotensive or hypertensive subjects occurs at any time during the administration of the drug, cessation of medication is necessary.

Migraine and Headache: The onset or exacerbation of migraine or the development of headache of a new pattern that is recurrent, persistent or severe, requires discontinuation of oral contraceptives and evaluation of the cause.

Diabetes: Current low-dose oral contraceptives exert minimal impact on glucose metabolism. Diabetic patients, or those with a family history of diabetes, should be observed closely to detect any worsening of carbohydrate metabolism. Patients predisposed to diabetes who can be kept under close supervision may be given oral contraceptives. Young diabetic patients whose disease is of recent origin, well controlled, and not associated with hypertension or other signs of vascular disease such as ocular fundal changes, should be monitored more frequently while using oral contraceptives.

Ocular Disease: Patients who are pregnant or are taking oral contraceptives, may experience corneal edema that may cause visual disturbances and changes in tolerance to contact lenses, especially of the rigid type. Soft contact lenses usually do not cause disturbances. If visual changes or alterations in tolerance to contact lenses occur, temporary or permanent cessation of wear may be advised.

Breasts: Increasing age and a strong family history are the most significant risk factors for the development of breast cancer. Other established risk factors include obesity, nulliparity and late age for first full-term pregnancy. The identified groups of women that may be at increased risk of developing breast cancer before menopause are long-term users of oral contraceptives (more than 8 years) and starters at early age. In a few women, the use of oral contraceptives may accelerate

Table I—Alesse 21/Alesse 28

Drugs That May Decrease the Efficacy of Oral Contraceptives

Class of Compound	Drug	Proposed Mechanism	Suggested Management
Anticonvulsants	Carbamazepine Ethosuximide Phenobarbital Phenytoin Primidone	Induction of hepatic microsomal enzymes. Rapid metabolism of estrogen and increased binding of progestin and ethinyl estradiol to SHBG.	Use higher dose of oral contraceptives (50 µg ethinyl estradiol), another drug or another method.
Antibiotics	Ampicillin Cotrimoxazole Penicillin	Enterohepatic circulation disturbance, intestinal hurry.	For short course, use additional method or use another drug. For long course, use another method.
	Rifampin	Increased metabolism of progestins. Suspected acceleration of estrogen metabolism.	Use another method.
	Chloramphenicol Metronidazole Neomycin Nitrofurantoin Sulfonamides Tetracyclines	Induction of hepatic microsomal enzymes. Also disturbance of enterohepatic circulation.	For short course, use additional method or use another drug. For long course, use another method.
	Troleandomycin	May retard metabolism of oral contraceptives, increasing the risk of cholestatic jaundice.	
Antifungals	Griseofulvin	Stimulation of hepatic metabolism of contraceptive steroids may occur.	Use another method.
Cholesterol Lowering Agents	Clofibrate	Reduces elevated serum triglycerides and cholesterol; this reduces oral contraceptive efficacy.	Use another method.
Sedatives and Hypnotics	Benzodiazepines Barbiturates Chloral Hydrate Glutethimide Meprobamate	Induction of hepatic microsomal enzymes.	For short course, use additional method or another drug. For long course, use another method or higher dose of oral contraceptives.
Antacids		Decreased intestinal absorption of progestins.	Dose 2 hours apart.
Other Drugs	Phenylbutazone[b] Antihistamines[b] Analgesics[b] Antimigraine preparations[b] Vitamin E	Reduced oral contraceptive efficacy has been reported. Remains to be confirmed.	

[a]Adapted from Dickey, RP, ed.: Managing Contraceptive Pill Patients, 5th edition, Creative Informatics Inc., Durant, OK, 1987.
[b]Refer to Oral Contraceptives 1994, A Report by the Special Advisory Committee on Reproductive Physiology to the Drugs Directorate, Health Protection Branch, Health Canada.

Alesse (cont'd)

the growth of an existing but undiagnosed breast cancer. Since any potential increased risk related to oral contraceptive use is small, there is no reason to change prescribing habits at present (see Warnings).

Women receiving oral contraceptives should be instructed in self-examination of their breasts. Their physicians should be notified whenever any masses are detected. A yearly clinical breast examination is also recommended because, if a breast cancer should develop, drugs that contain estrogen may cause a rapid progression.

Vaginal Bleeding: Persistent irregular vaginal bleeding requires assessment to exclude underlying pathology.

Fibroids: Patients with fibroids (leiomyomata) should be carefully observed. Sudden enlargement, pain, or tenderness requires discontinuation of the use of oral contraceptives.

Emotional Disorders: Patients with a history of emotional disturbances, especially the depressive type, may be more prone to have a recurrence of depression while taking oral contraceptives. In cases of a serious recurrence, a trial of an alternate method of contraception should be made, which may help to clarify the possible relationship. Women with premenstrual syndrome (PMS) may have a varied response to oral contraceptives, ranging from symptomatic improvement to worsening of the condition.

Laboratory Tests: Results of laboratory tests should be interpreted in the light that the patient is on oral contraceptives. The following laboratory tests are modified:

A. Liver Function Tests: Bromsulphthalein Retention Test (BSP): moderate increase. AST and GGT: minor increase. Alkaline Phosphatase: variable increase. Serum Bilirubin: increased, particularly in conditions predisposing to or associated with hyperbilirubinemia.

B. Coagulation Tests: Factors II, VII, IX, X, XII and XIII: increased. Factor VIII: mild increase. Platelet Aggregation and Adhesiveness: mild increase in response to common aggregating agents. Fibrinogen: increased. Plasminogen: mild increase. Antithrombin III: mild decrease. Prothrombin Time: increased.

C. Thyroid Function Tests: Protein-bound Iodine (PBI): increased. Total Serum Thyroxine (T_4): increased. Thyroid Stimulating Hormone (TSH): unchanged.

D. Adrenocortical Function Tests: Plasma Cortisol: increased.

E. Miscellaneous Tests: Serum Folate: occasionally decreased. Glucose Tolerance Test: variable increase with return to normal after 6 to 12 months. Insulin Response: mild to moderate increase. c-Peptide Response: mild to moderate increase.

Tissue Specimens: Pathologists should be advised of oral contraceptive therapy when specimens obtained from surgical procedures and Pap smears are submitted for examination.

Return to Fertility: After discontinuing oral contraceptive therapy, the patient should delay pregnancy until at least one normal spontaneous cycle has occurred in order to date the pregnancy. An alternate contraceptive method should be used during this time.

Amenorrhea: Women having a history of oligomenorrhea, secondary amenorrhea, or irregular cycles may remain anovulatory or become amenorrheic following discontinuation of estrogen-progestin combination therapy.

Amenorrhea, especially if associated with breast secretion, that continues for 6 months or more after withdrawal, warrants a careful assessment of hypothalamic-pituitary function.

Thromboembolic Complications – Post-surgery: There is an increased risk of thromboembolic complications in oral contraceptive users after major surgery. If feasible, oral contraceptives should be discontinued and an alternative method substituted at least 1 month prior to **major** elective surgery. Oral contraceptive use should not be resumed until the first menstrual period after hospital discharge following surgery.

Drug Interactions: The concurrent administration of oral contraceptives with other drugs may result in an altered response to either agent. Reduced effectiveness of the oral contraceptive, should it occur, is more likely with the low-dose formulations. It is important to ascertain all drugs that a patient is taking, both prescription and nonprescription, before oral contraceptives are prescribed.

For possible drug interactions with oral contraceptives, see Table I (on previous page) and Table II.

Noncontraceptive Benefits of Oral Contraceptives: Several health advantages other than contraception have been reported.

1. Combination oral contraceptives reduce the incidence of cancer of the endometrium and ovaries.

Table II*—Alesse 21/Alesse 28

Modification of Other Drug Action by Oral Contraceptives

Class of Compound	Drug	Modification of Drug Action	Suggested Management
Alcohol		Possible increased levels of ethanol or acetaldehyde.	Use with caution.
Alpha-II Adrenoreceptor Agents	Clonidine	Sedation effect increased.	Use with caution.
Anticoagulants	All	Oral contraceptives increase clotting factors, decrease efficacy. However, oral contraceptives may potentiate action in some patients.	Use another method.
Anticonvulsants	All	Fluid retention may increase risk of seizures.	Use another method.
Antidiabetic Drugs	Oral Hypoglycemics and Insulin	Oral contraceptives may impair glucose tolerance and increase blood glucose.	Use low-dose estrogen and progestin oral contraceptive or another method. Monitor blood glucose.
Antihypertensive Agents	Guanethidine and Methyldopa	Estrogen component causes sodium retention, progestin has no effect.	Use low-dose estrogen oral contraceptive or use another method.
	beta-blockers	Increased drug effect (decreased metabolism).	Adjust dose of drug if necessary. Monitor cardiovascular status.
Antipyretics	Acetaminophen	Increased metabolism and renal clearance.	Dose of drug may have to be increased.
	Antipyrine	Impaired metabolism.	Decrease dose of drug.
	ASA	Effects of ASA may be decreased by the short-term use of oral contraceptives.	Patients on chronic ASA therapy may require an increase in ASA dosage.
Aminocaproic Acid		Theoretically, a hypercoagulable state may occur because oral contraceptives augment clotting factors.	Avoid concomitant use.
Betamimetic Agents	Isoproterenol	Estrogen causes decreased response to these drugs.	Adjust dose of drug as necessary. Discontinuing oral contraceptives can result in excessive drug activity.
Caffeine		The actions of caffeine may be enhanced as oral contraceptives may impair the hepatic metabolism of caffeine.	Use with caution.
Cholesterol Lowering Agents	Clofibrate	Their action may be antagonized by oral contraceptives. Oral contraceptives may also increase metabolism of clofibrate.	May need to increase dose of clofibrate.
Corticosteroids	Prednisone	Markedly increased serum levels.	Possible need for decrease in dose.
Cyclosporine		May lead to an increase in cyclosporine levels and hepatotoxicity.	Monitor hepatic function. The cyclosporine dose may have to be decreased.
Folic Acid		Oral contracepives have been reported to impair folate metabolism.	May need to increase dietary intake, or supplement.
Meperidine		Possible increased analgesia and CNS depression due to decreased metabolism of meperidine.	Use combination with caution.
Phenothiazine Tranquilizers	All Phenothiazines, Reserpine and similar drugs	Estrogen potentiates the hyperprolactinemia effect of these drugs.	Use other drugs or lower dose of oral contraceptives. If galactorrhea or hyperprolactinemia occurs, use other method.
Sedatives and Hypnotics	Chlordiazepoxide Lorazepam Oxazepam Diazepam	Increased effect (increased metabolism).	Use with caution.
Theophylline	All	Decreased oxidation, leading to possible toxicity.	Use with caution. Monitor theophylline levels.
Tricyclic Antidepressants	Clomipramine (possibly others)	Increased side effects: i.e., depression.	Use with caution.
Vitamin B_{12}		Oral contraceptives have been reported to reduce serum levels of Vitamin B_{12}.	May need to increase dietary intake, or supplement.

*Adapted from Dickey, RP, ed.: Managing Contraceptive Pill Patients, 5th edition, Creative Informatics Inc., Durant, OK, 1987.

2. Oral contraceptives reduce the likelihood of developing benign breast disease.
3. Oral contraceptives reduce the likelihood of development of functional ovarian cysts.
4. Pill users have less menstrual blood loss and have more regular cycles, thereby reducing the chance of developing iron-deficiency anemia.
5. The use of oral contraceptives may decrease the severity of dysmenorrhea and premenstrual syndrome, and may improve acne vulgaris, hirsutism, and other androgen-mediated disorders.
6. Other noncontraceptive benefits are outlined in Oral Contraceptives 1994, Health Canada.

Oral contraceptives **do not protect** against sexually transmitted diseases (STDs) including HIV/AIDS. For protection against STDs, it is advisable to use latex condoms **in combination with** oral contraceptives.

Adverse Effects: An increased risk of the following serious adverse reactions has been associated with the use of oral contraceptives: thrombophlebitis; arterial thromboembolism; pulmonary embolism; mesenteric thrombosis; neuro-ocular lesions (e.g., retinal thrombosis); myocardial infarction; cerebral thrombosis; cerebral hemorrhage; hypertension; benign hepatic tumors; Hepatic adenomas or benign liver tumors; gallbladder disease.

The following adverse reactions also have been reported in patients receiving oral contraceptives: nausea and vomiting, usually the most common adverse reaction, occurs in approximately 10% or fewer of patients during the first cycle. Other reactions, as a general rule, are seen less frequently or only occasionally.

Other Adverse Reactions: The following adverse reactions have been reported in patients receiving oral contraceptives and are believed to be drug related: gastrointestinal symptoms (such as abdominal cramps and bloating); breakthrough bleeding; spotting; change in menstrual flow; amenorrhea; temporary infertility after discontinuance of treatment; edema; melasma which may persist; breast changes: tenderness, enlargement, and secretion; change in weight (increase or decrease); change in cervical erosion and secretion; diminution in lactation when given immediately postpartum; cholestatic jaundice; migraine; rash (allergic); depression; reduced tolerance to carbohydrates; vaginal candidiasis; change in corneal curvature (steepening); intolerance to contact lenses; retinal thrombosis.

The following adverse reactions have been reported in users of oral contraceptives and the association has been neither confirmed nor refuted: congenital anomalies; premenstrual syndrome; cataracts; optic neuritis; changes in appetite, cystitis-like syndrome; headache; nervousness; dizziness; hirsutism; loss of scalp hair; erythema multiforme; erythema nodosum; hemorrhagic eruption; vaginitis; porphyria; impaired renal function; hemolytic uremic syndrome; Budd-Chiari syndrome; acne; changes in libido; colitis; sickle-cell disease; cerebrovascular disease with mitral valve prolapse; lupus-like syndrome.

Overdose: Symptoms: With levonorgestrel/ethinyl estradiol, acute doses in excess of clinical levels when administered to experimental animals, have been shown to have a minimal deleterious effect. The LD_{50} values for the combination of levonorgestrel and ethinyl estradiol in acute oral administration approximates 500 000 times the equivalent human oral dose (for an explanation of the relationship between norgestrel and levonorgestrel, see Pharmacology). In humans, however, the extent of ill effects to be expected following accidental ingestion of a large dose of any oral contraceptive has not been firmly established.

Depending upon the amount ingested, liver toxicity, temporary interference with the function of the seminiferous tubules, or in the case of females, possible withdrawal bleeding within a few days of consumption, are theoretically possible. However, case histories of both male and female children, some of whom ingested more than half a month's supply of oral contraceptive tablets, indicate that the effects are asymptomatic and without immediate consequence. Despite the frequency of nausea and vomiting in adult females during the first few cycles of use, none of these children presented such symptoms.

Treatment: Although the physiologic effects of oral contraceptives may be theoretically offset by concomitant administration of gonadotrophin preparations, there are no known chemotherapeutic agents which will neutralize their effects subsequent to accidental ingestion. In the practical management of an acute overdosage, gastric lavage may be of value if the offending agent has recently been swallowed. The general rules for observation and symptomatic resolution should be followed. Liver function tests should be conducted, particularly transaminase levels, 2 to 3 weeks after consumption.

Dosage: Alesse 21: 21-Day Regimen: Each cycle consists of 21 days on medication and a 7-day interval without medication (3 weeks on, 1 week off).

The dosage is 1 tablet daily for 21 consecutive days per menstrual cycle, according to prescribed schedule. For the first cycle of medication, the patient is instructed to take 1 tablet daily for 21 consecutive days beginning on Day 1 of her menstrual cycle, on Day 5, or on the first Sunday after her period begins. (For the first cycle only, the first day of menstrual flow is considered Day 1.) The tablets are then discontinued for 7 days (1 week). Withdrawal bleeding should usually occur within 3 days following discontinuation of Alesse.

The patient begins her next and all subsequent 21-day courses of tablets (following the same 21 days on, 7 days off) on the same day of the week that she began her first course. She begins taking her tablets 7 days after discontinuation, regardless of whether or not withdrawal bleeding is still in progress.

Alesse 28: 28-Day Regimen: Each cycle consists of 21 days of pink tablets followed by 7 days of light green inert tablets (3 weeks on, 1 week on inert tablets).

The dosage is 1 tablet daily for 21 consecutive days per menstrual cycle, according to prescribed schedule, followed by 1 inert tablet daily for 7 consecutive days according to prescribed schedule. For the first cycle of medication, the patient is instructed to take one pink tablet daily for 21 consecutive days beginning on Day 1 of her menstrual cycle, on Day 5, or on the first Sunday after her period begins. (For the first cycle only, the first day of menstrual flow is considered Day 1.) One light green tablet is taken daily for the following 7 consecutive days. Withdrawal bleeding should usually occur within 3 days following the discontinuation of pink Alesse tablets, i.e., during the week the patient is taking the light green inert tablets.

The patient begins her next and all subsequent 28-day courses of tablets on the same day of the week that she began her first course. She continues her next course of 28 tablets immediately after the last course, regardless of whether or not a period of withdrawal bleeding is still in progress. There is no need for the patient to count days between cycles because there are no "off-tablet days".

Special Notes on Administration: It is recommended that Alesse tablets be taken at the same time each day, preferably after the evening meal or at bedtime.

Alesse is effective from the first day of therapy if the tablets are begun on the first day of the menstrual cycle.

If Alesse tablets administration is initiated after Day 1 of the first menstrual cycle of medication or postpartum, contraceptive reliance should not be placed on Alesse until after the first 7 consecutive days of administration. The possibility of ovulation and conception prior to initiation of medication should be considered. Therefore, nonhormonal methods of contraception (with the exception of the rhythm or temperature methods) should be used for the next 7 days. In the nonlactating mother, Alesse may be prescribed in the postpartum period either immediately or at the first postpartum examination, whether or not menstruation has resumed.

If spotting or breakthrough bleeding occurs, the patient is instructed to continue on the same regimen. This type of bleeding usually is transient and without significance; however, if the bleeding is persistent or prolonged, the patient is advised to consult her physician. The patient should be instructed to use the following chart if she misses one or more of her birth control pills. She should be told to match the number of pills with the appropriate starting time for her type of pill.

Table III—Alesse 21/Alesse 28

What to Do if You Miss Pills

Sunday Start	**Other than Sunday Start**
Miss 1 Pill	**Miss 1 Pill**
Take it as soon as you remember, and take the next pill at the usual time. This means that you might take 2 pills in one day.	Take it as soon as you remember, and take the next pill at the usual time. This means that you might take 2 pills in one day.
Miss 2 Pills in a row	**Miss 2 Pills in a row**
First 2 Weeks: 1. Take 2 pills the day you remember and 2 pills the next day. 2. Then take 1 pill a day until you finish the pack. 3. Use a backup method of birth control if you have sex in the 7 days after you miss the pills.	First 2 Weeks 1. Take 2 pills the day you remember and 2 pills the next day. 2. Then take 1 pill a day until you finish the pack. 3. Use a backup method of birth control if you have sex in the 7 days after you miss the pills.
Third Week: 1. Keep taking 1 pill a day until Sunday. 2. On Sunday, safely discard the rest of the pack and start a new pack that day. 3. Use a backup method of birth control if you have sex in the 7 days after you miss the pills. 4. You may not have a period this month. **If you miss 2 periods in a row, call your doctor or clinic.**	**Third Week** 1. Safely dispose of the rest of the pill pack and start a new pack that same day. 2. Use a back-up method of birth control if you have sex in the 7 days after you miss the pills. 3. You may not have a period this month. **If you miss 2 periods in a row, call your doctor or clinic.**
Miss 3 or more pills in a row	**Miss 3 or more pills in a row**
Anytime in the Cycle: 1. Keep taking 1 pill a day until Sunday. 2. On Sunday, safely discard the rest of the pack and start a new pack that day. 3. Use a backup method of birth control if you have sex in the 7 days after you miss the pills. 4. You may not have a period this month. **If you miss 2 periods in a row, call your doctor or clinic.**	**Anytime in the Cycle:** 1. Safely dispose of the rest of the pill pack and start a new pack that same day. 2. Use a backup method of birth control if you have sex in the 7 days after you miss the pills. 3. You may not have a period this month. **If you miss two periods in a row, call your doctor or clinic.**

Information for the Patient: See Blue Section—Information for the Patient "Oral Contraceptives".

Supplied: Alesse 21: Each pink tablet contains: levonorgestrel 100 µg and ethinyl estradiol 20 µg. Nonmedicinal ingredients: hydroxypropyl methylcellulose, lactose, magnesium stearate, microcrystalline cellulose, polacrillin potassium, polyethylene glycol, synthetic red iron oxide, titanium dioxide and wax E. Blister packs for the 21-day regimen.

Alesse 28: Each pink tablet contains: levonorgestrel 100 µg and ethinyl estradiol 20 µg. The green tablets are inactive. Nonmedicinal ingredients: hydroxypropyl methylcellulose, lactose, magnesium stearate, microcrystalline cellulose, polacrillin potassium, polyethylene glycol, synthetic red iron oxide, titanium dioxide and wax E; green tablets: FD&C Blue No. 1 aluminum lake, hydroxypropyl methylcellulose, lactose, magnesium stearate, microcrystalline cellulose, polacrillin potassium, polyethylene glycol, synthetic yellow iron oxide, titanium dioxide and wax E. Blister packs for the 28-day regimen (21 active pink tablets and 7 inactive green tablets).

Store at 15 to 30°C. Protect from light source once opened using the protective covering provided.

(Shown in Product Recognition Section)

New Product 1998

ALFENTA® Ⓝ

Janssen-Ortho

Alfentanil HCl

Opioid Analgesic—Adjunct to Anesthesia

Pharmacology: Alfentanil is a potent opioid analgesic/anesthetic with a rapid onset and short duration of action. The analgesic potency of alfentanil is ¼ to ⅓ that of fentanyl. Low to moderate doses of alfentanil in short-stay surgical procedures provide good analgesic protection against hemodynamic responses to surgical stress and rapid recovery. Hemodynamic stability and duration of action increase with increasing dosage. At high doses followed by continuous infusion in general surgery, alfentanil provides hemodynamic stability, rapid recovery and a reduced need for postoperative analgesics.

Alfentanil has an immediate onset of action and plasma levels decay according to a 3 compartment model with sequential half-lives of 1 minute for the fast distribution phase, 12 minutes for the redistribution phase and 90 minutes for the terminal elimination phase. It is extensively metabolized in the liver and small intestine. Approximately 88% of the administered dose is excreted in the urine within 48 hours

Alfenta (cont'd)

with unchanged alfentanil accounting for only 0.2 to 0.5% of the recovered dose. The plasma protein binding of alfentanil is approximately 92%.

Pharmacokinetics: The pharmacokinetics of alfentanil are characterized by limited accumulation and extremely rapid elimination from tissue storage sites. The apparent volume of distribution is 0.59 to 1.0 L/kg and the plasma clearance is 5.1 to 7.7 mL/kg/min. This accounts for the rapid recovery seen following i.v. bolus injection or continuous infusion.

At dosages of 8 μg/kg to 40 μg/kg alfentanil produces analgesia in short-stay surgery. For longer procedures, doses up to 75 μg/kg in intubated patients provide better hemodynamic stability with recovery time comparable to fentanyl. A pre-intubation loading dose of 50 to 75 μg/kg attenuates the response to laryngoscopy, intubation and incision. Subsequent administration of alfentanil infusion administered at a rate of 0.5 to 1.5 μg/kg/min with nitrous oxide/oxygen dampens sympathetic responses to surgical stress and maintains hemodynamic stability, providing smooth and rapid postoperative recovery.

At doses of 105 to 119 μg/kg, alfentanil produces dependable hypnosis; an anesthetic ED_{90} of 182 μg/kg for alfentanil in unpremedicated patients has been determined, based upon the ability to block response to placement of a nasopharyngeal airway.

In one study of patients administered alfentanil with nitrous oxide/oxygen, a narrow range of alfentanil plasma concentrations, 312 to 338 ng/mL, was shown to provide adequate anesthesia for intra-abdominal surgery, while lower concentrations, approximately 250 ng/mL, blocked responses to abdominal closure. Levels from 100 to 200 ng/mL provide adequate anesthesia for superficial surgery.

Attenuation of the catecholamine response with alfentanil infusion was greater than or equal to that seen with a thiopental/enflurane technique.

Patients administered doses of up to 200 μg/kg of alfentanil have shown no elevation in plasma histamine levels and no indication of histamine release.

Indications: For Surgical Patients: As an analgesic adjunct to a barbiturate induction agent during short procedures. As an analgesic adjunct to barbiturate/nitrous oxide/oxygen anesthesia when given in incremental doses for the maintenance of anesthesia at dosages of 5 to 75 μg/kg in surgical procedures with an expected duration of up to 1 hour. As an analgesic adjunct given as a continuous infusion at a rate of 0.5 to 1.5 μg/kg/min with nitrous oxide/oxygen in the maintenance of general anesthesia (see Warnings and Precautions).

For Mechanically Ventilated Patients in the Intensive Care Unit: As an analgesic and suppressant of respiratory drive, to aid compliance with the ventilator and to facilitate toleration of the endotracheal tube, when given as a continuous infusion. As an additional analgesic during brief painful procedures, when given in bolus doses to supplement continuous infusion.

Contraindications: Patients with known hypersensitivity to the drug or to other morphinomimetics.

Warnings: As with other CNS depressants, patients who have received alfentanil should have appropriate surveillance. Resuscitation equipment and a narcotic antagonist should be readily available to manage apnea.

Intensive Care Patients: Alfentanil should not be used in spontaneously breathing patients in the Intensive Care Unit.

Alfentanil, even at the low doses used in the Intensive Care Unit, may cause skeletal muscle rigidity, particularly of the truncal muscles. The incidence and severity of muscular rigidity is related to dose and speed of administration of alfentanil, and may involve all skeletal muscles including those of the head and neck. A neuromuscular blocking agent may be necessary to allow intubation and mechanical ventilation. The onset of muscular rigidity occurs earlier with alfentanil than with other opioids.

The incidence may be reduced by 1) routine administration of neuromuscular blocking agents for balanced narcotic anesthesia; 2) administration of up to ¼ of the full paralyzing dose of a neuromuscular blocking agent just prior to administration of alfentanil at dosages up to 75 μg/kg. The neuromuscular blocking agent used should be compatible with the patient's cardiovascular status.

As with all potent opioids, profound analgesia is accompanied by marked respiratory depression, which may persist into or recur in the early postoperative or postinfusion period. **If alfentanil has been used for prolonged sedation in the Intensive Care Unit, close observation of respiration should continue for at least 12 hours after discontinuation of the infusion. Care should be taken after infusions or large bolus doses of alfentanil to ensure that adequate spontaneous breathing has been established and maintained in the absence of ventilatory support or stimulation before close monitoring of the patient is discontinued. The adjunctive use of sedative hypnotics or other anesthetic agents may result in significant respiratory depression even with small doses of alfentanil.**

Hyperventilation during anesthesia may alter the patient's responses to CO_2, thus affecting respiration postoperatively.

Adequate facilities should be available for monitoring and ventilation of all patients receiving alfentanil. It is essential that these facilities be fully equipped to handle all degrees of respiratory depression, including the use of neuromuscular blocking agents for tracheal intubation.

Nonepileptic myoclonic movements can occur.

Precautions: Alfentanil should be administered only by persons specifically trained in the use of i.v. anesthetics. Vital signs should be monitored routinely.

Skeletal muscle rigidity is related to the dose and speed of administration of alfentanil and administration of adequate doses of a muscle relaxant. At high doses, muscular rigidity will occur unless preventative measures are employed (see Warnings).

Geriatrics: In geriatric patients, the dose of alfentanil required to produce anesthesia, as determined by the appearance of delta waves in the EEG, was 40% lower than that needed in healthy young patients.

Patients with Impaired Hepatic Function: In patients with compromised liver function (and in geriatric patients), the plasma clearance of alfentanil may be reduced and postoperative recovery may be prolonged.

The initial dose of alfentanil should be appropriately reduced in elderly and debilitated patients. The effect of the initial dose should be considered in determining supplemental doses. In obese patients (more than 20% above ideal total body weight), the dosage should be determined on the basis of lean body weight.

Patients with Impaired Renal Function: Although the clearance of alfentanil does not appear to be altered in patients with renal impairment, it may be necessary to reduce dosage requirements due to an increased free fraction of the drug.

Patients with Impaired Respiration: Decreased respiratory drive and increased airway resistance occur with increasing doses of alfentanil. The degree and duration of respiratory depression is dose-related. At high doses, a pronounced decrease in pulmonary exchange and apnea may be produced. Alfentanil should be used with caution in patients with pulmonary disease, decreased respiratory reserve or potentially compromised respiration. In such patients, opioids may additionally decrease respiratory drive and increase airway resistance. During anesthesia, this can be managed by assisted or controlled respiration. Respiratory depression caused by opioid analgesics can be reversed by opioid antagonists such as naloxone. Because the duration of respiratory depression produced by alfentanil may last longer than the duration of the opioid antagonist action, appropriate surveillance should be maintained.

Patients with Compromised Cardiovascular Systems: Rapid administration may produce loss of vascular tone and hypotension. Management with fluid replacement should be considered in patients with compromised cardiovascular systems prior to induction.

In some patients administered alfentanil, bradycardia and possibly asystole can occur if the patient has received an insufficient amount of anticholinergic, or when alfentanil is combined with nonvagolytic muscle relaxants. Bradycardia can be treated with atropine.

Careful titration of dosage may be required in patients with special conditions, such as uncontrolled hypothyroidism or alcoholism (see Drug Interactions; alcohol can potentiate the respiratory depression of narcotics). In such cases, prolonged postoperative monitoring is required.

Patients on chronic opioid therapy or with a history of narcotic abuse, may require increased amounts of alfentanil.

Head Injuries: Alfentanil may obscure the clinical course of patients with head injuries.

In patients with compromised intracerebral compliance, the use of rapid bolus injections should be avoided. In such patients with opioid therapy, the decrease in mean arterial pressure has occasionally been accompanied by a short-lasting reduction of the cerebral perfusion pressure.

Pregnancy: There are no adequate well-controlled studies in pregnant women. Alfentanil should be used during pregnancy only if the potential benefits justify the potential risks.

Labor and Delivery: There are insufficient data to support the use of alfentanil in labor and delivery. Such use is not recommended.

Lactation: In one study of 9 women undergoing postpartum tubal ligation, minimal levels of alfentanil were detected in colostrum 4 hours after administration of 60 μg/kg alfentanil, with no detectable levels present after 28 hours. Caution should be exercised when alfentanil is administered to a nursing woman.

Children: There are insufficient data on the safety, efficacy and dosage regimen in children under 12 years of age, therefore the use of alfentanil is not recommended in this age group.

Drug Interactions: CNS Depressants: Both magnitude and duration of CNS and cardiovascular effects may be enhanced when alfentanil is administered to patients receiving barbiturates, tranquilizers, opioids, general anesthetics or other CNS depressants (e.g., alcohol). When patients have received such drugs, the dose of alfentanil required will be less than usual. Likewise, following the administration of alfentanil the dose of other CNS-depressant drugs should be reduced.

MAO Inhibitors: It is usually recommended to discontinue MAO inhibitors 2 weeks prior to any surgical or anesthetic procedure.

Diazepam: Administration of i.v. diazepam immediately prior to or following high doses of alfentanil has been shown to produce decreases in blood pressure that may be secondary to vasodilation; recovery may also be prolonged.

Hepatic Enzyme Inhibitors: The concomitant use of erythromycin with alfentanil can significantly inhibit the clearance of alfentanil and may increase the risk of prolonged or delayed respiratory depression. The concomitant use of cimetidine with a prolonged infusion of alfentanil may reduce clearance and extend the elimination half-life of alfentanil due to the inhibitory effects of cimetidine on microsomal enzymes. Therefore smaller doses of alfentanil may be required.

Drug Abuse and Dependence: Alfentanil can produce drug dependence of the morphine type and, therefore, has the potential for being abused.

Occupational Hazards: Effect on Driving Ability and Use of Machinery: Patients should be advised to allow sufficient time to elapse before operating a car or heavy machinery. Individual reactions vary. On average, the patient should wait 3 to 6 hours after doses of 1 to 3 mL and 12 to 24 hours after higher doses and infusions.

Adverse Effects: The most frequent adverse reactions experienced in patients administered alfentanil were: Cardiovascular: bradycardia 2%, hypertension 2%, hypotension 2%.

Gastrointestinal: nausea 5%, vomiting 4%.

Musculoskeletal: chest wall rigidity 33% (incremental administration) and 22.5% (continuous infusion).

This incidence of chest wall rigidity can be significantly reduced by pretreatment with a nonparalyzing dose of a neuromuscular blocking agent (i.e., nondepolarizing muscle relaxant).

Other adverse reactions reported in ≤1% of the patients were:

Cardiovascular: tachycardia.

Respiratory: apnea, laryngospasm, postoperative respiratory depression.

CNS: dizziness, sleepiness.

Musculoskeletal: skeletal muscle movements.

In postmarketing data, myoclonic movements and respiratory depression have been reported.

Allergic reactions (such as anaphylaxis, bronchospasm, pruritus, urticaria) and asystole have been reported; since several drugs were coadministered during anesthesia, it is uncertain whether there is a causal relationship to the drug.

Overdose: Symptoms: There has been no clinical experience of overdosage with alfentanil in clinical trials to date. As with other potent opioid analgesics, overdosage is expected to be manifested by an extension of the pharmacological actions of alfentanil. The i.v. LD_{50} of alfentanil in male rats is 43.0 to 50.9 mg/kg.

An overdose of alfentanil injection is manifested as an extension of its pharmacologic actions.

Treatment: In the event of overdosage, oxygen should be administered and ventilation assisted or controlled as indicated for hypoventilation or apnea. A patent airway must be maintained and an oropharyngeal airway or endotracheal tube may be indicated.

I.V. administration of an opioid antagonist such as naloxone should be employed as a specific antidote to manage respiratory depression. The duration of respiratory depression following overdosage with alfentanil may be longer than the duration of action of the opioid antagonist; additional doses of the latter may be required. Administration of an opioid antagonist should not preclude more immediate countermeasures.

Table I—Alfenta

Dosage Chart—Surgical Use

Indication	Approximate Duration of Anesthesia	Initial Dose	Increments/ Infusion	Total Dose	Effects
Incremental Injection	≤30 min	5–20 μg/kg (ventilated or spontaneously breathing)	2.5 μg/kg	5–40 μg/kg	Minimal hemodynamic changes with some attenuation of sympathetic response to surgical stress. More rapid recovery than fentanyl. At doses >11 μg/kg transient apnea may occur which may require assisted ventilation.
Incremental Injection	30–60 min	20–50 μg/kg (ventilated)	5–15 μg/kg	up to 75 μg/kg	Minimal hemodynamic changes with attenuation of response to laryngoscopy and intubation. Recovery times better than or equal to fentanyl.
Continuous Infusion	>45 min	50–75 μg/kg (ventilated)	0.5–1.5 μg/ kg/min	dependent on duration of procedure	Attenuation of cardiovascular response to intubation and incision, intraoperative stability and faster recovery than thiopental/inhalation.

Infusion Dosage: Continuous Infusion: 0.5 to 1.5 μg/kg/min administered with nitrous oxide/oxygen in patients undergoing general anesthesia. When the infusion is started at 0.5 μg/kg/min and there are changes in vital signs that indicate surgical stress or lightening of anesthesia, these may be controlled by increasing the rate up to 1.5 μg/kg/min or administering up to 3 bolus doses of 7 μg/kg given over a 5- to 10-minute period. Infusion rates should be adjusted downward in the absence of these signs until the minimum infusion rate is reached. An average alfentanil infusion rate of 1.5 μg/kg/min has been shown to maintain cardiovascular stability, dampen sympathetic responses to surgical stress and to provide rapid recovery with some postoperative analgesia. Administration of alfentanil should be discontinued 10 to 15 minutes prior to the end of surgery.

Table II—Alfenta

Dosage Chart—Intensive Care Use

Treatment		Dosage
Alfentanil	initial loading dose	0–50 μg/kg
	infusion: initial rate	0.5 μg/kg/min
	increment/decrement	0.25 μg/kg/min
	maximum rate	2.0 μg/kg/min
	minimum rate	0 μg/kg/min
	bolus dose prior to painful procedures	10–20 μg/kg
Other Supplements	sedative/hypnotic agents neuromuscular blocking agents	

If depressed respiration is associated with muscular rigidity, a neuromuscular blocking agent may be required to facilitate assisted or controlled ventilation. I.V. fluids and vasopressors for the treatment of hypotension and other supportive measures may be employed.

Dosage: Adults: The dosage should be individualized according to body weight, physical status, underlying pathological condition, concomitant medication, and type and duration of surgical procedure and anesthesia. In obese patients (more than 20% above ideal total body weight), the dosage of alfentanil should be determined on the basis of lean body weight. The dose of alfentanil should be reduced in geriatric patients.

Vital signs should be monitored routinely.

Alfentanil may be administered: 1) by incremental injection as an analgesic adjunct with barbiturate/nitrous oxide/oxygen anesthesia for short surgical procedures (expected duration of less than 1 hour); 2) as an analgesic adjunct to barbiturate induction for general surgical procedures followed by continuous infusion as a maintenance analgesic with nitrous oxide/oxygen for general surgical procedures. See Table I.

Dosage for Mechanically Ventilated Patients in the Intensive Care Unit: The dosage of alfentanil required in intensive care patients will depend on many factors including the underlying pathological condition, the severity of the pain, the type of mechanical ventilation, the individual patient's response to the drug, and the use of concomitant medications, especially sedative hypnotics or major tranquilizers (see Table II).

Continuous Infusion: The recommended initial infusion rate of alfentanil in mechanically ventilated adult patients is 0.5 μg/kg/min. The rate of infusion should be reassessed regularly and individualized to ensure that it is kept at the minimum necessary to achieve the desired clinical effect. The optimal infusion rate varies considerably from patient to patient. However, in the majority of patients, infusion rates in the range of 0.2 to 2.0 μg/kg/min effectively prevent pain and aid compliance with mechanical ventilation.

An initial loading dose of up to 50 μg/kg may be required in some patients, depending on their status prior to initiation of the infusion as well as previous analgesic or anesthetic therapy.

Supplemental Bolus Doses: Supplemental bolus doses of 10 to 20 μg/kg may be given during periods of increased stimulation due to painful procedures such as physiotherapy or endotracheal suction.

Patients should be closely monitored for at least 12 hours following cessation of the infusion to detect any evidence of respiratory depression. Care should be taken to ensure that adequate spontaneous ventilation has been established and maintained in the absence of ventilatory support or stimulation.

At the recommended dosage, alfentanil provides analgesia and suppression of respiratory drive but it may not provide sedation or induce sleep. The addition of an anxiolytic such as a benzodiazepine may be required to achieve sedation. Neuromuscular blocking agents may also be necessary for intubation or to settle patients who are difficult to manage on mechanical ventilation.

There is no clinical experience with infusions of more than 5 consecutive days.

Children: Not recommended, see Precautions.

Premedication: The selection of preanesthetic medication should be based upon the needs of the individual patient.

Neuromuscular Blocking Agents: The neuromuscular blocking agent selected should be compatible with the patient's condition, taking into account the hemodynamic effects of a particular muscle relaxant and the degree of skeletal muscle relaxation required (see Pharmacology, Warnings and Precautions).

Supplied: Each mL of colorless, sterile, preservative-free aqueous solution contains: alfentanil HCl equivalent to 500 μg of alfentanil base and water for injection. Sodium chloride is added to produce an isotonic solution. pH range of 4.0 to 6.0. Ampuls of 2 and 5 mL (packages of 10), ampuls of 20 mL (packages of 5). Store at room temperature protected from light.

Reviewed 1999

ALIMENTUM®

Abbott

Infant Feeding Formula

Indications: A nutritionally complete formula for infants and children with milk and/or soy protein allergy, severe food allergies, colic due to milk sensitivity, select cases of chronic diarrhea or maldigestion/malabsorption.

Precautions: Shake very well to assure proper blending. Because of the special nutritional characteristics of Alimentum, it does not look or taste like milk or soy formulations. This is a ready-to-feed formula; if diluted with additional water, it may not provide proper nutrition and repeated use of such feeding could cause illness.

Dosage: As directed by the physician.

Supplied: Each 945 mL can contains: water, sucrose, casein hydrolysate (enzymatically hydrolyzed and charcoal treated), modified tapioca starch, fractionated coconut oil (medium-chain triglycerides), safflower oil, minerals (calcium citrate calcium phosphate dibasic, potassium phosphate dibasic, calcium hydroxide, magnesium chloride, potassium chloride, sodium chloride, potassium citrate, ferrous sulfate, zinc sulfate, cupric sulfate, manganese sulfate, sodium selenite, potassium iodide), soy oil, carrageenan, vitamins (ascorbic acid, alpha-tocopheryl acetate, niacinamide, calcium pantothenate, vitamin A palmitate, thiamine hydrochloride, riboflavin, pyridoxine hydrochloride, folic acid, phylloquinone, biotin, vitamin D_3, cyanocobalamin), L-cystine dihydrochloride, L-tyrosine, L-tryptophan, choline chloride, taurine, myoinositol and L-carnitine. See Table I.

Energy Distribution: 285 kJ/100 mL.

Table I—Alimentum

Analysis	100 mL	
Energy	285 (68)	kJ (kcal)
Carbohydrate	6.89	g
Fat	3.75	g
Protein	1.86	g
Linoleic Acid	1.08	g
Ash	0.5	g
Vitamin A	203	IU
Vitamin D_3	30.4	IU
Vitamin E	2.0	IU
Vitamin C	6.0	mg
Niacin	0.9130	mg
d-Pantothenic Acid	0.5070	mg
Riboflavin	0.0610	mg
Thiamine	0.0410	mg
Vitamin B_6	0.0410	mg
Folic Acid	0.0100	mg
Vitamin K_1	0.0100	mg
Biotin	0.0030	mg
Vitamin B_{12}	0.0003	mg
Sodium	30	mg
Potassium	80	mg
Chloride	54	mg
Calcium	71	mg
Phosphorus	51	mg
Magnesium	5.1	mg
Zinc	0.51	mg
Iron	1.2	mg
Copper	0.0510	mg
Iodine	0.0100	mg
Manganese	0.0200	mg
Selenium	0.0019	mg
Choline	8.5	mg
Carnitine	1.48	mg
Taurine	5.19	mg
Myoinositol	3.4	mg

Liquid ready-to-feed (prediluted); cans of 945 mL, cases of 12; for hospital use, bottles of 104 mL, cases of 48. Store unopened liquid at room temperature. Prepared bottles and opened cans (covered) should be refrigerated and used within 48 hours.

ALKERAN® ℞

Glaxo Wellcome

Melphalan

Antineoplastic

Pharmacology: Melphalan is an alkylating agent of the bischloroethylamine type. As a result, its cytotoxicity appears to be

Alkeran (cont'd)

related to the extent of its interstrand cross-linking with DNA, probably by binding at the N^7 position of guanine. Like other bifunctional alkylating agents, it is active against both resting and rapidly dividing tumor cells.

Pharmacokinetics: The pharmacokinetics of melphalan after i.v. administration have been extensively studied in adult patients, and linear pharmacokinetics were observed over a broad dose range (5 to 220 mg/m²). Following injection, drug plasma concentrations declined rapidly in a biexponential manner with distribution phase and terminal elimination phase half-lives of approximately 10 and 70 minutes, respectively. Estimates of average total body clearance varied among studies, but typical values of approximately 7 to 9 mL/min/kg (250 to 325 mL/min/m²) were observed. Mean (±SD) peak melphalan plasma concentrations in myeloma patients given melphalan i.v. at doses of 10 or 20 mg/m² were 1.2±0.4 and 2.8±1.9μg/mL, respectively. Studies in children as young as 1 year showed results similar to adults.

The steady-state volume of distribution of melphalan is 0.5 L/kg and approximates total body water. Penetration into cerebrospinal fluid (CSF) is low, with plasma/CSF concentration ratios reported from 10:1 to greater than 100:1. The extent of melphalan binding to plasma proteins is moderately high with reports ranging from 60 to 90%. Serum albumin is the major binding protein, while α-acid glycoprotein appears to account for about 20% of the plasma protein binding. Interaction with immunoglobulins have been found to be negligible.

Melphalan is eliminated from plasma primarily by chemical hydrolysis to monohydroxy- and dihydroxy-melphalan. Aside from these hydrolysis products, no other melphalan metabolites have been observed in man. Although the contribution of renal elimination to melphalan clearance is low and most investigators have observed no relationship between renal dysfunction and melphalan pharmacokinetics, one study noted an increase in the occurrence of severe leukopenia in patients with elevated BUN after 10 weeks of therapy.

The pharmacokinetics of melphalan administered by closed circuit limb perfusion have been studied by several investigators. Melphalan concentrations declined rapidly and biexponentially from circulating perfusate with average terminal half-lives reported from 26 min (n=4) to 53 min (n=48). Systemic exposure to melphalan during limb perfusion is generally very low. Peak melphalan concentrations in the closed circuit perfusate are typically 10 to 100 times greater than peak concentrations in plasma observed following standard dose systemic i.v. therapy for multiple myeloma.

Indications:

> **Caution: There are many reports of patients with multiple myeloma who have developed acute, non-lymphatic leukemia or myeloproliferative syndrome following therapy with alkylating agents (including melphalan). Evaluation of published reports strongly suggests that melphalan is leukemogenic in patients with multiple myeloma.**
>
> **There is a greatly increased incidence of acute, non-lymphatic leukemia in women with ovarian carcinoma treated with alkylating agents (including melphalan).**
>
> **Melphalan is a carcinogen in animals and must be presumed to be so in humans. Although the palliation to be anticipated from the use of melphalan in multiple myeloma and ovarian carcinoma is generally felt to greatly outweigh the possible induction of a second neoplasm, the potential benefits and the potential risk of carcinogenesis must be evaluated on an individual basis.**
>
> **Melphalan has been observed to produce chromosomal aberrations in human cells in vitro and in vivo. Melphalan is potentially mutagenic and teratogenic in humans, although the extent of the risk is unknown.**

Melphalan is indicated for the palliative treatment of multiple myeloma and for the palliation of non-resectable epithelial carcinoma of the ovary.

Malignant Melanoma: Melphalan for injection has been administered by hyperthermic isolated limb perfusion as an adjuvant to surgery. However, there have been no prospective controlled or uncontrolled trials evaluating dose and its relationship to disease response and/or toxicity.

Contraindications: Melphalan should not be used in patients whose disease has demonstrated a prior resistance to this agent. Patients who have demonstrated hypersensitivity to melphalan should not be given the drug. There may be cross-sensitivity (skin rash) between melphalan and chlorambucil.

Melphalan should not be given if other similar chemotherapeutic agents or radiotherapy have been administered to the patient recently or if neutrophil and/or platelet counts are depressed.

Melphalan should not be administered concurrently with radiotherapy.

Warnings:

> Melphalan should be administered in carefully adjusted dosages by or under the supervision of experienced physicians who are familiar with the drug's actions and the possible complications of its use.
>
> The major acute toxicities are related to bone marrow suppression, hypersensitivity reactions including anaphylaxis, gastrointestinal disturbances and pulmonary toxicity. The major long-term toxicities are related to infertility and secondary malignancies. Melphalan is leukemogenic and potentially mutagenic in humans.
>
> Careful attention should be paid to the monitoring of blood counts. Patients with renal impairment should be closely observed as they may have uremic marrow suppression.

The drug should not be administered by hyperthermic isolated limb perfusion unless the clinician is experienced and well-trained in this technique.

As with other nitrogen mustard drugs, excessive dosage will produce marked bone marrow suppression. Bone marrow suppression is the most significant toxicity associated with melphalan for injection in most patients. Therefore, the following tests should be performed at the start of therapy and prior to each subsequent dose of melphalan: platelet count, hemoglobin, WBC count and differential. The occurrence of a platelet count below 50 000/mm³ or an absolute neutrophil count below 500/mm³ is an indication to withhold further therapy until the blood counts have sufficiently recovered. Frequent blood counts are essential to determine optimal dosage and to avoid toxicity.

Acute hypersensitivity reactions, including anaphylaxis, have occurred infrequently (see Adverse Effects). Treatment is symptomatic. The infusion should be terminated immediately, followed by the administration of volume expanders, pressor agents, corticosteroids, or antihistamines at the discretion of the physician.

Secondary malignancies, including acute nonlymphocytic leukemia, myeloproliferative syndrome, and carcinoma, have been reported in patients with cancer treated with alkylating agents (including melphalan). Some patients also received other chemotherapeutic agents or radiation therapy. Precise quantitation of the risk of actue leukemia, myeloproliferative syndrome or carcinoma is not possible. Published reports of leukemia in patients who have received melphalan (and other alkylating agents) suggest that the risk of leukemogenesis increases with chronicity of treatment and with cumulative dose. In one study, the 10-year cumulative risk of developing acute leukemia or myeloproliferative syndrome after melphalan therapy was 19.5% cumulative doses ranging from 730 mg to 9 652 mg. In this same study, as well as in an additional study, the 10-year cumulative risk of developing acute leukemia or myeloproliferative syndrome after melphalan therapy was less than 2% for cumulative doses under 600 mg. This does not mean that there is a cumulative dose below which there is no risk of the induction of secondary malignancy. The potential benefits from melphalan therapy must be weighed on an individual basis against the possible risk of the induction of a second malignancy.

Melphalan has been shown to cause chromatid or chromosome damage in man. Melphalan causes suppression of ovarian function in premenopausal women, resulting in amenorrhea in a significant number of patients. Reversible and irreversible testicular suppression have also been reported.

Lactation: It is not known whether this drug is excreted in human milk. Because many drugs are excreted in human milk and because of the potential for serious adverse reactions in nursing infants from melphalan, a decision should be made whether to discontinue nursing or to discontinue the drug, taking into account the importance of the drug to the mother.

Precautions: General: In all instances where the use of melphalan for injection is considered for chemotherapy, the physician must evaluate the need and usefulness of the drug against the risk of adverse events. Melphalan should be used with extreme caution in patients whose bone marrow reserve may have been compromised by prior irradiation or chemotherapy, or whose marrow function is recovering from previous cytotoxic therapy. Dose reduction should be considered in patients with renal insufficiency receiving i.v. melphalan. In one trial, increased bone marrow suppression was observed in patients with BUN levels ≥30 mg/dL. A 50% reduction in the i.v. melphalan dose decreased the incidence of severe bone marrow suppression in the later portion of this study.

If the leukocyte count falls below 3 000 cells/μL, or the platelet count below 100 000/μL, the drug should be discontinued until the blood picture has had a chance to recover.

Blood counts may continue to fall for 6 to 8 weeks after initiation of treatment, So, at the first sign of an abnormally large fall in leukocyte or platelet counts, treatment should be temporarily interrupted.

Patients with azotemia should be closely observed, however, in order to make dosage reductions, if required, at the earliest possible time.

Laboratory Tests: Periodic complete blood counts with differentials should be performed during the course of treatment with melphalan. At least one determination should be obtained prior to each dose. Patients should be observed closely for consequences of bone marrow suppression, which include severe infections, bleeding, and symptomatic anemia (see Warnings).

Pregnancy: Safe use of melphalan has not been established with respect to adverse effects on fetal development. Therefore, it should be used in women of childbearing potential and particularly during early pregnancy only when, in the judgment of the physician, the potential benefits outweigh the possible hazards.

Children: The safety and effectiveness in children have not been established.

Geriatrics: Clinical experience with melphalan has not identified differences in responses between the elderly and younger patients. In general, dose selection for an elderly patient should be cautious, usually starting at the low end of the dosing range, reflecting the greater frequency of decreased hepatic, renal, or cardiac function, and of concomitant disease or other drug therapy.

Adverse Effects: The following information on adverse reactions is based on data from both oral and i.v. administration of melphalan as a single agent, using several different dose schedules for treatment of a wide variety of malignancies.

Hematologic: Leukopenia, neutropenia and hemolytic anemia were observed. The most common side effect is bone marrow suppression. Irreversible bone marrow failure has been reported. Bone marrow suppression is uncommon after limb perfusion.

Blood Chemistry: Elevation in liver function enzymes is usually mild. An increase in urea and creatinine levels has been observed.

Gastrointestinal: Gastrointestinal effects such as nausea and vomiting occur in up to 30% of patients receiving conventional oral doses of melphalan and in up to 50% of patients receiving i.v. doses of melphalan. Diarrhea is noted to occur 1 week post high dose melphalan therapy. Oral ulceration and hepatic toxicity including veno-occlusive disease have been reported.

Hypersensitivity: Acute hypersensitivity reactions, including anaphylaxis, were reported in 2.4% of 425 patients receiving melphalan for injection for myeloma (see Warnings). These reactions were characterized by urticaria, pruritus, edema, and in some patients, tachycardia, bronchospasm, dyspnea, and hypotension. These patients appeared to respond to antihistamine and corticosteroid therapy. Treatment with melphalan should be discontinued if a hypersensitivity reaction occurs.

Local Reactions: Mild pain and/or irritation at, or near, the site of injection occurred after approximately half of the infusions, resolving within a few hours after the end of the injection, without a need for treatment. Skin ulceration at injection site and flushing were reported.

Miscellaneous: Other reported adverse reactions include: skin hypersensitivity, vasculitis, alopecia, allergic reaction, pulmonary fibrosis, and interstitial pneumonitis. Flushing sensations were reported at high doses of melphalan.

Hyperthermic Isolated Limb Perfusion: Adverse reactions may be attributable to the surgical procedure as well as the heated perfusion with melphalan for injection. Systemic complications are uncommon, with reversible bone marrow suppression occurring in <5% of patients. Wound complications, such as delayed healing or infection, occur in 5 to 10% of patients. The local toxicity of hyperthermic perfusion appears to increase with increasing drug dose, duration of perfusion, and temperature. Severe nerve or muscle damage, severe skin or soft tissue reaction, or arterial thrombosis requiring amputation are rare, occurrring in less than 1% of patients.

Overdose: Symptoms: Overdose as high as 290 mg/m² resulting in death has been reported. It has also been reported that a pediatric patient survived a 254 mg/m² overdose treated with standard supportive care. The immediate effects are severe nausea and vomiting. Decreased consciousness, convulsions, muscular paralysis and cholinomimetic effects are less frequently seen. Severe mucositis, stomatitis, colitis, diarrhea, and hemorrhage of the gastrointestinal tract occur at high dose (>100 mg/m²). Elevations in liver enzymes and veno-occlusive disease occur infrequently. Nephrotoxicity and adult respiratory distress syndrome have been reported rarely. The principal effect is bone marrow suppression.

Treatment: Hematologic parameters should be closely followed for 3 to 6 weeks. Administration of autologous bone marrow or hematopoietic growth factors (i.e., sargramostim, filgrastim) may shorten the period of pancytopenia. General supportive measures together with appropriate blood transfusions and antibiotics should be instituted as deemed necessary by the physician. This drug is not removed from plasma to any significant degree by hemodialysis or hemoperfusion.

Dosage: Oral: Multiple Myeloma: The usual oral dose is 6 mg daily. The entire daily dose may be given at one time. It is adjusted, as required, on the basis of blood counts done at approximately weekly intervals. After 2 to 3 weeks of treatment, the drug should be discontinued for up to 4 weeks, during which time the blood count should be followed carefully. When the white blood cell and platelet counts are rising, a maintenance dose of 2 mg daily may be instituted. Because of the patient-to-patient variation in melphalan plasma levels following oral administration of the drug, several investigators have recommended that melphalan dosage be cautiously escalated until some myelosuppression is observed, in order to assure that potentially therapeutic levels of the drug have been reached.

Other dosage regimens have been used by various investigators. Osserman and Takatsuki have used an initial course of 10 mg/day for 7 to 10 days. They report that maximal suppression of the leukocyte and platelet counts occurs within 3 to 5 weeks and recovery within 4 to 8 weeks. Continuous maintenance therapy with 2 mg/day is instituted when the white blood cell count is greater than 4 000 and the platelet count is greater than 100 000. Dosage is adjusted to between 1 and 3 mg/day depending upon the hematological response. It is desirable to try to maintain a significant degree of bone marrow depression so as to keep the leukocyte count in the range of 3 000 to 3 500 cells/µL.

Hoogstraten et al have started treatment with 0.15 mg/kg/day for 7 days. This is followed by a rest period of at least 14 days, but it may be as long as 5 to 6 weeks. Maintenance therapy is started when the white blood cell and platelet counts are rising. The maintenance dose is 0.05 mg/kg/day or less and is adjusted according to the blood count.

Available evidence suggests that about one-third to one-half of the patients with multiple myeloma show a favorable response to oral administration of the drug. It is to be emphasized that response may be very gradual over many months; it is important that repeated courses or continuous therapy be given since improvement may continue slowly over many months and the maximum benefit may be missed if treatment is abandoned too soon.

Epithelial Ovarian Cancer: One commonly employed regimen for the treatment of ovarian carcinoma has been to administer melphalan at a dose of 0.2 mg/kg p.o. daily for 5 days as a single course. Courses are repeated every 4 to 5 weeks depending upon hematologic tolerance.

I.V.: Multiple Myeloma: The usual i.v. dose is 16 mg/m². Dosage reduction of up to 50% should be considered in patients with renal insufficiency (BUN ≥30 mg/dL). The drug is administered in one dose and the length of infusion should be from 15 to 90 minutes. Melphalan is repeated at 2-week intervals initially for 4 doses, then at 4-week intervals after adequate recovery from toxicity. Available evidence suggests about one-third to one-half of the patients with multiple myeloma show a favorable response to the drug. Experience with oral melphalan suggests that repeated courses should be given since improvement may continue slowly over many months, and the maximum benefit may be missed if treatment is abandoned prematurely. Dose adjustment on the basis of blood cell counts at the nadir prior to each dose should be considered.

Perfusion Method: Malignant Melanoma: Only physicians experienced and well-trained in hyperthermic isolated limb perfusion should administer the drug in this fashion. The recommended dose of melphalan for injection for hyperthermic limb perfusion for the treatment of locally advanced malignant melanoma of the extremity is 1.0 mg/kg body weight for upper extremity and 1.5 mg/kg for lower extremity. The total dose for a perfusion should not exceed 80 mg for upper extremity and 120 mg for lower extremity. As soon as hyperthermic conditions are achieved, melphalan for injection is administered into the arterial line of the perfusion in 3 equally divided doses at 5-minute intervals. The hyperthermic perfusion is continued for one hour after the administration of melphalan for injection. The surgical technique and procedure have been well-described. To exclude or minimize perfusion-related complications, the key perfusion variables should be followed: Temperature: perfusate and i.m./s.c. tissue should not exceed 42.5 and 42°C, respectively. Flow Rate: 250 to 400 mL/minute are generally used for auxiliary perfusions, 400 to 600 mL/minute for iliac perfusions. Perfusate: 650 to 750 mL volume consisting of either heparinized whole blood (2 000 units/500 mL) or a heparinized (2 000 units/500 mL) 50:50 mixture of Lactated Ringer's and washed packed red blood cells. Perfusion Duration: not to exceed 1 hour. Dose: not to exceed 1 mg/kg for upper extremity (total dose ≤80 mg) and 1.5 mg/kg for lower extremity (total dose ≤120 mg) of melphalan for injection.

Preparation for Administration/Stability: I.V.: Reconstitute melphalan for injection, as directed, with 10 mL of the supplied diluent. This provides a 5 mg/mL solution of melphalan. Immediately dilute the dose to be administered in 0.9% sodium chloride injection, USP, to a concentration not greater than 2 mg/mL. Administer the diluted product over a minimum of 15 minutes. Complete administration within 50 minutes of reconstitution. Discard any reconstituted and diluted solutions remaining after 50 minutes of reconstitution.

The reconstituted product is stable for up to 2 hours at 30°C. A precipitate forms if the solution is stored at 5°C. **Do not refrigerate.**

Solutions diluted to a concentration of 0.1 mg/mL to 0.45 mg/mL in 0.9% sodium chloride injection are stable for up to 50 minutes at 30°C and 3 hours at 20°C.

Perfusion: Reconstitute melphalan for injection, as directed, with 10 mL of the supplied diluent. This provides a 5 mg/mL solution of melphalan. Administer the reconstituted melphalan directly into the arterial line of the perfusion in 3 equally divided doses at 5-minute intervals. Complete administration within 2 hours of reconstitution. Discard any portion remaining after 2 hours of reconstitution.

The reconstituted product is stable for up to 2 hours at 30°C. A precipitate forms if the solution is stored at 5°C. **Do not refrigerate.**

Reconstituted Solutions: Melphalan for injection must be reconstituted, at room temperature, by rapidly transferring 10 mL of the supplied solvent-diluent directly into the vial of lyophilized powder using a sterile needle (20 gauge or larger needle diameter) and syringe. Immediately shake vial vigorously until a clear solution is obtained. Rapid addition of the diluent followed by immediate vigorous shaking is important for proper dissolution. The pH of resulting solution is approximately 6.5. See Table I.

Table I—Alkeran

Reconstitution

Vial Size	Volume of Diluent to be Added to Vial	Approximate Available Volume	Nominal Concentration per mL
50 mg	10 mL	10 mL	5 mg/mL

Melphalan injection solution has limited stability and should be prepared immediately before use. Any unused solution should be discarded. The reconstituted solution should be used immediately and should not be refrigerated as this will cause precipitation. It is stable for up to 2 hours at 30°C.

Melphalan injection solution has reduced stability when further diluted in an infusion solution and the rate of degradation increases rapidly with rise in temperature. In that case, only Sodium Chloride Infusion, 0.9% w/v should be used. Solutions diluted to a concentration of 0.1 mg/mL to 0.45 mg/mL in 0.9% Sodium Chloride Infusion should be used immediately and are stable for up to 50 minutes at 30°C and 3 hours at 20°C.

Administration Precautions: Parenteral drug products should usually be inspected for particulate matter and discoloration prior to administration whenever solution and container permit. If either occurs, do not use this product.

As with other toxic compounds, caution should be exercised when handling and preparing the solution of melphalan. Skin reactions associated with accidental exposure may occur. The use of gloves is recommended. If the solution of melphalan contacts the skin or mucosa, immediately wash the skin or mucosa thoroughly with soap and water.

Information for the Patient: See Blue Section—Information for the Patient "Alkeran".

Supplied: Injection: Each vial of sterile, white to cream-colored, freeze-dried powder contains: melphalan HCl equivalent to melphalan 50 mg and povidone 20 mg. Each vial of solvent-diluent provides 10 mL of buffer solution containing sodium citrate 0.20 g, ethanol 0.52 mL, propylene glycol 6 mL and water for injection, q.s. Component packs of 2 comprising a vial containing a freeze-dried powder and a vial of solvent-diluent. Store at controlled room temperature (15 to 30°C). Protect from light.

Tablets: Each white, scored tablet, imprinted ALKERAN and A2A on each side of the score, contains: melphalan 2 mg. Bottles of 50. Nonmedicinal ingredients: lactose, magnesium stearate, potato starch, povidone and sucrose. Store between 15 and 25°C, protected from light. Keep dry and dispense in glass.

(Shown in Product Recognition Section)

ALLEGRA™

Hoechst Marion Roussel

Fexofenadine HCl

Histamine H_1-Receptor Antagonist

Pharmacology: Fexofenadine, the predominant human and animal active metabolite of terfenadine, is a selective histamine H_1-receptor antagonist. In laboratory animals, there is no evidence of local anesthetic, analgesic, anticonvulsant, antidepressant, antidopaminergic, antiserotonergic, anticholinergic, sedative, H_2-receptor antagonist, or α_1-adrenergic receptor blocking activity. Fexofenadine inhibits antigen-induced bronchospasm in sensitized guinea pigs and histamine release from peritoneal mast cells of the rat. It does not cross the blood-brain barrier in the rat.

Fexofenadine inhibits histamine induced skin wheal and flare responses. Following single and twice daily oral dose administration, antihistaminic effects occur within 1 hour, achieve a maximum at 6 hours, and last a minimum of 12 hours. There is no evidence of tolerance to these effects after 28 days of dosing

At steady-state with 60 mg b.i.d. dosing, the average per cent inhibition of skin wheal was 45.8% and 53.6% for fexofenadine and terfenadine, respectively. The average maximum inhibition and average area under effect curve was similar for both drugs at equivalent doses. Although higher doses, i.e., 180 mg b.i.d. produced somewhat greater inhibition, the average difference was only 10 to 12%. At 12 hours postdose, the average percent inhibition was approximately 30%.

Similar results were observed with the skin flare response, although the average percent inhibition was somewhat higher—69% and 75%, for 60 mg b.i.d. fexofenadine and terfenadine, respectively. Equivalent doses of both drugs produced comparable maximum inhibition and area under effect curve. The flare area was inhibited greater than 55% at 12 hours postdose.

There was no clear-cut relationship between plasma concentrations of fexofenadine or dose of either fexofenadine or terfenadine. Maximum inhibition was achieved at plasma fexofenadine concentrations of 200 ng/mL.

In randomized, double-blind, placebo-controlled trials, a daily dose of fexofenadine 60 mg b.i.d. was shown to be effective in relieving the symptoms of seasonal allergic rhinitis (trees and grasses in the spring or ragweed pollen in the fall). These symptoms consisted of sneezing, rhinorrhea, itchy nose/palate/throat and itchy, watery, red eyes. There was no statistically significant difference in the treatment effect in subgroups defined by age, gender, race or weight.

There was no direct comparison with terfenadine. However, in studies with similar trial design, the effectiveness of fexofenadine appears to be comparable to that of the parent compound.

Preclinical and clinical evidence indicates that fexofenadine does not prolong the QTc interval (the mechanism underlying the arrhythmias associated with elevated levels of terfenadine). The evidence is derived from in vitro electrophysiological studies, in vivo preclinical studies in dogs and rabbits and a number of clinical trials consisting of 2 definitive QTc studies (n=24 and 40), 2 dose escalation studies (n=24 and 66), 2 drug interaction studies investigating the effects of erythromycin and ketoconazole (n=24 for each study), 2 randomized Phase III clinical trials in patients with fall allergic rhinitis (n=870 subjects treated with fexofenadine), 2 long-term safety studies (n=234 and 217 subjects treated with fexofenadine), and single dose (80 mg) studies in special populations (individuals over 65 years of age, patients with various degrees of renal and hepatic impairment).

Allegra (cont'd)

Pharmacokinetics: Fexofenadine is rapidly absorbed following oral administration. The single and multiple dose pharmacokinetics of fexofenadine were linear from 20 mg to 120 mg doses. T_{max} occurs at approximately 2.6 hours and C_{max} is approximately 209 ng/mL following oral administration of a single 60 mg dose.

Following multiple dosing, fexofenadine has an apparent elimination half-life of 11 to 16 hours. Steady-state pharmacokinetic parameters following 60 mg b.i.d. dosing are: $AUC_{ss\ (0\text{-}12h)}$=1 367 ng/mL·h, C_{max}=299 ng/mL, C_{min}=29 ng/mL, T_{max}=1 h.

The pharmacokinetics of fexofenadine in seasonal allergic rhinitis patients are similar to that of otherwise healthy subjects. Peak fexofenadine plasma concentrations were similar between adolescent (12 to 16 years of age) and adult patients.

Metabolism of fexofenadine is negligible. The methyl ester of fexofenadine (3.6% of the dose) and MDL 4829 (1.5% of the dose) were the only potential metabolites of fexofenadine detected.

Following a single 60 mg oral dose, 80% and 11% of the total [^{14}C] fexofenadine dose is recovered in the feces and urine, respectively. The principal elimination pathways of fexofenadine are biliary and renal. Fecal excretion of fexofenadine is comprised of biliary excretion and gastrointestinal secretion processes as well as nonabsorbed drug. The contribution of each component is unknown.

The absolute bioavailability of fexofenadine has not been established but is estimated to be approximately 33%. The capsule and tablet formulations are considered to be bioequivalent but the tablet formulation exhibits a greater food effect. The AUC and C_{max} of the tablet formulation in the presence of food was reduced to 76% (83% for the capsule) and 75% (89% of the capsule) of the fasted values.

Current theory suggests that fexofenadine absorption is incomplete due to the gate-keeping function of the p-glycoprotein transport system in the intestinal epithelium which reduces both fexofenadine absorption, explaining the low bioavailability, as well as secretes absorbed drug back into the gastrointestinal tract. Since approximately 80% of an orally administered dose is recovered in the feces, primarily as unchanged drug, rather than 67% (100%−33%), this difference is believed to represent fexofenadine secretion from the systemic circulation into the gastrointestinal lumen.

Fexofenadine is 60 to 80% bound to plasma proteins, including serum albumin and α-acid glycoprotein. Protein binding is decreased to 56 to 68% and 56 to 75% in renally and hepatically impaired patients, respectively.

Special Populations: Pharmacokinetics in special populations were determined following a single 80 mg oral dose of fexofenadine. The pharmacokinetics were compared to those from normal subjects in a separate study of similar design. While subjects' weights were relatively uniform between the studies, the special population patients were older than the healthy, young volunteers. Thus, an age effect may be confounding the pharmacokinetic differences observed.

Renal Impairment: Following a single 80 mg oral dose, renal clearance is decreased to 68, 15 and 3% of the control value (3.63 L/h) in patients with mild to moderate impairment (creatinine clearance 41 to 80 mL/min; n=9), moderate to severe impairment (creatinine clearance 11 to 40 mL/min; n=10) and dialysis patients (creatinine clearance <10 mL/min; n=10). The corresponding $AUC_{0-\infty}$ and C_{max} were increased by 80, 154 and 88%, respectively (control value=1 788.1 ng/mL·h), and by 58, 78 and 54%, respectively (control value=248.7 ng/mL). The half-life increased from 13.7 h to 22.8, 24.8 and 18.9 h, respectively. Based on these increases in bioavailability and half-life, a dose of 60 mg once daily is recommended as the starting dose in patients with decreased renal function.

Hepatic Impairment: The pharmacokinetics of fexofenadine in 14 patients with hepatic disease (moderate, n=9; moderate to severe, n=5), did not differ substantially from that observed in healthy subjects. The lack of effect may be explained by the fact that none of the patients investigated suffered from complete biliary obstruction, as biliary excretion is one of the major elimination pathways for fexofenadine.

Effect of Age: The pharmacokinetics of fexofenadine in healthy elderly individuals (>65 years old, n=20) were different from those observed in healthy younger individuals following a single oral dose of 80 mg fexofenadine. Mean AUC was 63% higher (control value=1 788 ng/mL·h), oral clearance 30% lower (control value=48 L/h), renal clearance 24% less (control value=3.6 L/h), C_{max} 68% higher (control value=248.7 ng/mL) and half-life 10% longer (15.2 h).

Effect of Gender: The steady-state AUC and C_{max} values in female subjects (n=20) were 33% and 46% higher, respectively, than those observed in male subjects (n=20). Renal clearance was equivalent. There was no indication of any difference in safety or efficacy.

<u>Drug Interactions</u>: During multiple dose coadministration (fexofenadine 120 mg b.i.d. for 6.5 days plus erythromycin 500 mg t.i.d. for 6.33 days) erythromycin increased $AUC_{ss(0\text{-}12\ h)}$ of fexofenadine from 2 422 to 5 055 ng/mL·h (109%), reduced oral clearance by 51%, extended t_{max} from 2.2 to 3.7 hours and increased C_{max} from 410 to 744 ng/mL (80%) in 20 healthy volunteers. Renal clearance was increased from 3.6 to 4 L/h. Fexofenadine had no effect on the pharmacokinetics of erythromycin.

Ketoconazole coadministration (fexofenadine 120 mg b.i.d. plus ketoconazole 400 mg daily for 7 days) increased $AUC_{ss\ (0\text{-}12h)}$ of fexofenadine from 2 100 to 5 547 ng/mL·h (164%), reduced oral clearance by 61% and increased C_{max} from 388 to 914 ng/mL (136%) in 24 healthy volunteers. Fexofenadine had no effect on the pharmacokinetics of ketoconazole.

The increased systemic exposure to fexofenadine as a result of erythromycin or ketoconazole co-administration is below that observed with 240 or 400 mg b.i.d. doses (AUC_{ss} of 6 935 and 13 578 ng/mL·h, respectively) of fexofenadine, neither of which was associated with any adverse effects.

Indications: For the relief of symptoms associated with seasonal allergic rhinitis, such as sneezing, rhinorrhea, lacrimation, itchy, red eyes or itchy nose/palate/throat in adults and children 12 years of age and older.

Contraindications: In patients with known hypersensitivity to any of its ingredients.

Precautions: <u>*Drug Interactions*</u>: Since fexofenadine does not undergo hepatic biotransformation, it is unlikely to interact with drugs that rely upon hepatic metabolism.

Fexofenadine at twice the recommended dose (120 mg b.i.d.), has been safely coadministered with erythromycin (500 mg q8h) and ketoconazole (400 mg daily) under steady-state conditions in healthy volunteers. No differences in adverse events were reported whether fexofenadine was administered alone or in combination. The coadministration of fexofenadine with erythromycin or ketoconazole resulted in no significant increases in daily mean or maximum QTc interval when analyzed by machine or a cardiologist.

The mechanism(s) underlying the interaction with ketoconazole and erythromycin have not been conclusively established. Preliminary evidence suggests that both ketoconazole and erythromycin decrease fexofenadine secretion into the gastrointestinal tract. Secondarily, erythromycin also appears to decrease biliary clearance. Ketoconazole appears to have negligible effects on biliary or renal clearance of fexofenadine.

The administration of a single 20 mL dose of Maalox suspension followed 15 minutes later by a single oral dose of 120 mg fexofenadine resulted in a significant reduction in fexofenadine bioavailability (41% reduction in $AUC_{(0\text{-}30h)}$; 43% reduction in C_{max}). This interaction has been explained on the basis that up to 27.8% of fexofenadine is physically bound to Maalox in the stomach at pH of 4 or greater.

Pretreatment with omeprazole (20 mg 10 hour prior to and 40 mg 1 hour prior to a single dose of 120 mg fexofenadine) did not alter the bioavailability of fexofenadine.

Pregnancy: The reproduction toxicology data for fexofenadine rely solely upon those that have been obtained with terfenadine (Seldane) and linked by appropriate bridging pharmacokinetic studies. There was no evidence of teratogenicity in rats or rabbits at fexofenadine plasma AUC values 4 and 37 times the human therapeutic value, respectively. Dose-related decreases in pup weight gain and survival were observed in rats exposed to fexofenadine plasma AUC values equal to or greater than 3 times the human therapeutic value (obtained at steady state with 60 mg b.i.d. dosing).

There are no adequate and well-controlled studies in pregnant women. Fexofenadine should be used during pregnancy only if the potential benefit justifies the potential risk to the fetus.

Lactation: There are no adequate and well controlled studies in women during lactation. However, when terfenadine was administered to nursing mothers, fexofenadine was found to cross into human breast milk. Therefore, fexofenadine is not recommended for breast-feeding women.

Children: The safety and effectiveness of fexofenadine in children under 12 years of age have not been established. In a randomized, controlled, clinical trial setting, a total of 205 subjects between the ages of 12 to 16 years were administered doses of fexofenadine ranging from 20 to 240 mg b.i.d. for 2 weeks. Adverse events were similar in this group compared to subjects above 16 years of age.

Geriatrics: In randomized, controlled, clinical trials, 42 patients age 60 to 68 years were administered doses of fexofenadine ranging from 20 to 240 mg b.i.d. for 2 weeks. Adverse events are similar in this group compared to patients under 60 years of age. Nevertheless, the pharmacokinetics of fexofenadine are altered (increased bioavailability) in individuals over 65 years of age (see Pharmacology, Pharmacokinetics).

Special Populations: The pharmacokinetics of fexofenadine are altered in individuals with renal impairment (see Pharmacology, Pharmacokinetics). Based on increases in bioavailability and half-life, a dose of 60 mg once daily is recommended as the starting dose in patients with decreased renal function.

Moderate to severe hepatic disease does not affect the pharmacokinetics of fexofenadine substantially.

In surgically manipulated intestinal tissue (e.g., bowel resection) as well as in inflamed intestinal tissue, p-glycoprotein expression is actually increased. Thus, the oral bioavailability of fexofenadine could possibly be reduced in these disease states.

Adverse Effects: In 4, 2-week, placebo-controlled trials involving seasonal allergic rhinitis (SAR) patients, adverse events were similar in fexofenadine and placebo-treated patients. There was no dose-related increase in adverse events, including drowsiness, when administered up to 4 times the recommended therapeutic dose. Adverse event rates were similar among subgroups defined by age, gender, and race. The rate of premature withdrawal because of adverse events was 2% (48/2 346) with fexofenadine vs 3.2% (22/685) with placebo. See Table I.

Table I—Allegra

Percentage of Patients Reporting Adverse Events (>1%) in Placebo-Controlled Seasonal Allergic Rhinitis Clinical Trials

Adverse Event	Placebo (n=671)	Allegra 60 mg b.i.d. (n=679)	Total Allegra 20-240 mg b.i.d. (n=2 319)
Headache	3.1	3.1	2.9
Nausea	1.0	1.3	0.8
Drowsiness	0.9	1.3	0.8
Fatigue	0.9	1.0	1.0

In addition to the above, the following infrequent (≥0.1 to <1%) adverse events were reported at rates similar to placebo in the controlled SAR studies with doses from 20 to 240 mg b.i.d.:

Central and Peripheral Nervous Systems: insomnia, dizziness.

Gastrointestinal: diarrhea, dyspepsia, abdominal pain, flatulence, vomiting.

Respiratory: epistaxis, throat irritation.

Metabolic and Nutritional: thirst.

Psychiatric: appetite increase, nervousness, agitation, nightmares.

Autonomic Nervous System: dry mouth, dryness of mucous membranes.

Skin and Appendages: pruritus, rash.

Urinary: urinary frequency.

Heart Rate and Rhythm: tachycardia, palpitation.

Infectious Disease: viral infection.

Vision: blurred vision.

Musculoskeletal: chest pain.

Hearing and Vestibular: earache.

The frequency and magnitude of laboratory abnormalities were similar with fexofenadine and placebo.

Two double-blind, placebo-controlled, parallel group, long-term safety studies were conducted in healthy volunteers. In 1 study, 217 subjects received 60 mg fexofenadine b.i.d. for 6 months, and in the other, 234 subjects received 240 mg fexofenadine once daily for 12 months. The nature and incidence of adverse events observed were similar for fexofenadine and placebo, and the types of adverse events reported in these 2 long-term studies were not different from those observed in the Phase III clinical trials. There were no particular patterns observed in the occurrence of treatment related adverse events in demographic subgroups with respect to gender, age and race. There were no statistically significant changes in measured ECG parameters or vital signs from baseline to the last visit in subjects treated with fexofenadine vs placebo.

In U.S. postmarketing surveillance, 1 case of congestive heart failure has been reported. One case of atrial fibrillation has been reported in clinical studies. A definite cause and effect relationship has not been established.

Overdose: Symptoms: There is no clinical experience with fexofenadine overdose. Single doses of fexofenadine up to 800 mg (n=6 healthy male volunteers; highest C_{max}= 12 250 ng/mL; mean C_{max} and AUC=6 383 ng/mL and 28 396 ng/mL·h, respectively) and doses up to 690 mg b.i.d. (n=3 healthy male volunteers; mean AUC_{ss}=21 706 ng/mL·h; mean $C_{max,ss}$=4 677 ng/mL) for 1 month were investigated without the development of clinically significant adverse events. The maximum tolerated dose of fexofenadine was not reached. Overall, there was no evidence of QT_c prolongation at doses 11 times the recommended therapeutic dose.

Treatment: In the event of overdose, standard measures to remove any unabsorbed drug should be considered. Symptomatic and supportive treatment is recommended.

Hemodialysis did not effectively remove fexofenadine from blood (up to 1.7% removed) following terfenadine administration.

Information for the Patient: See Blue Section—Information for the Patient "Allegra".

Dosage: Adults and Children 12 years and older: The recommended dose is 60 mg twice daily.

A dose of 60 mg daily is recommended as a starting dose in individuals with decreased renal function.

Children under 12 years: Safety and effectiveness of fexofenadine in children under the age of 12 have not been established.

Supplied: Each peach, round, double convex tablet, plain on one side and debossed on the other side with "00", contains fexofenadine HCl 60 mg. Nonmedicinal ingredients: croscarmellose sodium, gelatin, hydroxypropyl methylcellulose, lactose, magnesium stearate, microcrystalline cellulose, pink and yellow iron oxide blend, povidone, polyethylene glycol, silicon dioxide, starch and titanium dioxide. Blister packs of 12, 24 and 36.

Store at 15 to 30°C in a dry place.

(Shown in Product Recognition Section)

Reviewed 1998

ALLENBURYS® BASIC SOAP
Roberts

Skin Cleanser

Supplied: A nonmedicated, natural-based, quality soap formulated for dry skin types or skin sensitive to irritation, very low free-alkali content, delicately scented with oils of natural herbs. Near neutral pH, biodegradable, long-lasting. Individually cartoned oval blue, pink (with extra moisturizers) and white bars of 100 g.

ALLERDRYL®
ICN

Diphenhydramine HCl

Antihistaminic

Supplied: 25 mg: Each light blue and pink, hard gelatin capsule branded ICN A17 contains: diphenhydramine HCl USP 25 mg. Bottles of 100 and 500.

50 mg: Each pink and white, hard gelatin capsule branded ICN A18 contains: diphenhydramine HCl USP 50 mg. Bottles of 100 and 500.

ALLERNIX
Technilab

Diphenhydramine HCl

Antihistamine

Supplied: Caplets: 25 mg: Each pink coated caplet contains: diphenhydramine HCl USP 25 mg. Nonmedicinal ingredients: FD&C red #3 aluminum lake, hydroxypropylcellulose, hydroxypropyl methylcellulose, magnesium stearate, microcrystalline cellulose, polyethylene glycol, povidone, sodium croscarmellose, sorbitol and titanium dioxide. Bottles of 100. Blister packs of 20. Keep bottle tightly closed and protect from light.

50 mg: Each white coated caplet contains: diphenhydramine HCl USP 50 mg. Nonmedicinal ingredients: hydroxypropylcellulose, hydroxypropyl methylcellulose, magnesium stearate, microcrystalline cellulose, polyethylene glycol, povidone, sodium croscarmellose, sorbitol and titanium dioxide. Bottles of 100. Blister packs of 20. Keep bottle tightly closed and protect from light.

Elixir: Each 5 mL of red, cinnamon-flavored elixir contains: diphenhydramine HCl USP 12.5 mg. Nonmedicinal ingredients: alcohol, artificial coloring and flavoring, citric acid, glycerin, purified water, sodium benzoate and sucrose. Bottles of 100 and 450 mL. Keep bottle tightly closed and protect from light and freezing.

Store between 15 and 30°C.

ALLOPURINOL Ⓟ
General Monograph, CPhA

Xanthine Oxidase Inhibitor

This monograph has been compiled by CPhA. It may contain information different from that approved by Therapeutic Products Programme, Health Canada, and the pharmaceutical manufacturers' approval has not been requested.

Pharmacology: Allopurinol and its active metabolite, oxypurinol, inhibit xanthine oxidase, the enzyme responsible for the conversion of hypoxanthine to xanthine and of xanthine to uric acid. Inhibition of this enzyme accounts for the major pharmacological effects of allopurinol. In addition, allopurinol increases reutilization of hypoxanthine and xanthine for nucleotide and nucleic acid synthesis, via an action involving the enzyme hypoxanthine-guanine phosphoribosyltransferase (HGPRTase). The resultant increase in nucleotide concentration leads to feedback inhibition of de novo purine synthesis. Allopurinol thereby decreases uric acid concentrations in both serum and urine.

Accompanying the decrease in uric acid produced by allopurinol is an increase in serum and urine concentrations of hypoxanthine and xanthine. Plasma concentrations of these oxypurines are only slightly increased, and renal clearance is rapid and greater than that of uric acid. In the absence of allopurinol, normal urinary output of oxypurines is almost solely in the form of uric acid. After administration of allopurinol, it is composed of hypoxanthine, xanthine and uric acid. Since each has its independent solubility, the concentration of uric acid in plasma is reduced without exposing the urinary tract to an excessive load of uric acid, thus decreasing the risk of crystalluria. By lowering the uric acid concentration in plasma below its limits of solubility, allopurinol facilitates dissolution of tophi.

Pharmacokinetics: See Table I.

Table I—Allopurinol

Pharmacokinetics	
Absorption	80 to 90% of single 300 mg dose from gastrointestinal tract
Biotransformation	Hepatic[a]
Protein binding	None
Distribution	Total tissue water, except brain (concentration approximately 50% compared to other tissues)
Half-life	Allopurinol: 1 to 3 h Oxypurinol 12 to 30 h (average 15 h)[b]
Onset of action	2 to 3 days[c]
Time to peak serum concentrations	Allopurinol: 0.5 to 2 h Oxypurinol: 4.5 to 5 h
Time to peak effect	↓ Serum uric acid to normal in 1 to 3 weeks[d]
Duration of action	1 to 2 weeks after discontinuation of therapy
Elimination	Renal: Allopurinol 10% unchanged, oxypurinol 70% Fecal: 20% within 48 to 72 h Dialyzable: yes

[a] Approximately 70% of a dose is metabolized to the active metabolite, oxypurinol.
[b] May be prolonged in patients with renal impairment.
[c] Allopurinol's ability to lower serum uric acid levels is dose-related.
[d] Because of continued mobilization of urate deposits, substantial decrease in uric acid may be delayed 6 to 12 months or may not occur in some patients, particularly those with tophaceous gout and those who are underexcretors of uric acid.

Indications: The treatment of gout, either primary, or secondary to hyperuricemia which occurs in polycythemia vera, myeloid metaplasia or other blood dyscrasias.

Allopurinol is also indicated in the treatment of primary or secondary uric acid nephropathy, with or without accompanying symptoms of gout.

Allopurinol may be useful in patients with gouty nephropathy, in those who form renal urate stones, and in those with unusually severe disease.

Allopurinol may be given prophylactically to prevent tissue urate deposition or renal calculi as well as acute urate nephropathy and resultant renal failure in patients with leukemias, lymphomas or other malignancies who are receiving radiation therapy or antineoplastic drugs that will result in elevated serum uric acid concentrations.

To prevent the occurrence and recurrence of uric acid stones and renal calcium lithiasis in patients with hyperuricemia and/or hyperuricosuria.

Contraindications: Allopurinol should not be given to patients who are hypersensitive to it or who have previously developed a severe reaction to this drug.

Warnings: Allopurinol should be discontinued at first appearance of skin rash or any sign of adverse reactions. The skin rash may be, in some instances, followed by more severe hypersensitivity reactions such as exfoliative, urticarial or purpuric lesions, as well as Stevens-Johnson syndrome (erythema multiforme) and, very rarely, a generalized vasculitis which may lead to irreversible hepatotoxicity and death. Hypersensitivity reactions, frequently marked by fever and eosinophilia, usually begin 2 to 4 weeks after start of therapy and appear related to pre-existing renal dysfunction, elevated oxypurinol plasma levels and/or concurrent thiazide therapy.

Periodic liver function tests, renal function tests and complete blood cell counts should be performed in all patients on allopurinol. Alterations in liver function test results, including transient elevations of serum alkaline phosphatase, urinary urobilinogen, and serum AST and ALT, have occurred in some patients. Reversible hepatomegaly, hepatocellular damage (including necrosis), granulomatous changes, hepatitis and jaundice have also occurred.

Observe patients with impaired renal or hepatic functions carefully during the early stages of allopurinol administration and withdraw the drug if increased abnormalities in hepatic or renal function appear.

Precautions: Allopurinol is not effective for the treatment of acute gouty attacks since it has no anti-inflammatory action and may intensify and prolong inflammation during the acute phase.

Acute gouty attacks may be precipitated at the start of treatment with allopurinol in new patients, and these may continue even after serum uric acid concentrations begin to fall, usually for the first 6 to 12 months (see Dosage).

Because therapy with allopurinol is not without some serious risks, the drug is used for the management of gout when uricosurics cannot be used because of adverse effects, allergy, renal insufficiency or inadequate response, when there are visible tophi or radiographic evidence of uric acid deposits and stones, when urinary uric acid excretion is greater than 5.35 mmol/day, or when serum urate concentrations are greater than 510 to 540 µmol/L (8.5 to 9 mg/100 mL) and a family history of tophi and low urate excretion exists.

In conditions where the body's miscible urate pool is greatly increased (e.g., malignant disease and its treatment; Lesch-Nyhan syndrome), the reduction of urate formation by allopurinol is accompanied by a relative rise in the xanthine and hypoxanthine fractions. In these circumstances, the absolute concentration of xanthine could rise to a level at which deposition in the urinary tract may occur. This risk may be minimized by adequate hydration to achieve maximum diuresis. Alkalinization, of considerable benefit in relation to urate stones, may be less so in relation to xanthine stones.

Drug Interactions: Amoxicillin or Ampicillin: Concurrent ampicillin or amoxicillin and allopurinol therapy has resulted in an increased incidence of drug-induced skin rash. It is not clear whether this is due to allopurinol therapy.

Antacids: Concurrent administration may reduce gastrointestinal absorption of allopurinol. It is advisable that allopurinol be given at least 3 hours before an antacid.

Angiotensin Converting Enzyme Inhibitors: Isolated case reports indicate that concurrent administration of captopril and allopurinol may predispose to hypersensitivity reactions, e.g., Stevens-Johnson syndrome. Patients on the combination should be monitored, and if a reaction occurs, the drugs should be discontinued.

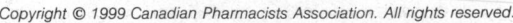

Azathioprine and Mercaptopurine: Allopurinol increases the pharmacologic and toxic effects of thiopurines by increasing their half-lives. Concomitant administration of azathioprine or

Allopurinol (cont'd)

mercaptopurine and with allopurinol requires that initial thiopurine doses be reduced to 25% or 33% of the recommended initial dose. Subsequent doses should be adjusted according to clinical response.
Chlorpropamide: In the presence of allopurinol, there may be competition with chlorpropamide for renal tubular secretion. When renal function is poor, the recognized risk of chlorpropamide's prolonged hypoglycemic activity may be increased if allopurinol is given concomitantly.
Oral Anticoagulants: Occasionally patients on oral anticoagulants and allopurinol develop an enhanced anticoagulant effect. Prothrombin times should be monitored, and the oral anticoagulant dosage should be adjusted as needed.
Cyclophosphamide: Concurrent cyclophosphamide and allopurinol therapy may increase the incidence of bone marrow depression as compared with cyclophosphamide alone, but the mechanism for this interaction is not known.
Theophylline: Doses exceeding 600 mg/day of allopurinol may decrease theophylline clearance when both drugs are used for longer than 2 weeks. Since increases in serum theophylline concentrations of 25% have been reported, some patients may require monitoring for signs of possible theophylline toxicity and dosage adjustments during concurrent allopurinol therapy.
Diuretics: Thiazides and ethacrynic acid, when given with allopurinol, may increase serum oxypurinol concentrations and may thereby increase the risk of serious allopurinol toxicity, including hypersensitivity reactions, particularly in patients with decreased renal function.
Uricosurics: Concomitant administration of a uricosuric agent and allopurinol may alter the disposition of both drugs. The combination usually results in an additive lowering of the serum uric acid level.
Occupational Hazards: Drowsiness may occur. Patients should be cautioned not to engage in activities where alertness is mandatory until their response to the drug is known.
Children: Allopurinol should not be given to children except those with hyperuricemia secondary to malignancy or with Lesch-Nyhan syndrome, because safety and effectiveness have not been established in other conditions.
Pregnancy: Allopurinol is not recommended for use during pregnancy or in women of childbearing potential unless the potential benefits outweigh the possible risks.
Lactation: Allopurinol and oxypurinol are distributed into milk. Use with caution in nursing women.

Adverse Effects: Dermatologic: Skin rash, usually maculopapular, is the most commonly reported adverse effect. Incidence of skin rash may be increased in the presence of renal disorders. In some instances, rashes have been followed by severe hypersensitivity reactions. Withdraw allopurinol immediately if such reactions occur (see Warnings). Exfoliative, urticarial or purpuric lesions, Stevens-Johnson syndrome (erythema multiforme), bullae and toxic epidermal necrolysis have also been reported. A few cases of alopecia with or without accompanying dermatitis have been reported. After recovery from **mild** reactions allopurinol may, if desired, be reintroduced at a low dose (e.g., 50 mg/day) and gradually increased. If the rash recurs, withdraw allopurinol permanently. The drug should not be reinstituted in patients who have had a severe reaction.
Generalized Hypersensitivity: Skin reactions associated with exfoliation, fever, chills, nausea and vomiting, lymphadenopathy, arthralgia and/or eosinophilia have occurred. These reactions may occur at any time during therapy and necessitate the immediate and permanent withdrawal of allopurinol. A generalized hypersensitivity vasculitis has rarely led to irreversible hepatotoxicity and death. Corticosteroids may be beneficial in managing such reactions.

When generalized hypersensitivity reactions have occurred, renal and/or hepatic dysfunction have usually been present.
Gastrointestinal: Diarrhea, intermittent abdominal pain, nausea and vomiting were reported. Gastrointestinal symptoms may be decreased by taking allopurinol with meals.
Hematologic: There have been occasional reports of reduction in the number of circulating formed elements of the blood, including bone marrow suppression, granulocytopenia and thrombocytopenia, usually in association with renal and/or hepatic disorders or in whom concomitant drugs have been administered which have a potential for causing these reactions.
Miscellaneous: The following adverse effects have been reported occasionally: fever, general malaise, headache, vertigo, somnolence, taste perversion, hepatic necrosis, granulomatous hepatitis, abnormal liver function tests, rise in urea, hyperlipidemia, visual disorder, cataracts, macular changes, neuropathy, impotence, diabetes mellitus, furunculosis, hypertension, hematuria, edema, drowsiness, peripheral neuritis.

Overdose: Symptoms: Nausea and vomiting.

Treatment: No treatment is normally required provided allopurinol is withdrawn and adequate hydration is maintained to facilitate the drug's excretion.

Dosage: Dosage of allopurinol varies with the severity of the disease and should be adjusted according to the response and tolerance of the patient.
Adults: Dosage range of 100 to 800 mg daily divided into 1 to 3 doses. Single dose should not exceed 300 mg. Allopurinol is better tolerated when taken with meals.

In all patients receiving allopurinol, a high fluid intake (e.g., 2.5 to 3 L) and the maintenance of a neutral or, preferably, slightly alkaline urine are recommended.
Gout: Some investigators have reported an increase in acute attacks of gout during the early stages of allopurinol administration. Accordingly, allopurinol should be initiated at a dose of 100 to 200 mg daily and inreased by 100 mg daily at weekly intervals, until a serum uric acid concentration of about 360 µmol/L (6 mg/dL) or less is attained, or until the maximum recommended dosage of 800 mg/day (in patients with normal renal function) is reached. In addition, concurrent administration of colchicine (0.6 mg twice daily) or a nonsteroidal anti-inflammatory drug is recommended as prophylaxis during the first 3 to 6 months of allopurinol therapy. Serum urate concentrations are often reduced more slowly with allopurinol and minimum concentrations may not be reached for 1 to 3 weeks.

After serum urate concentrations are controlled, it may be possible to reduce dosage; the minimum effective dose is 100 to 200 mg/day. The average maintenance dosage is 200 to 300 mg/day for patients with mild gout, 400 to 600 mg/day for patients with moderately severe tophaceous gout, and 700 to 800 mg/day in severe conditions.
Dosage in Renal Impairment: Since allopurinol and its metabolites are excreted by the kidney, drug accumulation can occur in renal failure and the initial dose of allopurinol should consequently be reduced. With a creatinine clearance of 0.33 to 0.17 mL/s, a daily dosage of 200 mg of allopurinol is suitable. When the creatinine clearance is less than 0.17 mL/s, the daily dosage should not exceed 100 mg. With extreme renal impairment (creatinine clearance less than 0.05 mL/s), the interval between doses may also need to be lengthened. Some clinicians recommend the following maintenance dosages of allopurinol based on the patient's creatinine clearance (see Table I). Refer to the Clin-Info Section for estimation of creatinine clearance.

Table I—Allopurinol

Maintenance Dosage

Creatinine Clearance (mL/s)	Creatinine Clearance (mL/min)	Dose
0	0	100 mg every 3 days
0.17	10	100 mg every 2 days
0.33	20	100 mg daily
0.67	40	150 mg daily
1.00	60	200 mg daily
1.33	80	250 mg daily
1.67	100	300 mg daily
2.00	120	350 mg daily
2.33	140	400 mg daily

Because allopurinol concentrations are difficult to determine and because serum concentrations may not adequately reflect the amount of drug bound to xanthine oxidase in the tissues, serum urate concentrations should be used to monitor therapy. The upper limit of normal is about 430 µmol/L for men and postmenopausal women and 345 µmol/L for premenopausal women. By the selection of the appropriate dose, together with the use of uricosuric agents in certain patients, it is possible to reduce the serum uric acid concentration to normal and, if desired, to hold it as low as 120 to 180 µmol/L. Combined therapy of allopurinol and uricosurics will often result in a dosage reduction of both agents.

In patients who are being treated with uricosuric agents, colchicine and/or anti-inflammatory agents, it is wise to continue this therapy while adjusting the allopurinol dosage until a normal serum uric acid concentration and freedom from acute attacks have been maintained for several months. If desired, the patient may then be transferred to allopurinol therapy exclusively. When a uricosuric agent is being withdrawn, dosage of the uricosuric agent should be gradually reduced over several weeks.

Prevention of Uric Acid Nephropathy during Aggressive Therapy of Neoplastic Disease: Treatment with 600 to 800 mg daily for 2 or 3 days prior to chemotherapy or irradiation is advisable. When allopurinol is used with mercaptopurine or azathioprine, dosage of the latter drugs must be reduced (see Precautions). Continue treatment at a dosage adjusted to the serum uric acid concentration until there is no longer a threat of hyperuricemia and hyperuricosuria. Allopurinol treatment can be maintained during cancer therapy for prophylaxis of hyperuricemia which may arise during the natural crises of the disease. In prolonged treatment, 300 to 400 mg of allopurinol daily is usually enough to control the serum uric acid concentration.
Prophylaxis of Renal Calcium Lithiasis: 200 to 300 mg daily. Therapy should be continued indefinitely. Some patients have received maintenance doses of 200 to 300 mg daily for more than 7 years. In some patients, the maintenance dose may be reduced to 100 to 200 mg daily.
Children: For the treatment of secondary hyperuricemia associated with malignancies (6 to 10 years of age): 300 mg/day. (<6 years of age): 150 mg/day. For Lesch-Nyhan syndrome (6 to 10 years of age): 10 mg/kg/day.

Response should be evaluated after approximately 48 hours by monitoring serum uric acid and/or urinary uric acid concentrations and adjusting the dose if necessary.

Reviewed 1997

ALOMIDE® Ⓟ

Alcon

Lodoxamide Tromethamine

Anti-allergy Agent

Pharmacology: Lodoxamide, a mast cell stabilizer inhibits the in vivo type I immediate hypersensitivity reaction in animals and man.

In vitro studies have demonstrated the ability of lodoxamide to stabilize mast cells and prevent the antigen specific induced release of histamine. In addition, lodoxamide prevents the release of other mast cell inflammatory mediators (i.e., SRS-A, slow reacting substances of anaphylaxis also known as the peptido-leukotrienes) and appears to inhibit eosinophil chemotaxis. Lodoxamide inhibits histamine release in vitro by preventing the movement of calcium into the mast cell after stimulation.

Indications: Treatment of the ocular signs and symptoms associated with vernal keratoconjunctivitis, giant papillary conjunctivitis, and allergic/atopic conjunctivitis.

Contraindications: Hypersensitivity to any component of this product.

Precautions: General: As with all ophthalmic medications containing benzalkonium chloride, patients should be advised to remove their contact lenses to instill lodoxamide ophthalmic solution and wait at least 15 minutes before reinserting the lenses.
Pregnancy: Reproduction studies with lodoxamide administered orally to rats and rabbits have not shown any effect of the product on fertility or reproductive performance, or any evidence of embryotoxicity or pre- and postnatal toxicity. However, there are no adequate and well controlled studies in pregnant women. Since animal reproduction studies are not always predictive of human response, lodoxamide should be used during pregnancy only if clearly needed.
Lactation: It is not known whether lodoxamide is excreted in human milk. Caution should be exercised when it is given to a nursing mother.
Children: The safety and effectiveness of lodoxamide ophthalmic solution in children below the age of 4 years have not been established.

Adverse Effects: Lodoxamide has been generally well tolerated. In controlled clinical studies the most common side effect reported was mild and transient discomfort upon instillation (8.7% of patients) expressed as burning, stinging, itching or tearing.

Overdose: Symptoms and Treatment: Overdosage in the use of topical ophthalmic preparations is a remote possibility. Discontinue medication when heavy or protracted use is suspected.

Dosage: Adults and children is 1 or 2 drops in each eye 4 times a day at regular intervals.

Patients should be advised that the effect of lodoxamide therapy is dependent upon its administration at regular intervals, as directed.

The safety and effectiveness of lodoxamide ophthalmic solution in children below the age of 4 years have not been established.

Improvements in signs and symptoms in response to lodoxamide therapy (decreased discomfort, itching, foreign body sensation, photophobia, acute ocular pain, tearing, discharge, erythema/swelling, bulbar conjunctivae, limbus, epithelial disease, ptosis) are usually evident within a few days, but longer treatment for up to 4 weeks is sometimes required. Once symptomatic improvement has been established, therapy should be continued for as long as needed to sustain improvement.

Patients should be instructed to avoid contamination of the dropper tip.

Information for the Patient: See Blue Section—Information for the Patient "Alomide".

Supplied: Each mL of sterile isotonic solution contains: lodoxamide 0.1% (lodoxamide tromethamine 0.178%). Nonmedicinal ingredients: benzalkonium chloride 0.007% (as preservative), citric acid, edetate disodium, hydroxypropyl methylcellulose, mannitol, purified water, sodium citrate and tyloxapol. Natural plastic ophthalmic Drop-Tainer dispensers of 10 mL. Store at room temperature.

ALPHAGAN™ ℞

Allergan

Brimonidine Tartrate

Elevated Intraocular Pressure Therapy

Pharmacology: Mechanism of Action: Brimonidine is a relatively selective alpha adrenergic receptor agonist that in radioligand binding assays and in functional assays, is approximately 1 000 times more selective for the alpha-2 adrenoceptor than the alpha-1 adrenoceptor. This selectivity results in the absence of vasoconstriction in microvessels associated with human retinal xenografts.

Topical administration of brimonidine decreases intraocular pressure (IOP) in humans. When used as directed, brimonidine ophthalmic solution reduces elevated IOP with minimal effect on cardiovascular parameters.

Brimonidine has a rapid onset of action, with the peak ocular hypotensive effect occurring at approximately 2 hours postdosing. The duration of effect is 12 hours or greater.

Fluorophotometric studies in animals and humans suggest that brimonidine has a dual mechanism of action. Brimonidine lowers IOP by reducing aqueous humor production and increasing uveoscleral outflow.

Pharmacodynamics: Brimonidine has no effect on pulmonary function or exercise-induced tachycardia. The cardiovascular effects of brimonidine during exercise in normal volunteers were found to be limited to a slight suppression of systolic blood pressure, which was clinically insignificant, during the recovery period following a treadmill test.

Pharmacokinetics: After ocular administration of brimonidine 0.2% twice daily (both eyes) in humans for 10 days, plasma concentrations were low (mean C_{max}=0.06 ng/mL). Plasma brimonidine levels peaked within 1 to 4 hours and declined with a systemic half-life of approximately 3 hours.

In humans, brimonidine is eliminated rapidly via extensive systemic metabolism; there is no marked systemic accumulation after multiple dosing. It is metabolized primarily by the liver. Urinary excretion is the major route of elimination of the drug and its metabolites. Approximately 87% of an orally-administered radioactive dose was eliminated within 120 hours, with 74% found in the urine in the first 96 hours.

Clinical Studies: Brimonidine lowers intraocular pressure with minimal effect on cardiovascular parameters (heart rate, systolic and diastolic blood pressure) and no apparent effect on pulmonary parameters (spirometry, respiratory rate).

The long-term efficacy of brimonidine 0.2% dosed b.i.d. was demonstrated in two 1-year multicenter studies in subjects with open angle glaucoma or ocular hypertension. In these trials brimonidine 0.2% lowered IOP by mean values of 4.3 mm Hg at trough and 6.7 mm Hg at peak. IOP decreases were maintained for the duration of the studies in the majority of patients; no tachyphylaxis was observed. Nine percent of subjects were discontinued from the studies due to inadequately controlled intraocular pressure.

Indications: For the control of intraocular pressure in patients with chronic open-angle glaucoma or ocular hypertension.

Contraindications: Patients with hypersensitivity to brimonidine or any component of this medication. It is also contraindicated in patients receiving monoamine oxidase (MAO) inhibitor therapy.

Warnings: For topical ophthalmic use only.

Children: The use of brimonidine in pediatric patients is currently not recommended. Several serious adverse reactions have been reported in association with the administration of brimonidine to infants in the age range of 28 days to 3 months (see Adverse Effects).

Precautions: General: Brimonidine ophthalmic solution 0.2% should be used with caution in patients with known hypersensitivity to other alpha-adrenoceptor agonists.

Although brimonidine had minimal effect on blood pressure and heart rate of patients in clinical studies, caution should be exercised in treating patients with severe cardiovascular disease.

Brimonidine has not been studied in patients with hepatic or renal impairment; caution should be exercised in treating such patients.

Brimonidine should be used with caution in patients with depression, cerebral or coronary insufficiency, Raynaud's phenomenon, orthostatic hypotension or thromboangiitis obliterans.

Drug Interactions: Although specific drug interaction studies have not been conducted with brimonidine, the possibility of an additive or potentiating effect with CNS depressants (alcohol, barbiturates, opiates, sedatives, or anesthetics) should be considered.

Brimonidine did not have clinically significant effects on pulse and blood pressure in chronic clinical studies. However, since alpha-agonists, as a class, may reduce pulse and blood pressure, caution in the concomitant use of drugs such as beta-blockers (ophthalmic and/or systemic), antihypertensives and/or cardiac glycosides is advised.

Tricyclic antidepressants have been reported to blunt the hypotensive effect of systemic clonidine. It is not known whether the concurrent use of these agents with brimonidine can lead to an interference in IOP lowering effect. No data are available on the level of circulating catecholamines after brimonidine is instilled. Caution, however, is advised in patients taking tricyclic antidepressants which can affect the metabolism and uptake of circulating amines.

Carcinogenesis, Mutagenesis, Impairment of Fertility: No compound-related carcinogenic effects were observed in 21-month and 2-year studies in mice and rats given oral doses of 2.5 mg base/kg/day and 1.0 mg base/kg/day, respectively. These oral doses are approximately 830 and 330 times greater, respectively, than the maximum recommended human daily ophthalmic dosage for brimonidine (0.003 mg base/kg/day) based on a 60 kg human.

Brimonidine was not mutagenic or cytogenic in a series of in vitro and in vivo studies including the Ames test, host-mediated assay, chromosomal aberration assay in Chinese Hamster Ovary (CHO) cells, cytogenic studies in mice and dominant lethal assay.

Pregnancy: Teratogenicity studies showed no adverse effects in rats and rabbits when oral doses (1.65 mg base/kg/day and 3.33 mg base/kg/day) were administered at approximately 550 and 1 110 times, respectively, the maximum recommended human daily ophthalmic dosage for brimonidine (based on a 60 kg human).

There are no studies of brimonidine in pregnant women; however, in animal studies, brimonidine crossed the placenta and entered into the fetal circulation to a limited extent (ratio of drug-related material in fetal:maternal blood = 0.1 to 0.3). Drug-derived material was eliminated from fetal tissues by 24 hours postdose. Brimonidine should be used during pregnancy only if the potential benefit to the mother justifies the potential risk to the fetus.

Lactation: It is not known whether brimonidine is excreted in human milk; although in animal studies, brimonidine has been shown to be excreted in breast milk. During treatment with brimonidine, a decision should be made whether to discontinue nursing or to discontinue the drug, taking into account the importance of the drug to the mother.

Children: **The use of brimonidine in pediatric patients is currently not recommended.** Several serious adverse reactions have been reported in association with the administration of brimonidine ophthalmic solution to infants in the age range of 28 days to 3 months (see Adverse Effects).

Information to be Provided to the Patient: Occupational Hazards: Brimonidine, as with other similar medications, can potentially cause fatigue and/or drowsiness in some patients. Patients who engage in hazardous activities should be cautioned of the potential for a decrease in mental alertness.

The preservative in Alphagan, benzalkonium chloride, may be absorbed by soft contact lenses. Patients wearing soft contact lenses should be instructed to wait at least 15 minutes after instilling the product to insert soft contact lenses.

Adverse Effects: In clinical studies including 717 patients on brimonidine, the most frequently reported adverse events were oral dryness [25.8%], ocular hyperemia [24.8%], burning and stinging [22.5%], blurring [17.3%], headache [16.3%], foreign body sensation [15.5%], fatigue/drowsiness [15.2%], corneal staining/erosion [10.0%], ocular allergic reactions [9.9%], and ocular pruritus [9.8%], and conjunctival follicles [9.6%].

Events occurring less frequently included photophobia [7.4%], ocular dryness [7.0%], eyelid erythema [6.1%], ocular ache/pain [6.0%], upper respiratory symptoms [6.0%], tearing [5.6%], conjunctival edema [5.3%], eyelid edema [4.9%], dizziness [4.2%], conjunctival blanching [3.8%], blepharitis [3.6%], ocular irritation [3.1%], gastrointestinal symptoms [3.1%], asthenia [2.8%], abnormal vision [2.6%], abnormal taste [1.4%], conjunctival discharge [1.4%] conjunctival papillae [1.0%], and nasal dryness [1.0%].

The following adverse reactions were reported infrequently (<1%): depression [0.8%], systemic allergic reactions [0.8%], and palpitations [0.4%].

Serious Reports of Adverse Reactions in Pediatric Patients: Several serious adverse reactions have been reported in association with the administration of brimonidine ophthalmic solution to infants in the age range of 28 days to 3 months. These reactions included: bradycardia, hypotension, hypothermia, hypotonia, apnea, dyspnea, hypoventilation, cyanosis and lethargy resulting in hospitalization. Upon discontinuation of brimonidine the infants recovered without sequelae.

Overdose: Symptoms and Treatment: No data are available on overdosage of brimonidine ophthalmic solution in humans. Treatment of an oral overdose includes supportive and symptomatic therapy; a patent airway should be maintained. Evacuation of the stomach should be considered during the first few hours after an overdosage.

Dosage: The recommended dose is 1 drop of ophthalmic solution in the affected eye(s) twice daily (doses taken approximately 12 hours apart).

Information for the Patient: See Blue Section—Information for the Patient "Alphagan".

Supplied: Each mL of sterile ophthalmic solution contains: brimonidine tartrate 2 mg (0.2%). Nonmedicinal ingredients: benzalkonium chloride (as preservative), citric acid, hydrochloric acid and/or sodium hydroxide (to adjust pH), polyvinyl alcohol, purified water, sodium chloride and sodium citrate. White, opaque plastic dropper bottles of 5 and 10 mL with C Cap Compliance Cap b.i.d. (twice daily). Store at 15 to 25°C.

New Product 1998

ALPRAZOLAM ℞

General Monograph, CPhA

see BENZODIAZEPINES

ALSOY™

Nestlé, Carnation

Soy Infant Formula

Indications: A nutritionally complete iron fortified soya brand formula for routine feeding of infants from birth if breastfeeding is not an option or if a supplement is required. For milk-free feeding if a soy supplement is required.

Dosage: As determined by the individual infant's needs for the first year of life. Consult the physician for specific feeding recommendations.

Preparation: Concentrated Liquid: Bring clean bottles, nipples, rings and preparation utensils to a full boil and cool before using. Do not use a microwave to sterilize utensils or to warm formula. In a separate container, bring water to a boil. Allow water to cool to 40°C or for approximately 20 to 30 minutes before using. Clean can top. Shake well, and open. After opening, can may be covered and stored in refrigerator to be used within 48 hours. Mix equal amounts of formula and warm water in a sterilized bottle, cap and shake well. Bottled formula may be covered and stored in refrigerator to be used within 48 hours. Formula should be at body temperature before feeding. Formula is at the right temperature if you do not feel a temperature difference when placing a drop on your own hand. Discard unused formula left in bottle after feeding.

Powder: Bring clean bottles, nipples, rings and preparation utensils to a full boil and cool before using. Do not use a microwave to sterilize utensils or to warm formula. In a separate container, bring water to a boil. Allow water to cool to

Alsoy (cont'd)

40°C or for approximately 20 to 30 minutes before using. Poor desired amount of water into bottle. Add one unpacked level scoop (8.9 g), enclosed, of powder for each 60 mL of water in bottle. Cap bottle and shake well. Feed immediately or bottled formula may be covered and stored in refrigerator to be used within 24 hours. Formula should be at body temperature before feeding. Formula is at the right temperature if you do not feel a temperature difference when placing a drop on your own hand. Discard unused formula left in bottle after feeding.

One can will make approximately 3.1 L of formula.

Supplied: Concentrated Liquid: Each can contains: water, corn maltodextrin, soy protein isolate, palm olein, sucrose, soybean oil, coconut oil, minerals (calcium citrate, potassium chloride, tricalcium phosphate, potassium citrate, magnesium phosphate, ferrous sulfate, zinc sulfate, copper sulfate, potassium iodide, sodium selenate), high monounsaturate safflower oil, soy lecithin, vitamins (sodium ascorbate, choline bitartrate, inositol, alpha-tocopheryl acetate, niacinamide, calcium pantothenate, vitamin A acetate, riboflavin, thiamine HCl, pyridoxine HCl, folic acid, phytonadione, beta-carotene, biotin, vitamin D_3, vitamin B_{12}), calcium carrageenan, l-methionine, taurine, l-carnitine. Lactose-free. See Table I.

Cans of 385 mL, cases of 12. Store unopened cans at room temperature. Avoid excessive temperatures. Use before date shown on top of can.

Table I—Alsoy, Concentrated Liquid

Dilution Analysis

Average Composition	Concentrate/ 100 mL	Units	Standard Dilution/ 100 mL
Energy	560 (134)	kJ (kcal)	280 (67)
Carbohydrate	15	g	7.5
Fat	6.6	g	3.3
Protein	3.8	g	1.9
Ash	0.74	g	0.37
Linoleic Acid	1.2	g	0.6
Linolenic Acid	0.12	g	0.06
Vitamin A	416	IU	208
Vitamin D	84	IU	42
Vitamin E	4	IU	2
Vitamin K	0.011	mg	0.0055
Vitamin C	20	mg	10
Thiamine	0.08	mg	0.04
Riboflavin	0.13	mg	0.06
Vitamin B_6	0.08	mg	0.04
Vitamin B_{12}	0.0004	mg	0.0002
Niacin	1.8	mg	0.9
Folacin	0.02	mg	0.01
Pantothenic Acid	0.64	mg	0.32
Biotin	0.01	mg	0.005
Choline	16	mg	8
Taurine	10.8	mg	5.4
Inositol	25	mg	12.4
L-Carnitine	4	mg	2
L-Methionine	46	mg	23
Calcium	140	mg	70
Phosphorus	82	mg	41
Magnesium	14.9	mg	7.4
Iron	2.4	mg	1.2
Zinc	1.2	mg	0.6
Manganese	0.044	mg	0.022
Selenium	0.0026	mg	0.0013
Copper	0.16	mg	0.08
Iodine	0.0108	mg	0.0054
Sodium	46	mg	23
Potassium	154	mg	77
Chloride	94	mg	47

Powder: Each can contains: corn maltodextrin, soy protein isolate, palm olein, sucrose, soybean oil, coconut oil, minerals (calcium citrate, potassium chloride, tricalcium phosphate, potassium citrate, magnesium phosphate, ferrous sulfate, zinc sulfate, copper sulfate, potassium iodide, sodium selenate), high monounsaturate safflower oil, soy lecithin, vitamins (sodium ascorbate, choline bitartrate, inositol, alpha-tocopheryl acetate, niacinamide, calcium panthothenate, vitamin A acetate, riboflavin, thiamine HCl, pyridoxine HCl, folic acid, phylloquinone, beta-carotene, biotin, vitamin D_3, vitamin B_{12}), l-methionine, taurine, l-carnitine. Lactose-free. See Table II.

Cans of 396 g, cases of 6. Cover opened can and store in a cool dry place. Use within 1 month after opening. Use before date shown on bottom of can.

Table II—Alsoy, Powder

Dilution Analysis

Average Composition	Powder/ 100 g	Units	Standard Dilution/ 100 mL
Energy	2 100 (501)	kJ (kcal)	280 (67)
Carbohydrate	56	g	7.5
Fat	25	g	3.3
Protein	14	g	1.9
Ash	2.8	g	0.37
Linoleic Acid	4.6	g	0.6
Linolenic Acid	0.46	g	0.06
Vitamin A	1 600	IU	208
Vitamin D	320	IU	42
Vitamin E	15	IU	2
Vitamin K	0.041	mg	0.0055
Vitamin C	80	mg	10
Thiamine	0.3	mg	0.04
Riboflavin	0.47	mg	0.06
Vitamin B_6	0.3	mg	0.04
Vitamin B_{12}	0.0016	mg	0.0002
Niacin	6.5	mg	0.9
Folacin	0.08	mg	0.01
Pantothenic Acid	2.4	mg	0.32
Biotin	0.04	mg	0.005
Choline	60	mg	8
Taurine	40	mg	5.4
Inositol	90	mg	12.4
L-Carnitine	15	mg	2
L-Methionine	220	mg	23
Calcium	525	mg	70
Phosphorus	305	mg	41
Magnesium	55	mg	7.4
Iron	9	mg	1.2
Zinc	4.5	mg	0.6
Manganese	0.17	mg	0.022
Selenium	0.01	mg	0.0013
Copper	0.6	mg	0.08
Iodine	0.04	mg	0.0054
Sodium	165	mg	23
Potassium	580	mg	77
Chloride	355	mg	47

Reviewed 1998

ALTACE® 🄿

Hoechst Marion Roussel

Ramipril

Angiotensin Converting Enzyme Inhibitor

Pharmacology: Ramipril is an angiotensin-converting enzyme (ACE) inhibitor, which is used in the treatment of essential hypertension, and following acute myocardial infarction in stabilized patients with clinically confirmed heart failure.

Following oral administration, ramipril is rapidly hydrolyzed to ramiprilat, its principal active metabolite.

Angiotensin-converting enzyme catalyzes the conversion of angiotensin I to the vasoconstrictor substance, angiotensin II. Angiotensin II also stimulates aldosterone secretion by the adrenal cortex. Inhibition of ACE activity leads to decreased levels of angiotensin II thereby resulting in decreased vasoconstriction and decreased aldosterone secretion. The latter decrease may result in a small increase in serum potassium (see Precautions). Decreased levels of angiotensin II and the accompanying lack of negative feedback on renal renin secretion result in increases in plasma renin activity.

ACE is identical to kininase II. Thus, ramipril may also block the degradation of the vasodepressor peptide bradykinin, which may contribute to its therapeutic effect.

Pharmacokinetics: Following oral administration, ramipril is rapidly absorbed with peak plasma concentrations occurring within 1 hour. The extent of absorption of ramipril is 50 to 60% and is not significantly altered by the presence of food in the gastrointestinal tract, although the rate of absorption is reduced. Following absorption, ramipril is rapidly hydrolyzed in the liver to its active metabolite, ramiprilat. Peak plasma concentrations of ramiprilat are reached 2 to 4 hours after drug intake. The serum protein binding of ramipril is about 73% and that of ramiprilat is 56%.

Ramipril is almost completely metabolized to the active metabolite ramiprilat, and to the diketopiperazine ester, the diketopiperazine acid, and the glucuronides of ramipril and ramiprilat, all of which are inactive. After oral administration of ramipril, about 60% of the parent drug and its metabolites are excreted in the urine, and about 40% are found in the feces. Drug recovered in the feces may represent both biliary excretion of metabolites and/or unabsorbed drug. Less than 2% of the administered dose is recovered in urine as unchanged ramipril.

Plasma concentrations of ramipril and ramiprilat increase with increased dose, but are not strictly dose-proportional. The 24-hour AUC for ramiprilat, however, is dose-proportional over the recommended dose range. The absolute bioavailabilities of ramipril and ramiprilat were 28 and 44% respectively when 5 mg of oral ramipril was compared to 5 mg given i.v.

Plasma concentrations of ramiprilat decline in a triphasic manner. The initial rapid decline, which represents distribution of the drug, has a half-life of 2 to 4 hours. Because of its potent binding to ACE and slow dissociation from the enzyme, ramiprilat shows two elimination phases. The apparent elimination phase has a half-life of 9 to 18 hours, and the terminal elimination phase has a prolonged half-life of >50 hours. After multiple daily doses of ramipril 5 to 10 mg, the half-life of ramiprilat concentrations was 13 to 17 hours, but was considerably prolonged at 2.5 mg (27 to 36 hours).

After once daily dosing, steady-state plasma concentrations of ramiprilat are reached by the fourth dose. Steady-state concentrations of ramiprilat are higher than those seen after the first dose of ramipril especially at low doses (2.5 mg).

The urinary excretion of ramipril, ramiprilat, and their metabolites is reduced in patients with impaired renal function. In patients with creatinine clearance <40 mL/min/1.73 m², increases in C_{max} and AUC of ramipril and ramiprilat compared to normal subjects were observed following multiple dosing with 5 mg ramipril (see Dosage).

In patients with impaired liver function, plasma ramipril levels increased about 3-fold, although peak concentrations of ramiprilat in these patients were not different from those seen in patients with normal hepatic function.

A single-dose pharmacokinetic study conducted in a limited number of elderly patients indicated that peak ramiprilat levels and the AUC for ramiprilat are higher in older patients (see Precautions).

Pharmacodynamics: Administration of ramipril to patients with mild to moderate essential hypertension results in a reduction of both supine and standing blood pressure usually with little or no orthostatic change or change in heart rate. Symptomatic postural hypotension is infrequent, although this may occur in patients who are salt and/or volume-depleted (see Warnings).

In single-dose studies, doses of 5 to 20 mg of ramipril lowered blood pressure within 1 to 2 hours, with peak reductions achieved 3 to 6 hours after dosing. At recommended doses given once daily, antihypertensive effects have persisted over 24 hours.

The effectiveness of ramipril appears to be similar in the elderly (over 65 years of age) and younger adult patients given the same daily doses.

In studies comparing the same daily dose of ramipril given as a single morning dose or as a twice daily dose, blood pressure reductions at the time of morning trough blood levels were greater with the divided regimen.

While the mechanism through which ramipril lowers blood pressure appears to result primarily from suppression of the renin-angiotensin-aldosterone system, ramipril has an antihypertensive effect even in patients with low-renin hypertension.

The antihypertensive effect of angiotensin converting enzyme inhibitors is generally lower in black patients than in nonblacks.

The antihypertensive effect of ramipril and thiazide diuretics used concurrently is greater than that seen with either agent used alone.

Abrupt withdrawal of ramipril has not resulted in rapid increase in blood pressure.

Indications: Essential Hypertension: In the treatment of essential hypertension. It may be used alone or in association with thiazide diuretics.

Ramipril should normally be used in patients in whom treatment with a diuretic or a beta blocker was found ineffective or has been associated with unacceptable adverse effects.

Ramipril can also be tried as an initial agent in those patients in whom use of diuretics and/or beta blockers are contraindicated or in patients with medical conditions in which these drugs frequently cause serious adverse effects.

The safety and efficacy of ramipril in renovascular hypertension have not been established and therefore, its use in this condition is not recommended.

The safety and efficacy of concurrent use of ramipril with antihypertensive agents other than thiazide diuretics have not been established.

Treatment Following Acute Myocardial Infarction: Ramipril is indicated following acute myocardial infarction in clinically stable patients with signs of left ventricular dysfunction to improve survival and reduce hospitalizations for heart failure.

Sufficient experience in the treatment of patients with severe (NYHA class IV) heart failure immediately after myocardial infarction is not yet available (see Warnings, Hypotension).

General: In using ramipril consideration should be given to the risk of angioedema (see Warnings).

Pregnancy: **When used in pregnancy during the second and third trimesters, ACE inhibitors can cause injury or even death of the developing fetus. When pregnancy is detected ramipril should be discontinued as soon as possible (see Warnings, Pregnancy, and Information for the Patient).**

Contraindications: Patients who are hypersensitive to this drug, or to any ingredient in the formulation, or in those patients who have a history of angioedema.

Warnings: Angioedema: Angioedema has been reported in patients with ACE inhibitors, including ramipril. Angioedema associated with laryngeal involvement may be fatal. If laryngeal stridor or angioedema of the face, tongue, or glottis occurs, ramipril should be discontinued immediately, the patient treated appropriately in accordance with accepted medical care, and carefully observed until the swelling disappears. In instances where swelling is confined to the face and lips, the condition generally resolves without treatment, although antihistamines may be useful in relieving symptoms. Where there is involvement of tongue, glottis, or larynx, likely to cause airway obstruction, appropriate therapy (including, but not limited to 0.3 to 0.5 mL of s.c. epinephrine solution 1:1 000) should be administered promptly (see Adverse Effects).

The incidence of angioedema during ACE inhibitor therapy has been reported to be higher in blacks than in nonblacks.

Patients with a history of angioedema unrelated to ACE inhibitor therapy may be at increased risk of angioedema while receiving an ACE inhibitor (see Contraindications).

Hypotension: Symptomatic hypotension has occurred after administration of ramipril, usually after the first or second dose or when the dose was increased. It is more likely to occur in patients who are volume depleted by diuretic therapy, dietary salt restriction, dialysis, diarrhea, or vomiting. In patients with ischemic heart disease or cerebrovascular disease, an excessive fall in blood pressure could result in a myocardial infarction or cerebrovascular accident (see Adverse Effects). Because of the potential fall in blood pressure in these patients, therapy with ramipril should be started under close medical supervision. Such patients should be followed closely for the first weeks of treatment and whenever the dose of ramipril is increased. In patients with severe congestive heart failure, with or without associated renal insufficiency, ACE inhibitor therapy may cause excessive hypotension and has been associated with oliguria, and/or progressive azotemia, and rarely, with acute renal failure and/or death.

If hypotension occurs, the patient should be placed in a supine position and, if necessary, receive an i.v. infusion of 0.9% sodium chloride. A transient hypotensive response may not be a contraindication to further doses which usually can be given without difficulty once the blood pressure has increased after volume expansion in hypertensive patients. However, lower doses of ramipril and/or reduced concomitant diuretic therapy should be considered.

In patients receiving treatment following acute myocardial infarction, consideration should be given to discontinuation of ramipril (see Adverse Effects, Treatment Following Acute Myocardial Infarction and Dosage, Treatment Following Acute Myocardial Infarction).

Neutropenia/Agranulocytosis: Agranulocytosis and bone marrow depression have been caused by ACE inhibitors. Several cases of agranulocytosis, neutropenia or leukopenia have been reported in which a causal relationship to ramipril cannot be excluded. Current experience with the drug shows the incidence to be rare. Periodic monitoring of white blood cell counts should be considered, especially in patients with collagen vascular disease and/or renal disease.

Pregnancy: ACE inhibitors can cause fetal and neonatal morbidity and mortality when administered to pregnant women. Several dozen cases have been reported in the world literature. When pregnancy is detected, ramipril should be discontinued as soon as possible.

In rare cases (probably less than one in every thousand pregnancies) in which no alternative to ACE inhibitor therapy will be found, the mother(s) should be apprised of the potential hazard(s) to their fetus(es). Serial ultrasound examinations should be performed to assess fetal development and well-being and the volume of amniotic fluid.

If oligohydramnios is observed, ramipril should be discontinued unless it is considered life-saving for the mother. A non-stress test (NST), and/or a biophysical profiling (BPP) may be appropriate, depending upon the week of pregnancy. If concerns regarding fetal well-being still persist, a contraction stress testing (CST) should be considered. Patients and physicians should be aware, however, that oligohydramnios may not appear until the fetus has sustained irreversible injury.

Infants with a history of in utero exposure to ACE inhibitors should be closely observed for hypotension, oliguria and hyperkalemia. If oliguria occurs, attention should be directed toward support of blood pressure and renal perfusion. Exchange transfusion or dialysis may be required as a means of reversing hypotension and/or substituting for impaired renal function; however, limited experience with those procedures has not been associated with significant clinical benefit. It is not known if ramipril or ramiprilat can be removed from the body by hemodialysis.

Human Data: It is not known whether exposure limited to the first trimester of pregnancy can adversely affect fetal outcome. The use of ACE inhibitors during the second and third trimesters of pregnancy has been associated with fetal and neonatal injury including hypotension, neonatal skull hypoplasia, anuria, reversible or irreversible renal failure, and death. Oligohydramnios has also been reported, presumably resulting from decreased fetal renal function; oligohydramnios in this setting has been associated with fetal limb contractures, craniofacial deformation and hypoplastic lung development. Prematurity and patent ductus arteriosus have also been reported, although it is not clear whether these occurrences were due to the ACE-inhibitor exposure.

Animal Data: No teratogenic effects of ramipril were seen in studies of pregnant rats, rabbits, and cynomolgus monkeys. The doses used were: 10, 100 or 1 000 mg/kg in rats (2 500 times maximum human dose), 0.4, 1 or 2.5 mg/kg in rabbits (6.25 times maximum human dose), and 5, 50 or 500 mg/kg in cynomolgus monkeys (1 250 times maximum human dose). In rats, the highest dose caused reduced food intake in the dams, with consequent reduced birthweights of the pups and weight development during the lactation period. In rabbits, maternal effects were mortalities (high and middle dose) and reduced body weight. In monkeys, maternal effects were mortalities (high and middle dose), vomiting, and reduced weight gain.

Precautions: Renal Impairment: As a consequence of inhibiting the renin-angiotensin-aldosterone system, changes in renal function have been seen in susceptible individuals. In patients whose renal function may depend on the activity of the renin-angiotensin-aldosterone system, such as patients with bilateral renal artery stenosis, unilateral renal artery stenosis to a solitary kidney, or severe congestive heart failure, treatment with agents that inhibit this system has been associated with oliguria, progressive azotemia, and rarely, acute renal failure and/or death. In susceptible patients, concomitant diuretic use may further increase risk.

Use of ramipril should include appropriate assessment of renal function.

Ramipril should be used with caution in patients with renal insufficiency as they may require reduced or less frequent doses (see Dosage). Close monitoring of renal function during therapy should be performed as deemed appropriate in patients with renal insufficiency.

Anaphylactoid Reactions during Membrane Exposure: Anaphylactoid reactions have been reported in patients dialyzed with high-flux membranes (e.g., polyacrylonitrile [PAN]) and treated concomitantly with an ACE inhibitor. Dialysis should be stopped immediately if symptoms such as nausea, abdominal cramps, burning, angioedema, shortness of breath and severe hypotension occur. Symptoms are not relieved by antihistamines. In these patients consideration should be given to using a different type of dialysis membrane or a different class of antihypertensive agents.

Anaphylactoid Reactions during Desensitization: There have been isolated reports of patients experiencing sustained life-threatening anaphylactoid reactions while receiving ACE inhibitors during desensitization treatment with hymenoptera (bees, wasps) venom. In the same patients, these reactions have been avoided when ACE inhibitors were temporarily withheld for at least 24 hours, but they have reappeared upon inadvertent rechallenge.

Hyperkalemia and Potassium-Sparing Diuretics: Elevated serum potassium (greater than 5.7 mEq/L) was observed in approximately 1% of hypertensive patients in clinical trials treated with ramipril. In most cases these were isolated values which resolved despite continued therapy. Hyperkalemia was not a cause of discontinuation of therapy in any hypertensive patient. Risk factors for the development of hyperkalemia may include renal insufficiency, diabetes mellitus, and the concomitant use of agents to treat hypokalemia or other drugs associated with increases in serum potassium (see Precautions, Drug Interactions).

Surgery/Anesthesia: In patients undergoing surgery or anesthesia with agents producing hypotension, ramipril may block angiotensin II formation secondary to compensatory renin release. If hypotension occurs and is considered to be due to this mechanism, it may be corrected by volume repletion.

Aortic Stenosis: There is concern, on theoretical grounds, that patients with aortic stenosis might be at particular risk of decreased coronary perfusion when treated with vasodilators because they do not develop as much afterload reduction.

Patients with Impaired Liver Function: Hepatitis (hepatocellular and/or cholestatic), elevations of liver enzymes and/or serum bilirubin have occurred during therapy with ACE inhibitors in patients with or without pre-existing liver abnormalities. In most cases the changes were reversed on discontinuation of the drug.

Elevations of liver enzymes and/or serum bilirubin have been reported with ramipril (see Adverse Effects). Should the patient receiving ramipril experience any unexplained symptoms particularly during the first weeks or months of treatment, it is recommended that a full set of liver function tests and any other necessary investigations be carried out. Discontinuation of ramipril should be considered when appropriate.

There are no adequate studies in patients with cirrhosis and/or liver dysfunction. Ramipril should be used with particular caution in patients with pre-existing liver abnormalities. In such patients baseline liver function tests should be obtained before administration of the drug and close monitoring of response and metabolic effects should apply.

Lactation: Ingestion of a single 10 mg oral dose of ramipril resulted in undetectable amounts of ramipril and its metabolites in breast milk. However, because multiple doses may produce low milk concentrations that are not predictable from single doses, ramipril should not be administered to nursing mothers.

Children: The safety and effectiveness of ramipril in children have not been established; therefore, use in this age group is not recommended.

Geriatrics: Although clinical experience has not identified differences in response between the elderly (>65 years) and younger patients, greater sensitivity of some older individuals cannot be ruled out (see Pharmacology, Pharmacokinetics).

Occupational Hazards: Ramipril may lower the state of patient alertness and/or reactivity, particularly at the start of treatment (see Adverse Effects).

Cough: A dry, persistent cough, which usually disappears only after withdrawal or lowering of the dose of ramipril, has been reported. Such possibility should be considered as part of the differential diagnosis of cough.

Drug Interactions: Concomitant Diuretic Therapy: Patients concomitantly taking ACE inhibitors and diuretics, and especially those in whom diuretic therapy was recently instituted, may occasionally experience an excessive reduction of blood pressure after initiation of therapy. The possibility of hypotensive effects after the first dose of ramipril can be minimized by either discontinuing the diuretic or increasing the salt intake prior to initiation of treatment with ramipril. If it is not possible to discontinue the diuretic, the starting dose of ramipril should be reduced, and the patient should be closely observed for several hours following the initial dose and until blood pressure has stabilized (see Warnings and Dosage).

Agents Increasing Serum Potassium: Since ramipril decreases aldosterone production, elevation of serum potassium may occur. Potassium sparing diuretics such as spironolactone, triamterene or amiloride, or potassium supplements should be given only for documented hypokalemia and with caution and frequent monitoring of serum potassium, since they may lead to a significant increase in serum potassium. Salt substitutes which contain potassium should also be used with caution.

Agents Causing Renin Release: The antihypertensive effect of ramipril is augmented by antihypertensive agents that cause renin release (e.g., diuretics).

Lithium: Increased serum lithium levels and symptoms of lithium toxicity have been reported in patients receiving ACE inhibitors during therapy with lithium. These drugs should be administered with caution, and frequent monitoring of serum lithium levels is recommended. If a diuretic is also used, the risk of lithium toxicity may be further increased.

Antacids: In one open-label, randomized, cross-over single dose study in 24 male subjects, it was determined that the bioavailability of ramipril and the pharmacokinetic profile of ramiprilat were not affected by concomitant administration of the antacid, magnesium and aluminum hydroxides.

Altace (cont'd)

Digoxin: In one open-label study in 12 subjects, administered multiple doses of both ramipril and digoxin, no changes were found in serum levels of ramipril, ramiprilat and digoxin.

Warfarin: The coadministration of ramipril with warfarin did not alter the anticoagulant effects.

Acenocoumarol: In a multi-dose double-blind, placebo-controlled, pharmacodynamic interaction study with 14 patients with mild hypertension administered both ramipril and therapeutic doses of acenocoumarol, blood pressure, thrombotest time and coagulation factors were not significantly changed.

Nonsteroidal Anti-inflammatory Agents: The antihypertensive effects of ACE inhibitors may be reduced with concomitant administration of nonsteroidal anti-inflammatory agents (e.g., indomethacin).

Information for the Patient: Angioedema: Angioedema, including laryngeal edema, may occur especially following the first dose of ramipril. Patients should be so advised and told to report immediately any signs or symptoms suggesting angioedema, such as swelling of face, extremities, eyes, lips, tongue, difficulty in swallowing or breathing. They should immediately stop taking ramipril and consult with their physician (see Warnings).

Hypotension: Patients should be cautioned to report lightheadedness, especially during the first few days of ramipril therapy. If actual syncope occurs, the patients should be told to discontinue the drug and consult with their physician.

All patients should be cautioned that excessive perspiration and dehydration may lead to an excessive fall in blood pressure because of reduction in fluid volume. Other causes of volume depletion such as vomiting or diarrhea may also lead to a fall in blood pressure, patients should be advised to consult with their physician.

Agranulocytosis/Neutropenia: Patients should be told to report promptly to their physician any indication of infection (e.g., sore throat, fever) as this may be a sign of neutropenia (see Warnings and Adverse Effects).

Impaired Liver Function: Patients should be advised to return to their physician if they experience any symptoms possibly related to liver dysfunction. This would include "viral-like symptoms" in the first weeks to months of therapy (such as fever, malaise, muscle pain, rash or adenopathy which are possible indicators of hypersensitivity reactions), or if abdominal pain, nausea or vomiting, loss of appetite, jaundice, itching or any other unexplained symptoms occur during therapy.

Hyperkalemia: Patients should be told not to use salt substitutes containing potassium without consulting their physician (see Precautions).

Pregnancy: Since the use of ramipril during pregnancy can cause injury and even death of the developing fetus, patients should be advised to report promptly to their physician if they become pregnant.

Adverse Effects: Ramipril has been evaluated for safety in over 4 000 hypertensive patients. Almost 500 elderly patients have participated in controlled trials. Long-term safety has been assessed in almost 700 patients treated for 1 year or more. There was no increase in the incidence of adverse events in elderly patients given the same daily dose. The overall frequency of adverse events was not related to duration of therapy or total daily dose.

Serious adverse events occurring in North American controlled clinical trials with ramipril monotherapy in hypertension (n=972) were: hypotension (0.1%); myocardial infarction (0.3%); cerebrovascular accident (0.1%); edema (0.2%); syncope (0.1%). Among all North American ramipril patients (n=1 244), angioedema occurred in (0.1%) patients treated with ramipril and a diuretic.

The most frequent adverse events occurring in these trials with ramipril monotherapy in hypertensive patients that were treated for at least 1 year (n=651) were: headache (15.1%); dizziness (3.7%); asthenia (3.7%); chest pain (2%); nausea (1.8%); peripheral edema (1.8%); somnolence (1.7%); impotence (1.5%); rash (1.4%); arthritis (1.1%); dyspnea (1.1%). Discontinuation of therapy due to clinical adverse events was required in 5 patients (0.8%).

In placebo-controlled trials, an excess of upper respiratory infection and flu syndrome was seen in the ramipril group. As these studies were carried out before the relationship of cough to ACE inhibitors was recognized, some of these events may represent ramipril-induced cough. In a later 1-year study, increased cough was seen in almost 12% of ramipril patients, with about 4% of these patients requiring discontinuation of treatment. Approximately 1% of patients treated with ramipril monotherapy in North American controlled clinical trials (n=972) have required discontinuation because of cough.

Treatment Following Acute Myocardial Infarction: 1 004 post-AMI patients received ramipril in a controlled clinical trial. In both the ramipril and placebo groups, myocardial infarction, heart failure, atrial fibrillation, peripheral vascular disease and urinary tract infection were more common in elderly than in younger patients. Gastrointestinal disturbances were more frequent in elderly patients on ramipril. Cough and hypotension were more frequent in women receiving ramipril.

Adverse events (except laboratory abnormalities) considered possibly/probably related to study drug that occurred in more than one percent of stabilized patients with clinical signs of heart failure treated with ramipril following an acute myocardial infarction are shown in Tables I and II. The incidences represent the experiences from the AIRE (Acute Infarction Ramipril Efficacy) study. The follow-up time was between 6 and 48 months for this study (mean follow up = 15 months).

Table I—Altace

Percentage of Patients with Adverse Events Possibly/Probably Related to Study Drug Placebo-Controlled (AIRE) Mortality Study

Adverse Event	Ramipril n=1 004 %	Placebo n=982 %
Hypotension	10.7	4.7
Cough increased	7.6	3.7
Dizziness/Vertigo	5.6	3.9
Nausea/Vomiting	3.8	1.9
Angina pectoris	2.9	2.0
Postural hypotension	2.2	1.4
Syncope	2.1	1.4
Heart failure	2.0	2.2
Severe/resistant heart failure	2.0	3.0
Myocardial infarct	1.7	1.7
Vomiting	1.6	0.5
Headache	1.2	0.8
Abnormal kidney function	1.2	0.5
Abnormal chest pain	1.1	0.9
Diarrhea	1.1	0.4

Table II—Altace

Percentage of Patients with Serious Adverse Events Possibly related to Study Drug Placebo-Controlled (AIRE) Mortality Study

Adverse Event	Ramipril n=1 004 %	Placebo n=982 %
Hypotension	3.0	1.1
Angina pectoris	2.0	1.2
Severe/resistant heart failure	1.9	2.9
Myocardial infarct	1.7	1.7
Heart failure	1.5	1.5
Syncope	1.3	0.8
Chest pain	0.7	0.9
Nausea	0.6	0.5
Vomiting	0.5	0.1
Dizziness	0.5	0.5
Abnormal kidney function	0.5	0.2
Chest infection	0.2	—
Postural hypotension	0.2	0.2
Headache	0.1	—

Isolated cases of death have been reported with the use of ramipril that appear to be related to hypotension (including first dose effects), but many of these are difficult to differentiate from progression of underlying disease (see Warnings, Hypotension).

Discontinuation of therapy due to adverse reactions was required in 368/1 004 post-AMI patients taking ramipril (36.7%), compared to 401/982 patients receiving placebo (40.8%).

Clinical Adverse Events by Body System: Clinical adverse events occurring in less than 1% of patients treated with ramipril in controlled clinical trials, or seen in postmarketing experience, are listed below by body system: Body as a Whole: anaphylactoid reactions, angioneurotic edema.

Cardiovascular: symptomatic hypotension, syncope, angina pectoris, arrhythmia, chest pain, palpitations, myocardial infarction, cerebrovascular disorders.

Respiratory: increased cough.

CNS: anxiety, amnesia, convulsions, depression, hearing loss, insomnia, nervousness, neuralgia, neuropathy, paresthesia, polyneuritis, somnolence, tinnitus, tremor, vertigo, vision disturbances.

Dermatologic: apparent hypersensitivity reactions (with manifestations of urticaria, pruritus, or rash, with or without fever), photosensitivity, purpura, erythema multiforme, pemphigus, Stevens-Johnson syndrome.

Gastrointestinal: abdominal pain (sometimes with enzyme changes suggesting pancreatitis), pancreatitis, anorexia, constipation, diarrhea, dry mouth, dyspepsia, dysphagia, gastroenteritis, hepatitis, nausea, increased salivation, taste disturbance, vomiting.

Renal: increases in blood urea nitrogen (BUN) and serum creatinine.

Hematologic: leukopenia, eosinophilia, thrombocytopenia, pancytopenia and hemolytic anemia.

Other: arthralgia, arthritis, dyspnea, edema, epistaxis, impotence, increased sweating, malaise, myalgia, weight gain.

A symptom complex has been reported which may include fever, vasculitis, myalgia, arthralgia/arthritis, a positive ANA, elevated ESR, eosinophilia and leukocytosis. Rash, photosensitivity or other dermatologic manifestations may also occur.

Clinical Laboratory Test Findings: increased creatinine; increases in blood urea nitrogen (BUN); decreases in hemoglobin or hematocrit; hyponatremia; elevations of liver enzymes, serum bilirubin, uric acid, blood glucose; proteinuria and significant increases in serum potassium.

Overdose: Symptoms and Treatment: Limited data are available regarding overdosage of ramipril in humans. Two cases of overdosage have been reported. In the case of an overdose with ramipril, the most likely clinical manifestation would be symptoms attributable to severe hypotension, which should normally be treated by i.v. volume expansion with normal saline. It is not known if ramipril or ramiprilat can be removed from the body by hemodialysis.

Dosage: Essential Hypertension: Dosage of ramipril must be individualized. Initiation of therapy requires consideration of recent antihypertensive drug treatment, the extent of blood pressure elevation and salt restriction. The dosage of other antihypertensive agents being used with ramipril may need to be adjusted.

Monotherapy: The recommended initial dosage of ramipril in patients not on diuretics is 2.5 mg once daily. Dosage should be adjusted according to blood pressure response, generally, at intervals of at least 2 weeks. The usual dose range is 2.5 to 10 mg once daily. A daily dose of 20 mg should not be exceeded.

In some patients treated once daily, the antihypertensive effect may diminish towards the end of the dosing interval. This can be evaluated by measuring blood pressure just prior to dosing to determine whether satisfactory control is being maintained for 24 hours. If it is not, either twice daily administration with the same total daily dose, or an increase in dose should be considered. If blood pressure is not controlled with ramipril alone, a diuretic may be added. After the addition of a diuretic, it may be possible to reduce the dose of ramipril.

Concomitant Diuretic Therapy: Symptomatic hypotension occasionally may occur following the initial dose of ramipril and is more likely in patients who are currently being treated with a diuretic. The diuretic should, if possible, be discontinued for 2 to 3 days before beginning therapy with ramipril to reduce the likelihood of hypotension (see Warnings). If the diuretic cannot be discontinued, an initial dose of 1.25 mg ramipril should be used with careful medical supervision for several hours and until blood pressure has stabilized. The dosage of ramipril should subsequently be titrated (as described above) to the optimal response.

Renal Impairment: For patients with a creatinine clearance below 40 mL/min/1.73 m² (serum creatinine above 2.5 mg/dL), the recommended initial dose is 1.25 mg ramipril once daily. Dosage may be titrated upward until blood pressure is controlled or to a maximum total daily dose of 5 mg. In patients with severe renal impairment (creatinine clearance below 10 mL/min/1.73 m²), the maximum dose of 2.5 mg ramipril should not be exceeded.

Treatment Following Acute Myocardial Infarction: Dosage of ramipril must be individualized. Initiation of therapy requires consideration of concomitant medication and baseline blood pressure and should be instituted under close medical supervision, usually in a hospital, 3 to 10 days following an acute myocardial infarction in hemodynamically stable patients with clinical signs of heart failure.

The recommended initial dosage of ramipril is 2.5 mg given twice a day (b.i.d.), 1 in the morning and 1 in the evening. If tolerated, and depending on the patient's response, dosage may be increased by doubling at intervals of 1 to 3 days. The maximum daily dose of ramipril should not exceed 5 mg twice daily (b.i.d.).

After the initial dose of ramipril, the patient should be observed under medical supervision for at least 2 hours and until blood pressure has stabilized for at least an additional hour. If a patient becomes hypotensive at this dosage, it is recommended that the dosage be lowered to 1.25 mg b.i.d. following effective management of the hypotension (see Warnings, Hypotension).

Patients who have been fluid or salt depleted, or treated with diuretics are at an increased risk of hypotension (see Warnings, Hypotension). An excessive fall in blood pressure may occur particularly in the following: after the initial dose of ramipril; after every first increase of dose of ramipril; after the first dose of a concomitant diuretic and/or when increasing the dose of the concomitant diuretic. If appropriate, the dose of any concomitant diuretic should be reduced which may diminish the likelihood of hypotension (see Precautions, Drug Interactions). Consideration should be given to reducing the initial dose to 1.25 mg of ramipril in these patients.

Renal Impairment: In patients with impaired renal function (creatinine clearance of 20 to 50 mL/min/1.73 m^2 body surface area), the initial recommended dosage is generally 1.25 mg of ramipril once daily. This dosage may be increased with caution up to 1.25 mg of ramipril twice daily, depending upon clinical response and tolerability.

Insufficient data are available concerning the use of ramipril following acute myocardial infarction in patients with heart failure and severe renal failure (see Pharmacology, Pharmacokinetics and Precautions, Renal Impairment).

Hepatic Impairment: Insufficient data are available concerning the use of ramipril following acute myocardial infarction in patients with heart failure and hepatic dysfunction. Dose reduction and careful monitoring of these patients is required (see Pharmacology, Pharmacokinetics and Precautions, Patients with Impaired Liver Function).

Information for the Patient: See Blue Section—Information for the Patient "Altace".

Supplied: 1.25 mg: Each no. 4 hard gelatin capsule, with white opaque body, imprinted with "Altace" and yellow opaque cap, imprinted with "1.25", contains: ramipril 1.25 mg. Nonmedicinal ingredients: gelatin NF, pregelatinized starch NF, titanium dioxide and yellow iron oxide.

2.5 mg: Each no. 4 hard gelatin capsule, with white opaque body, imprinted with "Altace" and orange opaque cap, imprinted with "2.5", contains: ramipril 2.5 mg. Nonmedicinal ingredients: FD&C red No. 3, gelatin NF, pregelatinized starch NF, titanium dioxide and yellow iron oxide.

5 mg: Each no. 4 hard gelatin capsule, with white opaque body, imprinted with "Altace" and red opaque cap, imprinted with "5", contains: ramipril 5 mg. Nonmedicinal ingredients: FD&C blue No. 2, FD&C red No. 3, gelatin NF, pregelatinized starch NF and titanium dioxide.

10 mg: Each No. 4 hard gelatin capsule, with white opaque body, imprinted with "Altace" and blue opaque cap, imprinted with "10", contains: ramipril 10 mg. Nonmedicinal ingredients: black iron oxide, FD&C blue No. 2, FD&C red No. 3, gelatin NF, pregelatinized starch NF and titanium dioxide.

Cartons of 30 (2×15 blister-packed). Capsules of 2.5 mg or 5 mg are also available in white, high-density polyethylene (HDPE) bottles of 100 (for hospital use). Store in original container at room temperature, below 25°C and not beyond the date indicated on the container.

(Shown in Product Recognition Section)

Reviewed 1998

ALTI-ACYCLOVIR

AltiMed

Acyclovir

Antiviral

Supplied: 200 mg: Each blue, round, scored tablet, imprinted Alti 200 on one side, contains: acyclovir 200 mg. Nonmedicinal ingredients: cellulose, indigotine, lactose, magnesium stearate, povidone and sodium starch glycolate. Bottles of 100 and 500.

400 mg: Each pink, round, scored tablet, imprinted Alti 400 on one side, contains: acyclovir 400 mg. Nonmedicinal ingredients: cellulose, magnesium stearate, povidone, red iron oxide and sodium starch glycolate. Bottles of 100.

800 mg: Each blue, oval, scored tablet, imprinted Alti 800 on one side, contains: acyclovir 800 mg. Nonmedicinal ingredients: cellulose, indigotine, magnesium stearate, povidone and sodium starch glycolate. Bottles of 100 and 250.

Store between 15 and 25°C. Keep dry and protect from light.

ALTI-ALPRAZOLAM

AltiMed

Alprazolam

Anxiolytic—Sedative

Supplied: Each white, scored, ovoid-shaped tablet branded "K29" contains: alprazolam 0.25 mg. Each peach, scored, ovoid-shaped tablet branded "K55" contains: alprazolam 0.5 mg. Nonmedicinal ingredients: cornstarch, docusate sodium, lactose, magnesium stearate, microcrystalline cellulose, silicon dioxide. 0.50 mg tablet also contains FD&C Yellow No. 6. Gluten-free. Bottles of 100 and 1 000.

ALTI-AMILORIDE HCTZ

AltiMed

Hydrochlorothiazide—Amiloride HCl

Diuretic—Antihypertensive

Supplied: Each peach-colored, diamond-shaped, single-scored tablet, engraved "SYC" above and "AM" below the score line and engraved "SYC-AM" on unscored side, contains: hydrochlorothiazide 50 mg and amiloride HCl 5 mg. Also contains lactose. Gluten- and tartrazine-free. Bottles of 100 and 1 000.

ALTI-AZATHIOPRINE

AltiMed

Azathioprine

Immunosuppressive Agent

Supplied: Each yellow to off-white, dumbbell-shaped tablet, imprinted "ALTI 50" on one side and with converging scored lines on the other, contains: azathioprine 50 mg. Nonmedicinal ingredients: lactose, magnesium stearate, potato starch, povidone and stearic acid. Bottles of 100. Store in a dry place between 15 and 25°C, protected from light.

New Product 1998

ALTI-BECLOMETHASONE Aqueous Suspension

AltiMed

Beclomethasone Dipropionate

Corticosteroid

Supplied: Each spray delivered by the nasal applicator contains: beclomethasone dipropionate 50 µg. Nonmedicinal ingredients: avicel, benzalkonium chloride, dextrose, phenylethyl alcohol, polysorbate 80 and purified water. Amber glass bottles of 200 doses, fitted with a metered atomizing pump and a nasal applicator. Protect from light. Do not refrigerate. Discard 3 months after first use. Store between 15 and 30°C.

ALTI-BECLOMETHASONE Inhalation Aerosol

AltiMed

Beclomethasone Dipropionate

Anti-inflammatory Corticosteroid

Supplied: Each depression of the metered dose aerosol valve delivers: beclomethasone dipropionate 50 µg. Nonmedicinal ingredients: dichlorodifluoromethane (propellant), oleic acid and trichlorofluoromethane (propellant). Each unit is housed in a suitable actuater/adaptor. Aluminum canisters of 200 doses fitted with metering valves.

Caution: Container may explode if heated. Contents under pressure. Do not place in hot water or near radiators, stoves or other sources of heat. Even when empty do not puncture or incinerate container. Store at a temperature below 30°C. Protect from direct sunlight and freezing.

As with most inhaled medications in aerosol canisters, the therapeutic effect of this medication may decrease when the canister is cold.

ALTI-BENZYDAMINE

AltiMed

Benzydamine HCl

Local Analgesic

Supplied: Each mL of clear yellow-green liquid contains: benzydamine HCl 0.15%. Nonmedicinal ingredients: D&C yellow #10, ethyl alcohol, FD&C blue #1, flavor, glycerin, methyl- and propylparabens, polysorbate 80 and purified water. Alcohol: 10%. Tartrazine-free. Bottles of 100 and 250 mL.

ALTI-BROMAZEPAM

AltiMed

Bromazepam

Anxiolytic—Sedative

Supplied: 1.5 mg: Each cylindrical, biplane, white tablet, single score on one side, engraved with "SYC-BMZ" over "1.5" on the other side, contains: bromazepam 1.5 mg. Nonmedicinal ingredients: lactose, magnesium stearate, microcrystalline cellulose and talc. Gluten-, paraben-, sodium-, sulfite- and tartrazine-free. Bottles of 100.

3 mg: Each cylindrical, biplane, pink tablet, single score on one side, engraved with "SYC-BMZ" over "3" on the other side, contains: bromazepam 3 mg. Nonmedicinal ingredients: erythrosine aluminum lake, lactose, magnesium stearate, microcrystalline cellulose and talc. Gluten-, paraben-, sodium-, sulfite- and tartrazine-free. Bottles of 100 and 500.

6 mg: Each cylindrical, biplane, pale green tablet, single score on one side, engraved with "SYC-BMZ" over "6" on the other side, contains: bromazepam 6 mg. Nonmedicinal ingredients: indigotine aluminum lake, iron oxide, lactose, magnesium stearate, microcrystalline cellulose and talc. Gluten-, paraben-, sodium-, sulfite- and tartrazine-free. Bottles of 100 and 500.

Store at 15 to 30°C.

ALTI-CAPTOPRIL

AltiMed

Captopril

Angiotensin Converting Enzyme Inhibitor

Supplied: 12.5 mg: Each white, slightly mottled, flat-faced, capsule-shaped tablet, with beveled edge and partial bisect bars on both sides, engraved with SYC on one side and C12.5 on the other, contains: captopril 12.5 mg. Nonmedicinal ingredients: cornstarch, hydroxypropyl cellulose, hydroxypropyl methylcellulose, lactose, microcrystalline cellulose and stearic acid. Bottles of 100.

25 mg: Each white, square, quadrisect tablet, scored on one side and imprinted SYC/C25 on the other, contains: captopril 25 mg. Nonmedicinal ingredients: cornstarch, hydroxypropyl cellulose, hydroxypropyl methylcellulose, lactose, microcrystalline cellulose and stearic acid. Bottles of 100 and 1 000.

50 mg: Each white, oval, biconvex tablet, with a partial bisecting score and SYNCARE imprinted on one side and imprinted SYC/C50 on the other, contains: captopril 50 mg. Nonmedicinal ingredients: cornstarch, hydroxypropyl cellulose, hydroxypropyl methylcellulose, lactose, microcrystalline cellulose and stearic acid. Bottles of 100 and 500.

100 mg: Each white, oval, biconvex tablet, with a partial bisecting score and SYNCARE imprinted on one side and imprinted SYC/C100 on the other, contains: captopril 100 mg. Nonmedicinal ingredients: cornstarch, hydroxypropyl cellulose, hydroxypropyl methylcellulose, lactose, microcrystalline cellulose and stearic acid. Bottles of 100.

Store at room temperature (15 to 30°C). Protect from moisture. Keep bottles tightly closed.

ALTI-CHOLESTYRAMINE LIGHT

AltiMed

Cholestyramine Resin

Antidiarrheal—Antihypercholesterolemic

Supplied: Each packet (1 dose) of powder contains: anhydrous cholestyramine resin 4 g. Nonmedicinal ingredients:

Alti-Cholestyramine Light (cont'd)

aspartame, citric acid, D&C Yellow #10, FD&C Red # 40, flavor, propylene glycol alginate, silicon dioxide, sucrose and xanthan gum. Sodium- and tartrazine-free. Cartons of 30. Store at room temperature (15 to 30°C). Protect from temperatures above 30°C. Protect from moisture.

ALTI-CLOBETASOL

AltiMed

Clobetasol 17-propionate

Topical Corticosteroid

Supplied: Cream: Each g contains: clobetasol 17-propionate 0.05% w/w in a white, water miscible cream. Nonmedicinal ingredients: beeswax substitute, cetostearyl alcohol, chlorocresol, citric acid hydrous, glycerol monostearate, propylene glycol, purified water and sodium citrate. Paraben- and lanolin-free. Tubes of 50 g. Do not dilute the cream.

Ointment: Each g contains: clobetasol 17-propionate 0.05% w/w in a water repellent ointment base. Nonmedicinal ingredients: propylene glycol, sorbitan sesquiolate and soft white paraffin. Tubes of 50 g.

Scalp Lotion: Each mL of hydroalcoholic solution for application on the scalp contains: clobetasol 17-propionate 0.05% in an aqueous alcohol base. Nonmedicinal ingredients: carbopol 934P, isopropyl alcohol, purified water and sodium hydroxide. Bottles of 60 mL.

Store below 30°C.

ALTI-CLONAZEPAM

AltiMed

Clonazepam

Anticonvulsant

Supplied: 0.5 mg: Each orange, cylindrical, biplane, beveled-edge tablet, engraved "SYC-CL 0.5" on one face and single score on the other, contains: clonazepam 0.5 mg. Nonmedicinal ingredients: cornstarch, iron oxide, lactose, magnesium stearate, potato starch and talc. Gluten-, paraben-, sodium-, sulfite- and tartrazine-free. Bottles of 100 and 500.

2 mg: Each white, cylindrical, biplane, beveled-edge tablet, engraved on one side with "SYC-CL 2" and cross-scored on the other, contains: clonazepam 2 mg. Nonmedicinal ingredients: cornstarch, lactose, magnesium stearate and microcrystalline cellulose. Gluten-, paraben-, sodium-, sulfite- and tartrazine-free. Bottles of 100 and 500.

Keep in a tightly closed, light-resistant container. Store at 15 to 30°C.

ALTI-CPA

AltiMed

Cyproterone Acetate

Antiandrogen

Supplied: Each white, round, flat-sided, beveled-edged tablet, scored on one side, contains: cyproterone acetate 50 mg. Nonmedicinal ingredients: aerosil (colloidal silicic acid), cornstarch, lactose, magnesium stearate and polyvinylpyrrolidone. Gluten- and tartrazine-free. Bottles of 60.

New Product 1998

ALTI-CYCLOBENZAPRINE

AltiMed

Cyclobenzaprine HCl

Skeletal Muscle Relaxant

Supplied: Each butterscotch yellow, film-coated, D-shaped tablet, engraved "SYC" on one side and "CY10" on the other, contains: cyclobenzaprine HCl 10 mg. Also contains lactose. Gluten- and tartrazine-free. Bottles of 100 and 500.

ALTI-DESIPRAMINE

AltiMed

Desipramine

Antidepressant

Supplied: 10 mg: Each blue, round, biconvex, sugar-coated tablet, branded K20, contains: desipramine HCl 10 mg. Nonmedicinal ingredients: acacia, beeswax, blue FD&C No. 1, calcium carbonate, carnauba wax, cornstarch, gelatin, hydrogenated vegetable oil, magnesium stearate, mannitol, mineral oil, polyethylene glycol, povidone, sodium benzoate, sucrose and talc. Tartrazine-free. Bottles of 100.

25 mg: Each yellow, round, film-coated tablet, branded K108, contains: desipramine HCl 25 mg. Nonmedicinal ingredients: cellulose, cornstarch, hydrogenated vegetable oil, hydroxypropyl methylcellulose, magnesium stearate, mannitol, polyethylene glycol, polysorbate, titanium dioxide, yellow D&C No. 10 and yellow FD&C No. 6. Tartrazine-free. Bottles of 100 and 500.

50 mg: Each green, round, film-coated tablet, branded K109, contains: desipramine HCl 50 mg. Nonmedicinal ingredients: blue FD&C No. 1, cellulose, cornstarch, hydrogenated vegetable oil, hydroxypropyl methylcellulose, magnesium stearate, mannitol, polyethylene glycol, polysorbate, titanium dioxide, yellow D&C No. 10 and yellow FD&C No. 6. Tartrazine-free. Bottles of 100 and 500.

75 mg: Each orange, round, sugar-coated tablet, branded K110, contains: desipramine HCl 75 mg. Nonmedicinal ingredients: acacia, beeswax, calcium carbonate, carnauba wax, cornstarch, gelatin, hydrogenated vegetable oil, magnesium stearate, mannitol, methylparaben, mineral oil, polyethylene glycol, povidone, propylparaben, red D&C No. 30, sodium benzoate, sucrose, talc, titanium dioxide and yellow D&C No. 10. Tartrazine-free. Bottles of 50.

Store at room temperature in a tightly closed container. Avoid extreme heat.

ALTI-DILTIAZEM
ALTI-DILTIAZEM CD

AltiMed

Diltiazem HCl

Antianginal

Antianginal—Antihypertensive

Supplied: Alti-Diltiazem: 30 mg: Each green, unscored tablet, engraved with "SYC-D30" on one side and 30 on the other, contains: diltiazem HCl 30 mg. Nonmedicinal ingredients: Blue FD&C No. 1, hydroxypropyl cellulose, hydroxypropyl methylcellulose, hydrogenated vegetable oil, lactose, magnesium stearate, polyethylene glycol, povidone, sodium methylparaben, talc and Yellow D&C No. 10. Bisulfites-, gluten- and tartrazine-free. Bottles of 100 and 500.

60 mg: Each yellow, scored tablet, engraved with "SYC-D60" on one side and 60 on the other, contains: diltiazem HCl 60 mg. Nonmedicinal ingredients: hydroxypropyl cellulose, hydroxypropyl methylcellulose, hydrogenated vegetable oil, lactose, magnesium stearate, polyethylene glycol, povidone, sodium methylparaben, talc. Yellow D&C No. 10 and Yellow FD&C No. 6. Bisulfites-, gluten- and tartrazine-free. Bottles of 100 and 500.

Alti-Diltiazem CD: 120 mg: Each light turquoise blue, controlled delivery capsule, imprinted with Alti-Dilt CD 120 mg, contains: diltiazem HCl 120 mg. Nonmedicinal ingredients: acetyltributyl citrate, beeswax, Blue FD&C No. 1, castor oil, cornstarch, ethylcellulose, fumaric acid, gelatin, polymethyl methacrylate, silica, simethicone, sucrose, stearic acid, talc and titanium dioxide. Bisulfites-, gluten- and tartrazine-free. Bottles of 100, 250 and 500.

180 mg: Each light blue/light turquoise blue, controlled delivery capsule, imprinted with Alti-Dilt CD 180 mg, contains: diltiazem HCl 180 mg. Nonmedicinal ingredients: acetyltributyl citrate, beeswax, Blue FD&C No. 1, castor oil, cornstarch, ethylcellulose, fumaric acid, gelatin, polymethyl methacrylate, silica, simethicone, sucrose, stearic acid, talc and titanium dioxide. Bisulfites-, gluten- and tartrazine-free. Bottles of 100, 250 and 500.

240 mg: Each light blue/light blue, controlled delivery capsule, imprinted with Alti-Dilt CD 240 mg, contains: diltiazem HCl 240 mg. Nonmedicinal ingredients: acetyltributyl citrate, beeswax, Blue FD&C No. 1, castor oil, cornstarch, ethylcellulose, fumaric acid, gelatin, polymethyl methacrylate, silica, simethicone, sucrose, stearic acid, talc and titanium dioxide. Bisulfites-, gluten- and tartrazine-free. Bottles of 100, 250 and 500.

300 mg: Each light blue/light gray, controlled delivery capsule, imprinted with Alti-Dilt CD 300 mg, contains: diltiazem HCl 300 mg. Nonmedicinal ingredients: acetyltributyl citrate, beeswax, Blue FD&C No. 1, castor oil, cornstarch, ethylcellulose, fumaric acid, gelatin, iron oxide, polymethyl methacrylate, silica, simethicone, stearic acid, sucrose, talc and titanium dioxide. Bisulfites-, gluten- and tartrazine-free. Bottles of 100, 250 and 500.

Store between 15 and 30°C.

ALTI-DOMPERIDONE

AltiMed

Domperidone Maleate

Upper Gastrointestinal Motility Modifier

Supplied: Each white to faintly cream film-coated tablet, branded "K113", contains: domperidone maleate 12.72 mg (equivalent to domperidone 10 mg). Nonmedicinal ingredients: cornstarch, hydroxypropyl methylcellulose, lactose, magnesium stearate, microcrystalline cellulose, polysorbate, povidone, pregelatinized potato starch, propylene glycol and colloidal silicon dioxide. Bisulfite-, gluten- and tartrazine-free. HDPE bottles of 500. Store at room temperature between 15 and 30°C. Protect from light and moisture.

ALTI-DOXEPIN

AltiMed

Doxepin HCl

Antidepressant

Supplied: 10 mg: Each pink/scarlet capsule, imprinted "K715", contains: doxepin HCl equivalent to doxepin 10 mg. Nonmedicinal ingredients: cornstarch, magnesium stearate and sodium lauryl sulfate; capsule shell: D&C Yellow No. 10, FD&C Blue No. 1 FD&C Red No. 2, FD&C Red No. 3, FD&C Yellow No. 6, gelatin silicon dioxide, sodium lauryl sulfate and titanium dioxide. Tartrazine-free. Bottles of 500.

25 mg: Each pink/blue capsule, imprinted "K716", contains: doxepin HCl equivalent to doxepin 25 mg. Nonmedicinal ingredients: cornstarch, magnesium stearate and sodium lauryl sulfate; capsule shell: FD&C Blue No. 1, FD&C Red No. 3, gelatin, silicon dioxide, sodium lauryl sulfate and titanium dioxide. Tartrazine-free. Bottles of 100 and 500.

50 mg: Each flesh/pink capsule, imprinted "K717", contains: doxepin HCl equivalent to doxepin 50 mg. Nonmedicinal ingredients: cornstarch, magnesium stearate and sodium lauryl sulfate; capsule shell: D&C Yellow No. 10, FD&C Blue No. 1, FD&C Red No. 3, gelatin, silicon dioxide, sodium lauryl sulfate and titanium dioxide.Tartrazine-free. Bottles of 100 and 500.

75 mg: Each flesh/flesh capsule, imprinted "K718", contains: doxepin HCl equivalent to doxepin 75 mg. Nonmedicinal ingredients: cornstarch, magnesium stearate and sodium lauryl sulfate; capsule shell: D&C Yellow No. 10, FD&C Red No. 3, gelatin, silicon dioxide, sodium lauryl sulfate and titanium dioxide. Tartrazine-free. Bottles of 100.

ALTI-DOXYCYCLINE

AltiMed

Doxycycline Hyclate

Antibiotic

Supplied: Capsules: Each blue, hard gelatin capsule, imprinted "K750", contains: doxycycline hyclate equivalent to doxycycline 100 mg. Nonmedicinal ingredients: microcrystalline cellulose, magnesium stearate/sodium lauryl sulfate; capsule shell: gelatin, sulfur dioxide, titanium dioxide and FD&C blue #1. Bottles of 200.

Tablets: Each orange, film-coated tablet, embossed "K124", contains: doxycycline hyclate equivalent to doxycycline 100 mg. Nonmedicinal ingredients: aluminum hydroxide, ethylcellulose, FD&C yellow #6, hydroxypropylmethylcellulose, magnesium stearate, microcrystalline cellulose, propylene glycol, sodium lauryl sulfate, talc and titanium dioxide. Bottles of 100 and 250.

Store between 15 and 30°C. Protect from light.

ALTI-FLURBIPROFEN Pr
AltiMed

Flurbiprofen

Anti-inflammatory—Analgesic

Supplied: 50 mg: Each white, elliptical, film-coated tablet, branded "K104", contains: flurbiprofen 50 mg. Nonmedicinal ingredients: carnauba wax, colloidal silicon dioxide, croscarmellose sodium, film-coat white, hydroxypropyl methylcellulose, lactose, magnesium stearate and microcrystalline cellulose. Gluten free. Bottles of 100.

100 mg: Each blue, elliptical, film-coated tablet, branded "K105", contains: flurbiprofen 100 mg. Nonmedicinal ingredients: carnauba wax, colloidal silicon dioxide, croscarmellose sodium, hydroxypropyl methylcellulose, lactose, magnesium stearate, microcrystalline cellulose and Opaspray blue. Gluten free. Bottles of 100 and 500.

ALTI-FLUVOXAMINE Pr
AltiMed

Fluvoxamine Maleate

Antidepressant—Antiobsessional Agent

Supplied: 50 mg: Each film-coated, biconvex, round, scored, white tablet, stamped "50" over score and stamped "MG" under score and "FLUVOX" arced on the other side, contains: fluvoxamine maleate 50 mg. Gluten-, lactose-, sodium metabisulfite- and tartrazine-free. Bottles of 100.

100 mg: Each film-coated, biconvex, oval, scored, white tablet, stamped "100" to the left of the score and stamped "MG" to the right of the score and "FLUVOX" on the other side, contains: fluvoxamine maleate 100 mg. Gluten-, lactose-, sodium metabisulfite- and tartrazine-free. Bottles of 100.

Preserve in well closed containers. Store in a dry place between 0 and 30°C.

ALTI-IBUPROFEN Pr
AltiMed

Ibuprofen

Anti-inflammatory—Analgesic

Supplied: 300 mg: Each white, film-coated tablet, branded "K300" contains: ibuprofen 300 mg. Nonmedicinal ingredients: branding ink, carnauba wax, cornstarch, hydroxymethylcellulose, pregelatinized starch, propylene glycol, silicon dioxide and stearic acid. Gluten- and lactose-free. Bottles of 100 and 1 000.

400 mg: Each orange, film-coated tablet, branded "K400" contains: ibuprofen 400 mg. Nonmedicinal ingredients: carnauba wax, cornstarch, hydroxymethylcellulose, opaspray dark orange, pregelatinized starch, propylene glycol, silicon dioxide and stearic acid. Gluten- and lactose-free. Bottles of 100 and 1 000.

600 mg: Each peach, film-coated tablet, branded "K600" contains: ibuprofen 600 mg. Nonmedicinal ingredients: carnauba wax, cornstarch, hydroxymethylcellulose, opaspray orange, pregelatinized starch, propylene glycol, silicon dioxide and stearic acid. Gluten- and lactose-free. Bottles of 100 and 1 000.

ALTI-IPRATROPIUM Pr
AltiMed

Ipratropium Bromide

Bronchodilator

Supplied: Bottles: Each mL of clear, colorless or almost colorless solution contains: ipratropium bromide 250 µg (0.025%). Nonmedicinal ingredients: benzalkonium chloride, edetate disodium, purified water and sodium chloride. Amber glass bottles of 20 mL with screwcap.

Unit Dose Vials: 125 µg: Each mL of clear, colorless solution contains: ipratropium bromide 125 µg (0.0125%). Nonmedicinal ingredients: hydrochloric acid, purified water and sodium chloride. Plastic single use vials of 2 mL.

250 µg: Each mL of clear, colorless solution contains: ipratropium bromide 250 µg (0.025%). Nonmedicinal ingredients: hydrochloric acid, purified water and sodium chloride. Plastic single use vials of 1 and 2 mL.

ALTI-MEXILETINE Pr
AltiMed

Mexiletine HCl

Antiarrhythmic

Supplied: 100 mg: Each orange/scarlet, hard, gelatin capsule, imprinted "Alti" and "100 mg", contains: mexiletine HCl 100 mg. Nonmedicinal ingredients: colloidal silica, magnesium stearate and maize starch. Blister packs, boxes of 100.

200 mg: Each scarlet, hard, gelatin capsule, imprinted "Alti" and "200 mg", contains: mexiletine HCl 200 mg. Nonmedicinal ingredients: colloidal silica, magnesium stearate and maize starch. Blister packs, boxes of 100.

Store between 15 and 30°C in an air-tight container.

New Product 1998

ALTI-MINOCYCLINE Pr
AltiMed

Minocycline HCl

Antibiotic

Supplied: 50 mg: Each orange, hard-shell capsule, printed "AltiMed M2" and "MIN 50 mg", contains: minocycline HCl equivalent to minocycline 50 mg. Nonmedicinal ingredients: magnesium stearate, mineral oil and starch; empty capsule: FD&C Yellow 6, gelatin, silicon dioxide, sodium lauryl sulfate and titanium dioxide. Energy: <4.2 kJ (1 kcal). Tartrazine-free. Bottles of 100.

100 mg: Each orange-purple, hard-shell capsule, printed "AltiMed M4" and "MIN 100 mg", contains: minocycline HCl equivalent to minocycline 100 mg. Nonmedicinal ingredients: magnesium stearate, mineral oil and starch; empty capsule: FD&C Blue 1, FD&C Red 3, FD&C Yellow 6, gelatin, silicon dioxide, sodium lauryl sulfate and titanium dioxide. Energy: <4.2 kJ (1 kcal). Tartrazine-free. Bottles of 100.

ALTI-MOCLOBEMIDE Pr
AltiMed

Moclobemide

Antidepressant

Supplied: Each pale yellow, biconvex, film-coated tablet, single-scored on one side, MOC/150 imprinted on the other, contains: moclobemide 150 mg. Nonmedicinal ingredients: cornstarch, ethylcellulose, lactose, magnesium stearate, methylhydroxypropyl cellulose, polyethylene glycol, povidone, red iron oxide, sodium starch glycolate, talc, titanium dioxide and yellow iron oxide. Gluten-, parabens-, sucrose-, sulfites- and tartrazine-free. Bottles of 100. Store at 15 to 30°C.

New Product 1998

ALTI-MPA Pr
AltiMed

Medroxyprogesterone Acetate

Progestin

Supplied: 2.5 mg: Each orange, round, scored, compressed tablet, embossed "K6", contains: medroxyprogesterone acetate 2.5 mg. Nonmedicinal ingredients: calcium stearate, cornstarch, FD&C Yellow #6, lactose, mineral oil, sucrose and talc. Gluten-free. Bottles of 100 and 500.

5 mg: Each blue, round, scored, compressed tablet, embossed "K1", contains: medroxyprogesterone acetate 5 mg. Nonmedicinal ingredients: calcium stearate, cornstarch, FD&C Blue #2, lactose, mineral oil, sucrose and talc. Gluten-free. Bottles of 100 and 500.

10 mg: Each white, round, scored, compressed tablet, embossed "K3", contains: medroxyprogesterone acetate 10 mg. Nonmedicinal ingredients: calcium stearate, cornstarch, lactose, mineral oil, sucrose and talc. Gluten-free. Bottles of 100 and 500.

Store at controlled room temperature (15 to 30°C).

ALTI-NADOLOL Pr
AltiMed

Nadolol

Antianginal—Antihypertensive

Supplied: 40 mg: Each off-white, round, biconvex tablet, scored on one side and engraved with SYC/N40 on the other, contains: nadolol 40 mg. Nonmedicinal ingredients: citric acid, cornstarch, magnesium stearate, microcrystalline cellulose and povidone. Bottles of 100 and 500.

80 mg: Each off-white, round, biconvex tablet, engraved with SYNCARE and a partial bisect bar on one side and SYC/N80 on the other, contains: nadolol 80 mg. Nonmedicinal ingredients: citric acid, cornstarch, magnesium stearate, microcrystalline cellulose and povidone. Bottles of 100 and 500.

160 mg: Each blue, flat, capsule-shaped tablet, scored on both sides with a partial bisect bar and engraved with SYNCARE on one side and SYC/N160 on the other, contains: nadolol 160 mg. Nonmedicinal ingredients: citric acid, cornstarch, FD&C Blue #2 and Blue #2 aluminum lake, magnesium stearate, microcrystalline cellulose and povidone. Bottles of 100.

Store tightly closed, at room temperature (15 to 30°C). Protect from heat, light and moisture.

ALTI-ORCIPRENALINE Pr
AltiMed

Orciprenaline Sulfate

Bronchodilator

Supplied: Each 5 mL of clear, sugar-free, woodruff-flavored syrup contains: orciprenaline sulfate 10 mg. Nonmedicinal ingredients: disodium edetate, glycerol, hydrochloric acid, hydroxyethylcellulose, methyl parahydroxybenzoate, propyl parahydroxybenzoate, purified water, sorbitol and essence of woodruff. Energy: 0.76 kJ (0.18 kcal). Sodium: <1 mmol (<10 mg)/5 mL. Bottles of 250 mL.

ALTI-PIROXICAM Pr
AltiMed

Piroxicam

Anti-inflammatory—Analgesic

Supplied: 10 mg: Each No. 2, maroon/blue, opaque, hard gelatin capsule, printed with "K713", contains: piroxicam 10 mg. Nonmedicinal ingredients: cornstarch, lactose and magnesium stearate/sodium lauryl sulfate; capsule shell: gelatin, silicon dioxide, titanium dioxide and dyes FD&C Red No. 3 and FD&C Blue No 1. Tartrazine-free. Bottles of 100.

20 mg: Each No. 2, maroon, opaque, hard gelatin capsule, printed with "K714", contains: piroxicam 20 mg. Nonmedicinal ingredients: cornstarch, lactose and magnesium stearate/sodium lauryl sulfate; capsule shell: gelatin, silicon dioxide, titanium dioxide and dyes FD&C Red No. 3 and FD&C Blue No 1. Tartrazine-free. Bottles of 100 and 500.

Store between 15 and 30°C.

ALTI-PRAZOSIN Pr
AltiMed

Prazosin HCl

Antihypertensive

Supplied: 1 mg: Each orange, scored tablet, branded "K17", contains: prazosin HCl equivalent to prazosin 1 mg. Nonmedicinal ingredients: calcium phosphate, cornstarch, FD&C yellow #6, magnesium stearate, microcrystalline cellulose and sodium lauryl sulfate. Tartrazine-free. Bottles of 500.

2 mg: Each white, round, scored tablet, branded "K18", contains: prazosin HCl equivalent to prazosin 2 mg. Nonmedicinal

Alti-Prazosin (cont'd)

ingredients: calcium phosphate, cornstarch, magnesium stearate, microcrystalline cellulose and sodium lauryl sulfate. Tartrazine-free. Bottles of 500.

5 mg: Each white, diamond-shaped, scored tablet, branded "K19", contains: prazosin HCl equivalent to prazosin 5 mg. Nonmedicinal ingredients: calcium phosphate, cornstarch, magnesium stearate, microcrystalline cellulose and sodium lauryl sulfate. Tartrazine-free. Bottles of 100.

Store between 15 and 30°C.

ALTI-RANITIDINE Ⓟ
AltiMed
Ranitidine HCl
Histamine H_2-Receptor Antagonist

Supplied: 150 mg: Each white, round, biconvex, film-coated tablet, branded "K101", contains: ranitidine HCl 168 mg (equivalent to ranitidine anhydrous free base 150 mg). Nonmedicinal ingredients: magnesium stearate and microcrystalline cellulose; film-coating suspension: dichloromethane, hydroxypropyl methylcellulose, isopropyl alcohol and Opaspray K-1-7000. Gluten- and tartrazine-free. Packs of 60 in foil. Dispensers of 12 bottles of 60 tablets. Bottles of 100 and 500.

300 mg: Each white, capsule-shaped, film-coated tablet, branded "K100", contains: ranitidine HCl 336 mg (equivalent to ranitidine anhydrous free base 300 mg). Nonmedicinal ingredients: croscarmellose sodium, magnesium stearate and microcrystalline cellulose; film-coating suspension: dichloromethane, hydroxypropyl methylcellulose, isopropyl alcohol and Opaspray K-1-7000. Gluten- and tartrazine-free. Packs of 30 in foil. Bottles of 100.

Store between 2 and 30°C. Protect from light.

ALTI-SALBUTAMOL Ⓟ
ALTI-SALBUTAMOL SULFATE Ⓟ
AltiMed
Salbutamol
Salbutamol Sulfate
Bronchodilator

Supplied: Alti-Salbutamol: Inhalation Aerosol: Each valve depression of the metered-dose aerosol delivers: salbutamol 100 µg. Nonmedicinal ingredients: dichlorodifluoromethane (propellant), oleic acid and trichloromonofluoromethane (propellant). Containers of 200 doses. Store at a temperature between 2 to 30°C. Protect from direct sunlight. The canister should not be punctured, broken or burnt, even when apparently empty.

Alti-Salbutamol Sulfate: Respirator Solution: Bottles: Each mL of isotonic solution contains: salbutamol sulfate, equivalent to salbutamol base 5 mg. Adjusted to pH 3.4 to 4.4. Preserved with benzalkonium chloride 0.01% w/v. Amber colored glass bottles of 10 mL. Store below 25°C. Protect from light.

Unit Dose Ampuls: Each ampul of sterile, isotonic solution contains: salbutamol sulfate equivalent to salbutamol base 2.5 mg in 2.5 mL. Adjusted to pH 3.5 to 4.5. Boxes of 20. Overwrapped nebule: store below 25°C. Nebule removed from overwrap: store below 25°C. Protect from light. Use within 3 months.

ALTI-SOTALOL Ⓟ
AltiMed
Sotalol HCl
Antiarrhythmic

Supplied: 80 mg: Each light blue, biconvex, capsule-shaped tablet, engraved with "SYC80" on one side and a bisect bar on the other, contains: sotalol HCl 80 mg. Nonmedicinal ingredients: colloidal silicon dioxide, FD&C Blue No. 2, lactose, magnesium stearate, microcrystalline cellulose, starch and stearic acid. Bottles of 100.

160 mg: Each light blue, biconvex, capsule-shaped tablet, engraved with "SYC160" on one side and a bisect bar on the other, contains: sotalol HCl 160 mg. Nonmedicinal ingredients: colloidal silicon dioxide, FD&C Blue No. 2, lactose, magnesium stearate, microcrystalline cellulose, starch and stearic acid. Bottles of 100.

Store at room temperature (15 to 30°C).

ALTI-SULFASALAZINE Ⓟ
AltiMed
Sulfasalazine
Anti-inflammatory

Supplied: Tablets: Each orange, round, biconvex, tablet, embossed "107" and scored, contains: sulfasalazine 500 mg USP. Tartrazine-free. Bottles of 100 and 300.

Enteric-coated Tablets: Each orange, elliptical, biconvex, enteric film-coated tablet, embossed "104" on one side, contains: sulfasalazine 500 mg USP. Tartrazine-free. Bottles of 100 and 300.

ALTI-TERAZOSIN Ⓟ
AltiMed
Terazosin HCl
Antihypertensive—Symptomatic Treatment of Benign Prostatic Hyperplasia (BPH)

Supplied: 1 mg: Each white, round tablet, imprinted "74" on one side and "ZA" on the other, contains: terazosin 1 mg (as terazosin HCl dihydrate). Nonmedicinal ingredients: cornstarch, lactose, magnesium stearate, povidone and talc. Alcohol-, gluten-, paraben-, sodium-, sucrose-, sulfite- and tartrazine-free. Bottles of 100.

2 mg: Each orange, round tablet, imprinted "74" on one side and "ZB" on the other, contains: terazosin 2 mg (as terazosin HCl dihydrate). Nonmedicinal ingredients: cornstarch, FD&C yellow No. 6, lactose, magnesium stearate, povidone and talc. Alcohol-, gluten-, paraben-, sodium-, sucrose-, sulfite- and tartrazine-free. Bottles of 100.

5 mg: Each tan, round tablet, imprinted "74" on one side and "ZC" on the other, contains: terazosin 5 mg (as terazosin HCl dihydrate). Nonmedicinal ingredients: cornstarch, iron oxide, lactose, magnesium stearate, povidone and talc. Alcohol-, gluten-, paraben-, sodium-, sucrose-, sulfite- and tartrazine-free. Bottles of 100.

10 mg: Each blue, round tablet, imprinted "74" on one side and "ZD" on the other, contains: terazosin 10 mg (as terazosin HCl dihydrate). Nonmedicinal ingredients: cornstarch, FD&C Blue No. 2, lactose, magnesium stearate and talc. Alcohol-, gluten-, paraben-, sodium-, sucrose-, sulfite- and tartrazine-free. Bottles of 100.

Store at controlled room temperature (15 to 30°C).

New Product 1998

ALTI-TRAZODONE Ⓟ
ALTI-TRAZODONE DIVIDOSE Ⓟ
AltiMed
Trazodone HCl
Antidepressant

Supplied: Alti-Trazodone: 50 mg: Each orange, round, scored tablet, one side debossed with the SYC logo, the other side with T50, contains: trazodone HCl 50 mg. Nonmedicinal ingredients: cornstarch, dibasic calcium phosphate, FD&C yellow #6 aluminum lake, lactose, magnesium stearate, microcrystalline cellulose, povidone and sodium starch glycolate. May or may not contain castor oil and ethylcellulose. Bottles of 100 and 250.

100 mg: Each white, round, film-sealed, scored tablet, one side debossed with the SYC logo, the other side with T100, contains: trazodone HCl 100 mg. Nonmedicinal ingredients: cornstarch, dibasic calcium phosphate, lactose, magnesium stearate, microcrystalline cellulose, povidone and sodium starch glycolate. May or may not contain castor oil and ethylcellulose. Bottles of 100.

Alti-Trazodone Dividose: Each orange, rectangular-shaped tablet, with bisects and one side debossed with SYC-T, the other with 75 on each segment, contains: trazodone HCl 150 mg. Nonmedicinal ingredients: FD&C yellow #6 aluminum lake, magnesium stearate, microcrystalline cellulose, pregelatinized starch and stearic acid. Bottles of 100. Each tablet can be broken accurately to provide any of the following dosages: 75 mg (½ of a tablet), 150 mg (the entire tablet). To break a Dividose tablet accurately and easily, hold the tablet between your thumbs and index fingers close to the appropriate tablet score (groove). Then with the tablet score facing you, apply pressure and snap the tablet segments apart.

ALTI-TRIAZOLAM Ⓟ
AltiMed
Triazolam
Hypnotic

Supplied: 0.125 mg: Each violet, scored tablet, branded "K/8", contains: triazolam 0.125 mg. Nonmedicinal ingredients: cellulose, cornstarch, docusate sodium, erythrosine sodium, FD&C Blue No. 2, lactose, magnesium stearate and silicon dioxide. Gluten-free. Blister packs of 7.

0.25 mg: Each powder blue, scored tablet, branded "K/4", contains: triazolam 0.25 mg. Nonmedicinal ingredients: cellulose, cornstarch, docusate sodium, FD&C Blue No. 2, lactose, magnesium stearate and silicon dioxide. Gluten-free. Blister packs of 7.

Store at controlled room temperature (15 to 30°C).

ALTI-TRYPTOPHAN Ⓟ
AltiMed
L-Tryptophan
Adjunct in the Management of Affective Disorders

Supplied: Each white, oval, film-coated tablet, embossed "ALTI-TRYP" on top and "1 g" underneath on one side, contains: L-tryptophan USP 1 g. Nonmedicinal ingredients: calcium phosphate, croscarmellose sodium, magnesium stearate, methylcellulose, Opaspray white and wax solution; film-coating base solution: acetylated monoglyceride, hydroxypropylmethyl cellulose, povidone and titanium dioxide. Bottles of 100 and 250. Store at controlled room temperature (15 to 30°C). Protect from heat and light.

New Product 1998

ALTI-VALPROIC Ⓟ
AltiMed
Valproic Acid
Anticonvulsant

Supplied: Capsules: 250 mg: Each orange, soft gelatin capsule, imprinted with "K", contains: valproic acid 250 mg. Also contains methylparaben and propylparaben. Alcohol-, gluten-, lactose-, sucrose-, sulfite- and tartrazine-free. Bottles of 100 and 500.

500 mg: Each pale-yellow, oval, soft gelatin, enteric-coated capsule contains: valproic acid 500 mg. Also contains methylparaben, propylparaben and tartrazine. Alcohol-, gluten-, lactose-, sucrose- and sulfite-free. Bottles of 100 and 500.

Syrup: Each 5 mL of red syrup contains: the equivalent of 250 mg valproic acid, as the sodium salt. Also contains methylparaben, propylparaben, red amaranth and sucrose. Energy: 74.08 kJ (17.70 kcal/5mL). Alcohol-, gluten-, lactose-, sulfite- and tartrazine-free. Bottles of 450 mL.

ALTI-VERAPAMIL Ⓟ
AltiMed
Verapamil HCl
Antianginal—Antiarrhythmic—Antihypertensive

Supplied: 80 mg: Each round, yellow, sugar-coated tablet contains: verapamil HCl 80 mg. Nonmedicinal ingredients: acacia, calcium carbonate, carnauba wax, cellulose, cornstarch, gelatin, lactose, magnesium stearate, povidone, quinoline yellow lake, silicon dioxide, sodium carboxymethylcellulose, sucrose, talc and titanium dioxide. Bottles of 250 and 1 000.

120 mg: Each round, white, sugar-coated tablet contains: verapamil HCl 120 mg. Nonmedicinal ingredients: acacia, calcium carbonate, carnauba wax, cellulose, cornstarch, gelatin, lactose, magnesium stearate, povidone, silicon dioxide, sodium carboxymethylcellulose, sucrose, talc and titanium dioxide. Bottles of 250.

ALUPENT® Preparations

Boehringer Ingelheim

Orciprenaline Sulfate

Bronchodilator

Pharmacology: Orciprenaline is a bronchodilating agent. The bronchospasm associated with various pulmonary diseases—chronic bronchitis, pulmonary emphysema, bronchial asthma, silicosis, tuberculosis, sarcoidosis and carcinoma of the lung, has been successfully reversed by therapy with orciprenaline.

Orciprenaline has the following major characteristics: The action of orciprenaline is one of beta stimulation. Receptor sites in the bronchi and bronchioles are more sensitive to the drug than those in the heart and blood vessels, so that the ratio of bronchodilating to cardiovascular effects is favorable. Consequently, it is usually possible clinically to produce good bronchodilation at dosage levels which are unlikely to cause cardiovascular side effects.

The efficacy of the bronchodilator after both oral and inhalation administration has been demonstrated by pulmonary function studies (spirometry, and by measurements of airways resistance by body plethysmography).

Rapid onset of action follows administration of orciprenaline inhalants, and the effect is usually noted immediately. Following oral administration, the effect is usually noted within 30 minutes.

The peak effect of bronchodilator activity following orciprenaline generally occurs within 60 to 90 minutes, and this activity lasts for 3 to 6 hours.

Orciprenaline taken orally potentiates the action of a bronchodilator inhalant administered 90 minutes later, whereas no additive effect occurs when the drugs are given in reverse order.

Patients have not developed tolerance to the drug during prolonged therapy.

No toxic effects on the liver, kidneys or hematologic system have been reported in the long-term use of orciprenaline in man.

Indications: Orciprenaline has been found useful in the following conditions: bronchial asthma, chronic bronchitis, pulmonary emphysema.

Orciprenaline is also useful in sarcoidosis, silicosis, carcinoma of the lung and tuberculosis when bronchospasm contributes to the disability.

Patients with chronic airways obstructive disease require long-term therapy with bronchodilators as an essential part of overall management aimed at lowering airways resistance and facilitating bronchial drainage. Orciprenaline has been shown to fulfill the basic requirements of such continued therapy in that it is effective both orally and as an inhalant, has a rapid and prolonged action, and has a low incidence of side effects.

Inhalation Aerosol: The efficacy of orciprenaline administered as an aerosol has been demonstrated by increased flow rates (FEV_1, MMFR, MEFR, MBC) decreased airways resistance (body plethysmography), and decreased functional residual capacity (body plethysmography).

In one study the effect of 4.5 mg of orciprenaline has been compared with the effect of 0.45 mg of isoproterenol each drug being given as an aerosol over a period of 8 minutes. Although the improvement in pulmonary function was consistently better with orciprenaline, 1 hour, 3 hours, and 6 hours following inhalation, changes in pulse rate and blood pressure were less pronounced with orciprenaline. This indicated a more favorable ratio of bronchodilating to cardiovascular effects for orciprenaline.

In another study, orciprenaline 2% solution, racemic epinephrine 2.25% and isoproterenol 1% were each administered as aerosols on separate days. The aerosols were administered by hand nebulizer for 30 minutes or until cardiovascular side effects appeared.

The immediate effect of orciprenaline on airways resistance in this study was similar to that produced by isoproterenol and by racemic epinephrine. However, the reduction in airways resistance after orciprenaline was significantly greater than that seen with isoproterenol in 30 minutes after inhalation, and after 90 minutes the effect of orciprenaline was superior to both isoproterenol and racemic epinephrine.

Whereas isoproterenol aerosol and epinephrine aerosol produced only transient reductions in the **functional residual capacity** of less than 30 minutes duration, the effect of orciprenaline on this parameter remained significant up to 90 minutes after inhalation.

Syrup: The efficacy of orciprenaline has been demonstrated by improvement of flow rates (FEV_1, MMFR, MEFR) and airways resistance measurements (body plethysmography). Repeated measurements of pulmonary function made over a 4-hour period show that orciprenaline 20 mg orally gives a generally better result regarding duration of action and magnitude of response than placebo, 100 mg methoxyphenamine, 30 mg ephedrine by mouth, or 10 mg isoproterenol sublingually.

The effect of an inhalant bronchodilator may be potentiated by oral administration of 20 mg of orciprenaline 90 minutes prior to use of the inhalant. No additive effect occurs when the drugs are given in reverse order. The probable reason for this is that a bronchodilator delivered to the lungs via the vascular system (i.v. or oral medication) acts upon bronchioles whether or not they are occluded. Such an effect causes a wider distribution in the lungs of a subsequently given drug, and consequently the bronchodilation is more intense. Knowledge of this interaction is of value when instructing patients in the combined use of oral and inhalant forms of orciprenaline.

Orciprenaline may be given orally in dosages ranging from 60 to 120 mg daily. **An effective clinical response in adults and children above 12 years can be achieved by 20 mg orciprenaline 3 times daily, and at this dosage side effects are not significantly different from those following placebo. Orciprenaline at a dosage of 20 mg 4 times daily is well tolerated and side effects are usually mild.** Only at dosages of 100 mg daily and above, do palpitations and tremulousness become troublesome. If high doses of orciprenaline are necessary, it may be possible to eliminate the side effects whilst continuing the same total daily dose, by administering 10 mg single doses at more frequent intervals.

General: The low incidence of side effects together with effective bronchodilation make orciprenaline acceptable to patients with chronic **bronchial asthma** for continuous use either alone or concurrently with corticosteroids. Some of these patients may be controlled with orciprenaline as the sole medication, and it may be possible to avoid the use of steroid therapy. In a proportion of individuals who are already taking corticosteroids, it may be possible to withdraw this medication and continue with orciprenaline alone. However, caution should be observed in this regard as many patients, particularly those with severe bronchial asthma, can be managed satisfactorily only if steroids and bronchodilators are given together.

Prolonged studies have shown that patients with bronchitis and emphysema respond to continuous therapy with orciprenaline. The frequency and severity of acute attacks decrease, and patients experience relief of wheezing, chest congestion and shortness of breath. A close association is apparent between objective measurements of pulmonary function and the subjective response.

Contraindications: Known sensitivity to the drug or other sympathomimetic amines. The use of orciprenaline and other beta stimulators is generally considered to be contraindicated in patients with cardiac arrhythmias associated with tachycardia.

Beta blocking agents, (e.g. propranolol) effectively antagonize the action of orciprenaline. Their concomitant use, except in the treatment of accidental overdosage, is therefore contraindicated.

Warnings: Inhalation Aerosol: Like other β_2-agonist inhalers, orciprenaline should not be used on a regular daily basis without appropriate concomitant anti-inflammatory therapy (see Dosage).

General: *Pregnancy:* Orciprenaline should not be administered to pregnant women or to women of childbearing potential unless in the opinion of the physician the expected benefits outweigh the possible risks to the fetus. In rabbits, high oral doses (100 mg/kg) and low s.c. doses (0.2 mg/kg) have resulted in malformed offspring in some experiments, but not in others. Studies in the rat, mouse and rhesus monkey have shown no adverse effects on the developing fetus. Other sympathomimetic drugs tested, viz., ephedrine and phenylephrine, produced teratogenic effects in the rabbit when given orally at high doses as did isoproterenol given s.c. at low doses. The significance of these findings is not known.

However, clinical evidence presently available from the use of orciprenaline in pregnancy is limited. β_2-agonists should be used with caution before childbirth in view of their inhibiting effect on uterine contractions.

Care should be taken in patients suffering from myocardial insufficiency, cardiac arrhythmias, recent myocardial infarction, severe organic heart and/or other vascular disorders, hypertension, hyperthyroidism or diabetes mellitus.

Occasional patients have been reported to have developed severe paradoxical airway resistance with repeated excessive use of sympathomimetic inhalation preparations. The cause of this refractory state is unknown. It is advisable that in such instances the use of the preparation be discontinued immediately and alternate therapy instituted since, in reported cases, the patients did not respond to other forms of therapy until the drug was withdrawn. **Fatalities have been reported following excessive use of isoproterenol inhalation preparations and the exact cause is unknown. Cardiac arrest was noted in several instances.**

Patients should be advised to seek medical aid in the event that they do not respond to their **usual dose** of a sympathomimetic amine aerosol. The failure to respond may be due to retention of viscid bronchial secretions, associated with an allergic or infective exacerbation of the patient's condition. Increased airways resistance on the basis of bronchospasm alone is reversed promptly by bronchodilators and, if this does not occur, a more serious condition should be suspected. Admission to hospital for intensive support of the cardiovascular and respiratory systems may be necessary.

Potentially serious hypokalemia may result from β_2-agonist therapy, mainly from parenteral and nebulized administration. Particular caution is advised in acute severe asthma as this may be potentiated by concomitant treatment with xanthine derivatives, steroids and diuretics; the adverse effects of hypokalemia may be exacerbated by hypoxia. It is recommended that serum potassium levels be monitored in such situations. Hypokalemia will increase the susceptibility of digitalis-treated patients to cardiac arrhythmias.

Precautions: Inhalation Aerosol: If therapy does not produce a significant improvement or if the patient's condition gets worse, medical advice must be sought in order to determine a new plan of treatment. In the case of acute or rapidly worsening dyspnea, a doctor should be consulted immediately.

Increasing use of β_2-agonists to control symptoms of bronchial obstruction, especially administration on a regular basis or in high amounts, indicates deterioration of asthma control. Under these conditions, the patient's therapy plan has to be revised. It is inadequate simply to increase the use of bronchodilators under these circumstances, in particular over extended periods of time (see Dosage).

General: Concomitant use of orciprenaline with other sympathomimetic agents is not recommended since the combined use may lead to deleterious cardiovascular effects. If concomitant use is necessary, this should take place only under strict medical supervision.

In acute tests, orciprenaline has been shown to have minimal effect on blood pressure and pulse. The drug should be used with care, however, in asthmatic or emphysematous patients who also have systemic hypertension, coronary artery disease, acute and recurring congestive heart failure, diabetes mellitus, glaucoma or hyperthyroidism, or in patients sensitive to sympathomimetic amines. Extreme care must also be exercised in the concomitant use of orciprenaline with epinephrine or MAO inhibitors.

Adverse Effects: In the recommended dosage, adverse reactions to orciprenaline, such as tremor or palpitation have been infrequent. Mild tachycardia, nausea, vomiting, minimal hypertension, nervousness and bad taste have been reported. Potentially serious hypokalemia may result from β_2-agonist therapy.

Overdose: Symptoms and Treatment: The symptoms of overdosage are those of excess beta stimulation listed under Adverse Effects. It has been shown that the beta blocker propranolol effectively antagonizes the action of orciprenaline, and the use of this agent should be considered under these circumstances.

Dosage: Dosage should be individualized, and patient response should be monitored by the prescribing physician on an ongoing basis.

Inhalation Aerosol: If a previous effective dosage regimen fails to provide the usual relief, medical advice should be sought immediately, this is a sign of seriously worsening asthma that requires reassessment of therapy.

In accordance with the present practice for asthma treatment, concomitant anti-inflammatory therapy should be part of the regimen if the β_2-agonist needs to be used on a regular daily basis.

Inhalation Aerosol: 1 or 2 inhalations will usually provide control of an acute attack of bronchospasms for periods of up to 5 hours or longer. As a general rule, patients should not exceed a total of 12 inhalations/day.

Syrup: The following recommended dosages represent general guidelines which will be found suitable for the majority of

Alupent Preparations (cont'd)

patients. Adults: 20 mg (10 mL) t.i.d. or q.i.d. Children: 4 to 12 years: 10 mg (5 mL) t.i.d.; over 12: 20 mg (10 mL) t.i.d.
Stability and Storage: Inhalation Aerosol: The aerosol canisters should be stored at room temperature (below 30°C); the contents are stable up to the expiration date stamped on the label. Caution: Contents under pressure. Do not place in hot water or near radiators, stoves, or other sources of heat. Do not puncture or incinerate container or store at temperatures over 30°C.
Syrup: The syrup should be stored at controlled room temperature (approximately 25°C). In the original bottle, it is stable up to the expiration date stamped on the label.

Information for the Patient: See Blue Section—Information for the Patient "Alupent Preparations".

Supplied: Inhalation Aerosol: Each 15 mL metal canister (with disposable mouthpiece) contains 300 individual doses. Each depression of the valve releases 0.75 mg of orciprenaline sulfate as a micronized powder. Nonmedicinal ingredients: fluorocarbon propellants (difluorodichloromethane, monofluorotrichloromethane, tetrafluorodichloroethane) with sorbitan trioleate as a dispersing agent.

Syrup: Each 5 mL of clear, sugar-free, woodruff-flavored syrup contains: orciprenaline sulfate 10 mg. Nonmedicinal ingredients: edetate disodium, essence of woodruff, glycerol, hydrochloric acid, hydroxyethylcellulose, methyl parahydroxybenzoate, propyl parahydroxybenzoate, purified water and sorbitol. Energy: 0.76 kJ (0.18 kcal). Sodium: <1 mmol (<10 mg)/5 mL. Bottles of 250 mL.

Reviewed 1999

AMATINE® Ⓟ

Knoll

Midodrine HCl

Vasopressor

Pharmacology: Midodrine is a postsynaptic alpha adrenergic receptor stimulant with little effect on the beta-adrenergic receptors in the heart. The actions of midodrine on the cardiovascular and other organ systems are essentially identical with those of other alpha-adrenergic receptor stimulants, such as phenylephrine or methoxamine. The most prominent effects of midodrine are on the cardiovascular system, consisting of a rise in systolic and diastolic blood pressures, accompanied by a marked reflex bradycardia. The increase in blood pressure is due almost entirely to an increase in peripheral resistance. Midodrine slightly decreases cardiac output and renal blood flow; it increases the tone of the internal bladder sphincter and delays the emptying of the bladder.

Midodrine is a prodrug, i.e., the therapeutic effect of orally administered midodrine is due to and directly related to its conversion after absorption to desglymidodrine which differs chemically from methoxamine only by lacking in a methyl group on the side chain.

Pharmacokinetics: After oral administration, midodrine is rapidly and almost completely absorbed, with a mean absolute bioavailability (as desglymidodrine) of 93% for the oral tablets.

After the oral administration of 2.5 mg midodrine in a single dose to 12 volunteers, the mean peak concentration of unchanged midodrine is approximately 10 ng/mL and occur after 20 to 30 minutes, with a terminal plasma half-life of 0.4 to 0.5 hours. The mean plasma concentration of the active metabolite, desglymidodrine, peaks in approximately 1 hour, with a plasma half-life of approximately 3 hours after the oral administration of 2.5 mg midodrine.

Midodrine is poorly diffused across the blood-brain barrier. Both midodrine and desglymidodrine are quickly eliminated from the body, mostly by the kidneys. Approximately 91% of the administered dose is excreted in the urine in 24 hours. Of the urinary material, 50 to 60% is present as desglymidodrine and approximately 2%, as non-metabolized midodrine. Unidentified breakdown products do not exceed 3.9% of the urinary material.

Indications: Midodrine may be added to an established treatment regimen in order to attenuate symptoms in the primary neurogenic types of idiopathic orthostatic hypotension, that is in the Bradbury-Eggleston or Shy-Drager syndromes, in those cases when the response to the standard therapy is not adequate. The initiation of midodrine therapy should be undertaken under close medical supervision in a controlled clinical setting such as in hospital, in clinic or in the office.

Contraindications: In patients with severe organic heart disease, acute renal disease, urinary retention, pheochromocytoma, thyrotoxicosis or known hypersensitivity to midodrine.

Warnings: Supine Hypertension: The most serious and frequent (see Adverse Effects) adverse reaction to midodrine in patients suffering from primary neurogenic hypotension is the unacceptable elevation of supine arterial blood pressure (supine hypertension), which, if sustained, may cause stroke, myocardial infarction, congestive heart failure, renal insufficiency or similar disorders which individually or collectively may be fatal. Symptoms of supine hypertension are more frequently detected at the initiation of midodrine therapy and during the titration period.

Control of supine blood pressure has been obtained by an adjustment in midodrine dosage with or without a 45-degree elevation of the patient's head. If supine hypertension persists, treatment with midodrine should be discontinued, and appropriate therapy (e.g., phentolamine, a specific antagonist of midodrine pressor activity) instituted immediately.

To minimize the incidence of supine hypertension, instruction how to initiate midodrine therapy should strictly be followed (see Dosage). Patients should be cautioned to report symptoms of supine hypertension immediately. Symptoms may include cardiac awareness, pounding in the ears, headache, blurred vision, etc. If these occur, the patient should discontinue the drug and consult with the prescribing physician.

Bradycardia: Bradycardia may occur after midodrine administration, primarily due to vagal reflex. Caution should be exercised when midodrine is used concomitantly with cardiac glycosides (such as digitalis), psychopharmacologic agents, beta blockers or other agents which directly or indirectly reduce heart rate. Patients who experience bradycardia should be told to report immediately any signs or symptoms suggesting bradycardia (pulse slowing, increased dizziness, syncope, cardiac awareness) and to take no more drug until they have consulted with the prescribing physician.

Midodrine should not be administered in the presence of uncorrected tachyarrhythmias or ventricular fibrillation.

Precautions: Urinary Retention: Midodrine may induce an increase in the tone of the internal sphincter of the urinary bladder which may lead to urinary retention. Midodrine also may effect the bladder trigone which may result in a delayed response to bladder filling. Initial signs of urinary retention are manifested clinically as hesitancy or change in frequency of micturition. Patients should be told to report promptly any indication of urinary retention (e.g., hesitancy or frequency of micturition) which may be a sign of urinary retention.

When midodrine is used concomitantly with other vasoconstrictor sympathomimetic pressor agents, monitoring of blood pressure is necessary.

Midodrine should be used with caution in patients with urinary tract outflow obstruction, neurogenic bladder or similar conditions, since midodrine is eliminated by the kidneys and accumulation may occur in such patients.

Laboratory Tests: Evaluation of the patient should include assessment of renal and hepatic function prior to initiation of therapy, and during treatment, when appropriate.

Pregnancy: No teratogenic effects have been observed in studies in animals. At very high doses (20 mg/kg/day) the drug was toxic to dams and fetal loss occurred. There are no data on the use of midodrine on pregnant women. Therefore, midodrine should be used during pregnancy only when the benefit to the mother exceeds the possible harm to the fetus.

Lactation: It is not known if midodrine is excreted in human milk. Caution should be exercised when midodrine is administered to nursing mothers.

Children: Safety and effectiveness in children have not been established.

Drug Interactions: When administered concomitantly with midodrine, cardiac glycosides may enhance or precipitate bradycardia, block or arrhythmia.

The use of drugs which stimulate alpha adrenergic receptors (e.g., phenylephrine, phenylpropanolamine or dihydroergotamine) may enhance or potentiate the pressor effects of midodrine. Therefore, when midodrine is used concomitantly with vasoconstrictor sympathomimetic agents, use caution.

Patients on salt-retaining steroids (e.g., fludrocortisone), with or without salt supplementation, may experience an excessive pressor effect after midodrine therapy, especially in the supine posture. The possibility of hypertensive effects with midodrine can be minimized by either reducing the dose of fludrocortisone or decreasing the salt intake prior to initiation of treatment with midodrine.

Alpha adrenergic blocking agents antagonize the vasopressor effect of midodrine.

Adverse Effects: In 305 patients treated with midodrine for primary neurogenic types of idiopathic orthostatic hypotension (Bradbury-Eggleston or Shy-Drager Syndrome), the overall adverse reaction rate was 34%, and the drop out rate due to adverse reactions was 6.9%. The most serious and frequent adverse reaction to midodrine is supine hypertension (17.5%). The other frequent adverse reaction to midodrine (>10%) is pruritus (11.5%). The adverse reactions to midodrine grouped according to organ systems, are given in Table I.

Table I—Amatine

Adverse Effects

Organ System	Adverse Reaction	No. of Patients	(%) n=305
Cardiovascular	Supine Hypertension	48*	(17.5)
	Palpitation/Tachycardia	1	(0.3)
	Chest Pain	1	(0.3)
	Angiitis	1	(0.3)
Gastrointestinal	Nausea/Vomiting	3	(1.0)
	Abdominal Discomfort	1	(0.3)
	Diarrhea	1	(0.3)
Integumentary	Pruritus	35	(11.5)
	Paresthesia (Scalp/Other)	22	(7.2)
	Piloerection	16	(5.2)
Urinary	Urge/Full Bladder	14	(4.6)
	Dysuria	2	(0.7)
	Frequency	2	(0.7)
	Urinary Retention	2	(0.7)
CNS	Weakness/Fatigue	3	(1.0)
	Headache	2	(0.7)
	Tremor	1	(0.3)
	Depression	1	(0.3)
Body as a Whole	Flushing/Heat	1	(0.3)
	Chills/Cold	1	(0.3)

*n=275.

Overdose: Symptoms and Treatment: We have had no reports of overdose with midodrine. However, symptoms of overdose could include piloerection (goose flesh), a sensation of coldness and urinary retention. The effects of midodrine can be treated with alpha sympatholytic drugs (e.g., phentolamine). In cutaneous hypersensitivity reactions, H_1-antihistamines should be administered.

Dosage: Adults and Adolescents: Treatment with midodrine should be started under close medical supervision in a controlled clinical setting such as in hospital, in clinic, or in the office. Hourly measurements of blood pressure (supine and sitting or standing, if possible) should be made for 3 hours following the first dose and also the second dose of a three times daily dosage regimen.

It is recommended that treatment begin at the lowest level and be titrated at intervals of 3 to several days until the optimal response is obtained. Upon escalating the dosage, the supine and standing blood pressure should be closely monitored in hospital, in clinic or in the office as for the initiation of therapy, hourly for 3 hours following the first 2 doses.

The usual starting dose is 2.5 mg 3 times daily. Single doses of 2.5, 5 and 10 mg have been successfully employed. Most patients are controlled at or below 30 mg/day given in 3 or 4 divided doses. Midodrine can be given up to 6 times/day. Some patients require a morning dose that is higher than that taken later in the day. In some instances midodrine has been given on a 3 times/day schedule as follows: 1 to 2 hours before arising in the morning, mid-morning and mid-afternoon. In order to reduce the potential for supine hypertension, it may be recommended that midodrine doses not be given after the evening meal. The maximum recommended dose should not exceed 30 mg daily.

During the period of close medical supervision, the patient or a relative should be trained to measure blood pressures. Supine and sitting blood pressures should be measured daily for at least a month after initiation of treatment and twice per week afterwards.

The administration of midodrine should be stopped and the attending physician notified immediately, if the blood pressure in either position increases above 180/100 mmHg.

Children: In view of the lack of experience in children, this drug is not recommended for patients under 12 years of age.

Supplied: 2.5 mg: Each oral, white tablet, scored on one side contains: midodrine HCl 2.5 mg. Nonmedicinal ingredients: colloidal anhydrous silica, magnesium stearate, maize starch, microcrystalline cellulose and talc. Glass bottles of 100 with plastic cap to cap LDPE closures.

5 mg: Each oral, orange tablet, scored on one side contains: midodrine HCl 5 mg. Nonmedicinal ingredients: colloidal anhydrous silica, magnesium stearate, maize starch, microcrystalline cellulose, sunset Yellow col. lake and talc. Glass bottles of 100 with plastic cap to cap LDPE closures.

Store between 15 to 25°C.

(Shown in Product Recognition Section)

AMCINONIDE

General Monograph, CPhA

see CORTICOSTEROIDS: TOPICAL

AMERGE®

Glaxo Wellcome

Naratriptan HCl

5-HT₁ Receptor Agonist—Migraine Therapy

Pharmacology: Naratriptan has been demonstrated to be a selective agonist for a vascular 5-hydroxytryptamine$_1$ receptor subtype (probably a member of the 5-HT$_{1B/1D}$ family) with little or no binding affinity for 5-HT$_{2/3}$ receptor subtypes, alpha$_1$-, alpha$_2$-, or beta-adrenergic; dopamine$_1$; dopamine$_2$, muscarinic; or benzodiazepine receptors. Naratriptan did not exhibit agonist or antagonist activity in ex vivo assays of 5-HT$_4$ and 5-HT$_7$ receptor-mediated activities.

The therapeutic activity of naratriptan in migraine is generally attributed to its agonist activity at 5-HT$_{1B}$/5-HT$_{1D}$ receptors. Two current theories have been proposed to explain the efficacy of 5-HT$_1$ receptor agonists in migraine. One theory suggests that activation of 5-HT$_1$ receptors located on intracranial blood vessels, including those on the arteriovenous anastomoses, leads to vasoconstriction, which is believed to be correlated with the relief of migraine headache. The other hypothesis suggests that activation of 5-HT$_1$ receptors on perivascular fibers of the trigeminal system results in the inhibition of pro-inflammatory neuropeptide release. These theories are not mutually exclusive.

Pharmacokinetics: Absorption: Naratriptan is well absorbed, with 74% oral bioavailability in females and 63% in males. After oral administration, the absorption is rapid and peak concentrations are obtained in 2 to 5 hours. A 2-period crossover study was performed in 15 female migraine patients who received naratriptan as a single 2.5 mg tablet during a migraine attack, followed 3 to 7 days later by another 2.5 mg treatment during a non-migraine period. During a migraine attack, absorption is slower, although exposure (AUC) and elimination half-life are not significantly affected. See Table I.

Table I—Amerge

Pharmacokinetic Parameters in Female Migraine Patients After Receiving 2.5 mg Amerge Tablets*

Parameter	Migraine Attack (N=15)	Non-Migraine Period (N=15)
C_{max} (ng/mL)	7.66 (3.07)	9.50 (3.63)
t_{max} (h)	3.8 (2.1)	2.0 (1.0)
AUC (ng/mL·h)	86.7 (32.5)	92.0 (33.7)
Cl/F (mL/min)	467.5 (126.4)	520.7 (222.6)
$t_{1/2}$ (h)	6.75 (1.44)	7.02 (2.39)

*Values quoted are arithmetic mean (standard deviation).

Legend: C_{max}: Maximum concentrations.
Cl/f: Apparent clearance.
AUC: Area under the curve of concentration vs time extrapolated to infinity.
t_{max}: Time to maximum concentration.
$t_{1/2}$: Elimination half-life.

Plasma levels of naratriptan increase in a dose-proportional manner consistent with linear pharmacokinetics over a 1 to 10 mg dose range. The absorption and elimination are independent of the dose. Administration with food does not appreciably influence the pharmacokinetics of naratriptan. Repeat administration of naratriptan (up to 10 mg once daily for 5 days) does not result in drug accumulation.

Metabolism and Distribution: In vitro, naratriptan is metabolized by a wide range of cytochrome P450 isoenzymes into a number of inactive metabolites. Naratriptan is a poor inhibitor of cytochrome P450 isoenzymes, and does not inhibit monoamine oxidase (MAO) enzymes; metabolic interactions between naratriptan and drugs metabolized by P450 or MAO are, therefore, unlikely. According to a population pharmacokinetic estimate, naratriptan is distributed into a volume of approximately 261 L.

Protein Binding: Plasma protein binding is low (29%).

Elimination: The elimination half-life generally ranges from 5 to 8 hours. Oral clearance is 509 mL/min in females and 770 mL/min in males. The renal clearance (220 mL/min) exceeds the glomerular filtration rate, suggesting that the drug undergoes active tubular secretion. Naratriptan is predominantly eliminated in urine, with 50% of the dose recovered unchanged and 30% as metabolites.

Special Populations: Age Effects: A study was performed to compare the pharmacokinetics of naratriptan in young (6 female/6 male, 24 to 44 years) and elderly (6 female/ 6 male, 65 to 77 years) subjects. The subjects received 2 doses each of placebo, 1 mg naratriptan, and 2.5 mg naratriptan separated by 4-hour intervals. A minimum 96-hour period intervened between consecutive treatment days.

Elderly subjects experienced a higher degree of exposure to naratriptan than did younger subjects. Mean C_{max} and area under the plasma concentration time curve values were 28% and 38% higher, respectively, for the 1 mg treatment group and 15% and 32% higher, respectively, for the 2.5 mg group. Total and renal clearance were decreased by about 30%, while the elimination half-life was increased by about 1 hour.

Elevations in systolic blood pressure at the 2.5 mg dose were more pronounced in the elderly subjects than in the young subjects (mean peak increases 12 mmHg in elderly versus 2 mmHg in young subjects).

Renal Impairment: Renal excretion is the major route for elimination of naratriptan. A study to compare male and female subjects with mild to moderate renal impairment (n=15; 31 to 58 years, screening creatinine clearance: median 41.2 mL/min, range 18 to 115 mL/min,) to gender-matched healthy subjects (n=8, 21 to 47 years) showed a decrease in oral clearance (mean decreased by 50%) resulting in a longer mean half-life (approximately 11 hours, range, 7 to 20 hours) and an increase in the mean C_{max} (approximately 40%). In this study, blood pressure measurements suggested that increased exposure in renally-impaired subjects may be associated with increases in blood pressure which are larger than those seen in healthy subjects receiving the same dose (5 mg) (see Dosage).

Hepatic Impairment: Liver metabolism plays a limited role in the clearance of naratriptan. The pharmacokinetics of a single 2.5 mg dose of naratriptan were determined in subjects with moderate hepatic impairment (Child-Pugh grade A or B, n=8) and gender- and age-matched healthy subjects (n=8). Subjects with hepatic impairment showed a moderate decrease in clearance (approximately 30%) resulting in increases of approximately 40% in the half-life (range, 8 to 16 hours) and the area under the plasma concentration time curve (see Dosage).

Clinical Studies: Therapeutic Clinical Trials: Four double-blind, placebo-controlled, dose-ranging clinical trials evaluated the safety and efficacy of naratriptan at oral doses ranging from 0.1 to 10 mg in a total of 3 160 adult patients with migraine attacks characterized by moderate or severe pain. The minimal effective dose was 1.0 mg. In 3 of the 4 clinical trials, a higher overall rate of headache relief was achieved with a 2.5 mg dose. Single doses of 5 mg and higher are not recommended due to an increased incidence of adverse events. Onset of significant headache relief (defined as no or mild pain) became apparent at 60 to 120 minutes after these doses. Naratriptan also relieved the nausea, phonophobia, and photophobia associated with migraine attacks.

Table II shows the 4-hour efficacy results obtained for the recommended doses of naratriptan in 2 of the 4 dose-ranging efficacy studies. In study 1, patients were randomised to receive placebo or a particular dose of naratriptan for the treatment of a single migraine attack according to a parallel group design, whereas, in study 2, patients were randomised to receive each of the treatments for separate migraine attacks according to a crossover design. In both studies, patients who achieved headache relief at 240 minutes post-dose, but experienced a worsening of severity between 4 and 24 hours post-dosing were permitted to take a second dose of double-blind medication identical to the first.

Significant headache relief was sustained over 24 hours. Data from four placebo controlled studies (n=3 160) showed that of the patients who achieved headache relief with naratriptan 2.5 mg, 72% to 83% did not experience recurrence of headache between 4 and 24 hours post-dosing.

Subgroup analyses of the overall population of patients participating in the placebo-controlled trials indicate that the efficacy of naratriptan was unaffected by migraine type (with/ without aura), gender, oral contraceptive use, or concomitant use of common migraine prophylactic drugs (e.g., beta-blockers, calcium channel blockers, tricyclic antidepressants).

In a long-term, repeat dose, open study of 417 patients (all were initiated on a 2.5 mg dose of naratriptan but were given the option to titrate down to a 1 mg dose if 2.5 mg was not well tolerated) a total of 15 301 attacks were treated (mean number of treated attacks/patient=36 for the 2.5 mg dose and 8 for the 1 mg dose) over a period of up to 12 months. Headache response was sustained (as judged by the proportion of attacks treated with naratriptan resulting in headache relief). The median percentage of attacks per patient requiring a second dose for headache recurrence was 8%. Of the 417 patients treating attacks, 10 patients opted for a dosage reduction.

Indications: For the acute treatment of migraine attacks with or without aura.

Naratriptan is not for use in the management of hemiplegic, basilar, or ophthalmoplegic migraine (see Contraindications). Safety and efficacy have not been established for cluster headache which is present in an older, predominantly male population.

Contraindications: Naratriptan is contraindicated in patients with history, symptoms, or signs of ischemic cardiac, cerebrovascular or peripheral vascular syndromes, valvular heart disease or cardiac arrhythmias (especially tachycardias). In addition, patients with other significant underlying cardiovascular diseases (e.g., atherosclerotic disease, congenital heart disease) should not receive naratriptan. Ischemic cardiac syndromes include, but are not limited to, angina pectoris of any type (e.g., stable angina of effort and vasospastic forms of angina such as the Prinzmetal's variant), all forms of myocardial infarction, and silent myocardial ischemia. Cerebrovascular syndromes include, but are not limited to, strokes of any type as well as transient ischemic attacks (TIAs). Peripheral vascular disease includes, but is not limited to, ischemic bowel disease, or Raynaud's syndrome (see Warnings).

Table II—Amerge

Results at 240 Minutes Post First Dose

	Study 1			Study 2		
Parameter	Placebo (n=107)	Amerge 1 mg (n=219)	Amerge 2.5 mg (n=209)	Placebo (n=602)	Amerge 1 mg (n=595)	Amerge 2.5 mg (n=586)
Pain Relief (0/1)[a]	27%	52%[e]	66%[e,f]	33%	57%[e]	68%[e,f]
Pain Free (0)[b]	10%	26%[e]	43%[e,f]	15%	33%[e]	45%[e]
Nausea Free	56%	71%[g]	77%[g]	54%	69%[e]	75%[e]
Photophobia Free	34%	57%[g]	67%[g]	33%	53%[e]	61%[e]
Phonophobia Free	d	d	d	36%	55%[e]	65%[e]
Clinical Disability[c] (0/1)	49%	62%[g]	72%[g]	50%	70%[e]	76%[e]

[a] Pain relief is defined as a reduction in headache severity from grade 3 or 2 (severe or moderate) to grade 1 or 0 (mild or no pain).
[b] Pain free is defined as a headache severity score of 0 (no pain).
[c] Clinical disability is measured on a 4-point scale (0=able to function normally, 1=ability mildly impaired, 2=ability severely impaired, 3=bed rest required).
[d] Photophobia and phonophobia collected as one measure.
[e] $p<0.01$ vs placebo.
[f] $p<0.01$ vs Amerge 1 mg. Note comparisons were not performed for any parameter other than pain relief and pain free in study 1 and for pain relief in study 2.
[g] Statistical comparisons not performed.

Amerge (cont'd)

Because naratriptan can give rise to increases in blood pressure, it is contraindicated in patients with uncontrolled or severe hypertension (see Warnings).

Ergot-containing drugs have been reported to cause prolonged vasospastic reactions. Because naratriptan may also cause coronary vasospasm and these effects may be additive, the use of naratriptan within 24 hours before or after treatment with other 5-HT$_1$ receptor agonists, or ergotamine-containing drugs or their derivatives (e.g., dihydroergotamine, methysergide) is contraindicated.

Naratriptan is contraindicated in patients with hemiplegic, basilar, or ophthalmoplegic migraine.

Naratriptan is contraindicated in patients with severe renal impairment (creatinine clearance <15 mL/min) (see Pharmacology and Dosage).

Naratriptan is contraindicated in patients with severe hepatic impairment (Child-Pugh grade C) (see Pharmacology and Dosage).

Naratriptan is contraindicated in patients with hypersensitivity to naratriptan or any component of the formulation.

Warnings: Naratriptan should only be used where a clear diagnosis of migraine has been established.

Risk of Myocardial Ischemia and/or Infarction and Other Adverse Cardiac Events: Amerge has been associated with transient chest and/or neck pain and tightness which may resemble angina pectoris. In rare cases, the symptoms have been identified as being the likely result of coronary vasospasm or myocardial ischemia. Rare cases of serious coronary events or arrhythmia have occurred following use of another 5-HT$_1$ agonist. Naratriptan should not be given to patients who have documented ischemic or vasospastic coronary artery disease (see Contraindications). It is strongly recommended that naratriptan not be given to patients in whom unrecognized coronary artery disease (CAD) is predicted by the presence of risk factors (e.g., hypertension, hypercholesterolemia, smoking, obesity, diabetes, strong family history of CAD, female who is surgically or physiologically postmenopausal, or male who is over 40 years of age) unless a cardiovascular evaluation provides satisfactory clinical evidence that the patient is reasonably free of coronary artery and ischemic myocardial disease or other significant underlying cardiovascular disease. The sensitivity of cardiac diagnostic procedures to detect cardiovascular disease or predisposition to coronary artery vasospasm is unknown. If, during the cardiovascular evaluation, the patient's medical history or electrocardiographic investigations reveal findings indicative of or consistent with coronary artery vasospasm or myocardial ischemia, naratriptan should not be administered (see Contraindications).

For patients with risk factors predictive of CAD who are considered to have a satisfactory cardiovascular evaluation, the first dose of naratriptan should be administered in the setting of a physician's office or similar medically staffed and equipped facility. Because cardiac ischemia can occur in the absence of clinical symptoms, consideration should be given to obtaining ECGs in patients with risk factors during the interval immediately following naratriptan administration on the first occasion of use. However, an absence of drug-induced cardiovascular effects on the occasion of the initial dose does not preclude the possibility of such effects occurring with subsequent administrations.

Intermittent long-term users of naratriptan who have or acquire risk factors predictive of CAD, as described above, should receive periodic interval cardiovascular evaluations over the course of treatment.

If symptoms consistent with angina occur after the use of naratriptan, ECG evaluation should be carried out to look for ischemic changes.

The systematic approach described above is intended to reduce the likelihood that patients with unrecognized cardiovascular disease will be inadvertently exposed to naratriptan.

Cardiac Events and Fatalities Associated With 5-HT$_1$ Agonists: Naratriptan can cause coronary artery vasospasm. Serious adverse cardiac events, including acute myocardial infarction, life-threatening disturbances of cardiac rhythm, and death have been reported within a few hours following the administration of 5-HT$_1$ agonists. Considering the extent of use of 5-HT$_1$ agonists in patients with migraine, the incidence of these events is extremely low.

Premarketing Experience With Naratriptan: Among approximately 3 500 patients with migraine who participated in premarketing clinical trials of naratriptan, 4 patients treated with single oral doses of naratriptan ranging from 1 to 10 mg experienced asymptomatic ischemic ECG changes with at least 1, who took 7.5 mg, likely due to coronary vasospasm.

Cerebrovascular Events and Fatalities With 5-HT$_1$ Agonists: Cerebral hemorrhage, subarachnoid hemorrhage, stroke, and other cerebrovascular events have been reported in patients treated with 5-HT$_1$ agonists, and some have resulted in fatalities. In a number of cases, it appears possible that the cerebrovascular events were primary, the agonist having been administered in the incorrect belief that the symptoms experienced were a consequence of migraine, when they were not. It should be noted that patients with migraine may be at increased risk of certain cerebrovascular events (e.g., stroke, hemorrhage, TIA).

Special Cardiovascular Pharmacology Studies: In subjects (n=10) with suspected coronary artery disease undergoing angiography, naratriptan at a s.c. dose of 1.5 mg produced an 8% increase in aortic blood pressure, an 18% increase in pulmonary artery blood pressure, and an 8% increase in systemic vascular resistance. In addition, mild chest pain or tightness was reported by 4 subjects. Clinically significant increases in blood pressure were experienced by 3 of the subjects (2 of whom also had chest pain/discomfort). Diagnostic angiogram results revealed that 9 subjects had normal coronary arteries and 1 had insignificant coronary artery disease.

Migraine patients (n=35) free of cardiovascular disease were subjected to assessments of myocardial perfusion by positron emission tomography while receiving s.c. naratriptan 1.5 mg in the absence of a migraine attack. Naratriptan was associated with a reduced coronary vasodilatory reserve (approximately 10%), increased coronary resistance (approximately 20%), and decreased hyperemic myocardial blood flow (approximately 10%). The relevance of these findings to the use of recommended oral doses of naratriptan is not known.

Hypersensitivity: Rare hypersensitivity (anaphylaxis/anaphylactoid) reactions may occur in patients receiving 5-HT$_1$ agonists such as naratriptan. Such reactions can be life threatening or fatal. In general, hypersensitivity reactions to drugs are more likely to occur in individuals with a history of sensitivity to multiple allergens (see Contraindications). Owing to the possibility of cross-reactive hypersensitivity reactions, naratriptan should not be used in patients having a history of hypersensitivity to sumatriptan or chemically-related 5-HT$_1$ receptor agonists. As naratriptan contains a sulfonamide component, there is a theoretical risk of hypersensitivity reactions in patients with known hypersensitivity to sulfonamides.

Other Vasospasm-Related Events: 5-HT$_1$ agonists may cause vasospastic reactions other than coronary artery vasospasm. Extensive postmarket experience has shown the use of another 5-HT$_1$ agonist to be associated with rare occurrences of peripheral vascular ischemia and colonic ischemia with abdominal pain and bloody diarrhea.

Increases in Blood Pressure: Elevations in blood pressure have been reported following use of naratriptan. At the recommended oral doses, the elevations are generally small (population average maximum increases of <5 mm Hg systolic and <3 mm Hg diastolic at the 2.5 mg dose). The effects may be more pronounced in the elderly and hypertensive patients. In a pharmacodynamic study conducted in normotensive patients (n=12) and in hypertensive patients controlled by antihypertensive treatment (n=12), the pressor effects of naratriptan were greater in hypertensive patients (weighted mean increases in systolic and diastolic blood pressure of 6 and 4 mm Hg in hypertensive subjects vs 3 and 2 mm Hg in normotensive patients receiving two 2.5 mg doses separated by a 2-hour time interval). Two hypertensive patients experienced 3 events of chest discomfort while receiving naratriptan. Significant elevation in blood pressure, including hypertensive crisis, has been reported on rare occasions in patients receiving 5-HT$_1$ agonists with and without a history of hypertension. Naratriptan is contraindicated in patients with uncontrolled or severe hypertension (see Contraindications).

Precautions: Cardiovascular: Discomfort in the chest, neck, throat, and jaw (including pain, pressure, heaviness, tightness) has been reported after administration of naratriptan. Because 5-HT$_1$ agonists may cause coronary artery vasospasm, patients who experience signs or symptoms suggestive of angina following naratriptan should be evaluated for the presence of CAD or a predisposition to variant angina before receiving additional doses, and should be monitored electrocardiographically if dosing is resumed and similar symptoms recur. Similarly, patients who experience other symptoms or signs suggestive of decreased arterial flow, such as ischemic bowel syndrome or Raynaud's syndrome following naratriptan administration should be evaluated for atherosclerosis or predisposition to vasospasm (see Contraindications and Warnings).

Neurologic Conditions: Care should be taken to exclude other potentially serious neurologic conditions before treating headache in patients not previously diagnosed with migraine or who experience a headache that is atypical for them. There have been rare reports where patients received 5-HT$_1$ agonists for severe headaches that were subsequently shown to have been secondary to an evolving neurologic lesion. For newly diagnosed patients or patients presenting with atypical symptoms, the diagnosis of migraine should be reconsidered if no response is seen after the first dose of naratriptan.

Seizures: Caution should be observed if naratriptan is to be used in patients with a history of epilepsy or structural brain lesions which lower the convulsion threshold.

Renal or Hepatic Impairment: Naratriptan should be administered with caution to patients with impaired renal or hepatic function (see Pharmacology, Contraindications and Dosage).

Occupational Hazards: Psychomotor Impairment: In a study of psychomotor function in healthy volunteers, single oral 5 and 10 mg doses of naratriptan were associated with sedation and decreased alertness. Although these doses are higher than those recommended for the treatment of migraine, patients should be cautioned that drowsiness may occur following treatment with naratriptan. They should be advised not to perform skilled tasks (e.g., driving or operating machinery) if drowsiness occurs.

Drug Interactions: The limited metabolism of naratriptan and the wide range of cytochrome P450 isoenzymes involved, as determined by in vitro studies, suggest that significant drug interactions with naratriptan are unlikely. Naratriptan did not inhibit MAO enzymes (MAO-A or MAO-B) in vitro. The possibility of pharmacodynamic in vivo interactions between naratriptan and MAO inhibitors has not been investigated.

Ergot-Containing Drugs: Ergot-containing drugs have been reported to cause prolonged vasospastic reactions. Because there is a theoretical basis for these effects being additive, ergot-containing or ergot-type medications (like dihydroergotamine or methysergide) are contraindicated within 24 hours of naratriptan administration (see Contraindications).

Other 5-HT$_1$ agonists: The administration of naratriptan with other 5-HT$_1$ agonists has not been evaluated in migraine patients. As an increased risk of coronary vasospasm is a theoretical possibility with coadministration of 5-HT$_1$ agonists, use of these drugs within 24 hours of each other is contraindicated.

Other Serotonergic Drugs: Rare postmarketing reports describe patients with weakness, hyperreflexia, and incoordination following the combined use of a selective serotonin reuptake inhibitor (SSRI) and 5-HT$_1$ agonists. If concomitant treatment with naratriptan and an SSRI (e.g., fluoxetine, fluvoxamine, paroxetine, sertraline), tricyclic antidepressant, MAO inhibitor, or other drugs with serotonergic activity is clinically warranted, appropriate observation of the patient for acute and long-term adverse events is advised.

Hormonal Contraceptives: In a population pharmacokinetic study in migraine patients, hormonal contraceptive use was associated with a 32% decrease in naratriptan clearance.

Tobacco: In a population pharmacokinetic study in migraine patients, tobacco use was associated with a 29% increase in naratriptan clearance.

Alcohol and Food: Clinical studies did not reveal any pharmacokinetic interaction when naratriptan was administered together with alcohol or food.

Pregnancy: The safety of naratriptan for use during human pregnancy has not been established. Naratriptan should be used during pregnancy only if the potential benefit justifies the potential risk to the fetus. To monitor fetal outcomes of pregnant women exposed to naratriptan, Glaxo Wellcome Inc. maintains a Naratriptan Pregnancy Registry. Health care providers are encouraged to register patients by calling (800) 722-9292, ext. 39441.

Lactation: Naratriptan and/or its metabolites are distributed into the milk of lactating rats (at 2 hours post oral gavage dosing, levels in milk were 3.5 times higher than maternal plasma levels). Therefore, caution should be exercised when considering the administration of naratriptan to nursing women.

Children: Safety and effectiveness of naratriptan have not been studied in children under 12 years of age. Use of the drug in this age group is, therefore, not recommended.

Adolescents: The efficacy of naratriptan at single doses of 0.25, 1.0 and 2.5 mg was not demonstrated to be greater than placebo in adolescents (12 to 17 years). Therefore, the use of the drug in adolescents is not recommended.

Geriatrics: The safety and effectiveness of naratriptan has not been adequately studied in individuals over 65 years of age. Naratriptan is known to be substantially excreted by the kidney, and the risk of adverse reactions to this drug may be greater in elderly patients who have reduced renal function. In addition, elderly patients are more likely to have decreased hepatic function; they are at higher risk for CAD; and blood pressure increases may be more pronounced in the elderly. Clinical studies of naratriptan did not include patients over 65 years of age. Its use in this age group is, therefore, not recommended.

Drug/Laboratory Test Interactions: Naratriptan is not known to interfere with commonly employed clinical laboratory tests.

Dependence Liability: In 1 clinical study enrolling 12 subjects, all of whom had experience using oral opiates and other psychoactive drugs, subjective responses typically associated with many drugs of abuse were produced with less intensity during treatment with naratriptan (1 to 5 mg) than with codeine (30 to 90 mg). Long-term studies (12 months) in migraine patients using naratriptan revealed no evidence of increased drug utilization.

Melanin Binding: In pigmented rats treated with a single oral dose (10 mg/kg) of radiolabeled naratriptan, radioactivity was detected in the eyes at 3 months postadministration, a finding which suggests that the drug or its metabolites may bind to the melanin of the eye. The possible clinical significance of this finding is unknown. No systematic monitoring of ophthalmologic function was undertaken in clinical trials. Prescribers should consider the possibility of long term ophthalmologic effects due to accumulation of naratriptan in melanin-rich tissues.

Adverse Effects: Serious cardiac events, including some that have been fatal, have occurred following the use of 5-HT_1 agonists. These events are extremely rare and most have been reported in patients with risk factors predictive of CAD. Events reported have included coronary artery vasospasm, transient myocardial ischemia, myocardial infarction, ventricular tachycardia, and ventricular fibrillation (see Contraindications, Warnings and Precautions).

Experience in Controlled Clinical Trials with Naratriptan: Typical 5-HT_1 Agonist Adverse Reactions: As with other 5-HT_1 agonists, naratriptan has been associated with sensations of heaviness, pressure, tightness or pain which may be intense. These may occur in any part of the body including the chest, throat, neck, jaw and upper limb.

Acute Safety: The safety and efficacy of the 1 and 2.5 mg doses of naratriptan were investigated in 4 placebo-controlled clinical trials in adult migraine patients. Two of these trials were of parallel group design and involved the treatment of a single migraine attack. A third study was of crossover design and involved the treatment of one migraine attack per dose group. The fourth study was a parallel group trial in which patients treated up to 3 migraine attacks. In all studies, patients who achieved headache relief at 240 minutes postdose, but experienced a worsening of severity between 4 and 24 hours postdosing, were permitted to take a second dose of double-blind medication identical to the first.

The overall incidence of adverse events following doses of naratriptan 1 mg or 2.5 mg (1 or 2 doses) were similar to placebo (28.5 and 30.2% vs 28.9% with placebo). Naratriptan is generally well tolerated and most adverse reactions were mild, transient and self-limiting. The most common adverse events to occur at a higher rate than in the corresponding placebo group were malaise/fatigue (2.4% vs 0.8% with placebo) and neck/throat/jaw sensations (2.1% vs 0.3% with placebo). Table III lists the most common adverse events that occurred in the 4 large placebo-controlled clinical trials. Only events that occurred at a frequency of 1% or more in the naratriptan 2.5 mg or 1 mg group and were more frequent in that group then in the placebo group are included in Table III. From this table, it appears that many of these adverse events are dose related.

Table III—Amerge

Treatment-Emergent Adverse Events in Placebo-Controlled Clinical Trials Reported by at Least 1% of Patients With Migraine*

	Placebo	Amerge 1 mg	Amerge 2.5 mg
Number of Patients	922	1 024	1 016
Number of Migraine Attacks Treated	1 059	1 387	1 368
Symptoms of Potentially Cardiac Origin			
neck/throat/jaw sensations*	0.3%	1.7%	2.1%
chest sensations*	1.1%	0.8%	1.2%
upper limb sensations*	0.3%	0.5%	1.4%
Neurological			
dizziness	1.5%	1.0%	2.2%
drowsiness/sleepiness	0.8%	0.9%	1.7%
paresthesia	0.8%	1.6%	1.5%
head/face sensations*	0.5%	0.5%	1.3%
headache	0.2%	0.4%	1.0%
Gastrointestinal			
nausea	6.2%	5.9%	6.3%
hyposalivation	0.3%	0.5%	1.0%
Non-Site Specific			
malaise and fatigue	0.8%	1.6%	2.4%

*The term "sensations" encompasses adverse events described as pain and discomfort, pressure, heaviness, constriction, tightness, heat/burning sensation, paresthesia, numbness, tingling, and strange sensations.

Long-Term Safety: In a long-term open study, 417 patients treated 15 301 migraine attacks with naratriptan over a period of up to 1 year. The most common adverse events in descending order of frequency were as follows: nausea (16%); malaise/fatigue (11%); drowsiness (10%); chest sensations* (8%); neck/throat/jaw sensations* (8%); paresthesia (7%); head/face sensations* (6%); vomiting (6%); and dizziness (5%). Due to the lack of a placebo arm in this study, the role of naratriptan in causation cannot be reliably determined (*see footnote for Table III).

Other Adverse Events Observed in Association with Naratriptan: In the paragraphs that follow, the frequencies of less commonly reported adverse clinical events are presented. Because some events were observed in open and uncontrolled studies, the role of naratriptan in their causation cannot be reliably determined. All reported events are included except those already listed in Table III, those too general to be informative, and those not reasonably associated with the use of the drug. Event frequencies are calculated as the number of patients reporting an event divided by the total number of patients (n=2 790) exposed to naratriptan. Events are further classified within body system categories and enumerated in order of decreasing frequency using the following definitions: frequent adverse events are defined as those occurring in at least 1/100 patients; infrequent adverse events are those occurring in 1/100 to 1/1 000 patients; rare adverse events are those occurring in fewer than 1/1 000 patients.

Cardiovascular: Infrequent: palpitations, increased blood pressure, tachyarrhythmias and abnormal ECGs. Rare: bradycardia, hypotension, varicosities and heart murmur.

Ear, Nose and Throat: Frequent: ear, nose and throat infections. Infrequent: phonophobia, sinusitis, and upper respiratory inflammation. Rare: allergic rhinitis, labyrinthitis, tinnitus, ear, nose and throat hemorrhage and hearing difficulty.

Endocrine and Metabolic: Infrequent: thirst and polydipsia, dehydration and fluid retention. Rare: hyperlipidemia, hypercholesterolemia, hypothyroidism, hyperglycemia, glycosuria and ketonuria and parathyroid neoplasm.

Eye: Infrequent: photophobia. Rare: eye hemorrhage, dry eyes and difficulty focusing.

Gastrointestinal: Frequent: vomiting. Infrequent: dyspeptic symptoms, diarrhea, hyposalivation, gastrointestinal discomfort and pain, gastroenteritis and constipation. Rare: abnormal liver function tests, abnormal bilirubin levels, salivary gland swelling, hemorrhoids, gastritis, esophagitis, oral itching and irritation, regurgitation and reflux and gastic ulcers.

Musculoskeletal: Infrequent: musculoskeletal/muscle pain, muscle cramps and spasms, arthralgia and articular rheumatism. Rare: joint and muscle stiffness, tightness and rigidity.

Neurology: Frequent: migraine. Infrequent: vertigo, tremors, sleep disorders, cognitive function disorders and hyperesthesia. Rare: disorders of equilibrium, decreased consciousness, confusion, sedation, coordination disorders, neuritis, dreams, altered sense of taste, motor retardation, muscle twitching and fasciculation.

Non-Site Specific: Frequent: paresthesia and heat sensations. Infrequent: chills and/or fever, descriptions of odor or taste and feelings of pressure/tightness/heaviness. Rare: allergies and allergic reactions, mobility disorders and faintness.

Psychiatry: Infrequent: anxiety and depressive disorders. Rare: aggression, agitation and detachment.

Reproduction: Rare: lumps of female reproductive tract and inflammation of the fallopian tube.

Skin: Infrequent: skin photosensitivity, skin rashes, pruritus, sweating and urticaria. Rare: skin erythema, dermatitis and dermatosis, and pruritic skin rash.

Urology: Infrequent: urinary infections. Rare: urinary tract hemorrhage, urinary urgency and pyelitis.

Overdose: Symptoms and Treatment: In clinical studies, numerous patients (n=222) and healthy subjects (n=196) have received naratriptan at doses of 5 to 25 mg. In the majority of cases, no serious adverse events were reported. One patient treated with a 7.5 mg dose experienced ischemic ECG changes which were likely due to coronary vasospasm. This event was not associated with a serious clinical outcome. A patient who was mildly hypertensive experienced a significant increase in blood pressure (baseline value of 150/98 to 204/144 mm Hg at 225 minutes) beginning 30 minutes after the administration of a 10 mg dose (4 times the maximum recommended single dose). The event resolved with antihypertensive treatment. Administration of 25 mg (10 times the maximum recommended single dose) in 1 healthy male subject increased blood pressure from 120/67 mm Hg pretreatment up to 191/113 mm Hg at approximately 6 hours postdose and resulted in adverse events including lightheadedness, tension in the neck, tiredness, and loss of coordination. Blood pressure returned to near baseline by 8 hours after dosing without any pharmacological intervention.

The elimination half-life of naratriptan is about 5 to 8 hours (see Pharmacology), and therefore monitoring of patients after overdose with naratriptan should continue for at least 24 hours or longer if symptoms or signs persist. Standard supportive treatment should be applied as required. If the patient presents with chest pain or other symptoms consistent with angina pectoris, ECG monitoring should be performed for evidence of ischemia. Appropriate treatment (e.g., nitroglycerin or other coronary artery vasodilators) should be administered as required.

It is unknown what effect hemodialysis or peritoneal dialysis has on the serum concentrations of naratriptan.

Dosage: Naratriptan is recommended only for the acute treatment of migraine attacks. Naratriptan should not be used prophylactically.

Adults: The minimal effective single adult dose of naratriptan is 1 mg. The maximum recommended single dose is 2.5 mg (see Clinical Studies in Table IV).

Table IV—Amerge

Percentage of Patients with Headache Relief at 4 Hours Postdosing[a]

	Placebo		Amerge 1 mg		Amerge 2.5 mg	
	%	(N)	%	(N)	%	(N)
Study 1	39	(91)	64	(85)	63[b]	(87)
Study 2	34	(122)	50[c]	(117)	60[b,c]	(127)
Study 3	27	(107)	52[c]	(219)	66[c,d]	(209)
Study 4	33	(602)	57[c]	(595)	68[c,d]	(586)

[a] Pain relief is defined as a reduction in headache severity from grade 3 or 2 (severe or moderate) to grade 1 or 0 (mild or no pain).

[b] Comparison between 1 and 2.5 mg Amerge doses was not performed.

[c] $p<0.05$ vs placebo.

[d] $p<0.01$ vs Amerge 1 mg.

In 3 of the 4 studies, optimal rates of headache relief were achieved with a 2.5 mg dose. As patients may vary in their dose-responsiveness, the choice of dose should be made on an individual basis, weighing the possible benefit of the 2.5 mg dose with the potential for a greater risk of adverse events.

If the migraine headache returns, or if a patient has a partial response, the initial dose may be repeated once after 4 hours, for a maximum dose of 5 mg in a 24-hour period.

The safety of treating, on average, more than 4 headaches in a 30-day period has not been established.

Naratriptan tablets should be swallowed whole with fluids. Naratriptan tablets should be taken as early as possible after the onset of a migraine headache, but are effective if taken at a later stage.

Amerge (cont'd)

If a patient does not respond to the first dose of naratriptan, a second dose should not be taken for the same attack, as it is unlikely to be of benefit.

Renal disease/functional impairment causes prolongation of the half-life of orally administered naratriptan. Consequently, if treatment is deemed advisable in the presence of renal impairment, a maximum single dose of 1 mg should be administered. No more than a total of 2 mg should be taken in any 24-hour period. Repeated dosing in renally impaired patients has not been evaluated (see Pharmacology). Administration of naratriptan in patients with severe renal impairment (creatinine clearance $<$15 mL/min) is contraindicated (see Contraindications).

Hepatic disease/functional impairment causes prolongation of the half-life of orally administered naratriptan. Consequently, if treatment is deemed advisable in the presence of hepatic impairment, a maximum single dose of 1 mg should be administered. No more than a total of 2 mg should be taken in any 24-hour period (see Pharmacology). Administration of naratriptan in patients with severe hepatic impairment (Child-Pugh grade C) is contraindicated (see Contraindications).

Hypertension: Naratriptan should not be used in patients with uncontrolled or severe hypertension. Patients with mild to moderate controlled hypertension should be treated cautiously at the lowest effective dose.

Information for the Patient: See Blue Section—Information for the Patient "Amerge".

Supplied: 1 mg: Each white film-coated, D-shaped tablet, embossed GXCE3 on one side, contains: naratriptan (base) 1 mg as the HCl salt. Nonmedicinal ingredients: croscarmellose sodium, hydroxypropyl methylcellulose, lactose, magnesium stearate, microcrystalline cellulose, titanium dioxide and triacetin. Blister packs of 2, cartons of 4 blisters.

2.5 mg: Each green film-coated, D-shaped tablet, embossed GXCE5 on one side, contains: naratriptan (base) 2.5 mg as the HCl salt. Nonmedicinal ingredients: croscarmellose sodium, hydroxypropyl methylcellulose, indigo carmine aluminium lake (FD&C Blue No. 2), iron oxide yellow, lactose, magnesium stearate, microcrystalline cellulose, titanium dioxide and triacetin. Blister packs of 2 and 6, cartons of 4 blisters.

Store below 30°C.

(Shown in Product Recognition Section)

New Product 1998

AMETOP™
Smith & Nephew

Tetracaine HCl

Topical Anesthetic

Pharmacology: Tetracaine is a local anesthetic of the ester type (para-amino benzoic acid derivative). Ametop has been formulated as the free base to allow the tetracaine to diffuse across the skin barrier and reach the pain receptors (nociceptors) located just below the stratum corneum.

It acts by inhibiting sodium ion flux across the axon membrane thus preventing the nociceptors signalling pain to the CNS.

Indications: Topical anesthetic for dermal analgesia.

Contraindications: Premature babies or full-term infants less than 1 month of age, in whom the metabolic pathway for tetracaine may not be fully developed.

Known hypersensitivity to local anesthetics of the ester type.

Do not apply gel to broken skin, mucous membranes or to the eyes or ears.

Do not use prior to immunization.

Warnings: If accidentally ingested, systemic toxicity may occur and signs will be similar to those observed after other local anesthetics.

As tetracaine can cause contact sensitization reactions, particularly with repeated exposure, healthcare professionals should take care to minimize contact with the gel during application and removal.

Precautions: Only apply to intact, unbroken skin. Not to be taken internally. Tetracaine gel, like other local anesthetics may be ototoxic and should not be instilled into the middle ear or used for procedures which might involve penetration into to the middle ear. Repeated exposure to tetracaine gel may increase the risk of sensitization reactions to tetracaine.

Pregnancy and *Lactation:* There is no specific information as to the safety of tetracaine in pregnancy. It is not known whether tetracaine or its metabolites are secreted in breast milk. Therefore the product is not recommended for use by pregnant women or by breast-feeding mothers.

Adverse Effects: Slight erythema is frequently seen at the site of application and is due to the pharmacological action of tetracaine dilating capillary vessels. This may help in delineating the anesthetized area.

Slight edema or itching are less frequently seen at the site of application.

More severe erythema, edema and/or itching have rarely been reported.

Dosage: Adults (including geriatrics) and children over 1 month of age: Apply the contents of the tube to the skin starting from the centre of the area to be anesthetized and cover wih an occlusive dressing. The contents expellable from 1 tube (approximately 1 g) are sufficient to cover and anesthetize an area of up to 30 cm² (6×5 cm). Smaller areas of anesthetized skin may be adequate in infants and small children.

Adequate anesthesia can usually be achieved for venepuncture following a 30-minute application time, and for venous cannulation following a 45-minute application time; after which the gel should be removed with a gauze swab and the site prepared with an antiseptic wipe in the normal manner.

It is not necessary to apply tetracaine gel for longer than the above recommended times and anesthesia is maintained for 4 to 6 hours in most patients after a single application.

Supplied: Each g of white, opalescent gel contains: tetracaine base 40 mg (4% w/w) (as tetracaine HCl). Nonmedicinal ingredients: purified water, potassium phosphate, sodium chloride, sodium hydroxide, sodium methyl-p-hydroxybenzoate, sodium propyl-p-hydroxybenzoate and xanthan gum. Tubes of 1.5 g. Keep refrigerated at 2 to 8°C. Within the shelf life of 2 years, the product may be stored after dispensing for up to 1 month at 25°C.

Reviewed 1998

AMICAR® Ⓟ
Wyeth-Ayerst

Epsilon Aminocaproic Acid

Antifibrinolytic Agent

Pharmacology: Epsilon aminocaproic acid is a monoaminocarboxylic acid which acts as an effective inhibitor of fibrinolysis. The beneficial fibrinolysis-inhibitory effects of aminocaproic acid appear to be principally via inhibition of plasminogen activator substances and to a lesser degree, through antiplasmin activity. The drug is absorbed rapidly following oral administration. Whether administered by the oral or i.v. route, a major portion of the compound is recovered unmetabolized in the urine. The renal clearance of aminocaproic acid is high (about 75 % of the creatinine clearance). Thus, the drug is excreted rapidly. After prolonged administration, aminocaproic acid distributes throughout both the extravascular and intravascular compartments of the body and readily penetrates human red blood and other tissue cells.

Indications: Aminocaproic acid is useful in enhancing hemostasis when fibrinolysis contributes to bleeding. In life-threatening situations, fresh whole blood transfusions, fibrinogen infusions and other emergency measures may be required.

Fibrinolytic bleeding may frequently be associated with surgical complications following heart surgery (with or without cardiac bypass procedures) and portocaval shunt, hematological disorders such as aplastic anemia, abruptio placentae, hepatic cirrhosis, neoplastic disease such as carcinoma of the prostate, lung, stomach and cervix.

Urinary fibrinolysis, usually a normal physiological phenomenon, may frequently be associated with life-threatening complications following severe trauma, anoxia and shock. Symptomatic of such complications is surgical hematuria (following prostatectomy and nephrectomy) or nonsurgical hematuria (accompanying polycystic or neoplastic diseases of the genitourinary system (see Warnings).

Increased fibrinolytic activity has been demonstrated in the cerebrospinal fluid of patients with proved aneurysmal subarachnoid hemorrhage. Studies indicate a significant reduction in incidence of both death and proven rebleeds when treatment with aminocaproic acid is started within 7 days and continued through 14 days following the initial bleed.

As an inhibitor of plasminogen activation and by impeding the natural process of clot lysis, aminocaproic acid has been shown to be an effective agent as an adjunct in replacement therapy in hemophiliac patients undergoing tooth extractions.

Contraindications: Aminocaproic acid should not be used when there is evidence of an active intravascular clotting process.

When there is uncertainty as to whether the cause of bleeding is primary fibrinolysis or disseminated intravascular coagulation (DIC), this distinction must be made before administering aminocaproic acid. The following tests can be applied to differentiate the two conditions: Platelet count is usually decreased in DIC but normal in primary fibrinolysis.

Protamine Paracoagulation test is positive in DIC; a precipitate forms when protamine sulfate is dropped in citrated plasma. The test is negative in the presence of primary fibrinolysis.

The euglobin clot lysis test is abnormal in primary fibrinolysis, but normal in DIC.

Aminocaproic acid must not be used in the presence of DIC without concomitant heparin.

Pregnancy: The effect on the fetus and transplacental passage of this drug is unknown. Therefore, its use during the first and second trimesters should be confined to instances where need outweighs possible hazards.

Warnings: The drug is offered for use only in potentially acute life-threatening situations where hemorrhage results from an overactivity of the fibrinolytic system.

Antifertility effects, consistent with the drug's antifibrinolytic activity, have been suggested in some rodent studies.

In patients with upper urinary tract bleeding, administration of aminocaproic acid has been known to cause intrarenal obstruction in the form of glomerular capillary thrombosis, or clots in the renal pelvis and ureters. For this reason, aminocaproic acid should not be used in hematuria of upper urinary tract origin, unless the possible benefits outweigh the risk.

Precautions: The use of aminocaproic acid should be accompanied by tests designed to determine the amount of fibrinolysis present. There are presently available (a) general tests, such as those for the determination of the lysis of a clot of blood or plasma and (b) more specific tests for the study of various phases of fibrinolytic mechanisms. These latter tests include both semi-quantitative and quantitative techniques for the determination of profibrinolysin, fibrinolysin and anti-fibrinolysin.

Animal experiments indicate particular caution should be taken in administering aminocaproic acid to patients with cardiac, hepatic or renal diseases.

Demonstrable animal pathology in some cases has shown endocardial hemorrhages and myocardial fat degeneration. The use of this drug should thus be restricted to patients in whom the benefit expected would outweigh the hazard.

Rapid i.v. administration of the drug should be avoided since this may induce hypotension, bradycardia and/or arrhythmia.

One case of cardiac and hepatic lesions observed in man has been reported. The patient received 2 g of aminocaproic acid every 6 hours for a total dose of 26 g. Death was due to continued cerebral vascular hemorrhage. Necrotic changes in the heart and liver were noted at autopsy.

Fibrinolysis is a normal process, potentially active at all times to ensure the fluidity of blood. Inhibition of fibrinolysis by aminocaproic acid may result in clotting or thrombosis. However, there is no definite evidence that administration of aminocaproic acid has been responsible for the few reported cases intravascular clotting which followed this treatment. Rather, it appears that such intravascular clotting was most likely due to the patient's pre-existing clinical condition, e.g., the presence of DIC.

It has been postulated that extravascular clots formed in vivo with incorporated aminocaproic acid may not undergo spontaneous lysis as do normal clots. However, it is the consensus of experts that the few reported cases of extravascular clotting could have occurred in the absence of aminocaproic acid treatment.

Adverse Effects: Occasionally nausea, cramps, diarrhea, dizziness, tinnitus, malaise, conjunctival suffusion, nasal stuffiness, headache, myopathy and skin rash have been reported as results of the administration of aminocaproic acid. Only rarely has it been necessary to discontinue or reduce medication because of one or more of these effects.

There have also been some reports of dry ejaculation during the period of aminocaproic acid treatment. These have been reported to date only in hemophiliac patients who received the drug after undergoing dental surgical procedures. However, this symptom resolved in all patients within 24 to 48 hours of completion of therapy.

One case of a convulsion occurring, following i.v. administration of aminocaproic acid, has been reported. However, definite association between the seizure and the drug has not been established.

Thrombophlebitis, a possibility with all i.v. therapy, should be guarded against by strict attention to the proper insertion of the needle and the fixing of its position.

Dosage: Therapy is recommended as follows for all indications other than subarachnoid hemorrhage and dental extractions in hemophiliacs: An initial priming dose of 5 g of aminocaproic acid administered either orally or i.v. followed by 1 to 1.25 g doses at hourly intervals thereafter should achieve and sustain plasma levels of 0.130 mg/mL of the drug. This is the concentration apparently necessary for the inhibition of fibrinolysis. Administration of more than 30 g in any 24-hour period is not recommended.

I.V.: Administer by infusion, utilizing the usual compatible i.v. vehicles (e.g., water for injection, physiologic saline, 5% dextrose or Ringer's solution). **Rapid injection of aminocaproic acid i.v. undiluted into a vein is not recommended.**

For the treatment of acute bleeding syndromes due to elevated fibrinolytic activity, it is suggested that 16 to 20 mL (4 or 5 g) of aminocaproic acid i.v. in 250 mL of diluent be administered by infusion during the first hour of treatment, followed by a continuing infusion at the rate of 4 mL (1 g)/hour in 50 mL of diluent. This method of treatment would ordinarily be continued for about 8 hours or until the bleeding situation has been controlled.

Oral Therapy: If the patient is able to take medication by mouth, an identical dosage regimen may be followed by administering the tablets or syrup as follows: For the treatment of acute bleeding syndromes due to elevated fibrinolytic activity, it is suggested that 10 tablets (5 g) or 20 mL of syrup (5 g) of aminocaproic acid be administered during the first hour of treatment, followed by a continuing rate of 2 tablets (1 g) or 5 mL of syrup (1.25g)/hour. This method of treatment would ordinarily be continued for about 8 hours or until the bleeding situation has been controlled.

Therapy for Subarachnoid Hemorrhage: 36 g/day i.v. by continuous infusion, administered as 18 g in 400 mL 5% dextrose every 12 hours for 10 days. Then continue with oral therapy of 3 g every 2 hours until surgery is performed.

If surgery is not performed, antifibrinolytic therapy may be continued for 21 days following the last bleed. Dosage should then be reduced to 24 g/day (2 g every 2 hours) for 3 days, followed by 1 g every 2 hours for 3 days, then discontinued.

Therapy for Hemophiliacs undergoing Dental Extractions: Following preoperative treatment with a loading dose of Factor VIII or IX to raise factor levels to at least 30 to 50%, administer 6 g orally as soon as possible postoperatively, followed by 6 g orally every 6 hours (total dose of 24 g/24 hours) for a 9- to 10-day period.

Supplied: Injectable: Each mL of aqueous solution contains: epsilon aminocaproic acid 250 mg with benzyl alcohol 0.9% as preservative. Vials of 20 mL, packages of 12.

Syrup: Each mL contains: epsilon aminocaproic acid 250 mg. Nonmedicinal ingredients: citric acid, flavor raspberry, hydrochloric acid, potassium sorbate, sodium benzoate, sodium hydroxide, sorbitol solution and water purified. Energy: 50.2 kJ (12.0 kcal)/5 mL. Sodium: <1 mmol (8 mg)/5 mL. Tartrazine-free. Bottles of 450 mL.

Tablets: Each round, scored, white tablet, engraved "LL" and "A10", contains: epsilon aminocaproic acid 500 mg. Energy: <4.2 kJ (1 kcal). Tartrazine-free. Bottles of 100.

Reviewed 1998

AMIKIN® Pr

Bristol

Amikacin Sulfate

Antibiotic

Pharmacology: Amikacin is a semi-synthetic bactericidal aminoglycoside antibiotic affecting bacterial growth by specific inhibition of protein synthesis in susceptible bacteria and is active primarily against gram negative organisms, including Pseudomonas. A 30 μg amikacin sensitivity disc should give a zone inhibition of 17 mm or greater to be sensitive, using the Kirby-Bauer method of disc sensitivity for the causative organism.

The pharmacokinetics of amikacin and kanamycin are virtually identical. Amikacin is readily available and rapidly absorbed following i.v. or i.m. administration. The mean serum half-life is 2.2 hours with a mean renal clearance rate of 1.24 mL/kg/minute. No accumulation is associated with dosing at 12 hour intervals in individuals with a normal renal function.

Amikacin is not metabolized. Small amounts (1 to 2% of the dose) are excreted in the bile, while the remainder (98 to 99%) is excreted in the urine via glomerular filtration. The mean human serum protein binding is 11% over a concentration range of 5 to 50 μg/mL of serum. The apparent volume of distribution of drug is approximately 0.25 L/kg of body weight. Amikacin pharmacokinetics remain linear over the entire dosage range studied (0.5 μg/kg to 9 mg/kg).

Tolerance studies in normal volunteers revealed amikacin to be well tolerated locally following repeated i.m. dosing.

Amikacin has been found in the cerebrospinal fluid, pleural fluid, and peritoneal cavity following parenteral administration.

Spinal fluid concentrations in normal infants are approximately 10 to 20% of the serum concentrations and may reach 50% when the meninges are inflamed. Amikacin crosses the placental barrier and yields significant concentrations in amniotic fluid. The peak fetal serum concentration is about 16% of the peak maternal serum concentration and maternal and fetal serum half-life values are about 2 and 3.7 hours, respectively.

Indications: The short-term treatment of serious infections due to amikacin susceptible strains of Pseudomonas species, E. coli, Proteus species, Klebsiella-Enterobacter-Serratia species, Providencia species, Salmonella species, Citrobacter species and S. aureus.

Clinical studies have shown Amikin to be effective in bacteremia, septicemia (including neonatal sepsis), osteomyelitis, septic arthritis, respiratory tract, urinary tract, intra-abdominal (including peritonitis) infections and soft tissue abscesses. Appropriate bacteriological studies should be performed in order to identify and determine the susceptibility of the causative organism. Perform relevant surgical procedures when indicated.

Contraindications: Allergy to amikacin.

Warnings: Patients receiving amikacin should be under close observation and evaluation because of the potential toxicity associated with its use. Ototoxicity mainly at the auditory portion of the 8th nerve, occurs primarily in patients with preexisting or subsequently developing renal impairment and those receiving higher doses than recommended. This effect has been permanent in a significant proportion of the patients developing varying degrees of hearing loss and assessment of the renal and, where possible, auditory functions should be made before and during treatment in order that appropriate action may be taken to minimize the risk of permanent impairment.

Since the risk of ototoxicity, irreversible deafness and nephrotoxicity is increased when amikacin is used in conjunction with rapidly acting diuretic, nephrotoxic or ototoxic drugs, avoid such therapy whenever possible.

If amikacin is used concurrently with other antibacterial agents to treat mixed or superinfections, it should not be physically mixed. Each agent should be administered separately in accordance with its recommended route of administration and dosage schedule.

Precautions: Perform a pretreatment audiogram in patients with renal and pre-existing 8th nerve impairment and repeat an audiogram during therapy. If tinnitus or subjective hearing loss occurs in patients, the discontinuation of amikacin treatment should be strongly considered.

Because of high amikacin concentrations in the urinary excretory system, patients should be well hydrated to prevent damage to renal tubular cells. Kidney function should be assessed prior to starting therapy and periodically during the course of treatment.

If signs of renal damage appear, such as casts, white or red cells, and albumin, hydration should be increased and a reduction in dosage may be desirable. However, if azotemia or a progressive decrease in urine output occurs, stop treatment. One suggested method for estimating dosage in patients with known or suspected diminished renal function is to multiply the serum creatinine concentration (mg/100 mL) by 9 and to use the resulting figure as the interval (in hours) between doses; e.g.: if the creatinine concentration is 2.0 mg/100 mL, the recommended dose (7.5 mg/kg) should be administered every 18 hours. Such calculations cannot be used safely in the elderly where dosage should be based on creatinine clearance. If the creatinine clearance is available, determine the maintenance dose in elderly patients as follows: the maintenance dose to be administered every 12 hours equals the calculated loading dose multiplied by the ratio of the observed creatinine clearance to the normal creatinine clearance. Since renal function may alter appreciably during therapy, the serum creatinine should be checked frequently. Changes in the concentration necessitate changes in the dosage frequency.

Animal studies have demonstrated that amikacin is capable of producing neuromuscular blockade. Although proof that this adverse effect can be produced in man does not exist, exercise caution when anesthetic or muscle relaxant drugs are to be administered to patients receiving amikacin.

Pregnancy: Although studies in pregnant animals have not revealed any teratogenic effects, amikacin is not recommended during pregnancy unless the benefit outweighs the risk.

Cross allergenicity among aminoglycosides has been demonstrated. If superinfection occurs with the use of amikacin, institute appropriate therapy.

Adverse Effects: Nephrotoxicity: renal failure, abnormal urinalysis, including albuminuria, presence of red and white cells and granular casts; azotemia, hemoglobinuria, oliguria, elevated BUN or serum creatinine levels or a decrease in creatinine clearance. In most cases, these changes are reversible when amikacin is discontinued.

Ototoxicity: tinnitus, vertigo, dizziness, nystagmus, fullness in the ear, staggering, and partial (reversible to irreversible) deafness have been reported, usually associated with higher than recommended dosage. Rapid development of hearing loss may occur in patients with poor kidney function treated concurrently with amikacin and one of the rapidly acting diuretic agents given i.v. These have included ethacrynic acid, furosemide and mannitol.

Miscellaneous: skin rash, drug fever, nausea, headache, paresthesia. With i.m. administration, mild to severe pain at injection sites, as well as localized burning and erythema. Induration and sterile ulcers have been noted on rare occasions. The following adverse effects have been observed although it is felt they are not drug related: hematological changes including decrease in hematocrit and hemoglobin, thrombocytopenia, granulo-cytopenia/lymphocytosis, anemia and increase in eosinophils; hepatic changes, including increased serum bilirubin, serum transaminases [AST, ALT], hepatic enzymes, and alkaline phosphatase; pruritus, upper gastrointestinal bleeding, vomiting, diarrhea, fatigue, weakness, loss of appetite, weight loss, diplopia, sterile abscess, multifocal premature nodal and ventricular contractions, vasoconstriction, hypotension, seizures, Parkinson-like tremor, Bell's palsy, phlebitis and thrombophlebitis.

Overdose: Symptoms and Treatment: In the event of overdosage or toxic reactions, peritoneal dialysis or hemodialysis should be considered. These procedures are of particular importance in patients with impaired renal function.

Dosage: A maximum total adult dose of 15 g during a course of treatment by all routes of administration should not be exceeded. Treatment should not exceed 1.5 g/day and should not be administered for longer than 10 days. In the unusual circumstance, where treatment beyond 10 days or a dose larger than 1.5 g daily or 15 g total is considered, the use of amikacin should be reevaluated. If amikacin administration is prolonged, monitor renal and auditory functions daily.

In patients with impaired renal function, the interval between doses should be prolonged. The dosage interval may be calculated by the following formula: Serum creatinine (mg/100 mL)×9=dosage interval (in hours). This formula should not be used to calculate dosage for elderly patients.

If there is evidence of progressive renal dysfunction during therapy, consider discontinuation of amikacin.

Infants and neonates: In order to insure adequate therapeutic concentrations, which may be critical, while at the same time avoiding potentially toxic concentrations, serum concentrations should be monitored.

The usual dosage in adults, children and neonates is 15 mg/kg/day administered as 7.5 mg/kg every 12 hours i.m., or i.v. over a 30 to 60 minute period.

The solution for i.v. use is prepared by adding the contents of a 500 mg/2 mL vial to 250 mL of sterile diluent. Use solutions for i.v. administration within 12 hours after preparation.

Stability/Compatibility: Amikin is supplied as a colorless solution which requires no refrigeration. It is stable at room temperature for 18 months. At times the solution becomes pale yellow; this does not indicate a loss of potency. Discard dark colored solutions.

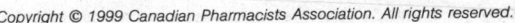

Amikin in concentrations of 0.25 or 5 mg/mL has been found to be compatible for 12 hours at 25°C in the following i.v. solutions: normal saline, 0.25% sodium chloride in water,

Amikin (cont'd)

sterile water for injection USP, 5% dextrose USP, 2.5% dextrose and 0.9% sodium chloride, 5% dextrose and 0.33% sodium chloride, 5% dextrose in Ringer's Injection, 10% invert sugar in 0.9% sodium chloride, lactated Ringer's injection USP, Ringer's injection USP, Ionosol D-CM (Abbott).

If Amikin solution is used concurrently with other antibacterial agents, it should not be physically mixed. Each agent should be administered separately in accordance with its recommended route of administration and dosage schedule.

Supplied: Each mL of aqueous solution contains: amikacin sulfate 250 mg, sodium bisulfite 0.66%, and sodium citrate 2.5% with pH adjusted to 4.5 with sulfuric acid. Nonmedicinal ingredients: sodium bisulfite 0.66% w/v (preservative), sodium citrate 2.5% w/v (buffer), sulfuric acid 7.7% w/v, water for injection. Sodium: <1 mmol (8.0 mg)/vial. 2 mL single dose vials of 500 mg.

AMINO-CERV
Milex

Amino Acids—Sodium Propionate—Urea
Cervical Therapy

Pharmacology: Methionine and cystine are amino-acids necessary for wound healing and forming of epithelial tissue.

Inositol acts as an essential growth factor and promotes epithelialization.

Urea aids in debridement, dissolves the coagulum and promotes epithelialization. Its solvent action on fibroblasts prevents the formation of excessive tissue, thus preventing stenosis when used as directed.

Benzalkonium chloride serves to lower surface tension and thus aids in spreading the medication. Along with sodium propionate it also exerts a bacteriostatic effect.

Amino-Cerv is geared to the higher pH of the healthy cervix in contrast with pH 4 vaginal preparations. With its pH factor of 5.5 it promotes faster healing of the cervix, yet will not adversely affect a healthy vagina.

Indications: For cervical treatment: cervicitis (mild), postpartum cervicitis, postpartum cervical tears and post surgical cervical procedures.

Contraindications: Deleterious side effects have not been a problem at the doses recommended. The usual precautions against allergic reactions should be observed.

Dosage: When immediate postpartum bleeding has subsided (usually from 24 to 48 hours after delivery), 1 Milex-Jector full of cream should be applied nightly for 4 weeks. In mild cervicitis (not requiring cautery or cryosurgery), 1 applicatorful of cream should be injected into the vagina nightly upon retiring for 2 weeks. A small amount should be applied immediately following a surgical cervical procedure with the exception of a cold coning procedure. One applicatorful should be injected nightly upon retiring for 2 to 4 weeks (the duration of treatment depends on extent of the surgical procedure). In each of the post surgical visits, the physician should again apply a small amount of the cream with a probe or applicator. The canal is to be completely probed on the last visit.

After cold coning, 1 applicatorful should be injected upon retiring about 24 hours after surgery and nightly thereafter for 4 weeks. During the 4 weekly office visits following cold coning, a small amount of cream should be applied with a probe or applicator into the canal by the physician. The canal is to be completely probed on the last visit.

Reasons for Variation of Directions: After most surgical procedures, cauterization, cryosurgery and laser surgery, immediate use of Amino-Cerv is indicated to aid in dissolving dead or burned tissue.

After cold coning, there is no dead tissue to slough off. Therefore, a wait of 24 hours or longer is desirable for normal healing to take place and for some fibroblasts to be laid down before applying the Amino-Cerv (which has a solvent action on both the fibroblasts and the absorbable sutures). When **nonabsorbable** sutures are used, Amino-Cerv can be used immediately.

Supplied: Each g of cream contains: urea 8.34%, sodium propionate 0.5%, methionine 0.83%, cystine 0.35%, inositol 0.83% and benzalkonium chloride buffered to pH of 5.5 in a water-miscible cream base. Tubes of 78 g with or without Milex-Jector (2 weeks' supply, 14 applications). Tubes of 142 g with Milex-Jector (4 weeks' supply, 28 applications)—hospital use only. Store at room temperature.

AMINOHIPPURATE SODIUM
MSD

Determination of Renal Function

Pharmacology: Aminohippurate Sodium (PAH) is filtered by the glomeruli and is actively secreted by the proximal tubules. At low plasma concentrations (1 to 2 mg/100 mL), an average of 90% of PAH is cleared by the kidneys from the renal blood stream in a single circulation. It is ideally suited for measurement of ERPF since it has a high clearance, is essentially nontoxic at the plasma concentrations reached with recommended doses, and its analytical determination is relatively simple and accurate.

PAH is also used to measure the functional capacity of the renal tubular secretory mechanism or transport maximum (Tm_{PAH}). This is accomplished by elevating the plasma concentration to levels (40 to 60 mg/100 mL) sufficient to saturate the maximal capacity of the tubular cells to secrete PAH.

Inulin clearance is generally measured during Tm_{PAH} determinations since glomerular filtration rate (GFR) must be known before calculations of secretory Tm measurements can be done (see Dosage, Calculations).

Indications: Estimation of Effective Renal Plasma Flow (ERPF).

Measurement of the functional capacity of the renal tubular secretory mechanism.

Contraindications: Hypersensitivity to this product or to its components.

Precautions: General: I.V. solutions must be given with caution to patients with low cardiac reserve, since a rapid increase in plasma volume can precipitate congestive heart failure.

For measurement of ERPF, small doses of PAH are used. However, in research procedures to measure Tm_{PAH}, high plasma levels are required to saturate the capacity of the tubular cells. During these procedures the i.v. administration of PAH solutions should be carried out slowly and with caution. The patient should be continuously observed for any adverse reactions.

Children: Safety and effectiveness in children have not been established.

Pregnancy: Animal reproduction studies have not been done with PAH. It is also not known whether PAH can cause fetal harm when given to a pregnant woman or can affect reproduction capacity. PAH should be given to a pregnant woman only if clearly needed.

Lactation: It is not known whether this drug is excreted in human milk. Because many drugs are excreted in human milk, caution should be exercised when PAH is administered to a nursing woman.

Drug Interactions: Renal clearance measurements of PAH cannot be made with any significant accuracy in patients receiving sulfonamides, procaine or thiazolesulfone. These compounds interfere with chemical color development essential to the analytical procedures.

Probenecid depresses tubular secretion of certain weak acids such as PAH. Therefore, patients receiving probenecid will have erroneously low ERPF and Tm_{PAH} values.

Carcinogenesis, Mutagenesis, Impairment of Fertility: Long-term studies in animals have not been done to evaluate any effects upon fertility or carcinogenic potential of PAH.

Adverse Effects: Vasomotor disturbances, flushing, tingling, nausea, vomiting and cramps may occur.

Patients may have a sensation of warmth or the desire to defecate or urinate during or shortly following initiation of infusion.

Overdose: Symptoms and Treatment: The i.v. LD_{50} in female mice is 7.22 g/kg.

Dosage: For i.v. use only.

Clearance measurements using single injection techniques are generally inaccurate, particularly in the measurement of ERPF. For this reason, i.v. infusions at fixed rates are used to sustain the plasma PAH concentration at the desired level.

To measure ERPF, the concentration of PAH in the plasma should be maintained at 2 mg/100 mL, which can be achieved with a priming dose of 6 to 10 mg/kg and an infusion dose of 10 to 24 mg/min.

As a research procedure for the measurement of Tm_{PAH}, the plasma level of PAH must be sufficient to saturate the capacity of the tubular secretory cells. Concentrations of from 40 to 60 mg/100 mL are usually necessary.

Technical details of these tests may be found in references available from the manufacturer.

Parenteral drug products should be inspected visually for particulate matter and discoloration prior to use, whenever solution and container permit. **Note:** The normal color range for this product is a colorless to yellow/brown solution. The efficacy is not affected by color changes within this range.

Calculations: Effective Renal Plasma Flow (ERPF): The clearance of PAH, which is extracted almost completely from the plasma during its passage through the renal circulation, constitutes a measure of ERPF. Hence:

$$ERPF = \frac{U_{PAH}V}{P_{PAH}}$$

Where U_{PAH} = concentration of PAH (mg/mL) in the urine

V = rate of urine excretion (mL/min), and

P_{PAH} = plasma concentration of PAH (mg/mL).

Example: U_{PAH} = 8.0 mg/mL

V = 1.5 mL/min

P_{PAH} = 0.02 mg/mL

$$ERPF = \frac{8.0 \times 1.5}{0.02} = 600 \text{ mL/min}$$

Based on PAH clearance studies, the normal values for ERPF are: men 675±150 mL/min and women 595±125 mL/min.

Maximum Tubular Secretory (Tm_{PAH}) Mechanism: The quantity of PAH secreted by the tubules (Tm_{PAH}) is given by the difference between the total rate of excretion ($U_{PAH}V$) and the quantity filtered by the glomeruli ($GFR \times P_{PAH}$). Hence: $Tm_{PAH} = U_{PAH}V - (GFR \times P_{PAH} \times 0.83)$.

The factor, 0.83, corrects for that portion of PAH which is bound to plasma protein and hence is unfilterable.

Example: U_{PAH} = 9.55 mg/mL

V = 16.68 mL/min

GFR = 120 mL/min

P_{PAH} = 0.60 mg/mL

Then Tm_{PAH} = 9.55×16.68−(120×0.60×0.83)

= 100 mg/min

Average normal values of Tm_{PAH}, are 80 to 90 mg/min.

The value of the expression $U_{PAH}V$, used in calculations of ERPF and Tm_{PAH}, may be found by determining the amount of PAH in a measured volume of urine excreted within a specific period of time.

These calculations are based on a body surface area of 1.73 m². Corrections for variations in surface area are made by multiplying the values obtained for ERPF and Tm_{PAH} by $\frac{1.73}{A}$, where A is the subject surface area.

Supplied: Each 10 mL of sterile, nonpreserved aqueous solution for injection, with a pH of 6.7 to 7.6 contains: aminohippurate sodium 2 g (20%), sodium hydroxide to adjust pH and water for injection, q.s. Vials of 10 mL. Avoid storage at temperatures below −20°C and above 40°C. **Discard any unused portion.**

AMINOPHYLLINE Ⓟ
General Monograph, CPhA

see THEOPHYLLINE and its Salts

AMINOPHYLLINE Ⓟ
Abbott

Bronchodilator

Supplied: Each mL contains: 25 or 50 mg aminophylline. Nonmedicinal ingredients: ethylenediamine. Ampuls of 10 mL.

AMINOSALICYLATE SODIUM Ⓟ
General Monograph, CPhA

see PAS SODIUM

For a list of Canadian manufacturers who do not use tartrazine in their products, see the CLIN-INFO SECTION.

AMITRIPTYLINE

General Monograph, CPhA

Antidepressant

This monograph has been compiled by CPhA. It may contain information different from that approved by Therapeutic Products Programme, Health Canada, and the pharmaceutical manufacturers' approval has not been requested.

Pharmacology: Amitriptyline is a tertiary amine tricyclic antidepressant. The manner in which the tricyclic antidepressants exert their clinical antidepressant effect is uncertain but they have been shown to block, in different degrees, the reuptake of various neurotransmitters including serotonin and norepinephrine at the neuronal membrane. This action potentiates the effects of these neurotransmitters.

Amitriptyline exhibits strong anticholinergic activity, cardiovascular effects including orthostatic hypotension, changes in heart rhythm and conduction, and a lowering of the seizure threshold. As with other antidepressants, several weeks of therapy may be required in order to realize the full clinical benefit of amitriptyline.

Pharmacokinetics: Amitriptyline is well absorbed from the gastrointestinal tract with peak plasma concentrations occurring between 2 and 12 hours after administration. Bioavailability of the drug is between 30 and 60% due to extensive first pass metabolism of the drug in the liver. Amitriptyline is demethylated in the liver to its primary active metabolite, nortriptyline.

Amitriptyline is over 90% protein bound. Its elimination half-life varies from 10 to 50 hours, with an average of 15 hours. Within 24 hours, approximately 25 to 50% of a dose of amitriptyline is excreted in the urine as inactive metabolites; small amounts are excreted in the bile.

Routine serum drug concentration monitoring is not warranted but may be useful to assess compliance or suspected toxicity. Recommended therapeutic trough levels, i.e., the sum of both amitriptyline and its metabolite nortriptyline, vary widely and range from 260 to 900 nmol/L (60 to 250 ng/mL). Ideally, the trough level should be taken 12 hours following administration of the last dose.

Indications: In the pharmacologic management of depressive illness.

Amitriptyline may be used in depressed phase of bipolar affective disorder or in melancholic or psychotic depression. The use of amitriptyline in patients with bipolar illness may precipitate a hypomanic or manic state.

Patients with transient mood disturbances or normal grief reaction are not expected to benefit from tricyclic antidepressants.

Although not a labelled indication, amitriptyline and other antidepressants are widely used in the management of chronic nonmalignant pain (e.g., post-herpetic neuralgia, fibromyalgia).

Contraindications: Amitriptyline is contraindicated in patients who have shown hypersensitivity to the drug. Cross-sensitivity between amitriptyline and related tricyclic antidepressants is possible.

Hyperpyretic crises, severe convulsions, and deaths have occurred in patients receiving tricyclic antidepressants and MAO inhibiting drugs simultaneously; however, patients with refractory depression have received combination therapy without significant adverse effects, under certain strict conditions and under the supervision of prescribers experienced with such therapy.

Amitriptyline is not recommended during the acute recovery phase following myocardial infarction or in the presence of congestive heart failure (see Precautions).

Warnings: Anticholinergic Effects: Because of its strong anticholingergic properties, amitriptyline must be used with caution in patients with urinary retention, benign prostatic hypertrophy, angle-closure glaucoma or increased intraocular pressure.

Cardiovascular: Orthostatic hypotension, arrhythmias and conduction abnormalities have occurred during therapy with amitriptyline. Caution is advised if tricyclic antidepressants are used in patients with pre-existing cardiovascular disease.

Sedation: Patients should be warned about the possible sedation and mental or motor impairment associated with amitriptyline therapy and advised of the potential danger of operating machinery or driving a motor vehicle if this occurs.

Suicide: The potential for attempted suicide must always be considered in depressed patients. It is considered prudent to provide a limited supply of amitriptyline to patients known to be suicidal.

Precautions: Bipolar Illness: The use of antidepressants during the depressed phase of bipolar illness may precipitate a hypomanic or manic state.

CNS: Sedation is the most common CNS effect of tricylic antidepressants. Other reactions have occurred such as agitation, confusion, nightmares, restlessness, hostility, exacerbation of psychosis and extrapyramidal symptoms. Elderly patients may be more susceptible to some of these effects.

Hematologic: Rarely, blood dyscrasias have occurred in patients taking tricyclic antidepressants. A leukocyte and differential count should be performed in patients who develop symptoms such as sore throat and fever while taking these drugs.

Hypersensitivity: Allergic reactions have included rash, edema, drug fever and photosensitivity. The possibility of cross-sensitivity among the tricyclic agents must be considered.

Seizures: Tricyclic antidepressants can lower the seizure threshold and should be used with caution in patients with a history of seizures or those who may be predisposed to seizures.

Thyroid: Tricyclic antidepressants should be used with caution in patients who are hyperthyroid or receiving thyroid medication, because of the possibility of cardiac arrhythmias.

Drug Interactions: Anticholinergics: Concurrent use of tricyclic antidepressants and other drugs with anticholinergic activity may necessitate dosage adjustments to minimize the additive effects. Elderly patients may be particularly susceptible to excessive anticholinergic effects.

Antihypertensives: Tricyclic antidepressants may antagonize the antihypertensive effects of clonidine or guanethidine.

Carbamazepine: Plasma concentrations of tricyclic antidepressants may be decreased because of induction of hepatic enzymes by carbamazepine.

Cimetidine: Plasma concentrations of amitriptyline may be increased because of inhibition of hepatic enzymes by cimetidine.

CNS Depressants: The concomitant use of tricylcic antidepressants and other CNS depressants may result in additive depressant effects.

Lithium: There is some evidence that concurrent use of lithium and tricyclic antidepressants may increase the risk of neurotoxicity, particularly in the elderly. It has been suggested that reducing the dose of lithium in elderly patients may reduce the risk of neurotoxicity without compromosing its clinical effect. Elderly patients should be monitored carefully for signs of neurotoxicity (e.g., tremor, ataxia, seizures) when on combined therapy.

MAO Inhibitors: Because of the additive serotonergic effects, combination therapy with tricyclic antidepressants and MAO inbibitors is not recommended, except under certain conditions (see Contraindications).

Sympathomimetics: Tricyclic antidepressants can significantly enhance the pressor response to norepinephrine and may ptoentiate the cardiovascular effects (e.g., arrhythmia) of sympathomimetics in general.

Selective Serotonin Reuptake Inhibitors (SSRIs): Amitriptyline toxicity may occur if used concurrently with fluoxetine, because of inhibition of the hepatic mirosomal enzyme responsible for the metabolism of amitriptyline. Reduction of amitriptyline dose by as much as 75% may be necessary. The potential for this interaction occurring with other SSRIs must be considered. Because of the extremely long elimination half-life of fluoxetine, the potential for interacting with other drugs remains for several weeks after its discontinuation.

Thyroid Medications: Concomitant use of amitriptyline and levothyroxine may potentiate the cardiovascular effects (e.g., arrhythmias) of both drugs.

Pregnancy: Amitriptyline has not been proven to be without risk to the developing fetus; however, it is often continued during pregnancy when the need to treat an underlying depression justifies the potential risk to the fetus.

Lactation: Amitriptyline and its metabolite are excreted into breast milk, although levels have not been detected in infants' serum. Amitriptyline's effect in breast-feeding is unknown.

Children: Not recommended for treatment of depression in children under 12 years of age.

Geriatrics: Elderly patients may be more susceptible to the anticholinergic, cardiovascular and CNS effects of tricyclic antidepressants. Lower initial dosages with more gradual increases are warranted.

Adverse Effects: The more common adverse reactions involve anticholinergic effects such as dry mouth, disturbances of visual accommodation, constipation and urinary retention. Also commonly seen are light headedness, drowsiness, increased perspiration and mild tremors as well as insomnia. Adverse reactions of the cardiovascular system may be much more serious; however, these occur less frequently.

Note: Included in this listing are a few adverse reactions reported with other tricyclics but not specifically with amitriptyline. Pharmacological similarities among the tricyclic antidepressant drugs require that each reaction be considered when amitriptyline is administered.

Autonomic: Frequently: dry mouth and rarely associated sublingual adenitis, blurred vision, disturbances of accommodation, constipation, perspiration, flushing. Occasionally: delayed micturition, dilation of the urinary tract. In isolated cases: mydriasis, glaucoma, paralytic ileus, urinary frequency.

Behavioral: Occasionally: confusional states (especially in the elderly) with hallucinations, disorientation, delusions, anxiety, agitation, insomnia, restlessness, nightmares, hypomania, mania, exacerbation of psychosis, decrease in memory, feeling of unreality. In isolated cases: feeling of weakness, aggressiveness.

Cardiovascular: Frequently: hypotension, particularly orthostatic hypotension with associated vertigo, tachycardia, ECG changes (including flattening or inversion of T waves). Occasionally: arrhythmia, disturbances in cardiac conduction, palpitation, syncope. In isolated cases: hypertension, congestive heart failure, myocardial infarction, heart block, asystole, stroke, peripheral vasospastic reactions.

CNS: Frequently: drowsiness, fatigue, tremors. Occasionally: insomnia, dizziness, headache, paresthesia (numbness, tingling sensation, symptoms suggestive of peripheral neuropathy). Rarely: seizures. In isolated cases: tinnitus, incoordination, ataxia, alterations in EEG patterns, extrapyramidal symptoms, myoclonus, speech disorders.

Endocrine: Frequently: weight gain. Occasionally: increased or decreased libido, impotence. In isolated cases: gynecomastia in the male, breast enlargement and galactorrhea in the female, testicular swelling, elevation or depression of blood sugar levels, weight loss, syndrome of inappropriate antidiuretic hormone secretion (SIADH).

Hematologic: In isolated cases: agranulocytosis, eosinophilia, leukopenia, purpura and thrombocytopenia may occur as an idiosyncratic response.

Hypersensitivity: Occasionally: skin rash, urticaria. In isolated cases: petechiae, itching, photosensitization (avoid excessive exposure to sunlight), edema (general or of face and tongue), drug fever, obstructive jaundice, nasal congestion, alopecia, allergic alveolitis (pneumonia) with or without eosinophilia.

Gastrointestinal: Occasionally: nausea, vomiting, anorexia. Rarely: elevated transaminases. In isolated cases: diarrhea, bitter taste, stomatitis, epigastric distress, abdominal cramps, black tongue, dysphagia, increased salivation, hepatitis with or without jaundice.

Withdrawal: If treatment is terminated abruptly, withdrawal symptoms, such as gastrointestinal discomfort, nervousness, anxiety and muscle twitching may occur.

Overdose: Symptoms: Overdose of tricyclic antidepressants may be manifest with doses as small as 50 mg in a child. Of patients who are alive at initial presentation, a mortality rate of between 0 and 15% has been reported. Symptoms of overdose of tricyclic antidepressants may begin within several hours of oral ingestion. Symptoms and signs may include: blurred vision, confusion, restlessness, dizziness, hyporeflexes, dilated pupils, fever, rapid heart rate, decreased bowel sounds, dry mouth, inability to void, myoclonic jerks, seizures, respiratory depression, myoglobinuric renal failure, nystagmus, ataxia, dysarthria, choreoathetosis, coma, hypotension and cardiac arrhythmias. An effect on cardiac conduction similar to that of quinidine may be seen with slowing of conduction, prolongation of the QRS complex and QT intervals, right bundle branch and AV block, ventricular tachyarrhythmias (including torsades de pointes and fibrillation) and death. Prolongation of the QRS duration to more than 0.1 seconds is predictive of more severe toxicity. The absence of sinus tachycardia does not ensure a benign course. Hypotension may be caused by vasodilation, central and peripheral alpha adrenergic blockade, and cardiac depression. In an otherwise healthy young person, prolonged resuscitation may be effective.

Treatment: In managing overdose, consider the possibility of multiple drug overdose, interactions among drugs, and unusual drug kinetics. Protect the patient's airway and support ventilation and perfusion. Meticulously monitor and maintain the patient's vital signs, blood gases, serum electrolytes, and acid-base balance. Absorption of drugs from the gastrointestinal tract may be decreased by giving activated charcoal. The usual dose in adults is 50 to 100 g and in children 1 to 2 g/kg. One dose of a saline or sorbitol cathartic may be administered with the charcoal or separately. If gastric lavage is performed, an endotracheal tube with cuff inflated should be in place to prevent aspiration of gastric contents.

Amitriptyline (cont'd)

Ventricular arrhythmias, especially when accompanied by lengthened QRS intervals, may respond to alkalinization by hyperventilation or administration of sodium bicarbonate. It is important to monitor and manage serum electrolyte levels. Refractory arrhythmias may respond to propranolol, bretylium or lidocaine. Propranolol should be used with caution. Its negative inotropic effect may cause hypotension. Quinidine and procainamide usually should not be used because they may exacerbate arrhythmias and conduction already slowed by the overdosage.

Seizures may respond to diazepam. Phenytoin has pharmacologic properties that may be helpful in dealing with both the seizures and cardiac rhythm disturbances of tricyclic antidepressant overdose. Although the prophylactic use of phenytoin has been suggested, it is not of proven value.

In some patients, physostigmine may be used to antagonize some of the effects of tricyclic antidepressant overdose, such as atrial tachycardia, gut immotility, myoclonic jerks and somnolence. It is less effective for seizures and ventricular arrhythmias. When giving physostigmine, the patient's condition should be carefully monitored and ventilation and cardiac rhythm should be supported. Cholinergic toxicity from physostigmine may include bronchospasm, bronchorrhea, bradycardia, asystole, diaphoresis, incontinence and seizures. Most clinicians caution against the routine use of physostigmine in tricyclic antidepressant overdose and many feel it should be reserved only for life-threatening anticholinergic symptoms not responding to other measures. If physostigmine is used, give it slowly because rapid injection may cause seizures. The effects of physostigmine may be short-lived; repeated doses may lead to continued improvement.

Diuresis and dialysis remove little of the tricyclic antidepressant present in the body of a patient who has taken an overdose. Hemoperfusion is of unproven benefit. The patient who has taken a tricyclic overdose should be monitored closely, at least until the QRS duration is normal.

Dosage: Depression: Dosage should be initiated at a low level and increased gradually, noting carefully the clinical response and any evidence of adverse effects.

Initial dose for adults: 25 mg 3 times daily. The dose may be gradually increased, if necessary, to the level providing maximal clinical benefit with minimal toxicity, to a maximum of 300 mg daily.

Hospitalized patients may require higher initial or overall dosage.

Adolescents: An initial dose of 10 mg 3 times daily with 20 mg at bedtime is recommended. The dose may be increased to a maximum of 100 mg daily, either in divided doses or as a single bedtime dose.

Geriatrics: Recommended initial dose is 10 to 25 mg at bedtime. May be increased by 10 to 25 mg daily, at weekly intervals, up to 150 mg daily.

Maintenance: When satisfactory improvement has been achieved, dosage should be reduced to the lowest amount that will maintain relief of symptoms. The usual maintenance dose is 50 to 100 mg/day in divided doses; however, in suitable patients, the total daily dosage may be given in a single dose, preferably at bedtime. It is appropriate to continue maintenance therapy throughout the active phase of the depression and for the expected duration of the depressive episode, in order to lessen the possibility of relapse.

Chronic Nonmalignant Pain (see Indications): 10 to 25 mg at bedtime or 2 to 3 hours before bedtime.

Reviewed 1999

AMOBARBITAL ◇

General Monograph, CPhA

see BARBITURATES

The database, reporting form and procedures for monitoring adverse events from vaccines are separate from those of other drug products. See the CLIN-INFO SECTION for a description of the program and a copy of the reporting form.

AMOXICILLIN Ⓟ

General Monograph, CPhA

Amoxycillin

Antibiotic

This monograph has been compiled by CPhA. It may contain information different from that approved by Therapeutic Products Programme, Health Canada, and the pharmaceutical manufacturers' approval has not been requested.

Pharmacology: Amoxicillin, a semisynthetic penicillin of the aminopenicillin group, is bactericidal against sensitive organisms. It acts through the inhibition of mucopeptide synthesis in the bacterial cell wall.

The spectrum of activity of amoxicillin includes H. influenzae, E. coli, P. mirabilis, Salmonella and some Shigella species while also retaining activity against penicillin-sensitive gram-positive bacteria (see Penicillin G/Penicillin V, General Monograph). However, many Enterobacteriaceae, H. Influenzae, Salmonella and Shigella species are resistant to amoxicillin because these organisms produce beta-lactamase. Amoxicillin has the same in vitro activity as ampicillin but has slightly better activity against E. faecalis, E. coli and Salmonella species. Combining amoxicillin with a ß-lactamase inhibitor such as clavulanic acid effectively broadens its spectrum of activity to include many strains of ß-lactamase-producing bacteria.

Pharmacokinetics: Amoxicillin is rapidly absorbed by the gastrointestinal tract after oral administration and is stable in the presence of gastric acid. Peak serum concentrations are usually attained within 1 to 2 hours following oral administration and are generally 2 to 2.5 times greater than those obtained with an equivalent dose of oral ampicillin. Amoxicillin diffuses readily into most body tissue and fluids, with the exception of the cerebrospinal fluid, although higher concentrations of the drug may be attained in patients with inflamed meninges. Amoxicillin is not highly protein bound. Its elimination half-life ranges from 0.7 to 1.4 hours in patients with normal renal function. Amoxicillin is partially metabolized to microbiologically inactive metabolites and both are then rapidly excreted in urine. Small amounts of the compounds are excreted in feces and bile.

Indications: Amoxicillin is indicated for the treatment of: bronchitis, acute otitis media, pharyngitis, pneumonia, sinusitis and urinary tract infections caused by susceptible organisms; chlamydial infections in pregnant women who cannot tolerate erythromycin; gastritis and peptic ulcer disease caused by H. pylori (in combination with metronidazole and bismuth subsalicylate); Lyme disease caused by B. burgdorferi; typhoid fever caused by S. typhi.

Amoxicillin is recommended for prophylaxis against endocarditis in patients undergoing certain dental, oral, upper respiratory tract or esophageal procedures, who have any of the following conditions: congenital cardiac malformations, rheumatic and other acquired valvular lesions, prosthetic heart valves, previous history of bacterial endocarditis, hypertrophic cardiomyopathy, surgically constructed systemic pulmonary shunts or conduits, mitral valve prolapse with valvular regurgitation or mitral valve prolapse without valvular regurgitation but associated with thickening and/or redundancy of the valve leaflets. Amoxicillin is also included in prophylactic regimens for certain genitourinary and non-esophageal gastrointestinal procedures.

Contraindications: History of allergic reaction to penicillins.

Warnings: Serious and occasionally fatal hypersensitivity reactions have been reported in patients on penicillin therapy. Although anaphylaxis is more frequent following parenteral therapy, it has occurred in patients on oral penicillins. These reactions are more apt to occur in individuals with a history of sensitivity to multiple allergens.

Careful inquiry should be made concerning previous hypersensitivity reactions to penicillins, other β-lactam antibiotics or other allergens. The incidence of cross-sensitivity between penicillins and other ß-lactam antibiotics such as cephalosporins or carbapenems is not precisely known. The possibility of cross-sensitivity must be considered in all patients reporting an allergic reaction to a ß-lactam antibiotic.

If an allergic reaction occurs, discontinue amoxicillin and institute appropriate therapy. Serious anaphylactic reactions require immediate emergency treatment with epinephrine, oxygen, i.v. corticosteroids and airway management, including intubation, as indicated.

Precautions: If suprainfections with fungal or bacterial pathogens occur (usually involving Enterobacter, Candida or Pseudomonas), amoxicillin should be discontinued and appropriate therapy instituted.

Because amoxicillin is excreted mostly by the kidney, dosage reduction is important in patients with a creatinine clearance less than 0.5 mL/s and it should be reduced in proportion to the degree of loss of renal function (see Dosage).

Amoxicillin should not be used if infectious mononucleosis is suspected due to an increased incidence of maculopapular rash (see Adverse Effects).

Drug Interactions: Concurrent use of probenecid or other inhibitors of the renal acid secretory system decrease renal secretion of amoxicillin and increase and prolong blood amoxicillin concentrations. Allopurinol may increase the possibility of skin rash. Tetracyclines, chloramphenicol and other bacteriostatic drugs may interfere with the bactericidal effects of amoxicillin.

Whether amoxicillin decreases the effectiveness of oral contraceptives is controversial. Some clinicians recommend adding an alternative method of contraception for the duration of the cycle when amoxicillin is taken.

Pregnancy: Amoxicillin readily crosses the placenta. Amoxicillin's safety in the treatment of infections during pregnancy has not yet been established. However harmful effects have not been documented. The benefits of amoxicillin therapy must be weighed against its possible hazards to the mother and child.

Lactation: Amoxicillin appears in milk in low concentrations. See Drugs in Lactation in the Clin-Info Section for more information.

Adverse Effects: Gastrointestinal: nausea, vomiting, diarrhea, anorexia, epigastric distress and gastritis. Black hairy tongue, glossitis and stomatitis have also been noted. Diarrhea is generally less frequent than with ampicillin. Antibiotic-associated pseudomembranous colitis has been reported. Severe abdominal pain and bloody diarrhea associated with acute, transient enterocolitis, but without evidence of pseudomembranous colitis, has also been reported.

Renal: Acute interstitial nephritis has been reported rarely.

Hematologic: Anemia, thrombocytopenia, thrombocytopenic purpura, eosinophilia, leukopenia, neutropenia and agranulocytosis have been reported during therapy with amoxicillin. These reactions are usually reversible on discontinuation of therapy.

Hypersensitivity: A morbilliform, erythematous, urticarial rash, similar to those reported with other penicillins, may occur. In addition, aminopenicillins may cause an erythematous, maculopapular rash which may or may not be immunologically mediated. The overall incidence of rash in patients taking amoxicillin is 1.4 to 10%, with greater than 65% being of the maculopapular type.

Hepatic: Moderate rise in serum aspartate transferase (AST), alkaline phosphatase and lactic dehydrogenase has been noted, but the significance of these findings is unknown.

Overdose: Symptoms: Serious toxicity is unlikely following large doses of amoxicillin. Acute ingestion of large doses of amoxicillin may cause nausea, vomiting, diarrhea and abdominal pain. Acute oliguric renal failure and hematuria may occur following large doses.

Treatment: Empty stomach only if a very large amount has been ingested and if the patient is conscious and not experiencing seizures. Activated charcoal may be administered to decrease further absorption. Monitor fluid and electrolyte status and renal function in patients with severe vomiting and/or diarrhea.

Dosage: Amoxicillin is stable in the presence of gastric acid and may be given without regard to meals. For upper respiratory tract infections, including otitis media, due to susceptible strains of streptococci, nonpenicillinase producing staphylococci or H. influenzae, genitourinary tract infections caused by susceptible strains of E. coli, P. mirabilis or E. faecalis, or skin and soft tissue infections involving susceptible streptococci, nonpenicillinase-producing staphylococci, or E. coli: Adults and children $>$20 kg: 250 mg every 8 hours. Children $<$20 kg: 20 mg/kg/day in divided doses every 8 hours, not to exceed the recommended adult dose.

For severe infections or those caused by less susceptible organisms: 500 mg every 8 hours for adults and children $>$20 kg; 40 mg/kg/day in divided doses every 8 hours for children $<$20 kg, not to exceed the recommended adult dosage.

For lower respiratory tract infections due to streptococci, nonpenicillinase-producing staphylococci or H. influenzae: Adults and children $>$20 kg: 500 mg every 8 hours. Children $<$20 kg: 40 mg/kg/day in divided doses every 8 hours, not to exceed the recommended adult dosage.

Amoxicillin is not included in the Canadian guidelines for treatment of N. gonorrhoeae (Can Commun Dis Rep 1995; 21 Suppl 4). However, some clinicians recommend it for acute, uncomplicated gonorrhea when the infecting strain has been tested and found to be susceptible: Adults and children >45 kg: 3 g as a single dose; 1 g of oral probenecid should be administered concomitantly, as well as appropriate therapy (doxycycline or tetracycline) for presumptive or proven infection with C. trachomatis. Children <45 kg: a single 50 mg/kg dose of amoxicillin (maximum 3 g) given with a single 25 mg/kg (up to 1 g) dose of probenecid. However, probenecid is not recommended in children under 2 years of age. Appropriate therapy of presumptive or proven infection with C. trachomatis should be included as well.

For prophylaxis of bacterial endocarditis in selected patients: Adults: 2 g 1 hour before the procedure. Children: 50 mg/kg 1 hour before the procedure, to a maximum of 2 g. For more information, see Endocarditis Prophylaxis in the Clin-Info section.

In chronic urinary tract infections, frequent bacteriologic and clinical appraisals are necessary. Do not use doses smaller than those recommended above for the treatment of genitourinary tract infections. In persistent infections, therapy may be required for several weeks, sometimes at higher doses than recommended above. Concurrent bacteriologic sensitivity monitoring is recommended. It may be necessary to continue clinical and/or bacteriologic follow up for several months after cessation of therapy.

For treatment of H. pylori infection in adults with associated peptic ulcer disease, amoxicillin 1 g twice daily is given for 7 days with a proton pump inhibitor plus clarithromycin.

For most infections, except gonorrhea, continue treatment for a minimum of 48 to 72 hours beyond the time the patient becomes asymptomatic or evidence of bacterial eradication has been obtained. Although natural penicillins are generally preferred, if amoxicillin is used in the treatment of infections caused by group A beta-hemolytic streptococci, at least 10 days of treatment is recommended to prevent acute rheumatic fever or glomerulonephritis.

Dosage in Renal Failure: ClCr 0.83 to 0.17 mL/s: increase dosing interval from 8 hours to 12 hours; ClCr <0.17 mL/s: increase dosing interval to 12 to 24 hours.

Hemodialysis: 250 to 500 mg orally every 16 to 24 hours. An additional 250 mg may be given after each dialysis period.

Reviewed 1999

AMOXIL® ℞

Wyeth-Ayerst

Amoxicillin Trihydrate

Antibiotic

Supplied: Capsules: 250 mg: Each red and gold dry powder capsule, imprinted with strength, contains: amoxicillin trihydrate equivalent to amoxicillin 250 mg. Nonmedicinal ingredients: lactose anhydrous (may be added), magnesium stearate and magnesium sulfate anhydrous. Empty capsule: D&C Red 33, D&C Yellow 10, FD&C Blue 1, FD&C Red 3, FD&C Yellow 6, gelatin, silicon dioxide, sodium lauryl sulfate and titanium dioxide. Energy: 0.84 kJ (0.2 kcal). Alcohol-, gluten-, sulfites- and tartrazine-free. Bottles of 100 and 500.

500 mg: Each red and gold dry powder capsule, imprinted with strength, contains: amoxicillin trihydrate equivalent to amoxicillin 500 mg. Nonmedicinal ingredients: lactose anhydrous (may be added), magnesium stearate and magnesium sulfate anhydrous. Empty capsule: D&C Red 33, D&C Yellow 10, FD&C Blue 1, FD&C Red 3, FD&C Yellow 6, gelatin, silicon dioxide, sodium lauryl sulfate and titanium dioxide. Energy: 1.67 kJ (0.4 kcal). Alcohol-, gluten-, sulfites- and tartrazine-free. Bottles of 100 and 250.

Chewable Tablets: 125 mg: Each oval, mottled, rose colored tablet with cherry flavor, embossed AMOXIL with 2 score lines on one side and 125 on the other, contains: amoxicillin trihydrate equivalent to 125 mg of amoxicillin. Nonmedicinal ingredients: aminoacetic acid, citric acid anhydrous, Dye D&C Red 36, Dye D&C Red 7 Lake Conc, flavor banana imit., flavor cherry imit., magnesium stearate, mannitol, sodium cyclamate, sucrose extra ground starch free and syloid. Energy: 2.1 kJ (0.5 kcal). Sodium: <1 mmol (0.3543 mg). Alcohol-, gluten-, lactose-, parabens-, sulfites- and tartrazine-free. Bottles of 100 and 500.

250 mg: Each oval, mottled, rose colored tablet with cherry flavor, embossed AMOXIL with 1 score line on one side and 250 on the other, contains: amoxicillin trihydrate equivalent to 250 mg of amoxicillin. Nonmedicinal ingredients: aminoacetic acid, citric acid anhydrous, Dye D&C Red 36, Dye D&C Red 7 Lake Conc, flavor banana imit., flavor cherry imit., magnesium stearate, mannitol, sodium cyclamate, sucrose extra ground starch free and syloid. Energy: 4.2 kJ (1 kcal). Sodium: <1 mmol (0.7086 mg). Alcohol-, gluten-, lactose-, parabens-, sulfites- and tartrazine-free. Bottles of 100 and 500.

Oral Suspension: 125 mg/5 mL: After reconstitution, each 5 mL of strawberry flavored suspension contains: amoxicillin trihydrate equivalent to 125 mg of amoxicillin. Nonmedicinal ingredients: citric acid anhydrous, flavor strawberry imit., seaspen, sodium benzoate, sodium carboxymethylcellulose, sodium cyclamate, sucrose granulated verifine and syloid. Energy: 8.37 kJ (2.0 kcal)/5 mL. Sodium: <1 mmol (5.85 mg)/5 mL. Alcohol-, gluten-, lactose-, parabens-, sulfites- and tartrazine-free. Bottles of 75, 100 and 150 mL. Keep bottle tightly closed. The reconstituted suspension is stable for 7 days at room temperature (20°C) or 14 days refrigerated at 4.5°C.

250 mg/5 mL: After reconstitution, each 5 mL of bubble gum flavored suspension contains: amoxicillin trihydrate equivalent to 250 mg of amoxicillin. Nonmedicinal ingredients: citric acid anhydrous, Dye D&C Yellow 10, Dye FD&C Yellow 6, flavor bubble gum imit., seaspen, sodium benzoate, sodium carboxymethylcellulose, sodium cyclamate, sucrose granulated verifine and syloid. Energy: 6.7 kJ (1.6 kcal)/5 mL. Sodium: <1 mmol (5.95 mg)/5 mL. Alcohol-, gluten-, lactose-, parabens-, sulfites- and tartrazine-free. Bottles of 75, 100 and 150 mL. Keep bottle tightly closed. The reconstituted suspension is stable for 7 days at 20°C or 14 days at 4.5°C.

(Shown in Product Recognition Section)

AMPHOJEL®

Axcan Pharma

Aluminum Hydroxide

Antacid

Supplied: Liquid: Each 5 mL of white, mint-flavored, sugar-free suspension contains: aluminum hydroxide 320 mg. Nonmedicinal ingredients: artificial flavor, glycerin, methocel, methylparaben, peppermint oil, propylparaben, simethicone emulsion, sodium cyclamate, sorbitol solution and spearmint oil. Energy: 12.54 kJ (3.0 kcal). Tartrazine-free. Bottles of 350 and 500 mL.

Tablets: Each white, mint-flavored, scored tablet, imprinted AMPHOJEL on one face, contains: aluminum hydroxide 600 mg. Nonmedicinal ingredients: artificial flavor, calcium cyclamate, magnesium stearate, mannitol powder, microcrystalline cellulose, peppermint oil, spearmint oil, starch, vanilla flavor and talc. Energy: 6.28 kJ (1.5 kcal) and has an antacid effect equal to 10 mL of Amphojel liquid. Gluten- and tartrazine-free. Bottles of 50.

AMPICILLIN SODIUM ℞

Bioniche

Antibiotic

Supplied: Each dry filled vial contains: sterile ampicillin 250 mg (as the sodium salt). pH range: 8 to 10. Vials of 10 mL. Trays of 25. Store vials at room temperature (15 to 30°C). Reconstituted solutions should be used within 1 hour of reconstitution and should not be frozen.

AMPICIN® ℞

Bristol

Ampicillin Sodium

Antibiotic

Pharmacology: Ampicillin is a broad-spectrum penicillin, indicated for the treatment of a wide range of bacterial infections caused by ampicillin-sensitive organisms.

Ampicillin is similar to benzyl penicillin in its bactericidal action against susceptible organisms during the stage of active multiplication. It acts through the inhibition of cell wall mucopeptide biosynthesis. Ampicillin has a broad spectrum of bactericidal activity against many gram-positive and gram-negative aerobic and anaerobic bacteria. (Ampicillin is, however, degraded by beta-lactamases and therefore the spectrum of activity does not normally include organisms which produce these enzymes.)

Ampicillin diffuses readily into most body tissue and fluids. However, penetration into the cerebrospinal fluid and brain occurs only when the meninges are inflamed. Ampicillin is excreted largely unchanged in the urine and its excretion can be delayed by concurrent administration of probenecid. The active form appears in the bile in higher concentrations than those found in the serum. Ampicillin is the least serum-bound of all the penicillins, averaging about 20% compared to approximately 60 to 90% for other penicillins.

Most strains of the following organisms have been shown in in vitro studies to be susceptible to ampicillin: gram-positive organisms: hemolytic and nonhemolytic streptococci, S. pneumoniae, nonpenicillinase-producing staphylococci, Clostridia sp., B. anthracis, Listeria monocytogenes, C. xerosis and most strains of enterococci; gram-negative organisms: H. influenzae, B. funduliformis, N. Gonorrhea, N. meningitides, Br. abortus, Br. melitensis, Proteus mirabilis and many strains of Salmonella, Shigella and E. coli.

Indications: Ampicillin is indicated in the treatment of respiratory tract infections, urinary tract infections, gonorrhea, gastrointestinal infections and bacterial meningitis, septicemia and endocarditis caused by susceptible organisms such as:

Gram-positive Bacteria: S. aureus (nonpenicillinase-producing), S. epidermidis (nonpenicillinase-producing), S. saprophyticus (nonpenicillinase-producing), Enterobacter faecalis, S. pneumoniae, S. pyogenes and S. viridans.

Gram-negative Bacteria: H. influenzae (nonpenicillinase-producing), B. catarrhalis (nonpenicillinase-producing), E. coli (nonpenicillinase-producing), P. mirabilis (nonpenicillinase-producing), P. vulgaris, Providencia rettgeri, Providencia stuartii, M. morganii, and N. gonorrhea (nonpenicillinase-producing), Shigellae, S. typhosa and other Salmonellae.

Anerobes: Clostridium species, Peptococcus species, Peptostreptococcus species, Bacteroides species, including B. fragilis.

Bacteriology studies to determine the causative organisms and their susceptibility to ampicillin should be performed. Therapy may be instituted prior to obtaining results of susceptibility testing.

Contraindications: Ampicillin is contraindicated in patients with a history of hypersensitivity to any penicillin or cephalosporin.

Warnings: Serious and occasional fatal hypersensitivity (anaphylaxis) reactions have been reported in patients on penicillin therapy especially following parenteral administration. These reactions are more apt to occur in individuals with a history of sensitivity to multiple allergens.

There have been well-documented reports of individuals with a history of penicillin hypersensitivity reactions who have experienced severe hypersensitivity reactions when treated with a cephalosporin. Before therapy with a penicillin, careful inquiry should be made concerning previous hypersensitivity reactions to penicillins, cephalosporins, and other allergens.

If an allergic reaction occurs, the drug should be discontinued and the patient treated with the usual agents (e.g., pressor amines, antihistamines, and corticosteroids). Serious anaphylactoid reactions are not controlled by antihistamines alone, and require such emergency measures as the immediate use of epinephrine, aminophylline, oxygen, and i.v. corticosteroids.

Precautions: General: A high percentage of patients with infectious mononucleosis or lymphatic leukemia who receive ampicillin develop a skin rash, and the drug should not be administered to such patients. In most cases, the rash is maculopapular, pruritic, and generalized.

Prolonged use of antibiotics may promote overgrowth of nonsusceptible organisms. Should superinfections occur, appropriate measures should be taken.

Drug Interactions: The concurrent administration of allopurinol and ampicillin increases substantially the incidence of rashes in patients receiving both drugs as compared to patients receiving ampicillin alone. It is not known whether this potentiation of ampicillin rashes is due to allopurinol or to hyperuricemia present in these patients. Ampicillin and aminoglycosides should not be reconstituted together due to the in vitro inactivation of the aminoglycosides by the ampicillin.

Drug/Laboratory Test Interactions: Following administration of ampicillin to pregnant women, a transient decrease in plasma concentration of total conjugated estriol, estriol-glucuronide, conjugated estrone and estradiol has been noted.

With high urine concentrations of ampicillin, false-positive urinary glucose reactions may occur if copper reduction methods are used. Therefore, it is recommended that glucose tests based on enzymatic glucose oxidase reactions be employed.

Ampicin (cont'd)

Pregnancy: Animal studies with ampicillin have shown no teratogenic effects. There are, however, no adequate and well-controlled studies in pregnant women. Because animal reproduction studies are not always predictive of human response, this drug should be used during pregnancy only if clearly needed.

Labor and Delivery: It is not known whether use of ampicillin-class antibiotics in humans during labor or delivery has immediate or delayed adverse effects on the fetus, prolongs the duration of labor, or increases the likelihood that forceps delivery or other obstetrical intervention or resuscitation of the newborn will be necessary.

Lactation: Ampicillin is excreted in trace amounts in human milk. Therefore caution should be exercised when ampicillin is administered to a nursing mother.

Geriatrics: There are no known specific precautions for the use of ampicillin in the elderly.

Adverse Effects: As with other penicillins, presumably, the most common untoward reactions will be related to sensitivity phenomena. Hypersensitivity reactions are more likely to occur in individuals who have previously demonstrated hypersensitivity to penicillins and in those with a history of allergy, asthma, hay fever or urticaria. The following adverse reactions have been reported with the use of ampicillin.

Gastrointestinal: glossitis, stomatitis, black "hairy" tongue, nausea, vomiting, enterocolitis and diarrhea. Severe pseudomembranous colitis has been reported in some patients.

Hypersensitivity: Skin rashes and urticaria have been reported frequently. A few cases of exfoliative dermatitis and erythema multiforme have been reported. Anaphylaxis is the most serious reaction experienced and has usually been associated with the parenteral dosage forms.

Note: Urticaria, other skin rashes, and serum sickness-like reactions may be controlled with antihistamines, and if necessary, systemic corticosteroids. Whenever such reactions occur, ampicillin should be discontinued unless, in the opinion of the physician, the condition is life-threatening and amenable only to ampicillin therapy.

Liver: A moderate rise in AST has been noted, but the significance of this finding is unknown. Mild transitory AST elevations have been observed in individuals receiving larger (2 to 4 times) than usual and oft-repeated i.m. injections. Evidence indicates that AST is released at the site of the i.m. injection of ampicillin sodium, and the presence of increased amounts of this enzyme in the blood does not necessarily indicate liver involvement.

Hematologic: Anemia, thrombocytopenia, thrombocytopenic purpura, hemorrhagic diathesis, eosinophilia, leukopenia and agranulocytosis have been reported rarely in association with ampicillin therapy. These reactions are usually reversible on discontinuation of therapy and are believed to be hypersensitivity phenomena.

Renal: Interstitial nephritis has been reported.

Ototoxicity: Ampicillin may be ototoxic when given i.v. in very high doses.

Overdose: Symptoms and Treatment: The treatment of overdosage would likely be needed only in patients with severely impaired renal function, since patients with normal kidneys excrete penicillins at a rapid rate (90% unchanged, normal renal excretion, with half-life of 1.5 hours).

In case of overdosage, discontinue medication, treat symptomatically and institute supportive measures as required. In patients with renal function impairment, ampicillin-class antibiotics can be removed by hemodialysis but not by peritoneal dialysis.

Dosage: Ear, Nose, Throat and Lower Respiratory Tract Infections: Adults and children 40 kg or over: 250 to 500 mg every 6 hours. Children under 40 kg: 25 to 50 mg/kg/day in equally divided doses at 6- to 8-hour intervals.

Gastrointestinal and Genitourinary Tract Infections (including genitourinary infections caused by N. gonorrhea in females): Adults and children 40 kg or over: 500 mg every 6 hours. Children under 40 kg: 50 mg/kg/day in equally divided doses at 6- to 8-hour intervals.

The children's dosage is intended for individuals whose weights will not cause a dosage to be calculated greater than that recommended for adults.

In the treatment of chronic urinary tract and intestinal infections, frequent bacteriological and clinical appraisal is necessary. Smaller doses than those recommended above should not be used. Higher doses should be used for stubborn or severe infections. In stubborn infections, therapy may be required for several weeks. It may be necessary to continue clinical and/or bacteriological follow up for several months after cessation of therapy.

Urethritis in males due to N. gonorrhea: Adults: 2 doses of 500 mg each at an interval of 8 to 12 hours. Treatment may be repeated if necessary or extended if required.

In the treatment of complications of gonorrheal urethritis, such as prostatitis and epididymitis, prolonged and intensive therapy is recommended. Cases of gonorrhea with a suspected primary lesion of syphilis should have darkfield examinations before receiving treatment. In all other cases where concomitant syphilis is suspected, monthly serological tests should be made for a minimum of 4 months.

The parenteral doses for the preceding infections may be given by either the i.m. or i.v. route. A change to oral ampicillin may be made when appropriate.

Bacterial Meningitis: Adults and children with bacterial meningitis (caused by N. meningitides or H. influenzae) have been sucessfully treated with doses of 150 to 200 mg/kg/day in divided doses every 3 or 4 hours. A few adults have been successfully treated for bacterial meningitis with doses ranging from 8 to 14 g daily. This treatment has been initiated with i.v. drip therapy and continued with frequent (every 3 to 4 hours) i.m. therapy.

Septicemia: Adult and children: 150 to 200 mg/kg/day in equally divided doses every 3 to 4 hours. Start with i.v. administration for at least 3 days, and continue with either the i.v. or i.m. route.

Treatment of all infections should be continued for a minimum of 48 to 72 hours beyond the time that the patient becomes asymptomatic or evidence of bacterial eradication has been obtained. A minimum of 10 days' treatment is recommended for any infection caused by Group A beta-hemolytic streptococci.

Reconstitution: Use only freshly prepared solutions. I.M. and I.V. injections should be administered within 1 hour after preparation, since the potency may decrease significantly after this period.

I.M.: Using sterile Water for Injection, USP, Ampicin for Injection may be reconstituted as follows (see Table I).

Table I—Ampicin

Reconstitution—I.M.

Vial	Diluent Added	Available Volume	Concentration mg/mL
125 mg	1.2 mL	1.0 mL	125
250 mg	2.0 mL	2.0 mL	125
500 mg	1.8 mL	2.0 mL	250
1 g	3.5 mL	4.0 mL	250

Direct I.V. Use: Use Sterile Water for Injection, USP. Add 5 mL to the 125, 250 or 500 mg vial, withdraw contents, and administer slowly over a period of 3 to 5 minutes. Add 10 mL to the 1 g vial and withdraw the entire contents. Inject slowly over a period of at least 10 to 15 minutes. **Caution:** More rapid administration may result in convulsive seizures.

I.V. Infusion: Reconstitute the 1 or 2 g vial with 10 mL of Sterile Water for Injection, USP prior to dilution with the i.v. solution. Stability studies on ampicillin sodium, at concentrations of 2 mg/mL and 30 mg/mL in various i.v. solutions, indicate the drug will lose less than 10% activity at room temperature (15 to 30°C) for the time periods stated (see Table II).

Table II—Ampicin

Reconstitution—I.V.

Diluent	Concentration	Stability Periods
Isotonic Sodium Chloride	30 mg/mL	8 hours
5% Dextrose in Water	2 mg/mL	4 hours
5% Dextrose in 0.4% Sodium Chloride Solution	2 mg/mL	4 hours
10% Invert Sugar in Water	2 mg/mL	4 hours
M/6 Sodium Lactate Solution	30 mg/mL	4 hours

Only those solutions listed above should be used for the i.v. infusion of ampicillin. The concentrations should fall within the range specified. The drug concentration and the rate and volume of the infusion should be adjusted so that the total dose of ampicillin is administered before the drug loses its stability in the solution in use.

Supplied: Each dry filled vial contains: ampicillin 125 mg, 250 mg, 500 mg, 1 g and 2 g (as the sodium salt). Nonmedicinal ingredients: none. Sodium: 2.9 mEq/g.

AMSA P-D™ ℞

Parke-Davis

Amsacrine

Antineoplastic

Pharmacology: Amsacrine is a potent cytotoxic agent. In in vitro studies, the LD_{50} against cultured L1210 cells is 0.04 µg/mL and 0.2 µg/mL against cultured Novikoff cells at 6 hours. Higher concentrations or longer exposure produce cell destruction. A 3 hour exposure of Novikoff cells to 2 µg of AMSA P-D indicated 62% inhibition of DNA synthesis (incorporation of radioactive thymidine) while RNA synthesis was not affected (incorporation of radioactive uridine). Essentially the same results were obtained in vivo when L1210-inoculated mice were treated with a dose of 0.1 mg/mouse. AMSA P-D binds to DNA both through intercalation and external binding and has base specificity for A-T pairs.

Cycling cells are 2 to 4 times more sensitive to AMSA P-D than are resting cells. Cycling cells initially in S and G2 phases were grossly delayed in their capacity for normal progression, leading to a transitory (approximately 8 hours) accumulation of cells in S phase, followed at later times by arrest in G2 phase. A limited degree of mitotic nondisjunction and a high degree of polyploidization was seen. Examination of chromosome damage indicated incomplete condensation and chromosome stickiness, which are characterisitics of DNA intercalators.

Amsacrine is active against a wide spectrum of murine tumors. These include the ascitic form of L1210 and P388 leukemias, Lewis lung carcinoma, spontaneous C_3H mammary adenocarcinoma, mammary tumor in CD8F mice, and the commonly resistant B16 melanoma. No antitumor activity was detected in intra-cerebrally inoculated L1210 leukemia, which suggests that the drug penetration across the blood-brain barrier in mice did not achieve significant levels.

The effect of amsacrine on the immune system was also investigated. The production of hemolytic plaque-forming cells (PFC) in mice in response to immunization with sheep red blood cells (SRBC) was used as the indicator of activity. In contrast to the 95% inhibition of PFC formation caused by Actinomycin D, cyclophosphamide, cytosine arabinoside, thioguanine and vinblastine, amsacrine produced no such inhibition when administered at the same time as SRBC. However, when given 28 hours following SRBC immunization, the drug caused a 99% suppression of immune activity. After six days, the inhibition was still strongly evident.

Following a 90 mg/m² infusion of amsacrine over 60 minutes, the plasma concentration showed a biphasic decrease with an alpha phase half-life of 10 to 15 minutes and a beta phase half-life of 8 to 9 hours. Peak plasma levels were dose dependent, increasing from 0.47 to 12.3 µM as the patient's dose was escalated from 10 to 90 mg/m². In 2 studies, 15 of 54 (27.8%) evaluable patients achieved remission (7 were complete remissions and 8 were partial remissions). Duration of amsacrine remissions is brief and variable if not followed by consolidation or maintenance regimens.

Indications: For induction of remission in acute adult leukemia refractory to conventional therapy.

Contraindications: In patients who have pre-existing drug-induced or radiotherapy-induced bone marrow suppression.

Amsacrine treatment is **not** contraindicated in patients who have received previous treatment with doxorubicin or daunorubicin.

Warnings: Amsacrine is a potent bone marrow suppressant. In some patients prolonged bone marrow aplasia may occur, necessitating intensive supportive therapy. Patients receiving the drug must be under close medical supervision by physicians skilled in cancer chemotherapy. During induction therapy, leukocyte and platelet count determinations are mandatory and should be performed frequently. With recommended dose schedules, leukopenia is usually transient, reaching its nadir at 11 to 13 days after treatment, with recovery usually occurring by the 17th to 25th day (see Dosage). Leukocyte counts as low as 1 000/mm³ can be expected during drug therapy. Red cell and platelet concentrations should be monitored because they also may be depressed. Doses higher than those recommended may produce more severe or more prolonged marrow suppression.

Facilities should be available for management of complications of bone marrow suppression (infection resulting from granulocytopenia and other impaired body defenses, and hemorrhage secondary to thrombocytopenia). Periodic monitoring of bone marrow should be performed. Hematologic toxicity may require dose reduction, suspension, or delay of amsacrine therapy.

Toxicity at recommended doses of the drug is enhanced by hepatic or renal impairment. Laboratory evaluation of hepatic and renal function is necessary prior to and during administration. Liver metabolism and biliary excretion appear to be the major routes of Amsacrine elimination in man. Therefore, dose reduction is recommended in patients with significant hepatic dysfunction (bilirubin>2 mg%). The same recommendation applies in cases of significant renal impairment (BUN>20 mg%, creatinine>1.2 mg%), since 35% of the total dose is excreted by the kidney within 72 hours after administration (20% as intact drug).

There is no clear evidence from animal studies and clinical trials that amsacrine is cardiotoxic. There have been eight documented cases in which an acute arrhythmia developed during or immediately after amsacrine infusion. Several of these patients had received prior anthracycline treatment or were hypokalemic. An additional seven cases have been reported but no documentation is available. Therefore, careful monitoring of cardiac rhythm, during and after drug administration, is strongly recommended.

Pregnancy: Safe use of amsacrine in pregnancy has not been established. Reproduction studies have not been performed in animals. Thus, there is no evidence as to whether this drug may adversely affect fertility in either men or women or have teratogenic or other adverse effects on the fetus and embryo. Therefore, benefit/risk considerations should be carefully weighed in using the drug in pregnant women or in patients of either sex in the reproductive age group.

Precautions: Like other cytotoxic drugs, amsacrine may induce hyperuricemia secondary to rapid lysis of neoplastic cells. Careful monitoring of the patient's blood uric acid level should be performed.

Pregnancy: See Warnings.

Drug Interactions: Data available suggest that AMSA P-D does not potentiate the increased risk of doxorubicin-induced cardiac toxicity.

Although animal studies suggested cross resistance between the anthracyclines and AMSA P-D, clinical studies indicate that this is not true.

Sufficient data are not available to prove or disprove AMSA P-D potentiation of the toxicities of other anticancer drugs.

Adverse Effects: The major toxicities associated with amsacrine have been myelosuppression and mucositis. Other target organ systems of toxicity are the gastrointestinal tract and CNS. Evidence of cumulative toxicity has not been observed.

Myelosuppression: Using recommended doses and schedules, leukopenia occurs in most patients. Mild to severe anemia and mild to moderate thrombocytopenia also develop in the majority of patients.

Patients with leukemia have pancytopenia due to the disease state as well as to prior therapy. While the goal of amsacrine therapy is myelosuppression, this can become an untoward effect if therapy is prolonged.

Gastrointestinal: Effects reported in over 10% of patients in decreasing order of frequency are: nausea, vomiting, stomatitis, diarrhea, perirectal abscess, and abdominal pain. Other effects are: anorexia, dysphagia, hematemesis, jaundice, gum hemorrhage, and gingivitis.

Mucositis has been reported as a serious side effect at higher dose levels.

CNS: headache, confusion, paresthesias, and dizziness. Seizures occurred in several patients, all of whom had metabolic conditions that may have caused the seizures or made these patients more susceptible to them.

Integumentary: rashes (purpuric or maculopapular), alopecia, and urticaria.

Hepatotoxicity: Rarely occurred as evidenced by jaundice and increased bilirubin. These effects are usually transient and return to normal after cessation of drug therapy. One death has been attributed to progressive liver failure.

Cardiovascular: See Warnings regarding ventricular arrhythmias. Other effects are phlebitis and inflammation at the injection site, hypotension, and tachycardia. Phlebitis, related to the concentration of amsacrine administered, is reduced by infusing the diluted drug over a period of 60 to 120 minutes (see Dosage).

Systemic: Other effects reported are: asthenia, lethargy, and musculoskeletal pain.

Dosage: Caution: AMSA P-D must be mixed with the L-lactic acid diluent provided. The resultant solution must be further diluted in 500 mL dextrose injection, USP. Do not use saline solutions. AMSA P-D is incompatible with solutions containing chloride ions.

For i.v. infusion only.

The following schedules are recommended for acute adult leukemia:

Induction: The total recommended dose for each 5-day course of therapy is 375 to 625 mg/m². Each course is repeated at 3-to-4-week intervals. Two courses may be necessary to achieve induction. This may be given according to the following schedules: 75mg/m²/d×5 d; 100 mg/m²/d×5 d; and 125 mg/m²/d×5 d (the preferred regimen).

The dose of amsacrine should be increased by 20% in the second and each subsequent course if the patient has had no significant toxicity in the preceding course, and if marrow hypoplasia has not been achieved. If patients have had life-threatening infection or hemorrhage during the preceding course, consideration should be given to decreasing the dose by 20%. Second and subsequent courses should not be initiated until recovery from drug-induced myelosuppression or evidence of residual leukemic infiltrate is evident.

Maintenance: Once remission has been achieved the maintenance dose should be about one half that described above, repeated every 4 to 8 weeks depending upon the peripheral blood counts and bone marrow recovery from myelosuppression.

Administration: Because of phlebitis that may occur at doses greater than 70 mg/m², AMSA P-D must be diluted in 500 mL 5% Dextrose Injection USP and infused over 60 to 90 minutes. Care must be taken that no extravasation occurs which might produce severe irritation or necrosis.

Method of Preparation: Step 1: Each ampul contains 75 mg (1.5 mL) of AMSA P-D for infusion. Aseptically transfer 1.5 mL from the ampul to the 13.5 mL vial of L-lactic Acid diluent (use only the diluent provided). The resulting orange-red solution contains 5 mg AMSA P-D per mL. It is preferable to use glass syringes for step one, however, plastic syringes can be used, providing the AMSA P-D solution remains in the syringe for no more than 15 minutes. The stock solution is chemically stable for 24 hours at room temperature when protected from exposure to direct sunlight. Since this solution does not contain a preservative, any unused portion should be discarded.

Step Two: Prepare the i.v. infusion solution by aseptically transferring the total daily dose of Stock Solution to 500 mL Dextrose Injection USP. **Do not use saline solution.** The freshly prepared i.v. infusion is chemically stable for up to 7 days when using an Abbott plastic container or glass bottle.

As with all i.v. admixtures containing no preservatives (microbiological) the solution should be used within 24 hours when stored at room temperature or 72 hours, when refrigerated.

Caution in the handling and preparation of the solution should be exercised, and the use of gloves is recommended. If AMSA P-D solution contacts the skin or mucosa, immediately wash thoroughly with soap and water.

General Information for the Safe Handling of Cytotoxic Agents:

Preparation of all antineoplastic agents should be done in a vertical laminar flow hood (Biological Safety Cabinet—Class II).

Personnel preparing parenteral antineoplastic agents should wear PVC gloves, safety glasses, disposable gowns and masks.

All needles, syringes, vials, ampuls, and other materials which have come in contact with cytotoxic drugs should be segregated and incinerated at 1 000° C or more. Sealed containers may explode sealed.

Intact vials or ampuls, unopened bottles, or oral medication should be **returned to the manufacturer for destruction.** Proper precautions should be taken in packaging these materials for transport. If incineration is not available, neutralization should be done (the manufacturer can supply this information), usually with the use of 5% sodium hypochlorite and/or 5% sodium thiosulfate.

Personnel regularly involved in the preparation and handling of cytotoxic agents should have bi-annual blood examinations.

Supplied: Each ampul (75 mg/1.5 mL ampul) contains: amsacrine 50 mg/mL. Nonmedicinal ingredients: n,n-dimethylacetamide. Packages of 5 ampuls with 13.5 mL vials of L-lactic acid diluent. Contains no preservatives. Store at controlled room temperature.

AMYL NITRITE Ⓟ

Roberts

Vasodilator

Indications: Amyl nitrite is administered by inhalation in the immediate treatment of patients with definite cyanide poisoning. Amyl nitrite induces formation of methemoglobin which combines with the cyanide to form nontoxic cyanmethemoglobin.

Supplied: Each vitriole contains: amyl nitrite 0.3 mL. Packages of 12.

AMYTAL® ◈

Lilly

Amobarbital Sodium

Sedative—Hypnotic

Supplied: Each vial contains: amobarbital sodium 500 mg without diluent. Nonmedicinal ingredients: none. Boxes of 10.

ANACIN®
ANACIN® EXTRA STRENGTH

Whitehall-Robins

ASA—Caffeine

Analgesic—Antipyretic—Anti-inflammatory

Indications: For fast relief of headaches, aches and fever of colds, arthritic and rheumatic pain, toothache and menstrual pain.

Contraindications: Sensitivity to salicylates, bleeding ulcers and patients with blood coagulation defects, hemophilia, anemia, vitamin K deficiency, renal function impairment, asthma, sensitivity to caffeine and cardiac disease.

Warnings: All salicylates should be kept out of reach of children to avoid accidental poisoning. Children and teenagers with influenza or chickenpox should not use this product due to possible association with Reye's Syndrome.

Precautions: Patients with asthma, allergy to salicylates, blood coagulation problems or receiving anticoagulation therapy, with severe anemia, in the last 3 months of pregnancy or breast-feeding should not take salicylate-containing drugs unless monitored with caution.

Children: Pediatric patients are susceptible to caffeine and its adverse CNS effects.

Drug Interactions: Alcohol and nonsteroidal anti-inflammatory drugs administered with salicylates may increase the potential for gastrointestinal bleeding.

Diabetics under therapy should be monitored if salicylates are administered.

Patients taking valproic acid, furosemide, methotrexate, nifedipine, vancomycin, blood coagulation inhibitors and sulfinpyrazone are **not** recommended to take salicylates concurrently.

Adverse Effects: Nausea, vomiting, diarrhea, heartburn, bleeding or irritation of stomach, loss of hearing including ringing or buzzing in the ear, skin rashes, hives or itching, breathing difficulties. Additionally, caffeine may cause nervousness, insomnia, palpitations, vertigo and muscle tremor.

Overdose: Symptoms: Rapid and deep breathing, nausea, vomiting, vertigo, tinnitus, flushing, sweating and thirst. In severe overdose situations patients may have fever, blood in urine, hemorrhage, excitement, confusion, convulsions, coma, breathing difficulties and acid-base disturbances e.g., metabolic acidosis and respiratory alkalosis. CNS stimulation due to caffeine (trouble in sleeping, nervousness or jitters).

Treatment: Induce emesis or perform gastric lavage, then administer activated charcoal. If hyperthermia is present, sponge the patient with tepid water. Maintain appropriate fluid therapy based on the patient's fluid, acid-base and electrolyte status. Also monitor blood gases, blood glucose, serum creatinine and urea, urinary output and pH. Draw blood for determination of serum salicylate level. Sodium bicarbonate i.v. should be used cautiously to correct metabolic acidosis. Care should be taken to avoid sodium overload or alkalosis. Hypokalemia may require administration of i.v. potassium chloride. If present, hypoglycemia may be managed with dextrose solutions. Seizures may be treated with i.v. diazepam. Alkalinization of the urine to enhance urinary excretion of salicylates may be useful in severe intoxication but should be performed very cautiously in selected patients. Vitamin K may be administered to patients with hemorrhagic complications or prolonged PT. Peritoneal or hemodialysis may be required if serum salicylate concentrations are greater than 6.5 mmol/L 6 hours after ingestion, in complex acid-base disturbances unresponsive to conventional therapy, if the patient is in renal failure, or if the patient is deteriorating clinically despite appropriate care.

Dosage: Adults: Anacin: 1 or 2 tablets or caplets every 4 hours as required. Do not exceed 12 tablets (caplets) in 24 hours. Anacin Extra Strength: 1 or 2 tablets or caplets every 4 hours as required. Do not exceed 8 tablets (caplets) in 24 hours.

Anacin (cont'd)

Supplied: Anacin: Caplets: Each white caplet, printed "Anacin", contains: ASA 325 mg and caffeine 32 mg. Nonmedicinal ingredients: cellulose, cornstarch, ethoxyethanol, iron oxide, lecithin, pharmaceutical glaze, polyethylene glycol, propylene glycol, simethicone and sodium lauryl sulfate. Energy: 0.18 kJ (0.04 kcal). Sodium: <1 mmol (<0.1 mg). Bottles of 50 and 100.

Tablets: Each white tablet, embossed "Anacin", contains: ASA 325 mg and caffeine 32 mg. Nonmedicinal ingredients: cellulose, cornstarch, polyethylene glycol and sodium lauryl sulfate. Energy: 0.18 kJ (0.04 kcal). Tins of 12. Bottles of 30, 50, 100 and 200.

Anacin Extra Strength: Caplets: Each white caplet, printed "Anacin 500", contains: ASA 500 mg and caffeine 32 mg. Nonmedicinal ingredients: cellulose, cornstarch, ethoxyethanol, iron oxide, lecithin, pharmaceutical glaze, polyethylene glycol, propylene glycol, simethicone and sodium lauryl sulfate. Energy: 0.13 kJ (0.03 kcal). Sodium: <1 mmol (<0.1 mg). Bottles of 50.

Tablets: Each white tablet, embossed "Anacin 500", contains: ASA 500 mg and caffeine 32 mg. Nonmedicinal ingredients: cellulose, cornstarch, polyethylene glycol and sodium lauryl sulfate. Energy: 0.13 kJ (0.03 kcal). Sodium: <1 mmol (<0.1 mg). Bottles of 30 and 50.

Store at room temperature (15 to 30°C).

Reviewed 1997

ANAFRANIL® Ⓟ

Novartis Pharmaceuticals

Clomipramine HCl

Antidepressant—Antiobsessional

Pharmacology: Clomipramine is a tricyclic agent with both antidepressant and antiobsessional properties. Like other tricyclics, clomipramine inhibits norepinephrine and serotonin uptake into central nerve terminals, possibly by blocking the membrane-pump of neurons, thereby increasing the concentration of transmitter monoamines at receptor sites. Clomipramine is presumed to influence depression and obsessive and compulsive behavior through its effects on serotonergic neurotransmission. The actual neurochemical mechanism is unknown, but clomipramine's capacity to inhibit serotonin reuptake is thought to be important. Clomipramine appears to have a mild sedative effect which may be helpful in alleviating the anxiety component often accompanying depression.

As with other tricyclic compounds, clomipramine possesses anticholinergic properties which are responsible for certain side effects. It also has weak antihistamine and antiserotonin properties, lowers the convulsive threshold, potentiates the effect of norepinephrine and other drugs acting on the CNS, has a quinidine-like effect on the heart and may impair cardiac conduction.

The action of clomipramine on the human EEG is one of desynchronization. Clomipramine causes a persistent increase in the frequency of shifts into stage I sleep and produces marked reduction or suppression of rapid eye movement sleep (REM or paradoxical sleep). Partial recovery occurs within 3 to 4 weeks as does a rebound after drug withdrawal which appears to last approximately the same time. In normal human volunteers tricyclic antidepressants tend to produce a sedative effect accompanied by atropine-like symptoms and may produce some difficulty in concentrating and thinking.

Pharmacokinetics: Clomipramine is rapidly and completely absorbed after oral administration in humans. Peak plasma levels are usually reached 2 hours after dosage but much individual variation occurs. The plasma half-life after a single oral dose is approximately 21 hours. After 28 days of oral administration to patients in a daily dosage of 75 mg, plasma concentrations of clomipramine ranged from 17 to 70 ng/mL (mean=35.7 ng/mL). The concentration of the active metabolite, desmethylclomipramine, was about twice as high.

The binding of clomipramine to serum proteins is very high at 96 to 97% and is practically concentration-independent within the therapeutic range. Clomipramine has a volume of distribution of approximately 12 L/kg.

Clomipramine is extensively metabolized in the body with hydroxylation, demethylation and N-oxidation being the quantitatively more important routes of metabolism.

Owing to the lower clearance of clomipramine in plasma, elderly patients require lower doses of clomipramine than patients in younger age groups.

As expected, the metabolites of clomipramine are quite similar to those of imipramine, all retaining the benzazepine structure. Two-thirds of clomipramine is excreted as water-soluble conjugates in the urine and approximately one-third in the feces. After a 25 mg radiolabeled dose of clomipramine in 2 subjects, the urinary recoveries of clomipramine and desmethylclomipramine were about 2% and 0.5% of the total radioactivity, respectively.

Indications: For the treatment of depression. Clomipramine also appears to have a mild sedative effect which may be helpful in alleviating the anxiety component often accompanying depression.

For the treatment of obsessions and compulsions in patients with obsessive compulsive disorder (OCD). The obsessions and compulsions must cause marked distress, be time-consuming, or significantly interfere with social or occupational functioning.

The effectiveness of clomipramine for long-term use (e.g., for more than 10 weeks) has not been systematically evaluated in placebo-controlled trials. The physician who elects to use clomipramine for extended periods should periodically re-evaluate the long-term usefulness of the drug for the individual patient.

Contraindications: Patients who have known or suspected hypersensitivity to the drug or its excipients, or have known or suspected hypersensitivity to tricyclic antidepressants belonging to the dibenzazepine group.

Clomipramine should not be given in conjunction with or within 14 days before or after treatment with a MAO inhibitor (see Drug Interactions). The concomitant treatment with selective, reversible MAO-A inhibitors, such as moclobemide, is also contraindicated. Hypertensive crises, hyperactivity, hyperpyrexia, spasticity, severe convulsions or coma, and death have been reported in patients receiving such combinations.

It is contraindicated during the acute recovery phase following myocardial infarction and in the presence of acute congestive heart failure.

Clomipramine is contraindicated in patients with existing liver or kidney damage and should not be administered to patients with a history of blood dyscrasias.

Clomipramine is contraindicated in patients with glaucoma, as the condition may be aggravated due to the atropine-like effects of the drug.

Warnings: Seizures: Tricyclic agents are known to lower the convulsive threshold and clomipramine should, therefore, be used with extreme caution in patients with a history of convulsive disorders and other predisposing factors, e.g., brain damage of varying etiology, concomitant use of neuroleptics, alcoholism and withdrawal from alcohol, and concomitant use with other drugs that lower the seizure threshold. It appears that the occurrence of seizures is dose dependent. Therefore, the recommended total daily doses should not be exceeded (see Dosage).

Concurrent administration of ECT and clomipramine may be hazardous and such treatment should be limited to patients for whom it is essential. Physicians should discuss with patients the risk of taking clomipramine while engaging in activities in which a sudden loss of consciousness could result in serious injury to the patient or others, e.g., the operation of complex machinery, driving, swimming, or climbing.

Cardiovascular: Tricyclic antidepressants, particularly in high doses, have been reported to produce sinus tachycardia, changes in conduction time and arrhythmias. A few instances of unexpected death have been reported in patients with cardiovascular disorders. Myocardial infarction and stroke have also been reported with drugs of this class. Therefore, clomipramine should be administered with extreme caution to patients with a history of cardiovascular disorders, especially those with cardiovascular insufficiency, conduction disorders (e.g., atrioventricular block grades I to III) or other arrhythmias, those with circulatory lability and elderly patients. Clomipramine also has a hypotensive action which may be detrimental in these circumstances. In such cases, treatment should be initiated at low doses with progressive increases only if required and tolerated, and the patients should be under close surveillance at all dosage levels. Monitoring of cardiac function and the ECG is indicated in such patients as well as in the elderly.

Use in Concomitant Illness: Caution should be observed in prescribing clomipramine in hyperthyroid patients or for patients receiving thyroid medication. Transient cardiac arrhythmias have occurred in rare instances in patients who have been receiving other tricyclic compounds concomitantly with thyroid medication.

Because of its anticholinergic properties, clomipramine should be used with caution in patients with increased intraocular pressure, narrow angle glaucoma or urinary retention, particularly in the presence of prostatic hypertrophy.

Tricyclic antidepressants may give rise to paralytic ileus, particularly in the elderly and in hospitalized patients. Therefore, appropriate measures should be taken if constipation occurs.

Caution is called for when employing clomipramine in patients with tumors of the adrenal medulla (e.g., pheochromocytoma, neuroblastoma) in whom the drug may provoke hypertensive crisis.

Clomipramine should be kept in a safe place, well out of the reach of children.

Pregnancy: The safety of use in pregnant women has not been established. Therefore, clomipramine should not be administered to women of childbearing potential, or during pregnancy, unless, in the opinion of the physician, the expected benefit to the patient outweighs the potential risk to the fetus. Withdrawal symptoms including tremors, dyspnea, lethargy, colic, irritability, hypotonia/hypertonia, convulsions, and respiratory depression have been reported in neonates whose mothers received tricyclic antidepressants during the third trimester of pregnancy. To avoid such symptoms, clomipramine should, if possible, be gradually withdrawn at least 7 weeks before the calculated date of confinement.

Lactation: Since clomipramine passes into breast milk, the drug should be gradually withdrawn or the infant weaned if the patient is breast-feeding.

Precautions: Suicide: The possibility of a suicide attempt is inherent in depression with or without obsessive compulsive disorder. These patients should be carefully supervised during treatment with clomipramine, and hospitalization or concomitant ECT may be required. To minimize the risk of an intentional overdose by a depressed patient, prescriptions for clomipramine should be written for the smallest possible quantity of the drug consistent with good patient management.

Psychosis, Mania-Hypomania, and other Neuropsychiatric Phenomena: In patients treated with tricyclic antidepressants, activation of latent schizophrenia or aggravation of existing psychotic manifestations in schizophrenic patients may occur. Patients with manic-depressive tendencies may experience hypomanic or manic shifts. Hyperactive or agitated patients may become over-stimulated. A reduction in dose or discontinuation of clomipramine should be considered under these circumstances.

In predisposed and elderly patients, tricyclic antidepressants may, particularly at night, provoke pharmacogenic (delirious) psychoses that disappear within a few days of withdrawing the drug.

Occupational Hazards: Since clomipramine may produce sedation, particularly during the initial phase of therapy, patients should be cautioned about the danger of engaging in activities requiring mental alertness, judgement and physical coordination.

Cardiovascular: Before initiating treatment, it is advisable to check the patient's blood pressure, because individuals with hypotension or a labile circulation may react to the drug with a fall in blood pressure. Regular measurements of blood pressure should be performed in susceptible patients. Postural hypotension may be controlled by reducing the dosage or administering circulatory stimulants.

ECG abnormalities have been observed in patients treated with clomipramine. The most common ECG changes were premature ventricular contractions (PVCs), ST-T wave changes, and abnormalities in intraventricular conduction. These changes were rarely associated with significant clinical symptoms. Nevertheless, caution is necessary when treating patients with heart disease, as well as elderly subjects. In these patients cardiac function should be monitored and ECG examinations performed during long-term therapy. Gradual dose titration is also recommended.

Hepatic Changes: Clomipramine has occasionally been associated with elevations in AST and ALT of potential clinical significance (e.g., values greater than 3 times the upper limit of normal). In the majority of cases, these enzyme elevations were not associated with other clinical findings suggestive of hepatic injury.

Isolated cases of obstructive jaundice have been reported. Caution is indicated in treating patients with known liver disease, and periodic monitoring of hepatic function is recommended in such patients.

Hematologic Changes: Isolated cases of bone marrow depression with agranulocytosis have been reported. Leukocyte and differential blood cell counts are recommended in patients receiving treatment with clomipramine over prolonged periods, and should be performed for patients who develop fever, an influenzal infection, or sore throat. In the event of an allergic skin reaction, clomipramine should be withdrawn.

CNS: More than 30 cases of hyperthermia have been recorded by nondomestic post-marketing surveillance systems. Most cases occurred when clomipramine was used in combination with other drugs. When clomipramine and a neuroleptic were used concomitantly, the cases were sometimes considered to be examples of a neuroleptic malignant syndrome.

Withdrawal Symptoms: A variety of withdrawal symptoms has been reported in association with abrupt discontinuation of clomipramine, including dizziness, nausea, vomiting, headache, malaise, sleep disturbance, hyperthermia and irritability. In addition, such patients may experience a worsening of psychiatric status. While the withdrawal effects of clomipramine have not been systematically evaluated in controlled trials, they are well known with closely related tricyclic antidepressants. It is recommended that the dosage be tapered gradually and the patient monitored carefully during discontinuation.

Metabolic Effects: Tricyclic antidepressants have been associated with porphyrinogenicity in susceptible patients.

Renal Function: It is also advisable to monitor renal function during long-term therapy with tricyclic antidepressants.

Dental Effects: Lengthy treatment with tricyclic antidepressants can lead to an increased incidence of dental caries.

Lacrimation: Decreased lacrimation and accumulation of mucoid secretions, due to the anticholinergic properties of tricyclic antidepressants, may cause damage to the corneal epithelium in patients with contact lenses.

Endocrine Effects: As with certain other psychotherapeutic drugs, clomipramine elevates prolactin levels. Tissue culture experiments indicate that approximately one-third of human breast cancers are prolactin dependent in vitro, a factor of potential importance if the prescription of clomipramine is contemplated in a patient with a previously detected breast cancer. Although disturbances such as galactorrhea, amenorrhea, gynecomastia, and impotence have been reported, the clinical significance of elevated serum prolactin levels is unknown for most patients. An increase in mammary neoplasms has been found in rodents after chronic administration of neuroleptic drugs. Neither clinical studies nor epidemiologic studies conducted to date, however, have shown an association between chronic administration of these drugs and mammary tumorigenesis: the available evidence is considered too limited to be conclusive at this time.

Children: As clomipramine has not been studied in patients under 10 years of age, specific recommendations for use in this age group cannot be provided. The long-term effects of clomipramine on childhood growth and development have not been determined.

Drug Interactions: Patients should be warned that, while taking clomipramine, their responses to alcoholic beverages, other CNS depressants (e.g., barbiturates, benzodiazepines or general anesthetics) or anticholinergic agents (e.g., atropine, antihistamines, biperiden, levodopa) may be exaggerated.

When tricyclic antidepressants are given in combination with anticholinergics or neuroleptics with an anticholinergic action, hyperexcitation states or delirium may occur, as well as attacks of glaucoma.

Tricyclic antidepressants should not be employed in combination with antiarrhythmic agents of the quinidine type (see Warnings, Cardiovascular).

Since clomipramine may diminish or abolish the antihypertensive effects of guanethidine, bethanidine, clonidine, reserpine, or alpha-methyldopa, patients requiring concomitant treatment for hypertension should be given antihypertensives of a different type (e.g., diuretics, vasodilators, betablockers).

Clomipramine may potentiate the cardiovascular effects of norepinephrine or epinephrine, amphetamine, as well as nasal drops and local anesthetics containing sympathomimetics (e.g., isoprenaline, ephedrine, phenylephrine).

Fluoxetine, fluvoxamine and other selective serotonin reuptake inhibitors (SSRIs) may increase the activity and plasma concentrations of tricyclic antidepressants with corresponding adverse effects.

Caution should be exercised if clomipramine is administered together with cimetidine or methylphenidate since these drugs have been shown to inhibit the metabolism of several tricyclic antidepressants. Clinically significant increases in plasma levels of clomipramine may occur, necessitating a dosage reduction.

Substances which activate the hepatic mono-oxygenase enzyme system (e.g., barbiturates, carbamazepine, phenytoin, nicotine and oral contraceptives) may lower plasma concentrations of tricyclic antidepressants and so reduce their antidepressive effects. In addition, clomipramine may increase plasma levels of phenytoin and carbamazepine, therefore, it may be necessary to adjust the dosage of these drugs.

Clomipramine should not be administered for a period of at least 14 days after the discontinuation of treatment with MAO inhibitors due to the potential for severe interactions (see Contraindications). The same caution should also be observed when administering an MAO inhibitor after previous treatment with clomipramine.

Clomipramine should be discontinued prior to elective surgery for as long as is clinically feasible, since little is known about the interaction with general anesthetics.

Concomitant treatment with neuroleptic agents (e.g., phenothiazines and butyrophenones) may result in increased plasma concentrations of clomipramine, a lowered convulsion threshold and seizures. Combination with thioridazine may produce cardiac arrhythmias. No such effects are known to occur in combination with diazepam but it might be necessary to lower the dosage of clomipramine if administered concomitantly with alprazolam or disulfiram.

Tricyclic antidepressants may potentiate the anticoagulant effect of coumarin drugs by inhibiting hepatic metabolism of these drugs. Careful monitoring of plasma prothrombin is therefore advised.

If administered concomitantly with estrogens, the dose of clomipramine should be reduced since steroid hormones inhibit the metabolism of clomipramine.

Teratology: No teratogenic effects were observed in rats and mice at doses up to 20 times the maximum daily human dose. Slight nonspecific fetotoxic effects were seen in the offspring of pregnant mice given doses 10 times the maximum daily human dose. Slight nonspecific embryotoxicity was observed in rats given doses 5 to 10 times the maximum daily human dose.

Animal Toxicology: As with tricyclic compounds, clomipramine has been associated with changes in testicular and lung tissue in long-term animal toxicology studies. In 1- and 2-year studies in rats, a dose 4 times the maximum daily human dose was associated with phospholipidosis in the lungs and changes in the testes (atrophy, aspermatogenesis, and calcification). In a 1-year toxicity study in dogs, testicular atrophy was detected in animals receiving 10 times the maximum recommended daily human dose.

Adverse Effects: The most commonly observed adverse events associated with the use of clomipramine and not seen at an equivalent incidence among placebo-treated patients were gastrointestinal complaints, including dry mouth, constipation, nausea, dyspepsia, and anorexia; nervous system complaints, including somnolence, tremor, dizziness, nervousness and myoclonus; genitourinary complaints including changed libido, ejaculatory failure, impotence and micturition disorder; and other miscellaneous complaints, including fatigue, sweating, increased appetite, weight gain, and visual changes.

If severe neurological or psychiatric reactions occur, clomipramine should be withdrawn.

Elderly patients are particularly susceptible to anticholinergic, psychiatric, neurological and cardiovascular effects.

The following adverse reactions have also been reported with clomipramine or other tricyclic antidepressants. (Frequency estimates: Frequent: $>10\%$; Occasional: $>1\text{-}10\%$; Rare: $>0.01\text{-}1\%$; Isolated cases: $<0.01\%$).

Neurological: Occasional: headache, paresthesia (numbness, tingling sensation, symptoms suggestive of peripheral neuropathy), delirium, muscle hypertonia. Rare: epileptic seizures. Isolated cases: tinnitus, incoordination, ataxia, alterations in EEG patterns, extrapyramidal symptoms, speech disorders, weakness, hyperpyrexia.

Behavioral: Occasional: drowsiness, insomnia, confusional states with hallucinations (particularly in geriatric patients and patients suffering from Parkinson's disease), anxiety, agitation, restlessness, nightmares, aggravated depression, hypomania, mania, decrease in memory, feeling of unreality, yawning. Rare: activation of latent psychosis. Isolated cases: aggressiveness.

Anticholinergic: Frequent: dry mouth and rarely associated sublingual adenitis, disturbances of visual accommodation, hot flushes. Occasional: dilation of the urinary tract. Isolated cases: mydriasis, glaucoma, paralytic ileus.

Cardiovascular: Frequent: hypotension, particularly orthostatic hypotension with associated vertigo, sinus tachycardia, ECG changes (including flattening or inversion of T wave, depressed S-T segments) in patients of normal cardiac status. Occasional: arrhythmia, disturbances in cardiac conduction (e.g., widening of QRS complex, PQ changes, bundle-branch block), palpitation, syncope. Isolated cases: hypertension, congestive heart failure, myocardial infarction, heart block, asystole, stroke, peripheral vasospastic reactions.

Hematologic: Isolated cases: agranulocytosis, eosinophilia, leukopenia, purpura and thrombocytopenia may occur as an idiosyncratic response. One case of pancytopenia has been reported.

Gastrointestinal: Occasional: vomiting, abdominal cramps. Rare: diarrhea, elevated transaminases. Isolated cases: bitter taste, stomatitis, epigastric distress, black tongue, dysphagia, increased salivation, hepatitis with or without jaundice.

Respiratory: Isolated cases: bronchospasm.

Endocrine: Isolated cases: gynecomastia in the male, breast enlargement and galactorrhea in the female, testicular swelling, elevation or depression of blood sugar levels, weight loss, inappropriate antidiuretic hormone (SIADH) secretion syndrome, increase in prolactin levels, menstrual irregularity.

Allergic or Toxic: Occasional: skin rash, urticaria. Isolated cases: petechiae, itching, photosensitization (avoid excessive exposure to sunlight), edema (general or of face and tongue), drug fever, obstructive jaundice, nasal congestion, alopecia, allergic alveolitis (pneumonia) with or without eosinophilia, systemic analphylactic/anaphylactoid reactions including hypotension.

Withdrawal Symptoms: Abrupt cessation of treatment with tricyclic antidepressants after prolonged administration may occasionally produce nausea, vomiting, abdominal pain, diarrhea, insomnia, nervousness, anxiety, headache and malaise. These symptoms are not indicative of addiction.

Overdose: Since children may be more sensitive than adults to acute overdosage with tricyclic antidepressants, and since fatalities in children have been reported, effort should be made to avoid potential overdose particularly in this age group.

Symptoms: These may vary in severity depending on various factors such as the amount of drug absorbed, the interval between drug ingestion and start of treatment, and the age of the patient. Accidental ingestion in children should be regarded as serious and potentially fatal.

Symptoms generally appear within 4 hours of ingestion and reach maximum severity after 24 hours. Owing to delayed absorption (increased anticholinergic effect due to overdose), long half-life and enterohepatic recycling of the drug, the patient may be at risk for up to 4 to 6 days.

Symptoms may include drowsiness, stupor, ataxia, vomiting, cyanosis, restlessness, agitation, delirium, severe perspiration, hyperactive reflexes, muscle rigidity, athetoid and choreiform movements, and convulsions. Hyperpyrexia, mydriasis, bowel and bladder paralysis, and respiratory depression may occur.

Hypotension and initial hypertension may occur. However, the usual finding is increasing hypotension which may lead eventually to shock. Serious cardiovascular disturbances are frequently present, including tachycardia, cardiac arrhythmias (flutter, atriofibrillation, premature ventricular beats and ventricular tachycardia) as well as impaired myocardial conduction, atrioventricular and intraventricular block, ECG abnormalities (such as widened QRS complexes and marked S-T shifts), signs of congestive heart failure and cardiac arrest. Coma may ensue.

Treatment: Patients in whom overdosage is suspected should be admitted to hospital without delay. No specific antidote is available and treatment is essentially symptomatic and supportive.

Gastric lavage or aspiration should be performed promptly and is recommended up to 12 hours or even more after the overdose, since the anticholinergic effect of the drug may delay gastric emptying. Administration of activated charcoal may help to reduce absorption of the drug. As clomipramine is largely protein bound, forced diuresis, peritoneal dialysis and hemodialysis are unlikely to be of value.

Treatment should be designed to insure maintenance of the vital functions. An open airway should be maintained in comatose patients and assisted ventilation instituted, if necessary, but respiratory stimulants should not be used. Hyperpyrexia should be controlled by external measures, such as ice packs and cooling sponge baths. Acidosis may be treated by cautious administration of sodium bicarbonate. Adequate renal function should be maintained.

ECG monitoring in an intensive care unit is recommended in all patients, particularly in the presence of ECG abnormalities, and should be maintained for several days after the cardiac rhythm has returned to normal. Unexpected deaths attributed to cardiac arrhythmias have been reported several days following an apparent recovery from tricyclic antidepressant overdose. Correction of hypoxia and acidosis, if present, may be beneficial. Correction of metabolic acidosis and low potassium concentrations by means of bicarbonate i.v. and potassium substitution may also be effective for treatment of arrhythmias. If bradyarrhythmia or AV-block occur, consider temporary insertion of a cardiac pacemaker. Because of its

Anafranil (cont'd)

effect on cardiac conduction, digitalis should be used only with caution. If rapid digitalization is required for the treatment of congestive heart failure, special care should be exercised in using the drug.

External stimulation should be minimized to reduce the tendency to convulsions. If convulsions occur, anticonvulsants (preferably i.v. diazepam) should be administered. Barbiturates may intensify respiratory depression, particularly in children, and aggravate hypotension and coma. Paraldehyde may be used in some children to counteract muscular hypertonus and convulsions with less likelihood of causing respiratory depression. If the patient fails to respond rapidly to anticonvulsants, artificial ventilation should be instituted. Prompt control of convulsions is essential since they aggravate hypoxia and acidosis and may thereby precipitate cardiac arrhythmias and arrest.

Shock should be treated with supportive measures, such as i.v. fluids, plasma expanders and oxygen. The use of corticosteroids in shock is controversial and may be contraindicated in tricyclic antidepressant overdose. Hypotension usually responds to elevation of the foot of the bed. Pressor agents (but **not** epinephrine) should be given cautiously, if indicated. In the event of reduced myocardial function, consider recourse to treatment with dopamine or dobutamine by i.v. drip.

Since it has been reported that physostigmine may cause severe bradycardia, asystole and seizures, its use is not recommended in cases of overdosage with clomipramine.

Deaths by deliberate or accidental overdosage have occurred with this class of drugs. Since the propensity for suicide is high in depressed patients, a suicide attempt by other means may occur during the recovery phase. The possibility of simultaneous ingestion of other drugs should also be considered.

Dosage: Dosage should be individualized according to the requirements of each patient. Treatment should be initiated at the lowest recommended dose and increased gradually, noting carefully the clinical response and any evidence of intolerance. During the initial dose titration phase, the total daily dose of clomipramine should be divided and administered with meals to reduce gastrointestinal side effects.

Owing to the long elimination half-lives of clomipramine and its active metabolite, desmethylclomipramine, steady-state plasma levels may not be achieved until 2 to 3 weeks after a dosage adjustment. It may thus be advisable to wait 2 to 3 weeks after the initial dose titration phase, before attempting further dosage adjustments. It should be kept in mind that a lag in therapeutic response usually occurs at the onset of therapy, lasting from several days to a few weeks. Increasing the dosage does not normally shorten this latent period and may increase the incidence of side effects.

Depression: Initial Dosage: Adults: Clomipramine therapy should be initiated at daily doses of 25 mg. Dosage may be increased by 25 mg increments, as tolerated, at 3- to 4-day intervals up to a total daily dose of 150 mg by the end of 2 weeks. Thereafter, the dose may be gradually increased over a period of several weeks to 200 mg. Doses in excess of 200 mg daily are not recommended for outpatients. Occasionally, in more severely depressed hospitalized patients, dosages up to 300 mg daily may be required.

Elderly and Debilitated Patients: In general, lower dosages are recommended for these patients. Initially, 20 to 30 mg daily in divided doses is suggested, with very gradual increments, depending on tolerance and response. Blood pressure and cardiac rhythm should be checked frequently, particularly in patients who have unstable cardiovascular function.

Maintenance Dosage: Dosage during maintenance therapy should be kept at the lowest effective level. To minimize daytime sedation during maintenance treatment, the total daily dosage may be given as a single dose at bedtime. Medication should be continued for the expected duration of the depressive episode in order to minimize the possibility of relapse following clinical improvement.

Obsessive Compulsive Disorders: Initial Dosage: Adults: Clomipramine therapy in adult obsessive compulsive patients should be initiated at daily doses of 25 mg. Dosage may be increased by 25 mg increments, as tolerated, at 3- to 4-day intervals up to a total daily dose of 100 or 150 mg by the end of 2 weeks. Thereafter, the dose may be gradually increased over a period of several weeks to 200 mg. Doses in excess of 200 mg/day are not generally recommended for outpatients. However, in the treatment of severe cases of Obsessive Compulsive Disorder, daily doses of up to 250 mg may be required.

Children and Adolescents: In children aged 10 to 17 years, an initial dose of 25 mg/day is recommended. Dosage may be increased by 25 mg increments, as tolerated, at 3- to 4-day intervals. By the end of 2 weeks, patients may be titrated up to 100 to 150 mg/day or 3 mg/kg, whichever is lower. Thereafter, the dose may be gradually increased to 200 mg or 3 mg/kg whichever is lower. A total daily dose above 200 mg should not be used in children or adolescents.

Elderly and Debilitated Patients: In general, lower dosages are recommended for these patients. Initially, 20 to 30 mg daily in divided doses is suggested, with very gradual increments, depending on tolerance and response. Blood pressure and cardiac rhythm should be checked frequently, particularly in patients who have unstable cardiovascular function.

Maintenance Dosage (Adults, Children, and Adolescents): Double blind extension phase studies of clomipramine therapy in patients with Obsessive Compulsive Disorder have followed patients for up to 52 weeks. Although placebo enrollment in these studies was inadequate to permit a controlled comparison, data suggest that clomipramine therapy can be continued for up to a year without loss of efficacy.

Dosage adjustments may be made during maintenance therapy with the objective of maintaining the patient at the lowest effective dose. To minimize daytime sedation during maintenance treatment, the total daily dosage may be given as a single dose at bedtime. If symptoms recur, the dosage should be increased until the symptoms are controlled. Patients should be reassessed periodically to determine the need for continued treatment. To avoid withdrawal symptoms upon discontinuation of therapy, a gradual decrease in dosage and careful patient monitoring are recommended.

Supplied: 10 mg: Each cream-colored, triangular, sugar-coated tablet, contains: clomipramine HCl 10 mg. Nonmedicinal ingredients: cellulose compounds, cornstarch, gelatin, glycerin, iron oxide, lactose, magnesium stearate, polyethylene glycol, polyvinylpyrrolidone, sucrose, talc and titanium dioxide. Bottles of 100 and 500.

25 mg: Each cream-colored, round, biconvex, sugar-coated tablet, branded GEIGY on one side and FH on the other side in black, contains: clomipramine HCl 25 mg. Nonmedicinal ingredients: cellulose compounds, colloidal silicon dioxide, cornstarch, glycerin, iron oxide, lactose, magnesium stearate, polyethylene glycol, polyvinylpyrrolidone, stearic acid, sucrose, talc and titanium dioxide. Bottles of 100 and 500.

50 mg: Each white, round, beveled edge, film-coated tablet, engraved GEIGY on one side and LP on the other side, contains: clomipramine HCl 50 mg. Nonmedicinal ingredients: cellulose compounds, colloidal silicon dioxide, lactose, magnesium stearate, polysorbates, talc and titanium dioxide. Bottles of 100 and 500.

Protect from heat. Store between 2 and 30°C. Keep out of reach of children.

(Shown in Product Recognition Section)

Reviewed 1997

ANA-KIT®

Bayer

Epinephrine—Chlorpheniramine Maleate

Allergy Therapy

Pharmacology: Epinephrine: The most valuable drug for the emergency treatment of severe allergic reactions is epinephrine. The vasoconstrictor effect of epinephrine on the capillary directly antagonizes the generalized vasodilation produced by histamine. Epinephrine reverses the increased permeability of dilated capillaries to plasma. The shock of severe allergic reactions is due to the loss of circulating blood volume by pooling in the dilated capillary beds and loss of plasma into the tissues. Epinephrine quickly restores circulating blood volume and blood pressure by constricting the capillary bed. The itching during episodes of hives or angioedema is promptly relieved by epinephrine. Epinephrine is a powerful relaxer of the smooth muscle of the bronchioles, stomach, intestine, pregnant uterus and urinary bladder wall. The bronchospasm, wheezing and dyspnea of the acute allergic reactions are relieved. Where abdominal cramping, defecation or involuntary urination have occurred during severe allergic attacks, epinephrine rapidly produces relief. S.C. or i.m. administered epinephrine has a rapid onset and short duration of action. S.C. administration during asthmatic attacks may produce bronchodilation within 5 to 10 minutes, and maximal effects may occur within 20 minutes.

Chlorpheniramine: Chlorpheniramine is an effective agent in nullifying the characteristic effects of histamine and is especially valuable in the prophylaxis and relief of many allergic symptoms. It is readily absorbed from the intestinal tract and released into the tissues from the bloodstream. This action is both prompt and sustained. Elimination of the drug is such that there is a low incidence of side effects.

Indications: For use by adults and pediatric patients under the following situations: 1. Allergic reactions including anaphylactic shock due to stinging insects (primarily of the Hymenoptera order, which includes bees, wasps, hornets, yellow jackets, bumble bees, and fire ants). 2. Severe allergic or anaphylactoid reactions due to allergy injections, exposures to pollens, dusts, molds, foods, drugs, and exercise or unknown substances (so-called idiopathic anaphylaxis).

In the sensitive patient, severe allergic reactions and anaphylactic shock may occur within minutes of the insect sting or exposure to an allergenic substance.

Symptoms may include bronchoconstriction, wheezing, sneezing, hoarseness, urticaria, angioedema, erythema, pruritus, tachycardia, thready pulse, falling blood pressure, sense of oppression or impending doom, disorientation, cramping abdominal pain, incontinence, faintness, and loss of consciousness.

The Ana-Kit is compactly designed to be carried and used by patients when severe symptoms arise, and the patient is out of reach of immediate attention by a doctor or hospital.

Contraindications: Epinephrine must not be given intra-arterially as marked vasoconstriction may result in gangrene.

This unit is not intended for i.v. use. Further dilution would be necessary and is not practical with this emergency syringe.

Epinephrine Injection USP (1:1 000) must not be used if there is hypersensitivity to any of the components.

Epinephrine is contraindicated in narrow-angle glaucoma; cardiogenic, traumatic, or hemorrhagic shock; cardiac dilation; cerebral arteriosclerosis; and organic brain damage.

Epinephrine should not be used to counteract circulatory collapse or hypotension due to phenothiazines, since such agents may reverse the pressor effect of epinephrine, leading to a further lowering of blood pressure.

Epinephrine should not be administered concomitantly with other sympathomimetic agents, since the effects are additive and may be detrimental to the patient.

Chlorpheniramine: No known contraindications.

Warnings: Epinephrine: Overdosage or accidental i.v. administration of conventional s.c. doses may induce severe or fatal hypertension, or cerebrovascular hemorrhage. Fatalities may also occur from pulmonary edema resulting from peripheral constriction and cardiac stimulation. The marked pressor effects may be counteracted by use of rapidly acting vasodilators, such as the nitrites and alpha-adrenergic blockers.

Deaths have been reported in asthmatics treated with epinephrine following the use of isoproterenol or orciprenaline.

Epinephrine is the preferred treatment for serious allergic or other emergency situations even though this product contains sodium bisulfite, a sulfite that may in other products cause allergic-type reactions including anaphylactic symptoms or life-threatening or less severe asthmatic episodes in certain susceptible persons. The alternatives to using epinephrine in a life-threatening situation may not be satisfactory. The presence of a sulfite(s) in this product should not deter administration of the drug for treatment of serious allergic or other emergency situations.

Epinephrine must be administered with great caution, if at all, in patients with cardiac arrhythmias, coronary artery or organic heart disease and hypertension. In patients with coronary insufficiency or ischemic heart disease, epinephrine may precipitate or aggravate angina pectoris as well as produce potentially fatal ventricular arrhythmias. Epinephrine should be administered only with great caution to elderly patients, those with diabetes mellitus, hyperthyroidism, or psychoneurotic disorders; also to those with long-standing bronchial asthma or emphysema if such individuals may also have degenerative heart disease, and to pregnant women (see Pregnancy). Patients with Parkinson's disease may notice a temporary worsening of symptoms.

Chlorpheniramine: Chlorpheniramine should be used with extreme caution in patients with stenosing peptic ulcer, pyloroduodenal obstruction, prostatic hypertrophy, or bladder neck obstruction. These compounds have an atropine-like action and therefore should be used with caution in patients with a history of increased intraocular pressure, cardiovascular disease, or hypertension. The asthmatic patient should take the chlorpheniramine tablets with caution.

Precautions: Ana-Kit is not intended to be a substitute for medical attention or hospital care. The kit is designed to be compact and easy to carry, and to provide emergency treatment when medical care is not immediately available. Highly sensitive individuals should have the kit readily available at all times. Because of its small size it can be carried by outdoor sportsmen, golfers, gardeners, or any sensitive individual who may be exposed to stinging insects (wasps, hornets, yellow jackets, fire ants or bees) or other potentially life-threatening allergens. The drugs in the Ana-Kit, when used as directed immediately following exposure to an allergen, may prove life-saving. Certain changes in the emergency instructions and in the kit itself may be made by the doctor according to the needs of the patient. **In all cases the physician should instruct the patient, and/or any other person who might be in a position to administer the epinephrine, in the proper use of the syringe and the other components of this kit.**

Drug Interactions: Caution is indicated in patients receiving cardiac glycosides or mercurial diuretics, since these agents may sensitize the myocardium to beta-adrenergic stimulation and make cardiac arrhythmias more likely.

The effects of epinephrine may be potentiated by tricyclic antidepressants, sodium levothyroxine, and certain antihistamines, notably chlorpheniramine, tripelennamine, and diphenhydramine.

The cardiostimulating and bronchodilating effects of epinephrine are antagonized by beta-adrenergic blocking drugs, such as propranolol. The vasoconstricting and hypertensive effects are antagonized by alpha-adrenergic blocking drugs, such as phentolamine. Ergot alkaloids and phenothiazines may also reverse the pressor effects of epinephrine.

Diabetic patients receiving epinephrine may require an increased dose of insulin or oral hypoglycemic drugs.

Carcinogenesis, Mutagenesis, Impairment of Fertility: There are no data from either animal or human studies regarding the carcinogenicity or mutagenicity of epinephrine or chlorpheniramine, and no studies have been conducted to determine their potential for the impairment of fertility.

Pregnancy: Teratogenic Effects. Epinephrine has been shown to be teratogenic in rats and hamsters at dose levels hundreds of times as high as the maximal human dose. Although there are no adequate or well-controlled studies in pregnant women, epinephrine crosses the placenta and its use during pregnancy may cause anoxia in the fetus. Epinephrine should be used in pregnancy only if the potential benefit justifies the potential risk to the fetus.

Children: Administered epinephrine or chlorpheniramine with caution to infants and children (see Dosage). Syncope has occurred following the administration of epinephrine to asthmatic children.

Adverse Effects: Epinephrine: Adverse reactions include transient, moderate anxiety, apprehensiveness, restlessness, tremor, weakness, dizziness, sweating, palpitations, pallor, nausea and vomiting, headache, and respiratory difficulties. These symptoms occur in some persons receiving therapeutic doses of epinephrine, but are more likely to occur, or to occur in exaggerated form, in those with hypertension or hyperthyroidism. Excessive doses cause acute hypertension. Arrhythmias, including fatal ventricular fibrillation, have been reported, particularly in patients with underlying cardiac disease or those receiving certain drugs (see Drug Interactions).

Rapid rises in blood pressure have produced cerebral hemorrhage, particularly in elderly patients with cerebrovascular disease. Angina may occur in patients with coronary-artery disease.

Chlorpheniramine: Drowsiness, dizziness, blurred vision, dry mouth and gastrointestinal upsets may occur.

Occupational Hazards: Patients should not drive or operate machinery after taking chlorpheniramine. Large doses produce CNS depression and occasionally tremors or convulsions.

Reports of hematological disorders are rare.

Overdose: Symptoms and Treatment: Epinephrine: Epinephrine is rapidly inactivated in the body, and treatment is primarily supportive. If necessary, pressor effects may be counteracted by rapidly acting vasodilators or alpha-adrenergic blocking drugs. If prolonged hypotension follows such measures, it may be necessary to administer another pressor drug, such as levarterenol.

Overdosage of epinephrine may produce extremely elevated arterial pressure, which may result in cerebrovascular hemorrhage, particularly in elderly patients.

If an epinephrine overdose induces pulmonary edema that interferes with respiration, treatment consists of a rapidly acting alpha-adrenergic blocking drug such as phentolamine and/or intermittent positive-pressure respiration.

Epinephrine overdosage can also cause transient bradycardia followed by tachycardia, and these may be accompanied by potentially fatal cardiac arrhythmias. Ventricular premature contractions may appear within 1 minute after injection and may be followed by multilocal ventricular tachycardia (prefibrillation rhythm). Subsidence of the ventricular effects may be followed by atrial tachycardia and occasionally by atrioventricular block. Treatment of arrhythmias consists of administration of a beta-adrenergic blocking drug such as propranolol.

Overdosage sometimes also results in extreme pallor and coldness of the skin, metabolic acidosis, and kidney failure. Suitable corrective measures must be taken.

Chlorpheniramine: Overdose symptoms may be sedation, apnea, cardiovascular collapse to stimulation, insomnia, hallucinations, tremors or convulsions. Also there may be dizziness, tinnitus, ataxia, blurred vision, hypotension, dry mouth, flushing and abdominal symptoms.

The patient should be induced to vomit, preferably with ipecac syrup and large amounts of water. Prevent aspiration of vomitus. Gastric lavage may be necessary using activated charcoal and saline. Hyperosmotic cathartics such as Milk of Magnesia may hasten elimination of residual cling. Vasopressors can be used to correct hypotension. Diazepam may be used to control seizures. Hyperpyrexia can be treated with cool sponges or a hypothermic blanket.

Dosage: Parenteral drug products should be inspected visually for particulate matter and discoloration prior to administration, whenever solution and container permit. Do not use Epinephrine Injection if it has a pinkish or darker than slightly yellow color or contains a precipitate.

The physician who prescribes the Ana-Kit should review the package insert in detail with the patient. This review should include the proper use of the 2-dose epinephrine syringe to insure that s.c. or i.m. injections are given into the deltoid region of the arm or the anteriolateral aspect of the thigh. See also Information for the Patient.

Epinephrine: For s.c. or i.m. injection only.

Adults and children over 12 years: 0.3 mL; 6 to 12 years: 0.2 mL; 2 to 6 years: 0.15 mL; Infants to 2 years: 0.05 to 0.1 mL.

When syringe is properly set up, as directed in the Patient Directions (see Information for the Patient), a 0.3 mL dose is administered when plunger is pushed until it stops. Syringe barrel has 0.1 mL graduations so that smaller doses can be measured. (Operation of syringe is explained in the Patient Directions For Use—see Information for the Patient.)

If after 10 minutes from the first injection symptoms are not noticeably improved, administer a second dose of epinephrine from the syringe.

Chlorpheniramine: Tablets are chewable antihistamines. Adults and children over 12 years: 4 tablets; children 6 to 12 years: 2 tablets; children under 6 years: 1 tablet.

Information for the Patient: See Blue Section—Information for the Patient "Ana-Kit".

Supplied: Each kit contains: 1 syringe containing 2 single doses of epinephrine USP 1:1 000; 4 tablets of chlorpheniramine maleate USP 2 mg; 2 sterilizing swabs of isopropyl alcohol 70 %; 1 tourniquet and complete instruction sheet. Epinephrine injection contains sodium bisulfite. Store at room temperature (approximately 25°C).

ANALGESIC BALM

Warner-Lambert Consumer Healthcare

Menthol—Methyl Salicylate

Topical Analgesic

Indications: For the local treatment of muscular and joint pains.

Contraindications: Any sensitivity to the components.

Precautions: Avoid contact with eyes, mucous membranes or broken skin. Keep out of reach of children. In case of accidental swallowing, seek medical advice.

Dosage: Apply by thoroughly rubbing into the skin to promote absorption. To prolong the effect, cover the surface with a piece of gauze or linen.

Supplied: Each g of amber-yellow ointment contains: menthol 20% and methyl salicylate 20% in a petrolatum base. Nonmedicinal ingredients: ceresin, lanolin, petrolatum and wax. Tubes of 30 g.

ANANDRON® Ⓟ

Hoechst Marion Roussel

Nilutamide

Nonsteroidal Antiandrogen

Pharmacology: Nilutamide is a pure, nonsteroidal antiandrogen which blocks androgens binding at receptor target cells. Nilutamide is specific and does not bind to any other steroidal receptors; therefore, it does not have any other hormonal or antihormonal activity.

Nilutamide demonstrates potent antiandrogenic effects by inhibiting androgen uptake and/or inhibiting nuclear binding of androgen in target tissues. In adult male rats, ventral prostate and seminal vesicle weights were markedly reduced by daily administration of nilutamide.

Androgen-sensitive prostatic carcinoma cells respond to treatment that counteracts the effect of androgen and/or removes the source of androgen e.g., castration. Combined with castration, nilutamide exerts a total peripheral antiandrogenic activity by antagonizing the action of androgens of adrenal origin which otherwise may maintain the proliferation of prostatic cancer cells.

Nilutamide also inhibits the consequences of the initial rise of testosterone plasma levels observed after treatment with LHRH agonists.

Clinical studies with nilutamide have demonstrated improvement in metastatic bone pain, diminished consumption of analgesics, regression of the cancer together with reduced rate of objective progression and higher survival actuarial rate of patients with metastatic prostate cancer.

Nilutamide is rapidly and completely absorbed as indicated by the low level of fecal radioactivity measured after administration of radiolabeled nilutamide. Unchanged nilutamide represents the major active compound. In patients, nilutamide has a long half-life of 56 hours (range from 23 to 87 hours). Nilutamide is 84% bound to plasma proteins. The plasma concentrations are dose-related and steady-state levels are reached approximately 2 weeks after initiation of treatment. No evidence of accumulation has been demonstrated.

Nilutamide is mainly excreted in the urine as metabolites. Using radiolabeled nilutamide, unchanged drug accounts for only 3% of recovered urinary radioactivity. Fecal excretion accounts for 1.4 to 7% of the total administered dose after 4 to 5 days. The major metabolic pathway is by reduction of the nitro group and the amino derivative of nilutamide represents the major metabolite. Among the metabolites of nilutamide only the hydroxymethylnitro derivative shows some androgen receptor binding affinity.

Indications: In the treatment of metastatic prostatic carcinoma (Stage D_2) in conjunction with surgical castration.

Contraindications: Patients with known hypersensitivity to the drug or to any constituents of the drug product and in patients with severe hepatic dysfunction or with severe respiratory insufficiency.

Nilutamide is contraindicated in women and children.

Warnings: The hepatic and respiratory state of the patient should be evaluated and the necessity to report any respiratory symptoms as soon as they appear should be emphasized.

Cases of interstitial lung disease have been reported with the use of nilutamide. If dyspnea or worsening of dyspnea occurs, treatment should be interrupted and a chest x-ray performed immediately. If interstitial pneumopathy is diagnosed, nilutamide must be discontinued and corticosteroid treatment may be considered.

Cases of hepatic dysfunction have been reported with the use of nilutamide. If clinical symptoms give rise to a suspicion of liver dysfunction, transaminases should be measured. If an increase in serum transaminases above 3 times the upper limit of normal laboratory range is shown, treatment must be interrupted.

Precautions: Information for the Patient: Patients should be informed that they should not interrupt their dosing or stop taking nilutamide without consulting their physician(s).

Occupational Hazards: Where patients are participating in activities such as driving an automobile or operating machinery, attention should be drawn to possible visual disturbances mainly due to an increase in adaptation time when passing from a well lit area to a more dimly lit area. These disturbances, should they occur, can decrease even if treatment is continued and can be ameliorated with the use of sunglasses.

Patients should be informed about signs/symptoms suggestive of liver dysfunction (e.g., right upper quadrant tenderness, dark urine, persistent anorexia, nausea, vomiting, jaundice, pruritus or unexplained flu-like symptoms) and be advised to contact their physician should these occur.

Patients administered nilutamide should be warned against consuming alcohol because of a possible disulfiram-like reaction.

Drug Interactions: Nilutamide, apparently through an effect on certain oxidative microsomal enzymes, may reduce the hepatic metabolism of warfarin-type anticoagulants, phenytoin, propranolol, chlordiazepoxide, lidocaine, diazepam and theophylline, thereby delaying elimination and increasing blood

Anandron (cont'd)

levels of these drugs. Benzodiazepines that are not oxidized by the hepatic system do not exhibit this effect.

Dosage of the drugs mentioned above, and other similarly metabolized drugs, may require adjustment when starting or stopping concomitantly administered nilutamide, to maintain safe optimum therapeutic blood levels.

In case of associated treatment with warfarin-type anticoagulants, close monitoring of prothrombin time is recommended and adjustment of the anticoagulant dose may be necessary.

Alcohol intolerance (disulfiram-like reaction) may occur if alcohol is consumed during treatment with nilutamide.

Specific Patient Populations: In an uncontrolled pilot study conducted in a Japanese population, interstitial pneumonitis was reported and was considered possibly or probably related to nilutamide in 6 out of 47 patients (12.8%). This incidence figure is higher than the incidence of interstitial pneumonitis available from the international database of placebo-controlled trials in orchiectomized patients (1.1%; see Adverse Effects). In concurrent pharmacokinetics/metabolism investigations in Japanese vs Caucasian patients, no differences in the results could account for the higher incidence of this event in this race. The incidence rate of raised transaminases in the Japanese study was 19%. Special care should be observed when treating Asian patients.

Adverse Effects: Clinical Trials: Adverse Drug Reactions: Table I lists the possibly or probably drug-related adverse events (adverse reactions) most frequently reported during placebo-controlled clinical trials of nilutamide in conjunction with surgical castration. Hot flushes, decreased libido and impotence are known to occur with surgical castration.

Table I—Anandron

Adverse Effects

Adverse Reaction	Percentage of Patients Nilutamide (n=560)	Placebo (n=558)
Hot flushes	13.8	9.7
Impaired adaptation to darkness	10.5	0.7
Nausea	4.3	1.1
Alcohol intolerance	4.1	0.2
Dizziness	2.9	0.5
Chromatopsia	2.5	0
ALT increased	2.0	0.7
Abnormal vision	1.8	0.5
AST increased	1.4	0.4
Photophobia	1.4	0
Hyperglycemia	1.3	1.6
Impotence	1.3	0.5
Dyspnea	1.1	0.2
Gynecomastia	1.1	1.3
Impaired light adaptation	1.1	0
Interstitial lung disease	1.1	0
Eye disorder	0.9	0.4
Libido decreased	0.9	0
Sweating increased	0.9	0.5
Vomiting	0.9	0
Anorexia	0.7	0
Blurred vision	0.7	0
Hepatitis	0.7	0
Hypertension	0.7	0.2
Anemia	0.5	0.2
Asthenia	0.5	0.4
Gastrointestinal pain	0.5	0.2
Lung disorder	0.5	0
Malaise	0.5	0

Adverse Events Irrespective of Relationship with Nilutamide: Other adverse events reported overall in clinical trials (of which most occurred with similar frequencies in patients receiving placebo), others known to commonly occur in elderly patients or expected in patients with metastatic prostate cancer included:

Cardiovascular: cerebrovascular accident (1.4%), heart failure (1.0%). Rare cases of tachycardia.

Digestive: constipation (2.6%), gastrointestinal disorder (2.0%). Rare cases of diarrhea.

Metabolic and Nutritional: peripheral edema (1.5%).

Nervous System: headache (2.6%), depression (1.1%), insomnia (1.1%). Rare cases of drowsiness and anxiety.

Skin and Appendages: pruritus (1.1%). Rare cases of maculopapular rash and hirsutism.

Special Senses: rare cases of dazzle and dry mouth.

Urogenital: urinary tract infection (1.3%).

No causal relationship of these experiences with drug treatment has been established.

Post-Marketing Surveillance: The adverse events which have been spontaneously reported worldwide further to marketing of nilutamide and which are considered possibly or probably related to the drug (adverse reactions) include the following: interstitial pneumonitis (most of the cases showed a favorable outcome after treatment discontinuation, however, there have been reports of fatality), hepatocellular or mixed liver injury, and unspecified vision disorders. Isolated cases of angina pectoris, anxiety dyspnea palpitation, cold extremities, dizziness, headache, gynecomastia, maculopapular rash, urticaria, vomiting and weight increase have been reported.

Aplastic anemia (including 1 fatality) has been reported rarely in patients treated with nilutamide but no specific relationship to the drug product has been ascertained.

Overdose: Symptoms and Treatment: At the dose of 900 mg (3 to 6 times the recommended daily dose), nilutamide caused malaise, dizziness, nausea and vomiting which disappeared upon discontinuation of treatment.

The effects of ingestion of a very high dose of nilutamide have been described in 1 case report. A 79-year-old man was admitted 2 hours after the ingestion of 13 g of nilutamide (170 mg/kg or 43 times the therapeutic dose). He had been receiving nilutamide 300 mg/day for 2 weeks. On admission, he underwent gastric lavage immediately, followed by administration of a 20 g oral dose of activated charcoal. Clinical and biological parameters were monitored. There were no changes in the biological parameters as compared to the pre-treatment values either early post ingestion or upon control on days 4, 9 and 30. The clinical manifestations were limited to moderate vomiting and diarrhea during the first 12 hours post ingestion and the patient recovered. Plasma and serum concentrations were measured. The initial level reached 6 times the usual therapeutic range of 4.4 to 8.5 mg/L. Levels 3.5 times greater than the normal range were measured 72 hours post-ingestion.

The ingested dose (170 mg/kg) is close to the lethal dose in animals, the oral LD_{50} being 215 mg/kg (180 to 240) in mice and 195 mg/kg (160 to 230) in rats. However, the extent of absorption was probably limited by early therapeutic intervention. The lethal dose in man has not been established.

Dosage: Treatment with nilutamide should be initiated immediately after surgical castration.

Initial Dosage: 300 mg once daily for the first month of treatment. Maintenance treatment may be started earlier should intolerance occur.

Maintenance Dosage: 150 mg once daily.

Nilutamide should be taken before breakfast, until more information is available.

Discontinuation of nilutamide should be considered once objective evidence of disease progression is noted.

Information for the Patient: See Blue Section—Information for the Patient "Anandron".

Supplied: 50 mg: Each biconvex, white tablet about 7 mm in diameter, engraved "ANANDRON" on one side and the strength "50" on the other, contains: nilutamide 50 mg. Nonmedicinal ingredients: lactose, magnesium stearate, maize starch, povidone, sodium docusate and talc. Lactose: 30 mg. Bottles of 90.

100 mg: Each biconvex, white tablet about 9 mm in diameter, scored, engraved "ANANDRON" on one side and the strength "100" on the other, contains: nilutamide 100 mg. Nonmedicinal ingredients: lactose, magnesium stearate, maize starch, povidone, sodium docusate and talc. Lactose: 60 mg. Bottles of 90.

Store at room temperature and protect from light.

(Shown in Product Recognition Section)

ANAPROX® Ⓟ
ANAPROX® DS Ⓟ
Roche

Naproxen Sodium

Analgesic—Anti-inflammatory

Pharmacology: Naproxen sodium, has demonstrated analgesic, anti-inflammatory and antipyretic properties in human clinical studies and in classical animal test systems. It exhibits an anti-inflammatory effect even in adrenalectomized animals and therefore its action is not mediated through the pituitary-adrenal axis. It is not a corticosteroid. It inhibits prostaglandin synthetase, as do certain other nonsteroidal analgesic/anti-inflammatory agents. As with other agents, however, the exact mechanism of its anti-inflammatory and analgesic actions is not known.

Blood loss and gastroscopy studies with normal volunteers showed that daily administration of 1 100 mg of naproxen sodium caused significantly less gastric bleeding and erosion than 3 250 mg of ASA.

At the recommended dosage, the analgesic effect was shown to be comparable to that observed using 650 mg of ASA. The analgesic effect is obtained within 1 hour and can last at least 7 hours.

Naproxen sodium is freely soluble in water and is completely absorbed from the gastrointestinal tract. Plasma levels are obtained in patients within 20 minutes and peak levels in approximately 1 hour. It is extensively bound to plasma protein and has a plasma half-life of approximately 13 hours. The preferred route of excretion is via the urine with only 1% of the dose excreted in the feces.

Indications: The relief of mild to moderately severe pain, accompanied by inflammation in conditions such as musculoskeletal trauma and postdental extraction. It is also indicated for the relief of pain associated with postpartum cramping and dysmenorrhea.

Contraindications: Patients with active ulcers or active inflammatory diseases of the gastrointestinal tract. Patients who have shown hypersensitivity to it or to naproxen. Since cross-sensitivity has been demonstrated, naproxen sodium should not be given to patients in whom ASA or other nonsteroidal anti-inflammatory drugs induce the syndrome of asthma, rhinitis, or urticaria. Sometimes severe and occasionally fatal anaphylactoid reactions have occurred in such individuals.

Warnings: Peptic ulceration, perforation and gastrointestinal bleeding, sometimes severe and occasionally fatal have been reported during therapy with nonsteroidal anti-inflammatory drugs (NSAIDs) including naproxen sodium.

Naproxen sodium should be given under close medical supervision to patients prone to gastrointestinal tract irritation particularly those with a history of peptic ulcer, diverticulosis or other inflammatory disease of the gastrointestinal tract. In these cases the physician must weigh the benefits of treatment against the possible hazards.

Patients taking any NSAID including this drug should be instructed to contact a physician immediately if they experience symptoms or signs suggestive of peptic ulceration or gastrointestinal bleeding. These reactions can occur without warning symptoms or signs and at any time during the treatment.

Elderly, frail and debilitated patients appear to be at higher risk from a variety of adverse reactions from nonsteroidal anti-inflammatory drugs (NSAIDs). For such patients, consideration should be given to a starting dose lower than usual, with individual adjustment when necessary and under close supervision (see Precautions).

Pregnancy and *Lactation:* Safety in pregnancy and lactation has not been established and its use during these events is therefore not recommended. Reproduction studies have been performed in rats, rabbits and mice. In rats, pregnancy was prolonged when naproxen sodium was given before the onset of labor; when it was given after the delivery process had begun, labor was protracted. Similar results have been found with other nonsteroidal anti-inflammatory agents and the evidence suggests that this may be due to decreased uterine contractility resulting from the inhibition of prostaglandin synthesis. Moreover, because of the known effect of drugs of this class on the human fetal cardiovascular system (closure of ductus arteriosus), use during late pregnancy should be avoided.

The naproxen anion readily crosses the placental barrier. It has been found in the milk of lactating women at a concentration approximately 1% of that found in the plasma.

Precautions: Naproxen sodium should not be used concomitantly with the related drug naproxen since they circulate in plasma as the naproxen anion.

Gastrointestinal: If peptic ulceration is suspected or confirmed, or if gastrointestinal bleeding or perforation occurs naproxen sodium should be discontinued, an appropriate treatment instituted and patient closely monitored.

There is no definitive evidence that the concomitant administration of histamine H_2-receptor antagonists and/or antacids will either prevent the occurrence of gastrointestinal side effects or allow continuation of naproxen sodium therapy when and if these adverse reactions appear.

Renal Effects: As with other nonsteroidal anti-inflammatory drugs, long-term administration of naproxen sodium to animals has resulted in renal papillary necrosis and other abnormal renal pathology. In humans, there have been reports of acute interstitial nephritis with hematuria, proteinuria and occasionally nephrotic syndrome.

A second form of renal toxicity has been seen in patients with prerenal conditions leading to the reduction in renal blood flow or blood volume, where the renal prostaglandins have a supportive role in the maintenance of renal perfusion. In these patients, administration of a nonsteroidal anti-inflammatory drug may cause a dose-dependent reduction in prostaglandin formation and may precipitate overt renal decompensation. Patients at greatest risk of this reaction are those with impaired renal function, extracellular volume depletion, sodium restrictions, heart failure, liver dysfunction, those taking diuretics and the elderly. Assessment of renal function in these patients before and during therapy with naproxen sodium is recommended. Discontinuation of nonsteroidal anti-inflammatory therapy is typically followed by recovery to the pretreatment state.

Naproxen sodium and its metabolites are eliminated primarily by the kidneys, therefore, the drug should be used with great caution in patients with significantly impaired renal function and the monitoring of serum creatinine and/or creatinine clearance is advised in these patients. A reduction in daily dosage should be anticipated to avoid the possibility of excessive drug accumulation.

Naproxen sodium should not be used chronically in patients having baseline creatinine clearance less than 20 mL/minute. During long-term therapy, kidney function should be monitored periodically.

Fluid and Electrolyte Balance: Peripheral edema has been observed in some patients receiving naproxen sodium. Therefore, as with many other nonsteroidal anti-inflammatory drugs, the possibility of precipitating congestive heart failure in elderly patients or those with compromised cardiac function should be borne in mind. Although sodium retention has not been reported in metabolic studies, the drug should be used with caution in patients with fluid retention, hypertension or heart failure.

Serum electrolytes should be monitored periodically during long-term therapy, especially in those patients at risk.

Each Anaprox tablet contains approximately 25 mg of sodium and each Anaprox DS tablet contains approximately 50 mg of sodium. This should be considered in patients whose overall intake of sodium must be markedly restricted.

It is possible that patients with questionable or compromised cardiac function may be at greater risk when taking naproxen sodium.

Anaphylactoid reactions to naproxen or naproxen sodium, whether of the true allergic type or the pharmacologic idiosyncratic (e.g., syndrome associated with the use of ASA) type, usually but not always occur in patients with a known history of such reactions. Therefore, careful questioning of patients for such things as asthma, nasal polyps, urticaria and hypotension associated nonsteroidal anti-inflammatory drugs before starting therapy is important. In addition, if such symptoms occur during therapy, treatment should be discontinued.

Geriatrics: One study indicates that although total plasma concentration of naproxen is unchanged, the unbound plasma fraction of naproxen is increased in the elderly. The implication of this finding for naproxen sodium dosing is unknown, but caution is advised when high doses are required. As with other drugs used in the elderly, it is prudent to use the lowest effective dose.

Patients with Impaired Liver Function: As with other nonsteroidal anti-inflammatory drugs, borderline elevations of one or more liver tests may occur in up to 15% of patients. These abnormalities may progress, may remain essentially unchanged, or may be transient with continued therapy. A patient with symptoms and/or signs suggesting liver dysfunction, or in whom an abnormal liver test has occurred, should be evaluated for evidence of the development of more severe hepatic reaction while on therapy with this drug. Severe hepatic reactions including jaundice and cases of fatal hepatitis have been reported with this drug as with other nonsteroidal anti-inflammatory drugs. Although such reactions are rare, if abnormal liver tests persist or worsen, if clinical signs and symptoms consistent with liver disease develop, or if systemic manifestations occur (e.g. eosinophilia, rash, etc.), this drug should be discontinued.

During long-term therapy, liver function tests should be monitored periodically. If this drug is to be used in the presence of impaired liver function, it must be done under strict observation.

Chronic alcoholic liver disease and probably also other forms of cirrhosis reduce the total plasma concentration of naproxen, but the plasma concentration of unbound naproxen is increased. The implication of this finding for naproxen sodium dosing is unknown, but caution is advised when high doses are required. It is prudent to use the lowest effective dose.

Hematology: Drugs inhibiting prostaglandin biosynthesis do interfere with platelet function to some degree; therefore, patients who may be adversely affected by such an action should be carefully observed when naproxen sodium is administered.

Blood dyscrasias associated with the use of nonsteroidal anti-inflammatory drugs are rare, but could be associated with severe consequences.

Patients with initial hemoglobin values of 10 g or less who are to receive long-term therapy should have hemoglobin values determined frequently.

Infection: The anti-inflammatory, antipyretic and analgesic effects of naproxen sodium may mask the usual signs of infection and the physician should be alert for development of infection in patients receiving naproxen sodium.

Ophthalmology: Because of adverse eye findings in animal studies with drugs of this class it is recommended that ophthalmic studies be carried out within a reasonable period of time after starting therapy and at periodic intervals thereafter if the drug is to be used for an extended period of time.

CNS: Caution should be exercised by patients whose activities require alertness if they experience drowsiness, dizziness, vertigo or depression during therapy with the drug.

Drug Interactions: The naproxen anion may displace from their binding sites other drugs which are also albumin-bound and may lead to drug interactions. For example, in patients receiving bishydroxycoumarin or warfarin, the addition of naproxen sodium could prolong the prothrombin time. These patients should, therefore, be under careful observation. Similarly, patients receiving naproxen sodium and a hydantoin, sulfonamide or sulfonylurea should be observed for signs of toxicity to these drugs.

The natriuretic effect of furosemide has been reported to be inhibited by some drugs of this class. Inhibition of renal lithium clearance leading to increases in plasma lithium concentrations have also been reported.

Naproxen sodium and other nonsteroidal anti-inflammatory drugs can reduce the antihypertensive effect of propranolol and other beta blockers.

The rate of absorption of naproxen sodium is altered by concomitant administration of antacids but is not adversely influenced by the presence of food. Probenecid given concurrently increases naproxen anion plasma levels and extends its plasma half-life significantly.

Caution is advised in the concomitant administration of naproxen sodium and methotrexate since naproxen and other nonsteroidal anti-inflammatory agents have been reported to reduce the tubular secretion of methotrexate in an animal model, thereby possibly enhancing its toxicity.

Laboratory Tests: Naproxen sodium decreases platelet aggregation and prolongs bleeding time. This effect should be kept in mind when bleeding times are determined.

The administration of naproxen sodium may result in increased urinary values for 17-ketogenic steroids because of an interaction between the drug and/or its metabolites with m-dinitrobenzene used in this assay. Although 17-hydroxy corticosteroid measurements (Porter-Silber test) do not appear to be artifactually altered, it is suggested that naproxen sodium therapy be temporarily discontinued 48 hours before adrenal function tests are performed.

The drug may interfere with some urinary assays of 5-hydroxy indoleacetic acid (5HIAA).

Children: The safety and efficacy of this drug in children has not been established and its use in children is therefore not recommended.

Adverse Effects: The most common adverse reactions encountered with nonsteroidal anti-inflammatory drugs are gastrointestinal, of which peptic ulcer, with or without bleeding is the most severe. Fatalities have occurred on occasion, particularly in the elderly.

Adverse reactions reported in controlled clinical trials are listed below. (1) Denotes incidence of reported reaction between 3% and 9%. (2) Denotes incidence of reported reactions between 1% and 3%. Reactions occurring in less than 1% of the patients during controlled clinical trials and through voluntary reports since marketing are unmarked.

Gastrointestinal: heartburn (1), constipation (1), abdominal pain (1), nausea (1), diarrhea (2), dyspepsia (2), stomatitis (2), diverticulitis (2), gastrointestinal bleeding, hematemesis, melena, peptic ulceration with or without bleeding and/or perforation, vomiting, ulcerative stomatitis.

CNS: headache (1), dizziness (1), drowsiness (1), lightheadedness (2), vertigo (2), depression (2) and fatigue (2). Occasionally patients had to discontinue treatment because of the severity of some of these complaints (headache and dizziness). Other adverse effects were inability to concentrate, malaise, myalgia, insomnia and cognitive dysfunction (i.e. decreased attention span, loss of short-term memory, difficulty with calculations).

Skin: pruritus (1), ecchymoses (1), skin eruptions (1), sweating (2), purpura (2), alopecia, urticaria, skin rash, erythema multiforme, Stevens-Johnson syndrome, epidermal necrolysis, photosensitive dermatitis, exfoliative dermatitis and erythema nodosum.

Hepatic Changes: abnormal liver function tests, jaundice, cholestasis and hepatitis.

Cardiovascular Reactions: dyspnea (1), peripheral edema (1), palpitations (2), congestive heart failure and vasculitis.

Renal: glomerular nephritis, hematuria, interstitial nephritis, nephrotic syndrome, nephropathy and tubular necrosis.

Hematologic: eosinophilia, granulocytopenia, leukopenia, thrombocytopenia, agranulocytosis, aplastic anemia and hemolytic anemia.

Special Senses: tinnitus (1), hearing disturbances (2), hearing impairment and visual disturbances.

Others: thirst (2), muscle weakness, anaphylactoid reactions, menstrual disorders, pyrexia (chills and fever), angioneurotic edema, hyperglycemia, hypoglycemia, hepatitis and eosinophilic pneumonitis.

Overdose: Symptoms and Treatment: Significant overdosage may be characterized by drowsiness, heartburn, indigestion, nausea or vomiting. No evidence of toxicity or late sequelae have been reported 5 to 15 months after ingestion for 3 to 7 days of doses up to 3 000 mg of naproxen. One patient ingested a single dose of 25 g naproxen and experienced mild nausea and indigestion. It is not known what dose of the drug would be life threatening. The oral LD_{50} of the drug is 543 mg/kg in rats, 1 234 mg/kg in mice, 4 110 mg/kg in hamsters and greater than 1 000 mg/kg in dogs.

Should a patient ingest a large number of naproxen sodium tablets, the stomach may be emptied and usual supportive measures employed. Animal studies suggest that the prompt administration of 5 g of activated charcoal would tend to reduce markedly the absorption of the drug. In dogs, 0.5 g/kg of charcoal was effective in reducing the plasma levels of naproxen when given after the drug. Hemodialysis does not decrease the plasma concentration of naproxen because of the high degree of its protein binding. However, hemodialysis may still be appropriate in the management of renal failure.

Dosage: The recommended starting dose of Anaprox for adults is two 275 mg tablets, followed by one 275 mg tablet every 6 to 8 hours, as required. The total daily dose should not exceed 1 375 mg. Alternatively, one Anaprox DS tablet (550 mg) given twice daily may be used.

Information for the Patient: See Blue Section—Information for the Patient ''Anaprox/Anaprox DS''.

Supplied: Anaprox: Each oval-shaped, blue film-coated tablet, engraved on one side NPS-275, contains: naproxen sodium 275 mg. Nonmedicinal ingredients: FD&C Blue No. 2 aluminum lake, hydroxypropyl methylcellulose, magnesium stearate, microcrystalline cellulose, polyethylene glycol, povidone, talc and titanium dioxide. Bisulfite-, erythrosine-, gluten-, lactose-, sorbitol-, tartrazine- and xylitol-free. Bottles of 100 and 500.

Anaprox DS: Each oblong, dark blue, film-coated tablet, engraved on one side NPS 550, break scored on both sides, contains: naproxen sodium 550 mg. Nonmedicinal ingredients: FD&C Blue No. 2 aluminum lake, hydroxypropyl methylcellulose, magnesium stearate, microcrystalline cellulose, polyethylene glycol, povidone, talc and titanium dioxide. Bisulfite-, erythrosine-, gluten-, lactose-, sorbitol-, tartrazine- and xylitol-free. Bottles of 100 and 500.

Store at room temperature (15 to 30°C) in a well-closed container, protected from light.

(Shown in Product Recognition Section)

ANBESOL® Preparations

Whitehall-Robins

Benzocaine Compound

Topical Anesthetic

Indications: Anbesol: For temporary pain relief of toothache, denture irritation, brace pain, minor mouth irritations, cold sores, sun and fever blisters and canker sores.

Anbesol Baby: For temporary relief from the pain and irritation associated with teething.

Anbesol Preparations (cont'd)

Contraindications: Anbesol: Known sensitivity to any of the ingredients.
Anbesol Baby: Known sensitivity to any of the ingredients.

Precautions: Not for prolonged use. If condition persists or irritation develops, discontinue use. Avoid contact with eyes. Anbesol: Use under dentures or other dental work only as directed below. Flammable. Do not use near fire or flame. Avoid smoking during application and until product has dried.

Dosage: Anbesol: To be applied topically to the affected area.
For denture irritation: Apply thin layer to the affected area and do not reinsert dental work until irritation/pain is relieved. Rinse mouth before reinserting dentures.
Anbesol Baby: Apply a small amount on the infant's irritated gums with a cotton swab or finger tip. Reapply as necessary up to 4 times daily.

Supplied: Anbesol: Extra Strength Gel: Each plastic tube contains: benzocaine 20%. Nonmedicinal ingredients: alcohol, carbomer, D&C Yellow No. 10, FD&C Blue No. 1, FD&C Red No. 40, flavor, polyethylene glycol and saccharin. Tubes of 7 g.

Gel: Each plastic tube contains: benzocaine 6.4% and phenol 0.5%. Nonmedicinal ingredients: alcohol, camphor, carbopol, D&C Red No. 33, D&C Yellow No. 10, FD&C Blue No. 1, FD&C Yellow No. 6, flavor and glycerin. Tubes of 7 g.

Liquid: Each glass bottle contains: benzocaine 6.5%, phenol 0.45%, camphor 0.25%, menthol 0.25%. Nonmedicinal ingredients: alcohol, FD&C Blue No. 1, FD&C Yellow No. 6, flavor and glycerin. Bottles of 10 mL.

Maximum Strength Liquid: Each glass bottle contains: benzocaine 20%, phenol 0.45%, camphor 0.25%, menthol 0.25%. Nonmedicinal ingredients: alcohol, FD&C Blue No. 1, FD&C Yellow No. 6, flavor and polyethylene glycol. Bottles of 10 mL.

Anbesol Baby: Gel: Each plastic tube contains: benzocaine 7.5%. Nonmedicinal ingredients: calcium cyclamate, carbomer, clove oil, D&C Red No. 33, disodium edetate, flavor, glycerin, polyethylene glycol and water. Tubes of 7 g.

Grape Gel: Each plastic tube contains: benzocaine 7.5%. Nonmedicinal ingredients: benzoic acid, carbomer, D&C Red No. 33, disodium edetate, FD&C Blue No. 1, flavor, glycerin, parabens, polyethylene glycol, saccharin and water. Tubes of 7 g.

ANCEF® Ⓟ

SmithKline Beecham

Cefazolin Sodium

Antibiotic

Pharmacology: Cefazolin sodium is a cephalosporin antibiotic for parenteral administration. It exerts its bactericidal action through inhibition of bacterial cell wall synthesis.

Indications: In the treatment of the following infections when caused by susceptible strains of the following organisms:

Respiratory tract infections caused by S. pneumoniae (formerly D. pneumoniae), K. pneumoniae, H. influenzae, S. aureus (penicillin-sensitive and penicillin-resistant) and group A beta-hemolytic streptococci.

Genitourinary tract infections caused by E. coli, P. mirabilis, K. pneumoniae and some strains of enterobacter and enterococci.

Skin and soft tissue infections caused by S. aureus (penicillin-sensitive and penicillin-resistant), group A beta-hemolytic streptococci and other strains of streptococci.

Bone and joint infections caused by S. aureus.

Septicemia caused by S. pneumoniae (formerly D. pneumoniae), S. aureus (penicillin-sensitive and penicillin-resistant), P. mirabilis, E. coli and K. pneumoniae.

Endocarditis caused by S. aureus (penicillin-sensitive and penicillin-resistant) and group A beta-hemolytic streptococci.

Appropriate culture and susceptibility studies should be performed to determine susceptibility of the causative organism to cefazolin.

Most strains of indole positive Proteus (P. vulgaris), E. cloacae, M. morganii, P. rettgeri and methicillin-resistant staphylococci are resistant. Serratia, Pseudomonas, Mima and Herellea species are almost uniformly resistant to cefazolin.

Perioperative Prophylaxis: Preoperative, intraoperative and postoperative administration in patients undergoing potentially contaminated surgical procedures, and in patients in whom infection would pose a serious risk (e.g., during open-heart surgery and prosthetic arthroplasty).

Should signs of infection occur, identification of the causative organisms should be made by culture so that appropriate therapy may be instituted.

Contraindications: Patients with known allergy to the cephalosporin group of antibiotics.

Warnings: In penicillin allergic patients, cephalosporin derivatives should be used with caution. There is clinical and laboratory evidence of partial cross-allergenicity of the penicillins and the cephalosporins, and there are instances of patients who have had reactions to both drug classes (including fatal anaphylaxis after parenteral use).

Any patient who has demonstrated some form of allergy, particularly to drugs, should receive cefazolin cautiously and then only when absolutely necessary. Serious anaphylactoid reactions require immediate emergency treatment with epinephrine. Oxygen, i.v. steroids, and airway management, including intubation, should also be administered as indicated.

Pseudomembranous colitis has been reported with the use of cephalosporins; therefore, it is important to consider this diagnosis in patients who develop diarrhea in association with antibiotic use.

Precautions: Prolonged use of cefazolin may result in the overgrowth of nonsusceptible organisms. Careful clinical observation of the patient is essential.

Cefazolin should be prescribed with caution in patients with a history of lower gastrointestinal disease, particularly colitis. Although cefazolin has not shown evidence of nephrotoxicity, caution should be exercised in treating patients with preexisting renal damage.

When cefazolin is administered to patients with low urinary output due to impaired renal function, daily dosage should be reduced (see Dosage in Patients with Reduced Renal Function). Blood levels of cefazolin remain fairly high in spite of dialysis, and should be monitored in such patients.

Drug Interactions: Probenecid may decrease renal tubular secretion of cefazolin when used concurrently, resulting in increased and prolonged cefazolin blood levels.

Positive direct and indirect Coombs' tests have been reported during treatment with cefazolin; these may also occur in neonates whose mothers received cephalosporins before delivery. The clinical significance of this effect has not been established.

A false-positive reaction for glucose in the urine of patients on cefazolin may occur with Clinitest tablets but not with enzyme-based tests such as Clinistix and Tes-Tape.

In beta-hemolytic streptococcal infections, treatment should be continued for at least 10 days, to minimize possible complications associated with the disease.

Pregnancy: Safety for use during pregnancy has not been established.

Children: Safety for use in premature infants and in infants under 1 month of age has not been established.

Lactation: Cefazolin is present in very low concentrations in the milk of nursing mothers. Caution should be exercised when cefazolin is administered to a nursing woman.

Adverse Effects: The following reactions have been reported:
Gastrointestinal: diarrhea, oral candidiasis (oral thrush), vomiting, nausea, stomach cramps, anorexia. Symptoms of pseudomembranous colitis can appear during antibiotic treatment. Nausea and vomiting have been reported rarely.
Allergic: anaphylaxis, eosinophilia, itching, drug fever, skin rash.
Hematologic: neutropenia, anemia, leukopenia, thrombocythemia, positive direct and indirect antiglobulin (Coombs') tests.
Hepatic and Renal: Transient increases in AST, ALT, BUN and alkaline phosphatase levels have been observed without clinical evidence of renal or hepatic impairment.
Local Reactions: Rare instances of phlebitis have been reported at the site of injection. Pain at the site of injection after i.m. administration has occurred infrequently. Some induration has occurred.
Other Reactions: vulvar pruritus, genital moniliasis, vaginitis and anal pruritus.

Overdose: Symptoms and Treatment: There is a lack of experience with acute cefazolin overdosage. In cases of suspected overdosage, supportive therapy should be instituted according to symptoms.

Dosage: Cefazolin may be administered i.m. or i.v. after reconstitution. Total daily dosages are the same in both cases.

Adults: Adult Dosage Guide (see Table I).

Table I—Ancef

Adult Dosage Guide

Type of Infection	Dose	Frequency
Mild infections caused by susceptible gram+ cocci	250 to 500 mg	q 8 h
Acute, uncomplicated urinary tract infections*	1 g	q 12 h
Moderate to severe infections	500 mg to 1 g	q 6 to 8 h

* This dosage recommendation applies to i.m. use. The efficacy of Ancef when administered i.v. at 12-hour intervals has not been established.

Ancef has been administered in dosages of 6 g/day in serious infections such as endocarditis.

Patients with Reduced Renal Function: The reduced dosage schedule in Table II is recommended after an initial loading dose appropriate to the severity of the infection.

Table II—Ancef

Dosage Schedule for Patients with Reduced Renal Function

Creatinine Clearance (mL/s)	Serum Creatinine (μmol/L)	Dosage
≥0.91	≤140	250 mg–1 g every 6 to 12 hours
0.58 to 0.90	141 to 273	250 mg–1 g every 8 to 12 hours
0.18 to 0.57	274 to 406	125–500 mg every 12 hours
≤0.17	≥407	125–500 mg every 18 hours

Perioperative Prophylaxis: To prevent postoperative infection in contaminated or potentially contaminated surgery, the recommended dosage regimen is: a) 1 g i.v. or i.m. administered 0.5 hour to 1 hour prior to the start of surgery so that adequate antibiotic levels are present in the serum and tissues at the time of the initial surgical incision. b) For lengthy operative procedures (e.g., 2 hours or more) 0.5 to 1 g, i.v. or i.m. during surgery. (Administration should be modified according to the duration of the operative procedure and the time of greatest exposure to infective organisms). c) 0.5 g to 1 g i.v. or i.m. every 6 to 8 hours for 24 hours postoperatively. In surgery where the occurrence of infection may be particularly devastating (e.g., open-heart surgery and prosthetic arthroplasty), the prophylactic administration of cefazolin may be continued for 3 to 5 days following the completion of surgery.

Children: In children, a total daily dosage of 25 to 50 mg/kg of body weight, divided into 3 or 4 equal doses, is effective for most mild to moderately severe infections [see Tables III and IV (on following page)].

Table III—Ancef

Pediatric Dosage Guide—25 mg/kg/day

Weight (kg)	25 mg/kg/day Divided into 3 Doses		25 mg/kg/day Divided into 4 Doses	
	Approximate Single Dose mg/q8h	Volume Needed of 125 mg/mL* Solution	Approximate Single Dose mg/q6h	Volume Needed of 125 mg/mL* Solution
4.5	40 mg	0.35 mL	30 mg	0.25 mL
9.0	75 mg	0.60 mL	55 mg	0.45 mL
13.6	115 mg	0.90 mL	85 mg	0.70 mL
18.1	150 mg	1.20 mL	115 mg	0.90 mL
22.7	190 mg	1.50 mL	140 mg	1.10 mL

* 125 mg/mL concentration may be obtained by reconstituting the 500 mg vial with 3.8 mL of diluent.

Total daily dosage may be increased to 100 mg/kg of body weight for severe infections. Since safety for use in premature infants and in infants under 1 month has not been established, the use of cefazolin in these patients is not recommended.

Children with mild to moderate renal impairment (CCr 0.67 to 1.17 mL/s) may be treated with 60% of the normal daily dose given in divided doses every 12 hours. Children with moderate renal impairment (CCr 0.33 to 0.87 mL/s) should be given 25% of the normal daily dose in equally divided doses every 12 hours, and patients with severe renal impairment (CCr 0.08 to 0.33 mL/s) should receive 10% of the normal daily dose every 24 hours.

Table IV—Ancef

Pediatric Dosage Guide—50 mg/kg/day

Weight (kg)	50 mg/kg/day Divided into 3 Doses		50 mg/kg/day Divided into 4 Doses	
	Approximate Single Dose mg/q8h	Volume Needed of 225 mg/mL* Solution	Approximate Single Dose mg/q6h	Volume Needed of 225 mg/mL* Solution
4.5	75 mg	0.35 mL	55 mg	0.25 mL
9.0	150 mg	0.70 mL	110 mg	0.50 mL
13.6	225 mg	1.00 mL	170 mg	0.75 mL
18.1	300 mg	1.35 mL	225 mg	1.00 mL
22.7	375 mg	1.70 mL	285 mg	1.25 mL

* 225 mg/mL solution may be obtained by reconstituting the 500 mg vial with 2 mL of diluent.

Administration: I.M.: Inject the reconstituted solution into a large muscle mass. Pain on injection is infrequent with cefazolin.

I.V.: Direct (bolus) injection: Inject the appropriately diluted reconstituted solution slowly over 3 to 5 minutes directly into vein or through tubing for patients receiving parenteral fluids (see list of solutions for i.v. infusion).

Intermittent or Continuous Infusion: The reconstituted solution can be administered along with primary i.v. fluid management programs in a volume control set or in a separate secondary i.v. bottle (see list of solutions for i.v. infusion).

Reconstitution: Single Dose Vials: See Table V.

Table V—Ancef

Reconstitution for Single Dose Vial

Vial Size (mg)	Diluent	Volume to be Added to Vial (mL)	Approximate Available Volume (mL)	Nominal Concentration (mg/mL)
500	Sodium Chloride Injection	2.0	2.2	225
	OR			
	Sterile Water for Injection	3.8	4.0	125
1 000	Sterile Water for Injection	2.5	3.0	334

Shake well and inspect visually for particulate matter prior to administration. If particulate matter is evident in reconstituted fluids, the drug solutions should be discarded.

I.M. Injection: Reconstitute as directed in Table V. **Shake well.**

I.V. Direct (Bolus) Injection: Reconstitute as directed in Table V. **Shake well.** Dilute the reconstituted solution in a minimum of 10 mL of Sterile Water for Injection.

Intermittent or Continuous I.V. Infusion: Reconstitute as directed in Table V. **Shake well.** Then further dilute reconstituted Ancef in 50 to 100 mL of Sterile Water for Injection or one of the Solutions for I.V. Infusion.

Solutions for I.V. Infusion: Sodium Chloride Injection, Dextrose Injection 5% or 10%, Dextrose 5% in Lactated Ringer's Injection, Dextrose 5% and Sodium Chloride Injection 0.9% (also may be used with Dextrose 5% and Sodium Chloride Injection 0.45% or 0.2%), Lactated Ringer's Injection, Invert Sugar 5% or 10% in Sterile Water for Injection, Ringer's Injection, Sodium Bicarbonate 5% in Sterile Water for Injection.

Stability and Storage of Parenteral Solutions: When reconstituted or diluted according to the instructions above, Ancef is stable for 24 hours at room temperature or for 96 hours if stored under refrigerated temperatures (2 to 8°C). Reconstituted solutions may range in color from pale yellow to yellow without a change in potency.

Pharmacy Bulk Vials: The Pharmacy Bulk Vial is intended for multiple dispensing for i.v. use **only** employing a single puncture. Any unused stock solution remaining after a period of 8 hours should be discarded (see Table VI).

Table VI—Ancef

Reconstitution for Pharmacy Bulk Vial

Vial Size	Volume to be Added to Vial (mL)	Approximate Available Volume (mL)	Nominal Concentration (mg/mL)
10 g	45	50	200
	96	100	100

Shake well and inspect visually for particulate matter prior to administration. If particulate matter is evident in reconstituted fluids, the drug solutions should be discarded.

Extended Use of I.V. Admixtures: Although i.v. admixtures may often be physically and chemically stable for longer periods, **due to microbiological considerations, they are usually recommended for use within 24 hours at room temperature or 72 hours when refrigerated. (2 to 8°C).**

Hospitals and institutions that have recognized admixture programs and use validated aseptic techniques for preparation of i.v. solutions, may extend the storage times for Ancef in admixtures with 5% Dextrose Injection or 0.9% Sodium Chloride Injection in Viaflex bags, in concentrations of 5 to 80 mg/mL, for 21 days when stored under refrigeration at 2 to 8°C.

Warning: As with all parenteral products, i.v. admixtures should be inspected visually for clarity, particulate matter, precipitate, discoloration and leakage prior to administration, whenever solution and container permit. Solutions showing haziness, particulate matter, precipitate, discoloration or leakage should not be used.

Supplied: Each 10 mL vial contains: cefazolin sodium equivalent to 500 mg or 1 g of cefazolin. Each 100 mL pharmacy bulk vial contains: cefazolin sodium equivalent to 10 g of cefazolin. Sodium: 46 mg/g of cefazolin. Preservative-free. Boxes of 10.

Store vials at normal room temperature. Protect from light. Under normal conditions of storage, the lyophilized form has a shelf life of 24 months.

ANDRIOL ◇

Organon

Testosterone Undecanoate

Androgen

Pharmacology: Testosterone undecanoate, an orally active testosterone preparation, is a fatty acid ester of the natural androgen testosterone. Unlike other oral testosterone preparations, testosterone undecanoate is able to by-pass the liver via the lymphatic system and is therefore orally bioavailable.

Therapy with Andriol increases plasma levels of testosterone and its active metabolites, leading to a regular therapeutic effect. In eugonadal men, peak testosterone levels are reached in approximately 4 to 5 hours after ingestion returning to basal levels after about 10 hours. In volunteers and hypogonadal men, 77 to 93% of an orally administered dose of testosterone undecanoate was excreted in the urine and feces within 3 to 4 days.

Indications: For replacement therapy in males in conditions associated with symptoms of deficiency or absence of endogenous testosterone: for the management of congenital or acquired primary hypogonadism and hypogonadotropic hypogonadism; to develop and maintain secondary sexual characteristics in males with testosterone deficiency. Testosterone undecanoate is also indicated to stimulate puberty in carefully selected males with clearly delayed puberty not secondary to pathological disorder.

It is also used as replacement therapy in impotence or for male climacteric symptoms when the conditions are due to a measured or documented androgen deficiency.

Contraindications: Known hypersensitivity to any of the components of the product; males with carcinoma of the breast; males with known or suspected carcinoma of the prostate gland; patients with serious cardiac, hepatic or renal disease; hypercalcemia; impaired liver function; prepubertal males; patients easily stimulated sexually. Androgens are also contraindicated in patients with nephrosis or the nephrotic phase of nephritis.

Warnings: Hypercalcemia may occur in immobilized patients and in patients with breast cancer. If this occurs, the drug should be discontinued.

Prolonged use of high doses of androgens (principally the 17-alpha-alkyl-androgens) has been associated with development of hepatic adenomas, hepatocellular carcinoma and peliosis hepatis—all potentially life-threatening complications.

Cholestatic hepatitis and jaundice may occur with 17-alpha-alkyl-androgens. Should this occur, the drug should be discontinued. This is reversible with discontinuation of the drug. Geriatric patients treated with androgens may be at an increased risk of developing prostatic hypertrophy and prostatic carcinoma although conclusive evidence to support this concept is lacking.

Edema, with or without congestive heart failure, may be a serious complication in patients with pre-existing cardiac, renal or hepatic disease. In addition to discontinuation of the drug, diuretic therapy may be required.

Gynecomastia may develop and occasionally persists in patients being treated for hypogonadism. Androgen therapy should be used cautiously in males with delayed puberty. Androgens can accelerate bone maturation without producing compensatory gain in linear growth. The effect on bone maturation should be monitored by assessing bone age of the wrist and hand every 6 months. These adverse effects may result in compromised adult stature. The younger the child the greater the risk of compromising final mature height.

Precautions: Patients with benign prostatic hypertrophy may develop acute urethral obstruction. Priapism or excessive sexual stimulation may develop. Oligospermia may occur after prolonged administration or excessive dosage. If any of these effects appear, the androgen should be stopped and if restarted, a lower dosage should be utilized.

Drug Interactions: Androgens may increase sensitivity to oral anticoagulants. Dosage of the anticoagulant may require reduction in order to maintain satisfactory therapeutic hypoprothrombinemia. Patients receiving oral anticoagulant therapy require close monitoring, especially when androgens are started and stopped.

In diabetic patients, the metabolic effects of androgens may decrease blood glucose and, therefore, insulin requirements.

May potentiate cyclosporine and increase risk of nephrotoxicity.

Concurrent use of somatrem or somatropin with androgens in prepubertal males may accelerate epiphyseal maturation.

Increased serum oxyphenbutazone concentrations have been reported with concurrent administration of androgen and oxyphenbutazone.

May interact with adrenocorticoids, glucocorticoids, especially with significant mineralocorticoid activity, mineralocorticoids, or corticotropins, especially prolonged use, or sodium-containing medications or foods.

Laboratory Test Interference: Alterations may occur in the following clinical laboratory tests: metyrapone test, fasting blood sugar (FBS) and glucose tolerance test, thyroid function tests (decrease in thyroxine-binding capacity and radioactive iodine uptake, and an increase in T3 uptake by the red blood cells or resin; free thyroxine levels remain unchanged); electrolytes (retention of sodium chloride, water, potassium, calcium, and inorganic phosphates), blood coagulation tests (suppression of clotting factors II, V, VII, and X), alteration to liver function tests, increased serum cholesterol and miscellaneous laboratory tests (decreased creatinine and creatine excretion lasting up to 2 weeks after discontinuing therapy). Androgens enhance blood fibrinolytic activity and increase hematocrit and serum hemoglobin levels; effects on plasma lipids are variable. Administration of testosterone, but not the 17-alpha-alkyl substituted derivatives, elevates the level of urinary 17-ketosteroids.

Laboratory Tests: Because of the hepatotoxicity associated with the use of 17-alpha-alkylated androgens, liver function tests should be obtained periodically.

Hemoglobin and hematocrit levels (to detect polycythemia) should be checked periodically in patients receiving long-term androgen administration.

Serum cholesterol may increase during androgen therapy.

Periodic (every 6 months) x-ray examinations of bone age should be made during treatment of prepubertal males to determine the rate of bone maturation and the effect of androgen therapy on the epiphyseal centers.

Adverse Effects: The following adverse reactions have occurred with androgen therapy: inhibition of testicular function, testicular atrophy and oligospermia, impotence, gynecomastia, epididymitis and bladder irritability, excessive frequency and duration of penile erections, nausea, cholestatic jaundice, peliosis hepatis, polyerythemia, headache, anxiety, depression, generalized paresthesia and rarely anaphylactoid reaction. In addition, the following reactions are known to occur with anabolic steroids: increased or decreased libido, flushing of the skin, acne, habituation, excitation and sleeplessness, chills, leukopenia, and bleeding in patients on concomitant anticoagulant therapy. There have been rare reports of hepatocellular carcinoma, particularly in association with long-term therapy, in patients receiving methyltestosterone or other androgenic and anabolic steroids.

Overdose: Symptoms and Treatment: No experience with overdosage has been reported. No specific antidote is available.

Dosage: The dosage should be adjusted according to the response of the individual patient.

Usually, an initial dosage of 120 to 160 mg daily in 2 divided doses for 2 to 3 weeks is adequate, followed by a maintenance dosage of 40 to 120 mg daily.

The capsules should be taken after meals and swallowed without chewing.

Andriol (cont'd)

Storage: Pharmacist: Refrigerate at 2 to 8°C. Protect from light and moisture. Do not freeze. Patient: Store between 15 and 25°C. Protect from light and moisture. Use within 90 days.

Information for the Patient: See Blue Section—Information for the Patient "Andriol".

Supplied: Each oval, reddish-brown, soft gelatin capsule, marked D_3V, contains: testosterone undecanoate 40 mg in oleic acid. Nonmedicinal ingredients: gelatin, glycerol, iron oxide red (E172), karion 83, sodium ethyl hydroxybenzoate, sodium propyl hydroxybenzoate and titanium dioxide. Bottles of 60.

(Shown in Product Recognition Section)

ANDROCUR® ℞
ANDROCUR® DEPOT ℞
Berlex Canada

Cyproterone Acetate
Antiandrogen

Pharmacology: Cyproterone is a steroid which clinically demonstrates 2 distinct properties: Antiandrogenic: Cyproterone blocks the binding of dihydrotestosterone—the active metabolite of testosterone—to the specific receptors in the prostatic carcinoma cell. Progestogenic/antigonadotrophic: Cyproterone exerts a negative feed-back on the hypothalamo-pituitary axis, by inhibiting the secretion of LH leading to diminished production of testicular testosterone.

The absorption of cyproterone following oral administration is complete. Peak plasma levels are reached 3 to 4 hours after administration. Plasma levels fall rapidly during the first 24 hours as a result of tissue distribution and excretion, and plasma half-life was 38±5 hours.

Most of the cyproterone is excreted unchanged in the feces (60%) or urine (33%) within 72 hours.

Cyproterone is eliminated in the urine mainly in the form of unconjugated metabolites and in the bile via feces in the form of glucuronidized metabolites.

The principal metabolite identified was 15 β-hydroxy-cyproterone acetate.

Androcur Depot: Following i.m. administration, mean maximum blood levels are attained 3.4 days after injection. The mean elimination half-life was found to be 4 days.

Indications: For the palliative treatment of patients with advanced prostatic carcinoma.

Contraindications: Known hypersensitivity to the drug. Active liver disease and hepatic dysfunction. Renal insufficiency.

Warnings: Liver Function: Direct hepatic toxicity, including jaundice, hepatitis and hepatic failure, which has been fatal in some cases, has been reported in patients treated with 200 to 300 mg cyproterone. Most reported cases are in men with prostatic cancer. Toxicity is dose-related and develops usually, several months after treatment has begun. Liver function tests should be performed before treatment and whenever any symptoms or signs suggestive of hepatotoxicity occur. If hepatotoxicity is confirmed, cyproterone should normally be withdrawn, unless the hepatotoxicity can be explained by another cause, e.g., metastatic disease, in which case cyproterone should be continued only if the perceived benefit outweighs the risk.

Inhibition of Spermatogenesis: The sperm count and the volume of ejaculate are reduced at oral doses of 50 to 300 mg/day. Infertility is usual, and there may be azoospermia after 8 weeks of therapy, which is associated with atrophy of seminiferous tubules.

Follow-up examinations on discontinuation of therapy have shown these changes to be reversible.

Spermatogenesis usually reverts to its previous level about 3 to 5 months after stopping cyproterone, or in some patients, after up to 20 months. Production of abnormal spermatozoa during cyproterone therapy has been observed; their relationship to abnormal fertilization or malformed embryos is not known.

Gynecomastia: Benign nodules (hyperplasia) of the breast have been reported, these generally subside 1 to 3 months after discontinuation of therapy and/or after a reduction of dosage. The reduction of dosage should be weighed against the risk of inadequate tumor control.

Depression: Cyproterone therapy has occasionally been associated with an increased incidence of depressive mood changes, especially during the first 6 to 8 weeks of therapy. Similar mood changes have also been seen following surgical castration and are considered to be due to androgen deprivation. Patients with tendencies to depressive reaction should be carefully observed.

Precautions: Thromboembolism: Clinical investigations have shown that when cyproterone is used alone it has a minor effect on blood clotting factors. However, when cyproterone was combined with ethinyl estradiol, changes were found in increased coagulation capability. There is an inherent risk for those patients with a history of thrombophlebitis or thromboembolism for recurrence of the disease. Cyproterone should be discontinued at the first sign of thrombophlebitis or thromboembolism, and the patient should be carefully re-evaluated if manifestations of thrombotic disorders (thrombophlebitis, cerebrovascular complications, retinal thrombosis or pulmonary embolism) occur.

Adrenocortical Function: Suppression of adrenocortical function tests have occurred in patients receiving high doses (100 mg/m²) of cyproterone.

Reduced response to endogenous ACTH was noted by metyrapone test; furthermore, reduced ACTH and cortisol blood levels determined by the Mattingly method were also found.

It is therefore recommended that adrenocortical function tests should be monitored periodically by serum cortisol assay.

Diabetes: Cyproterone may impair carbohydrate metabolism. Parameters of carbohydrate metabolism, fasting blood glucose and glucose tolerance test, should be examined carefully in all patients and particularly in all diabetics before and regularly during therapy with cyproterone.

Hematology: Hypochromic anemia has been observed rarely during therapy with cyproterone. Regular hematological assessment is recommended.

Nitrogen Balance: A negative nitrogen balance is usual at the start of therapy, but does generally correct itself within 3 months of continued therapy.

Metabolic Effects: Fluid retention, hypercalcemia and changes in plasma lipid profile may occur. Accordingly, cyproterone should be used with caution in patients with cardiac disease.

Skin: Cyproterone therapy may cause a reduction of sebum production leading to dryness of the skin, and transient patchy loss of body hair.

Concomitant Alcohol: Alcohol may reduce the antiandrogenic effect of cyproterone in hypersexuality. The relevance of this in prostatic carcinoma is not known, however, it would be prudent to inform the patients that the use of alcohol during cyproterone therapy is not advisable.

Patients should be informed that fatigue and lassitude are common in the first few weeks of therapy, but usually becomes much less pronounced from the third month on.

Marked lassitude and asthenia necessitate special care when driving or operating machinery.

Adverse Effects: The adverse events associated most frequently with the use of cyproterone are those related to the hormonal effects of the drug. These reactions usually disappear upon discontinuation of therapy or reduction of dose: increased libido, breast enlargement, breast tenderness, benign nodular hyperplasia of the breast, galactorrhea, gynecomastia, abnormal spermatozoa, impotence and inhibition of spermatogenesis.

Other adverse events which have been reported are listed below:

Cardiovascular: hypotension, tachycardia, heart failure, syncope, myocardial infarct, hemorrhage, cerebrovascular accident, cardiovascular disorder, retinal vascular disorder, embolus, pulmonary embolism, superficial and deep thrombophlebitis, thrombosis, retinal vein thrombosis, phlebitis, vascular headache and shock.

Gastrointestinal: constipation, diarrhea, indigestion, anorexia, nausea, vomiting, cholestatic jaundice, cirrhosis of liver, hepatic coma, hepatitis, hepatoma, hepatomegaly, jaundice, liver carcinoma, liver failure, abnormal liver function test, liver necrosis, pancreatitis and glossitis.

Hematology: increased fibrinogen, decreased prothrombin, thrombocytopenia, anemia, hemolytic anemia, hypochromic anemia, normocytic anemia, leukopenia and leukocytosis.

Metabolism: negative nitrogen balance, decreased response to ACTH, hyperglycemia, lowered cortisol, hypercalcemia, increased AST, increased ALT, increased creatinine, hypernatremia, edema, weight gain, weight loss and diabetes mellitus.

Musculoskeletal: myasthenia, osteoporosis.

Nervous System: fatigue, lassitude, weakness, hot flashes, increased sweating, aphasia, coma, depression, dizziness, encephalopathy, hemiplegia, personality disorder, psychotic depression, abnormal gait and headache.

Respiratory: asthma, increased cough, dyspnea, hyperventilation, respiratory disorder, shortness of breath on effort and lung fibrosis.

Skin: eczema, urticaria, erythema nodosum, exfoliative dermatitis, rash, maculopapular rash, dryness of the skin, pruritus, alopecia, hirsutism, skin discolouration, photosensitivity reactions and scleroderma.

Sensory System: ear disorder, optic atrophy, optic neuritis, abnormality of accommodation, abnormal vision, blindness and retinal disorder.

Urogenital: enlarged uterine fibroids, uterine hemorrhage, increased urinary frequency, bladder carcinoma, kidney failure, hematuria, urate crystalluria, urine abnormality.

Other: ascites, allergic reaction, asthenia, chills, fetal chromosome abnormality, death, fever, hernia, malaise and injection site reaction.

Adverse reactions are rarely of sufficient severity to require dosage reduction or discontinuation of treatment.

If reactions are severe, it may be beneficial to reduce the dosage.

Overdose: Symptoms and Treatment: There have been no reports of fatal overdosage in man with cyproterone. There are no specific antidotes and treatment should be symptomatic. If oral overdosage is discovered within 2 to 3 hours, gastric lavage can safely be used if indicated.

Dosage: Androcur: The usual daily initial and maintenance dose is 200 to 300 mg (4 to 6 tablets) divided into 2 to 3 doses and taken after meals.

After orchiectomy a lower daily dose of 100 to 200 mg (2 to 4 tablets) is recommended.

Androcur Depot: The usual initial and maintenance dose is one weekly i.m. injection of 300 mg (3 mL). For orchiectomized patients, the recommended dose is one i.m. injection of 300 mg (3 mL) every 2 weeks.

Androcur or Androcur Depot therapy should not be discontinued when remission or improvement occurs.

Because of their pharmacokinetic properties, the oral and i.m. depot can be interchanged in the course of long-term treatment. The dosage may be reduced if side effects are intolerable but should be kept within the oral range of 100 to 300 mg daily (2 to 6 tablets) or i.m. injections of 300 mg (3 mL) at weekly intervals, or every 2 weeks.

Supplied: Androcur: Each white, round, flat-sided tablet with beveled edges, imprinted one side "BV" in a regular hexagon, other side scored, contains: cyproterone acetate 50 mg. Nonmedicinal ingredients: aerosil (colloidal silicic acid), cornstarch, lactose, magnesium stearate and polyvinylpyrrolidone. Gluten- and tartrazine-free. Bottles of 60.

Androcur Depot: Each ampul contains: cyproterone acetate 100 mg/mL in a castor oil solution. Nonmedicinal ingredients: benzyl benzoate and castor oil. Ampuls of 3 mL. Boxes of 4.

(Shown in Product Recognition Section)

ANECTINE® ℞
Glaxo Wellcome

Succinylcholine Chloride
Neuromuscular Blocking Agent

Pharmacology: Succinylcholine is an ultra short-acting depolarizing-type, skeletal muscle relaxant. As does acetylcholine, it combines with the cholinergic receptors of the motor end plate to produce depolarization. This depolarization may be observed as fasciculations. Subsequent neuromuscular transmission is inhibited so long as adequate concentration of succinylcholine remains at the receptor site. Onset of flaccid paralysis is rapid, (less than 1 minute after i.v. administration), and with single administration lasts approximately 4 to 6 minutes.

Succinylcholine is rapidly hydrolyzed by plasma cholinesterase to succinylmonocholine (which possesses clinically insignificant depolarizing muscle relaxant properties) and then more slowly to succinic acid and choline (see Precautions). About 10% of the drug is excreted unchanged in the urine. The paralysis following administration of succinylcholine chloride is progressive, initially involving consecutively the levator muscles of the face, muscles of the glottis and finally the intercostals and the diaphragm and all other skeletal muscles.

Succinylcholine has no direct action on the uterus or other smooth muscle structures. Because it is highly ionized and has low fat solubility, it does not readily cross the placenta.

Tachyphylaxis occurs with repeated administration (see Precautions).

Depending on the dose and duration of succinylcholine administration, the characteristic depolarizing neuromuscular block (Phase I block) may change to a block with characteristics superficially resembling a nondepolarizing block (Phase II block). This may be associated with prolonged respiratory muscle paralysis or weakness in patients who manifest the transition to Phase II block. When this diagnosis is confirmed by peripheral nerve stimulation, it may sometimes be reversed with anticholinesterase drugs such as neostigmine (see Precautions). Anticholinesterase drugs may not always be effective. If given before succinylcholine is metabolized by cholinesterase, anticholinesterase drugs may prolong rather than shorten paralysis.

Succinylcholine has no direct effect on the myocardium. Succinylcholine stimulates both autonomic ganglia and muscarinic receptors which may cause changes in cardiac rhythm, predominantly bradycardia and occasional asystoles. Changes in rhythm including cardiac arrest, may also result from vagal stimulation, which may occur during surgical procedures, or from hyperkalemia, particularly in children (see Precautions, Children). These effects are enhanced by halogenated anesthetics.

Succinylcholine causes an increase in intraocular pressure immediately after its injection and during the fasciculation phase, and causes slight increases which may persist after onset of complete paralysis (see Warnings).

Succinylcholine may cause slight increases in intracranial pressure immediately after its injection and during the fasciculation phase (see Precautions).

As with other neuromuscular blocking agents, the potential for releasing histamine is present following succinylcholine administration. Signs and symptoms of histamine-mediated release such as flushing, hypotension and bronchoconstriction are, however, uncommon in normal clinical usage.

Succinylcholine has no effect on consciousness, pain threshold or cerebration, It should be used only with adequate anesthesia (see Warnings).

Indications: As an adjunct to general anesthesia, to facilitate tracheal intubation, and to provide skeletal muscle relaxation during surgery or mechanical ventilation.

Contraindications: In persons with personal or familial history of malignant hyperthermia, skeletal muscle myopathies and known hypersensitivity to the drug. It is also contraindicated in patients after the acute phase of injury following major burns, multiple trauma, extensive denervation of skeletal muscle, or upper motor neuron injury, because succinylcholine administered to such individuals may result in severe hyperkalemia which may result in cardiac arrest (see Warnings). The risk of hyperkalemia in these patients increases over time and usually peaks at 7 to 10 days after the injury. The risk is dependent on the extent and location of the injury. The precise time of onset and the duration of the risk period are not known. Acute rhabdomyolysis with hyperkalemia can occur when used in individuals with a skeletal muscle myopathy such as Duchenne's muscular dystrophy (see Precautions, Children).

Warnings: In infants and children, especially in boys under 8 years of age, the rare possibility of inducing life-threatening hyperkalemia in undiagnosed myopathies by the use of succinylcholine must be balanced against the risk of alternative means of securing the airway.

Succinylcholine should be used only by those skilled in the management of artificial respiration and only when facilities are instantly available for tracheal intubation and for providing adequate ventilation of the patient, including the administration of oxygen under positive pressure and the elimination of carbon dioxide. The clinician must be prepared to assist or control respiration.

To avoid distress to the patient, succinylcholine should not be administered before unconsciousness has been induced. In emergency situations, however, it may be necessary to administer succinylcholine before unconsciousness is induced.

Succinylcholine is metabolized by plasma cholinesterase and should be used with caution, if at all, in patients known to be or suspected of being homozygous for the atypical plasma cholinesterase gene.

Hyperkalemia: Succinylcholine should be administered with **great caution** to patients suffering from hyperkalemia because in these circumstances succinylcholine may induce serious cardiac arrhythmias or cardiac arrest due to hyperkalemia.

Great caution should be observed if succinylcholine is administered to patients during the acute phase of injury following major burns, multiple trauma, extensive denervation of skeletal muscle, or upper motor neuron injury (see Contraindications). The risk of hyperkalemia in these patients increases over time and usually peaks at 7 to 10 days after the injury. The risk is dependent on the extent and location of the injury. The precise time of onset and the duration of the risk period are undetermined. Patients with chronic abdominal infection, subarachnoid hemorrhage, or conditions causing degeneration of central and peripheral nervous systems should receive succinylcholine with **great caution** because of the potential for developing severe hyperkalemia.

Immediate treatment of hyperkalemia should include hyperventilation, i.v. calcium, i.v. sodium bicarbonate and i.v. glucose (with or without insulin).

Malignant Hyperthermia: Succinylcholine administration has been associated with acute onset of malignant hyperthermia, a potentially fatal hypermetabolic state of skeletal muscle. The risk of developing malignant hyperthermia following succinylcholine administration increases with the concomitant administration of volatile anesthetics. Malignant hyperthermia frequently presents as intractable spasm of the jaw muscles (masseter spasm) which may progress to generalized rigidity, increased oxygen demand, tachycardia, tachypnea and profound hyperpyrexia. Successful outcome depends on recognition of early signs, such as jaw muscle spasm, increase of end-tidal carbon dioxide concentrations, or generalized rigidity to initial administration of succinylcholine for tracheal intubation, or failure of tachycardia to respond to deepening anesthesia. Skin mottling, rising temperature and coagulopathies may occur later in the course of the hypermetabolic process. In short procedures, these symptoms and signs may not appear until the patient is in the recovery room. Recognition of the syndrome is a signal for discontinuance of anesthesia, attention to increased oxygen consumption, requirement for a marked increase in minute ventilation to correct respiratory acidosis, supplementary i.v. bicarbonate to control metabolic acidosis, support of circulation, assurance of adequate urinary output and institution of measures to control rising temperature. Dantrolene sodium i.v., is recommended as an adjunct to supportive measures in the management of this problem. Consult literature references and the dantrolene prescribing information for additional information about the management of malignant hyperthermic crisis. Continuous monitoring of temperature and expired CO_2 is recommended as an aid to early recognition of malignant hyperthermia.

Other: In adults the incidence of bradycardia, which may progress to asystole, is greater after a second dose of succinylcholine. In infants and young children, bradycardia and transient asystole may occur after one dose of succinylcholine. The incidence and severity of bradycardia is greater in infants and children than in adults. Pretreatment with anticholinergic agents (e.g., atropine), in most cases, will reduce the occurrence of bradyarrhythmias.

Succinylcholine causes an increase in intraocular pressure. It should not be used in instances in which an increase in intraocular pressure is undesirable (e.g., narrow-angle glaucoma, penetrating eye injury) unless the potential benefit of this use outweighs the potential risk.

Succinylcholine is acidic (pH=3.5) and should not be mixed with alkaline solutions having a pH greater than 8.5 (e.g., barbiturate solutions).

Precautions: General: When succinylcholine is given over a prolonged period of time, the characteristic depolarization block of the myoneural junction (Phase I block) may change to a block with characteristics superficially resembling a nondepolarizing block (Phase II block). Prolonged respiratory muscle paralysis or weakness may be observed in patients manifesting this transition to Phase II block. The transition from Phase I to Phase II block has been reported in 7 of 7 patients studied under halothane anesthesia after an accumulated dose of 2 to 4 mg/kg succinylcholine (administered in repeated, divided doses). The onset of Phase II block coincided with the onset of tachyphylaxis and prolongation of spontaneous recovery. In another study, using balanced anesthesia (N_2O/O_2/narcotic/thiopental) and succinylcholine infusion, the transition was less abrupt, with great individual variability in the dose of succinylcholine required to produce Phase II block. Of 32 patients studied, 24 developed Phase II block. Tachyphylaxis was not associated with the transition to Phase II block, and 50% of the patients who developed Phase II block experienced prolonged recovery.

When Phase II block is suspected in cases of prolonged neuromuscular blockade, positive diagnosis should be made by peripheral nerve stimulation, prior to administration of any anticholinesterase drug. Reversal of Phase II block is a medical decision which must be made upon the basis of the individual clinical pharmacology and the experience and judgment of the physician. The presence of Phase II block is indicated by fade of responses to successive stimuli (preferably "train of four"). The use of an anticholinesterase drug to reverse Phase II block should be accompanied by appropriate doses of an anticholinergic drug to prevent disturbances of the cardiac rhythm. After adequate reversal of Phase II block with an anticholinesterase agent, the patient should be continually observed for at least 1 hour for signs of return of muscle relaxation. Reversal should not be attempted unless: (1) a peripheral nerve stimulator is used to determine the presence of Phase II block (since anticholinesterase agents will potentiate succinylcholine chloride-induced Phase I block), and (2) spontaneous recovery of muscle twitch has been observed for at least 20 minutes and has reached a plateau with further recovery proceeding slowly; this delay is to ensure complete hydrolysis of succinylcholine by cholinesterase prior to administration of the anticholinesterase agent. Should the type of block be misdiagnosed, depolarization of the type initially induced by succinylcholine, (i.e., Phase I block), will be prolonged by an anticholinesterase agent.

Succinylcholine should be employed with caution in patients with fractures or muscle spasm because the initial muscle fasciculations may cause additional trauma.

Succinylcholine may cause a transient increase in intracranial pressure; however, adequate anesthetic induction prior to administration of succinylcholine will minimize this effect.

Succinylcholine may increase intragastric pressure, which could result in regurgitation and possible aspiration of stomach contents.

Neuromuscular blockade may be prolonged in patients with hypokalemia or hypocalcemia.

Reduced Plasma Cholinesterase Activity: Succinylcholine should be used carefully in patients with reduced plasma cholinesterase (pseudocholinesterase) activity. The likelihood of prolonged neuromuscular block following administration of succinylcholine must be considered in such patients (see Dosage).

Plasma cholinesterase activity may be diminished in the presence of genetic abnormalities of plasma cholinesterase (e.g., patients heterozygous or homozygous for atypical plasma cholinesterase gene), pregnancy, severe liver or kidney disease, malignant tumors, infections, burns, anemia, decompensated heart disease, peptic ulcer, or myxedema. Plasma cholinesterase activity may also be diminished by chronic administration of oral contraceptives, glucocorticoids, or certain MAO inhibitors and by irreversible inhibitors of plasma cholinesterase, (e.g., organophosphate insecticides, echothiophate, and certain antineoplastic drugs).

Patients homozygous for atypical plasma cholinesterase gene (1 in 2 500 patients) are extremely sensitive to the neuromuscular blocking effect of succinylcholine. In these patients, a 5 to 10 mg test dose of succinylcholine may be administered, or neuromuscular blockage may be produced by the cautious administration of a 1 mg/mL solution of succinylcholine by i.v. drip. Apnea or prolonged muscle paralysis should be treated with controlled respiration.

Drug Interactions: Drugs which may enhance the neuromuscular blocking action of succinylcholine include: promazine, oxytocin, aprotinin, certain non-penicillin antibiotics, quinidine, β-adrenergic blockers, procainamide, lidocaine, trimethaphan, lithium carbonate, magnesium salts, quinine, chloroquine, diethylether, isoflurane, desflurane, metoclopramide and terbutaline. The presence of an inhalational anesthetic may exacerbate the side effects of succinylcholine in infants and children (see Adverse Effects).

The neuromuscular blocking effect of succinylcholine may be enhanced by drugs that reduce plasma cholinesterase activity (e.g., chronically administered oral contraceptives, glucocorticoids, or certain MAO inhibitors) or by drugs that irreversibly inhibit plasma cholinesterase (see Precautions).

If other neuromuscular blocking agents are to be used during the same procedure, the possibility of a synergistic or antagonistic effect should be considered.

Carcinogenesis, Mutagenesis, Impairment of Fertility: There have been no long-term studies performed in animals to evaluate carcinogenic potential.

Pregnancy: Teratogenic effects: Animal reproduction studies have not been conducted with succinylcholine. It is also not known whether succinylcholine can cause fetal harm when administered to a pregnant woman or can affect reproduction capacity. Succinylcholine should be given to a pregnant woman only if clearly needed.

Nonteratogenic Effects: Plasma cholinesterase levels are decreased by approximately 24% during pregnancy and for several days postpartum. Therefore, a higher proportion of patients may be expected to show increased sensitivity (prolonged apnea) to succinylcholine when pregnant than when nonpregnant.

Labor and Delivery: Succinylcholine is commonly used to provide muscle relaxation during delivery by cesarean section.

Anectine (cont'd)

While small amounts of succinylcholine are known to cross the placental barrier, under normal conditions the quantity of drug that enters fetal circulation after a single dose of 1 mg/kg to the mother should not endanger the fetus. However, since the amount of drug that crosses the placental barrier is dependent on the concentration gradient between the maternal and fetal circulations, residual neuromuscular blockade (apnea and flaccidity) may occur in the newborn after repeated high doses to, or in the presence of atypical plasma cholinesterase in, the mother.

Lactation: It is not known whether succinylcholine is excreted in human milk. Because many drugs are excreted in human milk, caution should be exercised following succinylcholine administration to a nursing woman.

Children: There are rare reports of ventricular dysrhythmias and cardiac arrest secondary to acute rhabdomyolysis with hyperkalemia in apparently healthy infants and children who receive succinylcholine (see Warnings). Several of these individuals were subsequently found to be suffering from a myopathy such as Duchenne's muscular dystrophy whose clinical signs were not obvious. When a healthy appearing infant or child suddenly develops cardiac arrest soon after administration of succinylcholine, immediate treatment of hyperkalemia should include hyperventilation, i.v. calcium, i.v. sodium bicarbonate and i.v. glucose (with or without insulin). Treatment for acute rhabdomyolysis, including a single dose of dantrolene, should also be considered.

Unlike in adults, the incidence of bradycardia in infants and young children is common after one dose of succinylcholine. The incidence and severity of bradycardia is greater in infants and children than in adults. Pre-treatment with anticholinergic agents, e.g., atropine, in most cases, will reduce the occurrence of bradyarrhythmias.

Adverse Effects: Adverse reactions to succinylcholine consist primarily of an extension of its pharmacological actions. Succinylcholine causes profound muscle relaxation resulting in respiratory depression to the point of apnea; this effect may be prolonged. Hypersensitivity reactions, including anaphylaxis may occur in rare instances. The following additional adverse reactions have been reported: cardiac arrest, malignant hyperthermia, arrhythmias, bradycardia, tachycardia, hypertension, hypotension, hyperkalemia, prolonged respiratory depression or apnea, increased intraocular pressure, muscle fasciculation, jaw rigidity, postoperative muscle pain, rhabdomyolysis with possible myoglobinuric acute renal failure, excessive salivation, and rash.

Overdose: Symptoms: Overdosage with succinylcholine may result in neuromuscular block beyond the time needed for surgery and anesthesia. This may be manifested by skeletal muscle weakness, decreased respiratory reserve, low tidal volume or apnea.

Treatment: The primary treatment is maintenance of a patent airway and respiratory support until recovery of normal respiration is assured. Depending on the dose and duration of succinylcholine administration, the characteristic depolarizing neuromuscular block (Phase I) may change to a block with characteristics superficially resembling a nondepolarizing block (Phase II) (see Precautions).

The decision to use neostigmine to reverse a Phase II succinylcholine-induced block depends on the judgement of the clinician in the individual case. Valuable information in regard to this decision will be gained by monitoring neuromuscular function. If neostigmine is used, its administration should be accompanied by appropriate doses of an anticholinergic agent such as atropine.

Dosage: The dosage of succinylcholine should be individualized and should always be determined by the clinician after careful assessment of the patient (see Warnings).

Parenteral drug products should be inspected visually for particulate matter and discoloration prior to administration whenever solution and container permit. Solutions which are not clear and colorless should not be used.

Adults: For Short Surgical Procedures: The average dose required to produce neuromuscular blockade and to facilitate tracheal intubation is 0.6 mg/kg succinylcholine given i.v. The optimum dose will vary among individuals and may be from 0.3 to 1.1 mg/kg. Following administration of doses in this range, neuromuscular blockade develops in about 1 minute; maximum blockade may persist for about 2 minutes, after which recovery takes place within 4 to 6 minutes. However, very large doses may result in more prolonged blockade. A 5 to 10 mg test dose may be used to determine the sensitivity of the patient and the individual recovery time (see Precautions).

For Long Surgical Procedures: The dosage of succinylcholine administered by infusion depends upon the duration of the surgical procedure and the need for muscle relaxation. The average rate for an adult ranges between 2.5 and 4.3 mg/min. (The sterile powder is supplied in a Flo-Pack for i.v. solutions only.)

Solutions containing from 1 to 2 mg/mL succinylcholine have commonly been used for continuous infusion. The more dilute solution (1 mg/mL) is probably preferable from the standpoint of ease of control of the rate of administration of the drug and hence, of relaxation. This i.v. solution containing 1 mg/mL may be administered at the rate of 0.5 mg (0.5 mL) to 10 mg (10 mL)/minute to obtain the required amount of relaxation. The amount required/minute will depend upon the individual response as well as the degree of relaxation required. Avoid overburdening the circulation with a large volume of fluid. It is recommended that neuromuscular function be carefully monitored with a peripheral nerve stimulator when using succinylcholine by infusion in order to avoid overdose, detect development of Phase II block, follow its rate of recovery, and assess the effects of reversing agents (see Precautions).

Children: The i.v. dose of succinylcholine is 2 mg/kg for infants and small children; for older children and adolescents the dose is 1 mg/kg (see Warnings and Precautions, Children).

Rarely, i.v. bolus administration of succinylcholine in infants and children may result in malignant ventricular arrhythmias and cardiac arrest secondary to acute rhabdomyolysis with hyperkalemia. In such situations, an underlying myopathy should be suspected.

I.V. bolus administration of succinylcholine in infants and young children may result in profound bradycardia or, rarely, asystole. Unlike in adults, the incidence of bradycardia in infants and children is greater after a single dose of succinylcholine. The occurrence of bradyarrhythmias, in most cases, will be reduced by pretreatment with an anticholinergic drug (e.g., atropine) (see Precautions, Children).

I.M.: If necessary, succinylcholine may be given i.m. to infants, older children or adults when a suitable vein is inaccessible. A dose of up to 3 or 4 mg/kg may be given, but not more than 150 mg total dose should be administered by this route. The onset of effect of succinylcholine given i.m. is usually observed in about 2 to 3 minutes.

Reconstituted Solutions: Flo-Pack: Succinylcholine is acidic (pH 3.5) and should not be mixed with alkaline solutions having a pH greater than 8.5 (e.g., barbiturate solutions).

Preparations containing 1 to 2 mg/mL may be prepared by adding 1 000 mg succinylcholine (the contents of 2 Anectine Sterile Powder Flo-Pack units containing 500 mg succinylcholine chloride) to 1 L or 500 mL of either of the following diluents: 5% Dextrose Injection USP; 0.9% Sodium Chloride Injection USP.

Aseptic techniques should be used to prepare the diluted product. Solutions must be used within 24 hours after preparation. Discard unused portions.

Supplied: Injection: Each mL of sterile nonpyrogenic solution for i.v. use contains: succinylcholine chloride 20 mg and water for injection. The solution is made isotonic with 4.5 mg sodium chloride. The pH is adjusted to 3.5 with hydrochloric acid. Single-dose ampuls of 5 mL. Multiple-dose vials of 10 and 20 mL (also contains methylparaben 0.1% as preservative), boxes of 25. Store in refrigerator at 2 to 8°C. The multiple-dose vials are stable for up to 14 days at room temperature without significant loss of potency.

Flo-Pack: Each vial sterile powder contains: succinylcholine chloride 500 mg for preparation of i.v. solutions only. Powder does not require refrigeration. Store at 15 to 30°C.

ANEXATE®
Roche

Flumazenil

Benzodiazepine Antagonist

Pharmacology: Flumazenil, an imidazobenzodiazepine, is a benzodiazepine antagonist which blocks the central effects of agents that act via the benzodiazepine receptor, by competitive inhibition. The antagonism is specific, since in animal experiments the effects of compounds which have no affinity for the benzodiazepine receptor (e.g., barbiturates, meprobamate, ethanol, GABA-mimetics, and adenosine receptor agonists) were not affected by flumazenil.

Following the i.v. administration of radiolabeled flumazenil to human volunteers, the distribution of radioactivity corresponded closely to the distribution of benzodiazepine receptors as determined by positron emission tomography.

The hypnotic-sedative effects of benzodiazepines are rapidly reversed by flumazenil. However, the residual effects may reappear gradually within a few hours, depending on the dose of flumazenil, the time elapsed since the benzodiazepine agonist was given, and the dose and elimination half-life of the previously administered benzodiazepine. Flumazenil has shown some weak intrinsic agonistic (e.g., anticonvulsant) activity without therapeutic relevance.

Pharmacokinetics: In young male volunteers, the pharmacokinetics of i.v. flumazenil were linear over a dose range of 2 to 100 mg. Increasing doses of flumazenil were accompanied by a corresponding increase in the area under the plasma concentration-time curve (AUC: 37 ng/mL•hour at 2 mg and 1 906 ng/mL•hour at 100 mg), and maximum plasma concentration (C_{max}: 55 ng/mL at 2 mg and 3 332 ng/mL at 100 mg). However, elimination half-life, volume of distribution at steady-state and plasma clearance were independent of dose over the entire range studied. The mean elimination half-life of flumazenil following the administration of single i.v. doses to healthy subjects was approximately 1 hour.

In patients with cirrhosis, the pharmacokinetics of flumazenil were altered, particularly in patients with severely impaired liver function. Elimination half-life was prolonged and plasma clearance markedly decreased. Since plasma protein binding is lower in cirrhotic patients than in healthy subjects, the levels of free drug are substantially increased, namely from 55% in controls to 64% and 79% in patients with moderate and severe liver dysfunction, respectively.

In patients with chronic stabilized renal failure (creatinine clearance <10 mL/min) in the absence and presence of dialysis, the pharmacokinetics of flumazenil remained essentially unaltered.

There were no statistically significant differences between the distribution and elimination parameters of 12 elderly (8 males and 4 females) and 6 young (4 males and 2 females) healthy volunteers, following the administration of a 2 mg i.v. dose.

Flumazenil undergoes rapid and extensive hepatic metabolism; less than 0.2% of the administered dose is eliminated unchanged in the urine. The major metabolites of flumazenil identified in the urine are the free acid and its glucuronide conjugate. In healthy volunteers, approximately 70% of an i.v. dose of flumazenil was excreted within the first 2 hours after dosing and another 16% during the next 2 hours. Elimination was essentially complete within 72 hours, with 90 to 95% of the total radioactivity appearing in the urine and 5 to 10% in the feces.

Plasma protein binding is rather low. Over a concentration range of 24 to 570 ng/mL, flumazenil was found to be 50% bound to human plasma proteins. Albumin accounts for approximately two-thirds of the plasma protein binding. The binding of flumazenil was not affected by a high concentration of diazepam (10 μg/mL), and flumazenil did not interfere with the binding of diazepam.

When administered together with the benzodiazepines midazolam, flunitrazepam or lormetazepam, the pharmacokinetic parameters of flumazenil were not affected. Similarly, the pharmacokinetics of benzodiazepines remained unaltered in the presence of the antagonist flumazenil.

Table I (on following page) summarizes the ranges of mean pharmacokinetic parameters reported in a series of studies, after single i.v. doses of flumazenil.

Indications: For the complete or partial reversal of the central sedative effects of benzodiazepines. It may therefore be used in anesthesia and intensive care in the following situations: termination of general anesthesia induced and/or maintained with benzodiazepines, reversal of benzodiazepine sedation in short diagnostic and therapeutic procedures, for the diagnosis and/or management of deliberate or accidental benzodiazepine overdosage.

Contraindications: Patients with known hypersensitivity to flumazenil or to benzodiazepines.

Epileptic patients who have been receiving benzodiazepine treatment for a prolonged period. The abrupt suppression of the protective effect of benzodiazepines may induce convulsions in epileptic patients.

In patients who are showing signs of serious cyclic antidepressant overdose (see Precautions).

Warnings: In view of the short duration of action of flumazenil and the possible need for repeat doses, the patient should remain closely monitored until all possible central benzodiazepine effects have subsided.

Table I—Anexate

Pharmacokinetics

Subjects	**Dose (mg)**	**Elimination Half-life ($t_{1/2}\beta$) (min)**	**Volume of Distribution at Steady-state (Vd_{ss})(L/kg)**	**Plasma Clearance (Cl_{pl}) (L/h)**
Male volunteers 23-26 years	2–100	48–55	0.83–0.86	55–57
Male volunteers 28–42 years	2.5	42–72	0.63	41
Volunteers 39 years	2	46	0.62	74
Cirrhosis – moderate 45 years	2	76	0.68	29
– severe 45 years	2	142	0.85	19
Volunteers 37 years	1	51	0.91	60
Chronic renal failure – without dialysis 36 years	1	38	0.94	75
– with dialysis 55 years	1	43	1.07	75
Age volunteers:				
Male:				
20–28 years	2	54	0.87	56
65–77 years	2	66	0.93	56
Female:				
24–30 years	2	48	0.96	66
63–67 years	2	54	0.78	44

The immediate availability of oxygen, resuscitative equipment and skilled personnel for the maintenance of airway, ventilation and cardiac function should be ensured before the administration of any benzodiazepine or flumazenil.

Resedation: Flumazenil is a competitive inhibitor of benzodiazepines at the receptor site and does not affect the pharmacokinetics of benzodiazepines. Thus, when the effect of flumazenil wears off, the patient returns to the point of residual sedation that would have been present at that time had flumazenil not been given. In patients administered large doses of long-acting benzodiazepines or in critically ill patients, this could be deep sedation. In a U.S. clinical study in patients with benzodiazepine intoxication, 90/133 (67.7%) patients became resedated. **Therefore, flumazenil should be administered only when the continued observation of patients for recurrence of sedation can be assured.**

Respiration: When used in anesthesiology at the end of surgery, flumazenil should not be given until the effects of neuromuscular blockade have been completely antagonized and careful monitoring of the respiratory depressant effect of opiate analgesics has been assured. After the benzodiazepine has been antagonized with flumazenil, any residual respiratory depressant effect of other agents, such as opiates, should be appropriately treated.

The ability of flumazenil to reverse benzodiazepine-induced respiratory depression is equivocal; in some studies residual effects of benzodiazepines on respiration were still present despite reversal of sedation.

Seizures: In patients treated for long periods of time with high doses of benzodiazepines, flumazenil may trigger withdrawal symptoms (e.g., convulsions); rapid i.v. injections should therefore be avoided.

Precautions: General: In high-risk patients, the advantages of counteracting benzodiazepine-related sedation should be weighed against the drawbacks of rapid awakening.

Postoperative pain must be taken into account. Following a major intervention, it may be preferable to maintain a moderate degree of sedation.

Anxiety: The dosage of flumazenil should be adjusted carefully in patients suffering from pre-operative anxiety or having a history of chronic or episodic anxiety. In anxious patients, particularly those with coronary heart disease, it is preferable to maintain a degree of sedation throughout the early postoperative period rather than bring about complete arousal.

Instruction to Patients Upon Discharge: Occupational Hazards: Patients who have received flumazenil to reverse the effects of benzodiazepine sedation should be instructed, if possible in writing, not to drive, to operate machinery or to engage in any other physically or mentally demanding activity for 24 hours or until the effects of the benzodiazepine have subsided, since the effect of the benzodiazepine may return. Patients should also be warned not to take alcohol, or drugs not prescribed by their physician, until the effects of the benzodiazepines have subsided.

Children: The safety and effectiveness of flumazenil in children below the age of 18 has not been established.

Geriatrics: In the absence of data on the use of flumazenil in elderly patients, it should be borne in mind that this population is generally more sensitive to the effects of drugs and should be treated with due caution.

Pregnancy and *Lactation:* Although studies in animals have not shown evidence of embryotoxicity or teratogenicity, flumazenil should be used during pregnancy only, if in the opinion of the treating physician, the possible benefit to the patient outweighs the potential risks to the fetus.

It is not known whether flumazenil is excreted in human milk. For this reason, breast-feeding should be interrupted for 24 hours when flumazenil is used during lactation.

Hepatic and Renal Impairment: In patients with liver insufficiency, the elimination of flumazenil can be delayed (see Pharmacology, Pharmacokinetics). No dosage adjustments are necessary in patients with renal impairment.

Acute Myocardial Infarction or Cardiac Arrhythmias: Flumazenil abruptly terminates the effects of benzodiazepines. As a result, sympathetic tone may be increased and thus, cardiac electrical instability enhanced. Consequently, caution is advised when administering flumazenil to patients with mycordial infarction or cardiac arrhythmias.

Use in Patients with Increased Intracranial Pressure Receiving Benzodiazepines (e.g., head injury, brain tumor, intracranial hemorrhage): In patients with increased intracranial pressure, flumazenil may further increase intracranial pressure, cerebral perfusion pressure, or precipitate convulsions. In such patients, flumazenil should be used with extreme caution and only by practitioners prepared to manage such complications, should they occur.

Drug Interactions: Flumazenil blocks the central effects of benzodiazepines by competitive interaction at the receptor level; the effects of non-benzodiazepines which act via the benzodiazepine receptor, such as zopiclone, are also blocked. However, flumazenil does not reverse the effects of drugs that do not act via this route.

The pharmacokinetics of flumazenil are unaltered in the presence of benzodiazepines, and similarly, flumazenil does not affect the kinetics of benzodiazepines.

Multiple Drug Overdosage: Particular caution is necessary when using flumazenil in cases of multiple drug overdosage, since the toxic effects (cardiac arrhythmias and/or convulsions) of other psychotropic drugs, especially tricyclic antidepressants, may increase as the effects of benzodiazepines subside.

Patients should be evaluated for the signs and symptoms of a tricyclic antidepressant overdose. A diagnostic ECG can be used to confirm the presence of these agents; a QRS duration of 0.1 seconds or greater indicates a serious overdosage with tricyclic antidepressants, which should be treated with appropriate measures. Depending on the extent of involvement of benzodiazepines in the multiple drug overdose, this may or may not include flumazenil.

ICU: Flumazenil should be used with caution in the Intensive Care Unit because of the increased risk of unrecognized benzodiazepine dependence in such settings. Flumazenil may produce convulsions in patients physically dependent on benzodiazepine (see Warnings).

Adverse Effects: Flumazenil is generally well tolerated. In postoperative use, nausea and/or vomiting are observed, particularly if opiates have also been employed. Flushing has also been noted. If patients are awakened too rapidly, they may become agitated, anxious or fearful. Transient increases in blood pressure and heart rate may also occur.

Excessively and/or rapidly injected doses of flumazenil may induce benzodiazepine withdrawal symptoms such as anxiety attacks, tachycardia, dizziness and sweating in patients on long-term benzodiazepine treatment.

Although clinical experience with flumazenil is limited, seizures and/or cardiac arrhythmias have been observed in patients who are physically dependent on benzodiazepines, and in multiple drug overdose, particularly in the presence of tricyclic antidepressants.

Table II summarizes the adverse reactions which occurred with an incidence of >1%.

Table II—Anexate

Clinical Adverse Events >1%

		Frequency (%)	
Organ System	**Adverse Event**	**General Anesthesia/ Sedation n=7 365**	**Known or Suspected Benzodiazepine Overdose n=764**
CNS	Agitation	0.2	5.8
	Crying/Tears	0.5	3.5
	Headache	0.5	1.6
	Anxiety/Anxious Feeling	0.3	1.4
	Seizures/ Convulsions	—	1.3
	Dizziness	1.4	1.2
Gastrointestinal	Nausea	4.3	2.2
	Vomiting	2.6	2.0
Cardiovascular	Hypertension	0.1	1.4
	Tachycardia	0.1	1.2
Miscellaneous	Shivering/Cold Sensation/Chills	0.5	1.2

Other clinical adverse events which occurred with an incidence of <1% are as follows: Cardiovascular: ventricular premature beats, arrhythmia, palpitations, bradycardia, flush, hypotension.

Respiratory: dyspnea, hypopnea, nasal congestion, cough, subjective suffocation.

CNS/Neuromuscular: startle reaction, fear, nervousness, restlessness, excitation, aggressiveness, anger; euphoria, hallucinations, vertigo, confusion, tiredness/drowsiness, depression; involuntary/spontaneous movement, tremor, mouth movement, tetany.

Gastrointestinal: salivation, dry mouth, hiccoughs.

Dermatological: urticaria, pruritus.

Miscellaneous: pain, allergic reaction, strabismus, sweating.

Local Tolerance: Slight to moderate pain at the site of injection occurred in 2.5% of patients and redness was observed in 1.3% of patients 1 hour after the administration of flumazenil.

Overdose: Symptoms and Treatment: Flumazenil, administered i.v. to healthy volunteers at a dosage of 100 mg, did not produce symptoms of overdosage.

Dosage: Flumazenil should be administered i.v. by a physician with experience in anesthesiology.

The dose should always be individually titrated to the desired response to avoid abrupt awakening. Particular care is needed with patients who are physically dependent on benzodiazepines, patients who have ingested multiple drugs, and patients who are prone to anxiety (see Warnings and Precautions).

Flumazenil may be used concurrently with other resuscitative procedures.

Flumazenil may be diluted with sodium chloride 0.9%, sodium chloride 0.45% + dextrose 2.5%, or dextrose 5% for infusion. Infusion solutions containing flumazenil should be used within 24 hours, and unused portions discarded.

General Anesthesia/Sedation: The recommended initial dose is 0.2 mg administered i.v. over 15 seconds. If the desired level of consciousness is not obtained within 60 seconds, a further dose of 0.1 mg can be injected and repeated at 60 second intervals, up to a maximum total dose of 1 mg. The usual dose is between 0.3 and 0.6 mg.

Known or Suspected Benzodiazepine Overdose: For the reversal of excessive sedative effects of benzodiazepines in overdose cases, titrate flumazenil as described below, until the patient clearly responds or until the maximum recommended dose has been reached.

The recommended initial dose is 0.3 mg administered i.v. over 30 seconds, followed by a series of 0.3mg injections, each administered over a 30 second period, at 60 second intervals. The maximum recommended dose is 2.0 mg.

If a significant improvement in the level of consciousness and respiratory function is not achieved after repeated injections of flumazenil, a non-benzodiazepine etiology must be assumed.

If drowsiness recurs, an i.v. infusion of 0.1 to 0.4 mg/hr may be useful. The rate of the infusion should be individually adjusted to the desired level of arousal.

Anexate (cont'd)

Supplied: Each mL of the colorless aqueous solution contains: flumazenil 0.1 mg. Nonmedicinal ingredients: acetic acid, disodium edetate, methylparaben, propylparaben and sodium chloride. Sodium hydroxide and hydrochloric acid added to adjust pH to approximately 4. Multidose vials of 10 mL, packs of 10. Store at 15 to 30°C.

ANILERIDINE Ⓝ
General Monograph, CPhA

see OPIOID ANALGESICS

ANODAN™-HC Ⓟ
Odan

Hydrocortisone Acetate—Zinc Sulfate Monohydrate

Anorectal Therapy

Supplied: Ointment: Each g contains: hydrocortisone acetate 0.5% and zinc sulfate monohydrate 0.5% in a petrolatum ointment base. Nonmedicinal ingredients: petrolatum and purified water. Tubes of 15 and 30 g with rectal applicator.

Suppositories: Each suppository contains: zinc sulfate monohydrate 10 mg, hydrocortisone acetate 10 mg in a triglyceride base. Nonmedicinal ingredients: methylparaben, propylparaben and triglyceride. Boxes of 12 and 24. Store between 8 and 15°C. Avoid freezing.

ANSAID® Ⓟ
Pharmacia & Upjohn

Flurbiprofen

Anti-inflammatory—Analgesic

Pharmacology: Flurbiprofen, a phenylalkanoic acid derivative, is a nonsteroidal anti-inflammatory agent which also possesses analgesic and antipyretic activities. Its mode of action, like that of other nonsteroidal anti-inflammatory agents, is not known. However, its therapeutic action is not due to pituitary-adrenal stimulation. Flurbiprofen is an inhibitor of prostaglandin synthesis. The resulting decrease in prostaglandin synthesis may partially explain the drug's anti-inflammatory effect at the cellular level.

Pharmacokinetics: In bioavailability studies in normal volunteers, flurbiprofen reached peak blood levels in about 1.5 hours (range of 0.5 to 4 hours). Its plasma half-life is 5.7 hours (range of 3 to 9 hours). Administration with food does not alter total drug availability but delays absorption. Excretion is 88 to 98% complete within 24 hours after the last dose.

Flurbiprofen is rapidly metabolized and excreted in the urine as free and unaltered intact drug (20%) and hydroxylated metabolites (50%). About 90% of the flurbiprofen in urine is present as conjugates. In animal models of inflammation the metabolites showed no activity. Flurbiprofen is extensively bound (99%) to human plasma protein such as albumin, but less than 10% of the primary albumin binding sites would be occupied by the drug. Flurbiprofen binds to a different primary site on albumin than do anticoagulants, sulfonamides and phenytoin. Mean peak serum concentrations of flurbiprofen were higher in the elderly female patients.

Indications: For the relief of signs and symptoms of rheumatoid arthritis, osteoarthritis and ankylosing spondylitis.

For the relief of pain associated with dysmenorrhea.

For the relief of mild to moderate pain accompanied by inflammation (e.g., bursitis, tendinitis, soft-tissue trauma).

Contraindications: Flurbiprofen should not be used in patients with active, or recent history of inflammatory diseases of the gastrointestinal tract such as peptic ulcer, gastritis, regional enteritis or ulcerative colitis.

It is contraindicated in patients with a history of hypersensitivity to the drug.

It should not be used in patients in whom acute asthmatic attacks, urticaria, rhinitis or other allergic manifestations are precipitated by ASA or other nonsteroidal anti-inflammatory agents. Fatal anaphylactoid reactions have occurred in such individuals.

Warnings: General: ulceration, perforation and bleeding of the stomach, small intestine, large intestine, sometimes severe and occasionally fatal have been reported during therapy with nonsteroidal anti-inflammatory drugs (NSAIDs) including flurbiprofen.

Flurbiprofen should be given under close medical supervision to patients prone to gastrointestinal tract irritation particularly those with a history of peptic ulcer, diverticulosis or other inflammatory disease of the gastrointestinal tract. In these cases the physician must weigh the benefits of treatment against the possible hazards.

Patients taking nonsteroidal anti-inflammatory drugs including flurbiprofen should be instructed to contact a physician immediately if they experience symptoms or signs suggestive of peptic ulceration or gastrointestinal bleeding. These reactions can occur without warning symptoms or signs and at any time during treatment.

Elderly, frail and debilitated patients appear to be at higher risk from a variety of adverse reactions from NSAIDs. For such patients, consideration should be given to a starting dose lower than usual, with individual adjustment when necessary and under close supervision (see Precautions).

Pregnancy and *Lactation:* Safe use in pregnancy and lactation has not been established. Although no teratogenic effects were seen in animal studies, parturition was delayed and prolonged, and there was an increase in the number of stillbirths. Flurbiprofen has been found to cross the placental barrier, and it is secreted in breast milk. Therefore, the use of this drug is not recommended during pregnancy and lactation.

Children: Safety and efficacy has not been established in children, and therefore the use in this age group is not recommended.

Pre-existing asthma: About 10% of patients with asthma may have ASA-sensitive asthma. The use of ASA in patients with ASA-sensitive Asthma has been associated with severe bronchospasm which can be fatal. Since cross-reactivity, including bronchospasm, between ASA and other NSAIDs has been reported in such ASA-sensitive patients, flurbiprofen should not be administered to patients with this form of ASA-sensitivity and should be used with caution in all patients with pre-existing asthma.

Precautions: As with all NSAIDs, flurbiprofen should be used with caution in the elderly particularly women and the dosage should be adjusted individually.

Gastrointestinal: If peptic ulceration is suspected or confirmed, or if gastrointestinal bleeding or perforation occurs, flurbiprofen should be discontinued, an appropriate treatment instituted and patient closely monitored.

There is no definite evidence that the concomitant administration of histamine H_2-receptor antagonists and/or antacids will either prevent the occurrence of gastrointestinal side effects or allow continuation of flurbiprofen therapy when and if these adverse reactions appear.

Renal Function: As with other NSAIDs, long-term administration of flurbiprofen to animals has resulted in renal papillary necrosis and other abnormal renal pathology. In humans, there have been reports of acute interstitial nephritis with hematuria, proteinuria, and occasionally nephrotic syndrome.

A second form of renal toxicity has been seen in patients with prerenal conditions leading to the reduction in renal blood flow or blood volume, where the renal prostaglandins have a supportive role in the maintenance of renal perfusion.

In these patients, administration of a NSAID may cause a dose-dependent reduction in prostaglandin formation and may precipitate overt renal decompensation. Patients at greatest risk of this reaction are those with impaired renal function, heart failure, liver dysfunction, those taking diuretics, and the elderly. Discontinuation of nonsteroidal anti-inflammatory therapy is usually followed by recovery to the pretreatment state.

Flurbiprofen and its metabolites are eliminated primarily by the kidneys, therefore the drug should be used with great caution in patients with impaired renal function. In these cases lower doses of flurbiprofen should be anticipated and patients carefully monitored.

During long-term therapy kidney function should be monitored periodically.

Hepatic Function: As with other NSAIDs, borderline elevations of one or more liver tests may occur. These abnormalities may progress, may remain essentially unchanged, or may be transient with continued therapy.

A patient with symptoms and/or signs suggesting liver dysfunction, or in whom an abnormal liver test has occurred, should be evaluated for evidence of the development of more severe hepatic reaction while on therapy with this drug. Severe hepatic reactions including jaundice and cases of fatal hepatitis have been reported with this drug as with other NSAIDs. Although such reactions are rare, if abnormal liver tests persist or worsen, if clinical signs and symptoms consistent with liver disease develop, or if systemic manifestations occur (e.g., eosinophilia, rash, etc.), this drug should be discontinued.

During long-term therapy, liver function tests should be monitored periodically. If this drug is to be used in the presence of impaired liver function, it must be done under strict observation.

Fluid and Electrolyte Balance: Fluid retention and edema have been observed in patients treated with flurbiprofen. Therefore, as with many other nonsteroidal anti-inflammatory drugs, the possibility of precipitating congestive heart failure in elderly patients or those with compromised cardiac function should be born in mind. Flurbiprofen should be used with caution in patients with heart failure, hypertension or other conditions predisposing to fluid retention.

Serum electrolytes should be monitored periodically during long-term therapy, especially in those patients at risk.

Hematology: NSAIDs, including flurbiprofen, can increase the risk of bleeding in patients receiving anticoagulants, and should be given with caution.

NSAIDs including flurbiprofen can cause reductions in hemoglobin and should be used with caution in patients who are anemic.

Flurbiprofen inhibits collagen-induced platelet aggregation, and patients who may be adversely affected by prolonged bleeding time should be carefully observed when flurbiprofen is administered.

Blood dyscrasias associated with the use of NSAIDs are rare, but could be with severe consequences.

Infection: In common with other anti-inflammatory drugs, flurbiprofen may mask the usual signs of infection.

Ophthalmology: Blurred and/or diminished vision has been reported with the use of flurbiprofen and other NSAIDs. If such symptoms develop this drug should be discontinued and an ophthalmologic examination performed; ophthalmic examination should be carried out at periodic intervals in any patient receiving this drug for an extended period of time.

Drug Interactions: Anticoagulants, Sulfonamides, Phenytoin: Flurbiprofen affects bleeding parameters and serious clinical bleeding has been reported. Caution is advised.

Flurbiprofen is extensively protein bound (99%) to human serum albumin. Less than 10% of the primary binding sites were estimated to be occupied at therapeutic drug concentrations. In vitro studies suggest that it binds to a different primary site on albumin (Type II) than drugs such as anticoagulants, sulfonamides and phenytoin (Type I). However, patients with such combination therapy should be monitored.

ASA: Concomitant oral administration of flurbiprofen and ASA indicates that flurbiprofen has no significant effect on the pharmacokinetics and metabolism of ASA. However, concomitant administration of ASA decreases flurbiprofen peak serum levels, as well as the rate and amount of flurbiprofen absorbed.

Antacids: In geriatric subjects antacid suspensions caused a reduction in the rate but not the extent of flurbiprofen absorption.

ß-adrenergic Blocking Agents: Flurbiprofen pretreatment attenuated the hypotensive effect of propranolol but did not appear to affect the β-blocker mediated reduction in heart rate.

Cimetidine, Ranitidine: A small but statistically significant increase in flurbiprofen serum concentration may result with administration of these agents.

Digoxin: Concurrent administration of digoxin with flurbiprofen did not reveal a change in steady-state serum levels of either drug.

Diuretics: Flurbiprofen can interfere with the effects of furosemide. NSAIDs have been shown to interfere with the action of thiazide diuretics and potassium-sparing diuretics.

Oral Hypoglycemic Agents: Concomitant administration of flurbiprofen and hypoglycemic agents revealed a slight reduction in blood sugar concentrations but no signs or symptoms of hypoglycemia.

Adverse Effects: In clinical trials of flurbiprofen a total of 2 820 patients were treated. Gastrointestinal adverse reactions were those most commonly seen, the most severe of which were gastrointestinal bleeding and ulceration.

Gastrointestinal (24.3%): abdominal pain 6.8%; dyspepsia 6.0%; diarrhea 5.7%; nausea 4.5%; constipation 2.6%; gastrointestinal bleeding 1.7%; flatulence 1.4%; emesis 1.2%; elevated liver enzymes 1.4%. Incidence 0.1 to 1.0%: increased appetite, stomatitis, gastrointestinal distress, gastritis, gastroenteritis, ulcer (peptic, gastric or duodenal), melena (includes rectal bleed, bloody diarrhea), oral inflammation, eructation, dry mouth, esophagitis, hematemesis, colitis, hepatitis, rectal discomfort, periodontal abscess, gingivitis,

glossitis, anorexia, vomiting. Incidence less than 0.1%: gums bleeding, cholecystitis.
CNS (8.0%): headache 2.6%; asthenia 1.0%. Incidence 0.1% to 1.0%: somnolence, hypertonia, insomnia, nervousness, paresthesia, depression, mood changes, tremors, anxiety, amnesia, migraine, ataxia, cerebrovascular accident, confusion, cerebral ischemia, malaise, increased reflex. Incidence less than 0.1%: EEG abnormalities, neuralgia, convulsions, meningitis, speech disorder, twitch, euphoria, decreased libido.
Respiratory (9.6%): pharyngitis 6.1%; infection 1.2%; rhinitis 1.3%; sinusitis 1.6%. Incidence 0.1 to 1.0%: bronchitis, epistaxis, increase in cough, dyspnea, laryngitis, lung disorder, asthma, voice alterations. Incidence less than 0.1%: hyperventilation, pleural distress, pulmonary infarct, pulmonary embolism, pneumonia.
General Body (6.7%): edema 2.6%; pain 1.9%; flu syndrome 2.0%. Incidence 0.1 to 1.0%: fever, abdominal enlargement, chills, infection, allergic reaction, death. Incidence less than 0.1%: injury.
Special Senses (5.2%): Ear: dizziness 1.5%; tinnitus 1.2%; vertigo 0.6%; pain 0.3%; disorder 0.2%. Incidence less than 0.1%: vestibular disturbances.
Eye: ocular inflammations 0.3%; amblyopia 0.6%; vision disturbances 0.4%; blepharitis 0.1%; conjunctivitis 0.5%; keratoconjunctivitis 0.1%; photophobia 0.1%. Incidence less than 0.1%: diplopia, visual field problems, corneal opacity, lacrimal distress, glaucoma, pain, scleritis.
Others: taste changes 0.2%; parosmia <0.1%
Urogenital (4.9%): urinary tract infections 1.5%. Incidence 0.1 to 1.0%: urine abnormalities, hematuria, cystitis, frequency, vaginitis, breast pain, kidney function abnormalities. Incidence less than 0.1%: dysuria, albuminuria, pyuria, pain, kidney stones, kidney failure, incontinence, ejaculatory abnormality, leukorrhea, urethritis, retention, dysmenorrhea, menstrual distress, impotence.
Cardiovascular (2.2%): Incidence 0.1 to 1.0%: hypertension, arrhythmias, inotropic problems, palpitations, vasodilatation, angina, phlebitis, vascular distress, extrasystoles, right heart failure, myocardial infarction, vasculitis. Incidence less than 0.1%: tachycardia, syncope.
Metabolic (1.1%): Incidence 0.1 to 1.0%: weight changes, hyperuricemia. Incidence less than 0.1%: electrolyte changes (Ca++, K+), increased CPK, thirst.
Musculoskeletal (0.7%): Incidence 0.1 to 1.0%: arthritis, injury, myalgia. Incidence less than 0.1%: myasthenia, tenosynovitis, joint disease.
Skin (3.5%): rash 1.9%. Incidence 0.1 to 1.0%: herpetic infections, alopecia, dry skin, eczema, nail discoloration, pruritus, sweating, skin ulcerations, urticaria. Incidence less than 0.1%: seborrhea, angioedema, exfoliation.
Hemic/Lymphatic (6.6%): Decrease in hemoglobin and hematocrit 4.6%. Incidence 0.1 to 1.0%: iron deficiency anemia, ecchymosis, eosinophilia, leukopenia, lymphadenopathy, neutropenia. Incidence less than 0.1%: anemia, leukocytosis, petechia, thrombocytopenia, WBC abnormality.

Rare events are derived principally from worldwide marketing experience and the literature. Accurate rate estimates are generally impossible. These include the following: cholestatic and non-cholestatic jaundice, exacerbation of inflammatory bowel disease, small intestine inflammation with loss of blood and protein, photosensitivity, toxic epidermal necrolysis, interstitial nephritis and anaphylaxis.

Overdose: Symptoms and Treatment: Information on flurbiprofen overdosage is available for 13 children and 12 adults; all persons receiving only a flurbiprofen overdose and all but one person exposed to more than 1 drug recovered. Manifestations of flurbiprofen overdose have included decreased mental status, coma, diminished muscle tone, headache, diplopia, elevated liver enzymes, respiratory depression, nausea, and epigastric pain.

Dosage: Rheumatoid Arthritis, Osteoarthritis, Ankylosing Spondylitis: 200 mg/day given in divided doses. Some patients may require up to 300 mg/day. The dose should be adjusted until the minimum effective maintenance dose is established. During the course of treatment, the maximum daily dose of 300 mg should be used only during symptom exacerbations and not for maintenance therapy (see Adverse Effects).
Dysmenorrhea: 50 mg given 4 times daily.
Mild to Moderately Severe Pain: 50 mg given every 4 to 6 hours as needed.

Information for the Patient: See Blue Section—Information for the Patient "Ansaid".

Supplied: 50 mg: Each white, elliptical, film-coated tablet imprinted with Ansaid logo contains: flurbiprofen 50 mg. Nonmedicinal ingredients: carnauba wax, colloidal silicon dioxide, croscarmellose sodium, film-coat white, hydroxypropyl methylcellulose, lactose, magnesium stearate, microcrystalline cellulose. Gluten-free. Bottles of 100 and 500.

100 mg: Each blue, elliptical, film-coated tablet imprinted with Ansaid logo contains: flurbiprofen 100 mg. Nonmedicinal ingredients: carnauba wax, colloidal silicon dioxide, croscarmellose sodium, hydroxypropyl methylcellulose, lactose, magnesium stearate, microcrystalline cellulose, Opaspray blue. Gluten-free. Bottles of 100 and 500.

(Shown in Product Recognition Section)

ANTABUSE® ℞

Wyeth-Ayerst

Disulfiram

Alcohol Deterrent

Pharmacology: Disulfiram produces a sensitivity to alcohol which results in a highly unpleasant reaction when the patient under treatment ingests even small amounts of alcohol. Disulfiram blocks the oxidation of alcohol at the acetaldehyde stage. During alcohol metabolism after disulfiram intake, the concentration of acetaldehyde occurring in the blood may be 5 to 10 times higher than that found during metabolism of the same amount of alcohol alone.

Accumulation of acetaldehyde in the blood produces a complex of highly unpleasant symptoms referred to as the disulfiram-alcohol reaction. This reaction, which is proportional to the dosage of both disulfiram and alcohol, will persist as long as alcohol is being metabolized. Disulfiram does not appear to influence the rate of alcohol elimination from the body.

Disulfiram plus even small amounts of alcohol produces flushing, throbbing in head and neck, throbbing headache, respiratory difficulty, nausea, copious vomiting, sweating, thirst, chest pain, palpitation, dyspnea, hyperventilation, tachycardia, hypotension, syncope, marked uneasiness, weakness, vertigo, blurred vision, and confusion. In severe reactions, there may be respiratory depression, cardiovascular collapse, arrhythmias, myocardial infarction, acute congestive heart failure, unconsciousness, convulsions, and death. The intensity of the reaction may vary with each individual but is generally proportional to the amount of disulfiram and alcohol ingested. In the sensitive individual, mild reactions may occur when the blood alcohol concentration is increased to as little as 5 to 10 mg/100 mL. At a concentration of 50 mg/100 mL symptoms are usually fully developed, and when the concentration reaches 125 to 150 mg/100 mL unconsciousness may occur.

The duration of the reaction is variable, from 30 to 60 minutes in mild cases, up to several hours in more severe cases or as long as there is alcohol remaining in the blood. In severe reactions, supportive measures to restore blood pressure and treat shock should be instituted. Other measures such as the administration of oxygen or carbogen (95% oxygen, 5% carbon dioxide), massive i.v. doses of vitamin C (1 g), ephedrine sulfate, or antihistamines i.v. might be indicated. Potassium levels should be monitored particularly in patients on digitalis since hypokalemia has been reported.

Disulfiram is slowly absorbed from the gastrointestinal tract and is slowly eliminated from the body. Ingestion of alcohol may produce unpleasant symptoms 1 or even 2 weeks after a patient has taken his last dose of disulfiram.

Prolonged administration of disulfiram does not produce tolerance. The longer a patient remains on therapy the more sensitive he becomes to alcohol.

Pharmacokinetic data are not clearly established; however, it has been shown that 80 to 95% of an ingested dose is absorbed from the gastrointestinal tract and rapidly distributed to tissues and organs: liver, spleen, adrenals, fatty tissues, and brain. It is then metabolized to diethyldithiocarbamate or mixed disulfides, one of the end products being carbon disulfide. The unabsorbed fraction is excreted in the feces, the intermediate and final metabolites are excreted in the urine, and the volatile metabolites in the breath.

Indications: As an aid in the management of selected chronic alcoholic patients who **want** to remain in a state of enforced sobriety so that supportive and psychotherapeutic treatment may be applied to best advantage. (Used alone, without proper motivation and without supportive therapy, disulfiram is not a cure for alcoholism, and it is unlikely that it will have more than a brief effect on the drinking pattern of the chronic alcoholic.)

Contraindications: Patients who are receiving or have recently received metronidazole, paraldehyde, alcohol, or alcohol-containing preparations such as cough syrups, elixirs, should not be given disulfiram.

Disulfiram is also contraindicated in the presence of severe myocardial disease or coronary occlusion; diabetes mellitus; hepatic cirrhosis or insufficiency; hypothyroidism; epilepsy; cerebral damage; chronic and acute nephritis; psychoses; and hypersensitivity to disulfiram or other thiuram derivatives used in the manufacture of items such as pesticides or vulcanized rubber.

Warnings: Disulfiram should never be administered to a patient without his full knowledge or when he is in a state of alcohol intoxication. The attending physician should instruct those tending the patient accordingly.

Patients must be fully informed about the disulfiram-alcohol reaction. They must be strongly cautioned against surreptitious drinking while taking the drug and must be fully aware of possible consequences. They should be warned to avoid alcohol in disguised form, i.e., in sauces, vinegars, cough and cold mixtures, and even aftershave lotions or liniments. They should also be warned that reactions may occur with alcohol up to 14 days after ingestion of disulfiram.

For recommendations regarding management of the disulfiram-alcohol reaction, see Pharmacology.

Precautions: Patients should be informed of the type of reaction which will be encountered if alcohol is taken overtly or as a component of food or other products (see Pharmacology).

Patients having a history of industrial contact dermatitis who currently work or have previously worked in the rubber industry should be evaluated for hypersensitivity to thiuram derivatives before receiving disulfiram (see Contraindications).

Patients exposed to organic solvents which may contain alcohol, acetaldehyde, paraldehyde or structural analogues are at risk of experiencing disulfiram-alcohol reactions. Such exposure should be eliminated prior to treatment.

It is suggested that every patient under treatment carry an identification card stating that he is receiving disulfiram and describing the symptoms most likely to occur as a result of the disulfiram-alcohol reaction. In addition, this card should identify the attending physician or institution to be contacted in emergency. (Cards may be obtained from Wyeth-Ayerst Canada Inc. upon request.)

Alcoholism may be associated or followed by dependence on narcotics or sedatives. Barbiturates have been administered concurrently with disulfiram without untoward effects, but the possibility of initiating a new dependence should be considered. Patients taking disulfiram should not be exposed to ethylene dibromide or its vapors. This precaution is based on animal studies which have suggested a possible toxic reaction between inhaled dibromide and ingested disulfiram. Rats exposed to this regimen have shown a higher incidence of tumors and mortality. Correlation of this finding in humans however has not been demonstrated.

Since disulfiram-alcohol reactions could aggravate some medical conditions such as diabetes mellitus, hypothyroidism, epilepsy, cerebral damage, chronic and acute nephritis, hepatic cirrhosis or hepatic insufficiency, disulfiram should be used with extreme care in patients having such a medical history. Baseline and follow-up transaminase tests (10 to 14 days) are suggested to detect any hepatic dysfunction that may be associated with disulfiram therapy. In addition, a complete blood count and a sequential multiple analysis-12 test (SMA-12) should be carried out every 6 months.

Disulfiram inhibits enzyme induction and may thus interfere with the metabolism of drugs taken concomitantly. It enhances the effects of the coumarin anticoagulants and phenytoin. Consequently, in patients on oral anticoagulants, such dosage should be adjusted. In patients on phenytoin therapy, a baseline phenytoin serum level should be obtained before initiation of disulfiram therapy. After initiation of therapy, serum levels should be reevaluated on different days for evidence of an increase or continuing rise in levels. Appropriate dosage adjustment should be made, if elevated levels are found. Disulfiram should be discontinued in patients taking isoniazid if an unsteady gait develops or there are marked changes in mental state.

Carcinogenicity and mutagenicity data are not clearly established. In rats, simultaneous ingestion in the diet of disulfiram and nitrite for 78 weeks has been reported to cause tumors. It has been suggested that conversion of nitrite to nitrosamines in the stomach could be responsible for the development of the tumors. Disulfiram alone did not lead to tumor development. The relevance of these findings to humans is not known at this time. In one study, disulfiram had deleterious effects on the reproductive cycle and reproductive capabilities of female rats, and the growth of their pups. In another study, no adverse effect on fertility was noted. Studies in the hamster, rat, and mouse have not produced any teratogenic effect in the offspring.

Antabuse (cont'd)

Pregnancy and *Lactation:* It is not known whether disulfiram can cause fetal harm when administered during pregnancy, but one report of limb reduction anomalies in infants born to disulfiram-treated mothers has been published. Because of these findings, extreme care should be exercised before administering disulfiram during pregnancy.

It is not known whether this drug is excreted in human milk. Since many drugs are, and because of the potential for serious adverse reactions in the nursing infants, before administering disulfiram to a nursing mother it would appear advisable to discontinue nursing.

Adverse Effects: Optic neuritis, peripheral neuritis, polyneuritis may occur following administration of disulfiram. Multiple cases of both cholestatic and fulminant hepatitis have been reported following administration of the drug. Occasional skin eruptions have been reported. In a small number of patients, a transient mild drowsiness, fatigue, impotence, headache, acneiform eruptions, allergic dermatitis, or a metallic or garlic-like aftertaste may be experienced during the first 2 weeks of therapy. These complaints usually disappear later during therapy or with reduced dosage.

Psychotic reactions have been noted, in most cases attributable to high dosage, associated toxicity with other drugs (metronidazole or isoniazid), or the unmasking of underlying psychoses in patients stressed by withdrawal of alcohol.

Hepatotoxicity has been observed in a few patients.

Overdose: Symptoms and Treatment: Severe cases of disulfiram poisoning have been reported mainly in children. Within a few hours of ingestion of a large amount, drowsiness followed by coma develop accompanied by persistent nausea, vomiting, aggressive and psychotic behavior, and ascending flaccid paralysis which can reach the cranial nerves.

Treatment consists of administration of oxygen therapy, glucose 5% i.v., and sodium ascorbate 1 g i.v. Patient should be kept in bed and as quiet as possible with appropriate symptomatic treatment.

Dosage: Disulfiram should never be administered until the patient has abstained from alcohol for at least 12 hours.
Initiation of therapy: A **maximum** of 500 mg daily in a single dose should be given for 1 to 2 weeks, preferably taken in the morning. Patients experiencing a sedative effect may take the drug at bedtime or, if necessary, dosage may be adjusted downward.

Average maintenance dose is 250 mg daily (range 125 to 500 mg) but should not exceed 500 mg daily.
Note: Some patients, while seemingly on adequate maintenance doses, report that they are able to drink with impunity. Such patients must be presumed to be disposing of their tablets in some manner without actually taking them. Until it has been reliably confirmed that these patients have been taking their daily tablets (preferably crushed and well mixed with liquid), it cannot be concluded that disulfiram is ineffective.
Duration of Therapy: Daily, uninterrupted administration of disulfiram must be continued until the patient has established a basis for permanent self-control. Depending on the individual patient, maintenance therapy may be required for months or even years.

Supplied: 250 mg: Each white to off-white tablet, embossed with the letter A on one side and a double score line on the other, contains: disulfiram USP 250 mg. Nonmedicinal ingredients: cornstarch, magnesium stearate, povidone and Veegum. Alcohol-, gluten-, lactose-, parabens-, sugar-, sulfites- and tartrazine-free. Energy: 0.54 kJ (0.13 kcal). Bottles of 100.

500 mg: Each white to off-white tablet, embossed with the letter A on one side and a double score line on the other, contains: disulfiram USP 500 mg. Nonmedicinal ingredients: cornstarch, magnesium stearate, povidone and Veegum. Alcohol-, gluten-, lactose-, parabens-, sugar-, sulfites- and tartrazine-free. Energy: 1.13 kJ (0.27 kcal). Bottles of 50.

(Shown in Product Recognition Section)

ANTHRAFORTE®
Medican

Anthralin

Psoriasis Therapy

Supplied: Each g contains: anthralin USP 1% (Anthraforte 1) or anthralin USP 2% (Anthraforte 2) in a petrolatum base. Nonmedicinal ingredients: ascorbyl palmitate, butylated hydroxytoluene, dl-alpha tocopherol, microcrystalline wax, salicylic acid and white soft petrolatum. Tubes of 50 g. Store between 15 and 25°C.

ANTHRANOL®
Medican

Anthralin

Psoriasis Therapy

Supplied: Each g contains: anthralin USP 0.1% (Anthranol 0.1), 0.2% (Anthranol 0.2) or 0.4% (Anthranol 0.4) in a vanishing cream type base. Nonmedicinal ingredients: aluminum monostearate, ascorbyl palmitate, butylated hydroxytoluene, citric acid anhydrous, dl-alpha tocopherol, edetate disodium, methyl paraben, mineral oil light 90, octyldodecanol, paraffin wax, polyglyceryl 4 oleate, propyl paraben, purified water USP, salicylic acid, sodium bisulfite and white soft petrolatum. Tubes of 50 g. Store between 15 and 25°C.

ANTHRASCALP®
Medican

Anthralin

Psoriasis Therapy

Supplied: Each g contains: anthralin USP 0.4% in a vanishing lotion base. Nonmedicinal ingredients: ascorbyl palmitate, butylated hydroxytoluene, citric acid anhydrous, dl-alpha tocopherol, glyceryl monostearate, methyl paraben, mineral oil, polysorbate 60, propyl paraben, purified water USP, sodium bisulfite and sodium EDTA. Tubes of 50 mL, with special applicator cap. Store between 15 and 25°C.

ANTIBIOTIC COLD SORE OINTMENT
Novartis Consumer Health

Polymyxin B Compound

Cold Sore Therapy

Indications: Symptomatic treatment of cold sores and fever blisters. Prevention of secondary bacterial infection.

Contraindications: Hypersensitivity to any of the components.

Warnings: It is dangerous to apply any product containing menthol or camphor to the nostrils of an infant. To do so may cause difficulty in breathing and collapse.

Precautions: For external use only. Avoid contact with eyes. Do not use inside nose. If symptoms persist or become more severe, or if hypersensitivity or adverse reaction to the product occurs, discontinue use and consult a physician. Prolonged use may result in the overgrowth of non-susceptible organisms. If this occurs, the use of this preparation should be discontinued, and appropriate therapy instituted.

Keep out of reach of children.

Dosage: Adults and children over 12 years: Apply ointment every 3 hours to cold sore until healing is complete.
Children 6 to 12 years: Use only on the advice of a physician.
Do not use on children under 6 years.
Pregnancy and *Lactation:* Use only on the advice of a physician.

Supplied: Each g of ointment contains: polymyxin B (as sulfate) 500 IU, tyrothricin 0.5 mg, camphor 20 mg, menthol 1 mg and benzocaine 50 mg. Nonmedicinal ingredients: mineral oil and white petrolatum. Tubes of 3.5 g. Store between 15 and 25°C. Protect from heat and moisture.

ANTIPHLOGISTINE RUB A-535
Carter Horner

Methyl Salicylate—Camphor—Menthol—Eucalyptus Oil

Topical Analgesic

Indications: External counterirritant cream for temporary pain relief of stiff and sore muscles, backache, strains, arthritic and rheumatic pain, sciatica, lumbago and bursitis.

Contraindications: Salicylate hypersensitivity.

Precautions: For external use only. Do not apply to wounds or damaged skin and avoid contact with eyes and mucous membranes. Discontinue use if rash or irritation occurs. If condition persists for more than 7 days, consult physician. Do not bandage after application and avoid external sources of heat such as heating pads. Do not use if you are allergic to salicylates or are taking anticoagulant medications. Keep out of reach of children. Store in a cool place.

Dosage: Adults and Children over 2 years of age: Massage into affected area until completely absorbed, not more than 3 or 4 times daily.

Supplied: Regular Strength: Each g contains: methyl salicylate 12.5%, camphor 1%, menthol 0.75% and eucalyptus oil 0.5% w/w. Nonmedicinal ingredients: anhydrous lanolin, beeswax, glycerin, isobornyl acetate, light mineral oil, paraffin, propylene glycol stearate, salicylic acid, trolamine, stearic acid, water and white petrolatum. Tubes of 50 and 100 g. Jars of 450 g.

Extra Strength: Each g contains: methyl salicylate 18%, camphor 1%, menthol 0.75% and eucalyptus oil 0.5% w/w. Nonmedicinal ingredients: anhydrous lanolin, beeswax, glycerin, isobornyl acetate, light mineral oil, paraffin, propylene glycol stearate, salicylic acid, trolamine, stearic acid, water and white petrolatum. Tubes of 100 g. Jars of 160 g.

Reviewed 1997

ANTIPHLOGISTINE RUB A-535 CAPSAICIN
Carter Horner

Capsaicin

Topical Analgesic

Supplied: Each g of cream contains: capsaicin 0.05% w/w. Nonmedicinal ingredients: benzyl alcohol, light mineral oil, sodium citrate dihydrate, stearyl alcohol, steareth-2, steareth-21 and water. Tubes of 45 and 85 g.

New Product 1998

ANTIPHLOGISTINE RUB A-535 ICE
Carter Horner

Menthol

Topical Analgesic

Supplied: Each g of penetrating gel contains: menthol 4% w/w. Nonmedicinal ingredients: carbomer 934, FD&C Blue #1, isopropyl alcohol, polyethylene glycol, polysorbate 20, propylene glycol, trolamine and water. Tubes of 100 g. Jars of 250 g. Glide-on applicator containers of 100 g.

ANTIPHLOGISTINE RUB A-535 NO ODOUR
Carter Horner

Triethanolamine Salicylate

Topical Analgesic

Supplied: Each g contains: triethanolamine salicylate 13.3% w/w. Nonmedicinal ingredients: acetylated lanolin alcohol, caprylic/capric triglyceride, carbomer 980, cetyl alcohol, diazolidinyl urea, diethanolamine cetyl phosphate, isopropylpalmitate, methylparaben, perfume, propylene glycol, propylparaben, stearic acid, trolamine and water. Tubes of 50 and 100 g.

ANTIVENIN
Wyeth-Ayerst

Crotalid Serum

Antivenin

Supplied: Each vial contains: sufficient vacuum dried material of Neartic Crotalidae, polyvalent to yield 10 mL of pure concentrated serum, when reconstituted with water for injection. Combination package contains: 1 vial of dried serum, one

10 mL vial of bacteriostatic water for injection, one 1 mL vial of normal horse serum (1:10 strength) for sensitivity testing.

ANTIVENIN (Latrodectus Mactans)

MSD

Black Widow Spider Antivenin

Indications: Used to treat patients suffering from symptoms due to bites from the black widow spider. Early use of the antivenin is emphasized for prompt relief.

Warnings: Prior to treatment with any product prepared from horse serum, a careful review of the patient's history should be taken emphasizing prior exposure to horse serum or any allergies. Serious sickness and even death could result from the use of horse serum in a sensitive patient. A skin or conjunctival test should be performed prior to administration of Antivenin.

Skin Test: Inject into (not under) the skin not more than 0.02 mL of the test material (1:10 dilution of normal horse serum in physiologic saline). Evaluate result in 10 minutes. A positive reaction is an urticarial wheal surrounded by a zone of erythema. A control test using Sodium Chloride Injection facilitates interpretation of the results.

Conjunctival Test: For adults instill into the conjunctival sac one drop of a 1:10 dilution of horse serum and for children one drop of 1:100 dilution. Itching of the eye and reddening of the conjunctiva indicate a positive reaction, usually within 10 minutes.

Patients should be observed for serum sickness for an average of 8 to 12 days following administration of Antivenin.

Desensitization should be attempted only when the administration of Antivenin is considered necessary to save life. Epinephrine must be available in case of untoward reaction.

Desensitization: If the history is positive or the results of the sensitivity tests are mildly or questionably positive, Antivenin should be administered as follows to reduce the risk of an immediate severe allergic reaction:

1. In separate sterile vials or syringes prepare 1:10 or 1:100 dilutions of Antivenin in Sodium Chloride for Injection.
2. Allow at least 15 but preferably 30 minutes between injections and only proceed with the next dose if no reactions occurred following the previous dose.
3. Using a tuberculin syringe, inject s.c. 0.1, 0.2 and 0.5 mL of the 1:100 dilution at 15 or 30 minute intervals; repeat with the 1:10 dilution, and finally the undiluted Antivenin.
4. If there is a reaction after any of the injections, place a tourniquet proximal to the sites of injection and administer epinephrine, 1:1 000 (0.3 to 1.0 mL s.c., 0.05 to 0.1 mL i.v.), proximal to the tourniquet or into another extremity. Wait at least 30 minutes before giving another injection of Antivenin, the amount of which should be the same as the last one not evoking a reaction.
5. If no reaction has occurred after 0.5 mL of undiluted Antivenin has been given, it is probably safe to continue the dose at 15 minute intervals until the entire dose has been injected.

Precautions: Carcinogenesis, Mutagenesis, Impairment of Fertility: No long-term studies in animals have been performed to evaluate the potential for carcinogenesis, mutagenesis, or impairment of fertility.

Pregnancy: Pregnancy Category C. Animal reproduction studies have not been conducted with Black Widow Spider Antivenin. It is also not known whether Black Widow Spider Antivenin can cause fetal harm when administered to a pregnant woman or can affect reproduction capacity. Black Widow Spider Antivenin should be given to a pregnant woman only if clearly needed.

Lactation: It is not known whether this drug is excreted in human milk. Because many drugs are excreted in human milk, caution should be exercised when Black Widow Spider Antivenin is administered to a nursing woman.

Children: Controlled clinical studies for safety and effectiveness in children have not been conducted; however, there have been virtually no adverse effects reported in those children who have received the product.

Adverse Effects: Anaphylaxis and serum sickness have been reported following use of Antivenin.

Dosage: Using a sterile syringe, remove from the accompanying vial 2.5 mL of Sterile Diluent for Antivenin and inject into the vial of Antivenin. With the needle still in the rubber stopper, shake the vial to dissolve the contents completely.

Parenteral drug products should be inspected visually for particulate matter prior to administration, whenever solution and container permit.

The dose for adults and children is the entire contents of a restored vial (2.5 mL) of Antivenin. It may be given i.m., preferably in the region of the anterolateral thigh so that a tourniquet may be applied in the event of a systemic reaction. Symptoms usually subside in 1 to 3 hours. Although one dose of Antivenin usually is adequate, a second dose may be necessary in some cases.

Antivenin also may be given i.v. in 10 to 50 mL of saline solution over a 15-minute period. It is the preferred route in severe cases, or when the patient is under 12, or in shock. One restored vial usually is enough.

Supplied: Each vial of white to gray crystalline powder contains not less than 6 000 Antivenin units. Thimerosal (mercury derivative) 1:10 000 is added as preservative. A 2.5 mL vial of Sterile Diluent for Antivenin is included. A 1 mL vial of normal horse serum (1:10 dilution) for sensitivity testing is also included. Thimerosal (mercury derivative) 1:10 000 is added as preservative.

Antivenin must be stored and shipped at 2 to 8°C. When reconstituted as directed, the color of Antivenin ranges from light (straw) to very dark (iced tea), but the color has no effect on potency. **Do not freeze.**

ANTIVERT™ Ⓟ

Pfizer

Meclizine HCl—Nicotinic Acid

Vertigo Therapy

Pharmacology: Meclizine has antihistaminic and anticholinergic properties. Nicotinic acid is a vasodilator agent which has been found effective in the treatment of vertigo due to Ménière's syndrome and to cerebral arteriosclerosis.

The site and mechanism of action of meclizine in controlling vertigo arising from various conditions, have not been clearly defined. Pharmacological studies conducted with other antihistamines show that the peripheral labyrinthine structure may be the site of action.

Indications: For the treatment of vertigo, whether due to cerebral arteriosclerosis, Ménière's syndrome, labyrinthitis, vestibular dysfunction or other related conditions. Also useful in treating vascular headaches and radiation sickness.

Contraindications: Hypersensitivity to either meclizine or nicotinic acid.

Because of the vasodilation produced by nicotinic acid, severe hypotension and hemorrhage are contraindications to Antivert therapy.

Warnings: Occupational Hazards: Patients should be warned that Antivert may occasionally cause drowsiness and that when taking it they should take the necessary precautions against driving or operating dangerous machinery or when taking part in activities requiring mental alertness.

Patients suffering from glaucoma or prostatic enlargement should take Antivert only under the direction of a physician.

Precautions: Patients should be made aware of the frequent, short-lived reactions experienced with nicotinic acid therapy such as cutaneous flushing, sensations of warmth, tingling and itching, burning of the skin, increased gastrointestinal motility and sebaceous gland activity. These reactions are coincidental to the vasodilatation produced by nicotinic acid.

Pregnancy: One of the components of this combination product meclizine, as many other drugs of this class, has shown certain teratogenic effects (i.e., cleft palates) in the rat at doses of 25 to 50 times the human dose. These abnormalities have not been observed in other experimental animals, including the monkey.

The use of Antivert by women who are pregnant or may become pregnant requires that the potential benefits be weighed against the potential risks.

Drug Interactions: There may be increased CNS depression when Antivert is administered concomitantly with other CNS depressants, including barbiturates, alcohol, tranquilizers, and sedatives.

MAO inhibitors may prolong and intensify the anticholinergic effects of Antivert.

Adverse Effects: Drowsiness, dry mouth, vomiting, fatigue and, on rare occasions, blurred vision have been reported with Antivert therapy.

Adverse effects associated with nicotinic acid include cutaneous flushing, sensations of warmth, tingling and itching, burning of the skin, increased gastrointestinal motility and sebaceous gland activity. These reactions are coincidental to the vasodilatation produced by nicotinic acid.

Overdose: Symptoms: In adults, the usual signs of meclizine overdose are CNS depression with drowsiness, coma and convulsions. Hypotension may also occur, particularly in the elderly. In children, anticholinergic effects and CNS stimulation (hallucinations, seizures, trouble sleeping) are more likely to occur.

Signs of nicotinic acid overdose are flushing, gastrointestinal upset, and pruritus.

Treatment: There is no specific antidote for treatment of meclizine overdosage. Symptomatic and supportive treatment should be employed. If ingestion is recent (within 1 hour), induce emesis (syrup of ipecac is recommended; precautions against aspiration are required, especially in infants and children) or empty stomach by gastric lavage if patient has been unable to vomit within 3 hours of ingestion. Activated charcoal may also be used. Keep patient calm to minimize excitation. Vasopressors (norepinephrine or phenylephrine) may be used to correct hypotension. Physostigmine may be useful to counteract the CNS anticholinergic effects of meclizine. Do not use stimulants. If vasopressors are indicated do not use epinephrine, because it may lower blood pressure further. Diazepam i.v. may be given for treatment of seizures that do not respond to physostigmine.

Dosage: One tablet 3 times a day before each meal. If excess flushing occurs, take Antivert immediately after meals.

Supplied: Each blue, scored tablet contains: meclizine HCl 12.5 mg and nicotinic acid 50 mg. Nonmedicinal ingredients: calcium phosphate, cornstarch, magnesium stearate, polyethylene glycol, sucrose, talc and dye FD & C Blue #1. Tartrazine-free. Bottles of 100 and 500. Store between 15 and 30°C.

(Shown in Product Recognition Section)

ANTURAN® Ⓟ

Novartis Pharmaceuticals

Sulfinpyrazone

Platelet Inhibitory Agent—Uricosuric Agent—Prophylactic Agent for Reduction of Mortality Post-myocardial Infarction

Pharmacology: Sulfinpyrazone inhibits thrombotic processes that are associated with platelet adhesion, aggregation and reduced platelet survival.

Sulfinpyrazone reduces serum urate levels, prevents formation of new tophi, and promotes resorption of existing tophi by increasing clearance of uric acid and water through the kidneys.

Sulfinpyrazone has been shown to reduce cardiac mortality during the second through the seventh month after myocardial infarction. Whether benefits can be expected after this period is unknown. The exact mechanism by which this is achieved is unclear.

Indications: Clinical states in which abnormal platelet behavior is a causative or associated factor, as demonstrated by: recurrent venous thrombosis, arteriovenous shunt thrombosis.

Chronic phases of gout, both the intercritical or silent stage and the gouty arthritis stage.

Prophylactic use post-myocardial infarction.

Contraindications: Initiation of sulfinpyrazone therapy during an acute attack of gout. Active peptic ulcer. Known or suspected hypersensitivity to sulfinpyrazone and other pyrazolone derivatives. A history of severe parenchymal lesions of the liver or kidneys (e.g., hepatitis, cirrhosis or acute interstitial nephritis). Patients in whom attacks of asthma, urticaria or acute rhinitis are precipitated by ASA or other prostaglandin-synthase inhibitors. Porphyria. A history of blood dyscrasis. Hemorrhagic diatheses (e.g., blood coagulation disorders).

Warnings: Especially in patients with elevated plasma uric acid levels and/or those with a history of nephrolithiasis or renal colic, and in patients receiving concomitant diuretic medication, particular care should be taken in initiating sulfinpyrazone therapy by ensuring adequate fluid intake, alkalinizing the urine if necessary, and using an incremental dosage regimen. Frequent determinations of BUN and serum creatinine should be done, especially during early drug treatment and in patients with significant renal impairment. When resuming treatment after interruption of the medication, the incremental dosage regimen should be adopted.

Avoid salicylate therapy, unless administered under careful supervision: Salicylates and citrates antagonize the uricosuric action of sulfinpyrazone and may therefore interfere with uric acid excretion and thus exacerbate gout.

Anturan (cont'd)

Salicylates may cause unpredictable and, at times, serious prolongation of the bleeding time and in combination with sulfinpyrazone may cause bleeding episodes. If, during sulfinpyrazone therapy, ASA or other related substances which may affect hemostasis (e.g., NSAIDs) must be used, patients should be urged to report immediately any undue bleeding episode.

As salicylates compete with sulfinpyrazone not only for protein binding but also for renal tubular secretion, the plasma concentrations of both drugs may rise if co-administered.

Sulfinpyrazone should be administered with care to patients having a history of gastric disorder or healed peptic ulcer.

Should allergic skin reactions occur, discontinue sulfinpyrazone.

Pregnancy: The safe use of sulfinpyrazone in pregnancy has not been established. Sulfinpyrazone should not be used during pregnancy, especially in the first trimester, unless, in the opinion of the treating physician, the expected benefits outweigh the potential risks.

Lactation: It is not known whether sulfinpyrazone can be found in breast milk. The benefits of drug treatment for the mother and that of breast-feeding must be weighed against the risk for the child.

Precautions: As with all pyrazole compounds, patients receiving sulfinpyrazone should be kept under close medical supervision. Periodic blood counts are recommended.

As with any long-term treatment with uricosuric agents, renal function tests should be performed regularly, especially if the patient has pre-existing renal insufficiency.

Since sulfinpyrazone may lead to sodium and water retention, caution is indicated in patients with overt or latent heart failure.

At the start of treatment, attacks of gout may occur more frequently when urate is mobilized from affected joints. Patients should therefore be cautioned to maintain an adequate fluid intake (see Warnings). If an attack of gout occurs, sulfinpyrazone should be continued but supplemented by other treatments, e.g., colchicine or nonsteroidal antirheumatic drugs—but not salicylates (see Warnings). Prophylactic treatment with these agents may also be indicated when commencing treatment with sulfinpyrazone.

Initiation of treatment with Anturan during an acute attack of gout is contraindicated (see Contraindications).

Drug Interactions: Sulfinpyrazone should be used with caution in conjunction with oral anticoagulants (especially vitamin K antagonists such as nicoumalone and warfarin) since there may be an increased risk of hemorrhage. Sulfinpyrazone not only modifies platelet behavior and therefore interferes with the coagulation process, but also potentiates the action of anticoagulants by inhibiting their metabolism by microsomal liver enzymes. As a result, anticoagulant dosage must be adjusted according to the prothrombin time, which should be checked daily for a few days prior to initiating or withdrawing treatment. Regular estimates of bleeding time should be performed.

Displacement of sulfonamides from their plasma protein binding sites by pyrazoles may lead to a rise in their plasma concentrations and thus potentiate their action.

Sulfinpyrazone increases the half-lives and plasma concentrations of sulfonylureas (e.g., tolbutamide), both by displacement from serum albumin binding sites and by inhibiting metabolism by microsomal liver enzymes. Sulfinpyrazone may therefore potentiate the hypoglycemic effects of sulfonylureas. As with other pyrazole compounds (e.g., phenylbutazone), sulfinpyrazone may also potentiate the hypoglycemic effect of insulin.

Displacement of phenytoin by sulfinpyrazone from its plasma protein binding sites as well as inhibition of microsomal liver enzymes delays the metabolism of phenytoin, thus prolonging its half-life and raising its plasma concentration.

Sulfinpyrazone may raise the plasma concentration of penicillin by competing for serum albumin binding sites and renal tubular secretion.

Sulfinpyrazone lowers the plasma concentration of theophylline by inducing hepatic enzymes.

Sulfinpyrazone should not be administered with salicylates or related substances that interfere with hemostatis (see Warnings).

Adverse Effects: The most frequently reported adverse reactions to sulfinpyrazone have been gastric complaints or disturbances, such as nausea, vomiting and diarrhea. Sulfinpyrazone may aggravate or reactivate peptic ulcer. There have been isolated cases of gastrointestinal bleeding and ulcers.

Impairment of renal function with accompanying changes in electrolytes has been reported. As well, occasional overt acute renal failure has been reported. A clear causal relationship could not be established. These events occurred with high initial doses of sulfinpyrazone; renal function returned to normal upon withdrawal of the drug.

Sodium and water retention have been reported.

Allergic skin rashes e.g., drug rash, urticaria, have been reported in rare instances. In cases of urticaria, the drug should be withdrawn (see Warnings).

Blood dyscrasias (anemia, leukopenia, agranulocytosis, thrombocytopenia, aplastic anemia) have rarely been associated with the administration of sulfinpyrazone.

Isolated cases of hepatic dysfunction (elevated transaminases and alkaline phosphatase), jaundice, and hepatitis have been reported (see Contraindications).

Overdose: Symptoms: (based on overdosage with pyrazolidine analogues): nausea, vomiting, pain in the upper abdomen, diarrhea, ataxia, gastrointestinal hemorrhage, hypotension, cardiac arrhythmias, hyperventilation, respiratory disorders, impairment of consciousness, coma, convulsions, oliguria or anuria, acute renal failure, renal colic and jaundice.

Treatment: There is no specific antidote for sulfinpyrazone. Induce emesis and/or gastric lavage; give activated charcoal; administer saline cathartic if deemed appropriate; administer i.v. glucose infusion; give symptomatic supportive treatment (see below). Dialysis is indicated in severe poisoning. Note that forced diuresis is of no value.

Symptomatic Management: Keep a close watch on the patient's vital functions (level of consciousness, cardiovascular, respiratory, hepatic and renal functions). If necessary provide supportive measures.

Respiration: Analeptic therapy if respiration is affected. Endotracheal intubation and artificial respiration to combat respiratory failure.

Metabolic Acidosis: Sodium bicarbonate.

Acute renal colic due to high uric acid excretion and intraluminal urate crystallization in distal tubules and collecting ducts: Increase the solubility of uric acid by alkalinizing the urine (to pH 7 or above), by giving sodium bicarbonate and/or a carbonic anhydrase inhibitor such as acetazolamide. Administer fluid and a potent diuretic (e.g., furosemide or mannitol) to increase urine volume.

Prolonged renal failure: hemodialysis.

Gastrointestinal hemorrhage: Appropriate measures for early diagnosis and treatment if necessary.

Dosage: Since sulfinpyrazone has a potent uricosuric effect, treatment should be initiated with an incremental dosage regimen, as follows: 1st and 2nd day: 100 mg twice daily or 200 mg once daily; 3rd and 4th day: 200 mg twice daily; 5th and 6th day: 200 mg 3 times daily; from 7th day onwards: 200 mg 4 times daily.

Recurrent Venous Thrombosis and Arteriovenous Shunt Thrombosis: Maintenance daily dose is 600 to 800 mg in 3 to 4 divided doses and should be titrated to meet the patient's needs.

Gout: Daily maintenance dose is 200 to 400 mg. The dosage may be increased up to 800 mg if necessary, or reduced to 200 mg when the urate blood level has been satisfactorily controlled. Minimum effective dose should be maintained without interruption even during acute attacks. The change from other uricosuric agents to sulfinpyrazone does not have to follow an incremental dosing regimen.

Reduction of Cardiac Mortality During the 2nd Through the 7th Month, after Myocardial Infarction: Daily maintenance dose is 200 mg q.i.d. Treatment following myocardial infarction should not be started until at least 2 weeks after the acute event.

Whenever possible, distribute the total dose over the 24-hour period. Sulfinpyrazone should be taken with meals or milk. The maximum recommended dosage is 800 mg daily.

Supplied: Each white, round, biconvex, sugar-coated tablet, branded in blue with GEIGY on one side and ANTURAN on the other side, contains: sulfinpyrazone 200 mg. Nonmedicinal ingredients: carnauba wax, cellulose compounds, cerulean blue, gelatin, lactose, magnesium stearate, polyethylene glycol, silicon dioxide, starches (corn and synthetic), sugar, talc and titanium dioxide. Energy: 3.1 kJ (0.73 kcal). Sodium: <1 mmol (0.03 mg). Alcohol-, bisulfite-, gluten-, parabens- and tartrazine-free. Bottles of 100 and 1 000. Protect from heat. Store between 15 and 30°C.

(Shown in Product Recognition Section)

Reviewed 1997

ANUGESIC®-HC Ⓟ

Parke-Davis

Pramoxine HCl—Hydrocortisone Acetate—Zinc Sulfate

Anorectal Therapy

Supplied: Ointment: Each tube contains: pramoxine HCl 1%, hydrocortisone acetate 0.5%, zinc sulfate monohydrate 0.5% in a petroleum ointment base. Nonmedicinal ingredients: calcium phosphate, methylparaben, mineral oil, petrolatum, poloxyl 2 oleyl ether and propylparaben. Tubes of 15 and 30 g with plastic applicator. Store in a cool place under 22°C.

Suppositories: Each white-colored suppository contains: pramoxine HCl 20 mg, hydrocortisone acetate 10 mg, zinc sulfate monohydrate 10 mg, in a base of triglycerides. Nonmedicinal ingredients: calcium phosphate, magnesium stearate, methylparaben, propylparaben and triglyceride base. Boxes of 12. Store in a cool place under 22°C.

ANUSOL®
ANUSOL® PLUS

Warner-Lambert Consumer Healthcare

Zinc Sulfate Monohydrate

Pramoxine HCl—Zinc Sulfate Monohydrate

Anorectal Therapy

Indications: Symptomatic relief of pain and discomfort as in: external and internal hemorrhoids, proctitis, papillitis, cryptitis, fissures, incomplete fistulas and relief of local pain following anorectal surgery.

Contraindications: History of sensitivity to any component.

Precautions: In case of rectal bleeding, consult physician promptly.

Adverse Effects: An occasional patient may experience burning upon application, especially if the anoderm is not intact. Discontinue medication if irritation or sensitivity is suspected.

Dosage: Ointment: Bathe and dry the affected anal area. Apply ointment freely to the affected area every 4 hours or as needed and after each bowel movement.

Suppositories: Bathe and dry the affected anal area. Insert 1 suppository morning and evening and after each bowel movement.

Supplied: Anusol: Ointment: A smooth, colorless, translucent ointment contains: zinc sulfate monohydrate 0.5%. Nonmedicinal ingredients: calcium phosphate, mineral oil, oleth-2, parabens and petrolatum. Tubes of 30 g with applicator. Store in a cool place under 22°C.

Suppositories: Each white, opaque suppository contains: zinc sulfate monohydrate 10 mg. Nonmedicinal ingredients: calcium phosphate, magnesium stearate, parabens and vegetable oil. Boxes of 12 and 24. Store in a cool place under 22°C.

Anusol Plus: Ointment: Each tube of smooth, colorless, translucent ointment contains: pramoxine HCl 1% and zinc sulfate monohydrate 0.5%. Nonmedicinal ingredients: calcium phosphate, mineral oil, oleth-2, parabens and petrolatum. Tubes of 30 g with applicator. Store in a cool place under 22°C.

Suppositories: Each white, opaque suppository contains: pramoxine HCl 20 mg and zinc sulfate monohydrate 10 mg. Nonmedicinal ingredients: calcium phosphate, magnesium stearate, parabens and vegetable oil. Boxes of 12 and 24. Store in a cool place under 22°C.

ANUSOL®-HC Ⓟ

Parke-Davis

Hydrocortisone Acetate—Zinc Sulfate

Anorectal Therapy

Supplied: Ointment: Each tube contains: zinc sulfate monohydrate 0.5% and hydrocortisone acetate 0.5% in a petroleum ointment base. Nonmedicinal ingredients: calcium phosphate, methylparaben, mineral oil, petrolatum, poloxyl 2 oleyl ether and propylparaben. Tubes of 15 and 30 g with applicator. Store in a cool place under 22°C.

Suppositories: Each suppository contains: zinc sulfate monohydrate 10 mg, hydrocortisone acetate 10 mg in a triglyceride base. Nonmedicinal ingredients: calcium phosphate, magnesium stearate, methylparaben, propylparaben and triglyceride base. Boxes of 12 and 24. Store in a cool place under 22°C.

ANUZINC®
Technilab

Zinc Sulfate
Anorectal Therapy

Supplied: Ointment: Each tube contains: zinc sulfate monohydrate 0.5%. Nonmedicinal ingredients: light mineral oil and petrolatum. Tubes of 30 g with applicator.

Suppositories: Each suppository contains: zinc sulfate monohydrate 10 mg. Nonmedicinal ingredients: semisynthetic glycerides. Boxes of 12 and 24.

Store in a cool place under 22°C. Protect from freezing.

ANZEMET™ Ⓟ
Hoechst Marion Roussel

Dolasetron Mesylate
Antiemetic

Pharmacology: Dolasetron and its active metabolite, hydrodolasetron (MDL 74156), are selective 5-HT_3 receptor antagonists shown not to have activity at other known serotonin receptors and with low affinity for dopamine receptors. The serotonin 5-HT_3 receptors are located on the nerve terminals of the vagus in the periphery and centrally in the chemoreceptor trigger zone of the area postrema. It is thought that chemotherapeutic agents produce nausea and vomiting by releasing serotonin from the enterochromaffin cells of the small intestine, and that serotonin then activates the 5-HT_3 receptors located on vagal afferents to initiate the vomiting reflex.

Acute, reversible, ECG changes (PR and QTc; QRS widening), caused by dolasetron, have been observed in controlled clinical trials. Dolasetron appears to prolong both depolarization and, to a lesser extent, repolarization time. Although QTc prolongation is primarily due to QRS widening, JT prolongation has also been observed. The magnitude and frequency of the ECG changes increased with dose (related to the peak plasma concentration of hydrodolasetron but not the parent compound). These ECG changes usually returned to baseline within 6 to 8 hours, but in some patients have lasted 24 hours or longer. Dolasetron administration has little or no effect on blood pressure.

In healthy volunteers (N=4), dolasetron in single i.v. doses up to 5 mg/kg produced no effect on pupil size or meaningful changes in EEG tracings. Results from neuropsychiatric tests revealed that dolasetron does not alter mood or concentration. Multiple daily doses of dolasetron have no effect on colonic transit in humans. Dolasetron has no effect on plasma prolactin concentrations.

Pharmacokinetics: Pharmacokinetics in Humans (I.V. Administration): I.V. dolasetron is rapidly eliminated ($t_{1/2}$ <10 min) and completely metabolized to the most clinically relevant species, hydrodolasetron. Hydrodolasetron appears rapidly in plasma, with a maximum concentration occurring approximately 0.6 hours after the end of i.v. treatment, and is eliminated with a mean half-life of 7.3 hours (CV=24%, n=30) in adult cancer patients. Hydrodolasetron is eliminated by multiple routes, including renal excretion, after metabolism mainly by glucuronidation and hydroxylation. Hydrodolasetron exhibits linear pharmacokinetics over the i.v. dose range of 50 to 200 mg and they are independent of infusion rate. Doses lower than 50 mg have not been studied. Two-thirds of the administered dose is recovered in the urine and one-third in the feces. Hydrodolasetron is widely distributed in the body with a mean apparent volume of distribution of 5.8 L/kg (CV=25%; n=24) in adults.

Sixty-nine to 77% of hydrodolasetron is bound to plasma proteins. In a study with ^{14}C-labeled dolasetron, the distribution of radioactivity to blood cells was not extensive. The binding of hydrodolasetron to α1-acid glycoprotein is approximately 51%. The pharmacokinetics are similar in men and women. The pharmacokinetics of hydrodolasetron, in special and targeted patient populations following i.v. administration of dolasetron, are summarized in Table I. The pharmacokinetics of hydrodolasetron are similar in adult healthy volunteers and adult cancer patients receiving chemotherapeutic agents. The apparent clearance of hydrodolasetron is not affected by age in adult cancer patients. Following i.v. administration, the apparent clearance of hydrodolasetron remains unchanged with severe hepatic impairment and decreases 47% with severe renal impairment.

Table I—Anzemet

Pharmacokinetic Values for Hydrodolasetron Following I.V. Administration of Dolasetron Mesylate (1.8 mg/kg)

	Age (years)	Cl_{app} (mL/min/kg)	$t_{1/2}$ (h)	AUC∞ (ng/mL×h)	C_{max} (ng/mL)
Young healthy volunteers (n=24)	19-40	9.4 (28%)	7.3 (24%)	2 567*	457*
Elderly healthy volunteers (n=15)	65-75	8.3 (30%)	6.9 (22%)	3 021*	465*
Cancer patients (n=273)	19-87	10.2 (34%)	7.5 (43%)	3 640 (32%)	505 (26%)

Legend:
Cl_{app}: Apparent clearance.
C_{max}: Maximal serum concentration.
$t_{1/2}$: Terminal elimination half-life.
*: Results dose-normalized to the recommended dose assuming linear kinetics.
Values in brackets ( ) represent the coefficient of variation in %.

Table II—Anzemet

Pharmacokinetic Values for Hydrodolasetron Following Oral Administration of Dolasetron Mesylate (100 mg)

	Age (years)	Cl_{app} (mL/min/kg)	$t_{1/2}$ (h)	AUC∞ (ng/mL×h)	C_{max} (ng/mL)
Young healthy volunteers (n=24)	19-45	10.5 (32%)	8.2 (21%)	1 605[a]	299[a]
Elderly healthy volunteers (n=14)	65-75	9.5 (36%)	7.2 (32%)	2 106[a]	402[a]
Cancer patients (n=17)	30-84	11.5 (47%)	7.9 (33%)	—[b]	—[b]

Legend:
Cl_{app}: Apparent oral clearance.
C_{max}: Maximal serum concentration.
$t_{1/2}$: Terminal elimination half-life.
[a]: Results dose-normalized to the recommended dose assuming linear kinetics.
[b]: Sampling times did not allow for determination.
Values in brackets ( ) represent the coefficient of variation in %.

Pharmacokinetics in Humans (Oral Administration): Oral dolasetron is well absorbed, although the parent drug is rarely detected in plasma due to rapid and complete metabolism to the most clinically relevant species, hydrodolasetron. Hydrodolasetron appears rapidly in plasma, with a maximum concentration occurring approximately 1 hour after dosing, and is eliminated with a mean half-life of 8.1 hours (CV=18%; n=30). The apparent absolute bioavailability of oral dolasetron, determined by the major active metabolite hydrodolasetron, is about 75%. Food does not affect the apparent bioavailability of dolasetron taken by mouth. Hydrodolasetron is eliminated by multiple routes, including renal excretion, after metabolism, mainly glucuronidation and hydroxylation. Two-thirds of the administered dose is recovered in the urine and one-third in the feces. Hydrodolasetron is widely distributed in the body with a mean apparent volume of distribution of 5.8 L/kg (CV=25%; n=24). Sixty-nine to 77% of hydrodolasetron is bound to plasma proteins. The binding of hydrodolasetron to α1-acid glycoprotein is approximately 51%. In a study with ^{14}C-labeled dolasetron, the distribution of radioactivity to blood cells was not extensive. The pharmacokinetics of hydrodolasetron are linear and similar in men and women.

The pharmacokinetics of hydrodolasetron following oral administration, in special and targeted patient populations, are summarized in Table II. The pharmacokinetics of hydrodolasetron are similar between adult healthy volunteers and cancer patients receiving chemotherapeutic agents. The apparent clearance of hydrodolasetron following oral administration of dolasetron is not affected by age in adult cancer patients. The apparent clearance of hydrodolasetron decreases 42% with severe hepatic impairment and 44% with severe renal impairment.

Clinical Trials: I.V. Administration: One thousand nine hundred and seventeen patients receiving emetogenic chemotherapy (including high dose cisplatin ≥70 mg/m^2) were studied in 5 randomized, double blind trials in which 597 patients were treated with the recommended dose of 1.8 mg/kg dolasetron injection (see Table III). Efficacy was based on complete response rates (no emetic episodes and no rescue medication). Dolasetron administered i.v. at a dose of 1.8 mg/kg gave similar results in preventing nausea and vomiting as the other selective 5-HT_3 receptor antagonists studied as active comparators. Dolasetron injection was more effective than metoclopramide.

Table III—Anzemet

Prevention of Chemotherapy-Induced Nausea and Emesis in Cisplatin[a] Chemotherapy with Anzemet Injection (1.8 mg/kg)

Response over 24 hours	Patients responding (%) (n=597)
Complete Response[b]	313 (52.4%)
Nausea Score[c]	10.5
Total Response[d]	223 (37.4%)

[a]Cisplatin was used at moderately and highly emetogenic doses; cyclophosphamide, doxorubicin, fluorouracil, epirubicin and vincristine were used at moderately emetogenic doses and were the most commonly used chemotherapeutic agents in these trials.
[b]No emetic episodes and no rescue medication.
[c]Median 24-hour change from baseline nausea score using visual analog scale (VAS); score range 0="none" to 100="nausea as bad as it could be".
[d]Complete response plus no nausea (VAS <5 mm).

Oral Administration: One thousand and twenty-six patients receiving emetogenic chemotherapy were studied in 3 randomized, double blind trials in which 227 patients were treated with 100 mg oral dolasetron (see Table IV). Efficacy was based on complete response rates (no emetic episodes and no rescue medication). Dolasetron administered at an oral dose of 100 mg gave similar results in preventing nausea and vomiting as the other selective 5-HT_3 receptor antagonists studied as active comparators.

Table IV—Anzemet

Prevention of Chemotherapy-Induced Nausea and Vomiting in Moderately Emetogenic Chemotherapy with Anzemet Tablets (100 mg)[a]

Response over 24 hours	Patients responding (%) (n=227)
Complete Response[b]	147 (64.8%)
Nausea Score[c]	2.5
Total Response[d]	111 (48.9%)

[a]Cisplatin, carboplatin, doxorubicin and cyclophosphamide were used at moderately emetogenic doses.
[b]No emetic episodes and no rescue medication.
[c]Median 24-hour change from baseline nausea score using visual analog scale (VAS); score range 0="none" to 100="nausea as bad as it could be".
[d]Complete response and no nausea (VAS <5 mm).

Anzemet (cont'd)

Indications: For the prevention of nausea and vomiting associated with initial and repeat courses of emetogenic cancer chemotherapy, including high dose cisplatin.

Contraindications: In patients with known hypersensitivity to the drug or any components of its formulations (see Supplied).

Warnings: Dolasetron can cause ECG interval changes (PR and QTc prolongations and QRS widening) in healthy volunteers and patients. In patients receiving chemotherapy or undergoing surgery, JT prolongations have also been observed following dolasetron, active comparator or placebo. JT prolongations have not been observed in healthy volunteers receiving dolasetron. ECG interval changes are related in magnitude and frequency to blood levels of the active metabolite, hydrodolasetron. These changes are self-limiting with declining blood levels. Some patients have interval prolongations for 24 hours or longer. Interval prolongations could lead to cardiovascular consequences, including heart block or cardiac arrhythmias. These have been rarely reported in patients receiving dolasetron.

Complete heart block was observed interoperatively in a 61-year-old woman who received 200 mg dolasetron oral tablet for the prevention of postoperative nausea and vomiting. This patient was also taking verapamil. A 66-year-old man receiving chemotherapy was found dead 6 hours after receiving 1.8 mg/kg (119 mg) i.v. dolasetron injection and concomitant anthracycline therapy. Vital signs taken at 1 and 4.5 hours after dolasetron injection indicated an adequate blood pressure and increasing heart rate. This patient had other potential risk factors including substantial exposure to doxorubicin and concomitant cyclophosphamide.

Precautions: General: **Dolasetron should be administered with caution in patients who have or may develop prolongation of cardiac conduction intervals, particularly QTc. These include patients with hypokalemia or hypomagnesemia, patients taking diuretics with potential for inducing electrolyte abnormalities, patients with congenital QT syndrome, patients taking antiarrhythmic drugs or other drugs which lead to QT prolongation, and cumulative high dose anthracycline therapy.**

Because dolasetron affects cardiac conductivity, the recommended doses should not be exceeded.

Children: Due to insufficient safety and efficacy data, dolasetron is not recommended for use in pediatric patients at this time.

Renal Impairment: Dosage adjustment is not necessary in mild to moderate renal impairment. However, dolasetron is not recommended in patients with severe renal impairment because of the possibility of prolonged QTc intervals and other cardiac conduction abnormalities from elevated hydrodolasetron levels.

Hepatic Impairment: Dosage adjustment is not necessary in mild to moderate hepatic impairment. The oral formulation of dolasetron is not recommended in patients with severe hepatic impairment because of the possibility of prolonged QTc intervals and other cardiac conduction abnormalities from elevated hydrodolasetron levels.

Pregnancy: There are no adequate and well-controlled studies in pregnant women. This drug is not recommended for use during pregnancy.

Lactation: It is not known whether dolasetron is excreted in human milk. Dolasetron should not be administered to a nursing woman.

Geriatrics: Dosage adjustment is not needed in patients over 65.

Carcinogenicity: In a 24-month carcinogenicity study in CD-1 mice, there was a statistically significant (p=0.001) increase in the incidence of combined hepatocellular adenomas and carcinomas in male mice treated orally with 150 mg/kg/day dolasetron and above. No increase in liver tumors was observed at a dose of 75 mg/kg/day in male mice and at doses up to 300 mg/kg/day in female mice.

In a 24-month carcinogenicity study in Sprague-Dawley rats, oral dolasetron mesylate was not tumorigenic at doses up to 150 mg/kg/day in males and 300 mg/kg/day in females.

Drug Interactions: The potential for clinically significant drug-drug interactions posed by dolasetron and hydrodolasetron appears to be low for drugs commonly used in chemotherapy or surgery (see Warnings for information about potential interaction with other drugs that prolong QTc intervals). Blood levels of hydrodolasetron increased 24% when dolasetron was coadministered with cimetidine (nonselective inhibitor of cytochrome P450) for 7 days, and decreased 28% with coadministration of rifampin (potent inducer of cytochrome P450) for 7 days. Dolasetron injection has been safely coadministered with drugs used in chemotherapy and surgery. In patients taking furosemide, nifedipine, diltiazem, ACE inhibitors, verapamil, glyburide, propranolol, and various chemotherapy agents, no effect was shown on the clearance of hydrodolasetron. Clearance of hydrodolasetron decreased by about 27% when dolasetron was administered concomitantly with atenolol. Dolasetron does not influence anesthesia recovery time in patients. Dolasetron did not inhibit the antitumor activity of 4 chemotherapeutic agents (cisplatin, 5-fluorouracil, doxorubicin, cyclophosphamide) in 4 murine models.

Adverse Effects: The safety of dolasetron has been evaluated in over 7 000 patients in North American and European clinical trials. Dolasetron was well tolerated, with headache being the most frequently reported adverse event. The incidence of adverse events from pivotal controlled clinical trials is presented in Tables V and VI.

Injection: In controlled and uncontrolled clinical trials, 2 265 adult patients received dolasetron injection of which 731 patients were treated at the recommended therapeutic dose (1.8 mg/kg). The most frequently reported adverse events (≥2%) in patients receiving dolasetron injection are presented in Table V. Patients were receiving chemotherapy (primarily cisplatin) and i.v. fluids. Adverse events were recorded for at least 24 hours following dolasetron injection administration.

Table V—Anzemet

Anzemet I.V. Adverse Events ≥2% in Chemotherapy-Induced Nausea and Vomiting

Event	Anzemet Injection 1.8 mg/kg (n=731)
Headache	188 (25.7%)
Diarrhea	93 (12.7%)
Fever	36 (4.9%)
Hepatic Function Abnormal*	28 (3.8%)
Fatigue	25 (3.4%)
Abdominal Pain	23 (3.1%)
Tachycardia	21 (2.9%)
Chills/Shivering	20 (2.7%)
Hypertension	20 (2.7%)
Extrasystoles	19 (2.6%)
Pain	18 (2.5%)
Dizziness	15 (2.1%)

*Includes events coded as AST- or ALT-increased.

Oral Administration: In controlled clinical trials, 943 patients received oral dolasetron of which 227 patients were treated at the recommended therapeutic dose (100 mg). These patients were receiving concurrent chemotherapy, predominantly cyclophosphamide and doxorubicin regimens. Table VI lists adverse events occurring in ≥2% of patients in comparative clinical trials.

Table VI—Anzemet

Oral Anzemet Adverse Events Occurring ≥2% in Chemotherapy-Induced Nausea and Vomiting Patients

	Anzemet 100 mg (n=227)
Headache	52 (22.9%)
Diarrhea	12 (5.3%)
Fatigue	13 (5.7%)
Bradycardia	9 (4.0%)
Pain	7 (3.1%)
Dizziness	7 (3.1%)
Tachycardia	6 (2.6%)
T Wave Change	6 (2.6%)
ST-T Wave Change	6 (2.6%)
Chills/Shivering	5 (2.2%)
Dyspepsia	5 (2.2%)

Less frequently occurring adverse events: Injection: In controlled and uncontrolled clinical trials the following adverse events occurred at a frequency of 0.3 to 2.0% in patients treated with dolasetron injection at the recommended dose (1.8 mg/kg): Autonomic Nervous System: dry mouth, flushing.

Body as a Whole: malaise.

Cardiovascular (general): chest pain, edema, edema peripheral, fluid overload, hypotension.

Central and Peripheral Nervous System: drowsiness, paresthesia, tremor, vertigo.

GastroIntestinal: abdominal distension, anorexia, appetite increased, constipation, dyspepsia, flatulence, hiccup, nausea, stomatitis.

Hearing, Taste, and Vision: taste perversion.

Heart Rate and Rhythm: atrial arrhythmia, sinus arrhythmia, atrial flutter/fibrillation, first degree AV block, bradycardia, cardiac arrest, ECG abnormal specific, QT/QTc prolonged, ST-T wave change, T wave change.

Hematologic: bone marrow aplasia, epistaxis.

Musculoskeletal: myalgia.

Psychiatric: agitation, anxiety, confusion, sleep disorder.

Resistance Mechanism: sepsis.

Respiratory System: abnormal breath sounds, bronchospasm, cough, dyspnea, pneumonia, pulmonary congestion, throat irritation, upper respiratory congestion.

Skin and Appendages: facial edema, increased sweating.

Urinary System: urinary retention.

Oral Administration: In controlled clinical trials the following adverse events occurred at a frequency of 0.9 to 2.0% in patients treated with oral dolasetron at the recommended dose (100 mg): Application Site: injection site pain.

Autonomic Nervous System: dry mouth, flushing.

Body as a Whole: fever.

Cardiovascular (general): dependent edema, hypotension.

Central and Peripheral Nervous System: drowsiness.

GastroIntestinal: abdominal pain, anorexia, increased appetite, constipation, eructation, flatulence, nausea.

Hearing, Taste, and Vision: taste perversion.

Heart Rate and Rhythm: atrial arrhythmia, sinus arrhythmia, extrasystoles.

Liver and Biliary System: AST increased.

Metabolic and Nutritional: dehydration.

Resistance Mechanism: influenza-like symptoms.

Respiratory System: dyspnea, nasal irritation, sneezing, throat irritation.

Overdose: Symptoms and Treatment: A 59-year-old male with metastatic melanoma (otherwise healthy) developed severe hypotension and dizziness 40 minutes after receiving a 15-minute infusion of 1 000 mg (13 mg/kg) of dolasetron. Treatment for overdose consisted of infusion of 500 mL of a plasma expander, dopamine, and atropine. The patient had normal sinus rhythm and prolongation of PR, QRS, and QTc intervals on an ECG recorded 2 hours after the infusion. The patient's blood pressure was normal 3 hours after the event and the ECG intervals returned to baseline on follow-up. The patient was released from the hospital 6 hours after the event.

A 7-year-old boy received 6 mg/kg of dolasetron orally before surgery. No symptoms occurred and no treatment was required.

It is not known if dolasetron is removed by hemodialysis or peritoneal dialysis.

Following a suspected overdose of dolasetron, a patient found to have second-degree or higher AV conduction block should undergo cardiac telemetry monitoring.

There is no known specific antidote for dolasetron, and patients with suspected overdose should be managed with supportive therapy. Individual doses as large as 5 mg/kg i.v. or 400 mg orally have been safely given to healthy volunteers or cancer patients.

Single i.v. doses of dolasetron at 160 mg/kg in male mice and 140 mg/kg in female mice and rats of both sexes were lethal. Symptoms of acute toxicity were tremors, depression and convulsions.

Dosage: The following recommended doses should not be exceeded due to the effects on cardiac conductivity (see Warnings and Precautions).

I.V. Administration: Adults: The recommended i.v. dosage is 1.8 mg/kg given as a single dose approximately 30 minutes before chemotherapy. Most patients can be adequately treated with 100 mg. For light patients (<56 kg) or heavy patients (>90 kg), 1.8 mg/kg should be used.

The injection can be infused as rapidly as 100 mg over 30 seconds, or it can be diluted in a compatible i.v. solution such as normal saline or 5% dextrose to 50 mL and infused over 15 minutes. Dolasetron should not be mixed with other drugs. Flush the infusion line before and after administration of dolasetron.

Oral Administration: Adults: The recommended oral dosage is one 100 mg tablet given within 1 hour prior to chemotherapy.

Geriatrics: It is not necessary to adjust the dose of dolasetron in elderly patients.

Children: Due to insufficient safety and efficacy data, dolasetron is not recommended for use in pediatric patients at this time.

Hepatic Impairment: No dosage adjustment is necessary in mild to moderate hepatic impairment. However, oral dolasetron is not recommended in patients with severe hepatic impairment because of the possibility of prolonged QTc intervals and other cardiac conduction abnormalities from elevated hydrodolasetron levels.

Table VII—Anzemet

Dilution

Diluent Volume	Quantity of Anzemet Injection	Final Concentration	Administration*	
			Dose	Infusion Rate
50 mL	100 mg (5 mL)	1.82 mg/mL	100 mg/15 min	55 mL/15 min

*Anzemet Injection can also be injected over 30 seconds.

Renal Impairment: No dosage adjustment is necessary in mild to moderate renal impairment. However, dolasetron is not recommended in patients with severe renal impairment because of the possibility of prolonged QTc intervals and other cardiac conduction abnormalities from elevated hydrodolasetron levels.

Parenteral Products: Administration of I.V. Infusion Solutions: Compatibility with I.V. Solutions: Dolasetron injection should only be admixed with the following recommended infusion fluids: 0.9% w/v Sodium Chloride Injection, 5% w/v Glucose Injection, 10% w/v Mannitol Injection, 0.45% w/v Sodium Chloride and 5% w/v Glucose Injection, Lactated Ringer's Injection, 5% w/v Glucose Injection and Lactated Ringer's Injection.

Dolasetron is compatible with polypropylene syringes, i.v. bags, and associated tubing.

Compatibility with Other Drugs: Dolasetron should not be mixed with other drugs. Flush the infusion line before and after administration of dolasetron.

Note: As with all parenteral drug products, i.v. admixtures should be inspected visually for clarity, particulate matter, precipitate, discoloration and leakage prior to administration, whenever solution and container permit. Solutions showing haziness, particulate matter, precipitate, discoloration or leakage should not be used.

Dilution: To prepare dolasetron injection for i.v. infusion, aseptically transfer the appropriate amount of dolasetron injection to the desired volume of infusion fluid. See Table VII.

Stability and Storage of Diluted Solutions: Dilutions of i.v. fluids should be used immediately after preparation or stored for no more than 24 hours at 2 to 8°C.

Information for the Patient: See Blue Section—Information for the Patient "Anzemet".

Supplied: Injection: Each mL of clear, colorless, sterile, nonpyrogenic solution for i.v. injection contains: dolasetron mesylate monohydrate 20 mg. Nonmedicinal ingredients: glacial acetic acid, mannitol, sodium acetate trihydrate and water for injection. pH: 3.2 to 3.8. Clear glass vials of 5 mL.

Tablets: 50 mg: Each pale pink, round, film-coated tablet, printed with "ANZEMET" around "50" centered on one side and plain on the other, contains: dolasetron mesylate monohydrate 50 mg. Nonmedicinal ingredients: carnauba wax, croscarmellose sodium, hydroxypropyl methylcellulose, lactose, magnesium stearate, polyethylene glycol, polysorbate 80, pregelatinized starch, red iron oxide, titanium dioxide and white wax. Bottles of 15.

100 mg: Each pink, oval, film-coated tablet, printed with "ANZEMET" on one side and "100" on the other, contains: dolasetron mesylate monohydrate 100 mg. Nonmedicinal ingredients: carnauba wax, croscarmellose sodium, hydroxypropyl methylcellulose, lactose, magnesium stearate, polyethylene glycol, polysorbate 80, pregelatinized starch, red iron oxide, titanium dioxide and white wax. Bottles of 15.

Store at controlled temperature (15 to 30°C) and protect from light.

Reviewed 1998

A.P.L.® ℞

Wyeth-Ayerst

Chorionic Gonadotropin

Gonadotropin

Supplied: Each mL of reconstituted solution contains: chorionic gonadotropin 1 000 USP units. Nonmedicinal ingredients: hydrochloric acid, lactose, phenol and sodium hydroxide.

A.P.L. is a glycoprotein preparation secreted by placenta and obtained from pregnant women's urine. The finished dosage form is prepared by cryodesiccation and must be stored at 2 to 8°C.

To reconstitute, add 10 mL of accompanying sterile diluent to obtain an approximate withdrawable volume of 10 mL. The reconstituted colorless solution so obtained must be refrigerated and is stable for 30 days.

One vial of A.P.L. Dry Powder containing 10 000 USP units of active material and packaged with 10 mL of sterile diluent. Note: USP units are equivalent to international units. Chorionic gonadotropin used in A.P.L. has an approximate potency of 2 000 units/mg.

APO®-ACEBUTOLOL ℞

Apotex

Acebutolol HCl

Antihypertensive—Antianginal

Supplied: 100 mg: Each white, round, biconvex, film-coated tablet, scored and engraved "APO" over "100" on one side, contains: acebutolol HCl equivalent to acebutolol 100 mg. Nonmedicinal ingredients: colloidal silicon dioxide, dextrates and magnesium stearate. Energy: <1 kJ (0.10 kcal). Gluten-, lactose-, sodium-, sulfite- and tartrazine-free. Bottles of 100 and 500.

200 mg: Each white, oval, biconvex, film-coated tablet, scored and engraved "APO 200" on one side, contains: acebutolol HCl equivalent to acebutolol 200 mg. Nonmedicinal ingredients: colloidal silicon dioxide, dextrates and magnesium stearate. Energy: <1 kJ (0.21 kcal). Gluten-, lactose-, sodium-, sulfite- and tartrazine-free. Bottles of 100 and 500.

400 mg: Each white, capsule-shaped, biconvex, film-coated tablet, scored and engraved "APO 400" on one side, contains: acebutolol HCl equivalent to acebutolol 400 mg. Nonmedicinal ingredients: colloidal silicon dioxide, dextrates and magnesium stearate. Energy: 1.73 kJ (0.41 kcal). Gluten-, lactose-, sodium-, sulfite- and tartrazine-free. Bottles of 100 and 500.

Store at 15 to 30°C. Protect from light.

APO®-ACETAMINOPHEN

Apotex

Acetaminophen

Analgesic—Antipyretic

Supplied: 325 mg: Each white, round, flat-faced with beveled edge, scored tablet, identified APO over 325, contains: acetaminophen 325 mg. Nonmedicinal ingredients: croscarmellose sodium, hydroxypropyl cellulose, magnesium stearate and purified water. Energy: <1 kJ (0.11 kcal). Sodium: <1 mmol (0.39 mg). Gluten-, lactose-, sulfite- and tartrazine-free. Bottles of 100 and 1 000. Unit dose packages of 100. Apo Long-Term Care (LTC) Pak.

500 mg: Each white, round, flat-faced with beveled edge, scored tablet, identified APO over 500, contains: acetaminophen 500 mg. Nonmedicinal ingredients: croscarmellose sodium, hydroxypropyl cellulose and magnesium stearate. Energy: <1 kJ (0.16 kcal). Sodium: <1 mmol (0.58 mg). Gluten-, lactose-, sulfite- and tartrazine-free. Bottles of 100 and 1 000. Unit dose packages of 100. Apo Long-Term Care (LTC) Pak.

APO®-ACETAZOLAMIDE ℞

Apotex

Acetazolamide

Carbonic Anhydrase Inhibitor—Diuretic

Supplied: Each round, white, double scored, biconvex tablet identified APO over 250, contains: acetazolamide 250 mg. Nonmedicinal ingredients: colloidal silicon dioxide, magnesium stearate and microcrystalline cellulose. Energy: 3.30 kJ (0.79 kcal). Gluten-, lactose-, sodium-, sulfite- and tartrazine-free. Bottles of 100 and 500.

APO®-ACYCLOVIR ℞

Apotex

Acyclovir

Antiviral Agent

Pharmacology: Acyclovir, a synthetic acyclic purine nucleoside analog, is a substrate with a high degree of specificity for herpes simplex and varicella-zoster specified thymidine kinase. Acyclovir is a poor substrate for host cell-specified thymidine kinase. Herpes simplex and varicella-zoster specified thymidine kinase transform acyclovir to its monophosphate which is then transformed by a number of cellular enzymes to acyclovir diphosphate and acyclovir triphosphate. Acyclovir triphosphate is both an inhibitor of, and a substrate for, herpesvirus-specified DNA polymerase. Although the cellular α-DNA polymerase in infected cells may also be inhibited by acyclovir triphosphate, this occurs only at concentrations of acyclovir triphosphate which are higher than those which inhibit the herpesvirus-specified DNA polymerase. Acyclovir is selectively converted to its active form in herpesvirus-infected cells and is thus preferentially taken up by these cells. Acyclovir has demonstrated a very much lower toxic potential in vitro for normal uninfected cells because: 1) less is taken up; 2) less is converted to the active form; 3) cellular α-DNA polymerase has a lower sensitivity to the action of the active form of the drug. A combination of the thymidine kinase specificity, inhibition of DNA polymerase and premature termination of DNA synthesis results in inhibition of herpesvirus replication. No effect on latent nonreplicating virus has been demonstrated. Inhibition of the virus reduces the period of viral shedding, limits the degree of spread and level of pathology, and thereby facilitates healing. During suppression there is no evidence that acyclovir prevents neural migration of the virus. It aborts episodes of recurrent herpes due to inhibition of viral replication following reactivation.

Pharmacokinetics: The pharmacokinetics of acyclovir after oral administration have been evaluated in 6 clinical studies involving 110 adult patients. In 1 study of 35 immunocompromised patients with herpes simplex or varicella-zoster infection given acyclovir capsules in doses of 200 to 1 000 mg every 4 hours, 6 times daily for 5 days, the bioavailability was estimated to be 15 to 20%. In this study, steady-state plasma levels were reached by the second day of dosing. Mean steady-state peak and trough concentrations following the last 200 mg dose were 0.49 μg/mL (0.47 to 0.54 μg/mL) and 0.31 μg/mL (0.18 to 0.41 μg/mL), respectively and following the last 800 mg dose were 2.8 μg/mL (2.3 to 3.1 μg/mL) and 1.8 μg/mL (1.3 to 2.5 μg/mL). In another study, 20 immunocompetent patients with recurrent genital herpes simplex infections given acyclovir capsules in doses of 800 mg every 6 hours, 4 times daily for 5 days, the mean steady-state peak and trough concentrations were 1.4 μg/mL (0.66 to 1.8 μg/mL) and 0.55 μg/mL (0.14 to 1.1 μg/mL).

Indications: For the following conditions: the treatment of initial episodes of herpes genitalis; the suppression of unusually frequent recurrences of herpes genitalis (6 or more episodes per year); the acute treatment of herpes zoster (shingles).

The results of clinical studies suggest that some patients with recurrent genital herpes may derive clinical benefit from the administration of oral acyclovir if taken at the first sign of an impending episode. Those most likely to benefit are patients who experience severe, prolonged recurrences; such intermittent therapy may be more appropriate than suppressive therapy when these recurrences are infrequent.

Early treatment of acute herpes zoster (shingles) in immune competent individuals with oral acyclovir resulted in decreased viral shedding; decreased time to healing; less dissemination; and alleviation of acute pain.

Contraindications: In patients who develop hypersensitivity or who are hypersensitive to the components of the formulation (see Supplied).

Warnings: Suppressive therapy of herpes genitalis with acyclovir should be considered only for severely affected patients. Periodic evaluation of the need for continued suppressive therapy is recommended. In some patients, there is a tendency for the first recurrent episode to be more severe following cessation of suppressive therapy.

In severely immunocompromised patients, the physician should be aware that prolonged or repeated courses of acyclovir may result in selection of resistant viruses associated with infections which may not respond.

Precautions: General: The recommended dosage and length of treatment should not be exceeded (see Dosage). Acyclovir

Apo-Acyclovir (cont'd)

has caused mutagenesis in some acute studies at high concentrations of drug. Also, decreased spermatogenesis was observed in some animals at high parenteral doses. However, no adverse effects on sperm counts were reported in humans given recommended oral doses of acyclovir.

The decision to prescribe a course of suppressive therapy should be weighed in the light of present knowledge about the long-term effects of acyclovir and must clearly relate to the condition of the patient.

It is suggested that periodic discontinuation of the suppressive regimen occur so that the patient's status and need for continued suppressive therapy can be monitored.

Whereas cutaneous lesions associated with herpes simplex infections are often pathognomonic, Tzanck smears prepared from lesion exudate or scrapings may assist in the diagnosis. Positive cultures for herpes simplex virus offer the only absolute means for confirmation of the diagnosis. Appropriate examinations should be performed to rule out other sexually transmitted diseases. All patients should be advised to take particular care to avoid potential transmission of virus if active lesions are present while they are on therapy.

Caution should be exercised when administering to patients receiving potentially nephrotoxic agents since this may increase the risk of renal dysfunction.

Pregnancy: Teratology studies carried out to date in animals have been negative in general. However, in a nonstandard test in rats, there were fetal abnormalities such as head and tail anomalies, and maternal toxicity; since such studies are not always predictive of human response, acyclovir should not be used during pregnancy unless the physician feels the potential benefit justifies the risk of possible harm to the fetus. The potential for high concentrations of acyclovir to cause chromosome breaks in vitro should be taken into consideration in making this decision.

Lactation: Acyclovir is excreted in human milk. Caution should therefore be exercised when acyclovir is administered to a nursing mother.

Children: Safety and effectiveness in children less than 2 years of age have not been adequately studied.

Drug Interactions: Coadministration of probenecid with i.v. acyclovir has been shown to increase the mean half-life and the area under the concentration-time curve. Urinary excretion and renal clearance were correspondingly reduced.

Adverse Effects: Treatment of Herpes Simplex: Short-term Administration (5 to 10 days): The most frequent adverse reactions reported during clinical trials of treatment of genital herpes with oral acyclovir in 298 patients are listed in Table I.

Table I—Apo-Acyclovir

Adverse Reactions—Treatment of Herpes Simplex (Short-term Administration)

Adverse Reactions	Total	(%)
Nausea and/or vomiting	8	2.7
Headache	2	0.6

Less frequent adverse reactions, each of which occurred in 1 of 298 patient treatments (0.3%), included: diarrhea, dizziness, anorexia, fatigue, edema, skin rash, leg pain, inguinal adenopathy, medication taste and sore throat.

Suppression: Long-term Administration: The most frequent adverse events reported in a clinical trial for the prevention of recurrences with continuous administration of 400 mg (two 200 mg capsules) 2 times daily are shown in Table II.

Table II—Apo-Acyclovir

Adverse Reactions—Treatment of Herpes Simplex (Long-term Administration)

	1st Year (n=586) (%)	2nd Year (n=390) (%)	3rd Year (n=329) (%)
Nausea	4.8		
Diarrhea	2.4		
Headache	1.9	1.5	0.9
Rash	1.7	1.3	
Paresthesia		0.8	1.2
Asthenia			1.2

Evidence so far from clinical trials suggests that the severity and frequency of adverse events is unlikely to necessitate discontinuation of therapy.

Herpes Zoster: The most frequent adverse reactions reported during 3 clinical trials of treatment of herpes zoster (shingles) with 800 mg of oral acyclovir 5 times daily for 7 or 10 days or placebo are shown in Table III.

Table III—Apo-Acyclovir

Adverse Reactions—Treatment of Herpes Zoster

Adverse Reactions	Acyclovir (n=323) (%)	Placebo (n=323) (%)
Malaise	11.5	11.1
Nausea	8.0	11.5
Headache	5.9	11.1
Vomiting	2.5	2.5
Diarrhea	1.5	0.3
Constipation	0.9	2.4

Overdose: Symptoms and Treatment: Overdosage of acyclovir during oral use is unlikely because of incomplete bioavailability from the gastrointestinal tract. Doses as high as 800 mg 6 times daily for 5 days have been administered to humans without untoward effects. In clinical studies, the highest plasma concentration observed in a single patient at these doses was 10.0 μg/mL.

I.V. doses administered to humans have been as high as 1 200 mg/m² (28 mg/kg) 3 times daily for up to 2 weeks. Peak plasma concentrations have reached 80 μg/mL. No acute massive overdosage of acyclovir has been reported; however, in the case of an excessively high ingestion of acyclovir, precipitation of acyclovir in renal tubules may occur if the solubility (2.5 mg/mL) in the intratubular fluid is exceeded. In the event of renal failure and anuria, the patient may benefit from hemodialysis until renal function is restored.

Dosage: Herpes Genitalis: Treatment of Initial Infection: 200 mg every 4 hours, 5 times daily, for a total of 1 g daily for 10 days. Therapy should be initiated as early as possible following onset of signs and symptoms.

Suppressive Therapy for Recurrent Disease: The initial dose recommended is 200 mg 3 times daily. This can be increased if breakthrough occurs up to a dosage of 200 mg 5 times daily. If necessary, a dose of one 400 mg tablet (two 200 mg tablets) given twice daily may be considered. Periodic re-evaluation of the need for therapy is recommended.

Administration of acyclovir for intermittent therapy is one 200 mg tablet every 4 hours 5 times daily for 5 days. Therapy should be initiated at the earliest sign or symptom (prodrome) of recurrence.

Herpes Zoster: 800 mg every 4 hours, 5 times daily for 7 to 10 days. Treatment should be initiated within 72 hours of the onset of lesions. In clinical trials, the greatest benefit occurred when treatment was begun within 48 hours of the onset of lesions.

Patients with Acute or Chronic Renal Impairment: Comprehensive pharmacokinetic studies have been completed following i.v. acyclovir infusions in patients with renal impairment.

Based on these studies, dosage adjustments are recommended in Table IV for genital herpes and herpes zoster indications.

Hemodialysis: For patients who require hemodialysis, the mean plasma half-life of acyclovir during hemodialysis is approximately 5 hours. This results in a 60% decrease in plasma concentrations following a 6-hour dialysis period. Therefore, the patient's dosing schedule should be adjusted so that an additional dose is administered after each dialysis.

Peritoneal Dialysis: No supplement dose appears to be necessary after adjustment of the dosing interval.

Supplied: 200 mg: Each blue, round, flat-faced, beveled-edged, compressed tablet, engraved "APO" over "200" on one side, contains: acyclovir 200 mg. Nonmedicinal ingredients: colloidal silicon dioxide, croscarmellose sodium, lactose, magnesium stearate, microcrystalline cellulose; coloring agent: indigotine lake. Bottles of 100, 250, 500 and 1 000.

400 mg: Each pink, round, flat-faced, beveled-edged, compressed tablet, engraved "APO" over "400" on one side, contains: acyclovir 400 mg. Nonmedicinal ingredients: colloidal silicon dioxide, croscarmellose sodium, magnesium stearate, microcrystalline cellulose; coloring agent: red ferric oxide. Bottles of 100, 250, 500 and 1 000. Unit dose packages of 56 and 100.

800 mg: Each blue, biconvex, oval, scored, compressed tablet, engraved "APO 800" on one side, contains acyclovir 800 mg. Nonmedicinal ingredients: colloidal silicon dioxide, croscarmellose sodium, magnesium stearate, microcrystalline cellulose; coloring agent: indigotine lake (Blue #2) and brilliant Blue FCF lake. Bottles of 100, 250 and 500. Unit dose packages of 50 and 100.

Store at controlled room temperature (20 to 25°C) in a dry place and protected from light.

New Product 1998

Table IV—Apo-Acyclovir

Dosage Adjustments Recommended for Genital Herpes and Herpes Zoster

Normal Dosage Regimen (5×daily)	Creatinine Clearance (mL/min/1.73m²)	Adjusted Dosage Regimen: Dose (mg)	Adjusted Dosage Regimen: Dosing Interval (hours)
200 mg every 4 hours	>10	200	every 4 hours, 5× daily
	0-10	200	every 12 hours
400 mg every 12 hours	>10	400	every 12 hours
	0-10	200	every 12 hours
800 mg every 4 hours	>25	800	every 4 hours, 5× daily
	10-25	800	every 8 hours
	0-10	800	every 12 hours

APO®-ALLOPURINOL ℞

Apotex

Allopurinol

Xanthine Oxidase Inhibitor

Supplied: 100 mg: Each round, white, biconvex, scored tablet, identified APO over 100, contains: allopurinol 100 mg. Nonmedicinal ingredients: colloidal silicon dioxide, croscarmellose sodium, lactose monohydrate, magnesium stearate and microcrystalline cellulose. Energy: 3.72 kJ (0.89 kcal). Sodium: <1 mmol (0.13 mg). Gluten-, sulfite- and tartrazine-free. Bottles of 100 and 1 000.

200 mg: Each round, peach, biconvex, scored tablet, identified APO over 200, contains: allopurinol 200 mg. Nonmedicinal ingredients: colloidal silicon dioxide, croscarmellose sodium, lactose, magnesium stearate, microcrystalline cellulose and sunset yellow aluminum lake 40. Energy: <1 kJ (<0.01 kcal). Sodium: <1 mmol (<0.01 mg). Gluten-, sulfite- and tartrazine-free. Bottles of 100 and 500.

300 mg: Each round, orange, biconvex, scored tablet, identified APO over 300, contains: allopurinol 300 mg. Nonmedicinal ingredients: colloidal silicon dioxide, croscarmellose sodium, lactose, magnesium stearate, microcrystalline cellulose and sunset yellow aluminum lake 40. Energy: <1 kJ (<0.01 kcal). Sodium: <1 mmol (<0.01 mg). Gluten-, sulfite- and tartrazine-free. Bottles of 100 and 500.

APO®-ALPRAZ ℞

Apotex

Alprazolam

Anxiolytic—Sedative

Supplied: 0.25 mg: Each white, oval, biconvex, compressed tablet, scored and identified APO over .25 on one side, contains: alprazolam 0.25 mg. Nonmedicinal ingredients: croscarmellose sodium, lactose monohydrate, magnesium stearate and microcrystalline cellulose. Energy: 2.25 kJ (0.54 kcal). Sodium: <1 mmol (0.14 mg). Gluten-, sulfite- and tartrazine-free. Bottles of 100 and 1 000.

0.5 mg: Each peach, oval, biconvex, compressed tablet, scored and identified APO over 0.5 on one side, contains: alprazolam 0.5 mg. Nonmedicinal ingredients: croscarmellose sodium, lactose monohydrate, magnesium stearate, microcrystalline cellulose and sunset yellow lake (FD&C yellow #6). Energy: 2.33 kJ (0.56 kcal). Sodium: <1 mmol (0.14 mg). Gluten-, sulfite- and tartrazine-free. Bottles of 100 and 1 000.

Store at room temperature.

APO®-AMILZIDE ℞

Apotex

Hydrochlorothiazide—Amiloride HCl

Diuretic—Antihypertensive

Supplied: Each peach colored, diamond-shaped tablet, scored and identified APO above the score, 5/50 below the score, contains: hydrochlorothiazide 50 mg and amiloride HCl 5 mg. Nonmedicinal ingredients: colloidal silicon dioxide, croscarmellose sodium, lactose monohydrate, magnesium stearate, microcrystalline cellulose, sodium bicarbonate and sunset yellow aluminum lake 40. Energy: 2.90 kJ (0.69 kcal). Sodium: <1 mmol (2.93 mg). Gluten-, sulfite- and tartrazine-free. Bottles of 100 and 1 000.

APO®-AMITRIPTYLINE ℞

Apotex

Amitriptyline HCl

Antidepressant

Supplied: 10 mg: Each round, blue, biconvex, film-coated tablet, identified 10, contains: amitriptyline HCl 10 mg. Nonmedicinal ingredients: colloidal silicon dioxide, croscarmellose sodium, FD&C blue #1 aluminum lake, hydroxypropyl methylcellulose, magnesium stearate, microcrystalline cellulose, polyethylene glycol and titanium dioxide. Energy: 1.46 kJ (0.35 kcal). Sodium: <1 mmol (0.18 mg). Gluten-, lactose-, sulfite- and tartrazine-free. Bottles of 100 and 1 000. Unit dose packages of 100. Apo Long-Term Care (LTC) Pak.

25 mg: Each round, yellow, biconvex, film-coated tablet, identified 25, contains: amitriptyline HCl 25 mg. Nonmedicinal ingredients: carnauba wax, colloidal silicon dioxide, croscarmellose sodium, D&C yellow #10 lake 16%, hydroxypropyl methyl-cellulose, magnesium stearate, microcrystalline cellulose, polyethylene glycol and titanium dioxide. Energy: 1.21 kJ (0.29 kcal). Sodium: <1 mmol (0.18 mg). Gluten-, lactose-, sulfite- and tartrazine-free. Bottles of 100, 1 000 and 3 000. Unit dose packages of 100. APO Long-Term Care (LTC) Pak.

50 mg: Each round, brown, biconvex, film-coated tablet, identified 50, contains: amitriptyline HCl 50 mg. Nonmedicinal ingredients: colloidal silicon dioxide, croscarmellose sodium, hydroxypropyl methylcellulose, indigotine aluminum lake (Blue #2), magnesium stearate, microcrystalline cellulose, polyethylene glycol, sunset yellow lake (FD&C yellow #6) and titanium dioxide. Energy: 2.39 kJ (0.57 kcal). Sodium: <1 mmol (0.37 mg). Gluten-, lactose-, sulfite- and tartrazine-free. Bottles of 100 and 1 000. Unit dose packages of 100. APO Long-Term Care (LTC) Pak.

75 mg: Each round, orange, biconvex, film-coated tablet, identified APO over 75, contains: amitriptyline HCl 75 mg. Nonmedicinal ingredients: carnauba wax, colloidal silicon dioxide, croscarmellose sodium, hydroxypropyl methylcellulose, magnesium stearate, microcrystalline cellulose, polyethylene glycol, sunset yellow lake and titanium dioxide. Energy: 3.61 kJ (0.84 kcal). Sodium: <1 mmol (0.55 mg). Gluten-, lactose-, sulfite- and tartrazine-free. Bottles of 100.

APO®-AMOXI ℞

Apotex

Amoxicillin Trihydrate

Antibiotic

Supplied: Capsules: 250 mg: Each scarlet and gold no. 2 capsule, identified APO 250, contains: amoxicillin trihydrate equivalent to 250 mg amoxicillin. Nonmedicinal ingredients: capsule #2 gold scarlet, colloidal silicon dioxide, D&C red #28, D&C red #40, D&C yellow #10, FD&C blue #1, FD&C yellow #6, stearic acid and titanium dioxide. Energy: <1 kJ (0.21 kcal). Alcohol-, gluten-, lactose-, sodium- and tartrazine-free. Bottles of 100 and 1 000.

500 mg: Each scarlet and gold no. 0 capsule, identified APO 500, contains: amoxicillin trihydrate equivalent to 500 mg amoxicillin. Nonmedicinal ingredients: capsule #2 gold scarlet, colloidal silicon dioxide, D&C red #28, D&C red #40, D&C yellow #10, FD&C blue #1, FD&C yellow #6, stearic acid and titanium dioxide. Energy: 1.52 kJ (0.36 kcal). Alcohol-, gluten-, lactose-, sodium- and tartrazine-free. Bottles of 100 and 500.

Oral Suspensions (regular): 125 mg: After reconstitution each 5 mL of strawberry-flavored suspension contains: amoxicillin trihydrate equivalent to 125 mg amoxicillin. Nonmedicinal ingredients: guar gum, sodium benzoate, sodium citrate and sucrose. Energy: 38.21 kJ (9.12 kcal)/5 mL. Sodium: <1 mmol (2.18 mg)/5 mL. Alcohol-, gluten-, lactose-, sulfite- and tartrazine-free. Bottles of 75, 100 and 150 mL.

250 mg: After reconstitution each 5 mL of banana-flavored suspension contains: amoxicillin trihydrate equivalent to 250 mg amoxicillin. Nonmedicinal ingredients: D&C yellow #10 aluminum lake, guar gum, sodium benzoate, sodium citrate and sucrose. Energy: 37.30 kJ (8.91 kcal)/5 mL. Sodium: <1 mmol (2.60 mg)/5 mL. Alcohol-, gluten-, lactose-, sulfite- and tartrazine-free. Bottles of 75, 100 and 150 mL.

Oral Suspensions (sugar-free): 125 mg: After reconstitution, each 5 mL of strawberry-flavored suspension contains: amoxicillin trihydrate equivalent to 125 mg amoxicillin. Nonmedicinal ingredients: aspartame, collodial silicon dioxide, sodium benzoate, sodium citrate and xanthan gum. Energy: 0.54 kJ (0.13 kcal)/5 mL. Alcohol-, gluten-, lactose-, sulfite- and tartrazine-free. Bottles of 75, 100 and 150 mL.

250 mg: After reconstitution, each 5 mL of banana-flavored suspension contains: amoxicillin trihydrate equivalent to 250 mg amoxicillin. Nonmedicinal ingredients: aspartame, colloidal silicon dioxide, D&C yellow #10 aluminum lake, sodium benzoate, sodium citrate and xanthan gum. Energy: 0.54 kJ (0.13 kcal)/5 mL. Alcohol-, gluten-, lactose-, sulfite- and tartrazine-free. Bottles of 75, 100 and 150 mL.

The reconstituted suspension is stable for 7 days at room temperature or 14 days refrigerated. Keep bottles tightly closed.

APO®-AMPI ℞

Apotex

Ampicillin Trihydrate

Antibiotic

Supplied: Capsules: 250 mg: Each red and black no. 2 capsule, identified APO 250, contains: ampicillin trihydrate equivalent to 250 mg ampicillin. Nonmedicinal ingredients: croscarmellose sodium, silicon dioxide and stearic acid. Energy: <1 kJ (0.22 kcal). Sodium: <1 mmol (0.13 mg). Gluten-, lactose- and tartrazine-free. Bottles of 100 and 1 000.

500 mg: Each red and black no. 0 capsule, identified APO 500, contains: ampicillin trihydrate equivalent to 500 mg ampicillin. Nonmedicinal ingredients: croscarmellose sodium, silicon dioxide and stearic acid. Energy: 1.62 kJ (0.39 kcal). Sodium: <1 mmol (0.25 mg). Gluten-, lactose- and tartrazine-free. Bottles of 100 and 500.

Oral Suspensions: 125 mg: After reconstitution each 5 mL of cherry-flavored suspension contains: ampicillin trihydrate equivalent to 125 mg ampicillin. Nonmedicinal ingredients: erythrosine supra (red #3), guar gum, sodium benzoate, sodium citrate and sucrose. Energy: 38.04 kJ (9.09 kcal)/5 mL. Sodium: <1 mmol (3.19 mg)/5 mL. Alcohol-, gluten-, lactose-, sulfite- and tartrazine-free. Bottles of 60, 100 and 150 mL.

250 mg: After reconstitution each 5 mL of cherry-flavored suspension contains: ampicillin trihydrate equivalent to 250 mg ampicillin. Nonmedicinal ingredients: FD&C red #40, guar gum, sodium benzoate, sodium citrate and sucrose. Energy: 35.61 kJ (8.50 kcal)/5 mL. Sodium: <1 mmol (6.20 mg)/5 mL. Alcohol-, gluten-, lactose-, sulfite- and tartrazine-free. Bottles of 60, 100 and 150 mL.

Store in refrigerator. Do not freeze. Refrigerated suspension is stable for 3 weeks.

APO®-ASA

Apotex

ASA

Analgesic—Antipyretic—Anti-inflammatory

Supplied: Each round, white, biconvex, film-coated tablet, identified 325, contains: ASA 325 mg. Nonmedicinal ingredients: cornstarch. Energy: < 1 kJ (0.09 kcal). Gluten-, lactose-, sodium-, sulfite- and tartrazine-free. Bottles of 100, 500 and 1 000.

APO®-ATENOL ℞

Apotex

Atenolol

Antihypertensive—Antianginal Agent

Supplied: 50 mg: Each white, round, biconvex, scored tablet, identified APO over A50 on one side, contains: atenolol 50 mg. Nonmedicinal ingredients: colloidal silicon dioxide, croscarmellose sodium, lactose, magnesium stearate, microcrystalline cellulose and stearic acid. Energy: 1.91 kJ (0.46 kcal). Sodium: <1 mmol (0.63 mg). Gluten-, sulfite- and tartrazine-free. Bottles of 30, 100 and 500. Unit dose packages of 30 and 100. Apo Long-Term Care (LTC) Pak.

100 mg: Each white, round, biconvex, scored tablet, identified APO over A100 on one side, contains: atenolol 100 mg. Nonmedicinal ingredients: colloidal silicon dioxide, croscarmellose sodium, lactose, magnesium stearate, microcrystalline cellulose and stearic acid. Energy: 3.82 kJ (0.91 kcal). Sodium: <1 mmol (1.27 mg). Gluten-, sulfite- and tartrazine-free. Bottles of 30, 100 and 500. Unit dose packages of 30 and 100.

Protect from light and moisture. Store between 15 and 30°C.

APO®-BACLOFEN ℞

Apotex

Baclofen

Muscle Relaxant—Antispastic

Supplied: 10 mg: Each white, oval, scored tablet, imprinted with "APO B10", contains: baclofen 10 mg. Nonmedicinal ingredients: cornstarch, lactose, magnesium stearate and microcrystalline cellulose. Energy: 3.15 kJ (0.75 kcal). Gluten-, sodium-, sulfite- and tartrazine-free. Bottles of 100 and 500.

20 mg: Each white, capsule-shaped, scored tablet, imprinted with "APO B20", contains: baclofen 20 mg. Nonmedicinal ingredients: cornstarch, lactose, magnesium stearate and microcrystalline cellulose. Energy: 6.29 kJ (1.50 kcal). Gluten-, sodium-, sulfite- and tartrazine-free. Bottles of 100.

Store in tight containers between 15 and 30°C.

APO®-BENZTROPINE ℞

Apotex

Benztropine Mesylate

Antiparkinsonian Agent

Supplied: Each round, white, flat-faced with beveled edge, double-scored tablet, identified APO over 2, contains: benztropine mesylate 2 mg. Nonmedicinal ingredients: cornstarch, lactose, magnesium stearate and microcrystalline cellulose. Energy: 2.12 kJ (0.51 kcal). Gluten-, sodium-, sulfite- and tartrazine-free. Bottles of 100 and 1 000. Unit dose packages of 100. Apo Long-Term Care (LTC) Pak.

APO®-BISACODYL

Apotex

Bisacodyl

Laxative

Supplied: Suppositories: Each white, bullet-shaped, foil-wrapped suppository contains: bisacodyl 10 mg. Nonmedicinal ingredients: hydrogenated vegetable oil. Strips of 6 and 100.

Tablets: Each round, yellow, biconvex, enteric-coated tablet, marked "5", contains: bisacodyl 5 mg. Nonmedicinal ingredients: D&C yellow #10, eudragit, FD&C yellow #6, guar gum, lactose, magnesium stearate, microcrystalline cellulose, talc, titanium dioxide and triethyl citrate. Energy: 1.99 kJ (0.48 kcal). Gluten-, sodium-, sulfite- and tartrazine-free. Bottles of 30, 100 and 1 000. Unit dose packages of 100. Apo Long-Term Care (LTC) Pak.

APO®-BROMAZEPAM 🄿

Apotex

Bromazepam

Anxiolytic—Sedative

Supplied: 1.5 mg: Each white, round, flat-faced, beveled-edge, scored tablet, engraved APO over B-1.5 on one side, contains: bromazepam 1.5 mg. Nonmedicinal ingredients: cornstarch, lactose, magnesium stearate and microcrystalline cellulose. Gluten-, sulfite- and tartrazine-free. Bottles of 100, 250, 500 and 1 000.

3 mg: Each pink, round, flat-faced, beveled-edge, scored tablet, engraved APO over B-3 on one side, contains: bromazepam 3 mg. Nonmedicinal ingredients: cornstarch, D&C red #30 aluminum lake 30, D&C red #7 calcium lake 50%, lactose, magnesium stearate and microcrystalline cellulose. Gluten-, sulfite- and tartrazine-free. Bottles of 100, 250, 500 and 1 000.

6 mg: Each green, round, flat-faced, beveled-edge, scored tablet, engraved APO over B-6 on one side, contains: bromazepam 6 mg. Nonmedicinal ingredients: brilliant blue aluminum lake 12%, cellulose, cornstarch, D&C yellow #10 aluminum lake, ferric-ferrous oxide, lactose and magnesium stearate. Gluten-, sulfite- and tartrazine-free. Bottles of 100, 250, 500 and 1 000.

Store at temperatures between 15 and 30°C.

APO®-BROMOCRIPTINE 🄿

Apotex

Bromocriptine Mesylate

Prolactin Inhibitor—Growth Hormone Suppressant in Acromegaly—Adjunctive Medication in Parkinson's Disease

Supplied: 2.5 mg: Each white, oval-shaped tablet, scored and engraved APO 2.5, contains: bromocriptine 2.5 mg (as mesylate). Nonmedicinal ingredients: cellulose, croscarmellose sodium, lactose and magnesium stearate. Energy: ≤2.29 kJ (≤0.55 kcal). Sodium: <1 mmol (0.16 mg). Gluten-, sulfite- and tartrazine-free. Bottles of 100. Store between 15 and 30°C. Protect from light and moisture.

5 mg: Each white and caramel capsule, imprinted APO 5, contains: bromocriptine 5 mg (as mesylate). Nonmedicinal ingredients: cornstarch, gelatin, lactose, red iron oxide, silicon dioxide, sodium lauryl sulfate, stearic acid, talc, titanium dioxide and yellow iron oxide. Bottles of 100. Store between 15 and 30°C. Protect from light.

APO®-BUSPIRONE 🄿

Apotex

Buspirone HCl

Anxiolytic

Supplied: Each white, pillow-shaped, scored tablet, engraved "BU 10" on one side and "APO" on the other, contains: buspirone HCl 10 mg. Nonmedicinal ingredients: cellulose, croscarmellose sodium, lactose, magnesium stearate and silicon dioxide. Gluten-, sulfite- and tartrazine-free. Bottles of 100. Store at room temperature (15 to 30°C) in tight, light-resistant containers.

APO®-C

Apotex

Ascorbic Acid

Vitamin Supplement

Supplied: 100 mg: Each round, white, biconvex, scored tablet contains: ascorbic acid 100 mg. Nonmedicinal ingredients: magnesium stearate and microcrystalline cellulose. Energy: <1 kJ (0.03 kcal). Sodium: <1 mmol (0.04 mg). Gluten-, lactose-, sulfite- and tartrazine-free. Bottles of 100, 250 and 500.

250 mg: Each round, white, biconvex, scored tablet contains: ascorbic acid 250 mg. Nonmedicinal ingredients: croscarmellose sodium, magnesium stearate and microcrystalline cellulose. Energy: <1 kJ (0.06 kcal). Sodium: <1 mmol (0.09 mg). Gluten-, lactose-, sulfite- and tartrazine-free. Bottles of 100 and 500.

500 mg: Each round, white, biconvex, scored tablet contains: ascorbic acid 500 mg. Nonmedicinal ingredients: magnesium stearate and microcrystalline cellulose. Energy: <1 kJ (0.13 kcal). Sodium: <1 mmol (0.17 mg). Gluten-, lactose-, sulfite- and tartrazine-free. Bottles of 100 and 250.

1 000 mg: Each round, white, biconvex, scored tablet contains: ascorbic acid 1 000 mg. Nonmedicinal ingredients: magnesium stearate and microcrystalline cellulose. Energy: 1.07 kJ (0.26 kcal). Sodium: <1 mmol (0.35 mg). Gluten-, lactose-, sulfite- and tartrazine-free. Bottles of 100.

APO®-CAL

Apotex

Calcium Carbonate

Calcium Supplement

Supplied: 250 mg: Each round, light green, biconvex, film-coated tablet, identified APO over CAL, contains: calcium 250 mg as calcium carbonate. Nonmedicinal ingredients: brilliant blue (FD&C blue #1), carnauba wax, croscarmellose sodium, D&C yellow #10, hydroxypropyl methylcellulose, magnesium stearate, polydextrose, polyethylene glycol, sodium lauryl sulfate and titanium dioxide. Energy: <1 kJ (0.15 kcal). Sodium: <1 mmol (0.42 mg). Gluten-, lactose-, sulfite- and tartrazine-free. Bottles of 100 and 500.

500 mg: Each capsule-shaped, light green, biconvex, film-coated tablet, identified APO-CAL, contains: calcium 500 mg as calcium carbonate. Nonmedicinal ingredients: brilliant blue (FD&C blue #1), carnauba wax, croscarmellose sodium, D&C yellow #10, hydroxypropyl methylcellulose, magnesium stearate, polydextrose, polyethylene glycol, sodium lauryl sulfate and titanium dioxide. Energy: 1.23 kJ (0.29 kcal). Sodium: <1 mmol (0.84 mg). Gluten-, lactose-, sulfite- and tartrazine-free. Bottles of 100 and 500.

APO®-CAPTO 🄿

Apotex

Captopril

Angiotensin-Converting Enzyme Inhibitor

Supplied: 6.25 mg: Each round, white, flat-faced, beveled edge tablet, both sides plain, contains: captopril 6.25 mg. Nonmedicinal ingredients: colloidal silicon dioxide, croscarmellose sodium, lactose, magnesium stearate and microcrystalline cellulose. Energy: <1 kJ (0.07 kcal). Sodium: <1 mmol (0.02 mg). Gluten-, sulfite- and tartrazine-free. Bottles of 100.

12.5 mg: Each oblong, white, flat-faced, beveled edge tablet, partially bisected on both sides, one side identified APO, the other side identified 12.5, contains: captopril 12.5 mg. Nonmedicinal ingredients: colloidal silicon dioxide, croscarmellose sodium, lactose, magnesium stearate and microcrystalline cellulose. Energy: <1 kJ (0.14 kcal). Sodium: <1 mmol (0.03 mg). Gluten-, sulfite- and tartrazine-free. Bottles of 100 and 500.

25 mg: Each square, white, biconvex tablet, quadrisected on one side and identified APO over 25 on the other side, contains: captopril 25 mg. Nonmedicinal ingredients: colloidal silicon dioxide, croscarmellose sodium, lactose, magnesium stearate and microcrystalline cellulose. Energy: 1.16 kJ (0.28 kcal). Sodium: <1 mmol (0.06 mg). Gluten-, sulfite- and tartrazine-free. Bottles of 100 and 1 000.

50 mg: Each oval, white, biconvex tablet, partially bisected and identified APO-50 on one side, contains: captopril 50 mg. Nonmedicinal ingredients: colloidal silicon dioxide, croscarmellose sodium, lactose, magnesium stearate and microcrystalline cellulose. Energy: 2.32 kJ (0.56 kcal). Sodium: <1 mmol (0.13 mg). Gluten-, sulfite- and tartrazine-free. Bottles of 100 and 500.

100 mg: Each oval, white, biconvex tablet, partially bisected and identified APO-100 on one side, contains: captopril 100 mg. Nonmedicinal ingredients: colloidal silicon dioxide, croscarmellose sodium, lactose, magnesium stearate and microcrystalline cellulose. Energy: 4.65 kJ (1.11 kcal). Sodium: <1 mmol (0.25 mg). Gluten-, sulfite- and tartrazine-free. Bottles of 100.

Store at room temperature. Protect from moisture. Keep bottles tightly closed.

APO®-CARBAMAZEPINE 🄿

Apotex

Carbamazepine

Anticonvulsant—Trigeminal Neuralgia Therapy

Supplied: Each round, white, double-scored, flat-faced, beveled-edge tablet, identified APO over 200, contains: carbamazepine 200 mg. Nonmedicinal ingredients: colloidal silicon dioxide, croscarmellose sodium, magnesium stearate and microcrystalline cellulose. Energy: 1.47 kJ (0.35 kcal). Sodium: <1 mmol (0.25 mg). Gluten-, lactose-, sulfite- and tartrazine-free. Bottles of 100 and 500. Unit dose packages of 100. Apo Long-Term Care (LTC) Pak.

APO®-CEFACLOR 🄿

Apotex

Cefaclor

Antibiotic

Pharmacology: Like other β-lactam antibiotics, cefaclor owes its antibacterial activity to its ability to bind to and inhibit the action of certain bacterial cell wall synthetic enzymes, the penicillin-binding proteins.

Cefaclor is well absorbed after oral administration to fed and fasted subjects. Following doses of 250 mg, 500 mg, and 1 g to fasted subjects, average peak serum levels of approximately 7, 13 and 23 mg/L respectively were obtained within 0.5 to 1 hour. Total absorption is the same whether the drug is given before or after meals. However, when it is taken after food, the peak concentration achieved is 50 to 75% of that observed when the drug is administered to fasted subjects and is delayed by 0.8 to 1 hour. Approximately 25% of cefaclor is bound to human plasma.

Within 8 hours, 60 to 85% of the drug is excreted unchanged in the urine, the greater portion being excreted within the first 2 hours. During this 8-hour period, peak urine concentrations following the 250 mg, 500 mg and 1 g doses were approximately 600, 900 and 1 900 mg/L respectively.

The serum half-life in normal subjects is 0.6 to 0.9 hour. In patients with reduced renal function, the serum half-life of cefaclor is slightly prolonged. In those with complete absence of renal function, the plasma half-life of the intact molecule is 2.3 to 2.8 hours. Excretion pathways in patients with markedly impaired renal function have not been determined. Hemodialysis shortens the half-life by 25 to 30%.

Probenecid administered with a 500 mg dose of cefaclor increased the peak serum concentration only slightly, from 12.4 to 13.9 mg/L, and urine levels were predictably diminished. The mean half-life among 5 fasted volunteers with normal renal function was 0.8 hour, and probenecid significantly prolonged the half-life to a mean of 1.3 hours.

Indications: In the treatment of the following infections caused by S. pyogenes and S. pneumoniae, Staphylococci, including coagulase-positive, coagulase-negative and penicillinase-producing strains, E. coli, P. mirabilis, K. pneumoniae, H. influenzae, including ampicillin-resistant strains: otitis media; lower respiratory tract infections, including pneumonia, bronchitis, and pulmonary complications resulting from cystic fibrosis; upper respiratory tract infections, including pharyngitis and tonsillitis; skin and soft-tissue infections; urinary tract infections. Appropriate culture and susceptibility studies should be performed.

Contraindications: Persons who have shown hypersensitivity to the cephalosporin antibiotics.

Warnings: Before therapy with cefaclor is instituted, careful inquiry should be made concerning previous hypersensitivity reactions to cefaclor, cephalosporins, penicillins or other drugs. If these products are to be given to penicillin-sensitive patients, caution should be exercised because cross-hypersensitivity, including anaphylaxis, among β-lactam antibiotics has been clearly documented.

Antibiotics including cefaclor should be administered with caution, and then only when absolutely necessary, to any patient who has demonstrated some form of allergy, particularly to drugs.

As is the case with all new drugs, patients should be followed carefully so that adverse reactions or unusual manifestations of drug idiosyncrasy may be detected. If an allergic reaction to cefaclor occurs, the drug should be discontinued and the patient treated with the usual agents (e.g., epinephrine, antihistamines, pressor amines or corticosteroids).

Pseudomembranous colitis has been reported with virtually all broad-spectrum antibiotics, including cefaclor; therefore, it is important to consider its diagnosis in patients who develop diarrhea in association with the use of antibiotics. Such colitis may range in severity from mild to life-threatening. Treatment with broad-spectrum antibiotics alters the normal flora of the colon and may permit overgrowth of clostridia. Studies indicate that a toxin produced by C. difficile is one primary cause of antibiotic-associated colitis. Mild cases of pseudomembranous colitis usually respond to drug discontinuance alone. In moderate to severe cases, management should include sigmoidoscopy, appropriate bacteriologic studies, and fluid, electrolyte and protein supplementation. When the colitis does not improve after the drug has been discontinued, or when it is severe, oral vancomycin is the drug of choice for antibiotic-associated pseudomembranous colitis produced by C.difficile. Other causes of colitis should be ruled out.

Precautions: If an allergic reaction to cefaclor occurs, the drug should be discontinued and the patient treated appropriately.

Pregnancy: The safety of cefaclor in the treatment of infections during pregnancy has not been established. Reproduction studies in rats have revealed no evidence of impaired fertility.

Lactation: Small amounts of cefaclor, up to 0.21 mg/L, have been detected in mother's milk following administration of single 500 mg doses. The effect on nursing infants is not known. Caution should be exercised when cefaclor is administered to a nursing woman.

Prolonged use of cefaclor may result in the overgrowth of nonsusceptible organisms. Careful observation of the patient is essential. If superinfection occurs during therapy, administration of cefaclor should cease and appropriate measures should be taken.

Positive direct Coombs' tests have been reported during treatment with cephalosporin antibiotics. In hematologic studies or in transfusion cross-matching procedures, when antiglobulin tests are performed on the minor side or in Coombs' testing of newborns whose mothers have received cephalosporin antibiotics before parturition, it should be recognized that a positive Coombs' test may be due to the drug.

Cefaclor should be administered with caution in the presence of markedly impaired renal function. Since the half-life of cefaclor in anuria is 2.3 to 2.8 hours, dosage adjustments for patients with moderate or severe renal impairment are not usually required. Clinical experience with cefaclor under such conditions is limited; therefore, careful clinical observation and laboratory studies should be made.

In patients treated with cefaclor, a false-positive reaction for glucose in the urine may occur with Benedict's or Fehling's solution or with Clinitest tablets but not with Tes-Tape.

There have been rare reports of increased prothrombin time with or without clinical bleeding in patients receiving cefaclor and warfarin concomitantly.

As with many other β-lactam antibiotics, the renal excretion of cefaclor is inhibited by probenecid.

Adverse Effects: During clinical trials in 8 346 patients (4 626 adults and 3 720 children under the age of 16) treated with cefaclor, the adverse reactions listed below were observed. The majority of these adverse reactions were mild and transient. The incidence rates were less than 1 in 100 (less than 1%), except as otherwise noted.

Gastrointestinal: The most frequent side effect has been diarrhea ($\leq$1.5%). It was rarely severe enough to warrant cessation of therapy. Nausea, vomiting and dyspepsia have been reported. As with some penicillins and some other cephalosporins, transient hepatitis and cholestatic jaundice have been reported. Colitis, including rare instances of pseudomembranous colitis, has been reported in conjunction with or after therapy with cefaclor has stopped.

Hypersensitivity: Allergic reactions, such as urticaria and morbilliform eruptions (1%), have been observed, as have pruritus and positive Coombs' tests. These reactions usually subsided upon discontinuation of the drug. Eosinophilia (2%), genital pruritus or vaginitis, and rarely, thrombocytopenia or reversible interstitial nephritis have also occurred.

Cases of serum sickness-like reactions have been reported. In contrast to classic serum sickness, signs and symptoms of serum sickness-like reactions involving cefaclor appear to be primarily confined to findings including erythema multiforme or other skin manifestations accompanied by arthritis/arthralgia, with or without fever. Serum sickness-like reactions are apparently due to hypersensitivity and more often occur during or following a second (or subsequent) course of therapy with cefaclor. Such reactions have been reported more frequently in children than in adults with an overall occurrence ranging from 1 in 200 (0.5%) in one focused trial to 2 in 8 346 (0.024%) in overall clinical trials (with an incidence in children in clinical trials of 0.055%) to 1 in 38 000 (0.003%) in spontaneous event reports. Signs and symptoms usually occur a few days after initiation of therapy and subside within a few days after cessation of therapy; occasionally these reactions have resulted in hospitalization, usually of short duration (median hospitalization = 2 to 3 days, based on postmarketing surveillance studies). In those requiring hospitalization, the symptoms have ranged from mild to severe at the time of admission with more of the severe reactions occuring in children. Antihistamines and glucocorticoids appear to enhance resolution of the signs and symptoms. No serious sequelae have been reported.

More severe hypersensitivity reactions, including Stevens-Johnson syndrome, toxic epidermal necrolysis and anaphylaxis have been reported rarely. Anaphylaxis may be more common in patients with a history of penicillin allergy.

CNS: Rarely, reversible hyperactivity, nervousness, insomnia, confusion, hypertonia, headache, dizziness or somnolence have been reported.

Genitourinary: Vaginal moniliasis and vaginitis have been reported.

Other: Transitory abnormalities in clinical laboratory test results have been reported. Although they were of uncertain etiology, they are listed here to serve as alerting information for the physician.

Hepatic: Slight elevations of AST, ALT or alkaline phosphatase values have been reported.

Hematopoietic: Transient lymphocytosis, leukopenia, eosinophilia and, rarely, hemolytic anemia, aplastic anemia, agranulocytosis and reversible neutropenia of possible clinical significance were observed.

There have been rare reports of increased prothrombin time with or without clinical bleeding in patients receiving cefaclor and warfarin concomitantly.

Renal: Slight and transient evelations in BUN or serum creatinine or abnormal urinalysis have been observed with cefaclor.

In addition to the adverse reactions listed above, renal dysfunction and toxic nephropathy have been reported in patients treated with β-lactam antibiotics.

Several β-lactam antibiotics have been implicated in triggering seizures, particularly in patients with renal impairment when the dosage was not reduced. If seizures associated with drug therapy should occur, the drug should be discontinued. Anticonvulsant therapy can be given if clinically indicated.

Overdose: Symptoms: The toxic symptoms following an overdose of cefaclor may include nausea, vomiting, epigastric distress and diarrhea. The severity of the epigastric distress and the diarrhea are dose related. If other symptoms are present, it is probable that they are secondary to an underlying disease state, an allergic reaction, or the effects of other intoxication.

Treatment: In managing overdosage, consider the possibility of multiple drug overdoses, interaction among drugs, and unusual drug kinetics in your patient. Unless 5 times the normal dose of cefaclor has been ingested, gastrointestinal decontamination will not be necessary.

Protect the patient's airway and support ventilation and perfusion. Meticulously monitor and maintain, within acceptable limits, the patient's vital signs, blood gases, serum electrolytes, etc. Absorption of drugs from the gastrointestinal tract may be decreased by giving activated charcoal, which, in many cases, is more effective than emesis or lavage; consider charcoal instead of or in addition to gastric emptying. Repeated doses of charcoal over time may hasten elimination of some drugs that have been absorbed. Safeguard the patient's airway when employing gastric emptying or charcoal.

Forced diuresis, peritoneal dialysis, hemodialysis or charcoal hemoperfusion have not been established as beneficial for an overdose of cefaclor.

Dosage: Cefaclor is administered orally, without regard to meals.

Adults: The usual adult dosage is 250 mg every 8 to 12 hours. For more severe infections or those caused by less susceptible organisms, larger doses may be needed. The maximum recommended dosage is 2 g/day, although doses of 4 g/day have been administered safely for 28 days.

For lower respiratory tract infections, the dosage should be administered 3 times daily.

For skin and soft-tissue infections, the dosage is 250 mg administered 2 or 3 times daily.

Children: The usual recommended daily dosage for children is 20 mg/kg/day in divided doses every 8 to 12 hours. For streptococcal pharyngitis or tonsillitis and soft-tissue infections, the total daily dosage may be divided and administered every 12 hours.

In more serious infections, otitis media and those infections caused by less susceptible organisms, 40 mg/kg/day is recommended, up to 1 g/day.

For otitis media, the total daily dosage may be divided and administered every 12 hours. For lower respiratory tract infections, the total daily dosage should be divided and administered 3 times daily.

In the treatment of beta-hemolytic streptococcal infections, a therapeutic dosage of cefaclor should be administered for at least 10 days.

Most clinical studies were performed with a duration of therapy between 5 and 14 days.

Supplied: Capsules: 250 mg: Each opaque purple and white, size #2 capsule, imprinted "APO 250", contains: cefaclor 250 mg. Nonmedicinal ingredients: colloidal silicon dioxide, croscarmellose sodium and stearic acid; capsule shell: D&C Red #28, FD&C Blue #1, FD&C Yellow #6, gelatin, silicon dioxide, sodium lauryl sulfate and titanium dioxide; edible black ink (on the capsule shell): n-butyl alcohol, ammonium hydroxide, black iron oxide, D&C Yellow #10, ethyl alcohol, FD&C Blue #1, FD&C Blue #2, FD&C Red #40, isopropyl alcohol, propylene glycol and shellac. Bottles of 100 and 500. Store at room temperature 15 to 30°C. Keep tightly closed.

500 mg: Each opaque purple and grey, size #0 capsule, imprinted "APO 500", contains: cefaclor 500 mg. Nonmedicinal ingredients: colloidal silicon dioxide, croscarmellose sodium and stearic acid; capsule shell: D&C Red #28, FD&C Blue #1, FD&C Yellow #6, gelatin, red and yellow iron oxide, Sicomet black oxide, silicon dioxide, sodium lauryl sulfate and titanium dioxide; edible black ink (on the capsule shell): n-butyl alcohol, ammonium hydroxide, black iron oxide, D&C Yellow #10, ethyl alcohol, FD&C Blue #1, FD&C Blue #2, FD&C Red #40, isopropyl alcohol, propylene glycol and shellac. Bottles of 100. Store at room temperature 15 to 30°C. Keep tightly closed.

Suspension: 125 mg/5 mL: Each mL of strawberry-flavored suspension contains: cefaclor 25 mg. Nonmedicinal ingredients: artificial strawberry flavoring, carboxymethylcellulose sodium, citric acid, colloidal silicon dioxide, FD&C Red #40, maltodextrin, polydimethylsiloxane, silica, sodium lauryl sulfate, sucrose and xanthan gum. Bottles of 100 and 150 mL. Reconstitute by adding 78 mL to each 100 mL bottle or 117 mL to each 150 mL bottle. Store powder for oral suspension at room temperature 15 to 30°C. After reconstitution, oral suspension must be refrigerated and used within 14 days. Shake well before using. Keep tightly closed.

250 mg/5 mL: Each mL of strawberry-flavored suspension contains: cefaclor 50 mg. Nonmedicinal ingredients: artificial strawberry flavoring, carboxymethylcellulose sodium, citric acid, colloidal silicon dioxide, FD&C Red #40, maltodextrin, polydimethylsiloxane, silica, sodium lauryl sulfate, sucrose and xanthan gum. Bottles of 100 and 150 mL. Reconstitute by adding 76 mL to each 100 mL bottle or 114 mL to each 150 mL bottle. Store powder for oral suspension at room temperature 15 to 30°C. After reconstitution, oral suspension must be refrigerated and used within 14 days. Shake well before using. Keep tightly closed.

375 mg/5 mL: Each mL of strawberry-flavored suspension contains: cefaclor 75 mg. Nonmedicinal ingredients: artificial strawberry flavoring, carboxymethylcellulose sodium, citric acid, colloidal silicon dioxide, FD&C Red #40, maltodextrin, polydimethylsiloxane, silica, sodium lauryl sulfate, sucrose and xanthan gum. Bottles of 70 and 100 mL. Reconstitute by adding 53 mL to each 70 mL bottle or 75 mL to each 100 mL bottle. Store powder for oral suspension at room temperature 15 to 30°C. After reconstitution, oral suspension must be refrigerated and used within 14 days. Shake well before using. Keep tightly closed.

Reviewed 1999

APO®-CEPHALEX ℞

Apotex

Cephalexin

Antibiotic

Supplied: 250 mg: Each capsule-shaped, orange, film-coated tablet, identified APO-250, contains: cephalexin 250 mg. Nonmedicinal ingredients: carnauba wax, colloidal silicon dioxide, hydroxypropyl methylcellulose, magnesium stearate, microcrystalline cellulose, polyethylene glycol, stearic acid, sunset yellow lake 16%, sunset yellow lake 40% and titanium dioxide. Energy: 2.14 kJ (0.51 kcal). Gluten-, lactose-, sodium-, sulfite- and tartrazine-free. Bottles of 100 and 1 000.

500 mg: Each capsule-shaped, orange, film-coated tablet, scored and identified APO 500, contains: cephalexin 500 mg. Nonmedicinal ingredients: carnauba wax, colloidal silicon

Apo-Cephalex (cont'd)

dioxide, hydroxypropyl methylcellulose, magnesium stearate, microcrystalline cellulose, polyethylene glycol, stearic acid, sunset yellow lake 16%, sunset yellow lake 40% and titanium dioxide. Energy: 4.18 kJ (1.02 kcal). Gluten-, lactose-, sodium-, sulfite- and tartrazine-free. Bottles of 100 and 500.

APO®-CHLORAX ℞
Apotex

Chlordiazepoxide HCl—Clidinium Bromide
Anticholinergic—Anxiolytic

Supplied: Each green No. 4 capsule contains: chlordiazepoxide HCl 5 mg and clidinium bromide 2.5 mg. Nonmedicinal ingredients: lactose, microcrystalline cellulose and stearic acid. Energy: 2.83 kJ (0.68 kcal). Gluten-, sodium- and tartrazine-free. Bottles of 100 and 500.

APO®-CHLORDIAZEPOXIDE ℞
Apotex

Chlordiazepoxide HCl
Anxiolytic

Supplied: 5 mg: Each yellow and green, no. 4 capsule, identified APO 5, contains: chlordiazepoxide HCl 5 mg. Nonmedicinal ingredients: cornstarch, lactose and stearic acid. Energy: 2.82 kJ (0.67 kcal). Gluten-, sodium- and tartrazine-free. Bottles of 100 and 500.

10 mg: Each green and black, no. 4 capsule, identified APO 10, contains: chlordiazepoxide HCl 10 mg. Nonmedicinal ingredients: cornstarch, lactose, stearic acid and talc. Energy: 2.74 kJ (0.65 kcal). Gluten-, sodium- and tartrazine-free. Bottles of 100 and 1 000.

25 mg: Each white and green, no. 4 capsule, identified APO 25, contains: chlordiazepoxide HCl 25 mg. Nonmedicinal ingredients: cornstarch, lactose, stearic acid and talc. Energy: 2.52 kJ (0.60 kcal). Gluten-, sodium- and tartrazine-free. Bottles of 100 and 500.

APO®-CHLORPROPAMIDE ℞
Apotex

Chlorpropamide
Oral Hypoglycemic

Supplied: 100 mg: Each white, round, flat-faced with beveled edge, scored tablet, identified APO over 100, contains: chlorpropamide 100 mg. Nonmedicinal ingredients: calcium hydroxide, colloidal silicon dioxide, croscarmellose sodium, magnesium stearate and microcrystalline cellulose. Energy: 1.46 kJ (0.35 kcal). Sodium: <1 mmol (0.22 mg). Gluten-, lactose-, sulfite- and tartrazine-free. Bottles of 100 and 500.

250 mg: Each white, oval, biconvex, scored tablet, identified APO 250, contains: chlorpropamide 250 mg. Nonmedicinal ingredients: calcium hydroxide, colloidal silicon dioxide, croscarmellose sodium, magnesium stearate and microcrystalline cellulose. Energy: 3.66 kJ (0.87 kcal). Sodium: <1 mmol (0.54 mg). Gluten-, lactose-, sulfite- and tartrazine-free. Bottles of 100 and 1 000. Unit dose packages of 100. Apo Long-Term Care (LTC) Pak.

APO®-CHLORTHALIDONE ℞
Apotex

Chlorthalidone
Diuretic—Antihypertensive

Supplied: 50 mg: Each yellow, round, flat-faced with beveled edge, scored tablet, identified APO over 50, contains: chlorthalidone 50 mg. Nonmedicinal ingredients: colloidal silicon dioxide, D&C yellow #10 aluminum lake, magnesium stearate, microcrystalline cellulose and sunset yellow aluminum lake 40. Energy: 1.22 kJ (0.29 kcal). Gluten-, lactose-, sodium-, sulfite- and tartrazine-free. Bottles of 100 and 1 000.

100 mg: Each white, round, flat-faced with beveled edge, scored tablet, identified APO over 100, contains: chlorthalidone 100 mg. Nonmedicinal ingredients: colloidal silicon dioxide and magnesium stearate and microcrystalline cellulose. Energy: <1 kJ (0.13 kcal). Gluten-, lactose-, sodium-, sulfite- and tartrazine-free. Bottles of 100 and 500.

APO®-CIMETIDINE ℞
Apotex

Cimetidine
Histamine H_2-Receptor Antagonist

Supplied: 200 mg: Each round, pale green, biconvex, film-coated tablet, identified APO over 200, contains: cimetidine 200 mg. Nonmedicinal ingredients: colloidal silicon dioxide, croscarmellose sodium, D&C yellow #10 lake 16%, ferric ferrous oxide, hydroxypropyl methylcellulose, magnesium stearate, microcrystalline cellulose, polyethylene glycol and titanium dioxide. Energy: 3.11 kJ (0.74 kcal). Sodium: <1 mmol (0.11 mg). Gluten-, lactose-, sulfite- and tartrazine-free. Bottles of 100 and 500. Apo Long-Term Care (LTC) Pak.

300 mg: Each round, pale green, biconvex, film-coated tablet, identified APO over 300, contains: cimetidine 300 mg. Nonmedicinal ingredients: colloidal silicon dioxide, croscarmellose sodium, D&C yellow #10 lake 16%, ferric ferrous oxide, hydroxypropyl methylcellulose, magnesium stearate, microcrystalline cellulose, polyethylene glycol and titanium dioxide. Energy: 3.59 kJ (0.86 kcal). Sodium: <1 mmol (0.17 mg). Gluten-, lactose-, sulfite- and tartrazine-free. Bottles of 100 and 1 000. Unit dose packages of 100. Apo Long-Term Care (LTC) Pak.

400 mg: Each oblong, pale green, biconvex, film-coated tablet, identified APO-400, contains: cimetidine 400 mg. Nonmedicinal ingredients: colloidal silicon dioxide, croscarmellose sodium, D&C yellow #10 lake 16%, ferric ferrous oxide, hydroxypropyl methylcellulose, magnesium stearate, microcrystalline cellulose, polyethylene glycol and titanium dioxide. Energy: 4.26 kJ (1.02 kcal). Sodium: <1 mmol (0.23 mg). Gluten-, lactose-, sulfite- and tartrazine-free. Bottles of 100 and 500. Unit dose packages of 100. Apo Long-Term Care (LTC) Pak.

600 mg: Each oblong, pale green, biconvex, film-coated tablet, identified APO-600, contains: cimetidine 600 mg. Nonmedicinal ingredients: colloidal silicon dioxide, croscarmellose sodium, D&C yellow #10 lake 16%, ferric ferrous oxide, hydroxypropyl methylcellulose, magnesium stearate, microcrystalline cellulose, polyethylene glycol and titanium dioxide. Energy: 5.85 kJ (1.40 kcal). Sodium: <1 mmol (0.34 mg). Gluten-, lactose-, sulfite- and tartrazine-free. Bottles of 100 and 500. Unit dose packages of 100. Apo Long-Term Care (LTC) Pak.

800 mg: Each oblong, pale green, biconvex, film-coated tablet, identified APO-800, contains: cimetidine 800 mg. Nonmedicinal ingredients: colloidal silicon dioxide, croscarmellose sodium, D&C yellow #10 lake 16%, ferric ferrous oxide, hydroxypropyl methylcellulose, magnesium stearate, microcrystalline cellulose, polyethylene glycol and titanium dioxide. Energy: 7.55 kJ (1.80 kcal). Sodium: <1 mmol (0.46 mg). Gluten-, lactose-, sulfite- and tartrazine-free. Bottles of 100 and 500.

APO®-CLOMIPRAMINE ℞
Apotex

Clomipramine HCl
Antidepressant—Antiobsessional

Supplied: 10 mg: Each triangular, pale yellow, biconvex, film-coated tablet, engraved "10" on one side, contains: clomipramine HCl 10 mg. Nonmedicinal ingredients: carnauba wax, colloidal silicon dioxide, hydroxypropyl methylcellulose, lactose, magnesium stearate, microcrystalline cellulose, polyethylene glycol, titanium dioxide and yellow ferric oxide. Energy: <1 kJ (0.08 kcal). Gluten-, sodium-, sulfite- and tartrazine-free. Bottles of 100 and 500.

25 mg: Each round, pale yellow, biconvex, film-coated tablet, engraved "25" on one side, contains: clomipramine HCl 25 mg. Nonmedicinal ingredients: carnauba wax, colloidal silicon dioxide, hydroxypropyl methylcellulose, lactose, magnesium stearate, microcrystalline cellulose, polyethylene glycol, titanium dioxide and yellow ferric oxide. Energy: <1 kJ (0.20 kcal). Gluten-, sodium-, sulfite- and tartrazine-free. Bottles of 100 and 500.

50 mg: Each white, round, biconvex, film-coated tablet, engraved "APO" over "50" on one side, contains: clomipramine HCl 50 mg. Nonmedicinal ingredients: carnauba wax, colloidal silicon dioxide, hydroxypropyl methylcellulose, lactose, magnesium stearate, microcrystalline cellulose, polyethylene glycol and titanium dioxide. Energy: 1.71 kJ (0.41 kcal). Gluten-, sodium-, sulfite- and tartrazine-free. Bottles of 100 and 500.

Store between 15 and 25°C. Protect from heat and moisture.

APO®-CLONAZEPAM ℞
Apotex

Clonazepam
Anticonvulsant

Supplied: 0.5 mg: Each round, orange, flat-faced, beveled-edge tablet, scored and engraved APO over C-0.5 on one side, other side plain, contains: clonazepam 0.5 mg. Nonmedicinal ingredients: croscarmellose sodium, D&C yellow #10 aluminum lake, lactose, magnesium stearate, microcrystalline cellulose, polyethylene glycol and sunset yellow aluminum lake 40. Gluten-, sulfite- and tartrazine-free. Bottles of 100 and 500.

2 mg: Each round, white, flat-faced, beveled-edge tablet, scored and engraved APO over C-2 on one side, other side plain, contains: clonazepam 2 mg. Nonmedicinal ingredients: croscarmellose sodium, D&C yellow #10 aluminum lake, lactose, magnesium stearate, microcrystalline cellulose, polyethylene glycol and sunset yellow aluminum lake 40. Gluten-, sulfite- and tartrazine-free. Bottles of 100 and 500.

Store at controlled room temperature (15 to 30°C), in tightly-closed, light-resistant containers.

APO®-CLONIDINE ℞
Apotex

Clonidine HCl
Antihypertensive Agent

Supplied: 0.1 mg: Each white, round, flat-faced with beveled edge tablet, scored and identified APO over 0.1 on one side, contains: clonidine HCl 0.1 mg. Nonmedicinal ingredients: cornstarch, lactose, magnesium stearate and microcrystalline cellulose. Energy: 2.46 kJ (0.59 kcal). Gluten-, sodium-, sulfite- and tartrazine-free. Bottles of 100 and 500.

0.2 mg: Each orange, round, flat-faced with beveled edge tablet, scored and identified APO over 0.2 on one side, contains: clonidine HCl 0.2 mg. Nonmedicinal ingredients: cornstarch, lactose, magnesium stearate, microcrystalline cellulose and sunset yellow aluminum lake 40. Energy: 4.90 kJ (1.17 kcal). Gluten-, sodium-, sulfite- and tartrazine-free. Bottles of 100 and 500.

APO®-CLORAZEPATE ℞
Apotex

Clorazepate Dipotassium
Anxiolytic—Sedative

Supplied: 3.75 mg: Each no. 4 capsule, gray body with white cap, identified APO 3.75, contains: clorazepate dipotassium 3.75 mg. Nonmedicinal ingredients: cornstarch, lactose and stearic acid. Energy: 1.63 kJ (0.39 kcal). Gluten-, sodium- and tartrazine-free. Bottles of 100 and 500.

7.5 mg: Each no. 4 capsule, gray body with maroon cap, identified APO 7.5, contains: clorazepate dipotassium 7.5 mg. Nonmedicinal ingredients: cornstarch, lactose and stearic acid. Energy: 2.70 kJ (0.64 kcal). Gluten-, sodium- and tartrazine-free. Bottles of 100 and 500.

15 mg: Each no 3. capsule, gray body with gray cap, identified APO 15, contains: clorazepate dipotassium 15 mg. Nonmedicinal ingredients: cornstarch, lactose and stearic acid. Energy: 4.95 kJ (1.18 kcal). Gluten-, sodium- and tartrazine-free. Bottles of 100.

APO®-CLOXI ℞
Apotex

Cloxacillin Sodium
Antibiotic

Supplied: Capsules: 250 mg: Each orange and black No. 2 capsule, identified APO 250, contains: cloxacillin sodium equivalent to cloxacillin 250 mg. Nonmedicinal ingredients: colloidal silicon dioxide, stearic acid and talc. Energy: <1 kJ (0.21 kcal). Sodium: <1 mmol (≤13.88 mg). Gluten-, lactose- and tartrazine-free. Bottles of 100 and 1 000.

500 mg: Each orange and black No. 0 capsule, identified APO 500, contains: cloxacillin sodium equivalent to cloxacillin 500 mg. Nonmedicinal ingredients: amaranth, colloidal silicon dioxide, D&C yellow #10, FD&C blue #1, FD&C yellow #6, stearic acid, talc and titanium dioxide. Energy: 1.37 kJ (0.33 kcal). Sodium: ≤1.20 mmol (≤27.76 mg). Gluten-, lactose- and tartrazine-free. Bottles of 100 and 500.

Oral Solution: After reconstitution each 5 mL cherry flavored suspension contains: cloxacillin sodium equivalent to cloxacillin 125 mg. Nonmedicinal ingredients: artificial flavoring, FD&C red #40, sodium benzoate, sodium citrate, sodium cyclamate and sucrose. Energy: ≤37.45 kJ (≤8.94 kcal)/5 mL. Sodium: <1 mmol (≤14.08 mg)/5 mL. Alcohol-, gluten-, lactose-, sulfite- and tartrazine-free. Bottles of 60, 100 and 200 mL.

APO®-CROMOLYN ℞
Apotex

Sodium Cromoglycate
Seasonal Rhinitis Prophylaxis

Pharmacology: In the immediate allergic reaction (Type I) the union of antigen with reaginic antibody leads to the formation and release of spasmogens and other mediators of the anaphylactic reaction. Sodium cromoglycate appears to block a step in the chain of events triggered by this union. This property accounts for the prophylactic rather than symptomatic approach to the management of seasonal rhinitis.

Sodium cromoglycate has no antihistaminic, anti-inflammatory or decongestant activity.

Indications: For the prophylaxis of seasonal rhinitis.

Contraindications: Hypersensitivity to any of the components of the product.

Warnings: The number of sprays to be administered per day should be specified to the patient. Regular dosage is important—treatment must not be discontinued abruptly, especially when benefit has been obtained.

Patients with nasal polyps should not use this product except on advice of a doctor. If you do not obtain relief of your symptoms within 7 days consult a doctor.

Precautions: The experience in patients with nasal polyps is limited and therefore these patients should be carefully observed while undergoing treatment.

Possible immunologic changes resulting in reactions such as polymyositis, pneumonitis and heart failure, urticaria and anaphylaxis, have been reported.

Children: Clinical experience in children under 5 years of age is limited.

Pregnancy: During clinical use there have been, to date, no reports of adverse effects on the mother or the fetus which could be ascribed to the use of sodium cromoglycate. Nevertheless, as with all medications, caution must be exercised during pregnancy.

Adverse Effects: Occasionally, slight irritation of the nasal mucosa may occur. Cases of erythema, urticaria or maculopapular rash have been reported and these have cleared within a few days on withdrawal of the drug. Occasional headache, sneezing, cough and unpleasant taste in the mouth have been reported. Eosinophilic pneumonia has been reported rarely.

Overdose: Symptoms and Treatment: There have been no reported cases in humans of overdosage of the drug. Symptomatic treatment is suggested should overdosage occur.

Dosage: It is recommended that treatment be instituted prior to the time at which the seasonal symptoms normally occur, and continued through the season. This medication is a preventative measure, not a treatment.

Adults and Children over 5 Years of Age: One mist into each nostril 6 times daily. One mist delivers approximately 0.13 mL (2.6 mg) of sodium cromoglycate 2% solution.

Maintenance Therapy: When adequate response has been obtained, the frequency of inhalations may be reduced to one spray to each nostril every 8 to 12 hours.

Concomitant Therapy: Other rhinitis therapy should be used as required.

Withdrawal of Therapy: **Patients should be warned against suddenly discontinuing therapy when symptoms have been partially or completely controlled by sodium cromoglycate.**

As the action of sodium cromoglycate is essentially preventative, continuity of therapy is important in patients who have gained benefit.

If for any reason sodium cromoglycate is withdrawn, a suggested regimen for withdrawal is to reduce the dosage gradually over a period of 1 week. It should be borne in mind that symptoms of rhinitis may recur when sodium cromoglycate is discontinued.

Supplied: Each mL of clear, colorless to slightly yellowish solution, contains: sodium cromoglycate 2% w/v. Nonmedicinal ingredients: benzalkonium chloride, edetate disodium, purified water and sodium hydroxide. High density polyethylene bottle containing not less than 26 mL (or not less than 13 mL) of solution; with a pump attached to the bottle. The pump delivers approximately 2.6 mg of sodium cromoglycate (0.13 mL of the 2% w/v solution) per mist. Store at controlled room temperature (20 to 25°C). Preserve in tight, light-resistant containers.

New Product 1998

APO®-CROMOLYN STERULES ℞
Apotex

Cromolyn Sodium
Asthma Prophylaxis

Pharmacology: In vitro and in vivo animal studies have shown that cromolyn sodium inhibits sensitized mast cell degranulation which occurs after exposure to specific antigens. It acts by inhibiting the release of mediators from mast cells. Studies show that cromolyn sodium indirectly blocks calcium ions from entering the mast cell, thereby preventing mediator release.

Cromolyn sodium inhibits both the immediate and nonimmediate bronchoconstrictive reactions to inhaled allergens. Cromolyn sodium also attenuates bronchospasm caused by exercise, toluene diisocyanate, ASA, cold air, sulfur dioxide and environmental pollutants in some patients.

Cromolyn sodium has no intrinsic bronchodilator, antihistaminic, or anti-inflammatory activity.

Indications: As an adjunct in the management of intrinsic and extrinsic asthma. It is used on a continuous basis to prevent symptoms associated with asthma.

Also indicated for use in the prevention of bronchospasm induced by known precipitating factors such as exercise, cold air, allergens and environmental pollutants.

Contraindications: Hypersensitivity to components of this product.

Warnings: Cromolyn sodium has no role in the treatment of an acute attack of asthma, especially status asthmaticus.

Severe anaphylactic reactions can occur after cromolyn sodium administration. The recommended dosage should be decreased in patients with decreased renal or hepatic function. Cromolyn sodium should be discontinued if the patient develops eosinophilic pneumonia (or pulmonary infiltrates with eosinophilia).

The number of cromolyn sodium sterules to be inhaled per day should be specified to the patient. **Regular dosage is important and treatment must not be discontinued abruptly, especially when benefit has been obtained. If troublesome symptoms occur,** particularly breathlessness at rest, no benefit is likely to be obtained by increasing the dosage above 8 sterules a day and the **patient should be advised to consult a physician immediately,** so that additional measures can be instituted if necessary.

Precautions: Mild throat irritation, coughing and transient bronchospasm may occur. Very rarely, severe bronchospasm associated with a marked fall in pulmonary function has been reported. In such cases, treatment should be stopped and should not be reintroduced.

Possible immunologic changes resulting in reactions such as polymyositis, pneumonitis and heart failure, urticaria and anaphylaxis have been reported.

Pregnancy: There are no adequate and well controlled studies in pregnant women. However, during clinical use there have been, to date, no reports of adverse effects on the fetus which could be ascribed to the use of cromolyn sodium. Nevertheless as with all medications, caution must be exercised during pregnancy.

Lactation: It is not known whether this drug is excreted in human milk; therefore, caution should be exercised when cromolyn sodium is administered to a nursing woman, and the attending physician must make a benefit/risk assessment in regard to its use in this situation.

Adverse Effects: In controlled clinical studies, the most frequently reported adverse reactions attributed to cromolyn sodium treatment were: throat irritation or dryness, bad taste, cough, wheeze and nausea.

Bronchospasm [sometimes severe, associated with precipitous fall in pulmonary function (FEV_1)], laryngeal edema (rare), nasal congestion (sometimes severe) and pharyngeal irritation have been reported.

Adverse reactions which occur infrequently and are associated with administration of the drug are: anaphylaxis, angioedema, dizziness, dysuria and urinary frequency, joint swelling and pain, lacrimation, headache, rash, swollen parotid gland, urticaria, pulmonary infiltrates with eosinophilia, substernal burning and myopathy.

The following adverse reactions have been reported as rare events and it is unclear whether they are attributable to the drug: anemia, exfoliative dermatitis, hemoptysis, hoarseness, myalgia, nephrosis, periarteritic vasculitis, pericarditis, peripheral neuritis, photodermatitis, sneezing, drowsiness, nasal itching, nasal bleeding, nasal burning, serum sickness, stomach ache, polymyositis, vertigo and liver disease.

Overdose: Symptoms and Treatment: There have been no reported cases in humans of overdosage of the drug. Symptomatic treatment is suggested should overdosage occur.

Dosage: Cromolyn sodium in a plastic sterule contains 2 mL of a sterile 1% cromolyn sodium USP solution in water (20 mg cromolyn sodium in 2 mL water). It is recommended for use in a power operated nebulizer operated at an air flow rate of 6 to 8 L per minute and equipped with a suitable face mask.

The sterules are an alternative presentation of cromolyn sodium for those patients (including young children) who are unable to inhale the drug in powder form.

Adults and Children: The sterules are used on a continuous basis to prevent the symptoms of asthma and have no role in the treatment of acute attacks.

Initial Treatment: 1 sterule 4 times daily at 4 to 6 hourly intervals. In more severe cases, or during periods of high antigen challenge, the interval between doses may be reduced to 3 hours (i.e., up to 8 sterules daily may be taken).

For protection against bronchospasm induced by exercise, cromolyn sodium should be used 15 to 30 minutes beforehand.

Maintenance Therapy: When adequate response has been obtained, the frequency of inhalations may be reduced to 1 sterule every 8 to 12 hours (i.e., 2 or 3 sterules per day). If chest symptoms are troublesome at night, it is important that the final dose be taken, if awakened during the night.

Patients should be warned against suddenly discontinuing therapy when symptoms have been partially or completely controlled by the sterules.

Concomitant Therapy: Other asthma therapy should be continued until clinical improvement permits a progressive reduction in dosage. However, cromolyn sodium therapy alone may prevent symptoms of mild to moderate asthma, especially in children and young adults.

In severe asthma, particularly in older patients, cromolyn sodium therapy alone is insufficient to prevent symptoms. In a proportion of such cases, significant improvement can be obtained by combining cromolyn sodium with corticosteroid therapy even when inadequate relief is obtained from either drug alone.

In steroid-dependent patients, the addition of cromolyn sodium to the regimen may permit a slow, progressive and significant reduction in the maintenance dose of steroids.

Reduction or Withdrawal of Corticosteroids: The dangers of sudden withdrawal of corticosteroids are well recognized, particularly in steroid treated patients who have received long-term administration of oral steroids or injections of adrenocorticotrophic hormone (ACTH).

When the physician attempts to reduce the corticosteroid dosage, it is important that the reduction should be gradual and that close surveillance and frequent examination of the patient is maintained. It should be remembered that the adrenal cortex is suppressed by the administration of oral steroids, and that in both oral steroid and ACTH therapy, the ability of the patient to react to stress is usually impaired. In such patients, acute renal insufficiency and severe asthma can be precipitated by an increase in stress and/or reduction or withdrawal of either steroid or ACTH therapy. In order to

Apo-Cromolyn Sterules (cont'd)

identify such a risk in patients who have received long-term steroid therapy and where substantial reduction or complete withdrawal of corticosteroids is contemplated, it is advisable to assess adrenal and pituitary function.

Method of Reducing Steroid Dosage: The reduction in the daily maintenance dose of steroids should be stepwise at a suggested rate equivalent to about 1% per day (e.g., a maintenance dose of 10 mg prednisolone per day is reduced to 9 mg/day after 1 week). The gradual reduction should be continued until either the patient cannot tolerate a further reduction or it is found possible to withdraw corticosteroids completely.

Note: If troublesome symptoms recur during the period of reduction, the daily dose should be raised immediately. A larger increase in the steroid dose may be essential at times as a temporary measure, to control a severe relapse induced by antigen challenge, infections or stress. The **increased physical or mental activity resulting from subjective improvement can also constitute a stress.** When symptoms are brought under control, a progressive reduction may be attempted as before.

Method of Withdrawing ACTH: The same principles apply as discussed above. In practice, either the number of units of ACTH per injection can be reduced, or the interval between injections can be extended (e.g., from 1 per day, to 1 on alternate days, to 1 biweekly).

Withdrawal of Therapy: As the action of cromolyn sodium is essentially preventive, continuity of therapy is important in patients who have gained benefit. If for any reason cromolyn sodium is withdrawn, a suggested regimen for withdrawal is to reduce the cromolyn sodium dosage gradually over a period of 1 week. It should be borne in mind that symptoms of asthma may recur when the drug is discontinued.

Caution: In such cases where cromolyn sodium has permitted a reduction in the maintenance dose of steroids, it is recommended that the steroid dose first be restored to at least the pre-cromolyn sodium level at the commencement of withdrawal of cromolyn sodium, followed by a slow reduction of the steroid dose to tolerance. This is to avoid risk of acute relapse. It is also recommended that adrenal function be assessed before restoring the pre-cromolyn sodium steroid dose.

Administration of Sterules: Administration by inhalation of the contents of an sterule is only possible with the use of the nebulizer unit.

Supplied: Each mL of sterile solution contains: cromolyn sodium 1%. Nonmedicinal ingredients: purified sterile water. Sterules of 2 mL, cartons of 50. Store at room temperature (15 to 25°C) and protect from direct sunlight. Discard any unused sterules in opened foil packs after 3 months.

New Product 1998

APO®-CYCLOBENZAPRINE ℞

Apotex

Cyclobenzaprine HCl

Skeletal Muscle Relaxant

Supplied: Each butterscotch yellow, biconvex, film-coated, D-shaped tablet, engraved APO over 10 on one side, contains: cyclobenzaprine HCl 10 mg. Nonmedicinal ingredients: carnauba wax, colloidal silicon dioxide, cornstarch, hydroxypropyl methylcellulose, lactose, magnesium stearate, microcrystalline cellulose, polyethylene glycol, titanium dioxide and yellow ferric oxide. Gluten-, sulfite- and tartrazine-free. Bottles of 100 and 500. Store in well-closed containers at room temperature (15 to 30°C).

APO®-DESIPRAMINE ℞

Apotex

Desipramine HCl

Antidepressant

Supplied: 10 mg: Each blue, round, biconvex, film-coated tablet, engraved "10" on one side, contains: desipramine HCl 10 mg. Nonmedicinal ingredients: colloidal silicon dioxide, dextrate and magnesium stearate; film-coating: brilliant blue FCF aluminum lake 12%, carnauba wax, hydroxypropyl methylcellulose, polyethylene glycol and titanium dioxide. Bottles of 100. Blister packs of 100.

25 mg: Each yellowish-orange, round, biconvex, film-coated tablet, engraved "25" on one side, contains: desipramine HCl 25 mg. Nonmedicinal ingredients: colloidal silicon dioxide, dextrate and magnesium stearate; film-coating: carnauba wax, D&C Yellow #10 aluminum lake, hydroxypropyl methylcellulose, polyethylene glycol, sunset yellow and titanium dioxide. Bottles of 100 and 500. Blister packs of 100.

50 mg: Each green, round, biconvex, film-coated tablet, engraved "50" on one side, contains: desipramine HCl 50 mg. Nonmedicinal ingredients: colloidal silicon dioxide, dextrate and magnesium stearate; film-coating: brilliant blue FCF aluminum lake 12%, carnauba wax, D&C Yellow #10 aluminum lake, ferric-ferrous oxide, hydroxypropyl methylcellulose, polyethylene glycol and titanium dioxide. Bottles of 100 and 500. Blister packs of 100.

75 mg: Each orange, round, biconvex, film-coated tablet, engraved "75" on one side, contains: desipramine HCl 75 mg. Nonmedicinal ingredients: colloidal silicon dioxide, dextrate and magnesium stearate; film-coating: carnauba wax, hydroxypropyl methylcellulose, polyethylene glycol and sunset yellow lake 40%. Bottles of 100. Blister packs of 100.

100 mg: Each peach, round, biconvex, film-coated tablet, engraved "100" on one side, contains: desipramine HCl 100 mg. Nonmedicinal ingredients: colloidal silicon dioxide, dextrate and magnesium stearate; film-coating: carnauba wax, hydroxypropyl methylcellulose, polyethylene glycol, sunset yellow lake 40% and titanium dioxide. Bottles of 100.

Store at room temperature (15 to 30°C).

APO®-DIAZEPAM ℞

Apotex

Diazepam

Anxiolytic—Sedative

Supplied: 2 mg: Each round, white, flat-faced with beveled edge, scored tablet, identified APO over 2, contains: diazepam 2 mg. Nonmedicinal ingredients: cornstarch, lactose, magnesium stearate and microcrystalline cellulose. Energy: 2.61 kJ (0.62 kcal). Gluten-, sodium-, sulfite- and tartrazine-free. Bottles of 100 and 1 000. Unit dose packages of 100. Apo Long-Term Care (LTC) Pak.

5 mg: Each round, yellow, flat-faced with beveled edge, scored tablet, identified APO over 5, contains: diazepam 5 mg. Nonmedicinal ingredients: cornstarch, D&C yellow #10 aluminum lake, lactose, magnesium stearate, microcrystalline cellulose and sunset yellow aluminum lake 40. Energy: 2.55 kJ (0.61 kcal). Gluten-, sodium-, sulfite- and tartrazine-free. Bottles of 100, 1 000 and 5 000. Unit dose packages of 100. Apo Long-Term Care (LTC) Pak.

10 mg: Each round, blue, flat-faced with beveled edge, scored tablet, identified APO over 10, contains: diazepam 10 mg. Nonmedicinal ingredients: brilliant blue FCF aluminum lake 12%, cornstarch, indigotine aluminum lake, lactose, magnesium stearate and microcrystalline cellulose. Energy: 2.47 kJ (0.59 kcal). Gluten-, sodium-, sulfite- and tartrazine-free. Bottles of 100 and 1 000. Unit dose packages of 100. Apo Long-Term Care (LTC) Pak.

APO®-DICLO ℞
APO®-DICLO SR ℞

Apotex

Diclofenac Sodium

Anti-inflammatory—Analgesic

Supplied: Apo-Diclo: 25 mg: Each yellow, round, biconvex, enteric-coated tablet, identified 25 on one side, contains: diclofenac sodium 25 mg. Nonmedicinal ingredients: colloidal silicon dioxide, D&C yellow #10 aluminum lake, dextrates, hydroxypropyl methylcellulose, magnesium stearate, methylcellulose, polyethylene glycol, polyvinyl acetate pthalate, stearic acid, sunset yellow lake 40%, titanium dioxide, triethyl citrate and yellow ferric oxide. Energy: 1.99 kJ (0.47 kcal). Sodium: <1 mmol (1.81 mg). Gluten-, lactose-, sulfite- and tartrazine-free. Bottles of 100 and 500.

50 mg: Each light brown, round, biconvex, enteric-coated tablet, identified 50 on one side, contains: diclofenac sodium 50 mg. Nonmedicinal ingredients: colloidal silicon dioxide, D&C yellow #10 aluminum lake, dextrates, hydroxypropyl methylcellulose, magnesium stearate, methylcellulose, polyethylene glycol, polyvinyl acetate pthalate, stearic acid, sunset yellow lake 40%, titanium dioxide, triethyl citrate and yellow ferric oxide. Energy: 3.97 kJ (0.95 kcal). Sodium: <1 mmol (3.62 mg). Gluten-, lactose-, sulfite- and tartrazine-free. Bottles of 100 and 500.

Apo-Diclo SR: 75 mg: Each white, triangular, film-coated, slow-release tablet, identified APO over 75 on one side, contains: diclofenac sodium 75 mg. Nonmedicinal ingredients: carnauba wax, dextrates, hydroxyethyl cellulose, hydroxypropyl methylcellulose, magnesium stearate, microcrystalline cellulose, polyethylene glycol and titanium dioxide. Energy: 2.03 kJ (0.49 kcal). Sodium: <1 mmol (5.43 mg). Gluten-, lactose-, sulfite- and tartrazine-free. Bottles of 100 and 500.

100 mg: Each white, round, biconvex, film-coated, slow-release tablet, identified APO over 100 on one side, contains: diclofenac sodium 100 mg. Nonmedicinal ingredients: carnauba wax, dextrates, hydroxyethyl cellulose, hydroxypropyl methylcellulose, magnesium stearate, microcrystalline cellulose, polyethylene glycol, red ferric oxide and titanium dioxide. Energy: 2.71 kJ (0.65 kcal). Sodium: <1 mmol (7.24 mg). Gluten-, lactose-, sulfite- and tartrazine-free. Bottles of 100 and 250.

Store at room temperature and protect from humidity.

APO®-DIFLUNISAL ℞

Apotex

Diflunisal

Analgesic—Anti-inflammatory

Supplied: 250 mg: Each light-orange, capsule-shaped, film-coated, biconvex tablet, engraved "APO" on one side, "D250" on the other side, contains: diflunisal 250 mg. Nonmedicinal ingredients: carnauba wax, colloidal silicon dioxide, croscarmellose sodium, hydroxypropyl methylcellulose, magnesium stearate, microcrystalline cellulose, polyethylene glycol, pregelatinized starch, sunset yellow lake 40% and titanium dioxide. Energy: 2.51 kJ (0.60 kcal). Sodium: <1 mmol (0.51 mg). Alcohol-, gluten-, lactose-, sulfite- and tartrazine-free. Bottles of 100. Unit dose packages of 100.

500 mg: Each orange, capsule-shaped, film-coated, biconvex tablet, engraved "APO" on one side, "D500" on the other side, contains: diflunisal 500 mg. Nonmedicinal ingredients: carnauba wax, colloidal silicon dioxide, croscarmellose sodium, hydroxypropyl methylcellulose, magnesium stearate, microcrystalline cellulose, polyethylene glycol, pregelatinized starch, sunset yellow lake 40% and titanium dioxide. Energy: 5.01 kJ (1.20 kcal). Sodium: <1 mmol (1.01 mg). Alcohol-, gluten-, lactose-, sulfite- and tartrazine-free. Bottles of 100 and 500. Unit dose packages of 100.

Store at room temperature 15 to 30°C. Protect from light and moisture.

APO®-DILTIAZ ℞
APO®-DILTIAZ SR ℞
APO®-DILTIAZ CD ℞

Apotex

Diltiazem HCl

Antianginal

Antihypertensive—Antianginal

Antihypertensive—Antianginal

Supplied: Apo-Diltiaz: 30 mg: Each round, biconvex, light green, film-coated tablet, plain one side, identified APO over D30 on the other side, contains: diltiazem HCl 30 mg. Nonmedicinal ingredients: colloidal silicon dioxide, D&C Yellow #10, FD&C Blue #1, hydroxypropyl methylcellulose, lactose, magnesium stearate, polyethylene glycol and titanium dioxide. Energy: 2.91 kJ (0.69 kcal). Gluten-, sodium-, sulfite- and tartrazine-free. Bottles of 100 and 500.

60 mg: Each round, biconvex, yellow, scored, film-coated tablet, plain one side, identified APO over D60 on the other side, contains: diltiazem HCl 60 mg. Nonmedicinal ingredients: colloidal silicon dioxide, D&C Yellow #10, FD&C Blue #1, FD&C Yellow #6, hydroxypropyl methylcellulose, lactose, magnesium stearate, polyethylene glycol and titanium dioxide. Energy: 5.82 kJ (1.39 kcal). Gluten-, sodium-, sulfite- and tartrazine-free. Bottles of 100 and 500.

Apo-Diltiaz SR (Twice-a-day): 60 mg: Each hard gelatin #4 capsule with an ivory body and a chocolate brown cap, imprinted APO 60, contains: diltiazem HCl 60 mg. Nonmedicinal ingredients: eudragit, methylcellulose, microcrystalline cellulose, polysorbate, talc and tributyl citrate; shell: D&C Yellow #10, FD&C Blue #1, FD&C Red #40, FD&C Yellow #6, gelatin, silicon dioxide, sodium lauryl sulfate and titanium dioxide. Gluten-, lactose-, sulfite- and tartrazine-free. Bottles of 100, 250 and 500. Unit dose packages of 100 (10×10). Apotex Long-Term Care unit dose packages (Apo-LTC Paks) of 620 (20×31) and 700 (20×35).

90 mg: Each hard gelatin #3 capsule with a gold body and a chocolate brown cap, imprinted APO 90, contains: diltiazem HCl 90 mg. Nonmedicinal ingredients: eudragit, methylcellulose, microcrystalline cellulose, polysorbate, talc and tributyl citrate; shell: D&C Yellow #10, FD&C Blue #1, FD&C Red #40, FD&C Yellow #6, gelatin, silicon dioxide, sodium, lauryl sulfate and titanium dioxide. Gluten-, lactose-, sulfite- and tartrazine-free. Bottles of 100, 250 and 500. Unit dose packages of 100 (10×10). Apotex Long-Term Care unit dose packages (Apo-LTC Paks) of 620 (20×31) and 700 (20×35).

120 mg: Each hard gelatin #2 capsule with a caramel body and a chocolate brown cap, imprinted APO 120, contains: diltiazem HCl 120 mg. Nonmedicinal ingredients: eudragit, methylcellulose, microcrystalline cellulose, polysorbate, talc and tributyl citrate; shell: D&C Yellow $10, FD&C Blue #1, FD&C Red #40, FD&C Yellow #6, gelatin, silicon dioxide, sodium lauryl sulfate and titanium dioxide. Gluten-, lactose-, sulfite- and tartrazine-free. Bottles of 100, 250 and 500. Unit dose packages of 100 (10×10). Apotex Long-Term Care unit dose packages (Apo-LTC Paks) of 620 (20×31) and 700 (20×35).

Apo-Diltiaz CD (Once-a-day): 120 mg: Each hard gelatin #1 capsule with a light turquoise body and a light turquoise cap, marked with APO 120, contains: diltiazem HCl 120 mg. Nonmedicinal ingredients: eudragit, methylcellulose, microcrystalline cellulose, polysorbate, talc and tributyl citrate; shell: FD&C Blue #1, gelatin, silicon dioxide, sodium lauryl sulfate and titanium dioxide. Gluten-, lactose-, sulfite- and tartrazine-free. Bottles of 100 and 500. Unit dose packages of 30 and 100 (10×10). Apotex Long-Term Care unit dose packages (Apo-LTC Paks) of 620 (20×31) and 700 (20×35).

180 mg: Each hard gelatin #1 capsule with a light turquoise body and a light blue cap, marked with APO 180, contains: diltiazem HCl 180 mg. Nonmedicinal ingredients: eudragit, methylcellulose, microcrystalline cellulose, polysorbate, talc and tributyl citrate; shell: FD&C Blue #1, gelatin, silicon dioxide, sodium lauryl sulfate and titanium dioxide. Gluten-, lactose-, sulfite- and tartrazine-free. Bottles of 100 and 500. Unit dose packages of 30 and 100 (10×10). Apotex Long-Term Care unit dose packages (Apo-LTC Paks) of 620 (20×31) and 700 (20×35).

240 mg: Each hard gelatin #0 capsule with a light blue body and a light blue cap, marked with APO 240, contains: diltiazem HCl 240 mg. Nonmedicinal ingredients: eudragit, methylcellulose, microcrystalline cellulose, polysorbate, talc and tributyl citrate; shell: FD&C Blue #1, gelatin, silicon dioxide, sodium lauryl sulfate and titanium dioxide. Gluten-, lactose-, sulfite- and tartrazine-free. Bottles of 100 and 500. Unit dose packages of 30 and 100 (10×10). Apotex Long-Term Care unit dose packages (Apo-LTC Paks) of 620 (20×31) and 700 (20×35).

300 mg: Each hard gelatin #0 elongated capsule with a light grey body and a light blue cap, marked with APO 300, contains: diltiazem HCl 300 mg. Nonmedicinal ingredients: eudragit, methylcellulose, microcrystalline cellulose, polysorbate, talc and tributyl citrate; shell: black iron oxide, FD&C Blue #1, gelatin, silicon dioxide, sodium lauryl sulfate and titanium dioxide. Gluten-, lactose-, sulfite- and tartrazine-free. Bottles of 100, 250 and 500. Unit dose packages of 100 (10×10). Apotex Long-Term Care unit dose packages (Apo-LTC Paks) of 620 (20×31) and 700 (20×35).

Store between 15 and 30°C. Protect unit dose and Apo-LTC Paks packages from humidity.

APO®-DIMENHYDRINATE

Apotex

Dimenhydrinate

Antiemetic

Supplied: Each round, orange, flat-faced with beveled-edge, double-scored tablet, identified APO over 50, contains: dimenhydrinate 50 mg. Nonmedicinal ingredients: croscarmellose sodium, lactose, magnesium stearate, microcrystalline cellulose and sunset yellow aluminum lake 40. Energy: 1.74 kJ (0.42 kcal). Sodium: <1 mmol (0.06 mg). Gluten-, sulfite- and tartrazine-free. Bottles of 100 and 1 000. Unit dose packages of 100. Apo Long-term Care (LTC) Pak.

APO®-DIPYRIDAMOLE FC Ⓟ

Apotex

Dipyridamole

Platelet Inhibitor—Vasodilator

Supplied: 25 mg: Each round, orange, biconvex, film-coated (identified 25) tablet contains: dipyridamole 25 mg. Nonmedicinal ingredients: colloidal silicon dioxide, magnesium stearate, microcrystalline cellulose; film-coating: hydroxypropyl methylcellulose, polyethylene glycol, sunset yellow lake 40%, titanium dioxide; sugar-coating: sucrose, sunset yellow lake 40% and titanium dioxide. Energy: <1 kJ (0.11 kcal). Gluten-, lactose-, sodium-, sulfite- and tartrazine-free. Bottles of 100.

50 mg: Each round, brown, biconvex, film-coated (identified D50) tablet contains: dipyridamole 50 mg. Nonmedicinal ingredients: colloidal silicon dioxide, magnesium stearate, microcrystalline cellulose; film-coating: hydroxypropyl methylcellulose, polyethylene glycol, sunset yellow lake 40% and titanium dioxide; sugar-coating: red ferric oxide, sucrose, sunset yellow lake 40%, titanium dioxide and yellow ferric oxide. Energy: <1 kJ (0.21 kcal). Gluten-, lactose-, sodium-, sulfite- and tartrazine-free. Bottles of 100.

75 mg: Each round, red, biconvex, film-coated (identified D75) tablet contains: dipyridamole 75 mg. Nonmedicinal ingredients: colloidal silicon dioxide, magnesium stearate, microcrystalline cellulose; film-coating: D&C Red #7 calcium lake, hydroxypropyl methylcellulose, polyethylene glycol, sunset yellow lake 40% and titanium dioxide; sugar-coating: sucrose, sunset yellow lake 40% and titanium dioxide. Energy: 1.39 kJ (0.33 kcal). Gluten-, lactose-, sodium-, sulfite- and tartrazine-free. Bottles of 100.

APO®-DOMPERIDONE Ⓟ

Apotex

Domperidone Maleate

Modifier of Upper Gastrointestinal Motility

Pharmacology: Domperidone is a peripheral dopamine antagonist structurally related to the butyrophenones with antiemetic and gastroprokinetic properties.

Domperidone effectively increases esophageal peristalsis and lower esophageal sphincter pressure (LESP), increases gastric motility and peristalsis, enhances gastroduodenal coordination and consequently facilitates gastric emptying and decreases small bowel transit time.

The mechanism of action of domperidone is related to its peripheral dopamine-receptor-blocking properties. Emesis induced by apomorphine, hydergine, morphine or levodopa through stimulation of the chemoreceptor trigger zone (situated outside the blood-brain barrier) can be blocked by domperidone. There is indirect evidence that emesis is also inhibited at the gastric level, since domperidone also inhibits emesis induced by oral levodopa, and local gastric wall concentrations following oral domperidone are much greater than those of the plasma and other organs. Domperidone does not readily cross the blood-brain barrier and therefore is not expected to have central effects.

Domperidone elevates serum prolactin levels but has no effect on circulating aldosterone levels.

Pharmacokinetics: In man, peak plasma levels of domperidone occur within 10 to 30 minutes following i.m. injection and 30 minutes after oral (fasted) administration. Plasma concentrations 2 hours after oral administration are lower than following i.m. injection, and this is likely the result of hepatic first-pass and gut wall metabolism. Peak plasma concentrations are 40 ng/mL following an i.m. injection of 10 mg, 20 ng/mL after a single 10 mg tablet, and 70 to 100 ng/mL after oral doses of 60 mg (tablets or oral drops). The half-life was calculated as approximately 7 hours in each case. The degree of human plasma protein binding was calculated from tritiated domperidone concentrations of 10 and 100 ng/mL as 91.7 and 93%, respectively. The major metabolic pathways for domperidone in man are hydroxylation and oxidative N-dealkylation, the products of which are hydroxy-domperidone and 2,3 dihydro-2-oxo-1-H-benzimidazole-1-propionic acid, respectively. After oral administration of 40 mg ^{14}C-domperidone to healthy volunteers, 31% of the radioactivity is excreted in the urine and 66% in the feces over a period of 4 days.

Indications: In the symptomatic management of upper gastrointestinal motility disorders associated with chronic and subacute gastritis and diabetic gastroparesis. Domperidone may also be used to prevent gastrointestinal symptoms associated with the use of dopamine agonist antiparkinsonian agents.

Contraindications: In patients with known sensitivity or intolerance to the drug. Domperidone should not be used whenever gastrointestinal stimulation might be dangerous, i.e., gastrointestinal hemorrhage or mechanical obstruction.

Warnings: Dopamine-receptor-blocking agents elevate prolactin levels; the elevation persists during chronic administration. Tissue culture experiments indicate that approximately one third of human breast cancers are prolactin dependent in vitro, a factor of potential importance if the prescription of these drugs is contemplated in a patient with a previously detected breast cancer. Although disturbances such as galactorrhea, amenorrhea, gynecomastia, and impotence have been reported, the clinical significance of elevated serum prolactin levels is unknown for most patients. An increase in mammary neoplasms has been found in rodents after chronic administration of dopamine-receptor-blocking agents. Neither clinical studies nor epidemiologic studies conducted to date, however, have shown an association between chronic administration of these drugs and mammary tumorigenesis. The available evidence is considered too limited to be conclusive at this time.

Pregnancy: While animal studies have not shown drug related teratogenic or primary embryotoxic effects on animal fetuses, comparable studies have not been performed in pregnant women. For this reason, domperidone should not be used in pregnant women unless the expected benefit outweighs the potential hazard.

Lactation: Domperidone is excreted in breast milk in very low concentrations. Caution should be exercised when domperidone is administered to nursing mothers.

Children: The safety and efficacy of domperidone in children have not been established. Therefore, domperidone should not be used in children.

Precautions: In the event that the patient develops galactorrhea and/or gynecomastia, withdrawal of the drug will result in alleviation of these symptoms.

Drug Interactions: The concomitant administration of anticholinergic drugs may compromise the beneficial effects of domperidone.

Since domperidone enhances gastric and small intestinal motility, it may accelerate absorption of drugs from the small bowel while slowing absorption of drugs taken up from the stomach.

Care should be exercised when domperidone is administered in combination with MAO inhibitors.

The concomitant administration of domperidone with antacids or H_2-receptor blockers does not decrease the absorption of domperidone.

Adverse Effects: In clinical studies with oral domperidone the overall incidence of side effects was <7%. Some of these side effects are an extension of the dopamine antagonist properties of domperidone. Most side effects resolve spontaneously during continued therapy or are easily tolerated. The more serious or troublesome side effects (galactorrhea, gynecomastia, menstrual irregularities) are dose-related and gradually resolve after lowering the dose or discontinuing therapy.

CNS (4.6%): dry mouth (1.9%), headache/migraine (1.2%), insomnia, nervousness, dizziness, thirst, lethargy, irritability (all <1%).

Gastrointestinal (2.4%): abdominal cramps, diarrhea, regurgitation, changes in appetite, nausea, heartburn, constipation (all <1%).

Endocrinological (1.3%): hot flushes, mastalgia, galactorrhea, gynecomastia, menstrual irregularities.

Mucocutaneous (1.1%): rash, pruritus, urticaria, stomatitis, conjunctivitis.

Urinary (0.8%): urinary frequency, dysuria.

Cardiovascular (0.5%): edema, palpitations.

Musculoskeletal (0.1%): leg cramps, asthenia.

Miscellaneous (0.1%): drug intolerance.

Laboratory parameters: elevated serum prolactin, elevation of AST, ALT and cholesterol (all <1%).

Overdose: Symptoms: There has been no experience with overdosage of domperidone. However, based on the pharmacological properties of domperidone, CNS effects (dyskinesias) and cardiovascular effects (arrhythmia, hypotension) might possibly occur.

Apo-Domperidone (cont'd)

Treatment: Treatment is gastric lavage with close observation and supportive therapy.

Dosage: Upper Gastrointestinal Motility Disorders: The usual dosage in adults is 10 mg orally 3 to 4 times a day, 15 to 30 minutes before meals and at bedtime if required. In severe or resistant cases the dose may be increased to a maximum of 20 mg 3 to 4 times a day.

Nausea and Vomiting Associated with Dopamine Agonist Antiparkinsonian Agents: The usual dosage in adults is 20 mg orally 3 to 4 times a day. Higher doses may be required to achieve symptom control while titration of the antiparkinsonian medication is occurring.

Supplied: Each white, round, biconvex, film-coated tablet engraved "APO" over "10" on one side, contains: domperidone maleate equivalent to domperidone 10 mg. Nonmedicinal ingredients: colloidal silicon dioxide, croscarmellose sodium, fumaric acid, hydroxypropyl methylcellulose, magnesium stearate, microcrystalline cellulose, polyethylene glycol and titanium dioxide. Bottles of 100 and 500. Store at room temperature 15 to 30°C. Protect from light and moisture.

New Product 1998

APO®-DOXEPIN ℞
Apotex

Doxepin HCl
Antidepressant—Anxiolytic

Supplied: 10 mg: Each No. 4, pink and scarlet capsule, identified "APO 10", contains: doxepin HCl equivalent to doxepin base 10 mg. Nonmedicinal ingredients: colloidal silicon dioxide, croscarmellose sodium, lactose, microcrystalline cellulose and stearic acid. Energy: <1 kJ (0.11 kcal). Sodium: <1 mmol (0.06 mg). Gluten-, sulfite- and tartrazine-free. Bottles of 100 and 500.

25 mg: Each No. 4, pink and blue capsule, identified "APO 25", contains: doxepin HCl equivalent to doxepin base 25 mg. Nonmedicinal ingredients: colloidal silicon dioxide, croscarmellose sodium, lactose, microcrystalline cellulose and stearic acid. Energy: 1.16 kJ (0.28 kcal). Sodium: <1 mmol (0.16 mg). Gluten-, sulfite- and tartrazine-free. Bottles of 100 and 500.

50 mg: Each No. 2, flesh and pink capsule, identified "APO 50", contains: doxepin HCl equivalent to doxepin base 50 mg. Nonmedicinal ingredients: colloidal silicon dioxide, croscarmellose sodium, lactose, microcrystalline cellulose and stearic acid. Energy: 2.33 kJ (0.56 kcal). Sodium: <1 mmol (0.32 mg). Gluten-, sulfite- and tartrazine-free. Bottles of 100 and 500.

75 mg: Each No. 2, flesh and flesh capsule, identified "APO 75", contains: doxepin HCl equivalent to doxepin base 75 mg. Nonmedicinal ingredients: colloidal silicon dioxide, croscarmellose sodium, lactose, microcrystalline cellulose and stearic acid. Energy: 3.49 kJ (0.83 kcal). Sodium: <1 mmol (0.48 mg). Gluten-, sulfite- and tartrazine-free. Bottles of 100.

100 mg: Each No. 1, flesh and blue capsule, identified "APO 100", contains: doxepin HCl equivalent to doxepin base 100 mg. Nonmedicinal ingredients: colloidal silicon dioxide, croscarmellose sodium, lactose, microcrystalline cellulose and stearic acid. Energy: 4.66 kJ (1.11 kcal). Sodium: <1 mmol (0.63 mg). Gluten-, sulfite- and tartrazine-free. Bottles of 100.

150 mg: Each No. 0, pink and pink capsule, identified "APO 150", contains: doxepin HCl equivalent to doxepin base 150 mg. Nonmedicinal ingredients: colloidal silicon dioxide, croscarmellose sodium, lactose, microcrystalline cellulose and stearic acid. Energy: 6.98 kJ (1.67 kcal). Sodium: <1 mmol (0.95 mg). Gluten-, sulfite- and tartrazine-free. Bottles of 100.

Store at room temperature 15 to 30°C.

APO®-DOXY ℞
APO®-DOXY-TABS ℞
Apotex

Doxycycline Hyclate
Antibiotic

Supplied: Capsules: Each pale blue, hard gelatin no. 2 capsule, identified APO 100, contains: doxycycline hyclate equivalent to doxycycline base 100 mg. Nonmedicinal ingredients: croscarmellose sodium, lactose, magnesium stearate, stearic acid and talc. Energy: 3.09 kJ (0.74 kcal). Sodium: <1 mmol (0.25 mg). Gluten- and tartrazine-free. Bottles of 100 and 250.

Tablets: Each round, orange, biconvex, film-coated tablet, identified APO-DOXY 100, contains: doxycycline hyclate equivalent to doxycycline base 100 mg. Nonmedicinal ingredients: colloidal silicon dioxide, croscarmellose sodium, magnesium stearate and microcrystalline cellulose; film-coating: hydroxypropyl methylcellulose, polyethylene glycol, sunset yellow lake (FD&C yellow #6) and titanium dioxide. Energy: 1.86 kJ (0.44 kcal). Sodium: <1 mmol (0.23 mg). Gluten-, lactose-, sulfite- and tartrazine-free. Bottles of 100 and 250.

APO®-ERYTHRO BASE ℞
Apotex

Erythromycin
Antibiotic

Supplied: Each oval, pink, biconvex, film-coated tablet, identified APO-250, contains: erythromycin base 250 mg. Nonmedicinal ingredients: colloidal silicon dioxide, croscarmellose sodium, D&C red 30 lake, hydroxypropyl methylcellulose, magnesium stearate, microcrystalline cellulose, polyethylene glycol, stearic acid and titanium dioxide. Energy: ≤5.63 kJ (≤1.34 kcal). Sodium: <1 mmol (1.52 mg). Gluten-, lactose-, sulfite- and tartrazine-free. Bottles of 100 and 1 000.

APO®-ERYTHRO E-C ℞
Apotex

Erythromycin Enteric-Coated
Antibiotic

Supplied: 250 mg: Each orange and clear no. 0 capsule, identified APO 250, contains: erythromycin 250 mg (as white and orange enteric-coated pellets). Nonmedicinal ingredients: D&C yellow #10 lake, hydroxypropyl methylcellulose, polyethylene glycol, sunset yellow lake and titanium dioxide. Energy: 1 kJ (0.2 kcal). Gluten-, lactose- and tartrazine-free. Bottles of 100 and 500.

333 mg: Each yellow and clear no. 0 capsule, identified APO 333, contains: erythromycin 333 mg (as white and orange enteric-coated pellets). Nonmedicinal ingredients: D&C yellow #10 lake, hydroxypropyl methylcellulose, polyethylene glycol, sunset yellow lake and titanium dioxide. Gluten-, lactose- and tartrazine-free. Bottles of 100 and 500.

APO®-ERYTHRO-ES ℞
Apotex

Erythromycin Ethylsuccinate
Antibiotic

Supplied: Each oval, yellow, film-coated tablet identified APO-600 contains: erythromycin (as ethylsuccinate) 600 mg. Nonmedicinal ingredients: colloidal silicon dioxide, croscarmellose sodium, D&C yellow #10, hydroxypropyl methylcellulose, magnesium stearate, microcrystalline cellulose, polyethylene glycol, stearic acid and titanium dioxide. Energy: ≤5.81 kJ (≤1.39 kcal). Sodium: <1 mmol (3.09 mg). Gluten-, lactose- and tartrazine-free. Bottles of 100 and 500.

APO®-ERYTHRO-S ℞
Apotex

Erythromycin Stearate
Antibiotic

Supplied: 250 mg: Each round, bright pink, film-coated tablet, identified APO over 250, contains: erythromycin stearate 250 mg. Nonmedicinal ingredients: colloidal silicon dioxide, croscarmellose sodium, magnesium stearate, methylcellulose and microcrystalline cellulose; film-coating: erythrosine lake, hydroxypropyl methylcellulose, polyethylene glycol and titanium dioxide. Energy: ≤3.62 kJ (≤0.87 kcal). Sodium: <1 mmol (0.19 mg). Gluten-, lactose- and tartrazine-free. Bottles of 100 and 1 000.

500 mg: Each oval, white, film-coated tablet, identified APO-500, contains: erythromycin stearate 500 mg. Nonmedicinal ingredients: colloidal silicon dioxide, croscarmellose sodium, magnesium stearate, methylcellulose and microcrystalline cellulose; film-coating: hydroxypropyl methylcellulose, polyethylene glycol and titanium dioxide. Energy: ≤7.24 kJ (≤1.73 kcal). Sodium: <1 mmol (0.38 mg). Gluten-, lactose- and tartrazine-free. Bottles of 100.

APO®-ETODOLAC ℞
Apotex

Etodolac
Anti-inflammatory

Pharmacology: Etodolac is a nonsteroidal anti-inflammatory drug (NSAID) that exhibits anti-inflammatory, analgesic and antipyretic properties in animal models. The pharmacological actions of etodolac are thought to be related to inhibition of prostaglandin biosynthesis at the site of inflammation.

Etodolac is a racemic mixture of R- and S-etodolac. As with other NSAIDs, it has been demonstrated in animals that the S-form is biologically active and the R-form is not. Both enantiomers are stable and there is no R-to-S conversion in vivo.

According to in vitro studies of human chondrocytes, etodolac may preserve collagen phenotype while still inhibiting prostaglandin (PGE_2) biosynthesis. The results demonstrated that normal chondrocyte function remained unaffected by etodolac, as assessed by the rate of DNA synthesis, proteoglycan synthesis, type II collagen production, and collagenase production. Etodolac maintained type II collagen synthesis and partially blocked the effects of interleukin-1 (IL-1). Nevertheless, PGE_2 synthesis was significantly decreased in the presence of etodolac. These results need to be verified through in vivo testing.

Pharmacokinetics: Etodolac is well absorbed following oral administration. The systemic availability of etodolac is at least 80%, and the drug does not undergo significant first-pass metabolism. The dose-proportionality based on AUC (the area under the plasma concentration-time curve) is linear following doses up to 600 mg every 12 hours. Etodolac is more than 99% bound to plasma proteins.

Mean peak plasma concentrations range from approximately 14±4 to 37±9 μg/mL after 200 to 600 mg single doses and are reached in 80±30 minutes. The mean plasma clearance of etodolac is 47 (±16) mL/h/kg, and terminal disposition half-life is 7.3 (±4.0) hours (see Table I).

Table I—Apo-Etodolac

Table of Etodolac Steady-state Pharmacokinetic Parameters (n=267)

Kinetic Parameters	Scientific Notation (Units)	Mean±SD
Extent Of Oral Absorption (Bioavailability)	F(%)	≥80
Peak Concentration Time	t_{max} (h)	1.7±1.3
Oral-Dose Clearance	CL/F (mL/h/kg)	47±16
Central Compartment Volume	V_c/F (mL/kg)	132±47
Steady-state Volume	V_{ss}/F (mL/kg)	362±129
Distribution Half-life	$t_{1/2}\ \alpha$ (h)	0.71±0.50
Terminal Half-life	$t_{1/2}\ \beta$ (h)	7.3±4.0

Etodolac is extensively metabolized in the liver, with renal elimination of etodolac and its metabolites being the primary route of excretion. Approximately 72% of the administered dose is recovered in the urine as the following, indicated as % of the administered dose: etodolac, unchanged 1%; etodolac glucuronide 13%; hydroxylated metabolites (6-, 7- and 8-OH) 5%; hydroxylated metabolite glucuronides 20% and unidentified metabolites 33%.

Fecal excretion accounted for 16% of the dose. Therefore, enterohepatic circulation, if present, is not extensive.

The extent of absorption of etodolac is not affected when it is administered after a meal or with an antacid. Food intake, however, reduces the peak concentration reached by approximately one-half, and increases the time-to-peak concentration by 1.4 to 3.8 hours. Coadministration with an antacid decreases the peak concentration reached by about 15 to 20%, with no measurable effect on time-to-peak.

Geriatrics: In studies in the elderly, age was found to have no effect on etodolac half-life or protein binding, and there was no drug accumulation. Etodolac clearance was reduced by about 15%. Because the reduction in clearance is small, no dosage adjustment is generally necessary in the elderly on the basis of pharmacokinetics. The elderly may need dosage adjustment, however, on the basis of body size, and they may be more sensitive to antiprostaglandin effects than younger patients.

In studies of the effects of mild to moderate renal impairment, no significant differences in the disposition of total and free etodolac were observed. In patients undergoing hemodialysis, there was a 50% greater apparent clearance of total etodolac, due to a 50% greater unbound fraction. Free etodolac clearance was not altered, indicating the importance of protein binding in etodolac's disposition. Nevertheless, etodolac is not dialyzable. No adjustment of etodolac is generally required in patients with mild to moderate renal impairment; however, etodolac should be used with caution in such patients because, as with other NSAIDs, it may further decrease renal function in some patients with impaired renal function.

In patients with compensated hepatic cirrhosis, the disposition of total and free etodolac is not altered. Although no dosage adjustment is generally required in this patient population, etodolac clearance is dependent on hepatic function and could be reduced in patients with severe hepatic failure.

Indications: For acute or long-term use in the relief of signs and symptoms of rheumatoid arthritis and osteoarthritis (degenerative joint disease).

Contraindications: Should not be used in patients who have previously shown hypersensitivity to etodolac. Due to possible cross-reactivity, etodolac should not be administered to patients who experience asthma, rhinitis, urticaria or other allergic reactions during therapy with ASA or other NSAIDs. Fatal anaphylactoid reactions have occurred in such individuals.

Etodolac should not be used in patients with an active peptic ulcer or inflammatory diseases of the gastrointestinal tract.

Warnings: Peptic ulceration, perforation and gastrointestinal bleeding, sometimes severe and occasionally fatal have been reported during therapy with NSAIDs including etodolac.

Etodolac should be given under close medical supervision to patients prone to gastrointestinal tract irritation, particularly those with a history of peptic ulcer, melena, diverticulosis or other inflammatory disease of the gastrointestinal tract (such as ulcerative colitis or Crohn's disease). In these cases the physician must weigh the benefits of treatment against the possible hazards (see Contraindications and Adverse Effects).

Patients taking any NSAID including this drug should be instructed to contact a physician immediately if they experience symptoms or signs suggestive of peptic ulceration or gastrointestinal bleeding. These reactions can occur at any time during treatment, without warning symptoms or signs.

Elderly, frail and debilitated patients appear to be at higher risk from a variety of adverse reactions from NSAIDs. As with other NSAIDs, etodolac should be used with special caution and under close supervision in these patients and consideration should be given to a starting dose lower than usual, with individual adjustment when necessary.

Pregnancy and *Lactation*: The safety of etodolac during pregnancy and lactation has not been established and therefore its use during pregnancy and lactation is not recommended.

In teratology studies, isolated occurrences of alterations in limb development were found and included polydactyly, oligodactyly, syndactyly, and unossified phalanges in rats and oligodactyly and synostosis of metatarsal in rabbits. These were observed at dose levels (2 to 14 mg/kg/day) close to human clinical doses. However, the frequency and the dosage group distribution of these findings in initial or repeated studies did not establish a clear drug-or dose-response relationship.

In rat studies with etodolac, as with other drugs known to inhibit prostaglandin synthesis, an increased incidence of dystocia, delayed parturition, and decreased pup survival occurred. The effects of etodolac on labor and delivery in pregnant women are unknown.

It is not known whether etodolac is excreted in human milk. Caution should be exercised if etodolac is administered to a nursing woman because many drugs are excreted in human milk.

Children: The safety and effectiveness of etodolac in children have not been established and therefore, the drug is not recommended in this age group.

Precautions: Gastrointestinal: If peptic ulceration is suspected or confirmed or if gastrointestinal bleeding or perforation occurs in patients under treatment with etodolac, the drug should be immediately withdrawn, an appropriate treatment initiated and the patient closely monitored.

There is no definitive evidence that the concomitant administration of histamine H_2-receptor antagonists and/or antacids will either prevent the occurrence of gastrointestinal side effects or allow continuation of etodolac therapy when and if the adverse reactions appear.

Renal Function: As with other NSAIDs, long-term administration of etodolac to animals has resulted in renal papillary necrosis and other abnormal renal pathology. In humans there have been reports of acute interstitial nephritis with hematuria, proteinuria, and occasionally nephrotic syndrome.

In patients with prerenal conditions leading to reduction in renal blood flow or blood volume, where renal prostaglandins have a supportive role in the maintenance of renal perfusion, administration of nonsteroidal anti-inflammatory agents may precipitate overt renal decompensation due to a dose-dependent reduction in prostaglandin formation. Patients at greatest risk are those with impaired renal function, heart failure, liver dysfunction, those taking diuretics, and the elderly. Discontinuation of NSAID therapy is usually followed by recovery to the pretreatment state.

Etodolac and its metabolites are eliminated primarily by the kidneys; therefore, the drug should be used with great caution in patients with impaired renal function. In these cases, lower doses of etodolac should be considered and patients carefully monitored. During long-term therapy, kidney function should be monitored periodically.

Hepatic Function: As with other NSAIDs, borderline elevations of one or more liver tests may occur in up to 15% of patients. These abnormalities may progress, may remain essentially unchanged, or may be transient with continued therapy. Meaningful (3 times the upper limit of normal) elevations of ALT or AST occurred in controlled clinical trials with etodolac in approximately 1% of patients. A patient with symptoms and/or signs suggesting liver dysfunction, or in whom an abnormal liver test has occurred, should be evaluated for evidence of the development of more severe hepatic reaction while on therapy with this drug. Severe hepatic reactions including jaundice and cases of fatal hepatitis have been reported with this drug as with other NSAIDs. Although such reactions are rare, if abnormal liver tests persist or worsen, if clinical signs and symptoms consistent with liver disease develop, or if systemic manifestations occur (e.g., eosinophilia, rash, etc.), this drug should be discontinued.

During long-term therapy, liver function tests should be monitored periodically. If this drug is to be used in the presence of impaired liver function, it must be done under strict observation.

Fluid and Electrolyte Balance: Fluid retention and edema have been reported; therefore, as with many other NSAIDs, the possibility of precipitating congestive heart failure in elderly patients or those with compromised cardiac function should be borne in mind. Etodolac should be used with caution in patients with heart failure, hypertension and renal diseases and in those recovering from surgical operations under general anesthesia and other conditions predisposing to fluid retention. With NSAID treatment, there is a potential risk of hyperkalemia, particularly in patients with conditions such as diabetes mellitus or renal failure, elderly patients or in patients receiving concomitant therapy with β-adrenergic blockers, angiotensin converting enzyme inhibitors or some diuretics.

Serum electrolytes should be monitored periodically during long-term therapy, especially in those patients at risk.

Hematology: Drugs inhibiting prostaglandin biosynthesis do interfere with platelet function and vascular response to bleeding to some degree; therefore, patients who may be adversely affected by such an action should be carefully observed when etodolac is administered.

Blood dyscrasias associated with the use of NSAIDs are rare, but could be with severe consequences.

Anemia is commonly observed in rheumatoid arthritis and is sometimes aggravated by NSAIDs, which may produce fluid retention or minor gastrointestinal blood loss in some patients. Therefore, patients with initial hemoglobin values of 10 g/dL or less who are to receive long-term therapy, should have hemoglobin values determined frequently.

Infection: In common with other anti-inflammatory drugs, etodolac may mask the usual signs of infection.

Ophthalmology: Blurred and/or diminished vision has been reported with the use of etodolac and other NSAIDs. If such symptoms develop, this drug should be discontinued and an ophthalmologic examination performed; ophthalmic examination should be carried out at periodic intervals in any patient receiving this drug for an extended period of time.

Hypersensitivity: As with other NSAIDs, allergic reactions, including anaphylactic/anaphylactoid reactions, can occur without prior exposure to drug; therefore, careful questioning of patients for a history of asthma, nasal polyps, urticaria, and hypotension associated with NSAIDs before starting therapy is important.

Drug Interactions: Antacids: The concomitant administration of antacids has no apparent effect on the extent of absorption of etodolac. However, antacids can decrease the peak concentration reached by 15 to 20% but have no detectable effect on the time-to-peak.

ASA: When etodolac is administered with ASA, its protein binding is reduced although the clearance of free etodolac is not altered. The clinical significance of this interaction is not known; however, as with other NSAIDs, concomitant administration of etodolac and ASA is not generally recommended because of potential of increased adverse effects.

Warfarin: Concomitant administration of warfarin and etodolac results in reduced protein binding of warfarin, but there is no change in the clearance of free warfarin. There is no significant difference in the pharmacodynamic effect of warfarin administered alone and warfarin administered with etodolac as measured by prothrombin time. Thus, concomitant therapy with warfarin and etodolac should not require dosage adjustment of either drug. Caution should be exercised, nevertheless, because interactions have been seen with other NSAIDs.

Phenytoin: Etodolac has no apparent pharmacokinetic interaction when administered with phenytoin.

Glyburide: Etodolac has no apparent pharmacokinetic or pharmacodynamic interaction when administered with glyburide.

Diuretics: Etodolac has no apparent pharmacokinetic interaction when administered with furosemide or hydrochlorothiazide, nor does etodolac attenuate the diuretic response of either of these drugs in normal volunteers. Etodolac, and other NSAIDs nevertheless, should be used with caution in patients receiving diuretics or who have cardiac, renal or hepatic failure (see Renal Function).

Antihypertensive Agents: NSAIDs can reduce the antihypertensive effect of propranolol and other β-blockers as well as other antihypertensive agents.

Cyclosporine, Digoxin, Lithium, Methotrexate: Etodolac, like other NSAIDs, through effects on renal prostaglandins may cause changes in the elimination of these drugs leading to elevated serum levels of digoxin, lithium, and methotrexate and increased toxicity. Nephrotoxicity associated with cyclosporine may also be enhanced. Patients receiving these drugs who are given etodolac, or any other NSAID, and particularly those patients with altered renal function, should be observed for the development of the specific toxicities of these drugs (monitoring of plasma drug levels).

Protein Binding: Data from in vitro studies using peak serum concentrations at reported therapeutic doses in humans show that the etodolac free fraction is not significantly altered by ibuprofen, acetaminophen, phenytoin, probenecid, indomethacin, chlorpropamide, glyburide, naproxen, glipizide or piroxicam.

In contrast, phenylbutazone causes an increase (by about 80%) in the free fraction of etodolac. Although in vivo studies have not been done to see if etodolac clearance is changed by coadministration of phenylbutazone, it is not recommended that they be coadministered.

Laboratory Test Interactions: The urine of patients who take etodolac can give a false-positive reaction for urinary bilirubin (urorubin) due to the presence of phenolic metabolites of etodolac.

Diagnostic dip-stick methodology, used to detect ketone bodies in urine, has resulted in false-positive findings in some patients treated with etodolac. Generally, this phenomenon has not been associated with other clinically significant events. No dose-relationship has been observed.

Etodolac treatment is associated with a small decrease in serum uric acid levels. In clinical trials, mean decreases of 1 to 2 mg% were observed in arthritic patients receiving etodolac (600 to 1 000 mg/day) after 4 weeks of therapy. These levels then remained stable for up to 1 year of therapy.

Adverse Effects: The most common adverse reactions encountered with NSAIDs are gastrointestinal, of which peptic ulcer, with or without bleeding, is the most severe. Fatalities have occurred on occasion, particularly in the elderly.

Adverse reaction information for etodolac was derived from 2 629 arthritic patients treated with etodolac in double-blind and open-label clinical trials of 4 to 320 weeks in duration and worldwide postmarketing surveillance studies in approximately 60 000 patients.

In clinical studies, etodolac was generally well tolerated. Most adverse reactions were mild and transient. The discontinuation rate in controlled clinical trials because of adverse events, was 9% for patients treated with etodolac.

Listed below are the patient complaints with an incidence of greater than, equal to, or less than 1% which occurred in clinical trials and postmarketing experience with etodolac at doses up to 1 000 mg/day.

Incidence ≥ 1%: Gastrointestinal: nausea, diarrhea, epigastric pain, heartburn, indigestion, flatulence, abdominal pain,

Apo-Etodolac (cont'd)

gastrointestinal cramps, abdominal distention, constipation, vomiting, dyspepsia, gastritis, melena.
CNS: headache, dizziness, drowsiness, insomnia, nervousness/anxiety, depression.
Dermatologic: dermatitis manifested as skin rash (erythematous, vesicular, maculopapular, morbilliform, petechial, or eczematous), or pruritus.
General Illness: fatigue, weakness/malaise.
Genitourinary: urinary frequency, dysuria.
Metabolic System: fluid retention/edema.
Eye, Ear, Nose and Throat: tinnitus, blurred vision.
Incidence <1%: Gastrointestinal: peptic ulcer with/without gastrointestinal hemorrhage and/or perforation; hematemesis; rectal bleeding; stool changes (loose, with mucus, or increase in number and/or frequency); taste abnormalities including loss of taste; eructation; stomatitis; hepatitis; cholestasis; jaundice; esophagitis with or without erosions or stricture or cardiospasm; colitis; pancreatitis.
CNS: restlessness, confusion, vertigo, syncope, nightmares, listlessness, inability to concentrate, somnolence.
Dermatologic: urticaria, angioedema, alopecia, sore, dry, inflamed or swollen mucous membranes including mouth, tongue, and lips, photosensitivity, peeling, easy bruising, brittle nails, exfoliative dermatitis, Stevens-Johnson syndrome, cutaneous vasculitis with purpura, erythema multiforme.
Eye, Ear, Nose and Throat: hearing loss, visual disturbances including teichopsia, epistaxis, ear ache, pressure/throbbing in ears, burning sensation of eyes/nose, twinging behind eyes, photophobia, conjunctivitis.
Extremities: paresthesias, muscle cramps, muscular fatigue, involuntary muscle movement, pain in arms/hands/shoulders, hand tremor, tenderness, s.c. nodule/first metatarsophalangeal joint.
General Illness: pyrexia, chills, lethargy, vasculitis, general deterioration, breast tenderness.
Genitourinary: dysuria, urinary urgency, hematuria, nocturia, vaginal bleeding, difficulty maintaining erection, rectopubic pain, cystitis, leukorrhea, renal calculus, interstitial nephritis, papillary necrosis, renal failure, uterine bleeding irregularities.
Metabolic System: change in weight, change in appetite, flushing, anorexia, excessive thirst, hot flashes, diaphoresis.
Cardiovascular: hypertension, congestive heart failure, palpitations, tachycardia, chest pain (costal, costochondral or retrosternal), arrhythmias, myocardial infarction, and chest tightness or fullness.
Respiratory: dyspnea, asthma, bronchospasm, hyperventilation, sneezing and sighing, bronchitis, pharyngitis, rhinitis, sinusitis.
Hypersensitivity: anaphylactic/anaphylactoid reaction, laryngeal edema.
Hematology: agranulocytosis, pancytopenia, decreased hemoglobin, decreased hematocrit, anemia, hemolytic anemia, thrombocytopenia, leukopenia, neutropenia, eosinophilia, atypical lymphocytes, increased bleeding time.
Laboratory: elevated hepatic enzymes, increased serum creatinine.

Overdose: Symptoms: Symptoms following acute NSAID overdose are usually limited to lethargy, drowsiness, nausea, vomiting and epigastric pain which are generally reversible with supportive care. Gastrointestinal bleeding can occur and coma has occurred following massive ibuprofen or mefenamic acid overdose. Hypertension, acute renal failure, and respiratory depression may occur, but are rare. Anaphylactoid reactions have been reported with therapeutic ingestion of NSAIDs, and may occur following overdose.

Treatment: Patients should be managed by symptomatic and supportive care following an NSAID overdose. There are no specific antidotes. Gut decontamination may be indicated in patients seen within 4 hours with symptoms or following a large overdose (5 to 10 times the usual dose). This should be accomplished via emesis and/or activated charcoal (60 to 100 g in adults, 1 to 2 g/kg in children) with an osmotic cathartic. Forced diuresis, alkalinization of the urine, hemodialysis or hemoperfusion would probably not be useful due to etodolac's high protein binding.

One case of intentional etodolac overdosage has been reported. This 53-year-old female ingested from 15 to 46 two hundred mg etodolac capsules (3 to 8.6 g). Plasma etodolac concentrations were measured frequently over the next 4 days. At 5 hours after ingestion (3 hours after gastric lavage) the plasma etodolac level was 22 μg/mL. These plasma levels and her subsequent recovery with no signs or symptoms of etodolac toxicity were consistent with systemic absorption of 600 to 800 mg. Her laboratory tests on admission showed a prolonged prothrombin time and a false-positive urine bilirubin (attributed to the phenolic etodolac metabolites).

Dosage: Adults: The recommended dosage of etodolac in the treatment of rheumatoid arthritis and osteoarthritis is 200 to 300 mg twice daily. Patients may also respond to a single daily (400 mg or 600 mg) dose administered in the evening.

The safety of doses in excess of 1 000 mg/day for extended periods has not been established. In order to maximize the effectiveness of therapy, the dosage must be individualized for each patient.

Geriatrics: As with any NSAID, caution should be exercised in treating the elderly, and when individualizing their dosage, extra care should be taken when increasing the dose because the elderly seem to tolerate NSAID side effects less well than younger patients. In otherwise healthy patients 65 years and older, no substantial differences in the side-effects profile of etodolac were seen.

Supplied: 200 mg: Each hard gelatin, light grey/dark grey, size #1 capsule, imprinted "APO 200", contains: etodolac 200 mg. Nonmedicinal ingredients: black iron oxide, colloidal silicon dioxide, croscarmellose sodium, D&C Red No. 7 Calcium Lake, ethylene glycol monoethyl ether, FD&C Yellow No. 6 Aluminum Lake, gelatin, lactose, n-butyl alcohol, pharmaceutical shellac, SDA-3A alcohol, silicon dioxide, sodium lauryl sulfate, stearic acid, talc, titanium dioxide and yellow iron oxide. Bottles of 60, 100, 250, 500 and 1 000. Unit dose packages of 30 and 100. Apotex Long-Term Care Packages (Apo-LTC Paks) of 620 and 700.

300 mg: Each hard gelatin, light grey/light grey, size #0 capsule, imprinted APO 300, contains: etodolac 300 mg. Nonmedicinal ingredients: black iron oxide, colloidal silicon dioxide, croscarmellose sodium, D&C Red No. 7 Calcium Lake, ethylene glycol monoethyl ether, FD&C Yellow No. 6 Aluminum Lake, gelatin, lactose, n-butyl alcohol, pharmaceutical shellac, SDA-3A alcohol, silicon dioxide, sodium lauryl sulfate, stearic acid, talc, titanium dioxide and yellow iron oxide. Bottles of 60, 100, 250 and 500. Unit dose packages of 30 and 100. Apotex Long-Term Care Packages (Apo-LTC Paks) of 620 and 700.

Store at room temperature (15 to 30°C) and protect from moisture.

New Product 1998

APO®-FAMOTIDINE ℞
Apotex

Famotidine

Histamine H_2 Receptor Antagonist

Supplied: 20 mg: Each beige, D-shaped, biconvex, film-coated tablet, identified APO over 20, contains: famotidine 20 mg. Nonmedicinal ingredients: colloidal silicon dioxide, croscarmellose sodium, dextrates, hydroxypropyl methylcellulose, magnesium stearate, polyethylene glycol, red ferric oxide, stearic acid, titanium dioxide and yellow ferric oxide. Energy: 3.23 kJ (0.77 kcal). Sodium: <1 mmol (0.44 mg). Gluten-, lactose-, sulfite- and tartrazine-free. Bottles of 30, 100 and 500. Unit dose packages of 30 and 100.

40 mg: Each light brown, D-shaped, biconvex, film-coated tablet, identified APO over 40, contains: famotidine 40 mg. Nonmedicinal ingredients: colloidal silicon dioxide, croscarmellose sodium, dextrates, hydroxypropyl methylcellulose, magnesium stearate, polyethylene glycol, red ferric oxide, stearic acid, titanium dioxide and yellow ferric oxide. Energy: 2.90 kJ (0.69 kcal). Sodium: <1 mmol (0.44 mg). Gluten-, lactose-, sulfite- and tartrazine-free. Bottles of 30, 100 and 500. Unit dose packages of 30 and 100.

Store at room temperature 15 to 30°C. Protect from light and moisture. Keep container tightly closed.

APO®-FENOFIBRATE ℞
Apotex

Fenofibrate

Antihyperlipidemic Agent

Supplied: Each opaque, white, #2 hard gelatin capsule, marked "APO 100", contains: fenofibrate 100 mg. Nonmedicinal ingredients: cornstarch, lactose and stearic acid. Bottles of 100 and 500. Store at controlled room temperature (15 to 25°C).

APO®-FERROUS GLUCONATE
Apotex

Ferrous Gluconate

Anemia Therapy

Supplied: Each pale green, film-coated, round, biconvex tablet, identified APO over 300, contains: ferrous gluconate 300 mg. Nonmedicinal ingredients: brilliant blue FCF aluminum lake, carnauba wax, croscarmellose sodium, hydroxypropyl methylcellulose, magnesium stearate, polydextrose, polyethylene glycol, titanium dioxide and yellow ferric oxide. Energy: <1 kJ (0.05 kcal). Sodium: <1 mmol (0.29 mg). Gluten-, lactose-, sulfite- and tartrazine-free. Bottles of 100 and 500.

APO®-FERROUS SULFATE
Apotex

Ferrous Sulfate

Anemia Therapy

Supplied: Each round, red, film-coated tablet, marked with "300", contains: ferrous sulfate 300 mg. Nonmedicinal ingredients: croscarmellose sodium, D&C red #7 lake, hydroxypropyl methylcellulose, magnesium stearate, microcrystalline cellulose, polyethylene glycol and sunset yellow lake. Energy: 1.25 kJ (0.30 kcal). Sodium: <1 mmol (0.46 mg). Gluten-, lactose-, sulfite- and tartrazine-free. Bottles of 100 and 1 000. Unit dose packages of 100.

APO®-FLUOXETINE ℞
Apotex

Fluoxetine HCl

Antidepressant—Antiobsessional—Antibulimic

Supplied: Capsules: 10 mg: Each green/grey, opaque, size #4 capsule, imprinted "APO 10", contains: fluoxetine HCl equivalent to fluoxetine 10 mg. Nonmedicinal ingredients: cornstarch, D&C Yellow #10, FD&C Blue #1, FD&C Yellow #6, lactose, sicomet-85 black iron oxide, stearic acid and talc. Bottles of 100, 250, 500 and 1 000. Blisters of 100.

20 mg: Each ivory, opaque, size #3 capsule, imprinted "APO 20", contains: fluoxetine HCl equivalent to fluoxetine 20 mg. Nonmedicinal ingredients: cornstarch, D&C Yellow #10, FD&C Blue #1, FD&C Yellow #6, lactose, stearic acid and talc. Bottles of 100 and 500. Blisters of 100.

Syrup: Each 5 mL of clear, colorless syrup solution, with an odor of mint, contains: fluoxetine HCl equivalent to fluoxetine 20 mg. Nonmedicinal ingredients: benzoic acid, glycerin, natural mint flavor and sucrose. Brown opaque bottles of 120 mL.

Store at controlled room temperature (15 to 30°C).

APO®-FLUPHENAZINE ℞
Apotex

Fluphenazine HCl

Antipsychotic—Antianxiety

Supplied: 1 mg: Each bright pink, round, biconvex, film-coated tablet, identified 1, contains: fluphenazine HCl 1 mg. Nonmedicinal ingredients: cornstarch, erythrosine lake, hydroxypropyl methylcellulose, lactose, magnesium stearate, microcrystalline cellulose, polyethylene glycol and titanium dioxide. Energy: 1.51 kJ (0.36 kcal). Gluten-, sodium-, sulfite- and tartrazine-free. Bottles of 100 and 500.

2 mg: Each pink, round, biconvex, film-coated tablet, identified 2, contains: fluphenazine HCl 2 mg. Nonmedicinal ingredients: cornstarch, D&C Red #30 lake, hydroxypropyl methylcellulose, lactose, magnesium stearate, microcrystalline cellulose, polyethylene glycol and titanium dioxide. Energy: 2.08 kJ (0.50 kcal). Gluten-, sodium-, sulfite- and tartrazine-free. Bottles of 100 and 500.

5 mg: Each white, round, biconvex, film-coated tablet, identified 5, contains: fluphenazine HCl 5 mg. Nonmedicinal ingredients: cornstarch, hydroxypropyl methylcellulose, lactose, magnesium stearate, microcrystalline cellulose, polyethylene glycol and titanium dioxide. Energy: 2.95 kJ (0.70 kcal). Gluten-, sodium-, sulfite- and tartrazine-free. Bottles of 100 and 500.

APO®-FLURAZEPAM ℞
Apotex
Flurazepam HCl
Hypnotic

Supplied: 15 mg: Each no. 2, orange/ivory capsule, identified APO 15, contains: flurazepam HCl 15 mg. Nonmedicinal ingredients: cornstarch, lactose and stearic acid; shell: D&C Yellow #10, FD&C Red #40, FD&C Yellow #6, gelatin, silicon dioxide, sodium lauryl sulfate and titanium dioxide. Energy: 5.37 kJ (1.28 kcal). Gluten-, sodium- and tartrazine-free. Bottles of 100 and 1 000. Unit dose packages of 100. Apo Long-Term Care (LTC) Pak.

30 mg: Each no. 2, red/ivory capsule, identified APO 30, contains: flurazepam HCl 30 mg. Nonmedicinal ingredients: cornstarch, lactose and stearic acid; shell: D&C Yellow #10, FD&C Yellow #6, FD&C Yellow #40, gelatin, silicon dioxide, sodium lauryl sulfate and titanium dioxide. Energy: 5.12 kJ (1.22 kcal). Gluten-, sodium- and tartrazine-free. Bottles of 100 and 1 000. Unit dose packages of 100. Apo Long-Term Care (LTC) Pak.

APO®-FLURBIPROFEN ℞
Apotex
Flurbiprofen
Anti-inflammatory—Analgesic

Supplied: 50 mg: Each white, oval, biconvex, film-coated tablet, identified APO-50 on one side, contains: flurbiprofen 50 mg. Nonmedicinal ingredients: colloidal silicon dioxide, croscarmellose sodium, hydroxypropyl methylcellulose, lactose, microcrystalline cellulose, polyethylene glycol, stearic acid and titanium dioxide. Energy: 2.63 kJ (0.63 kcal). Sodium: <1 mmol (1.01 mg). Gluten-, sulfite- and tartrazine-free. Bottles of 100 and 500.

100 mg: Each blue, oval, biconvex, film-coated tablet, identified APO-100 on one side, contains: flurbiprofen 100 mg. Nonmedicinal ingredients: colloidal silicon dioxide, croscarmellose sodium, hydroxypropyl methylcellulose, indigotine lake, lactose, microcrystalline cellulose, polyethylene glycol, stearic acid and titanium dioxide. Energy: 5.26 kJ (1.26 kcal). Sodium: <1 mmol (2.03 mg). Gluten-, sulfite- and tartrazine-free. Bottles of 100 and 500.

Store at controlled room temperature 15 to 30°C.

APO®-FLUVOXAMINE ℞
Apotex
Fluvoxamine Maleate
Antidepressant—Antiobsessional Agent

Supplied: 50 mg: Each round, white, biconvex, film-coated tablet, engraved "APO" on one side and "50" on the other, contains: fluvoxamine maleate 50 mg. Nonmedicinal ingredients: carnauba wax, hydroxypropyl methylcellulose, magnesium stearate, mannitol, polydextrose, polyethylene glycol, titanium dioxide and yellow ferric oxide. Bottles of 100 and 250.

100 mg: Each oval, white, biconvex, film-coated tablet, engraved "APO" on one side and "100" on the other, contains: fluvoxamine maleate 100 mg. Nonmedicinal ingredients: carnauba wax, hydroxypropyl methylcellulose, magnesium stearate, mannitol, polydextrose, polyethylene glycol, titanium dioxide and yellow ferric oxide. Bottles of 100 and 250.

Preserve in well-closed containers. Store in a dry place at room temperature (15 to 30°C).

APO®-FOLIC ℞
Apotex
Folic Acid
Hematopoietic—Anemia Therapy

Supplied: Each round, yellow, flat-faced with beveled edge, scored tablet, identified APO over 5, contains: folic acid 5 mg. Nonmedicinal ingredients: lactose, magnesium stearate and microcrystalline cellulose. Energy: 1.58 kJ (0.38 kcal). Gluten-, sodium-, sulfite- and tartrazine-free. Bottles of 100 and 1 000. Unit dose packages of 100. Apo Long-Term Care (LTC) Pak.

APO®-FUROSEMIDE ℞
Apotex
Furosemide
Diuretic

Supplied: 20 mg: Each white, round, flat-faced with beveled edge tablet, identified APO over 20, contains: furosemide 20 mg. Nonmedicinal ingredients: colloidal silicon dioxide, croscarmellose sodium, lactose, magnesium stearate and microcrystalline cellulose. Energy: <1 kJ (0.24 kcal). Sodium: <1 mmol (0.04 mg). Gluten-, sulfite- and tartrazine-free. Bottles of 100 and 1 000. Unit dose packages of 100. Apo Long-Term Care (LTC) Pak. Protect from light.

40 mg: Each yellow, round, flat-faced with beveled edge tablet, scored and identified APO over 40, contains: furosemide 40 mg. Nonmedicinal ingredients: colloidal silicon dioxide, croscarmellose sodium, D&C Yellow #10 aluminum lake, lactose, magnesium stearate, microcrystalline cellulose and sunset yellow aluminum lake. Energy: 1.96 kJ (0.47 kcal). Sodium: <1 mmol (0.08 mg). Gluten-, sulfite- and tartrazine-free. Bottles of 100, 1 000 and 5 000. Unit dose packages of 100. Apo Long-Term Care (LTC) Pak. Protect from light.

80 mg: Each yellow, capsule-shaped, flat-faced with beveled edge tablet, partial score and identified APO 80, contains: furosemide 80 mg. Nonmedicinal ingredients: colloidal silicon dioxide, croscarmellose sodium, D&C Yellow #10 aluminum lake, lactose, magnesium stearate, microcrystalline cellulose and sunset yellow aluminum lake. Energy: 3.93 kJ (0.93 kcal). Sodium: <1 mmol (0.15 mg). Gluten-, sulfite- and tartrazine-free. Bottles of 100 and 500. Protect from light.

APO®-GAIN ℞
Apotex
Minoxidil
Hair Growth Stimulant

Supplied: Each mL of topical solution contains: minoxidil 20 mg (2%). Nonmedicinal ingredients: alcohol, propylene glycol and water. Bottles of 60 mL. The following metered disposable applicators are available: pump spray, extended-spray-tip and rub-on. **For external use only.** Keep container tightly closed. Store at controlled room temperature, between 15 to 30°C.

APO®-GEMFIBROZIL ℞
Apotex
Gemfibrozil
Antihyperlipidemic Agent

Supplied: 300 mg: Each No. 1, maroon and white capsule identified "APO 300", contains: gemfibrozil 300 mg. Nonmedicinal ingredients: colloidal silicon dioxide, croscarmellose sodium, magnesium stearate, microcrystalline cellulose, polysorbate 80 and povidone; shell: D&C Red #33, FD&C Blue #1, FD&C Yellow #6, gelatin, methylparaben, propylparaben, sodium lauryl sulfate and titanium dioxide; film-coating: hydroxypropyl cellulose, hydroxypropyl methylcellulose, polyethylene glycol and titanium dioxide. Gluten-, lactose- and tartrazine-free. Energy: 2 kJ (0.48 kcal). Sodium: <1 mmol (0.38 mg). Bottles of 100 and 500. Unit dose packages of 100. Store at room temperature 15 to 30 °C.

600 mg: Each white, oval, biconvex, film-coated tablet, identified "APO 600" on one side and plain on the other, contains: gemfibrozil 600 mg. Nonmedicinal ingredients: colloidal silicon dioxide, croscarmellose sodium, magnesium stearate, microcrystalline cellulose, polysorbate 80 and povidone; shell: D&C Red #33, FD&C Blue #1, FD&C Yellow #6, gelatin, methylparabens, propylparabens, sodium lauryl sulfate and titanium dioxide; film-coating: hydroxypropyl cellulose, hydroxypropyl methylcellulose, polyethylene glycol and titanium dioxide. Gluten-, lactose- and tartrazine-free. Energy: 1.9 kJ (0.45 kcal). Sodium: <1 mmol (0.76 mg). Bottles of 100 and 500. Store between 15 and 25 °C. Protect from moisture.

APO®-GLYBURIDE ℞
Apotex
Glyburide
Oral Hypoglycemic

Supplied: 2.5 mg: Each white, round tablet, flat-faced with beveled edges, one side plain, other side single scored and identified APO 2.5, contains: glyburide 2.5 mg. Nonmedicinal ingredients: croscarmellose sodium, lactose, magnesium stearate and microcrystalline cellulose. Energy: 1.30 kJ (0.31 kcal). Sodium: <1 mmol (0.13 mg). Gluten-, sulfite- and tartrazine-free. Bottles of 100 and 500. Patient packages of 30. Apo Long-Term Care (LTC) Pak.

5 mg: Each white, capsule-shaped tablet, flat-faced with beveled edges, one side identified APO 5, other side single scored, contains: glyburide 5 mg. Nonmedicinal ingredients: croscarmellose sodium, lactose, magnesium stearate and microcrystalline cellulose. Energy: 2.59 kJ (0.62 kcal). Sodium: <1 mmol (0.25 mg). Gluten-, sulfite- and tartrazine-free. Bottles of 100 and 500. Patient packages of 30. Apo Long-Term Care (LTC) Pak.

Store at controlled room temperature 15 to 30°C.

APO®-HALOPERIDOL ℞
Apotex
Haloperidol
Antipsychotic—Antiemetic

Supplied: Tablets: 0.5 mg: Each round, white, flat-faced with beveled edge tablet, scored and identified APO over 0.5, contains: haloperidol 0.5 mg. Nonmedicinal ingredients: cornstarch, magnesium stearate and microcrystalline cellulose. Energy: 1.53 kJ (0.37 kcal). Gluten-, lactose-, sodium-, sulfite- and tartrazine-free. Bottles of 100 and 1 000. Unit dose packages of 100. Apo Long-Term Care (LTC) Pak.

1 mg: Each round, yellow, flat-faced with beveled edge tablet, scored and identified APO over 1, contains: haloperidol 1 mg. Nonmedicinal ingredients: cornstarch, D&C yellow #10 aluminum lake, magnesium stearate, microcrystalline cellulose and sunset yellow aluminum lake. Energy: 1.43 kJ (0.34 kcal). Gluten-, lactose-, sodium-, sulfite- and tartrazine-free. Bottles of 100 and 1 000. Unit dose packages of 100. Apo Long-Term Care (LTC) Pak.

2 mg: Each round, pink, flat-faced with beveled edge tablet, scored and identified APO over 2, contains: haloperidol 2 mg. Nonmedicinal ingredients: cornstarch, D&C red #7 calcium lake, magnesium stearate and microcrystalline cellulose. Energy: 1.43 kJ (0.34 kcal). Gluten-, lactose-, sodium-, sulfite- and tartrazine-free. Bottles of 100 and 1 000. Unit dose packages of 100. Apo Long-Term Care (LTC) Pak.

5 mg: Each round, green, flat-faced with beveled edge tablet, scored and identified APO over 5, contains: haloperidol 5 mg. Nonmedicinal ingredients: brilliant blue FCF aluminum lake, cornstarch, D&C yellow #10 aluminum lake, magnesium stearate and microcrystalline cellulose. Energy: 1.26 kJ (0.33 kcal). Gluten-, lactose-, sodium-, sulfite- and tartrazine-free. Bottles of 100 and 1 000. Unit dose packages of 100. Apo Long-Term Care (LTC) Pak.

10 mg: Each round, light-green, flat-faced with beveled edge tablet, scored and identified APO over 10, contains: haloperidol 10 mg. Nonmedicinal ingredients: brilliant blue FCF aluminum lake, cornstarch, D&C yellow #10 aluminum lake, magnesium stearate and microcrystalline cellulose. Energy: 2.75 kJ (0.66 kcal). Gluten-, lactose-, sodium-, sulfite- and tartrazine-free. Bottles of 100 and 500. Unit dose packages of 100. Apo Long-Term Care (LTC) Pak.

Oral Solution: Each mL of colorless, odorless solution contains: haloperidol 2 mg. Nonmedicinal ingredients: lactic acid, methylparaben and purified water. Energy: <1 kJ (<0.01 kcal)/mL. Alcohol-, gluten-, lactose-, sodium-, sugar-, sulfite- and tartrazine-free. Bottles of 15 mL with droppers, 100 mL with calibrated droppers and 500 mL.

...SYMBOLS:
℞ denotes "Prescription required."
◈ denotes "Controlled Drug."
Ⓝ denotes "Narcotic."

APO®-HEXA
Apotex
Hexavitamins
Vitamin Supplement

Supplied: Each red, biconvex, film-coated tablet contains: vitamin A 5 000 IU, vitamin B_1 2 mg, vitamin B_2 3 mg, niacinamide 20 mg, vitamin C 75 mg and vitamin D 400 IU. Nonmedicinal ingredients: carnauba wax, colloidal silicon dioxide, FD&C red #40, FD&C yellow #6 aluminum lake, glycerin, hydroxypropyl methylcellulose, magnesium stearate, microcrystalline cellulose and titanium dioxide. Gluten-, lactose-, sulfite- and tartrazine-free. Bottles of 100 and 1 000.

APO®-HYDRALAZINE ℞
Apotex
Hydralazine HCl
Antihypertensive

Supplied: 10 mg: Each round, yellow, biconvex, scored tablet, identified APO over H10, contains: hydralazine HCl 10 mg. Nonmedicinal ingredients: cornstarch, D&C yellow #10 aluminum lake, magnesium stearate, microcrystalline cellulose and sunset yellow lake. Energy: 2.43 kJ (0.58 kcal). Gluten-, lactose-, sodium-, sulfite- and tartrazine-free. Bottles of 100 and 500.

25 mg: Each round, blue, film-coated, biconvex tablet, identified 25, contains: hydralazine HCl 25 mg. Nonmedicinal ingredients: brilliant blue lake, croscarmellose sodium, D&C yellow #10 lake, hydroxypropyl methylcellulose, magnesium stearate, microcrystalline cellulose, polyethylene glycol and titanium dioxide. Energy: 1.64 kJ (0.39 kcal). Sodium: <1 mmol (0.02 mg). Gluten-, lactose-, sulfite- and tartrazine-free. Bottles of 100 and 500.

50 mg: Each round, pink, film-coated, biconvex tablet, identified 50, contains: hydralazine HCl 50 mg. Nonmedicinal ingredients: croscarmellose sodium, erythrosine lake, hydroxypropyl methylcellulose, magnesium stearate, microcrystalline cellulose, polyethylene glycol and titanium dioxide. Energy: 1.16 kJ (0.28 kcal). Sodium: <1 mmol (0.03 mg). Gluten-, lactose-, sulfite- and tartrazine-free. Bottles of 100 and 500.

APO®-HYDRO ℞
Apotex
Hydrochlorothiazide
Diuretic—Antihypertensive

Supplied: 25 mg: Each round, pale pink, flat-faced with beveled edge tablet, scored and identified APO over 25, contains: hydrochlorothiazide 25 mg. Nonmedicinal ingredients: colloidal silicon dioxide, cornstarch, lactose, magnesium stearate, microcrystalline cellulose and sunset yellow aluminum lake (FD&C yellow #6). Energy: 1.20 kJ (0.29 kcal). Gluten-, sodium-, sulfite- and tartrazine-free. Bottles of 100 and 1 000. Unit dose packages of 100. Apo Long-Term Care (LTC) Pak.

50 mg: Each round, pale pink, flat-faced with beveled edge tablet, scored and identified APO over 50, contains: hydrochlorothiazide 50 mg. Nonmedicinal ingredients: colloidal silicon dioxide, cornstarch, lactose, magnesium stearate, microcrystalline cellulose and sunset yellow aluminum lake (FD&C yellow #6). Energy: 2.07 kJ (0.49 kcal). Gluten-, sodium-, sulfite- and tartrazine-free. Bottles of 100, 1 000 and 5 000. Unit dose packages of 100. Apo Long-Term Care (LTC) Pak.

100 mg: Each round, pale pink, flat-faced with beveled edge tablet, scored and identified APO over 100, contains: hydrochlorothiazide 100 mg. Nonmedicinal ingredients: colloidal silicon dioxide, cornstarch, lactose, magnesium stearate, microcrystalline cellulose and sunset yellow aluminum lake (FD&C yellow #6). Energy: 4.13 kJ (0.99 kcal). Gluten-, sodium-, sulfite- and tartrazine-free. Bottles of 100.

...Seeking additional product information? Ask the manufacturers. Their addresses appear in full in the YELLOW SECTION.

APO®-HYDROXYZINE ℞
Apotex
Hydroxyzine HCl
Anxiolytic—Antihistamine

Supplied: 10 mg: Each oval, orange, soft gelatin capsule, identified 10, contains: hydroxyzine HCl 10 mg. Nonmedicinal ingredients: beeswax, ethyl venalyn, FD&C yellow #6, gelatin, glycerin, lecithin, methylparaben, propylparaben, soyabean oil, titanium dioxide and vegetable shortening. Energy: 1.97 kJ (0.47 kcal). Gluten-, lactose-, sodium- and tartrazine-free. Bottles of 100 and 500.

25 mg: Each oval, green, soft gelatin capsule, identified 25, contains: hydroxyzine HCl 25 mg. Nonmedicinal ingredients: beeswax, D&C yellow #10, ethyl venalyn, FD&C blue #1, gelatin, glycerin, lecithin, methylparaben, propylparaben, soyabean oil, titanium dioxide and vegetable shortening. Energy: 1.84 kJ (0.44 kcal). Gluten-, lactose-, sodium- and tartrazine-free. Bottles of 100 and 500.

50 mg: Each oval, red, soft gelatin capsule, identified 50, contains: hydroxyzine HCl 50 mg. Nonmedicinal ingredients: beeswax, ethyl venalyn, gelatin, glycerin, lecithin, methylparaben, propylparaben, red coloring, soyabean oil, titanium dioxide and vegetable shortening. Energy: 1.83 kJ (0.44 kcal). Gluten-, lactose-, sodium- and tartrazine-free. Bottles of 100 and 500.

APO®-IBUPROFEN ℞*
Apotex
Ibuprofen
Anti-inflammatory—Analgesic

Supplied: Caplets: Each yellow, capsule-shaped, biconvex, film-coated tablet, identified 200 on one side, contains: ibuprofen 200 mg. Nonmedicinal ingredients: colloidal silicon dioxide, croscarmellose sodium, magnesium stearate and microcrystalline cellulose; film-coating: hydroxypropyl methylcellulose, polyethylene glycol and titanium dioxide. Energy: 3.51 kJ (0.84 kcal). Sodium: <1 mmol (0.36 mg). Gluten-, lactose-, sulfite- and tartrazine-free. Bottles of 50 and 100.

Tablets: 200 mg: Each yellow, round, biconvex, film-coated (identified APO over 200) tablet, contains: ibuprofen 200 mg. Nonmedicinal ingredients: colloidal silicon dioxide, croscarmellose sodium, magnesium stearate and microcrystalline cellulose; film-coating: D&C Yellow #10 lake, FD&C Yellow #6, hydroxypropyl methylcellulose, polyethylene glycol and titanium dioxide. Energy: 3.51 kJ (0.84 kcal)/film-coated tablet. Sodium: <1 mmol (0.36 mg)/film-coated tablet. Gluten-, lactose-, sulfite- and tartrazine-free. Bottles of 50, 100 and 1 000. Unit dose packages of 100. Apo Long-Term Care (LTC) Pak.

300 mg: Each white, round, biconvex, film-coated (identified APO over 300) tablet, contains: ibuprofen 300 mg. Nonmedicinal ingredients: colloidal silicon dioxide, croscarmellose sodium, magnesium stearate and microcrystalline cellulose; film-coating: hydroxypropyl methylcellulose, polyethylene glycol and titanium dioxide. Energy: 3.90 kJ (0.93 kcal)/film-coated tablet. Sodium: <1 mmol (0.53 mg)/film-coated tablet. Gluten-, lactose-, sulfite- and tartrazine-free. Bottles of 100 and 1 000. Unit dose packages of 100. Apo Long-Term Care (LTC) Pak.

400 mg: Each orange, round, biconvex, film-coated (identified APO over 400) or sugar-coated (unidentified) tablet, contains: ibuprofen 400 mg. Nonmedicinal ingredients: colloidal silicon dioxide, croscarmellose sodium, magnesium stearate and microcrystalline cellulose; film-coating: FD&C Yellow #6, hydroxypropyl methylcellulose, polyethylene glycol and titanium dioxide. Energy: 5.32 kJ (1.27 kcal)/film-coated tablet; 8.55 kJ (2.04 kcal)/sugar-coated tablet. Sodium: <1 mmol (0.71 mg)/film-coated tablet; <1 mmol (0.71 mg)/sugar-coated tablet. Gluten-, lactose-, sulfite- and tartrazine-free. Bottles of 100 and 1 000. Unit dose packages of 100. Apo Long-Term Care (LTC) Pak.

600 mg: Each light orange, oval, biconvex, film-coated tablet, identified APO-600, contains: ibuprofen 600 mg. Nonmedicinal ingredients: colloidal silicon dioxide, croscarmellose sodium, magnesium stearate and microcrystalline cellulose; film-coating: FD&C Yellow #6, hydroxypropyl methylcellulose, polyethylene glycol and titanium dioxide. Energy: 7.90 kJ (1.89 kcal). Sodium: <1 mmol (1.07 mg). Gluten-, lactose-, sulfite- and tartrazine-free. Bottles of 100 and 1 000. Unit dose packages of 100. Apo Long-Term Care (LTC) Pak.

*200 mg strength available without prescription.

APO®-IMIPRAMINE ℞
Apotex
Imipramine HCl
Antidepressant

Supplied: 10 mg: Each round, light brown, biconvex, film-coated tablet, identified 10, contains: imipramine HCl 10 mg. Nonmedicinal ingredients: FD&C Yellow #6, hydroxypropyl methylcellulose, magnesium stearate, microcrystalline cellulose, polyethylene glycol, red ferric oxide, titanium dioxide and yellow ferric oxide. Energy: <1 kJ (0.10 kcal). Gluten-, lactose-, sodium-, sulfite- and tartrazine-free. Bottles of 100 and 1 000. Unit dose packages of 100. Apo Long-term Care (LTC) Pak.

25 mg: Each round, light brown, biconvex, film-coated tablet, identified 25, contains: imipramine HCl 25 mg. Nonmedicinal ingredients: FD&C Yellow #6, hydroxypropyl methylcellulose, lactose, magnesium stearate, microcrystalline cellulose, polyethylene glycol, red ferric oxide, titanium dioxide and yellow ferric oxide. Energy: <1 kJ (0.15 kcal). Gluten-, sodium-, sulfite- and tartrazine-free. Bottles of 100 and 1 000. Unit dose packages of 100. Apo Long-term Care (LTC) Pak.

50 mg: Each round, light brown, biconvex, film-coated tablet, identified 50, contains: imipramine HCl 50 mg. Nonmedicinal ingredients: FD&C Yellow #6, hydroxypropyl methylcellulose, lactose, magnesium stearate, microcrystalline cellulose, polyethylene glycol, red ferric oxide, titanium dioxide and yellow ferric oxide. Energy: 1.23 kJ (0.29 kcal). Gluten-, sodium-, sulfite- and tartrazine-free. Bottles of 100 and 1 000. Unit dose packages of 100. Apo Long-term Care (LTC) Pak.

75 mg: Each round, light brown, biconvex, film-coated tablet, scored and identified APO over 75, contains: imipramine HCl 75 mg. Nonmedicinal ingredients: FD&C Yellow #6, hydroxypropyl methylcellulose, lactose, magnesium stearate, microcrystalline cellulose, polyethylene glycol, red ferric oxide, titanium dioxide and yellow ferric oxide. Energy: 1.82 kJ (0.44 kcal). Gluten-, sodium-, sulfite- and tartrazine-free. Bottles of 100.

APO®-INDAPAMIDE ℞
Apotex
Indapamide
Diuretic—Antihypertensive

Supplied: Each pink, round, biconvex, film-coated tablet, engraved "2.5" on one side and plain on the other, contains: indapamide 2.5 mg. Nonmedicinal ingredients: croscarmellose sodium, D&C red #30 aluminum lake, hydroxypropyl methylcellulose, lactose, magnesium stearate, microcrystalline cellulose, polyethylene glycol and titanium dioxide. Gluten– and tartrazine–free. Bottles of 30 and 100. Store at room temperature (15 to 30°C) in tightly-closed containers.

APO®-INDOMETHACIN ℞
Apotex
Indomethacin
Anti-inflammatory—Analgesic

Supplied: 25 mg: Each blue and white no. 3 capsule, identified APO 25, contains: indomethacin 25 mg. Nonmedicinal ingredients: cornstarch, lactose and stearic acid. Energy: 3.45 kJ (0.82 kcal). Gluten-, sodium- and tartrazine-free. Bottles of 100 and 1 000.

50 mg: Each blue and white no. 1 capsule, identified APO 50, contains: indomethacin 50 mg. Nonmedicinal ingredients: cornstarch, lactose and stearic acid. Energy: 7.55 kJ (1.80 kcal). Gluten-, sodium- and tartrazine-free. Bottles of 100 and 500.

APO®-IPRAVENT ℞

Apotex

Ipratropium Bromide

Bronchodilator

Supplied: Each mL of clear, colorless or almost colorless solution contains: ipratropium bromide 250 µg (0.025%) in isotonic solution preserved with benzalkonium chloride 0.025% and EDTA-disodium 0.05% at pH 3.4. Amber glass bottles of 20 mL with screwcap.

APO®-ISDN

Apotex

Isosorbide Dinitrate

Antianginal Agent—Coronary Vasodilator

Supplied: Sublingual Tablets: Each pink, round, flat-faced with beveled edge tablet, identified 5, contains: isosorbide dinitrate 5 mg. Nonmedicinal ingredients: colloidal silicon dioxide, croscarmellose sodium, D&C Red #30, lactose, magnesium stearate and microcrystalline cellulose. Energy: <1 kJ (0.06 kcal). Sodium: <1 mmol (0.05 mg). Gluten-, sulfite- and tartrazine-free. Bottles of 100 and 500.

Oral Tablets: 10 mg: Each white, round, flat-faced with beveled edge tablet, scored and identified APO over 10, contains: isosorbide dinitrate 10 mg. Nonmedicinal ingredients: croscarmellose sodium, lactose, magnesium stearate and microcrystalline cellulose. Energy: 2.19 kJ (0.52 kcal). Sodium: <1 mmol (0.02 mg). Gluten-, sulfite- and tartrazine-free. Bottles of 100, 1 000 and 5 000. Unit dose packages of 100. Apo Long-Term Care (LTC) Pak.

30 mg: Each white, round, flat-faced with beveled edge tablet, scored and identified APO over I30, contains: isosorbide dinitrate 30 mg. Nonmedicinal ingredients: colloidal silicon dioxide, croscarmellose sodium, D&C Red #30 aluminum lake, lactose, magnesium stearate and microcrystalline cellulose. Energy: 2.83 kJ (0.67 kcal). Sodium: <1 mmol (0.06 mg). Gluten-, sulfite- and tartrazine-free. Bottles of 100, 1 000 and 3 000. Unit dose packages of 100. Apo Long-Term Care (LTC) Pak.

APO®-K

Apotex

Potassium Chloride

Potassium Replacement Therapy

Supplied: Each orange, round, film-coated slow release tablet identified APO-K over 600 contains: potassium chloride 600 mg (8 mEq K). Nonmedicinal ingredients: colloidal silicon dioxide, D&C Yellow #10 lake, ethyl cellulose, FD&C Yellow #6, hydroxypropyl methylcellulose, magnesium stearate and titanium dioxide. Energy: 11.45 kJ (2.73 kcal). Gluten-, lactose-, sodium-, sulfite- and tartrazine-free. Bottles of 100, 1 000 and 3 000.

APO®-KETO ℞
APO®-KETO-E ℞
APO®-KETO SR ℞

Apotex

Ketoprofen

Anti-inflammatory—Analgesic

Supplied: Apo-Keto: Each dark green and ivory, hard gelatin no. 2 capsule, identified APO 50, contains: ketoprofen 50 mg. Nonmedicinal ingredients: colloidal silicon dioxide, croscarmellose sodium, D&C Yellow #10, edible red ink, FD&C Green #3, FD&C Yellow #6, gelatin, lactose, magnesium stearate, sodium lauryl sulfate and titanium dioxide. Energy: 5.02 kJ (1.20 kcal). Sodium: <1 mmol (0.38 mg). Gluten- and tartrazine-free. Bottles of 100 and 500.

Apo-Keto-E: 50 mg: Each round, biconvex, yellow, enteric-coated tablet, identified 50, contains: ketoprofen 50 mg. Nonmedicinal ingredients: cellulose acetate phthalate, colloidal silicon dioxide, croscarmellose sodium, D&C Yelow #10, dextrates, diethyl phthalate, FD&C Yellow #6, hydroxypropyl methylcellulose, magnesium stearate, methylcellulose, polyethylene glycol, strong ammonia solution and titanium dioxide. Energy: 1.70 kJ (0.41 kcal). Sodium: <1 mmol (0.27 mg). Gluten-, lactose-, sulfite- and tartrazine-free. Bottles of 100 and 500.

100 mg: Each round, biconvex, yellow, enteric-coated tablet, identified APO over 100, contains: ketoprofen 100 mg. Nonmedicinal ingredients: cellulose acetate phthalate, colloidal silicon dioxide, croscarmellose sodium, D&C Yellow #10, dextrates, diethyl phthalate, FD&C Yellow #6, hydroxypropyl methylcellulose, magnesium stearate, methylcellulose, polyethylene glycol, strong ammonia solution and titanium dioxide. Energy: 3.39 kJ (0.81 kcal). Sodium: <1 mmol (0.54 mg). Gluten-, lactose-, sulfite- and tartrazine-free. Bottles of 100 and 500.

Apo-Keto SR: Each round, biconvex, white, slow release tablet, identified APO on one side and 200 on the other, contains: ketoprofen 200 mg. Nonmedicinal ingredients: colloidal silicon dioxide, dextrates, hydroxypropyl cellulose, hydroxypropyl methylcellulose, magnesium stearate, methanol, polyethylene glycol, polyvinyl acetate phthalate, stearic acid, titanium dioxide and triethyl citrate. Energy: 2.15 kJ (0.52 kcal). Gluten-, lactose-, sodium-, sulfite- and tartrazine-free. Bottles of 100 and 500.

APO®-KETOCONAZOLE ℞

Apotex

Ketoconazole

Antifungal

Pharmacology: In vitro studies suggest that the antifungal properties of ketoconazole may be related to its ability to impair the synthesis of ergosterol, a component of fungal and yeast cell membranes. Without the availability of this essential sterol, there are morphological alterations of the fungal and yeast cell membranes manifested as abnormal membranous inclusions between the cell wall and the plasma membrane. The inhibition of ergosterol synthesis has been attributed to interference with the reactions involved in the removal of the 14-α-methyl group of the precursor of ergosterol, lanosterol.

Indications: For the treatment of serious or life threatening systemic fungal infections in normal, predisposed, or immunocompromised patients where alternate therapy is considered inappropriate or has been unsuccessful: systemic candidiasis, chronic mucocutaneous candidiasis, coccidioidomycosis and paracoccidioidomycosis, histoplasmosis and chromomycosis.

The use of ketoconazole may also be considered in the treatment of severe, recalcitrant dermatophytoses unresponsive to other forms of therapy.

The type of organism responsible for the infection should be identified; however, therapy may be initiated prior to obtaining these results, when clinically warranted.

Note: The treatment of fungal infections of the CNS is not recommended; ketoconazole penetrates poorly into the CNS.

Contraindications: Patients with known hypersensitivity to the drug, and patients with hepatic dysfunction. Ketoconazole is contraindicated in women of child-bearing potential unless effective forms of contraception are employed.

Concurrent therapy of ketoconazole tablets together with terfenadine is contraindicated. Ketoconazole may inhibit the metabolism of terfenadine, causing increased plasma levels of terfenadine. Increased plasma levels of terfenadine can result in prolonged QT intervals. Cases of severe cardiovascular events including death, cardiac arrest, torsades de pointes and other ventricular dysrhythmias have been reported in patients taking terfenadine in combination with ketoconazole.

Concurrent therapy of astemizole with oral ketoconazole is contraindicated. Pharmacokinetic data indicate that oral ketoconazole inhibits the metabolism of astemizole, resulting in elevated plasma levels of astemizole and its active metabolite desmethylastemizole which may prolong QT intervals.

Concomitant administration of oral ketoconazole and cisapride is contraindicated because it has resulted in markedly elevated cisapride plasma concentrations and prolonged QT intervals. This interaction has been rarely associated with ventricular arrhythmia and torsades de pointes.

Oral midazolam and triazolam should not be used by patients treated with ketoconazole tablets. Pharmacokinetic data revealed higher and prolonged midazolam concentrations when oral midazolam was administered concomitantly with oral ketoconazole versus placebo. A more pronounced and prolonged hypnotic effect of midazolam was also observed. Metabolism of both ketoconazole and midazolam by the same cytochrome P450 3A isozyme may explain this interaction. Similar pharmacokinetic and pharmacodynamic effects have been observed with triazolam which is primarily metabolized by the same P450 3A isozyme (see Precautions, Drug Interactions).

Pharmacokinetic data indicate that another oral antifungal, itraconazole inhibits the metabolism of HMG-CoA reductase inhibitors such as lovastatin. Coadministration of Itraconazole and lovastatin resulted in elevated and prolonged plasma concentrations of lovastatin and its active metabolite, lovastatin acid, which may increase the risk of diffuse myalgia and rhabdomyolysis. Based on the chemical resemblance of itraconazole and ketoconazole, HMG-CoA reductase inhibitors such as lovastatin should not be used during treatment with itraconazole.

Warnings: Cases of idiosyncratic hepatocellular dysfunction have been reported during ketoconazole treatment. It is important to recognize that liver disorders can occur during therapy with ketoconazole. The occurrence of liver disorders while on ketoconazole could be fatal unless properly recognized and managed. Liver function tests such as SGGT, alkaline phosphatase, AST, ALT and bilirubin should be performed before treatment, after 2 weeks and at periodic intervals during treatment (monthly or more frequently) particularly in patients who are expected to be on prolonged therapy (>2 weeks) or who have a history of significant alcohol consumption. The concurrent use of ketoconazole with potentially hepatotoxic drugs should be most carefully monitored, especially in patients who are expected to be on prolonged therapy or who have a history of significant alcohol consumption. Other factors increasing the risk of hepatitis are: women over 50, history of liver disease and known drug intolerance.

A mild transient asymptomatic increase of transaminases or alkaline phosphatase sometimes occurs. This asymptomatic reaction is harmless and does not necessarily require a discontinuation of the therapy but these patients should be monitored. It should be emphasized, however, that the occurrence of symptoms of hepatotoxicity, even with minor elevations of liver enzymes, is an indication for termination of therapy. Deaths have been reported with therapeutic doses of ketoconazole associated with evidence of hepatotoxicity.

Clinical studies in men have shown that single doses of ketoconazole at 200, 400 and 600 mg caused a dose-related decrease in serum testosterone levels, which returned to baseline values 8 to 24 hours later. During chronic administration (12 months) of 200 mg ketoconazole daily, testosterone levels were not significantly suppressed. However, at high doses (1 200 mg a day), administration of ketoconazole resulted in a reduction of serum testosterone to the castrate level (24 ng/dL) within 24 hours; this reduction was maintained for the duration of therapy (3-10 months). Oligospermia and azoospermia have been reported at therapeutic doses and above. In 6 healthy females receiving 400 mg once in the late follicular phase and once in the luteal phase, ketoconazole produced a 38% drop in 17-β-estradiol along with a 50% increase in progesterone during the follicular phase as well as a 61% drop in 17-β-estradiol and a 94% increase in progesterone during the luteal phase. Since ketoconazole influences steroid synthesis, the potential for a deleterious effect on puberty and/or fertility must be carefully considered when long-term therapy is contemplated in children.

A single 200 mg oral dose of ketoconazole had no effect on human cortisol levels. After a single dose of 400 or 600 mg, ketoconazole caused a slight nonsignificant fall in basal cortisol levels from 11.7 to 9.3 and 8.1 µg/dL, respectively. There was a significant blunting of cortisol response to ACTH which was reversible; following a single dose of 400 mg or 600 mg ketoconazole, cortisol levels fell from 25.4 to 15.7 and 13.5 µg/dL, respectively. Chronic (1 to 34 months) administration of 800 or 1200 mg ketoconazole impaired the ability of the adrenal gland to produce cortisol, although evidence of frank adrenal insufficiency was not observed. In patients predisposed to adrenal insufficiency, in those having marginal adrenal function or during periods of prolonged stress, such as in the intensive care unit, cortisol levels should be monitored regularly. Administration of ketoconazole to males at a dose of 1 200 mg/day resulted in a rapid and significant decline in adrenal androgens (androstenedione and dehydroepiandrosterone).

Because the effects of ketoconazole on hormonal pathways are incompletely understood, judicious consideration is recommended before ketoconazole is prescribed on a long-term basis.

Toxicity studies in rats receiving ketoconazole admixed in the diet at doses of 160 mg/kg have indicated that ketoconazole leads to increased bone fragility in females. Therefore, therapeutic doses (400 mg/day) should not be exceeded in

Apo-Ketoconazole (cont'd)

patients such as postmenopausal women and elderly patients, susceptible to increased bone fragility. In view of the ability of ketoconazole to interfere with steroid synthesis and vitamin D metabolism, careful consideration should be given prior to the use of ketoconazole in children. During long-term treatment, calcium and phosphorus serum levels should be monitored.

Studies in pregnant rats and in guinea pigs with ^{3}H-ketoconazole indicate that ketoconazole crosses the placental barrier. Whereas in the rat, fetal levels of total radioactivity were 6 times lower than those of the placenta, unchanged drug levels were 3.5 times lower in the fetuses. Concentrations of radioactivity in the fetal membrane indicate that ketoconazole is only very slowly eliminated from this membrane. In the pregnant patient, the implications of placental transfer of ketoconazole must be carefully considered.

Precautions: Patients should be instructed to report any signs and symptoms which may suggest liver dysfunction so that appropriate biochemical testing can be done. Such signs and symptoms would include unusual fatigue, anorexia, nausea and/or vomiting, jaundice, dark urine or pale stools. Patients who receive ketoconazole concomitantly with potentially hepatotoxic drugs, those who are expected to be on long-term therapy (>2 weeks) as well as those with a history of significant alcohol intake or suspicion of liver disorder should have liver function tests performed before and during the initial days of treatment and at periodic intervals during treatment (monthly or more frequently [see Warnings]).

Since ketoconazole influences steroid synthesis, the potential for a deleterious effect on puberty and/or fertility must be carefully considered when long-term therapy is contemplated in children.

Anaphylactic reactions to ketoconazole with severe angioedema have been reported in 2 cases. Cross sensitivity with miconazole may exist and caution is suggested when ketoconazole is administered to patients with a known sensitivity to miconazole.

Patients with Decreased Gastric Acidity: Absorption of ketoconazole is impaired when gastric acidity is decreased. In patients also receiving acid neutralizing medicines (eg. aluminum hydroxide) these should be administered at least 2 hours after the intake of ketoconazole. In patients with achlorhydria such as certain AIDS patients and patients on acid secretion suppressors (eg. H_2-antagonists, proton pump inhibitors) it is advisable to administer ketoconazole with a cola beverage.

Women of Child-bearing Age: In women of child-bearing potential, an effective form of contraception must be used during therapy with ketoconazole.

Pregnancy: Ketoconazole has been shown to be teratogenic (syndactyly, oligodactyly, abnormal head and leg formation) in the rat when given at 80 mg/kg administered in the diet. When ketoconazole was given to rats by gavage, evidence of maternal toxicity and embryotoxicity was seen with doses as low as 10 mg/kg. There is no experience with the use of ketoconazole in pregnant women, but animal experiments in pregnant rats and guinea pigs indicate that ketoconazole crosses the placental barrier and that ketoconazole is only very slowly eliminated from fetal membranes.

Very careful consideration should be given to the implications for both mother and fetus before using ketoconazole in pregnant patients.

Lactation: Ketoconazole is excreted in the milk. When treatment with ketoconazole is deemed necessary for the lactating patient, nursing should be stopped before therapy with ketoconazole is initiated.

Children: Although ketoconazole has been used in children under 2 years of age, the number of instances is limited and monitoring was not comprehensive. Caution should be exercised when ketoconazole is administered to children and careful hepatic and hematological monitoring is indicated. In view of the ability of ketoconazole to interfere with steroid synthesis and vitamin D metabolism, careful consideration should be given prior to the use of ketoconazole in children. There has been a report of hypoparathyroidism developing in a 6 year old during long-term treatment with ketoconazole. During long-term treatment, calcium and phosphorus serum levels should be monitored.

Drug Interactions: Since ketoconazole inhibits certain hepatic P450 enzymes, especially of the CYP 3A family, it may decrease the elimination of coadministered drugs whose metabolism depends on such enzymes. Increased levels of such drugs, when used together with ketoconazole, have been associated with an increase and/or a prolongation of their effects, including side effects. Known examples of potentially serious interactions are: Ketoconazole has been reported to increase plasma concentrations of cyclosporine. When ketoconazole and cyclosporine are used concomitantly, the dose requirement for cyclosporine may be substantially reduced in order to achieve appropriate plasma trough levels. Blood levels of cyclosporine should be monitored when the two drugs are given concomitantly.

Ketoconazole inhibits the metabolism of terfenadine, resulting in an increased plasma concentration of terfenadine and a delay in the elimination of its acid metabolite. The increased plasma concentration of terfenadine or its metabolite may result in prolonged QT intervals (see Contraindications).

Pharmacokinetic data indicate that oral ketoconazole inhibits the metabolism of astemizole, resulting in elevated plasma levels of astemizole and its active metabolite desmethylastemizole which may prolong QT intervals (see Contraindications).

Human pharmacokinetic data indicate that oral ketoconazole potently inhibits the metabolism of cisapride, increasing its half life and plasma concentration and resulting in a mean 8-fold increase in its AUC. Data suggest that co-administration of oral ketoconazole and cisapride can result in prolongation of the QT interval on the ECG (see Contraindications).

After the co-administration of 200 mg oral ketoconazole twice daily and one 20 mg dose of loratadine to 11 subjects, the AUC and C_{max} of loratadine averaged 302% (±142 S.D.) and 251% (±68 S.D.), respectively, of those obtained after co-treatment with placebo. The AUC and C_{max} of descarboethoxyloratadine, an active metabolite, averaged 155% (±27 S.D.) and 141% (±35 S.D.), respectively. However, no related changes were noted in the QT_c on ECG taken at 2, 6 and 24 hours after the co-administration. Also, there were no clinically significant differences in adverse events when loratadine was administered with or without ketoconazole.

Pharmacokinetic data suggest that oral ketoconazole may inhibit the metabolism of oral midazolam. In 9 subjects, pretreatment with 400 mg ketoconazole once daily for 4 days resulted in a 15-fold increase in midazolam $AUC_{0-\infty}$, an approximate 4-fold increase in C_{max}, and an approximate 3-fold increase in $t_{1/2}$. Enhanced and prolonged sedative effects were also observed. Similar pharmacokinetic and pharmacodynamic effects have been observed for triazolam which is primarily metabolized by the same P450 3A isozyme. In 9 subjects, pretreatment with 400 mg ketoconazole for 4 days resulted in a 22-fold increase in triazolam $AUC_{0-\infty}$, a 3-fold increase in C_{max} and a 6-fold increase in $t_{1/2}$. Midazolam and triazolam should not be used by patients treated with ketoconazole (see Contraindications). If midazolam is administered i.v., special precaution is required since the sedative effect may be prolonged.

Pharmacokinetic data demonstrate that when co-administered, another oral antifungal, itraconazole inhibits the metabolism of lovastatin, resulting in increased plasma concentrations of lovastatin, and its active metabolite lovastatin acid, and a 20-fold increase in AUC for both compounds. These increased plasma levels potentially elevate the risk of skeletal muscle toxicity such as diffuse myalgia and rhabdomyolysis. Based on the chemical resemblance of itraconazole and ketoconazole, concomitant administration of itraconazole with HMG-CoA reductase inhibitors such as lovastatin is contraindicated (see Contraindications).

Ketoconazole may increase the plasma levels of methylprednisolone and possibly busulphane and tacrolimus. The dosage of such drugs, if coadministered with ketoconazole, should be reduced if necessary.

There have also been reports of decreased insulin needs in diabetic patients treated with ketoconazole. Because of a possible insulin-sparing effect of ketoconazole, insulin requirements should be assessed more frequently when ketoconazole is used concomitantly with insulin.

Since administration of rifampin and/or enzyme inducers such as isoniazid in conjunction with ketoconazole reduced the blood levels of the latter, these drugs should not be administered concomitantly.

There has been a report of an interaction between ketoconazole and phenytoin in patients receiving concomitant therapy. This interaction is complex and is a result of the opposing actions of both agents on cytochrome P450 enzymes: while ketoconazole tends to inhibit this enzymatic system, phenytoin induces it, resulting in a decrease or an increase of either drug in the plasma.

Rare cases of a disulfiram-like reaction to alcohol, characterized by flushing, rash, peripheral edema, nausea and headache have been reported. All symptoms completely resolved within a few hours.

Adverse Effects: Some deaths have occurred during clinical trials with ketoconazole. These may or may not be drug related.

Gastrointestinal: dyspepsia, nausea and/or vomiting (3%), gastrointestinal hemorrhage (<1%), abdominal pain (1.2%), diarrhea (<1%).

Dermatological: pruritus (1.5%), alopecia (<1%), purpura (<1%), rash (<1%), dermatitis (<1%).

CNS: headache, dizziness, somnolence, tremors, nervousness, paresthesia (<1% in all cases).

Endocrinological: gynecomastia (<1%), dose-dependent decrease in testosterone serum levels, decrease in basal and ACTH-induced cortisol levels, increased serum levels of 17-OH progesterone and decreased urinary levels of 17-ketosteroids, hypoparathyroidism.

Genitourinary: oligospermia and azoospermia, impotence, loss of libido, menstrual irregularities.

Hematological: thrombocytopenia, eosinophilia, decreased hematocrit, anemia, leukopenia, neutropenia (<1%).

Hepatic: idiosyncratic hepatocellular dysfunction (<0.01%; see Warnings); transient increases in liver enzymes. Three patients have died in hepatic coma; two when ketoconazole therapy was continued despite icteric symptoms, and the third despite discontinuation of therapy.

Miscellaneous: fever and chills, photophobia, idiosyncratic allergic reactions, anaphylactic shock, pronounced dyspnea, arthralgia, sensation of detachment (at 800 mg/day), corneal deposits, cataract enlargement (<1%).

Postmarketing: In rare instances, cases of exanthema, urticaria and reversible increased intracranial pressure (e.g., papiloedema, bulging fontanelle in infants) have been reported in association with ketoconazole treatment.

Overdose: Symptoms and Treatment: In the event of accidental overdosage with ketoconazole, supportive measures, including gastric lavage (within the first hour) with sodium bicarbonate, may be employed. Activated charcoal may be given if considered appropriate. It has been reported that ketoconazole cannot be removed by hemodialysis.

Dosage: When ketoconazole therapy may be indicated, the type of organism responsible for the infection should be identified, although therapy may be initiated prior to obtaining these results, when clinically warranted.

Table I—Apo-Ketoconazole

General Guidelines for the Duration of Ketoconazole Treatment in Patients with Severe or Recalcitrant Fungal Infections

Condition	Recommended Treatment[a]	Response Time[b]
Dermal and Cutaneous Mycoses		
Dermatomycosis	4-8 weeks	4 weeks
Hair or scalp mycoses	4-8 weeks	4 weeks
Pityriasis versicolor	3-6 weeks	3 weeks
Oral thrush	1-2 weeks	1 week
Chronic mucocutaneous candidiasis	6-12 months	4 months
Onychomycosis	6-12 months	3 months
Deep Mycoses[c]		
Systemic candidiasis	2-4 weeks	4 weeks
Paracoccidioidomycosis	2-4 months	2 months
Coccidioidomycosis	>6 months	6 months
Histoplasmosis	2-4 months	2 months
Chromomycosis	>6 months	3 months

[a] The final decision on length of therapy in individual patients should be based on clinical and mycological response whenever possible.

[b] If no response is seen during this period, dosage can be increased up to the maximum recommended dose.

[c] In deep mycoses, treatment should continue for at least 1 week after apparent eradication of the infecting fungus.

Note: Refer to Warnings and Precautions.

Adults: Ketoconazole should be administered at a dose of 200 mg once a day. Patients who fail to show a response (see Table I on previous page) may have inadequate blood levels (<1 μg/mL) as determined by bioassay and the dose may be increased to 400 mg. Ketoconazole blood levels can also be determined by an HPLC assay.

A maximum daily dose of 400 mg should not be exceeded.

Children: Weighing 20 kg or less: 50 mg once daily. Weighing 20 to 40 kg: 100 mg once daily. Weighing over 40 kg: 200 mg once daily.

A maximum daily dose of 100 to 400 mg should not be exceeded.

Ketoconazole should be taken once daily with a meal. Concomitant administration of agents which inhibit gastric secretion should be avoided since ketoconazole requires adequate gastric acidity for dissolution. In patients also receiving acid neutralizing medicines (e.g., aluminum hydroxide), these should be administered at least 2 hours after intake of ketoconazole. In patients with achlorhydria such as certain AIDS patients and patients on acid secretion suppressors (e.g., H_2-antagonists, proton pump inhibitors) it is advisable to administer ketoconazole with a cola beverage.

Supplied: Each round, white to slightly grey, flat-faced, beveled-edged tablet, engraved "APO-200" above the partial bisect on one side, plain on the other, contains: ketoconazole 200 mg. Nonmedicinal ingredients: colloidal silicon dioxide, croscarmellose sodium, dextrates and magnesium stearate. Bottles of 100, 250, 500 or 1 000. Unit dose packages of 100. Store at room temperature (15 to 30°C) in well closed containers.

New Product 1998

APO®-KETOTIFEN

Apotex

Ketotifen Fumarate

Pediatric Asthma Prophylactic Agent—Antiallergic Agent

Supplied: Each 5 mL of oral syrup contains: ketotifen fumarate 1 mg. Nonmedicinal ingredients: artificial strawberry flavor, glycerin, methylparaben, propylparaben, sodium citrate, sorbitol and sucrose. Bottles of 250 mL. Store at room temperature (15 to 30°C).

APO®-LEVOCARB

Apotex

Levodopa—Carbidopa

Antiparkinson Agent

Supplied: 100 mg/10 mg: Each blue, oval, biconvex tablet, with one side scored and engraved "100 10", and the other side engraved "APO", contains: levodopa 100 mg and carbidopa 10 mg expressed as anhydrous carbidopa. Nonmedicinal ingredients: brilliant blue FCF aluminum lake 12%, croscarmellose sodium, indigotine aluminum lake 12%, magnesium stearate, microcrystalline cellulose and sorbitol. Gluten-, sulfite- and tartrazine-free. Bottles of 100.

100 mg/25 mg: Each yellow, oval, biconvex tablet, with one side scored and engraved "100 25", and the other side engraved "APO", contains: levodopa 100 mg and carbidopa 25 mg expressed as anhydrous carbidopa. Nonmedicinal ingredients: croscarmellose sodium, D&C yellow #10 aluminum lake, magnesium stearate, microcrystalline cellulose and sorbitol. Gluten-, sulfite- and tartrazine-free. Bottles of 100 and 500.

250 mg/25 mg: Each blue, oval, biconvex tablet, with one side scored and engraved "250 25", and the other side engraved "APO", contains: levodopa 250 mg and carbidopa 25 mg expressed as anhydrous carbidopa. Nonmedicinal ingredients: brilliant blue FCF aluminum lake 12%, croscarmellose sodium, indigotine aluminum lake 12%, magnesium stearate, microcrystalline cellulose and sorbitol. Gluten-, sulfite- and tartrazine-free. Bottles of 100 and 500.

Store at controlled room temperature (15 to 30°C), in well-closed, light-resistant containers.

APO®-LISINOPRIL

Apotex

Lisinopril

Angiotensin Converting Enzyme Inhibitor

Supplied: Each pink, oval, biconvex tablet, engraved APO over L5 on one side and scored on the other, contains: lisinopril 5 mg. Nonmedicinal ingredients: lactose, red ferric oxide and zinc stearate. Bottles of 100 and 500. Store at room temperature 15 to 30°C.

APO®-LOPERAMIDE

Apotex

Loperamide

Antidiarrheal

Supplied: Each light green, capsule-shaped tablet, scored and engraved "APO 2" on one side, contains: loperamide HCl 2 mg. Nonmedicinal ingredients: brilliant blue FCF aluminum lake 12%, cornstarch, D&C yellow #10 aluminum lake, lactose, magnesium stearate and microcrystalline cellulose. Gluten-, sulfite- and tartrazine-free. Bottles of 100 and 500. Store at room temperature 15 to 30°C. Protect from light and high humidity.

APO®-LORAZEPAM

Apotex

Lorazepam

Anxiolytic—Sedative

Supplied: 0.5 mg: Each white, round, flat-faced with beveled edge, tablet identified APO on one side and 0.5 on the other contains: lorazepam 0.5 mg (500 μg). Nonmedicinal ingredients: croscarmellose sodium, lactose, magnesium stearate and microcrystalline cellulose. Energy: <1 kJ (0.19 kcal). Sodium: <1 mmol (0.06 mg). Gluten-, sulfite- and tartrazine-free. Bottles of 100 and 500. Unit dose packages of 100. Apo Long-Term Care (LTC) Pak.

1 mg: Each white, capsule-shaped, flat-faced with beveled edge, scored tablet identified APO 1 contains: lorazepam 1 mg. Nonmedicinal ingredients: croscarmellose sodium, lactose, magnesium stearate and microcrystalline cellulose. Energy: 1.57 kJ (0.38 kcal). Sodium: <1 mmol (0.13 mg). Gluten-, sulfite- and tartrazine-free. Bottles of 100, 1 000 and 3 000. Unit dose packages of 100. Apo Long-Term Care (LTC) Pak.

2 mg: Each white, oval, flat-faced with beveled edge, scored tablet identified APO 2 contains: lorazepam 2 mg. Nonmedicinal ingredients: croscarmellose sodium, lactose, magnesium stearate and microcrystalline cellulose. Energy: 1.96 kJ (0.47 kcal). Sodium: <1 mmol (0.16 mg). Gluten-, sulfite- and tartrazine-free. Bottles of 100, 1 000 and 3 000. Unit dose packages of 100. Apo Long-Term Care (LTC) Pak.

APO®-LOVASTATIN

Apotex

Lovastatin

Lipid Metabolism Regulator

Supplied: 20 mg: Each light blue, octagonal, flat-faced, beveled-edged tablet, engraved APO on one side, scored and engraved LOVA over 20 on the other side, contains: lovastatin 20 mg. Nonmedicinal ingredients: brilliant blue FCF aluminum lake, croscarmellose sodium, indigotine aluminum lake, lactose monohydrate, magnesium stearate and microcrystalline cellulose. Bottles of 100 and 500.

40 mg: Each light green, octagonal, flat-faced, beveled-edged tablet, engraved APO on one side and LOVA over 40 on the other side, contains: lovastatin 40 mg. Nonmedicinal ingredients: croscarmellose sodium, D&C yellow #10 aluminum lake, indigotine aluminum lake, lactose monohydrate, magnesium stearate and microcrystalline cellulose. Bottles of 100 and 250.

Store at room temperature (15 to 30°C). Protect from light.

APO®-LOXAPINE

Apotex

Loxapine

Antipsychotic

Pharmacology: Loxapine, a tricyclic dibenzoxazepine antipsychotic agent, which is clinically distinct from the phenothiazines, thioxanthenes and butyrophenones, produces pharmacologic responses in various animal species which are characteristic of those seen with the majority of antipsychotic drugs.

Loxapine is an antipsychotic drug which exhibits many of the actions common to this broad class of drugs. Loxapine has proven to be of value in the management of both acute and chronic schizophrenia. As in the case of other antipsychotics, the mode of action has not been clearly established, but is postulated to involve changes in synaptic transmission at the subcortical level of the brain, resulting in strong inhibition of spontaneous motor activity.

Absorption of orally administered loxapine tablets in man is rapid and virtually complete following a single 25 mg dose. Signs of sedation in normal volunteers appear generally within 30 minutes. Duration of sedation may last through a 12-hour period. The duration and intensity of sedation produced in normal volunteers average close to 3 hours. When multiple doses were given initially, sedation occurred within 1.5 hours of the dose and lasted 8 hours: thereafter the duration was shortened to 1 to 2.5 hours. Loxapine is metabolized extensively, essentially no unchanged parent drug being excreted in urine or feces. The serum half-life of loxapine is approximately 3 hours. The serum concentration time curve of total drug related materials (loxapine plus metabolites), as shown by studies with radio-labeled drug, is biphasic in nature and shows larger half-lives, i.e., 5 hours for the α-phase and 19 hours for the β-phase.

Five metabolites have been identified in the urine—loxapine N-oxide, 8-hydroxyloxapine, 7-hydroxyloxapine, 8-hydroxyamoxapine and 7-hydroxyamoxapine. The phenolic metabolites are excreted in the urine largely in the form of conjugates and in the feces primarily in the free form. In man, the greater proportion of the dose (56 to 70%) is excreted in the urine.

Indications: In the management of the manifestations of schizophrenia.

Contraindications: Comatose or severe, drug-induced depressed states (alcohol, barbiturates, narcotics, etc.); individuals with known hypersensitivity to the drug; patients with circulatory collapse.

Warnings: Tardive Dyskinesia: A syndrome consisting of potentially irreversible, involuntary, dyskinetic movements may develop in patients treated with conventional antipsychotic drugs. Although the prevalence of tardive dyskinesia with conventional antipsychotics appears to be highest among the elderly, especially elderly women, it is impossible to rely upon prevalence estimates to predict, at the beginning of treatment, which patients are likely to develop the syndrome.

Both the risk of developing tardive dyskinesia and the likelihood that it will become irreversible are believed to increase as the duration of treatment and the total cumulative dose of antipsychotic drugs administered to the patient increase. However, the syndrome can develop, although much less commonly, after relatively brief treatment periods at low doses. There is no known treatment for established cases of tardive dyskinesia, although the syndrome may remit, partially or completely, if antipsychotic drug treatment is withdrawn. Antipsychotic drug treatment itself, however, may suppress (or partially suppress) the signs and symptoms of tardive dyskinesia and thereby may possibly mask the underlying process. The effect that symptom suppression has upon the long-term course of the syndrome is unknown.

Given this consideration, loxapine should be prescribed in a manner that is most likely to minimize the risk of the occurrence of tardive dyskinesia. As with any antipsychotic drug, chronic loxapine use should be reserved for patients who appear to be obtaining substantial benefit from the drug. In such patients, the smallest dose and the shortest duration of treatment should be sought. The need for continued treatment should be reassessed periodically.

If signs and symptoms of tardive dyskinesia appear in a patient on loxapine, drug discontinuation should be considered. However, some patients may require treatment with loxapine despite the presence of the syndrome.

Neuroleptic Malignant Syndrome (NMS): A potentially fatal symptom complex sometimes referred to as Neuroleptic Malignant Syndrome (NMS) has been reported in association with antipsychotic drugs. Clinical manifestations of NMS are

Apo-Loxapine (cont'd)

hyperpyrexia, muscle rigidity, altered mental status and evidence of autonomic instability (irregular pulse or blood pressure, tachycardia, diaphoresis and cardiac dysrhythmias).

The diagnostic evaluation of patients with this syndrome is complicated in arriving at a diagnosis. It is important to identify cases where the clinical presentation includes both serious medical illness (e.g., pneumonia, systemic infection, etc.) and untreated or inadequately treated extrapyramidal signs and symptoms (EPS). Other important considerations in the differential diagnosis include central anticholinergic toxicity, heat stroke, drug fever and primary CNS pathology.

The management of NMS should include 1) immediate discontinuation of antipsychotic drugs and other drugs not essential to concurrent therapy, 2) intensive symptomatic treatment and medical monitoring, and 3) treatment of any concomitant serious medical problem for which specific treatment is available. There is no general agreement about specific pharmacological treatment regimens for uncomplicated NMS.

If a patient requires antipsychotic drug treatment after recovery from NMS, the potential reintroduction of drug therapy should be carefully considered. The patient should be carefully monitored, since recurrences of NMS have been reported.

Pregnancy and *Lactation:* Safe use of loxapine during pregnancy or lactation has not been established; therefore, its use in pregnancy, in nursing mothers or in women of childbearing potential requires that the benefits of treatment be weighed against the possible risks to mother and child.

Children: Studies have not been performed in children; therefore, this drug is not recommended for use in children below the age of 16.

Occupational Hazards: Loxapine, like other antipsychotics may impair mental and/or physical abilities, especially during the first few days of therapy. Therefore, ambulatory patients should be warned about activities requiring alertness (e.g., operating vehicles or machinery) and about concomitant use of alcohol and other CNS depressants.

This drug is not recommended for use in patients suffering from blood dyscrasias or liver disease of significant severity.

Loxapine has not been evaluated for the management of behavioral complications in patients with mental retardation, and therefore cannot be recommended in these patients.

Precautions: Loxapine should be used with extreme caution in patients with a history of convulsive disorders, since it lowers the convulsive threshold. Seizures have been reported in epileptic patients receiving loxapine at antipsychotic dose levels, and may occur even with maintenance of routine anticonvulsant drug therapy.

Loxapine has an antiemetic effect in animals. Since this effect may also occur in man, loxapine may mask signs of overdosage of toxic drugs and may obscure conditions such as intestinal obstruction and brain tumor.

Loxapine should be used with caution in patients with cardiovascular disease. Increased pulse rate and transient hypotension have both been reported in patients receiving antipsychotic doses. In the presence of severe hypotension requiring vasopressor therapy, the preferred drugs would be norepinephrine or phenylephrine. The use of epinephrine in these cases should be avoided.

Although clinical experience has not demonstrated ocular toxicity, careful observation should be made for pigmentary retinopathy and lenticular pigmentation, since these have been observed in some patients receiving certain other antipsychotic drugs for prolonged periods.

Because of possible anticholinergic action, the drug should be used with caution in patients with glaucoma or a tendency to urinary retention, particularly with concomitant administration of an anticholinergic type of antiparkinson medication.

Neuroleptic drugs elevate prolactin levels; the elevation persists during chronic administration. Tissue culture experiments indicate that approximately one-third of human breast cancers are prolactin-dependent in vitro, a factor of potential importance if the prescription of these drugs is contemplated in a patient with a previously detected breast cancer. Although disturbances such as galactorrhea, amenorrhea, gynecomastia and impotence have been reported, the clinical significance of elevated serum prolactin levels is unknown for most patients. An increase in mammary neoplasms has been found in rodents after chronic administration of neuroleptic drugs. Neither clinical studies, nor epidemiologic studies conducted to date, however, have shown an association between chronic administration of these drugs and mammary tumorigenesis; the available evidence is considered too limited to be conclusive at this time.

Withdrawal Emergent Neurological Signs: Abrupt withdrawal after short-term administration of antipsychotic drugs does not generally pose problems. However, transient dyskinetic signs are experienced by some patients on maintenance therapy after abrupt withdrawal. The signs are very similar to those described under Tardive Dyskinesia, except for duration. Although it is not known whether gradual withdrawal of antipsychotic drugs will decrease the incidence of withdrawal emergent neurological signs, gradual withdrawal would appear to be advisable.

Adverse Effects: CNS Effects: The incidence of sedation following loxapine administration has been less than that of certain aliphatic phenothiazines and slightly more than the piperazine phenothiazines. Drowsiness, usually mild, may occur at the beginning of therapy or when dosage is increased. It usually subsides with continued loxapine therapy. Dizziness, faintness, headache, staggering gait, shuffling gait, muscle twitching, weakness, insomnia, agitation, tension, seizures, akinesia, slurred speech, numbness, paresthesia and confusional states have been reported. Neuroleptic malignant syndrome has been reported (see Warnings).

Extrapyramidal Reactions: Neuromuscular (extrapyramidal) reactions during the administration of loxapine have been reported frequently, often during the first few days of treatment. In most patients, these reactions involved Parkinson-like symptoms such as tremor, rigidity, excessive salivation and masked facies. Akathisia (motor restlessness) also has been reported relatively frequently. These symptoms are usually not severe and can be controlled by reduction of loxapine dosage or by administration of antiparkinson drugs in usual doses.

Dystonic and dyskinetic reactions have occurred less frequently, but may be more severe and may occur during the first few days of treatment. Dystonias include spasms of muscles of the neck and face, tongue protrusion and oculogyric movement. Dyskinetic reaction has been described in the form of choreoathetoid movements. These reactions sometimes require reduction or temporary withdrawal of loxapine dosage in addition to appropriate counter-active drugs.

Tardive Dyskinesia: As with all antipsychotic agents, tardive dyskinesia may appear in some patients on long-term therapy or may appear after drug therapy has been discontinued. The risk appears to be greater in elderly patients on high-dose therapy, especially females. The symptoms are persistent and, in some patients, appear to be irreversible. The syndrome is characterized by rhythmical involuntary movement of the tongue, face, mouth or jaw (e.g., protrusion of tongue, puffing of cheeks, puckering of mouth, chewing movements). Sometimes these may be accompanied by involuntary movements of the extremities.

There is no known effective treatment for tardive dyskinesia; antiparkinson agents usually do not alleviate the symptoms of this syndrome. It is suggested that all antipsychotic agents be discontinued if these symptoms appear. Should it be necessary to reinstitute treatment, or increase the dosage of the agent, or switch to a different antipsychotic agent, the syndrome may be masked. The physician may be able to reduce the risk of this syndrome by minimizing the unnecessary use of neuroleptic drugs and reducing the dose or discontinuing the drug, if possible, when manifestations of this syndrome are recognized, particularly in patients over the age of 50. It has been reported that fine vermicular movements of the tongue may be an early sign of the syndrome and if the medication is stopped at that time the syndrome may not develop.

Autonomic Reactions: Dry mouth, nasal congestion, constipation and blurred vision, urinary retention and paralytic ileus have occurred.

Cardiovascular Effects: Tachycardia, hypotension, hypertension, lightheadedness and syncope have been reported. A few cases of ECG changes similar to those seen with phenothiazines have been reported. It is not known whether these were related to loxapine administration.

Hematologic Effects: Rarely, agranulocytosis, thrombocytopenia and leukopenia.

Gastrointestinal Effects: Nausea and vomiting have been reported in some patients. Hepatocellular injury (i.e., AST/ALT elevation) has been reported in association with loxapine administration and rarely, jaundice and/or hepatitis questionably related to loxapine treatment.

Dermatological Effects: Dermatitis, edema (puffiness of face), pruritus and seborrhea have been reported with loxapine. The possibility of photosensitivity and/or phototoxicity occurring has not been excluded; skin rashes of uncertain etiology have been observed in a few patients during the hot summer months.

Endocrine Effects: Rarely, galactorrhea, amenorrhea, gynecomastia and menstrual irregularity of uncertain etiology have been reported.

Other Adverse Reactions: Weight gain, weight loss, dyspnea, ptosis, hyperpyrexia, flushed facies, and polydipsia have been reported in some patients.

Overdose: Symptoms and Treatment: Signs and symptoms of overdosage of loxapine would be expected to range from mild depression of the CNS and cardiovascular systems to profound hypotension, respiratory depression and unconsciousness. The possibility of occurrence of extrapyramidal symptoms and/or convulsive seizures should be kept in mind.

No specific antidote is known. The treatment of overdosage would be essentially symptomatic and supportive. Early gastric lavage would be expected to be beneficial as might be extended dialysis. Additional supportive measures include the administration of oxygen and i.v. fluids. Centrally acting emetics may have little effect because of the antiemetic action of loxapine. In addition, emesis should be avoided because of the possibility of aspiration of vomitus. Avoid analeptics, which may cause convulsions.

Severe hypotension might be expected to respond to the administration of norepinephrine or phenylephrine. **Epinephrine should not be used since its use in a patient with partial adrenergic blockage may further lower the blood pressure.** Severe extrapyramidal reactions should be treated with anticholinergic antiparkinson agents or diphenhydramine HCl, and anticonvulsant therapy should be initiated as indicated.

Renal failure following loxapine overdosage has also been reported.

Dosage: Loxapine is administered orally, usually in divided doses 2 to 4 times a day. Daily dosage should be adjusted to the individual patient's needs, as assessed by the severity of symptoms and previous history of response to antipsychotic drugs. Initial dosage of 10 mg twice daily is recommended, although, in severely disturbed patients, initial dosage up to a total of 50 mg daily may be desirable. Based on initial response to the drug, dosage may then be increased fairly rapidly over the first 7 to 10 days until there is effective control of psychotic symptoms. The usual therapeutic range is 60 to 100 mg daily. However, as with other antipsychotic drugs, some patients respond to lower dosage and others require higher dosage for optimal benefit. Daily dosage higher than 250 mg is not recommended. For maintenance therapy, dosage should be reduced to the lowest level compatible with symptom control; many patients have been maintained satisfactorily at dosages in the range of 20 mg to 60 mg daily.

Supplied: 5 mg: Each round, yellow, film-coated, biconvex tablet, engraved "APO" on one side, scored and engraved "LOX" over 5 on the other, contains: loxapine succinate equivalent to loxapine 5 mg. Nonmedicinal ingredients: colloidal silicon dioxide, croscarmellose sodium, D&C yellow #10, FD&C yellow #6, hydroxypropyl methylcellulose, lactose, magnesium stearate, microcrystalline cellulose, polyethylene glycol and titanium dioxide. Bottles of 100, 250, 500 and 1 000. Unit dose packages of 100.

10 mg: Each round, green, film-coated, biconvex tablet, engraved "APO" on one side, scored and engraved "LOX" over 10 on the other, contains: loxapine succinate equivalent to loxapine 10 mg. Nonmedicinal ingredients: colloidal silicon dioxide, croscarmellose sodium, D&C yellow #10, FD&C blue #1, hydroxypropyl methylcellulose, lactose, magnesium stearate, microcrystalline cellulose, polyethylene glycol and titanium dioxide. Bottles of 100, 250, 500 and 1 000.

25 mg: Each round, pink, film-coated, biconvex tablet, engraved "APO" on one side, scored and engraved "LOX" over 25 on the other, contains: loxapine succinate equivalent to loxapine 25 mg. Nonmedicinal ingredients: colloidal silicon dioxide, croscarmellose sodium, D&C red #30, hydroxypropyl methylcellulose, lactose, magnesium stearate, microcrystalline cellulose, polyethylene glycol and titanium dioxide. Bottles of 100, 250, 500 and 1 000.

50 mg: Each round, white, film-coated, biconvex tablet, engraved "APO" on one side, scored and engraved "LOX" over 50 on the other, contains: loxapine succinate equivalent to loxapine 50 mg. Nonmedicinal ingredients: colloidal silicon dioxide, croscarmellose sodium, hydroxypropyl methylcellulose, lactose, magnesium stearate, microcrystalline cellulose, polyethylene glycol and titanium dioxide. Bottles of 100, 250, 500 and 1 000.

Store at room temperature (15 to 25°C).

New Product 1998

APO®-MEFENAMIC ℞

Apotex

Mefenamic Acid

Analgesic

Supplied: Each yellow and blue no. 1 capsule, identified APO 250, contains: mefenamic acid 250 mg. Nonmedicinal ingredients: colloidal silicon dioxide, D&C yellow #10, FD&C blue #1, FD&C yellow #6, gelatin, lactose, polysorbate, povidone, stearic acid and titanium dioxide. Bottles of 100 and 500. Store at room temperature (15 to 30°C). Protect from moisture.

APO®-MEGESTROL ℞

Apotex

Megestrol Acetate

Antineoplastic—Progestogen

Supplied: 40 mg: Each light blue, round, flat-faced, beveled-edge, scored tablet, engraved "APO" over "40" on one side, contains: megestrol acetate 40 mg. Nonmedicinal ingredients: brilliant blue FCF aluminum lake 12%, colloidal silicon dioxide, croscarmellose sodium, lactose, magnesium stearate and microcrystalline cellulose. Gluten-, sulfite- and tartrazine-free. Bottles of 100 and 250, and unit dose packages of 100 tablets.

160 mg: Each white, oval, biconvex, scored tablet engraved "APO 160" on one side, contains: megestrol acetate 160 mg. Nonmedicinal ingredients: colloidal silicon dioxide, croscarmellose sodium, lactose, magnesium stearate and microcrystalline cellulose. Gluten-, sulfite- and tartrazine-free. Bottles of 100 and 250, and unit dose packages of 100 tablets.

Store at room temperature (15 to 30°C) in well-closed containers.

APO®-MEPROBAMATE ℞

Apotex

Meprobamate

Antianxiety

Supplied: Each round, white, biconvex, scored tablet contains: meprobamate 400 mg. Nonmedicinal ingredients: colloidal silicon dioxide, croscarmellose sodium, magnesium stearate, microcrystalline cellulose and stearic acid. Energy: <1 kJ (0.22 kcal). Sodium: <1 mmol (0.57 mg). Gluten-, lactose-, sulfite- and tartrazine-free. Bottles of 100 and 1 000.

APO®-METFORMIN ℞

Apotex

Metformin HCl

Antihyperglycemic Agent

Supplied: 500 mg: Each white, round, biconvex, partially scored tablet, engraved APO on one side and M500 on the other, contains: metformin HCl 500 mg. Nonmedicinal ingredients: magnesium stearate and methylcellulose. Gluten-, sulfite- and tartrazine-free. Bottles of 100, 250, 500 and 1 000.

850 mg: Each white, capsule-shaped tablet, engraved APO on one side and 850 on the other, contains: metformin HCl 850 mg. Nonmedicinal ingredients: magnesium stearate and methylcellulose. Gluten-, sulfite- and tartrazine-free. Bottles of 100.

Store at controlled room temperature (15 to 30°C) in tightly closed containers.

APO®-METHAZIDE ℞

Apotex

Methyldopa—Hydrochlorothiazide

Antihypertensive

Supplied: Apo-Methazide 15: Each round, dark pink, biconvex, film-coated tablet, identified APO over 15, contains: methyldopa 250 mg and hydrochlorothiazide 15 mg. Nonmedicinal ingredients: hydroxypropyl methylcellulose, magnesium stearate, microcrystalline cellulose, polyethylene glycol and red ferric oxide. Energy: 2.73 kJ (0.65 kcal). Gluten-, lactose-, sodium-, sulfite- and tartrazine-free. Bottles of 100 and 500.

Apo-Methazide 25: Each round, white, biconvex, film-coated tablet, identified APO over 25, contains: methyldopa 250 mg and hydrochlorothiazide 25 mg. Nonmedicinal ingredients: carnauba wax, hydroxypropyl methylcellulose, magnesium stearate, microcrystalline cellulose, polydextrose and polyethylene glycol. Energy: 2.73 kJ (0.65 kcal). Gluten-, lactose-, sodium-, sulfite- and tartrazine-free. Bottles of 100 and 500.

APO®-METHYLDOPA ℞

Apotex

Methyldopa

Antihypertensive

Supplied: 125 mg: Each round, yellow, biconvex, film-coated tablet, identified APO over 125, contains: methyldopa 125 mg. Nonmedicinal ingredients: carnauba wax, croscarmellose sodium, D&C Yellow #10 lake 16%, hydroxypropyl methylcellulose, magnesium stearate, microcrystalline cellulose, polydextrose, polyethylene glycol, titanium dioxide and yellow ferric oxide. Energy: <1 kJ (0.23 kcal). Sodium: <1 mmol (0.04 mg). Gluten-, lactose-, sulfite- and tartrazine-free. Bottles of 100 and 500. Unit dose packages of 100. Apo Long-Term Care (LTC) Pak.

250 mg: Each round, yellow, biconvex, film-coated tablet, identified APO over 250, contains: methyldopa 250 mg. Nonmedicinal ingredients: carnauba wax, croscarmellose sodium, D&C Yellow #10 lake 16%, hydroxypropyl methylcellulose, magnesium stearate, microcrystalline cellulose, polydextrose, polyethylene glycol, titanium dioxide and yellow ferric oxide. Energy: 1.91 kJ (0.46 kcal). Sodium: <1 mmol (0.08 mg). Gluten-, lactose-, sulfite- and tartrazine-free. Bottles of 100 and 1 000. Unit dose packages of 100. Apo Long-Term Care (LTC) Pak.

500 mg: Each, round, yellow, biconvex, film-coated tablet, identified APO over 500, contains: methyldopa 500 mg. Nonmedicinal ingredients: carnauba wax, croscarmellose sodium, D&C Yellow #10 lake 16%, hydroxypropyl methylcellulose, magnesium stearate, microcrystalline cellulose, polydextrose, polyethylene glycol, titanium dioxide and yellow ferric oxide. Energy: 3.82 kJ (0.91 kcal). Sodium: <1 mmol (0.15 mg). Gluten-, lactose-, sulfite- and tartrazine-free. Bottles of 100 and 500. Unit dose packages of 100.

APO®-METOCLOP ℞

Apotex

Metoclopramide HCl

Upper Gastrointestinal Motility Modifier—Antiemetic

Supplied: 5 mg: Each square, white, biconvex tablet, identified APO over M5 on one side, contains: metoclopramide monohydrochloride 5 mg. Nonmedicinal ingredients: croscarmellose sodium, lactose, magnesium stearate and microcrystalline cellulose. Energy: 1.58 kJ (0.38 kcal). Sodium: <1 mmol (0.06 mg). Gluten-, sulfite- and tartrazine-free. Bottles of 100 and 500. Unit dose packages of 100.

10 mg: Each round, white, biconvex tablet, scored and identified APO over M10 on one side, contains: metoclopramide monohydrochloride 10 mg. Nonmedicinal ingredients: croscarmellose sodium, lactose, magnesium stearate and microcrystalline cellulose. Energy: 3.16 kJ (0.76 kcal). Sodium: <1 mmol (0.11 mg). Gluten-, sulfite- and tartrazine-free. Bottles of 100 and 500. Unit dose packages of 100.

APO®-METOPROLOL ℞
APO®-METOPROLOL (Type L) ℞

Apotex

Metoprolol Tartrate

Antianginal—Antihypertensive

Supplied: Apo-Metoprolol: 50 mg: Each white, scored, biconvex, round tablet, identified APO over M50, contains: metoprolol tartrate 50 mg. Nonmedicinal ingredients: colloidal silicon dioxide, croscarmellose sodium, lactose and magnesium stearate. Energy: 1.44 kJ (0.35 kcal). Sodium: <1 mmol (1.02 mg). Gluten-, sulfite- and tartrazine-free. Bottles of 100 and 1 000. Unit dose packages of 100.

100 mg: Each white, scored, biconvex, round tablet, identified APO over M100, contains: metoprolol tartrate 100 mg. Nonmedicinal ingredients: colloidal silicon dioxide, croscarmellose sodium, lactose and magnesium stearate. Energy: 2.89 kJ (0.69 kcal). Sodium: <1 mmol (2.05 mg). Gluten-, sulfite- and tartrazine-free. Bottles of 100 and 1 000. Unit dose packages of 100.

Apo-Metoprolol (Type L): 50 mg: Each pink, film-coated, capsule-shaped, biconvex tablet, scored on one side and identified 50 on the other, contains: metoprolol tartrate 50 mg. Nonmedicinal ingredients: colloidal silicon dioxide, croscarmellose sodium, D&C Red #30 aluminum lake 30%, FD&C Yellow #6, hydroxypropyl methylcellulose, lactose, magnesium stearate, microcrystalline cellulose, polyethylene glycol and titanium dioxide. Energy: 1.74 kJ (0.41 kcal). Sodium: <1 mmol (0.81 mg). Gluten-, sulfite- and tartrazine-free. Bottles of 100 and 1 000. Unit dose packages of 100. Apo Long-Term Care (LTC) Pak.

(Type L): 100 mg: Each blue, film-coated, capsule-shaped, biconvex tablet, scored on one side and identified 100 on the other, contains: metoprolol tartrate 100 mg. Nonmedicinal ingredients: colloidal silicon dioxide, croscarmellose sodium, hydroxypropyl methylcellulose, indigotine lake 13%, lactose, magnesium stearate, microcrystalline cellulose, polyethylene glycol and titanium dioxide. Energy: 3.50 kJ (0.84 kcal). Sodium: <1 mmol (1.72 mg). Gluten-, sulfite- and tartrazine-free. Bottles of 100 and 1 000. Unit dose packages of 100. Apo Long Term Care (LTC) Pak.

APO®-METRONIDAZOLE ℞

Apotex

Metronidazole

Trichomonacide

Supplied: Each round, white, biconvex tablet, identified APO over 250, contains: metronidazole 250 mg. Nonmedicinal ingredients: colloidal silicon dioxide, croscarmellose sodium, magnesium stearate and microcrystalline cellulose. Energy: 3.99 kJ (0.95 kcal). Sodium: <1 mmol (0.16 mg). Gluten-, lactose-, sulfite- and tartrazine-free. Bottles of 100 and 500.

APO®-MINOCYCLINE ℞

Apotex

Minocycline HCl

Antibiotic

Supplied: 50 mg: Each No. 4, orange capsule, identified APO 50, contains: minocycline HCl equivalent to minocycline 50 mg. Nonmedicinal ingredients: croscarmellose sodium, D&C yellow #10, edible black ink, FD&C blue #1, FD&C blue #2, FD&C red #40, lactose, magnesium stearate and stearic acid; shell: FD&C yellow #6, gelatin, sodium lauryl sulfate and titanium dioxide. Energy: 1.16 kJ (0.28 kcal). Sodium: <1 mmol (0.13 mg). Gluten- and tartrazine-free. Bottles of 100 and 250.

100 mg: Each No. 2, orange and purple capsule, identified APO 100, contains: minocycline HCl equivalent to minocycline 100 mg. Nonmedicinal ingredients: croscarmellose sodium, edible white ink, FD&C blue #1, FD&C red #3, lactose, magnesium stearate and stearic acid; shell: FD&C yellow #6, gelatin, sodium lauryl sulfate and titanium dioxide. Energy: 2.33 kJ (0.56 kcal). Sodium: <1 mmol (0.25 mg). Gluten- and tartrazine-free. Bottles of 100 and 250.

Store at controlled room temperature 15 to 30°C. Protect from light.

APO®-MOCLOBEMIDE ℞

Apotex

Moclobemide

Antidepressant

Pharmacology: Moclobemide is a short-acting, reversible inhibitor of monoamine oxidase type A (RIMA). It is a benzamide derivative which inhibits the deamination of serotonin, noradrenaline and dopamine. This action leads to increased concentrations of these neurotransmitters, which may account for the antidepressant activity of moclobemide.

Apo-Moclobemide (cont'd)

Monoamine oxidases are currently subclassified into 2 types, A and B, which differ in their substrate specificity. Moclobemide preferentially inhibits MAO-A; at a 300 mg dose, the inhibition of MAO-A is approximately 80%, while that of MAO-B is approximately 20 to 30%. The estimated MAO-A inhibition is short-lasting (maximum 24 hours) and reversible.
Pharmacokinetics: Volunteers: General: Following oral administration, moclobemide is 98% absorbed from the gastrointestinal tract. Due to hepatic first pass effect, absolute bioavailability is approximately 55% after single doses, but 90% after multiple doses. The apparent volume of distribution is approximately 1.2 L/kg, indicating extensive tissue distribution.

Moclobemide is extensively metabolized, 95% of the administered dose is excreted in the urine. The metabolites are pharmacologically inactive. Moclobemide is 50% bound to plasma proteins, mainly to albumin.

The presence of food reduces the rate, but not the extent of moclobemide absorption.

Single Dose: Following the administration of a 100 mg single oral dose of moclobemide to healthy subjects, peak plasma concentrations ranged from 488 ng/mL to 1 450 ng/mL (mean C_{max}: 849 ng/mL) and were reached in 0.5 to 3.5 hours (mean T_{max}: 49 min). The elimination half-life is 1.5 hours. Up to 200 mg, the pharmacokinetics of moclobemide are linear. At higher doses, nonlinear pharmacokinetics are observed. In a dose range of 400 mg to 1 200 mg, maximum plasma concentrations increased and clearance decreased in a non dose-proportional manner. With increasing doses, the elimination half-life also becomes prolonged.

Multiple Dose: During the second week of a 100 mg t.i.d. dosing regimen in healthy subjects, the steady-state trough concentrations of moclobemide ranged between 114 and 517 ng/mL. An increase in the dose to 150 mg t.i.d. resulted in a greater than proportional increase in moclobemide steady-state trough concentrations, namely to concentrations ranging between 346 and 1 828 ng/mL.

Patients: Hepatic Impairment, Single Dose: In patients with liver cirrhosis, the administration of a single 100 mg dose of moclobemide resulted in approximately a 3-fold increase in peak plasma concentrations (C_{max}: 1 607 ng/mL) and elimination half-life ($t_{1/2}\beta$: 4.0 h), while clearance decreased about 4-fold (Cl: 337 mL/min).

Renal Impairment, Single Dose: In patients with renal insufficiency, the administration of a single 100 mg dose of moclobemide did not appreciably alter the pharmacokinetics of the drug, except for an increase in absorption time.

Elderly Patients, Single and Multiple Dose: Following a 100 mg t.i.d. dosing regimen in elderly subjects (65 to 77 years old), C_{max} and AUC values were somewhat higher than in young subjects (21 to 34 years old), namely 1 498 vs 950 ng/mL and 5 571 vs 3 102 ng·h/mL, respectively. Clearance in the elderly was reduced (19.7 versus 32.3 L/h).

Slow Metabolisers: Approximately 2% of the caucasian population and 15% of the Asian population can be genetically phenotyped as slow metabolisers with respect to oxidative hepatic metabolism. It was found that the AUC measurement in slow metaboliser subjects was approximately 1.5 times greater than in extensive metaboliser subjects for the same dose of moclobemide. This increase is within the normal range of variation (up to 2-fold) typically seen in patients.

Indications: For the symptomatic relief of depressive illness.

Contraindications: In patients with a known hypersensitivity to the drug. As with any other exogenous compound the possibility of hypersensitivity reaction should be considered in susceptible patients. Moclobemide is also contraindicated in patients in an acute confusional state.

In a clinical study designed to test the interaction between moclobemide and a tricyclic antidepressant (clomipramine), severe adverse reactions emerged and the study was terminated. Data involving other tricyclic antidepressants are limited. Consequently, the concomitant use of moclobemide and tricyclic antidepressants is contraindicated.

Clinical data are not available on the concomitant use of moclobemide and selective serotonin reuptake inhibitors or conventional MAO inhibitors. Therefore, until such data become available, moclobemide should not be administered in combination with these agents.

There is no experience with the concomitant use of moclobemide and narcotics. However, death has occurred in patients receiving a conventional MAO inhibitor and meperidine given concomitantly. Therefore, moclobemide should not be used in combination with meperidine.

Children: As safety and effectiveness of moclobemide in children below the age of 18 have not been established, pediatric use is not recommended.

Precautions: General: The possibility of suicide in depressed patients is inherent in their illness and may persist until remission occurs. Therefore, patients must be carefully supervised during all phases of treatment with moclobemide. Prescriptions for potentially suicidal patients should be written for a limited supply only.

In patients with thyrotoxicosis or pheochromocytoma, conventional MAO inhibitors may precipitate a hypersensitive reaction. Because there are no data available on the use of moclobemide in such patients, caution is advised when prescribing moclobemide to these subjects.

Occupational Hazards: Patients should be cautioned against driving an automobile or performing hazardous tasks until they are certain of the effect that moclobemide has on them.

Pregnancy: Safety of use in pregnancy has not been established. Therefore, moclobemide is not recommended in women who may be pregnant, unless, in the opinion of the physician, the expected benefits to the patient markedly outweigh the possible risk to the fetus.

Lactation: Clinical data suggest that small quantities of moclobemide are excreted in human milk. Therefore, moclobemide is not recommended in nursing mothers unless the anticipated benefits outweigh the potential harm to the infant.

Hepatic Dysfunction: In patients with severe liver dysfunction, the daily dose of moclobemide should be substantially reduced to one-third or one-half of the standard dose (see Pharmacology, Pharmacokinetics).

Renal Dysfunction: Single dose pharmacokinetic data suggest that no dosage adjustment may be required in patients with impaired renal function (see Pharmacology, Pharmacokinetics). However, multiple dose studies with moclobemide have not been performed in patients with renal dysfunction, therefore, moclobemide should be used with caution in this patient population. In normal volunteers, the absolute bioavailability almost doubles following multiple dosing as compared to a single dose.

Drug Interactions: Cimetidine: Cimetidine doubles the AUC (area under the plasma concentration-time curve) of moclobemide and is expected to approximately double moclobemide steady-state concentrations.

In patients receiving moclobemide concomitantly with cimetidine, a 50% reduction in the dosage of moclobemide may be necessary.

Tyramine: During studies conducted at the maximum recommended moclobemide dose of 600 mg/day, the mean dose of tyramine required to produce a 30 mm Hg increase in systolic blood pressure was 148±50 mg (76 to 200 mg) when moclobemide was administered immediately after tyramine. The threshold dose of tyramine was reduced to 84±23 mg (54 to 112 mg) when the sequence of administration was reversed so that moclobemide was administered 1 hour before tyramine. These findings indicate that the potentiation of tyramine may be minimized by administering moclobemide after, instead of prior to, a tyramine-enriched meal. There is limited experience in patients who took moclobemide before meals. Most clinical trial protocols specified that the drug be taken immediately after meals. Therefore, patients should be instructed to take moclobemide immediately after meals.

Treatment with moclobemide does not necessitate special dietary restrictions. In clinical studies, it was demonstrated that up to 100 mg tyramine can be safely ingested during treatment with moclobemide 600 mg/day when moclobemide was given after meals. This amount of tyramine, 100 mg, corresponds to 1 000 to 2 000 g mild or 200 g strong cheese, or to 70 g Marmite yeast extract.

As a safety measure, patients should be urged to report immediately the abrupt occurrence of any of the following symptoms: occipital headache, palpitations, neck stiffness, tachycardia or bradycardia or other atypical or unusual symptoms not previously experienced.

Other Antidepressants: Concomitant Use: Clinical interaction studies between moclobemide and a tricyclic antidepressant (clomipramine) resulted in severe adverse reactions (see Contraindications). Data involving other tricyclic antidepressants are limited. Therefore, the concomitant use of moclobemide and tricyclic antidepressants is contraindicated.

Clinical data are not available on the concomitant use of moclobemide and selective serotonin reuptake inhibitors, or conventional MAO inhibitors. Therefore, until clinical data become available, moclobemide should not be administered in combination with these agents.

Sequential Use: Treatment with a tricyclic antidepressant may be initiated following the discontinuation of moclobemide with a short washout period of no less than 2 days.

When switching patients from serotonergic antidepressants to a conventional MAO inhibitor, it is standard practice to allow for a washout period equivalent to at least 4 to 5 half-lives of the previously administered drug or any active metabolites. This recommendation also applies to moclobemide.

Fluoxetine: An exception is fluoxetine; at least 5 weeks should elapse between its discontinuation and initiation of treatment with moclobemide.

Buspirone: To date, there is no experience regarding the coadministration of moclobemide and buspirone. Therefore, patients should be carefully monitored should concomitant administration be implemented.

Antipsychotics: In depressed patients with schizophrenic or schizoaffective disorder, psychotic symptoms may be exacerbated during treatment with moclobemide. There is little experience regarding the concomitant use of moclobemide and antipsychotic drugs. Therefore, patients should be carefully monitored should concomitant treatment be undertaken.

Alcohol: Excessive alcohol consumption should be avoided. Alcohol interaction studies were performed at blood alcohol concentrations of 0.05%. However, no studies were conducted at blood alcohol concentrations recognized as legally intoxicating.

Anesthetic Agents: While specific data on the use of moclobemide in patients undergoing anesthesia are not available, based on its reversible action and short elimination half-life (see Pharmacology), moclobemide should be discontinued no less than 2 days before the administration of anesthetic agents, especially spinal or local anesthetic agents that contain epinephrine.

Sympathomimetics: Following multiple oral doses of moclobemide (total dose: 600 mg/day), a phenylephrine-induced increase in systolic blood pressure was potentiated (1.6 times) after i.v. administration. Patients should be advised to avoid the concomitant use of sympathomimetic amines (e.g., amphetamine and ephedrine like compounds contained in many proprietary cold, hay fever or weight-reducing preparations), until further studies have been conducted.

Dextromethorphan: In isolated cases, the coadministration of moclobemide and dextromethorphan resulted in adverse events, including vertigo, tremor, nausea and vomiting. Since cough and cold medicines may contain dextromethorphan, they should not be taken without prior consultation with the physician, such that nondextromethorphan containing alternatives may be given.

Antihypertensive Agents: Clinical trials with moclobemide have shown inconsistent effects on the blood pressure of hypertensive patients. Therefore, careful monitoring is recommended during initial treatment.

Adverse Effects: Table I (on following page) lists the adverse events reported during clinical trials in which 1 922 patients were treated with 50 to 600 mg/day moclobemide for depressive illness. Limited experience in 60 patients treated with 601 to 750 mg/day of moclobemide suggests that the incidence of adverse reactions may increase at higher doses.

Other clinical adverse events with an incidence of < 1% are as follows: Psychiatric: difficulties falling asleep, nightmares/dreams, hallucinations, memory disturbances, confusion, disorientation, delusions, increased depression, excitation/irritability, hypomanic symptoms, aggressive behavior, apathy, tension.

Central and Peripheral Nervous System: migraine, extrapyramidal effects, tinnitus, paresthesia, dysarthria.

Gastrointestinal: heartburn, gastritis, meteorism, indigestion.

Cardiovascular: hypertension, bradycardia, extrasystoles, angina/chest pain, phlebitic symptoms.

Dermatological/Mucocutaneous: exanthema/rash, allergic skin reaction, itching, gingivitis, stomatitis, dry skin, conjunctivitis.

Genitourinary: disturbances of micturition (dysuria, polyuria, tenesmus) metrorrhagia, prolonged menstruation.

Miscellaneous: general malaise, skeletal/muscular pain, altered taste sensations, hot flushes/cold sensation, photopsia, dyspnea.

Laboratory Abnormalities: Laboratory examinations were performed in a total of 1 401 patients during clinical trials with moclobemide. Reductions were observed in leukocyte, AST and ALT values, however, these reductions were not considered clinically relevant. No other laboratory abnormalities were noted.

Overdose: Symptoms: Signs and symptoms of overdosage with moclobemide include nausea, drowsiness, mild disorientation, slurred speech, amnesia and reduced reflexes. One patient remained stuporous for 36 hours following an overdose of 1 550 mg moclobemide. All abnormal laboratory values and vital signs returned to within normal range one to five days after overdosage. No organ toxicity was reported.

Table I—Apo-Moclobemide

Clinical Adverse Events >1%

Organ System	Adverse Event	% Moclobemide (n=1 922)	% Placebo (n=271)
CNS	headache, pressure in head	8.0	11.1
	insomnia, sleep disturbances	7.3	4.8
	dizziness	5.1	8.1
	tremor	5.0	3.0
	increased agitation	4.5	2.6
	restlessness, nervousness	4.1	2.6
	sleepiness, somnolence	3.7	5.5
	tiredness, sedation	3.0	4.1
	increased anxiety, acute anxiety state	2.8	2.2
	weakness or faintness	1.2	1.8
Gastrointestinal	nausea	5.2	4.8
	constipation	3.9	3.3
	gastrointestinal pain, epigastric discomfort	2.3	2.6
	sickness	1.9	1.1
	diarrhea	1.8	1.1
	abdominal fullness, abdominal pain	1.6	1.5
	vomiting	1.6	0.4
Cardiovascular	tachycardia, palpitations	3.8	3.3
	hypotension	3.0	0.4
	orthostatic, reactive hypotension	2.3	3.3
Anticholinergic	dry mouth	9.2	10.7
Miscellaneous	sweating	2.4	2.2
	blurred vision	1.8	1.1
	increase/loss of appetite	1.3	1.8

Treatment: The treatment of overdosage should consist of general supportive measures. Gastric lavage or induction of emesis, activated charcoal and fluid control may be of benefit.

Dosage: Note: Moclobemide should always be taken after meals (see Precautions, Drug Interactions).

Usual Adult Dosage: The administration of moclobemide should be initiated at 300 mg daily (in 2 to 3 divided doses), and increased gradually to a maximum of 600 mg/day if needed, noting carefully the clinical response and any evidence of intolerance. As with other antidepressants, it should be kept in mind that there may be a lag time in therapeutic response. There is no evidence that increasing the dosage rapidly shortens this latent period and may, in fact, increase the incidence of side effects.

Liver Dysfunction: In patients with severe liver dysfunction, the daily dose of moclobemide should be reduced to one-third or one-half of the standard dose.

Renal Dysfunction: Single dose pharmacokinetic data suggest that no dosage adjustment may be required in patients with impaired renal function. However, multiple dose studies with moclobemide have not been performed in patients with renal dysfunction, therefore, moclobemide should be used with caution in this patient population. In normal volunteers, the absolute bioavailability almost doubles following multiple dosing as compared to a single dose.

Geriatrics: No dosage adjustments are necessary in elderly patients.

Cimetidine: Cimetidine doubles the AUC (area under the plasma concentration-time curve) of moclobemide and is expected to approximately double moclobemide steady-state concentrations (see Precautions, Drug Interactions).

In patients receiving moclobemide concomitantly with cimetidine, a 50% reduction in the dosage of moclobemide may be necessary.

Supplied: 100 mg: Each orange, oval, biconvex, film-coated tablet, scored on one side and engraved APO over 100 on the other, contains: moclobemide 100 mg. Nonmedicinal ingredients: carnauba wax, colloidal silicon dioxide, croscarmellose sodium, dextrates, hydroxypropyl methylcellulose, magnesium stearate, polydextrose, polyethylene glycol (carbowax), red ferric oxide, titanium dioxide and yellow ferric oxide. Bottles of 100 and 500.

150 mg: Each pale yellow, oval, biconvex, film-coated tablet, scored on one side and engraved APO over 150 on the other, contains: moclobemide 150 mg. Nonmedicinal ingredients: carnauba wax, colloidal silicon dioxide, croscarmellose sodium, dextrates, hydroxypropyl methylcellulose, magnesium stearate, polydextrose, polyethylene glycol (carbowax), titanium dioxide and yellow ferric oxide. Bottles 100 and 500.

Store at room temperature 15 to 30°C.

New Product 1998

APO®-NADOL Ⓟ
Apotex

Nadolol

Antianginal—Antihypertensive Agent

Supplied: 40 mg: Each round, white, biconvex tablet, scored and identified APO over N40 on one side, contains: nadolol 40 mg. Nonmedicinal ingredients: colloidal silicon dioxide, croscarmellose sodium, lactose, magnesium stearate and microcrystalline cellulose. Energy: 2.59 kJ (0.62 kcal). Sodium: <1 mmol (0.18 mg). Gluten-, sulfite- and tartrazine-free. Bottles of 100 and 500.

80 mg: Each round, white, biconvex tablet, scored and identified APO over N80 on one side, contains: nadolol 80 mg. Nonmedicinal ingredients: colloidal silicon dioxide, croscarmellose sodium, lactose, magnesium stearate and microcrystalline cellulose. Energy: 5.19 kJ (1.24 kcal). Sodium: <1 mmol (0.37 mg). Gluten-, sulfite- and tartrazine-free. Bottles of 100 and 500.

160 mg: Each blue, capsule-shaped, biconvex tablet, scored and identified APO 160 on one side, contains: nadolol 160 mg. Nonmedicinal ingredients: brilliant blue FCF aluminum lake 12%, colloidal silicon dioxide, croscarmellose sodium, indigotine aluminum lake 12%, lactose, magnesium stearate and microcrystalline cellulose. Energy: 10.38 kJ (2.48 kcal). Sodium: <1 mmol (0.81 mg). Gluten-, sulfite- and tartrazine-free. Bottles of 100.

Store tightly closed, at room temperature.

APO®-NAPRO-Na Ⓟ
APO®-NAPRO-Na DS Ⓟ
Apotex

Naproxen Sodium

Analgesic—Anti-inflammatory

Supplied: Apo-Napro-Na: Each blue, oval, biconvex, film-coated tablet, identified APO-275, contains: naproxen sodium 275 mg. Nonmedicinal ingredients: colloidal silicon dioxide, dextrates, hydroxypropyl cellulose, hydroxypropyl methylcellulose, indigotine lake 13%, magnesium stearate, microcrystalline cellulose, polyethylene glycol, stearic acid and titanium dioxide. Energy: 2.45 kJ (0.59 kcal). Sodium: 1.17 mmol (26.95 mg). Gluten-, lactose-, sulfite- and tartrazine-free. Bottles of 100 and 500.

Apo-Napro-Na DS: Each blue, oval, biconvex, film-coated tablet, identified APO-550 on one side, contains: naproxen sodium 550 mg. Nonmedicinal ingredients: colloidal silicon dioxide, dextrates, hydroxypropyl cellulose, hydroxypropyl methylcellulose, indigotine lake 13%, magnesium stearate, microcrystalline cellulose, polyethylene glycol, stearic acid and titanium dioxide. Energy: 4.46 kJ (1.07 kcal). Sodium: 2.34 mmol (53.90 mg). Gluten-, lactose-, sulfite- and tartrazine-free. Bottles of 100 and 500.

APO®-NAPROXEN Ⓟ
Apotex

Naproxen

Anti-inflammatory—Analgesic

Supplied: 125 mg: Each light green, oval, biconvex tablet, identified APO-125, contains: naproxen 125 mg. Nonmedicinal ingredients: colloidal silicon dioxide, croscarmellose sodium, D&C yellow #10 aluminum lake, indigotine aluminum lake 13%, magnesium stearate, methylcellulose and microcrystalline cellulose. Energy: <1 kJ (0.19 kcal). Sodium: <1 mmol (0.17 mg). Gluten-, lactose-, sulfite- and tartrazine-free. Bottles of 100 and 500. Unit dose packages of 100.

250 mg: Each yellow, oval, biconvex tablet, identified APO-250, contains: naproxen 250 mg. Nonmedicinal ingredients: colloidal silicon dioxide, croscarmellose sodium, D&C yellow #10 aluminum lake, FD&C yellow #6, magnesium stearate, methylcellulose and microcrystalline cellulose. Energy: 1.60 kJ (0.38 kcal). Sodium: <1 mmol (0.34 mg). Gluten-, lactose-, sulfite- and tartrazine-free. Bottles of 100 and 1 000. Unit dose packages of 100. Apo Long-Term Care (LTC) Pak.

375 mg: Each peach, capsule-shaped, biconvex tablet, scored and identified APO 375 contains: naproxen 375 mg. Nonmedicinal ingredients: colloidal silicon dioxide, croscarmellose sodium, FD&C yellow #6, magnesium stearate, methylcellulose and microcrystalline cellulose. Energy: 2.43 kJ (0.58 kcal). Sodium: <1 mmol (0.51 mg). Gluten-, lactose-, sulfite- and tartrazine-free. Bottles of 100 and 500. Unit dose packages of 100. Apo Long-Term Care (LTC) Pak.

500 mg: Each yellow, capsule-shaped, biconvex tablet, scored and identified APO 500, contains: naproxen 500 mg. Nonmedicinal ingredients: colloidal silicon dioxide, croscarmellose sodium, D&C yellow #10 aluminum lake, FD&C yellow #6, magnesium stearate, methylcellulose and microcrystalline cellulose. Energy: 3.20 kJ (0.76 kcal). Sodium: <1 mmol (0.68 mg). Gluten-, lactose-, sulfite- and tartrazine-free. Bottles of 100 and 500. Unit dose packages of 100. Apo Long-Term Care (LTC) Pak.

APO®-NIFED Ⓟ
Apotex

Nifedipine

Antianginal Agent

Supplied: 5 mg: Each mustard-colored, opaque, soft gelatin capsule, identified 5, contains: nifedipine 5 mg. Nonmedicinal ingredients: benzyl alcohol, FD&C Yellow #6, gelatin, glycerin, lemon oil, mannitol, methylparaben, polyethylene glycol, propylparaben, sorbitol, titanium dioxide and yellow iron oxide. Energy: 3.51 kJ (0.84 kcal). Gluten-, lactose-, sodium-, sulfite- and tartrazine-free. Bottles of 100 and 500.

10 mg: Each mustard-colored, opaque, soft gelatin capsule, identified APO 10, contains: nifedipine 10 mg. Nonmedicinal ingredients: benzyl alcohol, FD&C Yellow #6, gelatin, glycerin, lemon oil, mannitol, methylparaben, polyethylene glycol, propylparaben, sorbitol, titanium dioxide and yellow iron oxide. Energy: 7.64 kJ (1.82 kcal). Gluten-, lactose-, sodium-, sulfite- and tartrazine-free. Bottles of 100 and 500.

Store between 15 and 25°C. Avoid freezing. Protect from light.

APO®-NIFED PA Ⓟ
Apotex

Nifedipine

Antihypertensive Agent

Supplied: 10 mg: Each greyish-pink, round, biconvex, film-coated, prolonged action tablet, engraved APO on one side and 10 on the other, contains: nifedipine 10 mg. Nonmedicinal ingredients: carnauba wax, hydroxypropyl methylcellulose, polyethylene glycol, red ferric oxide, stearic acid and titanium dioxide. Gluten-, sulfite- and tartrazine-free. Bottles of 100 and

Apo-Nifed PA (cont'd)

500, unit dose packages of 100 (10×10s) and Apotex Long-Term Care (Apo-LTC) Paks of 620 (20×31s) and 700 (20×35s).

20 mg: Each greyish-pink, round, biconvex, film-coated, prolonged action tablet, engraved APO on one side and 20 on the other, contains: nifedipine 20 mg. Nonmedicinal ingredients: carnauba wax, hydroxypropyl methylcellulose, polyethylene glycol, red ferric oxide, stearic acid and titanium dioxide. Gluten-, sulfite- and tartrazine-free. Bottles of 100 and 500, unit dose packages of 100 (10×10s) and Apotex Long-Term Care (Apo-LTC) Paks of 620 (20×31s) and 700 (20×35s).

Store between 15 and 30°C. Protect from light. Broken tablets should not be used.

APO®-NITROFURANTOIN

Apotex

Nitrofurantoin

Urinary Antibacterial

Supplied: 50 mg: Each round, yellow, biconvex, scored, unidentified tablet contains: nitrofurantoin 50 mg. Nonmedicinal ingredients: croscarmellose sodium, lactose, magnesium stearate and microcrystalline cellulose. Energy: 1.65 kJ (0.39 kcal). Sodium: <1 mmol (0.10 mg). Gluten-, sulfite- and tartrazine-free. Bottles of 100 and 500.

100 mg: Each round, yellow, biconvex, scored, unidentified tablet contains: nitrofurantoin 100 mg. Nonmedicinal ingredients: croscarmellose sodium, lactose, magnesium stearate and microcrystalline cellulose. Energy: 3.30 kJ (0.79 kcal). Sodium: <1 mmol (0.19 mg). Gluten-, sulfite- and tartrazine-free. Bottles of 100 and 500.

Protect from light.

APO®-NIZATIDINE

Apotex

Nizatidine

Histamine H_2-Receptor Antagonist

Supplied: 150 mg: Each pale yellow and dark yellow no. 2 capsule contains: nizatidine 150 mg. Nonmedicinal ingredients: colloidal silicon dioxide, croscarmellose sodium, lactose and stearic acid; shell: D&C Red #33, D&C Yellow #10, FD&C Red #40, FD&C Yellow #6, gelatin, methylparaben, propylparaben, sodium lauryl sulfate, titanium dioxide and yellow iron oxide. Bottles of 100 and 500. Unit dose packages of 30 and 100.

300 mg: Each pale yellow and reddish-brown no. 1 capsule contains: nizatidine 300 mg. Nonmedicinal ingredients: colloidal silicon dioxide, croscarmellose sodium, lactose and stearic acid; shell: D&C Red #33, D&C Yellow #10, FD&C Blue #1, FD&C Red #40, gelatin, methylparaben, propylparaben, sodium lauryl sulfate and titanium dioxide. Bottles of 100 and 500. Unit dose packages of 30 and 100.

Keep bottle tightly closed. Store at room temperature 15 to 30°C. Protect from exposure to high humidity.

APO®-NORTRIPTYLINE

Apotex

Nortriptyline HCl

Antidepressant

Supplied: 10 mg: Each No. 4 capsule with white opaque body and yellow opaque cap, imprinted APO 10, contains: nortriptyline HCl equivalent to nortriptyline base 10 mg. Nonmedicinal ingredients: cornstarch, D&C yellow #10, FD&C yellow #6, gelatin, lactose, silicon dioxide, sodium lauryl sulfate, stearic acid, talc and titanium dioxide. Tartrazine-free. Bottles of 100.

25 mg: Each No. 2 capsule with white opaque body and yellow opaque cap, imprinted APO 25, contains: nortriptyline HCl equivalent to nortriptyline base 25 mg. Nonmedicinal ingredients: cornstarch, D&C yellow #10, FD&C yellow #6, gelatin, lactose, silicon dioxide, sodium lauryl sulfate, stearic acid, talc and titanium dioxide. Tartrazine-free. Bottles of 100 and 500. Blisters of 100.

Keep tightly closed. Store at room temperature (15 to 30°C).

APO®-OFLOX

Apotex

Ofloxacin

Antibacterial

Pharmacology: Ofloxacin is a broad-spectrum, synthetic fluoroquinolone antibacterial agent for oral administration.

Ofloxacin is thought to exert a bactericidal effect on susceptible bacterial cells by inhibiting the essential bacterial enzyme DNA gyrase, a critical catalyst in the duplication, transcription and repair of bacteria.

The bioavailability of ofloxacin in the tablet formulation is approximately 98%. Ofloxacin is rapidly and completely absorbed from the upper small bowel following oral administration. The pharmacokinetic parameters of ofloxacin following single doses of 200, 300 and 400 mg and multiple doses of 400 mg to healthy males are summarized in Table I.

Table I—Apo-Oflox

Pharmacokinetic Parameters

Dose	C_{max} µg/mL ±S.D.	$AUC_{0\text{-last point}}$ µg×hr/mL±S.D.	T_{max}±S.D.	$t_{1/2}$
200 mg—single dose	1.7±0.3	14.1±2.3	1.5±0.3	4.9
300 mg—single dose	2.6±0.4	21.2±2.5	1.7±0.5	4.6
400 mg—single dose	3.7±0.7	31.4±4.7	1.8±0.6	3.8
400 mg—steady state	5.0±1.0	62.9±14.5	1.7±0.5	5.2

Elimination is mainly by renal excretion. Ofloxacin undergoes minimal biotransformation.

Indications: For the treatment of adults with the following infections caused by susceptible strains of the designated microorganisms: Lower Respiratory Tract Infections: including pneumonia and acute exacerbation of chronic bronchitis due to H. influenzae, S. pneumoniae, or M. catarrhalis.

Urinary Tract Infections: **Uncomplicated cystitis** due to E. coli, K. pneumoniae or P. mirabilis.

Complicated urinary tract infections due to E. coli, K. pneumoniae or P. mirabilis.

Prostatitis: due to E. coli.

Sexually Transmitted Diseases (see Warnings): acute, uncomplicated urethral and cervical gonorrhea due to N. gonorrhoeae. Urethritis/cervicitis due to C. trachomatis or mixed infections due to N. gonorrhoeae and C. trachomatis.

Note: Ofloxacin is not effective in the treatment of syphilis. All patients with gonorrhea should have an initial serologic test for syphilis and a follow-up serologic test after 3 months (see Warnings).

Skin and Skin Structure Infections: uncomplicated skin and skin structure infections due to S. aureus or S. pyogenes.

Appropriate culture and susceptibility tests should be performed before treatment in order to isolate and identify organisms causing the infection and to determine their susceptibility to ofloxacin. Therapy with ofloxacin may be initiated before results of these tests are known; once the results of bacteriological testing become known, therapy should be adjusted if required.

As with other drugs of this class, some strains of P. aeruginosa may develop resistance fairly rapidly during treatment with ofloxacin tablets. Culture and susceptibility testing performed periodically during therapy will provide information not only on the therapeutic effect of the antimicrobial agent but also on the possible emergence of bacterial resistance.

If anaerobic organisms are suspected of or known to be contributing to the infection, appropriate therapy for anaerobic pathogens should be considered.

Contraindications: Persons with a history of hypersensitivity to ofloxacin or members of the quinolone group of antibacterial agents.

Warnings: The safety and efficacy of ofloxacin in children, adolescents (under the age of 18 years), pregnant women and lactating women has not been established (see Precautions; Children, Pregnancy and Lactation).

The oral administration of ofloxacin has produced lesions in weight bearing articular cartilage and lameness in several species of immature animals. Consequently, ofloxacin should not be used in pre-pubertal patients.

Syphilis: **Ofloxacin is not effective in the treatment of syphilis.** Antimicrobial agents used in high doses for short periods of time to treat gonorrhea may mask or delay the symptoms of incubating syphilis. All patients with gonorrhea should have a serologic test for syphilis at the time of diagnosis. Patients treated with ofloxacin should have a follow-up serologic test for syphilis after 3 months.

Hypersensitivity Reactions: Serious and occasionally fatal hypersensitivity (anaphylactic/anaphylactoid) reactions have been reported in patients receiving therapy with quinolones, including ofloxacin. These reactions often occur following the first dose. Some reactions were accompanied by cardiovascular collapse, hypotension/shock, seizure, loss of consciousness, tingling, angioedema (including tongue, laryngeal, throat or facial edema/swelling, etc.), airway obstruction (including bronchospasm, shortness of breath, and acute respiratory distress), dyspnea, urticaria/hives, itching and other serious skin reactions. A few patients had a history of hypersensitivity reactions. The drug should be discontinued immediately at the first appearance of a skin rash or any other sign of hypersensitivity. Serious acute hypersensitivity reactions may require treatment with epinephrine and other resuscitative measures, including oxygen, i.v. fluids, antihistamines, corticosteroids, pressor amines and airway management, as clinically indicated (see Precautions and Adverse Effects).

Serious and sometimes fatal events of uncertain etiology have been reported in patients receiving therapy with quinolones including, extremely rarely, ofloxacin. These events may be severe and generally occur following the administration of multiple doses. Clinical manifestations may include one or more of the following: fever, rash or severe dermatologic reactions (e.g., toxic epidermal necrolysis, Stevens-Johnson syndrome, etc.); vasculitis, arthralgia, myalgia, serum sickness; allergic pneumonitis; interstitial nephritis, acute renal insufficiency/failure; hepatitis, jaundice, acute hepatic necrosis/failure; anemia including hemolytic and aplastic, thrombocytopenia including thrombotic thrombocytopenic purpura, leukopenia, agranulocytosis, pancytopenia, and/or other hematologic abnormalities. The administration of ofloxacin should be discontinued immediately after appearance of a skin rash or any other sign of hypersensitivity and supportive measures instituted (see Adverse Effects).

CNS Effects: Convulsions, increased intracranial pressure, and toxic psychosis have been reported in patients receiving quinolones, including ofloxacin. Quinolones, including ofloxacin, may also cause CNS stimulation, which may lead to tremors, restlessness/agitation, nervousness/anxiety, lightheadedness, confusion, hallucinations, paranoia and depression, nightmares, insomnia, and rarely suicidal thoughts or acts. These reactions may occur following the first dose. If these reactions occur in patients receiving ofloxacin, the drug should be discontinued and appropriate measures instituted. As with all quinolones, ofloxacin should be used with caution in patients with a known or suspected CNS disorder that may predispose to seizures or lower the seizure threshold (e.g., severe cerebral arteriosclerosis, epilepsy, etc.) or in the presence of other risk factors that may predispose to seizures or lower the seizure threshold (e.g., certain drug therapy, renal dysfunction, etc.) (see Precautions and Adverse Effects).

Gastrointestinal Effects: Pseudomembranous colitis has been reported with nearly all antibacterial agents, including ofloxacin, and may range in severity from mild to life-threatening. Therefore, it is important to consider this diagnosis in patients who present with diarrhea subsequent to the administration of antibacterial agents.

Treatment with antibacterial agents alters the normal flora of the colon and may permit overgrowth of clostridia. Studies indicate that a toxin produced by C. difficile is one primary cause of antibiotic-associated colitis. After the diagnosis of pseudomembranous colitis has been established, therapeutic measures should be initiated. Mild cases of pseudomembranous colitis usually respond to drug discontinuation alone. In moderate to severe cases, consideration should be given to management with fluids and electrolytes, protein supplementation and treatment with an oral antibacterial drug effective against C. difficile (see Adverse Effects).

Precautions: General: Periodic assessment of organ system functions, including renal, hepatic and hematopoietic, is advisable during prolonged therapy (see Warnings and Adverse Effects).

Adequate hydration of patients receiving ofloxacin should be maintained to prevent the formation of highly concentrated urine.

Renal/Hepatic: Administer ofloxacin with caution in the presence of renal or hepatic insufficiency/impairment. In patients with known or suspected renal or hepatic insufficiency/impairment, careful clinical observation and appropriate laboratory studies should be performed prior to and during therapy since elimination of ofloxacin may be reduced. Alteration of the dosage regimen is necessary for patients with impairment of renal function (creatinine clearance ≤50 mL/min) (see Dosage).

Allergic Reactions: Moderate to severe phototoxicity reactions have been observed in patients who are exposed to direct sunlight while receiving some drugs in this class including ofloxacin. Excessive sunlight should be avoided. Therapy should be discontinued if phototoxicity (e.g., a skin eruption, etc.) occurs.

Pregnancy: Doses equivalent to 50 and 10 times the maximum therapeutic dose of ofloxacin (based on mg/kg) were fetotoxic (i.e., decreased fetal body weight and increased fetal mortality) in rats and rabbits, respectively. Minor skeletal variations were reported in rats receiving doses of 810 mg/kg/day, which is more than 10 times higher than the maximum intended human dose (based on mg/m²).

Safety and efficacy have not been established in pregnant women. Ofloxacin should not be used during pregnancy unless the potential benefit justifies the potential risk to the fetus (see Warnings).

Lactation: In nursing females a single 200 mg dose resulted in concentrations of ofloxacin in milk which were similar to those found in plasma. Because of the potential for serious adverse reactions from ofloxacin in nursing infants, a decision should be made whether to discontinue nursing or to discontinue the drug, taking into account the importance of the drug to the mother (see Warnings and Adverse Effects).

Children: Safety and effectiveness in children and adolescents below the age of 18 years have not been established. Ofloxacin causes arthropathy (arthrosis) and osteochondrosis in juvenile animals of several species (see Warnings).

Patients with Special Diseases and Conditions: CNS Disorders: As with all quinolones, ofloxacin should be used with caution in any patient with a known or suspected CNS disorder that may predispose to seizures or lower the seizure threshold (e.g., severe cerebral arteriosclerosis, epilepsy, etc.) or in the presence of other risk factors that may predispose to seizures or lower the seizure threshold (e.g., certain drug therapy, renal dysfunction, etc.) (see Warnings and Precautions, Drug Interactions).

Disturbances of Blood Glucose: As with other quinolones, disturbances of blood glucose including symptomatic hyper- and hypoglycemia have been reported, usually in diabetic patients receiving concomitant treatment with an oral hypoglycemic agent (e.g., glyburide/glibenclamide, etc.) or with insulin. In these patients careful monitoring of blood glucose is recommended. If a hypoglycemic reaction occurs in a patient being treated with ofloxacin, the patient should discontinue ofloxacin immediately and appropriate ancillary measures should be instituted (see Precautions, Drug Interactions and Adverse Effects).

Drug Interactions: Antacids, Sucralfate, Metal Cations and Multivitamins: Quinolones have the potential to form stable complexes with many metal ions. Administration of oral quinolones with antacids containing calcium, magnesium, or aluminum; sucralfate; divalent or trivalent cations such as iron; or multivitamins containing zinc may substantially interfere with the absorption of oral quinolones resulting in systemic levels considerably lower than desired. These agents should not be taken within the 2-hour period before or within the 2-hour period after ofloxacin administration.

Cimetidine: Cimetidine has demonstrated interference with the elimination of some quinolones. This interference has resulted in significant increases in half-life and AUC of some quinolones. The potential for interaction between ofloxacin and cimetidine had not been studied.

Cyclosporine: Elevated serum levels of cyclosporine have been reported following concomitant use with some other quinolones. The potential for interaction between ofloxacin and cyclosporine has not been studied.

Drugs Metabolized by Cytochrome P450 Enzymes: Most quinolone antimicrobial drugs inhibit cytochrome P450 enzyme activity. This may result in a prolonged half-life for some drugs that are also metabolized by this system (e.g., cyclosporine, theophylline/methylxanthines, warfarin, etc.) when co-administered with quinolones. The extent of this inhibition varies among different quinolones (see other Drug Interactions).

Nonsteroidal Anti-inflammatory Drugs: The concomitant administration of a nonsterodial anti-inflammatory drug with a quinolone, including ofloxacin, may increase the risk of CNS stimulation and convulsive seizures (see Warnings).

Probenecid: The concomitant use of probenecid with certain other quinolones has been reported to affect renal tubular secretion. The effect of probenecid on the elimination of ofloxacin has not been studied.

Theophylline: Steady-state theophylline levels may increase when ofloxacin and theophylline are given concurrently. As with other quinolones, concomitant administration of ofloxacin may prolong the half-life of theophylline, elevate serum theophylline levels, and increase the risk of theophylline-related adverse reactions. Theophylline levels should be closely monitored and theophylline dosage adjustments made when ofloxacin and theophylline are co-administered. Adverse reactions (including seizures, etc.) may occur with or without an elevation in the serum theophylline level (see Warnings and Precautions, General).

Warfarin: Some quinolones have been reported to enhance the effects of the oral anticoagulant warfarin or its derivatives. Therefore, if a quinolone antibiotic is administered concomitantly with warfarin or its derivatives, the prothrombin time (PT) (or other appropriate test(s) of coagulation) should be monitored and the dose of warfarin modified as appropriate.

Antidiabetic Agents (e.g., insulin, glyburide/glibenclamide, etc.): Since disturbances of blood glucose including hyperglycemia and hypoglycemia have been reported in patients treated concurrently with quinolones and an antidiabetic agent, careful monitoring of blood glucose is recommended when these agents are used concomitantly.

Adverse Effects: Clinical Trials Experience: The following is a compilation of the data for ofloxacin based on clinical experience with both the oral and i.v. formulations. The incidence of drug-related adverse reactions in patients during Phase 2 and 3 clinical trials was 11%. Among patients receiving multiple-dose therapy, 4% discontinued ofloxacin due to adverse experiences.

In clinical trials, the following events were considered likely to be drug related in patients receiving multiple doses of ofloxacin: nausea 3%, insomnia 3%, rash 1%, external genital pruritus in women 1%, diarrhea 1%, vomiting 1%, dizziness 3%, pruritus 1%, vaginitis 1%, headache 3% and dysgeusia 1%.

In clinical trials, the most frequently reported adverse events, regardless of relationship to drug, were: nausea 10%, vomiting 4%, diarrhea 4%, external genital pruritus in women 6%, insomnia 7%, headache 9%, vaginitis 5% and dizziness 5%.

Additional events occurring in clinical trials at rates of 1 to 3% and less than 1% regardless of relationship to drug or route of administration are shown in Table II.

The following laboratory abnormalities appeared in ≥ 1% of patients receiving multiple doses of ofloxacin. It is not known whether these abnormalities were caused by the drug or the underlying conditions being treated.

Hematopoietic: anemia, leukopenia, leukocytosis, neutropenia, neutrophilia, increased band forms, lymphocytopenia, eosinophilia, lymphocytosis, thrombocytopenia, thrombocytosis, elevated ESR.

Hepatic: elevated: alkaline phosphatase, AST, ALT.

Serum Chemistry: hyperglycemia, hypoglycemia, elevated creatinine, elevated BUN.

Urinary: glucosuria, proteinuria, alkalinuria, hyposthenuria, hematuria, pyuria.

Worldwide Marketing Experience: Additional adverse events regardless of relationship to drug were reported from worldwide marketing experience with quinolones, including ofloxacin. See Table III (on following page).

In clinical trials using multiple-dose therapy, ophthalmologic abnormalities including cataracts and multiple punctate lenticular opacities have been noted in patients undergoing treatment with other quinolones. The relationship of the drugs to these events is not presently established.

Overdose: Symptoms and Treatment: Information on overdosage with ofloxacin is limited. One incident of accidental overdosage has been reported. In this case, an adult female received 3 g of ofloxacin i.v. over 45 minutes. A blood sample obtained 15 minutes after the completion of the infusion revealed an ofloxacin level of 39.3 μg/mL. In 7 hours, the level had fallen to 16.2 μg/mL, and by 24 hours to 2.7 μg/mL. During the infusion, the patient developed drowsiness, nausea, dizziness, hot and cold flushes, subjective facial swelling and numbness, slurring of speech, and mild to moderate disorientation. All complaints except the dizziness subsided within 1 hour after discontinuation of infusion. The dizziness, most bothersome while standing, resolved in approximately 9 hours. Laboratory testing reportedly revealed no clinically significant changes in routine parameters in this patient.

In the event of acute overdose, the patient should be observed and appropriate hydration maintained. Ofloxacin is not efficiently removed by hemodialysis or peritoneal dialysis.

Dosage: General: The dosing recommendations apply to patients with normal renal function (i.e., creatinine clearance >50 mL/min). For patients with altered renal function (i.e., creatinine clearance ≤50 mL/min), see Dosage Adjustment for Renal Impairment.

The usual dose of ofloxacin is 200 to 400 mg orally every 12 hours as described in the Dosage Chart (see Table IV on following page).

Antacids containing calcium, magnesium, or aluminum; sucralfate; divalent or trivalent cations such as iron; or multivitamins containing zinc should not be taken within the 2-hour period before, or within the 2-hour period after oral administration of ofloxacin (see Precautions).

Dosage Adjustment for Renal Impairment: Dosage should be adjusted in patients with a creatinine clearance value of less

Table II—Apo-Oflox

Adverse Events

	Adverse Event Without Regard to Relationship to Drug or Route of Administration	
Body System	**<1%**	**1-3%**
Body as a Whole	asthenia, chills, extremity pain, malaise, pain, epistaxis	chest pain, fatigue, abdominal pain and cramps, trunk pain and pharyngitis
Nutritional/Metabolic	thirst, weight loss	decreased appetite, dry mouth, dysgeusia
Special Senses	decreased hearing acuity, photophobia, tinnitus	visual disturbances
Nervous System	anxiety, cognitive change, confusion, depression, dream abnormality, euphoria, hallucinations, paresthesia, seizures, syncope, vertigo, tremor	nervousness, sleep disorders, somnolence
Cardiovascular	cardiac arrest, edema, hypertension, hypotension, palpitations, vasodilation	—
Respiratory	cough, respiratory arrest, rhinorrhea	—
Gastrointestinal	dyspepsia	flatulence, gastrointestinal distress, constipation
Genital/Reproductive	burning, irritation, pain and rash of the female genitalia, dysmenorrhea, menorrhagia, metrorrhagia	vaginal discharge
Urinary	dysuria, urinary frequency, urinary retention	—
Skin/Hypersensitivity	angioedema, diaphoresis, urticaria, vasculitis	pruritus, fever, rash
Musculoskeletal	arthralgia, myalgia	—

Apo-Oflox (cont'd)

Table III—Apo-Oflox

Adverse Events

Body System	Adverse Event
Special Senses	diplopia, nystagmus, blurred vision, disturbances of: taste, smell, hearing and equilibrium, usually reversible following discontinuation
Nervous System	nightmares; suicidal thoughts or acts, disorientation, psychotic reactions, paranoia; phobia, agitation, restlessness, aggressiveness/hostility, manic reaction, emotional lability; peripheral neuropathy, ataxia, incoordination; possible exacerbation of: myasthenia gravis and extrapyramidal disorders; dysphasia, lightheadedness (see Warnings and Precautions)
Cardiovascular	cerebral thrombosis, pulmonary edema, tachycardia, hypotension/shock, syncope
Respiratory	bronchospasm, dyspnea, allergic pneumonitis, stridor
Gastrointestinal	hepatic dysfunction including: hepatic necrosis, hepatitis, jaundice (cholestatic or hepatocellular); intestinal perforation; pseudomembranous colitis, gastrointestinal hemorrhage; hiccough; painful oral mucosa, pyrosis (see Warnings)
Genital/Reproductive	vaginal candidiasis
Urinary	anuria, polyuria, renal failure, renal calculi, urinary retention, interstitial nephritis, hematuria (see Warnings and Precautions)
Skin/Hypersensitivity	anaphylactic/toid reactions/shock; purpura, serum sickness, erythema multiforme/Stevens-Johnson syndrome, exfoliative dermatitis, photosensitivity, toxic epidermal necrolysis, erythema nodosum, hyperpigmentation, conjunctivitis, vesiculobullous eruption (See Warnings and Precautions)
Endocrine/Metabolic	hyper- or hypoglycemia, especially in diabetic patients on insulin or oral hypoglycemic agents (see Precautions, General and Drug Interactions)
Hematopoietic	anemia, including hemolytic and aplastic; hemorrhage, pancytopenia, agranulocytosis, leukopenia, reversible bone marrow depression, thrombocytopenia, thrombotic thrombocytopenic purpura, petechiae, ecchymosis/bruising (see Warnings)
Musculoskeletal	tendonitis/rupture; weakness
Laboratory Abnormalities	Hematopoietic: prolongation of prothrombin time Serum Chemistry: acidosis, elevation of: serum triglycerides, serum cholesterol, serum potassium, liver function tests including: GGTP, LDH, bilirubin Urinary: albuminuria, candiduria

Table IV—Apo-Oflox

Dosage Chart (Patients with Normal Renal Function)

Infection	Description	Unit Dose	Frequency	Duration*	Daily Dose
Lower Respiratory Tract Infections	Exacerbation of chronic bronchitis or pneumonia	400 mg	q12h	10 days	800 mg
Sexually Transmitted Diseases	Acute, uncomplicated gonorrhea	400 mg	single dose	1 day	400 mg
	Cervicitis/urethritis due to C. trachomatis or mixed infections due to C. trachomatis and N. gonorrhoeae	300 mg	q12h	7 days	600 mg
Skin and Skin Structure Infections	Uncomplicated/Complicated	400 mg	q12h	10 days	800 mg
Urinary Tract	Acute cystitis	200 mg	q12h	3 days	400 mg
	Uncomplicated UTI	200 mg	q12h	7 days	400 mg
	Complicated UTI	200 mg	q12h	10 days	400 mg
Prostatitis		300 mg	q12h	6 weeks	600 mg

*Total therapy duration. When appropriate, patients may be converted from ofloxacin i.v. to an equivalent dose of ofloxacin tablets. As an example, patients receiving 400 mg i.v. q12h may be converted to 400 mg p.o. q12h or b.i.d.

than or equal to 50 mL/min. After a normal initial dose, the dosing interval should be adjusted as shown in Table V.

Table V—Apo-Oflox

Dosage Adjustment for Renal Impairment

Creatinine Clearance	Maintenance Unit Dose	Frequency
20-50 mL/min	as recommended in the Dosage Chart	q24h
<20 mL/min	½ recommended dose in Dosage Chart	q24h

When only the serum creatinine is known, the following formula may be used to estimate creatinine clearance. The serum creatinine should represent steady-state renal function.

$$\text{Men: } \frac{\text{Creatinine clearance}}{\text{(mL/min)}} = \frac{\text{Weight (kg)} \times \text{(140-age)}}{72 \times \text{serum creatinine (mg/dL)}}$$

Women: 0.85×the value calculated in men.

Patients with Cirrhosis: The excretion of ofloxacin may be reduced in patients with severe liver function disorders (e.g., cirrhosis with or without ascites). A maximum dose of 400 mg of ofloxacin per day should therefore not be exceeded.

Supplied: 200 mg: Each light yellow, oval, biconvex, film-coated tablet, engraved APO on one side and 200 on the other, contains: ofloxacin 200 mg. Nonmedicinal ingredients: carnauba wax, colloidal silicon dioxide, croscarmellose sodium, hydroxypropyl methylcellulose, magnesium stearate, methylcellulose, microcrystalline cellulose, polydextrose, polyethylene glycol, titanium dioxide and yellow ferric oxide. Bottles of 100 and 250. Unit dose packages of 100. Apotex Long-Term Care Packages (Apo-LTC Paks) of 620 and 700.

300 mg: Each white, oval, biconvex, film-coated tablet, engraved APO on one side and 300 on the other, contains: ofloxacin 300 mg. Nonmedicinal ingredients: carnauba wax, colloidal silicon dioxide, croscarmellose sodium, hydroxypropyl methylcellulose, magnesium stearate, methylcellulose, microcrystalline cellulose, polydextrose, polyethylene glycol and titanium dioxide. Bottles of 100 and 250. Unit dose packages of 100. Apotex Long-Term Care Packages (Apo-LTC Paks) of 620 and 700.

400 mg: Each yellow, oval, biconvex, film-coated tablet, engraved APO on one side and 400 on the other, contains; ofloxacin 400 mg. Nonmedicinal ingredients: carnauba wax, colloidal silicon dioxide, croscarmellose sodium, hydroxypropyl methylcellulose, magnesium stearate, methylcellulose, microcrystalline cellulose, polydextrose, polyethylene glycol, titanium dioxide and yellow ferric oxide. Bottles of 100 and 250. Unit dose packages of 100. Apotex Long-Term Care Packages (Apo-LTC Paks) of 620 and 700.

Store in well closed containers at room temperature (15 to 30°C). Protect from light.

New Product 1998

APO®-OXAZEPAM Ⓟ

Apotex

Oxazepam

Antianxiety

Supplied: 10 mg: Each round, pale yellow, flat-faced with beveled edge tablet, scored and identified APO over 10, contains: oxazepam 10 mg. Nonmedicinal ingredients: cornstarch, D&C Yellow #10 aluminum lake, FD&C Yellow #6, lactose, magnesium stearate and microcrystalline cellulose. Energy: 2.93 kJ (0.70 kcal). Gluten-, sodium-, sulfite- and tartrazine-free. Bottles of 100 and 1 000. Unit dose packages of 100. Apo Long-Term Care (LTC) Pak.

15 mg: Each round, orange-yellow, flat-faced with beveled edge tablet, scored and identified APO over 15, contains: oxazepam 15 mg. Nonmedicinal ingredients: cornstarch, D&C Yellow #10 aluminum lake, FD&C Yellow #6, lactose, magnesium stearate and microcrystalline cellulose. Energy: 2.80 kJ (0.67 kcal). Gluten-, sodium-, sulfite- and tartrazine-free. Bottles of 100 and 1 000. Unit dose packages of 100. Apo Long-Term Care (LTC) Pak.

30 mg: Each round, white, flat-faced with beveled edge tablet, scored and identified APO over 30, contains: oxazepam 30 mg. Nonmedicinal ingredients: colloidal silicon dioxide, croscarmellose sodium, lactose, magnesium stearate and microcrystalline cellulose. Energy: 2.81 kJ (0.67 kcal). Sodium: <1 mmol (0.49 mg). Gluten-, sulfite- and tartrazine-free. Bottles of 100 and 1 000. Unit dose packages of 100. Apo Long-Term Care (LTC) Pak.

APO®-OXTRIPHYLLINE Ⓟ

Apotex

Oxtriphylline

Bronchodilator

Supplied: 100 mg: Each round, pink, biconvex, film-coated tablet, identified APO over 100, contains: oxtriphylline 100 mg (equivalent to 64 mg anhydrous theophylline). Nonmedicinal ingredients: colloidal silicon dioxide, croscarmellose sodium, D&C Red #30 aluminum lake, hydroxypropyl methylcellulose, magnesium stearate, microcrystalline cellulose, polyethylene glycol and titanium dioxide. Energy: 3.25 kJ (0.78 kcal). Sodium: <1 mmol (0.06 mg). Gluten-, lactose-, sulfite- and tartrazine-free. Bottles of 100.

200 mg: Each round, yellow, biconvex, film-coated tablet, identified APO over 200, contains: oxtriphylline 200 mg (equivalent to 128 mg anhydrous theophylline). Nonmedicinal ingredients: colloidal silicon dioxide, croscarmellose sodium, D&C yellow #10 lake 15%, FD&C Yellow #6, hydroxypropyl methylcellulose, magnesium stearate, microcrystalline cellulose, polyethylene glycol and titanium dioxide. Energy: 6.60 kJ (1.58 kcal). Sodium: <1 mmol (0.13 mg). Gluten-, lactose-, sulfite- and tartrazine-free. Bottles of 100 and 500.

300 mg: Each round, blue, biconvex, film-coated tablet, identified APO over 300, contains: oxtriphylline 300 mg (equivalent to 192 mg anhydrous theophylline). Nonmedicinal ingredients: brilliant blue FCF lake 12%, hydroxypropyl methylcellulose, microcrystalline cellulose, polyethylene glycol and titanium dioxide. Energy: 7.00 kJ (1.67 kcal). Gluten-, lactose-, sodium-, sulfite- and tartrazine-free. Bottles of 100.

APO®-OXYBUTYNIN Ⓟ

Apotex

Oxybutynin Chloride

Anticholinergic—Antispasmodic Agent

Supplied: Syrup: Each 5 mL of green colored syrup contains: oxybutynin chloride 5 mg. Nonmedicinal ingredients: artificial berry flavor, citric acid monohydrate, FD&C Green #3, glycerin, methylparaben, sodium citrate dihydrate and sucrose. Alcohol-, gluten- and tartrazine free. Bottles of 473 mL.

Tablets: Each scored, biconvex, blue tablet engraved with APO over 5, contains: oxybutynin chloride 5 mg. Nonmedicinal ingredients: brilliant blue FCF aluminum lake 12%, lactose, magnesium stearate and microcrystalline cellulose. Gluten-, sulfite- and tartrazine-free. Bottles of 100 and 500.

Store at room temperature (15 to 30°C) in tight, light-resistant containers.

APO®-PENTOXIFYLLINE SR Ⓟ

Apotex

Pentoxifylline

Vasoactive Agent

Supplied: Each bright pink, capsule-shaped, biconvex, film-coated, sustained-release tablet, identified APO-400, contains: pentoxifylline 400 mg. Nonmedicinal ingredients: carnauba wax, colloidal silicon dioxide, erythrosine, hydroxypropyl methylcellulose, magnesium stearate, polyethylene glycol and titanium dioxide. Bottles of 100 and 500. Unit dose packages of 60. Store at room temperature 15 to 30°C.

APO®-PEN VK Ⓟ

Apotex

Phenoxymethyl Penicillin Potassium

Antibiotic

Supplied: Oral Solution: 125 mg: After reconstitution each 5 mL light pink, cherry-flavored suspension contains: penicillin V potassium 125 mg (200 000 IU). Nonmedicinal ingredients: artificial cherry flavor, FD&C Red #40, sodium benzoate, sodium citrate, sodium cyclamate and sucrose. Energy: 16.92 kJ (4.04 kcal)/5 mL. Sodium: <1 mmol (3.34 mg)/ 5 mL. Alcohol-, gluten-, lactose-, sulfite- and tartrazine-free. Bottles of 100 mL.

300 mg: After reconstitution each 5 mL light pink, cherry-flavored suspension contains: penicillin V potassium 300 mg (500 000 IU). Nonmedicinal ingredients: artificial cherry flavor, FD&C Red #40, sodium benzoate, sodium citrate, sodium cyclamate and sucrose. Energy: 52.49 kJ (12.53 kcal)/5 mL. Sodium: <1 mmol (10.35 mg)/5 mL. Alcohol-, gluten-, lactose-, sulfite- and tartrazine-free. Bottles of 60 and 100 mL.

Tablets: Each orange, film-coated, round, biconvex, scored tablet identified APO over 300 contains: penicillin V potassium 300 mg (500 000 IU). Nonmedicinal ingredients: colloidal silicon dioxide, croscarmellose sodium, D&C Yellow #10, FD&C Yellow #6, hydroxypropyl methylcellulose, magnesium stearate, methylcellulose, polyethylene glycol and titanium dioxide. Energy: <1 kJ (0.09 kcal). Sodium: <1 mmol (0.19 mg). Gluten-, lactose-, sulfite- and tartrazine-free. Bottles of 100 and 1 000.

APO®-PERPHENAZINE Ⓟ

Apotex

Perphenazine

Antipsychotic—Antiemetic—Antianxiety

Supplied: 2 mg: Each round, white, biconvex, film-coated tablet, identified 2, contains: perphenazine 2 mg. Nonmedicinal ingredients: cornstarch, hydroxypropyl methylcellulose, lactose, magnesium stearate, microcrystalline cellulose, polyethylene glycol and titanium dioxide. Energy: 1.56 kJ (0.37 kcal). Gluten-, sodium-, sulfite- and tartrazine-free. Bottles of 100 and 500.

4 mg: Each round, white, biconvex, film-coated tablet, identified 4, contains: perphenazine 4 mg. Nonmedicinal ingredients: cornstarch, hydroxypropyl methylcellulose, lactose, magnesium stearate, microcrystalline cellulose, polyethylene glycol and titanium dioxide. Energy: 2.04 kJ (0.49 kcal). Gluten-, sodium-, sulfite- and tartrazine-free. Bottles of 100 and 500.

8 mg: Each round, white, biconvex, film-coated tablet, identified 8, contains: perphenazine 8 mg. Nonmedicinal ingredients: cornstarch, hydroxypropyl methylcellulose, lactose, magnesium stearate, microcrystalline cellulose, polyethylene glycol and titanium dioxide. Energy: 2.72 kJ (0.65 kcal). Gluten-, sodium-, sulfite- and tartrazine-free. Bottles of 100 and 500.

16 mg: Each round, white, biconvex, film-coated tablet, identified 16, contains: perphenazine 16 mg. Nonmedicinal ingredients: cornstarch, hydroxypropyl methylcellulose, lactose, magnesium stearate, microcrystalline cellulose, polyethylene glycol and titanium dioxide. Energy: 3.50 kJ (0.84 kcal). Gluten-, sodium-, sulfite- and tartrazine-free. Bottles of 100 and 500.

APO®-PHENYLBUTAZONE Ⓟ

Apotex

Phenylbutazone

Anti-inflammatory—Antiarthritic

Supplied: Each round, red, biconvex, film-coated tablet contains: phenylbutazone 100 mg. Nonmedicinal ingredients: colloidal silicon dioxide, croscarmellose sodium, D&C Red #7 lake 50%, FD&C Yellow #6, hydroxypropyl methylcellulose, lactose, magnesium stearate and polyethylene glycol. Energy: 1.77 kJ (0.42 kcal). Sodium: <1 mmol (0.51 mg). Gluten-, sulfite- and tartrazine-free. Bottles of 100 and 1 000.

APO®-PINDOL Ⓟ

Apotex

Pindolol

Antihypertensive—Antianginal Agent

Supplied: 5 mg: Each round, white, flat-faced with beveled-edge tablet, scored and identified APO over P5 on one side, contains: pindolol 5 mg. Nonmedicinal ingredients: croscarmellose sodium, lactose, magnesium stearate and microcrystalline cellulose. Energy: 1.25 kJ (0.30 kcal). Sodium: <1 mmol (0.09 mg). Gluten-, sulfite- and tartrazine-free. Bottles of 100 and 500.

10 mg: Each round, white, biconvex, tablet, scored and identified APO over P10 on one side, contains: pindolol 10 mg. Nonmedicinal ingredients: croscarmellose sodium, lactose, magnesium stearate and microcrystalline cellulose. Energy: 2.49 kJ (0.60 kcal). Sodium: <1 mmol (0.07 mg). Gluten-, sulfite- and tartrazine-free. Bottles of 100 and 500.

15 mg: Each round, white, flat-faced with beveled-edge tablet, scored and identified APO over P15 on one side, contains: pindolol 15 mg. Nonmedicinal ingredients: croscarmellose sodium, lactose, magnesium stearate and microcrystalline cellulose. Energy: 3.74 kJ (0.89 kcal). Sodium: <1 mmol (0.27 mg). Gluten-, sulfite- and tartrazine-free. Bottles of 100.

APO®-PIROXICAM Ⓟ

Apotex

Piroxicam

Anti-inflammatory—Analgesic

Supplied: 10 mg: Each no. 2, maroon and blue, hard gelatin capsule, identified APO 10, contains: piroxicam 10 mg. Nonmedicinal ingredients: cornstarch, lactose, microcrystalline cellulose and stearic acid. Energy: 4.66 kJ (1.11 kcal). Gluten-, sodium- and tartrazine-free. Bottles of 100 and 500.

20 mg: Each no. 2, maroon, hard gelatin capsule, identified APO 20, contains: piroxicam 20 mg. Nonmedicinal ingredients: cornstarch, lactose, microcrystalline cellulose and stearic acid. Energy: 4.49 kJ (1.07 kcal). Gluten-, sodium- and tartrazine-free. Bottles of 100 and 500.

APO®-PRAZO Ⓟ

Apotex

Prazosin HCl

Antihypertensive Agent

Supplied: 1 mg: Each capsule-shaped, peach, flat-faced with beveled edge tablet, scored and identified APO P1 on one side, contains: prazosin HCl equivalent to prazosin 1 mg. Nonmedicinal ingredients: croscarmellose sodium, D&C Yellow #10 aluminum lake, FD&C Yellow #6, lactose, magnesium stearate and microcrystalline cellulose. Energy: 2.31 kJ (0.55 kcal). Sodium: <1 mmol (0.16 mg). Gluten-, sulfite- and tartrazine-free. Bottles of 100 and 500.

2 mg: Each round, white, biconvex tablet, scored and identified APO over P2 on one side, contains: prazosin HCl equivalent to prazosin 2 mg. Nonmedicinal ingredients: croscarmellose sodium, lactose, magnesium stearate and microcrystalline cellulose. Energy: 2.63 kJ (0.63 kcal). Sodium: <1 mmol (0.19 mg). Gluten-, sulfite- and tartrazine-free. Bottles of 100 and 500.

5 mg: Each diamond-shaped, white, biconvex tablet, scored and identified APO over P5 on one side, contains: prazosin HCl equivalent to prazosin 5 mg. Nonmedicinal ingredients: croscarmellose sodium, lactose, magnesium stearate and microcrystalline cellulose. Energy: 6.57 kJ (1.57 kcal). Sodium: <1 mmol (0.48 mg). Gluten-, sulfite- and tartrazine-free. Bottles of 100.

APO®-PREDNISONE Ⓟ

Apotex

Prednisone

Glucocorticoid

Supplied: 1 mg: Each round, white, flat-faced with beveled edge tablet, identified APO over 1, contains: prednisone 1 mg. Nonmedicinal ingredients: croscarmellose sodium, lactose, magnesium stearate and microcrystalline cellulose. Energy: <1 kJ (0.00 kcal). Sodium: <1 mmol (0.02 mg). Gluten-, sulfite- and tartrazine-free. Bottles of 100.

5 mg: Each round, white, flat-faced with beveled edge tablet, scored and identified APO over 5, contains: prednisone 5 mg. Nonmedicinal ingredients: croscarmellose sodium, lactose, magnesium stearate and microcrystalline cellulose. Energy: 1.57 kJ (0.38 kcal). Sodium: <1 mmol (0.16 mg). Gluten-, sulfite- and tartrazine-free. Bottles of 100, 1 000 and 5 000. Unit dose packages of 100. Apo Long-Term Care (LTC) Pak.

50 mg: Each round, white, biconvex tablet, scored and identified APO over 50, contains: prednisone 50 mg. Nonmedicinal ingredients: croscarmellose sodium, lactose, magnesium stearate and microcrystalline cellulose. Energy: 5.77 kJ (1.38 kcal). Sodium: <1 mmol (0.16 mg). Gluten-, sulfite- and tartrazine-free. Bottles of 100.

APO®-PRIMIDONE Ⓟ

Apotex

Primidone

Anticonvulsant

Supplied: 125 mg: Each round, white, flat-faced with beveled edge, scored tablet, identified APO over 125, contains: primidone 125 mg. Nonmedicinal ingredients: colloidal silicon dioxide, croscarmellose sodium, magnesium stearate and methylcellulose. Energy: <1 kJ (0.17 kcal). Sodium: <1 mmol (0.19 mg). Gluten-, lactose-, sulfite- and tartrazine-free. Bottles of 100 and 500.

250 mg: Each round, white, flat-faced with beveled edge, scored tablet, identified APO over 250, contains: primidone 250 mg. Nonmedicinal ingredients: colloidal silicon dioxide, croscarmellose sodium, magnesium stearate and methylcellulose. Energy: 1.44 kJ (0.34 kcal). Sodium: <1 mmol (0.38 mg). Gluten-, lactose-, sulfite- and tartrazine-free. Bottles of 100 and 1 000.

APO®-PROCAINAMIDE Ⓟ

Apotex

Procainamide HCl

Antiarrhythmic Agent

Supplied: 250 mg: Each yellow, No. 2 capsule, identified APO 250, contains: procainamide HCl 250 mg. Nonmedicinal ingredients: colloidal silicon dioxide, D&C yellow #10, edible grey ink, FD&C yellow #6, gelatin, methylparaben, propylparaben, sodium lauryl sulfate, stearic acid and titanium dioxide. Energy: <1 kJ (0.21 kcal). Gluten-, lactose-, sodium- and tartrazine-free. Bottles of 100 and 500.

375 mg: Each orange and white, No. 1 capsule, identified APO 375, contains: procainamide HCl 375 mg. Nonmedicinal ingredients: colloidal silicon dioxide, edible grey ink, FD&C yellow #6, gelatin, methylparaben, propylparaben, sodium

Apo-Procainamide (cont'd)

lauryl sulfate, stearic acid and titanium dioxide. Energy: 1.10 kJ (0.26 kcal). Gluten-, lactose-, sodium- and tartrazine-free. Bottles of 100 and 500.

500 mg: Each orange and yellow, No. 0 capsule, identified APO 500, contains: procainamide HCl 500 mg. Nonmedicinal ingredients: colloidal silicon dioxide, D&C yellow #10, edible black ink, FD&C yellow #6, gelatin, methylparaben, propylparaben, sodium lauryl sulfate, stearic acid and titanium dioxide. Energy: 1.37 kJ (0.33 kcal). Gluten-, lactose-, sodium- and tartrazine-free. Bottles of 100 and 500.

APO®-PROPRANOLOL Ⓟ
Apotex

Propranolol HCl

Beta-Adrenergic Receptor Blocking Agent

Supplied: 10 mg: Each round, orange, biconvex tablet, scored and identified APO over 10, contains: propranolol HCl 10 mg. Nonmedicinal ingredients: cornstarch, D&C yellow #10 aluminum lake, FD&C Yellow #6, lactose, magnesium stearate and microcrystalline cellulose. Energy: 2.41 kJ (0.58 kcal). Gluten-, sodium-, sulfite- and tartrazine-free. Bottles of 100 and 1 000. Unit dose packages of 100. Apo Long-term Care (LTC) Pak.

20 mg: Each hexagonal, blue, biconvex tablet, scored and identified APO over 20, contains: propranolol HCl 20 mg. Nonmedicinal ingredients: brilliant blue FCF aluminum lake, cornstarch, indigotine aluminum lake, lactose, magnesium stearate and microcrystalline cellulose. Energy: 2.65 kJ (0.63 kcal). Gluten-, sodium-, sulfite- and tartrazine-free. Bottles of 100 and 1 000. Apo Long-Term Care (LTC) Pak.

40 mg: Each round, green, biconvex tablet, scored and identified APO over 40, contains: propranolol HCl 40 mg. Nonmedicinal ingredients: cornstarch, croscarmellose sodium, D&C yellow #10 aluminum lake, indigotine aluminum lake 12%, lactose, magnesium stearate and microcrystalline cellulose. Energy: 2.80 kJ (0.67 kcal). Sodium: <1 mmol (0.03 mg). Gluten-, sulfite- and tartrazine-free. Bottles of 100 and 1 000. Unit dose packages of 100. Apo Long-Term Care (LTC) Pak.

80 mg: Each round, yellow, biconvex tablet, scored and identified APO over 80, contains: propranolol HCl 80 mg. Nonmedicinal ingredients: colloidal silicon dioxide, cornstarch, croscarmellose sodium, D&C yellow #10 aluminum lake, FD&C yellow #6, lactose, magnesium stearate and microcrystalline cellulose. Energy: 3.93 kJ (0.94 kcal). Sodium: <1 mmol (0.07 mg). Gluten-, sulfite- and tartrazine-free. Bottles of 100 and 1 000. Apo Long-Term Care (LTC) Pak.

120 mg: Each round, deep rose, biconvex tablet, scored and identified APO over 120, contains: propranolol HCl 120 mg. Nonmedicinal ingredients: colloidal silicon dioxide, croscarmellose sodium, lactose, magnesium stearate, microcrystalline cellulose and red ferric oxide. Energy: 5.44 kJ (1.30 kcal). Sodium: <1 mmol (0.03 mg). Gluten-, sulfite- and tartrazine-free. Bottles of 100.

APO®-QUINIDINE
Apotex

Quinidine Sulfate

Antiarrhythmic

Supplied: Each round, white, biconvex, scored tablet, identified APO over 200, contains: quinidine sulfate 200 mg. Nonmedicinal ingredients: colloidal silicon dioxide, croscarmellose sodium, magnesium stearate and methylcellulose. Energy: <1 kJ (0.04 kcal). Sodium: <1 mmol (0.14 mg). Gluten-, lactose-, sulfite- and tartrazine-free. Bottles of 100 and 1 000. Unit dose packages of 100.

APO®-RANITIDINE Ⓟ
Apotex

Ranitidine HCl

Histamine H_2-Receptor Antagonist

Supplied: 150 mg: Each round, white, film-coated tablet, identified APO over 150, contains: ranitidine 150 mg (as the hydrochloride). Nonmedicinal ingredients: colloidal silicon dioxide, croscarmellose sodium, hydroxypropyl methylcellulose, magnesium stearate, microcrystalline cellulose, polydextrose, polyethylene glycol and titanium dioxide. Energy: 2.54 kJ (0.61 kcal). Sodium: <1 mmol (0.37 mg). Gluten-, lactose-, sulfite- and tartrazine-free. Bottles of 100 and 500. Patient packs of 60 and 100.

300 mg: Each capsule-shaped, white, film-coated tablet, identified APO-300, contains: ranitidine 300 mg (as the hydrochloride). Nonmedicinal ingredients: colloidal silicon dioxide, croscarmellose sodium, hydroxypropyl methylcellulose, magnesium stearate, microcrystalline cellulose, polydextrose, polyethylene glycol and titanium dioxide. Energy: 5.07 kJ (1.21 kcal). Sodium: <1 mmol (0.73 mg). Gluten-, lactose-, sulfite- and tartrazine-free. Bottles of 100 and 500. Patient packs of 30 and 100.

APO®-SALVENT Ⓟ
Apotex

Salbutamol

Bronchodilator

Supplied: Inhaler: Each depression of the valve delivers: salbutamol 100 µg (as a micronized suspension of salbutamol base in an inert propellant mixture of trichlorofluoromethane, dichlorodifluoromethane and oleic acid). Each canister contains 200 doses.

The contents of the inhaler are under pressure. Do not puncture. Do not use or store near heat or open flame. Store between 15 and 30°C. Exposure to temperatures above 50°C may cause bursting. Never throw container into fire or incinerator. Keep out of reach of children.

Respirator Solution: Each mL of solution contains: salbutamol sulfate, equivalent to salbutamol base 5 mg. Nonmedicinal ingredients: benzalkonium chloride and sulfuric acid. Bottles of 10 mL.

Sterules: 1 mg/mL: Each sterule contains: salbutamol sulfate 2.5 mg in normal saline 2.5 mL. Preservative-free. Prediluted unit-doses, packs of 20 (4 trays of 5). Store between 15 and 25°C. Protect from light.

2 mg/mL: Each sterule contains: salbutamol sulfate 5.0 mg in normal saline 2.5 mL. Preservative-free. Prediluted unit-doses, packs of 20 (4 trays of 5). Store between 15 and 25°C. Protect from light.

Tablets: 2 mg: Each light purple, round, flat-faced with beveled edge tablet, scored and engraved APO over 2 on one side, contains: salbutamol sulfate equivalent to 2 mg of salbutamol. Nonmedicinal ingredients: cornstarch, D&C Red #30 aluminum lake, ferric-ferrous oxide, lactose, magnesium stearate and microcrystalline cellulose. Energy: 1.45 kJ (0.35 kcal). Gluten-, sodium-, sulfite- and tartrazine-free. Bottles of 100 and 500.

4 mg: Each light purple, round, flat-faced with beveled edge tablet, scored and engraved APO over 4 on one side, contains: salbutamol sulfate equivalent to 4 mg of salbutamol. Nonmedicinal ingredients: cornstarch, D&C Red #30 aluminum lake, ferric-ferrous oxide, lactose, magnesium stearate and microcrystalline cellulose. Energy: 2.90 kJ (0.69 kcal). Gluten-, sodium-, sulfite- and tartrazine-free. Bottles of 100 and 500.

APO®-SELEGILINE Ⓟ
Apotex

Selegiline HCl

Antiparkinsonian Agent

Supplied: Each round, white, flat-faced, beveled-edged tablet, engraved "S5" on one side, contains: 5 mg of the l-isomer of selegiline HCl. Nonmedicinal ingredients: cornstarch, lactose, magnesium stearate and microcrystalline cellulose. Bottles of 100 and 500. Store at room temperature 15 to 30°C. Protect from light. Unit dose packages should also be protected from high humidity.

APO®-SOTALOL Ⓟ
Apotex

Sotalol HCl

Antiarrhythmic

Supplied: 80 mg: Each blue, capsule-shaped, biconvex tablet, identified "APO-80" on one side and scored on the other, contains: sotalol HCl 80 mg. Nonmedicinal ingredients: colloidal silicon dioxide, dextrates, FD&C blue #2, magnesium stearate and methylcellulose. Gluten-, sulfite- and tartrazine-free. Bottles of 100, 250, 500 and 1 000.

160 mg: Each blue, capsule-shaped, biconvex tablet, identified "APO-160" on one side and scored on the other, contains: sotalol HCl 160 mg. Nonmedicinal ingredients: colloidal silicon dioxide, dextrates, FD&C blue #2, magnesium stearate and methylcellulose. Gluten-, sulfite- and tartrazine-free. Bottles of 100, 250, 500 and 1 000.

Store at room temperature (15 to 30°C). Protect from light.

APO®-SUCRALFATE Ⓟ
Apotex

Sucralfate

Gastroduodenal Cytoprotective Agent

Supplied: Each white, capsule-shaped tablet, engraved "APO-1g" on one side, contains: sucralfate 1 g. Nonmedicinal ingredients: colloidal silicon dioxide, croscarmellose sodium and magnesium stearate. Energy: <1 kJ (0.05 kcal). Sodium: <1 mmol (0.76 mg). Gluten-, lactose-, sulfite- and tartrazine-free. Bottles of 100 and 500. Store at room temperature 15 to 25°C. Protect from humidity in container tightly closed.

APO®-SULFATRIM Ⓟ
Apotex

Sulfamethoxazole—Trimethoprim

Antibacterial

Supplied: Adult Tablets: Each white, round, scored tablet, one side convex, identified APO over 400—80, other side flat and plain, contains: sulfamethoxazole 400 mg and trimethoprim 80 mg. Nonmedicinal ingredients: colloidal silicon dioxide, croscarmellose sodium, magnesium stearate and methylcellulose. Energy: <1 kJ (0.15 kcal). Sodium: <1 mmol (0.25 mg). Gluten-, lactose-, sulfite- and tartrazine-free. Bottles of 100 and 1 000. Unit dose packages of 100.

DS Tablets: Each white, capsule-shaped tablet, one side scored and identified APO DS contains: sulfamethoxazole 800 mg and trimethoprim 160 mg. Nonmedicinal ingredients: colloidal silicon dioxide, croscarmellose sodium, magnesium stearate and methylcellulose. Energy: 1.27 kJ (0.30 kcal). Sodium: <1 mmol (0.51 mg). Gluten-, lactose-, sulfite- and tartrazine-free. Bottles of 100 and 500.

Pediatric Tablets: Each white, round, flat-faced, beveled-edge tablet, scored and identified APO over PED, contains: sulfamethoxazole 100 mg and trimethoprim 20 mg. Nonmedicinal ingredients: colloidal silicon dioxide, croscarmellose sodium, magnesium stearate and methylcellulose. Energy: <1 kJ (0.04 kcal). Sodium: <1 mmol (0.06 mg). Gluten-, lactose-, sulfite- and tartrazine-free. Bottles of 100.

Oral Suspension: Each 5 mL of pink, cherry flavored suspension contains: sulfamethoxazole 200 mg and trimethoprim 40 mg. Nonmedicinal ingredients: artificial cherry flavor, carboxymethylcellulose, carboxymethylcellulose sodium, FD&C red #2, FD&C yellow #6, glycerin, methylparaben, microcrystalline cellulose, polysorbate, sodium cyclamate, sorbitol and water. Energy: 51.67 kJ (12.34 kcal)/5 mL. Sodium: <1 mmol (0.93 mg)/5 mL. Alcohol-, gluten-, lactose-, sugar-, sulfite- and tartrazine-free. Bottles of 100, 400 and 800 mL.

Store tablets and suspension in light-resistant containers. Store suspension at room temperature (15 to 30°C).

APO®-SULFINPYRAZONE Ⓟ
Apotex

Sulfinpyrazone

Platelet Inhibitor—Uricosuric

Supplied: 100 mg: Each white, round, flat-faced with beveled-edge tablet, scored and identified APO over 100, contains: sulfinpyrazone 100 mg. Nonmedicinal ingredients: carnauba wax, colloidal silicon dioxide, croscarmellose sodium, lactose and magnesium stearate. Energy: 3.62 kJ (0.86 kcal). Sodium: <1 mmol (0.19 mg). Gluten-, sulfite- and tartrazine-free. Bottles of 100.

200 mg: Each white, round, biconvex, film-coated tablet, identified APO over 200, contains: sulfinpyrazone 200 mg. Nonmedicinal ingredients: carnauba wax, colloidal silicon dioxide, croscarmellose sodium and magnesium stearate. Energy: 3.22 kJ (0.77 kcal). Gluten-, lactose-, sodium-, sulfite- and tartrazine-free. Bottles of 100 and 500.

APO®-SULIN ℞
Apotex

Sulindac

Anti-inflammatory—Analgesic

Supplied: 150 mg: Each hexagonal, yellow, biconvex tablet, scored and identified APO over 150 on one side and plain on the other side, contains: sulindac 150 mg. Nonmedicinal ingredients: colloidal silicon dioxide, croscarmellose sodium, lactose, magnesium stearate and microcrystalline cellulose. Energy: 1.19 kJ (0.28 kcal). Sodium: <1 mmol (0.04 mg). Gluten-, sulfite- and tartrazine-free. Bottles of 100 and 500.

200 mg: Each hexagonal, yellow, biconvex tablet, scored and identified APO over 200 on one side and plain on the other side, contains: sulindac 200 mg. Nonmedicinal ingredients: colloidal silicon dioxide, croscarmellose sodium, lactose, magnesium stearate and microcrystalline cellulose. Energy: 1.50 kJ (0.36 kcal). Sodium: <1 mmol (0.05 mg). Gluten-, sulfite- and tartrazine-free. Bottles of 100 and 500.

APO®-TAMOX ℞
Apotex

Tamoxifen Citrate

Antineoplastic Agent

Supplied: 10 mg: Each white, round, biconvex tablet, identified APO over T10, contains: tamoxifen 10 mg (as tamoxifen citrate 15.2 mg). Nonmedicinal ingredients: cornstarch, croscarmellose sodium, magnesium stearate and mannitol. Energy: 2.63 kJ (0.63 kcal). Sodium: <1 mmol (0.38 mg). Gluten-, lactose-, sulfite- and tartrazine-free. Bottles of 100 and 500. Patient packs of 60.

20 mg: Each white, octagonal, biconvex tablet, identified APO over T20 on one side and scored on the other, contains: tamoxifen 20 mg (as tamoxifen citrate 30.4 mg). Nonmedicinal ingredients: cornstarch, croscarmellose sodium, magnesium stearate and mannitol. Energy: 5.25 kJ (1.25 kcal). Sodium: <1 mmol (0.76 mg). Gluten-, lactose-, sulfite- and tartrazine-free. Bottles of 100 and 250. Patient packs of 30.

Protect from heat and light.

APO®-TEMAZEPAM ℞
Apotex

Temazepam

Hypnotic

Supplied: 15 mg: Each maroon and flesh capsule, imprinted "APO 15", contains: temazepam 15 mg. Nonmedicinal ingredients: ammonium hydroxide, croscarmellose sodium, D&C red #28, FD&C blue #1, FD&C red #40, gelatin, isopropyl alcohol, lactose anhydrous, magnesium stearate, microcrystalline cellulose, N-butyl alcohol, pharmaceutical glaze, propylene glycol, red iron oxide T, simethicone, sodium lauryl sulfate and titanium dioxide. Bottles of 100 and 500. Blister packs of 100.

30 mg: Each maroon and blue capsule, imprinted "APO 30", contains: temazepam 30 mg. Nonmedicinal ingredients: ammonium hydroxide, croscarmellose sodium, D&C red #28, FD&C blue #1, FD&C red #40, gelatin, isopropyl alcohol, lactose anhydrous, magnesium stearate, microcrystalline cellulose, N-butyl alcohol, pharmaceutical glaze, propylene glycol, simethicone, sodium lauryl sulfate and titanium dioxide. Bottles of 100 and 500.

Store at room temperature (15 to 25°C) in well-closed, light-resistant containers.

APO®-TENOXICAM ℞
Apotex

Tenoxicam

Anti-inflammatory—Analgesic

Supplied: Each yellow, oval, biconvex, film-coated tablet, engraved APO on one side and 20 and partially bisected on the other side, contains: tenoxicam 20 mg. Nonmedicinal ingredients: colloidal silicon dioxide, croscarmellose sodium, hydroxypropyl methylcellulose, lactose, magnesium stearate, microcrystalline cellulose, polydextrose, polyethylene glycol, titanium dioxide and yellow ferric oxide. Bottles of 100 and 500. Blisters of 100. Store at 15 to 30°C.

APO®-TERAZOSIN ℞
Apotex

Terazosin HCl

Antihypertensive Agent—Symptomatic Treatment of Benign Prostatic Hyperplasia (BPH)

Pharmacology: Hypertension: The antihypertensive effect of terazosin is believed to be a direct result of peripheral vasodilation. Although the exact mechanism by which the lowering of blood pressure is achieved is not known, the relaxation of the vessels appears to be produced mainly by selective blockade of α_1-adrenoceptors.

Benign Prostatic Hyperplasia (BPH): The reduction in the symptoms associated with BPH following administration of terazosin may be related to the changes in muscle tone produced by a blockade of α_1-adrenoceptors in the smooth muscle of the bladder neck and prostate.

Pharmacodynamics: Hypertension: Systolic and diastolic blood pressure is lowered in both the supine and standing positions. In clinical trials, blood pressure responses were measured at the end of the dosing interval (24 hours), with the usual supine response 5 to 10 mmHg systolic and 3.5 to 8 mmHg diastolic. The response in the standing position tended to be larger by 1 to 3 mmHg.

Limited measurements of peak response (2 to 3 hours after dosing) during chronic terazosin administration indicate that this response is somewhat greater than the trough (24 hours) response, suggesting some attenuation of response at 24 hours, presumably due to a fall in blood terazosin concentrations at the end of the dose interval.

The greater blood pressure effect associated with peak plasma concentrations appears to be more position-dependent (greater in the standing position) than the effect of terazosin at 24 hours; in the standing position there is also a 6 to 10 beats/min increase in heart rate in the first few hours after dosing. During the first 3 hours after dosing, 12.5% of patients had a systolic pressure fall of 30 mmHg or more from supine to standing, or standing systolic pressure below 90 mmHg with a fall of at least 20 mmHg.

During controlled clinical studies, patients receiving terazosin monotherapy had a small but statistically significant decrease (a 3% fall) compared to placebo in total cholesterol and the combined low-density and very low-density lipoprotein fractions. No significant changes were observed in high-density lipoprotein fraction and triglycerides compared to placebo.

Benign Prostatic Hyperplasia (BPH): The symptoms associated with BPH are related to bladder outlet obstruction. The bladder outlet obstruction is comprised of a static obstruction due to the enlarged prostate and a dynamic obstruction which is dependent upon the sympathetically controlled tone of the smooth muscle in the prostate and the bladder neck. Stimulation of α_1-adrenoceptors in the smooth muscle of the bladder neck and the prostate causes smooth muscle contraction and an increase in muscle tone.

In 3 placebo-controlled studies in men with symptomatic BPH, symptom evaluation and uroflowmetric measurements were performed approximately 24 hours following dosing. Results from these studies indicated that terazosin significantly improved symptoms and peak urine flow rates over placebo.

In 30 to 70% of patients with symptomatic BPH, placebo has also shown a remarkable and sometimes dramatic effect in controlled short-term studies. The symptoms may subside or fade away without treatment in approximately 20% of patients.

Pharmacokinetics: Orally-administered terazosin hydrochloride is essentially completely absorbed in man. Nearly all of the circulating dose is in the form of parent drug. Food has little or no effect on the bioavailability. The plasma levels of the free base peak in about 1 hour and then decline with a half-life of approximately 12 hours. Approximately 90 to 94% of the drug is bound to plasma proteins and binding is constant over the clinically-observed concentration range.

Hepatic metabolism is extensive with major biliary elimination. Approximately 10% of an orally-administered dose is excreted as parent drug in the urine and approximately 20% is excreted in the feces. The remainder is eliminated as metabolites. Overall, approximately 40% of the administered dose is excreted in the urine and approximately 60% in the feces.

Indications: Hypertension: In the treatment of mild to moderate hypertension. It is employed in a general treatment program in conjunction with a thiazide diuretic and/or other antihypertensive drugs as needed for proper patient response. Terazosin may be tried as a sole therapy in those patients in whom other agents caused adverse effects or are inappropriate.

Benign Prostatic Hyperplasia (BPH): Terazosin is also indicated for the treatment of symptoms of benign prostatic hyperplasia (BPH). The onset of effect is rapid, with improvement in peak flow rate and symptoms observed at 2 weeks. The effect on these variables was well maintained throughout the study duration (18 months). Terazosin does not retard or stop the progression of BPH. The long-term effects of terazosin on the incidence of surgery, acute urinary obstruction or other complications of BPH, are yet to be determined.

A number of clinical conditions can mimic symptomatic BPH (i.e., stricture of urethra, stricture of bladder neck, urinary bladder stones, neurogenic bladder dysfunction secondary to diabetes, Parkinsonism, etc.). These conditions should therefore be ruled out before terazosin therapy is initiated.

Contraindications: Individuals who have shown hypersensitivity to terazosin or its analogs.

Warnings: Syncope and First-dose Effect: Terazosin can cause marked hypotension, especially postural hypotension, and syncope in association with the first dose or first few doses of therapy. A similar effect can occur if therapy is reinstated following interruption for more than a few doses. Syncope has also occurred in association with rapid dosage increases or the introduction of another antihypertensive agent into the regimen of a patient taking high doses of terazosin.

Syncope is believed to be due to an excessive postural hypotensive effect, although occasionally the syncopal episode has been preceded by a bout of severe supraventricular tachycardia with heart rates of 120 to 160 beats/min.

In studies of terazosin, the incidence of syncopal episodes was approximately 1% in hypertensive patients and 0.7% in patients with BPH.

The likelihood of syncopal episodes or excessive hypotension can be minimized by limiting the initial dose of the drug to 1 mg of terazosin given at bedtime, by increasing the dosage slowly, and by introducing any additional antihypertensive drugs into the patient's regimen with caution (see Dosage).

Occupational Hazards: Patients should be advised of the possibility of syncopal and orthostatic symptoms, and to avoid driving or hazardous tasks for 12 hours after the initial dose of terazosin, after the dose is increased and after interruption of therapy when treatment is resumed. They should be cautioned to avoid situations where injury could result should syncope occur.

If syncope occurs, place the patients in the recumbent position and institute supportive measures as necessary.

Patients with a history of micturition syncope should not receive terazosin.

Concomitant administration of terazosin with verapamil to hypertensive patients may result in symptomatic hypotension and in some cases tachycardia (see Precautions).

Anaphylactoid-like Reactions: Anaphylactoid-like reactions manifested by angioedema of the lips, tongue, pharynx, and/or laryngeal spasm have been rarely reported in patients treated with terazosin (see Adverse Effects). In such cases, terazosin should be promptly discontinued and appropriate therapy and monitoring should be provided until complete and sustained resolution of signs and symptoms has occurred.

Precautions: General: Terazosin therapy does not modify the natural history of benign prostatic hyperplasia (BPH). It does not retard or stop the progression of BPH, nor does it improve urine flow sufficiently to significantly reduce the residual urine volume. However, significant reduction of the mean residual volume have been shown in patients with baseline residual volumes of >50 mL. The patient may continue to be at risk

Apo-Terazosin (cont'd)

of developing urinary retention and other BPH complications during terazosin therapy.

Prostatic Cancer: Carcinoma of the prostate and BPH cause many of the same symptoms. These two diseases frequently coexist. Therefore, patients thought to have BPH should be examined prior to starting terazosin therapy to rule out the presence of carcinoma of the prostate.

Orthostatic Hypotension: While syncope is the most severe orthostatic effect of terazosin (see Warnings), other symptoms of lowered blood pressure, such as dizziness, light-headedness and palpitations are more common with one or more of these occurring in 28% of patients in clinical trials of hypertension. In BPH clinical trials, 21% of the patients experienced one or more of the following: dizziness, hypotension, postural hypotension, syncope and vertigo. Patients should be advised to lie down when these symptoms occur and then wait for a few minutes before standing to prevent their recurrence.

Patients with occupations in which such events represent potential problems should be treated with particular caution.

There is evidence that the orthostatic effect of terazosin is greater, even in chronic use, shortly after dosing.

Concomitant Conditions: Terazosin should not be prescribed to patients with symptomatic BPH who have the following concomitant conditions: chronic urinary retention, high residual urine (over 200 mL), peak urine flow of 5 mL/s or less, history of prior prostatic surgery, chronic fibrous or granulomatous prostatitis, urethral stricture, history of pelvic irradiation, presence of prostatic calculi, presence of large median lobe of prostate, presence of calculi in urinary bladder, recent history of epididymitis, gross hematuria, presence of neurogenic bladder dysfunction (diabetes mellitus, Parkinsonism, uninhibited neurogenic bladder, etc.), hydronephrosis, presence of carcinoma of the prostate, patients with clinically significant renal or hepatic impairment (i.e., serum creatinine >2 mg/dL or AST >1.5 times the upper limit of normal (or equivalent level on the international scale).

Carcinogenesis, Mutagenesis, Impairment of Fertility: Terazosin was devoid of mutagenic potential when evaluated in vivo and in vitro.

Terazosin, administered in the feed to rats at doses of 8, 40 and 250 mg/kg/day for 2 years, was associated with a statistically significant increase in benign adrenal medullary tumors of male rats exposed to the 250 mg/kg dose. Female rats were unaffected. Terazosin was not oncogenic in mice when administered in feed for 2 years at a maximum tolerated dose of 32 mg/kg/day.

Effect on fertility was assessed in a standard fertility/reproductive performance study in which male and female rats were administered oral doses of 8, 30 and 120 mg/kg/day. Four of 20 male rats given 30 mg/kg and 5 of 19 male rats given 120 mg/kg failed to sire a litter. Testicular weights and morphology were unaffected by treatment. Vaginal smears at 30 and 120 mg/kg, however, appeared to contain less sperm than smears from control matings and good correlation was reported between sperm count and subsequent pregnancy.

Oral administration of terazosin hydrochloride for 1 or 2 years elicited a statistically significant increase in the incidence of testicular atrophy in rats exposed to 40 and 250 mg/kg/day, but not in rats exposed to 8 mg/kg/day. Testicular atrophy was also observed in dogs dosed with 300 mg/kg/day for 3 months, but not after 1 year when dosed with 20 mg/kg/day.

Geriatrics: Terazosin should be used cautiously in elderly patients because of the possibility of orthostatic hypotension. There was an age-related trend towards an increased incidence of dizziness, blurred vision and syncope in elderly patients treated with this drug. Patients over 75 years of age may have limited benefit from terazosin therapy.

Children: The use of terazosin in children is not recommended since safety and efficacy have not been established.

Renal Impairment: The use of terazosin in patients with impaired renal function requires careful monitoring. Limited pharmacokinetic studies using low doses (1 mg) showed no difference in the pharmacokinetics of terazosin as compared to patients with normal renal function. Approximately 40% of an oral terazosin dose is excreted by the kidney as parent drug or metabolites.

Liver Impairment: No information is available on the use of terazosin in patients with impaired liver function.

Peripheral Edema: Fluid retention resulting in weight gain may occur during terazosin therapy. In placebo-controlled monotherapy trials, male and female patients receiving terazosin gained a mean 0.8 and 1 kg, respectively, compared to losses of 0.1 and 0.5 kg, respectively, in the placebo group. Both differences are significant.

Pregnancy: The safety of terazosin in pregnancy has not been established. Terazosin is not recommended during pregnancy unless potential benefits justify potential risks to mother and fetus.

In animal studies there was no teratogenic effect. In peri- and postnatal development studies in rats, significantly more pups died in the group dosed with 120 mg/kg/day than in the control group during the 3-week postpartum period.

Lactation: It is not known whether terazosin is excreted in human milk. Because of possible adverse reactions in nursing infants, an alternate method of infant feeding should be considered when the use of drug is essential.

Drug Interactions: In controlled trials, terazosin has been added to diuretics and several α-adrenergic blockers; except for the additive hypotensive effect, no unexpected interactions were observed. Terazosin has also been used in patients on a variety of concomitant therapies. While these were not formal interaction studies, no interactions were observed. Terazosin has been used concomitantly in at least 50 patients on the following drugs or drug classes: analgesic/anti-inflammatory (e.g., acetaminophen, ASA, codeine, ibuprofen, indomethacin); antibiotics (e.g., erythromycin, trimethoprim and sulfamethoxazole); anticholinergic/sympathomimetics (e.g., phenylephrine HCl, phenylpropanolamine HCl, pseudoephedrine HCl); antigout (e.g., allopurinol); antihistamines (e.g., chlorpheniramine); cardiovascular agents (e.g., atenolol, hydrochlorothiazide, methyclothiazide, propranolol); corticosteroids; gastrointestinal agents (e.g., antacids); hypoglycemics; sedatives and tranquilizers (e.g., diazepam).

Concomitant administration of terazosin with verapamil to hypertensive patients resulted in significant increases in AUC, C_{max} and C_{min} of terazosin. The pharmacokinetics of verapamil were not altered. Symptomatic hypotension, and in some cases tachycardia, were observed. Caution should therefore be exercised when these drugs are administered concomitantly (see Warnings).

Laboratory Tests: Long-term (6 months or longer) administration of terazosin has produced no pattern of clinically significant changes attributable to the drug in the following clinical laboratory measurements: glucose, uric acid, creatinine, BUN, liver function tests and electrolytes.

Small but statistically significant decreases in hematocrit, hemoglobin, white blood cells, total protein and albumin were observed in controlled clinical trials. These laboratory findings suggested the possibility of hemodilution. Treatment with terazosin for up to 24 months had no significant effect on prostate specific antigen (PSA) levels.

Adverse Effects: Hypertension: The incidence of adverse reactions was derived from clinical trials involving 1 986 hypertensive patients on terazosin monotherapy or combination therapy.

The most serious adverse reaction encountered with terazosin is syncope occurring in approximately 1% of patients.

The most common reactions were dizziness (18.9%), headache (14.1%), asthenia (11%), somnolence (4.8%), nasal congestion (4.6%) and palpitation (4.6%).

The most frequently reported adverse effects which resulted in termination of terazosin were dizziness (3.5%), asthenia (2.1%) and headache (1.8%).

The following events were reported in less than 1% of cases except as indicated in brackets. The order of presentation corresponds within each heading to the relative frequency of occurrence.

Body as a Whole: headache (14.1%), asthenia (11%), peripheral edema (3.6%), chest pain (2.2%), abdominal pain (1.5%), edema (1.3%), facial edema (1.0%), back pain, weight gain, allergic reactions, malaise.

Cardiovascular: palpitation (4.6%), tachycardia (2.9%), syncope (1%), postural hypotension, angina pectoris, arrhythmias, cerebrovascular accident, heart failure, hypotension (at times severe), migraine.

Digestive: nausea (3.9%), dry mouth (1.7%), diarrhea (1.3%), dyspepsia, vomiting, anorexia, gastritis, liver function abnormality, jaundice.

Nervous System: dizziness (18.9%), somnolence (4.8%), nervousness (2.2%), paresthesia (1.5%), insomnia (1.2%), incoordination, abnormal dreams, confusion, speech disorder, tremor, vertigo, seizure, depression.

Respiratory: nasal congestion (4.6%), dyspnea (2.8%), rhinitis (1.2%), sinusitis, cold symptoms, pharyngitis, asthma, increased cough, laryngeal spasm.

Skin and Appendages: sweating (1.1%), pruritus, rash, photosensitivity.

Special Senses: blurred vision (1.4%), eye disorder (1.2%), tinnitus, taste perversion.

Urogenital: impotence (1.1%), urinary frequency, dysuria.

Miscellaneous: pain in extremities (1.8%), hypokalemia, hypophosphatemia, decreased libido.

At least 2 cases of severe anaphylactoid reactions were reported to be associated with administration of terazosin (see Warnings).

Postmarketing Experience: Body as a Whole: fever, neck pain, and shoulder pain.

Cardiovascular: Vasodilation and atrial fibrillation have been reported; however, a cause and effect relationship has not been established.

Digestive: constipation and flatulence.

Nervous System: anxiety.

Respiratory: bronchitis, epistaxis and flu symptoms.

Special Senses: conjunctivitis.

Urogenital: priapism, urinary tract infection, and urinary incontinence primarily reported in postmenopausal women.

Musculoskeletal: arthralgia, arthritis, joint disorder, and myalgia.

Hemapoietic: Thrombocytopenia has been reported.

Metabolic/Nutritional: gout.

Benign Prostatic Hyperplasia (BPH): In clinical trials involving 1 171 patients with BPH, syncope was reported in 0.7% of patients following treatment with terazosin.

The most common reactions (≥1%) were dizziness (14.0%), asthenia (9.0%), headache (6.4%), somnolence (4.5%), postural hypotension (3.8%), impotence (3.5%), urinary tract infection (3.1%), pharyngitis (2.7%), dyspnea (2.5%), rhinitis (2.2%), dysuria (2%), back pain (1.8%), nausea (1.8%), flu syndrome (1.7%), rash (1.7%), sinusitis (1.7%), hypotension (1.5%), chest pain (1.5%), vertigo (1.3%), dyspepsia (1.1%), diarrhea (1%), palpitation (1%), abdominal pain (1%) and amblyopia (1%).

Postmarketing Experience: Thrombocytopenia has been reported. Atrial fibrillation has been reported; however, a cause and effect relationship has not been established. Priapism has also been reported.

Overdose: Symptoms and Treatment: Should administration of terazosin lead to hypotension, support of the cardiovascular system is of first importance. Restoration of blood pressure and normalization of heart rate may be accomplished by keeping the patient in the supine position. If this measure is inadequate, shock should first be treated with volume expanders. If necessary, vasopressors should then be used and the renal function should be monitored and supported as needed. Laboratory data indicate that terazosin is highly protein bound; therefore, dialysis may not be of benefit.

Dosage: Hypertension: The dose and the dosing intervals (12 to 24 hours) of terazosin should be adjusted to the patient's individual blood pressure response.

When terazosin is being added to the existing antihypertensive therapy, the patient should be carefully monitored for the occurrence of hypotension. If a diuretic or other antihypertensive agent is being added to the terazosin regimen, dosage reduction of terazosin and retitration with careful monitoring may be necessary. The following is a guide to its administration:

Initial Dose: 1 mg of terazosin at bedtime is the starting dose for all patients and this dose should not be exceeded; compliance with this initial dosage recommendation should be strictly observed to minimize the potential for acute hypotensive episodes.

Subsequent Doses: The dose may be slowly increased to achieve the desired blood pressure response. The usual dose range is 1 to 5 mg once a day. Some patients may benefit from doses up to 20 mg/day which is the maximum recommended daily dose.

The blood pressure should be monitored at the end of the dosing interval to assure that control is maintained. It is also helpful to measure the blood pressure 2 to 3 hours after dosing to see if the maximum and minimum responses are similar and to evaluate symptoms.

If response to terazosin is substantially diminished at 24 hours, patients may be tried on a larger dose or twice daily dosage regimen. The latter should also be considered if adverse effects such as dizziness, palpitations or orthostatic complaints are seen 2 to 3 hours after dosing.

If terazosin administration is discontinued for several days or longer, therapy should be reinstituted using the initial dosing regimen.

Benign Prostatic Hyperplasia (BPH): The dose of terazosin should be adjusted to the patient's individual response.

Initial Dose: 1 mg of terazosin at bedtime is the starting dose for all patients, and this dose should not be exceeded for the first week. Compliance with this initial dosage should be strictly observed to minimize to potential for acute hypotensive episodes.

Subsequent Doses: The dose should be increased in stepwise fashion at weekly intervals to 2, 5, or 10 mg once daily to achieve the desired improvement of symptoms and/or flow rates. Maintenance doses of 5 to 10 mg once daily are generally required for the clinical response. The duration and dosage of treatment should be carefully titrated. Four weeks of terazosin therapy may be required before statistically significant improvement in the objective parameters of flowmetry (peak urine flow) are obtained. Improvement in the symptoms may appear as early as 2 weeks, but may be delayed as late as 6 weeks or more. Some patients may not achieve a clinical response despite appropriate titration. Following 18 months of treatment, a complete re-evaluation of the patient's condition should be made.

Following the administration of the maximum recommended dosage, terazosin should be discontinued if improvement in uroflowmetry is not clinically significant from baseline level or improvement in the American Urology Association (AUA) Scores are not translated into improvements in quality of life. Terazosin therapy should also be discontinued if terazosin side effects are more bothersome than BPH symptoms or if the patient develops a urinary complication while on terazosin therapy.

If terazosin administration is discontinued for several days or longer, therapy should be reinstituted using the initial dosing regimen.

Supplied: 1 mg: Each white, round, flat-faced, beveled-edged tablet, engraved "APO" on one side and "T1" on the other, contains: terazosin HCl dihydrate equivalent to terazosin 1 mg. Nonmedicinal ingredients: cornstarch, lactose, magnesium stearate and microcrystalline cellulose. Bottles of 100, 250, 500 and 1 000.

2 mg: Each orange, round, flat-faced, beveled-edged tablet, engraved "APO" on one side and "T2" on the other, contains: terazosin HCl dihydrate equivalent to terazosin 2 mg. Nonmedicinal ingredients: cornstarch, D&C yellow #10, lactose, magnesium stearate, microcrystalline cellulose and Sunset Yellow. Bottles of 100, 250, 500 and 1 000.

5 mg: Each tan, round, flat-faced, beveled-edged tablet, engraved "APO" on one side and "T5" on the other, contains: terazosin HCl dihydrate equivalent to terazosin 5 mg. Nonmedicinal ingredients: cornstartch, ferric-ferrous oxide, lactose, magnesium stearate, microcrystalline cellulose and red ferric oxide-Orange Shade. Bottles of 100, 250, 500 and 1 000.

10 mg: Each green, round, flat-faced, beveled-edged tablet, engraved "APO" on one side and "T10" on the other, contains: terazosin HCl dihydrate equivalent to terazosin 10 mg. Nonmedicinal ingredients: cornstarch, D&C yellow #10, indigotine (blue #2), lactose, magnesium stearate and microcrystalline cellulose. Bottles of 100, 250, 500 and 1 000.

Store at room temperature (15-30°C).

New Product 1998

APO®-TERFENADINE ℞

Apotex

Terfenadine

Histamine H_1-Receptor Antagonist

Supplied: 60 mg: Each white, round, flat-faced, beveled edge tablet, identified APO over 60 on one side, contains: terfenadine 60 mg. Nonmedicinal ingredients: cornstarch, croscarmellose sodium, lactose, magnesium stearate and sodium bicarbonate. Energy: 3.59 kJ (0.86 kcal). Sodium: <1 mmol (16.78 mg). Gluten-, sulfite- and tartrazine-free. Bottles of 100.

120 mg: Each white, capsule-shaped tablet, identified APO-120 on one side, contains: terfenadine 120 mg. Nonmedicinal ingredients: cornstarch, croscarmellose sodium, lactose, magnesium stearate and sodium bicarbonate. Energy: 7.19 kJ (1.72 kcal). Sodium: 1.46 mmol (33.57 mg). Gluten-, sulfite- and tartrazine-free. Bottles of 100.

Store at room temperature 15 to 30°C.

APO®-TETRA ℞

Apotex

Tetracycline HCl

Antibiotic

Supplied: Each orange and yellow No. 2 capsule, identified APO 250, contains: tetracycline HCl 250 mg. Nonmedicinal ingredients: colloidal silicon dioxide, croscarmellose sodium, D&C yellow #10, FD&C red #40, FD&C yellow #6, magnesium stearate, microcrystalline cellulose, stearic acid and titanium dioxide. Energy: <1 kJ (0.21 kcal). Gluten-, lactose-, sodium- and tartrazine-free. Bottles of 100, 1 000 and 3 000.

APO®-THEO LA ℞

Apotex

Theophylline

Bronchodilator

Supplied: 100 mg: Each white, round, biconvex, sustained-release tablet, scored and identified APO over 100 on one side, contains: anhydrous theophylline 100 mg. Nonmedicinal ingredients: colloidal silicon dioxide, hydroxypropyl methylcellulose, lactose and magnesium stearate. Energy: 2.98 kJ (0.71 kcal). Gluten-, sodium-, sulfite- and tartrazine-free. Bottles of 100.

200 mg: Each white, oval, biconvex, sustained-release tablet, scored and identified APO 200 on one side, contains: anhydrous theophylline 200 mg. Nonmedicinal ingredients: colloidal silicon dioxide, hydroxypropyl methylcellulose, lactose and magnesium stearate. Energy: 3.13 kJ (0.75 kcal). Gluten-, sodium-, sulfite- and tartrazine-free. Bottles of 100.

300 mg: Each white, capsule-shaped, biconvex, sustained-release tablet, scored and identified APO 300 on one side, contains: anhydrous theophylline 300 mg. Nonmedicinal ingredients: colloidal silicon dioxide, hydroxypropyl methylcellulose, lactose and magnesium stearate. Energy: 5.08 kJ (1.21 kcal). Gluten-, sodium-, sulfite- and tartrazine-free. Bottles of 100.

Do not break, chew or crush tablets. Store at controlled room temperature 15 to 30°C.

APO®-THIORIDAZINE ℞

Apotex

Thioridazine HCl

Antipsychotic—Antianxiety

Supplied: 10 mg: Each round, light green, biconvex, film-coated tablet, identified 10, contains: thioridazine HCl 10 mg. Nonmedicinal ingredients: D&C yellow #10 lake, hydroxypropyl methylcellulose, indigotine lake 13%, magnesium stearate, microcrystalline cellulose, polyethylene glycol and titanium dioxide. Energy: <1 kJ (0.19 kcal). Gluten-, lactose-, sodium-, sulfite- and tartrazine-free. Bottles of 100 and 1 000. Unit dose packages of 100. Apo Long-Term Care (LTC) Pak.

25 mg: Each round, brown, biconvex, film-coated tablet, identified 25, contains: thioridazine HCl 25 mg. Nonmedicinal ingredients: ferric-ferrous oxide, hydroxypropyl methylcellulose, magnesium stearate, microcrystalline cellulose, polyethylene glycol, red ferric oxide, titanium dioxide and yellow ferric oxide. Energy: 1.47 kJ (0.35 kcal). Gluten-, lactose-, sodium-, sulfite- and tartrazine-free. Bottles of 100 and 1 000. Unit dose packages of 100. Apo Long-Term Care (LTC) Pak.

50 mg: Each round, white, biconvex, film-coated tablet, identified 50, contains: thioridazine HCl 50 mg. Nonmedicinal ingredients: hydroxypropyl methylcellulose, magnesium stearate, microcrystalline cellulose, polyethylene glycol and titanium dioxide. Energy: 1.56 kJ (0.37 kcal). Gluten-, lactose-, sodium-, sulfite- and tartrazine-free. Bottles of 100 and 1 000. Unit dose packages of 100. Apo Long-Term Care (LTC) Pak.

100 mg: Each round, dark green, biconvex, film-coated tablet, identified 100, contains: thioridazine HCl 100 mg. Nonmedicinal ingredients: D&C yellow #10 lake, ferric-ferrous oxide, hydroxypropyl methylcellulose, indigotine lake 13%, magnesium stearate, microcrystalline cellulose, polyethylene glycol and titanium dioxide. Energy: 1.58 kJ (0.38 kcal). Gluten-, lactose-, sodium-, sulfite- and tartrazine-free. Bottles of 100 and 500.

APO®-TIAPROFENIC ℞

Apotex

Tiaprofenic Acid

Anti-inflammatory—Analgesic Agent

Supplied: 200 mg: Each round, white, film-coated, biconvex tablet, bisected and engraved "APO" over "200" on one side contains: tiaprofenic acid 200 mg. Nonmedicinal ingredients: colloidal silicon dioxide, hydroxypropyl cellulose, hydroxypropyl methylcellulose, magnesium stearate, microcrystalline cellulose, polyethylene glycol and titanium dioxide. Energy: 1.56 kJ (0.37 kcal). Gluten-, lactose-, sodium-, sulfite- and tartrazine-free. Bottles of 100.

300 mg: Each round, white, film-coated, biconvex tablet, bisected and engraved "APO" over "300" on one side contains: tiaprofenic acid 300 mg. Nonmedicinal ingredients: colloidal silicon dioxide, hydroxypropyl cellulose, hydroxypropyl methylcellulose, magnesium stearate, microcrystalline cellulose, polyethylene glycol and titanium dioxide. Energy: 2.35 kJ (0.56 kcal). Gluten-, lactose-, sodium-, sulfite- and tartrazine-free. Bottles of 100 and 500.

Protect from excessive heat, light and humidity. Store at room temperature 15 to 30°C.

APO®-TICLOPIDINE ℞

Apotex

Ticlopidine HCl

Inhibitor of Platelet Function

Pharmacology: Ticlopidine is an inhibitor of platelet aggregation. It causes a time and dose-dependent inhibition of platelet aggregation and release of platelet factors, as well as prolongation of bleeding time. The drug has no significant in vitro activity. The exact mechanism of action is not fully characterized, but does not involve inhibition of the prostacyclin/thromboxane pathways or platelet cAMP. Ticlopidine interferes with platelet membrane function by inhibiting ADP-induced platelet-fibrinogen binding and subsequent platelet-platelet interactions. The effect of ticlopidine on platelet function is irreversible. Template bleeding time is usually prolonged by 2 to 5-fold of baseline values with the therapeutic dose of ticlopidine hydrochloride. Upon discontinuation of ticlopidine hydrochloride dosing, bleeding time and other platelet function tests return to normal within 1 week in the majority of patients. The correlation between ticlopidine plasma levels and activity is still under investigation. Much of the following data was obtained from older patients corresponding to the age of patients participating in clinical trials (mean age: 63 years). After oral administration of the therapeutic dose of ticlopidine hydrochloride, rapid absorption occurs, with peak plasma levels occurring at approximately 2 hours after dosing. Absorption is at least 80% complete. Administration of ticlopidine hydrochloride after meals results in an increased (20%) level of ticlopidine in plasma. Steady-state plasma levels of ticlopidine in plasma are obtained after approximately 14 days of dosing at 250 mg b.i.d. The terminal elimination half-life is 4 to 5 days. However, inhibition of platelet aggregation is not correlated with plasma drug levels. Ticlopidine binds reversibly (98%) to plasma proteins, mainly to serum albumin and lipoproteins in a nonsaturable manner. Ticlopidine is metabolized extensively by the liver; no intact ticlopidine is detected in the urine. Unmetabolized ticlopidine is a minor component in plasma after a single dose, but at steady-state, ticlopidine is the major component. Impaired hepatic function resulted in higher than normal plasma levels of unchanged ticlopidine after single doses or after multiple doses. Inhibition of platelet aggregation is detected within 2 days of administration with 250 mg b.i.d. Maximum platelet aggregation inhibition is achieved 8 to 11 days following dosing with 250 mg b.i.d.

Indications: For reduction of the risk of first or recurrent stroke for patients who have experienced at least one of the following events: complete thromboembolic stroke, minor stroke, reversible ischemic neurological deficit (RIND), or transient ischemic attack (TIA) including transient monocular blindness (TMB).

Considerations in the selection of stroke prevention therapy should include the patients' current medical status and history, and their ability to comply with the required blood monitoring instructions concerning the use of ticlopidine.

Contraindications: Known hypersensitivity to drug or its excipients. Presence of hematopoietic disorders (such as neutropenia and/or thrombocytopenia). Presence of hemostatic disorder. Conditions associated with active bleeding, such as bleeding peptic ulcer or intracranial bleeding. Severe liver dysfunction.

Warnings: The following warnings were developed from clinical trial experience with over 2 000 patients with cerebrovascular disease who were treated with ticlopidine hydrochloride for as long as 5.8 years.

Apo-Ticlopidine (cont'd)

Hematological Complications: About 2.4% of ticlopidine patients in clinical trials developed neutropenia (defined as an absolute neutrophil count [ANC] below 1.2×10^9 cells/L). The incidence of severe neutropenia (ANC $<0.45 \times 10^9$ cells/L) was 0.8%. Severe neutropenia occurs during the first 3 to 12 weeks of therapy, and may develop quickly over a few days. The bone marrow shows a reduction in myeloid precursors. The condition may be life-threatening. It is usually reversible, and recovery occurs within 1 to 3 weeks after discontinuation of the drug but may take longer on occasion. In clinical trials, thrombocytopenia (defined as a platelet count of $<0.8 \times 10^{11}$ cells/L) has been observed in 0.4% of ticlopidine patients. The incidence of thrombocytopenia in patients on ASA or placebo was 0.3% or 0.4%, respectively. The thrombocytopenia may occur as an isolated finding or in combination with neutropenia.

Thrombocytopenia occurs during the first 3 to 12 weeks of therapy, and recovery usually occurs after drug discontinuation. All patients should have a white blood cell count with a differential count and platelet count performed every 2 weeks starting at baseline, before treatment is initiated, to the end of the third month of therapy with ticlopidine. When the neutrophil count shows a declining trend or the neutrophil numbers have fallen below 30% of the baseline, the values should be confirmed. If the presence of neutropenia (ANC $<1.2 \times 10^9$ cells/L) or thrombocytopenia ($<0.8 \times 10^{11}$ cells/L) is confirmed, the drug should be discontinued. Because of the long plasma half-life of ticlopidine, it is recommended that any patient who discontinues ticlopidine for any reason within the first 90 days have an additional CBC with white cell differential count obtained 2 weeks after discontinuation of therapy (see Precautions).

All forms of hematological adverse reactions are potentially fatal. Rarely, cases of pancytopenia, aplastic anemia or thrombocytopenia have been reported. Most cases were reversible, but some of them have been fatal. Thrombocytopenia may occur in isolation or together with neutropenia. Thrombotic thrombocytopenic purpura (TTP) has been reported, therefore careful attention to diagnosis should be made to guide treatment; platelet transfusion may be harmful in these patients.

Hemorrhagic Complications: Prolongation of bleeding time occurs in subjects treated with ticlopidine hydrochloride. Purpura and a few cases of more serious hemorrhagic events such as hematemesis, melena, hemothorax and intracranial bleeding have been reported. Patients must be instructed to watch for signs of bleeding disorders and to report any abnormality to their physician immediately. Ticlopidine therapy has to be stopped by the patient if a physician is not immediately available for consultation.

Anticoagulant Drugs: Anticoagulant drugs should be avoided as tolerance and safety of simultaneous administration with ticlopidine have not been established.

Hepatic Abnormalities: Most patients receiving ticlopidine showed some increase of their alkaline phosphatase values above their baseline and in one-third the increase exceeded the upper reference range. In 6%, the value was greater than twice the upper reference range. These increases in alkaline phosphatase were nonprogressive and asymptomatic. In clinical trials, 2 cases (0.1%) of cholestatic jaundice accompanied by elevated transaminases, alkaline phosphatase and bilirubin levels above 43 µmol/L have been observed. Both patients recovered promptly upon drug discontinuation.

Pregnancy: The safety of ticlopidine in pregnancy has not been established. It should not be used in pregnant patients.

Children: Safety in children has not been studied. Do not use in pediatric patients.

Precautions: Selection of Patients: Ticlopidine should be used only for the established indications (see Indications) and should not be given to patients with hematopoietic disorders, hemostatic disorders, patients suffering from conditions associated with active bleeding (see Contraindications) and patients anticipating elective surgery. In clinical trials elderly patients tolerated the drug well, but safety in children and pregnant women have not been established.

Clinical Monitoring: All patients have to be carefully monitored for clinical signs and symptoms of adverse drug reactions (see Adverse Effects). The signs and symptoms possibly related to neutropenia (fever, chills, sore throat, ulcerations in oral cavity), thrombocytopenia and abnormal hemostasis (prolonged or unusual bleeding, bruising, purpura, dark stool), jaundice (including dark urine, light colored stool) and allergic reactions should be explained to the patients who should be advised to stop medication and consult their physician immediately if any of these occur.

Laboratory Monitoring: All patients should have a WBC count with a differential and platelet count performed every 2 weeks starting at baseline, before treatment is initiated, to the end of the third month of therapy with ticlopidine. When the neutrophil count shows a declining trend or the neutrophil numbers have fallen below 30% of the baseline, the value should be confirmed. If the presence of neutropenia (ANC $<1.2 \times 10^9$ cells/L) or thrombocytopenia ($<0.8 \times 10^{11}$ cells/L) is confirmed, the drug should be discontinued. Because of the long plasma half-life of ticlopidine, it is recommended that any patient who discontinues ticlopidine for any reason within the first 90 days have an additional CBC with white cell differential obtained 2 weeks after discontinuation of therapy (see Warnings). Thereafter, the WBC counts need only be repeated for symptoms or signs suggestive of neutropenia. Liver function tests should be conducted during therapy with ticlopidine in response to signs and symptoms suggestive of hepatic dysfunction.

Elective Surgery: Ticlopidine should be discontinued 10 to 14 days prior to elective surgery or dental extraction, and bleeding time and thrombocyte count performed before the procedure if clinically indicated.

Emergency Surgery: Prolonged bleeding during surgery may be a problem in ticlopidine-treated patients. Transfusions of fresh platelets would be expected to improve hemostasis in such patients, but there are no data from clinical trials to confirm this expectation. There are data from clinical pharmacology trials that indicate treatment with glucocorticosteroids can normalize bleeding time in ticlopidine subjects, but there is no experience with ticlopidine hydrochloride surgical patients to show that such treatment improves hemostasis.

Specific Precautions: Liver: Ticlopidine is contraindicated in patients with severe liver dysfunction or cholestatic jaundice. Mild increase of alkaline phosphatase may be seen for the duration of the treatment and is inconsequential in the majority of patients (see Warnings and Contraindications).

Kidneys: Ticlopidine has been well tolerated in patients with moderately decreased renal function. In severe renal disease, caution and close monitoring are recommended.

Gastrointestinal: Conditions associated with active bleeding, such as bleeding ulcers, constitute contraindications for ticlopidine. Clinical judgment and monitoring of stool for occult blood are required for patients with a history of ulcerative lesions.

Trauma: Ticlopidine should be discontinued temporarily until the danger of abnormal bleeding is eliminated. A single fatal case of intracranial bleeding following head trauma has been reported. The extent to which ticlopidine may have contributed to the severity of the bleeding is unknown.

Drug Interactions: Since ticlopidine is metabolized by the liver, dosing of ticlopidine or other drugs metabolized in the liver may require adjustment upon starting or stopping therapy.

Table I outlines the agents which have been concomitantly administered with ticlopidine and the observed interaction if any.

Table I—Apo-Ticlopidine

Drug Interactions

Agents	Observed Interaction
NSAIDs including ASA	Ticlopidine potentiates the effect of ASA or NSAIDs on platelet aggregation. The safety of use of ticlopidine with ASA or NSAIDs is not established.
Antipyrine and products metabolized by hepatic microsomal enzymes	30% increase in t½ of antipyrine. Dose of products metabolized by hepatic microsomal enzymes to be adjusted when starting or stopping concomitant therapy with ticlopidine.
Theophylline	t½ of theophylline increased from 8.6 to 12.2 hours along with a comparable reduction in its total plasma clearance.
Digoxin	Approximately 15% reduction in digoxin plasma levels (little or no change in digoxin's efficacy expected).
Cimetidine	Chronic administration of cimetidine induced a 50% reduction in clearance of a single dose of ticlopidine.
Antacids	20% decrease in ticlopidine plasma level when administered after antacids.
Phenobarbital	No interaction reported.

Other Concomitant Therapy: Although specific interaction studies were not performed, in clinical studies, ticlopidine was used concomitantly with β-blockers, calcium channel blockers and diuretics without evidence of clinically significant adverse interactions.

Adverse Effects: Most adverse effects with ticlopidine are mild, transient and occur early in the course of treatment. In controlled clinical trials of 1 to 5 years duration, discontinuation of ticlopidine due to one or more adverse effects was required in 20.9% of patients. In these same trials, ASA and placebo led to discontinuation in 14.5% and 6.7% of patients, respectively. The incidence rates of adverse reactions listed in Table II were derived from multicenter, controlled clinical trials comparing ticlopidine, placebo and ASA over study periods of up to 5 years. The rates are based on adverse reactions considered probably drug-related by the investigator. Adverse experiences occurring in greater than 1% of patients treated with ticlopidine in controlled clinical trials are shown in Table II.

Table II—Apo-Ticlopidine

Adverse Experiences

	Percent of Patients in Controlled Studies		
	Ticlopidine HCl (n=2 048)	ASA (n=1 527)	Placebo (n=536)
Event	Incidence	Incidence	Incidence
Diarrhea	12.5 (6.3)*	5.2 (1.8)	4.5 (1.7)
Nausea	7.0 (2.6)	6.2 (1.9)	1.7 (0.9)
Dyspepsia	7.0 (1.1)	9.0 (2.0)	0.9 (0.2)
Rash	5.1 (3.4)	1.5 (0.8)	0.6 (0.9)
Gastrointestinal Pain	3.7 (1.9)	5.6 (2.7)	1.3 (0.4)
Neutropenia	2.4 (1.3)	0.8 (0.1)	1.4 (0.4)
Purpura	2.2 (0.2)	1.6 (0.1)	0.0 (0.0)
Vomiting	1.9 (1.4)	1.4 (0.9)	0.9 (0.4)
Flatulence	1.5 (0.1)	1.4 (0.3)	0.0 (0.0)
Pruritus	1.3 (0.8)	0.3 (0.1)	0.0 (0.0)
Dizziness	1.1 (0.4)	0.5 (0.4)	0.0 (0.0)
Anorexia	1.0 (0.4)	0.5 (0.4)	0.0 (0.0)

*Percent of patients (in parentheses) discontinuing clinical trials due to event.

The incidence of thrombocytopenia in these controlled studies was 0.4% in the ticlopidine and placebo groups of patients and 0.3% in the ASA patient population. The following rare events have been reported and their relationship to ticlopidine is uncertain. Pancytopenia, hemolytic anemia with reticulocytosis, thrombocytopenic thrombotic purpura, jaundice, allergic pneumonitis, systemic lupus (positive ANA), peripheral neuropathy, vasculitis, serum sickness, arthropathy, hepatitis, nephrotic syndrome, myositis, angioedema, fever, hyponatremia, bleeding increased (spontaneous, posttraumatic or postoperative), cholestatic jaundice, colitis, erythema multiforme, hepatic necrosis, hepatocellular jaundice, peptic ulcer, Stevens-Johnson syndrome, renal failure and sepsis.

Gastrointestinal: Ticlopidine therapy has been associated with a variety of gastrointestinal complaints including diarrhea and nausea. The majority of cases are mild and transient in nature and occur within 3 months of initiation of therapy. Typically, events are resolved within 1 to 2 weeks without discontinuation of therapy. If the effect is severe or persistent, therapy should be discontinued.

Hemorrhagic: Ticlopidine has been associated with a number of bleeding complications such as ecchymosis, epistaxis, hematuria, conjunctival hemorrhage, gastrointestinal bleeding and postoperative bleeding. Intracerebral bleeding was rare in clinical trials with ticlopidine, and was no more than that seen with comparator agents (ASA, placebo).

Rash: Ticlopidine has been associated with a maculopapular or urticarial rash (often with pruritus). Rash usually occurs within 3 months of initiation of therapy, with a mean time to onset of 11 days. If drug is discontinued, recovery should occur within several days. Many rashes do not recur on drug rechallenge. There have been rare reports of more severe rashes.

Altered Laboratory Findings: Hematological: Agranulocytosis, eosinophilia, neutropenia, pancytopenia, thrombocytopenia and thrombocytosis have been associated with ticlopidine administration (see Warnings).

Liver: Ticlopidine therapy has been associated with elevations of alkaline phosphatase (see Warnings). Maximal changes occur within 1 to 4 months of therapy initiation. No further progressive increases are seen with continuous therapy. Occasionally patients developed deviations in bilirubin, AST, ALT and GGTP.

Cholesterol: Chronic ticlopidine therapy has been associated with increased serum cholesterol and triglycerides. Serum levels of HDL-C, LDL-C, VLDL-C, and triglycerides are increased 8 to 10% after 1 to 4 months of therapy. No further progressive elevations are seen with continuous therapy. The ratios of the lipoprotein subfractions are unchanged. The effect is not correlated with age, sex, alcohol use or diabetes.

Overdose: Symptoms and Treatment: One case of deliberate overdosage with ticlopidine has been reported in a foreign postmarketing surveillance program. A 38-year-old male took a single 6 000 mg dose of ticlopidine (equivalent to 24 standard 250 mg tablets). The only abnormalities reported were increased bleeding time and increased ALT. No special therapy was instituted and the patient recovered without sequelae. Based on animal studies, overdosage may result in severe gastrointestinal intolerance. In the case of excessive bleeding after injury or surgery, standard supportive measures should be carried out if indicated, including gastric lavage, platelet transfusion and use of corticosteroids.

Dosage: The recommended dose of ticlopidine is 250 mg twice daily with food. Ticlopidine should be taken with meals to minimize gastrointestinal intolerance.

Information for the Patient: See Blue Section—Information for the Patient "Apo-Ticlopidine".

Supplied: Each oval, white, biconvex, film-coated tablet, engraved APO on one side and 250 on the other side, contains: ticlopidine HCl 250 mg. Nonmedicinal ingredients: carnauba wax, croscarmellose sodium, hydroxypropyl methylcellulose, mirocrystalline cellulose, polyethylene glycol, stearic acid and titanium dioxide. Bottles of 30 and 100. Two-and Four-Week Patient Packs of 28 (2 blister strips of 14 tablets each) and 56 (4 × 14) tablets, respectively. Store at room temperature (15 to 30°C) and protect from light.

For the first 3 months of therapy, only request or dispense the 14-day supply of tablets (see Precautions).

New Product 1998

APO®-TIMOL ℞
Apotex

Timolol Maleate

Antihypertensive—Antianginal Agent

Supplied: 5 mg: Each white, round, flat-faced with beveled-edge tablet, scored and identified APO over T5, contains: timolol maleate 5 mg. Nonmedicinal ingredients: croscarmellose sodium, lactose, magnesium stearate and microcrystalline cellulose. Energy: 1.58 kJ (0.38 kcal). Sodium: <1 mmol (0.06 mg). Gluten-, sulfite- and tartrazine-free. Bottles of 100 and 500.

10 mg: Each light-blue, round, flat-faced with beveled-edge tablet, scored and identified APO over T10, contains: timolol maleate 10 mg. Nonmedicinal ingredients: brilliant blue FCF lake, croscarmellose sodium, indigotine (FD&C blue #2), lactose, magnesium stearate and microcrystalline cellulose. Energy: 3.16 kJ (0.75 kcal). Sodium: <1 mmol (0.13 mg). Gluten-, sulfite- and tartrazine-free. Bottles of 100 and 500.

20 mg: Each light-blue, capsule-shaped tablet, scored and identified APO T20, contains: timolol maleate 20 mg. Nonmedicinal ingredients: brilliant blue FCF lake, croscarmellose sodium, indigotine (FD&C blue #2), lactose, magnesium stearate and microcrystalline cellulose. Energy: 6.32 kJ (1.51 kcal). Sodium: <1 mmol (0.25 mg). Gluten-, sulfite- and tartrazine-free. Bottles of 100.

APO®-TIMOP ℞
Apotex

Timolol Maleate

Glaucoma Therapy

Supplied: 2.5 mg/mL: Each mL of clear, colorless to light yellow, sterile, isotonic, buffered aqueous ophthalmic solution contains: timolol maleate equivalent to timolol 2.5 mg (0.25%). Nonmedicinal ingredients: benzalkonium chloride (as preservative), dibasic sodium phosphate, monobasic sodium phosphate, sodium hydroxide (to adjust pH) and water for injection. Clear, colorless, plastic ophthalmic dispensers of 5 and 10 mL with controlled drop tips.

5 mg/mL: Each mL of clear, colorless to light yellow, sterile, isotonic, buffered aqueous ophthalmic solution contains: timolol maleate equivalent to timolol 5 mg (0.5%). Nonmedicinal ingredients: benzalkonium chloride (as preservative), dibasic sodium phosphate, monobasic sodium phosphate, sodium hydroxide (to adjust pH) and water for injection. Clear, colorless, plastic ophthalmic dispensers of 5 and 10 mL with controlled drop tips.

Stable at room temperature.

APO®-TOLBUTAMIDE ℞
Apotex

Tolbutamide

Oral Hypoglycemic

Supplied: Each round, white, biconvex, scored tablet, identified APO over TOL, contains: tolbutamide 500 mg. Nonmedicinal ingredients: colloidal silicon dioxide, croscarmellose sodium and magnesium stearate. Energy: <1 kJ (0.02 kcal). Sodium: <1 mmol (0.50 mg). Gluten-, lactose-, sulfite- and tartrazine-free. Bottles of 100 and 1 000.

APO®-TRAZODONE ℞
APO®-TRAZODONE D ℞
Apotex

Trazodone HCl

Antidepressant

Supplied: Apo-Trazodone: 50 mg: Each round, pale orange, biconvex tablet, scored and engraved APO over T50 on one side, contains: trazodone HCl 50 mg. Nonmedicinal ingredients: colloidal silicon dioxide, FD&C yellow #6, magnesium stearate, microcrystalline cellulose, pregelatinized starch, sodium lauryl sulfate and sodium starch glycolate. Energy: 1.62 kJ (0.39 kcal). Sodium: <1 mmol (<0.26 mg). Gluten-, lactose-, sulfite- and tartrazine-free. Bottles of 100 and 250.

100 mg: Each round, white, biconvex tablet, scored and engraved APO over T100 on one side, contains: trazodone HCl 100 mg. Nonmedicinal ingredients: colloidal silicon dioxide, magnesium stearate, microcrystalline cellulose, pregelatinized starch, sodium lauryl sulfate and sodium starch glycolate. Energy: 3.23 kJ (0.77 kcal). Sodium: <1 mmol (<0.53 mg). Gluten-, lactose-, sulfite- and tartrazine-free. Bottles of 100 and 500.

Apo-Trazodone D: Each pale orange, rectangular, flat-faced tablet with beveled edges, trisected on both sides and marked APO on one side and 50 50 50 on the other, contains: trazodone HCl 150 mg. Nonmedicinal ingredients: colloidal silicon dioxide, FD&C yellow #6, magnesium stearate, microcrystalline cellulose, pregelatinized starch, sodium lauryl sulfate and sodium starch glycolate. Energy: 4.85 kJ (1.16 kcal). Sodium: <1 mmol (<0.79 mg). Gluten-, lactose-, sulfite- and tartrazine-free. The design of the Apo Trazodone D tablet makes dosage adjustments easy. Each tablet can be broken accurately to provide any of the following dosages: 50 mg (⅓ of a tablet), 75 mg (½ of a tablet), 100 mg (⅔ of a tablet), 150 mg (entire tablet). To break the Apo-Trazodone D tablet accurately and easily, hold the tablet between your thumb and index fingers close to the appropriate tablet score (groove). Then with the tablet score facing you, apply pressure and snap the tablet segments apart. Bottles of 100, 250 and 500.

Store at controlled room temperature 15 to 30°C. Protect from light.

APO®-TRIAZIDE ℞
Apotex

Triamterene—Hydrochlorothiazide

Diuretic—Antihypertensive

Supplied: Each round, flat-faced with beveled edge, scored, dark yellow tablet identified APO over 50-25 contains: triamterene 50 mg and hydrochlorothiazide 25 mg. Nonmedicinal ingredients: colloidal silicon dioxide, croscarmellose sodium, FD&C Yellow #6, lactose and magnesium stearate. Energy: 3.69 kJ (0.88 kcal). Sodium: <1 mmol (1.52 mg). Gluten-, sulfite- and tartrazine-free. Bottles of 100, 1 000 and 3 000. Unit dose packages of 100. Apo Long-Term Care (LTC) Pak.

APO®-TRIAZO ℞
Apotex

Triazolam

Hypnotic

Supplied: 0.125 mg: Each violet, oval, flat-faced with beveled edge, scored tablet, identified APO over .125, contains: triazolam 0.125 mg. Nonmedicinal ingredients: croscarmellose sodium, erythrosine lake 40%, indigotine lake 13%, lactose, magnesium stearate and microcrystalline cellulose. Energy: 1.58 kJ (0.38 kcal). Sodium: <1 mmol (0.32 mg). Gluten-, sulfite- and tartrazine-free. Cartons of 70×7 strip packs.

0.25 mg: Each light blue, oval, flat-faced with beveled edge, scored tablet, identified APO over 0.25, contains: triazolam 0.25 mg. Nonmedicinal ingredients: croscarmellose sodium, indigotine lake 13%, lactose, magnesium stearate and microcrystalline cellulose. Energy: 1.57 kJ (0.38 kcal). Sodium: <1 mmol (0.32 mg). Gluten-, sulfite- and tartrazine-free. Cartons of 70×7 strip packs.

Store at controlled room temperature 15 to 30°C.

APO®-TRIFLUOPERAZINE ℞
Apotex

Trifluoperazine HCl

Antipsychotic—Antiemetic—Antianxiety

Supplied: 1 mg: Each round, deep blue, biconvex, film-coated tablet, identified 1, contains: trifluoperazine HCl 1 mg. Nonmedicinal ingredients: cornstarch, hydroxypropyl methylcellulose, indigotine aluminum lake, lactose, magnesium stearate, microcrystalline cellulose, polyethylene glycol and titanium dioxide. Energy: 1.34 kJ (0.32 kcal). Gluten-, sodium-, sulfite- and tartrazine-free. Bottles of 100 and 1 000. Unit dose packages of 100. Apo Long-Term Care (LTC) Pak.

2 mg: Each round, deep blue, biconvex, film-coated tablet, identified 2, contains: trifluoperazine HCl 2 mg. Nonmedicinal ingredients: cornstarch, hydroxypropyl methylcellulose, indigotine aluminum lake, lactose, magnesium stearate, microcrystalline cellulose, polyethylene glycol and titanium dioxide. Energy: 1.75 kJ (0.42 kcal). Gluten-, sodium-, sulfite- and tartrazine-free. Bottles of 100 and 1 000. Unit dose packages of 100. Apo Long-Term Care (LTC) Pak.

5 mg: Each round, deep blue, biconvex, film-coated tablet, identified 5, contains: trifluoperazine HCl 5 mg. Nonmedicinal ingredients: croscarmellose sodium, hydroxypropyl methylcellulose, indigotine aluminum lake, lactose, magnesium stearate, microcrystalline cellulose, polyethylene glycol and titanium dioxide. Energy: 2.04 kJ (0.49 kcal). Sodium: <1 mmol (0.24 mg). Gluten-, sulfite- and tartrazine-free. Bottles of 100 and 1 000. Unit dose packages of 100. Apo Long-Term Care (LTC) Pak.

10 mg: Each round, deep blue, biconvex, film-coated tablet, identified 10, contains: trifluoperazine HCl 10 mg. Nonmedicinal ingredients: croscarmellose sodium, hydroxypropyl methylcellulose, indigotine aluminum lake, lactose, magnesium stearate, microcrystalline cellulose, polyethylene glycol and titanium dioxide. Energy: 3.64 kJ (0.87 kcal). Sodium: <1 mmol (0.48 mg). Gluten-, sulfite- and tartrazine-free. Bottles of 100 and 1 000.

20 mg: Each round, deep blue, biconvex, film-coated tablet, identified APO over 20, contains: trifluoperazine HCl 20 mg. Nonmedicinal ingredients: croscarmellose sodium, hydroxypropyl methylcellulose, indigotine aluminum lake, lactose, magnesium stearate, microcrystalline cellulose, polyethylene glycol and titanium dioxide. Energy: 4.90 kJ (1.17 kcal). Sodium: <1 mmol (0.68 mg). Gluten-, sulfite- and tartrazine-free. Bottles of 100 and 500.

APO®-TRIHEX ℞
Apotex

Trihexyphenidyl HCl

Antispasmodic

Supplied: 2 mg: Each round, white, flat-faced with beveled edge, scored tablet, identified APO over TRM, contains: trihexyphenidyl HCl 2 mg. Nonmedicinal ingredients: croscarmellose sodium, lactose, magnesium stearate and microcrystalline cellulose. Energy: 2.47 kJ (0.59 kcal). Sodium: <1

Apo-Trihex (cont'd)

mmol (0.10 mg). Gluten-, sulfite- and tartrazine-free. Bottles of 100 and 500.

5 mg: Each round, white, flat-faced with beveled edge, scored tablet, identified APO over 5, contains: trihexyphenidyl HCl 5 mg. Nonmedicinal ingredients: croscarmellose sodium, lactose, magnesium stearate and microcrystalline cellulose. Energy: 3.67 kJ (0.88 kcal). Sodium: <1 mmol (0.16 mg). Gluten-, sulfite- and tartrazine-free. Bottles of 100 and 500.

APO®-TRIMIP

Apotex

Trimipramine Maleate

Antidepressant

Supplied: Capsules: Each buff and pink No. 1 capsule identified APO 75, contains: trimipramine maleate equivalent to trimipramine 75 mg. Nonmedicinal ingredients: croscarmellose sodium, D&C yellow #10, FD&C blue #1, FD&C red #3, gelatin, lactose, magnesium stearate, sodium lauryl sulfate, sodium metabisulfite, stearic acid and titanium dioxide; capsule shell (edible black printing ink): alcohol, D&C yellow #10, FD&C blue #1, FD&C blue #2, FD&C red #40, pharmaceutical glaze, propylene glycol and synthetic black iron oxide. Energy: <5.74 kJ (<1.37 kcal). Sodium: <1 mmol (<0.01 mg). Alcohol-, gluten- and tartrazine-free. Bottles of 100 and 500.

Tablets: 12.5 mg: Each pink, round, biconvex, film-coated tablet, identified A, contains: trimipramine maleate equivalent to trimipramine 12.5 mg. Nonmedicinal ingredients: colloidal silicon dioxide, croscarmellose sodium, FD&C red #3, hydroxypropyl methylcellulose, magnesium stearate, microcrystalline cellulose, polyethylene glycol and titanium dioxide. Energy: <1 kJ (0.03 kcal). Sodium: <1 mmol (<0.01 mg). Gluten-, lactose-, sulfite- and tartrazine-free. Bottles of 100 and 500.

25 mg: Each pink, round, biconvex, film-coated tablet, identified 25, contains: trimipramine maleate equivalent to trimipramine 25 mg. Nonmedicinal ingredients: colloidal silicon dioxide, croscarmellose sodium, FD&C red #3, hydroxypropyl methylcellulose, magnesium stearate, microcrystalline cellulose, polyethylene glycol and titanium dioxide. Energy: <1 kJ (0.05 kcal). Sodium: <1 mmol (0.02 mg). Gluten-, lactose-, sulfite- and tartrazine-free. Bottles of 100 and 500. Unit dose packages of 100.

50 mg: Each pink, round, biconvex, film-coated tablet, identified APO over 50, contains: trimipramine maleate equivalent to trimipramine 50 mg. Nonmedicinal ingredients: colloidal silicon dioxide, croscarmellose sodium, FD&C red #3, hydroxypropyl methylcellulose, magnesium stearate, microcrystalline cellulose, polyethylene glycol and titanium dioxide. Energy: <1 kJ (0.10 kcal). Sodium: <1 mmol (0.04 mg). Gluten-, lactose-, sulfite- and tartrazine-free. Bottles of 100 and 500. Unit dose packages of 100.

100 mg: Each pink, round, biconvex, film-coated tablet, scored and identified APO over 100, contains: trimipramine maleate equivalent to trimipramine 100 mg. Nonmedicinal ingredients: colloidal silicon dioxide, croscarmellose sodium, FD&C red #3, hydroxypropyl methylcellulose, magnesium stearate, microcrystalline cellulose, polyethylene glycol and titanium dioxide. Energy: <1 kJ (0.21 kcal). Sodium: <1 mmol (0.07 mg). Gluten-, lactose-, sulfite- and tartrazine-free. Bottles of 100 and 500.

APO®-VERAP

Apotex

Verapamil HCl

Antianginal—Antiarrhythmic—Antihypertensive

Supplied: 80 mg: Each yellow, round, biconvex, film-coated tablet identified APO over V80 on one side contains: verapamil HCl 80 mg. Nonmedicinal ingredients: colloidal silicon dioxide, croscarmellose sodium, D&C yellow #10 lake, FD&C yellow #6, hydroxypropyl methylcellulose, lactose, magnesium stearate, microcrystalline cellulose, polyethylene glycol and titanium dioxide. Energy: 3.07 kJ (0.73 kcal). Sodium: <1 mmol (0.19 mg). Gluten-, sulfite- and tartrazine-free. Bottles of 100 and 500. Unit dose packages of 100.

120 mg: Each white, round, biconvex, film-coated tablet identified APO over V120 on one side contains: verapamil HCl 120 mg. Nonmedicinal ingredients: colloidal silicon dioxide, croscarmellose sodium, hydroxypropyl methylcellulose, lactose, magnesium stearate, microcrystalline cellulose, polyethylene glycol and titanium dioxide. Energy: 4.59 kJ (1.10 kcal). Sodium: <1 mmol (0.29 mg). Gluten-, sulfite- and tartrazine-free. Bottles of 100 and 500. Unit dose packages of 100.

APO®-ZIDOVUDINE

Apotex

Zidovudine

Antiretroviral Agent

Supplied: Each no. 3 capsule, identified APO 100, contains: zidovudine 100 mg. Nonmedicinal ingredients: colloidal silicon dioxide, cornstarch, microcrystalline cellulose, stearic acid and talc; capsule: edible black ink, gelatin, methylparaben, propylparaben, sodium lauryl sulfate and titanium dioxide. Energy: 1.45 kJ (0.35 kcal). Gluten-, lactose-, sodium- and tartrazine-free. Bottles of 100 and 500. Unit dose packages of 100. Store between 15 and 25°C. Protect from light and moisture.

APO®-ZOPICLONE

Apotex

Zopiclone

Hypnotic

Supplied: Each oval, blue, biconvex, film-coated tablet, scored and engraved "APO 7.5" on one side, contains: zopiclone 7.5 mg. Nonmedicinal ingredients: brilliant blue FCF lake, D&C yellow #10 lake, hydroxypropyl methylcellulose, lactose, magnesium stearate, microcrystalline cellulose, polyethylene glycol and titanium dioxide. Bottles of 100 and 500. Store at room temperature 15 to 30°C. Protect from light.

APRESOLINE®

Novartis Pharmaceuticals

Hydralazine HCl

Antihypertensive

Pharmacology: Although the precise mechanism of action of hydralazine is not fully understood, the major effects are on the cardiovascular system. Hydralazine apparently lowers blood pressure by exerting a peripheral vasodilating effect through a direct relaxation of vascular smooth muscle. Hydralazine, by altering cellular calcium metabolism, interferes with the calcium movements within the vascular smooth muscle that are responsible for initiating or maintaining the contractile state.

The peripheral vasodilating effect of hydralazine results in decreased arterial blood pressure (diastolic more than systolic); decreased peripheral vascular resistance; and an increased heart rate, stroke volume, and cardiac output. The vasodilating effect is much greater on arterioles than on veins and vascular resistance decreases more in the coronary, cerebral, splanchnic and renal circulations than in skin and muscle.

Hydralazine usually increases renin activity in plasma presumably as a result of increased secretion of renin by the renal juxtaglomerular cells in response to reflex sympathetic discharge. This increase in renin activity leads to the production of angiotensin II, which then causes stimulation of aldosterone and consequent sodium reabsorption and fluid retention.

Sodium retention and excessive sympathetic stimulation of the heart caused by hydralazine may be precluded by coadministration of a thiazide diuretic and a beta-blocker. Beta-adrenergic blocking drugs and hydralazine are complementary in their pharmacologic effects, a beta-adrenergic blocking agent minimizes hydralazine-induced increases in cardiac rate and ouput, and hydralazine prevents the reflex increase in peripheral resistance induced by beta-blockers.

Pharmacokinetics: Hydralazine is rapidly and fairly completely absorbed after oral administration. In the plasma only small amounts of the free drug can be traced, the bulk circulating in conjugated form, i.e., pyruvic acid hydrazone. Peak serum concentrations are reached within 1 to 2 hours after a dose.

Plasma levels of hydralazine vary widely among individuals. Orally administered hydralazine undergoes extensive, saturable first-pass metabolism (systemic availability: 26 to 55%), this first-pass effect being dependent on the individual's acetylator status. In response to the same oral dose, slow-acetylators show higher apparent plasma hydralazine levels than rapid acetylators and require lower doses to maintain control of blood pressure.

After i.v. administration of hydralazine no first-pass effect occurs; acetylator status therefore has no influence on the plasma levels.

Hydralazine is widely distributed in the body. The apparent volume of distribution of hydralazine is approximately 50% body weight. Binding to plasma proteins (chiefly albumin) is 88 to 90%.

Hydralazine crosses the placental barrier and is excreted in the breast milk.

The pattern of the metabolites depends on the subject's acetylator and presumably hydroxylator status. The main metabolite, NAc-HPZ (N-acetyl-hydrazine-phthalazinone), was found to be the relevant indicator for the drug-related phenotype.

The plasma half-life generally ranges between 1.7 and 3.0 hours in most subjects, but in rapid acetylators it is shorter, averaging 45 minutes.

Hydralazine and its metabolites are rapidly excreted by the kidney and 80% of the oral dose appears in the urine within 48 hours. The bulk of hydralazine excreted is in the form of acetylated and hydroxylated metabolites, some of which are conjugated with glucuronic acid; 2 to 14% is excreted as apparent hydralazine.

Indications: Oral: Essential hypertension. Hydralazine is used in conjunction with other antihypertensives such as beta-blockers and diuretics.

Parenteral: Severe hypertension when the drug cannot be given orally or when there is an urgent need to lower blood pressure (e.g., toxemia of pregnancy).

Contraindications: Hypersensitivity to hydralazine or other hydrazinophthalazine derivatives. Idiopathic systemic lupus erythematosus (SLE) and related diseases. Severe tachycardia and heart failure with a high cardiac output (e.g., in thyrotoxicosis). Myocardial insufficiency due to mechanical obstruction (e.g., in the presence of aortic or mitral stenosis or constrictive pericarditis). Isolated right-ventricular heart failure due to pulmonary hypertension (cor pulmonale). Acute dissecting aneurysm of the aorta. Coronary artery disease.

Warnings: Hydralazine may provoke in a few patients a clinical picture simulating SLE including glomerulonephritis. In its mild form this syndrome is reminiscent of rheumatoid arthritis (arthralgia, sometimes associated with fever and skin rash). When fully developed a syndrome resembling disseminated lupus erythematosus occurs.

Should this SLE-like syndrome develop, treatment should be discontinued immediately. Symptoms and signs usually regress when the drug is discontinued but residua have been detected many years later. Long-term treatment with adrenocorticosteroids may be necessary.

The frequency of these untoward effects increases with dosage and duration of exposure to the drug and is higher in slow than in fast acetylators. When treated with the same dosage, slow acetylators have higher serum concentrations than fast acetylators. The lowest effective dosage should therefore be used for maintenance therapy. If 100 mg daily fails to elicit an adequate clinical effect, the patient's acetylator status should be evaluated.

Slow acetylators and women run a greater risk of developing this SLE-like syndrome. In such cases dosage should be kept below 100 mg daily and the patients carefully monitored for clinical signs and symptoms suggestive of this syndrome.

Complete blood counts, examination of LE cell preparations, antinuclear antibody titre determinations and urine analysis are indicated before and periodically (e.g., every 6 months) during prolonged therapy with hydralazine even though the patient is asymptomatic. These tests are also indicated if the patient develops arthralgia, fever, chest pain, continued malaise or other unexplained signs or symptoms. If the test results are abnormal, treatment should be discontinued.

Antinuclear antibody may be found in the blood of as many as 50% of patients receiving hydralazine who remain asymptomatic. A positive antinuclear antibody titre requires that the physician carefully weigh the implications of the test results against the benefits to be derived from antihypertensive therapy with hydralazine. Microhematuria and/or proteinuria, in particular together with positive titres of antinuclear antibodies, may be initial signs of immune-complex glomerulonephritis associated with the SLE-like syndrome.

The chronotropic and inotropic effects of hydralazine increase myocardial oxygen requirements. It can cause ECG changes of myocardial ischemia, and in patients with coronary artery disease may precipitate angina pectoris or congestive heart failure. Hydralazine has been implicated in the production of myocardial infarction.

Hydralazine must therefore be used with caution in patients with suspected coronary artery disease. It should be given in combination with a beta-blocker or other suitable sympatholytic agents. The beta-blocker medication should be commenced a few days before the start of treatment with hydralazine.

Patients who have survived a myocardial infarction should not receive hydralazine until postinfarction stabilization has been achieved.

The hyperdynamic circulation caused by hydralazine may accentuate specific cardiovascular inadequacies (e.g., hydralazine may increase pulmonary artery pressure in patients with mitral valvular disease).

Pregnancy: Animal studies indicate that high doses of hydralazine are teratogenic in mice, possibly in rabbits, but not in rats. Teratogenic effects observed were cleft palate and malformation of facial and cranial bones. There are no adequate and well-controlled studies in pregnant women. Although clinical experience does not include any positive evidence of adverse effects on the human fetus, hydralazine should be used during pregnancy only if the benefit clearly justifies the potential risk to the fetus.

Precautions: Postural hypotension may result from hydralazine, but is less common than with ganglionic blocking agents. The drug should be used with caution in patients with cerebral vascular disease since abrupt decreases in blood pressure should be avoided in these patients.

Occupational Hazards: A pronounced lowering of the blood pressure may adversely affect the patient's reactions (e.g., as in driving or operating machinery).

In hypertensive patients with normal kidneys who are treated with hydralazine, there is evidence of increased renal blood flow and a maintenance of glomerular filtration rate. In some instances, improved renal function has been noted where control values were below normal prior to hydralazine administration. However, as with any antihypertensive agent, hydralazine should be used with caution in patients with advanced renal damage.

In patients with renal impairment, serum levels of hydralazine increased as compared to those in patients with normal renal function, therefore the dose or the dosing interval has to be adapted according to the clinical response, in order to avoid accumulation of the apparent active substance.

In patients with hepatic dysfunction, serum levels of hydralazine increased as compared to those in patients with normal hepatic function, therefore the dose or the dosing interval has to be adapted according to the clinical response, in order to avoid accumulation of the apparent active substance.

Peripheral neuritis, evidenced by paresthesias, numbness and tingling in the extremities has been observed. Published evidence suggests an antipyridoxine effect and the addition of pyridoxine to the regimen if symptoms develop.

Blood dyscrasias consisting of reduction in hemoglobin and red cell count, leukopenia, agranulocytosis and purpura have been reported. Periodic blood counts are advised during therapy. If such abnormalities develop, therapy should be discontinued.

Tumorigenicity and Mutagenicity: Hydralazine in chronic toxicity studies has been shown to increase the incidence of some tumors in aging rodents. A mutagenic potential was observed in some but not all mutagenicity tests. The extent to which these findings indicate a risk to man is uncertain. While long-term clinical observations have not suggested that human cancer is associated with hydralazine use, epidemiologic studies have so far been insufficient to arrive at any conclusion.

Lactation: Hydralazine passes into breast milk. Alternatives to hydralazine should be considered in nursing mothers.

Geriatrics: The elderly may be more sensitive to the hypotensive effects. In addition the risk of hydralazine-induced hypothermia may be increased in elderly patients.

Children: Although there is some experience with the use of hydralazine in children, controlled clinical trials to establish safety and effectiveness in this age group have not been conducted.

Drug Interactions: Concomitant treatment with other vasodilators, calcium antagonists, ACE inhibitors, diuretics, antihypertensives, tricyclic antidepressants and major tranquilizers, as well as the consumption of alcohol, may potentiate the hypotensive effect of hydralazine.

Administration of hydralazine shortly before or after diazoxide may lead to marked hypotension. When potent antihypertensive drugs, such as diazoxide, are used in combination with hydralazine, patients should be continuously observed for several hours for any excessive fall in blood pressure.

Concurrent administration of hydralazine with beta-blockers subject to a strong first-pass effect (e.g., propranolol) may increase their bioavailability. Downward dosage adjustment of these drugs may be required when they are given concomitantly.

MAO inhibitors should be used with caution in patients receiving hydralazine.

Hydralazine may reduce the pressor responses to epinephrine.

Adverse Effects: The most common adverse reactions are tachycardia, palpitation, anginal symptoms, flushing, headache, and gastrointestinal disturbances. These are more frequent at the start of treatment, especially if the dosage is raised rapidly. However, such reactions generally subside in the further course of treatment or following a reduction of dosage.

The most severe reactions are neuropathy, blood dyscrasias and an acute rheumatoid state resulting in a syndrome resembling disseminated lupus erythematosus (see Warnings and Precautions).

Cardiovascular: tachycardia, palpitation, flushing, hypotension, anginal symptoms, edema, heart failure, paradoxical pressor responses.

Central and Peripheral Nervous System: headache, dizziness, peripheral neuritis as evidenced by paresthesia numbness and tingling, polyneuritis, tremor, agitation, anorexia, anxiety, depression, hallucinations, disorientation, sleep disturbances.

Musculoskeletal: arthralgia, joint swelling, myalgia, muscle cramps.

Skin and Appendages: rash.

Urogenital: proteinuria, increased plasma creatinine, hematuria sometimes in association with glomerulonephritis, acute renal failure, urinary retention, difficulty in micturition.

Gastrointestinal: gastrointestinal disturbances, diarrhea, constipation, nausea, vomiting, jaundice, liver enlargement, abnormal liver function sometimes in association with hepatitis, paralytic ileus.

Blood: anemia, leukopenia, neutropenia, thrombocytopenia with or without purpura, hemolytic anemia, leukocytosis, lymphadenopathy, pancytopenia, splenomegaly, agranulocytosis, antinuclear antibodies.

Sense Organs: increased lacrimation, conjunctivitis, nasal congestion, blurred vision.

Hypersensitivity Reactions: SLE-like syndrome (see Warnings), chills, eosinophilia, hypersensitivity reactions such as pruritus, urticaria, vasculitis, hepatitis.

Respiratory: dyspnea, pleural pain.

Miscellaneous: fever, weight decrease, malaise, exophthalmos, decreased libido, pancreatitis. Hyperuricemia, hyperglycemia and hypokalemia have been reported.

Overdose: Symptoms: hypotension, tachycardia, headache, generalized skin flushing, sweating, nausea and dizziness. Myocardial ischemia with angina pectoris, cardiac arrhythmia, and profound shock can develop.

Further signs may include impairment of consciousness, vomiting, tremor, convulsions, oliguria and hypothermia.

Treatment: No known specific antidote.

Evacuate gastric contents by induction of emesis or gastric lavage, taking adequate precautions against aspiration and for protection of the airway. If general conditions permit, administer activated charcoal slurry and possibly an osmotic cathartic. These procedures may have to be omitted or carried out after cardiovascular status has been stabilized, since they might precipitate cardiac arrhythmias or increase the depth of shock.

Support of the cardiovascular system is of primary importance. Shock should be treated with volume expanders without resorting to use of vasopressors. The use of dopamine to elevate systolic blood pressure to 90 mmHg may be considered in an emergency. If a vasopressor is required, a type that is least likely to precipitate or aggravate cardiac arrhythmia should be used, and the ECG should be monitored while they are being administered. Digitalization may be necessary. Renal function must be monitored and supported as required.

No experience has been reported with extracorporeal or peritoneal dialysis.

Dosage: The dose must always be individualized and adjusted according to the patient's blood pressure response.

Oral: Initially, one 10 mg tablet 4 times daily for the first 2 to 4 days. The dose is increased to 25 mg 4 times daily for the remainder of the first week. Dosage is then increased to 50 mg 4 times daily for the second and subsequent weeks of treatment.

For maintenance, adjust dosage to lowest effective levels. The incidence of toxic reactions, particularly the lupus erythematosus syndrome, is highest in the group of patients receiving large doses of hydralazine.

The usual effective maintenance daily dose ranges from 50 to 200 mg. However, the dose should not be increased above 100 mg/day without determining the acetylator phenotype.

After the titration period, some patients may be maintained on a twice daily schedule.

The influence of food on the bioavailability of hydralazine is uncertain. Contradictory results have been obtained.

Note: Geriatric patients may be more sensitive to the effects of the usual adult dose. Response should be monitored and the dosage adjusted accordingly to lowest effective levels.

In patients with renal impairment the dose or the dosing interval should be adapted according to the clinical response, in order to avoid accumulation of the apparent active substance.

In patients with hepatic dysfunction the dose or the dosing interval should be adapted according to the clinical response, in order to avoid accumulation of the apparent active substance.

Parenterally: Patients should be hospitalized. The parenteral administration of hydralazine should always be carried out cautiously and under strict medical supervision.

Blood pressure and heart rate should be checked frequently (every 5 minutes). Blood pressure levels may begin to fall within a few minutes after injection, with an average maximal decrease occurring in 10 to 80 minutes. A satisfactory response can be defined as a decrease in diastolic blood pressure to 90 to 100 mmHg.

The initial dose is 5 to 10 mg, administered by slow i.v. injection in order to avoid precipitous decreases in mean arterial pressure with a critical reduction in cerebral or uteroplacental perfusion. In hypertensive crises other than pre-eclampsia/eclampsia, initial doses of up to 40 mg have been used. If necessary, the dose can be repeated after an interval of 20 to 30 minutes.

Apresoline may also be given by continuous i.v. infusion, beginning with a flow rate of 200 to 300 μg/min. Maintenance flow rates must be determined individually and are usually within the range of 50 to 150 μg/min.

Patients with marked renal damage may require a lower dosage. In cases where there is a previously existing increased intra-cranial pressure, lowering the blood pressure may increase cerebral ischemia.

Most patients can be transferred to oral hydralazine within 24 to 48 hours.

Reconstitution: Ampuls (see Table I).

Table I—Apresoline

Reconstitution for Ampuls

Vial Size	Volume of Diluent to be Added to Ampul	Approximate Available Volume	Concentration on Reconstitution
20 mg	1 mL sterile water for injection	1.0 mL	approximately 19.7 mg/mL

The freshly prepared solution should be used immediately and any remainder discarded.

Direct Injection: Administer the reconstituted solution by slow i.v. injection. For ease of administration the reconstituted solution may be further diluted with physiological saline.

I.V. Infusion: For administration by i.v. infusion, freshly reconstituted hydralazine ampul(s) should be further diluted by the addition of physiological saline, 5% sorbitol solution or Ringer solution. Such admixtures should be used within 24 hours because of the risk of microbial contamination during preparation.

Glucose solution is not suitable for further dilution.

Apresoline (cont'd)

Dilution and Administration: Each mL reconstituted solution contains approximately 19.7 mg hydralazine HCl (see Table II).

Table II—Apresoline

Dilution and Administration

To 500 mL Add	Final Concentration	Flow Rate (mL/hr) 60	65	70	75
		Dosage Delivered (μg/min)			
1 mL	39 μg/mL	39	42	45	49
2 mL	79 μg/mL	79	86	92	99
3 mL	118 μg/mL	118	128	138	148
4 mL	158 μg/mL	158	171	184	198
5 mL	197 μg/mL	197	213	230	246
6 mL	236 μg/mL	236	256	275	295

Supplied: Ampuls: Each mL of sterile lyophilized solution contains: hydralazine HCl 20 mg. Alcohol-, bisulfite-, gluten-, lactose-, sodium-, parabens- and tartrazine-free. Ampuls of 1 mL, cartons of 10. Protect from heat (store below 30°C) and light.

Tablets: 10 mg: Each yellow, uncoated, biconvex, scored tablet, imprinted FA on one side and CIBA on the other, contains: hydralazine HCl 10 mg. Nonmedicinal ingredients: colloidal silicon dioxide, cornstarch, edetate disodium, FD&C Yellow No. 5, magnesium stearate, mannitol and talc. Energy: 0.54 kJ (0.13 kcal). Sodium: <1 mmol (0.14 mg). Alcohol-, bisulfite-, gluten-, lactose- and parabens-free. Bottles of 100. Protect from heat (store below 30°C) and humidity.

25 mg: Each blue, coated tablet, contains: hydralazine HCl 25 mg. Nonmedicinal ingredients: acacia, FD&C Blue No. 1, carnauba wax, cornstarch, gelatin, hydroxypropylmethylcellulose, lactose, magnesium stearate, polyethylene glycol, povidone, sucrose, talc, titanium dioxide and white ink. Energy: 2 kJ (0.48 kcal). Alcohol-, bisulfite-, gluten-, parabens- and tartrazine-free. Bottles of 100. Protect from heat (store below 30°C) and humidity.

50 mg: Each pink, coated tablet, contains: hydralazine HCl 50 mg. Nonmedicinal ingredients: acacia, carnauba wax, cornstarch, FD&C Red No. 3, gelatin, hydroxypropylmethylcellulose, lactose, magnesium stearate, polyethylene glycol, povidone, sucrose, talc, titanium dioxide and white ink. Energy: 1.67 kJ (0.4 kcal). Alcohol-, bisulfite-, gluten-, parabens- and tartrazine-free. Bottles of 100. Protect from heat (store below 30°C) and humidity.

(Shown in Product Recognition Section)

AQUACORT® Ⓟ

Spectropharm Dermatology

Hydrocortisone

Topical Corticosteroid

Pharmacology: Topical corticosteroids are synthetic derivatives of cortisone which are effective when applied locally to control many types of inflammatory, allergic and pruritic dermatoses.

They are thought to act by controlling the rate of synthesis of proteins. The primary action of the corticosteroid is to interfere with the synthesis of arachidonic acid by inhibiting the phospholipase A_2 synthesis. The overall effect of corticosteroids is a catabolic one.

Corticosteroid responsive dermatoses may be divided into those which are very responsive and those which require higher concentrations of corticosteroids, occlusion of the drug under a plastic film or intralesional administration. Attention must be paid to the concentration of topical corticosteroid used.

Although effectiveness is enhanced by the application of the corticosteroid preparation under a transparent plastic wrapping, systemic absorption is also enhanced, occasionally sufficiently to suppress the pituitary-adrenal axis.

Indications: For inflammatory manifestations of corticosteroid responsive dermatoses, where an anti-inflammatory, anti-allergenic and antipruritic activity in topical management is required.

Contraindications: Untreated tubercular, bacterial and fungal infections involving the skin and in certain viral diseases such as herpes simplex, chickenpox and vaccinia. Hypersensitivity to any of the components of the preparation. Not for ophthalmic use.

Warnings: *Pregnancy* and *Lactation:* The safety of topical corticosteroids during pregnancy and lactation has not been established. The potential benefit should be weighed in these conditions against possible hazard to the fetus or the nursing infant.

Adrenal suppression and other systemic effects may occur after application to extensive areas and prolonged usage.

Should not be used under occlusive dressings.

Precautions: Topical corticosteroids should be used with caution on lesions close to the eye.

Although hypersensitivity reactions have been rare with topically applied steroid products, the drug should be discontinued and appropriate therapy initiated if there are signs of reaction.

Prolonged use of topical corticosteroid products may produce atrophy of the skin and subcutaneous tissues, particularly on flexor surfaces and on the face. If this is noted, discontinue the use of these products. In cases of bacterial infections of the skin, appropriate antibacterial agents should be used as primary therapy. If necessary, the topical corticosteroid may be used as an adjunct to control inflammation, erythema and itching.

These products should be used with caution in patients with stasis dermatitis and other skin diseases associated with impaired circulation. If a symptomatic response is not noted within a few days to a week, the local applications of corticosteroid should be discontinued and the patient re-evaluated.

During the use of topical corticosteroids secondary infections may occur.

Significant systemic absorption may occur when corticosteroids are applied over large areas of the body. To minimize this possibility, when long-term therapy is anticipated, interrupt treatment periodically or treat one area of the body at a time.

Advise patients to inform subsequent physicians of the prior use of corticosteroids.

Not for ophthalmic use.

Adverse Effects: The following adverse skin reactions have been reported with the use of topical corticosteroids; dryness, itching, burning, local irritation, striae, skin atrophy, atrophy of subcutaneous tissues, telangiectasia, hypertrichosis, change in pigmentation and secondary infection.

Adrenal suppression has also been reported following topical corticosteroid therapy.

Posterior subcapsular cataracts have been reported following use of corticosteroids.

These side effects have been very rarely observed, even under occlusive conditions, with low potency topical glucocorticosteroid preparations such as hydrocortisone.

Dosage: Apply sparingly to affected areas 2 to 3 times daily. When favorable response is obtained, reduce frequency of application and eventually discontinue altogether.

Supplied: Each mL of white, odorless, washable lotion contains: hydrocortisone 2.5%. Nonmedicinal ingredients: amphisol, carbopol, cetyl alcohol, coconut oil, EDTA, glyceryl stearate, Germall, isopropyl myristate, panthenol, propylene glycol and water. Plastic bottles of 60 mL. Protect from excessive heat. Store at room temperature. Avoid freezing.

AQUAPHOR®

Smith & Nephew

Petrolatum

Dermatological Base

Indications: A neutral, anhydrous base for compounding smooth, stable emulsions; highly miscible with both aqueous solutions and other oil-based substances. For severely dry skin. Also helps promote healing of minor skin irritations.

Precautions: For external use only. Avoid contact with eyes. If this occurs, rinse thoroughly with water. If rash or irritation occurs or worsens, discontinue use and consult a physician. Do not place on open wounds.

Supplied: Each g of odorless ointment contains: petrolatum 41% w/w. Fragrance- and preservative-free. Jars of 396 g.

AQUASITE™

CIBA Vision

Polyethylene Glycol 400—Dextran 70

Eye Lubricant

Supplied: Each mL contains: 0.2% w/w polyethylene glycol 400 and 0.1% w/w dextran 70 in DuraSite (polycarbophil, purified water, sodium chloride, edetate disodium and sodium hydroxide to adjust pH). Preservative-free. Single-use containers of 0.6 mL, boxes of 24. Store at room temperature.

AQUASOL® E

Novartis Consumer Health

Vitamin E

Vitamin

Pharmacology: Vitamin E is a fat soluble vitamin which is present in many foods and exists in a variety of forms. It is considered an essential element of human nutrition, with many of its actions related to its antioxidant properties.

Indications: A nutritional supplement for the treatment of vitamin E deficiency.

Vitamin E deficiency states are rare, but have been noted in premature and some full-term infants and in patients with impaired fat absorption.

Precautions: Vitamin E may increase the hypoprothrombinemic response to oral anticoagulants, and can intensify an existing coagulation defect produced by vitamin K deficiency that is the result of either malabsorption or anticoagulant therapy. Doses in excess of recommended daily nutrient intakes should be avoided in patients on oral anticoagulants. Vitamin K status should be monitored in cases of malabsorption.

Adverse Effects: Diarrhea and intestinal cramps have been reported with daily doses of 3 200 IU of vitamin E.

Dosage: Standard oral doses are variable and empirical.

Supplied: Capsules: Each clear, oblong shaped, yellowish green, soft gel capsule contains: water-solubilized natural vitamin E (as d-alpha tocopheryl acetate) 100 IU. Nonmedicinal ingredients: D&C Yellow #10, FD&C Blue #1, FD&C Yellow #6, gelatin, glycerin, methylparaben, polysorbate, propylparaben and water. Tartrazine-free. Bottles of 100.

Drops: Water solubilized vitamin E (as dl-alpha tocopheryl acetate) 50 IU/mL. Caramel odor, clear yellow color. Nonmedicinal ingredients: anise oil, flavor, polysorbate, propylene glycol and water. Tartrazine-free. Dropper bottles of 25 mL.

AQUASOL® E TPGS

Novartis Consumer Health

Water Soluble Vitamin E

Nutritional Supplement

Pharmacology: Vitamin E is a fat soluble vitamin which is present in many foods, and exists in a variety of forms, the most active of which is d-alpha tocopherol (natural source vitamin E). It is considered an essential element of human nutrition, with many of its actions related to its antioxidant properties.

Absorption of standard fat soluble forms of vitamin E from the gastrointestinal tract is dependent upon the presence of bile. D-alpha tocopheryl polyethylene glycol 1 000 succinate is a water soluble form of vitamin E which forms micelles at low concentrations and is absorbed without the need for bile salt activity.

Indications: A nutritional supplement for the treatment of vitamin E deficiency.

Precautions: Due to polyethylene glycol content, individuals with impaired renal function, should consult a physician before taking this vitamin supplement.

Vitamin E may increase the hypoprothrombinemic response to oral anticoagulants, and can intensify an existing coagulation defect produced by vitamin K deficiency that is the result of either malabsorption or anticoagulant therapy. Doses in excess of recommended daily nutrient intakes, should be avoided in patients on oral anticoagulants. Vitamin K status should be monitored in cases of malabsorption.

Dosage: 5 mL daily, or as directed by a physician. Lower doses may be dispensed at 77 IU/mL.

Supplied: Each mL of clear tasteless liquid contains: natural source vitamin E 77 IU as d-alpha tocopheryl polyethylene glycol 1 000 succinate. Nonmedicinal ingredients: citric acid, methyl parahydroxybenzoate, propyl parahydroxybenzoate, potassium sorbate, sodium citrate and water. Alcohol-, gluten-, sulfite- and tartrazine-free. Bottles of 150 mL. Keep out of reach of children. Replace cap after use, and store at room temperature.

AQUATAIN®
Whitehall-Robins

Emollient

Indications: Emollient for dry, chapped, rough skin.

Dosage: Apply as needed several times daily or as prescribed.

Supplied: Cream: Each tube of unscented, hypoallergenic cream contains: benzyl alcohol, polawax, isopropyl palmitate, glycerin, sorbitol, lactic acid and water. Tartrazine-free. Tubes of 75 g.

Lotion: Each bottle of unscented, hypoallergenic lotion contains: benzyl alcohol, polawax, isopropyl palmitate, glycerin, sorbitol, lactic acid and water. Tartrazine-free. Bottles of 200 and 350 mL.

ARALEN® Ⓟ
Sanofi

Chloroquine Phosphate

Antimalarial—Antiparasitic

Pharmacology: Chloroquine has been found to be highly active against the erythrocytic forms of Plasmodium vivax, ovale and malariae and many strains of Plasmodium falciparum (but not the gametocytes of Plasmodium falciparum). The precise mechanism of plasmodicidal action of the drug is not known. While the drug can inhibit certain enzymes, its effect is believed to result, in part, from its interaction with DNA.

Chloroquine does not prevent vivax malariae infection when administered prophylactically. It acts on the erythrocytic forms of the parasite, inhibiting parasite development in the red blood cell thus preventing or suppressing clinical symptoms. Chloroquine does not prevent relapses in patients with vivax or malariae malaria because it is not effective against exo-erythrocytic forms of the parasite. It is highly effective as a suppressive agent in patients with vivax or malariae malaria, in terminating acute attacks, and significantly lengthening the interval between treatment and relapse. In patients with a susceptible strain of falciparum malaria, it abolishes the acute attack and effects complete cure of the infection.

In vitro studies with trophozoites of Entamoeba histolytica have demonstrated that chloroquine also possesses amebicidal activity comparable to that of emetine.

Chloroquine is rapidly and almost completely absorbed from the gastrointestinal tract. Approximately 55% of the drug in the plasma is bound to nondiffusible plasma constituents. Chloroquine is deposited in tissues in considerable amounts. In animals, from 200 to 700 times the plasma concentration may be found in the liver, spleen, kidney and lung; leukocytes also concentrate the drug. The brain and spinal cord, in contrast, contain only 10 to 30 times the amount present in plasma.

Chloroquine undergoes appreciable degradation in the body. The main metabolite is desethylchloroquine. Bisdesethylchloroquine, a carboxylic acid derivative, and other uncharacterized metabolites are found in small amounts. Slightly more than half of the urinary drug products can be accounted for as unchanged chloroquine and about one fourth is desethylchloroquine. Excretion is quite slow, but can be increased by acidification of urine.

Indications: The suppressive treatment and for acute attacks of malaria due to P. vivax, P. malariae, P. ovale, and susceptible strains of P. falciparum. The drug is also indicated for treatment of extraintestinal amebiasis.

(Although chloroquine has been used in the treatment of rheumatoid arthritis and discoid lupus erythematosus, it is considered that the potential toxicity of the drug outweighs any anticipated benefits.)

Contraindications: The presence of retinal or visual field changes either attributable to 4-aminoquinoline compounds or to any other etiology, and in patients with known hypersensitivity to 4-aminoquinoline compounds. However, in the treatment of acute attacks of malaria caused by susceptible strains of plasmodia, the physician may elect to use this drug after carefully weighing the possible benefits and risks to the patient.

Precautions: In recent years it has been found that certain strains of P. falciparum have become resistant to 4-aminoquinoline compounds (including chloroquine and hydroxychloroquine) as shown by the fact that normally adequate doses have failed to prevent or cure clinical malaria or parasitemia. Treatment with quinine or other specific forms of therapy is therefore advised for patients infected with a resistant strain of parasites.

Irreversible retinal damage has been observed in some patients who had received long-term or high-dosage 4-aminoquinoline therapy. Retinopathy has been reported to be dose-related.

When prolonged therapy with any antimalarial compound is contemplated, initial (base line) and periodic ophthalmologic examinations (including visual acuity, expert slit lamp, funduscopic, and visual field tests) should be performed.

If there is any defect in the visual acuity, visual field, or retinal macular areas (such as pigmentary changes, loss of foveal reflex), or any visual symptoms (such as light flashes and streaks) which are not fully explainable by difficulties of accommodation or corneal opacities the drug should be discontinued immediately and the patient closely observed for possible progression. Retinal changes (and visual disturbances) may progress even after cessation of therapy.

All patients on long-term therapy with this preparation should be questioned and examined periodically, including testing skeletal muscle function and tendon reflexes, (knee and ankle reflexes), to detect any evidence of muscular weakness. If weakness occurs, discontinue the drug.

A number of fatalities have been reported following the accidental ingestion of chloroquine. One case involved the ingestion of a relatively small dose (1 g of chloroquine in a 3 year old child). Patients should be strongly warned to keep this drug out of the reach of children because they are especially sensitive to the 4-aminoquinoline compounds.

Use of chloroquine in patients with psoriasis may precipitate a severe attack of psoriasis. When used in patients with porphyria, the condition may be exacerbated. The drug should not be used in these conditions unless in the judgment of the physician the benefit to the patient outweighs the possible hazard.

In patients with pre-exisiting auditory damage, chloroquine should be administered with caution. In case of any defect in hearing, chloroquine should be immediately discontinued, and the patient closely observed.

Patients with a history of epilepsy should be advised about the risk of chloroquine provoking seizures.

Pregnancy. Usage of this drug during pregnancy should be avoided except in the suppression or treatment of malaria when in the judgment of the physician the benefit outweighs the possible hazard. It should be noted that radioactively tagged chloroquine administered i.v. to pregnant pigmented CBA mice passed rapidly across the placenta, accumulated selectively in the melanin structures of the fetal eyes and was retained in the ocular tissues for 5 months after the drug had been eliminated from the rest of the body.

Lactation: Chloroquine crosses the placenta and is excreted in human breast milk. Because of the potential of chloroquine to produce serious adverse reactions in nursing infants, a decision should be made whether to discontinue breast-feeding or to discontinue the drug, taking into account the importance of the therapy to the mother.

Since the drug is known to concentrate in the liver, it should be used with caution in patients with hepatic disease or alcoholism or in conjunction with known hepatotoxic drugs.

Complete blood cell counts should be made periodically if patients are given prolonged therapy. If any severe blood disorder appears which is not attributable to the disease under treatment, discontinuance of the drug should be considered. The drug should be administered with caution to patients having G-6-PD (glucose-6-phosphate dehydrogenase) deficiency.

Drug Interactions: Antacids and kaolin can reduce the absorption of chloroquine. An interval of at least 4 hours between intake of these agents and chloroqine should be observed.

Cimetidine can inhibit the metabolism of chloroquine, increasing its plasma level.

Chloroquine significantly reduces the bioavailability of ampicillin. An interval of at least 2 hours between ingestion of ampicillin and chloroquine should be observed.

Cyclosporine serum level has been reported to suddenly increase following the ingestion of chloroquine. Close monitoring of serum cyclosporine level is recommended following ingestion of chloroquine. Chloroquine should be discontinued if necessary.

Caution should be observed in prescribing chloroquine concomitantly with any known hepatotoxic agent (see Precautions).

Adverse Effects: Chloroquine is generally well tolerated when given in antimalarial doses. Adverse effects are rare.

Ocular: With long-term therapy, particularly if high doses are used, retinopathy may occur. This is generally irreversible and sometimes progressive. Rarely, it may be delayed.

Retinal changes include narrowing of the arterioles, macular lesions such as areas of edema, atrophy and abnormal pigmentation with loss of foveal reflex, pallor of the optic disk, optic atrophy and patchy retinal pigmentation.

Initially patients with retinal changes may be asymptomatic, or they may complain of nyctalopia and scotomatous vision with paracentral, pericentral ring types and typically temporal scotomas.

Rarely, scotomatous vision may occur without observable retinal changes.

Reversible corneal changes may develop, including transient edema or opaque deposits in the epithelium. These changes may be asymptomatic or cause visual haloes, focusing difficulties or blurred vision.

Transient and reversible blurring of vision or difficulty of focusing or accommodation may also occur.

Cardiovascular: Rarely, electrocardiographic changes, particularly inversion or depression of the T-wave with widening of the QRS complex, have been noted.

Hypotension has also been noted in case of high doses.

There have been rare reports of cardiomyopathy.

Neuromuscular: Skeletal muscle myopathy leading to progressive weakness and atrophy of proximal muscle groups has been noted. Myopathy is reversible after discontinuation of chloroquine, but recovery may take many months.

Associated mild sensory changes, depression of tendon reflexes and abnormal nerve conduction studies suggesting an associated peripheral neuropathy have also been observed.

There have been rare reports of myasthenia gravis-like signs and symptoms.

Auditory: Side effects such as tinnitus, vertigo and hearing loss have been noted. Severe and permanent hearing losses which normally occur following high-dose prolonged therapy have also been reported following the administration of small doses of the drug.

Chloroquine-induced hearing loss may progress or even develop after discontinuation.

CNS: Mild and transient headache has been reported. The occurrence of headache is usually reversible upon withdrawal of chloroquine.

Mental changes including psychic stimulation, psychosis, anxiety and personality changes although uncommon have been observed.

Convulsions have also been reported.

Hematological: Blood dyscrasias are rare and include aplastic anemia, reversible agranulocytosis, thrombocytopenia and neutropenia.

Chloroquine may exacerbate porphyria.

Patients with G-6-PD deficiency may present with severe hemolysis in case of treatment with chloroquine.

Dermatologic: Pruritus and rashes are usually reversible upon withdrawal of chloroquine.

Other uncommon adverse effects from prolonged use include: skin and mucosal pigment changes (bluish-black), photosensitivity, lichen planus-like eruptions, exfoliative dermatitis, hair loss and bleaching of hair pigment.

Chloroquine may precipitate attacks of psoriasis.

Gastrointestinal: Gastrointestinal disturbances which are usually reversible upon withdrawal of chloroquine therapy include: anorexia, nausea, vomiting, diarrhea and abdominal cramps.

Overdose: Symptoms and Treatment: As chloroquine is rapidly and completely absorbed after ingestion, and in accidental overdosage, or rarely with lower doses in hypersensitive patients, toxic doses may be fatal. As little as 1 g may be fatal in children. Toxic symptoms may occur within minutes. These consist of headache, drowsiness, visual disturbances, nausea, vomiting, cardiovascular collapse, and convulsions followed by sudden and early respiratory and cardiac arrest. The ECG may reveal atrial standstill, nodal rhythm, prolonged intraventricular conduction time, and progressive bradycardia leading to ventricular fibrillation and/or arrest. Treatment with early gastric lavage is indicated if ingestion has occurred recently. In order to avoid sudden cardiac arrest and lung aspiration lavage should be preceded by appropriate symptomatic treatment and intubation with artificial respiration.

Symptomatic and prompt measures which may be taken include immediate evacuation of the stomach by emesis (at home, before transportation to the hospital) and/or gastric lavage until the stomach is completely emptied. Finely-powdered, activated charcoal, if introduced by the stomach tube after lavage within 30 minutes after ingestion of the antimalarial, may inhibit further intestinal absorption of the drug. To be effective, the dose of activated charcoal should be at least 5 times the estimated dose of chloroquine ingested.

Convulsions, if present, should be controlled before attempting gastric lavage. If due to cerebral stimulation, cautious administration of an ultra short-acting barbiturate may

Aralen (cont'd)

be tried but, if due to anoxia it should be corrected by oxygen administration and artificial respiration. In shock with hypotension, vasopressor therapy such as phenylephrine and other means of circulatory support may also be indicated.

Diazepam also may be used to treat convulsions. It may decrease the cardiotoxicity of chloroquine. Because of the importance of supporting respiration, tracheal intubation or tracheostomy, followed by gastric lavage, may also be necessary.

A patient who survives the acute phase and is asymptomatic should be closely observed for at least 6 hours. Fluids may be forced, and ammonium chloride (8 g daily in divided doses for adults) may be administered for a few days to acidify the urine to help promote urinary excretion in cases of both overdosage or sensitivity.

Dosage: The dosage of chloroquine phosphate is often expressed or calculated as the base. Each 250 mg tablet of Aralen is equivalent to 150 mg base. In infants and children the dosage is preferably calculated by body weight.

Malaria: Suppression: In adults, 500 mg (300 mg base) on exactly the same day of each week. In infants and children the weekly suppressive dosage is 5 mg/kg (calculated as base), but should not exceed the adult dose regardless of weight.

If circumstances permit, suppressive therapy should begin 2 weeks prior to exposure. However, failing this in adults, an initial double (loading) dose of 1 g (600 mg base) may be taken; or in children 10 mg base/kg may be given in 2 divided doses, 6 hours apart. The suppressive therapy should be continued for 8 weeks after leaving the endemic area.

Treatment of the acute attack: In adults, an initial dose of 1 g (600 mg base) followed by an additional 500 mg (300 mg base) after 6 to 8 hours and then a single dose of 500 mg (300 mg base) on each of 2 consecutive days. This represents a total dose of 2.5 g chloroquine phosphate or 1.5 g base in 3 days.

The dosage for adults may also be calculated on the basis of body weight; this method is preferred for infants and children. In children, a total dose representing 25 mg/kg (calculated as base) is administered in 3 days, as follows:

First dose: 10 mg base/kg (but not exceeding a single dose of 600 mg base).

Second dose: 5 mg base/kg (but not exceeding a single dose of 300 mg base) 6 hours after 1st dose.

Third dose: 5 mg base/kg 18 hours after 2nd dose.

Fourth dose: 5 mg base/kg 24 hours after 3rd dose.

For radical cure of vivax and malariae concomitant therapy with an 8-aminoquinoline compound is necessary.

Extraintestinal amebiasis: Adults, 1 g (600 mg base) daily for 2 days, followed by 500 mg (300 mg base) daily for at least 2 to 3 weeks. Treatment is usually combined with an effective intestinal amebicide.

Supplied: Each white, round tablet, W on one side, scored on other, contains: chloroquine phosphate USP 250 mg (equivalent to 150 mg chloroquine base). Nonmedicinal ingredients: calcium phosphate (dibasic, dihydrate), cornstarch, magnesium stearate and talc. Energy: 0.4 kJ (0.10 kcal). Gluten-, lactose-, sucrose- and tartrazine-free. Bottles of 100.

(Shown in Product Recognition Section)

Reviewed 1999

AREDIA® ℞

Novartis Pharmaceuticals

Pamidronate Disodium

Bone Metabolism Regulator

Pharmacology: Pamidronate belongs to a class of bisphosphonates (previously termed diphosphonate), which inhibit bone resorption. The therapeutic activity of pamidronate is attributable to its potent anti-osteoclastic activity on bone. In animal studies, at therapeutic doses, pamidronate inhibits bone resorption apparently without inhibiting bone formation and mineralization.

The predominant means by which pamidronate reduces bone turnover both in vitro and in vivo appears to be through the local, direct antiresorptive effect of bone-bound bisphosphonate. Pamidronate binds to calcium phosphate (hydroxyapatite) crystals and directly inhibits the formation and dissolution of this bone mineral component in vitro. In vitro studies indicate that pamidronate is a potent inhibitor of osteoclastic bone resorption. Pamidronate also suppresses the migration of osteoclast precursors onto the bone and their subsequent transformation into the mature resorbing osteoclast.

Tumor-induced Hypercalcemia: In tumor-induced hypercalcemia, pamidronate normalizes plasma calcium between 3 and 7 days following the initiation of treatment irrespective of the type of malignancy or presence of detectable metastases. This effect is dependent on initial calcium levels.

Pamidronate improves symptoms associated with hypercalcemia, e.g., anorexia, nausea, vomiting and diminished mental status.

The kidneys play a prominent role in calcium homeostasis. In addition to skeletal osteolysis, renal dysfunction contributes to the pathogenesis of tumor-induced hypercalcemia. When diagnosed, most hypercalcemic patients are significantly dehydrated. Elevated plasma calcium antagonizes antidiuretic hormone-induced renal concentration, and thus results in polyuria and excessive fluid loss. Hydration status is further compromised by reduced fluid intake due to nausea, vomiting and diminished mental status. Furthermore, dehydration often leads to a fall in glomerular filtration rate (GFR).

Before pamidronate therapy is initiated, patients should be adequately rehydrated with isotonic saline (0.9%) (see Precautions). Normalization of plasma calcium levels by pamidronate in adequately hydrated patients may also normalize plasma parathyroid hormone (PTH) which is suppressed by hypercalcemia.

The duration of normocalcemia following pamidronate treatment varies in patients with tumor-induced hypercalcemia because of early mortality, and the heterogeneity of diseases and cancer therapies. In general, recurrences tend to occur preferentially after treatment with lower doses: at doses of 30 mg or less, plasma calcium levels tend to increase after approximately 1 week, while at high doses (total treatment doses of 45 to 90 mg) plasma calcium levels remained normal for at least 2 weeks and up to several months. One study has shown a clear relationship between recurrence rates and pamidronate dose: in patients treated with single i.v. infusions of 30, 45, 60 and 90 mg pamidronate, recurrence rates were lower for the higher dose group 9 months after initial treatment. The duration of response tends to be more prolonged in patients in whom the underlying disease is well controlled by cancer therapy.

Clinical experience with pamidronate in relapsed tumor-induced hypercalcemia is limited. In general, with retreatment, the response is similar to that with the first pamidronate treatment, unless the cancer has progressed significantly. Therefore, pamidronate treatment appears effective for recurrent hypercalcemia at doses established for the initial treatment course (see Dosage). The mechanisms underlying possible decreased effects of repeat treatment with pamidronate in advanced cancer are unknown.

In severe forms of hypercalcemia the dose of pamidronate may be increased, or eventually, a combination drug therapy should be considered (see Warnings).

Bone Metastases and Multiple Myeloma: Lytic bone metastases in cancer patients are caused by increased osteoclast activity. Metastatic tumor cells secrete paracrine factors which stimulate neighboring osteoclasts to resorb bone. By inhibiting osteoclast function, bisphosphonates interrupt the cascade of events which lead to tumor-induced osteolysis. Lytic bone destruction causes significant complications and associated morbidity.

Clinical trials in patients with predominantly lytic bone metastases or multiple myeloma showed that pamidronate prevented or delayed skeletal-related events, (SREs: hypercalcemia, pathologic fractures, radiation therapy to bone, orthopedic surgery, spinal cord compression) and decreased bone pain. When used in combination with standard anticancer treatment, pamidronate led to a delay in progression of bone metastases. In addition, osteolytic bone metastases which have proved refractory to cytotoxic and hormonal therapy may show radiological evidence of disease stabilization or sclerosis.

A significant reduction in bone pain was also demonstrated, which in some patients led to decreased analgesic intake and increased mobility. Greater deteriorations in ECOG performance status and Spitzer quality of life scores were seen in the placebo patients compared to pamidronate-treated patients.

Paget's Disease: Paget's Disease of bone, which is characterized by local areas of increased bone resorption and formation with qualitative changes in remodeling, responds well to treatment with pamidronate. Repeated infusions of pamidronate do not lead to reduced efficacy. In addition, patients resistant to etidronate and calcitonin respond well to pamidronate infusions. In long-term follow-up to clinical trials, bone fracture rate does not appear to be increased following treatment with pamidronate relative to the normally occurring rate in patients with Paget's disease.

Clinical and biochemical remission of Paget's disease has been demonstrated by bone scintigraphy, by decreases in urinary hydroxyproline and serum alkaline phosphatase, and by symptomatic improvement. Bone scans show that pamidronate reduces the number of bones and the percentage of the skeleton affected and that bone scintigraphy significantly improves. Bone biopsies consistently show histological and histomorphometric improvement indicating the reversal of the disease process. Symptoms improve even in those with severe disease.

Pharmacokinetics: Plasma concentrations of pamidronate rise rapidly after infusion is started and fall rapidly when the infusion is stopped. The apparent plasma half-life is about 0.8 hours. Apparent steady state is therefore achieved with infusions of >2 to 3 hours' duration. When infused i.v. at 60 mg/hour, the peak plasma concentration is about 10 nmol/mL and the apparent total plasma clearance is about 180 mL/min.

As pamidronate has a strong affinity for calcified tissues, total elimination is not observed within the time frame of experimental studies.

After an i.v. infusion, about 20 to 55% of the dose is recovered in the urine within 72 hours as unchanged pamidronate, the majority being excreted within the first 24 hours. Pamidronate does not appear to be metabolized, and the remaining fraction of the dose is retained in the body (within the time frame of the studies). The percentage of the dose retained is independent of both the dose (range 15 to 180 mg) and the infusion rate (range 1.25 to 60 mg/hour).

Retention is similar after each dose of pamidronate. Thus, accumulation in bone is not capacity limited and is dependent solely on the cumulative dose.

Urinary elimination is biphasic ($t_{1/2\alpha}$=1.6 hours; $t_{1/2\beta}$=27.2 hours). The apparent renal clearance is about 54 mL/min and there is a tendency for renal clearance to correlate with creatinine clearance.

Pamidronate binding to human serum proteins is relatively low (about 54%) but increases to approximately 5 mmol when exogenous 95% calcium is added to human plasma.

Hepatic Impairment: Impaired liver function is not expected to influence pamidronate pharmacokinetics as hepatic and metabolic clearance of pamidronate are insignificant. Pamidronate thus displays little potential for drug interactions at either the metabolic or protein binding level.

Renal Impairment: The mean plasma AUC is approximately doubled in cancer patients (n=19) with severe renal impairment (creatinine clearance <30 mL/min). Urinary excretion rate decreases with decreasing creatinine clearance, although the total amount excreted in the urine is not greatly influenced by renal function. Body retention of pamidronate is therefore similar in patients with and without impaired renal function. Adverse experiences were not found to be related to changes in renal clearance of pamidronate. Dose adjustment does not appear to be necessary in these patients when using the recommended dose schedule (see Dosage).

Indications: Tumor-induced hypercalcemia following adequate saline rehydration. Prior to treatment with pamidronate, renal excretion of excess calcium should be promoted by restoring and maintaining adequate fluid balance and urine output.

Conditions associated with increased osteoclast activity: predominantly lytic bone metastases and multiple myeloma.

Symptomatic Paget's disease of bone.

Contraindications: Known or suspected hypersensitivity to pamidronate, to any of its components (see Supplied), or to other bisphosphonates.

Warnings: Pamidronate must never be given as a bolus injection since severe local reactions and thrombophlebitis may result from high local concentrations.

Pamidronate should always be diluted and administered as a slow i.v. infusion (see Dosage). Regardless of the volume of solution in which pamidronate is diluted, slow i.v. infusion is absolutely necessary for safety.

Pamidronate should not be given together with other bisphosphonates to treat hypercalcemia since the combined effects of these agents are unknown.

Pamidronate should not be mixed with calcium-containing i.v. infusions.

Precautions: It is essential in the initial treatment of tumor-induced hypercalcemia that i.v. rehydration be instituted to restore urine output. Patients should be hydrated adequately throughout treatment but overhydration must be avoided.

In patients with cardiac disease, especially in the elderly, additional saline overload may precipitate cardiac failure (left ventricular failure or congestive heart failure). Fever (influenza-like symptoms) may also contribute to this deterioration.

Although pamidronate is excreted unchanged by the kidney (see Pharmacology), the drug has been used without apparent increase in adverse effects in patients with significantly elevated plasma creatinine levels (including patients undergoing renal replacement therapy with both hemodialysis and peritoneal dialysis). However, experience with pamidronate in patients with severe renal impairment (serum creatinine >440 μmol/L, or 5 mg/dL in TIH patients; >180 μmol/L, or 2 mg/dL in multiple myeloma patients) is limited. If clinical judgment determines that the potential benefits outweigh the risk in such cases, pamidronate should be used cautiously and renal function carefully monitored.

Patients with Paget's disease of the bone, who are at risk of calcium or vitamin D deficiency, should be given oral calcium supplements and vitamin D to minimize the risk of hypocalcemia.

Patient Monitoring: Patients should have standard laboratory (serum creatinine and BUN) and clinical renal function parameters periodically evaluated, especially those receiving frequent pamidronate infusions over a prolonged period of time, and those with pre-existing renal disease or a predisposition to renal impairment (e.g., patients with multiple myeloma and/or tumor-induced hypercalcemia). Fluid balance (urine output, daily weights) should also be followed carefully. If there is deterioration of renal function during pamidronate therapy, the infusion must be stopped.

Serum electrolytes, calcium and phosphate should be monitored following initiation of therapy with pamidronate. Patients with anemia, leukopenia or thrombocytopenia should have regular hematology assessments. Occasional cases of mild, transient hypocalcemia, usually asymptomatic, have been reported. Symptomatic hypocalcemia occurs rarely and can be reversed with calcium gluconate. Patients who have undergone thyroid surgery may be particularly susceptible to develop hypocalcemia due to relative hypoparathyroidism.

In tumor-induced hypercalcemia, either ionized calcium or total serum calcium corrected (adjusted) for albumin should be monitored during treatment with pamidronate. Serum calcium levels in patients who have hypercalcemia of malignancy may not reflect the severity of hypercalcemia, since hypoalbuminemia is commonly present. Corrected serum calcium values should be calculated using established algorithms, such as:

$cCa = tCa + (0.02 \times [40 - ALB])$

where:

cCa = adjusted calcium concentration (mmol/L)

tCa = measured total calcium concentration (mmol/L)

ALB = measured albumin concentration (g/L)

Drug Interactions: Pamidronate has been used concomitantly with the following medications without evidence of significant adverse interactions (see Pharmacology): aminoglutethimide, cisplatin, corticosteroids, cyclophosphamide, cytarabine, doxorubicin, etoposide, fluouracil, loop diuretics, megestrol, melphalan, methotrexate, mitoxantrone, paclitaxel, tamoxifen, vinblastine, vincristine, and, in patients with severe hypercalcemia, calcitonin or mithramycin.

Pregnancy: There is no clinical evidence to support the use of pamidronate in pregnant women. Therefore, pamidronate should not be administered during pregnancy except for life-threatening hypercalcemia.

In animal experiments, pamidronate was not teratogenic and did not affect general reproductive performance or fertility. In rats, prolonged parturition and reduced pup survival were probably caused by a decrease in maternal serum calcium levels. The fertility of the pups was also reduced. Pamidronate crosses the placental barrier and accumulates in fetal bone.

Lactation: There is no clinical experience with pamidronate in lactating women and it is not known whether pamidronate passes into breast milk. A study in lactating rats has shown that pamidronate passes into the milk. Mothers treated with pamidronate should therefore not breast-feed their infants.

Children: The safety and efficacy of pamidronate in children have not been established. Until further experience is gained, pamidronate is only recommended for use in adult patients.

Occupational Hazards: In rare cases, somnolence and/or dizziness may occur, in which case the patient should not drive, operate potentially dangerous machinery or engage in other activities that may be hazardous.

Adverse Effects: Adverse reactions with pamidronate are usually mild and transient. The most common adverse reactions are influenza-like symptoms and mild fever (an increase in body temperature of >1°C, which may last up to 48 hours). Fever usually resolves spontaneously and does not require treatment. Acute "influenza-like" reactions usually occur only with the first pamidronate infusion. Tables I and II below shows the incidence of the more commonly observed adverse effects overall and by indication.

Adverse experiences by body system (Frequency estimate: Frequent: >10%; Occasional: >1% to ≤10%; Rare: >0.001% to ≤1%; Isolated cases: <0.001%).

Body as a Whole: Frequent: fever and influenza-like symptoms sometimes accompanied by malaise, rigor, fatigue and flushes.

Isolated cases: allergic reaction (swollen and itchy eyes, runny nose and scratchy throat).

Local Reactions: Occasional: reactions at the infusion site: pain, redness, swelling, induration, phlebitis, thrombophlebitis.

Musculoskeletal: Occasional: transient bone pain, arthralgia, myalgia, generalized pain, skeletal pain. Rare: muscle cramps.

Gastrointestinal: Occasional: nausea, vomiting. Rare: anorexia, abdominal pain, diarrhea, constipation, dyspepsia. Isolated cases: gastritis.

CNS: Occasional: headache. Rare: symptomatic hypocalcemia (paresthesia, tetany), agitation, confusion, dizziness, insomnia, somnolence, lethargy. Isolated cases: seizures, visual hallucinations in one case.

Blood: Occasional: lymphocytopenia. Rare: anemia, leukopenia. Isolated cases: thrombocytopenia. One case of acute lymphoblastic leukemia has been reported in a patient with Paget's disease. The causal relationship to the treatment or the underlying disease is unknown.

Cardiovascular: Rare: hypotension, hypertension. Isolated cases: left ventricular failure (dyspnea, pulmonary edema), congestive heart failure (edema) due to fluid overload.

Respiratory: Isolated cases: adult respiratory distress syndrome, interstitial pneumonitis.

Renal: Isolated cases: hematuria, acute renal failure, deterioration of pre-existing renal disease.

Skin: Rare: rash, pruritus.

Special Senses: Isolated cases: conjunctivitis, uveitis (iritis, iridocyclitis), scleritis, episcleritis, xanthopsia.

Others: Isolated cases: reactivation of herpes simplex and herpes zoster.

Biochemical Changes: Frequent: hypocalcemia, hypophosphatasemia. Occasional: hypomagnesemia. Rare: hyperkalemia, hypokalemia, hypernatremia, symptomatic hypocalcemia. Isolated cases: abnormal liver function test results, increase in serum creatinine and urea.

Many of these adverse events may have been related to the underlying disease.

Other adverse reactions reported rarely in postmarketing use include: allergic reaction, anaphylactic shock (very rare), anaphylactic reactions, bronchospasm (dyspnea) and Quincke's edema.

Tumor-induced Hypercalcemia and Paget's Disease: Adverse experiences considered to be related to pamidronate occurring in ≥1% patients in the specified indication: See Table I.

Table I—Aredia

Adverse Experiences Considered to be Related to Pamidronate Occurring in ≥1% Patients in the Specified Indication

Adverse Experiences	Tumor-induced Hypercalcemia	Paget's Disease
No. of patients	**n=910 (%)**	**n=395 (%)**
Fever	6.9	8.9
Headache	0.0	4.8
Hypocalcemia	3.2	0.8
Influenza-like symptoms	0.0	11.9
Infusion site reaction	1.7	1.8
Malaise	0.0	5.8
Myalgia	0.0	2.0
Nausea	0.9	2.0
Pain (bone)	0.0	8.9
Pain (unspecified)	0.0	7.9
Rigors	0.0	2.8

Deterioration of renal function has been noted in patients treated with bisphosphonates. Since many patients with tumor-induced hypercalcemia have compromised renal function prior to receiving antihypercalcemia therapy (see Precautions), it is difficult to estimate the role of individual bisphosphonates in subsequent changes in renal function. Deterioration of renal function (elevation of serum creatinine of >20% above baseline) which could not be readily explained in terms of pre-existing renal disease, prior nephrotoxic chemotherapies or compromised intravascular volume status has been noted in 7 cases of 404 patients treated with pamidronate where these data have been reported. The role of pamidronate in these changes in renal function is unclear, but merits cautious observation.

Bone Metastases and Multiple Myeloma: The most commonly reported adverse experiences regardless of relationship to therapy are shown in Table II.

Deterioration of renal function (including renal failure) has been reported following long-term treatment with pamidronate in patients with multiple myeloma. However, underlying disease progression and/or concomitant complications were also present and therefore a causal relationship with pamidronate is unproven.

Table II—Aredia

Commonly Reported Adverse Experiences in 3 Controlled Trials (regardless of causality)

Bone Metastases and Multiple Myeloma Patients

Adverse Event	Aredia 90 mg n=572	Placebo n=573
General		
Asthenia	16.4	15.4
Fatigue	30.4	35.5
Fever	35.5	30.5
Metastases	14.0	13.6
Digestive System		
Anorexia	20.8	18.0
Constipation	27.6	00.0
Diarrhea	24.3	26.2
Dyspepsia	13.6	12.4
Nausea	48.4	46.4
Pain Abdominal	17.3	14.0
Vomiting	30.9	28.1
Hemic and Lymphatic System		
Anemia	35.1	32.6
Granulocytopenia	16.8	17.3
Thrombocytopenia	11.0	13.1
Musculoskeletal System		
Myalgias	22.6	16.9
Skeletal Pain	59.4	69.1
CNS		
Headache	24.0	19.7
Insomnia	18.2	17.3
Respiratory System		
Coughing	21.2	18.8
Dyspnea	23.3	18.7
Upper Respiratory Infection	19.8	20.9
Urogenital System		
Urinary Tract Infection	14.5	10.8

Overdose: Symptoms and Treatment: Patients who have received doses higher than those recommended should be carefully monitored. Clinically significant hypocalcemia with paresthesia, tetany and hypotension, may be reversed by an infusion of calcium gluconate. Acute hypocalcemia is not expected to occur with pamidronate since plasma calcium levels fall progressively for several days after treatment.

Dosage: Dosing recommendations differ for tumor-induced hypercalcemia, lytic bone metastases and multiple myeloma, and Paget's disease. For patients suffering from TIH and multiple myeloma, see the TIH dosage guidelines.

Pamidronate must never be given as a bolus injection (see Warnings). Pamidronate should be administered in a compatible calcium-free i.v. solution (e.g., sterile normal saline or dextrose 5% in water). Pamidronate should be infused slowly.

To minimize local reactions the cannula should be carefully inserted in a relatively large vein.

The infusion rate should never exceed 60 mg/h (1 mg/min), and the concentration of pamidronate in the infusion solution should not exceed 90 mg/250 mL. A dose of 90 mg should normally be administered as a 2-hour infusion in 250 mL infusion solution. **However, in patients with multiple myeloma and in patients with tumor-induced hypercalcemia it is recommended not to exceed 90 mg in 500 mL over 4 hours (i.e., an infusion rate of 22.5 mg/h).**

Renal Impairment: Pharmacokinetic studies indicate that no dose adjustment is necessary in patients with any degree of renal impairment when pamidronate is administered as recommended. However, until further experience is gained a maximum infusion rate of 22.5 mg/h is recommended in renally impaired patients (see Pharmacology and Precautions).

Aredia (cont'd)

Table III—Aredia

Dosing Guidelines for Tumor-induced Hypercalcemia

Initial Serum Calcium (mmol/L)	(mg%)	Total Dose (mg)	Concentration of Infusate (mg/mL)	Maximum Infusion Rate (mg/h)
Up to 3.0	Up to 12.0	30	30/125	22.5
			30/125	22.5
3.0–3.5	12.0–14.0	30 or 60	60/250	22.5
			60/250	22.5
3.5–4.0	14.0–16.0	60 or 90	90/500	22.5
>4.0	>16.0	90	90/500	22.5

Dosing Guidelines for Tumor-induced Hypercalcemia: The recommended total dose of pamidronate for a treatment course depends upon initial plasma calcium levels. Doses should be adapted to the degree of severity of hypercalcemia to ensure normalization of plasma calcium and to optimize the duration of response. Rehydration with normal saline before treatment is recommended (see Precautions). **A dose of 90 mg should be administered in 500 mL of infusion solution. The infusion rate should not exceed 22.5 mg/h.**

The total dose for a treatment course may be given as a single infusion, or in multiple infusions spread over 2 to 4 consecutive days. The **maximum dose** of pamidronate per treatment course is 90 mg whether for initial or repeat treatment courses. Higher doses have not been associated with increased clinical effect.

Table III presents dosing guidelines for pamidronate derived from clinical data on uncorrected calcium values. These dose ranges also apply for calcium corrected for serum protein.

Decreases in serum calcium levels are generally observed within 24 to 48 hours after drug administration, with maximum lowering occurring by 3 to 7 days. If hypercalcemia recurs, or if plasma calcium does not decrease within 2 days, repeat infusions of pamidronate may be given, according to the dosing guidelines. The limited clinical experience available to date has suggested the possibility that pamidronate may produce a weaker therapeutic response with repeat treatment in patients with advanced cancer.

Dosing Guidelines for Bone Metastases and Multiple Myeloma: The recommended dose of pamidronate for the treatment of predominantly lytic bone metastases and multiple myeloma is 90 mg administered as a single infusion every 4 weeks. In patients with bone metastases who receive chemotherapy at 3-weekly intervals, pamidronate 90 mg may also be given every 3 weeks. A dose of 90 mg should normally be administered as a 2-hour infusion in 250 mL of infusion solution. However, in patients with multiple myeloma it is recommended not to exceed 90 mg in 500 mL over 4 hours (see Table IV).

Radiotherapy is the treatment of choice for patients with solitary lesions in weight bearing bones.

Table IV—Aredia

Dosing Guidelines for Bone Metastases

Disease State	Dosing Schedule	Concentration of infusate (mg/mL)
Bone metastases	90 mg/2 hours every 3*-4 weeks	90/250
Multiple myeloma	90 mg/4 hours every 4 weeks	90/500

* for patients receiving chemotherapy every 3 weeks.

Dosing Guidelines for Paget's Disease of Bone: The recommended total dose of pamidronate for a treatment course is 180 to 210 mg. This may be administered either as 6 doses of 30 mg once a week (total dose 180 mg). Alternatively, 3 doses of 60 mg may be administered every second week, but treatment should be initiated with a 30 mg dose (total dose 210 mg) as influenza-like reactions are common only with the first infusion. Each dose of 30 or 60 mg should be diluted in at least 250 or 500 mL, respectively, or normal saline or D5W. An infusion rate of 15 mg/h is recommended. This regimen, omitting the initial dose, can be repeated after 6 months until remission of disease is achieved, and when relapse occurs (see Table V).

Reconstitution of Lyophilized Vials: Each vial of sterile lyophilized powder should be reconstituted with sterile water for injection prior to dilution as given in Table VI.

Table VI—Aredia

Reconstitution Table

Vial size mg/mL	Volume of Diluent to be Added to the Vial (mL)	Approximate Available Volume (mL)	Nominal Concentration (mg/mL)
30/10	10	10	3
60/10	10	10	6
90/10	10	10	9

Dilution of Reconstituted Solution for I.V. Infusion: Reconstituted solutions that have been prepared with sterile water for injection should be further diluted with either 0.9% sodium chloride or 5% dextrose injection prior to i.v. infusion administration. Diluted solutions prepared in this manner should be used within 24 hours from the time of initial entry (reconstitution) when stored at room temperature (15 to 30°C) due to the possibility of microbial contamination during preparation. Discard the unused portion.

All parenteral products should be visually inspected for particulate matter and discoloration prior to administration. Any solution found to have particulate matter or discoloration should be discarded.

Incompatibilities: Pamidronate must not be mixed with calcium-containing infusion solutions, such as Ringer's solution.

Information for the Patient: See Blue Section—Information for the Patient "Aredia".

Supplied: 30 mg: Each vial of sterile, white to practically white lyophilized powder contains: pamidronate disodium (anhydrous) 30 mg and mannitol 470 mg. Phosphoric acid is employed to adjust the pH to 6.3. Preservative-free. Vials of 10 mL, cartons of 2.

60 mg: Each vial of sterile, white to practically white lyophilized powder contains: pamidronate disodium (anhydrous) 60 mg and mannitol 400 mg. Phosphoric acid is employed to adjust the pH to 6.3. Preservative-free. Vials of 10 mL, cartons of 1.

90 mg: Each vial of sterile, white to practically white lyophilized powder contains: pamidronate disodium (anhydrous) 90 mg and mannitol 375 mg. Phosphoric acid is employed to adjust the pH to 6.3. Preservative-free. Vials of 10 mL, cartons of 1.

Protect vials from heat (store below 30°C).

(Shown in Product Recognition Section)

Reviewed 1998

Table V—Aredia

Recommended Treatment Regimens for Paget's Disease

Regimen	Dosing Schedule	Concentration of Infusate (mg/mL)	Infusion Rate (mg/hr)
	Recommended Total Dose/Treatment Course (Paget's Disease): 180-210 mg		
Regimen 1 Total dose 180 mg	30 mg once weekly for 6 weeks	30/≥250–500	15
Regimen 2 Total Dose 210 mg	Infusions administered every 2 weeks. Initial dose (week 1)=30 mg; Subsequent doses (weeks 3, 5 & 7)=60 mg	30 or 60/≥250–500	15
Retreatment Regimen Total dose 180 mg	60 mg every 2 weeks for a total of 3 infusions	60/500	15

ARICEPT™ ℞

Pfizer

Donepezil HCl

Cholinesterase Inhibitor

Pharmacology: Donepezil is a piperidine-based, reversible inhibitor of the enzyme acetylcholinesterase.

A consistent pathological change in Alzheimer's disease is the degeneration of cholinergic neuronal pathways that project from the basal forebrain to the cerebral cortex and hippocampus. The resulting hypofunction of these pathways is thought to account for some of the clinical manifestations of dementia. Donepezil is postulated to exert its therapeutic effect by enhancing cholinergic function. This is accomplished by increasing the concentration of acetylcholine (ACh) through reversible inhibition of its hydrolysis by acetylcholinesterase (AchE). If this proposed mechanism of action is correct, donepezil's effect may lessen as the disease process advances and fewer cholinergic neurons remain functionally intact.

There is no evidence that donepezil alters the course of the underlying dementing process.

Pharmacokinetics: Absorption: Donepezil is well absorbed with a relative oral bioavailability of 100% and reaches peak plasma concentrations (C_{max}) approximately 3 to 4 hours after dose administration. Plasma concentrations and area under the curve (AUC) were found to rise in proportion to the dose administered within the 1 to 10 mg dose range studied. The terminal disposition half-life ($t_{1/2}$) is approximately 70 hours and the mean apparent plasma clearance (Cl/F) is 0.13L/h/kg. Following multiple dose administration, donepezil accumulates in plasma by 4- to 7-fold and steady-state is reached within 15 days. The minimum, maximum and steady-state plasma concentrations (C) and pharmacodynamic effect (E, percent inhibition of acetylcholinesterase in erythrocyte membranes) of donepezil in healthy adult male and female volunteers are given in Table I (on following page).

The range of inhibition of erythrocyte membrane acetylcholinesterase noted in Alzheimer's disease patients in controlled clinical trials was 40 to 80% and 60 to 90% for the 5 mg/day and 10 mg/day doses, respectively.

Pharmacokinetic parameters from healthy adult male and female volunteers participating in a multiple-dose study where single daily doses of 5 or 10 mg of donepezil were administered each evening are summarized in Table II (on following page). Treatment duration was 1 month. However, volunteers randomized to the 10 mg/day dose group initially received 5 mg daily doses of donepezil for 1 week before receiving the 10 mg daily dose for the next 3 weeks in order to avoid acute cholinergic effects.

Neither food nor time of dose administration (i.e., morning vs evening dose) have an influence on the rate and extent of donepezil absorption.

The effect of achlorhydria on the absorption of donepezil is unknown.

Distribution: Donepezil is about 96% bound to human plasma proteins, mainly to albumins (~75%) and α_1-acid glycoprotein (~21%) over the concentration range of 2 to 1 000 ng/mL.

Metabolism/Excretion: Donepezil is extensively metabolized and is also excreted in the urine as parent drug. The rate of metabolism of donepezil is slow and does not appear to be saturable. There are 4 major metabolites – 2 of which are known to be active – and a number of minor metabolites, not all of which have been identified. Donepezil is metabolized by CYP450 isoenzymes 2D6 and 3A4 and undergoes glucuronidation. Following administration of a single 5 mg dose of ^{14}C-labelled donepezil, plasma radioactivity, expressed as a percent of the administered dose, was present primarily as unchanged donepezil (53%), and as 6-O-desmethyl donepezil (11%) which has been reported to inhibit AChE to the same extent as donepezil in vitro and was found in plasma at concentrations equal to about 20% of donepezil. Approximately 57% of the total administered radioactivity was recovered from the urine and 15% was recovered from the feces (total recovery of 72%) over a period of 10 days. Approximately 28% of the labelled donepezil remained uncovered, with about

Table I—Aricept

Plasma Concentrations and Pharmacodynamic Effect of Donepezil at Steady-state (Mean±S.D.)

Dose (mg/day)	C_{min} (ng/mL)	C_{max} (ng/mL)	C_{ss}[a] (ng/mL)	E_{min} %	E_{max} %	E_{ss}[b] %
5	21.4±3.8	34.1±7.3	26.5±3.9	62.2±5.8	71.8±4.3	65.3±5.2
10	38.5±8.6	60.5±10.0	47.0±8.2	74.7±4.4	83.6±1.9	77.8±3.0

[a]C_{ss}: Plasma concentration at steady-state.
[b]E_{ss}: Inhibition of erythrocyte membrane acetylcholinesterase at steady-state.

Table II—Aricept

Pharmacokinetic Parameters of Donepezil at Steady-state (Mean±S.D.)

Dose (mg/day)	t_{max} (h)	AUC_{0-24} (ng·h/mL)	Cl_T/F (L/h/kg)	V_z/F (L/kg)	$t_{1/2}$ (h)
5	3.0±1.4	634.8±92.2	0.110±0.02	11.8±1.7	72.7±10.6
10	3.9±1.0	1127.8±195.9	0.110±0.02	11.6±1.9	73.5±11.8

Legend: t_{max}: Time to maximal plasma concentration.
AUC_{0-24}: Area under the plasma concentration vs time curve from 0 to 24 hours.
Cl_T/F: Mean apparent plasma clearance.
V_z/F: Apparent volume of distribution.
$t_{1/2}$: Elimination half-life.

17% of the donepezil dose recovered in the urine as parent drug.

Age and Gender: No formal pharmacokinetic study was conducted to examine age and gender related differences in the pharmacokinetic profile of donepezil. However, mean plasma donepezil concentrations measured during therapeutic drug monitoring of elderly male and female patients with Alzheimer's disease are comparable to those observed in young healthy volunteers.

Renal: In a study of 4 patients with moderate to severe renal impairment (Cl_{cr} <22 mL/min/1.73 m²) the clearance of donepezil did not differ from that of 4 age and sex matched healthy subjects.

Hepatic: In a study of 10 patients with stable alcoholic cirrhosis, the clearance of donepezil was decreased by 20% relative to 10 healthy age and sex matched subjects.

Race: No specific pharmacokinetic study was conducted to investigate the effects of race on the disposition of donepezil. However, retrospective pharmacokinetic analysis indicates that gender and race (Japanese and Caucasians) did not affect the clearance of donepezil.

Clinical Trial Data: Two randomized, double-blind, placebo-controlled, clinical trials, in patients with Alzheimer's disease (diagnosed by DSM III-R and NINCDS criteria, Mini-Mental State Examination ≥10 and ≤26 as well as a Clinical Dementia Rating of 1 or 2) provided efficacy data for donepezil in this patient population. In these studies, the mean age of patients was 73 years with a range of 50 to 94 years. Approximately 64% of the patients were women and 38% were men. The racial distribution was as follows: white: 95%, black: 3% and other races: 2%.

In each study, the effectiveness of treatment with donepezil was evaluated using a dual outcome assessment strategy. The ability of donepezil to improve cognitive performance was assessed with the cognitive subscale of the Alzheimer's Disease Assessment Scale (ADAS-cog), a widely used and well validated multi-item instrument which samples cognitive domains affected by the disease.

The ability of donepezil to produce an overall clinical effect was assessed using the semi-structured CIBIC Plus (Clinician's Interview Based Impression of Change that required the use of caregiver information). The CIBIC Plus evaluates four major areas of functioning: general, cognition, behavior and activities of daily living.

The data shown below for the 2 primary outcome measures in donepezil clinical trials were obtained from the Intent-to-Treat population (ITT analysis, i.e., all patients who were randomized to treatment, regardless of whether or not they were able to complete the study. For patients unable to complete the study, their last observation while on treatment was carried forward and used at endpoint).

Fifteen-Week Study (12 weeks of treatment + 3-week placebo washout): In this study 468 patients were randomized to receive single daily doses of placebo, 5 or 10 mg/day of donepezil for 12 weeks, followed by a 3-week placebo washout period. To reduce the likelihood of cholinergic effects, the 10 mg/day treatment group received 5 mg/day for the first week prior to receiving their first 10 mg daily dose.

Effects on ADAS-cog: Patients treated with donepezil showed significant improvements in ADAS-cog score from baseline, and when compared with placebo. The difference in mean ADAS-cog change scores for the donepezil treated patients compared to the patients on placebo, for the intent-to-treat population, at week 12 were 2.44±0.43 and 3.07±0.43 units each, for the 5 mg/day and 10 mg/day donepezil treatment groups, respectively. These differences were statistically significant. The difference between active treatments was not statistically significant. Following a 3-week placebo washout period, the ADAS-cog scores for both donepezil treatment groups increased, indicating that discontinuation of donepezil resulted in a loss of its treatment effect. The duration of this placebo washout period was not sufficient to characterize the rate of loss of the treatment effect, but, the 30-week study (see below) demonstrated that treatment effects associated with the use of donepezil abate within 6 weeks of treatment discontinuation.

Effects on the CIBIC Plus: The CIBIC Plus showed significant improvement with donepezil treatment versus placebo. The differences in mean scores for donepezil treated patients compared to those on placebo for the intent-to-treat population at Week 12 were 0.29±0.08 and 0.34±0.08 units for the 5 mg/day and 10 mg/day treatment groups, respectively. These differences from placebo were statistically significant. There was no significant difference between the 2 active treatments.

Thirty-Week Study (24 weeks of treatment + 6-week placebo washout): In this study, 473 patients were randomized to receive single daily doses of placebo, 5 or 10 mg/day of donepezil for 24 weeks of double-blind active treatment followed by a 6-week single-blind placebo washout period. As in the 15-week study to avoid acute cholinergic effects, the 10 mg/day treatment group received 5 mg/day for the first week prior to receiving their first 10 mg daily dose.

Effects on the ADAS-cog: Patients treated with donepezil showed significant improvements in ADAS-cog score from baseline, and when compared with placebo. The mean differences in the ADAS-cog change scores for donepezil treated patients compared to the patients on placebo for the intent-to-treat population at Week 24 were 2.49±0.51 and 2.88±0.51 units for the 5 mg/day and 10 mg/day treatments, respectively. These differences were statistically significant. The difference between the 2 active treatments was not statistically significant. Over the 24-week treatment period, 80% (5 mg) and 81% (10 mg) of donepezil treated patients versus 58% placebo treated patients showed no evidence of deterioration or an improvement. A 4 point improvement in ADAS-cog was observed in 38% (5 mg) and 54% (10 mg) of donepezil treated patients vs 27% for placebo. A 7 point improvement was observed in 15% (5 mg) and 25% (10 mg) of donepezil treated patients vs 8% for placebo. Following 6 weeks of placebo washout, scores on the ADAS-cog for both the donepezil treatment groups were indistinguishable from those patients who had received only placebo for 30 weeks. This suggests that the beneficial effects of donepezil abate over 6 weeks following discontinuation of treatment and therefore do not represent a change in the underlying disease. There was no evidence of a rebound effect 6 weeks after abrupt discontinuation of therapy. This is in line with the pharmacokinetics of donepezil (i.e., approximately 70 hour half-life) which preclude an abrupt reduction in drug plasma levels.

Effects on the CIBIC Plus: After 24 weeks of treatment, the mean drug-placebo differences were 0.36±0.09 and 0.44±0.07 units for 5 mg/day and 10 mg/day of donepezil, respectively. These differences were statistically significant. There was no statistically significant difference between the 2 active treatments.

Data from these controlled clinical trials showed that the beneficial symptomatic effects of donepezil vs placebo was more consistently apparent after 12 weeks of continuous treatment. Once treatment is discontinued, the effects of donepezil were shown to abate within 6 weeks of treatment discontinuation.

Indications: For the symptomatic treatment of patients with mild to moderate dementia of the Alzheimer's type. Donepezil has not been studied in controlled clinical trials for longer than 6 months.

Donepezil should only be prescribed by (or following consultation with) clinicians who are experienced in the diagnosis and management of Alzheimer's disease.

Contraindications: Patients with known hypersensitivity to donepezil or to piperidine derivatives.

Warnings: Anesthesia: Donepezil, as a cholinesterase inhibitor, is likely to exaggerate succinylcholine-type muscle relaxation during anesthesia.

Neurological Conditions: Seizures: Some cases of seizures have been reported with the use of donepezil in clinical trials and from spontaneous Adverse Reaction reporting. Cholinomimetics can cause a reduction of seizure threshold, increasing the risk of seizures. However, seizure activity may also be a manifestation of Alzheimer's disease. The risk/benefit of donepezil treatment for patients with a history of seizure disorder must therefore be carefully evaluated.

Donepezil has not been studied in patients with moderately severe or severe Alzheimer's disease, non-Alzheimer dementias or individuals with Parkinsonian features. The efficacy and safety of donepezil in these patient populations is unknown.

Pulmonary Conditions: Because of their cholinomimetic action, cholinesterase inhibitors should be prescribed with care to patients with a history of asthma or obstructive pulmonary disease. Donepezil has not been studied in patients under treatment for these conditions and should therefore be used with particular caution in such patients.

Cardiovascular: Because of their pharmacological action, cholinesterase inhibitors may have vagotonic effects on heart rate (e.g., bradycardia). The potential for this action may be particularly important to patients with "sick sinus syndrome" or other supraventricular cardiac conduction conditions. In clinical trials, most patients with significant cardiovascular conditions were excluded, except for patients with: controlled hypertension (DBP <95 mmHg), right bundle branch blockage, and pacemakers. Therefore, caution should be taken in treating patients with active coronary artery disease and congestive heart failure. Syncopal episodes have been reported in association with the use of donepezil. It is recommended that donepezil should not be used in patients with cardiac conduction abnormalities (except for right bundle branch block) including sick sinus syndrome and those with unexplained syncopal episodes.

Gastrointestinal: Through their primary action, cholinesterase inhibitors may be expected to increase gastric acid secretion due to increased cholinergic activity. Therefore, patients at increased risk for developing ulcers, e.g., those with a history of ulcer disease or those receiving concurrent NSAIDs including high doses of ASA, should be monitored closely for symptoms of active or occult gastrointestinal bleeding. Clinical studies of donepezil have shown no increase, relative to placebo in the incidence of either peptic ulcer disease or gastrointestinal bleeding (see Adverse Effects).

Donepezil, as a predictable consequence of its pharmacological properties, has been shown to produce, in controlled clinical trials in patients with Alzheimer's disease, diarrhea, nausea and vomiting. These effects, when they occur, appear more frequently with the 10 mg dose than with the 5 mg dose. In most cases, these effects have usually been mild and transient, sometimes lasting 1 to 3 weeks and have resolved during continued use of donepezil (see Adverse Effects). A treatment with the 5 mg/day dose for over 6 weeks prior to initiating treatment with the 10 mg/day dose is associated with a lower incidence of gastrointestinal intolerance.

Genitourinary: Although not observed in clinical trials of donepezil, cholinomimetics may cause bladder outflow obstruction.

Precautions: Concomitant Use with Other Drugs: Anticholinergics: Because of their mechanism of action, cholinesterase inhibitors have the potential to interfere with the activity of anticholinergic medications.

Cholinomimetics and Other Cholinesterase Inhibitors: A synergistic effect may be expected when cholinesterase inhibitors

Aricept (cont'd)

are given concurrently with succinylcholine, similar neuromuscular blocking agents or cholinergic agonists such as bethanechol.

Other Psychoactive Drugs: Few patients in controlled clinical trials received neuroleptics, antidepressants or anticonvulsants, there is thus limited information concerning the interaction of donepezil with these drugs.

Patients ≥85 years old: In controlled clinical studies with 5 and 10 mg of donepezil, 536 patients were between the ages of 65 to 84, and 37 patients were aged 85 years or older. In Alzheimer's disease patients, nausea, diarrhea, vomiting, insomnia, fatigue and anorexia increased with dose and age and the incidence appeared to be greater in female patients. Since cholinesterase inhibitors as well as Alzheimer's disease can be associated with significant weight loss, caution is advised regarding the use of donepezil in low body weight elderly patients, especially in those ≥85 years old.

Geriatrics with Comorbid Disease: There is limited safety information for donepezil in patients with mild to moderate Alzheimer's Disease and significant comorbidity. The use of donepezil in Alzheimer's disease patients with chronic illnesses common among the geriatric population, should be considered only after careful risk/benefit assessment and include close monitoring for adverse events. Caution is advised regarding the use of donepezil doses above 5 mg in this patient population.

Renally and Hepatically Impaired: There is limited information regarding the pharmacokinetics of donepezil in renally and hepatically impaired Alzheimer disease patients (see Pharmacokinetics). Close monitoring for adverse effects in Alzheimer disease patients with renal or hepatic disease being treated with donepezil is therefore recommended.

Drug Interactions: Pharmacokinetic studies, limited to short-term, single-dose studies in young subjects evaluated the potential of donepezil for interaction with theophylline, cimetidine, warfarin and digoxin administration. No significant effects on the pharmacokinetics of these drugs were observed. Similar studies in elderly patients were not done.

Drugs Highly Bound to Plasma Proteins: Drug displacement studies have been performed in vitro between donepezil, a highly bound drug (96%) and other drugs such as furosemide, digoxin, and warfarin. Donepezil at concentrations of 0.3 to 10 μg/mL did not affect the binding of furosemide (5 μg/mL), digoxin (2 ng/mL) and warfarin (3 μg/mL) to human albumin. Similarly, the binding of donepezil to human albumin was not affected by furosemide, digoxin and warfarin.

Effect of Donepezil on the Metabolism of Other Drugs: No in vivo clinical trials have been conducted to investigate the effect of donepezil on the clearance of drugs metabolized by CYP 3A4 (e.g., cisapride, terfenadine) or by CYP 2D6 (e.g., imipramine). However, in vitro studies show a low rate of binding to these enzymes (mean Ki about 50 to 130 μM), that, given the therapeutic plasma concentrations of donepezil (164 nM), indicates little likelihood of interferences.

It is not known whether donepezil has any potential for enzyme induction.

Effect of Other Drugs on the Metabolism of Donepezil: Ketoconazole and quinidine, inhibitors of CYP450, 3A4 and 2D6, respectively, inhibit donepezil metabolism in vitro. Whether there is a clinical effect of these inhibitors is not known. Inducers of CYP 2D6 and CYP 3A4 (e.g., phenytoin, carbamazepine, dexamethasone, rifampin and phenobarbital) could increase the rate of elimination of donepezil.

Pharmacokinetic studies demonstrated that the metabolism of donepezil is not significantly affected by concurrent administration of digoxin or cimetidine.

Pregnancy and *Lactation:* The safety of donepezil during pregnancy and lactation has not been established and therefore, it should not be used in women of childbearing potential or in nursing mothers unless, in the opinion of the physician, the potential benefits to the patient outweigh the possible hazards to the fetus or the infant.

Teratology studies conducted in pregnant rats at doses of up to 16 mg/kg/day and in pregnant rabbits at doses of up to 10 mg/kg/day did not disclose any evidence for a teratogenic potential of donepezil.

Children: There are no adequate and well-controlled trials to document the safety and efficacy of donepezil in any illness occurring in children. Therefore, donepezil is not recommended for use in children.

Adverse Effects: A total of 747 patients with mild to moderate Alzheimer's disease were treated in controlled clinical studies with donepezil. Of these patients, 613 (82%) completed the studies. The mean duration of treatment for all donepezil groups was 132 days (range 1 to 356 days).

Adverse Events Leading to Discontinuation: The rates of discontinuation from controlled clinical trials of donepezil due to adverse events for the donepezil 5 mg/day treatment groups were comparable to those of placebo-treatment groups at approximately 5%. The rate of discontinuation of patients who received the 10 mg/day dose after only a 1 week initial treatment with 5 mg/day donepezil was higher at 13%.

The most common adverse events leading to discontinuation, defined as those occurring in at least 2% of patients and at twice the incidence seen in placebo patients, are shown in Table III.

Table III—Aricept

Most Frequent Adverse Events Leading to Withdrawal from Controlled Clinical Trials by Dose Group

Dose Group	Placebo	5 mg/day Aricept	10 mg/day Aricept
Number of Patients Randomized	**355**	**350**	**315**
Events/% Discontinuing			
Nausea	1%	1%	3%
Diarrhea	0%	<1%	3%
Vomiting	<1%	<1%	2%

Most Frequent Adverse Clinical Events Seen in Association with the Use of Donepezil: The most common adverse events, defined as those occurring at a frequency of at least 5% in patients receiving 10 mg/day and twice the placebo rate, are largely predicted by donepezil's cholinomimetic effects. These include nausea, diarrhea, insomnia, vomiting, muscle cramp, fatigue and anorexia. These adverse events were often of mild intensity and transient, resolving during continued donepezil treatment without the need for dose modification.

There is evidence to suggest that the frequency of these common adverse events may be affected by the duration of treatment with an initial 5 mg daily dose prior to increasing the dose to 10 mg/day. An open-label study was conducted with 269 patients who received placebo in the 15- and 30-week studies. These patients received a 5 mg/day dose for 6 weeks prior to initiating treatment with 10 mg/day. The rates of common adverse events were lower than those seen in controlled clinical trial patients who received 10 mg/day after only a 1 week initial treatment period with a 5 mg daily dose, and were comparable to the rates noted in patients treated only with 5 mg/day.

The comparison of the most common adverse events following 1- and 6-week initial treatment periods with 5 mg/day donepezil is shown in Table IV.

Adverse Events Reported in Controlled Trials: The events cited reflect experience gained under closely monitored conditions of clinical trials in a highly selected patient population. In actual clinical practice or in other clinical trials, these frequency estimates may not apply, as the conditions of use, reporting behavior, and the kinds of patients treated may differ. Table V lists treatment emergent signs and symptoms (TESS) that were reported in at least 2% of patients from placebo-controlled clinical trials who received donepezil and for which the rate of occurrence was greater for donepezil than placebo assigned patients. In general, adverse events occurred more frequently in female patients and with advancing age.

Table IV—Aricept

Comparison of Rates of Adverse Events in Patients Treated With 10 mg/day After 1 and 6 weeks of Initial Treatment with 5 mg/day

	No Initial Treatment		1-Week Initial Treatment with 5 mg/day	6-Week Initial Treatment with 5 mg/day
Adverse Event	Placebo (N=315) %	5 mg/day (N=311) %	10 mg/day (N=315) %	10 mg/day (N=269) %
Nausea	6	5	19	6
Diarrhea	5	8	15	9
Insomnia	6	6	14	6
Fatigue	3	4	8	3
Vomiting	3	3	8	5
Muscle Cramps	2	6	8	3
Anorexia	2	3	7	3

Table V—Aricept

Events Reported in Controlled Clinical Trials in at Least 2% of Patients Receiving Aricept and at a Higher Frequency than Placebo-Treated Patients

Body System/ Adverse Events	Placebo n=355	Aricept n=747
Percent of patients with any adverse event	72	74
Body as a Whole		
Headache	9	10
Pain, various locations	8	9
Accident	6	7
Fatigue	3	5
Cardiovascular		
Syncope	1	2
Digestive		
Nausea	6	11
Diarrhea	5	10
Vomiting	3	5
Anorexia	2	4
Hemic and Lymphatic		
Ecchymosis	3	4
Metabolic and Nutritional		
Weight decrease	1	3
Musculoskeletal		
Muscle cramps	2	6
Arthritis	1	2
Nervous System		
Insomnia	6	9
Dizziness	6	8
Depression	<1	3
Abnormal dreams	0	3
Somnolence	<1	2
Urogenital		
Frequent urination	1	2

Other Adverse Events Observed During Clinical Trials: Donepezil has been administered to over 1 700 individuals for various lengths of time during clinical trials worldwide. Approximately 1 200 patients have been treated for at least 3 months, and more than 1 000 patients have been treated for at least 6 months. Controlled and uncontrolled trials in the US included approximately 900 patients. In regards to the highest dose of 10 mg/day, this population includes 650 patients treated for 3 months, 475 patients treated for 6 months and 115 patients treated for over 1 year. The range of patient exposure is from 1 to 1 214 days.

Treatment emergent signs and symptoms that occurred during three controlled clinical trials and 2 open-label trials were recorded as adverse events by the clinical investigators using terminology of their own choosing. To provide an overall estimate of the proportion of individuals having similar types of events, the studies were integrated and the events were grouped into a smaller number of standardized categories using a modified COSTART dictionary and event frequencies were calculated across all studies. These categories are used in the listing below. The frequencies represent the proportion of 900 patients from these trials who experienced that event while receiving donepezil. All adverse events occurring at least twice are included. Adverse events already listed in Tables IV and V are not repeated here (i.e., events occurring at an incidence >2%). Also excluded are COSTART terms too general to be informative, or events less likely to be drug caused. Events are classified by body system and listed as occurring in ≥1% and <2% of patients (i.e., in 1/100 to 2/100 patients:

frequent) or in <1% of patients (i.e., in 1/100 to 1/1000 patients: infrequent). These adverse events are not necessarily related to donepezil treatment and in most cases were observed at a similar frequency in placebo-treated patients in the controlled studies.

Adverse events occurring in ≥1% and <2% or <1% of patients receiving donepezil:

Body as a Whole:(≥1% and <2%) influenza, chest pain, toothache; (<1%) fever, edema face, periorbital edema, hernia hiatal, abscess, cellulitis, chills, generalized coldness, head fullness, head pressure, listlessness.

Cardiovascular: (≥1% and <2%) hypertension, vasodilation, atrial fibrillation, hot flashes, hypotension; (<1%) angina pectoris, postural hypotension, myocardial infarction, premature ventricular contraction, arrhythmia, AV Block (first degree), congestive heart failure, arteritis, bradycardia, peripheral vascular disease, supraventricular tachycardia, deep vein thromboses.

Digestive: (≥1% and <2%) fecal incontinence, gastrointestinal bleeding, bloating, epigastric pain; (<1%) eructation, gingivitis, increased appetite, flatulence, periodontal abscess, cholelithiasis, diverticulitis, drooling, dry mouth, fever sore, gastritis, irritable colon, tongue edema, epigastric distress, gastroenteritis, increased transaminases, hemorrhoids, ileus, increased thirst, jaundice, melena, polydipsia, duodenal ulcer, stomach ulcer.

Endocrine: (< 1%) diabetes mellitus, goiter.

Hemic and Lymphatic: (<1%) anemia, thrombocythemia, thrombocytopenia, eosinophilia, erythrocytopenia.

Metabolic and Nutritional Disorders: (≥1% and <2%) dehydration; (<1%) gout, hypokalemia, increased creatine kinase, hyperglycemia, weight increase, increased lactate dehydrogenase.

Musculoskeletal: (≥1% and <2%) bone fracture; (<1%) muscle weakness, muscle fasciculation.

Nervous System: (≥1% and <2%) delusions, tremor, irritability, paresthesia, aggression, vertigo, ataxia, libido increased, restlessness, abnormal crying, nervousness, aphasia; (<1%) cerebrovascular accident, intracranial hemorrhage, transient ischemic attack, emotional lability, neuralgia, coldness (localized), muscle spasm, dysphoria, gait abnormality, hypertonia, hypokinesia, neurodermatitis, numbness (localized), paranoia, dysarthria, dysphasia, hostility, decreased libido, melancholia, emotional withdrawal, nystagmus, pacing, seizures.

Respiratory: (≥1% and <2%) dyspnea, sore throat, bronchitis; (<1%) epistaxis, postnasal drip, pneumonia, hyperventilation, pulmonary congestion, wheezing, hypoxia, pharyngitis, pleurisy, pulmonary collapse, sleep apnea, snoring.

Skin and Appendages: (≥1% and <2%) abrasion, pruritus, diaphoresis, urticaria; (<1%) dermatitis, erythema, skin discoloration, hyperkeratosis, alopecia, fungal dermatitis, herpes zoster, hirsutism, skin striae, night sweats, skin ulcer.

Special Senses: (≥1% and <2%) cataract, eye irritation, blurred vision; (<1%) dry eyes, glaucoma, earache, tinnitus, blepharitis, decreased hearing, retinal hemorrhage, otitis externa, otitis media, bad taste, conjunctival hemorrhage, ear buzzing, motion sickness, spots before eyes.

Urogenital: (≥1% and <2%) urinary incontinence, nocturia; (< 1%) dysuria, hematuria, urinary urgency, metrorrhagia, cystitis, enuresis, prostate hypertrophy, pyelonephritis, inability to empty bladder, breast fibroadenosis, fibrocystic breast, mastitis, pyuria, renal failure, vaginitis.

Overdose: Symptoms: Overdosage with cholinesterase inhibitors can result in cholinergic crisis characterized by severe nausea, vomiting, salivation, sweating, bradycardia, hypotension, respiratory depression, collapse and convulsions. Increasing muscle weakness is a possibility and may result in death if respiratory muscles are involved.

Treatment: The elimination half-life of donepezil at recommended doses is approximately 70 hours, thus, in the case of overdose, it is anticipated that prolonged treatment and monitoring of adverse and toxic reactions will be necessary. As in any case of overdose, general supportive measures should be utilized.

Tertiary anticholinergics such as atropine may be used as an antidote for donepezil overdosage. I.V. atropine sulfate titrated to effect is recommended: an initial dose of 1 to 2 mg i.v. with subsequent doses based upon clinical response. Atypical responses in blood pressure and heart rate have been reported with other cholinomimetics when coadministered with quaternary anticholinergics such as glycopyrrolate. It is not known whether donepezil and/or its metabolites can be removed by dialysis (hemodialysis, peritoneal dialysis, or hemofiltration).

Dose-related signs of toxicity observed in animals included reduced spontaneous movement, prone position, staggering gait, lacrimation, clonic convulsions, depressed respiration, salivation, miosis, fasciculation, and lower body surface temperature.

Dosage: Should only be prescribed by (or following consultation with) clinicians who are experienced in the diagnosis and management of Alzheimer's disease.

The recommended initial dose of donepezil is 5 mg taken once daily. Therapy with the 5 mg dose should be maintained for 4 to 6 weeks before considering a dose increase, in order to avoid or decrease the incidence of the most common adverse reactions to the drug (see Adverse Effects) and to allow plasma levels to reach steady-state.

For those patients who do not respond adequately to the 5 mg daily dose after 4 to 6 weeks of treatment, the 10 mg daily dose may then be considered.

The maximum recommended dose is 10 mg taken once daily.

Following initiation of therapy or any dosage increase, patients should be closely monitored for adverse effects. Adverse events are more common in individuals of low body weight, in patients ≥ 85 years old and in females. It is recommended that donepezil be used with caution in elderly women of low body weight and that the dose should not exceed 5 mg/day.

Donepezil should be taken once daily in the evening, before retiring. It may be taken with or without food.

In a population of cognitively-impaired individuals, safe use of this and all other medications may require supervision.

Information for the Patient: See Blue Section—Information for the Patient "Aricept".

Supplied: 5 mg: Each white, film-coated tablet contains: donepezil HCl 5 mg equivalent to donepezil free base 4.56 mg. Nonmedicinal ingredients: cornstarch, hydroxypropylcellulose, lactose monohydrate, magnesium stearate and microcrystalline cellulose; film-coating: hydroxypropyl methylcellulose, polyethylene glycol, talc and titanium dioxide. HDPE bottles of 30 and 100. Boxed blister strips of 7, 14 and 28 (2 strips of 14).

10 mg: Each yellow, film-coated tablet contains: donepezil HCl 10 mg equivalent to donepezil free base 9.12 mg. Nonmedicinal ingredients: cornstarch, hydroxypropylcellulose, lactose monohydrate, magnesium stearate and microcrystalline cellulose; film-coating: hydroxypropyl methylcellulose, iron oxide, polyethylene glycol, talc and titanium dioxide. HDPE bottles of 30 and 100. Boxed blister strips of 7, 14 and 28 (2 strips of 14).

Store at controlled room temperature, 15 to 30°C and away from moisture.

(Shown in Product Recognition Section)

Reviewed 1998

ARIMIDEX® Ⓟ

Zeneca

Anastrozole

Nonsteroidal Aromatase Inhibitor

Pharmacology: Many breast cancers have estrogen receptors and growth of these tumors can be stimulated by estrogens. In postmenopausal women, the principal source of circulating estrogen (primarily estrone) is conversion of adrenally-generated androstenedione to estrone by aromatase in peripheral tissues, such as adipose tissue, with further conversion of estrone to estradiol. Many breast cancers also contain aromatase; the importance of tumor-generated estrogens is uncertain.

Treatment of breast cancer has included efforts to decrease estrogen levels by ovariectomy premenopausally and by use of anti-estrogens and progestational agents both pre- and postmenopausally, and these interventions lead to decreased tumor mass or delayed progression of tumor growth in some women.

Anastrozole is a potent and selective nonsteroidal aromatase inhibitor. It significantly lowers serum estradiol concentrations and has no detectable effect on formation of adrenal corticosteriods or aldosterone.

The relationship between dose and response, measured as suppression of serum estradiol, was studied in postmenopausal women. Daily doses of anastrozole at 1 mg for 14 days produced estradiol suppression of greater than 80%. Suppression of serum estradiol was maintained for up to 6 days after cessation of daily dosing with 1 mg anastrozole.

The selectivity of anastrozole to the aromatase enzyme, rather than other cytochrome P_{450} enzymes controlling glucocorticoid and mineralocorticoid synthesis in the adrenal gland, has been established. Furthermore, provocative stimulation of the adrenal glands by ACTH in subjects under treatment with anastrozole up to 10 mg, produced a normal response in terms of cortisol and aldosterone secretion. Therefore, patients treated with anastrozole do not require glucocorticoid or mineralocorticoid replacement therapy.

Anastrozole does not possess direct progestogenic, androgenic or estrogenic activity and does not interfere with secretion of thyroid stimulating hormone (TSH).

Pharmacokinetics: Inhibition of aromatase activity is primarily due to anastrozole, the parent drug. Absorption of anastrozole is rapid and maximum plasma concentrations typically occur within 2 hours of dosing under fasted conditions. Studies with radiolabeled drug have demonstrated that orally administered anastrozole is well absorbed into the systemic circulation. Food reduces the rate but not the overall extent of anastrozole absorption.

Anastrozole is eliminated slowly with a plasma elimination half-life of approximately 50 hours in postmenopausal women. The pharmacokinetics of anastrozole are linear over the dose range of 1 to 20 mg and do not change with repeated dosing. Consistent with the 50 hour plasma elimination half-life, plasma concentrations of anastrozole approach steady-state concentrations after 7 days of once daily dosing and are approximately 3- to 4-fold higher than the concentrations observed after a single dose of anastrozole. The protein binding of anastrozole to plasma proteins is about 40% and independent of concentration over a range which includes therapeutic concentrations.

Studies in postmenopausal women with radiolabeled anastrozole demonstrated that elimination occurs primarily via metabolism (approximately 85%) and to a lesser extent renal excretion of unchanged anastrozole (approximately 11%). Metabolism of anastrozole occurs by N-dealkylation, hydroxylation and glucuronidation. Three metabolites of anastrozole (triazole, a glucuronide conjugate of hydroxy-anastrozole, and a glucuronide conjugate of anastrozole itself) have been identified in human plasma or urine. Several minor (less than 5% of the radioactive dose) metabolites excreted in the urine have not been identified. The major metabolite of anastrozole in the circulation, triazole, lacks pharmacologic activity.

Special Populations: Geriatrics: Anastrozole pharmacokinetics have been investigated in postmenopausal female volunteers and patients with breast cancer. The pharmacokinetics were similar in volunteers and in patients and no age related effects were seen.

Race: Anastrozole pharmacokinetic differences due to race have not been studied.

Renal Insufficiency: Anastrozole pharmacokinetics have been investigated in subjects with renal insufficiency. Anastrozole renal clearance decreased proportionately with creatinine clearance and was approximately 50% lower in volunteers with severe renal impairment (creatinine clearance less than 30 mL/min/1.73 m²) compared to controls. Because renal clearance is not a significant pathway of elimination, the apparent oral clearance of anastrozole is unchanged even in severe renal impairment. Dosage adjustment in patients with renal dysfunction is not necessary (see Dosage).

Hepatic Insufficiency: Anastrozole pharmacokinetics have been investigated in subjects with stable hepatic cirrhosis related to alcohol abuse. The apparent oral clearance of anastrozole was approximately 30% lower in subjects with hepatic cirrhosis than in control subjects with normal liver function. However, plasma anastrozole concentrations in the subjects with hepatic cirrhosis are within the range of concentrations seen in normal subjects across all clinical trials. Dosage adjustment in patients with hepatic dysfunction is not necessary (see Dosage).

Drug Interactions: Anastrozole inhibits reactions catalyzed by cytochrome P_{450} 1A2, 2C8/9, and 3A4 in vitro with Ki values which are approximately 30 times higher than the mean plasma steady-state C_{max} values observed following a 1 mg daily dose. Anastrozole has no inhibitory effect on reactions catalyzed by cytochrome P_{450} 2A6 or 2D6 in vitro. Administration of a single 30 mg or multiple 10 mg doses of anastrozole to subjects had no effect on the clearance of antipyrine or urinary recovery of antipyrine metabolites. Based on these in vitro and in vivo results, it is unlikely that the administration of anastrozole 1 mg will result in clinically significant inhibition of cytochrome P_{450}-mediated metabolism of coadministered drugs.

Clinical Experience: Anastrozole was studied in 2 well-controlled clinical trials (0004, a North American study; 0005, a predominantly European study) in postmenopausal women

Arimidex (cont'd)

with advanced breast cancer who had disease progression following tamoxifen therapy. Most patients were estrogen receptor-positive; a smaller fraction was estrogen receptor-unknown or estrogen receptor-negative. Eligible patients were randomized to receive either a single daily dose of 1 or 10 mg of anastrozole, or megestrol acetate 40 mg 4 times a day. The studies were double-blinded with respect to anastrozole. Approximately 1/3 of the patients in each treatment group in both studies had either an objective response or stabilization of their disease for greater than 24 weeks. Hazard ratios for time to progression and odds ratios for response rates were calculated for the pooled studies were shown to be similar. After analysis of mature data involving 473 patients among 764 randomized participants, the hazard ratios for survival demonstrated a significant prolongation of survival in the 1 mg anastrozole group compared to hormonal treatment with megestrol acetate. See Table I.

Table I—Arimidex

Analysis of Time to Death for Patients in Trials 0004 and 0005 Combined

Time to death	Trial treatment: Anastrozole 1 mg	Anastrozole 10 mg	MA	Hazard ratio[a], (97.5% CI), and p-values[b]: Anastrozole 1 mg vs MA	Anastrozole 10 mg vs MA
Number of patients who died (%)	151 of 263 (57.4)	151 of 248 (60.9)	171 of 253 (67.6)		
2-year survival rate	56.1%	54.6%	46.3%		
Median time to death (months)	26.7	25.5	22.5	0.78 (0.6040 to 0.9996) p=0.0248[c]	0.83 (0.6452 to 1.0662) p=0.0951[c]

[a]Hazard ratio greater than 1.00 indicated that the first treatment is associated with shorter time to death than is the second treatment.
[b]The critical p-value for statistical significance is 0.025.
[c]Calculated using Cox's regression model.
Legend: CI Confidence interval.
MA Megestrol acetate.

Patients with estrogen receptor-negative disease rarely responded to anastrozole, but there were too few patients in this group for a meaningful analysis.

Indications: For hormonal treatment of metastatic breast cancer in postmenopausal women with disease progression following tamoxifen therapy. Because of its pharmacological action, patients with estrogen receptor-positive disease and patients who responded to previous anti-estrogen therapy are more likely to respond to anastrozole.

Contraindications: Patients with hypersensitivity to the drug or any of its components.

Pregnancy and *Lactation:* Anastrozole is contraindicated in pregnant or lactating women.

Warnings: Premenopausal Women: Anastrozole is not recommended for use in premenopausal women as safety and efficacy have not been established in this group of patients.

Pregnancy: There are no adequate and well-controlled studies in pregnant women using anastrozole. If the patient becomes pregnant while receiving this drug, the patient should be apprised of the potential hazard to the fetus or potential risk for loss of the pregnancy (see Contraindications).

Reproductive Toxicology: Anastrozole has been found to cross the placenta following oral administration of 0.1 mg/kg in rats and rabbits. Studies in both rats and rabbits at doses equal to or greater than 0.1 and 0.02 mg/kg/day, respectively (about ¾ and ⅓, respectively, the recommended human dose on a mg/m² basis), administered during the period of organogenesis showed that anastrozole increased pregnancy loss (increased pre- and/or postimplantation loss, increased resorption and decreased numbers of live fetuses). Effects were dose related in rats. Placental weights were significantly increased in rats at doses of 0.1 mg/kg/day or more.

Evidence of fetotoxicity, including delayed fetal development (i.e., incomplete ossification and depressed fetal body weights), was observed in rats administered doses of 1 mg/kg/day (about 7 times the recommended human dose on a mg/m² basis). There was no evidence of teratogenicity in rats administered doses up to 1 mg/kg/day. In rabbits, anastrozole caused pregnancy failure at doses equal to or greater than 1 mg/kg/day (about 16 times the recommended human dose on a mg/m² basis). There was no evidence of teratogenicity in rabbits administered 0.2 mg/kg/day (about 3 times the recommended human dose on a mg/m² basis).

Children: The safety and efficacy of anastrozole in pediatric patients have not been established.

Severe Hepatic/Renal Impairment: Anastrozole has not been investigated in patients with severe hepatic or severe renal impairment. The potential risk/benefit to such patients should be carefully considered before administration of anastrozole (see Pharmacology, Special Populations—Renal Insufficiency and Hepatic Insufficiency and Dosage).

Other: Anastrozole has not been investigated in patients with any degree of brain or leptomeningeal involvement or with pulmonary lymphangitic disseminated disease.

Precautions: General: Anastrozole should be administered under the supervision of a qualified physician experienced in the use of anti-cancer agents.

Drug Interactions: Antipyrine and cimetidine clinical interaction studies indicate that the co-administration of anastrozole with other drugs is unlikely to result in clinically significant drug interactions mediated by cytochrome P_{450} (see Pharmacology, Drug Interactions).

Drug/Laboratory Test Interactions: Anastrozole has not been observed to interfere with routine clinical laboratory tests results.

Occupational Hazards: Effect on Ability to Drive and Use Machinery: Anastrozole is unlikely to impair the ability of patients to drive and operate machinery. However, asthenia and somnolence have been reported with the use of anastrozole and caution should be observed when driving or operating machinery while such symptoms persist.

Adverse Effects: Anastrozole was generally well tolerated in two controlled clinical trials, with less than 3.3% of the anastrozole-treated patients and 4% of the megestrol acetate-treated patients withdrawing due to an adverse event.

The pharmacological action of anastrozole may give rise to certain expected effects. These include hot flushes, vaginal dryness and hair thinning. Anastrozole may also be associated with gastrointestinal disturbances (anorexia, nausea, vomiting and diarrhea), asthenia, somnolence, headache or rash.

Hepatic changes (elevated gamma-GT or less commonly alkaline phosphatase) have been reported in patients with advanced breast cancer, many of whom had liver and/or bone metastases. A causal relationship for these changes has not been established. Slight increases in total cholesterol have also been observed in clinical trials with anastrozole.

Adverse events reported in greater than 5% of the patients in any of the treatment groups in these two controlled clinical trials, regardless of causality, are presented in Table II.

Other less frequent (2 to 5%) adverse experiences reported in patients receiving anastrozole 1 mg in the 2 pivotal clinical trials are listed below. These adverse experiences are listed by body system and are in order of decreasing frequency within each body system regardless of assessed causality.

Body as a Whole: flu syndrome, fever, neck pain, malaise, accidental injury, infection.

Cardiovascular: hypertension, thrombophlebitis.

Hepatic: gamma GT increased, ALT increased, AST increased.

Hematologic: anemia, leukopenia.

Metabolic and Nutritional: alkaline phosphatase increased, weight loss.

Mean serum total cholesterol levels increased by 0.5 mmol/L among patients receiving anastrozole. Increases in LDL cholesterol have been shown to contribute to these changes.

Musculoskeletal: myalgia, arthralgia, pathological fracture.

Table II—Arimidex

Number (n) and Percentage of Patients with Adverse Event*

Adverse Event	Arimidex 1 mg (n=262) n	(%)	Arimidex 10 mg (n=246) n	(%)	Megestrol Acetate 160 mg (n=253) n	(%)
Asthenia	42	(16.0)	33	(13.4)	47	(18.6)
Nausea	41	(15.6)	48	(19.5)	28	(11.1)
Headache	34	(13.0)	44	(17.9)	24	(9.5)
Hot Flushes	32	(12.2)	29	(10.6)	21	(8.3)
Pain	28	(10.7)	38	(15.4)	29	(11.5)
Back Pain	28	(10.7)	26	(10.6)	19	(7.5)
Dyspnea	24	(9.2)	27	(11.0)	53	(20.9)
Vomiting	24	(9.2)	26	(10.6)	16	(6.3)
Cough Increased	22	(8.4)	18	(7.3)	19	(7.5)
Diarrhea	22	(8.4)	18	(7.3)	7	(2.8)
Constipation	18	(6.9)	18	(7.3)	21	(8.3)
Abdominal Pain	18	(6.9)	14	(5.7)	18	(7.1)
Anorexia	18	(6.9)	19	(7.7)	11	(4.3)
Bone Pain	17	(6.5)	26	(11.8)	19	(7.5)
Pharyngitis	16	(6.1)	23	(9.3)	15	(5.9)
Dizziness	16	(6.1)	12	(4.9)	15	(5.9)
Rash	15	(5.7)	15	(6.1)	19	(7.5)
Dry Mouth	15	(5.7)	11	(4.5)	13	(5.1)
Peripheral Edema	14	(5.3)	21	(8.5)	28	(11.1)
Pelvic Pain	14	(5.3)	17	(6.9)	13	(5.1)
Depression	14	(5.3)	6	(2.4)	5	(2.0)
Chest Pain	13	(5.0)	18	(7.3)	13	(5.1)
Paresthesia	12	(4.6)	15	(6.1)	9	(3.6)
Vaginal Hemorrhage	6	(2.3)	4	(1.6)	13	(5.1)
Weight Gain	4	(1.5)	9	(3.7)	30	(11.9)
Sweating	4	(1.5)	3	(1.2)	16	(6.3)
Increased Appetite	0	(0)	1	(0.4)	13	(5.1)

*A patient may have more than 1 adverse event.

Nervous: somnolence, confusion, insomnia, anxiety, nervousness.

Respiratory: sinusitis, bronchitis, rhinitis.

Skin and Appendages: hair thinning, pruritus.

Urogenital: urinary tract infection, breast pain.

The incidence of the following adverse event groups, potentially causally related to one or both of the therapies because of their pharmacology, were statistically analyzed: weight gain, edema, thromboembolic disease, gastrointestinal disturbance, hot flushes and vaginal dryness. These 6 groups, and the adverse events captured in the groups, were prospectively defined. The results are shown in Table III.

Table III—Arimidex

Number (n) and Percentage of Patients

Adverse Event Group	Arimidex 1 mg (n=262) n	(%)	Arimidex 10 mg (n=246) n	(%)	Megestrol Acetate 160 mg (n=253) n	(%)
Gastrointestinal Disturbance	77	(29.4)	81	(32.9)	54	(21.3)
Hot Flushes	33	(12.6)	29	(11.8)	35	(13.8)
Edema	19	(7.3)	28	(11.4)	35	(13.8)
Thromboembolic Disease	9	(3.4)	4	(1.6)	12	(4.7)
Vaginal Dryness	5	(1.9)	3	(1.2)	2	(0.8)
Weight Gain	4	(1.5)	10	(4.1)	30	(11.9)

More patients treated with megestrol acetate reported weight gain as an adverse event compared to patients treated with anastrozole 1 mg ($p<0.0001$). Other differences were not statistically significant.

An examination of the magnitude of change in weight in all patients was also conducted. Thirty-four percent (87/253) of the patients treated with megestrol acetate experienced weight gain of 5% or more and 11% (27/253) of the patients treated with megestrol acetate experienced weight gain of 10% or more. Among patients treated with anastrozole 1 mg, 13% (33/262) experienced weight gain of 5% or more and 3% (6/262) experienced weight gain of 10% or more. On average, this 5 to 10% weight gain represented between 6 and 12 pounds.

No patients receiving anastrozole or megestrol acetate discontinued treatment due to drug-related weight gain.
Postmarketing Fxperience: Vaginal bleeding has been reported infrequently, mainly in patients during the first few weeks after changing from existing hormonal therapy to treatment with anastrozole. If bleeding persists, further evaluation should be considered.

Overdose: Symptoms and Treatment: There is no clinical experience of accidental overdosage. In animal studies, anastrozole demonstrated low acute toxicity. Clinical trials have been conducted with various dosages of anastrozole, up to 60 mg in a single dose given to healthy male volunteers and up to 10 mg daily given to postmenopausal women with advanced breast cancer; these dosages were well tolerated. A single dose of anastrozole that results in life-threatening symptoms has not been established.

There is no specific antidote to overdosage and treatment must be symptomatic. In the management of an overdose, consideration should be given to the possibility that multiple agents may have been taken. Vomiting may be induced if the patient is alert. Dialysis may be helpful because anastrozole is not highly protein bound. General supportive care, including frequent monitoring of vital signs and close observation of the patient, is indicated.

Dosage: Anastrozole should be administered 1 mg orally, once a day. **Concomitant administration of steroid therapy is not necessary.**
Patients with Hepatic Impairment: Although the apparent oral clearance of anastrozole was decreased in subjects with cirrhosis due to alcohol abuse, plasma anastrozole concentrations remained within the range seen across all clinical trials in subjects without liver disease. Therefore, no changes in dose are recommended for patients with mild-to-moderate hepatic impairment, although patients should be monitored for side effects. Anastrozole has not been studied in patients with severe hepatic impairment (see Pharmacology, Special Populations—Hepatic Insufficiency).
Patients with Renal Impairment: No changes in dose are necessary for patients with renal impairment (see Pharmacology, Special Populations—Renal Insufficiency).

Information for the Patient: See Blue Section—Information for the Patient "Arimidex".

Supplied: Each white, biconvex, film-coated tablet, intagliated with "Adx 1" on one side and a logo on the other side ("A" for Arimidex), contains: anastrozole 1 mg. Nonmedicinal ingredients: lactose, macrogol 300, magnesium stearate, methylhydroxypropylcellulose, polyvidone, sodium starch glycolate and titanium dioxide. Calendar packs of 30. Store at room temperature (15 to 30°C).

(Shown in Product Recognition Section)

Reviewed 1998

ARISTOCORT® Parenteral

Stiefel/Glades

Triamcinolone Diacetate

Corticosteroid

Indications: Intralesional Injection: For intralesional or sublesional use in local therapy of various skin diseases, e.g. psoriasis, alopecia areata, neurodermatitis, atopic dermatitis, acne, synovial and sebaceous cysts, pruritus ani, contact and nummular dermatoses. Not for i.v. use.
Forte Parenteral: For i.m., intrasynovial or intra-articular injection. Not for i.v. use. May be used in the treatment of asthma, allergies, ulcerative colitis, collagen diseases, and various dermatoses including psoriasis, contact dermatitis and urticaria. Also in the treatment of rheumatoid arthritis, bursitis, fibromyositis, peritendinitis, intermittent hydrarthrosis, epicondylitis, and related conditions, and may be used in any accessible joint except the intervertebrals.

Contraindications: See Aristospan. Local contraindications for the use of intrarectal steroids, include obstruction, abscess, perforation, peritonitis, extensive fistulas and sinus tracts. It must be remembered that infected joints should not be injected with corticosteroids.

Precautions: See Aristospan. Strict asepsis should be observed since exacerbation of symptoms of flare-up from septic joint have been reported in the literature following intra-articular administration. Should this condition develop it should receive early and adequate treatment. Unstable joints should not be injected. X-ray follow up is suggested in selected cases to detect deterioration. During rectal administration, caution should be exercised in patients with severe ulcerative disease because these individuals are predisposed to perforation of the bowel wall.

Adverse Effects: See Aristospan. Rare cases of anaphylactoid reactions have been reported following parenteral triamcinolone therapy. Appropriate precautions are advised. Flushing of the face may occur but it is not considered serious. In contrast to euphoria seen with other glucocorticoids, a mild depression may occur. Occasional patients manifest reversible weakness or atrophy of the quadriceps or gastrocnemius muscle groups when on large doses. The development of myopathy has been demonstrated by electromyographic abnormalities and biopsy findings. The effect may be reversed by discontinuation of the drug.

A "side effect" sometimes observed with intralesional or sublesional or i.m. use is a local loss of tissue substance or depression of the treated area called "atrophy" by some physicians. In this condition the injected site appears thinned out and is shiny. In certain conditions, keloids for example, atrophy and sloughing of tissue may be a desirable "complication". Administration of smaller amounts of the drug should lessen this effect. Changes in pigmentation and a papule at the injection site may occur. Injection given too deeply or in doses greater than 75 mg per week may lead to systemic manifestations.

For the first few hours following intrasynovial or intra-articular injection there may be local discomfort in the joint but this is usually rapidly followed by effective relief of pain and improvement of local function.

Dosage: Parenteral-Intralesional: Intra-articular or intrasynovial, 5 to 40 mg. Intralesional, from 5 mg divided over several locations in small lesions up to 50 mg total in large psoriatic plaques. May also be used to replace or supplement oral therapy. In general, a single parenteral dose 4 to 7 times the oral daily dose may be expected to control the patient from 4 to 7 days up to 3 to 4 weeks.
Forte Parenteral: I.M.: 40 mg once a week. Single doses over 80 mg are seldom indicated. Intra-articular and intrasynovial, 5 to 40 mg every 1 to 8 weeks.

Supplied: Parenteral-Intralesional: Each mL contains: triamcinolone diacetate 25 mg suspended in a vehicle of polysorbate 80 USP 0.2%, polyethylene glycol 4 000 USP 3%, sodium chloride 0.85%, benzyl alcohol 0.9%, water for injection q.s. to 100%, hydrochloric acid to pH 6. Vials of 5 mL.

Forte Parenteral: Each mL contains: triamcinolone diacetate 40 mg suspended in a vehicle of polysorbate 80 USP 0.2%, polyethylene glycol 4 000 USP 3%, sodium chloride 0.85%, benzyl alcohol 0.9%, water for injection q.s. to 100%, hydrochloric acid to pH 6. Vials of 5 mL. Boxes of 5.

ARISTOCORT® Tablets

Stiefel/Glades

Triamcinolone

Corticosteroid

Indications: Endocrine Disorders: Primary or secondary adrenocortical insufficiency (hydrocortisone or cortisone are the drugs of choice although synthetic analogs may be used in conjunction with mineralocorticoids where applicable; mineralocorticoid supplementation is of particular importance when treating this condition in infants); nonsuppurative thyroiditis; hypercalcemia associated with cancer.
Rheumatic Disorders: As adjunctive therapy for short-term administration (to tide the patient over an acute episode or exacerbation) in psoriatic arthritis; rheumatoid arthritis (selected cases may require low dose maintenance therapy); ankylosing spondylitis; acute and subacute bursitis; acute nonspecific tenosynovitis; and acute gouty arthritis, synovitis of osteoarthritis, epicondylitis.
Collagen Diseases: for use during an exacerbation or as maintenance therapy in selected cases of systemic lupus erythematosus and acute rheumatic carditis.
Dermatologic Diseases: pemphigus, bullous dermatitis herpetiformis, severe erythema multiforme (Stevens-Johnson syndrome), exfoliative dermatitis, mycosis fungoides, and severe psoriasis. Severe seborrheic dermatitis.
Allergic States: control of seasonal or perennial allergic rhinitis, bronchial asthma, contact dermatitis, atopic dermatitis, serum sickness, drug hypersensitivity reactions and urticaria when they are severe or incapacitating, and intractable to adequate trials of conventional treatment.
Ophthalmic Diseases: severe acute and chronic allergic and inflammatory processes involving the eye and its associated anatomic parts such as allergic conjunctivitis, keratitis, allergic corneal marginal ulcers, herpes zoster ophthalmicus, iritis and iridocyclitis, chorioretinitis, anterior segment inflammation, diffuse posterior uveitis and choroiditis, optic neuritis, and sympathetic ophthalmia.
Respiratory Diseases: symptomatic sarcoidosis, Löffler's syndrome not manageable by other means, berylliosis, fulminating or disseminated pulmonary tuberculosis when concurrently accompanied by appropriate antituberculous chemotherapy, aspiration pneumonitis.
Hematologic Disorders: idiopathic and secondary thrombocytopenia in adults, acquired (autoimmune) hemolytic anemia, erythroblastopenia (RBC anemia), and congenital (erythroid) hypoplastic anemia.
Neoplastic Diseases: palliative management of leukemias and lymphomas in adults and acute leukemia of childhood.
Edematous States: to induce a diuresis or remission of proteinuria in the nephrotic syndrome (nonuremic, the idiopathic type, or that which is due to lupus erythematosus) and, in conjunction with diuretic agents, to induce a diuresis in refractory congestive heart failure and in cirrhosis of the liver with refractory ascites.
Gastrointestinal Diseases: to tide the patient over a critical period of the disease in ulcerative colitis, regional enteritis.
Nervous System: exacerbations of multiple sclerosis.
Miscellaneous: Tuberculous meningitis with subarachnoid block or impending block when concurrently accompanied by appropriate antituberculous chemotherapy. Trichinosis with neurologic or myocardial involvement.

Contraindications: Acute psychosis; ocular herpes simplex, fungal or viral infections for which adequate anti-infective therapy is lacking; untreated acute or chronic infection, including tuberculosis.

Precautions: When patients who are receiving corticosteroid therapy are subjected to unusual stress (trauma, surgery or severe illness), increased dosage of rapidly acting corticosteroids is indicated before, during and after the stressful situation.

Corticosteroids may mask some signs of infection, and new infections may appear during their use. There may be decreased resistance and inability to localize infection when corticosteroids are used. If an infection occurs during corticosteroid therapy, it should be promptly controlled by suitable antimicrobial therapy.

Pregnancy: Weigh the potential hazards of corticosteroid therapy to the embryo or fetus carefully against possible benefits when using the drug during pregnancy. The observation of fetal abnormalities in experimental animals indicates a potential hazard during the first trimester. If corticosteroids were given during pregnancy, watch the newborn infant closely for signs of hypoadrenalism and institute appropriate therapy if such signs are present.

Do not vaccinate patients receiving corticosteroids against smallpox. Avoid other immunization procedures because of the possible hazards of neurological complication and lack of antibody response.

If corticosteroids are indicated in patients with latent tuberculosis or tuberculin reactivity, close observation is necessary as reactivation of the disease may occur. During prolonged corticosteroid therapy, these patients should receive chemoprophylaxis. The employment of triamcinolone may be a life-saving measure to control the acute toxicity associated with overwhelming tuberculous infection. Its use must be accompanied by appropriate, specific antituberculous therapy. Triamcinolone should not be used to alleviate joint pain arising from infectious states such as gonococcal or tuberculous arthritis.

If corticosteroids are considered for use in the following conditions, weigh the risks carefully against possible benefits: myasthenia gravis, metastatic carcinoma, diverticulitis, fresh intestinal anastomoses, active or latent peptic ulcer, hypertension, Cushing's syndrome, renal insufficiency, chronic nephritis, thromboembolic tendencies, thrombophlebitis, osteoporosis, diabetes mellitus and psychotic tendencies.

Systemic steroid administration for prolonged periods may produce posterior subcapsular cataracts, glaucoma with possible damage to the optic nerve or may enhance the establishment of secondary ocular infection due to fungi and viruses.

Average and large doses of hydrocortisone or cortisone can cause elevation of blood pressure, salt and water retention, and increased potassium excretion. These effects are less likely to occur with the synthetic derivatives except when they are used in large doses; dietary salt restriction and potassium supplementation may be necessary. Edema may occur in the presence of renal disease with a fixed or decreased glomerular filtration rate. All corticosteroids increase calcium excretion.

Triamcinolone should be administered only with full knowledge of characteristic activity of, and varied responses to,

Aristocort Tablets (cont'd)

adrenocortical hormones. Use corticosteroids under close clinical supervision.

Unlike other corticosteroids, triamcinolone and its derivatives do not stimulate the appetite. During prolonged therapy, a liberal protein intake is essential, and administration of anabolic steroids may be useful for counteracting the tendency to gradual weight loss, sometimes associated with negative nitrogen balance and wasting or weakness of skeletal muscles.

There is an enhanced corticosteroid effect in patients with hyperthyroidism and in those with cirrhosis of the liver. Corticosteroids should be used only with caution in patients with acute glomerulonephritis, convulsive disorders and congestive heart failure.

Exercise caution when using ASA in conjunction with corticosteroids in hypoprothrombinemia.

When bacterial infections are present, corticosteroid therapy is not recommended but may be employed with caution and only in conjunction with appropriate antibiotic or chemotherapeutic medication. Corticosteroids may mask signs of infection and enhance dissemination of the infecting organism. Hence, all patients receiving corticosteroids should be watched for evidence of intercurrent infection. Should infection occur, initiate vigorous, appropriate anti-infective therapy. If possible, avoid abrupt cessation of steroids because of the danger of superimposing adrenocortical insufficiency on the infectious process.

Psychic derangements may appear when corticosteroids are used. These may range from euphoria, insomnia, mood swings, personality changes, and severe depression, to frank psychotic manifestations. Existing emotional instability or psychotic tendencies may also be aggravated by corticosteroids.

Use corticosteroids cautiously in patients with nonspecific ulcerative colitis if there is a probability of impending perforation, abscess, or other pyogenic infection.

Glucocorticoids may aggravate diabetes, so that higher dosages of insulin or oral hypoglycemic agents may become necessary; or, steroid therapy may precipitate the manifestations of latent diabetes mellitus.

The use of steroids in myasthenia gravis may aggravate myasthenic symptoms and should, therefore, be given with proper precautions.

In peptic ulcer, recurrence may be asymptomatic until perforation or hemorrhage occurs. Long-term adrenocorticoid therapy may evoke hyperacidity or peptic ulcer; therefore, as a prophylactic measure, an ulcer regimen and the administration of an antacid are highly recommended. Take x-rays in peptic ulcer patients complaining of gastric distress or when therapy is prolonged. Whether or not changes are observed, an ulcer regimen is recommended.

With corticosteroids, consider the possibility of other severe reactions, including anaphylactoid reactions. Take precautionary measures prior to administration, especially with patients having a history of drug allergy.

Reductions or discontinuation of dosage should be gradual. Continued supervision of the patient after termination of steroid therapy is essential, since there may be a sudden reappearance of severe manifestations of the disease for which the patient was treated. Relative adrenocortical insufficiency may persist for months after cessation of therapy; therefore, in any stress situation reinstitute hormone therapy. Since mineralocorticoid secretion may be impaired in such cases, administer salt and/or a mineralocorticoid concurrently.

Growth and development of children should be carefully followed due to the possibility of growth suppression after prolonged therapy.

Menstrual irregularities may occur, and this possibility should be mentioned to female patients past menarche.

Use the lowest possible corticosteroid dose to control the condition being treated. A gradual dosage reduction should be made when possible.

Advise patients to inform subsequent physicians of the prior use of corticosteroids.

Adverse Effects: Watch patients receiving triamcinolone closely for the following adverse effects which may be associated with any corticosteroid therapy:

Fluid and Electrolyte Disturbances: sodium retention, fluid retention, congestive heart failure in susceptible patients, potassium loss, cardiac arrhythmias or ECG changes due to potassium deficiency, hypokalemic alkalosis, hypertension.

Musculoskeletal: muscle weakness, fatigue, steroid myopathy, loss of muscle mass, osteoporosis, vertebral compression fractures, delayed healing of fractures, aspectic necrosis of femoral and humeral heads, pathologic fractures of long bones, spontaneous fractures.

Gastrointestinal: peptic ulcer with possible subsequent perforation and hemorrhage, pancreatitis, abdominal distention, ulcerative esophagitis.

Dermatologic: impaired wound healing, thin fragile skin, petechiae and ecchymoses, facial erythema, increased sweating, purpura, striae, hirsutism, acneiform eruptions, lupus erythematosus like lesions, suppressed reactions to skin tests.

Neurological: convulsions, increased intracranial pressure with papilledema (pseudotumor cerebri) usually after treatment, vertigo, headache, neuritis or paresthesias, aggravation of pre-existing psychiatric conditions.

Endocrine: menstrual irregularities; development of the Cushingoid state; suppression of growth in children; secondary adrenocortical and pituitary unresponsiveness, particularly in times of stress (e.g. trauma, surgery or illness); decreased carbohydrate tolerance; manifestations of latent diabetes mellitus; increased requirements for insulin or oral hypoglycemic agents in diabetics.

Ophthalmic: posterior subcapsular cataracts, increased intraocular pressure, glaucoma, exophthalmos.

Metabolic: hyperglycemia, glycosuria, negative nitrogen balance due to protein catabolism.

Others: necrotizing angiitis, thrombophlebitis, thromboembolism, aggravation or masking of infections, insomnia, syncopal episodes, anaphylactoid reactions.

Dosage: The physician should individualize the dosage for the patient and the disease under treatment. In adults and children over 34 kg with the common diseases amenable to steroid therapy, the usual initial dose ranges from 8 to 20 mg per day divided into 3 or 4 doses. When a satisfactory response is obtained, the initial dose should be reduced gradually by decrements of 2 mg over 2 to 3 days until the smallest dose is obtained which will adequately maintain the patient. 4 mg of triamcinolone is approximately equivalent to: cortisone 25 mg, prednisolone or prednisone 5 mg, methylprednisolone 4 mg, hydrocortisone 20 mg, dexamethasone 0.75 mg, paramethasone 2 mg.

Specific Dosage Recommendations: see Table I.

Table I—Aristocort Tablets

Dosage Recommendations

Indications	Initial Suppressive	Daily Maintenance
Rheumatoid Arthritis	8 to 16 mg/day for 2 to 7 days	2 to 16 mg
Respiratory Allergies	8 to 16 mg/day to achieve control within 24 to 48 hours	
Dermatoses (Allergic and Inflammatory)	8 to 16 mg/day	1 to 2 mg
Acute Bursitis	2 to 16 mg/day	by response
Rheumatic Fever	16 to 20 mg/day	6 to 20 mg
Neoplastic Disease (Acute Leukemia and Other Lymphomatous Diseases)	Children: 1 to 2 mg/kg/day Adults: 16 to 40 mg/day	by response
Lupus Erythematosus (Disseminated)	20 to 30 mg/day	3 to 30 mg
Pulmonary Emphysema and Fibrosis	8 to 12 mg/day	2 to 4 mg
Nephrotic Syndrome	16 to 20 mg/day until diuresis occurs	Continue until full remission then gradually discontinue
Vasomotor and Allergic Rhinitis	8 to 12 mg/day	2 to 6 mg

Supplied: 2 mg: Each oblong pink, scored tablet, engraved ''LL'' and ''A2'', contains: triamcinolone 2 mg. Nonmedicinal ingredients: calcium phosphate dibasic, docusate sodium, dye D&C Red 30 Lake (talc), dye D&C Yellow 10 Al Lake, lactose, magnesium stearate, microcrystalline cellulose, sodium starch glycolate and starch. Tartrazine-free. Bottles of 100.

4 mg: Each oblong white, scored tablet, engraved ''LL'' and ''A4'', contains: triamcinolone 4 mg. Nonmedicinal ingredients: calcium phosphate dibasic, docusate sodium with sodium benzoate, lactose, magnesium stearate, microcrystalline cellulose, sodium starch glycolate and starch. Tartrazine-free. Bottles of 100.

ARISTOCORT® Topicals ℞

Stiefel/Glades

Triamcinolone Acetonide

Topical Corticosteroid

Indications: In management of certain dermatoses, e.g., atopic dermatitis, eczematous dermatitis, nummular eczema, contact dermatitis, pruritus vulvae and ani, generalized erythrodermia, external otitis, seborrheic dermatitis, eczematized psoriasis, neurodermatitis.

Contraindications: Tuberculosis of skin, fungal and viral dermal lesions, herpes simplex, chickenpox and vaccinia. Hypersensitivity to any of the components.

Warnings: *Pregnancy* and *Lactation:* The safety of topical corticosteroids during pregnancy and lactation has not been established. The potential benefit of topical corticosteroids, if used during pregnancy and lactation, should be weighed against possible hazard to the fetus or the nursing infant.

If used under an occlusive dressing, particularly over extensive areas, sufficient absorption may take place to give rise to adrenal suppression and other systemic effects.

Topical corticosteroids are not for ophthalmic use.

Precautions: Should not be used in the eyes. Although untoward effects associated with the use of topical corticosteroids are uncommon and not to be expected from ordinary use, sensitization, irritation and failure of therapeutic response have been noted in rare instances. Application to extensive areas, too frequent application, or application under occlusive dressings may result in systemic absorption with symptoms of adrenal suppression, localized atrophy and striae. If infection of the tissues is present, the use of a systemic broad spectrum antibiotic may be desirable.

Pregnancy: While topical corticosteroids have not been reported to have an adverse effect on pregnancy, the safety of their use on pregnant females, has not absolutely been established. Therefore, they should not be used extensively on pregnant patients, in large amounts or for prolonged periods of time.

Adverse Effects: The following local adverse reactions have been reported rarely with the use of topical corticosteroids: burning, itching, irritation, dryness, folliculitis, hypertrichosis, hypopigmentation.

The following may occur more frequently with occlusive dressings: maceration of the skin, secondary infection, skin atrophy, striae, miliaria, pustules, pyoderma.

Dosage: Apply in small quantities to the affected areas 3 or 4 times daily. Some cases of psoriasis and certain other refractory dermatoses may be treated more effectively by the application of triamcinolone acetonide topicals under an occlusive nonpermeable dressing such as Saran Wrap.

Supplied: Cream: Aristocort ''C'' (0.5%), concentrate, 15 g tubes; Aristocort ''R'' (0.1%), regular, 30 g tubes and 500 g jars; Aristocort ''D'' (0.025%) dilute, 30 g tubes. Nonmedicinal ingredients: benzyl alcohol, emulsifying wax, glycerin, isopropyl palmitate, lactic acid, sorbitol solution and water purified.

Ointment: Aristocort ''R'' (0.1%) regular, 30 g tubes. No preservatives. Nonmedicinal ingredients: white petrolatum.

ARISTOSPAN® ℞

Stiefel/Glades

Triamcinolone Hexacetonide

Glucocorticoid

Pharmacology: The hexacetonide ester of triamcinolone is relatively insoluble (0.0002% at 25°C in water). When injected intra-articularly it can be expected to be absorbed slowly from the injection site. The pharmacological action of triamcinolone hexacetonide is less intense and more prolonged, but qualitatively the same as triamcinolone acetonide. Triamcinolone hexacetonide's activity is ascribable to the slow release of triamcinolone acetonide through hydrolysis. Following this reaction, the pharmacology is identical to that of the parent compound, triamcinolone acetonide.

Indications: Adjunctive therapy for short-term administration in synovitis of osteoarthritis, acute and subacute bursitis, epicondylitis, post-traumatic osteoarthritis, rheumatoid arthritis, acute gouty arthritis, acute nonspecific tenosynovitis.

Since triamcinolone hexacetonide has low solubility, if a more immediate therapeutic effect is desired, then a more soluble corticosteroid should be administered locally or systemically.

Contraindications: Systemic fungal infection.

Warnings: Should not be given i.v.

Active, latent or questionably healed tuberculosis, ocular herpes simplex and acute psychosis are considered to be conditions which require caution when glucocorticoid therapy is utilized.

Pregnancy: In pregnancy, particularly during the first trimester, steroids should be considered only when the benefits outweigh the risks involved, since fetal abnormalities have been observed in experimental animals.

Steroids should be used with caution in cases of psychic disturbances, in acute glomerulonephritis, active or latent peptic ulcer, myasthenia gravis, osteoporosis, fresh intestinal anastomoses, diverticulitis, thrombophlebitis, diabetes mellitus, hyperthyroidism, acute coronary artery disease, hypertension, limited cardiac reserve or systemic infections including exanthematous diseases.

Caution regarding vaccination against smallpox and other immunization procedures is advised.

Ophthalmic complications during prolonged corticosteroid therapy have been observed. These include posterior subcapsular cataract, glaucoma and possible damage to optic nerves and enhancement of secondary ocular infections due to fungi or virus.

Calcium excretion is increased during corticosteroid therapy.

Patients should be advised to inform subsequent physicians of the prior use of corticosteroids.

Appropriate examination of any joint fluid present is necessary to avoid a septic process.

Precautions: See Aristocort monograph.

The prolonged and repeated use of glucocorticoids in weight bearing joints may result in further joint degeneration. This may be related to increased use of still diseased joints following relief of pain and other symptoms, or it may be due to inhibition by corticosteroids of protein synthesis in articular cartilage. It is inadvisable to inject unstable joints; repeated injections may, in some cases, result in instability of the joint.

Inadvertent injection into the soft tissues around the joint may lead to an increased incidence of systemic effect. As with all intra-articular injections, take care to avoid entering a blood vessel.

A marked increase in pain, accompanied by local swelling, further restriction of joint motion, fever and malaise occurring after intra-articular injection is suggestive of septic arthritis. If this complication appears and the diagnosis of sepsis is confirmed, institute antimicrobial therapy immediately and continue for at least 7 to 10 days after clinical evidence of infection has disappeared.

Avoid over distension of the joint capsule and deposition of the steroid along the needle track.

Advise patients not to overuse treated joints in which symptomatic benefit has been obtained as long as the inflammatory process remains active.

Adverse Effects: Systemic effects have occurred infrequently with triamcinolone hexacetonide, but, nevertheless, the patient should be observed for the following:

Specific triamcinolone effects: Certain systemic effects may occur that do not occur or may occur less frequently with other corticosteroids. These include:

A depression of appetite, in contrast to voracious appetite ordinarily encountered with other glucocorticoids.

Most common corticosteroids may cause euphoria whereas triamcinolone may cause a mood depression.

Common glucocorticoids cause sodium retention and edema, but triamcinolone may produce a mild early diuresis, making edema uncommon.

A myopathy with muscle weakness involving the muscles of the thighs, pelvis and lower back may occur more frequently with triamcinolone than with other corticosteroids.

Calcium excretion is increased during corticosteroid therapy.

Since systemic absorption may occasionally occur with intra-articular administration, watch patients closely for adverse reactions which may be associated with any corticosteroid therapy (see Aristocort monograph).

Intra-articular corticosteroid administration may produce an exacerbation of symptoms or "flare-up" following injection. Local atrophy, Charcot-like arthropathy, burning, flushing, pain and swelling may occur. Blindness associated with therapy around the face and head have been reported following intra-articular corticosteroid administration.

Dosage: Not for i.v. use. Strict aseptic administration technique is mandatory. Topical ethyl chloride spray may be used locally before injection.

Before each use gently agitate the vial to achieve a uniform suspension. A small bore needle (25 to 26 gauge) may be used for administration.

Average intra-articular dose is 2 to 20 mg. Dosage is dependent on the size of the joint to be injected, the degree of inflammation and the amount of fluid present. In general, large joints (such as knee, hip, shoulder) require 10 to 20 mg. For small joints (such as interphalangeal, metacarpophalangeal) 2 to 6 mg may be employed. When the amount of synovial fluid is increased, aspiration may be performed before administering Aristospan. Subsequent dosage and frequency of injections can best be judged by clinical response.

The usual frequency of injection into a single joint is every 3 or 4 weeks, and injection more frequently than that is generally not advisable. To avoid possible joint destruction from repeated use of intra-articular corticosteroids, injection should be as infrequent as possible, consistent with adequate patient care. Avoid deposition of drug along the needle path, which might produce atrophy.

Supplied: Each mL of suspension contains: micronized triamcinolone hexacetonide 20 mg, polysorbate 80 USP 0.4% w/v, sorbitol solution USP 50% v/v and water for injection q.s. Preserved with benzyl alcohol 0.9% w/v. Tartrazine-free. Vials of 1 and 5 mL.

ARLIDIN® Ⓟ
ARLIDIN® FORTE Ⓟ
Rhône-Poulenc Rorer

Nylidrin HCl

Peripheral Vasodilator—Organic Brain Syndrome Therapy

Pharmacology: Nylidrin acts predominantly by beta receptor stimulation. It has been shown to dilate arterioles in skeletal muscle and to increase cardiac output. An increase in cerebral blood flow and a decrease in vascular resistance has also been reported. The result of this combination of actions is a greater blood supply to ischemic tissues, with usually minimal change in blood pressure.

The mechanism whereby nylidrin may provide relief of selected symptoms in some elderly patients with organic brain disorders is not known.

Indications: May be of benefit in elderly patients with mild to moderate symptoms that are commonly associated with organic mental disorders. Short-term (3-month duration) and long-term (12-month duration) clinical studies have demonstrated a modest improvement in ability to perform general activities of daily living, self care and in a capability for social interactions.

Although the patients appeared to be less confused, more alert, and more aware of their surroundings, an objective improvement in cognitive function has not been quantitatively determined.

Nylidrin has been shown to be of possible benefit in peripheral vascular disorders. It increases walking ability and promotes healing of trophic ulcers associated with: arteriosclerosis obliterans, thromboangiitis obliterans (Buerger's disease), diabetic vascular disease, night leg cramp, Raynaud's phenomenon, ischemic ulcers, frost bite, thrombophlebitis.

While improvement does occur in advanced cases, experience has shown that the better the condition of the vascular bed the greater the degree of early therapeutic benefit.

Contraindications: Acute myocardial infarctions, paroxysmal tachycardia, progressive angina pectoris, thyrotoxicosis.

Warnings: Nylidrin should not be initiated before a careful diagnosis of chronic organic brain syndrome or organic mental disorder is established since it is essential to identify the many treatable or reversible conditions or mental changes in those patients that will benefit from specific therapy.

Among the most common causes of reversible or treatable organic mental disorders are drug induced mental changes and those due to alcohol, metabolic imbalances, nutritional deficiencies, hepatic cardiovascular and pulmonary conditions, trauma, tumors and particularly depressive and other emotional disorders.

Nylidrin is not indicated in the management of normal aging or of patients with presenile dementia (Alzheimer's Disease).

Precautions: *Pregnancy* and *Lactation:* Safety during pregnancy and lactation has not been established; therefore, it should not be administered to women of child bearing potential unless the expected benefit to the patient outweighs the potential hazard to the fetus.

In patients with cardiac disease such as tachyarrhythmias and uncompensated congestive heart failure the benefit to risk ratio should be weighed prior to therapy and reassessed periodically during treatment.

Adverse Effects: Trembling, nervousness, weakness, dizziness (not associated with labyrinthine artery insufficiency), palpitations, nausea and vomiting may occur. Postural hypotension and allergic manifestations may also occur.

Overdose: Symptoms: Transient headache, flushing, shortness of breath, palpitation, or increased cardiac awareness, sinus tachycardia, transient loss of diastolic pressure and transient non radiating chest pain.

Treatment: Administer a mild sedative or beta blocking drug titrated against cardiovascular response.

Dosage: Relief of manifestations of peripheral vascular disorders: 12 to 48 mg/day in 3 to 4 divided doses.

Relief of selected symptoms in patients with organic mental disorders: 12 to 24 mg/day in 3 to 4 divided doses.

Supplied: Arlidin: Each white, round, biconvex tablet, imprinted with "A" in shield on one side and bisected and marked with RPR on the other side, contains: nylidrin HCl 6 mg Nonmedicinal ingredients: cellulose, cornstarch, gelatin, lactose, magnesium stearate and pregelatinized starch. Tartrazine-free. Bottles of 100.

Arlidin Forte: Each white, round, biconvex tablet, imprinted with "A" in shield on one side and bisected and marked with RPR on the other side, contains: nylidrin HCl 12 mg Nonmedicinal ingredients: cellulose, cornstarch, gelatin, lactose, magnesium stearate and pregelatinized starch. Tartrazine-free. Bottles of 100.

(Shown in Product Recognition Section)

ARTHROTEC® Ⓟ
Searle

Diclofenac Sodium—Misoprostol

Anti-inflammatory—Analgesic—Mucosal Protective Agent

Pharmacology: Arthrotec is a combination of a nonsteroidal anti-inflammatory drug (NSAID) with analgesic properties and a mucosal protective synthetic analog of prostaglandin E_1.

Arthrotec has been shown to be as effective as diclofenac in reducing the signs and symptoms of rheumatoid arthritis and osteoarthritis. In addition, Arthrotec has been associated with a lower incidence of gastroduodenal erosions and ulcers than diclofenac.

Diclofenac inhibits prostaglandin synthesis by interfering with the action of prostaglandin synthetase. This inhibitory effect may partially explain its actions, both therapeutic and adverse. From a clinical efficacy standpoint, diclofenac (150 mg daily) is similar in activity to equivalent dosages of 3.6 to 4.8 g daily of ASA. Diclofenac is similar in activity to equivalent dosages of indomethacin (75 to 150 mg daily). Although diclofenac does not alter the course of the underlying disease, it has been found to relieve pain, reduce fever, swelling and tenderness, and increase mobility in patients with rheumatic disorders of the types listed under Indications.

Studies in healthy subjects indicate that misoprostol enhances several of the factors implicated in maintaining gastroduodenal mucosal integrity. Misoprostol has been shown to inhibit both basal and stimulated gastric acid secretion. In addition, increases in gastric mucosal blood flow, duodenal bicarbonate secretion and gastric mucus secretion have all been observed following treatment with misoprostol. The ability of misoprostol to protect the gastric and duodenal mucosa has been confirmed in studies in both healthy subjects and patients with rheumatoid arthritis or osteoarthritis. Endoscopic examination and measurement of fecal blood loss have shown that coadministration of misoprostol prevents mucosal injury induced by a variety of NSAIDs, including, ASA, ibuprofen, piroxicam, naproxen, tolmetin and diclofenac.

Pharmacokinetics: Following administration of a single dose of Arthrotec 50 to 36 healthy male subjects, the mean Cmax, AUC (0 to 24) and Tmax for diclofenac were 1.13 μg/mL, 1.63 μg·h/mL and 3.9 h, respectively, while the mean Cmax, AUC (0 to 4) and Tmax for the principal active metabolite of misoprostol (misoprostol acid) were 136 pg/mL, 238 pg·h/mL and 0.87 h, respectively.

Following a single dose of Arthrotec 75 to 35 healthy male and female subjects, the mean Cmax, AUC (0 to 12) and Tmax for diclofenac were 2.03 μg/mL, 2.77 μg·h/mL and 1.96 h,

Arthrotec (cont'd)

respectively. The mean Cmax, AUC (0 to 4) and Tmax for the principal metabolite of misoprostol (misoprostol acid) were 304 pg/mL, 177 pg·h/mL and 0.26 h, respectively.

Orally administered diclofenac is rapidly and almost completely absorbed. Forty to 60% of the drug and its metabolites are eliminated in the urine and the balance in the bile.

Orally administered misoprostol is also rapidly and extensively absorbed, and undergoes rapid metabolism to misoprostol acid, which is thereafter quickly eliminated (elimination half-life of approximately 30 minutes). Approximately 70% of the dose is excreted in the urine, mainly as biologically inactive metabolites.

Influence of Food: With Arthrotec the effect of food on the bioavailability of the diclofenac and misoprostol components is similar to that reported for the individual drugs. The times of peak concentration (Tmax) for diclofenac and misoprostol are prolonged by approximately 50 and 100% respectively, while the peak concentrations (Cmax) are decreased by about 25% for diclofenac and 50% for misoprostol: the AUC for diclofenac is decreased by approximately 60%, while that of misoprostol is increased by about 25%.

Clinical Use: In 2 multicentre, double-blind, controlled clinical trials of 12 weeks duration involving a total of 346 and 339 patients respectively, patient global assessments of the arthritic condition revealed no statistically significant differences between Arthrotec 50 and a fixed-combination of diclofenac/placebo.

In 2 multicentre, double-blind, controlled trials of 4 weeks duration in 455 and 361 patients with osteoarthritis, patient global assessments of the arthritic condition revealed no overall differences between Arthrotec 50 and diclofenac/placebo.

A multicentre, double-blind, controlled trial of 6 weeks duration involving a total of 572 patients (154 in the diclofenac group, 152 in the Arthrotec 50 group, 175 in the Arthrotec 75 group and 91 in the placebo group) showed that Arthrotec 50 three times daily and Arthrotec 75 twice daily were equivalent to diclofenac/placebo in relieving the signs and symptoms of osteoarthritis.

A multicentre, double-blind, controlled trial of 12 weeks duration involving a total of 380 patients (107 in the diclofenac group, 107 in the Arthrotec 50 group, 111 in the Arthrotec 75 group and 55 in the placebo group) showed that Arthrotec 50 three times daily and Arthrotec 75 twice daily were equivalent to diclofenac/placebo in relieving the signs and symptoms of rheumatoid arthritis.

Misoprostol has been compared to placebo in the prevention of clinically significant and serious gastrointestinal events associated with NSAID use. In a 6-month, double-blind study of 8 843 patients (4 404 in the misoprostol group, 4 439 in the placebo group, mean age 68 years) with rheumatoid arthritis, misoprostol significantly reduced the incidence of serious complications, such as gastrointestinal bleeding and ulcer perforation, by 40 to 50%.

Arthrotec is associated with a low incidence of gastroduodenal lesions relative to diclofenac/placebo.

Indications: For acute and chronic use in the relief of the signs and symptoms of rheumatoid arthritis and osteoarthritis.

Contraindications: The contraindications of Arthrotec are those of the components of the product.

Diclofenac is contraindicated in the following conditions: active peptic ulcer, a history of recurrent ulceration or active inflammatory disease of the gastrointestinal system.

Known or suspected hypersensitivity to the drug or other nonsteroidal anti-inflammatory drugs (NSAIDs). The potential for cross-reactivity between different NSAIDs must be kept in mind. Diclofenac should not be used in patients in whom asthma, anaphylaxis, urticaria, rhinitis or other allergic manifestations are precipitated by ASA or other nonsteroidal anti-inflammatory agents. Fatal anaphylactoid reactions have occurred in such individuals. As well, individuals with the above medical problems are at risk of a severe reaction even if they have taken NSAIDs in the past without any adverse effects.

Significant hepatic impairment or active liver disease.

Severely impaired or deteriorating renal function (creatinine clearance <30 mL/min). Individuals with lesser degrees of renal impairment are at risk of deterioration of their renal function when prescribed NSAIDs and must be monitored.

Diclofenac is not recommended for use with other NSAIDs because of the absence of any evidence demonstrating synergistic benefits and the potential for additive side effects.

Pregnancy: Arthrotec is contraindicated in pregnancy. Women should be advised not to become pregnant while taking Arthrotec. If pregnancy is suspected, use of the product should be discontinued, and the pregnancy followed closely.

Warnings: Gastrointestinal: The presence of misoprostol in the product may protect against the mucosal damaging effects of the other component, diclofenac.

However, serious gastrointestinal toxicity, such as peptic ulceration, perforation and gastrointestinal bleeding, **sometimes severe and occasionally fatal** can occur at any time, with or without symptoms in patients treated with NSAIDs including diclofenac.

Minor upper gastrointestinal problems, such as dyspepsia, are common, usually developing early in therapy. Physicians should remain alert for ulceration and bleeding in patients treated with NSAIDs, even in the absence of previous gastrointestinal tract symptoms.

In clinical trials, 3 549 arthritic patients have been treated with Arthrotec, 506 of whom received Arthrotec for more than 1 year. A total of 285 patients have been treated with Arthrotec 75 in clinical trials for a duration of up to 12 weeks.

In patients observed in clinical trials with Arthrotec, upper gastrointestinal ulcers occurred as follows: See Table I.

Table I—Arthrotec

Occurrence of Gastrointestinal Ulcers

	A50 b.i.d. N=391	A50 t.i.d. N=692	A50 b.i.d./t.i.d. N=750	D50 b.i.d./t.i.d. N=754	A75 b.i.d. N=285	D75 b.i.d. N=260
upper gastrointestinal ulcers	0.8	1.8	0.8	2.1	3.9	9.6

Diclofenac should be given under close medical supervision to patients prone to gastrointestinal tract irritation, particularly those with a history of peptic ulcer; diverticulosis or other inflammatory disease of the gastrointestinal tract such as ulcerative colitis and Crohn's disease. In these cases the physician must weigh the benefits of treatment against the possible hazards.

Physicians should inform patients about the signs and/or symptoms of serious gastrointestinal toxicity and instruct them to contact a physician immediately if they experience persistent dyspepsia or other symptoms or signs suggestive of gastrointestinal ulceration or bleeding.

Because serious gastrointestinal tract ulceration and bleeding can occur without warning symptoms, physicians should follow chronically treated patients by checking their hemoglobin periodically and by being vigilant for the signs and symptoms of ulceration and bleeding and should inform the patients of the importance of this followup.

If ulceration is suspected or confirmed, or if gastrointestinal bleeding occurs, Arthrotec should be discontinued immediately, appropriate treatment instituted and the patient monitored closely.

No studies, to date, have identified any group of patients **not** at risk of developing ulceration and bleeding. A prior history of serious gastrointestinal events and other factors such as excess alcohol intake, smoking, age, female gender and concomitant oral steroid and anticoagulant use have been associated with increased risk.

Studies to date show that all NSAIDs can cause gastrointestinal tract adverse events. Although existing data does not clearly identify differences in risk between various NSAIDs, this may be shown in the future.

Geriatrics: Patients older than 65 years and frail or debilitated patients are most susceptible to a variety of adverse reactions from NSAIDs, their incidence increases with dose and duration of treatment. In addition, these patients are less tolerant of ulceration and bleeding, and most reports of fatal gastrointestinal events are in this population. Older patients are also at risk of lower esophageal ulceration and bleeding.

For such patients, consideration should be given to a starting dose lower than usual, with individual adjustment when necessary and under close supervision.

Cross Sensitivity: Patients sensitive to one of the nonsteroidal anti-inflammatory drugs may be sensitive to any of the other NSAIDs also.

Aseptic Meningitis: In occasional cases, with some NSAIDs, the symptoms of aseptic meningitis (stiff neck, severe headaches, nausea and vomiting, fever or clouding of consciousness) have been observed. Patients with autoimmune disorders (systemic lupus erythematosus, mixed connective tissues diseases, etc.) seem to be predisposed. Therefore, in such patients, the physician must weigh the benefits of therapy against the possible hazards before prescribing and must be vigilant to the development of this complication.

Lactation: It is not recommended that Arthrotec be administered to nursing mothers. Diclofenac has been found in human milk. It is unlikely that misoprostol is secreted in human milk since it is rapidly metabolized throughout the body. It is not known if the active metabolite of misoprostol (misoprostol acid) is secreted in human milk. However, the potential presence of misoprostol acid in human milk could cause diarrhea in nursing infants.

Women of Childbearing Potential: Arthrotec should not be used in women of childbearing potential unless they use effective contraception (i.e., oral contraceptives or intrauterine devices) and have been advised of the risks of taking Arthrotec if pregnant.

Children: The safety and effectiveness of Arthrotec in children below the age of 18 years have not been established.

Precautions: Renal Function: As with other NSAIDs, long-term administration of diclofenac to animals has resulted in renal papillary necrosis and other abnormal renal pathology. In humans, there have been reports of acute interstitial nephritis with hematuria, proteinuria, and occasionally nephrotic syndrome.

A second form of renal toxicity has been seen in patients with prerenal conditions leading to the reduction in renal blood flow or blood volume, where the renal prostaglandins have a supportive role in the maintenance of renal perfusion. In these patients, administration of an NSAID may cause a dose dependent reduction in prostaglandin formation and may precipitate overt renal decompensation. Patients at greatest risk of this reaction are those with impaired renal function, heart failure, liver dysfunction, those taking diuretics, and the elderly. Discontinuation of nonsteroidal anti-inflammatory therapy is usually followed by recovery to the pretreatment state.

Diclofenac and its metabolites are eliminated primarily by the kidneys, therefore the drug should be used with great caution in patients with impaired renal function. In these cases, lower dose of diclofenac should be anticipated and patients carefully monitored.

During long-term therapy kidney function should be monitored periodically.

Genitourinary Tract: Some NSAIDs are known to cause persistent urinary symptoms (bladder pain, dysuria, urinary frequency) hematuria or cystitis. The onset of these symptoms may occur at any time after the initiation of therapy with an NSAID. Some cases have become severe on continued treatment. Should urinary symptoms occur, treatment with Arthrotec **must be stopped immediately** to obtain recovery. This should be done before any urological investigations or treatments are carried out.

Hepatic Function: As with other NSAIDs, borderline elevations of one or more liver function tests may occur in up to 15% of patients. These abnormalities may progress, may remain essentially unchanged, or may be transient with continued therapy. A patient with symptoms and/or signs suggesting liver dysfunction, or in whom an abnormal liver test has occurred, should be evaluated for evidence of the development of more severe hepatic reaction while on therapy with this drug. Severe hepatic reactions including jaundice and cases of fatal hepatitis have been reported with this drug as with other NSAIDs.

Although such reactions are rare, if abnormal liver tests persist or worsen, if clinical signs and symptoms consistent with liver disease develop, or if systemic manifestations occur (e.g., eosinophilia, rash, etc.), this drug should be discontinued.

During long-term therapy, liver function tests should be monitored periodically. If this drug needs to be used in the presence of impaired liver function, it must be done under strict observation.

Fluid and Electrolyte Balance: Fluid retention and edema have been observed in patients treated with Arthrotec. Therefore, as with many other NSAIDs, the possibility of precipitating congestive heart failure in elderly patients or those with compromised cardiac function should be borne in mind.

Arthrotec should be used with caution in patients with heart failure, hypertension or other conditions predisposing to fluid retention. With NSAID treatment, there is a potential risk of hyperkalemia particularly in patients with conditions such as diabetes mellitus or renal failure; elderly patients; or in patients receiving concomitant therapy with beta-adrenergic blockers, angiotensin converting enzyme inhibitors or some diuretics.

Serum electrolytes should be monitored periodically during long-term therapy, especially in those patients who are at risk.

Hematology: Drugs inhibiting prostaglandin biosynthesis do interfere with platelet function to varying degrees. Therefore, patients who may be adversely affected by such an action should be carefully observed when Arthrotec is administered.

The addition of misoprostol does not exacerbate the effect of diclofenac on platelet function. In clinical trials, there has been no evidence that Arthrotec affects hemostasis.

Blood dyscrasias (such as neutropenia, leukopenia, thrombocytopenia, aplastic anemia and agranulocytosis) associated with the use of NSAIDs are rare, but could occur with severe consequences.

Infection: In common with other anti-inflammatory drugs, Arthrotec may mask the usual signs of infection.

Ophthalmology: Blurred and/or diminished vision has been reported with the use of NSAIDs. If such symptoms develop Arthrotec should be discontinued and an ophthalmologic examination performed; ophthalmic examination should be carried out at periodic intervals in any patient receiving this drug for an extended period of time.

CNS: Some patients may experience drowsiness, dizziness, vertigo, insomnia or depression with the use of diclofenac. If patients experience these side effects, they should exercise caution in carrying out activities that require alertness.

Allergies: Allergic reactions have been reported in individuals without prior exposure to diclofenac.

Drug Interactions: No drug-drug interactions for Arthrotec have been observed. However, the following information is known for the components.

Misoprostol has been used concomitantly with at least 44 different classes of drugs, including more than 150 drugs. There were no reports of any clinically significant drug interactions.

In laboratory studies, misoprostol has shown no significant effect on the cytochrome P450-linked hepatic mixed function oxidase system, and therefore should not affect the metabolism of theophylline, warfarin, benzodiazepines or other drugs normally metabolized by this system.

ASA or Other NSAIDs: When diclofenac and ASA are taken simultaneously, the bioavailability of each is reduced. Concomitant administration of Arthrotec and ASA is not recommended because diclofenac is displaced from its binding sites by ASA, resulting in lower plasma concentrations, peak plasma levels and AUC values. Misoprostol does not affect the kinetics of other NSAIDs (e.g., ibuprofen, indomethacin and piroxicam). The use of Arthrotec and any other NSAIDs, including over the counter ones (such as ASA and ibuprofen) is not recommended due to the possibility of additive side effects.

Antacids: The concomitant administration of aluminum hydroxide or magnesium hydroxide antacids may delay the absorption of diclofenac but does not affect the total amount of the drug absorbed. The total availability of misoprostol acid is reduced by antacids in large doses. Only aluminum-based antacids should be used with Arthrotec as magnesium-based antacids may increase the potential for diarrhea (see Adverse Effects).

Digoxin: Diclofenac may increase the plasma concentration of digoxin. Dosage adjustment of the digoxin may be required with Arthrotec. Serum digoxin levels should be monitored.

Diuretics/Antihypertensives: NSAIDs have been reported to inhibit the activity of diuretics. Concomitant treatment of Arthrotec with potassium-sparing diuretics may be associated with increased serum potassium levels, thus making it necessary to monitor the latter. The antihypertensive effect of hydrochlorothiazide and other agents may be decreased by diclofenac in patients with essential hypertension.

Anticoagulants: Numerous studies have shown that concomitant use of NSAIDs and anticoagulants increases the risk of gastrointestinal adverse events such as ulceration and bleeding. Pharmacodynamic studies have shown no potentiation of anticoagulant drugs due to concurrent administration with diclofenac. However, other NSAIDs have been shown to interact with anticoagulant agents. Although clinical investigations would appear to indicate that diclofenac has no influence on the effect of anticoagulants, there are isolated reports of an increased risk of hemorrhage with the combined use of diclofenac and nicoumalone anticoagulant therapy. Special caution is therefore recommended and frequent laboratory tests should be performed to check that the desired response to the anticoagulant is being maintained. Because prostaglandins play an important role in hemostasis and NSAIDs affect platelet function as well, concurrent therapy of Arthrotec with warfarin requires close monitoring to be certain no change in anticoagulant dosage is necessary.

Table II—Arthrotec

Adverse Reactions Reported in ≥1% of Patients

	A50 b.i.d. N=391	A50 t.i.d. N=692	A50 b.i.d./t.i.d. N=750	D50 b.i.d./t.i.d. N=754	A75 b.i.d.* N=285	D75 b.i.d.* N=260
Gastrointestinal						
Abdominal Pain	19.4	19.4	23.2	19.5	24.6	24.2
Diarrhea	15.9	17.8	19.9	11.3	20.4	16.2
Dyspepsia	7.2	14.5	11.3	7.8	33.3	34.6
Nausea	10.2	10.0	11.7	6.5	14.0	9.2
Flatulence	6.1	8.7	8.0	3.1	18.2	9.2
Gastritis	2.8	2.3	3.6	6.8	7.4	13.1
Vomiting	2.6	3.3	3.1	1.3	3.9	5.4
Constipation	1.8	2.6	2.1	2.9	4.9	6.9
Eructation	2.6	0.3	2.0	0.8	2.1	0.4
Esophagitis	0.8	1.7	1.1	0.8	3.9	1.9
Duodenitis	2.3	0.9	0.9	2.3	3.5	5.0
Gastroesophageal Reflux	0.0	1.0	0.4	1.7	1.1	1.2
Duodenal Ulcer	0.0	1.2	0.1	0.4	0.7	2.7
Gastric Ulcer	0.8	0.6	0.7	1.7	3.2	6.9
Tooth Disorder	0.3	0.6	0.0	0.0	1.1	0.8
CNS						
Headache	9.2	6.4	7.3	9.2	12.3	15.8
Dizziness	2.6	2.0	3.5	5.3	3.9	4.2
Migraine	1.3	0.6	0.4	0.9	1.4	0.8
Paresthesia	0.3	0.3	0.7	0.7	1.1	0.4
Dermatologic						
Rash	0.8	1.4	1.5	1.1	2.1	3.5
Pruritus	1.0	0.4	1.2	0.9	2.1	1.9
Skin Ulceration	0.0	0.0	0.1	0.0	1.1	0.1
Cardiovascular						
Hypertension	0.0	0.5	0.0	0.1	1.1	2.3
Edema	0.8	0.7	0.0	0.3	1.1	1.2
Dependent Edema	0.0	0.3	0.4	0.5	1.1	0.4
Leg Edema	0.0	0.1	0.0	0.1	1.1	0.8
Hepatic						
ALT Increase	0.5	0.6	0.1	0.7	2.5	2.3
AST Increase	0.5	0.4	0.0	0.5	1.1	2.3
Respiratory						
Upper Respiratory Tract Infection	1.0	2.7	1.1	2.1	2.8	3.8
Pharyngitis	0.5	1.9	1.1	1.9	3.5	1.5
Rhinitis	0.8	2.6	0.3	0.9	3.2	4.2
Sinusitis	0.0	0.9	0.1	0.1	6.0	2.7
Coughing	0.3	1.2	0.4	1.2	1.8	3.5
Bronchitis	0.0	0.4	0.7	1.1	2.1	1.5
Dyspnea	0.3	0.4	0.4	0.7	1.4	0.4
Urogenital						
Menorrhagia	0.9	0.6	1.3	0.0	0.0	0.5
Vaginitis	0.0	0.9	0.0	0.0	1.0	1.1
Perineal Pain, male	0.6	0.0	0.0	0.0	1.1	0.0
Psychiatric						
Insomnia	1.3	0.4	0.9	1.2	2.5	1.9
Somnolence	0.8	0.6	0.7	0.9	1.1	0.8
Body as a Whole						
Influenza-Like Symptoms	1.0	0.6	2.0	1.5	1.1	2.3
Pain	0.5	1.0	0.7	0.8	4.2	1.9
Back Pain	0.8	0.6	1.2	1.1	3.2	3.5
Chest Pain	1.0	0.3	1.1	0.5	0.7	3.1
Fever	0.0	0.6	0.7	1.1	1.4	0.0
Asthenia	0.0	0.1	0.1	0.7	1.1	0.4
Myalgia	0.8	0.7	0.8	0.3	1.1	0.4
Arthralgia	0.0	0.7	0.3	0.3	2.8	3.5
Arthrosis	0.0	0.1	0.3	0.0	1.4	1.2

Legend: A50=Arthrotec 50.
D50=Diclofenac 50 mg.
A75=Arthrotec 75.
D75=Diclofenac 75 mg.

* Patients must have experienced ulceration in order to enter study. This represents an extremely high risk cohort.

Oral Hypoglycemic Agents: Pharmacodynamic studies have shown no potentiation of oral hypoglycemic drugs due to concurrent administration with diclofenac. However, other NSAIDs have been shown to interact with oral hypoglycemic agents.

Methotrexate: Rare cases of fatal renal toxicity have been reported in patients receiving methotrexate and diclofenac. Thus, caution should be taken when administering Arthrotec and methotrexate.

Lithium: Diclofenac, when administered concomitantly with lithium, increases the lithium plasma concentration through an effect on lithium renal clearance. Lithium toxicity may develop in these patients. Dosage adjustment of lithium may be required with Arthrotec.

Glucocorticoids: Numerous studies have shown that the concomitant use of NSAIDs and oral glucocorticoids increases the risk of gastrointestinal side effects such as ulceration and bleeding. This is especially the case in older (>65 years old) individuals.

Clinical Laboratory Tests: Diclofenac increases platelet aggregation time but does not affect bleeding time, plasma prothrombin clotting time, plasma fibrinogens, or factors V and VII to XII. Statistically significant changes in prothrombin and partial thromboplastin times have been reported in normal volunteers. The mean changes were observed to be less than 1 second in both instances, and are unlikely to be clinically important.

Arthrotec (cont'd)

Persistently abnormal or worsening renal, hepatic or hematological test values should be followed up carefully since they may be related to therapy.

Adverse Effects: The most common adverse reactions encountered with NSAIDs are gastrointestinal, of which peptic ulcer, with or without bleeding, is the most severe. Fatalities have occurred, particularly in the elderly.

In clinical trials, 3 549 arthritic patients have been treated with Arthrotec, 506 of whom received Arthrotec for more than 1 year. A total of 285 patients have been treated with Arthrotec 75 in clinical trials for a duration of up to 12 weeks.

The following adverse reactions occurred with an incidence of 1% or greater with at least one of the Arthrotec dosing regimens presented below: See Table II (on previous page).

The following adverse events were reported by 1% or less of the subjects receiving Arthrotec. Causal relationships between Arthrotec and these events have not been established but cannot be excluded.

Gastrointestinal: abdomen enlarged, esophageal ulceration, gall bladder disorder, glossitis, hematemesis, hiccup and melena.

CNS/Psychiatric: anorexia, anxiety, concentration impaired, depression, hypoesthesia, mouth dry, speech disorder and vertigo.

Dermatologic: angioedema, erythematous rash, sweating increased and urticaria.

Cardiovascular: palpitation and syncope.

Special Senses: earache, eye pain, taste loss, taste abnormalities, tinnitus and vision abnormal.

Hematologic: leukopenia and thrombocytopenia.

Hepatic: bilirubinemia, abnormal hepatic function, LDH increased, and alkaline phosphatase increased.

Metabolic: BUN increased and glycosuria.

Respiratory: hyperventilation and sputum increased.

Gynecological: menstrual disorder, intermenstrual bleeding, dysmenorrhea, leukorrhea, and vaginal bleeding. (Postmenopausal vaginal bleeding may be related to Arthrotec administration. If this occurs, diagnostic workup should be undertaken to rule out gynecological pathology.)

Body as a Whole: hot flushes, malaise, rigors.

Urinary: dysuria and urine abnormal.

Overdose: Symptoms and Treatment: Diclofenac Sodium: Worldwide reports on overdosage with diclofenac cover 27 cases. In 10 of these 27 cases, diclofenac was the only drug taken; all of these patients recovered. The highest dose of diclofenac was 2.5 g in a 20-year-old male who suffered acute renal failure as a consequence, and who was treated with dialysis sessions and recovered in 2 days. The next highest dose was 2.35 g in a 17-year-old female who experienced vomiting and drowsiness. A dose of 2 g of diclofenac was taken by a woman of unspecified age who remained asymptomatic.

There is no specific antidote for diclofenac. In cases of overdosage, absorption should be prevented as soon as possible by means of induction of vomiting, gastric lavage or treatment with activated charcoal.

Supportive and symptomatic treatment should be given for complications such as drowsiness, confusion, general hypotonia, hypotension, renal failure, convulsions, gastrointestinal irritation and respiratory depression. Measures to accelerate elimination (forced diuresis, hemoperfusion, dialysis) may be considered, but may be of limited use because of the high (99%) protein-binding and extensive metabolism.

Misoprostol: The toxic dose of misoprostol in humans has not been determined. Cumulative total daily doses of 1 600 µg have been tolerated with only symptoms of gastrointestinal discomfort being reported.

In animals, the acute toxic effects are similar to those reported for other prostaglandins: relaxation of smooth muscle, respiratory difficulties, and depression of the CNS. Clinical signs that may indicate an overdose are sedation, tremor, convulsions, dyspnea, abdominal pain, diarrhea, fever, palpitations, hypotension, or bradycardia. Symptoms should be treated with supportive therapy.

It is not known if misoprostol acid is dialyzable. However, because misoprostol is metabolized like a fatty acid, it is unlikely that dialysis would be appropriate treatment for overdosage.

The use of oral activated charcoal may help to reduce the absorption of diclofenac and misoprostol.

Dosage: Adults: The recommended oral dose for treating the signs and symptoms of rheumatoid arthritis and osteoarthritis is Arthrotec 50: 1 tablet 2 or 3 times daily; Arthrotec 75: 1 tablet twice daily.

Arthrotec should be taken **immediately after a meal or with food or milk.**

Arthrotec should be swallowed whole.

No adjustment of dosage is necessary in patients with hepatic impairment or in mild to moderate renal failure as the pharmacokinetic parameters for Arthrotec are not altered to any clinically relevant extent. If Arthrotec must be used in patients with severe renal or hepatic impairment, these patients must be closely monitored.

Geriatrics: The dosage should be reduced to the lowest dose that will provide control of symptoms, adjusted when necessary, and closely supervised.

Information for the Patient: See Blue Section—Information for the Patient "Arthrotec".

Supplied: Arthrotec 50: Each white to off-white, round and biconvex tablet, engraved "SEARLE" over "1411" on one side, 4 × "A" around the circumference of the reverse side, contains: an enteric-coated core of diclofenac sodium 50 mg, surrounded by an outer mantle containing misoprostol 200 µg. Nonmedicinal ingredients: castor oil, cellulose, cellulose acetate phthalate, colloidal silicon dioxide, cornstarch, crospovidone, diethyl phthalate, hydroxypropyl methylcellulose, lactose, magnesium stearate and povidone. Bottles of 250.

Arthrotec 75: Each white to off-white, round and biconvex tablet, engraved "SEARLE" over "1421" on one side, 4 × "A" around the circumference of the reverse side with a "75" in the middle, contains: an enteric-coated core of diclofenac sodium 75 mg, surrounded by an outer mantle containing misoprostol 200 µg. Nonmedicinal ingredients: castor oil, cellulose, colloidal silicon dioxide, cornstarch, crospovidone, hydroxypropyl methylcellulose, lactose, magnesium stearate, methacrylic acid copolymer, povidone, sodium hydroxide and triethyl citrate. Bottles of 250.

Protect tablets from heat and humidity. Store at 15 to 25°C. Pharmacist: Dispense with patient insert.

(Shown in Product Recognition Section)

Reviewed 1998

ARTIFICIAL TEARS

Rivex Ophthalmics

Polyvinyl Alcohol

Ocular Lubricant

Supplied: Each mL of sterile ophthalmic solution contains: polyvinyl alcohol 1.4%. Nonmedicinal ingredients: benzalkonium chloride, dibasic sodium phosphate, edetate disodium, monobasic sodium phosphate, phosphoric acid, purified water, sodium chloride and sodium hydroxide. Plastic squeeze bottles of 15 mL with controlled tip applicators.

ASA

General Monograph, CPhA

Acetylsalicylic Acid

Analgesic—Antipyretic—Anti-inflammatory—Platelet Aggregation Inhibitor

This monograph has been compiled by CPhA. It may contain information different from that approved by Therapeutic Products Programme, Health Canada, and the pharmaceutical manufacturers' approval has not been requested.

Pharmacology: ASA interferes with the production of prostaglandins in various organs and tissues through acetylation and inactivation of the enzyme cyclooxygenase. The main action of the drug is thought to be peripheral; however, it may have similar activity in the CNS. The reduction in tissue levels of prostaglandins may be responsible for the analgesic and anti-inflammatory effects of the drug. ASA is most effective in the management of pain of low to moderate intensity associated with inflammation.

ASA is also a potent antipyretic and lowers body temperature in patients with fever, mainly by inhibition of prostaglandin-E_1 synthesis in the brain. Heat production is not affected but dissipation of heat is enhanced by increased blood flow through the skin and sweating.

ASA has antiplatelet activity through inhibition of thromboxane A_2 synthesis. Thromboxane A_2 plays an essential role in platelet aggregation. ASA prevents thromboxane A_2 formation by acetylation of platelet cyclooxygenase. ASA's effect on the platelet is irreversible and persists for the life of the platelet (7 to 10 days). At higher doses, ASA prolongs bleeding time by altering the hepatic synthesis of certain blood coagulation factors. The increase in prothrombin time is dose dependent and rarely occurs with doses less than 6 g/day.

Pharmacokinetics: Following oral administration, ASA is rapidly absorbed from the stomach and proximal small intestine, although there is some evidence that absorption may be substantially impaired during the febrile phase of Kawasaki syndrome (mucocutaneous lymph node syndrome). Absorption in the small intestine occurs at a significantly faster rate than in the stomach. Optimum absorption of salicylate occurs in the pH range of 2.15 to 4.10. Enteric-coating resists disintegration at a pH less than 3.5 for a period of at least 2 hours but is capable of disintegrating at a pH of greater than 5.5 in 10 to 30 minutes. Enteric-coating therefore inhibits the release of ASA in the stomach. Absorption of enteric-coated tablets takes place primarily in the duodenum.

Rectal absorption is slow, usually incomplete and variable, and may be associated with rectal mucosal irritation.

Peak blood levels occur approximately 2 hours after ingestion of regular tablets and 6 to 8 hours after the ingestion of enteric-coated tablets.

ASA is widely distributed in most body tissues and fluids. After oral absorption, ASA is rapidly hydrolyzed to salicylic acid. The plasma protein binding of salicylate is concentration dependent. The bound fraction decreases as the plasma concentration of salicylate increases; at low concentrations of less than 0.75 mmol/L about 90% of the drug is bound and at concentrations between 0.76 and 2.9 mmol/L, approximately 70 to 85% is bound. Because of capacity-limited metabolism, serum concentrations of salicylate increase more than proportionally with an increase in dose.

The elimination half-life of ASA is 14 to 20 minutes, 3 to 6 hours for the salicylate (after low doses of 325 mg to 1.3 g of ASA) and up to 15 to 30 hours after anti-inflammatory doses of ASA. The salicylate then undergoes hepatic metabolism. Salicylate and its metabolites are rapidly and almost completely excreted in the urine. Only about 1% of ASA is excreted in the urine unchanged. This proportion is extremely variable and depends on dose and urinary pH.

Indications: The relief of mild to moderate pain, fever and inflammation.

ASA is indicated for the relief of the signs and symptoms of osteoarthritis, rheumatoid arthritis, ankylosing spondylitis, bursitis and other forms of rheumatism and musculoskeletal disorders. It is also indicated in the treatment of rheumatic fever; however, penicillin and other appropriate therapy should be administered concomitantly.

Based on its platelet aggregation inhibitory properties, ASA is also indicated for secondary prevention after a myocardial infarction, reducing the risk of myocardial infarction and mortality in unstable angina, reducing the risk of transient ischemic attacks (TIA), stroke and death in patients with a history of TIA, preventing graft occlusion after coronary artery bypass and preventing thromboembolism after hip replacement surgery.

Enteric-coated tablets are indicated whenever gastric intolerance to ASA is suspected.

ASA is currently the drug of choice for the management of Kawasaki syndrome. When anti-inflammatory doses of ASA are used, the duration of fever may be reduced by several days and coronary involvement may be reduced or prevented, especially if ASA is given in conjunction with high dose i.v. immune globulin.

Contraindications: Salicylate sensitivity: patients who have had a bronchospastic reaction, generalized urticaria, angioedema, severe rhinitis, laryngeal edema or shock precipitated by ASA or nonsteroidal anti-inflammatory drugs. Some patients sensitive to ASA, may be cross-sensitive to other nonsteroidal anti-inflammatory drugs as well as tartrazine dye. Patients with asthma associated nasal poylps have an increased risk of sensitivity to ASA.

ASA should not be used in patients with active peptic ulcer (see Warnings, Precautions).

Warnings: ASA is one of the most frequent causes of accidental poisoning in toddlers and infants. ASA-containing products should be kept well out of the reach of children.

Authorities advise that ASA not be used in children, teenagers or young adults with varicella or influenza.

A strong association between development of Reye's syndrome and ingestion of salicylates (almost exclusively ASA) has been found although a causal relationship has not been established. Most evidence to date, including a decline in the use of ASA in children accompanied by a continuing decline in reported cases of Reye's syndrome, supports such an association.

As with other nonsteroidal anti-inflammatory drugs, serious gastrointestinal toxicity, such as peptic ulceration, perforation and bleeding, sometimes severe and occasionally fatal, can occur at any time, with or without symptoms, in patients treated with ASA (see Precautions).

Precautions: Gastrointestinal toxicity may occur with the use of ASA (see Warnings). No studies, to date, have identified any group of patients not at risk of ulceration and bleeding. A history of serious gastrointestinal events and other factors such as ASA dosage, excessive alcohol intake, smoking, advanced age, female gender and concomitant corticosteroid or anticoagulant use have been associated with increased risk. Patients should be informed about the signs and symptoms of serious gastrointestinal toxicity and advised to contact their physician immediately if they occur. Because serious events can occur without warning symptoms, patients on long-term therapy should have periodic hemoglobin determinations in conjunction with vigilant follow up.

ASA should be used with extreme caution in patients with decreased renal function, bleeding tendencies, significant anemia, hypoprothrombinemia, thrombocytopenia, vitamin K deficiency or severe hepatic disease.

ASA should be discontinued at least one week prior to elective surgery because of increased risk of bleeding.

Drug Interactions: Analgesics: Concurrent long-term use of ASA and other analgesic-antipyretic agents such as acetaminophen may be associated with analgesic nephropathy (papillary necrosis and tubulointerstitial inflammation).

Antacids: Chronic high-dose use of antacids may increase renal elimination of salicylates through alkalinization of the urine.

Anticoagulants: Concomitant use of ASA and anticoagulants increases the risk of bleeding. Large doses of ASA may enhance the hypoprothrombinemic response to warfarin.

Anticonvulsants: Large doses of ASA may increase phenytoin serum levels by inhibition of phenytoin metabolism.

Valproic acid may cause hypoprothrombinemia and inhibit platelet aggregation. Concomitant use of ASA and valproic acid may cause increased valproic acid levels and may lead to an increased risk of bleeding.

Antihyperglycemic Agents: ASA increases the antihyperglycemic response to sulfonylureas, especially chlorpropamide. Large doses of ASA may cause a decrease in blood glucose, which may alter the insulin requirements of diabetic patients.

Corticosteroids: Corticosteroids may decrease the serum salicylate concentrations through increased excretion. Concomitant use may also increase the risk of gastrointestinal side effects.

Methotrexate: Concurrent use of ASA and methotrexate may lead to higher methotrexate serum levels, mainly through competition for renal excretion.

Nonsteroidal Anti-inflammatory Drugs (NSAIDs): Concomitant use of ASA and NSAIDs increases the risk of gastrointestinal side effects while providing no additional therapeutic benefit.

Uricosuric agents: ASA may decrease the uricosuric effects of sulfinpyrazone and probenecid.

Vancomycin: Use of vancomycin with ASA may increase the risk of ototoxicity.

Vitamin C: Large doses of vitamin C may decrease the excretion of ASA through acidification of the urine.

Zidovudine: ASA may increase the risk of zidovudine toxicity by decreasing the hepatic metabolism of zidovudine.

Drug/Lab Test Interactions: Bleeding time: ASA may prolong bleeding time for 4 to 7 days due to its effects on platelet aggregation.

Copper sulfate urine sugar tests: Daily doses of ASA greater than 2.4 g may cause false positive results.

Thyroid function tests: Large doses of salicylates may increase T_3 resin uptake and decrease serum concentrations of T_3 and T_4 when determined by radioimmunoassay. Salicylates may also affect TRH-induced TSH release determinations.

Pregnancy: Salicylates cross the placenta. Administration during the third trimester increases the risk of maternal, fetal and neonatal hemorrhage. It may also cause premature closure of the fetal ductus arteriosus and lengthen the duration of pregnancy and parturition time.

Lactation: Salicylates are excreted into breast milk. No adverse effects have been reported in infants of mothers taking usual analgesic doses; however, close supervision of the infant is advised with chronic dosing. Moderate amounts in the breast milk may increase the risk of bleeding in the infant by decreasing the prothrombin time or interfering with platelet function. Breast feeding is generally not recommended for women on high dose, long-term ASA therapy.

Geriatrics: Patients over 65 years of age and frail or debilitated patients are more susceptible to many adverse effects of ASA, including gastrointestinal toxicity. Consideration should be given to using lower initial dosages in this patient group.

Adverse Effects: Gastrointestinal: Ulcer, hemorrhage, dyspepsia, heartburn, epigastric distress, nausea, vomiting, diarrhea or abdominal pain may occur with increasing incidence at higher dosages (see Warnings, Precautions).

Hematologic: Leukopenia, thrombocytopenia, pancytopenia, agranulocytosis, aplastic anemia, purpura, eosinophilia associated with ASA-induced hepatoxicity have been reported rarely. Hematocrit and plasma iron concentration may be decreased with daily doses of 3 to 4 g.

Cardiovascular: Pulmonary edema may occur with chronic or acute ingestion of large doses.

Hypersensitivity: Urticaria, angioedema, bronchospasm, severe rhinitis or shock may occur rarely. The incidence of these reactions appear to be higher in patients with chronic urticaria, asthma and chronic rhinitis.

Hepatic: Reversible hepatoxicity particularly in patients with juvenile rheumatoid arthritis and systemic lupus erythematosus has been reported rarely.

Otic: Tinnitus and hearing loss, usually completely reversible, may occur in patients receiving large doses of ASA or with long-term use and are dose related.

Dermatologic: Skin eruptions and lesions have been reported. Stevens-Johnson syndrome has rarely been associated with ASA.

Chronic salicylate intoxication may result from high doses or from prolonged therapy with high doses. Tinnitus and hearing loss are the most frequent signs of chronic intoxication. Other manifestations such as dimness of vision, headache, dizziness, mental confusion, drowsiness, sweating, thirst, hyperventilation, tachycardia, nausea, vomiting and sometimes diarrhea may occur.

Overdose: Symptoms: Symptoms of acute toxicity with ASA may occur with doses greater than 150 mg/kg. Doses greater than 500 mg/kg are potentially fatal. Acid-base and electrolyte disturbances, dehydration, hyperpyrexia, hyperglycemia or hypoglycemia are the principal physiologic manifestations of acute ASA toxicity. Other symptoms of toxicity include burning pain in the mouth or throat, dizziness, tinnitus and sweating. In more severe cases, presence of CNS symptoms such as lethargy, disorientation, or confusion may be a predictor for the development of pulmonary edema. Coma and convulsions may be delayed for 24 to 48 hours. Cardiac arrhythmias have been reported. Bleeding disorders, cerebral edema, oliguria are also possible.

Treatment: Treatment is largely symptomatic and supportive. Induce emesis or perform gastric lavage, then administer activated charcoal. If hyperthermia is present, sponge the patient with tepid water or use a cooling blanket. Maintain appropriate fluid therapy based on the patient's fluid, acid-base and electrolyte status. Monitor blood gases, blood glucose, serum creatinine and urea, urinary output and pH. Draw blood for determination of serum salicylate level. Sodium bicarbonate i.v. should be used cautiously to correct metabolic acidosis and to enhance renal elimination of salicylate. Care should be taken to avoid sodium overload or alkalosis. Hypokalemia may require administration of i.v. potassium chloride. If present, hypoglycemia may be managed with dextrose solutions. Seizures may be treated with i.v. diazepam. Alkalinization of the urine to enhance urinary excretion of salicylates may be useful in severe intoxication but should be performed very cautiously in selected patients. Vitamin K may be administered to patients with hemorrhagic complications or prolonged PT. Peritoneal or hemodialysis may be required if serum salicylate concentrations are greater than 6.5 mmol/L 6 hours after ingestion, in complex acid-base disturbances unresponsive to conventional therapy, if the patient is in renal failure, or if the patient is deteriorating clinically despite appropriate care.

Dosage: Oral: Analgesic/Antipyretic: Adults: 325 to 650 mg 4 to 6 times daily as necessary.

Children: **Authorities advise that ASA should not be used in children, teenagers and young adults with varicella or influenza.** 10 to 15 mg/kg every 4 to 6 hours as needed up to a maximum of 65 mg/kg/day. Alternatively, Table I gives dosage recommendation for children.

Table I—ASA

Dosage Recommendation for Children[a,b]

Age (yrs)	Single Dose (mg)	Max. Daily Dose (mg)
Under 2	Recommendation of physician	
2 to under 4	160	800
4 to under 6	240	1 200
6 to under 9	320	1 600
9 to under 11	400	2 000
11 to under 12	480	2 400

[a]The recommended dose may be given every 4 hours as necessary. Do not administer more than 5 doses to children in any 24 hour period.
[b]See Warnings.

ASA should not be used for self-medication of marked fever (greater than 39.5°C), fever persisting longer than 3 days, or recurrent fever, unless directed by a physician since such fevers may indicate serious illness requiring prompt medical attention.

ASA should not be used for self-medication of pain for longer than 10 days in adults or 5 days in children, unless directed by a physician, since pain of such intensity and duration may indicate a pathological condition requiring medical evaluation.

Anti-inflammatory: Because the anti-inflammatory effect of salicylates is achieved with higher doses of ASA, the appearance of signs and symptoms of salicylate toxicity is often a limiting factor to its use. Most patients will tolerate blood salicylate levels in the range of 1.45 to 1.80 mmol/L.

Adults: Usual initial anti-inflammatory dose is 2.4 to 3.6 g daily in divided doses. Doses up to 6 g daily may be needed.

Children (see Warnings): Usual initial anti-inflammatory dose is 60 to 90 mg/kg daily in divided doses, up to 100 mg/kg daily.

Subsequently, adjust dosage slowly according to patient's tolerance to achieve optimal therapeutic response.

Serum salicylate concentration determinations are recommended if high dosage regimens are used, due to wide variations in pharmacokinetics. Usual serum salicylate concentrations for anti-inflammatory effect range from 1.1 to 2.2 mmol/L.

Enteric-coated preparations are not recommended for use in fever or in children under 2 years.

Kawasaki syndrome: Initial (febrile phase): 80 to 100 mg/kg per day in 4 divided doses with serum level monitoring. Some patients may require higher doses to achieve thereapeutic levels, because of impaired absorption during the febrile phase of the disease. When fever subsides, the dose should be reduced to 8 to 10 mg/kg once daily until 6 to 10 weeks after initial onset of illness. In patients with coronary involvement, ASA is often continued due to the potential benefit of its antithrombotic effects.

Acute Rheumatic Fever: Usual adult dose is 5 to 8 g daily and for children, 90 to 130 mg/kg/day administered in 4 to 6 divided doses for 1 to 2 weeks; then decreased to 60 to 70 mg/kg/day for 1 to 6 weeks or until required; then gradually withdrawn over 1 to 2 weeks.

Platelet Antiaggregant: The optimal dose has not been determined. The following doses have been shown to be effective: secondary prevention of myocardial infarction, 162.5 to 1 500 mg daily; prevention of occlusion of coronary artery grafts, 100 to 975 mg daily; secondary prevention of transient ischemic attacks, 1 300 mg daily in 2 to 4 divided doses.

Rectal: Adults: 650 mg 4 to 6 times a day as required. Usual dosage range: 325 mg to 8 g daily.

Children: As for oral analgesic/antipyretic dose outlined above.

Reviewed 1998

A.S.A.

WestCan

Acetylsalicylic Acid

Analgesic—Antipyretic—Anti-inflammatory

Supplied: Each tablet contains: acetylsalicylic acid 325 mg. Bottles of 48, 100, 120, 125, 200, 250, 300 and 500 (child resistant caps supplied for 100, 120, 125, 200, 250).

ASACOL® Ⓟ

Procter & Gamble Pharmaceuticals

5-ASA

Lower Gastrointestinal Anti-inflammatory

Pharmacology: The active ingredient in Asacol, mesalamine (5-aminosalicylic acid, also referred to as 5-ASA), is the major active component of sulfasalazine for the treatment of inflammatory bowel disease. The available evidence suggests that mesalamine has a topical anti-inflammatory effect on the colon, where it inhibits prostaglandin and leukotriene synthesis.

Asacol tablets have a special acrylic-based resin coating which delays release of mesalamine until the tablets reach the terminal ileum and colon. Once released in the colon, mesalamine is minimally absorbed and plasma levels are similar to those found following rectal administration of mesalamine. Approximately 20% of the administered dose released in the colon is absorbed, with about 80% being excreted in the feces. The absorbed mesalamine is rapidly acetylated through the gut mucosal wall and by the liver. It is mainly excreted by the kidney, as N-acetyl-5-aminosalicylic acid.

Pharmacokinetics: Mesalamine release from Asacol is delayed until the terminal ileum as reflected by t_{max}'s of about 7 hours for mesalamine and its metabolite, N-acetyl-5-ASA. The $t^1/_{2elim.}$'s were about 3 hours for mesalamine and 10 hours for N-acetyl-5-ASA.

Human studies conducted using radiological and serum markers showed that the Asacol coating delayed release of mesalamine until the terminal ileum was reached. Other studies compared mesalamine absorption when administered as an enema (a readily available dosage form) and when released for absorption in the stomach, small intestine, and colon relative to an i.v. dose. Once released in the colon, mesalamine was minimally absorbed and plasma levels were similar to those found following rectal administration. Approximately 20% of the administered dose released was absorbed, with about 80% available for topical activity in the colon. The absorbed mesalamine was rapidly acetylated through the gut mucosal wall and by the liver. It was mainly excreted by the kidney as N-acetyl-5-ASA.

Serum levels and urinary excretion of mesalamine and N-acetyl-5-ASA following single and multiple equimolar Asacol and sulfasalazine doses to healthy subjects and to patients were compared. There was no consistent trend for greater serum mesalamine or metabolite levels following Asacol dosage. Based on urinary dose recoveries, the extent of mesalamine absorption for Asacol was no greater than that for sulfasalazine. Overall, there were no meaningful differences in the extents of mesalamine absorption following equimolar Asacol and sulfasalazine doses.

In another study, there was a dose response in serum mesalamine and metabolite levels at Asacol doses of 1.2 and 2.4 g/day. In other studies when Asacol was administered at higher or lower doses than 1.2 and 2.4 g/day, serum mesalamine and N-acetyl-5-ASA concentrations differed from those for the 1.2 and 2.4 g/day doses as would be expected following a linear dose response relationship. The effects of coadministration of Asacol with cimetidine, an antacid containing activated simethicone and aluminum hydroxide, and antacid with a high fat meal were addressed in another study. There were no significant in vivo effects on mesalamine release or the extent of drug absorption from Asacol by any of the three treatments.

Clinical Trials: In a randomized, double-blind, placebo controlled clinical trial it was shown that Asacol (4.8 g/day of mesalamine in divided doses) was highly effective in inducing remission in ulcerative colitis patients with active disease.

Additional double-blind clinical trials of 16-, 24-, and 52-weeks duration have shown Asacol, in doses ranging from 0.8 to 4.4 g/day to be as effective as sulfasalazine for maintenance of remission. It is particularly noteworthy that most patients intolerant or allergic to sulfasalazine can be effectively maintained in remission on Asacol, as demonstrated in open-labeled clinical trials. In addition, male infertility resulting from sulfasalazine therapy has been shown to be reversible upon treatment with Asacol.

Indications: The treatment of mild to moderate active ulcerative colitis. In the long-term management of ulcerative colitis patients, repeat dosing may be required. Abrupt discontinuation may result in relapse.

Contraindications: In patients with a history of sensitivity to salicylates; existing gastric or duodenal ulcer; urinary tract obstruction; and in infants under 2 years of age.

Warnings: If toxic or hypersensitivity reactions occur, the drug should be discontinued. In assessing liver and joint complications, it should be kept in mind that these are frequently associated with ulcerative colitis (see Precautions).

Precautions: Caution should be exercised in patients with impaired renal function and/or hepatic dysfunction.

Patients with pyloric stenosis may have prolonged gastric retention of Asacol tablets which could delay release of mesalamine in the colon.

Drug Interactions: There are no known drug interactions. The effects of coadministration of Asacol with cimetidine, with an antacid containing activated dimethicone and aluminum hydroxide, or with an antacid accompanied by a high fat meal were addressed in a clinical study. There were no significant in vivo effects on mesalamine release or the extent of drug absorption from Asacol by any of the 3 treatments. It has been reported that simultaneous administration of famotidine, a potent H_2-antagonist, and Asacol does not influence the absorption and urinary excretion of mesalamine.

Asacol should not be administered with preparations which lower the stool pH, such as lactulose.

Interactions similar to ASA cannot be excluded.

Pregnancy: In reproduction studies, mesalamine was administered orally at a dosage of 480 mg/kg/day to pregnant rats and rabbits. No evidence of impaired female fertility or harm to the fetus due to therapy with 5-ASA was observed. There are, however, no adequate and well-controlled studies in pregnant women. Because animal reproduction studies are not always predictive of human response, this drug should be used during pregnancy only if clearly needed.

Lactation: It has been reported in one case, that small amounts of 5-ASA and higher concentrations of acetyl-5-ASA are found in breast milk. Caution should be exercised when Asacol is administered to a nursing woman.

Children: Safety and effectiveness of 5-ASA therapy in children have not been established.

Information to be Provided to the Patient: 1. Swallow tablets whole, taking care not to break the outer coating. The outer coating is designed to remain intact, to protect the active ingredient until it reaches the terminal ileum, where the tablet coating dissolves and the contents of the tablet are released into the terminal ileum and colon.

2. Take Asacol tablets only as prescribed. Do not change the number or frequency of tablets ingested without first consulting your physician.

3. What appears to be intact or partially intact tablets may infrequently appear in the stool. If this occurs repeatedly, consult your physician.

Adverse Effects: 5-ASA is generally well tolerated. Adverse events seen in clinical trials with 5-ASA have generally been mild and reversible, and have seldom resulted in discontinuation of treatment. Because Asacol does not contain a sulfa moiety, sulfa-related side effects are avoided. Many patients with a history of sulfasalazine intolerance are able to tolerate 5-ASA as demonstrated in open-label clinical trials.

The most frequently reported side effects (5% of the patients or greater) have been headache, rhinitis, fever, chills, weakness, dizziness, nausea, abdominal pain, dyspepsia, diarrhea, joint pain and rash. Other less frequently reported events (fewer than 5% of patients) include alopecia, pruritus, urticaria, acne, anxiety, insomnia, depression, tinnitus, vertigo, paresthesia, muscle cramps, anorexia, dyspnea and flatulence.

The relationship of the reported events to 5-ASA is unclear in many cases, particularly for reported events which could be considered part of the clinical presentation of ulcerative colitis.

Allergic: An acute hypersensitivity reaction characterized by cramping, abdominal pain, bloody diarrhea and occasionally by fever, headache, malaise, pruritus, rash and conjunctivitis has been infrequently reported to occur shortly after the initiation of mesalamine. If these symptoms occur, therapy should be discontinued. Symptoms usually abate promptly after discontinuation.

Hepatic: Asymptomatic elevations of liver function tests have occurred in patients taking 5-ASA. These elevations usually resolve during continued therapy or with the discontinuation of administration of 5-ASA. When any elevations in liver enzymes are assessed, it should be kept in mind that hepatic complications are frequently associated with inflammatory bowel disease.

Rare Events: The following events have been reported rarely during mesalamine use: pancreatitis, pericarditis, transverse myelitis, peripheral neuropathy, intestinal perforation, hepatitis, interstitial pneumonitis, leukopenia, agranulocytosis, minimal change nephropathy, and acute and chronic interstitial nephritis.

Overdose: Symptoms and Treatment: There is no experience with acute overdosage in humans. The drug is not metabolized to salicylate. If the amount ingested is considered dangerous or excessive, induce vomiting with ipecac syrup unless the patient is convulsing, comatose, or has lost the gag reflex, in which case perform gastric lavage using a large bore tube. If indicated, follow with activated charcoal and a saline cathartic. There is no specific antidote and treatment is symptomatic and supportive.

Dosage: Usual daily adult dose is 2 to 8 Asacol 400 mg tablets, taken orally in divided doses. In patients with severe active disease, the dose may be increased to 12 tablets daily. Abrupt discontinuation is not recommended. Prolonged treatment may be required.

Supplied: Each brown-red capsule-shaped, enteric coated, colon-targeted tablet contains: 5-ASA 400 mg (mesalamine), coated with a special acrylic-based resin, Eudragit S (methacrylic acid copolymer Type B), which delays release of the 5-ASA until the tablet reaches the terminal ileum. Nonmedicinal ingredients: dibutyl phthalate, iron oxide red, iron oxide yellow, lactose, magnesium stearate, Eudragit S (methacrylic acid copolymer Type B), polyethylene glycol, polyvinylpyrrolidone, sodium starch glycolate and talc. Bisulfite-, gluten-, paraben-, and tartrazine-free. Blister packs of 10, cartons of 10. Store at controlled room temperature (15 to 30°C).

Reviewed 1999

A.S.A. ENTERIC COATED

WestCan

Acetylsalicylic Acid

Analgesic—Antipyretic—Anti-inflammatory

Supplied: Each enteric-coated tablet contains: ASA 650 mg. Bottles of 100, 200, 500 and 1 000 (child resistant caps supplied for 100).

ASAPHEN
ASAPHEN E.C.

Pharmascience

ASA

Analgesic—Antipyretic

Supplied: Asaphen: Each chewable tablet contains: ASA USP 80 mg. Bottles of 24, 30 and 100.

Asaphen E.C.: Each enteric-coated white tablet contains: ASA USP 80 mg. Bottles of 24 and 120.

ASASANTINE® Ⓟ

Boehringer Ingelheim

Dipyridamole—ASA

Inhibitor of Platelet Adhesion and Aggregation

Pharmacology: The combined use of dipyridamole and ASA causes a significant reduction in the incidence of new fatal and nonfatal coronary events in patients with a previously documented myocardial infarction.

In a randomized, double blind study, the effects of combined dipyridamole and ASA treatment were compared to ASA alone and to placebo in 2 026 patients who had suffered a myocardial infarction 8 weeks to 5 years previously.

Combined treatment with dipyridamole 75 mg and ASA 325 mg 3 times daily reduced the life-table rates for coronary incidence over a range of 37.0 to 66.7% when compared to placebo in the 4- to 24-month period after starting treatment. Similarly, for ASA alone, these reductions ranged from 29.1 to 52.4% over the same period. The differences between combined treatment and placebo were statistically significant at each 4-month evaluation. Differences between ASA alone and placebo were statistically significant only at 8 and 24 months. At the end of the follow-up, 41 months later, essentially no differences were found between ASA and dipyridamole-ASA treatments, but both drug treated groups showed 21 to 25% lower coronary mortality and coronary incidence compared to placebo. This was no longer statistically significant.

Hospitalization longer than 2 weeks for recurrent myocardial infarction was significantly reduced in both drug treatment groups compared to the placebo group.

The patient sub-group (447 or about 20% of the total sample) entering the trial within 6 months after their last myocardial infarction showed the largest reduction in total and coronary mortality. However, the only statistically significant finding was a 63.6% reduction in life-table rates for coronary death in the dipyridamole/ASA group compared to placebo after 36 months of treatment.

A randomized, double blind trial comparing dipyridamole (begun 2 days before operation) plus ASA (begun 7 hours after operation) against placebo, in 407 patients undergoing coronary bypass, showed a statistically significant reduction in the rate of graft occlusion in patients receiving dipyridamole and ASA. Long-term follow-up (median 12 months) showed that treatment with dipyridamole and ASA continued to be effective in preventing late development of vein-graft occlusion after operation, and such treatment should be continued for at least 1 year.

Dipyridamole: When given to man, dipyridamole normalizes increased platelet adhesiveness and tendency to aggregate (Hellem's method). Dose-related increases in platelet survival time in patients with prosthetic heart valves have been observed: 400 mg/day, or 100 mg/day plus 1 g ASA, normalizes pathologically-shortened platelet survival. In combination with anticoagulants, 400 mg/day of dipyridamole causes a significant reduction in the postoperative incidence of thromboembolic phenomena associated with prosthetic heart valves (mitral and/or aortic valve replacement) without increasing hemorrhagic complications. Use of dipyridamole preoperatively in the prevention of bypass vein grafts has not been associated with an increase of chest tube blood loss or transfusion requirements following coronary bypass surgery.

In vitro, dipyridamole potentiates the aggregation-inhibiting effects of adenosine and prostaglandin E_1, inhibits platelet uptake of adenosine, serotonin and glucose and increases platelet cyclic AMP levels. At higher concentrations dipyridamole inhibits platelet aggregation induced by ADP or collagen.

Myocardial blood flow increases in a dose-dependent fashion after i.v. or oral dipyridamole, with flows 170% or more above normal. Maximal increases are achieved at about 2.0 μg/mL with 0.8 μg/mL being the threshold serum level. Single oral doses of 150 mg dipyridamole produce the maximal response. At normal therapeutic doses, no significant alterations of peripheral blood flow, systemic blood pressure or heart rate have been observed.

Dipyridamole is readily absorbed from the gastrointestinal tract, reaching peak plasma levels in man 1 to 3 hours following oral administration. Peak plasma levels are dose-dependent and range from about 0.5 μg/mL after a 25 mg dose to 1.6 μg/mL after a 75 mg dose. Blood levels are quite variable depending on food intake and gastrointestinal peristalsis. Ingestion on an empty stomach may result in higher blood levels.

Following i.v. administration, the half-life in man is about 25 minutes and after oral administration about 3 hours. When plasma levels of drug are followed for up to 60 hours after i.v. administration of 20 mg, 3 exponential components of the decline in plasma levels are detectable with half-lives of 5 minutes, 53 minutes and 11.3 hours. The volume of distribution is about 140 litres with about 92 to 99% binding to plasma proteins, primarily α_1-acid glycoprotein.

ASA: ASA interferes with the production of prostaglandins in various organs and tissues through the acetylation of the enzyme cyclo-oxygenase. Prostaglandins are powerful irritants and sensitize pain receptors to histamine and bradykinin. Thus, ASA acts as an analgesic and anti-inflammatory agent by reducing tissue levels of prostaglandins. Its antipyretic activity is due to inhibition of prostaglandin E_1 in the brain.

In vitro, ASA inhibits platelet aggregation induced by ADP, collagen and adrenaline. The release of ADP by platelets which leads to the second wave of aggregation is suppressed by ASA. The number of platelet aggregates in the myocardial microcirculation found distal to an electrically induced coronary thrombus is significantly reduced by ASA. It can normalize the increased tendency to platelet aggregation in some patients as determined by in vitro platelet function tests. Bleeding time is prolonged by ASA but platelet survival or half-life is not influenced. ASA combined with dipyridamole, however, was restricted to post-operative drug administration in the prevention of bypass graft occlusion because of the heightened risk of perioperative bleeding in humans.

Orally ingested ASA is absorbed partly from the stomach but primarily from the upper small intestine, with peak serum concentration of salicylate reached at about 2 hours. The drug is distributed throughout most body tissues and transcellular fluids by pH-dependent passive processes. It has been detected in synovial, spinal and peritoneal fluid and in saliva and milk. It crosses the blood-brain barrier relatively slowly because the largest fraction of drug is in the ionized form. Salicylate readily crosses the placental barrier.

Following absorption ASA is rapidly hydrolyzed to salicylate by esterases in the gastrointestinal mucosa, liver, plasma and erythrocytes. By 30 minutes after dosing, only 27% of total plasma salicylate is in the acetylated form. The plasma half-life of ASA is approximately 30 minutes. Due to the rapid hydrolysis of ASA, plasma concentrations of salicylate rarely exceed 20 μg/mL at therapeutic doses. Eighty to 90% of plasma salicylate is protein-bound, primarily to albumin.

Biotransformation takes place primarily in the liver where the salicylate is conjugated with glycine to form salicyluric acid, or with glucuronic acid by an ether (phenolic) or ester (acyl) bond.

A small fraction is oxidized to gentisic acid. Salicylates are excreted mainly by the kidney. In man, the urine contains free salicyclic acid (10%), salicyluric acid (75%), salicylic phenolic (10%) and acyl (5%) glucuronides, and gentisic acid (1%). The excretion of free salicylate can be increased to 85% of the ingested drug by alkalinization of urine or decreased to 5% in acidic urine.

The plasma half-life of salicylate is 2 to 3 hours in low doses and 15 to 30 hours in high doses due to saturated metabolic processes in the liver.

Indications: Combined therapy with dipyridamole and ASA is indicated in patients who are recovering from a myocardial infarction. The rate of re-infarction is significantly reduced by such therapy.

Combined treatment with dipyridamole and ASA is indicated for the prevention of occlusion of saphenous vein coronary artery bypass grafts.

Contraindications: Known sensitivity to salicylates or to other nonsteroidal anti-inflammatory agents, hypersensitivity to dipyridamole, diagnosed ulcers of the gastrointestinal tract, pathological risk of increased bleeding.

Pregnancy: The use of **ASA containing products** is contraindicated during the last trimester of pregnancy. Salicylates interfere with maternal and infant blood clotting and lengthen the duration of pregnancy and parturition time (see Precautions).

Lactation: The use of **ASA containing products** is contraindicated during lactation (see Precautions).

Warnings: Patients should be cautioned about the possibility of additive toxic effects of ASA if they are taking over-the-counter ASA containing remedies, including cough and cold medications.

Since excessive doses of dipyridamole can produce peripheral vasodilation, dipyridamole should be used with caution in patients with hypotension, rapidly worsening angina, subvalvular aortic stenosis, or hemodynamic instability. In rare cases, such patients may be at risk for developing myocardial ischemia and infarction.

Precautions: ASA should be administered cautiously to patients with asthma and other allergic conditions, a history of gastrointestinal ulcerations, significant anemia or hypoprothrombinemia.

Products containing salicylates should be used cautiously in patients with impaired renal function since salicylate and its metabolites are excreted almost exclusively in the urine. Hematocrit and renal function should be monitored periodically in patients receiving prolonged salicylate therapy or high salicylate doses since iron deficiency or adverse renal effects may occur. Because of increased risk of hepatotoxicity, hepatic function should also be monitored in patients with juvenile arthritis, active systemic lupus erythematosus, rheumatic fever or pre-existing hepatic impairment.

Since salicylates may cause or aggravate hemolysis in patients with pyruvate kinase deficiency or with rare variants of glucose-6-phosphate dehydrogenase, Asasantine should be used cautiously in such patients.

The use of ASA containing products should be avoided in teenagers and young adults with varicella or influenza-like illnesses as the use of salicylates in such conditions has been associated with an increased risk of developing Reye's syndrome.

Salicylates can produce changes in thyroid function tests.

Children: Not recommended for use in children.

Pregnancy: Reproductive studies have been performed in mice, rats, and rabbits at doses of up to 125 mg/kg and have not revealed evidence of impaired embryonic development attributable to **dipyridamole.** However, there have not been adequate, well-controlled studies in pregnant women and the drug should be used during pregnancy only if the expected benefits outweigh the potential risks.

Lactation: **Dipyridamole** is excreted in human milk. Caution should therefore be used when this drug is administered to nursing mothers.

Drug Interactions: Patients taking 2 to 3 g of ASA daily are at an increased risk of developing severe gastrointestinal bleeding following the ingestion of alcohol.

Caution is necessary when salicylates and dipyridamole are used concurrently with anticoagulants or thrombolytics as the combined use of such agents may result in an increased risk of hemorrhage.

ASA induced hypoprothrombinemia, gastrointestinal ulceration, or hemorrhage may be potentiated by the following medications; some cephalosporins (e.g., cefamandole, cefoperazone, moxalactam), some penicillins (e.g., carbenicillin, piperacillin, ticarcillin), dextran, divalproex and valproic acid.

Patients receiving concurrent salicylates and hypoglycemic therapy should be monitored closely, since reduction of the hypoglycemic drug dosage may be necessary.

Although salicylates in large doses are uricosuric agents, smaller amounts may depress uric acid clearance and thus decrease the uricosuric effects of probenecid, sulfinpyrazone, oxyphenbutazone and phenylbutazone.

Caution should be exercised when corticosteroids and salicylates are used concurrently.

Salicylate ingestion should be restricted in patients receiving indomethacin (and perhaps other NSAIDs) for conditions such as rheumatoid arthritis.

Sodium excretion produced by spironolactone may be decreased by salicylate administration.

Concomitant ingestion of salicylates and aminosalicylic acid (PAS) or aminobenzoic acid (PABA) in normal doses may lead to increased toxicity and salicylism.

Salicylates reportedly displace sulfonylureas, penicillins and methotrexate from their binding sites on plasma proteins. Salicylates also retard the renal elimination of methotrexate.

The use of oral maintenance xanthines (e.g., theophylline, aminophylline) or xanthine derivatives (e.g., found in coffee, tea) may weaken the effect of Asasantine.

Adverse Effects: In a recurrent myocardial infarction trial of 2 026 patients, the most common patient complaints, except for headaches, were those associated with ASA administration. In order of frequency of occurrence, these were stomach pain, headaches, heartburn, dizziness, constipation, hematemesis, bloody stools and/or black, tarry stools, nausea and vomiting. An increased frequency of elevations of serum urea nitrogen, uric acid and creatinine were noted in the active treatment groups but increases for individual patients were small and not associated with clinical problems. There was also a slightly greater frequency of elevated systolic blood pressure readings in the active treatment groups.

When dipyridamole has been used alone, headache, dizziness, nausea, flushing, syncope or weakness and skin rash have occurred during initiation of therapy. In most cases, these tend to be minimal and transient. Gastric irritation, emesis and abdominal cramping may occur at high dosage levels. Rare cases of what appears to be an aggravation of angina pectoris have been reported, usually at the initiation of therapy. On those uncommon occasions when adverse reactions have been persistent or intolerable to the patient, withdrawal of medication has been followed promptly by cessation of the undesirable symptoms.

For ASA alone the following side effects have been reported:

Gastrointestinal: nausea, vomiting, diarrhea, gastrointestinal bleeding and/or ulceration.

Ear: tinnitus, vertigo, hearing loss.

Hematologic: leukopenia, thrombocytopenia, purpura.

Dermatologic and Hypersensitivity: urticaria, angioedema, pruritus, skin eruptions, asthma, anaphylaxis.

Miscellaneous: acute, reversible hepatotoxicity, mental confusion, drowsiness, sweating, thirst.

Overdose: Symptoms: Hypotension, as a result of high serum levels of dipyridamole, is likely to be of short duration if it occurs but vasopressor substances may be used if necessary.

Salicylate overdosage symptoms may include rapid and deep breathing, nausea, vomiting, vertigo, tinnitus, flushing, sweating, thirst and tachycardia. In more severe cases, acid-base disturbances including respiratory alkalosis and metabolic acidosis can occur. Severe cases may show fever, hemorrhage, excitement, confusion, convulsions or coma and respiratory failure.

Treatment: Treatment of salicylate overdosage consists of prevention and management of acid-base and fluid and electrolyte disturbances. Renal clearance is increased by increasing urine flow and by alkaline diuresis but care must be taken in this approach to not further aggravate metabolic acidosis and hypokalemia. Acidemia should be prevented by

Asasantine (cont'd)

administration of adequate sodium containing fluids and sodium bicarbonate.

Hypoglycemia is an occasional accompaniment of salicylate overdosage and can be managed by glucose solutions. If a hemorrhagic diathesis is evident, give Vitamin K. Hemodialysis may be useful in complex acid base disturbances particularly in the presence of abnormal renal function.

Dosage: Prevention of recurrent myocardial infarction: The recommended oral dose is 1 capsule, containing dipyridamole 75 mg and ASA 330 mg, 3 times a day, in patients who have suffered a previous myocardial infarction.
For prevention of occlusion of saphenous vein coronary artery bypass grafts:
For 2 days preoperatively: Persantine 100 mg (oral) q.i.d.
Day of surgery: morning of operation: Persantine 100 mg (oral); 1 hour postop: Persantine 100 mg (via nasogastric tube); 7 hours postop: Asasantine (Persantine/ASA) 1 capsule.
Daily maintenance dosage: (for the next 12 months): Asasantine (Persantine/ASA) 1 capsule t.i.d.

Supplied: Each opaque orange and yellow hard gelatin capsule contains: dipyridamole 75 mg and ASA 330 mg. Nonmedicinal ingredients: acacia, aluminum stearate, gelatin, lactose, magnesium stearate, maize starch, polyvinylpyrrolidone, sodium starch glycollate, sucrose and talc. Energy: 1.39 kJ (0.33 kcal). Packages of 100 and bottles of 500. Store at room temperature (15 to 30°C).

ASCOFER®
Desbergers
Ferrous Ascorbate
Hematinic

Indications: Ferrous ascorbate, a synthetic molecule of ascorbic acid and iron, is indicated in the treatment of iron deficiency anemia.

Contraindications: Hemosiderosis, hemochromatosis, hemolytic anemia.

Precautions: Oral iron preparations may aggravate existing peptic ulcer, regional enteritis and ulcerative colitis.

Iron compounds taken orally can impair the absorption of tetracycline antibiotics. Antacids given concomitantly with iron compounds decrease iron absorption.

Adverse Effects: The treatment of a neurotic patient was interrupted because of nausea and regurgitation. In pregnant women, the incidence of pyrosis and chronic constipation is slightly increased. In children, a clinical investigator reported 3 cases of slight diarrhea which disappeared within a few days. In 1 case, slightly curdled stools were observed, although this could not be definitely attributed to the product. In the final case studies, clay colored stools were noted.

Overdose: Iron poisoning is rare in adults but serious acute poisoning in children can result from ingestion of doses in excess of 1 g. Doses of 1 g should be considered as toxic in children and therapy instituted as soon as possible. Serum iron levels above 500 μg/100 mL can be taken as presumptive evidence of poisoning; severe poisoning is usually associated with levels well above 1 000 μg/100 mL.

Symptoms: May occur within 30 minutes or may be delayed several hours. They are largely those of gastrointestinal irritation and necrosis with vomiting, diarrhea, tarry stools, hematemesis, fast and weak pulse, lethargy, low blood pressure, coma and signs of peripheral circulatory collapse. There may be a transient period of apparent recovery after 4 to 6 hours followed by a second crisis characterized by cyanosis, pulmonary edema, circulatory collapse, convulsion, and coma may then occur followed by death in 12 to 48 hours.

Treatment: Milk should be given immediately and vomiting induced. Eggs and milk should be fed (to form iron-protein complexes) until it is possible to perform gastric lavage with 1% sodium bicarbonate solution (to convert the iron to a less soluble form). Gastric lavage should not be performed after the first hour of iron ingestion because of the danger of perforation due to gastric necrosis. If an iron-chelating agent such as deferoxamine mesylate is available, it should be utilized. BAL (dimercaprol) should not be used because it may form a toxic complex. Measures to combat shock, dehydration, blood loss and respiratory failure may be necessary.

Dosage: Adults and children over 12: 275 mg twice daily with meals for treatment of mild iron deficiency anemia; 275 mg 4 times daily for severe anemia.
Infants and young children: 275 mg daily, divided into 3 equal doses for treatment of mild iron deficiency; 550 mg divided into 3 equal doses for severe anemia. Open the capsule and empty its contents into a small quantity of liquid (fruit juice, milk), or semiliquid food such as pureed baby foods.

Supplied: Each No. 2, black capsule with red cap printed with the Desbergers logo contains: hydrated ferrous ascorbate 275 mg equivalent to 33 mg of elemental iron. Energy: 36.96 kJ (8.8 kcal). Bottles of 100.

ASCORBIC ACID
General Monograph, CPhA
see VITAMIN C

ASCORBIC ACID
Roberts
Vitamin C
Vitamin Supplement

Supplied: Each ¼ teaspoon of fine powdered crystals contains: ascorbic acid 1 g. Cartoned bottles of 25 and 100 g.

ASENDIN® Ⓟ
Wyeth-Ayerst
Amoxapine
Antidepressant

Pharmacology: Amoxapine is a tricyclic antidepressant of the dibenzoxazepine class. The mechanism of clinical action of amoxapine in man is not well understood. Amoxapine is not a monoamine oxidase (MAO) inhibitor. In animals, amoxapine inhibits the re-uptake of norepinephrine and, to a lesser degree, of serotonin, at adrenergic nerve endings and blocks the response of dopamine receptors to dopamine. Its major metabolite, 8-hydroxyamoxapine, has similar norepinephrine uptake inhibiting activity but greater serotonin blocking effect than the parent compound, while the other major metabolite, 7-hydroxyamoxapine, has a dopamine receptor blocking effect.

Amoxapine is absorbed rapidly and reaches peak blood levels approximately 90 minutes after ingestion. It has a serum elimination half-life of 8 hours and is almost completely metabolized in the liver to 7-hydroxyamoxapine and 8-hydroxyamoxapine. The major active metabolite, 8-hydroxyamoxapine, has a serum half-life of 30 hours, while 7-hydroxyamoxapine is present in serum only in low concentrations with a half-life of 6.5 hours. Most of the drug is excreted in the urine and smaller amounts in the feces. The urinary metabolites appear in conjugated form as glucuronides with 33% of the dose accounted for as the 8-hydroxy metabolite and 25% as the 7-hydroxy metabolite. Only 2% is excreted unchanged. In vitro tests show that amoxapine binding to human serum protein is approximately 90%. The drug crosses the placental barrier and is excreted in human milk. The initial clinical effect usually occurs within 2 weeks of administration, but may be seen in some patients within 4 to 7 days.

Indications: The relief of symptoms of depression. Patients who have failed to respond satisfactorily to other antidepressants may show response to amoxapine.

Contraindications: Hypersensitivity to dibenzoxazepine compounds. It should not be given concomitantly with MAO inhibitors. When replacing MAO inhibitors with amoxapine, a minimum of 14 days should be allowed to elapse after the former is discontinued. Amoxapine should then be initiated cautiously with gradual increase in dosage until optimum response is achieved. Amoxapine is also contraindicated during the acute recovery phase following myocardial infarction and in the presence of acute congestive heart failure.

Warnings: Tardive Dyskinesia: Tardive dyskinesia is known to occur in patients treated with neuroleptics with antipsychotic properties and other drugs with substantial neuroleptic activity. It has also been observed with amoxapine administration (see Adverse Effects). Although the dyskinetic syndrome may remit partially or completely if the medication is withdrawn, it is irreversible in some patients. At the present time there is uncertainty as to whether neuroleptic drugs differ in their potential to cause tardive dyskinesia.

Since there is a significant prevalence of this syndrome associated with the use of neuroleptic drugs, and since there is no known effective treatment, chronic use of these drugs should generally be restricted to patients for whom neuroleptics are known to be effective and for whom there is no alternative therapy available with better risk acceptability. If manifestations of tardive dyskinesia are detected during the use of amoxapine, the drug should be discontinued. The risk of a patient developing tardive dyskinesia and of the syndrome becoming irreversible appear to increase with the duration of treatment and the total amount of drugs administered, although, in some instances, tardive dyskinesia may develop after relatively short periods of treatment at low doses. The risk of developing tardive dyskinesia may, therefore, be minimized by reducing the dose of the neuroleptic drug used and its duration of administration, consistent with the effective management of the patient's condition. Continued use of neuroleptics should be periodically reassessed.

Withdrawal Emergent Neurological Signs: As with antipsychotic agents, withdrawal emergent dyskinetic signs have been reported in some patients on maintenance therapy with amoxapine following its discontinuation. The signs are very similar to those described under Tardive Dyskinesia (see Adverse Effects), except that they are usually less persistent. Although it is not known whether gradual withdrawal will decrease the incidence of withdrawal emergent neurological signs, gradual withdrawal would appear to be advisable.

Since tricyclic agents are known to reduce the seizure threshold and since grand mal seizures have occurred at therapeutic dosage levels, extreme caution should be taken in administering the drug to patients with a history of convulsive disorders. Concurrent administration of ECT and amoxapine may be hazardous and, therefore, such treatment should be limited to patients for whom it is essential.

Because of its anticholinergic properties, amoxapine should be used with extreme caution in patients with a history of urinary retention, angle closure glaucoma or increased intraocular pressure.

Tricyclic antidepressant drugs, particularly when given in high doses, can induce sinus tachycardia, changes in conduction time and arrhythmias. A few instances of unexpected death have been reported in patients with cardiovascular disorders. Myocardial infarction and stroke have also been reported with drugs of this class. Therefore, amoxapine should be administered with extreme caution to patients with a history of cardiovascular disease, those with circulatory lability and elderly patients. In such cases, treatment should be initiated with low doses with progressive increases only if required and tolerated, and the patients should be under close surveillance at all dosage levels.

Close supervision is required when amoxapine is given to hyperthyroid patients or those receiving thyroid medication because of the possibility of cardiovascular toxicity. Tricyclic drugs may also block the antihypertensive effects of guanethidine and related compounds.

Pregnancy and *Lactation:* Safety during pregnancy and lactation has not been established. It should not be used in women of childbearing potential or nursing mothers, unless, in the opinion of the physician, the potential benefits to the patient outweigh the possible hazards to the fetus. Amoxapine is excreted in breast milk.

Children: Amoxapine is not recommended for use in children since safety and efficacy in this age group have not been established.

Precautions: Occupational Hazards: Since amoxapine has a sedative component to its action, patients should be advised against driving or engaging in activities requiring mental alertness and physical coordination until their response to the drug has been well established.

Patients should be warned that the effects of other drugs acting on the CNS, such as alcohol, barbiturates and other CNS depressants, may be potentiated by amoxapine.

The possibility of suicide in seriously depressed patients may remain until significant remission occurs. Such patients should be closely supervised throughout therapy and consideration should be given to the possible need for hospitalization. This type of patient should not have easy access to large quantities of amoxapine.

Tricyclic antidepressants may precipitate or aggravate psychotic manifestations in schizophrenic patients and hypomanic or manic episodes in manic-depressive patients. This may require a reduction of dosage, discontinuation of the drug, and/or administration of an antipsychotic agent.

Tricyclic antidepressants may also give rise to paralytic ileus, particularly in the elderly and in hospitalized patients. Therefore, appropriate measures should be taken if constipation occurs.

When amoxapine is given concomitantly with anticholinergic or sympathomimetic drugs, close supervision and careful adjustment of dosages are required.

Amoxapine should be discontinued prior to elective surgery for as long as the clinical situation will allow.

Amoxapine should be used with caution in patients with impaired liver function or with a history of hepatic damage or blood dyscrasias. Periodic blood counts and liver function tests should be performed when patients receive amoxapine in large doses or over prolonged periods.

As with other dopamine antagonists, amoxapine elevates serum prolactin levels. Tissue culture experiments indicate that approximately one-third of human breast cancers are prolactin-dependent in vitro, a factor of potential importance if the prescription of amoxapine is contemplated in a patient with a previously detected breast cancer. Although disturbances such as galactorrhea, amenorrhea, gynecomastia and impotence have been reported, the clinical significance of elevated serum prolactin levels is unknown for most patients. An increase in mammary neoplasms has been found in rodents after chronic administration of neuroleptic drugs. Neither clinical studies, nor epidemiologic studies conducted to date, however, have shown an association between chronic administration of these drugs and mammary tumorigenesis; the available evidence is considered too limited to be conclusive at this time.

Caution should be exercised if amoxapine is administered together with cimetidine since cimetidine inhibits tricyclic antidepressant metabolism, and clinically significant increases in plasma levels of amoxapine may occur.

Adverse Effects: Although some of the adverse reactions included in the following list have not been reported with amoxapine, pharmacological similarities among the tricyclic antidepressants require that each of the reactions be considered when prescribing amoxapine. With amoxapine, as with other tricyclic antidepressant drugs, the side effects most often reported are sedation and anticholinergic effects.

Behavioral: drowsiness, fatigue, excitement, agitation, restlessness, insomnia, nightmares, hypomania, anxiety, confusion, disorientation, disturbed concentration, delusions, hallucinations, activation of latent psychosis.

Neurological: seizures, alteration in EEG patterns, dizziness, tremors, extrapyramidal symptoms, numbness, tingling, paresthesias of the extremities, peripheral neuropathy, tinnitus, syndrome of inappropriate ADH (antidiuretic hormone) secretion.

Extrapyramidal symptoms reported with amoxapine include: akinesia, akathisia, chorea, cogwheel rigidity, dysarthria, mask-like facies, oculogyric crisis, torticollis and dyskinesia, including tardive dyskinesia. Although most of these symptoms have been reported infrequently, the possibility of their occurrence should be borne in mind when prescribing amoxapine.

As with antipsychotic agents, tardive dyskinesia may appear in some patients on long-term therapy with amoxapine or may appear after drug therapy has been discontinued (withdrawal tardive dyskinesia). The risk appears to be greater in elderly patients on high-dose therapy, especially females. The symptoms are persistent and in some patients may be irreversible. The syndrome is usually characterized by rhythmical involuntary movements of the tongue, face, mouth or jaw (e.g. protrusion of tongue, puffing of cheeks, puckering of mouth, chewing movements), but may also be manifested by abnormal involuntary movements of extremities and other extrapyramidal symptoms, such as akathisia.

There is, at present, no known effective treatment for tardive dyskinesia; anticholinergic agents may worsen the symptoms of this syndrome and the results from studies with other agents (e.g. dopamine agonists, cholinergics, GABA agonists) are not clear. Therefore, it is suggested that amoxapine be discontinued if symptoms of tardive dyskinesia appear, and the patient be switched to a different antidepressant.

On no account should the dosage be increased in an attempt to mask the syndrome. It has been reported that fine vermicular movements of the tongue may be an early sign of the syndrome, and, if the medication is stopped at that time, the syndrome may not develop.

Cardiovascular: hypotension, hypertension, tachycardia, palpitations, syncope, atrial arrhythmias (including premature atrial contractions and fibrillation), heart block, stroke and cardiac arrest have been reported with amoxapine. A quinidine-like effect and other reversible ECG changes such as flattening or inversion of T waves, bundle branch block, depressed ST segments, prolonged conduction time and asystole have been reported with other tricyclic antidepressants.

Autonomic: dry mouth, blurred vision, disturbances of accommodation, mydriasis, constipation, nasal stuffiness, delayed micturition, sublingual adenitis, paralytic ileus, urinary retention, dilation of the urinary tract, precipitation of latent and aggravation of existing glaucoma, vertigo.

Endocrine: increased or decreased libido, impotence, menstrual irregularity, testicular swelling, painful ejaculation, inhibition of orgasm, breast enlargement and galactorrhea in the female, gynecomastia in the male, elevation and lowering of blood sugar levels, and increased prolactin levels.

Allergic or toxic: pruritus, skin rash, photosensitization, edema, drug fever, leukopenia, urticaria, petechiae, obstructive jaundice, bone marrow depression, including agranulocytosis, eosinophilia, purpura and thrombocytopenia, toxic epidermal necrolysis and neuroleptic malignant syndrome.

Gastrointestinal: nausea, epigastric distress, vomiting, flatulence, abdominal pain, diarrhea, peculiar taste, stomatitis.

Miscellaneous: weakness, headache, weight gain or loss, excessive appetite, anorexia, increased perspiration, urinary frequency, lacrimation, alopecia, parotid swelling, black tongue, hepatitis.

Withdrawal Symptoms: Abrupt cessation of treatment with tricyclic antidepressants after prolonged administration may produce nausea, headache and malaise. These symptoms are not indicative of addiction. Withdrawal emergent dyskinesia has been reported with amoxapine.

Overdose: Symptoms: Toxic manifestations of overdosage differ significantly from those of other tricyclic antidepressants. CNS effects such as drowsiness, delirium, lethargy with diminished deep tendon reflexes and particularly grand mal convulsions, occur frequently, and treatment should be directed primarily toward prevention or control of seizures. Status epilepticus may develop and constitutes a neurologic emergency. Coma and acidosis are other serious complications of substantial overdosage in some cases.

Fatalities have resulted from amoxapine overdosage and permanent neurologic damage has occurred in some patients who recovered after prolonged status epilepticus and severe acidosis.

Renal failure may develop 2 to 5 days after toxic overdosage in patients who may appear otherwise recovered. Acute tubular necrosis with rhabdomyolysis and myoglobinuria is the most common renal complication in such cases. This reaction typically occurs in those who have experienced multiple seizures, and most patients recover with appropriate treatment.

Cardiovascular effects, when they occur, are usually limited to sinus tachycardia and transient minor ECG changes. Hence, prolongation of the QRS interval beyond 100 milliseconds within the first 24 hours is **not** a useful guide to the severity of overdosage with amoxapine. Serious hypotension, hypertension, incomplete bundle branch block and cardiac arrhythmias have been rarely observed with amoxapine.

The smallest estimated lethal overdoses reported with amoxapine in adults have been 1.5 to 2 g. A 15-month old child died after ingesting approximately 250 mg. On the other hand, some patients have survived much larger overdoses. Age and physical condition of the patient, concomitant ingestion of other drugs, and especially the interval between drug ingestion and initiation of emergency treatment, are important determining factors in the probability of survival.

Symptoms of overdosage reported with other tricyclic antidepressants include: drowsiness, mydriasis, dysarthria, general weakness, excitement, agitation, hyperactive reflexes, muscle spasms and rigidity, hypothermia, hyperpyrexia, vomiting, perspiration, rapid thready pulse, convulsions, severe hypotension, hypertension, tachycardia, disturbances of cardiac conduction, arrhythmia, congestive heart failure, circulatory collapse, respiratory depression and coma. In patients with glaucoma, even average doses may precipitate an attack.

Treatment: Treatment should be symptomatic and supportive, but with special attention to prevention or control of seizures. Renal failure may develop a few days after substantial amoxapine overdosage in patients who may appear otherwise recovered. Therefore, patients who may have ingested an overdosage of amoxapine, particularly children, should be hospitalized and kept under close surveillance.

In all comatose patients basic life support measures must be instituted, including establishment of an adequate airway and assisted ventilation, if necessary. Emesis should be induced only in conscious, asymptomatic patients. In all other patients, gastric lavage, with appropriate precautions to prevent pulmonary aspiration, should be performed as soon as possible. These measures are recommended up to 12 hours or even more after the overdose since the anticholinergic effect of the drug may delay gastric emptying. Following lavage or emesis activated charcoal may be administered to reduce absorption, and repeated administration may facilitate drug elimination. Acidosis may be treated by cautious administration of sodium bicarbonate. Treatment of renal impairment is the same as that for non-drug-induced renal dysfunction. The value of dialysis is doubtful due to the extensive plasma protein binding of amoxapine.

External stimulation should be minimized to reduce the tendency to convulsions. Convulsions, when they occur, typically begin within 12 hours after ingestion of amoxapine. Because seizures may occur precipitously in some overdosage patients who appear otherwise relatively asymptomatic, the treating physician may wish to consider prophylactic administration of anticonvulsant medication during this period. Standard anticonvulsants, such as i.v. diazepam and/or phenytoin should be administered. Barbiturates may intensify respiratory depression, particularly in children, and aggravate hypotension and coma. Paraldehyde may be used in some children to counteract muscular hypertonus and convulsions with less likelihood of causing respiratory depression. Prompt control of convulsions, including status epilepticus, is essential since they aggravate hypoxia and acidosis and may thereby precipitate cardiac arrhythmias and arrest, as well as cause permanent neurological damage.

ECG monitoring in an intensive care unit is recommended in all patients with tricyclic antidepressant overdosage, although cardiac complications do not appear to be as serious a problem with amoxapine overdosage as with some other tricyclic antidepressants, and the ECG typically remains within normal limits except for sinus tachycardia.

Shock should be treated with supportive measures such as i.v. fluids, oxygen and corticosteroids. Pressor agents, such as norepinephrine (but **not** epinephrine) are rarely indicated and should be given only after careful consideration and under continuous monitoring.

The slow i.v. administration of physostigmine salicylate has been reported to reverse most of the cardiovascular and CNS effects of tricyclic overdosage, such as cardiac arrhythmias and convulsions; however, it should not be used routinely because of its short duration of action and potentially serious adverse effects. The recommended dosage in adults has been 1 to 2 mg in **very slow** i.v. injection (avoid rapid injection to reduce the possibility of physostigmine-induced convulsions). In children, the initial dosage should not exceed 0.5 mg and should be adjusted to age and response. Since physostigmine has a short duration of action, administration may have to be repeated at 30 to 60 minute intervals.

Deaths by deliberate or accidental overdosage have occurred with this class of drugs. Since the propensity for suicide is high in depressed patients, a suicide attempt by other means may occur during the recovery phase. The possibility of simultaneous ingestion of other drugs should also be considered.

Dosage: The dosage must be individualized according to the requirements of each patient. Treatment should be initiated at the lowest recommended dose and increased gradually with careful assessment of clinical response and any evidence of intolerance. Once effective dosage is well established, the total daily dosage may be given in a single daily dose (not to exceed 300 mg) at bedtime. Total daily dosages higher than 300 mg should be given in divided doses. Care should be taken not to increase the dosage of amoxapine if manifestations of extrapyramidal effects occur, as there is a possibility of development of tardive dyskinesia with this drug.

Adults: Initially, 50 mg twice daily. Depending on the patient's tolerance and response, this should be increased to 50 mg 3 times daily as early as the third day of treatment. In severely depressed hospitalized patients or patients under close supervision, a higher initial dose of 50 mg 3 times daily may be indicated, and this may be increased to 100 mg 2 or 3 times daily. The usual optimum dose is 150 to 300 mg daily, but some patients may require higher doses, up to 400 mg or more daily, depending on tolerance and response of each individual patient. Some hospitalized patients have received doses up to 600 mg daily in divided doses. When higher doses are used, it is essential to exclude history of convulsive disorders.

Elderly or Debilitated Patients: The total experience with amoxapine in elderly patients is limited. Therefore, if there is a valid indication for use of amoxapine in an elderly patient, the dosage should be titrated very carefully. As with other drugs of this class, it is recommended to initiate treatment with lower doses and to increase dosage gradually. The recommended starting dosage is 12.5 mg, 3 times daily. This should be increased very gradually, depending on tolerance and response, to 50 mg 2 or 3 times daily.

Maintenance Dosage: The recommended maintenance dosage is the lowest dose that will sustain remission. Medication

Asendin (cont'd)

should be continued for the expected duration of the depressive episode in order to minimize the possibility of relapse following clinical improvement. If symptoms reappear, dosage should be increased to the level which previously induced remission, until symptoms are again controlled.

When a maintenance dosage has been established as described above, amoxapine may be administered in a single dose before bedtime provided such a dosage regimen is well tolerated. However, if the total daily dose exceeds 300 mg, it should be administered in divided doses.

When amoxapine therapy is discontinued, the withdrawal of the drug should be gradual.

Supplied: 25 mg: Each heptagonal, white, scored tablet engraved "LL25" and "A13" contains: amoxapine 25 mg. Nonmedicinal ingredients: calcium phosphate dibasic, magnesium stearate, starch, starch pregelatinized and stearic acid. Tartrazine-free. Bottles of 100.

50 mg: Each heptagonal, mottled, orange, scored tablet engraved "LL50" and "A15" contains: amoxapine 50 mg. Nonmedicinal ingredients: calcium phosphate dibasic, FD&C Yellow No. 6 aluminum lake, magnesium stearate, starch, starch pregelatinized and stearic acid. Tartrazine-free. Bottles of 100 and 500.

100 mg: Each heptagonal, mottled, blue, scored tablet engraved "LL100" and "A17" contains: amoxapine 100 mg. Nonmedicinal ingredients: calcium phosphate dibasic dihydrate, FD&C Blue No. 2 aluminum lake, magnesium stearate, starch, starch pregelatinized and stearic acid. Tartrazine-free. Bottles of 100.

ASMAVENT® P

Technilab

Salbutamol Sulfate

Bronchodilator

Supplied: Respirator Solution: Each mL of isotonic solution contains: salbutamol sulfate equivalent to salbutamol base 5 mg. Nonmedicinal ingredients: benzalkonium chloride and sulfuric acid. Bottles of 10 mL.

Respirator Solution Unit Dose Nebules P.F.: Each nebule of sterile, isotonic solution contains: salbutamol sulfate equivalent to salbutamol base 1.25, 2.5 or 5.0 mg in 2.5 mL. Nonmedicinal ingredients: sulfuric acid and sodium chloride. Adjusted to pH 3.5 to 4.5. Boxes of 20.

Store between 15 and 25°C. Protect from light.

ASPIRIN®

Bayer Consumer

ASA

Analgesic—Anti-inflammatory—Antipyretic—Platelet Aggregation Inhibitor

Pharmacology: ASA interferes with the production of prostaglandins in various organs and tissues through acetylation of the enzyme cyclo-oxygenase. Prostaglandins are themselves powerful irritants and produce headaches and pain on injection in man. Prostaglandins also appear to sensitize pain receptors to other noxious substances such as histamine and bradykinin. By preventing the synthesis and release of prostaglandins in inflammation, ASA may avert the sensitization of pain receptors.

The antipyretic activity of ASA is due to its ability to interfere with the production of prostaglandin E_1 in the brain. Prostaglandin E_1 is one of the most powerful pyretic agents known.

The inhibition of platelet aggregation by ASA is due to its ability to interfere with the production of thromboxane A_2 within the platelet. Thromboxane A_2 is largely responsible for the aggregating properties of platelets.

When ASA is taken orally, it is rapidly absorbed from the stomach and proximal small intestine. The gastric mucosa is permeable to the non-ionized form of ASA, which passes through the stomach wall by a passive diffusion process.

Optimum absorption of salicylate in the human stomach occurs in the pH range of 2.15 to 4.10. Absorption in the small intestine occurs at a significantly faster rate than in the stomach. After an oral dose of 650 mg Aspirin, the plasma acetylsalicylate concentration in man usually reaches a level between 0.6 and 1.0 mg% in 20 minutes after ingestion and drops to 0.2 mg% within an hour. Within the same period of time, half or more of the ingested dose is hydrolyzed to salicylic acid by esterases in the gastrointestinal mucosa and the liver, the total plasma salicylate concentration reaching a peak between 1 or 2 hours after ingestion, averaging between 3 and 7 mg%. Many factors influence the speed of absorption of ASA in a particular individual at a given time; tablet disintegration, solubility, particle size, gastric emptying time, psychological state, physical condition, nature and quantity of gastric contents, etc., all affect absorption.

Distribution of salicylate throughout most body fluids and tissues proceeds at a rapid rate after absorption. Aside from the plasma itself, fluids which have been found to contain substantial amounts of salicylate after oral ingestion include spinal, peritoneal and synovial fluids, saliva and milk. Tissues containing high concentrations of the drug are the kidney, liver, heart and lungs. Concentrations in the brain are usually low, and are minimal in feces, bile and sweat.

The drug readily crosses the placental barrier. At clinical concentrations, from 50% to 90% of the salicylate is bound to plasma proteins especially albumin, while ASA itself is bound to only a very limited extent. However, ASA has the capacity of acetylating various proteins, hormones, DNA, platelets and hemoglobin, which at least partly explains its wide-ranging pharmacological actions.

The liver appears to be the principal site for salicylate metabolism, although other tissues may also be involved. The three chief metabolic products of salicylic acid are salicyluric acid, the ether or phenolic glucuronide and the ester or acyl glucuronide. A small fraction is also converted to gentisic acid and other hydroxybenzoic acids. The half-life of Aspirin in the circulation is from 13 to 19 minutes so that the blood level drops quickly after absorption is complete. However, the half-life of the salicylate ranges between 3.5 and 4.5 hours, which means that 50% of the ingested dose leaves the circulation within that time.

Excretion of salicylates occurs principally via the kidney, through a combination of glomerular filtration and tubular excretion, in the form of free salicylic acid, salicyluric acid, as well as phenolic and acyl glucuronides. Salicylate can be detected in the urine shortly after its ingestion but the full dose requires up to 48 hours for complete elimination. The rate of excretion of free salicylate is extremely variable, reported recovery rates in human urine ranging from 10% to 85%, depending largely on urinary pH. In general, it can be stated that acid urine facilitates reabsorption of salicylate by renal tubules, while alkaline urine promotes excretion of the drug.

Indications: The relief of pain, fever and inflammation of a variety of conditions such as influenza, common cold, low back and neck pain, dysmenorrhea, headache, toothache, sprains and strains, myositis, neuralgia, synovitis, arthritis, bursitis, burns, injuries, following surgical and dental procedures.

ASA is also indicated for the following uses, based on its platelet aggregation inhibitory properties:

For reducing the risk of morbidity and death in patients with unstable angina and in those with previous myocardial infarction.

For reducing the risk of transient ischemic attacks (TIA) and for secondary prevention of atherothrombotic cerebral infarction.

Prophylaxis of venous thromboembolism after total hip replacement in men.

Reduction in the adhesive properties of the platelets in patients following carotid endarterectomy to prevent recurrence of TIA and in hemodialysis patients with a silicone rubber arteriovenous cannula.

Contraindications: Salicylate sensitivity, active peptic ulcer.

Warnings: ASA is one of the most frequent causes of accidental poisonings in toddlers and infants. Tablets should be kept well out of the reach of children.

A possible association between Reye's syndrome and the use of salicylates has been suggested but not established. Reye's syndrome has also occurred in many patients not exposed to salicylates. However, caution is advised when prescribing salicylate-containing medications for children and teenagers with influenza or chickenpox.

Precautions: Salicylates should be administered cautiously to patients with asthma and other allergic conditions, a history of gastrointestinal ulcerations, bleeding tendencies, significant anemia or hypoprothrombinemia.

Patients taking ASA daily are at an increased risk of developing gastrointestinal bleeding following the ingestion of alcohol.

Caution is necessary when salicylates and anticoagulants are prescribed concurrently, as salicylates can depress the concentration of prothrombin in the plasma.

Diabetics receiving concurrent salicylate-hypoglycemic therapy should be monitored closely: reduction of the sulfonylurea hypoglycemic drug dosage may be necessary; insulin requirements may change.

Pregnancy: High doses (3 g daily) of ASA during pregnancy may lengthen the gestation and parturition time.

Salicylates can produce changes in thyroid function tests.

Sodium excretion produced by spironolactone may be decreased by salicylate administration.

Salicylates in large doses are uricosuric agents, smaller amounts may depress uric acid clearance and thus decrease the uricosuric effects of other drugs.

Salicylates also retard the renal elimination of methotrexate.

Adverse Effects: Gastrointestinal: (the frequency and severity of these adverse effects are dose related) nausea, vomiting, diarrhea, gastrointestinal bleeding and/or ulceration, dyspepsia, heartburn.

Ear: tinnitus, vertigo, hearing loss.

Hematologic: leukopenia, thrombocytopenia, purpura, anemia.

Dermatologic and hypersensitivity: urticaria, angioedema, pruritus, skin eruptions, asthma, anaphylaxis.

Miscellaneous: mental confusion, drowsiness, sweating, thirst.

Overdose: Symptoms: In mild overdosage these may include rapid and deep breathing, nausea, vomiting, vertigo, tinnitus, flushing, sweating, thirst and tachycardia. In more severe cases, acid-base disturbances including respiratory alkalosis and metabolic acidosis can occur. Severe cases may show fever, hemorrhage, excitement, confusion, convulsions or coma and respiratory failure.

Treatment: Treatment consists of prevention and management of acid-base and fluid and electrolyte disturbances. Renal clearance is increased by increasing urine flow and by alkaline diuresis but care must be taken in this approach to not further aggravate metabolic acidosis and hypokalemia. Acidemia should be prevented by administration of adequate sodium containing fluids and sodium bicarbonate. Hypoglycemia is an occasional accompaniment of salicylate overdosage and can be managed by glucose solutions. If a hemorrhagic diathesis is evident, give vitamin K. Hemodialysis may be useful in complex acid base disturbances particularly in the presence of abnormal renal function.

Dosage: Analgesic and Antipyretic: Adults: 1 to 2 tablets (325 to 650 mg) orally every 4 hours. Children under 12: 10 to 15 mg/kg every 6 hours, not to exceed total daily dose of 2.4 g.

Anti-inflammatory: Adults: 3 tablets (975 mg) 4 to 6 times a day, up to 30 tablets daily, may be required for optimal anti-inflammatory effect. A blood level between 15 and 30 mg/100 mL is in the desirable therapeutic range.

Children: 60 to 125 mg/kg daily in 4 to 6 divided doses.

For reducing the risk of morbidity and death in patients with unstable angina and in those with previous myocardial infarction: 80 to 325 mg daily according to the individual needs of the patient, as determined by the physician. Coated Aspirin Daily Low Dose is specifically indicated for these uses.

For reducing the risk of transient ischemic attacks (TIA) and for secondary prevention of atherothrombotic cerebral infarction: 80 to 325 mg daily according to the individual needs of the patient, as determined by the physician. Coated Aspirin Daily Low Dose is specifically indicated for these uses.

For prophylaxis of venous thromboembolism after total hip replacement: 650 mg twice a day (1 300 mg daily), started 1 day before surgery and continued for 14 days.

For other platelet aggregation inhibitory uses: 325 to 1 300 mg daily according to individual needs and generally accepted standards of care for each indication.

Supplied: Tablets: 325 mg: Each white tablet with the Bayer Cross on both sides contains: ASA 325 mg USP. Nonmedicinal ingredients: cornstarch, FD&C Blue #2, hydroxypropyl methylcellulose, potassium sorbate, titanium dioxide, triacetin and xanthan gum. Energy: 1.4 kJ (0.336 kcal). Alcohol-, lactose-, paraben-, sodium-, sulfite- and tartrazine-free. Packages of 12, 24, 50, 100 and 200.

Extra Strength, 500 mg: Each white tablet with the Bayer Cross in red ink on one side contains: ASA 500 mg USP. Nonmedicinal ingredients: cornstarch, D&C Red #7, FD&C Blue #2, FD&C Red #40, hydroxypropyl methylcellulose, titanium dioxide and triacetin. Energy: 2.18 kJ (0.52 kcal). Alcohol-, lactose-, paraben-, sodium-, sulfite- and tartrazine-free. Packages of 30, 60 and 100.

Caplets: Each white capsule-shaped tablet (caplet) with Bayer on one side and score on the other, contains: ASA 325 mg. Nonmedicinal ingredients: cornstarch, FD&C Blue #2, hydroxypropyl methylcellulose, potassium sorbate, titanium dioxide, triacetin and xanthan gum. Alcohol-, lactose-, parabens-, sodium-, sulfite- and tartrazine-free. Packages of 50 and 100.

Children's Size Aspirin Tablets: Each peach colored tablet, with a pleasant orange taste, with Bayer Cross on one side and Aspirin on the other, contains: ASA 80 mg USP. Nonmedicinal ingredients: cornstarch, dextrose, FD&C Yellow #6, orange juice flavor and sodium cyclamate. Energy: 2.24 kJ (0.537 kcal). Sodium: <1 mmol (0.32 mg). Alcohol-, lactose-, paraben-, sulfite- and tartrazine-free. Bottles of 24 and 90.

Coated Aspirin Daily Low Dose: Each pale blue colored enteric coated tablet, with 81 in dark blue ink on one side, contains: ASA 81 mg. Alcohol-, paraben-, sulfite- and tartrazine-free. Bottles of 24 and 120.

(Shown in Product Recognition Section)

ASPIRIN® BACKACHE
Bayer Consumer
ASA—Methocarbamol
Analgesic—Muscle Relaxant

Indications: Provides effective relief of back pain by reducing muscle spasms and relaxing tense back and neck muscles, thereby increasing mobility.

Precautions: Consult a physician or pharmacist before taking this medication if you: have a predisposition to asthma, stomach problems, peptic ulcer, severe liver disease, gout, severe anemia or allergy to salicylates; have a history of blood coagulation defects; are receiving anticoagulant drugs; are scheduled for surgery within 7 days; are taking anti-inflammatory drugs, anticonvulsants, antidiabetic or gout medicine or other medications containing salicylates or acetaminophen.

Caution: This package contains enough medication to seriously harm a child. Keep out of children's reach. Children and teenagers should not use this medicine for chickenpox or flu symptoms before a doctor is consulted about Reye's Syndrome, a rare but serious illness reported to be associated with ASA.

Pregnancy and *Lactation:* Consult a physician before taking when pregnant or nursing. It is especially important not to use this drug during the last 3 months of pregnancy unless specifically directed to do so by a physician because it may cause problems in the unborn child or complications during delivery.

Occupational Hazards: This medication may cause drowsiness. Do not drive or engage in activities requiring alertness. Avoid alcohol.

Adverse Effects: Like all medicines, ASA may occasionally produce unwanted side effects. A physician should be contacted if any of the following reactions develop during treatment: bleeding or irritation of stomach, nausea, vomiting, pain; any loss of hearing, including ringing or buzzing in the ears; skin rashes, hives or itching; breathing difficulties.

Overdose: Symptoms and Treatment: In case of accidental overdose, contact a physician or Poison Control Centre at once, even in the absence of symptoms.

Dosage: Adults: Take 1 or 2 caplets every 4 hours as necessary, up to 8 caplets daily. May be taken with milk or water, if desired. It is hazardous to exceed the maximum recommended dose unless advised by a physician. If these doses do not bring relief, and pain persists for more than 5 days, this is an indication that the advice of a physician is required. Use only as directed by a doctor.

Supplied: Each pale green, oblong caplet, with embossed "BAYER" on one side, contains: ASA 500 mg and methocarbamol 400 mg. Nonmedicinal ingredients: carnauba wax, colloidal silicon dioxide, cornstarch, croscarmellose sodium, FD&C blue No. 2, hydrogenated vegetable oil, hydroxypropyl methylcellulose, microcrystalline cellulose, polyethylene glycol, polysorbate 80, polyvinylpyrrolidone, sodium lauryl sulfate, synthetic yellow iron oxide and titanium dioxide. Lactose-, parabens-, sucrose- and tartrazine-free. Bottles of 18 and 40.

(Shown in Product Recognition Section)

Reviewed 1998

ASPIRIN®, COATED
Bayer Consumer
see COATED ASPIRIN

ASPIRIN® WITH STOMACH GUARD™
Bayer Consumer
ASA Compound
Analgesic—Anti-inflammatory—Antipyretic

Supplied: Regular Strength: Each round, white, film-coated tablet, with BAYER PLUS in blue ink on one side, contains: ASA 325 mg, calcium carbonate 160 mg, magnesium carbonate 34 mg and magnesium oxide 63 mg. Nonmedicinal ingredients: acacia, carnauba wax, cornstarch, croscarmellose sodium, FD&C Blue #2, hydrogenated vegetable oil, hydroxypropyl methylcellulose, magnesium stearate, microcrystalline cellulose, polysorbate 80, polyvinylpyrrolidone, propylene glycol, silicon dioxide, sodium lauryl sulfate, talc, titanium dioxide and triacetin. Lactose-, parabens-, sulfite- and tartrazine-free. Packages of 36.

Extra Strength: Each, white, film-coated caplet, with BAYER PLUS over 500 on one side in blue ink, contains: ASA 500 mg, calcium carbonate 246.2 mg, magnesium carbonate 52.3 mg and magnesium oxide 96.9 mg. Nonmedicinal ingredients: acacia, carnauba wax, cornstarch, croscarmellose sodium, FD&C Blue #2, hydrogenated vegetable oil, hydroxypropyl methylcellulose, magnesium stearate, microcrystalline cellulose, polysorbate 80, polyvinylpyrrolidone, propylene glycol, silicon dioxide, sodium lauryl sulfate, talc, titanium dioxide and triacetin. Lactose-, parabens-, sulfite- and tartrazine-free. Packages of 30 and 60.

(Shown in Product Recognition Section)

ASTRACAINE®
ASTRACAINE® FORTE
Astra
Articaine HCl—Epinephrine
Local Anesthetic

Pharmacology: Articaine is a local anesthetic of the amide type. As with other local anesthetics, it prevents the generation and conduction of the nerve impulse by interfering with the large transient increase in the permeability of the membrane to sodium ions.

Epinephrine acts on alpha-adrenergic receptors in the vasculature of the mucous membranes to produce vasoconstriction, thereby decreasing blood flow in the area of injection. This results in a reduction in the rate of local clearance of articaine which prolongs its duration of action, lowers the peak serum concentration, decreases the risk of systemic toxicity and increases the frequency of complete conduction blocks with low concentrations of the local anesthetic.

Following intraoral injection of a 240 mg dose of articaine 4% with epinephrine 5 μg/mL in healthy volunteers, peak plasma levels (C_{max}) of 1.17$\pm$0.14 μg/mL were reached at approximately 17 minutes. The elimination half-life ($T_{1/2}\beta$) was 25.28$\pm$3.3 minutes.

Articaine is excreted mainly by the kidneys. Of an epidural dose, approximately 2 to 5% is excreted unchanged, 40 to 70% is excreted as articainic acid and 4 to 15% as articainic acid glucuronide.

When used for infiltration or nerve block anesthesia, the onset of action for articaine hydrochloride with epinephrine is 1 to 2 minutes.

The duration of anesthesia varies depending on the type of block and the amount injected.

Indications: For infiltration anesthesia and nerve block anesthesia in clinical dentistry.

Contraindications: Patients with a known hypersensitivity to local anesthetics of the amide type. As with all vasoconstrictors, epinephrine is contraindicated in hypertension, thyrotoxicosis, or severe heart disease, particularly when tachycardia is present. Local anesthetics should not be used in severe shock or heart block. They should also not be used when there is inflammation or sepsis in the region of the proposed injection.

Warnings: Resuscitative equipment and drugs should be immediately available when any local anesthetic is used.

As with other local anesthetics, articaine is capable of producing methemoglobinemia. This has been observed with epidural anesthesia, but not when used as directed in dental procedures.

Methemoglobinemia values of less than 20% usually do not produce any clinical symptoms. The usual clinical signs of methemoglobinemia are cyanosis of the nail beds and lips. Although the possibility of methemoglobinemia occurring in dental patients is extremely rare it can be rapidly reversed by the use of 1 to 2 mg/kg body weight of methylene blue administered i.v. over a 5 minute period.

Because Astracaine contains a vasoconstrictor, it should be used with extreme caution in patients receiving drugs known to produce blood pressure alterations (for example MAO inhibitors, tricyclic antidepressants, phenothiazines), as either severe and sustained hypotension or hypertension may occur.

Precautions: General: The safety and effectiveness of local anesthetics depend upon proper dosage, correct technique, adequate precautions and readiness for emergencies.

The lowest dose that results in effective anesthesia should be used to avoid high plasma levels and serious undesirable adverse effects. Injections should be made slowly, with frequent aspirations before and during the injection. If blood is aspirated, the needle should be relocated. Tolerance varies with the status of the patient. Debilitated or elderly patients, acutely ill patients and children should be given reduced doses commensurate with their age and physical status.

Pregnancy: Safe use of articaine in pregnant women has not been established; however, animal studies have not demonstrated teratogenic or embryotoxic effects.

Lactation: Articaine is rapidly metabolized and eliminated and is therefore unlikely to be transferred to the mother's milk.

Patients with Special Diseases and Conditions: Astracaine contains a vasoconstrictor and should therefore be used with caution in the presence of diseases which may adversely affect the patient's cardiovascular system.

The drug should be used with caution in persons with known drug sensitivities. Astracaine contains sodium metabisulfite. Sulfates may cause allergic reactions in susceptible people. The prevalence of sulfite sensitivity in the general population is unknown and probably low, but it is seen more frequently in patients with bronchial asthma. Reactions can include anaphylactic symptoms and life-threatening or less severe asthmatic episodes.

Many drugs used during the conduct of anesthesia are considered potential triggering agents for familial malignant hyperthermia. It has been shown that the use of amide local anesthetics in malignant hyperthermia patients is safe. However, there is no guarantee that neural blockade will prevent the development of malignant hyperthermia during surgery. It is also difficult to predict the need for supplemental general anesthesia. Therefore, a standard protocol for the management of malignant hyperthermia should be available.

Drug Interactions: Serious cardiac arrhythmias may occur if preparations containing a vasoconstrictor are employed in patients during or following the administration of chloroform, halothane, cycloproprane, trichloroethylene or other related agents.

Caution should be exercised when administering articaine concomitantly with other medications which are potential producers of methemoglobin (e.g., sulfonamides).

Adverse Effects: Reactions to articaine are characteristic of those associated with amide-type local anesthetics.

Adverse reactions may result from high plasma levels due to excessive dosage, rapid absorption or inadvertent intravascular injection, or may result from a hypersensitivity, idiosyncrasy or diminished tolerance on the part of the patient. Such reactions are systemic in nature and involve the CNS and/or the cardiovascular system.

CNS: CNS manifestations are excitatory and/or depressant and may be characterized by nervousness, dizziness, blurred vision and tremors, followed by drowsiness, convulsions, unconsciousness and possibly respiratory arrest. The excitatory reactions may be very brief or may not occur at all, in which case, the first manifestations of toxicity may be drowsiness, merging into unconsciousness and respiratory arrest.

Cardiovascular: Cardiovascular reactions are depressant and may be characterized by hypotension, myocardial depression, bradycardia and possibly cardiac arrest.

Allergic: Allergic reactions are characterized by cutaneous lesions, urticaria, edema or anaphylactoid reactions. The detection of sensitivity by skin testing is of doubtful value.

Astracaine (cont'd)

Swelling and persistent paresthesia of the lips and oral tissues have been reported after blocking the inferior alveolar nerve.

Overdose: Symptoms and Treatment: Treatment of a patient with toxic manifestations consists of assuring and maintaining a patent airway and supporting ventilation using oxygen and assisted or controlled respiration as required. This will be sufficient in the management of most reactions. Should circulatory depression occur, vasopressors, such as ephedrine or metaraminol, and i.v. fluids may be used. Should a convulsion persist despite oxygen therapy, small increments of an ultrashort acting barbiturate (thiopental or thiamylal) or a short-acting barbiturate (pentobarbital or secobarbital) may be given i.v.

Dosage: As with all local anesthetics, the dosage varies and depends on the area to be anesthetized, the vascularity of the tissues, the number of neuronal segments to be blocked, individual tolerance and the technique of anesthesia. The lowest dosage needed to provide effective anesthesia should be administered. See Table I.

Table I—Astracaine 4%/Astracaine 4% Forte

Dosage

	Astracaine 4% and Astracaine 4% Forte	
Procedure	**Volume (mL)**	**Total Dose (mg)**
Infiltration	0.5-2.5	20-100
Nerve block	0.5-3.6	20-144
Oral surgery	1.0-5.4	40-216

Adults: It is recommended that the dosage should not exceed 7 mg/kg body weight in adults and, in general, the maximum total dose should not exceed 500 mg (12.5 mL or 7 cartridges).

Children: Dosages in children should be reduced commensurate with their age and weight. Experience in children younger than 4 years of age has not been documented. The dosage should not exceed 5 mg/kg body weight in children between the ages of 4 and 12.

Supplied: Astracaine 4%: Each mL of solution contains: articaine HCl 40 mg and epinephrine 5 μg (1:200 000). Nonmedicinal ingredients: sodium chloride, sodium hydroxide and/or hydrochloric acid to adjust pH range to 2.7 to 4.5, sodium metabisulfite and water for injection. Dental cartridges of 1.8 mL, boxes of 50.

Astracaine 4% Forte: Each mL of solution contains: articaine HCl 40 mg and epinephrine 10 μg (1:100 000). Nonmedicinal ingredients: sodium chloride, sodium hydroxide and/or hydrochloric acid to adjust pH range to 2.7 to 4.5, sodium metabisulfite and water for injection. Dental cartridges of 1.8 mL, boxes of 50.

Store at controlled room temperature (15 to 30°C). Protect from light. Do not use if solution is pinkish or darker than slightly yellow or if it contains a precipitate. Solutions are without preservative and are for single use only. Discard unused portion.

New Product 1998

ATARAX™ 🅿

Pfizer

Hydroxyzine HCl

Anxiolytic—Antihistamine

Indications: Oral: The management of anxiety and tension as in the preparation for dental procedures and in acute emotional problems. Also used in the management of anxiety associated with organic disturbances and as adjunctive therapy in alcoholism and allergic conditions with strong emotional overlay, such as in asthma. Useful in the management of pruritus due to allergic conditions such as chronic urticaria and atopic and contact dermatoses. Useful in the control of nausea and vomiting, excluding nausea and vomiting of pregnancy (see Contraindications).

I.M.: The treatment of the following types of patients when this route of administration is desirable: the acutely disturbed or hysterical patient; the acute or chronic alcoholic with anxiety, withdrawal symptoms or delirium tremens; as pre and postoperative and pre and postpartum adjunctive medication to allay anxiety and to permit substantial reduction in narcotic dosage and to control emesis, excluding nausea and vomiting of pregnancy (see Contraindications).

Patients may be started on parenteral therapy when indicated by the clinical situation. They should be maintained on oral therapy whenever this route is again practicable.

Contraindications: In patients with known hypersensitivity to the drug.

Pregnancy: Hydroxyzine, when administered to the pregnant mouse, rat and rabbit, induced fetal abnormalities in the rat at doses substantially above the human therapeutic range. Clinical data in humans are inadequate to establish safety in early pregnancy. Until such data are available, hydroxyzine is contraindicated in early pregnancy.

Warnings: *Lactation:* It is not known whether this drug is excreted in human milk. Since many drugs are so excreted, hydroxyzine should not be given to nursing mothers.

Precautions: The potentiating effect of hydroxyzine must be considered when the drug is used in conjunction with CNS depressants such as narcotics, non-narcotic analgesics, hypnotics, sedatives, psychotherapeutic agents, barbiturates or alcohol. Therefore, when CNS depressants are administered concomitantly with hydroxyzine, their dosage should be reduced.

Administer hydroxyzine cautiously to epileptic patients.

Occupational Hazards: Since drowsiness may occur with use of this drug, patients should be cautioned against driving a car or operating dangerous machinery while taking hydroxyzine.

Adverse Effects: Side effects reported with the administration of hydroxyzine are usually mild and transitory in nature.

Anticholinergic: Dry mouth may be encountered at higher dosages.

CNS: drowsiness.

Involuntary motor activity, including rare instances of tremor and convulsions, has been reported usually with doses considerably higher than those recommended.

Overdose: Symptoms and Treatment: Gastric lavage, when necessary.

Dosage: Oral: Dosage is dependent upon the intensity of the emotional disturbance, rather than upon the weight of the patient.

Adults: 25 to 100 mg 3 or 4 times a day.

Children: under 6 years, 30 to 50 mg daily in divided doses; over 6 years, 50 to 100 mg daily in divided doses.

I.M.: Psychiatric and emotional emergencies, including acute alcoholism: adults, 50 to 100 mg initially, repeated every 4 to 6 hours as needed. Pre and postoperative adjunctive medication: adults, 25 to 100 mg; children, 1 mg/kg body weight. Pre and postpartum adjunctive therapy: 25 to 100 mg. Nausea and vomiting: adults, 25 to 100 mg; children, 1 mg/kg body weight.

When hydroxyzine i.m. is used as preoperative or prepartum adjunctive medication, narcotic requirements may be reduced by as much as 50%. Thus, when 50 mg of hydroxyzine is administered i.m., meperidine dosage may be reduced from 100 mg to 50 mg.

Atarax I.M. is intended only for i.m. administration and should not, under any circumstances, be injected s.c., intra-arterially or i.v.

Atarax I.M. may be administered without further dilution. It should be injected deep into the body of a relatively large muscle such as the upper outer quadrant of the buttock or the lateral thigh.

Adults: The preferred site is the upper outer quadrant of the buttock, (i.e., gluteus maximus) or the mid-lateral thigh.

Children: It is recommended that i.m. injections be given preferably in the mid-lateral muscles of the thigh. In younger children, the periphery of the upper outer quadrant of the gluteal region should be used only when necessary, such as in burn patients, in order to minimize the possibility of damage to the sciatic nerve. The deltoid area should be used only if well developed such as in certain adults and older children, and then only with caution to avoid radial nerve injury. I.M. injections should not be made into the lower and mid-third of the upper arm.

Aspiration and proper anatomical selection of injection sites should be observed as a precaution against inadvertent injection into a blood vessel or major nerve.

Atarax I.M. is physically compatible with parenteral solutions of morphine, atropine, papaverine, codeine, meperidine and scopolamine.

Supplied: Capsules: 10 mg: Each soft orange gelatin capsule contains: hydroxyzine HCl 10 mg. Nonmedicinal ingredients: hydrogenated vegetable oil, lecithin, soybean oil, vegetable shortening and yellow wax; capsule shell: D&C Yellow #10, FD&C Yellow #6, FD&C Red #3, gelatin, glycerin, methylparabens, propylparabens and titanium dioxide. Tartrazine-free. Bottles of 100.

25 mg: Each soft green gelatin capsule contains: hydroxyzine HCl 25 mg. Nonmedicinal ingredients: hydrogenated vegetable oil, lecithin, soybean oil, vegetable shortening and yellow wax; capsule shell: D&C Yellow #10, FD&C Blue #1, FD&C Yellow #6, gelatin, glycerin, methylparabens, propylparabens and titanium dioxide. Tartrazine-free. Bottles of 100.

50 mg: Each soft red gelatin capsule contains: hydroxyzine HCl 50 mg. Nonmedicinal ingredients: hydrogenated vegetable oil, lecithin, soybean oil, vegetable shortening and yellow wax; capsule shell: FD&C Red #40, FD&C Yellow #6, gelatin, glycerin, methylparabens, propylparabens and titanium dioxide. Tartrazine-free. Bottles of 100.

I.M.: Each mL contains: hydroxyzine HCl 50 mg with benzyl alcohol 0.9%, sodium hydroxide to adjust to optimum pH, and water for injection, q.s. Vials of 10 mL and vials of 1 mL, boxes of 10.

Syrup: Each 5 mL of vanilla-flavored syrup contains: hydroxyzine HCl 10 mg. Nonmedicinal ingredients: alcohol, menthol, sodium benzoate 1.5 mg, sucrose and purified water. Energy: 67 kJ (16 kcal). Tartrazine-free. Bottles of 500 mL.

(Shown in Product Recognition Section)

ATASOL®-8, -15, -30 Ⓝ

Carter Horner

Acetaminophen—Codeine Phosphate—Caffeine Citrate

Analgesic—Antipyretic

Indications: The relief of mild to moderate pain of various causes as in headache, migraine, dental pain, dysmenorrhea, myalgias and neuralgias. As an antipyretic when fever accompanies painful conditions.

Contraindications: Acetaminophen and/or codeine hypersensitivity.

Precautions: See Atasol Preparations.

Adverse Effects: Codeine: Adverse reactions due to codeine phosphate may include drowsiness, nausea, vomiting and constipation. Infrequent adverse effects include palpitation, pruritus and, rarely, hyperhidrosis and agitation have been reported. Respiratory depression is seen in higher dosage and the potential for habituation may occur.

Overdose: Symptoms: See Atasol Preparations. Codeine overdosage is manifested by marked respiratory depression, significant miosis (pinpoint pupils), sweating, itching, lightheadedness, headache, nausea, vomiting, insensibility to pain. In severe cases: deep coma and significant CNS depression. Death is usually produced by respiratory failure.

Treatment: See Atasol Preparations.

Codeine: Gastric lavage, intubation measures aimed at supporting respiration and the administration of a narcotic antagonist, e.g., naloxone.

Dosage: Atasol-8: Adults: 1 to 2 tablets every 4 hours (maximum: 2 tablets 6 times daily). Children: 12 to 14 years: only when recommended by a physician or dentist: 1 tablet 3 times daily (maximum: 1 tablet 4 times daily).

Atasol-15 and Atasol-30: Adults: 2 to 4 tablets daily or as prescribed by a physician or dentist.

Supplied: Atasol-8: Each light peach, round, biconvex tablet bisected on one side, imprinted ATASOL on one section, and 8 on the other, plain on other side, contains: acetaminophen 325 mg, codeine phosphate 8 mg, caffeine citrate 30 mg (equivalent to 15 mg caffeine). Nonmedicinal ingredients: alumina, cellulose, D&C Yellow No. 10, FD&C Yellow 6, magnesium stearate, povidone, silicon dioxide, starch (corn) and stearic acid. Energy: 0.4 kJ (0.1 kcal). Gluten- and tartrazine-free. Bottles of 30, 100 and 500. Unit dose packages of 500.

Atasol-15: Each light yellow, round, biconvex tablet bisected on one side, imprinted ATASOL on one section, and 15 on the other, plain on the other side, contains: acetaminophen 325 mg, codeine phosphate 15 mg, caffeine citrate 30 mg (equivalent to 15 mg caffeine). Nonmedicinal ingredients: alumina, cellulose, D&C Yellow No. 10, FD&C Yellow No. 6, magnesium stearate, povidone, silicon dioxide, starch (corn) and stearic acid. Energy: 0.4 kJ (0.1 kcal). Gluten- and tartrazine-free. Bottles of 50, 100 and 500. Hospital Control Packs of 1 000. Unit dose packs of 500.

Atasol-30: Each pale green, round, biconvex tablet bisected on one side, imprinted ATASOL on one section, and 30 on the other section, plain on the other side, contains: acetaminophen 325 mg, codeine phosphate 30 mg, caffeine citrate 30 mg (equivalent to 15 mg caffeine). Nonmedicinal ingredients: alumina, cellulose, D&C Yellow No. 10, D&C Green No. 5, FD&C Yellow No. 6, magnesium stearate, povidone, silicon dioxide, starch (corn) and stearic acid. Energy: 0.4 kJ (0.1 kcal). Gluten- and tartrazine-free. Bottles of 50, 100 and 500. Hospital Control Packs of 1 000. Unit dose packs of 500.

(Shown in Product Recognition Section)

ATASOL® Preparations

Carter Horner

Acetaminophen

Analgesic—Antipyretic

Indications: As an analgesic for the relief of pain in headache, dysmenorrhea, myalgias and neuralgias; arthritis, sprains, toothache, and fever caused by cold or flu. As an antipyretic when fever accompanies painful conditions.

Contraindications: Acetaminophen hypersensitivity.

Precautions: The incidence of gastrointestinal upset is less than after salicylate administration. If a rare sensitivity reaction occurs, discontinue the drug. Hypersensitivity to acetaminophen is usually manifested by a rash or urticaria.

Regular use of acetaminophen has been shown to produce a slight increase in prothrombin time in patients receiving oral anticoagulants. Chronic, high-dose administration of acetaminophen may potentiate the anticoagulant effect of warfarin. Patients stabilized on oral anticoagulants should be advised to limit their intake of acetaminophen to not more than 2 g daily for no more than a few days at a time.

Acetaminophen poisoning can result in severe hepatic damage. Phenobarbital increases the activity of microsomal enzymes which produce a toxic metabolite and therefore acetaminophen's hepatotoxicity may be enhanced. Thus, concomitant ingestion of phenobarbital may increase the likelihood of liver necrosis in acetaminophen overdose. The chronic ingestion of alcohol may be implicated in the increasing potential for hepatic toxicity.

Lactation: Acetaminophen is excreted in human breast milk, but may be used without danger, in therapeutic dosages, for short-term treatment. Peak concentrations in breast milk occur 1 to 2 hours after a dose.

Pregnancy: Acetaminophen crosses the placenta and is apparently safe for short-term use when therapeutic doses are used.

Adverse Effects: In therapeutic doses, acetaminophen is relatively nontoxic. Chronic use of large doses of acetaminophen may produce more significant toxicity.

Hepatic: Hepatic toxicity has been associated with acetaminophen in overdose. Chronic use of high doses, e.g., ≥5 g daily for several weeks in adults or 150 mg/kg/day for 2 to 4 days in children, has also been associated with hepatotoxicity. Alcoholics, patients with liver disease, the malnourished and patients taking drugs that induce hepatic microsomal enzymes, may be at increased risk for hepatic toxicity.

Renal: Nephropathy, including papillary renal failure has been reported following consumption of large amounts of acetaminophen. Renal tubular necrosis has been associated occasionally with hepatic injury produced by acetaminophen overdose.

Hematologic: Neutropenia and thrombocytopenia purpura have been reported and rarely agranulocytosis.

Hypersensitivity: Laryngeal edema, angioedema and anaphylactoid reactions may occur rarely.

Overdose: In adults, hepatotoxicity may occur after ingestion of a single dose of more than 7.5 g (adults) or 150 mg/kg (children) of acetaminophen; a dose of 10 g or more is potentially fatal. However, reports have indicated hepatic necrosis with a single dose of 6 g and death occurring with a single dose of 13 g. Nonfatal overdoses of 12.5 to 31.5 g have also been reported.

Symptoms: Symptoms during the first 2 days of acute poisoning by acetaminophen do not reflect the potential seriousness of the intoxication. Nausea, vomiting, anorexia and abdominal pain occur during the initial 24 hours and may persist for a week or more. Liver injury may become manifest the second day, initially by elevation of serum transaminase and lactic dehydrogenase activity, increased serum bilirubin concentration and prolongation of prothrombin time. Alkaline phosphatase activity and serum albumin concentration may remain normal. The hepatotoxicity may progress to encephalopathy, coma and death. Liver biopsy reveals centrilobular necrosis with sparing of the periportal area. In nonfatal cases, the hepatic lesions are reversible over a period of weeks or months. Transient azotemia is apparent in most patients and acute renal failure occurs in some. Hypoglycemia may occur, but glycosuria and impaired glucose tolerance have also been reported. Both metabolic acidosis and metabolic alkalosis have been noted; cerebral edema and nonspecific myocardial depression have also occurred.

In addition to hepatic damage, clotting defects, and myocardial damage with ST segment abnormalities, T wave flattening and pericarditis have been reported.

Since acetaminophen is metabolized primarily by the liver, in cases of acute poisoning, prolongation of the plasma half-life beyond 3 hours may be indicative of liver injury. Hepatic necrosis should be anticipated if the half-life exceeds 4 hours, and hepatic coma is likely if the half-life is greater than 12 hours. A single determination of serum acetaminophen concentration is a less reliable predictor of hepatic injury. However, only minimal liver damage has developed when the serum concentration was below 120 μg/mL at 4 hours or less than 50 μg/mL at 12 hours after ingestion of the drug. Encephalopathy should also be anticipated if serum bilirubin concentration exceeds 4 mg/100 mL during the first 5 days.

Treatment: Treatment of acute acetaminophen overdosage is symptomatic; vigorous supportive therapy is essential in severe intoxication. Since the hepatic injury is dose dependent and occurs early in the course of intoxication, procedures to limit continuing absorption of the drug must be initiated promptly. Gastric lavage or emesis can be used if the drug has been recently ingested. Persistent vomiting induced by ipecac may interfere with acetylcysteine administration. If activated charcoal has been administered prior to initiation of acetylcysteine therapy, gastric lavage should be performed before the first dose of oral acetylcysteine is given, as charcoal may interfere with acetylcysteine absorption and reduces its effectiveness.

Although appropriate i.v. administration of cysteine or cysteamine may decrease the risk of acetaminophen-induced hepatic necrosis, these drugs are not readily available in Canada at this time. Current evidence suggests that oral N-acetylcysteine may exert a protective effect against hepatic necrosis. Call the nearest Poison Control Centre for the most recent information on treatment.

Dosage: Adults: 325 to 650 mg every 4 to 6 hours, not to exceed 4 000 mg/24 hours.

Children: 10 to 15 mg/kg every 4 to 6 hours, not to exceed 65 mg/kg/24 hours. Alternatively, see Table I.

Table I—Atasol Preparations

Dosage in Children

Age	Single Dose (mg)	Max. Daily Dose (mg)
0 to under 4 months	40	200
4 months to under 1 year	80	400
1 year to under 2	120	600
2 to under 4	160	800
4 to under 6	240	1 200
6 to under 9	320	1 600
9 to under 11	400	2 000
11 to under 12	480	2 400

Supplied: Caplets: Atasol: Each white, elongated, clear, film-coated, biconvex caplet, bisected on one side and imprinted ATASOL on the other side, contains: acetaminophen 325 mg. Nonmedicinal ingredients: alumina, cellulose, cornstarch, FD&C Blue No. 2, magnesium stearate, polyethylene glycol, povidone, stearic acid and titanium dioxide. Alcohol-, sucrose- and tartrazine-free. Bottles of 24 and 100.

Atasol Forte: Each white, elongated, clear, film-coated, biconvex caplet, imprinted ATASOL on one side and FORTE on the other, contains: acetaminophen 500 mg. Nonmedicinal ingredients: alumina, cellulose, cornstarch, FD&C Blue No. 2, magnesium stearate, polyethylene glycol, povidone, stearic acid and titanium dioxide. Alcohol-, sucrose- and tartrazine-free. Bottles of 24 and 100.

Drops: Each mL of red, fruit-flavored solution contains: acetaminophen 80 mg. Nonmedicinal ingredients: citric acid, dibasic sodium phosphate, FD&C Red No. 2 and No. 40, flavor, glycerin, parabens, polyethylene glycol, sodium cyclamate, sorbitol and sucrose. Alcohol- and tartrazine-free. Energy: 10 kJ (2.4 kcal). Sodium: <1 mmol (0.9 mg). Plastic bottles of 24 mL with graduated dropper.

Oral Solution: Each 5 mL of orange, fruit-flavored solution contains: acetaminophen 80 mg. Nonmedicinal ingredients: citric acid, dibasic sodium phosphate, FD&C Yellow No. 6, flavor, parabens, polyethylene glycol, sodium benzoate, sodium cyclamate and sorbitol. Alcohol-, sucrose- and tartrazine-free. Energy: 10 kJ (2.4 kcal) Sodium: <1 mmol (3.4 mg). Plastic bottles of 100 mL.

Tablets: Atasol: Each white, round, biconvex tablet, bisected on one side and imprinted ATASOL in one section and plain on the other side, contains: acetaminophen 325 mg. Nonmedicinal ingredients: cellulose, cornstarch, povidone and stearic acid. Alcohol-, sucrose- and tartrazine-free. Energy: 1.3 kJ (0.3 kcal). Sodium: <1 mmol (0.1 mg). Bottles of 24, 100 and 500. Unit dose packages of 500.

Atasol Forte: Each white, shield-shaped tablet, biconvex, diagonally scored on one side, imprinted ATASOL FORTE and plain on the other side, contains: acetaminophen 500 mg (Atasol Forte). Nonmedicinal ingredients: cellulose, cornstarch, povidone and stearic acid. Alcohol-, sucrose- and tartrazine-free. Energy: 1.3 kJ (0.3 kcal). Sodium: <1 mmol (0.1 mg). Bottles of 30, 100, 120 and 1 000.

(Shown in Product Recognition Section)

ATGAM®

Pharmacia & Upjohn

Lymphocyte Immune Globulin—Anti-Thymocyte Globulin (Equine)

Immunosuppressant

Pharmacology: Atgam is the purified, concentrated, and sterile gamma globulin, primarily monomeric IgG, from hyperimmune plasma of horses immunized with human thymus lymphocytes.

Atgam is a lymphocyte-selective immunosuppressant as is demonstrated by its ability to reduce the number of circulating, thymus-dependent lymphocytes that form rosettes with sheep erythrocytes. This antilymphocyte effect is believed to reflect an alteration of the function of the T-lymphocytes, which are responsible in part for cell-mediated immunity and are involved in humoral immunity. In addition to its antilymphocyte activity, Atgam contains low concentrations of antibodies against other formed elements of the blood. In rhesus and cynomolgus monkeys, Atgam reduces lymphocytes in the thymus-dependent areas of the spleen and lymph nodes. It also decreases the circulating sheep-erythrocyte-rosetting lymphocytes that can be detected, but does not cause severe lymphopenia.

In general, when Atgam is given with other immunosuppressive therapy, such as antimetabolites and corticosteroids, the patient's own antibody response to horse gamma globulin is minimal. In a small clinical study, Atgam administered with other immunosuppressive therapy and measured as horse IgG had a serum half-life of 5.7±3 days.

Indications: For any patient in whom reduction of peripheral T-lymphocyte function as measured by rosette-forming cell assay could be desirable.

During controlled clinical trials, this immunosuppression has been demonstrated in renal allograft recipients treated with Atgam. When administered with conventional therapy at the time of rejection, it increases the frequency of resolution of the acute rejection episode. The drug has also been administered as an adjunct to other immunosuppresssive therapy to delay the onset of the first rejection episode.

In noncontrolled clinical studies, Atgam has been administered to other patients in whom reduction of T-cell function could be desirable. They had aplastic anemia, T-cell malignancies, or graft-versus-host disease, or had received skin, cardiac, liver, or bone marrow transplants. Anecdotal reports of benefit have been published, but to date controlled studies to establish safety and efficacy in circumstances other than renal transplantation have not been completed.

Contraindications: Should not be administered to a patient who has had a severe systemic reaction during prior administration of the drug or any other equine gamma globulin preparation.

Warnings: Only physicians experienced in immunosuppressive therapy and management of renal transplant patients should use Atgam.

Patients receiving Atgam should be managed in facilities equipped and staffed with adequate laboratory and supportive medical resources.

Treatment with Atgam should be discontinued if any of the following occurs: anaphylaxis (see Adverse Effects); severe and unremitting thrombocytopenia; severe and unremitting leukopenia.

Atgam (cont'd)

This product is manufactured using components of human blood which may contain the causative agent of hepatitis and other viral disease. Prescribed manufacturing procedures utilized in blood collection centres and the plasma testing laboratories are designed to reduce the risk of transmitting viral infection. However the risk of viral infectivity from this product cannot be totally excluded.

Precautions: Because Atgam is an immunosuppressive agent ordinarily given with corticosteroids and antimetabolites, patients should be monitored carefully for signs of leukopenia, thrombocytopenia or concurrent infection. If infection occurs, appropriate adjunctive therapy should be instituted promptly. The physician should decide whether or not to continue therapy with Atgam depending on clinical circumstances.

Some studies have suggested an increase in the incidence of cytomegalovirus infection in patients receiving Atgam. Some physicians have found that it may be possible to reduce this by decreasing the dosage of other immunosuppressive agents which might be administered concomitantly with Atgam.

Dilution of Atgam in dextrose infusion solutions is not recommended, as low salt concentrations may result in precipitation. The use of highly acidic infusion solutions is also not recommended because of possible physical instability over time.

Drug Interactions: When the dose of corticosteroids and other immunosuppressants is being reduced, some previously masked reactions to Atgam may appear. Under these circumstances, observe patients especially carefully during therapy with Atgam.

Pregnancy and *Lactation:* Atgam has not been evaluated in either pregnant or lactating women.

Children: Experience with children has been limited. Atgam has been administered safely to a small number of pediatric renal, liver and bone marrow allograft recipients and aplastic anemia patients at dosage levels comparable to those in adults.

Adverse Effects: The primary clinical experience with Atgam has been in renal allograft patients, who were also receiving concurrent standard immunosuppressive therapy (azathioprine, corticosteroids).

In controlled clinical trials, the following adverse reactions have been reported:

Incidence greater than 5%: fever (33%), chills (14%), leukopenia (14%), thrombocytopenia (11%), dermatological reactions such as rash, pruritus, urticaria, wheal and flare (12.5%).

Incidence of 1 to 5%: arthralgia, chest and/or back pain, clotted A/V fistula, diarrhea, dyspnea, headache, hypotension, nausea and/or vomiting, night sweats, pain at the infusion site, peripheral thrombophlebitis and stomatitis.

The incidence of adverse reactions has been higher in patients being treated for aplastic anemia. Frequently reported adverse reactions among patients enrolled in aplastic anemia studies were arthralgia, chills, fever, skin rashes and thrombocytopenia. The high incidence of skin rashes and arthralgia was believed by investigators to represent serum sickness. In patients with aplastic anemia and other hematologic abnormalities who have received Atgam, abnormal tests of liver function (AST, ALT, alkaline phosphatase) and renal function (serum creatinine) have been observed. In some trials, clinical and laboratory findings of serum sickness have been seen in a majority of patients.

Other reactions reported in renal allograft or aplastic anemia patients receiving therapy have included: back pain, chest pain, clotted A/V fistula, diarrhea, dyspnea, headache, hypotension, nausea, night sweats, pain at the infusion site, peripheral thrombophlebitis, stomatitis and vomiting.

Reactions reported **rarely** have been: agitation, anaphylaxis, dizziness, edema, epigastric pain or hiccups, herpes simplex reactivation, hyperglycemia, hypertension, iliac vein obstruction, infection, laryngospasm, lymphadenopathy, malaise, paresthesia, periorbital edema, pleural effusions, possible encephalitis, proteinuria, pulmonary edema, renal artery thrombosis, seizure, tachycardia, toxic epidermal necrosis, weakness or faintness, and wound dehiscence.

Postmarketing Experience: During approximately 5 years of postapproval marketing experience, the frequency of adverse reactions in voluntarily reported cases is as follows; chills (16%), fever (51%), leukopenia (14%), rashes (27%), systemic infection (13%), thrombocytopenia (30%).

Events reported with a frequency of 5 to 10% include: abnormal renal function tests, arthralgia, chest, back or flank pain, diarrhea, dyspnea/apnea, nausea and/or vomiting and serum sickness-like symptoms.

Events reported with a frequency of <5% include: abnormal involuntary movement or tremor, abnormal liver function tests, abdominal pain, acute renal failure, anaphylaxis, anemia, aplasia or pancytopenia, confusion or disorientation, cough, deep vein thrombosis, dizziness, edema, enlarged or ruptured kidney, eosinophilia, epigastric or stomach pain, faintness, gastrointestinal bleeding or perforation, hemolysis or hemolytic anemia, headache, herpes simplex infection, hyperglycemia, hypertension, hypotension, localized infection, lymphadenopathy, malaise, myalgias or leg pains, neutropenia or granulocytopenia, nosebleed, pain, swelling or redness at infusion site, paresthesias, pulmonary edema or congestive heart failure, renal artery thrombosis, rigidity, seizures, sore mouth-throat, sweating, laryngospasm/edema, tachycardia, thrombophlebitis, vasculitis, and viral hepatitis.

The recommended management for some of the adverse reactions that could occur during treatment with Atgam follows: Anaphylaxis is uncommon but serious and may occur during therapy with Atgam. If this condition does occur, infusion of Atgam should be discontinued immediately; 0.3 mL aqueous epinephrine (1:1 000 dilution) should be administered i.m. along with steroids. Respiration should be assisted and other resuscitative measures provided. **Do not** resume therapy with Atgam.

Hemolysis can usually be detected only in the laboratory. Fulminant hemolysis has been reported rarely. Appropriate treatment of hemolysis often includes transfusion of erythrocytes; if necessary, administer i.v. mannitol, furosemide, sodium bicarbonate, and fluids. Severe and unremitting hemolysis may necessitate discontinuation of therapy with Atgam.

Thrombocytopenia and leukopenia are usually transient. Platelet and white cell counts generally return to adequate levels without interrupting therapy and without transfusions. If thrombocytopenia and leukopenia become severe, it may be helpful to decrease the dose of concomitant immunosuppressant (particularly azathioprine). If after 1 or 2 days the situation does not improve, the dose of Atgam may also be reduced (see Warnings).

Respiratory distress may indicate an anaphylactoid reaction. Infusion of Atgam should be discontinued. If distress persists, antihistamine, epinephrine, corticosteroid, or some combination of the three should be administered.

Pain in chest, flank or back may indicate anaphylaxis or hemolysis. Treatment is the same as for respiratory distress or, if hemolysis has occurred, as for hemolysis.

Hypotension may indicate anaphylaxis. Infusion of Atgam should be discontinued and blood pressure stabilized with pressor agents if necessary.

Chills and fever occur frequently in patients receiving Atgam. Atgam may release endogenous leukocyte pyrogens. Prophylactic and/or therapeutic administration of antihistamines or corticosteroids generally controls this reaction.

Chemical phlebitis can be caused by infusion of Atgam through peripheral veins. This often can be avoided by administering the infusion solution into a high-flow vein. A s.c. arterialized vein produced by a Brescia fistula is also a useful administration site.

Itching and erythema probably result from the effect of Atgam on blood elements. Antihistamines generally control the symptoms.

Serum sickness-like symptoms in aplastic anemia patients that have been treated with oral and i.v. corticosteroids. Resolution of symptoms has generally been prompt and long-term sequelae have not been observed. Prophylactic administration of corticosteroids may decrease the frequency of this reaction.

Overdose: Symptoms and Treatment: Because of its mode of action and because it is a biologic substance, the maximum tolerated dose of Atgam would be expected to vary from patient to patient. To date, the largest single daily dose administered to a patient (renal transplant recipient) was 7 000 mg administered at a concentration of approximately 10 mg/mL of saline, 7 times the recommended total dose and infusion concentration. In this patient, the administration of Atgam was not associated with any signs of acute intoxication or late sequelae.

The greatest number of doses (10 to 20 mg/kg/dose) that can be administered to a single patient has not yet been determined. Some renal transplant patients have received up to 50 doses in 4 months, and others have received 28-day courses of 21 doses followed by as many as 3 more courses for the treatment of acute rejection. The incidence of toxicologic manifestations did not increase with any of these regimens.

Dosage: Renal-Allograft Recipients: Adult renal allograft patients have received Atgam 10 to 30 mg/kg daily. The few children studied received 5 to 25 mg/kg daily. Atgam has been used to delay the onset of the first rejection episode and at the time of the first rejection episode. Most patients who received Atgam for the treatment of acute rejection had not received it starting at the time of transplantation.

Usually, Atgam is used concomitantly with azathioprine and corticosteroids, which are commonly used to suppress the immune response. Exercise caution during repeat courses of Atgam; carefully observe patients for signs of allergic reactions.

Delaying the Onset of Allograft Rejection: The recommended dose is 15 mg/kg daily for 14 days, then every other day for 14 days for a total of 21 doses in 28 days. The first dose should be administered within 24 hours before or after the transplant.

Treatment of Rejection: The first Atgam dose can be delayed until the diagnosis of the first rejection episode. The recommended dose is 10 to 15 mg/kg daily for 14 days. Additional alternate-day therapy up to a total of 21 doses can be given.

Other Allograft Recipients: Atgam has been used in liver transplant recipients at daily doses of 8 to 15 mg/kg. The duration of therapy averaged 13 days. In heart transplant patients, intermittent daily doses averaged 8 mg/kg (range: 5 to 11 mg/kg), duration of therapy averaged 4 months, and the number of doses averaged 29 (range: 7 to 49). In burn patients who had received temporary skin allografts, Atgam dosage ranged from 10 to 15 mg/kg for up to 24 doses. All patients received the first Atgam dose in the 24-hour period immediately before or after the surgical procedure.

Bone Marrow Transplantation: Several different Atgam dosage regimens have been used in patients receiving bone marrow transplants. Generally patients received Atgam 7 to 20 mg/kg for 3 to 14 doses. The first dose was given 9 days before transplant for pre-conditioning, 7 to 30 days after transplant for prophylaxis of graft-versus-host disease or when graft-versus-host disease was diagnosed.

Aplastic Anemia: Patients with aplastic anemia have received Atgam in several regimens, generally 10 to 20 mg/kg for 8 to 21 doses.

Other Indications: Atgam has also been used in patients with Sezary syndrome, T-cell leukemia, and nephrotic syndrome. Although some patients have received multiple high doses intermittently over long periods, a standard dosage regimen has not been established.

Preparation and Administration: Skin Testing: Before the first i.v. infusion of Atgam, it is **strongly** recommended that skin testing potential recipients take place before commencing treatment. First the patient should receive an epicutaneous (prick) testing with undiluted Atgam. If a wheal does not develop 10 minutes after pricking, then proceed to intradermal testing with 0.02 mL of a 1:1 000 v/v saline dilution of Atgam with a separate saline control injection of similar volume. After 10 minutes read the results. A wheal at the Atgam site of 3 mm or larger in diameter compared to the saline control site suggests clinical sensitivity and an increased possibility of a systemic allergic reaction. Where an Atgam skin test causes a locally positive reaction, serious consideration should be given to alternative forms of therapy. The risk to benefit ratio must be carefully weighed. If therapy with Atgam is deemed appropriate following a locally positive skin test, treatment should be administered in a setting where intensive life support facilities are immediately available and a physician familar with the treatment of potentially life-threatening allergic reactions is in attendance.

A systemic reaction such as generalized rash, tachycardia, dyspnea, hypotension, or anaphylaxis precludes an additional administration of Atgam.

Note: The predictive value of this test has not been clinically proven. Allergic reactions can occur in the presence of a negative skin test (see Warnings, Precautions and Adverse Effects).

Infusion Instruction: Parenteral drug products should be inspected visually for particulate matter and discoloration prior to administration whenever solution and container permit. Because Atgam is a gamma globulin product, it can be transparent to slightly opalescent, colorless to light brown, and may develop a slight granular or flaky deposit during storage. Atgam (diluted or undiluted) should not be shaken because excessive foaming and/or denaturation of the protein may occur.

Atgam should be diluted for i.v. infusion in an inverted bottle of sterile vehicle, so that the undiluted Atgam does not contact the air inside. Add the total daily dose of Atgam to the sterile vehicle, with a concentration not exceeding 4 mg of Atgam Sterile Solution per mL. The diluted solution should be gently rotated or swirled to effect complete mixing. Once diluted, Atgam has been shown to be physically and chemically stable for up to 24 hours at concentration of up to 4 mg/mL in the following diluents: 0.9% Sodium Chloride Injection, 5%

Dextrose and 0.225% Sodium Chloride Injection, 5% Dextrose and 0.45% Sodium Chloride Injection.

Adding Atgam to dextrose injection is not recommended, as low salt concentrations can cause precipitation. Highly acidic infusion solutions can also contribute to physical instability over time.

Atgam should not be kept in a diluted form for more than 24 hours (including actual infusion time). It is recommended that diluted Atgam be stored in a refrigerator if it is prepared prior to time of infusion. The diluted Atgam solution should be allowed to reach room temperature before infusion.

During the clinical trials, most investigators chose to infuse Atgam into a vascular shunt, arterial venous fistula, or a high-flow central vein through an in-line filter with a pore size of 0.2 to 1.0 micron. The in-line filter should be used with all i.v. infusions to prevent the inadvertent administration of any insoluble material that may develop in the product during storage.

Using high-flow veins will minimize the occurrence of phlebitis and thrombosis.

Do not infuse a dose of Atgam in less than 4 hours.

Always keep a tray containing epinephrine, antihistamines, corticosteroids, syringes, and an airway at the patient's bedside while Atgam is being administered.

Observe the patient continuously for possible allergic reactions throughout the infusion (see Adverse Effects).

Supplied: Each mL contains: horse gamma globulin 50 mg stabilized in glycine to a pH of approximately 6.8. Cartons of 5 ampuls of 5 mL. Store in refrigerator at 2 to 8°C. **Do not freeze.** Protect from light; store ampuls in carton.

Reviewed 1998

ATIVAN® ℞

Wyeth-Ayerst

Lorazepam

Anxiolytic—Sedative

Pharmacology: Lorazepam is a benzodiazepine with CNS depressant, anxiolytic and sedative properties. Lorazepam has also been shown to possess anticonvulsant activity. Peak plasma concentrations of free lorazepam after oral administration are reached at 2 hours (range 1 to 6 hours). Peak concentrations are reached in 60 to 90 minutes after i.m. administration and in 60 minutes after sublingual administration. Lorazepam is 85% bound to plasma proteins. Lorazepam is rapidly conjugated to an inactive glucuronide. Very small amounts of other metabolites have also been isolated in man. The serum half-life of lorazepam is approximately 12 to 15 hours while the half-life of the conjugate is 16 to 20 hours. Most of the drug (88%) is excreted in the urine with 75% excreted as the glucuronide.

Anterograde amnesia, decreased or lack of recall of events during period of drug action, has been reported after administration of lorazepam and appears to be dose-related.

Indications: The short-term relief of manifestations of excessive anxiety in patients with anxiety neurosis. Adjunct for the relief of excessive anxiety that might be present prior to surgical procedures.

Anxiety and tension associated with the stresses of everyday life usually do not require treatment with anxiolytic drugs.

Injectable lorazepam is useful as an initial anticonvulsant medication for the control of status epilepticus.

Contraindications: Myasthenia gravis, acute narrow angle glaucoma, known hypersensitivity to benzodiazepines. Lorazepam injectable is also contraindicated in patients with known hypersensitivity to polyethylene glycol, propylene glycol or benzyl alcohol.

Lorazepam should not be injected intraarterially and care should be taken to prevent its extravasation into tissue adjacent to an artery because of the danger of producing arteriospasm resulting in gangrene which may require amputation.

Warnings: Lorazepam is not recommended for use in depressive neurosis or in psychotic reactions. Because of the lack of sufficient clinical experience, lorazepam is not recommended for use in patients less than 18 years of age. Since lorazepam has a CNS depressant effect, patients should be advised against the simultaneous use of other CNS depressant drugs. Patients should also be cautioned not to take alcohol during the administration of lorazepam because of the potentiation of effects that may occur.

Occupational Hazards: Excessive sedation has been observed with lorazepam at standard therapeutic doses. Therefore, patients should be warned against engaging in hazardous activities requiring mental alertness and motor coordination, such as operating dangerous machinery or driving motor vehicles.

Prior to i.v. use, lorazepam injection should be diluted with an equal amount of compatible diluent (see Dosage). I.V. injection should be made slowly and with repeated aspiration. Care should be taken to determine that any injection will not be intraarterial and that perivascular extravasation will not take place. Partial airway obstruction may occur in heavily sedated patients. I.V. lorazepam, when given alone in greater than the recommended dose, or at the recommended dose and accompanied by other drugs used during the administration of anesthesia, may produce heavy sedation; therefore, equipment necessary to maintain a patent airway and to support respiration/ventilation should be available.

As with any premedicant, extreme care must be used in administering lorazepam injection to elderly or very ill patients and to those with limited pulmonary reserve, because of the possibility that apnea and/or cardiac arrest may occur. Because of the lack of sufficient clinical experience lorazepam injection is not recommended for use in patients less than 18 years of age.

Clinical trials have shown that patients over the age of 50 years may have a more profound and prolonged sedation with i.v. lorazepam. Ordinarily an initial dose of 2 mg may be adequate, unless a greater degree of lack of recall is desired.

There is no evidence to support the use of lorazepam injection in coma, shock or acute alcohol intoxication at this time. When lorazepam injection is used in patients with mild to moderate hepatic or renal disease, the lowest effective dose should be considered since drug effect may be prolonged.

As is true of other similar CNS acting drugs, patients receiving injectable lorazepam should not operate machinery or engage in hazardous occupations or drive a motor vehicle for a period of 24 to 48 hours. Impairment of performance may persist for greater intervals because of extremes of age, concomitant use of other drugs, stress of surgery or the general condition of the patient.

The addition of scopolamine to injectable lorazepam is not recommended, since their combined effect may result in increased incidence of sedation, hallucination and irrational behaviour.

Care should be exercised when administering lorazepam to patients with status epilepticus, especially when the patient has received other CNS depressants or is severely ill. The possibility that respiratory arrest may occur or that the patient may have partial airway obstruction should be considered. Proper resuscitation equipment should be available.

Pregnancy: The safety of the use of lorazepam in pregnancy has not been established. Therefore, it is not recommended for use during pregnancy or lactation. Several studies have suggested an increased risk of congenital malformations associated with the use of the benzodiazepines, chlordiazepoxide and diazepam, and meprobamate, during the first trimester of pregnancy. Since lorazepam is also a benzodiazepine derivative, its administration is rarely justified in women of childbearing potential. If the drug is prescribed to a woman of childbearing potential, she should be warned to contact her physician regarding discontinuation of the drug if she intends to become or suspects that she is pregnant.

In women, blood levels obtained from umbilical cord blood indicate placental transfer of lorazepam and lorazepam glucuronide. Lorazepam injection should not be used during pregnancy. There are insufficient data regarding obstetrical safety of parenteral lorazepam, including use in cesarean section. Such use, therefore, is not recommended.

Precautions: Elderly and debilitated patients, or those with organic brain syndrome, have been found to be prone to CNS depression after even low doses of benzodiazepines. Therefore, medication should be initiated in these patients with very low initial doses, and increments should be made gradually, depending on the patient's response, in order to avoid oversedation or neurological impairment. Extreme care must be used in administering lorazepam injection to elderly patients, very ill patients, and to patients with limited pulmonary reserve, because of the possibility that underventilation and/or hypoxic cardiac arrest may occur. Resuscitative equipment for ventilatory support should be readily available.

Dependence Liability: Lorazepam should not be administered to individuals prone to drug abuse.

Observe caution in patients who are considered to have potential for psychological dependence. Lorazepam should be withdrawn gradually if it has been used in high dosage.

As with other benzodiazepines, lorazepam injection has a low potential for abuse and may lead to limited dependence. Although there are no clinical data available for injectable lorazepam in this respect, physicians should be aware that repeated doses over a prolonged period of time may result in limited physical and psychological dependence.

Lorazepam is not recommended for the treatment of psychotic or depressed patients. Since excitement and other paradoxical reactions can result from the use of these drugs in psychotic patients, they should not be used in ambulatory patients suspected of having psychotic tendencies.

As with other anxiolytic-sedative drugs, lorazepam should not be used in patients with nonpathological anxiety. These drugs are also not effective in patients with characterological and personality disorders or those with obsessive-compulsive neurosis.

When using lorazepam, it should be recognized that suicidal tendencies may be present and that protective measures may be required.

Since the liver is the most likely site of conjugation of lorazepam and since excretion of conjugated lorazepam is a renal function, the usual precautions should be taken if lorazepam is used in patients who may have some impairment of renal or hepatic function. In such cases, the dose should be very carefully titrated.

In patients for whom prolonged lorazepam therapy is indicated, periodic blood counts and liver function tests should be carried out.

When injectable lorazepam is used in patients with mild to moderate hepatic or renal disease, the lowest effective dose should be considered since drug effect may be prolonged.

While lorazepam has been shown to control status epilepticus promptly, it is not recommended for maintenance treatment of epilepsy. After seizures are controlled, agents useful in the prevention of further seizures should be administered. In the treatment of status epilepticus due to acute reversible metabolic derangement (e.g., hypoglycemia, hypocalcemia, hyponatremia etc.) immediate efforts should be made to correct the specific defect.

<u>Drug Interactions:</u> If lorazepam is to be combined with other drugs acting on the CNS, careful consideration should be given to the pharmacology of the agents to be employed because of the possible potentiation of drug effects. The benzodiazepines, including lorazepam, produce CNS depressant effects when administered with such medications as barbiturates or alcohol.

Lorazepam injection, like other injectable benzodiazepines, also produces depression of the CNS when administered with ethyl alcohol, phenothiazines, barbiturates, MAO inhibitors and other antidepressants. When scopolamine is used concomitantly with injectable lorazepam, an increased incidence of sedation, hallucinations and irrational behavior has been observed.

When lorazepam injection is used i.v. as the premedicant prior to regional or local anesthesia, the possibility of excessive sleepiness or drowsiness may interfere with patient cooperation to determine levels of anesthesia. This is most likely to occur when a dose greater than 0.05 mg/kg is given and when narcotic analgesics are used concomitantly with the recommended dose.

Adverse Effects: Drowsiness is the most frequently reported adverse effect. Other reported adverse effects are dizziness, weakness, fatigue and lethargy, disorientation, ataxia, anterograde amnesia, nausea, change in appetite, change in weight, depression, blurred vision and diplopia, psychomotor agitation, sleep disturbance, vomiting, sexual disturbance, headache, skin rashes, gastrointestinal, ear, nose and throat, musculoskeletal and respiratory disturbances.

Release of hostility and other paradoxical effects, such as irritability and excitability have occurred with benzodiazepines. In addition, hypotension, mental confusion, slurred speech, oversedation and abnormal liver and kidney function tests and hematocrit values have been reported with these drugs.

The most frequent adverse effects seen with injectable lorazepam are an extension of the CNS depressant effects of the drug. Excessive sleepiness and drowsiness are the main side effects: the incidences reported depended on the dosage, route of administration, concomitant use of other CNS depressants and the investigators' expectations concerning the degree and duration of sedation.

When injectable lorazepam was given i.v., patients over 50 years of age had a higher incidence of excessive sedation than patients under 50 years of age. Restlessness, confusion, depression, crying, sobbing, delirium, hallucinations, dizziness, diplopia have been reported. Hypertension and hypotension have occasionally been observed after injectable lorazepam.

Respiratory depression and partial airway obstruction have been observed after injectable lorazepam. Skin rash, nausea and vomiting have been noted occasionally in patients who have received injectable lorazepam combined with other drugs during anesthesia and surgery.

Ativan (cont'd)

Pain at the injection site, a sensation of burning, and redness in the same area have been reported after i.m. administration of injectable lorazepam. Pain in the immediate postinjection period and redness at the 24 hour observation period also have been reported after i.v. administration of injectable lorazepam.

Overdose: Symptoms: With benzodiazepines, including lorazepam, symptoms of mild overdosage include drowsiness, mental confusion and lethargy. In more serious overdosage, symptoms may include ataxia, hypotonia, hypotension, hypnosis, stages I to III coma and, very rarely, death.

Treatment: In the case of an oral overdose, if vomiting has not occurred spontaneously and the patient is fully awake, emesis may be induced with 20 to 30 mL of ipecac syrup USP. Institute gastric lavage as soon as possible, and introduce 50 to 100 g of activated charcoal to the stomach and allow it to remain there. Institute general supportive therapy as indicated. Vital signs and fluid balance should be carefully monitored. An adequate airway should be maintained and assisted respiration used as needed. With normally functioning kidneys, forced diuresis with i.v. fluids and electrolytes may accelerate elimination of benzodiazepines from the body. In addition, osmotic diuretics such as mannitol may be effective as adjunctive measures. In more critical situations, renal dialysis and exchange blood transfusions may be indicated. Published reports indicate that i.v. infusion of 0.5 to 4 mg of physostigmine at the rate of 1 mg/minute may reverse symptoms and signs suggestive of central anticholinergic overdose (confusion, memory disturbance, visual disturbances, hallucinations, delirium); however, hazards associated with the use of physostigmine (i.e., induction of seizures) should be weighed against its possible clinical benefit.

Dosage: Dosage must be individualized and carefully titrated in order to avoid excessive sedation or mental and motor impairment. As with other anxiolytic sedatives, short courses of treatment should usually be the rule for the symptomatic relief of disabling anxiety in psychoneurotic patients and the initial course of treatment should not last longer than 1 week without reassessment of the need for a limited extension. Initially, not more than 1 week's supply of the drug should be provided and automatic prescription renewals should not be allowed. Subsequent prescriptions, when required, should be limited to short courses of therapy.

Generalized anxiety disorder: The recommended initial adult daily oral dosage is 2 mg in divided doses of 0.5 mg, 0.5 mg and 1 mg, or of 1 mg and 1 mg. The daily dosage should be carefully increased or decreased by 0.5 mg depending upon tolerance and response. The usual daily dosage is 2 to 3 mg. However, the optimal dosage may range from 1 to 4 mg daily in individual patients. Usually, a daily dosage of 6 mg should not be exceeded.

The initial daily dose in elderly and debilitated patients should not exceed 0.5 mg and should be very carefully and gradually adjusted, depending upon tolerance and response.

Excessive anxiety prior to surgical procedures: Adults: Usually 50 μg/kg to a maximum of 4 mg given sublingually (1 to 2 hours before surgery) or i.m. (2 to 3 hours before surgery). As with all premedicant drugs, the dose should be individualized. Doses of other CNS depressant drugs should ordinarily be reduced.

When a rapid onset of action is required, lorazepam may be given i.v., 15 to 20 minutes before surgery. The usual i.v. dose is 44 μg/kg or 2.0 mg total, whichever is smaller.

I.V. doses in excess of 2 mg should be restricted to patients of unusual size. A dose of 2 mg should not ordinarily be exceeded in patients over 50 years of age. Doses of other CNS depressants should ordinarily be reduced.

Equipment necessary to maintain a patent airway should be immediately available prior to i.v. administration of lorazepam.

Status Epilepticus: Adults: The usual recommended initial dose of lorazepam is 0.05 mg/kg up to a maximum of 4 mg given by slow i.v. injection. If seizures are terminated, no additional lorazepam is required. If seizures continue or recur after a 10 to 15 minute observation period, an additional i.v. dose of 0.05 mg/kg may be administered. If the second dose does not result in seizure control after another 10 to 15 minute observation period, other measures to control status epilepticus should be employed. A maximum of 8 mg only, of lorazepam, should be administered during a 12 hour period.

Administration: The sublingual tablet, when placed under the tongue, will dissolve in approximately 20 seconds. The patients should not swallow for at least 2 minutes to allow sufficient time for absorption.

When given i.m., lorazepam injection, undiluted, should be injected deep into a muscle mass.

Lorazepam injectable can be used with atropine sulfate, narcotic analgesics, other parenterally used analgesics, commonly used anesthetics and muscle relaxants. The use of scopolamine with lorazepam injection is not recommended since this combination has been associated with a higher incidence of adverse reactions.

Immediately prior to i.v. use, lorazepam injection must be diluted with an equal volume of compatible solution. When properly diluted the drug may be injected directly into the vein or into the tubing of an existing i.v. infusion. The rate of injection should not exceed 2 mg/minute. Parenteral drug products should be inspected visually for particulate matter and discoloration prior to administration. Do not use if solution is discolored or contains a precipitate.

Lorazepam injection is compatible for dilution purposes with the following solutions: Sterile Water for Injection, USP, Sodium Chloride Injection, USP, 5% Dextrose Injection, USP, Bacteriostatic Sodium Chloride Injection, USP with benzyl alcohol, Bacteriostatic Water for Injection, USP with parabens, Bacteriostatic Water for Injection, USP with benzyl alcohol.

Directions for dilution for i.v. use: Aspirate the desired amount of lorazepam injection into the syringe, then slowly aspirate the desired volume of diluent. Pull back slightly on the plunger to provide additional mixing space. Immediately mix contents thoroughly by gently inverting the syringe repeatedly until a homogenous solution results. Do not shake vigorously since this will result in air entrapment.

Supplied: Injection: Each mL contains: lorazepam 4 mg. Nonmedicinal ingredients: benzyl alcohol, polyethylene glycol and propylene glycol. Single use vials of 1 mL, boxes of 10. Keep refrigerated and protect from light. Do not use if solution is discolored or contains a precipitate. Discard unused portion.

Oral Tablets: 0.5 mg: Each white, round tablet, imprinted 0.5 on one side and W on the other, contains: lorazepam 0.5 mg. Nonmedicinal ingredients: lactose, magnesium stearate, microcrystalline cellulose and polacrilin potassium. Energy: 0.84 kJ (0.20 kcal). Gluten- and tartrazine-free. Bottles of 100, 500 and 1 000.

1 mg: Each white, scored, oblong tablet, imprinted 1 on one side and ATIVAN on the other, contains: lorazepam 1 mg. Nonmedicinal ingredients: lactose, magnesium stearate, microcrystalline cellulose and polacrilin potassium. Energy: 1.63 kJ (0.39 kcal). Gluten- and tartrazine-free. Bottles 100, 1 000 and 2 500.

2 mg: Each white, scored, ovoid tablet, imprinted 2 on one side and ATIVAN on the other, contains: lorazepam 2 mg. Nonmedicinal ingredients: lactose, magnesium stearate, microcrystalline cellulose and polacrilin potassium. Energy: 2.05 kJ (0.49 kcal). Gluten- and tartrazine-free. Bottles of 100, 1 000 and 2 500.

Sublingual Tablets: 0.5 mg: Each pale green, round, flat tablet, imprinted W on one side and 0.5 on the other side contains: lorazepam 0.5 mg. Nonmedicinal ingredients: cornstarch, dye D&C Yellow 10 Aluminum Lake, dye FD&C Blue 1 Aluminum Lake, dye FD&C Yellow 6 Aluminum Lake, lactose, magnesium stearate and microcrystalline cellulose. Energy: 0.59 kJ (0.14 kcal). Gluten- and tartrazine-free. Bottles of 100.

1 mg: Each white, round, flat, tablet, imprinted W on one side and 1 on the other, contains: lorazepam 1 mg. Nonmedicinal ingredients: cornstarch, lactose, magnesium stearate and microcrystalline cellulose. Energy: 0.59 kJ (0.14 kcal). Gluten- and tartrazine-free. Bottles of 100.

2 mg: Each blue, round, flat tablet, imprinted W on one side and 2 on the other, contains: lorazepam 2 mg. Nonmedicinal ingredients: cornstarch, dye FD&C Blue 2 Aluminum Lake, lactose, magnesium stearate and microcrystalline cellulose. Energy: 0.80 kJ (0.19 kcal). Gluten- and tartrazine-free. Bottles of 100.

(Shown in Product Recognition Section)

Look in the YELLOW SECTION for the addresses and telephone numbers of the pharmaceutical manufacturers participating in the *CPS*.

ATRACURIUM BESYLATE INJECTION
Abbott

I.V. Skeletal Neuromuscular Blocking Agent

Supplied: Ampuls: Each mL of sterile, nonpyrogenic aqueous solution contains: atracurium besylate 10 mg. Nonmedicinal ingredients: benzenesulfonic acid to adjust the pH to 3.25 to 3.65 and water for injection. Ampuls of 5 mL.

Multiple-dose Vials: Each mL of sterile, nonpyrogenic aqueous solution contains: atracurium besylate 10 mg. Nonmedicinal ingredients: benzenesulfonic acid to adjust the pH to 3.25 to 3.65, benzyl alcohol (as preservative) and water for injection. Multiple-dose Fliptop vials of 10 mL.

Store under refrigeration (2 to 8°C) to preserve potency. **Do not freeze.** Upon removal from refrigeration, stable for up to 14 days at room temperature (25°C) without significant loss of potency. The injection slowly loses potency with time at the rate of approximately 6% per year under refrigeration (2 to 8°C). Rate of loss in potency increases to approximately 5% per month at 25°C.

New Product 1998

ATRACURIUM BESYLATE INJECTION Ⓟ
Faulding

I.V. Skeletal Neuromuscular Blocking Agent

Pharmacology: Atracurium is a nondepolarizing, intermediate-duration, skeletal neuromuscular blocking agent. Nondepolarizing agents antagonize the neurotransmitter action of acetylcholine by binding competitively to cholinergic receptor sites on the motor endplate. This antagonism is inhibited, and neuromuscular block reversed by acetylcholinesterase inhibitors such as neostigmine, edrophonium and pyridostigmine.

The duration of neuromuscular blockade produced by atracurium is approximately one-third to one-half the duration seen with d-tubocurarine, metocurine and pancuronium at equipotent doses. As with other nondepolarizing neuromuscular blockers, the time to onset of paralysis decreases and the duration of maximum effect increases with increasing atracurium doses.

Pharmacokinetics: The pharmacokinetics of atracurium in man are essentially linear within the 0.3 to 0.6 mg/kg dose range. The elimination half-life is approximately 20 minutes. The duration of neuromuscular blockade produced by atracurium does not correlate with plasma pseudocholinesterase levels and is not altered by the absence of renal function.

Indications: As an adjunct to general anesthesia, to facilitate endotracheal intubation and to provide skeletal muscle relaxation during surgery or mechanical ventilation. It can be used most advantageously if muscle twitch response to peripheral nerve stimulation is monitored.

Contraindications: In patients known to have a hypersensitivity to it.

Warnings: Atracurium should be used only by those skilled in the management of artificial respiration and only when facilities are instantly available for endotracheal intubation and for providing adequate ventilation of the patient, including the administration of oxygen under positive pressure and the elimination of carbon dioxide. The clinician must be prepared to assist or control respiration and anticholinesterase reversal agents should be immediately available. Do not give atracurium i.m.

Atracurium has no known effect on consciousness, pain threshold or cerebration. It should be used only with adequate anesthesia.

The injection, which has an acid pH, should not be mixed with alkaline solutions (e.g., barbiturate solutions) in the same syringe or administered simultaneously during i.v. infusion through the same needle. In such mixtures, the resultant pH may cause inactivation of the drug and precipitation of the free acid.

Atracurium 10 mL multiple-dose vials contain benzyl alcohol. Benzyl alcohol has been associated with an increased incidence of neurological and other complications in newborn infants which are sometimes fatal.

The 5 mL vials do not contain benzyl alcohol.

Precautions: Histamine Release: The possibility of substantial histamine release with consequent bronchospasm or anaphylaxis in sensitive individuals must be considered. Special caution should be exercised in administering atracurium to those patients in whom substantial histamine release would be especially hazardous (e.g., patients with clinically significant cardiovascular disease) and in patients with any history (e.g., severe anaphylactoid reactions or asthma) suggesting a greater risk of histamine release. In these patients, the recommended initial dose is lower (0.3 to 0.4 mg/kg) than for other patients and should be administered slowly or in divided doses over 1 minute. Limited clinical experience indicates that mean arterial pressure decreases in a substantial percentage of patients with a history of cardiovascular disease even at these doses.

Pregnancy: Atracurium has been shown to be potentially teratogenic at up to half the human dose when given to nonventilated rabbits by the s.c. route at sub-paralyzing doses. Therefore, atracurium should not be used during pregnancy unless, in the opinion of the physician, the potential benefits outweigh the unknown hazards.

Obstetrics: It is not known whether muscle relaxants administered during vaginal delivery have immediate or delayed adverse effects on the fetus or increase the likelihood that resuscitation of the newborn will be necessary. The possibility that a forceps delivery will be necessary may increase.

In an open study, atracurium has been administered (0.3 mg/kg) to 26 pregnant women during delivery by cesarean section. No harmful effects were attributable to the drug in any of the newborn infants, although small amounts were shown to cross the placental barrier. The possibility of respiratory depression in the newborn infant should always be considered following cesarean section during which a neuromuscular blocking agent has been administered. In patients receiving magnesium sulfate, the reversal of neuromuscular blockade may be unsatisfactory and atracurium dose should be lowered as indicated.

Lactation: It is not known whether this drug is excreted in human milk. Because many drugs are excreted in human milk, caution should be exercised when atracurium is administered to a nursing woman.

Patients with Special Disease and Conditions: Atracurium may have profound effects in patients with myasthenia gravis, Eaton-Lambert syndrome, or other neuromuscular diseases in which potentiation of nondepolarizing agents has been noted. The use of a peripheral nerve stimulator is especially important for assessing neuromuscular blockade in these patients. Similar precautions should be taken in patients with severe electrolyte disorders of carcinomatosis.

The safety of atracurium has not been established in patients with bronchial asthma.

Obesity: Ideal body weight should be considered in dosage calculations for obese patients with appropriate attention to the attendant risk of underdosing. Severe obesity may pose airway or ventilatory problems before, during, or after the use of nondepolarizing neuromuscular blockers.

Hypothermia: Hypothermia (25 to 28°C) has been associated with a decreased requirement for nondepolarizing blocking agents.

Cardiovascular Effects: Since atracurium has no clinically significant effects on heart rate at the recommended dosage range, it will not counteract the bradycardia produced by many anesthetic agents or vagal stimulation.

Malignant Hyperthermia: Multiple factors in anesthesia practice are suspected of triggering malignant hyperthermia (MH), a potentially fatal hypermetabolic state of skeletal muscle. Halogenated anesthetic agents and succinylcholine are recognized as the principal pharmacologic triggering agents in MH susceptible patients; however, since MH can develop in the absence of established triggering agents, the clinician should be prepared to recognize and treat MH in any patient scheduled for general anesthesia. Reports of MH have been rare in cases in which Atracurium Besylate Injection has been used. In a clinical study of MH-susceptible patients, Atracurium Besylate Injection did not trigger this syndrome.

Burns: Resistance to nondepolarizing neuromuscular blocking agents may develop in burn patients. Increased doses of nondepolarizing muscle relaxants may be required in burn patients and are dependent on the time elapsed since the burn injury and the size of the burn.

Electrolyte Abnormalities: Electrolyte abnormalities may antagonize or potentiate the action of neuromuscular blocking agents. For example, hyperkalemia has been reported to antagonize nondepolarizing agents, while hypokalemia has been associated with an enhancement of their activity.

The action of neuromuscular blocking agents may be enhanced by magnesium salts administered for the management of toxemia of pregnancy.

Long-Term Use in Intensive Care Unit (ICU): There is only limited information available on the efficacy and safety of long-term (days to weeks) i.v. atracurium infusion to facilitate mechanical ventilation in the ICU. These data suggest that dosage requirements show wide interpatient variability and may decrease or increase with time. When there is a need for long-term mechanical ventilation, the benefits-to-risk ratio of neuromuscular blockade must be considered.

Little information is available on the plasma levels or clinical consequences of atracurium metabolites that may accumulate during days to weeks of atracurium administration in ICU patients. Laudanosine, a major biologically active metabolite of atracurium without neuromuscular blocking activity, produces transient hypotension and, in higher doses, cerebral excitatory effects (generalized muscle twitching and seizures) when administered to several species of animals. There have been rare reports of seizures in ICU patients who have received atracurium or other agents. These patients usually had predisposing causes (such as head trauma, cerebral edema, hypoxic encephalopathy, viral encephalitis, uremia). There are insufficient data to determine whether or not laudanosine contributes to seizures in ICU patients.

Whenever the use of atracurium or any neuromuscular blocking agent is contemplated in the ICU, it is recommended that neuromuscular transmission be monitored continuously during administration with the help of a nerve stimulator. Additional doses of atracurium or any other neuromuscular blocking agent should not be given before there is a definite response to T_1 or the first twitch. If no response is elicited, infusion administration should be discontinued until a response returns.

The effects of hemodialysis, hemoperfusion and hemofiltration on plasma levels of atracurium and its metabolites are unknown.

Drug Interactions: Atracurium is potentiated by isoflurane and by enflurane anesthesia, and marginally potentiated by halothane (see Dosage).

Drugs which may enhance the neuromuscular blocking action of atracurium include: certain antibiotics, especially the aminoglycosides and polymyxins, lithium, magnesium salts, procainamide and quinidine. If other muscle relaxants are used during the same procedure, the possibility of a synergistic or antagonistic effect should be considered.

The prior administration of succinylcholine does not enhance the duration, but quickens the onset and may increase the depth of neuromuscular blockade induced by atracurium. Atracurium should not be administered until a patient has recovered from succinylcholine-induced neuromuscular blockade.

Adverse Effects: Atracurium was well tolerated and produced few adverse reactions during extensive clinical trials and as observed in clinical practice. Most adverse reactions were suggestive of histamine release. Fully developed anaphylactic or anaphylactoid reactions have been reported, and in rare instances these were severe (e.g., cardiac arrest). Skin flush and decreases in mean arterial pressure were the most common reactions seen in the recommended dose range. The incidences of decreases in mean arterial pressure were substantially increased in patients with a history of cardiovascular disease.

Observed in Controlled Clinical Studies: In 27 studies including 875 patients, atracurium was discontinued in 1 patient (who required treatment for bronchial secretions). Six other patients required treatment for adverse reactions attributable to the drug (wheezing in 1, hypotension in 5). Of the 5 patients who required treatment for hypotension, three had a history of significant cardiovascular disease. The overall incidence rate for clinically important adverse reactions, therefore, was 7 in 875 or 0.8%. Table I includes all adverse reactions reported attributable to atracurium during clinical trials with 875 patients.

Table I—Atracurium Besylate Injection

% of Patients Reporting Adverse Reactions

	Initial Dose (mg/kg) (Total = 875 Patients)			
Adverse Reaction	**0.00-0.30 n=485**	**0.31-0.40 n=236**	**0.46-0.50 n=127**	**≥0.56 n=27**
Skin Flush	0.8	5.5	15.0	26.0
Erythema	0.4	0.0	2.4	0.0
Itching				
Wheezing/ Bronchial	0.4	0.0	0.0	0.0
Secretions	0.2	0.0	0.8	0.0
Hives	0.2	0.0	0.0	0.0

Most adverse reactions were of little clinical significance unless they were associated with significant hemodynamic changes. Table II summarizes the incidences of substantial vital sign changes noted during atracurium clinical trials with 530 patients in whom these parameters were assessed.

Table II—Atracurium Besylate Injection

% of Patients with Vital Sign Changes (ASA 1 and 2)*

		Initial Dose (mg/kg)			
Vital Sign Change		**0.00-0.30 n=365**	**0.36-0.40 n=124**	**0.50 n=20**	**≥0.60 n=21**
Mean Arterial Pressure					
Decrease	≥40	0.3	0.0	10.0	5.0
Decrease	≥30	1.1	0.0	15.0	15.0
Decrease	≥20	2.5	2.4	15.0	30.0
Increase	≥20	7.4	7.3	5.0	0.0
Increase	≥30	1.9	3.2	0.0	0.0
Increase	≥40	0.8	1.6	0.0	0.0
Heart Rate					
Decrease	≥40	0.3	0.0	0.0	0.0
Decrease	≥30	0.8	0.0	0.0	0.0
Decrease	≥20	3.0	1.6	0.0	5.0
Increase	≥20	4.9	4.0	5.0	10.0
Increase	≥30	1.6	2.4	5.0	5.0
Increase	≥40	1.4	1.6	0.0	0.0

*American Society of Anesthesiologist Classification of Physical Status:
1. A normal healthy patient
2. A patient with a mild systemic disease.

In a small group of patients with cardiovascular disease (n=34) the changes in vital signs were more predominant, even at the lower doses (see Table III).

Table III—Atracurium Besylate Injection

Patients with Cardiovascular Disease with Vital Sign Changes (%)

		Initial Dose (mg/kg)	
Vital Sign Change		**0.00-0.30 n=18**	**0.36-0.40 n=16**
Mean Arterial Pressure			
Decrease	≥40	0.0	1 (6.3)
Decrease	≥30	2 (11.1)	6 (37.5)
Decrease	≥20	7 (38.9)	11 (68.8)
Increase	≥20	0.0	2 (12.5)
Increase	≥30	0.0	0.0
Heart Rate			
Decrease	≥30	0.0	0.0
Decrease	≥20	2 (11.0)	1 (6.3)
Increase	≥20	2 (11.0)	0.0
Increase	≥30	0.0	0.0

Three large prospective postmarketing surveillance studies have been reported, tabulating the incidence of adverse reactions associated with atracurium; they did not uncover any new events attributable to the drug.

Observed in Clinical Practice: Based on initial clinical practice experience in approximately 11 million patients who received atracurium, spontaneously reported adverse reactions were uncommon (0.006%). The following adverse reactions are among the most frequently reported, but there are insufficient data to support an estimate of their incidence.

General: Allergic reactions (anaphylactic or anaphylactoid responses) which, in rare instances, were severe (e.g., cardiac arrest).

Musculoskeletal: inadequate block, prolonged block.

Cardiovascular: hypotension, vasodilation (flushing), tachycardia, bradycardia.

Respiratory: dyspnea, bronchospasm, laryngospasm.

Integumentary: rash, urticaria, reaction at injection site.

There have been rare reports of seizures in ICU patients following long-term infusion of atracurium to support mechanical ventilation. There are insufficient data to define the contribution, if any, of atracurium and/or its metabolite laudanosine (see Precautions, Long-term Use in the Intensive Care Unit).

Overdose: Symptoms and Treatment: There has been limited experience with atracurium overdosage. The possibility of limited iatrogenic overdosage can be minimized by carefully monitoring muscle twitch response to peripheral nerve stimulation. Excessive doses can be expected to produce enhanced pharmacological effects. Overdosage may increase the risk of histamine release and cardiovascular effects, especially hypotension. If cardiovascular support is necessary, this should include proper positioning, fluid administration, and the use of vasopressor agents if necessary. The patient's

Atracurium Besylate Injection (cont'd)

airway should be assured, with manual or mechanical ventilation maintained as necessary. A longer duration of neuromuscular blockade may result from overdosage and a peripheral nerve stimulator should be used to monitor recovery. Recovery may be facilitated by administration of an anticholinesterase-reversing agent such as neostigmine, edrophonium, or pyridostigmine, in conjunction with an anticholinergic agent such as atropine or glycopyrrolate.

Three pediatric patients (3 weeks, 4 and 5 months of age) unintentionally received doses of 0.8 to 1 mg/kg of atracurium. The time to 25% recovery (50 to 55 minutes) following these doses, which were 5 to 6 times the ED_{95} dose, was moderately longer than the corresponding time observed following doses 2 to 2.5 times the atracurium ED_{95} dose in infants (22 to 36 minutes). Cardiovascular changes were minimal. Nonetheless, the possibility of cardiovascular changes must be considered in the case of overdose.

An adult patient (17 years of age) unintentionally received an initial dose of 1.3 mg/kg of atracurium. The time from injection to 25% recovery (83 minutes) was approximately twice that observed following maximum recommended doses in adults (35 to 45 minutes). The patient experienced moderate hemodynamic changes (13% increase in mean arterial pressure and 27% increase in heart rate) which persisted for 40 minutes and did not require treatment.

Dosage: To avoid distress to the patient, atracurium should not be administered before unconsciousness has been induced. It should not be mixed in the same syringe, or administered simultaneously through the same needle, with alkaline solutions (e.g., barbiturate solutions).

Atracurium should be administered i.v. **Do not give atracurium i.m.** I.M. administration may result in tissue irritation and there are no clinical data to support this route of administration.

The use of a peripheral nerve stimulator to monitor muscle twitch suppression and recovery will permit the most advantageous use of the drug and minimize the possibility of overdosage.

Bolus Injection for Intubation and Maintenance of Neuromuscular Blockade: Adults: A dose of 0.4 to 0.5 mg/kg (1.7 to 2.2 times the ED_{95}), given as an i.v. bolus injection, is the recommended initial dose for most patients. With this dose, good or excellent conditions for nonemergency intubation can be expected in 2 to 2.5 minutes in most patients, with maximum neuromuscular blockade being achieved approximately 3 to 5 minutes after injection. Clinically effective neuromuscular blockade generally lasts to 20 to 35 minutes under balanced anesthesia. Recovery to 25% of control is achieved approximately 35 to 45 minutes after injection, and recovery is usually 95% complete 60 minutes after injection.

Atracurium is potentiated by isoflurane or enflurane anesthesia. The same initial dose of 0.4 to 0.5 mg/kg may be used for intubation prior to administration of these inhalation agents; however, if atracurium is first administered under steady-state isoflurane or enflurane anesthesia, the initial dose may be reduced by approximately one-third, i.e., to 0.25 to 0.35 mg/kg, to adjust for the potentiating effects of these anesthetic agents. With halothane, which has only a marginal (approximately 20%) potentiating effect on atracurium, smaller dosage reductions may be considered.

Doses of 0.08 to 0.10 mg/kg are recommended for maintenance of neuromuscular blockade during prolonged surgical procedures. The first maintenance dose will generally be required 20 to 45 minutes after the initial atracurium injection, but the need for maintenance doses should be determined by clinical criteria. Because atracurium lacks cumulative effects, maintenance doses may be administered at relatively regular intervals for each patient, ranging approximately from 15 to 25 minutes under balanced anesthesia, slightly longer under isoflurane or enflurane. Higher doses (up to 0.2 mg/kg) permit maintenance dosing at longer intervals.

Children: No dosage adjustments are required for pediatric patients 2 years of age or older. A dose of 0.3 to 0.4 mg/kg is recommended as the initial dose for infants (1 month to 2 years of age) under halothane anesthesia. Maintenance doses may be required with slightly greater frequency in children than in adults.

Reversal: Reversal of neuromuscular blockade produced by atracurium can be achieved with an anticholinesterase agent such as neostigmine, edrophonium, or pyridostigmine, in conjunction with an anticholinergic agent such as atropine or glycopyrrolate. Under balanced anesthesia, reversal can usually be attempted approximately 20 to 35 minutes after an initial dose of 0.4 to 0.5 mg/kg, or approximately 10 to 30 minutes after a 0.08 to 0.10 mg/kg maintenance dose, when recovery of muscle twitch has started. Complete reversal is usually accomplished within 8 to 10 minutes of the administration of reversing agents. Rare incidences of breathing difficulties, possibly related to incomplete reversal have been reported following attempted pharmacologic antagonism of atracurium-induced neuromuscular blockade. As with other agents in this class, the tendency for residual neuromuscular block is increased if reversal is attempted at deep levels of blockade or if inadequate doses of reversal agents are employed.

Special Considerations: An initial dose of 0.3 to 0.4 mg/kg, given slowly or in divided doses over 1 minute, is recommended for adults or children with significant cardiovascular disease (an increased incidence of hypotensive episodes has been seen in these patients) and for adults or children with any history (e.g., several anaphylactoid reactions or asthma) suggesting a greater risk of histamine release.

Dosage reductions must be considered also in patients with neuromuscular disease, severe electrolyte disorders, or carcinomatosis in which potentiation of neuromuscular blockade or difficulties with reversal have been demonstrated. There has been no clinical experience with atracurium in these patients, and no specific dosage adjustments can be recommended.

No atracurium dosage adjustments are required for patients with renal disease.

An initial dose of 0.3 to 0.4 mg/kg is recommended for adults following the use of succinylcholine for intubation under balanced anesthesia. Further reductions may be desirable with the use of potent inhalation anesthetics. The patient should be permitted to recover from the effects of succinylcholine prior to atracurium administration. Insufficient data are available for recommendation of a specific initial atracurium dose for administration following the use of succinylcholine in children and infants.

As with other parenteral drug products, atracurium should be inspected visually for particulate matter and discoloration prior to administration, whenever solution and container permit.

Infusion: After administration of a recommended initial bolus dose of atracurium (0.3 to 0.5 mg/kg), a diluted solution can be administered by continuous infusion to adults and children aged 2 or more years for maintenance of neuromuscular blockade during extended surgical procedures.

Long-term i.v. infusion to support mechanical ventilation in the intensive care unit has not been studied sufficiently to support dosage recommendations (see Precautions, Long-term Use in Intensive Care Unit).

Infusion should be individualized for each patient. The rate of administration should be adjusted according to the patient's response as determined by peripheral nerve stimulation. Accurate dosing is best achieved using a precision infusion pump.

Infusion should be initiated only after evidence of spontaneous recovery from the bolus dose. An initial infusion rate of 9 to 10 µg/kg/min may be required to rapidly counteract the spontaneous recovery of neuromuscular function. Thereafter, a rate of 5 to 9 µg/kg/min should be adequate to maintain continuous neuromuscular blockade in the range of 89 to 99% in most pediatric and adult patients under balanced anesthesia. Occasional patients may require infusion rates as low as 2 µg/kg/min or as high as 15 µg/kg/min.

The neuromuscular blocking effect of atracurium administered by infusion is potentiated by enflurane or isoflurane and, to a lesser extent, by halothane. Reduction in the infusion rate of atracurium should, therefore, be considered for patients receiving inhalation anesthesia. The rate of infusion should be reduced by approximately one-third in the presence of steady-state enflurane or isoflurane anesthesia; smaller reductions should be considered in the presence of halothane.

In patients undergoing cardiopulmonary bypass with induced hypothermia, the rate of infusion required to maintain adequate surgical relaxation during hypothermia (25 to 28°C) has been shown to be approximately half the rate required during normothermia.

Spontaneous recovery from neuromuscular blockage following discontinuation of infusion may be expected to proceed at a rate comparable to that following administration of a single bolus dose.

The amount of infusion solution required per minute will depend upon the concentration of atracurium in the infusion solution, the desired dose and the patient's weight. Tables IV and V provide guidelines for delivery in mL/h (equivalent to microdrops/min when 60 microdrops = 1 mL) of drug solutions in concentrations of 0.2 mg/mL (20 mg in 100 mL) or 0.5 mg/mL (50 mg in 100 mL) with an infusion pump or a gravity flow device.

Table IV—Atracurium Besylate Injection

Atracurium Infusion Rates for a Concentration of 0.2 mg/mL

Patient Weight (kg)	Drug Delivery Rate (µg/kg/min) 5	6	7	8	9	10
	Infusion Delivery Rate (mL/h)					
30	45	54	63	72	81	90
35	53	63	74	84	95	105
40	60	72	84	96	108	120
45	68	81	95	108	122	135
50	75	90	105	120	135	150
55	83	99	116	132	149	165
60	90	108	126	144	162	180
65	98	117	137	156	176	195
70	105	126	147	168	189	210
75	113	135	158	180	203	225
80	120	144	168	192	216	240
90	135	162	189	216	243	270
100	150	180	210	240	270	300

Table V—Atracurium Besylate Injection

Atracurium Infusion Rates for a Concentration of 0.5 mg/mL

Patient Weight (kg)	Drug Delivery Rate (µg/kg/min) 5	6	7	8	9	10
	Infusion Delivery Rate (mL/h)					
30	18	22	25	29	32	36
35	21	25	29	34	38	42
40	24	29	34	38	43	48
45	27	32	38	43	49	54
50	30	36	42	48	54	60
55	33	40	46	53	59	66
60	36	43	50	58	65	72
65	39	47	55	62	70	78
70	42	50	59	67	76	84
75	45	54	63	72	81	90
80	48	58	67	77	86	96
90	54	65	76	86	97	108
100	60	72	84	96	108	120

Stability and Storage: Atracurium slowly loses potency with time at the rate of approximately 6%/year under refrigeration (2 to 8°C). The injection **should be stored under refrigeration (2 to 8°C)** to preserve potency. **Protect from freezing.**

Compatability and Admixtures: Infusion solutions may be prepared by admixing atracurium with an appropriate diluent such as 5% Dextrose Injection USP, 0.9% Sodium Chloride Injection USP, or 5% Dextrose and 0.9% Sodium Chloride Injection USP. Solutions containing 0.2 or 0.5 mg/mL atracurium in these diluents may be stored either under refrigeration or at room temperature for 24 hours without significant loss of potency. Infusion solutions should be used within 24 hours of preparation. Unused solutions should be discarded.

In Lactated Ringer's Injection minor degradation was observed at room temperature. However, the product is stable at 2 to 8°C protected from light for 24 hours.

Care should be taken during admixture to prevent inadvertent contamination. As with other parenteral drug products, the admixtures should be inspected visually for discoloration, haziness, particulate matter and leakage prior to administration, whenever a solution and container permit. Discard unused portions.

Supplied: Single Dose Vials: Each mL of sterile, nonpyrogenic aqueous solution contains: atracurium besylate 10 mg. pH adjusted to 3.25 to 3.65 with benzene sulfonic acid. Single dose vials of 5 mL.

Multidose Vials: Each mL of sterile, nonpyrogenic aqueous solution contains: atracurium besylate 10 mg. Nonmedicinal ingredients: benzyl alcohol (preservative). pH adjusted to 3.25 to 3.65 with benzene sulfonic acid. Multidose vials of 10 mL.

New Product 1998

Can't find information on a particular drug? Check the CPhA General Monograph index at the beginning of the WHITE SECTION.

ATROMID-S® ℞
Wyeth-Ayerst

Clofibrate

Antihyperlipidemic Agent

Supplied: 500 mg: Each orange, oblong, soft gelatin capsule, imprinted "Ayerst" in white script, contains: clofibrate USP 500 mg. Also contains methyl- and propylparabens. Energy: 1.67 kJ (0.4 kcal). Sodium: <1 mmol (0.0023 mg). Alcohol-, gluten, lactose-, sulfites- and tartrazine-free. Bottles of 100 and 1 000.

1 g: Each light red, oblong, soft gelatin capsule, imprinted "Ayerst" in white script, contains: clofibrate USP 1 g. Also contains methyl- and propylparabens. Energy: 3.35 kJ (0.8 kcal). Sodium: <1 mmol (0.0023 mg). Alcohol-, gluten, lactose-, sulfites- and tartrazine-free. Bottles of 100.

Protect from light and excessive heat.

(Shown in Product Recognition Section)

ATROPINE ℞
CIBA Vision

Atropine Sulfate

Mydriatic—Cycloplegic

Supplied: Each bottle of ophthalmic solution contains: atropine sulfate 1% in a sterile aqueous vehicle of hydroxypropyl methylcellulose with a borate buffer and benzalkonium chloride as preservative. Plastic bottles of 10 mL with dropper tip.

ATROPINE ℞
Dioptic

Atropine Sulfate

Mydriatic—Cycloplegic

Supplied: Each mL of sterile ophthalmic solution contains: atropine sulfate 1%. Nonmedicinal ingredients: benzalkonium chloride, dibasic potassium phosphate, disodium edetate, hydroxypropyl methylcellulose, monobasic sodium phosphate, sodium bisulfite and purified water. Hydrochloric acid may be used to adjust pH. Plastic dropper bottles of 5 mL. Store at controlled room temperature (15 to 30°C).

ATROPINE INJECTION ℞
Bioniche

Parasympatholytic

Supplied: 0.4 mg: Each mL of sterile solution contains: atropine sulfate 0.4 mg, sodium chloride 8.9 mg and sulfuric acid (to adjust pH). Ampuls of 1 mL, boxes of 10.

0.6 mg: Each mL of sterile solution contains: atropine sulfate 0.6 mg, sodium chloride 8.9 mg and sulfuric acid (to adjust pH). Ampuls of 1 mL, boxes of 10.

Store at room temperature (15 to 30°C).

ATROPINE™ OINTMENT ℞
Alcon

Atropine Sulfate

Mydriatic—Cycloplegic—Anticholinergic

Supplied: Each 3.5 g of sterile ointment contains: atropine sulfate 1%, white petrolatum, anhydrous lanolin, purified water and hydrochloric acid with methylparaben 0.05% and propylparaben 0.01% as preservatives. Also available in solution form (Isopto Atropine).

ATROPINE SULFATE ℞
Abbott

Anticholinergic

Supplied: Each mL contains: atropine sulfate, 0.4 mg (400 μg), 0.6 mg (600 μg) or 1 mg. Nonmedicinal ingredients: sodium chloride, sulfuric acid and/or sodium hydroxide and water for injection. Boxes of 50 and 100. Also supplied in 5 mL and 10 mL syringes of 0.1 mg/mL. Boxes of 10.

ATROPINE SULFATE ℞
Rivex Ophthalmics

Mydriatic—Cycloplegic

Supplied: Each mL of sterile ophthalmic solution contains: atropine sulfate 1%. Nonmedicinal ingredients: benzalkonium chloride, boric acid, hydrochloric acid, hydroxypropyl methylcellulose, purified water and sodium hydroxide. Plastic squeeze bottles of 5 mL with controlled tip applicators.

ATROPINE SULFATE INJECTION USP ℞
Astra

Atropine Sulfate

Parasympatholytic

Pharmacology: Atropine is commonly classified as an anticholinergic or antiparasympathetic (parasympatholytic) drug. More precisely, however, it is termed an antimuscarinic agent since it antagonizes the muscarine-like actions of acetylcholine and other choline esters.

Atropine inhibits the muscarinic actions of acetylcholine on structures innervated by postganglionic cholinergic nerves, and on smooth muscles which respond to endogenous acetylcholine but are not so innervated. As with other antimuscarinic agents, the major action of atropine is a competitive or surmountable antagonism which can be overcome by increasing the concentration of acetylcholine at receptor sites of the effector organ (e.g., by using anticholinesterase agents which inhibit the enzymatic destruction of acetylcholine). The receptors antagonized by atropine are the peripheral structures that are stimulated or inhibited by muscarine (i.e., exocrine glands and smooth and cardiac muscle). Responses to postganglionic cholinergic nerve stimulation also may be inhibited by atropine but this occurs less readily than with responses to injected (exogenous) choline esters.

Atropine-induced parasympathetic inhibition may be preceded by a transient phase of stimulation, especially on the heart where small doses first slow the rate before characteristic tachycardia develops due to paralysis of vagal control. Atropine exerts a more potent and prolonged effect on heart, intestine and bronchial muscle than scopolamine, but its action on the iris, ciliary body and certain secretory glands is weaker than that of scopolamine. Unlike the latter, atropine in clinical doses does not depress the CNS but may stimulate the medulla and higher cerebral centres. Although mild vagal excitation occurs, the increased respiratory rate and (sometimes) increased depth of respiration produced by atropine are probably the result of bronchiolar dilatation. Accordingly, atropine is an unreliable respiratory stimulant and large or repeated doses may depress respiration.

Adequate doses of atropine abolish various types of reflex vagal cardiac slowing or asystole. The drug also prevents or abolishes bradycardia or asystole produced by injection of choline esters, anticholinesterase agents or other parasympathomimetic drugs, and cardiac arrest produced by stimulation of the vagus. Atropine also may lessen the degree of partial heart block when vagal activity is an etiologic factor. In some patients with complete heart block, the idioventricular rate may be accelerated by atropine; in others, the rate is stabilized. Occasionally a large dose may cause atrioventricular (AV) block and nodal rhythm.

Atropine Sulfate Injection USP in clinical doses counteracts the peripheral dilation and abrupt decrease in blood pressure produced by choline esters. However, when given by itself, atropine does not exert a striking or uniform effect on blood vessels or blood pressure. Systemic doses slightly raise systolic and lower diastolic pressures and can produce significant postural hypotension. Such doses also slightly increase cardiac output and decrease central venous pressure. Occasionally, therapeutic doses dilate cutaneous blood vessels, particularly in the blush area (atropine flush), and may cause atropine fever due to suppression of sweat gland activity in infants and small children.

Atropine disappears rapidly from the blood following injection and is distributed throughout the body. Much of the drug is destroyed by enzymatic hydrolysis, particularly in the liver; from 13 to 50% is excreted unchanged in the urine. Traces are found in various secretions, including milk. Atropine readily crosses the placental barrier and enters the fetal circulation.

Sodium chloride added to render the solution isotonic for injection of the active ingredient is present in amounts insufficient to affect serum electrolyte balance of sodium and chloride ions.

Indications: As an antisialagogue for preanesthetic medication to prevent or reduce secretions of the respiratory tract. To restore cardiac rate and arterial pressure during anesthesia when vagal stimulation produced by intra-abdominal surgical traction causes a sudden decrease in pulse rate and cardiac action. To lessen the degree of AV heart block when increased vagal tone is a major factor in the conduction defect as in some cases due to digitalis. To overcome severe bradycardia and syncope due to a hyperactive carotid sinus reflex. As an antidote (with external massage) for cardiovascular collapse from the injudicious use of a choline ester (cholinergic) drug. In the treatment of anticholinesterase poisoning from organophosphorus insecticides. As an antidote for the rapid type of mushroom poisoning due to the presence of the alkaloid, muscarine, in certain species of fungus such as Amanita muscaria.

Contraindications: Glaucoma, pyloric stenosis or prostatic hypertrophy, except in doses ordinarily used for preanesthetic medication.

Warnings: Atropine is a highly potent drug and due care is essential to avoid overdosage, especially with i.v. administration. Not for pediatric use. Children are more susceptible than adults to the toxic effects of anticholinergic agents.

Precautions: Use with caution in all individuals over 40 years of age. Conventional systemic doses may precipitate acute glaucoma in susceptible patients, convert partial organic pyloric stenosis into complete obstruction, lead to complete urinary retention in patients with prostatic hypertrophy or cause inspissation of bronchial secretions and formation of dangerous viscid plugs in patients with chronic lung disease.

Pregnancy: Animal reproduction studies have not been conducted with atropine. It also is not known whether atropine can cause fetal harm when given to a pregnant woman or can affect reproduction capacity. Atropine should be given to a pregnant woman only if clearly needed.

Adverse Effects: Most of the side effects of atropine are directly related to its antimuscarinic action. Dryness of the mouth, blurred vision, photophobia and tachycardia commonly occur with chronic administration of therapeutic doses. Anhidrosis also may occur and produce heat intolerance or impair temperature regulation in persons living in a hot environment. Constipation and difficulty in micturition may occur in elderly patients. Occasional hypersensitivity reactions have been observed, especially skin rashes which in some instances progressed to exfoliation.

Adverse effects following single or repeated injections of atropine are most often the result of excessive dosage. These include palpitation, dilated pupils, difficulty in swallowing, hot dry skin, thirst, dizziness, restlessness, tremor, fatigue and ataxia. Toxic doses lead to marked palpitation, restlessness and excitement, hallucinations, delirium and coma. Depression and circulatory collapse occur only with severe intoxication. In such cases, blood pressure declines and death due to respiratory failure may ensue following paralysis and coma.

Overdose: Symptoms and Treatment: In the event of toxic overdosage (see Adverse Effects), a short-acting barbiturate or diazepam may be given as needed to control marked excitement and convulsions. Large doses for sedation should be avoided because central depressant action may coincide with the depression occurring late in atropine poisoning. Central stimulants are not recommended. Physostigmine, given as an atropine antidote by slow i.v. injection of 1 to 4 mg (0.5 to 1.0 mg in children), rapidly abolishes delirium and coma caused by large doses of atropine. Since physostigmine is rapidly destroyed, the patient may again lapse into coma after 1 to 2 hours, and repeated doses may be required. Artificial respiration with oxygen may be necessary. Ice bags and alcohol sponges help to reduce fever, especially in children.

The fatal adult dose of atropine is not known; 200 mg doses have been used and doses as high as 1 000 mg have been given.

In children, 10 mg or less may be fatal. With a dose as low as 0.5 mg, undesirable minimal symptoms or responses of overdosage may occur. These increase in severity and extent with larger doses of the drug (excitement, hallucinations, delirium and coma with a dose of 10 mg or more).

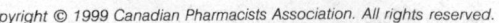

Dosage: May be administered s.c., i.m. or i.v. The average adult dose is 0.5 mg with a range of 0.4 to 0.6 mg. As an antisialagogue it is usually injected i.m. prior to induction of anesthesia. This produces only minimal blocking of vagal activity. During surgery, the drug is given i.v. when reduction in pulse rate and cessation of cardiac action are due to

Atropine Sulfate Injection USP (cont'd)

increased vagal activity; however, if the anesthetic is cyclopropane, doses less than 0.4 mg should be used and should be given slowly to avoid the possible production of ventricular arrhythmia. Usual doses are used to reduce severe bradycardia and syncope associated with hyperactive carotid sinus reflex. For bradyarrhythmias the usual i.v. adult dosage ranges from 0.4 to 1 mg every 1 to 2 hours as needed; larger doses up to a maximum of 2 mg may be required.

Atropine is also a specific antidote for cardiovascular collapse resulting from injudicious administration of choline ester. When cardiac arrest has occurred, external cardiac massage or other method of resuscitation is required to distribute the drug after i.v. injection.

In anticholinesterase poisoning from exposure to insecticides, large doses of at least 2 to 3 mg should be administered parenterally and repeated until signs of atropine intoxication appear. In the rapid type of mushroom poisoning, atropine should be given in doses sufficient to control parasympathomimetic signs before coma and cardiovascular collapse supervene.

Supplied: Each mL of sterile, nonpyrogenic solution contains: atropine sulfate monohydrate 0.4 mg or 0.6 mg in water for injection with sodium chloride sufficient to render the solution isotonic and sodium hydroxide and/or sulfuric acid to adjust pH to 3 to 6.5. No bacteriostat, antimicrobial agent or added buffer (except to adjust pH between 3 and 6.5). Polyamp Duofit units of 1 mL. When smaller doses are required the unused portion should be discarded.

Solutions should be stored at controlled room temperature, 15 to 30°C. Do not use if solution is cloudy or contains a precipitate.

ATROPISOL® Ⓟ

CIBA Vision

Atropine Sulfate

Mydriatic—Cycloplegic

Supplied: Each bottle contains: atropine sulfate 1% (w/v). Nonmedicinal ingredients: benzalkonium chloride 0.01% w/v (preservative), boric acid, disodium edetate, potassium chloride, purified water and sodium carbonate. Plastic squeeze bottles of 5 mL with dropper tip. Store at 15 to 30°C. Keep bottle tightly closed when not in use.

ATROVENT® Inhalation Aerosol Ⓟ

Boehringer Ingelheim

Ipratropium Bromide

Bronchodilator

Pharmacology: Ipratropium, a quaternary ammonium derivative of atropine is an anticholinergic drug having bronchodilator properties. On inhalation the onset of action is noted within 5 to 15 minutes with a peak response between 1 and 2 hours, lasting about 2 additional hours with subsequent decline. An inhaled dose of 40 μg induces bronchodilator effect lasting for some 6 hours.

In maintenance therapy of chronic reversible airways obstruction ipratropium has been shown to provide additive bronchodilating effects to theophylline and β-adrenoceptor agonists (sympathomimetic amines). Repeated inhalation of ipratropium has not been linked to tolerance towards bronchodilating effects. Significant alterations in mucociliary clearance of sputum were not observed in short term clinical trials. Systemic absorption is poor and the blood levels reached are very low. Metabolic studies in healthy volunteers show an average elimination half-life of 3.5 hours (range 1.5 to 4 hours), the drug is transformed to some 8 metabolites with little or no anticholinergic activity.

Pharmacokinetics: In man, inhalation of 555 μg of radiolabeled ipratropium bromide, about 14 times the recommended therapeutic dose, produced peak plasma levels of 0.06 ng/mL after 3 hours. The plasma concentration-versus-time curve was similar to that seen after oral administration, likely reflecting the large fraction of inhaled dose which is deposited on the pharyngeal mucosae and swallowed. I.V. administration of 1 mg in man showed a rapid distribution into tissues (half-life of α phase approximately 5 minutes), and a terminal half-life (β phase) of 3 to 4 hours. Plasma concentrations after inhaled ipratropium were about 1 000 times lower than equipotent oral or i.v. doses (15 and 0.15 mg, respectively).

Up to 8 metabolites of ipratropium have been detected in man, rat and dog. In man, about 70% of the drug is excreted unchanged after i.v. administration and only 1 metabolite exceeds 10% of the total radioactivity. The elimination occurs primarily via the kidney with less than 10% of the total i.v. dose excreted via the biliary or fecal route. After oral or inhaled doses, however, up to 90% of the dose is detectable in the feces, suggesting poor absorption.

A wide variety of challenge studies have been conducted utilizing ipratropium as a protective agent. In pharmacologically induced bronchospasm, ipratropium, in clinical doses, was very effective against methacholine and acetylcholine, moderately effective against propranolol but had little or no effect against histamine or serotonin. Studies in exercise induced bronchospasm have yielded variable results. Some investigations have indicated that the drug has little or no effect but other studies have shown that some patients, at least, are protected against bronchospasm induced by exercise. Likewise, the protective effects against cold air induced bronchospasm have been variable.

Antigen challenge studies have demonstrated that ipratropium offers some protection against the early allergic asthma response, but has no effect on the late response.

Indications: For the maintenance therapy of responsive cases of chronic reversible airways obstruction, such as chronic bronchitis and asthma.

Contraindications: In patients with a history of hypersensitivity to soya lecithin or related food products such as soybean and peanut. It should also not be taken by patients hypersensitive to ipratropium bromide, atropinics or any other aerosol components.

Warnings: Ipratropium should not be used for the abatement of the acute asthmatic attack, since the drug has a slower onset of effect than that of an adrenergic β_2 agonist aerosol.

Care should be taken to ensure that ipratropium does not reach the eye. There have been isolated reports of ocular complications (i.e., mydriasis, increased intraocular pressure, glaucoma and eye pain) when aerosolized ipratropium has been released into the eyes. Ocular events have occurred when the aerosol was used with the standard mouthpiece or with a spacing device. In the event that glaucoma is precipitated or worsened, treatment should include standard measures for this condition.

Precautions: General: To ensure optimal delivery to the bronchial tree, the patient should be properly instructed by the physician or other health professional in the use of the inhaler.

Caution is advised against the release of the aerosol into the eyes. Due care should be taken when a spacing device is employed.

In patients with glaucoma, prostatic hypertrophy or urinary retention ipratropium should be used with caution.

If a reduced response to ipratropium becomes apparent, the patient should seek medical advice.

Like other pressurized aerosol formulations, Atrovent contains fluorocarbon propellants trichloromonofluoromethane, dichlorodifluoromethane, 1,2- dichlorotetrafluoroethane. Such propellants may be hazardous if they are deliberately abused. Inhalation of high concentrations of aerosol sprays has brought about toxic cardiovascular effects and even death, especially under conditions of hypoxia. **However, evidence attests to the relative safety of aerosols when used properly and with adequate ventilation.** The recommended dose should not be exceeded and the patient should be so informed.

Pregnancy: The safety in pregnancy has not been established. The benefits of using ipratropium when pregnancy is present or suspected must be weighed against the possible hazards caused to the fetus. Studies in rats, mice and rabbits showed no embryotoxic nor teratogenic effects.

Lactation: No specific studies have been conducted on excretion of this drug in breast milk. Benefits during lactation should therefore be weighed against possible effects on the infant.

Children: Efficacy and safety in children younger than 12 years has not been established.

Drug Interactions: In patients receiving other anticholinergic drugs, ipratropium should be used with caution because of possible additive effects.

Xanthine derivatives and β_2 adrenergic agents may enhance the effect of ipratropium.

Adverse Effects: The frequency of side effects reported after repeated dosing in 605 patients: dry mouth or throat (9.4%), headache (7.9%), bad taste (3.8%), blurred vision (3.1%), tremor (2.8%), palpitations (2.1%), urinary hesitation or retention (1.5%), dizziness (1.5%), stuffy nose (1.2%), difficulty in expectoration (0.7%), dyspnea (0.7%), nausea (0.5%).

There have been isolated reports of ocular events such as mydriasis, increased intraocular pressure, glaucoma and eye pain associated with the release of aerosolized ipratropium into the eyes.

Overdose: Symptoms and Treatment: Doses of ipratropium up to 1.2 mg (60 puffs) have been administered by inhalation without the appearance of serious systemic anticholinergic effects.

Should signs of serious anticholinergic toxicity appear, cholinesterase inhibitors may be considered.

Dosage: The optimal maintenance dosage must be individually determined. The recommended dosage is 2 metered doses (actuations) (40 μg) 3 or 4 times daily. Some patients may need up to 4 metered doses (actuations) (80 μg) at a time to obtain maximum benefit during early treatment. The maximum daily dose should not exceed 8 metered doses (actuations) (160 μg) and the minimum interval between doses should not be less than 4 hours.

Stability and Storage: The aerosol canister should be stored at room temperature (15 to 30°C); the contents are stable up to the expiration date stamped on the label. Caution: contents under pressure. Container may explode if heated. Do not place in hot water or near radiators, stoves or other sources of heat. Do not puncture or incinerate container or store at temperatures over 30°C. Keep out of reach of children.

Information for the Patient: See Blue Section—Information for the Patient ''Atrovent Inhalation Aerosol''.

Supplied: Each 10 mL metal canister with mouthpiece (oral adaptor) contains: ipratropium bromide 140 or 200 doses. Each valve depression delivers 20 μg. Nonmedicinal ingredients: propellants (difluorodichloromethane, monofluorotrichloromethane, tetrafluorodichloroethane) and soya lecithin. Store between 15 and 30°C.

(Shown in Product Recognition Section)

ATROVENT® Inhalation Solution Ⓟ

Boehringer Ingelheim

Ipratropium Bromide

Bronchodilator

Pharmacology: Ipratropium, a quaternary ammonium derivative of atropine, is an anticholinergic drug which has bronchodilator properties. On inhalation, the onset of action is noted within 5 to 15 minutes, with a peak response between 1 and 2 hours, lasting about 2 additional hours, with subsequent decline from the peak. Bronchodilation is still evident 8 hours after inhalation.

In acute and maintenance therapy of chronic reversible airways obstruction, ipratropium has been shown to provide additive bronchodilating effects to theophylline and beta-adrenoceptor agonists (sympathomimetic amines). Repeated inhalation of ipratropium has not been linked to tolerance towards bronchodilating effects.

In controlled 12-week studies in patients with bronchospasm associated with chronic obstructive pulmonary disease (chronic bronchitis and emphysema), significant improvements in pulmonary function (FEV_1 and $FEF_{25-75\%}$ in increases of 15% or more) occurred within 15 minutes, reached a peak in 1 to 2 hours, and persisted for periods of 4 to 5 hours in the majority of patients, with 25 to 38% of the patients demonstrating increases of at least 15% at 7 to 8 hours. Continued effectiveness of ipratropium solution was demonstrated throughout the 12-week period. In addition, significant changes in forced vital capacity (FVC) have been demonstrated.

Additional controlled 12-week studies were conducted to evaluate the safety and efficacy of ipratropium solution administered concomitantly with bronchodilator solutions of orciprenaline or salbutamol, compared with the administration of each of the beta agonists alone.

Combined therapy produced significant additional responses in FEV_1, FVC and $FEF_{25-75\%}$. On combined therapy, the median duration of 15% improvement in FEV_1 was 5 to 7 hours, compared with 3 to 4 hours in patients receiving a beta agonist alone.

Significant alterations in mucociliary clearance of tracheobronchial secretions (sputum) were not observed in short-term clinical trials. Systemic absorption of ipratropium is poor and the blood levels reached are very low. Metabolic studies with ipratropium in healthy volunteers show an average elimination half-life of 3.5 hours (range 1.5 to 4 hours). The drug is transformed to some 8 metabolites with little or no anticholinergic activity.

Indications: Ipratropium solution administered either alone or with a β_2-adrenergic stimulant solution is indicated as a bronchodilator for the maintenance treatment of bronchospasm associated with, or for the therapy of, acute exacerbations of chronic obstructive pulmonary disease, including chronic bronchitis and emphysema. Ipratropium solution, when used in conjunction with a β_2-adrenergic stimulant solution such as fenoterol or salbutamol, is indicated for acute asthmatic attacks. Ipratropium solution is to be administered by compressed air or oxygen driven nebulizers.

Contraindications: Known hypersensitivity to ipratropium, to any of the product's ingredients or to atropinics.

Warnings: Ipratropium solution in the 20 mL multidose bottle contains preservatives (benzalkonium chloride and disodium ethylene diamine tetraacetic acid—EDTA-disodium). It has been reported that these preservatives may cause bronchoconstriction in some patients with hyperreactive airways.

The unit dose vials do not contain preservatives.

Ipratropium should not be used alone for the abatement of an acute asthmatic attack since the drug has a slower onset of effect than that of an adrenergic β_2 agonist.

Patients with cystic fibrosis may be more prone to gastrointestinal motility disturbances.

Glaucoma, Angle-Closure: Care should be taken to ensure that the nebulizer mask fits the patient's face properly and that nebulized solution does not escape into the eyes. In patients with glaucoma or narrow anterior chambers, the administration by nebulizer of a combined ipratropium/β_2-agonist solution should be avoided unless measures (e.g., use of swimming goggles or use of a nebulizer with a mouth piece) are taken to ensure that nebulized solution does not reach the eye. There have been isolated reports of ocular complications (i.e., mydriasis, increased intraocular pressure, angle closure glaucoma) when nebulized ipratropium either alone or in combination with an adrenergic β_2 agonist solution has escaped into the eyes. In the event that glaucoma is precipitated or worsened, treatment should include standard measures for this condition.

Pregnancy: The safety of ipratropium in pregnancy has not been established. The benefits of using ipratropium when pregnancy is confirmed or suspected must be weighed against possible hazards to the fetus. Studies in rats, mice and rabbits showed no embryotoxic nor teratogenic effects.

Lactation: No specific studies have been conducted on excretion of this drug in breast milk. Benefits of ipratropium use during lactation should therefore be weighed against the possible effects on the infant.

Children: The efficacy and safety in children younger than 5 years has not been established.

Precautions: Ipratropium solution is intended only for inhalation with suitable nebulizing devices and should not be taken orally or administered parenterally.

Patients should be instructed in the proper use of the nebulizer.

Caution is advised against accidental release of the solution into the eyes.

In patients with glaucoma, prostatic hypertrophy or urinary retention, ipratropium should be used with caution.

If a reduced response to ipratropium becomes apparent, the patient should seek medical advice.

Ipratropium solution, when administered to patients with acute severe asthma, should be used with concomitant β_2-adrenergic stimulant therapy.

Immediate hypersensitivity reactions may occur after administration of ipratropium inhalation solution, as demonstrated by rare cases of urticaria, angioedema, rash, bronchospasm and oropharyngeal edema.

Use with other drugs: In patients receiving other anticholinergic drugs, ipratropium should be used with caution because of possible additive effects.

Ipratropium solution with preservatives (i.e., from the 20 mL multidose bottle) should not be mixed with sodium cromoglycate, as this produces a cloudy solution caused by complexation between the preservatives and sodium cromoglycate. If the patient's condition requires the administration of sodium cromoglycate, it should be given in combination with ipratropium solution without preservatives (i.e., from the unit dose vial).

Adverse Effects: Because of the low systemic absorption of ipratropium, anticholinergic side effects, such as tachycardia and palpitations, ocular accommodation disturbances, gastrointestinal motility disturbances and urinary retention, are rare and reversible, although the risk of urinary retention may be increased in patients with pre-existing outflow tract obstruction.

Acute Administration: The frequency of adverse reactions recorded in 214 patients receiving ipratropium solution was as follows: dry mouth or throat 9.3%, bad taste 5.1%, tremor 4.2%, exacerbation of symptoms 4.2%, burning eyes 0.9%, nausea 0.9%, sweating 0.9%, cough 0.9%, headache 0.5%, palpitations 0.5%.

The adverse effect judged to be most severe was exacerbation of bronchospasm. This occurred in 8 patients treated with ipratropium solution alone, 6 of whom withdrew from the clinical studies.

Bronchospasm occurred in 3 patients with acute severe asthma who received ipratropium solution alone. In 2 patients, this was reversed after therapy with a β_2 sympathomimetic solution. The third patient received no other therapy.

Table I compares the incidence of adverse effects of the combination of Atrovent and a β_2 agonist (either fenoterol or salbutamol) solution with that of the β_2 agonist alone.

Table I—Atrovent Inhalation Solution

Comparision of Adverse Effects

Adverse Effect	Atrovent+β_2 Agonist (% of 94 patients)	β_2 Agonist (% of 96 patients)
Tremor	31.9	26.0
Dry mouth	16.0	28.1
Bad taste	16.0	13.5
Vomiting	2.1	2.1
Palpitations	2.1	1.0
Headache	1.1	2.1
Cough	1.1	0.0
Flushing	1.1	0.0
Dizziness	0.0	1.0
Numbness in leg	0.0	1.0

Chronic Administration: The frequency of adverse reactions reported as possibly related to ipratropium treatment in 219 COPD patients participating in long-term (12-week) controlled clinical trials was as follows: dry mouth 2.7%, coughing 1.8%, dyspnea 1.8%, headache 1.8%, urinary retention 1.4%, tremor 0.9%, nausea 0.9%, palpitation 0.9%, sputum increased 0.9%, rhinitis 0.9%, eye pain 0.9%.

The following other adverse events were reported as possibly related to drug treatment in 1 patient each: bronchitis, bronchospasm, chest pain, depression, fatigue, flu-symptoms, hypoesthesia, increased saliva, insomnia, nervousness, pain, paresthesia, pharyngitis, somnolence, tachycardia and urticaria.

The frequency of adverse reactions reported as possibly related to drug treatment in greater than 1% of COPD patients participating in long-term (12-week) controlled clinical trials that compared the efficacy and safety of Atrovent+β_2-agonists (metaproterenol or salbutamol) versus the β_2-agonist alone, was as follows: see Table II.

Table II—Atrovent Inhalation Solution

Comparison of Adverse Effects

Adverse Effect	Atrovent+β_2-Agonist (% of Patients) (n=208)	β_2-Agonist (% of Patients) (n=417)
Headache	4.3	1.7
Tremor	3.8	3.4
Nervousness	3.8	1.9
Dyspnea	2.4	3.4
Dry mouth	2.4	1.0
Bronchitis	2.9	2.9
Dizziness	1.4	1.9
Coughing	1.4	1.0
Taste perversion	1.9	1.2
Insomnia	1.9	0.2
Dysuria	1.0	0.2
Nausea	1.0	1.7
Abnormal vision	0.5	1.2
Chest pain	1.4	0.7
Constipation	1.4	0.0
Dysphonia	1.0	0.2
Dyspepsia	1.0	0.0
Bronchospasm aggravated	1.0	0.7
Micturition frequency	1.0	0.2

There have been isolated reports of ocular effects such as mydriasis, increased intraocular pressure, and acute glaucoma associated with the escape of nebulized ipratropium alone or in combination with a β_2-agonist solution into the eyes.

Overdose: Symptoms and Treatment: Doses of ipratropium up to 1.2 mg (approximately 30 times the therapeutic dose) have been administered by ipratropium inhaler without the appearance of serious systemic anticholinergic effects.

Should signs of serious anticholinergic toxicity appear, cholinesterase inhibitors may be considered.

Dosage: Counselling by physicians on smoking cessation should be the first step in treating patients with chronic obstructive pulmonary disease (COPD), who smoke, independent of the clinical presentation i.e. chronic bronchitis (with or without airflow limitation) or emphysema. Cessation of smoking produces dramatic symptomatic benefits and has been shown to confer a survival advantage.

Adults: The average single dose is 250 to 500 μg of ipratropium. Children 5 to 12 years: The recommended dose is 125 to 250 μg of ipratropium. In most cases, dilution of the dose with sterile preservative-free saline is not necessary. However, volumes of ipratropium solution less than 2 mL are not appropriate for nebulization and must be diluted with saline or another suitable nebulizer solution to make up a total fill volume of 2 to 5 mL (see Stability and Storage).

Nebulization should take place using a gas flow (oxygen or compressed air) of 6 to 10 L/minute and the solution nebulized to dryness over a 10 to 15 minute period. The Hudson Updraft, Bennett Twin Jet, DeVilbiss, Pari Compressors and Inspiron Mini-Neb nebulizers, with facemask or mouthpiece have been used. The manufacturer's instructions concerning cleaning and maintenance of the nebulizer should be strictly followed.

Treatment with ipratropium solution may be repeated every 4 to 6 hours as necessary.

Daily doses exceeding 2 mg in adults should be given under medical supervision.

For the maintenance treatment of bronchospasm associated with chronic obstructive pulmonary disease, the recommended dose is 500 μg of ipratropium solution given 3 to 4 times/day.

Stability and Storage: **Bottles:** Unopened bottles of the solution should be stored at controlled room temperature (between 15 and 30°C). Solutions diluted with preservative-free sterile Sodium Chloride Inhalation Solution, USP 0.9% should be used within 24 hours from time of dilution when stored at room temperature and within 48 hours when stored in the refrigerator.

A controlled Preservative Challenge test, done in accordance with the current USP guideline for Preservative Efficacy Testing, indicated that bottles of ipratropium inhalation solution, opened and closed several times, simulating patient use, were stable for up to 28 days when stored at room temperature 15 to 30°C.

Controlled laboratory experiments using mixtures of the solution with Alupent, Berotec or salbutamol sulfate (6 mg/mL preserved with benzalkonium chloride) solutions and diluted with a sterile bacteriostatic sodium chloride solution 0.9% (i.e., normal saline), preserved with benzalkonium chloride, indicated that such mixtures were stable for 7 days at room temperature. For the preparation of such mixtures, it is recommended that only sterile solutions of bacteriostatic sodium chloride 0.9% preserved with 0.01% benzalkonium chloride be used to maintain the level of preservative in the mixture.

The safety of preservatives other than benzalkonium chloride has not been established.

Incompatibilities: Ipratropium solution with preservatives (i.e., from the 20 mL multidose bottle) should not be mixed with sodium cromoglycate solution, as this produces a cloudy solution caused by complexation between the preservatives and sodium cromoglycate. If the patient's condition requires the administration of sodium cromoglycate, it should be given in combination with ipratropium solution without preservatives (i.e., from the unit dose vial).

Unit Dose Vials: Unopened unit dose vials of ipratropium solution should be stored at controlled room temperature (between 15 and 30°C) and protected from light. If required, the solution should be diluted with a preservative-free sterile sodium chloride solution 0.9% and used immediately. Any solution remaining in the vial must be discarded.

The solution is physically compatible with Alupent, Berotec or salbutamol sulfate (6 mg/mL) solutions. If such mixtures are prepared, they should be diluted with preservative-free sterile sodium chloride solution 0.9% and used immediately. Any unused portion of such combined solutions must be discarded.

Information for the Patient: See Blue Section—Information for the Patient "Atrovent Inhalation Solution".

Supplied: Bottles: Each mL of clear, colorless or almost colorless solution contains: ipratropium bromide 250 μg (0.025%). Nonmedicinal ingredients: benzalkonium chloride, edetate

Atrovent Inhalation Solution (cont'd)

disodium, purified water and sodium chloride. Amber glass bottles of 20 mL with screwcap.

Unit Dose Vials: 125 μg/mL: Each mL of clear, colorless solution contains: ipratropium bromide 125 μg (0.0125%). Nonmedicinal ingredients: hydrochloric acid, purified water and sodium chloride. Plastic single use vials of 2 mL.

250 μg/mL: Each mL of clear, colorless solution contains: ipratropium bromide 250 μg (0.025%). Nonmedicinal ingredients: hydrochloric acid, purified water and sodium chloride. Plastic single use vials of 1 and 2 mL.

Reviewed 1998

ATROVENT® Nasal Spray ℞

Boehringer Ingelheim

Ipratropium Bromide

Topical Anticholinergic

Pharmacology: Ipratropium, a quaternary ammonium derivative of atropine, is an anticholinergic drug. Ipratropium administered intranasally has a localized parasympathetic blocking action which reduces watery hypersecretion from mucosal glands in the nose.

Two nasal provocation trials in perennial rhinitis patients (n=44) using ipratropium nasal spray showed a dose-dependent increase in inhibition of methacholine-induced nasal secretion with an onset of action within 15 minutes. The duration of action of the nasal spray was also dose-dependent.

Ipratropium administration via nasal aerosol had no marked effect on sense of smell, nasal mucociliary transport, ciliary beat frequency or the air-conditioning capacity of the nose.

Ipratropium is not readily absorbed into the systemic circulation from the nasal mucosa as confirmed by blood level measurements and renal excretion studies with ipratropium nasal spray 0.03%, 0.06% and 0.12%. The plasma half-life in man is less than 2 hours after i.v. administration of ipratropium. Serum protein binding is less than 20%. In placebo-controlled pharmacokinetic trials in a total of 17 volunteers, 0.03%, 0.06%, and 0.12% concentrations of ipratropium nasal spray exhibited linear kinetics up to a total dose of 336 μg. One clinical trial has shown that the rate of ipratropium absorption was accelerated in a limited number of perennial rhinitis patients (n=4) using ipratropium nasal spray 0.06% chronically versus normal patients (cross trial comparison). This is presumably due to an inflamed nasal mucosa which is, therefore, more permeable. However, the extent of absorption was the same for patients and normal volunteer groups. Since there was no increase in the frequency of systemic adverse events, the clinical significance of this increased rate of absorption is not known.

Studies in rats have shown that ipratropium does not cross the blood-brain barrier.

In double-blind, placebo-controlled, crossover, single dose pharmacokinetic trials (n=17), ipratropium nasal spray 0.03%, 0.06%, and 0.12% (84 μg, 168 μg and 336 μg total nasal dose, respectively) did not significantly affect pupillary diameter, or have any systemic anticholinergic physiologic effect (i.e., changes in heart rate or systolic/diastolic blood pressure) or adverse events (e.g., dry mouth, blurred vision, constipation, difficulty urinating, etc.).

Indications: Nasal Spray 0.03%: For the symptomatic relief of rhinorrhea associated with allergic or nonallergic perennial rhinitis.

Nasal Spray 0.06%: For the symptomatic relief of rhinorrhea associated with the common cold.

Contraindications: Known hypersensitivity to ipratropium, atropinics or to any of the ingredients of the nasal spray (see Supplied).

Warnings: Care should be taken to ensure that the nasal spray does not reach the eye. There have been isolated reports of ocular complications (i.e., mydriasis, increased intraocular pressure, angle-closure glaucoma and eye pain) when aerosolized ipratropium has been released into the eyes.

Eye pain or discomfort, blurred vision, visual halos or colored images in association with red eyes from conjunctival and corneal congestion may be signs of acute angle-closure glaucoma. Should any combination of these symptoms develop, treatment with miotic drops should be initiated and specialist advice sought immediately.

Patients must be instructed in the correct administration of the nasal spray. Care must be taken not to allow the aqueous spray into the eyes. Patients who may be predisposed to glaucoma should be warned specifically to protect their eyes.

Precautions: Caution should be taken to avoid accidental release of the nasal spray into the eyes.

Patients with or predisposed to narrow-angle glaucoma, prostatic hypertrophy or bladder neck obstruction should use ipratropium nasal spray with caution.

Pregnancy: The safety of ipratropium nasal spray administration during pregnancy has not yet been established. The benefits of using ipratropium when pregnancy is confirmed or suspected must be weighed against possible hazards to the fetus. Studies in rats, mice and rabbits showed no embryotoxic effects nor teratogenic effects.

Lactation: No specific studies have been conducted on excretion of ipratropium in breast milk. Benefits of nasal spray use during lactation should therefore be weighed against possible effects on the infant.

Children: There is insufficient evidence available at present to recommend ipratropium nasal spray for use in children under 12 years of age.

Drug Interactions: If patients are receiving other anticholinergic drugs, ipratropium nasal spray should be used with caution because of possible additive effects.

Although the open-label, long-term studies to date have not shown a drug-drug interaction, ipratropium nasal spray should be used with caution in patients concomitantly using intranasal steroids because of the possible adverse local effects, (e.g., epistaxis, etc.). Any patient who experiences the above adverse effect should contact their doctor and a reduction in dose or frequency of ipratropium nasal spray or the nasal steroid should be considered.

Adverse Effects: Nasal Spray 0.03%: Adverse reaction information concerning Atrovent nasal spray 0.03% in patients with perennial rhinitis is derived from 5 multicentre, placebo-controlled clinical trials involving 854 patients (454 patients on Atrovent and 400 patients on placebo), and a 1-year open-label, follow-up trial. In 3 of the placebo-controlled trials, patients received Atrovent nasal spray, 42 μg per nostril, or placebo 3 times daily, for 8 weeks. In the other 2 placebo-controlled trials, Atrovent nasal spray, 21 or 42 μg per nostril, was administered to patients 2 or 3 times daily for 4 weeks. Of the 285 patients who entered the open-label, follow-up trial, 232 were treated for 3 months, 200 for 6 months, and 159 up to 1 year, with the majority (>86%) of patients going 1 year being maintained on 42 μg per nostril, 2 or 3 times daily, of Atrovent nasal spray.

Adverse events reported for patients who received Atrovent nasal spray 0.03%, 42 μg per nostril, or placebo 2 or 3 times daily where the prevalence in the Atrovent group is 2% or greater and exceeds the prevalence in placebo group appear in Table I.

Adverse events were usually mild to moderate and transient in the 5 placebo-controlled trials, resulting in discontinuation of treatment for 5.3% of the Atrovent nasal spray 0.03% and 5.3% of the placebo-treated patients. There was no evidence of nasal rebound (i.e., a clinically significant increase in rhinorrhea, posterior nasal drip, sneezing or nasal congestion severity compared to baseline) upon discontinuation of double-blind therapy in these trials. There were no drug-related serious or anticholinergic adverse events (with the exception of dry mouth reported for 1% of the Atrovent and 0.5% of the placebo-treated patients) during the placebo-controlled trials or the 1-year open-label, follow-up trial in patients on Atrovent nasal spray 0.03%.

Nasal adverse events were reported for 84 (29.5%) of the 285 patients in the 1-year open-label, follow-up trial; 16.5% of these events were considered drug-related by the physicians conducting the trial. The incidence (and assessment of drug relationship) for the most frequently reported nasal adverse events were nasal congestion 11.6% (1.4% drug-related), nasal dryness 10.2% (9.5% drug-related), and epistaxis 4.9% (4.2% drug-related). Nasal dryness and/or epistaxis occurred in 45 patients. It resolved with continued treatment or dose reduction in 40 of these patients (89%), and required discontinuation of treatment in 5 patients (11%).

Adverse events, reported as possibly related to drug treatment, which were found in less than 2% of perennial rhinitis patients receiving Atrovent nasal spray 0.03% in the 5 multicentre, placebo-controlled clinical trials and 1 year open-label follow-up trial were: paresthesia, fatigue, dizziness, insomnia, dysphonia, migraine, vertigo, rash, furunculosis, urticaria, generalized edema, diarrhea, abdominal pain, taste perversion, conjunctivitis and xerophthalmia.

There have been isolated reports of ocular events such as mydriasis, increased intraocular pressure, glaucoma and eye pain associated with the release of aerosolized ipratropium into the eyes. These ocular events have not been reported with the use of Atrovent nasal spray.

Nasal Spray 0.06%: Adverse reaction information concerning Atrovent nasal spray 0.06% in patients with the common cold is derived from 2 multicentre, placebo-controlled clinical trials involving 1 276 patients (195 patients on Atrovent nasal spray 0.03%, 352 patients on Atrovent nasal spray 0.06%, 189 patients on Atrovent nasal spray 0.12%, 351 patients on placebo and 189 patients receiving no treatment). The adverse events reported for patients receiving Atrovent nasal spray 0.06% administered 3 or 4 times daily, where the incidence in the Atrovent group is 1% or greater and exceeds the prevalence in the placebo group appear in Table II.

Table II—Atrovent Nasal Spray

Adverse Events Associated with 0.06% Spray

	% of Patients Reporting Events*	
	Atrovent Nasal Spray 0.06% (n=352)	Placebo (n=351)
Epistaxis or nosebleed	5.4%	1.4%
Nasal dryness	4.8%	2.8%
Blood-tinged nasal mucus	2.8%	0.9%
Dry mouth/throat	1.4%	0.3%
Nasal congestion	1.1%	0.0%

* This table includes only those adverse events for which the frequency in the Atrovent group was 1% or greater and exceeds the frequency in the placebo group.

Adverse events, reported as possibly related to drug treatment, which were found in less than 1% of patients with the common cold receiving Atrovent nasal spray 0.06% in 2 multicentre, placebo-controlled clinical trials were: paresthesia, dizziness, dysphonia, tachycardia, taste perversion, conjunctivitis and abnormal vision.

Table I—Atrovent Nasal Spray

Adverse Events Associated with 0.03% Spray

	% of Patients Reporting Events[a]			
	Atrovent Nasal Spray 0.03% (n=356)		Placebo Spray (n=347)	
	Incidence %	Discontinued %	Incidence %	Discontinued %
Headache	9.8	0.6	9.2	0
Upper respiratory tract infection	9.8	1.4	7.2	1.4
Epistaxis	9.0	0.3	4.6	0.3
Rhinitis[b]				
Nasal dryness	5.1	0	0.9	0.3
Nasal irritation[c]	2.0	0	1.7	0.6
Other nasal symptoms[d]	3.1	1.1	1.7	0.3
Pharyngitis	8.1	0.3	4.6	0
Nausea	2.2	0.3	0.9	0

[a] This table includes only adverse events for which the prevalence in the Atrovent group was 2% or greater and exceeds the prevalence in the placebo group.

[b] All events are listed by their WHO term; rhinitis has been presented by descriptive terms for clarification.

[c] Nasal irritation includes reports of nasal itching, nasal burning, nasal irritation and rhinitis ulcerative.

[d] Other nasal symptoms include reports of nasal congestion, increased rhinorrhea, increased rhinitis, posterior nasal drip, sneezing, nasal polyps and nasal edema.

Atrovent nasal spray 0.06% was well tolerated by the patients, with the most frequently reported adverse events being minor local nasal adverse events. The majority of the adverse events were mild to moderate in nature, none were considered serious, none resulted in hospitalization and no patient receiving Atrovent nasal spray 0.06% was discontinued from the trial due to a drug-related adverse event. There was no evidence of rebound of nasal symptoms.

There have been isolated reports of ocular events such as mydriasis, increased intraocular pressure, glaucoma and eye pain associated with the release of aerosolized ipratropium into the eyes. These ocular events have not been reported with the use of Atrovent nasal spray.

Overdose: Symptoms and Treatment: Acute overdosage by intranasal administration is unlikely since ipratropium is not well absorbed systemically after intranasal or oral administration.

Should signs of serious anticholinergic toxicity appear, cholinesterase inhibitors may be considered.

Dosage: The dose of nasal spray 0.03% for symptomatic relief of rhinorrhea associated with allergic or nonallergic perennial rhinitis is 2 sprays (42 µg) per nostril 2 or 3 times a day (total dose 168 to 252 µg/day). Optimum dosage varies with the response of the individual patient.

The dose of nasal spray 0.06% is 2 sprays (84 µg) per nostril 3 or 4 times daily (total doses 504 to 672 µg/day) as required for symptomatic relief of rhinorrhea associated with the common cold.

Treatment in the common cold has only been studied up to 4 days. Efficacy and safety of treatment beyond 4 days has not been established, although there has been no evidence of adverse safety effects with longer treatment in perennial rhinitis patients.

Children: Not recommended for use in children under 12 years of age.

Information for the Patient: See Blue Section—Information for the Patient "Atrovent Nasal Spray".

Supplied: 0.03%: Each spray is designed to deliver 0.07 mL which contains: ipratropium bromide 21 µg. Nonmedicinal ingredients: benzalkonium chloride, edetate disodium, hydrochloric acid, sodium chloride, sodium hydroxide and purified water. Bottles of 30 mL, fitted with a metered nasal spray pump, a safety clip to prevent accidental discharge of the spray and a clear plastic dust cap. The 30 mL bottle is designed to deliver 345 sprays of 0.07 mL each or 28 days of therapy at the maximum recommended dose (2 sprays per nostril 3 times a day).

0.06%: Each spray is designed to deliver 0.07 mL which contains: ipratropium bromide 42 µg. Nonmedicinal ingredients: benzalkonium chloride, edetate disodium, hydrochloric acid, sodium chloride, sodium hydroxide and purified water. Bottles of 15 mL, fitted with a metered nasal spray pump, a safety clip to prevent accidental discharge of the spray and a clear plastic dust cap. The 15 mL bottle is designed to deliver 165 sprays of 0.07 mL each or 10 days of therapy at the maximum recommended dose (2 sprays per nostril 4 times a day).

Store tightly closed between 15 and 30°C. The contents are stable up to the expiration date stamped on the label. Avoid excessive heat or freezing. Keep out of reach of children.

(Shown in Product Recognition Section)

Reviewed 1997

AURALGAN®
Whitehall-Robins

Antipyrine—Benzocaine

Analgesic—Antiphlogistic

Indications: As an analgesic and decongestant for pain and inflammation in the ear, swimmer's ear; adjunctive treatment of otitis media.

Contraindications: Hypersensitivity to any of the components.

Precautions: Do not rinse dropper with water. Keep dry. Keep well closed.

Dosage: Warm Auralgan slightly and fill ear canal. Saturate cotton plug with Auralgan and insert in ear. Repeat several times daily as required.

Supplied: Each mL of otic solution contains: benzocaine 14 mg, antipyrine 54 mg. Nonmedicinal ingredients: glycerin and oxyquinoline sulfate. Does not contain alcohols, gluten, parabens, sugars, sulfites or tartrazine. Plastic dropper bottles of 14 mL.

AUREOMYCIN® Ⓟ
Wyeth-Ayerst

Chlortetracycline HCl

Topical Antibiotic

Supplied: Each g of topical ointment contains: chlortetracycline HCl 30 mg (3%). Nonmedicinal ingredients: lanolin anhydrous and petrolatum white. Tartrazine-free. Tubes of 30 g.

AVAPRO™ Ⓟ
Bristol-Myers Squibb/Sanofi Canada

Irbesartan

Angiotensin II AT$_1$ Receptor Blocker

Pharmacology: Irbesartan antagonizes angiotensin II by blocking AT$_1$ receptors.

Angiotensin II is the primary vasoactive hormone in the renin-angiotensin system. Its effects include vasoconstriction and the stimulation of aldosterone secretion by the adrenal cortex.

Irbesartan blocks the vasoconstrictor and aldosterone-secreting effects of angiotensin II by selectively blocking in a noncompetitive manner the binding of angiotensin II to the AT$_1$ receptor found in many tissues. Irbesartan has no agonist activity at the AT$_1$ receptor. AT$_2$ receptors have been found in many tissues, but to date they have not been associated with cardiovascular homeostasis. Irbesartan has essentially no affinity for the AT$_2$ receptors.

Irbesartan does not inhibit angiotensin converting enzyme, also known as kininase II, the enzyme that converts angiotensin I to angiotensin II and degrades bradykinin, nor does it affect renin or other hormone receptors or ion channels involved in cardiovascular regulation of blood pressure and sodium homeostasis.

Pharmacokinetics: Irbesartan is an orally active agent . The oral absorption of irbesartan is rapid and complete with an average absolute bioavailability of 60 to 80%. Irbesartan exhibits linear pharmacokinetics over the therapeutic dose range with an average terminal elimination half-life of 11 to 15 hours. Following oral administration, peak plasma concentrations are attained at 1.5 to 2 hours after dosing. Steady-state concentrations are achieved within 3 days.

Irbesartan is 90% protein-bound in the plasma, primarily to albumin and α_1-acid glycoprotein.

The average volume of distribution of irbesartan is 53 to 93 L. Total plasma and renal clearances are in the range of 157 to 176 and 3 to 3.5 mL/minute, respectively.

Irbesartan is metabolized via glucuronide conjugation, and oxidation by the cytochrome P-450 system. Following either oral or i.v. administration of ^{14}C-labeled irbesartan, more than 80% of the circulating plasma radioactivity is attributable to unchanged irbesartan. The primary circulating metabolite is the inactive irbesartan glucuronide (approximately 6%). The remaining oxidative metabolites do not add appreciably to the pharmacologic activity.

Irbesartan and its metabolites are excreted by both biliary and renal routes. Following either oral or i.v. administration of ^{14}C-labeled irbesartan, about 20% of radioactivity is recovered in the urine and the remainder in the feces. Less than 2% of the dose is excreted in urine as unchanged irbesartan.

In vitro studies of irbesartan indicate that the oxidation of irbesartan is primarily by cytochrome P-450 isoenzyme CYP 2C9. Metabolism of irbesartan by CYP 3A4 is negligible. Irbesartan is neither metabolized, nor does it substantially induce or inhibit the following isoenzymes: CYP 1A1, 1A2, 2A6, 2B6, 2D6, 2E1. There was no induction or inhibition of CYP 3A4.

In subjects over the age of 65 years, irbesartan elimination half-life was not significantly altered, but AUC and C_{MAX} values were about 20 to 50% greater than those of young subjects.

The mean AUC and C_{max} were not altered in patients with any degree of renal impairment, including patients on hemodialysis. However, a wide variance was seen in patients with severe renal impairment.

The pharmacokinetics of irbesartan following repeated oral administration were not significantly affected in patients with mild to moderate cirrhosis of the liver. No data are available in patients with severe liver disease.

Pharmacodynamics: In healthy subjects, single oral doses of irbesartan up to 300 mg produced dose-dependent inhibition of the pressor effect of angiotensin II infusions. The pressor effect of angiotensin II was completely blocked (≥90%) at the time of peak irbesartan concentrations; 60% and 40% inhibition persisted for 24 hours following doses of 300 mg and 150 mg, respectively.

In hypertensive patients, angiotensin II receptor inhibition following chronic administration of irbesartan causes a 1.5 to 2 fold rise in angiotensin II plasma concentration and a 2 to 3 fold increase in plasma renin levels. Aldosterone plasma concentrations generally decline following irbesartan administration; however, serum potassium levels are not significantly affected at recommended doses.

During clinical trials, minimal incremental blood pressure response was observed at doses greater than 300 mg.

The blood pressure lowering effect of irbesartan is apparent after the first dose and substantially present within 1 to 2 weeks, with the maximal effect occurring by 4 to 6 weeks. In long-term studies, the effect of irbesartan appeared to be maintained for more than 1 year. There was essentially no change in average heart rate in patients treated with irbesartan in controlled trials.

There is no rebound effect after withdrawal of irbesartan.

Black hypertensive patients had a smaller blood pressure response to irbesartan monotherapy than caucasians.

Indications: For the treatment of essential hypertension.

Irbesartan may be used alone or concomitantly with thiazide diuretics.

Irbesartan should normally be used in those patients in whom treatment with diuretic or beta-blocker was found ineffective or has been associated with unacceptable adverse effects. Irbesartan can also be tried as an initial agent in those patients in whom the use of diuretics and/or beta-blockers is contraindicated or in patients with medical conditions in which these drugs frequently cause serious adverse effects.

The safety and efficacy of concurrent use with angiotensin converting enzyme inhibitors have not been established.

Contraindications: In patients who are hypersensitive to any component of this product.

Warnings: *Pregnancy:* Drugs that act directly on the renin-angiotensin system can cause fetal and neonatal morbidity and death when administered to pregnant women. When pregnancy is detected, irbesartan should be discontinued as soon as possible.

The use of drugs that act directly on the renin-angiotensin system during the second and third trimesters of pregnancy has been associated with fetal and neonatal injury, including hypotension, neonatal skull hypoplasia, anuria, reversible or irreversible renal failure, and death. Oligohydramnios has also been reported, presumably resulting from decreased fetal renal function; oligohydramnios in this setting has been associated with fetal limb contractures, craniofacial deformation, and hypoplastic lung development. Prematurity, intrauterine growth retardation, and patent ductus arteriosus have also been reported, although it is not clear whether these occurrences were due to exposure to the drug. These adverse effects do not appear to have resulted from intrauterine drug exposure that has been limited to the first trimester.

Mothers whose embryos and fetuses are exposed to an angiotensin II receptor antagonist only during the first trimester should be so informed. Nonetheless, when patients become pregnant, physicians should have the patient discontinue the use of irbesartan as soon as possible.

Rarely (probably less often than once in every thousand pregnancies), no alternative to an angiotensin II receptor antagonist will be found. In these rare cases, the mothers should be apprised of the potential hazards to their fetuses, and serial ultrasound examinations should be performed to assess the intra-amniotic environment.

If oligohydramnios is observed, irbesartan should be discontinued unless it is considered life-saving for the mother. Contraction stress testing (CST), a nonstress test (NST), or biophysical profiling (BPP) may be appropriate, depending upon the week of pregnancy. Patients and physicians should be aware, however, that oligohydramnios may not appear until after the fetus has sustained irreversible injury.

Infants with histories of in utero exposure to an angiotensin II receptor antagonist should be closely observed for hypotension, oliguria, and hyperkalemia. If oliguria occurs, attention should be directed toward support of blood pressure and renal perfusion. Exchange transfusion may be required as means of reversing hypotension and/or substituting for disordered renal function. Irbesartan is not removed by hemodialysis.

Hypotension: Occasionally, symptomatic hypotension has occurred after administration of irbesartan, in some cases after the first dose. It is more likely to occur in patients who are volume depleted by diuretic therapy, dietary salt restriction, dialysis, diarrhea or vomiting. In these patients, because of the potential fall in blood pressure, therapy should be started under close medical supervision (see Dosage). Similar

Avapro (cont'd)

considerations apply to patients with ischemic heart or cerebrovascular disease, in whom an excessive fall in blood pressure could result in myocardial infarction or cerebrovascular accident.

Precautions: Renal Impairment: As a consequence of inhibiting the renin-angiotensin-aldosterone system, changes in renal function have been seen in susceptible individuals. In patients whose renal function may depend on the activity of the renin-angiotensin-aldosterone system, such as patients with bilateral renal artery stenosis, unilateral renal artery stenosis to a solitary kidney, or severe congestive heart failure, treatment with agents that inhibit this system has been associated with oliguria, progressive azotemia, and rarely, acute renal failure and/or death. In susceptible patients, concomitant diuretic use may further increase risk.

Use of irbesartan should include appropriate assessment of renal function.

Valvular Stenosis: There is concern on theoretical grounds that patients with aortic stenosis might be at particular risk of decreased coronary perfusion when treated with vasodilators because they do not develop as much afterload reduction.

Lactation: It is not known whether irbesartan is excreted in human milk, but measurable levels of radioactivity was shown to be present in milk of lactating rats. Because many drugs are excreted in human milk, and because of their potential for affecting the nursing infant adversely, a decision should be made whether to discontinue nursing or discontinue the drug, taking into account the importance of the drug to the mother.

Children: Safety and effectiveness have not been established.

Geriatrics: Of the 4 140 hypertensive patients receiving irbesartan in clinical studies, 793 patients were 65 years of age and over. No overall age-related differences were seen in the adverse effect profile but greater sensitivity in some older individuals cannot be ruled out.

Drug Interactions: Diuretics: Patients on diuretics, and especially those in whom diuretic therapy was recently instituted, may occasionally experience an excessive reduction of blood pressure after initiation of therapy with irbesartan. The possibility of symptomatic hypotension with the use of irbesartan can be minimized by discontinuing the diuretic prior to initiation of treatment and/or lowering the initial dose of irbesartan (see Warnings, Hypotension and Dosage). No drug interaction of clinical significance has been identified with thiazide diuretics.

Agents Increasing Serum Potassium: Since irbesartan decreases the production of aldosterone, potassium-sparing diuretics or potassium supplements should be given only for documented hypokalemia and with frequent monitoring of serum potassium. Potassium-containing salt substitutes should also be used with caution.

Lithium Salts: As with other drugs which eliminate sodium, lithium clearance may be reduced. Therefore, serum lithium levels should be monitored carefully if lithium salts are to be administered.

Warfarin: When irbesartan was administered as 300 mg once daily under steady-state conditions, no pharmacodynamic effect on PT was demonstrated in subjects stabilized on warfarin.

Digoxin: When irbesartan was administered as 150 mg once daily under steady-state conditions, no effect was seen on the pharmacokinetics of digoxin at steady-state.

Adverse Effects: Irbesartan has been evaluated for safety in more than 4 100 patients with essential hypertension including approximately 1 300 patients for over 6 months and 400 patients for 1 year or more.

In placebo-controlled clinical trials, therapy was discontinued due to a clinical adverse event in 3.3% of patients treated with irbesartan, versus 4.5% of patients given placebo.

The following potentially serious adverse reactions have been reported rarely with irbesartan in controlled clinical trials: syncope, hypotension.

Adverse events occurring in 1% or more of the 2 606 hypertensive patients in placebo-controlled clinical trials include those shown in Table I.

The incidence of hypotension or orthostatic hypotension occurred in 0.4% of irbesartan treated patients, unrelated to dosage, and in 0.2% of patients receiving placebo.

In addition, the following potentially important events occurred in less than 1% of patients receiving irbesartan, regardless of drug relationship: Body as a Whole: fever.

Cardiovascular: flushing, hypertension, myocardial infarction, angina pectoris, arrhythmic/conduction disorder, cardiorespiratory arrest, heart failure, hypertensive crisis.

Table I—Avapro

Adverse Events

Body System/Reaction	Avapro n=1 965 Incidence (%)	Placebo n=641 Incidence (%)
General		
Abdominal Pain	1.4	2.0
Chest pain	1.8	1.7
Edema	1.5	2.3
Fatigue	4.3	3.7
Cardiovascular		
Tachycardia	1.2	0.9
Dermatologic		
Rash	1.3	2.0
Gastrointestinal		
Diarrhea	3.1	2.2
Dyspepsia/Heartburn	1.7	1.1
Nausea/Vomiting	2.1	2.8
Musculoskeletal/Connective Tissue		
Musculoskeletal pain	6.6	6.6
Nervous System		
Anxiety/Nervousness	1.1	0.9
Headache	12.3	16.7
Dizziness	4.9	5.0
Respiratory		
Cough	2.8	2.7
Urogenital System		
Urinary Tract Infection	1.1	1.4

Dermatologic: pruritus, dermatitis, ecchymosis, erythema, urticaria, photosensitivity.

Endocrine: sexual dysfunction, libido change, gout.

Gastrointestinal: constipation, gastroenteritis, flatulence, distention abdomen, hepatitis.

Musculoskeletal: muscle cramp, arthritis, myalgia, muscle weakness.

Nervous System: sleep disturbance, numbness, somnolence, vertigo, depression, paresthesia, tremor, transient ischemic attack, cerebrovascular accident.

Renal/Genitourinary: abnormal urination.

Respiratory: epistaxis, tracheobronchitis, pulmonary congestion, dyspnea, wheezing.

Special Senses: visual disturbance, hearing abnormality, conjunctivitis, taste disturbance.

Angioedema (involving swelling of the face, lips, and/or tongue) has been reported rarely in postmarketing use.

Laboratory Test Findings: In controlled clinical trials, clinically important differences in laboratory tests were rarely associated with irbesartan.

Liver Function Tests: In placebo-controlled trials, elevations of AST and ALT ≥3 times upper limit of normal occurred in 0.1% and 0.2%, respectively, of irbesartan treated patients compared to 0.3% and 0.3%, respectively, of patients receiving placebo. The cumulative incidence of AST and/or ALT elevations ≥3 times upper limit of normal was 0.4% in patients treated with irbesartan for a mean duration of over 1 year.

Hyperkalemia: In placebo-controlled trials, greater than a 10% increase in serum potassium was observed in 0.4% of irbesartan treated patients compared to 0.5% of patients receiving placebo.

Creatinine, Blood Urea Nitrogen: Minor increases in blood urea nitrogen (BUN) or serum creatinine were observed in less than 0.7% of patients with essential hypertension treated with irbesartan alone versus 0.9% on placebo.

Hemoglobin: Mean decreases in hemoglobin of 0.16g/dL were observed in patients receiving irbesartan. No patients were discontinued due to anemia.

Neutropenia: Neutropenia (<1 000 cells/mm³) was observed in 0.3% of irbesartan treated patients compared to 0.5% of patients receiving placebo.

In clinical trials, the following were noted to occur with an incidence of <1%, regardless of drug relationship: anemia, thrombocytopenia, lymphocytopenia and increased CPK.

Overdose: Symptoms and Treatment: No data are available in regard to overdosage in humans. The most likely manifestations of overdosage would be hypotension and/or tachycardia; bradycardia might also occur in this setting.

Irbesartan is not removed by hemodialysis.

Dosage: Initiation of therapy requires consideration of recent antihypertensive drug treatment, the extent of blood pressure elevation, salt restriction and other pertinent clinical factors. The dosage of other antihypertensive agents used with irbesartan may need to be adjusted.

Irbesartan may be administered with or without food.

The recommended dose is 150 mg once daily. In patients whose blood pressure is not adequately controlled, the daily dose may be increased to 300 mg.

No initial dosage adjustment is required in the elderly or in patients with renal impairment (see Pharmacology, Pharmacokinetics and Precautions, Geriatrics). However, due to the apparent greater sensitivity of hemodialysis patients, an initial dose of 75 mg is recommended in this group of patients.

No initial dosage adjustment is required in patients with mild-to-moderate hepatic impairment (see Pharmacology, Pharmacokinetics).

Concomitant Diuretic Therapy: In patients receiving diuretics, irbesartan therapy should be initiated with caution, since these patients may be volume-depleted and thus more likely to experience hypotension following initiation of additional antihypertensive therapy. Whenever possible, all diuretics should be discontinued 2 to 3 days prior to the administration of irbesartan to reduce the likelihood of hypotension (see Warnings, Hypotension and Precautions, Drug Interactions). If this is not possible because of the patient's condition, irbesartan should be administered with caution and the blood pressure monitered closely. The recommended starting dose of irbesartan is 75 mg once daily in hypovolemic patients (see Warning, Hypotension). Thereafter, the dosage should be adjusted according to the individual response of the patient.

Supplied: 75 mg: Each white to off-white biconvex, oval tablet, with a heart shape debossed on one side and the digits 2771 on the other, contains: irbesartan 75 mg. Nonmedicinal ingredients: croscarmellose sodium, lactose, magnesium stearate, microcrystalline cellulose, poloxamer 188, pregelatinized starch and silicon dioxide. Bottles of 90.

150 mg: Each white to off-white biconvex, oval tablet, with a heart shape debossed on one side and the digits 2772 on the other, contains: irbesartan 150 mg. Nonmedicinal ingredients: croscarmellose sodium, lactose, magnesium stearate, microcrystalline cellulose, poloxamer 188, pregelatinized starch and silicon dioxide. Bottles of 90.

300 mg: Each white to off-white biconvex, oval tablet, with a heart shape debossed on one side and the digits 2773 on the other, contains: irbesartan 300 mg. Nonmedicinal ingredients: croscarmellose sodium, lactose, magnesium stearate, microcrystalline cellulose, poloxamer 188, pregelatinized starch and silicon dioxide. Bottles of 90.

Store at room temperature (15 to 30°C).

(Shown in Product Recognition Section)

New Product 1998

AVC® Ⓟ

Hoechst Marion Roussel

Sulfanilamide

Vaginitis Therapy

Pharmacology: Sulfanilamide has been an ingredient of vaginal formulations for about four decades. It blocks certain metabolic processes essential for the growth of susceptible bacteria.

AVC Cream is buffered to the pH of the normal healthy vagina (approximately 4.3) to encourage the presence of normally occurring Döderlein's bacilli of the vagina.

Indications: For the treatment of vulvovaginitis caused by C. albicans. Diagnosis of Candida should be confirmed by vaginal smears and/or cultures prior to initiating therapy.

Contraindications: AVC should not be used in patients known to be sensitive to the sulfonamides, or to AVC Cream.

Precautions: General: Because sulfonamides are absorbed from the vaginal mucosa, the usual precautions for oral sulfonamides apply. Patients should be observed for manifestations such as skin rash or other evidence of systemic toxicity, and if these develop, the medication should be discontinued.

If clinical symptoms persist microbiological tests should be repeated to rule out other pathogens and to confirm the diagnosis.

Deaths associated with administration of oral sulfonamides have reportedly occurred from hypersensitivity reactions, agranulocytosis, aplastic anemia, and other blood dyscrasias. Goiter production, diuresis, and hypoglycaemia have reportedly occurred rarely in patients receiving oral sulfonamides. Cross-sensitivity may exist with these agents. Rats appear to be especially susceptible to the goitrogenic effects of sulfonamides, and long-term administration has reportedly produced thyroid malignancies in this species.

Pregnancy: Vaginal applicators should be used with caution after the seventh month of pregnancy.

It is not known whether sulfanilamide can cause fetal harm when administered to a pregnant woman or can affect reproductive capability. Sulfanilamide should be administered to a pregnant woman only if clearly needed.

Sulfonamides, including sulfanilamide, readily pass through the placenta and reach fetal circulation. The concentration in the fetus is from 50 to 90% of that in the maternal blood and if high enough, can cause toxic effects. The safe use of sulfonamides, including sulfanilamide, in pregnancy has not been established. The teratogenic potential of most sulfonamides has not been thoroughly investigated in either animals or humans. However, a significant increase in the incidence of cleft palate and other bony abnormalities of offspring has been observed when certain sulfonamides of the short, intermediate, and long-acting types (including sulfanilamide) were given to pregnant rats and mice at high oral doses (7 to 25 times the human therapeutic oral dose).

Lactation: Sulfanilamide should be avoided in nursing mothers because absorbed sulfonamides will appear in maternal milk and have caused kernicterus in the newborn. Because of the potential for serious adverse reactions in nursing infants from sulfonamides, a decision should be made whether to discontinue nursing or to discontinue the drug.

Children: Safety and effectiveness of sulfanilamide in children have not been established.

Adverse Effects: Although absorption of sulfanilamide occurs through the vaginal mucosa, systemic manifestations attributable to this drug are infrequent. Local sensitivity reactions such as increased discomfort or a burning sensation have occasionally been reported following the use of topical sulfonamides. Treatment should be discontinued if either local or systemic manifestations of sulfonamide toxicity or sensitivity occur.

Overdose: Symptoms and Treatment: There have been no reports of accidental overdosage with sulfanilamide. The acute oral LD_{50} of sulfonamide is 3 700 to 4 200 mg/kg in mice. The minimum human lethal dose of sulfanilamide has not been established. It is not known if sulfanilamide is dialyzable.

Dosage: 1 applicatorful (about 6 g) intravaginally once or twice daily. Improvement will often be apparent within a few days. Exacerbation may occur during menses; therefore, it is advisable to continue the applications for 1 month, or through 1 complete menstrual cycle.

Douching with a suitable solution before insertion may be recommended for hygienic purposes. A pad may be used to protect underclothing if necessary.

Supplied: Each tube contains: sulfanilamide 15%. Nonmedicinal ingredients: lactose, in a water-miscible, non-staining base made from propylene glycol, stearic acid, diglycol stearate, methylparaben, propylparaben, lactic acid and triethanolamine. Buffered with lactic acid to an acid pH of approximately 4.3. Tubes of 100 g with applicator. Store at room temperature (15 to 30°C).

AVENTYL® Ⓟ

Lilly

Nortriptyline HCl

Antidepressant

Pharmacology: The mechanism of mood elevation of tricyclic antidepressants is at present unknown. Nortriptyline is not an MAO inhibitor. It inhibits the activity of such diverse agents as histamine, 5-hydroxytryptamine, and acetylcholine. It increases the pressor effect of norepinephrine but blocks the pressor response of phenethylamine. Studies suggest that nortriptyline interferes with the transport, release, and storage of catecholamines.

Indications: The relief of symptoms of depression. Endogenous depressions are more likely to be alleviated than are other depressive states.

Contraindications: The concurrent use of nortriptyline or other tricyclic antidepressants with an MAO inhibitor is contraindicated. Hyperpyretic crises, severe convulsions, and fatalities have occurred when similar tricyclic antidepressants were used in such combinations. Discontinue the MAO inhibitor at least 2 weeks before nortriptyline treatment is started. Patients hypersensitive to nortriptyline should not be given the drug.

Cross-sensitivity between nortriptyline and other dibenzazepines is a possibility.

Nortriptyline is contraindicated during the acute recovery period after myocardial infarction.

Warnings: Patients with cardiovascular disease should be given nortriptyline only under close supervision because of the tendency of the drug to produce sinus tachycardia and to prolong the conduction time. Myocardial infarction, arrhythmia, and strokes have occurred. The antihypertensive action of guanethidine and similar agents may be blocked. Because of its anticholinergic activity, use nortriptyline with great caution in patients with glaucoma or a history of urinary retention. Patients with a history of seizures should be followed closely when nortriptyline is administered because this drug is known to lower the convulsive threshold. Great care is required if nortriptyline is administered to hyperthyroid patients or those receiving thyroid medication, because cardiac arrhythmias may develop.

Occupational Hazards: Nortriptyline may impair the mental and/or physical abilities required for the performance of hazardous tasks, such as operating machinery or driving a car; therefore, warn the patient accordingly.

Pregnancy and *Lactation:* Safe use of nortriptyline during pregnancy and lactation has not been established; therefore, when the drug is administered to pregnant patients, nursing mothers, or women of childbearing age, the potential benefits must be weighed against the possible hazards. Animal reproduction studies have yielded inconclusive results.

Precautions: The use of nortriptyline in schizophrenic patients may result in an exacerbation of the psychosis or may activate latent schizophrenic symptoms. If the drug is given to overactive or agitated patients, increased anxiety and agitation may occur. In manic depressive patients, nortriptyline may cause symptoms of the manic phase to emerge.

Troublesome patient hostility may be aroused by the use of nortriptyline. Epileptiform seizures may accompany its administration, as may happen with other drugs of its class.

Close supervision and careful adjustment of the dosage are required when nortriptyline is used with other anticholinergic drugs and sympathomimetic drugs.

Inform the patient that the response to alcohol may be exaggerated. Excessive consumption of alcohol in combination with nortriptyline therapy may have a potentiating effect, which may lead to the danger of increased suicidal attempts or overdosage, especially in patients with histories of emotional disturbances or suicidal ideation.

When it is essential, the drug may be administered concurrently with electroconvulsive therapy, although the hazards may be increased. Discontinue the drug for several days, if possible, prior to elective surgery.

The possibility of a suicidal attempt by depressed patients remains after the initiation of treatment; in this regard, it is important that the least possible quantity of drug be dispensed at any given time.

Both elevation and lowering of blood sugar levels have been reported. A case of significant hypoglycemia has been reported in a Type II diabetic patient maintained on chlorpropamide (250 mg/day) after the addition of nortriptyline (125 mg/day).

<u>*Drug Interactions:*</u> Steady-state serum concentrations of the tricyclic antidepressants are reported to fluctuate significantly as cimetidine is either added or deleted from the drug regimen. Serious anticholinergic symptoms (severe dry mouth, urinary retention, blurred vision) have been associated with elevations in the serum levels of the tricyclic antidepressant when cimetidine is added to the drug regimen. In addition, higher than expected steady-state serum concentrations of the tricyclic antidepressant have been observed when therapy is initiated in patients already taking cimetidine.

In well-controlled patients undergoing concurrent therapy with cimetidine, a decrease in the steady-state serum concentrations of the tricyclic antidepressants may occur when cimetidine therapy is discontinued. The therapeutic efficacy of the tricyclic antidepressant may be compromised in these patients as the cimetidine is discontinued. Several of the tricyclic antidepressants have been cited in these reports.

There have been greater than 2-fold increases in previously stable plasma levels of other antidepressants including nortriptyline, when fluoxetine has been administered in combination with these agents. Fluoxetine and its active metabolite, norfluoxetine, have a long half-life (4 to 16 days for norfluoxetine) which might affect strategies during conversion from one drug to another.

Administration of reserpine during therapy with a tricyclic antidepressant has been shown to produce a stimulating effect in some depressed patients.

Close supervision and careful adjustment of the dosage are required when nortriptyline is used with other anticholinergic drugs or sympathomimetic drugs.

The patient should be informed that the response to alcohol may be exaggerated.

Drugs Metabolized by P450IID6: A subset (3 to 10%) of the population has reduced activity of certain drug metabolizing enzymes such as the cytochrome P450 isoenzyme P450IID6. Such individuals are referred to as "poor metabolizers" of drugs such as debrisoquin, dextromethorphan, and the tricyclic antidepressants. These individuals may have higher than expected plasma concentrations of tricyclic antidepressants when given usual doses. In addition, certain drugs that are metabolized by this isoenzyme, including many antidepressants (tricyclic antidepressants, selective serotonin reuptake inhibitors, and others), may inhibit the activity of this isoenzyme, and thus may make normal metabolizers resemble poor metabolizers with regard to concomitant therapy with other drugs metabolized by this enzyme system, leading to drug interactions.

Concomitant use of tricyclic antidepressants with other drugs metabolized by cytochrome P450IID6 may require lower doses than usually prescribed for either the tricyclic antidepressant or the other drug. Therefore, coadministration of tricyclic antidepressants with other drugs that are metabolized by this isoenzyme, including other antidepressants, phenothiazines, carbamazepine, and Type 1C antiarrhythmics (e.g., propafenone, flecainide, and encainide), or that inhibit this enzyme (e.g., quinidine), should be approached with caution.

Adverse Effects: Note: Included in the following list are a few adverse reactions that have not been reported with this specific drug. However, the pharmacologic similarities among the tricyclic antidepressant drugs require that each of these reactions be considered when nortriptyline is administered.

Cardiovascular: hypotension, hypertension, tachycardia, palpitation, myocardial infarction, arrhythmias, heart block, stroke.

Psychiatric: confusional states (especially in the elderly) with hallucinations, disorientation, delusions; anxiety, restlessness, agitation; insomnia, panic, nightmares; hypomania; exacerbation of psychosis.

Neurologic: numbness, tingling, paresthesias of extremities; incoordination, ataxia, tremors; peripheral neuropathy, extrapyramidal symptoms; seizures, alteration of EEG patterns; tinnitus.

Anticholinergic: dry mouth and, rarely, associated sublingual adenitis or gingivitis; blurred vision, disturbance of accommodation, mydriasis; constipation, paralytic ileus; urinary retention, delayed micturition, dilation of the urinary tract.

Allergic: skin rash, petechiae, urticaria, itching, photosensitization (avoid excessive exposure to sunlight); edema (general or of face and tongue), drug fever, cross-sensitivity with other tricyclic drugs.

Hematologic: bone-marrow depression, including agranulocytosis, aplastic anemia; eosinophilia; purpura; thrombocytopenia.

Gastrointestinal: nausea and vomiting, anorexia, epigastric distress, diarrhea; peculiar taste, stomatitis, abdominal cramps, black tongue, constipation, paralytic ileus.

Endocrine: gynecomastia in the male; breast enlargement and galactorrhea in the female; increased or decreased libido, impotence; testicular swelling; elevation or depression of blood sugar levels; syndrome of inappropriate ADH (antidiuretic hormone) secretion.

Other: jaundice (simulating obstructive); altered liver function, hepatitis, and liver necrosis; weight gain or loss; perspiration; flushing; urinary frequency, nocturia; drowsiness, dizziness, weakness, fatigue; headache; parotid swelling; alopecia.

Withdrawal Symptoms: Though these are not indicative of addiction, abrupt cessation of treatment after prolonged therapy may produce nausea, headache, and malaise.

Overdose: Deaths may occur from overdosage with this class of drugs. Multiple drug ingestion (including alcohol) is common in deliberate tricyclic antidepressant overdose. As the management is complex and changing, it is recommended that the physician contact a Poison Control Centre for current information on treatment. Signs and symptoms of toxicity develop rapidly after tricyclic antidepressant overdose; therefore, hospital monitoring is required as soon as possible.

Symptoms: Critical manifestations of overdose include: cardiac dysrhythmias, severe hypotension, convulsions, and CNS depression, including coma. Changes in the ECG, particularly in QRS axis or width, are clinically significant indicators of tricyclic antidepressant toxicity.

Other signs of overdose may include: confusion, disturbed concentration, transient visual hallucinations, dilated pupils, agitation, hyperactive reflexes, stupor, drowsiness, muscle

Aventyl (cont'd)

rigidity, vomiting, hypothermia, hyperpyrexia, or many of the symptoms listed under Adverse Effects.

Treatment: General: Obtain an ECG and immediately initiate cardiac monitoring. Protect the patient's airway, establish an i.v. line and initiate gastric decontamination. A minimum of 6 hours of observation with cardiac monitoring and observation for signs of CNS or respiratory depression, hypotension, cardiac dysrhythmias and/or conduction blocks, and seizures is necessary. If signs of toxicity occur at any time during this period, extended monitoring is required. There are case reports of patients succumbing to fatal dysrhythmias later after overdose; these patients had clinical evidence of significant poisoning prior to death and most received inadequate gastrointestinal decontamination. Monitoring of plasma drug levels should not guide management of the patient.

Gastrointestinal Decontamination: All patients suspected of tricyclic antidepressant overdose should receive gastrointestinal decontamination. This should include large volume gastric lavage followed by activated charcoal. If consciousness is impaired, the airway should be secured prior to lavage. Emesis is contraindicated.

Cardiovascular: A maximal limb-lead QRS duration of ≥0.10 seconds may be the best indication of the severity of the overdose. I.V. sodium bicarbonate should be used to maintain the serum pH in the range of 7.35 to 7.45. If the pH response is inadequate, hyperventilation may also be used. Concomitant use of hyperventilation and sodium bicarbonate should be done with extreme caution, with frequent pH monitoring. A pH >7.60 or a pCO_2 <20 mm Hg is undesirable. Dysrhythmias unresponsive to sodium bicarbonate therapy/hyperventilation may respond to lidocaine, bretylium or phenytoin. Type 1A and 1C antiarrhythmics are generally contraindicated (e.g., quinidine, disopyramide, and procainamide).

In rare instances, hemoperfusion may be beneficial in acute refractory cardiovascular instability in patients with acute toxicity. However, hemodialysis, peritoneal dialysis, exchange transfusions, and forced diuresis generally have been reported as ineffective in tricyclic antidepressant poisoning.

CNS: In patients with CNS depression, early intubation is advised because of the potential for abrupt deterioration. Seizures should be controlled with benzodiazepines, or if these are ineffective, other anticonvulsants (e.g., phenobarbital, phenytoin). Physostigmine is not recommended except to treat life-threatening symptoms that have been unresponsive to other therapies, and then only in consultation with a Poison Control Centre.

Psychiatric Follow-up: Since overdosage is often deliberate, patients may attempt suicide by other means during the recovery phase. Psychiatric referral may be appropriate.

Pediatric Management: The principles of management of child and adult overdosage are similar. It is strongly recommended that the physician contact the local Poison Control Centre for specific pediatric treatment.

Dosage: Nortriptyline is not recommended for children. Nortriptyline is administered orally in the form of capsules. Lower than usual dosages are recommended for elderly patients and adolescents. The use of lower dosages for outpatients is more important than for hospitalized patients who will be treated under close supervision. The physician should initiate dosages at a low level and increase it gradually, checking the clinical response carefully and noting any evidence of intolerance. Following remission, maintenance medication may be required for a long period of time at the lowest dose that will maintain remission. If a patient develops minor side effects, the dosage should be reduced. The drug should be discontinued promptly if adverse effects of a serious nature or allergic manifestations occur.

Adults: 25 mg 3 or 4 times daily; dosage should begin at a low level and be increased as required. As an alternate regimen, the total daily dose may be given once a day. When doses above 100 mg daily are administered, plasma levels of nortriptyline should be monitored and maintained in the optimum range of 50 to 150 ng/mL. Doses above 150 mg/day are not recommended.

Geriatric and Adolescent Patients: 30 to 50 mg/day, in divided doses.

Plasma Levels: Optimal responses to nortriptyline have been associated with plasma concentrations of 50 to 150 ng/mL. Higher concentrations may be associated with more adverse experiences. Plasma concentrations are difficult to measure, and physicians should consult with the laboratory professional staff. Larger plasma concentrations of the active nortriptyline metabolite 10-hydroxynortriptyline have been reported in older patients. In one case, such a condition was associated with apparent cardiotoxicity despite the fact that nortriptyline concentrations were within the therapeutic range. Clinical findings should predominate over plasma concentrations as primary determinants of dosage changes.

Supplied: 10 mg: Each No. 3 Pulvule capsule with white, opaque body and yellow, opaque cap with Identi-Code H 17, contains: equivalent of 10 mg nortriptyline base. Nonmedicinal ingredients: butylparaben, benzyl alcohol, D&C Yellow No. 10, dimethicone, edetate calcium disodium, FD&C Yellow No. 6, gelatin, methylparaben, propylparaben, sodium lauryl sulfate, sodium propionate, starch and titanium dioxide. Tartrazine-free. Bottles of 100.

25 mg: Each No. 1 Pulvule capsule with white, opaque body and yellow, opaque cap with Identi-Code H 19, contains: equivalent of 25 mg nortriptyline base. Nonmedicinal ingredients: butylparaben, benzyl alcohol, D&C Yellow No. 10, dimethicone, edetate calcium disodium, FD&C Yellow No. 6, gelatin, methylparaben, propylparaben, sodium lauryl sulfate, sodium propionate, starch and titanium dioxide. Tartrazine-free. Bottles of 100.

Store at controlled room temperature (15 to 30°C).

Reviewed 1998

AVIRAX™ ℞

Fabrigen

Acyclovir

Antiviral

Pharmacology: Acyclovir, a synthetic acyclic nucleoside analog, is a substrate with a high degree of specificity for herpes simplex and varicella-zoster specified thymidine kinase. Acyclovir is a poor substrate for host cell-specified thymidine kinase. Herpes simplex and varicella-zoster specified thymidine kinase transform acyclovir to its monophosphate which is then transformed by a number of cellular enzymes to acyclovir diphosphate and acyclovir triphosphate. Acyclovir triphosphate is both an inhibitor of, and a substrate for, herpesvirus-specified DNA polymerase. Although the cellular α-DNA polymerase in infected cells may also be inhibited by acyclovir triphosphate, this occurs only at concentrations of acyclovir triphosphate which are higher than those which inhibit the herpesvirus-specified DNA polymerase. Acyclovir is selectively converted to its active form in herpesvirus-infected cells and is thus preferentially taken up by these cells. Acyclovir has demonstrated a very much lower toxic potential in vitro for normal uninfected cells because: 1) less is taken up; 2) less is converted to the active form; 3) cellular α-DNA polymerase has a lower sensitivity to the action of the active form of the drug. A combination of the thymidine kinase specificity, inhibition of DNA polymerase and premature termination of DNA synthesis results in inhibition of herpesvirus replication. No effect on latent nonreplicating virus has been demonstrated. Inhibition of the virus reduces the period of viral shedding, limits the degree of spread and level of pathology, and thereby facilitates healing. During suppression therapy there is no evidence that acyclovir prevents neural migration of the virus. It aborts episodes of recurrent herpes due to inhibition of viral replication following reactivation.

Pharmacokinetics: The pharmacokinetics of acyclovir after oral administration have been evaluated in 6 clinical studies involving 110 adult patients. In one study of 35 immunocompromised patients with herpes simplex or varicella-zoster infection given acyclovir capsules in doses of 200 to 1 000 mg every 4 hours, 6 times daily for 5 days, the bioavailability was estimated to be 15 to 20%. In this study, steady-state plasma levels were reached by the second day of dosing. Mean steady-state peak and trough concentrations following the last 200 mg dose were 0.49 µg/mL (0.47 to 0.54 µg/mL) and 0.31 µg/mL (0.18 to 0.41 µg/mL), respectively and following the last 800 mg dose were 2.8 µg/mL (2.3 to 3.1 µg/mL) and 1.8 µg/mL (1.3 to 2.5 µg/mL). In another study, 20 immunocompetent patients with recurrent genital herpes simplex infections given acyclovir capsules in doses of 800 mg every 6 hours, 4 times daily for 5 days, the mean steady-state peak and trough concentrations were 1.4 µg/mL (0.66 to 1.8 µg/mL) and 0.55 µg/mL (0.14 to 1.1 µg/mL).

In general, the pharmacokinetics of acyclovir in children is similar to adults. Mean half-life after oral doses of 300 mg/m² and 600 mg/m², in children ages 7 months to 7 years, was 2.6 hours (range 1.59 to 3.74 hours).

Orally administered acyclovir in children less than 2 years of age has not yet been fully studied.

Indications: May be indicated for the following conditions:

The treatment of initial episodes of herpes genitalis.

The suppression of unusually frequent recurrences of herpes genitalis (6 or more episodes/year).

The acute treatment of herpes zoster (shingles) and varicella (chickenpox).

The results of clinical studies suggest that some patients with recurrent genital herpes may derive clinical benefit from the administration of oral acyclovir if taken at the first sign of an impending episode. Those most likely to benefit are patients who experience severe, prolonged recurrences; such intermittent therapy may be more appropriate than suppressive therapy when these recurrences are infrequent.

Early treatment of acute herpes zoster (shingles) in immune competent individuals with oral acyclovir resulted in decreased viral shedding; decreased time to healing; less dissemination; and alleviation of acute pain.

Treatment of varicella (chickenpox) in immune competent patients with oral acyclovir reduced the total number of lesions, accelerated the progression of lesions to the crusted and healed stages, and decreased the number of residual hypopigmented lesions. In addition it decreased fever and constitutional symptoms associated with chickenpox.

The prophylactic use of acyclovir in chickenpox has not been established.

Contraindications: For patients who develop hypersensitivity or who are hypersensitive to the components of the formulation (see Supplied).

Warnings: Suppressive therapy of herpes genitalis with acyclovir should be considered only for severely affected patients. Periodic evaluation of the need for continued suppressive therapy is recommended. In some patients, there is a tendency for the first recurrent episode to be more severe following cessation of suppressive therapy.

In severely immunocompromised patients, the physician should be aware that prolonged or repeated courses of acyclovir may result in selection of resistant viruses associated with infections which may not respond.

Precautions: General: The recommended dosage and length of treatment should not be exceeded (see Dosage). Acyclovir has caused mutagenesis in some acute studies at high concentrations of drug. Also, decreased spermatogenesis was observed in some animals at high parenteral doses. However, no adverse effects on sperm counts were reported in humans given recommended oral doses of acyclovir.

The decision to prescribe a course of suppressive therapy should be weighed in the light of our present knowledge about the long-term effects of acyclovir and must clearly relate to the condition of the patient.

It is suggested that periodic discontinuation of the suppressive regimen occur so that the patient's status and need for continued suppressive therapy can be monitored.

Whereas cutaneous lesions associated with herpes simplex infections are often pathognomonic, Tzanck smears prepared from lesion exudate or scrapings may assist in the diagnosis. Positive cultures for herpes simplex virus offer the only absolute means for confirmation of the diagnosis. Appropriate examinations should be performed to rule out other sexually transmitted diseases. All patients should be advised to take particular care to avoid potential transmission of virus if active lesions are present while they are on therapy.

Caution should be exercised when administering to patients receiving potentially nephrotoxic agents since this may increase the risk of renal dysfunction.

Chickenpox: Although chickenpox in otherwise healthy children is usually a self-limited disease of mild to moderate severity, adolescents and adults tend to have more severe disease. Treatment was initiated within 24 hours of the typical chickenpox rash in the controlled studies, and there is no information regarding the effects of treatment begun later in the disease course. It is unknown whether the treatment of chickenpox in childhood has any effect on long-term immunity. However, there is no evidence to indicate that acyclovir treatment of chickenpox would have any effect on either decreasing or increasing the incidence or severity of subsequent recurrences of herpes zoster (shingles) later in life.

Pregnancy: Teratology studies carried out to date in animals have been negative in general. However, in a nonstandard test in rats, there were fetal abnormalities such as head and tail anomalies, and maternal toxicity; since such studies are not always predictive of human response, acyclovir should not be used during pregnancy unless the physician feels the potential benefit justifies the risk of possible harm to the fetus. The potential for high concentrations of acyclovir to cause chromosome breaks in vitro should be taken into consideration in making this decision.

Lactation: Acyclovir is excreted in human milk. Caution should therefore be exercised when it is administered to a nursing mother.

Children: Safety and effectiveness in children less than 2 years of age have not been adequately studied.

Drug Interactions: Coadministration of probenecid with i.v. acyclovir has been shown to increase the mean half-life and the area under the concentration-time curve. Urinary excretion and renal clearance were correspondingly reduced.

Adverse Effects: Treatment of Herpes Simplex: Short-term administration (5 to 10 days): The most frequent adverse reactions reported during clinical trials of treatment of genital herpes with oral acyclovir in 298 patients are listed in Table I.

Table I—Avirax

Adverse Effects: Herpes Simplex: Long-Term Administration

Adverse Reactions	Total	%
Nausea and/or vomiting	8	2.7
Headache	2	0.6

Less frequent adverse reactions, each of which occurred in 1 of 298 patient treatments (0.3%), included: diarrhea, dizziness, anorexia, fatigue, edema, skin rash, leg pain, inguinal adenopathy, medication taste and sore throat.

Suppression: Long-term administration: The most frequent adverse events reported in a clinical trial for the prevention of recurrences with continuous administration of 400 mg (two 200 mg capsules) 2 times daily are listed in Table II.

Table II—Avirax

Adverse Effects: Herpes Simplex: Long-Term Administration

	1st Year (n=586) (%)	2nd Year (n=390) (%)	3rd Year (n=329) (%)
Nausea	4.8		
Diarrhea	2.4		
Headache	1.9	1.5	0.9
Rash	1.7	1.3	
Paresthesia	0.8		1.2
Asthenia			1.2

Evidence so far from clinical trials suggests that the severity and frequency of adverse events is unlikely to necessitate discontinuation of therapy.

Herpes Zoster: The most frequent adverse reactions reported during 3 clinical trials of treatment of herpes zoster (shingles) with 800 mg of oral acyclovir 5 times daily for 7 or 10 days or placebo were as shown in Table III.

Table III—Avirax

Adverse Effects: Herpes Zoster

Adverse Reactions	Acyclovir (n=323) (%)	Placebo (n=323) (%)
Malaise	11.5	11.1
Nausea	8.0	11.5
Headache	5.9	11.1
Vomiting	2.5	2.5
Diarrhea	1.5	0.3
Constipation	0.9	2.4

Chickenpox: The most frequent adverse events reported during 3 clinical trials of treatment of chickenpox with oral acyclovir or placebo are listed in Table IV.

Table IV—Avirax

Adverse Effects: Chickenpox

Adverse Reactions	Acyclovir (n=495) (%)	Placebo (n=498) (%)
Diarrhea	3.2	2.2
Abdominal Pain	0.6	0.2
Rash	0.6	0.2
Vomiting	0.6	0.2
Flatulence	0.4	0.8
Urticaria	0.2	0.2
Spasmodic Hand Movement	0.2	0.2
Insomnia	0.2	0.4

Observed During Clinical Practice: Based on clinical practice experience in patients treated with oral acyclovir in the U.S., spontaneously reported adverse events are uncommon. Data are insufficient to support an estimate of their incidence or to establish causation. These events may also occur as part of the underlying disease process. Voluntary reports of adverse events which have been received since market introduction include: General: fever, headache, pain, peripheral edema, and rarely, anaphylaxis.

Nervous: confusion, dizziness, hallucinations, paresthesia, somnolence (these symptoms may be marked, particularly in older adults).

Digestive: diarrhea, elevated liver function tests, gastrointestinal distress, nausea.

Hemic and Lymphatic: leukopenia, lymphadenopathy.

Musculoskeletal: myalgia.

Skin: alopecia, pruritus, rash, urticaria.

Special Senses: visual abnormalities.

Urogenital: elevated creatinine.

Overdose: Symptoms and Treatment: Overdosage with acyclovir during oral use is unlikely because of incomplete bioavailability from the gastrointestinal tract. Doses as high as 800 mg 6 times daily for 5 days have been administered to humans without acute untoward effects. In clinical studies, the highest plasma concentration observed in a single patient at these doses was 10 μg/mL.

I.V. doses administered to humans have been as high as 1 200 mg/m² (28 mg/kg) 3 times daily for up to 2 weeks. Peak plasma concentrations have reached 80 μg/mL. No acute massive overdosage of acyclovir has been reported; however, in the case of an excessively high ingestion of acyclovir, precipitation of acyclovir in renal tubules may occur if the solubility (2.5 mg/mL) in the intratubular fluid is exceeded. In the event of renal failure and anuria, the patient may benefit from hemodialysis until renal function is restored.

Dosage: Herpes Genitalis: Treatment of Initial Infection: 200 mg every 4 hours, 5 times daily for a total of 1 g daily for 10 days. Therapy should be initiated as early as possible following onset of signs and symptoms.

Suppressive Therapy for Recurrent Disease: The initial recommended dose is 200 mg 3 times daily. This can be increased if breakthrough occurs up to a dosage of 200 mg 5 times daily. If necessary, a dose of 400 mg given twice daily may be considered. Periodic re-evaluation of the need for therapy is recommended.

Administration of acyclovir for intermittent therapy is 200 mg every 4 hours, 5 times daily for 5 days. Therapy should be initiated at the earliest sign or symptom (prodrome) of recurrence.

Herpes Zoster: 800 mg every 4 hours, 5 times daily for 7 to 10 days. Treatment should be initiated within 72 hours of the onset of lesions. In clinical trials, the greatest benefit occurred when treatment was begun within 48 hours of the onset of lesions.

Treatment of Chickenpox: 20 mg/kg (not to exceed 800 mg) orally, 4 times daily for 5 days. Therapy should be initiated within 24 hours of the appearance of rash.

Patients with Acute or Chronic Renal Impairment: Comprehensive pharmacokinetic studies have been completed following i.v. acyclovir infusions in patients with renal impairment.

Based on these studies, dosage adjustments are recommended in Table V for genital herpes and herpes zoster indications.

Hemodialysis: For patients who require hemodialysis, the mean plasma half-life of acyclovir during hemodialysis is approximately 5 hours. This results in a 60% decrease in plasma concentrations following a 6-hour dialysis period. Therefore, the patient's dosing schedule should be adjusted so that an additional dose is administered after each dialysis.

Peritoneal Dialysis: No supplement dose appears to be necessary after adjustment of the dosing interval.

Information for the Patient: See Blue Section—Information for the Patient "Avirax".

Supplied: 200 mg: Each blue, round-shaped, single-scored, compressed tablet, imprinted "ACV 200" on one side, contains: acyclovir 200 mg. Nonmedicinal ingredients: cellulose, indigotine, lactose, magnesium stearate, povidone and sodium starch glycolate. Bottles of 100 and 500. Store between 15 and 25°C. Keep dry and protect from light.

400 mg: Each pink, round-shaped, single-scored, compressed tablet, imprinted with "ACV 400" on one side, contains: acyclovir 400 mg. Nonmedicinal ingredients: cellulose, magnesium stearate, povidone, red iron oxide and sodium starch glycolate. Bottles of 100. Store between 15 and 25°C. Keep dry and protect from light.

800 mg: Each blue, oval, biconvex, elongated, single-scored, compressed tablet, imprinted with "ACV 800" on one side, contains: acyclovir 800 mg. Nonmedicinal ingredients: cellulose, indigotine, magnesium stearate, povidone and sodium starch glycolate. Bottles of 100 and 250. Store between 15 and 25°C. Keep dry and protect from light.

(Shown in Product Recognition Section)

Table V—Avirax

Patients with Acute or Chronic Renal Impairment: Dosage Adjustments

Normal Dosage Regimen	Creatinine Clearance (mL/min/1.73 m²)	Adjusted Dosage Regimen Dose (mg)	Dosing Interval (hours)
200 mg every 4 hours (5×daily)	>10	200	every 4 hours, 5×daily
	0–10	200	every 12 hours
400 mg every 12 hours	>10	400	every 12 hours
	0–10	200	every 12 hours
800 mg every 4 hours (5×daily)	>25	800	every 4 hours, 5×daily
	10–25	800	every 8 hours
	0–10	800	every 12 hours

AVLOSULFON® Ⓟ

Wyeth-Ayerst

Dapsone

Antibacterial Sulfone

Indications: Leprosy; dermatitis herpetiformis; actinomycotic mycetoma.

Contraindications: Sulfones are contraindicated in patients with advanced amyloidosis of the kidneys.

Precautions: Dapsone should be used with caution in patients with cardiac, pulmonary, hepatic or renal disease. Routine hematologic analysis should be carried out during long-term therapy with sulfones, because of the danger of hemolytic anemia. The hemolytic effect of sulfones may be exaggerated in glucose-6-phosphate dehydrogenase deficient individuals.

Drug Interactions: Rifampicin has been reported to increase the plasma clearance of dapsone, and probenecid has been reported to decrease excretion of dapsone. Administration of dapsone with chloroquine and/or primaquine may lead to an increase of methemoglobin levels in individuals predisposed to methemoglobinemia.

Pregnancy and Lactation: The sulfone drugs are generally contraindicated in pregnancy and therefore the use of dapsone during pregnancy should be avoided unless, in the judgment of the physician, potential benefit outweighs the risk. Dapsone in high doses has been reported to be carcinogenic in rats and mice, but negative in salmonella mutagenicity assays. The relevance of this finding to human exposure is unclear. Dapsone is excreted in breast milk in therapeutic amounts. Sulfones may cause hemolytic anemia in glucose-6-phosphate dehydrogenase deficient neonates.

Reaction States: Leprosy patients receiving effective chemotherapy may suffer episodes of acute or chronic inflammation. Generally, antileprosy chemotherapy should be continued unchanged but these reactions must be adequately treated since they may result in crippling deformity.

Nonlepromatous Lepra Reactions: Complications may include severe peripheral neuritis with accompanying cutaneous sensory loss and paralysis. In the management of acute neuritis corticosteroids may be considered.

Lepromatous Lepra Reactions: Complications may include neuritis, an increase in muscle weakness, lymphadenitis, Iridocyclitis, orchitis and more rarely nephritis and large-joint arthritis. In the management of these reactions, corticosteroids, and clofazimine may be considered.

Adverse Effects: Most adverse reactions are dose-related and uncommon at dosages up to 100 mg daily. They include anorexia, nausea, vomiting, headache, dizziness, tachycardia, nervousness, insomnia and skin disorders. Agranulocytosis, peripheral neuritis and psychosis have also been reported. Varying degrees of dose-related hemolysis and methemoglobinemia occur in most individuals given more than 200 mg daily. Dosages up to 100 mg daily are unlikely to cause hemolysis, but individuals with glucose-6-dehydrogenase deficiency

Avlosulfon (cont'd)

may be affected by dosages above 50 mg daily. Rare reactions include the "dapsone syndrome" and hypoalbuminemia.

The "dapsone syndrome" is hypersensitivity reactions which develop rarely and tend to occur during the first 6 weeks of therapy. Symptoms may include fever, eosinophilia, mononucleosis, lymphadenopathy, leukopenia, jaundice with hepatitis, and exanthematous skin eruptions which may progress to exfoliative dermatitis, toxic epidermal necrolysis, or Stevens-Johnson syndrome. Although patients usually improve if dapsone is withdrawn fatalities have occurred. Fixed drug eruptions occur in dark-skinned people. Although agranulocytosis has been reported rarely for dapsone when used alone, reports have been more common when the drug has been used with other agents in the prophylaxis of malaria. Other miscellaneous reactions such as peripheral neuropathy, nephrotic syndrome and renal papillary necrosis have been reported.

Overdose: Symptoms and Treatment: In cases of severe overdosage the stomach should be emptied by aspiration and lavage. There is no specific antidote and therefore treatment should be symptomatic e.g., i.v. methylene blue 1 to 2 mg/kg body weight, i.v. ascorbic acid 0.5 to 1 g and oxygen for the methemoglobinemia plus general supportive measures. The repeated administration of activated charcoal has been reported to increase the elimination rate of dapsone and its metabolite following overdosage.

Dosage: Leprosy: Adults: The standard dose is 100 mg daily (1 to 2 mg/kg body weight).

Children: Dosage should be adjusted according to body weight.

The modern treatment of leprosy involves the use of multiple drug regimens to avoid the development of resistant strains. The World Health Organization has made the following recommendations for standard adult treatment regimens (with dosage adjustments according to body weight): Multibacillary leprosy: rifampicin: 600 mg once-monthly, supervised; dapsone: 100 mg daily, self-administered; clofazimine: 300 mg once-monthly, supervised and 50 mg daily, self-administered. Paucibacillary Leprosy: rifampicin: 600 mg once a month for 6 months, supervised; dapsone: 100 mg daily for 6 months, self-administered.

Further information on treatment regimens is contained in "Chemotherapy of Leprosy for Control Programmes" W.H.O. Technical Report Series 675 (1982).

Dermatitis Herpetiformis: Adults: The usual maintenance dosage is 50 to 100 mg daily, but as little as 50 mg weekly may be adequate. Dosages of up to 300 mg daily may be considered, but efforts should be made to reduce this to the minimal maintenance dosage as soon as possible.

Actinomycotic Mycetoma: Adults: Published reports suggest that a dose of 100 mg should be given twice daily and continued for some months after the clinical symptoms have disappeared.

Supplied: Each round, biconvex, white tablet, embossed Ayerst on one side with a score line on other side, contains: dapsone USP 100 mg. Nonmedicinal ingredients: calcium carbonate, cornstarch and magnesium stearate. Energy: 0.5 kJ (0.12 kcal). Alcohol-, gluten-, lactose-, parabens-, sugar-, sulfites- and tartrazine-free. Bottles of 100. Store at room temperature. Protect from light.

(Shown in Product Recognition Section)

AXID® Ⓟ

Lilly

Nizatidine

Histamine H_2 Receptor Antagonist

Pharmacology: Nizatidine is a competitive, reversible inhibitor of the histamine H_2 receptor of gastric-acid secreting cells. Nizatidine is not an anticholinergic agent. It inhibits nocturnal gastric-acid secretion and gastric-acid secretion stimulated by food, caffeine, betazole and pentagastrin. Pepsin output is reduced in proportion to the reduced volume of gastric secretions. Nizatidine has little or no effect on basal serum gastrin or food induced hypergastrinemia.

In man nizatidine is absorbed rapidly, peak plasma concentrations occur from 0.5 to 3 hours after an oral dose. Absorption is unaffected by food or propantheline; however, antacids consisting of aluminum and magnesium hydroxide with simethicone decrease the absorption of nizatidine by about 10%. The absolute oral bioavailability of nizatidine is 70.9% ± 6.4. Approximately 35% of nizatidine is bound to plasma protein, primarily α1-glycoprotein. This binding is not influenced by other drugs such as warfarin, diazepam, acetaminophen, propranolol, or phenobarbital. Approximately 90% of an oral dose of nizatidine is excreted in the urine within 12 hours. About 60% of an oral dose and 77% of an I.V. dose of nizatidine is excreted as unchanged drug.

The elimination half-life is 1 to 2 hours and the systemic plasma clearance is about 50 L/hour. The volume of distribution is 0.8 to 1.5 L/kg.

Since nizatidine is primarily excreted in the urine, renal impairment significantly prolongs the half-life and decreases the clearance of nizatidine. In anephric individuals with creatinine clearance less than 10 mL/min the half-life is 3.5 to 11 hours, and the plasma clearance is 7 to 14 L/hour. The pharmacokinetic profile for nizatidine in the elderly was not significantly different from the profile in younger normal subjects.

Gastric acid suppression correlates directly with nizatidine doses from 75 to 350 mg. Oral doses of 100 mg or 1.3 mg/kg suppressed gastric acid secretion in sham fed volunteers for 3 hours after the dose. The duration of acid suppression directly correlates with the nizatidine dose. 300 mg nizatidine suppressed acid secretion almost entirely early in the day, and the suppression persisted about 10 hours. Nocturnal acid was suppressed for 10 to 12 hours after 300 mg nizatidine.

Treatment for up to 2 weeks with nizatidine 600 mg daily did not influence the serum concentrations of gonadotropins, prolactin, growth hormone, antidiuretic hormone, cortisol, triiodothyronine, thyroxin, testosterone, 5α-dihydrotestosterone, androstenedione or estradiol.

Indications: In the treatment of conditions where a controlled reduction of gastric acid secretion is required such as, ulcer healing and/or pain relief: acute duodenal ulcer, acute benign gastric ulcer, gastroesophageal reflux disease, and prophylactic use in duodenal ulcer.

Contraindications: Patients with known hypersensitivity to the drug. Because cross-sensitivity in this class of compounds has been observed, H_2-receptor antagonists, including nizatidine, should not be administered to individuals with a history of previous hypersensitivity to other agents.

Precautions: Gastric ulcer: Where gastric ulcer is suspected the possibility of malignancy should be excluded before therapy with nizatidine is instituted.

Pregnancy: Safety during pregnancy has not been established. Reproduction studies performed in rats and rabbits at doses up to 300 times the human dose have revealed no evidence of impaired fertility or teratogenicity. If the administration of nizatidine is considered to be necessary, its use requires that the potential benefits be weighed against possible hazards to the patient and to the fetus.

Lactation: Nizatidine is secreted in human breast milk in proportion to maternal plasma concentration (<0.1%) and caution should be exercised when it is administered to nursing mothers.

Impaired Renal Function: As nizatidine is excreted via the kidney, dosage should be adjusted in patients with moderately or severely impaired renal function (see Dosage).

Hepatic Dysfunction: Nizatidine is partially metabolized in the liver; however, in patients with mild to moderate hepatic dysfunction, disposition of nizatidine is similar to that of normal subjects.

Geriatrics: Ulcer healing rates in elderly patients are similar to those in younger age groups. The incidence rates of adverse events and laboratory test abnormalities are also similar to those seen in other age groups. Age alone is not an important factor in the disposition of nizatidine. However, elderly patients may have reduced renal function (see Dosage).

Children: Safety and effectiveness in children has not been established.

Laboratory Tests: False positive tests for urobilinogen with Multistix may occur during therapy with nizatidine.

<u>*Drug Interactions:*</u> No interactions have been observed between nizatidine and theophylline, chlordiazepoxide, lorazepam, lidocaine, phenytoin, warfarin, aminophylline, diazepam, metoprolol. Nizatidine does not inhibit the cytochrome P450-linked drug-metabolizing enzyme system; therefore, drug interactions mediated by inhibition of hepatic metabolism are not expected to occur. In patients given very high doses (3 900 mg) of ASA daily, increases in serum salicylate levels were seen when nizatidine, 150 mg twice daily, was administered concurrently.

Adverse Effects: Clinical trials of nizatidine included almost 5 000 patients given nizatidine in studies of varying durations. North American placebo-controlled trials included over 1 900 patients given nizatidine and over 1 300 given placebo. Among the more common adverse events in these placebo-controlled trials, sweating (1% vs 0.2%), urticaria (0.5% vs <0.01%) and somnolence (2.4% vs 1.3%) were significantly more common in the nizatidine group. A variety of less common events were also reported; it was not possible to determine whether these were caused by nizatidine.

Hepatic: Hepatocellular injury, evidenced by elevated liver enzyme tests (AST, ALT, or alkaline phosphatase), occurred in some patients possibly or probably related to nizatidine. In some cases there was marked elevation of AST, ALT enzymes (greater than 500 IU/L) and in a single instance ALT was greater than 2 000 IU/L. The overall rate of occurrences of elevated liver enzymes and elevations to 3 times the upper limit of normal, however, did not significantly differ from the rate of liver enzyme abnormalities in placebo treated patients. Hepatitis and jaundice have been reported. All abnormalities were reversible after discontinuation of nizatidine.

Cardiovascular: In clinical pharmacology studies, short episodes of asymptomatic ventricular tachycardia occurred in 2 individuals administered nizatidine and in 3 untreated subjects.

CNS: Rare cases of reversible mental confusion have been reported.

Endocrine: Clinical pharmacology studies and controlled clinical trials showed no evidence of antiandrogenic activity due to nizatidine. Impotence and decreased libido were reported with equal frequency by patients who received nizatidine and by those given placebo. Rare reports of gynecomastia occurred.

Hematologic: Fatal thrombocytopenia was reported in a patient who was treated with nizatidine and another H_2-receptor antagonist. On previous occasions, this patient had experienced thrombocytopenia while taking other drugs. Rare cases of thrombocytopenic purpura have been reported.

Integumental: Sweating and urticaria were reported significantly more frequently in nizatidine than in placebo patients. Rash and exfoliative dermatitis were also reported.

Hypersensitivity: As with other H_2-receptor antagonists, rare cases of anaphylaxis following administration of nizatidine have been reported. Because cross-sensitivity in this class of compounds has been observed, H_2-receptor antagonists should not be administered to individuals with a history of previous hypersensitivity to these agents. Rare episodes of hypersensitivity reactions (e.g., bronchospasm, laryngeal edema, rash, and eosinophilia) have been reported.

Other: Hyperuricemia unassociated with gout or nephrolithiasis was reported. Eosinophilia, fever and nausea related to nizatidine administration have been reported.

Overdose: Symptoms and Treatment: There is little clinical experience with deliberate overdosage of nizatidine in humans. Test animals that received large doses of nizatidine have exhibited cholinergic-type effects, including lacrimation, salivation, emesis, miosis, and diarrhea. Should overdosage occur, use of activated charcoal, emesis, or lavage should be considered along with clinical monitoring and supportive therapy. Renal dialysis does not substantially increase clearance of nizatidine due to its large volume of distribution.

Dosage: Duodenal or Gastric Ulcer: One 300 mg capsule or two 150 mg capsules once daily at bedtime. Alternatively, 150 mg twice daily may be used. Healing occurs within 4 weeks in most cases of duodenal ulcer; but if healing is not documented or has not occurred, therapy should be given for 8 weeks.

Maintenance Dosage in Duodenal Ulcer: One 150 mg capsule once daily at bedtime for 6 to 12 months depending on the severity of the condition.

Gastroesophageal Reflux Disease: One 150 mg capsule twice daily for the treatment of erosions, ulcerations, and associated heartburn.

Antacids may be given concomitantly if needed.

Dosage Adjustment in Renal Impairment (see Table I).

Table I—Axid

Dosage Adjustment in Renal Impairment

Renal Function	Creatinine Clearance (mL/min)	Dosage Acute	Dosage Maintenance
Normal	>50	300 mg/day	150 mg/day
Moderate Impairment	20–50	150 mg/day	150 mg/2nd day
Severe Impairment	<20	150 mg/2nd day	150 mg/3rd day

Supplied: 150 mg: Each pale yellow and dark yellow Pulvule 3144 contains: nizatidine 150 mg. Nonmedicinal ingredients: magnesium stearate, silicone and starch; capsule shell may contain: gelatin, iron oxide yellow and titanium dioxide. Bottles of 100.

300 mg: Each pale yellow and brown Pulvule 3145 contains: nizatidine 300 mg. Nonmedicinal ingredients: carboxymethylcellulose sodium, povidone, silicone, starch and talc; capsule shell may contain: gelatin, iron oxide red, iron oxide yellow and titanium dioxide. Bottles of 100.

AZATHIOPRINE SODIUM FOR INJECTION, USP ℞

Novopharm

Immunosuppressive Agent

Supplied: Each glass vial of lyophilized powder contains: the equivalent of azathioprine 100 mg as the sodium salt. Nonmedicinal ingredients: hydrochloric acid (qs to adjust pH) and sodium hydroxide.

New Product 1998

AZMACORT® ℞

Rhône-Poulenc Rorer

Triamcinolone Acetonide

Corticosteroid

Pharmacology: Triamcinolone is a potent anti-inflammatory steroid with strong topical and weak systemic activity. When inhaled at therapeutic dosages, it has a direct anti-inflammatory action on the bronchial mucosa. Since the minute amounts absorbed do not exert any significant systemic effect, inhaled triamcinolone can replace oral steroids with the elimination of the untoward effects of systemic therapy.

Indications: Only for patients requiring chronic treatment with corticosteroids for symptomatic control of bronchial asthma. Such patients would include: steroid-dependent asthmatic patients to replace oral medication with this product through gradual withdrawal of systemic corticosteroids and selected patients who are inadequately controlled on a nonsteroid regimen and in whom steroid therapy has been withheld because of concern over potential adverse effects.

Contraindications: For the primary treatment of status asthmaticus or other acute asthmatic episodes where intensive therapeutic measures are required, or in patients with moderate to severe bronchiectasis.

Hypersensitivity to any of the ingredients of this preparation contraindicates its use.

It is also contraindicated in active or quiescent untreated pulmonary tuberculosis or untreated fungal, bacterial or viral infections.

Warnings: Particular care is needed in patients who are transferred from systemic corticosteroids to Azmacort, because **deaths due to adrenal insufficiency have occurred in asthmatic patients during and after transfer from systemic corticosteroids to aerosolized steroids** in recommended doses. After withdrawal from systemic corticosteroids, a number of months is usually required for recovery of hypothalamic pituitary-adrenal (HPA) function.

For some patients who received large doses of oral steroids for long periods of time before therapy with inhaled triamcinolone was initiated, recovery was delayed for 1 year or longer. During this period of HPA suppression, patients may exhibit signs and symptoms of adrenal insufficiency when exposed to trauma, surgery or infection, particularly gastroenteritis or other conditions with acute electrolyte loss. Although inhaled triamcinolone may provide control of asthmatic symptoms during these episodes, it supplies systemically only normal physiological amounts of corticosteroid in recommended doses and does **not** provide the increased systemic steroid needed for coping with these emergencies.

During periods of stress or a severe asthmatic attack, patients who have recently been withdrawn from systemic corticosteroids should be instructed to resume systemic steroids (in large doses) immediately and to contact their physician for further instructions. These patients should also be instructed to carry a warning card indicating that they may need supplementary systemic steroids during periods of stress or a severe asthmatic attack.

To assess the risk of adrenal insufficiency in emergency situations, routine tests of adrenal cortical function, including measurement of early morning and evening cortisol levels, should be performed periodically in all patients. An early morning resting cortisol level may be accepted as normal only if it falls at or near the normal mean level.

Localized infections with C. albicans have occurred infrequently in the mouth and pharynx. These areas should be examined by the treating physician at each patient visit. The percentage of positive mouth and throat cultures for C. albicans did not change during a year of continuous therapy. The incidence of clinically apparent infection was low (2.5%). **The development of pharyngeal and laryngeal candidiasis is cause for concern because the extent of its penetration of the respiratory tract is unknown. These infections may require treatment with appropriate antifungal therapy and/or discontinuance or treatment with inhaled triamcinolone, depending on the severity of the infection.** Azmacort is not to be regarded as a bronchodilator and is not indicated for rapid relief of bronchospasm.

Patients should be instructed to contact their physician immediately when episodes of asthma not responsive to bronchodilators occur during the course of treatment with inhaled triamcinolone. During such episodes, patients may require systemic corticosteroid therapy.

There is no evidence that control of asthma can be achieved by the administration of inhaled triamcinolone in amounts greater than the recommended doses, which appear to be the therapeutic equivalent of approximately 10 mg/day of oral prednisone.

Theoretically, the use of inhaled corticosteroids with alternate day oral prednisone therapy should be accompanied by more HPA suppression than a therapeutically equivalent regimen of either alone.

Transfer of patients from systemic steroid therapy to inhaled triamcinolone may unmask allergic conditions previously suppressed by the systemic steroid therapy, e.g., rhinitis, conjunctivitis, and eczema.

Precautions: It is essential that the patient be instructed that inhaled triamcinolone is a preventative agent which must be taken at regular intervals and is not to be used during an asthmatic attack.

During withdrawal from oral steroids, some patients may experience symptoms of systemically active steroid withdrawal, e.g., joint and/or muscular pain, lassitude and depression, despite maintenance or even improvement of respiratory function (see Dosage). Although steroid withdrawal effects are usually transient and not severe, severe and even fatal exacerbations of asthma can occur if the previous daily oral corticosteroid requirement significantly exceeded 10 mg/day of prednisone or equivalent.

In responsive patients, inhaled corticosteroids will often permit control of asthmatic symptoms with less suppression of HPA function than therapeutically equivalent oral doses of prednisone. Since triamcinolone is absorbed into the circulation and can be systemically active, the beneficial effects of the drug in minimizing or preventing HPA dysfunction may be expected only when recommended dosages are not exceeded.

Suppression of HPA function has been reported in volunteers who received 4 000 µg daily of triamcinolone. In addition, suppression of HPA function has been reported in some patients who have received recommended doses for as little as 6 to 12 weeks. Since the response of HPA function to inhaled corticosteroids is highly individualized, the physician should consider this information when treating patients.

Because of the possibility of systemic absorption of inhaled corticosteroids, patients treated with such drugs should be observed carefully for evidence of systemic corticosteroid effects including suppression of growth in children. Particular care should be taken in observing patients postoperatively or during periods of stress for evidence of a decrease in adrenal function.

The long-term effects of triamcinolone in human subjects are not completely known, therefore during long-term therapy pituitary-adrenal function and hematological status should be periodically assessed.

While there have been no clinical reports of adverse experience, the local effects of the agent on developmental or immunologic processes in the mouth, pharynx, trachea and lung are also unknown.

The potential effects of inhaled triamcinolone on acute, recurrent, or chronic pulmonary infections, including active or quiescent tuberculosis, are not known. For this reason, since systemic administration of corticosteroids may mask some signs of fungal, bacterial or viral infection, the same caution should be observed when treating patients with inhaled triamcinolone. The potential effects of the long-term administration on lung or other tissues are unknown. However, pulmonary infiltrates with eosinophilia have occurred in patients receiving other inhaled corticosteroids.

Pregnancy: Triamcinolone has been shown to be teratogenic in rats and rabbits when given in doses comparable to the highest recommended dose for human use (approximately 0.032 mg/kg/day). Administration by aerosol inhalation to pregnant rats and rabbits produced embryotoxic and fetotoxic effects which were compared to those produced by administration by other routes.

Teratogenic effects in both species included a low incidence of cleft palate and/or internal hydrocephaly and axial skeletal defects. These findings represent known effects of glucocorticoids in laboratory animals.

There are no well-controlled studies in pregnant women. Experience with other dosage forms of triamcinolone does not include positive evidence of adverse effects on the fetus. However, since such experience cannot exclude the possibility of fetal damage, the drug should be used during pregnancy only if the benefit clearly justifies the potential risk to the fetus. Infants born to mothers who have received substantial doses of corticosteroids during pregnancy should be carefully observed for hypoadrenalism.

Lactation: It is not known whether this drug is excreted in human milk. Because of the potential for tumorigenicity shown by triamcinolone in animal studies, a decision should be made whether to discontinue nursing or to discontinue the drug, taking into account the importance of the drug to the mother.

Corticosteroids may mask some signs of infections and new infections may appear. A decreased resistance to localized infection has been observed during corticosteroid therapy. During long-term therapy, pituitary-adrenal function and hematological status should be periodically assessed.

Fluorocarbon propellants may be hazardous if they are deliberately abused. Inhalation of high concentrations of aerosol sprays has brought about toxic cardiovascular effects and even death, especially under conditions of hypoxia. However, evidence attests to the safety of aerosols when used properly and with adequate ventilation.

There is an enhanced effect of corticosteroids in patients with hypothyroidism and in those with cirrhosis.

ASA should be used cautiously in conjunction with corticosteroids in hypoprothrombinemia.

Patients should be advised to inform subsequent physicians of the prior use of corticosteroids.

To ensure the proper dosage and administration of the drug, the patient must be instructed by a physician or other health professional in the use of the inhaler.

Adequate oral hygiene is of primary importance in minimizing overgrowth of microorganisms such as C. albicans (see Dosage).

Adverse Effects: Oral candidiasis has been reported (see Warnings). In addition, some patients receiving inhaled triamcinolone have experienced hoarseness, dry throat, irritated throat and dry mouth. Increased wheezing and cough have been infrequently reported, as has facial edema. These adverse effects have generally been mild and transient. Symptoms of rhinitis and eczema may become apparent during therapy after withdrawal of systemic corticosteroids.

Overdose: Symptoms and Treatment: Overdosage may cause systemic steroid effects such as adrenal suppression and hypercorticism. Decreasing the dose will diminish these effects.

Dosage: All patients should be instructed that Azmacort must be used on a regular daily basis rather than prn. Reliable dosage delivery cannot be assured after 240 actuations and patients should be cautioned against longer use of individual canisters.

Patients must be instructed in the correct method of using the inhaler (see Information for the Patient).

Good oral hygiene including rinsing of the mouth after inhalation is recommended.

Adults: The usual adult dosage is 2 inhalations (approximately 400 µg) given 3 to 4 times a day. **The maximal daily intake should not exceed 16 inhalations (3 200 µg) for adults.** Higher initial doses (12 to 16 inhalations/day) may be advisable in patients with more severe asthma, with dosage when being adjusted downward according to patient response. In some patients maintenance can be accomplished when the total daily dose is given on a twice a day schedule.

Each actuation releases approximately 200 µg of triamcinolone from the metered valve, of which approximately 100 µg are delivered from the mouthpiece (in vitro testing). The dosages expressed in this product monograph are based on 200 µg of drug being released from the metered valve upon each actuation.

Children 6 to 12 years of age: The usual dosage is 1 to 2 inhalations (200 to 400 µg) given 3 to 4 times a day according to the response of the patient. **The maximal daily intake should not exceed 12 inhalations (2 400 µg) in children**

Azmacort (cont'd)

6 to 12 years of age. Insufficient clinical data exist with respect to the administration of Azmacort to children below the age of 6. The long-term effects of inhaled steroids on growth are still under evaluation.

Patients receiving bronchodilators by inhalation should be advised to use them before using this product, in order to enhance penetration of triamcinolone into the bronchial tree. After use of an aerosol bronchodilator, several minutes should elapse before use of inhaled triamcinolone in order to reduce potential toxicity from inhaled fluorocarbon propellants in the 2 aerosols.

Different considerations must be given to the following groups of patients in order to obtain the full therapeutic benefit of inhaled triamcinolone.

Patients not receiving systemic steroids: The use of Azmacort is straightforward in patients inadequately controlled with nonsteroidal medications, but in whom systemic steroid therapy has been withheld because of concern for potential adverse reactions. In patients who respond to inhaled triamcinolone, an improvement in pulmonary function is usually apparent within 1 to 2 weeks of the start.

Patients receiving systemic steroids: In those patients dependent on systemic steroids, transfer to Azmacort and subsequent management may be more difficult because recovery from impaired adrenal function is usually slow. Such suppression has been known to last for up to 12 months or longer. Clinical studies, however, have demonstrated that Azmacort may be effective in the management of these asthmatic cases and may permit replacement or significant reduction in dosage of the systemic corticosteroids.

The patient's asthma should be reasonably stable before treatment with inhaled triamcinolone is started. Initially, the inhaler should be used concurrently with the usual maintenance dose of systemic steroid. After approximately 1 week, gradual withdrawal of the systemic steroid is started with an initial reduction in dosage, and close supervision.

The next reduction is made after an interval of 1 or 2 weeks, depending on response of the patient. Generally, these decrements should not exceed 2.5 mg of prednisone or its equivalent. **If continuous supervision is not feasible, the withdrawal of the systemic steroid should be slower.** A slow rate of withdrawal cannot be overemphasized. During this process, some patients may experience systemic symptoms of active steroid withdrawal, e.g., joint and/or muscle pain, lassitude and depression, despite maintenance or even improvement in respiratory function. Such patients should be encouraged to continue with the inhaler but should be watched carefully for objective signs of adrenal insufficiency, such as hypotension and weight loss. If evidence of adrenal insufficiency occurs, the systemic steroid dose should be boosted temporarily and thereafter, further withdrawal should continue more slowly. No clinical studies have been conducted evaluating Azmacort with alternate day prednisone regimens. However, based on the results of such a study with another corticosteroid inhaler, these products are generally not recommended for chronic use with alternate day prednisone regimens (see Warnings).

During periods of stress or a severe asthma attack, withdrawal patients will require supplementary treatment with systemic steroids.

Exacerbations of asthma which can occur during the course of treatment with inhaled triamcinolone, should be treated with a short course of systemic steroid and gradually tapered as the symptoms subside. There is no evidence that control of asthma can be achieved by the administration of inhaled triamcinolone in amounts greater than the recommended doses.

Under stressful conditions or when the patient has a severe exacerbation of bronchial asthma, after complete withdrawal of the systemic steroid, use of the latter must be resumed in order to avoid relative adrenocortical insufficiency. There are some patients who cannot completely discontinue the oral corticosteroid. In these cases, a minimum maintenance dosage should be given in addition to inhaled triamcinolone.

Information for the Patient: See Blue Section—Information for the Patient "Azmacort".

Supplied: Each metered-dose aerosol unit contains: a microcrystalline suspension of triamcinolone acetonide 60 mg. Nonmedicinal ingredients: alcohol and dichlorodifluoromethane. Each actuation releases approximately 200 µg triamcinolone acetonide, of which approximately 100 µg are delivered from the unit (in vitro testing). Canisters of at least 240 oral inhalations. The device should not be used after 240 inhalations, since the amount delivered thereafter may be less than consistent. Boxes of 1 supplied with an oral adapter and patient's leaflet of instructions.

Store at room temperature. Caution: container may explode if heated. Contents under pressure. Do not place in hot water or near radiators, stoves or other sources of heat. Even when empty do not puncture or incinerate containers or store at temperatures over 50°C.

CANADIAN *in* CHARACTER

CRYSTAAL
CORPORATION

PAAB
98C001E

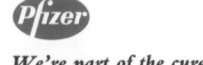

B

BABY'S OWN™ GRIPE WATER
Block Drug

Sodium Bicarbonate Compound

Antacid—Antiflatulent

Indications: For fast soothing relief from minor stomach upset, colic, cramps, flatulence and hiccups due to indigestion.

Dosage: Shake before using. Newborn infant: 2.5 mL; 1 to 6 months: 5 mL; over 6 months: 10 mL. May be repeated up to 4 times daily as required. If symptoms persist, consult physician.

Supplied: Each 5 mL contains: sodium bicarbonate 72 mg, oil of dill 3 mg, oil of anise 1.8 mg and oil of fennel 0.9 mg. Nonmedicinal ingredients: ethyl alcohol, purified water and sucrose. Unbreakable plastic bottles of 200 mL. Store in a cool place.

BABY'S OWN™ INFANT DROPS
Block Drug

Simethicone

Antiflatulent

Indications: To relieve infant colic, bloating and flatulence due to gas.

Warnings: Keep this and all drugs out of the reach of children. Do not take for more than 2 weeks unless directed by a physician. If symptoms recur consult a physician.

Dosage: Shake well before using. Use only on the advice of a physician. Infants (under 2 years): orally 0.3 mL up to 3 times daily. May be mixed with liquids or given directly from the dropper. Children (2 to 12 years): 0.6 mL orally up to 4 times daily with meals and at bedtime.

Supplied: Each 0.6 mL contains: simethicone 40 mg in a natural orange flavored base (1 mL=simethicone 66.7 mg). Nonmedicinal ingredients: carbomer, citric acid, hydroxypropyl methylcellulose, natural orange flavor, polyoxyethylene 8 stearate, sodium citrate and water. Alcohol-, artificial flavor-, color-, lactose- and sugar-free. Bottles of 30 mL with a graduated dropper.

BABY'S OWN™ OINTMENT
Block Drug

Zinc Oxide

Skin Protective

Indications: Prevention and relief of diaper rash.

Warnings: For external use only. Avoid contact with eyes. If eye contact occurs, rinse thoroughly with water. Discontinue use if rash occurs or worsens. Keep out of the reach of children.

Dosage: To relieve diaper rash apply 3 or more times daily at first sign of redness. To prevent diaper rash apply liberally, especially at bedtime and when exposure to wet diapers may be prolonged.

Supplied: Each g of emollient ointment contains: zinc oxide 11.3%. Tubes of 57 g.

Reviewed 1998

BABY'S OWN™ TEETHING GEL
Block Drug

Benzyl Alcohol

Topical Analgesic

Indications: For quick relief from teething pain by its topical anesthetic effect on sore gums.

Warnings: Keep this and all medications out of the reach of children.

Dosage: Wash hands. Apply small amount directly to sore gums. Repeat, if necessary, every 4 hours. If symptoms persist, consult physician.

Supplied: Each pleasantly flavored g of gel contains: benzyl alcohol 2.5%. Aluminum tubes of 15 g.

BACID®
Rhône-Poulenc Rorer

Lactobacillus acidophilus

Flora Modifier

Indications: To assist in the restoration and maintenance of the normal physiological and bacterial flora of the oral and intestinal tracts. Has been used in the prevention and treatment of postantibiotic stomatitis and microbial diarrheas; also in aphthous and herpetic stomatitis.

Precautions: Should be stored in a refrigerator at a temperature of 10°C, or below to maintain potency. Not to be used in the preparation of yogurt or acidophilus milk.

Dosage: 2 capsules 2 to 4 times daily, taken preferably with milk or lactose. For infants or others unable to take capsules, the contents of the capsules may be added to semi-solid food.

Supplied: Each light orange, hard gel capsule, contains: a viable human strain of Lactobacillus acidophilus. Nonmedicinal ingredients: butylated hydroxytoluene, FD&C Yellow No 10, FD&C Yellow No 6, gelatin, magnesium stearate, mineral oil, skim-milk powder and sodium carboxymethylcellulose. Tartrazine-free. Odor similar to milk powder. Bottles of 50 and 100.

(Shown in Product Recognition Section)

BACIGUENT®
Johnson & Johnson • Merck

Bacitracin

Topical Antibiotic

Indications: For the treatment and prevention of infection in minor cuts, wounds and burns.

Warnings: For external use only. Avoid contact with eyes. If contact occurs, wash thoroughly with water. Use should be discontinued if condition worsens. No refrigeration required.

Precautions: Discontinue if sensitization occurs. Prolonged use may result in the overgrowth of nonsusceptible organisms, particularly monilia. If this occurs, discontinue therapy and institute appropriate measures.

Dosage: Clean affected area, then apply liberally one or more times daily to injured skin surface and cover with a dry, sterile, surgical gauze dressing.

Supplied: Each g of topical ointment contains: bacitracin 500 IU. Nonmedicinal ingredients: mineral oil, white petrolatum and wool fat. Paraben-free. Tubes of 7.5, 15 and 25 g.

BACITRACIN
Pharmacia & Upjohn

Antibiotic

Pharmacology: Bacitracin, an antibiotic substance derived from cultures of B. subtilis (Tracey), exerts pronounced antibacterial action in vitro against a variety of gram-positive and a few gram-negative organisms.

However, among systemic diseases, only staphylococcal infections qualify for consideration of bacitracin therapy. Bacitracin is assayed against a standard and its activity is expressed in units, 1 mg having a potency of not less than 50 units.

Susceptibility Plate Testing: If the Kirby-Bauer method of disc susceptibility is used, a 10-unit bacitracin disc should give a zone over 13 mm when tested against a bacitracin-susceptible strain of S. aureus. Absorption of bacitracin following i.m. injection is rapid and complete. A dose of 200 or 300 units/kg every 6 hours gives serum levels of 0.2 to 2 μg/mL in individuals with normal renal function. The drug is excreted slowly by glomerular filtration. It is widely distributed in all body organs and is demonstrable in ascitic and pleural fluids after i.m. injection.

Indications: The use of i.m. bacitracin is indicated in the treatment of infants with pneumonia and empyema caused by staphylococci shown to be susceptible to the drug.

Bacitracin solutions, applied locally in the form of compresses or instillations, may be used once or twice daily in secondarily infected wounds, ulcers, pyodermas and other superficial skin infections and in superficial infections of the eye caused by bacitracin-susceptible organisms. Bacitracin solutions may be instilled into the nasal cavities or administered by inhalation as an aerosol in the treatment of bacitracin-susceptible infections of the upper and lower respiratory tract. In severe or extensive infections, appropriate antibacterial therapy should be given in addition to local treatment with bacitracin.

Contraindications: In those individuals with a history of previous hypersensitivity or toxic reaction to it.

Warnings: I.M.: Nephrotoxicity: Bacitracin in parenteral (i.m.) therapy may cause renal failure due to tubular and glomerular necrosis. Its use should be restricted to infants with staphylococcal pneumonia and empyema when due to organisms shown to be susceptible to bacitracin. It should be used only where adequate laboratory facilities are available and when constant supervision of the patient is possible.

Renal function should be carefully determined prior to and daily during therapy. The recommended daily dose should not be exceeded and fluid intake and urinary output maintained at proper levels to avoid kidney toxicity. If renal toxicity occurs, the drug should be discontinued. The concurrent use of other nephrotoxic drugs, particularly streptomycin, kanamycin, polymyxin B, polymyxin E (colistin), neomycin, and viomycin, should be avoided.

Precautions: See Warnings for precautions in regard to kidney toxicity associated with i.m. use of bacitracin.

Adequate fluid intake should be maintained orally or, if necessary, by parenteral method.

As with other antibiotics, use of this drug may result in overgrowth of nonsusceptible organisms, including fungi. If superinfection occurs, appropriate therapy should be instituted.

Adverse Effects: Nephrotoxic: albuminuria, cylindruria, azotemia, rising blood levels without any increase in dosage.

Others: nausea and vomiting. Pain at site of injection. Skin rashes.

Dosage: To be administered i.m.

Infants: For infants under 2 500 g: 900 units/kg/24 hours in 2 or 3 divided doses. For infants over 2 500 g: 1 000 units/kg/24 hours in 2 or 3 divided doses. I.M. injections of the solution should be given in the upper outer quadrant of the buttocks, alternating right and left and avoiding multiple injections in the same region because of the transient pain following injection.

Preparation of Solutions: Should be dissolved in sodium chloride injection containing 2% procaine. The concentration of the antibiotic in the solution should not be less than 5 000 units/mL nor more than 10 000 units/mL.

Diluents containing parabens should not be used to reconstitute bacitracin; cloudy solutions and precipitate formation have occurred. Reconstitution of the 50 000 unit vial with 9.8 mL of diluent will result in a concentration of 5 000 units/mL.

To be administered topically.

Preparation of Solution: Solutions for topical application are prepared by dissolving bacitracin in Sterile Water for Injection or Sodium Chloride Injection in amounts to give the following concentrations: skin, 500 units/mL; ophthalmic solutions, 500 to 1 000 units/mL; intranasal therapy, 250 units/mL; aerosol, 500 to 1 000 units/mL.

Supplied: Each vial contains: bacitracin 50 000 units. Store unreconstituted bacitracin in a refrigerator 2 to 8°C. Solutions are rapidly inactivated at room temperature but are stable for 1 week when stored in a refrigerator 2 to 8°C.

BACITRACIN ZINC
Roberts

Bacitracin

Topical Antibiotic

Supplied: Each g of ointment contains: bacitracin (as zinc) 500 USP units in lanolin-free mineral oil, white petrolatum. Cartoned tubes of 15 and 25 g; jars of 450 g.

BACLOFEN ℞
BDH

Muscle Relaxant—Antispasticity Agent

Supplied: 10 mg: Each flat, white, beveled-edged tablet, marked BN breakline 10 on one side and G on the reverse, contains: baclofen 10 mg. Alcohol-, bisulfite-, parabens- and tartrazine-free. Bottles of 100 and 500.

20 mg: Each flat, white, beveled-edged tablet, scored and marked BN breakline 20 on one side and G on the reverse, contains: baclofen 20 mg. Alcohol-, bisulfite, parabens- and tartrazine-free. Bottles of 100.

BACTIGRAS®
Smith & Nephew

Chlorhexidine Acetate

Topical Antibacterial

Pharmacology: Chlorhexidine inhibits the growth of vegetative gram-positive and gram-negative organisms in vitro. Acid fast bacilli and heat resistant bacterial spores are not susceptible to the lethal action of chlorhexidine even in strong concentrations at room temperature. Chlorhexidine has greater activity in alkaline media. Adsorption of chlorhexidine on organic matter, pus, serum, blood, etc. will cause a reduction in the amount of chlorhexidine available for reaction with bacterial cells. Less than 0.25% of the chlorhexidine administered is absorbed into the body. With systemic doses, rats passed 85% of the amount administered in the feces and urine within 48 hours and 95% within 144 hours.

Indications: For adjunctive treatment and prevention of infection in skin loss lesions, including wounds, burns and ulcers.

Contraindications: In patients with a known, or suspected, sensitivity to chlorhexidine.

Precautions: Due to the cationic properties of chlorhexidine, Bactigras is incompatible with anionic surfactants and other anionic compounds. One layer of Tulle Gras dressing only should be applied directly to the surface of lesions being treated, and this should be done with forceps under sterile conditions. Bactigras should not be used if the seal or wrapper is broken.

Adverse Effects: Photosensitivity, hypersensitivity and contact eczema have been observed, but the incidence has been very low. Since its introduction on the market in the U.K., reports indicate that the tulle presentation of chlorhexidine acetate causes only slight skin irritation or sensitization and that there is no pain on application.

Overdose: Symptoms and Treatment: As a topical preparation, there have been no reports of chlorhexidine acetate overdosage by a systemic route. Accidental systemic administration of chlorhexidine solutions have failed to yield any specific ill effects which were attributed to chlorhexidine.

Reports indicate that chlorhexidine soaks have been used in the U.K. on body area wounds of up to 50% with no evidence of toxicity. Cases of accidental systemic administration of chlorhexidine of 6 to 40 mg have been reported and no symptoms of toxicity were evident.

Dosage: Adults and Children: Dressings may be changed daily but frequency of application will depend upon the clinical circumstances (average: every 2 to 4 days).

It is intended that the dressing will be principally used on up to 15% body area wounds for adults, (10% body area wounds for children). Although there is insufficient evidence to establish the safety of more extensive use, such use on larger area wounds may be considered when in the opinion of the physician, the expected benefit outweighs the potential risks. (Reports indicate that chlorhexidine acetate 0.1% solutions have been used on body area wounds of up to 50% without ill effect.) The dressing is to be applied directly to the wound surface, 1 layer only, with forceps, under sterile conditions.

Duration of administration will range from a few days to several months in extreme cases, depending upon the nature and severity of the wound. Treatment should be continued until satisfactory healing has occurred or until the wound site is ready for grafting. The drug should not be withdrawn from the therapeutic regimen while there remains the possibility of infection unless overt infection occurs, requiring specific alternative therapy, or a significant adverse reaction occurs.

Supplied: Tulle Gras as a gauze of leno weave impregnated with soft paraffin USP containing 0.5% chlorhexidine acetate BP. Dressings are available in an individually wrapped, sterile format of 10 cm×10 cm, 15 cm×20 cm in cartons of 10, and 5 cm×5 cm, 10 cm×10 cm in cartons of 50. Store flat at controlled room temperature (15 to 25°C).

BACTRIM™ ROCHE® ℞
Roche

Trimethoprim—Sulfamethoxazole

Antibacterial

Pharmacology: Trimethoprim plus sulfamethoxazole block 2 consecutive steps in the biosynthesis of nucleic acids and proteins essential to many bacteria. Sulfamethoxazole inhibits bacterial synthesis of dihydrofolic acid by competing with para-aminobenzoic acid. Trimethoprim blocks the production of tetrahydrofolic acid from dihydrofolic acid by reversibly inhibiting the required enzyme, dihydrofolate reductase.

The effect of the dual consecutive action is to reduce the minimum inhibitory concentration of each agent (synergism) and to convert a bacteriostatic action to a bactericidal action.

Indications: For treatment of the following infections when associated with the gram-positive and gram-negative organisms: H. influenzae, N. gonorrhoeae, E. coli, Klebsiella, E. aerogenes, P. mirabilis, P. vulgaris, S. typhi, S. paratyphi, S. typhimurium, S. enteritidis, Shigella species, S. pyogenes, S. viridans, S. albus, S. aureus and S. pneumoniae.

Upper and lower respiratory tract infections (particularly chronic bronchitis and including acute and chronic otitis media).

Acute, recurrent, and chronic urinary tract infections.

Genital tract infections (uncomplicated gonococcal urethritis).

Gastrointestinal tract infections.

P. carinii pneumonitis.

The local prevalence of resistance to Bactrim among bacteria relevant to the infection should be known when Bactrim is prescribed on an empiric basis to exclude resistance, especially in infections likely to be caused by a partially sensitive pathogen, the isolate should be tested for sensitivity. Sensitivity to Bactrim can be determined by standardized methods such as the disk or dilution tests recommended by the National Committee for Clinical Laboratory Standards (NCCLS). The following criteria (see Table I) for susceptibility are recommended by the NCCLS.

Table I—Bactrim Roche

Criteria for Susceptibility

	Disk test[a], diameter of inhibition zone (mm)	Dilution test[b], MIC (μg/mL) TMP	SMZ
Sensitive	≥16	≤2	≤38
Partially sensitive	11-15	4	76
Resistant	≤10	≥8	≥152

[a] Disk: 1.25 μg trimethoprim (TMP) and 23.75 μg sulfamethoxazole (SMZ).

[b] TMP and SMZ in a ratio of 1 to 19.

Bactrim for Infusion is indicated for the treatment of serious systemic infections such as meningitis and septicemia caused by susceptible organisms as well as in the treatment of Pneumocystis carinii pneumonitis, when oral administration is not practical.

The combination of trimethoprim plus sulfamethoxazole is not indicated in infections associated with Pseudomonas, Mycoplasma or viruses. It should not be used in the treatment of group A beta-hemolytic streptococcal pharyngitis.

Contraindications: In patients with evidence of known hypersensitivity to trimethoprim or sulfonamides or any of the excipients, marked liver parenchymal damage, blood dyscrasias or marked renal impairment when measurements of drug concentrations cannot be done (see Warnings and Precautions).

Bactrim should not be given to premature neonates or infants less than 2 months of age (see Precautions).

Pregnancy and *Lactation:* Not to be used in pregnancy or during nursing. If pregnancy cannot be excluded, the possible risks should be balanced against the expected therapeutic effect.

Warnings: Fatalities associated with the administration of sulfonamides, although rare, have occurred due to severe reactions, including Stevens-Johnson syndrome, toxic epidermal necrolysis, fulminant hepatic necrosis, agranulocytosis, aplastic anemia and other blood dyscrasias.

There is an increased risk of severe adverse reactions in elderly patients, particularly when complicating conditions exist, for example, impaired kidney and/or liver function or concomitant use of other drugs (in which case the risk may be related to the dosage and duration of treatment). Severe skin reactions, generalized bone marrow suppression or a specific decrease in platelets (with or without purpura) are the most frequently reported severe adverse reactions in elderly patients. In elderly patients concurrently receiving certain diuretics, primarily thiazides, an increased incidence of thrombocytopenia with purpura has been reported.

Patients with Acquired Immunodeficiency Syndrome (AIDS) may not tolerate or respond to the combination of trimethoprim plus sulfamethoxazole in the same manner as non-AIDS patients because of their unique immune dysfunction. The incidence of side effects, particularly rash, fever and leukopenia, with trimethoprim plus sulfamethoxazole therapy in AIDS patients who are being treated for Pneumocystis carinii pneumonitis has been reported to be greatly increased compared with the incidence normally associated with the use of trimethoprim plus sulfamethoxazole in non-AIDS patients.

In glucose-6-phosphate dehydrogenase deficient individuals, hemolysis may occur. This reaction is frequently dose-related. Therefore, Bactrim should not be given to patients with G6PD deficiency unless absolutely essential, and then only in minimal doses.

Precautions: As with other sulfonamide preparations, critical appraisal of benefit versus risk should be done in patients with liver or renal damage, urinary obstruction, blood dyscrasias, allergies or bronchial asthma. Clinical signs such as rash, sore throat, fever, pallor, purpura or jaundice may be early indications of severe reactions such as Stevens-Johnson syndrome, toxic epidermal necrolysis, fulminant hepatic necrosis, agranulocytosis, aplastic anemia or other blood dyscrasias. In rare instances, a skin rash may be followed by a severe reaction. Therefore, Bactrim should be discontinued immediately at the first appearance of skin rash or any sign of serious adverse reaction. As a general precaution, complete blood counts should be done frequently in patients receiving sulfonamides.

Urinalysis and renal function tests should be performed regularly in patients undergoing long-term treatment wiht Bactrim (particularly in patients with kidney failure). During treatment, adequate fluid intake and urinary output should be ensured to prevent crystalluria and stone formation.

Interference with folate metabolism is possible in patients on long-term therapy, in patients predisposed to folate deficiency (i.e., the elderly, chronic alcoholics and rheumatoid arthritics), in malabsorption syndromes, in malnutrition states or during the treatment of epilepsy with anticonvulsant drugs such as phenytoin, primidone or barbiturates. Regular blood counts are advised in these patients. Changes indicative of folic acid impairment have, in certain specific situations, been reversed by folinic acid therapy.

In order to minimize the risk of undesirable reactions, the duration of treatment with Bactrim should be as short as possible, particularly in elderly patients.

If Bactrium is given over a prolonged period, regular blood counts are required. If a significant reduction in the count of any formed blood element is noted, Bactrim should be discontinued. Other than in exceptional cases, Bactrim should not be given to patients with serious hematological disorders.

The possibility of superinfection with a non-sensitive organism should be borne in mind.

Local irritation and inflammation due to extravascular infiltration have been observed with Bactrim for Infusion. If these occur, the infusion should be discontinued and restarted at another site.

Neonatal Infants: If Bactrim for Infusion is administered on an emergency basis to neonatal infants, a potential complication in this age group is kernicterus.

Pregnancy and *Lactation:* Because both trimethoprim and sulfamethoxazole cross the placental barrier and thus may interfere with folic acid metabolism, Bactrim should only be used during pregnancy if the potential benefit justifies the potential risk to the fetus. It is recommended that pregnant women who are being treated with Bactrim should be given 5 to 10 mg of folic acid daily. During the last stage of pregnancy, treatment with Bactrim should be avoided because of the risk of kernicterus in the neonate.

Both trimethoprim and sulfamethoxazole pass into breast milk. Although the quantity of Bactrim ingested by a breast-fed infant is small, possible risks for the infant (kernicterus, hypersensitivity) should be weighed against the expected therapeutic benefits for the mother.

Patients with Special Diseases and Conditions: In patients with renal impairment, a reduced or less frequent dosage is recommended in order to avoid accumulation of trimethoprim and sulfamethoxazole in the blood (see Dosage). For such patients, serum drug concentration measurements are necessary. Bactrim should not be used when the creatinine clearance is <15 mL/min in order to avoid possible permanent impairment of renal function.

Drug Interactions: PABA or its derivatives antagonize the action of sulfamethoxazole.

Plasma protein binding displacement and/or inhibition of hepatic metabolism may account for a number of interactions between Bactrim and other drugs. Phenylbutazone, oxyphenbutazone, salicylates, sulfinpyrazone, and highly bound oral anticoagulants and sulfonylurea hypoglycemics may increase sulfamethoxazole free plasma concentrations. Bactrim may increase the free plasma concentrations of lesser bound oral anticoagulants and sulfonylurea hypoglycemics and methotrexate. It has been reported that Bactrim may prolong the prothrombin time in patients who are receiving the anticoagulant warfarin. The coagulation time should be reassessed when Bactrim is administered to patients on anticoagulation therapy. Sulfonamides may enhance the hypoglycemic effects of sulfonylurea hypoglycemics.

An increased incidence of thrombocytopenia with purpura has been observed in elderly patients concurrently receiving certain diuretics, primarily thiazides (see Warnings).

Increased digoxin levels can occur with Bactrim therapy, especially in elderly patients. Serum digoxin levels should be monitored.

Bactrim given at common clinical dosage increased the half-life of phenytoin by 39% and decreased the metabolic clearance of phenytoin by 27%. When administering these drugs concurrently, one should be alert for possible excessive phenytoin effect.

Reversible deterioration of renal function, manifested by increased serum creatinine, has been observed in patients treated with trimethoprim-sulfamethoxazole and cyclosporin following renal transplantation. This combined effect is presumably due to the trimethoprim component. A reversible decrease in creatinine clearance in renal function has been observed in patients with normal renal function. This is probably due to reversible inhibition of the tubular secretion of creatinine.

The efficacy of tricyclic antidepressants can decrease when co-administered with Bactrim.

Sulfonamides, including sulfamethoxazole, can compete with protein binding and also with renal transport of methotrexate, thus increasing the free-methotrexate fraction and the systemic exposure to methotrexate.

Occasional reports suggest that patients receiving pyrimethamine as malaria prophylaxis in doses exceeding 25 mg weekly may develop megaloblastic anemia if Bactrim is prescribed concurrently.

Increased sulfamethoxazole blood levels may occur in patients who are also receiving indomethacin.

Increased sulfamethoxazole blood concentrations may occur in patients who are receiving urinary acidifiers.

Drug Laboratory Test Interactions: Bactrim, specifically the trimethoprim component, can interfere with a serum methotrexate assay as determined by the competitive binding protein technique when a bacterial dihydrofolate reductase is used as the binding protein. No interference occurs, however, if methotrexate is measured by a radioimmunoassay.

The presence of trimethoprim and sulfamethoxazole may also interfere with the Jaffe alkaline picrate reaction assay for creatinine, resulting in overestimations of about 10% of the range of normal values.

Adverse Effects: The most common adverse effects are gastrointestinal disturbances (nausea, vomiting, anorexia) and allergic skin reactions (such as skin rash and urticaria).

Gastrointestinal: Nausea, vomiting and gastric intolerance have been observed most frequently. Diarrhea, constipation, flatulence, anorexia, pyrosis, gastritis and gastroenteritis occur infrequently. Glossitis, stomatitis, dyspepsia, dry mouth and black tongue have been occasionally reported. Pseudomembranous enterocolitis, pancreatitis and abdominal pain have also been reported.

Allergic: Skin rash has been observed most frequently. Urticaria, erythema (including erythema multiforme), edema, angioneurotic edema, pruritus, toxicoderma, photosensitivity, dyspnea, drug fever and anaphylactoid reactions (sweating and collapse) have been occasionally reported. Stevens-Johnson syndrome, toxic epidermal necrolysis, allergic myocarditis, exfoliative dermatitis, angioedema, chills, Henoch-Schönlein purpura, serum sickness-like syndrome, generalized allergic reactions, hypersensitivity reactions, generalized skin eruptions, conjunctival and scleral injection, periarteritis nodosa and systemic lupus erythematosus have also been reported. Pulmonary infiltrates as occurs in eosinophilic or allergic alveolitis have been reported in rare instances. They may manifest themselves through symptoms such as cough or shortness of breath. Should such symptoms appear or unexpectedly worsen, the patient should be re-evaluated and discontinuation of Bactrim therapy considered.

Hematologic: Hematological changes have been observed in some patients, particularly the elderly. The great majority of these changes were mild, asymptomatic, and proved reversible on withdrawal of the drug. The reported changes were primarily neutropenia and thrombocytopenia. Those observed less frequently include: leukopenia, aplastic and hemolytic anemia, purpura, agranulocytosis and bone marrow depression. Megaloblastic anemia, hypoprothombinemia, methemoglobinemia, pancytopenia, purpura and eosinophilia have also been reported.

Hepatic: Liver changes (as indicated by abnormal elevations in alkaline phosphatase and serum transaminase levels) occur infrequently. Jaundice has been occasionally reported. Hepatic necrosis and elevation of bilirubin levels have also been reported. Rare cases of hepatitis and cholestasis have been reported.

Genitourinary: Dysuria, oliguria, anuria, hematuria, urgency and functional kidney changes (as indicated by abnormal elevations in blood urea nitrogen, blood non-protein nitrogen, serum creatinine and urine protein concentrations) have been reported occasionally. Renal failure, interstitial nephritis and toxic nephrosis have been reported. Diuresis has occurred rarely in patients receiving sulfonamides, particularly in patients with edema of cardiac origin. Crystalluria has also been reported.

CNS: Headache occurs infrequently. Tremor and vertigo have been occasionally reported. Aseptic meningitis or meningitis-like symptoms, convulsions, peripheral neuritis, ataxia, tinnitus, hallucinations, depression, apathy, nervousness and insomnia have also been reported.

Metabolic Disorders: High dose trimethoprim, as used in patients with P. carinii pneumonia, induces a progressive but reversible increase of serum potassium concentrations in a substantial number of patients. Even at recommended doses, trimethoprim may cause hyperkalemia when administered to patients with underlying disorders of potassium metabolism, renal insufficiency, or who are receiving drugs which induce hyperkalemia. Close monitoring of serum potassium is warranted in these patients. Cases of hypoglycemia in non-diabetic patients treated with trimethoprim-sulfamethoxazole are rarely seen, usually after a few days of therapy. Patients with impaired renal function, liver disease or malnutrition or receiving high doses of trimethoprim-sulfamethoxazole are particularly at risk.

Musculoskeletal: Arthalgia and myalgia have been reported.

Miscellaneous: Tiredness (fatigue), weakness, vision troubles, alopecia and epistaxis have been occasionally reported. Goiter and hypoglycemia have occurred rarely in patients receiving sulfonamides.

Local Tolerance with Bactrim Solution for Infusion: Local reaction, pain and slight irritation on i.v. administration are infrequent. Thrombophlebitis has rarely been observed.

Overdose: Symptoms: Symptoms of acute overdosage may include nausea, vomiting, diarrhea, headache, vertigo, dizziness, mental and visual disturbances; crystalluria, hematuria, and anuria may occur in severe cases. In chronic overdosage bone marrow depression, as manifested as thrombocytopenia or leukopenia, and other blood dyscrasias due to folinic acid deficiency may occur.

Treatment: Remove the drug from the stomach by gastric lavage and/or emesis. If renal function is normal, force fluids orally or parenterally to promote excretion (alkalinization of urine increases sulfamethoxazole excretion). Hemodialysis may be considered in patients with impaired renal function. Peritoneal dialysis is ineffective. The patient should be monitored with blood counts and appropriate blood chemistries. Blood dyscrasias and jaundice are potential late manifestations of overdosage.

There is no known antidote for sulfonamide poisoning; however, calcium folinate (3 to 6 mg i.m. for 5 to 7 days) is an effective antidote for adverse effects in the hemopoietic system caused by trimethoprim.

There has been no experience with deliberate or inadvertent overdosage in humans with Bactrim for Infusion. When repeated doses are required, large volumes of infusion solution may induce fluid overload. Appropriate therapy, e.g., diuretics, may be required.

Dosage: Oral: Bacterial Infections: Adults and children over 12 years: 2 adult tablets or 1 DS tablet twice daily. In severe infections, the dosage may be increased to 3 adult or 1.5 DS tablets twice daily.

Children under 12 years: 3 mg trimethoprim/kg+15 mg sulfamethoxazole/kg twice daily.

Therapy should be continued for at least 5 days or until the patient is asymptomatic for 48 hours or, in the case of urinary infections, until the urine becomes sterile.

As prophylaxis and for Salmonella carriers, 1 adult tablet or ½ DS tablet twice daily.

In acute salmonellosis, therapy should be continued for at least 7 days after defervescence. Carriers should continue therapy until repeated stool cultures are negative.

Uncomplicated Gonorrhea: Adults and children, 2 adult or 1 DS tablet 4 times daily for 2 days.

P. Carinii Pneumonitis: Adults and children, 5 mg trimethoprim/kg+25 mg sulfamethoxazole/kg 4 times daily for at least 14 days.

I.V. Infusion: Bactrim for Infusion may be used in patients who cannot take oral medication or need rapid attainment of high serum concentrations (see Table II).

Parenteral treatment should be terminated and oral treatment instituted as soon as possible.

Method of Dilution: Caution: Bactrim for Infusion must be diluted prior to infusion administration. Direct i.v. injection is not recommended. Do not mix the prepared infusion solution with other drugs or solutions.

Each mL should be diluted with 25 mL of 5% dextrose in water or Ringer's solution or sodium chloride 0.9% solution. The prepared solution must be kept at room temperature (15 to 30°C) and administration should be started within 1 hour of preparation. It should be infused over ½ to 1 hour (after proper dilution).

Note: In those instances where fluid restriction is desirable, each mL of Bactrim for Infusion may be added to 15 mL of 5% dextrose in water or Ringer's solution or sodium chloride 0.9% solution. Under these circumstances the solution should be mixed just prior to use and administration should be completed within 1 hour.

If upon visual inspection there is cloudiness or evidence of precipitation after mixing, the solution should be discarded and a fresh solution prepared.

P. Carinii Pneumonitis: Children and Adults: The recommended daily i.v. dosage is 20 mg trimethoprim/kg+100 mg sulfamethoxazole/kg. This daily dosage is to be divided into 4 equal doses and administered at 6 hour intervals, until oral therapy can be instituted.

Table II—Bactrim Roche

Volume of Undiluted Bactrim for Infusion per Body Weight* (conversion factor 1.25 mL/kg)

Body Weight (kg)	Volume of Undiluted Bactrim for Infusion (mL): Total Daily Dose	Volume of Undiluted Bactrim for Infusion (mL): Doses Every 6 hours (q.i.d.)
5	6.3	1.6
10	12.5	3.1
20	25.0	6.3
40	50.0	12.5
60	75.0	18.8
80	100.0	25.0

*Bactrim for Infusion must be properly diluted (see Method of Dilution) and administered at 6 hour intervals.

Serious Systemic Infections: Adults: The i.v. dosage depends on the severity of the infection. A dose of 160 to 240 mg trimethoprim+800 to 1 200 mg sulfamethoxazole (10 to 15 mL of undiluted solution) may be given every 6, 8 or 12 hours. The dosage must be properly diluted (see Method of Dilution) and infused.

Children: The recommended daily dosage for children is 5 to 10 mg trimethoprim/kg/day and 25 to 50 mg sulfamethoxazole/kg/day. This daily dosage is to be properly diluted and administered in equally divided doses by infusion (see Table III).

Table III—Bactrim Roche

Volume of Undiluted Bactrim for Infusion per Body Weight* (conversion factor 0.31 to 0.63 mL/kg)

Body Weight (kg)	Total Daily Dose	Doses Every 12 hours (b.i.d.)	Doses Every 8 hours (t.i.d.)	Doses Every 6 hours (q.i.d.)
5	1.6 to 3.2	0.8 to 1.6	0.5 to 1.1	0.4 to 0.8
10	3.1 to 6.3	1.6 to 3.2	1.0 to 2.1	0.8 to 1.6
20	6.2 to 12.6	3.1 to 6.3	2.1 to 4.2	1.6 to 3.2
40	12.4 to 25.2	6.2 to 12.6	4.1 to 8.4	3.1 to 6.3
60	18.6 to 37.8	9.3 to 18.9	6.2 to 12.6	4.7 to 9.5

(Table III column headings as printed: "Volume of Undiluted Bactrim for Infusion (mL)" spans all dose columns.)

*Bactrim for Infusion must be properly diluted (see Method of Dilution) and administered in equally divided doses.

Bactrim Roche (cont'd)

Impaired Renal Function: When renal function is impaired, a reduced dosage should be employed using Table IV.

Table IV—Bactrim Roche

Dosage—Impaired Renal Function

Creatinine Clearance (mL/s)	Recommended Dose Regimen
0.5 (Above 30 mL/min)	Usual standard regimen
0.25 to 0.5 (15 to 30 mL/min)	One half the usual regimen
0.25 (Below 15 mL/min)	Use not recommended

$$\text{Creatinine clearance corrected for body surface area} = \frac{\mu\text{mol/L (urine creatinine)}}{\mu\text{mol/L (serum creatinine)}} \times \text{mL/s} \times \frac{1.73}{A}$$

(where A is the body surface area in m²).

Supplied: Adult Tablets: Each white, round, biconvex, tablet with ROCHE on one face and indented score on the other, contains: trimethoprim 80 mg and sulfamethoxazole 400 mg. Nonmedicinal ingredients: magnesium stearate, povidone, sodium docusate and sodium starch glycolate. Energy: 0.9 kJ (0.2 kcal). Sodium: <1 mmol (2.8 mg). Paraben-, sulfite-, tartrazine-, lactose-, and gluten-free. Bottles of 100.

DS Tablets: Each film-coated, white, oval, biconvex tablet with ROCHE 800+160 on one face and indented score on the other, contains: trimethoprim 160 mg and sulfamethoxazole 800 mg. Nonmedicinal ingredients: hydroxypropylmethylcellulose, magnesium stearate, polyethylene glycol, povidone, sodium docusate, sodium starch glycolate, talc and titanium dioxide. Energy: 1.7 kJ (0.4 kcal). Sodium: <1 mmol (6.0 mg). Gluten-, lactose-, paraben-, sulfite- and tartrazine-free. Bottles of 100.

Solution for Infusion: Each mL contains: sulfamethoxazole 80 mg, trimethoprim 16 mg, benzyl alcohol 10 mg as preservative, propylene glycol 400 mg, alcohol 100 mg, sodium metabisulfite 1 mg, diethanolamine 3 mg, and sodium hydroxide to adjust the pH to 10, for infusion with 5% dextrose in water or Ringer's solution or sodium chloride 0.9% solution. Sodium: <1 mmol (8.1 mg)/mL. Paraben-free. Vials of 10 mL, packs of 10. Vials of 30 mL.

Suspension: Each 5 mL of sweet, pink, cherry-flavored suspension contains: trimethoprim 40 mg and sulfamethoxazole 200 mg. Nonmedicinal ingredients: amaranth, ethanol 0.24%, flavor, glycerin, methylparaben, microcrystalline cellulose, polysorbate 80, ponceau 4R, propylparaben, sodium carboxymethylcellulose, sodium cyclamate, sorbitol and water. Energy: 50.9 kJ (12.1 kcal). Sodium: <1 mmol. Gluten-, lactose-, sucrose-, sulfite- and tartrazine-free. Bottles of 400 mL. Shake well before using.

Store all dosage forms at 15 to 30°C in a light-resistant container. Protect from light.

(Shown in Product Recognition Section)

BACTROBAN®
SmithKline Beecham

Mupirocin

Topical Antibiotic

Pharmacology: Mupirocin exerts a bactericidal action against sensitive organisms by inhibiting bacterial protein synthesis. It reversibly and specifically binds to bacterial isoleucyl transfer-RNA synthetase.

Indications: For the topical treatment of the following when caused by sensitive strains of staphylococcus and streptococcus species: impetigo, superficially infected dermatoses, lesions which are moist and weeping.

For abrasions, minor cuts and wounds, the use of mupirocin may prevent the development of infection by sensitive Gram-positive organisms.

No cross-resistance has been shown between mupirocin and other commonly used antibiotics.

Contraindications: In patients with a history of hypersensitivity to mupirocin or to other ointments containing polyethylene glycols.

Warnings: This mupirocin ointment formulation is not suitable for ophthalmic or intranasal use, or in conjunction with cannulae.

When mupirocin ointment is used on the face, care should be taken to avoid the eyes.

Polyethylene glycol (PEG) can be absorbed from open wounds and damaged skin. It is excreted by the kidneys. As with other PEG based ointments, mupirocin ointment should not be used in conditions where absorption of large quantities of PEG is possible, especially if there is evidence of moderate or severe renal impairment.

In the rare event of a possible sensitization reaction or severe local irritation occurring with the use of mupirocin, treatment should be discontinued and appropriate alternative therapy for the infection instituted.

Precautions: Use of topical antibiotics occasionally allows overgrowth of non-susceptible organisms. If this occurs, or irritation or sensitization develop, treatment should be discontinued and appropriate therapy instituted.

Pregnancy and *Lactation:* Safety in the treatment of infections during pregnancy has not been established. If administration to pregnant patients is considered necessary, its potential benefits should be weighed against the possible hazards to the fetus. Caution should be exercised when mupirocin ointment is administered to nursing mothers.

If a cracked nipple is to be treated, lactation from the affected breast should be maintained by manual expression until the end of treatment. During this time, milk from the affected breast should be discarded.

Adverse Effects: The following local adverse reactions have been reported during therapy with mupirocin: itching, burning, erythema, stinging and dryness. It was not usually necessary to discontinue therapy due to these adverse reactions. Cutaneous sensitization reactions to mupirocin or the ointment base have been reported rarely.

Overdose: Symptoms and Treatment: Overdosage has not been known to occur during topical therapy with mupirocin ointment.

Dosage: A small amount of the ointment should be applied to the affected area 3 times daily for up to 10 days, depending on the response. The area treated may be covered with a gauze dressing if desired.

Supplied: Each g of ointment contains: mupirocin 20 mg (2%) in a bland water-soluble ointment base consisting of polyethylene glycol 400 and polyethylene glycol 3 350 (polyethylene glycol ointment, USP). Tubes of 15 and 30 g. Store at room temperature.

BALMINIL® CAMPHORUB
Rougier

Camphor—Menthol—Eucalyptol

Analgesic

Supplied: Each g of ointment contains: camphor 6.5%, menthol 2% and eucalyptol 1.4%. Nonmedicinal ingredients: petrolatum. Alcohol-, gluten-, lactose-, parabens-, sulfite- and tartrazine-free. Jars of 130 mL.

New Product 1998

BALMINIL® DECONGESTANT
Rougier

Pseudoephedrine HCl

Decongestant

Supplied: Each 5 mL of violet, grape-flavored syrup contains: pseudoephedrine HCl 30 mg. Also contains sodium. Energy: 40 kJ (9.4 kcal). Alcohol-, bisulfite-, gluten-, lactose-, parabens- and tartrazine-free. Bottles of 100, 250 and 2 000 mL.

BALMINIL® DM
Rougier

Dextromethorphan HBr

Antitussive

Supplied: Solution (sucrose-free): Each 5 mL of orange, melon-flavored solution contains: dextromethorphan HBr 15 mg. Energy: 29.8 kJ (7 kcal). Alcohol-, gluten-, parabens-, sucrose-, sulfite- and tartrazine-free. Bottles of 100, 250 and 2 000 mL.

Syrup: Each 5 mL of red, cherry-flavored syrup contains: dextromethorphan HBr 15 mg. Energy: 51 kJ (12 kcal). Alcohol-, gluten-, parabens-, sulfite- and tartrazine-free. Bottles of 100, 250 and 2 000 mL.

BALMINIL® DM CHILDREN
Rougier

Dextromethorphan HBr

Antitussive

Supplied: Each 5 mL of orange-colored, orange-flavored, transparent liquid contains: dextromethorphan HBr 7.5 mg. Energy: 40 kJ (9.4 kcal). Alcohol-, gluten-, lactose-, paraben-, sulfite- and tartrazine-free. Amber plastic bottles of 100 mL.

BALMINIL® DM + DECONGESTANT
Rougier

Pseudoephedrine HCl—Dextromethorphan HBr

Decongestant—Antitussive

Supplied: Each 5 mL of purple-colored, fruit-flavored syrup contains: pseudoephedrine HCl 30 mg and dextromethorphan HBr 15 mg. Energy: 40 kJ (9.4 kcal). Alcohol-, gluten-, parabens-, sulfite- and tartrazine-free. Bottles of 100 and 250 mL.

BALMINIL® DM + DECONGESTANT + EXPECTORANT
Rougier

Dextromethorphan HBr—Pseudoephedrine HCl—Guaifenesin

Antitussive—Decongestant—Expectorant

Supplied: Extra-Strength: Each 5 mL of reddish-pink, minty-raspberry and menthol flavored syrup contains: dextromethorphan HBr 15 mg, pseudoephedrine HCl 30 mg and guaifenesin 200 mg. Sweetened with glycerin and sodium saccharine. Energy: 29.75 kJ (7 kcal). Alcohol-, gluten-, parabens-, sulfite- and tartrazine-free. Bottles of 100 and 250 mL.

Regular Strength: Each 5 mL of reddish-pink, minty-raspberry and menthol flavored syrup contains: dextromethorphan HBr 15 mg, pseudoephedrine HCl 30 mg and guaifenesin 100 mg. Sweetened with glycerin and sodium saccharine. Energy: 29.75 kJ (7 kcal). Alcohol-, gluten-, parabens-, sulfite- and tartrazine-free. Bottles of 100 and 250 mL.

BALMINIL® DM + EXPECTORANT
Rougier

Dextromethorphan HBr—Guaifenesin

Antitussive—Expectorant

Supplied: Extra-Strength: Each 5 mL of reddish-pink, minty-grape and menthol flavored syrup contains: dextromethorphan HBr 15 mg and guaifenesin 200 mg. Sweetened with glycerin and sodium saccharine. Energy: 29.75 kJ (7 kcal). Alcohol-, gluten-, parabens-, sulfite- and tartrazine-free. Bottles of 100 and 250 mL.

Regular Strength: Each 5 mL of reddish-pink, wild cherry and menthol flavored syrup contains: dextromethorphan HBr 15 mg and guaifenesin 100 mg. Sweetened with sorbitol and sodium saccharine. Energy: 27.6 kJ (6.5 kcal). Alcohol-, gluten-, parabens-, sulfite- and tartrazine-free. Bottles of 100 and 250 mL.

BALMINIL® EXPECTORANT
Rougier

Guaifenesin

Expectorant

Supplied: Solution (sucrose-free): Each 5 mL of pink, wild cherry citrus flavored syrup contains: guaifenesin 100 mg. Energy: 34.5 kJ (8.1 kcal). Alcohol-, gluten-, parabens-, sucrose-, sulfite- and tartrazine-free. Bottles of 100, 250 and 2 000 mL.

Syrup: Each 5 mL of pink, menthol flavored syrup contains: guaifenesin 100 mg. Energy: 34.0 kJ (8.0 kcal). Alcohol-, gluten-, parabens-, sulfite- and tartrazine-free. Bottles of 100, 250 and 2 000 mL.

BALNETAR®

Westwood-Squibb

Coal Tar

Emollient—Antipruritic

Supplied: Each mL contains: coal tar solution (equivalent to 2.5% coal tar, USP) in a water-dispersible emollient base. Nonmedicinal ingredients: fragrance, lanolin oil, laureth-4, mineral oil, PEG-4 dilaurate and sodium dioctyl sulfosuccinate. Bottles of 230 mL.

BARBITURATES ◈

General Monograph, CPhA

Amobarbital
Butabarbital
Pentobarbital
Phenobarbital
Secobarbital

Anticonvulsant—Sedative-Hypnotic

This monograph has been compiled by CPhA. It may contain information different from that approved by Therapeutic Products Programme, Health Canada, and the pharmaceutical manufacturers' approval has not been requested.

Pharmacology: Barbiturates are nonselective central nervous system (CNS) depressants, capable of producing all degrees of depression from mild sedation and hypnosis to general anaesthesia, deep coma and death. The extent of CNS depression varies with the route of administration, dose and pharmacokinetic characteristics of the particular barbiturate. Patient specific factors such as age, physical or emotional state and the concomitant use of other drugs will also affect response.

The mechanism of action of barbiturates is not completely known. They may act by enhancing and/or mimicking the synaptic action of gamma-aminobutyric acid (GABA), an inhibitory neurotransmitter. The sedative-hypnotic action of barbiturates may be due to an inhibition of conduction in the reticular formation resulting in a decrease in the number of impulses reaching the cerebral cortex.

Anticonvulsant activity may result from a reduction in CNS synaptic transmission and an increase in the threshold for electrical stimulation of the motor cortex. Phenobarbital is the only barbiturate with anticonvulsant activity at subhypnotic doses.

The therapeutic index of barbiturates is narrow. Amounts needed to relieve anxiety and those causing general CNS depression are not greatly different. Therefore, the use of barbiturates as anxiolytics is almost always accompanied by some degree of impairment of cognitive function. Supratherapeutic doses lead to marked impairment of mental and motor faculties i.e. distortion of judgment, clouding of perception, slurring of speech and ataxia. In some patients however, (especially children and the elderly), drowsiness may be paradoxically preceded by transient euphoria, elation, excitement and confusion.

Pharmacokinetics: See Table I. After oral administration, absorption is usually rapid and relatively complete. The sodium salts undergo rapid dissolution and are absorbed more quickly than their corresponding free acids. The rate of absorption is increased when the barbiturate is formulated as a liquid, when the stomach is empty and when alcohol is ingested concurrently. The onset of action following rectal administration is similar to that following oral administration. After i.v. administration, the onset of action is immediate for amobarbital and pentobarbital and within 5 minutes for phenobarbital. The onset of action following i.m. administration is slightly faster than when the drugs are administered orally or rectally.

Once absorbed the barbiturates are rapidly distributed to all tissues and fluids. High concentrations appear in the brain, liver and kidneys. Secobarbital has the highest degree of lipid solubility and thus the fastest distribution, phenobarbital is the least lipid soluble and has the slowest distribution. Barbiturates readily cross the placenta and are excreted into breast milk. If administered i.v., fetal blood concentrations are approximately equal to maternal serum concentration; if administered orally fetal concentrations are less than maternal levels.

Barbiturates are slowly metabolized and/or conjugated in the liver and then excreted renally. Amobarbital, butabarbital, pentobarbital and secobarbital are almost completely metabolized. Due to its lower lipid solubility, phenobarbital is not metabolized as extensively and almost 25% is excreted unchanged in the urine. Metabolic elimination is influenced by age (being slower in the elderly and infants), chronic liver disease and other drugs.

Table I—Barbiturates

Pharmacokinetics

Drug	Onset of Action* (minutes)	Half-life (hours)	Duration of Action (hours)
Amobarbital	45-60	8-42	6-8
Butabarbital	45-60	34-42	6-8
Pentobarbital	10-15	15-48	3-4
Phenobarbital	60	80-120	10-12
Secobarbital	10-15	15-40	3-4

* oral administration.

Indications: Barbiturates are indicated as hypnotics in the treatment of insomnia and as sedatives in other conditions including use as preanesthetics in surgery or to relieve the symptoms of anxiety or tension resulting from emotional, physical or situational stress. They are indicated in certain cases of increased intracranial pressure and in the treatment of prolonged status epilepticus which is refractory to standard treatment.

Phenobarbital is indicated for the control of generalized tonic-clonic and complex partial seizures.

Contraindications: Not to be administered to patients who are known to be hypersensitive to barbituric acid derivatives. Patients with porphyria, severe respiratory depression or pulmonary insufficiency, renal impairment, hepatic impairment, sleep apnea, suicidal potential, alcoholism or drug dependence. Not to be used in the presence of uncontrolled pain as paradoxical excitement may be produced. Barbiturates should not be administered to elderly patients who exhibit nocturnal confusion or restlessness from sedative hypnotic drugs or to persons who are known to be, or are likely to become, dependent on sedative hypnotic medications.

Precautions: Prolonged use of barbiturates, even in therapeutic dosages, may result in psychologic and physiologic dependence. Patients may escalate dosage without medical advice. Withdrawal symptoms may occur following abrupt termination of hypnotic doses causing nightmares or insomnia, sweating, irritability, tremor, weight loss, anorexia or after chronic use of large doses, resulting in delirium, seizures, or death. Withdrawal should be cautious and gradual.

Rarely, rickets and osteomalacia have been reported following prolonged usage of barbiturates due to increased metabolism of vitamin D.

Barbiturates should be used with caution in patients with impaired liver function or in patients with a history of drug dependence or abuse. Caution is essential when the drug is administered in the presence of any respiratory difficulty. Special care should be taken when barbiturates are administered to patients in whom the hypnotic effect may be prolonged or intensified, as in those suffering from shock, hepatic dysfunction, uremia, or after recent administration of other respiratory depressants.

Since barbiturates are potent CNS depressants, i.v. administration should not be attempted without adequate provisions for supporting respiration and circulation. Rapid injection can cause cardiovascular collapse. Slow administration will usually prevent this occurrence but may cause apnea, laryngospasm, coughing, or other respiratory difficulties.

I.M. injection should not exceed a volume of 5 mL at any one site because of possible tissue damage.

Barbiturate solutions are highly alkaline. Extreme care should be exercised to avoid extravasation or intra-arterial injection. Extravascular injection may cause local tissue damage with subsequent necrosis. The consequences of intra-arterial injection may vary from transient pain along the course of the artery to gangrene of the limb. Signs of accidental injection by this route include, in addition to pain, delayed onset of hypnosis, pallor and cyanosis of the extremity and patchy discoloration of the skin. Any complaint of pain in the limb warrants stopping the injection.

Hypotension may result from i.v. administration of the drug, particularly in patients with hypertension. Slow administration will usually prevent this occurrence.

Solutions which appear cloudy or in which a precipitate has formed should not be used.

Occupational Hazards: Barbiturates may impair the mental and/or physical abilities required for the performance of potentially hazardous tasks such as driving a vehicle or operating machinery. The concomitant use of alcohol or other CNS depressants may have an additive effect. Patients should be warned accordingly. The incidence of fractures due to falls may be increased, particularly in the elderly. Following use of barbiturates in office procedures, warn patients against operating motor vehicles for the remainder of the day.

Drug Interactions: Most drug interactions have been documented with phenobarbital, however they are likely applicable to other barbiturates as well. The barbiturates are inducers of hepatic microsomal enzymes, and are capable of increasing the clearance of many hepatically metabolized drugs. This can result in two concerns: i) decrease in or loss of effectiveness of other drugs during barbiturate use; ii) increase in effect and even frank toxicity on discontinuation of the barbiturate.

When adding or deleting any barbiturate to or from the patient's therapeutic regimen, pharmacotherapy must be monitored closely as dosage adjustment may be necessary.

Anticonvulsants: Phenytoin: When phenobarbital is used with phenytoin, concentrations of either or both drugs may be increased, decreased or unchanged. While phenobarbital may induce the metabolism of phenytoin, it may also decrease it because both drugs compete for the same metabolic pathway. Plasma concentrations of both drugs should be monitored when any change in the therapeutic regimen occurs. Valproic Acid: Concomitant administration of valproic acid and phenobarbital usually results in increased levels of phenobarbital and resultant oversedation. There have been case reports of progression of CNS depression to coma. Plasma concentrations of both drugs should be monitored when any change in the therapeutic regimen occurs. Carbamazepine: When phenobarbital and carbamazepine are used together, the metabolism of carbamazepine is usually accelerated and plasma concentrations may be decreased. The clinical significance of this interaction is not known. Plasma concentrations of both drugs should be monitored when any change in the therapeutic regimen occurs.

Antidepressants, MAO Inhibitors: MAO inhibitors may inhibit barbiturate metabolism, resulting in increased CNS depressant effects. A reduction in barbiturate dosage may be required.

Antidepressants, Tricyclic: Barbiturates may increase metabolism of tricyclic antidepressants resulting in lack of effect. Plasma tricyclic concentrations should be monitored if possible, especially if the patient is not responding to standard dosages of antidepressant. The use of both drugs concomitantly may result in additive respiratory depressant effects.

CNS Depressants: Alcohol, benzodiazepines, other sedatives and hypnotics, antihistamines etc. when used concurrently with a barbiturate may result in excessive CNS depressant effects.

Corticosteroids: Barbiturates may increase the metabolism of corticosteroids. There have been several reports of exacerbation of asthma and other conditions when barbiturates were added to regimens containing corticosteroids.

Oral Anticoagulants: Metabolism of coumarin anticoagulants may be accelerated, resulting in decreased anticoagulant response. Correspondingly, if the barbiturate is discontinued from a stabilized dosage, the hypoprothrombinemic response may be greatly increased potentially resulting in hemorrhagic complications. Prothrombin times should be monitored closely when barbiturates are added to or deleted from a regimen that includes oral anticoagulants.

Oral Contraceptives: Barbiturates may accelerate the metabolism of both the estrogenic and progestagenic components of the contraceptive, resulting in decreased effectiveness which may or may not be signalled by breakthrough bleeding. There have been reports of pregnancy resulting from this combination. If the barbiturate is necessary it would be advisable to use some other form of contraception.

Miscellaneous: Barbiturates have been reported to increase the metabolism and correspondingly reduce the effectiveness of the following: griseofulvin, digitoxin and doxycycline. When ketamine is used for anesthesia following preoperative administration of a barbiturate, profound respiratory depression may result.

Pregnancy: Barbiturates readily cross the placental barrier.

Amobarbital: Amobarbital use during the first trimester has been associated with cardiovascular malformations, genitourinary malformations, inguinal hernia and club foot. This drug should be avoided in women of childbearing potential and particularly during early pregnancy.

Butabarbital, Pentobarbital and Secobarbital: The safe use of these drugs during pregnancy has not been established.

Phenobarbital: The great majority of mothers on antiepileptic medication deliver normal infants. It is important to note that antiepileptic drugs should not be discontinued in patients in whom the drug is administered to prevent major seizures

Barbiturates (cont'd)

because of the strong possibility of precipitating status epilepticus with attendant hypoxia and threat to life. In individual cases where the severity and frequency of the seizure disorder are such that the removal of medication does not pose a serious threat to the patient, discontinuation of the drug may be considered prior to and during pregnancy, although it cannot be said with any confidence that even minor seizures do not pose some hazard to the developing embryo or fetus.

In addition to reports of increased incidence of congenital malformations such as cleft lip/palate and heart malformations in children of women receiving phenobarbital and other antiepileptic drugs, there have been reports of fetal hydantoin syndrome. This consists of prenatal growth deficiency, microcephaly and mental deficiency in children born to mothers who have received barbiturates, phenytoin, alcohol or trimethadione. However, these features are all inter-related and are frequently associated with intrauterine growth retardation from other causes.

The prescribing physician should weigh these considerations in treating or counseling epileptic women of childbearing potential.

The serum level of anticonvulsants may decline during pregnancy requiring adjustments in dosage. Postpartum restoration of the original dosage will probably be indicated.

Neonatal coagulation defects have been reported within the first 24 hours in babies born to epileptic mothers receiving phenobarbital and/or phenytoin. Vitamin K has been shown to prevent or correct this defect and has been recommended to be given to the mother before delivery and to the neonate after birth.

Barbiturate withdrawal has occurred in newborns who were exposed to the drug in utero and may be characterized by hypotonia, irritability and vomiting.

Lactation: Breast milk concentrations are 35 to 50% maternal serum concentrations. Breast-fed infants should be observed for excessive drowsiness, feeding problems, rash or other adverse effects. If any of these occur, breast feeding should be discontinued. When breast-feeding is discontinued there exists a potential for withdrawal symptoms in infants. Barbiturates are eliminated slowly in neonates and the drug may accumulate. If possible serum concentrations in the infant may be monitored.

Adverse Effects: CNS: Drowsiness is frequent especially at initiation of therapy and may persist throughout the next day after hypnotic doses. Mild impairment of concentration, judgment, memory, and fine motor skills may occur. Disturbances of sleep, dizziness, vertigo, headache and depression may occur. Patients with uncontrolled pain may experience paradoxical euphoria, elation, excitement and confusion. In children, hyperactivity is not uncommon; behavioral disturbances and cognitive impairment may occur. Geriatric patients may experience excitation, confusion or depression.

Cardiovascular: Hypotension may be observed with i.v. administration and is generally related to the rate of administration (see Precautions).

Respiratory: respiratory depression (see Precautions).

Hypersensitivity: Facial edema, skin rash (1 to 2%) may be purpuric, vesicular or erythematous. Exfoliative dermatitis and erythema multiforme are rare. Hypersensitivity reactions have a greater tendency to occur in patients with a history of asthma, urticaria or angioedema.

Hepatic: Severe allergic reactions may result in jaundice due to degenerative changes in the liver. Toxic hepatitis is rare.

Hematologic: megaloblastic anemia (responds to folic acid therapy). Agranulocytosis and thrombocytopenia are rare.

Metabolic: Barbiturates may increase vitamin D requirements, possibly by increasing vitamin D metabolism via enzyme induction. Rarely, rickets and osteomalacia have been reported following prolonged use of barbiturates.

Gastrointestinal: nausea, vomiting, diarrhea and constipation.

Miscellaneous: Exacerbation of porphyria, pain at the injection site, withdrawal (see Precautions).

Overdose: Symptoms: Acute overdosage with barbiturates primarily involves the CNS and the cardiovascular system. Mild overdose resembles alcohol intoxication. Drowsiness, confusion, stupor, respiratory depression, ataxia, sluggish or absent reflexes, early hypothermia, late fever, cardiovascular depression with hypotension, renal failure, cardiac arrhythmias, pulmonary edema, aspiration pneumonia, bullae over pressure points and decreased gastrointestinal motility are all possible symptoms. Severe overdose may progress to shock, coma and death.

Doses that can result in toxicity vary widely between patients. A severe and potentially lethal dose (after acute intoxication) is about 10 times the usual hypnotic dose of amobarbital, pentobarbital and secobarbital (1 to 3 g). The lethal dose of phenobarbital is believed to be 5 g.

Chronic ingestion of barbiturates results in the development of tolerance and large doses can be ingested without overt toxicity. Serious toxicity can result at lower barbiturate levels if combined with alcohol or other CNS depressant drugs.

Treatment: Support hemodynamic and respiratory functions and monitor for pulmonary complications. If the drug has been ingested recently (within 4 hours), empty stomach. Take precautions to avoid aspiration. Administer activated charcoal and a cathartic. Charcoal may be repeated for ingestions involving phenobarbital. Administer i.v. fluids to correct hypovolemia, maintain blood pressure and body temperature. If renal and cardiac function are satisfactory and the patient is hydrated, forced diuresis and i.v. sodium bicarbonate may be used to enhance urinary excretion of phenobarbital. This will only result in a maximum increased elimination of 25% as this is the amount excreted unchanged in the urine. Urinary alkalinization is not indicated for amobarbital, pentobarbital and secobarbital. In the event of renal failure, hemodialysis should be instituted.

CNS stimulants are not indicated. They are not antidotes; mortality rates were much higher when CNS stimulants were used formerly in barbiturate overdose.

Dosage: The general use of barbiturates as sedatives or hypnotics has for the most part, been supplanted by other less toxic drugs (i.e., benzodiazepines). Decreased dosage is recommended in geriatrics or older individuals and in patients with decreased renal or hepatic function. For more information on pediatric dosages, consult specialized pediatric references. The barbiturates can be given orally or by deep i.m. or slow i.v. injection.

Amobarbital: Oral: Hypnotic: 65 to 200 mg at bedtime.
Sedative: 50 to 300 mg daily in divided doses. Children, 2 mg/kg 3 times a day.
Pre-operative: 200 mg 1 to 2 hours prior to surgery. Children, 2 to 6 mg/kg up to a maximum of 100 mg 1 to 2 hours prior to surgery.
Parenteral: Hypnotic: 65 to 200 mg daily i.v. or i.m. Children, 2 to 3 mg/kg i.m.
Sedative: 30 to 50 mg i.v. or i.m. 2 or 3 times a day.
Anticonvulsant: 65 to 500 mg i.v.

The rate of i.v. administration in adults should not exceed 100 mg/minute. The maximum i.m. dose is 500 mg and the maximum i.v. dose is 1 g.

Butabarbital: Oral: Hypnotic: 50 to 100 mg at bedtime.
Sedative: 15 to 30 mg 3 or 4 times a day. Children, 2 mg/kg 3 times a day.

Pentobarbital: Oral: Hypnotic: 100 mg at bedtime.
Sedative: 20 mg 3 or 4 times a day. Children, 2 to 6 mg/kg/day.
Pre-operative: 100 mg 30 minutes prior to surgery. Children, 2 to 6 mg/kg to a maximum of 100 mg per dose.
Parenteral: Hypnotic: 150 to 200 mg i.m. or 100 mg i.v. with additional doses if necessary at 1 minute intervals to a maximum daily dose of 500 mg. Children, 2 to 6 mg/kg i.m. to a maximum of 100 mg per dose or 50 mg i.v. with additional doses if necessary at 1 minute intervals.
Pre-operative: 150 to 200 mg i.m. prior to surgery. Children, 2 to 6 mg/kg i.m. to a maximum of 100 mg per dose.
Anticonvulsant: 100 mg i.v. with additional doses if necessary at 1 minute intervals to a maximum daily dose of 500 mg. Children, 50 mg i.v. with additional doses if necessary at 1 minute intervals.
Rectal: Hypnotic: 120 to 200 mg. Children, under 4 years, 3 to 6 mg/kg; over 4 years, 1.5 to 3 mg/kg/dose.

Phenobarbital: Oral: Hypnotic: 100 to 320 mg at bedtime.
Sedative: 30 to 120 mg daily in 2 or 3 divided doses. Children, 2 mg/kg 3 times a day.
Anticonvulsant: 60 to 250 mg daily in a single dose or in divided doses. Maximum daily dose should not exceed 600 mg. Children, 1 to 6 mg/kg/day in a single dose or in divided doses.
Parenteral: Hypnotic: 100 to 325 mg i.v. or i.m.
Sedative: 30 to 120 mg i.v. or i.m. daily in 2 or 3 divided doses.
Pre-operative: 130 to 200 mg 1 to 2 hours prior to surgery. Children, 1 to 3 mg/kg 1 to 2 hours prior to surgery.
Anticonvulsant: 100 to 320 mg i.v. with additional doses if necessary to a maximum daily dose of 600 mg. Children, 1 to 6 mg/kg/day.
Status epilepticus: 10 to 20 mg/kg by slow i.v. injection. Repeat if necessary at 20 minute intervals, until the seizure is controlled or a total dose of 1 to 2 g is given. Children, 10 to 20 mg/kg by slow i.v. injection. Repeat if necessary at a dose of 5 to 10 mg/kg every 20 minutes, until the seizure is controlled or a total dose of 40 mg/kg is given.

The rate of i.v. administration should not exceed 60 mg/minute.

Secobarbital: Oral: Hypnotic: 100 mg at bedtime.
Sedative: 30 to 50 mg 3 or 4 times a day. Children, 2 mg/kg 3 times a day.
Pre-operative: 200 to 300 mg 1 to 2 hours prior to surgery. Children, 2 to 6 mg/kg to a maximum of 100 mg, 1 to 2 hours prior to surgery.
Parenteral: Hypnotic: 100 to 200 mg i.m. or 50 to 250 mg i.v. Children, 3 to 5 mg/kg to a maximum of 100 mg.

The reader is referred to individual product monographs for more specific prescribing information.

Reviewed 1999

BARRIERE™

Roberts

Dimethylpolysiloxane

Skin Protectant

Supplied: Each g of vanishing cream contains: dimethylpolysiloxane 20%. Also contains parabens. Cartoned tubes of 50 and 100 g; jars of 450 g.

BARRIERE-HC® Ⓟ

Roberts

Hydrocortisone—Silicone

Dermatitis Therapy

Indications: Adjunctive treatment of allergic dermatoses and other inflammatory skin conditions amenable to topical corticosteroid therapy (e.g., contact, atopic and seborrheic dermatitis, neurodermatitis, psoriasis and anogenital pruritus).

Contraindications: Tuberculous and most fungal and viral lesions of the skin, herpes simplex, vaccinia and varicella particularly.

Precautions: Although untoward effects associated with the use of topical corticosteroids are uncommon and not to be expected from ordinary use, sensitization, irritation and failure of therapeutic response have been noted in rare instances. Application to extensive areas, too frequent application, or application under occlusive dressings may result in systemic absorption with symptoms of adrenal suppression, localized atrophy and striae. If secondary bacterial infection exists or supervenes, concomitant antimicrobial therapy is indicated. Do not apply in or near eyes.

Advise patients to inform subsequent physicians of the prior use of corticosteroids.

Pregnancy: Although topical corticosteroids have not been reported to have an adverse effect on pregnancy, the safety of their use during pregnancy has not been established. Therefore, they should not be used extensively on pregnant patients, or in large amounts, or for prolonged periods.

Adverse Effects: When occlusive dressings are used, pustules, miliaria, folliculitis and pyoderma may occur. The following adverse skin reactions have been reported rarely with the use of topical steroids: dryness, itching, burning, local irritation, striae, hypopigmentation, atrophy and secondary infection.

Dosage: Apply 3 or 4 times a day to affected area. For external use only.

Supplied: Each tube contains: hydrocortisone 1% in a silicone vanishing cream base. Also contains parabens. Cartoned tubes of 15 and 45 g.

BASALJEL®

Axcan Pharma

Aluminum Hydroxide

Gastrointestinal Phosphate Binder

Supplied: Each yellow and red capsule contains: dried aluminum gel 500 mg (aluminum hydroxide-sucrose 641 mg, equivalent to Al_2O_3 327 mg or $Al(OH)_3$ 500 mg based on an Al_2O_3 content of 51%). Nonmedicinal ingredients: magnesium stearate, microcrystalline cellulose and talc. Energy: 2.80 kJ (0.67 kcal)/capsule. Tartrazine-free. Bottles of 100.

BAYCOL® Ⓟ

Bayer

Cerivastatin Sodium

Lipid Metabolism Regulator

Pharmacology: Cerivastatin is an entirely synthetic, enantiomerically pure cholesterol-lowering agent and is structurally similar to the fungal derivatives of this therapeutic class.

Cerivastatin is a competitive inhibitor of 3-hydroxy-3methylglutaryl-coenzyme A (HMG CoA) reductase, the enzyme catalyzing the conversion of HMG-CoA to mevalonate, which is an early and rate-limiting step in the biosynthesis of cholesterol. The inhibition of cholesterol biosynthesis by cerivastatin reduces the level of cholesterol in hepatic cells, which stimulates the synthesis of low density lipoprotein (LDL) receptors, thereby increasing the uptake of cellular LDL particles. The end result of these biochemical processes is a reduction of plasma total cholesterol (Total-C) and low density lipoprotein cholesterol (LDL-C).

Pharmacokinetics: Cerivastatin is rapidly absorbed following oral dosing. The absolute bioavailability of cerivastatin sodium tablets is 60% compared to oral solution. The pharmacokinetics of cerivastatin are linear over the dose range of 0.05 to 0.4 mg. Cerivastatin is >99% bound to plasma proteins. The elimination half-life is in the range of 2 to 4 hours; consequently no drug accumulation with once daily dosing is observed. The pharmacokinetics of cerivastatin are similar under fed and fasted conditions.

When ^{14}C-cerivastatin was given as an oral solution, the mean urinary excretion of total radioactivity was 24% of dose, while a mean of 70% was excreted in the feces. Thus, biliary secretion is a major pathway of drug (or metabolite) elimination. Only negligible quantities of ^{14}C were associated with unchanged drug, indicating extensive metabolism. Cerivastatin is metabolized via a dual metabolic pathway utilizing at least 2 cytochrome P450 isoenzymes, CYP2C8 and CYP3A4. If one of the metabolic pathways (e.g., CYP3A4) is blocked, cerivastatin is metabolized, although not completely in some cases, by the alternate metabolic route. Three metabolites have been identified, and M1 and M23 are present in plasma, urine and feces, whereas M24 is present in urine and feces only. Plasma concentrations of all identified metabolites are substantially lower than those of parent drug, and the elimination half-lives are similar. Therefore, while some metabolites have pharmacologic (i.e., HMG-CoA reductase inhibitory) activity, they do not contribute significantly to the overall efficacy of cerivastatin.

Indications: As an adjunct to diet, at least equivalent to the American Heart Association (AHA) Step 1 diet, for the reduction of elevated Total-C and LDL-C levels in patients with primary hypercholesterolemia (Types IIa and IIb) when the response to dietary restriction of saturated fat and cholesterol and other nonpharmacological measures alone has been inadequate.

For the reduction of elevated cholesterol levels in patients with combined hypercholesterolemia and hypertriglyceridema, when the hypercholesterolemia is the abnormality of most concern.

Prior to initiating therapy with cerivastatin, secondary causes for hyperlipoproteinemia, such as obesity, poorly controlled diabetes mellitus, hypothyroidism, nephrotic syndrome, dysproteinemias, obstructive liver disease, other drug therapy (e.g., some antihypertensive agents) or alcoholism, should be excluded. A lipid profile should be performed to measure Total-C, high density lipoprotein cholesterol (HDL-C) and triglycerides.

For patients with total triglycerides less than 4.52 mmol/L (400 mg/dL), LDL-C can be estimated using the following equation:

$$\text{LDL-C (mmol/L)} = \text{Total-C} - [(0.37 \times \text{Trig}) + \text{HDL-C}]$$
$$\text{LDL-C (mg/dL)} = \text{Total-C} - [(0.16 \times \text{Trig}) + \text{HDL-C}]$$

When total triglyceride levels exceed 4.52 mmol/L (400 mg/dL), this equation is less accurate and LDL-C concentrations should be directly measured by preparative ultracentrifugation. In many hypertriglyceridemic patients, LDL-C may be low or normal despite elevated Total-C. In such cases, cerivastatin is not indicated.

Lipid determinations should be performed at intervals of no less than 4 weeks and dosage adjusted according to the patient's response to therapy.

Cerivastatin has not been studied in conditions where the major abnormality is elevation of chylomicrons, very low density lipoprotein (VLDL), or intermediate-density lipoprotein (IDL), i.e., hyperlipoproteinemia types I, III, IV, or V.

Contraindications: Hypersensitivity to any component of this medication.

Active liver disease or unexplained persistent elevations of serum transaminases exceeding 3 times the upper limit of normal (see Warnings).

Pregnancy and lactation (see Precautions).

Warnings: Pharmacokinetic Interactions: The use of HMG-CoA reductase inhibitors has been associated with severe myopathy, including rhabdomyolysis, which may be more frequent when they are co-administered with drugs that inhibit the cytochrome P450 enzyme system. Cerivastatin is metabolized via a dual metabolic pathway utilizing at least 2 cytochrome P450 isoenzymes, CYP2C8 and CYP3A4. If one of the metabolic pathways (e.g., CYP3A4) is blocked, cerivastatin is metabolized, although not completely in some cases, by the alternate metabolic route. (See Warnings, Muscle Effects and Precautions, Drug Interactions and Cytochrome P450 Inhibitors.)

For more information on the metabolism of cerivastatin in humans, see Pharmacology.

Hepatic Effects: **In clinical trials, persistent increases of serum transaminase values to more than 3 times the upper limit of normal (ULN) (occurring on 2 or more, not necessarily sequential, occasions) have been reported in <1% of patients treated with cerivastatin.** Most of these abnormalities occurred within the first 6 weeks of treatment, resolved after discontinuation of the drug, and were not associated with cholestasis. In most cases, these biochemical abnormalities were asymptomatic.

It is recommended that liver function tests be performed before the initiation of treatment, and within 12 weeks after initiation of therapy or elevation in dose, and periodically thereafter, e.g., semiannually. Special attention should be paid to patients who develop elevated serum transaminase levels, and in these patients, measurements should be repeated promptly and then performed more frequently. **If increases in alanine aminotransferase (ALT) or aspartate aminotransferase (AST) show evidence of progression, particularly if they rise to >3 times the ULN and are persistent, the dosage should be reduced or the drug discontinued.**

The drug should be used with caution in patients with a history of liver disease or heavy alcohol ingestion (>14 drinks/week).

Active liver disease or unexplained transaminase elevations are contraindications to the use of cerivastatin; if such conditions develop during therapy, the drug should be discontinued (see Contraindications).

Muscle Effects: Myopathy, defined as muscle aching or muscle weakness, associated with increases in plasma creatine phosphokinase (CPK) values to greater than 10 times the ULN was rare (<0.2%) in cerivastatin clinical trials. Myopathy should be considered in any patient with diffuse myalgias, muscle tenderness or weakness, and/or marked elevation of CPK. Patients should be advised to report promptly unexplained muscle pain, tenderness, or weakness, particularly if accompanied by malaise or fever.

The risk of myopathy and rhabdomylosis during treatment with HMG-CoA reductase inhibitors is increased if therapy with cyclosporine, fibric acid derivatives, erythromycin, niacin (nicotinic acid) in lipid-lowering doses, nefazodone or azole antifungals is administered concurrently. The benefits and risks of combined therapy should be carefully considered (see Precautions, Drug Interactions).

Rhabdomyolysis with renal dysfunction secondary to myoglobinuria have been reported with other HMG-CoA reductase inhibitors. This has not been reported with cerivastatin sodium to date. Cerivastatin therapy should be discontinued if markedly elevated CPK levels occur or myopathy is diagnosed or suspected. Cerivastatin should be temporarily withheld in any patient experiencing an acute or serious condition suggestive of a myopathy or having a risk factor predisposing to the development of renal failure secondary to rhabdomyolysis, e.g., sepsis; hypotension; major surgery; trauma; severe metabolic, endocrine or electrolyte disorders; or uncontrolled epilepsy.

Precautions: General: **The effects of cerivastatin-induced changes in lipoprotein levels, including reduction of serum cholesterol on cardiovascular morbidity or mortality or total mortality have not been established.**

Before instituting therapy with cerivastatin, an attempt should be made to control hypercholesterolemia with appropriate diet, exercise, weight reduction in obese patients, and treatment of underlying medical problems (see Indications). The patient should be advised to inform subsequent physicians of the prior use of cerivastatin or any other lipid lowering agent.

Effect on Lens: Current data from clinical trials do not indicate an adverse effect of cerivastatin on the human lens.

Homozygous Familial Hypercholesterolemia: Cerivastatin has not been evaluated in patients with rare homozygous familial hypercholesterolemia. Most HMG-CoA reductase inhibitors are less or not effective in this subgroup of hypercholesterolemic patients.

Effect on Lipoprotein (a): In some patients, the beneficial effect of lowered total cholesterol and LDL-C levels may be partly blunted by a concomitant increase in the Lipoprotein (a) [Lp(a)] levels. Therefore, until further experience is obtained from controlled clinical trials, it is suggested that measurements of serum Lp(a) be followed-up in patients placed on cerivastatin therapy.

Effect on CoQ_{10} Levels (Ubiquinone): Significant decreases in circulating ubiquinone levels in patients treated with other statins has been observed. The clinical significance of a potential long-term statin-induced deficiency of ubiquinone has not yet been established. It has been reported that a decrease in myocardial ubiquinone levels could lead to impaired cardiac function in patients with borderline congestive heart failure.

Hypersensitivity: An apparent hypersensitivity syndrome has been reported rarely with other HMG-CoA reductase inhibitors. This has included one or more of the following features: anaphylaxis, angioedema, lupus erythematous-like syndrome, polymyalgia rheumatica, vasculitis, purpura, thrombocytopenia, leukopenia, hemolytic anemia, positive antinuclear antibody (ANA), erythrocyte sedimentation rate (ESR) increase, eosinophilia, arthritis, arthralgia, urticaria, asthenia, photosensitivity, fever, chills, flushing, malaise, dyspnea, toxic epidermal necrolysis, erythema multiforme including Stevens-Johnson syndrome. Although to date hypersensitivity syndrome has not been described as such, cerivastatin should be discontinued if hypersensitivity is suspected.

Pregnancy: **Cerivastatin is contraindicated during pregnancy (see Contraindications).**

Safety in pregnant women has not been established. Atherosclerosis is a chronic process and discontinuation of lipid metabolism regulators during pregnancy should have little impact on the outcome of long-term therapy of primary hypercholesterolemia. Cholesterol and other products of cholesterol biosynthesis are essential components for fetal development (including synthesis of steroids and cell membranes). Since HMG-CoA reductase inhibitors decrease cholesterol synthesis and possibly the synthesis of other biologically active substances derived from cholesterol, they may cause fetal harm when administered to pregnant women. Cerivastatin should be administered to women of child-bearing age only when such patients are highly unlikely to conceive and have been informed of the potential hazards. If the patient becomes pregnant while taking this drug, cerivastatin should be discontinued and the patient should be apprised of the potential hazard to the fetus.

Lactation: Based on preclinical data, cerivastatin is present in breast milk in a 1.3:1 ratio (milk:plasma). It is not known whether cerivastatin is excreted in human milk. Because of the potential for serious adverse reactions in nursing infants, women taking cerivastatin should not nurse (see Contraindications).

Children: Limited experience with the use of other HMG-CoA reductase inhibitors is available in children. Safety and effectiveness of cerivastatin in children have not been established.

Geriatrics and Gender: The effect of age on the pharmacokinetics of cerivastatin was evaluated. Results indicate that for the general patient population, plasma concentrations of cerivastatin do not vary as a function of age. A slight increase in plasma cerivastatin levels was observed in females (approximately 12% higher for C_{max} and 16% higher for AUC).

Patients with Impaired Renal Function: No dose adjustment is necessary for patients with mild renal dysfunction (creatinine clearance 61 to 90 mL/min/1.73 m²). In patients with significant renal impairment (creatinine clearance <60 mL/min/1.73 m²), the lowest dosage should be used and implemented cautiously (see Warnings, Muscle Effects).

Endocrine Function: HMG-CoA reductase inhibitors interfere with cholesterol synthesis and lower cholesterol levels and, as such, might theoretically blunt adrenal or gonadal steroid hormone production. Cerivastatin demonstrated no effect

Baycol (cont'd)

upon nonstimulated cortisol levels and no effect on thyroid metabolism as assessed by TSH. Clinical studies with other HMG-CoA reductase inhibitors have suggested that these agents do not reduce plasma cortisol concentration or impair adrenal reserve and do not reduce plasma testosterone concentration. In rare cases, however, impotence may occur following their administration. The effects of HMG-CoA reductase inhibitors on male fertility have not been studied in adequate numbers of male patients. The effects, if any, on the pituitary-gonadal axis in premenopausal women are unknown.

Patients treated with cerivastatin who develop clinical evidence of endocrine dysfunction should be evaluated appropriately. Caution should be exercised if an HMG-CoA reductase inhibitor or other agent used to lower cholesterol levels is administered to patients also receiving other drugs, e.g., ketoconazole, spironolactone, or cimetidine, that may decrease the levels of endogenous steroid hormones (see Drug Interactions, Cytochrome Inhibitors).

Drug Interactions: Concomitant Therapy with Other Lipid Metabolism Regulators: Combined drug therapy should be approached with caution as information from controlled studies is limited.

Bile Acid Sequestrants: Coadministration of cerivastatin and cholestyramine resulted in a 22% decrease in cerivastatin plasma concentration (AUC). Administration of cholestyramine 1 hour before the evening meal and cerivastatin 4 hours after the same evening meal resulted in a decrease in the cerivastatin plasma concentration of less than 8%. Therefore, it would be expected that a dosing schedule of cerivastatin given at bedtime and cholestyramine administered before the evening meal would not result in a significant decrease in the clinical effect of cerivastatin.

Gemfibrozil, Fenofibrate and Niacin: Myopathy, including rhabdomyolysis, has occurred in patients receiving HMG-CoA reductase inhibitors with fibric acid derivatives and niacin (in lipid-lowering doses), particularly in subjects with pre-existing renal insufficiency (see Warnings, Muscle Effects).

Erythromycin: Coadministration of erythromycin 500 mg b.i.d., a known inhibitor of cytochrome P450 3A4, with cerivastatin 0.3 mg every day during 10 days in hypercholesterolemic patients resulted in a 50% increase in cerivastatin AUC and in a 24% increase in C_{max} (see Warnings, Pharmacokinetic Interactions and Muscle Effects, and Precautions, Inhibitors).

Azole Antifungals: Coadministration with the antifungal agent itraconazole 200 mg every evening, another potent CYP3A4 inhibitor, and cerivastatin 0.3 mg every evening during 10 days in hypercholesterolemic patients resulted in a 40% increase in cerivastatin steady-state plasma concentrations (see Warnings, Pharmacokinetic Interactions and Muscle Effects, and Precautions, Inhibitors).

Calcium Channel Blockers: Coadministration of a single dose of 60 mg nifedipine extended release and cerivastatin 0.3 mg to hypercholesterolemic patients did not show any effect on either nifedipine or cerivastatin plasma concentrations.

Coumarin Anticoagulants: Coadministration of warfarin and cerivastatin had no effect on the plasma concentration of either agent.

Digoxin: Coadministration of cerivastatin and digoxin resulted in a <10% increase in plasma digoxin levels. Patients taking digoxin should be monitored appropriately when cerivastatin therapy is initiated. Digoxin did not alter the pharmacokinetics of cerivastatin.

Antacid (Magnesium-Aluminum Hydroxide): Coadministration of antacid with cerivastatin resulted in an approximate 10% decrease in the cerivastatin plasma concentration.

Cimetidine: Coadministration of cerivastatin (0.2 mg) with cimetidine (400 mg) resulted in an 11% decrease in the cerivastatin plasma concentration.

Other Concomitant Therapy: Although specific interaction studies were not performed, in clinical studies cerivastatin sodium was used concomitantly with angiotensin converting enzyme (ACE) inhibitors, β-blockers, calcium-channel blockers, diuretics, estrogen replacement therapy, and nonsteroidal anti-inflammatory drugs (NSAIDs) without evidence to date of clinically significant adverse interactions.

Cytochrome P450 Inhibitors: Cerivastatin is metabolized via a dual metabolic pathway utilizing at least two cytochrome P-450 isoenzymes, CYP2C8 and CYP3A4. Although not complete in some cases, a compensatory effect is observed when one pathway is inhibited. When coadministered with erythromycin, a known inhibitor of cytochrome P450 isoform 3A4, cerivastatin plasma concentrations increased by 50%. Drugs or common agents such as grapefruit juice that inhibit this enzyme may represent a potential for drug interactions when combined with cerivastatin. Caution should thus be exercised with concomitant use of drugs such as immunosuppressants, antifungal agents (e.g., itraconazole, ketoconazole), macrolide antibiotics including erythromycin, antidepressants (e.g., nefazodone) or grapefruit juice (see Warnings, Muscle Effects and Precautions, Endocrine Function).

Patients with Severe Hypercholesterolemia: Higher drug dosages (0.3 mg/day) required for some patients with severe hypercholesterolemia are associated with increased plasma level of cerivastatin. **Caution should be exercised in such patients who are also significantly renally impaired, elderly, or are concomitantly being administered digoxin, erythromycin or other cytochrome P450 inhibitors (see Warnings, Muscle Effects and Precautions, Drug Interactions).**

Drug/Lab Interactions: HMG-CoA reductase inhibitors may elevate CPK and transaminase levels (see Adverse Effects, Laboratory Tests). In the differential diagnosis of chest pain in a patient on therapy with cerivastatin, cardiac and non-cardiac fractions of these enzymes should be determined.

Adverse Effects: Cerivastatin is generally well-tolerated. Adverse events have usually been mild and transient. In 1 394 patients treated in placebo-controlled clinical studies investigating doses of 0.2 mg and 0.3 mg, less than 2% of patients were discontinued due to adverse reactions attributable to cerivastatin, compared to 2.5% for placebo. Of these 1 394 patients, 855 were treated for ≥1 year.

Adverse experiences occurring at an incidence ≥1% in patients participating in placebo-controlled clinical studies of cerivastatin 0.2 or 0.3 mg/day and reported to be possibly, probably, or definitely drug related are shown in Table I.

Table I—Baycol

Associated Adverse Events Reported in ≥1% of Patients in Placebo-Controlled Clinical Trials of 0.2 and 0.3 mg Cerivastatin

	Placebo % (N=641)	Cerivastatin % (N=1 394)
Gastrointestinal		
Dyspepsia	2	2
Flatulence	1	2
Abdominal pain	2	1
Diarrhea	2	1
Constipation	1	<1
CNS		
Headache	2	2

Ophthalmological Observations: See Precautions, Effect on Lens.

Laboratory Tests: Increases of serum transaminases and CPK have been noted in clinical trials (see Warnings).

The following effects have been reported with drugs in this class. Not all the effects listed below have necessarily been associated with cerivastatin therapy: myopathy, muscle cramps, rhabdomyolysis, arthralgias, dysfunction of certain cranial nerves (including alteration of taste, impairment of extra-ocular movement, facial paresis), tremor, dizziness, memory loss, vertigo, paresthesia, peripheral neuropathy, peripheral nerve palsy, anxiety, insomnia, depression, pancreatitis, hepatitis, cholestatic jaundice, fatty change in liver, cirrhosis (rare), fulminant hepatic necrosis (rare), hepatoma (rare), anorexia, vomiting, alopecia, pruritus, gynecomastia, loss of libido, erectile dysfunction, progression of cataracts (lens opacities), ophthalmoplegia.

Hypersensitivity: anaphylaxis, angioedema, lupus erythematosus-like syndrome, polymyalgia rheumatica, vasculitis, purpura, thrombocytopenia, leukopenia, hemolytic anemia, positive ANA, ESR increase, eosinophilia, arthritis, arthralgia, urticaria, asthenia, photosensitivity, fever, chills, flushing, malaise, dyspnea, toxic epidermal necrolysis, erythema multiforme including Stevens-Johnson syndrome.

Laboratory Abnormalities: elevated transaminases, alkaline phosphatase, γ-glutamyl transpeptidase, and bilirubin; thyroid function abnormalities.

Overdose: Symptoms: The maximum single oral dose of cerivastatin received by healthy volunteers and patients is 0.8 mg.

Treatment: No specific recommendations concerning the treatment of an overdosage can be made. Should an overdose occur, it should be treated symptomatically and supportive measures should be undertaken as required.

The ability of cerivastatin and its metabolites to be dialyzed in humans is not known.

Dosage: The patient should be placed on a standard cholesterol-lowering diet [at least equivalent to the American Heart Association (AHA) Step 1 diet] before receiving cerivastatin and should continue on this diet during treatment with cerivastatin. If appropriate, a program of weight control and physical exercise should be implemented.

The recommended starting dose is 0.2 mg once daily in the evening. The recommended dosing range is 0.2 to 0.3 mg as a single dose in the evening. Cerivastatin may be taken with or without food since there are no apparent differences in the lipid lowering effects of cerivastatin administered with the evening meal or at bedtime. Dosages should be individualized according to the recommended goal of therapy and the patient's response.

Since the maximal effect of a given dose of cerivastatin is seen within 4 weeks, periodic lipid determinations should be performed at this time and the dosage adjusted to the patient's response to therapy and established treatment guidelines.

Consideration should be given to reducing the dosage of cerivastatin if cholesterol levels fall below the targeted range, such as that recommended by the Second Report of the U.S. National Cholesterol Education Program (NCEP) and/or the Canadian Consensus Conference Guidelines.

Severe Hypercholesterolemia: In patients with severe hypercholesterolemia, higher dosages (0.3 mg/day) may be required (see Warnings, Muscle Effects and Precautions, Drug Interactions).

Concomitant Therapy: See Precautions, Drug Interactions.

Patients with Renal Insufficiency: See Precautions.

Information for the Patient: See Blue Section—Information for the Patient "Baycol".

Supplied: 0.2 mg: Each light yellow-brown tablet, with 283 on one side and 200 MCG on the other, contains: cerivastatin sodium 0.2 mg. Nonmedicinal ingredients: crospovidone, ferric oxide, hydroxypropyl methylcellulose, magnesium stearate, mannitol, polyethylene glycol 4000, povidone 25, sodium hydroxide and titanium dioxide. Bottles of 100.

0.3 mg: Each yellow-brown tablet, with 284 on one side and 300 MCG on the other, contains: cerivastatin sodium 0.3 mg. Nonmedicinal ingredients: crospovidone, ferric oxide, hydroxypropyl methylcellulose, magnesium stearate, mannitol, polyethylene glycol 4000, povidone 25, sodium hydroxide and titanium dioxide. Bottles of 100.

Store at room temperature (15 to 25°C). Dispense in tight containers.

(Shown in Product Recognition Section)

New Product 1998

BAYGAM™

Bayer

Immune Globulin (Human), I.M.

Passive Immunizing Agent

Supplied: Immune Globulin (Human) treated with solvent/detergent is a sterile solution of immune globulin for i.m. administration; it contains no preservative. The product is prepared by cold ethanol fractionation from human plasma. The immune globulin is isolated from solubilized Cohn fraction II. The fraction II solution is adjusted to a final concentration of 0.3% tri-n-butyl phosphate (TNBP) and 0.2% sodium cholate. After the addition of solvent (TNBP) and detergent (sodium cholate), the solution is heated to 30°C and maintained at that temperature for not less than 6 hours. After the viral inactivation step, the reactants are removed by precipitation, filtration and finally ultrafiltration and diafiltration. Baygam is formulated as a 15 to 18% protein solution at a pH of 6.4 to 7.2 in 0.21 to 0.32 M glycine. The pH is adjusted with sodium bicarbonate. The product is then incubated in the final container for 21 to 28 days at 20 to 27°C.

The removal and inactivation of spiked model enveloped and nonenveloped viruses during the manufacturing process has been validated in laboratory studies. Human Immunodeficiency Virus, Type 1 (HIV-1), was chosen as the relevant virus for blood products; Bovine Viral Diarrhea Virus (BVDV) was chosen to model Hepatitis C virus; Pseudorabies virus (PRV) was chosen to model Hepatitis B virus and the Herpes viruses; and Reo virus type 3 (Reo) was chosen to model nonenveloped viruses and for its resistance to physical and chemical inactivation. Significant removal of model enveloped and nonenveloped viruses is seen in the Fraction II + IIIW to Effluent III step and significant removal of PRV and Reo virus is seen in the Effluent III to Filtrate III step. Significant inactivation of enveloped viruses is achieved at the time of treatment of solubilized Cohn Fraction II with solvent/detergent.

Single use vials of 2, 5 and 10 mL. Store at 2 to 8°C. Do not freeze. Do not use after expiration date. Once entered, discard any unused contents.

BAYHEP B™

Bayer

Hepatitis B Immune Globulin (Human)

Passive Immunizing Agent

Supplied: Hepatitis B Immune Globulin (Human) treated with solvent/detergent is a sterile solution of hepatitis B hyperimmune immune globulin for i.m. administration; it contains no preservative. The product is prepared by cold ethanol fractionation from the plasma of donors with high titers of antibody to the hepatitis B surface antigen (anti-HBs). The immune globulin is isolated from solubilized Cohn fraction II. The fraction II solution is adjusted to a final concentration of 0.3% tri-n-butyl phosphate (TNBP) and 0.2% sodium cholate. After the addition of solvent (TNBP) and detergent (sodium cholate), the solution is heated to 30°C and maintained at that temperature for not less than 6 hours. After the viral inactivation step, the reactants are removed by precipitation, filtration and finally ultrafiltration and diafiltration. It is formulated as a 15 to 18% protein solution at a pH of 6.4 to 7.2 in 0.21 to 0.32 M glycine. The pH is adjusted with sodium carbonate. The product is then incubated in the final container for 21 to 28 days at 20 to 27°C. Each vial contains HBs antibody equivalent to or exceeding the potency of anti-HBs (i.e., ≥217 IU/mL) in a U.S. reference hepatitis B immune globulin (Center for Biologics Evaluation and Research, FDA). The U.S. reference has been tested against the World Health Organization standard Hepatitis B Immune Globulin and found to be equal to 217 IU/mL.

The removal and inactivation of spiked model enveloped and nonenveloped viruses during the manufacturing process for Bayhep B has been validated in laboratory studies. Human Immunodeficiency Virus, Type 1 (HIV-1), was chosen as the relevant virus for blood products; Bovine Viral Diarrhea Virus (BVDV) was chosen to model Hepatitis C virus; Pseudorabies virus (PRV) was chosen to model Hepatitis B virus and the Herpes viruses; and Reo virus type 3 (Reo) was chosen to model nonenveloped viruses and for its resistance to physical and chemical inactivation.

Significant removal of model enveloped and nonenveloped viruses is seen in the Fraction II+IIIW to Effluent III step and significant removal of PRV and Reo virus is seen in the Effluent III to Filtrate III step. Significant inactivation of enveloped viruses is achieved at the time of treatment of solubilized Cohn Fraction II with solvent/detergent.

Neonatal single dose syringes of 0.5 mL with attached needle. The syringes are disposable and packaged with a prep swab. Single use vials of 1 and 5 mL. Store at 2 to 8°C . Do not freeze. Do not use after expiration date. Once entered, discard any unused contents.

BAYRAB™

Bayer

Rabies Immune Globulin (Human)

Passive Immunizing Agent

Supplied: Rabies Immune Globulin (Human) treated with solvent/detergent is a sterile solution of antirabies immune globulin for i.m. administration; it contains no preservative. It is prepared by cold ethanol fractionation from the plasma of donors hyperimmunized with rabies vaccine. The immune globulin is isolated from solubilized Cohn fraction II. The fraction II solution is adjusted to a final concentration of 0.3% tri-n-butyl phosphate (TNBP) and 0.2% sodium cholate. After the addition of solvent (TNBP) and detergent (sodium cholate), the solution is heated to 30°C and maintained at that temperature for not less than 6 hours. After the viral inactivation step, the reactants are removed by precipitation, filtration and finally ultrafiltration and diafiltration. The product is formulated as a 15 to 18% protein solution at a pH of 6.4 to 7.2 in 0.21 to 0.32 M glycine. The pH is adjusted with sodium carbonate and it is then incubated in the final container for 21 to 28 days at 20 to 27°C.

The removal and inactivation of spiked model enveloped and nonenveloped viruses during the manufacturing process has been validated in laboratory studies. Human Immunodeficiency Virus, Type 1 (HIV-1), was chosen as the relevant virus for blood products; Bovine Viral Diarrhea Virus (BVDV) was chosen to model Hepatitis C virus; Pseudorabies virus (PRV) was chosen to model Hepatitis B virus and the Herpes viruses; and Reo virus type 3 (Reo) was chosen to model nonenveloped viruses and for its resistance to physical and chemical inactivation. Significant removal of model enveloped and nonenveloped viruses is seen in the Fraction II+IIIW to Effluent III step and significant removal of PRV and Reo virus is also seen in the Effluent III to Filtrate III step. Significant inactivation of enveloped viruses is achieved at the time of treatment of solubilized Cohn Fraction II with solvent/detergent.

Single use vials of 2 and 10 mL with an average potency value of 150 IU/mL based on the U.S. Standard Rabies Immune Globulin. The 2 mL vial contains a total of 300 IU which is sufficient for a child weighing 15 kg. The 10 mL vial contains a total of 1 500 IU which is sufficient for an adult weighing 75 kg. Store under refrigeration (2 to 8°C). Do not freeze. Solution that has been frozen should not be used. Do not use beyond the expiration date. Once entered, discard any unused contents.

BAYTET™

Bayer

Tetanus Immune Globulin (Human)

Passive Immunizing Agent

Supplied: Tetanus Immune Globulin (Human) treated with solvent/detergent is a sterile solution of tetanus hyperimmune immune globulin for i.m. administration; it contains no preservative and is supplied as a single dose syringe or single dose vial. The product is prepared by cold ethanol fractionation from the plasma of donors immunized with tetanus toxoid. The immune globulin is isolated from solubilized Cohn fraction II. The fraction II solution is adjusted to a final concentration of 0.3% tri-n-butyl phosphate (TNBP) and 0.2% sodium cholate. After the addition of solvent (TNBP) and detergent (sodium cholate), the solution is heated to 30°C and maintained at that temperature for not less than 6 hours. After the viral inactivation step, the reactants are removed by precipitation, filtration and finally ultrafiltration and diafiltration. The product is formulated as a 15 to 18% protein solution at a pH of 6.4 to 7.2 in 0.21 to 0.32 M glycine. The pH is adjusted with sodium carbonate. It is then incubated in the final container for 21 to 28 days at 20 to 27°C. The product is standardized against the U.S. Standard Antitoxin and the U.S. Control Tetanus Toxin and contains not less than 250 tetanus antitoxin units per container.

The removal and inactivation of spiked model enveloped and nonenveloped viruses during the manufacturing process has been validated in laboratory studies. Human Immunodeficiency Virus, Type 1 (HIV-1), was chosen as the relevant virus for blood products; Bovine Viral Diarrhea Virus (BVDV) was chosen to model Hepatitis C virus; Pseudorabies virus (PRV) was chosen to model Hepatitis B virus and the Herpes viruses; and Reo virus type 3 (Reo) was chosen to model nonenveloped viruses and for its resistance to physical and chemical inactivation.

Significant removal of model enveloped and nonenveloped viruses is seen in the Fraction II and IIIW to Effluent III step and significant removal of PRV and Reo-virus is seen in the Effluent III to Filtrate III step. Significant inactivation of enveloped viruses is achieved at the time of treatment of solubilized Cohn Fraction II with solvent/detergent.

Prefilled disposable single dose syringes with attached needles of 250 units and single dose vials of 250 units. Store at 2 to 8°C. Do not freeze. Solution that has been frozen should not be used. Do not use beyond expiration date.

BCG VACCINE (Freeze Dried)

Connaught

Attenuated Tubercle Bacillus

Active Immunizing Agent

Pharmacology: BCG Vaccine (Freeze-Dried) for intracutaneous administration, as prepared by Connaught Laboratories Limited, is made from a culture of an attenuated strain of living bovine tubercle bacillus (Bacillus Calmette-Guérin). It is supplied as a freeze-dried product ready for immediate use following reconstitution with the accompanying diluent, which consists of sterile phosphate-buffered saline.

The manufacturing and testing procedures used by Connaught for freeze-dried BCG vaccine comply with the recommendations of WHO as stipulated in WHO Technical Report Series No. 638, 1979: Revised Requirements for Dried BCG Vaccine.

Indications: For the vaccination of tuberculin negative individuals against tuberculosis. Administer only to individuals who have **not** been infected by the tubercle bacillus or to individuals who are tuberculin negative.

BCG Vaccination has no value in the treatment of tuberculous disease.

Administration of BCG Vaccine (Freeze dried) is recommended only for tuberculin negative individuals who are repeatedly exposed to untreated or inadequately treated active tuberculosis; communities or groups of persons with high rates of infection, including Indian, Metis and Inuit children, in which other control measures have proven ineffective; health workers at considerable risk of exposure to unrecognized infectious pulmonary tuberculosis or who handle tubercle bacilli or potentially infectious specimens in a laboratory; newborn infants whose mothers have infectious tuberculosis at the time of delivery, although isoniazid prophylaxis is preferred to avoid the necessary separation of mother and infant when BCG is used. However, BCG is recommended if the infecting strain is isoniazid resistant or if compliance with a program of isoniazid prophylaxis cannot be assured. BCG may also be considered for the infant after isoniazid prophylaxis is completed, provided chest radiographs and tuberculin test are negative.

Contraindications: Do not vaccinate individuals suffering general malaise or conditions such as measles, whooping cough, eczema, furunculosis, atopic dermatitis or other exudative or inflammatory dermatologic conditions. BCG vaccination should not be combined with vaccination against other diseases. After vaccination with another antigen, there should be a sufficient time interval to allow any reaction that results to subside before BCG vaccine is administered. Conversely, if BCG vaccine is given first, vaccination with other antigens should not be carried out until the reaction to the BCG vaccine has subsided.

BCG Vaccine (Freeze-Dried) should not be administered to the following: (a) individuals with primary immunodeficiency e.g.: agammaglobulinemia, dysgammaglobulinemia, hypogammaglobulinemia, and symptomatic HIV (Human Immunodeficiency Virus [HTLV-III/LAV]) infections. (b) individuals undergoing treatment with immunosuppressive agents of any kind. (c) children and young adults who are immunosuppressed in association with AIDS or other clinical manifestation of HIV (Human Immunodeficiency Virus [HTLV-III/LAV]) infection.

Warnings: BCG vaccination has **no** value in the treatment of tuberculous disease.

Precautions: Administer BCG Vaccine (Freeze-Dried) intracutaneously. Do not inject s.c.

The vaccinated person should avoid contact with all known tuberculous contacts or suspects until the sensitivity to tuberculin is verified (usually within 3 months).

Pregnancy: Although no harmful effects on the fetus have been observed, use of BCG is not recommended during pregnancy unless there is an excessive risk or unavoidable exposure to infective tuberculosis.

Adverse Effects: Intracutaneous vaccination produces a small indurated papule in 1 to 3 weeks. In 39% of vaccinated newborns, this induration was 10 to 15 mm in diameter. Ulceration may follow, though with this strain and the proper administration technique ulceration is usually minimal and cold abscesses not observed. If small cold abscesses should appear, spontaneous resorption usually occurs. In a few instances, the abscess may soften and may open spontaneously producing an ulcer. If an abscess forms, it may be punctured with a syringe and a fine needle in order to avoid ulceration and scar formation.

Enlargement of the regional lymph glands may occasionally develop after vaccination. Some enlargement of the regional lymph nodes usually accompanies the lesions at the vaccination site. This was observed in 25% in a recent study in newborn infants. Spontaneous regression usually occurs after a period of several months. If, however, perforation and persistent suppuration accompany enlargement of the regional lymph glands, antituberculous chemoprophylaxis is indicated. Surgical excision of the lymph glands is not recommended.

Dosage: The freeze-dried vaccine is reconstituted by introducing the diluent supplied into the vial of vaccine (see instructions for reconstitution).

Cleanse the outer surface of the upper arm with alcohol and allow to dry. Using a 1 mL syringe with a 26 gauge needle,

BCG Vaccine (Freeze Dried) (cont'd)

inject the recommended dose of reconstituted vaccine indicated below into the most superficial layers of the skin (intracutaneously) at one site. The bevelled side of the needle should face upwards.

The recommended dose for newborns and infants is 0.05 mL (0.05 mg). Children over 12 months of age and adults should be given the 0.1 mL (0.1 mg) dose. **Do not inject s.c.**

Reconstitution of Freeze-Dried Vaccine and Withdrawal from Rubber-Stoppered Vial: **Do not remove the rubber stopper from the vial.**

Apply a sterile piece of cotton moistened with a suitable antiseptic to the surface of the rubber stoppers of the vials of diluent and vaccine. Allow the antiseptic to act for at least 5 minutes. Draw into a sterile syringe a volume of air equal to the volume of the diluent in the vial. Pierce the center of the rubber stopper in the vial containing the diluent with the sterile needle of the syringe, invert the vial, slowly inject into it the air contained in the syringe, and, keeping the point of the needle immersed, withdraw into the syringe 1.5 mL of the diluent supplied. Then holding the syringe-plunger steady, withdraw the needle from the vial. Inject this volume of diluent into the vial of freeze-dried vaccine. Shake the vial gently until a fine, even suspension results. Withdraw the required dose of the reconstituted vaccine into the syringe.

Revaccination: If an individual remains tuberculin negative to the Mantoux test for 3 months or longer after vaccination, it is advisable to repeat the vaccination. The development of tuberculin sensitivity as measured by the Mantoux test confirms that the vaccine has established a primary infection in that individual.

Where BCG vaccination has been followed by a satisfactory level of tuberculin sensitivity a few months after vaccination, there is no current indication that revaccination is necessary within 5 to 10 years. In areas where young children are vaccinated, a second vaccination is sometimes given between the ages of 12 to 15 years.

Interpretation of Tuberculin Test: "After BCG vaccination, it is usually not possible to distinguish between a tuberculin reaction caused by virulent supra-infection and one resulting from persistent postvaccination sensitivity. Therefore, caution is advised in attributing a positive skin test to BCG (except in the immediate postvaccination period), especially if the vaccinee has recently been exposed to infective tuberculosis."

Supplied: Multidose vial plus diluent. The freeze-dried vaccine should be kept in a refrigerator at a temperature of **not** more than 8°C. The vaccine should not be used after the expiration date marked on the vial, otherwise it may be inactive. The vaccine should be used immediately after reconstitution and any reconstituted vaccine not used within 8 hours **must** be discarded. The reconstituted vaccine should be maintained at 4°C. At no time should the freeze-dried or reconstituted vaccine be exposed to sunlight, direct or indirect. Exposure to artificial light should be kept to a minimum.

Reviewed 1998

BEANO®

Block Drug

Alpha-D-Galactosidase

Alpha Galactosidase Enzyme

Pharmacology: Hydrolysis converts raffinose, stachyose and verbascose into their digestible sugar components: glucose, galactose, sucrose and fructose. Raffinose yields sucrose+galactose; stachyose yields sucrose+galactose; verbascose yields glucose+fructose+galactose.

Indications: Helps prevent gas. Beano enzyme has been shown to be effective in both clinical and anecdotal studies with humans when consuming foods with high alpha-linked sugar content. Use results in substantially reduced breath hydrogen emissions and marked reduction or elimination of symptoms, compared with identical challenges without Beano.

Flatulence and/or bloat as a result of eating a variety of grains, cereals, nuts, seeds and vegetables containing the sugars raffinose, stachyose and/or verbascose. This includes all or most legumes and all or most cruciferous vegetables. Examples of such foods are oats, wheat, beans of all kinds, chickpeas, peas, lentils, peanuts, soy-content foods, broccoli, brussels sprouts, cabbage, carrots, corn, leeks, onions, parsnips, squash.

Note: Beano has no effect on fibre. Most vegetables also contain fibre, which is gas productive in some people, but usually far less so than the alpha-linked sugars.

Contraindications: Beano is made from a safe food-grade mold; however, if a rare sensitivity occurs, with allergic-type symptoms, discontinue use.

Precautions: Galactosemics should not use without their physicians' advice, since one of the breakdown sugars is galactose.

Adverse Effects: Reports to date include gastroenterological symptoms, such as cramping and diarrhea as well as allergic-type reactions including rash and pruritus. Rare reports of more serious allergic reactions have been received.

Dosage: Drops: Add 5 drops on the first bite of food serving. Tablets: 1 to 3, swallowed, chewed or crumbled onto food, should be enough for a meal of 1 to 3 servings of problem foods.

The optimum number of tablets or drops required is a function of the quantity of food eaten, the levels of alpha-linked sugars in the food and the gas-producing propensity of the person.

Beano enzyme is inactivated at high temperatures. It should be added to foods at a temperature of less than 54°C. If the food is too hot to eat, it is too hot for the enzyme. Do not cook with Beano as the enzyme will be inactivated. Beano will hydrolyze the complex sugars (raffinose, stachyose and verbascose) into the simple sugars—glucose, galactose and fructose, and the easily digestible disaccharide, sucrose. This happens simultaneously with normal digestion.

Supplied: Drops: Each 5 drops contains: not less than 150 GalU (galactose units) of alpha-D-galactosidase [following Food Chemical Codex (FCC) standards] derived from A. niger mold. Nonmedicinal ingredients: sorbitol and water. Bottles of 7.5 and 18.75 g (30 and 75 serving drops).

Tablets: Each tablet contains: not less than 150 GalU (galactose units) of alpha-D-galactosidase (following Food Chemical Codex (FCC) standards) derived from A. niger mold. Nonmedicinal ingredients: cornstarch, hydrogenated cottonseed oil, mannitol and sorbitol. Bottles of 30 and 60.

Store at room temperature (avoid heat).

New Product 1998

BEBEN® ℞

Parke-Davis

Betamethasone Benzoate

Topical Corticosteroid

Supplied: Each tube of gel contains: betamethasone 0.025% as 17-benzoate in a self-liquefying, clear gel base compounded with Carbopol 934, disodium edetate USP, propylene glycol USP, alcohol USP, diisopropanolamine and purified water. pH: 4.0 to 5.2. Tubes of 30 g with applicator.

BECLODISK® ℞
BECLODISK® DISKHALER®

Glaxo Wellcome

Beclomethasone Dipropionate

Corticosteroid for the Treatment of Bronchial Asthma

Pharmacology: Beclomethasone dipropionate is a potent anti-inflammatory steroid with strong topical and weak systemic activity. When inhaled at therapeutic dosages, it has a direct anti-inflammatory action on the bronchial mucosa. Since with therapeutic doses, the minute amounts absorbed do not exert any significant systemic effect, inhaled beclomethasone dipropionate can replace oral steroids with the elimination of the untoward reactions of systemic therapy.

Indications: Treatment of steroid-responsive bronchial asthma. Beclomethasone dipropionate can be used in: bronchial asthmatic patients who in the past have not been on steroids, but whose condition requires inhaled beclomethasone dipropionate; steroid-dependent patients to replace oral medication with beclomethasone dipropionate through gradual withdrawal of the systemic corticosteroids.

Contraindications: Not to be used in the presence of active or quiescent untreated pulmonary tuberculosis, or untreated fungal, bacterial and viral infections.

Not to be used in the primary treatment of status asthmaticus, or other acute episodes of asthma or in patients with moderate to severe bronchiectasis.

Also contraindicated in patients with a history of hypersensitivity to any of the ingredients of this preparation.

Warnings: Systemic Steroid Replacement by Inhaled Steroid: Particular care is needed in patients who are transferred from systemically active corticosteroids to beclomethasone dipropionate because **deaths due to adrenal insufficiency have occurred in asthmatic patients during and after transfer from systemic corticosteroids to aerosol beclomethasone dipropionate.**

After withdrawal from systemic corticosteroids, a number of months may be required for recovery of hypothalamic-pituitary-adrenal (HPA) function. During this period signs of HPA suppression may become manifest especially at times of physical or mental stress, trauma, surgery or infections, particularly gastroenteritis. Although beclomethasone dipropionate may provide control of asthmatic symptoms during these episodes, it does **not** provide the systemic steroid which is necessary for coping with these emergencies.

During periods of stress or a severe asthmatic attack, patients who have been withdrawn from systemic corticosteroids should be instructed to resume systemic steroids immediately and to contact their physician for further instruction. These patients should also be instructed to carry a warning card indicating that they may need supplementary systemic steroids during periods of stress or a severe asthma attack. To assess the risk of adrenal insufficiency in emergency situations, routine tests of adrenal cortical function, including measurement of early morning and evening cortisol levels, should be performed periodically in all patients. An early morning resting cortisol level may be accepted as normal only if it falls at or near the normal mean level. In the majority of patients no significant adrenal suppression occurs until doses of 1 500 μg/day, by inhalation, are exceeded. Reduction of plasma cortisol levels has been reported in some patients who received 2 000 μg/day of inhaled beclomethasone dipropionate. In such patients the risk of developing adrenal suppression should be balanced against the therapeutic advantages and precautions should be taken to provide systemic steroid cover in situations of prolonged stress. Prolonged suppression of the HPA axis may eventually lead to systemic effects including growth retardation in children and adolescents.

Transfer of patients from systemic steroid therapy to beclomethasone dipropionate may unmask allergic conditions previously suppressed by the systemic steroid therapy, e.g., rhinitis, conjunctivitis, and eczema. These allergies should be symptomatically treated with antihistamine and/or topical preparations, including topical steroids.

Studies have shown that the combined administration of alternate-day prednisone systemic treatment and orally inhaled beclomethasone increases the likelihood of HPA suppression compared to a therapeutic dose of either one alone. Therefore, beclomethasone dipropionate treatment should be used with caution in patients already on alternate-day prednisone regimens for any disease.

Systemic Absorption of Orally Inhaled Steroids: Because of the possibility of systemic absorption of orally inhaled corticosteroids, including beclomethasone, patients should be monitored for symptoms of systemic effects such as mental disturbances, increased bruising, weight gain, cushingoid features, acneiform lesions and cataracts. If such changes occur, beclomethasone dipropionate should be discontinued slowly, consistent with accepted procedures for discontinuing oral steroids.

Candidiasis: **The development of pharyngeal and laryngeal candidiasis is a cause of concern because the extent of its penetration into the respiratory tract is unknown. These infections may require treatment with appropriate antifungal therapy and/or the discontinuance of treatment with beclomethasone dipropionate depending on the severity of the infections.**

Monitoring Asthma Control: Beclomethasone dipropionate is not to be regarded as a bronchodilator and is not indicated for rapid relief of bronchospasm. Patients will require a fast and short acting inhaled bronchodilator (e.g., salbutamol) to relieve acute asthmatic symptoms.

Patients should be instructed to contact their physician immediately when episodes of asthma which are not responsive to bronchodilators occur during the course of treatment with beclomethasone dipropionate. During such episodes, patients may require therapy with systemic corticosteroids. There is no evidence that control of bronchial asthma can be achieved by the administration of beclomethasone dipropionate in amounts greater than the recommended dosages.

Precautions: General: It is essential that the patients be instructed that beclomethasone dipropionate is a preventative agent which must be taken daily at the intervals recommended by their doctor and is not to be used as acute treatment for an asthmatic attack.

Steroid Replacement by Beclodisk: The replacement of a systemic steroid with beclomethasone dipropionate has to be gradual and carefully supervised by the physician since upon withdrawal, systemic symptoms (e.g., joint and/or muscular pain, lassitude, depression) may occur despite maintenance or improvement of respiratory function. The guidelines under Dosage should be followed in all such cases.

Long-Term Effects: The long-term effects of beclomethasone dipropionate in human subjects are still unknown. In particular, the local effects of the agent on developmental or immunologic processes in the mouth, pharynx, trachea, and lung are unknown. There is also no information about the possible long-term systemic effects of the agent. During long-term therapy, HPA axis function and hematological status should be assessed periodically.

Discontinuance: Treatment with beclomethasone dipropionate should not be stopped abruptly, but tapered off gradually.

Pulmonary Infiltration by Eosinophils: Pulmonary infiltrates with eosinophilia may occur in patients on beclomethasone dipropionate therapy. Although it is possible that in some patients this state may become manifest because of systemic steroid withdrawal when inhalational steroids are administered, a causative role for beclomethasone dipropionate and/or its vehicle cannot be ruled out.

Pregnancy: Unnecessary administration of drugs during the first trimester of pregnancy is undesirable.

There is inadequate evidence of the safety of beclomethasone dipropionate use in human pregnancy. In animal reproduction studies adverse effects typical of potent corticosteroids are only seen at high systemic exposure levels; direct inhaled application ensures minimal systemic exposure. However, as with other drugs, the use of beclomethasone dipropionate during human pregnancy requires that the therapeutic benefits be weighed against the possible risks associated with the product. Infants born of mothers who have received substantial dosages of corticosteroids during pregnancy should be carefully observed for hypoadrenalism.

Lactation: Glucocorticoids are secreted in human milk. It is not known whether beclomethasone dipropionate would be secreted in human milk, but it is suspected to be likely. The use of beclomethasone dipropionate in pregnancy, nursing mothers, or women of childbearing potential requires that the possible benefits of the drug be weighed against the potential hazards to the mother and embryo or fetus.

Teratogenic Effects: Glucocorticoids are known teratogens in rodent species and beclomethasone dipropionate is no exception.

Teratology studies done in rats, mice and rabbits treated with s.c. beclomethasone dipropionate resulted in fetal resorption, cleft palate, agnathia, microstomia, absence of tongue, delayed ossification, and partial agenesis of the thymus. Well-controlled trials relating to fetal risk in humans are not available.

Effect on Infection: Patients who are on drugs that suppress the immune system are more susceptible to infections than healthy individuals. Chickenpox and measles, for example, can have a more serious or even fatal course in nonimmune children or adults on corticosteroids. In such children or adults who have not had these diseases, particular care should be taken to avoid exposure. How the dose, route, and duration of corticosteroid administration affects the risk of developing a disseminated infection is not known. The contribution of the underlying disease and/or prior corticosteroid treatment to the risk is also not known. If exposed to chickenpox, prophylaxis with varicella zoster immune globulin (VZIG) may be indicated. If exposed to measles, prophylaxis with pooled i.v. immunoglobulin (IVIG), as appropriate, may be indicated. If chickenpox develops, treatment with antiviral agents may be considered.

Corticosteroids may mask some signs of infection and new infections may appear. A decreased resistance to localised infection has been observed during corticosteroid therapy. During long-term therapy, pituitary-adrenal function and hematological status should be periodically assessed. Exacerbation of asthma caused by infections is usually controlled by appropriate antibiotic treatment, by increasing the dose of inhaled beclomethasone dipropionate and if necessary by giving a systemic steroid.

Hypothyroidism and Cirrhosis: There is an enhanced effect of corticosteroids on patients with hypothyroidism and in those with cirrhosis.

Corticosteroids and ASA: ASA should be used cautiously in conjunction with corticosteroids in hypoprothrombinemia.

Children: The application of beclomethasone dipropionate therapy in children from 6 years upwards depends on the ability of the individual child to learn the proper use of the Diskhaler. Assistance by an adult may be necessary.

Proper Use of Drug: To ensure the proper dosage and administration of the drug, the patient must be instructed by a physician or other health professional in the use of the Beclodisk Diskhaler. Patients should be advised to inform subsequent physicians of the prior use of corticosteroids. Treatment with beclomethasone dipropionate should not be stopped abruptly, but tapered off gradually.

Oral Hygiene: Adequate oral hygiene is of primary importance in minimizing overgrowth of microorganisms such as C. albicans (See Dosage).

In the presence of excessive mucus secretion, the drug may fail to reach the bronchioles. Therefore, if an obvious response is not obtained after 10 days, attempts should be made to remove the mucus with expectorants and/or with a short course of systemic corticosteroid treatment.

Adverse Effects: General: In general, inhaled corticosteroid therapy may be associated with dose dependent increases in the incidence of ocular complications, reduced bone density, suppression of HPA axis responsiveness to stress, and inhibition of growth velocity in children.

Glaucoma may be exacerbated by inhaled corticosteroid treatment for asthma or rhinitis. In patients with established glaucoma who require long-term inhaled corticosteroid treatment, it is prudent to measure intraocular pressure before commencing the inhaled corticosteroid and to monitor it subsequently. In patients without established glaucoma, but with a potential for developing intraocular hypertension (e.g., the elderly), intraocular pressure should be monitored at appropriate intervals.

In elderly patients treated with inhaled corticosteroids, the prevalence of posterior subcapsular and nuclear cataracts is probably low but increased in relation to the daily and cumulative lifetime dose. Cofactors such as smoking, ultraviolet B exposure, or diabetes may increase the risk. Children may be less susceptible.

A reduction in growth velocity in children or teenagers may occur as a result of inadequate control of chronic diseases such as asthma or from use of corticosteroids for treatment. Physicians should closely follow the growth of adolescents taking corticosteroids by any route and weigh the benefits of corticosteroid therapy and asthma control against the possibility of growth suppression if any adolescent's growth appears slowed.

Osteoporosis and fracture are the major complications of long-term asthma treatment with parenteral or oral steroids. Inhaled corticosteroid therapy is also associated with dose-dependent bone loss although the degree of risk is very much less than with oral steroid. This risk may be offset by estrogen replacement in postmenopausal women, and by titrating the daily dose of inhaled steroid to the minimum required to maintain optimal asthma control. It is not known yet whether the peak bone density achieved during youth is adversely affected if substantial amounts of inhaled corticosteroid are administered prior to 30 years of age. Failure to achieve maximal bone density during youth could increase the risk of osteoporotic fracture when these individuals reach 60 years of age and older.

Paradoxical Bronchospasm: As with other inhalation therapy, the potential for paradoxical bronchospasm should be kept in mind. If it occurs, the preparation should be discontinued immediately and alternative therapy instituted.

Adrenal Suppression: No indication of significant adrenal cortical suppression has been observed when the daily dosage was up to 1 mg. Above this dosage, reduction of plasma cortisol may occur indicating adrenal cortical suppression.

Gastrointestinal Tract: Therapeutic dosages frequently cause the appearance of C. albicans in the mouth and throat. Long-term studies have shown a dosage-dependent effect. Positive cultures for oral Candida may be present in up to 75% of patients, although the frequency of clinically apparent infection is considerably lower, varying between 0 and 43% with an average of l5%. In children, the incidence of oropharyngeal candidiasis is lower than in adults. In some studies, an overgrowth of A. niger has been found in conjunction with C. albicans. Such affected patients may find it helpful to rinse their mouths with water after using beclomethasone dipropionate.

A few patients on beclomethasone dipropionate therapy have complained of hoarseness, dry mouth or throat irritation. It may be helpful to rinse out the mouth with water immediately after inhalation.

Immunologic Reactions: The replacement of systemic steroids with beclomethasone dipropionate may unmask symptoms of allergies which were previously suppressed by the systemic drug. Conditions such as allergic rhinitis and eczema may thus become apparent during beclomethasone dipropionate therapy after the withdrawal of systemic corticosteroids.

Rare cases of immediate and delayed hypersensitivity reactions, including urticaria, angioedema, rash and bronchospasm, have been reported after the use of beclomethasone oral or intranasal inhalers; pruritus, erythema and edema of the eyes, face, lips and throat also have been reported.

Other Effects: Reports of headache, lightheadedness, dryness and irritation of the nose and throat, and unpleasant taste and smell have been received. There are rare reports of loss of taste and smell.

Overdose: Symptoms and Treatment: Acute: The acute toxicity of beclomethasone dipropionate is low. The only harmful effect that follows inhalation of large amounts of the drug over a short period of time is decreased hypothalamic-pituitary-adrenal (HPA) function. No special emergency action need be taken. Treatment with beclomethasone dipropionate should be continued at the recommended dose to control the asthma; HPA function recovers in a day or two.

Chronic: Chronic overdosage of beclomethasone dipropionate may cause systemic steroid effects such as adrenal suppression and hypercorticism. Decreasing the dose will abolish these side effects.

Dosage: Adults: For optimum benefit beclomethasone dipropionate and the Diskhaler must be used regularly. The usual dose of beclomethasone dipropionate is 200 µg 3 to 4 times daily. As a maintenance dose, many patients do well on 2 inhalations daily.

The optimal dosage of beclomethasone dipropionate may vary widely and must be individually determined, but **the total daily dose should not exceed 1 mg of beclomethasone dipropionate** or 5 blisters of beclomethasone dipropionate 200 µg or 10 blisters of beclomethasone dipropionate 100 µg. Beclomethasone dipropionate blisters are per inhalation use only, using a beclomethasone dipropionate Diskhaler.

Adolescents: Above 14 years of age, the adult dose applies.

Children: There is insufficient clinical experience with beclomethasone dipropionate in children below 6 years of age. Children from 6 to 14 years of age can be started on one 100 µg beclomethasone dipropionate 2 to 4 times daily. **The total daily dose should not exceed 500 µg of beclomethasone dipropionate.**

General: As a general rule, rinsing the mouth and gargling after each inhalation with water can help in preventing the occurrence of candidiasis. Cleansing dentures has the same effect.

Since the effect of beclomethasone dipropionate depends on its regular use and on the proper technique of inhalation, patients must be instructed to take the inhalations at regular intervals as prescribed by their physician and not as with other treatments-as they feel necessary. They must also be instructed in the correct method to use the Diskhaler which is described in the Section Information for the Patient to ensure that the drug reaches the target areas within the lungs.

Patients receiving bronchodilators by inhalation should be advised to use the bronchodilator before the beclomethasone dipropionate in order to enhance the penetration of beclomethasone dipropionate into the bronchial tree. Several minutes should elapse between treatments to allow some bronchodilation to occur.

Patients Receiving Systemic Steroids: Careful attention must be given to patients previously treated for prolonged periods with systemic corticosteroids, when transferred to beclomethasone dipropionate. Patients' bronchial asthma should be stable before transfer is started. Initially, beclomethasone dipropionate and the systemic steroid must be given concomitantly while the doses of the latter is gradually decreased. In adults, the usual rate of withdrawal of the systemic corticoid is the equivalent of 2.5 mg of prednisone every 4 days if the patient is under close observation. In children, the rate of withdrawal is 2.5 mg of prednisone every 8 days when under close supervision. **If continuous supervision is not feasible, the withdrawal of the systemic steroid should be slower,** approximately 2.5 mg of prednisone (or equivalent) every 10 days in adults and 20 days in children. A slow rate of withdrawal cannot be overemphasized. If withdrawal symptoms appear, the previous dose of the systemic drug should be resumed for a week before further decrease is attempted.

During withdrawal, some patients may experience symptoms of systemically active steroid withdrawal, e.g., joint and/or muscular pain, lassitude, and depression, despite maintenance or even improvement of respiratory function. Such patients should be encouraged to continue with the

Beclodisk (cont'd)

inhaler but should be watched carefully for objective signs of adrenal insufficiency such as hypotension and weight loss. If evidence of adrenal insufficiency occurs, the systemic steroid dosage should be boosted temporarily and thereafter further withdrawal should continue more slowly.

During periods of stress or a severe asthma attack, transfer patients will require supplementary treatment with systemic steroids.

Exacerbations of bronchial asthma which occur during the course of treatment with beclomethasone dipropionate should be treated with a short course of systemic steroid which is gradually tapered as these symptoms subside. There is no evidence that control of bronchial asthma can be achieved by the administration of beclomethasone dipropionate therapy in amounts greater than the recommended dosages. Under stressful conditions or when the patient has a severe exacerbation of bronchial asthma, after complete withdrawal of the systemic steroid, the use of the systemic steroids must be resumed in order to avoid relative adrenocortical insufficiency. There are some patients who cannot completely discontinue the use of oral corticosteroid. In these cases, a minimum maintenance dose should be given in addition to beclomethasone dipropionate.

The dosage of inhaled beclomethasone dipropionate should be increased in times of stress. Antibiotic treatment should be considered if the exacerbation of asthma is caused by infection.

Information for the Patient: See Blue Section—Information for the Patient "Beclodisk/Beclodisk Diskhaler".

Supplied: Beclodisk: Disks are circular, double foil blister packs with 8 regularly spaced blisters, each containing 100 μg or 200 μg of beclomethasone dipropionate and lactose. Each dosage strength is identified in the centre of the Beclodisk Disk as BECLODISK 100, 8 doses (beige) or BECLODISK 200, 8 doses (dark brown). Disks of 8 doses, cartons of 15. Store below 30°C in a dry place.

The Beclodisk Disk is intended only for use in a specific drug delivery device known as the Beclodisk Diskhaler. The contents of each Beclodisk blister are deposited into the beige Beclodisk Diskhaler device when pierced with the Beclodisk Diskhaler needle. The blisters must only be pierced immediately prior to use. The contents are then available to the patients to inhale by breath actuation.

Beclodisk Diskhaler: Available separately from the Beclodisk Disk.

(Shown in Product Recognition Section)

Reviewed 1999

BECLOFORTE® ℞

Glaxo Wellcome

Beclomethasone Dipropionate

Corticosteroid for the Treatment of Bronchial Asthma

Pharmacology: Beclomethasone dipropionate is a potent anti-inflammatory steroid with strong topical and weak systemic activity. When inhaled at therapeutic dosages, it has a direct anti-inflammatory action on the bronchial mucosa. Since with therapeutic doses the minute amounts absorbed do not exert any significant systemic effect, inhaled beclomethasone dipropionate can replace oral steroids with the elimination of the untoward effects of systemic therapy.

Indications: Treatment of steroid-responsive bronchial asthma. Beclomethasone dipropionate can be used in 2 conditions: in bronchial asthmatic patients who in the past have not been on steroids, but whose condition requires inhaled beclomethasone dipropionate; in steroid-dependent patients to replace oral steroid medication with beclomethasone dipropionate through gradual withdrawal of the systemic steroid.

Becloforte is only to be used when the total daily dosage of beclomethasone dipropionate required is 500 to 1 000 μg.

Contraindications: Active or quiescent pulmonary tuberculosis, or fungal, bacterial and viral infections.

Not to be used in primary treatment of status asthmaticus, or other acute episodes of asthma, or in patients with moderate to severe bronchiectasis.

Also contraindicated in patients with a history of hypersensitivity to any of the ingredients of this preparation.

Warnings: Systemic Steroid Replacement by Inhaled Steroid: Particular care is needed in patients who are transferred from systemically active corticosteroids to beclomethasone dipropionate because **deaths due to adrenal insufficiency have occurred in asthmatic patients during and after transfer from systemic corticosteroids to aerosol beclomethasone dipropionate.**

After withdrawal from systemic corticosteroids, a number of months is required for recovery of hypothalamic-pituitary-adrenal (HPA) function. During this period of HPA suppression, patients may exhibit signs and symptoms of adrenal insufficiency when exposed to trauma, surgery or infections, particularly gastroenteritis. Although beclomethasone dipropionate may provide control of asthmatic symptoms during these episodes, it does **not** provide the systemic steroid which is necessary for coping with these emergencies.

During periods of stress or a severe asthmatic attack, patients who have been withdrawn from systemic corticosteroids should be instructed to resume systemic steroids (in large dosages) immediately and to contact their physician for further instruction. These patients should also be instructed to carry a warning card indicating that they may need supplementary systemic steroids during periods of stress or a severe asthma attack. To assess the risk of adrenal insufficiency in emergency situations, routine tests of adrenal cortical function, including measurement of early morning and evening cortisol levels, should be performed periodically in all patients. An early morning resting cortisol level may be accepted as normal only if it falls at or near the normal mean level. In the majority of patients no significant adrenal suppression occurs until doses of 1 500 μg/day, by inhalation, are exceeded. Reduction of plasma cortisol levels has been reported in some patients who received 2 000 μg/day of inhaled beclomethasone dipropionate. In such patients the risk of developing adrenal suppression should be balanced against the therapeutic advantages and precautions should be taken to provide systemic steroid cover in situations of prolonged stress. Prolonged suppression of the HPA axis may eventually lead to systemic effects including growth retardation in children and adolescents.

Transfer of patients from systemic steroid therapy to beclomethasone dipropionate may unmask allergic conditions previously suppressed by the systemic steroid therapy, e.g., rhinitis, conjunctivitis, and eczema. These allergies should be symptomatically treated with antihistamine and/or topical preparations, including topical steroids.

Studies have shown that the combined administration of alternate-day prednisone systemic treatment and orally inhaled beclomethasone increases the likelihood of HPA suppression compared to a therapeutic dose of either one alone. Therefore, beclomethasone dipropionate treatment should be used with caution in patients already on alternate-day prednisone regimens for any disease.

Systemic Absorption of Orally Inhaled Steroids: Because of the possibility of systemic absorption of orally inhaled corticosteroids, including beclomethasone, patients should be monitored for symptoms of systemic effects such as mental disturbances, increased bruising, weight gain, cushingoid features, acneiform lesions and cataracts. If such changes occur, beclomethasone dipropionate should be discontinued slowly, consistent with accepted procedures for discontinuing oral steroids.

Candidiasis: **The development of pharyngeal and laryngeal candidiasis is cause for concern because the extent of its penetration into the respiratory tract is unknown. These infections may require treatment with appropriate antifungal therapy and/or discontinuance of treatment with beclomethasone dipropionate, depending on the severity of the infections.**

Monitoring Asthma Control: Beclomethasone dipropionate is not to be regarded as a bronchodilator and is not indicated for rapid relief of bronchospasm. Patients will require a fast and short acting inhaled bronchodilator (e.g., salbutamol) to relieve acute asthmatic symptoms.

Patients should be instructed to contact their physicians immediately when episodes of asthma which are not responsive to bronchodilators occur during the course of treatment with Becloforte. During such episodes, patients may require therapy with systemic corticosteroids. There is no evidence that control of bronchial asthma can be achieved by the administration of beclomethasone dipropionate in amounts greater than the recommended dosages.

Precautions: It is essential that the patients be instructed that beclomethasone dipropionate is a preventative agent which must be taken daily at the intervals recommended by their doctor and is not to be used as acute treatment for an asthmatic attack.

Steroid Replacement by beclomethasone dipropionate: The replacement of a systemic steroid with beclomethasone dipropionate has to be gradual and carefully supervised by the physician since upon withdrawal systemic symptoms (e.g., joint and/or muscular pain, lassitude, depression) may occur despite maintenance or improvement of respiratory function. The guidelines under Dosage should be followed in all such cases.

Long-term Effects: The long-term effects of beclomethasone dipropionate in human subjects are still unknown. In particular, the local effects of the agent on developmental or immunologic processes in the mouth, pharynx, trachea, and lungs are unknown. There is also no information about the possible long-term systemic effects of the agent. During long-term therapy, HPA axis function and hematological status should be assessed periodically.

Discontinuance: Treatment should not be stopped abruptly, but tapered off gradually.

Pulmonary Infiltration by Eosinophils: Pulmonary infiltration by eosinophils may occur in patients on Becloforte therapy. Although it is possible that in some patients this state may become manifest because of systemic steroid withdrawal when inhalational steroids are administered, a causative role for beclomethasone dipropionate and/or its vehicle cannot be ruled out.

Pregnancy: Unnecessary administration of drugs during the first trimester of pregnancy is undesirable. There is inadequate evidence of safety of beclomethasone dipropionate in human pregnancy. In animal reproduction studies adverse effects typical of potent corticosteroids are only seen at high systemic exposure levels; direct inhaled application ensures minimal systemic exposure. However, as with other drugs, the use of beclomethasone dipropionate during human pregnancy requires that the therapeutic benefits be weighed against the possible risks associated with the product. Infants born of mothers who have received substantial dosages of corticosteroids during pregnancy should be carefully observed for hypoadrenalism.

Lactation: Glucocorticoids are excreted in human milk. It is not known whether beclomethasone dipropionate would be excreted in human milk, but it is suspected to be likely. The use of beclomethasone dipropionate in pregnancy, nursing mothers, or women of childbearing potential requires that the possible benefits of the drug be weighed against the potential hazards to the mother, and embryo or fetus.

Teratogenic Effects: Glucocorticoids are known teratogens in rodent species and beclomethasone dipropionate is no exception.

Teratology studies done in rats, mice, and rabbits treated with s.c. beclomethasone dipropionate resulted in fetal resorptions, cleft palate, agnathia, microstomia, absence of tongue, delayed ossification, and partial agenesis of the thymus in both the mouse and rabbit. Well-controlled trials relating to fetal risk in humans are not available.

Effect on Infection: Patients who are on drugs that suppress the immune system are more susceptible to infections than healthy individuals. Chickenpox and measles, for example, can have a more serious or even fatal course in nonimmune children or adults on corticosteroids. In such children or adults who have not had these diseases, particular care should be taken to avoid exposure. How the dose, route, and duration of corticosteroid administration affects the risk of developing a disseminated infection is not known. The contribution of the underlying disease and/or prior corticosteroid treatment to the risk is also not known. If exposed to chickenpox, prophylaxis with varicella zoster immune globulin (VZIG) may be indicated. If exposed to measles, prophylaxis with pooled i.v. immunoglobulin (IVIG), as appropriate, may be indicated. If chickenpox develops, treatment with antiviral agents may be considered.

Corticosteroids may mask some signs of infections and new infections may appear. A decreased resistance to localized infection has been observed during corticosteroid therapy. During long-term therapy, pituitary-adrenal function and hematological status should be periodically assessed. Exacerbation of asthma caused by infections is usually controlled by appropriate antibiotic treatment, by increasing the dose of inhaled beclomethasone dipropionate and if necessary by giving a systemic steroid.

Abuse of Fluorocarbon Propellants: Fluorocarbon propellants may be hazardous if they are deliberately abused. Inhalation of high concentrations of aerosols sprays has brought about cardiovascular toxic effects and even death, especially under conditions of hypoxia. However, evidence attests to the safety of aerosols when used properly and with adequate ventilation.

Hypothyroidism and Cirrhosis: There is an enhanced effect of corticosteroids on patients with hypothyroidism and in those with cirrhosis.

Corticosteroids and ASA: ASA should be used cautiously in conjunction with corticosteroids in hypoprothrombinemia.

Proper Use of Drug: To ensure the proper dosage and administration of the drug, the patient must be instructed by a physician or other health professional in the proper use of the inhaler. Patients should be advised to inform subsequent physicians of the prior use of corticosteroids. Treatment with beclomethasone dipropionate should not be stopped abruptly, but tapered off gradually.

Oral Hygiene: Adequate oral hygiene is of primary importance in minimizing overgrowth of microorganisms such as C. albicans (see Dosage).

Adverse Effects: General: In general, inhaled corticosteroid therapy may be associated with dose dependent increases in the incidence of ocular complications, reduced bone density, suppression of HPA axis responsiveness to stress, and inhibition of growth velocity in children.

Glaucoma may be exacerbated by inhaled corticosteroid treatment for asthma or rhinitis. In patients with established glaucoma who require long-term inhaled corticosteroid treatment, it is prudent to measure intraocular pressure before commencing the inhaled corticosteroid and to monitor it subsequently. In patients without established glaucoma, but with a potential for developing intraocular hypertension (e.g., the elderly), intraocular pressure should be monitored at appropriate intervals.

In elderly patients treated with inhaled corticosteroids, the prevalence of posterior subcapsular and nuclear cataracts is probably low but increased in relation to the daily and cumulative lifetime dose. Cofactors such as smoking, ultraviolet B exposure, or diabetes may increase the risk. Children may be less susceptible.

A reduction in growth velocity in children or teenagers may occur as a result of inadequate control of chronic diseases such as asthma or from use of corticosteroids for treatment. Physicians should closely follow the growth of adolescents taking corticosteroids by any route and weigh the benefits of corticosteroid therapy and asthma control against the possibility of growth suppression if any adolescent's growth appears slowed.

Osteoporosis and fracture are the major complications of long-term asthma treatment with parenteral or oral steroids. Inhaled corticosteroid therapy is also associated with dose-dependent bone loss although the degree of risk is very much less than with oral steroid. This risk may be offset by estrogen replacement in postmenopausal women, and by titrating the daily dose of inhaled steroid to the minimum required to maintain optimal asthma control. It is not known yet whether the peak bone density achieved during youth is adversely affected if substantial amounts of inhaled corticosteroid are administered prior to 30 years of age. Failure to achieve maximal bone density during youth could increase the risk of osteoporotic fracture when these individuals reach 60 years of age and older.

Paradoxical Bronchospasm: As with other inhalation therapy, the potential for paradoxical bronchospasm should be kept in mind. If it occurs, the preparation should be discontinued immediately and alternative therapy instituted.

Adrenal Suppression: No indication of significant adrenal corticol suppression has been observed when the daily dosage was up to 1 mg (4 puffs). Above this dosage, reduction of plasma cortisol may occur.

Gastrointestinal Tract: Therapeutic dosages frequently cause the appearance of C. albicans in the mouth and throat. Long-term studies have shown a dosage-dependent effect. Positive cultures for oral Candida may be present in up to 75% of patients although the frequency of clinically apparent infection is considerably lower, varying between 0 and 43%, with an average of 15%. In some studies, an overgrowth of A. niger has been found in conjunction with C. albicans. Such affected patients may find it helpful to rinse their mouths with water after using Becloforte.

A few patients on beclomethasone dipropionate have complained of hoarseness, dry mouth or throat irritation. It may be helpful to rinse out the mouth with water immediately after inhalation.

Immunologic Reactions: The replacement of systemic steroids with beclomethasone dipropionate may unmask symptoms of allergies which were previously suppressed by the systemic drug. Conditions such as allergic rhinitis and eczema may thus become apparent during beclomethasone dipropionate therapy after the withdrawal of systemic corticosteroids.

Rare cases of immediate and delayed hypersensitivity reactions, including urticaria, angioedema, rash, and bronchospasm, have been reported after the use of beclomethasone oral or intranasal inhalers; pruritus, erythema, and edema of the eyes, face, lips and throat also have been reported.

Other Effects: Reports of headache, lightheadedness, dryness and irritation of the nose and throat, and unpleasant taste and smell have been received. There are rare reports of loss of taste and smell.

Overdose: Symptoms and Treatment: Acute: The acute toxicity of beclomethasone dipropionate is low. The only harmful effect that follows inhalation of large amounts of the drug over a short period of time is suppression of hypothalamic-pituitary-adrenal (HPA) function. No special emergency action need be taken. Treatment with beclomethasone dipropionate should be continued at the recommended dose to control the asthma; HPA function recovers in a day or two.

Chronic: The excessive use of beclomethasone dipropionate over a long period could lead to adrenal suppression. In such a case the patient should be transferred to oral corticosteroid therapy and when the condition has stabilized, be returned to inhaled therapy at the recommended dose. To guard against the unexpected event of adrenal suppression regular tests of adrenal function are advised. Oral steroids should then be slowly withdrawn, as for steroid-dependent patients.

Dosage: Becloforte is only to be used when the total daily dosage of beclomethasone dipropionate required is 500 to 1 000 μg.

Adults: One inhalation (250 μg) 2 to 4 times daily. Some patients may do well with 2 inhalations (500 μg) twice daily.

The total daily dosage should not exceed 1 mg of beclomethasone dipropionate (4 inhalations).

Adolescents: Above 16 years of age, the adult dosage applies.

Children: Not recommended for children under 16 years of age.

General: As a general rule, rinsing the mouth and gargling after each inhalation with water can help in preventing the occurrence of candidiasis. Cleansing dentures has the same effect.

Since the effect of Becloforte depends on its regular use and on the proper technique of inhalation, patients must be instructed to use their inhaler daily, as prescribed by their physician and not as with other aerosols, as they feel necessary. They must also be instructed in the correct method to use the Belcoforte inhalation aerosol which is described in the section Information for the Patient to ensure that the drug reaches the target areas within the lungs.

In the presence of excessive mucus secretion, the drug may fail to reach the bronchioles. Therefore, if an obvious response is not obtained after 10 days, attempts should be made to remove the mucus with expectorants and/or with a short course of systemic corticosteroid treatment. Continuation of treatment with inhaled beclomethasone dipropionate usually maintains the improvement achieved, the oral steroid being gradually withdrawn.

Patients receiving bronchodilators by inhalation should be advised to use the bronchodilator before the beclomethasone dipropionate inhalation aerosol in order to enhance the penetration of beclomethasone dipropionate into the bronchial tree. Several minutes should elapse between the use of the 2 inhalers to reduce the potential toxicity from the inhaled fluorocarbon propellants and to allow for some bronchodilation to occur.

Patients Receiving Systemic Steroids: Careful attention must be given to patients previously treated for prolonged periods with systemic corticosteroids, when transferred to beclomethasone dipropionate. Patients' bronchial asthma should be stable before transfer is started. Initially, Becloforte and the systemic steroid must be given concomitantly while the dosage of the latter is gradually decreased. In adults, the usual rate of withdrawal of the systemic corticosteroid is the equivalent of 1 mg of prednisone at no less than weekly intervals if the patient is under close observation. **If continuous supervision is not feasible, the withdrawal of the systemic steroid should be slower,** approximately 1 mg of prednisone (or equivalent) every 10 days. A slow rate of withdrawal cannot be overemphasized. If withdrawal symptoms appear, the previous dosage of the systemic drug should be resumed for a week before further decrease is attempted.

During withdrawal, some patients may experience symptoms of systemically active steroid withdrawal, e.g., joint and/or muscular pain, lassitude, and depression, despite maintenance or even improvement of respiratory function. Such patients should be encouraged to continue with beclomethasone dipropionate but should be watched carefully for objective signs of adrenal insufficiency such as hypotension and weight loss. If evidence of adrenal insufficiency occurs, the systemic steroid dosage should be boosted temporarily and thereafter further withdrawal should continue more slowly.

During periods of stress or a severe asthma attack, transfer patients will require supplementary treatment with systemic steroids.

Exacerbations of bronchial asthma which occur during the course of treatment should be treated with a short course of systemic steroid which is gradually tapered as these symptoms subside. There is no evidence that control of bronchial asthma can be achieved by the administration of beclomethasone dipropionate in amounts greater than the recommended dosages. Under stressful conditions or when the patient has a severe exacerbation of bronchial asthma, after complete withdrawal of the systemic steroid, use of the latter must be resumed in order to avoid relative adrenocortical insufficiency.

There are some patients who cannot completely discontinue the oral corticosteroid. In these cases, a minimum maintenance dosage should be given in addition to beclomethasone dipropionate.

Information for the Patient: See Blue Section—Information for the Patient "Becloforte".

Supplied: Each depression of the metered dose aerosol valve delivers: beclomethasone dipropionate 250 μg suspended in trichlorofluoromethane and dichlorodifluoromethane. Nonmedicinal ingredients: dichlorodifluoromethane, oleic acid and trichlorofluoromethane. Each unit is housed in a suitable actuator/adaptor. Aluminum canisters fitted with metering valves. Becloforte is available in 200 dose containers.

Caution: Container may explode if heated. Contents under pressure. Do not place in hot water or near radiators, stoves or other sources of heat. Even when empty, do not puncture or incinerate container or store at temperatures over 30°C. Protect from freezing and direct sunlight. As with most inhaled medications in aerosol canisters, the therapeutic effect of this medication may decrease when the canister is cold.

(Shown in Product Recognition Section)

Reviewed 1999

BECLOMETHASONE Ⓟ

General Monograph, CPhA

see CORTICOSTEROIDS: EYE EAR NOSE
see CORTICOSTEROIDS: INHALED

BECLOVENT® INHALER Ⓟ
BECLOVENT® ROTACAPS® Ⓟ
BECLOVENT® ROTAHALER®

Glaxo Wellcome

Beclomethasone Dipropionate

Corticosteroid for the Treatment of Bronchial Asthma

Pharmacology: Beclomethasone dipropionate is a potent anti-inflammatory steroid with strong topical and weak systemic activity. When inhaled at therapeutic doses it has a direct anti-inflammatory action on the bronchial mucosa. Since with therapeutic doses the minute amounts absorbed do not exert any significant systemic effect, inhaled beclomethasone dipropionate can replace oral steroids with the elimination of the untoward effects of systemic therapy.

Indications: Treatment of steroid-responsive bronchial asthma. Beclomethasone dipropionate can be used in 2 conditions: in bronchial asthmatic patients who in the past have not been on steroids, but whose condition requires inhaled beclomethasone dipropionate; in steroid-dependent patients to replace oral steroid medication through gradual withdrawal of the systemic steroid.

The effectiveness of Beclovent Rotacaps is dependent upon their regular use and proper inhalation technique. Beclovent Rotacap capsules are for inhalation use only, using a Beclovent Rotahaler inhaler.

Contraindications: Active or quiescent pulmonary tuberculosis, or fungal, bacterial and viral infections.

Not to be used in the primary treatment of status asthmaticus or other acute episodes of asthma, or in patients with moderate to severe bronchiectasis.

Also contraindicated in patients with a history of hypersensitivity to any of the ingredients of this preparation.

Warnings: Systemic Steroid Replacement by Inhaled Steroid: Particular care is needed in patients who are transferred from systemically active corticosteroids to inhaled beclomethasone dipropionate because **deaths due to adrenal insufficiency have occurred in asthmatic patients during and after transfer from systemic corticosteroids to aerosol beclomethasone dipropionate.**

Beclovent (cont'd)

After withdrawal from systemic corticosteroids, a number of months is required for recovery of hypothalamic-pituitary-adrenal (HPA) function. During this period of HPA suppression, patients may exhibit signs and symptoms of adrenal insufficiency when exposed to trauma, surgery or infections, particularly gastroenteritis. Although inhaled beclomethasone dipropionate may provide control of asthmatic symptoms during these episodes, it does **not** provide the systemic steroid which is necessary for coping with these emergencies.

During periods of stress or a severe asthmatic attack, patients who have been withdrawn from systemic corticosteroids should be instructed to immediately resume systemic steroids in dosages that were previously effective and to contact their physicians for further instruction. These patients should also be instructed to carry a warning card indicating that they may need supplementary systemic steroids during periods of stress or a severe asthma attack. To assess the risk of adrenal insufficiency in emergency situations, routine tests of adrenal cortical function, including measurement of early morning and evening cortisol levels, should be performed periodically in all patients. An early morning resting cortisol level may be accepted as normal only if it falls at or near the normal mean level. In the majority of patients no significant adrenal suppression occurs until doses of 1 500 μg/day, by inhalation, are exceeded. Reduction of plasma cortisol levels has been reported in some patients who received 2 000 μg/day of inhaled beclomethasone dipropionate. In such patients the risks of developing adrenal suppression should be balanced against the therapeutic advantages and precautions should be taken to provide systemic steroid cover in situations of prolonged stress. Prolonged suppression of the HPA axis may eventually lead to systemic effects including growth retardation in children and adolescents.

Transfer of patients from systemic steroid therapy to beclomethasone dipropionate may unmask allergic conditions previously suppressed by the systemic steroid therapy, e.g., rhinitis, conjunctivitis, and eczema. These allergies should be symptomatically treated with antihistamine and/or topical preparations, including topical steroids.

Studies have shown that the combined administration of alternate-day prednisone systemic treatment and orally inhaled beclomethasone increases the likelihood of HPA suppression compared to a therapeutic dose of either one alone. Therefore, beclomethasone dipropionate treatment should be used with caution in patients already on alternate-day prednisone regimens for any disease.

Systemic Absorption of Orally Inhaled Steroids: Because of the possibility of systemic absorption of orally inhaled corticosteroids, including beclomethasone, patients should be monitored for symptoms of systemic effects such as mental disturbances, increased bruising, weight gain, cushingoid features, acneiform lesions and cataracts. If such changes occur, beclomethasone dipropionate should be discontinued slowly, consistent with accepted procedures for discontinuing oral steroids.

Candidiasis: **The development of pharyngeal and laryngeal candidiasis is a cause of concern because the extent of its penetration into the respiratory tract is unknown. These infections may require treatment with appropriate antifungal therapy and/or discontinuation of treatment with beclomethasone dipropionate, depending on the severity of the infections.**

Monitoring Asthma Control: Beclomethasone dipropionate is not to be regarded as a bronchodilator and is not indicated for rapid relief of bronchospasm. Patients will require a fast and short acting inhaled bronchodilator (e.g., salbutamol) to relieve acute asthmatic symptoms.

Patients should be instructed to contact their physicians immediately when episodes of asthma which are not responsive to bronchodilators occur during the course of treatment with beclomethasone dipropionate. During such episodes, patients may require therapy with systemic corticosteroids. There is no evidence that control of bronchial asthma can be achieved by the administration of beclomethasone dipropionate in amounts greater than the recommended dosages.

Pregnancy: Administration of drugs during pregnancy should only be considered if the expected benefit to the mother is greater than any possible risk to the fetus (see Precautions).

Precautions: General: It is essential that the patients be instructed that beclomethasone dipropionate is a preventative agent which must be taken daily at the intervals recommended by their doctor and is not to be used as treatment for an acute asthmatic attack.

Steroid Replacement by Beclovent: The replacement of a systemic steroid with beclomethasone dipropionate has to be gradual and carefully supervised by the physician since upon withdrawal, systemic symptoms (e.g., joint and/or muscle pain, lassitude, depression) may occur despite maintenance or improvement of respiratory function. The guidelines under Dosage should be followed in all such cases.

Long-term Effects: The long-term effects of beclomethasone dipropionate in human subjects are still unknown. In particular, the local effects of the agent on developmental or immunologic processes in the mouth, pharynx, trachea and lungs are unknown. There is also no information about the possible long-term systemic effects of the agent. During long-term therapy, HPA axis function and hematological status should be assessed periodically.

Discontinuance: Treatment with beclomethasone dipropionate inhalation aerosol should not be stopped abruptly, but tapered off gradually.

Pulmonary Infiltration by Eosinophils: Pulmonary infiltrates with eosinophils may occur in patients on beclomethasone dipropionate therapy. Although it is possible that in some patients this state may become manifest because of systemic steroid withdrawal when inhalational steroids are administered, a causative role for beclomethasone dipropionate and/or its vehicle cannot be ruled out.

Pregnancy: There is inadequate evidence of safety during human pregnancy. In animal reproduction studies adverse effects typical of potent corticosteroids are only seen at high systemic exposure levels; direct inhaled application ensures minimal systemic exposure. However, as with other drugs, the use of beclomethasone dipropionate during human pregnancy requires that the therapeutic benefits be weighed against the possible risks associated with the product. Infants born of mothers who have received substantial dosages of corticosteroids during pregnancy should be carefully observed for hypoadrenalism.

Lactation: No specific studies examining the transference of beclomethasone dipropionate into the milk of lactating animals have been performed. It is reasonable to assume that beclomethasone dipropionate is excreted in human milk. The use of beclomethasone dipropionate in mothers breast-feeding their babies requires that the therapeutic benefits of the drug be weighed against the potential hazards to the mother and baby.

Teratogenic Effects: Glucocorticoids are known teratogens in rodent species and beclomethasone dipropionate is no exception.

Teratogenicity studies have been carried out by the inhaled and oral routes in mice, rats and rabbits. In mice and rabbits, beclomethasone dipropionate showed effects at high dose levels typical of a potent corticosteroid, e.g., retardation of fetal growth and cleft palate. Similarly in rats beclomethasone dipropionate induced early embryonic death and fetal growth retardation at very high dose levels; however, no fetus with cleft palate was detected. Well-controlled trials relating to fetal risk in humans are not available.

Effect on Infection: Patients who are on drugs that suppress the immune system are more susceptible to infections than healthy individuals. Chickenpox and measles, for example, can have a more serious or even fatal course in nonimmune children or adults on corticosteroids. In such children or adults who have not had these diseases, particular care should be taken to avoid exposure. How the dose, route, and duration of corticosteroid administration affects the risk of developing a disseminated infection is not known. The contribution of the underlying disease and/or prior corticosteroid treatment to the risk is also not known. If exposed to chickenpox, prophylaxis with varicella zoster immune globulin (VZIG) may be indicated. If exposed to measles, prophylaxis with pooled i.v. immunoglobulin (IVIG), as appropriate, may be indicated. If chickenpox develops, treatment with antiviral agents may be considered.

Corticosteroids may mask some signs of infections and new infections may appear. A decreased resistance to localized infection has been observed during corticosteroid therapy. During long-term therapy, pituitary-adrenal function and hematological status should be periodically assessed. Exacerbation of asthma caused by infections is usually controlled by appropriate antibiotic treatment, by increasing the dose of inhaled beclomethasone and if necessary, by giving a systemic steroid.

Abuse of Fluorocarbon Propellants: Fluorocarbon propellants may be hazardous if they are deliberately abused. Inhalation of high concentrations of aerosol sprays has brought about cardiovascular toxic effects and even death, especially under conditions of hypoxia. However, evidence attests to the safety of aerosols when used properly and with adequate ventilation.

Hypothyroidism and Cirrhosis: There is an enhanced effect of corticosteroids on patients with hypothyroidism and in those with cirrhosis.

Corticosteroids and ASA: ASA should be used cautiously in conjunction with corticosteroids in hypoprothrombinemia.

Children: The application of beclomethasone dipropionate therapy in children from 3 years upwards for the inhaler and 6 years upwards for the Rotahaler should depend on the ability of the individual child to learn the proper use of the device. These children should be assisted or supervised by an adult during inhalation.

Proper Use of Drug: To ensure the proper dosage and administration of the drug, the patient must be instructed by a physician or other health professional in the use of the inhaler or the Rotahaler. Patients should be advised to inform subsequent physicians of the prior use of corticosteroids. Treatment with beclomethasone dipropionate should not be stopped abruptly, but tapered off gradually.

Oral Hygiene: Adequate oral hygiene is of primary importance in minimizing overgrowth of microorganisms such as C. albicans (see Dosage).

Adverse Effects: General: In general, inhaled corticosteroid therapy may be associated with dose dependent increases in the incidence of ocular complications, reduced bone density, suppression of HPA axis responsiveness to stress, and inhibition of growth velocity in children.

Glaucoma may be exacerbated by inhaled corticosteroid treatment for asthma or rhinitis. In patients with established glaucoma who require long-term inhaled corticosteroid treatment, it is prudent to measure intraocular pressure before commencing the inhaled corticosteroid and to monitor it subsequently. In patients without established glaucoma, but with a potential for developing intraocular hypertension (e.g., the elderly), intraocular pressure should be monitored at appropriate intervals.

In elderly patients treated with inhaled corticosteroids, the prevalence of posterior subcapsular and nuclear cataracts is probably low but increased in relation to the daily and cumulative lifetime dose. Cofactors such as smoking, ultraviolet B exposure, or diabetes may increase the risk. Children may be less susceptible.

A reduction in growth velocity in children or teenagers may occur as a result of inadequate control of chronic diseases such as asthma or from use of corticosteroids for treatment. Physicians should closely follow the growth of adolescents taking corticosteroids by any route and weigh the benefits of corticosteroid therapy and asthma control against the possibility of growth suppression if any adolescent's growth appears slowed.

Osteoporosis and fracture are the major complications of long-term asthma treatment with parenteral or oral steroids. Inhaled corticosteroid therapy is also associated with dose-dependent bone loss although the degree of risk is very much less than with oral steroid. This risk may be offset by estrogen replacement in postmenopausal women, and by titrating the daily dose of inhaled steroid to the minimum required to maintain optimal asthma control. It is not known yet whether the peak bone density achieved during youth is adversely affected if substantial amounts of inhaled corticosteroid are administered prior to 30 years of age. Failure to achieve maximal bone density during youth could increase the risk of osteoporotic fracture when these individuals reach 60 years of age and older.

Paradoxical Bronchospasm: As with other inhalation therapy, the potential for paradoxical bronchospasm should be kept in mind. If it occurs, the preparation should be discontinued immediately and alternative therapy instituted.

Adrenal Suppression: In the majority of patients no significant adrenal suppression occurs until doses of 1 500 μg/day by inhalation are exceeded. Reduction of plasma cortisol levels has been reported in some patients who received 2 000 μg/day of inhaled beclomethasone dipropionate.

Gastrointestinal Tract: Therapeutic dosages frequently cause the appearance of C. albicans in the mouth and throat. Long-term studies have shown a dosage-dependent effect. Positive cultures for oral Candida may be present in up to 75% of patients, although the frequency of clinically apparent infection is considerably lower, varying between 0 and 43% with an average of 15%. In children, the incidence of oropharyngeal candidiasis is lower than in adults. In some studies, an overgrowth of A. niger has been found in conjunction with C. albicans. Such affected patients may find it helpful to rinse their mouths with water after using beclomethasone dipropionate.

A few patients on beclomethasone dipropionate have complained of hoarseness, dry mouth or throat irritation. It may be helpful to rinse out the mouth with water immediately after inhalation.

Immunologic Reactions: The replacement of systemic steroids with beclomethasone dipropionate may unmask symptoms of allergies which were previously suppressed by the systemic drug. Conditions such as allergic rhinitis and eczema may thus become apparent during beclomethasone dipropionate therapy after the withdrawal of systemic corticosteroids.

Rare cases of immediate and delayed hypersensitivity reactions, including urticaria, angioedema, rash and bronchospasm, have been reported after the use of beclomethasone oral or intranasal inhalers; pruritus, erythema, and edema of the eyes, face, lips and throat also have been reported.

Other Effects: Reports of headache, lightheadedness, dryness and irritation of the nose and throat, and unpleasant taste and smell have been received. There are rare reports of loss of taste and smell.

Overdose: Symptoms and Treatment: Acute: The acute toxicity of beclomethasone dipropionate is low. The only harmful effect that follows inhalation of large amounts of the drug over a short period of time is decreased hypothalamic-pituitary-adrenal (HPA) function. No special emergency action need be taken. Treatment with beclomethasone dipropionate should be continued at the recommended dose to control the asthma; HPA function recovers in a day or two.

Chronic: The excessive use of beclomethasone dipropionate over a long period could lead to adrenal suppression. In such a case the patient should be transferred to oral corticosteroid therapy and when the condition has stabilized, be returned to inhaled therapy at the recommended dose. To guard against the unexpected event of adrenal suppression, regular tests of adrenal function are advised. Oral steroids should then be slowly withdrawn, as for steroid-dependent patients.

Dosage: The optimal dosage may vary widely and must be individually determined. Treatment with Beclovent should not be stopped abruptly but tapered off gradually.

Inhaler: Adults: The usual dosage is 200 to 400 μg/day, divided into 2 to 4 administrations. As a maintenance dose, many patients do well on 100 μg twice daily. In more severe cases, dosage may be started at 800 μg/day and adjusted downward according to the individual patient's response. If control is not achieved at 800 μg/day the dosage may be increased to 1 000 μg/day. **The total daily dosage should not exceed 1 000 μg of beclomethasone dipropionate, i.e., 20 inhalations of the 50 μg/metered dose inhaler.**

Children: There is insufficient clinical experience with beclomethasone dipropionate in children below 3 years of age. Above 3 years of age those children who can learn the correct use of aerosol inhalers can be treated with assistance or supervision of an adult. Children from 3 to 5 years: The usual starting dose is 50 μg twice daily, i.e., 1 inhalation (1×50 μg of the 50 μg/metered dose inhaler) twice daily. If this gives no clinical response within a few days, the dosage can be increased to 3 times daily. The maintenance dosage is 1 inhalation 2 to 3 times daily. **The total daily dosage for children between 3 and 5 years of age should not exceed 150 μg of beclomethasone dipropionate.** From 6 to 14 years: Can be started on 100 μg of beclomethasone dipropionate 2 to 3 times daily, i.e., 2 inhalations (2×50 μg) of the 50 μg/metered dose inhaler, 2 to 3 times daily (200 to 300 μg total daily dose). This can be increased to a maximum of 100 μg 4 times daily (400 μg total daily dose). **The total daily dosage for children between 6 to 14 years of age should not exceed 500 μg of beclomethasone dipropionate.** Above 14 years of age, the adult dosage applies.

Rotacaps: Adults: The usual dose is one 200 μg Rotacap 3 to 4 times daily. Maintenance dose: Many patients do well on 2 Rotacaps daily. **The total daily dosage should not exceed 1 000 μg of beclomethasone dipropionate or 5 Beclovent Rotacaps 200 μg.**

Children: There is insufficient clinical experience with Beclovent Rotacaps in children below 6 years of age. Above 6 years of age, those children who can learn the correct use of the Rotahaler can be treated with the assistance or supervision of an adult. The usual starting dosage between 6 and 14 years of age is one 100 μg Rotacap twice daily. If this gives no clinical response within a few days, the dosage can be increased to 3 times daily. The maintenance dosage is 1 inhalation 2 to 3 times daily. **The total daily dose should not exceed 500 μg of beclomethasone dipropionate.** Above 14 years of age, the adult dosage applies.

General: As a general rule, rinsing the mouth and gargling with water after each inhalation can help in preventing the occurrence of candidiasis. Cleansing dentures has the same effect.

Since the effect of Beclovent depends on its regular use and on the proper technique of inhalation, the patient should be made aware of the prophylactic nature of therapy with inhaled beclomethasone dipropionate, and that Beclovent should be taken regularly, even when the patient is asymptomatic. The patient must also be instructed, as described in the section Information for the Patient, in the correct method to use the Beclovent Inhaler or Rotahaler to ensure that the drug reaches the target areas within the lungs.

Beclovent Rotacap capsules are for inhalation use only, using a Beclovent Rotahaler inhaler.

In the presence of excessive mucus secretion, the drug may fail to reach the bronchioles. Therefore, if an obvious response is not obtained after 10 days, attempts should be made to control the secretion of mucus and other inflammatory changes in the lung with expectorants and/or with a short course of systemic corticosteroid therapy. Continuation of treatment with inhaled beclomethasone dipropionate usually maintains the improvement achieved, the oral steroid being gradually withdrawn.

Patients receiving bronchodilators by inhalation should be advised to use the bronchodilator before the Beclovent in order to enhance the penetration of Beclovent into the bronchial tree. Several minutes should elapse between the use of the 2 medications to reduce the potential toxicity from the inhaled fluorocarbon propellants and to allow for some bronchodilation to occur.

Patients Receiving Systemic Steroids: The transfer of steroid-dependent patients to beclomethasone dipropionate and their subsequent management needs special care mainly because recovery from impaired adrenocortical function, caused by prolonged systemic therapy, is slow. Patients' bronchial asthma should be stable before being given beclomethasone dipropionate in addition to the usual maintenance dose of systemic steroid. After about a week, gradual withdrawal of the systemic steroid is started by reducing the daily dose by 1 mg of prednisone, or its equivalent of other corticosteroid, at not less than weekly intervals, if the patient is under close observation. In children, the usual rate of withdrawal is 1 mg of the daily dose of prednisone every 8 days when under close supervision. **If continuous supervision is not feasible the withdrawal of the systemic steroid should be slower,** approximately 1 mg of the daily dose of prednisone (or equivalent) every 10 and every 20 days in adults and in children, respectively. A slow rate of withdrawal cannot be over emphasized.

If withdrawal symptoms appear, the previous dose of the systemic drug should be resumed for a week before any further decrease is attempted. Patients who have been treated with systemic steroids for long periods of time or at a high dose may have adrenocortical suppression. With these patients adrenocortical function should be monitored regularly and their dose of systemic steroid reduced cautiously.

Some patients feel unwell during the withdrawal phase experiencing symptoms such as joint and/or muscular pain, lassitude, and depression, despite maintenance or even improvement of respiratory function. Such patients should be encouraged to persevere with beclomethasone dipropionate but should be watched carefully for objective signs of adrenal insufficiency such as hypotension and weight loss. If evidence of adrenal insufficiency occurs, the systemic steroid dosage should be boosted temporarily and thereafter further withdrawal should be continued more slowly.

Transferred patients whose adrenocortical function is impaired should carry a warning card indicating that they need supplementary treatment with systemic steroids during periods of stress, e.g., surgery, chest infection or severe asthma attack. Consideration should be given to supplying such patients with oral steroids to use in an emergency. The dose of inhaled beclomethasone dipropionate should be increased at this time and then reduced to the maintenance level after the systemic steroid has been discontinued.

Exacerbations of bronchial asthma which occur during the course of treatment with beclomethasone dipropionate should be treated with a short course of systemic steroid which is gradually tapered as these symptoms subside. Under stressful conditions or when the patient has a severe exacerbation of bronchial asthma, after complete withdrawal of the systemic steroid, use of the latter must be resumed in order to avoid relative adrenocortical insufficiency.

There are some patients who cannot completely discontinue the oral corticosteroid. In these cases, a minimum maintenance dosage should be given in addition to inhaled beclomethasone dipropionate.

Information for the Patient: See Blue Section—Information for the Patient "Beclovent Inhaler/Beclovent Rotacaps/Beclovent Rotahaler".

Supplied: Inhaler: A metered dose aerosol delivering beclomethasone dipropionate 50 μg with each depression of the valve. Nonmedicinal ingredients: dichlorodifluoromethane, oleic acid and trichlorofluoromethane. Each unit is housed in a suitable actuator/adaptor. Aluminum canisters fitted with metering valves. Available in 200 dose containers.

Caution: Container may explode if heated. Contents under pressure. Do not place in hot water or near radiators, stoves or other sources of heat. Even when empty, do not puncture or incinerate container. Store at temperatures below 30°C. Protect from freezing and direct sunlight.

As with most inhaled medications in aerosol canisters, the therapeutic effect of this medication may decrease when the canister is cold.

Rotacaps: Each Rotacap contains: microfine beclomethasone dipropionate 100 μg (buff-colored) or 200 μg (brown) and larger particle lactose in gelatin capsules. Polypropylene containers with polythene snap caps of 100.

Store below 30°C, in a dry place. The Rotacaps must only be inserted into the Rotahaler immediately prior to use. Failure to observe this instruction will affect the delivery of the drug.

Rotahaler: The contents of the Rotacaps are inhaled using a device called Beclovent Rotahaler which separates the capsule into halves and releases the drug, when the patient inhales, by breath actuation.

The Beclovent Rotahaler is available separately from the Rotacaps in a plastic box held in a carton.

(Shown in Product Recognition Section)

Reviewed 1999

BECONASE Aq® Ⓟ

Glaxo Wellcome

Beclomethasone Dipropionate

Corticosteroid for Nasal Use

Pharmacology: Beclomethasone dipropionate is a potent anti-inflammatory steroid with strong topical and weak systemic activity. When inhaled intranasally at therapeutic doses, it has a direct anti-inflammatory action within the nasal mucosa, the mechanism of which is not yet completely defined. The minute amount absorbed in therapeutic doses has not been shown to exert any apparent clinical systemic effects.

Indications: Treatment of perennial and seasonal allergic rhinitis, poorly responsive to conventional treatment. Beclomethasone dipropionate can significantly delay the recurrence of nasal polyps in those patients who have undergone nasal polypectomy. In those patients in whom polyps do recur, beclomethasone dipropionate nasal spray can prevent their increase in size.

Contraindications: Active or quiescent tuberculosis of the respiratory tract or untreated fungal, bacterial and viral infections.

Patients with a history of hypersensitivity to any of the ingredients of these preparations.

Warnings: Careful attention must be given to patients previously treated for prolonged periods with systemic corticosteroids. Transfer to beclomethasone dipropionate nasal spray may cause withdrawal symptoms e.g. joint and/or muscular pain, lassitude and depression. In severe cases, adrenal insufficiency may occur necessitating the temporary resumption of systemic steroids. This is particularly important in those patients who have associated asthma or other clinical conditions, in whom too rapid a decrease in systemic corticosteroids may cause a severe exacerbation of their symptoms. **Deaths due to adrenal insufficiency have occurred in asthmatic patients during and after transfer from systemic corticosteroids to aerosol beclomethasone dipropionate.** Therefore, systemic corticosteroid therapy should be withdrawn gradually.

If recommended doses of intranasal beclomethasone dipropionate are exceeded or if individuals are particularly sensitive or predisposed by virtue of recent systemic therapies, systemic effects may occur, including reduction in growth velocity and symptoms of hypercorticism, including very rare cases of menstrual irregularities, acneiform lesions, cataracts, and cushingoid features. If such changes occur, beclomethasone dipropionate should be discontinued slowly consistent with accepted procedures for discontinuing oral steroid therapy.

Pregnancy and Lactation: Glucocorticoids are known teratogens in rodent species and beclomethasone dipropionate is no exception. Teratogenicity studies were performed in the mouse and rabbit using beclomethasone dipropionate administered by the inhaled or oral route. At high dose levels of beclomethasone dipropionate fetuses were growth retarded and had cleft palate.

Beconase Aq (cont'd)

The safety of beclomethasone dipropionate nasal spray in human pregnancy and lactation has not been established. Administration of drugs during pregnancy should only be considered if the expected benefit to the mother is greater than any possible risk to the fetus.

Precautions: Beclomethasone dipropionate nasal spray is absorbed into the circulation. Use of excessive doses of beclomethasone dipropionate may suppress hypothalamic-pituitary-adrenal function. Therefore, larger than recommended doses should be avoided. Systemic effects have been minimal with recommended doses. Treatment should not be stopped abruptly but tapered off gradually.

Patients should be advised that beclomethasone dipropionate nasal spray must be used at regular intervals to be therapeutically effective. The patient should take the medication as directed, and the prescribed dosage should not be increased. For proper dosage and administration of the drug and to attain maximum improvement, the patient must be instructed by the physician or other health care professional in the correct use of this preparation. The physician should also advise the patient to read and follow the accompanying Information for the Patient insert carefully. The patient should contact the physician if the symptoms do not improve, or if the condition worsens, or if sneezing or nasal irritation occurs. An abnormally heavy challenge of summer allergens may, in certain instances, necessitate appropriate additional therapy, particularly to control eye symptoms. These patients should also be instructed to inform subsequent physicians of the prior use of corticosteroids.

Rare instances of increased intraocular pressure have been reported following intranasal application of aerosolised corticosteroids. Rare instances of nasal septum perforation have been spontaneously reported.

Steroid Replacement by Beconase Aq: The replacement of systemic steroids with beclomethasone dipropionate nasal spray has to be gradual and carefully supervised by the physician. During withdrawal from oral steroids, some patients may experience symptoms of withdrawal, e.g., joint and/or muscular pain, lassitude and depression. The guidelines under Dosage should be followed in all such cases.

During periods of stress or during a severe asthmatic attack, patients who have been withdrawn from systemic corticosteroids should be instructed to immediately resume systemic steroids in dosages that were previously effective and to contact their physicians for further instructions. These patients should also be instructed to carry a warning card indicating that they may need supplementary systemic steroids during periods of stress or a severe asthma attack. To assess the risk of adrenal insufficiency in emergency situations, routine tests of adrenal cortical function, including measurement of early morning and evening cortisol levels, should be performed periodically in all patients. An early morning resting cortisol level may be accepted as normal only if it falls at or near the normal mean level.

Studies in asthmatic patients have shown that the combined administration of alternate-day prednisone systemic treatment and orally inhaled beclomethasone dipropionate increases the likelihood of hypothalamic-pituitary-adrenal suppression compared to a therapeutic dose of either drug alone. Therefore, beclomethasone dipropionate nasal spray should be used with caution in patients already on an alternate day prednisone regimen for any disease.

Long-Term Effects: The long-term effects of beclomethasone dipropionate in human subjects have not been established. In particular, the local effects of the agent on the developmental or immunologic processes of the respiratory passageways are still unknown. During long-term therapy, pituitary-adrenal function and hematological status should be periodically assessed. In addition, as with any long-term treatment with a topical steroid, patients using beclomethasone dipropionate nasal spray over several months or longer should be examined periodically for possible changes in the nasal mucosa. The possibility of atrophic rhinitis should be kept in mind.

Effect on Infections: Patients on drugs that suppress the immune system are more susceptible to infections than healthy individuals. Chickenpox and measles, for example, can have a more serious or even fatal course in nonimmune children or adults on corticosteroids. In such children or adults who have not had these diseases, particular care should be taken to avoid exposure. How the dose, route, and duration of corticosteroid administration affects the risk of developing a disseminated infection is not known. The contribution of the underlying disease and/or prior corticosteroid treatment to the risk is also not known. If exposed to chickenpox, prophylaxis with varicella zoster immune globulin (VZIG) may be indicated. If exposed to measles, prophylaxis with pooled i.v. immunoglobulin (IVIG), as appropriate, may be indicated. If chickenpox develops, treatment with antiviral agents may be considered.

Corticosteroids may mask some signs of infection and new infections may appear. A decreased resistance to localized infections has been observed during corticosteroid therapy. The possibility of nasal, prenasal or pharyngeal candidiasis should be kept in mind. If any infection occurs during therapy, it requires appropriate treatment and/or discontinuance of beclomethasone dipropionate nasal spray, depending on the severity of the infection.

Inhibitory Effect on Wound Healing: Because of the inhibitory effect of corticosteroids on wound healing, patients who have experienced recent nasal septal ulcers, nasal surgery or trauma should not use a nasal corticosteroid until healing has occurred.

Hypothyroidism and Cirrhosis: There may be enhanced systemic effects of corticosteroids on patients with hypothyroidism and in those with cirrhosis.

Corticosteroids and ASA: ASA should be used cautiously in conjunction with corticosteroids in hypoprothrombinemia.

Pregnancy and *Lactation:* The safety of beclomethasone dipropionate nasal spray in pregnancy and in lactation has not been established. Unnecessary administration of drugs during the first trimester of pregnancy is undesirable.

Administration of drugs during pregnancy should only be considered if the expected benefit to the mother is greater than any possible risk to the fetus.

Glucocorticoids are secreted in human milk. It is not known whether beclomethasone dipropionate is secreted in human milk, but it is suspected to be likely.

The use of beclomethasone dipropionate in pregnancy, nursing mothers, or women of childbearing potential requires that the possible benefits of the drug be weighed against the potential hazards to the mother, and embryo or fetus. Infants born of mothers who have received substantial dosages of corticosteroids during pregnancy should be carefully observed for hypoadrenalism.

Teratogenic Effects: Glucocorticoids are known teratogens in rodent species and beclomethasone dipropionate is no exception.

Teratogenicity studies have been carried out by the inhaled and oral routes in mice, rats and rabbits. In mice and rabbits beclomethasone dipropionate showed effects at high dose levels typical of a potent corticosteroid, e.g. fetal growth retardation and cleft palate. Similarly, in rats beclomethasone dipropionate induced early embryonic death and fetal growth retardation at very high dose levels; however, no fetus with cleft palate was detected. Well controlled trials relating to fetal risk in humans are not available.

Adverse Effects: General: In general, inhaled corticosteroid therapy may be associated with dose dependent increases in the incidence of ocular complications, suppression of HPA axis responsiveness to stress, and inhibition of growth velocity in children.

Glaucoma may be exacerbated by inhaled corticosteroid treatment for asthma or rhinitis. In patients with established glaucoma who require long-term inhaled corticosteroid treatment, it is prudent to measure intraocular pressure before commencing the inhaled corticosteroid and to monitor it subsequently. In patients without established glaucoma, but with a potential for developing intraocular hypertension (e.g., the elderly), intraocular pressure should be monitored at appropriate intervals.

In elderly patients treated with inhaled corticosteroids, the prevalence of posterior subscapular and nuclear cataracts is probably low but increased in relation to the daily and cumulative lifetime dose. Cofactors such as smoking, ultraviolet B exposure, or diabetes may increase the risk. Children may be less susceptible.

A reduction in growth velocity in children or teenagers may occur as a result of inadequate control of chronic diseases such as asthma or from use of corticosteroids for treatment. Physicians should closely follow the growth of adolescents taking corticosteroids by any route and weigh the benefits of corticosteroid therapy and asthma control against the possibility of growth suppression if any adolescent's growth appears slowed.

Nasopharyngeal Effect: In general, side effects have been primarily associated with the nasal mucous membranes and are consistent with what one would expect from applying a topical medication to an already inflamed membrane.

Sensations of irritation and burning in the nose following the use of beclomethasone dipropionate nasal spray have been reported. Occasional sneezing attacks have occurred immediately following the use of intranasal beclomethasone dipropionate.

Other adverse nasopharyngeal effects of beclomethasone dipropionate use include nasal dryness or crusting and transient episodes of bloody discharge from the nose. Extremely rare instances of ulceration of the nasal mucosa and of nasal septum perforation have been reported following intranasal application of aerosol and aqueous corticosteroids. Localized infections of the nose and pharynx with C. albicans have occurred rarely (see Precautions, Effect on Infection). If persistent nasopharyngeal irritation occurs, it may be an indication for stopping beclomethasone dipropionate nasal spray.

Other Effects: Other less frequent adverse effects associated with beclomethasone dipropionate include: sore throat, cough, headache, rhinorrhea, nasal stuffiness, tearing eyes, dizziness, nausea, lightheadedness, lethargy and stomach pains. Rare cases of wheezing, cataracts, raised intraocular pressure or glaucoma in association with intranasal formulations of beclomethasone dipropionate have been reported. Reports of dryness and irritation of the throat, and unpleasant taste and smell have been received. There are rare reports of loss of taste and smell. Rare cases of immediate and delayed hypersensitivity reactions, including urticaria, angioedema, rash, pruritus, erythema, edema of the eyes, face, lips and throat and bronchospasm, have been reported after the use of beclomethasone dipropionate oral or intranasal inhalers.

When patients are transferred to beclomethasone dipropionate nasal spray from a systemic steroid, allergic conditions such as asthma, conjunctivitis or eczema may be unmasked.

Overdose: Symptoms and Treatment: When used at excessive dosages (above 600 μg or 12 applications/day), systemic steroid effects such as hypercorticism and adrenal suppression, may appear. Decreasing the dose will abolish these side effects.

The restoration of hypothalamic-pituitary-axis may be slow; during periods of pronounced physical stress (i.e., severe infections, trauma, surgery) a supplement with systemic steroids may be advisable.

Dosage: The safety and efficacy of the nasal spray in children under 6 years of age have not been established.

For administration by the intranasal route only.

The usual dosage for patients who have received no previous systemic steroid is 2 applications (100 μg) into each nostril twice daily. A dosage regimen of 1 application into each nostril 3 or 4 times daily may be preferred. When administered as 2 applications into each nostril, the first puff should be directed at the upper and the second at the lower part of the nasal cavity. Maximum daily dosage should not exceed 12 applications (600 μg) in adults and 8 applications (400 μg) in children.

When Beconase Aq is used concurrently with Beclovent, the combined total daily dosage should not exceed the maximum daily recommended dosage of beclomethasone dipropionate (1 000 μg in adults). Since the effectiveness of beclomethasone dipropionate nasal spray depends on its regular use, patients must be instructed to take the nasal inhalations at regular intervals and not as with other nasal sprays, as they feel necessary.

Patients should be instructed on the correct method of use, which is to blow the nose, then insert the nozzle firmly into the nostril, compress the opposite nostril and actuate the spray while inspiring through the nose, with the mouth closed (see Information for the Patient).

In order to ensure cooperation and continuation of treatment, patients must be advised that the therapeutic effects are not immediate and that some days may elapse before improvement is noted. Beclomethasone dipropionate nasal spray should not be continued beyond 3 weeks in the absence of significant symptomatic improvement.

In the presence of excessive nasal mucus secretion or edema of the nasal mucosa, the drug may fail to reach the site of action. In such cases, it is advisable to use a nasal vasoconstrictor for 2 to 3 days prior to beclomethasone dipropionate nasal spray.

Careful attention must be given to patients previously treated for prolonged periods with systemic corticosteroids when these patients are transferred to beclomethasone dipropionate nasal spray. Initially, the corticosteroid nasal spray and the systemic corticosteroid must be given concomitantly, while the dose of the latter is gradually decreased. In adults, the usual rate of withdrawal of the systemic corticosteroid is the equivalent of 1 mg of the daily dose of prednisone (or equivalent) at no less than weekly intervals if the patient is under close supervision. In children over 6 years of age, the rate of withdrawal is 1 mg of the daily dose of prednisone (or equivalent), every 8 days under close supervision. **If continuous supervision is not feasible, the withdrawal of the systemic steroid should be slower,** approximately 1 mg of prednisone (or equivalent) every 10 days and every 20 days, in adults and in children, respectively. A slow rate of withdrawal cannot be overemphasized. If withdrawal symptoms appear, the previous dose of the systemic steroid should be resumed for a week before a further decrease is attempted.

Information for the Patient: See Blue Section—Information for the Patient "Beconase Aq".

Supplied: Each spray of aqueous suspension delivered by the nasal applicator contains: beclomethasone dipropionate 50 μg. Nonmedicinal ingredients: avicel, benzalkonium chloride, dextrose, phenylethyl alcohol, polysorbate 80 and purified water. Glass bottles of 200 doses fitted with a metered atomizing pump and a nasal applicator. Protect from light. Do not refrigerate. Store between 15 and 30°C. Discard 3 months after first use.

Reviewed 1999

BELLERGAL® SPACETABS® ◈

Novartis Pharmaceuticals

Belladonna—Ergotamine Tartrate—Phenobarbital

Anticholinergic—Antispasmodic—Sedative

Indications: Functional symptoms such as hot flushes, perspiration, palpitations, dizzy spells, restlessness, apprehension, fatigue, insomnia, headache, for example in patients with anxiety-tension states associated with menopause.

Menopausal women who are treated with Bellergal, exhibiting atrophic vaginitis and/or osteoporosis, require specific therapy for these conditions if indicated.

Contraindications: Narrow-angle glaucoma, sepsis, occlusive vascular disease, hypertension, peripheral vascular disease, severe coronary insufficiency, myocardial lesions, pregnancy and lactation, severe disorders of renal or hepatic function, porphyria, malnutrition, prostatic hypertrophy, hypersensitivity to any of the components.

Precautions: Administer with caution to patients with pyloric obstruction or angina pectoris. Excessive dryness of the mouth and visual disturbances are signs of overdosage or sensitivity to belladonna alkaloids. Reduction of dosage may be necessary. If excessive or prolonged dosage is contemplated, the physician should be alert to possible peripheral vascular complications in patients highly sensitive to ergot. Due to presence of a barbiturate, Bellergal may be habit forming.

Occupational Hazards: Barbiturate containing preparations may impair the mental and/or physical abilities required for the performance of potentially hazardous tasks such as driving a vehicle or operating machinery.

Interactions: The concomitant use of alcohol or other CNS depressants may have an additive effect. Warn patients accordingly.

The prolonged ingestion of barbiturates gives rise to enzyme induction. This increases the rate of metabolism of certain drugs, including oral anticoagulants and oral contraceptives, thus reducing their effectiveness.

See also phenobarbital general monograph.

There is some evidence that the concomitant use of triacetyloleandomycin (troleandomycin) or erythromycin and ergotamine may lead to an elevated concentration of ergotamine in the plasma, thereby causing untoward peripheral vasoconstriction.

Like all drugs, Bellergal Spacetabs should be kept out of the reach of children.

Adverse Effects: Visual disturbances, dry mouth, flushing, drowsiness may occur.

Children: In children, behavioral disturbances and cognitive impairment may occur, due to the presence of phenobarbital.

Overdose: Symptoms: 1) Nausea, vomiting and abdominal discomfort, usually after an acute overdose of ergotamine (these symptoms may be masked by the action of the belladonna). 2) Numbness, tingling, pain and cyanosis of the extremities, with diminished or absent peripheral pulses. 3) Drowsiness, confusion, incoordination and coma (convulsions, while a feature of acute ergotamine and belladonna poisoning, may be masked by the depressant action of the barbiturate and hence may not be common in a theoretical Bellergal intoxication). 4) Respiratory depression, which may be early in onset, pronounced and persistent. 5) Hypotension, followed by a typical shock like state in more severe cases. 6) Respiratory complications and renal failure, which are not uncommon late sequelae of severe barbiturate intoxication. 7) Hypothermia or hyperthermia.

The danger of Bellergal intoxication is increased when the drug is ingested in the presence of alcohol, phenothiazines, minor tranquilizers and/or narcotics.

Treatment: Elimination of the drug by gastric lavage and administration of activated charcoal. Supportive symptomatic treatment with close monitoring of cardiovascular and respiratory systems. In the event of vasospasm, vasodilators such as nitroprusside sodium are indicated.

Special Features due to Ergotamine Overdosage: Marked peripheral vasospasm with coldness and poor or absent pulses in the hands and feet are commonly associated with acute ergotamine poisoning. Warmth, but not heat, and protection must be afforded the ischemic limbs. Vasopressors should be avoided.

Vasodilators, such as sodium nitroprusside or tolazoline, may be used with benefit.

Dosage: One Spacetab in the morning and 1 in the evening. Weekly maximum: 16 tablets.

Supplied: Each compressed tablet, speckled dark green, orange and light lemon yellow, embossed '⚠' on one side and double-scored on the other, contains: levorotatory belladonna alkaloids 0.2 mg, ergotamine tartrate USP 0.6 mg and phenobarbital USP 40 mg. Nonmedicinal ingredients: cornstarch, lactose and tartrazine. Bottles of 100.

(Shown in Product Recognition Section)

BEMINAL® with C FORTIS Injectable

Wyeth-Ayerst

Vitamin B Complex

Vitamin Supplement

Indications: Avitaminoses of the vitamin B complex and vitamin C. Pre- and postoperatively, when indicated, and in debilitated patients. Secondary deficiencies of the above vitamins caused by severe vomiting, chronic diarrhea, celiac disease, and other conditions interfering with normal absorption and metabolism.

Dosage: The reconstituted solution may be injected slowly into the vein or added to a saline or glucose infusion for convenient administration, according to the patient's requirements.

Note: Sensitivity to the i.v. use of thiamine has been reported in some persons. Any i.v. solution containing thiamine should therefore be used cautiously.

Reconstitution: Cleanse the rubber cap of vial with a suitable antiseptic. With sterile syringe inject 5 mL Sterile Water for Injection or Sterile Sodium Chloride Injection into a vial of Beminal. Shake the vial well and permit air bubbles to escape before filling the syringe.

Beminal may vary slightly in color, and the reconstituted solution may darken progressively. These changes in no way affect the potency or therapeutic value of the preparation.

Supplied: Each vial of sterile dry powder contains: thiamine 50 mg, riboflavin (as riboflavin 5′phosphate sodium) 5 mg, niacinamide 125 mg, pyridoxine 5 mg, pantothenic acid (as dl-panthenol) 10.68 mg and vitamin C 500 mg. Nonmedicinal ingredients: sodium hydroxide and water for injection. **Keep from light.** Prepared solution is stable for 2 days at room temperature or 2 weeks refrigerated.

BENADRYL® ALLERGY/SINUS/HEADACHE

Warner-Lambert Consumer Healthcare

Diphenhydramine HCl—Pseudoephedrine HCl—Acetaminophen

Antihistaminic—Decongestant—Analgesic

Indications: For relief of sneezing, runny nose, itchy watery eyes, sinus and nasal congestion, sinus pain and headache.

Precautions: Occupational Hazards: May cause drowsiness, use caution when driving a motor vehicle or operating machinery.

A physician should be consulted prior to using this product if patient has chronic alcoholism, serious kidney or liver disease, high blood pressure, heart or thyroid disease, diabetes, chronic lung disease, glaucoma or difficulty in urinating due to enlargement of the prostate gland, is elderly, or is taking other antihistamines or sedating drugs.

If symptoms do not improve in 5 days or are accompanied by a fever, a physician should be consulted.

Dosage: Adults and children 12 years and over: 2 caplets every 6 hours. Do not exceed 4 doses/day. Not recommended for children under 12 years.

Supplied: Each light-green caplet, printed "BENADRYL" on both sides, contains: diphenhydramine HCl 12.5 mg, pseudoephedrine HCl 30 mg and acetaminophen 500 mg. Nonmedicinal ingredients: cellulose, D&C Yellow No. 10, FD&C Blue No. 1, FD&C Yellow No. 6, PEG, polysorbate, starches, stearic acid, titanium dioxide, wax and zinc stearate. Blister packages of 20.

(Shown in Product Recognition Section)

Reviewed 1998

BENADRYL® Preparations

Warner-Lambert Consumer Healthcare

Diphenhydramine HCl

Antihistaminic

Indications: Antihistamine, antiemetic and antispasmodic. Allergic diseases such as hay fever, allergic rhinitis, urticaria, angioedema, atopic dermatitis, contact dermatitis, gastrointestinal allergy, pruritus, physical allergies, reactions to injection of contrast media, reactions to therapeutic preparations and allergic transfusion reactions; also postoperative nausea and vomiting, motion sickness, and quieting emotionally disturbed children.

Contraindications: Cream should not be applied to extensively denuded or weeping skin areas.

Warnings: Antihistamines should be used with considerable caution in patients with narrow-angle glaucoma, stenosing peptic ulcer, pyloroduodenal obstruction, symptomatic prostatic hypertrophy, or bladder-neck obstruction. Not recommended for children with chronic lung disease or glaucoma.

Topical: For external use only. Do not use on chickenpox, measles or extensive areas of skin. If condition worsens or persists for more than 7 days, consult a physician. Do not use other drugs containing diphenhydramine while using this product.

Children: In infants and children, especially, antihistamines in **overdosage** may cause hallucinations, convulsions, or death. As in adults, antihistamines may diminish mental alertness in children. In the young child, particularly, they may produce excitation.

Geriatrics (approximately 60 years or older): Antihistamines are more likely to cause dizziness, sedation and hypotension in elderly patients.

Precautions: *Pregnancy* and *Lactation:* Safety for use in pregnancy and lactation has not been established. Its use therefore in such patients should involve consideration of expected benefits and possible risks.

Avoid s.c. or perivascular injection. Single parenteral dosage greater than 100 mg should be avoided, particularly in hypertension and cardiac disease.

Use as Local Anesthetic: This drug should not be used as a local anesthetic due to the risk of local tissue necrosis.

Occupational Hazards: Patients should be cautioned not to operate vehicles or hazardous machinery until their response to the drug has been determined.

Since the depressant effects of antihistamines are additive to those of other drugs affecting the CNS, patients should be cautioned against drinking alcoholic beverages or taking hypnotics, sedatives, psychotherapeutic agents or other drugs with CNS depressant effects during antihistaminic therapy.

Diphenhydramine has an atropine-like action and therefore should be used with caution in patients with a history of bronchial asthma, increased intraocular pressure, hyperthyroidism, cardiovascular disease or hypertension.

Adverse Effects: Drowsiness, dizziness, dryness of mouth, nausea and nervousness may occur. Other infrequently reported effects are vertigo, palpitation, blurring of vision, headache, restlessness, insomnia and thickening of bronchial secretions. Allergic reactions, diarrhea, vomiting and excitation may also occur.

Dosage: Oral: Capsules or Caplets: Adults and children 12 years and over: 25 to 50 mg 3 or 4 times daily. Maximum 4 doses/day. Capsules and caplets are not recommended for children under 12.

Benadryl Preparations (cont'd)

Junior Strength Chewable Tablets: Adults and children 12 years and over: 2 to 4 tablets every 4 to 6 hours. Maximum 16 tablets/day. Children 6 to under 12 years: 1 to 2 tablets every 4 to 6 hours. Maximum 8 tablets/day. Chew tablets thoroughly before swallowing.

Elixir: Adults and children 12 years and over: 10 to 20 mL every 4 to 6 hours. Children, 6 to under 12 years: 5 to 10 mL every 4 to 6 hours. Maximum 4 doses/day.

Children's Liquid: Children under 2 years: 2.5 mL every 4 to 6 hours. Children 2 to 5 years: 5 mL every 4 to 6 hours. Children 6 to under 12 years: 10 to 20 mL every 4 to 6 hours. Maximum 4 doses/day.

Parenteral: 10 to 50 mg i.v. or deep i.m. Maximum daily dose: 400 mg in divided doses. High dosage for adults (300 to 400 mg daily) may be required in acute, generalized or chronic urticaria, and allergic eczema.

Topical: For relief of itching due to insect bites, mild cases of sunburn, poison ivy or oak, and other minor skin irritations. Apply locally 3 or 4 times daily.

Supplied: Caplets: Each, pink, film-coated caplet imprinted Benadryl on both sides contains: diphenhydramine HCl 25 mg. Nonmedicinal ingredients: celluloses, dicalcium phosphate, D&C Red No. 27, PEG, polysorbate, starch, stearic acid, titanium dioxide, wax and zinc stearate. Energy: 0.5 kJ (0.12 kcal). Gluten-, lactose-, paraben-, sodium-, sulfite- and tartrazine-free. Unit packages of 12 and 24. Bottles of 50 and 100.

Capsules: Each white capsule with pink cap contains: diphenhydramine HCl 50 mg. Nonmedicinal ingredients: lactose, talc; capsule shell: FD&C Blue No. 1, FD&C Red No. 3, gelatin, silicon dioxide, sodium lauryl sulfate and titanium dioxide. Energy: 2 kJ (0.47 kcal). Gluten-, paraben-, sodium-, sulfite- and tartrazine-free. Bottles of 100.

Cream: Each g of white emulsion for topical use contains: diphenhydramine 2% w/w. Nonmedicinal ingredients: alcohol, paraben, PEG, propylene glycol and water. Tubes of 30 g.

Elixir: Each 5 mL of red elixir contains: diphenhydramine HCl 12.5 mg. Nonmedicinal ingredients: alcohol, FD&C Red No. 2, flavoring agents, sugar and water. Energy: 42.7 kJ (10.2 kcal)/5 mL. Gluten-, lactose-, paraben-, sodium-, sulfite- and tartrazine-free. Plastic bottles of 100 mL.

Children's Liquid: Each 5 mL of colorless, bubble-gum flavored liquid contains: diphenhydramine HCl 6.25 mg. Nonmedicinal ingredients: artificial bubble gum flavor, carboxymethylcellulose, citric acid, glycerin, saccharin, sodium benzoate, sodium citrate, sorbitol, vanilla flavor and water. Energy: 43.68 kJ (10.4 kcal)/5 mL. Alcohol-, dye-, gluten-, lactose-, paraben-, sulfite- and tartrazine-free. Plastic bottles of 100 mL.

Injectable: Each mL of injectable solution contains: diphenhydramine HCl 50 mg. Nonmedicinal ingredients: hydrochloric acid solution and sodium hydroxide (to adjust pH) and water. Vials of 1 mL, packages of 10.

Junior Strength Chewable Tablets: Each light purple, mottled, grape-flavored, scored, round tablet, imprinted Benadryl 12.5 on one side contains: diphenhydramine HCl 12.5 mg. Nonmedicinal ingredients: aspartame, corn syrup solids, D&C Red No. 27, FD&C Blue No. 1, flavor, magnesium stearate, magnesium trisilicate, monoammonium glycyrrhizinate and tartaric acid. Energy: 9.83 kJ (2.34 kcal). Alcohol-, gluten-, lactose-, paraben-, sucrose-, sulfite- and tartrazine-free. Unit packages of 12.

(Shown in Product Recognition Section)

BENAZEPRIL Ⓟ
General Monograph, CPhA

see ACE INHIBITORS

BENEMID® Ⓟ
MSD

Probenecid

Uricosuric Agent

Pharmacology: Probenecid is a uricosuric and a blocking agent of tubular secretion of organic anions. It inhibits the tubular reabsorption of urate, thus increasing the urinary excretion of uric acid and decreasing serum urate levels. Effective uricosuria reduces the miscible urate pool, retards urate deposition and promotes resorption of urate deposits. Probenecid inhibits the tubular secretion of penicillin and usually increases penicillin plasma levels by any route the antibiotic is given. A 2-fold to 4-fold elevation has been demonstrated for various penicillins. Probenecid also inhibits the tubular excretion and increases blood levels of cephalosporins (other than cephaloridine).

Indications: For treatment of hyperuricemia associated with all stages of gout and gouty arthritis, except a presenting acute attack.

As an adjuvant to therapy with penicillin G or V, or with ampicillin, methicillin, oxacillin, cloxacillin, nafcillin, carbenicillin or the cephalosporins (other than cephaloridine), for elevation and prolongation of plasma levels by whatever route the antibiotic is given.

Asymptomatic hyperuricemia seems to occur in a significant percentage of relatives of gouty patients. Probenecid may be given prophylactically to these persons to forestall acute gouty attacks and urate deposition in tissues.

By virtue of its effective uricosuric activity, probenecid may be used to control the hyperuricemia induced or aggravated by the many diuretics employed for the treatment of edema and hypertension (e.g., thiazides and similar diuretics).

Contraindications: Hypersensitivity to probenecid or to any component of this medication. Children under 2 years of age. Not recommended in persons with known blood dyscrasias or uric acid kidney stones. Therapy with probenecid should not be started until an acute gouty attack has subsided.

Warnings: In patients on probenecid the use of salicylates in either small or large doses is contraindicated because it antagonizes the uricosuric action of probenecid. In patients on probenecid who require a mild analgesic agent the use of acetaminophen rather than small doses of salicylates would be preferred.

The appearance of hypersensitivity reactions requires cessation of therapy with probenecid.

Pregnancy: Probenecid crosses the placental barrier and appears in cord blood. The use of any drug in women of childbearing potential requires that the anticipated benefit be weighed against possible hazards.

Precautions: Hematuria, renal colic, costovertebral pain, and formation of urate stones associated with the use of probenecid in gouty patients may be prevented by alkalization of the urine and a liberal fluid intake. Sufficient sodium bicarbonate (3 to 7.5 g daily) or potassium citrate (7.5 g daily) is recommended to maintain alkaline urine. With such quantities of alkali, the acid-base balance of the patient should be watched.

Alkalization of the urine is recommended until the serum urate level returns to normal (upper normal limit in males is about 6 mg/100 mL and in females, it is about 5 mg/100 mL) and tophaceous deposits disappear, i.e., during the period when urinary excretion of uric acid is at high level. After the miscible pool of urates decreases to normal (about 1 g) and deposited urates are resorbed and eliminated, alkalization of the urine probably is unnecessary, since the urinary uric acid concentration is lower and less likely to cause crystallization.

Use with caution in patients with a history of peptic ulcer.

Probenecid has been used in patients with some renal impairment but dosage requirements may be increased. Probenecid may not be effective in chronic renal insufficiency particularly when the glomerular filtration rate is 30 mL/min or less. Because of its mechanism of action, probenecid is not recommended in conjunction with a penicillin in the presence of **known** renal impairment.

A reducing substance may appear in the urine of patients receiving probenecid. This disappears with discontinuance of therapy. Suspected glycosuria should be confirmed by using a test specific for glucose.

Lactation: It is not known whether this drug is excreted in human milk. Because many drugs are excreted in human milk, caution should be exercised when probenecid is administered to a nursing mother.

Drug Interactions: The use of ASA antagonizes the uricosuric action of probenecid (see Warnings). The uricosuric action of probenecid is also antagonized by pyrazinamide.

Since probenecid decreases the renal excretion of conjugated sulfonamides, plasma concentrations of the latter should be determined from time to time when a sulfa drug and probenecid are coadministered for prolonged periods. Probenecid may prolong or enhance the action or oral sulfonylureas and thereby increase the risk of hypoglycemia.

Caution should be used if probenecid is administered simultaneously with methotrexate. Probenecid has been reported to decrease the tubular secretion of methotrexate and to potentiate toxicity.

Probenecid increases the mean plasma elimination half-life of a number of other drugs which can lead to increased peak plasma concentrations. These drugs include acetaminophen, naproxen, indomethacin, ketoprofen, meclofenamate, lorazepam, rifampin, acyclovir, ganciclovir and zidovudine. The clinical significance of this effect on plasma elimination half-life is not known; however, adjustment in the usual dosage of these drugs may be required.

In addition to its effect on the excretion of uric acid, the penicillins, and the cephalosporins (other than cephaloridine), probenecid decreases the urinary excretion of p-aminosalicylic acid (PAS), p-aminohippuric acid (PAH), phenolsulfonphthalein (PSP), pantothenic acid, 17-ketosteroids, sodium iodomethamate and related iodinated organic acids. Probenecid decreases both hepatic and renal excretion of sulfobromophthalein (BSP). The renal tubular reabsorption of phosphorus is inhibited in hypoparathyroid but not in euparathyroid individuals.

Laboratory Test Interactions: A reducing substance may appear in the urine of patients receiving probenecid which may produce a false-positive Benedict's test leading to the possibility of a false diagnosis of glycosuria. However, this disappears with discontinuance of therapy.

Falsely high readings for theophylline have been reported in an in vitro study, using the Schack and Waxler technique, when therapeutic concentrations of theophylline and probenecid were added to human plasma.

Adverse Effects: Headache, gastrointestinal symptoms, (e.g., anorexia, nausea, vomiting), urinary frequency, hypersensitivity reactions (including anaphylaxis, dermatitis, pruritus, urticaria, fever and Stevens-Johnson syndrome), sore gums, flushing, alopecia, dizziness, and anemia have occurred; also hemolytic anemia which in some instances could be related to genetic deficiency of glucose-6-phosphate dehydrogenase in red blood cells. Toxic epidermal necrolysis has been reported rarely after combination therapy of colchicine and probenecid. Nephrotic syndrome, leukopenia, hepatic necrosis, and aplastic anemia occur rarely.

In gouty patients, exacerbation of gout, and uric acid stones with or without hematuria, renal colic, or costovertebral pain, have been observed.

Overdose: Symptoms and Treatment: In the event of overdosage, symptomatic and supportive measures should be employed along with gastric lavage. If signs of CNS excitation are present, a short-acting barbiturate may be given parenterally.

Dosage: Gout: Therapy with probenecid should not be initiated until an acute gouty attack has subsided. However, if an acute attack is precipitated during therapy, the drug may be continued without changing the dosage, and therapeutic doses of colchicine, indomethacin or other appropriate therapy should be given to control the acute attack.

The recommended dosage for adults is 0.25 g (½ tablet) twice a day for 1 week, followed by 0.5 g (1 tablet) twice a day thereafter.

Some degree of renal impairment is common in patients with gout, therefore, a daily dosage of 1 g may be adequate for many patients. If necessary, however, the daily dosage may be increased every 4 weeks by increments of 0.5 g (within tolerance, and usually not beyond 2 g daily) if symptoms of gouty arthritis are not controlled or the 24-hour uric acid excretion is not above 700 mg.

Probenecid may not be effective in chronic renal insufficiency particularly when the glomerular filtration rate is 30 mL/min or less.

Gastric intolerance may be indicative of overdosage, and may be corrected by reducing the dosage without losing the therapeutic response.

Probenecid should be continued at a dosage that will maintain a normal serum uric acid level. When acute attacks have been absent for 6 months or more and serum uric levels remain within normal limits, the daily dosage of probenecid may be decreased by 1 tablet every 6 months to a minimum effective dosage. The maintenance dosage should not be reduced to the point where serum uric acid levels tend to rise.

Penicillin Therapy of Gonorrhea: For the treatment of uncomplicated gonorrhea in men or women, a single 1 g (2 tablets) dose of probenecid should be given with adequate doses of either oral ampicillin or aqueous procaine penicillin G injected i.m. If oral ampicillin is used, probenecid should be administered simultaneously. If parenteral penicillin is administered, the dose of probenecid should be given preferably at least 30 minutes before the injection.

Treatment of Contacts: Patients with known exposure to gonorrhea should receive the same treatment as those known to have gonorrhea.

Penicillin and Cephalosporin Therapy (general): The recommended dosage for adults is 2 g (4 tablets) daily in divided doses, reduced in older patients suspected of having renal impairment. Because of its mechanism of action, probenecid is not recommended for concurrent use with penicillin in the presence of known renal impairment.

The recommended dosage for children 2 years of age or older is 25 mg/kg (or 0.7 g/m² body surface) of body weight initially, followed by 40 mg/kg (or 1.2 g/m² body surface) daily in divided doses every 6 hours (see Table I). The adult dosage, however is recommended for children weighing more than 50 kg.

Table I—Benemid

Dosage in Children

Children			Number of Tablets	
Approx. Age (years)	**Weight (kg)**	**Approx. Surface Area (m²)**	**Initial Dose**	**Daily Maintenance Dosage***
2–5	12–18	0.55–0.75	½–1	1–1½
5–10	18–32	0.75–1.10	1–1½	1½–2½
10–14	32–48	1.10–1.45	1½–2	2½–3

*In divided doses every 6 hours.

The phenolsulfonphthalein (PSP) excretion test may be used to determine the effectiveness of probenecid in retarding penicillin excretion and maintaining therapeutic levels. The renal clearance of PSP is reduced to about one-fifth of the normal rate when dosage of probenecid is adequate.

Supplied: Each white, discoid-shaped (round), uncoated tablet, flat with a beveled edge, bisected on one side, coded MCD 501 on the other, contains: probenecid 500 mg. Nonmedicinal ingredients: calcium stearate, cornstarch, gelatin and magnesium carbonate. Bottles of 100. Store at 15 to 30°C.

(Shown in Product Recognition Section)

Reviewed 1999

BENOXYL® 5% Lotion BENOXYL® 10% and 20% Lotion ℞

Stiefel

Benzoyl Peroxide

Keratolytic Agent—Acne Therapy

Supplied: Each mL of lotion contains: benzoyl peroxide 5%, 10% or 20% in a greaseless, washable lotion base. Nonmedicinal ingredients: glyceryl monostearate, imidurea NF, isopropyl palmitate, polyethylene glycol 1 000 monostearate, propylene glycol, purified water USP, stearic acid, xanthan gum (200 mesh) and zinc stearate. Plastic bottles of 30 and 60 mL with dispenser top. Protect from heat.

BENTYLOL®

Hoechst Marion Roussel

Dicyclomine HCl

Antispasmodic

Pharmacology: Dicyclomine relieves smooth muscle spasm of the gastrointestinal tract. Animal studies indicate that this action is achieved via a dual mechanism: 1) a specific anticholinergic effect (antimuscarinic) at the ACh-receptor sites with approximately 1/8 the mg potency of atropine (in vitro guinea pig ileum); 2) a direct effect upon smooth muscle (musculotropic) as evidenced by dicyclomine's antagonism of bradykinin- and histamine-induced spasms of the isolated guinea pig ileum. Atropine did not affect responses to these 2 agonists. Animal studies showed dicyclomine to be equally potent against ACh- or $BaCl_2$-induced intestinal spasm while atropine was at least 200 times more potent against the effects of ACh than against $BaCl_2$. Tests for mydriatic effects in mice showed that dicyclomine was approximately 1/500 as potent as atropine; antisialagogue tests in rabbits showed dicyclomine to be 1/300 as potent as atropine.

After a single oral 20 mg dose of dicyclomine in volunteers, peak plasma concentration reached a mean value of 58 ng/mL in 1 to 1.5 hours. The principal route of elimination is via the urine.

Indications: For the treatment of functional gastrointestinal tract conditions involving smooth muscle spasm such as irritable colon (mucous colitis, spastic colon, irritable bowel syndrome) and spastic constipation. It can also be used as adjunctive therapy in organic gastrointestinal conditions to relieve associated smooth muscle spasm such as in colitis, diverticulitis, regional enteritis, gastritis, and peptic ulcer.

Contraindications: Known idiosyncrasy to dicyclomine. Infants less than 6 months of age (see Warnings) and in nursing mothers (see Precautions). Should not be used in patients with obstructive uropathy, obstructive disease of the gastrointestinal tract, paralytic ileus and intestinal atony, severe ulcerative colitis, myasthenia gravis, reflux esophagitis, glaucoma, unstable cardiovascular status in acute hemorrhage.

Warnings: Infants: There are reports of infants who, in their first 3 months of life, were given dicyclomine syrup and evidenced respiratory symptoms (breathing difficulty, shortness of breath, breathlessness, respiratory collapse, apnea), as well as seizures, syncope, asphyxia, pulse rate fluctuations, muscular hypotonia, and coma. In some instances, these symptoms occurred within minutes of ingestion and lasted up to 20 to 30 minutes. The symptoms were reported in association with dicyclomine syrup therapy but a proven cause and effect relationship has not been established.

Worldwide, a few deaths have been reported in infants 3 months of age or less who had been given dicyclomine syrup. Two of these were reported to have been associated with excessively high dicyclomine blood levels.

Although no causal relationship between these effects, observed in infants, and dicyclomine administration has been established, dicyclomine is contraindicated in infants 6 months of age or less (see Contraindications).

Other: Diarrhea may be an early symptom of incomplete intestinal obstruction, especially in patients with ileostomy or colostomy. In this instance, treatment with this drug would be inappropriate and possibly harmful.

Occupational Hazards: Dicyclomine may produce drowsiness or blurred vision. The patient should be warned not to engage in activities requiring mental alertness, such as operating a motor vehicle or other machinery or performing hazardous work while taking this drug.

Psychosis has been reported in sensitive individuals given anticholinergic drugs. CNS signs and symptoms include confusion, disorientation, short-term memory loss, hallucinations, dysarthria, ataxia, coma, euphoria, decreased anxiety, fatigue, insomnia, agitation and mannerisms, and inappropriate affect. These CNS signs and symptoms usually resolve within 12 to 24 hours after discontinuation of the drug.

Precautions: General: Dicyclomine should be used with caution in any patient with, or suspected of having: prostatic hypertrophy, hiatal hernia associated with reflux esophagitis because anticholinergic drugs may aggravate the condition, autonomic neuropathy, hepatic or renal disease, hyperthyroidism, hypertension, coronary heart disease, congestive heart failure, cardiac tachyarrhythmia.

Pregnancy: Epidemiologic studies in pregnant women with products containing dicyclomine (at doses up to 40 mg/day) have not shown that dicyclomine increases the risk of fetal abnormalities if administered during the first trimester of pregnancy. There are however no adequate and well-controlled studies in pregnant women at the recommended doses (80 to 160 mg/day). Animal reproduction studies have revealed no evidence of impaired fertility or harm to the fetus due to dicyclomine. Because animal reproduction studies are not always predictive of human response, dicyclomine should be used during pregnancy only if required.

Lactation: Since dicyclomine has been reported to be excreted in human milk, its use is contraindicated in nursing mothers (see Contraindications).

Drug Interactions: The following agents may increase certain actions or side effects of anticholinergic drugs: amantadine, antiarrhythmic agents of class I (e.g., quinidine), antihistamines, antipsychotic agents (e.g., phenothiazines), benzodiazepines, MAO inhibitors, narcotic analgesics (e.g., meperidine), nitrates and nitrites, sympathomimetic agents, tricyclic antidepressants, and other drugs having anticholinergic activity.

Anticholinergics antagonize the effects of antiglaucoma agents. Anticholinergic drugs in the presence of increased intraocular pressure may be hazardous when taken concurrently with agents such as corticosteroids.

Anticholinergic agents may affect gastrointestinal absorption of various drugs, such as slowly dissolving dosage forms of digoxin; increased serum digoxin concentrations may result. Anticholinergic drugs may antagonize the effects of drugs that alter gastrointestinal motility such as metoclopramide. Because antacids may interfere with the absorption of anticholinergic agents, simultaneous use of these drugs should be avoided.

The inhibiting effects of anticholinergic drugs on gastric hydrochloric acid secretion are antagonized by agents used to treat achlorhydria and those to test gastric secretion.

Adverse Effects: Most adverse reactions reported in clinical trials conducted with dicyclomine were typically anticholinergic in nature and included, in decreasing order of frequency: dry mouth, dizziness, blurred vision, nausea, lightheadedness, drowsiness, weakness and nervousness.

Other adverse reactions reported with dicyclomine and pharmacologically similar drugs, e.g., other anticholinergics and antispasmodics, were the following:

Gastrointestinal: vomiting, constipation, bloated feeling, abdominal pain, taste loss, anorexia.

CNS: tingling, headache, numbness, mental confusion and/or excitement (especially in elderly persons), dyskinesia, lethargy, syncope, speech disturbance, insomnia.

Ophthalmologic: diplopia, mydrias, cycloplegia, increased ocular tension.

Dermatologic/Allergic: rash, urticaria, itching, and other dermal manifestations; severe allergic reaction or drug idiosyncrasies including anaphylaxis.

Genitourinary: urinary hesitancy, urinary retention.

Cardiovascular: tachycardia, palpitations.

Respiratory: dyspnea, apnea, asphyxia.

Other: decreased sweating, nasal stuffiness or congestion, sneezing, throat congestion, impotence, suppression of lactation (see Precautions).

Overdose: Symptoms: Signs and symptoms of dicyclomine overdosage are headache; nausea; vomiting; blurred vision; dilated pupils; hot, dry skin; dizziness; dry mouth; difficulty in swallowing; and CNS stimulation. A curare-like action may occur (i.e., neuromuscular blockage leading to muscular weakness and possible paralysis).

Treatment: Treatment should consist of gastric lavage, emetics and activated charcoal. Sedatives (e.g., short-acting barbiturates, benzodiazepines) may be used for management of overt signs of excitement. If indicated, an appropriate parenteral cholinergic agent may be used as an antidote. Dialysis: It is not known if dicyclomine is dialyzable.

Dosage: Dosage should be adjusted to individual patient needs.

Syrup and Tablets: Adults: 10 to 20 mg 3 to 4 times daily. Depending upon the patient's response during the first week of therapy, the dose should be increased to 160 mg/day unless side effects limit dose escalation. If efficacy is not achieved within 2 weeks or side effects require doses below 80 mg/day, the drug should be discontinued. Documented safety data are not available for doses above 80 mg daily for periods longer than 2 weeks.

Children (2 to 12 years): 10 mg 3 to 4 times daily.

Infants (6 months to 2 years): 5 to 10 mg 3 to 4 times daily, 15 minutes before feeding. Do not exceed 40 mg daily. Syrup should be diluted with equal volume of water.

Supplied: Syrup: Each 5 mL of clear red syrup contains: dicyclomine HCl USP 10 mg. Nonmedicinal ingredients: artificial and natural vanilla flavors, artificial blackcurrant flavor, artificial cherry flavor, artificial raspberry flavor, citric acid, glucose, methylparaben, propylene glycol, propylparaben, purified water, red no. 2, sodium citrate, sodium cyclamate and yellow FD&C #6. Energy: 57.4 kJ (14 kcal)/5 mL. Bottles of 250 mL. Store at room temperature, between 15 and 30°C. Protect from excessive heat.

Tablets: 10 mg: Each white, flat-faced, beveled edge, compressed tablet, with 10 on one side and M on the other with a double circle around it, contains: dicyclomine HCl USP 10 mg. Bottles of 100 and 500. Store at room temperature between 15 and 30°C. Protect from excessive heat and moisture.

20 mg: Each white, flat-faced, beveled edge, compressed tablet, with 20 on one side and M on the other with a double circle around it, contains: dicyclomine HCl USP 20 mg. Bottles of 100 and 500. Store at room temperature between 15 and 30°C. Protect from excessive heat and moisture.

(Shown in Product Recognition Section)

BENURYL™ ℞

ICN

Probenecid

Uricosuric

Supplied: Each white, round, scored tablet, imprinted ICN B11, contains: probenecid, USP 500 mg. Nonmedicinal ingredients: colloidal silicon dioxide, dibasic calcium phosphate, magnesium stearate, microcrystalline cellulose, starch and talc. Bottles of 100 and 500.

BENYLIN® CODEINE 3.3 mg-D-E (OTC) Ⓝ
BENYLIN® DM
BENYLIN® DM 12 HOUR
BENYLIN® DM FOR CHILDREN
BENYLIN® DM FOR CHILDREN 12 HOUR
BENYLIN® DM-D (ADULT)
BENYLIN® DM-D FOR CHILDREN
BENYLIN® DM-D-E
BENYLIN® DM-D-E EXTRA STRENGTH
BENYLIN® DM-E
BENYLIN® DM-E EXTRA STRENGTH
BENYLIN® E EXTRA STRENGTH
BENYLIN® 4 FLU

Warner-Lambert Consumer Healthcare

Codeine Phosphate—Pseudoephedrine HCl—Guaifenesin
Dextromethorphan HBr
Dextromethorphan HBr
Dextromethorphan HBr
Dextromethorphan HBr
Dextromethorphan HBr—Pseudoephedrine HCl
Dextromethorphan HBr—Pseudoephedrine HCl
Dextromethorphan HBr—Pseudoephedrine HCl—Guaifenesin
Dextromethorphan HBr—Pseudoephedrine HCl—Guaifenesin
Dextromethorphan HBr—Guaifenesin
Dextromethorphan HBr—Guaifenesin
Guaifenesin
Dextromethorphan HBr—Pseudoephedrine HCl—Guaifenesin—Acetaminophen

Antitussive—Decongestant—Expectorant
Antitussive
Antitussive
Antitussive
Antitussive
Antitussive—Decongestant
Antitussive—Decongestant
Antitussive—Decongestant—Expectorant
Antitussive—Decongestant—Expectorant
Antitussive—Expectorant
Antitussive—Expectorant
Expectorant
Antitussive—Decongestant—Expectorant—Analgesic

Indications: DM/Codeine: Antitussive Products (dextromethorphan)/(codeine): Suppression of dry hacking coughs.

E: Expectorant Products (guaifenesin): Loosens mucus/phlegm in coughs due to colds.

D: Decongestant Products (pseudoephedrine): Relieves nasal congestion.

A: Analgesic/Antipyretic (acetaminophen): Relieves pain, fever, chills, headache, body aches, and sore throat pain.

Contraindications: Hypersensitivity to any of the components.

DM or Codeine: Pre-existing respiratory depression.

DM or D (Decongestant): Patients receiving or having received MAO inhibitors in the preceding 3 weeks.

Warnings: Massive acetaminophen overdose can be toxic and potentially fatal. In adults, hepatotoxicity from acetaminophen is unlikely to occur with overdoses at less than 10 g ingested at one time and fatalities are unlikely to occur with overdoses of less than 15 g ingested at one time.

Precautions: Before prescribing medication to suppress or modify cough, it is important to ascertain that the underlying cause of the cough is identified, that modification of the cough does not increase the risk of clinical or physiologic complications, and that appropriate therapy for the primary disease is provided.

If cough worsens, lasts for more than 1 week or is accompanied by high fever, consult a physician. Do not exceed recommended dosage. Keep safely out of reach of children.

Caution should be exercised and dosage may need to be reduced when a codeine or dextromethorphan containing product is administered with other drugs which depress the CNS (including alcohol), phenothiazines or tricyclic antidepressants.

Codeine: In young children the respiratory centre is especially susceptible to the depressant action of narcotic cough suppressants. Benefit to risk ratio should be carefully considered especially in children with respiratory embarrassment, e.g., croup. Estimation of dosage relative to the child's age and weight is of great importance.

Dextromethorphan (DM) or Guaifenesin (E): Not recommended for patients with asthma unless directed by a physician.

Pseudoephedrine (D): This product should be used with caution in diabetics, hypertensive patients and patients with glaucoma, coronary artery disease, hyperthyroidism, urinary retention due to prostate enlargement.

Geriatrics, *Pregnancy* and *Lactation:* In elderly, pregnant or nursing patients, consult a physician before using these products.

Benylin DM-D For Children: In cases of overdose, the respiratory centre in young children is especially susceptible to depression. Estimation of dosage relative to the child's age and weight is of great importance.

Do not use in cases of high blood pressure, heart or thyroid disease, diabetes or asthma, except on the advice of a physician. Do not exceed recommended dosage. If cough worsens, lasts for more than 1 week or is accompanied by high fever, consult a physician. Keep safely out of reach of children.

Adverse Effects: Benylin DM (Adult and Children) or Benylin DM-E: Drowsiness, dizziness, constipation, nausea, vomiting and confusion have been encountered.

Benylin DM-D (Adult and Children), Benylin DM-D-E, Benylin Codeine 3.3 mg-D-E: Drowsiness, nausea, vomiting, constipation, palpitation, confusion, dizziness and tightness in the chest may be encountered.

Benylin E Extra Strength: Nausea, gastrointestinal upset and drowsiness occur infrequently.

Dosage: Benylin Codeine 3.3 mg-D-E (OTC): Adults: 10 mL every 4 hours. Up to a maximum of 4 doses/day.

Benylin DM: Adults and children 12 years and over: 10 mL every 6 to 8 hours. Children: 6 to 11 years: 5 mL every 6 to 8 hours; 2 to 5 years: 2.5 mL every 6 to 8 hours. Maximum 4 doses/day.

Benylin DM 12 Hour: Adults and children 12 years and over: 10 mL every 12 hours. Children 6 to 11 years: 5 mL every 12 hours. Children 2 to 5 years: 2.5 mL every 12 hours. Maximum 2 doses/day. Not recommended for children under 2 years of age except on the advice of a physician.

Benylin DM For Children: Children 6 to 11 years: 10 mL every 6 hours. 2 to 5 years: 5 mL every 6 hours. Maximum 4 doses/day. Not recommended for children under 2 years of age except on the advice of a physician.

Benylin DM For Children 12 Hour: Children 6 to 11 years: 10 mL every 12 hours. Children 2 to 5 years: 5 mL every 12 hours. Maximum 2 doses/day.

Benylin DM-D For Children: 6 to under 12 years: 10 mL every 6 hours. 2 to 5 years: 5 mL every 6 hours. Not recommended for children under 2 years of age except on the advice of a physician.

Benylin DM-E, Benylin DM-D (Adult), Benylin DM-D-E: Adults and children 12 years and over: 10 mL every 6 hours. Children: 6 to 11 years: 5 mL every 6 hours; 2 to 5 years: 2.5 mL every 6 hours. Maximum 4 doses/day.

Benylin DM-D-E Extra Strength: Adults and children over 12 years: 10 mL every 6 hours. Maximum 4 doses/day. Not recommended for children under 12 years.

Benylin DM-E Extra Strength: Adults and children 12 years and over: 10 mL every 6 hours. Maximum 4 doses/day. Not recommended for children under 12 years.

Benylin E Extra Strength: Adults and Children 12 years and over: 5 to 10 mL every 6 hours. Maximum 40 mL/day. Not recommended for children under 12 years.

Benylin 4 Flu: Adults and children 12 years and over: 30 mL or 2 caplets every 6 hours. Maximum 4 doses/day. Not recommended for children under 12 years.

Supplied: Benylin Codeine 3.3 mg-D-E (OTC) Syrup: Each 5 mL contains: codeine phosphate 3.3 mg, pseudoephedrine HCl 30 mg and guaifenesin 100 mg. Nonmedicinal ingredients: alcohol, D&C Red No. 33, citric acid, cellulose, FD&C Red No. 2, glycerin, menthol, PEG, propyl gallate, raspberry artificial flavor, sodium benzoate, sodium citrate, sodium cyclamate, sorbitol and water. Energy: 42.7 kJ (10.2 kcal)/5 mL. Sodium: <1.1 mmol (25mg)/5 mL. Gluten-, lactose-, paraben-, sucrose-, sulfite- and tartrazine-free. Bottles of 100 and 250 mL.

Benylin DM: Each 5 mL of syrup contains: dextromethorphan HBr 15 mg. Nonmedicinal ingredients: artificial sweetener, cellulose, citric acid, D&C Red No. 33, FD&C Red No. 40, glycerin, menthol, PEG, raspberry artificial flavor, sodium benzoate, sodium citrate, sodium cyclamate, sorbitol and water. Energy: 28 kJ (6.7 kcal)/5 mL. Sodium: <1 mmol (18.8 mg)/5 mL. Alcohol-, gluten-, lactose-, paraben-, sucrose-, sulfite- and tartrazine-free. Bottles of 100 and 250 mL.

Benylin DM 12 Hour: Each 5 mL of syrup contains: dextromethorphan polistirex in a controlled-release formula equivalent to dextromethorphan hydrobromide 30 mg. Nonmedicinal ingredients: D&C Red No. 33, menthol, parabens, PEG, polysorbate, raspberry artificial flavor, sorbitan monooleate, sorbitol, sucralose, tragacanth gum, water and xanthan gum. Energy: 12.6 kJ (3 kcal)/5 mL. Alcohol-, gluten-, lactose-, sucrose-, sulfite- and tartrazine-free. Bottles of 85 mL.

Benylin DM For Chldren: Each 5 mL of grape-flavored syrup contains: dextromethorphan HBr 7.5 mg. Nonmedicinal ingredients: cellulose, citric acid, FD&C Blue No. 1, FD&C Red No. 2, glycerin, grape artificial flavor, monoammonium glycyrrhizinate, sodium benzoate, sodium citrate, sodium cyclamate, sorbitol and water. Alcohol-, gluten-, lactose-, paraben-, sucrose-, sulfite- and tartrazine-free. Bottles of 100 mL.

Benylin DM For Children 12 Hour: Each 5 mL of syrup contains: dextromethorphan polistirex in a controlled-release formula equivalent to dextromethorphan hydrobromide 15 mg. Nonmedicinal ingredients: bubblegum flavor, D&C Red No. 33, maltol, parabens, PEG, polysorbate, sorbitan monooleate, sorbitol, sucralose, tragacanth gum, water and xanthan gum. Energy: 12.6 kJ (3 kcal)/5 mL. Alcohol-, gluten-, lactose-, sucrose-, sulfite- and tartrazine-free. Bottles of 85 mL.

Benylin DM-D (Adult): Each 5 mL of syrup contains: dextromethorphan HBr 15 mg and pseudoephedrine HCl 30 mg. Nonmedicinal ingredients: artificial sweetener, cellulose, citric acid, D&C Red No. 33, FD&C Red No. 40, glycerin, menthol, PEG, raspberry artificial flavor, sodium citrate, sodium cyclamate, sodium benzoate, sorbitol and water. Energy: 28 kJ (6.7 kcal)/5 mL. Sodium: <1 mmol (19 mg)/5 mL. Alcohol-, gluten-, lactose-, paraben-, sucrose-, sulfite- and tartrazine-free. Bottles of 100 mL.

Benylin DM-D For Children: Each 5 mL of grape-flavored syrup contains: dextromethorphan HBr 7.5 mg and pseudoephedrine HCl 15 mg. Nonmedicinal ingredients: cellulose, citric acid, FD&C Blue No. 1, FD&C Red No. 2, glycerin, artificial grape flavor, monoammonium glycyrrhizinate, sodium benzoate, sodium citrate, sodium cyclamate, sorbitol and water. Energy: 38.6 kJ (9.2 kcal)/5 mL. Sodium: <1 mmol (11.04 mg)/5 mL. Alcohol-, gluten-, lactose-, paraben-, sucrose-, sulfite- and tartrazine-free. Bottles of 100 and 250 mL.

Benylin DM-D-E: Each 5 mL of syrup contains: dextromethorphan HBr 15 mg, pseudoephedrine HCl 30 mg and guaifenesin 100 mg. Nonmedicinal ingredients: alcohol, artificial sweetener, cellulose, citric acid, D&C Red No. 33, FD&C Red No. 40, glycerin, menthol, PEG, raspberry artificial flavor, sodium benzoate, sodium citrate, sodium cyclamate, sorbitol and water. Energy: 34.7 kJ (8.3 kcal)/5 mL. Sodium: <1 mmol (20.6 mg)/5 mL. Gluten-, lactose-, paraben-, sucrose-, sulfite- and tartrazine-free. Bottles of 100 and 250 mL.

Benylin DM-D-E Extra Strength: Each 5 mL of syrup contains: dextromethorphan HBr 15 mg, pseudoephedrine HCl 30 mg and guaifenesin 200 mg. Nonmedicinal ingredients: alcohol, artificial cherry fruitti flavor, artificial sweetener, cellulose, citric acid, D&C Red No. 33, FD&C Red No. 40, glycerin, menthol, monoammonium glycyrrhizinate, PEG, sodium benzoate, sodium citrate, sodium cyclamate, sorbitol and water. Energy: 36 kJ (8.6 kcal)/5 mL. Sodium: <1 mmol (19.6 mg)/5 mL. Gluten-, lactose-, paraben-, sucrose-, sulfite- and tartrazine-free. Bottles of 100 and 250 mL.

Benylin DM-E: Each 5 mL of syrup contains: dextromethorphan HBr 15 mg and guaifenesin 100 mg. Nonmedicinal ingredients: alcohol, artificial sweetener, citric acid, D&C Red No. 33, FD&C Red No. 40, glycerin, menthol, PEG, raspberry artificial flavor, sodium benzoate, sodium citrate, sodium cyclamate, cellulose, sorbitol and water. Energy: 34.7 kJ (8.3 kcal)/5 mL. Sodium: <1 mmol (20.6 mg)/5 mL. Gluten-, lactose-, paraben-, sucrose-, sulfite- and tartrazine-free. Bottles of 100 and 250 mL.

Benylin DM-E Extra Strength: Each 5 mL of syrup contains: dextromethorphan HBr 15 mg, and guaifenesin 200 mg. Nonmedicinal ingredients: alcohol, artificial cherry-fruitti flavor, artificial sweetener, cellulose, citric acid, D&C Red No. 33, FD&C Red No. 40, glycerin, menthol, monoammonium glycyrrhizinate, PEG, sodium benzoate, sodium citrate, sodium cyclamate, sorbitol and water. Energy: 36 kJ (8.6 kcal)/5 mL. Sodium: <1 mmol (19.6 mg)/5 mL. Gluten-, lactose-, paraben-, sucrose-, sulfite- and tartrazine-free. Bottles of 100.

Benylin E Extra Strength: Each 5 mL of syrup contains: guaifenesin 200 mg. Nonmedicinal ingredients: alcohol, artificial cherry-fruitti flavor, artificial sweetener, cellulose, citric acid, D&C Red No. 33, FD&C Red No. 40, glycerin, menthol, monoammonium glycyrrhizinate, PEG, sodium benzoate, sodium citrate, sodium cyclamate, sorbitol and water. Energy: 36.12 kJ (8.6 kcal)/5 mL. Bottles of 100 and 250 mL.

Benylin 4 Flu: Caplets: Each green caplet, printed "BENYLIN" on both sides, contains: dextromethorphan HBr 15 mg, pseudoephedrine HCl 30 mg, guaifenesin 100 mg and acetaminophen 500 mg. Nonmedicinal ingredients: celluloses, D&C Yellow No. 10, FD&C Blue No. 1, PEG, polysorbate, silica, titanium dioxide, wax and zinc stearate. Energy: 0.76 kJ (0.18 kcal). Alcohol-, gluten-, lactose-, paraben-, sucrose-, sulfite- and tartrazine-free. Blister packages of 10.

Syrup: Each 15 mL of syrup contains: dextromethorphan HBr 15 mg, pseudoephedrine HCl 30 mg, guaifenesin 100 mg and acetaminophen 500 mg. Nonmedicinal ingredients: alcohol, artificial sweetener, cellulose, citric acid, D&C Red No. 33, glycerin, menthol, monoammonium glycyrrhizinate, PEG, raspberry artificial flavor, sodium benzoate, sodium citrate, sodium cyclamate, sodium saccharin, sorbitol and water. Energy: 82.35 kJ (19.7 kcal)/15 mL. Bottles of 180 mL.

(Shown in Product Recognition Section)

Reviewed 1997

BENZAC® AC 5
BENZAC® AC 10 Ⓟ
Galderma

Benzoyl Peroxide

Acne Therapy

Supplied: Each tube contains: benzoyl peroxide USP 5% or 10% in a water base gel. Nonmedicinal ingredients: acrylates copolymer, carbomer 940, docusate sodium, edetate disodium, glycerin, poloxamer 182, propylene glycol, purified water, silicon dioxide and sodium hydroxide. May contain citric acid to adjust pH. Plastic tubes of 60 g. Store at room temperature; avoid excessive heat.

BENZAC® W5
BENZAC® W10 Ⓟ
Galderma

Benzoyl Peroxide

Acne Therapy

Supplied: Each tube contains: benzoyl peroxide USP 5% or 10% in a water base gel. Nonmedicinal ingredients: carbomer 940, docusate sodium, edetate disodium, poloxamer 182, propylene glycol, purified water, silicon dioxide and sodium hydroxide. May contain citric acid to adjust pH. Plastic tubes of 60 g. Store at room temperature; avoid excessive heat.

BENZAC® W WASH 5
BENZAC® W WASH 10 Ⓟ
Galderma

Benzoyl Peroxide

Acne Therapy

Supplied: Each bottle contains: benzoyl peroxide USP 5% or 10% cleanser in a water base gel. Nonmedicinal ingredients: carbomer 940, citric acid, purified water and sodium C14-16 olefin sulfonate. Plastic bottles of 225 g. Store at room temperature; avoid excessive heat.

2.5 BENZAGEL® Acne Gel
5 BENZAGEL® Acne Gel
Novartis Consumer Health

Benzoyl Peroxide

Acne Vulgaris Therapy

Indications: A topical aid in the treatment of acne vulgaris.

Contraindications: Known sensitivity to any of the components.

Precautions: Avoid contact with eyes, nostrils, lips and mouth. Observe patients carefully for possible local irritation or sensitivity during long-term topical therapy. Apply with caution on neck, circumoral and/or other sensitive areas. If excessive dryness or irritation occurs, discontinue use. May bleach colored fabrics. For external use only.

Radiation from ultraviolet and cold quartz sources as well as abrasion may add to the desquamating effect produced by benzoyl peroxide and, therefore, should be reduced in intensity and/or frequency.

When using this product, avoid unnecessary or prolonged exposure to the sun.

Dosage: Wash face prior to application. Apply once or more daily to affected areas. Very fair individuals should begin with a single application at bedtime, allowing overnight medication.

Supplied: 2.5 Benzagel: Each plastic tube contains: benzoyl peroxide 2.5% w/w in a hydroalcoholic base. Nonmedicinal ingredients: alcohol, carbopol, dioctyl sodium sulfosuccinate, fragrance, methyl salicylate, sodium hydroxide and water. Tubes of 30 g. Store at room temperature.

5 Benzagel: Each plastic tube contains: benzoyl peroxide 5% w/w in a hydroalcoholic base. Nonmedicinal ingredients: alcohol, carbopol, dioctyl sodium sulfosuccinate, fragrance, methyl salicylate, sodium hydroxide and water. Tubes of 15, 30 and 60 g. Store at room temperature.

2.5 BENZAGEL® Acne Lotion
5 BENZAGEL® Acne Lotion
Novartis Consumer Health

Benzoyl Peroxide

Acne Therapy

Indications: An aid in the treatment of uncomplicated facial acne.

Precautions: Avoid contact with eyes, nostrils, lips and mouth. Slight stinging and redness may occur at the beginning of treatment. First test on a small area, if excessive dryness or irritation occurs then or during treatment, discontinue use and consult a physician. If there is not substantial improvement within 3 to 4 weeks, consult a physician. May bleach colored fabrics. Store at room temperature. For external use only.

When using this product avoid unnecessary or prolonged exposure to the sun.

Dosage: Shake well. Wash face with a non-medicated soap prior to application. Apply acne lotion to affected areas twice daily or as directed by your physician. Very fair skinned individuals should begin with a single application at bedtime allowing for overnight medication.

Supplied: 2.5 Benzagel: Each plastic, flip top bottle contains: benzoyl peroxide 2.5% w/w in a lotion base. Nonmedicinal ingredients: cetyl alcohol, citric acid, glyceryl stearate, methylparaben, propylparaben, sodium citrate and water. Bottles of 25 mL. Store at room temperature.

5 Benzagel: Each plastic, flip top bottle contains: benzoyl peroxide 5% w/w in a lotion base. Nonmedicinal ingredients: cetyl alcohol, citric acid, glyceryl stearate, methylparaben, propylparaben, sodium citrate and water. Bottles of 25 mL. Store at room temperature.

5 BENZAGEL® Acne Wash
Novartis Consumer Health

Benzoyl Peroxide

Acne Therapy

Indications: An effective aid in the treatment of uncomplicated facial acne.

Precautions: Avoid contact with eyes, nostrils, lips, mouth and hair. Slight stinging and redness may occur when beginning treatment. First, test a small area of the face. If excessive dryness or irritation develops then or during use, discontinue use and consult a physician. It is recommended that very fair skinned persons should start with one application. The product should not be used with other products for acne containing sulfur or resorcinol. May bleach fabrics. Store at room temperature. For external use only.

When using this product avoid unnecessary or prolonged exposure to the sun.

Dosage: Shake well before use. Wash face twice daily with 5 Benzagel Acne Wash and warm water using a gentle rubbing action. Rinse thoroughly and dry with a clean towel. After this treatment 2.5 or 5 Benzagel Acne Gel or Lotion may be applied directly to the acne pimples of the face.

Supplied: Each plastic, flip top bottle contains: benzoyl peroxide 5% w/w in a cleansing base. Nonmedicinal ingredients: cetyl alcohol, citric acid, methylparaben, propylene glycol, propylparaben, sodium citrate, sodium lauryl sulfate and water. Bottles of 85 mL. Store at room temperature.

10 BENZAGEL® Acne Gel Ⓟ
Dermik Laboratories Canada

Benzoyl Peroxide

Acne Vulgaris Therapy

Indications: A topical aid in the treatment of acne vulgaris.

Contraindications: Known sensitivity to any of the components.

Precautions: Avoid contact with eyes, nostrils, lips and mouth. Observe patients carefully for possible local irritation or sensitivity during long-term topical therapy. Apply with caution on neck, circumoral and/or other sensitive areas. If excessive dryness or irritation occurs, discontinue use. May bleach colored fabrics. For external use only.

Radiation from ultraviolet and cold quartz sources as well as abrasion may add to the desquamating effect produced by benzoyl peroxide and, therefore, should be reduced in intensity and/or frequency.

Dosage: Wash face prior to application. Apply once or more daily to affected areas. Very fair individuals should begin with a single application at bedtime, allowing overnight medication.

Supplied: Each plastic tube contains: benzoyl peroxide 10% w/w in a hydroalcoholic base. Nonmedicinal ingredients: alcohol, carboxypolymethylene, dioctyl sodium sulfosuccinate, lemon fragrance oil, methyl salicylate, purified water and sodium hydroxide. Alcohol 15% w/w. Tubes of 60 g. Store at room temperature.

BENZAMYCIN® Ⓟ
Dermik Laboratories Canada

Erythromycin—Benzoyl Peroxide

Acne Therapy

Pharmacology: Erythromycin is a bacteriostatic macrolide antibiotic, but may be bactericidal in high concentrations. Although the mechanism by which erythromycin acts in reducing inflammatory lesions of acne vulgaris is not fully elucidated, it is presumably due to its antibiotic action. It inhibits the growth of P. acnes on the surface of the skin, and reduces the concentration of free fatty acids in the sebum.

Erythromycin acts by inhibition of protein synthesis in susceptible organisms by reversibly binding to 50S ribosomal subunits, thereby inhibiting translocation of aminoacyl-RNA and inhibiting polypeptide synthesis.

Benzamycin (cont'd)

Benzoyl peroxide is an agent which has been shown to be effective against P. acnes, an anaerobe found in sebaceous follicles and comedones. The antibacterial action of benzoyl peroxide is believed to be due to the release of active oxygen. Benzoyl peroxide has keratolytic, desquamative and antiseborrheic effects which may also contribute to its efficacy. Benzoyl peroxide has been shown to be absorbed by the skin where it is converted to benzoic acid. Approximately 5% of the metabolite is excreted unchanged in the urine.

Indications: For the topical treatment of moderate acne vulgaris characterized by comedones, inflammatory papules/pustules, with or without an occasional cyst or nodule (Grade II to III*). Benzamycin is not indicated for the treatment of cystic acne (Grade IV*).

[*Pillsbury DM., Heaton C. Manual of Dermatology 1980.]

Contraindications: In those patients with a history of hypersensitivity to erythromycin, benzoyl peroxide or any of the ingredients in the preparation (see Supplied).

Warnings: For external use only.

Not for ophthalmic use. Avoid contact with eyes, nose, lips, mouth and other mucous membranes. If contact occurs, rinse thoroughly with water.

Benzamycin contains drying and peeling agents that are potential irritants. Therefore, reduction in frequency of application may be necessary to avoid excessive irritation. If severe irritation develops, discontinue use and institute appropriate therapy. Concomitant topical acne therapy should be used with caution because a possible cumulative irritancy effect may occur, especially with peeling, desquamating or abrasive agents.

Precautions: General: The use of antibiotic agents may be associated with the overgrowth of nonsusceptible organisms including fungi. If this occurs, administration of Benzamycin should be discontinued, and appropriate measures taken.

Pregnancy: The safety of Benzamycin in pregnancy has not been established, nor have any animal reproduction studies been conducted with Benzamycin. It is also not known whether Benzamycin can cause fetal harm when administered to a pregnant woman or can affect reproductive capacity. Benzamycin should be given to a pregnant woman only if clearly needed.

Lactation: It is not known whether Benzamycin is excreted in human milk after topical application. However, erythromycin is excreted in human milk following oral and parenteral administration. Therefore, caution should be exercised when erythromycin is administered to a nursing woman.

Children: The safety and effectiveness of Benzamycin in children below the age of 12 years have not been established.

Drug Interactions: Antagonism has been demonstrated in vitro between erythromycin, lincomycin, chloramphenicol and clindamycin. Therefore erythromycin, lincomycin, chloramphenicol and clindamycin should not be used concomitantly with Benzamycin, although no studies have been conducted testing for antagonism of Benzamycin with these antibiotics.

Adverse Effects: Local irritation reactions such as irritation of the skin including: peeling, itching, burning sensation, erythema, inflammation of the face, eyes and nose, irritation of the eyes, skin discoloration, oiliness, tenderness of the skin, pruritus and edema may occur while using Benzamycin.

In clinical trials conducted with Benzamycin, 5 of 155 patients experienced adverse reactions. Four of the adverse reactions were dryness, and 1 was an urticarial reaction which responded to symptomatic treatment.

Overdose: Symptoms and Treatment: Acute overdosage with the topical use of Benzamycin is unlikely. In the event of accidental ingestion, appropriate intervention should be initiated.

Dosage: Benzamycin should be applied as a thin layer to affected areas twice daily, morning and evening, or as directed by physician. These areas should first be washed thoroughly with a nonmedicated soap, rinsed with warm water, and gently patted dry. Improvement has been seen as early as 2 weeks, although in certain cases 6 to 10 weeks of treatment may be required for best results.

Compounding Directions: Benzamycin is supplied to the pharmacist in a package containing 20 g of benzoyl peroxide gel and 0.8 g of active erythromycin powder in a plastic vial. **Prior to dispensing, tap the vial of erythromycin until all powder flows freely. Add 3 mL of ethyl alcohol (70%) to the vial (to the mark) and immediately shake to completely dissolve the erythromycin.** Add this solution to the gel and stir until homogeneous in appearance (1 to 1½ minute).

Information for the Patient: See Blue Section—Information for the Patient "Benzamycin".

Supplied: Each g of topical gel contains: erythromycin 3% (30 mg/g) and benzoyl peroxide 5% (50 mg/g). Nonmedicinal ingredients: alcohol, carboxypolymethylene, dioctyl sodium sulfosuccinate, lemon fragance oil, methyl salicylate, purified water and sodium hydroxide.

Prior to dispensing, the package containing 20 g of benzoyl peroxide and 0.8 g of active erythromycin powder in a plastic vial should be stored at room temperature (15 to 25°C). Following compounding (see Compounding Directions), Benzamycin should be stored under refrigeration (2 to 8°C). Do not freeze. A 3-month expiration date is to be placed on the label.

Reviewed 1998

BENZODIAZEPINES ℞

General Monograph, CPhA

Alprazolam
Bromazepam
Chlordiazepoxide
Clobazam
Clonazepam
Clorazepate
Diazepam
Flurazepam
Lorazepam
Midazolam
Nitrazepam
Oxazepam
Temazepam
Triazolam

Anticonvulsant—Anxiolytic—Hypnotic—Sedative

> This monograph has been compiled by CPhA. It may contain information different from that approved by Therapeutic Products Programme, Health Canada, and the pharmaceutical manufacturers' approval has not been requested.

Pharmacology: Benzodiazepines are glycoproteins with an affinity for benzodiazepine receptors which act as specific binding sites for gamma aminobutyric acid (GABA), the major inhibitory neurotransmitter in the CNS. Although various mechanisms of action have been proposed, the precise sites and mechanisms of action have not been completely established. It is believed that benzodiazepines produce their effect within the CNS by interacting with a macromolecular protein complex in the neuronal membrane which includes $GABA_a$ receptors, high-affinity benzodiazepine receptors and chloride channels.

Occupation of the benzodiazepine receptor increases the affinity of the $GABA_a$ receptor for GABA. GABA potentiates the direct opening of the chloride ion channel, allowing an increased influx of chloride into the neuron. The inward shift of chloride ions hyperpolarizes and stabilizes the membrane, resulting in a net inhibitory effect on neuronal firing. Benzodiazepines alone have little effect on chloride ion channel permeability and depend upon the presence of GABA in the synapse for their actions.

Benzodiazepines with very similar chemical structures can differ in their potency, rate of absorption and other pharmacological parameters. The potency of a benzodiazepine is correlated with its affinity for its binding site, the benzodiazepine receptor. In therapeutic use, the benzodiazepines, while differing in potency, have similar pharmacologic profiles.

It is believed that there are different types of benzodiazepine receptors in different areas of the CNS which produce the various pharmacological actions of the drugs. As the dose of benzodiazepine is increased, anxiolytic effects are first produced, followed by anticonvulsant effects, a reduction in muscle tonus, and finally sedation and hypnosis.

Clinically, benzodiazepines are used in the management of anxiety disorders, insomnia, seizure disorders, skeletal muscle spasticity, alcohol withdrawal, panic disorder and as premedicants prior to surgical or diagnostic procedures. Benzodiazepines have also been used in the management of nausea and vomiting associated with emetogenic cancer chemotherapy.

Pharmacokinetics: Following oral administration, benzodiazepines are well absorbed from the gastrointestinal tract. Absorption of diazepam or chlordiazepoxide after i.m. injection is slow and erratic. Following i.m. administration of lorazepam or midazolam, absorption appears to be rapid and complete. Lorazepam is well absorbed after sublingual administration, reaching peak levels in 60 minutes.

Benzodiazepines are widely distributed in the body and accumulate preferentially in lipid rich areas such as the CNS and adipose tissue. The more lipophilic agents have the fastest rates of absorption and onset of clinical effects. Benzodiazepines and their metabolites are highly bound to plasma proteins.

Steady state plasma concentrations of benzodiazepines and their metabolites are reached after about 5 elimination half-lives, usually a few days to 2 weeks after initiation of therapy.

Benzodiazepines or active metabolites with very long elimination half-lives can accumulate with chronic dosing and produce prolonged effects, especially in elderly or obese patients, those with liver disease, or with concurrent use of other drugs that compete for hepatic oxidation. Benzodiazepines that undergo hepatic glucuronide conjugation and do not have active metabolites are unlikely to accumulate with chronic administration and require multiple daily dosing for sustained effects.

Most of the benzodiazepines are excreted almost entirely in the urine in the form of oxidized and glucuronide-conjugated metabolites. Benzodiazepines are not significantly removed by hemodialysis.

The primary differences among the benzodiazepines are in their pharmacokinetic properties, and these often are among the main factors considered in drug selection. Table I (on following page) reflects the major pharmacokinetic properties of these agents.

Indications: Benzodiazepines have similar pharmacologic actions; however, clinical applications of specific agents may reflect differences in their pharmacokinetic profiles, the availability of evidence-based data, or the labeled indications for a particular agent. Table II (on following page) outlines the current labeled indications of benzodiazepines available in Canada.

Contraindications: Patients with known hypersensitivity to this class of drugs or to any component of the product in question. The manufacturers advise against the use of benzodiazepines in patients with myasthenia gravis and acute closed angle glaucoma, but they may be used in patients receiving appropriate therapy for open angle glaucoma. Specific product monographs should be consulted as individual products may have additional contraindications to their use.

Warnings: Benzodiazepines are not recommended for use in patients with a major depressive disorder or psychosis in which anxiety is not a prominent feature.

Benzodiazepines should be used with extreme caution in patients with severe pulmonary insufficiency or sleep apnea, especially the elderly or very ill patients, and those with limited pulmonary reserve.

Resuscitative facilities and equipment should be available when benzodiazepines are administered parenterally, particularly i.v. These agents should not be administered i.v. to patients in shock, coma, acute alcohol intoxication, or to patients who have recently received other respiratory depressant drugs.

Benzodiazepines must be used with caution in severely depressed patients or those in whom there is any sign of impending depression with an associated anxiety disorder, particularly in patients at risk of increased suicidal tendencies. Appropriate protective measures may be necessary during benzodiazepine therapy in these patients. Consideration should be given to the quantity of medication prescribed at any one time.

Patients should be informed about possible negative effects on memory and advised to report to their physician any mental or behavioral changes that develop during benzodiazepine therapy (see Precautions).

Occupational Hazards: Patients should be warned about the potential impairment of mental alertness or physical coordination which may decrease their ability to perform hazardous tasks such as driving or operating machinery. Elderly patients may be at particular risk for these CNS depressant effects.

Dependence and Withdrawal: Tolerance and the risk of psychological and physical dependence may occur following prolonged use of benzodiazepines at therapeutic doses. The possibility that such effects also may occur following short-term use of benzodiazepines, particularly at higher doses, should also be considered. Tolerance to the hypnotic and sedative effects develops rapidly. In contrast, clinically significant tolerance to the anxiolytic effect usually does not occur even after prolonged use.

Table I—Benzodiazepines

Pharmacokinetic Properties[a]

Drug	Approximate Equivalent Oral Dose (mg)	Time to Peak Plasma Concentration (hours)	Onset of Action F=fast (<1 h) I=intermediate (1 to 3 h) S=slow (>3 h)	Active Metabolite(s)	Pathway of Metabolism	Approximate Half-life (hours, parent compound and active metabolite)
Long-acting						
Chlordiazepoxide	10	0.5 to 4	I	Yes	Oxidation	100
Clorazepate	7.5	0.5 to 2	F	Yes	Oxidation	100
Diazepam	5	0.5 to 2	F	Yes	Oxidation	100
Flurazepam	15	0.5 to 1	F	Yes	Oxidation	100
Intermediate-acting						
Alprazolam	0.5	1 to 2	I	Yes	Oxidation	12 to 15
Bromazepam	6	1 to 4	I	Yes	Conjugation	8 to 30
Clobazam	10	1 to 4	I	Yes	Oxidation	10 to 46
Clonazepam	1	1 to 2	I	No	Nitro reduction	20 to 80
Lorazepam	1	2 to 4	I	No	Conjugation	10 to 20
Nitrazepam	5	2 to 3	I	No	Nitro reduction	16 to 55
Oxazepam	15	2 to 4	S	No	Conjugation	5 to 15
Temazepam	15	2 to 3	I	No	Conjugation	10 to 20
Short-acting						
Midazolam[b]	Not applicable	See Onset of Action	I.M.: 5 to 15 min I.V.: 1.5 to 5 min[c]	Yes	Oxidation	1 to 4
Triazolam	0.25	1 to 2	F	No	Oxidation	1.5 to 5

[a]After oral administration.
[b]Parenteral use only.
[c]Onset of action may be faster if opioid premedicant administered concurrently.

Table II—Benzodiazepines

Labeled Indications[a]

Drug	Anxiety Disorders	Panic Disorder	Insomnia	Perioperative Medication	Seizure Disorders[b]	Skeletal Muscle Spasticity	Alcohol Withdrawal
Alprazolam	Yes	Yes	—	—	—	—	—
Bromazepam	Yes	—	—	—	—	—	—
Chlordiazepoxide	Yes	—	—	—	—	—	—
Clobazam	—	—	—	—	Yes	—	—
Clonazepam	—	—	—	—	Yes	—	—
Clorazepate	Yes	Yes	—	—	—	—	Yes
Diazepam	Yes	—	—	Yes	Yes	Yes	Yes
Flurazepam	—	—	Yes	—	—	—	—
Lorazepam	Yes	—	—	Yes	Yes	—	—
Midazolam	—	—	—	Yes	—	—	—
Nitrazepam	—	—	Yes	—	Yes	—	—
Oxazepam	Yes	—	—	—	—	—	Yes
Temazepam	—	-	Yes	—	—	—	—
Triazolam	—	—	Yes	—	—	—	—

[a]Refer to individual product monographs for more detailed information.
[b]Used in adults and children.

Risk of benzodiazepine dependence can be minimized by titrating the dose, close observation and follow up, proper screening for possible risk factors and education of the patient. Benzodiazepine use should be avoided in patients with a history of alcohol or substance abuse.

Abrupt withdrawal of benzodiazepines may lead to symptoms such as anxiety, insomnia, irritability, gastrointestinal discomfort, anorexia, diaphoresis, photophobia or increased sensitivity to noise. More severe symptoms may occur such as confusion, depersonalization, myoclonus, delirium, psychosis or seizures. Rebound insomnia may occur, particularly following abrupt discontinuation of a benzodiazepine with a short elimination half-life.

Withdrawal can also be precipitated by dosage tapering or inadvertent withdrawal, e.g., due to forgotten doses or admission to hospital. Such effects can also emerge in the early morning following bedtime administration of a short-acting agent. In addition, an increase in daytime anxiety and/or restlessness may be observed between doses of short-acting agents. Rebound or symptom re-emergence may occur after as little as 4 to 6 weeks therapy. It is more likely if the drug is short-acting, taken regularly for >3 months and abruptly discontinued. Symptoms may be similar to those experienced by the patient prior to initiation of the benzodiazepine, but may be more intense.

Choice of withdrawal regimen may depend on the setting of detoxification, severity of dependence and concurrent drug or substance abuse. Patients should follow a structured discontinuation program. When discontinuing benzodiazepines in patients on prolonged therapy, dosage should be gradually decreased over about 6 to 12 weeks, especially in patients with a history of seizures or epilepsy, regardless of their concomitant anticonvulsant drug therapy. If the patient had been taking a short-acting agent, a longer-acting benzodiazepine may be substituted, to provide a gradual decrease in drug concentration and decrease the possibility of withdrawal symptoms. Adjunctive agents such as propranolol, clonidine and carbamazepine have been useful in some patients in suppressing withdrawal symptoms which continue to be severe despite gradual reduction in benzodiazepine dosage.

Precautions: Benzodiazepines may cause psychologic or physical dependence (see Warnings).

Elderly or debilitated patients, children, and patients with liver disease or low serum albumin are most likely to experience CNS adverse effects. Generally it is recommended that therapy be initiated with low dosages and gradually titrated up to the lowest effective dose, to minimize the possibility of ataxia, dizziness and oversedation. Benzodiazepines can produce prolonged CNS depression in neonates because of the inability to convert the benzodiazepine into inactive metabolites. Reversible dementia has also been reported in the elderly after prolonged administration of benzodiazepines.

Differences in the degree of residual and cumulative CNS depressant effects among the benzodiazepines may be particularly important in elderly patients, in patients with potentially impaired elimination of drugs and in individuals whose occupation or life style requires unimpaired intellectual or psychomotor function. There is some evidence that ataxia and the risk of falling and associated hip fracture in elderly patients is greatest with the use of long-acting benzodiazepines as compared to short-acting agents.

Benzodiazepine therapy should be individualized and closely monitored in elderly patients, and the need for continued therapy with these drugs should be re-evaluated frequently.

Anterograde amnesia has occurred following therapeutic doses of benzodiazepines. The degree of severity and duration of effects may vary depending on the drug, dosage, route of administration or individual patient (e.g., elderly patients may be at particular risk). Although amnesic effects have been more commonly associated with midazolam, triazolam and lorazepam, these effects have occurred with other benzodiazepines. Data suggest that anterograde amnesia and next day memory loss occur at a higher rate with triazolam, generally at a 0.5 mg dose. Cases of transient global amnesia and "traveler's amnesia" have also been associated with triazolam in patients taking the drug to induce sleep while traveling. These amnesic effects are unpredictable and not necessarily dose related. The manufacturers advise warning patients not to take triazolam under circumstances in which a full night's sleep and clearance of the drug from the body are not possible before they will need to resume full activity and alertness, e.g., an overnight flight of less than 7 to 8 hours.

Paradoxical stimulant reactions have occurred in psychiatric patients and hyperactive, aggressive children. Such reactions include restlessness, anxiety, mania, insomnia, sleep disturbances, increased muscle spasticity, acute rage and hyperactivity, and have appeared early in therapy, usually in the first 2 weeks. Benzodiazepine therapy should be discontinued if CNS stimulation occurs.

Serious behavioral changes and abnormal thinking have occasionally been associated with benzodiazepine use. Some of these changes may be characterized by hallucinations, depersonalization, agitation, bizarre behavior and decreased inhibition manifested as aggression or excessive extroversion, similar to that seen with alcohol and other CNS depressants.

Caution is advised during parenteral administration of benzodiazepines to elderly patients as they may be more likely to experience apnea, hypotension, bradycardia or cardiac arrest.

Patients with compromised renal or hepatic function should be monitored and the dose carefully titrated to avoid accumulation of these agents.

Because of isolated reports of blood dyscrasias and abnormal liver function tests, periodic blood counts and liver function tests may be of benefit during long-term therapy.

Drug Interactions: Table III lists the more common interactions. Consult individual product monographs for more detailed information pertaining to specific agents.

Table III—Benzodiazepines

Drug Interactions

Drug(s) Interacting with Benzodiazepines	Potential Effect
Alcohol and other CNS depressants	Additive CNS depressant effects. Tolerance may develop with chronic alcohol use
Grapefruit Juice	Increased serum levels of benzodiazepines metabolized by CYP3A4 (e.g., alprazolam, triazolam and orally administered midazolam). Flavonoids found in grapefruit juice have been shown to inhibit the presystemic metabolism of certain drugs by intestinal CYP3A4.
Hepatic enzyme inducers (e.g., carbamazepine, rifampin)	Decreased serum concentrations and effects of benzodiazepines.*
Hepatic enzyme inhibitors (e.g., cimetidine, oral contraceptives, disulfiram, fluconazole, fluoxetine, fluvoxamine, isoniazid, macrolides, specifically erythromycin and clarithromycin, omeprazole, quinolones, ritonavir, indinavir)	Increase in pharmacologic effects of benzodiazepines, especially those which undergo oxidative metabolism (see Table I).
Phenytoin	Increased phenytoin serum concentrations.

*Cigarette smoking may have a similar effect.

Benzodiazepines (cont'd)

Pregnancy: Benzodiazepines should be avoided during pregnancy. Benzodiazepines have been associated with an increased risk of congenital malformations after first trimester exposure. Hypotonia, lethargy and sucking difficulties have been reported in infants whose mothers received benzodiazepines during labor. Chronic use of benzodiazepines during pregnancy has also been associated with neonatal withdrawal. **The use of benzodiazepines solely as hypnotics is contraindicated during pregnancy.** A women planning a pregnancy or who becomes pregnant should be encouraged to discontinue benzodiazepine therapy.

Lactation: Benzodiazepine use in lactating women is not recommended. Because the ability of neonates to metabolize these drugs is limited, accumulation may occur.

Occupational Hazards: Because of the CNS depressant effect of benzodiazepines, patients should be cautioned with regard to driving or performing other hazardous tasks which require mental alertness and physical coordination.

Adverse Effects: The most common adverse effects reported with the use of benzodiazepines are dose dependent CNS effects. Ataxia, dizziness, lightheadedness, drowsiness, including residual daytime drowsiness when used as a hypnotic, weakness, and fatigue usually occur in the first few days of therapy and may decrease with continued therapy. If these effects are persistent, a reduction in dosage may be necessary. Elderly or debilitated patients, children, and patients with liver disease or low serum albumin may be unusually sensitive to the CNS effects.

The more serious, occasionally reported adverse reactions are hypersensitivity reactions, mental depression, behavioral problems, paradoxical stimulant reactions, leukopenia, jaundice, hypotension, memory impairment, phlebitis or venous thrombosis, and seizures.

Other adverse effects less frequently reported include: abdominal or stomach cramps or pain, blurred vision or diplopia, sexual dysfunction, constipation, diarrhea, dry mouth or increased thirst, vertigo, syncope, confusion, vivid or disturbing dreams, slurred speech, euphoria, headache, increased bronchial secretions or watering of mouth, muscle spasm, nausea or vomiting, incontinence, urinary retention, tachycardia or palpitations, trembling and unusual tiredness or weakness.

Overdose: Symptoms: Symptoms of mild overdose include drowsiness, impaired coordination, diminished reflexes, confusion and lethargy. In more serious overdose, symptoms may include ataxia, hypotonia, hypotension, respiratory depression, seizures and coma. Although cardiac arrest has been reported, death from overdose of benzodiazepines in the absence of concurrent ingestion of alcohol or other CNS depressants is rare.

Treatment: Management consists of appropriate supportive and symptomatic therapy. In the case of a recent oral overdose, if vomiting has not occurred spontaneously and if the patient is fully conscious, emesis may be induced with ipecac. If the patient is unconscious, gastric lavage should be considered. Activated charcoal and a saline cathartic may be administered after gastric lavage and or emesis to remove any remaining drug. Vital signs and fluid balance should be monitored. With normal renal function, i.v. fluids may be administered. An adequate airway should be maintained and respiration assisted as required. Hypotension may be controlled by i.v. administration of vasopressors.

Flumazenil is used as an adjunct for the management of benzodiazepine overdosage and for the complete or partial reversal of benzodiazepine-induced sedation. The hypnotic-sedative effects of benzodiazepines are rapidly reversed. However, the residual effects may reappear gradually within a few hours, depending on the dose of flumazenil, the time elapsed since the benzodiazepine was administered, and elimination half-life of the benzodiazepine in question. Flumazenil should be administered only when continued observation of the patient, for recurrence of sedation, can be assured. Its effects on respiratory depression are inconsistent; in some studies residual respiratory depressant effects were still present despite reversal of sedation. Improved consciousness is expected within the first several minutes of flumazenil administration, but ventilatory support may be required for respiratory depression. Flumazenil does not consistently reverse benzodiazepine-associated amnesia. In patients treated for long periods of time with high doses of benzodiazepines (e.g., patients physically dependent, or those maintained on benzodiazepines for control of seizure disorders or intracranial pressure), flumazenil may trigger withdrawal symptoms including convulsions. Rapid i.v. injections should therefore be avoided. The flumazenil product monograph should be consulted for complete prescribing information.

Dialysis is of limited value in benzodiazepine overdose.

Dosage: The dosage of benzodiazepines should be individualized and carefully titrated to avoid excessive sedation and mental or motor impairment. The lowest effective dose should be used and the need for continued therapy reassessed frequently. The risk of dependence may increase with the dose and duration of treatment. Individual product monographs may contain recommendations for maximum duration of use or maximum quantity per prescription, e.g., in the treatment of insomnia or anxiety.

Geriatrics: Elderly patients may be particularly sensitive to the CNS effects of benzodiazepines, and may have longer elimination half-lives due to decreased hepatic metabolism. In general, dosages of benzodiazepines for elderly patients tend to be approximately one-third to one-half of the recommended dose for younger adults.

Please refer to individual product monographs for dosage recommendations for specific indications or specific patient groups such as children, elderly or debilitated patients, or those with hepatic or renal failure.

Reviewed 1999

BENZTROPINE MESYLATE ℞

General Monograph, CPhA

Antiparkinsonian Agent

This monograph has been compiled by CPhA. It may contain information different from that approved by Therapeutic Products Programme, Health Canada, and the pharmaceutical manufacturers' approval has not been requested.

Pharmacology: Benztropine is a synthetic tertiary amine with structural similarities to atropine and diphenhydramine. Benztropine exhibits anticholinergic, antihistaminic and local anesthetic properties. Its mechanism of action as an antiparkinsonian agent is not clearly known. The pharmacologic effects of the drug may not be apparent until 2 to 3 days after initiation of therapy and may persist for up to 24 hours after discontinuation of the drug.

Pharmacokinetics: When given orally, benztropine has an onset of action of between 1 and 2 hours. When given by i.m. or i.v. injection, the onset of action is within minutes.

Indications: The symptomatic treatment of all etiologic groups of parkinsonism and drug-induced extrapyramidal reactions.

Contraindications: Benztropine is contraindicated in patients with a known hypersensitivity to benztropine or to any of its excipients, in patients with angle-closure glaucoma, or in patients with tardive dyskinesia because it has been of little benefit and may actually aggravate this condition. Because of its adverse anticholinergic effects, this drug is contraindicated in children under 3 years of age and should be used with caution in older children.

Precautions: Since benztropine has cumulative action, continued supervision is advisable.

Patients with tachycardia and patients with prostatic hypertrophy should be closely observed during treatment.

The occurrence of glaucoma is possible. Although the drug does not appear to have any adverse effect on simple glaucoma, it should not be used in narrow angle glaucoma (see Contraindications).

Tardive dyskinesia may appear in some patients on long-term therapy with neuroleptics and related agents, or may occur after these drugs have been discontinued. Antiparkinsonian agents usually do not alleviate the symptoms of tardive dyskinesia and in some instances may aggravate or unmask such symptoms. Benztropine is not recommended in tardive dyskinesia (see Contraindications).

When benztropine is used to treat extrapyramidal symptoms caused by neuroleptic therapy in patients with a psychiatric illness, there may be an intensification of psychiatric illness. Although benztropine need not be discontinued when this occurs, the psychogenic potential of antiparkinsonian drugs should be considered when planning the management of patients with psychiatric illnesses. When using benztropine in these patients, they should be kept under careful observation, especially at the beginning of treatment or if dosage is increased.

Benztropine may produce anhidrosis. It should be given with caution during hot weather, especially to the elderly, chronically ill, alcoholics, those with CNS disease and those who do manual labor in a hot environment. Anhidrosis may be anticipated to occur more readily when some disturbance of sweating already exists. If there is evidence of anhidrosis, dosage should be decreased so that the ability to maintain body heat equilibrium by perspiration is not impaired. Severe anhidrosis and fatal hyperthermia have occurred.

Drug Interactions: Anticholinergics: Additive anticholinergic effects may occur when benztropine is used concurrently with drugs such as amantadine, atropine, MAO inhibitors, tricyclic antidepressants and phenothiazines. Paralytic ileus (sometimes fatal), hyperthermia and heat stroke may occur. Patients should be advised to report gastrointestinal problems, fever or heat intolerance promptly.

CNS depressants: Benztropine may enhance the CNS depressant effects of drugs including alcohol, anticonvulsants, barbiturates, MAO inhibitors, opioid analgesics, phenothiazines and tricyclic antidepressants.

Occupational Hazards: Benztropine may impair mental and/or physical abilities required for performance of hazardous tasks such as operating machinery or driving a motor vehicle.

Pregnancy: The safe use of this drug in pregnancy has not been established.

Lactation: It is not known if benztropine is excreted into breast milk.

Children: Benztropine is not recommended in children under 3 years of age (see Contraindications).

Adverse Effects: The adverse effects of benztropine are usually an extension of its pharmacologic action. They are usually dose related and may be reduced by lowering the dose.

CNS: nervousness, impaired memory, numbness of fingers, listlessness, depression. Mental confusion, excitement and visual hallucinations with high doses.

Gastrointestinal: dry mouth, constipation, nausea, vomiting, rarely paralytic ileus.

Ophthalmic: blurred vision, mydriasis.

Endocrine: hyperthermia, anhidrosis, heat stroke.

Genitourinary: urinary retention and/or dysuria.

Skeletomuscular: weakness and inability to move particular muscle groups.

Hypersensitivity: skin rash may occur occasionally.

Cardiovascular: tachycardia, arrhythmias.

Overdose: Symptoms: Symptoms of benztropine overdosage are related to an extension of its pharmacologic action. Severe anticholinergic side effects may include: clumsiness; unsteadiness, severe dryness of the mouth, nose or throat; tachycardia; shortness of breath; warmth, dryness and flushing of the skin. CNS depression or severe drowsiness may be preceded or followed by CNS stimulation including hallucinations, seizures and confusion. Toxic psychosis may occur in patients with psychiatric illness being treated with neuroleptic drugs. Other symptoms may include: nausea, vomiting, blurred vision, mydriasis, seizures, respiratory and circulatory failure.

Treatment: For oral overdoses, perform gastric lavage followed by administration of activated charcoal and a cathartic. Cathartics should not be administered to patients with an ileus or impaired renal function. Treatment is symptomatic and supportive. Monitor the patient for development of seizures, hypertension and arrhythmias. Maintain respiration, fluid and electrolyte balance. A local miotic for mydriasis and cycloplegia may be used and ice bags or sponging with tepid water for hyperpyrexia. Physostigmine is not routinely recommended for the treatment of anticholinergic toxicity because of its potential for adverse effects. Peritoneal dialysis and hemodialysis are of no value in the management of benztropine overdose.

Dosage: Benztropine should be used orally in all cases when patients are able to take oral medication. In other cases, where more rapid response is desired, benztropine mesylate may be administered i.v. or i.m.

Since there is no significant difference in onset of effect after i.v. and i.m. injection, usually there is no need to give benztropine i.v. It is quickly effective after either route, with improvement sometimes noticeable a few minutes after injection.

Because benztropine has cumulative action, therapy should be initiated with a low dose, which is increased gradually by 0.5 mg increments at 5- or 6-day intervals, to the smallest amount necessary for optimal relief without excessive adverse effects. The maximum adult dose is 6 mg. Generally, older patients, thin patients and those with arteriosclerotic parkinsonism cannot tolerate large doses. Most patients with postencephalic parkinsonism need fairly large doses and tolerate them well. Patients with dementia or mental confusion are usually poor candidates for therapy.

In arteriosclerotic, idiopathic, and post encephalitic parkinsonism, therapy may be initiated with a single daily dose of

0.5 to 1 mg at bedtime. In some patients, this will be adequate; in others 4 to 6 mg daily may be required.

Some patients experience optimal relief by taking the entire daily dose at bedtime; others respond more favorably to divided doses 2 to 4 times daily.

Therapy with other agents should not be terminated abruptly when therapy with benztropine is initiated, but may be reduced or discontinued gradually. Benztropine may be administered concomitantly with levodopa or a levodopa/carbidopa combination, in which case the dose of each may need adjustment.

Drug-induced Extrapyramidal Symptoms: In treating extrapyramidal disorders caused by neuroleptics, the recommended dosage is 1 to 4 mg once or twice daily, orally or parenterally. Dosage must be individualized according to the needs of the patient.

In acute dystonic reactions, 2 mg of benztropine given i.m./i.v. quickly relieves the condition. After that, 1 to 2 mg given orally twice daily for 2 to 3 days usually prevents recurrence.

When extrapyramidal disorders develop soon after initiation of treatment with neuroleptics, they are likely to be transient. One to 2 mg given orally 2 or 3 times daily usually provides relief within 1 or 2 days. After 1 or 2 weeks, the need for continued therapy with benztropine should be re-evaluated.

Benztropine mesylate should not be used beyond the period necessary to counteract the extrapyramidal manifestations. In the majority of patients, the use of anticholinergic agents is not required after 3 months of neuroleptic therapy. Although therapy with the drug causing parkinsonism can frequently be continued without change of dosage when adjunctive therapy with benztropine is used, a reduction in dosage of the psychotropic drug might be indicated.

Patients must be closely observed for severe reactions and benztropine discontinued temporarily if they appear (see Precautions and Adverse Effects).

Reviewed 1999

BEROTEC® Inhalation Aerosol ℞
BEROTEC® FORTE Inhalation Aerosol ℞

Boehringer Ingelheim

Fenoterol HBr

Bronchodilator

Pharmacology: The bronchodilating effect of fenoterol is produced primarily by stimulation of β_2 receptors in the bronchial smooth muscles. The effect has been measured by means of spirometry (FEV_1, FVC, MMFR), peak flow rates, flow volume curves, airway resistance (plethysmography) and oscillation mechanics.

Fenoterol, when administered by inhalation, exerts a significant increase in pulmonary function 5 minutes after administration and maximal effect in 30 to 60 minutes. This effect remains at the same level for 2 to 3 hours before gradually declining. A significant degree of bronchodilation has been detected in some studies for 6 to 8 hours.

Pharmacokinetics: In man, fenoterol is rapidly absorbed from the gastrointestinal tract, with an absorption level of 60%. After administration of tritium labelled fenoterol, peak plasma levels (2.5% of the oral dose) are reached in 2 hours, the half-life of radioactivity being 6 to 7 hours. When given from a pressurized container, absorption proceeds in 2 phases: the first one is essentially independent of the dose and apparently takes place between the first and fourth subdivision of the bronchial tree. A second phase appears to be identical to oral absorption. After inhalation, blood levels remain almost unchanged for 7 hours (0.3 to 0.4 ng/mL fenoterol).

Following i.v. administration, fenoterol is very rapidly taken up by the tissues where it is conjugated to the extent of 99% (as sulfates). Unlike isoproterenol, fenoterol is not metabolized by catechol-O-methyl transferase. The resulting metabolites are excreted via the kidneys (40% within 48 hours after oral administration) and the bile (fecal excretion: 40% of the oral dose).

Autoradiographic studies in gravid rats showed no detectable amounts of fenoterol in the fetus. Direct blood and tissue studies in several animal species and in man showed that the levels of fenoterol and its conjugates were 10 to 20 times lower in the fetus than in the maternal tissues.

Indications: For the symptomatic relief and acute prophylaxis of bronchial obstruction in asthma and other conditions in which reversible bronchospasm is a complicating factor, such as chronic bronchitis or emphysema.

Contraindications: Like other sympathomimetic amines, fenoterol inhalation aerosols should not be used in patients with tachyarrhythmias, hypertrophic obstructive cardiomyopathy or in patients with known hypersensitivity to fenoterol or to any of the product components (see Supplied).

Warnings: Like other β_2 agonists inhalers, fenoterol should not be used on a regular basis without appropriate concomitant anti-inflammatory therapy (see Dosage).

Children: Not currently indicated for use in children under 12 years of age as the dosing regimen and evidence concerning its safety in this age group have not been established.

Pregnancy and *Lactation:* The safety of fenoterol in pregnancy and lactation has not been established. β_2 agonists should be used with caution before childbirth in view of their inhibiting effect on uterine contractions.

General: Care should be taken in patients suffering from myocardial insufficiency, cardiac arrhythmias, recent myocardial infarction, severe organic heart and/or other vascular disorders, hypertension, hyperthyroidism or diabetes mellitus.

Fatalities, the exact cause of which is unknown, have been reported following excessive use of sympathomimetic amines by inhalation. Cardiac arrest was noticed in several instances.

Some patients receiving inhaled β-adrenergic agonists have developed severe paradoxical bronchospasm, which has been life-threatening. The cause of this refractory state is unknown. If it occurs, the preparation should be discontinued immediately and alternative therapy instituted.

In common with other β-adrenergic agents, fenoterol can induce reversible metabolic changes. These are most pronounced during **infusions** of the drug and include hyperglycemia and hypokalemia.

Potentially serious hypokalemia may result from β_2-agonist therapy, mainly from parenteral and nebulized administration. Particular caution is advised in acute severe asthma as hypokalemia may be potentiated by concomitant treatment with xanthine derivatives, steroids and diuretics; the adverse effects of hypokalemia may be exacerbated by hypoxia. It is recommended that serum potassium levels be monitored in such situations. Hypokalemia will increase the susceptibility of digitalis-treated patients to cardiac arrhythmias.

The bronchodilating action of sympathomimetic drugs may be antagonized by β-adrenergic blocking agents with the result that the respiratory status of patients may worsen when the 2 drugs are used concomitantly. In patients requiring concomitant treatment with fenoterol inhalation aerosols and a β-adrenergic blocking agent, the use of a relatively cardioselective β-blocker (e.g., metoprolol, atenolol, acebutolol) must be considered. During concomitant treatment, patients must be monitored carefully for possible deterioration in pulmonary function or for the need to adjust the dosage of either drug.

Precautions: General: If therapy does not produce a significant improvement or if the patient's condition gets worse, medical advice must be sought in order to determine a new plan of treatment. In the case of acute or rapidly worsening dyspnea, a doctor should be consulted immediately.

Increasing use of β_2 agonists to control symptoms of bronchial obstruction, especially administration on a regular basis or in high amounts, indicates deterioration of asthma control. Under these conditions, the patient's therapy plan has to be revised. It is inadequate simply to increase the use of bronchodilators under these circumstances, in particular over extended periods of time (see Dosage).

Concomitant use of fenoterol inhalation aerosols with other sympathomimetic agents is not recommended since the combined use may lead to deleterious cardiovascular effects. If concomitant use is necessary, this should take place only under strict medical supervision.

Fenoterol should be used with caution in asthmatic or emphysematous patients who also have acute and recurring congestive heart failure or glaucoma or in patients sensitive to sympathomimetic amines.

Like other pressurized aerosol formulations, fenoterol inhalation aerosols contain fluorocarbon propellants (monofluorotrichloromethane, tetrafluorodichloroethane and difluorodichloromethane). Such propellants may be hazardous if they are deliberately abused. Inhalation of high concentrations of aerosol sprays has brought about toxic cardiovascular effects and even death, especially under conditions of hypoxia. **However, evidence attests to the relative safety of aerosols when used properly and with adequate ventilation.** The recommended dose of fenoterol inhalation aerosol should not be exceeded and the patient should be so informed.

Three retrospective case-control studies, from one group in New Zealand, have suggested that there may be an increased risk of death in those patients using fenoterol whom the studies classified as severe asthmatics. These conclusions have not been confirmed by other studies and are subject to considerable debate and ongoing studies.

To ensure the proper dosage administration, the patient should be instructed by the physician or other health professional in the use of the inhaler.

Drug Interactions: Other β-adrenergic agents, anticholinergics, xanthine derivatives and corticosteroids may enhance the effect of fenoterol inhalation aerosol. Avoid concomitant use of fenoterol with monoamine oxidase inhibitors, tricyclic antidepressants or with other sympathomimetic agents since their combined effect on the cardiovascular system may be deleterious to the patient.

Beta-receptor blocking agents and fenoterol inhibit the effect of one another (see Warnings).

Labor and Delivery: Beta-adrenergic agents have been shown to delay preterm labor in some reports. There are no well controlled studies which demonstrate that such agents will stop preterm labor or prevent labor at term. Cautious use of β-adrenergics for the relief of bronchospasm is therefore required in pregnant patients to avoid interference with uterine contractility.

Adverse Effects: The following adverse reactions have been reported at therapeutic dosage levels of fenoterol inhalation aerosols: tremor, restlessness, palpitations, dizziness, headache, nausea, lightheadedness and weakness. Other occasional reactions include vomiting, heartburn, sweating, nervousness, bad taste, fatigue, prickling and tingling sensations over the body, and agitation. Local irritation or allergic reactions have been reported rarely. As with other bronchodilators, cough and, very rarely, paradoxical bronchospasm have been observed (see Warnings). Potentially serious hypokalemia may result from β_2 agonist therapy.

Overdose: Symptoms: Overdosage resulting in excessive β-adrenergic stimulation may cause tachycardia, cardiac arrhythmia, hypertension and, in extreme cases, sudden death.

Treatment: Symptomatic: Cardiac and respiratory support should be provided as required. If needed, to antagonize the effect of β-adrenergic stimulation, the use of a cardioselective β-adrenergic blocking agent, (e.g., metoprolol, atenolol, acebutolol) may be considered, bearing in mind however the potential danger of inducing an asthmatic attack.

Dosage: Dosage should be individualized, and patient response should be monitored by the prescribing physician on an ongoing basis.

Berotec (100 µg): Acute Symptoms: 1 puff will usually be adequate to relieve bronchospasm in the majority of patients, however, if required, a second puff may be taken preferably after waiting 5 minutes for the effect of the first puff to be obtained. This delay allows better assessment of the effectiveness of 1 puff and deeper penetration of the second puff.

If an attack has not been relieved by 2 puffs, further puffs may be required. In these cases, patients should immediately consult the doctor or the nearest hospital.

If, despite other adequate maintenance therapy, regular use of beta-agonists remains necessary for the control of bronchospasm, the recommended dose is 1 to 2 puffs of Berotec 100 µg 3 to 4 times daily. A maximum of 8 puffs/day should not be exceeded.

Berotec forte (200 µg): Acute symptoms: 1 puff should be adequate to relieve bronchospasm in the majority of patients. However, if required, a second puff may be taken, preferably after waiting 5 minutes for the effect of the first puff to be obtained. This dose of 1 or 2 inhalations may be repeated up to 3 times daily. Doses should not be taken more often than every 4 hours.

If an attack has not been relieved by 2 puffs, the patient should immediately consult the doctor or the nearest hospital.

If a previously effective dosage regimen fails to provide the usual relief, or the effects of a dose last for less than 3 hours, medical advice should be sought immediately; this is a sign of worsening asthma that requires reassessment of therapy.

Intermittent and Long-Term Treatment: Generally, long-term treatment with beta-agonists in bronchial asthma should be on demand, e.g., symptoms orientated.

Patients must not use them on a daily regular basis without using other concomitant anti-asthma medication(s) according to the present practice for asthma treatment to control airway inflammation.

The regular daily dose of fenoterol should not be increased without adequate reassessment of the therapy plan.

As with other beta-agonists increasing demand for fenoterol in bronchial asthma is a sign of poor asthma control and indicates that the treatment plan should be revised.

Berotec Inhalation Aerosol/Berotec Forte Inhalation Aerosol (cont'd)

Stability and Storage: The aerosol canister should be stored at room temperature (15 to 30°C); the contents are stable up to the expiration date stamped on the label. Caution. Contents under pressure. Do not place in hot water or near radiators, stoves, or other sources of heat. Do not puncture or incinerate container or store at temperatures over 30°C.

Information for the Patient: See Blue Section—Information for the Patient "Berotec/Berotec Forte Inhalation Aerosols".

Supplied: Berotec (100 μg) and Berotec forte (200 μg) are metered dose aerosol systems which contain a suspension of fenoterol HBr in fluorocarbon propellants (difluorodichloromethane, monofluorotrichloromethane, tetrafluorodichloroethane) with sorbitan trioleate as a dispersing agent.

Berotec (100 μg): Each valve depression (actuation) delivers 100 μg of fenoterol HBr as a micronized powder. Each canister is designed to deliver at least 200 metered doses.

Berotec forte (200 μg): Each valve depression (actuation) delivers 200 μg of fenoterol HBr as a micronized powder. One canister size for hospital use only, is designed to deliver at least 100 metered doses.

BEROTEC® Inhalation Solution Ⓟ

Boehringer Ingelheim

Fenoterol HBr

Bronchodilator

Pharmacology: The bronchodilating effect of fenoterol is produced primarily by stimulation of β_2-receptors in the bronchial smooth muscles. The effect has been measured by means of spirometry (FEV_1, FVC, MMFR), peak flow rates, flow volume curves, airway resistance (plethysmography) and oscillation mechanics.

Fenoterol, when administered by inhalation, exerts a significant increase in pulmonary function 5 minutes after administration and maximal effect in 30 to 60 minutes. This effect remains at the same level for 2 to 3 hours before gradually declining. A significant degree of bronchodilation has been detected in some studies for 6 to 8 hours.

Pharmacokinetics: In man, fenoterol is rapidly absorbed from the gastrointestinal tract, with an absorption level of 60%. After administration of tritium labelled fenoterol, peak plasma levels (2.5% of the oral dose) are reached in 2 hours, the half-life of radioactivity being 6 to 7 hours. When given from a pressurized container, absorption proceeds in 2 phases: the first one is essentially independent of the dose and apparently takes place between the first and fourth subdivision of the bronchial tree. A second phase appears to be identical to oral absorption. After inhalation, blood levels remain almost unchanged for 7 hours (0.3 to 0.4 ng/mL fenoterol).

Following inhalation, depending upon the method of inhalation and the system used, about 10 to 30% of the active ingredient released from the aerosol preparation reaches the lower respiratory tract, whereas the remainder is deposited in the upper respiratory tract and in the mouth. As a result, some of the fenoterol, which has been administered by inhalation, enters the gastrointestinal tract. After inhalation of one puff from a fenoterol metered aerosol, an absorption rate of 17% of the dose has been determined. Absorption then follows a biphasic course, 30% of fenoterol being rapidly absorbed with a half-life of 120 minutes.

Following i.v. administration, fenoterol is very rapidly taken up by the tissues where it is conjugated to the extent of 99% (as sulfates). Unlike isoproterenol, fenoterol is not metabolized by catechol-O-methyl transferase. The resulting metabolites are excreted via the kidneys (40% within 48 hours after oral administration) and the bile (fecal excretion: 40% of the oral dose).

Autoradiographic studies in gravid rats showed no detectable amounts of fenoterol in the fetus. Direct blood and tissue studies in several animal species and in man showed that the levels of fenoterol and its conjugates were 10 to 20 times lower in the fetus than in the maternal tissues.

Indications: For the treatment of acute severe bronchospasm, e.g. acute exacerbations of bronchial asthma or of severe chronic bronchitis. Fenoterol solution should be administered only by means of ultrasonic, motorized or compressed air nebulizers or in conjunction with intermittent positive pressure ventilation where IPPV is indicated.

Contraindications: Like other sympathomimetic amines, fenoterol should not be used in patients with tachyarrhythmias, hypertrophic obstructive cardiomyopathy, or in those with known hypersensitivity to fenoterol or to any of the product components (see Supplied).

Warnings: Like other B_2-agonist inhalation solutions, fenoterol should not be used on a regular daily basis without appropriate concomitant anti-inflammatory therapy (see Dosage).

Children: Not currently indicated for use in children under 12 years of age as the dosing regimen and evidence concerning its safety in this age group have not been established.

Pregnancy and *Lactation:* The safety of fenoterol in pregnancy and lactation has not been established. β_2-agonists should be used with caution before childbirth in view of their inhibiting effect on uterine contractions.

General: Care should be taken in patients suffering from myocardial insufficiency, cardiac arrhythmias, recent myocardial infarction, severe organic heart and/or other vascular disorders, hypertension, hyperthyroidism, pheochromocytoma or diabetes mellitus.

Fatalities, the exact cause of which is unknown, have been reported following excessive use of sympathomimetic amines by inhalation. Cardiac arrest was noticed in several instances.

Some patients receiving inhaled β-adrenergic agonists have developed severe paradoxical bronchospasm, which has been life-threatening. The cause of this refractory state is unknown. If it occurs, the preparation should be discontinued immediately and alternative therapy instituted.

Fenoterol solution in 20 mL bottles contains preservatives (benzalkonium chloride and edetate disodium) which may cause bronchoconstriction in some patients with hyperreactive airways.

The 2 mL unit dose vial **does not** contain preservatives.

In common with other β-adrenergic agents, fenoterol can induce reversible metabolic changes. These are most pronounced during **infusions** of the drug and include hyperglycemia and hypokalemia.

Potentially serious hypokalemia may result from β_2-agonist therapy, mainly from parenteral and nebulized administration. Particular caution is advised in acute severe asthma as hypokalemia may be potentiated by concomitant treatment with xanthine derivatives, steroids and diuretics; the adverse effects of hypokalemia may be exacerbated by hypoxia. It is recommended that serum potassium levels be monitored in such situations. Hypokalemia will increase the susceptibility of digitalis-treated patients to cardiac arrhythmias.

The bronchodilating action of sympathomimetic drugs may be antagonized by β-adrenergic blocking agents with the result that the respiratory status of patients may worsen when the 2 drugs are used concomitantly. In patients requiring concomitant treatment with fenoterol and a β-adrenergic blocking agent, the use of a relatively cardioselective β-blocker (e.g. metoprolol, atenolol, acebutolol) must be considered. During concomitant treatment, patients should be monitored carefully for possible deterioration in pulmonary function or for the need to adjust the dosage of either drug.

Fenoterol Solution in Conjunction with IPPV: It has been reported in several cases that the use of intermittent positive-pressure ventilation in acute asthma attacks was related to lethal episodes of hypoxia and pneumothorax. This method of drug administration may be ineffective in patients with severe obstruction and greatly increased airway resistance and it may induce severe hypercapnia and hypoxia. During intermittent positive-pressure ventilation therapy, the monitoring of arterial blood gases is highly desirable.

Precautions: Fenoterol solution is intended only for inhalation with suitable nebulizing devices and should not be taken orally or administered parenterally.

Instruct your patients to seek medical advice if therapy does not produce a significant improvement or if the patient's condition gets worse in order to determine a new plan of treatment. Instruct your patients to consult a doctor immediately in the case of acute or rapidly worsening dyspnea.

Increasing use of β_2 agonists to control symptoms of bronchial obstruction, especially administration on a regular basis or in high amounts, indicates deterioration of asthma control. Under these conditions, the patient's therapy plan has to be revised. It is inadequate simply to increase the use of bronchodilators under these circumstances, in particular over extended periods of time (see Dosage).

Concomitant use of fenoterol with other sympathomimetic agents is not recommended since the combined use may lead to deleterious cardiovascular effects. If concomitant use is necessary, this should take place only under strict medical supervision.

Fenoterol should be used with caution in asthmatic or emphysematous patients who also have acute and recurring congestive heart failure or glaucoma or in patients sensitive to sympathomimetic amines.

On-demand (symptom-oriented) treatment may be preferable to regular use. Patients should be evaluated for the addition or the increase of anti-inflammatory therapy (e.g., inhaled corticosteroids) to control airway inflammation and to prevent long term lung damage.

Three retrospective case-control studies, from one group in New Zealand, have suggested that there may be an increased risk of death in those patients using Berotec whom the studies classified as severe asthmatics. These conclusions have not been confirmed by other studies and are subject to considerable debate and ongoing studies.

To ensure the proper dosage administration, the patient should be instructed by the physician or other health professional on the proper use and maintenance of the nebulizer.

Drug Interactions: Other β-adrenergic agents, anticholinergics, xanthine derivatives (such as theophylline) and corticosteroids may enhance the effect of fenoterol. Avoid concomitant use of fenoterol with MAO inhibitors, tricyclic antidepressants or with other sympathomimetic agents since their combined effect on the cardiovascular system may be deleterious to the patient.

β-receptor blocking agents and fenoterol inhibit the effect of one another (see Warnings).

Concomitant anti-inflammatory therapy should be considered for patients with bronchial asthma and steroid responsive chronic obstructive pulmonary disease.

Inhalation of halogenated hydrocarbon anesthetics such as halothane, trichloroethylene and enflurane may increase the susceptibility to the cardiovascular effects of β-agonists.

Labor and Delivery: Beta-adrenergic agents have been shown to delay preterm labor in some reports. There are no well controlled studies which demonstrate that such agents will stop preterm labor or prevent labor at term. Cautious use of β-adrenergics for the relief of bronchospasm is therefore required in pregnant patients to avoid interference with uterine contractility.

Adverse Effects: At the most frequently used dosage of fenoterol of 0.5 to 1 mg, tremor occurred in 12% of patients. At higher doses of fenoterol solution (up to 2.5 mg) given for the treatment of severe asthma in a hospital emergency room, mild to moderate tremor occurred in 32% of patients. Other adverse reactions in decreasing order of frequency included nervousness, dizziness, headache, lightheadedness, and palpitations.

In 104 patients who received the highest recommended dosage of 2.5 mg of fenoterol, increases in heart rate of 10% or greater within 4 hours after drug administration were observed in 21% of the patients. However, at least an equal number of patients had decreased heart rate of a similar magnitude in the same time period. The remainder showed no significant pulse rate changes.

As with other β-mimetics, nausea, vomiting, sweating, weakness, and myalgia/muscle cramps may occur. In rare cases, decrease in diastolic blood pressure, increase in systolic blood pressure, arrhythmia, particularly after higher doses, may occur.

Local irritation or allergic reactions have been reported rarely. As with other bronchodilators, cough and, very rarely, paradoxical bronchospasm have been observed (see Warnings). Potentially serious hypokalemia may result from β_2-agonist therapy.

In individual cases, psychological alterations have been reported under inhalational therapy with β-mimetics.

Overdose: Symptoms: Overdosage resulting in excessive β-adrenergic stimulation (including exaggeration of the known pharmacological effects, i.e., any of the symptoms listed under adverse reactions) may cause flushing, palpitations, tremor, hypotension, widening of pulse pressure, anginal pain, tachycardia, arrhythmias, hypertension, and in extreme cases, sudden death.

Treatment: Symptomatic: Cardiac and respiratory support should be provided as required. If needed to antagonize the effect of β-adrenergic stimulation, the use of a β-adrenergic blocking agent, preferably one of the relatively cardioselective ones (e.g., metoprolol, atenolol, acebutolol) may be considered, bearing in mind, however, the potential danger of inducing an asthmatic attack. Administration of sedatives or tranquilizers may be appropriate in severe cases.

Dosage: Dosage should be individualized, and patient response should be monitored by the prescribing physician on an ongoing basis.

Fenoterol solution should be used only under medical supervision. On prolonged use, patients should be evaluated for the addition or the increase of anti-inflammatory therapy (e.g., inhaled corticosteroids) to control airway inflammation and to prevent long-term lung damage.

In most cases, dilution of the dose with sterile preservative-free saline is not necessary. However, volumes of fenoterol solution less than 2 mL are not appropriate for nebulization and must be diluted with saline or another suitable nebulizer solution to make-up a total fill volume of 2 to 5 mL.

Motorized, Compressed Air or Ultrasonic Nebulizers: These nebulizers generate low pressure, low velocity aerosols. The average single dose is 0.5 to 1 mg of fenoterol. In more refractory cases, up to 2.5 mg of fenoterol may be given. Optimal deposition in the lungs is achieved with the patient breathing quietly and slowly. Treatment may be repeated every 6 hours if necessary.

Intermittent Positive Pressure Ventilation: Fenoterol solution may be used in conjunction with Intermittent Positive Pressure Ventilation (IPPV) when such therapy is indicated (see Warnings). The average single dose is 0.5 to 1 mg of fenoterol. In more refractory cases, up to 2.5 mg of fenoterol may be given. The inspiratory pressure is usually 10 to 20 cm H_2O and optimal deposition of the drug in the lungs is achieved with the patient breathing quietly and slowly. Treatment may be repeated every 6 hours if necessary.

If a previously effective dosage regimen fails to provide the usual relief, or the effects of a dose last for less than 3 hours, medical advice should be sought immediately; this is a sign of seriously worsening asthma that requires reassessment of therapy.

In accordance with the present practice for asthma treatment, concomitant anti-inflammatory therapy should be part of the regimen if fenoterol inhalation solution needs to be used on a regular daily basis.

Stability and Storage: **Bottles:** The **undiluted** solution in its original, **unopened** amber glass bottle may be stored at room temperature (approximately 25°C) and will be stable up to the expiration date stamped on the label.

The **undiluted** solution in its original amber glass bottle, **opened and tightly recapped several times**, may be stored at room temperature (approximately 25°C) for 30 days.

The solution, **diluted with preservative-free, sterile sodium chloride inhalation solution, USP 0.9% (normal saline)** may be stored at room temperature (approximately 25°C) for 24 hours.

The effects of refrigeration on the stability of undiluted or diluted solution is not known.

Controlled laboratory experiments using a mixture of fenoterol solution with ipratropium solution diluted with a sterile bacteriostatic sodium chloride 0.9% preserved with benzalkonium chloride (i.e., preserved normal saline), indicated that such a mixture was stable for 7 days at room temperature. For the preparation of such a mixture, it is recommended that only sterile solutions of bacteriostatic sodium chloride 0.9% preserved with 0.01% benzalkonium chloride be used to maintain the level of preservative in the mixture.

The safety of saline-preservatives other than benzalkonium chloride has not been established.

Unit Dose Vials: Unopened unit dose vials of fenoterol solution should be stored at controlled room temperature (approximately 25°C) and protected from heat and light. If required, the solution should be diluted with a preservative-free sterile sodium chloride solution 0.9% and used immediately. Any solution remaining in the vial must be discarded.

The physical compatibility of fenoterol solution in unit dose vials with other inhalation solutions will not be affected by the absence of preservatives from the solution. If a mixture is prepared, dilute the mixture with preservative free sterile sodium chloride solution 0.9% and use immediately.

Any unused portion of such combined solutions must be discarded.

Information for the Patient: See Blue Section—Information for the Patient "Berotec Inhalation Solution".

Supplied: Bottles: Each mL of aqueous solution contains: fenoterol HBr 1 mg. Nonmedicinal ingredients: benzalkonium chloride and edetate disodium in an aqueous solution. Sodium: <1 mmol (0.0805 mg)/mL. Amber glass, screw cap bottles of 20 mL. Bottles supplied individually in cartons.

Unit Dose Vials: 0.625 mg/mL: Each mL of aqueous solution contains: fenoterol HBr 0.625 mg. Nonmedicinal ingredients: hydrochloric acid, sodium chloride and water. Plastic single use vials of 2 mL.

0.25 mg/mL: Each mL of aqueous solution contains: fenoterol HBr 0.25 mg. Nonmedicinal ingredients: hydrochloric acid, sodium chloride and water. Plastic single use vials of 2 mL.

Reviewed 1999

BETADERM Ⓟ

Taro

Betamethasone Valerate

Topical Corticosteroid

Supplied: Cream: Each g contains: betamethasone as betamethasone 17-valerate 0.1% (regular) or 0.05% (mild) in a water washable aqueous base of mineral oil, white petrolatum, polyethylene glycol 1 000, polyoxyethylene stearyl cetyl ether, cetyl and stearyl alcohol, propylene glycol, chlorocresol, purified water, sodium hydroxide and phosphoric acid. Tubes of 15 g and jars of 454 g.

Ointment: Each g contains: betamethasone as betamethasone 17-valerate 0.1% (regular) or 0.05% (mild) in a base consisting of fractionated coconut oil and white petrolatum and chlorocresol as a preservative. Tubes of 15 g and jars of 454 g.

Scalp Lotion: Each g contains: betamethasone as betamethasone 17-valerate 0.1% in a base of carbomer, isopropyl alcohol, purified water and sodium hydroxide. Plastic bottles of 30 and 75 mL.

BETADINE® Topical Preparations

Purdue Frederick

Povidone-Iodine

Antiseptic

Pharmacology: Betadine is iodine complexed with povidone (polyvinyl-pyrrolidone). The compound is soluble in water forming a golden brown solution. Like iodine, the solution of the iodine complex is bactericidal, fungicidal, virucidal and trichomonacidal. However, unlike solutions of iodine, it is nonstaining to natural fabrics. The antiseptic action of povidone-iodine is due to the available iodine present in the complex.

Indications: Aerosol Spray: Prophylaxis or treatment of infection in minor wounds, burns and skin lesions. Skin preparation prior to surgery or injections.

Gauze Pads: For disinfection of wounds, cutaneous ulcers, lacerations, abrasions and first, second and third degree burns.

Mouth Wash/Gargle: As a mouth wash for routine use. Eliminates or reduces offensive mouth odors. As a gargle or mouth wash, as primary or adjunctive therapy in infections of the mouth and throat such as aphthous stomatitis, Vincent's infection, pharyngitis, oral moniliasis, tonsillitis, laryngitis, tongue ulcers, stomatitis, bronchitis, sinusitis and following oral surgery and dental procedures.

Ointment: For the prevention of infection in burns, cuts, abrasions, poison ivy rash, poison oak rash and insect bites. The treatment of skin infections, including infections of varicose and decubitus ulcers.

Shampoo: For seborrheic conditions of the scalp associated with erythema, scaling, exfoliation, pityriasis and pruritus. As a germicidal skin cleanser for prophylaxis of recurrent furunculosis and acute inflammatory skin lesions.

Skin Cleanser: Useful as a topical antimicrobial in preventing infections in lacerations, minor cuts, abrasions and burns caused by iodine-susceptible pathogenic organisms. Helps prevent acute and chronic inflammatory infections such as in acne vulgaris. In pyodermas, as a topical adjunct to systemic antimicrobial therapy. Prophylaxis of recurrent furunculosis and acute inflammatory skin lesions.

Solution: Use full strength for pre- and postoperative skin and mucous membrane antisepsis, prophylaxis and treatment of wounds, lacerations and burns, trichomonal, monilial and nonspecific vaginitis, cervicitis, oral infections, and dental procedures.

Surgical Scrub: Pre- and postoperative scrubbing or washing, pre- and postoperative use on patients, general use in physician's office.

Swab Aids: Disposable antiseptic germicide pad.

Precautions: Use with caution in patients known to be allergic to iodine. If irritation, redness or swelling develops, discontinue use of the product and institute appropriate measures. Blue stains on starched linen will wash off with soap and water.

Iodine absorption and subsequent excretion in breast milk may follow vaginal application of povidone-iodine.

Adverse Effects: Although rare, local hypersensitivity reactions have occurred. Serum PBI may increase temporarily in some patients after topical application of povidone-iodine.

Dosage: Aerosol Spray: Hold container about 25 cm from skin. Press valve firmly with index finger, spraying to cover desired area. Allow to dry. Replace cap after use. If actuator clogs, remove and soak in warm water. Treated area may be covered with gauze, adhesive bandage or plaster casts. Bottle operates in any position.

Gauze Pads: Apply as directed.

Mouth Wash/Gargle: As a routine mouth wash: use full strength or dilute to taste. Effective up to dilution of 1 part Betadine with 2 parts water. As a gargle or mouth wash: use full strength for 30 seconds, hourly, or as directed by physician or dentist.

Ointment: Apply directly to affected area as needed. May be bandaged.

Shampoo: Apply 10 mL to hair and scalp, using warm water to lather. Rinse and repeat, massaging gently into scalp. Allow lather to remain on scalp for at least 5 minutes. Work up lather, then rinse thoroughly. Repeat treatment twice weekly for 6 to 8 weeks, then weekly or as directed by physician.

Skin Cleanser: Wet the skin and apply a sufficient amount to cover the affected areas. Massage for 5 minutes, add a little water, continue to work up a lather, then rinse thoroughly. For oily skin and prevention of blemishes, wash face and neck or affected area several times weekly with Betadine Skin Cleanser and shampoo regularly with Betadine Shampoo.

Solution: Apply full strength as often as needed as a paint or wet soak. Allow to dry before applying surgical drapes and avoid "pooling" beneath the patient. Prolonged exposure to the solution may cause irritation or rarely, severe skin reaction. In rare instance of local irritation or sensitivity, discontinue use.

Surgical Scrub: A. Preoperative scrubbing by operating personnel: wet hands with water. Pour 5 mL on the palm of the hand and spread over both hands. Without adding more water, rub the scrub thoroughly over all areas for about 5 minutes. Use a soft brush if desired. Clean thoroughly under fingernails. Add a little water to develop copious suds. Rinse thoroughly under running water. Complete the wash by scrubbing with another 5 mL if desired.

B. Preoperative use on patients: wet the operative area with water. Apply scrub (1 mL is sufficient to cover an area of 125 to 200 cm²) and rub thoroughly for about 5 minutes. Then develop a lather and rinse off by aid of sterile gauze saturated with water. The area may then be painted with solution and allowed to dry.

C. Use in physician's office: Use for washing whenever a germicidal soap is required. For maximum degerming of the hands proceed as under (A). To prepare the patient's skin proceed as under (B).

Swab Aids: Prior to venipuncture and other injections, swab area to be cleansed. Allow to dry before inserting needle.

Supplied: Aerosol Spray: Each mL of mahogany colored solution contains: povidone-iodine USP 5% (0.5% available iodine). Contains no chlorofluorocarbons. Pump spray bottles of 88 mL.

Gauze Pads: Each 7.6×22.8 cm fine mesh gauze pad contains: povidone-iodine USP 450 mg as a 10% solution in a viscous base. Packages of 10 and 50.

Mouth Wash/Gargle: Each mL of mahogany colored solution contains: povidone-iodine USP 1% (0.1% available iodine) and alcohol 8%. pH: 4 to 6. Bottles of 250 mL.

Ointment: Each g contains: povidone-iodine USP 10% (1% available iodine) in a water-soluble polyethylene glycol ointment base. pH (5% solution): 3.5 to 4.5. Packettes of 1 g, cartons of 144. Tubes of 20 g. Jars of 500 g.

Shampoo: Each mL contains: povidone-iodine USP 7.5% (0.75% available iodine). pH 4.5 to 5.5. Forms a rich golden, perfumed lather. Plastic squeeze bottles of 114 mL.

Skin Cleanser: Each mL of sudsing, antiseptic liquid cleanser contains: povidone-iodine USP 7.5% (0.75% available iodine) and detergents. pH 4.5 to 5.5. Plastic squeeze bottles of 114 and 250 mL.

Solution: Each mL of mahogany colored solution contains: povidone-iodine USP 10% (1% available iodine) with surfactant. pH 4.5 to 5.5. Plastic bottles of 25 mL, cartons of 40. Plastic bottles of 100 mL, 500 mL and 5 L.

Betadine Topical Preparations (cont'd)

Surgical Scrub: Each mL of mahogany colored liquid contains: povidone-iodine USP 7.5% (0.75% available iodine) with sudsing agent. pH 4.5 to 5.5. Plastic bottles of 100 mL, 500 mL and 5 L.

Swab Aids: Each germicide pad contains: 1 mL povidone-iodine 10% solution (1% available iodine). Cartons of 100.

Protect from excessive heat. Check label for expiration date.

BETADINE® Vaginal Preparations
Purdue Frederick

Povidone-Iodine

Bactericidal—Trichomonacidal—Fungicidal

Pharmacology: Betadine is iodine complexed with povidone (polyvinyl-pyrrolidone). The compound is soluble in water forming a golden brown solution. Like iodine, the solution of the iodine complex is bactericidal, trichomonacidal, fungicidal and virucidal. Unlike solutions of iodine it is nonstaining to skin and natural fabrics. The antiseptic action is due to the available iodine present in the complex.

Indications: For treatment of vaginal infections including nonspecific vaginitis, vaginitis and vulvovaginitis associated with Trichomonas vaginalis and monilial infection. Douche only: also indicated for adjunctive use in preoperative vaginal prepping and for routine cleansing and deodorizing.

Contraindications: Hypersensitivity to iodine.

Warnings: Douching is reported to be associated with Pelvic Inflammatory Disease (PID), a serious infection of the reproductive system which can lead to infertility and/or tubal (ectopic) pregnancy. Symptoms of PID and a sexually transmitted disease (STD) include pain and tenderness in the lower part of the abdomen and pelvis; vaginal discharge and/or bleeding; nausea and/or fever; frequent urination; genital sores, and genital ulcers. If you suspect you have an STD or PID, stop using this product and see a doctor immediately.
When to stop use: If symptoms persist after 5 days of use, or redness, swelling or pain develops, discontinue use and consult a doctor.

Pregnancy and *Lactation:* Betadine is spermicidal and should not be used if pregnancy is desired. Douching does not prevent pregnancy, nor should it be used for self-treatment or prevention of an STD. Do not use during pregnancy, while breast-feeding, or when symptoms of PID or an STD are present, except with the approval of your doctor.

Serum PBI may increase temporarily in some patients after povidone-iodine application.

Adverse Effects: Although rare, local hypersensitivity reactions have occurred.

Dosage: Therapeutic Use: Use gel, suppositories or douche in the morning and in the evening. The products may be interchanged as desired.
Gel: 5 g application/dose.
Suppositories: 1 suppository/dose.
Douche: Therapeutic Use: Betadine Concentrate 25 mL in 1 L of lukewarm water/dose. Routine cleansing and deodorizing: 6 to 12 mL in 1 L, no more than once or twice a week.

Treatment should be continued for up to 14 days and should be continued during menstruation. Since Betadine may stain synthetic fabrics, use of a feminine hygiene pad is recommended.

Supplied: Gel: Each g of mahogany-colored gel contains: povidone-iodine USP 10% (1% available iodine) in a base of diffusible, water-soluble polyethylene glycols. pH: 3.5 to 4.5. Tubes of 85 g complete with applicator.

Suppositories: Each suppository contains: povidone-iodine USP 200 mg (20 mg available iodine) in a polyethylene glycol base. Packages of 14, complete with applicator.

Douche: Each mL of scented mahogany-colored solution contains: povidone-iodine USP 10% (1% available iodine). pH diluted: 3.0 to 3.5. May be used with any type of douching apparatus (purchased separately). Bottles of 100 and 250 mL. Protect from excessive heat.

BETAGAN® Ⓟ
Allergan

Levobunolol HCl

Glaucoma Therapy

Pharmacology: Levobunolol is a noncardioselective beta-adrenoceptor antagonist, equipotent at both $beta_1$ and $beta_2$ receptors. Levobunolol is approximately 60 times more potent than the dextro isomer in its beta-blocking activity, yet equipotent in its potential for direct myocardial depression. Accordingly, the levo isomer, levobunolol, is used. Levobunolol does not have significant local anesthetic (membrane-stabilizing) effect or intrinsic sympathomimetic activity.

Beta-adrenergic receptor blockade reduces cardiac output in both healthy subjects and patients with heart disease. In patients with severe impairment of myocardial function, beta-adrenergic receptor blockade may inhibit the stimulatory effect of the sympathetic nervous system necessary to maintain adequate cardiac function.

Beta-adrenergic receptor blockade in the bronchi and bronchioles results in increased airway resistance from unopposed parasympathetic activity. Such an effect in patients with asthma or other bronchospastic conditions is potentially dangerous.

Levobunolol, when instilled into the eye, will lower elevated intraocular pressure (IOP), as well as normal IOP, whether or not accompanied by glaucoma. Elevated IOP is a major risk factor in the pathogenesis of glaucomatous visual field loss. The higher the level of intraocular pressure, the greater the likelihood of optic nerve damage and visual field loss.

The onset of action with 1 drop of levobunolol can be detected within 1 hour after treatment, with maximum effect seen between 2 and 6 hours. A significant decrease in IOP can be maintained for up to 24 hours with once daily dosing of levobunolol 0.5%.

Measurements of aqueous flow and total outflow facility suggest that levobunolol lowers IOP primarily by decreasing aqueous humor production. Levobunolol reduces IOP with little or no effect on pupil size or accommodation, in contrast to the miosis which cholinergic agents are known to produce. The blurred vision and night blindness often associated with miotics would not be expected. This is particularly important in patients with central lens opacities who would experience decreased visual acuity with pupillary constriction.

Levobunolol has been shown to be as effective as timolol in lowering intraocular pressure.

In controlled clinical studies of up to 2 years duration, IOP was well controlled in approximately 80% of subjects treated with levobunolol 0.5% b.i.d. The mean IOP decreases from baseline were between 6.87 and 7.81 mm Hg. No significant effects on pupil size, tear production or corneal sensitivity were observed. Topically applied levobunolol at concentrations of 0.5 and 1%, decreased heart rate and blood pressure in some patients. The IOP-lowering effect of levobunolol was well maintained over the course of these studies.

In a 3-month controlled clinical study, once-daily application of levobunolol 0.5% controlled the IOP of 72% of subjects, producing an overall mean decrease in IOP of 7.0 mm Hg. Once-daily application of timolol 0.5% controlled the IOP of 64% of subjects, producing a mean decrease in IOP of 4.5 mm Hg. The difference in overall mean decreases in IOP was statistically significant.

In 2 subsequent 3-month trials comparing levobunolol 0.5% with timolol 0.5% administered once daily, overall differences between the 2 drugs were not significant. A greater percentage of subjects in both the levobunolol groups and the timolol groups maintained adequately lowered intraocular pressure in the latter 2 studies, probably because subjects with severe ocular hypertension, unlikely to be controlled by therapy with a beta-blocker alone, were excluded from the study.

In one 3-month study and one 1-year study, levobunolol 0.25% twice daily controlled the IOP of approximately 63 and 70% of the subjects, respectively. The overall mean decreases from baseline were 5.4 and 5.1 mm Hg respectively.

In another 3-month clinical study, the mean decrease in IOP was significantly greater (more than 2 mm Hg) in the 0.25 and 0.5% levobunolol twice-daily treatment groups than in the betaxolol 0.5% twice-daily treatment group.

The prophylactic effect of topical 0.5% levobunolol HCl on IOP elevations after neodymium: YAG laser posterior capsulotomies was investigated in a controlled study. One drop was administered 30 to 120 minutes prior to the capsulotomy. Eight subjects (38%) in the vehicle treatment group and none in the levobunolol group experienced increases from baseline in IOP of 10 mm Hg or greater. Mean reductions in IOP from baseline ranged from 2.1 to 2.9 mm Hg in the levobunolol group, while in the vehicle treatment group, IOP increases (4.4 to 6.4 mm Hg) were observed at hours 1, 2, and 3 following capsulotomy.

In a controlled study, 0.5% levobunolol or placebo were administered immediately after a unilateral extracapsular cataract extraction and implantation of a posterior chamber intraocular lens. Treatment continued on a once-daily basis for 7 days. The incidence of IOP elevations from baseline ≥10 mm Hg was 8 subjects (40%) in the vehicle group and 4 subjects (19%) in the levobunolol group. Mean IOP increased from baseline up to 8.6 mm Hg at 24 hours in the vehicle group and up to 2 mm Hg at 24 hours in the levobunolol group.

In another controlled study, levobunolol 0.5% was significantly more effective than betaxolol 0.5% or placebo in preventing increased IOP after cataract extraction and posterior chamber lens placement. Two drops of the assigned medication were administered to the study eye after surgery. A significant mean increase in intraocular pressure from the preoperative to the early postoperative period was noted in the groups treated with betaxolol (6.73 mm Hg), placebo (5.35 mm Hg) and timolol (3.83 mm Hg). Levobunolol-treated eyes showed a mean decrease in pressure of 0.43 mm Hg.

An IOP of 30 mm Hg or greater was found in 3 placebo-treated eyes (15%), 4 betaxolol-treated eyes (20%), 1 timolol-treated eye (5%), and none of the levobunolol-treated eyes. Five placebo-treated eyes (25%), 6 betaxolol-treated eyes (30%), 5 timolol-treated eyes (25%), and 1 levobunolol-treated eye (5%) experienced a pressure rise of 10 mm Hg or greater.

Indications: The control of intraocular pressure in patients with chronic open-angle glaucoma or mild to moderate ocular hypertension.

Contraindications: In those individuals with bronchial asthma or with a history of bronchial asthma, or severe chronic obstructive pulmonary disease; sinus bradycardia; second- and third-degree atrioventricular block; overt cardiac failure; cardiogenic shock; or hypersensitivity to any component of this product.

Warnings: As with other topically applied ophthalmic drugs, levobunolol may be absorbed systemically. The same adverse reactions found with systemic administration of beta-adrenergic blocking agents may occur with topical administration.

Contains sodium metabisulfite, a sulfite that may cause allergic-type reactions including anaphylactic symptoms and life-threatening or less severe asthmatic episodes in certain susceptible people. The overall prevalence of sulfite sensitivity in the general population is unknown and probably low. Sulfite sensitivity is seen more frequently in asthmatic than in non-asthmatic people.

Keep out of reach of children. For external use only. Do not touch dropper tip to any surface, since this may contaminate the solution. Protect from light and excessive heat. Discard any unused solution after end of treatment period.

Precautions: Use with caution in patients with known contraindications to systemic use of beta-adrenoceptor blocking agents. These include abnormally low heart rate and heart block more severe than first degree. Congestive heart failure should be adequately controlled before beginning therapy with levobunolol. In patients with a history of cardiac disease, especially arrhythmia and bradycardia, pulse rates should be monitored.

Use with caution in patients with known hypersensitivity to other beta-adrenoceptor blocking agents.

Use with caution in patients with known diminished pulmonary function.

Lactation: It is not known whether this drug is excreted in human milk. Systemic beta-blockers and topical timolol maleate are known to be excreted in human milk. Caution should be exercised when levobunolol is administered to a nursing woman.

Children: Safety and effectiveness in children have not been established.

Drug Interactions: Levobunolol may have additive effects in patients taking systemic antihypertensive drugs. These possible additive effects may include hypotension, including orthostatic hypotension, bradycardia, dizziness, and/or syncope. Conversely, systemic beta-adrenoceptor blocking agents may potentiate the ocular hypotensive effect of levobunolol.

Close observation of the patient is recommended when a beta-blocker is administered to patients receiving catecholamine-depleting drugs such as reserpine, because of possible additive effects and the production of hypotension and/or marked bradycardia, which may produce vertigo, syncope, or postural hypotension.

Adverse Effects: Transient burning, stinging or itching, blepharoconjunctivitis and decreases in heart rate and blood pressure have been reported occasionally with the use of levobunolol. Iridocyclitis, headache, transient ataxia, dizziness, lethargy, urticaria and pruritus have been reported rarely. Decreased corneal sensitivity has been noted in a small number of patients. The following additional adverse reactions have been reported with ophthalmic use of $beta_1$ and $beta_2$ (nonselective) adrenergic receptor blocking agents: Body as a whole: headache.

Cardiovascular: arrhythmia, syncope, heart block, cerebral vascular accident, cerebral ischemia, congestive heart failure, palpitation.

Digestive: nausea.

Psychiatric: depression.

Skin: hypersensitivity, including localized and generalized rash.

Respiratory: bronchospasm (predominantly in patients with pre-existing bronchospastic disease), respiratory failure.

Endocrine: masked symptoms of hypoglycemia in insulin-dependent diabetics.

Special Senses: signs and symptoms of keratitis, blepharoptosis, visual disturbances including refractive changes (due to withdrawal of miotic therapy in some cases), diplopia, ptosis.

Other reactions associated with the oral use of nonselective adrenergic receptor blocking agents should be considered potential effects with ophthalmic use of these agents.

Overdose: Symptoms and Treatment: Overdose has not been reported to date. Should accidental ocular overdosage occur, flush eye(s) with water or normal saline. If accidentally ingested, efforts to decrease further absorption may be appropriate (gastric lavage). The most common signs and symptoms to be expected with overdosage of a systemic beta-adrenergic blocking agent are symptomatic bradycardia, hypotension, bronchospasm, and acute cardiac failure. Should these symptoms occur, discontinue therapy and initiate appropriate supportive therapy.

Dosage: The recommended starting dose is 1 drop of levobunolol 0.25% twice a day in the affected eye(s). If the clinical response is not adequate, the dosage may be changed to 1 drop of levobunolol 0.5% twice a day in the affected eye(s). Levobunolol 0.5% once a day has been found to be effective in controlling IOP in many patients with mild to moderate open-angle glaucoma and ocular hypertension. As with any new medication, careful monitoring of patients is advised.

Dosages above 1 drop of levobunolol 0.5% twice a day are not generally more effective. If the patient's IOP is not at a satisfactory level on this regimen, concomitant therapy with dipivefrin and/or epinephrine, and/or pilocarpine and other miotics, and/or systemically administered carbonic anhydrase inhibitors, such as acetazolamide, can be instituted.

Supplied: 0.25%: Each mL of sterile ophthalmic solution contains: levobunolol HCl 2.5 mg. Nonmedicinal ingredients: benzalkonium chloride 0.004% (as preservative), edetate disodium, polyvinyl alcohol (Liquifilm), potassium phosphate monobasic, sodium chloride, sodium metabisulfite, sodium phosphate dibasic, sodium hydroxide or hydrochloric acid to adjust pH. Plastic dropper bottles of 5, 10 and 15 mL. Protect from light and excessive heat.

0.5%: Each mL of sterile ophthalmic solution contains: levobunolol HCl 5 mg. Nonmedicinal ingredients: benzalkonium chloride 0.004% (as preservative), edetate disodium, polyvinyl alcohol (Liquifilm), potassium phosphate monobasic, sodium chloride, sodium metabisulfite, sodium phosphate dibasic, sodium hydroxide or hydrochloric acid to adjust pH. Plastic dropper bottles of 3 mL (hospitals only), 5, 10 and 15 mL. Protect from light and excessive heat.

BETALOC® Ⓟ
BETALOC® DURULES® Ⓟ

Astra

Metoprolol Tartrate

β-Adrenoceptor Blocking Agent

Pharmacology: Metoprolol is a β-adrenoceptor blocking agent. In vitro and in vivo animal studies have shown that it has a preferential effect on β_1-adrenoreceptors, chiefly located in cardiac muscle. This preferential effect is not absolute, however, and at higher doses, metoprolol also inhibits β_2-adrenoreceptors, chiefly located in the bronchial and vascular musculature. It is used in the treatment of hypertension, angina pectoris and to reduce mortality in patients with myocardial infarction.

The mechanism of the **antihypertensive** effect has not been established. Among the factors that may be involved are: competitive ability to antagonize catecholamine-induced tachycardia at the beta-receptor sites in the heart, thus decreasing heart rate, cardiac contractility and cardiac output; inhibition of renin release by the kidneys; inhibition of the vasomotor centres.

By blocking catecholamine-induced increases in heart rate, in velocity and extent of myocardial contraction and in blood pressure, metoprolol reduces the oxygen requirements of the heart at any given level of effort, thus making it useful in the long-term management of **angina pectoris.** However, in patients with heart failure, β-adrenoceptor blockade may increase oxygen requirements by increasing left ventricular fibre length and end-diastolic pressure.

The mechanisms involved in **reducing mortality in patients with acute myocardial infarction** are not fully understood.

Pharmacokinetics: In man, absorption of metoprolol is rapid and complete. Plasma levels following oral administration, however, approximate 50% of levels following i.v. administration, indicating about 50% first-pass metabolism.

Intersubject plasma levels achieved are highly variable after oral administration, although they show good reproducibility within each individual. Peak plasma concentrations are attained after approximately 1.5 to 2 hours with conventional metoprolol formulations, and after approximately 4 to 5 hours with sustained-release formulations. Upon repeated oral administration, the percentage of the dose systemically available is higher than after a single dose and also increases dose-dependently. Ingestion together with food may raise the systemic availability of an oral dose by approximately 30 to 40%. Only a small fraction of the drug (about 12%) is bound to human serum albumin. Elimination is mainly by biotransformation in the liver, and the plasma half-life averages 3.5 hours (extremes: 1 and 9 hours). The total clearance rate is approximately 1 L/min and the protein binding rate is approximately 5 to 10%. Less than 5% of an oral dose of metoprolol is recovered unchanged in the urine; the rest is excreted by the kidneys as metabolites that appear to have no clinical significance.

The systemic availability and half-life of metoprolol in patients with renal failure do not differ to a clinically significant degree from those in normal subjects. The excretion of metabolites, however, is reduced. Significant accumulation of metabolites was observed in patients with a GFR of approximately 5 mL/min, but this accumulation does not influence the β-blocking effects of metoprolol. Consequently, no reduction in dosage is usually needed in patients with chronic renal failure.

Elderly subjects show no significant changes in the plasma concentrations of metoprolol as compared with young persons. However, plasma concentrations of the major pharmacologically active metabolites were higher in the elderly.

Liver cirrhosis may increase the bioavailability of metoprolol and reduce its total clearance.

Pharmacodynamics: Significant β-blocking effect (as measured by reduction of exercise heart rate) occurs within 1 hour after oral administration, and its duration is dose-related. For example, a 50% reduction of the maximum registered effect after single oral doses of 20, 50 and 100 mg occurred at 3.3, 5.0 and 6.4 hours, respectively, in normal subjects. After repeated oral dosages of 100 mg twice daily, a significant reduction in exercise systolic blood pressure was evident at 12 hours.

Following i.v. administration of metoprolol, the half-life of the distribution phase is approximately 12 minutes; the urinary recovery of unchanged drug is approximately 10%. When the drug was infused over a 10 minute period, in normal volunteers, maximum β-blockade was achieved at approximately 20 minutes. Doses of 5 and 15 mg yielded a maximal reduction in exercise-induced heart rate of approximately 10 and 15%, respectively. The effect on exercise heart rate decreased linearly with time at the same rate for both doses, and disappeared at approximately 5 hours and 8 hours for the 5 mg and 15 mg doses, respectively.

Equivalent maximal beta-blocking effect is achieved with oral and i.v. doses in the ratio of approximately 2.5:1.

There is a linear relationship between the log of plasma levels and reduction of exercise heart rate. However, antihypertensive activity does not appear to be related to plasma levels. Because of variable plasma levels attained with a given dose and lack of a consistent relationship of antihypertensive activity to dose, selection of proper dosage requires individual titration.

In several studies of patients with acute myocardial infarction, i.v. followed by oral administration of metoprolol caused a reduction in heart rate, systolic blood pressure and cardiac output. Stroke volume, diastolic blood pressure, and pulmonary artery end diastolic pressure remained unchanged.

Studies in hypertensive and angina patients have shown plasma levels of 28 to 46 ng/mL 12 hours after regular tablets and 19 to 45 ng/mL 24 hours after Durules and were comparable to the peak levels after 100 mg regular tablets.

Indications: Hypertension: In patients with mild or moderate hypertension. It may be used alone or in combination with other antihypertensive agents (see Dosage).

The combination of metoprolol with a diuretic or peripheral vasodilator has been found to be compatible and generally more effective than metoprolol alone. Limited experience with other antihypertensive agents has not shown evidence of incompatibility with metoprolol.

Not recommended for the emergency treatment of hypertensive crises.

Angina Pectoris: For the long-term treatment of angina pectoris due to ischemic heart disease.

Myocardial Infarction: In the treatment of hemodynamically stable patients with definite or suspected acute myocardial infarction to reduce cardiovascular mortality.

Treatment with i.v. metoprolol can be initiated as soon as the patient's clinical condition allows (see Dosage, Contraindications and Warnings). Alternatively, in patients with proven myocardial infarction, oral treatment can begin within 3 to 10 days of the acute event (see Dosage). Data are not available as to whether benefit would ensue if the treatment is initiated later.

Clinical trials have shown that patients in whom the myocardial infarction was unconfirmed, received no benefit from early metoprolol therapy.

Contraindications: Known hypersensitivity to metoprolol and related derivatives; sinus bradycardia; sick sinus syndrome; second- and third-degree AV block; right ventricular failure secondary to pulmonary hypertension; overt heart failure; cardiogenic shock; severe peripheral arterial circulatory disorders; anesthesia with agents that produce myocardial depression, e.g. ether. The i.v. form is also contraindicated in the presence of asthma and other obstructive respiratory diseases (for oral treatment, see Precautions, Bronchospastic Diseases).

Myocardial Infarction Patients: Additional Contraindications: Metoprolol is contraindicated in patients with a heart rate <45 beats/min; significant heart block greater than first degree (PR interval ≥ 0.24 s); systolic blood pressure <100 mmHg; or moderate-to-severe cardiac failure (see Warnings).

Warnings: Cardiac Failure: Special caution should be exercised when administering metoprolol to patients with a history of heart failure. Sympathetic stimulation is a vital component supporting circulatory function in congestive heart failure, and inhibition with beta-blockade always carries the potential hazard of further depressing myocardial contractility and precipitating cardiac failure. The positive inotropic action of digitalis may be reduced by the negative inotropic effect of metoprolol when the two drugs are used concomitantly. The effects of beta-blockers and digitalis are additive in depressing AV conduction. This also applies to combinations with calcium antagonists of the verapamil type or some antiarrhythmics (see Precautions, Drug Interactions).

In patients without a history of cardiac failure, continued depression of the myocardium over a period of time can, in some cases, lead to cardiac failure and/or hypotension (systolic blood pressure ≤ 90 mmHg). Therefore, at the first sign or symptom of impending cardiac failure, patients should be fully digitalized and/or given a diuretic and the response observed closely. If cardiac failure continues, despite adequate digitalization and diuretic therapy, therapy should be reduced or withdrawn.

Abrupt Cessation of Therapy: Patients with angina should be warned against abrupt discontinuation of metoprolol. There have been reports of severe exacerbation of angina and of myocardial infarction or ventricular arrhythmias occurring in patients with angina pectoris, following abrupt discontinuation of beta-blocker therapy. The last 2 complications may occur with or without preceding exacerbation of angina pectoris. Therefore, when discontinuation is planned in patients with angina pectoris or previous myocardial infarction, the dosage should be gradually reduced over a period of at least 10 to 14 days, in diminishing doses, to 25 mg once a day for the last 6 days. During this period the patient should be carefully observed. In situations of greater urgency, metoprolol therapy should be discontinued stepwise and under conditions of closer observation. If angina markedly worsens or acute coronary insufficiency develops, it is recommended that treatment with metoprolol should be reinstituted promptly, at least temporarily.

Betaloc (cont'd)

Patients should be warned against interruption or discontinuation of therapy without the physician's advice. Because coronary artery disease is common and may be unrecognized, it may be prudent not to discontinue metoprolol therapy abruptly even in patients treated only for hypertension.

Oculomucocutaneous Syndrome: Various skin rashes and conjunctival xerosis have been reported with beta-blockers, including metoprolol. Oculomucocutaneous syndrome, a severe syndrome whose signs include conjunctivitis sicca and psoriasiform rashes, otitis and sclerosing serositis, has occurred with chronic use of one β-adrenergic-blocking agent (practolol). This syndrome has not been observed with metoprolol or any other such agent. However, physicians should be alert to the possibility of such reactions and should discontinue treatment in the event that they occur.

Severe Sinus Bradycardia: Severe sinus bradycardia may occur with the use of metoprolol from unopposed vagal activity remaining after blockade of β_1-adrenergic receptors. Very rarely a pre-existing AV conduction disorder of moderate degree may become aggravated, possibly leading to AV block. In such cases, dosage should be reduced. Atropine, isoproterenol or dobutamine should be considered in patients with acute myocardial infarction.

Thyrotoxicosis: Although metoprolol has successfully been used for the symptomatic (adjuvant) therapy of thyrotoxicosis, possible deleterious effects from long-term use of metoprolol have not been adequately appraised. β-blockade may mask the clinical signs of continuing hyperthyroidism or complications and give a false impression of improvement. Therefore, abrupt withdrawal of metoprolol may be followed by an exacerbation of the symptoms of hyperthyroidism, including thyroid storm.

Myocardial Infarction Patients: Additional Warnings: Acute Intervention: During acute intervention in myocardial infarction, i.v. metoprolol should only be used by experienced staff under circumstances where resuscitation and monitoring equipment are available.

Cardiac Failure: Depression of the myocardium with metoprolol may lead to cardiac failure (see general Warnings). Special caution should be exercised when administering metoprolol to patients with a history of cardiac failure or those with a minimal cardiac reserve. Should failure occur, treatment should be as described in Warnings.

Severe Sinus Bradycardia: See general Warnings for severe sinus bradycardia.

AV Conduction: Metoprolol slows AV conduction and may produce significant first- (PR interval $\geq$ 0.26 s), second-, or third-degree heart block. Acute myocardial infarction also produces heart block.

If heart block occurs, metoprolol should be discontinued and atropine (0.25 to 0.5 mg) should be administered i.v. If treatment with atropine is not successful, cautious administration of isoproterenol or installation of a cardiac pacemaker should be considered.

Hypotension: If hypotension (systolic blood pressure $\leq$90 mmHg) occurs, metoprolol should be discontinued, and the hemodynamic status of the patient and the extent of myocardial damage carefully assessed. Invasive monitoring of central venous, pulmonary capillary wedge, and arterial pressures may be required. Appropriate therapy with fluids, positive inotropic agents, balloon counterpulsation, or other treatment modalities should be instituted. If hypotension is associated with sinus bradycardia or AV block, treatment should be directed at reversing these (see above).

Precautions: Bronchospastic Diseases: **Patients with bronchospastic diseases should, in general, not receive beta-blockers.** Because of its relative β_1-selectivity, however, metoprolol may be used with caution in patients with bronchospastic disease who do not respond to, or cannot tolerate, other antihypertensive treatment. Since β_1-selectivity is not absolute, a β_2-stimulating agent should preferably be administered concomitantly, and the lowest possible dose of metoprolol should be used. In these circumstances it would be prudent initially to administer metoprolol in smaller doses 3 times daily, instead of larger doses 2 times daily, to avoid the higher plasma levels associated with the longer dosing interval (see Dosage).

Because it is unknown to what extent β_2-stimulating agents may exacerbate myocardial ischemia and the extent of infarction, these agents should not be used prophylactically in patients with proven or suspected acute myocardial infarction. If bronchospasm not related to congestive heart failure occurs, metoprolol should be discontinued. A theophylline derivative or a β_2-agonist may be administered cautiously, depending on the clinical condition of the patient. Both theophylline derivatives and β_2-agonists may produce serious cardiac arrhythmias.

Diabetes and Hypoglycemia: Metoprolol should be administered with caution to diabetic patients subject to spontaneous hypoglycemia (most of these patients are insulin treated). β-adrenergic blockers may mask the premonitory signs and symptoms of acute hypoglycemia, but this is mainly attributed to unselective β-adrenergic blockers.

Liver Function: Metoprolol should be used with caution in patients with impaired liver function. Liver function tests should be performed at regular intervals during long-term treatment. Dose adjustment is normally not needed in patients suffering from liver cirrhosis because metoprolol has low protein binding (5 to 10%). When there are signs of serious impairment of liver function (e.g., shunt-operated patients) a dose reduction should be considered.

Allergen Immunotherapy: There may be increased difficulty in treating an allergic type reaction in patients on β-blockers. In these patients, the reaction may be more severe due to pharmacologic effects of the β-blockers and problems with fluid changes. Epinephrine should be administered with caution since it may not have its usual effects in the treatment of anaphylaxis. On the one hand, larger doses of epinephrine may be needed to overcome the bronchospasm, while on the other these doses can be associated with excessive alpha-adrenergic stimulation with consequent hypertension, reflex bradycardia and heart-block, and possible potentiation of bronchospasm. Alternatives to the use of large doses of epinephrine include vigorous supportive care such as fluids and the use of β-agonists including parenteral salbutamol or isoproterenol to overcome bronchospasm and norepinephrine to overcome hypotension.

Patients Undergoing Surgery: It is not advisable to withdraw β-adrenoceptor blocking drugs prior to surgery in the majority of patients especially in those with risk of overt or silent coronary heart disease. However, care should be taken to avoid using anesthetic agents that may depress the myocardium. Vagal dominance, if it occurs, may be corrected with atropine (1 to 2 mg i.v.).

Some patients receiving β-blocking drugs have been subject to protracted severe hypotension during anesthesia. Difficulty in restarting and maintaining the heartbeat has also been reported.

Since metoprolol is a competitive inhibitor of β-adrenoceptor agonists, its effects may be reversed, if necessary, by sufficient doses of such antagonists as isoproterenol or dobutamine.

Peripheral Artery Disorders: Metoprolol may aggravate the symptoms of peripheral arterial circulatory disorders, mainly due to its blood pressure lowering effect.

Pheochromocytoma: Where a β-blocker is prescribed for a patient known to be suffering from a pheochromocytoma, an α-blocker should be given concomitantly.

Occupational Hazards: Reaction Time: β-blockers may adversely affect the patient's reaction time. Patients should be advised to avoid operating automobiles and machinery or engaging in other tasks requiring alertness until the patient's response to therapy with metoprolol has been determined.

Pregnancy: Metoprolol crosses the placental barrier. Since metoprolol has not been studied in human pregnancy, it should not be given to pregnant women. The use of any drug in patients of child-bearing potential requires that the anticipated benefit be weighed against possible hazards.

Lactation: Metoprolol is excreted in breast milk in very small quantities. Caution should be exercised when metoprolol is administered to a nursing woman.

Children: The safety and efficacy of metoprolol in children has not been established.

Geriatrics: Caution is indicated when using metoprolol in elderly patients. An excessively pronounced decrease in blood pressure or pulse rate may cause the blood supply to vital organs to fall to inadequate levels.

Drug Interactions: Antihypertensives: Dosage should be adjusted according to the individual requirements of the patient especially when used concomitantly with other antihypertensive agents (see Dosage).

MAO Inhibitors and Adrenergic Neuron Blockers: Patients receiving MAO inhibitors or catecholamine-depleting drugs, (such as reserpine or guanethidine), should be closely monitored because the added β-adrenergic-blocking action of metoprolol may produce an excessive reduction of sympathetic activity. Metoprolol should not be combined with other β-blockers.

Calcium Entry Blockers: As with other β-blockers metoprolol should not be given to patients receiving calcium antagonists of the verapamil type. However, in exceptional cases, when in the opinion of the physician concomitant use is considered essential, such use should be instituted gradually in a hospital setting under careful supervision. Negative inotropic, dromotropic, and chronotropic effects may occur when metoprolol is given together with calcium antagonists. Verapamil and diltiazem may reduce clearance of metoprolol.

Antiarrhythmic Agents: β-blockers may enhance the negative inotropic and negative dromotropic effect of antiarrhythmic agents such as quinidine and amiodarone.

Clonidine Withdrawal Syndrome: The hypertensive crisis which may follow the withdrawal of clonidine may be accentuated in the presence of β-blockade. It has been proposed that withdrawal of the β-blocker several days before the clonidine may reduce the danger of rebound effects.

Oral Antidiabetics: The dosage of oral antidiabetics may have to be readjusted in patients receiving β-blockers (see Precautions).

Indomethacin: Concurrent treatment with indomethacin may decrease the antihypertensive effect of β-blockers.

Hepatic Enzyme-Inducers and Enzyme-Inhibitors: Hepatic enzyme-inducing and enzyme-inhibiting substances may exert an influence on the plasma level of metoprolol. The plasma concentration of metoprolol is lowered by rifampin, and may be raised by cimetidine, ranitidine, propafenone and hydralazine.

Lidocaine: Metoprolol may reduce the clearance of lidocaine.

Adverse Effects: Adverse reactions have generally been mild and reversible. The following events have been reported as adverse events in clinical trials or reported from routine use. In many cases, a relationship to treatment with metoprolol has not been established.

The most common adverse events reported are exertional tiredness, gastrointestinal disorders and disturbances of sleep patterns. The most serious adverse events reported are congestive heart failure, bronchospasm and hypotension.

Reported adverse events according to organ systems are: Cardiovascular: congestive heart failure (see Warnings); secondary effects of decreased cardiac output, which include: syncope, vertigo, lightheadedness and postural hypotension; severe bradycardia; lengthening of PR interval; second and third degree AV block; sinus arrest; cardiac arrhythmias; palpitations; chest pains; edema; cold extremities; claudication; gangrene in patients with pre-existing severe peripheral circulatory disorders; hot flushes.

In a placebo controlled study in patients with acute myocardial infarction, the incidences of cardiovascular reactions are found in Table I.

Table I—Betaloc

Cardiovascular Reactions

	Metoprolol	Placebo
Hypotension (systolic BP < 90 mmHg)	27.4%	23.2%
Bradycardia (heart rate < 40 beats/min)	15.9%	6.7%
Second- or third-degree heart block	4.7%	4.7%
First-degree heart block (PR $\geq$ 0.26 sec)	5.3%	1.9%
Heart failure	27.5%	29.6%

CNS: headache, dizziness, mental depression, lightheadedness, concentration impaired, anxiety, weakness, fatigue, sedation, somnolence or insomnia, vivid dreams/nightmares, vertigo, paresthesia, hallucination, nervousness, impotence/sexual dysfunction, amnesia/memory impairment, confusion.

Gastrointestinal: diarrhea, constipation, flatulence, heartburn, nausea and vomiting, abdominal pain, dryness of mouth, hepatitis.

Respiratory: shortness of breath, wheezing, bronchospasm, status asthmaticus, rhinitis.

Allergic/Dermatological (see Warnings): skin rash (exanthema, urticaria, psoriasiform and dystrophic skin lesions); sweating; pruritus; photosensitivity.

Eye, Ear, Nose and Throat (EENT): blurred vision and nonspecific visual disturbances; dry and/or itching eyes; conjunctivitis; tinnitus; hearing difficulties in doses exceeding those recommended; taste disturbances.

Miscellaneous: muscle cramps; exertional tiredness; weight gain; loss of hair; arthritis; Peyronie's disease.

Clinical Laboratory: The following laboratory parameters have been rarely elevated: transaminases, BUN, alkaline phosphatase and bilirubin. Isolated cases of thrombocytopenia and leukopenia have been reported.

Overdose: Symptoms: The most common signs to be expected with overdosage of a β-adrenoceptor blocking agent are hypotension, bradycardia, congestive heart failure, bronchospasm and hypoglycemia. Atrioventricular block, cardiogenic shock and cardiac arrest may develop. In addition, impairment of consciousness (or even coma), nausea, vomiting and cyanosis may occur.

Concomitant ingestion of alcohol, antihypertensives, quinidine, or barbiturates aggravate the signs and symptoms.

The first manifestations of overdosage set in 20 minutes to 2 hours after drug administration.

Treatment: If overdosage occurs, in all cases therapy with metoprolol should be discontinued and the patient hospitalized and observed closely. Remove any drug remaining in the stomach by induction of emesis or gastric lavage. In addition, if required, the following therapeutic measures are suggested.

Bradycardia and Hypotension: Initially 1 to 2 mg of atropine sulfate should be given i.v. If a satisfactory effect is not achieved, norepinephrine or dopamine may be administered after preceding treatment with atropine (see Precautions concerning the use of epinephrine in β-blocked patients). In case of hypoglycemia glucagon (1 to 10 mg) can also be administered.

Heart Block (second- or third-degree): Isoproterenol or transvenous cardiac pacemaker.

Congestive Heart Failure: Conventional therapy.

Bronchospasm: I.V. aminophylline or β_2-agonist.

Hypoglycemia: I.V. glucose.

It should be remembered that metoprolol is a competitive antagonist of isoproterenol and hence, large doses of isoproterenol can be expected to reverse many of the effects of excessive doses of metoprolol. However, the complications of excess isoproterenol e.g., hypotension and tachycardia, should not be overlooked.

Dosage: Hypertension: Metoprolol is usually used in conjunction with other antihypertensive agents, particularly a thiazide diuretic, but may be used alone (see Indications).

The dose must always be adjusted to the individual requirements of the patient, in accordance with the following guidelines.

Metoprolol treatment should be initiated with doses of 50 mg b.i.d. If an adequate response is not seen after 1 week, dosage should be increased to 100 mg b.i.d. In some cases the daily dosage may need to be increased by further 100 mg increments at intervals of not less than 2 weeks up to a maximum of 200 mg b.i.d., which should not be exceeded. The usual maintenance dose is within the range of 100 to 200 mg daily.

When metoprolol is combined with another antihypertensive agent which is already being administered, metoprolol should be added initially at a dose of 50 mg b.i.d. After 1 or 2 weeks the daily dosage may be increased if required, in increments of 100 mg, at intervals of not less than 2 weeks, until adequate blood pressure control is obtained.

Angina pectoris: The recommended dosage range is 100 to 400 mg/day in divided doses.

Treatment should be initiated with 50 mg b.i.d. for the first week. If the response is inadequate, the daily dosage should be increased by 100 mg for the next week. The usual maintenance dose is 200 mg/day.

The need for further increases should be closely monitored at weekly intervals and the dosage increased in 100 mg increments to a maximum of 400 mg/day in 2 or 3 divided doses.

A metoprolol dose of 400 mg/day should not be exceeded.

Slow-release Durules: 200 mg slow-release tablets are intended only for maintenance dosing in those patients requiring doses of 100 to 400 mg/day. Treatment must always be initiated and individual titration of dosage carried out using the regular tablets. Dosing with half or whole Durules may be preferred for maintenance because of the convenience of once daily administration. One half Durules will provide 100 mg slow-release metoprolol. The following maintenance doses may now be accommodated: 100 mg is equal to one half Durules, 200 mg is equal to 1 Durules, 300 mg is equal to one and one half Durules, 400 mg is equal to 2 Durules.

Myocardial infarction: In addition to the usual contraindications: **Only patients with suspected acute myocardial infarction who meet the following criteria are suitable for therapy as described:** systolic blood pressure $\geq$100 mm Hg; heart rate* $\geq$45 beats/min; PR interval $<$0.24 s; rales* $<$10 cm and adequate peripheral circulation.

*Extreme caution should be exercised when giving i.v. metoprolol to patients with heart rates between 45 and 60 and/or pulmonary rales less than 10 cm. Therapy should be discontinued in patients if the heart rate drops below 45 or the systolic blood pressure drops below 100 mmHg.

Early Treatment: During the early phase of definite or suspected acute myocardial infarction, treatment with metoprolol can be initiated as soon as possible after the patient's arrival in the hospital. Such treatment should be initiated in a coronary care or similar unit immediately after the patient's hemodynamic condition has stabilized.

Treatment in this early phase should begin with the i.v. administration of 3 bolus injections of 5 mg each. The injections should be given at approximately 2 minute intervals. During the i.v. administration of metoprolol, blood pressure, heart rate, and electrocardiogram should be carefully monitored. If any of the injections are associated with adverse cardiovascular effects, i.v. administration should be stopped immediately and the patient should be observed carefully and appropriate therapy instituted.

In patients who tolerate the full i.v. dose (15 mg), metoprolol tablets, 50 mg every 6 hours should be initiated 15 minutes after the last i.v. dose and continued for 48 hours. Thereafter, patients should receive a maintenance dosage of 100 mg twice daily (see Late Treatment).

Patients who appear not to tolerate the full i.v. dose should be started on either 25 mg or 50 mg every 6 hours (depending on the degree of intolerance) 15 minutes after the last i.v. dose or as soon as their clinical condition allows. In patients with severe intolerance, treatment with metoprolol should be discontinued (see Warnings).

Late Treatment (for proven myocardial infarction patients only): Patients with contraindications to treatment during the early phase of myocardial infarction, patients who appear not to tolerate the full early treatment, and patients in whom the physician wishes to delay therapy for any other reason should be started on metoprolol tablets, 100 mg twice daily, as soon as their clinical condition allows. Treatment can begin within 3 to 10 days of the acute event. Therapy should be continued for at least 3 months. Although the efficacy of treatment with metoprolol beyond 6 months has not been conclusively established, data from studies with other beta-blockers suggest that the treatment should be continued for 1 to 3 years.

Impaired Liver Function: Dose adjustment is normally not needed in patients suffering from liver cirrhosis because metoprolol has low protein binding (5 to 10%). When there are signs of serious impairment of liver function (e.g., shunt-operated patients) a dose reduction should be considered.

Note: Parenteral drug products should be inspected visually for particulate matter and discoloration prior to administration whenever solution and container permit.

Supplied: Tablets: 50 mg: Each compressed, white, scored, biconvex, circular tablet, contains: metoprolol tartrate 50 mg (engraved A/βB). Nonmedicinal ingredients: colloidal silica, lactose, magnesium stearate, microcrystalline cellulose, polyvinyl pyrrolidone and sodium starch glycolate. Energy: 0.31 kJ (0.07 kcal). Gluten- and tartrazine-free. Bottles of 100 and 500. Store at 15 to 30°C.

100 mg: Each compressed, white, scored, biconvex circular tablet, contains: metoprolol tartrate 100 mg (engraved A/ME). Nonmedicinal ingredients: colloidal silica, lactose, magnesium stearate, microcrystalline cellulose, polyvinyl pyrrolidone and sodium starch glycolate. Energy: 0.61 kJ (0.15 kcal). Gluten- and tartrazine-free. Bottles of 100 and 500. Store at 15 to 30°C.

Durules: Each white, biconvex rod-shaped film-coated tablet contains: metoprolol tartrate 200 mg (scored and engraved A/MD). Nonmedicinal ingredients: aluminum silicate, ethylcellulose, hydroxypropyl methylcellulose, magnesium stearate, paraffin, polyethylene glycol and titanium dioxide. Gluten-, lactose- and tartrazine-free. Bottles of 100 and 500. Store at 15 to 30°C.

Injection: Each mL of aqueous injectable solution contains: metoprolol tartrate 1 mg. Also contains sodium chloride 45 mg (9 mg/mL). Glass vials of 5 mL. Store at 15 to 30°C, protected from light.

(Shown in Product Recognition Section)

Reviewed 1998

BETAMETHASONE

General Monograph, CPhA

see CORTICOSTEROIDS: EYE EAR NOSE
see CORTICOSTEROIDS: SYSTEMIC
see CORTICOSTEROIDS: TOPICAL

BETASERON®

Berlex Canada

Interferon beta-1b

Immunomodulator

Pharmacology: General: Interferons are a family of naturally occurring proteins, which have molecular weights ranging from 15 000 to 21 000 daltons. Three major classes of interferons have been identified: alpha, beta and gamma. Interferon beta-1b, interferon alpha, and interferon gamma have overlapping yet distinct biologic activities. The activities of interferon beta-1b are species-restricted and, therefore, the most pertinent pharmacological information on interferon beta-1b is derived from studies of human cells in culture and in vivo.

Biologic Activities: Interferon beta-1b has been shown to possess both antiviral and immunomodulatory activities. The mechanisms by which interferon beta-1b exerts its actions in multiple sclerosis (MS) are not clearly understood. However, it is known that the biologic response-modifying properties of interferon beta-1b are mediated through its interactions with specific cell receptors found on the surface of human cells. The binding of interferon beta-1b to these receptors induces the expression of a number of interferon-induced gene products (e.g., 2′, 5′-oligoadenylate synthetase, protein kinase and indoleamine 2, 3-dioxygenase) that are believed to be the mediators of the biological actions of interferon beta-1b. A number of these interferon induced products have been readily measured in the serum and cellular fractions of blood collected from patients treated with interferon beta-1b.

Clinical Trials: The effectiveness of interferon beta-1b in relapsing-remitting MS was evaluated in a double-blind, multiclinic (11 sites: 4 in Canada and 7 in the U.S.), randomized, parallel, placebo-controlled clinical investigation of 2 years' duration. The study included MS patients, aged 18 to 50, who were ambulatory (Kurtzke expanded disability status scale [EDSS] of $\leq$5.5), exhibited a relapsing-remitting clinical course, met Poser's criteria for clinically definite and/or laboratory supported definite MS and had experienced at least two exacerbations over 2 years preceding the trial without exacerbation in the preceding month. Patients who had received prior immunosuppressant therapy were excluded.

An exacerbation was defined, per protocol, as the appearance of a new clinical sign/symptom or the clinical worsening of a previous sign/symptom (one that had been stable for at least 30 days) that persisted for a minimum of 24 hours.

Patients selected for study were randomized to treatment with either placebo (n=123), 0.05 mg (1.6 MIU) of interferon beta-1b (n=125), or 0.25 mg (8 MIU) of interferon beta-1b (n=124) self-administered s.c. every other day. Outcome based on the first 372 randomized patients was evaluated after 2 years.

Patients who required more than three 28-day courses of corticosteroids were withdrawn from the study. Minor analgesics (e.g., acetaminophen), antidepressants and oral baclofen were allowed ad libitum, but chronic nonsteroidal anti-inflammatory drug (NSAID) use was not allowed.

The primary, protocol defined, outcome assessment measures were 1) frequency of exacerbations per patient and 2) proportion of exacerbation-free patients. A number of secondary outcome measures were also employed as described in Table I on following page.

In addition to clinical measures, annual magnetic resonance imaging (MRI) was performed and quantitated for extent of disease as determined by changes in total area of lesions. In a substudy of patients (n=52) at one site, MRI was performed every 6 weeks and quantitated for disease activity as determined by changes in size and number of lesions.

Results at the protocol designated endpoint of 2 years (see Table I): In the 2-year analysis, there was a 31% reduction in annual exacerbation rate, from 1.31 in the placebo group to 0.9 in the 0.25 mg (8 MIU) group. The p-value for this difference was 0.0001. The proportion of patients free of exacerbations was 16% in the placebo group, compared with 25% in the interferon beta-1b 0.25 mg (8 MIU) group.

Of the first 372 patients randomized, 72 (19%) failed to complete 2 full years on their assigned treatments. The reasons given for withdrawal varied with treatment assignment. Excessive use of steroids accounted for 11 of the 26 placebo withdrawals. In contrast, among the 25 withdrawals from the 0.25 mg (8 MIU) assigned group, excessive steroid use accounted for only one withdrawal. Withdrawals for adverse events attributed to study article, however, were more common among interferon beta-1b-treated patients: 1 and 10

Betaseron (cont'd)

withdrew from the placebo and 0.25 mg (8 MIU) groups, respectively.

Over the 2-year period, there were 25 MS-related hospitalizations in the 0.25 mg (8 MIU) interferon beta-1b-treated group compared to 48 hospitalizations in the placebo group. In comparison, non-MS hospitalizations were evenly distributed between the groups, with 16 in the 0.25 mg (8 MIU) interferon beta-1b group and 15 in the placebo group. The average number of days of MS-related steroid use was 41 days in the 0.25 mg (8 MIU) interferon beta-1b group and 55 days in the placebo group (p=0.004).

conditions. Approximately 80% of patients in each treatment group accepted. Although there was a trend toward patient benefit in the interferon beta-1b groups during the third year, particularly in the 0.25 mg (8 MIU) group, there was no statistically significant difference between the interferon beta-1b-treated vs placebo-treated patients in exacerbation rate, or in any of the secondary endpoints described in Table I. As noted above, in the 2-year analysis, there was a 31% reduction in exacerbation rate in the 0.25 mg (8 MIU) group, compared to placebo. The p-value for this difference was 0.0001. In the analysis of the third year alone, the difference between treatment groups was 28%. The p-value was 0.065. The lower number of patients may account for the loss of statistical significance, and lack of direct comparability among the

Table I—Betaseron

2-Year Study Results
Primary and Secondary Clinical Endpoints

Efficacy Parameters		**Treatment Groups**			**Statistical Comparisons p-value**		
Primary Clinical Endpoints		**Placebo (n=123)**	**0.05 mg (1.6 MIU) (n=125)**	**0.25 mg (8 MIU) (n=124)**	**Placebo vs 0.05 mg (1.6 MIU)**	**0.05 mg (1.6 MIU) vs 0.25 mg (8 MIU)**	**Placebo vs 0.25 mg (8 MIU)**
Annual exacerbation rate		1.31	1.14	0.90	0.005	0.113	0.0001
Proportion of exacerbation-free patients[a]		16%	18%	25%	0.609	0.288	0.094
Exacerbation frequency per patient	0[a]	20	22	29	0.151	0.077	0.001
	1	32	31	39			
	2	20	28	17			
	3	15	15	14			
	4	15	7	9			
	≥5	21	16	8			
Secondary Endpoints[b]							
Median number of months to first on-study exacerbation		5	6	9	0.299	0.097	0.010
Rate of moderate or severe exacerbations per year		0.47	0.29	0.23	0.020	0.257	0.001
Mean number of moderate or severe exacerbation days per patient		44.1	33.2	19.5	0.229	0.064	0.001
Mean change in EDSS score[c] at endpoint		0.21	0.21	−0.07	0.995	0.108	0.144
Mean change in Scripps score[d] at endpoint		−0.53	−0.50	0.66	0.641	0.051	0.126
Median duration per exacerbation (days)		36	33	35.5	ND	ND	ND
% change in mean MRI lesion area at endpoint		21.4%	9.8%	−0.9%	0.015	0.019	0.0001

Legend: ND Not done.

[a] 14 exacerbation-free patients (0 from placebo, 6 from 0.05 mg and 8 from 0.25 mg groups) dropped out of the study before completing 6 months of therapy. These patients are excluded from this analysis.

[b] Sequelae and Functional Neurologic Status, both required by protocol, were not analyzed individually but are included as a function of the EDSS.

[c] EDSS scores range from 0-10, with higher scores reflecting greater disability.

[d] Scripps neurologic rating scores range from 0-100, with smaller scores reflecting greater disability.

MRI data were also analyzed for patients in this study. A frequency distribution of the observed percent changes in MRI area at the end of 2 years was obtained by grouping the percentages in successive intervals of equal width. Figure 1 (not shown) displays a histogram of the proportions of patients who fell into each of these intervals. The median percent change in MRI area for the 0.25 mg (8 MIU) group was −1.1% which was significantly smaller than the 16.5% observed for the placebo group (p=0.0001).

Figure 1 (not shown): Distribution of Change in MRI Area: Fifty-two patients at one site had frequent MRI scans (every 6 weeks). The percentage of scans with new or expanding lesions was 29% in the placebo group and 6% in the 0.25 mg (8 MIU) treatment group (p=0.006).

MRI scanning is viewed as a useful means to visualize changes in white matter that are believed to be a reflection of the pathologic changes that, appropriately located within the CNS, account for some of the signs and symptoms that typify relapsing-remitting MS. The exact relationship between MRI findings and the clinical status of patients is unknown. Changes in lesion area often do not correlate with clinical exacerbations probably because many of the lesions affect so-called "silent" regions of the CNS. Moreover, it is not clear what fraction of the lesions seen on MRI become foci of irreversible demyelinization (i.e., classic white matter plaques). The prognostic significance of the MRI findings in this study has not been evaluated.

At the end of 2 years on assigned treatment, patients in the study had the option of continuing on treatment under blinded

patient groups in this extension study make the interpretation of these results difficult. The third-year MRI data did not show a trend toward additional benefit in the interferon beta-1b arm compared with the placebo arm.

Throughout the clinical trial, serum samples from patients were monitored for the development of antibodies to interferon beta-1b. In patients receiving 0.25 mg (8 MIU) of interferon beta-1b (n=124) every other day, 45% were found to have serum neutralizing activity on at least one occasion. One third had neutralizing activity confirmed by at least two consecutive positive titres. This development of neutralizing activity may be associated with a reduction in clinical efficacy, although the exact relationship between antibody formation and therapeutic efficacy is not yet known.

Indications: For use in ambulatory patients with relapsing-remitting multiple sclerosis to reduce the frequency of clinical exacerbations (see Pharmacology, Clinical Trials). Relapsing-remitting MS is characterized by recurrent attacks of neurologic dysfunction followed by complete or incomplete recovery. The safety and efficacy of interferon beta-1b in chronic progressive MS has not been evaluated.

Contraindications: Patients with a history of hypersensitivity to natural or recombinant interferon beta, albumin human USP or any other component of the formulation.

Warnings: One suicide and 4 attempted suicides were observed among 372 study patients during a 3-year period. All 5 patients received interferon beta-1b (three in the 0.05 mg [1.6 MIU] group and two in the 0.25 mg [8.0 MIU] group). There were no attempted suicides in patients on study who did not receive interferon beta-1b. Depression and suicide have been reported to occur in patients receiving interferon alpha, a related compound. Patients treated with interferon beta-1b should be informed that depression and suicidal ideation may be a side effect of the treatment and should report these symptoms immediately to the prescribing physician. Patients exhibiting depression should be monitored closely and cessation of therapy should be considered.

Precautions: General: Patients should be instructed in injection techniques to assure the safe self-administration of interferon beta-1b. See Information for the Patient, Instruction on Self-injection Technique and Procedure below and Information for the Patient in the Blue Section.

Information for the Patient: Instruction on Self-Injection Technique and Procedures: It is recommended that the first injection be administered by, or under the direct supervision of, a physician. Appropriate instructions for reconstitution of interferon beta-1b and self-injection, using aseptic techniques, should be given to the patient. A careful review of the Betaseron Information for the Patient in the Blue Section is also recommended.

Patients should be cautioned against the re-use of needles or syringes and instructed in safe disposal procedures. Information on how to acquire a puncture-resistant container for disposal of used needles and syringes should be given to the patient along with instruction for safe disposal of full containers.

Eighty-five percent of patients in the controlled MS trial reported injection site reactions at one or more times during therapy. Post-marketing experience has been consistent with this finding, with infrequent reports of injection site necrosis.

The onset of injection site necrosis usually appears early in therapy with most cases reported to have occurred in the first 2 to 3 months of therapy. The number of sites where necrosis has been observed was variable.

Rarely, the area of necrosis has extended to s.c. fat or fascia. Response to treatment of injection site necrosis with antibiotics and/or steroids has been variable. In some of these patients elective debridement and, less frequently, skin grafting took place to facilitate healing which could take from 3 to 6 months.

Some patients experienced healing of necrotic skin lesions while interferon beta-1b therapy continued. In other cases new necrotic lesions developed even after therapy was discontinued.

The nature and severity of all reported reactions should be carefully assessed. Patient understanding and use of aseptic self-injection technique and procedures should be periodically re-evaluated.

Flu-like symptoms are not uncommon following initiation of therapy with interferon beta-1b. In the controlled MS clinical trial, acetaminophen was permitted for relief of fever or myalgia.

Patients should be cautioned not to change the dosage or the schedule of administration without medical consultation.

Awareness of Adverse Reactions: Patients should be advised about the common adverse events associated with the use of interferon beta-1b, particularly, injection site reactions and the flu-like symptom complex (see Adverse Effects).

Patients should be cautioned to report depression or suicidal ideation (see Warnings).

Patients should be advised about the abortifacient potential of interferon beta-1b (see Precautions, Pregnancy).

Laboratory Tests: The following laboratory tests are recommended prior to initiating interferon beta-1b therapy and at periodic intervals thereafter: thyroid function test, hemoglobin, complete and differential white blood cell counts, platelet counts and blood chemistries including liver function tests. A pregnancy test, chest roentgenogram and ECG should also be performed prior to initiating interferon beta-1b therapy. In the controlled MS trial, patients were monitored every 3 months. The study protocol stipulated that interferon beta-1b therapy be discontinued in the event the absolute neutrophil count fell below 750/mm^3. When the absolute neutrophil count had returned to a value greater than 750/mm^3, therapy could be restarted at a 50% reduced dose. No patients were withdrawn or dose-reduced for neutropenia or lymphopenia.

Similarly, if AST/ALT levels exceeded 10 times the upper limit of normal, or if the serum bilirubin exceeded 5 times the upper limit of normal, therapy was discontinued. In each instance during the controlled MS trial, hepatic enzyme abnormalities returned to normal following discontinuation of therapy. When measurements had decreased to below these levels, therapy could be restarted at a 50% dose reduction, if clinically appropriate. Dose was reduced in two patients due to increased liver enzymes; one continued on treatment and one was ultimately withdrawn.

Drug Interactions: Interactions between interferon beta-1b and other drugs have not been fully evaluated. Although studies designed to examine drug interactions have not been done, it was noted that interferon beta-1b patients (n=180) have received corticosteroid or ACTH treatment of relapses for periods of up to 28 days.

Interferon beta-1b administered in 3 cancer patients over a dose range of 0.025 mg (0.8 MIU) to 2.2 mg (71 MIU) led to a dose-dependent inhibition of antipyrine elimination. The effect of alternate-day administration of 0.25 mg (8 MIU) of interferon beta-1b on drug metabolism in MS patients is unknown.

Impairment of Fertility: Studies in female rhesus monkeys with normal menstrual cycles, at doses up to 0.33 mg (10.7 MIU)/kg/day (equivalent to 32 times the recommended human dose based on body surface area comparison) showed no apparent adverse effects on the menstrual cycle or on associated hormonal profiles (progesterone and estradiol) when administered over 3 consecutive menstrual cycles. The extrapolability of animal doses to human doses is not known. Effects of interferon beta-1b on women with normal menstrual cycles are not known.

Pregnancy: Interferon beta-1b was not teratogenic at doses up to 0.42 mg (13.3 MIU)/kg/day in rhesus monkeys, but demonstrated dose-related abortifacient activity when administered at doses ranging from 0.028 mg (0.89 MIU)/kg/day (2.8 times the recommended human dose based on body surface area comparison) to 0.42 mg (13.3 MIU)/kg/day (40 times the recommended human dose based on body surface area comparison). The extrapolation of animal doses to human doses is not known. Lower doses were not studied in monkeys. Spontaneous abortions while on treatment were reported in patients (n=4) who participated in the interferon beta-1b MS clinical trial. Interferon beta-1b given to rhesus monkeys on gestation days 20 to 70 did not cause teratogenic effects; however, it is not known if teratogenic effects exist in humans. There are no adequate and well-controlled studies in pregnant women. Women of childbearing potential should take appropriate contraceptive measures. If the patient becomes pregnant or plans to become pregnant while taking interferon beta-1b, the patient should discontinue therapy.

Lactation: It is not known whether interferon beta-1b is excreted in human milk. Given that many drugs are excreted in human milk, there is a potential for serious adverse reactions in nursing infants, therefore a decision should be made as to whether to discontinue nursing or discontinue interferon beta-1b treatment.

Children: Safety and efficacy in children under 18 years of age has not been established.

Dependence Liability: No evidence or experience suggests that abuse or dependence occurs with interferon beta-1b therapy; however, the risk of dependence has not been systematically evaluated.

Adverse Effects: Experience with interferon beta-1b in patients with MS is limited to a total of 147 patients at the recommended dose of 0.25 mg (8 MIU) or more, every other day. Consequently, adverse events that are associated with the use of interferon beta-1b in MS patients at an incidence of 1% or less may not have been observed in premarketing studies. Clinical experience with interferon beta-1b in non-MS patients (e.g., cancer patients, HIV positive patients) provides additional safety data; however, this experience may not be fully applicable to MS patients.

Injection site reactions (85%) and injection site necrosis (5%) occurred after administration of interferon beta-1b. Inflammation, pain, hypersensitivity, necrosis and nonspecific reactions were significantly associated ($p<0.05$) with the 0.25 mg (8 MIU) interferon beta-1b-treated group. Only inflammation, pain and necrosis were reported as severe events. The incidence rate for injection site reactions was calculated over the course of 3 years. This incidence rate decreased over time, with 79% of patients experiencing the event during the first 3 months of treatment compared to 47% during the last 6 months. The median time to the first occurrence of an injection site reaction was 7 days. Patients with injection site reactions reported these events 183.7 days per year. Three patients withdrew from the 0.25 mg (8 MIU) interferon beta-1b-treated group for injection site pain.

Flu-like symptoms complex was reported in 76% of the patients treated with 0.25 mg (8 MIU) interferon beta-1b. A patient was defined as having a flu-like symptom complex if flu-like syndrome or at least two of the following symptoms were concurrently reported: fever, chills, myalgia, malaise or sweating. Only myalgia, fever and chills were reported as severe in more than 5% of the patients. The incidence rate for flu-like symptom complex was also calculated over the course of 3 years. The incidence rate of these events decreased over time, with 60% of patients experiencing the event during the first 3 months of treatment compared to 10% during the last 6 months. The median time to the first occurrence of flu-like symptom complex was 3.5 days and the median duration per patient was 7.5 days per year.

Laboratory abnormalities included: lymphocyte count <1 500/mm³ (82%), ALT >5 times baseline value (19%), absolute neutrophil count <1 500/mm³ (18%) (no patients had absolute neutrophil counts <500/mm³), WBC <3 000/mm³ (16%), and total bilirubin >2.5 times baseline value (6%).

Three patients were withdrawn from treatment with 0.25 mg (8 MIU) interferon beta-1b for abnormal liver enzymes including one following dose reduction (see Precautions, Laboratory Tests).

Twenty-one (28%) of the 76 females of childbearing age treated at 0.25 mg (8 MIU) interferon beta-1b and 10 (13%) of the 76 females of childbearing age treated with placebo reported menstrual disorders. All reports were of mild to moderate severity and included: intermenstrual bleeding and spotting, early or delayed menses, decreased days of menstrual flow, and clotting and spotting during menstruation.

Mental disorders such as depression, anxiety, emotional lability, depersonalization, suicide attempts and confusion were observed in this study. Two patients withdrew for confusion. One suicide and 4 attempted suicides were also reported. It is not known whether these symptoms may be related to the underlying neurological basis of MS, to interferon beta-1b treatment, or to a combination of both. Some similar symptoms have been noted in patients receiving interferon alpha and both interferons are thought to act through the same receptor. Patients who experience these symptoms should be monitored closely and cessation of therapy should be considered.

Additional common clinical adverse events and laboratory abnormalities associated with the use of interferon beta-1b are listed in the following paragraphs. These events occurred at an incidence of 5% or more in the 124 MS patients treated with 0.25 mg (8 MIU) of interferon beta-1b every other day for periods of up to 3 years in the controlled trial, and at an incidence that was at least twice that observed in the 123 placebo patients. Common clinical adverse events and laboratory abnormalities associated with the use of interferon beta-1b were: injection site reaction (85%), lymphocyte count <1 500/mm³ (82%), ALT >5 times baseline value (19%), absolute neutrophil count <1 500/mm³ (18%), menstrual disorder (17%), WBC <3 000/mm³ (16%), palpitation (8%), dyspnea (8%), cystitis (8%), hypertension (7%), breast pain (7%), tachycardia (6%), gastrointestinal disorders (6%), total bilirubin >2.5 times baseline value (6%), somnolence (6%), laryngitis (6%), pelvic pain (6%), menorrhagia (6%), injection site necrosis (5%) and peripheral vascular disorders (5%).

A total of 277 MS patients have been treated with interferon beta-1b in doses ranging from 0.025 mg (0.8 MIU) to 0.5 mg (16 MIU). During the first 3 years of treatment, withdrawals due to clinical adverse events or laboratory abnormalities not mentioned above included: fatigue (2%, 6 patients), cardiac arrhythmia (<1%, 1 patient), allergic urticarial skin reaction to injections (<1%, 1 patient), headache (<1%, 1 patient), unspecified adverse events (<1%, 1 patient) and "felt sick" (<1%, 1 patient).

Table II that follows enumerates adverse events and laboratory abnormalities that occurred at an incidence of 2% or more among the 124 MS patients treated with 0.25 mg (8 MIU) interferon beta-1b every other day for periods of up to 3 years in the controlled trial and at an incidence that was at least 2% more than that observed in the 123 placebo patients. Reported adverse events have been re-classified using the standard COSTART glossary to reduce the total number of terms employed in the table. In Table II, terms so general as to be uninformative, and those events where a drug cause was remote have been excluded.

It should be noted that the figures cited in Table II cannot be used to predict the incidence of side effects in the course of usual medical practice where patient characteristics and other factors differ from those that prevailed in the clinical trials. The cited figures do provide the prescribing physician with some basis for estimating the relative contribution of drug and nondrug factors to the side effect incidence rate in the population studied.

Other events observed during premarketing evaluation of various doses of interferon beta-1b in 1 440 patients are listed in the paragraphs that follow. Given that most of the events were observed in open and uncontrolled studies, the role of

Table II—Betaseron

Adverse Events and Laboratory Abnormalities

Adverse Event	Placebo n=123	0.25 mg (8 MIU) n=124
Body as a Whole		
Injection site reaction*	37%	85%
Headache	77%	84%
Fever*	41%	59%
Flu-like symptom complex*	56%	76%
Pain	48%	52%
Asthenia*	35%	49%
Chills*	19%	46%
Abdominal pain	24%	32%
Malaise*	3%	15%
Generalized edema	6%	8%
Pelvic pain	3%	6%
Injection site necrosis*	0%	5%
Cyst	2%	4%
Necrosis	0%	2%
Suicide attempt	0%	2%
Cardiovascular System		
Migraine	7%	12%
Palpitation*	2%	8%
Hypertension	2%	7%
Tachycardia	3%	6%
Peripheral vascular disorder	2%	5%
Hemorrhage	1%	3%
Digestive System		
Diarrhea	29%	35%
Constipation	18%	24%
Vomiting	19%	21%
Gastrointestinal disorder	3%	6%
Endocrine System		
Goiter	0%	2%
Hemic and Lymphatic System		
Lymphocytes <1 500/mm³	67%	82%
ANC <1 500/mm³*	6%	18%
WBC <3 000/mm³*	5%	16%
Lymphadenopathy	11%	14%
Metabolic and Nutritional Disorders		
ALT >5 times baseline*	6%	19%
Glucose <55 mg/dL	13%	15%
Total bilirubin >2.5 times baseline	2%	6%
Urine protein >1+	3%	5%
AST >5 times baseline*	0%	4%
Weight gain	0%	4%
Weight loss	2%	4%
Musculoskeletal System		
Myalgia*	28%	44%
Myasthenia	10%	13%
Nervous System		
Dizziness	28%	35%
Hypertonia	24%	26%
Depression	24%	25%
Anxiety	13%	15%
Nervousness	5%	8%
Somnolence	3%	6%
Confusion	2%	4%
Speech disorder	1%	3%
Convulsion	0%	2%
Hyperkinesia	0%	2%
Amnesia	0%	2%
Respiratory System		
Sinusitis	26%	36%
Dyspnea*	2%	8%
Laryngitis	2%	6%
Skin and Appendages		
Sweating*	11%	23%
Alopecia	2%	4%
Special Senses		
Conjunctivitis	10%	12%
Abnormal vision	4%	7%
Urogenital System		
Dysmenorrhea	11%	18%
Menstrual disorder*	8%	17%
Metrorrhagia	8%	15%
Cystitis	4%	8%
Breast pain	3%	7%
Menorrhagia	3%	6%
Urinary urgency	2%	3%
Fibrocystic breast	1%	3%
Breast neoplasm	0%	2%

*Significantly associated with interferon beta-1b treatment.

Betaseron (cont'd)

interferon beta-1b in their causation cannot be reliably determined.

Body as a Whole: abscess, adenoma, anaphylactoid reaction, ascites, cellulitis, hernia, hydrocephalus, hypothermia, infection, peritonitis, photosensitivity, sarcoma, sepsis and shock.

Cardiovascular: angina pectoris, arrhythmia, atrial fibrillation, cardiomegaly, cardiac arrest, cerebral hemorrhage, cerebral ischemia, endocarditis, heart failure, hypotension, myocardial infarct, pericardial effusion, postural hypotension, pulmonary embolus, spider angioma, subarachnoid hemorrhage, syncope, thrombophlebitis, thrombosis, varicose vein, vasospasm, venous pressure increased, ventricular extrasystoles and ventricular fibrillation.

Digestive: aphthous stomatitis, cardiospasm, cheilitis, cholecystitis, cholelithiasis, duodenal ulcer, dry mouth, enteritis, esophagitis, fecal impaction, fecal incontinence, flatulence, gastritis, gastrointestinal hemorrhage, gingivitis, glossitis, hematemesis, hepatic neoplasia, hepatitis, hepatomegaly, ileus, increased salivation, intestinal obstruction, melena, nausea, oral leukoplakia, oral moniliasis, pancreatitis, periodontal abscess, proctitis, rectal hemorrhage, salivary gland enlargement, stomach ulcer and tenesmus.

Endocrine: Cushing's Syndrome, diabetes insipidus, diabetes mellitus, hypothyroidism and inappropriate ADH.

Hemic and Lymphatic: chronic lymphocytic leukemia, hemoglobin less than 9.4 g/100 mL, petechia, platelets less than 75 000/mm^3 and splenomegaly.

Metabolic and Nutritional Disorders: alcohol intolerance, alkaline phosphatase greater than 5 times baseline value, BUN greater than 40 mg/dL, calcium greater than 11.5 mg/dL, cyanosis, edema, glucose greater than 160 mg/dL, glycosuria, hypoglycemic reaction, hypoxia, ketosis and thirst.

Musculoskeletal: arthritis, arthrosis, bursitis, leg cramps, muscle atrophy, myopathy, myositis, ptosis and tenosynovitis.

Nervous System: abnormal gait, acute brain syndrome, agitation, apathy, aphasia, ataxia, brain edema, chronic brain syndrome, coma, delirium, delusions, dementia, depersonalization, diplopia, dystonia, encephalopathy, euphoria, facial paralysis, foot drop, hallucinations, hemiplegia, hypalgesia, hyperesthesia, incoordination, intracranial hypertension, libido decreased, manic reaction, meningitis, neuralgia, neuropathy, neurosis, nystagmus, oculogyric crisis, ophthalmoplegia, papilledema, paralysis, paranoid reaction, psychosis, reflexes decreased, stupor, subdural hematoma, torticollis, tremor and urinary retention.

Respiratory: apnea, asthma, atelectasis, carcinoma of the lung, hemoptysis, hiccup, hyperventilation, hypoventilation, interstitial pneumonia, lung edema, pleural effusion, pneumonia and pneumothorax.

Skin and Appendages: contact dermatitis, erythema nodosum, exfoliative dermatitis, furunculosis, hirsutism, leukoderma, lichenoid dermatitis, maculopapular rash, psoriasis, seborrhea, skin benign neoplasm, skin carcinoma, skin hypertrophy, skin necrosis, skin ulcer, urticaria and vesiculobullous rash.

Special Senses: blepharitis, blindness, deafness, dry eyes, ear pain, iritis, keratoconjunctivitis, mydriasis, otitis externa, otitis media, parosmia, photophobia, retinitis, taste loss, taste perversion and visual field defect.

Urogenital: anuria, balanitis, breast engorgement, cervicitis, epididymitis, gynecomastia, hematuria, impotence, kidney calculus, kidney failure, kidney tubular disorder, leukorrhea, nephritis, nocturia, oliguria, polyuria, salpingitis, urethritis, urinary incontinence, uterine fibroids enlarged, uterine neoplasm and vaginal hemorrhage.

Dosage: For s.c. use only. The recommended dose for the treatment of ambulatory relapsing-remitting MS is 0.25 mg (8 MIU) injected s.c. every other day. Limited data regarding the activity of a lower dose are presented above (see Pharmacology, Clinical Trials).

Evidence of efficacy beyond 2 years is not known since the primary evidence of efficacy derives from a 2-year, double-blind, placebo-controlled clinical trial (see Pharmacology, Clinical Trials). Safety data are not available beyond the third year. Some patients were discontinued from this trial due to unremitting disease progression of 6 months or greater.

To reconstitute lyophilized interferon beta-1b for injection, use a sterile syringe and needle to inject 1.2 mL of the diluent supplied, Sodium Chloride, 0.54% Solution, into the vial. Gently swirl the vial of interferon beta-1b to dissolve the drug completely; do not shake. Inspect the reconstituted product visually and discard the product before use if it contains particulate matter or is discolored. After reconstitution with accompanying diluent, each mL of solution contains 0.25 mg (8 MIU) interferon beta-1b, 13 mg albumin human USP and 13 mg dextrose USP.

Withdraw 1 mL of reconstituted solution from the vial into a sterile syringe fitted with a 27-gauge needle and inject the solution s.c. Sites for self-injection include abdomen, buttocks and thighs. A vial is suitable for single use only; unused portions should be discarded 3 hours after reconstitution (see Information for the Patient).

Information for the Patient: See Blue Section—Information for the Patient "Betaseron".

Supplied: Betaseron is a purified, sterile, lyophilized protein product produced by recombinant DNA techniques and formulated for use by injection. Interferon beta-1b is manufactured by bacterial fermentation of a strain of E. coli that bears a genetically engineered plasmid containing the gene for human interferon beta$_{ser17}$. The native gene was obtained from human fibroblasts and altered in a way that substitutes serine for the cysteine residue found at position 17. Interferon beta-1b is a highly purified protein that has 165 amino acids and an approximate molecular weight of 18 500 daltons. It does not include the carbohydrate side chains found in the natural material.

The specific activity of Betaseron is approximately 32 million international units (IU)/mg interferon beta-1b. Each vial contains 0.3 mg (9.6 MIU) of interferon beta-1b. The unit measurement is derived by comparing the antiviral activity of the product to the World Health Organization (WHO) reference standard of recombinant human interferon beta. Dextrose and albumin human, USP (15 mg each/vial) are added as stabilizers. Prior to 1993, a different analytical standard was used to determine potency. It assigned 54 million IU to 0.3 mg interferon beta-1b.

Each 3 mL single-use vial of lyophilized powder contains: interferon beta-1b 0.3 mg (9.6 MIU). Nonmedicinal ingredients: albumin human USP and Dextrose USP as stabilizers. Preservative-free. Cartons of 15 vials of medication and 15 vials of diluent (2 mL of Sodium Chloride, 0.54% Solution/vial). If refrigeration is not possible, vials of Betaseron and diluent should be kept as cool as possible, below 30°C, away from heat and light, and **used within 7 days.** If not used immediately following reconstitution store under refrigeration at 2 to 8°C **and use within 3 hours.** Avoid freezing.

(Shown in Product Recognition Section)

Reviewed 1997

BETAXIN®
Sanofi

Thiamine HCl
Vitamin

Supplied: Each 10 mL multiple dose vial contains: thiamine HCl 1 000 mg. Nonmedicinal ingredients: chlorobutanol, distilled water for injection and mono-thioglycerol. Gluten-, lactose-, sulfite- and tartrazine-free.

BETNESOL® Preparations ℞
Roberts

Betamethasone Sodium Phosphate
Corticosteroid

Indications: Enema: For local use as a retention enema in ulcerative colitis.

Eye and Ear Drops: Inflammatory eye conditions (anterior segment) and inflammatory ear conditions, e.g., otitis externa.

Tablets: Acute asthma, intractable hay fever, severe eczema, other inflammatory skin diseases; rheumatoid arthritis, nephrotic syndrome, severe ulcerative colitis, collagen diseases.

Contraindications: Systemic infections, live virus immunization, hypersensitivity.

Precautions: In patients on corticosteroid therapy subjected to unusual stress, increased dosage of rapidly acting corticosteroids before, during and after the stressful situation is indicated. Corticosteroid treatment may reduce the response of the pituitary-adrenal axis to stress and relative insufficiency may persist for up to 1 year after withdrawal or prolonged therapy.

While on corticosteroid therapy patients should not be vaccinated against smallpox because of potential complications. Conversely, patients with vaccinia should not receive corticosteroid therapy. Other immunization procedures should not be undertaken in patients who are on corticosteroids, especially on high doses, because of possible hazards of neurological complications and a lack of antibody response. Patients without a definite history of chickenpox should be advised to avoid close contact with chickenpox or herpes zoster. If exposed to chickenpox or herpes zoster, patients should seek urgent medical attention. If the patient is a child, then the parents must be aware that exposure to chickenpox must be avoided. Passive immunization with varicella/zoster immunoglobulin (VZIG) is needed by exposed nonimmune patients who are receiving systemic corticosteroids or who have used them within the previous 3 months. VZIG should be given not later than 10 days from exposure to chickenpox. If a diagnosis of chickenpox is confirmed, the illness warrants specialist care and urgent treatment. A diagnosis of chickenpox should be considered in any patient receiving corticosteroids who presents with a fever or systemic illness. Corticosteroids should not be stopped and a dose increase may be necessary.

Pregnancy and *Lactation:* Since adequate human reproduction studies have not been done with corticosteroids, the use of these drugs in pregnancy, nursing mothers or women of childbearing potential requires that the possible benefits of the drug be weighed against the potential hazards to the mother and embryo or fetus. Infants born of mothers who have received substantial doses of corticosteroids during pregnancy should be carefully observed for signs of hypoadrenalism.

The use of corticosteroids in active tuberculosis should be restricted to those cases of fulminating or disseminated tuberculosis in which the corticosteroid is used for the management of the disease in conjunction with an appropriate antituberculous regimen. If corticosteroids are indicated in patients with latent tuberculosis or tuberculin reactivity, close observation is necessary as reactivation of the disease may occur. During prolonged corticosteroid therapy, these patients should receive chemoprophylaxis.

Corticosteroids may mask some signs of infection and new infections may appear during their use. There may be impaired resistance to and inability to localize infection when corticosteroids are used. If corticosteroids have to be used in the presence of bacterial infections, institute appropriate vigorous anti-infective therapy.

Use corticosteroids cautiously in patients with ocular herpes simplex because of possible corneal ulceration and perforation. Corticosteroids may worsen diabetes mellitus, osteoporosis, hypertension, glaucoma and epilepsy.

Prolonged use of corticosteroids may produce posterior subcapsular cataracts, glaucoma with possible damage to the optic nerves, and may enhance the establishment of secondary ocular infections due to fungi or viruses.

Corticosteroid therapy may cause hyperacidity or peptic ulcer. Since appearance of peptic ulcer may be asymptomatic until perforation or hemorrhage occurs, take x-rays when treatment is prolonged or when there is gastric distress. An ulcer regimen including an antacid should be considered as a prophylactic measure during prolonged therapy.

Use the lowest possible dose of corticosteroid to control the condition under treatment, and when dosage reduction is possible, the reduction should be gradual.

Average and large doses of hydrocortisone or cortisone can cause elevation of blood pressure, salt, and water retention, and increased potassium excretion. These effects are less likely to occur with the synthetic derivatives except when used in large doses. Because of the possibility of fluid retention, care must be taken when corticosteroids are administered to patients with congestive heart failure. Dietary salt restriction and potassium supplementation may be necessary. All corticosteroids increase calcium excretion.

Drug induced secondary adrenocortical insufficiency may be minimized by gradual dosage reduction. This type of relative insufficiency may persist for months after discontinuation of therapy, therefore, in any stress situation occurring during that period, reinstitute hormone therapy. If the patient is receiving steroids already, the dosage may have to be increased. Since mineralocorticoid secretion may be impaired, salt and/or a mineralocorticoid should be administered concurrently.

Use ASA cautiously in conjunction with corticosteroids in hypoprothrombinemia.

Use steroids with caution in nonspecific ulcerative colitis if there is a probability of impending perforation, abscess or other pyogenic infection; diverticulitis, fresh intestinal anastomoses; active or latent peptic ulcer; renal insufficiency; hypertension; osteoporosis; and myasthenia gravis. Fat embolism has been reported as a possible complication of hypercorticonism.

There is an enhanced effect of corticosteroids on patients with hypothyroidism and in those with cirrhosis.

Psychic derangements may appear when corticosteroids are used, ranging from euphoria, insomnia, mood swings, personality changes, and severe depression, to frank psychotic manifestations. Also, existing emotional instability or psychotic tendencies may be aggravated by corticosteroids.

Growth and development of infants and children on prolonged corticosteroid therapy should be carefully observed.

Steroids may increase or decrease motility and number of spermatozoa in some patients.

Phenytoin may enhance the rate of metabolism and clearance of corticosteroids and this may increase steroid dosage requirements.

Advise patients to inform subsequent physicians of the prior use of corticosteroids.

Corticosteroids may suppress reactions to skin tests.

Enema: There is some systemic absorption of the steroid, which can be a therapeutic advantage, as combined systemic and local therapy has been beneficial, certainly in some cases. However, adrenal function can be affected; thus it is necessary to take such precautions as apply during and after systemic therapy.

Eye and Ear Preparations: Use with care in cases of perforated ear drum or in long standing cases of chronic otitis media because of possibility of ototoxicity. In diseases due to microorganisms, infection may be masked, enhanced or activated by the steroid. Extended use of topical corticosteroids may cause increased intraocular pressure in susceptible individuals. It is advisable that the intraocular pressure be checked frequently. In those diseases causing thinning of the cornea, perforation has been known to have occurred with the use of topical steroids. If infections which are present before use do not respond promptly, the preparation should be discontinued until the infection has been adequately controlled by other measures. If new infections due to bacteria or fungi appear during therapy, appropriate measures should be taken. If sensitivity or irritation develops, discontinue use.

Adverse Effects: Fluid and electrolyte disturbances: sodium retention; fluid retention; congestive heart failure in susceptible patients; potassium loss; hypokalemic alkalosis; hypertension. Musculoskeletal: muscle weakness; steroid myopathy; loss of muscle mass; osteoporosis; vertebral compression fractures; aseptic necrosis of femoral and humeral heads; pathologic fracture of long bones.

Gastrointestinal: peptic ulcer and possible subsequent perforation and hemorrhage; pancreatitis; abdominal distention; ulcerative esophagitis.

Dermatologic: impaired wound healing; thin fragile skin; petechiae and ecchymoses; erythema; increased sweating; may suppress reactions to skin tests.

Neurological: convulsions; increased intracranial pressure with papilledema (pseudotumor cerebri) usually after treatment; vertigo; headache.

Endocrine: menstrual irregularities, development of Cushingoid state; suppression of growth in children; secondary adrenocortical and pituitary unresponsiveness, particularly in times of stress, as in trauma, surgery or illness; decreased carbohydrate tolerance; manifestations of latent diabetes mellitus; increased requirements for insulin or oral hypoglycemic agents in diabetes.

Ophthalmic: posterior subcapsular cataracts; increased intraocular pressure; glaucoma; exophthalmos.

Metabolic: negative nitrogen balance due to protein catabolism.

Other: hypersensitivity, thromboembolism.

Dosage: Enema: Normally, 1 enema is used nightly, for 2 to 4 weeks. More prolonged treatment is permissible in patients showing progressive improvement. If the response is inadequate, it is undesirable to persist with medical treatment to a point where surgical measures are unduly delayed.

Drops: 1 or 2 drops into eye every 1 or 2 hours; or 2 or 3 drops into ear every 2 or 3 hours: in both cases until control is achieved, then frequency can be reduced.

Tablets: Depending upon the condition, 0.25 to 1 mg may be given 3 or 4 times daily.

Supplied: Enema: Each disposable plastic bag of 100 mL contains: betamethasone 5 mg (as betamethasone sodium phosphate) in buffered solution. Sodium: <1 mmol (0.31 mg)/mL. Tartrazine-free. Boxes of 7×100 mL.

Eye and Ear Drops: Each mL of sterile, isotonic, buffered solution contains: betamethasone 0.1% (as betamethasone sodium phosphate). Plastic dropper bottles of 5 mL.

Tablets: Each scored, soluble, effervescent tablet contains: betamethasone 0.5 mg (as betamethasone sodium phosphate). Tablets dissolve rapidly in water to form a tinted solution for oral administration. Sodium: <1 mmol (20.8 mg). Tartrazine-free. Bottles of 100.

(Shown in Product Recognition Section)

Reviewed 1999

BETNOVATE® Preparations

Roberts

Betamethasone-17-Valerate

Topical Corticosteroid

Supplied: Full-Strength Lotion: Each mL contains: betamethasone 0.1% (as betamethasone 17-valerate) in an aqueous lotion vehicle. Also contains parabens. Plastic squeeze bottles of 60 mL.

Half-Strength Ointment: Each g contains: betamethasone 0.05% (as betamethasone 17-valerate). Cartoned tubes of 15 g.

BETOPTIC® S

Alcon

Betaxolol HCl

Antiglaucoma Agent

Pharmacology: Betaxolol is a cardioselective (beta-1-adrenergic) receptor blocking agent. It does not have significant membrane-stabilizing (local anesthetic) activity and is devoid of intrinsic sympathomimetic action.

Ocular: When instilled in the eye, betaxolol reduces elevated as well as normal intraocular pressure, whether or not accompanied by glaucoma. When used as a solution, the onset of action occurs within 30 minutes and the maximal effect is usually attained approximately 2 hours after instillation. Although the time of onset of action, and time of maximal effect for the suspension have not been determined, controlled double masked studies show that the magnitude and duration of the ocular hypotensive effect of betaxolol 0.5% solution and betaxolol 0.25% suspension were clinically equivalent.

A single dose provides a 12-hour reduction in intraocular pressure (IOP) and twice daily administration maintains the IOP below 22 mm Hg in most patients.

Betaxolol has no effect on pupil size or accommodation.

Systemic: Ophthalmic betaxolol is virtually devoid of systemic effects. Following oral administration, the elimination half-life of betaxolol is 14 to 22 hours, and it is metabolized mainly to inactive substances which are excreted in the urine. Although betaxolol is absorbed systemically, ophthalmic doses do not ordinarily produce pharmacologically active tissue levels and thus, despite its cardioselective beta blocking activity, it has minimal, if any, effect on heart rate or blood pressure.

Betaxolol has a low affinity for β_2-adrenergic receptors, and ophthalmic doses have no significant effect on pulmonary function as measured by forced expiratory volume in one second (FEV_1), forced vital capacity (FVC) and FEV_1/FVC. Ophthalmic doses do not inhibit the effect of isoproterenol, a beta-adrenergic stimulant, on pulmonary function. Therefore, ophthalmic betaxolol may be used in the treatment of patients with glaucoma or ocular hypertension who have coexisting reactive airway disease.

Indications: For lowering intraocular pressure in the treatment of ocular hypertension or chronic open angle glaucoma. May be used alone or in combination with other IOP-lowering medication.

Contraindications: Hypersensitivity to any component of this product.

Although ophthalmic betaxolol has minimal systemic effects, as with all beta-adrenergic blocking agents, it should not be used in patients with sinus bradycardia, atrioventricular block greater than first degree, cardiogenic shock, or patients with overt cardiac failure.

Precautions: General: Patients who are receiving a beta adrenergic blocking agent orally and ophthalmic betaxolol should be observed for a potential additive effect either on the intraocular pressure or on the known systemic effects of beta blockade.

Although ophthalmic betaxolol has demonstrated a low potential for systemic effects, it should be used with caution in patients with bradycardia, and those with diabetes (especially labile diabetes) because of possible masking of hypoglycemia. Consideration should be given to the gradual withdrawal of all beta-adrenergic blocking agents in patients suspected of developing thyrotoxicosis, and also prior to general anesthesia, because of the reduced ability of the heart to respond to beta-adrenergically mediated sympathetic reflex stimuli (see Drug Interactions).

Betaxolol, a cardioselective beta-blocker, has produced only minimal effects in patients with reactive airway disease; however, caution should be exercised in the treatment of patients with excessive restriction of pulmonary function.

In patients with angle-closure glaucoma, the immediate treatment objective is to reopen the angle by constriction of the pupil with a miotic agent. Betaxolol has no effect on the pupil; therefore, ophthalmic betaxolol should be used with a miotic to reduce elevated intraocular pressure in angle-closure glaucoma.

As with the use of other antiglaucoma drugs, diminished responsiveness to ophthalmic betaxolol after prolonged therapy has been reported in some patients. However, in one long-term study in which 250 patients treated with betaxolol ophthalmic solution have been followed for up to 3 years, no significant difference in mean intraocular pressure has been observed after initial stabilization.

Drug Interactions: Although ophthalmic betaxolol used alone has little or no effect on pupil size, mydriasis resulting from concomitant therapy with epinephrine has been reported occasionally.

Close observation of the patient is recommended when a beta-blocker is administered to patients receiving oral beta-adrenergic blocking drugs, or catecholamine-depleting drugs such as reserpine, because of possible additive effects. Caution should be exercised in patients using concomitant adrenergic psychotropic drugs.

Pregnancy: There have been no adequate and well-controlled studies in pregnant women. Because animal reproduction studies are not always predictive of human response, this drug should be used during pregnancy only if clearly indicated.

Lactation: It is not known whether betaxolol is excreted in human milk. Because many drugs are excreted in human milk, caution should be exercised when ophthalmic betaxolol is administered to nursing women.

Children: Clinical studies to establish the safety and efficacy in children have not been performed.

Adverse Effects: The following adverse reactions have been reported in clinical trials of up to 3 years of patient experience with betaxolol ophthalmic preparations.

Ocular: Betaxolol has been well tolerated. Discomfort of short duration may be experienced by some patients upon instillation and occasional tearing has been reported. Instances of decreased corneal sensitivity, erythema, itching sensation, corneal punctate staining, keratitis, anisocoria and photophobia have been reported. Based on comparative studies, there is an increased incidence of blurred vision upon instillation of Betoptic S compared with Betoptic.

Systemic: Systemic reactions following topical administration of betaxolol have been reported rarely (e.g., CNS: insomnia and depressive neurosis).

Overdose: Symptoms: No data are available on overdosage of humans. However, anticipated symptoms include symptomatic bradycardia, hypotension, bronchospasm, acute cardiac failure and heart block (second or third degree).

A 10 mL container of 0.5% betaxolol ophthalmic solution would contain 50 mg of betaxolol. Betaxolol at 40 mg twice daily is reported to be an effective and safe systemic dosage for hypertension. Thus, an individual would ingest an amount of betaxolol from one container which is less than the maximum daily oral dose of betaxolol.

Since the oral LD_{50} in animals ranged from 350 to 1 050 mg/kg, a 10 kg child would only receive 5 mg/kg if the child ingested 10 mL of 0.5 % betaxolol ophthalmic solution. An acute toxic response is thus extremely remote.

Treatment: Should an overdosage occur, the following is suggested:

Ocular: Flush eye with lukewarm tap water.

Systemic: Gastric lavage.

Symptomatic bradycardia: Use atropine sulfate i.v. in a dosage of 0.25 mg to 2 mg to induce vagal blockage. If bradycardia persists, i.v. isoproterenol HCl should be administered cautiously. In refractory cases the use of a transvenous cardiac pacemaker may be considered.

Hypotension: Use sympathomimetic pressor drug therapy, such as dopamine, dobutamine or levarterenol. In refractory

Betoptic S (cont'd)

cases, the use of glucagon HCL has been reported to be useful.
Bronchospasm: Use isoproterenol HCl. Additional therapy with aminophylline may be considered.
Acute cardiac failure: Conventional therapy with digitalis, diuretics, and oxygen should be instituted immediately. In refractory cases the use of i.v. aminophylline is suggested. This may be followed if necessary by glucagon HCl which has been reported to be useful.
Heart block (second or third degree): use isoproterenol HCl or a transvenous cardiac pacemaker.

Dosage: The usual dose is 1 drop of betaxolol ophthalmic suspension in the affected eye(s) twice daily. In some patients, the intraocular pressure lowering response may require a few weeks to stabilize. Clinical follow-up should include a determination of the intraocular pressure during the first month of treatment. Thereafter, intraocular pressures should be determined on an individual basis at the judgment of the physician.

When a patient is transferred from a single antiglaucoma agent, continue the agent already used and add 1 drop of betaxolol in the affected eye(s) twice a day. On the following day, discontinue the previous antiglaucoma agent completely and continue with betaxolol ophthalmic solution or suspension.

Because of diurnal variations of intraocular pressure in individual patients, satisfactory response to twice a day therapy is best determined by measuring intraocular pressure at different times during the day. Intraocular pressure of less than 22 mm Hg may not be optimal for control of glaucoma in each patient; therefore, therapy should be individualized.

If the intraocular pressure of the patient is not adequately controlled on this regimen, concomitant therapy with pilocarpine, other miotics, epinephrine or systemically administered carbonic anhydrase inhibitors can be instituted.

When a patient is transferred from several concomitantly administered antiglaucoma agents, individualization is required. Adjustment should involve one agent at a time made at intervals of not less than 1 week. A recommended approach is to continue the agents being used and add 1 drop of betaxolol ophthalmic suspension in the affected eye(s) twice a day. On the following day, discontinue one of the other antiglaucoma agents. The remaining antiglaucoma agents may be decreased or discontinued according to the patient's response to treatment. The physician may be able to discontinue some or all of the other antiglaucoma agents.
Special Instructions: Patients should be instructed to avoid contamination of the dropper tip.

The Betoptic S suspension must be well shaken before use.

Supplied: Each mL of sterile, isotonic, aqueous suspension contains: betaxolol 0.25% (0.28% betaxolol HCl) with benzalkonium chloride (as preservative), mannitol, poly (styrene-divinyl benzene) sulfonic acid, carbomer 934P, edetate disodium, hydrochloric acid and/or sodium hydroxide (to adjust pH) and purified water. Drop-Tainer dispensers of 5 and 10 mL. Store at room temperature.

BEZALIP® Ⓟ

Roche

Bezafibrate

Lipid Metabolism Regulator

Pharmacology: The fibrates, including bezafibrate, lower elevated serum lipids by decreasing the low density lipoprotein (LDL) fraction rich in cholesterol and the very low density lipoprotein (VLDL) fraction rich in triglycerides. In addition, fibrates (including bezafibrate) increase the high density lipoprotein (HDL) cholesterol fraction.

Due to their major action on lipoprotein and hepatic triglyceride lipase, the fibrates appear to produce a greater reduction on the VLDL than on the LDL fraction. Therapeutic doses of bezafibrate produce variable elevations of HDL cholesterol, a reduction in the content of LDL cholesterol, and a substantial reduction in the triglyceride content of the VLDL fraction. Changes by bezafibrate in the lipid components (VLDL-triglycerides, VLDL-cholesterol, LDL-cholesterol, HDL-cholesterol) are usually paralleled by changes in the corresponding apolipoproteins: apolipoprotein B is reduced, while apolipoprotein A1 and A2 may be increased.

The mechanisms of action of the fibrates have not been definitely established. Work carried out to date, including the information derived from animal studies, suggests that the major modes of action of the fibrates likely encompass the following: VLDL catabolism by increased lipoprotein and hepatic triglyceride lipase activities; attenuation of triglyceride biosynthesis by acetyl-CoA carboxylase enzyme inhibition; attenuation of cholesterol biosynthesis by inhibition of the rate-limiting 3-hydroxy-3-methylglutaryl-coenzyme A reductase (HMG-CoA reductase).

Bezafibrate is rapidly and almost completely absorbed from the standard 200 mg immediate release. The relative bioavailability of bezafibrate 400 mg sustained-release tablet compared to the standard 200 mg form is about 70%. A peak plasma concentration of about 8 mg/L is reached after 1 to 2 hours following a single 200 mg dose in healthy volunteers. With the 400 mg sustained-release tablet, a peak concentration of about 6 mg/L is reached after 3 to 4 hours. In human serum, 94 to 96% of bezafibrate is bound to protein. The apparent volume of distribution is about 17 L. The elimination is rapid, with excretion almost exclusively renal. Within 48 hours, 95% of the activity of the ^{14}C-labeled drug is recovered in the urine and 3% in the feces. Fifty percent of the applied dose is recovered in the urine as unchanged drug and 20% in the form of glucuronides. The rate of renal clearance ranges from 3.4 to 6 L/hour. The elimination half-life of bezafibrate is 1 to 2 hours.

In patients with severe renal failure, important accumulation of fibrates are observed with large increases in the half-life. Therefore, the dose of bezafibrate may need to be reduced in such instances, depending on the rate of creatinine clearance (see Dosage).

Indications: As an adjunct to diet and other therapeutic measures for: treatment of patients with hypercholesterolemia Type IIa and IIb mixed hyperlipidemia, to regulate lipid and apoprotein levels (reduce serum TG, LDL cholesterol and apolipoprotein B, increase HDL cholesterol and apolipoprotein A); treatment of adult patients with high to very high triglyceride levels, Fredrickson classification Type IV and V hyperlipidemias, who are at a high risk of sequelae and complications (i.e., pancreatitis) from their dyslipidemia.

Bezafibrate may not be adequate therapy in some patients with familial combined hyperlipidemia with type IIb and type IV hyperlipoproteinemia.

Initial therapy for dyslipidemia should include at least an equivalent of the American Heart Association (AHA) step 1 diet.

Contraindications: Hepatic or renal dysfunction, including primary biliary cirrhosis. Pre-existing gallbladder disease (see Precautions). Hypersensitivity to fibrates. Pregnancy or lactation.

Bezafibrate is not indicated for the treatment of Type I hyperlipoproteinemia.

Warnings: Drug Interactions: Concomitant Anticoagulants: Caution should be exercised when oral anticoagulants are given with bezafibrate. The dosage of anticoagulants should be reduced up to 50% to maintain the prothrombin time at the desired level to prevent bleeding complications. Careful frequent (perhaps weekly) monitoring of prothrombin time is therefore recommended until it has been definitely determined that the prothrombin level has been stabilized.
Statins and Cyclosporine: Severe myositis and rhabdomyolysis have occurred when a statin or cyclosporine were administered with a fibrate. Therefore, the benefits and risks of using bezafibrate concomitantly with statins or cyclosporine should be carefully considered.

MAO inhibitors (with hepatotoxic potential) must not be administered together with bezafibrate.
Children: Limited experience is available in children at a dose of 10 to 20 mg/kg/day. Therefore, in the absence of adequate information concerning the long-term safety, bezafibrate should be used with caution in treating children.
Pregnancy: Strict birth control procedures must be exercised by women of childbearing potential. If pregnancy occurs despite birth control procedures, bezafibrate should be discontinued. Women planning a pregnancy should discontinue bezafibrate several months prior to conception.
Lactation: In the absence of data concerning the presence of bezafibrate in human breast milk, it should not be used by nursing mothers.
Cholelithiasis: Bezafibrate may increase cholesterol excretion into the bile, and may lead to cholelithiasis. If such is suspected, gallbladder studies are indicated. Bezafibrate therapy should be discontinued if gallstones are found.

Bezafibrate clinically, pharmacologically and chemically shows similarities with clofibrate. Physicians prescribing bezafibrate should also be familiar with the risks and benefits of clofibrate.

In long-term animal toxicity and carcinogenicity studies, bezafibrate has been shown to be hepatotoxic and possibly tumorigenic for the liver of rats. A drug-related dose-dependent increase in Leydig cell tumors was also observed in male rats. Administration of lipid-lowering agents of the fibrate class may cause peroxisome proliferation in animals. The phenomenon is species related and is more pronounced in small rodents.

Since a reduction of mortality from coronary artery disease and total mortality have not been established, bezafibrate should be administered only to those patients described in Indications. If a significant serum lipid response is not obtained in 3 months, bezafibrate should be discontinued. If bezafibrate is chosen for treatment, the prescribing physician should discuss the proposed therapy and inform the patient of the expected benefits and potential risks associated with long-term administration (see Precautions).

Precautions: Initial Therapy: Before instituting bezafibrate therapy, attempts should be made to control serum lipids with appropriate diet, exercise and weight loss in obese patients, as well as other medical problems, such as diabetes mellitus and hypothyroidism. In patients at high risk, consideration should be given to the control of other risk factors such as smoking, excessive alcohol intake, hormonal contraceptive use, and inadequately controlled hypertension.
Long-term Therapy: Since long-term administration of bezafibrate is recommended, the potential risks and benefits should be carefully weighed. Adequate pretreatment laboratory studies should be performed to ensure patients have elevated serum cholesterol and/or triglycerides with or without low HDL levels. Periodic determinations of serum lipids, fasting glucose, creatinine, ALT, CGT and CPK should be considered during bezafibrate treatment, particularly during the first months of therapy.
Reproduction Studies: Standard tests for teratology, fertility and peri- and post-natal effects in animals have shown a relative absence of risk, however, embryotoxicity has occurred in animals at toxic doses.
Hematologic Changes: Mild hemoglobin, leukocyte and platelet decreases have occurred occasionally following initiation of bezafibrate therapy. However, these levels stabilize during long-term administration. Periodic blood counts are recommended during the first 12 months of administration.
Liver Function: Abnormal liver function tests have been observed occasionally during bezafibrate administration, including elevated transaminases, and decreased or, rarely, increased alkaline phosphatase. However, these abnormalities are reversible upon discontinuation of the drug. Therefore, periodic liver function tests (AST, ALT and GGT [if originally elevated]) in addition to other baseline tests are recommended after 3 to 6 months and at least yearly thereafter. Bezafibrate therapy should be terminated if drug-related abnormalities persist.
Hepatobiliary Disease: In patients with a past history of jaundice or hepatic disorder, bezafibrate should be used with caution.
Skeletal Muscle: Treatment with drugs of the fibrate class including bezafibrate has been associated on rare occasions with myositis or rhabdomyolysis, usually in patients with impaired renal function. Myopathy should be considered in any patient with diffuse myalgias, muscle tenderness/weakness, or marked elevations in creatinine phosphokinase levels. Patients should be advised to report unexplained muscle pain, tenderness or weakness promptly, particularly if accompanied by malaise or fever. CPK levels should be assessed in patients reporting these symptoms, and bezafibrate therapy should be discontinued if markedly elevated CPK levels (10 times the upper limit of normal) occur or myopathy is diagnosed.
Drug Interactions (see also Warnings): Resins: When bezafibrate is used concurrently with cholestyramine or any other resin, an interval of at least 2 hours should be maintained between the 2 drugs, since the absorption of bezafibrate is impaired by cholestyramine.
Estrogens: Since estrogens may lead to a rise in lipid levels, the prescribing of bezafibrate in patients taking estrogens or estrogen-containing contraceptives must be critically considered on an individual basis.
Renal Function: In patients with hypoalbuminemia, e.g., nephrotic syndrome, and in patients with renal insufficiency, the dosage of bezafibrate must be reduced and renal function should be monitored regularly (see Precautions, Skeletal Muscle). In dialysis patients, the dosage must be reduced to one 200 mg tablet every third day (see Dosage).

Adverse Effects: In two separate double-blind placebo-controlled trials, a total of 88 patients on 200 mg bezafibrate t.i.d. and 87 patients on placebo were evaluated for adverse events. Listed in Table I (on following page) are those adverse events with a positive induced risk occurring during the first 2 months of bezafibrate treatment.

Table I—Bezalip

Adverse Events

Body System	2-month Cumulative Incidence (%) Bezafibrate 200 mg t.i.d. (n=88)	Placebo (n=87)	Induced Risk (%)
Body as a Whole	13.6	11.4	+2.6
Allergic Reaction	1.1	—	+1.1
Migraine	1.1	—	+1.1
Pain	1.1	—	+1.1
Digestive System	17.0	11.9	+5.9
Dyspepsia	3.4	—	+3.4
Flatulence	4.5	—	+4.5
Gastritis	5.7	4.6	+1.1
Hemic and Lymphatic System	1.1	—	+1.1
Anemia	1.1	—	+1.1
Nervous System	4.6	8.2	−3.9
Dizziness	2.3	—	+2.3
Insomnia	1.1	—	+1.1
Skin and Appendages	4.5	3.6	+1.0
Eczema	1.1	—	+1.1
Pruritus	3.4	—	+3.4

The most common adverse reactions observed in clinical trial patients treated for up to 2 years with bezafibrate and from surveillance studies in countries where bezafibrate has been marketed for up to 14 years include: gastrointestinal: epigastric distress, flatulence, nausea, diarrhea, constipation; dermatologic: pruritus, urticaria or erythema.

Less common adverse reactions observed include: musculoskeletal: muscular weakness, pain and muscle cramps; CNS: headache, dizziness, alopecia.

In isolated cases, the occurrence of gallstones and potency disorders have been reported.

Abnormal liver function tests have been observed occasionally during bezafibrate therapy including elevated transaminases and decreased or rarely increased alkaline phosphatase.

Mild decreases in hemoglobin, leukocytes and platelets have been observed occasionally in patients receiving bezafibrate therapy.

Slight increase in serum creatinine may occur. In patients with existing renal failure, if dosage recommendations are not followed, myositis and rhabdomyolysis may develop (see Precautions).

Bezafibrate also has the potential to provoke CPK elevations which generally subsides when the drug is discontinued (see Precautions).

Overdose: Symptoms and Treatment: While there has been no reported case of overdosage, symptomatic and supportive measures should be taken. Because bezafibrate is highly bound to plasma proteins, hemodialysis should not be considered.

In patients with existing impaired renal function, if dosage recommendations are not followed, overdosage may occur and severe rhabdomyolysis may develop. Administration of bezafibrate must be stopped immediately and renal function must be carefully monitored (see Precautions).

Dosage: Recommended Dosage: 200 mg: The standard dosage is one 200 mg immediate-release tablet 3 times daily. In cases of good therapeutic response, especially in hypertriglyceridemia, the dosage can be reduced to one 200 mg tablet twice daily. For patients with a history of gastric sensitivity, the dosage may be gradually increased to the maintenance level.

The dosage in patients with renal insufficiency/dialysis must be adjusted according to serum creatinine levels or creatinine clearance (see Table II).

It should be taken into account that creatinine clearance is a more reliable parameter than serum creatinine (especially in the elderly). The creatinine clearance can be estimated using the following equation (Cockroft and Gault equation) which is applicable to adults only:

Men:

$$CL_{cr} = \frac{(140-\text{age [years]}) \times \text{weight(kg)}}{72 \times C_{cr}(\text{mg/dL})} \text{(mL/min)}$$

CL_{cr} = creatinine clearance

C_{cr} = serum creatinine

For women, the value should be reduced to 85% of that estimated by this equation.

Administration: The 200 mg immediate-release tablet should be swallowed without chewing with sufficient fluid, with or after meals.

400 mg: The recommended dosage is one 400 mg sustained-release tablet once daily. Due to the necessary dosage reduction in cases of impaired renal function (serum creatinine >1.5 mg/100 mL, i.e., >135 μmol/L or creatinine clearance <60 mL/min) the 400 mg sustained-release tablet should be replaced by the 200 mg immediate-release tablets and dosed appropriately. Renal function should be monitored regularly (recommended dosage 200 mg tablet).

Administration: The 400 mg sustained release tablet should be taken in the morning or evening with or after meals. The sustained-release tablet should be swallowed without chewing with sufficient fluid.

When 200 or 400 mg tablets are administered concurrently with resins, an interval of 2 hours should be maintained between the two drugs (see Precautions).

Information for the Patient: See Blue Section—Information for the Patient "Bezalip".

Supplied: 200 mg: Each round, white, immediate-release film-coated tablet, printed on both sides: above BM, below G6, contains: bezafibrate 200 mg. Nonmedicinal ingredients: colloidal silicon dioxide, kaolin, lactose, macrogol 10 000, magnesium stearate, maize starch, microcrystalline cellulose, poly (ethylacrylate, methylmethacrylate), polysorbate 80, sodium citrate, sodium starch glycolate, talc and titanium dioxide. Blister packs of 90.

400 mg: Each round, white, sustained-release film-coated tablet, printed on both sides: above BM, below D9, contains: bezafibrate 400 mg. Nonmedicinal ingredients: colloidal silicon dioxide, lactose, macrogol 10 000, magnesium stearate, poly (ethylacrylate, methylmethacrylate), polysorbate 80, poly-02-hydroxypropyl, 0-methyl cellulose, polyvidone K25, sodium citrate, sodium lauryl sulfate, talc and titanium dioxide. Blister packs of 30.

Store at room temperature (15 to 30°C). Protect from high humidity.

(Shown in Product Recognition Section)

Table II—Bezalip

Dosage—Renal Insufficiency/Dialysis

Serum Creatinine	Creatinine Clearance	Dosage
up to 1.5 mg/100 mL up to 135 μmol/L	over 60 mL/min	3 immediate-release tablets/day (1 tablet 3 times daily)
1.6–2.5 mg/100 mL 136–225 μmol/L	60–40 mL/min	2 immediate-release tablets/day (1 tablet twice daily)
2.6–6 mg/100 mL 226–530 μmol/L	40–15 mL/min	1 immediate-release tablet every 1 or 2 days
over 6 mg/100 mL over 530 μmol/L	less than 15 mL/min	1 immediate-release tablet every third day (dialysis patients)

BIAXIN® Ⓟ

Abbott

Clarithromycin

Antibiotic

Note: When used in combination with acid antisecretory drugs and other antimicrobials for the eradication of helicobacter pylori, the product monograph for those agents should be consulted.

Pharmacology: General: Clarithromycin exerts its antibacterial action by binding to the 50S ribosomal subunit of susceptible bacteria and suppressing protein synthesis.

Eradication of H. pylori: H. pylori is now established as a major etiological factor in duodenal ulcer disease. The presence of H. pylori may damage the mucosal integrity due to the production of enzymes (catalase, lipases, phospholipases, proteases, and urease), adhesins and toxins; the generated inflammatory response contributes to mucosal damage.

The concomitant administration of an antimicrobial(s) such as clarithromycin and an antisecretory agent, improves the eradication of H. pylori as compared to individual drug administration. The higher pH resulting from antisecretory treatment, optimizes the environment for the pharmacologic action of the antimicrobial agent(s) against H. pylori.

Pharmacokinetics: Tablets: The absolute bioavailability of 250 mg and 500 mg clarithromycin tablets is approximately 50%. Food slightly delays the onset of clarithromycin absorption but does not affect the extent of bioavailability. Therefore, clarithromycin tablets may be given without regard to meals.

In fasting healthy human subjects, peak serum concentrations are attained within 2 hours after oral dosing. Steady-state peak serum clarithromycin concentrations, which are attained within 2 to 3 days, are approximately 1 mg/L with a 250 mg dose twice daily and 2 to 3 mg/L with a 500 mg dose twice daily. The elimination half-life of clarithromycin is about 3 to 4 hours with 250 mg twice daily dosing but increases to about 5 to 7 hours with 500 mg administered twice daily.

The nonlinearity of clarithromycin pharmacokinetics is slight at the recommended doses of 250 mg and 500 mg administered twice daily. With 250 mg twice daily, the principal metabolite, 14-OH clarithromycin attains a peak steady-state concentration of about 0.6 mg/L and has an elimination half-life of 5 to 6 hours. With a 500 mg twice daily dose, the peak steady-state of 14-OH concentrations of clarithromycin are slightly higher (up to 1 mg/L) and its elimination half-life is about 7 hours. With either dose, the steady-state concentration of this metabolite is generally attained within 2 to 3 days.

Steady-state concentrations of clarithromycin and 14-OH clarithromycin observed following administration of 500 mg doses of clarithromycin twice a day to adult patients with HIV infection were similar to those observed in healthy volunteers. However, at the higher clarithromycin doses which may be required to treat mycobacterial infections, clarithromycin concentrations can be much higher than those observed at 500 mg clarithromycin doses. In adult HIV-infected patients taking 2 000 mg/day in 2 divided doses, steady-state clarithromycin C_{max} values ranged from 5 to 10 mg/mL. C_{max} values as high as 27 mg/L have been observed in HIV-infected adult patients taking 4 000 mg/day in 2 divided doses of tablets.

Elimination half-lives appeared to be lengthened at these higher doses as well. The higher clarithromycin concentrations and longer elimination half-lives observed at these doses are consistent with the known nonlinearity in clarithromycin pharmacokinetics.

Clarithromycin 500 mg t.i.d. and omeprazole 40 mg once daily were studied in fasting healthy adult subjects. When clarithromycin was given alone as 500 mg q 8 h, the mean steady-state C_{max} value was approximately 3.8 μg/mL and the mean C_{min} value was approximately 1.8 μg/mL. The mean AUC_{0-8} for clarithromycin was 22.9 μg•h/mL. The T_{max} and half-life were 2.1 hours and 5.3 hours, respectively, when clarithromycin was dosed at 500 mg t.i.d.

Biaxin (cont'd)

When clarithromycin was administered with omeprazole, increases in omeprazole half-life and AUC_{0-24} were observed. For all subjects combined, the mean omeprazole AUC_{0-24} was 89% greater and the harmonic mean for omeprazole $t^1/_2$ was 34% greater when omeprazole was administered with clarithromycin than when omeprazole was administered alone. When clarithromycin was administered with omeprazole, the steady-state C_{max}, C_{min}, and AUC_{0-8} of clarithromycin were increased by 10%, 27%, and 15%, respectively over values achieved when clarithromycin was administered with placebo.

Pediatric Granules for Suspension: Single and multiple dose adult volunteer studies showed that the suspension formulation was not significantly different from the tablet formulation in terms of C_{max} of clarithromycin and AUC, although the onset and/or rate of absorption of the suspension formulation was slower than that of the tablet. As with the tablet formulation, steady state is achieved by the fifth dose of a 12-hour multiple dose suspension regimen.

In children taking 15 to 30 mg/kg/day in 2 divided doses, steady-state clarithromycin C_{max} values generally ranged from 8 to 20 μg/mL. C_{max} values as high as 23 μg/mL have been observed in HIV-infected pediatric patients taking 30 mg/kg/day in 2 divided doses.

In children requiring antibiotic therapy, administration of 7.5 mg/kg q 12 h doses of clarithromycin as the suspension generally resulted in steady-state peak plasma concentrations of 3 to 7 μg/mL for clarithromycin, and 1 to 2 μg/mL for 14-OH clarithromycin.

In HIV-infected children taking 15 mg/kg every 12 hours, steady-state clarithromycin peak concentrations generally ranged from 6 to 15 μg/mL.

A single and multiple dose study conducted in pediatric patients showed that food leads to a slight delay in the onset of absorption, but does not affect the overall bioavailability of clarithromycin.

Clarithromycin and its 14-OH metabolite penetrate into middle ear effusion (MEE) of patients with secretory otitis media.

For adult patients, the bioavailability of 10 mL of the 125 mg/5 mL suspension is similar to a 250 mg tablet.

Patients With Hepatic and Renal Impairment: The steady-state concentrations of clarithromycin in subjects with impaired hepatic function did not differ from those in normal subjects; however, the 14-OH clarithromycin concentrations were lower in the hepatically impaired subjects. The decreased formation of 14-OH clarithromycin was at least partially offset by an increase in renal clearance of clarithromycin in subjects with impaired hepatic function when compared to healthy subjects.

The pharmacokinetics of clarithromycin was also altered in subjects with impaired renal function (see Precautions and Dosage).

Indications: Tablets: In the treatment of mild to moderate infections caused by susceptible strains of the designated microorganisms in the diseases listed below:

Upper Respiratory Tract: Pharyngitis/tonsillitis, caused by S. pyogenes (Group A beta-hemolytic streptococci).

Acute maxillary sinusitis caused by S. pneumoniae. H. influenzae and M. (Branhamella) catarrhalis.

Lower Respiratory Tract: Acute bacterial exacerbation of chronic bronchitis caused by S. pneumoniae, H. influenzae (including beta-lactamase producing strains), M. (Branhamella) catarrhalis (including beta-lactamase producing strains).

Pneumonia caused by S. pneumoniae and M. pneumoniae.

Uncomplicated Skin and Skin Structure Infections: caused by S. pyogenes, S. aureus.

Mycobacterial Infections: For the prevention of disseminated M. avium complex (MAC) disease in patients with advanced HIV infection, and for the treatment of disseminated mycobacterial infections due to M. avium and M. intracellulare.

Eradication of H. pylori: In the presence of acid suppression (with omeprazole), with another antibiotic (amoxicillin) is indicated for the eradication of H. pylori that may result in decreased recurrence of duodenal ulcer in patients with active duodenal ulcers and who are H. pylori positive.

(For additional information on the use of clarithromycin in triple therapy for the treatment of H. pylori infection and active duodenal ulcer recurrence, refer to the Hp-PAC product monograph.)

Pediatric Granules for Suspension: Indicated for the treatment of infections due to susceptible organisms, in the following conditions: Upper Respiratory Tract: Pharyngitis caused by S. pyogenes (Group A ß-hemolytic streptococci). Acute otitis media caused by H. influenzae, M. catarrhalis or S. pneumoniae.

Lower Respiratory Tract: Mild to moderate community-acquired pneumonia caused by S. pneumoniae, C. pneumoniae or M. pneumoniae.

Uncomplicated Skin and Skin Structure Infections (i.e., impetigo and cellulitis) caused by S. aureus or S. pyogenes.

Mycobacterial Infections: Disseminated mycobacterial infections due to M. avium and M. intracellulare.

Contraindications: Patients with a known hypersensitivity to clarithromycin, erythromycin or other macrolide antibacterial agents.

Concurrent therapy with astemizole, terfenadine, cisapride or pimozide (see Precautions, Drug Interactions).

Warnings: Clarithromycin should be administered with caution to any patient who has demonstrated some form of drug allergy, particularly to structurally related drugs. If an allergic reaction to clarithromycin occurs, administration of the drug should be discontinued.

Serious hypersensitivity reactions may require epinephrine, antihistamines or corticosteroids.

Several studies of HIV positive patients receiving clarithromycin for treatment of M. avium complex infection (MAC) have shown poorer survival in those patients randomized to receive doses higher than 500 mg b.i.d. The explanation for the poorer survival associated with doses higher than 500 mg b.i.d. has not been determined. Treatment or prophylaxis of MAC infection with clarithromycin should not exceed the approved dose of 500 mg b.i.d.

Pregnancy: **Clarithromycin should not be used in pregnancy except where no alternative therapy is appropriate, particularly during the first 3 months of pregnancy. If pregnancy occurs while taking the drug, the patient should be apprised of the potential hazard to the fetus. Clarithromycin has demonstrated adverse effects on pregnancy outcome and/or embryo-fetal development in monkeys, mice, rats and rabbits at doses that produced plasma levels 2 to 17 times the serum levels obtained in humans treated at the maximum recommended doses.**

Pseudomembranous colitis has been reported with nearly all antibacterial agents, including macrolides, and may range in severity from mild to life-threatening. Therefore, it is important to consider this diagnosis in patients who present with diarrhea subsequent to the administration of antibacterial agents, including clarithromycin.

Treatment with antibacterial agents alters the normal flora of the colon and may permit overgrowth of clostridia. Studies indicate that a toxin produced by C. difficile is a primary cause of "antibiotic-associated colitis".

After the diagnosis of pseudomembranous colitis has been established, therapeutic measures should be initiated. Mild cases of pseudomembranous colitis usually respond to discontinuation of the drug alone. In moderate to severe cases, consideration should be given to management with fluids and electrolytes, protein supplementation, and treatment with an antibacterial drug effective against C. difficile.

Precautions: General: Clarithromycin is principally excreted by the liver and kidney (see Dosage). In patients with both hepatic and renal impairments or in the presence of severe renal impairment, decreased dosage of clarithromycin or prolonged dosing intervals might be appropriate.

The development of resistance (11 out of 19 breakthrough isolates in one study) has been seen in HIV positive patients receiving clarithromycin for prophylaxis and treatment of MAC infection.

H. pylori Eradication and Compliance: To avoid failure of the eradication treatment with a potential for developing antimicrobial resistance and a risk of failure with subsequent therapy, patients should be instructed to follow closely the prescribed regimen.

For the eradication of H. pylori, amoxicillin and clarithromycin should not be administered to patients with renal impairment since the appropriate dosage in this patient population has not yet been established.

Antibiotic Resistance in Relation to H. pylori Eradication: Triple and Dual Therapy with Omeprazole: Among the 113 triple therapy recipients with pretreatment H. pylori isolates susceptible to clarithromycin, 2/102 patients (2%) developed resistance after treatment with omeprazole, clarithromycin, and amoxicillin. Among patients who received triple therapy, 6/108 (5.6%) patients had pretreatment H. pylori isolates resistant to clarithromycin. Of these 6 patients, 3 (50%) had H. pylori eradicated at follow-up, and 3 (50%) remained positive after treatment. In 5/113 (4.4%) patients, no susceptibility data for clarithromycin pretreatment were available. Twenty-six patients 26/104 (25%) with pretreatment isolates susceptible to clarithromycin developed resistance after treatment with omeprazole and clarithromycin.

Development of clarithromycin resistance should be considered as a possible risk especially when less efficient treatment regimens are used.

__Drug Interactions:__ Theophylline: Clarithromycin use in patients who are receiving theophylline may be associated with an increase of serum theophylline concentrations. Monitoring of serum theophylline concentrations should be considered for patients receiving high doses of theophylline or with baseline concentrations in the upper therapeutic range.

Carbamazepine: Clarithromycin administration in patients receiving carbamazepine has been reported to cause increased levels of carbamazepine. Blood level monitoring of carbamazepine may be considered.

Terfenadine/Astemizole: Macrolides have been reported to alter the metabolism of terfenadine resulting in increased serum levels of terfenadine which has occasionally been associated with cardiac arrhythmias such as QT prolongation, ventricular tachycardia, ventricular fibrillation and torsades de pointes (see Contraindications).

In a study involving 14 healthy volunteers, the concomitant administration of clarithromycin tablets and terfenadine resulted in a 2- to 3-fold increase in the serum level of the acid metabolite of terfenadine, MDL 16, 455, and in prolongation of the QT interval which did not lead to any clinically detectable effect. Similar effects have been observed with concomitant administration of astemizole and other macrolides.

Cisapride/Pimozide: Elevated cisapride levels have been reported in patients receiving clarithromycin and cisapride concomitantly. This may result in QT prolongation and cardiac arrhythmias including ventricular tachycardia, ventricular fibrillation and torsades de pointes. Similar effects have been observed in patients taking clarithromycin and pimozide concomitantly (see Contraindications).

Zidovudine: Simultaneous oral administration of clarithromycin tablets and zidovudine to HIV-infected adult patients may result in decreased steady-state zidovudine concentrations. Clarithromycin appears to interfere with the absorption of simultaneously administered oral zidovudine, therefore this interaction can be largely avoided by staggering the doses of clarithromycin and zidovudine.

Didanosine: Simultaneous administration of clarithromycin tablets and didanosine to 12 HIV-infected adult patients resulted in no statistically significant change in didanosine pharmacokinetics.

Fluconazole: Concomitant administration of fluconazole 200 mg daily and clarithromycin 500 mg twice daily to 21 healthy volunteers led to increases in the mean steady-state clarithromycin C_{min} and AUC of 33% and 18%, respectively. Steady-state concentrations of 14-OH clarithromycin were not significantly affected by concomitant administration of fluconazole.

Digoxin: Elevated digoxin serum concentrations have been reported in patients receiving clarithromycin tablets and digoxin concomitantly. In postmarketing surveillance, some patients have shown clinical signs consistent with digoxin toxicity, including arrhythmias. Serum digoxin levels should be carefully monitored while patients are receiving digoxin and clarithromycin simultaneously.

Ritonavir: A pharmacokinetic study demonstrated that the concomitant administration of ritonavir 200 mg q 8 hours and clarithromycin 500 mg q 12 hours resulted in a marked inhibition of the metabolism of clarithromycin. The clarithromycin C_{max} increased by 31%, C_{min} increased 182% and AUC increased by 77% with concomitant administration of ritonavir. An essentially complete inhibition of the formation of 14-[R]-hydroxy-clarithromycin was noted. Because of the large therapeutic window for clarithromycin, no dosage reduction should be necessary in patients with normal renal function. However, for patients with renal impairment, the following dosage adjustments should be considered: For patients with CL_{CR} 30 to 60 mL/min the dose of clarithromycin should be reduced by 50%. For patients with $CL_{CR} < 30$ mL/min the dose of clarithromycin should be decreased by 75%. Doses of clarithromycin greater than 1 g/day should not be coadministered with ritonavir.

Lovastatin/Simvastatin: Rhabdomyolysis coincident with the coadministration of clarithromycin and the HMG-CoA reductase inhibitors, lovastatin and simvastatin, has rarely been reported.Combination Therapy With Omeprazole and/or Amoxicillin: For more information on drug interactions for omeprazole and amoxicillin, refer to their respective product monographs, under Precautions, Drug Interactions.

Others: As with other macrolide antibiotics, the use of clarithromycin in patients concurrently taking drugs metabolized by the cytochrome P450 system (e.g., warfarin, ergot alkaloids, triazolam, midazolam, lovastatin, disopyramide, phenytoin, cyclosporine and rifabutin) may be associated with elevations in serum levels of these other drugs.

There have been reports of drug interactions when erythromycin, another macrolide, has been given concomitantly with drugs metabolized by the cytochrome P450 system, such as hexobarbital, alfentanil, bromocriptine or valproate. Serum concentrations of drugs metabolized by the cytochrome P450 system should be monitored closely in patients concurrently receiving erythromycin.

Pregnancy: There are no adequate and well-controlled studies in pregnant women. The benefits against risk, particularly during the first 3 months of pregnancy should be carefully weighed by a physician (see Warnings). Four teratogenicity studies in rats (3 with oral doses and 1 with i.v. doses up to 160 mg/kg/day administered during the period of major organogenesis) and 2 in rabbits (at oral doses up to 125 mg/kg/day or i.v. doses of 30 mg/kg/day administered during gestation days 6 to 18) failed to demonstrate any teratogenicity from clarithromycin. Two additional oral studies in a different rat strain at similar doses and similar conditions demonstrated a low incidence of cardiovascular anomalies at doses of 150 mg/kg/day administered during gestation days 6 to 15. Plasma levels after 150 mg/kg/day were 2 times the human serum levels.

Four studies in mice revealed a variable incidence of cleft palate following oral doses of 1 000 mg/kg/day during gestation days 6 to 15. Cleft palate was also seen at 500 mg/kg/day. The 1 000 mg/kg/day exposure resulted in plasma levels 17 times the human serum levels. In monkeys, an oral dose of 70 mg/kg/day produced fetal growth retardation at plasma levels that were 2 times the human serum levels.

Embryonic loss has been seen in monkeys and rabbits.

Lactation: The safety of clarithromycin for use during breast-feeding of infants has not been established. Clarithromycin is excreted in human milk.

Preweaned rats, exposed indirectly via consumption of milk from dams treated with 150 mg/kg/day for 3 weeks, were not adversely affected, despite data indicating higher drug levels in milk than in plasma.

Children: Use of clarithromycin tablets in children under 12 years of age has not been studied.

Use of clarithromycin granules for suspension in children under 6 months has not been studied. In pneumonia, clarithromycin granules were not studied in children younger than 3 years.

The safety of clarithromycin has not been studied in MAC patients under the age of 20 months. Neonatal and juvenile animals tolerated clarithromycin in a manner similar to adult animals. Young animals were slightly more intolerant to acute overdosage and to subtle reductions in erythrocytes, platelets and leukocytes, but were less sensitive to toxicity in the liver, kidney, thymus and genitalia.

Increased valproate and phenobarbital concentrations and extreme sedation were noted in a 3-year-old patient coincident with clarithromycin therapy. Cause and effect relationship cannot be established. However, monitoring of valproate and phenobarbital concentrations may be considered.

Geriatrics: Dosage adjustment should be considered in elderly patients with severe renal impairment. In a steady-state study in which healthy elderly subjects (age 65 to 81 years old) were given 500 mg every 12 hours, the maximum concentrations of clarithromycin and 14-OH clarithromycin were increased. The AUC was also increased. These changes in pharmacokinetics parallel known age-related decreases in renal function. In clinical trials, elderly patients did not have an increased incidence of adverse events when compared to younger patients.

Adverse Effects: Tablets: Patients With Respiratory Tract or Skin Infections: The majority of side effects observed in clinical trials involving 3 563 patients treated with clarithromycin were of a mild and transient nature. Fewer than 3% of adult patients without mycobacterial infections discontinued therapy because of drug-related side effects.

The following adverse reactions were reported during these clinical studies or during postmarketing surveillance: Body as a Whole: headache (2%), asthenia, infection, back pain, pain and chest pain.

Digestive: nausea (4%), diarrhea (3%), abdominal pain (2%), dyspepsia (2%), vomiting (1%), constipation, flatulence, dry mouth, glossitis, stomatitis, gastrointestinal disorder, anorexia, oral moniliasis, tongue discoloration, hepatomegaly and pseudomembranous colitis. There have been reports of tooth discoloration in patients treated with clarithromycin. Tooth discoloration is usually reversible with professional dental cleaning.

As with other macrolides, hepatic dysfunction, including increased liver enzymes, and hepatocellular and/or cholestatic hepatitis, with or without jaundice, has been infrequently reported with clarithromycin. This hepatic dysfunction may be severe and is usually reversible. In very rare instances, hepatic failure with fatal outcome has been reported and generally has been associated with serious underlying diseases and/or concomitant medications.

Metabolic: There have been rare reports of hypoglycemia, some of which have occurred in patients on concomitant oral hypoglycemic agents or insulin.

Nervous System: dizziness, vertigo, tinnitus, nervousness, anxiety, insomnia, nightmares, somnolence, depression, confusion, disorientation, depersonalization, hallucinations and psychosis.

Respiratory: rhinitis, cough increased, dyspnea, pharyngitis and asthma.

Skin and Appendages: pruritus, rash, sweating; allergic reactions ranging from urticaria and mild skin eruptions to anaphylaxis and Stevens-Johnson syndrome have occurred with orally administered clarithromycin.

Special Senses: taste perversion (2%), ear disorder, abnormal vision and conjunctivitis. There have been reports of hearing loss with clarithromycin which is usually reversible upon withdrawal of therapy. Reports of alteration of the sense of smell, usually in conjunction with taste perversion have also been reported.

Urogenital: hematuria, vaginal moniliasis, vaginitis and dysmenorrhea.

Hemic and Lymphatic: eosinophilia, anemia, leukopenia and thrombocythemia. Isolated cases of thrombocytopenia have been reported.

Changes in Laboratory Values: Changes in laboratory values with possible clinical significance were as follows:

Hepatic: elevated ALT $<1\%$, AST $<1\%$, GGT $<1\%$, alkaline phosphatase $<1\%$, LDH $<1\%$ and total bilirubin $<1\%$.

Hematologic: decreased WBC $<1\%$ and elevated prothrombin time (1%).

Renal: elevated BUN (4%) and elevated serum creatinine $<1\%$.

Others: The following adverse reactions have not been observed in clinical trials with clarithromycin but they have been occasionally reported with erythromycin, another macrolide: cardiac arrhythmias such as ventricular tachycardia and torsades de pointes in individuals with prolonged QT intervals and CNS side effects (including seizures).

In studies of adults with pneumonia comparing clarithromycin to erythromycin base or erythromycin stearate, there were significantly fewer adverse events involving the digestive system in patients treated with clarithromycin.

Patients with Mycobacterial Infections: In AIDS and other immunocompromised patients treated with the higher doses of clarithromycin over long periods of time for prevention or treatment of mycobacterial infections, it was often difficult to distinguish adverse events possibly associated with clarithromycin administration from underlying signs of HIV disease or intercurrent illness.

(Other adverse reactions have been observed in different patient populations. Please also refer to Patients With Respiratory Tract or Skin Infections.)

Prophylaxis: Discontinuation due to adverse events was required in 18% of AIDS patients receiving clarithromycin 500 mg b.i.d., compared to 17% of patients receiving placebo in a randomized, double-blind study (561). Primary reasons for discontinuation in the clarithromycin-treated patients include headache, nausea, vomiting, depression and taste perversion. The most frequently reported adverse events with an incidence of 2% or greater, excluding those due to the patient's concurrent condition, are listed in Table I. Among these events, taste perversion was the only event that had significantly higher incidence in the clarithromycin-treated compared to the placebo-treated group.

Table I—Biaxin

Percentage of Adverse Events[a] in Immunocompromised Adult Patients Receiving Prophylaxis Against M. avium Complex

Body System[b] Adverse Event	Clarithromycin (n=339) %	Placebo (n=339) %
Digestive		
Nausea	11.2	7.1
Diarrhea	7.7	4.1
Vomiting	5.9	3.2
Dyspepsia	3.8	2.7
Flatulence	2.4	0.9
Special Senses		
Taste Perversion	8.0	0.3
Body as a Whole		
Abdominal Pain	5.0	3.5
Headache	2.7	0.9
Skin and Appendages		
Rash	3.2	3.5

[a] Includes those events possibly or probably related to study drug and excludes concurrent conditions.

[b] $\geq 2\%$ Adverse Event Incidence Rates for either treatment group.

Changes in Laboratory Values: In immunocompromised patients receiving prophylaxis against M. avium, those laboratory values outside the extreme high or low limit for the specified test were analyzed (see Table II).

Table II—Biaxin

Percentage of Patients[a] Exceeding Extreme Laboratory Value in Patients Receiving Prophylaxis Against M. avium Complex

		Clarithromycin 500 mg b.i.d.		Placebo	
Hemoglobin	<8 g/dL	4/118	3%	5/103	5%
Platelet Count	$<50\times10^9$/L	11/249	4%	12/250	5%
WBC Count	$<1\times10^9$/L	2/103	4%	0/95	0%
AST	>5×ULN[b]	7/196	4%	5/208	2%
ALT	>5×ULN[b]	6/217	3%	4/232	2%
Alkaline Phosphatase	>5×ULN[b]	5/220	2%	5/218	2%

[a] Includes only patients with baseline values within the normal range or borderline high (hematology variables) and within the normal range or borderline low (chemistry variables).

[b] ULN—Upper Limit of Normal.

Treatment of Patients with Mycobacterial Infections: Excluding those patients who discontinued therapy due to complications of their underlying nonmycobacterial diseases (including death), approximately 14% of the patients discontinued therapy due to drug-related adverse events.

In adult patients, the most frequently reported adverse events with an incidence of 3% or greater, excluding those due to the patient's concurrent condition, are listed in Table III (on following page) by the total daily dose the patient was receiving at the time of the event. A total of 867 patients were treated with clarithromycin for mycobacterial infections. Of these, 43% reported one or more adverse events. Most of these events were described as mild to moderate in severity, although 14% were described as severe.

Incidence of adverse events was higher in patients taking 4 000 mg doses compared to lower doses (see Table III on following page).

A limited number of pediatric AIDS patients have been treated with clarithromycin suspension for mycobacterial infections. The most frequently reported adverse events, excluding those due to the patient's concurrent condition, are listed in Table IV (on following page) by the total daily dose of clarithromycin the patient received.

Changes in Laboratory Values: In immunocompromised patients treated with clarithromycin for mycobacterial infections, evaluations of laboratory values were made by analyzing those values outside the seriously abnormal level (i.e., the extreme high or low limit) for the specified test (see Tables V and VI on following page).

Patients With H. pylori Infection: Triple Therapy: Clarithromycin/omeprazole/amoxicillin: Forty-four percent (60/137) of the patients in the triple therapy group and 43% (56/130) of the patients in the dual therapy group reported at least 1 adverse event; this difference between the two treatment groups was not statistically significant ($p > 0.999$).

Biaxin (cont'd)

Table III—Biaxin

Percentage of Adverse Events[a] in Immunocompromised Adult Patients Treated with Clarithromycin for Mycobacterial Infections

	Presented by Total Daily Dose at Time of the Event		
Adverse Event	**1 000 mg (n=463) (%)**	**2 000 mg (n=516) (%)**	**4 000 mg (n=87) (%)**
Nausea	11	16	40
Vomiting	7	9	24
Taste Perversion	6	7	29
Abdominal Pain	5	7	20
Diarrhea	4	6	17
Rash	4	3	2
AST Increased	2	2	11
Flatulence	1	2	7
Headache	2	2	7
Constipation	1	<1	5
ALT Increased	1	1	9
Dyspnea	<1	<1	7
Insomnia	<1	<1	6
Hearing Disturbance[b]	3	2	5
Dry Mouth	<1	0	5

[a] Related adverse events considered to be definitely, probably, possibly or remotely related to study events.
[b] Sum of patients with deafness, ear disorder, partial transitory deafness, and/or tinnitus.
n=Number of adverse events.

Table IV—Biaxin

Numbers of Pediatric AIDS Patients Treated with Clarithromycin for Mycobacterial Infections who Experienced Adverse Events

	Presented by Total Daily Dose at Time of the Event		
Adverse Event	**<15 mg/kg/day (n=19)**	**15-<25 mg/kg/day (n=13)**	**≥25 mg/kg/day (n=12)**
Tinnitus	2	0	0
Deafness	1	1	0
Vomiting	1	0	0
Nausea	1	0	0
Abdominal Pain	1	0	0
Purpuric Rash	1	0	0
Pancreatitis	1	0	0
Amylase Increased	0	0	1

Table V—Biaxin

Percentage of Immunocompromised Adult Patients Treated with Clarithromycin for Mycobacterial Infections who had on-Treatment Laboratory Values that Were Outside the Seriously Abnormal Level

		Presented by Total Daily Dose		
Parameter	**Seriously Abnormal Level**	**1 000 mg (%)**	**2 000 mg (%)**	**4 000 mg (%)**
AST	>5 × ULN*	3	2	4
ALT	>5 × ULN*	2	2	7
Platelets	<50 × 10⁹/L	2	2	4
WBC	<1 × 10⁹/L	0	2	0
BUN	>50 mg/dL	<1	<1	4

* ULN=Upper Limit of Normal.

Table VI—Biaxin

Number of Pediatric AIDS Patients Treated with Clarithromycin for Mycobacterial Infections who had on-Treatment Laboratory Values that Were Outside the Seriously Abnormal Level

		Presented by Total Daily Dose		
Parameter	**Seriously Abnormal Level**	**<15 mg/kg/day**	**15-<25 mg/kg/day**	**≥25 mg/kg/day**
ALT	>5 x ULN*	0	1	0
Total Bilirubin	>12 mg/dL	1	0	0
Platelets	<50 x 10⁹/L	0	1	0
BUN	>50 mg/dL	0	1	0

* ULN=Upper Limit of Normal.

Similarly, there was no statistically significant difference ($p > 0.999$) between the treatment groups for the number of patients reporting one or more drug-related adverse events. Thirty-three percent (33%; 45/137) of the patients in the triple therapy group reported adverse events considered possibly or probably related to study drug, compared with 32% (42/130) of the patients in the dual therapy group ($p > 0.999$). The rate of drug-related adverse events when evaluated by body system was very similar for both treatment groups. However, a trend toward statistical significance was noted for drug-related adverse events associated with special senses. The most common special sense adverse event was taste perversion, which was reported more frequently in patients treated with dual therapy as compared to triple therapy (18%, 23/130 vs 9%, 13/137, respectively; $p = 0.072$).

A summary of drug-related adverse event incidence rates by treatment group is presented in Table VII.

Table VII—Biaxin

Summary of Drug-related Adverse Event Incidence Rates by Body System

	Patients With Drug-Related Adverse Events (% of Patients Treated)[a]		
Body System	**Omeprazole + Clarithromycin + Amoxicillin (n=137)**	**Omeprazole + Clarithromycin (n=130)**	**p-value[b]**
Body as a Whole	6 (4%)	5 (4%)	>0.999
Cardiovascular	0 (0%)	1 (1%)	0.487
Digestive	24 (18%)	19 (15%)	0.618
Gastrointestinal	17 (12%)	10 (8%)	0.228
Other	7 (5%)	10 (8%)	0.457
Metabolic and Nutritional	7 (5%)	2 (2%)	0.174
Nervous	3 (2%)	4 (3%)	0.717
Respiratory	1 (1%)	0 (0%)	>0.999
Skin and Appendages	3 (2%)	1 (1%)	0.623
Special Senses	13 (9%)	24 (18%)	0.050
Urogenital	2 (1%)	0 (0%)	0.498
Overall[c]	45 (33%)	42 (32%)	>0.999

[a] Patients with more than one event within a body system are counted only once in the total for that body system; patients with events in more than one body system are counted only once in the overall total.
[b] 2 x 2 Fisher's Exact test result for comparing treatment groups.
[c] Number of patients with one or more adverse events.

Patients With H. pylori Infection: Dual Therapy: Clarithromycin/omeprazole: Of 346 patients, 156 (45%) reported at least one adverse event. Adverse events associated with the digestive, body as a whole, and special senses body systems were the most commonly reported adverse events among clarithromycin/omeprazole-treated patients. Eighty-three patients (24%) reported digestive system adverse events. The adverse events occurring most frequently in the digestive system were gastrointestinal events, of which nausea (5%), diarrhea (4%), vomiting (3%), and abdominal pain (3%) were the most common. Fifty-seven patients (16%) reported adverse events in the body as a whole body system. Headache (5%), infection (3%), and pain (2%) were the most frequently reported events in the body as a whole category. Fifty-four patients (16%) reported adverse events in the special senses body system; taste perversion was reported by 53 of these patients. Adverse events by body system for all patients treated with clarithromycin and omeprazole are presented in Table VIII.

(Other adverse reactions have been observed in different patient populations. Please also refer to Patients With Respiratory Tract or Skin Infections.)

The most commonly reported adverse events for the 346 patients who received clarithromycin and omeprazole were: taste perversion (15%), nausea (5%), headache (5%), diarrhea (4%), vomiting (3%), abdominal pain (3%), and infection (3%). Table IX presents adverse events reported by 1% or more of clarithromycin/omeprazole-treated patients.

Twelve (4%) of the clarithromycin/omeprazole-treated patients prematurely discontinued from study drug therapy due to adverse events. The most frequently reported adverse events leading to withdrawal included taste perversion, nausea, and headache.

Table VIII—Biaxin

Summary of Adverse Event Incidence by Body System All Patients Treated with Clarithromycin/Omeprazole

Body System[a]	**Number (%) of Patients (N=346)**
Body as a Whole	57 (16)
Cardiovascular	8 (2)
Digestive	83 (24)
Gastrointestinal	50 (14)
Other	42 (12)
Hemic and Lymphatic	1 (<1)
Metabolic and Nutritional	3 (<1)
Musculoskeletal	5 (1)
Nervous	23 (7)
Respiratory	15 (4)
Skin and Appendages	11 (3)
Special Senses	54 (16)
Urogenital	5 (1)
TOTAL[b]	156 (45)

[a] Patients with more than one event within a body system are only counted once in the total for that body system.
[b] Patients with event in more than one body system are counted only once in the total.

Table IX—Biaxin

Rank-Order of Adverse Events for Patients who Received Clarithromycin and Omeprazole

Adverse Event*	**Number (%) of Patients**
Taste Perversion	53 (15)
Nausea	18 (5)
Headache	16 (5)
Diarrhea	15 (4)
Vomiting	12 (3)
Abdominal Pain	11 (3)
Infection	9 (3)
Tongue Discoloration	8 (2)
Rhinitis	7 (2)
Dizziness	7 (2)
Pain	6 (2)
Constipation	5 (1)
Back Pain	5 (1)
Pharyngitis	5 (1)
Asthenia	4 (1)
Chills	4 (1)
Flu Syndrome	4 (1)
Dry Mouth	4 (1)
Rash	4 (1)

* Events reported in at least 1% of the clarithromycin/omeprazole population.

Three patients treated with clarithromycin and omeprazole died during follow-up periods; none of the deaths were considered by the investigator to be related to study drug administration.

Few laboratory abnormalities were observed among clarithromycin/omeprazole-treated patients. The incidence of possibly clinically significant hematology and serum chemistry variables was <1 % for any variable evaluated.

Pediatric Granules for Suspension: The safety profile of clarithromycin pediatric granules for suspension is similar to that of the 250 mg tablet in adult patients. (Please also refer to Patients With Respiratory Tract or Skin Infections).

As with other macrolides, hepatic dysfunction, including increased liver enzymes, and hepatocellular and/or cholestatic hepatitis, with or without jaundice, has been infrequently reported with clarithromycin. This hepatic dysfunction may be severe and is usually reversible. In very rare instances, hepatic failure with fatal outcome has been reported and generally has been associated with serious underlying diseases and/or concomitant medications.

Allergic reactions ranging from urticaria and mild skin eruptions to anaphylaxis and Stevens-Johnson syndrome have occurred with orally administered clarithromycin.

571/1 829 (31%) of the patients who received clarithromycin pediatric granules reported at least 1 adverse event. The adverse events reported are summarized in Table X (on following page).

The majority of the patients with adverse events reported events in the digestive (302; 17%) and body as a whole (168; 9%) body systems.

Table X—Biaxin

Adverse Events Reported in Pediatric Clinical Trials

Body System	**Number (%) of Patients (n=1 829)**
Body as a Whole	168 (9)
Cardiovascular	2 (<1)
Digestive	302 (17)
Gastrointestinal	285
Other	29
Hemic and Lymphatic	15 (1)
Metabolic and Nutritional	21 (1)
Musculoskeletal	2 (<1)
Nervous	21 (1)
Respiratory	120 (7)
Skin and Appendages	69 (4)
Special Senses	52 (3)
Urogenital	6 (<1)
TOTAL*	571 (31)

* Patients with more than one event within a body system are only counted once in the total for that body system. Patients with events in more than one body system are counted only once in the overall total.

The events occurring most frequently in the digestive system were gastrointestinal events of which diarrhea (7%), vomiting (7%), abdominal pain (3%), dyspepsia (3%) and nausea (1%) were the most common. Glossitis, stomatitis and oral monilia have also been reported with clarithromycin therapy.

Other adverse events included infection (3%), rhinitis (2.2%), rash (2.2%), increased cough (2.1%), fever (2.2%), headache (1.6%), conjunctivitis (1.1%), taste perversion (3%) and transient elevation of AST (0.9%).

The majority of adverse events were considered by the investigators to have either mild or moderate severity. 375/1 829 patients (21%) had a mild adverse events, 175/1 829 patients (10%) had moderate adverse events and 20/1 829 patients (1%) had severe adverse events.

In the 2 U.S. acute otitis media studies of clarithromycin vs antimicrobial/beta-lactamase inhibitor, the incidence of adverse events in all patients treated, primarily diarrhea (15% vs 38%) and diaper rash (3% vs 11%) in young children, was clinically or statistically lower in the clarithromycin arm vs the control arm.

In another U.S. otitis media study of clarithromycin vs cephalosporin, the incidence of adverse events in all patients treated, primarily diarrhea and vomiting, did not differ clinically or statistically for the two agents.

Overdose: Symptoms and Treatment: Reports indicate that the ingestion of large amounts of clarithromycin can be expected to produce gastrointestinal symptoms. Adverse reactions accompanying overdosage should be treated by the prompt elimination of unabsorbed drug and supportive measures.

Clarithromycin is protein bound (70%). No data are available on the elimination of clarithromycin by hemodialysis or peritoneal dialysis.

Dosage: May be given with or without meals.

Tablets: Adults with Respiratory Tract or Skin Infections: The usual adult dosage is 250 to 500 mg every 12 hours (see Table XI) for 7 to 14 days.

Table XI—Biaxin

Dosage Guidelines

Infection	**Dosage (b.i.d.)**
Upper Respiratory Tract	**250-500 mg**
Pharyngitis/tonsillitis	250 mg
Acute maxillary sinusitis	500 mg
Lower Respiratory Tract	**250-500 mg**
Acute exacerbation of chronic bronchitis and pneumonia	
Uncomplicated Skin and Skin Structure Infections	**250 mg**

For more severe infections or those caused by less susceptible organisms, the upper dosage should be used.

In the treatment of Group A streptococcus infections, therapy should be continued for 10 days. The usual drug of choice in the treatment of streptococcal infections and the prophylaxis of rheumatic fever is penicillin administered by either the i.m. or the oral route. Clarithromycin is generally effective in the eradication of S. pyogenes from the nasopharynx; however, data establishing the efficacy of clarithromycin in the subsequent prevention of rheumatic fever are not presently available.

In patients with renal impairment and a creatinine clearance less than 30 mL/min, the dosage of clarithromycin should be reduced by one-half, i.e., 250 mg once daily, or 250 mg twice daily in more severe infections. Dosage should not be continued beyond 14 days in these patients.

In patients with both hepatic and renal impairments or in the presence of severe renal impairment, decreased dosage of clarithromycin or prolonged dosing intervals may be appropriate. Clarithromycin may be administered without dosage adjustment in the presence of hepatic impairment if there is normal renal function.

Eradication of H. pylori: Triple Therapy: Clarithromycin/omeprazole/amoxicillin: The recommended dose is clarithromycin 500 mg b.i.d. in conjunction with amoxicillin 1 g b.i.d. and omeprazole 20 mg daily for 10 days.

For more information on omeprazole or amoxicillin, refer to their respective Product Monographs, under Dosage.

(For additional information on the use of clarithromycin in triple therapy for the treatment of H. pylori infection and active duodenal ulcer recurrence, refer to the Hp-PAC product monograph.)

Dual Therapy: Clarithromycin/omeprazole: In patients who are sensitive to penicillin-based therapy (e.g., amoxicillin), dual therapy with clarithromycin and omeprazole may provide a feasible alternative.

The recommended dose is clarithromycin 500 mg t.i.d plus omeprazole 40 mg daily for 14 days, followed by 20 mg omeprazole daily for 14 days.

Optimal therapeutic regimens consisting of a shorter treatment duration for the eradication of H. pylori are yet to be determined.

Adults with Mycobacterial Infections: Prophylaxis: The recommended dose of clarithromycin for the prevention of disseminated M. avium disease is 500 mg b.i.d.

Treatment: Clarithromycin is recommended as the primary agent for the treatment of disseminated infection due to M. avium complex. Clarithromycin should be used in combination with other antimycobacterial drugs which have shown in vitro activity against MAC, including ethambutol, clofazimine, and rifampin. Although no controlled clinical trial information is available for combination therapy with clarithromycin, the U.S. Public Health Service Task Force has provided recommendations for the treatment of MAC.

The recommended dose for mycobacterial infections in adults is 500 mg b.i.d.

Treatment of disseminated MAC infections in AIDS patients should continue for life if clinical and mycobacterial improvement are observed.

Pediatric Granules for Suspension: The recommended daily dosage of clarithromycin is 15 mg/kg/day, in divided doses every 12 hours, not to exceed 1 000 mg/day. The usual duration of treatment is for 5 to 10 days depending on the pathogen involved and the severity of the condition. Treatment for pharyngitis caused by Streptococcal spp. should be 10 days.

In children with renal impairment and a creatinine clearance less than 30 mL/min, the dosage of clarithromycin should be reduced by one-half, i.e., up to 250 mg once daily, or 250 mg twice daily in more severe infections. Dosage should not be continued beyond 14 days in these patients. Table XII is a suggested guide for determining dosage.

Table XII—Biaxin

Guide for Dosing of Children With Biaxin Suspension

Based on Body Weight in kg	
Weight[a]	**Dosage (mL) given twice daily**
8-11 kg (1-2 years)[b]	2.5
12-19 kg (2-4 years)	5
20-29 kg (4-8 years)	7.5
30-40 kg (8-12 years)	10

[a]Children <8 kg should be dosed on a per kg basis (approximately 7.5 mg/kg b.i.d.).
[b]Approximate ages.

The reconstituted suspension must not be refrigerated.

Children with Mycobacterial Infections: Clarithromycin is recommended as the primary agent for the treatment of disseminated infection due to M. avium complex. Clarithromycin should be used in combination with other antimycobacterial drugs which have shown in vitro activity against MAC, including ethambutol, clofazimine, and rifampin. Although no controlled clinical trial information is available for combination therapy with clarithromycin, the U.S. Public Health Service Task Force has provided recommendations for the treatment of MAC.

In children, the recommended dose is 7.5 mg/kg b.i.d. up to 500 mg b.i.d. clarithromycin/day in 2 divided doses. Dosing recommendations for children are in Table XII.

Treatment of disseminated MAC infections in AIDS patients should continue for life if clinical and mycobacterial improvement are observed.

Information for the Patient: See Blue Section—Information for the Patient "Biaxin".

Supplied: Pediatric Granules for Suspension: HDPE bottle which allows capacity for shaking consists of a: granulation of clarithromycin and carbopol which is coated with HP-55 polymer (hydroxypropylmethylcellulose phthalate). Nonmedicinal ingredients: castor oil, citric acid, flavor, potassium sorbate, povidone (K90), saccharine, silicon dioxide, sodium chloride, sucrose and xanthan gum. Water is added to reconstitute the suspension prior to use. When reconstituted, the concentration of clarithromycin is 125 mg/5 mL. HDPE bottles of 55, 105 and 150 mL. Store granules for suspension between 15 and 25°C in a tightly closed bottle. Protect from light. Do **not** refrigerate suspension.

Directions for reconstitution: 150 mL size: 80 mL of water should be added to the granules in the bottle and shaken to yield 150 mL of reconstituted suspension.

105 mL size: 56 mL of water should be added to the granules in the bottle and shaken to yield 105 mL of reconstituted suspension.

55 mL size: 29 mL of water should be added to the granules in the bottle and shaken to yield 55 mL of reconstituted suspension.

The reconstituted suspension must not be refrigerated. Any reconstituted unused medication should be discarded after 14 days.

Tablets: 250 mg: Each oval, debossed, yellow, film-coated tablet contains: clarithromycin 250 mg. Nonmedicinal ingredients: cellulosic polymers, crosscarmellose sodium, D&C Yellow No. 10, magnesium stearate, povidone, pregelatinized starch, propylene glycol, silicon dioxide, sorbic acid, sorbitan monooleate, stearic acid, talc, titanium dioxide and vanillin. Tartrazine-free. HDPE bottles of 100, 250 and 500.

500 mg: Each oval, debossed, pale yellow, film-coated tablet contains: clarithromycin 500 mg. Nonmedicinal ingredients: cellulosic polymers, crosscarmellose sodium, D&C Yellow No. 10, magnesium stearate, povidone, propylene glycol, silicon dioxide, sorbic acid, sorbitan monooleate, stearic acid, talc, titanium dioxide and vanillin. Tartrazine-free. HDPE bottles of 100 and 250.

Store tablets between 15 and 25°C in a tightly closed container. Protect from light.

Reviewed 1999

BICHLORACETIC ACID® ℞

Glenwood

Dichloroacetic Acid

Escharotic—Keratolytic

Pharmacology: Dichloroacetic acid rapidly penetrates and cauterizes skin, keratin and other tissues. Its cauterizing effect is comparable to that obtained with such methods as electrocautery or freezing.

Indications: For all types of verrucae; calluses; hard and soft corns; xanthoma palpebrarum; seborrheic keratoses; ingrown nails; cysts and benign erosion of the cervix including endocervicitis; epistaxis.

Contraindications: Should not be used for the treatment of malignant or premalignant lesions.

Warnings: Dichloroacetic acid is an extremely powerful keratolytic and cauterant. It should be restricted to those areas where these effects are desired.

Precautions and Adverse Effects: Before treating cervical lesions a careful diagnosis and possibly a biopsy may be required to rule out malignancy. Treatment is contraindicated in the event of positive findings.

Topical chemical cauterant-keratolytics should be applied only to the lesion being treated. To prevent them from spreading onto normal skin, petrolatum is painted around the area to be treated. If any acid is accidentally spilled on normal tissue or if too much acid is accidentally applied, it should be immediately wiped up with a cotton pledget and washed with water. Sodium bicarbonate may be applied as a local antidote.

Bichloracetic Acid (cont'd)

Prior to treatment with dichloroacetic acid the surfaces or cervical lesions must be well dried. If these surfaces have not been well dried or if too much acid is used, a fine trickle may be observed as a line of white moving downward on the cervix. If this occurs or if the vaginal wall is inadvertently touched with the applicator swab, immediately touch the affected area with a dry cotton swab following at once with a swab well moistened with water.

Overdose: Symptoms and Treatment: Skin Contact: Immediately remove contaminated clothing and wash affected area thoroughly with soap and water. In the event of massive exposure get immediate medical help.

Inhalation: Remove individual to fresh air. Get immediate medical help.

Eye Contact: Flush thoroughly with water for 15 minutes. Get immediate medical help.

Ingestion: If person is conscious, immediately give water or milk to dilute stomach contents (dilution of a least 100 mL/mL ingested). **Do not induce vomiting.** If breathing has stopped administer artificial respiration. Get immediate medical help.

Note: Contact lenses should not be worn when working with this chemical.

Dosage: The amount of dichloroacetic acid which should be applied varies with the nature of the lesion. Dense horny lesions such as corns, warts, calluses, plantar warts, etc. require repeated intensive treatment. Lesions of light density such as pedunculated warts, xanthoma palpebrarum, soft corns, seborrheic keratoses, condyloma acuminata, etc. should receive lighter applications.

Similarly, the technique for application will vary depending on the type of lesion being treated. Dense growths are treated by rubbing dichloroacetic acid into the lesion with a pointed wooden applicator or a cotton tipped applicator. Three or 4 office visits may be necessary before the desired result is achieved. Lesions of light density should receive a lighter application at each visit. Usually 1 or 2 such treatments is sufficient.

Administration is facilitated by use of the Treatment Kit (see Supplied) which contains in addition to the acid, petrolatum, pointed wooden applicators, 2 acid receptacles of differing capacity and a micro-dropper and holder. Both sealed-stem acid receptacles have flared funnel-shaped tops to simplify transfer of the acid from the bottle using the micro-dropper. Most kinds of lesions can be satisfactorily treated using the small-stemmed receptacle and 1 of the sharpened applicators. The large-stemmed receptacle is for use with cotton tipped applicators in the treatment of calluses or with gauze swabs in cauterization of the cervix uteri.

Typical Use: First a thin layer of petrolatum is applied to the normal tissue surrounding the lesion.

Next, the micro-dropper is used to transfer some dichloroacetic acid to the small-stemmed acid receptacle. The acid should not contact the neoprene bulb of the micro-dropper. Use the micro-dropper upright filling it no more than half way. Between uses store the micro-dropper in its holder.

A sharpened applicator stick is then moistened in the acid in the receptacle and drawn over the flared lip to remove any excess. There should never be a large excess drop of the liquid on the applicator.

Where it is desired to apply very small amounts, the applicator stick is held level or with the point up. By controlling the angle of application, a tiny fraction of one drop can be transferred to small lesions. Cauterization progress is followed by observing the change in color of the treated area to gray-white, using a loupe if necessary.

It is sometimes advantageous to apply the liquid by rolling the applicator over the surface of the lesion, using the point only at the edges.

When each treatment has been completed, rinse the receptacle with water, dry and return it to the Kit. To avoid contamination with foreign material, do not return any remaining acid from the receptacle to the bottle. Keep the bottle tightly capped except when removing acid. Applicators should be discarded after use.

Verrucae: Verrucae vulgaris will respond more quickly if surgically pared down before treatment with dichloroacetic acid. These warts require heavy treatments. After protecting the surrounding area with petrolatum, coat the entire lesion, including the sides, with acid. With the sharpened applicator work the acid into the center of the wart. Instruct the patient to return in 7 to 10 days. If any warty tissue remains, it will facilitate treatment to pare off the hard tissue with a scalpel. Try to avoid drawing blood. Repeat the application of dichloroacetic acid as outlined above. The results are permanent if all verrucous tissue has been destroyed.

Plantar warts are treated similarly to other warts but treatment will usually be of longer duration.

Venereal warts are best destroyed when the product is applied in light applications which should be repeated until the warts disappear.

Calluses: These dense lesions should first be surgically pared and the surrounding normal tissue protected with a thin layer of petrolatum. Dichloroacetic acid is then transferred to the large-stemmed acid receptacle. Dip a cotton tipped applicator into the acid in the receptacle and remove it permitting it to drain against the flared lip. Rub the acid into the callus lightly. In less than a week the patient will be able to remove the dead skin by soaking his feet in warm water, then rubbing the treated areas with a soft cloth. If complete removal is not obtained, make another application to the thickened areas and soak as before. Very thick dense calluses require further surgical paring before application of the acid.

Cervical Cauterization: First, the micro-dropper is used to transfer dichloroacetic acid to the large-stemmed acid receptacle. Two fairly large cotton or gauze swabs and a tightly-wound swab small enough to slip into the acid receptacle will also be needed (these swabs are not supplied in the Kit).

Next, use one of the large cotton swabs to wipe mucus or purulent material away from the cervical canal and from the eroded area.

Dip the small tightly-wound swab into the dichloroacetic acid in the receptacle then raise it and permit it to drain against the receptacle wall.

While the areas to be treated are still free of mucus, use the small well-drained swab to apply the product to all eroded areas. The swab may be rotated within the cervical canal if endocervicitis is found. The swab may be redipped in the acid or a fresh swab may be used if the first application does not cover the diseased area.

After a minute or two use the second large cotton swab to gently touch all the areas to which dichloroacetic acid has been applied. A slow rotating motion increases the efficiency of the swab in drying and removing any remaining acid.

Cauterization with dichloroacetic acid will often be followed for 5 to 10 days by a vaginal discharge, usually not profuse or foul smelling. In most cases the cervix will have completely healed after 10 days. If needed, additional courses of therapy with the acid may follow at 10 day intervals.

Nabothian cysts are usually destroyed concurrently with treatment of the areas of erosion. These cysts may be destroyed by puncturing them with a sharpened wooden applicator moistened with dichloroacetic acid.

In cases where electro-cautery has been used without satisfactory results, dichloroacetic acid may be used as a follow-up treatment. Properly used, dichloroacetic acid cauterization if far less drastic than electro-cauterization or conization.

Corns, Hard: With a scalpel or burr, surgically pare the corn as thoroughly as possible without drawing blood. Any slight bleeding which may occur will be stopped by application of the acid.

Apply dichloroacetic acid to all thickened areas and especially to the core. In a few minutes the acid will be absorbed. Make several more applications and instruct the patient to return in 4 or 5 days. At this second visit remove all hard, horny tissue with the scalpel or burr. If necessary, make several more applications of acid and pare off the hard tissue again after 5 days. The lesion will not recur if properly fitted shoes are worn.

Corns, Soft: Surgically pare down the corn and apply dichloroacetic acid. After 7 days remove the dead skin with a scalpel. Another application of the acid can then be made to the center of the corn and to the whitened skin. This is usually sufficient. A pad to separate the toes is helpful. Properly fitted shoes prevent recurrences.

Xanthoma Palpebrarum: Paint petrolatum around the xanthoma then carefully apply dichloroacetic acid with a sharpened applicator stick. In 7 to 10 days the crust falls off. Repeat application of the acid every 7 to 10 days until the xanthoma disappears. Very little scarring results.

Seborrheic Keratoses: These lesions yield very easily to dichloroacetic acid. Paint petrolatum around the abnormal tissue and apply the liquid until it whitens the lesion. A second treatment may be made in 7 to 10 days if needed. Very little scarring will result.

Ingrown Nails: Treat ingrown nails by applying dichloroacetic acid lightly to the granulation tissue associated with the lesion.

Epistaxis: The bleeding point is located, usually in Kiesselbach's area, and is lightly touched with dichloroacetic acid using a fine wooden applicator with cotton twisted on the end. Only the very tip of the applicator should be moistened with the acid. Cauterization is almost immediate.

Caution: Cauterize only the bleeding point.

Supplied: Treatment Kit: Each permanent, white plastic container contains: dichloroacetic acid 10 mL, petrolatum 16 g, approximately 100 applicators and directions. Also contains 2 sealed-stem acid receptacles of differing capacity, a micro-dropper and holder.

Replenishment Unit: Each unit contains: dichloroacetic acid 10 mL with approximately 100 pointed 7.5 cm applicators and directions.

Restocking Unit: Each unit contains: dichloroacetic acid 75 mL with approximately 200 pointed 7.5 cm applicators and directions.

BICILLIN® L-A ℞

Wyeth-Ayerst

Penicillin G Benzathine

Antibiotic

Pharmacology: Actions: Penicillin G exerts a bactericidal action against penicillin-sensitive microorganisms during the stage of active multiplication. It acts through the inhibition of biosynthesis of cell-wall mucopeptide. It is not active against the penicillinase-producing bacteria, which include many strains of staphylococci. Penicillin G exerts high in vitro activity against staphylococci (except penicillinase-producing strains), streptococci (Groups A,C,G,H,L and M) and pneumococci. Other organisms sensitive to penicillin G are: N. gonorrhoeae, C. diphtheriae, B. anthracis, Clostridia, A. bovis, S. moniliformis, L. monocytogenes, and Leptospira. T. pallidum is extremely sensitive to the bactericidal action of penicillin G.

Pharmacokinetics: I.M. penicillin G benzathine is absorbed very slowly into the bloodstream from the i.m. site and converted by hydrolysis to penicillin G. This combination of hydrolysis and slow absorption results in blood serum levels much lower but much more prolonged than other parenteral penicillins.

Approximately 60% of penicillin G is bound to serum protein. The drug is distributed throughout the body tissues in widely varying amounts. Highest levels are found in the kidneys with lesser amounts in the liver, skin, and intestines. Penicillin G penetrates into all other tissues to a lesser degree with a very small level found in the cerebrospinal fluid. With normal kidney function the drug is excreted rapidly by tubular excretion. In neonates and young infants and in individuals with impaired kidney function, excretion is considerably delayed.

Sensitivity Plate Testing: If the Kirby-Bauer method of disc sensitivity is used, a 10-unit penicillin disc should give a zone greater than 28 mm when tested against a penicillin-sensitive bacterial strain.

Indications: In the treatment of infections due to penicillin-G-sensitive microorganisms that are susceptible to the low and very prolonged serum levels common to this particular dosage form. Therapy should be guided by bacteriological studies (including sensitivity tests) and by clinical response.

The following infections will usually respond to adequate dosage of i.m. penicillin G benzathine.

Streptococcal infections (Group A without bacteremia): mild-to-moderate infections of the upper respiratory tract (e.g., pharyngitis).

Venereal infections: syphilis, yaws, bejel, and pinta.

Medical conditions in which penicillin G benzathine therapy is indicated as prophylaxis: Rheumatic fever and/or chorea: Prophylaxis with penicillin G benzathine has proven effective in preventing recurrence of these conditions. It has also been used as follow-up prophylactic therapy for rheumatic heart disease and acute glomerulonephritis.

Contraindications: A history of a previous hypersensitivity reaction to any of the penicillins is a contraindication.

Do not inject into or near an artery or nerve.

Warnings: Serious and occasionally fatal hypersensitivity (anaphylactoid) reactions have been reported in patients on penicillin therapy. Although anaphylaxis is more frequent following parenteral therapy, it has occurred in patients on oral penicillins. These reactions are more apt to occur in individuals with a history of sensitivity to multiple allergens.

There have been well-documented reports of individuals with a history of penicillin hypersensitivity reactions who have experienced severe hypersensitivity reactions when treated with a cephalosporin. Before therapy with a penicillin, careful inquiry should be made concerning previous hypersensitivity reactions to penicillins, cephalosporins and other allergens. If an allergic reaction occurs, the drug should be discontinued and the patient treated with the usual agents, e.g., pressor amines, antihistamines, and corticosteroids.

Inadvertent intravascular administration, including inadvertent direct intra-arterial injection or injection immediately adjacent to arteries, of penicillin G benzathine and other penicillin preparations has resulted in severe neurovascular damage, including transverse myelitis with permanent paralysis, gangrene requiring amputation of digits and more proximal portions of extremities, and necrosis and sloughing at and surrounding the injection site. Such severe effects have been reported following injections into the buttock, thigh, and deltoid areas.

Other serious complications of suspected intravascular administration which have been reported include immediate pallor, mottling or cyanosis of the extremity both distal and proximal to the injection site followed by bleb formation; severe edema requiring anterior and/or posterior compartment fasciotomy in the lower extremity. The above-described severe effects and complications have most often occurred in infants and small children. Prompt consultation with an appropriate specialist is indicated if any evidence of compromise of the blood supply occurs at, proximal to, or distal to the site of injection. See Contraindications, Precautions and Dosage.

Quadriceps femoris fibrosis and atrophy have been reported following repeated i.m. injections of penicillin preparations into the anterolateral thigh.

Injection into or near a nerve may result in permanent neurological damage.

Precautions: Penicillin should be used with caution in individuals with histories of significant allergies and/or asthma.

Care should be taken to avoid i.v. or intra-arterial administration, or injection into or near major peripheral nerves or blood vessels, since such injection may produce neurovascular damage. See Contraindications, Warnings and Dosage.

The use of antibiotics may result in overgrowth of nonsusceptible organisms. Constant observation of the patient is essential. If new infections due to bacteria or fungi appear during therapy, the drug should be discontinued and appropriate measures taken.

Whenever allergic reactions occur, penicillin should be withdrawn unless, in the opinion of the physician, the condition being treated is life-threatening and amenable only to penicillin therapy.

In streptococcal infections, therapy must be sufficient to eliminate the organism; otherwise, the sequelae of streptococcal disease may occur. Cultures should be taken following completion of treatment to determine whether streptococci have been eradicated.

Pregnancy: Penicillins readily cross the placenta. The effect, if any, on the fetus is not known. Although generally considered to be safe, penicillin G benzathine should be used during pregnancy only if clearly needed.

Lactation: Soluble penicillin G is excreted in breast milk. The effect on the infant, if any, is not known. Caution should be used when penicillin G benzathine is administered to a nursing woman.

Drug Interactions: Tetracycline, a bacteriostatic antibiotic, may antagonize the bactericidal effect of penicillin, and concurrent use of these drugs should be avoided. The rate of excretion of the penicillins is decreased by concomitant administration of probenecid; probenecid prolongs, as well as increases, blood levels of the penicillins.

Laboratory Tests: In prolonged therapy with penicillin and particularly with high-dosage schedules, periodic evaluation of the renal and hematopoietic systems is recommended.

Laboratory Test Interactions: Penicillins can interfere with the copper sulfate reagent method of testing for glycosuria, resulting in falsely elevated or falsely decreased readings. Such interference does not occur with the glucose oxidase method.

Adverse Effects: Penicillin is a substance of low toxicity but does possess a significant index of sensitization. The following hypersensitivity reactions associated with use of penicillin have been reported: skin rashes, ranging from maculopapular eruptions to exfoliative dermatitis; urticaria; laryngeal edema; serum-sickness like reactions, including chills, fever, edema, arthralgia, and prostration. Fever and eosinophilia may frequently be the only reaction observed. Severe and often fatal anaphylaxis has been reported (see Warnings).

Hemolytic anemia, leukopenia, thrombocytopenia, neuropathy and nephropathy are infrequent reactions and usually associated with high doses of parenteral penicillin.

As with other treatments for syphilis, the Jarisch-Herxheimer reaction has been reported.

Overdose: Symptoms and Treatment: There have been no reported overdosages. Usually, the penicillins have minimal direct toxicity to man. However, the viscous nature of penicillin G benzathine suspension may cause any of the local neurovascular effects described under Warnings. Since there is no antidote, treatment should be symptomatic and supportive.

Anaphylactic Shock: In adults, initially epinephrine HCl 0.5 mg (0.5 mL of a 1:1 000 solution) may be given by the s.c. or i.m. route followed by 0.025 to 0.05 mg (0.25 to 0.5 mL of a 1:10 000 solution) given i.v. in repeated doses every 5 to 15 minutes until relief of bronchospasm and hypotension has occurred, or excessive tachycardia induced.

In pediatrics, initially epinephrine HCl 0.01 mg/kg (0.01 mL/kg of a 1:1 000 solution) or 0.3 mg/m² (0.3 mL/m² of a 1:1 000 solution) may be given by the s.c. route. Single pediatric doses should not exceed 0.5 mg. Doses may be repeated every 20 minutes to 4 hours, depending on the severity of the condition and the response of the patient.

Aminophylline, oxygen and i.v. corticosteroids may also be required. Mild hypersensitivity reactions may respond to antihistamines, pressor amines or corticosteroids.

Dosage: The following dosages are recommended: Streptococcal Group A—upper respiratory infections (e.g., pharyngitis): Adults: a single dose of 1.2 million IU. Older children: a single dose of 900 000 IU. Children and infants under 27 kg: a single dose of 300 000 to 600 000 IU.

Venereal Infections: Syphilis—Primary, secondary, and latent: 2.4 million IU (1 dose).

Late (tertiary and neurosyphilis): 2.4 million IU at 7-day intervals for 3 doses.

Congenital: under 2 years of age: 50 000 IU/kg; ages 2 to 12 years: adjust dosage based on adult dosage schedule.

Yaws, Bejel, and Pinta: a single dose of 1.2 million IU.

Prophylaxis: for rheumatic fever and glomerulonephritis: Following an acute attack, penicillin G benzathine (parenteral) may be given in doses of 1 200 000 IU once a month or 600 000 IU every 2 weeks.

Directions for Use (see package insert for illustrations): Administer by **deep, i.m. injection** in the upper, outer quadrant of the buttock. In infants and small children, the midlateral aspect of the thigh may be preferable. When doses are repeated, vary the injection site. Care should be taken to avoid i.v. or intra-arterial administration, or injection into or near major peripheral nerves or blood vessels, since such injection may produce neurovascular damage. Discontinue delivery of the dose if the subject complains of severe immediate pain at the injection site or if, especially in infants and young children, symptoms or signs occur suggesting onset of severe pain.

The Wyeth-Ayerst Tubex cartridge for this product incorporates several features that are designed to facilitate the visualization of blood on aspiration if a blood vessel is inadvertently entered.

The design of this cartridge is such that blood which enters its needle will be quickly visualized as a red or dark-colored "spot". This "spot" will appear on the barrel of the glass cartridge immediately proximal to the blue hub. The Tubex is designed with 2 orientation marks, in order to determine where this "spot" can be seen. First insert and secure the cartridge in the Tubex injector in the usual fashion. Locate the yellow rectangle at the base of the blue hub. This yellow rectangle is aligned with the blood visualization "spot". An imaginary straight line, drawn from this yellow rectangle to the shoulder of the glass cartridge, will point to the area on the cartridge where the "spot" can be visualized. When the needle cover is removed, a second yellow rectangle will be visible. The second yellow rectangle is also aligned with the blood visualization "spot" to assist the operator in locating this "spot". The glass cartridge should be rotated by turning the plunger of the syringe clockwise until the yellow rectangle is visualized.

Thus, before the needle is inserted into the selected muscle, it is important for the operator to orient the yellow rectangles so that any blood which may enter after needle insertion and during aspiration can be visualized in the area on the cartridge where it will appear and not be obscured by any obstructions.

After selection of the proper site and insertion of the needle into the selected muscle, aspirate by pulling back on the plunger. While maintaining negative pressure for 2 to 3 seconds, carefully observe the barrel of the cartridge in the area previously identified (see above) for the appearance of a red or dark-colored "spot".

Blood or "typical blood color" may not be seen if a blood-vessel has been entered — only a mixture of blood and penicillin G benzathine. The appearance of any discoloration is reason to withdraw the needle and discard the glass Tubex cartridge. If it is elected to inject at another site, a new cartridge should be used. If no blood or discoloration appears, inject the contents of the cartridge slowly.

Some Tubex cartridges may contain a small air bubble which may be disregarded, since it does not affect administration of the product.

Because of the high concentration of suspended material in this product, the needle may be blocked if the injection is not made at a slow, steady rate.

Parenteral drug products should be inspected visually for particulate matter and discoloration prior to administration, whenever solution and container permit.

Tubex Injector: Note: The Tubex Injector is reusable: do not discard.

Directions for Use: Before proceeding, see important information above.

To load a Tubex Sterile Cartridge-Needle Unit into the Tubex Injector: 1) Turn the ribbed collar to the "Open" position until it stops. 2) Hold the Injector with the open end up and fully insert the Tubex Sterile Cartridge-Needle Unit. Firmly tighten the ribbed collar in the direction of the "Close" arrow. 3) Thread the plunger rod into the plunger of the Tubex Sterile Cartridge-Needle Unit until slight resistance is felt. The Injector is now ready for use in the usual manner.

To administer: Method of administration is the same as with conventional syringe. Remove needle cover by grasping it securely: twist and pull. Introduce needle into patient, aspirate by pulling back slightly on the plunger, and inject.

To remove empty Tubex Cartridge-Needle Unit and dispose into a vertical needle disposal container: 1) Do not recap the needle. Disengage the plunger rod. 2) Hold the Injector, needle down, over a vertical needle disposal container and loosen the ribbed collar. Tubex Cartridge-Needle Unit will drop into the container. 3) Discard the needle cover.

To remove empty Tubex Cartridge-Needle Unit and dispose into a horizontal (mailbox) needle disposal container: 1) Do not recap the needle. Disengage the plunger rod. 2) Open the horizontal (mailbox) needle disposal container. Insert Tubex Cartridge-Needle Unit, needle pointing down, halfway into container. Close the container lid on cartridge. Loosen ribbed collar; Tubex Cartridge Unit will drop into the container. 3) Discard the needle cover.

The Tubex Injector is reusable and should not be discarded. Used Tubex Cartridge-Needle Units should not be employed for successive injections or as multiple dose containers. They are intended to be used only once and discarded.

Note: Any graduated markings on Tubex Sterile Cartridge-Needle Units are to be used only as a guide in mixing, withdrawing, or administering measured doses.

Wyeth-Ayerst does not recommend and will not accept responsibility for the use of any cartridge-needle units other than Tubex Cartridge-Needle Units in the Tubex Injector.

Supplied: Each 2 mL of aqueous suspension contains: penicillin G benzathine 1 200 000 IU. Nonmedicinal ingredients: methylparaben, povidone, propylparaben, sodium carboxymethylcellulose, sodium citrate and water for injection. Boxes of 10 single use disposable Tubex Sterile Cartridge-Needle Units (20 gauge×1¼ inch needle) of 2 mL with a reusable Tubex Injector and one insert. Store under refrigeration (2 to 8°C). May be removed from refrigerator and stored for 7 days at a temperature not exceeding 30°C.

Reviewed 1990

BiCNU® Ⓟ

Bristol

Carmustine

Antineoplastic Agent

Pharmacology: Carmustine alkylates DNA and RNA and has been shown to inhibit several enzymes by carbamoylation of amino acids in proteins.

In a series of in vivo and in vitro experiments with formate ^{14}C, adenine-8-^{14}C and DL-leucine-4,5-^{3}H, Wheeler and Bowdon obtained results indicating that carmustine interferes with the de novo synthesis of purine nucleotides and with the conversion of purine nucleotides to components of DNA but to a much lesser extent of RNA. Inhibition of DNA synthesis occurred in the absence of inhibition of the synthesis of protein. In a more recent study, D.P. Groth et al confirmed that carmustine altered de novo purine biosynthesis. It is suggested that carmustine inhibits a reaction(s) involved with the insertion of the C-8 position of the purine ring. These biochemical effects are similar to those described by Wheeler and Alexander for the accepted biological alkylating agents like nitrogen mustards and suggest the inclusion of carmustine in this class of agents.

BiCNU (cont'd)

On the other hand, by chemical evaluation the alkylating properties of carmustine have been shown to be quite weak compared to the above mentioned alkylating agents and it is still an open question whether this activity is sufficient to account for the observed biological effects of carmustine.

Carmustine is not cross resistant with other alkylators.

Protein Binding: The average extent of binding of carmustine with human plasma proteins is about 80% at 0°C. (The experiments were carried out at 0°C because of carmustine's extreme instability in plasma.)

Plasma Level: Plasma samples taken as early as 5 minutes after oral or parenteral drug administration did not contain intact carmustine. Plasma levels of the radioactivity were prolonged with a half-life of about 34 hours for the orally and 67 hours for the i.v. administered ^{14}C carmustine.

CSF: After i.v. administration of ^{14}C carmustine, radioactive ^{14}C was found in the CSF of man equilibrating with plasma radioactivity in about 1 hour, showing 97 and 30% of plasma level in 2 men, respectively.

Urinary Excretion: Extremely small amounts of intact carmustine were detected in urine samples collected at one half hour following drug administration (i.v. or oral). After the second half hour urine samples did not contain unaltered carmustine.

Urinary excretion of the radioactivity was strikingly similar in all patients regardless of the route of administration (i.v. or oral) and quite comparable to monkeys. By 96 hours, an average of 65% of the isotope had been recovered in the urine.

Pulmonary Excretion: Over 24 hours, the radioactivity excretion of ^{14}C carmustine as $^{14}C\ O_2$ was approximately 10% of the dose after oral administration and 6% when given i.v. Although carmustine is well absorbed after oral, intraperitoneal and s.c. administration, it is mainly used by the i.v. route. The active moiety of carmustine is still unknown but the high degradation rate of carmustine in plasma suggests that the biological activity as well as the delayed toxicity of carmustine are related at least partly to its degradation products. The in vitro decomposition of carmustine has been studied quite extensively. However, to date, nothing is known on its biodegradation, except for the fact that part of it is excreted as CO_2 as determined with ^{14}C labeled carmustine.

Indications: As adjuvant therapy to surgery and radiotherapy or in combination therapy with other chemotherapeutic agents in the following: Primary Brain Tumors: Carmustine is a small molecule which is virtually un-ionized in aqueous solution at pH 7 and is therefore highly lipid soluble. These characteristics allow it to cross the blood brain barrier and make it attractive in the treatment of brain tumors. An overall 47% response rate with carmustine compares favorably with any other method of treating brain tumors, such as glioblastoma, brainstemglioma, medulloblastoma, astrocytoma, ependymoma, and metastatic brain tumors.

Malignant Lymphomas: Hodgkin's disease, non-Hodgkin's lymphomas either alone or in combination with other chemotherapeutic agents. Carmustine has a striking antineoplastic effect against Hodgkin's disease even when the tumor has become resistant to standard chemotherapeutic agents including radiotherapy.

Virtually all of these studies in which carmustine was used to treat patients with Hodgkin's disease resulted in a 40 to 50% response rate.

Multiple Myeloma: Carmustine is effective in the treatment of myeloma producing improvement in 30% of the patients. In combination with prednisone, it is particularly active in that it shows 70% response. Carmustine has been used as part of a five-drug regimen (melphalan, cyclophosphamide, prednisone and vincristine) in 29 patients with a 90% response rate.

Malignant Melanoma (disseminated): In combination with vincristine sulfate, carmustine has been shown to give response rates up to 45% in malignant melanoma.

Gastrointestinal Carcinoma: A 12.5% response rate was obtained with carmustine in the therapy of gastrointestinal cancer. Such a result suggests the use of carmustine only after other more appropriate agents have failed in advanced disease.

Contraindications: Carmustine should not be given to individuals who have demonstrated a previous hypersensitivity to it. Also, it is contraindicated in patients with decreased circulating platelets, leukocytes or erythrocytes either from previous chemotherapy or other causes, and severe hepatic and/or renal impairment.

Warnings: Caution: Carmustine is a potent drug and should be used only by physicians experienced with cancer chemotherapeutic drugs (see Precautions). Blood counts as well as renal and hepatic function tests should be taken regularly. Discontinue the drug if abnormal depression of bone marrow or abnormal renal or hepatic function is seen.

Bone marrow suppression, notably thrombocytopenia and leukopenia, which may contribute to bleeding and overwhelming infections in an already compromised patient, is the most common and severe of the toxic effects of carmustine.

Pulmonary toxicity from carmustine appears to be dose related. Patients receiving greater than 1 400 mg/m² cumulative dose are at significantly higher risk than those receiving less. Delayed pulmonary toxicity can occur years after treatment, and can result in death, particularly in patients treated in childhood (see Adverse Effects).

Nitrosourea therapy does have carcinogenic potential. The occurrence of acute leukemia and bone marrow dysplasias have been reported in patients following nitrosourea therapy.

Pregnancy: Safe use in pregnancy has not been established. Carmustine is embryotoxic and teratogenic in rats and embryotoxic in rabbits at dose levels equivalent to the human dose. Carmustine also affects fertility in male rats at doses somewhat higher than the human dose. Carmustine is carcinogenic in rats and mice, producing a marked increase in tumor incidence in doses approximating those employed clinically.

Precautions: Carmustine should be administered preferably by individuals experienced with antineoplastic therapy. Since delayed bone marrow toxicity is the major toxicity, complete blood counts should be monitored frequently for at least 6 weeks after a dose. Repeat doses of carmustine should not be given more frequently than every 6 weeks. The bone marrow toxicity of carmustine is cumulative, and therefore dosage adjustment must be considered on the basis of nadir blood counts from prior dose (see Table I).

It is recommended that liver and renal function tests also be monitored.

Baseline pulmonary function studies should be conducted along with frequent pulmonary function tests during treatment. Patients with a baseline below 70% of the predicted Forced Vital Capacity (FVC) or Carbon Monoxide Diffusing Capacity (DL_{co}) are particularly at risk.

Since pulmonary toxicity has been reported with increasing frequency, patients on carmustine therapy should be instructed to report immediately any signs of respiratory complications. In such cases, therapy should be discontinued and evaluation of respiratory gas exchange and spirometry should be performed. If necessary, patients should then be treated with corticosteroids.

Pregnancy: Safe use in pregnancy has not been established. Therefore the benefit to risk of toxicity must be carefully weighed.

Lactation: It is not known whether this drug is excreted in human milk. Because many drugs are excreted in human milk and because of the potential for serious adverse reactions in nursing infants from carmustine, a decision should be made whether to discontinue nursing or to discontinue the drug, taking into account the importance of the drug to the mother.

Children: Safety and effectiveness in children have not been established.

Adverse Effects: Hematopoietic: thrombocytopenia (platelets below 100 000/mm³) and leukopenia (leukocytes below 4 000/mm³).

The most frequent and most serious toxicity of carmustine is delayed myelosuppression. It usually occurs 4 to 6 weeks after drug administration and is dose-related. Myelosuppression is the major dose limiting factor with carmustine as is with so many drugs of this type. Thrombocytopenia is generally more severe than leukopenia; however, both may be dose-limiting toxicities. Anemia may also occur but it is generally less severe.

Carmustine may produce cumulative myelosuppression, manifested by more depressed indices or longer duration of suppression after repeated doses.

The occurrence of acute leukemia and bone marrow dysplasias have been reported in patients following long-term nitrosourea therapy.

Pulmonary Toxicity: Pulmonary toxicity characterized by pulmonary infiltrates and/or fibrosis has been reported to occur from 9 days to 43 months after treatment with carmustine and related nitrosoureas and appears to be dose related. Most of these patients were receiving prolonged therapy with total doses of carmustine greater than 1 400 mg/m². However, there have been reports of pulmonary fibrosis in patients receiving lower total doses. Other risk factors include past history of lung disease and duration of treatment. Cases of fatal pulmonary toxicity with carmustine have been reported.

In a long-term study of 17 patients who survived childhood brain tumors, very delayed onset pulmonary toxicity occurring up to 17 years after treatment with carmustine has been reported. These children ranged between 2 and 16 years of age when treated with carmustine at doses of 800 mg/m² or more. All received cranial irradiation and most received spinal radiotherapy. Chest radiographs and CT scans have demonstrated upper-zone fibrotic changes primarily. All children exhibited reduced pulmonary function and the toxicity was shown to be progressive, resulting in death in approximately 50% of cases. Severity was related to age at treatment. Five children treated at age less than 5 years died of pulmonary fibrosis.

Hepatic: Carmustine produces reversible hepatic toxicity which is manifested by increased transaminase, alkaline phosphatase and bilirubin levels when high doses are employed. It has been rarely noted at therapeutic doses. Hepatotoxicity is delayed **up to 60 days after dosing.**

Skin: Burning and hyperemia at the site of injection are common, but true thrombophlebitis is rare. Accidental contact of reconstituted carmustine with the skin has caused hyperpigmentation of the affected areas. Within 2 hours after rapid i.v. administration of carmustine, intense flushing of the skin and suffusion of the conjunctiva could last for about 4 hours. Skin rash has also been reported.

Renal: Renal abnormalities consisting of decreases in kidney size, progressive azotemia and renal failure have been reported in patients who receive large cumulative doses after prolonged therapy with carmustine and related nitrosoureas. Kidney damage has also been reported occasionally in patients receiving lower total doses.

Neurological: There have been rare instances of encephalopathy reported.

Gastrointestinal: Nausea and vomiting frequently appear within 2 hours and usually last 4 to 6 hours and are dose-related. Prior administration of antiemetics and sedatives is effective in diminishing and sometimes preventing nausea or vomiting.

Endocrine: Gynecomastia has been observed in a few rare cases.

Other: Muscular pain has been infrequently reported. Neuroretinitis has been reported.

Overdose: Symptoms and Treatment: In the case of overdosage, the patient should be treated symptomatically.

Dosage: The recommended dose of carmustine as a single agent in previously untreated patients is 200 mg/m² i.v. every 6 weeks. This may be given as a single dose or divided into daily injections such as 100 mg/m² on 2 successive days. When carmustine is used in combination with other myelosuppressive drugs or in patients in whom bone marrow reserve is depleted, the doses should be adjusted accordingly.

A repeat course of carmustine should not be given until circulating blood elements have returned to acceptable levels (platelets above 100 000/mm³, leukocytes above 4 000/mm³) and this is usually in 6 weeks. Blood counts should be monitored frequently and repeat courses should not be given before 6 weeks because of delayed toxicity.

Doses subsequent to the initial dose should be adjusted according to the hematologic response of the patient to the preceding dose. The schedule in Table I is suggested as a guide to dosage adjustment.

Table I—BiCNU

Dosage Adjustment

Nadir After Prior Dose: Leukocytes	Nadir After Prior Dose: Platelets	Percentage of Prior Dose to be Given
>4 000	>100 000	100%
3 000–3 999	75 000–99 999	100%
2 000–2 999	25 000–74 999	70%
<2 000	<25 000	50%

Reconstitution: Preparation of I.V. Solutions: To facilitate reconstitution, allow the supplied sterile diluent to come to controlled room temperature (15 to 30°C) before mixing.

Dissolve carmustine completely with 3 mL of the supplied sterile diluent and then aseptically add 27 mL of Sterile Water for Injection, USP, to the alcohol solution. Each mL of the resulting solution will contain 3.3 mg of carmustine in 10% ethanol having a pH of 5.6 to 6.0. (Solution in the ethanol must be complete before sterile water for injection is added.) Accidental contact of reconstituted carmustine with the skin has caused transient hyperpigmentation of the affected areas. If carmustine lyophilized material or solution contacts the skin, immediately wash thoroughly with soap and water. If carmustine lyophilized material or solution contacts mucosa, flush thoroughly with water.

Reconstitution as recommended results in a clear colorless solution which may be further diluted with Sodium Chloride for Injection, USP, or 5% Dextrose for Injection, USP. The reconstituted solution should be used i.v. only and should be administered by i.v. drip over a 1 to 2 hour period. Injection of carmustine over shorter periods of time may produce intense pain and burning at the site of injection.

Stability of Reconstituted Solutions: The lyophilized dosage formulation contains no preservatives and is not intended as a multiple dose vial.

After reconstitution as recommended carmustine is stable for 8 hours at or below 25°C, 3 hours at 30°C or 24 hours under refrigeration (4°C).

The reconstituted solution further diluted with 500 mL of 0.9% Sodium Chloride Injection, USP or 5% Dextrose Injection, USP, **in glass containers,** is stable for 24 hours under refrigeration (4°C). Further diluted carmustine should be used immediately if not refrigerated.

Note: Reconstituted vials stored under refrigeration should be examined for crystal formation prior to use. If crystals are observed, they may be redissolved by warming the vial to room temperature and agitation.

Handling and Disposal: Preparation of carmustine should be done in a vertical laminar flow hood (Biological Safety Cabinet—Class II). Personnel preparing carmustine should wear PVC gloves, safety glasses, disposable gowns and masks. All needles, syringes, vials and other materials which have come in contact with carmustine should be segregated and incinerated at 1 000°C or more. Sealed containers may explode. Intact vials should be returned to the manufacturer for destruction. Proper precautions should be taken in packaging these materials for transport. Personnel regularly involved in the preparation and handling of carmustine should have biannual blood examinations.

Supplied: Each 30 mL amber glass vial contains: carmustine 100 mg with a 3 mL vial of absolute ethanol as sterile diluent. Nonmedicinal ingredients: none. Boxes of 10.

The unopened vial may have a physical appearance ranging from lacy flakes to a congealed mass, with no evident degradation of the active ingredient, carmustine. Do not use if product has liquified.

Unopened vials of the dry powder must be stored in a refrigerator (2 to 8°C). This recommended storage of unopened vials prevents significant decomposition for 24 months. Normal room temperature storage (22°C) of the unopened vials will result in a slow decomposition of the drug (approximately 3%) in 36 days.

Note: Carmustine has a low melting point (approximately 30 to 32°C). Vials of the drug exposed to this temperature or above will cause the drug to liquify and appear as an oil film in the bottom of the vials. This is a sign of decomposition and vials should be discarded. For inspection, hold the vial to a bright light.

BILTRICIDE® Pr

Bayer

Praziquantel

Anthelmintic

Pharmacology: Mechanism of Action: Praziquantel induces a rapid contraction of schistosomes by a specific effect on the permeability of the cell membrane. The drug further causes vacuolization and disintegration of the schistosome tegument. The effect is more marked on adult worms compared to young worms. An increased calcium influx may play an important role.

Secondary effects are inhibition of glucose uptake, lowering of glycogen levels and stimulation of lactate release. The action of praziquantel is limited very specifically to trematodes and cestodes; nematodes (including filariae) are not affected.

After oral administration, praziquantel is rapidly absorbed (approximately 80%), subjected to a first pass effect, metabolized and eliminated by the kidneys. Maximal serum concentration is achieved 1 to 3 hours after dosing. The half-life of praziquantel in serum is 0.8 to 1.5 hours.

Indications: For the treatment of infections due to the following species of schistosoma: (S. haematobium, S. japonicum, S. mansoni, and S. mekongi), and infections due to the liver flukes C. sinensis/O. viverrini. (Approval of this indication was based on studies in which the two species were not differentiated.)

Contraindications: Patients who have previously shown hypersensitivity to the drug.

Since parasite destruction within the eye may cause irreparable lesions, ocular cysticercosis should not be treated with praziquantel.

Warnings: Information for the Patient: There may possibly be effects on vigilance. Patients should be warned not to drive a car and not to operate machinery on the day of praziquantel treatment and during the subsequent 24 hours as their ability to do so may be temporarily impaired by the use of praziquantel.

Children: Safety in children under 4 years of age has not been established.

Pregnancy: No adequate and well-controlled studies have been conducted with praziquantel in pregnant women (see Precautions).

Precautions: General: Nephrotoxic effects of praziquantel have not been observed. Since 80% of praziquantel and its derivatives are excreted in the kidneys, excretion may be delayed in patients with impaired renal function.

Caution should be taken in patients with uncompensated liver insufficiency or with hepatosplenic schistosomiasis. Because of reduced drug metabolization in the liver, considerably higher and longer lasting concentrations of unmetabolized praziquantel can occur in the vascular system and/or collateral circulation, leading to prolonged plasma half-life. If necessary, the patient may be hospitalized for the duration of treatment. Mild increases in liver enzymes have also been reported in some patients.

the infestation (no relation). It may be difficult to differentiate between the possible variations.

Overdose: Symptoms and Treatment: No data are available regarding overdosage in humans. In the event of an overdose, a fast-acting laxative is recommended. In rats and mice the acute oral LD_{50} was approximately 2 500 mg/kg and in dogs the oral LD_{50} was less than 200 mg/kg.

Dosage: Doses should be individualized depending on the diagnosis. Based on clinical experience, the following dosages are recommended.

Schistosomiasis: 3×20 mg/kg body weight as a 1-day treatment. Using Table I, the number of tablets to be taken 3 times on the same day can be determined.

The recommended dose for clonorchiasis and opisthorchiasis is 3×25 mg/kg body weight as a 1-day treatment. See Table II.

The tablets should be swallowed whole with a little liquid, preferably during or after meals. Keeping the tablets (or segments thereof) in the mouth may reveal a bitter taste which can cause gagging or vomiting.

Table I—Biltricide

Dosing in Schistosomiasis

Body Weight in kg	20-25	26-33	34-41	42-48	49-56	57-63	64-70	71-78	79-86
Dose (mg)	450	600	750	900	1 050	1 200	1 350	1 500	1 650
Number of tablets corresponding to 1×20 mg/kg*	3/4	1	1¼	1½	1¾	2	2¼	2½	2¾

*Each 600 mg oblong tablet has 3 scores. When broken, each of the 4 segments contains 150 mg of active ingredient.

Table II—Biltricide

Dosing in Clonorchiasis and Opisthorchiasis

Body Weight in kg	22-26	27-33	34-38	39-44	45-50	51-56	57-62	63-68	69-75
Dose (mg)	600	750	900	1 050	1 200	1 350	1 500	1 650	1 800
Number of tablets corresponding to 25 mg/kg*	1	1¼	1½	1¾	2	2¼	2½	2¾	3

*Each 600 mg oblong tablet has 3 scores. When broken, each of the 4 segments contains 150 mg of active ingredient.

Patients suffering from cardiac irregularities should be monitored during treatment.

When schistosomiasis or fluke infection is found in patients living in or coming from areas with endemic human cysticercosis, it is advisable to hospitalize the patient for the duration of treatment.

Pregnancy: An increase in the abortion rate was found in rats at 3 times the single human therapeutic dose. Although animal reproduction studies have not brought to light any evidence that the mother or the unborn child might be harmed, these studies are not always predictive of human response. Praziquantel should not be used in pregnancy unless clearly needed.

Lactation: Praziquantel appears in the milk of nursing women at a concentration of 20 to 25% that of maternal serum. Breast-feeding should be suspended for the day(s) of treatment and the following 72 hours.

Drug Interactions: Dexamethasone, when taken simultaneously, can lead to lower concentrations of praziquantel in blood.

Concomitant administration of drugs increasing the activity of drug metabolizing liver enzymes (cytochrome P450), i.e., antiepileptic drugs, may reduce plasma levels of praziquantel.

Adverse Effects: Adverse reactions vary according to dose and duration of praziquantel medication. Furthermore, they are dependent on the parasite species, extent of parasitization, duration of infection and localization of the parasites in the body.

Apart from these conditions, abdominal pain, inappetence, nausea, vomiting, headache, vertigo, weakness, dizziness, drowsiness, malaise, myalgia, urticaria or elevated temperature may occur occasionally to frequently.

Depending on the kind of infection the following additional adverse reactions have been observed in single cases: bloody diarrhea, seizure, arrhythmia, generalized hypersensitivity (including polyserositis).

Mild increases in liver enzymes have been reported in some patients.

It is often not clear whether the complaints reported by patients or the undesired effects recorded by the physician are caused by praziquantel itself (direct relation), or may be considered to be an endogenous reaction to the death of the parasites (indirect relation) or are symptomatic observations of

With single daily doses it is recommended to take the tablets in the evening. If ingestion of tablets several times a day is prescribed, the interval between administration should be at least 4 hours and not more than 6 hours.

When broken, each of the 4 segments contains 150 mg of active ingredient so that the dosage can be easily adjusted to the patient's body weight.

Children: Safety and efficacy in children under 4 years of age has not been established (see Warnings).

Information for the Patient: See Blue Section—Information for the Patient "Biltricide".

Supplied: Each white, film-coated, oblong tablet, with three scores on both sides and engraved BAYER on one side and LG on the other, contains: praziquantel 600 mg. Nonmedicinal ingredients: cornstarch, magnesium stearate, microcrystalline cellulose, polyvidone 25, sodium lauryl sulfate, polyethylene glycol 4000, methylhydroxypropylcellulose and titanium dioxide. When broken, each of the four segments contains 150 mg of the active ingredient so that the dosage can be easily adjusted to the patient's body weight. Segments are broken off by pressing the score (notch) with thumbnails. If one quarter of a tablet is required, this is best achieved by breaking the segment from the outer end. Bottles of 6. Store at room temperature below 30°C. Protect from light and excessive humidity.

(Shown in Product Recognition Section)

Reviewed 1998

BIOBASE™
BIOBASE-G™

Odan

Ethyl Alcohol
Glycolic Acid—Ethyl Alcohol

Antiseptic Vehicle for Topical Preparations

Supplied: Biobase: Each mL of unscented solution contains: ethyl alcohol 70% and cetyl steryl ethylene oxide. Nonmedicinal ingredients: cetomacrogol and purified water. Plastic bottles of 50 and 100 mL with a brushed nylon applicator to prevent clogging and control flow.

Biobase (cont'd)

Biobase-G: 6%: Each mL of unscented solution contains: glycolic acid 6% w/v and ethyl alcohol 20%. Nonmedicinal ingredients: citric acid, ethyl alcohol, laureth-4, purified water and sodium hydroxide. pH 3.5. Plastic bottles of 50 and 100 mL with a brushed nylon applicator to prevent clogging and control flow.

8%: Each mL of unscented solution contains: glycolic acid 8% w/v and ethyl alcohol 20%. Nonmedicinal ingredients: citric acid, ethyl alcohol, laureth-4, purified water and sodium hydroxide. pH 3.5 Plastic bottles of 50 and 100 mL with a brushed nylon applicator to prevent clogging and control flow.

BIODERM®
Odan
Polymyxin B Sulfate—Bacitracin
Antibiotic

Supplied: Each g of ointment contains: polymyxin B sulfate 10 000 units and bacitracin 500 units. Nonmedicinal ingredients: white petrolatum. Tubes of 15 and 30 g.

BIOLON™
Ophtapharma
Sodium Hyaluronate
Ophthalmosurgical Aid

Pharmacology: Sodium hyaluronate is a physiological material found in both animal and human tissues. It is a polysaccharide consisting of a repeating disaccharide of N-acetylglucosamine and sodium glucuronate, linked by alternating β-1,3 and β-1,4 glycosidic bonds. Chemically identical in all species, hyaluronate can be found in the vitreous and aqueous humor of the eye, in synovial fluid, in skin and in the umbilical cord. Biolon is a sterile 1% solution of highly purified, high molecular weight viscoelastic sodium hyaluronate in phosphate-buffered saline.

When introduced into the anterior segment of the eye during surgical procedures, Biolon maintains a deep anterior chamber throughout surgery, facilitates surgery and reduces trauma to the corneal endothelium and surrounding tissues.

Its viscoelasticity also helps to repel the vitreous face and discourage formation of a postoperative flat chamber. Biolon creates a clear field of vision during and after surgery. It does not interfere with epithelization and normal wound healing. Any traces of Biolon left in the anterior segment of the eye after surgery dissipate through Schlemm's canal within a week.

Indications: Eye surgery, including intraocular lens insertion, intracapsular and extracapsular lens extraction, glaucoma surgery, corneal graft surgery for accidental trauma.

Contraindications: When used as recommended, there are no known contraindications.

Precautions: Precautions are limited to those normally associated with the surgical procedures being performed.

Instilling excessive amounts of Biolon into the anterior segments of the eye may increase intraocular pressure. Increased postoperative intraocular pressure may also be caused by a pre-existing glaucoma condition or by compromised outflow and by operative procedures and sequelae thereto, including enzymatic zonulysis, absence of an iridectomy, trauma to filtration structures, and by blood and lenticular remnants in the anterior chamber.

Because these factors vary from case to case and are difficult to predict, the following precaution is recommended: Do not overfill the eye with Biolon.

At the end of surgery, all remaining Biolon should be removed by irrigation or aspiration.

Carefully monitor the intraocular pressure, especially during the immediate postoperative period. If a significant increase in pressure is observed, treat appropriately.

Avoid the trapping of air bubbles behind Biolon. Biolon is a very highly purified substance extracted from bacterial cells. Since the presence of minute quantities of impurities (proteins, etc.) cannot be totally excluded, the physician should be aware of immunological, allergic and other potential risks associated with the injection of biological substances. On rare occasions, viscoelastic products containing sodium hyaluronate have been observed to become slightly opaque or to form a slight precipitate upon instillation into the eye. The clinical significance, if any, of this phenomenon is not known. The physician should, however, be aware of this possibility, and, should it be observed, the cloudy or precipitated material should be removed by irrigation and/or aspiration. Avoid re-use of the cannula.

<u>Drug Interactions:</u> None currently known.

Adverse Effects: Biolon is well tolerated in the human eye. Transient rises of postoperative intraocular pressure have been reported in some cases. A causal relationship has not been established between Biolon use and postoperative inflammatory reactions (iritis), corneal edema and corneal decompensation.

Dosage: Dosage varies with type of surgery. Usually a dose of 0.2 to 0.6 mL is injected into the anterior segment of the eye.

Examples of Surgical Applications: Cataract Surgery: Before lens extraction, Biolon is introduced into the anterior chamber to protect the corneal endothelium and to maintain a deep anterior chamber. Additional amounts may also be introduced before implantation of an intraocular lens, and to coat the artificial lens, the surgical instruments and the corneal surface.

Glaucoma Surgery: Biolon is instilled before the trabeculectomy in order to reconstitute the anterior chamber. At the close of surgery, further instillation of Biolon may be required to achieve good subconjunctiva filtration and to prevent tissue adherences.

Corneal Transplant Surgery: In trepanation of the cornea, the anterior chamber is filled with Biolon. The donor graft should be placed on the surface of the solution and sutured into position. Additional amounts of Biolon may be injected to maintain a deep anterior chamber. Biolon may also be used in the anterior chamber of the donor eye to protect the corneal endothelial cells of the graft prior to trepanation, and to protect the exposed endothelial layer of the donor button during preparation of the recipient eye.

Incompatibilities: Mixing of quaternary ammonium salts such as benzalkonium chloride with sodium hyaluronate solutions results in formation of a precipitate. Biolon should not be administered through a cannula previously used with medical solutions containing benzalkonium chloride.

Supplied: Each mL contains: sodium hyaluronate 10 mg. Nonmedicinal ingredients: disodium hydrogen phosphate, sodium chloride, sodium dihydrogen phosphate and water for injection. Sterile disposable syringes of 0.5 and 1 mL. Store in a cold dark place (2 to 8°C). May be kept at 25°C for up to 1 month. Protect from freezing.

Reviewed 1997

BIONET®
Carter Horner
Benzocaine—Bicetonium
Local Anti-infective—Analgesic

Indications: The symptomatic treatment of mild infection and relief of pain in gum, pharyngeal, tonsillar and other oral disorders such as aphthous ulcers, stomatitis and gingivitis. May also be used postoperatively in tonsillectomy, dental surgery and tooth extraction.

Contraindications: Benzocaine sensitivity.

Precautions: Severe or persistent sore throat accompanied by high fever, headache, nausea and vomiting may be serious, consult a physician promptly. Do not use for more than 2 days or administer to children under 2 years of age unless directed by a physician.

If benzocaine sensitization develops, discontinue Bionet administration.

Overdose: Benzocaine has a low toxicity while the probable human lethal dose for Bicetonium is estimated to lie in the range of 50 to 500 mg/kg.

Symptoms: Overdosage of benzocaine will produce giddiness, motor unrest, cardiac palpitations, respiratory difficulties, tremors, clonic convulsions, arterial hypotension, dilated pupils and pallor. Quaternary ammonium salts ingested in large quantities evince the following symptomatology: burning of mouth and throat, apprehension, restlessness, confusion, weakness, CNS depression, muscular weakness with asphyxia.

Treatment: If respiration fails, start artificial respiration. 0.5 mL of 1:1 000 epinephrine given i.v. may be needed to improve circulation, or large quantities of milk or gastric lavage, if it can be performed promptly. In children, induce emesis and if there is no immediate response, use gastric lavage. Avoid alcohol.

Dosage: Allow lozenge to dissolve slowly in the mouth. Repeat every 2 hours or as required, until infection subsides.

Supplied: Each white, round, even, biconvex, uncoated, peppermint flavored lozenge, contains: Bicetonium 5 mg (cetyldimethyl benzyl ammonium chloride) and benzocaine 7.5 mg. Nonmedicinal ingredients: flavor, magnesium stearate, povidone, sucrose and tragacanth. Energy: 22 kJ (5.2 kcal). Alcohol-, gluten-, sodium- and tartrazine-free. Push-through packages of 16. Bottles of 500.

(Shown in Product Recognition Section)

BION TEARS®
Alcon
Dextran 70—Hydroxypropyl Methylcellulose
Artificial Tears

Supplied: Each mL of sterile solution contains: 0.1% dextran 70 and hydroxypropyl methylcellulose 0.3%. Nonmedicinal ingredients: calcium chloride, carbon dioxide, hydrochloric acid and/or sodium hydroxide (to adjust pH), magnesium chloride, potassium chloride, purified water, sodium bicarbonate, sodium chloride and zinc chloride. Preservative-free. Unit dose containers of 0.4 mL. Packs of 5. Boxes of 25.

BIQUIN DURULES®
Astra
Controlled Release Quinidine Bisulfate
Antiarrhythmic Agent

Pharmacology: Quinidine is a class IA antiarrhythmic agent according to the modified Vaughan-Williams classification. Quinidine is considered a myocardial depressant. Direct actions on the heart include: decreased myocardial excitability; prolongation of the atrial, ventricular and Purkinje refractory periods; decreased atrial, Purkinje and ventricular conduction velocities; substantially decreased firing rate of cardiac Purkinje fibres by direct action; decreased myocardial contractility.

The primary indirect action of quinidine on the heart is through its vagal blocking effect. This effect tends to antagonize some of the depressant actions of quinidine on the heart by increasing the conductivity through the atrioventricular node. Quinidine has a peripheral vasodilating effect and may reduce arterial blood pressure, particularly when given parenterally.

Quinidine is rapidly absorbed from the small intestine. The maximum plasma concentration occurs within 4 hours after administration of a single dose. At therapeutic plasma concentrations, the plasma protein binding of quinidine varies between 70 and 95%. Approximately 10 to 20% is excreted unchanged in the urine within 24 hours. Decreased liver function does not seem to have a significant effect on the plasma clearance of quinidine.

The slow release mechanism of Durules results in a more gradual climb to the peak plasma concentration which then remains unchanged for a significantly longer time than after the administration of regular tablets. The plasma concentration can thus be kept constant for a longer period of time. Administration of Durules also results in higher morning plasma concentrations than conventional quinidine tablets.

Electrocardiographic Effects: The most common effect of quinidine on the ECG is an increased QT interval. Large doses may cause QRS prolongation. Such changes may precede the development of ventricular arrhythmias. In patients with normal conduction time, a 50% increase in QRS duration is dangerous and therefore the QRS should not exceed 25% of the control value.

Hemodynamics: In normal subjects, oral quinidine causes a fall in systemic arterial blood pressure due to vasodilatation of the systemic arterioles. Right ventricular pressure and cardiac output remain unchanged. However, in patients with cardiovascular disease, quinidine may lower blood pressure significantly. The decrease in peripheral vascular resistance appears to be due to depression of sympathetic receptors and direct vasodilatory action. Peripheral dilatation may contribute to the syncope encountered in some patients taking the drug.

Indications:

> No antiarrhythmic drug has been shown to reduce the incidence of sudden death in patients with asymptomatic ventricular arrhythmias. Most antiarrhythmic drugs have the potential to cause dangerous arrhythmias; some have been shown to be associated with an increased incidence of sudden death. In light of the above, physicians should carefully consider the risks and benefits of antiarrhythmic therapy for all patients with ventricular arrhythmias.

Ventricular Arrhythmias: For the treatment of documented life-threatening ventricular arrhythmias, such as sustained ventricular tachycardia. Quinidine may also be used for the treatment of patients with documented symptomatic ventricular arrhythmias when the symptoms are of sufficient severity to require treatment. Because of the proarrhythmic effects of quinidine its use should be reserved for patients in whom, in the opinion of the physician, the benefit of treatment clearly outweighs the risks.

For patients with sustained ventricular tachycardia, quinidine therapy should be initiated in the hospital. Hospitalization may also be required for certain other patients depending on their cardiac status and underlying cardiac disease.

The effects of quinidine in patients with recent myocardial infarction have not been adequately studied and, therefore, its use in this condition cannot be recommended.

Supraventricular Arrhythmias: For the treatment of premature atrial or AV junctional contractions, paroxysmal atrial or AV junctional tachycardia, atrial flutter, atrial fibrillation when this therapy is appropriate and maintenance therapy after electrical conversion of atrial fibrillation and/or flutter to sinus rhythm.

Contraindications: Second-degree or complete atrioventricular block in the absence of a pacemaker, junctional or idioventricular conduction disturbance that might be aggravated by quinidine, uncompensated heart failure, digitalis intoxication, prolonged QT interval (see also Warnings), patients manifesting either clinical signs or having a past history of idiosyncrasy or hypersensitivity to quinidine (e.g. febrile reactions, skin eruptions, thrombocytopenic purpura, SLE syndrome, etc.), myasthenia gravis.

Warnings: Mortality: The results of the Cardiac Arrhythmia Suppression Trial (CAST) in postmyocardial infarction patients with asymptomatic ventricular arrhythmias showed a significant increase in mortality and in nonfatal cardiac arrest rate in patients treated with encainide or flecainide compared with a matched placebo-treated group. CAST was continued using a revised protocol with the moricizine and placebo arms only. The trial was prematurely terminated because of a trend towards an increase in mortality in the moricizine treated group.

The applicability of these results to other populations or other antiarrhythmic agents is uncertain, but at present it is prudent to consider these results when using any antiarrhythmic agent.

Control of Ventricular Rate: Particular attention should be given to the following conditions: In the treatment of atrial fibrillation with rapid ventricular response, ventricular rate should be controlled with digitalis glycosides, β-blockers or verapamil prior to administration of quinidine.

In the treatment of atrial flutter with quinidine, reversion to sinus rhythm may be preceded by progressive reduction in the degree of AV block to 1:1 ratio resulting in an extremely high ventricular rate. This potential hazard may be reduced by digitalization prior to administration of quinidine.

Digitalis Intoxication: Recent reports have described increased, potentially toxic, digoxin plasma levels when quinidine is administered concurrently. When concurrent use is necessary, digoxin dosage should be reduced by approximately 50% and plasma concentration should be monitored and patients observed closely for digitalis intoxication.

Cardiotoxicity: Quinidine cardiotoxicity may be manifested by increased PR and QT intervals, 50% widening of QRS and/or ventricular ectopic beats or tachycardia. Appearance of these toxic signs during quinidine administration mandates immediate discontinuation of the drug, and/or close clinical and electrocardiographic monitoring. Note: Quinidine effect is enhanced by potassium and reduced in the presence of hypokalemia.

Syncopal Episodes: Quinidine Syncope may occur as a complication of long-term therapy. It is manifested by sudden loss of consciousness and ventricular arrhythmias with bizarre QRS complexes of the torsades de pointes type. This syndrome does not appear to be related to dose or plasma levels, but occurs more often with prolonged QT intervals.

Vagal Stimulation: Because quinidine antagonizes the effect of vagal excitation upon the atrium and the AV node, the administration of parasympathomimetic drugs (choline esters) or the use of any other procedure to enhance vagal activity may fail to terminate paroxysmal supraventricular tachycardia in patients receiving quinidine.

Hepatotoxicity: A few cases of hepatotoxicity, including granulomatous hepatitis, due to quinidine hypersensitivity have been reported in patients taking quinidine. Unexplained fever and/or elevation of hepatic enzymes, particularly in the early stages of therapy, warrant consideration of possible hepatotoxicity. Monitoring liver function during the first 4 to 8 weeks should be considered. Cessation of quinidine in these cases usually results in the disappearance of toxicity.

Quinidine should be used with extreme caution in: the presence of incomplete AV block, since a complete block and asystole may result. Quinidine may cause unpredictable abnormalities of rhythm in digitalized hearts; partial bundle branch block; severe congestive heart failure, cardiogenic shock, severe bradycardia and hypotensive states. Quinidine may have a depressant effect on myocardial contractility and arterial pressure; poor renal function, especially renal tubular acidosis, because of the potential accumulation of quinidine in plasma leading to toxic concentrations.

Precautions: Test for Hypersensitivity: A test dose of 0.2 g quinidine sulfate should be given by mouth initially in order to ascertain any possible hypersensitivity to quinidine.

Large Quinidine Doses: Hospitalization for close clinical observation, ECG monitoring, and possibly plasma quinidine levels, is indicated when large doses are used or with patients at increased risk when starting therapy, such as those with a history of syncope or presyncope due to ventricular arrhythmias.

Matrix: Due to the matrix structure of Durules, there is the potential for the matrix to pass through the digestive system apparently unchanged.

Drug Interactions: Drugs Affecting Quinidine: The effects of quinidine are enhanced by potassium and reduced by hypokalemia.

Quinidine, a weak base, may have its half-life prolonged in patients who are concurrently taking drugs that can alkalize the urine, such as thiazide diuretics, sodium bicarbonate, and carbonic anhydrase inhibitors. Quinidine and drugs which alkalize the urine should be used together cautiously.

Cimetidine: It has been reported that the histamine H_2-antagonist cimetidine reduces renal clearance of quinidine resulting in higher plasma concentrations.

Rifampin: Rifampin induces the metabolism of quinidine, thereby reducing the plasma concentration to sub-therapeutic levels if the normal dosage is maintained.

Phenobarbital and Phenytoin: Bioavailability studies in healthy volunteers have indicated that phenobarbital and phenytoin reduce the half-life of quinidine by approximately 50% and increase the rate of plasma clearance, probably through an increase in the rate of metabolism. Quinidine dosage may require adjustment in patients in whom the concomitant administration of phenobarbital or phenytoin is initiated or discontinued.

Verapamil, Amiodarone, Nifedipine: Concomitant administration of verapamil or amiodarone can produce clinically important increases in serum quinidine concentrations. Simultaneous administration of nifedipine has resulted in reports about reduced as well as increased plasma quinidine levels. The clinical relevance is not clear. Appropriate quinidine dose changes and ECG monitoring should be carried out when these drugs are added or discontinued during quinidine therapy. A 30 to 50% change in quinidine dosage may be required in order to avoid systemic toxicity or lack of efficacy.

Desipramine and Imipramine: Quinidine inhibits the metabolism of desipramine and imipramine in the so-called rapid hydroxylators resulting in increased plasma concentrations. In addition they have additive antiarrhythmic properties. The combination should be avoided.

Procainamide: One case report indicates that the plasma concentration of procainamide and its main metabolite, N-acetylprocainamide, may increase significantly if quinidine is given simultaneously.

Metoprolol: In the so-called rapid hydroxylators, quinidine may inhibit the metabolism of metoprolol resulting in increased plasma concentrations of metoprolol.

Propranolol: By reducing cardiac output, propranolol can reduce hepatic blood flow and decrease the clearance of quinidine, causing a tendency to higher plasma concentrations than predicted.

Drugs Affected by Quinidine: Quinidine potentiates the neuromuscular blocking effect of certain skeletal muscle relaxants, specifically the curariform and depolarizing types, and the neuromuscular blocking effect of antibiotics such as neomycin, kanamycin and streptomycin. Respiratory depression may cause apnea. Curare-like effects may occur when quinidine is administered at a later time.

Quinidine, by depressing prothrombin formation or inhibiting synthesis of vitamin K sensitive clotting factors in the liver, tends to potentiate the anticoagulant effect of coumarin derivatives, thus increasing any hemorrhagic tendencies.

In patients with myasthenia gravis who are well controlled by neostigmine, quinidine causes symptoms to return. Quinidine antagonizes neostigmine, physostigmine and related drugs.

Digoxin: In digitalized patients quinidine may increase the concentration of digoxin in plasma by up to 100%. Therefore, when starting quinidine therapy in patients who are taking digoxin, the clinical course, ECG and, if possible, serum digoxin levels should be followed closely. It may be necessary to reduce the dose of digoxin in these patients (see Warnings).

Digitoxin: The interaction between digitoxin and quinidine is a controversial issue. Several studies indicate, however, that quinidine increases the plasma concentration of digitoxin.

Quinidine exhibits a distinct anticholinergic activity in the myocardial tissues. An additive vagolytic effect may be seen when quinidine and drugs having anticholinergic blocking activity are used together. Drugs having cholinergic activity may be antagonized by quinidine.

Caution is indicated in combined therapy with other class I antiarrhythmic drugs and β-blockers due to possible additive cardiac depressant effects. Myocarditis or severe myocardial damage also requires caution.

Pregnancy: The use of quinidine in pregnancy should be reserved only for those cases in which the benefits outweigh the possible hazards to the patient and fetus. There have been no teratogenic effects reported since the introduction of quinidine in the early 1930's. No clinical or epidemiological studies have however been made. In a single case report, similar maternal and fetal serum concentrations were observed at delivery.

Monitoring of quinidine concentrations in the mother is warranted to avoid adverse effects. Theoretically, changes in protein binding during pregnancy may result in lower total drug concentration that will underestimate the free (unbound) quinidine concentration. Judicious adjustment of dosage may be done if clinically indicated.

Lactation: Quinidine is secreted in milk with concentrations in milk similar to those in maternal serum. The amount of drug consumed by the infant however, is small when therapeutic doses are used and effects on the child are therefore unlikely. The benefit/risk ratio for continued nursing should be considered for each infant.

Adverse Effects: The most frequent adverse reactions occurring in approximately 30% of patients are gastrointestinal disorders (diarrhea, nausea and vomiting). The central and peripheral nervous system is rarely affected. The most common cardiovascular adverse reaction is ventricular tachycardia, mostly of the torsades de pointes type or ventricular fibrillation. Rarely are there signs of hypotension and bradycardia, which may lead to cardiac arrest. There have been isolated cases of hepatitis, thrombocytopenia, pancytopenia, agranulocytosis, photosensitization, lupus erythematosis-like syndrome, myalgia, and arthralgia.

Reported adverse effects according to organ system are: Gastrointestinal: diarrhea, nausea, vomiting, anorexia, or combinations of the above.

Central and Peripheral Nervous System: Cinchonism: tinnitus, vertigo, blurred vision, headache, dizziness.

Cardiac: Arrhythmias or Alterations in Conduction: sino-atrial node depression, sinus arrest (with Xylocaine), sino-atrial block, acceleration of the SA node, AV block, acceleration of ventricular response to atrial tachyarrhythmias, junctional rhythm, increase in His Purkinje conduction time, ventricular premature beats, ventricular tachycardia, including torsades de pointes, ventricular fibrillation, sudden death, potentiation of digitalis intoxication.

Decreased Contractility.

Reduction in Blood Pressure.

ECG Abnormality (marked increase in PR, QRS and QT intervals).

Hypersensitivity Reactions: Fever: with hepatic granulomas, with transient leukopenia.

Hematologic: potentiation of coumarin anticoagulants, hemolytic anemia, immunohemolytic anemia and thrombocytopenia, hemolysis in Caucasian with G6PD deficiency,

Biquin Durules (cont'd)

pancytopenia, thrombocytopenia, thrombocytopenia with leukopenia, reversible hypoplastic anemia with agranulocytosis, leukopenia with fever.
Dermatologic: urticaria, scarlatinoform or morbilliform eruptions, localized or generalized pruritus, flushing, fixed lichenoid lesions, eczema progressing to generalized scarlatinoform eruption, erythrodermic exacerbation of psoriasis, exfoliative dermatitis, contact dermatitis, photosensitivity reaction, SLE-like syndrome, angioneurotic edema.
Hepatic: hepatitis.
Miscellaneous: fatigue.

Overdose: Symptoms: Large doses may cause cinchonism, paradoxical tachycardia, ventricular tachycardia, cardiac standstill, ventricular fibrillation, embolism. Serious hypersensitivity reactions are manifested by respiratory embarrassment or vascular collapse.
Antidote: Cinchonism—same as for quinidine or quinine.

Treatment: Inasmuch as quinidine is rapidly destroyed in the body, the longer the patient survives the better the prognosis becomes. Absorption may be slow if fairly insoluble salts have been ingested. Therefore, the stomach should be copiously lavaged with water through the gastric tube, and alkaloid precipitants employed if they are readily available. Hypertonic sodium sulfate solution should be introduced in the stomach to hasten the passage of the unabsorbed quinidine through the bowel. The blood pressure should be supported and symptomatic measures employed to maintain renal function and overcome central depression. Caffeine, ephedrine, oxygen, and even artificial respiration may be needed to combat respiratory failure. Body temperature should be maintained. Hemoglobinuria may necessitate blood transfusion, and the use of alkali to prevent renal blockade may prove helpful. Angioneurotic or asthmatic phenomena may require the use of epinephrine and antiasthmatics. Residual visual impairment occasionally yields to vasodilators such as nitrates and methacholine; in the acute phase of toxic amaurosis caused by quinidine, sodium nitrate administered i.v. may have a salutary effect.

Dosage: Note: 0.25 g Biquin Durules is equivalent to 0.2 g quinidine sulfate.

Initiation of treatment, as with other antiarrhythmic agents used to treat life-threatening ventricular arrhythmias, should be carried out in hospital.

A test dose of 0.2 g quinidine sulfate should be administered in the morning to ascertain whether or not any hypersensitivity to quinidine exists. If no signs of a reaction occur, administer 2 Durules in the evening. Beginning the following day, 2 to 3 Durules can be given every 12 hours.

The usual maintenance dose is 2 to 5 Durules (0.5 to 1.25 g) morning and evening. The determination of dosage for maintenance of sinus rhythm should include assay of the serum concentration, beginning after about 1 week of treatment. The therapeutic serum concentration range of quinidine varies with the assay technique used; for the Abbott TDx assay the range is 2 to 5 mg/L (6 to 15 μmol/L). Due to interindividual variation of serum concentration versus response to quinidine, serum concentrations must be interpreted in the context of clinical parameters of efficacy and toxicity. The lowest effective maintenance dose which gives a morning level within the therapeutic range is the usual objective. The QT-time should be checked before and during treatment.

Concomitant food intake may decrease the likelihood of gastrointestinal side effects.

The tablets should not be broken or chewed but swallowed whole with liquid.

Patients with atrial fibrillation or flutter who are scheduled for elective cardioversion may be given the regimen described above for 2 days before the anticipated cardioversion. Appropriate doses of digoxin or verapamil may be needed to control ventricular response. About 33% of patients with atrial fibrillation and a similar proportion of patients with atrial flutter may convert to sinus rhythm on this dose of quinidine without DC shock. Others will require DC shock, but the required energy level may be reduced because of premedication with quinidine. Maintenance doses of quinidine according to the schedule given above may help to prevent recurrence of atrial fibrillation following cardioversion. The starting dose for maintenance treatment after conversion of atrial fibrillation is 3 Durules morning and evening.

Supplied: Each white, oval, sustained release Biquin Durules tablet contains: quinidine bisulfate 0.25 g, equivalent to quinidine sulfate 0.2 g. Nonmedicinal ingredients: hydroxypropyl methylcellulose 6 cps, magnesium stearate, paraffin powder, polyethylene glycol 6000, polyvinyl acetate, polyvinyl chloride and titanium dioxide. Gluten- and tartrazine-free. Bottles of 100 and 500. Store at room temperature (15 to 30°C). Protect from light.

(Shown in Product Recognition Section)

Reviewed 1998

BISACODYL
Technilab

Laxative

Supplied: Adults: Each rectal suppository contains: bisacodyl 10 mg. Nonmedicinal ingredients: semisynthetic glycerides. Boxes of 100. Preserve in well-closed containers at a temperature not exceeding 30°C.

BISMUTAL
Technilab

Bismuth Camphocarbonate—Guaifenesin

Sore Throat Treatment

Supplied: Each rectal suppository contains: bismuth camphocarbonate 150 mg and guaifenesin 250 mg. Nonmedicinal ingredients: semisynthetic glycerides. Boxes of 2.

New Product 1998

BLACK WIDOW SPIDER ANTIVENIN
MSD

see ANTIVENIN (Lactrodectus Mactans)

BLENOXANE® Ⓟ
Bristol

Bleomycin Sulfate

Antineoplastic—Antibiotic

Pharmacology: Although the exact mechanism of action of bleomycin is unknown, available evidence indicates that the main mode of action is inhibition of DNA synthesis with some evidence of inhibition of RNA and protein synthesis.

The major route of excretion of bleomycin is the kidney, with 60 to 70% of an administered dose recovered in the urine as active bleomycin. Renal dysfunction can significantly prolong excretion.

In patients with a creatinine clearance of >35 mL/minute, the serum or plasma terminal elimination half-life of bleomycin is approximately 115 minutes. In patients with a creatinine clearance of <35 mL/minute, the plasma or serum terminal elimination half-life increases exponentially as the creatinine clearance decreases.

When administered intrapleurally in the treatment of malignant pleural effusion, bleomycin acts as a sclerosing agent. Following intrapleural administration, resultant bleomycin plasma concentrations suggest a systemic absorption rate of approximately 45%.

Indications: Bleomycin should be considered an adjuvant to surgery and radiation therapy. It has been shown to be useful in the management of the following neoplasms:
Squamous Cell Carcinoma: head and neck including mouth, tongue, tonsil, nasopharynx, oropharynx, sinus, palate, lip, buccal mucosa, gingiva and epiglottis; skin; larynx and paralarynx.

Bleomycin is also indicated in squamous cell carcinomas of the penis, cervix, and vulva.

The response to bleomycin is poorer in patients with head and neck cancer who have received previous irradiation.
Lymphomas: Hodgkin's disease and non-Hodgkin's lymphoma.
Testicular Carcinoma: embryonal cell carcinoma, choriocarcinoma and teratocarcinoma. Studies to date have revealed that the use of vinblastine sulfate with bleomycin increases the response rate of testicular tumors.
Malignant Pleural Effusion: When administered by intrapleural injection, bleomycin has been shown to be useful in the treatment of malignant pleural effusion and in the prevention of recurrence.
Other Malignancies: Bleomycin has been shown to produce responses in some renal carcinomas and soft tissue sarcomas.

Contraindications: In patients who have demonstrated hypersensitivity to the drug.

Warnings: Bleomycin should be administered under the supervision of a qualified physician experienced in the use of cancer chemotherapeutic agents. Adequate diagnostic and treatment facilities should be available to allow appropriate management of therapy and possible complications.

Patients receiving bleomycin must be observed carefully and frequently during and after therapy. It should be used with extreme caution in patients with significant impairment of renal function or compromised pulmonary function.

Pulmonary toxicities occur in 10% of treated patients. In approximately 1% of treated patients, nonspecific pneumonitis induced by bleomycin progresses to pulmonary fibrosis, and death. Pulmonary toxicity is more frequent in patients over 70 years of age and in those receiving total doses greater than 400 units. Although pulmonary toxicity is age and dose related, the toxicity is unpredictable. Renal impairment is a risk factor in the development of pulmonary toxicity. Frequent monitoring is essential (see Adverse Effects).

Idiosyncratic reactions similar to anaphylaxis have been reported in 1% of patients with lymphoma who were treated with bleomycin. Since these reactions usually occur after the first or second dose, careful monitoring is essential after these doses (see Adverse Effects).

Renal and hepatic toxicity, beginning as a deterioration in renal or liver function tests, have been reported infrequently. These toxicities may occur, however, at any time after initiation of therapy.

Pregnancy: Bleomycin may cause fetal harm when administered to a pregnant woman. Women of childbearing potential should be advised to avoid becoming pregnant during therapy with bleomycin. If bleomycin is used during pregnancy or if the patient becomes pregnant while receiving this drug, the patient should be apprised of the potential hazard.
Lactation: It is not known if bleomycin is excreted in human milk. Because many drugs are excreted in human milk and because of the potential for serious adverse reactions in nursing infants from bleomycin, a decision should be made to discontinue nursing or to discontinue the drug, taking into account the importance of the drug to the mother. The benefits and risks of nursing against discontinuing the drug must be weighed carefully.

Precautions: Bleomycin should be used as indicated. The physician must carefully weigh the therapeutic benefit versus risk of toxicity.

Bleomycin should be administered preferably to patients who are hospitalized and who can be observed carefully and frequently during and after therapy. It should be used with extreme caution in patients with significant impairment of renal function or compromised pulmonary function due to disease other than malignancy, and in patients over 70 years of age because of the apparent increased danger of pulmonary toxicity.

To monitor the onset of pulmonary toxicity, x-rays of the chest should be taken every 1 to 2 weeks. If pulmonary changes are noted, treatment should be discontinued until it can be determined whether the cause is drug related. Pneumonitis due to bleomycin should be treated with corticosteroids in an effort to prevent progression to pulmonary fibrosis. Infectious pneumonitis should receive appropriate antibiotic therapy.

An association between decreased renal function and enhanced bleomycin-related toxicities has been reported. Dosage reductions of 40 to 75% have been recommended for patients with creatinine clearance values ≤40 mL/min.

Adverse Effects: Pulmonary: Pulmonary toxicity is potentially the most serious side effect of bleomycin (see Warnings).

The identification of patients with pulmonary toxicity due to bleomycin has been extremely difficult. The reason for this is the lack of specificity of the clinical syndrome, the x-ray changes and even the tissue changes seen on examination of biopsy and autopsy specimens.

Bleomycin-induced pneumonitis apparently produces dyspnea and fine rales that are in no way different from those produced by infectious pneumonias, or the signs and symptoms produced by primary or metastatic lung disease in some patients.

On x-ray, bleomycin-induced pneumonitis produces patchy opacities, usually of the lower lung fields, that look the same as infectious bronchopneumonia or even lung metastases in some patients.

The microscopic tissue changes due to bleomycin toxicity are frequently present as bronchiolar squamous metaplasia, reactive macrophages, atypical alveolar epithelial cells, fibrinous edema and interstitial fibrosis. The acute stage may involve capillary changes and subsequent fibrinous exudation into alveoli producing a change similar to hyaline membrane formation and progressing to a diffuse interstitial fibrosis resembling the Hamman-Rich syndrome. These microscopic findings are non specific and are similar to the changes produced in radiation pneumonitis, Pneumocystis pneumonitis, and at times reaction to long-standing malignant pulmonary disease.

Serial pulmonary function tests in 156 patients receiving bleomycin therapy revealed some demonstrable alteration in approximately 20%. The most common changes were a decrease in total lung volume and a decrease in vital capacity. However, no predictive correlation between these changes and the development of pulmonary fibrosis could be ascertained.

To monitor the onset of pulmonary toxicity, x-rays of the chest should be taken every 1 to 2 weeks. If pulmonary changes are noted, treatment should be discontinued until it can be determined if they are drug related. Studies have suggested that sequential measurement of the pulmonary diffusion capacity for carbon monoxide (DL_{co}) during treatment with bleomycin may be an indicator to subclinical pulmonary toxicity. It is recommended that the DL_{co} be monitored monthly if it is to be employed to detect pulmonary toxicities, and thus the drug should be discontinued when the DL_{co} falls below 30 to 35% of the pretreatment value.

Patients who have received bleomycin are at greater risk of developing pulmonary toxicity when oxygen is administered at surgery. While long exposure to very high oxygen concentrations is a known cause of lung damage, after bleomycin administration, lung damage can occur at lower concentrations than usually would be considered safe. Suggestive preventive measures are: maintain $FI\ O_2$ at concentrations approximately that of room air (25%) during surgery and the postoperative period; carefully monitor fluid replacement, focusing more on colloid administration than crystalloid administration.

Sudden onset of an acute chest pain syndrome suggestive of pleuropericarditis has been rarely reported during bleomycin infusion. Although each patient must be individually evaluated, further courses of bleomycin do not appear to be contraindicated.

Pulmonary adverse events have been reported rarely following the intrapleural administration of bleomycin.

Skin and Mucous Membranes: Cutaneous effects are the most frequent side effects occurring in approximately 50% of treated patients. Cutaneous reactions include stomatitis, alopecia, hyperpigmentation, thickening, ulceration, erythema, hyperkeratosis, nail changes, rash, vesiculation, tenderness, pruritus, hyperesthesia, peeling, striae and bleeding. In 2% of treated patients it was necessary to discontinue bleomycin therapy because of these toxicities. Cutaneous toxicity is a relatively late manifestation developing usually in the 2nd and 3rd week of treatment after 150 to 200 units of bleomycin had been administered and, in general, was related to total cumulative dose.

Idiosyncratic Reactions: In approximately 1% of patients with lymphoma who were treated with bleomycin, an idiosyncratic reaction, similar clinically to anaphylaxis, has been reported. The reaction may be immediate or delayed for several hours and occurs usually after the first or second dose. It consists of hypotension, fever, chills, mental confusion and wheezing. Treatment is symptomatic, including volume expanders, pressor agents, antihistamines, and corticosteroids.

Other: Fever, chills and vomiting were frequently reported side effects. Anorexia and weight loss are common and may persist long after termination of bleomycin. Pain at the tumor site, phlebitis, and other local reactions were reported infrequently.

Vascular toxicities coincident with the use of bleomycin in combination with other antineoplastic agents have been reported rarely. The events are clinically heterogeneous and may include myocardial infarction, cerebrovascular accident, thrombotic microangiopathy (hemolytic-uremic syndrome) or cerebrovascular arteritis.

There are also reports of Raynaud's phenomenon occurring in patients treated with bleomycin in combination with vinblastine with or without cisplatin or, in few cases, with bleomycin as a single agent. It is currently unknown if the cause of Raynaud's phenomenon in these cases is the disease, underlying vascular compromise, bleomycin, vinblastine, hypomagnesemia, or a combination of any of these factors.

Bleomycin occasionally has been associated with local pain following intrapleural administration. Hypotension requiring symptomatic treatment has been reported infrequently. Very rarely death has been reported in association with bleomycin pleurodesis in very seriously ill patients.

Toxicity to the renal, hepatic and central nervous systems are rare, but as with any potent drug, these symptoms should be monitored. It is noteworthy that there has been no evidence of bone marrow or immunological depression. This is contrary to the currently available antineoplastic drugs.

Dosage: The following dosage schedule is recommended:
Squamous Cell Carcinoma, Non-Hodgkin's Lymphoma, Testicular Carcinoma: 0.25 to 0.50 units/kg (10 to 20 units/m^2) given i.v. or i.m. weekly or twice weekly.
Hodgkin's Disease: 0.25 to 0.50 units/kg (10 to 20 units/m^2) i.v., i.m. or s.c. weekly or twice weekly. After a 50% response, the maintenance dose of 1 unit daily or 5 units weekly i.v. or i.m. should be given.
Malignant Pleural Effusion: 60 units administered as a single intrapleural injection (see Reconstitution).

Because of the possibility of an anaphylactoid reaction, patients with lymphoma should be started with 2 units or less for the first 2 doses. If no acute reaction occurs, then the regular dose schedule may be followed.

Pulmonary toxicity from bleomycin appears to be dose related with a striking increase when the total dose is over 400 units. Total doses over 400 units should be given with great caution.

Improvement or responses in testicular carcinoma and Hodgkin's lymphoma are usually prompt and noted within 2 weeks. When responses are not seen within this period of time, continued therapy with bleomycin should be re-evaluated.

Responses in patients with squamous cell cancers are slow, requiring up to 3 weeks before onset of response is noted.
Note: When bleomycin is used in combination with other antineoplastic agents, pulmonary toxicities may occur at lower doses. Bleomycin-related toxicities also may be more frequent in patients with impaired renal function and dose modification has been suggested. Dosage reductions of 40 to 75% have been recommended for patients with creatinine clearance values ≤ 40 mL/min.

Bleomycin may be given by i.m., i.v., intra-arterial, s.c. or intrapleural routes.
Reconstitution: I.M. or S.C.: Dissolve the contents of a bleomycin vial in 1 to 5 mL of Sterile Water for Injection, Sodium Chloride for Injection or Bacteriostatic Water for Injection.
I.V. or Intra-arterial: Dissolve the contents of the vial in 5 to 20 mL of Sodium Chloride Injection 0.9 % and administer slowly over a period of 10 minutes.
Intrapleural Infusion: Dissolve 60 units of bleomycin in 50 to 100 mL of Sodium Chloride Injection 0.9%, and administer as a rapid push through a thoracostomy tube following drainage of excess pleural fluid and the confirmation of complete lung expansion. The thoracostomy tube is then clamped and the patient is moved from the supine to the left and right lateral positions during the next 4 hours. The clamp is then removed and suction re-established. The amount of time the thoracostomy tube remains in place following sclerosis is based on individual patient requirements.

In general, intrapleural injection of local anesthetics or systemic narcotic analgesia is not required.
Stability of Reconstituted Solutions: Reconstituted bleomycin solution may be stored in refrigerator above freezing point for up to 48 hours.

Diluted bleomycin is stable at 25°C for 24 hours in 0.9% Sodium Chloride Injection and for up to 8 hours in 20% w/v Mannitol in Water. Discard the solution if precipitate forms in Mannitol.
Special Instructions for Handling and Disposal: 1. Preparation of bleomycin should be done in a vertical laminar flow hood (Biological Safety Cabinet-Class II). 2. Personnel preparing bleomycin should wear PVC gloves, safety glasses, disposable gowns and masks. 3. All needles, syringes, vials and other materials which have come in contact with bleomycin should be segregated and incinerated at 1 000°C or more. Sealed containers may explode. Intact vials should be returned to the Manufacturer for destruction. Proper precautions should be taken in packaging these materials for transport. 4. Personnel regularly involved in the preparation and handling of bleomycin should have biannual blood examinations.

Supplied: Each vial contains: sterile bleomycin sulfate equivalent to bleomycin 15 units. Nonmedicinal ingredients: none. Note: A unit of bleomycin is equal to the formerly used milligram activity. Store the dry powder at 2 to 8°C.

Reviewed 1998

BLEOMYCIN SULFATE USP

Faulding

Antineoplastic

Pharmacology: Experiments with isolated DNA have shown that bleomycin binds to the DNA molecule and cleaves it. This results in the inhibition of DNA synthesis. There is also evidence of lesser inhibition of RNA and protein synthesis.

Bleomycin exhibits a wide spectrum of in vitro and in vivo activity. It demonstrates inhibition of DNA synthesis in E. coli, B. subtilis, Ehrlich ascites cells, HeLa cells, PHA stimulated lymphocytes, L-929 fibroblasts, L5178Y cells and Novikoff hepatoma ascites cells, at concentrations within a general range of 4 to 20 μg/mL under typical incubation conditions.

The activity of bleomycin seems to be cell phase specific. Cyclic and continuous administration of bleomycin has been shown to be more effective than bolus dosing in in-vivo systems.

Bleomycin is well absorbed after parenteral, (i.v., s.c., i.m. and intrapleural) but not after oral administration. Tissue distribution was evaluated in mice and was found to be high in skin, kidney, lung, peritoneum, lymphatics and solid tumor and tumor cells in ascites. Bleomycin does not cross the blood-brain barrier.

Several tissues have demonstrated a capacity to degrade bleomycin. The liver and gastrointestinal tract show the highest rate of inactivation. The skin, lungs and kidney show a lower rate which may account for the site-specific toxicity of the drug.

Bleomycin half-life varies with creatinine clearance and is of 2 to 5 hours after i.v. administration **to patients with normal kidney function.**

Bleomycin is rapidly absorbed after i.m. administration. Bleomycin peak concentration is obtained after approximately 45 minutes with a half-life clearance of about 2.5 hours.

In patients with creatinine clearances greater than 50 mL/min, the composite intraperitoneal (I.P.) plasma half-life, approximately 5.3 hours, is significantly longer than the intrapleural (I.Pl.) and i.v. half-lives, approximately 3.4 and 4.0 hours respectively.

With continuous i.v. infusion, the terminal half-life of bleomycin is 9 hours for adults and about 2.3 hours for children. In children less than 3 years of age, the terminal half-life of bleomycin administered by rapid i.v. injection is 3 hours.

In patients with normal renal function, bleomycin excretion during the first 24 hours is lower in most cases following intracavitary (I.C.) administration than following i.v. administration.

Approximately 45% of bleomycin administered by the I.C. route is absorbed into the systemic circulation.
Pharmacokinetics: Patients with Impaired Renal Function: The serum half-life of bleomycin is markedly prolonged in patients with renal dysfunction. The bleomycin half-life increases as the creatinine clearance decreases.

Indications: Bleomycin should be used as first line therapy and/or adjuvant to surgery and radiation therapy. It has been shown to be useful in the following neoplasms:
Squamous Cell Carcinoma: skin, larynx and paralarynx, penis, cervix, vulva. Bleomycin in combination with radiotherapy shows improved results in lung cancer and cervical carcinoma.
Lymphomas: Hodgkin's lymphoma and non-Hodgkin's lymphoma including reticulum cell sarcoma, and lymphosarcoma.

BACOP, M-BACOP, COP-BLAM and MACOP-B are used as first line therapy in the treatment of diffuse large cell lymphoma.

MOOP/ABVD is used as first line therapy for Hodgkin's lymphoma. Bleomycin is useful in Hodgkin's patients with disseminated disease (stage IV) no longer treatable by bone marrow depressant agents. Bleomycin added to the widely used MOPP regimen increases the responses as well as survival rates of patients with advanced Hodgkin's disease; furthermore, bleomycin does not show cross-resistance to MOPP.
Testicular Carcinoma: embryonal cell carcinoma, choricocarcinoma, and teratocarcinoma. PEB, PVB and VAB-6 are used as first line therapy for testicular cancer.
Pleurodysis and Pleural Fluid Accumulation: Bleomycin is effectively used in the prevention of pleurodysis and pleural

Bleomycin Sulfate USP (cont'd)

fluid accumulation due to metastatic carcinoma, metastatic melanoma, esophageal carcinoma and ovarian cancer.

Other: Bleomycin has been shown to produce responses in some renal carcinomas and soft tissue sarcomas.

Contraindications: Patients who have demonstrated a hypersensitive or an idiosyncratic reaction to the drug. When used as indicated, the physician must weigh carefully the therapeutic benefit versus risk of toxicity which may occur.

Warnings: Idiosyncratic reactions similar to anaphylaxis have been reported in 1% of lymphoma patients treated with bleomycin. Since these usually occur after the first or second dose, careful monitoring is essential after these doses.

It is recommended that bleomycin be administered under the supervision of a qualified physician experienced in the use of cancer chemotherapeutic agents. Since facilities for necessary laboratory studies must be available, hospitalization of patients is recommended.

Patients receiving bleomycin must be observed carefully and frequently during and after therapy. It should be used with extreme caution in patients with significant impairment of renal function or compromised pulmonary function. Patients who are undergoing bleomycin treatment are predisposed to respiratory failure following exposure to high concentrations of O_2 (general anesthesia). Since this effect may be observed for up to 1 year after treatment with bleomycin, the oxygen administration to these patients should be kept at the lowest possible concentrations in order to minimize the risk of severe pneumonitis.

Pulmonary toxicities occur in approximately 10% of treated patients. In approximately 1%, the nonspecific pneumonitis induced by bleomycin progresses to pulmonary fibrosis and death. Although this is age and dose related, the toxicity is unpredictable.

A method suggested to lower the incidence of pulmonary toxicity is the continuous i.v. administration of bleomycin.

Renal or hepatic toxicity, beginning as a deterioration in renal or liver function tests, have been reported, infrequently. These toxicities may occur, however, at any time after initiation of therapy.

Pregnancy: Safe use of bleomycin in pregnant women has not been established.

Precautions: General: Bleomycin should be administered preferably to patients who are hospitalized and who can be observed carefully and frequently during and after therapy. It should be used with extreme caution in patients with significant impairment of renal function or compromised pulmonary function due to disease other than malignancy, and in patients over 70 years of age because of the apparent increased danger of pulmonary toxicity.

Frequent roentgenograms are not a preferable method of follow-up or detection of pulmonary toxicity from bleomycin. Current practice consists of frequent physical examination (cough, basal rales and pleuritic chest pain are frequently first signs of toxicity) and baseline evaluation of carbon monoxide diffusion capacity which also allows for the exclusion of patients with low pulmonary reserve, as well as for follow-up of progression of the pneumonitis after cessation of bleomycin therapy.

If pulmonary changes are noted, treatment should be discontinued until it can be determined whether the cause is drug related. Pneumonitis due to bleomycin should be treated with corticosteroids in an effort to prevent progression to pulmonary fibrosis. Infectious pneumonitis should receive appropriate antibiotic therapy.

Adverse Effects: Skin: 50% of the patients develop either hyperpigmentation of the skin, hyperkeratosis of hands and nails and edema and erythema of the hands and feet. The skin toxicity occurred more frequently at higher doses: 200 to 300 unit range and can be dose limiting. Rash forms on the pressure areas of the body and abdominal skin creases. It is a common side effect (due to accumulation of the bleomycin in the skin) and is reported to occur in 8% of treated patients within a few days to 2 to 3 weeks at doses of 1.25 to 35 mg/m².

Pulmonary: Pulmonary toxicity is potentially the most serious side effect, occurring in approximately 10% of treated patients. The most frequent manifestation is pneumonitis occasionally progressing to pulmonary fibrosis which may result in death.

Approximately 1% of patients treated succumb to pulmonary toxicity. Pulmonary toxicity is usually both dose and age related, being more common in patients over 70 years of age receiving over 400 units total dose; however, this toxicity is unpredictable and has been seen occasionally in young patients receiving low doses.

The identification of patients with pulmonary toxicity due to bleomycin has been extremely difficult, due to the lack of specificity of the clinical syndrome, the x-ray changes and even the tissue changes seen on examination of biopsy and autopsy specimens.

Bleomycin-induced pneumonitis apparently produces dyspnea and fine rales that are in no way different from those produced by infectious pneumonias, or the signs and symptoms produced by primary or metastatic lung disease in some patients.

The microscopic tissue changes due to bleomycin toxicity are frequently present as bronchiolar squamous metaplasia, reactive macrophages, atypical alveolar epithelial cells, fibrinous edema and interstitial fibrosis and are in line with interstitial pneumonitis. These microscopic findings are nonspecific.

Serial pulmonary function tests in patients receiving bleomycin therapy reveal some demonstrable alteration in approximately 20%. The most common changes are decrease in total lung volume and decrease in vital capacity. However, there are no predictive correlations between these changes and the development of pulmonary fibrosis.

Frequent roentgenograms are not a preferable method of follow-up or detection of pulmonary toxicity from bleomycin. Current practice consists of frequent physical examination (cough, basal rales and pleuritic chest pain are frequently first signs of toxicity) and baseline evaluation of carbon monoxide diffusion capacity which also allows for the exclusion of patients with low pulmonary reserve, as well as for follow-up of progression of the pneumonitis after cessation of bleomycin therapy.

If pulmonary changes are noted, treatment should be discontinued until it can be determined if they are drug related. Sequential measurement of the pulmonary diffusion capacity for carbon monoxide (DL_{CO}) during treatment with bleomycin may be an indicator of subclinical pulmonary toxicity. It is recommended that the DL_{CO} be monitored monthly if it is to be employed to detect pulmonary toxicities, and thus the drug should be discontinued when the DL_{CO} falls below 30 to 35% of the pretreatment value.

Concurrent or prior lung irradiation will also predispose patients to increased pulmonary toxicity.

The reaction which may be immediate or after several hours delay occurs only after the first or second dose. It consists of hypotension, fever, chills, mental confusion and wheezing.

In order to minimize the incidence of pneumonitis due to bleomycin therapy, it is recommended not to exceed total dose 200 units/m², not to exceed 100 units/m² if concurrent lung irradiation is also given, not to exceed 100 units/m² in patients over the age of 70 and to use continuous infusion to avoid peak serum levels.

Fever: Pretreatment with antipyretics or antihistamines is frequently given as fever occurs in 50% of patients with i.v. administration and 25% with i.m. administration.

Gastrointestinal Toxicity: Mucositis and stomatitis occur in 30% of patients.

Other: Fever, chills and vomiting are frequently reported side effects. Anorexia and weight loss are common and may persist long after termination of this medication. Pain at tumor site, phlebitis, and other local reactions are reported infrequently.

There are also isolated reports of Raynaud's phenomenon occurring in patients with testicular carcinomas treated with a combination of bleomycin and vinblastine. It is currently unknown if the cause for the Raynaud's phenomenon in these cases is the disease, either drug, or a combination of any or all of these.

Toxicity to the renal, hepatic and CNS is rare, but as with any potent drug, these symptoms should be monitored. It is noteworthy that there has been little evidence of bone marrow or immunological depression to date. This is contrary to the currently available antineoplastic drugs.

Dosage: Each mg of bleomycin contains 1.5 to 2.0 units of sterile bleomycin.

Because of the possibility of anaphylaxis, all lymphoma patients should be started with 2 units or less for the first 2 doses. If no acute reaction occurs, then the regular dose schedule may be followed.

Bleomycin may be given by the i.m., i.v., intra-arterial, intracavitary or s.c. routes.

The following dose schedule is recommended: Squamous Cell Carcinoma, Lymphosarcoma, Reticulum Cell Sarcoma, Testicular Carcinoma: 0.25 to 0.50 units/kg (10 to 20 units/m²) given i.v. or i.m. weekly or twice weekly.

Hodgkin's Disease: 0.25 to 0.50 units/kg (10 to 20 units/m²) i.v. or i.m. weekly or twice weekly. After a 50% response, a maintenance dose of 1 unit daily s.c. or 5 units weekly i.v. or i.m. should be given.

Toxicity of bleomycin appears to be dose related with a striking increase when the total dose is over 400 units. Total doses over 400 units should be given with great caution.

Hodgkin's and testicular improvement are prompt and noted within 2 weeks. If no improvement is seen by this time, chances of improvement are very low. Squamous cell cancers respond more slowly, sometimes requiring as long as 3 weeks before improvement is noted.

Note: When bleomycin is used in combination with other antineoplastic agents, pulmonary toxicities may occur at lower doses. In order to decrease pulmonary toxicities, administration by continuous infusion rather than i.v. bolus is recommended.

Intra-arterial: For intra-arterial infusion/perfusion where increased drug concentrations at the cancer site are desired, the suggested dosage schedule is 30 to 60 units once or twice a week until a total recommended dosage of 300 units has been administered.

Intracavitary: The following dosage schedule is recommended when used as a sclerosing agent to control pleural effusions due to metastatic tumours or to manage pneumothorax (associated with acquired immunodeficiency syndrome and pneumocytis pneumonia): 50 to 60 units of bleomycin diluted with 0.9% Sodium Chloride Injection or 5% Dextrose Injection (not exceeding 1 unit/kg or 40 units/m² in the case of geriatric patients.). The solution is instilled into the chest through a thoracostomy tube, the tube is then clamped, the patient rotated periodically and the fluid subsequently removed after 24 hours.

Note: Prior to the above administration to patients with effusions, the pleural cavity is drained via the thoracostomy tube (by gravity or suction) since efficacy may be reduced if the bleomycin solution is instilled into the pleural cavity while fluid drainage exceeds 100 mL/24 hours.

Impaired Renal Function: For patients with impaired renal function, the following dosage schedule is recommended.

Patients With Moderate Renal Failure (GFR 10 to 50 mL/min): Reduce to 75% of normal dose at the normal dosage interval.

Patients With Severe Renal Failure (GFR <10 mL/min): Reduce to 50% of normal dose at the normal dosage interval.

Patients With GFR Greater than 50 mL/min: No dosage adjustment is required.

Stability and Storage: Store vials between 2 to 8°C, protected from light.

Preparation for Use: Reconstitution: I.M. or S.C.: Dissolve the contents of the vial in 1 to 5 mL of Sterile Water for Injection or 0.9% Sodium Chloride Injection.

I.V. or Intra-arterial: Dissolve the contents of the vial in 5 to 10 mL of either Sterile Water for Injection or 0.9% Sodium Chloride Injection.

Intracavitary: Intrapleural: Dissolve the contents of 1 to 8 vials (15 to 120 units) in 100 mL of 0.9% Sodium Chloride Injection or 5% Dextrose Injection.

Intraperitoneal: Dissolve the contents of 4 to 8 vials (60 to 120 units) in 100 mL of 0.9% Sodium Chloride Injection.

Reconstituted solutions may be stored at room temperature for 24 hours or refrigerated at 2 to 8°C for up to 48 hours. Unused portions should be discarded after that time.

Warning: As with all parenteral drug products, i.v. admixtures should be inspected visually for clarity, particulate matter, precipitate, discoloration and leakage prior to administration, whenever solution and container permit. Solutions showing haziness, particulate matter, precipitate, discoloration or leakage should not be used.

Handling and Disposal: 1) Preparation of cytotoxic agents such as bleomycin should be done in a vertical laminar flow hood (Biological Safety Cabinet—Class II). 2) Personnel preparing cytotoxic agents should wear PVC gloves, safety glasses, disposable gowns and masks. 3) All needles, syringes, vials and other materials which have come in contact with bleomycin should be segregated and incinerated at 1 000°C or more. Sealed containers may explode. 4) Personnel regularly involved in the preparation and handling of cytotoxic agents should have biannual blood examinations.

Supplied: Each vial of sterile lyophilized powder contains: bleomycin activity 15 units (as bleomycin sulfate). Single dose, conventional glass vials, boxes of 1. Store between 2 to 8°C, protected from light.

New Product 1998

BLEPHAMIDE® Ⓟ

Allergan

Sulfacetamide Sodium—Prednisolone Acetate

Antibacterial—Anti-inflammatory

Supplied: Each mL of sterile ophthalmic suspension contains: sulfacetamide sodium 10% and prednisolone acetate 0.2%. Nonmedicinal ingredients: benzalkonium chloride 0.0044% (as preservative), edetate disodium, polysorbate 80, polyvinyl alcohol (Liquifilm), potassium phosphate monobasic, sodium phosphate dibasic and sodium thiosulfate. Plastic dropper bottles of 5 and 10 mL.

BLOCADREN® Ⓟ

Frosst

Timolol Maleate

Antihypertensive—Antianginal Agent

Pharmacology: Timolol is a beta-adrenergic receptor blocking agent. The mechanism of the antihypertensive effect of beta-adrenergic receptor blocking agents has not yet been established. Among the factors that may be involved are: competitive ability to antagonize catecholamine-induced tachycardia at the beta receptor sites in the heart, thus decreasing cardiac output, inhibition of renin release by the kidneys; inhibition of the vasomotor centres.

The exact mechanism by which timolol exercises its antianginal effect is not certain but it may reduce the oxygen requirements of the heart by blocking catecholamine-induced increases in heart rate, systolic blood pressure and the velocity and extent of myocardial contraction. However oxygen requirements may be increased by such actions as increases in left ventricular fibre length, end diastolic pressure and the systolic ejection period. When the net physiological effect is advantageous in anginal patients it manifests itself during exercise or stress by delaying the onset of pain and reducing the incidence and severity of anginal attacks. Timolol can therefore increase the capacity for work and exercise in such patients. In a multi-clinic study, two-thirds of the patients treated with timolol maleate benefitted to some degree.

Timolol has been found effective in prophylactic use for secondary prevention in patients with ischemic heart disease who have survived the acute phase of a myocardial infarction. At the present time, the mechanism of this protective effect of timolol is unknown.

Indications: For patients with mild or moderate hypertension. Timolol is usually used in combination with other drugs, particularly a thiazide diuretic. However, timolol may be tried alone, as an initial agent in those patients in whom, in the judgment of the physician, treatment should be started with a beta-blocker rather than a diuretic.

The combination of timolol maleate with a diuretic or peripheral vasodilator has been found to be compatible and generally more effective than timolol alone. Limited experience with other antihypertensive agents has not shown evidence of incompatibility with timolol.

Timolol is not indicated in the treatment of hypertensive emergencies.

Angina pectoris due to ischemic heart disease.

Patients who have survived the acute phase of a myocardial infarction, and are clinically stable, to reduce cardiovascular mortality and the risk of re-infarction. In the study which showed these benefits, treatment with timolol was begun 7 to 28 days after the acute phase. Data are not available as to whether benefit would ensue if the treatment is initiated later.

Prophylactic treatment of migraine. Timolol is not indicated in the management of acute migraine attacks.

Contraindications: Congestive heart failure (see Warnings); right ventricular failure secondary to pulmonary hypertension; significant cardiomegaly; sinus bradycardia; AV block; cardiogenic shock; allergic rhinitis, bronchospasm (including asthma), or a history of bronchospasm or severe chronic obstructive pulmonary disease (including severe chronic bronchitis and emphysema) (see Warnings); anesthesia with agents that produce myocardial depression, e.g., ether; hypersensitivity to any component of this product.

Warnings: Cardiac Failure: Special caution should be exercised when administering timolol to patients with a history of heart failure. Sympathetic stimulation is a vital component supporting circulatory function in congestive heart failure, and inhibition with beta blockade always carries a potential hazard of further depressing myocardial contractility and precipitating cardiac failure.

In patients without a history of cardiac failure, continued depression of the myocardium over a period of time can, in some cases, lead to cardiac failure. In rare instances this has been observed during therapy with timolol.

Therefore, at the first sign or symptom of impending cardiac failure occurring during drug therapy, patients should be fully digitalized and/or given a diuretic, and the response observed closely. Timolol acts selectively without blocking the inotropic action of digitalis on the heart muscle. However, the positive inotropic action of digitalis may be reduced by the negative inotropic effect of timolol when the 2 drugs are used concomitantly. The effects of timolol and digitalis are additive in depressing AV conduction. If cardiac failure persists, therapy with timolol should be discontinued (see below).

Abrupt Cessation of Therapy: Patients with ischemic heart disease should be warned against stopping timolol abruptly. Hypersensitivity to catecholamines has been observed in patients withdrawn from beta-blocker therapy. Myocardial infarction, ventricular arrhythmias, or sudden death has been reported in such patients following abrupt discontinuation of therapy with beta-adrenergic receptor blocking agents, with or without preceding exacerbation of angina pectoris. Therefore, in angina and postmyocardial infarction, the dosage of timolol should be gradually reduced over about 2 weeks (maintaining the same frequency of administration) and the patient should be carefully observed. In patients with angina pectoris, if the angina still markedly worsens, or in any patient if acute coronary insufficiency develops, it is recommended that timolol be reinstated, at least temporarily.

Since ischemic heart disease may be unrecognized, the above advice should be followed in patients considered to be at risk of having asymptomatic ischemic heart disease.

Patients with chronic obstructive pulmonary disease (e.g., chronic bronchitis, emphysema) of mild to moderate severity should in general not receive beta-blockers, particularly the nonselective beta-blockers such as timolol (see Contraindications). If timolol must be given to such patients, it should be given with caution and under careful medical supervision since it may block bronchodilation produced by endogenous catecholamine stimulation of beta receptors (see Precautions).

Various skin rashes and conjunctival xerosis have been reported with beta-blockers including timolol. A severe syndrome (oculomucocutaneous syndrome) whose signs include conjunctivitis sicca and psoriasiform rashes, otitis and sclerosing serositis have occurred with the chronic use of one beta-adrenergic blocking agent. This syndrome has not been observed with timolol. However, physicians should be alert to the possibility of such reactions and should discontinue treatment in the event that they occur.

Severe sinus bradycardia due to unopposed vagal activity may result from the administration of timolol; in such cases, consider the use of i.v. atropine, and, if no improvement is seen, i.v. isoproterenol.

In patients with thyrotoxicosis, timolol may give a false impression of improvement by diminishing peripheral manifestations of hyperthyroidism without improving thyroid function. Special considerations should be given to the potential of timolol to aggravate congestive heart failure. Timolol does not alter thyroid function tests. Patients suspected of developing thyrotoxicosis should be managed carefully to avoid abrupt withdrawal of beta blockade which might precipitate a thyroid storm.

Precautions: There may be increased difficulty in treating an allergic-type reaction in patients on beta-blockers. In these patients, the reaction may be more severe due to pharmacologic effects of the beta-blocker and problems with fluid changes. Epinephrine should be administered with caution since it may not have its usual effects in the treatment of anaphylaxis. On the one hand, larger doses of epinephrine may be needed to overcome the bronchospasm, while on the other, these doses can be associated with excessive alpha-adrenergic stimulation with consequent hypertension, reflex bradycardia, heart block and possible potentiation of bronchospasm. Alternatives to the use of large doses of epinephrine include vigorous supportive care such as fluids and the use of beta-agonists including parenteral salbutamol or isoproterenol to overcome bronchospasm and norepinephrine to overcome hypotension.

Timolol should be administered with caution to patients subject to spontaneous hypoglycemia, or to diabetic patients (especially those with labile diabetes) who are receiving insulin or oral hypoglycemic agents. Beta-adrenergic blockers may mask the premonitory signs and symptoms of acute hypoglycemia.

Timolol dosage should be individually adjusted when used concomitantly with other antihypertensive agents (see Dosage).

Suitable laboratory tests should be carried out at appropriate intervals and caution should be observed in patients with impaired renal or hepatic function. Since timolol is partially metabolized in the liver and excreted mainly by the kidneys, dosage reduction may be necessary when hepatic or renal insufficiency is present. Marked hypotension has been observed in patients with severe renal insufficiency undergoing renal hemodialysis following oral administration of 20 mg of timolol.

Beta-adrenergic blockade has been reported to potentiate muscle weakness consistent with certain myasthenic symptoms (e.g., diplopia, ptosis and generalized weakness). Timolol has been reported rarely to increase muscle weakness in some patients with myasthenic symptoms.

Because of potential effects of beta-adrenergic blocking agents relative to blood pressure and pulse, these agents should be used with caution in patients with cerebrovascular insufficiency. If signs or symptoms suggesting reduced cerebral blood flow are observed, consideration should be given to discontinuing these agents.

Patients Undergoing Elective or Emergency Surgery: The management of patients with angina, being treated with beta-blockers and undergoing elective or emergency surgery, is controversial because beta-adrenergic receptor blockade impairs the ability of the heart to respond to beta-adrenergically mediated reflex stimuli, but abrupt discontinuation of therapy may be followed by severe complications (see Warnings). Some patients receiving beta-adrenergic blocking agents have been subject to protracted severe hypotension during anesthesia. Difficulty in restarting and maintaining the heartbeat has also been reported.

For these reasons, in patients with angina undergoing elective surgery, timolol should be withdrawn gradually following the recommendation given under Abrupt Cessation of Therapy (see Warnings). According to available evidence, all clinical and physiologic effects of beta blockade are no longer present 48 hours after cessation of medication.

In emergency surgery, since timolol is a competitive inhibitor of beta-adrenergic receptor agonists, its effects may be reversed, if necessary, by sufficient doses of such agonists as isoproterenol, levarterenol, dopamine or dobutamine.

Pregnancy: Since timolol has not been studied in human pregnancy, the drug should not be given to pregnant women. The use of any drug in patients of childbearing potential requires that the anticipated benefit be weighed against possible hazards.

Lactation: Timolol is detectable in human milk. Because of the potential for serious adverse reactions from timolol in infants, a decision should be made whether to discontinue nursing or to discontinue the drug, taking into account the importance of the drug to the mother.

Children: Safety and effectiveness in children have not been established.

Risk of Anaphylactic Reaction: While taking beta-blockers, patients with a history of atopy or a history of severe anaphylactic reaction to a variety of allergens may be more reactive to repeated challenge with such allergens, either accidental, diagnostic or therapeutic. Such patients may be unresponsive to the usual doses of epinephrine used to treat anaphylactic reactions.

Drug Interactions: Close observation of the patient is recommended when timolol is administered to patients receiving catecholamine-depleting drugs such as reserpine or guanethidine, because of possible additive effects and the production of hypotension and/or marked bradycardia, which may produce vertigo, syncope, or postural hypotension.

Attenuation of the antihypertensive effect of beta-adrenoceptor blocking agents by NSAIDs has been reported. When using these agents concomitantly, patients should be observed carefully to confirm that the desired therapeutic effect has been obtained.

The potential exists for hypotension, AV conduction disturbances and left ventricular failure to occur in patients receiving a beta-blocking agent and an oral calcium entry blocker concurrently. The nature of any cardiovascular adverse effect tends to depend on the type of calcium entry blocker used. The dihydropyridine derivatives such as nifedipine are more likely to lead to hypotension whereas verapamil and diltiazem have a greater propensity to lead to AV conduction disturbances or left ventricular failure when used with a beta-blocker. Oral calcium antagonists may be used with caution in combination with beta-adrenergic blocking agents when cardiac function is normal, but should be avoided in patients with impaired cardiac function. However in exceptional cases,

Blocadren (cont'd)

when in the opinion of the physician, concomitant use is considered essential in patients with impaired cardiac function, such use should be instituted gradually, in a hospital setting, under careful supervision.

I.V. calcium entry blockers should not be used in patients receiving beta-adrenoceptor blocking agents.

The concomitant use of beta-adrenergic blocking agents and digitalis with either diltiazem or verapamil may have additive effects in prolonging cardiac AV conduction time.

Adverse Effects: Adverse Reactions Reported During Clinical Trials: Cardiovascular: Congestive heart failure in 3 to 4% of patients (see Warnings). Secondary effects of decreased cardiac output, about 4%, which could include: syncope, vertigo, lightheadedness, postural hypotension; decreased renal perfusion. Severe bradycardia in about 1% of patients, lengthening of the PR interval, 2nd- and 3rd-degree A-V block, sinus arrest (if SA node previously diseased), cold extremities, Raynaud's phenomenon, claudication or paresthesia, hypotension.
Respiratory: dyspnea has occurred in about 10% of patients, bronchospasm in about 1% of patients, laryngospasm occurs rarely.
CNS: most frequently reported: headache, tinnitus. Less frequently: drowsiness, anxiety, vertigo, dizziness, weakness, insomnia, sedation, mental depression. Rarely: vivid dreams.
Integumentary (see Warnings): occasionally rashes, including one case of psoriasiform rash reported to date, and pruritus. Rarely: exfoliative dermatitis (one case).
Gastrointestinal: vomiting in about 4% of patients, diarrhea in about 5% of patients, constipation, epigastric distress, nausea.
Special Senses: dry eyes.
Adverse Reactions Reported Since the Drug was Marketed: Cardiovascular: cardiac arrest, cerebral vascular accident, palpitation, arrhythmia, edema, pulmonary edema, worsening of arterial insufficiency, worsening of angina pectoris, vasodilatation.
Hematologic: nonthrombocytopenic purpura.
Respiratory: rales, cough.
CNS: Rarely: nightmares, nervousness, diminished concentration, hallucinations, increased dreaming, decreased libido.
Integumentary (see Warnings): skin irritation, increased pigmentation, sweating.
Gastrointestinal: dyspepsia, hepatomegaly.
Special Senses: visual disturbances, diplopia, ptosis, eye irritation.
Urogenital: impotence, micturition difficulties.
Body as a Whole: asthenia, fatigue, chest pain, extremity pain, decreased exercise tolerance, weight loss.
Musculoskeletal: arthralgia.
Endocrine: hypoglycemia, hyperglycemia.
Clinical Laboratory: Slight increases in blood urea nitrogen, serum potassium, serum uric acid and triglycerides, and slight decreases in hemoglobin, hematocrit, and HDL-cholesterol have occurred, but were not progressive or associated with clinical manifestations. Slight increases in ALT have also occurred.

Overdose: Symptoms: The most common signs expected are bradycardia, hypotension, bronchospasm, or acute cardiac failure.

If overdosage occurs, in all cases therapy with timolol should be discontinued and the patient observed closely. In addition, the following therapeutic measures are suggested:

Treatment: Gastric lavage.
Bradycardia: Use atropine sulfate i.v. 0.25 mg to 2 mg to induce vagal blockade. If bradycardia persists, i.v. isoproterenol HCl should be administered cautiously. In refractory cases the use of a cardiac pacemaker may be considered.
Heart Block (second degree or complete): isoproterenol HCl or a cardiac pacemaker.
Acute Cardiac Failure: Conventional therapy with digitalis, diuretics, and oxygen should be instituted immediately. In refractory cases the use of i.v. aminophylline is suggested. This may be followed, if necessary, by glucagon HCl which has been reported to be useful.
Hypotension: Use sympathomimetic pressor drug therapy, such as levarterenol, epinephrine, dopamine or dobutamine. The response to epinephrine in such patients may be altered (see Precautions). In refractory cases the use of glucagon HCl has been reported to be useful.
Bronchospasm: Use isoproterenol HCl. Additional therapy with aminophylline may be considered.
Hypoglycemia: I.V. glucose and/or i.m. glucagon.

An in vitro hemodialysis study, using C^{14} timolol added to human plasma or whole blood, showed that timolol was readily dialyzed from these fluids; however, a study of patients with renal failure showed that timolol did not dialyze readily.

It should be remembered that timolol is a competitive antagonist of isoproterenol and hence large doses of isoproterenol can be expected to reverse many of the effects of excessive doses of timolol. However, the complications of excess isoproterenol, such as tachycardia, headache, flushing of the skin, arrhythmias, nausea, weakness, tremor and sweating, should not be overlooked.

Dosage: Hypertension: Timolol is usually used in conjunction with other antihypertensive agents, particularly a thiazide diuretic, but may be used alone (see Indications).

The dose must always be adjusted to the individual requirements of the patient, in accordance with the following guidelines.

When timolol is given to patients already receiving other antihypertensive agents, the initial dose should be 5 to 10 mg twice a day. If after 1 to 2 weeks an adequate response is not observed, dosage may be increased by increments of 5 mg twice daily, at intervals of 2 weeks. A 60 mg daily dose should not be exceeded.

When timolol is used alone the initial dose should be 10 mg twice a day and dosage increased if required, following the regimen described above.

In those patients who are found to be adequately controlled on daily doses of 20 mg or less, the administration of the total dose in the morning should be tried, as studies show adequate response to this dose regimen.

Angina: The recommended dosage range is 15 to 45 mg/day. The majority of patients respond to a daily dosage of 35 to 45 mg. Therapy should be initiated with 5 mg 2 or 3 times a day. Depending on response, increases in dosage may be necessary. The first increase should not exceed 10 mg/day in divided doses. Subsequent increases should not exceed 15 mg/day in divided doses. A total daily dose of 45 mg should not be exceeded. There should be an interval of at least 3 days between increases in dosage.

After the titration period, some patients may be maintained on a twice-daily schedule.

Preventive Use in Ischemic Heart Disease: For long-term preventive use in patients who have survived the acute phase of myocardial infarction, the maintenance dose is 10 mg twice daily. Therapy should be initiated with 5 mg twice daily and the patient observed carefully. If no adverse reaction occurs, the dosage should then be increased after 2 days to 10 mg twice daily. In the studies evaluating timolol following myocardial infarction, treatment was begun 7 to 28 days after the acute phase.

Migraine: Dosage must be individualized. The recommended dosage for prevention of migraine headache is 10 mg twice daily. The dosage range is 10 to 30 mg/day. If a satisfactory response is not obtained after 6 to 8 weeks of the maximum suggested dosage, therapy with timolol should be discontinued.

Supplied: Each light-blue, flat, beveled-edged tablet, scored on one side, marked Frosst on other, contains: timolol maleate 10 mg. Nonmedicinal ingredients: magnesium stearate, microcrystalline cellulose and pregelatinized starch. Gluten-, lactose- and tartrazine-free. Bottles of 100. Keep container tightly closed. Store between 15 and 30°C. Protect from light.

(Shown in Product Recognition Section)

Reviewed 1999

BONAMIL®

Wyeth-Ayerst

Milk Protein (Casein Predominant)

Infant Formula

Indications: A nutritionally complete iron-fortified cow's milk-based infant formula for routine feeding of infants for the first year of life if breast-feeding is not an option or if a supplement is required. Contains vitamin A in the form of beta-carotene.

Supplied: Protein: casein-predominant (18% whey: 82% casein). Carbohydrate: lactose. Fat: polyunsaturated 37%, monounsaturated 18%, saturated 45%. Vitamins and Minerals: at recommended levels.

Powder: Each can contains: lactose, skim milk, soybean oil, coconut oil, lecithin soybean, potassium bicarbonate, choline chloride, ferrous sulfate, ascorbic acid, taurine, alpha-tocopheryl acetate, zinc sulfate, niacinamide, cupric sulfate, calcium pantothenate, vitamin A palmitate, thiamine hydrochloride, riboflavin, manganese sulfate, pyridoxine hydrochloride, beta-carotene, folic acid, phytonadione, biotin, cholecalciferol and cyanocobalamin. Normal Dilution: 1 scoop of powder and 60 mL water. Scoop provided in each can. Cans of 450 g, cases of 6.

BONAMINE™ Ⓟ

Pfizer

Meclizine HCl

Antiemetic

Pharmacology: Meclizine has antihistaminic and anticholinergic properties. The site and mechanism of action of meclizine in controlling vertigo arising from various conditions, have not been clearly defined. Pharmacological studies conducted with other antihistamines show that the peripheral labyrinthine structures may be the site of action.

Indications: For prophylaxis and symptomatic relief of nausea, vomiting and vertigo associated with motion sickness, radiation sickness, Ménière's syndrome, labyrinthitis and other vestibular disturbances.

Contraindications: In patients with known hypersensitivity to meclizine.

Warnings: Occupational Hazards: Patients should be warned that meclizine may occasionally cause drowsiness and that when taking it they should take the necessary precautions against driving or operating dangerous machinery.

Patients suffering from glaucoma or prostatic enlargement should take meclizine only under the direction of a physician.

As with all antihistamines, meclizine may cause hyperexcitability in children.

Precautions: *Pregnancy:* Epidemiological studies with meclizine in women experiencing nausea and vomiting of pregnancy has revealed no evidence of a teratogenic effect attributable to the drug.

As with many other drugs of this class, certain teratogenic effects have been observed in the rat. In the rat meclizine at doses of 25 to 50 times the human dose has shown certain fetal abnormalities. These abnormalities have not been observed in other experimental animals, including the monkey.

The use of meclizine by women who are pregnant or may become pregnant requires that the potential benefits be weighed against the potential risks.

Drug Interactions: There may be increased CNS depression when meclizine is administered concurrently with other CNS depressants, including barbiturates, alcohol, tranquilizers and sedatives.

MAO inhibitors may prolong and intensify the anticholinergic effects of meclizine.

Adverse Effects: Drowsiness, dry mouth, fatigue, vomiting and, on rare occasions, blurred vision have been reported with meclizine therapy.

Overdose: Symptoms: In adults, the usual signs of meclizine overdose are CNS depression with drowsiness, coma and convulsions. Hypotension may also occur, particularly in the elderly. In children, anticholinergic effects and CNS stimulation (hallucinations, seizures, trouble sleeping) are more likely to occur.

Treatment: There is no specific antidote for treatment of meclizine overdosage. Symptomatic and supportive treatment should be employed. If ingestion is recent (within 1 hour), induce emesis (syrup of ipecac is recommended; precautions against aspiration are required, especially in infants and children) or empty stomach by gastric lavage if patient has been unable to vomit within 3 hours of ingestion. Activated charcoal may also be used. Keep patient calm to minimize excitation. Vasopressors (norepinephrine or phenylephrine) may be used to correct hypotension. Physostigmine may be useful to counteract the CNS anticholinergic effects of meclizine. Do not use stimulants. If vasopressors are indicated do not use epinephrine, because it may lower blood pressure further. Diazepam i.v. may be given for treatment of seizures that do not respond to physostigmine.

Dosage: Adults: The recommended dose for specific indications is: Motion Sickness: A single dose of 25 to 50 mg affords protection against motion sickness for approximately 24 hours. The initial dose should be taken at least 1 hour prior to traveling in order to insure absorption of the drug, as retention of the medication is uncertain in individuals who have already developed motion sickness. Thereafter, the dose may be repeated every 24 hours as indicated for the duration of the journey.

Labyrinthine and Vestibular Disturbances: The optimal dosage is usually 25 to 100 mg daily in divided doses, depending on the clinical response.

Radiation Sickness: 50 mg administered 2 to 12 hours prior to radiation treatment.
Children: Children require about one half the adult dose.

The fruit-flavored tablets may be chewed, swallowed whole or allowed to dissolve in the mouth.

Supplied: Each scored, white, fruit-flavored tablet contains: meclizine HCl 25 mg. Nonmedicinal ingredients: microcrystalline cellulose, cornstarch, lactose, magnesium stearate/sodium lauryl sulfate, raspberry flavor and sucrose. Tartrazine-free. Bottles of 100. Store between 15 and 30°C.

(Shown in Product Recognition Section)

BONEFOS® Ⓟ
Rhône-Poulenc Rorer

Clodronate Disodium

Bone Metabolism Regulator—Antihypercalcemic Agent

Pharmacology: Clodronate belongs to the class of bisphosphonates which bind to hydroxyapatite and inhibit formation and dissolution of calcium crystals in vitro.

Bisphosphonates including clodronate act on the bony skeleton causing reduction of normal and abnormal bone resorption. Clodronate alters the activitics of osteoclasts and osteoblasts and the balance of bone resorption and bone formation is changed resulting in reduction of bone turnover. In responsive patients, inhibition of abnormal bone resorption by clodronate leads to reduction of hypercalcemia of malignancy presenting with or without demonstrable skeletal metastases. During and also after i.v. administration of clodronate the elevated serum calcium decreases, in some instances to hypocalcemic levels.

Clodronate is not metabolized and absorbed drug is excreted unchanged by the kidneys. The kidneys have a prominent role in calcium homeostasis. In addition to skeletal osteolysis, renal dysfunction becomes a contributor to the pathogenesis of hypercalcemia. At the time of diagnosis most hypercalcemic patients are significantly dehydrated. The antagonistic effects of calcium on the action of antidiuretic hormone impair the renal concentration mechanisms resulting in polyuria and excessive fluid loss. Hydration status is further compromised by reduction of oral fluid intake due to nausea, vomiting and mental status. Prior to initiation of therapy with clodronate, the state of the negative fluid balance requires vigorous and adequate hydration with isotonic saline (0.9%). Normalization of blood calcium levels by clodronate in adequately hydrated patients may also normalize plasma parathyroid hormone (PTH) levels without resulting impairment of desired clodronate effects (decrease in urinary calcium, hydroxyproline and phosphate excretion).

After i.v. dose, clodronate exhibits a plasma concentration profile which fits a two-compartment model with $t_{1/2}\,\alpha$ approximately 0.3 hours and $t_{1/2\beta}$ approximately 2 hours, and a terminal elimination phase with $t_{1/2}$ approximately 13 hours. The latter accounts for 10 to 15% of renal excretion. Total clearance is about 110 mL/min and renal clearance is approximately 90 mL/min. Volume of distribution is approximately 20 L.

Following oral administration, absorption is estimated at 1 to 3% of the ingested dose. Unabsorbed drug is excreted unchanged in the feces.

The decrease in serum calcium concentration is rapid with significant reductions usually attained within 2 days after starting i.v. therapy and continuing for 5 to 6 days after discontinuing therapy.

Indications: For the management of hypercalcemia of malignancy.

Prior to treatment with clodronate renal excretion of excess calcium should be promoted by restoration and maintenance of adequate fluid balance and urine output.

In responsive patients i.v. infusion of clodronate decreases the flux of calcium from the bones by inhibiting the osteoclastic activity and bone resorption, thus reducing the calcium level in blood.

Treatment with oral clodronate following i v infusion has been found to prolong the duration of action (see Dosage).

Contraindications: Renal functional impairment when serum creatinine exceeds 440 μmol/L (5.0 mg/dL).
- Hypersensitivity to clodronate.
- Severe inflammation of the gastrointestinal tract.
- Pregnancy and lactation.

Warnings: Clodronate should not be given as a bolus injection since severe local reactions and thrombophlebitis may occur as the result of high local concentrations. The rapid bolus injection may also precipitate acute renal failure.

The recommended daily dose of clodronate should always be diluted and administered as a slow i.v. infusion over a minimum 2 hour period (see Dosage).

Administration of clodronate may aggravate renal function in some patients. Appropriate monitoring of the renal function during and after i.v. infusion is required. Since the drug is excreted by the kidneys it is essential to establish that the excretion of the fluid load and that of the drug would not present an excessive medical risk. The effect of the drug on the renal function of patients with serum creatinine in excess of 220 μmol/L has not been studied in controlled trials. In such situations dose reduction should be considered or the drug should be withheld (see Precautions).

If during therapy there is deterioration of renal function, the i.v. infusion must be stopped.

Clodronate should **not** be given together with other bisphosphonates to treat hypercalcemia since the combined effects of these agents are unknown.

Clodronate should not be mixed with calcium-containing i.v. infusions.

Precautions: Administration of I.V. Infusion: The daily dose must be diluted in 500 mL of 0.9% sodium chloride injection, USP or 5% dextrose injection, USP and administered by infusion lasting at least 2 hours. No other drugs or nutrients may be added to the diluted injection solution. Paravenous infiltration should be avoided. Local reaction may occur.

Administration of Oral Dosage Form: The drug should be taken at least 2 hours before or after food, because food may decrease the amount of clodronate absorbed by the body.

Metabolic and Fluid Balance: As many patients with hypercalcemia have other electrolyte abnormalities at presentation, appropriate attention must be given to maintaining electrolyte balance. Serum electrolytes should be monitored at least daily and supplementation provided as needed.

Patients must be adequately hydrated before and during the treatment period. Excess calcium impairs the renal concentrating mechanisms resulting in polyuria and excessive fluid loss. Nausea and lethargy caused by hypercalcemia can also reduce oral intake leading to profound negative fluid balance. Isotonic saline should be administered at a rate determined by the severity of hypercalcemia, the degree of dehydration and the cardiovascular status of the patient. Hypercalcemia may lead to impairment of renal function.

Patient Monitoring: Calcium levels should be monitored throughout the treatment. Corrected (adjusted) serum calcium values may be calculated using established algorithms, such as:

$Ca_{adj} = Ca_t - 0.71\ (A - A_m)$
Ca_{adj} = adjusted calcium concentration (mg/100 mL)
Ca_t = total calcium concentration (mg/100 mL)
A = albumin concentration (g/100 mL)
A_m = mean normal albumin concentration of the given laboratory (g/100 mL)

Serum creatinine and blood urea nitrogen should be monitored when the drug is administered i.v. in patients with impaired renal function.

Hypocalcemia: Infusion of clodronate may present a risk of hypocalcemia. The drug tends to chelate blood calcium during therapy which may contribute to hypocalcemia. Hypocalcemia was seen in 26 of 703 patients treated with oral or i.v. clodronate but was symptomatic in only one case. Symptomatic hypocalcemia can be reversed by the administration of calcium gluconate.

Serum Phosphate: Hyperphosphatemia has not been reported during clodronate therapy. However, transient hypophosphatemia can occur following therapy with clodronate.

Hyperparathyroidism: Increased serum parathyroid levels have been observed in patients receiving clodronate and are attributed to a homeostatic response to the fall in serum calcium. The clinical importance has not been established.

<u>*Drug Interactions:*</u> The use of clodronate with other agents indicated for reduction of calcium such as corticosteroids, phosphate, calcitonin, mithramycin, loop-diuretics may result in increased hypocalcemic effect depending on tumor type and pathophysiological situation.

Concurrent use of antacids or any drug containing calcium, iron, magnesium or aluminum may prevent absorption of oral clodronate.

Although bisphosphonates are not known to affect the antineoplastic activity of various anticancer agents including carmustine, cyclophosphamide, doxorubicin or fluorouracil, no study has been reported so far of the interaction of clodronate and anticancer agents.

Compatibility with I.V. Solutions: Clodronate forms complexes with bivalent ions and must not be mixed with calcium-containing solutions such as Ringer's solution.

It is compatible with 0.9% saline and 5% dextrose injections.

Pregnancy: The safety and efficacy of clodronate in pregnancy has not been established (see Contraindications).

Lactation: There is no clinical experience with clodronate in lactating women and it is not known whether it passes into breast milk (see Contraindications).

Children: The safety and efficacy of clodronate in children has not been established.

Laboratory Examinations: Since clodronate binds to bone, it may interfere with bone scintigraphy examinations.

Adverse Effects: The following adverse reactions have been observed with clodronate.

Gastrointestinal: Gastrointestinal disturbances including nausea, vomiting, gastric pain and diarrhea are the most frequently reported adverse events with oral clodronate and have occurred in approximately 10% of 453 patients studied. In rare cases, treatment had to be discontinued. Difficulties in swallowing the capsule, irritation of the mouth and ulcerative pharyngitis were also rarely reported.

Renal: Occasional mild to moderate abnormalities in renal function (increase in mean serum creatinine concentrations, transient proteinuria) occurred after i.v. clodronate therapy. Three cases of fatal renal failure which may have been related to the underlying hypercalcemia and dehydration have occurred in patients receiving i.v. clodronate.

Biochemical Changes: Hypocalcemia was seen in approximately 4% (26/703) of patients treated with oral or i.v. clodronate disodium; it was symptomatic in only one case. Although not reported yet during clodronate therapy, hyperphosphatemia has been known to occur with other bisphosphonates.

Endocrine: Secondary hyperparathyroidism may develop as a result of clodronate therapy. This is a homeostatic response to the fall in serum calcium and will reverse upon discontinuation of therapy.

Hematologic: Patient surveillance encompassing about 2 700 patient-years treated with clodronate detected 5 cases of acute non-lymphocytic leukemia or myelodysplasia in patients without multiple myeloma, and 2 cases in patients with multiple myeloma (2 patients with multiple myeloma also developed non-lymphocytic leukemia while receiving placebo). The causal relationship to clodronate or to the underlying disease has not been established.

Overdose: Symptoms and Treatment: There is lack of documented experience on acute overdosing with clodronate. An overdose of the i.v. preparation could provide renal damage. Renal function should be monitored. Overdosage may result in hypocalcemia. Careful monitoring for several days for signs and symptoms of hypocalcemia is recommended in cases where the dose given was too high in relation to initial serum calcium (see Precautions). Oral or parenteral calcium supplementation may be required to restore plasma calcium levels.

Gastric lavage may be used to remove unabsorbed drug following acute oral overdosage.

Dosage: I.V. Infusion: The recommended adult dose is 300 mg/day (one 5 mL ampul).

The contents of the ampul must be diluted in 500 mL of 0.9% sodium chloride injection or 5% dextrose injection and administered by infusion lasting at least 2 hours. Treatment should be continued until plasma calcium returns to normal, this generally being achieved after 2 to 5 days of treatment. Treatment should not be prolonged beyond 7 days.

Dosage should be reduced in patients with renal impairment (see Warnings).

Capsules: The oral recommended daily maintenance dose following i.v. therapy is in the range of 1 600 mg (4 capsules) to 2 400 mg (6 capsules) given in single or 2 divided doses. Maximal recommended daily dose is 3 200 mg (8 capsules).

Dosage should be reduced in patients with severe renal impairment (see Contraindications, Warnings and Precautions).

Retreatment: Controlled studies have not been undertaken for retreatment with clodronate. Limited clinical experience has suggested that patients with re-increased serum calcium after termination of therapy with clodronate or during oral administration may be retreated either with a higher oral dosage (up to 3 200 mg/day) or with the i.v. infusion preparation (300 mg/day).

Supplied: Capsules: Each yellow, hard gelatin capsule contains: anhydrous clodronate disodium (as the tetrahydrate) 400 mg. Nonmedicinal ingredients: calcium stearate, colloidal silicon dioxide, FD&C Red No. 3, gelatin, iron oxides, lactose,

Bonefos (cont'd)

talc and titanium dioxide. High density polyethylene bottles of 100. Store at room temperature.

I.V. Infusion: Each mL of i.v. infusion contains: clodronate disodium tetrahydrate equivalent to anhydrous clodronate disodium 60 mg. Nonmedicinal ingredients: sodium hydroxide and water for injection. Ampuls of 5 mL, packages of 5. Store at room temperature. Diluted product may be stored for up to 24 hours at room temperature.

(Shown in Product Recognition Section)

BOTOX®

Allergan

Botulinum Toxin Type A

Neuromuscular Paralytic Agent

Pharmacology: Botulinum toxin type A blocks neuromuscular conduction by binding to receptor sites on motor nerve terminals, entering the nerve terminals, and inhibiting the release of acetylcholine. When injected i.m. at therapeutic doses, botulinum toxin type A produces a partial chemical denervation of the muscle resulting in localized muscle paralysis.

When chemically denervated, the muscle may atrophy, axonal sprouting may occur, and extrajunctional acetylcholine receptors may develop. There is evidence that reinnervation of the muscle may occur, thus reversing muscle weakness produced by localized injection of botulinum toxin type A.

When injected into neck muscles, botulinum toxin type A reduces both objective signs and subjective symptoms of cervical dystonia (spasmodic torticollis). These improvements include reduced angle of head turning, reduced shoulder elevation, decreased size and strength of hypertrophic muscles, and decreased pain. Based on the results of well-controlled studies, 40 to 58% of patients with cervical dystonia would be expected to have a significant improvement in their symptoms.

The paralytic effect on muscles injected with botulinum toxin type A reduces the excessive, abnormal contractions of blepharospasm associated with dystonia.

When used for the treatment of strabismus, it has been postulated that the administration of botulinum toxin type A affects muscle pairs by inducing an atrophic lengthening of the injected muscle and a corresponding shortening of the antagonist muscle.

Following injection of botulinum toxin type A some distant muscles have shown increased electrophysiologic neuromuscular jitter. This effect is not associated with other types of electrophysiologic abnormalities, or with clinical signs of weakness or symptoms regarding either safety or efficacy.

Indications: To reduce the subjective symptoms and objective signs of cervical dystonia (spasmodic torticollis) in adults.

For the treatment of blepharospasm associated with dystonia, including benign essential blepharospasm or VII nerve disorders in patients 12 years of age or older.

For the treatment of strabismus in patients 12 years of age or older. Botulinum toxin type A is ineffective in chronic paralytic strabismus except to reduce antagonist contracture in conjunction with surgical repair.

Contraindications: In the presence of infection at the proposed injection site(s). In individuals with known hypersensitivity to any ingredient in the formulation.

Warnings: The recommended dosages and frequencies of administration for botulinum toxin type A should not be exceeded.

The effect of botulinum toxin may be potentiated by aminoglycoside antibiotics or spectinomycin, or other drugs that interfere with neuromuscular transmission (e.g., tubocurainetype muscle relaxants). Caution should be exercised when botulinum toxin type A is used with aminoglycosides (e.g., streptomycin, tobramycin, neomycin, gentamicin, netilmicin, kanamycin, amikacin), spectinomycin, polymyxins, tetracyclines, lincomycin or any other drugs that interfere with neuromuscular transmission. Caution should also be exercised when botulinum toxin type A is utilized for treatment of patients with myasthenia gravis, Eaton Lambert Syndrome, or other disorders that produce a depletion of acetylcholine.

Precautions: General: The safe and effective use of botulinum toxin type A depends upon proper storage of the product, selection of the correct dose, and proper reconstitution and administration techniques. Physicians administering botulinum toxin type A should be familiar with the relevant anatomy of the area involved and any alterations to the anatomy due to prior surgical procedures. An understanding of standard electromyographic techniques is also required for treatment of strabismus and may be useful for the treatment of cervical dystonia and blepharospasm.

As with all biologic products, an anaphylactic reaction may occur. Necessary precautions should be taken and epinephrine should be available.

Caution should be used when botulinum toxin type A is used in the presence of inflammation at the proposed injection site(s).

Cervical Dystonia (Spasmodic Torticollis): Botulinum toxin type A when injected for cervical dystonia may cause dysphagia ranging in severity from very mild to severe, with potential for aspiration, and in rare instances may require medical intervention (nasogastric tube feeding).

In one study, dysphagia appeared to be dose-related, occurring at frequencies of 8, 21 and 35% with mean dosages of 66, 129 and 253 U respectively. Dysphagia has been reported in clinical trials to occur less frequently with total doses below 200 U in one treatment session. Limiting the dose injected into the sternocleidomastoid to less than 100 U may decrease the occurrence of dysphagia. Patients with smaller neck muscle mass, or patients who require bilateral injections into the sternocleidomastoid muscle, have been reported to be at greater risk of dysphagia. Dysphagia may be attributable to distribution of the pharmacological effect of botulinum toxin type A resulting from spread of the toxin in the vicinity of the injection site.

Blepharospasm: Reduced blinking from botulinum toxin type A when injected into the orbicularis oculi muscle can lead to corneal exposure, persistent epithelial defects and corneal ulceration, especially in patients with VII nerve disorders. Careful testing of previously operated eyes for corneal sensation, avoidance of injection into the lower lid area to avoid ectropion, and vigorous treatment of any epithelial defect should be employed. This may require protective drops, ointment, therapeutic soft contact lenses, or closure of the eye by patching or other means.

Strabismus: The efficacy of botulinum toxin type A in deviations over 50 prism diopters, in restrictive strabismus, in Duane's syndrome with lateral rectus weakness, and in secondary strabismus caused by prior surgical over-recession of the antagonist is doubtful. In order to enhance efficacy, multiple injections over time may be required.

During the administration of botulinum toxin type A for the treatment of strabismus, retrobulbar hemorrhages sufficient to compromise retinal circulation have occurred from needle penetrations into the orbit. It is recommended that appropriate instruments to decompress the orbit be accessible. Ocular (globe) penetrations by needles have also occurred. An ophthalmoscope to diagnose this condition should be available.

Drug Interactions: The effect of botulinum toxin may be potentiated by aminoglycoside antibiotics, spectinomycin, or any other drugs that interfere with neuromuscular transmission. Caution should be exercised when botulinum toxin type A is used in patients taking any of these drugs (see Warnings).

Carcinogenesis, Mutagenesis, Impairment of Fertility: Studies in animals have not been performed to evaluate the carcinogenic potential of botulinum toxin type A. Botulinum toxin type A was not mutagenic in in vitro and in vivo mutagenicity studies. A fertility and reproductive toxicity study following i.m. injection of botulinum toxin type A in rats indicated the 'no observable effect level' (NOEL) on reproduction was at dosages of 4 U/kg (approximately 2/3 of the maximum recommended human dose) in male rats and at dosages of 8 U/kg in female rats.

Pregnancy: Pregnancy Category C: Teratogenic Effects: The teratogenic effects of botulinum toxin type A were evaluated in mice, rats and rabbits. No teratogenic effects were observed when presumed pregnant mice were injected i.m. with doses of 4 U/kg (approximately 2/3 of the maximum recommended human dose) and 8 U/kg on days 5 and 13 of gestation; however, dosages of 16 U/kg induced a slightly lower fetal body weight. No teratogenic effects were observed in rats when injected i.m. with doses of 16 U/kg on days 6 and 13 of gestation, and 2 U/kg/day on days 6 through 15 of gestation. In rabbits, daily injections at dosages of 0.5 U/kg/day (days 6 through 18 of gestation) and 4 and 6 U/kg (days 6 and 13 of gestation) caused death and abortions among surviving animals. External malformations were observed in the fetus in one 0.125 U/kg/day and one 2 U/kg dosage. The rabbit appears to be a more sensitive species to botulinum toxin type A.

Reproductive and Developmental Effects: The reproductive and developmental effects of botulinum toxin type A were evaluated in rats at dose levels of 4, 8 and 16 U/kg. Muscle atrophy at the injected site, reduced body weight gains and reduced absolute feed consumption were observed following i.m. injection of botulinum toxin type A at dosages of 4 U/kg and higher on days 5 and 13 of presumed gestation, and day 7 of lactation. No effects on maternal reproductive performance were observed at the highest dose tested, 16 U/kg (approximately 3 times the maximum recommended human dose). No adverse effects on development of the pups was observed at 4 U/kg; however, higher dosages were associated with reduced pup body weight and/or pup viability at birth.

There are no adequate and well-controlled studies of botulinum toxin type A administration in pregnant women. Because animal reproduction studies are not always predictive of human response, botulinum toxin type A should be administered during pregnancy only if the potential benefit justifies the potential risk to the fetus.

Lactation: It is not known whether this drug is excreted in human milk. Because many drugs are excreted in human milk, caution should be exercised when botulinum toxin type A is administered to a nursing woman.

Children: Safety and effectiveness in children below the age of 12 years has not been established.

Information for the Patient: Patients with cervical dystonia (spasmodic torticollis) should be informed of the possibility of experiencing dysphagia which may persist for 2 to 3 weeks after injection, but has been reported in one case of lasting 5 months post-injection. Patients should also be advised of the potential for experiencing malaise lasting up to 6 weeks after injection with botulinum toxic type A. Patients who are sedentary should be cautioned to resume activity gradually following the administration of botulinum toxin type A.

As with any treatment with the potential to allow previously sedentary patients to resume activities, the sedentary patient should be cautioned to resume activity gradually following the administration of botulinum toxin type A.

Adverse Effects: Cervical Dystonia: The safety of botulinum toxin type A used for the treatment of cervical dystonia was evaluated in 710 patients. The most frequently reported adverse reactions were dysphagia, pain, soreness and bruising at the injection site, local weakness, symptomatic general weakness, malaise and nausea as summarized in Table I.

Table I—Botox

Adverse Effects—Cervical Dystonia

	Botox N=710	Vehicle N=137
Dysphagia	15.8%	2.9%
Pain and soreness at injection site	16.3%	34.3%
Weakness, local	12.8%	6.6%
Weakness, general	2.7%	1.5%
Nausea	2.1%	1.5%
Malaise	2.0%	2.9%
Bruising of injection site	2.0%	3.6%

Dysphagia may be attributable to spread of the botulinum toxin type A in the vicinity of the site of injection and into surrounding muscles. Local weakness represents the expected pharmacological action of botulinum toxin. In general, adverse reactions occur within the first few days following injection and last approximately 2 weeks.

Other adverse reactions during clinical trials which were reported rarely (1%) with botulinum toxin type A injection for cervical dystonia include drowsiness, numbness, stiffness, diplopia, ptosis, headache, dyspnea, fever, and flu syndrome. A female patient developed brachial plexopathy 2 days after injection of 120 units of botulinum toxin type A for cervical dystonia, with recovery after 5 months.

Blepharospasm: In clinical studies, there were reports of 7 cases of diffuse skin rash and 2 cases of local swelling of the eyelid skin lasting for several days following eyelid injection.

In clinical studies of 1 684 patients who received 4 258 treatments (involving multiple injections) for blepharospasm, reported incidence rates of adverse reactions per treated eye are as listed: ptosis 11%; irritation/tearing (includes dry eye, lagophthalmos, and photophobia) 10%; ectropion, keratitis, diplopia and entropion were reported rarely (incidence less than 1%).

Ecchymosis may occur and can be prevented by applying pressure at the injection site immediately after the injection.

In 2 cases of VII nerve disorder (1 case of an aphakic eye), reduced blinking from botulinum toxin type A when injected into the orbicularis muscle led to serious corneal exposure, persistent epithelial defect, and corneal ulceration. Perforation requiring corneal grafting occurred in one case, an aphakic eye.

A patient suffered an attack of acute angle closure glaucoma one day after receiving an injection of botulinum toxin for blepharospasm, with recovery 4 months later after laser iridotomy and trabeculectomy.

Strabismus: Inducing paralysis in 1 or more extraocular muscles may produce spatial disorientation, double vision, or past-pointing. Covering the affected eye may alleviate these symptoms. Extraocular muscles adjacent to the injection site can be affected, causing ptosis or vertical deviation, especially with higher doses of botulinum toxin type A. The incidence rates of these adverse effects in 2 058 adults who received 3 650 injections for horizontal strabismus are: ptosis 15.7%; vertical deviation 16.9%.

The incidence of ptosis was 0.9% after inferior rectus injection and 37.7% after superior rectus injection.

The incidence rates of these adverse events persisting for over 6 months in a large series of 5 587 injections of horizontal muscles in 3 104 patients are: ptosis lasting over 180 days 0.3%; vertical deviation greater than 2 prism diopters lasting over 180 days 2.1%.

In these patients, the injection procedure itself caused nine scleral perforations. A vitreous hemorrhage occurred and later cleared in one case. No retinal detachment or visual loss occurred in any case. Sixteen retrobulbar hemorrhages occurred without visual loss. Decompression of the orbit after 5 minutes was done to restore retinal circulation in 1 case. Five eyes had pupillary change consistent with ciliary ganglion damage (Adies pupil).

The following events have been reported (<0.1%) since the drug has been marketed and a causal relationship to the botulinum toxin injected is unknown: skin rash (including erythema multiforme, urticaria and psoriasiforme eruption), pruritus, allergic reaction, and facial paralysis.

A patient developed anterior segment ischemia after receiving botulinum toxin type A into the medial rectus muscle under direct visualization for esotropia.

Overdose: Symptoms and Treatment: In the event of overdosage or injection error, additional information may be obtained by contacting Allergan, Inc. at (800) 433-8871.

No cases of systemic toxicity have been reported following accidental injection or oral ingestion of botulinum toxin type A. Should accidental injection or oral ingestion occur, the patient should be monitored for approximately 1 week for signs or symptoms of systemic weakness or muscle paralysis.

Dosage: General: **For i.m. use only.**

The use of 1 vial for more than 1 patient is not recommended because the product and diluent do not contain a preservative. Do not freeze reconstituted botulinum toxin type A. Once opened and reconstituted, use within 4 hours and discard remaining solution.

An injection of botulinum toxin type A is prepared by drawing into a sterile 1 mL tuberculin syringe an amount of the properly diluted toxin (see Dilution Table) slightly greater than the intended dose. Air bubbles in the syringe barrel are expelled and the syringe may be attached to the electromyographic injection needle, preferably a 1.5 inch, 27 gauge needle. Injection volume in excess of the intended dose is expelled through the needle into an appropriate waste container to assure patency of the needle and to confirm that there is no syringe-needle leakage. A new sterile needle and syringe should be used to enter the vial on each occasion for dilution or removal of botulinum toxin type A.

Cervical Dystonia (Spasmodic Torticollis): Several dosing regimens have been used in clinical trials for treatment of cervical dystonia with botulinum toxin type A. Dosing must be tailored to the individual patient based on the patient's head and neck position, localization of pain and muscle hypertrophy, patient's body weight, and patient response. In initial controlled clinical trials to establish safety and efficacy for cervical dystonia, doses of diluted botulinum toxin type A ranged from 140 to 280 U. However, in clinical practice a range of 200 to 360 U have been used effectively. In general, a total dose of 6 U/kg every 2 months should not be exceeded for treatment of cervical dystonia.

A 25, 27 or 30 gauge needle may be used for superficial muscles, and a 22 gauge needle may be used for deeper musculature. For cervical dystonia, localization of the involved muscles with electromyographic guidance may be useful.

Multiple injection sites allow botulinum toxin type A to have more uniform contact with the innervation areas of the dystonic muscle, and are especially useful in larger muscles. The optimal number of injection sites is dependent upon the size of the muscle to be chemically denervated.

Clinical improvement generally occurs within the first 2 weeks after injection. The maximum clinical benefit generally occurs approximately 6 weeks postinjection. Repeat doses should be administered when the clinical effect of a previous injection diminishes, but not more frequently than every 2 months. The interval between injections reported in the clinical trials showed substantial variation (from 2 to 32 weeks), with a typical duration of approximately 12 to 16 weeks, depending on patient's individual symptoms and responses.

Table II is intended to give dosing guidelines for injection of botulinum toxin type A in the treatment of cervical dystonia.

This information is provided as guidance for the initial injection. The extent of muscle hypertrophy and the muscle groups involved in the dystonic posture may change with time necessitating alterations in the dose of toxin and muscles to be injected. The exact dosage and sites injected must be individualized for each patient.

Blepharospasm: For blepharospasm, diluted botulinum toxin type A (see Table III on following page) is injected using a sterile, 27 to 30 gauge needle without electromyographic guidance. The initial recommended dose is 1.25 to 2.5 U (0.05 to 0.1 mL volume at each site) injected into the medial and lateral pretarsal orbicularis oculi of the upper lid and into the lateral pretarsal orbicularis oculi of the lower lid.

In general, the initial effect of the injections is seen within 3 days and reaches a peak at 1 to 2 weeks post-treatment. Treatment effects last approximately 3 months, following which the procedure can be repeated indefinitely.

At repeat treatment sessions, the dose may be increased up to two-fold if the response from the initial treatment is considered insufficient (i.e., defined as an effect that lasts no longer than 2 months). However there appears to be little benefit obtainable from injecting more than 5 units per site. Some tolerance may be found when botulinum toxin type A is used in treating blepharospasm if treatments are given more frequently than every 3 months, and it is rare to have the effect be permanent.

The cumulative dose of botulinum toxin type A for treatment of blepharospasm in a 2-month period should not exceed 200 U.

Strabismus: Botulinum toxin type A is intended for injection into extraocular muscles utilizing the electrical activity recorded from the tip of the injection needle as a guide to placement within the target muscle. Injection without surgical exposure or electromyographic guidance should not be attempted. Physicians should be familiar with electromyographic techniques.

To prepare the eye for botulinum toxin type A injection, it is recommended that several drops of a local anesthetic and an ocular decongestant be given several minutes prior to injection.

Note: The recommended volume of botulinum toxin type A injected for treatment of strabismus is 0.05 to 0.15 mL per muscle.

The initial listed doses of the diluted botulinum toxin type A (see Table III on following page) typically create paralysis of injected muscles beginning 1 to 2 days after injection and increasing in intensity during the first week. The paralysis lasts for 2 to 6 weeks and gradually resolves over a similar time period. Overcorrections lasting over 6 months have been rare. About one-half of patients will require subsequent doses because of inadequate paralytic response of the muscle to the initial dose, or because of mechanical factors such as large deviations or restrictions, or because of the lack of binocular motor fusion to stabilize the alignment.

I. Initial doses in units (abbreviated as U). Use the lower listed doses for treatment of small deviations. Use the larger doses only for large deviations.

A. For vertical muscles, and for horizontal strabismus of less than 20 prism diopters: 1.25 to 2.5 U in any one muscle.

B. For horizontal strabismus of 20 prism diopters to 50 prism diopters: 2.5 to 5.0 U in any one muscle.

C. For persistent VI nerve palsy of 1 month or longer duration: 1.25 to 2.5 U in the medial rectus muscle.

II. Subsequent doses for residual or recurrent strabismus.

A. It is recommended that patients be re-examined 7 to 14 days after each injection to assess the effect of that dose.

B. Patients experiencing adequate paralysis of the target muscle that require subsequent injections should receive a dose comparable to the initial dose.

C. Subsequent doses for patients experiencing incomplete paralysis of the target muscle may be increased up to 2-fold compared to the previously administered dose.

D. Subsequent injections should not be administered until the effects of the previous dose have dissipated as evidenced by substantial function in the injected and adjacent muscles.

E. The maximum recommended dose as a single injection for any one muscle is 25 U.

Lack of Response: There are several explanations for a lack or diminished response to an individual treatment with botulinum toxin type A. These may include inadequate dose selection, selection of inappropriate muscles for injection, muscles inaccessible to injection, underlying structural abnormalities such as muscle contractures or bone disorders, change in pattern of muscle involvement, patient perception of benefit compared with initial results, inappropriate storage or reconstitution, as well as neutralizing antibodies to botulinum toxin. A neutralizing antibody is defined as an antibody that inactivates the biological activity of the toxin. However, the proportion of patients that lose their response to botulinum toxin therapy and have demonstrable levels of neutralizing antibodies is small.

The reported incidence of neutralizing antibody measured by the mouse bioassay in patients treated with botulinum toxin, is estimated to be less than 5%. However, there were patients who continued to respond to therapy and demonstrated presence of neutralizing antibodies. For example, many cervical dystonia patients were injected with botulinum toxin at 2- to 3-week intervals with doses exceeding 300 units in a 30-day period.

The critical factors for neutralizing antibody production are the frequency and dose of injection. To reduce the potential for neutralizing antibody formation, it is recommended that injection intervals should be no more frequent than 2 months. The dose should not exceed 360 U in any 2-month period.

A suggested course of action when patients do not respond to botulinum toxin type A injections is: 1) wait the usual treatment interval; 2) consider reasons for lack of response listed above; 3) more than 1 treatment course should be considered before classification of a patient as a nonresponder; 4) test patient serum for neutralizing antibody presence.

Reconstituted Solutions: To reconstitute vacuum-dried botulinum toxin type A, use sterile normal saline **without** a preservative; 0.9% Sodium Chloride Injection is the recommended diluent. Draw up the proper amount of diluent in the appropriate size syringe (see Table III on following page). Since the product is denatured by bubbling or similar violent agitation, inject the diluent into the vial gently. Discard the vial if a vacuum does not pull the diluent into the vial. Record the date and time of reconstitution on the space on the label. It should be administered within 4 hours after reconstitution.

During this time period, reconstituted botulinum toxin type A should be stored in a refrigerator (2 to 8°C). Reconstituted botulinum toxin type A should be clear, colorless and free of

Table II—Botox

Dosage Guide

Classification of Cervical Dystonia	Muscle Groupings	Total Dosage; Number of Sites
Type I Head rotated toward side of shoulder elevations	Sternocleidomastoid Levator scapulae Scalene Splenius capitis Trapezius	50–100 U; at least 2 sites 50 U; 1–2 sites 25-50 U; 1-2 sites 25–75 U; 1–3 sites 25–100 U; 1–8 sites
Type II Head rotation only	Sternocleidomastoid	25–100 U; at least 2 sites if >25 U given
Type III Head tilted toward side of shoulder elevation	Sternocleidomastoid Levator scapulae Scalene Trapezius	25–100 U; at posterior border; at least 2 sites if >25 U given 25–100 U; at least 2 sites 25–75 U; at least 2 sites 25–100 U; 1–8 sites
Type IV Bilateral posterior cervical muscle spasm with elevation of the face	Splenius capitis and cervicis	50–200 U; 2–8 sites, treat bilaterally

Botox (cont'd)

particulate matter. Parenteral drug products should be inspected visually for particulate matter and discoloration prior to administration and whenever the solution and the container permit.

Table III—Botox

Dilution Table

Diluent Added (0.9% Sodium Chloride Injection)	Resulting Dose in Units/0.1 mL
1.0 mL	10.0 U
2.0 mL	5.0 U
4.0 mL	2.5 U
8.0 mL	1.25 U

Note: These dilutions are calculated for an injection volume of 0.1 mL. A decrease or increase in the botulinum toxin type A dose is also possible by administering a smaller or larger injection volume (i.e., 0.05 mL [50% decrease in dose] to 0.15 mL [50% increase in dose]).

Supplied: Each vial contains: Clostridium botulinum toxin type A 100 units (U), albumin (human) 0.5 mg and sodium chloride 0.9 mg in a sterile, vacuum-dried form without a preservative. One unit (U) corresponds to the calculated median lethal intraperitoneal dose (LD_{50}) in mice using reconstituted botulinum toxin type A and injected intraperitoneally.

Store the vacuum-dried product in a freezer at or below −5°C. Administer within 4 hours after the vial is removed from the freezer and reconstituted. During these 4 hours, reconstituted botulinum toxin type A should be stored in a refrigerator (2 to 8°C). Reconstituted botulinum toxin type A should be clear, colorless and free of particulate matter.

All vials, including expired vials or equipment used with the drug should be disposed of carefully as is done with all medical waste.

BOTULISM ANTITOXIN TRIVALENT TYPES A, B AND E (EQUINE)

Connaught

Antitoxin

Indications: Experimental evidence concerning the amount of circulating antitoxin needed to counteract botulism toxin poisoning by antitoxin therapy is not fully documented. The outcome of treatment depends, as it does in other comparable conditions, largely on the time interval elapsing after onset of symptoms before the peak of absorbed antitoxin is reached. This principle is illustrated in recently reported animal experiments.

Clinical trials of type E botulism antitoxin in Canada and in Japan showed that dosages of not more than 5 000 IU of type E antitoxin, administered as a rule i.v., proved remarkably efficacious. The product, as distributed, contains 8 500 IU of E per vial, an amount which, if evenly distributed without loss throughout the blood stream, theoretically provides an adequate circulating titre.

Since the mouse-protective value of one IU of types A and B antitoxin is several times that of one IU of type E antitoxin, the relative proportions of types A and B present in the mixture are believed to be adequate to establish a level of neutralizing capacity in the blood stream, against the homologous toxins, of several times the level shown to be clinically efficacious for type E antitoxin. **One or more vials of this mixture may be necessary to provide adequate circulating antibody of each type, depending upon the severity of the toxemia.**

Precautions: Precautionary Measures in the Administration of any Serum or Antitoxin: Before administering any serum or antitoxin to a patient, physicians are well advised to ascertain whether the patient has a history of asthma or hay fever and particularly whether the patient suffers distress when in proximity to horses. Patients with such a history may develop serious reactions of an anaphylactic character upon the administration of serum of equine origin either s.c., i.m. or i.v. It should be borne in mind, also, that a patient who has been given a previous injection of serum of equine origin may develop a marked reaction when given a second injection, especially if the previous injection was i.v. in character.

At the time of administering any serum or antitoxin to a patient, it is desirable to have 1 mL of epinephrine HCl Solution (1:1 000) immediately available.

Tests for Sensitivity to Serum or Antitoxin: A test for sensitivity to serum or antitoxin should be carried out each time a serum or antitoxin is administered, unless it is being given daily. Sensitivity to any particular serum or antitoxin may be gauged by one of the following methods:

Skin or eye tests for sensitivity should be done before any injection, regardless of whether or not the patient has had the serum previously. The skin test dose is 0.1 mL of a 1:100 saline dilution of the serum to be given intracutaneously. In persons with a history of allergy, the dose is reduced to 0.05 mL of a 1:1 000 dilution, intracutaneously. The reaction is read in 5 to 30 minutes and is positive if a wheal with a hyperaemic areola appears. (In a marked reaction the wheal is likely to have irregular projections.) The extent of the wheal and of its projections, and the dimensions of the hyperaemic area provide a rough index of the degree of the patient's sensitivity, and of the resultant likelihood of his reacting unfavorably to the injection of the particular serum or antitoxin concerned.

A negative skin test does not entirely preclude the possibility of the occurrence of serum reactions.

Except in small children, an eye test often is simpler and is less likely to show nonspecific reactions. A drop of a 1:10 dilution of serum in physiologic saline is instilled in one eye, controlled by a drop of physiologic saline solution in the other eye; a positive reaction consists of lacrimation and conjunctivitis appearing in 10 to 30 minutes.

Eye tests have not been known to be fatal, but skin tests have resulted in fatalities. Therefore, a serum should never be injected, nor a skin test performed unless a syringe containing 1 mL of epinephrine HCl solution (1:1 000) is within immediate reach.

Serum Reactions: 1. Anaphylactic Reaction: In the event of a reaction of an anaphylactic character, 0.5 mL of epinephrine HCl solution (1:1 000) should be administered by the s.c. or i.m. route.

2. Thermal Reaction: When this reaction occurs, it usually develops from 20 minutes to 1 hour after the injection of serum or antitoxin. It is characterized by a chilly sensation, slight dyspnea and a rapid rise in temperature.

3. Serum Sickness: The symptoms of serum sickness are fever, skin rashes, edema of the skin, glandular enlargement and pains in the joints. These symptoms may appear individually, or in combination, within 14 days after the administration of a serum or antitoxin. Urticarial reactions are usually relieved by a s.c. or i.m. injection of 0.5 mL of epinephrine HCl solution (1:1 000). In severe cases of serum sickness, ACTH or cortisone may be required.

It has been recommended that 0.3 mL of epinephrine HCl solution (1:1 000) be administered not only to every patient who gives a positive reaction to a sensitivity test, or has received serum or antitoxin before, or has a history of allergy, but to every patient before receiving serum irrespective of these factors.

Dosage: Prevention of Botulism Types A, B, and E: The recommended prophylactic dose for an individual who has eaten food suspected of being infected with C. botulinum is 1 500 to 7 500 IU of Type A, 1 100 to 5 500 IU of Type B and 1 600 to 8 500 IU. Type E given i.m. depending on the amount of food eaten (one-fifth to one vial). This may be followed in 12 to 24 hours by the injection of the contents of a second vial if any signs or symptoms of botulism appear.

Treatment of Botulism Types A, B and E: The best results in the treatment of botulism are likely to be obtained where very large doses of antitoxin are given early in the disease. The object is to provide an excess of circulating antitoxin as early as possible.

Patients who received antitoxin in the first 24 hours after onset of signs and symptoms (early antitoxin) had a lower fatality rate (10%) than those who received antitoxin more than 24 hours after onset (late antitoxin) (15%) or those who did not receive antitoxin at all (46%). Patients who received early antitoxin had fewer days in the hospital, fewer days on a ventilator, and fewer days to sustained improvement than patients who received late antitoxin.

I.V.: In order to ensure the quickest possible neutralization of all toxin in the tissue and fluids, it is advisable to give immediately 7 500 IU of Type A, 5 500 IU of Type B and 8 500 IU of Type E (1 vial) i.v. at a 1:10 dilution. It should be at ambient temperature before being injected.

I.M.: In order to provide a reservoir of antitoxin from which it may be absorbed, an additional 7 500 IU of Type A, 5 500 IU of Type B and 8 500 IU of Type E (1 vial) may be given by i.m. injection.

The administration of two 5 000 IU vials of anti-ABE (15 000 IU Type A, 11 000 IU Type B, 17 000 IU Type E) (1 vial given i.v. and 1 vial given i.m.) to human subjects results in high levels of circulating antitoxins that are capable of neutralizing from 12 to 1 500 times the amount of toxin that is found in the serum of patients with botulism.

Further doses may be indicated in 2 to 4 hours if the signs and symptoms worsen. Black and Gunn found that the incidence of serum sickness in patients treated with botulism antitoxin was highest for persons who received more than 4 vials (30 000 IU Type A, 22 000 IU Type B, 34 000 IU Type E).

Important Points in Injecting the Serum: I.V.: The serum is injected very slowly i.v. at a dilution of 1:10. It is advisable that the patient be tested for sensitivity to horse serum and, if necessary, initial i.v. doses should be small and well diluted (see below).

Administration of Antitoxin to Sensitive Persons: Whenever there is a history of allergy, sensitivity to horse serum or manifestations of sensitivity when in proximity to horses, or if the reaction to the skin test is positive, great care must be exercised in the administration of serum (or antitoxin).

No one method can be advised for the administration of serum or antitoxin for sensitive persons as each presents an individual problem. Desensitization of the patient should be carried out by serial injections of diluted antitoxin as indicated below at intervals of 20 minutes, provided no reactions occur.

Schedule for Desensitization: (a) 0.05 mL of 1:20 dilution s.c., (b) 0.1 mL of 1:10 dilution s.c., (c) 0.3 mL of 1:10 dilution s.c., (d) 0.1 mL undiluted serum s.c., (e) 0.2 mL undiluted serum s.c., (f) 0.5 mL undiluted serum s.c., (g) inject remaining therapeutic doses i.m.

After the patient can properly withstand these doses of serum or antitoxin, it is usually safe to inject larger doses (i.m.) at 20-minute intervals.

If a reaction occurs after a desensitizing dose, injections should be stopped for an hour, recommencing the schedule at 20-minute intervals by repeating the last dose which failed to cause a reaction.

If deemed imperative on clinical grounds, i.v. administration of a serum or antitoxin may be commenced after the purpose of the desensitization has been satisfactorily served. The first i.v. dose should be small, however, i.e., 0.1 mL diluted with 10 mL of sterile physiological saline, and it should be injected very slowly, 1 mL/minute. Increasingly larger doses may then be similarly given at half-hourly intervals.

A separate sterilized syringe and needle should be used for each individual patient to prevent transmission of homologous serum hepatitis and other infectious agents from one person to another.

Note: Following the administration of serum (or antitoxin), and particularly in those cases showing a positive skin test, the patient should be kept under close observation for 1 to 2 hours and under reasonably close surveillance for a period of 24 hours.

Supplied: A refined and concentrated preparation of horse globulins modified by enzymatic digestion. Preservative: phenol 0.4%. Trace amounts of blood substance A and residual porcine pepsin may be present. Each vial contains: Type A: 7 500 IU. Type B: 5 500 IU. Type E: 8 500 IU. The volume per vial varies depending on the potency of the antitoxin. Store at 2 to 8°C. **Do not freeze.**

Reviewed 1998

BRADOSOL®
BRADOSOL® EXTRA-STRENGTH

Novartis Consumer Health

Hexylresorcinol

Antiseptic

Indications: For the relief of sore throat.

Precautions: If symptoms persist for more than 7 days, consult a physician.

Dosage: 1 lozenge every 2 to 3 hours, as required. Not recommended for children under 3 years, unless on the advice of a physician.

Supplied: Bradosol: Each lozenge contains: hexylresorcinol 2.4 mg in a pleasant-tasting, candy-flavored base. Nonmedicinal ingredients: cherry flavor: FD&C blue No. 1, FD&C red No. 3, flavor, glucose, menthol, propylene glycol and sugar; mint flavor: D&C yellow No. 10, FD&C blue No. 1, FD&C red No. 3, flavor, glucose, peppermint oil and sugar; lemon menthol flavor: D&C yellow No. 10, FD&C red No. 3, glucose, lemon oil, menthol, propylene glycol and sugar; honey eucalyptus flavor: eucalyptus oil, glucose, menthol, peppermint oil, red oxide, sugar, titanium dioxide and yellow oxide; orange flavor: D&C yellow No. 10, FD&C red No. 3, flavor, glucose, menthol, propylene glycol and sugar. Alcohol-, bisulfite-, gluten-, lactose-, parabens- and tartrazine-free. Boxes of 18 (cherry, mint, lemon menthol, honey eucalyptus or orange flavors).

Bradosol Extra-Strength: Each lozenge contains: hexylresorcinol 3.5 mg in a pleasant-tasting, candy-flavored base. Nonmedicinal ingredients: cherry flavor: FD&C blue No. 1, FD&C red No. 3, flavor, glucose, menthol, propylene glycol and sugar; mint flavor: D&C yellow No. 10, FD&C blue No. 1, flavor, glucose, peppermint oil and sugar. Gluten-, lactose- and tartrazine-free. Boxes of 18 (cherry or mint flavors).

BRĀSIVOL®

Stiefel

Aluminum Oxide Compound

Acne Therapy

Supplied: Fused, synthetic aluminum oxide, a non-silicone abrasive in a hypoallergenic base of soap and synthetic detergent. Nonmedicinal ingredients: butylated hydroxytoluene, ethoxylated lauryl alcohol, ferric oxide, fragrance citrus bouquet, glycerin, lauric acid, myristic acid, polyethylene glycol, purified water USP, quaternium-15, sodium hydroxide, sodium lauryl sulfate solution and stearic acid triple pressed. Two grades: Fine (1) and Medium (2). Tubes of 75 g.

BRETYLATE® ℞

Glaxo Wellcome

Bretylium Tosylate

Antiarrhythmic

Pharmacology: Bretylium is an adrenergic-neurone blocking agent. The mechanism by which it exerts its antiarrhythmic action is not fully understood. Although evidence has indicated that the benefit of bretylium in abating tachyarrhythmias may be due to its antiadrenergic properties, this has still not been firmly established. Some reports have even indicated that there is a clear-cut dissociation between the neuron-blocking and the antiarrhythmic actions of the drug.

I.V. injection of bretylium initially causes a release of norepinephrine from sympathetic nerve endings, followed by a prolonged antiadrenergic action which prevents further discharge of neurotransmitter from sympathetic nerve endings. Bretylium is preferentially taken up by the adrenergic nerve terminals. The initial release of norepinephrine accounts for the transient increased automaticity and the initial rise in the systemic and, usually more markedly, the pulmonary blood pressure. The blood pressure will revert later to control levels or fall below them during the adrenergic blocking phase.

Bretylium increases both the action potential duration in the heart and the functional refractory period. Bretylium does not depress automaticity in the Purkinje-fibers. The effectiveness of the drug is primarily in ventricular and not in supraventricular arrhythmias and the direct effect of bretylium in increasing refractoriness also accounts for its usefulness in abolishing re-entrant arrhythmias. Bretylium exerts a positive inotropic effect in the heart, probably due to catecholamine release, since this inotropic action can be blocked by propranolol. There is also an increase in myocardial oxygen consumption associated with bretylium administration. The heart rate following bretylium administration has been found to be variable, increasing in some patients and decreasing in others.

There is no conclusive evidence that bretylium has any direct effects on myocardial tissue. Bretylium does not have quinidine-like actions on the myocardium and in this respect, and in the increased contractility produced, differs from other antiarrhythmic agents.

Pharmacokinetics: Judging by therapeutic effectiveness bretylium is adequately absorbed after i.m. administration, but no pharmacokinetic comparison with the i.v. route has been reported. In one study elimination half-lives ranging from 4.2 to 16 hours (mean of 9.8 hours) were found. The concentration of bretylium in plasma has not been correlated with the intensity of its antiarrhythmic action and cannot be used to guide individualization of dosage.

Bretylium is eliminated intact by the kidneys. No metabolites have been identified following the administration of bretylium. Within 24 hours, 70 to 80% of i.m. dose is excreted in the urine with an additional 10% excreted over the next 3 days.

Bretylium causes an initial increase in urinary excretion of norepinephrine, but generally has no other effects on the renal system. Renal blood flow, glomerular filtration rate and potassium excretion are unchanged. Only slight increases in sodium, chloride or water excretion are found.

Indications: Bretylium may be of value as a last resort in life-threatening ventricular arrhythmias, principally ventricular tachycardia and fibrillation, which are resistant to conventional antiarrhythmic drug treatment.

Bretylium should be used only in intensive care units in hospitals where facilities for monitoring and treating patients with serious cardiac dysrhythmias are available.

Following administration of bretylium there may be a delay from 20 minutes to as long as 6 hours before the onset of antidysrhythmic activity. For this reason, quick-acting drugs such as lidocaine or procainamide remain the treatment of choice in patients with serious ventricular dysrhythmias. If these continue or recur despite treatment with lidocaine and other antiarrhythmic agents, bretylium may be of value in restoring sinus rhythm.

Contraindications: There is no evidence that prophylactic administration of bretylium confers clinical benefit in patients with recent but uncomplicated myocardial infarction. In such patients the use of bretylium may lead to unpredictable cardiovascular effects. Therefore, this drug should not be used to prevent the development of arrhythmias in patients with recent myocardial infarction.

Bretylium may potentially cause a severe hypertensive response in patients with pheochromocytoma and is therefore contraindicated in this condition.

Warnings: Hypotension: Administration of bretylium regularly results in postural hypotension, subjectively recognized by dizziness, lightheadedness, vertigo and faintness. Orthostatic hypotension may occur 20 to 30 minutes after acute administration of bretylium, and in patients with poor cardiac function clinically significant hypotension may occur even in the supine position. Some degree of hypotension is present in about 50% of patients while they are supine. Hypotension may occur at doses lower than those needed to suppress arrhythmias. Additionally, hypotension has been reported after cardiac surgery.

Patients should be kept in the supine position until tolerance to the hypotensive effect of bretylium develops. Tolerance occurs unpredictably but may be present after several days. Hypotension with supine systolic pressure greater than 75 mm Hg need not be treated unless there are associated symptoms. Hypovolemia will augment the hypotensive response to bretylium. If the blood pressure does not respond to simple postural manoeuvers, i.v. fluid should be given. An infusion of dopamine or norepinephrine may also be required to raise blood pressure. When catecholamines are administered, a dilute solution should be employed and blood pressure monitored closely because the pressor effects of the catecholamines are enhanced by bretylium.

Transient Hypertension and Increased Frequency of Arrhythmias: Due to the initial release of norepinephrine from adrenergic postganglionic nerve terminals by bretylium, transient hypertension or increased frequency of premature ventricular contractions and other arrhythmias may occur in some patients. Such arrhythmias have been observed especially in persons receiving inotropic catecholamines.

Caution During Use With Digitalis Glycosides: The initial release of norepinephrine caused by bretylium may aggravate digitalis toxicity. When a life-threatening cardiac arrhythmia occurs in the digitalized patient, bretylium should be used only if the etiology of the arrhythmia does not appear to be digitalis toxicity and other antiarrhythmic drugs are not effective. Simultaneous initiation of therapy with digitalis glycoside and bretylium should be avoided.

Patients With Fixed Cardiac Output: In patients with fixed cardiac output (i.e., severe aortic stenosis or severe pulmonary hypotension), bretylium should be avoided since severe hypotension may result from a fall in peripheral resistance without a compensatory increase in cardiac output. If survival is threatened by the arrhythmia, bretylium may be used but vasoconstrictive catecholamines should be given promptly if severe hypotension occurs.

Pregnancy: Safety in human pregnancy has not been established. However, as the drug is intended for use only in life-threatening situations, it may be used in pregnant women when its benefits outweigh the potential risk to the fetus.

Lactation: It is not known if bretylium is excreted in breast milk.

Children: The safety and efficacy of this drug in children have not been established. Bretylium has been administered to a limited number of pediatric patients, but such use has been inadequate to define fully proper dosage and limitations for use.

Geriatrics: The use of bretylium in the elderly depends on the degree of reduction in cardiac and renal function. The decision to treat rests on whether the benefits of the antiarrhythmic effect outweigh the potential risks of inappropriate dosing.

Precautions: When used i.v., bretylium should be diluted and given slowly in all cases except when immediate life-threatening ventricular arrhythmia exists as in ventricular fibrillation (see Dosage). Rapid i.v. administration may cause severe nausea and vomiting.

Since bretylium is excreted principally via the kidney, dosage should be reduced in patients with impaired renal function (see Dosage).

Administration may aggravate sinus bradycardia and, therefore, should be used with caution in patients with this condition.

Drug Interactions: Patients should be carefully observed when bretylium is used in combination with drugs such as quinidine, procainamide and propranolol because the addition of bretylium to the above drugs may result in a significantly prolonged AV transmission time and could aggravate pre-existing AV block.

Hypersensitivity to infused catecholamines would be expected after bretylium administration because bretylium blocks the normal mechanism of cathecholamine metabolism, namely neuronal uptake and subsequent degradation by MAO. For this reason, when it is necessary to increase perfusion pressure to vital organs after bretylium-induced hypotension, norepinephrine or other sympathomimetics should only be given under expert supervision (see Warnings).

Adverse Effects: Hypotension and postural hypotension have been the most frequently reported adverse reactions (see Warnings). Nausea and vomiting occurred in about 3% of patients, primarily when bretylium was administered rapidly by the i.v. route. Vertigo, dizziness, lightheadedness and syncope, which sometimes accompanied postural hypotension, were reported in about 7 patients in 1 000.

Bradycardia, increased frequency of premature ventricular contractions, transitory hypertension, initial increase in arrhythmias (see Warnings), precipitation of anginal attacks, and sensation of substernal pressure have also been reported in a small number of patients, i.e., approximately 1 to 2 patients in 1 000.

Renal dysfunction, diarrhea, abdominal pain, hiccups, erythematous macular rash, flushing, hyperthermia, confusion, paranoid psychosis, emotional lability, lethargy, generalized tenderness, anxiety, shortness of breath, diaphoresis, nasal stuffiness and mild conjunctivitis have been reported in about 1 patient in 1 000. The relationship of bretylium administration to these reactions has not been clearly established.

Overdose: Symptoms: Bretylium overdose has been reported in a patient with recurrent ventricular fibrillation and tachycardia who was inadvertently given an i.v. bolus of 2 g (approximately 30 mg/kg body weight). The authors reported ultimately successful control of the ventricular tachyarrhythmias but the patient exhibited marked hypertension with peak blood pressure of 310/90 mm Hg, followed approximately an hour later by marked hypotension refractory to i.v. dobutamine and volume expansion therapy.

Symptoms of overdosage are blurred vision, headache, nausea, hypotension and circulatory failure.

Treatment: Should be symptomatic. Bretylium can be removed by hemodialysis.

Dosage: To be used clinically only for treatment of life-threatening ventricular arrhythmias under constant ECG monitoring. Since there is a delay in onset of its antiarrhythmic action, bretylium is not to be considered or used as a replacement for rapidly-acting antiarrhythmic agents currently in use. The clinical use is for short-term use only. Patients should either be kept supine during the course of therapy or be closely observed for postural hypotension. The optimal dose schedule for parenteral administration has not been determined. There is comparatively little experience with dosages greater than 30 mg/kg/day although such doses have been used without apparent adverse effects. The following dosage schedule is suggested:

Immediately Life-Threatening Ventricular Arrhythmia, as in Ventricular Fibrillation: Administer undiluted at a dosage of 5 mg/kg of body weight by rapid i.v. injection. Other usual cardiopulmonary resuscitative procedures, including electrical cardioversion, should be employed prior to and following the injection in accordance with good medical practice. If ventricular fibrillation persists, the dosage may be increased to 10 mg/kg and repeated at 15- to 30-minute intervals until a total dose of not more than 30 mg/kg of body weight has been given.

Bretylate (cont'd)

Other Ventricular Arrhythmias: I.V.: Must be diluted as follows before i.v. administration: Using aseptic technique, dilute contents of 10 mL ampul containing 500 mg bretylium tosylate to a minimum of 50 mL with Dextrose Injection USP, or Sodium Chloride Injection USP. Diluted solutions must be used within 24 hours from the time of preparation.

Administer the diluted solution at a dosage of 5 to 10 mg/kg of body weight by i.v. infusion over a period greater than 8 minutes. More rapid infusion may cause nausea and vomiting. A second dose may be given in 1 to 2 hours if the arrhythmia persists.

I.M.: Do not dilute prior to i.m. injection. Inject 5 to 10 mg/kg of body weight. Dosage may be repeated in 1 to 2 hours if the arrhythmia persists. Thereafter, maintain with same dosage every 6 to 8 hours.

When injected i.m. not more than 5 mL should be given in one site and injection sites should be varied since repeated i.m. injection into the same site may cause atrophy and necrosis of muscle tissue, fibrosis, vascular degeneration and inflammatory changes. Care should be taken not to inject directly into or near a major nerve.

Maintenance Dosage: The diluted solution should be administered by intermittent bolus infusion or by constant infusion. The solution must be used within 24 hours.

Intermittent Infusion: Infuse the diluted solution at a dose of 5 to 10 mg/kg of body weight over a period greater than 8 minutes every 6 hours. More rapid infusion may cause nausea and vomiting.

Constant Infusion: Infuse the diluted solution at a dosage of 1 to 2 mg/minute.

Dosage should be reduced and discontinued in 3 to 5 days under ECG monitoring. Other appropriate antiarrhythmic agents should be substituted if indicated.

Method of Preparation of Bretylium for I.V. Administration: Using Dextrose Injection, USP or Sodium Chloride Injection, USP, bretylium may be diluted as follows before i.v. administration: dilute contents of 10 mL ampul (500 mg bretylium tosylate) to a minimum of 50 mL.

Diluted solution must be used within 24 hours from the time of preparation.

Parenteral drug products should be inspected visually for particulate matter and discoloration prior to administration whenever solution and container permit. Should either be observed, the solution should be discarded and fresh solution prepared.

Bretylium causes an initial increase in urinary excretion of norepinephrine, but generally has no other effects on the renal system. Renal blood flow, glomerular filtration rate and potassium excretion are unchanged. Only slight increases in sodium, chloride or water excretion are found.

Supplied: Each mL contains: bretylium tosylate 50 mg. Nonmedicinal ingredients: water for injection. Ampuls of 10 mL. Boxes of 5. Store at 15 to 25°C and protect from light.

Reviewed 1999

BRETYLIUM TOSYLATE INJECTION Pr
BRETYLIUM TOSYLATE AND DEXTROSE INJECTION Pr

Abbott

Antiarrhythmic

Supplied: Bretylium Tosylate Injection: Each mL of sterile, nonpyrogenic solution contains: bretylium tosylate 50 mg. Also may contain hydrochloric acid and sodium hydroxide for pH adjustment. pH approximately 6. Osmolarity: 174 mOsm/L. For i.m. or i.v. injection. Single dose ampuls of 10 mL, boxes of 5. Single dose plastic flip top vials of 10 mL, boxes of 5. Single dose Abboject syringes of 10 mL, boxes of 5.

Bretylium Tosylate and Dextrose Injection: Each mL of sterile, nonpyrogenic solution contains: bretylium tosylate 2 or 4 mg and dextrose monohydrate 50 mg. May also contain hydrochloric acid and sodium hydroxide for pH adjustment. Approximate pH of solutions is 4.5. Osmolarity: 264 mOsm/L (2 mg/mL) and 278 mOsm/L (4 mg/mL). For i.v. infusion only. Single dose flexible containers of 250 mL.

BREVIBLOC® Pr

Zeneca

Esmolol HCl

Beta-adrenergic Receptor Blocking Agent

Pharmacology: Esmolol is a beta-adrenergic receptor blocking agent with predominant blocking effect on beta-1 receptors. It does not possess significant intrinsic sympathomimetic or membrane stabilizing activity. Esmolol, which is administered only i.v., has a rapid onset and a short duration of action.

Pharmacodynamics: In human electrophysiology studies, esmolol produced effects typical of a beta-blocker: a decrease in the heart rate, increase in sinus cycle length, prolongation of the sinus node recovery time, prolongation of the AH interval during normal sinus rhythm and during atrial pacing, and an increase in antegrade Wenckebach cycle length.

Studies in normal volunteers have confirmed the beta-blocking activity of esmolol, showing reduction in heart rate at rest and during exercise, and attenuation of isoproterenol-induced increases in heart rate. Blood levels of esmolol have been shown to correlate with extent of beta-blockade.

Bolus injections of 50 and 100 mg esmolol, given intraoperatively during general anesthesia, decreased heart rate by more than 20% within 2 minutes. Systolic blood pressure fell by 17% within 5 minutes. The effects lasted for up to 10 minutes.

When given 1.5 to 2 minutes before intubation, 100 and 200 mg bolus injections of esmolol attenuated the heart rate and blood pressure response to endotracheal intubation. No effects were detectable 5 minutes after the administration of esmolol.

The hemodynamics were studied during continuous i.v. infusions in patients with elevated heart rate and acute ischemic heart disease (e.g., unstable angina pectoris or acute myocardial infarction). Titrated infusions of esmolol, from 0.05 to 0.3 mg/kg/min, lowered heart rate and blood pressure. There were small increases in the left ventricular end diastolic pressure and pulmonary capillary wedge pressure, but were not considered to be clinically significant. Cardiac index, however, decreased. Cardiac index returned to pretreatment levels within 30 minutes after discontinuation of the infusion.

The relative cardioselectivity of esmolol was demonstrated in mildly asthmatic patients. Esmolol infusions (0.1, 0.2 and 0.3 mg/kg/min) produced no significant increases in specific airway resistance when compared to placebo. At 0.3 mg/kg/min, esmolol produced slightly enhanced bronchomotor sensitivity to dry-air stimulus but was not considered clinically significant.

Pharmacokinetics: Following bolus injections of esmolol to healthy volunteers, the distribution and elimination half-lives averaged 1.4 and 10.9 minutes respectively. The blood concentrations of esmolol were below quantifiable limits within 10 minutes.

Following a loading infusion of 0.5 mg/kg/min over 1 minute, esmolol infusions of 0.05 to 0.3 mg/kg/min reach steady-state blood levels within 5 minutes with corresponding blood levels from 1.56×10^{-4} to 9.93×10^{-4} mg/mL. Steady state blood levels increase linearly with dose over the dose range of 0.05 to 0.3 mg/kg/min. If a loading dose is not used, approximately 30 minutes are required to reach steady-state blood levels. Fifty-five percent of the amount in blood is bound to plasma proteins while the acid metabolite is only 10% bound. After cessation of the infusion, the blood levels of esmolol decrease rapidly with an elimination half-life of 9 minutes.

The total body clearance of esmolol is about 20 L/hr/kg. Since this is greater than cardiac output, the metabolism of esmolol is not limited by the rate of blood flow to metabolizing tissues such as the liver. The central and total volume of distribution were found to be 1.9 L/kg and 3.3 L/kg, respectively.

Esterases in the red blood cell cytosol hydrolyse the ester link of esmolol resulting in the formation of the corresponding free acid and methanol. This acid metabolite, which shows approximately 1/1 500th the beta-blocking activity of esmolol in animal studies, has an elimination half-life of about 3.7 hours and is excreted in the urine with a clearance approximately equivalent to the glomerular filtration rate. Excretion of the acid metabolite is significantly decreased in patients with renal disease, with elimination half-life increased to about 10-fold that of patients with normal renal function, and plasma level was considerably elevated.

After several hours of infusion, at rates up to 0.3 mg/kg/min, methanol blood levels approximated endogenous levels (<10 μg/mL) and were less than 2% of levels usually associated with methanol toxicity.

Less than 2% of esmolol is excreted unchanged in urine. After 24 hours, approximately 73 to 88% of the dose is recovered in the urine as the acid metabolite.

The pharmacokinetics of esmolol and of its major metabolite are unaltered in patients with hepatic cirrhosis. In patients with end-stage renal disease, on hemo- or peritoneal dialysis, the pharmacokinetics of esmolol were unchanged except for an increase in the volume of distribution in patients on peritoneal dialysis. The elimination half-life of the acid metabolite is increased about 10 times in patients with renal disease.

Indications: In the perioperative management of tachycardia and hypertension in patients in whom there is a concern for compromised myocardial oxygen balance and who, in the judgment of the physician, are clearly at risk of developing hemodynamically-induced myocardial ischemia.

Esmolol is also indicated for the rapid control of ventricular rate in patients with atrial fibrillation or atrial flutter in acute situations when the use of a short-acting agent is desirable.

Esmolol is not indicated for use in chronic settings.

Contraindications: In patients who require inotropic agents and/or vasopressors to maintain systemic blood pressure and cardiac output.

Esmolol is also contraindicated in patients with hypotension, sinus bradycardia, second and third degree AV block, right ventricular failure secondary to pulmonary hypertension, overt cardiac failure or cardiogenic shock (see Warnings).

Warnings: During the administration of esmolol patients should be carefully monitored, with particular attention to heart rate and blood pressure.

Hypotension: The administration of esmolol has been associated with excessive hypotension. The hypotensive effect of esmolol is dose related and may increase in the presence of both narcotic analgesics and inhalational anesthetics. In patients with low pretreatment blood pressure or with a propensity to develop hypotension (e.g., hypovolemic patients) esmolol should be used with special caution and only when in the physician's judgment, the potential benefits outweigh the risk. In the event of hypotension, the dosage of esmolol should be reduced or the drug should be discontinued.

Sinus Bradycardia: Severe bradycardia and cardiac arrest may occur with the use of esmolol. Therefore, in patients with low pretreatment heart rates esmolol should be used with special caution and only when in the physician's judgment, the potential benefits outweigh the risk. In the event of bradycardia, the dosage of esmolol should be reduced or the drug should be discontinued.

Cardiac Failure: Sympathetic stimulation is a vital component supporting circulatory function in patients with congestive heart failure. Inhibition with beta-blockade always carries the potential hazard of further depressing myocardial contractility. Therefore, special caution should be exercised when administering esmolol to patients with a history of heart failure. Beta-blockers act selectively without abolishing the inotropic action of digitalis on the heart muscle. The effects of beta-blockers and digitalis are additive in depressing AV nodal conduction. Even in patients with no history of cardiac failure, continued depression of the myocardium over a period of time can, in some cases, lead to cardiac failure. Therefore, at the first sign or symptom of impending cardiac failure, the dosage of esmolol should be reduced or the drug should be withdrawn. Because of the short elimination half-life of esmolol, these measures may be sufficient but specific treatment may also be considered.

Abrupt Cessation of Therapy: Abrupt cessation of esmolol in patients has not been reported to produce the withdrawal effects which may occur with abrupt withdrawal of beta-blockers following chronic use in coronary artery disease patients. However, caution should be used in discontinuing esmolol infusions abruptly in these patients.

Concurrent use of Esmolol with Verapamil: The use of i.v. verapamil with a beta-blocker may cause severe depression of ventricular function. Accordingly, patients with atrial fibrillation or atrial flutter who have received verapamil should only be administered esmolol if the benefits outweigh the risk.

Bronchospastic Diseases: Patients with bronchospastic diseases should not, in general, receive beta-blockers. Because of its relative beta-1 selectivity and titratability, esmolol may be used with caution in patients with bronchospastic diseases. Since beta-1 selectivity is not absolute, esmolol should be carefully titrated to obtain the lowest possible effective dose. In the event of bronchospasm, the infusion should be terminated immediately and a beta-2 stimulating agent may be administered if conditions warrant.

Precautions: Renal Impairment: The pharmacokinetics of esmolol are unchanged in kidney-impaired patients except that the volume of distribution is increased. However the acid metabolite of esmolol is primarily excreted unchanged by the kidney, thus esmolol should be administered with caution to patients with impaired renal function. The elimination half-life of the acid metabolite was prolonged tenfold and the plasma level was considerably elevated in patients with end-stage renal disease.

Diabetes Mellitus/Hypoglycemia: Esmolol should be administered with caution to patients subject to spontaneous hypoglycemia, or to diabetic patients (especially those with labile diabetes) who are receiving insulin or oral hypoglycemic agents. Beta-adrenergic blockers may mask the premonitory signs and symptoms of acute hypoglycemia.

Venous Irritation: Prolonged infusion concentrations of 20 mg/mL have been associated with significant venous irritation in humans and thrombophlebitis in animals. Therefore, concentrations greater than 10 mg/mL should be avoided.

Pregnancy: There are no studies in pregnant women. Esmolol should be used during pregnancy only if the potential benefit justifies the potential risk to the fetus.

Lactation: It is not known whether esmolol is excreted in human milk. Caution, however, should be exercised when esmolol is administered to a nursing mother.

Children: The safety and effectiveness of esmolol in children have not been established.

Drug Interactions: Catecholamine-depleting drugs, (e.g., reserpine) may have an additive effect when given with beta-blocking agents. Patients treated concurrently with esmolol and a catecholamine depletor should, therefore, be closely observed for evidence of hypotension or marked bradycardia.

When digoxin and esmolol were concomitantly administered i.v. to normal volunteers, a 10 to 20% increase in digoxin blood level was observed at some time points. Digoxin did not affect esmolol pharmacokinetics.

When the interaction of i.v. morphine and esmolol was studied in normal subjects, no effect on morphine blood level was seen. However the steady-state blood levels of esmolol were increased by 46% in the presence of morphine, but no other pharmacokinetic parameters were changed.

The effect of esmolol on the duration of succinylcholine-induced neuromuscular blockade was studied in patients undergoing surgery. The onset of neuromuscular blockade by succinylcholine was unaffected by esmolol, but the duration of neuromuscular blockade was prolonged from 5 to 8 minutes.

A study of interaction between esmolol and warfarin showed that concomitant administration of esmolol and warfarin does not alter warfarin plasma levels. Esmolol concentrations were equivocally higher when given with warfarin, but this is not likely to be clinically important.

For interaction with verapamil see Warnings.

Adverse Effects: During Management of Perioperative Tachycardia and Associated Hypertension: In clinical trials 763 patients were treated with esmolol in operative settings.

Esmolol as a bolus of 100 mg and 200 mg was given in a total of 367 patients during clinical studies. Hypotension was reported in 16% among esmolol treated patients compared to 8% in the placebo group (187 patients). Bradycardia occurred in 4% of patients, in both the esmolol and placebo groups.

Other adverse effects with a frequency of less than 1% occurred as frequently in the esmolol as it did with the placebo group. They were: bronchospasm, pain at injection and wheezing.

When esmolol was infused in 396 patients, hypotension was the most commonly observed side effect in 5% of patients. The other reported adverse effect was bradycardia (heart rate less than 50 beats/minute), observed in 1% of patients. Other adverse effects occurring with a less than 1% incidence were the following: ST segment depression, ECG changes, myocardial ischemia, junctional rhythm, hypertension, atrial fibrillation, bronchospasm, agitation, nausea, vomiting, urticaria and itching.

None of these side effects were judged to be severe, and all resolved after the discontinuation of esmolol.

During Management of Atrial Fibrillation and Atrial Flutter: Most adverse effects reported in clinical trials with esmolol in 390 patients with atrial fibrillation and atrial flutter have been mild and transient. The most serious adverse reaction observed was symptomatic hypotension (12%). Esmolol was discontinued in about 11% of the patients. Other adverse reactions, grouped by system, are: Cardiovascular: symptomatic hypotension (diaphoresis, dizziness) (12%), asymptomatic hypotension (25%), diaphoresis (9%), premature ventricular contraction and dyspnea (1%). Pallor, flushing, bradycardia (<50 beats/minute), chest pain, syncope, pulmonary edema, junctional rhythm, heart block, increased PAP, abnormal ECG, narrowed pulse pressure, recurrence of SVT, angina, ventricular ectopy, peripheral ischemia (<1%).

CNS: dizziness (3%), somnolence (3%), headache (3%), confusion, agitation (2%), fatigue (1%). Paraesthesia, asthenia, depression, abnormal thinking, anxiety, anorexia, one brief episode of grand mal seizure (30 seconds), lightheadedness, weakness, irritability, drowsiness (<1%).

Respiratory: bronchospasm, wheezing, dyspnea, nasal congestion, rhonchi, pharyngitis, rales, pleural effusion, atelectasis and common cold, pleural pain (<1%).

Gastrointestinal: nausea (6%), vomiting (1%), dyspepsia, constipation, dry mouth, abdominal discomfort (<1%).

Local Dermatological Reactions: inflammation (2%), induration (2%), i.v. infiltration (2%), clamminess, edema, erythema, skin discoloration, ecchymosis, burning, enlarged macular area (<1%).

Miscellaneous: urinary retention, dysuria, oliguria, speech disorder, abnormal vision, midscapular pain, rigors, fever (<1%).

Overdose: Symptoms and Treatment: Overdosage with esmolol can produce bradycardia, congestive heart failure, hypotension, bronchospasm, electromechanical dissociation, drowsiness, loss of consciousness, hypoglycemia and cardiac arrest.

Cases of massive accidental overdoses of esmolol have occurred due to dilution errors. Some of these overdoses have been fatal while others resulted in permanent disability. Bolus doses in the range of 625 to 3 500 mg (12.5 to 70 mg/kg) have been fatal. Patients have recovered completely from overdoses as high as 1 750 mg given over 1 minute or doses of 7 500 mg given over 1 hour for cardiovascular surgery. The patients who survived appear to be those whose cardiovascular circulation could be supported until the effects of esmolol were resolved.

The first step in the management of toxicity should be to discontinue the esmolol infusion. Then, because of its approximately 9-minute elimination half-life and based on the observed clinical effects, the following measures should also be considered.

1. General: Esmolol is a competitive antagonist of isoproterenol and hence larger doses of isoproterenol may be needed to reverse many of the effects of excessive dosage of esmolol. However, the complications of excessive isoproterenol should not be overlooked.
2. Bradycardia: atropine or another anticholinergic drug.
3. Heart Block (second or third degree): isoproterenol or transvenous cardiac pacemaker.
4. Congestive Heart Failure: conventional therapy such as diuretic and/or digitalis glycoside. In shock due to inadequate cardiac contractility: dopamine, dobutamine, isoproterenol.
5. Hypotension (depending on associated factors): Epinephrine, rather than isoproterenol, or norepinephrine may be useful in addition to atropine and digitalis.
6. Bronchospasm: aminophylline or isoproterenol or other beta-2 agonists.
7. Hypoglycemia: i.v. glucose.

Dosage: Esmolol 2 500 mg/10 mL ampuls are not for direct i.v. injection. These are concentrated solutions of a potent drug which must be diluted prior to its infusion. Esmolol should not be admixed with sodium bicarbonate. Esmolol should not be mixed with other drugs prior to dilution (see Reconstituted Solutions).

Infusions should be used within 24 hours of preparation due to the possibility of microbial contamination.

Management of Perioperative Tachycardia and Hypertension: Intubation: 10 mg/mL (100 mg/10 mL vial) should be administered by a bolus injection (over 30 seconds). For the management of postintubation tachycardia and hypertension, give 1.5 mg/kg (up to a maximum of 100 mg) as a bolus injection (over 30 seconds) 1 to 2 minutes before intubation.

For Intra- and Postoperative Tachycardia and Hypertension: For intraoperative and postoperative treatment of tachycardia and/or hypertension give 1.5 mg/kg as a bolus injection (over 30 seconds) followed by 0.15 mg/kg/min infusion. Adjust infusion rate as required up to 0.3 mg/kg/min to maintain desired heart rate and/or blood pressure.

Management of Atrial Fibrillation and Atrial Flutter: Responses to esmolol usually (over 95%) occur within the range of 0.05 to 0.2 mg/kg/min. The average effective dosage is approximately 0.1 mg/kg/min (7 mg/70 kg/min) although dosages as low as 0.025 mg/kg/min have been sufficient in some patients. Dosages as high as 0.3 mg/kg/min have been used but provided little added effect with an increased rate of adverse effects, and are not recommended. Dosage must be individualized by titration in which each step consists of a loading dose followed by a maintenance infusion.

To initiate treatment, administer a loading dose infusion of 0.5 mg/kg/min of esmolol for 1 minute followed by a 4-minute maintenance infusion of 0.05 mg/kg/min. If the therapeutic response is inadequate at this point, repeat the same loading dose and increase the maintenance infusion to 0.1 mg/kg/min.

Continue the titration procedure as above, repeating the loading dose (0.5 mg/kg/min for 1 minute), and increasing the maintenance infusion by increments of 0.05 mg/kg/min (for 4 minutes). As the desired heart rate or a safety end point (e.g., lowered blood pressure) is approached, omit the loading dose and reduce the incremental dose of the maintenance infusion from 0.05 mg/kg/min to 0.025 mg/kg/min or lower. Also if desired, increase the interval between titration steps from 5 to 10 minutes.

Maintenance dosages above 0.2 mg/kg/min have not been shown to have significantly increased benefits. The effectiveness of dosages above 0.3 mg/kg/min has not been studied.

If a safety end point is exceeded, discontinue the infusion of esmolol and re-start at a lower dose. In the event of an adverse reaction, the dosage infusion of esmolol should be discontinued. If a reaction occurs at the site of the local infusion, an alternate infusion site should be used. Avoid the use of butterfly needles. The use of esmolol infusions up to 24 hours has been well documented.

Stability and Storage: Infusions should be used within 24 hours of preparation due to the possibility of microbial contamination.

Direct I.V. Injection: Esmolol 10 mg/mL (100 mg/10 mL vial) does not require dilution.

Reconstituted Solutions: **Esmolol 250 mg/mL (2 500 mg/10 mL ampul) is not for direct i.v. injection. This is a concentrated solution of a potent drug which must be diluted prior to its infusion (see Table I).**

Continuous I.V. Infusion: Esmolol should be infused at concentrations of no greater than 10 mg/mL (see Precautions). To prepare solutions of 10 mg/mL, reconstitute each esmolol ampul (10 mL) in 240 mL of a suitable i.v. fluid (see Table I).

Table I Brevibloc

Reconstitution Table

Brevibloc Ampul Concentration	No. of Brevibloc Ampuls	Volume of I.V. Fluid	Volume after Reconstitution	Nominal Concentration per mL
250 mg/mL	1	240 mL	250 mL	10 mg/mL
250 mg/mL	2	480 mL	500 mL	10 mg/mL

Esmolol was tested for compatibility with 9 commonly used i.v. fluids at a final concentration of 10 mg/mL esmolol. It was found to be compatible with the following solutions and was stable for at least 24 hours at controlled room temperature (15 to 25°C) or under refrigeration: Dextrose (5%) Injection, USP; Dextrose (5%) in Ringer's Injection; Dextrose (5%) in lactated Ringer's Injection; Dextrose (5%) and Sodium Chloride (0.45%) Injection, USP; Dextrose (5%) and Sodium Chloride (0.9%) Injection, USP; Lactated Ringer's Injection, USP; Sodium Chloride (0.45%) Injection, USP; Sodium Chloride (0.9%) Injection, USP; Potassium Chloride (40 mEq/L) in Dextrose (5%), USP.

Esmolol injection is not compatible with sodium bicarbonate (5%).

Supplied: Ampuls: Each mL of solution **for continuous i.v. infusion** contains: esmolol HCl 250 mg. Nonmedicinal ingredients: alcohol, glacial acetic acid, hydrochloric acid or sodium hydroxide for pH adjustment, propylene glycol, sodium acetate and water for injection. Glass ampuls of 10 mL. Boxes of 10. **This solution is not for direct i.v. injection. It is a concentrated solution of a potent drug which must be diluted prior to its infusion.**

Vials: Each mL of solution for direct i.v. injection contains: esmolol HCl 10 mg. Nonmedicinal ingredients: glacial acetic acid, hydrochloric acid or sodium hydroxide for pH adjustment, sodium acetate and water for injection. Amber glass vials of 10 mL. Boxes of 20.

Store at controlled room temperature (15 to 25°C).

Reviewed 1997

BREVICON® 0.5/35 ℞

Searle

Norethindrone—Ethinyl Estradiol

Oral Contraceptive

Pharmacology: Estrogen-progestogen combinations act primarily through the mechanism of gonadotropin suppression due to the estrogenic and progestational activity of their components. Although the primary mechanism of action is inhibition of ovulation, alterations in the cervical mucus and the endometrium may also contribute to effectiveness.

Indications: Prevention of pregnancy.

Brevicon 0.5/35 (cont'd)

Contraindications: History of or actual thrombophlebitis or thromboembolic disorders; history of or actual cerebrovascular disorders; history of or actual myocardial infarction or coronary arterial disease; active liver disease or history of or actual benign or malignant liver tumors; history of or known or suspected carcinoma of the breast; history of or known or suspected estrogen-dependent neoplasia; undiagnosed abnormal vaginal bleeding; any ocular lesion arising from ophthalmic vascular disease, such as partial or complete loss of vision or defect in visual fields; when pregnancy is suspected or diagnosed.

Warnings: Predisposing Factors for Coronary Artery Disease: Cigarette smoking increases the risk of serious cardiovascular side effects and mortality. Birth control pills increase this risk, especially with increasing age. Convincing data are available to support an upper age limit of 35 years for oral contraceptive use in women who smoke.

Other women who are independently at high risk for cardiovascular disease include those with diabetes, hypertension, abnormal lipid profile, or a family history of these. Whether oral contraceptives accentuate this risk is unclear.

In low risk, nonsmoking women of any age, the benefits of oral contraceptive use outweigh the possible cardiovascular risks associated with low-dose formulations. Consequently, oral contraceptives may be prescribed for these women up to the age of menopause.

> Cigarette smoking increases the risk of serious adverse effects on the heart and blood vessels. This risk increases with age and becomes significant in oral contraceptive users over 35 years of age. Women should be counselled not to smoke.

Discontinue Medication at the Earliest Manifestation of the Following:

A. Thromboembolic and cardiovascular disorders such as: thrombophlebitis, pulmonary embolism, cerebrovascular disorders, myocardial ischemia, mesenteric thrombosis and retinal thrombosis.

B. Conditions that predispose to venous stasis and to vascular thrombosis, e.g., immobilization after accidents or confinement to bed during long-term illness. Other nonhormonal methods of contraception should be used until regular activities are resumed. For use of oral contraceptives when surgery is contemplated, see Precautions.

C. Visual defects, partial or complete.

D. Papilledema or ophthalmic vascular lesions.

E. Severe headache of unknown etiology or worsening of pre-existing migraine headache.

Precautions: Physical Examination and Followup: Before oral contraceptives are used, a thorough history and physical examination should be performed, including a blood pressure determination. Breasts, liver, extremities and pelvic organs should be examined and a Papanicolaou smear should be taken if the patient has been sexually active.

The first followup visit should be done 3 months after oral contraceptives are prescribed. Thereafter, examinations should be performed at least once a year or more frequently if indicated. At each annual visit, examination should include those procedures that were done at the initial visit as outlined above or per recommendations of the Canadian Workshop on Screening for Cancer of the Cervix. Their suggestion was that, for women who had 2 consecutive negative Pap smears, screening could be continued every 3 years up to the age of 69.

Pregnancy: Fetal abnormalities have been reported to occur in the offspring of women who have taken estrogen-progestogen combinations in early pregnancy. Rule out pregnancy as soon as it is suspected.

Lactation: The use of oral contraceptives during the period a mother is breast-feeding her infant may not be advisable. The hormonal components are excreted in breast milk and may reduce its quantity and quality. The long-term effects on the developing child are not known.

Hepatic Function: Patients who have had jaundice including a history of cholestatic jaundice during pregnancy should be given oral contraceptives with great care and under close observation.

The development of severe generalized pruritus or icterus requires that the medication be withdrawn until the problem is resolved.

If a patient develops jaundice that proves to be cholestatic in type, the use of oral contraceptives should not be resumed. In patients taking oral contraceptives, changes in the composition of the bile may occur and an increased incidence of gallstones has been reported.

Hepatic nodules have been reported to be associated with use of oral contraceptives, particularly in long-term users of oral contraceptives. These nodules include benign hepatic adenomas, focal nodular hyperplasia and other hepatic lesions. In addition, hepatocellular carcinoma has been reported. Although these lesions are extremely rare, they have caused fatal intra-abdominal hemorrhage and should be considered in women presenting with an abdominal mass, acute abdominal pain, or evidence of intra-abdominal bleeding.

Hypertension: Patients with essential hypertension whose blood pressure is well-controlled may be given oral contraceptives but only under close supervision. If a significant elevation of blood pressure in previously normotensive or hypertensive subjects occurs at any time during the administration of the drug, cessation of medication is necessary.

Migraine and Headache: The onset or exacerbation of migraine or the development of headache of a new pattern which is recurrent, persistent or severe requires discontinuation of oral contraceptives and evaluation of the cause.

Diabetes: Current low dose oral contraceptives exert minimal impact on glucose metabolism. Diabetic patients, or those with a family history of diabetes, should be observed closely to detect any worsening of carbohydrate metabolism. Patients predisposed to diabetes who can be kept under close supervision may be given oral contraceptives. Young diabetic patients whose disease is of recent origin, well-controlled, and not associated with hypertension or other signs of vascular disease such as ocular fundal changes should be monitored more frequently while using oral contraceptives.

Ocular Disorders: Patients who are pregnant or are taking oral contraceptives may experience corneal edema that may cause visual disturbances and changes in tolerance to contact lenses, especially of the rigid type. Soft contact lenses usually do not cause disturbances. If visual changes or alterations in tolerance to contact lenses occur, temporary or permanent cessation of wear may be advised.

Breasts: Increasing age and a strong family history are the most significant risk factors for the development of breast cancer. Other established risk factors include obesity, nulliparity and late age at first full-term pregnancy. The identified groups of women that may be at increased risk of developing breast cancer before menopause are long-term users of oral contraceptives (more than 8 years) and starters at early age. In a few women, the use of oral contraceptives may accelerate the growth of an existing but undiagnosed breast cancer. Since any potential increased risk related to oral contraceptive use is small, there is no reason to change prescribing habits at present.

Women receiving oral contraceptives should be instructed in selfexamination of their breasts. Their physicians should be notified whenever any masses are detected. A yearly clinical breast examination is also recommended because, if a breast cancer should develop, drugs that contain estrogen may cause a rapid progression.

Vaginal Bleeding: Persistent irregular vaginal bleeding requires assessment to exclude underlying pathology.

Fibroids: Patients with fibroids (leiomyomata) should be carefully observed. Sudden enlargement, pain, or tenderness requires discontinuance of the use of oral contraceptives.

Emotional Disorders: Patients with a history of emotional disturbances, especially the depressive type, may be more prone to have a recurrence of depression while taking oral contraceptives. In cases of a serious recurrence, a trial of an alternate method of contraception should be made which may help to clarify the possible relationship. Women with premenstrual syndrome (PMS) may have a varied response to oral contraceptives, ranging from symptomatic improvement to worsening of the condition.

Metabolic and Endocrine Diseases: In metabolic or endocrine diseases and when metabolism of calcium and phosphorus is abnormal, careful clinical evaluation should precede medication and a regular followup is recommended.

Connective Tissue Disease: The use of oral contraceptives in some women has been associated with positive lupus erythematous cell tests and with clinical lupus erythematous. In some instances, exacerbation of rheumatoid arthritis and synovitis have been observed.

Laboratory Tests: Results of laboratory tests should be interpreted in the light of the fact that the patient is on oral contraceptives. The laboratory tests listed below are modified.

A. Liver function tests: Aspartate serum transaminase (AST): variously reported elevations. Alkaline phosphatase and gamma glutamine transaminase (GGT): slightly elevated.

B. Coagulation tests: Minimal elevation of test values reported for such parameters as Factors VII, VIII, IX and X. Increased platelet aggregation. Decreased antithrombin III.

C. Thyroid function tests: Protein binding of thyroxine is increased as indicated by increased total serum thyroxine concentrations and decreased T_3 resin uptake.

D. Lipoproteins: Small changes of unproven clinical significance may occur in lipoprotein cholesterol fractions.

E. Gonadotropins: LH and FSH levels are suppressed by the use of oral contraceptives. Wait 2 weeks after discontinuing the use of oral contraceptives before measurements are made.

Tissue Specimens: Pathologists should be advised of oral contraceptive therapy when specimens obtained from surgical procedures and Pap smears are submitted for examination.

Return to Fertility: After discontinuing oral contraceptive therapy, the patient should delay pregnancy until at least 1 normal spontaneous cycle has occurred in order to date the pregnancy. An alternative contraceptive method should be used during this time.

Amenorrhea: Women having a history of oligomenorrhea, secondary amenorrhea, or irregular cycles may remain anovulatory or become amenorrheic following discontinuation of estrogen-progestin combination therapy.

Amenorrhea, especially if associated with breast secretion, that continues for 6 months or more after withdrawal, warrants a careful assessment of hypothalamic-pituitary function.

Thromboembolic Complications—Postsurgery: There is an increased risk of postsurgery thromboembolic complications in oral contraceptive users, after major surgery. If feasible, oral contraceptives should be discontinued and an alternative method substituted at least 1 month prior to **major** elective surgery. Oral contraceptives should not be resumed until the first menstrual period after hospital discharge following surgery.

Drug Interactions: The concurrent administration of oral contraceptives with other drugs may result in an altered response to either agent. Reduced effectiveness of the oral contraceptive, should it occur, is more likely with the low dose formulations. It is important to ascertain all drugs that a patient is taking, both prescription and nonprescription, before oral contraceptives are prescribed.

Refer to the revised 1994 Report on Oral Contraceptives, Health Canada, for possible drug interactions with oral contraceptives.

Noncontraceptive Benefits of Oral Contraceptives: Several health advantages other than contraception have been reported.

Effects on menses: Increased menstrual cycle regularity; decreased menstrual blood loss; decreased incidence of iron deficiency anemia secondary to reduced menstrual blood loss; decreased incidence of dysmenorrhea.

Effects related to ovulation inhibition: Decreased incidence of functional ovarian cysts; decreased incidence of ectopic pregnancy.

Effects on other organs of the reproductive tract: Decreased incidence of acute salpingitis; decreased incidence of endometrial cancer (50%); decreased incidence of ovarian cancer (40%); potential beneficial effects on endometriosis; improvement of acne vulgaris, hirsutism, and other androgen-mediated disorders.

Effects on breasts: Decreased incidence of benign breast disease (fibroadenomas and fibrocystic breast disease); decreased incidence of breast biopsies.

The noncontraceptive benefits of oral contraceptives should be considered in addition to the efficacy of these preparations when counselling patients regarding contraceptive method selection.

> Oral contraceptives **do not protect** against sexually transmitted diseases (STDs) including HIV/AIDS. For protection against STDs, it is advisable to use latex condoms **in combination with** oral contraceptives.

Adverse Effects: An increased risk of the following serious adverse reactions has been associated with the use of oral contraceptives: thrombophlebitis; pulmonary embolism; mesenteric thrombosis; neuro-ocular lesions, e.g., retinal thrombosis; myocardial infarction; cerebral thrombosis; cerebral hemorrhage; hypertension; benign hepatic tumors; gallbladder disease.

The following adverse reactions also have been reported in patients receiving oral contraceptives: Nausea and vomiting, usually the most common adverse reactions, occur in approximately 10% or less of patients during the first cycle. Other reactions, as a general rule, are seen less frequently or only occasionally.

Other Adverse Reactions: gastrointestinal symptoms (such as abdominal cramps and bloating); breakthrough bleeding; spotting; change in menstrual flow; dysmenorrhea; amenorrhea during and after treatment; infertility after discontinuance of treatment; edema; chloasma or melasma which may persist; breast changes: tenderness, enlargement, and secretion; change in weight (increase or decrease); endocervical hyperplasias; possible diminution in lactation when given immediately post-partum; cholestatic jaundice; migraine; increase in size of uterine leiomyomata; rash (allergic); mental depression; reduced tolerance to carbohydrates; vaginal candidiasis; premenstrual-like syndrome; intolerance to contact lenses; change in corneal curvature (steepening); cataracts; optic neuritis; retinal thrombosis; changes in libido; chorea; changes in appetite; cystitis-like syndrome; rhinitis; headache; nervousness; dizziness; hirsutism; loss of scalp hair; erythema multiforme; erythema nodosum; hemorrhagic eruption; vaginitis; porphyria; impaired renal function; Raynaud's phenomenon; auditory disturbances; hemolytic uremic syndrome; pancreatitis; arterial thromboembolism.

Overdose: Symptoms and Treatment: Numerous cases of the ingestion by children of estrogen-progestogen combinations have been reported. Although mild nausea may occur, there appears to be no other reaction. Treatment should be limited to a laxative such as citrate of magnesia with the aim of removing unabsorbed material as rapidly as possible.

Dosage: Information for the Patient on How to Take the Birth Control Pill:

1. **Read these directions:**
   - before you start taking your pills, and
   - any time you are not sure what to do.
2. **Look at your pill pack** to see if it has 21 or 28 pills:
   - 21-Pill Pack: 21 active pills (with hormones) taken daily for 3 weeks, and then take no pills for 1 week

     or
   - 28-Pill Pack: 21 active pills (with hormones) taken daily for 3 weeks, and then 7 "reminder" pills (no hormones) taken daily for 1 week.

   Also check the pill pack for instructions on (1) where to start and (2) directions to take pills (see package insert for illustrations).
3. It is recommended that you use a second method of birth control (e.g., latex condoms and spermicidal foam or gel) for the first 7 days of the first cycle of pill use. This will provide a back-up in case pills are forgotten while you are getting used to taking them.
4. **When receiving any medical treatment, be sure to tell your doctor that you are using birth control pills.**
5. **Many women have spotting or light bleeding or may feel sick to their stomach during the first 3 months on the pill.** If you do feel sick, do not stop taking the pill. The problem will usually go away. If it does not go away, check with your doctor or clinic.
6. **Missing pills also can cause some spotting or light bleeding,** even if you make up the missed pills. You also could feel a little sick to your stomach on the days you take 2 pills to make up for missed pills.
7. **If you miss pills at any time, you could get pregnant. The greatest risks for pregnancy are:**
   - when you start a pack late, or
   - when you miss pills at the beginning or at the very end of the pack.
8. **Always be sure you have ready:**
   - **another kind of birth control** (such as latex condoms and spermicidal foam or gel) to use as a backup in case you miss pills, and
   - **an extra, full pack of pills.**
9. **If you experience vomiting or diarrhea, or if you take certain medicines,** such as antibiotics, your pills may not work as well. Use a backup method, such as latex condoms and spermicidal foam or gel, until you can check with your doctor or clinic.
10. **If you forget more than 1 pill 2 months in a row,** talk to your doctor or clinic about how to make pill-taking easier or about using another method of birth control.
11. **If your questions are not answered here, call your doctor or clinic.**

When to start the first pack of pills: Be sure to read these instructions:

- before you start taking your pills, and
- any time you are not sure what to do.

Decide with your doctor or clinic what is the best day for you to start taking your first pack of pills. Your pills may be either a 21-day or a 28-day type.

A. 21-Day Combination: With this type of birth control pill, you are on pills for 21 days and off pills for 7 days. You must not be off the pills for more than 7 days in a row.

1. **The first day of your menstrual period (bleeding) is Day 1 of your cycle.** Your doctor may advise you to start taking the pills on Day 1, on Day 5, or on the first Sunday after your period begins. If your period starts on Sunday, start that same day.
2. Take 1 pill at approximately the same time every day for 21 days; **then take no pills for 7 days.** Start a new pack on the 8th day. You will probably have a period during the 7 days off the pill. (This bleeding may be lighter and shorter than your usual period.)

B. 28-Day Combination: With this type of birth control pill, you take 21 pills which contain hormones and 7 pills which contain no hormones.

1. **The first day of your menstrual period (bleeding) is Day 1 of your cycle.** Your doctor may advise you to start taking the pills on Day 1, on Day 5, or on the first Sunday after your period begins. If your period starts on Sunday, start that same day.
2. Take 1 pill at approximately the same time every day for 28 days. Begin a new pack the next day, **not missing any days on the pills.** Your period should occur during the last 7 days of using that pill pack.

What to do during the month:

1. **Take a pill at approximately the same time every day until the pack is empty.**
   - Try to associate taking your pill with some regular activity like eating a meal or going to bed.
   - Do not skip pills even if you have bleeding between monthly periods or feel sick to your stomach (nausea).
   - Do not skip pills even if you do not have sex very often.
2. **When you finish a pack.**
   - **21 pills: Wait 7 days** to start the next pack. You will have your period during that week.
   - **28 pills:** Start the next pack **on the next day.** Take 1 pill every day. Do not wait any days between packs.

What to do if you miss pills: Table I outlines the actions you should take if you miss 1 or more of your birth control pills. Match the number of pills missed with the appropriate starting time for your type of pill pack.

Dosage: A. 21-Day Pack: With this type of birth control pill, the patient is 21 days on pills with 7 days off pills. The patient must not be off the pills for more than 7 days in a row.

1. **The first day of the patient's menstrual period (bleeding) is day 1 of a cycle.** The doctor may advise the patient to start taking the pills on Day 1, on Day 5, or on the first Sunday after a period begins. If a period starts on Sunday, the patient starts that same day.
2. The pack must be labelled correctly before starting. The pack is pre-printed with a Sunday starting day. If the patient is starting on a day other than a Sunday, she should use the Flexi-start sticker labels provided. The patient peels off the label with the chosen starting day and applies it over the pre-printed days on top of the card.
3. The patient takes 1 pill at approximately the same time every day for 21 days; **then she takes no pills for 7 days.** She starts a new pack on the 8th day. She will probably have a period during the 7 days off the pill. (This bleeding may be lighter and shorter than a usual period.)

B. 28-Day Pack: With this type of birth control pill, the patient takes 21 pills which contain hormones and 7 pills which contain no hormones.

1. **The first day of the patient's menstrual period (bleeding) is day 1 of a cycle.** The doctor may advise the patient to start taking the pills on Day 1, on Day 5, or on the first Sunday after a period begins. If a period starts on Sunday, the patient starts that same day.
2. The pack must be labelled correctly before starting. The pack is pre-printed with a Sunday starting day. If the patient is starting on a day other than a Sunday, she should use the Flexi-start sticker labels provided. The patient peels off the label with the chosen starting day and applies it over the pre-printed days on top of the card.
3. The patient takes 1 pill at approximately the same time every day for 28 days. She begins a new pack the next day, **not missing any days on the pills.** The patient's period should occur during the last 7 days of using that pill pack.

Table I—Brevicon 0.5/35

What to Do If You Miss Pills

Sunday Start	**Other Than Sunday Start**
Miss 1 pill	**Miss 1 pill**
Take it as soon as you remember, and take the next pill at the usual time. This means that you might take 2 pills in one day.	Take it as soon as you remember, and take the next pill at the usual time. This means that you might take 2 pills in one day.
Miss 2 pills in a row	**Miss 2 pills in a row**
First 2 Weeks: 1. Take 2 pills the day you remember and 2 pills the next day. 2. Then take 1 pill a day until you finish the pack. 3. Use a backup method of birth control if you have sex in the 7 days after you miss the pills.	**First 2 Weeks:** 1. Take 2 pills the day you remember and 2 pills the next day. 2. Then take 1 pill a day until you finish the pack. 3. Use a backup method of birth control if you have sex in the 7 days after you miss the pills.
Third Week: 1. Keep taking 1 pill a day until Sunday. 2. On Sunday, safely discard the rest of the pack and start a new pack that day. 3. Use a backup method of birth control if you have sex in the 7 days after you miss the pills. 4. You may not have a period this month. **If you miss 2 periods in a row, call your doctor or clinic.**	**Third Week:** 1. Safely dispose of the rest of the pill pack and start a new pack that same day. 2. Use a backup method of birth control if you have sex in the 7 days after you miss the pills. 3. You may not have a period this month. **If you miss 2 periods in a row, call your doctor or clinic.**
Miss 3 or more pills in a row	**Miss 3 or more pills in a row**
Anytime in the Cycle: 1. Keep taking 1 pill a day until Sunday. 2. On Sunday, safely discard the rest of the pack and start a new pack that day. 3. Use a backup method of birth control if you have sex in the 7 days after you miss the pills. 4. You may not have a period this month. **If you miss 2 periods in a row, call your doctor or clinic.**	**Anytime in the Cycle:** 1. Safely dispose of the rest of the pill pack and start a new pack that same day. 2. Use a backup method of birth control if you have sex in the 7 days after you miss the pills. 3. You may not have a period this month. **If you miss 2 periods in a row, call your doctor or clinic.**

Note: 28-Day Pack: If you forget any of the 7 "reminder" pills (without hormones) in Week 4, just safely dispose of the pills you missed. Then keep taking 1 pill each day until the pack is empty. You do not need to use a backup method.

Always be sure you have on hand:

- a backup method of birth control (such as latex condoms and spermicidal foam or gel) in case you miss pills, and
- an extra, full pack of pills.

If you forget more than 1 pill 2 months in a row, talk to your doctor or clinic about ways to make pill-taking easier or about using another method of birth control.

What to do during the month:

1. **The patient takes a pill at approximately the same time every day until the pack is empty.**
   - The patient should try to associate taking the pill with some regular activity like eating a meal or going to bed.
   - The patient must not skip pills even if she has bleeding between monthly periods or feels sick to her stomach (nausea).
   - The patient must not skip pills even if she does not have sex very often.

Brevicon 0.5/35 (cont'd)

2. When a pack is finished:
- **21 Pills: The patient must wait 7 days** to start the next pack. A period will begin during that week.
- **28 Pills:** The patient starts the next pack **on the next day.** She takes 1 pill every day. She does not wait any days between packs.

Information for the Patient: See Blue Section—Information for the Patient "Oral Contraceptives".

Supplied: Each blue circular tablet, impressed "SEARLE" on one side and "BX" on the other, contains: norethindrone 0.5 mg and ethinyl estradiol 0.035 mg. Inert orange-colored tablets, impressed "SEARLE" on one side and "P" on the other. Nonmedicinal ingredients: active tablets: cornstarch, FD&C Blue No. 2, lactose hydrous, magnesium stearate and polyvidone; placebo tablets: FD&C Yellow No. 6 Lake, lactose, lactose monohydrate, magnesium stearate and microcrystalline cellulose. Dispensers of 21 (21 active tablets) and 28 (21 active and 7 inert tablets) days.

(Shown in Product Recognition Section)

Reviewed 1998

BREVICON® 1/35 ℞

Searle

Norethindrone—Ethinyl Estradiol

Oral Contraceptive

Supplied: Each white circular tablet, impressed "Syntex" on one side and "BX" on the other, contains: norethindrone 1 mg and ethinyl estradiol 0.035 mg. Inert orange-colored tablets are impressed "Syntex" on one side. Nonmedicinal ingredients: Active tablets: cornstarch, lactose, magnesium stearate and povidone. Placebo tablets: cornstarch, lactose, magnesium stearate, povidone and sunset yellow FCF **or** FD&C Yellow No. 6 lake, lactose, lactose hydrous, magnesium stearate and microcrystalline cellulose. Dispensers of 21 (21 active tablets) and 28 (21 active and 7 inert tablets) days.

For prescribing information, see Brevicon 0.5/35 monograph.

(Shown in Product Recognition Section)

BRICANYL® Tablets ℞
BRICANYL® TURBUHALER® ℞

Astra

Terbutaline Sulfate

Bronchodilator

Pharmacology: Terbutaline produces bronchodilation by stimulation of the β_2 adrenergic receptors in bronchial smooth muscle, thereby causing relaxation of muscle fibres. This action is manifested by an increase in pulmonary function as demonstrated by FEV_1 measurements. Terbutaline also produces a decrease in airway and pulmonary resistance.

Following inhalation of terbutaline Turbuhaler, a significant improvement in pulmonary function measurements is well established after 5 minutes. Twenty to 30% of the metered dose is deposited in the lungs with an inspiration flow rate of about 60 L/min.

The maximal response is usually attained between 15 and 60 minutes following administration. Significant bronchodilator activity has been observed to persist for 4 to 7 hours.

Following administration of terbutaline tablets, a measurable change in flow rate is usually observed in 30 minutes, and improvement in pulmonary function occurs in 60 to 120 minutes. The maximum effect usually occurs within 120 to 180 minutes, and significant bronchodilator activity has been observed to persist for 4 to 8 hours.

Indications: For the symptomatic relief of bronchial asthma and for relief of reversible bronchospasm which may occur in association with bronchitis and emphysema.

Contraindications: Known hypersensitivity to sympathomimetic amines and, like other sympathomimetic amines, should not be used in patients with tachyarrhythmias.

Warnings: Like other β_2-agonist inhalers, terbutaline should not be used on a regular daily basis without appropriate concomitant anti-inflammatory therapy (see Dosage).

Terbutaline should be used with caution in patients with diabetes, hypertension, hyperthyroidism and a history of seizures. As with other sympathomimetic bronchodilator agents, terbutaline should be administered cautiously to cardiac patients, especially those with associated arrhythmias, and coronary insufficiency, to elderly or to patients who are unusually responsive to sympathomimetic amines. Due to the hyperglycemic effects of β_2-agonists, additional blood glucose controls are recommended initially in diabetic patients.

Occasionally, patients have been reported to have developed severe paradoxical bronchospasm with repeated use of sympathomimetic inhalant preparations. In such instances, the preparation should be discontinued immediately and alternate therapy instituted. Fatalities, the exact cause of which are unknown, have been reported following excessive use of aerosol preparations containing sympathomimetic amines. Cardiac arrest was noted in several instances.

Beta-receptor blocking agents (including eye-drops), especially those which are noncardioselective, may partially or totally inhibit the effect of beta-receptor stimulants. Severe resistant bronchospasm may be produced with the use of beta-blockers in asthmatic patients.

Potentially serious hypokalemia may result from β_2-agonist therapy, mainly from parenteral or nebulized administration. Particular caution is advised in acute severe asthma as this may be potentiated by hypoxia and concomitant treatment with xanthine derivatives, steroids and diuretics; it is recommended that serum potassium levels be monitored in such situations.

Pregnancy: The safe use of terbutaline has not been established in human pregnancy. The use of this drug in pregnancy, lactation, or women of childbearing potential requires that the expected therapeutic benefit of the drug be weighed against its possible hazards to the mother or child. Animal reproductive studies have shown no adverse effects on fetal development.

Transient hypoglycemia has been reported in newborn preterm infants after maternal β_2-agonist treatment.

Systemic β_2-agonists should be used with caution before childbirth in view of their inhibiting effect on uterine contractions.

Lactation: Terbutaline is excreted in breast milk. Caution should be exercised when terbutaline is administered to nursing women.

Children: Terbutaline is not presently recommended for children below 6 years of age due to limited clinical data in this pediatric group.

Precautions: If therapy does not produce a significant improvement or if the patient's condition gets worse, medical advice must be sought in order to determine a new plan of treatment. In the case of acute or rapidly worsening dyspnea, a doctor should be consulted immediately.

Increasing use of β_2-agonists to control symptoms of bronchial obstruction, especially administration on a regular basis or in high amounts, indicates deterioration of asthma control. Under these conditions, the patient's therapy plan has to be revised. It is inadequate simply to increase the use of bronchodilators under these circumstances, in particular over extended periods of time (see Dosage). The revised treatment regimen should include concomitant use of other anti-asthma drugs, such as anti-inflammatory agents.

To ensure optimal delivery of drug to the bronchial tree, the patient should be properly instructed in the use of Turbuhaler.

In patients in whom terbutaline administration induces cardiac irregularities, the administration of the drug should be stopped.

The concomitant use of terbutaline **tablets** with other orally administered sympathomimetic agents is not recommended, since their combined effect on the cardiovascular system may be deleterious to the patient. However, an **inhaled** bronchodilator of the sympathomimetic type can be used for the relief of acute bronchospasm in patients receiving chronic oral therapy.

If a reduced response to terbutaline becomes apparent, the patient should seek medical advice.

In patients requiring concomitant treatment with terbutaline and a beta-blocker, it is recommended that a beta-blocker (e.g., metoprolol) with less predominant β_2-blocking effects be considered. If concomitant treatment is necessary, patients should be monitored carefully for possible deterioration in pulmonary function and the need to adjust the dosage of either drug (see Drug Interactions).

Immediate hypersensitivity reactions and exacerbation of bronchospasm have been reported after terbutaline administration.

<u>Drug Interactions:</u> Sympathomimetic Bronchodilators and Epinephrine: The concomitant use of terbutaline with other sympathomimetic bronchodilators is not recommended since their combined effect on the cardiovascular system may be deleterious to the patient. This recommendation does not preclude the judicious use of an **inhaled** bronchodilator of the sympathomimetic type in patients receiving terbutaline tablets. Such concomitant use, however, should be individualized and not given on a routine basis. If regular co-administration is required, alternative therapy should be considered.

MAO Inhibitors and Tricyclic Antidepressants: Terbutaline should be administered with caution in patients being treated with MAO inhibitors or tricyclic antidepressants, since the action of terbutaline on the vascular system may be potentiated.

Beta-Adrenergic Receptor Blockers: Beta-adrenergic receptor blocking agents not only block the pulmonary effect of terbutaline but may produce severe asthmatic attacks in asthmatic patients. Therefore, patients requiring treatment for both bronchospastic disease and hypertension should be treated with medication other than beta-adrenergic blocking agents for their hypertension.

Terbutaline Turbuhaler contains terbutaline sulfate which is sensitive to moisture. Patients should be instructed to avoid exhaling into the device and to replace the cover after using Turbuhaler.

Adverse Effects: When treatment is started, the following adverse reactions can be classified as frequent (i.e. $>1/100$): tremor, palpitations, restlessness, headache, muscle cramps, nervousness. Other reported reactions include increased heart rate, ectopic beats, drowsiness, nausea, vomiting, sweating and dizziness.

These adverse reactions are all characteristic of sympathomimetic amines and initial dose titrations will often reduce these reactions. With the possible exception of muscle cramps, all have been spontaneously reversible within the first 2 weeks of treatment. Urticaria and exanthema may also occur.

Sleep disturbances and behavioral disturbances, such as agitation, hyperactivity and restlessness, have been observed.

As with other inhalation therapy, the potential for paradoxical bronchospasm should be kept in mind with terbutaline Turbuhaler. If it occurs, the preparation should be discontinued immediately and alternative therapy instituted.

Potentially serious hypokalemia may result from β_2-agonist therapy.

Overdose: Symptoms and Treatment: The symptoms of overdosage are similar to those described under Adverse Effects, and are attributable to excessive β-adrenergic stimulation. To antagonize the effect of excessive stimulation, the judicious use of a β-adrenergic blocking agent such as propranolol may be considered, bearing in mind the danger of inducing an asthmatic attack.

Dosage: Dosage should be individualized, and patient response should be monitored by the prescribing physician on an ongoing basis.

Turbuhaler: Adults and children ≥ 6 years: The generally recommended dose is 1 inhalation (0.5 mg) taken **as required.** This will usually be adequate to relieve bronchospasm in the majority of patients; however, if required, a second dose may be taken, preferably after waiting 5 minutes for the effect of the first dose to be obtained. If a more severe attack has not been relieved by the second administration, higher doses may be required. In these cases, patients should immediately consult their doctor or the nearest hospital.

More than 6 doses (6 inhalations of Turbuhaler) should not be necessary in any 24 hour period.

If a previously effective dosage regimen fails to provide the usual relief, or the effects of a dose last for less than 3 hours, medical advice should be sought immediately; this is a sign of seriously worsening asthma that requires reassessment of therapy.

Treatment with β_2-agonists in bronchial asthma should be on demand, e.g., symptoms oriented. **Patients must not use them on a daily basis for control of bronchospasm without using other concomitant antiasthma medication(s) according to the present practice for asthma treatment to control airway inflammation.**

The daily dose of terbutaline Turbuhaler should not be increased without adequate reassessment of the therapy plan.

As with other β_2-agonists, increasing demand for terbutaline in bronchial asthma is a sign of poor asthma control and indicates that the treatment plan should be revised.

When prescribing terbutaline Turbuhaler to children, it is necessary to ascertain that they can follow the instructions for use. Terbutaline Turbuhaler is not recommended for use in children below the age of 6 years.

Note: The medication from terbutaline Turbuhaler is delivered to the lungs as the patient inhales and, therefore, it is important to instruct the patient to breathe in forcefully and deeply through the mouthpiece. The patient may not taste or feel any medication when using terbutaline Turbuhaler due to the small amount of drug dispensed.

Tablets: Terbutaline tablets must not be used for relief of acute symptoms or without concomitant optimal anti-inflammatory asthma medications(s). If in spite of other adequate maintenance therapy, regular use of oral β_2-agonists remains necessary, the recommended dose is:

Adults: The usual oral dose is 5 mg administered at approximately 6-hour intervals 3 times daily, during the hours the patient is usually awake. In the event of excessive side effects in individual patients, the dose may be reduced to 2.5 mg 3 times daily. In adults, a total dose of 15 mg should not be exceeded in a 24-hour period.

Children 12 to 15 years: Usual oral dose is 2.5 mg 3 times daily. A total of 7.5 mg should not be exceeded in a 24-hour period.

Children 6 to 11 years: In younger children the dose should be according to body weight i.e. 0.075 mg/kg body weight 3 times daily.

Suitable Dosage (2.5 mg tablets): <20 kg: ¼ to ½ tablet (0.625 to 1.25 mg) 3 times in 24 hours. 20 to 30 kg: ½ to 1 tablet (1.25 to 2.5 mg) 3 times in 24 hours. >30 kg: 1 tablet (2.5 mg) 3 times in 24 hours.

The tablets are not recommended for use in children below the age of 6 years.

Information for the Patient: See Blue Section—Information for the Patient "Bricanyl Turbuhaler".

Supplied: Tablets: 2.5 mg: Each white, scored tablet, engraved 2.5, contains: terbutaline sulfate 2.5 mg (equivalent to 2.05 mg free base). Nonmedicinal ingredients: cornstarch, lactose, magnesium stearate, microcrystalline cellulose and polyvinylpyrrolidone. Energy: 2.76 kJ (0.66 kcal). Gluten-, sodium- and tartrazine-free. Bottles of 100. Store at room temperature between 15 and 30°C.

5 mg: Each white, scored tablet, engraved 5, contains: terbutaline sulfate 5 mg (equivalent to 4.1 mg free base). Nonmedicinal ingredients: cornstarch, lactose, magnesium stearate, microcrystalline cellulose and polyvinylpyrrolidone. Energy: 2.72 kJ (0.65 kcal). Gluten-, sodium- and tartrazine-free. Bottles of 100. Store at room temperature between 15 and 30°C.

Turbuhaler: Each Turbuhaler contains: 50 or 200 doses of micronized terbutaline sulfate. Each inhalation from the multiple-dose powder inhaler contains: terbutaline sulfate 0.5 mg; no additives or carrier substances are included in the inhalation. Turbuhaler cannot be refilled and should be discarded when empty. Store with the cover tightened at room temperature between 15 and 30°C, in a dry place, away from moisture.

(Shown in Product Recognition Section)

Reviewed 1999

BRIETAL SODIUM® ⬦

Lilly

Methohexital Sodium

Anesthetic

Pharmacology: Compared with thiamylal and thiopental, methohexital is at least twice as potent on a weight basis, and its duration of action is only about half as long. Although the metabolic fate of methohexital in the body is not clear, the drug does not appear to concentrate in fat depots to the extent that other barbiturate anesthetics do. Thus, cumulative effects are fewer and recovery is more rapid with methohexital than with thiobarbiturates. In experimental animals, the drug cannot be detected in the blood 24 hours after administration.

Methohexital differs chemically from the established barbiturate anesthetics in that it contains no sulfur. Little analgesia is conferred by barbiturates; their use in the presence of pain may result in excitation.

I.V. administration of methohexital results in rapid uptake by the brain (within 30 seconds) and rapid induction of sleep. With single doses, the rate of redistribution determines duration of pharmacologic effect. Metabolism occurs in the liver through demethylation and oxidation. Side-chain oxidation is the most important biotransformation involved in termination of biologic activity. Excretion occurs via the kidneys through glomerular filtration.

Indications: For i.v. induction of anesthesia prior to the use of other general anesthetic agents.

For i.v. induction of anesthesia and as an adjunct to subpotent inhalational anesthetic agents (such as nitrous oxide in oxygen) for short surgical procedures; methohexital may be given by infusion or intermittent injection.

For use along with other parenteral agents, usually narcotic analgesics, to supplement subpotent inhalational anesthetic agents (such as nitrous oxide in oxygen) for longer surgical procedures.

As i.v. anesthesia for short surgical, diagnostic, or therapeutic procedures associated with minimal painful stimuli (see Precautions).

As an agent for inducing a hypnotic state.

Contraindications: In patients in whom general anesthesia is contraindicated, in those with latent or manifest porphyria, or in patients with a known hypersensitivity to barbiturates.

Warnings: This drug should be administered by persons qualified in the use of intravenous anesthetics. Cardiac life support equipment must be immediately available during use of methohexital.

As with all potent anesthetic agents and adjuncts, this drug should be administered only by those trained in the administration of general anesthesia, the maintenance of a patent airway and ventilation and the management of cardiovascular depression encountered during anesthesia and surgery.

Because the liver is involved in demethylation and oxidation of methohexital and because barbiturates may enhance preexisting circulatory depression, severe hepatic dysfunction, severe cardiovascular instability, or a shock-like condition may be reason for selecting another induction agent.

Psychomotor seizures may be elicited in susceptible individuals.

Prolonged administration may result in cumulative effects, including extended somnolence, protracted unconsciousness, and respiratory and cardiovascular depression. Respiratory depression in the presence of an impaired airway may lead to hypoxia, cardiac arrest and death.

The CNS-depressant effect of methohexital may be additive with that of other CNS depressants, including ethyl alcohol and propylene glycol.

Danger of Intra-arterial Injection: Unintended intra-arterial injection of barbiturate solutions may be followed by the production of platelet aggregates and thrombosis, starting in arterioles distal to the site of injection. The resulting necrosis may lead to gangrene, which may require amputation. The first sign in conscious patients may be a complaint of fiery burning that roughly follows the distribution path of the injected artery; if noted, the injection should be stopped immediately and the situation re-evaluated. **Transient** blanching **may** or may not be noted very early; blotchy cyanosis and dark discoloration may then be the first sign in anesthetized patients. There is no established treatment other than prevention. The following should be considered prior to injection: 1. The extent of injury is related to concentration. Concentrations of 1% methohexital will usually suffice; higher concentrations should ordinarily be avoided. 2. Check the infusion to ensure that the catheter is in the lumen of a vein before injection. Injection through a running i.v. infusion may enhance the possibility of detecting arterial placement; however, it should be remembered that the characteristic bright-red color of arterial blood is often altered by contact with drugs. The possibility of aberrant arteries should always be considered.

Postinjury arterial injection of vasodilators and/or arterial infusion of parenteral fluids are generally regarded to be of no value in altering outcome. Animal experiments and published individual case reports concerned with a variety of arteriolar irritants, including barbiturates, suggest that one or more of the following may be of benefit in reducing the area of necrosis: arterial injection of heparin at the site of injury, followed by systemic anticoagulation; sympathetic blockade (or brachial plexus blockade in the arm); intra-arterial glucocorticoid injection at the site of injury, followed by systemic steroids. A recent case report (nonbarbiturate injury) suggests that intra-arterial urokinase may promote fibrinolysis, even if administered late in treatment. If extravasation is noted during injection of methohexital, the injection should be discontinued until the situation is remedied. Local irritation may result from extravasation; s.c. swelling may also serve as a sign of arterial or periarterial placement of the catheter.

Precautions: General: Maintenance of a patent airway and adequacy of ventilation must be ensured during induction and maintenance of anesthesia with methohexital solution. Laryngospasm is common during induction with all barbiturates and may be due to a combination of secretions and accentuated reflexes following induction or may result from painful stimuli during light anesthesia. Transient apnea may be noted during induction, which may impair pulmonary ventilation; the duration of apnea may be longer than that produced by other barbiturate anesthetics. Cardiorespiratory arrest may occur. I.V. administration of methohexital is often associated with hiccups, coughing, and/or muscle twitching, which may also impair pulmonary ventilation.

Following induction, temporary hypotension and tachycardia may occur.

Recovery from methohexital anesthesia is rapid and smooth. The incidence of postoperative nausea and vomiting is low if the drug is administered to fasting patients. Postanesthetic shivering has occurred in a few instances.

The usual precautions taken with any barbiturate anesthetic should be observed with methohexital. The drug should be used with caution in patients with asthma, obstructive pulmonary disease, severe hypertension or hypotension, myocardial disease, congestive heart failure, severe anemia, or extreme obesity.

Methohexital should be used with extreme caution in patients with status asthmaticus.

Caution should be exercised in debilitated patients or in those with impaired function of respiratory, circulatory, renal, hepatic or endocrine systems.

Information for the Patient: Occupational Hazards: When appropriate, patients should be instructed as to the hazards of drowsiness that may follow use of methohexital. Outpatients should be released in the company of another individual, and no skilled activities, such as operating machinery or driving a motor vehicle, should be engaged in for 8 to 12 hours.

Laboratory Tests: BSP and liver function studies may be influenced by administration of a single dose of barbiturates.

Drug Interactions: Barbiturates may influence the absorption and elimination of other concomitantly used drugs, such as phenytoin, halothane, anticoagulants, corticosteroids, ethyl alcohol and propylene glycol-containing solutions.

Pregnancy: Reproduction studies have been performed in rabbits and rats at doses up to 4 and 7 times the human dose respectively and have revealed no evidence of impaired fertility or harm to the fetus due to methohexital. There are, however, no adequate and well-controlled studies in pregnant women. Because animal reproduction studies are not always predictive of human response, this drug should be used during pregnancy only if clearly needed.

Labor and Delivery: Methohexital has been used in cesarean section delivery but, because of its solubility and lack of protein binding, it readily and rapidly traverses the placenta.

Lactation: Caution should be exercised when methohexital is administered to a nursing woman.

Children: Safety and effectiveness in children have not been established.

Adverse Effects: Side effects associated with methohexital are extensions of pharmacologic effects and include: Cardiovascular: circulatory depression, thrombophlebitis, hypotension, peripheral vascular collapse and convulsions in association with cardiorespiratory arrest.

Respiratory: respiratory depression (including apnea), cardiorespiratory arrest, laryngospasm, bronchospasm, hiccups and dyspnea.

Neurologic: skeletal muscle hyperactivity (twitching), injury to nerves adjacent to injection site and seizures.

Psychiatric: emergence delirium, restlessness and anxiety may occur, especially in the presence of postoperative pain.

Gastrointestinal: nausea, emesis and abdominal pain.

Allergic: erythema, pruritus, urticaria, and cases of anaphylaxis have been reported rarely.

Other: Other adverse reactions include pain at injection site, salivation, headache and rhinitis.

Drug Abuse and Dependence: Methohexital is a Schedule G drug, it may be habit-forming.

Overdose: Symptoms: The onset of toxicity following an overdose of i.v. administered methohexital will be within seconds of the infusion. If methohexital is administered rectally or is ingested, the onset of toxicity may be delayed. The manifestations of an ultrashort-acting barbiturate in overdose include CNS depression, respiratory depression, hypotension, loss of peripheral vascular resistance and muscular hyperactivity ranging from twitching to convulsive-like movements. Other findings may include convulsions and allergic reactions. An acute allergic reaction to methohexital may include erythema, pruritus, urticaria, rhinitis, dyspnea, hypotension, anxiety, abdominal pain and peripheral vascular collapse. Following

Brietal Sodium (cont'd)

massive exposure to any barbiturate, pulmonary edema, circulatory collapse with loss of peripheral vascular tone, and cardiac arrest may occur.

Treatment: Establish an airway and ensure oxygenation and ventilation. Resuscitative measures should be initiated promptly. For hypotension, i.v. fluids should be administered and the patient's legs raised. If desirable increase in blood pressure is not obtained, vasopressor and/or inotropic drugs may be used as dictated by the clinical situation.

For convulsions, diazepam i.v. and phenytoin may be required. If the seizures are refractory to diazepam and phenytoin, general anesthesia and paralysis with a neuromuscular blocking agent may be necessary.

Protect the patient's airway and support ventilation and perfusion.

Meticulously monitor and maintain, within acceptable limits, the patient's vital signs, blood gases, serum electrolytes, etc. Absorption of drugs from the gastrointestinal tract may be decreased by giving activated charcoal, which, in many cases, is more effective than emesis or lavage; consider charcoal instead of or in addition to gastric emptying. Repeated doses of charcoal over time may hasten elimination of some drugs that have been absorbed. Safeguard the patient's airway when employing gastric emptying or charcoal.

Dosage: Preanesthetic medication is generally advisable. Methohexital sodium may be used with any of the recognized preanesthetic medications, but the phenothiazines are less satisfactory than the combination of an opiate and a belladonna derivative.

Facilities for assisting respiration and administering oxygen are necessary adjuncts for i.v. anesthesia.

Preparation of Solution: **Follow diluting instructions exactly.**
Diluents: **Do not use diluents containing bacteriostats.** Sterile Water for Injection is the preferred diluent. Five percent Dextrose Injection or 0.9% Sodium Chloride Injection may be used. (Brietal Sodium is not compatible with Ringer's Lactate Solution.)

Dilution Instructions: For a 1% solution (10 mg/mL), contents of vials should be diluted as follows: 500 mg vials—add 50 mL of diluent.

Solutions of methohexital should be freshly prepared and used promptly. Reconstituted solutions are chemically stable at room temperature for 24 hours.

For continuous drip anesthesia, prepare 0.2% solution by adding 500 mg of drug to 250 mL of diluent. For this dilution, recommended solvents are either 5% glucose solution or isotonic (0.9%) sodium chloride solution instead of distilled water in order to avoid extreme hypotonicity.

Administration: Methohexital is administered i.v. in a concentration of no higher than 1%. Higher concentrations markedly increase the incidence of muscular movements and irregularities in respiration and blood pressure. Dosage is highly individualized; the drug should be administered only by those completely familiar with its quantitative differences from other barbiturate anesthetics.

Methohexital may be dissolved in Sterile Water for Injection, 5% Dextrose Injection, or Sodium Chloride Injection. For induction of anesthesia, a 1% solution is administered at a rate of about 1 mL/5 seconds. Gaseous anesthetics and/or skeletal-muscle relaxants may be administered concomitantly. The dose required for induction may range from 50 to 120 mg or more but averages about 70 mg. The induction dose usually provides anesthesia for 5 to 7 minutes.

The usual dosage in adults ranges from 1 to 1.5 mg/kg. Data on dosage requirements in children are not available.

Maintenance of anesthesia may be accomplished by intermittent injections of the 1% solution or, more easily, by continuous i.v. drip of a 0.2% solution. Intermittent injections of about 20 to 40 mg (2 to 4 mL of a 1% solution) may be given as required, usually every 4 to 7 minutes. For continuous drip, the average rate of administration is about 3 mL of a 0.2% solution/minute (1 drop/second). The rate of flow must be individualized for each patient. For longer surgical procedures, gradual reduction in the rate of administration is recommended (see discussion of prolonged administration in Warnings). Other parenteral agents, usually narcotic analgesics, are ordinarily employed along with methohexital during longer procedures.

Parenteral drug products should be inspected visually for particulate matter and discoloration prior to administration, whenever solution and container permit.

Compatibility: Solutions of Brietal Sodium should not be mixed in the same syringe or administered simultaneously during i.v. infusion through the same needle with acid solutions, such as atropine sulfate, metocurine iodide injection and succinylcholine chloride.

Reduction of pH by addition of acidic compounds may cause free barbituric acid to be precipitated.

The soluble sodium salts of barbiturates are the forms used for i.v. administration. Solubility is maintained only at a relatively high (basic) pH.

Supplied: Each rubber-stoppered vial of dry powder contains: methohexital sodium 500 mg/50 mL formulated with anhydrous sodium carbonate 30 mg. Preservative-free.

BROMAZEPAM Ⓟ
General Monograph, CPhA
see BENZODIAZEPINES

BRONALIDE® Ⓟ
Boehringer Ingelheim
Flunisolide
Corticosteroid Aerosol

Pharmacology: Flunisolide has demonstrated marked anti-inflammatory and anti-allergic activity in classical test systems. It is a corticosteroid which is several hundred times more potent in animal anti-inflammatory assays than the cortisol standard. When inhaled at therapeutic doses it has potent anti-inflammatory activity locally on the bronchial mucosa.

Following i.v. administration in man of 2 mg flunisolide, plasma concentrations of 12 to 21 ng/mL were observed within 5 minutes. Plasma levels declined with time so that after 6 hours, levels of 1 ng/mL or less were circulating. The plasma half-life was estimated to be 80 to 150 minutes.

Flunisolide 1 mg administered by bronchial inhalation to volunteers produced peak or near peak plasma levels at 2 minutes which remained near this level throughout the first hour before declining at a rate similar to that observed after i.v. administration (plasma half-life of 1.6 to 2 hours). After oral inhalation the peak plasma levels (approximately 1.4 ng/mL) were observed in 1 to 2 hours.

In man, following oral administration of 2 mg flunisolide, peak plasma levels of 20 to 27 ng/mL were obtained in 30 to 60 minutes.

Gargling with an alcoholic mouthwash immediately after oral inhalation did not appreciably affect the systemic availability. Inhalation without using mouthwash resulted in a systemic availability of 39%, compared to 32% in the presence of the mouthwash.

The apparent volume of distribution for flunisolide, estimated after the i.v. administration of a single dose, ranged from approximately 3 L/kg in the rat to 8 L/kg in the mouse. These data indicated that flunisolide was extensively distributed into the body tissues. When 100% plasma was used as the source of protein, about 50% of the added flunisolide (2.5×10 to 50×10 M) was found to be protein-bound.

In man, orally-administered flunisolide was extensively metabolized during its first-pass through the liver; the systemic availability of a 1 mg oral dose was about 20%.

In man, flunisolide was excreted via both the kidney and the liver. The drug was rapidly metabolized with 95% recovered in the first 24 hours (53% in urine; 42% in stool). A major metabolite isolated from the urine of man was 6α, 11β, 16α, 17α, 21-pentahydroxypregna-1, 4-diene-3, 20-dione 16, 17-acetonide (6β -OH metabolite) which had only low corticoid activity and a half-life of 1 to 3 hours. In man, the 6β-OH metabolite accounted for 60 to 75% of the recovered drug in the urine.

The data offer metabolic explanations for the clinical observation that flunisolide can be administered by bronchial inhalation in therapeutically effective doses for extensive periods of time without production of systemic-corticosteroid side effects. After bronchial inhalation, much of the dose is eventually swallowed and metabolized to compounds having weak corticoid activity. The lack of systemic effects could result from the rapid conversion of flunisolide to metabolites having low corticoid activity.

Indications: For the control of the signs and symptoms of steroid-responsive bronchial asthma when tolerance to or effectiveness of conventional treatment is unsatisfactory. It is also indicated in steroid dependent asthmatics where a reduction of systemic steroids is desirable.

Contraindications: Hypersensitivity to any of the ingredients. Active or quiescent untreated pulmonary tuberculosis, or untreated fungal, bacterial, or viral infections. In status asthmaticus, or in patients with moderate to severe bronchiectasis.

Warnings: Patients should be instructed to contact their physician immediately when episodes of asthma which are not responsive to bronchodilators occur during the course of treatment. During such episodes, patients may require therapy with systemic corticosteroids.

Particular care is needed in patients who are transferred from systemic corticosteroids to flunisolide because deaths due to adrenal insufficiency have occurred in asthmatic patients during and after transfer from systemic to aerosolized corticosteroids. After withdrawal from systemic corticosteroids, a number of months are required for recovery of hypothalamic-pituitary-adrenal (HPA) function. During this period of HPA suppression, patients may exhibit signs and symptoms of adrenal insufficiency when exposed to trauma, surgery, or infections, particularly gastroenteritis. Although flunisolide may provide control of asthmatic symptoms during these episodes, it does not provide the systemic steroid which is necessary for coping with these emergencies. During periods of stress or severe asthmatic attack, patients who have been withdrawn from systemic corticosteroids should be instructed to resume systemic steroids immediately (in large doses) and to contact their physician for further instruction.

The development of pharyngeal and laryngeal candidiasis is cause for concern because the extent of its penetration of the respiratory tract is unknown. If candidiasis develops, discontinue the treatment and initiate appropriate antifungal therapy. The incidence of candidiasis can generally be held to a minimum by having patients rinse their mouths with water after each inhalation.

During withdrawal from oral corticosteroids, some patients may experience symptoms of steroid withdrawal, e.g. joint and/or muscle pain, lassitude and depression, despite maintenance or even improvement of respiratory function.

Pregnancy and *Lactation:* Controlled trials relating to fetal risk in humans have not been done. Flunisolide may be secreted in human milk. The use of flunisolide in pregnancy or nursing mothers requires that the possible benefits of the drug be weighed against the potential hazards to the mother, embryo, fetus or nursing infant. Infants born of mothers who have received substantial doses of corticosteroids during pregnancy or those infants nursed by mothers receiving corticosteroids, should be carefully observed for hypoadrenalism.

Children: Insufficient information is available to warrant use in children under the age of 4.

Precautions: The replacement of a systemic steroid with flunisolide has to be gradual and carefully supervised by the physician. The guidelines under Dosage should be followed in all such cases.

Pregnancy: Avoid unnecessary administration of drugs during the first trimester of pregnancy.

It is essential that the patient be instructed that the inhalant is a preventive agent which must be taken at regular intervals and is not to be used during an asthmatic attack.

Transfer of patients from systemic steroid therapy to flunisolide may unmask allergic conditions previously suppressed by the systemic steroid therapy, e.g. rhinitis, conjunctivitis and eczema.

Potential effects on acute, recurrent or chronic infection, including active or quiescent tuberculosis, are not known.

Local effects on developmental or immunologic processes in the mouth, pharynx, trachea, and lung are unknown.

Corticosteroids may mask some signs of infection and new infections may appear. A decreased resistance to localized infection has been observed during corticosteroid therapy.

During long-term therapy, pituitary-adrenal function and hematological status should be periodically assessed.

As with many other pressurized aerosol formulations, flunisolide contains a fluorocarbon propellant. In large doses, these propellants can produce cardiac arrhythmia in animals, as well as sensitize their hearts to adrenaline-induced arrhythmia. Data in humans are meager. Excessive inhalation of the aerosol should, however, be avoided as this carries a potential hazard, both from the propellant as well as from overdosage of the active therapeutic agent contained in the formulation. The recommended dose should not be exceeded and patients should be advised appropriately.

There is an enhanced effect of corticosteroids in patients with hypothyroidism and in those with cirrhosis.

Use ASA cautiously in conjunction with corticosteroids in hypoprothrombinemia.

Advise patients to inform subsequent physicians of the prior use of corticosteroids.

Adverse Effects: The most frequent adverse reactions in clinical studies were related to the respiratory tract. These were, in decreasing order of frequency: cough, hoarseness, sore throat and wheezing. These occurred in up to 1 in 14 patients. Less frequent reactions were: nausea, infection with candida, glossitis, headache, chest tightness, dry throat, gas, pruritus, loss of smell and taste, abdominal pain, diarrhea, heartburn and rash. These occurred in up to 1 in 50 patients.

Other adverse reactions which occurred less often than 1 in 100 patients were: dyspepsia, sore mouth, rhinitis, throat itch, vomiting, abdominal fullness, acne, capillary fragility, edema, and shortness of breath.

Overdose: Symptoms and Treatment: In case of hypercorticism and/or adrenal suppression, discontinue therapy.

Dosage: For oral inhalation only.
Adults: The recommended starting dose is 2 inhalations twice daily, morning and evening, for a total daily dose of 1 mg. The maximum daily dose should not exceed 4 inhalations twice daily for a total daily dose of 2 mg.
Children: Insufficient information is available to warrant use in children under age 4. For children 4 to 15 years of age, 2 inhalations may be administered twice daily for a total dose of 1 mg. Higher doses have not been studied.

There is no evidence that better control of asthma can be achieved by the administration of flunisolide in amounts greater than the recommended doses; higher doses may induce adrenal suppression.

Since the effect of flunisolide depends on its regular use and on the proper technique of inhalation, patients must be instructed to take the inhalations at regular intervals and not as with other aerosols, as they feel necessary. They should also be instructed in the correct method, which is to exhale completely, placing the lips tightly around the mouthpiece and actuate the aerosol early during the next inspiratory period.

In the presence of excessive mucus secretion, the drug may fail to reach the bronchioles. Therefore, if an obvious response is not obtained after 10 days, attempts should be made to remove the mucus with expectorants and/or with a short course of systemic corticosteroid treatment.

Careful attention must be given to patients previously treated for prolonged periods with systemic corticosteroids, when transferred to flunisolide.

Initially, flunisolide and the systemic steroid must be given concomitantly while the dose of the latter is gradually decreased. In adults, the usual rate of withdrawal of the systemic corticoid is the equivalent of 2.5 mg prednisone every 4 days if the patient is under close observation. In children, the rate of withdrawal is 2.5 mg prednisone every 8 days when under close supervision. If continuous supervision is not feasible, the withdrawal of the systemic steroid should be slower, approximately 2.5 mg prednisone (or equivalent) every 10 days in adults and 20 days in children. If withdrawal symptoms appear, the previous dose of the systemic drug should be resumed for a week before further decrease is attempted. Under stressful conditions or when the patient has a severe exacerbation of asthma, after complete withdrawal of the systemic steroid, use of the latter must be resumed in order to avoid relative adrenocortical insufficiency. There are some patients who cannot completely discontinue the oral corticosteroid. In these cases, a minimum maintenance dose should be given in addition to flunisolide.

Information for the Patient: See Blue Section—Information for the Patient "Bronalide".

Supplied: Each canister contains: 100 metered doses of flunisolide aerosol. Nonmedicinal ingredients: propellants (difluorodichloromethane, monofluorotrichloromethane, tetrafluorodichloroethane) and sorbitan trioleate. Each valve depression (actuation) delivers 250 µg of flunisolide.

BRONCHO-GRIPPOL-DM
Technilab
Dextromethorphan HBr
Symptomatic Relief of Nonproductive Cough

Supplied: Each 5 mL contains: dextromethorphan HBr USP 15 mg. Alcohol-, dyes- and sugar-free. Sweetened with sorbitol and saccharin. Bottles of 250 mL.

New Product 1998

BRONKAID® MISTOMETER®
Sanofi
Epinephrine
Bronchodilator

Pharmacology: Epinephrine is a sympathomimetic drug that acts on both alpha and beta receptors.

Indications: For temporary relief of acute paroxysms of bronchial asthma.

Warnings: For oral inhalation only. Do not use this product unless a diagnosis of asthma has been made by a physician, if you have heart disease, high blood pressure, thyroid disease, diabetes, or difficulty in urination due to enlargement of the prostate gland, if you have ever been hospitalized for asthma or if you are taking any prescription drug for asthma. Do not use this product more frequently or at higher doses than recommended, unless directed by a physician. Keep this and all drugs out of the reach of children. In case of accidental overdose, seek professional assistance or contact a poison control center immediately.
Pregnancy and *Lactation:* As with any drug, if you are pregnant or nursing a baby, seek the advice of a health professional before using this product.

Precautions: *Drug Interactions:* Do not use this product if you are presently taking a prescription drug for high blood pressure or depression, without first consulting your physician.

Adverse Effects: Excessive use may cause nervousness and rapid heartbeat, and possibly adverse effects on the heart. Do not continue to use this product but seek medical assistance immediately if symptoms are not relieved within 20 minutes or become worse.

Dosage: Inhalation dosage for adults and children 14 years of age and older. Start with 1 inhalation, then wait at least 1 minute. If not relieved, use once more. Do not use again for at least 3 hours. Children under 14 years of age: as directed by physician.

If symptoms are not relieved within 20 minutes or become worse, do not continue to use this product, but seek medical assistance.

During use, the Mistometer must always be held upside down as it does not operate properly in an upright position. **Run warm or cold water through the mouthpiece once daily to wash it.** You may sanitize it by immersing it in alcohol. Always protect your epinephrine inhalation aerosol by replacing the plastic mouthpiece and cap after each use. Before each use, remove cap and inspect mouthpiece for foreign objects.

Supplied: Each 15 mL plastic coated vial contains: epinephrine USP 0.5% (5.5 mg/mL) solution. Nonmedicinal ingredients: alcohol 33%, ascorbic acid, dichlorodifluoromethane, dischlorotetrafluoroethane and distilled water. The contents of the vial permits the delivery of 300 single oral inhalations. Each spray delivers approximately 0.25 mg epinephrine through the mouthpiece (0.275 mg through the valve). Metered dose aerosol inhalers of 15 mL with detachable plastic mouthpiece with built-in nebulizer and protective cap.

BSS®
Alcon
Balanced Salt Solution
Ocular Irrigation Therapy

Supplied: Each 15 mL self dispensing plastic squeeze bottle with adapter for Luer-Lok hub irrigating needles in sterile packaging (Steri Unit, single dose), or each polyvinyl chloride bag of 500 mL, in sterile packaging, contains: sodium chloride 0.64%, potassium chloride 0.075%, magnesium chloride 0.03%, calcium chloride 0.048%, sodium acetate 0.39%, sodium citrate 0.17%, sodium hydroxide and/or hydrochloric acid (to adjust pH) and water for injection. Contains no preservatives. Discard unused portions.

...Grateful acknowledgement is accorded to the "participating companies" whose support has facilitated the widespread distribution of CPS.

BSS® PLUS
Alcon
Balanced Salt Solution
Intraocular Irrigating Solution

Supplied: BSS PLUS is available in 250 and 500 mL, supplied in 2 packages for reconstitution prior to use: Part 1 consists of a sterile 250 or 500 mL single-dose bottle which contains 240 or 480 mL. Part 2 consists of a sterile 10 or 20 mL single-dose vial.
Each mL of part 1 contains: sodium chloride 7.44 mg, potassium chloride 0.395 mg, dibasic sodium phosphate 0.433 mg, sodium bicarbonate 2.19 mg, hydrochloric acid and/or sodium hydroxide (to adjust pH), in water for injection.
Each mL of part 2 contains: calcium chloride dihydrate 3.85 mg, magnesium chloride hexahydrate 5 mg, dextrose 23 mg, glutathione disulfide (oxidized glutathione) 4.6 mg, in water for injection.

The reconstituted product has a pH of approximately 7.4. Osmolality is approximately 305 mOsm/kg.

BUDESONIDE ℞
General Monograph, CPhA
see CORTICOSTEROIDS: EYE EAR NOSE
see CORTICOSTEROIDS: INHALED

BUPIVACAINE HYDROCHLORIDE INJECTION ℞
Abbott
Local Anesthetic

Supplied: 0.25 %: Each mL of sterile, isotonic solution contains: bupivacaine HCl anhydrous 2.5 mg in Water for Injection and sodium chloride to adjust tonicity. May contain sodium hydroxide and/or hydrochloric acid for pH adjustment. Preservative-free. Single dose vials of 10 and 20 mL, boxes of 5.

0.5 %: Each mL of sterile, isotonic solution contains: bupivacaine HCl anhydrous 5 mg in Water for Injection and sodium chloride to adjust tonicity. May contain sodium hydroxide and/or hydrochloric acid for pH adjustment. Preservative-free. Single dose vials of 10 and 20 mL, boxes of 5.

0.75 %: Each mL of sterile, isotonic solution contains: bupivacaine HCl anhydrous 7.5 mg in Water for Injection and sodium chloride to adjust tonicity. May contain sodium hydroxide and/or hydrochloric acid for pH adjustment. Preservative-free. Single dose vials of 10 and 20 mL, boxes of 5.

Do not use if color of solution is pinkish or darker than slightly yellow or if a precipitate is present. Store at controlled room temperature (15 to 30°C). Protect from freezing.

BURINEX® ℞
Leo
Bumetanide
Diuretic

Pharmacology: Bumetanide is a loop diuretic. The diuretic effect of bumetanide results largely from the inhibition of sodium reabsorption in the ascending limb of the loop of Henle. This is shown by a marked reduction in freewater clearance during hydration and tubular solute-free water reabsorption during hydropenia.

Bumetanide may have an additional action in the proximal tubule, since phosphaturia has been observed during bumetanide induced diuresis and the renal clearance of bumetanide is decreased by probenecid. The proximal tubular activity does not seem to be related to an inhibition of carbonic anhydrase. Potassium excretion is increased by bumetanide in a dose-related fashion.

Following oral administration to normal subjects, bumetanide is rapidly and almost completely (>80%) absorbed from the gastrointestinal tract. The time to reach peak blood levels is 0.5 to 2 hours. Plasma protein binding of bumetanide is approximately 95%.

Bumetanide is rapidly eliminated, the plasma half-life being 1.5 hours. The majority (approx. 80%) of an oral dose of bumetanide is recovered in the urine (about 60% of this as unchanged bumetanide, the remainder as metabolites).

Burinex (cont'd)

After oral administration of 1 mg of bumetanide diuresis begins within 30 minutes with a peak effect between 1 and 2 hours. Diuresis is nearly completed after 3 to 4 hours.

Pharmacological and clinical studies have shown that 1 mg bumetanide produces a diuretic response similar to that of approximately 40 mg furosemide.

Indications: For the treatment of edema associated with congestive heart failure, cirrhosis of the liver and renal disease including the nephrotic syndrome.

Contraindications: In patients who are anuric, in patients in hepatic coma and in states of severe electrolyte depletion until the condition is improved or corrected. Bumetanide is contraindicated in patients hypersensitive to bumetanide and other sulfonamide derivatives.

Warnings:

> Bumetanide is a potent diuretic which, if given in excessive amounts, can lead to profound diuresis with water and electrolyte depletion. Therefore, careful medical supervision is required and dose and dosage schedule have to be adjusted to the individual patient's needs (see Dosage).

The dose of bumetanide should be adjusted to patient's need. Excessive doses or too frequent administration can lead to profound water loss, electrolyte depletion, dehydration, reduction in blood volume and circulatory collapse with a possibility of vascular thrombosis and embolism, particularly in elderly patients.

Hypokalemia can occur as a consequence of bumetanide administration. Prevention of hypokalemia requires particular attention in the following conditions: patients receiving digitalis and diuretics for congestive heart failure, hepatic cirrhosis and ascites, states of aldosterone excess with normal renal function, potassium-losing nephropathy, certain diarrheal states, or other states where hypokalemia is thought to represent particular added risks to the patient, (i.e., history of ventricular arrhythmias).

In patients with hepatic cirrhosis and ascites, sudden alterations of electrolyte balance may precipitate hepatic encephalopathy and coma.

Serum electrolyte determination should be performed frequently.

Ototoxicity: In cats, dogs and guinea pigs, bumetanide has been shown to produce ototoxicity. In these test animals bumetanide was 5 to 6 times more potent than furosemide and, since the diuretic potency of bumetanide is about 40 to 60 times greater, it is anticipated that blood levels necessary to produce ototoxicity will rarely be achieved. The potential exists, however, and must be considered a risk particularly with therapy at high doses, repeated frequently in the face of renal excretory function impairment. Potentiation of aminoglycoside ototoxicity has not been tested for bumetanide. Like other members of this class of diuretics, bumetanide probably shares this risk.

Patients allergic to sulfonamides may show hypersensitivity to bumetanide.

Precautions: Serum potassium should be measured periodically and potassium supplements or potassium sparing diuretics may be required especially when high doses are used for prolonged periods. Particular caution with potassium concentration is necessary in patients receiving digitalis glycosides or potassium depleting steroids. Periodic determination of other electrolytes are also advised, particularly in patients on low salt diets.

It may be advisable to hospitalize patients with hepatic cirrhosis and ascites prior to initiating therapy. Sudden alterations of fluid and electrolyte balance in patients with cirrhosis may precipitate hepatic encephalopathy and coma; therefore, strict observation is necessary during the period of diuresis. Supplemental potassium chloride and, if required, an aldosterone antagonist are helpful in preventing hypokalemia and metabolic alkalosis.

It is essential to replace electrolyte losses and to maintain fluid balance so as to avoid any risk of electrolyte depletion, hypovolemia or hypotension.

Since rigid sodium restriction is conducive to both hyponatremia and hypokalemia, such restriction is not advisable in patients on bumetanide therapy.

Bumetanide may increase urinary calcium excretion with resultant hypocalcemia.

Reversible elevation of BUN and creatinine may occur, especially in association with dehydration and in patients with renal insufficiency. Marked increases in BUN and creatinine or the development of oliguria during treatment of patients with progressive renal disease is an indication for discontinuation.

Hyperuricemia may occur; it has been asymptomatic in cases reported to date.

Studies in normal subjects receiving bumetanide revealed no adverse effects on glucose tolerance, plasma insulin, glucagon and growth hormone levels but the possibility of an effect on glucose metabolism exists. Periodic determinations of blood sugar should be done, particularly in patients with diabetes or suspected of latent diabetes.

Patients under treatment should be observed regularly for possible occurrence of blood dyscrasias, liver damage, or idiosyncratic reactions which have been reported rarely in foreign marketing experience.

Drug Interactions: Drugs with Ototoxic Potential: Bumetanide may, in view of its ototoxic potential, enhance the ototoxic effect of aminoglycosides and simultaneous administration should generally be avoided especially in patients with impaired renal function.

Drugs with Nephrotoxic Potential: There has been no experience on the concurrent use of bumetanide with drugs known to have nephrotoxic potential. Simultaneous administration of these drugs should be avoided.

Cardiac Glycosides: Low serum potassium levels can occur as a consequence of bumetanide administration. Hypokalemia may increase the sensitivity of the myocardium to the toxic effects of digitalis. Thus correction of the hypokalemic state is required and the dose may need adjustment.

Lithium: Lithium should generally not be given with diuretics such as bumetanide. Concurrent administration of diuretics such as bumetanide and lithium may reduce lithium clearance. Adjustment of lithium dosage may be necessary. To minimize potential lithium toxicity close clinical observation and more frequent determination of serum lithium are required.

Probenecid: Pretreatment with probenecid reduces both the natriuresis and hyperreninemia produced by bumetanide. This antagonistic effect of probenecid on bumetanide natriuresis is not due to a direct action on sodium excretion but is probably secondary to its inhibitory effect on renal tubular secretion of bumetanide. Thus, probenecid should not be administered concurrently with bumetanide.

Indomethacin: Indomethacin blunts the increases in urine volume and sodium excretion seen during bumetanide treatment and inhibits the bumetanide-induced increase in plasma renin activity. Concurrent therapy with bumetanide is thus not recommended.

Antihypertensives: Bumetanide may potentiate the effect of antihypertensive drugs. Therefore, the dose of the latter may need adjustment when bumetanide is used to treat edema in hypertensive patients.

Pregnancy: Bumetanide is neither teratogenic nor embryotoxic in mice when given in doses up to 3 400 times the maximum human therapeutic dose.

Bumetanide has been shown to be nonteratogenic, but it has a slight embryotoxic effect in rats when given in oral doses of 100 mg/kg/day and in rabbits at doses of 0.1 mg/kg/day. In one study, moderate growth retardation and increased incidence of delayed ossification of sternebrae were observed in rats at oral doses of 100 mg/kg/day. These effects were associated with maternal weight reduction during dosing. No such adverse effects were observed at 30 mg/kg/day.

In rabbits, a dose-related decrease in litter size and an increase in resorption rate were noted at oral doses of 0.1 and 0.3 mg/kg/day. A slightly increased incidence of delayed ossification of sternebrae occurred at 0.3 mg/kg/day; however, no effects were seen at 0.03 mg/kg/day. The sensitivity of the rabbit to bumetanide parallels the marked pharmacologic and toxicologic effects of the drug in this species.

Bumetanide was not teratogenic in the hamster at an oral dose of 0.5 mg/kg/day.

There are no studies in pregnant women. Bumetanide should be given to a pregnant woman only if the potential benefit justifies the potential risk to the fetus.

Lactation: Since bumetanide passes into the breast milk, the drug should not be given to nursing mothers.

Children: The safety and effectiveness of bumetanide in the pediatric age group below the age of 18 have not been established.

Adverse Effects: The most frequent clinical adverse reactions observed with bumetanide are muscle cramps (1.1%), dizziness (1.1%), hypotension (0.8%), headache (0.6%), nausea (0.6%), and encephalopathy (in patients with preexisting liver disease) (0.6%). One or more of these adverse reactions have been reported in approximately 4.1% of bumetanide-treated patients.

Less frequent clinical adverse reactions to bumetanide are impaired hearing (0.5%), pruritus (0.4%), ECG changes (0.4%), weakness (0.2%), hives (0.2%), abdominal pain (0.2%), arthritic pain (0.2%), musculoskeletal pain (0.2%), rash (0.2%), and vomiting (0.2%). One or more of these adverse reactions have been reported in approximately 2.9% of bumetanide-treated patients.

Other clinical adverse reactions, which have each occurred in approximately 0.1% of patients, are vertigo, chest pain, ear discomfort, fatigue, dehydration, sweating, hyperventilation, dry mouth, upset stomach, renal failure, asterixis, itching, nipple tenderness, diarrhea, premature ejaculation and difficulty maintaining an erection.

Laboratory abnormalities reported have included hyperuricemia (18.4%), hypochloremia (14.9%), hypokalemia (14.7%), azotemia (10.6%), hyponatremia (9.2%), increased serum creatinine (7.4%), hyperglycemia (6.6%), and variations in phosphorus (4.5%), CO_2 content (4.3%), bicarbonate (3.1%) and calcium (2.4%). Although manifestations of the pharmacologic action of bumetanide, these conditions may become more pronounced by intensive therapy.

Diuresis induced by bumetanide may also rarely be accompanied by changes in LDH (1.0%), total serum bilirubin (0.8%), serum proteins (0.7%), AST (0.6%), ALT (0.5%), alkaline phosphatase (0.4%), cholesterol (0.4%) and creatinine clearance (0.3%). Also reported have been thrombocytopenia (0.2%) deviations in hemoglobin (0.8%), prothrombin time (0.8%), hematocrit (0.6%), WBC (0.3%), platelet counts (0.2%) and differential counts (0.1%). Increases in urinary glucose (0.7%) and urinary protein (0.3%) have also been seen.

Overdose: Symptoms: Profound water loss and electrolyte depletion, dehydration, reduction of blood volume and circulatory collapse with a possibility of vascular thrombosis and embolism. Electrolyte depletion may be manifested by weakness, dizziness, mental confusion, anorexia, lethargy, vomiting and cramps.

Treatment: Discontinue the drug. Institute water and electrolyte replacement with careful monitoring of urine and electrolyte output and serum electrolyte levels.

Dosage: Dosage should be individualized with careful monitoring of patient response.

The usual total oral daily dosage is 0.5 to 2.0 mg and in most patients may be given as a single dose.

If the diuretic response to an initial 1 mg dose is not adequate, a second or third dose may be given at 4 to 5 hour intervals. The maximum recommended daily dose is 10 mg.

An intermittent dose schedule, whereby bumetanide is given on alternate days or for 3 to 4 days with rest periods of 1 to 2 days in between is recommended as the safest and most effective method for the continued control of edema.

In patients with hepatic failure the dosage should be kept to a minimum, and if necessary, dosage increased very carefully. A maintenance dose as low as 0.5 mg daily should be considered and the daily dose should not exceed 5 mg (see Warnings).

Supplied: 1 mg: Each 8 mm, white, circular, scored tablet, marked 133 and with an Assyrian lion on the other side, contains: bumetanide 1 mg. Nonmedicinal ingredients: agar, colloidal anhydrous silica, lactose, magnesium stearate, maize starch, polysorbate 80, polyvidone and talc. Amber glass bottles of 100. Blister packs of 10 and 30.

2 mg: Each 9 mm, white, circular tablet, embossed with the number 155 on one face and an Assyrian lion on the reverse, contains: bumetanide 2 mg. Nonmedicinal ingredients: colloidal anhydrous silica, lactose, magnesium stearate, maize starch and microcrystalline cellulose. Amber glass bottles of 100. Blister packs of 10 and 30.

5 mg: Each 10 mm, white, circular, tablet, marked with a score line and 5 mg on one face, contains: bumetanide 5 mg. Nonmedicinal ingredients: agar, colloidal anhydrous silica, lactose, magnesium stearate, maize starch, polysorbate 80, polyvidone and talc. Amber glass bottles of 100. Blister packs of 10 and 30.

Store at room temperature protected from light.

(Shown in Product Recognition Section)

BURO-SOL®
TCD
Aluminum Acetate—Benzethonium Chloride
Antipruritic—Astringent

Supplied: Each 2.36 g powder packet dissolved in 450 mL water produces: a clear aluminum acetate solution 0.35% USP (1:15 Burow's Solution) with benzethonium chloride 0.023% stable for 90 days. Boxes of 10 and 100.

BURO-SOL® OTIC SOLUTION
TCD
Aluminum Acetate—Benzethonium Chloride
Antipruritic—Astringent

Supplied: Each bottle contains: aluminum acetate 0.5% and benzethonium chloride 0.03% in a dilute acetic acid solution. Plastic bottles with ear dropper of 15 and 60 mL.

BUSCOPAN®
Boehringer Ingelheim
Hyoscine Butylbromide
Antispasmodic

Pharmacology: Hyoscine is an antispasmodic agent which relaxes the smooth muscle of the gastrointestinal, biliary and urinary tracts. It is believed to act predominantly at the parasympathetic ganglia in the walls of the viscera of these organs. Structurally, hyoscine exists as a quaternary ammonium compound and as a single positively charged cation throughout the entire pH range.

Hyoscine undergoes rapid tissue absorption after oral administration. In the rat, it concentrates in the gastrointestinal tract, liver and kidney tissues.

The high tissue affinity of the substance is further reflected in the extremely short distribution half-life ($t_{1/2}\alpha$) in the plasma of approximately 2 to 3 minutes. Despite low systemic bioavailability, hyoscine remains available in high concentrations at the site of action. Plasma levels of radioactivity in man peak within 1 to 3 hours of enteral administration. Protein binding in the human plasma occurs at 8 to 13% and in a 4.4% human serum albumin solution at 3 to 11%. Hyoscine does not readily cross the blood brain barrier.

A high portion of the absorbed hyoscine (^{14}C) undergoes elimination in an unchanged form within the first few hours of administration in man and animals. Later in elimination, the metabolized portion predominates. In man, following the administration of i.v. ^{14}C-labeled substance, the elimination followed a 3-phase course: $t_{1/2}\alpha=3.5$ min., $t_{1/2}\beta=0.8$ hours; $t_{1/2}=14.0$ hours. Following oral administration, the terminal elimination half-life is 4.8 hours. Metabolites from rat urine detected in quantities ranging from 4 to 44% include 3 main metabolites (phenyl acetic acid-scopine ester-butochloride, 4-hydroxytropic acid-scopine ester-butochloride, scopine butobromide) and 4 minor metabolites (including AD 12 and Ba 790).

Indications: Tablets and Suppositories: For relief of smooth muscle spasm of the gastrointestinal and genitourinary systems.

Ampuls: For the relief of acute genitourinary or gastrointestinal spasm (e.g., renal or biliary colic), or to produce smooth muscle relaxation prior to radiological procedures such as pyelography or other diagnostic procedures where spasm may be a problem (e.g., gastroduodenal endoscopy).

Contraindications: Hypersensitivity to hyoscine or atropinics (see Warnings) or to any of the product excipients.

Hyoscine tablets and suppositories are contraindicated in patients with glaucoma or obstructive prostatic hypertrophy.

Parenteral administration is contraindicated in patients with glaucoma, prostatic hypertrophy with urinary retention, stenotic lesions of the gastrointestinal tract, tachycardia, angina, cardiac failure and megacolon.

Warnings: Therapy should be discontinued if the patient reports any unusual visual disturbances or pressure pain within the eye.

Patients intolerant of one belladonna alkaloid or derivative may also be intolerant of other belladonna alkaloids or derivatives such as hyoscine.

Precautions: General: Hyoscine should be used with caution in patients with prostatic enlargement. Hyoscine may precipitate or aggravate urinary retention in patients with the following conditions: nonobstructive prostatic hypertrophy, urinary retention (or the predisposition to) or obstructive uropathy such as a bladder neck obstruction due to prostatic hypertrophy (see Contraindications).

Occupational Hazards: The parenteral administration of hyoscine, particularly of higher doses, has been reported to cause transient disturbances of accommodation which recede spontaneously. Therefore, patients should be cautioned about potential visual problems and the need to exercise care while driving or operating machinery after receiving hyoscine ampuls.

As large doses of anticholinergics/systemic antispasmodics may cause an increase in heart rate, due care is necessary in patients with cardiac disease, especially cardiac arrhythmias, congestive heart failure, coronary artery disease and mitral stenosis. The increase in heart rate may also be undesirable in patients with unstable cardiovascular status in an acute hemorrhage situation.

Exercise caution in patients with reflux esophagitis or gastrointestinal tract obstructive disease (i.e., achalasia and pyloroduodenal stenosis) due to the ability of anticholinergics/systemic antispasmodics to decrease smooth muscle motility and tone resulting in gastric retention.

Anticholinergics may aggravate hiatal hernia associated with reflux esophagitis, myasthenia gravis or pyloric obstruction.

In patients with ulcerative colitis, large anticholinergic doses may suppress intestinal motility, possibly causing paralytic ileus or resulting in obstruction; also, use may precipitate or aggravate toxic megacolon.

The mydriatic effect of anticholinergics/systemic antispasmodics may result in increased intraocular pressure. In patients with angle-closure glaucoma or with this predisposition, anticholinergics/systemic antispasmodics may precipitate an acute angle-closure glaucoma attack (see Contraindications).

Geriatrics: Geriatric patients are especially susceptible to the anticholinergic side effects of constipation, dryness of mouth and urinary retention (especially in males). If these side effects continue or are severe, discontinuation of medication should be considered.

Due care is necessary when anticholinergics are administered to geriatric patients due to the danger of precipitating undiagnosed glaucoma.

Administration of anticholinergics/systemic antispasmodics to elderly patients with intestinal atony or in debilitated patients may result in obstruction.

Pregnancy: Safety during pregnancy has not yet been established. Limited preclinical data has not indicated a hazard; nevertheless, the usual precautions regarding the use of drugs during pregnancy, especially during the first trimester, should be observed.

Lactation: No specific studies have been conducted on the excretion of this drug in breast milk. The benefits of hyoscine use during lactation should therefore be weighed against possible effects on the infant.

Children: Hyoscine is not currently recommended for use in children.

Drug Interactions: As hyoscine can reduce the motility and secretory activity of the gastrointestinal system, the systemic absorption and pharmacologic effects of other oral medications may be delayed.

Tricyclic antidepressants, quinidine and amantadine can potentiate the anticholinergic effect of parenterally administered hyoscine.

Concurrent use with MAO inhibitors may result in intensified anticholinergic side effects of hyoscine. Also, concurrent use of MAO inhibitors may block detoxification of anticholinergics thus potentiating their action.

Concurrent use with anticholinergics may intensify anticholinergic effects.

Concurrent use with antacids or absorbent antidiarrheals may reduce the absorption of anticholinergics, resulting in decreased therapeutic effectiveness. Anticholinergics such as hyoscine should be given at least 1 hour before these medications.

The severity of potassium chloride induced gastrointestinal lesions may increase with concurrent anticholinergic therapy.

Adverse Effects: A slight increase in pulse rate may occur when hyoscine is administered i.v. In some cases hypersensitivity reactions, such as urticaria, angioedema and fixed drug eruptions have been described. Following parenteral administration very rare cases of shock reactions have been observed. Parenteral administration, especially of large doses, may occasionally cause a transient disturbance of accommodation which recedes spontaneously.

The following effects have been reported rarely for the tablets, suppositories and/or ampuls: Body as a Whole: anaphylactic shock, anaphylactoid reaction.

Heart Rate and Rhythm: tachycardia, pulse rate increased.

Autonomic Nervous System: hypotension.

Gastrointestinal: diarrhea, nausea.

Skin and Appendages: urticaria, rash, angioedema, fixed drug eruptions.

Vision: retinal pigmentation, accommodation abnormal, glaucoma.

Overdose: Symptoms: Single oral doses of up to 590 mg and quantities of active drug up to 1 090 mg within 5 hours have produced dry mouth, tachycardia, slight drowsiness and transient visual disorders. Other symptoms which occurred in animals and which may be encountered in humans include: shock, Cheyne-Stokes respiration, respiratory paralysis, clonic spasms, paresis of the striated muscle, coma, paralytic ileus and cystoparalysis.

Treatment: In the case of an oral overdose, perform gastric lavage with activated charcoal followed by magnesium sulfate (15%). Hyoscine overdose symptoms respond to parasympathomimetics.

For patients with glaucoma, administer pilocarpine locally.

Other overdosage symptoms should be treated with standard supportive therapy.

Dosage: Individual response to hyoscine may vary and doses should be adjusted accordingly.

Usual Adult Dose: Tablets: 1 to 2 tablets/day up to a maximum of 6 tablets/day. In prolonged illness which requires repeated dosing, 1 tablet 3 to 5 times a day is recommended. Tablets should be swallowed whole with a glass of water.

Ampuls: ½ (10 mg/0.5 mL) to 1 ampul (20 mg/1 mL) administered parenterally by i.m., s.c. or i.v. routes, at an injection rate of 1 mL/min. No dilution of the ampul is necessary prior to administration. The maximum dose should not exceed 100 mg/day (5 ampuls).

The rapid action of injected hyoscine is advantageous in acutely ill patients and in those situations where prompt spasmolytic activity facilitates diagnostic procedures such as radiological examinations. Hyoscine ampuls may also be used i.m. 10 to 15 minutes before radiological examinations of the stomach to slow peristaltic movements.

Suppositories: Unwrap and insert into the rectum 1 to 2 suppositories/day, up to a maximum of 6 suppositories/day.

Note: Suppositories should only be unwrapped from the foil **immediately** before rectal insertion.

Dilution and Stability of Parenteral Hyoscine: Although dilution prior to administration is not required, the solution is compatible with the following solutions, should dilution be desirable: Ringers Solution, Ringers Lactate, NaCl 0.9%, Levulose 5%, Glucose 10%.

Solutions must be mixed under sterile conditions and are stable for 8 hours.

Supplied: Ampuls: Each mL contains: hyoscine butylbromide 20 mg. Nonmedicinal ingredients: sodium chloride and water for injection. Sodium: <1 mmol (<10 mg)/dose. Ampuls of 1 mL. Packages of 10.

Suppositories: Each suppository contains: hyoscine butylbromide 10 mg. Nonmedicinal ingredients: purified water and Witepsol W45. Foil wrapped, in strips of 6.

Tablets: Each round, white, sugar coated tablet contains: hyoscine butylbromide 10 mg. Nonmedicinal ingredients: acacia, carnauba wax, castor oil, lactose, magnesium stearate, maize starch, polyethylene glycol, shellac, sucrose, talc, tartaric acid, titanium dioxide, and white wax. Energy: 1.64 kJ (0.39 kcal). Bottles of 100 and 500.

Protect from heat and light. Ampuls and suppositories should be protected from freezing. Store at room temperature.

BUSPAR® ℞
Bristol
Buspirone HCl
Anxiolytic

Pharmacology: Buspirone is a psychotropic drug with selective anxiolytic properties which belongs chemically to the class of compounds known as the azaspirodecanediones, not chemically or pharmacologically related to benzodiazepines.

Buspirone shares some of the properties of the benzodiazepines and the neuroleptics, as well as demonstrating other pharmacological action. Buspirone attenuates punishment suppressed behavior in animals and exerts a taming effect, but is devoid of anticonvulsant and muscle relaxant properties

BusPar (cont'd)

and does not bind to the benzodiazepine/GABA receptor complex. Buspirone affects a variety of dopamine mediated biochemical and behavioral events, but is free of cataleptic activity. Buspirone has an affinity for brain D_2-dopamine receptors, where it acts as an antagonist and agonist, and for the 5-HT_{1A} receptors, where it acts as an agonist. Buspirone does not block the neuronal reuptake of monoamines and, on chronic administration, it does not lead to changes in receptor density in the models investigated. However, the mechanism of action of buspirone remains to be fully elucidated.

Buspirone is rapidly absorbed in man and undergoes extensive first pass metabolism. Following oral administration, low peak plasma levels of unchanged drug, of 1 to 6 ng/mL were observed 40 to 90 minutes after a single 20 mg dose. In a number of studies performed in healthy volunteers, the mean half-life of buspirone ranged from 2 to 3 hours up to approximately 11 hours with considerable variation in individual values. Multiple dose studies suggest that steady-state plasma levels were usually achieved within a few days. Buspirone is metabolized primarily by oxidation, producing several hydroxylated derivatives and a pharmacologically active metabolite, 1-pyrimidinylpiperazine (1-PP). In animal models predictive of anxiolytic potential, 1-PP has about 25% or less of the activity of buspirone. Peak plasma levels of 1-PP have been found to be higher than those of its parent drug and its half-life to be approximately double that of unchanged buspirone. In a single dose study using ^{14}C labeled buspirone, 29 to 63% of the dose was excreted in the urine within 24 hours, primarily as metabolites, while fecal excretion accounted for 18 to 38% of the dose. In man, approximately 95% of buspirone is plasma protein bound. Other highly bound drugs, e.g., phenytoin, propranolol and warfarin, are not displaced by buspirone from plasma protein binding in vitro at clinically relevant concentrations. However, in vitro binding studies show that buspirone does displace digoxin.

The effects of food upon the bioavailability of buspirone have been studied in 8 subjects. The results of this study suggest that food does not significantly affect the absorption of buspirone, but it does decrease first-pass metabolism. This results in increased bioavailability of unchanged buspirone; the clinical significance of this finding is unknown.

Buspirone had no effect on hepatic microsomal enzyme activity when administered to rats for 5 days. In man, the effect of buspirone on drug metabolism or concomitant drug disposition has not been studied. Buspirone clearance is reduced in patients with hepatic impairment as well as in patients with impaired renal function. No significant difference in buspirone pharmacokinetics as a function of age and/or sex were found.

Indications: For the short-term symptomatic relief of excessive anxiety in patients with generalized anxiety disorder.

The effectiveness of buspirone in long-term use (e.g., more than 4 weeks) has not been evaluated in controlled clinical trials.

Eight 3-way short-term, controlled clinical trials involving buspirone, diazepam and placebo are considered central to the evaluation of buspirone as an anxiolytic agent. In 4 of the 8 clinical trials, buspirone demonstrated a significant difference from placebo. In the other 4 trials, there was no significant difference between buspirone and placebo, but a significantly greater improvement was observed with diazepam than with placebo. The adverse effect profiles of buspirone and diazepam in these clinical trials were, however, different.

Contraindications: In patients hypersensitive to buspirone or any of the inactive ingredients.

Buspirone is contraindicated in patients with severe hepatic or severe renal impairment.

Warnings: MAO Inhibitors: The occurrence of elevated blood pressure in patients receiving both buspirone and a MAO inhibitor has been reported. Therefore, it is recommended that buspirone should not be used concomitantly with a MAO inhibitor.

Extrapyramidal Symptoms: Since buspirone can bind to central dopaminergic receptors, the possibility of acute and chronic changes in dopamine mediated neurological function (e.g., dystonia, pseudo-parkinsonism, akathisia and tardive dyskinesia) should be considered (see Precautions).

Convulsive Disorders: Buspirone is not recommended for patients with a history of seizure disorders.

Use of Buspirone in Patients Previously Treated with a Benzodiazepine: Because buspirone does not exhibit cross-tolerance with benzodiazepines and other common sedative/hypnotic drugs, it will not block the withdrawal syndrome often seen with cessation of therapy with these drugs. Therefore, it is advisable to withdraw these drugs gradually, especially in patients who have been using a CNS-depressant drug chronically.

Patients who have previously taken benzodiazepines may be less likely to respond to buspirone than those who have not. In 2 clinical studies to date, substitution of buspirone did not ameliorate or prevent withdrawal symptoms in either abrupt or gradual withdrawal from various benzodiazepines following long-term use. Therefore, if it is considered desirable to switch a patient who has been receiving benzodiazepine therapy to buspirone, the benzodiazepine should first be withdrawn gradually. A drug-free interval is desirable between withdrawal of the benzodiazepine and initiation of buspirone, in order to increase the likelihood of distinguishing between benzodiazepine withdrawal effects and unrelieved anxiety due to possible failure of buspirone in this category of patients. In patients requiring continued therapy and where a benzodiazepine washout period is not feasible, gradual benzodiazepine taper/withdrawal may be overlapped by buspirone therapy over a few weeks. Buspirone should not, however, be used to detoxify patients addicted to benzodiazepines.

Benzodiazepine rebound or withdrawal symptoms may occur over varying time periods depending in part on the type of drug and its effective half-life of elimination. These symptoms may appear as any combination of irritability, anxiety, agitation, insomnia, tremor, abdominal cramps, muscle cramps, vomiting, sweating, flu-like symptoms without fever and, occasionally, seizures, and should be treated symptomatically.

Pregnancy and *Lactation:* The safety of buspirone during pregnancy and lactation has not been established and, therefore, it should not be used in women of childbearing potential or nursing mothers, unless, in the opinion of the physician, the potential benefits to the patient outweigh the possible hazards to the fetus. Buspirone and its metabolites are excreted in milk in rats. The extent of excretion in human milk has not yet been determined.

Labor and Delivery: The effect of buspirone on labor is unknown.

Precautions: Effects on Cognitive and Motor Performance: In controlled studies in healthy volunteers, single doses of buspirone up to 20 mg had little effect on most tests of cognitive and psychomotor function, although performance on a vigilance task was impaired in a dose-related manner. The effect of higher single doses of buspirone on psychomotor performance has not been investigated.

Ten mg of buspirone given 3 times daily for 7 days to healthy volunteers produced considerable subjective sedation but no significant effect on psychomotor performance (no vigilance tasks were used in this study). It also caused transient dizziness, especially on standing and walking.

Occupational Hazards: Until further experience is obtained with buspirone, patients should be warned not to operate an automobile or undertake activities requiring mental alertness, judgment and physical coordination, until they are reasonably certain that buspirone does not affect them adversely.

Significant Interactions: In laboratory studies in healthy volunteers, buspirone in doses up to 20 mg did not potentiate the psychomotor impairment produced by relatively modest doses of alcohol. However, decreased contentedness or dysphoria was observed with a combination of alcohol and a 20 mg single dose of buspirone. Since no data are available on concomitant use of higher doses of buspirone and alcohol, it is prudent to advise patients to avoid alcohol during buspirone therapy.

Food increased the bioavailability of unchanged buspirone in healthy subjects, possibly due to a reduced first-pass effect.

Concomitant use of MAO inhibitors and buspirone has been reported to cause an increase in blood pressure. Therefore, concomitant use of these medications is not recommended.

In a study in normal volunteers, no interaction of buspirone with amitriptyline was seen. A similar study with buspirone and diazepam showed an increase in the levels of nordiazepam.

In another study in normal volunteers, concomitant administration of buspirone and haloperidol resulted in increased serum haloperidol concentrations. The clinical significance of this finding is not clear.

There is 1 report suggesting that the concomitant use of trazodone and buspirone may have caused 3- to 6-fold elevations in ALT in a few patients. In a similar study, attempting to replicate this finding, no interactive effect on hepatic transaminases was identified.

The concomitant use of buspirone with other CNS active drugs should be approached with caution.

In vitro, buspirone does not displace from serum protein drugs like phenytoin, propranolol and warfarin that are highly protein-bound. However, there has been 1 report of prolonged prothrombin time when buspirone was added to the regimen of a patient treated with warfarin. The patient was also chronically receiving phenytoin, phenobarbital, digoxin and Synthroid. In vitro, buspirone may displace less firmly protein-bound drugs like digoxin. The clinical significance of this property is unknown.

Overall, there have been no major safety problems reported with the combination of buspirone and selective serotonin reuptake inhibitor antidepressants. Seizures have been reported rarely in patients taking this combination.

There have been no reports to date of interference of buspirone with commonly employed clinical laboratory tests.

Drug Abuse and Dependence: Preliminary animal and human investigations suggest that buspirone may be significantly devoid of potential for producing physical or psychological dependence, only extensive clinical experience with the drug will provide conclusive evidence. Meanwhile, physicians should carefully evaluate patients for a history of drug abuse and follow such patients closely, observing them for signs of buspirone misuse and abuse.

Patients with Impaired Hepatic or Renal Function: Since it is metabolized by the liver and excreted by the kidneys, buspirone should be used with caution in patients with a history of hepatic or renal impairment. It is contraindicated in patients with severe hepatic or renal impairment.

Children: The safety and effectiveness of buspirone in individuals below the age of 18 years have not been established.

Geriatrics: Buspirone has not been systematically evaluated in older patients. Although it would appear from limited pharmacokinetic and clinical studies that buspirone does not behave differently in the elderly, there is little known about the effects of buspirone in this age group at doses above 30 mg/day. Therefore, it is recommended that buspirone should be used in the elderly at doses not exceeding 30 mg/day for a duration not exceeding 4 weeks.

Neuroendocrine Effects: Single doses of 30 mg or higher of buspirone resulted in significantly elevated plasma prolactin and growth hormone concentrations in normal volunteers. No effect was seen at lower doses. In another study, no such increases were observed after buspirone was administered in divided doses (10 mg t.i.d.) for 28 days.

Long-term Toxicity: Buspirone can bind to central serotonin and dopamine receptors. A question has been raised about its potential to cause acute and chronic changes in dopamine mediated neurological function (e.g., dystonia, pseudoparkinsonism, akathisia, and tardive dyskinesia). Clinical experience in controlled trials has failed to identify any significant neuroleptic-like activity; however, a syndrome of restlessness, appearing shortly after initiation of treatment, has been reported in some small fraction of buspirone treated patients. The syndrome may be explained in several ways. For example, buspirone may increase central noradrenergic activity; alternatively, the effect may be attributable to dopaminergic effects (i.e., represent akathisia). Obviously, the question cannot be totally resolved at this point in time. Because its mechanism of action is not fully elucidated, long-term toxicity in the CNS or other organ systems cannot be predicted.

Adverse Effects: Commonly Observed: Side effects of buspirone, if they occur, are generally observed at the beginning of drug therapy and usually subside with use of the medication and/or decreased dosage.

When patients receiving buspirone were compared with patients receiving placebo, dizziness, headache, nervousness, lightheadedness, nausea, excitement, and sweating/clamminess were the only side effects occurring with significantly greater frequency ($p < 0.10$) in the buspirone group than in the placebo group.

Associated with discontinuation of treatment: During controlled clinical efficacy trials, approximately 10% of 2 200 anxious patients discontinued treatment due to an adverse event. The more common events associated with discontinuation included: CNS disturbances (3.4%), primarily dizziness, insomnia, nervousness, drowsiness and light-headed feeling; gastrointestinal disturbances (1.2%), primarily nausea; and miscellaneous disturbances (1.1%), primarily headache and fatigue.

Incidence in clinical trials: Adverse reactions reported in approximately 3 000 subjects who participated in premarketing trials are listed below by body system. Frequent adverse events are defined as those occurring in at least 1/100 patients. Infrequent adverse events are those occurring in less than 1/100 but at least 1/1 000 patients, while rare events are those occurring in less than 1/1 000 patients. In the absence of appropriate controls in some of the studies, a causal relationship to buspirone cannot be determined.

CNS: Frequent: dizziness, headache, drowsiness, lightheadedness, insomnia, fatigue, nervousness, decreased concentration, abnormal thinking, excitement, depression, confusion, nightmares/vivid dreams, anger/hostility. Infrequent: depersonalization, noise intolerance, euphoria/feeling high, dissociative reaction, fear, loss of interest, dysphoria, hallucinations, seizures, suicidal thoughts. Rare: slurred speech, claustrophobia, cold intolerance, stupor, psychosis.
Neurologic: Frequent: paresthesia, weakness, incoordination, tremor, numbness. Infrequent: muscle cramps and spasms, rigid/stiff muscles, involuntary movements, akathisia, slowed reaction time. Rare: tingling of limbs, stiff neck, rigidity of jaw.
Autonomic: Frequent: dry mouth, sweating/clamminess, blurred vision, constipation. Infrequent: urinary frequency, retention and burning, flushing.
Cardiovascular: Frequent: tachycardia/palpitations, chest pain. Infrequent: syncope, hypotension, hypertension. Rare: congestive heart failure, cerebrovascular accident, myocardial infarction, cardiomyopathy, bradycardia, ECG change.
Gastrointestinal: Frequent: nausea, gastrointestinal distress, diarrhea, vomiting. Infrequent: flatulence, increased appetite, anorexia, hypersalivation, rectal bleeding, irritable colon. Rare: burning tongue.
Respiratory: Frequent: nasal congestion. Infrequent: shortness of breath, chest congestion, hyperventilation. Rare: epistaxis.
Endocrine: Infrequent: decreased and increased libido, weight gain, weight loss, menstrual irregularity/breakthrough bleeding. Rare: delayed ejaculation, impotence, galactorrhea, amenorrhea, thyroid abnormality.
Allergic or Toxic: Frequent: skin rash, sore throat. Infrequent: edema/facial edema, pruritus, chills/fever. Rare: photophobia, erythema, flu-like symptoms.
Clinical Laboratory: Infrequent: increases in liver enzymes. Rare: eosinophilia, leukopenia, thrombocytopenia.
Miscellaneous: Frequent: tinnitus, muscle aches/pains, headache. Infrequent: redness/itching of eyes, altered taste/smell, roaring sensation in head, malaise, easy bruising, dry skin, arthralgia, blisters, hair loss. Rare: acne, thinning of nails, sore eyes, inner ear abnormality, pressure on eyes, nocturia, enuresis, hiccups, voice loss, alcohol abuse.
Postmarketing Experience: Although treatment conditions and duration vary greatly, and a causal relationship of adverse events to buspirone cannot always be determined, spontaneous adverse event reports have included rare occurrences (less than 1/10 000) of the following adverse events:
Body as a Whole: allergic reactions including urticaria, ecchymosis.
CNS/Neurological: extrapyramidal symptoms, including dyskinesias (acute and delayed), dystonic reactions and cogwheel rigidity; depersonalization; emotional lability; hallucinations; psychosis, ataxias, and seizures.
Miscellaneous: syncope; tunnel vision; urinary retention; and female galactorrhea.

Overdose: Symptoms: In clinical pharmacology trials, buspirone up to 400 mg/day was administered to healthy male volunteers. As this dose was approached, the following symptoms were observed in descending order of frequency: drowsiness, ataxia, nausea and vomiting, dizziness, clammy feeling, difficulty thinking, feeling high, rushing sensation, gastric distress, headache, itching, miosis, hypotension, tremor, incoordination, insomnia and hallucinations. In a dose-ranging study in acute psychotic patients, up to 2 400 mg/day was administered. Dizziness, nausea and vomiting were the most common adverse effects. One patient developed extrapyramidal symptoms at 600 mg/day.

Treatment: There is no specific antidote for buspirone. Management should, therefore, be symptomatic and supportive. Any patient suspected of having taken an overdose should be admitted to a hospital as soon as possible, and the stomach emptied by gastric lavage. Respiration, pulse and blood pressure should be monitored, as in all cases of drug overdosage. As with the management of intentional overdosage with any drug, the ingestion of multiple agents should be suspected. In 6 anuric patients, hemodialysis either had no effect on the pharmacokinetics of buspirone or decreased its clearance. The metabolite is partially removed by hemodialysis.

Dosage: Dosage should be individually adjusted, according to tolerance and response.

The recommended initial dose is 5 mg 2 to 3 times daily. This may be titrated according to the needs of the patient and the daily dose increased by 5 mg increments every 2 to 3 days up to a maximum of 45 mg daily in divided doses. The usual therapeutic dose is 20 to 30 mg daily in 2 or 3 divided doses.
Geriatrics: Limited pharmacokinetic and clinical data have shown no difference in the effects of buspirone between elderly patients and healthy adult volunteers. However, until more information has accumulated in the elderly, it is recommended that the maximum daily dose should not exceed 30 mg for a duration not exceeding 4 weeks.
Note: If buspirone is administered to patients with compromised hepatic or renal function, careful monitoring will be required together with appropriate dosage adjustment.

Supplied: Each white, biconvex, rectangular, pillow-shaped tablet with BusPar raised on one side and BL logo, bisect score and 10 on the other side, contains: buspirone HCl 10 mg. Nonmedicinal ingredients: lactose anhydrous, magnesium stearate, microcrystalline cellulose, silicon dioxide and sodium carboxymethyl starch. Bottles of 100. Store at controlled room temperature (15 to 30°C). Protect from light.

(Shown in Product Recognition Section)

Reviewed 1999

BUSPIREX ℞

Technilab

Buspirone HCl

Anxiolytic

Supplied: Each white, biconvex, oval tablet, with rectangular edges with TEC 90 engraved on one side and bisect score on the other side, contains: buspirone HCl 10 mg. Nonmedicinal ingredients: lactose, magnesium stearate, microcrystalline cellulose, silica and sodium croscarmellose. Bottles of 100. Store at controlled room temperature (15 to 30°C). Protect from light.

New Product 1998

BUSTAB® ℞

ICN

Buspirone HCl

Anxiolytic

Supplied: 5 mg: Each white, round, compressed tablet, scored on one side and marked "ICN B21" on the other, contains: buspirone HCl 5 mg, USP. Nonmedicinal ingredients: colloidal silicon dioxide, lactose, magnesium stearate, microcrystalline cellulose and sodium starch glycolate. Bottles of 100 and 500.

10 mg: Each white, round, compressed tablet, scored on one side and marked "ICN B22" on the other, contains: buspirone HCl 10 mg, USP. Nonmedicinal ingredients: colloidal silicon dioxide, lactose, magnesium stearate, microcrystalline cellulose and sodium starch glycolate. Bottles of 100 and 500.

New Product 1998

BUTABARBITAL ◈

General Monograph, CPhA

see BARBITURATES

BUTISOL® SODIUM ◈

Carter Horner

Butabarbital Sodium

Sedative—Hypnotic

Indications: A daytime sedative when mild sedation is required for relief of symptoms of anxiety or tension resulting from emotional, physical, or situational stress. May be used in such conditions as: neuroses and anxiety-tension states, functional gastrointestinal disorders, peptic ulcer, menopausal syndrome, premenstrual tension, hyperthyroidism, essential hypertension, coronary artery disease, congestive heart failure, preoperative apprehension and insomnia.

Contraindications: Barbiturate idiosyncrasy, patients with porphyria.

Precautions: Use with caution in patients with moderate to severe hepatic disease. Discontinue if urticaria, itching, or redness occurs.
Occupational Hazards: Barbiturates may impair the mental and/or physical abilities required for the performance of potentially hazardous tasks such as driving a vehicle or operating machinery. The concomitant use of alcohol or other CNS depressants may have an additive effect. Warn patients accordingly.

Barbiturates induce liver microsomal enzyme activity. This accelerates the biotransformation of various drugs and is probably part of the mechanism of the tolerance which is seen with barbiturates. Butabarbital may decrease the potency of coumarin anticoagulants so that patients receiving such concomitant therapy should have more frequent prothrombin determinations.

Prolonged use of barbiturates, even in therapeutic dosages, may result in psychic dependence. Withdrawal symptoms may occur after chronic use of large doses, resulting in delirium, convulsions, or death.

A reduced efficacy and increase in incidence of breakthrough bleeding have been reported in oral contraceptive users treated concomitantly with barbiturates.

Adverse Effects: Drowsiness at daytime sedative dose levels, skin rashes, hangover, and systemic disturbances may rarely occur. Elderly or debilitated patients may react to barbiturates with marked excitement or depression.

Overdose: In humans, the lethal dose is quite variable but is in the range of 100 mg/kg. There have been cases of survival following ingestion of as much as 10 g. The lethal dose may be lowered considerably in the presence of hepatic, renal or severe debilitating disease.

In children, the lethal dose will vary with the age, weight and physical condition. A 10-month-old child recovered after ingesting 270 mg and a 3-year-old child recovered after ingesting 540 mg.

The picture may be confused by prior consumption of alcohol or by the patient's possession of other CNS depressant drugs. Accurate differentiation depends upon identification of the compound in the blood or urine.

Symptoms: Moderate overdosage may resemble alcoholic inebriation. In more severe intoxication, the patient is comatose but the deep reflexes may be present. The pupils may be constricted and react to light, but late in the course show paralytic dilation. Respirations are usually depressed or Cheyne-Stokes respirations may be present. The blood pressure may fall and the patient may be in shock due to depression of the medullary vasomotor centres and to the peripheral effects on the myocardium and vascular smooth muscle. Complications of intoxication are pulmonary atelectasis, pulmonary edema or bronchopneumonia, and renal failure. Symptoms of butabarbital intoxication may be exaggerated in patients with liver disease since the drug is probably detoxified in the liver.

Chronic overdosage may lead to habituation and chronic poisoning. The symptoms include weakness, vertigo and malaise. Fever may occur. The mental functions are impaired, memory is defective and there may be delirium with visual hallucinations.

Treatment: Gastric lavage should be carried out or emesis induced if the patient is seen within 2 to 3 hours after ingestion of the drug. Pulmonary aspiration of gastric contents is a potential hazard. This may be reduced by inserting a cuffed endotracheal tube prior to gastric lavage. Maintain a patent airway through the use of an oropharyngeal airway or endotracheal tube. Tracheotomy should be performed if intubation is required for more than 24 hours. Artificial respiration or a mechanical respirator may be useful for respiratory depression. Analeptic drugs should not be used. The patient should receive oxygen and should be turned from side to side every 4 hours. If atelectasis develops, it should be treated by tracheobronchial suction or bronchoscopy. Shock may be counteracted by use of plasma, dextran, concentrated albumin, or vasopressor drugs such as dopamine, if necessary. If renal function is satisfactory, excretion of the drug may be hastened by forced diuresis and alkalinization of the urine with i.v. administration of sodium bicarbonate or lactate together with osmotic diuretics such as mannitol and urea. If renal failure occurs or if the patient does not respond to the above measures, carry out extracorporeal hemodialysis or peritoneal dialysis.

Dosage: Adults: As a daytime sedative, 15 to 30 mg 3 or 4 times daily. As a hypnotic, 50 to 100 mg daily. Children: As a daytime sedative, dose range is 7.5 to 30 mg depending upon age, weight, and the degree of sedation required.

Supplied: 15 mg: Each lavender, top bisected, round, uncoated tablet with convex top and bottom surfaces contains: butabarbital sodium 15 mg. Nonmedicinal ingredients: calcium phosphate, calcium stearate, cornstarch, FD&C Blue No. 1 and Red No. 3. Energy: 0.4 kJ (0.1 kcal). Sodium: <1 mmol (1.5 mg). Gluten-, lactose- and tartrazine-free. Bottles of 100.

30 mg: Each green, top bisected, round, uncoated tablet with convex top and bottom surfaces, contains: butabarbital ▶

Butisol Sodium (cont'd)

sodium 30 mg. Nonmedicinal ingredients: calcium phosphate, calcium stearate, cornstarch, FD&C Blue No. 1 and Yellow No. 5 (tartrazine). Energy: 0.4 kJ (0.1 kcal). Sodium: <1 mmol (3 mg). Gluten- and lactose-free. Bottles of 100.

100 mg: Each pink, top bisected, round, uncoated tablet with convex top and bottom surfaces, contains: butabarbital sodium 100 mg. Nonmedicinal ingredients: calcium phosphate, calcium stearate, cornstarch, FD&C Red No. 2 and Red No. 3. Energy: 1.7 kJ (0.4 kcal). Sodium: <1 mmol (10 mg). Gluten-, lactose- and tartrazine-free. Bottles of 100.

(Shown in Product Recognition Section)

BUTORPHANOL ®

General Monograph, CPhA

see OPIOID ANALGESICS

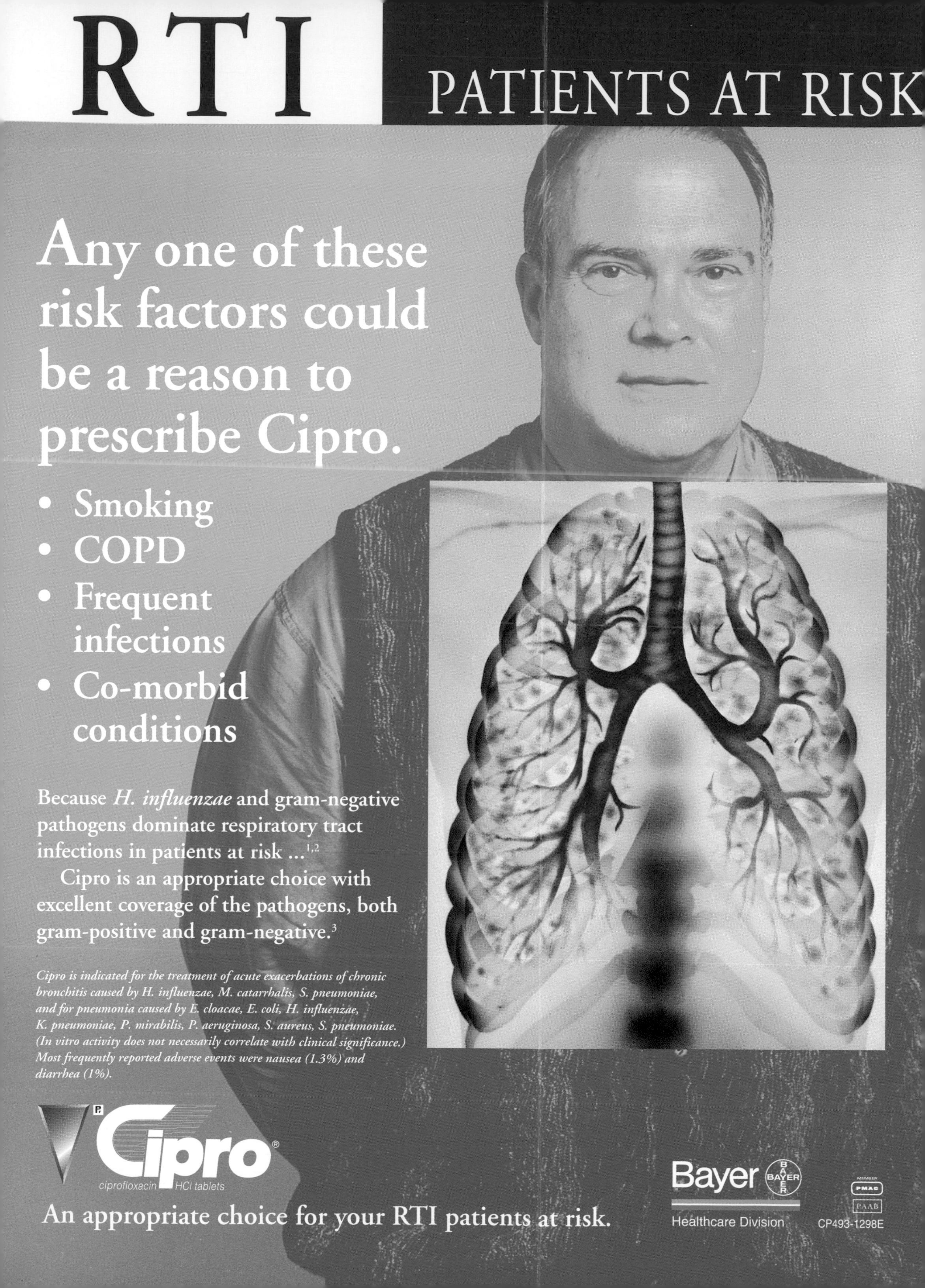
RTI
PATIENTS AT RISK
Any one of these risk factors could be a reason to prescribe Cipro.
• Smoking
• COPD
• Frequent infections
• Co-morbid conditions
Because *H. influenzae* and gram-negative pathogens dominate respiratory tract infections in patients at risk ...[1,2]
Cipro is an appropriate choice with excellent coverage of the pathogens, both gram-positive and gram-negative.[3]
Cipro is indicated for the treatment of acute exacerbations of chronic bronchitis caused by H. influenzae, M. catarrhalis, S. pneumoniae, and for pneumonia caused by E. cloacae, E. coli, H. influenzae, K. pneumoniae, P. mirabilis, P. aeruginosa, S. aureus, S. pneumoniae. (In vitro activity does not necessarily correlate with clinical significance.) Most frequently reported adverse events were nausea (1.3%) and diarrhea (1%).
Cipro®
ciprofloxacin HCl tablets
An appropriate choice for your RTI patients at risk.
Bayer
BAYER
Healthcare Division
MEMBER PMAC
PAAB
CP493-1298E

Memory loss is often the beginning of functional decline in patients with Alzheimer's disease.[1] Now you can bring light back into the lives of your Alzheimer's patients and their families with new once-a-day ARICEPT – a cholinesterase inhibitor for the symptomatic treatment of mild to moderate Alzheimer's disease.†

Enhances cognition: ***80% of patients on ARICEPT improved or did not deteriorate (vs 58% on placebo)***

- In a 30-week study, patients showed significant cognitive improvement vs placebo, including memory, reasoning, orientation, and language[2] (ADAS-cog, $p \leq 0.0001$)

Improves patient function

- In a 30-week study, clinician's global assessment with caregiver input demonstrated significant improvement vs placebo in patient function across these major areas: general function, cognition, behaviour, and activities of daily living[2] (CIBIC plus, $p \leq 0.0001$)

† ARICEPT has not been studied in patients with moderately severe or severe Alzheimer's disease. ARICEPT has not been studied in controlled clinical trials for longer than 6 months.

‡ It is recommended that patients with renal or hepatic disease be monitored for adverse effects. Caution is also advised when using ARICEPT in low body-weight elderly patients, especially in those ≥ 85 years old.

§ When used as recommended. For patients not responding after 4-6 weeks of therapy at 5 mg/day, a 10 mg once-daily dose may be considered.

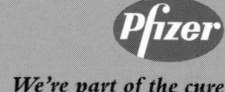

Quiet Power

Excellent Tolerability To Help Enhance Patient Compliance

Efficacy – Smooth, Effective 24-Hour Blood Pressure Control

Pr COZAAR® losartan potassium

Pr HYZAAR® losartan potassium and hydrochlorothiazide

Targeted A II* Receptor Blockade – Excellent Tolerability†

COZAAR® is indicated for the treatment of essential hypertension when beta blockers and diuretics are unsuitable.
HYZAAR® is indicated for the treatment of essential hypertension in patients for whom combination therapy is appropriate. HYZAAR® is not indicated for initial therapy.
HYZAAR® is not recommended for patients with severe renal impairment (creatinine clearance ≤ 30 mL/min).

* Angiotensin II

† In controlled clinical trials, dizziness was the only adverse experience, occurring in more than 1% of cases, that was reported as drug-related, and that occurred at a greater incidence in losartan-treated (2.4%) than placebo-treated (1.3%) patients and in losartan potassium-hydrochlorothiazide-treated (3.3%) than placebo-treated (2.1%) patients.

NOT RECOMMENDED DURING PREGNANCY.

BEFORE PRESCRIBING, PLEASE CONSULT THE APPROPRIATE ENCLOSED PRESCRIBING INFORMATION.

MERCK FROSST

MERCK SHARP & DOHME CANADA
DIV. OF MERCK FROSST CANADA INC.
KIRKLAND, QUEBEC

PAAB

CZR-98-CDN-4248-JA

C

CAFERGOT® ℞

Novartis Pharmaceuticals

Ergotamine Tartrate—Caffeine

Migraine Therapy

Pharmacology: Ergotamine is an alpha adrenergic blocking agent with a direct stimulating effect on the smooth muscle of peripheral and cranial blood vessels; it produces depression of the central vasomotor centers. Its properties also include serotonin antagonism. In comparison to dihydrogenated ergotamine, the adrenergic blocking actions of ergotamine tartrate are less pronounced and vasoconstrictive actions are greater. The addition of caffeine to ergotamine tartrate facilitates the absorption of ergotamine when administered orally or rectally, resulting in a more rapid onset of the vasoconstrictive effect and an increase in effectiveness. The migraine attack will be aborted in over 80% of the patients as long as the medication is taken early enough in the course of the attack.

Ergotamine is rapidly and incompletely (approximately 62% of the oral dose) absorbed by the gastrointestinal tract. Peak plasma levels are reached about 2 hours after ingestion. Ergotamine is extensively metabolized in the liver. The bioavailability of unchanged drug is about 2% when the drug is administered orally and 5% when it is administered by the rectal route. It has been suggested that the therapeutic effects of the drug are partially due to active metabolites. Protein binding amounts to 98%. Parent drug and metabolites are mainly excreted with the bile. Their elimination from plasma is biphasic with a half-life of 2.7 hours and 21 hours, respectively.

Caffeine is rapidly and almost completely absorbed; it is to a large extent metabolized. The metabolites are mainly excreted in the urine. Plasma elimination half-life is about 3.5 hours, protein binding 35%.

Indications: In acute attacks of migraine with or without aura.

The suppositories are available for the treatment of patients who have nausea and vomiting early in the attack and cannot retain or absorb anything taken orally. They have a faster onset of action due to by-pass of portal circulation.

Contraindications: Peripheral vascular disorders; obliterative vascular disease; coronary heart disease; severe hypertension and pregnancy, because of the vasoconstrictor action of ergotamine; hepatic insufficiency and septic conditions due to impaired inactivation of ergotamine; renal insufficiency; known hypersensitivity to ergot alkaloids or any other components of the formulation.

Lactation: Ergotamine is excreted in breast milk and may cause symptoms of vomiting, diarrhea, weak pulse and unstable blood pressure in infants. Thus, Cafergot is contraindicated in nursing mothers.

Precautions: Although signs and symptoms of ergotism rarely develop even after long-term intermittent use of the orally or rectally administered drugs, care should be exercised to remain within the limits of recommended dosage. Excessive or prolonged dosage is not recommended. Such symptoms as tingling in the fingers or toes should be reported to the physician immediately and the drug should be discontinued at once.

Cafergot is not recommended for the prophylaxis of migraine.

Like all drugs, Cafergot should be kept out of the reach of children.

The occurrence of drug-induced headaches has been reported during prolonged and uninterrupted treatment with Cafergot.

Rare cases of a solitary rectal or anal ulcer have occurred from abuse of ergotamine-containing suppositories, usually at higher than recommended doses or with continual use at the recommended dose for many years.

Drug Interactions: There is some evidence that the concomitant use of macrolide antibiotics such as troleandomycin, erythromycin or josamycin, and Cafergot can result in an elevated concentration of ergotamine in the plasma, thereby causing untoward peripheral vasoconstriction.

Among patients treated concomitantly with ergotamine-containing preparations and propranolol a few cases of vasospastic reactions have been reported. Concurrent use of vasoconstrictor agents including ergotamine, sumatriptan and nicotine may enhance the risk of vasoconstriction.

Adverse Effects: Non-migraine-related nausea and vomiting are the most commonly observed adverse events.

Paresthesia, pain and weakness in the extremities or peripheral vasoconstriction may occur in susceptible patients or following prolonged treatment, which is unadvisable. If ergotamine containing drugs are used excessively over years, they may induce fibrotic changes, in particular of the pleura and the retroperitoneum. There have also been rare reports of fibrotic changes of the cardiac valves.

Owing to its vasoconstrictor properties ergotamine may cause precordial pain, myocardial ischemia or, in rare cases, infarction, even in patients with no known history of coronary heart disease.

Overdose: Symptoms: In humans, the minimum lethal dose of ergotamine ranges from 15 to 20 mg. The following cases of ergotamine overdosage are cited to provide broad guidelines only:

An overdosage of 44 mg ergotamine taken by an adult female, presumably all absorbed, was followed by recovery on supportive therapy only.

A 14-month-old child died following the ingestion of 12 mg ergotamine. Although vomiting was induced shortly after ingestion, the child was not exposed to expert treatment for some 13 hours after ingestion.

Ergotamine poisoning results in nausea, vomiting, diarrhea, thirst, tingling and paresthesias of the extremities, muscle pain, cold and pale skin, itching, a rapid and weak pulse, bradycardia or tachycardia, pain suggestive of angina, rise and/or fall of blood pressure (usually in that order), mental confusion, dizziness, headache, depression, drowsiness and possible unconsciousness. The most prominent effects of ergotism are circulatory changes. CNS changes can rarely include convulsions and hemiplegia. Respiratory depression can occur.

Treatment: In the case of orally ingested drug, administration of activated charcoal is recommended. In the case of very recent oral intake gastric lavage may be considered.

Treatment should be symptomatic. In the event of severe vasospastic reactions, i.v. administration of a peripheral vasodilator such as nitroprusside, phentolamine or dihydralazine, local application of warmth to the affected area and nursing care to prevent tissue damage are recommended. In the event of coronary constriction, appropriate treatment such as nitroglycerine should be initiated.

Dosage: Should be given **at the first symptoms of an attack. Should not be administered prophylactically.**

Tablets: Adults: The first time Cafergot is taken, an initial dose of 2 tablets is recommended. If relief is not obtained within half an hour, a further tablet should be taken; this may be repeated at half-hourly intervals (see maximum daily dosage).

For **subsequent attacks** the initial dose may be increased up to 3 tablets, depending on the dose required in previous attacks. If necessary, additional doses may be taken at half-hourly intervals up to the maximum dosage indicated below.

Children (6 to 12 years): The initial dose is 1 tablet; additional doses of 1 tablet may be given twice only, if required, In the course of an attack.

Suppositories: Adults: Average dose: 1 suppository rectally at start of attack, followed by 1 after one hour, if required.

Children (6 to 12 years): The initial dose is half of a suppository; additional doses of half of a suppository may be given twice only, if required, in the course of an attack.

If supplemental antimigraine medication is required, a minimum of 6 to 8 hours should elapse before the use of any ergotamine or dihydroergotamine-containing preparations; and at least 24 hours should elapse before the use of sumatriptan. Conversely, Cafergot should not be taken until at least 6 hours have elapsed following the use of sumatriptan or ergotamine or dihydroergotamine-containing preparations.

Maximum dose per attack per day: Adults: 6 mg=6 tablets or 3 suppositories.

Children: 3 mg=3 tablets or 1½ suppositories.

Maximum weekly dose: Adults: 10 mg=10 tablets or 5 suppositories.

Children: 5 mg=5 tablets or 2½ suppositories.

Supplied: Suppositories: Each white, torpedo shaped suppository contains: ergotamine tartrate USP 2 mg and caffeine USP 100 mg. Nonmedicinal ingredients: cocoa butter. Boxes of 12. Store below 25°C in tight container (sealed foil). If soft, chill in refrigerator before opening foil wrapper.

Tablets: Each circular, flat-faced, yellowish-white mottled, compressed tablet, beveled-edged, 9 mm in diameter, with Cafergot imprint on one side, and single scored on the other, contains: ergotamine tartrate USP 1 mg and caffeine USP 100 mg. Nonmedicinal ingredients: cornstarch, iron oxide pigment yellow, magnesium stearate, microcrystalline cellulose, talc and tartaric acid. Bottles of 100.

(Shown in Product Recognition Section)

CAFERGOT-PB® ⊕

Novartis Pharmaceuticals

Ergotamine Tartrate—Belladonna—Caffeine—Pentobarbital

Migraine Therapy

Pharmacology: Ergotamine is an alpha adrenergic blocking agent with a direct stimulating effect on the smooth muscle of peripheral and cranial blood vessels; it produces depression of the central vasomotor centres. Its properties also include serotonin antagonism. In comparison to dihydrogenated ergotamine, the adrenergic blocking actions of ergotamine tartrate are less pronounced and vasoconstriction actions are greater. The addition of caffeine to ergotamine tartrate facilitates the absorption of ergotamine when administered orally or rectally, resulting in a more rapid onset of the vasoconstrictive effect and an increase in effectiveness. The migraine attack will be aborted in over 80% of the patients as long as the medication is taken early enough in the course of the attack.

Ergotamine is rapidly and incompletely (approximately 62% of the oral dose) absorbed by the gastrointestinal tract. Peak plasma levels are reached about 2 hours after ingestion. Ergotamine is extensively metabolized in the liver. The bioavailability of unchanged drug is about 2% when the drug is administered orally and 5% when it is administered by the rectal route. It has been suggested that the therapeutic effects of the drug are partially due to active metabolites. Protein bindings amounts to 98%. Parent drug and metabolites are mainly excreted with the bile. Their elimination from plasma is biphasic with a half-life of 2.7 hours and 21 hours, respectively.

Caffeine is rapidly and almost completely absorbed; it is to a large extent metabolized. The metabolites are mainly excreted in the urine. Plasma elimination half-life is about 3.5 hours, protein binding 35%.

Belladonna alkaloids and a small amount of pentobarbital sodium or pentobarbital have been added to that formulation for those patients who suffer excessively from nausea/vomiting or who have associated nervous tension, respectively.

Indications: In acute attacks of migraine with or without aura, especially where nausea, vomiting or nervous tension are prominent.

The suppositories are available for the treatment of patients who have nausea and vomiting early in the attack and cannot retain or absorb anything taken orally. They have a faster onset of action due to by-pass of portal circulation.

Contraindications: Peripheral vascular disorders; obliterative vascular disease; coronary heart disease; severe hypertension and pregnancy, because of the vasoconstrictor action of ergotamine; hepatic insufficiency and septic conditions due to impaired inactivation of ergotamine; renal insufficiency; urinary retention; elevated intraocular pressure; porphyria; known hypersensitivity to ergot alkaloids or any other components of the formulation.

Lactation: Ergotamine is excreted in breast milk and may cause symptoms of vomiting, diarrhea, weak pulse and unstable blood pressure in infants. Thus, Cafergot-PB is contraindicated in nursing mothers.

Precautions: Although signs and symptoms of ergotism rarely develop even after long-term intermittent use of the orally or rectally administered drugs, care should be exercised to remain within the limits of recommended dosage. Excessive or prolonged dosage is not recommended. Such symptoms as tingling in the fingers or toes should be reported to the physician immediately and the drug should be discontinued at once.

Cafergot-PB (cont'd)

Excessive dryness of the mouth and visual disturbances are signs of overdosage or of sensitivity to belladonna alkaloids. In such cases reduction of the dosage may be necessary. Cafergot-PB is not recommended for the prophylaxis of migraine.

Occupational Hazards: activities requiring mental alertness, such as operating hazardous equipment or driving a vehicle, should not be undertaken until the patient's response and sensitivity to the medication are established.

Cafergot-PB may be habit-forming due to the presence of a barbiturate.

Cafergot-PB should be kept out of the reach of children.

The occurrence of drug-induced headaches has been reported during prolonged and uninterrupted treatment with Cafergot-PB.

Rare cases of a solitary rectal or anal ulcer have occurred from abuse of ergotamine-containing suppositories, usually at higher than recommended doses or with continual use at the recommended dose for many years.

Drug Interactions: There is some evidence that the concomitant use of macrolide antibiotics such as troleandomycin, erythromycin or josamycin, and Cafergot-PB can result in an elevated concentration of ergotamine in the plasma, thereby causing untoward peripheral vasoconstriction.

Among patients treated concomitantly with ergotamine-containing preparations and propranolol a few cases of vasospastic reactions have been reported. Concurrent use of vasoconstrictor agents including ergotamine, sumatriptan and nicotine may enhance the risk of vasoconstriction.

The prolonged ingestion of barbiturates such as pentobarbital contained in Cafergot-PB on a regular daily basis gives rise to enzyme induction. This increases the rate of metabolism of certain drugs, including oral anticoagulants and oral contraceptives, thus reducing their effectiveness.

Adverse Effects: Nonmigraine-related nausea and vomiting are the most commonly observed adverse events.

Paresthesia, pain and weakness in the extremities or peripheral vasoconstriction may occur in susceptible patients or following prolonged treatment, which is unadvisable.

Drowsiness, as well as transient tachycardia or bradycardia may be experienced. Owing to its vasoconstrictor properties, ergotamine may cause precordial pain, myocardial ischemia or, in rare cases, infarction, even in patients with no known history of coronary heart disease. Localized edema and itching may occur rarely.

If ergotamine-containing drugs are used excessively over years, they may induce fibrotic changes, in particular of the pleura and the retroperitoneum. There have also been rare reports of fibrotic changes of the cardiac valves.

Overdose: Symptoms: In humans, the minimum lethal dose ranges from 15 to 20 mg. The following cases of ergotamine tartrate overdosage are cited to provide broad guidelines only.

An overdosage of 44 mg ergotamine taken by an adult female, presumably all absorbed, was followed by recovery on supportive therapy only.

A 14-month-old child died following the ingestion of 12 mg ergotamine. Although vomiting was induced shortly after ingestion, the child was not exposed to expert treatment for some 13 hours after ingestion.

Ergotamine poisoning results in nausea, vomiting, diarrhea, thirst, tingling and paresthesias of the extremities, muscle pain, cold and pale skin, itching, a rapid and weak pulse, bradycardia or tachycardia, pain suggestive of angina, rise and/or fall of blood pressure (usually in that order), mental confusion, dizziness, headache, depression, drowsiness and possible unconsciousness. The most prominent effects of ergotism are circulatory changes. CNS changes can rarely include convulsions and hemiplegia. Respiratory depression can occur.

Treatment: In the case of orally ingested drug, administration of activated charcoal is recommended. In the case of very recent oral intake gastric lavage may be considered.

Treatment should be symptomatic. In the event of severe vasospastic reactions, i.v. administration of a peripheral vasodilator such as nitroprusside, phentolamine or dihydralazine, local application of warmth to the affected area and nursing care to prevent tissue damage are recommended. In the event of coronary constriction, appropriate treatment such as nitroglycerine should be initiated.

Dosage: Should be given **at the first symptoms of an attack. Should not be administered prophylactically.**

Tablets; Adults: The first time Cafergot-PB is administered, an initial dose of 2 tablets is recommended. If relief is not obtained within half an hour a further tablet should be taken; this may be repeated at half-hourly intervals (see maximum daily dosage).

For **subsequent attacks** the initial dose may be increased up to 3 tablets, depending on the dose required in previous attacks. If necessary, additional doses may be taken at half-hourly intervals up to the maximum dosage indicated below.

Children (6 to 12 years): The initial dose is 1 tablet; additional doses of 1 tablet may be given twice only, if required, in the course of an attack.

Suppositories: Adults: Average dose: 1 suppository rectally at start of attack, followed by 1 after one hour, if required.

Children (6 to 12 years): The initial dose is half a suppository; additional doses of half a suppository may be given twice only, if required, in the course of an attack.

If supplemental antimigraine medication is required, a minimum of 6 to 8 hours should elapse before the use of any ergotamine or dihydroergotamine-containing preparations; and at least 24 hours should elapse before the use of sumatriptan. Conversely, Cafergot-PB should not be taken until at least 6 hours have elapsed following the use of sumatriptan or ergotamine or dihydroergotamine containing preparations.

Maximum dose per attack per day: Adults: 6 mg = 6 tablets or 3 suppositories.

Children: 3 mg = 3 tablets or 1½ suppositories.

Maximum weekly dose: Adults: 10 mg = 10 tablets or 5 suppositories.

Children: 5 mg = 5 tablets or 2½ suppositories.

Supplied: Suppositories: Each white, torpedo-shaped suppository contains: ergotamine tartrate USP 2 mg, caffeine USP 100 mg, levorotatory belladonna alkaloids 0.25 mg and pentobarbital USP 60 mg. Nonmedicinal ingredients: alcohol, malic acid and suppocire. Boxes of 12. Store below 25°C in tight container (sealed foil). Protect from heat. If soft, chill in refrigerator before opening foil wrapper.

Tablets: Each green, circular, sugar-coated tablet, 9 mm in diameter, contains: ergotamine tartrate USP 1 mg, caffeine USP 100 mg, levorotatory belladonna alkaloids 0.125 mg and pentobarbital USP 30 mg. Nonmedicinal ingredients: acacia, cornstarch, lactose, stearic acid, tartaric acid and tartrazine. Bottles of 100.

(Shown in Product Recognition Section)

Reviewed 1999

CALADRYL®

Warner-Lambert Consumer Healthcare

Calamine—Diphenhydramine HCl

Antipruritic

Indications: For temporary relief of itching due to insect bites, minor skin irritations, mild poison ivy and oak, mild sunburn, allergic itches and rashes.

Warnings: For external use only. Do not use on chickenpox, measles or extensive areas of skin. If condition worsens or if symptoms persist for more than 7 days or clear up and occur again within a few days, discontinue use and consult a physician. Do not use other drugs containing diphenhydramine while using this product without consulting a physician.

Precautions: Should not be applied to blistered, raw or oozing areas of the skin. If burning sensation results, discontinue and remove by washing skin with water.

Dosage: For external use only. Apply topically 3 or 4 times daily. Cleanse skin with soap and water and dry area before each application.

Supplied: Cream: Each g of flesh-colored cream contains: diphenhydramine HCl 1% and calamine 8%, in a water miscible cream base. Nonmedicinal ingredients: camphor, ceresin, cetyl alcohol, fragrance, paraben, polysorbate, propylene glycol, red ferric oxide, sorbitan monostearate, water and yellow ferric oxide. Tubes of 42 g.

Lotion: Each mL of flesh-colored lotion contains: diphenhydramine HCl 1% and calamine 8%. Nonmedicinal ingredients: alcohol, camphor, glycerin, fragrance, red ferric oxide, sodium carboxymethyl, water and yellow ferric oxide. Plastic bottles of 100 mL.

CALCIJEX® Ⓟ

Abbott

Calcitriol

Vitamin D_3 Metabolite

Supplied: Each mL of sterile, isotonic, clear, aqueous solution contains: calcitriol 1 or 2 μg, edetate disodium (stabilizer), polysorbate 20, sodium chloride and sodium ascorbate (stabilizer). Dibasic sodium phosphate, anhydrous and monobasic sodium phosphate, monohydrate as buffers. The pH of the solution is approximately 7. Preservative-free. Ampuls of 1 mL.

Store at room temperature; however, brief exposure up to 40°C does not adversely affect the product. Protect from light, excessive heat.

Parenteral drug products should be inspected visually for particulate matter and discoloration prior to administration, whenever solution and container permit. Discard unused portion.

CALCIMAR® Ⓟ

Rhône-Poulenc Rorer

Calcitonin Salmon

Paget's Disease Therapy—Hypercalcemia Treatment

Pharmacology: Calcitonin is a group of polypeptide hormones secreted by the thyroid gland in mammals and by the ultimobranchial gland of birds and fish. It is of physiological importance in the regulation of calcium metabolism in certain animal species, and may also have physiological importance in certain extra skeletal systems (e.g., gastrointestinal and renal function).

Only small amounts of the drug are absorbed after administration by buccal, oral, topical (to the skin) or inhalation routes, and no practical use of these non parenteral routes has been made thus far. The drug is given s.c. or i.m.

Calcitonin, particularly the salmon form, is extremely potent. As little as 1 nanogram given s.c. to young rats lowers the serum calcium by 1 to 2 mg%.

Calcitonin is rapidly absorbed from i.m. and s.c. sites into the blood, although absorption is slowed by the use of a gelatin vehicle. Its half-life in the circulation, like that of other peptide hormones, is measured in minutes rather than hours. Salmon calcitonin, however, has a relatively longer half life than does porcine or human calcitonin. Immediately after introduction into the circulation calcitonin is present in the free form. Later it is largely protein bound, but this does not appear to interfere with either its biological or immunological activity.

Salmon calcitonin participates in the regulation of the homeostasis of calcium by acting primarily on the bone. In Paget's disease, it is presumed to directly inhibit the accelerated bone resorption which characterizes the disease.

Calcitonin increases the excretion of filtered phosphate, calcium and sodium by decreasing their tubular reabsorption. In some patients the inhibition of bone resorption by calcitonin is of such magnitude that the consequent reduction of filtered calcium load more than compensates for the decrease in tubular reabsorption of calcium. The result in these patients is a decrease rather than an increase in urinary calcium.

Transient increases in sodium and water excretion may occur after the initial injection of calcitonin. In most patients, these changes return to pre treatment levels with continued therapy.

Short-term calcitonin administration results in marked transient decreases in the volume and acidity of gastric juice and in the volume and the trypsin and amylase content of pancreatic juice. Whether these effects continue to be elicited after each injection of calcitonin during chronic therapy has not been investigated.

Indications: Treatment of symptomatic Paget's disease of the bone. For early treatment of hypercalcemic emergencies, along with other appropriate agents, when a rapid decrease in serum calcium is required, until more specific treatment of the underlying disease can be accomplished. It also may be added to existing therapeutic regimens for hypercalcemia such as i.v. fluids and furosemide, oral phosphate or corticosteroids, or other agents. Calcitonin may be used in patients with azotemia and those with limited cardiac reserve in whom i.v. fluids may be contraindicated.

Contraindications: Known hypersensitivity to salmon calcitonin.

Warnings: *Pregnancy:* Reproduction studies in animals have revealed decreases in fetal birth weight. Data in humans are not available. Use of salmon calcitonin in women who are or may become pregnant requires that the potential benefit to the patient outweighs the possibility of risk to the fetus.
Lactation: Salmon calcitonin has been shown to inhibit lactation in animals and should not be administered to nursing mothers.
Children: The safety of the use of salmon calcitonin in children has not been established.

Precautions: Skin testing should be considered prior to treatment of patients with suspected sensitivity to calcitonin. The following procedure is suggested: Prepare a dilution of 10 IU/mL by withdrawing 0.05 mL of the reconstituted product in a tuberculin syringe and filling it to 1 mL with Dextrose Injection 5% USP (or Saline Injection USP). Mix well, discard 0.9 mL and inject intracutaneously 0.1 mL (approximately 1 IU) on the inner aspect of the forearm. Observe the injection site 15 minutes after injection. The appearance of more than mild erythema or wheal constitutes a positive response.

Because calcitonin is protein in nature, the possibility of a systemic allergic reaction must be considered. Administration of calcitonin salmon has been reported in a few cases to cause serious allergic-type reactions (e.g. bronchospasms, swelling of the tongue or throat, and anaphylactic shock), and in one case, death due to anaphylaxis. The usual provisions should be made for the emergency treatment of such a reaction should it occur. Allergic reactions should be differentiated from generalized flushing and hypotension.

Calcitonin administration could possibly lead to hypocalcemic tetany under special circumstances although no cases have yet been reported. Provisions for parenteral calcium administration should be available during the first several administrations of calcitonin.

Coarse granular casts and casts containing renal tubular epithelial cells were reported in young adult volunteers at bed rest who were given salmon calcitonin to study its effect on immobilization osteoporosis. There was no other evidence of renal abnormality and the urine sediment became normal after calcitonin was stopped. Urine sediment abnormalities have not been reported by other investigators, however, patients on chronic therapy should have periodic examinations of urine sediment.

Careful instruction in sterile injection technique should be given to the patient, and to other persons who may administer salmon calcitonin.

There are no known interactions with other drugs.

Adverse Effects: Nausea with or without vomiting has been noted in about 10% of patients treated. It is most evident when treatment is first initiated and tends to decrease or disappear with continued administration. Local inflammatory reactions at the injection site have been reported in about 10% of patients. Facial flushing occurs in about 2% of patients. Administration of calcitonin salmon has been reported in a few cases to cause serious allergic-type reactions (e.g. bronchospasms, swelling of the tongue or throat, and anaphylactic shock), and in one case, death due to anaphylaxis (see Precautions). Other systemic effects include anorexia, a metallic taste and tingling of the hands. These effects usually occur early in the treatment and tend to diminish with continued therapy.

Evidence of systemic allergic reactions is minimal and no anaphylactic reaction has been reported. In approximately one half the patients tested after 6 months or more of treatment, indications of circulating antibodies to calcitonin were obtained. In most of the patients the level of antibodies was not high enough to interfere with the effect of exogenous calcitonin. In a few patients, resistance to calcitonin was attributed to high levels of antibodies. Secondary hyperparathyroidism as a result of the transient hypocalcemia following calcitonin administration did not develop in patients with Paget's disease.

Overdose: Symptoms: Calcitonin administration can lead to antibody development. This is minimal when the hormone is injected in the absence of an adjuvant or when it is not complexed with a larger protein. Gelatin and acetate buffer solutions have been shown to have little or no adjuvant like action in comparison to Freund's adjuvant.

The antibodies which develop when calcitonin is administered repeatedly with Freund's adjuvant are measurable in the circulation by radio-immunoassay techniques. In no instance has any systemic allergic or anaphylactic effect been reported in animal studies with calcitonin, in spite of the known development of circulating antibodies.

Treatment: There is no specific antidote; however, additional symptoms other than those discussed under Adverse Effects have not been observed and no corrective action need be taken other than to discontinue treatment temporarily and maintain the patient under observation. Supportive treatment may be indicated.

Dosage: Paget's Disease: The recommended adult starting dose is 100 IU/day administered s.c. or i.m. Monitor drug effect by periodic measurement of serum alkaline phosphatase and 24 hour urinary hydroxyproline (if available) and evaluation of symptoms. A decrease toward normal of the biochemical abnormalities is usually seen, if it is going to occur, within the first few months. Bone pain may also decrease during that time. Improvement of neurologic lesions, when it occurs, requires a longer period of treatment, often more than 1 year.

In many patients, doses of 50 IU/day or alternate days are sufficient to maintain biochemical and clinical improvement. At the present time, however, there are insufficient data to determine whether this reduced dose will have the same effect as the higher dose on forming more normal bone structure. It appears preferable, therefore, to maintain the higher dose in any patient with serious deformity or neurological involvement.

In any patient with a good response initially who later relapses, either clinically or biochemically, explore the possibility of antibody formation. Although specialized tests for antibody titre are not widely available, the following test will detect titers that interfere with the action of calcitonin:

After overnight fasting, a sample of the patient's blood is taken for determination of serum calcium and 100 IU of Calcimar are injected i.m. The patient is then permitted to eat his usual breakfast. At 3 and 6 hours post injection, additional blood samples are drawn. The serum calcium values are then compared. A decrease of 0.5 mg % or more from fasting level at 3 and 6 hours is usually seen in the responsive patient. Decreases of 0.3 mg % or less constitute an inadequate response to calcitonin in the patient with active Paget's disease. If the hypocalcemic action of calcitonin is lost, further therapy will not be effective.

Assess patient compliance in the event of relapse. In patients who relapse, whether because of antibodies or for unexplained reasons, a dosage increase beyond 100 IU/day does not usually appear to elicit an improved response.
Hypercalcemia: The recommended starting dose of calcitonin in hypercalcemia is 4 IU/kg every 12 hours by s.c. or i.m. injection. If the response to this dose is not satisfactory after 1 or 2 days, the dose may be increased to 8 IU/kg every 12 hours. If the response remains unsatisfactory after 2 more days, the dose may be further increased to a maximum of 8 IU/kg every 6 hours.

If the volume to be injected exceeds 2 mL, i.m. injection is preferable and multiple sites of injection should be used.

In clinical trials, Calcimar has been shown to lower the elevated serum calcium of patients with carcinoma (with or without demonstrated metastases) multiple myeloma or primary hyperparathyroidism (lesser response). Patients with higher values for serum calcium tend to show greater reduction during Calcimar therapy. The decrease in calcium occurs about 2 hours after the first injection and lasts for about 6 to 8 hours. Calcimar given every 12 hours maintained a calcium lowering effect for about 5 to 8 days, the time period evaluated for most patients during the clinical studies. The average reduction of 8 hour post injection serum calcium during this period was about 9%.

The use of Calcimar Solution in the management of hypercalcemia should be limited to patients under close supervision in hospitals.

Supplied: Each mL of sterile solution contains: calcitonin salmon 200 IU. Nonmedicinal ingredients: acetic acid, phenol, sodium acetate, sodium chloride, sodium hydroxide and water for injection. Vials of 2 mL. Store refrigerated (2 to 8°C). Stable for 2 weeks at room temperature.

The database, reporting form and procedures for monitoring adverse events from vaccines are separate from those of other drug products. See the CLIN-INFO SECTION for a description of the program and a copy of the reporting form.

CALCITE 500
CALCITE D-500
Riva

Calcium Carbonate
Calcium Carbonate—Vitamin D

Calcium Supplement
Calcium-Vitamin D Supplement

Supplied: Calcite 500: Each yellow tablet embossed RIVA contains: calcium carbonate 1 250 mg from oyster shell which provides 500 mg (25 mEq) elemental calcium. Nonmedicinal ingredients: acacia, carnauba wax, cellulose, D&C Yellow, FD&C Blue, FD&C Yellow, hydroxypropylcellulose, hydroxypropyl methylcellulose, magnesium stearate, maltodextrin, polyethylene glycol, polysorbate 80, sodium croscarmellose and titanium dioxide. Alcohol-, gluten-, paraben-, sucrose-, sulfite- and tartrazine-free. Bottles of 100.

Calcite D-500: Each green tablet embossed RIVA contains: calcium carbonate 1 250 mg from oyster shell which provides 500 mg (25 mEq) elemental calcium and vitamin D 125 IU. Nonmedicinal ingredients: acacia, carnauba wax, cellulose, D&C Yellow, FD&C Blue, FD&C Yellow, hydroxypropyl methylcellulose, magnesium stearate, maltodextrin, polyethylene glycol, polydextrose, sodium croscarmellose, titanium dioxide and triacetin. Alcohol-, gluten-, paraben-, sucrose-, sulfite- and tartrazine-free. Bottles of 100.

CALCIUM CHLORIDE
Abbott

Calcium Therapy

Supplied: Each mL contains: calcium chloride 100 mg. May contain hydrochloric and/or sodium hydroxide. Ampuls of 10 mL providing 10% (1 g) calcium chloride, boxes of 25. Syringes of 10 mL, boxes of 10.

CALCIUM CHLORIDE INJECTION USP
Astra

Calcium Therapy

Pharmacology: Calcium plays important physiologic roles, many of which are not completely understood. Calcium is essential for the proper functioning of nerve and muscle, where it has a major influence on stimulation thresholds and the release of neurotransmitters. It is necessary for muscle contraction, maintenance of the integrity of membranes, coagulation of the blood, and cardiac function. Calcium also plays regulatory roles in the release and storage of neurotransmitters and hormones, in the uptake and binding of amino acids, and in cyanocobalamin (vitamin B_{12}) absorption and gastrin secretion.

Calcium is present in small quantities in the extracellular fluid and to a minor extent in the structure of cytoplasm of cells of soft tissue. To fulfill its vital function, ionized calcium must be available to the appropriate tissues in the proper concentrations. An endocrine control system ordinarily keeps the plasma concentrations of ionized calcium within narrow limits. Intracellular concentrations of ionized calcium are also strictly regulated by control of the exchange of ions between the cell and its environment and between intracellular compartments. The principal endocrine factors that control calcium metabolism are parathyroid hormone, calcitonin and vitamin D. Derangements in calcium metabolism may occasionally require the rapid restoration of calcium concentrations in body fluids by the infusion of i.v. calcium salts.

Indications: For the treatment of hypocalcemia for those conditions requiring a prompt increase in blood plasma calcium levels, such as neonatal tetany and tetany due to parathyroid deficiency, vitamin D deficiency and alkalosis. It is also indicated for the prevention of hypocalcemia during exchange transfusions.

Calcium chloride can be administered as adjunctive therapy in a number of conditions, including the following: insect bites or stings such as Black Widow Spider bites; sensitivity reactions, particularly when characterized by urticaria; magnesium intoxication due to overdosage of magnesium sulfate; as an aid in management of the acute symptoms in lead colic; in

Calcium Chloride Injection USP (cont'd)

cardiac resuscitation, particularly after open heart surgery, parenteral calcium can be used when epinephrine has failed to improve weak or ineffective myocardial contractions.

In hyperkalemia, calcium chloride injection may aid in antagonizing cardiac toxicity as measured by electrocardiographic (ECG), provided the patient is not receiving digitalis therapy.

Contraindications: Cardiac resuscitation in the presence of ventricular fibrillation; digitalized patients; hypercalcemia and hypercalciuria (e.g., in hyperparathyroidism, vitamin D overdosage, decalcifying tumors such as plasmocytoma, bone metastases); severe renal disease; calcium loss due to immobilization.

Warnings: For i.v. use only. Must not be injected i.m. or s.c.

Calcium chloride injection is irritating to veins and must not be injected into tissues, since severe necrosis and sloughing may occur. Great care should be taken to avoid extravasation or accidental injection into perivascular tissues (see Precautions).

Precautions: In mild hypercalciuria (exceeding 300 mg/24 hours) as well as in chronic renal failure, or where there is evidence of stone formation in the urinary tract, urinary calcium excretion should be monitored. If necessary, the dosage should be reduced or calcium therapy discontinued.

High vitamin D intake should be avoided during calcium therapy unless especially indicated.

Injections should be made slowly through a small needle into a large vein in order to avoid too rapid an increase in serum calcium and extravasation of calcium solution into surrounding tissue (see Warnings). It is particularly important to prevent a high concentration of calcium from reaching the heart because of the danger of cardiac syncope. If injected into the ventricular cavity in cardiac resuscitation, it must not be injected into the myocardial tissue.

Rapid injection of calcium chloride may cause vasodilation, decreased blood pressure, bradycardia, cardiac arrhythmias, syncope and cardiac arrest.

Drug Interactions: The ionotropic and toxic effects of cardiac glycosides and calcium are synergistic and arrhythmias may occur if these drugs are given together (particularly when calcium is given intravenously). I.V. administration of calcium should be avoided in patients receiving cardiac glycosides; if necessary, calcium should be given slowly in small amounts.

Calcium complexes tetracycline antibiotics rendering them inactive. The two drugs should not be given at the same time orally, nor should they be mixed for a parenteral administration.

Pregnancy: Animal reproduction studies have not been conducted with calcium chloride. It also is not known if calcium chloride can cause fetal harm when administered to a pregnant woman or can affect reproduction capacity. Calcium chloride should be given to a pregnant woman only if clearly needed.

Lactation: It is not known whether this drug is excreted in human milk. Because many drugs are excreted in human milk, caution should be exercised when calcium chloride is administered to a nursing woman.

Adverse Effects: Parenteral calcium may cause flushing, nausea, vomiting, drowsiness, sweating and hypotension. Vasomotor collapse may ensue if i.v. injection is too rapid.

Injections of calcium chloride are accompanied by peripheral vasodilatation as well as a local burning sensation.

Overdose: Untoward effects which may occur with parenterally administered calcium are related to the rate of injection.

Symptoms: Nausea, vomiting, diarrhea, sensations of heat and sweating, arrhythmias, hypotension, circulatory collapse.

Treatment: Persistent hypercalcemia from overdosage of calcium is unlikely because of rapid excretion. In the event of untoward effects from excessive calcium administration, the drug should be discontinued promptly, the patient re-evaluated and appropriate countermeasures instituted, if necessary.

Dosage: To aid in converting: 1 g of elemental calcium = 25 mmol elemental calcium = 50 mEq elemental calcium = 3.7 g calcium chloride = 37 mL of a 10% solution of calcium chloride.

Calcium chloride is administered only by **slow** i.v. injection (not to exceed 1 mL/min).

The usual precautions for i.v. therapy should be observed. If time permits, the solution should be warmed to body temperature. The injection should be halted if the patient complains of any discomfort; it may be resumed when symptoms disappear. Following injection, the patient should remain recumbent for a short time.

The usual adult dosage in hypocalcemic disorders ranges from 500 mg to 1 g (5 to 10 mL) at intervals of 1 to 3 days, depending on the response of the patient and/or results of serum calcium determinations. Repeated injections may be required because of rapid excretion of calcium.

In magnesium intoxication, an initial adult dose of 500 mg (5 mL) should be administered promptly and the patient observed for signs of recovery before further doses are given.

In hyperkalemic ECG disturbances of cardiac function, the dosage of calcium chloride injection should be titrated by constant monitoring of ECG changes during administration.

In cardiac resuscitation, the usual adult dosage ranges from 500 mg to 1 g (5 to 10 mL) i.v.

Supplied: Each mL of sterile, nonpyrogenic, hypertonic solution contains: calcium chloride dihydrate 100 mg (1.4 mEq/mL each of Ca^{++} and Cl^{-}) in water for injection. Single use glass vials of 10 mL.

The solution contains no bacteriostat, antimicrobial agent or added buffer and is intended only for use with a single dose injection. The pH is between 5.5 and 7.5 adjusted with hydrochloric acid. The osmolar concentration is 2.04 mOsmol/mL (calc.). Do not use if solution is unclear. Discard unused portion. Store at controlled room temperature between 15 and 30°C.

Reviewed 1999

CALCIUM DISODIUM VERSENATE™
3M Pharmaceuticals

Calcium Disodium Edetate

Chelating Agent

Supplied: Each mL of sterile solution contains: calcium disodium edetate 200 mg. Nonmedicinal ingredients: calcium carbonate, sodium hydroxide and water for injection. Ampuls of 5 mL, boxes of 6.

CALCIUM 500
CALCIUM D 500
Trianon

Calcium Carbonate

Calcium Carbonate—Vitamin D

Mineral Supplement

Vitamin—Mineral Supplement

Supplied: Calcium 500: Each green, biconvex, oblong shaped tablet contains: calcium carbonate 1 250 mg which provides calcium 500 mg (25 mEq) obtained from oyster shell. Nonmedicinal ingredients: carnauba wax, cellulose, colloidal silicon dioxide, magnesium stearate, Opadry green dye (D&C yellow 10 aluminum lake, FD&C blue 1 aluminum lake, hydroxypropyl methylcellulose, polydextrose, polyethylene glycol, titanium dioxide and triacetin). Alcohol, gluten-, sulfite- and tartrazine-free. Bottles of 100 and 500.

Calcium D 500: Each gray, biconvex, oblong shaped tablet contains: calcium carbonate 1 250 mg which provides calcium 500 mg (25 mEq) obtained from oyster shell and vitamin D 125 IU. Nonmedicinal ingredients: carnauba wax, cellulose, colloidal silicon dioxide, magnesium stearate, Opadry gray dye (FD&C blue 2 aluminum lake, FD&C red 40 aluminum lake, FD&C yellow 6 aluminum lake, hydroxypropyl methylcellulose, polyethylene glycol, polysorbate 80 and titanium dioxide). Alcohol, gluten-, sulfite- and tartrazine-free. Bottles of 100.

New Product 1998

...Seeking additional product information? Ask the manufacturers. Their addresses appear in full in the YELLOW SECTION.

CALCIUM GLUCONATE
Abbott

Calcium Therapy

Supplied: Each mL contains: calcium gluconate 100 mg with calcium dextrosaccharate 3 mg as a stabilizer. Nonmedicinal ingredients: water for injection. Ampuls of 10 mL providing 10% (1 g) calcium gluconate, boxes of 25.

CALCIUM GLUCONATE INJECTION USP
Astra

Electrolyte Replenisher

Pharmacology: Calcium plays important physiologic roles, many of which are not completely understood. Calcium is essential for the proper functioning of nerve and muscle, where it has a major influence on stimulation thresholds and the release of neurotransmitters. It is necessary for muscle contraction, renal function, maintenance of the integrity of membranes, coagulation of the blood, and cardiac function. Calcium also plays regulatory roles in the release and storage of neurotransmitters and hormones, in the uptake and binding of amino acids, and in cyanocobalamin (vitamin B_{12}) absorption and gastrin secretion.

Calcium is present in small quantities in the extracellular fluid and to a minor extent in the structure of cytoplasm of cells of soft tissue. To fulfill its vital function, ionized calcium must be available to the appropriate tissues in the proper concentrations. An endocrine control system ordinarily keeps the plasma concentrations of ionized calcium within narrow limits. Intracellular concentrations of ionized calcium are also strictly regulated by control of the exchange of ions between the cell and its environment and between intracellular compartments. The principal endocrine factors that control calcium metabolism are parathyroid hormone, calcitonin and vitamin D. Derangements in calcium metabolism may occasionally require the rapid restoration of calcium concentrations in body fluids by the infusion of i.v. calcium salts.

Indications: For the treatment of hypocalcemia for those conditions requiring a prompt increase in blood plasma calcium concentrations, such as neonatal tetany and tetany due to parathyroid deficiency, vitamin D deficiency and alkalosis. It is also indicated for the prevention of hypocalcemia during exchange transfusions.

Calcium gluconate has also been administered as adjunctive therapy in a number of conditions, including the following: rickets; osteomalacia; insect bites or stings such as Black Widow Spider bites; sensitivity reactions, particularly when characterized by urticaria; as an aid in the treatment of depression due to overdosage of magnesium sulfate; as an aid in management of the acute symptoms in lead colic; in cardiac resuscitation, particularly after open heart surgery when epinephrine has failed to improve weak or ineffective myocardial contractions.

In hyperkalemia, calcium gluconate may aid in antagonizing the cardiac toxicity provided the patient is not receiving digitalis therapy.

Contraindications: Hypercalcemia and hypercalciuria (e.g., in hyperparathyroidism, vitamin D overdosage, decalcifying tumors such as plasmocytoma, bone metastases); severe renal disease; calcium loss due to immobilization, ventricular fibrillation. The injection of calcium preparations is strictly contraindicated in digitalized patients.

Warnings: For i.v. use only.

The gluconate salt is not irritating to the veins but has been reported to cause skin necrosis and sloughing in infants. The i.m. route should not be used because it is irritating, painful, and may cause abscess formation.

Precautions: In mild hypercalciuria (exceeding 300 mg/24 hours) as well as in chronic renal failure, or where there is evidence of stone formation in the urinary tract, adequate checks must be kept on urinary calcium excretion. If necessary, the dosage should be reduced or calcium therapy discontinued.

High vitamin D intake should be avoided during calcium therapy unless especially indicated.

Tissue irritation and necrosis may occur with i.m. injection especially in infants and small children; this route should be avoided. High dose calcium therapy by any of the parenteral routes should always be accompanied by very careful monitoring of blood concentration and urinary calcium excretion, particularly in children. Treatment should be stopped at once if blood calcium exceeds 2.62 to 2.74 mmol/L (105 to 119 mg/L) or if more than 0.12 mmol/kg (5 mg/kg) is excreted in the urine in a period of 24 hours. Heart rhythm should also be monitored.

Injections should be made slowly through a small needle into a large vein in order to avoid too rapid an increase in serum calcium and extravasation of calcium solution into the surrounding tissue with resulting necrosis. It is particularly important to prevent a high concentration of calcium from reaching the heart because of the danger of cardiac syncope. If injected into the ventricular cavity in cardiac resuscitation, it must not be injected into the myocardial tissue.

Rapid injection of calcium gluconate may cause vasodilation, decreased blood pressure, bradycardia, cardiac arrhythmias, syncope and cardiac arrest.

Drug Interactions: The ionotropic and toxic effects of cardiac glycosides and calcium are synergistic and arrhythmias may occur if these drugs are given together (particularly when calcium is given i.v.). I.V. administration of calcium should be avoided in patients receiving cardiac glycosides; if necessary, calcium should be given slowly in small amounts.

Calcium complexes tetracycline antibiotics rendering them inactive. The 2 drugs should not be given at the same time orally, nor should they be mixed for a parenteral administration.

Calcium Gluconate Injection has been reported to be incompatible with i.v. solutions containing various drugs. Published data are too varied and/or limited to permit generalization, and specialized reference should be consulted for specific information.

Drug/Laboratory Test Interactions: Transient elevations of plasma 11-hydroxycorticosteroid levels (Glenn-Nelson technique) may occur when i.v. calcium is administered, but levels return to control values after 1 hour. In addition, i.v. calcium gluconate can produce false-negative for serum and urinary magnesium.

Pregnancy: Animal reproduction studies have not been conducted with calcium gluconate. It also is not known if calcium gluconate can cause fetal harm when administered to a pregnant woman or can affect reproduction capacity. Calcium gluconate should be given to a pregnant woman only if clearly needed.

Lactation: It is not known whether this drug is excreted in human milk. Because many drugs are excreted in human milk, caution should be exercised when calcium gluconate is administered to a nursing woman.

Adverse Effects: Parenteral calcium may cause flushing, nausea, vomiting, drowsiness, sweating and hypotension. Vasomotor collapse may ensue if i.v. injection is too rapid.

Overdose: Symptoms: Untoward effects which may occur with parenterally administered calcium are related to the rate of injection.

Nausea, vomiting, diarrhea, sensations of heat and sweating; arrhythmias, hypotension, circulatory collapse.

Treatment: The patient should be in the horizontal position. Treat shock in the usual fashion.

Dosage: The dose is dependent on the requirements of the individual patient. I.V. calcium gluconate injection must be administered slowly, e.g. approximately 1.5 mL over a period of 1 minute.

To aid in converting: 1 g of elemental calcium=25 mmol elemental calcium=50 mEq elemental calcium=11.1 g calcium gluconate=111 mL of a 10% solution of calcium gluconate.

Adults: Initially, 5 to 20 mL of a 10% solution (500 mg to 2 g) injected slowly i.v. This dose may be repeated until tetany is controlled. A 0.3 to 0.8% solution [30 to 40 mL of a 10% solution in 500 to 1 000 mL of sodium chloride injection or dextrose 5% in water (D5W)] may then be infused by slow drip within a 3 to 12-hour period. The maximum dosage for adults is 15 g (150 mL of a 10% solution).

Children: The usual dose is 200 to 500 mg/kg/day well diluted and administered slowly i.v. in divided doses. Doses above 500 mg/kg/day are not recommended.

Supplied: Each mL of sterile, nonpyrogenic, hypertonic solution contains: total calcium 0.465 mEq (9.3 mg), derived from calcium gluconate 94 mg and calcium D-saccharate tetrahydrate 4.5 mg (equivalent to calcium D-saccharate anhydrous 3.5 mg) in water for injection. Calcium D-saccharate provides 6% of the total calcium and stabilizes the supersaturated solution of calcium gluconate. Preservative-free. Single use vials of 10 mL.

Sodium hydroxide and/or hydrochloric acid is used to adjust pH to 6.0 to 8.2. The osmolality is 0.7 mOsmol/mL (calc.).

Supersaturated solutions are prone to precipitation. If precipitation is evident, vials may be heated to 80°C in a dry heat oven for a minimum of 1 hour. Shake vigorously. Allow to cool to room temperature before dispensing. The solution should not be used if the precipitate remains after following the above procedure.

Store at room temperature (15 to 30°C). Protect from freezing. Do not use if solution is unclear. Discard unused portion.

CALCIUM SALTS: ORAL

General Monograph, CPhA

Calcium Therapy

This monograph has been compiled by CPhA. It may contain information different from that approved by Therapeutic Products Programme, Health Canada, and the pharmaceutical manufacturers' approval has not been requested.

Pharmacology: Calcium is the most abundant mineral in the human body and is essential for maintaining the functional integrity of nervous and musculoskeletal systems as well as cell membrane and capillary permeability. The majority (99%) of body calcium is contained in bone with the remainder equally distributed between intra- and extracellular fluids. Calcium is an activator in many enzymatic reactions and is necessary for nerve impulse transmission, renal function, respiration and blood coagulation.

Pharmacokinetics: Calcium is actively absorbed, mainly in the duodenum and proximal jejunum. Calcium must be in a soluble, ionized form to be absorbed. Factors such as an acidic intestinal pH, the presence of Vitamin D, and pregnancy and lactation tend to favor calcium absorption. However, absorption may be impeded in the elderly, or by a deficiency of parathyroid hormone, calcitonin or Vitamin D, the presence of anions or fatty acids which may precipitate or complex with calcium, or in certain disease states such as achlorhydria, renal osteodystrophy, steatorrhea or uremia.

Once absorbed into the bloodstream, most calcium is rapidly incorporated into skeletal muscle; the remainder is equally distributed between intra- and extracellular fluids. Normal total serum calcium concentrations range from 2.2 to 2.6 mmol/L, although only the ionized fraction is physiologically active. Of the total serum calcium, 50% is ionized, 5% is complexed with anions such as phosphates or citrates and 45% is protein bound. Hyperproteinemia is associated with an increase in total serum calcium; hypoproteinemia has the opposite effect. Acidosis favors an increase in ionic calcium concentration, while alkalosis leads to a decrease in the ionized fraction.

CSF calcium concentrations tend to be similar to the serum concentration of ionized calcium, i.e., approximately 50% of total serum calcium.

Calcium crosses the placenta, reaching higher levels in fetal blood than in the mother. Calcium is excreted in breast milk.

Calcium is excreted mainly in the feces, either as a result of passing through the gut unabsorbed or through biliary or pancreatic secretion into the gut lumen. Very small amounts of calcium are excreted in the urine as most renally filtered calcium is reabsorbed. Urinary excretion of calcium is promoted by growth hormone, calcitonin and nonthiazide diuretics, whereas parathyroid hormone, Vitamin D, thiazide diuretics or a decrease in ionized calcium concentration tend to decrease the amount of calcium excreted in the urine. Calcium is also excreted in sweat.

Indications: As a dietary supplement where calcium intake may be inadequate: childhood and adolescence, pregnancy and lactation, postmenopausal females and in the aged.

In the treatment of calcium deficiency states which may occur in diseases such as: tetany of the newborn (as a supplement to parenterally administered calcium), hypoparathyroidism (acute and chronic), pseudohypoparathyroidism, postmenopausal and senile osteoporosis (as an adjunct to estrogen, exercise, etc.), rickets and osteomalacia.

Calcium carbonate is used in the management of dyspepsia, gastroesophageal reflux and peptic ulcer disease.

Contraindications: Hypercalcemia and hypercalciuria (e.g., in hyperparathyroidism, vitamin D overdosage, decalcifying tumors such as plasmocytoma, bone metastases); severe renal or cardiac disease; calcium loss due to immobilization.

Precautions: In mild hypercalciuria (exceeding 300 mg/24 hours) as well as in chronic renal failure, or where there is evidence of stone formation in the urinary tract, adequate checks must be kept on urinary calcium excretion. If necessary, the dosage should be reduced or calcium therapy discontinued.

Studies done in recent years have shown that many calcium supplements contain varying amounts of lead. Supplements derived from bone meal, fossil or oyster shells, or dolomite contain the highest amounts. Certain patients may be at higher risk such as children or patients who rely on supplementation to meet their daily calcium requirements. Patients on chronic calcium therapy, especially children, infants, pregnant or lactating women and chronic renal failure or dialysis patients, may be advised to avoid products derived from dolomite, fossil or oyster shells or bone meal, in favor of sources with lower lead content such as refined calcium carbonate or chelated calcium (gluconate and lactate salts).

Drug Interactions: Tetracyclines, Bisphosphonates (alendronate, clodronate, etidronate, pamidronate), Iron Supplements: Calcium decreases the absorption of these drugs and should be taken 3 hours after a dose of any of these agents.

Phenytoin: May form a nonabsorbable complex with calcium; calcium should be taken 3 hours after a phenytoin dose.

In addition to the specific medications mentioned in this monograph, the rate and/or extent of absorption of other oral medications may vary when taken concurrently with calcium supplements, especially the carbonate salt. Patients should generally be advised to take calcium supplements at least 3 hours after taking other oral medications.

Food Interactions: The absorption of calcium may be reduced in the presence of phosphorus (e.g., dairy products), oxalic acid (e.g., spinach, rhubarb) and phytic acid (e.g., bran and whole cereals).

Adverse Effects: Gastrointestinal: gastric irritation, constipation.

CNS: Irritability, lethargy, stupor and coma may occur with chronic ingestion.

Renal: Systemic alkalosis and hypercalcemia or the milk-alkali syndrome; generalized calcinosis leading to renal impairment may occur with chronic ingestion.

Overdose: Symptoms: Acute ingestion of calcium salts may cause mild gastric symptoms but has not caused hypercalcemia or other toxicity. Chronic ingestion of calcium salts may produce more significant toxicity (see Adverse Effects).

Treatment: Acute ingestion of calcium salts seldom requires treatment. Symptomatic hypercalcemia following chronic ingestion may require fluid resuscitation and general supportive care including cardiac monitoring, central venous pressure and wedge pressure measurement, pulmonary artery catheterization and monitoring of urinary output.

Dosage: Increased dietary intake of calcium is preferred over supplementation whenever possible. For information on food sources of calcium see Mineral Food Sources in the Clin-Info section. Table I lists the recommended daily calcium intake for various patient groups.

Table I—Calcium Salts: Oral

Recommended Calcium Intake (mg elemental Ca^{++}/day)[a]

Subgroup	Ages	Males	Females	Both
Infants	0–4 months			250[b]
	5–12 months			400
Children	1 year			500
	2–3 years			550
	4–6 years			600
	7–9 years			700
Adolescents	10–12 years	900	1 100	
	13–15 years	1 100	1 000	
	16–18 years	900	700	
Adults	19–49 years	800	700	
	>50 years			800
Additional Requirements	Pregnancy		500	
	Lactation		500	
	Post-menopause		300[c]	

[a] Adapted from: Health and Welfare Canada: Recommended Nutrient Intake for Canadians. 1990.

[b] Infant formula with high phosphorus should contain 375 mg calcium.

[c] For patients on estrogen replacement therapy. Recommended daily dose for postmenopausal women not taking estrogen is 1 500 mg.

Calcium replacement requirements can be estimated by clinical condition and/or serum calcium determinations. Prophylactic administration of calcium supplements may be necessary in some patients in order to maintain serum calcium

Calcium Salts: Oral (cont'd)

above 2.25 mmol/L (9 mg/dL). The average adult oral dosage of elemental calcium for prevention of hypocalcemia is 1 g daily, and the usual oral dosage for treatment of calcium depletion is 1 to 2 g or more daily. For the prevention of osteoporosis in women, elemental calcium intake of 1 to 1.5 g daily has been recommended.

Children: The usual supplemental dosage of elemental calcium is 45 to 65 mg/kg daily. In neonatal hypocalcemia, the daily dosage of elemental calcium is 50 to 150 mg/kg and should not exceed 1 g.

Oral calcium supplements are usually administered in 3 or 4 doses daily. Solid dosage forms should be taken with food (see Precautions, Food Interactions). Doses of syrup may be diluted in water, fruit juice or formula for children or infants.

With advancing age or in the presence of achlorhydria, calcium absorption from the gastrointestinal tract is reduced; calcium dosage may need to be adjusted accordingly.

Table II lists the various calcium salts and their elemental calcium content.

Table II—Calcium Salts: Oral

Elemental Calcium Content

Calcium Salt	% elemental Ca^{++}	Elemental Ca^{++}/g* (mg)	(mmol)
Calcium carbonate	40	400	10
Calcium citrate	21	210	5.3
Calcium glubionate	6.5	64	1.6
Calcium glucoheptonate	8	82	2.1
Calcium gluconate	9	90	2.3
Calcium lactate	13	130	3.3
Calcium phosphate dibasic anhydrous	29	290	7.3
Calcium phosphate dibasic dihydrate	23	230	5.8
Calcium phosphate tribasic	40	400	10

*Conversion: 1 g elemental calcium=25 mmol Ca^{++}= 50 mEq Ca^{++}.

Calcium supplements contain varying amounts of lead, depending on the source (see Precautions). Lead content should be among the many factors considered when recommending a calcium supplement to a patient.

Reviewed 1997

CALCIUM SALTS: PARENTERAL

General Monograph, CPhA

Calcium Therapy

This monograph has been compiled by CPhA. It may contain information different from that approved by Therapeutic Products Programme, Health Canada, and the pharmaceutical manufacturers' approval has not been requested.

Pharmacology: Calcium is the most abundant mineral in the human body and is essential for maintaining the functional integrity of nervous and musculoskeletal systems as well as cell membrane and capillary permeability. The majority (99%) of body calcium is contained in bone with the remainder equally distributed between intra- and extracellular fluids. Calcium is an activator in many enzymatic reactions and is necessary for nerve impulse transmission, renal function, respiration and blood coagulation.

Pharmacokinetics: Once absorbed into the bloodstream, most calcium is rapidly incorporated into skeletal muscle; the remainder is equally distributed between intra- and extracellular fluids. Normal total serum calcium concentrations range from 2.2 to 2.6 mmol/L, although only the ionized fraction is physiologically active. Of the total serum calcium, 50% is ionized, 5% is complexed with anions such as phosphates or citrates and 45% is protein bound. Hyperproteinemia is associated with an increase in total calcium; hypoproteinemia has the opposite effect. Acidosis favors an increase in ionic calcium concentration, while alkalosis leads to a decrease in the ionized fraction.

CSF calcium concentrations tend to be similar to the serum concentration of ionized calcium, i.e., approximately 50% of total serum calcium.

Calcium crosses the placenta, reaching higher levels in fetal blood than in the mother, and is excreted in breast milk.

Calcium is excreted mainly in the feces, either as a result of passing through the gut unabsorbed or through biliary or pancreatic secretion into the gut lumen. Very small amounts of calcium are excreted in the urine as most renally filtered calcium is reabsorbed. Urinary excretion of calcium is promoted by growth hormone, calcitonin and nonthiazide diuretics, whereas parathyroid hormone, Vitamin D, thiazide diuretics or a decrease in ionized calcium concentration tend to decrease the amount of calcium excreted in the urine. Calcium is also excreted in sweat.

Indications: The treatment of hypocalcemia for those conditions requiring a prompt increase in blood plasma calcium concentrations, such as neonatal tetany and tetany due to parathyroid deficiency, vitamin D deficiency and alkalosis. The prevention of hypocalcemia during exchange transfusions of citrated blood. In the treatment of hyperkalemia when there is ECG evidence of secondary cardiac toxicity.

Calcium salts have also been administered as adjunctive therapy in a number of conditions, including the following: insect bites or stings (e.g., black widow spider), sensitivity reactions characterized by urticaria or angioedema, magnesium sulfate overdosage, or lead colic.

The use of calcium is not recommended in cardiac arrest except in cases of calcium channel blocker overdose, hyperkalemia or severe hypocalcemia. For more information on the role of calcium in CPR, see Drugs Used in Cardiac Arrest in the Clin-Info section.

Contraindications: Hypercalcemia and hypercalciuria (e.g., in hyperparathyroidism, vitamin D overdosage, decalcifying tumors such as plasmocytoma, bone metastases); severe renal or cardiac disease; calcium loss due to immobilization.

Precautions: In mild hypercalciuria (exceeding 300 mg/24 hours) as well as in chronic renal failure, or where there is evidence of stone formation in the urinary tract, adequate checks must be kept on urinary calcium excretion. If necessary, the dosage should be reduced or calcium therapy discontinued.

Because concurrent use of i.v. calcium with digitalis glycosides may increase the risk of cardiac arrhythmias, the use of i.v. calcium in digitalized patients should be avoided. If absolutely necessary, i.v. calcium should be given slowly and in small amounts with ECG monitoring.

When severe hypocalcemia co-exists with hyperphosphatemia (>6 mmol/L), patients should be treated for hyperphosphatemia prior to the administration of i.v. calcium; the aim is to achieve a proper calcium/phosphate ratio in order to prevent extraskeletal deposition of calcium. Correction of hyperphosphatemia may require measures such as discontinuing exogenous phosphate, administration of oral aluminum hydroxide, or dialysis.

High dose calcium therapy by any of the parenteral routes should always be accompanied by very careful monitoring of serum concentration and urinary calcium excretion, particularly in children. Serum calcium concentrations should generally be maintained between 2.25 and 2.60 mmol/L. Cardiac monitoring is also recommended.

Drug Interactions: Digitalis glycosides (see Precautions). Parenteral calcium is precipitated by carbonates, bicarbonates, phosphates, sulfates and tartrates in addition to i.v. solutions containing various drugs. Specialized references should be consulted for compatability information.

Adverse Effects: Cardiovascular: Hypotension, bradycardia, cardiac arrhythmias, syncope and cardiac arrest may occur with too rapid i.v. administration.

Local: **Tissue irritation and necrosis may occur with i.m. or s.c. injection, or if extravasation occurs during i.v. administration, particularly with the chloride salt.**

Overdose: Symptoms: Markedly elevated plasma calcium level, weakness, lethargy, intractable nausea and vomiting, coma and sudden death.

Treatment: To rapidly lower serum calcium to safe levels, administer sodium chloride by i.v. infusion plus a potent natriuretic agent, e.g., furosemide, to increase renal clearance of calcium and reduce hypercalcemia.

Dosage: Table I lists the elemental calcium content of the available parenteral calcium salts.

Table I—Calcium Salts: Parenteral

Elemental Calcium Content

Calcium Salt	% elemental Ca^{++}	Elemental Ca^{++}/g* (mg)	(mmol)
Calcium chloride	27	270	6.8
Calcium gluconate	9	90	2.3

*Conversion: 1 g elemental calcium=25 mmol Ca^{++}= 50 mEq Ca^{++}.

I.V.: Calcium injections must be administered slowly, through a small needle into a large vein to minimize venous irritation. The rate of administration should not exceed 0.35 to 0.9 mmol/minute. Injection should be stopped if patient complains of discomfort. Patients should remain recumbent for a short period following injection.

Table II lists dosages of i.v. calcium for various indications as well as corresponding volumes of available calcium injection solutions.

Table II—Calcium Salts: Parenteral

Dosage

Indication	Dose of Elemental Calcium (mmol)	Volume (mL) of Calcium Chloride[a] 10% Injection, 0.68 mmol Ca^{++}/mL	Volume (mL) of Calcium Gluconate[b] 10% Injection, 0.23 mmol Ca^{++}/mL	Comments
Emergency treatment of hypocalcemia	Adults: 3.5 to 7 Children: 0.5 to 3.5 Infants: <0.5	—[b] —[b] —[b]	15 to 30 2 to 15 <2	May be repeated every 1 to 3 days depending on response.
Hyperkalemia-induced cardiac arrhythmias	Adults: 1.125 to 7	1.7 to 10.3	4.8 to 30	Monitor ECG. May repeat in 1 to 2 minutes if necessary.
Hypermagnesemia	Adults: 2.5 to 5	3.7 to 7.4	10.7 to 21.5	Repeat according to response.
Hypocalcemic tetany	Adults: 2.25 to 8	3.3 to 11.8	9.7 to 34.3	Once daily until tetany controlled.
	Children: 0.25 to 0.7/kg	0.4 to 1/kg	1.1 to 3/kg	Give 3 to 4 times daily until tetany controlled.
	Neonates: 1.2/kg/day	1.8/kg	5.5/kg	Give in divided doses.
Prevention of hypocalcemia during exchange transfusions	Adults: 0.68	1	—[a]	Concurrently with each 100 mL citrated blood.
	Neonates: 0.23	0.34	—[a]	After each 100 mL citrated blood.
Cardiopulmonary resuscitation[c]	Adults: 3.5 to 7	5.1 to 10.3	—[a]	Repeat at 10-minute intervals as necessary.
	Children: 0.135/kg	0.2/kg	—[a]	Repeat at 10-minute intervals as necessary.

[a] Calcium chloride is often recommended as the preferred salt when calcium is used in cardiopulmonary resuscitation or to prevent hypocalcemia during transfusions.

[b] Most clinicians consider calcium gluconate the preferred salt for the treatment of hypocalcemia, especially if acidosis is also present.

[c] Calcium should not be used in cardiopulmonary resuscitation except in the presence of hypocalcemia, hyperkalemia or calcium channel blocker overdose.

I.M.: Calcium chloride should never be injected i.m. as it may cause severe necrosis and sloughing when injected into tissue. Other calcium salts should only be administered i.m. when i.v. access cannot be established.

Intracardiac: 1.35 to 5.4 mmol (as Cl^-) into the ventricle cavity. **Not** to be injected into the myocardium.

Reviewed 1997

CALCIUM-SANDOZ®
Novartis Consumer Health

Calcium Preparations

Calcium Therapy

Indications: As a dietary supplement where calcium intake may be inadequate: childhood and adolescence, pregnancy and lactation, postmenopausal females and in the aged.

In the treatment of calcium deficiency states which may occur in diseases such as: tetany of the newborn (as a supplement to parenterally administered calcium), hypoparathyroidism (acute and chronic), pseudo-hypoparathyroidism, postmenopausal and senile osteoporosis, rickets and osteomalacia.

Contraindications: Hypercalcemia and hypercalciuria (e.g. hyperparathyroidism, vitamin D overdosage, decalcifying tumors such as plasmocytoma, bone metastases); severe renal disease; and in calcium loss due to immobilization. Hypersensitivity to any of the components of Calcium Sandoz.

Although no concrete evidence is available about the metabolic process leading from calcium glucono-galacto-gluconate to galactose, it is advisable not to administer to galactosemic patients.

Precautions: For diabetic patients, consideration should be given to the sucrose content of 719 mg/tablet of Calcium-Sandoz Forte. Gramcal and Calcium-Sandoz Syrup are suitable for sodium and potassium restricted diets. Calcium-Sandoz Forte is suitable for potassium restricted diets. Because of the presence of sodium (12 mmol), Calcium-Sandoz Forte is not suitable for sodium restricted diets.

In mild hypercalciuria (exceeding 300 mg/24 hours) as well as in chronic renal failure, or where there is evidence of stone formation in the urinary tract, adequate checks must be kept on urinary calcium excretion. If necessary the dosage should be reduced or calcium therapy discontinued. In patients prone to formation of calculi in the urinary tract an increased fluid intake is recommended.

Drug Interactions: Administration of corticosteroids may interfere with calcium absorption.

Calcium-Sandoz syrup and effervescent tablets should not be taken within 3 hours of oral tetracycline or fluoride administration (possible interference of absorption).

High vitamin D intake should be avoided during calcium therapy unless especially indicated.

Thiazide diuretics cause calcium retention and this may exacerbate hypercalcemia from $CaCo_3$ (calcium carbonate).

Administration of calcium may reduce the response to verapamil and possibly other calcium channel blockers.

Given in large doses to digitalized patients, calcium may increase the risk of cardiac arrhythmias.

Certain dietary substances interfere with the absorption of calcium. These include oxalic acid (found in large quantities in rhubarb and spinach), phytic acid (bran and whole cereals) and phosphorus (milk and other dairy products).

Adverse Effects: Occasional diarrhea or constipation may occur with high calcium intake.

Overdose: Symptoms and Treatment: Acute overdosage has not been reported. It would be expected to cause gastrointestinal disturbances but not to result in hypercalcemia, except in patients treated with an excessive dose of vitamin D.

Dosage: Calcium-Sandoz Forte: Children: completely dissolve 1 to 2 tablets in a glass of water daily. Adults: completely dissolve 1 to 2 tablets in a glass of water twice a day or as directed by the physician. Sugar can be added to taste or tablets can be dissolved in fruit juice.

Calcium-Sandoz Gramcal: Usual dose in osteoporosis, 1 or 2 tablets (dissolved in water) daily, or as prescribed.

Calcium-Sandoz Syrup: Infants: 0 to 3 years: 10 mL given 1 to 3 times daily. Children: 4 to 12 years: 15 mL given 1 to 3 times daily. Adults: 20 mL given 1 to 3 times daily. Pregnancy and nursing: 20 mL given 1 to 3 times daily.

Supplied: Calcium-Sandoz Forte: Each whitish, effervescent tablet contains: calcium lactate-gluconate 2 940 mg, calcium carbonate 300 mg and provides 500 mg (12.5 mmol) elemental calcium. Nonmedicinal ingredients: calcium cyclamate, citric acid, flavor, polyethylene glycol, sodium hydrogen carbonate and sucrose. Energy: 74.5 kJ (18 kcal). Sodium: 12 mmol (274 mg). Tubes of 20. Protect from heat and humidity.

Calcium-Sandoz Gramcal: Each whitish, effervescent tablet contains: calcium lactate-gluconate 2 327 mg, calcium carbonate 1 750 mg and provides 1 000 mg (25 mmol) of elemental calcium. Nonmedicinal ingredients: aspartame, citric acid, flavor and polyethylene glycol. Energy: 59.3 kJ (14.17 kcal). Potassium: 10 mEq. Sodium: 0.07 mmol (1.69 mg). Tubes of 20. Protect from heat and humidity.

Syrup: Each 5 mL of maize colored syrup contains: calcium lactobionate 295.0 mg, calcium glubionate 1 437.5 mg, elemental sodium: 0.007 mmol (0.162 mg) and provides 2.7 mmol (110 mg) elemental calcium. Nonmedicinal ingredients: benzoic acid, citric acid, flavors, malic acid, sodium saccharin, sorbitol and water. Energy: 28.4 kJ (6.77 kcal)/5 mL. Bottles of 230 mL.

(Shown in Product Recognition Section)

CALCIUM STANLEY
Stanley

Calcium Glucoheptonate—Calcium Gluconate

Calcium Therapy

Indications: As a dietary supplement where calcium intake may be inadequate: childhood and adolescence, pregnancy and lactation, postmenopausal females and in the aged.

In the treatment of calcium deficiency states which may occur in diseases such as: tetany of the newborn (as a supplement to parenterally administered calcium), hypoparathyroidism (acute and chronic), pseudohypoparathyroidism, postmenopausal and senile osteoporosis, rickets and osteomalacia. Since the product does not contain sugars, it is suitable for diabetics.

Contraindications: Hypercalcemia and hypercalciurea (e.g. in hyperparathyroidism, vitamin D overdosage, decalcifying tumors such as plasmocytoma, bone metastases); severe renal diseases; calcium loss due to immobilization.

Precautions: In mild hypercalciurea (exceeding 300 mg/24 hours) as well as in chronic renal failure, or where there is evidence of stone formation in the urinary tract, adequate checks must be kept on urinary calcium excretion. If necessary, the dosage should be reduced or calcium therapy discontinued. High vitamin D intake should be avoided during calcium therapy unless especially indicated. Administration of corticosteroids may interfere with calcium absorption.

Calcium compounds reduce blood concentrations of oral tetracyclines. Concomitant use should be avoided or doses of the drugs should not be taken within 1 hour of each other. Certain dietary substances interfere with the absorption of calcium. This include oxalic acid (found in large quantities in rhubarb and spinach), phytic acid (bran and whole cereals) and phosphorus (milk and other dairy products).

Calcium salts should be administered only with great caution, if at all, to patients a) receiving digitalis glycosides b) with impaired renal function and who have a history of formation of renal stones or (c) who are hypokalemic infants.

Adverse Effects: Gastrointestinal distress may occur. Overdosage may produce cardiac effects and give rise to anorexia, weakness, depression, polyuria, vomiting, and diarrhea or constipation.

Dosage: Adults: 10 mL 1 to 3 times daily. Children: 5 mL 3 times daily. Infants: 2.5 mL 3 times daily, mixed with formula.

Supplied: Each 5 mL of transparent, light yellow, fruit-flavored liquid contains: elemental calcium 100 mg from calcium glucoheptonate (132 mg/mL) and calcium gluconate (112 mg/mL). Nonmedicinal ingredients: FD&C Red No. 2, flavor, lactic acid, sodium benzoate, sodium cyclamate and water. Energy: <1 kJ (0.04 kcal)/mL. Bottles of 250 and 500 mL.

The safety of immunization programs is in part maximized through monitoring vaccine-associated adverse events. To report a vaccine-associated adverse event, complete the form "Report of Vaccine-associated Adverse Event" found in the CLIN-INFO SECTION.

CALDOMINE®-DH Ⓝ
Technilab

Hydrocodone Bitartrate—Pheniramine Maleate—Phenylpropanolamine HCl—Pyrilamine Maleate

Antihistaminic—Antitussive—Decongestant

Supplied: Caldomine-DH Forte: Each 5 mL contains: hydrocodone bitartrate 5 mg, phenylpropanolamine HCl 25 mg, pyrilamine maleate 12.5 mg and pheniramine maleate 12.5 mg. Nonmedicinal ingredients: alcohol, artificial flavorings, caramel, glycerin, menthol, methylparaben, propylparaben, purified water, simethicone and sucrose. Energy: 12.57 kcal/5 mL. Gluten-, lactose-, sodium- and tartrazine-free. Bottles of 500 mL.

Caldomine-DH Pediatric: Each 5 mL contains: hydrocodone bitartrate 1.667 mg, phenylpropanolamine HCl 12.5 mg, pyrilamine maleate 6.25 mg and pheniramine maleate 6.25 mg. Nonmedicinal ingredients: alcohol, artificial coloring and flavoring, glycerin, methylparaben, propylparaben, purified water and sucrose. Energy: 12.64 kcal/5 mL. Gluten-, lactose-, sodium- and tartrazine-free. Bottles of 500 mL.

Store between 15 and 30°C. Protect from freezing. Keep out of the reach of children.

CAL-MAG
Swiss Herbal

Vitamins—Minerals

Supplied: Each protein coated caplet contains: calcium (HVP chelated) 350 mg, magnesium (HVP chelated) 175 mg, vitamin C 25 mg, vitamin D 200 IU and zinc (citrate) 10 mg. Nonmedicinal ingredients: bromelain, cellulose, glutamic acid, magnesium stearate and rosehips. Bottles of 90, 180 and 360.

CALMURID®
Galderma

Urea

Emollient

Supplied: Each g of cream contains: urea 100 mg in an emulsified base formulated without lanolin or parabens. Nonmedicinal ingredients: betaine monohydrate, cholesterol, diethanolamine cetylphosphate complex, glyceryl monostearate, hard fat, lactic acid, purified water and sodium chloride. Plastic tubes of 100 g. Store in a cool place (8 to 15°C).

CALMURID® HC Ⓟ
Galderma

Hydrocortisone—Urea

Topical Corticosteroid—Emollient

Pharmacology: Topical corticosteroids are synthetic derivatives of cortisone which are effective when applied locally to control many types of inflammatory, allergic and pruritic dermatoses.

They are thought to act by controlling the rate of synthesis of proteins. The primary action of the corticosteroid is to interfere with the synthesis of arachidonic acid by inhibiting the phospholipase A_2 synthesis. The overall effect of corticosteroids is a catabolic one.

Corticosteroid responsive dermatoses may be divided into those which are very responsive and those which require higher concentrations of corticosteroids, occlusion of the drug under a plastic film or intralesional administration. Attention must be paid to the concentration of topical corticosteroid used. Although effectiveness is enhanced by the application of the corticosteroid preparation under a transparent plastic wrapping, systemic absorption is also enhanced, occasionally sufficiently to suppress the pituitary-adrenal axis.

Indications: For topical therapy of corticosteroid responsive acute and chronic skin disorders where an anti-inflammatory, antiallergic and antipruritic activity in the topical management is required.

Contraindications: Untreated tubercular, bacterial, and fungal infections involving the skin and in certain viral diseases such

Calmurid HC (cont'd)

as herpes simplex, chickenpox and vaccinia; hypersensitivity to any of the components of the preparation.

In concurrent mycotic infections, combine with antimycotic treatment.

Warnings: *Pregnancy* and *Lactation:* The safety of topical corticosteroids during pregnancy or lactation has not been established. The potential benefit of topical corticosteroids, if used during pregnancy or lactation, should be weighed against possible hazard to the fetus or the nursing infant.

If used under an occlusive dressing, particularly over extensive areas, sufficient absorption may take place to give rise to adrenal suppression and other systemic effects.

Not for ophthalmic use.

Precautions: Topical corticosteroids should be used with caution on lesions close to the eye.

Although hypersensitivity reactions have been rare with topically applied steroid products, this drug should be discontinued and appropriate therapy initiated if there are signs of reaction.

Prolonged use of topical corticosteroid products may produce atrophy of the skin and of subcutaneous tissues, particularly on flexor surfaces and on the face. However, this side effect is rarely seen when using hydrocortisone. If this is noted, discontinue the use of the drug.

In cases of bacterial infections of the skin, appropriate antibacterial agents should be used in primary therapy. If it is considered necessary, a topical corticosteroid may be used as an adjunct to control inflammation, erythema and itching.

The drug should be used with caution in patients with stasis dermatitis and other skin diseases associated with impaired circulation.

If a symptomatic response is not noted within a few days to a week, the local applications of corticosteroid should be discontinued and the patient re-evaluated. During the use of topical corticosteroids secondary infections may occur.

Significant systemic absorption may occur when corticosteroids are applied over large areas of the body. To minimize this possibility, when long-term therapy is anticipated, interrupt treatment periodically or treat one area of the body at a time.

Advise patients to inform subsequent physicians of the prior use of corticosteroids.

Adverse Effects: The following local adverse reactions have been reported with the use of topical corticosteroids: dryness, itching, burning, local irritation, striae, skin atrophy, atrophy of subcutaneous tissues, telangiectasia, hypertrichosis, change in pigmentation and secondary infection.

These side effects are very rarely observed, even under occlusive conditions, with low potency topical glucocorticosteroid preparations such as hydrocortisone creams.

Adrenal suppression has also been reported following topical corticosteroid therapy.

Overdose: Symptoms and Treatment: No cases of overdosage with this drug are known.

However, percutaneous absorption of topically applied corticosteroids can occur especially under occlusive conditions. When large amounts of corticosteroids are absorbed, toxic effects may be indicated by ecchymoses of the skin, peptic ulceration, hypertension, aggravation of the infection, hirsutism, acne, edema and muscle weakness due to protein depletion. No specific antidote is available. Toxic effects are nearly always manifestations of overdosage and should be treated symptomatically and dosage reduced or the drug withdrawn.

Dosage: Apply a thin layer of cream to the affected skin area(s), 3 to 4 times daily, until the skin has healed, or as prescribed by the physician.

Supplied: Each g of cream contains: hydrocortisone 1% and urea 10%. Nonmedicinal ingredients: betaine monohydrate, cholesterol, diethanolamine cetylphosphate complex, glyceryl monostearate, hard fat, lactic acid, purified water and sodium chloride. Noncollapsible propylene tubes of 30 and 100 g. Store in a cool place (8 to 15°C).

CALMYDONE® Ⓝ

Technilab

Hydrocodone Bitartrate—Etafedrine HCl—Sodium Citrate—Doxylamine Succinate

Antihistaminic—Antitussive—Decongestant

Supplied: Each mL contains: hydrocodone bitartrate 0.33 mg, etafedrine HCl 3.33 mg, sodium citrate 40 mg and doxylamine succinate 1.2 mg. Nonmedicinal ingredients: alcohol, artificial coloring and flavoring, caramel, FD&C yellow #6, glycerin, menthol, methylparaben, propylparaben, purified water and sucrose. Alcohol: 3.9% w/v. Sucrose: 0.6 g/mL. Bottles of 500 mL and 2 L. Store between 15 and 30°C.

CALMYLIN® ACE Ⓝ

Technilab

Guaifenesin—Codeine Phosphate—Pheniramine Maleate

Expectorant—Antitussive—Antihistamine

Supplied: Each 5 mL of cherry-flavored syrup contains: guaifenesin 100 mg, pheniramine maleate 7.5 mg and codeine phosphate 10 mg. Nonmedicinal ingredients: alcohol, artificial coloring and flavoring, caramel, citric acid, FD&C yellow #6, glycerin, menthol, propylene glycol, purified water, sodium benzoate, sodium citrate, sodium cyclamate and sucrose. Alcohol: 4.1 % v/v. Sucrose: 45 %. Bottles of 500 mL and 1 L. Store between 15 and 30°C. Protect from light.

CALMYLIN® EXPECTORANT

Technilab

Guaifenesin

Expectorant

Supplied: Each 5 mL of red, fruit flavored syrup contains: guaifenesin 100 mg. Nonmedicinal ingredients: alcohol, artificial coloring and flavoring, calcium cyclamate, glycerin, menthol, methylparaben, natural honey flavoring, propylparaben, purified water, sodium carboxymethylcellulose and sorbitol. Bottles of 250 mL. Store between 15 to 30°C. Protect from freezing.

CALMYLIN® ORIGINAL with Codeine Ⓝ
CALMYLIN® with Codeine Ⓝ

Technilab

Codeine Phosphate—Ammonium Chloride—Diphenhydramine HCl

Codeine Phosphate—Guaifenesin—Pseudoephedrine HCl

Antihistamine—Antitussive—Expectorant

Decongestant—Antitussive—Expectorant

Supplied: Calmylin Original with Codeine: Each 5 mL of red, raspberry-flavored syrup contains: codeine phosphate 3.3 mg, ammonium chloride 125 mg and diphenhydramine HCl 12.5 mg. Nonmedicinal ingredients: alcohol, artificial coloring and flavoring, FD&C Yellow #6, glycerin, menthol, methylparaben, propylparaben, purified water, simethicone, sorbitol and sucrose. Bottles of 100, 250 and 350 mL.

Calmylin with Codeine: Each 5 mL of red, raspberry-flavored syrup contains: codeine phosphate 3.3 mg, guaifenesin 100 mg and pseudoephedrine HCl 30 mg. Nonmedicinal ingredients: alcohol, artificial coloring and flavoring, citric acid, FD&C Yellow #6, glycerin, maltitol, menthol, methylparaben, propylparaben, propylene glycol, purified water, sodium chloride, sodium citrate, sodium cyclamate and sorbitol. Bottles of 100, 250 and 350 mL.

Store between 15 and 30°C. Protect from freezing.

New Product 1998

CALMYLIN® Preparations

Technilab

Dextromethorphan Compound

Analgesic—Antitussive—Decongestant—Expectorant Preparations

Supplied: Calmylin #1: Each 5 mL of red, raspberry flavored syrup contains: dextromethorphan HBr 15 mg. Nonmedicinal ingredients: artificial coloring and flavoring, calcium cyclamate, citric acid, D&C red #33, glycerin, menthol, methylparaben, natural honey flavoring, propylparaben, propylene glycol, purified water, sodium carboxymethylcellulose and sorbitol. Bottles of 250 mL.

Calmylin #2: Each 5 mL of red, raspberry flavored syrup contains: dextromethorphan HBr 15 mg and pseudoephedrine HCl 30 mg. Nonmedicinal ingredients: artificial coloring and flavoring, citric acid, glycerin, maltitol, menthol, methylparaben, natural honey flavoring, propylparaben, propylene glycol, purified water, sodium citrate, sodium cyclamate and sorbitol. Bottles of 250 mL.

Calmylin #3: Each 5 mL of red, fruit flavored syrup contains: dextromethorphan HBr 15 mg, pseudoephedrine HCl 30 mg and guaifenesin 100 mg. Nonmedicinal ingredients: alcohol, artificial coloring and flavoring, citric acid, glycerin, maltitol, menthol, methylparaben, natural honey flavoring, propylparaben, propylene glycol, purified water, sodium citrate, sodium cyclamate and sorbitol. Bottles of 250 mL.

Calmylin #4: Each 5 mL of red, raspberry flavored syrup contains: diphenhydramine HCl 12.5 mg, dextromethorphan HBr 15 mg and ammonium chloride 125 mg. Nonmedicinal ingredients: alcohol, artificial coloring and flavoring, glycerin, menthol, methylparaben, propylparaben, purified water, simethicone, sorbitol and sucrose. Bottles of 100 and 250 mL.

Calmylin Cough and Flu-Regular: Each 15 mL of dark red, blackberry flavored syrup contains: acetaminophen 325 mg, dextromethorphan HBr 15 mg, pseudoephedrine HCl 30 mg and guaifenesin 100 mg. Nonmedicinal ingredients: artificial coloring and flavoring, benzoic acid, caramel, citric acid, maltitol, polyethylene glycol, propylene glycol, purified water, sodium benzoate, sodium citrate and sodium cyclamate. Bottles of 250 mL.

Calmylin Pediatric: Each 5 mL of yellow, honey-lemon flavored syrup contains: dextromethorphan HBr 7.5 mg and pseudoephedrine HCl 15 mg. Nonmedicinal ingredients: artificial flavoring, citric acid, D&C yellow #10, FD&C yellow #6, glycerin, maltitol, menthol, methylparaben, natural honey and lemon flavoring, propylparaben, propylene glycol, purified water, sodium citrate, sodium cyclamate and sorbitol. Bottles of 250 mL.

Store between 15 to 30°C. Protect from freezing.

CALSAN®

Novartis Consumer Health

Calcium Carbonate

Calcium Supplement

Indications: As a dietary supplement where calcium intake may be inadequate: childhood, adolescence, adulthood, pregnancy, lactation, perimenopausal and postmenopausal women and in the aged.

In the treatment of calcium deficiency states which may occur in diseases such as hypoparathyroidism (acute and chronic), pseudohypoparathyroidism, postmenopausal and senile osteoporosis, rickets and osteomalacia.

Contraindications: Hypercalcemia and hypercalciuria (e.g. hyperparathyroidism, vitamin D overdosage, decalcifying tumors such as plasmocytoma, bone metastases); severe renal disease; and in calcium loss due to immobilization. Hypersensitivity to any of the components.

Precautions: In mild hypercalciuria (exceeding 300 mg/24 hours) as well as in chronic renal failure, or where there is evidence of stone formation in the urinary tract, adequate checks must be kept on urinary calcium excretion. If necessary, dosage should be reduced or calcium therapy discontinued. In patients prone to formation of calculi in the urinary tract, an increased fluid intake is recommended.

For phenylketonuric patients, consideration should be given to the aspartame content (5 mg/tablet) of Calsan chewable tablets. Calsan tablets and capsules are suitable for sodium and potassium restricted diets. Calsan preparations do not contain sugar and are therefore suitable for diabetic patients requiring calcium supplementation.

High vitamin D intake should be avoided during calcium therapy unless especially indicated.

<u>*Drug Interactions:*</u> Administration of corticosteroids may interfere with calcium absorption.

Calcium carbonate should not be taken within 3 hours of oral tetracycline or fluoride administration (possible interference of absorption).

Thiazide diuretics cause calcium retention and this may exacerbate hypercalcemia from $CaCO_3$ (calcium carbonate).

Administration of calcium may reduce the response to verapamil and possibly other calcium channel blockers.

Given in large doses to digitalized patients, calcium may increase the risk of cardiac arrhythmias.

Certain dietary substances interfere with the absorption of calcium. These include oxalic acid (found in large quantities in rhubarb and spinach), phytic acid (bran and whole cereals) and phosphorus (milk and other dairy products).

Adverse Effects: Occasional diarrhea or constipation may occur with high calcium intake.

Overdose: Symptoms and Treatment: Acute overdosage has not been reported. It would be expected to cause gastrointestinal disturbances but not to result in hypercalcemia, except in patients treated with an excessive dose of Vitamin D.

Dosage: Tablets: chew 1 to 3 chewable tablets/day or as directed by the physician.

Capsules: take 1 to 3 soft gelatin capsules/day with water or as directed by the physician.

Supplied: Capsules: Each off-white oblong soft gelatin capsule, imprinted 500 mg on one side and the CALSAN logo on the other (in green), contains: calcium carbonate 1 250 mg and provides 500 mg (12.5 mmol) elemental calcium. Nonmedicinal ingredients: FD&C blue No. 1, FD&C yellow No. 10, gelatin, glycerin, methyl paraben, polyethylene glycol, propyl paraben, sorbitol and titanium dioxide. Energy: 24.45 kJ (5.85 kcal). Potassium: 0.007 mmol (0.266 mg). Sodium: 0.16 mmol (3.79 mg). Bottles of 100. Keep in a cool, dry place.

Tablets: Each white, scored, double hexagonal chewable tablet, embossed "Ca++ 500" on one side and "CALSAN" on the other, contains: calcium carbonate 1 250 mg and provides 500 mg (12.5 mmol) elemental calcium. Nonmedicinal ingredients: aspartame, citric acid, flavors, magnesium stearate, mannitol, polyethylene glycol and povidone. Energy: 15.12 kJ (3.6 kcal). Potassium: 0.0017 mmol (0.065 mg). Sodium: 0.18 mmol (4.29 mg). Bottles of 100.

(Shown in Product Recognition Section)

CALTINE® Ⓟ

Ferring

Synthetic Calcitonin Salmon (Salcatonin)

Paget's Disease Therapy—Hypercalcemia Treatment

Pharmacology: Salmon calcitonin participates in the regulation of the homeostasis of calcium by acting primarily on the bone, in Paget's disease presumably by an initial blocking effect on accelerated bone resorption. The rate of bone turnover appears to be decreased.

The pharmacologic activity of salmon calcitonin is the same as that of the endogenously produced hormone, but salmon calcitonin is substantially more potent on a weight basis and has a longer duration of action. Calcitonin acts predominantly on bone to depress bone resorption, but also has direct effects on the kidneys and the gastrointestinal tract. As a result of the inhibition of release of calcium from bone, and the stimulation of urinary calcium excretion, calcitonin tends to lower blood calcium.

Following parenteral administration, the hypocalcemic effect of calcitonin is apparent in about 15 minutes, peaks at approximately 4 hours, and lasts for 8 to 24 hours.

The lowering of serum calcium with calcitonin can, under certain conditions, be as much as 3 to 4 mg%. Chronic administration of calcitonin results in a parallel diminution of 2 parameters of bone turnover, namely, serum alkaline phosphatase levels, and total hydroxyproline excretion in the urine. The extent to which calcitonin can inhibit bone resorption depends on the existing rate of bone resorption (the higher the rate of bone resorption, the more evident the inhibition of bone resorption following calcitonin administration). Thus, these biochemical effects are more prominent in patients with generalized Paget's disease, or hypercalcemia than in healthy adults, who have a relatively low rate of bone resorption.

Paget's disease is characterized by a mixed picture of bone resorption, increased vascularity, high bone turnover and irregular bone formation. One or more bones may be affected, and an increased alkaline phosphatase is often found on a routine laboratory screen. Clinical features can include bone pain, deformities, nerve and blood vessel compression, increased cardiac output, spontaneous fractures and osteogenic sarcoma. Immobilization of patients with Paget's disease may lead to hypercalcemia, hypercalciuria, and renal calculus formation.

Salmon calcitonin has been shown to be effective in relieving bone pain in 60 to 80% of patients with Paget's disease. A similar proportion show a parallel diminution of alkaline phosphatase levels in the serum (reflecting increased bone formation), and of total hydroxyproline excretion in the urine (reflecting breakdown of collagen-containing bone matrix) in the same proportions (average 50%). Significant pain relief is usually evident within 2 months after initiation of therapy, with the maximum relief being obtained within 6 to 12 months.

The biochemical changes produced by calcitonin have been shown to correlate with changes toward more normal bone, as evidenced by radiologic assessments showing slowing or even regression of resorption fronts in pagetic lesions, the observation of rapid healing of pathological fractures during treatment with the prevention of immobilization hypercalcemia, and the decreased fracture rate during therapy.

In Paget's disease, orthopedic surgery is associated with complications due to softness of bone and/or excessive bleeding in about 50% of cases. In patients pretreated with calcitonin prior to surgery, no complications were found.

Other symptoms of Paget's disease that may show a beneficial effect with calcitonin treatment are high output cardiac failure, and symptoms due to, or mimicking neurologic compression.

In most patients with hypercalcemia treated with calcitonin, the hypocalcemic response was partial, with the serum calcium decreasing from a dangerously high level to a more tolerable or mildly hypercalcemic range. Often, there was an accompanying clinical improvement, allowing resumption of eating and further improvement, and, where applicable, the institution of definitive treatment for the underlying disease. In patients with multiple myeloma, a stable normocalcemia was achieved in all those with mild hypercalcemia, and about half of those with severe hypercalcemia. Prolonged normocalcemia after cessation of calcitonin therapy has been reported.

Indications: Paget's Disease of Bone: For the management of symptomatic Paget's disease of bone (osteitis deformans).

Hypercalcemia: For the early treatment of hypercalcemic emergencies (eg. hypercalcemic patients with carcinoma—with or without metastases, multiple myeloma or primary hyperparathyroidism), along with other appropriate agents, in cases where a rapid reduction in serum calcium concentration is required, until more specific treatment of the underlying disorder is instituted. The drug may also be added to the existing therapeutic regimens for the treatment of hypercalcemia, such as i.v. fluids and furosemide, oral phosphates, corticosteroids or other agents.

Salmon calcitonin may be used in patients with azotemia and those with limited cardiac reserve in whom i.v. fluids may be contraindicated.

Contraindications: Hypersensitivity to salmon calcitonin.

Warnings: Administration of salmon calcitonin has been associated with serious allergic type reactions, such as bronchospasm, swelling of the tongue or throat, tachycardia, hypotension, collapse and anaphylactic shock and in 1 case death due to anaphylaxis (see Precautions).

Children: There are no adequate safety and efficacy data supporting the use of calcitonin in children. The relationship between juvenile Paget's disease to Paget's disease in adults has not been established and salmon calcitonin has been used only rarely in children.

Pregnancy: Salmon calcitonin has been shown to decrease fetal birth weights in rabbits when given in doses 14 to 56 times the human therapeutic doses. It is not known whether salmon calcitonin can cause fetal harm when administered to pregnant women. Therefore the drug should be used during pregnancy only when the potential benefits justify the possible risks to the fetus.

Lactation: Salmon calcitonin inhibits lactation in animals, and the drug should therefore not be administered to nursing mothers.

Precautions: The possibility of a systemic allergic reaction should be borne in mind, and appropriate measures of treatment of a hypersensitivity reaction should be readily available. Skin testing should be considered prior to initiating salmon calcitonin therapy and the drug should not be given to patients with a positive skin test. The following procedure is suggested for the skin test:

Prepare a dilution of 10 IU/mL by withdrawing 1/10 mL (0.1 mL) in a tuberculin syringe and filling it to 1 mL with Dextrose injection 5% USP (or Saline Injection, USP). Mix well, discard 0.9 mL and inject intracutaneously 0.1 mL (approximately 1 IU) on the inner aspect of the forearm. Observe the injection site 15 minutes after injection. The appearance of more than mild erythema or wheal constitutes a positive response.

The possibility of hypocalcemic tetany following salmon calcitonin administration should be considered, and calcium injection should be readily available, particularly during administration of the first several doses of salmon calcitonin.

Patients receiving salmon calcitonin for long periods should have periodic examinations of urine sediment as coarse granular casts and casts containing renal tubular epithelial cells were reported in some volunteers in a study of the effect of calcitonin salmon on immobilization osteoporosis.

Radiographic evidence of marked progressive pagetic lesions, possibly with some loss of definition of periosteal margins, must be evaluated carefully to rule out the possibility of osteogenic sarcoma since the frequency of this tumor is increased in patients with Paget's disease of bone.

Careful instructions in sterile injection technique should be given to the patient, and to other persons who may administer salmon calcitonin.

Adverse Effects: Adverse effects with salmon calcitonin are usually mild, although, in about 10% of patients adverse effects may be severe enough to require discontinuance of the drug.

Adverse effects of salmon calcitonin most frequently involve the gastrointestinal tract. Nausea, with or without vomiting, is the most common adverse effect (incidence of about 20 to 40%), but it usually disappears with continued use. Other less common adverse effects on the gastrointestinal tract include: anorexia, diarrhea, epigastric pain, abdominal pain and an unusual taste.

Three cases of hypertension have been reported following the use of salmon calcitonin.

Flushing of face, ears, hands, and feet may occur (incidence of 10 to 35%), usually within minutes after salmon calcitonin injection, but this effect is usually well tolerated. Tenderness and/or tingling of the palms and soles has also been reported.

A local inflammatory reaction may occur at the site of injection: swelling, pain, erythema, urticaria have been occasionally reported (incidence of about 10%). A few cases of generalized urticaria have been reported with both salmon and human forms of calcitonin.

During the first few days of the drug administration, some patients may experience diuresis and increased urinary sodium excretion but this usually returns to the baseline levels within 5 to 7 days. Urinary frequency may occur during this time.

Antibodies to salmon calcitonin have been reported in 30 to 50% of patients after 2 to 18 months of therapy, but in no instance have these elevated antibody titers been associated with any systemic allergic or anaphylactic effect, and only rarely have antibodies been associated with the development of clinical resistance to calcitonin.

One case of symptoms of hypocalcemic tetany accompanying administration of human calcitonin has been reported (paresthesia, increased irritability). These symptoms disappeared on administration of calcium salts.

Administration of salmon calcitonin has been associated with serious allergic type reactions, such as bronchospasm, swelling of the tongue or throat, tachycardia, hypotension, collapse and anaphylactic shock and in 1 case death due to anaphylaxis.

Overdose: Symptoms and Treatment: In general, no corrective action needs to be taken, other than to discontinue treatment temporarily and maintain the patient under observation. Supportive treatment may be indicated. Provisions for parenteral calcium administration should be available during the first several administrations of calcitonin in case of hypocalcemic tetany.

Dosage: Dosage is expressed in terms of IU (International Units). An International Unit for salmon calcitonin is defined as the activity contained in 0.02525 mg of the International Reference Preparation of Calcitonin, Salmon for Bioassay.

Paget's Disease: The recommended adult dosage in Paget's disease of bone is 100 IU (1 mL) daily administered s.c. or i.m. The effect of the drug should be monitored by determinations of serum alkaline phosphatase and urinary hydroxyproline excretion before initiating salmon calcitonin therapy and every 3 to 6 months during chronic therapy. Decreases in these parameters are usually seen within the first few months of therapy, as is relief of bone pain.

Adjustments in dosage should be guided by clinical and radiologic response and by changes in biochemical parameters. When clinical or biochemical improvement occurs, the patient can often be maintained at a dose of 50 IU/day or at 50 to 100 IU 3 times/week. A dose of 100 IU/day should be continued in more severe cases. Benefits of long-term calcitonin therapy generally persist for weeks or months after drug withdrawal, usually followed by return to the pretreatment status.

Caltine (cont'd)

The possibility of substantial antibody formation should be investigated. Although specialized tests for antibody titer are not widely available, the following test will detect titers that interfere with the action of calcitonin.

After overnight fasting, a sample of the patient's blood is taken for determination of serum calcium and 100 IU of salmon calcitonin are injected i.m. The patient is then permitted to eat his usual breakfast. At 3 and 6 hours post-injection, additional blood samples are drawn. The serum calcium values are then compared. A decrease of 0.5 mg% or more from fasting level at 3 and 6 hours is usually seen in the responsive patient. Decreases of 0.3 mg% or less constitute an inadequate response to calcitonin in the patient with active Paget's disease. If the hypocalcemic action of calcitonin is lost, further therapy with salmon calcitonin will not be effective. In these cases, patient compliance should also be assessed in the event of relapse.

Hypercalcemia: For the management of hypercalcemia, the recommended initial dosage is 4 IU/kg every 12 hours by s.c. or i.m. injection. If the response to this dosage is not satisfactory after 1 to 2 days, dosage may be increased up to 8 IU/kg every 12 hours. If there is no satisfactory improvement after another 2 days, dosage may be increased to a maximum of 8 IU/kg every 6 hours.

Administration: Calcitonin salmon may be administered s.c. or i.m. Prior to initiation of salmon calcitonin therapy, a skin test using calcitonin salmon should be performed (see Precautions). When the injection volume exceeds 2 mL, the i.m. route is preferable and multiple sites of injection should be used. The s.c. route of administration is preferred for self-administration. Patients and/or other individuals who are administering calcitonin salmon should be carefully instructed about proper techniques including aseptic precautions. Because treatment with salmon calcitonin is usually prolonged, injection sites should be alternated.

Information for the Patient: See Blue Section—Information for the Patient "Caltine".

Supplied: Each mL contains: salcatonin (B.P.) 100 IU, sodium acetate 0.489 mg, sodium chloride 0.067 mg, acetic acid and sodium hydroxide to adjust toxicity and pH. pH: 3.9 to 4.5. Prescored glass ampuls of either 100 IU (1 mL) or 50 IU (0.5 mL). Store at refrigerator temperature (2 to 8°C).

CALTRATE® 600
CALTRATE® 600 + D
CALTRATE® PLUS

Whitehall-Robins

Calcium Carbonate

Calcium Carbonate—Vitamin D

Calcium Carbonate—Vitamin D—Magnesium—Zinc—Copper—Manganese

Calcium Supplement

Indications: As a dietary supplement where calcium intake may be inadequate: during childhood, adolescence, pregnancy, lactation, and in postmenopausal women and the aged.

In the treatment of calcium deficiency states which may occur in diseases such as hypoparathyroidism (acute and chronic); pseudohypoparathyroidism, postmenopausal and senile osteoporosis, rickets and osteomalacia.

Contraindications: Hypercalcemia and hypercalciuria (e.g., hyperparathyroidism, vitamin D overdosage, decalcifying tumors such as plasmocytoma; bone metastases); severe renal disease; and in calcium loss due to immobilization.

Precautions: In mild hypercalciuria (exceeding 300 mg/24 hours) as well as in chronic renal failure, or where there is evidence of stone formation in the urinary tract, adequate checks must be kept on urinary calcium excretion. If necessary, dosage should be reduced or calcium therapy discontinued.

High vitamin D intake should be avoided during calcium therapy unless especially indicated.

Certain dietary substances interfere with the absorption of calcium. These include oxalic acid (found in large quantities in rhubarb and spinach), phytic acid (bran and whole cereals) and phosphorus (milk and other dairy products).

Administration of corticosteroids may interfere with calcium absorption.

Calcium compounds reduce blood concentrations of oral tetracyclines. Concomitant use should be avoided or doses of the drugs should not be taken within 3 hours of each other.

Adverse Effects: Occasional constipation may occur with high calcium carbonate intake.

Dosage: 1 or 2 tablets a day at mealtime or as recommended by a physician.

Supplied: Caltrate 600: Each white, oval, scored, film-coated tablet, engraved LL and C 600, contains: calcium carbonate USP 1 500 mg providing 600 mg (30 mEq) elemental calcium. Nonmedicinal ingredients: cellulose, crospovidone, FD&C blue no. 2, magnesium stearate, mineral oil, povidone, sodium croscarmellose, sodium lauryl sulfate and titanium dioxide. Energy: <4.2 kJ (1 kcal). Sugar-free. Bottles of 60 and 300.

Caltrate 600 + Vitamin D: Each light tan, oval, scored, film-coated tablet, engraved LL and C40, contains: calcium carbonate USP 1 500 mg providing 600 mg (30 mEq) elemental calcium and vitamin D 125 IU. Nonmedicinal ingredients: cellulose, crospovidone, FD&C blue no. 2, FD&C red no. 40, FD&C yellow no. 6, magnesium stearate, mineral oil, peanut oil, povidone, sodium croscarmellose, sodium lauryl sulfate and titanium dioxide. Energy: <4.2 kJ (1 kcal). Bottles of 60.

Caltrate Plus: Each dusty pink, oval, scored, film-coated tablet, engraved Caltrate and +600, contains: calcium carbonate USP 1 500 mg providing 600 mg (30 mEq) elemental calcium, vitamin D 200 IU, magnesium (as oxide) 50 mg, zinc (as oxide) 7.5 mg, copper (as oxide) 1 mg and manganese (as sulfate) 1.8 mg. Nonmedicinal ingredients: cellulose, crospovidone, FD&C blue no. 1, FD&C red no. 40, FD&C yellow no. 6, gelatin, magnesium stearate, maltodextrin, mineral oil, peanut oil, sodium lauryl sulfate, stearic acid and titanium oxide. Sugar-free. Energy: <4.2 kJ (1 kcal). Bottles of 60.

Bisulfite-, gluten-, lactose-, potassium-, preservative- and tartrazine-free. Suitable for sodium restricted diets. Store at controlled room temperature 15 to 30°C.

Reviewed 1999

CAMPTOSAR™ 🄿

Pharmacia & Upjohn

Irinotecan HCl Trihydrate

Antineoplastic

> Caution: Irinotecan should be administered only under the supervision of a physician who is experienced in the use of cancer chemotherapeutic agents.
>
> Irinotecan can cause both an early and late form of diarrhea. Both forms of diarrhea may be severe. Early diarrhea (occurring during or within 24 hours of irinotecan administration) may be preceded by sweats and abdominal cramping. Late diarrhea (occurring more than 24 hours after irinotecan administration) can be prolonged. It may lead to dehydration and electrolyte imbalance, and can be life-threatening.
>
> Irinotecan can cause severe myelosuppression, usually resulting in neutropenia.

Pharmacology: Irinotecan HCl trihydrate is an antineoplastic agent of the topoisomerase I inhibitor class. Irinotecan HCl is a semisynthetic derivative of camptothecin, an alkaloid extract from plants such as Camptotheca acuminata. Camptothecins interact specifically with the enzyme topoisomerase I, which relieves torsional strain in DNA by inducing reversible single-strand breaks. Irinotecan and its active metabolite SN-38 bind to the topoisomerase I-DNA complex and prevent religation of these single-strand breaks.

Irinotecan serves as a water-soluble precursor of the lipophilic metabolite SN-38, which is formed from irinotecan primarily by liver carboxylesterase enzymes. The SN-38 metabolite is approximately 1 000 times more potent than irinotecan as an inhibitor of topoisomerase I purified from human and rodent tumor cell lines. The precise contribution of SN-38 to the activity of irinotecan in humans has not been completely defined. Both irinotecan and SN-38 exist in an active lactone form and an inactive hydroxy acid anion form. An acidic pH promotes the formation of the lactone whereas a basic pH favors the hydroxy acid anion form.

Pharmacokinetics: After i.v. infusion of irinotecan in humans, irinotecan plasma levels decline in a multiexponential manner. A summary of mean irinotecan and SN-38 pharmacokinetic parameters in 64 patients with metastatic carcinoma of the colon and rectum (dosed at 125 mg/m²) is tabulated below in Table I.

Table I—Camptosar

Pharmacokinetic Parameters

	Irinotecan (±std deviation)	SN-38 (±std deviation)
C_{max} (ng/mL)	1 660 (±797)	26.3 (±11.9)
AUC_{0-24} (ng·hr/mL)	10 200 (±3 270)	229 (±108)
$t_{1/2}$ (hr)	5.8 (±0.7)	10.4 (±3.1)
V_{area} (L/m²)	110 (±48.5)	—
CL (L/hr/m²)	13.3 (±6.01)	—

Legend:
C_{max}: Maximum plasma concentration.
AUC_{0-24}: Area under plasma concentration-time curve from 0 to 24 hours after end of infusion.
$t_{1/2}$: Terminal elimination half-life.
V_{area}: Volume of distribution of terminal elimination phase.
CL: Total systemic clearance.

Over the dose range of 50 to 350 mg/m², the AUC of irinotecan increases linearly with dose. The AUC of SN-38 increases less than proportionally with dose. Irinotecan exhibits moderate plasma protein binding (30 to 68% bound). SN-38 is approximately 95% bound to human plasma proteins, mainly albumin.

The complete disposition of irinotecan in humans has not been fully elucidated. The metabolic conversion of irinotecan to SN-38 is mediated by carboxylesterase enzymes primarily in the liver. SN-38 subsequently undergoes conjugation to form a glucuronide metabolite (SN-38 glucuronide). The urinary excretion of irinotecan (11 to 20%), SN-38 (<1%), and SN-38 glucuronide (3%) is low.

The terminal half-life of irinotecan was 6 hours in patients who were 65 years or older, and 5.5 hours in patients younger than 65 years. Dose-normalized AUC_{0-24} for SN-38 in patients who were at least 65 years old was 11% higher than in patients younger than 65 years. The influence of renal or hepatic insufficiency on the pharmacokinetics of irinotecan has not been formally studied. Patients with hepatic metastases had somewhat higher irinotecan and SN-38 AUC values than patients without liver metastases.

There is no clinically important gender influence on the pharmacokinetics of irinotecan; the influence of race has not been studied.

Clinical Trials: Data from 3 single-agent studies, involving a total of 304 patients support the use of irinotecan in the treatment of patients with metastatic cancer of the colon or rectum that has recurred or progressed following treatment with 5-FU-based therapy. All of the patients had a performance status (PS) of 0 to 2, with the majority at 0 or 1. In each study, irinotecan was administered in repeated 6-week courses as a once weekly dose for 4 weeks, followed by a 2-week rest period. In these trials, the starting doses of irinotecan were 100, 125 or 150 mg/m².

Across all 3 studies, 193 of the 304 patients began therapy at the recommended starting dose of 125 mg/m². Among these 193 patients, 2 complete and 27 partial responses were observed for an overall response rate of 15.0% (95% confidence interval (CI), 10.0 to 20.1%). The majority of responses were observed within the first 2 courses of therapy. The median duration of response for patients beginning therapy at 125 mg/m² was 5.8 months (range, 2.6 to 15.1 months). An additional 53.4% (103/193) of the patients treated at a starting dose of 125 mg/m² achieved a best response of stable disease by formal response criteria.

Response to irinotecan was seen in both males and females of all ages. These patients responded to irinotecan regardless of whether prior 5-FU had been given as adjuvant therapy or for metastatic disease. Patients with cancer of the colon or rectum responded to the drug, and these responses occurred both in patients with single and multiple metastatic sites.

The Kaplan-Meier estimate of median survival time for patients on the 125 mg/m² starting dose was 8.9 months (range, 0.3 to 33.4 months). The majority of patients treated with irinotecan had an increase in, or stabilization of body weight, and an improvement or maintenance of performance status. Among responding patients with tumor-related symptoms, the majority experienced amelioration of these symptoms during irinotecan treatment.

Indications: For the treatment of patients with metastatic carcinoma of the colon or rectum whose disease has recurred or progressed following 5-fluorouracil-based therapy.

Contraindications: Patients with a known hypersensitivity to the product.

Warnings: Irinotecan should be administered only under the supervision of a physician who is experienced in the use of cancer chemotherapeutic agents. Appropriate management of complications is possible only when adequate diagnostic and treatment facilities are readily available.

Diarrhea: Irinotecan can induce both an early and a late form of diarrhea that appear to be mediated by different mechanisms. Early onset diarrhea (occurring during or within 24 hours of irinotecan administration) is cholinergic in nature. It can be severe but is usually transient. It may be preceded by complaints of diaphoresis and abdominal cramping. Early diarrhea may be alleviated by the use of atropine (see Precautions and Dosage).

Late onset diarrhea (occurring more than 24 hours after irinotecan administration) can be prolonged. It may lead to dehydration and electrolyte imbalance and can be life-threatening. **Late diarrhea should be treated promptly with loperamide** (see Precautions). Patients with severe diarrhea should be carefully monitored and given fluid and electrolyte replacement if they become dehydrated. If National Cancer Institute (NCI) grade 3 or 4 late diarrhea occurs, irinotecan administration should be delayed until the patient recovers. Subsequent doses should be decreased (see Dosage).

Myelosuppression: Therapy with irinotecan should be temporarily discontinued if neutropenic fever occurs or if the absolute neutrophil count drops below 0.5×10^9/L. The dose of irinotecan should be reduced if there is a clinically significant decrease in the total white blood cell count ($<2\times10^9$/L), neutrophil count ($<1\times10^9$/L), hemoglobin (<80 g/L), or platelet count ($<100\times10^9$/L) (see Dosage). Severe myelosuppression resulting in deaths due to sepsis have been reported in patients treated with irinotecan. Routine administration of a colony-stimulating factor (CSF) is not necessary. However, physicians may wish to consider using CSF in individual patients experiencing problems related to neutropenia.

Pregnancy: Irinotecan has been shown to be embryotoxic in rats and rabbits at a dose of 6 mg/kg/day. It is teratogenic in rats at doses greater than 1.2 mg/kg/day, and in rabbits at 6 mg/kg/day. Treatment-related changes in the fetuses included external and visceral abnormalities, skeletal variations and abnormalities. Irinotecan may cause fetal harm when administered to a pregnant woman. If the drug is used during pregnancy, or if the patient becomes pregnant while receiving this drug, the patient should be informed of the potential hazard to the fetus. Women of childbearing potential should be advised to avoid becoming pregnant while receiving irinotecan.

Lactation: It is not known whether irinotecan is excreted in human milk. Because many drugs are excreted in human milk and because of the potential for serious adverse reactions in nursing infants, it is recommended that nursing be discontinued when receiving therapy with irinotecan.

Children: The safety and effectiveness in the pediatric population have not been established.

Precautions: General: Careful monitoring of the white blood cell count with differential, hemoglobin, and platelet count is recommended before each dose of irinotecan. Physicians should use caution in particular when monitoring the effects of irinotecan in patients of 65 years or older as these patients may be more susceptible to the toxic effects of the drug.

The concurrent administration of irinotecan with irradiation is not recommended. Patients with prior pelvic or abdominal irradiation are at an increased risk of severe myelosuppression following irinotecan therapy.

Irinotecan is emetogenic. Premedication with antiemetic agents is recommended for patients receiving irinotecan. In clinical studies, this premedication has mostly consisted of 10 mg dexamethasone given in conjunction with another type of antiemetic agent. Antiemetic agents should be given on the day of treatment, starting at least 30 minutes before administration of irinotecan. Physicians should also consider providing patients with an antiemetic regimen for subsequent use as needed.

Irinotecan is administered by i.v. infusion. Care should be taken to avoid extravasation. The infusion site should be monitored for signs of inflammation or other adverse effects. If extravasation occurs, flushing the site with sterile water and/or applying ice to the area are recommended.

Treatment of Diarrhea: For the management of irinotecan-induced early onset diarrhea, the use of 0.25 to 1 mg of i.v. atropine should be considered (unless contraindicated) for patients experiencing diaphoresis, abdominal cramping, or diarrhea that occurs during or within 24 hours following administration of irinotecan.

For the management of irinotecan-induced late onset diarrhea (occurring more than 24 hours after irinotecan administration), the prompt use of oral loperamide for controlling and treating the diarrhea, is recommended. The median onset time for late diarrhea is 11 days following the first dose of irinotecan. The dosage of loperamide used in this situation is higher than the usual dosage recommendation. Pretreatment with loperamide before the onset of late diarrhea is not recommended. Instead, at the first episode of late-onset diarrhea (i.e., poorly formed stools or more frequent bowel movement), patients are to take 4 mg loperamide, followed by 2 mg loperamide every 2 hours until they are free of diarrhea for at least 12 hours. During the night, the dose of loperamide may be 4 mg administered every 4 hours.

Information to Be Conveyed to Patients and Care Givers: Patients and/or their care givers should be informed about the expected toxic effects of irinotecan, particularly its gastrointestinal side effects such as diarrhea, nausea and vomiting. Early onset diarrhea can be accompanied by sweating and abdominal cramping. Since this type of diarrhea can occur when the patient arrives home after the irinotecan dose, the patient and/or their care giver should be advised about this. They are to inform the physician promptly if diarrhea occurs.

For the treatment of late onset diarrhea, each patient should be instructed to have loperamide on hand. Premedication with loperamide is not recommended. Instead, the patient is instructed to begin treatment for late diarrhea at the first episode of poorly formed or loose stools; or at the earliest onset of more frequent than normally expected bowel movements for the patient. The dose and frequency of the loperamide regimen should be clearly explained to the patient. Once again, the patient and/or care giver should notify the physician about the occurrence of this late onset diarrhea.

Laxatives should be avoided. Patients are to consult their physician to discuss any laxative use.

Patients are to consult their physician if vomiting, fever or evidence of infection occurs; or if symptoms of dehydration such as fainting, light-headedness, or dizziness are noted following therapy with irinotecan.

Patients are to be alerted to the possibility of alopecia.

Drug Interactions: Adverse events due to irinotecan, such as myelosuppression and diarrhea, would be expected to be enhanced by combination with other antineoplastic agents having similar adverse effects.

Lymphocytopenia has been reported in patients receiving irinotecan. It is possible that the administration of dexamethasone as an antiemetic prophylaxis may have enhanced the likelihood of this effect.

Hyperglycemia has been reported in patients receiving irinotecan. This has usually been observed in patients with a history of diabetes mellitus or evidence of glucose intolerance prior to administration of irinotecan. It is probable that dexamethasone, given as antiemetic prophylaxis, contributed to hyperglycemia in some patients.

The incidence of akathisia in clinical trials was greater (8.5%, 4 of 47 patients) when prochlorperazine was administered on the same day as irinotecan than when these drugs were given on separate days (1.3%, 1 of 80 patients). However, the 8.5% incidence of akathisia is within the range reported for use of prochlorperazine when given as premedication for other chemotherapies.

It would be expected that laxative use during irinotecan therapy may worsen the incidence or severity of diarrhea.

The use of diuretics should be carefully monitored because of the potential risk of dehydration secondary to vomiting and/or diarrhea induced by irinotecan. The physician may wish to withhold diuretics during irinotecan dosing, and certainly during periods of active vomiting or diarrhea.

Laboratory Test Interactions: There are no known interactions between irinotecan and laboratory tests.

Adverse Effects: In 3 clinical studies, 304 patients with metastatic carcinoma of the colon or rectum that had recurred or progressed following 5-FU-based therapy were treated with irinotecan.

Seventeen of the patients died within 30 days of the administration of irinotecan. In 5 cases (1.6%, 5/304), the deaths were potentially drug-related. These 5 patients experienced a constellation of medical events that included known effects of irinotecan. One of these patients died of neutropenic sepsis without fever. Neutropenic fever, defined as NCI grade 4 neutropenia and grade 2 or greater fever, occurred in 9 (3%) other patients. These patients recovered with supportive care. Thirteen (4.3%) patients discontinued irinotecan treatment because of medical events.

The adverse events in Table II are based on the experience of the 304 patients enrolled in the 3 studies.

Table II—Camptosar

Adverse Events Occurring in >10% of 304 Patients with Previously Treated Metastatic Carcinoma of the Colon or Rectum

Body System and Event	% of Patients Reporting: NCI Grades 1-4	% of Patients Reporting: NCI Grades 3 and 4
Gastrointestinal		
Diarrhea (late)[a]	87.8	30.6
7-9 stools/day (grade 3)	—	(16.4)
10 stools/day (grade 4)	—	(14.1)
Nausea	86.2	16.8
Vomiting	66.8	12.5
Anorexia	54.9	5.9
Diarrhea (early)[b]	50.7	7.9
Constipation	29.9	2.0
Flatulence	12.2	0
Stomatitis	11.8	0.7
Dyspepsia	10.5	0
Hematologic		
Leukopenia	63.2	28.0
Anemia	60.5	6.9
Neutropenia	53.9	26.3
0.5 to $<1.0\times10^9$/L (grade 3)	—	(14.8)
$<0.5\times10^9$/L (grade 4)	—	(11.5)
Whole Body		
Asthenia	75.7	12.2
Abdominal Cramping/Pain	56.9	16.4
Fever	45.4	0.
Pain	23.7	2.3
Headache	16.8	0.7
Back Pain	14.5	1.6
Chills	13.8	0.3
Minor Infection[c]	14.5	0
Edema	10.2	1.3
Abdominal Enlargement	10.2	0.3
Metabolic and Nutritional		
↓ Body Weight	30.3	0.7
Dehydration	14.8	4.3
↑ Alkaline Phosphatase	13.2	3.9
↑ AST	10.5	1.3
Dermatologic		
Alopecia	60.5	NA[d]
Sweating	16.4	0
Rash	12.8	0.7
Respiratory		
Dyspnea	22.0	3.6
↑ Coughing	17.4	0.3
Rhinitis	15.5	0
Neurologic		
Insomnia	19.4	0
Dizziness	14.8	0
Cardiovascular		
Vasodilation (Flushing)	11.2	0

[a] Occurring >24 hours after administration of irinotecan.
[b] Occurring ≤24 hours after administration of irinotecan.
[c] Primarily upper respiratory infections.
[d] Not applicable; complete hair loss=NCI grade 2.

Gastrointestinal: Diarrhea, nausea and vomiting were common adverse events following treatment with irinotecan and could be severe. These events occurred early (during or within 24 hours of irinotecan administration) or late (more than 24 hours after irinotecan administration). The median time to onset of late diarrhea was 11 days following administration of irinotecan. For patients on the 125 mg/m² starting dose, the median duration of grades 1 to 4 diarrhea was 3 days. The median duration was 7 days for those patients reporting grades 3 or 4 diarrhea on this same starting dose.

Hematology: Typical adverse hematologic events of irinotecan included neutropenia, leukopenia (including lymphocytopenia) and anemia. Serious thrombocytopenia was uncommon. The frequency of grade 3 or 4 neutropenia was significantly increased in patients who had prior pelvic or abdominal irradiation. Neutropenic fever (concurrent NCI grade 4 neutropenia and fever of grade 2 or greater) occurred in 3% of the patients. Only 5.6% of patients received G-CSF for the treatment of

Camptosar (cont'd)

neutropenia. NCI grade 3 or 4 anemia was noted in 6.9% of the patients. Blood transfusions were given to 9.9% of the patients.

Whole Body: Asthenia, fever and abdominal pain were the most common events of this type.

Hepatic: NCI grade 3 or 4 liver enzyme abnormalities were observed in less than 10% of patients. These events typically occurred in patients with known hepatic metastases.

Dermatologic: Alopecia was reported during treatment with irinotecan. Rashes have also been reported but did not result in discontinuation of treatment.

Respiratory: Severe pulmonary events were infrequent. Over half the patients with dyspnea had lung metastases. The extent to which malignant pulmonary involvement or other pre-existing lung disease may have contributed to dyspnea in these patients is unknown. In the early Japanese trials, there is some information that patients with considerable ascites or pleural effusions were at increased risk for neutropenia or diarrhea.

A potentially life-threatening pulmonary syndrome, consisting of dyspnea, fever and reticulonodular pattern on chest x-ray, was observed in a small percentage of patients in these Japanese studies. The contribution of irinotecan to these preliminary events was difficult to assess because these patients also had lung tumors and some had pre-existing non-malignant pulmonary disease.

Neurologic: Insomnia and dizziness were observed, but were not usually considered to be directly related to the administration of irinotecan. Dizziness may sometimes have represented symptomatic evidence of orthostatic hypotension in patients with dehydration.

Cardiovascular: Vasodilation (flushing) has been observed during administration of irinotecan but has not required intervention.

Overdose: Symptoms and Treatment: In phase I trials, single doses of up to 345 mg/m² of irinotecan were administered to patients with various cancers. Single doses of up to 750 mg/m² of irinotecan have been given in some trials. There are reports of patients who received higher than recommended doses. The adverse events noted in these patients were similar to those reported from patients on the recommended dose, except for a worse level of severity. There is no known antidote for overdosage of irinotecan. Maximum supportive care should be instituted to prevent dehydration due to diarrhea and to treat any infectious complications.

Dosage: Patients should be monitored for toxicity. Careful monitoring of the white blood cell count with differential, hemoglobin and platelet count is recommended before each dose of irinotecan. It is recommended that patients receive pre-medication with antiemetic agents before each irinotecan dose.

Starting Dose: The recommended starting dose of irinotecan is 125 mg/m². All doses should be administered as an i.v. infusion over 90 minutes. The recommended treatment regimen (one treatment course) is 125 mg/m² administered once weekly for 4 weeks, followed by a 2-week rest period. Thereafter, additional courses of treatment may be repeated every 6 weeks (4 weeks on therapy followed by 2 weeks off therapy).

Dose Modifications: It is recommended that subsequent doses be adjusted to as high as 150 mg/m² or to as low as 50 mg/m², in increments of 25 to 50 mg/m² depending upon individual patient tolerance of treatment (see Table III). Provided intolerable toxicity does not develop, treatment with additional courses of irinotecan may be continued indefinitely in patients who attain a response or in patients whose disease remains stable.

Table III describes the recommended dose modifications during a course of therapy, and at the start of each subsequent course of therapy. Therapy with irinotecan should be interrupted when grade 3 or 4 late diarrhea occurs or when other intolerable toxicity is observed. All dose modifications should be based on the worst preceding toxicity. A new course of therapy should not begin until the granulocyte count has recovered to at least 1.5×10^9/L, and the platelet count has recovered to at least 100×10^9/L, and treatment-related diarrhea is fully resolved. If the patient has not recovered after a 2-week delay, discontinuing irinotecan should be considered (see Table III).

Hepatic Impairment: For patients having liver metastases without decreased hepatic function, no change in dosage and administration is recommended (see Pharmacology). The use of irinotecan in patients with significant hepatic dysfunction has not been established. In clinical trials, irinotecan was not administered to patients with serum bilirubin >35 μmol/L, or

Table III—Camptosar

Recommended Dose Modifications

Toxicity NCI Grade[a] (value)	During a Course of Therapy	At the Start of Subsequent Courses of Therapy
No toxicity	Maintain dose level	↑ 25 mg/m² up to a maximum dose of 150 mg/m²
Neutropenia		
1 (1.5 to 1.9×10^9/L)	Maintain dose level	Maintain dose level[b]
2 (1.0 to $<1.5 \times 10^9$/L)	↓ 25 mg/m²	Maintain dose level[b]
3 (0.5 to $<1.0 \times 10^9$/L)	Omit dose, then ↓ 25 mg/m² when resolved to ≤grade 2	↓ 25 mg/m²
4 ($<0.5 \times 10^9$/L)	Omit dose, then ↓ 50 mg/m² when resolved to ≤grade 2	↓ 50 mg/m²
Neutropenic fever (grade 4 neutropenia and ≥grade 2 fever)	Omit dose, then ↓ 50 mg/m² when resolved	↓ 50 mg/m²
Other hematologic toxicities	Dose modifications for leukopenia, thrombocytopenia and anemia during a course of therapy and at the start of subsequent courses of therapy are also based on NCI toxicity criteria and are the same as recommended for neutropenia above.	
Diarrhea		
1 (2-3 stools/day>pretx[c])	Maintain dose level	Maintain dose level[b]
2 (4-6 stools/day>pretx[c])	↓ 25 mg/m²	Maintain, if only grade 2 tox[d]
3 (7-9 stools/day>pretx[c])	Omit dose, then ↓ 25 mg/m² when resolved to ≤grade 2	↓ 25 mg/m², if only grade 3 tox[d]
4 (≥10 stools/day>pretx[c])	Omit dose, then ↓ 50 mg/m² when resolved to ≤grade 2	↓ 50 mg/m²
Other nonhematologic toxicities		
grade 1	Maintain dose level	Maintain dose level[b]
grade 2	↓ 25 mg/m²	↓ 25 mg/m²
grade 3	Omit dose, then ↓ 25 mg/m² when resolved to ≤grade 2	↓ 50 mg/m²
grade 4	Omit dose, then ↓ 50 mg/m² when resolved to ≤grade 2	↓ 50 mg/m²

[a] National Cancer Institute Common Toxicity Criteria.
[b] Refers to initial dose used in previous course.
[c] Pretreatment.
[d] Toxicity.

transaminase >3 times the upper limit of normal if no liver metastases, or transaminase >5 times the upper limit of normal with liver metastases.

Renal Impairment: The influence of renal insufficiency on the pharmacokinetics of irinotecan has not been evaluated. However, since renal excretion does not represent a major route of elimination for irinotecan and its metabolites, alterations in renal function would not be expected to have a major influence on the pharmacokinetics.

Geriatrics: No change in dosage and administration is recommended for geriatric patients (see Pharmacology and Precautions).

Management of Early Onset Diarrhea: The use of i.v. atropine is recommended (unless contraindicated) for the management of this (see Precautions).

Management of Late Onset Diarrhea: Besides the dosage modification, prompt use of oral loperamide is recommended in order to control and treat the diarrhea (see Precautions).

Management of Extravasation: Flushing the infusion site with sterile water and/or applying ice to the area are recommended.

Special Instructions for Preparation and Handling: As with other potentially toxic anticancer agents, care should be exercised in the handling and preparation of infusion solutions containing irinotecan. Preparation of irinotecan should be done in a vertical laminar flow hood. The use of gloves, safety glasses and protective clothing is recommended. If irinotecan solution contacts the skin, wash the skin immediately and thoroughly with soap and water. If irinotecan contacts the mucous membranes, flush thoroughly with water. All waste material that has come in contact with irinotecan should be properly segregated, sealed and incinerated.

Parenteral Products: The vial is for single use only. Unused portions must be discarded. Irinotecan must be diluted prior to infusion, using 5% Dextrose Injection USP (preferred) or 0.9% Sodium Chloride Injection USP to a final concentration range of 0.12 to 1.1 mg/mL. Other drugs should not be added to the infusion solution.

The infusion solution is physically and chemically stable for up to 24 hours at controlled room temperature (15 to 30°C) and in ambient fluorescent lighting. Solutions diluted in 5% Dextrose Injection USP and stored at refrigerated temperatures (2 to 8°C) and protected from light are physically and chemically stable for 48 hours. Refrigeration of admixtures using 0.9% Sodium Chloride Injection USP, is not recommended due to a low and sporadic incidence of visible particulates. **Freezing irinotecan and admixtures of irinotecan may result in precipitation of the drug and should be avoided.**

Because of possible microbial contamination during dilution, it is advisable to use the admixture prepared with 5% Dextrose Injection within 24 hours if refrigerated (2 to 8°C). In the case of admixtures prepared with 5% Dextrose Injection or 0.9% Sodium Chloride Injection, the solution should be used within 6 hours when kept at controlled room temperature (15 to 30°C).

Parenteral drug products should be inspected visually for particulate matter and discoloration prior to administration whenever solution and container permit.

Supplied: Each mL of sterile, pale yellow, clear, aqueous solution contains: irinotecan HCl trihydrate 20 mg. Nonmedicinal ingredients: lactic acid, sorbitol and water for injection. Sodium hydroxide and/or hydrochloric acid may be used to adjust the pH to 3.0 to 3.8. Single use vials of 5 mL. Store at controlled room temperature (15 to 30°C). Protect from light. The product is available in an amber glass vial that is packaged in plastic blister to protect from breakage. It is recommended that the vial (and plastic blister) remain in the carton until time of use. The vial should be inspected for damage and visible signs of leaks before removing the plastic blister. If there are signs of breakage or leakage from the vial, do not open the plastic blister. Incinerate the unopened package.

Reviewed 1998

CANDISTATIN®
Westwood-Squibb

Nystatin

Antifungal

Supplied: Each g contains: nystatin 100 000 units. Nonmedicinal ingredients: talc. Plastic squeeze bottles with directional top of 15 g.

CANESTEN® Topical
Bayer Consumer

Clotrimazole

Antifungal

Pharmacology: Clotrimazole acts primarily by damaging the permeability barrier in the cell membrane of fungi. Clotrimazole brings about inhibition of ergosterol biosynthesis, an essential constituent of fungal cell membranes. If ergosterol synthesis is completely or partially inhibited, the cell is no longer able to construct an intact cell membrane. This leads to death of the fungus.

Exposure of C. albicans to clotrimazole causes leakage of intracellular phosphorus compounds into the ambient medium with a concomitant breakdown of cellular nucleic acids and potassium efflux. The onset of these events is rapid and extensive after exposure of the organism to the drug, and causes a time-dependent and concentration-dependent inhibition of fungal growth.

Pharmacokinetics: Metabolism studies performed after oral or i.v. administration have shown that in most species studied, levels of clotrimazole in tissue and serum are low. The majority of the drug is excreted as metabolites in the feces, with small amounts excreted in the urine. Human studies indicate slow excretion following oral administration of ^{14}C-labeled clotrimazole (greater than 6 days). After intraperitoneal and s.c. administration, very low levels have been observed in the urine. The absorption and organ distribution of the drug is very poor when administered parenterally.

The pharmacokinetics of topically applied clotrimazole in human subjects have been evaluated by Duhm et al. who reported on the penetration of radioactive clotrimazole 1% cream and 1% solution into intact and acutely inflamed skin. Six hours after application of the drug, the concentration of clotrimazole found in skin layers varied from 100 μg/cm^3 in the stratum corneum to 0.5 to 1 μg/cm^3 in the stratum reticulare and $<$0.1 μg/cm^3 in the subcutis. No measurable amount of radioactivity (0.001 μg/mL) was found in the serum within 48 hours after application of 0.5 mL of the solution or 0.8 g of the cream.

In animal experiments, clotrimazole exerts an in vitro and in vivo, dose-dependent stimulating effect on certain microsomal enzyme systems which is approximately equal to that of phenobarbital in its inductive potential. However, this stimulating effect subsides rapidly when treatment is discontinued. The enzyme-inductive effect of clotrimazole has been found to be intact in adrenalectomized animals.

Results of 22 mycologically controlled double-blind, 1 mycologically controlled single blind, and 4 mycologically controlled open studies show that 1% solution and cream are effective in the treatment of tinea cruris, tinea corporis, tinea pedis, tinea versicolor and cutaneous candidiasis. For the cream, mycological cure rates were 80% for tinea cruris/tinea corporis, 67% for tinea pedis, 88% for tinea versicolor and 92% for cutaneous candidiasis as compared to 4.7%, 0%, 37.5% and 0%, respectively, for the vehicle control (total of 238 patients). The corresponding values for the solution are 92% for tinea cruris/tinea corporis, 64% for tinea pedis, 83% for tinea versicolor, 83% for cutaneous candidiasis, 100% for C. paronychia and 93% for mixed dermatophytoses as compared to 30%, 31%, 64%, 28% and 0%, respectively, (there is no corresponding value for mixed dermatophytoses) for the vehicle control (total of 874 patients).

Indications: For the topical treatment of the following dermal infections: tinea pedis, tinea cruris and tinea corporis due to T. rubrum, T. mentagrophytes and E. floccosum; candidiasis due to C. albicans; tinea versicolor due to M. furfur.

Contraindications: Hypersensitivity to clotrimazole.

Precautions: As with all topical agents, skin sensitization may result. Use of clotrimazole topical preparations should be discontinued should such reactions occur, and appropriate therapy instituted.

Pregnancy and *Lactation:* Although the topical application of clotrimazole has resulted in very low serum and tissue levels, the use of clotrimazole topical preparations by pregnant or lactating women is not recommended unless it is on the advice of a physician.

Clotrimazole topical preparations are not suitable for treating fungal infections of the nail or scalp.

Occlusive dressings should not be applied over clotrimazole topical preparations unless directed by a physician.

The topical preparations are not for ophthalmic use.

Adverse Effects: Experimental, therapeutic, and large scale clinical studies have shown clotrimazole to be well tolerated after topical application.

Erythema, stinging, blistering, peeling, edema, pruritus, urticaria and general irritation of the skin have been reported infrequently.

Out of a total of 184 patients treated with the 1% cream, irritation was reported in 12 and soreness in 1 patient; therapy was discontinued in 3 patients. In comparison, 1 case of increased inflammation and pruritus and 1 case of folliculitis was reported in the 54 patients treated with the vehicle control.

Out of 518 patients treated with the 1% solution, burning, itching or drying effect was reported in 2, burning and erythema in 1, irritation in 4, warm sensation or burning in 14, erythema in 1, itching in 5, stinging in 1, blisters in 1 and increased scaling and peeling in 2; therapy was discontinued in 4 patients. Of the 356 patients treated with the vehicle control, burning, itching or drying effect was reported in 3, irritation in 5, warm sensation or burning in 12, odor in 1, erythema in 1, itching in 4, stinging in 2, urticaria in 2, maculopapular rash in 1, and increased sweating in 1; therapy was discontinued in 4 patients.

Dosage: Thinly apply and gently massage sufficient solution or cream into the affected and surrounding skin areas twice daily, in the morning and evening. For the treatment to be completely successful, the solution or cream should be applied regularly and in sufficient quantities.

Clinical improvement with relief of pruritus, usually occurs within the first week of treatment. The symptoms of jock itch and ringworm usually resolve within 2 to 4 weeks. Athlete's foot may require at least 4 weeks. In mycoses of the foot, treatment should be continued—even when it has led to rapid subjective improvement—for about 2 weeks after all symptoms have disappeared so that relapses may be prevented. If the signs and symptoms of the infection have not been resolved after 4 weeks of treatment with clotrimazole, a physician should be consulted.

If a cure is not mycologically confirmed, treatment should, as a rule, be continued for 2 weeks after all clinical symptoms have disappeared. Candida infections are generally treated for only 2 weeks.

Added hygienic measures are of special importance in the management of the often refractory fungal diseases of the foot. After washing, the feet—particularly between the toes—should be dried thoroughly to avoid trapped moisture. Well-fitting, ventilated shoes and cotton or wool socks are recommended to ensure a successful treatment outcome and to help prevent a recurrence.

Information for the Patient: See Blue Section—Information for the Patient "Canesten Topical".

Supplied: Cream: Each g of topical cream contains: clotrimazole 10 mg in a vanishing cream base. Nonmedicinal ingredients: benzyl alcohol, cetostearyl alcohol, cetyl esters wax, 2-octyl dodecanol, polysorbate 60, purified water and sorbitan monostearate. Tubes of 15 and 30 g. Plastic tubs of 500 g.

Solution: Each mL of topical solution contains: clotrimazole 10 mg. Nonmedicinal ingredients: isopropanol, polyethylene glycol and propylene glycol. Plastic pump spray bottles of 40 mL.

Store below 30°C. Avoid freezing.

CANESTEN® Vaginal

Bayer Consumer

Clotrimazole

Antifungal

Pharmacology: Clotrimazole acts primarily by damaging the permeability barrier in the cell membrane of fungi. Clotrimazole brings about inhibition of ergosterol biosynthesis, an essential constituent of fungal cell membranes. If ergosterol synthesis is completely or partially inhibited, the cell is no longer able to construct an intact cell membrane. This leads to death of the fungus.

Exposure of C. albicans to clotrimazole causes leakage of intracellular phosphorus compounds into the ambient medium with a concomitant breakdown of cellular nucleic acids and potassium efflux. The onset of these events is rapid and extensive after exposure of the organism to the drug, and causes a time-dependent and concentration-dependent inhibition of fungal growth.

Pharmacokinetics: Metabolism studies performed after oral or i.v. administration have shown that in most species studied, levels of clotrimazole in tissue and serum are low. The majority of the drug is excreted as metabolites in the feces, with small amounts excreted in the urine. Human studies indicate slow excretion following oral administration of ^{14}C-labeled clotrimazole (greater than 6 days). After intraperitoneal and s.c. administration, very low levels have been observed in the urine. The absorption and organ distribution of the drug is very poor when administered parenterally.

The pharmacokinetics of topically applied clotrimazole in human subjects have been evaluated by Duhm et al. who reported on the penetration of radioactive clotrimazole 1% cream and 1% solution into intact and acutely inflamed skin. Six hours after application of the drug, the concentration of clotrimazole found in skin layers varied from 100 μg/cm^3 in the stratum corneum to 0.5 to 1 μg/cm^3 in the stratum reticulare and $<$0.1 μg/cm^3 in the subcutis. No measurable amount of radioactivity (0.001 μg/mL) was found in the serum within 48 hours after application of 0.5 mL of the solution or 0.8 g of the cream.

Intravaginal application of ^{14}C-labeled clotrimazole inserts containing 100 mg of active substance in human subjects has shown that the amount absorbed is less than 1/200 of that absorbed after the oral administration of 1.5 g of clotrimazole. The maximum serum concentration values were between 0.016 and 0.05 μg/mL from 1 to 3 days after intravaginal application. Intravaginal application in human subjects of 5 mL ^{14}C-labeled clotrimazole vaginal cream containing 50 mg of active substance has shown that the systemic absorption of clotrimazole from the vaginal cream is quantitatively proportional to that from the vaginal inserts.

In animal experiments, clotrimazole exerts an in vitro and in vivo, dose-dependent, stimulating effect on certain microsomal enzyme systems which is approximately equal to that of phenobarbital in its inductive potential. However, this stimulating effect subsides rapidly when treatment is discontinued. The enzyme-inductive effect of clotrimazole has been found to be intact in adrenalectomized animals.

In 11 double-blind and 1 large multicentre open study, treatment of 814 patients with the 100 mg insert for 6 to 7 days resulted in an average mycological cure rate of 79% (range of 67 to 91%). In studies comparing the 3- and 7-day regimen, 168 patients were treated with one clotrimazole vaginal insert (100 mg) daily for 7 days. Overall and mycological cure rates were 67 and 70%, respectively.

In 8 double-blind studies and one single-blind study involving 432 patients using the 1% cream for 7 days, the average mycological cure rate was 72% with a range of 55 to 90%.

Oral contraceptives did not significantly alter mycological cure rates and overall success. In a limited number of pregnant women, both the 1% cream and the 100 mg insert appeared to be effective, although the cure rates seemed to be somewhat lower.

In clinical trials involving 200 mg clotrimazole vaginal inserts, 498/611 patients (82%) had a negative culture for Candida sp. 4 weeks following treatment.

In clinical trials with clotrimazole 2% vaginal cream, 266/303 patients (88%) had a negative culture for Candida sp. 4 weeks following treatment.

In clinical trials with clotrimazole 500 mg vaginal inserts, 158/231 patients (68%) had a negative culture for Candida sp. 4 weeks following treatment.

In clinical trials with clotrimazole 10% vaginal cream, 592/726 patients (82%) had a negative culture for Candida sp. 4 weeks following treatment.

Indications: Canesten 1% Vaginal Cream: For the 6-day treatment of vaginal candidiasis.

Canesten 2% Vaginal Cream: For the 3-day treatment of vaginal candidiasis.

Canesten 10% Vaginal Cream: For the 1-day treatment of vaginal candidiasis.

Canesten Combi-Pak 3-Day Therapy: For the 3-day treatment of vaginal candidiasis.

Canesten Combi-Pak 1-Day Therapy: For the 1-day treatment of vaginal candidiasis.

Canesten 1 Day Cream Combi-Pak: For the 1-day treatment of vaginal candidiasis.

Contraindications: Hypersensitivity to clotrimazole.

Precautions: Clotrimazole vaginal inserts are not for oral use. Not for ophthalmic use.

As with all topical agents, skin sensitization may result. Use of clotrimazole topical preparations should be discontinued should such reactions occur, and appropriate therapy instituted.

Pregnancy: Although intravaginal application of clotrimazole has shown negligible absorption from both normal and inflamed human vaginal mucosa, clotrimazole vaginal preparations should not be used in the first trimester of pregnancy unless the physician considers it essential to the welfare of the patient.

The use of applicators may be undesirable in some pregnant patients and digital insertion of the inserts may be considered.

Adverse Effects: Experimental, therapeutic, and large scale clinical studies have shown clotrimazole to be well tolerated after topical application.

Erythema, stinging, blistering, peeling, edema, pruritus, urticaria and general irritation of the skin have been reported infrequently.

Two of 419 (0.5%) patients treated with the 1% vaginal cream experienced adverse reactions judged to be possibly drug related. These were intercurrent cystitis and vaginal burning. Neither necessitated discontinuation of treatment. None were of serious consequence and no complications occurred.

Canesten Vaginal (cont'd)

The 100 mg inserts were also well tolerated. Only a few cases consisting primarily of burning sensation and mild skin reactions were reported. In studies comparing the 3- and 7-day regimen, 4 of 212 patients (1.9%) in the 7-day group reported adverse reactions possibly related to treatment. These included: irritation, burning, cramping, itching, redness, abdominal bloating, bleeding and rash. In an additional 9 double-blind comparative studies, 5 out of 219 patients on the 7-day regimen with the 100 mg insert experienced similar types of adverse reactions, none of which necessitated discontinuation of treatment. In a large open multicentre and 2 double-blind studies employing the 100 mg insert in a 6-day regimen, 11 out of 595 (1.8%) patients complained of possible drug-related side effects. Mild burning occurred in 4 patients while other reactions such as skin rash, lower abdominal cramps, slight urinary frequency and burning or irritation in the sexual partner occurred rarely. In no case was it necessary to discontinue treatment.

In clinical trials involving 200 mg clotrimazole vaginal inserts, 24/832 patients (2.9%) experienced an adverse reaction. 2/217 patients (0.9%) who received 2% clotrimazole vaginal cream in clinical trials experienced an adverse reaction. In clinical trials involving 500 mg clotrimazole vaginal inserts, 12/515 patients (2.3%) experienced an adverse reaction. 26/796 (3.3%) of patients in clinical trials involving 10% clotrimazole vaginal cream experienced an adverse reaction. Most adverse reactions involved local itching and burning. Only rarely was it necessary to discontinue treatment.

Dosage: Canesten 1% Vaginal Cream: The recommended daily dose is 1 full applicator intravaginally for 6 consecutive days, preferably at bedtime.

Canesten 2% Vaginal Cream: The recommended daily dose is 1 full applicator intravaginally for 3 consecutive days preferably at bedtime.

Canesten 10% Vaginal Cream: The recommended dose is 1 full applicator intravaginally, (as a single dose therapy), preferably at bedtime.

Canesten Combi-Pak 3-Day Therapy: The recommended daily dose is 1 insert intravaginally for 3 consecutive days, preferably at bedtime. The cream should be spread onto the irritated area once or twice a day as needed, for up to 7 consecutive days.

Canesten Combi-Pak 1-Day Therapy: The recommended dose is 1 insert intravaginally for 1 day, preferably at bedtime. The cream should be spread onto the irritated area once or twice a day as needed, for up to 7 consecutive days.

Canesten 1-Day Cream Combi-Pak: The recommended dose is 1 full applicator intravaginally, (as a single dose therapy), preferably at bedtime. The topical cream should be spread onto the irritated area once or twice a day as needed, for up to 7 consecutive days.

Vaginal candidiasis may be accompanied by irritation in the vaginal area. Therefore, concomitant local treatment with vaginal cream (or topical cream) applied to the irritated vaginal area and as far as the anal region twice a day is advisable. Topical cream (or vaginal cream) applied on the glans penis may prevent re-infection by the partner.

Note: The cream or insert should be inserted deep intravaginally by means of the applicator (see Precautions). The plunger should then be depressed slowly.

General hygienic measures such as twice daily tub baths and avoidance of tight underclothing are important in vaginal infections.

Information for the Patient: See Blue Section—Information for the Patient: "Canesten Vaginal".

Supplied: Canesten 1% Vaginal Cream: Each g contains: clotrimazole 10 mg in a vanishing cream base. Nonmedicinal ingredients: benzyl alcohol, cetostearyl alcohol, cetyl esters wax, 2-octyl dodecanol, polysorbate 60, purified water and sorbitan monostearate. Tubes of 50 g in a carton with 6 disposable plastic applicators and patient instructions. 50 g of vaginal cream is sufficient for 6 intravaginal applications with additional cream for extravaginal use if required.

Canesten 2% Vaginal Cream: Each g contains: clotrimazole 20 mg in a vanishing cream base. Nonmedicinal ingredients: benzyl alcohol, cetostearyl alcohol, cetyl esters wax, 2-octyl dodecanol, polysorbate 60, purified water and sorbitan monostearate. Tubes of 25 g in a carton with 3 disposable plastic applicators and patient instructions. 25 g of vaginal cream is sufficient for 3 intravaginal applications with additional cream for extravaginal use if required.

Canesten 10% Vaginal Cream: Each g contains: clotrimazole 100 mg in a vanishing cream base. Nonmedicinal ingredients: benzyl alcohol, cetostearyl alcohol, cetyl palmitate, isopropyl myristate, polysorbate, purified water and sorbitan monostearate. Boxes containing one 5 g pre-filled applicator with a plunger in a blister pack and patient instructions.

Canesten Combi-Pak 3-Day Therapy: Each insert contains: clotrimazole 200 mg and each g of topical cream contains: clotrimazole 10 mg. Nonmedicinal ingredients: adipic acid, benzyl alcohol, cetostearyl alcohol, cetyl esters wax, colloidal silicon dioxide, cornstarch, lactose, magnesium stearate, 2-octyl dodecanol, polysorbate 60, polysorbate 80, sodium bicarbonate, sorbitan monostearate and stearic acid. Boxes of 1 strip of 3 Canesten 200 mg Vaginal Inserts with one plastic applicator and one 10 g tube of Canesten 1% Topical Cream.

Canesten Combi-Pak 1-Day Therapy: Each insert contains: clotrimazole 500 mg and each g of topical cream contains: clotrimazole 10 mg. Nonmedicinal ingredients: benzyl alcohol, calcium lactate, cetostearyl alcohol, cetyl esters wax, cornstarch, hydroxypropyl methylcellulose, lactic acid, lactose, magnesium stearate, microcrystalline cellulose, 2-octyl dodecanol, polysorbate 60, polyvinyl pyrrolidone, silicon dioxide and sorbitan monostearate. Boxes of 1 strip of 1 Canesten 500 mg Vaginal Insert with one plastic applicator and one 10 g tube of Canesten 1% Topical Cream.

Canesten 1-Day Cream Combi-Pak: Each g of vaginal cream contains: clotrimazole 100 mg and each g of topical cream contains: clotrimazole 10 mg. Nonmedicinal ingredients: benzyl alcohol, cetostearyl alcohol, cetyl esters wax, cetyl palmitate, isopropyl myristate, 2-octyl dodecanol, polysorbate 60, purified water and sorbitan monostearate. Boxes containing one 5 g pre-filled applicator with plunger of Canesten 10% Vaginal Cream and one 10 g tube of Canesten 1% Topical Cream.

Store below 30°C. Avoid freezing.

(Shown in Product Recognition Section)

Reviewed 1998

CANTHACUR®
Pharmascience

Cantharidin

Vesicant

Indications: For the topical use of removal of benign epithelial growths such as warts (verruca vulgaris) or molluscum contagiosum. Because of the absence of scarring, cantharidin is useful for treating exposed areas where cosmetic results are important. Painless application and the absence of instruments makes it especially useful for treating children.

Contraindications: Hypersensitivity to the ingredients. Avoid alcoholic beverages for several hours after treatment.

Precautions: Cantharidin is a potent vesicant and is to be applied only by the physician. It is recommended care be used in the selection of patients to be treated and method used. The physician should develop his own experience and technique. Care should be used in selection of site of application since residual pigmentation may occur (rarely). It is recommended patients be advised of effect and possible results of treatment. Do not use on mucosal tissue. Do not use if growth or surrounding tissue is inflamed or irritated. Do not use on diabetics, or people with poor blood-circulation, on moles, birthmarks, or unusual warts with hair growing from them. Larger areas should not be treated at one time since discomfort may be excessive and systemic absorption may result.

Pregnancy and *Lactation:* Use during pregnancy or in nursing mothers is not recommended since there have been no adequate and well controlled studies performed in these groups.

Adverse Effects: The development of annular warts following therapy has been reported in a small percentage of patients when the method of treatment was not properly followed. These lesions are superficial and, although they may alarm some patients, present little problem. Treatment consists of patient reassurance and re-treatment using either cantharidin or other procedures. There has been 1 report of chemical lymphangitis following use in combination with salicylic acid plaster.

Dosage: Without Curettage: No cutting or prior treatment is required. (Occasionally nails must be trimmed to expose subungual warts to medication.) Using a Q-Tip or applicator stick, apply cantharidin (1 layer only) to the wart and a 1 to 3 mm margin around the wart. Allow to dry for a few minutes. Cover with a piece of non-porous plastic adhesive tape. Instruct patient to keep the tape on for at least 4 hours (up to 24 hours). Within 24 hours a blister forms which is often painful and inflamed. Have the patient return for observation in 1 week. Remove necrotic tissue and treat as before if any viable wart tissue remains. Allow tissue to re-epithelialize before re-treatment.

With Curettage: Proceed as without curettage except have patient return in 1 day for curettage. (Local anesthesia may be necessary.) Advantages to this method include: Treatment prior to curettage enhances identification of tissue planes, increases separability of wart tissue and re-treatment is rarely necessary. Have the patient return for observation in 4 weeks. (The lesion normally heals completely within 1 to 3 weeks.) The use of a mild antibacterial agent until area heals is recommended.

Plantar Warts: Pare away keratin covering the wart, avoid bleeding. Using a Q-Tip or applicator stick, apply cantharidin to both the wart and a 1 to 3 mm margin around the wart. Allow a few minutes to dry. Secure with non-porous plastic adhesive tape. Leave in place for 1 week, then debride. If any viable wart tissue remains after debridement, re-apply a small amount of cantharidin and bandage as above. Three or more such treatments may be required for large lesions. When destruction of wart is complete, the healed site will appear smooth, with normal skin lines.

Palpebral Warts: Using a toothpick or fine probe, apply a small amount of cantharidin to the surface of the wart. Make certain that film is thoroughly dry. Avoid touching surrounding normal skin or applying inside the eye lashes. Leave lesion uncovered. Patient should be warned not to touch the eyelid. Removal of necrotic material should be done by the doctor. Repeat in a week or ten days if any growth remains and area is free of irritation or inflammation. After the removal of the growth, the use of a mild bacterial until area heals is advisable.

Molluscum contagiosum: Coat each lesion with a thin film of cantharidin. After 1 week, treat any new lesions the same way and re-treat any resistant lesions, covering with a small piece of occlusive tape. The tape should be removed in 6 to 8 hours.

Warn the patient that the blister may be painful. A mild analgesic, e.g. ASA with codeine, or acetaminophen with codeine may be used. The tape may be removed and the area soaked in cool water for 10 to 15 minute periods, as needed, provided sufficient time has been allowed for the medication to penetrate. Local anesthesia may be needed during curettage.

Note: Cantharidin is a strong vesicant and may produce blisters if it comes in contact with normal skin or mucous membrane. If spilled on skin, wipe off at once, using acetone, alcohol or tape remover. Then wash vigorously with warm soapy water and rinse well. If spilled on mucous membrane or in eyes, flush with water, remove the precipitated film, and flush with water for an additional 15 minutes. Patients vary in their sensitivity to cantharidin and in rare cases tingling, burning or extreme tenderness may develop. In these cases, patient should remove tape and soak the area in cool water for 10 to 15 minutes, repeating as required for relief. If soreness persists, puncture blister using sterile technique, apply antiseptic and cover with tape. It is advisable to treat only 1 or 2 lesions on the first visit, until the sensitivity of the patient is known.

Supplied: Each mL contains: cantharidin 0.7% in an adherent film-forming vehicle. Bottles of 7.5 mL with thin-tipped applicator attached to inside of cap. Flammable. Keep away from heat, fire and flame. Close tightly immediately after use. Store at room temperature away from heat.

CANTHACUR®-PS Ⓟ
Pharmascience

Cantharidin—Podophyllin—Salicylic Acid

Wart Remover

Indications: For the topical use of removal of benign epithelial growths such as warts (verruca vulgaris), especially plantar, mosaic, periungual, and molluscum contagiosum. Recommended for resistant and heavily keratinized warts. Because of the absence of scarring, the mixture is useful for treating exposed areas where cosmetic results are important.

Contraindications: Hypersensitivity to the ingredients. Avoid alcoholic beverages for several hours after treatment.

Precautions: Canthacur-PS is a potent vesicant and is to be applied only by the physician. It is recommended care be used in the selection of patients to be treated and method used. The physician should develop his own experience and technique. Care should be used in selection of site of application since residual pigmentation may occur (rarely). It is recommended patients be advised of effect and possible results of treatment. Do not use near eyes, on face, mucous membranes or ano-genital areas. Do not use if growth or surrounding tissue is inflamed or irritated. Do not use on diabetics, or people with poor blood-circulation, on moles, birthmarks, or unusual warts with hair growing from them. Larger areas should not be treated at one time since discomfort may be excessive and systemic absorption may result.

Pregnancy and *Lactation:* Use during pregnancy or in nursing mothers is not recommended since there has been no adequate and well controlled studies performed in these groups.

Children: Not recommended for use on young children due to difficulties in pain management.

Adverse Effects: The development of annular warts following therapy has been reported in a small percentage of patients when the method of treatment was not properly followed. These lesions are superficial and, although they may alarm some patients, present little problem. Treatment consists of patient reassurance and re-treatment using either Canthacur-PS or other procedures. There has been 1 report of chemical lymphangitis following use of Canthacur-PS in combination with salicylic acid plaster.

Dosage: Without Curettage: No cutting or prior treatment is required. (Occasionally nails must be trimmed to expose subungual warts to medication.) Using a Q-Tip or applicator stick, apply solution (1 layer only) to the wart and a 1 to 3 mm margin around the wart. Allow to dry for a few minutes. Cover with a piece of non-porous plastic adhesive tape. Instruct patient to keep the tape on for at least 4 hours (up to 24 hours). Within 24 hours a blister forms which is often painful and inflamed. Have the patient return for observation in 2 to 3 days. Remove necrotic tissue and treat as before if any viable wart tissue remains. Allow tissue to re-epithelialize before re-treatment.

With Curettage: Proceed as without curettage except have patient return in 1 day for curettage. (Local anesthesia may be necessary.) Advantages to this method include: Treatment prior to curettage enhances identification of tissue planes, increases separability of wart tissue and re-treatment is rarely necessary. Have the patient return for observation in 4 weeks. (The lesion normally heals completely within 1 to 3 weeks.) The use of a mild anti-bacterial agent until area heals is recommended.

Plantar Warts: Pare away keratin covering the wart, avoid bleeding. Using a Q-Tip or applicator stick, apply solution to both the wart and a 1 to 3 mm margin around the wart. Allow a few minutes to dry. Secure with non-porous plastic adhesive tape. Leave in place for 1 week, then debride. If any viable wart tissue remains after debridement, re-apply a small amount of solution and bandage as above. Three or more of such treatments may be required for large lesions. When destruction of wart is complete, the healed site will appear smooth, with normal skin lines.

Molluscum contagiosum: Coat each lesion with a thin film of solution. After 1 week, treat any new lesions the same way and retreat any resistant lesions, this time covering with a small piece of occlusive tape. The tape should be removed in 6 to 8 hours.

Warn the patient that the blister may be painful. A mild analgesic, e.g. ASA with codeine, or acetaminophen with codeine may be used. The tape may be removed and the area soaked in cool water for 10 to 15 minute periods, as needed, provided sufficient time has been allowed for the medication to penetrate. Local anesthesia may be needed during curettage.

Note: Canthacur-PS contains strong vesicants and may produce blisters if it comes in contact with normal skin or mucous membrane. If spilled on skin, wipe off at once, using acetone, alcohol or tape remover. Then wash vigorously with warm soapy water and rinse well. If spilled on mucous membrane or in eyes, flush with water, remove the precipitated film, and flush with water for an additional 15 minutes. Patients vary in their sensitivity to cantharidin and in rare cases tingling, burning or extreme tenderness may develop. In these cases, patient should remove tape and soak the area in cool water for 10 to 15 minutes, repeating as required for relief. If soreness persists, puncture blister using sterile technique, apply antiseptic and cover with tape. It is advisable to treat only 1 or 2 lesions on the first visit, until the sensitivity of the patient is known.

Supplied: Each mL contains: cantharidin 1%, podophyllin 5% and salicylic acid 30% in an adherent film-forming vehicle. Bottles of 7.5 mL with thin-tipped applicator attached to inside of cap. Flammable. Keep away from heat, fire and flame. Close tightly immediately after use. Store at room temperature away from heat.

CANTHARONE®
Dormer

Cantharidin

Vesicant

Supplied: Each bottle of 7.5 mL contains: cantharidin 0.7% in a film-forming vehicle of acetone, ethocol and flexible collodion, ether 35% and alcohol 11%. Close tightly immediately after use. Keep away from heat.

CANTHARONE PLUS® P
Dormer

Cantharidin—Salicylic Acid—Podophyllin

Vesicant

Supplied: Each bottle of 7.5 mL contains: salicylic acid 30%, podophyllin 2%, cantharidin 1% in a film-forming vehicle of octylphenylpolyethylene glycol, cellosolve, ethocel, collodion, castor oil and acetone. Close tightly. Highly flammable.

CAPOTEN™ P
Squibb

Captopril

Angiotensin Converting Enzyme Inhibitor

Pharmacology: Captopril is an angiotensin converting enzyme inhibitor which is used in the treatment of hypertension and heart failure.

The mechanism of action of captopril has not yet been fully elucidated. It appears to lower blood pressure and be an adjunct in the therapy of congestive heart failure primarily through suppression of the renin-angiotensin-aldosterone system; however, there is no consistent correlation between renin levels and response to the drug. Renin, an enzyme synthesized by the kidneys, is released into the circulation where it acts on a plasma globulin substrate to produce angiotensin I, a relatively inactive decapeptide. Angiotensin I is then converted by angiotensin converting enzyme (ACE) to angiotensin II, a potent endogenous vasoconstrictor substance. Angiotensin II also stimulates aldosterone secretion from the adrenal cortex, thereby contributing to sodium and fluid retention.

Captopril prevents the conversion of angiotensin I to angiotensin II by inhibition of ACE, a peptidyldipeptide carboxy hydrolase.

ACE is identical to "bradykininase", and captopril may also interfere with the degradation of the vasopressor peptide, bradykinin. However, the effectiveness of captopril in therapeutic doses appears to be unrelated to potentiation of the actions of bradykinin. Increased concentrations of bradykinin or prostaglandin E_2 may also have a role in the therapeutic effect of captopril, especially in low-renin hypertension.

Inhibition of ACE results in decreased plasma angiotensin II and increased plasma renin activity (PRA), the latter resulting from loss of negative feedback on renin release caused by reduction in angiotensin II. The reduction of angiotensin II leads to decreased aldosterone secretion, and, as a result, small increases in serum potassium may occur along with sodium and fluid loss.

The antihypertensive effects persist for a longer period of time than does demonstrable inhibition of circulating ACE. It is not known whether the ACE present in vascular endothelium is inhibited longer than the ACE in circulating blood.

Administration of captopril results in a reduction of peripheral arterial resistance in hypertensive patients with either no change, or an increase, in cardiac output. There is an increase in renal blood flow following administration of captopril and glomerular filtration rate is usually unchanged. In instances of rapid reduction of long-standing or severely elevated blood pressure, the glomerular filtration rate may decrease transiently.

Peak reductions of blood pressure usually occur within 60 to 90 minutes after oral administration of a single dose of captopril. The duration of effect appears to be dose related. The reduction in blood pressure may be progressive, so to achieve maximal therapeutic effects, several weeks of therapy may be required. The blood pressure lowering effects of captopril and thiazide-type diuretics appear to be additive. In contrast, captopril and beta-blockers have a less than additive effect.

Blood pressure is lowered to about the same extent in both standing and supine positions. Orthostatic effects and tachycardia are infrequent but may occur in volume-depleted patients. Abrupt withdrawal of captopril has not been associated with a rapid increase in blood pressure.

The antihypertensive effect of angiotensin converting enzyme inhibitors is generally lower in black patients than in non-blacks.

In patients with heart failure, captopril significantly decreased systemic vascular resistance (afterload), reduced pulmonary capillary wedge pressure (preload) and pulmonary vascular resistance, increased cardiac output (stroke index), and increased exercise tolerance time (ETT). Clinical improvement has been observed in some patients where acute hemodynamic effects were minimal.

Captopril has been studied in patients with diabetic nephropathy, most of whom had hypertension, with type I insulin-dependent diabetes mellitus, retinopathy and proteinuria ≥500 mg/day, in a multicenter, double-blind, placebo controlled trial. In this study, captopril has shown to decrease the rate of progression of renal insufficiency and to reduce associated clinical sequelae for the combined end-point of end-stage renal disease (dialysis or renal transplantation) or death (from all causes). The effect on reduction of all-cause mortality alone was not statistically significant. No dosage adjustment was made according to creatinine clearance. Patients who had already progressed to severe renal failure were not included in the clinical trial.

Studies in rats and cats indicate that captopril does not cross the blood-brain barrier to any significant extent.

Pharmacokinetics: Following oral administration of therapeutic doses of captopril, rapid absorption occurs with peak blood levels at about 1 hour. The presence of food in the gastrointestinal tract reduces absorption by about 30 to 40%. Based on C-14 labeling, average minimal absorption is approximately 70 to 75%. In a 24-hour period, over 95% of the absorbed dose is eliminated in the urine; 40 to 50% is unchanged drug although it appears this percentage may be smaller in patients with congestive heart failure; most of the remainder is the disulfide dimer of captopril and captopril-cysteine disulfide.

Approximately 25 to 30% of the circulating drug is bound to plasma proteins. The apparent elimination half-life for total radioactivity in blood is about 4 hours. The half-life of unchanged captopril is approximately 2 hours.

In patients with normal renal function, absorption and disposition of a labeled dose are not altered after 7 days of captopril administration. In patients with renal impairment, however, retention of captopril occurs (see Dosage).

Indications: For the treatment of essential or renovascular hypertension. It is usually administered in association with other drugs, particularly thiazide diuretics. The blood pressure lowering effects of captopril and thiazides are approximately additive.

In using captopril, consideration should be given to the risk of neutropenia/agranulocytosis (see Warnings).

Patients with Normal Renal Function: Captopril should normally be used in those patients in whom treatment with diuretics or beta-blockers was found ineffective or has been associated with unacceptable adverse effects.

Captopril can be tried as an initial agent in those patients with severe hypertension or in those in whom the use of diuretics and/or beta-blockers is contraindicated or in patients with medical conditions in which those drugs frequently cause serious adverse effects.

Patients with Impaired Renal Function: In these patients, particularly those with collagen vascular disease, captopril should be reserved for hypertensives who have either developed unacceptable side effects on other drugs, or have failed to respond satisfactorily to drug combinations (see Precautions).

Captopril is indicated in the treatment of congestive heart failure as concomitant therapy with a diuretic in patients who have not responded adequately to digitalis and diuretics or in whom the administration of digitalis is contraindicated or has been associated with unacceptable side effects. Captopril therapy must be initiated under close medical supervision.

Captopril is indicated to improve survival, delay the onset of symptomatic heart failure and reduce hospitalizations for heart failure following myocardial infarction in clinically stable patients with left ventricular dysfunction manifested as an ejection fraction of ≤40%.

Captopril is indicated for the treatment of diabetic nephropathy (proteinuria ≥500 mg/day) in patients with type I insulin-dependent diabetes mellitus and retinopathy.

Pregnancy: **When used in pregnancy during the second and third trimesters, ACE inhibitors can cause injury or even**

Capoten (cont'd)

death of the developing fetus. When pregnancy is detected, captopril should be discontinued as soon as possible (see Warnings, Pregnancy, and Precautions, Information for the Patient).

Contraindications: Patients with a history of hypersensitivity to the drug and in patients with a history of angioedema related to previous treatment with an ACE inhibitor.

Warnings: Angioedema: Angioedema has been reported in patients treated with ACE inhibitors, including captopril. Angioedema associated with laryngeal involvement may be fatal. If laryngeal stridor or angioedema of the face, tongue, or glottis occurs, captopril should be discontinued immediately, the patient treated appropriately in accordance with accepted medical care, and carefully observed until the swelling disappears. In instances where swelling is confined to the face and lips, the condition generally resolves without treatment, although antihistamines may be useful in relieving symptoms. Where there is involvement of the tongue, glottis or larynx, likely to cause airway obstruction, appropriate therapy (including but not limited to 0.3 to 0.5 mL of s.c. epinephrine solution 1:1 000) should be administered promptly (see Adverse Effects).

The incidence of angioedema during ACE inhibitor therapy has been reported to be higher in black than in non-black patients.

Patients with a history of angioedema unrelated to ACE inhibitor therapy may be at increased risk of angioedema while receiving an ACE inhibitor (see Contraindications).

Proteinuria: Total urinary proteins greater than 1 g/day were seen in less than 1% of patients receiving captopril. These have been predominantly in those who had prior renal disease, or in those receiving relatively high doses (in excess of 150 mg/day), or both. In patients without prior evidence of renal disease, the incidence of proteinuria was 0.5%. In those patients without prior evidence of renal disease receiving 150 mg or less per day, the incidence was 0.2%. Parameters of renal function, such as BUN and serum creatinine, were seldom altered in the patients with proteinuria. In most cases, proteinuria subsided or cleared within 6 months whether or not captopril was continued, but some patients had persistent proteinuria. Nephrotic syndrome occurred in about one-fifth of the proteinuric patients.

Membranous glomerulopathy was found in biopsies taken from proteinuric patients. A causal relationship to captopril has not been established since pretreatment biopsies were not taken and membranous glomerulopathy has been shown to occur in hypertensive patients not receiving captopril.

Since most cases of proteinuria occurred by the eighth month of therapy, patients with prior renal disease or those receiving captopril at doses greater than 150 mg/day should have urinary protein estimations (dipstick on first morning urine, or quantitative 24-hour urine) prior to therapy, at approximately monthly intervals for the first 9 months of treatment, and periodically thereafter. When proteinuria is persistent, 24-hour quantitative determinations provide greater precision. For patients who develop proteinuria exceeding 1 g/day, or proteinuria that is increasing, the benefits and risks of continuing captopril should be evaluated.

Neutropenia/Agranulocytosis: Neutropenia ($<1\,000/mm^3$) with myeloid hypoplasia has resulted from use of captopril. About half of the neutropenic patients developed systemic or oral cavity infections or other features of the syndrome of agranulocytosis.

The risk of neutropenia is dependent on the clinical status of the patient: In clinical trials in patients with hypertension who have normal renal function (serum creatinine less than 1.6 mg/dL and no collagen disease), neutropenia has been seen in 1 patient out of over 8 600 exposed.

In patients with some degree of renal failure (serum creatinine at least 1.6 mg/dL) but no collagen vascular disease, the risk of neutropenia in clinical trials was about 1 per 500, a frequency over 15 times that for uncomplicated hypertension. Daily doses of captopril were relatively high in these patients, particularly in view of their diminished renal function. In patients with renal failure, use of allopurinol concomitantly with captopril has been associated with neutropenia.

In patients with collagen vascular disease (e.g., systemic lupus erythematosus, scleroderma) and impaired renal function, neutropenia occurred in 3.7% of patients in clinical trials.

While none of the over 750 patients in formal clinical trials of heart failure developed neutropenia, it has occurred during the subsequent clinical experience. About half of the reported cases had serum creatinine >1.6 mg/dL and more than 75% were in patients also receiving procainamide. In heart failure, it appears that the same risk factors for neutropenia are present.

Neutropenia has been detected within 3 months after captopril was started. Bone marrow examinations in patients with neutropenia consistently showed myeloid hypoplasia, frequently accompanied by erythroid hypoplasia and decreased numbers of megakaryocytes (e.g., hypoplastic bone marrow and pancytopenia); anemia and thrombocytopenia were sometimes seen.

In general, neutrophils returned to normal in about 2 weeks after captopril was discontinued, and serious infections were limited to clinically complex patients. About 13% of the cases of neutropenia have ended fatally, but almost all fatalities were in patients with serious illness, having collagen vascular disease, renal failure, heart failure or immunosuppressant therapy, or a combination of these complicating factors.

Evaluation of the hypertensive or heart failure patient should always include assessment of renal function.

If captopril is used in patients with impaired renal function, white blood cell and differential counts should be evaluated prior to starting treatment and at approximately 2-week intervals for about 3 months, then periodically.

In patients with collagen vascular disease or who are exposed to other drugs known to affect the white cells or immune response, particularly when there is impaired renal function, captopril should be used only after an assessment of benefit and risk, and then with caution.

All patients treated with captopril should be told to report any signs of infection (e.g., sore throat, fever). If infection is suspected, white cell counts should be performed without delay.

Since discontinuation of captopril and other drugs has generally led to prompt return of the white count to normal, upon confirmation of neutropenia (neutrophil count $<1\,000/mm^3$) the physician should withdraw captopril and closely follow the patient's course.

Since captopril decreases aldosterone production, elevation of serum potassium may occur rarely, especially in patients with renal failure (see Precautions, Drug Interactions).

Hypotension: Excessive hypotension was seen in hypertensive patients but is a possible consequence of captopril use in severely salt/volume-depleted persons such as those treated vigorously with diuretics, for example patients with severe congestive heart failure (see Precautions, Drug Interactions).

In heart failure, where the blood pressure was either normal or low, decreases in mean blood pressure greater than 20% were recorded in about half of the patients. This transient hypotension may occur after any of the first several doses and produces either no symptoms or brief mild lightheadedness, although in rare instances, it has been associated with arrhythmia or conduction defects. Hypotension was the reason for discontinuation of drug in 3.6% of patients with heart failure.

Because of the potential fall in blood pressure in these patients, therapy should be started under close medical supervision. A low starting dose may minimize the hypotensive effect (see Dosage). Patients should be followed closely for the first 2 weeks of treatment and whenever the dose of captopril, or diuretic, is increased. Similar considerations may apply to patients with ischemic heart or cerebrovascular disease in whom an excessive fall in blood pressure could result in myocardial infarction or cerebrovascular accident. Hypotension in itself is not a reason to discontinue captopril. If associated symptoms are troublesome or persist, they are usually relieved by a reduction in the dose of either captopril or diuretic.

Pregnancy: ACE inhibitors can cause fetal and neonatal morbidity and mortality when administered to pregnant women. Several dozen cases have been reported in the world literature. When pregnancy is detected, captopril should be discontinued as soon as possible.

In rare cases (probably less than once in every thousand pregnancies) in which no alternative to ACE inhibitors therapy will be found, the mothers should be apprised of the potential hazards to their fetuses. Serial ultrasound examinations should be performed to assess fetal development and well-being and the volume of amniotic fluid.

If oligohydramnios is observed, captopril should be discontinued unless it is considered life-saving for the mother. A non-stress test (NST), and/or a biophysical profiling (BPP) may be appropriate, depending upon the week of pregnancy. If concerns regarding fetal well-being still persist, a contraction stress testing (CST) should be considered. Patients and physicians should be aware, however, that oligohydramnios may not appear until after the fetus has sustained irreversible injury.

Infants with a history of in utero exposure to ACE inhibitors should be closely observed for hypotension, oliguria, and hyperkalemia. If oliguria occurs, attention should be directed toward support of blood pressure and renal perfusion. Exchange transfusion or dialysis may be required as a means of reversing hypotension and/or substituting for impaired renal function, however, limited experience with those procedures has not been associated with significant clinical benefit. Captopril may be removed from the general circulation by hemodialysis.

Human Data: It is not known whether exposure limited to the first trimester of pregnancy can adversely affect fetal outcome. The use of ACE inhibitors during the second and third trimesters of pregnancy has been associated with fetal and neonatal injury including hypotension, neonatal skull hypoplasia, anuria, reversible or irreversible renal failure, and death. Oligohydramnios has also been reported, presumably resulting from decreased fetal renal function; oligohydramnios in this setting has been associated with fetal limb contractures, craniofacial deformation, and hypoplastic lung development. Prematurity and patent ductus arteriosus have also been reported, although it is not clear whether these occurrences were due to the ACE-inhibitor exposure.

Animal Data: Captopril was embryocidal in rabbits when given in doses 2 to 70 times (on a mg/kg basis) the maximum recommended human dose, and low incidences of craniofacial malformations were seen. These effects in rabbits were most probably due to the particularly marked decrease in blood pressure caused by the drug in this species. Captopril was also embryocidal in sheep when given in doses similar to those given in humans. Captopril given to pregnant rats at 400 times the recommended human dose continuously during gestation and lactation caused a reduction in neonatal survival.

No teratogenic effects have been observed after large doses of captopril were administered to hamsters and rats.

Precautions: Renal Impairment: As a consequence of inhibiting the renin-angiotensin-aldosterone system, changes in renal function have been seen in susceptible individuals. In patients whose renal function may depend on the activity of the renin-angiotensin-aldosterone system, such as patients with bilateral renal artery stenosis, unilateral renal artery stenosis to a solitary kidney, or severe congestive heart failure, treatment with agents that inhibit this system has been associated with oliguria, progressive azotemia, and rarely, acute renal failure and/or death. In susceptible patients, concomitant diuretic use may further increase risk.

Use of captopril should include appropriate assessment of renal function.

Hyperkalemia: Elevations in serum potassium have been observed in some patients treated with ACE inhibitors, including captopril. When treated with ACE inhibitors, patients at risk for the development of hyperkalemia include those with: renal insufficiency; diabetes mellitus; and those using concomitant potassium-sparing diuretics, potassium supplements or potassium-containing salt substitutes; or other drugs associated with increases in serum potassium (e.g., heparin). The incidence of hyperkalemia related or possibly related to therapy in the diabetic patients studied with nephropathy and proteinuria was 3.6% and was a reason for discontinuation of the drug in 1% of the patients. Hyperkalemia was defined as persistent elevation of serum potassium to 6.0 mg/dL or more in the absence of a remediable cause, such as other drugs, volume depletion, exogenous potassium supplements, etc.

Impaired Liver Function: Elevations of liver enzymes and/or serum bilirubin, cases of cholestatic jaundice, and of hepatocellular injury with or without secondary cholestasis, have occurred during therapy with captopril in patients without preexisting liver abnormalities. In most cases the changes were reversible on discontinuation of the drug. Should the patient receiving captopril experience any unexplained symptoms (see Information for the Patient), particularly during the first weeks or months of treatment, it is recommended that a full set of liver enzyme tests and other necessary investigations be carried out. Discontinuation of captopril should be considered when appropriate.

There are no adequate studies in patients with cirrhosis and/or liver dysfunction. Captopril should be used with particular caution in patients with pre-existent liver abnormalities. Such patients should have their baseline liver function tests obtained before administration of the drug. Close monitoring of response and metabolic effects should apply to these patients.

Cough: Cough has been reported with the use of captopril. Characteristically, ACE inhibitor-induced cough is nonproductive, persistent and resolves after discontinuation of therapy or lowering of the dose. Captopril-induced cough should be considered as part of the differential diagnosis of the cough.

Valvular Stenosis: There is concern, on theoretical grounds, that patients with aortic stenosis might be at particular risk of decreased coronary perfusion when treated with vasodilators because they do not develop as much afterload reduction.

Surgery/Anesthesia: In patients undergoing major surgery or during anesthesia with agents that produce hypotension, captopril will block angiotensin II formation secondary to compensatory renin release. This may lead to hypotension which can be corrected by volume expansion.

Anaphylactoid Reactions During Membrane Exposure: Anaphylactoid reactions have been reported in patients dialyzed with high-flux membranes (e.g., polyacrylonitrile [PAN] and treated concomitantly with an ACE inhibitor. Dialysis should be stopped immediately if symptoms such as nausea, abdominal cramps, burning, angioedema, shortness of breath and severe hypotension occur. Symptoms are not relieved by antihistamines. In these patients consideration should be given to using a different type of dialysis membrane or a different class of antihypertensive agents.

Anaphylactoid Reactions During Desensitization: There have been isolated reports of patients experiencing sustained life-threatening anaphylactoid reactions while receiving ACE inhibitors during desensitizing treatment with hymenoptera (bees, wasps) venom. In the same patients, these reactions have been avoided when ACE inhibitors were temporarily withheld for at least 24 hours, but they have reappeared upon inadvertent rechallenge.

Lactation: Following oral administration, concentrations of unchanged captopril in human milk are approximately 1% of those in maternal blood. The effect of low levels of captopril on the nursing infant has not been determined. Caution should be exercised when captopril is administered to a nursing woman, and, in general, nursing should be interrupted.

Children: Safety and effectiveness in children have not been established although there is limited experience with the use of captopril in children from 2 months to 15 years of age with secondary hypertension and varying degrees of renal insufficiency. Dosage, on a weight basis, was comparable to that used in adults. Captopril should be used in children only if other measures for controlling blood pressure have not been effective.

Information for the Patient: Patients should be told to report promptly any indication of infection (e.g., sore throat, fever), which may be a sign of neutropenia, or of progressive edema, which might be related to proteinuria and nephrotic syndrome.

All patients should be cautioned that excessive perspiration and dehydration may lead to an excessive fall in blood pressure because of reduction in fluid volume. Other causes of volume depletion such as vomiting or diarrhea may also lead to a fall in blood pressure; patients should be advised to consult with the physician.

Patients should be advised to return to the physician if he/she experiences any symptoms possibly related to liver dysfunction. This would include viral like symptoms in the first weeks to months of therapy (such as fever, malaise, muscle pain, rash or adenopathy which are possible indicators of hypersensitivity reactions), or if abdominal pain, nausea or vomiting, loss of appetite, jaundice, itching or any other unexplained symptoms occur during therapy.

Patients should be warned against interruption or discontinuation of antihypertensive medications without the physician's advice.

Patients treated for severe congestive heart failure should be cautioned to increase their physical activity slowly.

Pregnancy: Since the use of captopril during pregnancy can cause injury and even death of the developing fetus, patients should be advised to report promptly to their physician if they become pregnant.

Drug Interactions: Diuretic Therapy: Patients on diuretics and especially those in whom diuretic therapy was recently instituted, as well as those on severe dietary salt restriction or dialysis, may occasionally experience a precipitous reduction of blood pressure usually within the first hour after receiving the initial dose of captopril (see Warnings).

When feasible the hypotensive effects may be minimized by either discontinuing the diuretic or increasing the salt intake approximately 1 week prior to initiation of treatment with captopril. Alternatively, provide medical supervision for at least 1 hour after the initial dose. If hypotension occurs, the patient should be placed in a supine position and, if necessary, receive an i.v. infusion of normal saline. This transient hypotensive response is not a contraindication to further doses which can be given without difficulty once the blood pressure has increased after volume expansion.

Agents Having Vasodilator Activity: Data on the effect of concomitant use of other vasodilators in patients receiving captopril for heart failure are not available; therefore, nitroglycerin or other nitrates (as used for management of angina) or other drugs having vasodilator activity should, if possible, be discontinued before starting captopril. If resumed during captopril therapy, such agents should be administered cautiously, and perhaps at lower dosage.

Agents Causing Renin Release: Captopril's effect will be augmented by antihypertensive agents that cause renin release. For example, diuretics (e.g., thiazides) may activate the renin-angiotensin-aldosterone system.

Agents Affecting Sympathetic Activity: The sympathetic nervous system may be especially important in supporting blood pressure in patients receiving captopril alone or with diuretics. Therefore, agents affecting sympathetic activity (e.g., ganglionic blocking agents or adrenergic neuron blocking agents) should be used with caution. Beta-adrenergic blocking drugs add some further antihypertensive effect to captopril, but the overall response is less than additive.

In heart failure, special caution is necessary since sympathetic stimulation is a vital component supporting circulatory function and inhibition with beta-blockade always carries a potential hazard of further depressing myocardial contractility.

Agents Increasing Serum Potassium: Since captopril decreases aldosterone production, elevation of serum potassium may occur. Potassium-sparing diuretics such as spironolactone, triamterene, or amiloride or potassium supplements should be given only for documented hypokalemia, and then with caution, since they may lead to a significant increase of serum potassium. Salt substitutes which contain potassium should also be used with caution.

Inhibitors of Endogenous Prostaglandin Synthesis: It has been reported that indomethacin may reduce the antihypertensive effect of captopril, especially in cases of low renin hypertension. Other nonsteroidal anti-inflammatory agents (e.g., ASA) may also have this effect.

The blood pressure lowering effects of captopril and beta-blockers are less than additive.

In patients with renal failure, the use of allopurinol concomitantly with captopril has been associated with neutropenia.

In patients with heart failure, the use of procainamide concomitantly with captopril has been associated with neutropenia.

Drug/Laboratory Test Interaction: Captopril may cause false-positive reactions for urinary acetone and for dipstick tests for urinary ketones.

Adverse Effects: Reported incidences are based on clinical trials involving approximately 7 000 patients treated with captopril.

Renal: Approximately 1 of every 100 patients developed proteinuria (see Warnings).

Each of the following has been reported in approximately 1 to 2 of 1 000 patients and are of uncertain relationship to drug use: renal insufficiency, renal failure, polyuria, oliguria and urinary frequency.

Hematologic: Neutropenia/agranulocytosis has occurred (see Warnings). Cases of anemia, thrombocytopenia and pancytopenia have been reported.

Dermatologic: A rash occurred in 8.5% of patients with normal renal function and 13% of patients with evidence of prior renal functional impairment. It was dose related, having occurred in 7% of patients at doses of 150 mg or less per day. The rash is usually maculopapular, but rarely urticarial, and generally occurs during the first 4 weeks of therapy. The rash is usually mild and disappears within a few days of dosage reduction, short-term treatment with an antihistaminic agent, and/or discontinuing therapy; remission may occur even if captopril is continued. Pruritus, without rash, occurs in about 2 of 100 patients. Between 7 and 10% of patients with skin rash have shown an eosinophilia and/or positive ANA titers. A reversible associated pemphigoid-like lesion, and photosensitivity, have also been reported.

Allergic: Angioedema of the face, mucous membranes of the mouth, or of the extremities has been observed in approximately 1 of 1 000 patients and is reversible on discontinuance of captopril therapy. Serum sickness and bronchospasm have been reported. One case of laryngeal edema has been reported.

Cardiovascular: Hypotension may occur; see Warnings and Precautions (Drug Interactions) for discussion of hypotension on initiation of captopril therapy.

Tachycardia, chest pain, and palpitations have each been observed in approximately 1 of 100 patients.

Angina pectoris, myocardial infarction, Raynaud's syndrome and congestive heart failure have each occurred in 2 to 3 of 1 000 patients.

Flushing or pallor has been reported in 2 to 5 of 1 000 patients.

Alterations in Taste: 2% of patients receiving 150 mg or less per day of captopril developed a diminution or loss of taste perception. At doses in excess of 150 mg/day, 7% of patients experienced this effect. Taste impairment is reversible and usually self-limited (2 to 3 months) even with continued drug administration. Weight loss may be associated with the loss of taste.

The following have been reported in about 0.5 to 2% of patients:

Gastrointestinal: gastric irritation, abdominal pain, nausea, vomiting, diarrhea, anorexia, constipation, aphthous ulcers and peptic ulcer.

CNS: dizziness, headache, malaise, fatigue, insomnia and paresthesia.

Others: dry mouth, dyspnea, cough, alopecia, impotence, loss of libido, disturbed vision, and itching and/or dry eyes.

Other clinical adverse effects reported since the drug was marketed are listed below by body system. In many cases, an incidence or causal relationship cannot be accurately determined.

General: asthenia, gynecomastia.

Cardiovascular: cardiac arrest, cerebrovascular accident, syncope.

Dermatologic: bullous pemphigus, Stevens-Johnson syndrome.

Gastrointestinal: pancreatitis, glossitis.

Hematologic: anemia, including aplastic and hemolytic.

Hepatobiliary: hepatitis, including rare cases of necrosis, cholestasis (see Precautions).

Metabolic: symptomatic hyponatremia.

Musculoskeletal: myalgia, myasthenia.

Nervous/Psychiatric: ataxia, confusion, depression, nervousness, somnolence.

Respiratory: bronchospasm, eosinophilic pneumonitis, rhinitis.

Special Senses: blurred vision.

As with other ACE inhibitors, a syndrome has been reported which includes: fever, myalgia, arthralgia, rash or other dermatologic manifestations, eosinophilia and an elevated ESR. Findings have usually resolved with discontinuation of treatment.

Altered Laboratory Findings: Elevations of liver enzymes and/or serum bilirubin have occurred (see Precautions). Rare cases of cholestatic jaundice and hepatocellular injury with or without secondary cholestasis, have been reported in association with captopril administration.

Elevation of BUN and serum creatinine may occur, especially in patients who are volume-depleted or who have renovascular hypertension. In instances of rapid reduction of long-standing or severely elevated blood pressure, the glomerular filtration rate may decrease transiently, also resulting in transient rises in serum creatinine and BUN.

Small increases in the serum potassium concentration frequently occur, especially in patients with renal impairment (see Precautions).

Diabetic Nephropathy: In 400 patients treated with captopril, the overall adverse reactions profile appeared to be similar to the above. However, the following adverse reactions have occurred more frequently in women than in men: dizziness (31% vs 20%), cough (23% vs 17%) and pharyngitis (20% vs 14%). In 395 patients treated with placebo, the incidences were: dizziness (22%), cough (15%) and pharyngitis (11%) in women and men combined.

The incidence of hypotension or orthostatic hypotension was 5.3% and was a reason for discontinuation of the drug in 1.8% of the patients.

The incidence of hyperkalemia related or possibly related to therapy in the diabetic patients studied with nephropathy and proteinuria was 3.6% and was a reason of discontinuation of the drug in 1% of the patients.

Hyperkalemia was defined as persistent elevation of serum potassium to 6.0 mg/dL or more in the absence of a remediable cause, such as other drugs, volume depletion, exogenous potassium supplements, etc.

In patients with serum creatinine $\geq$1.5 mg/dL, the incidence of a marked abnormality in hemoglobin (a drop $>$3 g/dL) was 6% in patients treated with captopril versus 0% in those on placebo.

Overdose: Symptoms and Treatment: In the event of overdosage, correction of hypotension would be of primary concern. Volume expansion with an i.v. infusion of normal saline is the treatment of choice for restoration of blood pressure.

Captopril may be removed from the general circulation by hemodialysis.

Dosage: Captopril should be taken 1 hour before meals. **Dosage must be individualized.**

Capoten (cont'd)

Hypertension: Initiation of therapy requires consideration of recent antihypertensive drug treatment, the extent of blood pressure elevation, salt restriction, and other clinical circumstances. If possible, discontinue the patient's previous antihypertensive drug regimen for 1 week before starting captopril. If this is impossible, especially in severe hypertension, the diuretic should be continued.

Initial dose: 25 mg 2 or 3 times a day. If a satisfactory reduction of blood pressure has not been achieved after 1 or 2 weeks, the dose may be increased to 50 mg 2 or 3 times a day. The dose of captopril in hypertension usually does not exceed 150 mg daily. Therefore, if the blood pressure has not been satisfactorily controlled after 1 to 2 weeks at this dose (and the patient is not already receiving a diuretic), a modest dose of thiazide-type diuretic (e.g., hydrochlorothiazide 25 mg daily) should be added. The diuretic dose may be increased at 1 to 2 week intervals until its highest usual antihypertensive dose is reached.

If captopril is being started in a patient already receiving a diuretic, therapy should be initiated under close medical supervision (see Warnings and Precautions, Drug Interactions regarding hypotension), with dosage and titration of captopril as noted above.

In severe hypertension, if further blood pressure reduction is required, the dose of captopril may be increased to 100 mg 2 or 3 times a day, and then, if necessary, to 150 mg 2 or 3 times a day, while continuing the diuretic. The usual dose range is 25 to 150 mg 2 or 3 times a day. A maximum daily dose of 450 mg given in 3 equally divided doses should not be exceeded.

For patients with accelerated or malignant hypertension, when temporary discontinuation of current antihypertensive therapy is not practical or desirable, or when prompt titration to more normotensive blood pressure levels is indicated, the diuretic should be continued but other concurrent antihypertensive medication stopped and captopril dosage promptly initiated at 25 mg 3 times a day, under close medical supervision. When necessitated by the patient's clinical condition, the daily dose of captopril may be increased every 24 hours under continuous medical supervision until a satisfactory blood pressure response is obtained or the maximum dose of captopril is reached. In this regimen, addition of a more potent diuretic, e.g., furosemide, may also be indicated.

Beta-blockers may also be used in conjunction with captopril therapy (see Precautions, Drug Interactions), but the effects of the 2 drugs are less than additive.

Heart Failure: Initiation of therapy requires consideration of recent diuretic therapy and the possibility of severe salt/volume depletion. In patients with either normal or low blood pressure, who have been vigorously treated with diuretics and who may be hyponatremic and/or hypovolemic, a starting dose of 6.25 or 12.5 mg 3 times a day may minimize the magnitude or duration of the hypotensive effect (see Warnings, Hypotension). For these patients, titration to the usual daily dosage can then occur within the next several days.

For most patients the usual initial daily dosage is 25 mg 3 times daily. After a dose of 50 mg 3 times daily is reached, further increases in dosage should be delayed, where possible, for at least 2 weeks to determine if a satisfactory response occurs. Most patients studied have had a satisfactory clinical improvement at 50 or 100 mg 3 times daily. A maximum daily dose of 450 mg of captopril should not be exceeded.

Captopril is to be used in conjunction with a diuretic. Therapy must be initiated under very close medical supervision.

Left Ventricular Dysfunction after Myocardial Infarction: The recommended dose for long-term use in patients following a myocardial infarction is a target maintenance dose of 50 mg 3 times daily.

Therapy may be initiated as early as 3 days following a myocardial infarction. After a single dose of 6.25 mg, captopril therapy should be initiated at 12.5 mg 3 times daily. Captopril should then be increased to 25 mg 3 times daily during the next several days and to a target dose of 50 mg 3 times daily over the next several weeks as tolerated (see Pharmacology).

Captopril may be used in patients treated with other post-myocardial infarction therapies, e.g., thrombolytics, ASA, beta-blockers.

Diabetic Nephropathy: The recommended daily dose of captopril for long-term use to treat diabetic nephropathy is 25 mg 3 times daily.

If further blood pressure reduction is required, other antihypertensive agents such as diuretics, beta-adrenoceptor-blockers, centrally-acting agents or vasodilators may be used in conjunction with captopril.

Dosage Adjustment in Renal Impairment: Because captopril is excreted primarily by the kidneys, excretion rates are reduced in patients with impaired renal function. These patients will take longer to reach steady-state levels of captopril and will reach higher steady-state levels for a given daily dose than patients with normal renal function. Therefore, these patients may respond to smaller or less frequent doses.

Captopril is removed by hemodialysis.

Renal Impairment Due to Diabetic Nephropathy (With or Without Hypertension): Captopril at doses of 25 mg 3 times daily was well-tolerated in patients with diabetic nephropathy and mild to moderate renal impairment (see Precautions, Hyperkalemia). Accordingly, no dose adjustment based on creatinine clearance is recommended for these patients.

Captopril has not been studied in patients with diabetic nephropathy and severe renal impairment (creatinine clearance ≤30 mL/min/1.73m²). These patients can be expected to have a higher steady-state concentration for a given daily dose than those with normal or mild-moderate renal impairment, and therefore may respond to smaller or less frequent doses. Doses may be adjusted based on clinical observation.

Renal Impairment Not Due to Diabetic Nephropathy: For patients with significant renal impairment not due to diabetic nephropathy, initial daily dosage of captopril should be reduced, and smaller increments utilized for titration, which should be quite slow (1- to 2-week intervals). After the desired therapeutic effect has been achieved, the dose should be slowly back-titrated to determine the minimal effective dose. When concomitant diuretic therapy is required, a loop diuretic (e.g., furosemide), rather than a thiazide diuretic, is preferred in these patients with impaired renal function (see Precautions, Anaphylactoid Reactions During Membrane Exposure).

Table I is based on theoretical considerations and may be useful as a guide to minimize drug accumulation.

Table I—Capoten

Recommended Dosage Interval in Patients with Renal Impairment Not Due to Diabetic Nephropathy

Creatinine Clearance (mL/min/1.73 m²)	Dosage Interval (Hours)
>75	8
75 to 35	12 to 24
34 to 20	24 to 48
19 to 8	48 to 72
7 to 5	72 to 108 (3 to 4.5 days)

Supplied: 12.5 mg: Each white, capsule-shaped tablet with beveled edge, slightly mottled flat-faced, with partial bisect bars on both sides, engraved with CAPOTEN on one side and 12.5 on the other, contains: captopril 12.5 mg. Nonmedicinal ingredients: cornstarch, lactose, microcrystalline cellulose and stearic acid. May contain hydroxypropylcellulose and hydroxypropyl methylcellulose. Bottles of 100 and 500.

25 mg: Each white, square tablet, quadrisect scored on one side and imprinted CAPOTEN 25 on the other, contains: captopril 25 mg. Nonmedicinal ingredients: cornstarch, lactose, microcrystalline cellulose and stearic acid. May contain hydroxypropylcellulose and hydroxypropyl methylcellulose. Bottles of 1 000.

50 mg: Each white, oval tablet, biconvex with a full bisecting score on one side and imprinted CAPOTEN 50 on the other, contains: captopril 50 mg. Nonmedicinal ingredients: cornstarch, lactose, microcrystalline cellulose and stearic acid. May contain hydroxypropylcellulose and hydroxypropyl methylcellulose. Bottles of 100 and 500.

100 mg: Each white, oval tablet, biconvex with a full bisecting score on one side and imprinted CAPOTEN 100 on the other, contains: captopril 100 mg. Nonmedicinal ingredients: cornstarch, lactose, microcrystalline cellulose and stearic acid. May contain hydroxypropylcellulose and hydroxypropyl methylcellulose. Bottles of 100.

Store at room temperature (15 to 30°C). Protect from moisture. Keep bottles tightly closed.

(Shown in Product Recognition Section)

Reviewed 1998

Need a manufacturer's address? Use the YELLOW SECTION.

CAPSAICIN
CAPSAICIN HP
Stiefel/Glades

Topical Analgesic

Supplied: Capsaicin: Each g of cream contains: capsaicin 0.025% w/w. Nonmedicinal ingredients: Arlacel 165, benzoyl alcohol (as preservative), cetyl alcohol, isopropyl myristate, purified water, sorbitol and white petrolatum. Tubes of 42.5 and 85 g.

Capsaicin HP: Each g of cream contains: capsaicin 0.075% w/w. Nonmedicinal ingredients: Arlacel 165, benzoyl alcohol (as preservative), cetyl alcohol, isopropyl myristate, purified water, sorbitol and white petrolatum. Tubes of 42.5 g.

CAPTOPRIL ℞
General Monograph, CPhA

see ACE INHIBITORS

CAPTRIL ℞
Technilab

Captopril

Angiotensin Converting Enzyme Inhibitor

Supplied: 12.5 mg: Each tablet is a white, biconvex caplet, embossed with TEC 186A and scored on one side, contains: captopril 12.5 mg. Nonmedicinal ingredients: colloidal silicon dioxide, lactose, microcrystalline cellulose, palmitic acid, starch and talc. Bottles of 100 and 500.

25 mg: Each white, square, biconvex tablet, embossed with TEC 186B and double-scored on one side, contains: captopril 25 mg. Nonmedicinal ingredients: colloidal silicon dioxide, lactose, microcrystalline cellulose, palmitic acid, starch and talc. Bottles of 100 and 1 000.

50 mg: Each white, oval, biconvex tablet, embossed with TEC 186C and scored on one side, contains: captopril 50 mg. Nonmedicinal ingredients: colloidal silicon dioxide, lactose, microcrystalline cellulose, palmitic acid, starch and talc. Bottles of 100 and 500.

100 mg: Each white, oval, biconvex tablet, embossed with TEC 186D and scored on one side, contains: captopril 100 mg. Nonmedicinal ingredients: colloidal silicon dioxide, lactose, microcrystalline cellulose, palmitic acid, starch and talc. Bottles of 100.

Store at room temperature (15 to 30°C) and protect from moisture. Keep bottles tightly closed.

New Product 1998

CARBACHOL ℞
General Monograph, CPhA

Carbamylcholine Chloride

Parasympathomimetic—Miotic

This monograph has been compiled by CPhA. It may contain information different from that approved by Therapeutic Products Programme, Health Canada, and the pharmaceutical manufacturers' approval has not been requested.

Pharmacology: Carbachol is a parasympathomimetic agent that directly stimulates cholinergic receptors. Unlike acetylcholine, carbachol is resistant to inactivation by cholinesterase, resulting in a more prolonged action.

Carbachol is used primarily for its ocular hypotensive effect. Following ocular application, carbachol causes contraction of the ciliary muscle which pulls open the pores of the trabecular meshwork, facilitating aqueous humor outflow. Contraction of the ciliary muscle also causes accommodative spasm. Miosis is caused by the cholinergic stimulation of the papillary sphincter by the drug. Carbachol does not penetrate the cornea readily; benzalkonium chloride is used to enhance corneal penetration.

Pharmacokinetics: Following topical application of carbachol to the conjunctival sac, miosis occurs within 10 to 20 minutes, lasting 4 to 8 hours. Maximal reduction in intraocular pressure occurs in 4 hours and lasts for 8 hours.

Following intraocular administration, miosis occurs within 2 to 5 minutes and persists for about 24 hours. Reduction in intraocular pressure also lasts for approximately 24 hours.

Indications: Ophthalmic: 0.01% solutions have been used in ocular surgery to produce miosis following delivery of the lens in round pupil cataract extraction as well as in penetrating keratoplasty, iridectomy and anterior segment surgery where miosis is desired.

1.5 and 3% solutions are used for the reduction of intraocular pressure in chronic, primary, open-angle glaucoma.

Contraindications: Iritis, some secondary glaucomas and sensitivity to carbachol. Contraindicated for systemic use in acute cardiac failure, bronchial asthma, peptic ulcer.

Precautions: Patients requiring topical ophthalmic treatment should be advised about the transient ocular and frontal headache which usually accompanies the initial few days of therapy.

Pregnancy and *Lactation:* Safety has not been established.

Adverse Effects: The most frequent adverse effect following ophthalmic application is a burning or stinging sensation. Conjunctival hyperemia, blurred vision, twitching of eyelids, eye pain and headache frequently occur. Ophthalmic administration has rarely been associated with systemic cholinergic side effects.

Systemic side effects may include bradycardia, sweating, asthma, nausea, faintness, vomiting, diarrhea, salivation and abdominal cramps. Atropine may be required for serious toxicity.

Dosage: Ophthalmic: Topical: Instill 1 or 2 drops of carbachol 1.5% or 3% solution into the conjunctival sac 2 or 3 times daily, or as directed.

To minimize systemic absorption and drainage into the nose and throat, finger pressure may be applied to the lacrimal sac for 1 to 2 minutes following administration. Alternatively, simple lid closure for 2 to 5 minutes suspends the pumping action of fluid down the nasolacrimal system that occurs with blinking.

Following topical administration, excess solution should be removed from the hands and eye area.

Intraocular: Instill 0.1 to 0.5 mL carbachol 0.01% solution into the anterior chamber

Reviewed 1998

CARBACHOL ℞
Bioniche

Carbamylcholine Chloride
Parasympathomimetic

Supplied: Injection: Each mL of sterile solution contains: carbachol 0.25 mg, dextrose 50 mg and sodium hydroxide to adjust pH. Ampuls of 1 mL, boxes of 10. Store at room temperature (15 to 30°C).

Tablets: Each tablet contains: carbachol 2 mg. Bottles of 100. Store at room temperature (15 to 30°C).

CARBASTAT® ℞
CIBA Vision

Carbachol
Miotic

Supplied: Each mL contains: carbachol 0.01%. Nonmedicinal ingredients: calcium chloride dihydrate, magnesium chloride hexahydrate, potassium chloride, sodium acetate trihydrate, sodium chloride, sodium citrate dihydrate, sodium hydroxide and/or hydrochloric acid (to adjust pH) and water for injection. Sterile glass vials of 1.5 mL, cartons of 12. Store at controlled room temperature 15 to 30°C. Protect from freezing.

CARBOCAINE®
Sanofi

Mepivacaine HCl
Local Anesthetic

Pharmacology: Mepivacaine stabilizes the neuronal membrane and prevents the initiation and transmission of nerve impulses, thereby affecting local anesthesia. Its pharmacological properties are somewhat similar to those of lidocaine, which it resembles chemically. Its action is more rapid in onset and somewhat more prolonged than that of lidocaine. It has been employed for all types of infiltration and regional nerve block anesthesia.

Onset of anesthesia is rapid, the time of onset for sensory block ranging from about 3 to 20 minutes depending upon such factors as the anesthetic technique, the type of block, the concentration of the solution and the individual patient. The degree of motor blockade produced is dependent on the concentration of the solution. The 1% concentration will block sensory and sympathetic conduction without loss of motor function and will be effective in small superficial nerve blocks. The 2% concentration of mepivacaine will produce complete sensory and motor block of any nerve group.

The duration of anesthesia also varies depending upon the technique and type of block, the concentration and the individual. Mepivacaine will normally provide anesthesia which is adequate for 2 to 2½ hours of surgery. It has been reported that vasoconstrictors do not significantly prolong anesthesia with mepivacaine, but epinephrine (1:200 000) may be added to the mepivacaine solution to promote local hemostasis and to delay systemic absorption of the anesthetic.

The drowsiness and lassitude seen with lidocaine have not been commonly noted with mepivacaine. Mepivacaine has shown excellent tissue compatibility; irritation or tissue damage has not been observed.

Indications: For production of local or regional anesthesia by local infiltration, peripheral nerve block techniques, and central neural techniques including epidural and caudal blocks.

Contraindications: Hypersensitivity to mepivacaine or amide-type local anesthetics.

Warnings: Local anesthetics should only be employed by clinicians who are well versed in diagnosis and management of dose-related toxicity and other acute emergencies which might arise from the block to be employed, and then only after insuring the immediate availability of oxygen, other resuscitative drugs, cardiopulmonary resuscitative equipment, and the personnel resources needed for proper management of toxic reactions and related emergencies (see also Adverse Effects and Precautions). Delay in proper management of dose-related toxicity, underventilation from any cause, and/or altered sensitivity may lead to acidosis, cardiac arrest and, possibly death.

Local anesthetic solutions containing antimicrobial preservatives (i.e., those supplied in multiple-dose vials) should not be used for epidural or caudal anesthesia because safety has **not** been established with regard to intrathecal injection, either intentionally or inadvertently, of such preservatives.

It is essential that aspiration for blood or cerebrospinal fluid (where applicable) be done prior to injecting any local anesthetic, both the original dose and all subsequent doses, to avoid intravascular or subarachnoid injection. However, a negative aspiration does not ensure against an intravascular or subarachnoid injection.

Mepivacaine with epinephrine or other vasopressors should not be used concomitantly with ergot-type oxytocic drugs, because a severe persistent hypertension may occur. Likewise, solutions of mepivacaine containing a vasoconstrictor, such as epinephrine, should be used with extreme caution in patients receiving monoamine oxidase inhibitors (MAOI) or antidepressants of the triptyline or imipramine types, because severe prolonged hypertension may result.

Local anesthetic procedures should be used with caution when there is inflammation and/or sepsis in the region of the proposed injection.

Mixing or the prior or intercurrent use of any local anesthetic with mepivacaine cannot be recommended because of insufficient data on the clinical use of such mixtures.

These solutions are not intended for spinal anesthesia or dental use.

Precautions: General: During major regional nerve block, the patient should have i.v. fluids running via an indwelling catheter to assure a functioning i.v. pathway. Injections should be made slowly, with frequent aspirations before and during the injection to avoid intravascular injection. Current opinion favors fractional administration with constant attention to the patient, rather than rapid bolus injection. Syringe aspirations should also be performed before and during each supplemental injection in continuous (intermittent) catheter techniques. An intravascular injection is still possible even if aspirations for blood are negative.

During the administration of epidural anesthesia, it is recommended that a test dose be administered initially and the effects monitored before the full dose is given. When using a continuous catheter technique, test doses should be given prior to both the original and all reinforcing doses, because plastic tubing in the epidural space can migrate into a blood vessel or through the dura. When clinical conditions permit, an effective test dose should contain epinephrine (10 to 15 µg have been suggested) to serve as a warning of unintended intravascular injection. If injected into a blood vessel, this amount of epinephrine is likely to produce an epinephrine response within 45 seconds, consisting of an increase of pulse and blood pressure, circumoral pallor, palpitations, and nervousness in the unsedated patient. The sedated patient may exhibit only a pulse rate increase of 20 or more beats/minute for 15 or more seconds. Therefore, following the test dose, the heart rate should be monitored for a heart rate increase. The test dose should also contain an amide anesthetic to detect an unintended intrathecal administration. This will be evidenced within a few minutes by signs of spinal block. A negative outcome from the test dose does not guarantee that the epidural needle is accurately placed.

Injection of repeated doses of local anesthetics may cause significant increases in plasma levels with each repeated dose due to slow accumulation of the drug or its metabolites or to slow metabolic degradation. Tolerance to elevated blood levels varies with the status of the patient. Debilitated elderly patients, and acutely ill patients should be given reduced doses commensurate with their age and physical status. Local anesthetics should also be used with caution in patients with severe disturbances of cardiac rhythm, shock, heart block or hypotension.

Local anesthetic solutions containing a vasoconstrictor should be used cautiously and in carefully restricted quantities in areas of the body supplied by end arteries or having otherwise compromised blood supply such as digits, nose, external ear, penis. Patients with hypertensive vascular disease may exhibit exaggerated vasoconstrictor response. Ischemic injury or necrosis may result.

Mepivacaine should be used with caution in patients with known allergies and sensitivities.

Use mepivacaine cautiously in patients with hepatic and renal disease, and in patients with impaired cardiovascular function.

Serious dose-related cardiac arrhythmias may occur if preparations containing a vasoconstrictor such as epinephrine are employed in patients during or following the administration of potent inhalation anesthetics. In deciding whether to use these products concurrently in the same patient, the combined action of both agents upon the myocardium, the concentration and volume of vasoconstrictor used, and the time since injection, when applicable, should be taken into account. If epinephrine is used, a 1:200 000 concentration is preferred.

Many drugs used during the conduct of anesthesia are considered potential triggering agents for familial malignant hyperthermia. Because it is not known whether amide-type local anesthetics may trigger this reaction and because the need for supplemental general anesthesia cannot be predicted in advance, it is suggested that a standard protocol for management should be available.

Head and Neck Area: Small doses of local anesthetics injected into the head and neck area may produce adverse reactions similar to systemic toxicity seen with unintentional intravascular injections of larger doses. The injection procedures require the utmost care.

Pregnancy: Obstetrical anesthesia: Animal reproduction studies have not been conducted with mepivacaine. There are no adequate well-controlled studies in pregnant women of the effect of mepivacaine on the developing fetus. Mepivacaine should be used during pregnancy only if the potential benefit justifies the potential risk to the fetus. This does not preclude the use of mepivacaine at term for obstetrical anesthesia or analgesia.

Maternal hypotension has resulted from regional anesthesia. Local anesthetics produce vasodilation by blocking sympathetic nerves.

Epidural, paracervical, caudal, or pudendal anesthesia may alter the forces of parturition through changes in uterine contractility or maternal expulsive efforts. In one study, paracervical block anesthesia was associated with a decrease in the mean duration of first stage labor and facilitation of cervical dilation. Epidural anesthesia has been reported to prolong the second stage of labor by removing the parturient's reflex urge to bear down or by interfering with motor function. The use of obstetrical anesthesia may increase the need for forceps assistance.

The use of some local anesthetic drug products during labor and delivery may be followed by diminished muscle strength and tone for the first day or two of life. The long-term significance of these observations is unknown.

Fetal bradycardia may occur in 20 to 30% of patients receiving paracervical block anesthesia with the amide-type local anesthetics and may be associated with fetal acidosis.

Carbocaine (cont'd)

Fetal heart rate should always be monitored during paracervical anesthesia. Added risk appears to be present in prematurity, postmaturity, toxemia of pregnancy, and fetal distress. The physician should weigh the possible advantages against dangers when considering paracervical block in these conditions. Careful adherence to recommended dosage is of the utmost importance in obstetrical paracervical block. Failure to achieve adequate analgesia with recommended doses should arouse suspicion of intravascular or fetal intracranial injection.

Cases compatible with unintended fetal intracranial injection of local anesthetic solution have been reported following intended paracervical or pudendal block or both.

Case reports of maternal convulsions and cardiovascular collapse following use of some local anesthetics for paracervical block in early pregnancy (as anesthesia for elective abortion) suggest that systemic absorption under these circumstances may be rapid. Injection should be made slowly and with frequent aspiration. Allow a 5-minute interval between sides.

It is extremely important to avoid aortocaval compression by the gravid uterus during administration of regional block to parturients and the patient must be maintained in the left lateral decubitus position.

Lactation: It is not known whether local anesthetic drugs are excreted in human milk.

Adverse Effects: Reactions to mepivacaine are characteristic of those associated with other amide-type local anesthetics: A major cause of adverse reactions to this group of drugs is excessive plasma levels, which may be due to overdosage, inadvertent intravascular injection or slow metabolic degradation. Transient slight stinging on injection has been noted occasionally.

CNS reactions are characterized by excitation and/or depression. Disorientation, restlessness, anxiety, dizziness, tinnitus, blurred vision or tremors may occur, possibly proceeding to convulsions. However, excitement may be transient or absent, with depression being the first manifestation of an adverse reaction. This may quickly be followed by drowsiness merging into unconsciousness and respiratory arrest. Other CNS effects may be nausea, vomiting, chills and constriction of the pupils.

High doses or inadvertent intravascular injection may lead to high plasma levels and related depression of the myocardium, decreased cardiac output, heart block, hypotension (or sometimes hypertension) bradycardia, ventricular arrhythmias and possibly cardiac arrest.

Allergic-type reactions are rare and may occur as a result of sensitivity to the local anesthetic or to other formulation ingredients, such as the antimicrobial preservative methylparaben, contained in multiple-dose vials. Cross sensitivity among members of amide-type local anesthetic group has been reported. The usefulness of screening for sensitivity has not been definitely established.

Neurologic effects following epidural or caudal anesthesia may include spinal block of varying magnitude (including high or total spinal block); hypotension secondary to spinal block; urinary retention; fecal and urinary incontinence; loss of perineal sensation and sexual function; persistent anesthesia, paresthesia, weakness, paralysis of the lower extremities and loss of sphincter control, all of which may have slow, incomplete or no recovery; headache; backache; septic meningitis; meningismus, slowing of labor; increased incidence of forceps delivery; cranial nerve palsies due to traction on nerves from loss of cerebrospinal fluid; neuritis; numbness.

Overdose: Symptoms and Treatment: Toxic effects of local anesthetics require symptomatic treatment; there is no specific cure. The physician should be prepared to maintain an airway and to support ventilation with oxygen and assisted or controlled respiration as required. Supportive treatment of the cardiovascular system includes i.v. fluids and, when appropriate, vasopressors (preferably those that stimulate the myocardium).

Convulsions may be controlled with oxygen and i.v. administration, in small increments, of a barbiturate or muscle relaxant, as follows: preferably, an ultra short-acting barbiturate such as thiopental or thiamylal; if this is not available, a short-acting barbiturate (e.g. secobarbital or pentobarbital) or a short-acting muscle relaxant (succinylcholine). I.V. muscle relaxants and barbiturates should only be administered by those familiar with their use.

Dosage: The dose of any local anesthetic administered varies with the anesthetic procedure, the area to be anesthetized, the vascularity of the tissues, the number of neuronal segments to be blocked, the depth of anesthesia and degree of muscle relaxant required, the duration of anesthesia desired, individual tolerance and the physical condition of the patient. The recommended single adult dose should not exceed 400 mg. The following dosages have generally proved satisfactory and are therefore suggested as a guide. The smallest dose and concentration required to produce the desired result should be administered. The recommended dosage is based on requirements for the average adult and should be reduced for elderly or debilitated patients.

Nerve Block (e.g., **cervical, brachial, intercostal, pudendal**): From 5 to 40 mL of a 1% solution, or 5 to 20 mL of a 2% solution, depending on the area and extent of block. Pudendal block: one half of total dose injected each side.

Paracervical Block: Maximum of up to 20 mL of a 1% solution (half-dose injected slowly each side, 5 minutes between sides) per 90-minute period.

Transvaginal Block: Up to 30 mL of a 1% solution (half-dose injected each side).

Caudal and Epidural Block: From 15 to 30 mL of a 1% solution, from 10 to 20 mL of a 2% solution containing no preservative.

Infiltration: Up to 40 mL of a 1% solution (or an equivalent amount in a more dilute solution, depending on the area of the operative field).

Therapeutic Block (in management of pain): From 1 to 5 mL of a 1 or 2% solution.

Pediatric doses should be measured as a percentage of total adult dose based on body weight (not exceeding 5 to 6 mg/kg). In children under 3 years of age or weighing less than 14 kg, 1% solutions should be employed.

Mepivacaine solution may be diluted with an equal part of sodium chloride injection USP. Dosages in excess of the aforementioned amounts have been administered without serious side effects. Due caution should be exercised in the use of larger dosages and in general a total dosage of 7 mg/kg should not be exceeded. Under no circumstances should administration be repeated at intervals less than 1.5 hours. The total dose for 24 hours should not exceed 1 000 mg. For additional information, see package insert.

Supplied: Infiltration and Nerve Block: Each mL of solution contains: mepivacaine HCl 10 mg in water for injection. Nonmedicinal ingredients: sodium chloride and methylparaben. Gluten-, lactose-, preservative- and sulfite-free. Multiple dose vials of 50 mL (1%), boxes of 5.

Caudal and Epidural Block: Each mL of solution contains: mepivacaine HCl 10 mg in water for injection. Nonmedicinal ingredients: calcium chloride (dihydrate), potassium chloride and sodium chloride. Gluten-, lactose-, preservative- and sulfite-free. Single dose vials of 30 mL (1%), boxes of 5.

Caudal and Epidural Block: Each mL of solution contains: mepivacaine HCl 20 mg in water for injection. Nonmedicinal ingredients: calcium chloride (dihydrate), potassium chloride and sodium chloride. Gluten-, lactose-, preservative- and sulfite-free. Single dose vials of 20 mL (2%), boxes of 5.

CARBOLITH™ Ⓟ
ICN

Lithium Carbonate

Antimanic Agent

Pharmacology: Preclinical studies have shown that lithium alters sodium transport in nerve and muscle cells and effects a shift toward intraneuronal metabolism of catecholamines, but the specific biochemical mechanism of lithium action in mania is unknown.

Pharmacokinetics: Lithium ions are rapidly absorbed from the gastrointestinal tract and plasma lithium peaks are reached 2 to 4 hours after lithium administration. The distribution of lithium in the body approximates that of total body water, but its passage across the blood-brain barrier is slow and at equilibration the CSF lithium level reaches only approximately half the plasma concentration.

Lithium undergoes a biphasic elimination pathway with an alpha half-life of 5 hours and beta half-life of 18 hours.

Lithium is excreted primarily in urine with less than 1% being eliminated with the feces. Lithium is filtered by the glomeruli and 80% of the filtered lithium is reabsorbed in the tubules, probably by the same mechanism responsible for sodium reabsorption.

The renal clearance of lithium is proportional to its plasma concentration. About 50% of a single dose of lithium is excreted in 24 hours. A low salt intake resulting in low tubular concentration of sodium will increase lithium reabsorption and might result in retention or intoxication.

Renal lithium clearance tends to be remarkably constant in the same individual but decreases with age and when sodium intake is lowered. The dose necessary to maintain a given concentration of serum lithium depends on the ability of the kidney to excrete lithium. However, renal lithium excretion may vary greatly between individuals and lithium dosage must, therefore, be adjusted individually. In clinical reports, it has been noted that serum lithium may rise an average of 0.2 to 0.4 mEq or mmol/L after intake of 300 mg and 0.3 to 0.6 mEq or mmol/L after intake of 600 mg of lithium carbonate. It has been suggested that manic patients retain larger amounts of lithium during the active manic phase, but recent studies have been unable to confirm a clear difference in excretion patterns. However, patients in a manic state seem to have an increased tolerance to lithium.

Once daily administration: Clinical trials comparing once daily at bedtime dosing versus 2 to 4 times-a-day dosing have shown that urinary volume is significantly decreased with single daily dosing.

Total daily doses of lithium required to reach therapeutic levels were lower with the once-daily dosage schedule than with the divided dosage schedule.

In addition, administration of a single bedtime dose of lithium may result in initial post-absorptive symptoms—which are believed to be associated with rapid rise in serum lithium levels—to occur at night while the patient is sleeping.

In one study, significantly less sclerotic glomeruli, atrophic tubules and interstitial fibrosis were observed in patients on a single daily dosage regimen, as compared to patients on a multiple daily dosage regimen.

Indications: In the lithium treatment of manic episodes of manic-depressive illness. Maintenance therapy has been found to be useful in preventing or diminishing the frequency of subsequent relapses in bipolar manic-depressive patients (with a history of mania). Typical symptoms of mania, as an affective disorder, include pressure of speech, motor hyperactivity, reduced need for sleep, flight of ideas, grandiosity, or poor judgment, aggressiveness, and possibly hostility. When given to a patient experiencing a manic episode, lithium may produce a normalization of symptomatology within 1 to 3 weeks.

Contraindications: Lithium should generally not be given to patients with significant renal or cardiovascular disease, severe debilitation or dehydration, or sodium depletion, and to patients receiving diuretics, since the risk of lithium toxicity is very high in such patients. If the psychiatric indication is life-threatening, and if such a patient fails to respond to other measures, lithium treatment may be undertaken with extreme caution, including daily serum lithium determinations and adjustments to the usually low doses ordinarily tolerated by these individuals. In such instances, hospitalization is necessary.

Warnings: Lithium toxicity is closely related to serum lithium levels, and can occur at doses close to the therapeutic levels. Facilities for prompt and accurate serum lithium determinations should be available before initiating therapy.

The ability to tolerate lithium is greater during the acute manic phase and decreases when manic symptoms subside (see Dosage).

Impaired Renal Function: Chronic lithium therapy is frequently associated with a decrease in renal concentrating capacity with development of thirst, polyuria, micturia, weight gain and altered kidney function tests, occasionally presenting as nephrogenic diabetes insipidus. Such patients should be carefully managed to avoid dehydration with resulting lithium retention and toxicity. The evidence suggests that impaired renal function during chronic therapy may be in most instances, only partially reversible when lithium is discontinued.

Prevention of renal toxicity and other toxic effects of long-term therapy requires a firm diagnosis of bipolar manic depressive illness; careful screening for pre-existing renal and other diseases; establishment of standardized 12-hour serum lithium levels which are as low as possible yet clinically effective; maintaining control of treatment by monitoring serum lithium levels and exercising clinical and laboratory surveillance over possible side effects or signs of lithium intoxication; exercising maximum control of at-risk patients; insuring that long-term lithium therapy is maintained only when clinical response has been clearly established; and adjusting the dosage schedule and preparation used so as to obtain temporarily periods of lithium concentrations as low as possible in the kidney.

Glomerular sclerosis and interstitial fibrosis as well as tubular lesions have been reported in patients on chronic lithium therapy. When kidney function is assessed for baseline data prior to starting lithium therapy or thereafter, routine urinalysis and other tests may be used to evaluate tubular function (e.g., urine specific gravity or osmolality or 24-hour urine volume) and glomerular function (e.g., serum creatinine or creatinine clearance).

During lithium therapy, progressive or sudden changes in renal function, even within the normal range indicate the need for re-evaluation of treatment including dosage and frequency of lithium administration, and a reassessment of the risk-benefit of long-term lithium therapy.

Pregnancy: Data from lithium birth registries suggest an increase in cardiac and other anomalies, especially Ebstein's anomaly; nephrogenic diabetes insipidus, euthyroid goiter and hypoglycemia have occurred in infants born to women who took lithium during pregnancy. Therefore, lithium should not be used during pregnancy or in women of childbearing potential unless it cannot be substituted by other appropriate therapy and in the opinion of the physician the expected benefits outweigh the possible hazards to the fetus.

Lactation: Lithium is excreted in human milk. Nursing should not be undertaken during lithium therapy except in rare and unusual circumstances where, in the view of the physician, the potential benefits to the mother outweigh possible hazards to the child.

Children: Since information regarding the safety and effectiveness of lithium in children under 12 years of age is not available, the use of lithium carbonate in such patients is not recommended at this time.

Precautions: To maximize benefits, minimize the risks, and reduce as much as possible the adverse effects of lithium therapy, it is essential to provide proper information to patients and relatives about the treatment regimen and control procedures required during treatment, as well as an explanation of the expected benefits and the most commonly experienced immediate and long-term side effects. In most cases, appropriate written material should be provided to supplement verbal information.

Outpatients and their families should be warned that the patient must discontinue therapy and contact the physician if such clinical signs of lithium toxicity as diarrhea, vomiting, tremor, mild ataxia, drowsiness, or muscular weakness occur.

Occupational Hazards: Further, since lithium may impair mental and/or physical abilities, patients should be cautioned about undertaking activities requiring alertness (e.g., operating vehicles or machinery).

Previously existing underlying thyroid disorders do not necessarily constitute a contraindication to lithium therapy; where hypothyroidism exists, careful monitoring of the thyroid function during lithium stabilization and maintenance allows for correction of changing thyroid parameters, if any. Where hypothyroidism occurs during lithium stabilization and maintenance, supplemental thyroid treatment may be used.

Lithium decreases sodium re-absorption by the renal tubules which would lead to sodium depletion. Therefore, it is essential for the patient to maintain a normal diet, including salt, and an adequate fluid intake (2 500 to 3 000 mL), at least during the initial stabilization period. Decreased tolerance to lithium has been reported to ensue from protracted sweating or diarrhea and, if such occurs, supplemental fluid and salt should be administered. In addition to sweating and diarrhea, concomitant infection with elevated temperatures may also necessitate a temporary reduction or cessation of medication.

Drug Interactions: Combined use of haloperidol and lithium: An encephalopathy resembling the malignant neuroleptic syndrome (characterized by weakness, lethargy, fever, tremulousness and confusion, extrapyramidal symptoms, leukocytosis, elevated serum enzymes, BUN and FBS) followed by irreversible brain damage has occurred in a few patients treated with lithium plus haloperidol. A causal relationship between these events and concomitant administration of lithium and haloperidol has not been clearly established; however, patients receiving such combined therapy should be monitored closely for early evidence of neurological toxicity such as rigidity and/or hyperpyrexia and treatment discontinued promptly if such signs appear.

Combined use of phenothiazines and lithium: Both pharmacokinetic interactions and clinical toxicity with the combined use of these agents have been described. Lithium-induced reductions in plasma chlorpromazine levels, phenothiazine-induced increases in red cell uptake of lithium and chlorpromazine-induced increases in renal lithium excretion have been reported. Clinically, occasional cases of neurotoxicity have been reported and may be more likely to occur with thioridazine than other phenothiazines, when combined with lithium. Therefore, the clinician should be alert for altered response to either drug when used in combination and when either drug is withdrawn.

The action of neuromuscular blocking agents may be prolonged in patients receiving lithium. Therefore, caution should be exercised when the combination is required. A temporary omission of a few doses of lithium can reduce the risks of this interaction.

Indomethacin has been reported to increase steady-state plasma lithium levels by 30 to 59%. There is also evidence that other nonsteroidal anti-inflammatory agents may have a similar effect. When such combinations are used, increased frequency of monitoring plasma lithium levels is recommended.

There are reports that concurrent use of methyldopa or tetracycline may increase the risk of lithium toxicity.

Concurrent use of lithium and carbamazepine or phenytoin might result in an increased risk of CNS toxicity. The administration of aminophylline or theophylline to patients on lithium therapy may require increased lithium doses to maintain the psychotropic effect. Patients stabilized on lithium therapy who receive a thiazide diuretic may require a reduction of lithium dosage to avoid accumulation and toxicity, since there is often a 20 to 40% reduction of renal lithium clearance. Furosemide appears to be less likely to affect lithium clearance.

Adverse Effects: Mild side effects may be encountered even when serum lithium levels remain below 1 mEq/L. The most frequent side effects are the initial postabsorptive symptoms, believed to be associated with a rapid rise in serum lithium levels. They include nausea, abdominal pain, vomiting, diarrhea, vertigo, muscle weakness, sleepiness and a dazed feeling, and frequently disappear after stabilization of therapy. The more common and persistent adverse reactions are: fine tremor of the hands which is not responsive to antiparkinson drugs, and at times, fatigue, thirst and polyuria (renal toxicity). These side effects may subside with continued treatment or a temporary reduction or cessation of dosage. If persistent, a lowering or cessation of dosage and reassessment of lithium therapy is indicated.

Mild to moderate toxic reactions may occur at lithium levels from 1.5 to 2 mEq/L, and moderate to severe reactions at levels above 2 mEq/L. Permanent neurological damage has been reported after exposure to toxic levels of lithium.

A number of patients may experience lithium accumulation during initial therapy, increasing to toxic levels and requiring immediate discontinuation of the drug. Some elderly patients with lower renal clearances for lithium may also experience different degrees of lithium toxicity, requiring reduction or temporary withdrawal of medication. However, in patients with normal renal clearance the toxic manifestations appear to occur in a fairly regular sequence related to serum lithium levels. The usually transient gastrointestinal symptoms are the earliest side effects to occur. A mild degree of fine tremor of the hands may persist throughout therapy. Thirst and polyuria may be followed by increased drowsiness, ataxia, tinnitus and blurred vision, indicating early intoxication. As intoxication progresses the following manifestations may be encountered: confusion, increasing disorientation, muscle twitching, hyperreflexia, nystagmus, seizures, diarrhea, vomiting, and eventually coma and death.

The following toxic reactions have been reported and appear to be related to serum lithium levels, including levels within the therapeutic range.

Neuromuscular: tremor, muscle hyperirritability (fasciculations, twitching, clonic movements of whole limbs), ataxia choreoathetotic movements, hyperactive deep tendon reflexes.

CNS: blackout spells, epileptiform seizures, slurred speech, dizziness, vertigo, incontinence of urine or feces, somnolence, psychomotor retardation, restlessness, confusion, stupor, coma.

Cardiovascular: cardiac arrhythmia, hypotension, peripheral circulatory collapse.

Gastrointestinal: anorexia, nausea, vomiting, diarrhea.

Genitourinary: albuminuria, oliguria, polyuria, glycosuria.

Dermatologic: drying and thinning of hair, anesthesia of skin, acne, chronic folliculitis, xerosis cutis, alopecia and exacerbation of psoriasis.

Autonomic Nervous System: blurred vision, dry mouth.

Thyroid Abnormalities: euthyroid goiter and/or hypothyroidism (including myxedema) accompanied by lower T_3 and T_4 levels and elevated TSH. Iodine^{131} uptake may be elevated. On the average 5 to 15% of patients on long-term lithium therapy manifest clinical signs or have altered serum hormone levels (see Precautions). Paradoxically, rare cases of hyperthyroidism have been reported.

EEG Changes: diffuse slowing, widening of frequency spectrum, potentiation and disorganization of background rhythm.

ECG Changes: reversible flattening, isoelectricity or inversion of T waves.

Miscellaneous: fatigue, lethargy, transient scotomata, dehydration, weight loss, tendency to sleep.

Miscellaneous reactions frequently unrelated to dosage include: transient EEG and ECG changes, leukocytosis, headache, diffuse non-toxic goiter with or without hypothyroidism, transient hyperglycemia, generalized pruritus with or without rash, cutaneous ulcers, albuminuria, worsening of organic brain syndrome, excessive weight gain, edematous swelling of ankles or wrists, and thirst or polyuria, sometimes resembling diabetes insipidus, and metallic taste.

A single instance has been reported of the development of painful discoloration of fingers and toes and coldness of the extremities within one day of starting treatment with lithium. The mechanism through which these symptoms (resembling Raynaud's syndrome) developed is not known. Recovery followed discontinuance.

Serious reactions to long-term therapy: In addition to other possible adverse reactions, the main concern during chronic lithium therapy centres on the kidney function, the thyroid, parathyroid, the bones and skin.

Overdose: Symptoms: Lithium toxicity is closely related to the concentration of lithium in the blood and is usually associated with serum concentrations in excess of 1.5 mEq/L or mmol/L. Early signs of toxicity which may occur at lower serum concentrations were described under Adverse Effects and usually respond to reduction of dosage. Lithium intoxication has been preceded by the appearance of aggravation of the following symptoms: sluggishness, drowsiness, lethargy, coarse tremors or muscle twitchings, loss of appetite, vomiting, and diarrhea. Occurrence of these symptoms requires immediate cessation of medication and careful clinical reassessment and management. Signs and symptoms of lithium intoxication have already been described under Adverse Effects.

Treatment: No specific antidote for lithium poisoning is known. Early symptoms of lithium toxicity can usually be treated by reduction or cessation of dosage of the drug and resumption of the treatment at a lower dose after 24 to 48 hours. In severe cases of lithium poisoning, the first and foremost goal of treatment consists of elimination of this ion from the patient and supportive care.

Recommended treatment consists of: gastric lavage, correction of fluid and electrolyte imbalance and regulation of kidney function. Urea, mannitol and aminophylline all produce significant increases in lithium excretion. Hemodialysis is an effective and rapid means of removing the ion from the severely toxic patient. Infection prophylaxis, regular chest x-ray, and preservation of adequate respiration are essential.

Dosage: Selection of patients and approach to lithium therapy: The results of lithium therapy depend largely on the nature and course of the illness itself, rather than on the symptoms. The selection of patients for long-term treatment requires a clearcut diagnosis of primary affective disorder, the condition for which the stabilizing effects of lithium have been found useful. The variables that have been more consistently associated with response to lithium therapy in patients with a primary affective disorder are: the good quality of remissions with good function and no significant symptomatology during the free intervals between previous episodes of illness; low frequency of episodes, typically 1 or 2 (and not more than 3 or 4) per year; and symptomatology during the acute episodes that meet strict criteria for a primary affective disorder (DSM-III; Research Diagnosis Criteria).

Screening for lithium candidates should include at least, a medical history and physical examination with emphasis on the CNS, urinary, cardiovascular, gastrointestinal and endocrine systems and the skin. It should also include: routine 24-hour urine volume, serum creatinine, record of weight, and ECG, possibly electrolytes and TSH, and for long-term treatment, creatinine clearance and a urine concentration test. Other examinations and tests should be used when indicated. Monitoring lithium treatment should include, for each visit, mental status, physical examination, weight, 12-hour serum lithium and a check for lithium side effects and compliance. It should also include serum creatinine every 2 months, plasma thyroid hormone and TSH every 6 to 12 months, particularly in female patients, and attention to renal and thyroid function should be maintained throughout, with tests used for baseline screening repeated as required.

The first objective of treatment is to establish an effective and safe daily dosage of lithium with the aid of standardized 12-hour serum lithium levels maintained within the therapeutic range, as high as necessary for efficacy, and with the patient as much as possible free of significant side effects. Three daily doses should be used initially, at least until the daily dosage is established. The next aim is to move to an optimal

Carbolith (cont'd)

dose, which should be as low as possible, consistent with protection against relapse. During follow-up, an adjustment to lower dosages may be required to minimize adverse effects, and a change in the lithium preparation used and/or the frequency of dosing, either towards multiple doses or towards a single dose, may be necessary to handle absorption-related adverse effects or concern over possible renal toxicity. Intermittent lithium treatment in carefully selected patients has been recommended by some lithium experts, but should not be undertaken without careful planning and great caution. The cooperation of patients and relatives is required throughout. Before deciding on the institution of long-term treatment, it is essential to establish that the patient has clearly responded to a course of stabilizing lithium therapy and that the risk of such therapy is acceptable. Maintaining a patient with a lithium non-responsive condition on long-term therapy poses an unacceptable risk. A decision with regards to long-term therapy can be made during a time-limited trial of lithium therapy with frequent reassessment of outcome. The following are among the factors to be reassessed before a decision is made; careful reconfirmation of the diagnosis of primary affective disorder; the health status of the patient; the side effects of lithium therapy experienced by the patient, and the response to treatment. Assessment of response to treatment is based strictly on firm evidence of relapse prevention during a reasonable trial period, but can be assisted by consideration of the predictors of response outlined above. Great pains should be taken to exclude false responders and false non-responders. It should also be borne in mind that non-responders are more susceptible to the adverse effects of lithium.

Acute Mania: The therapeutic dose for the treatment of acute mania should be based primarily on the patient's clinical condition. It must be individualized for each patient according to blood concentrations and clinical response. The dosage should be adjusted to obtain serum concentrations between 0.8 and 1.2 mEq or mmol/L (in blood samples drawn before the patient has had his first lithium dose of the day).

In properly screened adult patients, with good renal function, the suggested initial daily dosage for acute mania is 900 to 1800 mg (15 to 20 mg/kg), divided into 3 doses. In view of the large variability of renal lithium excretion between individuals, it is suggested that lithium treatment be started at a dose between 600 and 900 mg/day, reaching gradually a level of 1 200 to 1 800 mg in 3 divided doses. Depending on the patient's clinical condition, the initial dosage should be adjusted to produce the desired serum lithium concentration. The weight of the patient should also influence the choice of the initial dose.

Geriatrics: Lithium should be used cautiously and in reduced doses in the elderly patient, usually in the range of 600 to 1 200 mg/day. Serum lithium concentrations should be monitored frequently and kept below 1.0 mEq/L or mmol/L.

Maintenance Therapy: After the acute manic episode subsides, the dosage should be rapidly reduced to achieve serum concentrations between 0.6 and 1.0 mEq or mmol/L, since there is evidence at this time of a decreased tolerance to lithium. The average suggested dosage at this stage is 900 mg/day (approximately 25 mEq), divided into 3 doses, with a range usually between 500 and 1 200 mg/day. If a satisfactory response to antimanic lithium is not obtained in 14 days, consider discontinuing lithium therapy. When the manic attack is controlled, maintain lithium administration during the expected duration of the manic phase, since early withdrawal might lead to relapse. It is essential to maintain clinical supervision of the patient and monitor lithium concentrations as required during treatment (see Precautions).

Once patients are stabilized on a maintenance dose with a multiple dosing schedule, and once stable therapeutic blood levels are reached, the dosage schedule may be changed to a once daily dosage administration.

The total daily dose, when administered as a single daily dose, may be approximately 5 to 30% lower than when given in divided doses over the day.

It is essential to maintain clinical supervision of the patient and to monitor serum lithium levels both when using the divided daily dosage regimen and when transferring to the once daily administration dosage regimen.

In uncomplicated cases receiving maintenance therapy during remission, serum lithium levels should be monitored at least every 2 months.

Patients abnormally sensitive to lithium may exhibit toxic signs at serum levels of 1 to 1.4 mEq/L.

Elderly patients often respond to reduced dosage and may exhibit signs of toxicity at serum levels ordinarily tolerated by other patients.

Note: Blood samples for serum lithium determination should be drawn immediately prior to the next dose when lithium concentrations are relatively stable (i.e., 12±1 hours after the previous dose of lithium). Total reliance must not be placed on serum levels alone. Adequate patient evaluation requires both clinical assessment and laboratory analysis.

Children: Lithium is not recommended for routine use in children under 12 years of age since information in this age group is not yet available.

Supplied: 150 mg: Each orange and white capsule printed ICN C11 contains: lithium carbonate USP 150 mg. Nonmedicinal ingredients: gelatin, lactose and starch. Bottles of 100 and 1 000.

300 mg: Each flesh-colored capsule printed ICN C12 contains: lithium carbonate USP 300 mg. Nonmedicinal ingredients: gelatin and starch. Lactose-free. Bottles of 100 and 1 000.

600 mg: Each aqua-blue opaque-colored capsule printed ICN C13 contains: lithium carbonate USP 600 mg. Nonmedicinal ingredients: lactose and talc. Bottles of 100.

CARBOPLATIN INJECTION Ⓟ

Faulding

Antineoplastic

Pharmacology: Carboplatin is a synthetic analogue of cisplatin. Like cisplatin, carboplatin interferes with DNA intrastrand and interstrand crosslinks in cells exposed to the drug. DNA reactivity has been correlated with cytotoxicity.

Following administration of carboplatin in man, linear relationships exist between dose and plasma concentrations of total and free ultrafilterable platinum.

The area under the plasma concentration versus time curve for total platinum also shows a linear relationship with the dose.

Repeated dosing during 4 consecutive days did not produce an accumulation of platinum in plasma.

Following administration of carboplatin, reported values for the terminal elimination half-lives of free ultrafilterable platinum and carboplatin in man were approximately 6 hours and 1.5 hours, respectively. During the initial phase, most of the free ultrafilterable platinum is present as carboplatin. The terminal half-life for total plasma platinum is 24 hours. Approximately 87% of the plasma platinum is protein bound within 24 hours following administration. Carboplatin is excreted primarily in the urine with recovery of approximately 70% of the administered platinum within 24 hours. Most of the drug is excreted in the first 6 hours.

Excretion of carboplatin is by glomerular filtration. Patients with poor renal function have a higher area under curve (AUC) for total platinum and a reduction in dosage is recommended (see Dosage).

Indications: For the treatment of ovarian cancer of epithelial origin in first line therapy and in second line therapy after other treatments have failed.

Contraindications: Severe myelosuppression.

Pre-existing severe renal impairment. Dosage adjustment may allow use in the presence of mild renal impairment (see Dosage).

History of severe allergic reactions to carboplatin, or other platinum-containing compounds. Patients allergic to mannitol may be given carboplatin injection.

Warnings: Caution: Carboplatin is a potent drug and should be used only by physicians experienced with cancer chemotherapeutic drugs (see Precautions). Blood counts as well as renal and hepatic function tests must be done regularly. Discontinue the drug if abnormal depression of bone marrow or abnormal renal or hepatic function is seen.

Myelosuppression as a result of carboplatin treatment is closely related to the renal clearance of the drug. Therefore in patients who have abnormal renal function or who are receiving concomitant therapy with nephrotoxic drugs, myelosuppression especially thrombocytopenia, may be more severe and prolonged.

The occurrence, severity and protraction of myelotoxicity is likely to be greater in patients who have received extensive prior treatment for their disease, have poor performance status and who are more than 65 years of age.

Renal function parameters should be assessed prior to, during and after therapy. Thrombocytopenia, leukopenia and anemia occur after administration of carboplatin. Peripheral blood counts (including platelets, white blood cells and hemoglobin) should be monitored frequently during and after therapy. Combination therapy with other myelosuppressive drugs may require modification of dosage and/or frequency of administration in order to minimize additive effects. Supportive transfusional therapy may be required in patients who suffer severe myelosuppression.

Carboplatin courses should not be repeated more frequently than monthly in most circumstances, in order to ensure that the nadir in blood counts has occurred and that there has been recovery to a satisfactory level.

Precautions: General: Carboplatin should only be administered to patients under the supervision of a qualified physician who is experienced in the use of chemotherapeutic agents. Diagnostic and treatment facilities should be readily available for appropriate management of therapy and possible complications.

Peripheral blood counts and renal function should be monitored closely. Blood counts should be performed prior to commencement of carboplatin therapy and weekly to assess hematologic nadir for subsequent dose adjustments. Lowest levels in white cells and platelets are seen between days 14 and 28, and days 14 and 21 respectively after initial therapy. A greater reduction in platelets is seen in patients who have received extensive myelosuppressive chemotherapy than in untreated patients. White blood cell counts less than 2 000 cells/mm³ or platelets less than 50 000 cells/mm³ may necessitate postponement of carboplatin therapy until bone marrow recovery is evident, usually within 5 to 6 weeks.

Dosage reduction or discontinuation may be necessary in the case of severe alteration of renal function tests.

Renal toxicity is not usually dose-limiting. Pretreatment and post-treatment hydration is not necessary. However about 25% of patients show decreases in creatinine clearance below 60 mL/min. and, less frequently, rises in serum creatinine and blood urea nitrogen may be seen in patients who have previously experienced nephrotoxicity as a result of cisplatin therapy.

Neurotoxicity, such as parasthesias and decreased deep tendon reflexes, and ototoxicity are more likely to be seen in patients who have received cisplatin previously to carboplatin therapy or who are undergoing combination therapy with other neurotoxic drugs such as vincristine. Neurological evaluations and an assessment of hearing should be performed prior to therapy and on a regular basis thereafter.

Conception Control: Carboplatin is mutagenic in in vitro tests. It is recommended that patients with child bearing or conceiving potential who are receiving carboplatin, exercise adequate conception control.

Pregnancy: Carboplatin produces embryotoxicity and teratogenicity in rats. Safe use of carboplatin in human pregnancy has not been established and its use in pregnancy is not recommended.

Lactation: It is not known whether carboplatin is excreted in breast milk. To avoid possible harmful effects in the infant, breast feeding is not advised during carboplatin therapy.

Geriatrics: For patients aged 65 and over, dosage adjustment, initially or subsequently, may be necessary, depending on the patient's physical status.

Patients with Impaired Renal Function: The optimal use of carboplatin in patients presenting with impaired renal function requires adequate dosage adjustments and frequent monitoring of both hematological nadirs and renal function.

Children: Sufficient use of carboplatin in pediatrics has not occurred to allow specific dosage recommendations to be made.

Interactions: Needles, syringes, catheters or i.v. administration sets that contain aluminum parts which may come in contact with carboplatin should not be used for preparation or administration of Carboplatin Injection. Carboplatin may interact with aluminum to form a black precipitate.

Concurrent therapy with nephrotoxic drugs may increase or exacerbate toxicity due to carboplatin-induced changes in renal clearance.

Combination therapy with other myelosuppressive drugs may necessitate changes in the dose or frequency of administration of carboplatin in order to minimize additive myelosuppressive effects.

Adverse Effects: Myelosuppression is the dose-limiting toxicity of carboplatin. It is usually reversible and is not cumulative when carboplatin is used as a single agent and at the recommended dosage regimens. Adverse reactions which have been observed include: Hematologic: leukopenia 55%, thrombocytopenia 32%, anemia 59%, bleeding 6%, infection 4%. Transfusional support has been required in about one-fifth of patients.

Gastrointestinal: nausea and vomiting 53%, nausea only 25%, diarrhea 6%, constipation 3%. Nausea and vomiting usually occur 6 to 12 hours after administration of carboplatin and disappear within 24 hours. It is readily controlled (or may be prevented) by antiemetic medication.

Renal: decrease in creatinine clearance 25%, increases in uric acid 25%, blood urea nitrogen 16% and serum creatinine 7%.

Serum Electrolytes: decreases in serum magnesium 37%, potassium 16% and calcium 5%. These changes have not caused clinical symptoms.

Neurological: peripheral neuropathy 6%, dysgeusia $<1\%$. Parasthesias present prior to treatment, especially if caused by cisplatin, may persist or worsen during carboplatin therapy (see Precautions).

Ototoxicity: subclinical decrease in hearing acuity as determined by audiogram in the high frequency (4 000 to 8 000 Hz) range, 15%, clinical ototoxicity usually manifested as tinnitus 1%. In patients who developed hearing loss as a result of cisplatin therapy, the impairment may persist or worsen after completion of therapy.

Hepatic: Increases in alkaline phosphatase 36%, AST 15%, ALT 16%, total bilirubin 4%. Increases in liver enzymes have been transient in the majority of cases.

Allergic Reactions: In less than 2% of patients, reactions similar to those seen after cisplatin have been observed, erythematous rash, fever and pruritus. However no cross-reactivity between cisplatin and carboplatin was seen.

Other: alopecia 2%, influenza-like syndrome 1%, reaction at injection site $<1\%$.

Overdose: Symptoms and Treatment: No cases of overdosage of carboplatin are known. Should it occur, the patient may need to be sustained through complications relating to myelosuppression, renal and hepatic impairment. From reports in which doses up to 1 600 mg/m² were used, patients were said to feel extremely unwell and developed diarrhea and alopecia.

Dosage: Adults: The recommended dose of carboplatin in previously untreated adults with normal renal function is 400 mg/m² given as a single i.v. infusion over 15 to 60 minutes. Therapy should not be repeated until 4 weeks after the previous carboplatin course.

Initial dosage should be reduced 20 to 25% in patients with risk factors such as previous myelosuppressive therapy and poor performance status. Initial and subsequent dose reduction may be required in elderly patients, depending upon their physical status.

Determination of hematologic nadir by weekly blood counts during initial courses is recommended for future dosage adjustment and scheduling of carboplatin.

Patients with Impaired Renal Function: Hematological nadir and renal function should be closely monitored.

A suggested dosage schedule based on creatinine clearance is shown in Table I.

Table I—Carboplatin Injection

Patients with Impaired Renal Function: Dosage Schedule

Creatinine Clearance	Dose of Carboplatin
>40 mL/min	400 mg/m²
20–39 mL/min	250 mg/m²
0–19 mL/min	150 mg/m²

Children: Specific dosage recommendations cannot be made due to insufficient use in pediatrics.

Stability and Storage: Store between 15 and 25°C, protected from light.

Dilution for I.V. Infusion: Vials of carboplatin may be further diluted with 5% Dextrose Injection or 0.9% Sodium Chloride Injection to give solutions containing approximately 0.3, 0.5 and 2 mg/mL carboplatin.

Diluted solutions are stable for 24 hours in glass or plastic containers, in light and dark storage conditions. Discard unused portion after 24 hours.

Dilutions prepared as directed with 5% Dextrose Injection or 0.9% Sodium Chloride Injection are stable for 48 hours under refrigeration from the time of initial reconstitution, after which time the unused portion should be discarded.

Special Instructions for Handling and Disposal: Carboplatin should be prepared for administration by professionals who have been trained in the safe use of cytotoxic drugs.

The personnel carrying out these procedures should be adequately protected with clothing, gloves, masks and eye protection.

Personnel regularly involved in the preparation and handling of carboplatin should have bi-annual blood examinations.

In the event of contact with the skin or eyes, the affected area should be washed with copious amounts of water or normal saline.

A bland cream may be used to treat the transient stinging of skin. Medical advice should be sought if the eyes are affected.

In the event of spillage, personnel wearing protective clothing should sponge up the spilled material. The area should be rinsed twice with water, and all solutions, and contaminated clothing and sponges put into a plastic bag and sealed. The bag should be disposed of as below.

Syringes, containers, absorbent materials, solution and any other material which has come into contact with carboplatin should be placed in a thick plastic bag or other impervious container and incinerated at 1 000°C. Tightly sealed containers may explode.

Supplied: Each mL of sterile aqueous solution contains: carboplatin 10 mg. Preservative-free. Single dose vials of 50 mg in 5 mL, 150 mg in 15 mL and 450 mg in 45 mL.

CARBOPLATIN INJECTION Pr

Novopharm

Antineoplastic

Supplied: Each mL of solution contains: carboplatin 10 mg and mannitol 10 mg. Amber glass vials of 5, 15 and 45 mL.

CARDENE® Pr

Roche

Nicardipine HCl

Antianginal—Antihypertensive

Pharmacology: Nicardipine is a calcium ion influx inhibitor (calcium entry blocker or calcium ion antagonist).

The therapeutic effect of this group of drugs is believed to be related to their specific cellular action of selectively inhibiting transmembrane influx of calcium ions into cardiac muscle and vascular smooth muscle. The contractile processes of these tissues are dependent upon the movement of extracellular calcium into the cells through specific ion channels. Nicardipine blocks transmembrane influx of calcium through the slow channel without affecting to any significant degree the transmembrane influx of sodium through the fast channel. This results in a reduction of free calcium ions available within cells of the above tissues. Nicardipine does not alter total serum calcium.

The precise mechanism by which nicardipine relieves angina has not been fully determined but it is believed to be brought about largely by its vasodilator action. In effort associated angina, it appears that the action of nicardipine is related to the reduction of myocardial oxygen demand. This is probably caused by a decrease in blood pressure brought about by the reduction of peripheral resistance.

The antihypertensive effect of nicardipine is believed to be brought about largely by its vasodilatory action on peripheral blood vessels with resultant decrease in peripheral vascular resistance.

In humans, nicardipine produces a significant decrease in systemic vascular resistance. In hypertensive patients, nicardipine reduces blood pressure at rest and during isometric and dynamic exercise. In normotensive patients, a small decrease in systolic and diastolic blood pressure may accompany the fall in peripheral resistance. An increase in heart rate may occur in response to the vasodilation and decrease in blood pressure, and in a few patients this heart rate increase may be pronounced.

In a study in patients with coronary artery disease, intracoronary administration of nicardipine caused no direct myocardial depression. Nicardipine does however have a negative inotropic effect in some patients with severe left ventricular dysfunction and could lead to worsened failure (see Warnings).

Nicardipine increased the heart rate when given i.v. during acute electrophysiological studies and prolonged the corrected QT interval to a minor degree. The sinus node recovery times and SA conduction times are not affected by the drug. The PA, AH and HV[a] intervals and the functional and effective refractory periods of the atrium were not prolonged by nicardipine and the relative and effective refractory periods of the His-Purkinje system were slightly shortened after i.v. nicardipine.

[a] PA=conduction time from high to low right atrium, AH=conduction time from low right atrium to His bundle deflection, or AV nodal conduction time, HV=conduction time through the His bundle and bundle branch-Purkinje system.

Nicardipine is rapidly and completely absorbed following oral administration and is subject to extensive first pass effect giving absolute bioavailability of about 35%. Nicardipine is highly protein bound (>95%) in human plasma over a wide concentration range.

Nicardipine is metabolized extensively by the liver, less than 1% of intact drug is detected in the urine and none of the metabolites possess significant biological activity. Following a radioactive oral dose in solution, 60% of the radioactivity was recovered in the urine and 35% in feces. Most of the dose (>90%) was recovered within 48 hours of dosing.

Of the dihydropyridine calcium channel blockers studied, all undergo biotransformation by the cytochrome P450 system, mainly via the CYP 3A4 isoenzyme. There are no studies done to indicate that nicardipine is also metabolized via this pathway.

Plasma levels of nicardipine are detectable 20 minutes following an oral dose and maximal plasma levels are observed between 30 minutes and 2 hours (mean T_{max}=1 hour). When given with a high fat meal, the mean C_{max} and area under the concentration-time curve were reduced by 30 and 20%, respectively.

Following oral administration, increasing doses result in a disproportionate increase in plasma levels. Steady state C_{max} value following 20, 30 and 40 mg (q8h) averaged 36, 88 and 133 ng/mL, respectively. Hence, increasing the dose from 20 to 30 mg (q8h) more than doubled C_{max} and increasing the dose from 20 to 40 mg (q8h) increased C_{max} more than 3-fold. A similar disproportionate increase in AUC with dose was observed. Steady state plasma levels are achieved after 2 to 3 days of dosing (at 20 or 30 mg q8h) and are 2- to 3-fold higher at steady state than after a single dose. No evidence of accumulation of nicardipine was observed with chronic dosing. However, considerable intersubject variability in plasma levels was observed. Postabsorption kinetics of nicardipine are also nonlinear although the terminal plasma half-life of nicardipine averaged 8.6 hours. The terminal half-life represents the elimination of less than 5% of the absorbed drug (measured by plasma concentrations). Elimination over the first 8 hours is much faster with a half-life of 2 to 4 hours.

The pharmacokinetics of nicardipine in elderly hypertensive patients are similar to those obtained in young normal adults. Pharmacokinetic parameters including the peak plasma concentration, time to peak plasma concentration, area under the concentration-time curve, terminal plasma half-life, and the extent of protein binding did not differ significantly between elderly hypertensive patients and healthy young volunteers after one week of nicardipine therapy (20 mg 3 times a day).

In patients with mild renal impairment (baseline serum creatinine concentration ranging from 1.2 to 5.5 mg/dL) nicardipine plasma levels were higher than in normal subjects. C_{max} and AUC were approximately 2-fold higher in these patients.

Indications: Chronic Stable Angina: For the management of chronic stable angina (effort-associated angina) in patients who remain symptomatic despite adequate doses of beta-blockers and/or organic nitrates or who cannot tolerate those agents. Nicardipine may be tried in combination with beta adrenergic blocking drugs in chronic stable angina in patients with normal ventricular function. When such concomitant therapy is introduced, care must be taken to monitor blood pressure closely since hypotension can occur from the combined effects of drugs (see Warnings).

Hypertension: The treatment of mild to moderate essential hypertension. Nicardipine should normally be used in those patients in whom treatment with diuretics or beta-blockers has been associated with unacceptable adverse effects.

Nicardipine can be tried as initial agent in those patients in whom the use of diuretics and/or beta-blockers is contraindicated or in patients with medical conditions in which these drugs frequently cause serious adverse effects.

Combination of nicardipine with a diuretic or a beta-blocker has been found to be compatible and showed additive antihypertensive effect.

Safety of concurrent use of nicardipine with other antihypertensive agents has not been established and such use cannot be recommended at this time.

Contraindications: Patients with hypersensitivity to the drug.

Since a major part of the effect of nicardipine is secondary to reduced afterload, the drug should not be given to patients with advanced valvular aortic stenosis. Reduction of diastolic pressure in these patients may worsen rather than improve myocardial oxygen balance.

In patients with severe hypotension (less than 90 mmHg systolic).

Cardene (cont'd)

Nicardipine is contraindicated in patients with acute myocardial infarction (see Warnings, Myocardial Infarction).

Warnings: Congestive Heart Failure: Because nicardipine has a negative inotropic effect in vitro and in some patients, it should be used with caution and under careful medical supervision in patients with congestive heart failure, particularly when used in combination with a beta-blocker (see Pharmacology).

Hypotension: Because nicardipine decreases peripheral resistance, careful monitoring of blood pressure during the initial administration and titration of nicardipine is suggested. Nicardipine like other calcium channel blockers, may occasionally produce symptomatic hypotension. Caution is advised to avoid systemic hypotension when administering the drug to patients who have sustained an acute cerebral infarction or hemorrhage. Because of prominent effects at the time of peak blood levels, initial titration should include measurements of blood pressure at peak effect (1 to 2 hours after dosing).

In patients with angina or arrhythmias using antihypertensive drugs, the additional hypotensive effect of nicardipine should be taken into consideration (see Indications).

Increased Angina: Approximately 5% of patients have developed increased frequency, duration or severity of angina on starting nicardipine or at the time of dosage increases, or during the course of treatment. The mechanism of this effect has not been established but could result from decreased coronary perfusion associated with decreased diastolic pressure and increased heart rate (see Adverse Effects).

Myocardial Infarction: Although there has not been a study of nicardipine in acute myocardial infarction reported, the use of nicardipine may have effects similar to those of the immediate-release formulation of the dihydropyridine, nifedipine, in acute myocardial infarction. Nicardipine should not be used within one week after myocardial infarction and not before the patient has stabilized.

Unstable Angina: Some clinical trials have shown that treatment with the immediate-release formulation of the dihydropyridine, nifedipine, in this setting increases the risk of myocardial infarction and recurrent ischemia.

Acute Reduction of Blood Pressure: Nicardipine should not be used for acute reduction of blood pressure. Strokes have occurred when immediate-release formulations of dihydropyridines were used in this setting.

Beta-blocker Withdrawal: Nicardipine gives no protection against the dangers of abrupt β-blocker withdrawal; any such withdrawal should be gradual reduction of the dose of beta-blockers.

Patients with Impaired Hepatic Function: 12 patients with severe liver disease given 20 mg of nicardipine b.i.d. for 6 days developed elevated blood levels (4 fold increase in AUC) and prolonged half-life (19 hours) of nicardipine. At this time there is insufficient data to recommend an appropriate dosing schedule in this group of patients. I.V. nicardipine at high doses (5 mg/20 minutes) has been reported to worsen portal vein hypertension and portal-systemic collateral blood flow index in cirrhotic patients.

Precautions: Peripheral Edema: Mild to moderate peripheral edema associated with arterial vasodilation has been reported to occur in patients treated with nicardipine (see Adverse Effects). Care should be taken to differentiate this peripheral edema from the effects of increasing left ventricular dysfunction.

Patients with Impaired Renal Function: Following a single dose or steady state treatment, patients with impaired renal function exhibited decreased nicardipine clearance, higher peak plasma concentrations and AUC which were approximately 2 fold that of healthy controls. Careful dose titration beginning with 20 mg nicardipine, thrice daily is advised when treating renally impaired patients. Medical supervision is recommended.

Pregnancy: The use of nicardipine has not been studied in pregnant women. Nicardipine should be used in pregnancy only if the potential benefit outweighs the potential risk to the fetus.

No adverse effects on mating, fertility or reproductive indices were found in rats. However, dystocia, reduced birth rate, reduced neonatal survival and reduced weight gains of pups were observed. Nicardipine was not teratogenic in rat or rabbit.

Lactation: Studies in rats reveal significant concentrations of nicardipine in maternal milk following oral administration. Nicardipine should not be given to nursing mothers.

Children: The safety of nicardipine in children has not been established.

Geriatrics: Pharmacokinetic parameters did not differ between elderly patients (65 years of age or older) and healthy adult subjects. However, since the elderly are less tolerant to side effects such as hypotension and dizziness, particular care in titration is advisable.

Interaction with Grapefruit Juice: Published data indicate that through inhibition of cytochrome P450, grapefruit juice can increase plasma levels and augment pharmacodynamic effects of dihydropyridine calcium channel blockers. Therefore, consumption of grapefruit juice prior to or during treatment with nicardipine should be avoided.

Drug Interactions: As with all drugs, care should be exercised when treating patients with multiple medications. Dihydropyridine calcium channel blockers undergo biotransformation by the cytochrome P450 system, mainly via the CYP 3A4 isoenzyme (see Pharmacology). Coadministration of nicardipine with other drugs which follow the same route of biotransformation may result in altered bioavailability. Dosages of similarly metabolized drugs, particularly those of low therapeutic ratio, and especially in patients with renal and/or hepatic impairment, may require adjustment when starting or stopping concomitantly administered nicardipine to maintain optimum therapeutic blood levels.

Drugs known to be inhibitors of the cytochrome P450 system include: azole antifungals, cimetidine, cyclosporine, erythromycin, quinidine, terfenadine, warfarin.

Drugs known to be inducers of the cytochrome P450 system include: phenobarbital, phenytoin, rifampin.

Drugs known to be biotransformed via P450 include: benzodiazepines, flecainide, imipramine, propafenone, theophylline.

Beta-blockers: When beta-adrenergic receptor blocking drugs are administered concomitantly with nicardipine, blood pressure and pulmonary signs and symptoms of congestive heart failure should be carefully monitored since the antihypertensive effect of beta-blockers may be augmented by nicardipine's reduction in peripheral vascular resistance.

Short-and Long-Acting Nitrates: The combination of nicardipine with short- or long-acting nitrates did not result in any unusual or unknown side effects.

Other Antihypertensives: The concomitant use of antihypertensives such as, diuretics and beta-blockers, with nicardipine was well tolerated. At this time no data are available for other antihypertensive agents (see Indications).

Cimetidine: Cimetidine increases nicardipine plasma levels. Patients receiving these 2 drugs concomitantly should be carefully monitored.

Digoxin: Since some increase in serum digoxin levels has been observed following concomitant therapy with nicardipine, patients should be monitored for increased digoxin levels.

Fentanyl Anesthesia: Severe hypotension has been reported during fentanyl anesthesia with concomitant use of a beta-blocker and a calcium channel blocker. Although such interactions were not seen during clinical studies with nicardipine, an increased volume of circulating fluids might be required if such an interaction were to occur.

Cyclosporine: Concomitant administration of nicardipine and cyclosporine results in elevated plasma cyclosporine levels. Plasma concentrations of cyclosporine should therefore be closely monitored, and its dosage reduced accordingly, in patients treated with nicardipine.

Carbamazepine: In healthy volunteers, concomitant administration with carbamazepine has been shown to result in increased plasma levels of carbamazepine (+28%) and reduced levels of nicardipine (−74%). Caution should be therefore exercised if these drugs are used concomitantly.

Adverse Effects: Angina: Adverse effects were derived from multicenter, controlled clinical trials in 520 angina patients. Adverse effects (regardless of drug relationship) were reported in 56% of the patients on nicardipine and required discontinuation of treatment in 9%.

The most common (incidence of at least 1%) adverse effects were: headache (13%), asthenia (13%), dizziness (11%), pedal edema (8%), flushing (7%), palpitation (6%), dyspepsia (5%), nausea (4%), myalgia (3%), nervousness (3%), somnolence (3%), tachycardia (3%), dyspnea (3%), rash (2%), dry mouth (2%), infection (2%), constipation (2%), diarrhea (2%), gastrointestinal pain (2%), arthralgia (2%), paresthesia (2%), insomnia (1%), vomiting (1%).

In addition, the following events were reported in less than 1% of cases: Cardiovascular: sustained tachycardia, syncope, atrial fibrillation, myocardial infarction, cerebral ischemia, sudden death, ventricular and supraventricular tachycardia, hypotension, atypical chest pain, peripheral vascular disorder, postural hypotension, ventricular extrasystoles, AV block, sinus node dysfunction, bigeminy, hypertension, vasodilatation.

CNS: tremor, apathy, abnormal dreams, ataxia, confusion, depression, hot flashes, paresthesia, impotence.

Gastrointestinal: flatulence, sore throat, anorexia, eructation, hepatitis, gastroenteritis.

Dermatologic: burning sensation, pruritus, dermatitis, dry skin.

Musculoskeletal: arthritis, bursitis.

Respiratory: upper respiratory infection, bronchitis, increased cough, pharyngitis, rhinitis.

Special Senses: abnormal or blurred vision, tinnitus, taste perversion, conjunctivitis.

Other: malaise, edema, polyuria, increased sweating, chills, allergic reaction, increased urinary frequency, nocturia, urinary retention, gout.

Hypertension: In 1 390 hypertensive patients treated in controlled clinical studies, with nicardipine, adverse effects (regardless of drug relationship) were reported in 61% of patients and required discontinuation of therapy in 10%.

The most common (incidence of at least 1%) adverse effects were: headache (19%), pedal edema (12%), flushing (11%), dizziness (8%), asthenia (8%), palpitation (6%), tachycardia (4%), nausea (4%), upper respiratory infection (4%), somnolence (2%), insomnia (2%), dyspepsia (2%), vomiting (2%), myalgia (2%), arthralgia (2%), dry mouth (1%), nervousness (1%), back pain (1%), atypical chest pain (1%), angina pectoris (1%), increased urinary frequency (1%), nocturia (1%), gastrointestinal pain (1%), diarrhea (1%), paresthesia (1%), arthritis (1%), rhinitis (1%), increased cough (1%), sinusitis (1%), dyspnea (1%), rash (1%), pruritus (1%).

In addition the following events were reported in less than 1% of cases: Cardiovascular: hypotension, postural hypotension, extrasystoles, ventricular extrasystoles, ventricular and supraventricular tachycardia, migraine, peripheral vascular disorder, bigeminy, pericardial effusion, syncope.

CNS: abnormal dreams, tremor, vertigo, hyperkinesia, agitation, confusion, hostility, anxiety, depression, hot flashes, decreased libido, impotence, abnormal gait, amnesia.

Gastrointestinal: constipation, flatulence, anorexia, gastrointestinal fullness, sore throat, gastroenteritis, gastritis, cholecystitis, eructation.

Dermatologic: rash, pruritus, dry skin, eczema, urticaria.

Musculoskeletal: bursitis, myasthenia.

Respiratory: epistaxis, bronchitis.

Special Senses: abnormal or blurred vision, taste perversion or loss, parosmia, scleritis, conjunctivitis, tinnitus.

Genitourinary: polyuria, urinary urgency, dysuria.

Other: malaise, chills, edema, increased sweating, allergic reaction, fever, purpura, gout.

Laboratory Tests: In rare instances, mild to moderate transient elevations of alkaline phosphatase, AST, ALT, LDH, CPK and hypokalemia have been noted during nicardipine therapy.

Thrombocytopenia has been rarely reported in association with the use of nicardipine.

Isolated cases of angioedema have been reported. Angioedema may be accompanied by breathing difficulty.

The following adverse reactions, possibly drug related, were observed with either oral or i.v. nicardipine: increased angina, sustained tachycardia, syncope, ventricular tachycardia, supraventricular tachycardia, myocardial infarction, intracranial hemorrhage, atrioventricular block, sinus node dysfunction, gingival hyperplasia, erythema multiforme, Stevens-Johnson syndrome.

Overdose: Symptoms and Treatment: Three cases of overdosage with nicardipine have been reported. Two occurred in adults, one of whom ingested 600 mg of nicardipine and the other 2 160 mg of nicardipine in a sustained release formulation. Symptoms included marked hypotension, bradycardia, palpitations, flushing, drowsiness, confusion and slurred speech. All symptoms resolved without sequelae. The second overdosage occurred in a 1 year old child who ingested half of the powder in a 30 mg nicardipine capsule. The child remained asymptomatic.

Based on results obtained in laboratory animals, overdosage may cause systemic hypotension, bradycardia (following initial tachycardia) and progressive atrioventricular conduction block. Hepatic function abnormalities and sporadic focal hepatic necrosis were noted in some animal species receiving very large doses of nicardipine.

For treatment of overdose standard measures (for example, evacuation of gastric contents, elevation of extremities, attention to circulating fluid volume and urine output) including monitoring of cardiac and respiratory functions should be implemented. The patient should be positioned so as to avoid cerebral anoxia. Frequent blood pressure determinations are essential. Vasopressors are clinically indicated for patients exhibiting profound hypotension. I.V. calcium gluconate may help reverse the effects of calcium entry blockade.

Dosage: Angina: The dose of nicardipine should be individually titrated for each patient beginning with 20 mg 3 times daily. Doses in the range of 20 to 40 mg 3 times daily have been shown to be effective. At least 3 days should be allowed before increasing the nicardipine dose to ensure achievement of steady state plasma drug concentration.

Hypertension: Therapy should be individualized for each patient according to the blood pressure response beginning with 20 mg 3 times daily. Doses of 20 to 40 mg 3 times a day have been effective in clinical trials. Because of the prominent difference in the peak and trough plasma levels of nicardipine, careful monitoring of blood pressure is required during initiation of therapy to ensure acceptable control of blood pressure during the entire dosing interval (see Warnings). At least 3 days should be allowed before increasing the nicardipine dose to ensure achievement of steady state plasma drug concentration.

Careful titration of nicardipine is advised when the drug is to be added to existing therapies with attention to the possibility of excessive blood pressure reduction (see Indications).

Special Patient Populations: Patients with Renal Insufficiency: In patients with renal impairment, careful dose titration beginning with 20 mg t.i.d. is advised. Medical supervision is recommended (see Precautions).

Hepatic Insufficiency: See Warnings.

Geriatrics: Particular care in titration is advisable (see Precautions).

Supplied: 20 mg: Each hard, opaque white/white, gelatin capsule, imprinted ROCHE on the body and "CARDENE 20 mg" on the cap, with a blue band around the capsule, contains: nicardipine HCl 20 mg. Nonmedicinal ingredients: FD&C Blue No. 2, magnesium stearate, pregelatinized cornstarch and titanium dioxide. Alcohol-, gluten-, lactose-, sugar-, sulfites- and tartrazine-free. Bottles of 100.

30 mg: Each hard, opaque dark blue/opaque light blue, gelatin capsule, imprinted ROCHE on the body and "CARDENE 30 mg" on the cap, with a blue band around the capsule, contains: nicardipine HCl 30 mg. Nonmedicinal ingredients: FD&C Blue No. 2, magnesium stearate, pregelatinized cornstarch and titanium dioxide. Alcohol-, gluten-, lactose-, sugar-, sulfites- and tartrazine-free. Bottles of 100.

Store at room temperature and dispense in light-resistant containers.

(Shown in Product Recognition Section)

CARDIOQUIN®

Purdue Frederick

Quinidine Polygalacturonate

Antiarrhythmic Agent

Pharmacology: Quinidine depresses excitability, conduction velocity and contractility of most cardiac tissues by a direct action on cardiac cells. Indirectly, cardiac tissues will also be affected by the anticholinergic and α-adrenoceptor blocking properties of quinidine.

According to Vaughan Williams antiarrhythmic drug classification, quinidine is a Class IA agent. Thus, quinidine reduces the maximal rate of phase 0 depolarization, prolongs repolarization and refractory periods and, in general, decreases automaticity of cardiac cells.

Pharmacokinetics: Absorption of oral quinidine sulfate is assumed to be essentially complete, though bioavailability is approximately 70% due to a first-pass removal by the liver. Peak plasma levels are variable among individuals. After a single dose given orally, quinidine can be detected in blood within 15 minutes and peak concentrations are achieved within 1 to 3 hours. Peak plasma levels during a multiple daily dose regimen may not be reached before the seventh day of administration. Quinidine concentrations are generally higher and appear earlier when the drug is administered on an empty stomach but the amount of drug absorbed is not diminished by the presence of food in the digestive tract.

Although quinidine is 80% bound to plasma constituents (mainly α-1 acid glycoprotein), its distribution in the body is predominantly extravascular. The terminal elimination half-life is approximately 7 hours and is primarily associated with its metabolism by the liver (50 to 90% of the dose administered). Quinidine half-life varies considerably between individuals, even among healthy subjects. Total body clearance is approximately 4 mL/kg/min and is also variable. The metabolites may be therapeutically active. Ten to 20% of an administered dose is excreted unchanged in urine. Renal excretion is due to glomerular filtration and secretion by proximal renal tubules and is dependent upon urinary pH; renal clearance diminishes as urinary pH increases. Fecal excretion accounts for less than 5% of the oral dose.

The average therapeutic range is between 6 to 15 μmol/L (2 and 5 μg/mL) of plasma. Toxic reactions are almost certain to appear at concentrations above 24.7 μmol/L (8 μg/mL). Levels may differ based on the assay method used.

Indications:

> No antiarrhythmic drug has been shown to reduce the incidence of sudden death in patients with asymptomatic ventricular arrhythmias. Most antiarrhythmic drugs have the potential to cause dangerous arrhythmias; some have been shown to be associated with an increased incidence of sudden death. In light of the above, physicians should carefully consider the risks and benefits of antiarrhythmic therapy for all patients with ventricular arrhythmias.

Ventricular Arrhythmias: For the treatment of documented life-threatening ventricular arrhythmias, such as sustained ventricular tachycardia. Quinidine may also be used for the treatment of patients with documented symptomatic ventricular arrhythmias when the symptoms are of sufficient severity to require treatment. Because of the proarrhythmic effects, its use should be reserved for patients in whom, in the opinion of the physician, the benefit of treatment clearly outweighs the risks.

For patients with sustained ventricular tachycardia, quinidine therapy should be initiated in the hospital. Hospitalization may be required for certain other patients depending on their cardiac status and underlying cardiac disease.

The effects of quinidine in patients with recent myocardial infarction have not been adequately studied and, therefore, their use in this condition cannot be recommended.

Supraventricular Arrhythmias: Quinidine is also indicated for premature atrial or AV junctional contractions, paroxysmal atrial or AV junctional tachycardia, atrial flutter, atrial fibrillation when this therapy is appropriate and maintenance therapy after electrical conversion of atrial flutter and/or fibrillation to sinus rhythm.

Contraindications: Hypersensitivity or idiosyncrasy to quinidine or other cinchona derivatives, history of thrombocytopenic purpura associated with previous quinidine administration, myasthenia gravis, digitalis intoxication manifested by AV conduction disorders, complete AV block with an AV nodal or idioventricular pacemaker, ectopic impulses and rhythms due to escape mechanisms and intraventricular conduction defects (especially with marked widening of the QRS complex).

Warnings: Mortality: The results of the Cardiac Arrhythmia Suppression Trial (CAST) in post-myocardial infarction patients with asymptomatic ventricular arrhythmias showed a significant increase in mortality and in non-fatal cardiac arrest rates in patients treated with encainide or flecainide compared with a matched placebo-treated group. CAST was continued using a revised protocol with the moricizine and placebo arms only. The trial was prematurely terminated because of a trend towards increase in mortality in the moricizine-treated group.

The applicability of these results to other populations or other antiarrhythmic agents is uncertain, but at present it is prudent to consider these results when using any antiarrhythmic agent.

Quinidine Cardiotoxicity: Manifestation of quinidine cardiotoxicity, such as excessive prolongation of the QT interval, widening of the QRS complex, and ventricular arrhythmias, mandates immediate discontinuation of the drug and/or close clinical and electrocardiographic monitoring.

Treatment should be discontinued if the duration of the QRS complex increases more than 50% or the P-waves disappear. A significant fall in blood pressure, the onset of ventricular or premature contractions or ventricular tachycardia due to quinidine requires the immediate discontinuation of treatment.

Atrial Flutter Treatment: In the treatment of atrial flutter, reversion to sinus rhythm may be preceded by a progressive reduction in the degree of AV block to a 1:1 ratio, resulting in an extremely rapid ventricular rate. This possible hazard may be reduced by digitalization prior to administration of quinidine.

Cardiac Depression: In predisposed individuals, such as those with marginally compensated cardiovascular disease, quinidine may produce clinically important depression of the cardiovascular system such as hypotension, bradycardia or heartblock. The depressant action of quinidine on cardiac contractility and arterial blood pressure limits its use in congestive heart failure and in hypotensive states unless these conditions are due to or aggravated by the arrhythmia. The potential disadvantages and benefits must be weighed.

Syncopal Episodes: Occasionally, patients taking quinidine have syncopal episodes which usually result from tachycardia or fibrillation. The syndrome has not been shown to be related to dose or plasma levels. Syncopal episodes frequently terminate spontaneously, but sometimes are fatal.

Incomplete AV block: Quinidine should be used with extreme caution in patients with incomplete AV block. This can lead to complete AV block and asystole.

Digitalis Intoxication: Quinidine may cause abnormalities of cardiac rhythm in digitalized patients and, therefore, should be closely monitored. Reports indicate that plasma concentrations of digoxin increase and may even double when quinidine is administered concurrently. Patients on concomitant therapy should be carefully monitored. Reduction of digoxin dosage may have to be considered.

Hepatotoxicity: A few cases of hepatotoxicity, including granulomatous hepatitis, due to quinidine hypersensitivity have been reported in patients taking quinidine. Unexplained fever and/or elevation of hepatic enzymes, particularly in the early stages of therapy, warrant consideration of possible hepatotoxicity. Monitoring of liver function during the first 4 to 8 weeks should be considered. Cessation of quinidine in these cases usually results in the disappearance of toxicity.

Precautions: Test for Hypersensitivity: A test dose of a single tablet of quinidine (275 mg) by mouth should be given initially in order to ascertain any possible hypersensitivity to quinidine. Hypersensitivity to quinidine, although rare, should be constantly considered, especially during the first week of therapy.

Large Doses: Continuous ECG monitoring and determination of plasma quinidine concentrations are indicated when large doses (>2 g/day) are used.

Serum Potassium: Quinidine's activity is enhanced by potassium and reduced if hypokalemia is present.

Established Atrial Fibrillation: The use of quinidine in established atrial fibrillation is controversial. Weigh the benefits of such use in each patient against the possible hazards.

Pregnancy: It is not known whether quinidine can cause fetal harm when administered to pregnant women. Quinine, the levostereoisomer of quinidine, has caused fetal blindness and has been implicated in congenital deafness. Quinidine should be used during pregnancy only when clearly indicated.

Lactation: Very small quantities pass into breast milk; no effects have been described in infants.

Children: Safety and efficacy of quinidine in children have not been determined.

Drug Interactions: See Table I.

Table I—Cardioquin

Drug Interactions

Quinidine with:	Effect:
Anticholinergic drugs	Additive, e.g., vagal block
Urine alkalinization	Increased quinidine blood level
Acidifying agents	Decreased quinidine blood level
Coumarin	Decreased coagulation
Neuromuscular blockers (including neomycin)	Potentiation of blockade
Phenothiazines, reserpine	Additive cardiac depression
Antihypertensives	Potentiation of blood pressure fall
Hepatic enzyme inducers, nifedipine	Reduction in plasma quinidine
Amiodarone, cimetidine	Increase in plasma quinidine
Digoxin	Increase in plasma digoxin
Quinine	Additive (all quinine/quinidine properties)
Verapamil	Hypotension
Potassium	Increased cardiotoxicity
Aluminum hydroxide	Decreased absorption
Drugs increasing QT	Additive or potentiation

Adverse Effects: Quinidine has a low therapeutic index. Adverse effects occur in as many as a third of cases.

The most frequent adverse reactions are gastrointestinal in nature: nausea, vomiting, diarrhea and abdominal pain.

Cinchonism: Symptoms of mild cases include tinnitus, dysphonia and occasionally loss of hearing, some blurring of vision and gastrointestinal upset; more severe cases show headache, photophobia, altered color perception and possibly confusion, delirium and psychosis. Other symptoms observed include palpitations, convulsions, faintness and flushing, localized edema, vertigo, tremor, light-headedness, excitement, apprehension, coma and even death.

Cardioquin (cont'd)

Idiosyncratic and Hypersensitivity Reactions: angioedema, febrile reactions, skin eruptions, acute asthmatic episodes, confusion, headache, anorexia, nausea, vomiting, diarrhea, precordial pain, abdominal pain, hepatic toxicity including granulomatous hepatitis, vascular collapse and respiratory arrest.

Cardiovascular: QRS widening, increased QT (and JT) interval, vasculitis, arterial embolism (following conversion of long standing atrial fibrillation to sinus rhythm), decreased cardiac contractility, hypotension (cardiac depression and vasodilatation), syncope (due to paroxysmal ventricular tachycardia or fibrillation), proarrhythmic effects (increased frequency of existing arrhythmia or development of new arrhythmias including ventricular tachycardia, fibrillation or torsades de pointes) and asystole.

Nervous System: apprehension, excitement, psychomotor agitation, hallucinations, delusions or paranoia, delirium, confusion, memory loss, depression, vertigo, disturbed hearing and/or vision.

Hematologic: thrombocytopenia including thrombotic purpura, hemolytic anemia, agranulocytosis, pancytopenia, hypoprothrombinemia and leukopenia.

Liver: moderate increase in enzyme levels, granulomatous hepatitis (see Warnings), hepatocellular necrosis and centrilobular cholestasis.

Kidney: nephrotic syndrome.

Skin: rash, flushing with pruritus, urticaria, photosensitivity and discoloration (bluish-gray).

Musculoskeletal: Very rare cases of lupus erythematosus, carpal tunnel syndrome and arthritis.

Overdose: Symptoms: Large doses may cause cinchonism, ventricular tachycardia, severe hypotension, cardiac standstill and ventricular fibrillation. Serious hypersensitivity reactions are manifested by respiratory embarrassment or cardiovascular collapse.

Treatment: If ingestion is recent, perform gastric lavage or induce emesis. (The use of an emetic may interfere with some of the following procedures.) Administration of 25 to 50 g of activated charcoal is indicated to reduce absorption of any remaining quinidine. Administration of a hypertonic cathartic (30 g sodium sulfate in 250 mL water) will hasten passage of unabsorbed quinidine through the gastrointestinal tract. If the charcoal preparation contains 70% sorbitol, the use of an additional hypertonic saline is not necessary. Maintain body temperature. Monitor electrolytes; especially potassium, calcium and magnesium. Support blood pressure and maintain renal function. Phenytoin or lidocaine may be used to control arrhythmias. Ventricular tachycardia may require DC cardioversion or pacing. Standard therapy for cardiac standstill should be employed. Refractory bradycardia or heart block that compromises blood pressure may require a temporary pacemaker. Angioneurotic or asthmatic phenomena may require the use of epinephrine and antihistamines. Hemoglobinuria may necessitate blood transfusion and attention to renal function. The use of an alkali to prevent precipitation in the tubules may prove helpful.

Dosage: Administer a preliminary test dose of a single tablet (275 mg) to determine whether the patient has a quinidine idiosyncrasy. Continuous ECG monitoring is recommended in all cases in which quinidine is used in large doses.

Gastrointestinal symptoms such as nausea, vomiting, diarrhea and colic may be minimized by giving the drug with food.

Dosage should be individualized.

Initially: 275 to 825 mg (1 to 3 tablets) may be used to terminate arrhythmia, and may be repeated in 3 or 4 hours. If, following 3 or 4 equal doses normal rhythm has not been restored, dosage may be increased by 137.5 to 275 mg (½ to 1 tablet) and should be administered 3 or 4 times before further dosage increases.

Maintenance: 550 to 825 mg (2 to 3 tablets) daily.

Quinidine polygalacturonate, 275 mg, may be substituted for each 200 mg of quinidine sulfate (or equivalent) previously administered.

Supplied: Each flat, uncoated, scored (one side), off-white tablet, engraved with $\frac{c}{275}$ on one side and PF on the other, contains: quinidine polygalacturonate 275 mg equivalent in quinidine content to quinidine sulfate 200 mg. Also contains cornstarch 20 mg and lactose 56 mg. Sodium-, sugar- and tartrazine-free. Bottles of 50. Store in tightly-closed, light-resistant containers.

CARDIZEM® ℞
CARDIZEM® SR ℞
CARDIZEM® CD ℞

Hoechst Marion Roussel

Diltiazem HCl

Antianginal

Antihypertensive—Antianginal

Antihypertensive—Antianginal

Pharmacology: Diltiazem is a calcium ion influx inhibitor (calcium entry blocker or calcium ion antagonist).

The therapeutic effect of this group of drugs is believed to be related to their specific cellular action of selectively inhibiting transmembrane influx of calcium ions into cardiac muscle and vascular smooth muscle. The contractile processes of these tissues are dependent upon the movement of extracellular calcium into the cells through specific ion channels. Diltiazem blocks transmembrane influx of calcium through the slow channel without affecting to any significant degree the transmembrane influx of sodium through the fast channel. This results in a reduction of free calcium ions available within cells of the above tissues. Diltiazem does not alter total serum calcium.

Angina: The precise mechanism by which diltiazem relieves angina has not been fully determined, but it is believed to be brought about largely by its vasodilator action.

In angina due to coronary spasm, diltiazem increases myocardial oxygen delivery by dilating both large and small coronary arteries and by inhibiting coronary spasm at drug levels which cause little negative inotropic effect. The resultant increases in coronary blood flow are accompanied by dose-dependent decreases in systemic blood pressure and decreases in peripheral resistance.

In angina of effort it appears that the action of diltiazem is related to the reduction of myocardial oxygen demand. This is probably caused by a decrease in blood pressure brought about by the reduction of peripheral resistance and of heart rate.

Hypertension: The antihypertensive effect of diltiazem is believed to be brought about largely by its vasodilatory action on peripheral blood vessels with resultant decrease in peripheral vascular resistance.

Hemodynamic and Electrophysiologic Effects: Diltiazem produces antihypertensive effects both in the supine and standing positions. Resting heart rate is usually slightly reduced. During dynamic exercise, increases in diastolic pressure are inhibited while maximum achievable systolic pressure is usually unaffected. Heart rate at maximum exercise is reduced.

Studies to date, primarily in patients with normal ventricular function, have shown that cardiac output, ejection fraction, and left ventricular end-diastolic pressure have not been affected.

Chronic therapy with diltiazem produces no change, or an increase, in circulating plasma catecholamines. However, no increased activity of the renin-angiotensin-aldosterone axis has been observed. Diltiazem inhibits the renal and peripheral effects of angiotensin II.

In man i.v. diltiazem in doses of 20 mg prolongs AH conduction time and AV node functional and effective refractory periods by approximately 20%. Chronic oral administration of diltiazem in doses up to 540 mg/day has resulted in small increases in PR interval. Second degree and third degree AV block have been observed (see Warnings). In patients with sick sinus syndrome, diltiazem significantly prolongs sinus cycle length (up to 50% in some cases).

Pharmacokinetics: Diltiazem is well absorbed from the gastrointestinal tract and is subject to an extensive first-pass effect giving absolute bioavailability (compared to i.v. dosing) of about 40%. Therapeutic blood levels appear to be in the 50 to 200 ng/mL range and the plasma elimination half-life (beta-phase) following single or multiple drug administration is approximately 3.5 to 6.0 hours. In vitro human serum binding studies revealed that 70 to 80% of diltiazem is bound to plasma proteins.

Cardizem undergoes extensive hepatic metabolism in which only 2 to 4% of the drug appears unchanged in the urine and 6 to 7% appears as metabolites. The metabolic pathways of Cardizem include N- and O-demethylation (via cytochrome P450), deacetylation (via plasma and tissue esterases), in addition to conjugation (via sulfation and glucuronidation). In vitro studies have demonstrated that CYP 3A4 is the principal CYP isoenzyme involved in N-demethylation. The major metabolite, desacetyl diltiazem, is present in the plasma at levels 10 to 20% of the parent drug and is 25 to 50% as potent as diltiazem in terms of coronary vasodilation.

Cardizem Tablets: Single oral doses of 30 to 120 mg of Cardizem tablets result in detectable plasma levels within 30 to 60 minutes and peak plasma levels 2 to 4 hours after drug administration. There is a departure from linearity of accumulation of diltiazem when Cardizem tablets are administered to steady-state in normal subjects. A 240 mg daily dose (60 mg q.i.d.) gave plasma levels 2.3 times higher than a 120 mg daily dose (30 mg q.i.d.) and a 360 mg daily dose (90 mg q.i.d.) had levels 1.7 times higher than the 240 mg daily dose.

Cardizem SR: Diltiazem is absorbed from the sustained release (SR) capsule formulation to about 93% of the tablet form at steady-state. A single 120 mg dose of the capsule resulted in detectable plasma levels within 2 to 3 hours and peak plasma levels at 7 to 11 hours. The apparent elimination half-life after single or multiple dosing is 5 to 7 hours. A departure from linearity similar to that observed with the Cardizem tablet is observed. As the dose of Cardizem SR capsules is increased from a daily dose of 120 mg (60 mg b.i.d.) to 240 mg (120 mg b.i.d.) daily, there is an increase in bioavailability of 2.6 times. When the dose is increased from 240 to 360 mg daily there is an increase in bioavailability of 1.8 times. The average plasma levels of the capsule dosed twice daily at steady-state are equivalent to the tablet dosed 4 times daily when the same total daily dose is administered.

Cardizem CD: When compared to a regimen of Cardizem tablets at steady-state, more than 95% of drug is absorbed from the Cardizem CD formulation. A single 360 mg dose of the capsule results in detectable plasma levels within 2 hours and peak plasma levels between 10 and 14 hours. When Cardizem CD was taken with a high fat content breakfast, the extent of diltiazem absorption was not affected but was delayed. Dose-dumping does not occur. The apparent elimination half-life after single or multiple dosing is 5 to 8 hours. A departure from linearity similar to that seen with Cardizem tablets and Cardizem SR capsules is observed. As the dose of Cardizem CD capsules is increased from a daily dose of 120 to 240 mg, there is an increase in the area under the curve (AUC) of 2.7 times. When the dose is increased from 240 to 360 mg there is an increase in AUC of 1.6 times.

A study which compared patients with normal hepatic function to liver cirrhosis patients noted an increase in half-life and a 69% increase in bioavailability in the hepatically impaired patients. A single dose study in patients with severely impaired renal function showed no difference in the half-life of diltiazem as compared to patients with normal renal function (see Precautions and Dosage).

Indications: Cardizem: Angina: In the management of angina resulting from coronary artery spasm.

For the management of chronic stable angina (effort-associated angina) without evidence of vasospasm in patients who remain symptomatic despite adequate doses of beta-blockers and/or organic nitrates or who cannot tolerate those agents.

Cardizem tablets may be useful in unstable angina when spasm of the coronary vessels is definitely a contributing factor (e.g., ST segment elevation). In the absence of objective evidence of a spastic component, nitrates or nitrates plus a beta-blocker are, at present, the treatment of choice. If, in the view of a cardiologist, the addition of Cardizem to this regimen is considered necessary and safe, then the use of Cardizem tablets might be considered. Generally, the patient should be hospitalized and treatment initiated under the supervision of a cardiologist.

Cardizem tablets may be tried in combination with beta-blockers in chronic stable angina in patients with normal ventricular function. When such concomitant therapy is introduced, patients must be monitored closely (see Warnings).

Cardizem SR: Angina: For maintenance therapy in the management of chronic stable angina. Treatment should be initiated and individual titration of dosage carried out using the regular tablets. The sustained release formulation may be substituted as maintenance, provided the dosage requirement is suitable (see also Pharmacology). When patients who have been stabilized on tablets are switched to SR capsules for maintenance, close medical supervision is recommended since in some patients the dosage of the SR formulation may require adjustment.

Since the safety and efficacy of SR capsules in the management of unstable or vasospastic angina has not been substantiated, use of this formulation for these indications is not recommended.

Hypertension: In the treatment of mild to moderate essential hypertension. Cardizem SR should normally be used in those patients in whom treatment with diuretics or beta-blockers has been associated with unacceptable adverse effects.

Cardizem SR can be tried as initial agent in those patients in whom the use of diuretics and/or beta-blockers is contraindicated or in patients with medical conditions in which these drugs frequently cause serious adverse effects.

Combination of Cardizem SR with a diuretic has been found to be compatible and showed additive antihypertensive effect. In a single clinical study, the concomitant use of Cardizem SR with captopril was also found to be compatible.

Safety of concurrent use of Cardizem SR with other antihypertensive agents has not been established.

Cardizem CD: Angina: For the management of chronic stable angina (effort-associated angina) without evidence of vasospasm in patients who remain symptomatic despite adequate doses of beta-blockers and/or organic nitrates or who cannot tolerate those agents.

Cardizem CD may be tried in combination with beta-blockers in chronic stable angina patients with normal ventricular function. When such concomitant therapy is introduced, patients must be monitored closely (see Warnings).

Since the safety and efficacy of CD capsules in the management of unstable or vasospastic angina have not been substantiated, use of this formulation for these indications is not recommended.

Hypertension: For the treatment of mild to moderate essential hypertension. Cardizem CD should normally be used in those patients in whom treatment with diuretics or beta blockers has been ineffective, or has been associated with unacceptable adverse effects.

Cardizem CD can be tried as an initial agent in those patients in whom the use of diuretics and/or beta-blockers is contraindicated, or in patients with medical conditions in which these drugs frequently cause serious adverse effects.

Safety of concurrent use of Cardizem CD with other antihypertensive agents has not been established.

Contraindications: In patients with sick sinus syndrome except in the presence of a functioning ventricular pacemaker; in patients with second or third degree AV block; in patients with known hypersensitivity to diltiazem; and in patients with severe hypotension (less than 90 mmHg systolic); in myocardial infarction patients who have left ventricular failure manifested by pulmonary congestion.

Pregnancy: In pregnancy and in women of childbearing potential. Fetal malformations and adverse effects on pregnancy have been reported in animals. In repeated dose studies a high incidence of vertebral column malformations were present in the offspring of mice receiving more than 50 mg/kg of diltiazem orally.

In the offspring of mice receiving a single oral dose of 50 or 100 mg/kg on day 12 of gestation, the incidence of cleft palate and malformed extremities was significantly higher. Vertebral malformations were most prevalent when they received the drug on day 9. In rats, a significantly higher fetal death rate was present when 200 and 400 mg/kg were given orally on days 9 to 14 of gestation. Single oral dose studies in rats resulted in a significant incidence of skeletal malformations in the offspring of the group receiving 400 mg/kg on day 11. In rabbits, all pregnant dams receiving 70 mg/kg orally from day 6 to 18 of gestation aborted; at 35 mg/kg, a significant increase in skeletal malformations was recorded in the offspring.

Warnings: Cardiac Conduction: Diltiazem prolongs AV node refractory periods without significantly prolonging sinus node recovery time, except in patients with sick sinus syndrome. This effect may rarely result in abnormally slow heart rates (particularly in patients with sick sinus syndrome) or second- or third-degree AV block (6 of 1 208 patients or 0.5%).

First degree AV block was observed in 5.8% of patients receiving Cardizem CD (see Adverse Effects).

Concomitant use of diltiazem with beta-blockers or digitalis may result in additive effects on cardiac conduction.

Congestive Heart Failure: Because diltiazem has a negative inotropic effect in vitro and it affects cardiac conduction, the drug should only be used with caution and under careful medical supervision in patients with congestive cardiac failure (see also Contraindications).

Use with Beta-blockers: The combination of diltiazem and beta-blockers warrants caution since in some patients additive effects on heart rate, AV conduction, blood pressure or left ventricular function have been observed. Close medical supervision is recommended.

Generally, diltiazem should not be given to patients with impaired left ventricular function while they receive beta-blockers. However, in exceptional cases when, in the opinion of the physician, concomitant use is considered essential, such use should be instituted gradually in a hospital setting.

Diltiazem gives no protection against the dangers of abrupt beta-blocker withdrawal and such withdrawal should be done by the gradual reduction of the dose of beta-blocker.

Hypotension: Since diltiazem lowers peripheral vascular resistance, decreases in blood pressure may occasionally result in symptomatic hypotension. In patients with angina or arrhythmias using antihypertensive drugs, the additional hypotensive effect of diltiazem should be taken into consideration.

Patients with Myocardial Infarction: Use of immediate release diltiazem at 240 mg/day started 3 to 15 days after a myocardial infarction was associated with an increase in cardiac events in patients with pulmonary congestion, and no overall effect on mortality. Although there has not been a study of Cardizem SR or Cardizem CD in acute myocardial infarction reported, their use may have effects similar to those of immediate release diltiazem in acute myocardial infarction.

Acute Hepatic Injury: In rare instances, significant elevations in alkaline phosphatase, CPK, LDH, AST, ALT and symptoms consistent with acute hepatic injury have been observed. These reactions have been reversible upon discontinuation of drug therapy. Although a causal relationship to diltiazem has not been established in all cases a drug induced hypersensitivity reaction is suspected (see Adverse Effects). As with any drug given over prolonged periods, laboratory parameters should be monitored at regular intervals.

Precautions: Impaired Hepatic or Renal Function: Because diltiazem is extensively metabolized by the liver and excreted by the kidney and in bile, monitoring of laboratory parameters and cautious dosage titration are recommended in patients with impaired hepatic or renal function (see Adverse Effects).

Children: The safety of diltiazem in children has not yet been established.

Lactation: Diltiazem has been reported to be excreted in human milk. One report suggests that concentrations in breast milk may approximate serum levels. Since diltiazem safety in newborns has not been established, it should not be given to nursing mothers.

Geriatrics: Administration of diltiazem to elderly patients (over or equal to 65 years of age) requires caution. The incidence of adverse reactions is approximately 13% higher in this group. Those adverse reactions which occur more frequently include: peripheral edema, bradycardia, palpitation, dizziness, rash and polyuria. Therefore, particular care in titration is advisable (see Dosage).

Drug Interactions: As with all drugs, care should be exercised when treating patients with multiple medications. Calcium channel blockers undergo biotransformation by the cytochrome P450 system. Coadministration of diltiazem with other drugs which follow the same route of biotransformation may result in altered bioavailability. Dosages of similarly metabolized drugs, particularly those of low therapeutic ratio, and especially in patients with renal and/or hepatic impairment, may require adjustment when starting or stopping concomitantly administered diltiazem to maintain optimum therapeutic blood levels.

Drugs known to be inhibitors of the cytochrome P450 system include: azole antifungals, cimetidine, cyclosporine, erythromycin, quinidine, warfarin.

Drugs known to be inducers of the cytochrome P450 system include: phenobarbital, phenytoin, rifampin.

Drugs known to be biotransformed via P450 include: benzodiazepines, flecainide, imipramine, propafenone, terfenadine, theophylline.

Anesthetics: The depression of cardiac contractility, conductivity, and automaticity as well as the vascular dilation associated with anesthetics may be potentiated by calcium channel blockers. When used concomitantly, anesthetics and calcium channel blockers should be titrated carefully.

Benzodiazepines: Diltiazem significantly increases peak plasma levels and the elimination half-life of triazolam and midazolam.

Beta-blockers: The concomitant administration of diltiazem with beta adrenergic blocking drugs warrants caution and careful monitoring. Such an association may have an additive effect on heart rate, on AV conduction or on blood pressure (see Warnings). Appropriate dosage adjustments may be necessary. A study in 5 normal subjects showed that diltiazem increased propranolol bioavailability by approximately 50%.

Carbamazepine: Concomitant administration of diltiazem with carbamazepine has been reported to result in elevated serum levels of carbamazepine (40 to 72% increase) resulting in toxicity in some cases. Patients receiving these drugs concurrently should be monitored for a potential drug interaction.

Cimetidine: A study in 6 healthy volunteers has shown a significant increase in peak diltiazem plasma levels (58%) and area under the curve (53%) after a 1-week course of cimetidine at 1 200 mg/day and a single dose of oral diltiazem 60 mg. Ranitidine produced smaller, nonsignificant increases. Patients currently receiving diltiazem therapy should be carefully monitored for a change in pharmacological effect when initiating and discontinuing therapy with cimetidine. An adjustment in the diltiazem dose may be warranted.

Cyclosporine: A pharmacokinetic interaction between diltiazem and cyclosporine has been observed during studies involving renal and cardiac transplant patients. In renal and cardiac transplant recipients, a reduction of cyclosporine dose ranging from 15 to 48% was necessary to maintain cyclosporine trough concentrations similar to those seen prior to the addition of diltiazem. If these agents are to be administered concurrently, cyclosporine concentrations should be monitored, especially when diltiazem therapy is initiated, adjusted or discontinued. The effect of cyclosporine on diltiazem plasma concentrations has not been evaluated.

Digitalis: Diltiazem and digitalis glycosides may have an additive effect in prolonging AV conduction. In clinical trials, concurrent administration of diltiazem and digoxin have resulted in increases in serum digoxin levels with prolongation of AV conduction. This increase may result from a decrease in renal clearance of digoxin. Patients on concomitant therapy, especially those with renal impairment, should be carefully monitored. The dose of digoxin may need downward adjustment.

Rifampin: Administration of diltiazem with rifampin markedly reduced plasma diltiazem concentrations and the therapeutic effect of diltiazem.

Short and Long-Acting Nitrates: Diltiazem may be safely coadministered with nitrates, but there have been few controlled studies to evaluate the antianginal effectiveness of this combination.

Other Calcium Antagonists: Limited clinical experience suggests that in certain severe conditions not responding adequately to verapamil or to nifedipine, using diltiazem in conjunction with either of these drugs may be beneficial.

Adverse Effects: See also Overall Cardizem Safety Profile.

Cardizem: A safety evaluation was carried out in controlled clinical trials with 1 208 North American angina patients, some of whom were severely ill and were receiving multiple concomitant therapy. Adverse effects were reported in 19.6% of patients and required discontinuation of treatment in 7.2%.

The most common occurrences and their frequency are: nausea (2.7%), swelling/edema (2.4%), arrhythmia (2.0%) (AV block, bradycardia, tachycardia and sinus arrest), headache (2.0%), rash (1.8%) and asthenia (1.1%).

In addition, the following events were reported in less than 1% of cases: Cardiovascular: angina, bradycardia, congestive heart failure, flushing, hypotension, palpitations, syncope. A patient with Prinzmetal's angina, experiencing episodes of vasospastic angina, developed periods of transient asymptomatic asystole approximately 5 hours after receiving a single 60 mg dose of diltiazem.

CNS: amnesia, confusion, depression, dizziness, drowsiness, gait abnormality, hallucinations, insomnia, nervousness, paresthesia, personality change, tremor, weakness.

Gastrointestinal: anorexia, constipation, diarrhea, dyspepsia, vomiting.

Dermatologic: petechiae, pruritus, urticaria.

Other: amblyopia, decreased sexual performance, dysgeusia, dyspnea, epistaxis, eye irritation, hyperglycemia, nocturia, osteo-articular pain, paresthesia, photosensitivity, polyuria, thirst, tinnitus, weight increase.

Rarely, reports of extremely elevated liver enzymes, cholestasis, hyperbilirubinemia, jaundice, epigastric pain, anorexia, nausea, vomiting, stool discoloration, dark urine and weight loss have been reported. The symptoms and laboratory test abnormalities have been reversible on drug discontinuation (see Warnings).

Two incidents of marked hyperglycemia, hyperkalemia, bradycardia, asthenia, hypotension and gastrointestinal disturbances have been reported in diabetic patients receiving diltiazem, glyburide and a beta-blocker along with several other medications. Drugs were discontinued and supportive measures were administered which resulted in the patients fully recovering within a few days.

Laboratory Tests: In rare instances, mild to moderate transient elevations of alkaline phosphatase, AST, ALT, LDH and CPK, have been noted during diltiazem therapy.

Cardizem SR: A safety evaluation was carried out in controlled and open label studies in 611 hypertensive patients treated with Cardizem SR either alone or in combination with other antihypertensive agents. Adverse effects were reported in 34.2% of patients and required discontinuation of therapy in 7.2%.

The most common adverse effects were: peripheral edema (8.3%), headache (4.9%), dizziness (4.7%), asthenia (3.9%), vasodilation (flushing) (2.3%) and bradycardia (2.1%).

Cardizem (cont'd)

The following percentage of adverse effects, divided by system, was reported: Cardiovascular: edema peripheral (8.3%), vasodilation (flushing) (2.3%), bradycardia (2.1%), AV block (first degree) (1.6%), palpitations (1.3%), arrhythmia (1.0%), heart failure right (0.5%).
CNS: headache (4.9%), dizziness (4.7%), asthenia (3.9%), somnolence (1.0%), nervousness (anxiety) (0.8%), paresthesia (0.7%), insomnia (0.5%), depression (0.5%), dream abnormality (0.5%), tinnitus (0.5%).
Gastrointestinal: dyspepsia (1.1%), nausea (1.1%), constipation (0.7%).
Dermatologic: rash (1.6%).
Laboratory Tests: increased alkaline phosphatase (0.7%).
Other: impotence (1.6%), musculoskeletal pain (1.5%), nocturia (1.1%), polyuria (1.0%), rhinitis (0.5%).

The following additional adverse effects have occurred with an incidence of less than 0.5% in clinical trials: syncope, AV block, postural hypotension, chest pain, dyspnea, tremor, gait abnormality, vertigo, taste alteration, anorexia, increased appetite, dry mouth, vomiting, diarrhea, increased saliva, acute hepatic injury, pruritus, urticaria, conjunctivitis, amblyopia, ejaculation abnormality, malaise, fever.

The following abnormal laboratory findings have been rarely reported: increased AST/ALT, bilirubinemia, hyperproteinemia, hypercholesteremia, hyperlipidemia, hyperglycemia, hypokalemia, urine abnormality (see Precautions).

Cardizem CD: Angina: The safety of Cardizem CD, administered at doses up to 360 mg a day, was evaluated in 365 patients with chronic stable angina treated in controlled and open-label clinical trials. Adverse events were reported in 21.1% of patients, and required discontinuation in 2.2% of patients.

The most common adverse effects reported were: first degree AV block (5.8%), dizziness (3.0%), headache (3.0%), asthenia (2.7%), bradycardia (2.5%), and angina pectoris (1.6%).

The following percentage of adverse effects, divided by system, was reported: Cardiovascular: first degree AV block (5.8%), bradycardia (2.5%), angina pectoris (1.6%), peripheral edema (1.4%), palpitations (1.1%), and ventricular extrasystoles (0.8%).
CNS: dizziness (3.0%), headache (3.0%), asthenia (2.7%), insomnia (1.1%), nervousness (0.8%).
Gastrointestinal: nausea (1.4%), diarrhea (0.5%).
Dermatological: rash (0.8%).
Other: amblyopia (0.5%).

The following additional adverse effects have occurred with an incidence of less than 0.5% in clinical trials: bundle branch block, ventricular tachycardia, ECG abnormality, supraventricular extrasystoles, chest pain, syncope, postural hypotension, paresthesia, tremor, depression, mental confusion, impotence, abdominal pain, constipation, gastrointestinal disorder, epistaxis, nuchal rigidity, myalgia.

Hypertension: A safety evaluation was carried out in controlled studies in 378 hypertensive patients treated with Cardizem CD at doses up to 360 mg a day. Adverse effects were reported in 30.7% of patients and required discontinuation of therapy in 2.1%.

The most common adverse effects were: headache (8.7%), edema (4.0%), bradycardia (3.7%), dizziness (3.4%), ECG abnormality (2.9%), asthenia (2.6%) and first degree AV block (2.1%).

The following percentage of adverse effects, divided by system, was reported: Cardiovascular: edema peripheral (4.0%), bradycardia (3.7%), ECG abnormalities (2.9%), first degree AV block (2.1%), arrhythmia (1.6%), vasodilation (flushing) (1.6%), bundle branch block (0.8%), cardiomegaly (0.5%), hypotension (0.5%).
CNS: headache (8.7%), dizziness (3.4%), asthenia (2.6%), somnolence (1.3%), nervousness (1.1%).
Gastrointestinal: constipation (1.3%), dyspepsia (1.3%), diarrhea (0.6%).
Laboratory Tests: ALT increase (0.8%).
Other: leukopenia (1.1%), nocturia (0.5%).

The following additional adverse effects have occurred with an incidence of less than 0.5% in clinical trials: systolic murmur, supraventricular extrasystoles, migraine, tachycardia, increased appetite, increase in weight, albuminuria, bilirubinemia, hyperuricemia, thirst, insomnia, vertigo, nausea, pruritus, rash, increased perspiration, polyuria, amblyopia, tinnitus, and elevations in creatine kinase, alkaline phosphatase, and AST.
Overall Cardizem Safety Profile: In clinical trials of Cardizem tablets, Cardizem SR capsules and Cardizem CD capsules involving over 3 300 patients, the most common adverse reactions were headache (4.6%), edema (4.6%), dizziness (3.5%), asthenia (2.7%), first degree AV block (2.4%), bradycardia (1.7%), flushing (1.5%), nausea (1.4%), rash (1.2%), and dyspepsia (1.0%).

In addition, the following events were reported with a frequency of less than 1.0%.
Cardiovascular: angina, arrhythmia, bundle branch block, tachycardia, ventricular extrasystoles, congestive heart failure, syncope, palpitations, AV block (second or third degree), hypotension, ECG abnormalities.
Nervous System: amnesia, depression, gait abnormality, nervousness, somnolence, hallucinations, paresthesia, personality change, tinnitus, tremor, abnormal dreams, insomnia.
Gastrointestinal: anorexia, diarrhea, dysgeusia, mild elevations of AST, ALT, LDH, and alkaline phosphatase (see Warnings), vomiting, weight increase, thirst, constipation.
Dermatological: petechiae, pruritus, photosensitivity, urticaria.
Other: amblyopia, CPK increase, dyspnea, epistaxis, eye irritation, hyperglycemia, sexual difficulties, nasal congestion, nocturia, osteo-articular pain, impotence, dry mouth, polyuria, hyperuricemia.

The following postmarketing events have been reported infrequently in patients receiving Cardizem: allergic reactions, alopecia, asystole, erythema multiforme (including Stevens-Johnson syndrome, toxic epidermal necrolysis), exfoliative dermatitis, extrapyramidal symptoms, gingival hyperplasia, hemolytic anemia, detached retina, increased bleeding time, leukopenia, purpura, retinopathy, and thrombocytopenia. Isolated cases of angioedema have been reported. Angioedema may be accompanied by breathing difficulty. In addition, events such as myocardial infarction have been observed which are not readily distinguishable from the natural history of the disease in these patients. A number of well-documented cases of generalized rash, some characterized as leukocytoclastic vasculitis, have been reported. However, a definitive cause and effect relationship between these events and Cardizem therapy is yet to be established.

Overdose: Symptoms and Treatment: There have been reports of diltiazem overdose in amounts ranging from <1 to 18 g. In cases with a fatal outcome, the majority involved multiple drug ingestion.

Events observed following diltiazem overdose included bradycardia, hypotension, heart block and cardiac failure. Most reports of overdose described some supportive medical measure and/or drug treatment. Bradycardia frequently responded favourably to atropine as did heart block, although cardiac pacing was also frequently utilized to treat heart block. Fluids and vasopressors were used to maintain blood pressure, and in cases of cardiac failure, inotropic agents were administered. In addition, some patients received treatment with ventilatory support, gastric lavage, activated charcoal, and i.v. calcium.

The effectiveness of i.v. calcium administration to reverse the pharmacological effects of diltiazem overdose has been inconsistent. In a few reported cases, overdose with calcium channel blockers associated with hypotension and bradycardia that was initially refractory to atropine became more responsive to atropine after the patients received i.v. calcium. In some cases i.v. calcium has been administered (1 g calcium chloride or 3 g calcium gluconate) over 5 minutes, and repeated every 10 to 20 minutes as necessary. Calcium gluconate has also been administrated as a continuous infusion at a rate of 2 g/hour for 10 hours. Infusions of calcium for 24 hours or more may be required. Patients should be monitored for signs of hypercalcemia.

In the event of overdosage or exaggerated response, appropriate supportive measures should be employed in addition to gastric lavage. Limited data suggest that plasmapheresis or charcoal hemoperfusion may hasten diltiazem elimination. The following measures may be considered: Bradycardia: Administer atropine. If there is no response to vagal blockade, administer isoproterenol cautiously.
High Degree AV Block: Treat as for bradycardia above. Fixed high degree AV block should be treated with cardiac pacing.
Cardiac Failure: Administer inotropic agents (isoproterenol, dopamine or dobutamine) and diuretics.
Hypotension: vasopressors (e.g., dopamine or norepinephrine).

Actual treatment and dosage should depend on the severity of the clinical situation.

Dosage: Cardizem: Angina: Chronic Stable Angina or Vasospastic Angina: Dosage must be adjusted to each patient's needs. Starting with 30 mg 4 times daily, before meals and at bedtime, dosage may be increased gradually to 240 mg a day (given in 3 to 4 equally divided doses) at 1 to 2 day intervals, until optimum response is obtained. Limited clinical experience in rare resistant cases suggests that dosage of up to 360 mg a day in 3 to 4 equally divided doses may be tried under careful supervision.

In patients with vasospastic angina, the last dose of the day may be given at bedtime to help minimize angina pain which, in such patients, frequently occurs in early morning.
Unstable Angina Pectoris: Dosage of Cardizem tablets should be carefully titrated in the Intensive Care Unit, up to 360 mg/day given in 3 to 4 equally divided doses. The titration should be done as rapidly as possible with consideration of concomitant therapy (see Precautions, Drug Interactions).
Geriatrics: Pharmacokinetics of diltiazem in elderly patients has not been fully elucidated. Preliminary results in elderly patients (over 65 years old) suggest that a lower dosage might be required in this age group (see Precautions).

There are few available data concerning dosage requirements in patients with impaired renal or hepatic function. If diltiazem must be used in these patients, the dosage should be carefully and gradually adjusted depending on patient tolerance and response (see Precautions).

Cardizem SR: Angina: Cardizem SR is intended for maintenance therapy in chronic stable angina patients requiring doses within the range of 120 to 360 mg/day. Initiation of treatment and individual titration of dosage should be carried out using the conventional tablets. Cardizem SR may be preferred for maintenance because of the convenience of twice daily dosage. Patients stabilized on a maintenance regimen between 120 and 360 mg of regular tablets may be changed to the same daily dose of Cardizem SR capsules divided into 2 equal doses and taken every 12 hours. When patients are switched to SR capsules, close medical supervision is recommended since in some patients the dosage of the SR formulation may require adjustment.
Hypertension: Dosage should be individualized depending on patient's tolerance and responsiveness to Cardizem SR capsules and to concurrent antihypertensive medications (see Indications and Precautions).

The adult dose range is 120 to 360 mg/day administered in 2 equally divided doses. Although individual patients may respond to any dosage level, the average optimum dosage range in clinical trials is between 240 and 360 mg/day. Maximum antihypertensive effect is usually observed by the second to fourth week of chronic therapy, therefore dosage adjustments should be scheduled accordingly.

A maximum daily dose of 360 mg should not be exceeded.

There is evidence that the effective dose in the elderly (over 65 years of age) is somewhat lower than in younger patients (average dose: 255 mg vs 288 mg respectively); therefore, Cardizem SR should be administered cautiously to elderly patients and the dosage should be carefully and gradually adjusted depending on patient tolerance and response (see Precautions).

Cardizem SR has an additive antihypertensive effect when used concomitantly with other antihypertensive agents. Therefore, it may be necessary to decrease the dose of Cardizem SR and/or the dose of the concomitant antihypertensive drug when adding one to the other (see Indications and Warnings).

Cardizem SR should not be used in severe hepatic or renal dysfunction.

Cardizem CD: Angina: Dosages for the treatment of angina should be adjusted to each patient's needs, starting with a dose of 120 mg to 180 mg once daily. Individual patients may respond to higher doses of up to 360 mg once daily. When necessary, titration should be carried out over a 7 to 14 day period.

Patients controlled on diltiazem alone or in combination with other medications may be safely switched to Cardizem CD capsules at the nearest equivalent total daily dose. Subsequent titration to higher or lower doses may be necessary and should be initiated as clinically warranted. There is limited experience with doses above 360 mg, however, the incidence of adverse reactions increases as the dose increases with first degree AV block, dizziness, and sinus bradycardia bearing the strongest relationship to dose. Therefore, doses greater than 360 mg are not recommended.
Hypertension: Dosage should be individualized depending on patient's tolerance and responsiveness to Cardizem CD capsules. When used as monotherapy, usual starting doses are 180 to 240 mg once daily, although some patients may respond to 120 mg once daily. Maximum antihypertensive effect is usually observed after approximately 2 to 4 weeks of therapy; therefore, dosage adjustments should be scheduled accordingly. The usual dosage range studied in clinical trials was 240 to 360 mg once daily.

A maximum daily dose of 360 mg once daily should not be exceeded.

The dosage of Cardizem CD or concomitant antihypertensive agents may need to be adjusted when adding one to the other (see Warnings and Precautions regarding use with beta-blockers).

Hypertensive patients controlled on Cardizem SR alone or in combination with other antihypertensive agents may be safely switched to Cardizem CD at the same total daily dose. Subsequent titration to higher or lower doses may be necessary and should be initiated as clinically warranted.

The tablets and capsules should not be chewed or crushed.

Supplied: Cardizem: 30 mg: Each green, unscored tablet, engraved with HMR on one side and 30 on the other, contains: diltiazem HCl 30 mg. Nonmedicinal ingredients: Blue FD&C No. 1, hydroxypropyl cellulose, hydroxypropyl methylcellulose, hydrogenated vegetable, oil, lactose, magnesium stearate, polyethylene glycol, povidone, sodium methylparaben, talc and Yellow D&C No. 10. Bisulfites-, gluten- and tartrazine-free. Bottles of 100 and 500. Blister packs of 100.

60 mg: Each yellow, scored tablet, engraved with HMR on one side and 60 on the other, contains: diltiazem HCl 60 mg. Nonmedicinal ingredients: hydroxypropyl cellulose, hydroxypropyl methylcellulose, hydrogenated vegetable oil, lactose, magnesium stearate, polyethylene glycol, povidone, sodium methylparaben, talc, Yellow D&C No. 10 and Yellow FD&C No. 6. Bisulfites-, gluten- and tartrazine-free. Bottles of 100 and 500. Blister packs of 100.

Cardizem SR: 60 mg: Each ivory/brown, sustained-release capsule, imprinted with the CARDIZEM logo on one end and CARDIZEM SR 60 mg on the opposite end, contains: diltiazem HCl 60 mg. Nonmedicinal ingredients: Blue FD&C No. 1, cornstarch, fumaric acid, gelatin, povidone, Red FD&C No. 40, shellac, sucrose, talc, titanium dioxide, Yellow D&C No. 10 and Yellow FD&C No. 6. Bisulfites-, gluten- and tartrazine-free. Bottles of 100. Blister packs of 100.

90 mg: Each gold/brown, sustained-release capsule, imprinted with the CARDIZEM logo on one end and CARDIZEM SR 90 mg on the opposite end, contains: diltiazem HCl 90 mg. Nonmedicinal ingredients: Blue FD&C No. 1, cornstarch, fumaric acid, gelatin, povidone, Red FD&C No. 40, shellac, sucrose, talc, titanium dioxide, Yellow D&C No. 10 and Yellow FD&C No. 6. Bisulfites-, gluten- and tartrazine-free. Bottles of 100 and 300. Blister packs of 100.

120 mg: Each caramel/brown, sustained-release capsule, imprinted with the CARDIZEM logo on one end and CARDIZEM SR 120 mg on the opposite end, contains: diltiazem HCl 120 mg. Nonmedicinal ingredients: Blue FD&C No. 1, cornstarch, fumaric acid, gelatin, povidone, Red FD&C No. 40, shellac, sucrose, talc, titanium dioxide, Yellow D&C No. 10 and Yellow FD&C No. 6. Bisulfites-, gluten- and tartrazine-free. Bottles of 100 and 300. Blister packs of 100.

Cardizem CD: 120 mg: Each light turquoise blue, controlled delivery capsule, imprinted with CARDIZEM CD 120 mg, contains: diltiazem HCl 120 mg. Nonmedicinal ingredients: acetyltributyl citrate, beeswax, Blue FD&C No. 1, castor oil, cornstarch, ethylcellulose, fumaric acid, gelatin, polymethyl methacrylate, silica, simethicone, sucrose, stearic acid, talc and titanium dioxide. Bisulfites-, gluten- and tartrazine-free. Bottles of 100. Blister packs 100.

180 mg: Each light blue/light turquoise blue, controlled delivery capsule, imprinted with CARDIZEM CD 180 mg, contains: diltiazem HCl 180 mg. Nonmedicinal ingredients: acetyltributyl citrate, beeswax, Blue FD&C No. 1, castor oil, cornstarch, ethylcellulose, fumaric acid, gelatin, polymethyl methacrylate, silica, simethicone, sucrose, stearic acid, talc and titanium dioxide. Bisulfites-, gluten- and tartrazine-free. Bottles of 100. Blister packs of 100.

240 mg: Each light blue/light blue, controlled delivery capsule, imprinted with CARDIZEM CD 240 mg, contains: diltiazem HCl 240 mg. Nonmedicinal ingredients: acetyltributyl citrate, beeswax, Blue FD&C No. 1, castor oil, cornstarch, ethylcellulose, fumaric acid, gelatin, polymethyl methacrylate, silica, simethicone, sucrose, stearic acid, talc and titanium dioxide. Bisulfites-, gluten- and tartrazine-free. Bottles of 100. Blister packs of 100.

300 mg: Each light blue/light gray, controlled delivery capsule, imprinted with CARDIZEM CD 300 mg, contains: diltiazem HCl 300 mg. Nonmedicinal ingredients: acetyltributyl citrate, beeswax, Blue FD&C No. 1, castor oil, cornstarch, ethylcellulose, fumaric acid, gelatin, iron oxide, polymethyl methacrylate, silica, simethicone, stearic acid, sucrose, talc and titanium dioxide. Bisulfites-, gluten- and tartrazine-free. Bottles of 100. Blister packs of 100.

Keep between 15 and 30°C.

(Shown in Product Recognition Section)

Reviewed 1999

CARDIZEM® INJECTABLE Ⓟ

Hoechst Marion Roussel

Diltiazem HCl

Antiarrhythmic

Pharmacology: Mechanism of Action: Diltiazem inhibits the influx of calcium ions during membrane depolarization of cardiac and vascular smooth muscle. The therapeutic benefits of diltiazem in supraventricular tachycardias are related to its ability to slow atrioventricular (AV) nodal conduction time and prolong AV nodal refractoriness. Diltiazem exhibits frequency (use) dependent effects on AV nodal conduction such that it may selectively reduce the heart rate during tachycardias involving the AV node with little or no effect on normal AV nodal conduction at normal heart rates.

Diltiazem slows the ventricular rate in patients with a rapid ventricular response during atrial fibrillation or atrial flutter (AF/FL). Diltiazem converts paroxysmal supraventricular tachycardia (PSVT) to normal sinus rhythm by interrupting the reentry circuit in AV nodal reentrant tachycardias and reciprocating tachycardias, e.g., Wolff-Parkinson-White syndrome (WPW).

Diltiazem prolongs the sinus cycle length. It has no effects on the sinus node recovery time or on the sinoatrial (SA) conduction time in patients without SA nodal dysfunction. Diltiazem has no significant electrophysiologic effects on tissues in the heart that are fast sodium channel dependent, e.g., His-Purkinje tissue, atrial and ventricular muscle and extranodal accessory pathways.

Like other calcium channel antagonists, because of its effect on vascular smooth muscle, diltiazem decreases total peripheral resistance resulting in a decrease in both systolic and diastolic blood pressure.

Hemodynamics: In patients with cardiovascular disease, diltiazem administered i.v. in single bolus doses, followed in some cases by a continuous infusion, reduced blood pressure, systemic vascular resistance, the rate-pressure product, and coronary vascular resistance and increased coronary blood flow. Following administration of 1 or 2 i.v. bolus doses of diltiazem, response usually occurs within 3 minutes and maximal heart rate reduction generally occurs in 2 to 7 minutes. Heart rate reduction may last from 1 to 3 hours. Upon discontinuation of infusion, heart rate reduction may last from 0.5 hours to more than 10 hours (median duration = 7 hours). Hypotension, if it occurs, may be similarly persistent.

In a limited number of studies of patients with compromised myocardiums (severe congestive heart failure, acute myocardial infarction, hypertrophic cardiomyopathy), administration of i.v. diltiazem produced no significant effect on contractility, left ventricular end diastolic pressure, or pulmonary capillary wedge pressure. The mean ejection fraction and cardiac output/index remained unchanged or increased. Maximal hemodynamic effects usually occurred within 2 to 5 minutes of an injection. However, in rare instances, worsening of congestive heart failure has been reported in patients with preexisting impaired ventricular function.

Pharmacodynamics: The prolongation of PR interval correlated significantly with plasma diltiazem concentration in normal volunteers using the Sigmoidal E_{max} model. Changes in heart rate, systolic blood pressure, and diastolic blood pressure did not correlate with diltiazem plasma concentrations in normal volunteers. Reduction in mean arterial pressure correlated linearly with diltiazem plasma concentration in a group of hypertensive patients.

In patients with atrial fibrillation and atrial flutter, a significant correlation was observed between the percent reduction in HR and plasma diltiazem concentration using the Sigmoidal E_{max} model. Based on this relationship, the mean plasma diltiazem concentration required to produce a 20% decrease in heart rate was determined to be 80 ng/mL. Mean plasma diltiazem concentrations of 130 ng/mL and 300 ng/mL were determined to produce reductions in heart rate of 30 and 40%.

Pharmacokinetics: Following a single i.v. injection in healthy male volunteers, diltiazem appears to obey linear pharmacokinetics over a dose range of 10.5 to 21 mg. The plasma elimination half-life is approximately 3.4 hours. The apparent volume of distribution of diltiazem is approximately 305 L. Diltiazem is extensively metabolized in the liver with a systemic clearance of approximately 65 L/h.

After constant rate i.v. infusion to healthy male volunteers, diltiazem exhibits nonlinear pharmacokinetics over an infusion range of 4.8 to 13.2 mg/h for 24 hours. Over this infusion range, as the dose is increased, systemic clearance decreases from 64 to 48 L/h while the plasma elimination half-life increases from 4.1 to 4.9 hours. The apparent volume of distribution remains unchanged (360 to 391 L).

In patients with AF/FL, diltiazem systemic clearance has been found to be decreased compared to healthy volunteers. In patients administered bolus doses ranging from 2.5 mg to 38.5 mg, systemic clearance averaged 36 L/h. In patients administered continuous infusions at 10 mg/h or 15 mg/h for 24 hours, diltiazem systemic clearance averaged 42 L/h and 31 L/h, respectively.

After oral administration, diltiazem undergoes extensive metabolism in man by deacetylation, N-demethylation, and O-demethylation via cytochrome P450 (oxidative metabolism) in addition to conjugation. Metabolites N-monodesmethyldiltiazem, desacetyldiltiazem, desacetyl-N-monodesmethyldiltiazem, desacetyl-O-desmethyldiltiazem, and desacetyl-N,O-desmethyldiltiazem have been identified in human urine. Following oral administration, 2 to 4% of the unchanged diltiazem appears in the urine. Drugs which induce or inhibit hepatic microsomal enzymes may alter diltiazem disposition.

Following single i.v. injection of diltiazem, however, plasma concentrations of N-monodesmethyldiltiazem and desacetyldiltiazem, 2 principal metabolites found in plasma after oral administration, are typically not detected. These metabolites are observed, however, following 24-hour constant rate i.v. infusion. Total radioactivity measurement following short i.v. administration in healthy volunteers suggests the presence of other unidentified metabolites which attain higher concentrations than those of diltiazem and are more slowly eliminated. Plasma half-life of total radioactivity is about 20 hours compared to 2 to 5 hours for diltiazem.

Diltiazem is 70 to 80% bound to plasma proteins.

Indications: Atrial Fibrillation or Atrial Flutter: Temporary control of rapid ventricular rate in atrial fibrillation or atrial flutter. It should not be used in patients with AF/FL associated with an accessory bypass tract such as in Wolff-Parkinson-White (WPW) syndrome, or short PR syndrome, e.g., Lown-Ganong-Levine syndrome. Diltiazem injectable rarely converts atrial fibrillation or atrial flutter to normal sinus rhythm.

Paroxysmal Supraventricular Tachycardia: Rapid conversion of paroxysmal supraventricular tachycardias to sinus rhythm. This includes AV nodal reentrant tachycardias, and reciprocating tachycardias associated with extranodal accessory pathway, such as the WPW syndrome, or short PR syndrome, e.g., Lown-Ganong-Levine syndrome. Unless otherwise contraindicated, appropriate vagal manoeuvres should be attempted prior to administration of diltiazem injectable.

The use of diltiazem injectable for control of ventricular response in patients with atrial fibrillation or atrial flutter or conversion to sinus rhythm in patients with paroxysmal supraventricular tachycardia should be undertaken with caution when the patient is compromised hemodynamically or is taking other drugs that decrease any or all of the following: peripheral resistance, myocardial filling, myocardial contractility, or electrical impulse propagation in the myocardium.

For either indication the setting should include continuous monitoring of the ECG and frequent measurement of blood pressure. A defibrillator and emergency equipment should be readily available.

Contraindications: In patients with sick sinus syndrome except in the presence of a functioning ventricular pacemaker. In patients with second- or third-degree AV block except in the presence of a functioning ventricular pacemaker. In patients with known hypersensitivity to diltiazem. In patients with severe hypotension or cardiogenic shock.

In patients with AF/FL associated with an accessory bypass tract such as in WPW syndrome, or short PR syndrome, e.g., Lown-Ganong-Levine syndrome. As with other agents which slow AV nodal conduction and do not prolong the refractoriness of the accessory pathway (e.g., verapamil, digoxin), in rare instances patients with AF/FL associated with an accessory bypass tract may experience a potentially life-threatening increase in heart rate accompanied by hypotension when treated with diltiazem injectable.

In patients with ventricular tachycardia. Administration of other calcium channel blockers to patients with wide complex tachycardia (QRS ≥ 0.12 seconds) has resulted in hemodynamic deterioration and ventricular fibrillation. It is important that an accurate pretreatment diagnosis distinguish wide complex QRS tachycardia of supraventricular origin from that of ventricular origin prior to administration of diltiazem injectable.

Pregnancy: In pregnancy and in women of childbearing potential. Fetal malformations and adverse effects on pregnancy have been reported in animals. In repeated dose studies, a

Cardizem Injectable (cont'd)

high incidence of vertebral column malformations was present in the offspring of mice receiving more than 50 mg/kg of diltiazem orally.

I.V. diltiazem and **i.v.** beta-blockers should not be administered together or in close proximity (within a few hours).

Warnings: Cardiac Conduction: Diltiazem prolongs AV nodal conduction and refractoriness that may rarely result in second- or third-degree AV block in sinus rhythm. Concomitant use of diltiazem with agents known to affect cardiac conduction may result in additive effects (see Precautions, Drug Interactions). If high-degree AV block occurs in sinus rhythm, i.v. diltiazem should be discontinued and appropriate supportive measures instituted (see Overdose: Symptoms and Treatment).

Congestive Heart Failure: Although diltiazem has a negative inotropic effect in isolated animal tissue preparations, hemodynamic studies in humans with normal ventricular function and in patients with a compromised myocardium, such as severe CHF, acute MI, and hypertrophic cardiomyopathy, have not shown a reduction in cardiac index nor consistent negative effects on contractility (dp/dt). Administration of **oral** diltiazem is contraindicated in myocardial infarction patients who have left ventricular failure manifested by pulmonary congestion. Experience with the use of diltiazem injectable in patients with impaired ventricular function is limited. Caution should be exercised when using the drug in such patients.

Hypotension: Decreases in blood pressure associated with diltiazem therapy may occasionally result in symptomatic hypotension (see Adverse Effects). In controlled clinical trials, 3.2% of patients required some form of intervention (use of i.v. fluids, or the Trendelenburg position) for blood pressure support following diltiazem injectable. The use of i.v. diltiazem for control of ventricular response in patients with supraventricular arrhythmias should be undertaken with caution when the patient is compromised hemodynamically. In addition, caution should be used in patients taking other drugs that decrease peripheral resistance, intravascular volume, myocardial contractility or conduction.

Acute Hepatic Injury: In rare instances, significant elevations of enzymes such as alkaline phosphatase, LDH, AST, ALT, and symptoms consistent with acute hepatic injury have been noted following oral diltiazem. Although a causal relationship to diltiazem has not been established in all cases, a drug induced hypersensitivity reaction is suspected (see Adverse Effects). Therefore, the potential for acute hepatic injury exists following administration of i.v. diltiazem.

Ventricular Premature Beats (VPBs): VPBs may be present on conversion of PSVT to sinus rhythm with i.v. diltiazem. These VPBs are transient, are typically considered to be benign and appear to have no clinical significance. Similar ventricular complexes have been noted during cardioversion, other pharmacologic therapy, and during spontaneous conversion of PSVT to sinus rhythm.

Precautions: Impaired Hepatic or Renal Function: Diltiazem is extensively metabolized by the liver and excreted by the kidneys and in bile. The drug should be used with caution in patients with impaired renal or hepatic function. Liver cirrhosis was shown to reduce apparent oral diltiazem clearance, prolong the half-life of orally administered diltiazem and increase its bioavailability by 69%.

In subacute and chronic dog and rat studies designed to produce toxicity, high oral doses of diltiazem were associated with hepatic damage. In special subacute hepatic studies, oral doses of 125 mg/kg and higher in rats were associated with histological changes in the liver, which were reversible when the drug was discontinued. In dogs, oral doses of 20 mg/kg were also associated with hepatic changes; however, these changes were reversible with continued dosing.

Dermatologic Disorders: Dermatologic events progressing to erythema multiforme and/or exfoliative dermatitis have been infrequently reported following oral diltiazem (see Adverse Effects). Therefore, the potential for these dermatologic reactions exists following exposure to i.v. diltiazem. Should a dermatologic reaction persist, the drug should be discontinued.

Drug Interactions: Due to potential for additive effects, caution is warranted in patients receiving diltiazem concomitantly with any agent(s) known to affect cardiac contractility and/or SA or AV node conduction (see Warnings).

As with all drugs, care should be exercised when treating patients with multiple medications. Calcium channel blockers undergo biotransformation by the cytochrome P450 system. Coadministration of diltiazem with other drugs which follow the same route of biotransformation may result in altered bioavailability. Dosages of similarly metabolized drugs, particularly those of low therapeutic ratio, and especially in patients with renal and/or hepatic impairment, may require adjustment when starting or stopping concomitantly administered diltiazem to maintain optimum therapeutic blood levels.

Drugs known to be inhibitors of the cytochrome P450 system include: azole antifungals, cimetidine, cyclosporine, erythromycin, quinidine, warfarin.

Drugs known to be inducers of the cytochrome P450 system include: phenobarbital, phenytoin, rifampin.

Drugs known to be biotransformed via P450 include: benzodiazepines, flecainide, imipramine, propafenone, terfenadine, theophylline.

Anesthetics: The depression of cardiac contractility, conductivity, and automaticity as well as the vascular dilation associated with anesthetics may be potentiated by calcium channel blockers. When used concomitantly, anesthetics and calcium blockers should be titrated carefully.

Benzodiazepines: Diltiazem significantly increases peak plasma levels and the elimination half-life of triazolam and midazolam.

Beta-blockers: I.V. diltiazem has been administered to patients on chronic oral beta-blocker therapy. The combination of the two drugs was generally well tolerated without serious adverse effects. If i.v. diltiazem is administered to patients receiving chronic oral beta-blocker therapy, the possibility of bradycardia, AV block, and/or depression of contractility should be considered (see Contraindications). Oral administration of diltiazem with propranolol in 5 normal volunteers resulted in increased propranolol levels in all subjects and bioavailability of propranolol was increased approximately 50%. In vitro, propranolol appears to be displaced from its binding sites by diltiazem.

Carbamazepine: Concomitant administration of diltiazem with carbamazepine has been reported to result in elevated serum levels of carbamazepine (40 to 72% increase) resulting in toxicity in some cases. Patients receiving these drugs concurrently should be monitored for a potential drug interaction.

Cimetidine: A study in 6 healthy volunteers has shown a significant increase in peak diltiazem plasma levels (58%) and area under the curve (53%) after a 1-week course of cimetidine at 1 200 mg/day and a single dose of oral diltiazem 60 mg. Ranitidine produced smaller, nonsignificant increases. Patients currently receiving diltiazem therapy should be carefully monitored for a change in pharmacological effect when initiating and discontinuing therapy with cimetidine. An adjustment in the diltiazem dose may be warranted.

Cyclosporine: A pharmacokinetic interaction between diltiazem and cyclosporine has been observed during studies involving renal and cardiac transplant patients. In renal and cardiac transplant recipients, a reduction of cyclosporine dose ranging from 15 to 48% was necessary to maintain cyclosporine trough concentrations similar to those seen prior to the addition of diltiazem. If these agents are to be administered concurrently, cyclosporine concentrations should be monitored, especially when diltiazem therapy is initiated, adjusted or discontinued. The effect of cyclosporine on diltiazem plasma concentrations has not been evaluated.

Digitalis: I.V. diltiazem has been administered to patients receiving either i.v. or oral digitalis therapy. The combination of the two drugs was well tolerated without serious adverse effects. However, since both drugs affect AV nodal conduction, patients should be monitored for excessive slowing of the heart rate and/or AV block.

Rifampin: Administration of diltiazem with rifampin markedly reduced plasma diltiazem concentrations and the therapeutic effect of diltiazem.

Short and Long-acting Nitrates: Diltiazem may be safely coadministered with nitrates, but there have been few controlled studies to evaluate the antianginal effectiveness of this combination.

Other Calcium Antagonists: Limited clinical experience suggests that in certain severe conditions not responding adequately to verapamil or to nifedipine, using diltiazem in conjunction with either of these drugs may be beneficial.

Lactation: Diltiazem is excreted in human milk. One report with oral diltiazem suggests that concentrations in breast milk may approximate serum levels. If use of diltiazem is deemed essential, an alternative method of infant feeding should be instituted.

Children: Safety and effectiveness in children have not been established.

Adverse Effects: Adverse reactions were derived from controlled clinical trials in 411 patients with paroxysmal supraventricular tachycardia, atrial fibrillation, or atrial flutter. Adverse reactions were reported in 17.3% of patients on diltiazem injectable, and required discontinuation of treatment in 1.5% of patients.

Worldwide experience in over 1 300 patients was similar.

The most common adverse reactions (incidence of at least 1%) were: hypotension 7.5%, symptomatic hypotension 3.2%, injection site reaction (e.g., itching, burning)—3.9%, vasodilation (flushing)—1.7%, and arrhythmia (junctional rhythm or isorhythmic dissociation)—1%.

In addition, the following events were reported in less than 1% of cases: Cardiovascular: atrial flutter, first-degree AV block, second-degree AV block, bradycardia, chest pain, congestive heart failure, sinus pause, sinus node dysfunction, syncope, ventricular arrhythmia, ventricular fibrillation, ventricular tachycardia.

Dermatologic: pruritus, sweating.

Gastrointestinal: constipation, elevated AST or alkaline phosphatase, nausea, vomiting.

Nervous system: dizziness, paresthesia.

Other: amblyopia, asthenia, dry mouth, dyspnea, general edema, headache, hyperuricemia.

Although not observed in clinical trials with diltiazem injectable, other reactions associated with oral diltiazem have been reported: Cardiovascular: third-degree AV block, bundle branch block, ECG abnormality, palpitations, syncope, tachycardia, ventricular extrasystoles.

Dermatologic: alopecia, erythema multiforme, exfoliative dermatitis, leukocytoclastic vasculitis, petechiae, photosensitivity, purpura, rash, urticaria.

Gastrointestinal: anorexia, diarrhea, dysgeusia, dyspepsia, mild elevations of ALT and LDH, thirst, weight increase.

Nervous system: abnormal dreams, amnesia, depression, extrapyramidal symptoms, gait abnormality, hallucinations, insomnia, nervousness, personality change, somnolence, tremor.

Other: CPK elevation, detached retina, epistaxis, eye irritation, gingival hyperplasia, hemolytic anemia, hyperglycemia, impotence, increased bleeding time, leukopenia, muscle cramps, nasal congestion, nocturia, osteoarticular pain, polyuria, retinopathy, sexual difficulties, thrombocytopenia, tinnitus.

Events such as myocardial infarction have been observed which are not readily distinguishable from the natural history of the disease for the patient.

Overdose: Symptoms and Treatment: Overdosage experience is limited. In the event of overdosage or an exaggerated response, appropriate supportive measures should be employed. The following measures may be considered:

Bradycardia: Administer atropine (0.6 to 1 mg). If there is no response to vagal blockade administer isoproterenol cautiously.

High-degree AV block: Treat as for bradycardia above. Fixed high-degree AV block should be treated with cardiac pacing.

Cardiac failure: Administer inotropic agents (isoproterenol, dopamine, or dobutamine) and diuretics.

Hypotension: vasopressors (e.g., dopamine or norepinephrine).

The effectiveness of i.v. calcium administration to reverse the pharmacological effects of diltiazem overdose has been inconsistent. In a few reported cases, overdose with calcium channel blockers associated with hypotension and bradycardia that was initially refractory to atropine became more responsive to atropine after the patients received i.v. calcium. In some cases i.v. calcium has been administrated (1 g calcium chloride or 3 g calcium gluconate) over 5 minutes, and repeated every 10 to 20 minutes as necessary. Calcium gluconate has also been administrated as a continuous infusion at a rate of 2 g/hour for 10 hours. Infusions of calcium for 24 hours or more may be required. Patients should be monitored for signs of hypercalcemia.

Actual treatment and dosage should depend on the severity of the clinical situation and the judgment and experience of the treating physician.

The i.v. LD_{50}'s in mice and rats were 58 to 61 and 38 to 39 mg/kg, respectively. The toxic dose in man is not known.

Dosage: Direct I.V. Single Injections (Bolus): The initial dose of diltiazem injectable should be **0.25 mg/kg** body weight as a bolus administered over **2** minutes. If response is inadequate, a second dose may be administered after **15** minutes. The second bolus dose of diltiazem injectable should be **0.35 mg/kg** body weight administered over **2** minutes. Subsequent i.v. bolus doses should be individualized for each

Table I—Cardizem Injectable

Dilution for I.V. Infusion

Diluent Volume	Quantity of Diltiazem Injectable	Final Concentration	Administration Dose	Administration Infusion Rate
100 mL	125 mg (25 mL)	1.0 mg/mL	5 mg/h*	5 mL/h
			10 mg/h	10 mL/h
			15 mg/h	15 mL/h
250 mL	250 mg (50 mL)	0.83 mg/mL	5 mg/h*	6 mL/h
			10 mg/h	12 mL/h
			15 mg/h	18 mL/h
500 mL	250 mg (50 mL)	0.45 mg/mL	5 mg/h*	11 mL/h
			10 mg/h	22 mL/h
			15 mg/h	33 mL/h

* The recommended initial infusion rate of diltiazem is 10 mg/h. An infusion rate of 5 mg/h may be appropriate for some patients.

patient. Some patients may respond to an initial dose of 0.15 mg/kg, although duration of action may be shorter.

Continuous I.V. Infusion: For continued reduction of the heart rate (up to 24 hours) in patients with AF/FL, an i.v. infusion of diltiazem may be administered. Immediately following bolus administration of 0.25 mg/kg or 0.35 mg/kg diltiazem injectable, and reduction in heart rate, begin an i.v. infusion of diltiazem. The recommended initial infusion rate of diltiazem is 10 mg/hour. The infusion rate may be increased 5 mg/hour to 15 mg/hour as needed, if further reduction in heart rate is required. Some patients may maintain response to an initial rate of 5 mg/hour. The infusion may be maintained for up to 24 hours.

Diltiazem shows dose-dependent, non-linear pharmacokinetics during continuous i.v. infusion. Duration of infusion longer than 24 hours and infusion rates greater than 15 mg/hour have not been studied. Therefore, infusion duration exceeding 24 hours and infusion rates exceeding 15 mg/hour are not recommended.

Dilution: To prepare diltiazem for continuous i.v. infusion, aseptically transfer the appropriate quantity (see Table I) of diltiazem injectable to the desired volume of either Normal Saline, D5W, or D5W/0.45% NaCl. Mix thoroughly. Use within 24 hours. Keep refrigerated until use.

Cardizem injectable was tested for compatibility with 3 commonly used i.v. fluids at a maximal concentration of 1 mg diltiazem/mL. Cardizem injectable was found to be physically compatible and chemically stable in the following parenteral solutions for at least 24 hours when stored in glass or in polyvinylchloride (PVC) bags at a controlled room temperature of 15 to 30°C or under refrigeration at 2 to 8°C: dextrose (5%) injection, USP; sodium chloride (0.9%) injection, USP; dextrose (5%) and sodium chloride (0.45%) injection, USP.

Because of potential physical incompatibilities, Cardizem injectable should not be mixed with any other drugs in the same container.

Therefore, it is recommended that Cardizem injectable not be co-infused in the same i.v. line.

Physical incompatibilities (precipitate formation or cloudiness) were observed when Cardizem injectable was infused in the same i.v. line with the following drugs: acetazolamide, acyclovir, aminophylline, ampicillin, ampicillin sodium/sulbactam sodium, cefamandole, cefoperazone, diazepam, furosemide, hydrocortisone sodium succinate, insulin (regular; 100 units/mL), methylprednisolone sodium succinate, mezlocillin, nafcillin, phenytoin, rifampin, and sodium bicarbonate.

Parenteral drug products should be inspected visually for particulate matter and discoloration prior to administration, whenever solution and container permit.

Transition to Further Antiarrhythmic Therapy: Experience in the use of antiarrhythmic agents following diltiazem injectable is limited. In controlled clinical trials, therapy with antiarrhythmic agents to maintain reduced heart rate in atrial fibrillation or atrial flutter, or for prophylaxis of paroxysmal supraventricular tachycardia was generally started within 3 hours after bolus administration. Patients should be dosed on an individual basis and reference should be made to the respective manufacturer's product monograph for information relative to dosage and administration of antiarrhythmic agents.

Supplied: Each mL contains: diltiazem HCl 5 mg. Nonmedicinal ingredients: citric acid, hydrochloric acid, purified water, sodium citrate, sodium hydroxide and sorbitol. Sodium hydroxide or hydrochloric acid may be used for pH adjustment. No preservatives. Vials of 5 mL, packages of 4. Vials of 10 mL, packages of 4. Single use container. Discard unused portion.

Store under refrigeration, at 2 to 8°C. Do not freeze. It may be stored at room temperature for up to 1 month. Destroy after 1 month at room temperature.

Dilution for Continous I.V. Infusion: To prepare diltiazem for continuous i.v. infusion refer to Dosage section for diluent volumes, compatibility with i.v. fluids and stability of dilutions.

I.V. admixtures should be inspected visually for clarity, particulate matter, precipitate, discoloration and leakage prior to administration whenever solution and container permit.

Reviewed 1999

CARDURA-1™ Ⓟ
CARDURA-2™ Ⓟ
CARDURA-4™ Ⓟ

Astra

Doxazosin Mesylate

Antihypertensive Agent—Symptomatic Treatment of Benign Prostatic Hyperplasia (BPH)

Pharmacology: The mechanism of action of doxazosin is selective blockade of $alpha_1$ subtype of post-synaptic, post-junctional alpha-adrenergic receptors.

Pharmacodynamics: Hypertension: Administration of doxazosin results in a reduction in systemic vascular resistance. In patients with hypertension there is little change in cardiac output. Maximum reductions in blood pressure usually occur 2 to 6 hours after dosing and are associated with a small increase in standing heart rate. Doxazosin has a greater effect on blood pressure and heart rate in the standing position. Tolerance has not been observed in long-term therapy.

Systolic and diastolic blood pressure is lowered in both the supine and standing positions. In clinical trials, blood pressure responses were measured at the end of the dosing interval (24 hours), with the usual supine response 6 to 11 mmHg systolic and 5 to 9 mmHg diastolic. The response in the standing position tended to be larger by 3 to 5 mmHg. Peak blood pressure effects (1 to 6 hours) were larger by about 50 to 75% (i.e., trough values were about 55 to 70% of peak effect), with the larger peak-trough differences seen in systolic pressures. There was no apparent difference in the blood pressure response of Caucasians and Blacks or of patients above and below age 65.

During controlled clinical studies, predominantly normocholesterolemic patients receiving doxazosin had small but statistically significant reductions in total serum cholesterol (2.7%) and LDL cholesterol (4.3%), and increase in the HDL/total cholesterol ratio (4.3%) relative to placebo. No significant changes were observed in high-density lipoprotein fraction and triglycerides compared to placebo.

Benign Prostatic Hyperplasia (BPH): Benign Prostatic Hyperplasia (BPH) is a common cause of urinary outflow obstruction in aging males. Severe BPH may lead to urinary retention and renal damage. A static and a dynamic component contribute to the symptoms and reduced urinary flow rate associated with BPH. The static component is related to an increase in prostate size caused, in part, by a proliferation of smooth muscle cells in the prostatic stroma. However, the severity of BPH symptoms and the degree of urethral obstruction do not correlate well with the size of the prostate. The dynamic component of BPH is associated with an increase in smooth muscle tone in the prostate and bladder neck. The degree of tone in this area is mediated by the $alpha_1$ adrenoceptor which is present in high density in the prostatic stroma, prostatic capsule and bladder neck. Blockage of the $alpha_1$ receptor decreases urethral resistance and may relieve the obstruction and BPH symptoms. In 30 to 70% of patients with symptomatic BPH, placebo has also shown a remarkable and sometimes dramatic effect in controlled short-term studies. The symptoms may subside or fade away without treatment in approximately 20% of patients.

Doxazosin antagonizes phenylephrine-induced contractions, in vitro, in the human prostate. Doxazosin is bound with high affinity to the $alpha_{1A}$-adrenoceptor subtype, thought to be the predominant functional type in the prostate.

The effect of doxazosin in BPH is thought to result from selective blockade of the $alpha_{1A}$-adrenoceptors located in the prostatic muscular stroma, capsule and bladder neck. This action results in relief of the urinary outlet obstruction and symptomatology associated with BPH.

In controlled clinical trials in over 900 patients, the efficacy of doxazosin was evaluated. In 2 studies doxazosin 4 to 8 mg once daily significantly improved maximum urinary flow rate (MFR) 2.3 to 3.3 mL/s (placebo 0.1 to 0.7 mL/s). Significant improvements were usually noticed within 2 weeks of commencing doxazosin treatment and a significantly larger proportion of patients (32 to 42%) responded with MFR improvements $\geq$3 mL/s (placebo 13 to 17%). As well, average flow rate also improved with doxazosin, 1.3 to 2.1 mL/s (placebo 0.2 to 0.3 mL/s). Doxazosin also resulted in a significant relief of the obstructive and irritative symptoms associated with BPH.

Using invasive urodynamics in a controlled clinical trial in 43 BPH patients, doxazosin 2 mg improved MFR 3.4 mL/s, and reduced urethral resistance 7.5 to 13.5 cmH_2O (placebo, MFR-0.6 mL/s and resistance of 3.3 cmH_2O).

In a 29 week controlled BPH trial in 100 patients, doxazosin was significantly more effective than placebo in improving urinary flow rates and reducing BPH symptoms; the effect was sustained over the entire treatment period. No tolerance to the effect of doxazosin on urodynamics or BPH symptomatology was observed in patients treated for up to 4 years in open-label studies.

Both hypertensive and normotensive BPH patients treated with doxazosin demonstrate statistically significant improvements in urodynamics and symptomatology compared to placebo.

Pharmacokinetics: After oral administration of therapeutic doses of doxazosin absorption occurs with peak blood levels at about 2 hours. Bioavailability is approximately 65%. Food has little or no effect on the bioavailability.

Approximately 98% of the circulating drug is bound to plasma proteins. Plasma elimination is biphasic with a terminal elimination half-life of about 22 hours. There is accumulation of plasma levels of doxazosin following steady state dosing, consistent with the terminal elimination half-life.

In a study of elderly hypertensive patients the pharmacokinetic parameters of doxazosin at steady state were similar to those observed in a previous study of young and elderly healthy subjects who received a single oral dose of doxazosin.

In a cross-over study in 24 normotensive subjects, the pharmacokinetics and safety of doxazosin were shown to be similar with morning and evening dosing regimens. Doxazosin may, therefore, be administered as a single daily morning or evening dose (see Dosage).

Doxazosin is extensively metabolized, mainly by 0-demethylation of the quinazoline nucleus or hydroxylation of the benzodioxan moiety. Excretion is mainly via the feces with 9% of the dose excreted in urine as doxazosin (<0.5%) or metabolites. Less than 5% is excreted as the unchanged drug, mainly in the feces.

The disposition of doxazosin in patients with renal insufficiency is similar to that in patients with normal renal function Only limited data are available in patients with liver impairment (see Precautions, Patients with Impaired Liver Function).

Indications: Hypertension: In the treatment of mild to moderate essential hypertension. It is employed in a general treatment program in association with a thiazide diuretic and/or other antihypertensive agents, as needed for proper patient response.

Doxazosin may be tried as a sole therapy in those patients in whom treatment with other agents caused adverse effects or is inappropriate.

Benign Prostatic Hyperplasia (BPH): Doxazosin is also indicated for the treatment of symptoms of benign prostatic hyperplasia (BPH). The onset of effect is rapid, with improvement in peak flow and symptoms observed within 1 to 2 weeks. The effect on these variables was maintained over the entire study duration (up to 4 years). Doxazosin may be used in BPH patients who are either hypertensive or normotensive.

Cardura (cont'd)

A number of clinical conditions can mimic symptomatic BPH (i.e. stricture of urethra, stricture of bladder neck, urinary bladder stones, neurogenic bladder dysfunction secondary to diabetes, Parkinsonism, etc.). These conditions should therefore be ruled out before doxazosin therapy is initiated.

Contraindications: Patients with a known sensitivity to doxazosin or quinazolines.

Warnings: Syncope and "First Dose" Effect: Doxazosin can cause marked hypotension, especially postural hypotension and syncope in association with the first dose or first few doses of therapy. A similar effect can occur if therapy is reinstated following interruption for more than a few doses. Postural effects are most likely to occur between 2 and 6 hours after dose.

In controlled studies of doxazosin the incidence of syncopal episodes was 0.7%. Initial dose of 1 mg/day resulted in a 4% incidence of postural side effects with no cases of syncope. In controlled clinical trials in BPH in normotensive patients, there was a 0.2% occurrence of syncope with doxazosin. In controlled trials in patients with both BPH and hypertension receiving doxazosin, the incidence of syncope was 0.8%.

The likelihood of syncopal episodes or excessive hypotension can be minimized by limiting the initial dose of doxazosin to 1 mg, by increasing the dosage slowly and by introducing any additional antihypertensive drugs into the patient's regimen with caution (see Dosage).

Occupational Hazards: Patients should be advised of the possibility of syncopal and orthostatic symptoms and to avoid driving or hazardous tasks for 24 hours after the initial dose of doxazosin after the dose is increased and after interruption of therapy when treatment is resumed. They should be cautioned to avoid situations where injury could result should syncope occur.

If syncope occurs, the patient should be placed in the supine position and if this measure is inadequate, volume expansion with i.v. fluids or vasopressor therapy may be used. A transient hypotensive response is not a contraindication to further doses of doxazosin.

Priapism: Rarely (probably less frequently than once in every several thousand patients), alpha$_1$-antagonists such as doxazosin have been associated with priapism. Because this condition can lead to permanent impotence if not promptly treated, patients should be advised about the seriousness of the condition.

Precautions: General: Doxazosin therapy does not modify the natural history of benign prostatic hyperplasia (BPH). It does not retard or stop the progression of BPH, nor does it improve urine flow sufficiently to significantly reduce the residual urine volume. However, significant reduction of the mean residual volume have been shown in patients with baseline residual volume of >50 mL. The patient may continue to be at risk of developing urinary retention and other BPH complications during doxazosin therapy.

Long-term Safety and Efficacy: The long-term safety and efficacy (i.e. >4 years) has not yet been established for the use of doxazosin in the treatment of benign prostatic hyperplasia.

Prostatic Cancer: Carcinoma of the prostate and BPH cause many of the same symptoms. These two diseases frequently coexist. Therefore, patients thought to have BPH should be examined prior to starting doxazosin therapy to rule out the presence of carcinoma of the prostate.

Doxazosin should not be used in patients with PSA >10 ng/mL unless cancer of the prostate has been ruled out.

Orthostatic Hypotension: While syncope is the most severe orthostatic effect of doxazosin (see Warnings), other symptoms of lowered blood pressure such as dizziness, lightheadedness or vertigo can occur. These were common in clinical trials in hypertension, occurring in up to 23% of all patients treated and causing discontinuation of therapy in about 2%. In placebo controlled titration trials there was an increased frequency of orthostatic effects in patients given 8 mg or more, 10% compared to 5% at 1 to 4 mg and 3% in the placebo group.

In placebo controlled trials in BPH, the incidence of orthostatic hypotension with doxazosin was ≤1%. With maintenance doses of up to 8 mg/day in normotensive patients with BPH, the average decreases in both sitting and standing blood pressure were small: 5/2 mm Hg with doxazosin and 1/1 mm Hg with placebo.

Patients with occupations in which such events represent potential problems should be treated with particular caution.

Patients should be advised of the need to lie down when symptoms of lowered blood pressure occur and to be careful when arising from a lying position. If dizziness, lightheadedness or palpitations are bothersome, they should be reported to the physician so that dose adjustment can be considered. Patients should also be told that drowsiness or somnolence can occur with doxazosin, requiring caution in people who must drive or operate heavy machinery.

If hypotension occurs, place the patient in the recumbent position and institute supportive measures as necessary.

Patients with Impaired Liver Function: As with any drug wholly metabolized by the liver, doxazosin should be administered with caution to patients with evidence of impaired hepatic function or to patients receiving drugs known to influence hepatic metabolism.

Patients with Impaired Renal Function: The use of doxazosin in patients with impaired renal function requires careful monitoring. Clinical studies indicate that the disposition of doxazosin in patients with renal insufficiency is similar to that in patients with normal renal function, however accumulation of the drug with chronic dosing may occur. Less than 10% of the dose of doxazosin is excreted in the urine as unchanged drug and metabolites.

Concomitant Conditions: Doxazosin should not be prescribed to patients with symptomatic BPH who have the following concomitant conditions:

Chronic urinary retention, high residual urine (over 200 mL), peak urine flow of 5 mL/s or less, history of prior prostatic surgery, chronic fibrous or granulomatous prostatitis, urethral stricture, history of pelvic irradiation, presence of prostatic calculi, presence of large median lobe of prostate, presence of calculi in urinary bladder, recent history of epididymitis, gross hematuria, presence of neurogenic bladder dysfunction (diabetes mellitus, parkinsonism, uninhibited neurogenic bladder, etc.), hydronephrosis, presence of carcinoma of the prostate.

Patients with recent history of myocardial infarction, transient ischemic attacks, or cerebrovascular accident within the past 6 months.

Pregnancy: There are no studies in pregnant women. Doxazosin is not recommended in pregnant women unless the potential benefit outweighs the potential risk to mother and fetus.

Doxazosin crosses the placental barrier.

Studies in pregnant rabbits and rats at daily oral doses of up to 40 and 20 mg/kg respectively have revealed no evidence of teratogenic effect. A dosage regimen of 82 mg/kg/day in the rabbit was associated with reduced fetal survival, an increase in embryomortality as well as increases in fetal and placental weights.

In peri-postnatal studies in rats, postnatal development at maternal doses of 40 or 50 mg/kg/day of doxazosin was delayed as evidenced by slower body weight gain and a slightly later appearance of anatomical features and reflexes.

Lactation: Studies in lactating rats indicate that doxazosin accumulates in rat breast milk. It is not known whether this drug is excreted in human milk. Caution should be exercised when doxazosin is administered to a nursing mother and in general, nursing should be interrupted.

Children: The use of doxazosin is not recommended in children since safety and efficacy have not been established.

Geriatrics: Doxazosin should be used cautiously in elderly patients because of the possibility of postural hypotension. There was an age-related trend towards an increased incidence of postural hypotension and postural dizziness in elderly hypertensive patients treated with this drug.

Peripheral Edema: Fluid retention resulting in weight gain may occur during doxazosin therapy. In placebo controlled monotherapy trials, patients receiving doxazosin gained a mean of 0.6 kg compared to a mean loss of 0.1 kg for placebo patients. The overall incidence of body weight gain reported as a side effect in controlled clinical trials was 0.8%.

Leukopenia/Neutropenia: Analysis of hematologic data from patients receiving doxazosin in controlled clinical trials showed that the mean white blood cell (WBC) (N=474) and mean neutrophil counts (N=419) were decreased by 2.4% and 1.0% respectively, compared to placebo. A search through a data base of 2 400 patients revealed 4 cases in which drug-related neutropenia could not be ruled out. Two had a single low value on the last day of treatment. Two had stable, non-progressive neutrophil counts in the 1 000/mm^3 range over periods of 20 and 40 weeks. No patients became symptomatic as a result of the low WBC or neutrophil counts.

In BPH patients the incidence of clinically significant WBC abnormalities was 0.4% with doxazosin.

Cardiac Toxicity in Animals: An increased incidence of myocardial necrosis or fibrosis was displayed by Sprague-Dawley rats after 6 months of dietary administration at concentrations calculated to provide 80 mg doxazosin/kg/day and after 12 months of dietary administration at concentrations calculated to provide 40 mg doxazosin/kg/day.

Myocardial fibrosis was observed in both rats and mice treated in the same manner with 40 mg doxazosin/kg/day for 18 months. No cardiotoxicity was observed at lower doses (up to 10 or 20 mg/kg/day, depending on the study) in either species.

These lesions were not observed after 12 months of oral dosing in dogs and Wistar rats at maximum doses of 20 and 100 mg/kg/day respectively. There is no evidence that similar lesions occur in humans.

Carcinogenesis, Mutagenesis and Impairment of Fertility: Chronic dietary administration (up to 24 months) of doxazosin at maximally tolerated concentrations (highest dose 40 mg/kg/day) revealed no evidence of carcinogenicity in rats. There was also no evidence of carcinogenicity in a similarly conducted study (up to 18 months of dietary administration) in mice. The mouse study, however, was compromised by the failure to use a maximally tolerated dose of doxazosin. A subsequent 24 month dietary study of doxazosin at maximally tolerated concentrations (highest dose 120 mg/kg/day) showed no carcinogenic effect in mice.

Mutagenicity studies revealed no drug or metabolite related effects at either chromosomal or subchromosomal levels.

Studies in rats showed reduced fertility in males treated with doxazosin at oral doses of 20 (but not 5 or 10) mg/kg/day. This effect was reversible within 2 weeks of drug withdrawal.

Drug Interactions: Doxazosin is highly (98%) bound to plasma protein. In vitro data in human plasma indicates that doxazosin has no effect on protein binding of digoxin, warfarin, phenytoin or indomethacin.

Doxazosin has been administered to patients receiving thiazide diuretics, beta-adrenergic blocking agents and nonsteroidal anti-inflammatory drugs. No unexpected interactions were reported. An additive hypotensive effect was observed when doxazosin was coadministered with thiazide diuretics and beta-adrenergic blocking agents. There is limited experience with doxazosin in combination with ACE inhibitors or calcium channel blockers.

Digoxin: Serum digoxin concentrations were not affected by treatment with doxazosin.

Cimetidine: In a randomized, open-label, cross-over study in 22 male subjects, the single coadministration of 1 mg doxazosin with 400 mg b.i.d. cimetidine resulted in a 10% increase in mean AUC of doxazosin (p=0.006) and a slight but not statistically significant increase in mean C_{max} and mean half-life of doxazosin. The effect of further administration of cimetidine has not been studied.

Adverse Effects: Hypertension: Doxazosin has been administered to approximately 4 000 patients in clinical trials of whom 1 679 patients were included in controlled trials. The most serious adverse reaction occurring in the controlled clinical trials was syncope occurring in 0.7% of patients and resulting in a discontinuation rate of 0.2%.

The most frequent adverse reactions in controlled clinical trials were: headache (16.5%), fatigue/malaise (14.8%), dizziness (14.6%), postural dizziness (8.7%) and edema (6.6%). Discontinuation of doxazosin due to adverse reactions was required in 7% of patients.

The following other adverse reactions occurred with an incidence of ≥0.5% in the controlled clinical trials program (n=1 679): Cardiovascular: palpitation (3.6%); vertigo (3.0%); tachycardia (1.6%); postural hypotension (0.9%); arrhythmia (0.8%); syncope (0.7%).

Skin and Appendages: rash (1.7%); pruritus (0.8%).

Musculoskeletal: myalgia (1.3%); arthralgia (0.8%).

Nervous System: somnolence (4.9%); sexual dysfunction (3.5%); dry mouth (3.4%); anxiety/nervousness (2.3%); insomnia (2.2%); paresthesia (1.7%); depression/apathy (1.6%); increased sweating (1.4%); hypoesthesia (1.6%); agitation (0.7%); flushing (0.7%); tremor (0.6%); paroniria (0.5%).

Special Senses: vision/accommodation abnormality (2.4%); conjunctivitis/eye pain (1.2%); tinnitus (0.8%).

Gastrointestinal: nausea (3.9%); diarrhea (2.9%); dyspepsia (2.1%) abdominal pain (1.6%); flatulence (1.4%); constipation (1.3%); vomiting (0.7%).

Respiratory: dyspnea (3.9%); rhinitis (3.0%); epistaxis (0.8%); sinusitis (0.6%); bronchospasm/bronchitis (0.5%).

Urinary: micturition frequency (1.2%); polyuria (1.0%); urinary incontinence (0.8%); urinary disorder (0.7%).

General Body: chest pain (2.7%); asthenia (2.7%); muscle cramps (1.7%); pain (1.3%); face edema (0.8%); weight increase (0.8%); general edema (0.5%).

Hematology: decreases in platelets (3.9%), white blood cell (2.4%), hematocrit (1.6%), hemoglobin (1.4%), neutrophil count (1.0%) (see Precautions).

The following additional adverse reactions were reported in at least 2 but <0.5% of 1 679 patients who received doxazosin in the controlled clinical trials program:

Cardiovascular: angina pectoris, peripheral ischemia, hypotension.

Nervous System: paresis, twitching, migraine, amnesia, movement disorders, emotional lability, abnormal thinking, depersonalization, pallor, hypertonia, ataxia.

Metabolic: thirst, gout, hypokalemia.

Hematopoietic: lymphadenopathy, purpura.

Reproductive: breast pain.

Skin Disorders: alopecia, dry skin, eczema.

Special Senses: taste perversion, photophobia, abnormal lacrimation.

Gastrointestinal: increased appetite, anorexia, fecal incontinence.

Respiratory: coughing, pharyngitis.

General Body: hot flushes, back pain, infection, fever/rigors, muscle weakness.

In uncontrolled trials or postmarketing experience the following occurred with an incidence of less than 0.5%: myocardial infarction, cerebrovascular accident, confusion, impaired concentration, pallor, parosmia, earache, tinnitus, renal calculus, influenza-like symptoms, priapism, jaundice.

No clinically relevant adverse effects were noted on serum potassium, serum glucose, uric acid, urea nitrogen or creatinine. Doxazosin has been associated with decreases in white blood cell count (see Precautions). Isolated cases of elevated liver transaminases have occurred.

Benign Prostatic Hyperplasia: Doxazosin has been administered once daily to 665 both hypertensive and normotensive patients with BPH in controlled clinical trials. The most serious adverse reaction occurring in the controlled trials was syncope (0.5%).

The most frequent adverse reactions in controlled trials were dizziness (15.6%), headache (9.8%) and fatigue (8%).

Discontinuation rate of doxazosin due to adverse reactions was 9%.

The following other adverse reactions occurred with an incidence of ≥0.5% in the controlled clinical BPH trials (n=665 doxazosin patients):

Cardiovascular: dizziness (15.6%); edema (2.7%); hypotension (1.7%); palpitation (1.2%); tachycardia (0.9%); angina (0.6%); syncope (0.5%); postural hypotension (0.3%).

Skin and Appendages: increased sweating (1.1%); pruritus (0.5%); rash (0.5%).

Musculoskeletal: myalgia (0.6%).

Central and Peripheral Nervous System: headache (9.8%); paresthesia (0.6%).

Autonomic: dry mouth (1.4%); flushing (0.6%).

Special Senses: abnormal vision (1.4%); conjunctivitis (0.5%); tinnitus (0.5%).

Psychiatric: somnolence (3.0%); insomnia (1.2%); anxiety (1.1%); libido decrease (0.8%); depression (0.6%); nervousness (0.5%).

Gastrointestinal: diarrhea (2.3%); abdominal pain (2.3%); dyspepsia (1.8%); nausea (1.5%); flatulence (0.8%).

Respiratory: dyspnea (2.6%); respiratory disorder (1.1%); rhinitis (0.8%); epistaxis (0.6%).

Reproductive Disorders: impotence (1.1%).

Neoplasm: carcinoma (0.5%).

Urinary: urinary tract infection (1.2%); dysuria (0.5%).

General: fatigue (8%); pain (2%); back pain (1.8%); chest pain (1.2%); asthenia (0.8%); influenza-like symptoms (0.8%); viral infection (0.6%); fever (0.5%); weight increase (0.5%); malaise (0.5%).

Additional adverse reactions have been reported, but these are, in general, not distinguishable from symptoms that might have occurred in the absence of exposure to doxazosin.

The following additional adverse reactions were reported by <0.5% of 665 patients who received doxazosin in controlled or open, short- or long-term clinical studies:

Cardiovascular: myocardial infarction, bradycardia, sudden death.

Autonomic Nervous System: pallor.

Metabolic: hyperglycemia, gout.

Hematopoietic: lymphadenopathy.

Reproductive: prostatic disorder, ejaculation failure, epididymitis.

Skin Disorders: dry skin, genital pruritus, urticaria, maculopapular rash, erythematous rash, aggravated psoriasis, eczema.

CNS: hypoesthesia, hypertonia, leg cramps, confusion, speech disorder, ataxia.

Psychiatric: abnormal thinking, depersonalization, paroniria, emotional lability, impaired concentration, amnesia.

Special Senses: earache, taste perversion, eye pain, visual field defect, cataract.

Gastrointestinal: melena, constipation, vomiting, gingivitis, increased appetite.

Respiratory: coughing, bronchospasm, bronchitis, upper respiratory tract infection, sinusitis, pneumonia.

Urinary: urinary retention, micturition disorder, abnormal urine, renal pain, urinary incontinence, cystitis.

Musculoskeletal: arthritis, tendon disorder, arthralgia, hernia.

General Body: rigors, hot flushes, allergy, sepsis, fungal infection.

Platelet Bleeding and Clotting Disorder: hematuria, subarachanoid hemorrhage.

Data from long-term (up to 50 months), open BPH studies (n=450) indicate a higher rate of dizziness in younger hypertensive (27%) and normotensive (22%) patients, impotence in younger hypertensive (8%) patients, and discontinuation rates in patients due to adverse events (16.7%) compared to data from short-term placebo-controlled BPH studies (n=665).

A summary of selected adverse events, with an incidence of 1.0%, experienced by patients treated with doxazosin in short-term placebo-controlled and long-term, open clinical trials is outlined in Table I.

Table I—Cardura

Summary of Adverse Event Data

The data listed in the table, "From Short-Term Placebo-Controlled Clinical Trials", was presented earlier in the product monograph. The data listed "From Long-Term Open Clinical Trials—BPH Only" was calculated from data generated in multicentre, open-label extensions of 3 double blind placebo-controlled BPH studies.

Adverse Events	From Short-Term[a], Placebo-Controlled Clinical Trials		From Long-Term[b], Open Clinical Trials
	Hypertensives Only (n=1 679)	BPH Only (normotensive and hypertensive patients) (n=665)	BPH Only (normotensive and hypertensive patients) (n=450)
Incidence of Adverse Events	49.0%	45.0%	66.0%
Dizziness	14.6%	15.6%	20.7%
Postural Dizziness	8.7%	NR	NR
Headache	16.5%	9.8%	12.2%
Fatigue	14.8%	8.0%	11.6%
Pain	1.3%	2.0%	5.1%
Somnolence	4.9%	3.0%	4.9%
Edema	6.6%	2.7%	3.6%
Impotence	NR	1.1%	4.9%
Sexual Dysfunction	3.5%	NR	<1.0%
Patients Discontinued (due to any adverse event)	7.0%	9.0%	16.7%

[a] Treated with doxazosin from 1 to 203 days (approx. 7 months).
[b] Treated with doxazosin from 1 to approx. 1 500 days (50 months).
Legend: NR=not reported.

Overdose: Symptoms and Treatment: No data are available in regard to overdosage with doxazosin in humans.

Should administration of doxazosin lead to hypotension, support of the cardiovascular system is of first importance. Restoration of blood pressure and normalization of heart rate may be accomplished by keeping the patient in the supine position. If this measure is inadequate, shock should first be treated with volume expanders. If necessary, vasopressors should be used. Renal function should be monitored and supported as needed. As doxazosin is highly protein bound, dialysis may not be of benefit.

Dosage: Dosage must be individualized.

The absorption of doxazosin is not affected by food.

When doxazosin is being added to the existing antihypertensive therapy, the patient should be carefully monitored for the occurrence of hypotension. If a diuretic or other antihypertensive agent is being added to doxazosin regimen, dosage reduction of doxazosin and retitration with careful monitoring may be necessary.

If doxazosin administration is discontinued for several days or longer, therapy should be reinstituted using the initial dosing regimen.

Hypertension: 1 to 16 mg Once Daily: The initial dose of doxazosin in patients with hypertension is 1 mg given once daily and this dose should not be exceeded. This starting dose is intended to minimize postural hypotensive effects. The maximum reduction in blood pressure normally occurs between 2 and 6 hours after a dose.

The dose may be slowly increased to achieve the desired blood pressure response. The usual dose range is 1 to 8 mg once daily. The maximum recommended daily dose is 16 mg once daily.

Increases in dose beyond 4 mg increased the likelihood of excessive postural effects including syncope, postural dizziness/vertigo and postural hypotension. At a titrated dose of 16 mg once daily, the frequency of postural effects is about 12% compared to 3% for placebo.

Benign Prostatic Hyperplasia: 1 to 8 mg Once Daily: The initial dosage of doxazosin is 1 mg given once daily. Depending on the individual patient's urodynamics and BPH symptomatology, dosage may then be increased to 2 mg and thereafter to 4 mg and 8 mg once daily, the maximum recommended dose. The recommended titration interval is 1 to 2 weeks. Blood pressure should be evaluated routinely in these patients.

Doxazosin should be discontinued if the drug has been increased to the maximum tolerated dose and improvement in urinary flowmetry is less than 25% or if doxazosin side effects are more bothersome than BPH symptoms or if the patient develops a urinary complication secondary to BPH while on doxazosin therapy.

Information for the Patient: See Blue Section—Information for the Patient "Cardura-1/Cardura-2/Cardura-4".

Supplied: 1 mg: Each white tablet, engraved ASTRA on one side and CARDURA with 1 on the other side, contains: doxazosin mesylate equivalent to doxazosin 1 mg. Nonmedicinal ingredients: lactose, magnesium stearate, microcrystalline cellulose, sodium lauryl sulfate and sodium starch glycolate. Gluten- and tartrazine-free. Opaque plastic (high density polyethylene) bottles of 100.

2 mg: Each white tablet, engraved ASTRA on one side and CARDURA with 2 on the other side, contains: doxazosin mesylate equivalent to doxazosin 2 mg. Nonmedicinal ingredients: lactose, magnesium stearate, microcrystalline cellulose, sodium lauryl sulfate and sodium starch glycolate. Gluten- and tartrazine-free. Opaque plastic (high density polyethylene) bottles of 100.

4 mg: Each white tablet, engraved ASTRA on one side and CARDURA with 4 on the other side, contains: doxazosin mesylate equivalent to doxazosin 4 mg. Nonmedicinal ingredients: lactose, magnesium stearate, microcrystalline cellulose, sodium lauryl sulfate and sodium starch glycolate. Gluten- and tartrazine-free. Opaque plastic (high density polyethylene) bottles of 100.

Store at room temperature, 15 to 30°C.

(Shown in Product Recognition Section)

Reviewed 1999

CARNITOR® Ⓟ

Sigma-Tau

Levocarnitine

Carnitine Replenisher

Pharmacology: Levocarnitine is a naturally occurring substance required in mammalian energy metabolism. It has been

Carnitor (cont'd)

shown to facilitate long-chain fatty acid entry into cellular mitochondria, therefore delivering substrate for oxidation and subsequent energy production. Fatty acids are utilized as an energy substrate in all tissues except the brain. In skeletal and cardiac muscle they serve as major fuel. Primary systemic carnitine deficiency is characterized by low plasma, RBC, and/or tissue levels. It has not been possible to determine which symptoms are due to carnitine deficiency and which are due to the underlying organic acidemia, as symptoms of both abnormalities may be expected to improve with carnitine. The literature reports that carnitine can promote the excretion of excess organic or fatty acids in patients with defects in fatty acid metabolism and/or specific organic acidopathies that bioaccumulate acyl CoA esters.

Secondary carnitine deficiency can be a consequence of inborn errors of metabolism. Levocarnitine may alleviate the metabolic abnormalities of patients with inborn errors that result in accumulation of toxic organic acids. Conditions for which this effect was demonstrated are: glutaric aciduria II, methylmalonic aciduria, propionic acidemia, and medium chain fatty acyl CoA dehydrogenase deficiency. Autointoxication occurs in these patients due to the accumulations of acyl CoA compounds that disrupt intermediary metabolism. The subsequent hydrolysis of the acyl CoA compound to its free acid results in acidosis that can be life threatening. Levocarnitine clears the acyl CoA compound by formation of acyl carnitine which is quickly excreted. Levocarnitine deficiency is defined biochemically as abnormally low plasma levels of free carnitine, less than 20 μmol/L at age greater than 1 week post-term and may be associated with low tissue and/or urine levels. Further, this condition may be associated with a ratio of plasma ester/free levocarnitine levels greater than 0.4 or abnormally elevated levels of esterified levocarnitine in the urine. In premature infants and newborns, secondary deficiency is defined as plasma free levocarnitine levels below age related normal levels.

Indications: In the treatment of primary systemic carnitine deficiency. In the reported cases, the clinical presentation consisted of recurrent episodes of Reye-like encephalopathy, hypoketotic hypoglycemia, and/or cardiomyopathy. Associated symptoms included hypotonia, muscle weakness and failure to thrive. A diagnosis of primary carnitine deficiency requires that serum, red cell and/or tissue carnitine levels be low and that the patient does not have a primary defect in fatty acid or organic acid oxidation (see Pharmacology). In some patients, particularly those presenting with cardiomyopathy, carnitine supplementation rapidly alleviated signs and symptoms. Treatment should include, in addition to carnitine, supportive and other therapy as indicated by the condition of the patient.

Levocarnitine is also indicated for acute and chronic treatments of patients with an inborn error of metabolism that results in a secondary carnitine deficiency.

Contraindications: None known.

Warnings: None.

Precautions: General: Oral Solution: For oral/internal use only. Gastrointestinal reactions may result from too rapid consumption of carnitine. The oral solution may be consumed alone, or dissolved in drinks or other liquid foods to reduce taste fatigue. It should be consumed slowly and doses should be spaced evenly throughout the day to maximize tolerance.

The injection is for i.v. use only.

Pregnancy: Category B: Reproductive studies have been performed in rats and rabbits at doses up to 3.8 times the human dose on the basis of surface area and have revealed no evidence of impaired fertility or harm to the fetus due to levocarnitine. There are, however, no adequate and well controlled studies in pregnant women. Because animal reproduction studies are not always predictive of human response, this drug should be used during pregnancy only if clearly needed.

Lactation: It is not known whether this drug is excreted in human milk. Because many drugs are excreted in human milk, a decision should be made whether to discontinue nursing or to discontinue the drug, taking into account the importance of the drug to the mother.

Adverse Effects: Seizures have been reported to occur in patients with or without pre-existing seizure activity receiving either oral or i.v. levocarnitine. In patients with pre-existing seizure activity, an increase in seizure frequency has been reported.

Injection: Transient nausea and vomiting have been observed. Less frequent adverse reactions are body odor, nausea, and gastritis. An incidence for these reactions is difficult to estimate due to the confounding effects of the underlying pathology.

Oral Solution and Tablets: Various mild gastrointestinal complaints have been reported during the long-term administration of oral L- or D,L-carnitine; these include transient nausea and vomiting, abdominal cramps, and diarrhea. Mild myasthenia has been described only in uremic patients receiving D,L-carnitine. Gastrointestinal adverse reactions with levocarnitine oral solution dissolved in liquids might be avoided by a slow consumption of the solution or by a greater dilution. Decreasing the dosage often diminishes or eliminates drug-related patient body odor or gastrointestinal symptoms when present. Tolerance should be monitored very closely during the first week of administration, and after any dosage increases.

Overdose: Symptoms and Treatment: There have been no reports of toxicity from carnitine overdosage. The oral LD_{50} of levocarnitine in mice is 19.2 g/kg. Carnitine may cause diarrhea. Overdosage should be treated with supportive care.

Dosage: Injection: Children and Adults: Administered i.v. The recommended dose is 50 mg/kg given as a slow 2 to 3 minute bolus injection or by infusion. Often a loading dose is given in patients with severe metabolic crisis followed by an equivalent dose over the following 24 hours. It should be administered q3h or q4h, and never less than q6h either by infusion or by i.v. injection. All subsequent daily doses are recommended to be in the range of 50 mg/kg or as therapy may require. The highest dose administered has been 300 mg/kg.

It is recommended that a plasma carnitine level be obtained prior to beginning this parenteral therapy. Weekly and monthly monitoring is recommended as well. This monitoring should include blood chemistries, vital signs, plasma carnitine concentrations (the plasma free carnitine level should be between 35 and 60 μmol/L at baseline) and overall clinical condition.

Parenteral drug products should be inspected visually for particulate matter and discoloration prior to administration, whenever solution and container permit.

Compatibility and Stability: Injection is compatible and stable when mixed in parenteral solutions of sodium chloride 0.9% or lactated Ringers' in concentrations ranging from 250 mg/500 mL (0.5 mg/mL) to 4 200 mg/500 mL (8 mg/mL) and stored at room temperature (25°C) for up to 24 hours in PVC plastic bags.

Oral Solution: For oral use only. **Not for parenteral use.**

Adults: 1 to 3 g/day for a 50 kg subject which is equivalent to 10 to 30 mL/day oral solution. Higher doses should be administered only with caution and only where clinical and biochemical considerations make it seem likely that higher doses will be of benefit. Dosage should start at 1 g/day, (10 mL/day), and be increased slowly while assessing tolerance and therapeutic response. Monitoring should include periodic blood chemistries, vital signs, plasma carnitine concentrations, and overall clinical condition.

Infants and Children: 50 to 100 mg/kg/day which is equivalent to 0.5 mL/kg/day oral solution. Higher doses should be administered only with caution and only where clinical and biochemical considerations make it seem likely that higher doses will be of benefit. Dosage should start at 50 mg/kg/day, and be increased slowly to a maximum of 3 g/day (30 mL/day) while assessing tolerance and therapeutic response. Monitoring should include periodic blood chemistries, vital signs, plasma carnitine concentrations, and overall clinical condition.

Oral solution may be consumed alone or dissolved in drinks or other liquid food. Doses should be spaced evenly throughout the day (every 3 or 4 hours) preferably during or following meals and should be consumed slowly in order to maximize tolerance.

Tablets: For oral administration only.

Adults: The recommended oral dosage is 990 mg 2 or 3 times a day using the 330 mg tablets, depending on clinical response.

Infants and Children: The recommended oral dosage is between 50 and 100 mg/kg/day in divided doses, with a maximum of 3 g/day. Dosage should begin at 50 mg/kg/day. The exact dosage will depend on clinical response.

Monitoring should include periodic blood chemistries, vital signs, plasma carnitine concentrations and overall clinical condition.

Supplied: Injection: Each mL of sterile, aqueous solution, **for i.v. use only,** contains: levocarnitine 200 mg. pH adjusted to 6.0 to 6.5 with hydrochloric acid. Preservative-free (levocarnitine will support microbial growth). Single dose ampuls of 2.5 and 5 mL, cartons of 5. Store at room temperature in the carton until use to protect from light. Avoid excessive heat. Protect from freezing. Discard unused portion after opening.

Oral Solution: Each 10 mL of clear, cherry flavored solution, **for oral use only,** contains: levocarnitine 1 g. Nonmedicinal ingredients: artificial cherry flavor, D,L-malic acid, methyl- and propylparaben (as preservatives), purified water and sucrose syrup. pH is approximately 5. Multiple-unit plastic containers of 118 mL, cases of 24. Store at room temperature. Avoid excessive heat. Protect from freezing. Store upright.

Tablets: Each white, biconvex tablet, embossed with "CARNITOR ST", **for oral use only,** contains: levocarnitine 330 mg. Nonmedicinal ingredients: magnesium stearate, microcrystalline cellulose and povidone. Single unit blisters of laminated aluminum foil in cards of 10, cartons of 90 (9 cards/carton). Store at room temperature. Avoid excessive heat. Protect from freezing. Do not store after removal from foil packaging: contents hygroscopic.

Reviewed 1997

CASODEX® ℞

Zeneca

Bicalutamide

Nonsteroidal Antiandrogen

Pharmacology: Bicalutamide is a nonsteroidal antiandrogen, devoid of other endocrine activity. Bicalutamide competitively inhibits the action of androgens by binding to cytosol androgen receptors in target tissue. This inhibition results in regression of prostatic tumors. Bicalutamide is a racemate and the (R)-enantiomer is primarily responsible for the antiandrogenic activity of bicalutamide.

Pharmacokinetics: The absorption, distribution, metabolism and excretion of bicalutamide has been investigated after administration of a single 50 mg oral dose to volunteers. The results indicated that the dose was extensively absorbed and was excreted almost equally in urine (36%) and feces (43%) over a 9-day collection period. There is no evidence of any clinically significant effect of food on bioavailability. Steady state plasma concentrations of the (R)-enantiomer of approximately 9 μg/mL are observed during daily administration of 50 mg doses of bicalutamide. At steady state, the active (R)-enantiomer accounts for 99% of the circulating plasma bicalutamide concentration. Bicalutamide is highly protein bound (96%). On daily administration, the (R)-enantiomer accumulates about 10-fold in plasma, consistent with an elimination half-life of approximately 1 week. The (S)-enantiomer is very rapidly cleared relative to the (R)-enantiomer. At the 50 mg/day dose, the pharmacokinetics of the (R)-enantiomer are unaffected by age, renal impairment or mild to moderate hepatic impairment. Patients with severe hepatic impairment eliminate the (R)-enantiomer from plasma more slowly. Bicalutamide is extensively metabolized via both oxidation and glucuronidation with approximately equal renal and biliary elimination of the metabolites.

Clinical Experience: In a large multicentre, controlled clinical trial, 813 patients with previously untreated advanced prostate cancer were randomized to receive bicalutamide 50 mg once daily (404 patients) or flutamide 250 mg (409 patients) 3 times a day, each in combination with LHRH analogues (either goserelin acetate implant or leuprolide acetate depot). At a median follow-up of 49 weeks, bicalutamide-LHRH analogue therapy was associated with a statistically significant ($p=0.005$) improvement in time to treatment failure. With a longer follow-up (median 95 weeks), improvement in time to treatment failure was no longer statistically significant ($p=0.10$). At the same timepoint, 130 (32%) patients treated with bicalutamide-LHRH analogue therapy and 145 (35%) patients treated with flutamide-LHRH analogue therapy had died.

Subjective responses, (including scores for pain, analgesic use and Eastern Oncology Cooperative Group (ECOG) performance status) assessed in patients with symptoms at entry were seen in 95 (52%) patients treated with bicalutamide and in 88 (54%) patients treated with flutamide, each in combination therapy with LHRH analogues. This small difference was not statistically significant between bicalutamide 50 mg combination therapy and flutamide combination therapy.

Indications: For use in combination therapy with either an LHRH analogue or surgical castration in the treatment of metastatic (Stage D2) prostate cancer.

Contraindications: In patients with hypersensitivity to the drug or any of its components.

Bicalutamide is contraindicated in females. The safety and effectiveness in women has not been studied.

Bicalutamide is contraindicated in children. The safety and effectiveness of bicalutamide in children has not been studied.

Precautions: Children: The safety and effectiveness of bicalutamide in children has not been established.

Pregnancy and *Lactation:* Bicalutamide is contraindicated in females. The drug may cause fetal harm when administered to pregnant women. The male offspring of rats (but not rabbits) receiving doses of 10 mg/kg/day and above, were observed to have reduced anogenital distance and hypospadias in reproductive toxicology studies. These pharmacological effects have been observed with other antiandrogens. No other teratogenic effects were observed in rabbits (receiving doses up to 200 mg/kg/day) or rats (receiving doses up to 250 mg/kg/day).

Patients with Hepatic Impairment: Bicalutamide is extensively metabolized in the liver. Data suggests that bicalutamide's elimination may be slower in subjects with severe hepatic impairment and this could lead to some accumulation of bicalutamide. Therefore, bicalutamide should be used with caution in patients with moderate to severe hepatic impairment.

Gynecomastia has been reported in patients receiving bicalutamide which may be reduced by concomitant castration.

Drug Interactions: Clinical studies with bicalutamide have not demonstrated any drug/drug interactions with LHRH analogues. Bicalutamide does not appear to interact with commonly prescribed drugs. There is no evidence of hepatic enzyme induction in patients receiving a daily dose of 150 mg. In vitro studies have shown that bicalutamide can displace the coumarin anticoagulant, warfarin, from its protein binding sites. It is recommended that if bicalutamide is started in patients who are already receiving coumarin anticoagulants prothrombin time should be closely monitored and adjustment of the anticoagulant dose may be necessary.

Laboratory Tests: Regular assessments of serum Prostate Specific Antigen (PSA) may be helpful in monitoring patients' responses.

Since transaminase abnormalities and, rarely, jaundice have been reported with the use of bicalutamide, periodic liver function tests should be considered. If clinically indicated, discontinuation of therapy should be considered. Abnormalities are usually reversible upon discontinuation.

Since bicalutamide may elevate plasma testosterone and estradiol levels, fluid retention could occur. Accordingly, bicalutamide should be used with caution in those patients with cardiac disease.

Information for the Patient: Patients should be informed that therapy with bicalutamide should be started at the same time as treatment with an LHRH analogue or surgical castration, and that patients should not interrupt or stop taking these medications without consulting their physician.

Adverse Effects: Bicalutamide, in general has been well tolerated with few withdrawals due to adverse events. The pharmacological action of bicalutamide may give rise to certain expected effects. These include hot flashes, pruritus, dry skin and in addition, breast tenderness and gynecomastia which may be reduced by concomitant castration. Bicalutamide may also be associated with the occurrence of diarrhea, nausea, vomiting and asthenia. In patients with advanced prostate cancer, treated with bicalutamide in combination with an LHRH analogue, the most frequent adverse experience was hot flashes (49%).

Diarrhea was the adverse event most frequently leading to treatment withdrawal with 6% of patients treated with flutamide-LHRH analogue and 0.5% of patients treated with bicalutamide-LHRH analogue withdrawing.

In the multicentre, double-blind controlled clinical trial comparing bicalutamide 50 mg once daily with flutamide 250 mg 3 times a day, each in combination with an LHRH analogue, the following adverse experiences with an incidence of more than 5%, regardless of causality have been reported. See Table I.

In addition, the following adverse experiences were reported in clinical trials (as possible adverse drug reactions in the opinion of investigating clinicians) with a frequency of ≥1% during treatment with bicalutamide plus an LHRH analogue. No causal relationship of these experiences to drug treatment has been made and some of the experiences reported are those that commonly occur in elderly patients.

Cardiovascular: heart failure.
Gastrointestinal: anorexia, dry mouth, dyspepsia, constipation, flatulence.
CNS: dizziness, insomnia, somnolence, decreased libido.
Respiratory: dyspnea.
Urogenital: impotence, nocturia.
Hematological: anemia.
Skin and Appendages: alopecia, rash, sweating, hirsutism.
Metabolic and Nutritional: hyperglycemia, edema, weight gain, weight loss, diabetes mellitus.

Table I—Casodex

Incidence of Adverse Events (≥ 5% in Either Treatment Group) Regardless of Causality

Adverse Event	**Treatment Group Number of Patients (%)** Casodex Plus LHRH Analogue (N=401)		Flutamide Plus LHRH Analogue (N=407)	
Hot flashes	196	(49)	202	(50)
Pain (general)	109	(27)	93	(23)
Constipation	67	(17)	50	(12)
Back pain	62	(15)	68	(17)
Asthenia	60	(15)	69	(17)
Pelvic pain	52	(13)	46	(11)
Nausea	44	(11)	45	(11)
Infection	41	(10)	35	(9)
Diarrhea	40	(10)	98	(24)
Nocturia	35	(9)	43	(11)
Peripheral edema	34	(8)	28	(7)
Abdominal pain	33	(8)	31	(8)
Dizziness	30	(7)	27	(7)
Dyspnea	30	(7)	24	(6)
Hematuria	30	(7)	20	(5)
Anemia[a]	29	(7)	35	(9)
Urinary tract infection	26	(6)	24	(6)
Increased liver enzyme test[b]	25	(6)	40	(10)
Rash	25	(6)	20	(5)
Paresthesia	24	(6)	27	(7)
Chest pain	24	(6)	20	(5)
Sweating	23	(6)	18	(4)
Flatulence	22	(5)	16	(4)
Hypertension	21	(5)	18	(4)
Impotence	20	(5)	29	(7)
Hyperglycemia	20	(5)	16	(4)
Insomnia	19	(5)	30	(7)
Gynecomastia	19	(5)	23	(6)
Bone pain	18	(4)	26	(6)
Headache	17	(4)	20	(5)
Flu syndrome	16	(4)	20	(5)
Weight loss	16	(4)	20	(5)
Vomiting	12	(3)	20	(5)
Urinary incontinence	9	(2)	20	(5)

[a]Anemia includes anemia, hypochromic and iron deficiency anemia.
[b]Increased liver enzyme test includes increases in ALT, AST or both.

Whole Body: abdominal pain, chest pain, headache, pain, pelvic pain, chills.

Abnormal Laboratory Test Values: Laboratory abnormalities including elevated AST, ALT, bilirubin, BUN, creatinine and decreased hemoglobin and white cell count have been reported in both bicalutamide-LHRH analogue treated and flutamide-LHRH analogue treated patients. Increased liver enzyme tests and decreases in hemoglobin were reported less frequently with bicalutamide-LHRH analogue therapy. Other changes were reported with similar incidence in both treatment groups.

Overdose: Symptoms and Treatment: A single dose of bicalutamide that results in symptoms of an overdose considered to be life-threatening has not been established. In animal studies, bicalutamide demonstrated a low potential acute toxicity. The LD_{50} in mice and rats was greater than 2 000 mg/kg. Long-term clinical trials have been conducted with doses up to 200 mg of bicalutamide daily and these doses have been well tolerated.

There is no specific antidote; treatment of an overdose should be symptomatic.

In the management of an overdose with bicalutamide, vomiting may be induced if the patient is alert. It should be remembered that in this patient population multiple drugs may have been taken. Dialysis is not likely to be helpful since bicalutamide is highly protein bound and is extensively metabolized. General supportive care, including frequent monitoring of vital signs and close observation of the patient, is indicated.

Dosage: The recommended dose for bicalutamide therapy in combination with an LHRH analogue or surgical castration is one 50 mg tablet once daily with or without food. Bicalutamide treatment should be started at the same time as treatment with an LHRH analogue or after surgical castration.

Renal or Hepatic Impairment: No dosage adjustment is necessary for patients with renal or mild hepatic impairment. Increased accumulation may occur in patients with moderate to severe hepatic impairment (see Precautions).

Information for the Patient: See Blue Section—Information for the Patient "Casodex".

Supplied: Each white, film-coated tablet, intagliated with CDX50 on one side and a logo on the other side, contains: bicalutamide 50 mg. Nonmedicinal ingredients: lactose, magnesium stearate, methylhydroxypropylcellulose, polyethylene glycol, polyvidone, sodium starch glycolate and titanium dioxide. Blisters of 30. Store between 15 and 30°C.

(Shown in Product Recognition Section)

Reviewed 1998

CATAPRES® Ⓟ

Boehringer Ingelheim

Clonidine HCl

Antihypertensive

Pharmacology: Clonidine is an α-adrenergic agonist which also has some α-adrenergic antagonist properties. The antihypertensive effect of clonidine is thought to be due to central α_2-adrenergic stimulation, which results in a decreased sympathetic outflow to the heart, kidneys, and peripheral vasculature and thus decreased peripheral vascular resistance, decreased systolic and diastolic blood pressure and decreased heart rate. Renal blood flow and glomerular filtration rate remain essentially unchanged. Normal postural reflexes are intact and therefore orthostatic symptoms are mild and infrequent. Acute studies with clonidine in humans have demonstrated a moderate reduction (15 to 20%) of cardiac output in the supine position with no change in the peripheral resistance; at a 45° tilt there is a smaller reduction in cardiac output and a decrease of peripheral resistance. During long-term therapy, cardiac output tends to return to control values, while peripheral resistance remains decreased. Slowing of the pulse rate has been observed in most patients given clonidine, but the drug does not alter normal hemodynamic response to exercise.

Clonidine acts relatively rapidly. The patient's blood pressure declines within 30 to 60 minutes after an oral dose, the maximum decrease occurring within 2 to 4 hours. The plasma level of clonidine peaks in approximately 3 to 5 hours and the plasma half-life ranges from 12 to 16 hours. The half-life increases up to 41 hours in patients with severe impairment of renal function. Following oral administration about 40 to 60% of the absorbed dose is recovered in the urine as unchanged drug in 24 hours. About 50% of the absorbed dose is metabolized in the liver.

Other studies in patients have provided evidence of a reduction in plasma renin activity and in the excretion of aldosterone and catecholamines, but the exact relationship of these pharmacologic actions to the antihypertensive effect has not been fully elucidated.

Prolonged treatment with clonidine in animals causes a decrease in the responsiveness of the vascular smooth muscle to catecholamines and angiotensin. The change in vascular response may be of importance in explaining the chronic hypotensive effect in man.

Acute administration of clonidine stimulates the release of growth hormone in children and adults, but the drug does not produce sustained elevation of growth hormone during chronic administration.

Indications: The treatment of hypertension. It may be used alone or in combination with thiazide diuretics. Clonidine should normally be used in those patients in whom treatment with diuretic or beta-blocker was found ineffective or has been associated with unacceptable adverse effects.

Clonidine can also be tried as an initial agent in those patients in whom use of diuretics and/or beta-blockers is contraindicated or in patients with medical conditions in which these drugs frequently cause serious adverse effects.

Contraindications: Hypersensitivity to clonidine or to any of the tablet excipients; patients with sinus node function impairment.

Warnings: Withdrawal: Patients should be instructed not to discontinue therapy without consulting their physician. A pronounced withdrawal reaction with symptoms suggesting sympathetic over-activity may develop within 12 to 48 hours when clonidine is discontinued. High serum levels of catecholamines have been found during such episodes (see Drug Interactions). When discontinuing clonidine therapy, the physician should reduce the dose gradually over 2 to 4 days to avoid a possible

Catapres (cont'd)

rapid rise in blood pressure and associated subjective symptoms such as nervousness, agitation, and headache. Rare instances of hypertensive encephalopathy and death have been recorded after abrupt cessation of clonidine therapy. A withdrawal reaction is most likely to occur in patients who have been receiving large doses (greater than 1.2 mg/kg) or in those who are continuing to receive a concomitant beta-blocker. If therapy is to be discontinued in patients receiving clonidine and a β-adrenergic blocking agent concomitantly, the β-blocker should be discontinued several days before clonidine therapy is discontinued.

It has been demonstrated that an excessive rise in blood pressure, should it occur, can be reversed by resumption of clonidine therapy or by i.v. phentolamine.

Perioperative Use: Administration of clonidine should be continued to within 4 hours of surgery and resumed as soon as possible thereafter. The blood pressure should be carefully monitored and appropriate measures instituted to control it as necessary.

Precautions: General: Because it lowers blood pressure, clonidine should be used with caution in patients with severe coronary insufficiency, recent myocardial infarction, cerebrovascular disease or chronic renal failure.

Depending on the dose given, clonidine can lower the heart rate and pulse rate. In patients with diseases affecting the rhythmic and AV conduction system of the heart, arrhythmias have been observed after high doses.

Tolerance may develop in some patients, necessitating a reevaluation of therapy. This usually consists of an increase in dosage or concomitant administration of a diuretic to enhance the hypotensive response to the drug.

Occupational Hazards: The dosage of clonidine should be increased gradually to minimize the sedative effect of the drug. This is of particular importance in those patients who operate automobiles and potentially dangerous machinery.

Patients with a known history of depression should be carefully supervised while under treatment with clonidine, as there have been occasional reports of further depressive episodes occurring in such patients.

In several studies clonidine produced a dose-dependent increase in the incidence and severity of spontaneously occurring retinal degeneration in albino rats treated for 6 months or longer. In view of this retinal degeneration, eye examinations were performed in 908 patients prior to the start of clonidine therapy, who were then examined periodically thereafter. In 353 of these 908 patients, examinations were performed for periods of 24 months or longer. Except for the dryness of the eyes, no drug-related abnormal ophthalmologic findings were recorded and clonidine did not alter retinal function as shown by specialized tests such as the electroretinogram and macular dazzle. It is recommended that as an integral part of their overall long-term care, patients treated with clonidine should receive periodic eye examinations.

As with any drug excreted primarily in the urine, smaller doses of the drug are often effective in treating patients with a degree of renal failure. In patients exhibiting renal failure, periodic determination of the BUN is indicated. If, in the physician's opinion, a rising BUN is significant, the drug should be stopped.

A few instances of a condition resembling Raynaud's phenomenon have been reported. Caution should therefore be observed if patients with Raynaud's disease or thromboangiitis obliterans are to be treated with clonidine.

Pheochromocytoma: Clonidine is not indicated in pheochromocytoma. However, **in contrast to guanethidine and reserpine the drug has no crisis-inducing properties,** in this condition.

Clonidine does not affect the urinary VMA and catecholamine excretion significantly in patients with pheochromocytoma, so that no false positive or false negative results will occur during the administration of the drug.

Pregnancy: Reproduction studies performed in rabbits at doses up to approximately 3 times the maximum recommended daily human dose (MRDHD) of clonidine has revealed no evidence of teratogenic or embryotoxic potential in rabbits. When rats were given clonidine alone in doses as low as one-third the MRDHD, some embryotoxicity was evident.

There are, however, no adequate and well-controlled studies in pregnant women. Because animal reproduction studies are not always predictive of human response, this drug should be used during pregnancy only if clearly needed.

Careful monitoring of the mother and child is recommended. Clonidine passes the placenta barrier and may lower the heart rate of the fetus. Postpartum a transient rise in blood pressure in the newborn cannot be excluded. There is no adequate experience regarding the long-term effect of prenatal exposure.

Lactation: Since clonidine is distributed into breast milk, the drug should be used with caution in nursing women.

Children: Safety and effectiveness in children have not been established.

<u>Drug Interactions:</u> Along with diuretics, vasodilators and β-blockers have the ability to enhance the blood pressure lowering effect of clonidine.

Concomitant use of β-blockers and/or cardiac glycosides can further lower heart rate (bradycardia) or cause dysrhythmia (AV-block) in isolated cases.

If clonidine and tricyclic antidepressants are administered as concurrent therapy, the effect of clonidine may be reduced, thus necessitating an increase in the dosage of clonidine. Amitriptyline in combination with clonidine enhances the manifestation of corneal lesions in rats.

Depending upon the dose administered, tolazoline can reduce or neutralize the effect of clonidine, and therefore, is suitable as an antidote.

Concurrent use of appetite suppressants (with the exception of fenfluramine) and clonidine may decrease the hypotensive effects of clonidine. Concurrent use of fenfluramine and clonidine may increase the hypotensive effects of clonidine.

Sympathomimetic amines, indomethacin and possibly other nonsteroidal anti-inflammatory agents may reduce the antihypertensive effects of clonidine. The patient should be carefully monitored to confirm that the desired effect is being obtained.

Clonidine may enhance the CNS-depressive effects of alcohol, barbiturates or other sedatives.

Withdrawal of clonidine may result in an excess of circulating catecholamines (see Warnings). Therefore, caution should be exercised in concomitant use of drugs which affect the metabolism, tissue uptake or pressor effects of these amines (MAO inhibitors, tricyclic antidepressants and beta-blocking agents, respectively).

Adverse Effects: Most adverse effects are mild and generally tend to diminish with continuation of therapy. The most common (which appear to be dose-related) are dry mouth (about 40%), drowsiness (about 33%), dizziness (about 16%), constipation and sedation (each in about 10%).

There have been isolated reports of continual dry mouth leading to an accelerated rate of dental caries, in patients receiving clonidine.

The most serious reactions have been reported upon abrupt discontinuation of the drug (see Warnings, Withdrawal).

The following less frequent adverse experiences have also been reported in patients receiving clonidine, but in many cases patients were receiving concomitant medication and a causal relationship has not been established.

Gastrointestinal: nausea and vomiting, about 5% of patients; anorexia and malaise, each about 1%; mild transient abnormalities in liver function tests, about 1%; rare reports of hepatitis; parotitis, rarely. In very rare cases pseudo-obstruction of the large bowel have been observed in predisposed patients.

Metabolic: weight gain, about 1% of patients; gynecomastia, about 0.1%, transient elevation of blood glucose or serum creatine phosphokinase, rarely.

CNS: nervousness and agitation, about 3% of patients, mental depression, about 1%; headache, about 1%; insomnia, about 0.5%. Vivid dreams or nightmares, other behavioral changes, restlessness, sleep disturbances, anxiety, visual and auditory hallucinations, perceptual disorders, confusion, disturbances of accommodation and delirium have been reported.

Cardiovascular: orthostatic symptoms, about 3% of patients; palpitations and tachycardia, bradycardia, each about 0.5%. Congestive heart failure and electrocardiographic abnormalities i.e., conduction disturbances and arrhythmias have been reported rarely. Rare cases of sinus bradycardia and atrioventricular block have been reported, both with and without the use of concomitant digitalis.

Dermatologic: rash, about 1% of patients; pruritus, about 0.7%; hives, angioneurotic edema and urticaria, about 0.5%; alopecia, about 0.2%.

Genitourinary: decreased sexual activity, impotence and loss of libido, about 3% of patients; nocturia, about 1%; difficulty in micturition, about 0.2%; urinary retention, about 0.1%.

Other: weakness, about 10% of patients; fatigue, about 4%; discontinuation syndrome, about 1%; muscle or joint pain, about 0.6% and cramps of the lower limbs, about 0.3%. Dryness, burning of the eyes, blurred vision, dryness of the nasal mucosa, pallor, weakly positive Coombs' test, increased sensitivity to alcohol and fever have been reported. Raynaud's phenomenon has been reported rarely.

Overdose: Symptoms and Treatment: The signs and symptoms of clonidine overdosage include hypotension, bradycardia, lethargy, irritability, weakness, somnolence, diminished or absent reflexes, miosis, vomiting and hypoventilation. With large overdoses, reversible cardiac induction defects or arrhythmias, apnea, seizures and transient hypertension have been reported. The oral LD_{50} of clonidine in rats was 465 mg/kg, and in mice 206 mg/kg.

In a patient who ingested 100 mg clonidine, plasma clonidine levels were 60 ng/mL (1 hour), 190 ng/mL (1.5 hours), 370 ng/mL (2 hours) and 120 ng/mL (5.5 and 6.5 hours). This patient developed hypertension followed by hypotension; bradycardia, apnea, hallucinations, semicoma, and premature ventricular contractions. The patient fully recovered after intensive treatment.

Clonidine overdosage usually responds to symptomatic treatment with careful cardiovascular monitoring. Gastric lavage is only worthwhile if it is guaranteed that part of the dose taken, which has not yet been absorbed, can be removed. Routine hemodialysis is of limited benefit since a maximum of 5% of circulating clonidine is removed.

I.V. tolazoline (an α-antagonist) and naloxone have each been used as antidotes to clonidine poisoning, with inconsistent results. If other efforts fail, these agents may provide some benefit in reversing the effects of clonidine.

Dosage: The dose must be adjusted according to the patient's individual blood pressure response.

Initial Dose: 0.1 mg tablet twice daily (morning and bedtime). (Elderly patients may benefit from a lower initial dose.)

Maintenance Dose: After a period of 2 to 4 weeks, further increments of 0.1 mg/day may be necessary until the desired response is achieved. In those instances where it is not possible to have equal amounts of drug at each of the dosing intervals, taking the larger portion of the total daily dose at bedtime may minimize transient adjustment effect of dry mouth and drowsiness. The therapeutic doses most commonly employed have ranged from 0.2 to 0.6 mg/day given in divided doses. Usually above 0.6 mg/day do not result in a further marked reduction in blood pressure.

Renal Insufficiency: Doses must be adjusted according to the degree of impairment and patients should be carefully monitored. Since only a minimal amount of clonidine is removed during routine hemodialysis, there is no need to give supplemental clonidine during dialysis.

Discontinuation of Treatment: If clonidine is to be discontinued, reduce dosage gradually (see Warnings).

Supplied: 0.1 mg: Each round, white, flat tablet with bevelled edges, one side scored with each half bearing the imprint 01C/01C, the reverse side bearing the Ingelheim Tower, contains: clonidine HCl 0.1 mg. Nonmedicinal ingredients: colloidal silica, dibasic calcium phosphate, lactose (fine), maize starch, polyvinylpyrrolidone, soluble starch and stearic acid. Bottles of 100 and 500.

0.2 mg: Each round, orange, flat tablet with bevelled edges, one side scored with each half bearing the imprint 02C/02C, the reverse side bearing the Ingelheim Tower, contains: clonidine HCl 0.2 mg. Nonmedicinal ingredients: colloidal silica, dibasic calcium phosphate, FD&C Yellow #6, lactose (fine), maize starch, polyvinylpyrrolidone, soluble starch and stearic acid. Bottles of 100 and 500.

Store at controlled room temperature (15 to 30°C).

CAVERJECT™ Ⓟ

Pharmacia & Upjohn

Alprostadil

Prostaglandin

Pharmacology: Alprostadil is a prostaglandin with various pharmacological actions that include vasodilatation and inhibition of platelet aggregation, inhibition of gastric secretion, stimulation of intestinal smooth muscle and stimulation of uterine smooth muscle.

Alprostadil, when given to impotent men by intracavernous injection, induces erections within 5 to 20 minutes after administration. The duration of erection is dose-dependent. The mechanism of penile erection involves a complex series of neurovascular events. Alprostadil injected intracavernosally causes tumescence by increasing cavernous blood flow through relaxation of trabecular smooth muscle and dilation of cavernosal arteries.

With regards to the action of alprostadil on penile structures, in most animal species tested, alprostadil had relaxant effects on retractor penis and corpus cavernosum urethra in vitro. Alprostadil also relaxed isolated preparations of human corpus cavernosum and spongiosum as well as cavernous arterial segments previously contracted by either norepinephrine or $PGF_{2}\alpha$. In pigtail monkeys (Macaca nemestrina), alprostadil increased cavernous arterial blood flow in vivo. The degree and duration of cavernous smooth muscle relaxation in this animal model was dose-dependent.

Other actions of PGE_1 involve the cardiovascular system, CNS, autonomic nervous system, respiratory system, gastrointestinal system and hematopoietic system.

Pharmacokinetics: Absorption: The absolute bioavailability of alprostadil following intracavernosal injection has not been determined.

Distribution: Following a 20 μg intracavernosal injection of alprostadil, mean peripheral plasma concentrations of alprostadil were 89 pg/mL and 102 pg/mL at 30 and 60 minutes post-injection respectively, which were not significantly greater than baseline levels of endogenous alprostadil at 96 pg/mL. Alprostadil is bound primarily to plasma albumin (81%) and to a lesser degree to γ-globulin IV-4 fraction (55%). No significant binding could be demonstrated with erythrocytes or white cells.

Metabolism: Alprostadil is rapidly converted to compounds, which are further metabolized prior to excretion. In man, a single pass through the lung effectively metabolizes approximately 80% of the available PGE_1 primarily by beta- and omega-oxidation. Therefore, any alprostadil that may enter the systemic circulation following intracavernosal injection is rapidly metabolized. However, pulmonary clearance of PGE_1 can be affected by disease states such as acute respiratory distress syndrome (ARDS), with a resultant reduction in the pulmonary extraction ratio.

After intracavernosal administration of 20 μg of alprostadil, peripheral levels of the primary metabolite 15-oxo-13,14-dihydro-PGE_1 increased, reaching a peak at 30 minutes and falling to predose levels by 60 minutes postinjection.

Excretion: The major route of elimination of the metabolites of alprostadil is through the kidney. Urinary excretion of an i.v. dose is essentially complete (90%) within 24 hours of administration. The remainder of the dose is excreted in the feces. There is no evidence to suggest any tissue retention of PGE_1 or its metabolites after an i.v. administration.

Pharmacokinetics in Special Populations: Geriatrics: The potential effect of age on the pharmacokinetics of alprostadil has not been formally evaluated. In patients with ARDS, the mean (±SD) pulmonary extraction of alprostadil was 72%±15% in 11 elderly patients aged 65 years or older (mean 71±6 years) and 65%±20% in 6 young patients aged 35 years or younger (mean 28±5 years).

Children: Plasma alprostadil concentrations were evaluated in 10 neonates (gestational age 34 weeks in 2 infants and 38 to 40 weeks in 8 infants) receiving steady-state i.v. infusions of alprostadil to treat underlying cardiac malformations. Alprostadil infusion rates ranged from 5 to 50 ng/kg/min (median 45 ng/kg/min), with resultant plasma concentrations in the range of 22 to 530 pg/mL (median 56 pg/mL). The individual clearance of alprostadil in neonates is highly variable as reflected by the wide range of plasma concentrations observed.

Gender: The influence of gender on the pharmacokinetics of alprostadil has not been formally studied. Two studies evaluated pulmonary extraction in 23 patients with ARDS following i.v. administration of alprostadil. The 17 males had a pulmonary extraction of 66% compared to 69% in the 6 female patients, suggesting no gender influence.

Race: The influence of race on the pharmacokinetics of alprostadil have not been formally studied.

Renal and Hepatic Insufficiency: The effects of renal and hepatic insufficiency on the pharmacokinetics of alprostadil have not been formally studied. Since systemic clearance of alprostadil is primarily by first-pass metabolism through the lungs, it is not expected that altered renal or hepatic function will have a major influence on the pharmacokinetics of alprostadil.

Pulmonary Disease: In one study, pulmonary extraction of alprostadil given i.v. was found to be reduced by 15% in patients with ARDS (66%) compared to patients with normal respiratory function (78%). In a second study of 14 patients with ARDS or at risk of developing ARDS, the mean extraction efficiency of alprostadil was 67% ranging from subnormal (11%) to normal (90%).

Indications: For the intracavernosal treatment of erectile dysfunction due to neurogenic, vasculogenic, psychogenic, or mixed etiology. Intracavernosal alprostadil may also be useful as an adjunct to diagnostic tests in the diagnosis of erectile dysfunction.

Contraindications: Patients with a known hypersensitivity to the drug. Patients who have any condition that may predispose them to priapism such as sickle cell anemia or trait, multiple myeloma or leukemia. Patients with anatomical deformations of the penis, such as angulation, cavernosal fibrosis, Peyronie's disease. Patients with penile implants.

Caverject should not be used in women or children and is **not for use in newborns.**

Alprostadil should not be used in men for whom sexual activity is inadvisable or contraindicated.

Warnings: Prolonged erection (4 to 6 hours) and/or priapism (>6 hours) are known to occur following intracavernosal administration of vasoactive substances, including alprostadil. In clinical studies, prolonged erection occurred in 4% of patients and 0.4% experienced priapism.

The patient should be instructed to immediately report to his physician, or if unavailable, to seek immediate medical assistance for an erection persisting for more than 3 hours. Treatment of prolonged erection/priapism should be according to established medical practice (see Overdose: Symptoms and Treatment). If priapism is not treated immediately, penile tissue damage and permanent loss of potency may result.

In the majority of cases, spontaneous detumescence occurred. To minimize the chances of prolonged erection or priapism, alprostadil should be titrated slowly to the lowest effective dose (see Dosage).

Precautions: General: Underlying treatable medical causes of erectile dysfunction must be diagnosed and treated prior to initiating therapy with alprostadil.

The results of clinical studies with alprostadil indicate an overall incidence of penile fibrosis, including Peyronie's disease, of 3% (55/1 861). In one long-term (up to 18 months duration) self-injection study, the incidence of fibrosis reported was 7.8% (53/683). Regular follow-up of patients, with careful examination of the penis, is strongly recommended to detect signs of penile fibrosis. Treatment with alprostadil should be discontinued in patients who develop penile angulation, cavernosal fibrosis or Peyronie's disease.

Patients on anticoagulants such as warfarin or heparin may have an increased propensity for bleeding after intracavernosal injection.

An injection of alprostadil can induce a small amount of bleeding at the injection site (see Adverse Effects, Hematoma Ecchymosis, Hemorrhage). In patients infected with blood-borne diseases, this may increase the transmission of blood-borne diseases between partners.

The safety and efficacy of combinations of alprostadil and other vasoactive agents have not been systematically studied. Therefore, the use of such combinations is not recommended.

Drug Interactions: The potential for pharmacokinetic drug-drug interactions between alprostadil and other agents has not been formally studied.

Information for the Patient: Patients using a self-injection program of therapy should receive proper instruction in both intracavernosal injection and aseptic technique (see Blue Section—Information for the Patient). Physicians should ensure that patients are able to demonstrate competence and skill with the injection procedure prior to initiating self-injection.

The initial treatment dose is established in the physicians office. The lowest effective dose sufficient to induce an erection lasting up to 1 hour should be used. The patient may expect an erection to occur within 5 to 20 minutes. Patients who require dosage adjustments and are self-injecting alprostadil, should not increase or decrease their dose without the advice of their physician. Generally, patients should not use alprostadil more than once a day and not more than 3 times a week, with at least 24 hours between each use.

Alprostadil is labelled for "single use only", patients should discard any unused solution after withdrawing the proper volume for their dose. The vial should not be shaken once reconstituted.

Reconstituted vials of alprostadil that on visual inspection appear cloudy, colored or contain particulate matter, should be discarded.

Patients who experience an erection lasting longer than 2 hours should attempt to detumesce using methods prescribed by their physician.

Patients should be advised on the possible adverse effects associated with the use of alprostadil; the most frequent being mild to moderate penile pain after injection. A patient should report to his physician if he complains of: any penile pain not previously present, an increased intensity of pain, nodules or hard tissue appearing in the penis, or curvature of the erect penis. There is the potential for infection with any type of injection, therefore patients should also report any occurrences of penile redness, swelling, or tenderness. The importance of regular physician visits to assess the continued safety and efficacy of alprostadil treatment should be stressed to the patient.

A potentially serious adverse reaction with intracavernosal therapy is priapism. Accordingly, the patient should be instructed to contact the physician's office immediately or, if unavailable, to seek immediate medical assistance if an erection persists for longer than 3 hours.

In clinical trials, the use of concomitant medicines such as antihypertensives, diuretics, antidiabetic agents (including insulin) or NSAIDs, did not affect the safety or efficacy of alprostadil.

The use of alprostadil intracavernosally does not offer any protection from the spread of sexually transmitted diseases. Individuals using alprostadil should be properly counselled with regards to protective measures to safeguard against the spread of sexually transmitted diseases, including human immunodeficiency virus (HIV) infection.

Patients should be instructed not to reuse or share needles or syringes. The patient should not allow anyone else to use this medicine. Patients should dispose of used needles, syringes, and vials, safely and properly (see Blue Section—Information for the Patient).

A patient administration guide, found in every package, provides a step-by-step method for proper preparation and administration of alprostadil. Patients should be instructed to carefully follow this guide for self-injection.

Carcinogenesis, Mutagenesis and Impairment of Fertility: Long-term carcinogenicity studies have not been conducted. Reproductive studies in the rat with alprostadil at doses of up to 0.2 mg/kg/day did not adversely affect or alter spermatogenesis, conferring a 200-fold margin of safety at usual human doses. A battery of mutagenicity assays including, bacterial mutation (Ames), alkaline elution, rat micronucleus, sister chromatid exchange, CHO/HGPRT mammalian cell forward gene mutation and unscheduled DNA synthesis (UDS), revealed no potential for mutagenesis.

A one-year irritancy study was conducted in male Cynomolgus monkeys. Three groups of 5 animals received twice weekly intracavernosal injections of either 3 or 8.25 μg alprostadil or vehicle. A further 2 groups of 6 animals were given 8.25 μg alprostadil or vehicle twice weekly, as above, and in addition, multiple doses during weeks 44, 48 and 52. Three monkeys receiving vehicle and 3 monkeys receiving 8.25 μg alprostadil were held for evaluation following a 4-week recovery period. No evidence of alprostadil-related penile or systemic tissue lesions were found. Local irritation noted in control and treated monkeys was considered to be related to the injection procedure itself and any penile lesions found were reversible. After the 4-week recovery period, a regression in histological changes in the penis was observed.

Adverse Effects: Local Adverse Events: The following local adverse events (see Table I) were reported from controlled and uncontrolled clinical trials, including an uncontrolled 18-month safety study.

Table I—Caverject

Local Adverse Events

Local Event (Reported in ≥1% of Patients)	**No. (%) of Patients (n=1 861)**	
Penile pain	696	(37)
Pain after injection	580	(31)
Pain at the injection site	370	(20)
Prolonged erection (4-6 h)	82	(4)
Penile fibrosis[a]	55	(3)
Injection site hematoma	63	(3)
Penis disorder[b]	46	(3)
Injection site ecchymosis	32	(2)
Penile rash	21	(1)
Penile edema	18	(1)

[a] Includes generalized or deep fibrosis, penile curvature/deviation, and Peyronie's disease.

[b] Includes numbness, yeast infection, irritation, sensitivity, phimosis, pruritus, erythema, venous leak, penile skin tear, strange feeling in penis, burning sensation in penis and itch at tip of penis.

Penile Pain: Penile pain after intracavernosal administration of alprostadil was reported at least once by 37% of patients in clinical studies up to 18 months in duration. The intensity of pain was rated mild or moderate in the majority of cases. Three percent of patients discontinued treatment because of penile pain. The frequency of penile pain was 2% in 294 patients who received 1 to 3 injections of placebo.

Prolonged Erection/Priapism: In clinical trials, prolonged erection was defined as an erection that lasted for 4 to 6 hours; priapism was defined as an erection that lasted 6 hours or longer (see Warnings).

Caverject (cont'd)

Hematoma/Ecchymosis: The frequency of hematoma and ecchymosis was 3 and 2 % respectively. In most cases, hematoma/ecchymosis was judged to be a complication of a faulty injection technique. Accordingly, proper instruction of the patient in self-injection is of importance to minimize the potential of hematoma/ecchymosis (see Dosage).

Local events observed in <1% of the patients include: balanitis, lack of efficacy, injection site hemorrhage, injection site inflammation, injection site itching, injection site reaction, injection site swelling, injection site edema, trauma, urethral bleeding, urethral disorder, penile hematoma, penile warmth, priapism (>6 h), numbness, yeast infection, irritation, sensitivity, phimosis, pruritus, erythema, venous leak, painful erection and abnormal ejaculation.

Systemic Adverse Events: The following systemic adverse event information (see Table II) was derived from controlled and uncontrolled studies, including an uncontrolled 18-month safety study.

Table II—Caverject

Systemic Adverse Events

Systemic Event[a] by Body System[b] (Reported in ≥1% of Patients)[c]	**No. (%) of Patients (n=1 861)**	
Body as a Whole	245	(13)
Upper respiratory infection	76	(4)
Flu syndrome	42	(2)
Headache	37	(2)
Trauma[d]	33	(2)
Localized pain[e]	32	(2)
Back pain	22	(1)
Localized abdominal pain	10	(<1)
Respiratory	123	(7)
Sinusitis	43	(2)
Nasal congestion	25	(1)
Cough	21	(1)
Bronchitis	18	(1)
Pharyngitis	16	(<1)
Urogenital	121	(7)
Prostatic disorder[f]	28	(2)
Urinary tract infection	16	(<1)
Testicular pain	16	(<1)
Hematuria	10	(<1)
Cardiovascular	80	(4)
Hypertension	39	(2)
CNS	66	(4)
Dizziness	22	(1)
Digestive	86	(5)
Nausea	14	(<1)
Tooth abscess	12	(<1)
Diarrhea	11	(<1)
Dyspepsia	11	(<1)
Skin and Appendages	49	(3)
Rash	11	(<1)

[a] Number (%) patients reporting the event, with patients reporting the same event more than once counted only once.
[b] Number (%) patients reporting a drug-related event within the body system, with patients reporting more than one event within the body system counted only once.
[c] No significant adverse events were reported by 294 patients who received 1 to 3 injections of placebo.
[d] Includes injuries, fractures, abrasions, lacerations, dislocations.
[e] Includes pain in various anatomical structures other than injection site.
[f] Includes prostatitis, pain, hypertrophy, enlargement.

Systemic events reported in 1% of patients and judged by investigators to be possibly related to the use of alprostadil include: testicular pain, scrotal disorder, scrotal edema, hematuria, testicular disorder, impaired urination, urinary frequency, pelvic pain, hypotension, vasodilation, peripheral vascular disorder, supraventricular extrasystole, vasovagal reactions, hypesthesia, nongeneralized weakness, diaphoresis, rash, nonapplication site pruritus, skin neoplasm, nausea, dry mouth, increased serum creatinine, leg cramps and mydriasis.

Hemodynamic changes, manifested as decreases in blood pressure and increases in pulse rate, were observed during clinical studies, principally at doses above 20 μg and above 30 μg of alprostadil respectively, and appeared to be dose-dependent. However, these changes were clinically unimportant; only 3 patients discontinued the treatment because of symptomatic hypotension.

Alprostadil had no clinically important effect on serum or urine laboratory tests.

Overdose: Symptoms and Treatment: The pharmacotoxic signs of alprostadil are similar in all animal species and include depression, soft stool or diarrhea and rapid breathing. In mice, the lowest acute LD_{50} was 12 mg/kg which is 12 000 times greater than the maximum recommended human dose of 60 μg.

In man, prolonged erection and/or priapism are known to occur following intracavernosal administration of vasoactive substances. Given the dose-response relationship of alprostadil with erection duration, the therapeutic dose range should be determined individually for each patient by his physician during the initial office instruction. Inadvertent or intentional overdosing is the most common cause of prolonged pharmacological erection. In clinical trials with alprostadil, overdosage was not observed. If intracavernous overdose of alprostadil occurs, the patient should be under medical supervision until any systemic effects have resolved and/or until penile detumescence has occurred. Symptomatic treatment of any systemic symptoms would be appropriate.

Patients should be instructed to report any erections persisting for more than 3 hours to a physician. The treatment of priapism/prolonged erection should be according to established medical practice. Physicians may refer to 2 suggested protocols for detumescence presented below.

Detumescence Protocols: 1. Aspirate 40 to 60 mL from either right or left corpora using vacutainer and holder as for drawing blood. Use landmarks as for intracavernosal injection. Patient will often detumesce while aspirating. Apply ice for 20 minutes post-aspiration if erection remains. If 1) unsuccessful then, 2. Have patient lie in supine postion. Dilute 10 mg phenylephrine into 20 mL water for injection (0.05%). With an insulin syringe, inject 0.1 to 0.2 mL (50 to 100 μg) into the corpora every 2 to 5 minutes, until detumescence occurs. The occasional patient may experience very transient bradycardia and hypertension when given phenylephrine injections, therefore monitor patient's blood pressure and pulse every 10 minutes. Patients at risk include those with cardiac arrhythmias and diabetics. Refer to the prescribing information for phenylephrine before use. **Do not** give to patients on MAOIs. When phenylephrine is used within the first 12 hours of erection, the majority of patients will respond. 3. If the above measures fail to detumesce the patient, a urologist should be consulted as soon as possible, especially if the erection has been present for many hours. If priapism is not treated immediately, penile tissue damage and/or permanent loss of potency may result.

Dosage: Administration: Alprostadil is administered by direct intracavernosal injection. A 0.5-inch 27- to 30-gauge needle is generally recommended. Alprostadil is injected into either of two corpora cavernosum along the dorso-lateral aspects of the proximal third of the penis. Avoid any area where there are visible veins. The injection site should be changed for each injection (i.e., alternate sides of penis). Within either area, the point of injection should also be changed each time and the injection site must be cleansed with an alcohol swab.

Therapeutic/Effective Dose: Appropriate initial doses and maintenance doses are recommended based on the etiology of the erectile dysfunction. In all cases, the dose should be titrated on an individual basis by the physician, and the lowest effective dose always employed as the therapeutic dose. An effective dose is defined as one that produces an erection sufficient for intercourse with an erection duration not exceeding 1 hour. The following guidelines for dose titration are recommended.

Initial Titration in Physician's Office: Erectile Dysfunction of Vasculogenic, Psychogenic or Mixed Etiology: Dosage titration should be initiated at 2.5 μg of alprostadil. If there is a partial response, the dose may be increased by 2.5 μg to a dose of 5 μg and then in increments of 5 to 10 μg, depending upon erectile response, until the effective dose is reached (see Therapeutic/Effective Dose). If there is no response to the initial 2.5 μg dose, the second dose may be increased to 7.5 μg, followed by increments of 5 to 10 μg. The patient must remain in the physician's office until complete detumescence is achieved. If there is no response, then the next higher dose may be given within 1 hour. If there is a response, then there should be at least a 24-hour interval before the next dose is given.

Erectile Dysfunction of Pure Neurogenic Etiology: Dosage titration should be initiated at 1.25 μg of alprostadil. The dose may be increased by 1.25 μg to a dose of 2.5 μg, followed by an increment of 2.5 μg to a dose of 5 μg and then in 5 μg increments until the effective dose is reached (see Therapeutic/Effective Dose). The patient must remain in the physician's office until complete detumescence is achieved. If there is no response, then the next higher dose may be given within 1 hour. If there is a response, then there should be at least a 24-hour interval before the next dose is given.

In one clinical study involving 579 patients, the majority of patients (56%) were titrated to doses of >5 μg but ≤20 μg. The mean dose at the end of the titration phase was 17.8 μg of alprostadil.

Maintenance Therapy: The initial injection of alprostadil must be delivered by a medically trained health care professional. Before beginning a self-injection program of therapy, the physician must ensure that the patient (or his partner) aptly demonstrates skill and competence with the injection procedure, and uses appropriate sterile technique. A patient package insert is available to patients for referral (see Blue Section—Information for the Patient).

The dose selected for self-injection therapy is established during dose titration in the physician's office. The correct dose is the lowest effective dose. The dose should be reduced if the erection persists for longer than 1 hour, however, the physician should take into consideration the patient's preferences when defining the dose for self-injection. An erection lasting >3 hours is to be treated as a medical emergency. A physician should be consulted for any dose adjustments, if required. The dose should be adjusted in accordance with the titration guidelines described above. Regular follow-up visits, at least every 3 months, are recommended in order to assess the safety and efficacy of the therapy.

Maximum Recommended Dose Limits: Daily dose should not exceed **60 μg. Not** more than once daily and **not** more than 3 times weekly, with at least 24 hours between each dose. Do not inject alprostadil into an erect penis.

There is no evidence that tolerance to the effects of alprostadil develops with continued use. The long-term use of alprostadil has been documented for up to 6 months in an uncontrolled self-injection study. The mean dose after 6 months was 20.7 μg.

A vial of Caverject delivers 1 dose only and is labelled **"single dose vial"**. Instructions for proper disposal of the syringe, needle and vial should be followed (see Blue Section—Information for the Patient).

Diagnostic Dose: Pharmacologic Testing: An initial dose of 2.5 μg is employed with subsequent upward titration in 2.5 μg increments. Patients are monitored for the occurrence of an erection following an intracavernosal injection of alprostadil.

Adjunct to Laboratory Investigations: A single dose of alprostadil sufficient to induce a rigid erection is used. For use with Doppler imaging/Duplex Ultrasonography, ^{133}Xenon washout tests, Radionuclide Phallography and Penile Arteriography for the visualization and assessment of the penile vasculature.

Reconstituted Solutions: See Table III. Alprostadil is reconstituted with the addition of 1 mL bacteriostatic water for injection (BWFI). Vial content after reconstitution is approximately 1.13 mL which allows 1.0 mL to be delivered to the patient. Approximately 0.5 μg/mL of alprostadil is lost due to adsorption to the vial and syringe. The resultant solution contains 10 or 20 μg/mL of alprostadil, 172 mg/mL lactose, 47 μg/mL sodium citrate, and 8.4 mg/mL benzyl alcohol. Once reconstituted, no additional substances should be injected into the vial.

Once reconstituted, the alprostadil solution must be used immediately. Do not freeze the reconstituted solution. A solution that appears cloudy, colored or contains particles should be discarded.

Table III—Caverject

Parenteral Products Reconstitution

Vial Amount	**Volume of Diluent Added**	**Nominal Concentration**
11.9 μg	1 mL	10 μg/mL
23.2 μg	BWFI	20 μg/mL

Legend: BWFI=bacteriostatic water for injection.

Information for the Patient: See Blue Section—Information for the Patient "Caverject".

Supplied: 10 μg: Each case contains: a single dose vial of alprostadil 10 μg sterile powder, 1 mL prefilled syringe of BWFI diluent, a 27-gauge (0.5 inch) needle, 2 alcohol swabs and Patient Administration Leaflet. These cases are fitted with a lock designed for safe and convenient disposal of the contents after use. Diagnostic vials of 10 μg. Cartons of 5.

20 μg: Each case contains: a single dose vial of alprostadil 20 μg sterile powder, 1 mL prefilled syringe of BWFI diluent, a 27-gauge (0.5 inch) needle, 2 alcohol swabs and Patient Administration Leaflet. These cases are fitted with a lock designed for safe and convenient disposal of the contents after use. Cartons of 5.

The unreconstituted lyophilized sterile powder (10 and 20 μg vials) should be stored between 2 to 30°C.

Reviewed 1997

CECLOR® ℞

Lilly

Cefaclor

Antibiotic

Pharmacology: Like other β-lactam antibiotics, cefaclor owes its antibacterial activity to its ability to bind to and inhibit the action of certain bacterial cell wall synthetic enzymes, the penicillin-binding proteins.

Cefaclor is well absorbed after oral administration to fed and fasted subjects. Following doses of 250 mg, 500 mg and 1 g to fasted subjects, average peak serum levels of approximately 7, 13 and 23 mg/L respectively were obtained within 0.5 to 1 hour. Total absorption is the same whether the drug is given before or after meals. However, when it is taken after food, the peak concentration achieved is 50 to 75% of that observed when the drug is administered to fasted subjects and is delayed by 0.8 to 1 hour. Approximately 25% of cefaclor is bound to human plasma.

Within 8 hours 60 to 85% of the drug is excreted unchanged in the urine, the greater portion being excreted within the first 2 hours. During this 8-hour period, peak urine concentrations following the 250 mg, 500 mg and 1 g doses were approximately 600, 900 and 1 900 mg/L respectively.

The serum half-life in normal subjects is 0.6 to 0.9 hours. In patients with reduced renal function, the serum half-life of cefaclor is slightly prolonged. In those with complete absence of renal function, the plasma half-life of the intact molecule is 2.3 to 2.8 hours. Excretion pathways in patients with markedly impaired renal function have not been determined. Hemodialysis shortens the half-life by 25 to 30%.

Probenecid administered with a 500 mg dose of cefaclor increased the peak serum concentration only slightly, from 12.4 to 13.9 mg/L, and urine levels were predictably diminished. The mean half-life among 5 fasted volunteers with normal renal function was 0.8 hour, and probenecid significantly prolonged the half-life to a mean of 1.3 hours.

Indications: May be used in the treatment of the following infections caused by S. pyogenes and S. pneumoniae, Staphylococci, (including coagulase-positive, coagulase-negative, and penicillinase producing strains), E. coli, P. mirabilis, K. pneumoniae, H. influenzae, including ampicillin resistant strains: otitis media; lower respiratory tract infections, including pneumonia, bronchitis, and pulmonary complications resulting from cystic fibrosis; upper respiratory tract infections, including pharyngitis and tonsillitis; skin and soft tissue infections; urinary tract infections. Appropriate culture and susceptibility studies should be performed.

Contraindications: Hypersensitivity to the cephalosporin antibiotics.

Warnings: Before therapy with cefaclor is instituted, careful inquiry should be made concerning previous hypersensitivity reactions to cefaclor, cephalosporins, penicillins or other drugs. If this product is to be given to penicillin-sensitive patients, caution should be exercised because cross-hypersensitivity, including anaphylaxis, among β-lactam antibiotics has been clearly documented.

Antibiotics including cefaclor should be administered with caution, and then only when absolutely necessary, to any patient who has demonstrated some form of allergy, particularly to drugs.

As is the case with all new drugs, patients should be followed carefully so that adverse reactions or unusual manifestations of drug idiosyncrasy may be detected. If an allergic reaction to cefaclor occurs, the drug should be discontinued and the patient treated with the usual agents (e.g., epinephrine, antihistamines, pressor amines or corticosteroids).

Pseudomembranous colitis has been reported with virtually all broad-spectrum antibiotics, including cefaclor; therefore, it is important to consider its diagnosis in patients who develop diarrhea in association with the use of antibiotics. Such colitis may range in severity from mild to life-threatening. Treatment with broad-spectrum antibiotics alters the normal flora of the colon and may permit overgrowth of clostridia. Studies indicate that a toxin produced by C. difficile is one primary cause of antibiotic-associated colitis. Mild cases of pseudomembranous colitis usually respond to drug discontinuance alone. In moderate to severe cases, management should include sigmoidoscopy, appropriate bacteriologic studies, and fluid, electrolyte, and protein supplementation. When the colitis does not improve after the drug has been discontinued, or when it is severe, oral vancomycin is the drug of choice for antibiotic-associated pseudomembranous colitis produced by C. difficile. Other causes of colitis should be ruled out.

Precautions: If an allergic reaction to cefaclor occurs, the drug should be discontinued and the patient treated appropriately.

Pregnancy: The safety of cefaclor in the treatment of infections during pregnancy has not been established. Reproduction studies in rats have revealed no evidence of impaired fertility.

Lactation: Small amounts of cefaclor, up to 0.21 mg/L, have been detected in mother's milk following administration of single 500 mg doses. The effect on nursing infants is not known. Caution should be exercised when cefaclor is administered to a nursing woman.

Prolonged use of cefaclor may result in the overgrowth of nonsusceptible organisms. Careful observation of the patient is essential. If super-infection occurs during therapy, administration of cefaclor should cease and appropriate measures should be taken.

Positive direct Coombs' tests have been reported during treatment with cephalosporin antibiotics. In hematologic studies or in transfusion cross matching procedures, when antiglobulin tests are performed on the minor side or in Coombs' testing of newborns whose mothers have received cephalosporin antibiotics before parturition, it should be recognized that a positive Coombs' test may be due to the drug.

Cefaclor should be administered with caution in the presence of markedly impaired renal function. Since the half-life of cefaclor in anuria is 2.3 to 2.8 hours, dosage adjustments for patients with moderate or severe renal impairment are not usually required. Clinical experience with cefaclor under such conditions is limited; therefore, careful clinical observation and laboratory studies should be made.

In patients treated with cefaclor, a false-positive reaction for glucose in the urine may occur with Benedict's or Fehling's solution or with Clinitest tablets but not with Tes-Tape.

<u>*Drug Interactions:*</u> There have been rare reports of increased prothrombin time with or without clinical bleeding in patients receiving cefaclor and warfarin concomitantly.

As with many other β-lactam antibiotics, the renal excretion of cefaclor is inhibited by probenecid.

Adverse Effects: During clinical trials in 8 346 patients (4 626 adults and 3 720 children under the age of 16) treated with cefaclor, the adverse reactions listed below were observed. The majority of these adverse reactions were mild and transient. The incidence rates were less than 1 in 100 (less than 1%), except as otherwise noted.

Gastrointestinal: The most frequent side effect has been diarrhea (≤1.5%). It was rarely severe enough to warrant cessation of therapy. Nausea, vomiting and dyspepsia have been reported. As with some penicillins and some other cephalosporins, transient hepatitis and cholestatic jaundice have been reported. Colitis, including rare instances of pseudomembranous colitis, has been reported in conjunction with or after therapy has stopped.

Hypersensitivity: Allergic reactions, such as urticaria and morbilliform eruptions 1%, have been observed, as have pruritus, rash and positive Coombs' tests. These reactions usually subsided upon discontinuation of the drug. Eosinophilia (2%), genital pruritus or vaginitis, and rarely, thrombocytopenia or reversible interstitial nephritis have also occurred.

Cases of serum sickness-like reactions have been reported. In contrast to classic serum sickness, signs and symptoms of serum sickness-like reactions involving cefaclor appear to be primarily confined to findings including erythema multiforme or other skin manifestations accompanied by arthritis/arthralgia, with or without fever. Serum sickness-like reactions are apparently due to hypersensitivity and more often occur during or following a second (or subsequent) course of therapy with cefaclor. Such reactions have been reported more frequently in children than in adults with an overall occurrence ranging from 1 in 200 (0.5%) in one focused trial to 2 in 8 346 (0.024%) in overall clinical trials (with an incidence in children in clinical trials of 0.055%) to 1 in 38 000 (0.003%) in spontaneous event reports. Signs and symptoms usually occur a few days after initiation of therapy and subside within a few days after cessation of therapy; occasionally these reactions have resulted in hospitalization, usually of short duration (median hospitalization=2 to 3 days, based on postmarketing surveillance studies). In those requiring hospitalization, the symptoms have ranged from mild to severe at the time of admission with more of the severe reactions occurring in children. Antihistamines and glucocorticoids appear to enhance resolution of the signs and symptoms. No serious sequelae have been reported.

More severe hypersensitivity reactions, including Stevens-Johnson syndrome, toxic epidermal necrolysis, angioedema and anaphylaxis have been reported rarely. Anaphylaxis may be more common in patients with a history of penicillin allergy.

CNS: Rarely, reversible hyperactivity, nervousness, insomnia, confusion, hypertonia, headache, dizziness, or somnolence have been reported.

Genitourinary: Vaginal moniliasis and vaginitis have been reported with cefaclor (≤1%).

Other: Transitory abnormalities in clinical laboratory test results have been reported. Although they were of uncertain etiology, they are listed here to serve as alerting information for the physician.

Hepatic: Slight elevations of AST, ALT, or alkaline phosphatase values have been reported.

Hematopoietic: Transient lymphocytosis, leukopenia, eosinophilia and, rarely, hemolytic anemia, aplastic anemia, agranulocytosis, and reversible neutropenia of possible clinical significance were observed.

There have been rare reports of increased prothrombin time with or without clinical bleeding in patients receiving cefaclor and warfarin concomitantly.

Renal: Slight and transient elevations in BUN or serum creatinine or abnormal urinalysis have been observed with cefaclor.

In addition to the adverse reactions listed above, renal dysfunction and toxic nephropathy have been reported in patients treated with β-lactam antibiotics.

Several β-lactam antibiotics have been implicated in triggering seizures, particularly in patients with renal impairment when the dosage was not reduced. If seizures associated with drug therapy should occur, the drug should be discontinued. Anticonvulsant therapy can be given if clinically indicated.

Overdose: Symptoms: The toxic symptoms following an overdose of cefaclor may include nausea, vomiting, epigastric distress, and diarrhea. The severity of the epigastric distress and the diarrhea are dose related. If other symptoms are present, it is probable that they are secondary to an underlying disease state, an allergic reaction, or the effects of other intoxication.

Treatment: In managing overdosage, consider the possibility of multiple drug overdoses, interaction among drugs, and unusual drug kinetics in your patient. Unless 5 times the normal dose of cefaclor has been ingested, gastrointestinal decontamination will not be necessary.

Protect the patient's airway and support ventilation and perfusion. Meticulously monitor and maintain, within acceptable limits, the patient's vital signs, blood gases, serum electrolytes, etc. Absorption of drugs from the gastrointestinal tract may be decreased by giving activated charcoal, which, in many cases, is more effective than emesis or lavage; consider charcoal instead of or in addition to gastric emptying. Repeated doses of charcoal over time may hasten elimination of some drugs that have been absorbed. Safeguard the patient's airway when employing gastric emptying or charcoal.

Forced diuresis, peritoneal dialysis, hemodialysis, or charcoal hemoperfusion have not been established as beneficial for an overdose of cefaclor.

Dosage: Administered orally, without regard to meals.

Adults: The usual adult dosage is 250 mg every 8 to 12 hours. For more severe infections or those caused by less susceptible organisms, larger doses may be needed. The maximum recommended dosage is 2 g/day, although doses of 4 g/day have been administered safely for 28 days.

For lower respiratory tract infections, the dosage should be administered 3 times daily.

For skin and soft tissue infections the dosage is 250 mg administered 2 or 3 times daily.

Children: The usual recommended daily dosage for children is 20 mg/kg/day in divided doses every 8 to 12 hours. For streptococcal pharyngitis or tonsillitis and soft tissue infections, the total daily dosage may be divided and administered every 12 hours.

In more serious infections, otitis media, and those infections caused by less susceptible organisms, 40 mg/kg/day is recommended, up to 1 g/day.

For otitis media, the total daily dosage may be divided and administered every 12 hours. For lower respiratory tract infections the total daily dosage should be divided and administered 3 times daily.

In the treatment of β-hemolytic streptococcal infections, a therapeutic dosage of cefaclor should be administered for at least 10 days.

Most clinical studies were performed with a duration of therapy between 5 and 14 days.

Ceclor (cont'd)

Directions for Reconstitution of Oral Suspensions: 125 mg: Add 60 mL of water to each 100 mL bottle or 90 mL to each 150 mL bottle in 2 portions. Shake well after each addition.

250 mg: Add 60 mL of water to each 100 mL bottle or 90 mL to each 150 mL bottle in 2 portions. Shake well after each addition.

375 mg: Add 44 mL of water to each 70 mL bottle or 62 mL to each 100 mL bottle in 2 portions. Shake well after each addition.

Supplied: Capsules: 250 mg: Each opaque purple and white capsule contains: cefaclor 250 mg. Nonmedicinal ingredients: cornstarch, FD&C Blue No. 1, FD&C Red No. 3, gelatin, magnesium stearate, silicone and titanium dioxide. Tartrazine-free. Bottles of 100 and 250.

500 mg: Each opaque purple and grey capsule contains: cefaclor 500 mg. Nonmedicinal ingredients: cornstarch, FD&C Blue No. 1, FD&C Red No. 3, gelatin, iron oxide, magnesium stearate, silicone and titanium dioxide. Tartrazine-free. Bottles of 30 and 100.

Oral Suspension: 125 mg: Each 5 mL dose of strawberry-flavored suspension contains: cefaclor 125 mg (25 mg/mL). Nonmedicinal ingredients: artificial strawberry flavor, cornstarch, FD&C Red No. 40, methylcellulose, silicone, sodium lauryl sulfate, sucrose and xantham gum. Energy: 52.9 kJ (12.6 kcal)/5 mL. Sodium: <1 mmol (0.06 mg)/5 mL. Bottles of 100 and 150 mL.

250 mg: Each 5 mL dose of strawberry-flavored suspension contains: cefaclor 250 mg (50 mg/mL). Nonmedicinal ingredients: artificial strawberry flavor, cornstarch, FD&C Red No. 40, methylcellulose, silicone, sodium lauryl sulfate, sucrose and xantham gum. Energy: 50.6 kJ (12.1 kcal)/5 mL. Sodium: <1 mmol (0.06 mg)/5 mL. Bottles of 100 and 150 mL.

375 mg: Each 5 mL dose of strawberry-flavored suspension contains: cefaclor 375 mg (75 mg/mL). Nonmedicinal ingredients: artificial strawberry flavor, cornstarch, FD&C Red No. 40, methylcellulose, silicone, sodium lauryl sulfate, sucrose and xantham gum. Energy: 47.0 kJ (11.2 kcal)/5 mL. Sodium: <1 mmol (0.06 mg)/5 mL. Bottles of 70 or 100 mL.

Store between 15 and 25°C. After reconstitution, oral suspensions must be refrigerated and used within 14 days. Shake well before using. Keep tightly closed.

Reviewed 1998

CEDOCARD® SR

Pharmascience

Isosorbide Dinitrate

Antianginal Agent

Pharmacology: The principal action of isosorbide dinitrate is that of all nitrates, the relaxation of vascular smooth muscle. The efficacy of nitrates in alleviating pain in angina pectoris is probably due primarily to reduction in myocardial oxygen demand rather than an increase in myocardial oxygen supply. This effect is thought to be brought about predominantly by a peripheral action. Although the venous effects predominate, nitrates produce dilation of both arterial and venous beds. Dilation of the post-capillary vessels, including large veins, promotes peripheral pooling of blood and decreases venous return to the heart, reducing left ventricular end-diastolic pressure (pre-load). Arteriolar relaxation reduces systemic vascular resistance and arterial pressure (after-load). The decrease in ventricular volume reduces intramyocardial tension and lessens myocardial oxygen demand.

Pharmacodynamics: Dosing regimens for most chronically used drugs are designed to provide plasma concentrations that are continuously greater than a minimally effective concentration. This strategy is inappropriate for organic nitrates. Prolonged administration of nitrate drugs according to traditionally recommended dosage regimens has been shown to produce tolerance. Tolerance results in a loss of efficacy. Several well-controlled clinical trials have used exercise testing to assess the antianginal efficacy of continuously delivered nitrates. In the large majority of these trials, nitrate effectiveness was indistinguishable from placebo after 24 hours (or less) of continuous therapy. Attempts to overcome tolerance by dose escalation, even to doses far in excess of those used acutely, have consistently failed.

Only after nitrates have been absent from the body for several hours has their antianginal efficacy been restored. Drug-free intervals sufficient to avoid tolerance to isosorbide dinitrate have not been completely defined. In the only regimen of twice-daily Cedocard SR, the 2 doses are given 6 hours apart. The eccentric twice-daily regimen provides antianginal efficacy for up to 14 hours (i.e., 6 hours between doses and 8 hours after second dose).

Pharmacokinetics: Radiotracer studies have shown that isosorbide is almost completely absorbed from the gastrointestinal tract and effectively metabolized in the liver by hepatic enzymes.

After the administration of a single oral dose of 20 mg Cedocard-SR tablets to 10 healthy volunteers mean peak plasma concentrations of 3.2 ng/mL were observed within 2 to 4 hours after dosing.

Plasma concentrations declined to about 1.7 ng/mL at 8 hours after drug administration but trace amounts of it were still detectable 12 hours after dosing.

Equilibrium dialysis experiments suggest that isosorbide is not extensively bound to plasma proteins. According to a recent study, the disposition of isosorbide showed a clear bi-exponential characteristic with half-lives of approximately 1.5 and 4 hours for the alpha and beta phases, respectively. According to this study plasma concentrations after chronic dosing were in general higher than those obtained after the comparable single doses.

Orally administered nitrates are rapidly metabolized in the liver by glutathion reductase. Recent investigations indicate that there is a wide interindividual variation in the pharmacokinetics of isosorbide and that some of the metabolites are also active. Two and 5-isosorbide mononitrate were found to exert a lesser but longer lasting hemodynamic effect than isosorbide dinitrate.

Thus, the active metabolites may contribute to the duration of action of isosorbide. Elimination occurs via the urine and is practically 100% within 24 hours post administration. Intact isosorbide is not found in urine. Twenty to 30% of the dose is excreted as 5-ISMN, 2-ISMN, isosorbide and isoiodide. The remainder is excreted primarily as the ether glucuronide of 5-ISMN and isosorbide.

Indications: For the prevention of anginal attacks in patients with chronic stable angina pectoris associated with coronary artery disease.

Not intended for the immediate relief of acute attacks of angina pectoris.

Contraindications: Known hypersensitivity to isosorbide dinitrate or to other nitrates or nitrites.

Acute circulatory failure associated with marked hypotension (shock and states of collapse).

Postural hypotension.

Myocardial insufficiency due to obstruction (e.g., in the presence of aortic or mitral stenosis or of constrictive pericarditis).

Increased intracranial pressure.

Increased intraocular pressure.

Severe anemia.

Warnings: The benefits and safety of isosorbide dinitrate in anginal patients with acute myocardial infarction or congestive heart failure have not been established. Because the effects of isosorbide dinitrate are difficult to terminate rapidly, this drug is not recommended in these settings.

Dependence on nitrates may occur with chronic use. To avoid possible withdrawal effects, the administration of isosorbide should not be abruptly discontinued but rather be gradually reduced. In industry workers continuously exposed to nitrates, chest pain, acute myocardial infarction, and even sudden death have occurred during temporary withdrawal of nitrate exposure.

Precautions: Headaches or symptoms of severe hypotension, such as weakness or dizziness, particularly when rising suddenly from a recumbent position, may occur. Caution should be exercised when using nitrates in patients prone to, or who might be affected by hypotension. Isosorbide dinitrate should therefore be used with caution in patients who may have volume depletion from diuretic therapy or in patients who have low systolic blood pressure (e.g., below 90 mmHg). Paradoxical bradycardia and increased angina pectoris may accompany nitrate-induced hypotension.

Nitrate therapy may aggravate the angina caused by hypertrophic cardiomyopathy.

In industrial workers who have had long-term exposure to unknown (presumably high) doses of organic nitrates, tolerance clearly occurs. There is, moreover, physical dependence since chest pain, acute myocardial infarction, and even sudden death have occurred during temporary withdrawal of nitrates from these workers. In clinical trials of anginal patients, there are reports of anginal attacks being more easily provoked and of rebound in the hemodynamic effects soon after nitrate withdrawal.

The importance of these observations to the routine, clinical use of oral isosorbide dinitrate has not been fully elucidated.

Caution should be exercised in patients with arterial hypoxemia due to anemia (see Contraindications). Similarly, caution is called for in patients with hypoxemia and a ventilation/perfusion imbalance due to lung disease or ischemic heart failure. Patients with angina pectoris, myocardial infarction or cerebral ischemia frequently suffer from abnormalities of the small airways (especially alveolar hypoxia). Under these circumstances, vasoconstriction occurs within the lung to shift perfusion from areas of alveolar hypoxia to better ventilated regions of the lung. As a potent vasodilator, isosorbide dinitrate could reverse this protective vasoconstriction and thus result in increased perfusion to poorly ventilated areas, worsening of the ventilation/perfusion imbalance, and a further decrease in the arterial partial pressure of oxygen.

Tolerance to isosorbide dinitrate with cross tolerance to other nitrates or nitrites may occur (see Pharmacology).

As tolerance to isosorbide dinitrate develops, the effects of sublingual nitroglycerin on exercise tolerance, although still observable, is somewhat blunted.

Occupational Hazards: As patients may experience faintness and/or dizziness, reaction time when driving or operating machinery may be impaired, especially at the start of treatment.

Pregnancy: No studies in pregnant women have been done. Studies in rabbits given isosorbide dinitrate in oral doses of 35 and 150 times the maximum daily recommended human dose have shown a dose-related increase in embryotoxicity. Isosorbide dinitrate should be used in pregnancy only if the potential benefit justifies the potential risk to the fetus.

Lactation: It is not known whether isosorbide dinitrate is excreted in breast milk. Although problems in humans have not been documented, caution should be exercised when isosorbide dinitrate is administered to a nursing mother.

Children: The safety and effectiveness in children have not been established. Therefore its use in children is not recommended.

Drug Interactions: Concomitant treatment with other vasodilators, calcium antagonists, ACE inhibitors, beta-blockers, diuretics, antihypertensives, tricyclic antidepressants and major tranquilizers may potentiate the blood pressure lowering effect of isosorbide dinitrate. Dose adjustment may be necessary. Alcohol may enhance sensitivity to the hypotensive effects of nitrates.

Adverse Effects: The most frequent adverse reaction following administration of isosorbide is vascular headache which may be severe and persistent. This adverse effect occurs most frequently at the beginning of therapy. Headache usually can be controlled by temporary dosage reduction, concomitant administration of commonly used analgesics or by administering the drug during meals. These headaches usually disappear within 1 week of continuous, uninterrupted therapy. It is usually best to advise the patient of their possible occurrence and of their importance in regard to the prevention of angina. Drug and/or exfoliative dermatitis occasionally occur.

Signs of cerebral ischemia associated with postural hypotension such as weakness, transient episodes of dizziness may occasionally develop. Cutaneous vasodilation with flushing may occur. Rarely a marked sensitivity to the hypotensive effects of the drug and severe response (nausea, vomiting, restlessness, perspiration and collapse) can occur and alcohol may enhance this effect. Isosorbide dinitrate can antagonize the effects of histamine or epinephrine, acetylcholine and similar agents.

Overdose: Symptoms: These may include the following: a prompt fall in blood pressure, persistent and throbbing headache, vertigo, palpitation, visual disturbances, flushed and perspiring skin (later becoming cold and cyanotic), nausea and vomiting (possibly with colic and even bloody diarrhea), syncope (especially in the upright position), methemoglobinemia with cyanosis and anoxia, initial hyperpnea, dyspnea and slow breathing, slow pulse (dicrotic and intermittent), heart block, increased intracranial pressure with cerebral symptoms of confusion and moderate fever, paralysis and coma followed by clonic convulsions and possibly death due to circulatory collapse.

Treatment: Prompt removal of the ingested material by gastric lavage is reasonable but not documented to be useful. Keep the patient recumbent in a shock position and comfortably warm. Passive movements of the extremities may aid venous return. Administer oxygen and artificial respiration if necessary.

Dosage: Cedocard SR tablets are administered orally twice daily, usually in the morning and in the early afternoon. The first and the second dose should be separated by approximately 6 hours, resulting in an interval between the second dose and the next first dose of about 18 hours. The recommended starting dose is 20 mg twice daily. This may be increased to a maximum of 40 mg twice daily depending on patient's tolerance and responsiveness to Cedocard SR.

While experiencing a reduction in the number of anginal episodes with Cedocard SR therapy, patients apprehensive of particularly stressful situations may still be prone to an attack. In such cases, the therapy should be supplemented with 1 or 2 sublingual isosorbide tablets 5 mg.

Supplied: Each yellow tablet, scored on one side and imprinted "CC-SR" on the other, contains: isosorbide dinitrate 20 mg in sustained release (SR) form. Nonmedicinal ingredients: D&C Yellow No. 10, FD&C Yellow No. 6, lactose, magnesium stearate, polyvinylacetate and talc. Bottles of 100.

CeeNU® ℞

Bristol

Lomustine

Antineoplastic Agent

Pharmacology: It is generally agreed that lomustine acts as an alkylating agent but, as with other nitrosoureas, it may also inhibit several key enzymatic processes.

Lomustine may be given orally. Following oral administration of radioactive lomustine at doses ranging from 30 mg/m² to 100 mg/m², about half of the radioactivity given was excreted within 24 hours. The serum half-life of the drug and/or metabolites ranges from 16 hours to 2 days. Tissue levels are comparable to plasma levels at 15 minutes after i.v. administration.

Because of the high lipid solubility and the relative lack of ionization at physiological pH, lomustine crosses the blood-brain barrier quite effectively. Levels of radioactivity in the CSF are 50% or greater than those measured concurrently in plasma.

Indications: Adjuvant therapy to surgery and radiotherapy or in combination therapy with other chemotherapeutic agents in the following: 1. Brain tumors: both primary and metastatic, in patients who have already received appropriate surgical and/or radiotherapeutic procedures. 2. Lung cancer: squamous cell, anaplastic large cell, and adenocarcinoma. Lomustine has been used alone and in combination with other appropriate antineoplastic drugs, such as cyclophosphamide. 3. Malignant melanoma: alone or in combination with other active drugs, such as vincristine. 4. Hodgkin's disease: alone or in combination with other active drugs. 5. Breast carcinoma: in advanced disease after conventional therapy has failed.

Lomustine has been used in renal cell carcinoma although the response rate is low in this resistant cancer. Responses have also been observed with non-Hodgkin's lymphoma, ovarian and pancreatic carcinoma but data are insufficient to make a definite recommendation.

Contraindications: Known hypersensitivity to lomustine. Severe leukopenia and/or thrombocytopenia.

Warnings: Caution: Lomustine is a potent drug and should be used only by physicians experienced with cancer chemotherapeutic drugs. Blood counts as well as renal and hepatic function tests should be taken regularly. Discontinue the drug if abnormal depression of bone marrow is seen.

Lomustine should be administered by individuals experienced in the use of antineoplastic therapy.

Delayed bone marrow suppression, notably thrombocytopenia and leukopenia, which may contribute to bleeding and overwhelming infections in an already compromised patient, is the most common and severe of the toxic effects of lomustine.

Blood counts should be monitored weekly for at least 6 weeks after a dose (see Adverse Effects). At the recommended dosage, courses of lomustine should not be given more frequently than every 6 weeks.

The bone marrow toxicity of lomustine is cumulative and therefore dosage adjustment must be considered on the basis of nadir blood counts from prior dose (see Table I).

Caution should be used in administering lomustine to patients with decreased circulating platelets, leukocytes or erythrocytes (see Dosage).

Pulmonary toxicity from lomustine appears to be dose related (see Adverse Effects).

Long-term use of nitrosoureas has been reported to be possibly associated with the development of secondary malignancies.

Liver and renal function tests should be monitored periodically (see Adverse Effects).

Pregnancy: Safe use in pregnancy has not been established. Lomustine is embryotoxic and teratogenic in rats and embryotoxic in rabbits at dose levels equivalent to the human dose. If this drug is used during pregnancy, or if the patient becomes pregnant while taking (receiving) this drug, the patient should be apprised of the potential hazard to the fetus. Women of childbearing potential should be advised to avoid becoming pregnant.

Carcinogenesis, Mutagenesis, Impairment of Fertility: Lomustine is carcinogenic in rats and mice, producing a marked increase in tumor incidence in doses approximating those employed clinically.

Nitrosourea therapy does have carcinogenic potential. The occurrence of acute leukemia and bone marrow dysplasias has been reported in patients following nitrosourea therapy.

Lomustine also affects fertility in male rats at doses somewhat higher than the human dose.

Lactation: It is not known whether this drug is excreted in human milk. Because many drugs are excreted in human milk and because of the potential for serious adverse reactions in nursing infants from lomustine, a decision should be made whether to discontinue nursing or to discontinue the drug, taking into account the importance of the drug to the mother.

Precautions: Due to delayed bone marrow suppression, blood counts should be monitored weekly for at least 6 weeks after a dose.

Baseline pulmonary function studies should be conducted along with frequent pulmonary function tests during treatment. Patients with a baseline below 70% of the predicted Forced Vital Capacity (FVC) or Carbon Monoxide Diffusing Capacity (DL_{CO}) are particularly at risk.

Since lomustine may cause liver dysfunction, it is recommended that liver function tests be monitored periodically.

Renal function tests should also be monitored periodically.

Adverse Effects: Gastrointestinal: Nausea and vomiting may occur 3 to 6 hours after an oral dose and usually lasts less than 24 hours. The frequency and duration may be reduced by the use of antiemetics prior to dosing and by the administration of lomustine to fasting patients.

Hematologic Toxicity: The most frequent and most serious toxicity of lomustine is delayed myelosuppression. It usually occurs 4 to 6 weeks after drug administration and is dose related. Thrombocytopenia occurs at about 4 weeks post-administration and persists for 1 to 2 weeks. Leukopenia occurs at 5 to 6 weeks after a dose of lomustine and persists for 1 to 2 weeks.

Approximately 65% of patients receiving 130 mg/m² develop white blood cell counts below 5 000 wbc/mm³. Thirty-six percent developed white blood cell counts below 3 000 wbc/mm³. Thrombocytopenia is generally more severe than leukopenia. However, both may be dose-limiting toxicities.

Lomustine may produce cumulative myelosuppression, manifested by more depressed indices or longer duration of suppression after repeated doses.

The occurrence of acute leukemia and bone marrow dysplasias have been reported in patients following long-term nitrosourea therapy. Anemia also occurs, but is less frequent and less severe than thrombocytopenia or leukopenia.

Pulmonary Toxicity: Pulmonary toxicity characterized by pulmonary infiltrates and/or fibrosis has been reported rarely with lomustine. Onset of toxicity has occurred after an interval of 6 months or longer from the start of therapy with cumulative dose of lomustine usually greater than 1 100 mg/m². There is one report of pulmonary toxicity at a cumulative dose of only 600 mg.

Delayed onset pulmonary fibrosis occurring up to 15 years after treatment has been reported in patients with intracranial tumors who received related nitrosoureas during their childhood and early adolescence.

Other Toxicities: Stomatitis, alopecia, anemia have been reported infrequently.

Neurological reactions such as disorientation, lethargy, ataxia and dysarthria have been noted in some patients receiving lomustine. However, the relationship to medication in these patients is unclear.

Nephrotoxicity: Renal abnormalities consisting of decrease in kidney size, progressive azotemia and renal failure have been reported in patients who receive large cumulative doses after prolonged therapy with lomustine and related nitrosoureas. Kidney damage has also been reported occasionally in patients receiving lower total doses.

Hepatotoxicity: A reversible type of hepatic toxicity, manifested by increased transaminase, alkaline phosphatase and bilirubin levels, has been reported in a small percentage of patients receiving lomustine.

Overdose: Symptoms and Treatment: In case of overdosage, treat the patient symptomatically.

Dosage: The recommended dose of lomustine in adults and children is 130 mg/m² as a single dose by mouth every 6 weeks.

In individuals with compromised bone marrow function, reduce the dose to 100 mg/m² every 6 weeks.

A repeat course of lomustine should not be given until circulating blood elements have returned to acceptable levels (platelets above 100 000/mm³; leukocytes above 4 000/mm³). Monitor blood counts weekly and do not give repeat courses before 6 weeks because the hematologic toxicity is delayed and cumulative.

Doses subsequent to the initial dose should be adjusted according to the hematologic response of the patient to the preceding dose. The schedule in Table I is suggested as a guide to dosage adjustments.

Table I—CeeNU

Dosage Adjustment Guide

Nadir After Prior Dose: Leukocytes	Platelets	Percentage of Prior Dose to be Given
>4 000	>100 000	100%
3 000-3 999	75 000-99 999	100%
2 000-2 999	25 000-74 999	70%
<2 000	<25 000	50%

When lomustine is used in combination with myelosuppressive drugs, the doses should be adjusted accordingly.

Supplied: 10 mg: Each capsule contains: lomustine 10 mg. Nonmedicinal ingredients: mannitol and magnesium stearate. Capsule shell: gelatin, printing ink and titanium dioxide. A desiccant packet is enclosed in each bottle of capsules. Bottles of 20.

40 mg: Each capsule contains: lomustine 40 mg. Nonmedicinal ingredients: mannitol and magnesium stearate. Capsule shell: FD&C blue No. 2, gelatin, printing ink, titanium dioxide and yellow iron oxide. A desiccant packet is enclosed in each bottle of capsules. Bottles of 20.

100 mg: Each capsule contains: lomustine 100 mg. Nonmedicinal ingredients: mannitol and magnesium stearate. Capsule shell: FD&C blue No. 2, gelatin, printing ink, titanium dioxide and yellow iron oxide. A desiccant packet is enclosed in each bottle of capsules. Bottles of 20.

Unopened bottles of lomustine capsules are stable for 24 months at room temperature. Protect from light and excessive heat (over 40°C).

(Shown in Product Recognition Section)

CEFAZOLIN SODIUM USP ℞

Novopharm

Antibiotic

Pharmacology: Cefazolin is a cephalosporin antibiotic for parenteral administration. Cefazolin exerts its bactericidal effect by inhibiting bacterial cell wall synthesis. Cefazolin is about 85% bound to serum protein. The peak level in serum is approximately 32 to 42 mg/mL after an i.m. injection of 500 mg. Over 80% of injected cefazolin is excreted in the urine during the first 24 hours after i.m. injection; most is excreted during the first 4 to 6 hours.

Indications: In the treatment of the following infections when caused by susceptible strains of the listed organisms:

Respiratory tract infections caused by S. pneumoniae, K. pneumoniae, H. influenzae, S. aureus (penicillin-sensitive and penicillin-resistant) and group A beta-hemolytic streptococci.

Urinary tract infections caused by E. coli, P. mirabilis, K. pneumoniae and some strains of enterobacter, and enterococci. See Note below.

Skin and soft tissue infections caused by S. aureus (penicillin-sensitive and penicillin-resistant), group A beta-hemolytic streptococci and other strains of streptococci.

Bone and joint infections caused by S. aureus.

Septicemia caused by S. pneumoniae, S. aureus (penicillin-sensitive and penicillin-resistant), P. mirabilis, E. coli and K. pneumoniae. See Note below.

Endocarditis caused by S. aureus (penicillin-sensitive and penicillin-resistant) and group A beta-hemolytic streptococci.

Cefazolin Sodium USP (cont'd)

Determine susceptibility of the causative organism to cefazolin by performing appropriate culture and susceptibility studies.

Note: Most strains of Enterococci, indole positive Proteus (P. vulgaris). E. cloacae, M. morganii, P. rettgeri and methicillin-resistant Staphylococci are resistant. Serratia, Pseudomonas and A. calcoaceticus (formerly Mima and Herellea species) are almost uniformly resistant to cefazolin.

Perioperative Prophylaxis: In patients undergoing potentially contaminated surgical procedures, and in patients in whom infection would pose a serious risk (e.g., during open-heart surgery and prosthetic arthroplasty), the preoperative, intraoperative and postoperative administration of cefazolin may reduce the incidence of certain postoperative infections.

Identification of the causative organisms should be made by culture should signs of infection occur, so that appropriate therapy may be instituted.

Contraindications: In patients with known allergy to the cephalosporin group of antibiotics.

Warnings: Use with caution in penicillin-allergic patients. There is clinical evidence of partial cross-allergenicity of the penicillins and the cephalosporins. There are instances of patients who have had reactions to both penicillins and cephalosporins (including fatal anaphylaxis after parenteral use). Clinical and laboratory evidence of partial cross-allergenicity of the 2 drug classes exists.

Cefazolin should be administered cautiously and then only when absolutely necessary to any patient who has demonstrated allergy, particularly to drugs. Immediate emergency treatment with epinephrine is indicated for serious anaphylactoid reactions. As indicated, oxygen, i.v. steroids, and airway management, including intubation, should also be employed.

There have been reports of pseudomembranous colitis with the use of cephalosporins. It is therefore important to consider its diagnosis in patients who develop diarrhea in association with antibiotic use.

Precautions: The overgrowth of nonsusceptible organisms may result from the prolonged use of cefazolin. It is essential that the patient be carefully observed.

In patients with a history of lower gastrointestinal disease, particularly colitis, cefazolin should be prescribed with caution. Clinitest tablets solution, but not enzyme-based tests such as Clinistix and Tes-Tape, may falsely indicate glucose in the urine of patients on cefazolin.

Positive direct and indirect Coombs' tests have been reported during treatment with cefazolin. These may also occur in neonates whose mothers received cephalosporins before delivery. The clinical significance of this effect has not been established.

Renal Impairment: Caution should be exercised in treating patients with pre-existing renal damage although cefazolin has not shown evidence of nephrotoxicity.

Patients with low urinary output due to impaired renal function should be administered reduced daily dosages of cefazolin. (See Dosage, Patients with Reduced Renal Function.) Blood levels of cefazolin in dialysis patients remain fairly high and should be monitored.

Probenecid may decrease renal tubular secretion of cefazolin when used concurrently with cefazolin, resulting in increased and prolonged cefazolin blood levels.

In beta-hemolytic streptococcal infections, treatment should be continued for at least 10 days, to minimize possible complications associated with the disease.

Pregnancy: The safety of the use of cefazolin during pregnancy has not been established.

Lactation: Very low concentrations of cefazolin are found in the milk of nursing mothers. Cefazolin should be administered with caution to a nursing woman.

Children: The safety of the use of cefazolin in prematures and infants under 1 month of age has not been established.

Drug Interactions: The renal tubular secretion of cefazolin may be decreased when probenecid is used concurrently, resulting in increased and prolonged cefazolin blood levels.

Adverse Effects: The following reactions have been reported: Gastrointestinal: diarrhea, oral candidiasis (oral thrush), vomiting, nausea, stomach cramps, anorexia. During antibiotic treatment symptoms of pseudomembranous colitis can appear. There have been rare reports of nausea and vomiting.

Allergic: Allergic reactions occur infrequently and include: anaphylaxis, eosinophilia, itching, drug fever, skin rash.

Hematologic: neutropenia, anemia, leukopenia, thrombocythemia, positive direct and indirect antiglobulin (Coombs') tests.

Hepatic and Renal: Without clinical evidence of renal or hepatic impairment transient increases in AST, ALT, BUN and alkaline phosphatase levels have been observed. Transient hepatitis and cholestatic jaundice have been reported rarely, as with some penicillins and some other cephalosporins.

Local: Phlebitis at the site of injection has occurred rarely. Infrequently there is pain at the site of injection following i.m. injection. Some induration has been reported.

Other: vulvar pruritus, genital moniliasis, vaginitis and anal pruritus.

Overdose: Symptoms and Treatment: There is a lack of experience with acute cefazolin overdosage. Supportive therapy should be instituted according to symptoms in cases of suspected overdosage.

Dosage: After reconstitution cefazolin may be administered either i.m. or i.v. In both cases total daily dosages are the same.

Adult Dosage Guide: See Table I.

Cefazolin has been administered in dosages of 6 g/day in serious infections such as endocarditis. Treatment should be continued for at least 10 days in beta-hemolytic streptococcal infections to minimize possible complications associated with the disease.

Patients with Reduced Renal Function: After an initial loading dose appropriate to the severity of the infection, the following reduced dosage schedule is recommended (see Table II).

Perioperative Prophylactic Use: The recommended dosage regimen to prevent postoperative infection in contaminated or potentially contaminated surgery is: a) 1 g i.v. or i.m. administered ½ hour to 1 hour prior to the start of surgery so that at the time of the initial surgical incision adequate antibiotic levels are present in the serum and tissues. b) For lengthy operative procedures (e.g., 2 hours or more) 0.5 to 1 g administered i.v. or i.m. during surgery. (Administration should be modified according to the duration of the operative procedure and the time of greatest exposure to infective organisms.) c) Postoperatively, 0.5 to 1 g i.v. or i.m. every 6 to 8 hours for 24 hours postoperatively. The prophylactic administration of cefazolin may be continued for 3 to 5 days following the completion of surgery in which the occurrence of infection may be particularly devastating (e.g., open-heart surgery and prosthetic athroplasty).

Children: A total daily dosage of 25 to 50 mg/kg of body weight, divided into 3 or 4 equal doses, is effective for most mild to moderately severe infections in children.

For severe infections total daily dosage may be increased to 100 mg/kg of body weight. The use of cefazolin in prematures and in infants under 1 month is not recommended since the safety for use in these patients has not been established.

Pediatric Dosage Guide: See Tables III and IV.

Treatment with 60% of the normal daily dose may be administered in divided doses every 12 hours to children with mild to moderate renal impairment (C_{cr} 0.67 to 1.17 mL/s). Children with moderate to severe renal impairment (C_{cr} 0.33 to 0.87 mL/s) should be given 25% of the normal daily dose in equally divided doses every 12 hours, and children with severe renal impairment (C_{cr} 0.08 to 0.33 mL/s) should receive 10% of the normal daily dose every 24 hours.

All dosage recommendations apply after an initial loading dose.

Administration: Note: See Reconstitution and Dilution directions below: I.M.: Inject the reconstituted solution into a large muscle mass. Pain on injection of cefazolin occurs infrequently.

I.V.: Direct (bolus) Injection: Inject the appropriately diluted reconstituted solution slowly over 3 to 5 minutes directly into a vein or through tubing for patients receiving parenteral fluids. (See list of solutions for i.v. infusion.)

Intermittent or Continuous Infusion: The reconstituted solution can be administered along with primary i.v. fluid management programs in a volume control set or in a separate secondary i.v. bottle. (See list of solutions for i.v. infusion.)

Reconstituted Solutions: Parenteral drug products should be **shaken well** when reconstituted, and inspected visually for particulate matter prior to administration. The drug solutions

Table I—Cefazolin Sodium USP

Adult Dosage Guide

Type of Infection	Dose	Frequency
Mild infections caused by susceptible Gram+ cocci	250 mg to 500 mg	Every 8 hours
Acute, uncomplicated urinary tract infections*	1 g	Every 12 hours
Moderate to severe infections	500 mg to 1 g	Every 6 to 8 hours

* This dosage recommendation applies to i.m. use. The efficacy of cefazolin when administered i.v. at 12-hour intervals has not been established.

Table II—Cefazolin Sodium USP

Dosage Guide for Patients with Renal Impairment

Creatinine Clearance (mL/s)	Serum Creatinine (mmol/L)	Dosage
≥0.91	≤140	250 mg to 1 g every 6–12 hours
0.58–0.90	141–273	250 mg to 1 g every 8–12 hours
0.18–0.57	274–406	125 mg to 500 mg every 12 hours
≤0.17	≥407	125 mg to 500 mg every 18 hours

Table III—Cefazolin Sodium USP

Pediatric Dosage Guide—25 mg/kg/day

	25 mg/kg/day Divided into 3 Doses		25 mg/kg/day Divided into 4 Doses	
Weight kg	Approximate Single Dose mg/q8h	Volume Needed of 125 mg/mL* Solution	Approximate Single Dose mg/q6h	Volume Needed of 125 mg/mL* Solution
4.5	40 mg	0.35 mL	30 mg	0.25 mL
9.0	75 mg	0.60 mL	55 mg	0.45 mL
13.6	115 mg	0.90 mL	85 mg	0.70 mL
18.1	150 mg	1.20 mL	115 mg	0.90 mL
22.7	190 mg	1.50 mL	140 mg	1.10 mL

* 125 mg/mL concentration may be obtained by reconstituting the 500 mg vial with 3.8 mL of diluent.

Table IV—Cefazolin Sodium USP

Pediatric Dosage Guide—50 mg/kg/day

	50 mg/kg/day Divided into 3 Doses		50 mg/kg/day Divided into 4 Doses	
Weight kg	Approximate Single Dose mg/q8h	Volume Needed of 225 mg/mL* Solution	Approximate Single Dose mg/q6h	Volume Needed of 225 mg/mL* Solution
4.5	75 mg	0.35 mL	55 mg	0.25 mL
9.0	150 mg	0.70 mL	110 mg	0.50 mL
13.6	225 mg	1.00 mL	170 mg	0.75 mL
18.1	300 mg	1.35 mL	225 mg	1.00 mL
22.7	375 mg	1.70 mL	285 mg	1.25 mL

* 225 mg/mL concentration may be obtained by reconstituting the 500 mg vial with 2 mL of diluent.

Table V—Cefazolin Sodium USP

Single Dose Vial Reconstitution

Strength (mg)	Diluent[a]	Volume to be Added to Vial (mL)	Approximate Available Volume (mL)	Nominal Concentration (mg/mL)
500	Sodium Chloride Injection or	2.0	2.2	225
	Sterile Water for Injection	3.8	4.0	125
1 000	Sterile Water for Injection	2.5	3.0	334[b]

[a]Bacteriostatic Water for Injection may also be used. Note: Dilution of the 10 g Pharmacy Bulk vial with Bacteriostatic diluent is not encouraged since a patient may receive an excessive amount of preservative if the entire container contents are given to 1 patient.

[b]Note: Under refrigeration, cefazolin of 334 mg/mL concentration precipitates. To redissolve, place vial between the palms of 2 hands and mix vial contents by a rotating action for 1 minute.

should be discarded if particulate matter is evident in reconstituted fluids.

Reconstituted solutions may range in color from pale yellow to yellow without a change in potency.

Reconstituted cefazolin may be stored for 24 hours at controlled room temperature not exceeding 25°C, or for 72 hours under refrigeration (2 to 8°C), protected from light.

Cefazolin solution reconstituted with bacteriostatic diluent and used for i.m. administration as multiple-dose containers should be used within 6 days when stored under refrigeration.

The pharmacy bulk vial is intended for multiple dispensing for i.v. use only, employing a single puncture. Following reconstitution, the solution should be dispensed and diluted for use within 8 hours. Any unused reconstituted solution should be discarded after 8 hours.

I.M. Injection: Single Dose Vials: Reconstitute according to Table V. **Shake well.**

Direct I.V. (bolus) Injection: Single Dose Vial: Reconstitute as directed above. **Shake well.** A minimum of 10 mL of Sterile Water for Injection should be used to dilute the reconstituted solution.

Pharmacy Bulk Vial: Pharmacy Bulk Vials should be used for i.v. use only. Add, according to Table VI, Sterile Water for Injection, Bacteriostatic Water for Injection, or Sodium Chloride Injection. **Shake well.**

Table VI—Cefazolin Sodium USP

Pharmacy Bulk Vial Reconstitution

Strength	Amount of Diluent (mL)	Approximate Available Volume (mL)	Approximate Concentration (mg/mL)
10 g	45	50	200
	96	100	100

The vial is intended for single puncture and multiple dispensing, and the vial contents should be used within 8 hours.

Intermittent or continous i.v. infusion, reconstituted cefazolin may be further diluted as follows: Single Dose Vials: Reconstitute according to Table V. **Shake well.** Further dilute the reconstituted cefazolin in 50 to 100 mL of Sterile Water for Injection or 50 to 100 mL of one of the following solutions: Sodium Chloride Injection 0.9%, Dextrose Injection 5% or 10%, Dextrose 5% in Lactated Ringer's Injection, Dextrose 5% and Sodium Chloride Injection 0.9% (also may be used with Dextrose 5% and Sodium Chloride Injection 0.45% or 0.2%), Lactated Ringer's Injection, Ringer's Injection, Sodium Bicarbonate 5% in Sterile Water for Injection.

Pharmacy Bulk Vial: Reconstitute according to Table VI. **Shake well.** Further dilute aliquots in 50 to 100 mL of Sterile Water for Injection or one of the solutions listed above.

The further diluted solutions above should be used within 24 hours at room temperature or 72 hours under refrigeration from the time of initial puncture.

Extended Use of I.V. Admixtures: Although i.v. admixtures may often be physically and chemically stable for longer periods, due to microbiological considerations, they are usually recommended for use within the maximum of 24 hours at room temperature or 72 hours when refrigerated (2 to 8°C).

Hospitals and institutions, that have recognized admixture programs and use validated aseptic techniques for preparation of i.v. solutions, may extend the storage times for cefazolin in admixtures with 5% Dextrose Injection or 0.9% Sodium Chloride Injection in Viaflex bags in 80 mg/mL concentrations to 30 days when stored under refrigeration (2 to 8°C) and in 5 mg/mL concentrations to 72 hours when stored under refrigeration (2 to 8°C).

Supplied: 500 mg: Each clear glass vial of sterile powder contains: cefazolin 500 mg. Preservative-free.

1 g: Each clear glass vial of sterile powder contains: cefazolin 1 g. Preservative-free.

10 g: Each pharmacy bulk vial of sterile powder contains: cefazolin 10 g. Preservative-free. **The availability of the pharmacy bulk vial is intended for hospitals with a recognized i.v. admixture program.**

Store between 15 and 25°C, protect from light.

Reviewed 1997

CEFIZOX® P

SmithKline Beecham

Ceftizoxime Sodium

Antibiotic

Pharmacology: In vitro studies indicate that the bactericidal action of ceftizoxime results from inhibition of cell-wall synthesis in aerobic and anaerobic gram-positive and gram-negative organisms. In vitro, ceftizoxime shows a strong affinity for penicillin-binding proteins 1a, 1bs and 3 of E. coli.

Indications: In the treatment of the infections listed below when caused by susceptible strains of the designated microorganisms:

Lower Respiratory Tract Infections caused by Streptococcus species (including S. pneumoniae but excluding enterococci); Klebsiella species; P. mirabilis; E. coli; H. influenzae (including ampicillin-resistant strains); S. aureus (including penicillinase-producing but excluding methicillin-resistant strains); Serratia species and Enterobacter species.

Urinary Tract Infections caused by E. coli; S. epidermidis; P. aeruginosa; P. mirabilis; Klebsiella species; S. marcescens and Enterobacter species.

Due to the nature of the underlying conditions which usually predispose patients to Pseudomonas infections of the urinary tract, a good clinical response accompanied by bacterial eradication may not be achieved despite evidence of in vitro sensitivity.

Intra-abdominal Infections caused by E. coli; S. epidermidis; Streptococcus species (excluding enterococci); Klebsiella species; Bacteroides species (including B. fragilis); Peptococcus species and Peptostreptococcus species.

Septicemia caused by Streptococcus species (excluding enterococci but including S. pneumoniae); S. aureus (excluding methicillin-resistant strains); E. coli; Bacteroides species (including B. fragilis); Klebsiella species and S. marcescens.

Skin Structure Infections caused by S. aureus (excluding methicillin-resistant strains); S. epidermidis; E. coli; Klebsiella species, (including K. pneumoniae); Streptococcus species (excluding enterococci but including Group A β-hemolytic Streptococcus pyogenes); P. mirabilis; Serratia species; Enterobacter species; Bacteroides species (including B. fragilis); Peptococcus species, and Peptostreptococcus species.

Bone and Joint Infections caused by S. aureus (excluding methicillin-resistant strains); P. mirabilis; Peptococcus species and Peptostreptococcus species.

Specimens for bacteriologic culture should be obtained prior to therapy in order to identify the causative organisms and to determine their susceptibilities to ceftizoxime. Therapy with ceftizoxime may be initiated before results of the susceptibility studies are known. However, modification of the treatment may be required once these results become available.

Contraindications: In persons who have shown hypersensitivity to ceftizoxime or other members of the cephalosporin group of antibiotics.

Warnings: Before therapy with ceftizoxime is instituted, careful inquiry should be made to determine whether the patient has had previous hypersensitivity reactions to cephalosporins, penicillins, or other drugs. Ceftizoxime should be given cautiously to penicillin-sensitive patients. Antibiotics, including ceftizoxime, should be administered with caution to any patient who has demonstrated some form of allergy, particularly to drugs. If an allergic reaction to ceftizoxime occurs, its administration should be discontinued. Serious acute hypersensitivity reactions may require epinephrine and other emergency measures.

Pseudomembranous colitis has been reported with the use of ceftizoxime (and other antibiotics). Therefore it is important to consider this diagnosis in patients administered ceftizoxime and who develop diarrhea.

Treatment with broad-spectrum antibiotics alters normal flora of the colon and may permit overgrowth of clostridia. Studies indicate a toxin produced by C. difficile is one primary cause of antibiotic-associated colitis.

Mild cases of colitis may respond to drug discontinuation alone. Moderate to severe cases should be managed with fluid, electrolyte and protein supplementation as indicated. When the colitis is not relieved by drug discontinuation or when it is severe, consideration may be given to the administration of oral vancomycin or other suitable therapy. Other possible causes of colitis should also be considered.

Precautions: Transient elevations of BUN and serum creatinine have been observed in clinical studies. However, there is no other evidence that ceftizoxime has produced alterations in renal function. Renal status should be periodically evaluated, especially in seriously ill patients.

Prolonged use of ceftizoxime may result in the overgrowth of nonsusceptible organisms including species originally sensitive to the drug. Careful observation of the patient is essential. If superinfection occurs during therapy, appropriate measures should be taken.

Ceftizoxime should be administered with caution to individuals with a history of gastrointestinal disease, particularly colitis.

Impaired Renal Function: Since ceftizoxime is excreted primarily in the urine, patients with impaired renal function (i.e., creatinine clearance $\leq$1.32 mL/s or $\leq$79 mL/min) should be placed on a special dosage schedule recommended under Dosage. Normal dosages in these individuals are likely to produce excessive serum concentrations of ceftizoxime.

Drug Interactions: The concomitant administration of some cephalosporins and aminoglycosides has caused nephrotoxicity. The effect of administering ceftizoxime concomitantly with aminoglycosides is not known.

Pregnancy: The safety of ceftizoxime in pregnancy has not been established. Its use in pregnant women requires that the likely benefit from the drug be weighed against the possible risk to the mother and fetus. The pharmacokinetics in pregnant patients have not been investigated. Reproduction studies performed in rats and rabbits have revealed no evidence of impaired fertility or harm to the fetus caused by ceftizoxime. Animal reproduction studies, however, are not always predictive of human response.

Labor and Delivery: The safety and efficacy of ceftizoxime use during labor and delivery has not been investigated.

Lactation: Ceftizoxime is excreted in human milk in low concentrations (less than 4% of serum concentrations at 1 hour after dosing). The clinical significance of this is unknown; therefore caution should be exercised if ceftizoxime is to be administered to a nursing woman.

Infants and Children: The safety in infants less than 6 months of age has not been established. In children 6 months of age and older, treatment with ceftizoxime has been associated with transient elevated levels of eosinophils, AST, ALT, and CPK (creatine phosphokinase). The CPK elevation may be related to i.m. administration.

Geriatrics: The elimination of ceftizoxime may be reduced due to an age-dependent reduction in renal function.

Adverse Effects: Ceftizoxime is generally well tolerated.

Hypersensitivity: Incidence > 1% but < 5%: rash, pruritus, fever.

Liver: Incidence > 1% but < 5%: transient elevation of AST, ALT and alkaline phosphatase.

Blood: Incidence ≤ 1%: neutropenia, leukopenia, thrombocytopenia. Incidence > 1% but < 5%: transient eosinophilia, thrombocytosis, positive direct Coombs' test.

Renal: Incidence ≤ 1%: transient elevation of BUN and creatinine.

Local: Incidence > 1% but < 5%: injection site: burning, cellulitis, phlebitis (with i.v. administration), pain, induration, tenderness, paresthesia.

Genitourinary: Incidence ≤ 1%: vaginitis.

Gastrointestinal: Incidence ≤ 1%: diarrhea, nausea, vomiting, pseudomembranous colitis.

Cefizox (cont'd)

No disulfiram-like reactions have been reported.

Overdose: Symptoms and Treatment: No case of acute overdosage has been reported to date; consequently there is no specific information available on symptoms or treatment. In cases of suspected overdosage, supportive therapy should be instituted according to symptoms. Serum ceftizoxime levels can be reduced by hemodialysis.

Dosage: Ceftizoxime may be administered either i.m. or i.v. after reconstitution.

Dosage and route of administration should be determined by the condition of the patient, severity of the infection and susceptibility of the causative organism(s). The i.v. route may be preferable for patients with bacterial septicemia, or other severe or life-threatening infections.

The usual course of treatment should be 7 to 14 days, and should normally continue at least 48 hours after evidence of bacterial eradication has been obtained. For β-hemolytic streptococcal infections, a minimum of 10 days of treatment is recommended.

Adults: The recommended daily dosage is 1 to 12 g administered in equally divided doses every 8 to 12 hours (see Table I).

Table I—Cefizox

Dosage in Adults

Type of Infection	Daily Dose (g)	Frequency and Route
Uncomplicated Urinary Tract	1	500 mg q12h, i.v. or i.m.
Other Sites	2–3	1 g q8h or q12h, i.v. or i.m.
Severe or Refractory	3–6	1 g q8h, i.v. or i.m. to 2 g q8h or q12h, i.v. or i.m.*
Life-Threatening	9–12	3 or 4 g q8h i.v.

* When administering 2 g i.m., the dose should be divided and injected into different large muscle masses.

Because of the serious nature of urinary tract infections due to P. aeruginosa and because many strains are only moderately susceptible to ceftizoxime, higher dosage may be appropriate when urinary tract infections are caused by these organisms. Other therapy should be instituted if the response is not prompt.

Adults with Impaired Renal Function: In patients in whom the creatinine clearance is 1.32 mL/s (79 mL/min) or less, the dosage must be reduced. Following an initial loading dose of 500 mg to 1.0 g i.m. or i.v., the maintenance dosing schedule presented in Table II should be followed in patients with reduced renal function.

Table II—Cefizox

Dosage in Adults with Impaired Renal Function

Renal Function	Creatinine Clearance mL/s	mL/min	Less Severe Infections	Life-Threatening Infections
Mild impairment	0.83–1.32	50–79	500 mg q8h	750 mg to 1.5 g q8h
Moderate to severe impairment	0.08–0.82	5–49	250 or 500 mg q12h	500 mg to 1.0 g q12h
Hemodialysis patients*	0–0.07	0–4	500 mg q48h or 250 mg q24h	500 mg to 1.0 g q48h or 500 mg q24h

* In patients undergoing hemodialysis no additional supplemental dosing is required. **Dosing, however, should be scheduled so that the patient receives the dose at the end of the dialysis.** When started 24 hours after administration of 1 g of ceftizoxime, hemodialysis has been shown to reduce serum levels by 50%.

When only the serum creatinine level is available, creatinine clearance may be calculated from the following formulas (for patients 18 years and over only). The serum creatinine level should represent renal function at the steady state:

Males:

$$\text{Creatinine clearance (mL/min)} = \frac{\text{Weight (kg)} \times (140-\text{age})}{72 \times \text{serum creatinine (mg/100 mL)}}$$

or

$$\text{Creatinine clearance (mL/s)} = \frac{\text{Weight (kg)} \times (140-\text{age})}{49 \times \text{serum creatinine } (\mu\text{mol/L})}$$

Females: 0.85 of the above values

Infants and Children: The dosage schedule in Table III is recommended.

Table III—Cefizox

Dosage in Infants and Children

Age Group	Unit Dosage	Frequency and Route
Infants (6 months–2 years) and Children (2–12 years)	50 mg/kg i.v. or i.m.	q6h or q8h, i.v. or i.m.

The pediatric dosage should not exceed the maximum adult dosage for serious infections.

I.M. Administration: The reconstituted solution of ceftizoxime should be injected well within the body of a relatively large muscle, such as the gluteus. When administering 2 g i.m. doses, the dose should be divided equally and then injected into different large muscle masses.

I.V. Administration: Injection (bolus): The reconstituted solution of ceftizoxime should be injected slowly over 3 to 5 minutes, directly or through the tubing system by which the patient is receiving another compatible i.v. solution. During administration of the solution containing ceftizoxime, it is desirable to temporarily discontinue administration of the other solution.

Intermittent or continuous infusion: The further diluted reconstituted solution of ceftizoxime should be administered over a 20 to 30 minute period.

Note: Ceftizoxime solutions should not be physically mixed with any other drug. There is a known incompatibility with aminoglycoside antibiotics. Therefore, they should not be physically mixed with ceftizoxime solutions nor administered at the same site.

Reconstitution: For I.M. Injection: Reconstitute with Sterile Water for Injection or Bacteriostatic Water for Injection (see Table IV).

Table IV—Cefizox

Reconstitution Table (I.M.)

Vial Size	Diluent to be Added to Vial	Approximate Available Volume	Approximate Average Concentration
1 g	3.0 mL	3.7 mL	270 mg/mL
2 g	6.0 mL	7.4 mL	270 mg/mL

Shake well until dissolved.

For I.V. Injection: Reconstitute only with Sterile Water For Injection (see Table V).

Table V—Cefizox

Reconstitution Table (I.V.)

Vial Size	Diluent to be Added to Vial	Approximate Available Volume	Approximate Average Concentration
1 g	10 mL	10.7 mL	95 mg/mL
2 g	20 mL	21.4 mL	95 mg/mL

Shake well until dissolved.

For I.V. Infusion: Reconstitute as for i.v. injection. Further dilute the reconstituted solution to 50 to 100 mL with one of the Solutions for I.V. Infusion (see below).

Solutions for I.V. Infusion: Sodium Chloride Injection; 5% or 10% Dextrose Injection; 5% Dextrose and 0.9%, 0.45% or 0.2% Sodium Chloride Injection; Ringer's Injection; Lactated Ringer's Injection; 10% Invert Sugar in Sterile Water for Injection; 5% Sodium Bicarbonate in Sterile Water for Injection; 5% Dextrose in Lactated Ringer's Injection **only** when reconstituted with 4% Sodium Bicarbonate Injection.

Extended Use of I.V. Admixtures: Although i.v. admixtures may often be physically and chemically stable for longer periods, **due to microbiological considerations, they are usually recommended for use within 24 hours at room temperature or 48 hours when refrigerated (2 to 8°C).**

Hospitals and institutions that have recognized admixture programs and use validated aseptic techniques for preparation of i.v. solutions may extend the storage times for ceftizoxime admixtures with 5% Dextrose Injection or 0.9% Sodium Chloride Injection in Viaflex bags in concentrations of 5 to 20 mg/mL to 14 days when stored under refrigeration at 2 to 8°C.

Warnings: As with all parenteral drug products, i.v. admixtures should be inspected visually for clarity, particulate matter, precipitate, discoloration and leakage prior to administration, whenever solution and container permit. Solutions showing haziness, particulate matter, precipitate, discoloration or leakage should not be used.

Stability and Storage: Ceftizoxime powder for injection should be stored at room temperature (15 to 30°C). Reconstituted solutions intended for i.m. injection (see Table IV) should be used within 16 hours when stored at room temperature or 48 hours when refrigerated (2 to 8°C). Reconstituted solutions intended for i.v. injection or solutions further diluted for i.v. infusion (see Table V) should be used within 24 hours when stored at room temperature or 48 hours when refrigerated (2 to 8°C) from the time of the initial reconstitution.

Solutions of ceftizoxime range from colorless to pale yellow, depending upon the diluent and volume used. The solution should be discarded if it becomes cloudy. The pH of freshly reconstituted solutions usually ranges from 6.0 to 8.0.

A solution of ceftizoxime 1 g in 13 mL Sterile Water for Injection is isotonic.

Incompatibility: Ceftizoxime should not be added to blood products, protein hydrolysates or amino acids. It should not be mixed together with an aminoglycoside.

Supplied: Each vial of sterile powder contains: ceftizoxime sodium (expressed in terms of free acid). Sodium: approx. 60 mg/g (2.6 mEq sodium ion). Standard vials of 1 and 2 g. Store unreconstituted product at room temperature (15 to 30°C).

CEFOTAN® Ⓟ

Wyeth-Ayerst

Cefotetan Disodium

Antibiotic

Pharmacology: Cefotetan disodium is a semisynthetic, beta-lactamase resistant, cephalosporin (cephamycin) antibiotic. In vitro studies indicate that the bactericidal action of cefotetan results from an interference of bacterial cell wall synthesis by inhibiting the cross-linking of peptidoglycan. Studies with ^{14}C-labeled cefotetan have shown that on reaching the target penicillin-binding proteins (PBPs) in the inner membrane, the radiolabeled antibiotic binds principally to PBP 3 followed by PBP 1A and 1B. Cefotetan, like other cephamycins, does not bind to PBP 2.

The plasma elimination half-life of cefotetan is 3 to 4.6 hours after either i.v. or i.m. administration. In normal patients, from 51 to 81% of the administered dose is excreted unchanged by the kidney in 24 hours. The biliary tract is the other major route of elimination.

Indications: Treatment: For the treatment of the following infections when caused by susceptible strains of the designated organisms: Urinary tract infections caused by E. coli and Klebsiella species (including K. pneumoniae), P. mirabilis and indole-positive Proteus.

Lower respiratory tract infections caused by S. pneumoniae (formerly D. pneumoniae), S. aureus (penicillinase and non-penicillinase-producing), H. influenzae (including ampicillin-resistant strains), Klebsiella species (including K. pneumoniae) and E. coli.

Skin and skin structure infections caused by S. aureus (penicillinase and non-penicillinase-producing), S. epidermidis, S. pyogenes, Streptococcus species (excluding Enterococci) and E. coli.

Gynecologic infections caused by S. aureus (penicillinase and non-penicillinase-producing), S. epidermidis, Streptococcus species (excluding Enterococci), E. coli, P. mirabilis, N. gonorrhoeae, anaerobic gram-positive cocci and gram-negative bacilli, Bacteroides species (excluding B. distasonis, B. ovatus and B. thetaiotaomicron).

Intra-abdominal infections caused by E. coli, anaerobic gram-negative bacilli, Bacteroides species (excluding B. distasonis, B. ovatus and B. thetaiotaomicron).

Bone and joint infections caused by S. aureus.

Specimens for bacteriological examination should be obtained prior to therapy in order to isolate and identify causative organisms and to determine their susceptibilities to cefotetan. Therapy may be instituted before results of susceptibility studies are known. However, once these results become available, the antibiotic treatment should be adjusted accordingly.

Prophylaxis: The preoperative administration of cefotetan may reduce the incidence of certain postoperative infections in patients undergoing surgical procedures that are classified as clean contaminated, or potentially contaminated (e.g., cesarean section, abdominal or vaginal hysterectomy, transurethral surgery, biliary tract surgery and gastrointestinal surgery).

The prophylactic dose of cefotetan should be administered 30 to 60 minutes prior to surgery. In patients undergoing cesarean section, cefotetan should be administered i.v. after the clamping of the umbilical cord.

If there are signs and symptoms of infection, specimens for culture should be obtained for identification of the causative organism so that appropriate therapeutic measures may be initiated.

Contraindications: In patients with a known allergy to the cephalosporin group of antibiotics and in those individuals who have experienced a cephalosporin associated hemolytic anemia.

Warnings: Before therapy with cefotetan is instituted, careful inquiry should be made to determine whether the patient has had previous hypersensitivity reactions to cefotetan, cephalosporins, penicillins or other drugs. Cefotetan should be given cautiously to penicillin-sensitive patients. Antibiotics, including cefotetan, should be administered with caution to any patient who has demonstrated some form of allergy, particularly to drugs. If an allergic reaction to cefotetan occurs, administration should be discontinued. Serious acute hypersensitivity reactions may require epinephrine and other emergency measures.

Pseudomembranous colitis has been reported with the use of cephalosporins, including cefotetan, (and other broad-spectrum antibiotics); therefore, it is important to consider this diagnosis in patients who develop diarrhea in association with antibiotic use.

An immune mediated hemolytic anemia has been observed in patients receiving cephalosporin class antibiotics. Rare cases of severe hemolytic anemia, including fatalities, have been reported in association with cefotetan and other cephalosporins. If a patient develops anemia anytime within 2 to 3 weeks subsequent to the administration of cefotetan, the diagnosis of a cephalosporin associated anemia should be considered and the drug stopped until the etiology is determined with certainty. Blood transfusions may be administered if considered to be necessary (see Contraindications).

Patients who receive prolonged courses of cefotetan for treatment of infections should have periodic monitoring for signs and symptoms of hemolytic anemia including a measurement of hematological parameters where appropriate.

Treatment with broad-spectrum antibiotics may alter normal flora of the colon and may permit overgrowth of clostridia. Studies indicate a toxin produced by C. difficile is one primary cause of antibiotic-associated colitis.

Mild cases of colitis may respond to drug discontinuance alone.

Moderate to severe cases should be managed with fluid, electrolyte and protein supplementation as indicated. When the colitis is not relieved by drug discontinuance or when it is severe, consideration should be given to the administration of oral vancomycin for antibiotic-associated pseudomembranous colitis produced by C. difficile. Other causes should also be considered.

Precautions: Prolonged use of cefotetan may result in overgrowth of nonsusceptible organisms and organisms initially sensitive to the drug. Careful observation of the patients is essential. If superinfection does occur during therapy, appropriate measures should be taken.

Cefotetan may be associated with a fall in prothrombin activity. Those at risk include patients with renal or hepatic impairment, poor nutritional state, the elderly and patients with cancer. Prothrombin times should be monitored in patients at risk and exogenous vitamin K administered as indicated.

Cefotetan should be used with caution in individuals with a history of gastrointestinal disease, particularly colitis.

A disulfiram-like reaction characterized by flushing, sweating, headache and tachycardia may occur when alcohol (beer, wine, etc.) is ingested within 72 hours after cefotetan administration. Patients should be cautioned about the ingestion of alcoholic beverages following the administration of cefotetan.

Patients with impaired renal function; i.e., creatinine clearance of 30 mL/min or less, should be placed on a special dosage schedule for cefotetan recommended under Dosage.

Drug Interactions: Renal function should be carefully monitored, especially if high dosages of the aminoglycosides are to be administered or if therapy is prolonged, because of the potential nephrotoxicity and ototoxicity of aminoglycosidic antibiotics. Although, to date, this has not been noted when cefotetan was given alone, increased nephrotoxicity has been reported following concomitant administration of cephalosporins and aminoglycoside antibiotics. However, at the recommended dose, enhancement of nephrotoxicity is unlikely to be a problem with cefotetan.

Drug/Laboratory Test Interactions: A false positive reaction for glucose in urine may occur with Benedict's or Fehling's solution.

High concentrations of cefotetan may interfere with measurement of serum and urine creatinine levels by Jaffe reaction and produce false increases in the levels of creatinine reported.

Pregnancy: The safety of cefotetan in the treatment of infection during pregnancy has not been established. The use of cefotetan in pregnant women requires that the likely benefit from the drug be weighed against the possible risks to the mother and fetus. Reproduction studies have been performed in rats and monkeys at doses up to 20 times the human dose and have revealed no evidence of impaired fertility or harm to the fetus due to cefotetan. There are, however, no adequate and well-controlled studies in pregnant women. Because animal reproductive studies are not always predictive of human response, cefotetan should be used during pregnancy only if clearly needed.

Lactation: Cefotetan is excreted in human milk in very low concentrations. Caution should be exercised when cefotetan is administered to a nursing woman.

Children: Safety and effectiveness in children have not been established.

Adverse Effects: In clinical studies, the following adverse effects were considered related to cefotetan therapy.

Gastrointestinal: Gastrointestinal symptoms occurred in 1.5% of patients, the most frequent were diarrhea (1 in 80) and nausea (1 in 700).

Hematologic: Hematologic laboratory abnormalities occurred in 1.4% of patients and included eosinophilia (1 in 200), positive direct Coombs' test (1 in 250) and thrombocytosis (1 in 300). Transient thrombocytopenia and leukopenia have been reported.

Hepatic: Hepatic enzyme elevations occurred in 1.2% of patients and included a rise in SGPT (1 in 150), SGOT (1 in 300), alkaline phosphatase (1 in 700) and LDH (1 in 700).

Hypersensitivity: Hypersensitivity reactions were reported in 1.2% of patients and included rash (1 in 150) and itching (1 in 700). During postmarketing experience with cefotetan, anaphylactic reactions have been reported.

Local Effects: Local effects were reported in less than 1% of patients and included phlebitis at the site of injection (1 in 300) and discomfort (1 in 500).

Overdose: Symptoms and Treatment: To date, there have been no documented cases of overdosage with cefotetan. If overdosage should occur, it should be treated symptomatically. Cefotetan may be removed by dialysis.

Dosage: Treatment: Adults: The usual adult dosage is 1 or 2 g administered i.v. or i.m. every 12 hours for 5 to 10 days. Proper dosage and route of administration should be determined by the condition of the patient, severity of the infection and susceptibility of the causative organism (see Table I). Therapy may be started while awaiting the results of susceptibility testing.

The i.v. route is preferable for patients with bacteremia, bacterial septicemia or other severe or life-threatening infections or for patients who may be at risk particularly if shock is present or impending.

Impaired Renal Function: When renal function is impaired, a reduced dosage schedule must be employed. The dosage guidelines in Table II may be used.

Alternatively, the dosing interval may remain constant at 12-hour intervals, but the dose reduced to one-half the usual recommended dose for patients with a creatinine clearance of 10 to 30 mL/min (0.17 to 0.50 mL/sec) and one-quarter the usual recommended dose for patients with a creatinine clearance of less than 10 mL/min (0.17 mL/sec).

When only serum creatinine levels are available, creatinine clearance may be calculated from the following formula. The serum creatinine level should represent a steady state of renal function.

Males:

$$\text{Creatinine clearance (mL/min)} = \frac{\text{Weight (kg)} \times (140-\text{age})}{72 \times \text{serum creatinine (mg/100 mL)}}$$

$$\text{Creatinine clearance (mL/s)} = \frac{\text{Weight (kg)} \times (140-\text{age})}{49 \times \text{serum creatinine } (\mu\text{mol/L})}$$

Females: 0.85×male value

Cefotetan is dialyzable and it is recommended that for patients undergoing intermittent hemodialysis, one-quarter of the usual recommended dose be given every 24 hours on days between dialysis and one-half the usual recommended dosage on the day of dialysis.

Children: The safety and effectiveness in children has not been established.

Prophylaxis: To prevent postoperative infection in clean contaminated or potentially contaminated surgery in adults, the recommended dosage is 1 to 2 g of cefotetan administered once, i.v., 30 to 60 minutes prior to surgery. In patients undergoing cesarean section, the dose should be administered as soon as the umbilical cord is clamped.

Administration: I.V.: For intermittent i.v. administration, a solution containing 1 g or 2 g of cefotetan in Sterile Water for Injection can be injected over a period of 3 to 5 minutes. Using an infusion system, it may also be given over a longer period of time through the tubing system by which the patient may be receiving other i.v. solutions.

Butterfly or scalp vein-type needles are preferred for this type of infusion. However, during infusion of the solution containing cefotetan, it is advisable to discontinue temporarily the administration of other solutions at the same site.

Note: Solutions of cefotetan must not be admixed with solutions containing aminoglycosides. If cefotetan and aminoglycosides are to be administered to the same patient, they must be administered separately and not as a mixed injection.

I.M.: Cefotetan should be injected well within the body of a relatively large muscle such as the upper outer quadrant of the buttock (i.e., gluteus maximus); aspiration is necessary to avoid inadvertent injection into a blood vessel.

Reconstitution: I.M.: Reconstitute with Sterile Water for Injection; Normal Saline, USP; 0.5% Lidocaine HCl or 1.0%

Table I—Cefotan

General Guidelines for Dosage of Cefotetan

Type of Infection	Daily Dose	Frequency and Route
Urinary Tract	1-4 g	500 mg every 12 hours i.v. or i.m. 1 or 2 g every 24 hours i.v. or i.m. 1 or 2 g every 12 hours i.v. or i.m.
Other Sites	2-4 g	1 or 2 g every 12 hours i.v. or i.m.
Severe	4 g	2 g every 12 hours i.v.
Life-Threatening	6 g*	3 g every 12 hours i.v.

*Maximum daily dosage should not exceed 6 g.

Table II—Cefotan

Dosage Guidelines for Patients with Impaired Renal Function

Creatinine Clearance mL/min	Creatinine Clearance mL/sec	Dose	Frequency
>30	>0.50	Usual Recommended Dose*	Every 12 hours
10-30	0.17-0.50	Usual Recommended Dose*	Every 24 hours
<10	<0.17	Usual Recommended Dose*	Every 48 hours

*Dose determined by the type and severity of infection, and susceptibility of the causative organism.

Cefotan (cont'd)

Lidocaine HCl. Shake to dissolve and let stand until clear. See Table III.

Table III—Cefotan

Reconstitution: I.M.

Vial Size	Amount of Diluent to be Added (mL)	Approximate Withdrawable Vol. (mL)	Approximate Average Concentration (mg/mL)
1 g	2	2.5	400
2 g	3	4.0	500

I.V.: Reconstitute with Sterile Water for Injection, 0.9% Sodium Chloride Injection or 5% Dextrose Injection. Shake to dissolve and let stand until clear. See Table IV.

Table IV—Cefotan

Reconstitution: I.V.

Vial Size	Amount of Diluent to be Added (mL)	Approximate Withdrawable Vol. (mL)	Approximate Average Concentration (mg/mL)
1 g	10	10.5	95
2 g	10-20	11-21	182-95

A solution prepared with sterile water for injection may be further diluted to the desired volume with any of the Solutions for I.V. Infusion listed below: Solutions for I.V. Infusion: 0.9% Sodium Chloride for Injection; 5% Dextrose Injection; 10% Dextrose Injection; Ringers Injection; Lactated Ringers Injection; 5% Dextrose and 0.9% Sodium Chloride Injection; 5% Dextrose and 0.225% Sodium Chloride Injection; 5% Dextrose and Ringers Injection; 5% Dextrose and Lactated Ringers Injection; 10% Invert Sugar Injection; 5% Sodium Bicarbonate Injection; Sodium Lactate Injection, ⅙ Molar; Isolyte-S Injection.

Compatibility and Stability: Cefotetan reconstituted as described above (Reconstitution) maintains satisfactory potency for 24 hours at room temperature (25°C), or 72 hours under refrigeration (5°C).

Any unused portions of the reconstituted solutions should be discarded.

Cefotetan should not be physically mixed with other antimicrobial agents.

Note: Parenteral drug products should be inspected visually for particulate matter and discoloration prior to administration, whenever solution and container permit.

Supplied: 1 g: Each vial of dry, white to pale yellow powder contains: cefotetan disodium equivalent to 1 g cefotetan activity for i.v. and i.m. administration. Nonmedicinal ingredients: sodium bicarbonate. Sodium: 3.4 mmol (78.7 mg). Vials of 10 mL.

2 g: Each vial of dry, white to pale yellow powder contains: cefotetan disodium equivalent to 2 g cefotetan activity for i.v. and i.m. administration. Nonmedicinal ingredients: sodium bicarbonate. Sodium: 6.8 mmol (157.4 mg). Vials of 20 mL.

Store below 25°C and protect from light.

CEFOXITIN SODIUM USP ℞

Novopharm

Antibiotic

Pharmacology: Cefoxitin is a cephamycin derived from cephamycin C. Evidence from in vitro studies suggests that cefoxitin exerts its bactericidal action through the inhibition of bacterial cell wall synthesis. Studies have indicated that the resistance of cefoxitin to degradation by bacterial beta-lactamases is due to the methoxy group in the 7α position.

After i.v. or i.m. administration of a 1 g dose, high serum concentrations are attained which rapidly decline to about 2 μg/mL at 3 hours in persons with normal renal function. The area under the plasma level-time curve is comparable after bolus injection or i.v. infusion over a period of 120 minutes.

Indications: Treatment: For the treatment of the following infections when due to susceptible organisms: intra-abdominal infections such as peritonitis and intra-abdominal abscess, gynecological infections such as endometritis and pelvic cellulitis, septicemia, urinary tract infections (including those caused by S. marcescens and Serratia spp.), lower respiratory tract infections, bone and joint infections caused by S. aureus, soft tissue infections such as cellulitis, abscesses and wound infections.

The susceptibility of the causative organism(s) to cefoxitin should be determined by conducting appropriate culture and susceptibility studies. Therapy may be initiated while awaiting these test results. Adjustments in treatment may be required once these results become available.

Organisms particularly appropriate for therapy with cefoxitin are: Gram-positive: staphylococci: penicillinase producing and nonproducing; streptococci excluding enterococci.

Gram-negative (beta-lactamase producing and nonproducing strains): E. coli; Klebsiella species (including K. pneumoniae); Proteus: indole positive and negative; H. influenzae; Providencia species.

Anaerobes: B. fragilis.

Cefoxitin may also be used for the treatment of infections involving both aerobic and anaerobic strains of susceptible bacteria.

Clinical evidence suggests that cefoxitin therapy may be administered to patients who are also receiving gentamicin, tobramycin, carbenicillin, or amikacin (see Precautions and Dosage).

Prophylactic Use: Cefoxitin may be administered perioperatively (preoperatively, intraoperatively, and postoperatively) in patients undergoing abdominal surgery and vaginal or abdominal hysterectomy when there is a significant risk of postoperative infection or where the occurrence of postoperative infection is considered to be especially serious.

Intraoperative (after clamping the umbilical cord) and postoperative administration of cefoxitin may reduce the incidence of surgery-related postoperative infections in patients undergoing cesarean section.

Cefoxitin should be administered 0.5 to 1 hour before the surgical procedure. Prophylactic administration should usually be stopped within 12 hours. Administration of any antibiotic continued beyond 24 hours following surgery has been reported to increase the possibility of adverse reactions, but, in the majority of surgical procedures, does not reduce the incidence of subsequent infection.

Should signs of postsurgical infection appear, specimens for culture should be obtained for identification of the causative organism(s) so that appropriate therapy can be instituted.

Contraindications: In patients who have previously shown hypersensitivity to cefoxitin or to other cephalosporin antibiotics.

Cefoxitin is not recommended for the treatment of meningitis. Appropriate antibiotic therapy should be instituted if meningitis is suspected.

Warnings: Before initiating therapy with cefoxitin it should be determined whether the patient has had previous hypersensitivity reactions to cefoxitin, cephalosporins, penicillins or other drugs. Exercise caution when administering cefoxitin to penicillin-sensitive patients.

There is clinical and laboratory evidence to suggest a partial cross-allergenicity between cephamycins and the other betalactam antibiotics, penicillins and cephalosporins. Severe reactions including anaphylaxis, have been observed with most beta-lactam antibiotics.

Exercise caution when administering cefoxitin and other antibiotics to patients who have demonstrated any form of allergy, particularly to drugs.

Discontinue treatment should an allergic reaction to cefoxitin occur. Serious hypersensitivity reactions may require treatment with epinephrine and other emergency measures.

Pseudomembranous colitis has been reported with the use of virtually all antibiotics including cefoxitin; therefore, it is important to consider its diagnosis in patients who develop diarrhea during the administration of cefoxitin. Antibiotics should be prescribed with caution in patients with a history of gastrointestinal disease, particularly colitis. This colitis can range from mild to life-threatening in severity. Studies have indicated that a toxin produced by C. difficile is one primary cause of antibiotic-associated colitis, however, other causes should also be considered.

Precautions: General: When cefoxitin is administered to patients with transient or persistent reduction of urinary output due to renal insufficiency, the total daily dose should be reduced because high and prolonged serum antibiotic concentrations may result from usual doses (see Dosage).

Prolonged cefoxitin treatment can result in the overgrowth of nonsusceptible organisms. Repeated evaluation of the patient's condition is essential. If superinfection occurs during therapy appropriate supportive measures should be taken. Resistance may develop during antibiotic therapy and in such cases another antibiotic may be substituted.

Laboratory Tests: A false-positive reaction to glucose in the urine may occur with Benedict's or Fehling's solutions in patients on cefoxitin therapy. No false-positive reactions have been observed with the use of specific glucose oxidase methods.

Analysis of serum creatinine levels using the Jaffe method may yield falsely high creatinine levels if the serum concentration of cefoxitin exceeds 100 μg/mL. Serum samples taken for analysis of creatinine levels from patients on cefoxitin therapy should not be analyzed if withdrawn within 2 hours of drug administration.

Drug Interactions: Increased nephrotoxicity has been reported following concomitant administration of cephalosporins and aminoglycoside antibiotics.

Pregnancy: The safety of cefoxitin in the treatment of infections during pregnancy has not been established. If the administration of cefoxitin to pregnant patients is considered necessary, its use requires that the anticipated benefits be weighed against possible hazards to the fetus. No evidence of impaired fertility or harm to the fetus has been reported from reproductive and teratogenic studies where cefoxitin was administered to both mice and rats.

Lactation: Cefoxitin has been found to be secreted in breast milk of nursing mothers.

Children: In children 3 months of age or older, higher doses of cefoxitin (100 mg/kg/day and above) have been associated with an increased incidence of eosinophilia and elevated AST.

Adverse Effects: Cefoxitin is generally well tolerated. Adverse reactions have been mild and transient and rarely require cessation of treatment.

Local Reactions: Thrombophlebitis has been reported after i.v. administration. Some degree of pain and tenderness is usually experienced after i.m. injections using water. Induration has occasionally been reported.

Allergic: Maculopapular rash, urticaria, pruritus, eosinophilia, fever and other allergic reactions including anaphylaxis have been reported.

Gastrointestinal: Symptoms of pseudomembranous colitis can appear during or after antibiotic treatment. Nausea and vomiting have been known to occur in rare cases.

Blood: Eosinophilia, leukopenia, neutropenia, hemolytic anemia, thrombocytopenia and bone marrow depression have been noted. During cefoxitin therapy, some individuals, particularly those with azotemia, may develop positive direct Coombs tests.

Liver Function: Transient elevations in AST, ALT, serum LDH and serum alkaline phosphatase have been reported. Jaundice has also been noted.

Cardiovascular: hypotension.

Kidney: Elevations in blood urea nitrogen and/or serum creatinine levels have been reported. Acute renal failure has been reported rarely, but is known to occur, as with other cephalosporins. Since factors predisposing to prerenal azotemia or to impaired renal function have been present, it is difficult to assess the role of cefoxitin in renal function test changes.

Overdose: Symptoms and Treatment: No specific antidote is known. In case of an overdose of cefoxitin, institute general supportive therapy. In patients with renal insufficiency dialysis may be performed to eliminate cefoxitin.

Dosage: Cefoxitin may be administered i.v. or i.m. as required (see Reconstitution below for each route).

I.V. Administration: I.V. administration is the preferred route for patients with bacteremia, bacterial septicemia, or other severe or life-threatening infections. The i.v. route is also preferred for patients who may be poor risks because of lowered resistance resulting from debilitating conditions such as malnutrition, trauma, surgery, diabetes, heart failure or malignancy, particularly if shock is present or impending.

Adults with Normal Renal Function: The usual adult dose is 1 to 2 g every 6 to 8 hours. Dosage and route of administration depend on severity of infection, susceptibility of the causative organisms, and the patient's condition. The usual adult dosages are shown in Table I (on following page).

Therapy may be initiated while awaiting the results of susceptibility tests.

Table I—Cefoxitin Sodium USP

Usual Adult Dosage

Type of Infection	Daily Dosage	Frequency and Route
Uncomplicated forms* of infections such as pneumonia, urinary tract infection, soft tissue infection	3-4 g	1 g every 6-8 h i.v. or i.m.
Moderately severe or severe infections	6-8 g	1 g every 4 h or 2 g every 6-8 h i.v.
Infections commonly needing antibiotics in higher dosage (e.g., gas gangrene	12 g	2 g every 4 h or 3 g every 6 h i.v.

*Including patients in whom bacteremia is absent or unlikely.

Antibiotic therapy for group A beta-hemolytic streptococcal infections should continue for a minimum of 10 days to guard against the risk of rheumatic fever or glomerulonephritis. In staphylococcal and other infections involving a collection of pus, surgical drainage should be carried out where indicated.

Adults with Impaired Renal Function: Patients with reduced renal function may require a reduced dose of cefoxitin. Serum levels should be monitored in patients with severe renal impairment.

In adults with renal insufficiency a loading dose of 1 to 2 g should be administered. In patients undergoing hemodialysis a loading dose should be given after each hemodialysis procedure. Table II presents recommended **maintenance doses** for patients with various levels of renal impairment and patients undergoing hemodialysis.

Table II—Cefoxitin Sodium USP

Maintenance Dosage in Adults with Reduced Renal Function

Renal Function	Creatinine Clearance mL/min	mL/s	Dose	Frequency
Mild impairment	50-30	0.83-0.50	1-2 g	every 8-12 h
Moderate impairment	29-10	0.48-0.17	1-2 g	every 12-24 h
Severe impairment	9-5	0.15-0.08	0.5-1 g	every 12-24 h
Essentially no function	<5	<0.08	0.5-1 g	every 24-48 h

Creatinine Clearance: When only the serum creatinine level is available, the following formula (based on sex, weight and age of the patient) may be used to convert this value into creatinine clearance (mL/s):

$$\text{Males: } \frac{\text{Weight (kg)}\times(140-\text{age})}{49\times\text{serum creatinine (mM/L)}}$$

Females: 0.85×above value.

Neonates (including Premature Infants, Infants and Children): See Table III.

Warning for Neonates: Solutions containing preservatives should not be used for injection or for flushing catheters in treating neonates.

Benzyl alcohol as a preservative in Bacteriostatic Water for Injection and Bacteriostatic Sodium Chloride Injection has been associated with toxicity in neonates. At present, data are unavailable on the toxicity of other preservatives in this age group. Therefore, any diluents used with cefoxitin in the treatment of neonates should not contain any preservatives.

Table III—Cefoxitin Sodium USP

Dosage in Neonates

Premature Infants with Body Weights Above 1 500 g	20-40 mg/kg every 12 h i.v.
Neonates	
0-1 week of age	20-40 mg/kg every 12 h i.v.
1-4 weeks of age	20-40 mg/kg every 8 h i.v.
Infants 1 month to 2 years of age	20-40 mg/kg every 6 h or every 8 h i.m. or i.v.
Children	20-40 mg/kg every 6 h or every 8 h i.m. or i.v.

The total daily dosage in infants and children with severe infections may be increased to 200 mg/kg, but should not exceed 12 g/day.

Cefoxitin is not recommended for the treatment of meningitis. Appropriate antibiotic therapy should be instituted if meningitis is suspected.

Sufficient data is not yet available to recommend a specific dosage schedule for children with renal impairment. If cefoxitin therapy proves to be necessary the dosage should be modified consistent with the recommendations for adults (see Table II).

Prophylactic Use: In Vaginal or Abdominal Hysterectomy and Abdominal Surgery: The first 2 g dose should be administered i.v. or i.m. just prior to surgery (approximately 0.5 to 1 hour before initial incision), followed by the second and third 2 g doses at 2- to 6-hour intervals.

Cesarean Section: 2 g administered i.v. as soon as the umbilical cord has been clamped. The second and third 2 g doses should be given at 4 and 8 hours after the first dose by i.v. or i.m. administration.

Administration: I.M.: I.M. administered cefoxitin should be injected into a large muscle mass such as the upper outer quadrant of the buttock (i.e., gluteus maximus). Maintain aspiration to avoid inadvertent injection into a blood vessel.

I.V.: The i.v. route is preferable for patients with severe life-threatening infection.

Cefoxitin may be administered by i.v. injection either by continuous or intermittent infusion. The reconstituted cefoxitin must be further diluted to the desired volume with any of the recommended diluents.

Intermittent I.V. Administration: A solution of cefoxitin in Sterile Water for Injection may be administered slowly over a period of 3 to 5 minutes. Using an infusion system cefoxitin may be given through the tubing by which the patient is receiving other parenteral solutions. However, during infusion of the solution containing cefoxitin it is advisable to temporarily discontinue administration of any other infusion solution at the same site (by using an appropriate i.v. infusion set). Any unused portions of cefoxitin must be discarded.

Continuous I.V. Infusions: A cefoxitin solution may be added to an i.v. bottle containing an appropriate i.v. infusion fluid in the amounts calculated to give the desired antibiotic dose. Butterfly or scalp vein-type needles are preferred for this type of infusion.

Reconstituted Solutions: As with all parenteral drug products, i.v. admixtures should be inspected visually for clarity, particulate matter, precipitate, discoloration and leakage prior to administration whenever solution and container permit.

For i.m. use, the following solutions can be used for reconstitution: Sterile Water for Injection or, if required Bacteriostatic Water for Injection. See Table IV.

Table IV—Cefoxitin Sodium USP

Reconstitution Table (I.M.)

Strength	Amount of Diluent to be Added (mL)*	Approximate Withdrawable Volume (mL)	Nominal Concentration (mg/mL)
1 g vial	2	2.5	400
2 g vial	4	5.0	400

*Shake to dissolve and let stand until clear.

For i.v. use, the following solutions can be used for reconstitution: Sterile Water for Injection or, if required, Sterile Sodium Chloride 0.9% or, Sterile Dextrose Injection 5% or 10%. See Table V.

Table V—Cefoxitin Sodium USP

Reconstitution Table (I.V.)

Strength	Amount of Diluent to be Added (mL)*	Approximate Withdrawable Volume (mL)	Nominal Concentration (mg/mL)
1 g vial	10	10.5	95
2 g vial	10 or 20	11.1 or 21.0	180 or 95

*Shake to dissolve and let stand until clear. The prepared solution may be further diluted to the desired volume with any of the solutions for i.v. infusion listed below.

For Direct I.V. Injection: Reconstitute as directed above.

For Intermittent I.V. Infusion: Reconstitute as directed above.

Parenteral Products: For continuous i.v. infusion: Reconstitute with Sterile Water for Injection. The reconstituted solution may be added to an appropriate i.v. bottle or bag containing any of the solutions for i.v. infusion listed below. A freshly reconstituted solution should be used for further dilution with solutions for i.v. infusion. The following solutions can be used for i.v. infusion: Sterile Water for Injection (see Dosage, Warning for Neonates), Sodium Chloride Injection 0.9%, Dextrose Injection 5% or 10%, Dextrose Injection 5% and Sodium Chloride Injection 0.2%, 0.45%, or 0.9%, Ringer's Injection, Lactated Ringer's Injection, Dextrose 5% in Lactated Ringer's Injection, Normosol-M in D5W.

Cefoxitin has also been found compatible when admixed in i.v. infusions with the following: Heparin 100 units/mL in Sodium Chloride Injection 0.9%; Heparin 100 units/mL in Dextrose Injection 5%; Heparin 0.1 unit/mL (at room temperature 8 hours) in Sodium Chloride Injection 0.9%; Heparin 0.1 unit/mL (at room temperature 8 hours) in Dextrose Injection 5%.

Stability of Reconstituted or Diluted Solutions: Reconstituted solution for i.m. injection and i.v. injection should be used within 8 hours if kept at room temperature or 72 hours if stored under refrigeration (2 to 8°C).

The further diluted solutions for i.v. infusions should be used within 12 hours if kept at room temperature or 24 hours if stored under refrigeration (2 to 8°C).

Incompatibility: Solutions of cefoxitin like those of most beta-lactam antibiotics, should not be added to aminoglycoside solutions (e.g., gentamicin sulfate, tobramycin sulfate, amikacin sulfate) because of potential interaction.

Supplied: Each vial of white to off-white sterile powder contains: cefoxitin 1 or 2 g as the sodium salt. Store at room temperature between 15 and 30°C. Protect from light. The dry material as well as solutions tend to darken, depending on storage conditions. Dark brown solution should not be used.

CEFTIN® Ⓟ

Glaxo Wellcome

Cefuroxime Axetil

Antibiotic

Pharmacology: Cefuroxime axetil is an orally active prodrug of cefuroxime. After oral administration, cefuroxime axetil is absorbed from the gastrointestinal tract and rapidly hydrolyzed by nonspecific esterases in the intestinal mucosa and blood to release cefuroxime into the blood stream. Conversion to cefuroxime, the microbiologically active form, occurs rapidly. The inherent properties of cefuroxime are unaltered after its administration as cefuroxime axetil.

Cefuroxime exerts its bactericidal effect by binding to an enzyme or enzymes referred to as penicillin-binding proteins (PBPs) involved in bacterial cell wall synthesis. This binding results in inhibition of bacterial cell wall synthesis and subsequent cell death. Specifically, cefuroxime shows high affinity for PBP 3, a primary target for cefuroxime in gram-negative organisms such as E. coli.

Indications: For the treatment of patients with mild to moderately severe infections caused by susceptible strains of the designated organisms in the following diseases:

Upper Respiratory Tract Infections: Pharyngitis and tonsillitis caused by S. pyogenes. Otitis Media caused by S. pneumoniae, S. pyogenes (group A beta-hemolytic streptococci), H. influenzae (beta-lactamase negative and beta-lactamase positive strains) or M. catarrhalis. Sinusitis caused by M. catarrhalis, S. pneumoniae or H. influenzae (including ampicillin-resistant strains).

Lower Respiratory Tract Infections: Pneumonia or bronchitis caused by S. pneumoniae, H. influenzae (including ampicillin-resistant strains), H. parainfluenzae, K. pneumoniae or M. catarrhalis.

Skin Structure Infections: Skin structure infections caused by S. aureus, S. pyogenes or S. agalactiae.

Gonorrhea: Acute uncomplicated urethritis and cervicitis caused by N. gonorrheae.

Bacteriologic studies to determine the causative organism and its susceptibility to cefuroxime should be performed. Once these results become available antibiotic treatment should be adjusted if required.

Contraindications: Type I hypersensitivity to cefuroxime or to any of the cephalosporin group of antibiotics.

Warnings: Before therapy with cefuroxime axetil is instituted, careful inquiry should be made to determine whether the patient has had previous hypersensitivity reactions to cefuroxime, cephalosporins, penicillin, or other drugs. Cefuroxime axetil should be administered with caution to any patient who has demonstrated some form of allergy, particularly to drugs. There is some clinical and laboratory evidence of partial cross allergenicity of the cephalosporins and penicillin. Special care is indicated in patients who have experienced anaphylactic reaction to penicillins. If an allergic reaction to cefuroxime axetil occurs, treatment should be discontinued and standard agents (e.g., epinephrine, antihistamines, corticosteroids) administered as necessary.

Ceftin (cont'd)

Pseudomembranous colitis has been reported to be associated with the use of cefuroxime axetil and other broad-spectrum antibiotics. Therefore, it is important to consider its diagnosis in patients administered cefuroxime axetil who develop diarrhea. Treatment with broad-spectrum antibiotics, including cefuroxime axetil, alters the normal flora of the colon and may permit overgrowth of Clostridia. Studies indicate that a toxin produced by C. difficile is one primary cause of antibiotic-associated colitis. Mild cases of colitis may respond to drug discontinuance alone. Moderate to severe cases should be managed with fluid, electrolyte, and protein supplementation as indicated. When the colitis is severe or not relieved by discontinuance of cefuroxime axetil administration, consideration should be given to the administration of oral vancomycin or other suitable therapy. Other possible causes of colitis should also be considered.

Precautions: Broad-spectrum antibiotics including cefuroxime axetil should be administered with caution to individuals with a history of gastrointestinal disease, particularly colitis.

The concomitant administration of aminoglycosides and some cephalosporins has caused nephrotoxicity. There is no evidence that cefuroxime axetil, when administered alone, is nephrotoxic, although transient elevations of BUN and serum creatinine have been observed in clinical studies. However, the effect of administering cefuroxime axetil concomitantly with aminoglycosides is not known.

Studies suggest that the concomitant use of potent diuretics, such as furosemide and ethacrynic acid, may increase the risk of renal toxicity with cephalosporins.

Prolonged treatment with cefuroxime axetil may result in the overgrowth of nonsusceptible organisms, including species originally sensitive to the drug. Repeated evaluation of the patient's condition is essential. If superinfection occurs during therapy, appropriate measures should be taken. Should an organism become resistant during antibiotic therapy, cefuroxime axetil should be discontinued and another appropriate antibiotic should be substituted.

Pregnancy: The safety of cefuroxime axetil in pregnancy has not been established. The use of cefuroxime axetil in pregnant women requires that the likely benefit from the drug be weighed against the possible risk to the mother and fetus. Animal studies following parenteral administration have shown cefuroxime to affect bone calcification in the fetus and to cause maternal toxicity in the rabbit. Reproduction studies that have been performed in mice and rats at oral doses of up to 50 to 160 times the human dose have revealed no evidence of impaired fertility or harm to the fetus due to cefuroxime axetil. There are, however, no adequate and well-controlled studies in pregnant women. Because animal reproduction studies are not always predictive of human response, this drug should be used during pregnancy only if clearly needed.

Lactation: Since cefuroxime is excreted in human milk, consideration should be given to discontinuing nursing temporarily during treatment with cefuroxime axetil.

Drug Interactions: Drugs which reduce gastric acidity may result in a lower bioavailability of cefuroxime axetil compared with that of the fasting state and tend to cancel the effect of post-prandial absorption.

Drug-Laboratory Test Interactions: A false-positive reaction for glucose in the urine may occur with copper reduction tests (Benedict's or Fehling's solution or with Clinitest Tablets) but not with enzyme-based tests for glycosuria (e.g., Clinistix, Tes-Tape). As a false-negative result may occur in the ferricyanide test, it is recommended that either the glucose oxidase or hexokinase method be used to determine blood plasma glucose levels in patients receiving cefuroxime axetil.

Cefuroxime does not interfere with the assay of serum and urine creatinine by the alkaline picrate method.

Cephalosporins as a class tend to be absorbed onto the surface of red cell membranes and react with antibodies directed against the drug to produce a positive Coombs' test (which can interfere with cross-matching of blood) and very rarely hemolytic anemia.

Adverse Effects: The following adverse reactions have been reported: Gastrointestinal (approximately 8% of patients): diarrhea (5.6%), nausea (2.4%), vomiting (2%), loose stools (1.3%). Reports of pseudomembranous colitis (see Warnings) have occurred.

Hepatic (3% of patients): transient elevations of AST (2%), ALT (1.6%) and LDH (1%). Jaundice has been reported very rarely.

CNS (2.2% of patients): headache and dizziness.

Hypersensitivity (1.3% of patients): rashes (0.6%), pruritus (0.3%), urticaria (0.2%), shortness of breath and rare reports of bronchospasm. Hypersensitivity reactions to cefuroxime axetil may occur in patients who report delayed hypersensitivity to penicillins (see Warnings). As with other cephalosporins, there have been rare reports of erythema multiforme, Stevens-Johnson syndrome, toxic epidermal necrolysis, serum sickness, drug fever and very rarely anaphylaxis.

Hematologic: thrombocytopenia and leukopenia (sometimes profound), increased erythrocyte sedimentation rate, eosinophilia, decreased hemoglobin and very rarely hemolytic anemia.

Miscellaneous: The following adverse reactions have been observed to occur, although infrequently, in association with parenteral cefuroxime sodium and may be potential adverse effects of oral cefuroxime axetil: drowsiness, vaginitis, positive direct Coombs' test, and transient increases in serum bilirubin, creatinine, alkaline phosphatase and urea nitrogen (BUN). In addition, the incidence of diaper rash (1.4%) has been associated with cefuroxime axetil suspension in children.

Overdose: Symptoms and Treatment: Other than general supportive treatment, no specific antidote is known. Excessive serum levels of cefuroxime can be reduced by dialysis. For treatment of hypersensitive reactions, see Warnings.

Dosage: Cefuroxime axetil may be given orally without regard to meals. Absorption is enhanced when cefuroxime axetil is administered with food. In comparative bioavailability studies in healthy adults, the suspension was not bioequivalent to the tablets. The area under the curve for the suspension averaged 91% of that for the tablet, while the C_{max} for the suspension averaged 71% of the C_{max} of the tablets.

Tablets: Adults and Children (12 Years of Age and Older): The usual recommended dosage is 250 mg twice a day. However, dosage may be modified according to the type of infection present as indicated in Table I.

Table I—Ceftin Tablets

Dosage According to the Type of Infection

Type of Infection	Dosage
pharyngitis, tonsillitis, sinusitis, bronchitis, skin structure infections	250 mg twice daily
more severe infections e.g., pneumonia	500 mg twice daily
uncomplicated gonorrhea	1 000 mg single dose

There is presently no data available on the effects of cefuroxime axetil in patients with renal impairment. However, in patients where there is significant impairment, a reduction in dosage may be required.

Infants and Children Less Than 12 Years of Age: Cefuroxime axetil tablets are not recommended for children.

Oral Suspension: Infants and Children 3 Months to 12 Years of Age: There is no experience in infants under the age of 3 months.

There is no clinical trial experience with the use of cefuroxime axetil suspension in the treatment of lower respiratory tract infections.

The recommended dosage of cefuroxime axetil suspension for various types of infections is indicated in Tables II, III and IV.

Table II—Ceftin Suspension

Recommended Dosage for Various Infections

Type of Infection	Dosage
otitis media, skin structure infections,	15 mg/kg twice daily Maximum dose 1 g/day
pharyngitis, tonsillitis	10 mg/kg twice daily Maximum dose 500 mg/day

Table III—Ceftin Suspension

Recommended Dosage for Pharyngitis and Tonsillitis Infections

Weight (kg)	mg/day	Doses/day	Dosage: Multidose Bottle mL/dose	Dosage: Sachets/ dose
6	125	2	2.5	—
13	250	2	5.0	—
19	375	2	7.5	—
25	500	2	10.0	1
>25	500	2	10.0	1

Table IV—Ceftin Suspension

Recommended Dosage for Otitis Media and Skin Structure Infections

Weight (kg)	mg/day	Doses/day	Dosage: Multidose Bottle mL/dose	Dosage: Sachets/ dose
4	125	2	2.5	—
8	250	2	5.0	—
13	375	2	7.5	—
17	500	2	10.0	1
21	625	2	12.5	—
25	750	2	15.0	—
29	875	2	17.5	—
33	1 000	2	20.0	2
>33	1 000	2	20.0	2

The usual duration of treatment for tablets and oral suspension is 7 to 10 days. For ß-hemolytic streptococcal infections, therapy should be continued for at least 10 days.

Directions for Constituting Suspension in Bottles: Prepare a suspension at time of dispensing as follows: 1. Shake the bottle to loosen the granules and remove the cap. 2. Add the total amount of water for reconstitution all at once (see Table V) and replace cap. 3 **Invert** the bottle and rock the bottle vigorously until the sound of the granules against the container disappears. 4. Turn the bottle into an upright position and shake vigorously. Each 5 mL provides 125 mg cefuroxime.

Note: Shake the bottle vigorously until the suspension can be heard moving in the bottle before each use. Replace cap securely after each opening. If desired, the dose of the reconstituted suspension may be added to one of the following cold beverages immediately prior to administration: milk (i.e. skim, 2% or homogenized), fruit juice (i.e. apple, orange, or grape) or lemonade.

Table V—Ceftin Suspension

Reconstitution Instructions

Labelled Volume (mL)	Amount of Water for Reconstitution (mL)
70	27
100	37

Directions for Constituting Suspension From Sachets: 1. Empty granules from sachet into a glass. 2. Add at least 10 mL of one of the following cold beverages: water, milk (i.e. skim, 2% or homogenized), juice (apple, orange, or grape) or lemonade. 3. Stir well and drink it all immediately.

Note: Ceftin granules should **not** be reconstituted in hot beverages.

Information for the Patient: See Blue Section—Information for the Patient "Ceftin".

Supplied: Suspension: Dry, white to pale yellow, tutti-frutti-flavored granules. After reconstitution each 5 mL contains: cefuroxime axetil equivalent to cefuroxime (base) 125 mg. The reconstituted suspension from the sachets contains: cefuroxime axetil equivalent to cefuroxime (base) 250 mg. Nonmedicinal ingredients: polyvinyl pyrrolidone, stearic acid, sucrose and tutti-frutti flavoring. Bottles of 70 and 100 mL. Sachets of 250 mg, boxes of 10 and 14. Store granules between 2 and 30°C. The reconstituted suspension should be stored between 2 and 25°C, preferably in a refrigerator, and discarded after 10 days. The reconstituted suspension from sachets should be taken immediately.

Tablets: 250 mg: Each white, capsule-shaped tablet, engraved with "250" on one side and "Glaxo" on the other, contains: cefuroxime axetil equivalent to 250 mg of cefuroxime (base). Nonmedicinal ingredients: colloidal silicon dioxide, croscarmellose sodium, hydrogenated vegetable oil, hydroxypropyl methylcellulose, methylparaben, microcrystalline cellulose, propylene glycol, propylparaben, sodium benzoate, sodium lauryl sulfate and titanium dioxide. Bottles of 60. Store between 15 and 30°C.

500 mg: Each white, capsule-shaped tablet, engraved with "500" on one side and "Glaxo" on the other, contains: cefuroxime axetil equivalent to 500 mg of cefuroxime (base). Nonmedicinal ingredients: colloidal silicon dioxide, croscarmellose sodium, hydrogenated vegetable oil, hydroxypropyl methylcellulose, methylparaben, microcrystalline cellulose, propylene glycol, propylparaben, sodium benzoate, sodium lauryl sulfate and titanium dioxide. Bottles of 60. Store between 15 and 30°C.

(Shown in Product Recognition Section)

Reviewed 1999

CEFUROXIME SODIUM USP, STERILE Ⓟ

Schein Pharmaceutical

Antibiotic

Supplied: Vials: 750 mg/10 mL: Each 10 mL vial (for i.m. or direct i.v. injection) contains: cefuroxime sodium powder equivalent to cefuroxime 750 mg. Nonmedicinal ingredients: none. Packs of 10.

1.5 g/20 mL: Each 20 mL vial (for i.v. injection) contains: cefuroxime sodium powder equivalent to cefuroxime 1.5 g. Nonmedicinal ingredients: none. Packs of 10.

Pharmacy Bulk Vials: Each 100 mL vial (for i.v. infusion) contains: cefuroxime sodium powder equivalent to cefuroxime 7.5 g. Nonmedicinal ingredients: none. Packs of 10.

New Product 1998

CEFZIL™ Ⓟ

Bristol-Myers Squibb

Cefprozil

Antibiotic

Pharmacology: Cefprozil is a semisynthetic broad spectrum cephalosporin antibiotic intended for oral administration. It has in vitro activity against a broad range of gram positive and gram negative bacteria. The bactericidal action of cefprozil results from inhibition of cell-wall synthesis.

Pharmacokinetics: Cefprozil is well absorbed following oral administration in both fasting and nonfasting subjects. The oral bioavailability of cefprozil is about 90%. The pharmacokinetics of cefprozil are not altered when administered with meals, or when coadministered with antacid. Average plasma concentrations after administration of cefprozil to fasting subjects are shown in Table I. Urinary recovery accounts for 60% of the administered dose.

Table I—Cefzil

Mean Plasma Concentrations

Dosage	Mean Plasma Cefprozil* Concentrations (µg/mL) Peak ~1.5 h	4 h	8 h	8-hour Urinary Excretion
250 mg	6.1	1.7	0.2	60%
500 mg	10.5	3.2	0.4	62%
1 g	18.3	8.4	1	54%

* Data represent mean values from 12 healthy, young male volunteers.

During the first 4-hour period after drug administration, the average urine concentrations following the 250 mg, 500 mg, and 1 g doses were approximately 170µg/mL, 450 µg/mL and 600 µg/mL, respectively.

The average plasma half-life in normal subjects is 1.3 hours. Plasma protein binding is approximately 36% and is independent of concentration in the range of 2 to 20 µg/mL. There is no evidence of accumulation of cefprozil in the plasma in individuals with normal renal function following multiple oral doses of up to 1 g every 8 hours for 10 days.

Renal Insufficiency: In patients with reduced renal function, the plasma half-life prolongation is related to the degree of the renal dysfunction and may be prolonged up to 5.2 hours. In patients with complete absence of renal function, the plasma half-life of cefprozil averaged 5.9 hours. The half-life is shortened during hemodialysis to 2.1 hours. Excretion pathways in patients with markedly impaired renal function have not been determined (see Precautions and Dosage).

Hepatic Insufficiency: In patients with impaired hepatic function, no differences in pharmacokinetic parameters were observed, when compared to normal control subjects.

Geriatrics: Following administration of a single 1 g dose of cefprozil, the average AUC observed in healthy elderly subjects (≥65 years of age) was approximately 35 to 60% higher than that of healthy young adults and the average AUC in females was approximately 15 to 20% higher than in males. The magnitude of these age and gender-related variations in the pharmacokinetics of cefprozil are not sufficient to necessitate dosage adjustments.

Children: Comparable pharmacokinetic parameters of cefprozil are observed between pediatric patients (6 months to 12 years) and adults following oral administration. The maximum plasma concentrations are achieved at 1 to 2 hours after dosing. The plasma elimination half-life is approximately 1.5 hours. The AUC of cefprozil to pediatric patients after 7.5, 15 and 30 mg/kg doses is similar to that observed in normal adult subjects after 250, 500 and 1 000 mg doses, respectively.

Indications: For the treatment of the following infections caused by susceptible strains of the designated microorganisms:

Upper Respiratory Tract: Pharyngitis/tonsillitis caused by group A β-hemolytic (GABHS) S. pyogenes. Substantial data establishing the efficacy of cefprozil in the subsequent prevention of rheumatic fever are not available at present, although no case was reported during its evaluation in over 978 pediatric and 831 adult patients in controlled clinical trials.

Otitis media caused by S. pneumoniae, H. influenzae. M. (Branhamella) catarrhalis.

Acute sinusitis caused by S. pneumoniae, H. influenzae, (beta-lactamase positive and negative strains), and M. (Branhamella) catarrhalis.

Skin and Skin Structure: Uncomplicated skin and skin-structure infections caused by S. aureus (including penicillinase-producing strains) and S. pyogenes.

Urinary Tract: Uncomplicated urinary tract infections (including acute cystitis) caused by E. coli, K. pneumoniae, P. mirabilis. Cultures and susceptibility studies should be performed when appropriate.

Contraindications: In patients with known allergy to the cephalosporin class of antibiotics or to any component of the cefprozil preparations.

Warnings: Before therapy with cefprozil is instituted, careful inquiry should be made to determine whether the patient has had previous hypersensitivity reactions to cefprozil, cephalosporins, penicillins, or other drugs. If this product is to be given to penicillin-sensitive patients, caution should be exercised because cross-sensitivity among beta-lactam antibiotics has been clearly documented and may occur in up to 10% of patients with a history of penicillin allergy.

If an allergic reaction to cefzil occurs, discontinue the drug. Serious acute hypersensitivity reactions may require treatment with epinephrine and other emergency measures, including oxygen, i.v. fluids, i.v. antihistamines, corticosteroids, pressor amines, and airway management, as clinically indicated.

Treatment with antibacterial agents alters the normal flora of the colon and may permit overgrowth of clostridia. Studies indicate that a toxin produced by C. difficile is one primary cause of "antibiotic-associated colitis". Pseudomembranous colitis is associated with the use of broad spectrum antibiotics (including macrolides, semisynthetic penicillins and cephalosporins) and may range in severity from mild to life-threatening. Therefore, it is important to consider this diagnosis in patients who present with diarrhea subsequent to the administration of antibacterial agents.

After the diagnosis of pseudomembranous colitis has been established, therapeutic measures should be initiated. Mild cases of pseudomembranous colitis usually respond to drug discontinuation alone. In moderate to severe cases, consideration should be given to management with fluids and electrolytes, protein supplementation, and treatment with an oral antibacterial drug effective against C. difficile (e.g., metronidazole).

Precautions: General: Evaluation of renal status before and during therapy is recommended, especially in seriously ill patients. In patients with known or suspected renal impairment (see Dosage), careful clinical observation and appropriate laboratory studies should be done prior to and during therapy. The total daily dose of cefprozil should be reduced in patients with creatinine clearance values ≤30 mL/min because high and/or prolonged plasma antibiotic concentrations can occur from usual doses in such individuals. Cephalosporins, including cefprozil, should be given with caution to patients receiving concurrent treatment with potent diuretics since these agents are suspected of adversely affecting renal function.

Prolonged use of cefprozil may result in the overgrowth of nonsusceptible organisms. Careful observation of the patient is essential. If superinfection occurs during therapy, appropriate measures should be taken.

Positive direct Coombs, tests have been reported during treatment with cephalosporin antibiotics.

Drug Interactions: Nephrotoxicity has been reported following concomitant administration of aminoglycoside antibiotics and cephalosporin antibiotics. Concomitant administration of probenecid doubled the area under the curve for cefprozil.

If an aminoglycoside is used concurrently with cefprozil, especially if high dosages of the former are used or if therapy is prolonged, renal function should be monitored because of the potential nephrotoxicity and ototoxicity of aminoglycoside antibiotics.

Drug/Laboratory Test Interactions: Cephalosporin antibiotics may produce a false positive reaction for glucose in the urine with copper reduction tests (Benedict's or Fehling's solution or with Clinitest tablets), but not with enzyme-based tests (glucose oxidase) for glycosuria. A false negative reaction may occur in the ferricyanide test for blood glucose. The presence of cefprozil in the blood does not interfere with the assay of plasma or urine creatinine by the alkaline picrate method.

Pregnancy: Reproduction studies have been performed in mice, rats, and rabbits at doses 14, 7 and 0.7 times the maximum human daily dose (1 000 mg) based upon mg/m^2, and have revealed no evidence of harm to the fetus due to cefprozil. There are, however, no adequate and well-controlled studies in pregnant women. Because animal reproduction studies are not always predictive of human response, this drug should be used during pregnancy only if the potential benefit justifies the potential risk.

Lactation: Less than 1% of a maternal dose is excreted in human milk. Caution should be exercised when cefprozil is administered to a nursing mother. Consideration should be given to temporary discontinuation of nursing and use of formula feeding.

Children: The use of cefprozil in the treatment of acute sinusitis in these age groups is supported by evidence from adequate and well-controlled studies of cefprozil in adults and from pediatric pharmacokinetic studies.

Safety and effectiveness in children below the age of 6 months have not been established. Accumulation of other cephalosporin antibiotics in newborn infants (resulting from prolonged drug half-life in this age group) has been reported.

Geriatrics: Cefprozil has not been studied in the chronically ill or institutionalized elderly subjects. In these subjects, drug clearance by the kidney may be reduced even with normal serum creatinine clearance. Reduction of dose or of frequency of administration may be indicated.

Adverse Effects: The adverse reactions to cefprozil are similar to those observed with other orally administered cephalosporins. Cefprozil was usually well tolerated in controlled clinical trials. Approximately 2% of patients discontinued cefprozil therapy due to adverse events.

The most common adverse events (of probable or unknown relationship to study drug) observed in 4 227 patients treated with cefprozil in clinical efficacy trials are:

Gastrointestinal: diarrhea (2.7%), nausea (2.3%), vomiting (1.4%) and abdominal pain (0.9%).

Hepatobiliary: As with some penicillins and some other cephalosporin antibiotics, cholestatic jaundice has been reported rarely.

Hypersensitivity: rash (1.2%), erythema (0.1%), pruritus (0.3%) and urticaria (0.07%). Such reactions have been reported more frequently in children than in adults. Signs and symptoms usually occur a few days after initiation of therapy and subside within a few days after cessation of therapy.

CNS: Dizziness, hyperactivity, headache, nervousness, insomnia, confusion, and drowsiness have been reported rarely (<1%) and causal relationship is uncertain. All were reversible.

Other: genital pruritus (0.8%) and vaginitis (0.7%).

Laboratory abnormalities: Transitory abnormalities in clinical laboratory test results of uncertain etiology have been reported during clinical trials as follows:

Hepatobiliary: elevations of AST, ALT, alkaline phosphatase, and bilirubin.

Hematopoietic: transiently decreased leukocyte count and eosinophilia.

Renal: slight elevations in BUN and serum creatinine.

Adverse reactions reported from postmarketing experience and which were not seen in the clinical trials include serum sickness, pseudomembranous colitis, Stevens-Johnson syndrome and exfoliative dermatitis. The association between these events and cefprozil administration is unknown.

In addition to the adverse reactions listed above which have been observed in patients treated with cefprozil, the following adverse reactions and altered laboratory tests have been reported for cephalosporin-class antibiotics. Anaphylaxis, erythema multiforme, toxic epidermal necrolysis, fever, renal

Cefzil (cont'd)

dysfunction, toxic nephropathy, aplastic anemia, hemolytic anemia, hemorrhage, prolonged prothrombin time, positive Coombs' tests, elevated LDH, pancytopenia, neutropenia, agranulocytosis, thrombocytopenia.

Several cephalosporins have been implicated in triggering seizures, particularly in patients with renal impairment, when the dosage was not reduced (see Dosage and Overdose). If seizures associated with drug therapy occur, the drug should be discontinued. Anticonvulsant therapy can be given if clinically indicated.

Overdose: Symptoms and Treatment: Since no case of overdosage has been reported to date, no specific information on symptoms or treatment of overdosage is available. In animal toxicology studies, single doses as high as 5 000 mg/kg were without serious or lethal consequences.

Cefprozil is eliminated primarily by the kidneys. In case of severe overdosage, especially in patients with compromised renal function, hemodialysis will aid in the removal of cefprozil from the body.

Dosage: Cefprozil is administered orally (with or without food), in the treatment of infections due to susceptible bacteria in the following doses:

Adults (13 years and older): Upper respiratory tract (pharyngitis/tonsillitis): 500 mg q24h. Acute sinusitis: 250 mg or 500 mg q12h. Skin and skin structure: 250 mg q12h or 500 mg q24h. Uncomplicated urinary tract: 500 mg q24h.

Children (2 to 12 years): skin and skin structure: 20 mg/kg q24h. See Table II.

Table II—Cefzil

Dosage in Children (2-12 years): Skin and Skin Structure (20 mg/kg q24h)

Age* (years)	Weight (kg)	Multi-dose bottle 125 mg/5 mL mL/dose	Multi-dose bottle 250 mg/5 mL mL/dose
2-3	11-14	10.0	5.0
4-6	15-21	15.0	7.5
7-8	22-26	—	10.0
9-10	28-31	—	12.5
11	35	—	15.0

*Ages given are a useful guide only. Correct dosage should be determined by weight.

Table III—Cefzil

Dosage in Infants and Children (6 months-12 years): Otitis Media (15 mg/kg q12h)

Age* (years)	Weight (kg)	Multi-dose bottle 125 mg/5 mL mL/dose	Multi-dose bottle 250 mg/5 mL mL/dose
6 months-1 year	7-9	5.0	2.5
2	11-12	7.5	3.75
3-4	14-15	—	5.0
5-6	17-21	—	6.25
7-8	22-26	—	7.5
9-10	28-31	—	8.75
11-12	35-39	—	10.0

*Ages given are a useful guide only. Correct dosage should be determined by weight.

Table IV—Cefzil

Dosage in Infants and Children (6 months-12 years): Upper Respiratory Tract (Pharyngitis/Tonsillitis) (7.5 mg/kg q12h)

Age* (years)	Weight (kg)	Multi-dose bottle 125 mg/5 mL mL/dose	Multi-dose bottle 250 mg/5 mL mL/dose
6 months-1 year	7-9	2.5	—
2-6	11-21	5.0	2.5
7-9	22-28	—	3.75
10-11	31-35	—	5.0
12	41	—	6.25

*Ages given are a useful guide only. Correct dosage should be determined by weight.

Table V—Cefzil

Reconstitution Table

Cefzil Powder for Oral Suspension	Bottle Size (mL)	Diluent (water) Added to Bottle (mL)	Approximate Available Volume (mL)	Final Concentration
125 mg/5 mL	75	54	75	125 mg/5 mL
	100	72	100	125 mg/5 mL
250 mg/5 mL	75	54	75	250 mg/5 mL
	100	72	100	250 mg/5 mL

Acute Sinusitis: 7.5 mg/kg q12h or 15 mg/kg q12h. Follow dosing instructions as for otitis media and upper respiratory tract presented in Tables III and IV.

The maximum pediatric daily dose should not exceed the maximum daily dose recommended for adults (e.g., 1 g/day).

Duration of Therapy: Duration of therapy in the majority of clinical trials was 10 to 15 days. The duration of treatment should be guided by the patient's clinical and bacteriological response. In the treatment of acute uncomplicated cystitis, a 7-day oral therapy is usually sufficient. In the treatment of infections due to S. pyogenes, a therapeutic dosage of cefprozil should be administered for at least 10 days.

Renal Impairment: Cefprozil may be administered to patients with impaired renal function. No dosage adjustment is necessary for patients with creatinine clearance values >30 mL/min. For those with creatinine clearance values ≤30 mL/min, 50% of the standard dose should be given at the standard dosing interval. Cefprozil is in part removed by hemodialysis; therefore, cefprozil should be administered after the completion of hemodialysis.

Reconstitution: Prior to dispensing, the pharmacist must constitute the dry powder with water as described in Table V.

For ease in preparation, the water can be added in 2 portions. Shake well after each addition and prior to use.

Storage of Reconstituted Suspension: The constituted cefprozil oral suspension must be stored in the refrigerator (2 to 8°C) for up to 14 days. Keep container tightly closed. Discard unused portion after 14 days.

Supplied: Powder for Oral Suspension: 125 mg/5 mL: Each 5 mL of constituted, bubble-gum flavored solution contains: anhydrous cefprozil 125 mg. Nonmedicinal ingredients: aspartame, citric acid, colloidal silicone dioxide, FD&C red No. 3, flavors (natural and artificial), glycine, microcrystalline cellulose, polysorbate 80, simethicone, sodium benzoate, sodium carboxymethylcellulose, sodium chloride and sucrose. Energy 6.2 kJ (1.5 kcal)/mL. Bottles of 75 and 100 mL.

250 mg/5 mL: Each 5 mL of constituted, bubble-gum flavored solution contains: anhydrous cefprozil 250 mg. Nonmedicinal ingredients: aspartame, citric acid, colloidal silicone dioxide, FD&C red No. 3, flavors (natural and artificial), glycine, microcrystalline cellulose, polysorbate 80, simethicone, sodium benzoate, sodium carboxymethylcellulose, sodium chloride and sucrose. Energy 5.5 kJ (1.3 kcal)/mL. Bottles of 75 and 100 mL.

Tablets: 250 mg: Each light orange, caplet-shaped, film-coated tablet engraved with 7720 on one side and with 250 on the other side,contains: anhydrous cefprozil 250 mg. Nonmedicinal ingredients: FD&C yellow No. 6, hydroxypropylmethylcellulose, magnesium stearate, microcrystalline cellulose, polyethylene glycol, polysorbate 80, simethicone, sodium starch glycolate and titanium dioxide. Bottles of 100.

500 mg: Each white, caplet-shaped, film-coated tablet, engraved with 7721 on one side and with 500 on the other side, contains: anhydrous cefprozil 500 mg. Nonmedicinal ingredients: hydroxypropylmethylcellulose, magnesium stearate, microcrystalline cellulose, polyethylene glycol, polysorbate 80, simethicone, sodium starch glycolate and titanium dioxide. Bottles of 100.

Store the tablets and powder for oral suspension at room temperature (15 to 30°C) and protect from light and excessive humidity.

(Shown in Product Recognition Section)

Reviewed 1998

General monographs are developed by CPhA editorial staff and reviewed by the *CPS* Editorial Advisory Panel to provide additional therapeutic information.

CELESTODERM®-V Ⓟ
CELESTODERM®-V/2 Ⓟ

Schering

Betamethasone Valerate

Topical Corticosteroid

Indications: The topical management of allergic and inflammatory dermatoses responsive to corticosteroid therapy, such as psoriasis, atopic eczema, infantile eczema, nummular eczema, pruritus ani and vulvae, neurodermatitis (lichen simplex chronicus), intertrigo, contact dermatitis, seborrheic dermatitis, exfoliative dermatitis, solar dermatitis, stasis dermatitis and dyshidrosis. Refractory psoriasis may be treated with Celestoderm-V especially in conjunction with the hydration technique of occlusive dressings.

The ointment formulations may be preferred for the treatment of dry, scaling and fissured lesions.

Celestoderm-V/2 contains a lower concentration (half strength) of betamethasone and is indicated for maintenance therapy after the acute phase has been brought under control, for less severe conditions and for extensive lesions involving large areas of the body surface.

Contraindications: Tuberculosis of skin, herpes simplex, varicella, vaccinia, superficial fungus or yeast infections. Patients with a history of sensitivity reactions to any of its components. Application in or near the eyes should be avoided.

Precautions: Corticosteroids are known to be absorbed percutaneously in patients under prolonged treatment, with extensive body surface treatment or particularly in those using the occlusive dressing technique on large areas of the body. In such cases, it is recommended that kidney function studies such as BUN be carried out prior to treatment and regularly throughout the course of the treatment.

Pregnancy and *Lactation:* Since safety of topical corticosteroid use in pregnant women has not been established, drugs of this class should be used during pregnancy only if the potential benefit justifies the potential risk to the fetus. Drugs of this class should not be used extensively in large amounts or for prolonged periods of time in pregnant patients. Since it is not known whether topical administration of corticosteroids can result in sufficient systemic absorption to produce detectable quantities in breast milk, a decision should be made to discontinue nursing or to discontinue the drug, taking into account the importance of the drug to the mother.

Children: Any of the side effects that have been reported following systemic use of corticosteroids, including adrenal suppression, may also occur with topical corticosteroids, especially in infants and children.

Systemic absorption of topical corticosteroids will be increased if extensive body surface areas are treated or if the occlusive technique is used. Suitable precautions should be taken under these conditions or when long-term use is anticipated, particularly in infants and children. Pediatric patients may demonstrate greater susceptibility to topical corticosteroid-induced HPA axis suppression and Cushing's syndrome than mature patients because of a larger skin surface area to body weight ratio. HPA axis suppression, Cushing's syndrome, linear growth retardation, delayed weight gain, and intracranial hypertension have been reported in children receiving topical corticosteroids. Manifestations of adrenal suppression in children include low plasma cortisol levels and absence of response to ACTH stimulation. Manifestations of intracranial hypertension include a bulging fontanelle, headaches and bilateral papilledema. Use of topical corticosteroids in children should be limited to the least amount compatible with an effective therapeutic regimen.

When long-term topical treatment under occlusive dressings is necessary, small dosages, rotation of sites and intermittent therapy should be considered.

Patients should be advised to inform subsequent physicians of the prior use of corticosteroids.

In the presence of infection, Celestoderm-V preparations should be superseded by suitable antibacterial agents until the infection has cleared.

Adverse Effects: With use of topical corticosteroids, local reactions have been reported, namely, burning sensation, itching, irritation, dryness, hypertrichosis, acneiform eruptions, and hypopigmentation. Striae, secondary infection, atrophy, miliaria, folliculitis, and pyodermas also occur but more frequently with use of occlusive dressings. Contact sensitivity to a particular dressing material or adhesive may occur occasionally.

Overdose: Symptoms: Excessive or prolonged use of topical corticosteroids can suppress pituitary-adrenal function, resulting in secondary adrenal insufficiency, and produce manifestations of hypercorticism, including Cushing's disease.

Treatment: Appropriate symptomatic treatment is indicated. Acute hypercorticoid symptoms are usually reversible. Treat electrolyte imbalance, if necessary. In case of chronic toxicity, slow withdrawal of corticosteroids is advised.

Dosage: Apply a small amount on the affected skin 2 or 3 times daily. Refractory lesions of psoriasis and other deep seated dermatoses such as lichen simplex chronicus, hypertrophic lichen planus, atopic dermatitis, chronic eczematous and lichenified hand eruptions, and recalcitrant pustular eruptions on the palms and soles will respond better to topical corticosteroids when used with the hydration technique of occlusive dressing. This technique reduces evaporation from the skin by means of a closed impermeable dressing over the lesion.

Occlusive Dressing Technique: 1. Apply a thick layer of the cream or ointment over the entire surface of the lesion under a light gauze dressing and then cover it with a pliable, transparent, impermeable, plastic material well beyond the treated area.

2. Seal the edges to the normal skin by adhesive tape or other means.

3. Leave the dressing in place 1 to 3 days and repeat the procedure 3 or 4 times as needed. With this method of treatment, marked improvement often is seen in a few days. Occasionally, a miliary eruption or folliculitis develops in the skin under the occlusive dressing requiring removal of the plastic covering.

Supplied: Celestoderm-V: Cream: Each g of cream contains: betamethasone 1 mg (as valerate USP) in a water-miscible base. Nonmedicinal ingredients: cetostearyl alcohol, chlorocresol, mineral oil, monobasic sodium phosphate, phosphoric acid, polyethylene glycol 1 000 monocetyl ether, purified water, sodium hydroxide and white petrolatum. Tubes of 15 g; jars of 450 g.

Ointment: Each g of ointment contains: betamethasone 1 mg (as valerate USP) in white petrolatum. Nonmedicinal ingredients: white petrolatum. Jars of 450 g.

Celestoderm-V/2: Cream: Each g of cream contains: betamethasone 0.5 mg (as valerate USP) in a water-miscible base. Nonmedicinal ingredients: cetostearyl alcohol, chlorocresol, mineral oil, monobasic sodium phosphate, phosphoric acid, polyethylene glycol 1 000 monocetyl ether, purified water, sodium hydroxide and white petrolatum. Jars of 450 g.

Ointment: Each g of ointment contains: betamethasone 0.5 mg (as valerate USP) in white petrolatum. Nonmedicinal ingredients: white petrolatum. Jars of 450 g.

CELESTONE® Ⓟ

Schering

Betamethasone

Glucocorticoid

Indications: Betamethasone is used orally in the management of disorders responsive to adrenocortical hormone therapy such as:

Endocrine Disorders: primary or secondary adrenocortical insufficiency (hydrocortisone or cortisone is the first choice; synthetic analogs may be used in conjunction with mineralocorticoids where applicable; in infancy, mineralocorticoid supplementation is of particular importance); congenital adrenal hyperplasia; nonsuppurative thyroiditis; hypercalcemia associated with cancer.

Musculoskeletal Disorders: as adjunctive therapy for short-term administration (to tide the patient over an acute episode or exacerbation) in psoriatic arthritis, rheumatoid arthritis (selected cases may require low dose maintenance therapy), ankylosing spondylitis, acute and subacute bursitis, acute nonspecific tenosynovitis, acute gouty arthritis.

Collagen Diseases: during an exacerbation or as maintenance therapy in selected cases of systemic lupus erythematosus and acute rheumatic carditis.

Dermatologic Disease: pemphigus, bullous dermatitis herpetiformis, severe erythema multiforme (Stevens-Johnson syndrome), exfoliative dermatitis, mycosis fungoides, severe psoriasis.

Allergic States: control of severe or incapacitating allergic conditions intractable to adequate trials of conventional treatment such as seasonal or perennial allergic rhinitis, bronchial asthma (including status asthmaticus), contact dermatitis, atopic dermatitis, serum sickness, angioedema and urticaria.

Ophthalmic Diseases: severe, acute and chronic allergy and inflammatory processes involving the eye and its adnexa such as allergic conjunctivitis, keratitis, allergic corneal marginal ulcers, herpes zoster ophthalmicus (but **not** herpes simplex), iritis and iridocyclitis, chorioretinitis, anterior segment inflammation, diffuse posterior uveitis and choroiditis, optic neuritis, retrobulbar neuritis, sympathetic ophthalmia.

Respiratory Diseases: symptomatic sarcoidosis, Löeffler's syndrome not manageable by other means, berylliosis, fulminating or disseminated pulmonary tuberculosis when concurrently accompanied by appropriate antituberculous chemotherapy, pulmonary emphysema where bronchospasm or bronchial edema plays a significant role, diffuse interstitial pulmonary fibrosis (Hamman-Rich syndrome).

Hematologic Disorders: idiopathic and secondary thrombocytopenia in adults, acquired (autoimmune) hemolytic anemia, erythroblastopenia (RBC anemia), congenital (erythroid) hypoplastic anemia.

Neoplastic Diseases: for palliative management of leukemias and lymphomas in adults, acute leukemia of childhood.

Edematous States: to induce a diuresis or remission of proteinuria in the nephrotic syndrome, without uremia, of the idiopathic type or that due to lupus erythematosus. In conjunction with diuretic agents, to induce a diuresis in cirrhosis of the liver with refractory ascites, refractory congestive heart failure.

Gastrointestinal Diseases: to tide the patient over a critical period of the disease in ulcerative colitis, regional enteritis, intractable sprue.

Miscellaneous: tuberculous meningitis with subarachnoid block or impending block when concurrently accompanied by appropriate antituberculous chemotherapy, dental postoperative inflammatory reactions.

Contraindications: Systemic fungal infections; hypersensitivity to betamethasone or to other corticosteroids or to any component of the tablets.

Precautions: In patients on corticosteroid therapy subjected to unusual stress, increased dosage of rapidly acting corticosteroids before, during and after the stressful situation is indicated.

Patients who are on immunosuppressant doses of corticosteroids should be warned to avoid exposure to chickenpox or measles and, if exposed, to obtain medical advice. This is of particular importance in children.

While on corticosteroid therapy patients should not be vaccinated against smallpox because of potential complications. Conversely, patients with vaccinia should not receive corticosteroid therapy. Other immunization procedures should not be undertaken in patients who are on corticosteroids, especially on high doses, because of possible hazards of neurological complications and a lack of antibody response.

Pregnancy and *Lactation:* Since adequate human reproduction studies have not been done with corticosteroids, the use of these drugs in pregnancy, nursing mothers or women of childbearing potential requires that the possible benefits of the drug be weighed against the potential hazards to the mother and embryo or fetus. Infants born of mothers who have received substantial doses of corticosteroids during pregnancy should be carefully observed for signs of hypoadrenalism.

The use of corticosteroids in active tuberculosis should be restricted to those cases of fulminating or disseminated tuberculosis in which the corticosteroid is used for the management of the disease in conjunction with an appropriate antituberculous regimen. If corticosteroids are indicated in patients with latent tuberculosis or tuberculin reactivity, close observation is necessary as reactivation of the disease may occur. During prolonged corticosteroid therapy, these patients should receive chemoprophylaxis.

Corticosteroids may mask some signs of infection and new infections may appear during their use. There may be decreased resistance and inability to localize infection when corticosteroids are used. If corticosteroids have to be used in the presence of bacterial infections, institute appropriate vigorous anti-infective therapy.

Use corticosteroids cautiously in patients with ocular herpes simplex because of possible corneal ulceration and perforation.

Prolonged use of corticosteroids may produce subcapsular cataracts, glaucoma with possible damage to the optic nerves, and may enhance the establishment of secondary ocular infections due to fungi or viruses.

Corticosteroid therapy may cause hyperacidity or peptic ulcer. Since appearance of peptic ulcer may be asymptomatic until perforation or hemorrhage occurs, take x-rays when treatment is prolonged or when there is gastric distress. An ulcer regimen including an antacid should be considered as a prophylactic measure during prolonged therapy.

Use the lowest possible dose of corticosteroid to control the condition under treatment, and when dosage reduction is possible, the reduction should be gradual.

Average and large doses of hydrocortisone or cortisone can cause elevation of blood pressure, salt and water retention, and increased potassium excretion. These effects are less likely to occur with the synthetic derivatives except when used in large doses. Dietary salt restriction and potassium supplementation may be necessary. All corticosteroids increase calcium excretion.

Drug induced secondary adrenocortical insufficiency may be minimized by gradual dosage reduction. This type of relative insufficiency may persist for months after discontinuation of therapy, therefore, in any stress situation occurring during that period, reinstitute hormone therapy. If the patient is receiving steroids already, the dosage may have to be increased. Since mineralocorticoid secretion may be impaired, salt and/or a mineralocorticoid should be administered concurrently.

Use ASA cautiously in conjunction with corticosteroids in hypoprothrombinemia.

Use steroids with caution in: nonspecific ulcerative colitis if there is a probability of impending perforation, abscess or other pyogenic infection; diverticulitis, fresh intestinal anastomoses; active or latent peptic ulcer; renal insufficiency; hypertension; osteoporosis; and myasthenia gravis. Fat embolism has been reported as a possible complication of hypercortisonism.

There is an enhanced effect of corticosteroids on patients with hypothyroidism and in those with cirrhosis.

Psychic derangements may appear when corticosteroids are used, ranging from euphoria, insomnia, mood swings, personality changes, and severe depression to frank psychotic manifestations. Also, existing emotional instability or psychotic tendencies may be aggravated by corticosteroids.

Growth and development of infants and children on prolonged corticosteroid therapy should be carefully observed.

Steroids may increase or decrease motility and number of spermatozoa in some patients.

Phenytoin may enhance the rate of metabolism and clearance of corticosteroids and this may increase steroid dosage requirements.

Advise patients to inform subsequent physicians of the prior use of corticosteroids.

Corticosteroids may suppress reactions to skin tests.

Drug Interactions: Concurrent use of phenobarbital, phenytoin, rifampin or ephedrine may enhance the metabolism of corticosteroids, reducing their therapeutic effects.

Adverse Effects: Fluid and electrolyte disturbances: sodium retention; fluid retention; congestive heart failure in susceptible patients; potassium loss; hypokalemic alkalosis; hypertension.

Musculoskeletal: muscle weakness; steroid myopathy; loss of muscle mass; aggravation of myasthenic symptoms in myasthenia gravis; osteoporosis; vertebral compression fractures; aseptic necrosis of femoral and humeral heads; pathologic fracture of long bones.

Gastrointestinal: hiccups; peptic ulcer with possible perforation and hemorrhage; pancreatitis; abdominal distention; ulcerative esophagitis.

Dermatologic: impaired wound healing; thin fragile skin; petechiae and ecchymoses; facial erythema; increased sweating; may suppress reactions to skin tests; reactions such as allergic dermatitis, urticaria and angioneurotic edema.

Neurological: convulsions; increased intracranial pressure with papilledema (pseudotumor cerebri) usually after treatment; vertigo; headache.

Endocrine; menstrual irregularities, development of Cushingoid state; suppression of growth in children; secondary adrenocortical and pituitary unresponsiveness, particularly in times of stress, as in trauma, surgery or illness; decreased carbohydrate tolerance; manifestations of latent diabetes mellitus; increased requirements of insulin or oral hypoglycemic agents in diabetes.

Celestone (cont'd)

Ophthalmic: posterior subcapsular cataracts; increased intraocular pressure; glaucoma; exophthalmos.
Metabolic: negative nitrogen balance due to protein catabolism.
Other: hypersensitivity, thromboembolism, anaphylactoid and hypotensive or shock-like reactions.

Overdose: Symptoms: Acute overdosage with glucocorticosteroids, including betamethasone, is not expected to lead to a life-threatening situation. Except at the most extreme dosages, a few days of excessive glucocorticosteroid dosing is unlikely to produce harmful results in the absence of specific contraindications, such as in patients with diabetes mellitus, glaucoma, or active peptic ulcer, or in patients on medications such as digitalis, coumarin-type anticoagulants or potassium-depleting diuretics.

Treatment: Acute overdosage should be treated immediately by inducing emesis or by the administration of gastric lavage. Otherwise complications resulting from the metabolic effects of the corticosteroid or from deleterious effects of the basic or concomitant illnesses or resulting from drug interactions should be handled as appropriate.

Dosage: Dosage must be determined and adjusted to the individual requirements of the patient, i.e. severity of the condition, anticipated duration of therapy, tolerance to the steroid and response obtained. The lowest dose that will produce the desired clinical effect should be employed. Starting dose should vary from 1 to 8 mg daily in divided doses. Should the physician prefer, total daily intake may be given in a single dose once every 24 to 48 hours.

Supplied: Each blue, scored tablet contains: betamethasone USP 500 µg. Nonmedicinal ingredients: cornstarch, dye, FD & C Blue No. 2, gelatin, lactose and magnesium stearate. Tartrazine-free. Bottles of 100. Store between 2 and 30°C. Protect from light.

(Shown in Product Recognition Section)

CELESTONE® SOLUSPAN® ℞
Schering

Betamethasone Sodium Phosphate—Betamethasone Acetate
Injectable Glucocorticoid

Indications: (1) I.M. injection in allergic, dermatologic, rheumatic, and other conditions responsive to systemic corticosteroids, including bursitis; (2) injection directly into the affected tissues in bursitis and associated inflammatory disorders of tendons such as tenosynovitis, and inflammatory disorders of muscle such as fibrositis and myositis; (3) intra-articular and periarticular injection in rheumatoid arthritis and osteoarthritis; (4) intralesional injection in various dermatologic conditions; and (5) local injection in certain inflammatory and cystic disorders of the foot.

Contraindications: Herpes simplex of the eye. Regional corticosteroid therapy is contraindicated in areas that are locally infected, although infection elsewhere in the body is not a contraindication to the use of corticosteroids regionally.

Precautions: See Celestone oral preparations. Following intra-articular injection, a portion of the administered dose of Celestone Soluspan is absorbed systemically. In patients being treated concomitantly with peroral or parenteral corticosteroids, especially those receiving large doses, the systemic absorption of the drug should be considered in determining intra-articular dosage.

Adverse Effects: See Celestone oral preparations. There have been a few cases of crystal deposition but no reports of dimpling of the skin after intradermal injection. Nevertheless, because dimpling of the skin is attributable to atrophy of subcutaneous fat and is seen with other injectable corticosteroids, s.c. injection should be avoided. Gastrointestinal side effects have not been reported, nor has pain or the "secondary flare" which sometimes occur after intra-articular injection of corticosteroids.

Dosage: Shake well before using. Dosage must be adjusted according to the severity of the condition, the response obtained, and the patient's tolerance of the corticosteroid. For systemic effect, treatment is initiated with 1 mL i.m. in most conditions and repeated weekly, or more often, if necessary. In severe illnesses such as status asthmaticus or disseminated lupus erythematosus, 2 mL might be required initially. In dermatologic disorders, including neurodermatitis, psoriasis, hypertrophic lichen planus, lichen simplex, eczema, contact dermatitis, and dermatitis medicamentosa, i.m. dosage is usually 1 mL at intervals of 3 days to a week. In respiratory tract disorders, including bronchial asthma, hay fever, allergic bronchitis, and perennial allergic rhinitis, i.m. dosage is usually 1 to 2 mL at weekly intervals. Bursitis may be treated with i.m. injections of 1 mL repeated weekly if necessary.

For local effect, in acute bursitis, 1 intrabursal injection of 1 mL may relieve pain and restore full range of movement in a few hours. Several intrabursal injections at intervals of 1 to 2 weeks are usually required in recurrent acute bursitis and in acute bursitis superimposed on chronic bursitis. Partial relief of pain and some increase in mobility may be expected in both conditions after 1 or 2 injections. In tenosynovitis and tendinitis, 3 or 4 injections of 1 mL each at intervals of 1 to 2 weeks between injections are given in most cases. Injection should be made into the affected tendon sheaths rather than into the tendons themselves. In ganglions of joint capsules and tendon sheaths, 0.5 mL is injected into the ganglion cysts. In rheumatoid arthritis and osteoarthritis, relief of pain, soreness, and stiffness may be experienced in 2 to 4 hours after intra-articular injection. Using sterile technique, a 20 to 24 gauge needle on a syringe for aspiration is inserted into the synovial cavity, and a few drops of synovial fluid are withdrawn to confirm that the needle is in the joint. The aspirating syringe is replaced by a syringe containing Celestone Soluspan, and injection is then made into the joint (see Table I).

Table I—Celestone Soluspan

Intra-articular Injection

Size of Joint	Location	Dose (mL)
Very Large	Hip	1.0 to 2.0
Large	Knee Ankle Shoulder	1.0
Medium	Elbow Wrist	0.5 to 1.0
Small (Metacarpophalangeal, interphalangeal) (Sternoclavicular)	Hand Chest	0.25 to 0.5

Pain with intra-articular injection of Celestone Soluspan has not been a problem. However, should the physician want to administer it with a local anesthetic, it can be mixed in the syringe with an equal volume of 1% procaine HCl or of 1% lidocaine HCl before injection. The required dose of Celestone Soluspan is first withdrawn from the vial into the syringe. The local anesthetic is then drawn in, and the syringe shaken briefly. Do not inject local anesthetics into the vial of Celestone Soluspan.

Dermatologic conditions that have responded to intralesional treatment with Celestone Soluspan include: localized neurodermatitis, psoriasis, nummular eczema, alopecia areata, hypertrophic lichen planus, circumscribed lichen simplex, keloids, and chronic discoid lupus erythematosus. In intralesional treatment, 0.2 mL of Celestone Soluspan is injected intradermally (not s.c.) per square centimeter of lesion using a tuberculin syringe with a 25 gauge, 13 mm needle. Care should be taken to deposit a uniform depot of medication intradermally. A total of no more than 1 mL at weekly intervals is recommended.

Disorders of the foot responsive to corticosteroids injected locally: For most injections into the foot, a tuberculin syringe with a 25 gauge, 2 cm needle is used. Treatment is given at intervals of 3 days to a week. In bursitis under heloma durum (hard corn), bursitis under heloma molle (soft corn), synovial cysts, and Morton's neuralgia (metatarsalgia) 0.25 to 0.5 mL are recommended. For bursitis under calcaneal spurs, bursitis over hallux rigidis (flexion deformity of the great toe), bursitis over digiti quinti varus (inward deviation of the fifth toe), tenosynovitis, and periostitis of the cuboid, 0.5 mL is recommended; in acute gouty arthritis, 0.5 to 1 mL are recommended.

Supplied: Each mL of aqueous suspension contains: betamethasone acetate USP 3 mg and betamethasone sodium phosphate USP equivalent to 3 mg betamethasone USP. Nonmedicinal ingredients: benzalkonium chloride, disodium edetate, sodium phosphate dibasic and sodium phosphate monobasic. Vials of 1 mL. Boxes of 10 and multiple dose vials of 5 mL. Store between 2 and 25°C. Protect from light.

CellCept® ℞
Roche

Mycophenolate Mofetil
Immunosuppressant Agent

Warnings: Increased susceptibility to infection and the possible development of lymphoma may result from immunosuppression. Only physicians experienced in immunosuppressive therapy and management of solid organ transplant patients should use mycophenolate mofetil. Patients receiving the drug should be managed in facilities equipped and staffed with adequate laboratory and supportive medical resources. The physician responsible for maintenance therapy should have complete information requisite for the follow-up of the patient.

Pharmacology: Mechanism of Action: Mycophenolate mofetil has been demonstrated in experimental animal models to prolong the survival of allogeneic transplants (kidney, heart, liver, intestine, limb, small bowel, pancreatic islets, and bone marrow). Mycophenolate mofetil has also been shown to reverse ongoing acute rejection in the canine renal and rat cardiac allograft models. Mycophenolate mofetil also inhibited proliferative arteriopathy in experimental models of aortic and heart allografts in rats, as well as in primate cardiac xenografts. Mycophenolate mofetil was used alone or in combination with other immunosuppressive agents in these studies. Mycophenolate mofetil has been demonstrated to inhibit immunologically-mediated inflammatory responses in animal models and to inhibit tumor development and prolong survival in murine tumor transplant models.

Mycophenolate mofetil is rapidly absorbed following oral administration and hydrolyzed to form MPA, which is the active metabolite. MPA is a potent, selective, uncompetitive and reversible inhibitor of inosine monophosphate dehydrogenase (IMPDH), and therefore inhibits the de novo pathway of guanosine nucleotide synthesis without incorporation into DNA. Because T- and B-lymphocytes are critically dependent for their proliferation on de novo synthesis of purines whereas other cell types can utilize salvage pathways, MPA has potent cytostatic effects on lymphocytes. MPA inhibits proliferative responses of T- and B-lymphocytes to both mitogenic and allospecific stimulation. Addition of guanosine or deoxyguanosine reverses the cytostatic effects of MPA on lymphocytes. MPA also suppresses antibody formation by B-lymphocytes. MPA prevents the glycosylation of lymphocyte and monocyte glycoproteins that are involved in intercellular adhesion to endothelial cells and may inhibit recruitment of leukocytes into sites of inflammation and graft rejection. Mycophenolate mofetil did not inhibit early events in the activation of human peripheral blood mononuclear cells, such as the production of interleukin-1 (IL-1) and interleukin-2 (IL-2), but did block the coupling of these events to DNA synthesis and proliferation.

Pharmacokinetics: Following oral administration, mycophenolate mofetil undergoes rapid and extensive absorption and complete presystemic metabolism to MPA, the active metabolite. Mycophenolate mofetil is not measurable systemically in plasma following oral administration.

Absorption: In 12 healthy volunteers, the mean absolute bioavailability of oral mycophenolate mofetil relative to i.v. mycophenolate mofetil (based on MPA AUC) was 94%. The area under the plasma-concentration time curve (AUC) for MPA appears to increase in a dose-proportional fashion in renal transplant patients receiving multiple doses of mycophenolate mofetil up to a daily dose of 3 g (see Table I).

Immediately post-transplant (<40 days), mean AUC and C_{max} are approximately 50% lower in renal transplant patients than that observed in healthy volunteers or in stable renal transplant patients.

Effect of Food: Food (27 g fat, 650 calories) had no effect on the extent of absorption (MPA AUC) of mycophenolate mofetil when administered at doses of 1.5 g b.i.d. to renal transplant patients. However, MPA C_{max} was decreased by 40% in the presence of food (see Dosage).

Distribution: The mean (±SD) apparent volume of distribution of MPA in 12 healthy volunteers is approximately 3.6 (±1.5) and 4.0 (±1.2) L/kg following i.v. and oral administration, respectively. MPA, at clinically relevant concentrations, is 97% bound to plasma albumin. MPAG is 82% bound to plasma albumin at MPAG concentration ranges that are normally seen in stable renal transplant patients; however, at higher MPAG concentrations (observed in patients with renal impairment or delayed graft function), the binding of MPA may be reduced as a result of competition between MPAG and MPA for protein binding. Mean blood to plasma ratio of radioactivity concentrations was approximately 0.6 indicating that MPA and MPAG do not extensively distribute into the cellular fractions of blood.

In vitro studies to evaluate the effect of other agents on the binding of MPA to human serum albumin (HSA) or plasma proteins showed that salicylate (at 25 mg/dL with HSA) and MPAG (at ≥460 μg/mL with plasma proteins) increased the free fraction of MPA. At concentrations exceeding those encountered clinically, cyclosporine, digoxin, naproxen, prednisone, propranolol, tacrolimus, theophylline, tolbutamide, and warfarin did not increase the free fraction of MPA. MPA at concentrations as high as 100 μg/mL had little effect on the binding of warfarin, digoxin or propranolol, but decreased the binding of theophylline from 53 to 45% and phenytoin from 90 to 87%.

Metabolism: Mycophenolate mofetil undergoes complete presystemic metabolism to MPA, the active metabolite. MPA is metabolized principally by glucuronyl transferase to form the phenolic glucuronide of MPA (MPAG) which is not pharmacologically active. The following metabolites of the 2-hydroxyethyl-morpholino moiety are also recovered in the urine following oral administration of mycophenolate mofetil to healthy subjects: N-(2-carboxymethyl)-morpholine, N-(2-hydroxyethyl)-morpholine, and the N-oxide of N-(2-hydroxyethyl)-morpholine.

Secondary peaks in the plasma MPA concentration-time profile are usually observed 6 to 12 hours postdose. The coadministration of cholestyramine (4 g t.i.d.) resulted in approximately a 40% decrease in the MPA AUC (largely as a consequence of lower concentrations in the terminal portion of the profile). These observations suggest that enterohepatic recirculation contributes to MPA plasma concentrations.

Renal insufficiency has no consistent effect on MPA pharmacokinetics. Mean MPA AUC was increased by 50% in severe renal impairment (GFR <25 mL/min/1.73 m²), however, there was considerable variation about the mean. For MPAG, there is an increase (3- to 6-fold) in mean AUC (see Pharmacology, Special Populations).

Excretion: Negligible amount of drug is excreted as MPA (<1% of dose) in the urine. Orally administered radiolabeled mycophenolate mofetil resulted in complete recovery of the administered dose; with 93% of the administered dose recovered in the urine and 6% recovered in feces. Most (about 87%) of the administered dose is excreted in the urine as MPAG. At clinically encountered concentrations MPA is not removed by hemodialysis. Similarly, MPAG concentrations normally encountered are unaffected by hemodialysis, however, at high MPAG plasma concentrations (>100 μg/mL), small amounts of this metabolite are removed.

Mean (±SD) apparent half-life and plasma clearance of MPA are 17.9 (±6.5) hours and 193 (±48) mL/min following oral administration and 16.6 (±5.8) hours and 177 (±31) mL/min following i.v. administration, respectively.

Pharmacokinetics in Healthy Volunteers and Renal Transplant Patients: Shown in Table I are the mean (±SD) pharmacokinetic parameters for MPA following the administration of oral mycophenolate mofetil given as single doses to healthy volunteers and multiple doses to renal transplant patients. As noted below, MPA AUC and C_{max} in early transplant patients (<40 days post-transplant) are approximately 50% lower when compared with healthy volunteers or to stable renal transplant patients.

It has been demonstrated that the 500 mg tablet (×2) is bioequivalent to the 250 mg capsule (×4) with respect to the extent of absorption (AUC), and with respect to the rate of absorption (Cmax). Shown in Table II are the pharmacokinetic parameters for MPA following the administration of oral mycophenolate mofetil in renal transplant patients.

Table I—CellCept

Pharmacokinetic Parameters for MPA [mean (±SD)] Following Administration of Mycophenolate Mofetil to Healthy Volunteers (Single dose) and Renal Transplant Patients (Multiple Doses)

Healthy Volunteers (no. of subjects)	Dose	T_{max} (h)	C_{max} (μg/mL)	Total AUC (μg·h/mL)
(n=129) (n=117)	1 g	0.80 (±0.36)	24.5 (±9.5)	63.9 (±16.2)
Time After Renal Transplantation (no. of patients)	**Dose**	**T_{max} (h)**	**C_{max} (μg/mL)**	**Interdosing Interval AUC_{0-12} (μg·h/mL)**
Early (<40 days) (n=25)	1 g b.i.d.	1.31 (±0.76)	8.16 (±4.50)	27.3 (±10.9)
Early (<40 days) (n=27)	1.5 g b.i.d.	1.21 (±0.81)	13.5 (±8.18)	38.4 (±15.4)
Late (>3 months) (n=23)	1.5 g b.i.d.	0.90 (±0.24)	24.1 (±12.1)	65.3 (±35.4)

Table II—CellCept

Summary Table of Measured Comparative Bioavailability Date for MPA Following Administration of Mycophenolate Mofetil 2×500 mg Tablet vs 4×250 mg Capsule in Renal Transplant Patients

Parameter	Geometric Mean and Arithmetic Mean (CV%) Test (500 mg tablet)	Reference (250 mg capsule)	Ratio of Geometric Means (%)
AUC_{0-12} (μg·h/mL)	31.7 33.5 (33.8)	31.2 33.4 (38.2)	102.1
C_{max} (μg/mL)	10.3 11.5 (46.8)	10.6 12.2 (48.1)	99.5
C_{min} (μg/mL)	1.40 (75)	1.35 (81.5)	110.3
T_{max}* (h)	1.09 (75.8)	1.15 (70.5)	—
Fluctuations*	378 (51.3)	404 (52.5)	—

*Expressed as arithmetic mean (CV%) only.

Special Populations: Shown in Table III are the mean (±SD) pharmacokinetic parameters for MPA following the administration of oral mycophenolate mofetil given as single doses to subjects with renal and hepatic impairment.

Table III—CellCept

Pharmacokinetic Parameters for MPA [mean (±SD)] Following Single Doses of Mycophenolate Mofetil in Chronic Renal and Hepatic Impairment

Renal Impairment (no. of patients)	Dose (g)	T_{max} (h)	C_{max} (μg/mL)	AUC_{0-96} (μg·h/mL)
Healthy Volunteers GFR >80 mL/min/1.73m² (n=6)	1	0.75 (±0.27)	25.3 (±7.99)	45.0 (±22.6)
Mild Renal Impairment GFR 50-80 mL/min/1.73m² (n=6)	1	0.75 (±0.27)	26.0 (±3.82)	59.9 (±12.9)
Moderate Renal Impairment GFR 25-49 mL/min/1.73m² (n=6)	1	0.75 (±0.27)	19.0 (±13.2)	52.9 (±25.5)
Severe Renal Impairment GFR <25 mL/min/1.73m² (n=7)	1	1.00 (±0.41)	16.3 (±10.8)	78.6 (±46.4)
Hepatic Impairment (no. of patients)	**Dose (g)**	**T_{max} (h)**	**C_{max} (μg/mL)**	**$AUC_{(0-48)}$ (μg·h/mL)**
Healthy Volunteers (n=6)	1	0.63 (±0.14)	24.3 (±5.73)	29.0 (±5.78)
Alcoholic cirrhosis (n=18)	1	0.85 (±0.58)	22.4 (±10.1)	29.8 (±10.7)

Renal Insufficiency: In a single-dose study (6 volunteers/group), the mean plasma MPA AUC observed in volunteers with severe chronic renal impairment [glomerular filtration rate (GFR) <25 mL/min/1.73 m²] was about 75% higher relative to the mean observed in healthy volunteers (GFR >80 mL/min/1.73 m²). However, the mean single dose plasma MPAG AUC was 3- to 6-fold higher in volunteers with severe renal impairment than in volunteers with mild renal impairment or healthy volunteers, consistent with the known renal elimination of MPAG. Multiple dosing of mycophenolate mofetil in patients with severe chronic renal impairment has not been studied. No data are available on the safety of long-term exposure to this level of MPAG (see Precautions, General, and Dosage).

In patients with delayed graft function post-transplant, mean MPA AUC_{0-12} was comparable to that seen in post-transplant patients without delayed graft function. Mean plasma MPAG AUC_{0-12} was 2- to 3-fold higher than in post-transplant patients without delayed graft function (see Precautions, General, and Dosage).

Hemodialysis: At clinically encountered concentrations, MPA is not removed by hemodialysis. Similary, MPAG concentrations normally encountered are unaffected by hemodialysis, however, at high MPAG concentrations (>100 μg/mL), hemodialysis removes only small amounts of MPAG.

Hepatic Insufficiency: In a single dose (1 g) study of 18 volunteers with alcoholic cirrhosis and 6 healthy volunteers, hepatic MPA glucuronidation processes appeared to be relatively unaffected by hepatic parenchymal disease when pharmacokinetic parameters of healthy volunteers and alcoholic cirrhosis patients within this study were compared. However, it should be noted that for unexplained reasons, the healthy volunteers in this study had about a 50% lower AUC as compared to healthy volunteers in other studies, thus making comparisons between volunteers with alcoholic cirrhosis and healthy volunteers difficult. Effects of hepatic disease on this process probably depend on the particular disease. Hepatic disease with other etiologies may show a different effect.

Children: Very limited pharmacokinetic data are available for pediatric renal transplant recipients. Data on these patients collected on day 21 post-transplant are presented in Table IV (on following page).

Gender: Data obtained from several studies were pooled to examine any gender-related differences in the pharmacokinetics of MPA (data were adjusted to 1 g dose). Mean (±SD) MPA AUC_{0-12} for males (n=79) was 32.0 (±14.5) and for females (n=41) was 36.5 (±18.8) μg·h/mL while mean (±SD) MPA C_{max} was 9.96 (±6.19) in the males and 10.6 (±5.64) μg/mL in the females. These differences are not of clinical significance.

Clinical Studies: The safety and efficacy of mycophenolate mofetil as adjunctive therapy for the prevention of organ rejection following allogeneic renal transplants was assessed in 3 randomized, double-blind, multicenter trials.

Prevention of Rejection: These studies compared 2 dose levels of mycophenolate mofetil (1.0 g b.i.d. and 1.5 g b.i.d.) with azathioprine (two studies) or placebo (one study) when administered in combination with cyclosporine and corticosteroids to prevent acute rejection episodes. One study also included antithymocyte globulin (Atgam) induction therapy. The three studies are described by geographic location of the investigational sites. One study was conducted in the U.S. at 14 sites, one study was conducted in Europe at 20 sites, and one study was conducted in Europe, Canada, and Australia at a total of 21 sites.

The primary efficacy endpoint was the proportion of patients in each treatment group who experienced biopsy-proven acute rejection or treatment failure (defined as early termination from the study for any reason without prior biopsy-proven rejection) within the first 6 months after transplantation. Mycophenolate

CellCept (cont'd)

Table IV—CellCept

Pharmacokinetic Parameters for MPA [mean ± (SD)] Following Multiple Oral Doses of Mycophenolate Mofetil in Pediatric Renal Transplant Patients

Age Range	Dose	T_{max} (h)	C_{max} (μg/mL)	AUC_{0-12} (μg·h/mL)
≥3 mo to <6 yr (Mean=2.75) (n=4)	15 mg/kg b.i.d	1.25 (±0.87)	3.70 (±2.08)	13.6 (±8.69)
≥6 yr to <12 yr (Mean=9.0) (n=4)	15 mg/kg b.i.d	0.50 (±0.00)	13.5 (±4.48)	23.4 (±2.84)
≥12 yr to 18 yr (Mean=15.6) (n=5)	15 mg/kg b.i.d	0.50 (±0.00)	13.2 (±6.86)	30.0 (±8.34)
≥12 yr to 18 yr (Mean=14.0) (n=7)	23 mg/kg b.i.d	1.14 (±0.80)	10.6 (±9.59)	28.3 (±12.8)

mofetil, when administered with antithymocyte globulin (Atgam) induction (1 study) and with cyclosporine and corticosteroids (all 3 studies), was shown to be superior to the following three therapeutic regimens: (1) antithymocyte globulin (Atgam) induction/azathioprine/cyclosporine/corticosteroids, (2) azathioprine/cyclosporine/corticosteroids, and (3) cyclosporine/corticosteroids.

Mycophenolate mofetil, in combination with corticosteroids and cyclosporine reduced (statistically significant at the <0.05 level) the incidence of treatment failure within the first 6 months following transplantation. Table V summarizes the results of these studies. Table V shows (1) the proportion of patients experiencing treatment failure, (2) the proportion of patients who experienced biopsy-proven acute rejection on treatment, and (3) early termination, for any reason other than graft loss or death, without a prior biopsy-proven acute rejection episode. Patients who prematurely discontinued treatment were followed for the occurrence of death or graft loss, and the cumulative incidence of graft loss and patient death are summarized separately. Patients who prematurely discontinued treatment were not followed for the occurrence of acute rejection after termination. More patients discontinued receiving mycophenolate mofetil (without prior biopsy-proven rejection, death or graft loss) than discontinued in the control groups, with the highest rate in the mycophenolate mofetil 3 g/day group. Therefore, the acute rejection rates may be underestimates, particularly in the mycophenolate mofetil 3 g/day group.

Cumulative incidence of 12-month graft loss and patient death are presented in Table VI. No advantage of mycophenolate mofetil with respect to graft loss and patient death was established. Numerically, patients receiving mycophenolate mofetil 2 g/day and 3 g/day experienced a better outcome than controls in all three studies; patients receiving mycophenolate mofetil 2 g/day experienced a better outcome than mycophenolate mofetil 3 g/day in 2 of the 3 studies. Patients in all treatment groups who terminated treatment early were found to have a poor outcome with respect to graft loss and patient death at 1 year.

Indications: For the prophylaxis of organ rejection in patients receiving allogeneic renal transplants. Mycophenolate mofetil should be used concomitantly with cyclosporine and corticosteroids.

Contraindications: Allergic reactions to mycophenolate mofetil have been observed, therefore, mycophenolate mofetil is contraindicated in patients with a hypersensitivity to mycophenolate mofetil, mycophenolic acid or any component of the drug product (see Supplied).

Table V—CellCept

Incidence of Treatment Failure (Biopsy-Proven Rejection or Early Termination for Any Reason)

U.S. Study (n=499)	**CellCept 2 g/day % (n=167)**	**CellCept 3 g/day % (n=166)**	**Azathioprine 1-2 mg/kg/day % (n=166)**
All treatment failures	31.1	31.3	47.6
Early termination without prior acute rejection*	9.6	12.7	6.0
Biopsy-proven rejection episode on treatment	19.8	17.5	38.0
Europe/Canada/ Australia Study (n=503)	**CellCept 2 g/day % (n=173)**	**CellCept 3 g/day % n=164)**	**Azathioprine 100-150 mg/day % (n=166)**
All treatment failures	38.2	34.8	50.0
Early termination without prior acute rejection*	13.9	15.2	10.2
Biopsy-proven rejection episode on treatment	19.7	15.9	35.5
Europe Study (n=491)	**CellCept 2 g/day % (n=165)**	**CellCept 3 g/day % (n=160)**	**Placebo % (n=166)**
All treatment failures	30.3	38.8	56.0
Early termination without prior acute rejection*	11.5	22.5	7.2
Biopsy-proven rejection episode on treatment	17.0	13.8	46.4

* Does not include death and graft loss as reason for early termination.

Table VI—CellCept

Cumulative Incidence of Combined Graft Loss and Patient Death at 12 Months

	CellCept 2 g/day	**CellCept 3 g/day**	**Control (Azathioprine or Placebo)**
U.S.	8.5%	11.5%	12.2%
Europe/ Canada/ Australia	11.7%	11.0%	13.6%
Europe	8.5%	10.0%	11.5%

Warnings: Increased susceptibility to infection and the possible development of lymphoma may result from immunosuppression. Only physicians experienced in immunosuppressive therapy and management of solid organ transplant patients should use mycophenolate mofetil. Patients receiving the drug should be managed in facilities equipped and staffed with adequate laboratory and supportive medical resources. The physician responsible for maintenance therapy should have complete information requisite for the follow-up of the patient.

Patients receiving immunosuppressive regimes involving combinations of drugs, including mycophenolate mofetil, as part of an immunosuppressive regimen are at increased risk of developing lymphomas and other malignancies, particularly of the skin. The risk appears to be related to the intensity and duration of immunosuppression rather than to the use of any specific agent. Oversuppression of the immune system can also increase susceptibility to infection. Mycophenolate mofetil has been administered in combination with the following agents in clinical trials: antithymocyte globulin (Atgam) induction, cyclosporine, and corticosteroids. The efficacy and safety of the use of mycophenolate mofetil in combination with other immunosuppressive agents has not been determined. The long-term risk of mycophenolate mofetil is unknown.

Lymphoproliferative disease or lymphoma developed in patients receiving mycophenolate mofetil with other immunosuppressive agents in approximately 1% of patients in the pivotal studies of prevention of rejection (see Adverse Effects).

In the three pivotal studies for prevention of rejection, similar rates of fatal infections (<2%) have occurred in patients receiving mycophenolate mofetil or control therapy in combination with other immunosuppressive agents (see Adverse Effects).

Up to 2.0% of patients receiving mycophenolate mofetil for prevention of rejection have developed severe neutropenia [absolute neutrophil count (ANC) $<0.5\times10^3/\mu L$ (see Adverse Effects).

Patients receiving mycophenolate mofetil should be monitored for neutropenia (see Precautions, Laboratory Tests). The development of neutropenia may be related to mycophenolate mofetil itself, concomitant medications, viral infections, or some combination of these causes. If neutropenia develops (ANC $<1.3\times10^3/\mu L$), dosing with mycophenolate mofetil should be interrupted or the dose reduced, appropriate diagnostic tests performed, and the patient managed appropriately. Neutropenia has been observed most frequently in the period from 31 to 180 days post-transplant for patients treated for prevention of rejection.

Pregnancy: Adverse effects on fetal development (including resorptions and malformations) occurred when pregnant rats and rabbits were dosed during organogenesis. These responses occurred at doses (6 mg/kg/day in rat and 90 mg/kg/day in rabbit) lower than those associated with maternal toxicity, and at doses 0.03 to 0.92 times the recommended clinical dose on a BSA basis. In a female fertility and reproduction study conducted in rats, oral doses of 4.5 mg/kg/day caused malformations (principally of the head and eyes) in the first generation offspring in the absence of maternal toxicity. This dose was 0.02 times the recommended clinical dose when corrected for BSA.

There are no adequate and well-controlled studies in pregnant women. However, as mycophenolate mofetil has been shown to have teratogenic effects in animals, it may cause fetal harm when administered to a pregnant woman. Therefore, mycophenolate mofetil should not be used in pregnant women unless the potential benefit justifies the potential risk to the fetus.

Women of childbearing potential should have a negative serum or urine pregnancy test with a sensitivitiy of at least 50 mIU/mL within 1 week prior to beginning therapy. It is recommended that mycophenolate mofetil therapy should not be initiated by the physician until a report of a negative pregnancy test has been obtained.

Effective contraception must be used before beginning mycophenolate mofetil therapy, during therapy, and for 6 weeks following discontinuation of therapy, even where there has been a history of infertility, unless due to hysterectomy. Two reliable forms of contraception must be used simultaneously unless abstinence is the chosen method. If pregnancy does occur during treatment, the physician and patient should discuss the desirability of continuing the pregnancy (see Precautions, Information for the Patient and Blue Section—Information for the Patient).

Lactation: Studies in rats have shown mycophenolate mofetil is excreted in milk. It is not known whether this drug is excreted in human milk. Because many drugs are excreted in human milk and because of the potential for serious adverse reactions in nursing infants from mycophenolate mofetil, a decision should be made whether to discontinue nursing or to discontinue the drug, taking into account the importance of the drug to the mother (see Blue Section—Information for the Patient).

Precautions: Mycophenolate mofetil should be administered with caution in patients with active serious digestive system disease. Gastrointestinal tract hemorrhage has been observed in approximately 3% of patients treated with mycophenolate mofetil. Mycophenolate mofetil has been associated with an increased incidence of digestive system adverse events, including infrequent cases of gastrointestinal tract ulceration, and rarely perforation. Most patients receiving mycophenolate mofetil were also receiving other drugs that are known to be associated with these complications. Patients with active peptic ulcer disease were excluded from enrollment in studies with mycophenolate mofetil.

Administration of doses of mycophenolate mofetil greater than 1 g b.i.d. in severe chronic renal impairment (GFR <25 mL/min/1.73m²) should be avoided and patients should be carefully observed (see Pharmacology, Pharmacokinetics and Dosage).

Subjects with severe chronic renal impairment who have received single doses of mycophenolate mofetil showed higher mean plasma MPA and MPAG AUCs relative to subjects with lesser degrees of renal impairment or normal healthy subjects.

In patients with delayed graft function post-transplant, mean MPA AUC_{0-12} was comparable, but MPAG AUC_{0-12} was 2- to 3-fold higher, compared to that seen in post-transplant patients without delayed graft function. In the three pivotal studies of prevention of rejection, 298 of 1 483 patients (20%) experienced delayed graft function. Although patients with delayed graft function have a higher incidence of certain adverse events (anemia, thrombocytopenia, hyperkalemia) than patients without delayed graft function, these events were not more frequent in patients receiving mycophenolate mofetil than azathioprine or placebo. No dose adjustment is recommended for these patients, however, they should be carefully observed (see Pharmacology, Pharmacokinetics).

It is recommended that mycophenolate mofetil not be administered concomitantly with azathioprine because such concomitant administration has not been studied clinically.

In view of the significant reduction in the AUC of MPA by cholestyramine, caution should be used in the concomitant administration of mycophenolate mofetil with drugs that interfere with enterohepatic recirculation because of the potential to reduce the efficacy of mycophenolate mofetil (see Drug Interactions).

Information for the Patient: Patients should be informed of the need for repeated appropriate laboratory tests while they are receiving mycophenolate mofetil. Patients should be given complete dosage instructions and informed of the increased risk of lymphoproliferative disease and certain other malignancies. Women of childbearing potential should be instructed of the potential risks during pregnancy, and that they should use effective contraception before beginning mycophenolate mofetil therapy, during therapy and for 6 weeks after mycophenolate mofetil has been stopped (see Warnings, Pregnancy and Blue Section—Information for the Patient).

Laboratory Tests: Complete blood counts should be performed weekly during the first month, twice monthly for the second and third months of treatment, then monthly through the first year (see Warnings and Dosage).

Drug Interactions: Drug interaction studies with mycophenolate mofetil have been conducted with acyclovir, antacids, cholestyramine, cyclosporine A, ganciclovir, oral contraceptives, and trimethoprim/sulfamethoxazole. Drug interaction studies have not been conducted with other drugs that may

Table VII—CellCept

Adverse Events in Prevention of Renal Allograft Rejection

		U.S. Study Combined with Europe/Canada/Australia Study	
	CellCept 2 g/day % (n=336)	**CellCept 3 g/day % (n=330)**	**Azathioprine 1 - 2 mg/kg/day or 100-150 mg/day % (n=326)**
Body as a Whole			
Pain	33.0	31.2	32.2
Abdominal pain	24.7	27.6	23.0
Fever	21.4	23.3	23.3
Headache	21.1	16.1	21.2
Infection	18.2	20.9	19.9
Sepsis	17.6	19.7	15.6
Asthenia	13.7	16.1	19.9
Chest pain	13.4	13.3	14.7
Back pain	11.6	12.1	14.1
Hemic and Lymphatic			
Anemia	25.6	25.8	23.6
Leukopenia	23.2	34.5	24.8
Thrombocytopenia	10.1	8.2	13.2
Hypochromic anemia	7.4	11.5	9.2
Leukocytosis	7.1	10.9	7.4
Urogenital			
Urinary tract infection	37.2	37.0	33.7
Hematuria	14.0	12.1	11.3
Kidney tubular necrosis	6.3	10.0	5.8
Cardiovascular			
Hypertension	32.4	28.2	32.2
Metabolic and Nutritional			
Peripheral edema	28.6	27.0	28.2
Hypercholesteremia	12.8	8.5	11.3
Hypophosphatemia	12.5	15.8	11.7
Edema	12.2	11.8	13.5
Hypokalemia	10.1	10.0	8.3
Hyperkalemia	8.9	10.3	16.9
Hyperglycemia	8.6	12.4	15.0
Digestive			
Diarrhea	31.0	36.1	20.9
Constipation	22.9	18.5	22.4
Nausea	19.9	23.6	24.5
Dyspepsia	17.6	13.6	13.8
Vomiting	12.5	13.6	9.2
Nausea and vomiting	10.4	9.7	10.7
Oral moniliasis	10.1	12.1	11.3
Respiratory			
Infection	22.0	23.9	19.6
Dyspnea	15.5	17.3	16.6
Cough increased	15.5	13.3	15.0
Pharyngitis	9.5	11.2	8.0
Skin and Appendages			
Acne	10.1	9.7	6.4
Rash	7.7	6.4	10.4
CNS			
Tremor	11.0	11.8	12.3
Insomnia	8.9	11.8	10.4
Dizziness	5.7	11.2	11.0

		Europe Study	
	CellCept 2 g/day % (n=165)	**CellCept 3 g/day % (n=160)**	**Placebo % (n=166)**
Body as a Whole			
Sepsis	21.8	17.5	13.9
Infection	12.7	15.6	13.3
Abdominal pain	12.1	11.9	11.4
Hemic and Lymphatic			
Leukopenia	11.5	16.3	4.2
Urogenital			
Urinary tract infection	45.5	44.4	37.3
Urinary tract disorder	6.7	10.6	4.2
Cardiovascular			
Hypertension	17.6	16.9	19.3
Digestive			
Diarrhea	16.4	18.8	13.9
Respiratory			
Infection	15.8	13.1	9.0
Bronchitis	8.5	11.9	8.4
Pneumonia	3.6	10.6	10.8

CellCept (cont'd)

be commonly administered to renal transplant patients. Mycophenolate mofetil has not been administered concomitantly with azathioprine.

Acyclovir: Coadministration of mycophenolate mofetil (1 g) and acyclovir (800 mg) to 12 healthy volunteers resulted in no significant change in MPA AUC and C_{max}. However, MPAG and acyclovir plasma AUCs were increased 10.6% and 21.9%, respectively. Because MPAG plasma concentrations are increased in the presence of renal impairment, as are acyclovir concentrations, the potential exists for the 2 drugs to compete for tubular secretion, further increasing the concentrations of both drugs.

Antacids with Magnesium and Aluminum Hydroxides: Absorption of a single dose of mycophenolate mofetil (2.0 g) was decreased when administered to rheumatoid arthritis patients also taking Maalox TC (10 mL q.i.d.). The C_{max} and AUC values for MPA were 38% and 17% lower, respectively, than when mycophenolate mofetil was administered alone under fasting conditions. Mycophenolate mofetil may be administered to patients who are also taking antacids containing magnesium and aluminum hydroxides; however, it is recommended that mycophenolate mofetil and the antacid not be administered simultaneously.

Cholestyramine: Following single dose administration of 1.5 g mycophenolate mofetil to normal healthy subjects pretreated with 4 g t.i.d. of cholestyramine for 4 days, there was a mean 40% reduction in the AUC of MPA. This decrease is consistent with interruption of enterohepatic recirculation by irreversible binding, in the intestine, of recirculating MPAG with cholestyramine. Mycophenolate mofetil is not recommended to be given with cholestyramine or other agents that may interfere with enterohepatic recirculation.

Cyclosporine: Mycophenolate mofetil has been investigated with Sandimmune but not with the Neoral formulation. Cyclosporine (Sandimmune) pharmacokinetics (at doses of 275 to 415 mg/day) were unaffected by single and multiple doses of 1.5 g b.i.d. of mycophenolate mofetil in 10 stable renal transplant patients. The mean (±SD) AUC_{0-12} and C_{max} of cyclosporine after 14 days of multiple doses of mycophenolate mofetil were 3 290 (±822) ng·h/mL and 753 (±161) ng/mL, respectively, compared to 3 245 (±1 088) ng·h/mL and 700 (±246) ng/mL, respectively, 1 week before administration of mycophenolate mofetil. The effect of cyclosporine on mycophenolate mofetil pharmacokinetics could not be evaluated in this study, however, plasma concentrations of MPA were similar to that for healthy volunteers.

Ganciclovir: Following single-dose administration to 12 stable renal transplant patients, no pharmacokinetic interaction was observed between mycophenolate mofetil (1.5 g) and i.v. ganciclovir (5 mg/kg). Mean (±SD) ganciclovir AUC and C_{max} (n=10) were 54.3 (±19.0) μg·h/mL and 11.5 (±1.8) μg/mL, respectively after coadministration of the 2 drugs, compared to 51.0 (±17.0) μg·h/mL and 10.6 (±2.0) μg/mL, respectively after administration of i.v. ganciclovir alone. The mean (±SD) AUC and C_{max} of MPA (n=12) after coadministration were 80.9 (±21.6) μg·h/mL and 27.8 (±13.9) μg/mL, respectively compared to values of 80.3 (±16.4) μg·h/mL and 30.9 (±11.2) μg/mL, respectively after administration of mycophenolate mofetil alone. Because MPAG plasma concentrations are increased in the presence of renal impairment, as are ganciclovir concentrations, the potential exists for the 2 drugs to compete for tubular secretion and thus further increases in concentrations of both drugs may occur.

Oral Contraceptives: Following single dose administration to healthy women, no pharmacokinetic interaction was observed between mycophenolate mofetil (1.0 g) and 2 tablets of Ortho-Novum 7/7/7 (1 mg norethindrone and 35 μg ethinyl estradiol). This single dose study demonstrates the lack of a gross pharmacokinetic interaction, but cannot exclude the possibility of changes in the pharmacokinetics of the oral contraceptive under long-term dosing conditions with mycophenolate mofetil which might adversely affect the efficacy of the oral contraceptive.

Trimethoprim/Sulfamethoxazole: Following single dose administration of mycophenolate mofetil (1.5 g) to 12 healthy male volunteers on day 8 of a 10 day course of Bactrim DS (trimethoprim 160 mg/sulfamethoxazole 800 mg) administered b.i.d., no effect on the bioavailability of MPA was observed. The mean (±SD) AUC and C_{max} of MPA after concomitant administration were 75.2 (±19.8) μg·h/mL and 34.0 (±6.6) μg/mL, respectively compared to 79.2 (±27.9) and 34.2 (±10.7), respectively after administration of mycophenolate mofetil alone.

Table VIII—CellCept

Malignancies Observed in Prevention of Renal Rejection Trials

	CellCept 2 g/day % (n=501)	CellCept 3 g/day % (n=490)	Placebo % (n=166)	Azathioprine 1-2 mg/kg/day or 100–150 mg/day % (n=326)
Lymphoma/lymphoproliferative disease	0.6	1.0	0.0	0.3
Nonmelanoma skin carcinoma	4.0	1.6	0.0	2.4
Other malignancy	0.8	1.4	1.8	1.8

Table IX—CellCept

Opportunistic Infections in Prevention of Renal Rejection Trials

	U.S. Study Combined with Europe/Canada/Australia Study		
	CellCept 2 g/day % (n=336)	CellCept 3 g/day % (n=330)	Azathioprine 1-2 mg/kg/day or 100-150 mg/day % (n=326)
Herpes simplex	16.7	20.0	19.0
CMV			
viremia/syndrome	13.4	12.4	13.8
tissue invasive disease	8.3	11.5	6.1
Herpes zoster	6.0	7.6	5.8
Candida			
fungemia/disseminated	0.6	0.6	0.3
tissue invasive	0.6	0.6	0.3
Aspergillus/Mucor invasive disease	0.3	0.9	0.3
P. carinii	0.3	0.0	1.2

	Europe Study		
	CellCept 2 g/day % (n=165)	CellCept 3 g/day % (n=160)	Placebo % (n=166)
Herpes simplex	15.2	12.5	6.0
CMV			
viremia/syndrome	15.2	15.0	13.3
tissue invasive disease	3.6	7.5	2.4
Herpes zoster	6.7	6.9	2.4
Candida			
fungemia/disseminated	0.0	0.6	0.0
tissue invasive	0.0	0.6	0.0
P. carinii	0.0	0.0	2.4

Other Interactions: The measured value for renal clearance of MPAG indicates removal occurs by renal tubular secretion as well as glomerular filtration. Consistent with this, coadministration of probenecid, a known inhibitor of tubular secretion, with mycophenolate mofetil in monkeys raises plasma AUC of MPAG by 3-fold. Thus, other drugs known to undergo renal tubular secretion may compete with MPAG and thereby raise plasma concentrations of MPAG or the other drug undergoing tubular secretion.

Drugs that alter the gastrointestinal flora may interact with mycophenolate mofetil by disrupting enterohepatic recirculation. Interference of MPAG hydrolysis may lead to less MPA available for absorption.

Carcinogenesis, Mutagenesis, Impairment of Fertility: In a 104-week oral carcinogenicity study in mice, mycophenolate mofetil in daily doses up to 180 mg/kg was not tumorigenic. The highest dose tested was 0.5 times the recommended clinical dose (2 g/day) when corrected for differences in body surface area (BSA). In a 104-week oral carcinogenicity study in rats, mycophenolate mofetil in daily doses up to 15 mg/kg was not tumorigenic. The highest dose was 0.08 times the recommended clinical dose when corrected for BSA. While these animal doses were lower than those given to patients, they were maximal in those species and were considered adequate to evaluate the potential for human risk (see Warnings).

Mycophenolate mofetil was not genotoxic, with or without metabolic activation, in several assays: the bacterial mutation assay, the yeast mitotic gene conversion assay, the mouse micronucleus aberration assay, or the Chinese hamster ovary cell (CHO) chromosomal aberration assay.

Mycophenolate mofetil had no effect on fertility of male rats at oral doses up to 20 mg/kg/day. This dose represents 0.1 times the recommended clinical dose when corrected for BSA. In a female fertility and reproduction study conducted in rats, oral doses of 4.5 mg/kg/day caused malformations (principally of the head and eyes) in the first generation offspring in the absence of maternal toxicity. This dose was 0.02 times the recommended clinical dose when corrected for BSA. No effects on fertility or reproductive parameters were evident in the dams or in the subsequent generation.

Children: Safety and efficacy in children have not been established. Very limited pharmacokinetic data are available in pediatric patients (see Pharmacology, Pharmacokinetics).

Adverse Effects: The adverse event profile associated with the use of immunosuppressive drugs is often difficult to establish owing to the presence of underlying disease and the concurrent use of many other medications. The principal adverse reactions associated with the administration of mycophenolate mofetil include diarrhea, leukopenia, sepsis and vomiting, and there is evidence of a higher frequency of certain types of infections.

The incidence of adverse events for mycophenolate mofetil was determined in three randomized comparative double-blind trials in prevention of rejection in renal transplant patients. Because of the lower overall reporting of events in the European placebo-controlled prevention of rejection study, these data were not combined with the other 2 active-controlled prevention trials, but are instead presented separately.

Safety data are summarized below for all patients in the double-blind prevention studies while receiving treatment; approximately 53% of these patients have been treated for more than 1 year. Adverse events, whether or not deemed to be causally associated with the study medication, which were reported in ≥10% of patients in any treatment group are presented in Table VII (on previous page) for the 2 active-controlled studies combined (U.S. and Europe/Canada/Australia) and for the 1 European placebo-controlled study. Opportunistic infections are summarized separately.

Table VII (on previous page) demonstrates that in 3 pivotal trials for prevention of rejection, patients receiving 2 g/day of mycophenolate mofetil had an overall better safety profile than did patients receiving 3 g/day of mycophenolate mofetil. Sepsis, which was generally CMV viremia, was slightly more common in patients treated with mycophenolate mofetil, with an incidence of 18 to 22%, compared to 16% in patients receiving azathioprine and 14% in patients receiving placebo. In the digestive system, diarrhea was most clearly increased in patients receiving mycophenolate mofetil with an incidence of up to 36%, compared 21% for patients receiving azathioprine and 14% for patients receiving placebo.

The incidence of malignancies among the 1 483 patients enrolled in controlled trials for the prevention of rejection who were followed for ≥1 year was similar to the incidence reported in the literature for renal allograft recipients. There was a slight increase in the incidence of lymphoproliferative disease in the mycophenolate mofetil treatment groups compared to the placebo and azathioprine groups (see Warnings). Table VIII (on previous page) summarizes the incidence of malignancies observed in the prevention of rejection trials.

Up to 2% of patients receiving mycophenolate mofetil for prevention of rejection have developed severe neutropenia [absolute neutrophil count (ANC) $<0.5\times10^3/\mu L$] (see Warnings, Precautions: Laboratory Tests and Dosage).

Table IX (on previous page) shows the incidence of opportunistic infections that occurred in the transplant population in the prevention of rejection trials:

In the 3 controlled studies for prevention of rejection, similar rates of fatal infections (<2%) have occurred in patients receiving mycophenolate mofetil or control therapy in combination with other immunosuppressive agents (see Warnings).

The following adverse events, not mentioned in any of the tables above, were reported with ≥3% incidence in patients treated with mycophenolate mofetil.

Body As a Whole: abdomen enlarged, accidental injury, chills and fever, cyst, face edema, flu syndrome, hemorrhage, hernia, malaise, pelvic pain.

Hemic and Lymphatic: ecchymosis, polycythemia.

Urogenital: albuminuria, dysuria, hydronephrosis, impotence, pain, pyelonephritis, urinary frequency, urinary tract disorder.

Cardiovascular: angina pectoris, atrial fibrillation, cardiovascular disorder, hypotension, palpitation, peripheral vascular disorder, postural hypotension, tachycardia, thrombosis, vasodilatation.

Metabolic and Nutritional: acidosis, alkaline phosphatase increased, creatinine increased, dehydration, gamma glutamyl transpeptidase increased, hypercalcemia, hyperlipemia, hyperuricemia, hypervolemia, hypocalcemia, hypoglycemia, hypoproteinemia, lactic dehydrogenase increased, AST increased, ALT increased, weight gain.

Digestive: anorexia, esophagitis, flatulence, gastritis, gastroenteritis, gastrointestinal hemorrhage, gastrointestinal moniliasis, gingivitis, gum hyperplasia, hepatitis, ileus, infection, liver function tests abnormal, mouth ulceration, rectal disorder.

Respiratory: asthma, lung disorder, lung edema, pleural effusion, rhinitis, sinusitis.

Skin and Appendages: alopecia, fungal dermatitis, hirsutism, pruritus, skin benign neoplasm, skin disorder, skin hypertrophy, skin ulcer, sweating.

Nervous: anxiety, depression, hypertonia, paresthesia, somnolence.

Endocrine: diabetes mellitus, parathyroid disorder.

Musculoskeletal: arthralgia, joint disorder, leg cramps, myalgia, myasthenia.

Special Senses: cataract (not specified), conjunctivitis, visual disturbance.

The following adverse events, not mentioned above, were reported in clinical trials and in postmarketing experience in patients treated with mycophenolate mofetil.

Digestive: colitis.

Resistance Mechanism Disorders: There is evidence of a higher frequency of certain types of serious infections such as meningitis, infectious endocarditis, pulmonary and extrapulmonary tuberculosis and other mycobacterial infections.

Overdose: Symptoms and Treatment: There has been no reported experience of overdosage of mycophenolate mofetil in humans. The highest dose administered to renal transplant patients has been 4 g/day. In limited experience with cardiac and hepatic transplant patients, the highest doses used were 4 or 5 g/day. At doses of 4 or 5 g/day, there appears to be a higher rate, compared to the use of 3 g/day or less, of gastrointestinal intolerance (nausea, vomiting, and/or diarrhea), and occasional hematologic abnormalities, principally neutropenia, leading to a need to reduce or discontinue dosing.

In acute oral toxicity studies, no deaths occurred in adult mice at doses up to 4 000 mg/kg or in adult monkeys at doses up to 1 000 mg/kg; these were the highest doses of mycophenolate mofetil tested in these species. These doses represent 11 times the recommended clinical dose when corrected for BSA. In adult rats, deaths occurred after single oral doses of 500 mg/kg of mycophenolate mofetil. The dose represents 3 times the recommended clinical dose when corrected for BSA.

At clinically encountered concentrations, MPA and MPAG are not removed by hemodialysis. However, at high MPAG plasma concentrations (>100 μg/mL), small amounts of MPAG are removed. By interfering with enterohepatic recirculation of the drug, bile acid sequestrants, such as cholestyramine reduce the MPA AUC.

Dosage: The initial dose should be given within 72 hours following transplantation. A dose of 1.0 g administered twice a day (daily dose of 2 g) is recommended for use in combination with corticosteroids and cyclosporine in renal transplant patients. Although a dose of 1.5 g administered twice daily (daily dose of 3 g) was used in clinical trials and was shown to be safe and effective, no efficacy advantage could be established. Patients receiving 2 g per day demonstrated an overall better safety profile than did patients receiving 3 g per day. Food had no effect on MPA AUC, but has been shown to decrease MPA C_{max} by 40%. It is recommended that mycophenolate mofetil be administered on an empty stomach.

Dosage Adjustments: In patients with severe chronic renal impairment (GFR <25mL/min/1.73m²) outside of the immediate post-transplant period, doses greater than 1 g administered twice a day should be avoided. These patients should also be carefully observed. No dose adjustments are needed in patients experiencing delayed graft function postoperatively (see Pharmacology, Pharmacokinetics and Precautions, General).

If neutropenia develops (ANC $<1.3\times10^3/\mu L$), dosing with mycophenolate mofetil should be interrupted or the dose reduced, appropriate diagnostic tests performed, and the patient managed appropriately (see Warnings, Adverse Effects and Precautions, Laboratory Tests).

Handling and Disposal: Because mycophenolate mofetil has demonstrated teratogenic effects in rats and rabbits, mycophenolate mofetil capsules should not be opened or crushed. Avoid inhalation or direct contact with skin or mucous membranes of the powder contained in mycophenolate mofetil capsules. If such contact occurs, wash thoroughly with soap and water; rinse eyes with plain water.

Information for the Patient: See Blue Section—Information for the Patient "CellCept".

Supplied: Capsules: Each oblong, blue/brown, two-piece hard gelatin capsule, printed in black with "CellCept 250" on the blue cap and "ROCHE" on the brown body, contains: mycophenolate mofetil 250 mg. Nonmedicinal ingredients: croscarmellose sodium, magnesium stearate, povidone (K-90) and pregelatinized starch; capsule: black iron oxide, FD&C blue #2, gelatin, potassium hydroxide, red iron oxide, shellac, sodium lauryl sulfate, titanium dioxide and yellow iron oxide. May also contain silicon dioxide. Blister packs of 10, boxes of 10. Store at 15 to 30°C.

Tablets: Each lavender-colored, caplet-shaped, film-coated tablet, printed in black with "CellCept 500" on one side and "ROCHE" on the other, contains: mycophenolate mofetil 500 mg. Nonmedicinal ingredients: croscarmellose sodium, FD&C blue #2 aluminum lake, hydroxypropyl cellulose, hydroxypropyl methylcellulose, iron oxide, magnesium stearate, microcrystalline cellulose, polyethylene glycol 400, povidone (K-90), talc and titanium dioxide. May also contain propylene glycol and shellac. Blister strips of 10, boxes of 5. Store at 15 to 30°C. Protect from light.

(Shown in Product Recognition Section)

Reviewed 1999

CELLUFRESH®
CELLUFRESH® M-D™
Allergan

Carboxymethylcellulose Sodium

Ocular Lubricant

Supplied: Unit Dose: Each unit-dose container of 0.4 mL contains: carboxymethylcellulose sodium 0.5%. Nonmedicinal ingredients: calcium chloride, magnesium chloride, potassium chloride, sodium chloride and sodium lactate. Preservative-free. Boxes of 30.

Multi-dose: Each mL of sterile solution contains: carboxymethylcellulose sodium 0.5%. Nonmedicinal ingredients: boric acid, calcium chloride, magnesium chloride, potassium chloride, purified water, Purite (stabilized oxychloro complex) and sodium chloride. Plastic bottles of 15 mL and boxes of 12×3 mL.

CELLUVISC™
Allergan

Carboxymethylcellulose Sodium

Ocular Lubricant

Supplied: Each unit-dose container of 0.4 mL contains: carboxymethylcellulose sodium 1%. Nonmedicinal ingredients: calcium chloride, potassium chloride, sodium chloride and sodium lactate. Preservative-free.

CELONTIN® Ⓟ
Parke-Davis

Methsuximide

Anticonvulsant

Pharmacology: Methsuximide elevates seizure threshold in the cortex and basal ganglia and reduces synaptic response to low frequency repetitive stimulation. The peroxisomal spike and wave pattern of the EEG, common in petit mal seizure, is suppressed.

Pharmacokinetics: Methsuximide is absorbed from the gastrointestinal tract and peak plasma levels are achieved in 1 to 3 hours. The plasma half-life of methsuximide is slightly less than 3 hours. In one study, mean peak serum levels were 3 μg/mL following a single 600 mg dose and 6 to 7 μg/mL following a single 1.2 g dose of methsuximide.

Limited studies indicate that the drug is metabolized via N-demethylation to N-demethylmethsuximide (NDM). Profound CNS depression following methsuximide overdose has been attributed to this metabolite, and it is probable that the anticonvulsant effects of the drug are due to NDM. In one study, which measured methsuximide and NDM levels simultaneously in plasma of patients who were receiving methsuximide chronically, the concentration of NDM was 700 times greater than the concentration of methsuximide. On the basis of this study, a tentative therapeutic plasma level of 10 to 40 μg/mL of NDM has been proposed.

Less than 1% of a dose of methsuximide is excreted unchanged in the urine, although a number of as yet unidentified metabolites are excreted in urine.

Indications: The control of absence (petit mal) seizures refractory to other drugs.

Contraindications: Methsuximide should not be used in patients with a history of hypersensitivity to succinimides.

Precautions: Blood dyscrasias, including some with fatal outcome, have been reported to be associated with the use of succinimides; therefore, periodic blood counts should be performed.

It has been reported that succinimides have produced morphological and functional changes in animal liver. For this reason, administer methsuximide with extreme caution to patients with known liver or renal disease. Periodic urinalysis and liver function studies are advised for all patients receiving the drug.

Cases of systemic lupus erythematosus have been reported with the use of succinimides. The physician should be alert to this possibility.

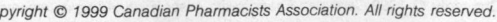

Pregnancy: Recent reports indicate an association between the use of anticonvulsant drugs and an elevated incidence of

Celontin (cont'd)

birth defects in children born to epileptic women taking such medications during pregnancy. The incidence of congenital malformations in the general population is regarded to be approximately 2%; in children of treated epileptic women this incidence may be increased 2- to 3-fold. The increase is largely due to specific defects, e.g., congenital malformations of the heart, and cleft lip and/or palate. Nevertheless, the great majority of mothers receiving anticonvulsant medications deliver normal infants.

Data are more extensive with respect to phenytoin and phenobarbital, but these drugs are also the most commonly prescribed anticonvulsants. Some reports indicate a possible similar association with the use of other anticonvulsants, including trimethadione and paramethadione. However, the possibility also exists that other factors, e.g., genetic predisposition or the epileptic condition itself may contribute to or may be mainly responsible for the higher incidence of birth defects.

Anticonvulsant drugs should not be discontinued in patients in whom the drug is administered to prevent major seizures, because of the strong possibility of precipitating status epilepticus with attendant hypoxia and risk to both the mother and the unborn child. With regard to drugs given for minor seizures, the risk of discontinuing medications prior to or during pregnancy should be weighed against the risk of congenital defects in the particular case and with the particular family history.

Epileptic women of childbearing age should be encouraged to seek professional counsel and should report the onset of pregnancy promptly to their physician. Where the necessity for continued use of the antiepileptic medication is in doubt, appropriate consultation might be indicated.

The preceding considerations should be borne in mind and methsuximide should be used in women of childbearing potential only when the expected benefits to the patients warrant the possible risk to a fetus.

Lactation: Mothers receiving methsuximide should not breast-feed their infants.

Occupational Hazards: Methsuximide may impair the mental and/or physical abilities required for the performance of potentially hazardous tasks, such as driving a motor vehicle or other such activities requiring alertness; therefore, caution the patient accordingly.

Withdraw the drug slowly on the appearance of unusual depression, aggression, or other behavioral alterations.

Proceed slowly when increasing or decreasing dosage, as well as when adding or eliminating other medication. Abrupt withdrawal of anticonvulsant medications may precipitate petit mal status.

Methsuximide, when used alone in mixed types of epilepsy, may increase the frequency of grand mal seizures in some patients.

Adverse Effects: Gastrointestinal: Gastrointestinal symptoms occur frequently and have included nausea or vomiting, anorexia, diarrhea, weight loss, epigastric and abdominal pain, and constipation.

Hemopoietic: eosinophilia, leukopenia, monocytosis, pancytopenia.

Nervous System: Neurologic and sensory reactions reported during therapy with methsuximide have included drowsiness, ataxia or dizziness, irritability and nervousness, headache, blurred vision, photophobia, hiccups, and insomnia.

Drowsiness, ataxia, and dizziness have been the most frequent adverse effects noted.

Psychological abnormalities have included confusion, instability, mental slowness, depression, hypochondriacal behavior, and aggression. There have been rare reports of psychosis, suicidal behavior and auditory hallucinations.

Integumentary System: Dermatologic manifestations which have occurred in the administration of methsuximide have included urticaria, Stevens-Johnson syndrome, and pruritic erythematous rashes.

Miscellaneous: periorbital edema, hyperemia.

Dosage: Optimal dosage (that which is just sufficient to control seizures without causing disturbing side effects) must be determined by trial and should be individualized according to the needs of each patient. A suggested schedule is 300 mg daily for the first week. If required, the daily dosage may be increased at weekly intervals by 300 mg/day for the 3 weeks following to a daily dosage of 1 200 mg.

Supplied: Each yellow capsule with orange cap contains: methsuximide USP 300 mg. Nonmedicinal ingredients: cornstarch; capsule shell: D&C Yellow No. 10, FD&C Red No. 3, FD&C Yellow No. 6 and gelatin. Energy: 1.57 kJ (0.38 kcal). Gluten-, lactose-, paraben-, sodium-, sulfite- and tartrazine-free. Bottles of 100.

(Shown in Product Recognition Section)

Reviewed 1998

CENTRUM®
CENTRUM® FORTE
CENTRUM® PROTEGRA
CENTRUM® SELECT

Whitehall-Robins

Multiple Vitamins—Minerals

Vitamin-Mineral Supplement

Indications: For use as a nutritional supplement.

Contraindications: In the presence of hemochromatosis, hemosiderosis, hemolytic anemia.

Precautions: Oral iron preparations may aggravate existing peptic ulcer, regional enteritis and ulcerative colitis. Oral iron preparations can impair the absorption of tetracycline antibiotics. Antacids given concomitantly with iron compounds decrease iron absorption.

Adverse Effects: Rarely, in iron sensitive patients, mild gastrointestinal upset may occur.

Dosage: Centrum, Centrum Forte, Centrum Select: 1 tablet daily.

Centrum Protegra: 2 tablets daily.

Supplied: Centrum: Each light peach, scored, oval, film-coated tablet, engraved W-R and U7 contains: vitamins: beta-carotene (a source of vitamin A) 3 000 IU, vitamin A 2 000 IU, vitamin E 25 IU, vitamin C 90 mg, folic acid 0.4 mg, vitamin B_1 2.25 mg, vitamin B_2 3.2 mg, niacinamide 40 mg, vitamin B_6 3 mg, vitamin B_{12} 9 μg, vitamin D 400 IU, biotin 45 μg, pantothenic acid 10 mg; minerals: calcium 175 mg, phosphorus 125 mg, iodine 0.15 mg, iron 10 mg, magnesium 100 mg, copper 2 mg. Nonmedicinal ingredients: ascorbyl palmitate, BHT, cellulose, citric acid, cornstarch, crospovidone, FD&C Yellow #6, gelatin, hydrolyzed protein, lactose, magnesium stearate, mineral oil, peanut oil, polysorbate 80, silicon dioxide, sodium aluminum silicate, sodium ascorbate, sodium benzoate, sodium citrate, sodium lauryl sulfate, sorbic acid, stearic acid, sucrose, titanium dioxide and triethyl citrate. Energy: <4.2 kJ (1 kcal). Sodium: <0.22 mmol (5 mg). Bottles of 60 and 100.

Centrum Forte: Each orange, scored, oval, film-coated tablet, engraved W-R and U10 contains: vitamins: beta-carotene (a source of vitamin A) 3 000 IU, vitamin A 2 000 IU, vitamin E 30 IU, vitamin C 90 mg, folic acid 0.4 mg, vitamin B_1 2.25 mg, vitamin B_2 3.2 mg, niacinamide 40 mg, vitamin B_6 3 mg, vitamin B_{12} 9 μg, vitamin D 400 IU, biotin 45 μg, pantothenic acid 10 mg; minerals: calcium 175 mg, phosphorus 125 mg, iodine 0.15 mg, iron 10 mg, magnesium 100 mg, copper 2 mg, manganese 5 mg, potassium 40 mg, chlorine 36 mg, chromium 25 μg, molybdenum 25 μg, selenium 25 μg, zinc 15 mg, nickel 5 μg, tin 10 μg, vanadium 10 μg, silicon 10 μg. Nonmedicinal ingredients: ascorbyl palmitate, BHT, cellulose, citric acid, cornstarch, crospovidone, FD&C Yellow #6, gelatin, hydrolyzed protein, lactose, magnesium stearate, mineral oil, peanut oil, polysorbate 80, silicon dioxide, sodium aluminum silicate, sodium ascorbate, sodium benzoate, sodium citrate, sodium lauryl sulfate, sorbic acid, stearic acid, sucrose, titanium dioxide and triethyl citrate. Energy: <4.2 kJ (1 kcal). Sodium: <0.22 mmol (5 mg). Bottles of 60 and 100.

Centrum Protegra: Each light peach, scored, oval, film-coated tablet, engraved W-R and U12 contains: vitamins: beta-carotene (a source of vitamin A) 5 000 IU, vitamin A 500 IU, vitamin E 100 IU, vitamin C 125 mg, folic acid 200 μg, vitamin B_1 1.15 mg, vitamin B_2 1.6 mg, niacinamide 20 mg, vitamin B_6 1.5 mg, vitamin B_{12} 4.5 μg, vitamin D 200 IU, biotin 22.5 μg, pantothenic acid 5 mg; minerals: calcium 87.5 mg, phosphorus 62.5 mg, iodine 75 μg, iron 5 mg, magnesium 50 mg, copper 1 mg, manganese 2.5 mg, potassium 20 mg, chlorine 18 mg, chromium 12.5 μg, molybdenum 12.5 μg, selenium 12.5 μg, zinc 7.5 mg, nickel 2.5 μg, tin 5 μg, vanadium 5 μg, silicon 5 μg. Nonmedicinal ingredients: ascorbyl palmitate, BHT, cellulose, citric acid, cornstarch, crospovidone, FD&C Yellow #6, gelatin, hydrolyzed protein, lactose, magnesium stearate, mineral oil, peanut oil, polysorbate 80, silicon dioxide, sodium aluminum silicate, sodium ascorbate, sodium benzoate, sodium citrate, sodium lauryl sulfate, sorbic acid, stearic acid, sucrose, titanium dioxide and triethyl citrate. Energy: <4.2 kJ (1 kcal). Sodium: <0.22 mmol (5 mg). Bottles of 80.

Centrum Select: Each orange, scored, oval, film-coated tablet, engraved W-R and U23 contains: vitamins: beta-carotene (a source of vitamin A) 3 000 IU, vitamin A 3 000 IU, vitamin E 45 IU, vitamin C 90 mg, folic acid 0.4 mg, vitamin B_1 2.25 mg, vitamin B_2 3.2 mg, niacinamide 40 mg, vitamin B_6 3 mg, vitamin B_{12} 25 μg, vitamin D 400 IU, biotin 45 μg, pantothenic acid 10 mg; minerals: calcium 200 mg, phosphorus 125 mg, iodine 0.15 mg, iron 4 mg, magnesium 100 mg, copper 2 mg, manganese 5 mg, potassium 80 mg, chlorine 72 mg, chromium 100 μg, molybdenum 25 μg, selenium 25 μg, zinc 15 mg, nickel 5 μg, tin 10 μg, vanadium 10 μg, silicon 10 μg. Nonmedicinal ingredients: ascorbyl palmitate, BHT, cellulose, citric acid, cornstarch, crospovidone, FD&C Yellow #6, gelatin, hydrolyzed protein, lactose, magnesium stearate, mineral oil, peanut oil, polysorbate 80, silicon dioxide, sodium aluminum silicate, sodium ascorbate, sodium benzoate, sodium citrate, sodium lauryl sulfate, sorbic acid, stearic acid, sucrose, titanium dioxide and triethyl citrate. Energy: <4.2 kJ (1 kcal). Sodium: <0.22 mmol (5 mg). Bottles of 60 and 100.

CENTRUM® JUNIOR COMPLETE
CENTRUM® JUNIOR REGULAR

Whitehall-Robins

Multiple Vitamins—Minerals

Vitamin-Mineral Supplement

Indications: For use as a nutritional supplement for children.

Contraindications: Centrum Junior Complete: In the presence of hemochromatosis, hemosiderosis, hemolytic anemia.

Precautions: Centrum Junior Complete contains iron. Oral iron preparations may aggravate existing peptic ulcer, regional enteritis and ulcerative colitis. Oral iron preparations can impair the absorption of tetracycline antibiotics. Antacids given concomitantly with iron compounds decrease iron absorption.

Phenylketonurics: contains phenylalanine.

Dosage: Chew 1 tablet daily.

Supplied: Centrum Junior Complete: Each oval, partially scored tablet, engraved Centrum Jr and U21, contains: vitamin A 5 000 IU, vitamin E 10 IU, vitamin C 50 mg, folic acid 0.1 mg, vitamin B_1 1.5 mg, vitamin B_2 1.7 mg, niacinamide 20.0 mg, vitamin B_6 2.0 mg, vitamin B_{12} 4.0 μg, vitamin D 400 IU, biotin 30 μg, pantothenic acid 10.0 mg, calcium 162 mg, phosphorus 125 mg, iodine 0.15 mg, iron 4 mg, copper 1 mg. Nonmedicinal ingredients: aspartame, butylated hydroxytoluene, citric acid, cornstarch, FD&C Red No. 40, FD&C Yellow No. 6, flavors, gelatin, glycerides of fatty acids, hydrogenated soybean oil, hydrolysed protein, hydrolysed cellulose, magnesium stearate, microcrystalline cellulose, peanut oil, prosweet, silicon dioxide, sodium aluminum silicate, sodium benzoate, sodium citrate, sorbic acid and sucrose. Energy: <4.2 kJ (1 kcal). Bottles of 60, assorted flavors and colors.

Centrum Junior Regular: Each oval, partially scored tablet, engraved Centrum Jr and U22, contains: vitamin A 5 000 IU, vitamin C 50 mg, folic acid 0.1 mg, vitamin B_1 1.5 mg, vitamin B_2 1.7 mg, niacinamide 20.0 mg, vitamin B_6 2.0 mg, vitamin B_{12} 4.0 μg, vitamin D 400 IU, pantothenic acid 10.0 mg, calcium 162 mg, phosphorus 125 mg. Nonmedicinal ingredients: aspartame, butylated hydroxytoluene, citric acid, cornstarch, FD&C Red No. 40, FD&C Yellow No. 6, flavors, gelatin, glycerides of fatty acids, hydrogenated soybean oil, hydrolysed protein, hydrolysed cellulose, magnesium stearate, microcrystalline cellulose, peanut oil, prosweet, silicon dioxide, sodium aluminum silicate, sodium benzoate, sodium citrate, sorbic acid and sucrose. Energy: <4.2 kJ (1 kcal). Bottles of 60, assorted flavors and colors.

CEPORACIN® ℞

Bioniche

Cephalothin Sodium

Antibiotic

Supplied: Each vial of sterile dry powder contains: cephalothin sodium equivalent to cephalothin 1 g. Vials of 10 mL, trays of 25. Store below 25°C. After reconstitution, the solution retains its potency for 72 hours when refrigerated. At room temperature, the solution should be used within 6 hours. The concentrated solution darkens after a few hours, especially when kept at room temperature. If the solution becomes brown, it should be discarded.

CEPTAZ® ℞

Glaxo Wellcome

Ceftazidime

Antibiotic

Pharmacology: In vitro studies indicate that the bactericidal action of ceftazidime, a semisynthetic cephalosporin antibiotic, results from inhibition of bacterial cell wall synthesis.

Ceftazidime has a high affinity for the Penicillin-Binding Protein-3 (PBP-3) and moderate affinity for the PBP-1a of certain gram negative organisms such as E. coli and P. aeruginosa. The affinity for PBP-1b is much less than that for either PBP-3 or PBP-1a. PBP-3 is involved in the process of cross-wall formation (septation). Binding to this protein results in formation of filaments and eventual death of the bacterium. PBP-1a and PBP-1b are involved in longitudinal wall synthesis (elongation) prior to septation. Binding to these proteins results in spheroplast formation followed by rapid lysis.

Ceftazidime has high affinity for PBP-1 and PBP-2 of S. aureus. However, the drug's affinity for PBP-3 is very much less in this organism.

Indications: For the treatment of patients with infections caused by susceptible strains of the designated organisms in the following diseases:

Lower Respiratory Tract Infections: Pneumonia caused by P. aeruginosa; H. influenzae including ampicillin-resistant strains; Klebsiella species; Enterobacter species; P. mirabilis; E. coli, Serratia species, S. pneumoniae, and S. aureus including ampicillin-resistant (but not methicillin-resistant) strains.

Urinary Tract Infections: Caused by P. aeruginosa; Enterobacter species; Proteus species (indole positive and negative); Klebsiella species, and E. coli.

Due to the nature of the underlying conditions which usually predispose patients to Pseudomonas infections of the lower respiratory and urinary tracts, a good clinical response accompanied by bacterial eradication may not be achieved despite evidence of in vitro sensitivity.

Skin Structure Infections: Caused by P. aeruginosa; Klebsiella species; E. coli; P. mirabilis; Enterobacter species; S. aureus, including ampicillin-resistant (but not methicillin-resistant) strains; and S. pyogenes.

Bacteremia/Septicemia: Caused by P. aeruginosa; Klebsiella species; E. coli; Serratia species; S. pneumoniae; S. aureus, including ampicillin-resistant (but not methicillin-resistant) strains; and S. epidermidis.

Bone Infections: Caused by P. aeruginosa; P. mirabilis; Enterobacter species; and S. aureus, including ampicillin-resistant (but not methicillin-resistant) strains.

Peritonitis: Caused by E. coli; Klebsiella species; and Peptostreptococcus species. Patients infected with Bacteroides species have also responded.

Meningitis: Caused by H. influenzae and N. meningitidis. Ceftazidime has also been used successfully in a limited number of cases of meningitis due to P. aeruginosa.

Specimens for bacteriologic culture should be obtained prior to therapy in order to identify the causative organisms and to determine their susceptibilities to ceftazidime. Therapy may be instituted before results of susceptibility testing are known. However, modification of the treatment may be required once these results become available.

Contraindications: Patients who have shown hypersensitivity to ceftazidime or the cephalosporin group of antibiotics.

Warnings: Before therapy with ceftazidime is instituted, careful inquiry should be made to determine whether the patient has had previous hypersensitivity reactions to ceftazidime, cephalosporins, penicillins, or other drugs. Ceftazidime should be administered with caution to any patient who has demonstrated some form of allergy, particularly to drugs. Ceftazidime should be given with caution to patients with Type 1 hypersensitivity reactions to penicillin. If an allergic reaction to ceftazidime occurs, treatment should be discontinued and standard agents (e.g. epinephrine, antihistamines, corticosteroids) administered as necessary.

Pseudomembranous colitis has been reported to be associated with treatment with ceftazidime (and other broad-spectrum antibiotics). Therefore, it is important to consider its diagnosis in patients administered ceftazidime who develop diarrhea. Treatment with broad-spectrum antibiotics, including ceftazidime, alters the normal flora of the colon and may permit overgrowth of Clostridia. Studies indicate that a toxin produced by C. difficile is one primary cause of antibiotic-associated colitis. Mild cases of colitis may respond to drug discontinuance alone. Moderate to severe cases should be managed with fluid, electrolyte, and protein supplementation as indicated. When the colitis is not relieved by discontinuance of ceftazidime administration or when it is severe, consideration should be given to the administration of vancomycin or other suitable therapy. Other possible causes of colitis should also be considered.

Precautions: Ceftazidime should be administered with caution to individuals with a history of gastrointestinal disease, particularly colitis.

Patients with impaired renal function (i.e. creatinine clearance of 50 mL/min/1.73 m² or less) should be placed on the special dosage schedule for ceftazidime recommended in the Dosage section. Normal dosages in these individuals are likely to produce excessive serum concentrations of ceftazidime. Elevated levels of ceftazidime in these patients could lead to convulsions.

The concomitant administration of aminoglycosides and some cephalosporins has caused nephrotoxicity. Although transient elevations of BUN and serum creatinine have been observed in clinical studies, there is no evidence that ceftazidime, when administered alone, is significantly nephrotoxic. However, the effect of administering ceftazidime concomitantly with aminoglycosides is not known. Studies suggest that the concomitant use of potent diuretics such as furosemide and ethacrynic acid, may increase the risk of renal toxicity with cephalosporins.

Ceftazidime is eliminated via the kidneys, therefore the dosage should be reduced according to the degree of renal impairment.

Neurological sequelae have occasionally been reported when the dose has not been reduced appropriately (see Dosage in Impaired Renal Function).

Prolonged treatment with ceftazidime may result in the overgrowth of nonsusceptible organisms, including species originally sensitive to the drug. Repeated evaluation of the patient's condition is essential. If superinfection occurs during therapy, appropriate measures should be taken.

Development of resistance during the administration of ceftazidime has been observed for S. aureus, members of the Enterobacteriaceae family, Acinetobacter species and Pseudomonas species.

Chloramphenicol is antagonistic in vitro with ceftazidime and other cephalosporins. The clinical relevance of this finding is unknown, but if concurrent administration of ceftazidime with chloramphenicol is proposed, the possibility of antagonism should be considered.

Pregnancy: The safety of ceftazidime in pregnancy has not been established. The use of ceftazidime in pregnant women requires that the likely benefit from the drug be weighed against the possible risk to the mother and fetus.

Reproduction studies have been performed in mice and rats employing ceftazidime doses of up to 25 times those usually administered to humans. These studies have revealed no evidence of impaired fertility or harm of the fetus caused by ceftazidime.

Animal reproduction studies, however, are not always predictive of human response.

Lactation: Ceftazidime is excreted in human milk in low concentrations (3.8 to 5.2 mg/L). The clinical significance of this is unknown, therefore, caution should be exercised when ceftazidime is administered to a nursing mother.

Children: The safety and efficacy of ceftazidime has not been established in infants (1 month of age or younger) and children (≤12 years).

Geriatrics: The elimination of ceftazidime may be reduced due to impairment of renal function.

Drug-Laboratory Test Interactions: Ceftazidime may cause a false-positive reaction for glucose in the urine with copper reduction tests (Benedict's or Fehling's solution). As a false-negative result may occur in the ferricyanide test, it is recommended that either the glucose oxidase or hexokinase method be used to determine blood plasma glucose levels in patients receiving ceftazidime.

Ceftazidime does not interfere in the alkaline picrate assay for creatinine.

A positive Coombs' test has been reported during treatment with cephalosporins. This phenomenon can interfere with cross matching of blood.

Adverse Effects: The most common adverse effects have been local reactions following i.v. injection, allergic reactions and gastrointestinal reactions. Other adverse effects have been encountered less frequently.

Local (2.8% of patients): thrombophlebitis or phlebitis and pain with i.v. administration. Pain and/or inflammation after i.m. injection.

Hypersensitivity (2.7% of patients): pruritus, urticaria, allergic exanthema, and fever. There have been rare reports of toxic epidermal necrolysis. Angioedema and anaphylaxis including (bronchospasm and/or hypotension) have been reported very rarely.

Gastrointestinal (<4% of patients): diarrhea, nausea, vomiting, colitis and abdominal pain. Pseudomembranous colitis has been reported (see Warnings). Oral thrush has been reported very rarely.

CNS (<1% of patients): headache, dizziness, hallucinations and lethargy. There have been reports of neurological sequelae including tremor, myoclonia, convulsions and encephalopathy occurring in patients with renal impairment in whom the dose of ceftazidime has not been appropriately reduced.

Renal (<1% of patients): transient elevations of blood urea, blood urea nitrogen (BUN) and serum creatinine.

Hepatic (<4% of patients): transient elevations of serum bilirubin, alkaline phosphatase, LDH, AST, ALT and GGT.

Hematopoietic: eosinophilia (3.4%), positive Direct Coombs' Test (5.1%), and with an incidence of <1%: thrombocytosis, transient leukopenia, neutropenia, agranulocytosis, thrombocytopenia, lymphocytosis and very rarely hemolytic anemia.

Miscellaneous (<1% of patients): paresthesia, blurred vision, bad taste, flushing, candidiasis and vaginitis.

Overdose: Symptoms and Treatment: Overdosage of cephalosporins can lead to neurological sequelae including encephalopathy, convulsions and coma. Excessive serum levels of ceftazidime can be reduced by hemodialysis or peritoneal dialysis.

Dosage: Ceftazidime may be administered either i.v. or i.m. after reconstitution.

Dosage and route of administration should be determined by severity of infection, susceptibility of the causative organism(s) and condition of the patient. The i.v. route is preferable for patients with septicemia, peritonitis or other severe or life-threatening infections, or for patients who may be poor risks because of lowered resistance resulting from such debilitating conditions as malnutrition, trauma, surgery, diabetes, heart failure, or malignancy, particularly if shock is present or pending.

The usual duration of treatment is 7 to 14 days. For Streptococcal infections, therapy should be continued for at least 10 days.

Adults: The recommended daily dosage is 0.5 to 6 g administered in equally divided doses every 8 to 12 hours (see Table I).

Table I—Ceptaz

Adult Dosage

Type of Infection	Daily Dose (g)	Frequency and Route
uncomplicated pneumonia or skin structure infection	1.5–3.0	0.5–1.0 g i.m. or i.v. q8h
uncomplicated urinary tract infections	0.5	250 mg i.m. or i.v. q12h
complicated urinary tract infections	1.0–1.5	500 mg i.m. or i.v. q8h or q12h
bone infections	4.0	2 g i.v. q12h
peritonitis or septicemia	6.0	2 g i.v. q8h
meningitis	6.0	2 g i.v. q8h

For the treatment of infections caused by Staphylococcus species, a dosage of 1 or 2 g administered every 8 hours is recommended. For the treatment of infections (except those confined to the urinary tract) caused by Enterobacter species, a dosage of at least 1 g administered every 8 hours is recommended.

Geriatrics: In acutely ill elderly patients with reduced renal clearance of ceftazidime, the daily dosage should not exceed 3 g.

Children: The safety and efficacy of ceftazidime has not been established in infants (1 month of age or younger) and children (≤12 years).

Impaired Hepatic Function: No adjustment in dosage is required for patients with hepatic dysfunction provided renal function is not impaired (see Pharmacology).

Adults with Impaired Renal Function: Ceftazidime is excreted almost exclusively by glomerular filtration. In patients in whom the glomerular filtration rate (GFR) is less than or equal to 50 mL/min (0.83 mL/s), the dosage of ceftazidime must be reduced to compensate for its slower excretion. After an initial

Ceptaz (cont'd)

loading dose of 1 g of ceftazidime, a maintenance dosage schedule should be followed (see Table II).

Table II—Ceptaz

Recommended Maintenance Doses of Ceptaz In Renal Insufficiency

Creatinine Clearance mL/min/ 1.73m²	mL/s/ 1.73m²	Recommended Unit Dose of Ceptaz Moderate Infections	Severe Infections	Frequency* of Dosing
31–50	0.51–0.83	1 g	1.5 g	q12h
16–30	0.26–0.50	1 g	1.5 g	q24h
6–15	0.10–0.25	500 mg	750 mg	q24h
<5	<0.09	500 mg	750 mg	q48h

*If the severity of the infection necessitates an increase in the dosing frequency, serum concentrations of ceftazidime should be used as guidelines.

When only serum creatinine levels are known, the following formula may be used to estimate creatinine clearance. The serum creatinine must represent a steady state of renal function:

Males:

$$\text{Creatinine clearance (mL/s)} = \frac{\text{Weight (kg)} \times (140-\text{age})}{49 \times \text{serum creatinine } (\mu\text{mol/L})}$$

or

$$\text{Creatinine clearance (mL/min)} = \frac{\text{Weight (kg)} \times (140-\text{age})}{72 \times \text{serum creatinine (mg/dL)}}$$

Females: 0.85×above value

Mean serum half-life of ceftazidime in patients with no kidney function was reduced from a range of 24 to 35.4 hours between dialysis sessions to a range of 2.8 to 4.6 hours during hemodialysis. Therefore a loading dose of 1 g is recommended followed by 0.5 to 1 g after each hemodialysis period. Serum concentrations of ceftazidime should be carefully monitored and used as a basis to adjust the dosage.

Ceftazidime can also be used in patients undergoing peritoneal dialysis and continuous ambulatory peritoneal dialysis. In such patients, a loading dose of ceftazidime (1 g) is suggested, followed by 500 mg every 24 hours. Serum concentrations of ceftazidime should be carefully monitored and used as a basis to adjust the dosage.

Administration: I.M.: Ceftazidime may be administered by deep i.m. injection into a large muscle mass such as the upper outer quadrant of the gluteus maximus or vastus lateralis. The maximum dose of ceftazidime should be 1 g for a single i.m. injection.

Intermittent I.V. Administration: The reconstituted solution may be slowly injected into the vein over a period of 3 to 5 minutes or given through the tubing of an administration set. During the infusion of the solution containing ceftazidime, the administration of other solutions should be discontinued temporarily.

Continuous I.V. Infusion: Ceftazidime may also be administered over a longer period of time.

Note: If therapy with ceftazidime is carried out in combination with an aminoglycoside antibiotic, each should be administered at different sites because of a physical incompatibility. An aminoglycoside should not be mixed with ceftazidime in the same container.

Reconstitution: Note: Vials of ceftazidime as supplied are under a slightly reduced pressure. This may assist entry of the diluent. No gas relief needle is required when adding the diluent. No evolution of gas occurs on constitution. When the vial contents are dissolved, vials may still be under a reduced pressure. This reduced pressure is particularly noticeable for the 10 g pharmacy bulk package.

I.M. Use: Solutions for Reconstitution: Sterile Water for Injection, 0.5% w/v and 1% w/v Lignocaine Hydrochloride Injection, Bacteriostatic Water for Injection preserved with Benzyl Alcohol or Parabens. See Table III.

Table III—Ceptaz

Reconstitution Table: I.M.

Vial Size	Diluent to be Added to Vial	Approximate Available Volume	Approximate Average Concentration
1 g	3.0 mL	4.2 mL	250 mg/mL

Shake well until dissolved.

I.V. Use: Solutions for Reconstitution: Sterile Water for Injection.

Reconstitute as shown in Table IV.

Table IV—Ceptaz

Reconstitution Table: I.V.

Vial Size	Diluent to be Added to Vial	Approximate Available Volume	Approximate Average Concentration
1 g	10 mL	11.2 mL	90 mg/mL
2 g	10 mL	12.0 mL	170 mg/mL

Shake well until dissolved. The prepared solution may be further diluted to the desired volume with any of the solutions listed under "Solutions for I.V. Infusion".

Direct I.V. Injection: Reconstitute as directed in Table IV.

Intermittent I.V. Infusion: Reconstitute as directed in Table IV for 1 g and 2 g vials of Ceptaz.

Continuous I.V. Infusion: 1 g and 2 g Vials: Reconstitute 1 g and 2 g vials of Ceptaz with 10 mL Sterile Water for Injection. The appropriate quantity of the reconstituted solution may be added to an i.v. bottle containing any of the solutions listed under "Solutions for I.V. Infusion".

Pharmacy Bulk Vial: **The availability of the pharmacy bulk vial is restricted to hospitals with a recognized i.v. admixture program.**

Ceptaz for injection does not contain any preservatives. The pharmacy bulk vial is intended for multiple dispensing for i.v. use only, employing a single puncture. Reconstitute with 40 mL Sterile Water for Injection. See Table V.

Table V—Ceptaz

Reconstitution Table: Pharmacy Bulk Vial

Vial Size	Diluent to be Added to Vial	Approximate Available Volume	Approximate Average Concentration
10 g	40 mL	51.6 mL	200 mg/mL

Shake well until dissolved. Following reconstitution with Sterile Water for Injection, the solution should be dispensed and diluted for use within 8 hours at room temperature (not exceeding 25°C). Any unused reconstituted solution should be discarded after 8 hours. The appropriate quantity of the reconstituted solution may be added to an i.v. bottle containing any of the solutions listed below.

Solutions for I.V. Infusion: 0.9% Sodium Chloride Injection, 1/6 Molar Sodium Lactate Injection, Ringers Injection USP, Lactated Ringers Injection USP, 5% Dextrose Injection, 5% Dextrose and 0.225% Sodium Chloride Injection, 5% Dextrose and 0.45% Sodium Chloride Injection, 5% Dextrose and 0.9% Sodium Chloride Injection, 10% Dextrose Injection, 10% Invert Sugar (Fructose/Dextrose) in Water for Injection, Normosol-M and 5% Dextrose Injection, Sterile Water for Injection.

Stability of Solutions: Storage: Reconstituted solutions should be administered within 12 hours when stored at room temperature (not exceeding 25°C), and within 72 hours when refrigerated, from the time of reconstitution, both when prepared as bolus injections, i.m. or i.v., and as infusion admixtures with recommended i.v. diluents.

Incompatibility: Ceftazidime should not be added to blood products, protein hydrolysates or amino acids. It should not be mixed together with an aminoglycoside. Ceftazidime is less stable in Sodium Bicarbonate Injection than in other i.v. fluids; therefore it is not recommended as a diluent.

Precipitation has been reported when vancomycin has been added to ceftazidime in solution. Therefore, it would be prudent to flush giving sets and i.v. lines between administration of these two agents.

Supplied: I.M. or Direct I.V. Injection: Each vial contains: the equivalent of ceftazidime 1 g. Nonmedicinal ingredients: L-arginine. Packs of 10.

I.V. Injection or Infusion: Each vial contains: the equivalent of ceftazidime 1 and 2 g. Nonmedicinal ingredients: L-arginine. Packs of 10.

Each vial contains: the equivalent of ceftazidime 10 g. Nonmedicinal ingredients: L-arginine. Packs of 6.

Ceptaz in the dry state should be stored between 15 and 30°C protected from light.

CEREBYX® Ⓟ

Parke-Davis

Fosphenytoin Sodium

Antiepileptic

Pharmacology: Introduction: Following parenteral administration of fosphenytoin, fosphenytoin is converted to the anticonvulsant phenytoin. For every mmol of fosphenytoin administered, 1 mmol of phenytoin is produced. The pharmacological and toxicological effects of fosphenytoin include those of phenytoin. However, the hydrolysis of fosphenytoin to phenytoin yields 2 metabolites, phosphate and formaldehyde. Formaldehyde is subsequently converted to formate, which is in turn metabolized via a folate dependent mechanism. Although phosphate and formaldehyde (formate) have potentially important biological effects, these effects typically occur at concentrations considerably in excess of those obtained when fosphenytoin is administered under conditions of use recommended in this labeling.

Mechanism of Action: Fosphenytoin is a prodrug of phenytoin and accordingly, its anticonvulsant effects are attributable to phenytoin.

After i.v. administration to mice, fosphenytoin blocked the tonic phase of maximal electroshock seizures at doses equivalent to those effective for phenytoin. In addition to its ability to suppress maximal electroshock seizures in mice and rats, phenytoin exhibits anticonvulsant activity against kindled seizures in rats, audiogenic seizures in mice, and seizures produced by electrical stimulation of the brainstem in rats. The cellular mechanisms of phenytoin thought to be responsible for its anticonvulsant actions include modulation of voltage-dependent sodium channels of neurons, inhibition of calcium flux across neuronal membranes, modulation of voltage-dependent calcium channels of neurons, and enhancement of the sodium-potassium ATPase activity of neurons and glial cells. The modulation of sodium channels may be a primary anticonvulsant mechanism because this property is shared with several other anticonvulsants in addition to phenytoin.

Pharmacokinetics and Drug Metabolism: Fosphenytoin: Absorption/Bioavailability: I.V.: When fosphenytoin is administered by i.v. infusion, maximum plasma fosphenytoin concentrations are achieved at the end of the infusion. Fosphenytoin has a half-life of approximately 15 minutes.

I.M.: Fosphenytoin is completely bioavailable following i.m. administration of fosphenytoin. Peak concentrations occur at approximately 30 minutes postdose. Plasma fosphenytoin concentrations following i.m. administration are lower but more sustained than those following i.v. administration due to the time required for absorption of fosphenytoin from the injection site.

Distribution: Fosphenytoin is extensively bound (95 to 99%) to human plasma proteins, primarily albumin. Binding to plasma proteins is saturable with the result that the percent bound decreases as total fosphenytoin concentrations increase. Fosphenytoin displaces phenytoin from protein binding sites. The volume of distribution of fosphenytoin increases with fosphenytoin dose and rate, and ranges from 4.3 to 10.8 L.

Metabolism and Elimination: The conversion half-life of fosphenytoin to phenytoin is approximately 15 minutes. The mechanism of fosphenytoin conversion has not been determined, but phosphatases probably play a major role. Fosphenytoin is not excreted in urine. Each mmol of fosphenytoin is metabolized to 1 mmol of phenytoin, phosphate, and formate (see Introduction and Precautions, Phosphate Load for Renally Impaired Patients).

Phenytoin (after Fosphenytoin Administration): In general, i.m. administration of fosphenytoin generates systemic phenytoin concentrations that are similar enough to oral phenytoin sodium to allow essentially interchangeable use.

The pharmacokinetics of fosphenytoin following i.v. administration of fosphenytoin, however, are complex, and when used in an emergency setting (e.g., status epilepticus), differences in rate of availability of phenytoin could be critical. Studies have therefore empirically determined an infusion rate for fosphenytoin that gives a rate and extent of phenytoin systemic availability similar to that of a 50 mg/min phenytoin sodium infusion.

A dose of 15 to 20 mg PE/kg of fosphenytoin infused at 100 to 150 mg PE/min yields plasma free phenytoin concentrations over time that approximate those achieved when an equivalent dose of phenytoin sodium (e.g., parenteral phenytoin sodium) is administered at 50 mg/min (see Dosage and Warnings).

Following administration of single i.v. fosphenytoin doses of 400 to 1 200 mg PE, mean maximum total phenytoin concentrations increase in proportion to dose, but do not change appreciably with changes in infusion rate. In contrast, mean maximum unbound phenytoin concentrations increase with both dose and rate.

Absorption/Bioavailability: Fosphenytoin is completely converted to phenytoin following i.v. administration, with a half-life of approximately 15 minutes. Fosphenytoin is also completely converted to phenytoin following i.m. administration and plasma total phenytoin concentrations peak in approximately 3 hours.

Distribution: Phenytoin is highly bound to plasma proteins, primarily albumin, although to a lesser extent than fosphenytoin. In the absence of fosphenytoin, approximately 12% of total plasma phenytoin is unbound over the clinically relevant concentration range. However, fosphenytoin displaces phenytoin from plasma protein binding sites. This increases the fraction of phenytoin unbound (up to 30% unbound) during the period required for conversion of fosphenytoin to phenytoin (approximately 0.5 to 1 hour postinfusion).

Metabolism and Elimination: Phenytoin derived from administration of fosphenytoin is extensively metabolized in the liver and excreted in urine primarily as 5-(p-hydroxy-phenyl)-5-phenylhydantoin and its glucuronide; little unchanged phenytoin (1 to 5% of the fosphenytoin dose) is recovered in urine. Phenytoin hepatic metabolism is saturable, and following administration of single i.v. fosphenytoin doses of 400 to 1 200 mg PE, total and unbound phenytoin AUC values increase disproportionately with dose. Mean total phenytoin half-life values (12 to 28.9 hours) following fosphenytoin administration at these doses are similar to those after equal doses of parenteral Dilantin and tend to be greater at higher plasma phenytoin concentrations.

Special Populations: Patients with Renal or Hepatic Disease: Due to an increased fraction of unbound phenytoin in patients with renal or hepatic disease, or in those with hypoalbuminemia, the interpretation of total phenytoin plasma concentrations should be made with caution (see Dosage). Unbound phenytoin concentrations may be more useful in these patient populations. After i.v. administration of fosphenytoin to patients with renal and/or hepatic disease, or in those with hypoalbuminemia, fosphenytoin clearance to phenytoin may be increased without a similar increase in phenytoin clearance. This has the potential to increase the frequency and severity of adverse events (see Precautions).

Age: The effect of age was evaluated in patients 5 to 98 years of age. Patient age had no significant impact on fosphenytoin pharmacokinetics. Phenytoin clearance tends to decrease with increasing age (20% less in patients over 70 years of age relative to that in patients 20 to 30 years of age). Phenytoin dosing requirements vary between patients and must be individualized (see Dosage).

Gender and Race: Gender and race have no significant impact on fosphenytoin or phenytoin pharmacokinetics.

Clinical Studies: Infusion tolerance was evaluated in clinical studies. One double-blind study assessed infusion-site tolerance of equivalent loading doses (15 to 20 mg PE/kg) of fosphenytoin infused at 150 mg PE/min or phenytoin infused at 50 mg/min. The study demonstrated better local tolerance (pain and burning at the infusion site), fewer disruptions of the infusion, and a shorter infusion period for fosphenytoin-treated patients (see Table I).

Table I—Cerebyx

Infusion Tolerance of Equivalent Loading Doses of I.V. Fosphenytoin and I.V. Phenytoin

	I.V. Fosphenytoin N=90	**I.V. Phenytoin N=22**
Local Intolerance	9%*	90%
Infusion Disrupted	21%	67%
Average Infusion Time	13 min	44 min

*Percent of patients.

Fosphenytoin-treated patients, however, experienced more systemic sensory disturbances (see Precautions, Sensory Disturbances). Infusion disruptions in fosphenytoin-treated patients were primarily due to systemic burning, pruritus, and/or paresthesia while those in phenytoin-treated patients were primarily due to pain and burning at the infusion site (see Table I).

In a double-blind study investigating temporary substitution of fosphenytoin for oral phenytoin, i.m. fosphenytoin was as well-tolerated as i.m. placebo. I.M. Fosphenytoin resulted in a slight increase in transient, mild to moderate local itching (23% of patients versus 11% of i.m. placebo-treated patients at any time during the study). This study also demonstrated that equimolar doses of i.m. fosphenytoin may be substituted for oral phenytoin sodium with no dosage adjustments needed when initiating i.m. or returning to oral therapy. In contrast, switching between i.m. and oral phenytoin requires dosage adjustments because of slow and erratic phenytoin absorption from muscle.

Indications: For short-term parenteral administration when other means of phenytoin administration are unavailable, inappropriate or deemed less advantageous. The safety and effectiveness of fosphenytoin in this use has not been systematically evaluated for more than 5 days.

Fosphenytoin can be used for the control of generalized convulsive status epilepticus and prevention and treatment of seizures occurring during neurosurgery. It can also be substituted, short-term, for oral phenytoin.

Contraindications: Patients who have demonstrated hypersensitivity to fosphenytoin or its ingredients, or phenytoin or other hydantoins.

Because of the effect of parenteral phenytoin on ventricular automaticity, fosphenytoin is contraindicated in patients with sinus bradycardia, sino-atrial block, second-and third-degree AV block, and Adams-Stokes syndrome.

Warnings: Doses of fosphenytoin are expressed as their phenytoin sodium equivalents in this monograph (PE=phenytoin sodium equivalent).

Do not, therefore, make any adjustment in the recommended doses when substituting fosphenytoin for phenytoin sodium or vice versa.

The following warnings are based on experience with fosphenytoin or phenytoin.

Status Epilepticus Dosing Regimen: **Do not administer fosphenytoin at a rate greater than 150 mg PE/min.**

The dose of i.v. fosphenytoin (15 to 20 mg PE/kg) that is used to treat status epilepticus is administered at a maximum rate of 150 mg PE/min. The typical fosphenytoin infusion administered to a 50 kg patient would take between 5 and 7 minutes. Note that the delivery of an identical molar dose of phenytoin using parenteral Dilantin or generic phenytoin sodium injection cannot be accomplished in less than 15 to 20 minutes because of the untoward cardiovascular effects that accompany the direct i.v. administration of phenytoin at rates greater than 50 mg/min. If rapid phenytoin loading is a primary goal, i.v. administration of fosphenytoin is preferred because the time to achieve therapeutic plasma phenytoin concentrations is greater following i.m. than that following i.v. administration (see Dosage).

Withdrawal Precipitated Seizure, Status Epilepticus: Antiepileptic drugs should not be abruptly discontinued because of the possibility of increased seizure frequency, including status epilepticus. When, in the judgment of the clinician, the need for dosage reduction, discontinuation, or substitution of alternative antiepileptic medication arises, this should be done gradually. However, in the event of an allergic or hypersensitivity reaction, rapid substitution of alternative therapy may be necessary. In this case, alternative therapy should be an antiepileptic drug not belonging to the hydantoin chemical class.

Cardiovascular Depression: Hypotension may occur, especially after i.v. administration at high doses and high rates of administration. Following administration of phenytoin, severe cardiovascular reactions and fatalities have been reported with atrial and ventricular conduction depression and ventricular fibrillation. Severe complications are most commonly encountered in elderly or gravely ill patients. Therefore, careful cardiac monitoring is needed when administering i.v. loading doses of fosphenytoin. Reduction in rate of administration or discontinuation of dosing may be needed.

Fosphenytoin should be used with caution in patients with hypotension and severe myocardial insufficiency.

Rash: Fosphenytoin should be discontinued if a skin rash appears. If the rash is exfoliative, purpuric, or bullous, or if lupus erythematosus, Stevens-Johnson syndrome, or toxic epidermal necrolysis is suspected, use of this drug should not be resumed and alternative therapy should be considered. If the rash is of a milder type (measles-like or scarlatiniform), therapy may be resumed after the rash has completely disappeared. If the rash recurs upon reinstitution of therapy, further fosphenytoin or phenytoin administration is contraindicated.

Hepatic Injury: Cases of acute hepatotoxicity, including infrequent cases of acute hepatic failure, have been reported with phenytoin. These incidents have been associated with a hypersensitivity syndrome characterized by fever, skin eruptions, and lymphadenopathy, and usually occur within the first 2 months of treatment. Other common manifestations include jaundice, hepatomegaly, elevated serum transaminase levels, leukocytosis, and eosinophilia. The clinical course of acute phenytoin hepatotoxicity ranges from prompt recovery to fatal outcomes. In patients with acute hepatotoxicity, fosphenytoin should be immediately discontinued and not readministered.

Hemopoietic System: Hemopoietic complications, some fatal, have occasionally been reported in association with administration of phenytoin. These have included thrombocytopenia, leukopenia, granulocytopenia, agranulocytosis, and pancytopenia with or without bone marrow suppression.

There have been a number of reports that have suggested a relationship between phenytoin and the development of lymphadenopathy (local or generalized), including benign lymph node hyperplasia, pseudolymphoma, lymphoma, and Hodgkin's disease. Although a cause and effect relationship has not been established, the occurrence of lymphadenopathy indicates the need to differentiate such a condition from other types of lymph node pathology. Lymph node involvement may occur with or without symptoms and signs resembling serum sickness, e.g., fever, rash, and liver involvement. In all cases of lymphadenopathy, follow-up observation for an extended period is indicated and every effort should be made to achieve seizure control using alternative antiepileptic drugs.

Alcohol Use: Acute alcohol intake may increase plasma phenytoin concentrations while chronic alcohol use may decrease plasma concentrations.

Pregnancy: Clinical: Risks to Mother: An increase in seizure frequency may occur during pregnancy because of altered phenytoin pharmacokinetics. Periodic measurement of plasma phenytoin concentrations may be valuable in the management of pregnant women as a guide to appropriate adjustment of dosage (see Precautions, Laboratory Tests). However, postpartum restoration of the original dosage will probably be indicated.

Risks to the Fetus: If this drug is used during pregnancy, or if the patient becomes pregnant while taking the drug, the patient should be apprised of the potential harm to the fetus.

Prenatal exposure to phenytoin may increase the risks for congenital malformations and other adverse developmental outcomes. Increased frequencies of major malformations (such as orofacial clefts and cardiac defects), minor anomalies (dysmorphic facial features, nail and digit hypoplasia), growth abnormalities (including microcephaly), and mental deficiency have been reported among children born to epileptic women who took phenytoin alone or in combination with other antiepileptic drugs during pregnancy. There have also been several reported cases of malignancies, including neuroblastoma, in children whose mothers received phenytoin during pregnancy. The overall incidence of malformations for children of epileptic women treated with antiepileptic drugs (phenytoin and/or others) during pregnancy is about 10%, or 2- to 3-fold that in the general population. However, the relative contribution of antiepileptic drugs and other factors associated with epilepsy to this increased risk are uncertain and in most cases it has not been possible to attribute specific developmental abnormalities to particular antiepileptic drugs.

Patients should consult with their physicians to weigh the risks and benefits of phenytoin during pregnancy and to select the regimen which would provide the least risk to mother and fetus.

Postpartum Period: A potentially life-threatening bleeding disorder related to decreased levels of vitamin K-dependent clotting factors may occur in newborns exposed to phenytoin in utero. This drug-induced condition can be prevented with vitamin K administration to the mother before delivery and to the neonate after birth.

Precautions: General (Fosphenytoin Specific): Sensory Disturbances: Severe burning, itching, and/or paresthesia were reported by 7 of 16 normal volunteers administered i.v. fosphenytoin at a dose of 1 200 mg PE at the maximum rate of administration (150 mg PE/min). The severe sensory disturbance lasted from 3 to 50 minutes in 6 of these subjects and for 14 hours in the seventh subject. In some cases, milder sensory disturbances persisted for as long as 24 hours. The location of the discomfort varied among subjects with the groin mentioned most frequently as an area of discomfort. In a separate cohort of 16 normal volunteers (taken from 2 other studies) who were administered i.v. fosphenytoin at a dose of 1 200 mg PE at the maximum rate of administration (150 mg PE/min), none experienced severe disturbances, but most experienced mild to moderate itching or tingling.

Patients administered fosphenytoin at doses of 20 mg PE/kg at 150 mg PE/min are expected to experience discomfort of some degree. The occurrence and intensity of the discomfort can be lessened by slowing or temporarily stopping the infusion.

The effect of continuing infusion unaltered in the presence of these sensations is unknown. No permanent sequelae have been reported thus far. The pharmacologic basis for these positive sensory phenomena is unknown, but other phosphate ester drugs, which deliver smaller phosphate loads, have been associated with burning, itching, and/or tingling predominantly in the groin area.

Phosphate Load: The phosphate load provided by fosphenytoin (0.0037 mmol phosphate/mg PE fosphenytoin) should be considered when treating patients who require phosphate restriction, such as those with severe renal impairment.

I.V. Loading in Renal and/or Hepatic Disease or in Those With Hypoalbuminemia: After i.v. administration to patients with

Cerebyx (cont'd)

renal and/or hepatic disease, or in those with hypoalbuminemia, fosphenytoin clearance to phenytoin may be increased without a similar increase in phenytoin clearance. This has the potential to increase the frequency and severity of adverse events (see Pharmacology, Special Populations and Dosage, Dosing in Special Populations).

General (Phenytoin Associated): Fosphenytoin is not indicated for the treatment of absence seizures.

A small percentage of individuals who have been treated with phenytoin have been shown to metabolize the drug slowly. Slow metabolism may be due to limited enzyme availability and lack of induction; it appears to be genetically determined.

Phenytoin and other hydantoins are contraindicated in patients who have experienced phenytoin hypersensitivity. Additionally, caution should be exercised if using structurally similar (e.g., barbiturates, succinimides, oxazolidinediones, and other related compounds) in these same patients.

Phenytoin has been infrequently associated with the exacerbation of porphyria. Caution should be exercised when fosphenytoin is used in patients with this disease.

Hyperglycemia, resulting from phenytoin's inhibitory effect on insulin release, has been reported. Phenytoin may also raise serum glucose concentrations in diabetic patients. Plasma concentrations of phenytoin sustained above the optimal range may produce confusional states referred to as "delirium", "psychosis", or "encephalopathy", or rarely, irreversible cerebellar dysfunction. Accordingly, at the first sign of acute toxicity, determination of plasma phenytoin concentrations is recommended (see Precautions, Laboratory Tests). Fosphenytoin dose reduction is indicated if phenytoin concentrations are excessive; if symptoms persist, administration of fosphenytoin should be discontinued.

The liver is the primary site of biotransformation of phenytoin; patients with impaired liver function, elderly patients, or those who are gravely ill may show early signs of toxicity. Phenytoin and other hydantoins are not indicated for seizures due to hypoglycemic or other metabolic causes. Appropriate diagnostic procedures should be performed as indicated.

Phenytoin has the potential to lower serum folate levels.

Laboratory Tests: Phenytoin doses are usually selected to attain therapeutic plasma total phenytoin concentrations of 40 to 80 μmol/L (10 to 20 μg/mL), (unbound phenytoin concentrations of 4 to 8 μmol/L (1 to 2 μg/mL)). Following fosphenytoin administration, it is recommended that phenytoin concentrations not be monitored until conversion to phenytoin is essentially complete. This occurs within approximately 2 hours after the end of i.v. infusion and 4 hours after i.m. injection.

Prior to complete conversion, commonly used immunoanalytical techniques, such as TDx/TDxFLx (fluorescence polarization) and Emit 2 000 (enzyme multiplied), may significantly overestimate plasma phenytoin concentrations because of cross-reactivity with fosphenytoin. The TDx/TDxFLx assay is not recommended while unconverted fosphenytoin is present in plasma, due to an unacceptable margin of error (overestimation) in the phenytoin measurement. The difference between predicted and actual phenytoin concentrations at 4 hours postdose is ≤20μmol/L (5 μg/mL). The error is dependent on plasma phenytoin and fosphenytoin concentration (influenced by fosphenytoin dose, route and rate of administration, and time of sampling relative to dosing), and analytical method. Chromatographic assay methods accurately quantitate phenytoin concentrations in biological fluids in the presence of fosphenytoin. Prior to complete conversion, blood samples for phenytoin monitoring should be collected in tubes containing EDTA as an anticoagulant to minimize ex vivo conversion of fosphenytoin to phenytoin. However, even with specific assay methods, phenytoin concentrations measured before conversion of fosphenytoin is complete will not reflect phenytoin concentrations ultimately achieved.

Drug Interactions: No drugs are known to interfere with the conversion of fosphenytoin to phenytoin. Conversion could be affected by alterations in the level of phosphatase activity, but given the abundance and wide distribution of phosphatases in the body it is unlikely that drugs would affect this activity enough to affect conversion of fosphenytoin to phenytoin. Drugs highly bound to albumin could increase the unbound fraction of fosphenytoin. Although, it is unknown whether this could result in clinically significant effects, caution is advised when administering fosphenytoin with other drugs that significantly bind to serum albumin.

The most significant drug interactions following administration of fosphenytoin are expected to occur with drugs that interact with phenytoin. Phenytoin is extensively bound to plasma proteins and is prone to competitive displacement. Phenytoin is metabolized by hepatic cytochrome P450 enzymes and is particularly susceptible to inhibitory drug interactions because it is subject to saturable metabolism. Inhibition of metabolism may produce significant increases in circulating phenytoin concentrations and enhance the risk of drug toxicity. Phenytoin is a potent inducer of hepatic drug-metabolizing enzymes.

The most commonly occurring drug interactions are listed below.

Drugs that may increase plasma phenytoin concentrations include: acute alcohol intake, amiodarone, chloramphenicol, chlordiazepoxide, cimetidine, diazepam, dicumarol, disulfiram, estrogens, ethosuximide, fluoxetine, H_2-antagonists, halothane, isoniazid, methylphenidate, phenothiazines, phenylbutazone, salicylates, succinimides, sulfonamides, tolbutamide, trazodone.

Drugs that may decrease plasma phenytoin concentrations include: carbamazepine, chronic alcohol abuse, reserpine, vigabatrin.

Drugs that may either increase or decrease plasma phenytoin concentrations include: phenobarbital, valproic acid, and sodium valproate. Similarly, the effects of phenytoin on phenobarbital, valproic acid and sodium plasma valproate concentrations are unpredictable.

Although not a true drug interaction, tricyclic antidepressants may precipitate seizures in susceptible patients and fosphenytoin dosage may need to be adjusted.

Drugs whose efficacy is impaired by phenytoin include: anticoagulants, corticosteroids, coumarin, digitoxin, doxycycline, estrogens, furosemide, oral contraceptives, rifampin, quinidine, theophylline, vitamin D.

Coadministration of phenytoin with lamotrigine doubles the plasma clearance and reduces the elimination half-life of lamotrigine by 50%. This clinically important interaction requires dosage adjustment.

Monitoring of plasma phenytoin concentrations may be helpful when possible drug interactions are suspected (see Laboratory Tests).

Drug/Laboratory Test Interactions: Phenytoin may decrease serum concentrations of T_4. It may also produce artifactually low results in dexamethasone or metyrapone tests. Phenytoin may cause increased serum concentrations of glucose, alkaline phosphatase, and gamma glutamyl transpeptidase (GGT).

Care should be taken when using immunoanalytical methods to measure plasma phenytoin concentrations following fosphenytoin administration (see Laboratory Tests).

Lactation: It is not known whether fosphenytoin is excreted in human milk.

Following administration of Dilantin, phenytoin appears to be excreted in low concentrations in human milk. Therefore, breast-feeding is not recommended for women receiving fosphenytoin.

Children: The safety of fosphenytoin in pediatric patients has not been established. Only limited pharmacokinetic data are available in children (N=8; age 5 to 10 years). In these patients with status epilepticus who received loading doses of fosphenytoin, the plasma fosphenytoin, total phenytoin, and unbound phenytoin concentration-time profiles did not signal any major differences from those in adult patients with status epilepticus receiving comparable doses.

Geriatrics: No systematic studies in geriatric patients have been conducted. Phenytoin clearance tends to decrease with increasing age (see Pharmacology, Special Populations).

Adverse Effects: The more important adverse clinical events caused by the i.v. use of fosphenytoin or phenytoin are cardiovascular collapse and/or CNS depression. Hypotension can occur when either drug is administered rapidly by the i.v. route. The rate of administration is very important; for fosphenytoin, it should not exceed 150 mg PE/min.

The adverse clinical events most commonly observed with the use of fosphenytoin in clinical trials were nystagmus, dizziness, pruritus, paresthesia, headache, somnolence, and ataxia. With 2 exceptions, these events are commonly associated with the administration of i.v phenytoin. Paresthesia and pruritus, however, were seen much more often following fosphenytoin administration and occurred more often with i.v. fosphenytoin administration than with i.m fosphenytoin administration. These events were dose and rate related; most alert patients (41 of 64; 64%) administered doses of ≥15 mg PE/kg at 150 mg PE/min experienced discomfort of some degree. These sensations, generally described as itching, burning, or tingling, were usually not at the infusion site. The location of the discomfort varied with the groin mentioned most frequently as a site of involvement. The paresthesia and pruritus were transient events that occurred within several minutes of the start of infusion and generally resolved within 10 minutes after completion of fosphenytoin infusion. Some patients experienced symptoms for hours. These events did not increase in severity with repeated administration. Concurrent adverse events or clinical laboratory change suggesting an allergic process were not seen (see Precautions, Sensory Disturbances).

Approximately 2% of the 859 individuals who received fosphenytoin in premarketing clinical trials discontinued treatment because of an adverse event. The adverse events most commonly associated with withdrawal were pruritus (0.5%), hypotension (0.3%), and bradycardia (0.2%).

Dose and Rate Dependency of Adverse Events Following I.V. Fosphenytoin: The incidence of adverse events tended to increase as both dose and infusion rate increased. In particular, at doses of ≥15 mg PE/kg and rates ≥150 mg PE/min, transient pruritus, tinnitus, nystagmus, somnolence, and ataxia occurred 2 to 3 times more often than at lower doses or rates.

Incidence in Controlled Clinical Trials: All adverse events were recorded during the trials by the clinical investigators using terminology of their own choosing. Similar types of events were grouped into standardized categories using modified fosphenytoin dictionary terminology. These categories are used in the tables and listings below with the frequencies representing the proportion of individuals exposed to fosphenytoin or comparative therapy. The prescriber should be aware that these figures cannot be used to predict the frequency of adverse events in the course of usual medical practice where patient characteristics and other factors may differ from those prevailing during clinical studies. Similarly, the cited frequencies cannot be directly compared with figures obtained from other clinical investigations involving different treatments, uses or investigators. An inspection of these frequencies, however, does provide the prescribing physician with one basis to estimate the relative contribution of drug and nondrug factors to the adverse event incidences in the population studied.

Incidence in Controlled Clinical Trials—I.V. Administration To Patients With Epilepsy or Neurosurgical Patients: Table II (on following page) lists treatment-emergent adverse events that occurred in at least 2% of patients treated with i.v. fosphenytoin at the maximum dose and rate in a randomized, double-blind, controlled clinical trial where the rates for phenytoin and fosphenytoin administration would have resulted in equivalent systemic exposure to phenytoin.

Incidence in Controlled Trials—I.M. Administration to Patients With Epilepsy: Table III (on following page) lists treatment-emergent adverse events that occurred in at least 2% of fosphenytoin-treated patients in a double-blind, randomized, controlled clinical trial of adult epilepsy patients receiving either i.m. fosphenytoin substituted for oral Dilantin or continuing oral Dilantin. Both treatments were administered for 5 days.

Adverse Events During All Clinical Trials: Fosphenytoin has been administered to 859 individuals during all clinical trials. All adverse events seen at least twice are listed in the following, except those already included in previous tables and listings. Events are further classified within body system categories and enumerated in order of decreasing frequency using the following definitions: frequent adverse events are defined as those occurring in greater than 1/100 individuals; infrequent adverse events are those occurring in 1/100 to 1/1 000 individuals.

Body As a Whole: Frequent: fever, injection-site reaction, infection, chills, face edema, injection-site pain. Infrequent: sepsis, injection-site inflammation, injection-site edema, injection-site hemorrhage, flu syndrome, malaise, generalized edema, shock, photosensitivity reaction, cachexia, cryptococcosis.

Cardiovascular: Frequent: hypertension. Infrequent: cardiac arrest, migraine, syncope, cerebral hemorrhage, palpitation, sinus bradycardia, atrial flutter, bundle branch block, cardiomegaly, cerebral infarct, postural hypotension, pulmonary embolus, QT interval prolongation, thrombophlebitis, ventricular extrasystoles, congestive heart failure.

Digestive: Frequent: constipation. Infrequent: dyspepsia, diarrhea, anorexia, gastrointestinal hemorrhage, increased salivation, liver function tests abnormal, tenesmus, tongue edema, dysphagia, flatulence, gastritis, ileus.

Endocrine: Infrequent: diabetes insipidus.

Hematologic and Lymphatic: Infrequent: thrombocytopenia, anemia, leukocytosis, cyanosis, hypochromic anemia, leukopenia, lymphadenopathy, petechia.

Metabolic and Nutritional: Frequent: hypokalemia. Infrequent: hyperglycemia, hypophosphatemia, alkalosis, acidosis, dehydration, hyperkalemia, ketosis.

Table II—Cerebyx

Treatment-emergent Adverse Event Incidence Following I.V. Administration at the Maximum Dose and Rate to Patients With Epilepsy or Neurosurgical Patients

(Events in at Least 2% of Fosphenytoin-treated Patients)

Body System Adverse Event	I.V. Fosphenytoin N=90	I.V. Phenytoin N=22
Body as a Whole		
Pelvic Pain	4.4	0.0
Asthenia	2.2	0.0
Back Pain	2.2	0.0
Headache	2.2	4.5
Cardiovascular		
Hypotension	7.7	9.1
Vasodilatation	5.6	4.5
Tachycardia	2.2	0.0
Digestive		
Nausea	8.9	13.6
Tongue Disorder	4.4	0.0
Dry Mouth	4.4	4.5
Vomiting	2.2	9.1
Nervous		
Nystagmus	44.4	59.1
Dizziness	31.1	27.3
Somnolence	20.0	27.3
Ataxia	11.1	18.2
Stupor	7.7	4.5
Incoordination	4.4	4.5
Paresthesia	4.4	0.0
Extrapyramidal Syndrome	4.4	0.0
Tremor	3.3	9.1
Agitation	3.3	0.0
Hypesthesia	2.2	9.1
Dysarthria	2.2	0.0
Vertigo	2.2	0.0
Brain Edema	2.2	4.5
Skin and Appendages		
Pruritus	48.9	4.5
Special Senses		
Tinnitus	8.9	9.1
Diplopia	3.3	0.0
Taste Perversion	3.3	0.0
Amblyopia	2.2	9.1
Deafness	2.2	0.0

Table III—Cerebyx

Treatment-emergent Adverse Event Incidence Following Substitution of I.M. Fosphenytoin for Oral Dilantin in Patients With Epilepsy

(Events in at Least 2% of Fosphenytoin-treated Patients)

Body System Adverse Event	I.M. Fosphenytoin N=179	Oral Dilantin N=61
Body as a Whole		
Headache	8.9	4.9
Asthenia	3.9	3.3
Accidental Injury	3.4	6.6
Digestive		
Nausea	4.5	0.0
Vomiting	2.8	0.0
Hematologic and Lymphatic		
Ecchymosis	7.3	4.9
Nervous		
Nystagmus	15.1	8.2
Tremor	9.5	13.1
Ataxia	8.4	8.2
Incoordination	7.8	4.9
Somnolence	6.7	9.8
Dizziness	5.0	3.3
Paraesthesia	3.9	3.3
Reflexes Decreased	2.8	4.9
Skin and Appendages		
Pruritus	2.8	0.0

Musculoskeletal: Frequent: myasthenia. Infrequent: myopathy, leg cramps, arthralgia, myalgia.

Nervous: Frequent: reflexes increased, speech disorder, dysarthria, intracranial hypertension, thinking abnormal, nervousness, hypaesthesia. Infrequent: confusion, twitching, Babinski sign positive, circumoral paresthesia, hemiplegia, hypotonia, convulsion, extrapyramidal syndrome, insomnia, meningitis, depersonalization, CNS depression, depression, hypokinesia, hyperkinesia, brain edema, paralysis, psychosis, aphasia, emotional lability, coma, hyperesthesia, myoclonus, personality disorder, acute brain syndrome, encephalitis, subdural hematoma, encephalopathy, hostility, akathisia, amnesia, neurosis.

Respiratory: Frequent: pneumonia. Infrequent: pharyngitis, sinusitis, hyperventilation, rhinitis, apnea, aspiration pneumonia, asthma, dyspnea, atelectasis, cough increased, sputum increased, epistaxis, hypoxia, pneumothorax, hemoptysis, bronchitis.

Skin and Appendages: Frequent: rash. Infrequent: maculopapular rash, urticaria, sweating, skin discoloration, contact dermatitis, pustular rash, skin nodule.

Special Senses: Frequent: taste perversion. Infrequent: deafness, visual field defect, eye pain, conjunctivitis, photophobia, hyperacusis, mydriasis, parosmia, ear pain, taste loss.

Urogenital: Infrequent: urinary retention, oliguria, dysuria, vaginitis, albuminuria, genital edema, kidney failure, polyuria, urethral pain, urinary incontinence, vaginal moniliasis.

Overdose: There is no experience with fosphenytoin overdosage in humans. The median lethal dose of fosphenytoin given i.v. in mice and rats was 156 mg PE/kg and approximately 250 mg PE/kg, or about 0.6 and 2 times, respectively, the maximum human loading dose on a mg/m² basis. Signs of acute toxicity in animals included ataxia, labored breathing, ptosis, and hypoactivity.

Symptoms: Because fosphenytoin is a prodrug of phenytoin, the following information may be helpful. Initial symptoms of acute phenytoin toxicity are nystagmus, ataxia and dysarthria. Other signs include tremor, hyperreflexia, lethargy, slurred speech, nausea, vomiting, coma and hypotension. Depression of respiratory and circulatory systems leads to death. There are marked variations among individuals with respect to plasma phenytoin concentrations where toxicity occurs. Lateral gaze nystagmus usually appears at 80 µmol/L (20 µg/mL), ataxia at 119 µmol/L (30 µg/mL), and dysarthria and lethargy appear when the plasma concentration is over 159 µmol/L (40 µg/mL). However, phenytoin concentrations as high as 198 µmol/L (50 µg/mL) have been reported without evidence of toxicity. As much as 25 times the therapeutic phenytoin dose has been taken, resulting in plasma phenytoin concentrations over 396 µmol/L (100 µg/mL), with complete recovery.

Treatment: Treatment is nonspecific since there is no known antidote to fosphenytoin or phenytoin overdosage. The adequacy of the respiratory and circulatory systems should be carefully observed, and appropriate supportive measures employed. Hemodialysis can be considered since phenytoin is not completely bound to plasma proteins. Total exchange transfusion has been used in the treatment of severe intoxication in children. In acute overdosage the possibility of other CNS depressants, including alcohol, should be borne in mind.

Formate and phosphate are metabolites of fosphenytoin and therefore may contribute to signs of toxicity following overdosage. Signs of formate toxicity are similar to those of methanol toxicity and are associated with severe anion-gap metabolic acidosis. Large amounts of phosphate, delivered rapidly, could potentially cause hypocalcemia with paresthesia, muscle spasms, and seizures. Ionized free calcium levels can be measured and, if low, used to guide treatment.

Dosage: The dose, concentration in dosing solutions, and infusion rate of i.v. fosphenytoin is expressed as phenytoin sodium equivalents (PE) to avoid the need to perform molecular weight-based adjustments when converting between fosphenytoin and phenytoin sodium doses. Fosphenytoin should always be prescribed and dispensed in phenytoin sodium equivalent units (PE). Fosphenytoin has important differences in administration from those for parenteral phenytoin sodium (see below).

Phenytoin doses are usually selected to attain therapeutic plasma total phenytoin concentrations of 40 to 80 µmol/L (10 to 20 µg/mL), (unbound phenytoin concentrations of 4 to 8 µmol/L (1 to 2 µg/mL)). Following fosphenytoin administration, it is recommended that phenytoin concentrations not be monitored until conversion to phenytoin is essentially complete. This occurs within approximately 2 hours after the end of i.v. infusion and 4 hours after i.m. injection.

Prior to complete conversion, commonly used immunoanalytical techniques, such as TDx/TDxFLx (fluorescence polarization) and Emit 2 000 (enzyme multiplied), may significantly overestimate plasma phenytoin concentrations because of cross-reactivity with fosphenytoin. The TDx/TDxFLx assay is not recommended due to an unacceptable margin of error. The difference between predicted and actual phenytoin concentrations at 4 hours postdose is ≤20 µmol/L (5 µg/mL). The error is dependent on plasma phenytoin and fosphenytoin concentration (influenced by fosphenytoin dose, route and rate of administration, and time of sampling relative to dosing), and analytical method. Chromatographic assay methods accurately quantitate phenytoin concentrations in biological fluids in the presence of fosphenytoin. Prior to complete conversion, blood samples for phenytoin monitoring should be collected in tubes containing EDTA as an anticoagulant to minimize ex vivo conversion of fosphenytoin to phenytoin. However, even with specific assay methods, phenytoin concentrations measured before conversion of fosphenytoin is complete will not reflect phenytoin concentrations ultimately achieved. Products with particulate matter or discoloration should not be used. Prior to i.v infusion, dilute fosphenytoin in 5% dextrose or 0.9% saline solution for injection to a concentration ranging from 1.5 to 25 mg PE/mL.

Status Epilepticus: The loading dose of fosphenytoin is 15 to 20 mg PE/kg administered at 100 to 150 mg PE/min.

Because of the risk of hypotension, fosphenytoin should be administered no faster than 150 mg PE/min. Continuous monitoring of the ECG, blood pressure, and respiratory function is essential and the patient should be observed throughout the period where maximal serum phenytoin concentrations occur, approximately 10 to 20 minutes after the end of fosphenytoin infusions.

Because the full antiepileptic effect of phenytoin, whether given as fosphenytoin or parenteral phenytoin, is not immediate, other measures, including concomitant administration of an i.v. benzodiazepine, will usually be necessary for the control of status epilepticus.

The loading dose should be followed by maintenance doses of fosphenytoin, or phenytoin, either orally or parenterally.

If administration of fosphenytoin does not terminate seizures, the use of other anticonvulsants and other appropriate measures should be considered.

I.M. fosphenytoin should not be used in the treatment of status epilepticus because therapeutic phenytoin concentrations may not be reached as quickly as with i.v. administrations. If i.v. access is impossible, loading doses of fosphenytoin have been given by the i.m. route for other indications.

Nonemergent Loading and Maintenance Dosing: The loading dose of fosphenytoin is 10 to 20 mg PE/kg given i.v. or i.m. The rate of administration for i.v fosphenytoin should be no greater than 150 mg PE/min. Continuous monitoring of the ECG, blood pressure, and respiratory function is essential and the patient should be observed throughout the period where maximal serum phenytoin concentrations occur, approximately 10 to 20 minutes after the end of fosphenytoin infusions.

The initial daily maintenance dose of fosphenytoin is 4 to 6 mg PE/kg/day.

I.M. or I.V. Substitution For Oral Phenytoin Therapy: Fosphenytoin can be substituted for oral phenytoin sodium therapy at the same total daily dose.

Dilantin capsules are approximately 90% bioavailable by the oral route. Phenytoin, supplied as fosphenytoin, is 100% bioavailable by both the i.m. and i.v. routes. For this reason, plasma phenytoin concentrations may increase modestly when i.m. or i.v. fosphenytoin is substituted for oral phenytoin sodium therapy.

The rate of administration for i.v. fosphenytoin should be no greater than 150 mg PE/min.

In controlled trials, i.m. fosphenytoin was administered as a single daily dose utilizing either 1 or 2 injection sites. Some patients may require more frequent dosing.

Dosing in Special Populations: Patients with Renal or Hepatic Disease: Due to an increased fraction of unbound phenytoin in patients with renal or hepatic disease, or in those with hypoalbuminemia, the interpretation of total phenytoin plasma concentrations should be made with caution (see Pharmacology, Special Populations). Unbound phenytoin concentrations may be more useful in these patient populations. After i.v. fosphenytoin administration to patients with renal and/or hepatic disease, or in those with hypoalbuminemia, fosphenytoin clearance to phenytoin may be increased without a similar increase in phenytoin clearance. This has the potential to increase the frequency and severity of adverse events (see Precautions).

Geriatrics: Age does not have a significant impact on the pharmacokinetics of fosphenytoin following administration. Phenytoin clearance is decreased slightly in elderly patients and lower or less frequent dosing may be required.

Cerebyx (cont'd)

Children: The safety of fosphenytoin in pediatric patients has not been established.
Compatibility: Fosphenytoin added to 5% dextrose or 0.9% saline solution for injection in a concentration range from 2.5 to 40 mg/mL is stable for 8 hours at room temperature or 24 hours when stored under refrigeration (2 to 8°C).

Fosphenytoin is for parenteral use only. As with all parenteral formulations, fosphenytoin vials should be inspected visually for particulate matter and discoloration before administration whenever solution and container permit. Products with particulate matter or discoloration should be discarded.

Supplied: Each mL of injection contains: fosphenytoin sodium 75 mg as heptahydrate, equivalent to phenytoin sodium 50 mg after administration. Nonmedicinal ingredients: tromethamine buffer (12 mg/mL) adjusted to pH 8.6 to 9.0 with either hydrochloric acid or sodium hydroxide and water for injection. Single-dose vials of 2 mL, packages of 5. Single-dose vials of 10 mL, packages of 1. Store under refrigeration at 2 to 8°C. The product should not be stored at room temperature for more than 48 hours. Vials that develop particulate matter should be discarded.

New Product 1998

CERUBIDINE® Ⓟ

Rhône-Poulenc Rorer

Daunorubicin

Antimitotic—Antibiotic

Pharmacology: Daunorubicin inhibits the synthesis of nucleic acids; its effect on desoxyribonucleic acid is particularly rapid and marked. Ribonucleic acid is more gradually affected.

It appears that the action of the drug is the result of the formation of a complex with desoxyribonucleic acid in the cell nucleus; this blocks the site of action of the polymerases and gives daunorubicin a cytostatic activity.

Daunorubicin displays an immunosuppressive action.

Daunorubicin has no effect on respiration or cellular glycolysis up to elevated concentrations which would inhibit cell growth.

It exerts an antiviral effect on the herpes and on the vaccine viruses of the desoxyribonucleic acid group, but not on the polio or influenza virus of the ribonucleic acid group.

Daunorubicin is inactive when administered orally.
Teratogenicity: No teratogenic effects have been observed in the chicken embryo, even at embryotoxic doses. In the mouse, prolonged treatment at a dose of 1.15 mg/kg s.c. daily did not interfere with gestation or produce any teratogenic effects.

In rabbits, doses of 90 µg/kg and 250 µg/kg i.v. induced 66% and 100% abortions respectively; in some fetuses, abnormalities which could not be attributed to the drug, were observed.

Indications: The initial treatment of myeloblastic and acute lymphoblastic leukemias. Daunorubicin can also induce a remission in patients suffering from chronic myeloid leukemia, reticulosarcoma, Ewing or Wilms' tumors and lymphosarcoma.

Precautions: Daunorubicin induces medullary aplasia and leukopenia. **It is therefore imperative that patients be protected against infection during the period of aplasia.**

At the start of therapy, the increase in uric acid in the blood due to leukocyte degradation can be controlled by administering allopurinol and liquids to stimulate urine excretion. Caution must be exercised in patients with renal insufficiency.

Daunorubicin can cause tissue necrosis, thus great care must be taken to inject the product directly into the vein.

When daunorubicin is employed in association with other anticancer agents, the dosage of each should be reduced so as to minimize the total toxic effect.

Some instances of cardiotoxicity may be observed when a cumulative dose of 25 mg/kg has been reached; in general, this dose must not be exceeded except in certain desperate cases where 30 mg/kg can be administered. Likewise, because of possible cardiotoxicity, the drug must not be administered to patients who exhibit myocardial lesions or to those above 75 years of age.

Before initiating treatment with daunorubicin, physical examination, appropriate x-rays and ECG should be performed and repeated at regular intervals thereafter, particularly when the cumulative dose has reached 15 mg/kg.

Daunorubicin should be employed only as a treatment to induce a remission, and not as maintenance therapy.

Adverse Effects: At the start of treatment, the patient may experience anorexia, nausea and vomiting. These are transient effects and generally do not require an interruption of treatment. Antiemetics may help relieve vomiting.

Abdominal pain, constipation or diarrhea, alopecia, rash, petechiae or purpura may be observed during therapy.

Some cases of thrombocytopenia and anemia have been reported during the first or second week of treatment. These phenomena are transient and corrective measures such as blood or platelet transfusions are rarely required.

During the aplastic phase, cases of localized infection have occurred, particularly in the buccal cavity and pharynx. Septicemia not responsive to antibiotics has also been reported.

Some cases of cardiopathy attended by rhythm abnormalities, electrical modifications and indications of cardiac insufficiency have been observed in patients receiving a cumulative dose exceeding 30 mg/kg.

In young patients, the urine occasionally acquires a red tint. This coloration is due to the presence of daunorubicin and its metabolites and has no clinical significance.

During treatment with combinations of daunorubicin with other antileukemic agents, there have been occurrences of myalgia and neuropathy. These symptoms, already associated with the use of other agents, have not been directly attributed to daunorubicin.

Dosage: Daunorubicin is reserved mainly for the initial therapy of acute leukemia and other forms of malignant tumors which are sensitive to the drug.

It is administered by the i.v. route only. After dilution in 4 mL of sterile water for injection, daunorubicin is injected into the tubing of a running infusion of 100 or 250 mL of isotonic solution. The infusion is performed rapidly to avoid local stasis.

Freshly prepared solution may be kept for a period of 24 hours at room temperature or 48 hours in a refrigerator.
Initial treatment: A) Daunorubicin Alone: Acute Lymphoblastic Leukemia: Daunorubicin is instituted at a daily dose of 1 mg/kg (30 mg/m²) over a period of from 3 to 6 days. If, after this first administration, the number of white cells is less than 1 500, maintenance therapy is begun. However, if a partial remission is obtained, but the number of leukocytes is greater than 1 500, treatment should be repeated 1 or more times, as necessary, based on the hematological response. As soon as the remission is obtained, maintenance treatment can be started. The total dose during the initial treatment should not, as a rule, exceed 20 mg/kg.
Acute Myeloblastic, Granulocytic and Promyelocytic Leukemias: A daily dose of 2 mg/kg (60 mg/m²) is administered for a period of from 3 to 6 days, plus 1 or 2 supplementary injections which are given a few days after a remission is obtained if the blasts have not completely disappeared from the peripheral blood or marrow. The total dose varies from 3 to 22.5 mg/kg (90 to 600 mg/m²). During the initial therapy, blood should be examined every day and marrow 2 or 3 times a week.
B) Combination Therapy: When daunorubicin is given in association with other antileukemic medication, it must be given every 2 or 3 days to avoid complete marrow aplasia; the treatment extends for a period of 2 to 4 weeks. Hemograms should be conducted before each injection and if they manifest a severe perturbation of the blood count, the medication should be stopped.

The dosage is from 1 mg/kg per injection every 2 or 3 days up to a total of 12 mg/kg. If only an incomplete remission is obtained after this treatment, daunorubicin can be continued up to the maximum dose of 20 mg/kg which must not be exceeded during any one treatment period. As soon as a complete remission is obtained the drug is withdrawn and maintenance treatment instituted.
Maintenance Treatment: Any standard chemotherapeutic agent may be employed during maintenance therapy. If the marrow is not completely ablastic in the course of 4 weeks, a weekly injection of 1 mg/kg daunorubicin may be given.
Cumulative Doses: As a rule the total cumulative dose should not exceed 25 mg/kg, e.g., approximately 500 mg/m² for a child of 10 kg; 600 mg/m² for a child of 20 kg; 750 mg/m² for a child of 30 kg and 900 mg/m² for an adult of 60 kg. In patients who have become resistant to all therapy and for whom a final effort is required to induce a remission, the total cumulative dose can be extended to 30 mg/kg.
Chronic Myeloid Leukemia: Injections of 1 to 2 mg/kg may be administered every day or every other day up to a total dose of 6 to 12 mg/kg.

Supplied: Each vial contains: daunorubicin 20 mg. Nonmedicinal ingredients: D-mannitol. Boxes of 1.

CERUMENEX®

Purdue Frederick

Triethanolamine Polypeptide Oleate-condensate

Cerumenolytic

Indications: For removal of impacted cerumen. Cleansing prior to aural examination, treatment, or audiometry. Should not be used for routine wax removal or cleaning of the ears.

Contraindications: Perforated eardrum. Middle ear infection or severe inflammatory or atopic dermatitis in the external ear. Positive patch test. History of untoward reaction to Cerumenex.

Precautions: Should be used with extreme caution in patients with demonstrable dermatologic idiosyncrasies or with a history of allergic reactions in general.

In case of doubt as to the safety of use, a patch test should be performed by placing a drop of Cerumenex Drops on the flexor surface of the arm (or forearm) and covering with a small bandage strip. The test results are read and interpreted after 24 hours. A positive reaction indicates the probability of an allergic reaction following instillation in the ear.

Patients should be instructed **not** to exceed a 15 to 20 minute exposure of the ear canal to the medication, nor to use the drops more frequently than prescribed. If an untoward reaction occurs, the drops should be discontinued.

When administering care should be taken to avoid undue exposure of the periaural skin during the instillation and the flushing out of the medication. If the medication comes in contact with the skin, the area should be washed with soap and water. Use of proper technique will help avoid such undue exposure.

Adverse Effects: Localized dermatitis reactions were reported in about 1% of 2 700 patients treated, ranging from a very mild erythema and pruritus of the external canal to a severe eczematoid reaction involving the external ear and periauricular tissue, generally with duration of 2 to 10 days. In all cases, complete and uneventful resolution occurred without supplemental therapy. Such therapy may consist of only symptomatic relief in mild cases and may include anti-inflammatory agents when indicated.

Dosage: Fill ear canal with Cerumenex Drops, insert cotton plug and allow to remain **only 15 to 20 minutes,** then gently flush ear with warm water (avoid excessive pressure).

Information for the Patient: See Blue Section—Information for the Patient "Cerumenex".

Supplied: Each mL of clear solution contains: triethanolamine polypeptide oleate-condensate 10% in propylene glycol with chlorbutanol 0.5%. Bottles of 8 and 15 mL with blunt end dropper.

CERUMOL®

Solvay Pharma

Paradichlorobenzene—Chlorbutol—Oil of terebinth

Cerumenolytic

Indications: Removal of cerumen from the external auditory meatus.

Contraindications: Perforated ear drum, otitis externa, seborrheic dermatitis or eczema affecting the external ear. Hypersensitivity to any of the components.

Precautions: Cerumol contains peanut oil, and although there have been no reports of any reaction, patients allergic to peanuts should use Cerumol only under the advice of their physician. For external use only.

Dosage: Instill 5 drops into the ear with head inclined when lying down. If necessary plug the ear with cotton wool moistened with the preparation. This may be repeated 2 or 3 times a day for several days. Unless the earwax is unusually hard it should run out of its own accord. If condition persists or worsens, consult your physician.

Supplied: Each mL of clear oily preparation contains: paradichlorobenzene 2%, chlorbutol 5% and oil of terebinth 10%. Nonmedicinal ingredients: peanut oil. Bottles of 11 mL, packaged with a separate dropper assembly in a tamper evident carton. After dropper is inserted, use within 6 months. Store at controlled room temperature (15 to 30°C).

CERVIDIL™ Ⓟ

Ferring

Dinoprostone

Prostaglandin

Pharmacology: Dinoprostone (PGE_2) is a naturally occurring biomolecule. It is found in low concentrations in most tissues of the body and functions as a local hormone. As with any local hormone, it is very rapidly metabolized in the tissues of synthesis. The rate limiting step for inactivation is regulated by the enzyme 15-hydroxyprostaglandin dehydrogenase (PGDH). Any PGE_2 that escapes local inactivation is rapidly cleared to the extent of 95% on the first pass through the pulmonary circulation.

In pregnancy, PGE_2 is secreted continuously by the fetal membranes and placenta and plays an important role in the final events leading to the initiation of labor. It is known that PGE_2 stimulates the production of $PGF_{2\alpha}$ which in turn sensitizes the myometrium to endogenous or exogenously administrated oxytocin. Although PGE_2 is capable of initiating uterine contractions and may interact with oxytocin to increase uterine contractility, the available evidence indicates, that in the concentrations found during the early part of labor, PGE_2 plays an important role in cervical ripening without affecting uterine contractions. This distinction serves as the basis for considering cervical ripening and induction of labor, usually by the use of oxytocin, as two separate processes.

PGE_2 plays an important role in the complex set of biochemical and structural alterations involved in cervical ripening. Cervical ripening involves a marked relaxation of the cervical smooth muscle fibers of the uterine cervix which must be transformed from a rigid structure to a softened, yielding and dilated configuration to allow passage of the fetus through the birth canal. This process involves activation of the enzyme collagenase, which is responsible for digestion of some of the structural collagen network of the cervix. This is associated with a concomitant increase in the amount of hydrophilic glycosaminoglycan, hyaluronic acid, and a decrease in dermatan sulfate. Failure of the cervix to undergo these natural physiologic changes, usually assessed by the method described by Bishop, prior to the onset of effective uterine contractions, results in an unfavorable outcome for successful vaginal delivery and may result in fetal compromise. It is estimated that in approximately 5% of the pregnancies the cervix does not ripen normally. In an additional 10 to 11% of pregnancies, labor must be induced for medical or obstetric reasons prior to the time of cervical ripening.

Clinical Studies: Treatment success in 3 double-blind, placebo-controlled studies was defined as Bishop score increase at 12 hours of ≥ 3, vaginal delivery within 12 hours or Bishop score at 12 hours ≥ 6. Results in a total of 603 (283 active, 320 placebo) qualified patients demonstrated success rates of 69.4% and 71.7% for primips and multips, respectively compared to placebo values of 29.7% for both groups.

Of the 658 patients evaluable for safety in the double-blind trials (320 active, 338 placebo), 9 patients (2.8%) who received the active insert experienced maternal hyperstimulation associated with fetal distress, while 15 patients (4.7%) experienced hyperstimulation without fetal distress. Removal of the insert resulted in relief of the symptomatology and in no case was there evidence of a neonatal adverse event.

Indications: For the initiation and/or continuation of cervical ripening in patients at or near term in whom there is a medical or obstetrical indication for the induction of labor.

Contraindications: Patients with known hypersensitivity to prostaglandins. Patients in whom there is clinical suspicion or definite evidence of fetal distress where delivery is not imminent. Patients with unexplained vaginal bleeding during this pregnancy. Patients in whom there is evidence or strong suspicion of marked cephalopelvic disproportion. Patients in whom oxytocic drugs are contraindicated or when prolonged contraction of the uterus may be detrimental to fetal safety or uterine integrity (previous cesarean section or major uterine surgery). Multipara with 6 or more previous term pregnancies. Patients with a history of difficult labor and/or traumatic delivery. Patients with overdistention of uterus (multiple pregnancy, polyhydramnios). Patients with ruptured membranes. Patients with fetal malpresentation. Patients with a history of epilepsy whose seizures are poorly controlled. Dinoprostone vaginal insert should not be used simultaneously with other oxytocics (see Warnings). Dinoprostone vaginal insert should not be used when there is a history of, or current pelvic inflammatory disease, unless adequate prior treatment has been instituted.

Warnings: For hospital use only. Dinoprostone vaginal insert should be administered only by trained obstetrical personnel in a hospital setting with appropriate obstetrical care facilities.

Precautions: General: Since prostaglandins potentiate the effect of oxytocin, dinoprostone vaginal insert must be removed before oxytocin administration is initiated and the patient's uterine activity carefully monitored for uterine hyperstimulation.

If uterine hyperstimulation is encountered or if labor commences, the vaginal insert should be removed. Dinoprostone vaginal insert should also be removed prior to amniotomy. The vaginal insert should be removed if there is evidence of maternal systemic adverse PGE_2 effects such as nausea, vomiting, hypotension or tachycardia.

Caution should be exercised in the administration of dinoprostone for cervical ripening in patients with a history of previous uterine hypertonicity, glaucoma, or a history of childhood asthma, even though there have been no asthma attacks in adulthood.

Uterine activity, fetal status and the progression of cervical dilatation and effacement should be carefully monitored whenever the dinoprostone vaginal insert is in place. Any evidence of uterine hyperstimulation, sustained uterine contractions, fetal distress, or other fetal or maternal adverse reactions, should be a cause for consideration of removal of the insert. The possibility of uterine rupture and/or cervical laceration should be borne in mind where hypertonic myometrial contractions are sustained.

Cephalopelvic relationships should be carefully evaluated before the use of dinoprostone vaginal insert.

Prolonged treatment of newborn infants with prostaglandin E_1 can induce proliferation of bone. There is no evidence that short-term administration of prostaglandin E_2 can cause similar bone effects.

Patients with severe renal disease and/or severe hepatic disease accompanied by metabolic aberrations should be dosed with caution.

Drug Interactions: Dinoprostone may augment the activity of oxytocic agents and their concomitant use is not recommended. A dosing interval of at least 30 minutes is recommended for the sequential use of oxytocin following the removal of the dinoprostone vaginal insert. No other drug interactions have been identified.

Dependence Liability: No drug abuse or dependence has been seen with the use of the dinoprostone vaginal insert.

Carcinogenicity: Long-term carcinogenicity and fertility studies have not been conducted with dinoprostone vaginal insert. No evidence of mutagenicity has been observed with prostaglandin E_2 in the Unscheduled DNA Synthesis Assay, the Micronucleus Test, or Ames Assay.

Pregnancy: Animal studies indicate that the prostaglandins may be teratogenic. No effect would be expected clinically, when used as indicated, since dinoprostone is administered after the period of organogenesis. Any dose of the drug that produces sustained increased uterine tone could put the embryo or fetus at risk.

Adverse Effects: Dinoprostone is well tolerated. In placebo-controlled trials in which 658 women were entered and 320 received active therapy (218 without retrieval system, 102 with retrieval system), the following events were reported in Table I.

Table I—Cervidil

Total Drug Related Adverse Events

	Controlled Studies[a]		Study 101-801[b]	
	Active (%)	Placebo (%)	Active (%)	Placebo (%)
Uterine hyperstimulation with fetal distress	2.8	0.3	2.9	0
Uterine hyperstimulation without fetal distress	4.7	0	2.0	0
Fetal distress without uterine hyperstimulation	3.8	1.2	2.9	1.0
N	320	338	102	104

[a] Controlled studies (with and without retrieval system).
[b] Controlled study (with retrieval system).

Drug related fever, nausea, vomiting, diarrhea, and abdominal pain were noted in less than 1% of patients who received dinoprostone.

In Study 101 to 801 (with the retrieval system) all cases of hyperstimulation reversed within 2 to 13 minutes of removal of the product. Tocolytics were required in 1 of the 5 cases.

In cases of fetal distress, when product removal was thought advisable, there was a return to normal rhythm and no neonatal sequelae.

Five-minute Apgar scores were 7 or above in 98.2% (646/658) of studied neonates whose mothers participated in placebo-controlled studies with dinoprostone vaginal insert. A 3-year pediatric follow-up study in 121 infants whose mothers received PGE_2, found no significant differences from a control group on physical examination or psychomotor evaluation.

Overdose: Symptoms and Treatment: Dinoprostone vaginal insert is used as a single dosage in a single application. Overdosage is usually manifested by uterine hyperstimulation which may be accompanied by fetal distress and is responsive to removal of the insert. Other treatment must be symptomatic, since to date, clinical experience with prostaglandin antagonists is insufficient.

The use of beta-adrenergic agents should be considered in the event of undesirable increased uterine activity.

Dosage: The dosage of dinoprostone in the vaginal insert is 10 mg designed to be released at approximately 0.3 mg/h over a 12-hour period. The vaginal insert should be removed upon onset of active labor or 12 hours after insertion.

One vaginal insert is placed transversely in the posterior fornix of the vagina immediately after removal from its foil package. The insertion of the vaginal insert does not require sterile conditions. The vaginal insert must not be used without its retrieval system. There is no need for previous warming of the product. A minimal amount of K-Y jelly (or other water-miscible lubricant) may be used to assist in insertion of the vaginal insert. Care should be taken not to permit excess contact or coating with the lubricant and thus prevent optimal swelling and release of dinoprostone from the vaginal insert. Patients should remain in the supine position for 2 hours following insertion, but thereafter may be ambulatory.

Supplied: Each vaginal insert contains: dinoprostone 10 mg (prostaglandin E_2) dispersed throughout its matrix described as 236 mg of a cross-linked polyethylene oxide/urethane polymer which is a semi-transparent, beige colored, flat, 0.8 mm thick rectangular slab with rounded corners measuring 29 mm by 9.5 mm, releasing approximately 0.3 mg/h PGE_2 over a 12-hour period. The reservoir of 10 mg dinoprostone serves to maintain constant release. The retrieval system consists of a one-piece knitted polyester pouch and withdrawal tape. This ensures easy and reliable removal of the insert when the patient's requirement for PGE_2 has been fulfilled or an obstetric event makes it necessary to stop further drug administration. The insert and its retrieval system, made of polyester yarn, are nontoxic and when placed in a moist environment, absorb water, swell, and release dinoprostone. Cartons of 1. The retrieval system is wound around the insert and the product is enclosed in an aluminum sleeve which is contained in a foil (aluminum/polyethylene) pack. Vaginal inserts exposed to high humidity will absorb moisture from the air and thereby alter the release characteristics of dinoprostone. Once used, the vaginal insert should be discarded. Store in a freezer between −20 and −10°C.

Reviewed 1998

C.E.S.® Ⓟ

ICN

Conjugated Estrogens

Estrogens

Pharmacology: Conjugated estrogens are a mixture of estrogens derived from plant sterols and contain the sodium salts of water-soluble estrogen sulfates. C.E.S. is derived from plant sterols, only. Conjugated estrogens contain estrone, equilin, 17-α-dihydroequilin, 17-α estradiol, equilenin and 17 α dihydroequilenin as salts of their sulfate esters.

Actions: Metabolic and Somatic Effects: Estrogens are responsible for the development and maintenance of the female reproductive system and secondary sex characteristics. Estrogens cause growth and development of the vagina, uterus and fallopian tubes, and the enlargement of the breasts. Indirectly, estrogens contribute to the shaping of the skeleton, maintenance of tone and elasticity of urogenital structures, cause changes in the epiphyses of the long bones producing pubertal growth spurt and termination, axillary and pubic hair growth, and pigmentation of the nipples and genitals. Estrogens affect calcium and phosphorus metabolism and are involved in maintaining normal bone structure. In prolonged estrogen deficiency states, the administration of estrogens may alter associated degenerative bone changes.

C.E.S. (cont'd)

Effect on Menstruation: An ebb and rise of the female gonadal hormone produces the normal menstrual cycle. In the pre- and anovulatory cycle, estrogens are the primary determinants for the onset of menstruation. Estrogens do not induce ovulation. Estrogen levels rise during the first half of the menstrual cycle. At midpoint in the second half of the cycle, the corpus luteum produces high levels of both estrogens and progesterone. Decline of estrogenic activity at the end of the menstrual cycle commonly brings on menstruation, although the cessation of progesterone secretion is the most important factor in this phase of the mature ovulatory cycle.
Effects on Nervous System: Estrogens also affect the psychologic and emotional aspects of feminine behavior. As estrogen levels increase during the menstrual cycle, women experience a sense of well-being and vigor. In the postmenopausal period, after the decline of endogenous estrogen production, estrogen administration aids in relieving nervous symptoms, such as anxiety, depression and irritability.

Indications: Replacement therapy in naturally occurring or surgically induced estrogen deficiency states associated with the climacteric, including the menopausal and postmenopausal syndromes; senile vaginitis and kraurosis vulvae, with or without pruritus; female hypogonadism; amenorrhea; primary ovarian failure; and for estrogen deficiency-induced osteoporosis, when combined with other important therapeutic measures such as a diet, calcium, physiotherapy, and good general health-promoting measures. For abnormal uterine bleeding due to hormonal imbalance in the absence of organic pathologic changes such as submucosal fibroids or uterine cancer. For inoperable progressing prostatic cancer (for palliation only when castration is not feasible, or when castration failures or delayed escape following a response to castration have occurred); breast cancer (for palliation only in women more than 5 years past the menopause with progressing inoperable or roentgen-resistant disease).

Contraindications: Should not be administered to patients with active hepatic dysfunction or disease, especially of the obstructive type; or a personal history of breast or endometrial cancer, except in special circumstances.

Endometrial hyperplasia is also a contraindication for estrogen therapy without accompanying progestogen.

Also contraindicated in the following situations: undiagnosed vaginal bleeding; a history of cerebrovascular accident, coronary thrombosis or in the presence of classical migraine; a history of thrombophlebitis or thromboembolic disease; partial or complete loss of vision or diplopia due to ophthalmic vascular disease; when pregnancy is suspected.

Warnings: Before conjugated estrogen is administered, the patient should have a complete physical examination including a blood pressure determination. Breast and pelvic organs should be examined and a Papanicolaou smear should be taken.

The first follow-up examination should be done preferably within 6 months after initiation of treatment. Thereafter, examinations should be made once a year. At each annual visit, examination should include those procedures outlined above that were done at the initial visit.

If any surgical procedures are performed, the pathologist should be advised of the patient's therapy when specimens are sent for examination. Liver function tests should be made periodically in subjects who have, or are suspected of having, hepatic disease.

If abnormal vaginal bleeding occurs during therapy, suction aspiration or curettage should be performed to rule out the possibility of uterine malignancy.

Although the estrogen content of oral contraceptive therapy has been associated with an increased risk of various thromboembolic, thrombotic and vascular diseases, to date no such increased risk in postmenopausal users of estrogens has been detected. Nevertheless, the physician should be alert to the earliest manifestations of thrombotic disorders (thrombophlebitis, retinal thrombosis, cerebral embolism, and pulmonary embolism). If these occur or are suspected, estrogen therapy should be discontinued immediately.

In patients with metastatic carcinoma and hypercalcemia, estrogen medication should be used with caution. Three independent retrospective studies have reported an association between postmenopausal oral estrogen therapy and an increased risk of endometrial carcinoma. These studies however, lacked information regarding certain important intrinsic risk factors of the patients (especially pretreatment endogenous hormonal status) and the mode of administration of estrogen. The potential relationship of estrogen to endometrial carcinoma under clinical conditions has to be considered. However, a cause and effect relationship between estrogen administration and endometrial carcinoma cannot be established by these data at this time.

Precautions: Development of sudden enlargement, pain, or tenderness of uterine fibroid requires discontinuation of medication.

Estrogen may cause sodium and water retention. Where this may be undesirable such as in cardiac or renal dysfunction, epilepsy, or asthma, particular caution is indicated.

Elevation of blood pressure in previously normotensive or hypertensive patients necessitates cessation of medication.

Diabetic patients or those with a predisposition to diabetes should be observed closely to detect any alterations in carbohydrate metabolism.

When liver or endocrine function tests are indicated, the results should not be considered reliable unless therapy has been discontinued for 2 to 4 months.

Adverse Effects: The following adverse reactions have been reported with the use of estrogens in general. Some of these (indicated in brackets) have been documented with oral contraceptives specifically, and have not, up to now, been associated with cyclic menopausal or postmenopausal conjugated estrogen therapy.
Gastrointestinal: nausea, (anorexia, vomiting, abdominal cramps, bloating), cholestatic jaundice and increase in body weight.
Genitourinary: sodium and water retention, breakthrough bleeding, spotting and withdrawal bleeding, increased cervical mucus, endometrial hyperplasia, reactivation of endometriosis, (cystitis-like syndrome).
Endocrine and Metabolic: breast swelling and tenderness, increased blood sugar levels, and decreased glucose tolerance. If product is indicated in males add: gynecomastia, reduced potency and feminization.
CNS: headaches, mental depression, increase or decrease of libido, (mental depression, nervousness, dizziness, fatigue, irritability).
Dermatologic—Hypersensitivity: allergic reactions and rashes, chloasma, (hemorrhagic eruption, itching, erythema nodosum, and erythema multiforme, pigmentation of the skin, loss of scalp hair).
Cardiovascular: an increase in blood pressure in susceptible individuals and aggravation of migraine headaches.
Hematologic: A statistically significant association has been demonstrated between the use of oral contraceptive preparations containing estrogens and the following serious reactions: thrombophlebitis, pulmonary embolism and cerebral thrombosis. Although available evidence is suggestive of an association, such a relationship has been neither confirmed nor refuted for the following serious reactions: coronary thrombosis and neuro-ocular lesions (e.g., retinal thrombosis and optic neuritis); altered coagulation tests (increase in prothrombin and Factors VII, VIII, IX, X).

Overdose: Symptoms and Treatment: Excessive doses may result in nausea, vomiting and abdominal cramps, headaches, dizziness and general malaise. All of the ingested drug should be removed by gastric lavage and symptomatic treatment given.

Dosage: In general, estrogen should be given cyclically (21 to 25 days followed by a 5 to 7 day rest period) and in some cases with progestogen or androgen to avoid overstimulation of breast and endometrial tissues. The addition of sufficient progestogen to promote conversion of the endometrium is mandatory in those patients who are receiving sufficient unopposed estrogen to cause vaginal bleeding or endometrial hyperplasia. Obviously, abnormal vaginal bleeding in such patients is an indication for prompt diagnostic measures.

The dosage should be carefully adjusted to the individual needs of the patient, the lowest effective dosage should be used, and the requirement for estrogen therapy should be reassessed periodically.
Menopausal Symptoms: 0.3 to 1.25 mg daily, cyclically. Adjust dosage upward or downward according to severity of symptoms and response of the patient. For maintenance, adjust dosage to lowest level providing effective control. If the patient has not menstruated within the last 2 months or more, cyclic administration is started arbitrarily. If the patient is menstruating, cyclic administration is started on day 5 of bleeding. If breakthrough bleeding (bleeding or spotting during estrogen therapy) occurs, the C.E.S. dosage should be increased as needed to stop bleeding. In the following cycle, the same dosage should be administered as that used to stop breakthrough bleeding in the previous cycle. In subsequent cycles, the dosage should be gradually reduced to the lowest level which will maintain the patient symptom-free. If planned withdrawal bleeding is desirable, a progestogen may be added during the last 5 to 10 days of the usual recommended C.E.S. regimen.
Postmenopause: For the treatment of estrogen deficiency-induced degenerative changes (e.g., osteoporosis, atrophic vaginitis, kraurosis vulvae): 0.3 to 1.25 mg daily and cyclically. Adjust dosage to lowest effective level.
Hypogenitalism: In an attempt to attain sexual and somatic maturation: 2.5 to 7.5 mg daily, in divided doses for 21 days, followed by a rest period of 10 days' duration. If bleeding does not occur at the end of this period, the same dosage schedule is repeated. The number of courses of C.E.S. therapy necessary to produce bleeding may vary depending on the responsiveness of the endometrium. If bleeding occurs before the end of the 10-day period, a 20-day C.E.S.-progestogen cyclic regimen, as in amenorrhea, is recommended.
Amenorrhea: To reproduce the hormone pattern of the ovary, i.e., bleeding from a progestational endometrium, begin a 20-day C.E.S.-progestogen cyclic regimen: 2.5 to 7.5 mg daily in divided doses, for 20 days. During the last 5 days of estrogen therapy, oral progestogen is added. If bleeding occurs before this regimen is concluded, therapy is discontinued and may be resumed on the fifth day of bleeding.
Mammary Carcinoma: (for palliation in women with progressive inoperable or roentgen-resistant disease more than 5 years after the menopause) suggested dosage: 10 mg 3 times daily for a period of at least 3 months.
Prostatic Carcinoma: (for palliation when castration is not feasible or when castration failure or delayed escape has occurred: suggested dosage: 1.25 to 2.5 mg 3 times daily). The effectiveness of therapy can be judged by phosphatase determination as well as by symptomatic improvement of the patient.

Supplied: 0.3 mg: Each oval, green tablet contains: conjugated estrogens CSD 0.3 mg. Nonmedicinal ingredients: calcium phosphate, colloidal silicon dioxide, lactose, magnesium carbonate, microcrystalline cellulose, starch and stearic acid. Bottles of 100.

0.625 mg: Each oval, maroon tablet contains: conjugated estrogens CSD 0.625 mg. Nonmedicinal ingredients: calcium phosphate, colloidal silicon dioxide, lactose, magnesium carbonate, microcrystalline cellulose, starch and stearic acid. Bottles of 100 and 1 000.

0.9 mg: Each oval, pink tablet contains: conjugated estrogens CSD 0.9 mg. Nonmedicinal ingredients: calcium phosphate, colloidal silicon dioxide, lactose, magnesium carbonate, microcrystalline cellulose, starch and stearic acid. Bottles of 100.

1.25 mg: Each oval, yellow tablet contains: conjugated estrogens CSD 1.25 mg. Nonmedicinal ingredients: calcium phosphate, colloidal silicon dioxide, lactose, magnesium carbonate, microcrystalline cellulose, starch and stearic acid. Bottles of 100 and 1 000.

Reviewed 1998

CESAMET® Ⓝ
Lilly

Nabilone

Antiemetic

Pharmacology: Nabilone is a synthetic cannabinoid with antiemetic properties which have been found to be of value in the management of some patients with nausea and vomiting associated with cancer chemotherapy. It also has sedative and psychotropic effects.

After oral administration, comparable peak plasma levels of nabilone and of its carbinol metabolite were attained within 2 hours. The combined plasma concentrations of nabilone and of its carbinol metabolite accounted for, at most, 10 to 20% of the total radio-carbon concentration in plasma. The plasma half life of nabilone was approximately 2 hours, while that of the total radiocarbon was of the order of 35 hours.

Of the 2 major possible metabolic pathways, stereo-specific enzymatic reduction and direct enzymatic oxidation, the latter appears to be the more important in man.

The drug and its metabolites are eliminated mainly in the feces (approximately 65%) and to a lesser extent in the urine (approximately 20%). The major excretory pathway is the biliary system.

Indications: For the management of severe nausea and vomiting associated with cancer chemotherapy.

Contraindications: Sensitivity to marijuana or other cannabinoid agents, and in patients with a history of psychotic reactions.

Warnings: Nabilone should be used with extreme caution in patients with severe liver dysfunction and in those with a history of non-psychotic emotional disorders.

Nabilone should not be taken with alcohol, sedatives, hypnotics, or other psychotomimetic substances.

Pregnancy, Lactation and Children: Nabilone should not be used during pregnancy, in nursing mothers or in pediatric patients, since its safety under these conditions has not been established.

Precautions: Occupational Hazards: Since nabilone will often impair the mental and/or physical abilities required for the performance of potentially hazardous tasks, such as driving a car and operating machinery, the patient should be warned accordingly and should not be permitted to drive or engage in dangerous tasks until the effects of nabilone are no longer present.

Adverse psychiatric reactions can persist for 48 to 72 hours following cessation of treatment.

Since nabilone elevates supine and standing heart rates and causes postural hypotension, it should be used with caution in the elderly and in patients with hypertension or heart disease.

Drug Interactions: Potential interactions between nabilone, and diazepam; sodium secobarbital; alcohol or codeine were evaluated. The depressant effects of the combinations were additive. Psychomotor function was particularly impaired with concurrent use of diazepam.

Adverse Effects: The most frequently observed adverse reactions to nabilone and their incidences reported in the course of clinical trials were as follows: drowsiness (66.0%), vertigo (58.8%), psychological high (38.8%), dry mouth (21.6%), depression (14.0%), ataxia (12.8%), blurred vision (12.8%), sensation disturbance (12.4%), anorexia (7.6%), asthenia (7.6%), headache (7.2%), orthostatic hypotension (5.2%), euphoria (4.0%) and hallucinations (2.0%).

The following adverse reactions were observed in less than 1% of the patients who were administered nabilone in the course of the clinical trials: tachycardia, tremors, syncope, nightmares, distortion in the perception of time, confusion, dissociation, dysphoria, psychotic reactions and seizures.

Spontaneously Reported Adverse Events: The following adverse reactions listed in order of decreasing frequency by body system have been reported since nabilone has been marketed. All events are listed regardless of causality assessment.

Blood and Hematopoietic: leukopenia.

Cardiovascular: hypotension and tachycardia.

Eye and Ear: visual disturbances.

Gastrointestinal: dry mouth, nausea, vomiting and constipation.

CNS: hallucinations, CNS depression, CNS stimulation, ataxia, stupor, vertigo, convulsion and circumoral paresthesia.

Psychiatric: somnolence, confusion, euphoria, depression, dysphoria, depersonalization, anxiety, psychosis and emotional lability.

Miscellaneous and Ill-Defined Conditions: dizziness, headache, insomnia, abnormal thinking, chest pain, lack of effect, and face edema.

Overdose: Symptoms: Signs and symptoms which might be expected to occur are psychotic episodes including hallucinations, anxiety reactions, respiratory depression and coma (experience with cases of overdosage of more than 10 mg/day has not yet been reported).

Treatment: Overdose may be considered to have occurred, even at prescribed dosages, if disturbing psychiatric symptoms are present. In these cases, the patient should be observed in a quiet environment and supportive measures, including reassurance, should be used. Subsequent doses should be withheld until patients have returned to their baseline mental status; routine dosing may then be resumed if clinically indicated. In such instances, a lower initiating dose is suggested.

If psychotic episodes occur, the patient should be managed conservatively, if possible. For moderate psychotic episodes and anxiety reactions, verbal support and comforting may be sufficient. In more severe cases, antipsychotic drugs may be useful; however, the utility of antipsychotic drugs in cannabinoid psychosis has not been systematically evaluated. Support for their use is drawn from limited experience using antipsychotic agents to manage cannabis overdoses. Because of the potential for drug-drug interactions (e.g., additive CNS depressant effects due to nabilone and chlorpromazine), such patients should be closely monitored.

Protect the patient's airway and support ventilation and perfusion. Meticulously monitor and maintain, within acceptable limits, the patient's vital signs, blood gases, serum electrolytes, etc. Absorption of drugs from the gastrointestinal tract may be decreased by giving activated charcoal, which, in many cases, is more effective than emesis or lavage; consider charcoal instead of or in addition to gastric emptying. Repeated doses of charcoal over time may hasten elimination of some drugs that have been absorbed. Safeguard the patient's airway when employing gastric emptying or charcoal.

The use of forced diuresis, peritoneal dialysis, hemodialysis, charcoal hemoperfusion or cholestyramine has not been reported. In the presence of normal renal function, most of a dose of nabilone is eliminated through the biliary system.

Treatment for respiratory depression and comatose state consists of symptomatic and supportive therapy. Particular attention should be paid to the occurrence of hypothermia. If the patient becomes hypotensive, consider fluids, inotropes and/or vasopressors.

Dosage: Adults: 1 mg or 2 mg twice a day. The first dose should be given the night before initiating administration of the chemotherapeutic medication. The second dose is usually administered 1 to 3 hours before chemotherapy. If required, administration of nabilone can be continued up to 24 hours after the chemotherapeutic agent is given. The maximum recommended daily dose is 6 mg in divided doses.

Supplied: Each No. 2, opaque, blue and white pulvule, Identi-Code 3101, contains: nabilone 1 mg. Nonmedicinal ingredients: povidone and starch flowable; capsule shell and printing ink: gelatin, indigo carmine, red iron oxide, sodium lauryl sulfate and titanium dioxide; Colorcon S-1-8159 (antifoam DC 1510, black iron oxide E172, N-butyl alcohol, IMS 74 OP BP, purified water, shellac and soya lecithin) or Tek SW-9008 (ammonium hydroxide, black iron oxide E172, N-butyl alcohol, ethyl alcohol, isopropyl alcohol, potassium hydroxide, propylene glycol, purified water and shellac). Bottles of 20.

CETAMIDE™ Ⓟ
Alcon

Sodium Sulfacetamide

Ophthalmic Antibacterial

Supplied: Each tube of sterile ointment contains: sodium sulfacetamide 10% in a base of white petrolatum, mineral oil and anhydrous lanolin with methylparaben and propylparaben as preservatives. Tubes of 3.5 g.

CHARCODOTE®
CHARCODOTE®, AQUEOUS
CHARCODOTE® TFS
Pharmascience

Activated Charcoal

Poison Antidote

Supplied: Charcodote: Each mL contains: micronized activated charcoal 200 mg in sorbitol solution USP. Bottle contains micronized activated charcoal 50 g and approximately 180 g of sorbitol without preservatives, flavoring, or suspending agents. Thin walled oversized squeeze bottles of 250 mL with special spout for oral or nasogastric routes of administration.

Pediatric Charcodote: Each mL contains: micronized activated charcoal 200 mg in sorbitol solution USP. Bottle contains 25 g of micronized activated charcoal and approximately 90 g of sorbitol without preservatives, flavoring, or suspending agents. Thin walled oversized squeeze bottles of 125 mL with special spout for oral or nasogastric routes of administration. Bottle is half filled allowing for dilution with water.

Aqueous Charcodote: Each mL contains: micronized activated charcoal 200 mg in purified water. Bottle contains 50 g of micronized activated charcoal without preservatives, flavoring or suspending agents. Thin walled oversized squeeze bottles of 250 mL with special spout for oral or nasogastric routes of administration.

Aqueous Pediatric Charcodote: Each mL contains: micronized activated charcoal 200 mg in purified water. Bottle contains 25 g of micronized activated charcoal without preservatives, flavoring or suspending agents. Thin walled oversized squeeze bottles of 125 mL with special spout for oral or nasogastric routes of administration. Bottle is half filled allowing for dilution with water.

Charcodote TFS-25: Each mL contains: micronized activated charcoal 200 mg and sorbitol 200 mg in purified water. Bottle contains 25 g of micronized activated charcoal and 25 g of sorbitol without preservatives, flavoring or suspending agents. Thin walled oversized squeeze bottles of 125 mL with special spout for oral or nasogastric routes of administration.

Charcodote TFS-50: Each mL contains: micronized activated charcoal 200 mg and sorbitol 200 mg in purified water. Bottle contains 50 g of micronized activated charcoal and 50 g of sorbitol without preservatives, flavoring or suspending agents. Thin walled oversized squeeze bottles of 250 mL with special spout for oral or nasogastric routes of administration.

Store in a cool place 15 to 30°C away from direct light.

CHERACOL® Ⓝ
Roberts

Codeine Phosphate—Guaifenesin—Ammonium Chloride

Antitussive—Expectorant

Indications: To facilitate expectoration and control cough associated with inflamed mucosa and tenacious sputum which does not respond to products of lesser potency.

Contraindications and Precautions: In patients with asthma or pulmonary emphysema, indiscriminate use may precipitate respiratory insufficiency resulting from increased viscosity of bronchial secretions and suppression of the cough reflex.

Use with caution in sedated or debilitated patients, in patients who have undergone thoracotomies or laparotomies, since suppression of the cough reflex may lead to retention of secretions postoperatively in these patients.

Caution should be exercised and dosage may need to be reduced when codeine is administered with other drugs which depress the CNS (including alcohol), with MAO inhibitors, phenothiazines or tricyclic antidepressants.

Use with caution in cases of hypertension, severe organic diseases or known sensitivity to the drug.

A metabolite of guaifenesin has been found to produce an apparent increase in urinary 5-hydroxyindoleacetic acid, and guaifenesin could thus interfere with the diagnosis of the carcinoid syndrome. Asthmatic patients being evaluated for the carcinoid syndrome should therefore discontinue any preparation containing guaifenesin for 24 hours before the collection of urine specimens for the determination of 5-hydroxyindoleacetic acid.

Occupational Hazards: Warn patients against driving or operating machinery if they become drowsy or show impaired mental and/or physical abilities while taking this product.

Prolonged use of codeine may prove habit-forming. In case of persistent cough and/or fever, consult a physician.

Before prescribing medication to suppress or modify cough, it is important to ascertain that the underlying cause of the cough is identified, that modification of the cough does not increase the risk of clinical or physiologic complications, and that appropriate therapy for the primary disease is provided.

Children: In young children the respiratory centre is especially susceptible to the depressant action of narcotic cough suppressants. Benefit to risk ratio should be carefully considered especially in children with respiratory embarrassment, e.g., croup. Estimation of dosage relative to the child's age and weight is of great importance.

Pregnancy: Since codeine crosses the placental barrier, its use in pregnancy is not recommended.

As codeine may inhibit peristalsis, patients with chronic constipation should be given this product only after weighing the potential therapeutic benefit against the hazards involved.

Dosage: Adults: 5 to 15 mL every 2 to 4 hours as required. Infants: 1 month: 2 to 3 drops; 3 months: 4 to 6 drops. Children over 1 year: 2.5 to 5 mL according to age.

Supplied: Each 5 mL of red, cherry flavored syrup contains: codeine phosphate 10 mg, guaifenesin 100 mg, ammonium chloride 91 mg. Alcohol 3%. Energy: 50 kJ (12 kcal)/5 mL. Gluten-free. Plastic bottles of 500 mL.

CHILDREN'S ACETAMINOPHEN ELIXIR DROPS
WestCan

Acetaminophen

Analgesic—Antipyretic

Supplied: Each mL of cherry-flavored, elixir drops contains: acetaminophen USP 80 mg. Dropper bottles of 24 mL with child resistant cap.

CHILDREN'S ACETAMINOPHEN ORAL SOLUTION
WestCan

Acetaminophen

Analgesic—Antipyretic

Supplied: Each 5 mL of oral solution contains: acetaminophen USP 80 mg. Bottles of 100 mL with child resistant cap.

CHILDREN'S CHEWABLE ACETAMINOPHEN
WestCan

Acetaminophen

Analgesic—Antipyretic

Supplied: Each chewable, fruit-flavored tablet contains: acetaminophen 80 mg. Bottles (child resistant caps) of 24.

CHILDREN'S CHOICE™ SUPER MULTI-VITAMINS and MINERALS
Swiss Herbal

Vitamins—Minerals

Supplied: Each fruit flavored chewable tablet contains: beta carotene 5 000 IU, vitamin D_3 400 IU, vitamin E 25 IU, vitamin C 75 mg, thiamine 5 mg, riboflavin 5 mg, pyridoxine 5 mg, vitamin B_{12} 10 μg, biotin 50 μg, folic acid 0.5 mg, niacinamide 20 mg, pantothenic acid 15 mg, choline bitartrate 5 mg, inositol 5 mg, calcium 125 mg, magnesium 50 mg, iodine 0.05 mg, iron 4 mg, zinc 1 mg, manganese 2 mg, copper 1 mg, and potassium 1 mg. Nonmedicinal ingredients: cellulose, citric acid, color, dextrose, flavor, fructose, kelp, magnesium stearate and silicon dioxide. Bottles of 60.

CHLORAL HYDRATE
General Monograph, CPhA

Sedative—Hypnotic

> This monograph has been compiled by CPhA. It may contain information different from that approved by Therapeutic Products Programme, Health Canada, and the pharmaceutical manufacturers' approval has not been requested.

Pharmacology: Chloral hydrate has general CNS depressant effects believed to be due to its active metabolite, trichloroethanol.

In doses used for hypnosis, chloral hydrate produces mild cerebral depression and quiet, deep sleep, usually with little or no hangover effects. Chloral hydrate decreases sleep latency and nighttime awakenings with minimal effects on REM sleep. REM rebound does not occur with drug withdrawal. Tolerance to the sedative effects may develop over a 5- to 14-day period of continued use.

At therapeutic doses, chloral hydrate has little effect on respiration and blood pressure. Higher doses may lead to depression of respiratory and vasomotor centres. Chloral hydrate has little analgesic activity and may produce excitement or delirium in the presence of pain. Sedative or hypnotic doses have little anticonvulsant activity.

Pharmacokinetics: Chloral hydrate is rapidly absorbed following oral or rectal administration. Following a hypnotic dose, drowsiness occurs within 10 to 15 minutes and sleep usually occurs within 30 to 60 minutes, which lasts about 4 to 8 hours. When used as a premedicant in children and infants, sedation usually occurs within 15 minutes and sleep by 40 minutes, with most fully awake within 2 hours.

Chloral hydrate is rapidly and extensively metabolized in the liver and erythrocytes by alcohol dehydrogenase to its major active metabolite, trichloroethanol. A small amount of chloral hydrate and a larger portion of trichloroethanol are oxidized to a minor, less active metabolite, trichloroacetic acid, in the liver and kidneys. This metabolite is excreted in the urine and bile, together with trichloroethanol in free or conjugated form.

The average half-life of trichloroethanol in adults is 8 hours, ranging from 4 to 12 hours. The half-life is prolonged in children (10 hours), preterm neonates (37 hours) and term neonates (28 hours). Trichloroethanol is 70 to 80% bound to plasma proteins and is widely distributed to all body tissues including CSF, breast milk and placenta.

The half-life of trichloroacetic acid is longer, up to 100 hours. It is highly plasma protein bound (94%), primarily to albumin and may be responsible for interactions with other highly protein bound drugs. Upon multiple dosing, trichloracetic acid can displace bilirubin or warfarin from binding sites, potentially resulting in hyperbilirubinemia or hypoprothrombinemia.

Indications: For short-term use as a sedative or hypnotic. Tolerance to these effects often develops after a 2-week period. Chloral hydrate has also been used prior to surgery or other procedures to allay anxiety or to produce sedation or sleep, without depressing respiration or cough reflex. In postoperative care and control of pain, chloral hydrate may be used as an adjunct to opiates and analgesics. There is some evidence that chloral hydrate may alleviate the symptoms of alcohol or drug withdrawal.

Contraindications: Patients with severe impairment of renal or hepatic function, or a history of idiosyncrasy or hypersensitivity to chloral hydrate.

Warnings: Abuse and Dependence: Chloral hydrate should be used as a hypnotic only for short-term use, usually 2 to 7 days. Prolonged use of chloral hydrate may produce tolerance and physical and/or psychological dependence. Sudden withdrawal after prolonged use may result in hallucinations and symptoms similar to delirium tremens (sometimes fatal), therefore chloral hydrate should be tapered gradually. Chloral hydrate should be used with caution in patients who are mentally depressed, suicidal or have a history of drug abuse or dependence.

Cardiac Disorders: In patients with severe cardiac disease, chloral hydrate should be avoided due to the possibility of cardiac arrhythmias and hypotension associated with larger doses.

Gastrointestinal: Because of its irritant properties, oral use of chloral hydrate should be avoided in patients with gastritis, esophagitis or gastric or duodenal ulcer. Rectal use should be avoided in patients with proctitis or colitis.

Children: Patients should be monitored for CNS and respiratory depressive effects. Deaths associated with the use of chloral hydrate for sedation prior to diagnostic or therapeutic procedures have been reported, particularly in pediatric patients. In addition, particular care must be taken in calculating and administering the proper dose.

Sedation with chloral hydrate in children with adenoidal hypertrophy and obstructive sleep apnea has been reported to cause episodes of life-threatening respiratory obstruction. Children with obstructive sleep apnea from other causes may be at risk as well. Laryngeal edema resulting in severe respiratory difficulty in a child has also been reported.

Precautions: Occupational Hazards: Due to chloral hydrate's sedative effects, patients should be warned against driving, operating dangerous machinery or engaging in other activities requiring mental alertness and physical coordination after taking the drug.

Drug Interactions: Ethanol: The combination of ethanol and chloral hydrate produces additive and possibly synergistic CNS depressant effects. A disulfiram-like reaction may occur, including tachycardia, facial flushing and dysphoria. Additive CNS effects may occur when chloral hydrate is given concurrently with other CNS depressants such as paraldehyde or barbiturates.

Oral Anticoagulants: Chloral hydrate may transiently enhance the hypoprothrombinemic response to warfarin, especially within the first 2 weeks of therapy, by displacing warfarin from plasma protein binding sites. When chloral hydrate is added or removed from the therapeutic regimen, or when dosage changes are made, frequent prothrombin time determinations are recommended.

Drug-Laboratory Test Interactions: Chloral hydrate may interfere with fluorometric determinations of urine catecholamines. Chloral hydrate should not be administered within 48 hours prior to the test. Chloral hydrate may cause elevations in urine 17-hydroxycorticosteroid. Administration of chloral hydrate can result in erroneously high values for vitamin B_{12} in some radioassay procedures.

Pregnancy: Chloral hydrate crosses the placenta. Safety has not been established. Chronic use during pregnancy may cause withdrawal symptoms in the neonate.

Lactation: Small amounts of chloral hydrate are excreted in breast milk. Use by nursing mothers may cause drowsiness in the infant.

Children: Gastric irritation and vomiting may occur following administration of the oral liquid. It should be well diluted with water or other liquid such as fruit juice or ginger ale.

Due to the prolonged half-lives of chloral hydrate's metabolites, excessive CNS depression may occur due to accumulation following repeated dosing. The degree of sedation should be monitored and caregivers cautioned against exceeding prescribed dosage.

Neonates should be monitored for increased bilirubin concentrations as hyperbilirubinemia may occur due to competition of chloral hydrate metabolites with bilirubin for hepatic glucuronidation.

Geriatrics: In elderly patients likely to have age-related hepatic/renal function impairment, and in debilitated patients or those patients prone to CNS depression, reduction of dose may be necessary to avoid oversedation or other adverse effects.

Respiratory: Careful monitoring is required in patients with respiratory insufficiency.

Adverse Effects: Gastrointestinal: The most frequent adverse effect of chloral hydrate is gastrointestinal irritation, manifested by nausea, vomiting, diarrhea and stomach pain. Unpleasant taste and flatulence may also occur. These effects can be minimized by taking chloral hydrate with a full glass of fluid. Ileus in an infant has been reported.

CNS: Adverse effects of chloral hydrate due to CNS depressant effects include: lightheadedness, ataxia, nightmares, drowsiness, vertigo, headache, confusion, and malaise. Most CNS effects occur infrequently. Hangover effect can occur, although it is less commonly observed than with barbiturates and some benzodiazepines. Rarely, paradoxical and idiosyncratic reactions (hallucinations, delirium, unusual excitement, disorientation, incoherence, paranoia) have occurred.

Cardiovascular: Large doses of chloral hydrate have been reported to produce hypotension, ventricular and atrial arrhythmias, torsades de pointes, depression of myocardial contractility, and shortening of refractory period.

Respiratory: Life-threatening respiratory obstruction episodes have been reported in young children (see Warnings).

Dermatologic: Dermatologic reactions are not common, but include: erythematous rash, urticaria, angioedema, eczematoid dermatitis, scarlatiniform exanthema, bullous lesions, non-thrombocytopenic purpura and erythema multiform. Some cutaneous reactions are accompanied by fever. Chloral hydrate is an irritant when applied to the skin and mucous membranes.

Metabolic: Chloral hydrate has been reported to precipitate attacks of acute intermittent porphyria. Rarely, ketonuria has been reported.

Hematologic: Leukopenia and eosinophilia have been reported.

Ophthalmologic: Chloral hydrate has produced oculotoxicities manifesting as ptosis, allergic conjunctivitis or keratoconjunctivitis.

Other: Increases in middle ear pressure in infants and children have been reported.

Overdose: Symptoms: Acute poisoning resembles barbiturate intoxication, producing symptoms of CNS depression and deep coma, respiratory depression, hypotension and cardiac arrhythmias. Death may result from respiratory or cardiovascular failure. Resistent cardiac arrhythmias account for most of the mortality. Individuals with known cardiac dysfunction are highly susceptible to toxicity.

Gastritis, nausea and vomiting are common. Gastric necrosis, perforation, gastrointestinal hemorrhage and esophageal stricture have also been reported. Other signs may include pinpoint pupils, cyanosis, hypothermia, muscle flaccidity and pulmonary edema. Renal damage (albuminuria) and hepatic damage (jaundice) may occur.

The usual lethal dose is 10 g; however, fatalities have occurred with as little as 4 g and survival has been documented after the ingestion of 30 g of chloral hydrate.

Chronic poisoning may manifest with symptoms of gastritis, skin rash, peripheral vasodilation, hypotension, renal damage and myocardial depression.

Treatment: Supportive therapy includes respiratory and cardiovascular assistance and maintenance of body temperature and circulation. Gastric lavage may be indicated if performed soon after ingestion or in patients who are comatose or at risk of convulsing. The airway should be protected in obtunded or unconscious patients. Activated charcoal may be administered.

Cardiac monitoring is important, especially in patients with pre-existing cardiac disease. Hypotension should be treated with appropriate i.v. fluids and electrolytes; dopamine or norepinephrine may be required. Baseline hepatic and renal function tests should be obtained.

Hemodialysis removes both the parent drug and the trichloroethanol metabolite.

Dosage: Dosage must be individualized. Doses for oral and rectal routes are equivalent. Chloral hydrate can be administered rectally by moistening capsules or as a retention enema by dissolving liquid in cottonseed or olive oil or in a hydrophilic polyethylene glycol base.

Capsules should be taken with a full glass (240 mL) of water, milk, fruit juice or ginger ale; they must not be crushed or chewed. The liquid formulation should be diluted with approximately 120 mL of water or other liquid to reduce gastric irritation.

Chloral hydrate should be avoided in patients with moderate to severe renal failure (creatinine clearance <0.8 mL/s), or in patients with severe hepatic dysfunction. No dosage adjustment is necessary for patients with mild renal failure.

Hypnotic: Adults: 500 to 1 000 mg, 15 to 30 minutes before bedtime.
Geriatrics: Initial 250 mg, 15 to 30 minutes before bedtime.
Children: 50 mg/kg at bedtime, maximum 1 000 mg per single dose.

Sedative: Adults: 250 mg 3 times daily after meals, maximum 2 000 mg/day.
Children: 25 mg/kg/day divided into 3 to 4 doses (after meals), maximum 500 mg/dose.

Premedicant: Adults: 500 to 1 000 mg, 30 minutes prior to procedure.
Children: 25 to 50 mg/kg, 30 minutes prior to procedure. May repeat in 30 minutes using half the dose. Maximum 1 000 mg per single dose.

Ethanol Withdrawal: For management of withdrawal symptoms, a dose of 500 mg to 1 g, repeated at 6-hour intervals, has been used. Single or daily dose should not exceed 2 g.

Reviewed 1999

CHLORAMPHENICOL Ⓟ

General Monograph, CPhA

Antibiotic

This monograph has been compiled by CPhA. It may contain information different from that approved by Therapeutic Products Programme, Health Canada, and the pharmaceutical manufacturers' approval has not been requested.

Pharmacology: Chloramphenicol, which was originally isolated from Streptomyces venezuelae and is now synthetically produced, exerts mainly a bacteriostatic effect on a wide range of gram-positive and gram-negative organisms and is active against Rickettsia, Chlamydia (psittacosis-lymphogranuloma organisms), and Mycoplasma. It is particularly effective against H. influenzae, S. pneumoniae, S. typhi and Neisseria species. The palmitate and sodium succinate esters are inactive until hydrolyzed to free chloramphenicol which occurs rapidly in vivo. The mechanism of action of chloramphenicol is through inhibition of protein synthesis by binding to the 50S ribosomal subunit. There is some evidence that chloramphenicol inhibits protein synthesis in rapidly proliferating mammalian cells which may be the cause of reversible bone marrow depression. Both natural and acquired resistance to chloramphenicol has been seen in strains of P. aeruginosa, Staphyloccus, and Enterobacteriacea particularly Shigella, Salmonella, and Escherichia. The type of resistance exhibited by gram-negative organisms involves acetylation of chloramphenicol, which is a plasmid-mediated trait.

Pharmacokinetics: Chloramphenicol palmitate is hydrolyzed in the gastrointestinal tract and rapidly absorbed as free chloramphenicol. The peak serum level after an oral dose of chloramphenicol occurs in 1 to 3 hours. Chloramphenicol sodium succinate is hydrolyzed to free chloramphenicol following i.v. administration, presumably by esterases in the liver, kidneys and lungs. The rate and extent of hydrolysis and renal elimination of the succinate ester are subject to a high degree of interindividual variation.

Chloramphenicol is approximately 60% bound to serum proteins and is widely distributed in the body. CSF concentrations range from 21 to 50% of serum concentrations with uninflamed meninges and 45 to 89% of serum concentrations with inflamed meninges. The drug crosses the placenta and is distributed into breast milk.

Chloramphenicol is metabolized in the liver, mainly by conjugation with glucuronic acid; only about 5 to 15% of an oral dose is excreted unchanged in the urine. The half-life of chloramphenicol is 1.5 to 4 hours in adults with normal renal and hepatic function. The plasma half-life is increased in patients with markedly reduced hepatic function. In patients with impaired renal function, the half-life of chloramphenicol itself is not significantly altered although the half-life of the inactive metabolites may be prolonged. Following i.v. administration, patients with renal impairment may achieve higher chloramphenicol concentrations due to decreased renal excretion of the succinate ester.

Since the processes for glucuronide conjugation and renal excretion in neonates may be immature, the half-life of the drug in neonates less than 3 days old may be in excess of 24 hours and about 10 hours for infants 10 to 16 days old. In these cases the dosage and administration interval should be adjusted using measured serum concentrations.

Plasma concentrations of chloramphenicol are not affected by peritoneal dialysis and only small amounts of the drug are removed by hemodialysis.

Indications: The use of chloramphenicol should be reserved for the treatment of serious infections caused by susceptible organisms when less toxic antimicrobials are ineffective or contraindicated.

Chloramphenicol is used in the acute treatment of typhoid fever caused by S. typhi, as well as invasive salmonellosis. It should not be used to eliminate the carrier state.

Chloramphenicol is used as an alternate for the treatment of bacterial meningitis caused by H. influenzae, S. pneumoniae and N. meningitidis when a cephalosporin or penicillin is not suitable. It is also used to treat brain abscesses caused by B. fragilis or other susceptible organisms.

Chloramphenicol is used as an alternative in the treatment of rickettsial infections, such as typhus or Rocky Mountain spotted fever, when tetracyclines cannot be given. It can also be used to treat severe H. influenzae infections other than meningitis, e.g., epiglottitis.

Chloramphenicol may be used locally in the treatment of superficial infections of the eye, external ear or skin, when caused by susceptible organisms.

Contraindications: Chloramphenicol is contraindicated in individuals with a history of previous hypersensitivity or toxic reaction to it.

Warnings: Serious and sometimes fatal reactions have occurred in patients taking chloramphenicol, even during short-term systemic therapy or after long-term local application. These include blood dyscrasias such as aplastic anemia, hypoplastic anemia, thrombocytopenia and granulocytopenia. While hematologic studies may detect early peripheral blood changes, they are not useful in predicting irreversible bone marrow depression which precedes the development of aplastic anemia.

A severe and potentially fatal reaction known as the gray syndrome has occurred in premature and newborn infants receiving large doses of chloramphenicol. Most commonly, chloramphenicol therapy had been initiated in the first 48 hours after birth; however, it has occurred in children as old as 2 years and in infants born to mothers who received chloramphenicol in the final stages of labor. Symptoms include failure to feed, abdominal distention, vomiting, blue-gray skin color, hypothermia, irregular breathing and cardiovascular collapse. Death can occur within hours. The syndrome has been attributed to excessive serum concentrations of chloramphenicol due to immature hepatic and renal elimination processes. If the syndrome is detected early and chloramphenicol is stopped, the infant may recover completely.

Chloramphenicol must not be used when less toxic agents may be expected to be effective.

Precautions: It is essential that hematologic studies be conducted prior to and frequently during therapy with chloramphenicol. The drug should be discontinued if reticulocytopenia, leukopenia, thrombocytopenia, anemia or other hematologic abnormalities occur (see Warnings).

Chloramphenicol has a narrow therapeutic index. In infants, or in patients with renal or hepatic impairment, plasma concentrations should be monitored and maintained in the range of 5 to 20 μg/mL.

Ocular symptoms such as a bilateral decrease in visual acuity or central scotomas may herald the onset of chloramphenicol-induced optic neuritis which rarely may result in blindness. Chloramphenicol must be discontinued immediately if optic or peripheral neuritis occurs.

Natural or plasmid-mediated resistance to chloramphenicol is known to occur in strains of staphylococci, Salmonella, Shigella, E. coli and rarely, H. influenzae.

As with other antibiotics, therapy with chloramphenicol may result in the overgrowth of nonsusceptible organisms including bacteria, viruses or fungi.

Repeated courses of chloramphenicol should be avoided whenever possible.

Otic preparations should not be used in patients with a perforated tympanic membrane.

When chloramphenicol is used topically in combination with corticosteroids, the signs of suprainfection may be masked.

Pregnancy: Chloramphenicol readily crosses the placenta. Birth defects in humans have not been documented; however, it should not be used in pregnancy at term or during labour because of potential toxicity in premature or full-term infants, including gray syndrome (see Warnings).

Lactation: Chloramphenicol is excreted in human breast milk and should not be used in nursing mothers because of the possibility of adverse effects (bone marrow depression) in the infant.

Neonates: Caution should be used in therapy of premature and full-term infants to avoid toxicity including gray syndrome (see Warnings). Serum drug levels should be monitored.

Drug Interactions: Hepatic drug clearance: Chloramphenicol inhibits hepatic microsomal enzymes and may interfere with the metabolism of alfentanil, chlorpropamide, phenobarbital, phenytoin, tolbutamide, warfarin or other drugs metabolized by the microsomal system. Dosages of these drugs may need to be adjusted accordingly. Conversely, drugs such as rifampin or phenobarbital which induce microsomal enzymes may increase the metabolism and reduce serum concentrations of chloramphenicol.

Anticoagulants: Chloramphenicol may prolong the prothrombin time in patients receiving anticoagulant therapy by interfering with vitamin K production by intestinal bacteria.

Anemia agents: Concurrent therapy with chloramphenicol may delay the clinical response to iron preparations, Vitamin B_{12} or folic acid in the treatment of anemias.

Antibacterial agents: Chloramphenicol has been reported to antagonize the bactericidal activity of penicillins and aminoglycosides in vitro and some clinicians recommend that these antibiotics not be used concomitantly. However, in vivo antagonism has not been demonstrated and chloramphenicol has been used successfully with ampicillin or penicillin G or aminoglycosides with no apparent decrease in activity.

Radiation Therapy or Myelosuppressive Drugs: Concomitant administration of chloramphenicol may result in additive bone marrow suppression.

Adverse Effects: Hematologic: Serious and sometimes fatal blood dyscrasias including aplastic anemia, hypoplastic anemia, thrombocytopenia and granulocytopenia have occurred during systemic or topical therapy with chloramphenicol. Two types of bone marrow suppression may occur. One is dose-related and generally reversible, tending to occur when serum levels exceed 25 μg/mL. Aplastic anemia, however, is an irreversible, idiosyncratic reaction occurring in approximately 1 in 25 000 to 40 000 patients treated and is not related to dose or duration of therapy. The onset of aplastic anemia may not occur until weeks or months following the discontinuation of chloramphenicol. See Warnings and Precautions.

Gastrointestinal: nausea, vomiting and diarrhea. Following oral administration, disturbances of the oral and intestinal flora may cause stomatitis, glossitis and enterocolitis. An unpleasant taste has been reported following rapid i.v. administration.

CNS: Headache, mild depression, mental confusion and delirium have been described in patients receiving chloramphenicol.

Optic and peripheral neuritis have been reported, usually following long-term therapy. If this occurs, the drug should be promptly discontinued.

Hypersensitivity: Fever, macular and vesicular rashes, angioedema and urticaria may occur, especially after topical use. Herxheimer-like reactions have occurred during therapy for typhoid fever.

Gray Syndrome: A toxic reaction which can occur in premature and newborn infants receiving large doses of chloramphenicol. It is characterized by abdominal distention, vomiting, blue-gray skin color, hypothermia, irregular breathing and cardiovascular collapse, followed by death in few hours or days. If chloramphenicol is stopped early after the onset of symptoms, the infant may recover completely (see Warnings and Precautions).

Local: Transient burning or stinging may occur upon instillation of ophthalmic preparations.

Overdose: Symptoms: Hypersensitivity reactions including anaphylaxis may occur. Nausea and vomiting may occur, particularly after oral ingestion. Metabolic acidosis may occur after acute or chronic ingestion and may precede the onset of hypotension, hypothermia and abdominal distention. Sustained high serum levels may be associated with many other adverse effects (see Warnings, Precautions and Adverse Effects).

Chloramphenicol (cont'd)

Treatment: Management of anaphylaxis may require the use of antihistamines, epinephrine, oxygen supplementation, airway management and i.v. fluids, depending on the severity of the reaction.

In cases of recent oral ingestion, induction of emesis or administration of activated charcoal with or without a cathartic may be indicated in certain cases.

Dosage: Where possible, chloramphenicol should be administered orally.

Oral and I.V.: Adults: 50 mg/kg/day in divided doses at 6 hour intervals. Patients with infections due to moderately resistant organisms or CNS infections may require higher doses of up to 100 mg/kg/day to achieve therapeutic serum or CSF levels, but the dose should be decreased as soon as possible to 50 mg/kg daily. Adults with impairment of hepatic or renal function may have reduced ability to metabolize and excrete the drug. In instances of impaired metabolic processes, dosages should be adjusted appropriately (see Precautions).

Children: Dosage of 50 mg/kg/day divided at 6 hour intervals is effective against most susceptible organisms. Severe infections (e.g., septicemia or meningitis): up to 100 mg/kg/day divided at 6 or 12 hour intervals.

Children with impaired hepatic or renal function require dosage adjustment with serum level monitoring where possible.

Infants: Premature infants or full-term infants up to 2 weeks of age: 6.25 mg/kg every 6 hours. Full-term infants over 2 weeks of age: 12.5 mg/kg every 6 hours or 25 mg/kg every 12 hours. **Appropriate dosing is extremely important in neonates with immature metabolic processes as severe toxicity such as gray syndrome may occur (see Warnings and Precautions).**

I.M. administration is controversial because studies have reported varying serum levels.

Local: Ophthalmic: Preparations (e.g., a thin strip of ointment approximately 1 cm long or 1 drop of solution) may be applied in the conjunctival sac every 3 hours for the first 48 hours, at which time the dosing interval may be increased.

Otic: Instil 2 or 3 drops into the ear canal every 6 to 8 hours.

Topical: Cream may be applied to the skin 3 or 4 times daily.

Reviewed 1999

CHLORDIAZEPOXIDE ℞

General Monograph, CPhA

see BENZODIAZEPINES

CHLOROMYCETIN® INJECTION ℞

Parke-Davis

Chloramphenicol

Antibiotic

Indications: In accordance with the concepts in the Contraindications section and this Indications section, chloramphenicol should be used only in those conditions for which it may be the antibiotic of choice. These would include:

1. Acute infections caused by Salmonella typhi. It is not recommended for the routine treatment of the typhoid carrier state.
2. Serious infections caused by susceptible strains: (a) Salmonella species with systemic involvement. (b) H. influenzae, specifically meningeal infections. (c) Rickettsia; psittacosis in children. (d) Various gram-negative bacteria causing bacteremia, meningitis or other serious gram-negative infections. (e) Other susceptible organisms which have been demonstrated to be resistant to other appropriate antimicrobial agents.
3. Cystic fibrosis regimens.

Contraindications: Chloramphenicol is contraindicated in individuals with a history of previous hypersensitivity and/or toxic reaction to it.

Warnings: Serious and fatal blood dyscrasias (aplastic anemia, hypoplastic anemia, thrombocytopenia, granulocytopenia and bone marrow depression) are known to occur after the administration of chloramphenicol. In addition, there have been reports of aplastic anemia attributed to chloramphenicol which later terminated in leukemia. Blood dyscrasias have occurred after both short term and prolonged therapy with this drug. Chloramphenicol must not be used when less potentially dangerous agents will be effective. It must not be used in the treatment of trivial infections or where it is not indicated as in colds, influenza, infections of the throat, or as a prophylactic agent to prevent bacterial infections.

Precautions: It is essential that appropriate blood studies be made during treatment with chloramphenicol. While blood studies may detect early peripheral blood changes, such as leukopenia, reticulocytopenia, or granulocytopenia, before they become irreversible, such studies cannot be relied on to detect bone marrow depression prior to development of aplastic anemia.

Baseline blood studies should be followed by periodic blood studies at intervals during therapy. The drug should be discontinued upon appearance of reticulocytopenia, leukopenia, thrombocytopenia, anemia, or other blood alterations attributable to chloramphenicol. However, it should be noted that such studies do not exclude the possible later appearance of the irreversible type of bone marrow depression.

Repeated courses of the drug should be avoided, if at all possible. Treatment should not be continued longer than required to produce a cure with little or no risk of relapse of the disease.

Concurrent therapy with other drugs that may cause bone marrow depression should be avoided.

Excessive blood levels may result from administration of the recommended dose to patients with impaired liver or kidney function, including that due to immature metabolic processes in the infant. The dosage should be adjusted accordingly and the blood concentration should be determined at appropriate intervals, if possible.

Caution should be used in therapy of premature and full-term neonates to avoid gray syndrome toxicity (see Adverse Effects). Serum drug levels should be carefully followed during therapy of the neonate.

Pregnancy and *Lactation:* There are no studies which establish the safety of this drug for use in pregnancy. Benefit to the mother must be weighed against a possible risk to the fetus. Use of the drug at term or during labor may pose an additional hazard to the fetus. One case of 'gray syndrome' has been reported in a neonate born to a mother having received chloramphenicol i.v. during labor. Chloramphenicol is excreted in human breast milk. Precaution should be used in therapy during lactation because of the possibility of toxic effects on the nursing infant.

The use of this antibiotic, as with other antibiotics, may result in an overgrowth of nonsusceptible organisms, including fungi. If infections caused by nonsusceptible organisms appear during therapy, appropriate measures should be taken.

Adverse Effects: Blood Dyscrasias: The most serious adverse effect of chloramphenicol is bone marrow depression. Serious and fatal blood dyscrasias (aplastic anemia, hypoplastic anemia, thrombocytopenia, and granulocytopenia) are known to occur rarely after the administration of chloramphenicol. A generally irreversible type of marrow depression leading to aplastic anemia with a high rate of mortality is characterized by the appearance weeks or months after therapy of bone marrow aplasia or hypoplasia. Peripherally, pancytopenia is most often observed, but in a small number of cases only 1 or 2 of the 3 major cell types (erythrocytes, leukocytes, platelets) may be depressed. There have been reports of aplastic anemia attributed to chloramphenicol later terminating in leukemia.

A reversible type of bone marrow depression which is dose related, may occur. This type of marrow depression is characterized by vacuolization of the erythroid cells, reduction of reticulocytes and leukopenia, and responds to withdrawal of chloramphenicol. Paroxysmal nocturnal hemoglobinuria has also been reported.

Gastrointestinal Reactions: Nausea, vomiting, glossitis and stomatitis, diarrhea and enterocolitis may occur in low incidence.

Neurotoxic Reactions: Headache, mild depression, mental confusion and delirium have been described in patients receiving chloramphenicol. Optic and peripheral neuritis have been reported, usually following long-term therapy. If this occurs, the drug should be promptly discontinued.

Hypersensitivity Reactions: Fever, macular and vesicular rashes, angioedema, urticaria and anaphylaxis may occur.

The Herxheimer reaction has occurred during therapy for typhoid fever.

Gray Syndrome: Toxic reactions including fatalities have occurred in premature infants and neonates. The signs and symptoms associated with these reactions have been referred to as the 'gray syndrome'. The following summarizes the clinical and laboratory studies that have been made on these patients.

In most cases therapy with chloramphenicol had been instituted within the first 48 hours of life.

Symptoms first appeared after 3 to 4 days of continued treatment with high doses of chloramphenicol.

The symptoms appeared in the following order: abdominal distension with or without emesis; progressive pallid cyanosis; vasomotor collapse, frequently accompanied by irregular respiration; death within a few hours of onset of these symptoms.

The progression of symptoms from onset to death was accelerated with higher dose schedules. Blood serum level studies revealed unusually high concentrations of chloramphenicol (over 90 µg/mL after repeated doses). Termination of therapy upon early evidence of the associated symptomatology frequently reversed the process with complete recovery.

<u>*Drug Interactions:*</u> Chloramphenicol has been shown to retard the biotransformation of tolbutamide, phenytoin, and dicumarol in man.

Chloramphenicol should be used with caution if administered concomitantly with lincomycin, clindamycin, or erythromycin. In vitro experiments have demonstrated that binding sites for erythromycin, lincomycin, clindamycin and chloramphenicol overlap and competitive inhibition may occur. Rifampin therapy can reduce chloramphenicol concentrations.

Dosage: Chloramphenicol must be prescribed in adequate dosage. Inhibition of the majority of sensitive organisms may be expected at blood levels of 5 to 20 µg/mL. Levels of the order of 10 µg/mL are usually achieved following oral doses of 50 mg/kg daily.

Where possible, chloramphenicol should be administered orally. Consequently, patients started on i.v. chloramphenicol sodium succinate should be changed to the oral form as soon as practicable. The use of the i.m. route should be restricted to those patients where oral dosing is not possible and i.v. use is impossible or impracticable. Blood levels achieved following i.m. administration of 50 mg/kg/day may be inadequate. If i.m. administration is deemed essential, it is advisable to give 75 mg/kg/day in divided doses in order to achieve desired blood levels.

I.V. dosage—Adults should receive 50 mg/kg/day in divided doses at 6 hour intervals. In exceptional cases patients with infections due to moderately resistant organisms may require increased dosage up to 100 mg/kg/day to achieve blood levels inhibiting the pathogen, but these high doses should be decreased as soon as possible.

Adults with impairment of hepatic or renal function or both may have reduced ability to metabolize and excrete the drug. In instances of impaired metabolic processes, dosages should be adjusted accordingly (see discussion under Neonates).

Children: Dosage of 50 mg/kg/day divided at 6 hour intervals is effective against most susceptible organisms. Severe infections (e.g. septicemia or meningitis) especially when adequate cerebrospinal fluid concentrations are desired, require dosage up to 100 mg/kg/day divided at 6 or 12 hour intervals; however, it is recommended that dosage be reduced to 50 mg/kg/day as soon as possible.

Children with impaired liver or kidney functions or both may retain excessive amounts of the drug.

Neonates: A total of 25 mg/kg/day in 4 equal doses at 6 hour intervals usually produces and maintains concentrations in blood and tissues adequate to control most infections for which the drug is indicated. Increased dosage in these individuals demanded by severe infections, should be given only to maintain the blood concentration within a therapeutically effective range. After the first 2 weeks of life, full term neonates ordinarily may receive up to a total of 50 mg/kg/day equally divided into 4 doses at 6 hour intervals. **These dosage recommendations are extremely important because blood concentration in all premature neonates and full term neonates under 2 weeks of age differs from that of other infants.** This difference is due to variations in the maturity of the metabolic functions of the liver and kidneys.

When these functions are immature (or seriously impaired in adults) high concentrations of the drug are found which tend to increase with succeeding doses.

See section titled Gray Syndrome under Adverse Effects.

Infants and Children with Immature Metabolic Processes: In young infants and other children in whom immature metabolic functions are suspected, a dose of 25 mg/kg/day will usually produce therapeutic concentrations of the drug in the blood. In this group particularly, the concentration of the drug in the blood should be carefully followed by microbiological techniques where possible.

Supplied: Each vial contains: chloramphenicol sodium succinate equivalent to 1 g of chloramphenicol for i.m., i.v. or s.c. use. Cartons of 10.

CHLORPROMANYL Ⓟ

Technilab

Chlorpromazine HCl

Antipsychotic—Antiemetic

Supplied: Chlorpromanyl-20: Each mL contains: chlorpromazine base 20 mg (as HCl). Nonmedicinal ingredients: anise oil, artificial flavoring, ascorbic acid, FD&C yellow #5 and #6, glycerin, methylparaben, peppermint oil, propylparaben, purified water, sodium metabisulfite, sodium sulfite, sucrose and vanillin. Energy: 3.4 kcal/mL. Bottles of 500 mL.

Chlorpromanyl-40: Each mL contains: chlorpromazine base 40 mg (as HCl). Nonmedicinal ingredients: anise oil, artificial flavoring, ascorbic acid, FD&C yellow #5 and #6, glycerin, methylparaben, peppermint oil, propylparaben, purified water, sodium metabisulfite, sodium sulfite, sucrose and vanillin. Energy: 3.6 kcal/mL. Bottles of 100 mL with calibrated dropper.

Protect from light or discoloration may occur. Discard if markedly discolored.

CHLORPROMAZINE Ⓟ

General Monograph, CPhA

Antipsychotic—Antiemetic

> This monograph has been compiled by CPhA. It may contain information different from that approved by Therapeutic Products Programme, Health Canada, and the pharmaceutical manufacturers' approval has not been requested.

Pharmacology: Chlorpromazine is an aliphatic phenothiazine. Phenothiazines are thought to elicit their antipsychotic and antiemetic effects via interference with central dopaminergic pathways in the mesolimbic and medullary chemoreceptor trigger zone areas of the brain, respectively. Extrapyramidal side effects are a result of interaction with dopaminergic pathways in the basal ganglia. Although often termed dopamine blockers, the exact mechanism of dopaminergic interference responsible for the drugs antipsychotic activity has not been determined.

The aliphatic phenothiazines are highly sedating. This is often apparent at the start of therapy; however, with time some tolerance to this effect develops. Chlorpromazine has strong alpha-adrenergic blocking activity and can cause orthostatic hypotension. Infrequently, prolongation of the QT interval may occur. Chlorpromazine has moderate anticholinergic activity.

Chlorpromazine increases prolactin secretion due to its dopamine receptor blocking action in the pituitary and hypothalamus.

Pharmacokinetics: Chlorpromazine is readily absorbed from the gastrointestinal tract; however, its bioavailability is variable due to considerable first pass metabolism by the liver. Liquid concentrates may have greater bioavailability than tablets. Food does not appear to affect bioavailability consistently. I.M. administration bypasses much of the first pass effect and higher plasma concentrations are achieved. The onset of action after i.m. administration is usually 15 to 30 minutes and after oral administration 30 to 60 minutes. Rectally administered chlorpromazine usually takes longer to act than oral.

Chlorpromazine is highly bound to plasma proteins (>90%), principally albumin. It is not dialyzable. It is distributed widely throughout the body; it crosses the blood brain barrier and the placenta and is distributed into breast milk. Volume of distribution is approximately 20 L/kg.

Chlorpromazine is metabolized extensively and at least 12 different metabolites are known. Less than 1% is excreted unchanged. Most metabolites are excreted in the urine as unconjugated or conjugated forms. The half-life of chlorpromazine is variable at approximately 30 hours.

Indications: The management of psychotic disorders including manifestations of the manic phase of bipolar depressive disorder and severe behavioral problems in children. Chlorpromazine is also used for the prevention and treatment of nausea and vomiting, for the treatment of acute intermittent porphyria, as an adjunct in the treatment of tetanus and for relief of intractable hiccups.

Contraindications: Chlorpromazine is contraindicated in patients who have a known hypersensitivity to the drug. Cross-sensitivity between chlorpromazine and other phenothiazine drugs may occur.

Chlorpromazine should not be used in patients who are comatose, in patients with severe CNS depression secondary to the use of CNS depressant medications and in patients with blood dyscrasias or bone marrow depression.

Phenothiazines are contraindicated in patients with suspected or established subcortical brain damage with or without hypothalamic damage, since a hyperthermic reaction with temperatures in excess of 40°C may occur in such patients, sometimes not until 14 to 16 hours after drug administration.

Warnings: The antiemetic effect of phenothiazines may mask vomiting as a sign of toxicity due to overdosage of other drugs or may obscure the cause of vomiting in various disorders such as brain tumor, intestinal obstruction or Reye's syndrome.

Precautions: During the first month of therapy, routine blood counts, renal and hepatic function tests are advised as blood dyscrasias and cholestatic jaundice may occur. Renal function should be monitored in patients on long-term therapy.

Chlorpromazine may cause agranulocytosis. Most reported cases of agranulocytosis associated with the administration of phenothiazine derivatives have occurred between the fourth and tenth week of treatment. Therefore, observe patients on prolonged therapy with particular care during that time for the appearance of such signs as sore throat, fever and weakness. If these symptoms appear, discontinue the drug and perform WBC and differential counts.

Chlorpromazine may cause hypotension. It should be used with caution in the elderly, alcoholics and in patients with cardiovascular disease or in patients undergoing surgery. The dosage of anaesthetics and CNS depressants may have to be reduced in the perioperative period. Epinephrine should not be used to treat chlorpromazine-induced hypotension (see Drug Interactions).

ECG changes have been associated with the administration of phenothiazines. These changes appear to be reversible and related to a disturbance in repolarization. Use chlorpromazine with caution in patients with cardiovascular disease.

Chlorpromazine should be used with caution in patients who have impaired liver function or alcoholic liver disease. CNS depression may be potentiated. If bilirubinemia or icterus occurs, discontinue the drug and perform liver function tests.

Use cautiously in patients with respiratory difficulties as CNS depression may cause some respiratory failure in these patients.

Paralytic ileus resulting from the anticholinergic action of chlorpromazine may occur, especially in the elderly. Administer with caution also in patients with glaucoma or prostatic hypertrophy.

Chlorpromazine may lower the seizure threshold. Use the drug cautiously in patients with a history of seizures.

Phenothiazines affect thermoregulation. Use chlorpromazine with caution in patients who may be exposed to extreme heat or cold.

Photosensitivity may occur. Patients should utilize sunscreens when exposed to sunlight for significant lengths of time.

Administer chlorpromazine with caution to patients exposed to organophosphate insecticides.

Use with caution in patients with hypocalcemia. These individuals are more susceptible to dystonic reactions.

Phenothiazines have been associated with retinopathy. Discontinue chlorpromazine if retinal changes are observed.

Neuroleptic drugs elevate prolactin levels; the elevation persists during chronic administration. Although disturbances such as galactorrhea, amenorrhea, gynecomastia, and impotence have been reported, the clinical significance of elevated serum prolactin levels is unknown for most patients.

Abrupt Withdrawal: In general, phenothiazines do not produce psychic dependence; however, gastritis, nausea and vomiting, dizziness, and tremulousness have been reported following abrupt cessation of high dose therapy. Therefore, therapy should be gradually withdrawn over 1 to 2 weeks. Reports suggest that these symptoms can be reduced if concomitant antiparkinsonian agents are continued for several weeks after the phenothiazine is withdrawn.

Occupational Hazards: Where patients are participating in activities requiring complete mental alertness such as driving an automobile or operating machinery, administer the phenothiazine cautiously, forewarn the patient and increase the dosage gradually.

Drug Interactions: Anticholinergics: Anticholinergic drugs such as antihistamines, antiparkinsonian drugs, atropine, MAO inhibitors and tricyclic antidepressants may have additive anticholinergic effects when administered with chlorpromazine. Concomitant use of these drugs may increase the predisposition of patients treated with phenothiazines to heat stroke and paralytic ileus.

Anticonvulsants: Chlorpromazine may lower the seizure threshold. It may also decrease phenytoin metabolism. Anticonvulsant therapy should be monitored closely and may require dosage adjustment.

Antidepressants, tricyclic: Concomitant use of chlorpromazine and tricyclic antidepressants may result in increased plasma concentrations of both drugs. The risk of neuroleptic malignant syndrome may also be increased.

Antihypertensives: Concomitant use of chlorpromazine and antihypertensives may result in additive hypotensive effects and an increase risk of orthostatic hypotension or syncope. Chlorpromazine may block the antihypertensive effects of guanethidine by preventing its uptake into sympathetic nerves.

Antithyroid agents: Concomitant use of chlorpromazine and antithyroid agents such as methimazole and propylthiouracil may increase the risk of agranulocytosis.

Cigarette Smoking: Hepatic metabilism may be induced by smoking, leading to decreased plasma concentrations of chlorpromazine. Conversely, levels may increase if smoking is discontinued during therapy.

CNS depressants: Chlorpromazine may enhance the CNS depressant effects of drugs including alcohol, anticonvulsants, antihistamines, barbiturates, benzodiazepines, MAO inhibitors, narcotic analgesics and tricyclic antidepressants. Monitor to avoid excessive sedation or respiratory depression.

Epinephrine: Epinephrine should not be used to treat chlorpromazine-induced hypotension. Chlorpromazine blocks peripheral alpha-adrenergic receptors, thereby inhibiting alpha-agonist effects of epinephrine such as vasoconstriction and increased blood pressure. The beta-agonist effects of epinephrine (vasodilation) may be left unopposed and a further fall in blood pressure may result. Agents such as phenylephrine, methoxamine or norepinephrine may be suitable alternatives to raise blood pressure.

Haloperidol: Concomitant use of chlorpromazine and haloperidol may increase the risk of extrapyramidal reactions.

Levodopa: Chlorpromazine may inhibit the antiparkinsonian effects of levodopa as a result of its dopamine blocking effects in the CNS.

Lithium: Patients receiving lithium and chlorpromazine for treatment of acute mania should be monitored closely for signs of adverse neurologic effects, especially if serum concentrations of lithium are in the upper range. Rare cases of severe neurotoxicity have been reported.

Metoclopramide: Concomitant use of chlorpromazine and metoclopramide may increase the risk of extrapyramidal reactions.

Metrizamide: Chlorpromazine should not be used in patients receiving the radiopaque contrast agent metrizamide. Concomitant use increases the risk of seizures.

Pregnancy: Safe use of phenothiazines in pregnancy has not been established. Most studies indicate these agents are not teratogenic but there are reports of defects in infants exposed to these drugs during the first trimester. Toxic effects observed after high doses near term include: hypotonia, lethargy, depressed reflexes, paralytic ileus, jaundice, and persistent extrapyramidal syndrome. Phenothiazines are not recommended for use during pregnancy.

Lactation: Phenothiazines are distributed into breast milk. Use with caution during lactation because of possible sedative and anticholinergic side effects on the infant.

Geriatrics: Use reduced dosages. Chlorpromazine may adversely affect many of the conditions commonly occurring in the aged, including cardiovascular problems, parkinsonian extrapyramidal effects and anticholinergic effects (e.g., constipation, blurred vision).

Children: The safety and efficacy of chlorpromazine in children less than 6 months of age has not been established.

Adverse Effects: Adverse effects with different phenothiazines vary in type, frequency and mechanism of occurrence, i.e., some are dose-related, while others involve individual patient sensitivity. Some adverse effects may be more likely to occur, or occur with greater intensity, in patients with special medical problems, i.e., hypotension may be a particular problem in patients with pheochromocytoma or mitral insufficiency. Severe hypotension has occurred with usual dosages of phenothiazines in these patients.

In general, members of the aliphatic group of phenothiazines have strong sedative, hypotensive and anticholinergic properties and mild to moderate extrapyramidal effects.

Not all of the following adverse reactions have been observed with every phenothiazine derivative, but they have been reported with one or more and should be borne in mind when drugs of this class are administered.

Autonomic Nervous System: dry mouth, blurred vision, constipation, ileus, nasal stuffiness, photophobia. Syncope and impaired temperature regulation have also occurred (see Precautions).

Chlorpromazine (cont'd)

Behavioral Reactions: oversedation; impaired psychomotor function; paradoxical effects, such as agitation, excitement, insomnia, bizarre dreams, aggravation of psychotic symptoms; toxic confusional states.

Cardiovascular: hypotension, tachycardia, ECG changes (see Precautions).

CNS: extrapyramidal reactions, including pseudoparkinsonism (with motor retardation, rigidity, mask-like facies, pill rolling and other tremors, drooling, shuffling gait, etc.); dystonic reactions (including perioral spasms, trismus, tics, torticollis, oculogyric crises, protrusion of the tongue, difficulty swallowing, carpopedal spasm, opisthotonos of the back muscles); and akathisia. In addition, slowing of the EEG rhythm, disturbed body temperature and lowering of the convulsive threshold have occurred. Dizziness has been reported.

Tardive Dyskinesia: Tardive dyskinesia may appear in some patients on long-term antipsychotic therapy or may appear after drug therapy has been discontinued. The risk appears to be greater in elderly patients on high-dose therapy, especially females. The symptoms are persistent and in some patients appear to be irreversible. The syndrome is characterized by rhythmical involuntary movements of the tongue, face, mouth or jaw (e.g., protrusion of the tongue, puffing of the cheeks, puckering of the mouth and chewing movements). Sometimes these may be accompanied by involuntary movements of the extremities.

There is no known effective treatment for tardive dyskinesia; antiparkinsonian agents usually do not alleviate the symptoms of this syndrome. All antipsychotic agents should be discontinued if these symptoms appear. Should it be necessary to reinstitute treatment, or increase the dosage of the agent, or switch to a different antipsychotic agent, the syndrome may be masked. The physician may be able to reduce the risk of this syndrome by minimizing the unnecessary use of neuroleptics and reducing the dose or discontinuing the drug, if possible, when manifestations of this syndrome are recognized, particularly in patients over the age of 50. In general, the lowest effective dose of phenothiazine should be used for the shortest duration of therapy that produces an adequate clinical response. The need for continued therapy should be reassessed periodically. Fine vermicular movements of the tongue may be an early sign of the syndrome. If the medication is stopped at that time, the syndrome may not develop.

Neuroleptic Malignant Syndrome: As with other neuroleptic drugs, a symptom complex sometimes referred to as neuroleptic malignant syndrome (NMS) has been reported. Cardinal features of NMS are hyperpyrexia, muscle rigidity, altered mental status (including catatonic signs) and evidence of autonomic instability (irregular pulse or unstable blood pressure). Additional signs may include elevated CPK, myoglobinuria (rhabdomyolysis), acute renal failure and leukocytosis. The syndrome seems to occur more frequently in young males. Other predisposing factors include dehydration, organic brain disease and use of depot injections of phenothiazines. NMS is rare but potentially fatal and therefore requires intensive symptomatic and supportive treatment and immediate discontinuation of neuroleptic treatment.

Dermatologic: itching, rash, hypertrophic papillae of the tongue, angioneurotic edema, erythema, allergic purpura, exfoliative dermatitis, photosensitivity, skin-eye syndrome (see Ophthalmologic). Contact dermatitis has occurred in personnel handling solutions or injections of chlorpromazine.

Endocrine: increased prolactin secretion; gynecomastia, galactorrhea, mastalgia, altered libido, menstrual irregularities, weight gain, alterations in glucose tolerance and false positive pregnancy tests have occurred.

Gastrointestinal: nausea, vomiting, increase or decrease in appetite, gastric irritation, constipation, paralytic ileus, rarely diarrhea.

Genitourinary: urinary retention, priapism, inhibition of ejaculation.

Hematologic: agranulocytosis, leukopenia, granulocytopenia, eosinophilia, thrombocytopenia, anemia, aplastic anemia, pancytopenia. Agranulocytosis occurs in fewer than 1 in 10 000 patients receiving chlorpromazine.

Hepatic: cholestatic jaundice; symptoms generally subside following discontinuance of the drug but cholestasis may be prolonged.

Ophthalmologic: A skin-eye syndrome has been recognized as an adverse effect following long-term treatment with phenothiazines. This reaction is marked by progressive pigmentation of areas of skin or conjunctiva and/or discoloration of the exposed sclera and cornea. Opacities of the anterior lens and cornea described as irregular or stellate in shape have also been reported. Patients expected to receive higher doses of phenothiazines for prolonged periods should have complete eye examinations at baseline and every 6 to 12 months.

General Systemic Events: Sudden death has occasionally been reported in patients who have received phenothiazines. In some cases, the death was apparently due to cardiac arrest; in others, the cause appeared to be asphyxia due to failure of the cough reflex. In some patients, the cause could not be determined nor could it be established that the death was due to the phenothiazine.

Overdose: Symptoms: Symptoms of chlorpromazine overdosage are related to an extension of its pharmacologic action. The primary symptoms observed are severe extrapyramidal reactions, hypotension and sedation. Mild or early intoxication may cause restlessness, confusion and excitement. CNS sedation may progress to coma. Other symptoms may include: tachycardia, cardiac arrhythmias, seizures, miosis, hypothermia and respiratory and/or vasomotor collapse.

Treatment: Empty stomach using gastric lavage. Administer one dose of activated charcoal and a saline cathartic.Support respiratory and cardiac functions as needed. Maintain fluid and electrolyte balance. Treat hypotension with i.v. fluids and by placing the patient Trendelenburg position. If unresponsive, dopamine or norepinephrine may be required. Do not use epinephrine (see Precautions, Drug Interactions). Seizures may be treated with i.v. diazepam or lorazepam. If seizures are uncontrolled or recur, use i.v. phenytoin or phenobarbital. Treat arrhythmias with phenytoin. Extrapyramidal reactions may be treated with i.v. diphenydramine or benztropine followed by maintenance therapy for 48 hours. Manage hypothermia with external warming. Hemodialysis is of little value in enhancing the elimination of phenothiazines.

Dosage: Oral: Dosage should be initiated at a low level and increased gradually, noting carefully the clinical response. Patients on long-term therapy should be evaluated periodically to determine the need for continued therapy. Elderly and debilitated patients are more susceptible to adverse effects of the drug and usually require lower dosages. See Precautions, Adverse Effects.

Psychotic Disorders: Adults: 25 to 75 mg daily in 2 to 4 divided doses. The daily dose may be increased twice weekly by 20 to 50 mg until symptoms are controlled. Optimum therapeutic response may not occur for weeks or months. The usual maximum recommended daily dose is 1 g. Therapy should be continued for 2 weeks at the same dose once optimum response is achieved. The dose should then be reduced to the lowest amount that will maintain relief of symptoms. The drug can be administered once or twice daily with the largest dose at bedtime during maintenance therapy.

Acute Intermittent Porphyria: Adults: 25 to 50 mg 3 to 4 times daily.

Intractable Hiccups: Adults: 25 to 50 mg 3 to 4 times daily. If not controlled in 2 to 3 days, 25 to 50 mg may be given i.m.

Relief of Nausea and Vomiting: 10 to 25 mg every 4 hours. Increase dose as needed and tolerated.

Children: 0.55 mg/kg/dose every 4 to 6 hours as necessary.

Parenteral: The i.m. route is used primarily when rapid action is required to control acute severe symptomatology. Elderly or debilitated patients may require lower dosages. The i.v. route is sometimes used. I.M. injections should be administered slowly, deep into the upper quadrant of the buttock. Oral administration should be substituted as soon as possible. To minimize the occurrence of hypotension, keep the patient lying down for at least 30 minutes following injection.

Chlorpromazine ampuls should be protected from light. Pink or discolored solutions should be discarded.

Psychotic Disorders: Adults: 25 mg i.m. followed by doses of 25 to 50 mg i.m. in 1 hour if required. Doses can be increased over several days to a maximum of 400 mg every 4 to 6 hours.

Acute Intermittent Porphyria: 25 mg i.m. 3 or 4 times daily.

Adjunctive Treatment of Tetanus: Adults: 25 to 50 mg i.m. 3 to 4 times daily; may be given direct i.v. Children: 0.55 mg/kg i.m. or i.v. Maximum dose if child's weight $<$22.7 kg is 40 mg daily; if 22.7 to 45.5 kg, 75 mg daily.

Intractable Hiccups: If oral therapy not effective, 25 to 50 mg i.m. If still not effective, 25 to 50 mg may be diluted in 500 to 1 000 mL normal saline and infused slowly i.v.

Relief of Nausea and Vomiting: 25 to 50 mg every 3 to 4 hours.

Children: 0.55 mg/kg/dose every 6 to 8 hours as necessary.

Rectal: Relief of Nausea and Vomiting: Adults: 50 to 100 mg every 6 to 8 hours as necessary.

Children: 1 mg/kg/dose every 6 to 8 hours as necessary.

Reviewed 1999

CHLORPROMAZINE HCl INJECTION ℞

Bioniche

Antipsychotic—Antiemetic

Supplied: Each mL of sterile solution contains: chlorpromazine HCl 25 mg (equivalent to 22.4 mg of base), ascorbic acid 0.3 mg, sodium metabisulfite 1 mg, sodium sulfite 2 mg and sodium chloride (for isotonicity). Ampuls of 2 mL, boxes of 10. Store at room temperature (15 to 30°C). Protect from light. Pink or discolored solutions should be discarded.

CHLORPROPAMIDE ℞

General Monograph, CPhA

see SULFONYLUREAS

CHLORTETRACYCLINE ℞

General Monograph, CPhA

see TETRACYCLINES

CHLOR-TRIPOLON®

Schering

Chlorpheniramine Maleate

Antihistamine

Indications: The symptomatic relief of allergic states generally responsive to antihistamines, such as hay fever, urticaria, angioedema, vasomotor rhinitis, allergic eczema, serum sickness and drug reactions; also in allergic conjunctivitis, dermographism, gastrointestinal allergy, physical allergy, and exanthematous eruptions such as measles and chickenpox. Useful in atopic dermatitis, contact dermatoses (including poisoning by ivy or oak), insect bites, neurodermatitis, pruritus ani and vulvae and generalized pruritus; may be of value in some cases of allergic migraine and spasmodic bronchial cough.

Precautions: Since the depressant effects of antihistamines are additive to those of other drugs affecting the CNS, patients should be cautioned against drinking alcoholic beverages or taking hypnotics, sedatives, psychotherapeutic agents or other drugs with CNS depressant effects during antihistaminic therapy.

Persons with chronic lung disease, glaucoma or difficulty in urination due to enlargement of the prostate gland should only take this product under the advice and supervision of a physician.

Should not be used by persons who are allergic or sensitive to any of the components of the product. May cause excitability in children; children should be observed by parents.

Occupational Hazards: Patients should be cautioned not to operate vehicles or hazardous machinery until their response to the drug has been determined.

Pregnancy and *Lactation:* The safe use of this product during pregnancy and lactation has not been established and therefore the compound should be used only if the potential benefit justifies the potential risk to the fetus or infant.

Antihistamines should be discontinued approximately 48 hours prior to skin testing procedures since these may prevent or diminish otherwise positive reactions to dermal reactivity indicators.

Adverse Effects: Slight to moderate drowsiness occurs relatively infrequently. Other untoward effects include restlessness, dry mouth, dizziness, weakness, anorexia, nausea, headache, nervousness, polyuria, heartburn, diplopia, dysuria, and very rarely dermatitis.

Overdose: Symptoms and Treatment: If accidental overdose occurs, seek medical assistance immediately.

Dosage: Syrup: Adults: 1 to 2 teaspoonsful every 6 to 8 hours. Children 6 to 12 years: ½ adult dosage. Children under 6 years: only as directed by a physician. Do not exceed the recommended dosage.

Tablets: Adults: 1 tablet (4 mg) every 4 to 6 hours. Children 6 to 12 years: ½ tablet every 6 to 8 hours.

Repetabs: Adults and children 12 years and over: 1 tablet (12 mg) every 12 hours. Do not exceed 2 tablets a day, or as directed by a physician.

Supplied: Repetabs: Each orange red, 12 mg Repetabs contains: chlorpheniramine maleate USP 6 mg in the outer layer, and 6 mg in the inner core. Nonmedicinal ingredients: cornstarch, lactose, magnesium stearate, povidone and dye, FD & C Yellow No. 6; coating: acacia, carnauba wax, cornstarch, dye-Opalux AO-2024 Orange, gum rosin, oleic acid, soap powder (white, neutral), sucrose, talc, terra alba (calcium sulfate), tribasic calcium phosphate, white wax and zein-F-200. Tartrazine-free. Packages of 12 and 24. Bottles of 60.

Syrup: Each 5 mL contains: chlorpheniramine maleate USP 2.5 mg. Nonmedicinal ingredients: alcohol (<7%); benzaldehyde; dye, FD & C Blue No. 1; dye, FD & C Yellow No. 10; flavor, peach imitation; glycerin; menthol; methylparaben; propylene glycol; propylparaben; sucrose; vanillin and water. Energy: 90 kJ (21.5 kcal). Tartrazine-free. Bottles of 100 mL.

Tablets: Each yellow, scored tablet contains: chlorpheniramine maleate USP 4 mg. Nonmedicinal ingredients: cornstarch, dyes, FD & C Yellow No. 6, No. 10, gelatin, lactose and magnesium stearate. Tartrazine-free. Packages of 12 and 24. Bottles of 60.

(Shown in Product Recognition Section)

CHLOR-TRIPOLON® DECONGESTANT Syrup CHLOR-TRIPOLON® DECONGESTANT Tablets

Schering

Chlorpheniramine Maleate—Phenylpropanolamine HCl
Chlorpheniramine Maleate—Pseudoephedrine Sulfate

Antihistamine—Decongestant

Indications: Symptomatic relief of upper respiratory mucosal congestion in seasonal and perennial nasal allergies, acute rhinitis and rhinosinusitis, acute and subacute sinusitis, eustachian tube blockage and secretory otitis media.

Contraindications: Patients receiving or having received MAO inhibitors in the preceding 2 weeks; known hypersensitivity to pressor amines or antihistamines.

Precautions: Although pseudoephedrine causes practically no pressor effect in normotensive individuals, it should be used with caution in patients with hypertension, diabetes, chronic lung disease, latent or clinically recognized angle closure glaucoma, coronary artery disease, congestive heart failure, urinary retention, prostatic hypertrophy and hyperthyroidism.

Since the depressant effects of antihistamines are additive to those of other drugs affecting the CNS, caution patients against drinking alcoholic beverages or taking hypnotics, sedatives, psychotherapeutic agents or other drugs with CNS depressant effects during antihistaminic therapy.

Should not be used by persons who are allergic or sensitive to any of the components of the product. May cause excitability in children; children should be observed by parents.
Occupational Hazards: Caution patients not to operate vehicles or hazardous machinery until their response to the drug has been determined.
Pregnancy and *Lactation:* The safe use of this product during pregnancy and lactation has not been established and therefore the compound should be used only if the potential benefit justifies the potential risk to the fetus or infant.

Antihistamines should be discontinued approximately 48 hours prior to skin testing procedures since these may prevent or diminish otherwise positive reactions to dermal reactivity indicators.

Adverse Effects: Slight to moderate drowsiness occurs relatively infrequently. Other untoward effects include restlessness, dry mouth, dizziness, weakness, anorexia, nausea, headache, nervousness, polyuria, heartburn, diplopia, dysuria, and very rarely dermatitis.

Other known possible adverse effects of sympathomimetic (i.e., pseudoephedrine) origin include anxiety, tension, restlessness, nervousness, tremor, weakness, insomnia, headache, palpitation, tachycardia, angina, elevated blood pressure, sweating, mydriasis, anorexia, nausea, vomiting, dizziness, constipation and dysuria due to vesicle sphincter spasm.

Overdose: If accidental overdose occurs, seek medical assistance immediately.

Symptoms: Pseudoephedrine sulfate: nervousness, insomnia, headaches, palpitations, nausea, vomiting, precordial pain.

Chlorpheniramine maleate: sedation, lassitude, muscular weakness, palpitations, dry mouth, gastrointestinal disturbances, dermatitis.

Treatment: No specific antidote. Follow the established principles of treatment of any drug overdosage. Specific therapy will depend on the predominant symptoms observed.

Dosage: Syrup: Adults: 5 to 10 mL every 6 to 8 hours. Children: 6 to 12 years: ½ adult dosage. Children under 6 years: only as directed by a physician. Do not exceed the recommended dosage.

Tablets: Adults and children 12 years and over: 1 extra strength tablet every 12 hours. Do not exceed 2 tablets a day. Prolonged use only as directed by a physician.

Supplied: Syrup: Each 5 mL of syrup contains: chlorpheniramine maleate USP 2 mg and phenylpropanolamine HCl USP 12.5 mg. Nonmedicinal ingredients: alcohol, benzaldehyde, dyes (FD & C Blue No. 1, Yellow No. 6, Green No. 3), flavor (peach imitation), glycerin, menthol, methylparaben, propylparaben, propylene glycol, sucrose, vanillin and water. Alcohol: <7%. Energy: 90 kJ (21.5 kcal). Tartrazine-free. Bottles of 100 mL.

Tablets: Each purple, coated extra-strength tablet contains: chlorpheniramine maleate USP 12 mg and pseudoephedrine sulfate USP 120 mg, divided equally between an outer coat for rapid absorption and an inner core for repeat action. Nonmedicinal ingredients: cornstarch, lactose, povidone and magnesium stearate; coating: acacia, calcium sulfate, carnauba wax, dye-Opalux AS-4705 Purple, gelatin, gum rosin, oleic acid, soap powder (white, neutral), sucrose, talc, white wax and zein F-200. Tartrazine-free. Packages of 10.

(Shown in Product Recognition Section)

CHLOR-TRIPOLON N.D.®

Schering

Loratadine—Pseudoephedrine Sulfate

Histamine H_1-Receptor Antagonist—Sympathomimetic Amine

Pharmacology: Loratadine is a long-acting tricyclic antihistamine with selective peripheral H_1 receptor antagonistic activity. It exhibits a dose-related inhibition of the histamine-induced skin wheal and flare response in humans which is rapid in onset, is apparent at 2 hours and persists throughout the 24 hour observation period. Single oral doses up to 160 mg and repeat daily doses of 40 mg for up to 13 weeks were well tolerated with the incidence of sedation and dry mouth being no different from placebo.

^{14}C-loratadine is rapidly absorbed reaching C_{max} values (4.7, 10.8 and 26.1 ng/mL) at 1.5, 1.0 and 1.3 hours for the 10, 20 and 40 mg dose, respectively. The loratadine elimination half-life ($T_{1/2\beta}$) ranged from 7.8 to 11.0 hours.

Descarboethoxyloratadine, the major active metabolite, reached C_{max} values (4.0, 9.9 and 16.0 ng/mL) at 3.7, 1.5 and 2.0 hours after a dose of 10, 20 and 40 mg, respectively. Its $T_{1/2\beta}$ ranged from 17 to 24 hours. The accumulation indices, calculated by C_{max} and the area under the curve (AUC) ratios did not change after the 5th day, indicating little or no accumulation of either loratadine or its metabolite after a multiple once per day dosage regimen. The $T_{1/2\beta}$ at steady state levels for loratadine and its active metabolite were 14.4 and 18.7 hours, respectively, similar to that reported following a single oral dose.

Approximately 82% of the ^{14}C-loratadine dose is excreted in the urine (40%) and feces (42%) over a 10-day period. Approximately 27% of the dose is eliminated in the urine during the first 24 hours largely in the conjugated form. Unchanged drug is present only in trace quantities in the urine and the active metabolite descarboethoxyloratadine represents only 0.4 to 0.6% of the administered loratadine dose.

Pseudoephedrine, one of the naturally occurring alkaloids of Ephedra and an orally administered vasoconstrictor, produces a gradual but sustained decongestant effect facilitating shrinkage of congested mucosa in upper respiratory areas. The mucous membrane of the respiratory tract is decongested through the action of the sympathetic nerves.

Indications: For the relief of nasal and ocular symptoms of upper respiratory mucosal congestion, such as in allergic rhinitis. They are intended for short-term use only unless taken under medical supervision.

Contraindications: Patients who have shown sensitivity or idiosyncrasy to their components, to adrenergic agents or to other drugs of similar chemical structures. They are also contraindicated in patients receiving MAO inhibitor therapy or within 14 days of discontinuing such treatment and in patients with narrow-angle glaucoma, urinary retention, hypertension, severe coronary artery disease and hyperthyroidism.

Precautions: General: Sympathomimetics should be used with caution in patients with stenosing peptic ulcer, pyloroduodenal obstruction, prostatic hypertrophy or bladder neck obstruction, cardiovascular disease, increased intraocular pressure or diabetes mellitus.

Sympathomimetics should be used with caution in patients receiving digitalis.

Sympathomimetics may cause CNS stimulation and convulsions or cardiovascular collapse with accompanying hypotension.

Patients with severe liver impairment should be administered a lower dose because they may have reduced clearance of loratadine; an initial dose of 1 tablet daily is recommended.
Geriatrics: In patients 60 years of age or older, sympathomimetics are also more likely to cause adverse reactions such as confusion, hallucination, convulsions, CNS depression and death. Consequently, caution should be exercised when administering a repeat-action formulation to this patient group.
Dependence Liability: There are no data available to indicate that abuse or dependency occurs with loratadine.

Pseudoephedrine, like other CNS stimulants, has been abused. At high doses, subjects commonly experience mood elevation, decreased appetite and a sense of increased energy, physical strength, mental capacity and alertness. Anxiety, irritability and loquacity also have been reported. With continued use, tolerance develops; the user increases the dose and ultimately toxicity occurs. Depression may follow rapid withdrawal.
Children: Safety and efficacy in children younger than 12 years of age have not yet been established.
Pregnancy: Safe use during pregnancy or lactation has not been established and therefore, this product should be used only if the potential benefit justifies the potential risk to fetus or infant.
Lactation: Loratadine and its active metabolite are eliminated in the breast milk of lactating women with milk concentrations being similar to plasma concentrations. Through 48 hours after dosing, only 0.029% of the loratadine dose is eliminated in the milk as unchanged loratadine and its active metabolite, descarboethoxyloratadine.

Pseudoephedrine has been reported to be excreted into breast milk of lactating women.
Other: Because of the lack of experience with long-term use of this drug, its use should be limited to 3 months unless recommended by a physician.
Drug Interactions: When administered concomitantly with alcohol, loratadine has no potentiating effect as measured by psychomotor performance studies.

When sympathomimetic drugs are given to patients receiving MAO inhibitors, hypertensive reactions, including hypertensive crises, may occur. The antihypertensive effects of methyldopa, mecamylamine, reserpine and veratrum alkaloids may be reduced by sympathomimetics. Beta-adrenergic blocking agents may also interact with sympathomimetics. Increased ectopic pacemaker activity can occur when pseudoephedrine is used concomitantly with digitalis. Antacids increase the rate of pseudoephedrine absorption; kaolin decreases it.

Increases in plasma concentrations of loratadine have been reported after concomitant use with ketoconazole, erythromycin or cimetidine in controlled clinical trials, but without clinically significant changes (including electrocardiographic). Other drugs known to inhibit hepatic metabolism should be coadministered with caution until definitive interaction studies can be completed.
Drug Laboratory Test Interactions: Loratadine should be discontinued approximately 48 hours prior to skin testing procedures since antihistamines may prevent or diminish otherwise positive reactions to dermal reactivity indicators.

Adverse Effects: During controlled clinical studies with the recommended dosage, the incidence of adverse effects associated with Chlor-Tripolon N.D. was comparable to that of

Chlor-Tripolon N.D. (cont'd)

placebo, with the exception of insomnia and dry mouth both of which were commonly reported. Other most frequently reported [≥5%] adverse reactions associated with Chlor-Tripolon N.D., their components and placebo are listed in Table I.

Rare adverse reactions in decreasing order of frequency included: nausea, abdominal distress, anorexia, thirst, tachycardia, pharyngitis, rhinitis, acne, prutitus, rash, urticaria, arthralgia, confusion, dysphonia, hyperkinesia, hypoesthesia, decreased libido, paresthesia, tremor, vertigo, flushing, postural hypotension, increased sweating, eye disorders, earache, tinnitus, taste abnormality, agitation, apathy, depression, euphoria, paroniria, increased appetite, change in bowel habits, dyspepsia, eructation, hemorrhoids, tongue discoloration, tongue disorder, vomiting, transient abnormal hepatic function, dehydration, increased weight, hypertension, palpitation, migraine, bronchospasm, coughing, dyspnea, epistaxis, nasal congestion, sneezing, nasal irritation, dysuria, micturition disorder, nocturia, polyuria, urinary retention, asthenia, back pain, leg cramps, malaise and rigors.

During the marketing of loratadine, alopecia, anaphylaxis and abnormal hepatic function have been reported rarely.

As with other sympathomimetic amines, CNS stimulation, muscular weakness, tightness in the chest and syncope may also be encountered.

used; however, as much as possible of the amount administered should be removed before the next instillation. Saline cathartics draw water into the bowel by osmosis and therefore may be valuable for their action in rapid dilution of bowel content. Loratadine is not removed by hemodialysis; it is not known if loratadine is removed by peritoneal dialysis. After emergency treatment, the patient should continue to be medically monitored.

Treatment of the signs and symptoms of overdosage is symptomatic and supportive. Stimulants (analeptic agents) should not be used. Vasopressors may be used to treat hypotension. Short-acting barbiturates, diazepam or paraldehyde may be administered to control seizures. Hyperpyrexia, especially in children, may require treatment with tepid water sponge baths or hypothermic blanket. Apnea is treated with ventilatory support.

Dosage: Adults and Children 12 years of age and over: 1 tablet twice a day.

Supplied: Each white to off-white, round, biconvex, coated tablet contains: loratadine 5 mg in the tablet coating and pseudoephedrine sulfate 120 mg equally distributed between the tablet coating and the barrier-coated core. The two active components in the coating are quickly liberated; release of the decongestant in the core is delayed for several hours. Nonmedicinal ingredients: lactose, starch, polyvinylpyrrolidone, magnesium stearate, microcrystalline cellulose, acacia, sucrose, calcium sulfate (terra alba), rosin, zein, oleic acid, soap, talc, titanium dioxide, white wax and carnauba wax. Gluten- and tartrazine-free. Blister packages of 12 and 24. Store between 2 and 25°C. Protect from exposure to excessive moisture.

(Shown in Product Recognition Section)

Reviewed 1997

Table I—Chlor-Tripolon N.D.

Number (%) of patients reporting adverse experiences (probably or possibly related to treatment) ≥5% incidence during treatment with Chlor-Tripolon N.D., either component alone (loratadine or pseudoephedrine sulfate) or placebo in clinical studies

Adverse Experience	A Chlortripolon N.D. (N=632)	B Loratadine (N=396)	C Pseudoephedrine (N=395)	D Placebo (N=532)
Dizziness	27 (4)	4 (1)	10 (5)	8 (2)
Dry mouth	93 (15)	17 (4)	41 (10)	21 (4)
Fatigue	26 (4)	22 (6)	14 (4)	13 (2)
Headache	64 (10)	48 (12)	34 (9)	52 (10)
Insomnia	113 (18)	16 (4)	66 (17)	20 (4)
Nervousness	33 (5)	11 (3)	30 (8)	5 (1)
Sedation	41 (6)	29 (7)	18 (5)	23 (4)

Overdose: In the event of overdosage, treatment, which should be started immediately, is symptomatic and supportive. Discontinuation of use, gastric lavage or induction of emesis (except in patients with impaired consciousness) and support of vital functions are advised.

Symptoms: They may vary from CNS depression (sedation, apnea, diminished mental alertness, cyanosis, coma, cardiovascular collapse) to stimulation (insomnia, hallucination, tremors or convulsions) to death. Other signs and symptoms may be euphoria, excitement, tachycardia, palpitations, thirst, perspiration, nausea, dizziness, tinnitus, ataxia, blurred vision and hypertension or hypotension. Stimulation is particularly likely in children, as are atropine-like signs and symptoms (dry mouth; fixed, dilated pupils; flushing; hyperthermia and gastrointestinal symptoms).

In large doses sympathomimetics may give rise to giddiness, headache, nausea, vomiting, sweating, thirst, tachycardia, precordial pain, palpitations, difficulty in micturition, muscular weakness and tenseness, anxiety, restlessness and insomnia. Many patients can present a toxic psychosis with delusions and hallucinations. Some may develop cardiac arrhythmias, circulatory collapse, convulsions, coma and respiratory failure.

Treatment: The patient should be induced to vomit, even if emesis has occurred spontaneously. Pharmacologically-induced vomiting by the administration of ipecac syrup is a preferred method. However, vomiting should not be induced in patients with impaired consciousness. The action of ipecac is facilitated by physical activity and by the administration of 240 to 360 mL of water. If emesis does not occur within 15 minutes, the dose of ipecac should be repeated. Precautions against aspiration must be taken, especially in children. Following emesis, adsorption of any drugs remaining in the stomach may be attempted by the administration of activated charcoal as a slurry with water. If vomiting is unsuccessful, or contraindicated, gastric lavage should be performed. Physiologic saline solution is the lavage solution of choice, particularly in children. In adults, tap water can be

CHOLECALCIFEROL
General Monograph, CPhA

see VITAMIN D

CHOLECYSTOKININ
Ferring

Diagnostic Cholecystokinetic

Pharmacology: Cholecystokinin (CCK) is a natural polypeptide, formed in the APUD cells of the proximal mucosa of the small intestine. It stimulates secretion of pancreatic digestive enzymes, the flow of bile and the secretion from the glands of Brunner. It stimulates contraction of the gallbladder, inhibits contraction of the lower esophageal sphincter and the sphincter of Oddi and increases motility of the stomach and intestine.

When injected i.v., cholecystokinin induces contraction of the contrast-filled gallbladder with good visualization of the bile ducts within 1 to 3 minutes, providing more immediate results than an egg fat meal. The effect persists for more than 2 hours. Choledochal concrement is also often expelled. If contrast medium does not penetrate into the duodenum an organic process should be suspected.

Bile collected by means of an indwelling duodenal catheter gives information about the presence of chronic cholecystitis, infection or cancer. Exfoliative cytology on the duodenal contents ad modum Papanicolaou represents a valuable addition to cancer diagnosis for demonstration of malignant processes in a gallbladder and bile ducts and, to some extent, primary processes in the liver. The gallbladder and stomach can be examined at the same time.

Indications: Cholecystography, preoperative cholangiography, secondary cholangiography, roentgenological studies of the small bowel, diagnosis of pancreatic insufficiency (complement to the secretin test).

To induce contraction of the gallbladder and relaxation of the sphincter of Oddi. During routine oral cholecystography, or preoperative cholangiography, cholecystokinin can be used to provide an evaluation of the contraction pattern of the gallbladder, filling of the bile ducts, flow of contrast medium into the duodenum, and localization of gallstones in the lower common bile duct in connection with cholecystectomy and/or bile duct surgery.

To increase small bowel motility during radiological investigation. Cholecystokinin can reduce transit time and flocculation of a barium meal.

To stimulate the output of enzymes in conjunction with secretin. Cholecystokinin can aid in the diagnosis of pancreatic insufficiency in the secretin-cholecystokinin test.

Contraindications: None known.

Warnings: As a result of the effect of CCK on the gallbladder and the motility of the intestine, stomach-ache and a feeling of discomfort in the epigastrium may occur. If CCK is given too rapidly flushing may occur.

Precautions: None.

Adverse Effects: No adverse reactions to CCK have so far been reported (see Warnings).

Overdose: Symptoms and Treatment: If cholecystokinin is given too rapidly flushing may occur. This side effect is rare provided the directions are followed.

Dosage: The contents of 1 bottle of cholecystokinin should be dissolved in 7.5 mL of physiological saline, giving a concentration of 10 Ivy dog units (IDU)/mL. Discard any unused portion of the reconstituted solution.

Cholecystography: For an ordinary cholecystokinin test the contents of one 75 IDU bottle of cholecystokinin should be dissolved in 7.5 mL of physiological saline and 1 IDU/kg body weight (0.1 mL) should be given by slow i.v. injection. Contraction of the gallbladder and filling of the bile ducts with "contrast bile" normally occurs within 1 to 3 minutes. The patient should be given contrast medium on the evening before the examination and fluoroscopy should be carried out before the x-ray examination. If the gallbladder is visible, cholecystokinin should be injected and x-ray films taken in the normal way. An advantage of the technique is that x-ray of the stomach may be carried out simultaneously as there is no interference from undigested food.

Preoperative Cholangiography: About 40 units (4 mL) of cholecystokinin solution should be injected i.v. immediately before the cholangiography. After about 1 minute, contrast medium should be injected into the common bile duct and x-ray plates taken in the normal way. As cholecystokinin increases enzyme activity in the pancreas, the amylase values should be monitored for the following 3 days.

Secondary Cholangiography: If concrement residues remain after the operation, 75 units should be given i.v. each day for 1 week and cholangiography should be performed in connection with the last cholecystokinin injection. If required, the treatment may be repeated for a further week. The amylase values should be monitored.

Roentgenological Studies of the Small Bowel: CCK can be used to facilitate the transit of the barium meal through the small bowel. After ingestion of 200 to 300 mL of barium mixture, the patient should lie on his right side for 10 to 15 minutes. If fluoroscopic control shows that most of the contrast medium has passed into the first part of the jejunum, 0.5 to 1 IDU CCK/kg body weight is injected slowly i.v. The examination is usually completed within 15 minutes, permitting fluoroscopy during the whole procedure if necessary.

Diagnosis of Pancreatic Insufficiency: As a complement to the secretin test, 0.5 to 1 IDU CCK/kg body weight administered as slow i.v. injection.

Supplied: Each injection bottle contains: cholecystokinin 75 IDU, L-cysteine 0.4 mg, L-cysteine HCl 0.1 mg and mannitol 20 mg. Packs of 1. The lyophilized powder should be stored at −20°C.

What foods are rich in vitamin K? To answer this and other vitamin food source questions, see the CLIN-INFO SECTION.

CHOLEDYL® ℞
Parke-Davis
Oxtriphylline
Bronchodilator

Pharmacology: Oxtriphylline contains 64% theophylline and has the properties attributed to theophylline.

Indications: The symptomatic treatment of reversible bronchoconstriction associated with bronchial asthma, chronic obstructive pulmonary emphysema, chronic bronchitis and related bronchospastic disorders.

Contraindications: Hypersensitivity to xanthines; active peptic ulcer; in coronary artery disease when myocardial stimulation might prove harmful.

Precautions: Parents should be cautioned against overdosage to children—children are very sensitive to xanthines; the margin of safety above therapeutic doses is small. Ensure that children receiving oral oxtriphylline are not also receiving xanthines by the rectal route.

There is a marked variation in blood concentrations achieved in different patients given the same dose of oxtriphylline. This may lead to serious adverse effects in some patients. This variability in blood concentrations is probably due to differences in drug distribution and metabolism. Therefore, it is advisable to individualize the dose regimens. Ideally, all individuals should have serum theophylline concentrations measured and a theophylline half-life calculated. This would enable doses and dosing regimens to be tailored to each patient to maintain a therapeutic concentration, to ensure optimal clinical response and to avoid toxicity. Concurrent administration of other drugs and xanthine containing beverages can affect assay results (Schack and Waxler method).

In patients with severe pulmonary or cardiovascular disease and in patients with hepatic dysfunction, oxtriphylline metabolism may be impaired and thus toxic concentrations may be reached with standard dose regimens.

Exercise caution when oxtriphylline is used concurrently with sympathomimetic amines or other xanthines. In general, oxtriphylline should not be given more frequently than every 6 hours or within 12 hours of the ingestion of other xanthines.

Oxtriphylline may cause an elevation of serum uric acid, urinary catecholamines and plasma free fatty acids.

<u>*Drug Interactions:*</u> Synergism with ephedrine has been documented and may occur with other sympathomimetic amines. Theophylline may cause increased excretion of lithium carbonate. Theophylline antagonizes the effect of propranolol. Theophylline potentiates the effects of diuretics and the cardiac effect of digitalis glycosides. The concomitant use of morphine, stilbamidine, curare may antagonize the effect of theophylline since these drugs stimulate histamine release and thereby induce bronchoconstriction.

Cigarette smoking and phenobarbital shorten, while alcohol consumption increases the half-life of theophylline.

Xanthines have been shown to be nephrotoxic with prolonged use at high dosage. Coincident toxicity should therefore be borne in mind when other potentially nephrotoxic drugs are administered concurrently.

Acidifying agents, by increasing urinary excretion of weak bases like the xanthines, inhibit theophylline action.

Alkalinizing agents, by decreasing urinary excretion of weak bases like the xanthines, potentiate theophylline action.

Combined use of several xanthines may cause excessive CNS stimulation.

Toxic reactions as a result of significant elevations of serum theophylline levels have been observed in patients after initiation of treatment with erythromycin preparations. Particular attention should therefore be directed toward monitoring the serum theophylline levels in such patients.

The methylxanthines increase blood levels of prothrombin and fibrinogen, shorten the prothrombin time and thus antagonize the effects of coumarin anticoagulants.

Xanthines antagonize the uricosuric action of probenecid and of sulfinpyrazone and uricosuric activity of pyrazolon derivatives.

Combined use of xanthines with sympathomimetics may cause excessive CNS stimulation.

Cimetidine, erythromycin, influenza vaccine and propranolol may increase the effect of theophylline by decreasing theophylline clearance.

Oxtriphylline potentiates the diuretic action of thiazide diuretics and the cardiac effect of digitalis glycosides. Oxtriphylline increases the ratio of clearances of lithium/ creatinine, and may thus decrease serum lithium to ineffective concentrations.

Adverse Effects: Toxicity of theophylline and its derivatives may present as follows:
Gastrointestinal: nausea, vomiting, diarrhea, abdominal cramps, epigastric pain, anorexia, reactivation of peptic ulcers, intestinal bleeding.
CNS: headache, nervousness, insomnia, dizziness, light- headedness, excitement, irritability, restlessness, convulsions.
Cardiovascular: palpitation, sinus tachycardia, increased pulse rate, peripheral vascular constriction and/or collapse.
Urinary tract: albuminuria, diuresis.
Skin: rarely urticaria, generalized pruritus, angioneurotic edema, contact dermatitis.
Blood: very rarely bone marrow suppression, leukopenia, thrombocytopenia, hemorrhagic diathesis.
Others: tachypnea, hyperglycemia and inappropriate ADH syndrome.

Overdose: Symptoms: The most consistent reactions observed with toxic overdoses of xanthine derivatives are:
Gastrointestinal: nausea, vomiting, epigastric pain, hematemesis, diarrhea.
CNS: In addition to those cited above, the patient may exhibit hyperreflexia, fasciculations and clonic and tonic convulsions. These are especially prone to occur in cases of overdosage in infants and small children.
Cardiovascular: In addition to those outlined above, marked hypotension and circulatory failure may be manifest.
Respiratory: Tachypnea and respiratory arrest may occur.
Renal: Albuminuria and microhematuria may occur. Increased excretion of renal tubular cells has been observed.
General systemic effects: syncope, collapse, fever and dehydration.

Treatment: 1. Discontinue drug immediately. 2. There is no known specific antidote. 3. Gastric lavage. 4. Emetic medication may be of value. 5. Avoid administration of sympathomimetic drugs. 6. I.V. fluids, oxygen and other supportive measures to prevent hypotension and overcome dehydration. 7. CNS stimulation and seizures may respond to i.v. diazepam, phenytoin sodium or phenobarbital sodium. 8. Monitor blood concentrations until below 20 μg/mL.

Dosage: Total daily dose should be individually titrated based on patient's clinical response and/or serum theophylline level which should be in the range of 8 to 20 μg/mL.

Adults: The average initial dose is 200 to 400 mg oxtriphylline. Usual daily maintenance dose will be between 800 to 1 200 mg oxtriphylline (512 to 768 mg expressed as anhydrous theophylline)/24 hours.

Children: Choledyl Elixir is not recommended for children under 10 years of age. Choledyl Pediatric Syrup may be preferred.
Children 10 to 14 years: Initial dose is 22 mg/kg of oxtriphylline in the first 24 hours divided into 4 equal doses. Usual maintenance dose will be 400 to 800 mg (15 to 22 mg/kg) oxtriphylline/24 hours (9.5 to 14 mg/kg expressed as anhydrous theophylline) divided into 4 equal doses, given at 6 hour intervals.
Children 5 to 9 years: Usual daily maintenance dose will be 200 to 400 mg/24 hours divided into 4 equal doses, given at 6 hour intervals.
Children under 5 years: Total daily dose should be between 24 to 36 mg/kg body weight/24 hours divided into 3 equal doses, given at 8 hour intervals.

This drug should be taken preferably prior to meals with a glass of water.

The following mg equivalents facilitate changing from one xanthine preparation to another: theophylline anhydrous 100 mg=aminophylline 118 mg=oxtriphylline 156 mg= theophylline sodium glycinate 200 mg.

Individual requirements may vary considerably and the patient's dose may have to be adjusted accordingly. To minimize gastric irritation, doses may be taken with milk, meals or antacids without altering drug absorption.

Because of the large intersubject variability, monitoring of plasma oxtriphylline concentrations is extremely important, especially in the initial stages of therapy (see Precautions).

Supplied: Elixir: Each 5 mL of clear, dark amber-colored liquid contains: oxtriphylline USP 100 mg. Nonmedicinal ingredients: alcohol, citric acid, D&C Green No. 5, D&C Yellow No. 10, FD&C Red No. 2, flavoring agents, glycerin, sodium chloride, sodium citrate, sodium cyclamate, sobitol and sugar Alcohol: 20%. Energy: 58.6 kJ (14 kcal)/5 mL. Sodium: <1 mmol (11.8 mg)/5 mL. Gluten-, lactose-, paraben-, sulfite- and tartrazine-free. Bottles of 500 mL.

Pediatric Syrup: Each 5 mL of clear, red colored, vanilla mint flavored syrup contains: oxtriphylline USP 50 mg. Nonmedicinal ingredients: caramel, citric acid, D&C Red No. 33, flavoring agents, glycerin, L-menthol, sodium citrate, sobitol and sugar. Energy: 76.6 kJ (18.3 kcal)/5 mL. Sodium: <1 mmol (3.7 mg)/5 mL. Alcohol-, gluten-, lactose-, paraben-, sulfite- and tartrazine-free. Bottles of 500 mL.

(Shown in Product Recognition Section)

CHOLEDYL® EXPECTORANT ℞
Parke-Davis
Oxtriphylline—Guaifenesin
Bronchodilator—Expectorant

Pharmacology: Oxtriphylline contains 64% theophylline and has the properties attributed to theophylline.

Indications: The symptomatic treatment of reversible bronchoconstriction associated with chronic obstructive pulmonary emphysema, bronchial asthma, chronic bronchitis and related bronchospastic disorders and where expectoration is required.

Precautions: Patients starting therapy should be carefully observed to determine if this fixed dose combination is suitable for them. The use of single drug preparations to allow for more accurate dose adjustment for each component may be preferable in some patients. The dose of oxtriphylline required to achieve therapeutic blood concentrations varies considerably among patients.

Should not be administered more often than every 4 hours or within 12 hours following oral, parenteral or rectal use of other xanthine containing preparations. Simultaneous use of additional xanthines by any route should be avoided in all patients, especially children.

Children are very sensitive to xanthines; the margin of safety above therapeutic doses is small.

<u>*Drug Interactions:*</u> Synergism with ephedrine has been documented and may occur with other sympathomimetic amines. Theophylline may cause increased excretion of lithium carbonate. Theophylline antagonizes the effect of propranolol. Theophylline potentiates the effects of diuretics and the cardiac effect of digitalis glycosides. The concomitant use of morphine, stilbamidine, curare may antagonize the effect of theophylline since these drugs stimulate histamine release and thereby induce bronchoconstriction.

Cigarette smoking and phenobarbital shorten, while alcohol consumption increases the half-life of theophylline.

Xanthines have been shown to be nephrotoxic with prolonged use at high dosage. Coincident toxicity should therefore be borne in mind when other potentially nephrotoxic drugs are administered concurrently.

Acidifying agents, by increasing urinary excretion of weak bases like the xanthines, inhibit theophylline action.

Alkalinizing agents, by decreasing urinary excretion of weak bases like the xanthines, potentiate theophylline action.

Combined use of several xanthines may cause excessive CNS stimulation.

Toxic reactions as a result of significant elevations of serum theophylline levels have been observed in patients after initiation of treatment with erythromycin preparations. Particular attention should therefore be directed toward monitoring the serum theophylline levels in such patients.

The methylxanthines increase blood levels of prothrombin and fibrinogen, shorten the prothrombin time and thus antagonize the effects of coumarin anticoagulants.

Xanthines antagonize the uricosuric action of probenecid and of sulfinpyrazone and uricosuric activity of pyrazolon derivatives.

Combined use of xanthines with sympathomimetics may cause excessive CNS stimulation.

Cimetidine, erythromycin, influenza vaccine and propranolol may increase the effect of theophylline by decreasing theophylline clearance.

Adverse Effects: Gastric distress, palpitation and CNS stimulation may occur occasionally.
Others: tachypnea, hyperglycemia and inappropriate ADH syndrome.

Overdose: Symptoms: Collapse, hypotension and excessive CNS stimulation. However, as with all theophylline products, marked gastric irritation occurs following overdosage and vomiting usually relieves the toxic level which may have been taken.
N.B.: Guaifenesin is a phenol (carbolic acid) derivative.

Treatment: Evacuate the stomach by lavage or emesis, followed by catharsis. Maintain blood pressure. Oxygen therapy as indicated. Usual measures for control of excessive CNS stimulation. See also Choledyl monograph.

Dosage: Usual maintenance doses: Patients over 14 years: 10 mL 4 times daily; 10 to 14 years: 5 mL 4 times daily.

Choledyl Expectorant (cont'd)

The following mg equivalents facilitate changing from one xanthine preparation to another: theophylline anhydrous 100 mg=aminophylline 118 mg=oxtriphylline 156 mg=theophylline sodium glycinate 200 mg.

Supplied: Each 5 mL of red, cherry-flavored liquid contains: oxtriphylline 100 mg and guaifenesin 50 mg. Nonmedicinal ingredients: alcohol, anethole, citric acid, FD&C Red No. 2, FD&C Yellow No. 6, flavoring agents, glycerin, sodium citrate, sodium cyclamate and sugar. Alcohol: 20%. Energy: 74.1 kJ (17.7 kcal)/5 mL. Sodium: <1 mmol (10.4 mg)/5 mL. Gluten-, lactose-, paraben-, sulfite- and tartrazine-free. Bottles of 250 and 500 mL.

(Shown in Product Recognition Section)

CHOLEDYL® SA ℞

Parke-Davis

Oxtriphylline

Bronchodilator

Pharmacology: Oxtriphylline is the theophylline salt of choline and contains 64% theophylline with the properties attributed to it. Choledyl SA is a sustained release tablet which produces peak blood levels of theophylline (8 to 12 µg/mL) between 2 and 4 hours. Once the steady-state level has been reached, the therapeutic blood levels persist for 12 hours.

Indications: For maintenance therapy in adult patients for the symptomatic relief of reversible bronchoconstriction associated with bronchial asthma, pulmonary emphysema, chronic bronchitis and related bronchospastic disorders.

Contraindications: In those patients who have shown hypersensitivity to it or to other theophylline derivatives; in coronary artery disease when in the physician's judgment myocardial stimulation might prove harmful. It should not be used in patients with peptic ulcer.

Warnings: Children are very sensitive to xanthines: the margin of safety above the therapeutic dose is small. The use of Choledyl SA tablets in children is not recommended at present as dose schedules for this age group have not been established. Use with caution in the presence of severe hypertension and other cardiovascular diseases.

Precautions: There is a marked variation in blood levels achieved in different patients given the same dose of theophylline. This may lead to serious side effects in some patients. This variability in blood levels is probably due to differences in the rate of metabolism. Therefore, it is advisable to individualize the dose regimens. Ideally all individuals should have serum theophylline levels measured and a theophylline half-life calculated which would enable doses and dosing regimens to be tailored to each patient to maintain a therapeutic level, to ensure optimal clinical response and to avoid toxicity. Concurrent tea, coffee or cocoa administration may affect assay results.The possibility of overdose must be considered in all patients and especially when large doses are used, because fatalities have been reported with theophylline-containing products. Overdoses of oxtriphylline may cause peripheral vascular collapse.

Caution should be exercised when theophylline is used concurrently with sympathomimetic amines or other xanthines, as such use may increase the incidence and severity of adverse reactions. Choledyl SA should not be given within 12 hours of the ingestion of other xanthines. Special caution is necessary in patients with severe pulmonary or cardiovascular disease and in patients with hepatic dysfunction as metabolism of theophylline may be impaired in these patients leading to the possibility of toxic blood levels on fixed dosage regimen.

Theophylline may cause an elevation of serum uric acid, urine catecholamines and plasma free fatty acids.

Pregnancy: Theophylline crosses the placental barrier and also passes freely into breast milk, where concentrations are similar to plasma levels. Safe use in pregnancy has not been established relative to possible adverse effects on fetal development, but neither have adverse effects on fetal development been established. Therefore, the use of theophylline in pregnant women should be balanced against the risk of uncontrolled asthma.

Drug Interactions: Synergism with ephedrine has been documented and may occur with other sympathomimetic amines. Theophylline may cause increased excretion of lithium carbonate. Theophylline antagonizes the effect of propranolol. Theophylline potentiates the effects of diuretics and the cardiac effect of digitalis glycosides. The concomitant use of morphine, stilbamidine, curare may antagonize the effect of theophylline since these drugs stimulate histamine release and thereby induce bronchoconstriction.

Cigarette smoking and phenobarbital shorten, while alcohol consumption increases the half-life of theophylline.

Xanthines have been shown to be nephrotoxic with prolonged use at high dosage. Coincident toxicity should therefore be borne in mind when other potentially nephrotoxic drugs are administered concurrently.

Acidifying agents, by increasing urinary excretion of weak bases like the xanthines, inhibit theophylline action.

Alkalinizing agents, by decreasing urinary excretion of weak bases like the xanthines, potentiate theophylline action.

Combined use of several xanthines may cause excessive CNS stimulation.

Toxic reactions as a result of significant elevations of serum theophylline levels have been observed in patients after initiation of treatment with erythromycin preparations. Particular attention should therefore be directed toward monitoring the serum theophylline levels in such patients.

The methylxanthines increase blood levels of prothrombin and fibrinogen, shorten the prothrombin time and thus antagonize the effects of coumarin anticoagulants.

Xanthines antagonize the uricosuric action of probenecid and of sulfinpyrazone and uricosuric activity of pyrazolon derivatives.

Combined use of xanthines with sympathomimetics may cause excessive CNS stimulation.

Cimetidine, erythromycin, influenza vaccine and propranolol may increase the effect of theophylline by decreasing theophylline clearance.

Adverse Effects: The most common adverse reactions are gastric irritation, nausea, vomiting, epigastric pain, and tremor. These are usually early signs of toxicity. However, with high doses ventricular arrhythmias or seizures may be the first signs to appear.

Adverse reactions reported with theophylline preparations include:

Gastrointestinal: nausea, vomiting, epigastric pain, anorexia, reactivation of peptic ulcers, abdominal cramps, diarrhea and intestinal bleeding.

CNS: headache, nervousness, insomnia, dizziness, lightheadedness, excitement, irritability, restlessness and convulsions.

Cardiovascular System: palpitation, hypotension, circulatory failure, tachycardia, extrasystole, life-threatening ventricular arrhythmias.

Urinary Tract: albuminuria, diuresis, hematuria.

Skin: urticaria, generalized pruritus, angioneurotic edema and contact dermatitis.

Blood: bone marrow suppression, leukopenia, thrombocytopenia and hemorrhagic diathesis.

Others: tachypnea, hyperglycemia and inappropriate ADH syndrome.

Overdose: Symptoms and Treatment: See Choledyl monograph.

Note: It is particularly important to administer a cathartic when the sustained release preparation (Choledyl SA), has been taken.

Dosage: Adults: The average recommended initial adult dose is one 400 or 600 mg tablet every 12 hours. If desired response is not achieved, and there are no adverse reactions, the dose may be increased by 3 to 4 mg/kg oxtriphylline daily at 3-day intervals. The maximum daily dose should not exceed 1 600 mg oxtriphylline. Tablets should not be chewed or crushed, but may be halved. Because of large differences in individual requirements, the physician should be prepared to adjust the dose according to the patient's clinical response and/or serum theophylline level which should be in the range of 8 to 20 µg/mL.

Children: Not recommended for children.

The following equivalents facilitate changing from one xanthine preparation to another: theophylline anhydrous 100 mg=aminophylline 118 mg=oxtriphylline 156 mg=theophylline sodium glycinate 200 mg.

Supplied: 400 mg: Each scored, glossy, pink-colored biconvex, ellipsoid, coated, sustained-release tablet contains: oxtriphylline 400 mg. Nonmedicinal ingredients: carnauba wax, hydrogenated soybean oil, magnesium stearate and sugar; coating: candelilla wax, hydroxypropyl cellulose, opaseal, opaspray pink and talc. Energy: 1.3 kJ (0.3 kcal).

600 mg: Each scored, glossy, tan-colored, biconvex, ellipsoid, coated, sustained-release tablet contains: oxtriphylline 600 mg. Nonmedicinal ingredients: carnauba wax, hydrogenated soybean oil, magnesium stearate and sugar; coating: candelilla wax, hydroxypropyl cellulose, opaseal, opaspray tan and talc. Energy: 2.5 kJ (0.6 kcal).

Both are gluten-, lactose-, paraben-, sodium-, sulfite- and tartrazine-free. Bottles of 100. Store between 15 to 30°C.

(Shown in Product Recognition Section)

CHOLERA VACCINE

Connaught

Cholera Prophylaxis

Indications: For immunization against cholera.

Precautions: As with any injection of biological materials, epinephrine HCl solution (1:1 000) should be immediately available as a precautionary measure should an acute anaphylactoid reaction occur.

Adverse Effects: Vaccination often results in discomfort at the site of injection for 1 or more days. The local reaction may be accompanied by fever, malaise and headache.

Dosage: Cholera vaccine is commonly given in 2 s.c. doses, as follows: Adults: first dose: 0.5 mL (approx. 4 000 million vibrios); second dose: 1 mL (approx. 8 000 million vibrios).

It is recommended that the second injection be given 3 to 4 weeks after the first injection. Where practicable, it is desirable to give a third (first booster) s.c. dose of 1 mL approximately 3 to 4 weeks after the second dose. When circumstances do not permit of an interval of from 3 to 4 weeks between doses, the interval may be shortened to 7 days.

Children: See Table I.

Table I—Cholera Vaccine

Dosage in Children

Dose Number	Age (Years) Under 5	5-10	Over 10
1	0.1 mL	0.3 mL	0.5 mL
2 & Boosters	0.3 mL	0.5 mL	1.0 mL

Booster Doses: The duration of immunity induced by the vaccine is relatively brief. Antibody titres reach a peak within 4 weeks of vaccination and are maintained for about 3 months. Protection against disease seems to last no more than 6 months after the primary series or a booster dose.

Booster injections should be given every 6 months as long as the likelihood of exposure exists. In areas where cholera only occurs in a 2 to 3 month "season", protection is optimal when the booster dose is given at the beginning of the season. The primary series need never be repeated for booster doses to be effective.

Administration: The preparation should be administered by s.c. injection. The injection may conveniently be made into s.c. tissue near the insertion of the deltoid muscle. The site of injection should be prepared with a suitable antiseptic.

Shake the vial vigorously until the vibrios are uniformly suspended in the vaccine.

Where sterile disposable syringes and needles are not used, syringes and needles should be sterilized in an autoclave at 121°C for 30 minutes. Failing that, they should be boiled for at least 20 minutes.

Withdrawing the preparation from a rubber-stoppered vial: **Do not remove the rubber stopper from the vial:** Shake the vial vigorously until the vibrios are uniformly suspended in the vaccine. Apply a sterile pledget of cotton moistened with a suitable antiseptic to the surface of the rubber stopper and allow it to act for at least 5 minutes. Draw into the sterile syringe a volume of air equal to the amount of the preparation to be withdrawn from the vial. Pierce the center of the rubber stopper with the sterile needle of the syringe, invert the vial, slowly inject into the air contained in the syringe, and, keeping the point of the needle immersed, withdraw into the syringe the required amount of the preparation. Then hold the syringe-plunger steady and withdraw the needle from the vial.

Carefully insert the needle into the s.c. tissue. In order to avoid i.v. injection, pull back the plunger of the syringe to make certain that no blood is withdrawn before injecting the desired dose.

Supplied: A saline suspension of killed cholera vibrios. Each mL contains: approximately 8 000 million killed V. cholerae. Vials of 2.5 and 10 mL. Store at 2 to 8°C. Do not freeze.

Reviewed 1998

CHOLOXIN® ℞
Knoll

Dextrothyroxine Sodium
Hypolipidemic Thyroactive Agent

Pharmacology: Dextrothyroxine reduces serum cholesterol levels in hyperlipidemic patients. Beta lipoprotein and triglyceride fractions may also be reduced from previously elevated levels.

Dextrothyroxine stimulates the liver to increase catabolism and excretion of cholesterol and its degradation products via the biliary route into the feces. Cholesterol synthesis is not inhibited and abnormal metabolic end-products do not accumulate in the blood.

Indications: Dextrothyroxine is an antilipidemic agent used as an adjunct to diet and other measures for the reduction of elevated serum cholesterol (low density lipoprotein) in euthyroid patients with no known evidence of organic heart disease.

Contraindications: Known organic heart disease, including angina pectoris; history of myocardial infarction; cardiac arrhythmia or tachycardia, either active or in patients with demonstrated propensity for arrhythmias; rheumatic heart disease; history of congestive heart failure, and decompensated or borderline compensated cardiac status.

Hypertensive states other than mild, labile systolic hypertension.

Advanced liver or kidney disease.

Pregnancy and *Lactation:* Contraindicated in pregnancy and lactation.

History of iodism.

Warnings: Several studies indicate that dextrothyroxine potentiates the effects of anticoagulants, such as warfarin or dicumarol, on prothrombin time.

Consequently, the dosage of anticoagulants should be reduced by one-third upon initiation of dextrothyroxine therapy and the dosage subsequently readjusted on the basis of prothrombin time, which should be monitored frequently during the first few weeks of treatment.

Dextrothyroxine has also apparently been shown to decrease the concentration of Factors VII, VIII, IX, and the platelet activity in some patients. Therefore, during anticoagulant therapy, attention should be paid to other clotting factors besides the one-step prothrombin time. Spontaneous bleeding has been observed in a dextrothyroxine-treated patient on warfarin who had a prothrombin time within the therapeutic range but whose prothrombin and Factor VII concentrations were greatly decreased.

Since the possibility of precipitating cardiac arrhythmias during surgery may be greater in patients treated with thyroid hormones, it may be wise to discontinue dextrothyroxine in euthyroid patients at least 2 weeks prior to an elective operation. During emergency surgery in euthyroid patients, in whom it may not be advisable to withdraw thyroid therapy, the patient should be carefully monitored.

Dextrothyroxine in diabetic patients is capable of increasing blood sugar levels with a resultant increase in requirements of insulin or oral hypoglycemic agents. Special attention should be paid to parameters necessary for good control of the diabetic state in dextrothyroxine-treated subjects and to dosage requirements of insulin or other antidiabetic drugs. If dextrothyroxine is later withdrawn from patients who had required an increase in the dosage of insulin or of other oral hypoglycemic agents during its administration, the dosage of antidiabetic drugs may again require adjustment to maintain good control of the diabetic state.

When impaired liver and/or kidney function are present, the advantages of dextrothyroxine therapy must be weighed against the possibility of deleterious results.

Precautions: General: Use of dextrothyroxine does not preclude consideration of dietary regulations in treatment of patients with hypercholesterolemia. Until more information is obtained on each effect in pediatric patients, use in children under 12 years of age is not recommended.

As with all dextrothyroxine thyroactive drugs, hypothyroid patients are more sensitive to any specified dose than euthyroid patients.

It is expected that patients on dextrothyroxine therapy will show increased serum thyronine levels. These increased serum thyronine values are evidence of absorption and transport of the drug, and should **not** be interpreted as evidence of hypermetabolism; therefore, they may not be used to determine the effective dose of dextrothyroxine. Thyroxine values in the range of 10 to 25 μg% in dextrothyroxine-treated patients are common.

If signs or symptoms of iodism develop during dextrothyroxine therapy, the drug should be discontinued.

The 2 mg tablets contain FD&C Yellow No. 5 (tartrazine) which may cause allergic-type reactions (including bronchial asthma) in certain susceptible individuals. Although the overall incidence of FD&C Yellow No. 5 (tartrazine) sensitivity in the general population is low, it is frequently seen in patients who also have aspirin hypersensitivity.

Carcinogenesis, Mutagenesis, Impairment of Fertility: Long-term studies in animals to evaluate carcinogenic potential have not been performed.

Pregnancy: Teratogenic Effects: Pregnancy Category B: Reproduction studies have been performed in rabbits and rats at doses up to 100 times the expected maximum daily dose for humans and have revealed no evidence of impaired fertility or harm to the fetus due to dextrothyroxine. There are, however, no adequate and well-controlled studies in pregnant women. Because animal reproduction studies are not always predictive of human response, this drug should be used during pregnancy only if clearly needed.

Women of childbearing age who require drug therapy for hypercholesterolemia should consider use of the bile acid secreting resins. Since pregnancy may occur despite use of birth control procedures, administration of dextrothyroxine to women of this age group should be undertaken only after weighing the possible risk to the fetus against the possible benefits to the mother.

Lactation: It is not known whether dextrothyroxine is excreted in human milk. Because many drugs are excreted in human milk, caution and careful monitoring of the nursing infant should be exercised when dextrothyroxine is administered to a nursing woman.

Children: Safety and effectiveness in children have not been established.

Drug Interactions: Additive metabolic effects may occur when dextrothyroxine is administered concomitantly with other thyroid preparations.

Dextrothyroxine may potentiate the anticoagulant effects of warfarin sodium or dicumarol. When either of these drugs is administered concurrently with dextrothyroxine, the dosage of the oral anticoagulant initially should be reduced by one-third to prevent hemorrhage. Frequent prothrombin time determinations should be performed (at least weekly during the first few weeks of therapy), and anticoagulant dosage should be adjusted as needed.

Dextrothyroxine may enhance the effects of cardiac glycosides on the myocardium, resulting in excessive myocardial stimulation.

Administration of catecholamines in patients with coronary artery disease may precipitate arrhythmias and/or coronary insufficiency. Because this reaction may be enhanced in patients receiving thyroid preparations, catecholamines should be given with extreme caution in patients with coronary artery disease who are receiving dextrothyroxine.

Cholestyramine resin, and possibly colestipol HCl, may decrease the absorption of concurrently administered thyroid preparations. Patients should be instructed to allow as long a time interval as possible between ingestion of dextrothyroxine and the resins. Some clinicians recommend that dextrothyroxine be administered at least 1 hour before or 4 hours after the resins.

Dextrothyroxine may increase blood glucose concentrations and cause glycosuria in patients with diabetes mellitus, thus necessitating close monitoring and possibly an increase in dosage of insulin or oral antidiabetic drugs during concomitant therapy. If dextrothyroxine is discontinued in a patient who required an increased dosage of hypoglycemic drugs, dosage of the hypoglycemic drug should be reduced and subsequently adjusted to maintain control of the diabetic state.

Adverse Effects: The side effects attributed to dextrothyroxine therapy may be minimized by following the recommended dosage schedule. Adverse effects are least commonly seen in euthyroid patients with no signs or symptoms of organic heart disease. The incidence of adverse effects is increased in hypothyroid patients and is highest in those patients with organic heart disease superimposed on the hypothyroid state.

The single side effect that has caused the most concern is the possibility of increased severity of frequency of angina in patients with coronary artery disease.

In the absence of known organic heart disease, some cardiac signs and symptoms have occurred during dextrothyroxine therapy. In addition to angina pectoris, arrhythmias consisting of extrasystoles, ectopic beats, or supraventricular tachycardia, ECG evidence of ischemic myocardial changes, and increase in heart size have been observed. Myocardial infarctions, both fatal and nonfatal, have occurred, but these are not unexpected in untreated patients in the age groups studied. It is not known whether any of these infarcts were drug related.

Changes in clinical status that may be related to the metabolic action of the drug include the development of insomnia, nervousness, palpitation, tremors, loss of weight, lid loss, sweating, flushing, hyperthermia, hair loss, diuresis, and menstrual irregularities. Gastrointestinal complaints during therapy have included dyspepsia, abdominal pain, nausea and vomiting, constipation, diarrhea, and decrease in appetite.

Other side effects reported to be associated with dextrothyroxine therapy include the development of headache, changes in libido (increase or decrease), hoarseness, tinnitus, dizziness, peripheral edema, malaise, tiredness, visual disturbances, psychological changes, paresthesia, muscle pain, and various bizarre subjective complaints. Skin rashes, including a few that appeared to be due to iodism, and itching, have been attributed to dextrothyroxine by some investigators.

Gallstones have been discovered in occasional dextrothyroxine-treated patients and cholestatic jaundice has occurred in 1 patient, although its relationship to dextrothyroxine therapy has not been established.

In several instances, the previously existing conditions of the patient appeared to continue or progress during the administration of dextrothyroxine. A worsening of peripheral vascular disease, sensorium, exophthalmos, and retinopathy have been reported.

Several clinicians have reported that dextrothyroxine potentiates the effect of anticoagulants, such as warfarin or dicoumarol on prothrombin time, thus indicating a decrease in the dosage requirements of the anticoagulants. On the other hand, dosage requirements of antidiabetic drugs have been reported to be increased during dextrothyroxine therapy (see Warnings).

Cerebrovascular accidents, thrombophlebitis, and gastrointestinal hemorrhages in patients who were not receiving anticoagulants have occurred but there appears to be no relationship between these developments and dextrothyroxine therapy.

Overdose: Symptoms and Treatment: Overdosage with dextrothyroxine may result in signs and symptoms of thyrotoxicosis. The dosage at which such symptoms may appear will depend on the previous thyroid status of the patient and his/her individual sensitivity to the drug. Dextrothyroxine is predominantly protein-bound and would not be expected to be appreciably dialyzable; however, no direct information is available. Treatment of overdosage is similar to that of thyrotoxic storm and may include hydration, sedation, and use of beta-adrenergic blocking agents.

Dosage: For most hypercholesterolemic patients, the recommended maintenance dose of dextrothyroxine is 4 to 6 mg administered as a single oral dose daily, although the effective dosage range is 2 to 8 mg/day. The initial daily dose should be 1 to 2 mg, to be increased in 1 to 2 mg increments at intervals of not less than 1 month, to a maximum level of 4 to 8 mg daily, if that dosage is indicated to effect the desired lowering of serum cholesterol.

If signs or symptoms of cardiac disease or iodism develop during the treatment period, the drug should be withdrawn.

Hypothyroid patients are more sensitive to any specified dose of dextrothyroxine than are euthyroid patients. The initial dose should not exceed 1 mg. Dosage may be increased by 1 mg increments at intervals of not less than 1 month. The maximum daily dose generally should not exceed 4 mg.

Information for the Patient: See Blue Section—Information for the Patient ''Choloxin''.

Supplied: 2 mg: Each orange, scored tablet, contains: dextrothyroxine sodium 2 mg. Nonmedicinal ingredients: acacia, confectioners' sugar, FD&C Yellow No. 5 (tartrazine), gelatin, lactose, magnesium stearate, polysorbate 80, povidone and talc. Packages of 100.

4 mg: Each white, scored tablet, contains: dextrothyroxine sodium 4 mg. Nonmedicinal ingredients: confectioners' sugar, gelatin, lactose, magnesium stearate, povidone and talc. Packages of 100.

Store at controlled room temperature 15 to 30°C. Dispense in well-closed containers as described in USP.

(Shown in Product Recognition Section)

Reviewed 1997

For information on Drug Exposure During Pregnancy and Lactation, see the CLIN-INFO SECTION.

CHRONOVERA® ℞

Searle

Verapamil HCl

Antihypertensive—Antianginal Agent

System Components and Performance: Chronovera is a formulation designed to initiate the release of verapamil approximately 4 to 5 hours after ingestion by means of a delay coating and thereafter to provide a constant rate of release over 12 hours. The tablet is comprised of a semipermeable membrane surrounding a drug core that is osmotically active. The core itself is divided into 2 layers: an "active" layer containing the drug, and a "push" layer containing pharmacologically inert, but osmotically active, components.

Delay in release of verapamil after ingestion is accomplished by the introduction of a coating between the active drug core and outer semipermeable membrane. As water from the gastrointestinal tract enters the tablet, this delay coating is solubilized and released. As tablet hydration continues, the osmotic layer expands and pushes against the drug layer, releasing drug through precision laser-drilled orifices in the outer membrane at a constant rate. This controlled rate of drug delivery in the gastrointestinal lumen is independent of posture, pH, gastrointestinal motility, and fed or fasting conditions.

The biologically inert components of the delivery system remain intact during gastrointestinal transit and are eliminated in the feces as an insoluble shell (see Warnings, Patients With Pre-existing Gastrointestinal Narrowing or Transit Disorders).

Pharmacology: Verapamil is a calcium ion influx inhibitor (calcium entry blocker or calcium ion antagonist) that exerts its pharmacological effects by modulating the influx of ionic calcium across the cell membrane of the arterial smooth muscle as well as in conducting and contractile myocardial cells.

Verapamil exerts antihypertensive effects by inducing vasodilation and reducing peripheral vascular resistance usually without reflex tachycardia. Verapamil does not blunt hemodynamic response to isometric or dynamic exercise.

Verapamil depresses AV nodal conduction and prolongs functional refractory periods. Verapamil does not alter the normal atrial action potential or intraventricular conduction time, but depresses amplitude, velocity of depolarization and conduction in depressed atrial fibres.

Verapamil may shorten the antegrade effective refractory period of the accessory bypass tract. Acceleration of ventricular rate and/or ventricular fibrillation has been reported in patients with atrial flutter or atrial fibrillation and a coexisting accessory AV pathway following administration of verapamil (see Warnings, Accessory Bypass Tract). Verapamil has a local anesthetic action that is 1.6 times that of procaine on an equimolar basis.

Verapamil is a potent smooth muscle relaxant with vasodilatory properties, as well as a depressant of myocardial contractility, and these effects are largely independent of autonomic influences.

Compared to baseline, verapamil does not affect electrolytes, glucose and creatinine. The hypotensive effect of verapamil is not blunted by an increase in sodium intake.

In hypertensive normolipidemic patients, verapamil had no effects on plasma lipoprotein fractions.

Pharmacodynamics: In a study in 5 healthy males, the S enantiomer of verapamil was found to be 8 to 20 times more active than the R enantiomer in slowing AV conduction. In another study using septal strips isolated from the left ventricle of 5 patients with mitral disease, the S enantiomer was 8 times more potent than the R enantiomer in reducing myocardial contractility.

Pharmacokinetics: Upon oral administration of verapamil, rapid stereoselective biotransformation occurs during the first pass through the portal circulation. The systemic concentrations of R and S enantiomers are dependent upon the route administration and the rate and extent of release from the dosage form.

The following bioavailability information was obtained from healthy volunteers and not from the populations most likely to be treated with verapamil.

In a study in 5 healthy volunteers with oral immediate-release verapamil, the systemic bioavailability varied from 33 to 65% for the R enantiomer and from 13 to 34% for the S enantiomer. The S enantiomer is pharmacologically more active than the R enantiomer (see Pharmacology, Pharmacodynamics).

There is a nonlinear correlation between the verapamil dose administered and verapamil plasma levels. In early dose titration with verapamil, a relationship exists between total verapamil (R and S combined) plasma concentration and prolongation of the PR interval. The mean elimination half-life in single-dose studies of immediate release verapamil ranged from 2.8 to 7.4 hours. In these same studies, after steady-state was reached, the half-life increased to a range from 4.5 to 12 hours (after less than 10 consecutive doses given 6 hours apart). Half-life of verapamil may increase during titration. Aging decreases the clearance and elimination of verapamil.

In healthy men, orally administered verapamil undergoes extensive metabolism by the cytochrome P450 system in the liver. The particular isoenzymes involved are CYP 3A4, CYP 1A2, CYP 2C family. Thirteen metabolites have been identified in urine. Norverapamil can reach steady-state plasma concentrations approximately equal to those of verapamil itself. The cardiovascular activity of norverapamil appears to be approximately 20% that of verapamil. Approximately 70% of an administered dose is excreted as metabolites in the urine and 16% or more in the feces within 5 days. About 3 to 4% is excreted in the urine as unchanged drug. R-verapamil is 94% bound to plasma albumin, while S-verapamil is 88% bound. In addition, R-verapamil is 92% and S-verapamil 86% bound to alpha-1 acid glycoprotein. The degree of biotransformation during the first pass of verapamil may vary according to the status of the liver in different patient populations. In patients with hepatic insufficiency, metabolism is delayed and elimination half-life prolonged up to 14 to 16 hours. (See Warnings—Hepatic Insufficiency and Dosage).

Verapamil crosses the placental barrier and can be detected in umbilical vein blood at delivery. Verapamil is excreted in human milk.

Formulation Specific Information: Racemic verapamil is released from Chronovera at a constant rate following solubilization of the delay coat (see System Components and Performance). This process produces a lag period in drug release of approximately 4 to 5 hours, followed by prolonged drug release over 12 hours. Peak plasma concentration (C_{max}) occurs in the morning hours approximately 11 hours after administration, to coincide with the normal circadian rise in blood pressure and heart rate, when Chronovera is administered at bedtime. Trough concentrations occur approximately 4 hours after bedtime dosing while the patient is sleeping.

The clinical benefit of presenting peak, rather than trough, plasma levels of verapamil in the morning has not been established.

Steady-state pharmacokinetics were reached by the third or fourth day of dosing, as determined in healthy volunteers (see Table I).

Table I—Chronovera

Steady-state Pharmacokinetics of Verapamil in Healthy Humans with Chronovera Administration

	Enantiomer	Chronovera Dose 180 mg	240 mg
Mean C_{max} (ng/mL)	R-verapamil	90.6	120
	S-verapamil	21.2	28.7
AUC (0-24h) (ng·mL/h)	R-verapamil	1 223	1 470
	S-verapamil	266	322

In older subjects (65 to 80 years), the C_{max} for S-verapamil increased by 1.7-fold and for R-verapamil increased by 1.45-fold, in comparison to values in younger subjects (19 to 53 years) when studied at 180 mg. The AUC for S-verapamil increased by 2-fold and for R-verapamil increased by 1.65-fold. Lean body weight also affects its pharmacokinetics inversely, but no gender difference was observed to date with Chronovera.

Consumption of a high fat meal just prior to dosing at night had no significant effect on the pharmacokinetics of Chronovera. The pharmacokinetics were also not affected by whether the volunteers were supine or ambulatory for the 8 hours following dosing. Administering Chronovera in the morning led to a slower rate of absorption and/or elimination, but did not affect the extent of absorption or extent of metabolism to norverapamil.

Indications: In the treatment of mild to moderate essential hypertension. Verapamil should normally be used in those patients in whom treatment with diuretics or β-blockers has been associated with unacceptable response or adverse effects.

Chronovera can be tried as an initial agent in those patients in whom the use of diuretics and/or β-blockers is contraindicated or in patients with medical conditions in which these drugs frequently cause serious adverse effects.

Verapamil should not be used concurrently with β-adrenoreceptor blockers in the treatment of hypertension (see Precautions, Drug Interactions).

Chronovera is also indicated in the treatment of chronic stable angina pectoris.

Contraindications: Complicated myocardial infarction (patients who have ventricular failure manifested by pulmonary congestion); severe congestive heart failure and/or severe left ventricular systolic dysfunction (i.e., ejection fraction <40%), unless secondary to a supraventricular tachycardia amenable to oral verapamil therapy; cardiogenic shock; severe hypotension; second- or third-degree AV block (except in patients with a functioning artificial ventricular pacemaker) (see Warnings, Conduction Disturbance); sick sinus syndrome (except in patients with a functioning artificial ventricular pacemaker); marked bradycardia; hypersensitivity to the drug; patients with atrial flutter or atrial fibrillation and an accessory bypass tract (e.g., Wolff-Parkinson-White, Lown-Ganong-Levine syndrome) (see Warnings, Accessory Bypass Tract).

Warnings: General: In hypertensive patients also using antianginal or antiarrhythmic agents, the additional hypotensive effect of verapamil should be taken into consideration.

Heart Failure: Because of the drug's negative inotropic effect, verapamil should not be used in patients with poorly compensated congestive heart failure, unless the failure is complicated by or caused by a dysrhythmia. If verapamil is used in such patients, they must be digitalized prior to treatment.

It has been reported that digoxin plasma levels may increase with chronic verapamil administration (see Precautions, Drug Interactions). The use of verapamil in the treatment of hypertension is not recommended in patients with heart failure caused by systolic dysfunction.

Patients with Pre-existing Gastrointestinal Narrowing or Transit Disorders: Since the Chronovera delivery system contains a nondeformable material, which is to be excreted, in general, its use should be avoided in patients with pre-existing gastrointestinal narrowing (pathologic or iatrogenic) or significant gastrointestinal motility disorders. There have been rare reports of obstructive symptoms in patients with known strictures in association with the ingestion of Chronovera tablets.

Hypotension: Hypotensive symptoms of lethargy and weakness with faintness have been reported following single oral doses and even after some months of treatment. In some patients it may be necessary to reduce the dose.

Conduction Disturbance: Verapamil slows conduction across the AV node and rarely may produce second or third degree AV block, bradycardia and in extreme cases, asystole.

Verapamil causes dose-related suppression of the SA node. In some patients, sinus bradycardia may occur, especially in patients with a sick sinus syndrome (SA nodal disease), which is more common in older patients (see Contraindications and Precautions, Geriatrics).

Bradycardia: The total incidence of bradycardia (ventricular rate less than 50 beats/min) was 1.4% in controlled studies. Asystole in patients other than those with sick sinus syndrome is usually of short duration (few seconds or less), with spontaneous return to AV nodal or normal sinus rhythm. If this does not occur promptly, appropriate treatment should be initiated immediately (see Overdose: Symptoms and Treatment).

Accessory Bypass Tract (Wolff-Parkinson-White or Lown-Ganong-Levine): Verapamil may result in significant acceleration of ventricular response during atrial fibrillation or atrial flutter in the Wolff-Parkinson-White (WPW) or Lown-Ganong-Levine syndromes after receiving i.v. verapamil. Although a risk of this occurring with oral verapamil has not been established, such patients receiving oral verapamil may be at risk and its use in these patients is contraindicated (see Contraindications).

Concomitant use with β-blockers: Generally, oral verapamil should not be given to patients receiving β-blockers since the depressant effects on myocardial contractility, heart rate and AV conduction may be additive. If combined therapy is used, close surveillance of vital signs and clinical status should be carried out and the need for continued concomitant treatment periodically assessed.

Verapamil gives no protection against the dangers of abrupt β-blocker withdrawal and such withdrawal should be done by the gradual reduction of the dose of β-blocker. Then verapamil may be started with the usual dose.

Patients with Hypertrophic Cardiomyopathy: In 120 patients with hypertrophic cardiomyopathy who received therapy with verapamil at doses up to 720 mg/day, a variety of serious adverse effects were seen. Three patients died in pulmonary edema; all had severe left ventricular outflow obstruction and a past history of left ventricular dysfunction. Eight other patients had pulmonary edema and/or severe hypotension; abnormally high (greater than 20 mmHg) pulmonary wedge pressure and a marked left ventricular outflow obstruction were present in most of these patients. Concomitant administration of quinidine (see Precautions, Drug Interactions) preceded the severe hypotension in 3 of the 8 patients (2 of whom developed pulmonary edema). Sinus bradycardia occurred in 11% of the patients, second-degree AV block in 4%, and sinus arrest in 2%. It must be appreciated that this group of patients had a serious disease with a high mortality rate. Most adverse effects responded well to dose reduction, and only rarely did verapamil use have to be discontinued.

Elevated Liver Enzymes: Elevations of transaminases with and without concomitant elevations in alkaline phosphatase and bilirubin have been reported. Several cases of hepatocellular injury related to verapamil have been proven by rechallenge. Clinical symptoms of malaise, fever, and/or right upper quadrant pain, in addition to elevation of AST, ALT, and alkaline phosphatase have been reported. Periodic monitoring of liver function in patients receiving verapamil is therefore prudent.

Hepatic Insufficiency: Because verapamil is extensively metabolized by the liver, it should be administered cautiously to patients with impaired hepatic function, since the elimination half-life of verapamil in these patients is prolonged 4-fold (from 3.7 to 14.2 hours). A decreased dosage should be used in patients with hepatic insufficiency and careful monitoring for abnormal prolongation of the PR interval or other signs of excessive pharmacologic effect should be carried out (see Pharmacology—Pharmacokinetics and Dosage).

Renal Insufficiency: About 70% of an administered dose of verapamil is excreted as metabolites in the urine. In one study in healthy volunteers, the total body clearance after i.v. administration of verapamil was 12.08 mL/min/kg, while in patients with advanced renal disease it was reduced to 5.33 mL/min/kg. This pharmacokinetic finding suggests that renal clearance of verapamil in patients with renal disease is decreased. In 2 studies with oral verapamil no difference in pharmacokinetics could be demonstrated. Until further data are available, verapamil should be administered cautiously to patients with impaired renal function. These patients should be carefully monitored for abnormal prolongation of the PR interval or other signs of overdosage (see Overdose: Symptoms and Treatment).

Precautions: Patients with Attenuated (Decreased) Neuromuscular Transmission: It has been reported that verapamil decreases neuromuscular transmission in patients with Duchenne's muscular dystrophy, and that verapamil prolongs recovery from the neuromuscular blocking agent vecuronium. It may be necessary to decrease the dosage of verapamil when it is administered to patients with attenuated neuromuscular transmission.

Geriatrics: Caution should be exercised when verapamil is administered to elderly patients (≥ 65 years) especially those prone to developing hypotension or those with a history of cerebrovascular insufficiency (see Dosage and Pharmacology—Pharmacokinetics). Serious adverse events associated with heart block have occurred in the elderly.

Pregnancy: Teratology and reproduction studies have been performed in rabbits and rats at oral doses up to 1.5 (15 mg/kg/day) and 6 (60 mg/kg/day) times the human oral daily dose, respectively, and have revealed no evidence of teratogenicity or impaired fertility. In rat, however, this multiple of the human dose was embryocidal and retarded fetal growth and development, probably because of adverse maternal effects reflected in reduced weight gains of the dams. This oral dose has also been shown to cause hypotension in rats.

There are no studies in pregnant women. However, verapamil crosses the placental barrier and can be detected in umbilical vein blood at delivery. Verapamil is not recommended for use in pregnant women unless the potential benefits outweigh potential risks to mother and fetus.

Labor and Delivery: It is not known whether the use of verapamil during labor or delivery has immediate or delayed adverse effects on the fetus, or whether it prolongs the duration of labor or increases the need for forceps delivery or other obstetric intervention.

Lactation: Verapamil is excreted in human milk. Because of the potential for adverse reactions in nursing infants from verapamil, nursing should be discontinued while verapamil is administered.

Children: The safety and dosage regimen of verapamil in children has not yet been established.

Information for the Patient: Chronovera tablets should be swallowed whole; do not break, crush, or chew. The medication in the Chronovera tablet is released slowly through an outer shell that does not dissolve. The patient should not be concerned if they occasionally observe this outer shell in their stool as it passes from the body.

Chronovera should be taken at bedtime.

Drug Interactions: As with all drugs, care should be exercised when treating patients with multiple medications. Calcium channel blockers undergo biotransformation by the cytochrome P450 system. Coadministration of verapamil with other drugs which follow the same route of biotransformation may result in altered bioavailability. Dosages of similarly metabolized drugs, particularly those of low therapeutic ratio, and especially in patients with renal and/or hepatic impairment, may require adjustment when starting or stopping concomitantly administered verapamil to maintain optimum therapeutic blood levels.

Drugs known to be inhibitors of the cytochrome P450 system include: azole antifungals, cimetidine, cyclosporine, erythromycin, quinidine, terfenadine, warfarin.

Drugs known to be inducers of the cytochrome P450 system include: phenobarbital, phenytoin, rifampin.

Drugs known to be biotransformed via P450 include: benzodiazepines, flecainide, imipramine, propafenone, theophylline.

Alcohol: Verapamil may increase blood alcohol concentrations and prolong its effects.

β-adrenergic Blockers: The concomitant administration of verapamil with β-blockers can result in severe adverse effects (see Warnings, Concomitant use with β-blockers).

Digoxin: Verapamil treatment increases serum digoxin levels by 50 to 75% during the first week of therapy, and this can result in digitalis toxicity. In patients with hepatic cirrhosis the influence of verapamil on digoxin kinetics is magnified. Verapamil may reduce total body clearance and extrarenal clearance of digitoxin by 27% and 29% respectively. Maintenance and digitalization doses should be reduced when verapamil is administered and the patient should be reassessed to avoid over- or underdigitalization. Whenever overdigitalization is suspected, the daily dose of digitalis should be reduced or temporarily discontinued. On discontinuation of verapamil use, the patient should be reassessed to avoid underdigitalization.

Antihypertensive: Verapamil administered concomitantly with oral antihypertensive agents (e.g., vasodilators, angiotensin-converting enzyme inhibitors, and diuretics) may have an additive effect on lowering blood pressure. Patients receiving these combinations should be appropriately monitored. Verapamil should not be combined with β-blockers for the treatment of hypertension. Concomitant use of agents that attenuate α-adrenergic function with verapamil may result in a reduction in blood pressure that is excessive in some patients. Such an effect was observed in one study following the concomitant administration of verapamil and prazosin.

Quinidine: In a small number of patients with hypertrophic cardiomyopathy (IHSS), concomitant use of verapamil and quinidine resulted in significant hypotension. Until further data are obtained, combined therapy of verapamil and quinidine in patients with hypertrophic cardiomyopathy should probably be avoided. The electrophysiologic effects of quinidine and verapamil on AV conduction were studied in 8 patients. Verapamil significantly counteracted the effects of quinidine and AV conduction. There has been a report of increased quinidine levels during verapamil therapy.

Disopyramide: Until data on possible interactions between verapamil and disopyramide are obtained, disopyramide should not be administered within 48 hours before or 24 hours after verapamil administration.

Flecainide: A study in healthy volunteers showed that the concomitant administration of flecainide and verapamil may have additive effects on myocardial contractility, AV conduction, and repolarization. Concomitant therapy with flecainide and verapamil may result in additive negative inotropic effect and prolongation of atrioventricular conduction.

Nitrates, Diuretics: No cardiovascular adverse effects have been attributed to any interaction between these agents and verapamil.

Neuromuscular Blocking Agents: Clinical data and animal studies suggest that verapamil may potentiate the activity of neuromuscular blocking agents (curare-like and depolarizing). It may be necessary to decrease the dose of verapamil and/or the dose of the neuromuscular blocking agent when the drugs are used concomitantly.

Carbamazepine: The concomitant oral administration of verapamil and carbamazepine may potentiate the effects of carbamazepine neurotoxicity. Symptoms include, diplopia, headache, ataxia or dizziness.

Cimetidine: Two clinical trials have shown a lack of significant verapamil interaction with cimetidine. A third study showed cimetidine reduced verapamil clearance and increased elimination half-life.

Lithium: Increased sensitivity to the effects of lithium (neurotoxicity) has been reported during concomitant verapamil-lithium therapy with either no change or an increase in serum lithium levels. However, the addition of verapamil has also resulted in the lowering of serum lithium levels in patients receiving chronic stable oral lithium. Patients receiving both drugs must be monitored carefully.

Rifampin: Therapy with rifampin may markedly reduce oral verapamil bioavailability.

Phenobarbital: Phenobarbital therapy may increase verapamil clearance.

Cyclosporine: Verapamil therapy may increase serum levels of cyclosporine.

Theophylline: Verapamil may inhibit the clearance and increase the plasma levels of theophylline.

Inhalation Anesthetics: Animal experiments have shown that inhalation anesthetics depress cardiovascular activity by decreasing the inward movement of calcium ions. When used concomitantly, inhalation anesthetics and calcium channel blocking agents, such as verapamil should each be titrated carefully to avoid excessive cardiovascular depression.

Sulfinpyrazone: Increased clearance and decreased bioavailability of verapamil may occur.

Antineoplastic Agents: Verapamil inhibits P-glycoprotein mediated transport of antineoplastic agents out of tumor cells, resulting in their decreased metabolic clearance. Dosage adjustments of antineoplastic agents should be considered when verapamil is administered concomitantly.

ASA: In a few reported cases, coadministration of verapamil with ASA uses led to an increased bleeding time.

Adverse Effects: Verapamil immediate release tablets have been studied in 4 826 patients in controlled and uncontrolled trials. The most common adverse reactions were: constipation, dizziness and nausea. The most serious adverse reactions reported with verapamil are heart failure (1.8%), 2° and 3° AV block (0.8%), hypotension (2.5%) and rapid ventricular response (see Warnings).

The following adverse reactions have been reported in controlled or uncontrolled clinical trials with immediate release verapamil.

Cardiovascular: hypotension 2.5%, edema 2.1%, CHF/Pulmonary Edema 1.9%, bradycardia (HR<50/min) 1.4%, AV Block Total (1°, 2°, 3°) 1.2%, 2° and 3° 0.8%.

CNS: dizziness 3.2%, headache 2.2%, fatigue 1.7%.

Gastrointestinal: constipation 7.3%, nausea 2.7%.

Other: rash 1.2%.

The following reactions to verapamil controlled-onset extended-release occurred at rates greater than 2% or occurred at lower rates but appeared drug-related in clinical trials in hypertension and angina (see Table II).

Table II—Chronovera

Adverse Reactions	**All Doses Studied n=572 (%)**	**Placebo n=261 (%)**
Constipation	11.7*	2.7
Headache	6.6	7.3
Dizziness	4.7	2.7
Fatigue	4.5	3.8
Edema	3.0	3.1
Nausea	2.1	1.9
AV block (1°)	1.7	0.0
Elevated liver enzymes	1.4	0.8
Bradycardia	1.4	0.4
Paresthesia	1.0	0.0
Flushing	0.8	0.3
Hypotension	0.7	0.0
Postural hypotension	0.4	0.3

*At a once daily dose of 240 mg, the observed incidence was 7.2%.

See Warnings for discussion of heart failure, hypotension, elevated liver enzymes, AV block, and rapid ventricular response.

Reversible (upon discontinuation of verapamil) nonobstructive, paralytic ileus has been infrequently reported in association with the use of verapamil.

Isolated cases of angioedema have been reported. Angioedema may be accompanied by breathing difficulties.

The following reactions, reported with orally administered verapamil in 2% or less of patients, occurred under conditions (open trials, marketing experience) where a causal relationship is uncertain; they are listed to alert the physician to a possible

Chronovera (cont'd)

relationship: Cardiovascular: angina pectoris, AV dissociation, pulmonary edema, chest pain, claudication, myocardial infarction, palpitations, syncope.
Gastrointestinal: dry mouth, gastrointestinal distress, gingival hyperplasia, vomiting, hepatitis.
Hematologic: purpura, petechiae, ecchymosis or bruising.
CNS: cerebrovascular accident, confusion, equilibrium disorders, insomnia, psychotic symptoms, shakiness, somnolence.
Dermatologic: arthralgia, exanthema, hair loss, sweating, pruritus, urticaria, Stevens-Johnson syndrome, erythema multiforme, and vasculitis.
Special Senses: blurred vision.
Urogenital: gynecomastia, galactorrhea/hyperprolactinemia, increased urination, spotty menstruation, impotence.
Other: allergy aggravated, dyspnea, myalgia.

Overdose: Symptoms: Based on reports of intentional overdosage of verapamil, the following symptoms have been observed. Hypotension occurs, varying from transient to severe. Conduction disturbances seen included: prolongation of AV conduction time, AV dissociation, nodal rhythm, ventricular fibrillation and ventricular asystole.

Treatment: Treatment of overdosage should be supportive. Gastric lavage should be undertaken, even later than 12 hours after ingestion, if no gastrointestinal motility is present. β-adrenergic stimulation or parenteral administration of calcium solutions may increase calcium ion influx across the slow channel.

These pharmacologic interventions have been effectively used in treatment of overdosage with verapamil. Clinically significant hypotensive reactions should be treated with vasopressor agents. AV block is treated with atropine and cardiac pacing. Asystole should be handled by the usual Advanced Cardiac Life Support measures including the use of vasopressor agents, e.g., isoproterenol HCl. Verapamil is not removed by hemodialysis.

In case of overdosage with large amounts of verapamil, it should be noted that the release of the active drug and the absorption in the intestine may take more than 48 hours. Depending on the time of ingestion, capsules may be present along the entire length of the gastrointestinal tract which function as active drug depots. Extensive elimination measures are indicated, such as induced vomiting, removal of the contents of the stomach and the small intestine under endoscopy, intestinal lavage and high enemas.

Suggested Treatment of Acute Cardiovascular Adverse Reactions: Actual treatment and dosage should depend on the severity of the clinical situation and the judgement of the treating physician. Patients with hypertrophic cardiomyopathy treated with verapamil should not be administered positive inotropic agents (marked by asterisks in Table III).

Dosage: Chronovera is a dosage form designed to deliver peak verapamil levels in the morning. Accordingly, Chronovera should be administered once daily at bedtime.

When Chronovera is administered at bedtime, office evaluation of blood pressure during morning and early afternoon hours is essentially a measure of peak effect. The usual evaluation of trough effect, which might be needed to evaluate the appropriateness of any given dose, would be just prior to bedtime.

Dosing should be individualized by titration.

Chronovera tablets should be swallowed whole and not chewed, broken or crushed.

Hypertension: Initiate therapy with 180 mg.

If an adequate response is not obtained with 180 mg, the dose may be titrated upward in the following manner: 240 mg each evening; 360 mg each evening (2×180 mg); 480 mg each evening (2×240 mg).

Chronic Stable Angina: Initiate therapy with 180 mg.

If an adequate response is not obtained with 180 mg, the dose may be titrated upward in the following manner: 240 mg each evening; 360 mg each evening (2×180 mg).

The majority of patients who will respond to therapy, will do so at a dosage of 180 to 360 mg once daily. However, some patients may respond to 480 mg once daily.

Geriatrics: In general, bioavailability of Chronovera is higher in the elderly and they tend to respond at lower dosages than those under 65. Dosage should be carefully individualized by titration (see Pharmacology—Pharmacokinetics and Precautions—Geriatrics).

Patients With Impaired Liver and Renal Function: Verapamil should be administered cautiously to patients with liver or renal function impairment. The dosage should be carefully and gradually adjusted depending on patient tolerance and response. These patients should be monitored carefully for abnormal prolongation of the PR interval or other signs of overdosage. Verapamil should not be used in severe hepatic dysfunction (see Warnings, Hepatic Insufficiency and Renal Insufficiency).

Supplied: 180 mg: Each controlled-onset extended-release, blue, round, film-coated tablet, with SEARLE 2011 printed on one side, contains: verapamil HCl 180 mg. Nonmedicinal ingredients: black ferric oxide, butylated hydroxytoluene, cellulose acetate, FD&C Blue No. 2 Lake, hydroxyethyl cellulose, hydroxypropyl cellulose, hydroxypropyl methylcellulose, magnesium stearate, polyethylene glycol, polyethylene oxide, polysorbate, povidone, sodium chloride and titanium dioxide. HDPE bottles of 100.

240 mg: Each controlled-onset extended-release, white, round, film-coated tablet with SEARLE 2021 printed on one side, contains: verapamil HCl 240 mg. Nonmedicinal ingredients: black ferric oxide, butylated hydroxytoluene, cellulose acetate, hydroxethyl cellulose, hydroxypropyl cellulose, hydroxypropyl methylcellulose, magnesium stearate, polyethylene glycol, polyethylene oxide, polysorbate, povidone, sodium chloride and titanium dioxide. HDPE bottles of 100.

Protect contents from light and high humidity. HDPE bottles should be stored at controlled room temperature (15 to 25°C).

(Shown in Product Recognition Section)

New Product 1998

Table III—Chronovera

Suggested Treatment of Acute Cardiovascular Adverse Reactions

Adverse Reaction	Proven Effective Treatment	Treatment with Good Theoretical Rationale	Supportive Treatment
Shock, cardiac failure, severe hypotension	calcium salt, e.g., calcium gluconate i.v.; i.v. metaraminol bitartrate*	i.v. dopamine HCl*; i.v. dobutamine HCl*	i.v. fluids; Trendelenburg position
Bradycardia, AV block, asystole	i.v. isoproterenol HCl*; i.v. atropine sulfate; cardiac pacing	—	i.v. fluids (slow drip)
Rapid ventricular rate (due to antegrade conduction in atrial flutter/fibrillation with WPW or LGL syndrome)	D.C. cardioversion (high energy may be required); i.v. procainamide; i.v. lidocaine HCl	—	i.v. fluids (slow drip)

CHYMODIACTIN®

Knoll

Chymopapain

Proteolytic Enzyme

Pharmacology: Chymopapain for intradiscal injection is injected into the herniated nucleus pulposus of the lumbar intervertabral disc resulting in rapid hydrolysis of the noncollagenous polypeptides or proteins that maintain the tertiary structure of the chondromucoprotein. This lessens the intradiscal osmotic activity, thereby decreasing fluid absorption and reducing intradiscal pressure. The foregoing mechanism of action is based on animal in vitro and in vivo data. Although the mechanism of action in the human has not been established directly, operative findings in patients who have come to surgery following injection have usually revealed the nucleus pulposus to be absent from its former site.

Indications: For the treatment of patients with documented herniated lumbar intervertebral discs whose symptoms and signs, particularly sciatica, have not responded to an adequate period or periods of conservative therapy. Chymopapain has not been studied in the treatment of herniated discs in areas other than the lumbar spine. **Chymopapain should only be used in hospitals by physicians who routinely care for the patients described above, who are qualified by training and experience to perform laminectomy, discectomy, or other spinal procedures and who have received specialized training in chemonucleolysis.** The appropriate use of chymopapain in chemonucleolysis requires precise diagnosis and the ability to employ skillfully all appropriate diagnostic and treatment modalities necessary, including surgical interventions other than chemonucleolysis (laminectomy/discectomy) and all aspects of pre- and postoperative patient management. Proper selection of patients for whom chemonucleolysis is applicable requires extensive training and experience in the diagnosis and management of all spinal disorders, since there are circumstances in which nerve root compression resulting from conditions other than herniated disc can produce similar signs and symptoms.

In hospitals where chymopapain is used, the supporting personnel, as well as physicians, should be qualified in the diagnosis and management of all potential complications of the use of chymopapain including anaphylaxis.

Clinical observations suggest that female patients are more likely to develop anaphylactic reactions secondary to chymopapain (see Warnings).

Contraindications: Patients with a known sensitivity to chymopapain, papaya or papaya derivatives, including papain containing contact lens cleaners, or meat tenderizer preparations.

Other contraindications are severe spondylolisthesis; severe, progressing paralysis as indicated by rapidly progressing neurologic dysfunction; and in patients with evidence of spinal cord tumor or other lesions producing spinal motor or sensory dysfunction (e.g. cauda equina lesion).

Patients who have previously been injected with any form of chymopapain.

Chymopapain has not been studied in regions of the spine other than the lumbar area; therefore, its use is contraindicated in any spinal region other than the lumbar area.

Children: Safety and effectiveness of chymopapain has not been studied in pediatric patients, therefore, the drug should not be used in children.

Pregnancy: Chymopapain has not been evaluated for possible teratogenic effects. Since animal reproduction studies have not been conducted, chymopapain is not recommended for use in pregnant women.

Warnings: Anaphylaxis of a severe to mild nature has been observed after injection of chymopapain in about 0.5% of patients and may be life threatening if not treated promptly and correctly. **At least 1 open i.v. line must always be in place to permit rapid and adequate management of such an occurrence.** The reaction can be immediate or delayed up to 2 hours after injection and can last for minutes to several hours or longer. The patient may present with almost immediate hypotension and/or bronchospasm, the former being more common. These may proceed to laryngeal edema, cardiac arrhythmia, cardiac arrest, coma and death. Speed in diagnosis and treatment is of the essence since the clinical signs, severity, progression, and duration of an anaphylactic reaction are highly unpredictable. Other signs of allergic response, such as erythema, pilomotor erection, rash, pruritic urticaria, conjunctivitis, vasomotor rhinitis, angioedema, or various gastrointestinal disturbances, must also be watched for.

U.S. post marketing surveillance data confirm that females are more likely to develop an anaphylactic reaction secondary to chymopapain (observed rate of 0.8% vs 0.3% in males). These data have also shown a statistically significant difference in the frequency of anaphylaxis in patients receiving local anesthesia vs those receiving general anesthesia (0.4% vs 0.6% respectively); however, a direct cause and effect relationship has not been established. In the population where race has been reported the incidence is statistically higher in black females.

Clinical judgment, speed of therapy, and choice of agents all enter into the treatment of anaphylaxis. **Epinephrine is the definitive therapeutic agent in the immediate treatment of anaphylaxis. Substitution of other agents such as steroids should be reserved for cases where epinephrine is not appropriate.**

In cases where the risk-benefit ratio of chemonucleolysis is dubious, allergy or immunology consultation before attempting this procedure is recommended. Documentation on the usefulness of in vitro chymopapain—specific IgE test or in vivo skin test as predictors for anaphylactic reactions is still inconclusive.

Acute transverse myelitis/acute transverse myelopathy has been reported in association with the injection of chymopapain at a rate of about 1 in 18 000. Although cause and effect relationship to the injection of chymopapain itself has not been established, the reported rate is significantly higher than the incidence reported in the medical literature. These patients are characterized clinically by the delayed (2 to 3 weeks) onset of paraplegia or paraparesis without prior signs or symptoms. Patients receiving injections at 2 or more disc spaces following discography appear to be at increased risk.

It is recommended that discography not be performed as part of the chemonucleolysis procedure unless the operating surgeon determines that the risks of discography are outweighed by the benefits in the particular clinical situation. Serious neurotoxicity from the injection of radiological contrast agents into the spinal fluid followed by chymopapain has been observed in studies with baboons. A water acceptance test or discometry may be used as an alternative to discography for assessment of the disc abnormality and to attempt reproduction of sciatic pain in the patients under local anesthesia. Certain radiopaque contrast media are neurotoxic. The toxicity of these materials may be enhanced by intrathecal bleeding. If chymopapain is then inadvertently administered intrathecally, disruption of the capillaries may occur, resulting in intrathecal bleeding.

Paraplegia/paraparesis (e.g., as are seen in the cauda equina syndrome), other serious neurologic adverse events, and subarachnoid and intracerebral hemorrhage and seizures have been observed soon (within hours or days) after chymopapain injection at a rate of about 1 in 2 000. Causal relationships to the drug when properly injected have not been established. Needle trauma and/or injection of chymopapain and contrast media into the spinal fluid may be causes in some of these reported cases. Other less severe neurologic reactions have included burning sacral, leg pain, hypalgesia, leg weakness, foot drop, cramping in both calves, pain in the opposite leg, paresthesia, tingling in legs, and numbness of legs/toes.

The drug is extremely toxic when injected intrathecally in animals. Therefore, great caution must be exercised in assuring the chymopapain is not injected intrathecally into dural canal.

Chemonucleolysis is not recommended during active inflammatory episodes and/or infections.

Patients using beta-blocking agents should be weaned from these agents prior to chemonucleolysis.

Precautions: Because of the potential for anaphylaxis resulting from the intradiscal injection of chymopapain the following precautions should be observed in the use of the drug:

Patient Selection: A careful history should be obtained to determine if the patient has multiple allergies, especially a known allergy to papaya or papaya derivatives. In patients allergic to iodine, discography must not be performed and absorbable iodine must not be used during myelography.

The use of chymopapain in a lumbar disc which has previously undergone surgical treatment has not been systematically studied. Therefore, chemonucleolysis at that disc level is not recommended.

Females, particularly black females, are more likely to develop anaphylactic reactions secondary to chymopapain (see Warnings).

In case of anaphylaxis, beta-blocker therapy may inhibit the action of epinephrine.

Pretreatment: Patients may be pretreated prior to the injection of chymopapain with histamine receptor (H_1 and H_2) antagonists to lessen the severity of an anaphylactic reaction. One regimen that is widely used is cimetidine 300 mg orally every 6 hours and diphenhydramine 50 mg orally every 6 hours for 24 hours prior to chemonucleolysis.

Because of the abrupt decrease in intravascular volume during anaphylaxis, patients should be well hydrated with oral or i.v. fluids prior to chemonucleolysis. **At least 1 open i.v. line must always be in place to permit rapid and adequate management of such an occurrence.**

Procedure: The choice of anesthetic for a specific patient should be made by the attending surgeon and anesthesiologist. However, **it is recommended that local or supplemented local anesthetic be used whenever possible.**

The advantages of local or supplemental local anesthesia are thought to be: a lower anaphylaxis rate (0.4%); possible ease of recognition of impending anaphylaxis because earliest symptoms can be reported by an awake patient; possible correlation of sciatic pain with a specific disc because the patient is awake; and possible decreased risk of experiencing a serious neurologic adverse event secondary to difficult needle placement (see Warnings).

The advantages of general anesthesia are thought to be: ease of airway management if anaphylaxis should develop; more precise patient positioning for injection; and less patient discomfort. A disadvantage of general anesthesia is a higher rate of anaphylaxis (0.5%). If halothane anesthesia is used, it should be noted that if epinephrine HCl is required for treatment of an anaphylactic reaction, there is a potential arrhythmogenic interaction of the 2 drugs.

Needle placement for the intradiscal administration of chymopapain should be made by physicians experienced in needle placement via the lateral approach to avoid puncture of the dura mater. Clinical trials have not been conducted using the posterior approach for needle placement and serious neurologic toxicity has been reported using the posterior transdural approach; therefore, this method of needle placement must be avoided. Surgeons performing chemonucleolysis may wish to consider the injection of saline or water into the nucleus pulposus (saline or water acceptance test) as an alternative to discography. The use of this test plus careful evaluation of high quality AP and lateral x-ray views of the disc are sufficient to confirm proper needle placement in the nucleus pulposus. If discography is performed (see Warnings) at least 15 minutes should elapse after the administration of radiopaque contrast media to allow for diffusion and absorption of the media before injection of chymopapain through the same needle after removal of the obturator. If high quality x-ray equipment including an image intensifier is not available to perform chemonucleolysis, the procedure should not be carried out. If there is any question about satisfactory needle placement or if needle placement is difficult, requiring repeated attempts, the procedure should be aborted.

Based on the increased frequency of neurological adverse reaction in patients with 2 or more disc level injections **chemonucleolysis should be limited to the 1 disc producing the patient's symptoms unless definitive signs, symptoms and diagnostic procedures indicate that more than 1 disc is at fault.**

For 3 minutes prior to chymopapain injection, 100% O_2 may be administered to the patient by the anesthesiologist to maximize oxygenation in case of anaphylaxis.

A test dose injection of 0.2 mL of chymopapain followed by a 10 to 15 minute wait is recommended prior to the injection of the full therapeutic dose. The purpose of the test dose is to help identify those patients who are most sensitive to chymopapain. Patients who develop signs and/or symptoms of anaphylaxis following the test dose must not receive the therapeutic dose. However, some patients have been reported who failed to react to the test dose, but developed anaphylaxis to the therapeutic dose suggesting that sensitivity to chymopapain may be dose related.

Patient Instructions: Patients should be instructed that after injection they may experience back pain or involuntary muscle spasm in the lower area of the back for several days. This is not uncommon nor is a residual stiffness or soreness of the low back which may persist for several months.

Patients should be instructed to anticipate the possibility of any of the following delayed allergic reactions which may occur as late as 15 days after injection: rash of any type, urticaria or itching. If any of these occur patients should contact their physician.

Patients should be adequately advised of the potential benefits and risks associated with chemonucleolysis using chymopapain.

Adverse Effects: The most serious adverse reactions encountered with the use of chymopapain have been anaphylactic in nature. Based on U.S. postmarketing surveillance reports, the overall frequency of anaphylaxis is 0.5% or 1 in 200 patients. The frequency in females is approximately 0.8%, in males approximately 0.3%. The frequency when general anesthesia is employed is 0.5%, when local anesthesia is employed 0.4%. These differences are statistically significant.

Several deaths have been reported in association with chymopapain injection. Some of these fatalities, such as those due to anaphylaxis or complications of anaphylaxis, disc space infection, or CNS hemorrhage, may be associated with either the drug or the procedure. Others appear to be coincidental. The overall mortality rate following chymopapain injection is approximately 1 in 5 000 patients (0.02%). For purposes of comparison, mortality associated with laminectomy has been reported to range from 0.02% to 0.1%.

Paraplegia/paraparesis (20 cases), other serious neurologic adverse events in 30 patients out of 80 000 treated with chymopapain, intracerebral hemorrhage (8 cases), quadriplegia (1 case) and hemiparesis (1 case). Causal relationships to the drug when properly injected have not been established. Needle trauma and/or injection of chymopapain and contrast media into the spinal fluid may be causes in some of these reported cases. Other less severe neurologic reactions have included burning sacral, leg pain, hypalgesia, leg weakness, foot drop, cramping in both calves, pain in the opposite leg, paresthesia, tingling in legs, and numbness of legs/toes.

Acute transverse myelitis/acute transverse myelopathy has been reported in association with the injection of chymopapain at a rate of about 1 in 18 000. Although cause and effect relationship to the injection of chymopapain itself has not been established, the reported rate is significantly higher than the incidence, reported in the medical literature. These patients are characterized clinically by the delayed (2 to 3 weeks) onset of paraplegia or paraparesis without prior signs or symptoms.

Discitis, both bacterial and aseptic, has been reported.

Less severe, but more frequent adverse reactions include back pain/stiffness/soreness in approximately 50% of treated patients and/or back spasm in approximately 30%. Less frequent adverse reactions, occurring in less than 1% of patients studied include rash, itching, urticaria, nausea, paralytic ileus, urinary retention, headache and dizziness.

Dosage: Each 2 mL vial of Chymodiactin contains 4 nKat units of enzyme and should be reconstituted with 2 mL sterile water for injection, USP. Each 5 mL vial of Chymodiactin contains 10 nKat units of the enzyme and should be reconstituted with 5 mL sterile water for injection, USP. The concentration of solution in the reconstituted vial is 2 nKat units of chymopapain per mL. Recommended dosage is 1 to 4 nKat units per disc, usually 3 nKat units per disc or a volume of injection of 0.5 to 2 mL, usually 1.5 mL per disc. Maximum dose in a single patient with multiple disc herniation is 8 nKat units. However, based on the increased frequency of neurological reaction in patients with two or more disc level injections (see Warnings), chemonucleolysis should be limited to the 1 disc producing the patient's symptoms, unless definitive signs, symptoms and diagnostic procedures indicate that more than 1 disc is at fault.

Note: Alcohol should be used to cleanse the vial stopper prior to insertion of needles into the vial. However, since residual alcohol may inactivate the enzyme, it should be allowed to air dry before continuing with the reconstitution process.

Bacteriostatic Water for Injection USP, must not be used because it may inactivate the enzyme.

As with all parenteral drug products, chymopapain should be visually inspected for particulate matter and discoloration prior to administration. Care should be exercised in the selection of proper size and use of needles inserted into the vials in the reconstitution process to reduce the possibility of coring the stopper. The manufacturing process results in a residual vacuum in the vial; therefore, the use of automatic filling syringes is not recommended. Chymodiactin should be stored under refrigeration (2 to 8°C) until it is reconstituted with sterile water for injection, USP and used. The drug must be used within 2 hours of its reconstitution with sterile water for injection, USP. Unused drug must be promptly discarded and not stored for future use.

Each herniated disc should be treated with a single injection of chymopapain after needle tip placement has been verified by image intensifier. If a discogram is performed (see Warnings), at least 15 minutes must elapse between discogram and drug administration to allow for dispersion and absorption of the contrast media.

Chymopapain is limited to use under the professional supervision of a physician with the following considerations:

The appropriate use of chymopapain in chemonucleolysis, as pointed out in the Indications section, requires precise diagnosis and the ability to skillfully employ all acceptable diagnostic and treatment modalities as necessary, including surgical intervention other than chemonucleolysis, e.g., laminectomy, including all aspects of pre- and postoperative patient care.

The proper selection of patients for whom chemonucleolysis is applicable is of the utmost importance. There are circumstances in which nerve root compression resulting from conditions other than the herniated disc can produce similar signs and symptoms, therefore, extensive training and experience in the diagnosis and management of all spinal disorders and diseases is required.

Chymopapain should only be used by physicians who routinely care for patients with herniated lumbar intervertebral discs, who are qualified by training and experience to perform laminectomy, discectomy, or other spinal procedures, and who have received specialized training in chemonucleolysis.

Chymopapain should be used only in a hospital setting with the assistance of trained personnel, and in such a manner as to assure immediate and proper management of all potential complications, especially anaphylaxis.

Chymodiactin (cont'd)

Supplied: Each glass vial of sterile and lyophilized powder contains: chymopapain 4 or 10 nKat units. Nonmedicinal ingredients: sodium L-cysteinate hydrochloride. Vials of 2 and 5 mL. Boxes of 1. Refrigerate at 2 to 8°C prior to reconstitution and use. Supplied to hospitals only.

CICATRIN® ℞
Glaxo Wellcome

Bacitracin—Neomycin Sulfate—Amino Acids

Antibiotic—Tissue Healant

Indications: As a prophylactic or treatment and healing agent for surface wounds, minor burns, and stasis ulcers. Not recommended for the treatment of superficial fungal infections. The use of the powder does not exclude concomitant systemic therapy with antibiotics where appropriate.

Contraindications: Patients who have demonstrated allergic hypersensitivity to the product or any of its constituents, or to cross-sensitizing substances such as framycetin, kanamycin, gentamicin and other related antibiotics.

The presence of preexisting nerve deafness is a contraindication to the use of powder in circumstances in which significant systemic absorption could occur.

The concurrent use of other aminoglycoside antibiotics in circumstances where significant systemic absorption of neomycin sulfate could occur is contraindicated.

A possibility of increased absorption of neomycin exists in neonates and infants, thus Cicatrin is not recommended for use in neonates and should be used at reduced dosages in infants.

Cicatrin powder should not be applied to the eyes.

Precautions: General: Ototoxicity and nephrotoxicity have been reported in association with large or prolonged doses of neomycin and nephrotoxicity has also been reported with inappropriate dosing with bacitracin. While these effects are normally reversible on cessation of therapy, the ototoxicity of neomycin is not. In consequence, the application of three 15 g insufflators of powder daily for 4 weeks should not be exceeded in adults. After such a course, treatment should not be repeated for at least 3 months.

As with any antibiotic product, overgrowth by nonsusceptible organisms may occur. If this occurs, institute appropriate measures. The possibility of allergies to neomycin in patients with stasis ulcers or eczema should be borne in mind. Following the application of powder to substantial areas of burnt or broken skin, significant systemic absorption of active ingredients may occur.

Geriatrics: Maximum dose should be reduced especially where decreased renal function exists.

Infants and Children: In neonates and infants, absorption of neomycin by immature skin may be enhanced. Immaturity of renal functions may predispose these patients to decreased elimination and increased blood levels of neomycin (see Contraindications). In children, the maximum dosage should be reduced in proportion to body weight.

Fertility: There is insufficient information available to determine whether any of the active ingredients can affect fertility.

Pregnancy and *Lactation:* There is little information to demonstrate the possible effect of topically applied neomycin in pregnancy and lactation. However, neomycin present in maternal blood can cross the placenta and may give rise to fetal toxicity thus use of Cicatrin powder is not recommended. No information is available regarding the excretion of the active ingredients in human milk.

Teratogenicity: There is insufficient information available to determine whether the active ingredients have teratogenic potential. Neomycin present in maternal blood can cross the placenta and may give rise to a theoretical risk of fetal ototoxicity.

Patients with Special Diseases and Conditions: In renal impairment the plasma clearance of neomycin is reduced; therefore, a reduction in dose should be made that relates to the degree of renal impairment.

Drug Interactions: Following significant systemic absorption, neomycin sulfate can intensify and prolong the respiratory depressant effect of neuromuscular blocking agents.

Adverse Effects: Allergic hypersensitivity to active ingredients has been reported. Anaphylactic reactions are rare.

Allergic hypersensitivity to neomycin following topical application may manifest itself as a reddening and scaling of the affected skin, as an eczematous exacerbation of the lesion, or as a failure of the lesion to heal.

Overdose: Symptoms and Treatment: No specific symptoms or signs have been associated with excessive use of Cicatrin powder. However, consideration should be given to significant systemic absorption (see Precautions).

In the event of signs of toxicity developing following significant absorption of the active ingredients, the patient's general status, hearing acuity and renal function should be monitored and blood levels of neomycin and zinc bacitracin determined. Serum levels of neomycin can be reduced by hemodialysis.

Dosage: Adults: Before use, the area of application should be cleaned gently. Debris such as pus or crusts should be removed from the affected area.

A light dusting of powder should be applied to affected area twice daily or as directed by a physician. Treatment should not be continued for more than 7 days without medical supervision (see Precautions).

Children: Cicatrin powder is suitable for use in children. In older children, dosage is as for adults, but in infants dosage should be reduced (see Contraindications and Precautions).

A possibility of increased absorption exists in neonates and infants thus Cicatrin powder is not recommended for use in neonates and should be used at reduced dosages in infants. Follow administration instructions as per adults.

Geriatrics: Cicatrin powder is suitable for use in the elderly (see Renal Impairment and Precautions).

Renal Impairment: Dosage should be reduced in patients with reduced renal function (see Precautions).

Supplied: Each g of white, free-flowing powder contains: zinc bacitracin 250 units, neomycin sulfate equivalent to 3.3 mg of neomycin base, l-cysteine 2 mg, glycine 10 mg, dl-threonine 1 mg and cornstarch. Polyethylene insufflators of 15 g. Store between 15 to 30°C and keep dry.

Reviewed 1998

CIDOMYCIN® ℞
Hoechst Marion Roussel

Gentamicin

Antibiotic

Pharmacology: Gentamicin is a bactericidal antibiotic which affects bacterial growth by specific inhibition of normal protein synthesis in susceptible bacteria.

Gentamicin Serum Levels Via the I.M. Route in Adults and Children: In patients with normal renal function, peak serum concentrations, bactericidal for susceptible bacteria, occur between 30 and 90 minutes after injection. The peak serum level (mg/L) is usually 4 times the single dose (mg/kg).

The mean serum half-life is approximately 2 hours.

Gentamicin Serum Levels Via the I.M. Route in Infants and Neonates: Peak serum concentrations of 2.2 to 8.6 mg/L (mean 4.0 mg/L) are observed ½ to 1 hour after 2.5 mg/kg of gentamicin are administered i.m. to infants 7 days of age and under.

The mean serum gentamicin half-life is approximately 5 hours in neonates under 72 hours of age. This may be considerably prolonged in infants weighing less than 1 500 g. In low birth weight infants, prolonged half-life values may extend through the second week of life. In contrast, values of 3 to 3½ hours are usually observed in full-term infants who are 7 days of age and older.

Concentrations of gentamicin in serum of infants 2 to 24 months of age following i.m. doses of 2.0 and 2.5 mg/kg were shown to be in the range of 2.5 to 7.5 mg/L.

Gentamicin Serum Levels via the I.V. Route in Adults and Children: After a 2 hour infusion of a dose of 1 mg/kg to a group of patients, peak gentamicin concentrations were reached at the end of the infusion and averaged 4.5 mg/L (range 0.5 to 8 mg/L).

Slow i.v. injection in patients gave average serum levels of 5 to 9 mg/L after 10 minutes.

The mean serum half-life is similar to that for i.m. injection.

Gentamicin Serum Levels via the I.V. Route in Infants and Neonates: Levels in serum and half-life values after i.v. infusion of gentamicin were similar to those after i.m. administration.

Gentamicin Excretion: In man, about 25 to 30% of the administered dose of gentamicin is bound by serum protein; it is released as the drug is excreted. Gentamicin is excreted principally in the urine by glomerular filtration, thus resulting in high urinary concentration of the antibiotic. After initial administration to patients with normal renal function, 30 to 100% of the drug is recoverable in the urine in 24 hours. Renal clearance of gentamicin is similar to that of endogenous creatinine.

In patients with impaired renal function, the clearance of gentamicin is decreased; the more severe the impairment, the slower the clearance.

In the newborn, approximately 30% of the administered dose is excreted in 12 hours.

Gentamicin Penetration: Following parenteral administration gentamicin is detected in tissues and body fluids. Concentrations in bile in general have been low and have suggested minimal biliary excretion. Gentamicin has been found in the cerebrospinal fluid after i.m. injection; however, concentrations have been low and may be inadequate for treatments of certain CNS infections.

Concentrations of gentamicin in CSF of infants with purulent meningitis range from 0.2 to 3.5 mg/L after a dose of 1.5 to 2.5 mg/kg. Peak values are found 4 to 6 hours after the dose and are dependent on degree of meningeal inflammation and dosage.

Gentamicin has also been found in the sputum, pleural fluid and peritoneal cavity. Gentamicin crosses the peritoneum as well as the placental membranes.

Gentamicin at considerably higher doses than normally recommended, like other aminoglycoside antibiotics, causes neuromuscular blockade in animals. This phenomenon is antagonized by neostigmine or calcium (see Precautions).

Minimal amounts of gentamicin are absorbed following oral administration; therefore, oral administration is not recommended.

Indications: Clinically effective in serious infections due to susceptible gram-negative and gram-positive bacteria, including: P. aeruginosa, indole negative and indole positive Proteus species, E. coli, K. pneumoniae, E. aerogenes, S. marcescens and Staphylococcus species (including strains resistant to other antibiotics).

The use of gentamicin is indicated in the treatment of serious infections caused by laboratory determined susceptible bacteria, with due regard for relative antibiotic toxicity. The drug, therefore, should be considered for treatment of: bacteremia, respiratory tract infections, urinary tract infections, infected wounds—surgical and traumatic, bone and soft tissue infections, including peritonitis and burns complicated by sepsis.

In the majority of cases, bacteriologic cultures should be obtained initially to identify the causative organism and to determine its sensitivity to gentamicin. Sensitivity discs of 10 μg are available for this purpose.

In suspected or documented gram-negative septicemia, particularly when shock or hypotension are present, gentamicin injection should be considered for initial antimicrobial therapy. Gentamicin should also be considered in serious Staphylococcus infections when other conventional antimicrobial therapy is inappropriate or when bacterial susceptibility testing and clinical judgment indicate its use. If anaerobic organisms are suspected, additional antimicrobial therapy should be added to the gentamicin regimen.

The decision to continue therapy with gentamicin injection should be based on results of the sensitivity tests, clinical response of the patient, and consideration of relative antibiotic toxicity.

Gentamicin injection has frequently been life-saving in serious infections with poor prognosis, particularly when therapy was begun promptly.

Clinical studies have shown that organisms previously sensitive to gentamicin have become resistant during therapy. Although this has occurred infrequently, the possibility should nevertheless be considered. There is evidence that cross-resistance between gentamicin and aminoglycoside antibiotics may occur since bacteria made resistant to aminoglycoside antibiotics artificially in the laboratory are also resistant to gentamicin; however, gentamicin may be active against clinical isolates of bacteria resistant to other aminoglycosides. Conversely, organisms resistant to gentamicin may be sensitive to other aminoglycoside antibiotics.

If susceptibility tests indicate the causative organism is resistant to gentamicin, other or additional antimicrobial therapy should be instituted.

Combined therapy with gentamicin and a penicillin type of drug has been used in suspected sepsis until bacteriological studies have identified the etiological organism.

Contraindications: A history of hypersensitivity or toxic reactions to gentamicin.

Pregnancy: Although studies in pregnant animals have not revealed teratogenic effects, gentamicin is not recommended during pregnancy except in life-threatening situations.

Newborns: Until further experience is gained, gentamicin injection should not be used in the newborn except for infections which threaten life. Although followup in these cases has been limited, no adverse reactions have been revealed.

Precautions: Ototoxicity: Gentamicin, in common with the antibiotics streptomycin, neomycin and kanamycin, has produced ototoxicity in experimental animals and man. This adverse reaction, which may be delayed in onset, is manifested primarily by damage to vestibular function. The reversibility of this adverse reaction is frequently contingent upon early recognition of potential ototoxicity. In all patients developing tinnitus, dizziness or loss of hearing, the attending physician should strongly consider discontinuing this antibiotic except in those cases where gentamicin appears to be the only proven course of therapy.

Complete damage has occurred mainly in patients who were uremic, had renal dysfunction, had prior therapy with ototoxic drugs or received higher doses and longer courses of therapy than those recommended.

In patients who have previously been treated with drugs likely to affect eighth cranial nerve function (e.g. streptomycin, neomycin, kanamycin, etc.), gentamicin should be used with caution and with the understanding that toxic effects may be cumulative with these agents.

Potent diuretics such as ethacrynic acid and furosemide have been associated with eighth cranial nerve dysfunction, and the concomitant use of either of these drugs with gentamicin should be avoided. It is believed that i.v. diuretics may cause fairly rapid rise in gentamicin serum levels and potentiate ototoxicity.

In patients with impaired renal function, the frequency of gentamicin administration should be reduced (see Dosage), and renal function should be monitored along with evaluation of auditory and vestibular function. Serum concentrations of gentamicin should be monitored whenever feasible; prolonged concentrations above 12 mg/L should be avoided.

Nephrotoxicity: Nephrotoxicity manifested by an elevated BUN or serum creatinine level or a decrease in the creatinine clearance has been reported with gentamicin. In most cases, these changes have been reversible when the drug has been discontinued.

The administration of other potentially nephrotoxic agents prior to, or in conjunction with, gentamicin may increase the risk of nephrotoxicity.

Superinfection: As with other antibiotics, treatment with gentamicin may occasionally result in overgrowth of nonsensitive organisms. If superinfection occurs, appropriate measures should be taken.

Neuromuscular Blocking Action: Neuromuscular blockage and respiratory paralysis have been reported in the cat receiving high doses (40 mg/kg) of gentamicin. The possibility of these phenomena occurring in man should be considered if gentamicin is administered to patients receiving general anesthesia and/or neuromuscular blocking agents such as succinylcholine and tubocurarine.

In patients with myasthenia gravis, use of drugs with potential neuromuscular blocking action may be dangerous.

Neuromuscular blocking action produced by gentamicin in animals may be antagonized by neostigmine or calcium.

Adverse Effects: In addition to the **ototoxicity** and **nephrotoxicity** discussed under Precautions, other adverse reactions reported infrequently and possibly related to gentamicin include increased serum transaminase AST, ALT, increased reticulocyte count, and increased serum bilirubin, anemia, rash, granulocytopenia, urticaria, thrombocytopenia, headache, vomiting and muscle twitching.

Adverse reactions reported rarely and possibly related to gentamicin are nausea, increased salivation, lethargy and decreased appetite, weight loss, pulmonary fibrosis, purpura, splenomegaly, transient hepatomegaly, itching, numbness, skin tingling, laryngeal edema and spasm, joint pain, drug fever, convulsions, hypotension, hypertension, decreased serum calcium, decreased hemoglobin and hematocrit, fifth nerve paresthesia and gastrointestinal hemorrhage. One case of neuromuscular blocking action has been reported in the literature.

Overdose: Symptoms and Treatment: In the event of overdosage or toxic reactions, peritoneal dialysis or hemodialysis will aid in the removal of gentamicin from the blood. These procedures are of particular importance in patients with impaired renal function.

Dosage: Gentamicin is usually administered i.m. The i.v. route generally is reserved for special indications (see I.V. Administration).

I.M.: Patients with Normal Renal Function: Urinary Tract Infections: Gentamicin is highly concentrated in urine and renal tissue. In patients with **lower** urinary tract infection particularly if chronic or recurrent and without evidence of impairment of renal function, gentamicin may be administered i.m. either in a dose of 160 mg once a day or 80 mg twice daily for 7 to 10 days. For adults weighing less than 60 kg, the single daily dose should be 3.0 mg/kg of body weight.

Upper urinary tract infections, such as pyelonephritis, and more particularly if there are signs of systemic involvement, should be treated according to one of the dosage schedules for systemic infections.

Since gentamicin activity is increased at pH 7.5, it may be advantageous to alkalinize the urine of patients treated for urinary tract infections.

Systemic Infections: Adults with serious infections and normal renal function: 3 mg/kg/day administered i.m. in 3 equal doses. For patients weighing over 60 kg, the usual dosage is 80 mg 3 times daily. For patients weighing 60 kg or less, the usual dosage is 60 mg 3 times a day.

The usual duration of treatment is 7 to 10 days. In difficult and complicated infections, a longer course of therapy may be necessary. In such cases, monitoring of renal, auditory and vestibular functions is advisable.

Life-threatening Infections: Dosages up to 5 mg/kg/day should be administered in 3 or 4 equally divided doses. This dosage should be reduced to 3 mg/kg/day as soon as clinically indicated.

Children: The precautions for the treatment of infection in children are the same as those for adults.

In severe infections, the recommended dosage is 3 to 6 mg/kg/day administered in 3 equal doses, every 8 hours. If a dosage greater than 3 mg/kg/day is administered initially, it should be reduced to 3 mg/kg/day when clinically indicated.

Infants and Neonates (see Contraindications): In premature and full-term neonates, 1 week of age or less, a dosage of 6 mg/kg/day may be administered in 2 equal doses every 12 hours. In infants older than 1 week, gentamicin may be administered in 3 equal doses every 8 hours. Using the recommended doses, considerable variation in the serum levels between individual patients has been observed. In order to insure adequate therapeutic levels which may be critical, while at the same time avoiding potentially toxic concentrations, serum levels should be monitored. A serum level in excess of 10 to 12 mg/L following i.m. administration should be considered potentially toxic.

The usual duration of treatment is 7 to 10 days. In difficult and complicated infections, a longer course of therapy may be necessary. In such cases, monitoring of renal, auditory and vestibular functions is advisable.

Patients with Impaired Renal Function: Dosage must be adjusted in patients with impaired renal function (see Table I). Since the creatinine clearance rate and serum creatinine concentration have high correlation with the serum half-life of gentamicin, these laboratory tests may provide the guidance necessary for adjustment of the interval between doses of gentamicin sulfate injection. The serum half-life (in hours) of gentamicin may be estimated by multiplying the serum creatinine (mg/100 mL) by 4. The frequency of administration (in hours) may be approximated by doubling the serum half-life.

In patients with renal failure who are undergoing 14 hour hemodialysis twice weekly, administration of gentamicin 1 mg/kg, at the end of each dialysis period has been suggested.

In those instances when only BUN concentration is available, this value may be utilized initially; however, it should be supplemented with a serum creatinine level or creatinine clearance rate whenever possible.

This dosage schedule (see Table I) is not intended as a rigid recommendation but is provided as a guide to dosage when the measurement of gentamicin serum levels is not feasible.

It should be used in conjunction with close clinical and laboratory observations of the patients and modified as deemed necessary by the treating physician.

I.V.: For use when the i.m. route is not feasible, e.g. patients in shock, with hemorrhagic disorders, severe burns, or reduced muscle mass.

The recommended dose of gentamicin administered i.v. is 3 mg/kg/day in 3 equally divided doses, identical to that recommended for i.m. use.

For i.v. administration, gentamicin injection may be administered either undiluted into the i.v. tubing or diluted in an infusion fluid.

Undiluted, a single dose may be given directly into the sidearm of an i.v. tubing set, slowly over a period of 2 to 3 minutes and repeated every 8 hours.

For infusion, a single dose (1 mg/kg) may be diluted in 100 to 200 mL of sterile normal saline or sterile dextrose 5% in water, the solution infused over a period of 1 to 2 hours and repeated every 8 hours.

Compatibility: Gentamicin sulfate injection should not be physically premixed with other drugs, but should be administered separately in accordance with the recommended route of administration and dosage schedule.

Supplied: Cidomycin Injectable Pediatric: Each mL of sterile, aqueous solution (pH 3.0 to 4.5) contains: gentamicin (as sulfate BP) 10 mg. Also contains methylparaben 1.3 mg, propylparaben 200 µg (as preservatives) and disodium edetate 100 µg. Sodium: <1 mmol/mL. Multiple dose vials of 2 mL, packages of 5.

Prefilled Disposable Syringes: Each 2 mL prefilled disposable syringe contains: gentamicin base 80 mg (as sulfate). Packs of 12. Each 1.5 mL prefilled disposable syringe contains: gentamicin base 60 mg (as sulfate). Packs of 12.

CILAZAPRIL ℞

General Monograph, CPhA

see ACE INHIBITORS

CILOXAN® ℞

Alcon

Ciprofloxacin HCl

Antibacterial Agent

Pharmacology: The bactericidal action of ciprofloxacin results from inhibition of the enzyme, DNA gyrase, which is required for the synthesis of bacterial DNA.

Pharmacokinetics: Topically applied ciprofloxacin ophthalmic solution is absorbed systemically with ciprofloxacin plasma concentrations approaching steady state at the end of dosing each day. Ciprofloxacin plasma concentrations following a routine ophthalmic treatment regimen were in the range of nonquantifiable to 4.7 ng/mL with the majority of levels falling between 1.5 to 2.5 ng/mL. Maximum serum concentration following a single oral administration of a 250 mg ciprofloxacin tablet is about 1 200 ng/mL.

Indications: Ointment: For the treatment of the following infections of the eye and its adnexae when caused by susceptible strains of the designated bacteria.

Corneal Ulcers: P. aeruginosa, S. aureus, S. epidermidis.

Conjunctivitis: S. aureus, S. epidermidis, Streptococcus (Viridans group), S. pneumoniae, H. influenzae.

Table I—Cidomycin

Approximate Dosage Guidelines in Adult Patients Based on Renal Function

		Renal Function Tests			
Body Weight Adults	**Dose**	**Creatinine Clearance Rate (mL/min)**	**Serum Creatinine (mg%)**	**Blood Urea Nitrogen (mg%)**	**Frequency of Administration**
Over 60 kg	80 mg (2 mL)	Over 70	Less than 1.4	Less than 18	q 8 hours
		35–70	1.4–1.9	18–29	q 12 hours
		24–34	2.0–2.8	30–39	q 18 hours
		16–32	2.9–3.7	40–49	q 24 hours
		10–15	3.8–5.3	50–74	q 36 hours
		5–9	5.4–7.2	75–100	q 48 hours
60 kg or less	60 mg (1.5 mL)	Same as above			

Ciloxan (cont'd)

Solution: For the treatment of the following infections of the eye and its adnexae when caused by susceptible strains of the designated bacteria.
Corneal Ulcers: P. aeruginosa, S. aureus, S. epidermidis, S. pneumoniae.
Conjunctivitis: S. aureus, S. epidermidis, Streptococcus (Viridans group), S. pneumoniae, H. influenzae.

Contraindications: A history of hypersensitivity to ciprofloxacin, other quinolones including nalidixic acid, or any other component of the medication.

Warnings: Not for injection into the eye.

Precautions: General: Prolonged use of ciprofloxacin ophthalmic solution or ointment may result in overgrowth of nonsusceptible organisms, including fungi. If superinfection occurs, appropriate therapy should be initiated. Whenever clinical judgment dictates, the patient should be examined with the aid of magnification, such as slit lamp biomicroscopy and, where appropriate, fluorescein staining.

Anaphylactic reactions following the first dose, have been reported in patients receiving therapy with quinolones by systemic administration. Some reactions were accompanied by cardiovascular collapse, loss of consciousness, tingling, pharyngeal or facial edema, dyspnea, urticaria and itching. Only a few patients had a history of hypersensitivity reaction. Anaphylactic reactions may require epinephrine and other emergency measures. Ciprofloxacin should be discontinued at the first sign of hypersensitivity or allergy and the patient monitored until the risk of anaphylaxis is no longer present. Severe hypersensitivity reactions characterized by rash, fever, eosinophilia, jaundice and hepatic necrosis with fatal outcome have been reported rarely (less than 1 per million prescriptions) in patients receiving systemically administered ciprofloxacin along with other drugs. One report exists of anaphylaxis in a patient treated with topical ciprofloxacin concomitantly with several other antibiotics and medications. The possibility that these reactions were related to ciprofloxacin cannot be excluded. Ciprofloxacin should be discontinued at the first appearance of a skin rash or any other sign of hypersensitivity reaction.

In clinical studies of patients with bacterial corneal ulcer, a white crystalline precipitate located in the superficial portion of the corneal defect was observed in 29 (18.8%) out of 154 patients administered ciprofloxacin ophthalmic solution and in 32 (12.6%) of 253 patients administered ciprofloxacin ophthalmic ointment. The onset of the precipitate was within 24 hours to 7 days (solution) and 13 days (ointment) after starting therapy. In 16 patients administered ciprofloxacin ophthalmic solution, resolution of the precipitate was seen in 1 to 8 days (7 within the first 24 to 72 hours), in 4 patients, resolution was noted in 10 to 13 days. In 1 patient, the precipitate was immediately irrigated out upon its appearance.

In 6 patients, exact resolution days were unavailable, however, at follow-up examinations 18 to 44 days after onset of the event, complete resolution of the precipitate was noted. In 2 patients, outcome information was unavailable. The presence of the white precipitate did not preclude continued use of ciprofloxacin ophthalmic solution or ointment, nor did it adversely affect the clinical course of the ulcer or visual outcome. A literature report exists of a single case of ciprofloxacin-associated dense precipitate apparently interfering with re-epithelialization.

Dosage regimens involving both solution and ointment formulations of ciprofloxacin 0.3% have not been studied. A controlled study of the efficacy and safety of ciprofloxacin ointment versus ciprofloxacin solution 0.3% has not been conducted.

In patients with large (>4 mm) and/or deep stromal ulcers, the clinical success rate was lower for both ciprofloxacin and standard (fortified antibiotics) therapy.

Drug Interactions: Specific drug interaction studies have not been conducted with ciprofloxacin ophthalmic solution or ointment. However, the systemic administration of some quinolones has been shown to elevate plasma concentrations of theophylline, interfere with the metabolism of caffeine, enhance the effects of oral coagulant, warfarin and its derivatives, and has been associated with transient elevations in serum creatinine in patients receiving cyclosporine concomitantly.

Pregnancy: There are no adequate and well controlled studies of ciprofloxacin ophthalmic solution or ointment in pregnant women. This drug should be used in pregnant women only if in the physician's opinion, the benefit clearly outweighs any potential unknown risks.

Reproduction studies have been performed in rats and mice at doses up to 6 times the usual daily human dose and have revealed no evidence of impaired fertility or harm to the fetus due to ciprofloxacin. In rabbits, as with most antimicrobial agents, ciprofloxacin (30 and 100 mg/kg orally) produced gastrointestinal disturbances resulting in maternal weight loss and an increased incidence of abortion. No teratogenicity was observed at either dose. After i.v. administration in rabbits, at doses up to 20 mg/kg, no maternal toxicity was produced and no embryotoxicity or teratogenicity was observed.

Lactation: It is not known whether topically applied ciprofloxacin ophthalmic solution or ointment is excreted in human milk, however, it is known that orally administered ciprofloxacin is excreted in milk of lactating rats and that other drugs of this class are excreted in human milk. For this reason, and because of the potential for serious adverse reactions from ciprofloxacin in nursing infants, a decision should be made to discontinue nursing or to discontinue the drug, taking into consideration the importance of the drug to the mother.

Children: Safety and efficacy of ciprofloxacin ophthalmic solution or ointment in children less than 1 year of age have not been demonstrated. Ciprofloxacin ophthalmic solution has been used in 123 children between the ages of 1 and 12 years and ciprofloxacin ophthalmic ointment has been used in 182 children between the ages of 1 and 12 years. No serious adverse event was reported in these patients.

Ciprofloxacin and quinolone-related drugs have been shown to cause arthropathy in immature animals of most species tested following oral administration. Topical ocular administration of ciprofloxacin to immature animals (Beagle dogs) did not cause arthropathy or demonstrate any articular lesions and there is no evidence that the ophthalmic dosage form has any effect on the weight bearing joints.

In 634 children treated orally with ciprofloxacin, clinical and radiologic monitoring did not reveal any skeletal toxicity felt to be quinolone-related. However, there are a small number of reports of arthralgia in children, associated with oral ciprofloxacin therapy. This arthralgia has been shown to be reversible on discontinuation of the systemic medication.

Adverse Effects: During clinical studies, treatment related adverse events to ciprofloxacin ophthalmic solution and ointment were mild, infrequent in occurrence and nonserious in nature, and did not lead to premature discontinuation of therapy. The most frequently reported adverse events that were considered related or possibly related to ciprofloxacin ophthalmic solution were: transient discomfort, i.e., stinging, burning, irritation (8.6%), noticeable taste (4.5%), foreign body sensation (1.8%), and itching (1.2%). Treatment-related or possibly related medical events occurring between 0.5 and 1% incidence were: lid margin crusting, crystals/scales, erythema/redness, dryness, discharge, corneal staining, keratopathy/keratitis, hyperemia/congestion and tearing.

In clinical trials in which 154 patients were treated for bacterial corneal ulcers, the most frequently reported adverse event related or possibly related to therapy was a white crystalline precipitate seen in 29 (18.8%) patients. The precipitate required no adjunctive therapy and resolved spontaneously with continued ciprofloxacin use.

Other rarely reported events related or possibly related to ciprofloxacin ophthalmic solution included: ocular congestion, photophobia, pain, vision decrease, chemosis, corneal infiltrate, inflammation, blurred vision, corneal toxicity, allergy, intolerance, lid edema, heavy sensation, swelling, conjunctival reaction, numbing sensation, conjunctivitis, punctate epithelial erosion, and worsened infiltrate and headache.

The most commonly reported drug adverse reactions in patients with conjunctivitis treated with ciprofloxacin ophthalmic ointment were discomfort (1.3%), pruritus (1.3%), and hyperemia (1.3%), and in patients with corneal ulcers were white precipitate (12.6%), discomfort (2.0%), and blurred vision (1.2%). Other reactions associated with ciprofloxacin ophthalmic ointment occurring in less than 1.0% of patients included hyperemia, pruritus, eye pain, tearing, photophobia, allergic reactions, dry eye, decreased visual acuity, lid erythema, corneal staining, keratoconjunctivitis, keratopathy, corneal lesion, epitheliopathy, ocular edema, irritation, foreign body sensation, nausea, dermatitis and metallic taste.

Overdose: Symptoms and Treatment: A topical overdosage of ciprofloxacin is considered to be a remote possibility. Discontinue medication when heavy or protracted use is suspected. A topical overdosage may be flushed from the eye(s) with warm tap water.

Dosage: Ointment: Conjunctivitis: Adults and Children (above the age of 1 year): Apply a 1.25 cm ribbon of ophthalmic ointment into the conjunctival sac 3 times a day on the first 2 days and then apply a 1.25 cm ribbon 2 times a day for the next 5 days.
Corneal ulcer: Adults and Children (above the age of 12 years): Apply a 1.25 cm ribbon of ophthalmic ointment into the conjunctival sac every 1 to 2 hours around the clock on the first 2 days, then apply a 1.25 cm ribbon every 4 hours for up to 12 days. If corneal re-epithelialization has not occurred after 12 days, the continuation of the dosing regimen is at the discretion of the attending physician.
Special Instructions: Patients should be advised to avoid contamination of the dispensing tip. As with other ophthalmic ointments, transient blurred vision may be experienced with the use of ciprofloxacin ointment.
Solution: Conjunctivitis: Adults and Children (above the age of 1 year): Instill 1 or 2 drops of ophthalmic solution into the conjunctival sac(s) every 2 hours while awake for 2 days and then 2 drops every 4 hours while awake for 5 days.
Corneal Ulcer: Adults and Children (above the age of 12 years): Instill 2 drops of ophthalmic solution into the affected eye every 15 minutes for the first 6 hours and then 2 drops into the affected eye every 30 minutes for the remainder of the first day. On the second day, instill 2 drops in the affected eye hourly. On the third through the fourteenth day, place 2 drops in the affected eye every 4 hours. If corneal re-epithelialization has not occurred after 14 days, the continuation of the dosing regimen is at the discretion of the attending physician.
Special Instructions: Patients should be advised to avoid contamination of the dispensing tip.

Supplied: Ointment: Each g of ophthalmic ointment contains: ciprofloxacin HCl 3.5 mg equivalent to 3 mg base. Nonmedicinal ingredients: mineral oil and white petrolatum. Metal ophthalmic ointment tubes of 3.5 g.

Solution: Each mL of ophthalmic solution contains: ciprofloxacin HCl 3.5 mg equivalent to ciprofloxacin base 3 mg. Also contains benzalkonium chloride 0.006% as preservative. Nonmedicinal ingredients: acetic acid, edetate disodium, hydrochloric acid and/or sodium hydroxide, mannitol, purified water, and sodium acetate. Plastic Drop-Tainer dispensers of 5 and 10 mL.

Store in the carton at room temperature (2 to 30°C).

Reviewed 1999

CIPRO® Ⓟ
CIPRO® I.V. Ⓟ
CIPRO® Oral Suspension Ⓟ

Bayer

Ciprofloxacin HCl
Ciprofloxacin
Ciprofloxacin

Antibacterial

Pharmacology: Ciprofloxacin, a synthetic fluoroquinolone, has a bactericidal mode of action. This action is achieved through inhibition of DNA gyrase, an essential component of the bacterial DNA replication system. Inhibition of the alpha subunit of the DNA gyrase blocks the resealing of the nicks on the DNA strands induced by this alpha subunit, leading to the degradation of the DNA by exonucleases. This bactericidal activity persists not only during the multiplication phase, but also during the resting phase of the bacterium.

Ciprofloxacin retained some of its bactericidal activity after inhibition of RNA and protein synthesis by rifampin and chloramphenicol, respectively. These observations suggest ciprofloxacin may possess two bactericidal mechanisms, one mechanism resulting from the inhibition of DNA gyrase and a second mechanism which may be independent of RNA and protein synthesis.

Ciprofloxacin and metronidazole have been studied in combination and serum levels of ciprofloxacin are not significantly altered by metronidazole at the doses studied. Serum levels of metronidazole when administered orally at a dose of 500 mg q6h in combination with ciprofloxacin 500 mg po q12h are: $AUC_{0\rightarrow6}$ 156.3 mg·h/L, C_{max} 31.3 mg/L and T_{max} 1.71 hours. Serum levels of metronidazole when administered i.v. at a dose of 500 mg i.v. q6h in combination with ciprofloxacin 400 mg i.v. q12h are: $AUC_{0\rightarrow6}$ 153.0 mg·h/L, C_{max} 33.6 mg/L and T_{max} 1.0 hours (see Dosage and Pharmacokinetics).

With oral administration, one 500 mg dose is bioequivalent to a 5 mL volume of the 10% ciprofloxacin oral suspension (containing 500 mg ciprofloxacin/5 mL) (see Dosage).

Following infusion of 400 mg i.v. ciprofloxacin every 8 hours in combination with 50 mg/kg i.v. piperacillin sodium every 4 hours, mean serum ciprofloxacin concentrations were 3.02 μg/mL at 30 minutes and 1.18 μg/mL between 6 and 8 hours after the end of infusion. The mean serum ciprofloxacin concentration given alone at 400 mg i.v. every 8 hours was 3.67 μg/mL at 30 minutes and 1.10 μg/mL at 0 hours after the end of infusion.

Pharmacokinetics: The relative bioavailability of oral ciprofloxacin given as a tablet, is between 70 and 80% compared to an equivalent dose of i.v. ciprofloxacin.

Following oral administration of single doses of 250, 500 and 750 mg of ciprofloxacin respectively to groups of 3 healthy male volunteers (age: 22.8±3.5 years, weight: 68.5±9.4 kg), ciprofloxacin was absorbed rapidly and extensively from the gastrointestinal tract.

Maximum serum concentrations (C_{max}) increased dose-proportionally and were attained 1 to 2 hours after oral dosing. The total areas under the serum concentration time curves (AUC) were also increased in proportion to dose. Mean concentrations 12 hours after dosing with 250, 500 or 750 mg were 0.1, 0.2, and 0.4 mg/L, respectively. The serum elimination half-lives ($t_{1/2}$) were between 4 and 6 hours.

With oral administration, a 500 mg dose, given as 10 mL of the 5% suspension (containing 250 mg ciprofloxacin/5 mL) is bioequivalent to the 500 mg tablet. A 10 mL volume of the 5% suspension (containing 250 mg ciprofloxacin/5 mL) is bioequivalent to a 5 mL volume of the 10% suspension (containing 500 mg ciprofloxacin/5 mL) (see Table I).

patients who display clinical improvement despite evidence of in vitro sensitivity. In patients requiring subsequent courses of therapy, ciprofloxacin should be used alternately with other antipseudomonal agents. Some strains of P. aeruginosa may develop resistance during treatment. Therefore, susceptibility testing should be performed periodically during therapy to detect the emergence of bacterial resistance.

Urinary Tract Infections: Upper and lower urinary tract infections, such as complicated and uncomplicated cystitis, pyelonephritis, and pyelitis, caused by: C. diversus, C. freundii, E. cloacae, E. coli, K. pneumoniae, K. oxytoca, M. morganii, P. mirabilis, P. aeruginosa, S. marcescens, S. aureus, S. epidermidis, S. saprophyticus, S. faecalis.

Chronic Bacterial Prostatitis: caused by: E. coli.

Skin and Soft Tissue Infections: caused by: E. cloacae, E. coli, K. pneumoniae, P. mirabilis, P. vulgaris, P. aeruginosa, S. aureus, S. epidermidis, S. pyogenes.

Bone and Joint Infections: caused by: E. cloacae, P. aeruginosa, S. marcescens, S. aureus,

Infectious Diarrhea (when antibacterial therapy is indicated): caused by: C. jejuni, E. coli (enterotoxigenic strains), S. dysenteriae, S. flexneri, S. sonnei.

Meningococcal Carriers: Treatment of asymptomatic carriers of N. meningitidis to eliminate meningococci from the nasopharynx. An MIC determination on the isolate from the index case should be performed as soon as possible. **Ciprofloxacin is not indicated for the treatment of meningococcal meningitis.**

Table I—Cipro Oral Suspension/Cipro Tablets

Summary Table of the Comparative Bioavailability Data

Ciprofloxacin Oral Suspension vs Tablet
Geometric Mean and Arithmetic Mean (CV%)*
Single Doses In Healthy Volunteers

Parameter	500 mg Oral Suspension	500 mg Tablet	% Ratio of Geometric Means
$AUC_{0-\infty}$	11.81	12.04	0.98
(μg·h/mL)	12.19 (22.6)	12.28 (19.4)	
AUC_I	11.29	11.51	0.98
(μg·h/mL)	11.68 (23.1)	11.75 (19.9)	
C_{max} (μg/mL)	2.18	2.36	0.92
	2.23 (23.1)	2.39 (17.9)	
T_{max} (h)*	1.62	1.22	—

*arithmetic mean only.

Following a 60-minute i.v. infusion of 200 and 400 mg ciprofloxacin to 13 healthy male volunteers (18 to 40 years), the mean maximum serum concentrations achieved were 2.14 and 4.60 mg/L respectively; the concentrations at 12.0 hours were 0.11, 0.23 mg/L respectively.

The pharmacokinetics of ciprofloxacin were linear over the dose range of 200 and 400 mg administered i.v. At steady-state, the serum elimination half-life was approximately 5 to 6 hours and the total clearance around 35 L/hour was observed. Comparison of the pharmacokinetic parameters following the 1st and 5th i.v. dose on a 12-hour regimen indicated no evidence of drug accumulation.

An i.v. infusion of 400 mg ciprofloxacin given over 60 minutes every 12 hours, for 6 doses, to 12 healthy male volunteers (18 to 40 years) has been shown to produce an area under the serum concentration time curve (AUC) equivalent to that produced by a 500 mg oral dose given every 12 hours. The 400 mg i.v. dose administered over 60 minutes every 12 hours resulted in a C_{max} similar to that observed with a 750 mg oral dose.

An infusion of 200 mg ciprofloxacin given every 12 hours produces an AUC equivalent to that produced by a 250 mg oral dose every 12 hours.

Pharmacokinetics were dose proportioned with no significant changes in clearance or half-life occurring over this dose range.

Indications: Oral: Treatment of patients with the following infections caused by susceptible strains of the indicated microorganisms:

Respiratory Tract Infections: Acute exacerbation of chronic bronchitis caused by: H. influenzae, M. catarrhalis, S. pneumoniae.

Acute pneumonia caused by: E. cloacae, E. coli, H. influenzae, K. pneumoniae, P. mirabilis, P. aeruginosa, S. aureus, S. pneumoniae.

Acute sinusitis caused by: H. influenza, M. catarrhalis, S. pneumoniae.

Due to the nature of the underlying conditions which usually predispose patients to pseudomonas infections of the respiratory tract, bacterial eradications may not be achieved in

Typhoid Fever: (enteric fever) caused by: S. paratyphi, S. typhi.

Uncomplicated Gonorrhea: Cervical/urethral/rectal/pharyngeal infections caused by N. gonorrhoea. Because co-infection with C. trachomatis is common, consideration should be given to treating presumptively with an additional regimen that is effective against C. trachomatis.

I.V.: For the treatment of patients with the following infections caused by susceptible strains of the indicated microorganisms:

Respiratory Tract Infections: Acute pneumonia caused by: E. cloacae, E. coli, H. influenzae, H. parainfluenzae, K. pneumoniae, P. mirabilis, P. aeruginosa, S. aureus, S. pneumoniae.

Due to the nature of the underlying conditions which usually predispose patients to Pseudomonas infections of the respiratory tract, bacterial eradications may not be achieved in patients who display clinical improvement despite evidence of in vitro sensitivity. In patients requiring subsequent courses of therapy, ciprofloxacin should be used alternately with other antipseudomonal agents. Some strains of P. aeruginosa may develop resistance during treatment. Therefore, susceptibility testing should be performed periodically during therapy to detect the emergence of bacterial resistance.

Urinary Tract Infections: Upper and lower complicated urinary tract infections including pyelonephritis caused by: C. diversus, E. coli, K. pneumoniae, P. mirabilis, P. aeruginosa.

Skin or Skin Structure Infections: caused by: E. cloacae, E. coli, K. pneumoniae, M. morganii, P. mirabilis, P. vulgaris, P. aeruginosa, S. aureus, S. pyogenes.

Septicemia: caused by: E. coli, S. typhi.

Bone: caused by: E. cloacae, P. aeruginosa.

Complicated Intra-abdominal infections only when used in combination with metronidazole (see Dosage): caused by: E. coli, P. aeruginosa, K. pneumoniae, B. fragilis.

Note: Most anaerobic bacteria, including B. fragilis, are resistant to ciprofloxacin. Therefore, ciprofloxacin should not be used as single agent therapy for complicated intra-abdominal infections. Efficacy against Enterococcus sp. in clinical trials has been shown to be only 75%.

Empiric Therapy in Febrile Neutropenic Patients (in combination with piperacillin sodium): (see Dosage).

Appropriate culture and susceptibility tests should be performed prior to initiating treatment in order to isolate and identify organisms causing the infection and to determine their susceptibilities to ciprofloxacin. Therapy with ciprofloxacin may be initiated before results of these tests are known. However, modification of this treatment may be required once results become available or if there is no clinical improvement. Culture and susceptibility testing performed periodically during therapy will provide information on the possible emergence of bacterial resistance. If anaerobic organisms are suspected to be contributing to the infection, appropriate therapy should be administered.

Contraindications: In patients who have shown hypersensitivity to ciprofloxacin or other quinolone antibacterial agents.

Warnings: Children: The safety of ciprofloxacin in children has not yet been established. Damage to juvenile weight-bearing joints and lameness were observed both in rat and dog studies but not in weaned piglets. Histopathological examination of the weight-bearing joints in immature dogs revealed permanent lesions of the cartilage.

Consequently, ciprofloxacin should not be used in prepubertal patients. Experience in pubertal patients below 18 years of age is limited.

Pregnancy: The safety of ciprofloxacin in the treatment of infections in pregnant women has not yet been established (see Precautions).

General: Convulsions have been reported in patients receiving ciprofloxacin. Convulsions, increased intracranial pressure, and toxic psychosis have been reported in patients receiving drugs in this class. Quinolones may also cause CNS stimulation, which may lead to tremors, restlessness, lightheadedness, confusion and hallucinations. If these reactions occur in patients receiving ciprofloxacin, the drug should be discontinued and appropriate measures instituted. As with all quinolones, ciprofloxacin should be used with caution in patients with known or suspected CNS disorders, such as severe cerebral arteriosclerosis, epilepsy, and other factors that predispose to seizures (see Adverse Effects).

Precautions: General: Anaphylactic reactions including cardiovascular collapse have occurred rarely in patients receiving therapy with ciprofloxacin. These reactions may occur within the first 30 minutes following the first dose and may require epinephrine and other emergency measures.

Serious and fatal reactions have been reported in patients receiving concurrent administration of ciprofloxacin i.v. and theophylline. These reactions include cardiac arrest, seizure, status epilepticus and respiratory failure. Similar serious adverse events have been noted with administration of theophylline alone, however, the possibility that ciprofloxacin may potentiate these reactions cannot be eliminated. If concomitant use cannot be avoided, the plasma levels of theophylline should be monitored and appropriate dosage adjustments should be made.

Severe hypersensitivity reactions characterized by rash, fever, eosinophilia, jaundice and hepatic necrosis with fatal outcome have also been reported to occur very rarely in patients receiving ciprofloxacin in combination with other drugs. The possibility that these reactions were related to ciprofloxacin cannot be excluded. Ciprofloxacin should be withdrawn at the first appearance of a skin rash or other signs of hypersensitivity.

Tendon rupture (predominantly achilles tendon) has been reported predominantly in the elderly on prior systemic treatment with glucocorticoids. At any sign of tendonitis (i.e., painful swelling), the administration of ciprofloxacin should be discontinued, physical exercise avoided, and a physician consulted.

Crystalluria related to ciprofloxacin has been reported only rarely in man because human urine is usually acidic. Crystals have been observed in the urine of laboratory animals, usually from alkaline urine. Patients receiving ciprofloxacin should be well hydrated and alkalinity of the urine should be avoided. The recommended daily dose should not be exceeded.

Pseudomembranous colitis has been reported with virtually all antibacterial agents, including ciprofloxacin, and may range in severity from mild to life-threatening. Therefore, it is important to consider this diagnosis in patients with diarrhea subsequent to the administration of antibacterial agents. Subsequent to diagnosis of pseudomembranous colitis, therapeutic measures should be initiated. Mild cases will usually respond to discontinuation of drug alone. In moderate to severe cases, consideration should be given to the management with fluids,

Cipro (cont'd)

electrolytes, protein supplementation and treatment with an antibacterial drug effective against C. difficile.

Ciprofloxacin has been shown to produce photosensitivity reactions. Patients taking ciprofloxacin should avoid direct exposure to excessive sunlight or UV light. Therapy should be discontinued if photosensitization (i.e., sunburn-like skin reactions) occurs.

I.V. infusion should be administered by slow infusion over a period of 60 minutes. Local i.v. reactions have been reported with the i.v. administration of ciprofloxacin. These reactions are more frequent if infusion time is 30 minutes or less, or if small veins of the hand are used.

Prolonged use of ciprofloxacin may result in the overgrowth of nonsusceptible organisms. Careful observation of the patient is therefore essential, and if superinfection should occur during therapy, appropriate measures should be taken.

Pregnancy: The safety of ciprofloxacin in pregnancy has not yet been established. Ciprofloxacin should not be used in pregnant women unless the likely benefits outweigh the possible risk to the fetus. Ciprofloxacin has been shown to be non-embryotoxic and nonteratogenic in animal studies.

Lactation: Ciprofloxacin is excreted in human milk. A decision should be made to discontinue nursing or to discontinue the administration of ciprofloxacin, taking into account the importance of the drug to the mother and the possible risk to the infant.

Drug Interactions: Concurrent administration of ciprofloxacin with theophylline may lead to an elevated plasma concentration and prolongation of elimination half-life of theophylline. This may result in increased risk of theophylline-related adverse reactions. If concomitant use cannot be avoided, plasma concentrations of theophylline should be monitored and dosage adjustments made as appropriate.

Ciprofloxacin has been shown to interfere with the metabolism and pharmacokinetics of caffeine. Excessive caffeine intake should be avoided.

Some quinolones, including ciprofloxacin, have been associated with transient increases in serum creatinine levels in patients who are concomitantly receiving cyclosporine.

Quinolones have been reported to increase the effects of the oral anticoagulant warfarin and its derivatives. During concomitant administration of these drugs, the prothrombin time or other appropriate coagulation tests should be closely monitored.

Probenecid blocks renal tubular secretion of ciprofloxacin and has been shown to produce an increase in the level of ciprofloxacin in the serum.

Concomitant administration of a nonsteroidal anti-inflammatory drug (fenbufen) with a quinolone (enoxacin) has been reported to increase the risk of CNS stimulation and convulsive seizures.

Antacids containing aluminum or magnesium hydroxide have been shown to reduce the absorption of ciprofloxacin. Concurrent administration with these agents should be avoided.

Administration of sucralfate prior to ciprofloxacin resulted in a 30% reduction in absorption of ciprofloxacin. Concurrent administration with ciprofloxacin should be avoided.

Oral ferrous sulfate at therapeutic doses decreases the bioavailability of oral ciprofloxacin, therefore concomitant therapy is not advised.

The use of calcium supplement and highly buffered drugs such as antiretrovirals reduces the absorption of ciprofloxacin, therefore concomitant administration is not advised.

In particular cases, concurrent administration of ciprofloxacin and glyburide can intensify the action of glyburide (hypoglycemia).

Renal Impairment: Since ciprofloxacin is eliminated primarily by the kidney, ciprofloxacin should be used with caution and at a reduced dosage in patients with impaired renal function (see Dosage).

Hepatic Impairment: In preliminary studies in patients with stable chronic liver cirrhosis, no significant changes in ciprofloxacin pharmacokinetics were observed. The kinetics of ciprofloxacin in patients with acute hepatic insufficiency, however, have not been fully elucidated. An increased incidence of nausea, vomiting, headache and diarrhea were observed in this patient population.

Adverse Effects: Ciprofloxacin is generally well tolerated. During worldwide clinical investigation, 16 580 courses of ciprofloxacin treatment were evaluated for drug safety.

Adverse events, possibly, probably or highly probably related to ciprofloxacin occurred in 1 395 (8.8%) of patients. The adverse reactions according to treatment (oral, i.v. and sequential therapy) show that the incidence of adverse reactions was 8% for the group treated orally, 17% for the group treated with ciprofloxacin i.v. and 15.3% for the group treated sequentially. The difference between the oral and i.v. group relates to adverse vascular reactions which are known to be associated with i.v. administration.

In orally treated patients enrolled in clinical trials, the most frequently reported events, possibly, probably drug-related were: nausea (1.3%) and diarrhea (1%).

In patients treated with ciprofloxacin i.v., the most frequently reported events, possibly, probably drug-related were: rash (1.8%), diarrhea (1%) and injection site pain (1%).

Local i.v. site reactions have been reported. These reactions are more frequent if the infusion time is 30 minutes or less. These may appear as local skin reactions which resolve rapidly upon completion of the infusion. Subsequent i.v. administration is not contraindicated unless the reactions recur or worsen.

Events possibly, probably drug-related occurring at a frequency of less than 1% with ciprofloxacin oral and i.v. treatment during clinical trials and subsequent postmarketing surveillance are as follows: Gastrointestinal: vomiting, dyspepsia, abdominal pain, flatulence, dysphagia, enlarged abdomen, dry mouth, stomatitis, gastrointestinal moniliasis, anorexia, jaundice. The following have been reported very rarely: constipation, tooth discoloration, ulcerative stomatitis, pseudomembranous colitis, intestinal perforation, esophagitis, increased appetite, gastrointestinal hemorrhage, melena, liver damage, tenesmus, ileus, toxic megacolon, hepatomegaly, glossitis.

Cardiovascular: palpitation, tachycardia, phlebitis. The following have been reported very rarely: hypertension, hot flashes, cerebrovascular disorder, syncope, kidney vasculitis, vasodilation, atrial fibrillation, cardiac arrest, angina pectoris, electrocardiogram abnormality, myocardial infarct, substernal chest pain, pulmonary embolus, pericarditis, hypotension.

Nervous System: increased sweating, dizziness, agitation, tremor, somnolence, insomnia, confusion, hallucinations, convulsion, headache. The following have been reported very rarely: anxiety, depression, nervousness, apathy, depersonalization, abnormal dreams, hemiplegia, sleep disorder, neuritis, paresthesia, polyneuritis, diplopia, meningism, migraine, increase of intracranial pressure. In some instances these reactions occurred after the first administration of ciprofloxacin. In these instances, ciprofloxacin has to be discontinued and the doctor should be informed immediately.

Respiratory: dyspnea. The following have been reported very rarely: hiccup, increased cough, stridor, larynx edema, voice alteration, lung edema, pharyngitis, hyperventilation, lung hemorrhage.

Skin and Appendages: rash, pruritus. The following have been reported very rarely: urticaria, photosensitive dermatitis, angioedema, alopecia.

Special Senses: tinnitus, abnormal vision, taste perversion. The following have been reported very rarely: conjunctivitis, corneal opacity, eye pain, color blindness, chromatopsia, diplopia, ear pain.

Urogenital: albuminuria, hematuria. The following have been reported rarely: leukorrhea, dysuria, urinary retention, acute kidney failure, abnormal kidney function, nephritis, vaginitis.

Hypersensitivity: rash. The following have been reported rarely: pruritus, drug fever, anaphylactic/anaphylactoid reactions including facial, vascular and laryngeal edema, serum sickness, petechiae, hemorrhagic bullae and small nodules (papules) with crust formation showing vascular involvement (vasculitis), Stevens-Johnson syndrome, interstitial nephritis, hepatitis; very rarely, major liver disorders including hepatic necrosis, Lyell's syndrome, erythema nodosum, erythema multiforme (minor).

Musculoskeletal: The following have been reported rarely: arthralgia (joint pain), joint swelling, achiness, pain in the extremities, tendonitis (predominantly achillotendonitis); partial or complete tendon rupture (achilles tendon) and very rarely back pain,

Blood and Blood Constituents: eosinophilia, leukocytopenia, leukocytosis, anemia, granulocytopenia, pancytopenia, agranulocytosis. Very rarely: hemolytic anemia, thrombocytopenia, thrombocytosis, altered prothrombin levels.

I.V. Infusion Site: thrombophlebitis: very rarely burning, pain, paresthesia, erythema and swelling.

Laboratory Values: increased alkaline phosphatase, Gamma-GT, transaminases, cholestatic parameters, lactic dehydrogenase, BUN, NPN, AST, ALT, decreased creatinine clearance, hypercholesteremia, albuminuria, bilirubinemia, hyperuricemia, increased sedimentation rate. The following have been reported rarely; electrolyte abnormality, hypercalcemia, hypocalcemia, acidosis, crystalluria and hematuria.

Other: very rarely, asthenia, death.

Most of the adverse events reported were described as only mild or moderate in severity.

There have been 54 reports of arthropathies with ciprofloxacin. Ten of these reports involved children. Arthralgia was usually the first symptom which led to rapid assessment and withdrawal of the drug. No irreversible arthropathies have been observed.

Adverse reactions noted during therapy with ciprofloxacin and metronidazole in clinical trials were similar to those already noted during therapy with ciprofloxacin alone with the following additions: Cardiovascular: peripheral edema.

Digestive: tongue discoloration, colitis, gastritis.

Hemic and Lymphatic: coagulation disorder, thrombocythemia.

Skin: fungal dermatitis, pustular rash, sweating.

Metabolic: hypernatremia, healing abnormal.

Nervous: dementia.

Urinary: kidney tumor necrosis, urinary incontinence.

Overdose: Symptoms and Treatment: In the event of acute, excessive oral overdosage, reversible renal toxicity, arthralgia, myalgia and CNS symptoms have been reported. Therefore, apart from routine emergency measures, it is recommended to monitor renal function and to administer magnesium- or calcium-containing antacids which reduce the absorption of ciprofloxacin and to maintain adequate hydration. Based on information obtained from subjects with chronic renal failure, only a small amount of ciprofloxacin (<10%) is removed from the body after hemodialysis or peritoneal dialysis.

Dosage: The determination of dosage for any particular patient must take into consideration the severity and nature of the infection, the susceptibility of the causative organism, the integrity of the patient's host-defence mechanisms and the status of renal function.

Oral: Ciprofloxacin may be taken before or after meals. Absorption is faster on an empty stomach. Patients should be advised to drink fluids liberally and not take antacids containing magnesium or aluminum.

Adults: The recommended dosages are shown in Table II.

Table II—Cipro Tablets

Dosage in Adults

Location of Infection	Type/Severity	Unit Dose	Frequency	Daily Dose
Urinary Tract	mild/moderate severe/complicated uncomplicated	250 mg 500 mg 100 mg	q12h q12h q12h	500 mg 1 000 mg 200 mg
Chronic Bacterial Prostatitis	asymptomatic/mild/moderate	500 mg	q12h	1 000 mg
Respiratory Tract Bone and Joint Skin and Soft Tissue	mild/moderate severe/complicated*	500 mg 750 mg	q12h q12h	1 000 mg 1 500 mg
Acute Sinusitis	moderate	500 mg	q12h	1 000 mg
Infectious Diarrhea	mild/moderate/severe	500 mg	q12h	1 000 mg
Urogenital and Extragenital Gonorrhea	uncomplicated	500 mg	once	500 mg
Typhoid Fever	mild/moderate	500 mg	q12h	1 000 mg
Neisseria Meningitidis Nasopharyngeal Colonization Acute Sinusitis	carrier state moderate	750 mg 500 mg	once q12h	750 mg 1 000 mg

*e.g., hospital-acquired pneumonia, osteomyelitis.

Oral Suspension: See Table III. One teaspoon (5 mL) of 10% oral ciprofloxacin suspension=500 mg of ciprofloxacin (see Instructions below for Use/Handling).

Table III—Cipro Oral Suspension

Dosage

Dosage	Volume (mL) of Oral Suspension 10%
250 mg	2.5 mL
500 mg	5 mL
750 mg	7.5 mL

Depending on the severity of the infections, as well as the clinical and bacteriological responses, the average treatment period should be approximately 7 to 14 days. Generally, treatment should last 3 days beyond the disappearance of clinical symptoms or until cultures are sterile. Patients with osteomyelitis may require treatment for a minimum of 6 to 8 weeks and up to 3 months. With infectious diarrhea, a 5-day treatment may be sufficient. Typhoid fever should be treated for 14 days. Acute sinusitis should be treated for 10 days with 500 mg q12h. With uncomplicated urinary tract infections such as acute cystitis, a 3-day treatment with 100 mg every 12 hours may be sufficient. Chronic bacterial prostatitis should be treated for 28 days with 500 mg every 12 hours.

Instructions to the Pharmacist for Use/Handling of Cipro Oral Suspension: Preparation of the suspension: 1. The small bottle contains the ciprofloxacin microcapsules; the large bottle contains the diluent. 2. Open both bottles. Child-proof cap: Press down according to the instructions on the cap while turning to the left. 3. Pour the microcapsules completely into the large bottle of diluent. **Do not add water to the suspension.** 4. Close the large bottle completely according to the instructions on the cap and shake vigorously for about 15 seconds. The suspension is ready for use.

Instructions to the Patient for Taking Cipro Oral Suspension: **Shake vigorously each time before use for approximately 15 seconds.** Swallow the prescribed amount of suspension. Do not chew the microcapsules. Reclose the bottle completely after use according to instruction on the cap. The suspension is stable for 14 days when stored in a refrigerator or at room temperature (5 to 25°C). Store in an upright position. After treatment has been completed, any remaining suspension should not be reused.

I.V.: Ciprofloxacin should be administered by i.v. infusion over a period of 60 minutes. Slow infusion into a large vein will minimize patient discomfort and reduce the risk of venous irritation.

Adults: The recommended adult dosages of ciprofloxacin injection are shown in Table IV.

Definitive clinical studies have not been completed for severe infections other than in the respiratory tract.

The duration of treatment depends upon the severity of infection. Generally ciprofloxacin should be continued for at least 3 days after the signs and symptoms of infection have disappeared. The usual duration is 7 to 14 days. However, for severe and complicated infections more prolonged therapy may be required. Bone and joint infections may require treatment for 4 to 6 weeks or longer.

Table IV—Cipro I.V.

Dosage in Adults—Cipro I.V.

Location of Infection	Type/Severity	Unit Dose	Frequency	Daily Dose
Urinary Tract	moderate/severe/complicated	200 to 400 mg	q12h	400 to 800 mg
Respiratory Tract	moderate/severe	400 mg	q8h to q12h	800 to 1 200 mg
Skin or Skin Structure Blood Bone	moderate	400 mg	q12h	800 mg
Intra-abdominal	complicated	400 mg	q12h	400 mg q12h only when used in combination with metronidazole 500 mg i.v. q6h*
Empiric Therapy in Febrile Neutropenic Patients	severe ciprofloxacin + piperacillin sodium	400 mg 50 mg/kg	q8h q4h	1 200 mg Not to exceed 24 g/day

* (1) Clinical success was demonstrated with a limited number of patients switched to oral therapy: (Cipro 500 mg orally q12h plus metronidazole 500 mg orally q6h) during day 3, 4 or 5 of therapy when able to take oral medication and having shown an initial clinical response to the i.v. therapy.

(2) See Metronidazole product monograph for Prescribing Information including cautionary statements.

(3) For information on Cipro plus metronidazole combination therapy, see Pharmacology and Adverse Effects.

Sequential I.V./Oral Therapy: In patients receiving i.v. ciprofloxacin, oral ciprofloxacin may be considered when clinically indicated at the discretion of the physician. Clinical studies evaluating the use of sequential i.v./oral therapy in septicemia, however, have not been completed.

Impaired Renal Function: Ciprofloxacin is eliminated primarily by renal excretion. However, the drug is also metabolized and partially cleared through the biliary system of the liver and through the intestine (see Pharmacology). This alternate pathway of drug elimination appears to compensate for the reduced renal excretion of patients with renal impairment. Nonetheless, some modification of dosage is recommended, particularly for patients with severe renal dysfunction. Table V provides a guideline for dosage adjustment. However, monitoring of serum drug levels provides the most reliable basis for dosage adjustments. Only a small amount of ciprofloxacin (<10%) is removed from the body after hemodialysis or peritoneal dialysis.

Table V—Cipro/Cipro I.V./Cipro Oral Suspension

Dosage Adjustment—Impaired Renal Function

Creatinine Clearance mL/min/1.73m²	Maximum Daily Dose Oral	Maximum Daily Dose I.V.	Serum Creatinine Concentration mg/100 mL
31-60	1 000 mg	800 mg	1.4-1.9
≤30	500 mg	400 mg	≥2.0

Maximum daily dose, not to be exceeded when either creatinine clearance or serum creatinine are in the ranges stated.

When only the serum creatinine concentration is available, the following formulas (based on sex, weight and age of the patient) may be used to convert this value into creatinine clearance. The serum creatinine should represent a steady state of renal function:

Creatinine Clearance mL/s =

$$\text{Males: } \frac{\text{Weight (kg)} \times (140-\text{age})}{49 \times \text{serum creatinine } (\mu\text{mol/L}).}$$

Females: 0.85×the above value.

In traditional units mL/min =

$$\text{Males: } \frac{\text{Weight (kg)} \times (140-\text{age})}{72 \times \text{serum creatinine (mg/100 mL).}}$$

Females: 0.85×the above value.

Children: The safety and efficacy of ciprofloxacin in children have not been established. Ciprofloxacin should not be used in prepubertal patients (see Warnings).

Parenteral Products: Intermittent I.V. Infusion: Ciprofloxacin injection should be administered only by i.v. infusion over a period of 60 minutes. The drug should not be given by rapid injection. Slow infusion of a dilute solution into a large vein will minimize patient discomfort and reduce the risk of venous irritation.

If ciprofloxacin i.v. is to be given concomitantly with another drug, each drug should be given separately in accordance with the recommended dosage and route of administration for each drug. Only ciprofloxacin injection in the 10 mg/mL vials should be diluted to 1 to 2 mg/mL with the following recommended i.v. solutions. Cipro I.V. Minibags contain ciprofloxacin at 2 mg/mL and should be administered as is.

Recommended I.V. Solutions for Dilution of Vials: Sterile Water for Injection, USP; 0.9% Sodium Chloride Injection, USP; 5% Dextrose Injection, USP; 5% Dextrose in 0.225% Sodium Chloride Injection, USP; 5% Dextrose in 0.45% Sodium Chloride Injection, USP; 5% Dextrose in Electrolyte #75 Injection; 10% Dextrose Injection; 10% Fructose Injection; Ringer's Injection; Lactated Ringer's Injection, USP.

Ciprofloxacin injection when diluted with the recommended i.v. solutions should be used within 24 hours at room temperature or 72 hours when refrigerated. Since ciprofloxacin is slightly light sensitive, the solutions should be protected from light during storage.

Dilution: See Table VI.

Table VI—Cipro I.V.

Dilution Table for Vials

Vial Size	Vial Strength	Volume of Diluent To Be Used Per Vial	Approximate Concentration of Diluted Products
20 mL	200 mg, 1%	80–180 mL	1–2 mg/mL
40 mL	400 mg, 1%	160–260 mL	1.3–2 mg/mL

Vials: The i.v. dose should be prepared by aseptically withdrawing the appropriate volume of concentrate from the vials of Cipro I.V. This should be diluted with the desired volume (80 to 260 mL) of a suitable i.v. solution (see Recommended I.V. Solution). The resulting solution should be infused over a period of 60 minutes by direct infusion or through a Y-type i.v. infusion set which may already be in place. If this method or the piggyback method of administration is used, it is advisable to discontinue temporarily the administration of any other solutions during the infusion of ciprofloxacin i.v.

As with all parenteral drug products, i.v. admixtures should be inspected visually for clarity, particulate matter, precipitate, discoloration and leakage prior to administration, whenever solution and container permit.

Supplied: Cipro: Oral Suspension: 10%: Each 100 mL of oral suspension contains: ciprofloxacin 10 g (10 %). The drug product is composed of 2 components (microcapsules and diluent) which are mixed prior to dispensing (see Dosage, Instructions to the Pharmacist for Use/Handling).

Reconstitution: See Table VII.

Table VII—Cipro Oral Suspension

Reconstitution Table

Total Volume After Reconstitution	Ciprofloxacin Contents After Reconstitution	Ciprofloxacin Contents/Bottle
100 mL	500 mg/5 mL	10 000 mg

Store at room temperature (15 to 25°C) in an upright position. Protect from freezing. Reconstituted product may be stored in a refrigerator or at room temperature (5 to 25°C) for 14 days. Store in an upright position. A teaspoon is provided for the patient.

Tablets: 100 mg: Each tablet, engraved CIPRO on one side and 100 on the other, contains: ciprofloxacin HCl equivalent to ciprofloxacin 100 mg. Nonmedicinal ingredients: colloidal silicon dioxide, crospovidone, hydroxypropyl methylcellulose 2910-15, magnesium stearate, maize starch, microcrystalline cellulose, polyethylene glycol, purified water, titanium dioxide. Lactose- and tartrazine-free. Unit dose packages of 6. Store below 30°C.

250 mg: Each tablet, engraved CIPRO on one side and 250 on the other, contains: ciprofloxacin HCl equivalent to ciprofloxacin 250 mg. Nonmedicinal ingredients: colloidal silicon dioxide, crospovidone, hydroxypropyl methylcellulose 2910-15, magnesium stearate, maize starch, microcrystalline cellulose, polyethylene glycol, purified water, titanium dioxide. Lactose- and tartrazine-free. Bottles of 100. Store below 30°C.

500 mg: Each tablet, engraved CIPRO on one side and 500 on the other, contains: ciprofloxacin HCl equivalent to ciprofloxacin 500 mg. Nonmedicinal ingredients: colloidal silicon dioxide, crospovidone, hydroxypropyl methylcellulose 2910-15, magnesium stearate, maize starch, microcrystalline cellulose, polyethylene glycol, purified water, titanium dioxide. Lactose- and tartrazine-free. Bottles of 100. Unit dose packages of 100. Store below 30°C.

750 mg: Each tablet, engraved CIPRO on one side and 750 on the other, contains: ciprofloxacin HCl equivalent to ciprofloxacin 750 mg. Nonmedicinal ingredients: colloidal silicon dioxide, crospovidone, hydroxypropyl methylcellulose 2910-15, magnesium stearate, maize starch, microcrystalline cellulose, polyethylene glycol, purified water, titanium dioxide.

Cipro (cont'd)

Lactose- and tartrazine-free. Bottles of 50. Unit dose packages of 100. Store below 30°C.

Cipro I.V.: Injection: Each mL contains: ciprofloxacin 10 mg. Nonmedicinal ingredients: hydrochloric acid, lactic acid and water for injection USP. Vials of 20 and 40 mL. Protect from light. Store at controlled room temperature (15 to 30°C).

Minibags: Each mL contains: ciprofloxacin 2 mg. Ready-to-use minibags of 100 and 200 mL.

(Shown in Product Recognition Section)

Reviewed 1999

CISPLATIN INJECTION

Faulding

Antineoplastic

Pharmacology: Cisplatin is thought to act by producing inter-strand and intra-strand cross-links of cellular DNA in a similar manner to bifunctional alkylating agents. It does not appear to be cell-cycle specific.

Using radioactive platinum, a high uptake of the drug was found in kidneys, liver and intestines with poor penetration of the CNS. An initial plasma half-life of 25 to 49 minutes and a terminal half-life of 58 to 73 hours was calculated. After initial i.v. injection, the radioactive platinum was rapidly cleared from the blood and more than 90% of the radioactive platinum in the post-distribution phase was protein-bound. The radioactive platinum was excreted primarily in the urine but only 27 to 45% of the dose was recovered in the first 5 days after administration. Excretion of platinum is slow and has been detected in tissue samples 4 months after administration.

Indications: As palliative therapy, to be employed in addition to other modalities, or in established combination therapy with other chemotherapeutic agents in the following:

Metastatic Testicular Tumors: In patients who have already received appropriate surgical and/or radiotherapeutic and/or chemotherapeutic procedures.

Metastatic Ovarian Tumors: As secondary therapy in patients refractory to standard chemotherapy.

It has also been used in advanced stage and refractory bladder carcinoma and in squamous cell carcinoma of the head and neck.

Contraindications: In patients with a history of allergic reaction to cisplatin or other platinum-containing compounds.

The physician should carefully weigh the therapeutic benefit expected versus the risk of toxicity which may occur when cisplatin is used as indicated.

Warnings: Caution: Cisplatin is a potent drug and should be used only by physicians experienced with cancer chemotherapy drugs. Blood counts as well as renal and hepatic function tests should be taken regularly. Discontinue the drug if abnormal depression of bone marrow or abnormal renal or hepatic function is seen (see Precautions).

Cisplatin has been shown to be cumulatively ototoxic and should not be given to patients with hearing impairment. It is recommended that hearing functions be monitored prior to and during treatment with cisplatin.

Cisplatin should be used cautiously in individuals with pre-existing renal impairment or with myelosuppressed patients.

Serum creatinine, BUN and creatinine clearance should be measured prior to initiating therapy and should be monitored throughout treatment with cisplatin, as cisplatin produces cumulative nephrotoxicity.

Anaphylactic-type reactions have been reported with cisplatin within minutes of administration to patients who have been previously exposed to cisplatin. The reactions have been alleviated by administration of epinephrine, steroids and antihistamines.

Pregnancy: Safe use in human pregnancy has not been established.

Cisplatin has been shown to be mutagenic in bacteria and to produce chromosome aberrations in animal cells in tissue culture and is teratogenic and embryotoxic in mice. Although cisplatin has not been definitely established as being carcinogenic, compounds with similar mechanisms of action have been reported to be carcinogenic.

Precautions: As with all potent antineoplastic drugs, cisplatin should be administered only by clinicians who are experienced in the use of antineoplastic therapy.

Because of the cumulative renal toxicity of cisplatin, it should not be administered more frequently than once every 3 to 4 weeks. In order to reduce nephrotoxicity, pretreatment hydration with 1 to 2 L of fluid infused over 8 to 12 hours, together with maintenance hydration and urinary output during the 24 hours following administration, is recommended.

Weekly peripheral blood counts should be carried out and liver function should be monitored periodically. As well, neurological examinations should be performed on a regular basis.

Cisplatin is incompatible with i.v. sets, needles and syringes which contain aluminum. In contact with aluminum, a visible black precipitate will form.

Adverse Effects: Nephrotoxicity: Renal toxicity has been shown to occur in 28 to 36% of patients treated with a single dose of cisplatin at a dose of 50 mg/m². Renal toxicity becomes more prolonged and severe with repeated courses of the drug. Renal function must be restored to normal before additional cisplatin therapy is given.

Nephrotoxicity is usually seen during the second week after a dose as elevations in BUN, creatinine, serum uric acid and/or a decrease in creatinine clearance.

Renal impairment has been associated with renal tubular damage. The administration of cisplatin with a 6 to 8 hour infusion with i.v. hydration and mannitol diuresis has been used to reduce nephrotoxicity.

Ototoxicity: This has occurred in up to 31% of patients treated with a single 50 mg/m² dose of cisplatin. The usual signs of ototoxicity are tinnitus and/or hearing loss in the high frequency range (4 000 to 8 000 Hz). Ototoxicity may be more severe in children and more frequent and severe with repeated administration. Hearing loss can be unilateral or bilateral and may not be reversible.

Hemotoxicity: Myelosuppression is observed in about 30% of patients treated with cisplatin. Changes in circulating platelets and leukocytes occur between days 18 to 23 (range 7.5 to 45) with most patients recovering by day 39 (range 13 to 62). Leukopenia and thrombocytopenia are more pronounced at doses in excess of 50 mg/m². Anemia, demonstrated as a decrease of greater than 2 g of hemoglobin/100 mL, occurs at approximately the same frequency and with the same timing as leukopenia and thrombocytopenia.

Gastrointestinal: Most patients treated with cisplatin will demonstrate marked nausea and vomiting which occasionally may be so severe that the drug must be discontinued. Gastrointestinal side effects usually occur 1 to 4 hours after treatment and last up to 24 hours. Various degrees of nausea and anorexia may persist for up to 1 week after treatment.

Hyperuricemia: The incidence of hyperuricemia is approximately the same as for increases in BUN and serum creatinine. The hyperuricemia is more pronounced after doses greater than 50 mg/m² and usually peaks 3 to 5 days after the initial dose. Allopurinol may be used to effectively reduce uric acid levels.

Neurotoxicity: Peripheral neuropathies have been reported in some patients following cisplatin administration. Loss of taste and seizures have been reported. Neuropathies may occur after prolonged therapy of 4 to 7 months, however, neurologic symptoms have been reported to occur after a single dose. As preliminary evidence suggests that peripheral neuropathies may be irreversible in some patients, cisplatin therapy should be discontinued when the symptoms are first observed.

Anaphylactic-like Reactions: Anaphylactic-like reactions have occasionally been reported in patients previously exposed to cisplatin. The reactions consist of facial edema, wheezing, tachycardia and hypotension within a few minutes of drug administration. Anaphylactic-like reactions may be controlled by the use of i.v. epinephrine, corticosteroids or antihistamines. Patients receiving cisplatin should be observed carefully for anaphylactic-like reactions and supportive equipment and medication should be available to treat such a complication, should it arise.

Other toxicities which have been reported to occur infrequently include cardiac abnormalities, anorexia and elevated AST.

Overdose: Symptoms and Treatment: In the event of overdosage or toxic reactions, symptomatic supportive measures should be taken. Complications to be anticipated include nephrotoxicity, ototoxicity, neurotoxicity and hemotoxicity. Patients should be monitored for 3 to 4 weeks in case of delayed toxicity.

Dosage: Adults and children 50 to 75 mg/m² as a single i.v. dose every 3 to 4 weeks, or 15 to 20 mg/m² i.v. daily for 5 days every 3 to 4 weeks (see Administration).

Do not give a repeat course of cisplatin until the serum creatinine is below 1.5 mg/100 mL and/or the BUN is below 25 mg/100 mL. A repeat course should not be given until circulating blood elements are at an acceptable concentration (platelets 100 000/mm³, WBC 4 000/mm³). Do not give subsequent doses of cisplatin until an audiometric analysis indicates that auditory acuity is within normal limits.

When employed in combination with other antitumor drugs, adjust the cisplatin dose appropriately.

Administration: Cisplatin is administered by intravenous infusion after dilution (see Dilution and Guidelines for Safe Handling of Cytotoxic Drugs).

Pretreatment hydration with 1 to 2 L of fluid infused for 8 to 12 hours prior to a cisplatin dose is advised. The diluted drug is then infused over a 6 to 8 hour period. Maintain adequate hydration and urinary output over the next 24 hours.

It is important that none of the injection components such as i.v. needles, syringes or sets have aluminum components, because these are incompatible with cisplatin.

Stability and Storage: Vials of cisplatin injection USP are stored at room temperature between 15 and 25°C. Do not refrigerate or freeze cisplatin solutions since a precipitate will form.

Preparation of I.V. solutions: **I.V. needles, syringes, or sets having aluminum components should not be employed in preparation or administration of cisplatin solutions.** An interaction will occur between aluminum and platinum from cisplatin causing a black precipitate which is visible in the cisplatin solution.

Dilution: Dilute the prepared cisplatin injection in 2 L of 5% dextrose in one half or one third N saline containing 37.5 g of mannitol.

Diluted cisplatin injection solution is suitable for i.v. infusion. This solution is not preserved; it should be used within 24 hours, and the unused portion discarded after that time, in order to avoid risk of microbial contamination.

Warning: **As with all parenteral drug products, i.v. admixtures should be inspected visually for clarity, particulate matter, precipitate, discoloration and leakage prior to administration, whenever solution and container permit. Solutions showing haziness, particulate matter, precipitate, discoloration or leakage should not be used.**

Guidelines for Safe Handling of Cytotoxic Drugs: Preparation of all antineoplastic agents should be done in a vertical laminar flow hood, when possible.

Personnel preparing parenteral antineoplastic agents should wear PVC gloves, safety glasses, disposable gowns, and masks.

All needles, syringes, vials, ampuls and other materials which have come in contact with cytotoxic drugs should be segregated and incinerated at 1 000°C or more. Sealed containers may explode. If incineration is not available, the waste material should be neutralized, usually with 5% sodium hypochlorite and/or 5% sodium thiosulfate, then placed in sealed containers and deposited in landfill sites, according to local regulations.

Personnel regularly involved in the preparation and handling of cytotoxic agents should have bi-annual blood examination.

Supplied: Cisplatin Injection (0.5 mg/mL): Each mL of sterile, unpreserved solution contains: cisplatin 0.5 mg with sodium chloride 9 mg and mannitol 1 mg in water for injection. Hydrochloric acid is added to adjust the pH. Single dose glass vials of 100 mL containing 50 mg of cisplatin. Do not refrigerate.

Cisplatin Injection (1 mg/mL): Each mL of sterile, unpreserved solution contains: cisplatin 1.0 mg with sodium chloride 9 mg and mannitol 1 mg in water for injection. Hydrochloric acid is added to adjust the pH. Single dose glass vials of 10, 50 and 100 mL containing 10, 50 and 100 mg of cisplatin, respectively. Do not refrigerate.

CITANEST® 4% PLAIN
CITANEST® 4% FORTE

Astra

Prilocaine HCl

Prilocaine HCl—Epinephrine

Local Anesthetic for Infiltration and Nerve Block

Pharmacology: Mechanism of Action: Prilocaine stabilizes the neuronal membrane and prevents the initiation and transmission of nerve impulses thereby, effecting local anesthetic action. Local anesthetics of the amide type are thought to act within sodium channels of the nerve membrane.

Onset of Action: When used for infiltration anesthesia in dental patients, the time of onset of Citanest 4% Forte averages

2 minutes with a duration of soft tissue anesthesia of approximately 2 hours. Operative anesthesia lasts up to 45 minutes. When used for infiltration anesthesia, Citanest 4% Plain has a rapid onset time of approximately 2 to 3 minutes and a duration of approximately 1 to 1.5 hours for soft tissue anesthesia. Citanest 4% Plain has a short duration for operative anesthesia of approximately 15 minutes.

When used for inferior alveolar nerve block the time of onset of Citanest 4% Forte averages approximately 2 to 4 minutes with an average duration of soft tissue anesthesia of approximately 3 hours providing 1.5 hours of operative anesthesia.

When used for mandibular block anesthesia, Citanest 4% Plain requires 5 minutes or more to take full effect. The duration of soft tissue anesthesia is approximately 2.5 hours while operative anesthesia has a duration of 1 to 1.5 hours.

Hemodynamics: Prilocaine, like other local anesthetics, may also have effects on excitable membranes in the brain and myocardium. If excessive amounts of drug reach systemic circulation rapidly, symptoms and signs of toxicity will appear, emanating from the central nervous and cardiovascular systems.

CNS toxicity (see Overdose: Symptoms and Treatment) usually precedes the cardiovascular effects since it occurs at lower plasma concentrations. Direct effects of local anesthetics on the heart include slow conduction, negative inotropism and eventually cardiac arrest.

Pharmacokinetics and Metabolism: Prilocaine is between 40 to 55% protein bound in plasma, mainly to alpha$_1$-acid glycoprotein.

Prilocaine redistributes rapidly from the blood and has a large apparent distribution volume of between 190 and 260 L. The terminal elimination half-life of prilocaine is 1.6 h.

Prilocaine readily passes the placenta and free plasma concentrations are similar in both fetus and mother. In the presence of fetal acidosis, plasma concentrations may be slightly higher in the fetus due to ion trapping. Information concerning the elimination half-life of prilocaine in neonates is not available.

In the liver, prilocaine is primarily metabolized by amide hydrolysis to o-toluidine and N-propylamine. o-Toluidine is subsequently hydroxylated to 2-amino-3-hydroxytoluene and 2-amino-5-hydroxytoluene, metabolites which are believed to be responsible for the occurrence of methemoglobinemia (see Contraindications).

Only a small proportion of prilocaine (<5%) is excreted unchanged in the urine. In vitro and animal studies have shown metabolism of prilocaine by lung and kidney tissues.

Indications: In dentistry for the production of local anesthesia by infiltration or nerve block.

Contraindications: Patients with a known history of hypersensitivity to local anesthetics of the amide type or to other components of the solution. Patients with congenital or idiopathic methemoglobinemia.

Warnings: Local anesthetics should only be employed by clinicians who are well versed in diagnosis and management of dose-related toxicity and other acute emergencies that might arise from the block to be employed and then only after ensuring the immediate availability of oxygen, other resuscitative drugs, cardiopulmonary equipment and the personnel needed for proper management of toxic reactions and related emergencies (see also Adverse Effects and Precautions). Delay in proper management of dose-related toxicity, underventilation from any cause, and/or altered sensitivity may lead to the development of acidosis, cardiac arrest and possibly, death.

To minimize the likelihood of intravascular injection, aspiration should be performed before the local anesthetic solution is injected. If blood is aspirated, the needle must be repositioned until no return of blood can be elicited by aspiration. Note, however, that the absence of blood in the syringe does not assure that intravascular injection will be avoided.

Citanest 4% Forte contains sodium metabisulfite, a sulfite that may cause allergic-type reactions including anaphylactic symptoms and life-threatening or less severe asthmatic episodes in certain susceptible people. Sulfite sensitivity is seen more frequently in asthmatic than in nonasthmatic people.

Precautions: The safety and effectiveness of prilocaine depends on proper dosage, correct technique, adequate precautions and readiness for emergencies. Standard textbooks should be consulted for specific techniques and precautions for various dental anesthetic procedures.

Resuscitative equipment, oxygen, and other resuscitative drugs should be available for immediate use (see Warnings and Overdose: Symptoms and Treatment). **The lowest dosage that results in effective anesthesia should be used to avoid high plasma levels and serious adverse effects. Injections should be made slowly, with frequent aspirations before and during the injection to avoid intravascular injection.**

Repeated doses of prilocaine may cause significant increases in blood levels with each repeated dose because of slow accumulation of the drug or its metabolites. Tolerance to elevated blood levels varies with the status of the patient. Debilitated, elderly patients, acutely ill patients and children should be given reduced doses commensurate with their age and physical condition. Prilocaine should also be used with caution in patients with epilepsy, impaired cardiac conduction, bradycardia, impaired hepatic function and in severe shock.

Because amide-type local anesthetics such as prilocaine are metabolized by the liver, these drugs, especially repeat doses, should be used cautiously in patients with hepatic disease. Patients with severe hepatic disease, because of their inability to metabolize local anesthetics normally, are at greater risk of developing toxic plasma concentrations. Prilocaine should also be used with caution in patients with impaired cardiovascular function since they may be less able to compensate for functional changes associated with the prolongation of AV conduction produced by these drugs.

Local anesthetic procedures should not be used when there is inflammation and/or sepsis in the region of the proposed injection.

Solutions containing epinephrine should be used with caution in patients whose medical history and physical evaluation suggest the existence of untreated hypertension, poorly controlled thyrotoxicosis, diabetes, ischemic heart disease, heart block, cerebral vascular insufficiency and peripheral vascular disorder. These solutions should also be used cautiously in areas of the body supplied by end arteries, such as digits, or otherwise having a compromised blood supply (see also Drug Interactions).

Careful and constant monitoring of cardiovascular and respiratory (adequacy of ventilation) vital signs and the patient's state of consciousness should be performed after each local anesthetic injection. It should be kept in mind at such times that restlessness, anxiety, incoherent speech, lightheadedness, numbness and tingling of the mouth and lips, metallic taste, tinnitus, dizziness, blurred vision, tremors, twitching, depression or drowsiness may be early warning signs of CNS toxicity.

Many drugs used during the conduct of anesthesia are considered potential triggering agents for familial malignant hyperthermia. It has been shown that the use of amide local anesthetics in malignant hyperthermia is safe. However, there is no guarantee that neural blockade will prevent the development of malignant hyperthermia during surgery. It is also difficult to predict the need for supplemental general anesthesia. Therefore a standard protocol for the management of malignant hyperthermia should be available.

Prilocaine should be used with caution in persons with known drug sensitivities. Patients allergic to para-aminobenzoic acid derivatives (procaine, tetracaine, benzocaine, etc.) have not shown cross-sensitivity to prilocaine.

Methemoglobinemia: A few instances of cyanosis have been reported following the administration of more than 400 mg of prilocaine. It would be necessary to inject 5 cartridges of Citanest 4% solution to produce an average methemoglobin value of 1%. Since methemoglobin values of less than 20% generally do not produce any clinical symptoms of hypoxia, the routine use of prilocaine solutions for normal dental procedures should not be associated with any side effects related to methemoglobinemia. The usual clinical signs of methemoglobinemia are cyanosis of the nail beds and lips. Although the possibility of methemoglobinemia occurring in dental patients is extremely rare, it should be remembered that methemoglobinemia can be treated easily and reversed rapidly by the use of 1 to 2 mg/kg body weight of methylene blue administered i.v. over a 5-minute period (see Adverse Effects and Overdose: Symptoms and Treatment).

Caution should be exercised when administering prilocaine concomitantly with other medications which are potential producers of methemoglobin (e.g., sulfonamides, antimalarials, and certain nitric compounds).

Head and Neck Area: Small doses of local anesthetics injected into the head and neck area, including retrobulbar, dental and stellate ganglion blocks, may produce adverse reactions caused by inadvertent injection to an artery. These reactions may be similar to systemic toxicity seen with unintentional intravascular injections of larger doses. Inadvertent injections into an artery can cause cerebral symptoms even at low doses. Confusion, convulsions, respiratory depression and/or respiratory arrest, and cardiovascular stimulation or depression leading to cardiac arrest have been reported. Patients receiving these blocks should have their circulation and respiration monitored and be constantly observed.

Drug Interactions: See also under Methemoglobinemia.

Prilocaine should be used with caution in patients receiving other agents structurally related to amide-type local anesthetics, since the toxic effects are additive.

Citanest 4% Forte, which contains epinephrine, should not be used concomitantly with ergot-type oxytocic drugs, because a severe persistent hypertension may occur and cerebrovascular and cardiac accidents are possible. Likewise, Citanest 4% Forte or solutions containing Citanest 4% Plain and another vasoconstrictor should be used with extreme caution in patients receiving MAO inhibitors or antidepressants of the triptyline or imipramine types, because severe prolonged hypertension may result. In situations when concurrent therapy is necessary, careful patient monitoring is essential. Phenothiazines and butyrophenones may reduce or reverse the pressor effect of epinephrine.

If sedatives are employed to reduce patient apprehension, they should be used in reduced doses, since local anesthetic agents, like sedatives, are CNS depressants which in combination may have an additive effect.

Solutions containing epinephrine should be used with caution in patients undergoing general anesthesia with inhalation agents such as halothane, due to the risk of serious cardiac arrhythmias.

Information for the Patient: The patient should be informed of the possibility of temporary loss of sensation and muscle function following infiltration or nerve block injections. The patient should be advised to exert caution to avoid inadvertent trauma to the lips, tongue, cheek mucosa or soft palate when these structures are anesthetized. The ingestion of food should therefore be postponed until normal function returns. The patient should be advised to consult the dentist if anesthesia persists, or if a rash develops.

Pregnancy: Although the safe use of prilocaine during pregnancy has not been established with respect to possible adverse effects upon fetal development, it is reasonable to assume that Citanest has been administered to a large number of pregnant women and women of childbearing age. No specific disturbances to the reproductive process have so far been reported, e.g., no increased incidence of malformations or other direct or indirect harmful effects on the fetus.

Methemoglobinemia in the neonate has been reported after the administration of prilocaine to the mother in doses exceeding 600 mg.

Lactation: Prilocaine may enter the breast milk, but in such small quantities that there is generally no risk of affecting the infant at therapeutic dose levels. It is not known whether epinephrine enters breast milk, but it is unlikely to affect the breast-fed infant.

Adverse Effects: Adverse experiences following the administration of prilocaine are similar in nature to those observed with other amide local anesthetic agents. These adverse experiences are, in general, dose-related and may result from high plasma levels caused by overdosage, rapid absorption, or inadvertent intravascular injection, or may result from a hypersensitivity, idiosyncrasy or diminished tolerance on the part of the patient.

Reactions to prilocaine are very rare in the doses used in dental procedures. Psychogenic reactions to anticipation of or during the dental procedures, are however, common and may mimic the symptoms of a generalized systemic reaction to local anesthetics.

Serious adverse experiences are generally systemic in nature. The following types are those most commonly reported:

CNS: CNS manifestations are excitatory and/or depressant and may be characterized by circumoral paresthesia, lightheadedness, nervousness, apprehension, euphoria, confusion, dizziness, drowsiness, hyperacusis, tinnitus, blurred vision, vomiting, sensations of heat, cold or numbness, twitching, tremors, convulsions, unconsciousness, respiratory depression and arrest. The excitatory manifestations may be very brief or may not occur at all, in which case the first manifestation of toxicity may be drowsiness merging into unconsciousness and respiratory arrest.

Drowsiness following the administration of prilocaine is usually an early sign of a high prilocaine plasma level and may occur as a consequence of rapid absorption.

Cardiovascular: Cardiovascular manifestations are usually depressant and are characterized by bradycardia, hypotension, arrhythmia, and cardiovascular collapse, which may lead to cardiac arrest.

Allergic: Allergic reactions are characterized by cutaneous lesions, urticaria, edema, or in the most severe instances, anaphylactic shock. Allergic reactions of the amide type are extremely rare and may occur as a result of sensitivity either

Citanest (cont'd)

to the local anesthetic agent or to other components in the formulation.

Neurologic: The incidence of adverse neurological reactions, e.g., persistent neurological deficit, associated with the use of local anesthetics is very low. Neurological reactions may be dependent upon the particular drug used, the route of administration and the physical status of the patient. Many of these effects may be linked to the injection technique, with or without a contribution by the drug. Neurological reactions following regional nerve blocks have included persistent paresthesia and sensory disturbances.

Methemoglobinemia: Cyanosis due to the formation of methemoglobin may occur after the administration of prilocaine. The repeated administration of prilocaine, even in relatively small doses, can lead to clinically overt methemoglobinemia.

The conversion of hemoglobin to methemoglobin is caused by the prilocaine metabolite, o-toluidine, which has a long half-life and tends to accumulate, and in turn, its conversion to 4- and 6-hydroxytoluidine. Methemoglobin has risen to clinically significant levels in patients receiving high doses of prilocaine. Cyanosis occurs when the methemoglobin concentration in the blood reaches 10 to 20 g/L (6 to 12% of the normal hemoglobin concentration). Methemoglobin oxidizes only slowly back to hemoglobin, but this process can be greatly accelerated by giving methylene blue i.v. (see Overdose: Symptoms and Treatment).

The reduction in the oxygen-carrying capacity in normal patients is marginal; hence cyanosis is usually symptomless. However, in severely anemic patients it may cause significant hypoxemia. It is important to rule out other more serious causes of cyanosis such as acute hypoxemia and/or heart failure. In using the recommended dosage of Citanest, 1 to 2 mL (40 to 80 mg prilocaine) (adult dosage), the occurrence of methemoglobinemia in dental practice appears remote. However, gross overdosage in dental practice has been reported to cause methemoglobinemia.

Note: Even low concentrations of methemoglobin may interfere with pulse oximetry readings, indicating a false low oxygen saturation.

Overdose: Since prilocaine is the least toxic of the amino-amide anesthetics, it is particularly useful in situations when high dosage may be needed. This advantage, however, should be weighed against the risk of causing methemoglobinemia.

Acute emergencies are, in general, dose-related and may result from high plasma levels caused by excessive dosage, rapid absorption (i.e., rate of increase of plasma concentration) or unintentional intravascular injection, or may result from hypersensitivity or diminished tolerance on the part of the patient.

Symptoms: Acute Systemic Toxicity: CNS reactions are excitatory or depressant and may be characterized by nervousness, tinnitus, twitching, euphoria, drowsiness, blurred or double vision, dizziness, convulsions, unconsciousness and possibly respiratory arrest. The excitatory reactions may be very brief or may not occur at all, in which case the first manifestation of toxicity is drowsiness merging into unconsciousness and even respiratory arrest.

Cardiovascular reactions are depressant and may be characterized by hypotension, myocardial depression, bradycardia and possibly cardiac arrest. Signs and symptoms of depressed cardiovascular function may commonly result from a vasovagal reaction, particularly if the patient is in an upright position. Less commonly, they may occur as a direct effect of the drug. Failure to recognize premonitory signs such as sweating, a feeling of faintness, changes in pulse or sensorium, may result in progressive cerebral hypoxia and seizure or serious cardiovascular collapse.

Cardiovascular effects are usually only seen in the most severe cases and are generally preceded by signs of toxicity in the central nervous system.

Acidosis or hypoxia in the patient may increase the risk and severity of toxic reactions. Such reactions involve the CNS and the cardiovascular system.

Treatment: Treatment of Acute Toxicity: The immediate treatment of acute systemic toxicity is as follows: a) Put the patient in a supine position. Raise the legs 30 to 45° above the horizontal level. b) Ensure a patent airway. If ventilation is inadequate, ventilate the patient, with oxygen if available. This is important since toxicity increases with acidosis. c) The treatment of convulsions consists in ensuring a patent airway and arresting convulsions. Should convulsions persist despite adequate ventilation, 5 to 15 mg diazepam or 50 to 200 mg thiopental should be administered i.v. to arrest the convulsions. Since this treatment may also depress respiration, the means of mechanically supporting or controlling ventilation should be available. d) Supportive treatment of circulatory depression may require the administration of i.v. fluids and, when appropriate, a vasopressor (e.g., ephedrine 5 to 10 mg i.v. and repeated, if necessary, after 2 to 3 minutes), as governed by the clinical situation. e) If the patient is unresponsive and the carotid pulse rate is totally absent, start external cardiac massage and mouth to mouth resuscitation.

Treatment of Acute Methemoglobinemia: If clinical methemoglobinemia occurs, it can be rapidly treated by a single i.v. injection of a 1% methylene blue solution, 1 mg/kg body weight, over a 5-minute period. Cyanosis will disappear in about 15 minutes. This dose should not be repeated as methylene blue in high concentrations acts as a hemoglobin oxidant.

Dosage: The dosage of Citanest 4% Plain and Citanest 4% Forte varies and depends on the area of the oral cavity to be anesthetized, the vascularity of the oral tissues and the technique of anesthesia. The total dose must be adjusted to the age, size and physical status of the patient. The lowest dosage that results in effective local anesthesia should be administered. Injections should be made slowly with careful aspiration before and intermittently during injection to avoid inadvertent intravascular injection, which may have toxic effects. For specific techniques and procedures of a local anesthesia in the oral cavity, refer to standard textbooks.

Citanest 4% Plain is recommended for use in maxillary infiltration anesthesia for procedures lasting approximately 15 minutes. Citanest 4% Plain is therefore especially suited to short procedures in the maxillary anterior teeth. For long procedures, or those involving maxillary posterior teeth where soft tissue numbness is not troublesome to the patient, Citanest 4% Forte is recommended.

Citanest 4% Plain is also recommended for those dental procedures in which it is desirable to use a local anesthetic that does not contain a vasoconstrictor agent, e.g., in those patients for whom vasoconstrictor agents are not indicated.

There are no practical clinical differences between Citanest 4% Plain and Citanest 4% Forte when used for inferior alveolar blocks.

Adults: For most routine dental procedures, initial dosages of 1 to 2 mL of Citanest 4% Plain or Citanest 4% Forte (40 to 80 mg prilocaine) will usually provide adequate infiltration or major nerve block anesthesia. No more than 400 mg (10 mL) should be administered per procedure.

Children: In children under 10 years of age it is rarely necessary to administer more than one-half cartridge (0.9 to 1 mL or 36 to 40 mg prilocaine) of Citanest 4% Plain or Citanest 4% Forte per procedure.

Due to the specific need for bone penetration, dental local anesthetics contain high concentrations of active drug, e.g., 40 mg/mL prilocaine for Citanest. A combination of high pressure induced by the use of a dental cartridge system and a rapid rate of injection may lead to complications (see Overdose: Symptoms and Treatment) even after the injection of small amounts of local anesthetic. This is due to the high concentration, especially following accidental intravascular injection, when the injected drug could travel in a retrograde manner along the vessel and, in cases of intra-arterial injection in the head and neck area, reach the brain without the same degree of dilution that occurs with an i.v. injection. It must also be noted that epinephrine, when added to a local anesthetic solution is less active as a localizing agent in the highly vascular oral environment than elsewhere in the body.

Aspiration is recommended since it reduces the possibility of intravascular injection, thereby keeping the incidence of side effects and anesthetic failures to a minimum.

For best results, it is important that cartridges be used with a syringe of appropriate size. The Astra Self-Aspirating Syringe has been designed especially for Astra cartridges.

Sterilization, Storage and Technical Procedures: Cartridges should not be autoclaved, because the rubber plunger will typically be extruded thus compromising container integrity.

If disinfection of the cartridge is desired, its immersion should be avoided due to the risk of undesirable effects on the rubber membrane and aluminum cap, and the risk of contamination of the solution. Disinfection of the rubber membrane or the entire dental cartridge should be accomplished by wiping it with a cotton pledget that has been moistened with a disinfectant. Isopropyl alcohol (91%) or ethyl alcohol (70%) is recommended. Many commercially available brands of rubbing alcohol, as well as solutions of ethyl alcohol not of USP grade, contain denaturants which are injurious to rubber and therefore are not to be used.

Quaternary ammonium salts, such as benzalkonium chloride, are electrolytically incompatible with aluminum. Cartridges which are sealed with aluminum caps should not be immersed in any solution containing these salts.

Anti-rust tablets usually contain sodium nitrate or other similar agents which may be capable of releasing metal ions from syringes, needles and aluminum sealed cartridges. Accordingly, cartridges should not be kept in such solutions.

Adequate precautions should be taken to avoid prolonged contact between local anesthetic solutions containing epinephrine (low pH) and metal surfaces (e.g., needles or metal parts of syringes), since dissolved metal ions, particularly copper ions, may cause severe local irritation (swelling, edema) at the site of injection and accelerate the degradation of epinephrine.

To avoid leakage of solutions during injection, be sure to penetrate the centre of the rubber diaphragm perpendicularly with the needle when loading the syringe. An off-centre penetration produces an oval shaped puncture that allows leakage around the needle.

In order to avoid traumatic nerve injuries leading to paresthesia in conjunction with dental nerve block, an atraumatic technique should be used. Dental cartridge systems may generate high pressures during injection, however, injected local anesthetics may travel in a retrograde manner along a nerve in cases of intraneural injection. If an accidental traumatic nerve injury has occurred, epinephrine, if present in the anesthetic solution, may aggravate the local neurotoxicity by decreasing the intraneural blood circulation. In order to minimize the risk of intraneural injection as well as fascicular injuries, the needle should always be withdrawn a little if paresthesia is elicited during injection. Furthermore, a short-bevelled needle should be considered for regional blocks (in which case a topical anesthetic may be used to reduce the pain of needle insertion), while a sharper (i.e., long-bevelled) needle can still be recommended for infiltration.

Citanest solutions should be stored at room temperature (15 to 30°C). Citanest 4% Forte should be protected from light. Do not use if solution is pinkish or darker than slightly yellow, or contains a precipitate.

Citanest 4% Plain and Citanest 4% Forte are preservative free and for single use only. Discard unused portion.

Supplied: Citanest 4% Plain: Each mL of sterile, aqueous, isotonic solution contains: prilocaine HCl 40 mg. Nonmedicinal ingredients: water for injection and sodium hydroxide and/or hydrochloric acid to adjust pH to 6 to 7. Preservative-free. Dental cartridges of 1.8 mL, boxes of 50.

Citanest 4% Forte: Each mL of sterile, aqueous, isotonic solution contains: prilocaine HCl 40 mg and epinephrine (1:200 000) 0.005 mg. Nonmedicinal ingredients: sodium metabisulfite, water for injection and sodium hydroxide and/or hydrochloric acid to adjust pH to 3.3 to 5.5. Preservative-free. Dental cartridges of 1.8 mL, boxes of 50.

Reviewed 1997

CITROCARBONATE®

Roberts

Bicarbonate—Tartrate Compound

Urinary Alkalizer

Indications: As a systemic and urinary alkalinizer, gastric antacid.

Precautions: Consider the sodium content in administration to patients on sodium free diets. Chronic, prolonged use may produce metabolic alkalosis.

Dosage: Adults: 1 to 2 teaspoonfuls of powder in a glass of cold water, 15 minutes to 2 hours after meals, or as directed by a physician.

Children: Gauge by weight: 18 kg, 1/4 adult dose or 0.98 to 1.95 g, given in one dose, in diluted solution, or as directed by a physician.

Supplied: Each 3.9 g, 1 teaspoonful of powder when dissolved provides approximately: sodium bicarbonate 0.78 g, sodium citrate anhydrous 1.82 g. Each teaspoon of powder contains: sodium bicarbonate 2.34 g, citric acid anhydrous 1.19 g, sodium citrate hydrous 254 mg, calcium lactate pentahydrate 151 mg, sodium chloride 79 mg, monobasic sodium phosphate anhydrous 44 mg, magnesium sulfate 42 mg. Each 3.9 g of powder contains 30.46 mEq or mmol (700.6 mg) of sodium. Gluten-free. Bottles of 227 g.

CITRO-MAG®

Rougier

Magnesium Citrate

Laxative

Indications: A laxative or purgative. Preparation of the colon for x-ray examination.

Contraindications: Abdominal pain, nausea or vomiting. Known or suspected intestinal obstruction.

Precautions: Frequent or prolonged use may result in dependence on laxatives.

Dosage: Adults: as a laxative: ¼ to ½ bottle; as a purgative: 1 bottle before breakfast or as prescribed before x-ray examination. Children (6 to 12 years): 30 to 60 mL according to age. Under 6 years: as prescribed. Dose may be repeated once if necessary. The solution should be served chilled and a glass of water should be consumed every hour before and after intake. Full x-ray preparation protocol available.

Supplied: Each bottle of lemon-flavored, carbonated solution contains: anhydrous magnesium citrate 15 g. Energy: 22.05 kJ (5.25 kcal)/5 mL. Sodium: <1 mmol (7.56 mg)/5 mL. Bottles of 300 mL.

CITROTEIN®

Novartis Nutrition

Therapeutic Nutrient

Indications: For patients requiring oral supplementation. It is lactose-free, low residue and is appropriate for fortification of the clear liquid diet.

Precautions: Not recommended for parenteral administration.

Dosage: 6 servings [1 520 mL or 4 264 kJ (1 018 kcal)] provides at least 100% of the Canadian RNI (adult males, 25 to 49) for protein and essential vitamins and minerals.

Supplied: Each 254 mL serving contains: water, sugar, dried egg white, maltodextrin, calcium glycerophosphate, citric acid, partially hydrogenated soybean oil, natural and artificial flavors, monoammonium phosphate, magnesium oxide, color, mono- and diglycerides, choline bitartrate, ascorbic acid, ferrous sulfate, zinc sulfate, niacinamide, propylene glycol, manganese sulfate, alpha tocopheryl acetate, copper gluconate, D-calcium pantothenate, pyridoxine hydrochloride, thiamine hydrochloride, vitamin A palmitate, riboflavin, folic acid, biotin, potassium iodide, vitamin D_3, cyanocobalamin. See Table I.

Energy Distribution: protein 25%, fat 2%, carbohydrate 73%; 280 kJ (67 kcal/100 mL).

Table I—Citrotein

Analysis	100 mL	
Energy	280 (67)	kJ (kcal)
Protein	4.1	g
Carbohydrate	12	g
Fat	0.21	g
Linoleic Acid	0.07	g
Potassium	54	mg
Sodium	83	mg
Vitamin A	256	IU
Vitamin C	4	mg
Thiamine	0.13	mg
Riboflavin	0.16	mg
Niacin	1.8	mg
Calcium	100	mg
Iron	1.6	mg
Vitamin D	20	IU
Vitamin E	1.3	IU
Vitamin B_6	0.18	mg
Folic Acid	0.04	mg
Vitamin B_{12}	0.0003	mg
Phosphorus	100	mg
Iodine	0.01	mg
Magnesium	35	mg
Zinc	1.3	mg
Copper	0.18	mg
Biotin	0.03	mg
Pantothenic Acid	0.88	mg
Choline	35	mg
Chloride	79	mg
Manganese	0.53	mg
Osmolality	500	mOsm/kg water

Cans of 402 g (9 servings), cases of 12. Store at room temperature. After powder is mixed with water, immediately consume or refrigerate up to 24 hours.

CLAFORAN® Pr

Hoechst Marion Roussel

Cefotaxime Sodium

Antibiotic

Pharmacology: Animal studies demonstrate that cefotaxime has no significant effect on the CNS, cardiovascular and respiratory systems, kidneys, blood clotting mechanisms and blood glucose levels.

There is a dose-dependent increase in serum levels after i.v. administration of 500 mg, 1 and 2 g of cefotaxime (38.9, 101.7 and 214.4 µg/mL respectively), without alteration in the elimination half-life.

The biological half-life was approximately 1 hour and the 24 hours urinary excretion of unchanged drug amounted to 62.6% of the administered dose (almost all of it in the first 6 hours).

In an in vitro study, approximately 51% (range 35 to 64%) of cefotaxime was bound to human serum proteins when concentrations ranged from 6.25 to 50 µg/mL. The bound percentage of the desacetyl metabolite was 16 to 32% which is approximately half of the parent compound.

In vitro studies indicate that the bacterial action of cefotaxime, a semi-synthetic cephalosporin antibiotic, results from inhibition of cell wall synthesis.

Cefotaxime is partially metabolized in humans by non-specific esterases which desacetylate the acetoxymethylside chain to form the desacetyl cefotaxime (DACM). Desacetylation is followed by formation of the lactone and subsequent conversion to open β-lactam ring structures (UP1) and (UP2).

Approximately 20 to 36% of an i.v. dose of ^{14}C cefotaxime is excreted by the kidney as unchanged drug and 15 to 25% as the DACM derivative, the major metabolite. Two other urinary metabolites (UP1 and UP2) account together for about 20 to 25%. Fecal recovery accounts for approximately 10% of the administered dose.

The DACM has been shown to contribute to 10 to 15% of the bactericidal activity of the parent compound. It has no activity against Pseudomonas. UP1 and UP2 lack antibacterial activity.

In a study conducted on 22 healthy volunteers administered cefotaxime and alcohol, there was no disulfiram-like reaction.

Indications: Cefotaxime may be indicated for the treatment of infections caused by susceptible strains of the designated microorganisms in the diseases listed below:

Lower respiratory tract infections: pneumonia and lung abscess caused by S. pneumoniae, other streptococci (excluding enterococci, e.g., S. faecalis), S. aureus (penicillinase and non-penicillinase producing), E. coli, H. influenzae, (including ampicillin resistant strains) and unspecified Klebsiella species.

Urinary tract infections: caused by E. coli, unspecified Klebsiella species (including K. pneumoniae), P. mirabilis, indole positive Proteus, S. marcescens and S. epidermidis. Also, uncomplicated gonorrhea caused by N. gonorrhoeae including penicillin resistant strains.

Bacteremia/Septicemia: caused by E. coli, unspecified Klebsiella strains and S. marcescens.

Skin infections: caused by S. aureus (penicillinase and non-penicillinase producing), S. epidermidis, Group A streptococci, E. coli, P. mirabilis and indole positive Proteus.

Intra-abdominal infections: caused by E. coli, and unspecified Klebsiella species.

Gynecological infections: including pelvic inflammatory disease, endometritis and pelvic cellulitis caused by E. coli, Group A streptococci and S. epidermidis; anaerobic bacteria including unspecified Peptococcus and Peptostreptococcus strains and some strains of B. fragilis. In several cases, although clinical cures were achieved, bacteriological follow-up was not available.

CNS infections: meningitis and ventriculitis caused by H. influenzae, N. meningitidis, S. pneumoniae, K. pneumoniae and E. coli. Cefotaxime is not active against L. monocytogenes.

Clinical experience in anaerobic infections is limited. It has been used with some success in wound and intra-abdominal infections against some strains of unidentified Bacteroides and anaerobic cocci.

Cefotaxime has been shown to be active against some strains of Pseudomonas.

In the treatment of infections encountered in immunosuppressed and granulocytopenic patients, results of therapy with cefotaxime have not been impressive.

Cefotaxime should not be considered in the treatment of enterococcal infections, i.e., S. faecalis.

Specimens for bacteriologic culture should be obtained prior to therapy in order to isolate and identify the causative organisms and to determine their susceptibilities to cefotaxime. Therapy may be instituted before results of susceptibility studies are known; antibiotic treatment should be re-evaluated once these results become available.

Prophylactic use: The administration of cefotaxime perioperatively (preoperatively, intraoperatively and postoperatively) may reduce the incidence of certain infections in patients undergoing elective surgical procedures (e.g., abdominal or vaginal hysterectomy, gastrointestinal and genitourinary tract surgery) that may be classified as contaminated or potentially contaminated.

In patients undergoing caesarian section who are considered to be at increased risk of infection, intraoperative (after clamping the umbilical cord) and postoperative use of cefotaxime may also reduce the incidence of certain postoperative infections.

Effective use for elective surgery depends on the time of administration (see Dosage).

For patients undergoing gastrointestinal surgery, preoperative bowel preparation by mechanical cleansing as well as with a nonabsorbable antibiotic (e.g., neomycin) is recommended.

If there are signs of infection, specimens for culture should be obtained for identification of the causative organism so that appropriate therapy may be instituted.

Contraindications: In patients who have shown hypersensitivity to cefotaxime sodium, the cephalosporin or the penicillin groups of antibiotics.

Warnings: Before therapy is instituted, it must be carefully determined whether the patient has had previous hypersensitivity reactions to cefotaxime, cephalosporins, penicillins or other drugs. Cefotaxime should be given with caution to patients with Type 1 hypersensitivity reactions to penicillin. Antibiotics, including cefotaxime should be administered with caution to any patient who has demonstrated some form of allergy, particularly to drugs. If an allergic reaction to cefotaxime occurs, the drug should be discontinued and the patient treated with the usual agents (e.g., epinephrine, antihistamine, pressor-amines or corticosteroids).

Pseudomembranous colitis has been reported with the use of cephalosporins (and other broad-spectrum antibiotics); therefore, it is important to consider its diagnosis in patients who develop diarrhea during the administration of cefotaxime. This colitis can range from mild to life-threatening in severity.

Treatment with broad-spectrum antibiotics, such as cefotaxime, alters the normal flora of the colon and may permit overgrowth of C. difficile or other clostridia. It has been established that a toxin produced by C. difficile is one primary cause of antibiotic-associated colitis.

Mild cases of colitis may respond to discontinuation of cefotaxime and replacement with a suitable specific antibiotic. Moderate to severe cases should be managed with fluid, electrolyte and protein supplementation as indicated. When the colitis is not relieved by discontinuance of cefotaxime administration or when it is severe, an antibiotic specifically effective in antibiotic-associated pseudomembranous colitis (e.g., vancomycin) or other suitable therapy may be indicated. Other possible causes of colitis should also be considered (see Adverse Effects).

Precautions: Cefotaxime should be prescribed with caution in individuals with a history of lower gastrointestinal disease, particularly colitis.

Pregnancy: Safety of cefotaxime in pregnancy has not been established. Consequently, use of the drug in pregnant women requires that the likely benefit from the drug be weighed against the possible risk to the mother and fetus.

Use of cefotaxime in women of childbearing potential requires that the anticipated benefits be weighed against the possible risks.

Lactation: Cefotaxime is excreted in human milk in low concentrations. Caution should be exercised when the drug is administered to nursing mothers.

Prolonged use may result in the overgrowth of nonsusceptible organisms. Constant evaluation of the patient's condition is essential. If superinfection occurs, therapy should be discontinued and appropriate measures taken.

Although cefotaxime rarely produces alterations in kidney function, evaluation of renal status is recommended, especially in severely ill patients receiving high doses.

Claforan (cont'd)

Patients with markedly impaired renal function should be placed on the special dosage schedule recommended under Dosage, because normal dosage in these individuals is likely to produce excessive and prolonged serum antibiotic concentrations.

Positive direct Coombs' test is known to develop in individuals during treatment with the cephalosporin group of antibiotics, including cefotaxime.

In laboratory tests a false-positive reaction to glucose may occur with reducing substances but not with the use of specific glucose oxidase methods.

As with other beta-lactam antibiotics, granulocytopenia and, more rarely, agranulocytosis may develop during treatment with cefotaxime, particularly if given over long periods. For courses of treatment lasting longer than 10 days, blood counts should therefore be monitored.

Adverse Effects: The most frequent adverse reactions with frequency of occurrence are:
Hypersensitivity (1.8%): rash, pruritus, fever.
Local (5%): injection site inflammation with i.v. administration. Pain, induration and tenderness after i.m. injection.
Gastrointestinal (1.7%): colitis, diarrhea, nausea and vomiting. Symptoms of pseudomembranous colitis can appear during or after cefotaxime treatment.
Hematologic System (<1%): Neutropenia, transient leukopenia, eosinophilia, thrombocytopenia and agranulocytosis have been reported. Some individuals have developed positive direct Coomb's test during treatment with cefotaxime and other cephalosporin antibiotics. Rare cases of hemolytic anemia have been reported.
Genitourinary System (<1%): moniliasis, vaginitis.
CNS (0.2%): headache.
Liver (<1%): Transient elevations in AST, ALT, serum LDH, and serum alkaline phosphatase levels have been reported.
Kidney (<1%): Increased serum creatinine and BUN have occasionally been observed.

Overdose: Symptoms and Treatment: Since no case of overdosage has been reported to date with cefotaxime, no specific information on symptoms or treatment is available. Treatment of overdosage should be symptomatic.

Dosage: Cefotaxime may be administered i.v. or i.m. after reconstitution (see Table with recommended mode of reconstitution according to route of administration).

Adults: Dosage should be determined by susceptibility of the causative organisms, severity of the infection and condition of the patient (see Table I).

Table I—Claforan

Dosage: Adults

Type of Infection	Daily Dose (g)	Frequency and Route
Uncomplicated Gonorrhea	1	1 g i.m. (single dose)
Uncomplicated infections	2	1 g every 12 hours i.m. or i.v.
Moderately severe to severe infections	3 to 6	1 to 2 g every 8 hours i.m. or i.v.
Very severe infections (e.g., septicemia, CNS)	6 to 8	2 g every 6 to 8 hours i.v.
Life-threatening infections	up to 12	2 g every 4 hours i.v.

To prevent postoperative infection in contaminated or potentially contaminated surgery, recommended doses are as follows: (a) 1 g i.m. or i.v. administered ½ to 1½ hours prior to the initial surgical incision to ensure that adequate antibiotic levels are present in the serum and tissues at the start of surgery; (b) 1 g i.m. or i.v. administered 1½ to 2 hours following the first dose; for lengthy operative procedures, additional intraoperative doses may be administered, if necessary, at appropriate intervals (1½ to 2 hours) during surgery; (c) 1 g i.m. or i.v. administered within 2 hours following completion of surgery.

The total cumulative prophylactic dose should not exceed 6 g in a 12-hour period.

Caesarian Section Patients: The first dose of 1 g is administered i.v. as soon as the umbilical cord is clamped. The second and third doses should be given as 1 g i.m. or i.v. at 6 and 12 hours after the first dose.

Neonates, Infants, and Children: The following dosage schedule is recommended. Neonates: 0 to 1 week of age; 50 mg/kg i.v. every 12 hours, 1 to 4 weeks of age; 50 mg/kg i.v. every 8 hours. Infants and children (1 month to 12 years): For body weights less than 50 kg, the recommended daily dose is 50 to 100 mg/kg i.m. or i.v. of body weight divided into 4 to 6 equal doses, or up to 180 mg/kg/day for severe infections (including CNS infections).

For body weights 50 kg or more, the usual adult dosage should be used.

The maximum daily dosage should not exceed 12 g.

Administration of cefotaxime should be continued for a minimum of 48 to 72 hours after the patient defervesces or after evidence of bacterial eradication has been obtained; a minimum of 10 days of treatment is recommended for infections caused by Group A beta-hemolytic streptococci in order to guard against the risk of rheumatic fever or glomerulonephritis; frequent bacteriologic and clinical appraisal is necessary during therapy of chronic urinary tract infections and may be required for several months after therapy has been completed; persistent infections may require prolonged treatment. Doses less than those recommended should not be employed.

Patients with Impaired Renal Function: In patients with estimated creatinine clearance of less than 20 mL/min/1.73 m², the dose should be halved (see Precautions).

If serum creatinine values alone are available, the following formulas (based on sex, weight, and age of the patient) may be used to convert these values into creatinine clearance.

Males:

$$\text{Creatinine clearance (mL/min)} = \frac{\text{Weight (kg)} \times (140-\text{age})}{72 \times \text{serum creatinine (mg/dL)}}$$

Females: 0.85×above value.

Administration: I.M.: Cefotaxime should be injected well within the body of a relatively large muscle such as the upper outer quadrant of the buttock (i.e., gluteus maximus); aspiration is necessary to avoid inadvertent injection into a blood vessel.

I.V.: The i.v. route is preferable for patients with bacteremia, bacterial septicemia, or other severe or life-threatening infections, or for patients who may be poor risks because of lowered resistance resulting from such debilitating conditions as malnutrition, trauma, surgery, diabetes, heart failure, or malignancy, particularly if shock is present or impending.

For bolus administration a solution containing 1 or 2 g of cefotaxime can be injected over a period of 3 to 5 minutes. Using an infusion system, it may also be given over a longer period of time through the tubing system by which the patient may be receiving other i.v. solutions. Butterfly or scalp vein type needles are preferred for this type of infusion. However, during infusion of the solution containing cefotaxime, it is advisable to discontinue temporarily the administration of other solutions at the same site.

Reconstitution: I.M.: Cefotaxime should be reconstituted with Sterile Water for Injection or Bacteriostatic Water for Injection in accordance with the volumes recommended in Table II.

Table II—Claforan

Reconstitution: I.M. Use

Strength	Volume To Be Added To Vial (mL)*	Approximate Available Volume (mL)	Approximate Average Concentration (mg/mL)
I.M.			
500 mg vial	2	2.2	230
1 g vial	3	3.4	300
2 g vial	5	6.0	330

*Shake to dissolve.

For direct i.v. injection (bolus) and/or continuous i.v. infusion: Conventional Flip-Top Vial: 500 mg, 1 and 2 g vials should be reconstituted with at least 10 mL of Sterile Water for Injection. Reconstituted solution may be further diluted with 50 to 1 000 mL of the fluids recommended for i.v. infusion.

Reconstitution: See Table III.

A solution of 1 g of cefotaxime in 14 mL of Sterile Water for Injection is isotonic.

Solutions for i.v. Infusion: Cefotaxime is compatible with the following infusion fluids: 0.9% NaCl injection; 5% dextrose injection; 0.9% NaCl and 5% dextrose injection; 0.45% NaCl and 5% dextrose injection; 0.2% NaCl and 5% dextrose injection; Sodium Lactate injection; 5% dextrose and 0.15% KCl injection; Plasma-Lyte 56 Electrolyte Solution in 5% dextrose injection; Ringer's injection; Lactated Ringer's solution; Lactated Ringer's with 5% dextrose injection. Cefotaxime is also compatible with 1% lignocaine.

Table III—Claforan

Reconstitution: I.V. Use

Strength	Volume To Be Added To Vial (mL)*	Approximate Available Volume (mL)	Approximate Average Concentration (mg/mL)
I.V.			
500 mg vial	10	10.2	50
1 g vial	10	10.4	95
2 g vial	10	11.0	180

*Shake to dissolve.

Stability and Storage: Solutions of cefotaxime range from light yellow to amber, depending on concentration and the diluent used. The solutions tend to darken depending on storage conditions and should be protected from elevated temperatures and excessive light.

Cefotaxime reconstituted in the original vial as described under Reconstitution maintains satisfactory potency for 24 hours at room temperature (25°C) and for 48 hours under refrigeration (0 to 5°C). Only freshly prepared reconstituted solutions may be further diluted with 50 to 1 000 mL of the recommended infusion fluids in Viaflex i.v. bags. Such solutions maintain satisfactory potency for 24 hours at room temperature (25°C) and for 72 hours under refrigeration (0 to 5°C). Any unused solutions should be discarded.

Cefotaxime reconstituted with 1% lignocaine maintains satisfactory potency for up to 24 hours at room temperature and 48 hours under refrigeration (reference to lignocaine restrictions is advisable).

Cefotaxime solutions exhibit maximum stability in the pH 5 to 7 range.

Special Instructions: Parenteral drug products should be inspected visually for particulate matter and discoloration prior to administration. Solutions of cefotaxime range from light yellow to amber, depending on concentration and diluent used. The dry powder as well as solutions tend to darken, depending on storage condition.

Incompatibilities: Solutions of cefotaxime must not be admixed with aminoglycoside solutions. If cefotaxime and aminoglycosides are to be administered to the same patient, they must be administered separately and not as a mixed injection.

Solutions of cefotaxime should not be prepared with diluents having a pH above 7.5 such as Sodium Bicarbonate Injection.

ADD-Vantage Vial: When administering cefotaxime using the ADD-Vantage Drug Delivery system, cefotaxime powder is added directly to a single-dose flexible plastic ADD-Vantage diluent container. Cefotaxime 1 g may be reconstituted in 50 to 100 mL of 5% Dextrose Injection USP or 0.9% Sodium Chloride Injection USP.

Reconstitution: See Table IV.

Table IV—Claforan

Reconstitution: ADD-Vantage Vials

ADD-Vantage Vial Size	Volume of ADD-Vantage Diluent (mL)	Approximate Average Concentration (mg/mL)
1 g	50	20
1 g	100	10

Stability: Solutions of cefotaxime reconstituted in 5% Dextrose Injection USP or 0.9% Sodium Chloride Injection USP in the ADD-Vantage flexible containers maintain satisfactory potency for 12 hours at room temperature.

Instructions for use, ADD-Vantage: (see package insert for diagrams).

To Open: Peel overwrap at corner and remove solution container. Some opacity of the plastic due to moisture absorption during the sterilization process may be observed. This is normal and does not affect the solution quality or safety. The opacity will diminish gradually.

To Assemble Vial and Flexible Diluent Container (Use Aseptic Technique): Remove the protective covers from the top of the vial and the vial port on the diluent container as follows: To remove the breakaway vial cap swing the pull ring over the top of the vial and pull down far enough to start the opening, then pull straight up to remove the cap. Note: Once the breakaway cap has been removed, do not access vial with syringe. To remove the vial port cover, grasp the tab on the pull ring, pull up to break the three tie strings, then pull back to remove the cover.

Screw the vial into the vial port until it will go no further. **The vial must be screwed in tightly to assure a seal.** This occurs approximately ½ turn after the first audible click. The clicking sound does not assure a seal, the vial must be turned as far as it will go. Note: Once vial is seated, do not attempt to remove.

Recheck the vial to assure that it is tight by trying to turn it further in the direction of assembly.

Label appropriately.

To Reconstitute the Drug: Squeeze the bottom of the diluent container gently to initiate the portion of the container surrounding the end of the drug vial.

With the other hand, push the drug vial down into the container telescoping the walls of the container. Grasp the inner cap of the vial through the walls of the container.

Pull the inner cap from the drug vial. Verify that the rubber stopper has been pulled out, allowing the drug and diluent to mix.

Mix container contents thoroughly and use within the specified time.

Immediately prior to administration, confirm that the contents of the vial have been dissolved by observing the inner cap/stopper in the flexible container.

Supplied: A sterile, white to pale yellow powder, in vials containing cefotaxime sodium 500 mg, 1 and 2 g and in ADD-Vantage Vials containing cefotaxime sodium 1 g (expressed as acid on a dry basis). In the dry state store at room temperature. Protect from light and heat.

CLARITIN®
Schering

Loratadine

Histamine H_1-Receptor Antagonist

Pharmacology: Loratadine is a long-acting tricyclic antihistamine with selective peripheral H_1-receptor antagonistic activity. It exhibits a dose-related inhibition of the histamine-induced skin wheal and flare response in humans which is rapid in onset, is apparent at 2 hours and persists throughout the 24-hour observation period. Single oral doses up to 160 mg and repeat daily doses of 40 mg for up to 13 weeks were well tolerated with the incidence of sedation and dry mouth being no different from placebo.

Pharmacokinetics: ^{14}C-loratadine is rapidly absorbed reaching C_{max} values (4.7, 10.8 and 26.1 ng/mL) at 1.5, 1.0 and 1.3 hours for the 10, 20 and 40 mg dose, respectively. The loratadine elimination half-life (t½ β) ranged from 7.8 to 11 hours. Descarboethoxyloratadine, the major active metabolite, reached C_{max} values (4.0, 9.9 and 16.0 ng/mL) at 3.7, 1.5 and 2.0 hours after a dose of 10, 20 and 40 mg, respectively. Its t½ β ranged from 17 to 24 hours. The accumulation indices, calculated by C_{max} and the area under the curve (AUC) ratios, did not change after the 5th day, indicating little or no accumulation of either loratadine or its metabolite after a multiple once per day dosage regimen. The t½ β at steady-state levels for loratadine and its metabolite were 14.4 and 18.7 hours, respectively, similar to that reported following a single oral dose.

The confidence intervals for C_{max} and $AUC_{0\text{-}\alpha}$ are within the 80 to 125% range indicating that the Claritin Rapid Dissolve Tongue Tablets were bioequivalent with respect to the active metabolite descarboethoxyloratadine.

After administration of a single 10 mg dose of loratadine as either the Rapid Dissolve Tongue Tablet, a conventional tablet, or the syrup formulation (1mg/mL), peak plasma concentrations of loratadine and its metabolite were achieved at approximately 1 and 2 hours, respectively; mean elimination half-life of the active metabolite ranged between 19 and 21 hours. See Tables I and II.

Since loratadine is extensively metabolized there was a high inter-subject variability in the plasma drug concentrations. Hence, the percent coefficient of variation of the pharmacokinetic parameters was large.

Following administration of 10 mg of loratadine once daily for 10 days as either a Rapid Dissolve Tongue tablet or a conventional tablet, plasma concentrations of loratadine and its active metabolite were at steady state by day 5 with both formulations. Mean peak plasma concentrations (T_{max}) of loratadine and its metabolite in both formulations were attained at 1.3 hours; peak to trough fluctuations observed for the Rapid Dissolve Tongue tablet and the conventional tablet were similar with respect to loratadine and its metabolite. Mean elimination half-life of the active metabolite was 20 hours for both formulations. See Table III.

In a single-dose, 2-way cross-over study with Claritin Rapid Dissolve Tongue Tablets, food increased the AUC of loratadine and descarboethoxyloratadine by 90% and 6% respectively. Food decreased the mean C_{max} of loratadine and descarboethoxyloratadine by 9% and 15% respectively. The time to peak plasma concentration (T_{max}) of loratadine and descarboethoxyloratadine were delayed by approximately 2.4 and 3.7 hours, respectively, when food was consumed prior to administration of Claritin Rapid Dissolve Tongue Tablets.

In a single-dose, randomized, 2-way cross-over study with 10 mg Claritin Rapid Dissolve Tongue Tablets in 24 subjects, under fasting condition, the mean AUC(tf) and C_{max} values were increased by 84% and 30%, respectively, when administered without water compared to administration with water, demonstrating that bioavailability was not attenuated when Claritin Rapid Dissolve Tongue Tablet was dissolved on the tongue and subsequently swallowed without concomitant consumption of a liquid. The bioavailability of descarboethoxyloratadine was not different when administered without water.

Approximately 82% of the ^{14}C-loratadine dose is excreted in the urine (40%) and feces (42%) over a 10-day period. Approximately 27% of the dose is eliminated in the urine during the first 24 hours largely in the conjugated form. Unchanged drug is present only in trace quantities in the urine and the active metabolite descarboethoxyloratadine represents only 0.4 to 0.6% of the administered loratadine dose.

In 2 randomized, multicentre, double-blind, placebo-controlled, parallel groups studies performed in patients with seasonal allergic rhinitis, the safety and efficacy of Claritin Rapid Dissolve Tongue Tablets and the conventional Claritin tablets vs placebo were evaluated. Claritin Rapid Dissolve Tongue Tablets administered as 10 mg once daily for 15 days, were significantly more effective than placebo in reducing physician-evaluated and patient daily-assessed total combined, total nasal, and total nonnasal symptoms in patients with seasonal allergic rhinitis. Claritin Rapid Dissolve Tongue Tablet had a clinical effect comparable to or greater than conventional Claritin tablet. Both of the drugs were safe and well tolerated in this patient population. From clinical studies conducted on healthy individuals with allergic rhinitis, no clinical consequences are anticipated in this population, whether or not Claritin Rapid Dissolve Tongue Tablets are administered with or without food.

Indications: Tablets and Rapid Dissolve Tongue Tablets: For the relief of symptoms associated with seasonal and perennial allergic rhinitis, such as sneezing, nasal discharge and itching, and ocular itching and burning, and for the relief of symptoms and signs of chronic urticaria and other allergic dermatologic disorders. Clinical studies to date support treatment for up to 6 months, thus medical recommendation is advised for longer-term use. The Rapid Dissolve Tongue Tablets should be taken on an empty stomach.

Syrup: For the relief of symptoms associated with seasonal allergic rhinitis, such as sneezing, nasal discharge and itching, and ocular itching and burning, and for the relief of symptoms and signs of chronic urticaria and other allergic dermatologic disorders. In children, it is intended for short-term use only unless taken under medical supervision.

Contraindications: In patients who have shown hypersensitivity or idiosyncrasy to the drug or its components.

Precautions: Patients with severe liver impairment should be administered a lower initial dose because they may have reduced clearance of loratadine; an initial dose of 5 mg once daily or 10 mg every other day is recommended.

Pregnancy and *Lactation:* The safe use of loratadine during pregnancy or lactation has not been established and therefore the compound should be used only if the potential benefit justifies the potential risk to fetus or infant.

Children: The safety and efficacy of loratadine in children younger than 2 years of age have not been established. Long-term safety and efficacy of loratadine in children between the ages of 2 and 12 have not been demonstrated. Therefore, it is desirable that loratadine not be administered to children between the ages of 2 and 12 for longer than 14 days, unless recommended by a physician.

Table I—Claritin

Mean (n=18) Pharmacokinetic Parameters for Loratadine and Descarboethoxyloratadine [(Claritin Rapid Dissolve Tongue 10 mg Tablet vs Claritin 10 mg Tablet (Conventional)]

	Mean (%CV)			
	Claritin Rapid Dissolve Tongue 10 mg Tablet		Claritin 10 mg Tablet (Conventional)	
Parameter	Loratadine	DCL*	Loratadine	DCL*
C_{max} (ng/mL)	2.56 (83)	3.72 (53)	2.11 (90)	3.66 (45)
T_{max} (h)	1.14 (72)	1.97 (129)	1.00 (34)	1.97 (98)
AUC (I) (ng.h/mL)	6.14 (100)	49.1 (50)	4.64 (106)	48.4 (44)

*DCL: Descarboethoxyloratadine.

Table II—Claritin

Mean (n=18) Pharmacokinetic Parameters for Loratadine and Descarboethoxyloratadine (Claritin Rapid Dissolve Tongue 10 mg Tablet vs Claritin 1 mg/mL)

	Mean (%CV[a])			
	Claritin Rapid Dissolve Tongue 10 mg Tablet		Loratadine Syrup (1 mg/mL) Tablet	
Parameter	Loratadine	DCL[b]	Loratadine	DCL[b]
C_{max} (ng/mL)	2.65 (193)	3.46 (44)	3.62 (150)	3.65 (35)
T_{max} (h)	1.00 (30)	1.42 (39)	0.86 (44)	0.94 (17)
AUC (I) (ng.h/mL)	6.33 (201)	40.8 (29)	10.1 (147)	38.8 (27)

[a]CV: Coefficient of variation.
[b]DCL: Descarboethoxyloratadine.

Table III—Claritin

Loratadine, Administered as Either Claritin Rapid Dissolve Tongue 10 mg Tablet or Claritin 10 mg Tablet (Conventional Tablet) to Healthy Subjects Once Daily for 10 Days

	Mean (%CV[a])					
	Loratadine			DCL[b]		
	Day 5	Day 7	Day 10	Day 5	Day 7	Day 10
Parameter	Claritin Rapid Dissolve Tongue 10 mg Tablet					
C_{max} (ng/mL)	3.79 (83)	3.35 (73)	4.04 (80)	4.65 (58)	4.69 (68)	4.69 (73)
AUC(r)[c] (ng.h/mL)	12.0 (76)	11.2 (75)	12.2 (71)	71.9 (88)	82.1 (93)	72.9 (103)
	Claritin 10 mg Tablet (Conventional tablet)					
C_{max} (ng/mL)	3.12 (77)	3.43 (64)	3.81 (67)	4.56 (63)	5.12 (68)	4.60 (81)
AUC(r)[c] (ng.h/mL)	10.6 (67)	11.6 (61)	11.3 (64)	75.4 (94)	85.0 (99)	73.5 (114)

[a]CV: Coefficient of variation.
[b]DCL: Descarboethoxyloratadine.
[c]Area under the plasma concentration-time curve from time 0 to 24 h (for day 10, using concentration time points matching those on day 5 and 7).

Claritin (cont'd)

Table IV—Claritin

Adverse Experiences Reported in Adult Patients

Claritin Tablets, 10 mg Once Daily vs Placebo and Comparatives

Number (%) of Adult Patients Reporting Frequently Occurring (> 2% of Loratadine-treated Patients) Adverse Experiences in Adults Possibly or Probably Related to Treatment: Patients Treated with Claritin, Placebo and Comparatives

Adverse Experience	Loratadine 10 mg once daily N=1 241	Placebo N=1 652	Clemastine 1 mg b.i.d. N=687	Terfenadine 60 mg b.i.d. N=506	Astemizole 10 mg once daily N=342
Fatigue	54 (4)	62 (4)	62 (9)	17 (3)	22 (6)
Headache	97 (8)	104 (6)	32 (5)	40 (8)	26 (7)
Dry mouth	49 (4)	32 (2)	22 (3)	15 (3)	2 (1)
Dryness in nose	9 (<1)	—	6 (<1)	3 (<1)	—
Sedation*	99 (8)	101 (6)	151 (22)	41 (8)	50 (15)

*Reported as somnolence, sleepiness, drowsiness, lethargy, slow or "drugged feeling."

Drug Interactions: When administered concomitantly with alcohol, loratadine has no potentiating effects as measured by psychomotor performance studies.

Increases in plasma concentrations of loratadine have been reported after concomitant use with ketoconazole, erythromycin or cimetidine in controlled clinical trials, but without clinically significant changes (including electrocardiographic). Other drugs known to inhibit hepatic metabolism should be coadministered with caution until definitive interaction studies can be completed.

Drug/Laboratory Test Interactions: Loratadine should be discontinued approximately 48 hours prior to skin testing procedures since antihistamines may prevent or diminish otherwise positive reactions to dermal reactivity indicators.

Adverse Effects: Adverse experiences reported with conventional loratadine in adults during the clinical trials were mild and consisted of fatigue, headache, dry mouth, sedation, gastrointestinal disorders such as nausea, gastritis, and also allergic symptoms like rash. The incidence of sedation was similar to that of the comparative agents terfenadine, astemizole and placebo, but statistically different ($p < 0.01$) from clemastine. See Table IV. In addition to those listed in Table IV, the following were reported less frequently (<1%): appetite increased, coughing, dizziness, and palpitations.

Table V—Claritin

Adverse Experiences

Claritin Rapid Dissolve Tongue Tablets vs Claritin Conventional Tablets vs Placebo

Number (%) of Patients Reporting Frequently Occurring (≥2% of Rapid Dissolve Tongue Tablet-treated patients) Adverse Experiences Possibly or Probably Related to Treatment in Seasonal Allergic Rhinitis Studies

Number (%) of Patients

Adverse Experience	Loratadine 10 mg Rapid Dissolve Tongue Tablet (N=495)	Loratadine 10 mg Tablet (N=328)	Placebo (N=497)
Dry Mouth	8 (2)	8 (2)	5 (1)
Fatigue	13 (3)	12 (4)	16 (3)
Headache	40 (8)	23 (7)	55 (11)
Somnolence	22 (4)	13 (4)	3 (3)

During the marketing of loratadine, alopecia, anaphylaxis, and abnormal hepatic function have been reported rarely.

Loratadine Rapid Dissolve Tongue Tablets were well tolerated and did not cause local irritation or taste abnormalities. The most frequently reported adverse experience was headache. Overall, the incidence of adverse reactions was comparable to that of conventional loratadine tablets and to that of placebo (see Table V).

Adverse experiences reported in pediatric patients are shown in Table VI. Nervousness and hyperkinesia were among the reported adverse experiences. One case of hyperkinesia was graded as severe and was judged by the physician to be possibly related to loratadine treatment. Gastrointestinal adverse reactions reported during pediatric trials may have been slightly more frequent in the younger patients (less than or equal to 30 kg), but in older children (greater than 30 kg) are similar to placebo (see Table VII).

Table VII—Claritin

Number of Patients Reporting Gastrointestinal Adverse Experiences in Placebo-controlled Clinical Trials Possibly or Probably Related to Study Medication, Grouped According to Treatment, Dose, Weight, in Pediatric Studies

Adverse Event	5 mg Dose Wt ≤ 30 kg (N=46)	10 mg Dose Wt > 30 kg (N=119)	Placebo Wt > 30 kg (N=168)
Diarrhea	1	0	0
Nausea	2	2	5
Dyspepsia	2	3	3
Vomiting	2	0	0
Abdominal pain	0	2	0
Total	7 (15%)	8 (6.8%)	8 (4.8%)

Overdose: Symptoms and Treatment: Somnolence, tachycardia and headache have been reported with overdoses of the conventional loratadine formulation. A single acute ingestion of 160 mg produced no adverse effects.

Treatment: In the event of overdosage, treatment, which should be started immediately, is symptomatic and supportive. Discontinuation of use, gastric lavage or induction of emesis (except in patients with impaired consciousness) and support of vital functions are advised.

The patient should be induced to vomit, even if emesis has occurred spontaneously. Pharmacologically induced vomiting by administration of ipecac syrup is a preferred method. However, vomiting should not be induced in patients with impaired consciousness. The action of ipecac is facilitated by physical activity and by the administration of 240 to 360 mL of water. If emesis does not occur within 15 minutes, the dose of ipecac should be repeated. Precautions against aspiration should be taken, especially in children.

Following emesis, adsorption of any drug remaining in the stomach may be attempted by the administration of activated charcoal as a slurry with water. If vomiting is unsuccessful, or contraindicated, gastric lavage should be performed. Physiologic saline solution is the lavage solution of choice, particularly in children. In adults, tap water can be used; however, as much as possible of the amount administered should be removed before the next instillation. Saline cathartics draw water into the bowel by osmosis and therefore may be valuable for their action in rapid dilution of bowel content.

Loratadine is not cleared by hemodialysis to any appreciable extent; it is not known if loratadine is removed by peritoneal dialysis.

Dosage: Syrup: Adults, children over 10 years of age (body weight greater than 30 kg): 10 mL of syrup once daily.
Children 2 through 9 years of age (body weight less than or equal to 30 kg): 5 mL of syrup once daily.
Tablets: Adults and Children 12 years of age and over: 1 tablet (10 mg) once daily. One Rapid Dissolve Tongue Tablet (10 mg), placed in the mouth once daily. The tablet disperses instantly and water or other liquid is not needed.

Supplied: Syrup: Each mL of clear, colorless to light yellow, peach-flavored syrup contains: loratadine 1 mg (as base). Nonmedicinal ingredients: artificial peach flavor, citric acid monohydrate, glycerin, propylene glycol, purified water, sodium benzoate and sucrose. Amber glass or amber plastic bottles of 100 mL. Store between 2 and 30°C.

Rapid Dissolve Tongue Tablets: Each white, round, tablet-shaped unit contains: micronized loratadine 10 mg (as base). Nonmedicinal ingredients: citric acid, gelatin, mannitol and mint flavor. Blister packages of 4, 8 and 12. Store between 2 and 30°C. Use within 6 months of opening sachet, immediately upon opening tablet blister. Protect from exposure to excessive moisture.

Tablets: Each white, oval, shallow, deep-scored tablet, with the flask and dish logo above the deep score and the number 10 below, contains: loratadine 10 mg (as base). Nonmedicinal ingredients: cornstarch, lactose and magnesium stearate. Blister packages of 6, 12 and 18. Bottles of 100. Store between 2 and 30°C. Protect from exposure to excessive moisture.

(Shown in Product Recognition Section)

Reviewed 1999

Table VI—Claritin

Adverse Experiences Reported in Pediatric Patients

Loratadine Syrup, 1 mg/mL, 5–10 mg Once Daily

Number (%) of Patients Reporting Frequently Occurring (≥ 2% of Loratadine-treated Patients) Treatment-related Adverse Experiences: Placebo-controlled Clinical Trials in Pediatric Studies in Seasonal Allergic Rhinitis and Allergic Skin Disorders Studies

Adverse Experience	Loratadine 5 mg N=46	Loratadine 10 mg N=119	Chlorpheniramine 2 mg N=48	Chlorpheniramine 4 mg N=122	Placebo N=168
Nervousness	2 (4)	5 (4)	1 (2)	2 (2)	2 (1)
Hyperkinesia	0 (0)	4 (3)	0 (0)	1 (1)	1 (0.6)
Sedation	2 (4)	6 (5)	4 (8)	13 (11)	9 (5)
Headache	3 (6)	4 (3)	4 (8)	5 (4)	13 (8)

CLARITIN® EXTRA

Schering

Loratadine—Pseudoephedrine Sulfate

Histamine H_1-Receptor Antagonist—Sympathomimetic Amine

Pharmacology: Loratadine is a long-acting tricyclic antihistamine with selective peripheral H_1 receptor antagonistic activity. It exhibits a dose-related inhibition of the histamine-induced skin wheal and flare response in humans which is rapid in onset, is apparent at 2 hours and persists throughout the 24 hour observation period. Single oral doses up to 160 mg and repeat daily doses of 40 mg for up to 13 weeks were well tolerated with the incidence of sedation and dry mouth being no different from placebo.

^{14}C-loratadine is rapidly absorbed reaching C_{max} values (4.7, 10.8 and 26.1 ng/mL) at 1.5, 1.0 and 1.3 hours for the 10, 20 and 40 mg dose, respectively. The loratadine elimination half-life ($t_{1/2\beta}$) ranged from 7.8 to 11 hours.

Descarboethoxyloratadine, the major active metabolite, reached C_{max} values (4.0, 9.9 and 16.0 ng/mL at 3.7, 1.5 and 2.0 hours after a dose of 10, 20 and 40 mg, respectively. Its $t_{1/2\beta}$ ranged from 17 to 24 hours. The accumulation indices, calculated by C_{max} and the area under the curve (AUC) ratios did not change after the 5th day, indicating little or no accumulation of either loratadine or its metabolite after a multiple once per day dosage regimen. The $t_{1/2\beta}$ at steady state levels for loratadine and its active metabolite were 14.4 and 18.7 hours, respectively, similar to that reported following a single oral dose.

Approximately 82% of the ^{14}C-loratadine dose is excreted in the urine (40%) and feces (42%) over a 10-day period.

Approximately 27% of the dose is eliminated in the urine during the first 24 hours largely in the conjugated form. Unchanged drug is present only in trace quantities in the urine and the active metabolite descarboethoxyloratadine represents only 0.4 to 0.6% of the administered loratadine dose.

Pseudoephedrine sulfate, one of the naturally occurring alkaloids of Ephedra and an orally administered vasoconstrictor, produces a gradual but sustained decongestant effect facilitating shrinkage of congested mucosa in upper respiratory areas. The mucous membrane of the respiratory tract is decongested through the action of the sympathetic nerves.

Indications: For the relief of nasal and ocular symptoms of upper respiratory mucosal congestion, such as in allergic rhinitis. For short-term use only unless taken under medical supervision.

Contraindications: In those patients who have shown sensitivity or idiosyncrasy to the components, to adrenergic agents or to other drugs of similar chemical structures. Also contraindicated in patients receiving MAO inhibitor therapy or within 14 days of discontinuing such treatment and in patients with narrow-angle glaucoma, urinary retention, hypertension, severe coronary artery disease and hyperthyroidism.

Precautions: General: Sympathomimetics should be used with caution in patients with stenosing peptic ulcer, pyloroduodenal obstruction, prostatic hypertrophy or bladder neck obstruction, cardiovascular disease, increased intraocular pressure or diabetes mellitus.

Sympathomimetics should be used with caution in patients receiving digitalis.

Sympathomimetics may cause central nervous system (CNS) stimulation and convulsions or cardiovascular collapse with accompanying hypotension.

Patients with severe liver impairment should be administered a lower dose because they may have reduced clearance of loratadine; an initial dose of 1 tablet daily is recommended.

Geriatrics: In patients 60 years of age or older, sympathomimetics are also more likely to cause adverse reactions such as confusion, hallucination, convulsions, CNS depression and death. Consequently, caution should be exercised when administering a repeat-action formulation to this patient group.

Dependence Liability: There are no data available to indicate that abuse or dependency occurs with loratadine.

Pseudoephedrine, like other CNS stimulants, has been abused. At high doses, subjects commonly experience mood elevation, decreased appetite and a sense of increases energy, physical strength, mental capacity and alertness. Anxiety, irritability and loquacity also have been reported. With continued use, tolerance develops; the user increased the dose and ultimately toxicity occurs. Depression may follow rapid withdrawal.

Children: Safety and efficacy in children younger than 12 years of age have not yet been established.

Pregnancy: The safe use of Claritin Extra during pregnancy or lactation has not been established and therefore, this product should be used only if the potential benefit justifies the potential risk to fetus or infant.

Lactation: Loratadine and its active metabolite are eliminated in the breast milk of lactating women with milk concentrations being similar to plasma concentrations.Through 48 hours after dosing, only 0.029% of the loratadine dose is eliminated in the milk as unchanged loratadine and its active metabolite, descarboethoxyloratadine.

Since loratadine and pseudoephedrine sulfate are excreted in breast milk, a decision should be made whether to discontinue nursing or to discontinue the use of this product.

Other: Because of the lack of experience with long-term use of this drug, its use should be limited to 3 months unless recommended by a physician.

Drug Interactions: When administered concomitantly with alcohol, loratadine has no potentiating effect as measured by psychomotor performance studies.

When sympathomimetic drugs are given to patients receiving MAO inhibitors, hypertensive reactions, including hypertensive crises, may occur. The antihypertensive effects of methyldopa, mecamylamine, reserpine and veratrum alkaloids may be reduced by sympathomimetics. Beta-adrenergic blocking agents may also interact with sympathomimetics. Increased ectopic pacemaker activity can occur when pseudoephedrine sulfate is used concomitantly with digitalis. Antacids increase the rate of pseudoephedrine sulfate absorption; kaolin decreases it.

Increases in plasma concentrations of loratadine have been reported after concomitant use with ketoconazole, erythromycin or cimetidine in controlled clinical trials, but without clinically significant changes (including electrocardiographic). Other drugs known to inhibit hepatic metabolism should be coadministered with caution until definitive interaction studies can be completed.

Antihistamines should be discontinued approximately 48 hours prior to skin testing procedures since these may prevent or diminish otherwise positive reactions to dermal reactivity indicators.

Adverse Effects: During controlled clinical studies with the recommended dosage, the incidence of adverse effects associated with Claritin Extra was comparable to that of placebo, with the exception of insomnia and dry mouth both of which were commonly reported. Other most frequently reported [≥5%] adverse reactions associated with Claritin Extra, the components and placebo are listed in Table I.

Rare adverse reactions in decreasing order of frequency included, nausea, abdominal distress, anorexia, thirst, tachycardia, pharyngitis, rhinitis, acne, prutitus, rash, urticaria, arthralgia, confusion, dysphonia, hyperkinesia, hypoesthesia, decreased libido, paresthesia, tremor, vertigo, flushing, postural hypotension, increased sweating, eye disorders, earache, tinnitus, taste abnormality, agitation, apathy, depression, euphoria, paroniria, increased appetite, change in bowel habits, dyspepsia, eructation, hemorrhoids, tongue discoloration, tongue disorder, vomiting, transient abnormal hepatic function, dehydration, increased weight, hypertension, palpitation, migraine, bronchospasm, coughing, dyspnea, epistaxis, nasal congestion, sneezing, nasal irritation, dysuria, micturition disorder, nocturia, polyuria, urinary retention, asthenia, back pain, leg cramps, malaise and rigors.

During the marketing of loratadine, alopecia, anaphylaxis and abnormal hepatic function have been reported rarely.

As with other sympathomimetic amines, CNS stimulation, muscular weakness, tightness in the chest and syncope may also be encountered.

Overdose: Symptoms: In the event of overdosage, treatment, which should be started immediately, is symptomatic and supportive. Discontinuation of use, gastric lavage or induction of emesis (except in patients with impaired consciousness) and support of vital functions are advised.

Manifestations: They may vary from CNS depression (sedation, apnea, diminished mental alertness, cyanosis, coma, cardiovascular collapse) to stimulation (insomnia, hallucination, tremors or convulsions) to death. Other signs and symptoms may be euphoria, excitement, tachycardia, palpitations, thirst, perspiration, nausea, dizziness, tinnitus, ataxia, blurred vision and hypertension or hypotension. Stimulation is particularly likely in children, as are atropine-like signs and symptoms (dry mouth; fixed, dilated pupils; flushing; hyperthermia; and gastrointestinal symptoms).

In large doses sympathomimetics may give rise to giddiness, headache, nausea, vomiting, sweating, thirst, tachycardia, precordial pain, palpitations, difficulty in micturition, muscular weakness and tenseness, anxiety, restlessness and insomnia. Many patients can present a toxic psychosis with delusions and hallucinations. Some may develop cardiac arrhythmias, circulatory collapse, convulsions, coma and respiratory failure.

Treatment: The patient should be induced to vomit, even if emesis has occurred spontaneously. Pharmacologically-induced vomiting by the administration of ipecac syrup is a preferred method. However, vomiting should not be induced in patients with impaired consciousness. The action of ipecac is facilitated by physical activity and by the administration of 240 to 360 mL of water. If emesis does not occur within 15 minutes, the dose of ipecac should be repeated. Precautions against aspiration must be taken, especially in children. Following emesis, adsorption of any drugs remaining in the stomach may be attempted by the administration of activated charcoal as a slurry with water. If vomiting is unsuccessful, or contraindicated, gastric lavage should be performed. Physiologic saline solution is the lavage solution of choice, particularly in children. In adults, tap water can be used; however, as much as possible of the amount administered should be removed before the next instillation. Saline cathartics draw water into the bowel by osmosis and therefore may be valuable for their action in rapid dilution of bowel content. Loratadine is not removed by hemodialysis; it is not known if loratadine is removed by peritoneal dialysis. After emergency treatment, the patient should continue to be medically monitored.

Treatment of the signs and symptoms of overdosage is symptomatic and supportive. Stimulants (analeptic agents) should not be used. Vasopressors may be used to treat hypotension. Short-acting barbiturates, diazepam or paraldehyde may be administered to control seizures. Hyperpyrexia, especially in children, may require treatment with tepid water sponge baths or hypothermic blanket. Apnea is treated with ventilatory support.

Dosage: Adults and Children 12 years of age and over: 1 tablet twice a day.

Supplied: Each white to off-white, round, biconvex, coated tablet contains: loratadine 5 mg in the tablet coating and pseudoephedrine sulfate 120 mg equally distributed between the tablet coating and the barrier-coated core. The two active components in the coating are quickly liberated; release of the decongestant in the core is delayed for several hours. Nonmedicinal ingredients: lactose, starch, polyvinylpyrrolidone, magnesium stearate, acacia, sucrose, calcium sulfate (terra alba), microcrystalline cellulose, rosin, zein, oleic acid, soap, talc, titanium dioxide, white wax and carnauba wax. Blister packages of 10 and 20. Bottles of 100. Store between 2 and 25°C. Protect from exposure to excessive moisture.

(Shown in Product Recognition Section)

Reviewed 1997

Table I Claritin Extra

Number (%) of patients reporting adverse experiences (probably or possibly related to treatment) ≥5% incidence during treatment with Claritin Extra, either component alone (loratadine or pseudoephedrine) or placebo in clinical studies

Adverse Experience	A Claritin Extra (N = 632)	B Loratadine (N = 396)	C Pseudoephedrine (N = 395)	D Placebo (N = 532)
Dizziness	27 (4)	4 (1)	10 (5)	8 (2)
Dry mouth	93 (15)	17 (4)	41 (10)	21 (4)
Fatigue	26 (4)	22 (6)	14 (4)	13 (2)
Headache	64 (10)	48 (12)	31 (9)	52 (10)
Insomnia	113 (18)	16 (4)	66 (17)	20 (4)
Nervousness	33 (5)	11 (3)	30 (8)	5 (1)
Sedation	41 (6)	29 (7)	18 (5)	23 (4)

CLAVULIN® Ⓟ

SmithKline Beecham

Amoxicillin—Clavulanate Potassium

Antibiotic—β-Lactamase Inhibitor

Pharmacology: Amoxicillin exerts a bactericidal action against sensitive organisms during the stage of active multiplication through the inhibition of the biosynthesis of bacterial cell wall mucopeptides. Clavulanic acid inhibits specific β-lactamases of some microorganisms and allows amoxicillin to inhibit amoxicillin (ampicillin) resistant organisms which produce clavulanic acid sensitive β-lactamases.

Indications: For the treatment of the following infections when caused by Clavulin-susceptible strains of the designated bacteria: Upper respiratory tract infections when caused by β-lactamase producing strains of S. aureus. Sinusitis when caused by β-lactamase producing strains of H. influenzae or M. (B.) catarrhalis. Otitis media when caused by β-lactamase producing strains of H. influenzae or M. (B.) catarrhalis.

Lower respiratory tract infections when caused by β-lactamase producing strains of H. influenzae, K. pneumoniae, S. aureus or M. (B.) catarrhalis. Skin and soft tissue infections when caused by β-lactamase producing strains of S. aureus. Urinary tract infections when caused by β-lactamase producing strains of E. coli, P. mirabilis or Klebsiella species.

While Clavulin is indicated only for the conditions listed above, infections caused by ampicillin (amoxicillin) susceptible organisms are also amenable to Clavulin treatment due to its amoxicillin content. Furthermore, mixed infections caused by organisms susceptible to ampicillin (amoxicillin) and β-lactamase producing organisms susceptible to Clavulin should not require the addition of another antibiotic.

Appropriate culture and susceptibility studies should be performed to identify the causative organism(s) and determine

Clavulin (cont'd)

the susceptibility to Clavulin. However, when there is reason to believe an infection may involve any of the β-lactamase producing organisms listed above, therapy may be instituted prior to obtaining the results from bacteriological and susceptibility studies. Once these results are known, therapy should be adjusted if appropriate.

Contraindications: In patients with a history of hypersensitivity to the penicillin, clavam, or cephalosporin group of β-lactams.

In patients where infectious mononucleosis is either suspected or confirmed.

In patients with a previous history of Clavulin-associated jaundice/hepatic dysfunction.

Warnings: Serious and occasionally fatal hypersensitivity reactions (anaphylaxis and angioedema) have been reported in patients on penicillin therapy. Although these reactions are more frequent following parenteral therapy, they have occurred in patients receiving penicillins orally. These reactions are most apt to occur in individuals with a history of sensitivity to multiple allergens. There have been reports of individuals with a history of cephalosporin hypersensitivity who have experienced severe reactions when treated with penicillins. Before initiating therapy with Clavulin, careful inquiry should be made concerning previous hypersensitivity reactions to penicillins, cephalosporins, clavams, or other allergens.

If an allergic reaction occurs the administration of Clavulin should be discontinued and appropriate therapy should be instituted. Serious anaphylactoid reactions require immediate emergency treatment with epinephrine. Oxygen, i.v. steroids, and airway management, including intubation, should also be used as indicated.

Clavulin should be used with caution in patients with evidence of hepatic dysfunction. Hepatic toxicity associated with the use of Clavulin is usually reversible. On rare occasions, deaths have been reported (less than 1 death reported per estimated 4 million prescriptions worldwide). These have generally been cases associated with serious underlying diseases or concomitant medications (see Contraindications and Adverse Effects, Liver).

Precautions: Periodic assessment of renal, hepatic, and hematopoietic function should be made during prolonged therapy.

Clavulin is excreted mostly by the kidney. There is insufficient data to make specific dosage recommendations for patients with renal dysfunction. However, either a reduction in dose level or an extension in dose interval in proportion to the degree of loss of renal function will be needed.

The possibility of superinfections with mycotic or bacterial pathogens should be kept in mind during therapy. If superinfection should occur (usually involving Aerobacter, Pseudomonas, or Candida), the administration of Clavulin should be discontinued and appropriate therapy instituted.

The occurrence of a morbilliform rash following the use of ampicillin in patients with infectious mononucleosis is well documented. This reaction has also been reported following the use of amoxicillin. A similar reaction would also be expected with Clavulin.

In common with other broad-spectrum antibiotics, Clavulin may reduce the efficacy of oral contraceptives and patients should therfore be advised accordingly.

Pregnancy: The safety of Clavulin in the treatment of infections during human pregnancy is unknown. As with all medicines, use should be avoided during pregnancy, especially during the first trimester, unless the anticipated benefit justifies the potential risk to the fetus.

Lactation: Penicillins (including ampicillin) have been shown to be excreted in human breast milk. It is not known whether clavulanic acid is excreted in human breast milk. Caution should be exercised if Clavulin is to be administered to a nursing mother.

Adverse Effects: Gastrointestinal: nausea, vomiting, diarrhea, abdominal cramps, flatulence, constipation, anorexia, colic pain, acid stomach, intestinal candidiasis and pseudomembranous colitis. If gastrointestinal reactions are evident, they may be reduced by taking Clavulin at the start of the meal. The incidence of gastrointestinal side effects tends to be proportional to dose and tends to be greater in children than in adults.

Hypersensitivity: erythematous maculopapular rash, urticaria, anaphylaxis, and pruritus. A morbilliform rash in patients with mononucleosis. Rarely erythema multiforme and Stevens-Johnson syndrome have been reported. Other reactions including angioedema, toxic epidermal necrolysis and exfoliative dermatitis, as in the case of other beta lactam antibiotics, have been seen rarely. Interstitial nephritis can occur rarely.

Note: Urticaria, other skin rashes, and serum sickness-like reactions may be controlled with antihistamines and if necessary systemic corticosteroids. Whenever such reactions occur, discontinue therapy unless, in the opinion of the physician, the condition being treated is life-threatening and amenable only to Clavulin therapy.

Liver: Transient hepatitis and cholestatic jaundice have been reported rarely. These events have been noted with other penicillins and cephalosporins. The hepatic events associated with Clavulin may be severe, and occur predominantly in adult and elderly patients. Signs and symptoms usually occur during or shortly after treatment, but in some cases may not become apparent until several weeks after treatment has ceased. The hepatic events are usually reversible. However, in extremely rare circumstances, deaths have been reported. These have almost always been cases associated with serious underlying disease or concomitant medications. Moderate rises in AST, alkaline phosphatase, lactic dehydrogenase and ALT have been noted in patients treated with ampicillin class antibiotics. The significance of these findings is unknown.

Hemic and Lymphatic Systems: As with other beta-lactams, anemia, hemolytic anemia, thrombocytopenia, thrombocytopenic purpura, eosinophilia, leukopenia, lymphocytopenia, basophilia, slight increase in platelets, neutropenia and agranulocytosis have been reported rarely during therapy with the penicillins. These reactions are usually reversible on discontinuation of therapy and are believed to be hypersensitivity phenomena. Prolongation of bleeding time and prothrombin time have also been reported rarely.

Other: vaginitis, headache, bad taste, dizziness, malaise, glossitis, black hairy tongue, and stomatitis.

Overdose: Symptoms and Treatment: There has been no reported overdosage. If a large overdose is consumed, the patient should be kept under observation and appropriate treatment undertaken as considered necessary.

Dosage: The absorption of Clavulin is optimized when taken at the start of a meal.

Adults: Note: Since both Clavulin-250 and Clavulin-500F contain the same amount of clavulanic acid (125 mg as the potassium salt) 2 tablets Clavulin-250 are not equivalent to 1 tablet Clavulin-500F. Therefore, 2 tablets Clavulin-250 should not be substituted for 1 tablet Clavulin-500F. See Table I.

Table I—Clavulin

Dosage for Adults

Infection	Severity	Dose
Urinary Tract Upper Respiratory Tract; Skin and Soft Tissue	mild to moderate	1 Clavulin-250 tablet every 8 hours
	severe	1 Clavulin-500F tablet every 8 hours
Lower Respiratory Tract		1 Clavulin-500F tablet every 8 hours

Children: See Table II.

Table II—Clavulin

Dosage for Children

Infection	Severity	Dose
Urinary Tract Upper Respiratory Tract; Skin and Soft Tissue	mild to moderate	25 mg/kg/day of Clavulin (20 mg of amoxicillin; 5 mg of clavulanic acid) in equally divided doses every 8 hours
	severe	50 mg/kg/day of Clavulin (40 mg of amoxicillin; 10 mg of clavulanic acid) in equally divided doses every 8 hours
Otitis Media; Lower Respiratory Tract; Sinusitis		50 mg/kg/day of Clavulin (40 mg of amoxicillin; 10 mg of clavulanic acid) in equally divided doses every 8 hours.

The children's dosage should not exceed that recommended for adults. Children weighing more than 38 kg should be dosed according to the adult recommendations.

Table III may be used as a guide to determine the dosage of oral suspension according to body weight.

Each 25 mg of Clavulin oral suspension is equivalent to 0.80 mL of reconstituted Clavulin-125F and 0.40 mL of reconstituted Clavulin-250F.

20 mL of reconstituted Clavulin-125F oral suspension or 10 mL of reconstituted Clavulin-250F oral suspension are equivalent to 1 Clavulin-500F tablet. **There is no equivalency between Clavulin oral suspensions and the Clavulin-250 tablet because of the different ratio of amoxicillin: clavulanic acid.**

A calibrated dropper should be used to measure the appropriate volume for dosing.

The normal duration of treatment is 7 to 10 days. However, in general, treatment should be continued for a minimum of 48 to 72 hours beyond the time that the patient becomes asymptomatic or evidence of bacterial eradication has been obtained. It is recommended that there be at least 10 days treatment for any infection caused by β-hemolytic streptococci to prevent the occurrence of acute rheumatic fever or glomerulonephritis.

Reconstitution: Reconstitute with purified water: Clavulin-125F Powder for Oral Suspension: The approximate average concentration after reconstitution is 125 mg of amoxicillin (as the trihydrate) and 31.25 mg of clavulanic acid (as the potassium salt) per 5 mL. See Table IV (on following page).

Clavulin-250F Powder for Oral Suspension: The approximate average concentration after reconstitution is 250 mg of amoxicillin (as the trihydrate) and 62.5 mg of clavulanic acid (as potassium salt) per 5 mL. See Table V (on following page).

Stability and Storage: Store powder in a dry place at room temperature. Use the powder only if its appearance is white to off-white. The reconstituted suspension should be stored under refrigeration and should be used within 10 days. Keep bottle tightly closed at all times.

Table III—Clavulin

Pediatric Dosage Schedule for Clavulin Oral Suspension*

Body Weight (kg)	Total Daily Dose (mg)*	Volume of Reconstituted Oral Suspension Every 8 Hours: Clavulin-125F	Clavulin-250F	Total Daily Dose (mg)*	Volume of Reconstituted Oral Suspension Every 8 Hours: Clavulin-125F	Clavulin-250F
5	125	1.3	0.7	250	2.7	1.3
7	175	1.9	0.9	350	3.7	1.9
10	250	2.7	1.3	500	5.3	2.7
12	300	3.2	1.6	600	6.4	3.2
14	350	3.7	1.9	700	7.5	3.7
16	400	4.3	2.1	800	8.5	4.3
18	450	4.8	2.4	900	9.6	4.8
20	500	5.3	2.7	1 000	10.7	5.3
25	625	6.7	3.3	1 250	13.3	6.7
30	750	8.0	4.0	1 500	16.0	8.0
35	875	9.3	4.7	1 750	18.7	9.3
38	950	10.1	5.1	1 900	20.3	10.1

* Dosages are expressed in terms of amoxicillin plus clavulanic acid. These 2 ingredients are in a ratio of 4:1 in both oral suspensions, Clavulin-125F and Clavulin-250F.

Table IV—Clavulin

Reconstitution—Clavulin-125F

Bottle Size	Volume to be added
100 mL	92 mL
150 mL	137 mL

Table V—Clavulin

Reconstitution—Clavulin-250F

Bottle Size	Volume to be added
100 mL	90 mL
150 mL	134 mL

Shake vigorously.

Supplied: Suspension: Clavulin-125F: Each 5 mL of reconstituted suspension contains: amoxicillin 125 mg as the trihydrate and clavulanic acid 31.25 mg as the potassium salt (in a ratio of 4:1). Nonmedicinal ingredients: aspartame, colloidal silica, flavors (golden syrup dry, orange dry 1, orange dry 2, raspberry dry), hydroxypropyl methylcellulose, silicon dioxide, succinic acid and xantham gum. Bottles of 100 and 150 mL.

Clavulin-250F: Each 5 mL of reconstituted suspension contains: amoxicillin 250 mg as the trihydrate and clavulanic acid 62.5 mg as the potassium salt (in a ratio of 4:1). Nonmedicinal ingredients: aspartame, colloidal silica, flavors (golden syrup dry, orange dry 1, orange dry 2, raspberry dry), hydroxypropyl methylcellulose, silicon dioxide, succinic acid and xantham gum. Bottles of 100 and 150 mL.

Tablets: Clavulin-250: Each white oval tablet contains: amoxicillin 250 mg as the trihydrate and clavulanic acid 125 mg as the potassium salt (in a ratio of 2:1). Nonmedicinal ingredients: colloidal silica, dimethicone 500, hydroxypropyl methylcellulose (methocel E5), hydroxypropyl methylcellulose (methocel E15), magnesium stearate, microcrystalline cellulose, polyethylene glycol 4 000, polyethylene glycol 6 000, sodium starch glycollate and titanium dioxide. Bottles of 100.

Clavulin-500F: Each white oval tablet contains: amoxicillin 500 mg as the trihydrate and clavulanic acid 125 mg as the potassium salt (in a ratio of 4:1). Nonmedicinal ingredients: colloidal silica, dimethicone 500, hydroxypropyl methylcellulose (methocel E5), hydroxypropyl methylcellulose (methocel E15), magnesium stearate, microcrystalline cellulose, polyethylene glycol 4 000, polyethylene glycol 6 000, sodium starch glycollate and titanium dioxide. Bottles of 30 and 100.

Clavulin Discs: Each disc is impregnated with: amoxicillin 20 µg as trihydrate and clavulanic acid 10 µg as the potassium salt (in a ratio of 2:1). Cartridges of 50 susceptibility discs.

(Shown in Product Recognition Section)

Reviewed 1999

CLIMACTERON® ◈
Sabex
Testosterone—Estradiol
Estrogen Androgen Therapy

Indications: As replacement therapy for the control of menopausal symptoms and for estrogen deficiency-induced osteoporosis where estrogen deficiency is naturally or surgically induced. It should be used only in patients available for reevaluation at periodic intervals. Each reevaluation should determine the need for continued therapy and, if continuing therapy is required, whether a downward readjustment of dosage can be made.

Contraindications: Esterified estrogens should not be administered to patients with active hepatic dysfunction or disease, especially of the obstructive type; or a personal history of breast or endometrial cancer.

Endometrial hyperplasia is also a contraindication for estrogen therapy without accompanying progestogen. The drug is also contraindicated in the following situations: undiagnosed vaginal bleeding; a history of cerebrovascular accident, coronary thrombosis or in the presence of classical migraine; a history of thrombophlebitis or thromboembolic disease; partial or complete loss of vision or diplopia, from ophthalmic vascular disease; suspected pregnancy. (A statistically significant association has been reported between maternal ingestion of diethylstilbestrol during pregnancy and the occurrence of vaginal carcinoma in the offspring. This occurred with the use of diethylstilbestrol for the treatment of threatened abortion or high risk pregnancies. Whether or not such an association is applicable to all estrogens is not known at this time. In view of this finding, however, the use of any estrogen in pregnancy is not recommended.)

Precautions: Three independent retrospective studies have reported an association between postmenopausal estrogen therapy and an increased risk of endometrial carcinoma. These studies, however, lacked information regarding certain important intrinsic risk factors of the patients (especially pretreatment endogenous hormonal status) and the mode of administration of estrogen. The potential relationship of estrogen to endometrial carcinoma under clinical conditions has to be considered. However, a cause and effect relationship between estrogen administration and endometrial carcinoma cannot be established by these data at this time.

Before estrogens are administered, the patient should have a complete physical examination including blood pressure determination. Breasts and pelvic organs should be examined and a Papanicolaou smear should be taken.

The first follow up examination should be done within 6 months after initiation of treatment. Thereafter, examinations should be made once a year. At each examination, repeat those procedures outlined above.

If any surgical procedures are performed, advise the pathologist of the patient's therapy when specimens are sent for examination. Liver function tests should be made periodically in subjects who have, or are suspected of having, hepatic disease.

If abnormal vaginal bleeding occurs during therapy, perform diagnostic aspiration biopsy or curettage to rule out the possibility of uterine malignancy.

Although the estrogen content of oral contraceptive therapy has been associated with an increased risk of various thromboembolic, thrombotic and vascular diseases, to date no such increased risk in postmenopausal users of estrogens has been detected. Nevertheless, the physician should be alert to the earliest manifestations of thrombotic disorders (thrombophlebitis, retinal thrombosis, cerebral embolism and pulmonary embolism). If these occur or are suspected, estrogen therapy should be discontinued immediately.

In patients with metastatic carcinoma and hypercalcemia, estrogen medication should be used with caution.

Development of sudden enlargement, pain, or tenderness of uterine fibroids requires discontinuation of medication.

Estrogen may cause sodium and water retention. Therefore, particular caution is indicated in cardiac or renal dysfunction, epilepsy, or asthma.

Elevation of blood pressure in previously normotensive or hypertensive patients necessitates cessation of medication.

Diabetic patients or those with a predisposition to diabetes should be observed closely to detect any alterations in carbohydrate metabolism.

When liver or endocrine function tests are indicated, the results should not be considered reliable unless therapy has been discontinued for 2 to 4 months.

Adverse Effects: Gastrointestinal: nausea, vomiting, anorexia, abdominal cramps, bloating.

Endocrine: Estrogenic effects: withdrawal and breakthrough bleeding; breast soreness.

Androgenic effect: If virilization occurs, discontinue therapy. Virilization appears to be reversible if detected early, except for some instances of voice changes.

Metabolic: Slight weight gain due to sodium retention or from increased appetite caused by the anabolic action of the preparation; alteration of carbohydrate metabolism.

Cardiovascular: High doses of estrogens may predispose the patient to the development of thrombophlebitis or thromboembolic disease (pulmonary embolism, cerebral thrombosis, coronary thrombosis, retinal thrombosis and optic neuritis). An increase in blood pressure in susceptible individuals has also been reported following use of estrogen.

Dermatologic: skin rash; hepatic cutaneous porphyria becoming manifest. There have been a few reported cases of a temporary growth of hair at the injection site. This adverse effect is believed caused by a direct stimulation of the hair follicle at the injection site. Since this may occur in either sex, it should not be considered as a masculinization symptom.

CNS: headache, aggravation of migraine headaches, nervousness.

Hematologic: Altered coagulation tests such as increase in prothrombin and Factor VII, VIII, IX, and X have been reported following use of preparations containing estrogen.

Miscellaneous: Cholestatic jaundice has been reported with estrogens and methyltestosterone. A few instances of coughing, dyspnea and chest constriction have been reported with preparations containing benzyl benzoate.

Climacteron should always be injected as a deep i.m. injection into the gluteus maximus. Reports of pain, redness, swelling and tenderness have been received following the injection into the deltoid muscle. This should be expected considering the relatively small size of this muscle for a depot injection.

Dosage: Climacteron should be used only in patients available for reevaluation at periodic intervals. Each reevaluation should determine the need for continued therapy and if continuing therapy is required, whether a downward dosage readjustment can be made. In making such reevaluation of long-term therapy, such reassessment should be based on an evaluation of the benefits of therapy versus risks.

Recommended Dose: 1 mL by deep i.m. injection into the gluteus maximus. Repeat every 4 to 8 weeks or less frequently as indicated by the patient's response.

Maximal Dose: 1 mL every 4 weeks. The patient's response should serve as a guide for the duration of use.

Supplied: Each mL of injectable solution contains: testosterone enanthate benzilic acid hydrazone 150 mg (equivalent to testosterone 69 mg), estradiol dienanthate 7.5 mg and estradiol benzoate 1 mg. Nonmedicinal ingredients: benzyl alcohol 7.5% as preservative in benzyl benzoate and corn oil. Ampuls of 1 mL, boxes of 3. Vials of 5 mL, boxes of 1. Store between 15 and 30°C.

CLIMARA® Ⓟ
Berlex Canada
Estradiol-17β
Estrogen

Pharmacology: Climara is composed of a translucent polyethylene film with an acrylate adhesive matrix containing estradiol-17β. Upon application to intact skin, Climara provides continuous systemic delivery of estrogen by releasing estradiol-17β, the major estrogenic hormone secreted by the human ovary.

Estradiol-17β is the predominant estrogen produced by the ovaries in premenopausal women. Administration of transdermal estradiol to postmenopausal women elevates plasma estradiol concentrations into the range observed in premenopausal women at the early to mid-follicular stage. As a result of the increased plasma estradiol concentrations, plasma concentrations of follicle-stimulating hormone and luteinizing hormone are decreased and vaginal cytology is converted to a pattern resembling that found in premenopausal women, with improvement of the maturation and karyopyknotic indices. Estrogens are effective in reducing the number and intensity of hot flushes associated with menopause.

Pharmacokinetics: When given orally, estrogens and their esters are extensively metabolized by the liver (first pass effect) and circulate primarily as estrone sulfate, with smaller amounts of other conjugated and unconjugated weaker estrogens. This results in limited oral potency.

In contrast, because the skin metabolizes estradiol only to a small extent, the transdermal administration of estradiol produces therapeutic serum levels of estradiol with lower circulating levels of estrone and estrone conjugates. Climara maintains the favorable estradiol/estrone ratio associated with transdermal application, which is comparable to that observed in premenopausal women during the early follicular phase.

Transdermal administration of estradiol offers several advantages over oral administration. It avoids the hepatic "first pass" effect thereby minimizing interpatient and intrapatient variations due to variable hepatic metabolism. Transdermal administration avoids gastrointestinal intolerance associated with oral administration of estrogens.

The Climara 50 and Climara 100 systems provide controlled delivery of approximately 0.05 mg and 0.1 mg of estradiol/day, respectively, into the systemic circulation. The expected 2:1 dose proportionality between the two strengths has been demonstrated. Consistent serum estradiol serum concentrations, within the desired therapeutic range, are maintained with both Climara systems over a 1 week application interval. On average, Climara 100 maintained mean steady-state serum estradiol levels of approximately 70 pg/mL, and Climara 50 maintained mean steady-state serum estradiol levels of approximately 35 pg/mL.

Climara does not produce an accumulation of estrogens following multiple 1-week applications. Because estradiol has a short half-life, transdermal administration of estradiol allows a rapid decline in blood levels after the Climara system is removed.

Indications: For the relief of menopausal and postmenopausal symptoms occurring in naturally or surgically induced estrogen deficiency states.

Climara (cont'd)

In patients with an intact uterus, Climara should always be supplemented by sequential administration of a progestin to prevent endometrial hyperplasia.

Contraindications: Should not be used in individuals with any of the following conditions: known or suspected estrogen-dependent neoplasia such as breast or endometrial cancer; endometrial hyperplasia; undiagnosed vaginal bleeding; known or suspected pregnancy; active liver dysfunction or disease, especially of the obstructive type; active thrombophlebitis, thrombosis or thrombotic disorders; a history of cerebrovascular accident, coronary thrombosis, or in the presence of classical migraine; a history of thrombophlebitis, thrombosis or thromboembolic disorders associated with previous estrogen use; partial or complete loss of vision from ophthalmic vascular disease; known or suspected hypersensitivity to any component of the patch.

Warnings: Before Climara is administered, the patient should have a complete physical examination. The breasts should be examined together with mammography where indicated. Pelvic organs should be examined, a Papanicolaou smear and an endometrial biopsy should be taken. Baseline tests should include measurement of blood glucose, calcium, triglycerides and cholesterol, and liver function tests.

The first followup examination should be done within 6 months after initiation of treatment to assess medical response to treatment. Thereafter, examinations should be made once a year and should include at least those procedures outlined above. It is important that patients are encouraged to practice frequent self-examination of the breasts.

If any surgical procedures are performed, the pathologist should be advised of the patient's therapy when specimens are sent for examination.

If unexpected or abnormal vaginal bleeding occurs during therapy, diagnostic aspiration biopsy or curettage should be performed to rule out the possibility of uterine malignancy.

Patients with acute hepatic disease, especially of the obstructive type, should not be given estrogens.

Patients who develop visual disturbances, classical migraine, transient aphasia, paralysis, or loss of consciousness should discontinue medication.

Although the estrogen content of oral contraceptive therapy has been associated with an increased risk of various thromboembolic, thrombotic and vascular disease, to date no such risk has been reported in epidemiological studies looking at currently prescribed doses of estrogen products used in menopause. Nevertheless, the physician should be alert to the earliest manifestations of thrombotic disorders (phlebitis, thrombophlebitis, retinal thrombosis, cerebral embolism and pulmonary embolism). If these occur or are suspected, estrogen therapy should be discontinued immediately. Women with a positive family history and women with a history of thromboembolic disorders during pregnancy or in association with estrogen use should be kept under special observation.

If feasible, estrogens should also be discontinued at least 4 weeks before surgery which may be associated with an increased risk of thromboembolism or during periods of prolonged immobilization.

Estrogen use, unopposed by progestins, has been reported to increase the risk of endometrial carcinoma in postmenopausal women. The incidence of endometrial hyperplasia is reported to be lowered with sequential coadministration of a progestin. Close clinical surveillance of all women taking estrogens is important. Adequate diagnostic measures, including endometrial sampling when indicated, should be undertaken to rule out malignancy in all cases of undiagnosed persistent or recurring abnormal vaginal bleeding.

Breast cancer is a multifactorial disease, which increases in frequency in older age. Much of the etiology of breast cancer is unknown. Several published epidemiological studies have documented an association between a modest increase in the risk of developing breast cancer and the use of hormone replacement therapy in menopause when given for periods exceeding 5 years. Information is still lacking to show whether the risks of combination estrogen-progestin therapy differ from those of estrogen used alone. There is a need for caution in prescribing estrogens for women with a strong family history of breast cancer or who present breast nodules, fibrocystic disease of the breast, or abnormal mammograms. Other known risk factors for the development of breast cancer such as nulliparity, obesity, early menarche, late age at full term pregnancy and at menopause should also be evaluated. It is recommended that a mammography be performed before starting treatment and repeated at regular intervals in patients at high risk for breast cancer.

The overall benefits and possible risks of hormone replacement therapy should be fully considered and discussed with patients. Instructions for self-examination of the breasts should be included in this counselling.

Contact sensitization is known to occur with topical applications. Although it is extremely rare, patients who develop contact sensitization to any component of the patch should be warned that a severe hypersensitivity reaction may occur with continuing exposure to the causative agent.

Benign hepatic adenomas have been associated with the use of combined estrogen and progestin oral contraceptives. Although benign and rare, these tumors may rupture and cause death from intra-abdominal hemorrhage. Such lesions have not yet been reported in association with other estrogen or progestin preparations, but they should be considered if abdominal pain and tenderness, abdominal mass, or hypovolemic shock occurs in patients receiving estrogen. Hepatocellular carcinoma has also been reported in women taking estrogen-containing oral contraceptives. The causal relationship of this malignancy to these drugs is not known.

Precautions: Pre-existing uterine leiomyoma may increase in size during estrogen use. Growth, pain or tenderness of uterine leiomyoma requires discontinuation of medication.

Symptoms of physical findings associated with a previous diagnosis of endometriosis may reappear or become aggravated with estrogen use.

Estrogens may cause fluid retention. Therefore, particular caution is indicated in cardiac or renal dysfunction, epilepsy or asthma.

Because the prolonged use of estrogens influences the metabolism of calcium or phosphorus, estrogens should be used with caution in patients with metabolic and malignant bone diseases associated with hypercalcemia and in patients with renal insufficiency.

In patients with a history of jaundice during pregnancy, there is an increased risk that jaundice will recur with the use of estrogen-containing oral contraceptives. If jaundice develops with the use of estrogens, the drug should be discontinued while the cause is investigated.

Women using oral estrogen and progestin contraceptives sometimes experience increased blood pressure which, in most cases, returns to normal upon discontinuing the drug. This may occur with the use of oral estrogens during menopause and blood pressure should be monitored during estrogen use. Elevation of blood pressure in previously normotensive or hypertensive patients should be evaluated and estrogen therapy may have to be discontinued.

A worsening of glucose tolerance has been observed in a significant percentage of patients on estrogen-containing oral contraceptives. Therefore, diabetic patients or those with a predisposition to diabetes should be observed closely to detect any alterations in carbohydrate or lipid metabolism, especially in triglyceride blood levels.

When liver or endocrine tests are indicated, the laboratory should be advised of the patient's therapy before specimens are forwarded.

Studies have reported a 2-to 4-fold increase in the risk of gallbladder disease requiring surgery in women receiving postmenopausal estrogens.

Drug Interactions: Estrogens may diminish the effectiveness of anticoagulants, antidiabetic and antihypertensive agents.

Preparations inducing liver enzymes (e.g., barbiturates, hydantoins, carbamazepine, meprobamate, phenylbutazone or rifampin) may interfere with the activity of orally administered estrogens. The extent of interference with transdermally administered estradiol-17β is not known.

Laboratory Tests: The results of certain endocrine and liver function tests may be affected by estrogen-containing products: increased sulfobromophthalein retention; increased prothrombin time and partial thromboplastin time; increased levels of fibrinogen and fibrinogen activity; increased coagulation factors VII, VIII, IX, X; increased norepinephrine-induced platelet aggregability; decreased antithrombin III; increased thyroxine-binding globulin (TBG), leading to increased circulating total thyroid hormone (T_4) as measured by column or radioimmunoassay; free T_3 resin uptake is decreased, reflecting the elevated TBG; free T_4 concentration is unaltered; other binding proteins may be elevated in serum, i.e., corticosteroid binding globulin (CBG), sex hormone-binding globulin (SHBG), leading to increased circulating corticosteroids and sex steroids respectively; free or biologically active hormone concentrations are unchanged; reduced response to the Metopirone test; reduced serum folate concentration; increased serum triglyceride and phospholipid concentration.

With transdermally administered estradiol-17β, no effect on fibrinogen, antithrombin III, TBG, CBG or SHBG and decreases in serum triglycerides have been observed.

The results of the above laboratory tests should not be considered reliable unless therapy has been discontinued for 2 to 4 months. The pathologist should be informed that the patient is receiving estrogen therapy when relevant specimens are submitted.

Adverse Effects: See Warnings and Precautions regarding the potential for induction of neoplasia and other effects of estrogens.

The most commonly reported adverse reaction to Climara in clinical trials was skin irritation at the application site. In 2 controlled clinical studies, the overall rate of discontinuation due to skin irritation at the application site was 6.8% (7.9% for the Climara 50 system and 5.3% for the Climara 100 system) compared with 11.5% for the placebo system.

The following additional adverse reactions have been reported with Climara and estrogens in general:

Genitourinary: changes in vaginal bleeding pattern and abnormal withdrawal bleeding or flow, breakthrough bleeding, spotting, increase in size of uterine leiomyomata, vaginal candidiasis, change in amount of cervical secretion, endometrial hyperplasia, premenstrual-like syndrome, reactivation of endometriosis, changes in cervical erosion, dysuria, cystitis.

Breasts: pain, tenderness, enlargement.

Gastrointestinal: nausea, vomiting, abdominal cramps, bloating, cholestatic jaundice, increased incidence of gallbladder disease.

Dermatological/Hypersensitivity: allergic contact dermatitis, reversible post-inflammatory pigmentation, general pruritus and exanthema, loss of scalp hair, chloasma, pigmentation of the skin, erythema nodosum, erythema multiforme, hemorrhagic skin eruptions, precipitation or aggravation of porphyria cutanea tarda in predisposed individuals.

Isolated cases of anaphylactoid reactions (some of the patients had a history of previous allergy or allergic disorders).

Eyes: steepening of corneal curvature, intolerance to contact lenses.

CNS: headache, migraine, dizziness, mental depression, chorea, neuro-ocular lesions (e.g., retinal thrombosis, optic neuritis).

Cardiovascular/Hematologic: palpitation, isolated cases of thrombophlebitis, pulmonary embolism and cerebral thrombosis, exacerbations of varicose veins, increase in blood pressure, coronary thrombosis, altered coagulation tests.

Miscellaneous: increase or decrease in weight, reduced carbohydrate tolerance, sodium retention, aggravation of porphyria, edema, changes in libido, musculoskeletal pain.

Overdose: Symptoms and Treatment: Overdosage with transdermal application of estradiol is unlikely. Serious ill effects have not been reported following acute ingestion of large doses of estrogen-containing products by young children. Overdosage of estrogen may cause nausea and vomiting, and withdrawal bleeding may occur in females. Symptomatic treatment should be given.

Dosage: In women who are not currently taking oral estrogens, treatment with estradiol-17β transdermal system can be initiated at once. In women who are currently taking oral estrogens, treatment with estradiol-17β transdermal system can be initiated on reappearance of menopausal symptoms, following discontinuation of oral therapy.

Therapy with estradiol-17β transdermal system is usually administered in a cyclic schedule (e.g., 3 weeks of therapy followed by 1 week without). In women with an intact uterus, a progestin should be sequentially coadministered for 12 to 14 days every month at a dose sufficient to prevent overstimulation of endometrial tissue. Unexpected or abnormal vaginal bleeding in such patients is an indication for prompt diagnostic measures. The lowest clinically effective (relief of symptoms) dose of each hormone should be used.

Continuous treatment at the lowest effective dose may be given to postmenopausal hysterectomized women.

Initiation of Therapy: Two Climara systems are available: Climara 50 (0.05 mg/day) and Climara 100 (0.1 mg/day). Treatment is usually initiated with Climara 50 applied to the skin once-weekly. The dose should be adjusted as necessary to control symptoms. Clinical response at the lowest effective dose should be the guide for establishing administration of Climara. Attempts to taper or discontinue the medication should be made at 3- to 6-month intervals.

Patch Application: The physician should discuss the most appropriate placement of the patch with the patient. Immediately after removal of a patch from the pouch and removal of the protective liner, the adhesive side of the Climara patch should be placed on a clean, dry area of intact skin. The area selected should not be oily, damaged or irritated, and not exposed to the sun. The site selected should also be one at which little wrinkling of the skin occurs during movement of the body, preferably the buttocks, lower abdomen or hip. The patch may also be placed on the side or lower back. The patch should be placed consistently on the same area of the body with each application (e.g., either the buttocks, lower abdomen, hip, side or lower back). Experience to date has shown that less irritation of the skin occurs on the buttocks than on other sites of application. Therefore, it is advisable to apply the patch to the buttocks. The waistline should be avoided, since tight clothing may dislodge the patch. The patch should be pressed firmly in place with the palm of the hand, making sure there is good contact, especially around the edges. In the event that a patch should fall off, it can be reapplied. If it fails to adhere then a new patch may be applied. In either case, the original treatment schedule should be continued. Patches should not be applied to the same skin site twice in succession.

Climara must not be applied to the breasts to avoid potentially harmful effects on the breast tissue.

Coadministration of Progestins: Studies of the addition of a progestin for 7 days or more days of estrogen administration have reported a lowered incidence of endometrial hyperplasia. Histological and biochemical studies of the endometrium suggest that at least 10 but most probably 12 to 14 days of progestin are needed to provide maximal maturation of the endometrium and to eliminate any hyperplastic changes. Whether this will provide protection from endometrial carcinoma has not been clearly established.

Wide interpatient variation in absorption occurs with progestins. The adequacy of the dose of progestin can be assessed by the bleeding patterns. Bleeding before day 11 of progestin administration indicates inadequate secretory transformation and the need for a higher dose of progestin.

The following regimens have been shown, in general, to produce histological and biochemical changes with uniform secretory pattern in the endometrium: norethindrone 0.7 mg/day orally administered sequentially for 12 days each cycle; medroxyprogesterone acetate (MPA) 10 mg/day orally administered sequentially for 12 days each cycle.

There are possible additional risks that may be associated with the inclusion of a progestin in estrogen replacement regimens. The potential risks include adverse effects on carbohydrate and lipid metabolism, mood changes and edema. The choice and dose of progestin may be important in minimizing these adverse effects and may differ among women.

Information for the Patient: See Blue Section—Information for the Patient "Climara".

Supplied: The Climara system is composed of 2 layers: a translucent polyethylene film with an acrylate adhesive matrix containing estradiol hemihydrate (Ph. Eur.) A protective liner is attached to the adhesive surface and must be removed before the system can be used. Other system components: low density polyethylene backing polyester film (release liner).

Climara 50: Each translucent 12.5 cm^2 system contains: estradiol hemihydrate 3.9 mg (Ph. Eur.) and provides controlled delivery of estradiol-17β 0.05 mg/day to the patient. Nonmedicinal ingredients: ethyl oleate, glyceryl monolaurate, isopropyl myristate, acrylate copolymer: acrylamide, isooctyl acrylate, vinyl acetate copolymer. Packages of 4.

Climara 100: Each translucent 25 cm^2 system contains: estradiol hemihydrate 7.8 mg (Ph. Eur.) and provides controlled delivery of estradiol-17β 0.1 mg/day to the patient. Nonmedicinal ingredients: ethyl oleate, glyceryl monolaurate, isopropyl myristate, acrylate copolymer: acrylamide, isooctyl acrylate, vinyl acetate copolymer. Packages of 4.

Store between 15 and 30°C. Store in sealed pouch. Apply immediately upon removal from the protective pouch. **Keep out of the reach of children and pets before and after use.**

(Shown in Product Recognition Section)

New Product 1998

CLINDAMYCIN PHOSPHATE INJECTION ℞

Abbott

Antibiotic

Supplied: Vials: Each mL of solution contains: clindamycin phosphate equivalent to clindamycin 150 mg. Each mL also contains: disodium edetate 0.5 mg (as stabilizer) and benzyl alcohol 9.45 mg (as preservative). It may also contain sodium hydroxide and/or hydrochloric acid for pH adjustment. pH is 6.4 (5.5 to 7.0). Vials of 60 mL.

Fliptop Vials: Each mL contains: clindamycin phosphate equivalent to clindamycin 150 mg. Each mL also contains: disodium edetate 0.5 mg (as stabilizer) and benzyl alcohol 9.45 mg (as preservative). It may also contain sodium hydroxide and/or hydrochloric acid for pH adjustment. pH is 6.4 (5.5 to 7.0). Fliptop vials of 2, 4 and 6 mL. For i.m. or i.v. use. These presentations must be diluted prior to i.v. use.

Store at room temperature (15 to 25°C). Protect from freezing and excessive heat.

CLOBAZAM ℞

General Monograph, CPhA

see BENZODIAZEPINES

CLOBETASOL ℞

General Monograph, CPhA

see CORTICOSTEROIDS: TOPICAL

CLOBETASONE ℞

General Monograph, CPhA

see CORTICOSTEROIDS: TOPICAL

CLOMID® ℞

Hoechst Marion Roussel

Clomiphene Citrate

Ovulatory Agent

Pharmacology: Clomiphene is an orally-administered, nonsteroidal agent which may induce ovulation in anovulatory women in appropriately selected cases. The ovulatory response to cyclic clomiphene therapy appears to be mediated through increased output of pituitary gonadotropins, which in turn stimulate the maturation and endocrine activity of the ovarian follicle and the subsequent development and function of the corpus luteum. The role of the pituitary is indicated by increased urinary excretion of gonadotropins and by the response of the ovary, as manifested by increased urinary estrogen excretion. Antagonism of competitive inhibition of endogenous estrogen may play a role in the action of clomiphene on the pituitary.

Clomiphene is a drug of considerable pharmacologic potency. Its administration should be preceded by careful evaluation and selection of the patient, and must be accompanied by close attention to the timing of the dose. With conservative selection and management of the patient, clomiphene has been demonstrated to be a useful therapy for the anovulatory patient.

Based on studies with C-14 labelled clomiphene, the drug is readily absorbed orally in humans, and is excreted principally in the feces. Excretion of C-14 averaged 51% of the dose after 5 days in 6 subjects given clomiphene C-14. After i.v. administration, 37% was excreted in 5 days. Since C-14 appeared in the feces 6 weeks after administration, available data suggested that the remaining drug/metabolites were being slowly excreted from a sequestered enterohepatic recirculation pool.

Indications: For induction of ovulation in patients with persistent ovulatory dysfunction who desire pregnancy. The work-up and treatment of candidates for clomiphene therapy should be supervised by physicians experienced in management of gynecologic or endocrine disorders. Patients should be chosen for therapy with clomiphene only after careful diagnostic evaluation. The work-up of the patient must begin with a careful and detailed history of menstrual and reproductive function, and a complete physical examination. It should be followed by a selective and careful laboratory investigation based on historical and physical findings.

The following considerations are appropriate: If any doubt exists as to the presence of early pregnancy, clomiphene therapy should be withheld until a diagnosis of pregnancy has been excluded.

The diagnosis of ovulatory dysfunction should be established by such standard techniques as basal body temperature curves, serial vaginal smears, cervical mucus, endometrial biopsy, and pregnanediol determination.

Appropriate diagnostic measures should be undertaken to exclude primary pituitary failure or primary ovarian failure. Intact pituitary and ovaries are required for successful therapy. Ovulatory dysfunction in the presence of abnormally high levels of pituitary gonadotropins is indicative of ovarian failure, and patients in this category cannot be expected to respond to clomiphene. Adequacy of endogenous estrogen, as estimated by vaginal smears, cervical mucus, endometrial biopsy, or urinary estrogen determination, furnishes a measure of ovarian function and indirectly of pituitary function. Bleeding after progesterone administration (progesterone alone, not combined with estrogen) furnishes evidence of an adequate level of endogenous estrogen. A good level of endogenous estrogen provides a favorable prognosis for treatment with clomiphene. A reduced estrogen level, although less favorable, does not always preclude successful therapy.

Mechanical impediments to conception, such as tubal obstruction, should be excluded or adequately treated, before undertaking clomiphene therapy.

When disorders such as diabetes, adrenal disease, or thyroid disease are identified during the investigation, specific treatment should be undertaken and subfertility therapy reconsidered only after the underlying disorder has been adequately treated. Clomiphene cannot be expected to substitute for specific therapy of these conditions.

The husband's potential fertility should be ascertained by semen analysis and other indicated examination.

Patients with abnormal or excessive bleeding should have particularly careful evaluation prior to clomiphene therapy. It is most important to ensure that neoplastic lesions are not overlooked.

Clinical evaluation of liver function should always precede clomiphene therapy.

Contraindications: *Pregnancy:* Although no causative evidence of a deleterious effect of clomiphene therapy on the human fetus has been seen, such evidence in regard to the rat and the rabbit has been presented. **Therefore, clomiphene should not be administered during pregnancy. To avoid inadvertent clomiphene administration during early pregnancy, careful pelvis examination must be done prior to each course of therapy, the basal body temperature must be recorded throughout all treatment cycles, and the patient should be carefully observed to determine whether ovulation occurs.** If the basal body temperature following clomiphene is biphasic and is not followed by menses, the patient should be examined carefully for the presence of an ovarian cyst and should have a pregnancy test. The next course of therapy should be delayed until the possibility of pregnancy has been excluded.

Liver Disease: Clomiphene therapy is contraindicated in patients with liver disease or a liver dysfunction.

Abnormal bleeding: Clomiphene is contraindicated in patients with abnormal bleeding of undetermined origin. Clomiphene is not indicated for the management of menstrual disorders.

Warnings: Visual Symptoms: Patients should be advised that blurring or other visual symptoms may occasionally occur during therapy with clomiphene. Patients should be warned that visual symptoms may render such activities as driving a car or operating machinery more hazardous than usual, particularly under conditions of variable lighting. The significance of these visual symptoms is not yet understood (see Adverse Effects). If the patient has any visual symptoms, treatment should be discontinued and complete ophthalmologic evaluation carried out.

Precautions: Diagnosis Prior to Clomiphene Therapy: Careful attention should be given to diagnosis in candidates for clomiphene therapy. Complete pelvic examination including cervical cytology is mandatory prior to treatment, and pelvic examination should be repeated before each subsequent course. Clomiphene should not be given in the presence of an ovarian cyst, since further enlargement of the ovary may occur.

Patients in later reproductive life have a greater tendency to endometrial carcinoma as well as a higher incidence of anovulatory disorders. Dilatation and curettage should always be done for diagnosis before starting clomiphene therapy in such patients. If abnormal bleeding is present, full diagnostic measures are mandatory.

Overstimulation of the Ovary During Clomiphene Therapy: In order to minimize the hazard associated with the occasional abnormal ovarian enlargement associated with clomiphene therapy (see Adverse Effects), the lowest dose consistent with expectation of good results should be used. The patient should be advised of the possibility of ovarian cyst formation and should be instructed to return for repeat pelvic examination between 2 and 3 weeks after starting each course of treatment. Some patients with polycystic ovary syndrome who are unusually sensitive to gonadotropin may have an exaggerated response to usual doses of clomiphene. It should be borne in mind that maximal enlargement of the ovary, whether physiologic or abnormal, does not occur until several days after discontinuation of the recommended dose of clomiphene. The

Clomid (cont'd)

patient who complains of pelvic pain after receiving clomiphene should be examined with care. If enlargement of the ovary occurs, additional clomiphene therapy should not be given until the ovaries have returned to pretreatment size, and the dosage or duration of the next course should be reduced. Experience has shown that the ovarian enlargement and cyst formation associated with clomiphene therapy regress spontaneously within a few days or weeks after discontinuing treatment. **Unless surgical indication for laparotomy exists, such cystic enlargement should always be managed conservatively.**

Multiple Pregnancy: The incidence of multiple pregnancy (including triplets, quadruplets and quintuplets) has been increased up to tenfold when conception takes place during a cycle in which clomiphene therapy is given. During clinical studies 353 infants were born of 163 multiple pregnancies. Of these infants, 293 survived, including 27 of 62 infants from triplet, quadruplet, and quintuplet pregnancies. The patient and her husband should be advised of the frequency and potential hazards of multiple pregnancy before starting treatment.

Adverse Effects: At recommended dosage, side effects are not prominent and infrequently interfere with treatment. Side effects tend to be dose related, occurring more frequently at the higher doses and longer duration of treatment courses used in some earlier studies. The more common side effects include hot flashes, abdominal discomfort (distention, bloating, pain, or soreness), ovarian enlargement, and visual blurring.

The vasomotor symptoms resembling menopausal "hot flashes" are not usually severe and disappear promptly after treatment is discontinued. Abdominal symptoms may be most often related to ovulatory (mittelschmerz) or premenstrual phenomena, or to ovarian enlargement. Nausea, and rarely vomiting, constipation or diarrhea have been described less often.

At recommended dosage, abnormal ovarian enlargement (see also Precautions) is infrequent, although the usual cyclic variation in ovarian size may be exaggerated. Similarly, cyclic ovarian pain (mittelschmerz) may be accentuated. With higher or prolonged dosage, more frequent ovarian enlargement and cyst formation (usually luteal) may occur, and the luteal phase of the cycle may be prolonged. Rare instances of massive ovarian enlargement are on record. Southam and Janovski described such an instance in a patient with polycystic ovary syndrome whose clomiphene therapy consisted of 100 mg daily for 14 days. Abnormal ovarian enlargement usually regresses spontaneously, and while laparotomy was performed on several such patients, investigators believe most of these patients should have been treated conservatively.

Visual symptoms (see also Warnings for further recommendations) described usually as "blurring" or spots or flashes, disappear within a few days or weeks after clomiphene is discontinued. These symptoms appear to be due to intensification and prolongation of after-images. Symptoms often first appear or are accentuated with exposure to a more brightly lit environment. While measured visual acuity has not generally been affected, one patient taking 200 mg daily developed visual blurring on the seventh day of treatment, which progressed to severe diminution of visual acuity by the tenth day. No other abnormality was found and the visual acuity returned to normal on the third day after treatment was stopped. Another patient treated during clinical studies developed scotomata during prolonged clomiphene administration, which disappeared on placebo. Monolateral exophthalmos associated with laboratory evidence of hyperthyroidism was observed in 1 patient concomitant with completion of the third course of clomiphene.

In a 34-year-old patient who had taken 3 courses of clomiphene, slit-lamp microscopic examination showed a mild amount of posterior cortical subcapsular opacity in each eye. Ophthalmoscopic examination revealed normal findings. The ocular diagnosis was posterior cortical senile cataracts.

Other less frequently reported symptoms during therapy have included nausea or vomiting, increased nervous tension, depression, fatigue, dizziness or lightheadedness, insomnia, headache, breast soreness, heavier menses, intermenstrual spotting, urticaria or allergic dermatitis, weight gain, and increased urinary frequency or volume. Moderate, reversible hair loss has been reported in a few patients, primarily on prolonged continuous therapy.

Clomiphene has not been reported to cause significant abnormality in the hematologic or renal systems, in protein bound iodine, or in serum cholesterol. Analysis by gas liquid chromatography (GLC) of serum sterols from patients on prolonged, continuous administration of clomiphene yields a peak compatible with an elevated level of desmosterol. This peak is indicative of an interference with cholesterol synthesis. However, the serum sterol GLC pattern from patients receiving recommended doses of clomiphene is not significantly altered.

Sulfobromophthalein (BSP) retention of greater than 5% has been reported in 32 of 141 patients in whom it was measured, including 5 of 43 patients who received approximately the dose of clomiphene now recommended. Retention was usually minimal unless associated with prolonged continuous clomiphene administration or with apparently unrelated liver disease. In some patients, pre-existing BSP retention decreased even though clomiphene therapy was continued. Other liver function tests were usually normal. In a later study in which patients were given 6 consecutive monthly courses of clomiphene (100 mg daily for 3 days) or matching placebo, BSP tests were done on 94 patients. Values in excess of 5% retention were recorded in 11 patients, 6 of whom had received drug and 5 placebo. One patient developed jaundice on the nineteenth day of treatment (50 mg/day); liver biopsy revealed bile stasis without evidence of hepatitis. A male prison subject who received 200 mg daily for 77 days developed the clinical picture of infectious hepatitis; his cellmate was discovered to have had infectious hepatitis 4 months earlier.

Birth Defects: From 2 339 completed pregnancies associated with clomiphene administration, 58 birth defects have been reported. They have been reported in 4 conceptions in the abortion/stillbirth category, 14 of 353 infants from multiple pregnancies, and 39 of 1 676 infants from single pregnancies. Three live-born infants failed to survive.

Reported defects were congenital heart lesions (8 infants), Down's syndrome (5 infants), club foot (4 infants), congenital gut lesions (4 infants), hypospadias (3 infants), microcephaly (2 infants), harelip and cleft palate (2 infants), congenital hip (2 infants), hemangioma (2 infants), undescended testes (2 infants), polydactyly (both of twins), conjoined twins with teratomatous malformation, patent ductus arteriosus, amaurosis (blindness), arteriovenous fistula, inguinal hernia, umbilical hernia, syndactyly, pectus excavatum, myopathy, dermoid cyst of scalp, omphalocele, spina bifida occulta, icthyosis, persistent lingual frenulum, and 7 infants with multiple somatic defects.

Eight of the entire group of 58 infants were born to 7 of 153 mothers who received a course of clomiphene during the first 6 weeks after conception.

An interval of 4, 4, and 10 months respectively elapsed between the last clomiphene therapy and conception in 3 mothers. In a 4th mother conception occurred during a subsequent ovulation induced by gonadotropin therapy.

Ovarian Cancer: Ovarian cancer has been reported in a very small number of infertile women who have been treated with fertility drugs. A causal relationship between treatment with fertility drugs and ovarian cancer has not been established.

Overdose: Symptoms and Treatment: There is no known antidote but gastric lavage should be performed.

Dosage: General Considerations: The work-up and treatment of candidates for clomiphene therapy should be supervised by physicians experienced in management of gynecologic or endocrine disorders. Patients should be chosen for therapy with clomiphene only after careful diagnostic evaluation (see Indications). The plan of therapy should be outlined in advance. Impediments to achieving the goal of therapy must be excluded or adequately treated before beginning clomiphene. Many patients will respond to 50 mg daily for 5 days (see Recommended Dosage). In the determination of a recommended starting dose schedule, efficacy must be balanced against potential side effects. For example, the data available so far suggest that ovulation and pregnancy are slightly more attainable on 100 mg/day for 5 days than on 50 mg/day for 5 days. As the dosage is increased, however, ovarian overstimulation and other side effects may be expected to increase. Furthermore, although the data do not yet establish a relationship between dosage and multiple births, it would seem reasonable on pharmacologic grounds that such a relationship does exist.

For these reasons, it would seem prudent to begin the treatment of the usual patient with a lower dose, 50 mg daily for 5 days, and to increase the dose only in those patients who do not respond to the first course (see Recommended Dosage). Special care in dosage is particularly recommended if unusual sensitivity to pituitary gonadotropin is suspected, such as in patients with polycystic ovary syndrome.

Recommended Dosage: The recommended dose for the first course of clomiphene is 50 mg (1 tablet) daily for 5 days. Therapy may be started at any time in the patient who has had no recent uterine bleeding. If progestin-induced bleeding is planned, or if spontaneous uterine bleeding occurs prior to therapy, the regimen of 50 mg daily for 5 days should be started on or about the fifth day of the cycle. When ovulation occurs at this dosage, there is no advantage to increasing the dose in subsequent cycles of treatment.

If ovulation appears not to have occurred after the first course of therapy, a second course of 100 mg (two 50 mg tablets) daily as a single daily dose for 5 days should be given. This course may be started as early as 30 days after the previous one. **Increasing the dosage or duration of therapy beyond 100 mg/day for 5 days should never be undertaken.**

The majority of patients who are going to respond will respond to the first course of therapy, and 3 courses should constitute an adequate therapeutic trial. If ovulatory menses have not yet occurred, the diagnosis should be re-evaluated. Treatment beyond this is not recommended in the patient who does not exhibit evidence of ovulation.

Pregnancy: The importance of properly timed coitus cannot be over-emphasized. In most patients, ovulation appears to occur from 6 to 12 days after completion of therapy. For regularity of cyclic ovulatory response it is also important that each course of clomiphene be started on or about the fifth cycle day, once ovulation has been established. In common with other therapeutic modalities, clomiphene therapy follows the rule of diminishing returns, such that likelihood of conception diminishes with each succeeding course of therapy. If pregnancy has not been achieved after 3 ovulatory responses to clomiphene, further treatment is not recommended. Patients should be advised of the possibility of multiple pregnancy and its potential hazards if conception occurs during a cycle in which clomiphene is given.

Long-term Cyclic Therapy Not Recommended: Since the relative safety of long-term cyclic therapy has not yet been conclusively demonstrated, and since the majority of patients will ovulate following 3 courses, long-term cyclic therapy is not recommended.

Supplied: Each white scored tablet contains: clomiphene citrate USP 50 mg. Nonmedicinal ingredients: cornstarch, lactose, magnesium stearate and sucrose. Energy: 4.5 kJ (1.1 kcal)/tablet. Bottles of 50. Protect from light and moisture.

(Shown in Product Recognition Section)

CLONAPAM ℞
ICN

Clonazepam

Anticonvulsant

Supplied: 0.5 mg: Each round, biconvex, yellow tablet, scored on one side and embossed C31 on the other side, contains: clonazepam USP 0.5 mg. Nonmedicinal ingredients: sunset yellow FCF Aluminum Lake, lactose, magnesium stearate and pregelatinized starch. Bottles of 100 and 500.

1 mg: Each round, biconvex, green tablet, scored on one side and embossed C32 on the other side, contains: clonazepam USP 1 mg. Nonmedicinal ingredients: sunset yellow FCF Aluminum Lake, lactose, magnesium stearate and pregelatinized starch. Bottles of 100 and 500.

2 mg: Each round, biconvex, white tablet, scored on one side and embossed C33 on the other side, contains: clonazepam USP 2 mg. Nonmedicinal ingredients: sunset yellow FCF Aluminum Lake, lactose, magnesium stearate and pregelatinized starch. Bottles of 100 and 500.

CLONAZEPAM ℞
General Monograph, CPhA

see BENZODIAZEPINES

CLOPIXOL® ℞
CLOPIXOL-ACUPHASE® ℞
CLOPIXOL® DEPOT ℞
Lundbeck

Zuclopenthixol Dihydrochloride
Zuclopenthixol Acetate
Zuclopenthixol Decanoate

Antipsychotic

Pharmacology: Zuclopenthixol, a thioxanthene derivative, has high affinity for both dopamine D_1 receptors and dopamine D_2

receptors. Zuclopenthixol also has high affinity for α_1-adrenergic and 5-HT_2 receptors. It has weaker histamine H_1 receptor blocking activity, and even lower affinity for muscarinic cholinergic and α_2-adrenergic receptors.

Pharmacokinetics: The pharmacokinetics of zuclopenthixol appear to be linear over the dosage range studied. A strong correlation exists between dose and steady-state serum level, and between dose and area under the serum concentration time curve. The apparent volume of distribution is 20 L/kg. Protein binding is approximately 98%.

The metabolism of zuclopenthixol is mainly by sulfoxidation, side chain N-dealkylation and glucuronic acid conjugation. The metabolites are devoid of pharmacological activity. Zuclopenthixol is excreted mainly in feces with about 10% excreted in the urine. Approximately 0.1% of a dose is excreted unchanged in the urine. The systemic clearance is approximately 0.9 L/min.

Zuclopenthixol acetate and zuclopenthixol decanoate are long-acting forms of zuclopenthixol that have been made more lipophilic by esterification with acetic and decanoic acid, respectively. Both esters of zuclopenthixol are dissolved in fractionated coconut oil and when injected i.m., diffuse slowly from the oil depot to the body water phase where they are rapidly hydrolyzed to the active substance, zuclopenthixol. Once hydrolyzed, zuclopenthixol is distributed, metabolized and excreted as described.

Clopixol: Maximum serum concentrations of zuclopenthixol are reached in approximately 4 hours (range 2 to 12 hours) following administration. The elimination half-life is approximately 20 hours (range 12 to 28 hours). The mean steady-state serum level of zuclopenthixol corresponding to a daily 20 mg dose of zuclopenthixol dihydrochloride is about 13 ng/mL (33 nmol/L).

Clopixol-Acuphase: Maximum serum concentrations of zuclopenthixol are reached, on average, 24 to 48 hours after i.m. injection, followed by a gradual decline. Average maximum serum concentration of zuclopenthixol corresponding to a 100 mg i.m. dose of zuclopenthixol acetate is 41 ng/mL (102 nmol/L). Three days after injection, serum levels are approximately one-third the maximum.

Clopixol Depot: Maximum serum concentrations of zuclopenthixol are reached 3 to 7 days following i.m. injection. The serum concentration time curve declines exponentially with a half-life of 19 days, reflecting the rate of release from the oil depot. Zuclopenthixol decanoate, when given at a dose of 200 mg every 2 weeks, results, on average, in a steady-state zuclopenthixol serum concentration of approximately 10 ng/mL (25 nmol/L), when measured immediately prior to the next injection.

Indications: For the management of the manifestations of schizophrenia.

Clopixol-Acuphase is intended for the initial treatment of acute psychotic episodes or exacerbation of psychosis associated with schizophrenia. Clopixol Depot is intended for maintenance treatment. Clopixol tablets may be used during either phase.

Contraindications: Patients with: acute alcohol, barbiturate or opiate intoxication; CNS depression due to any cause, comatose states, suspected or established subcortical brain damage, circulatory collapse, blood dyscrasias or pheochromocytoma; known hypersensitivity to the thioxanthenes, zuclopenthixol or any of the excipients of the product.

Warnings: Neuroleptic Malignant Syndrome: Neuroleptic malignant syndrome (NMS) is a rare, sometimes fatal, neurological disorder that has been reported in association with antipsychotic drugs including zuclopenthixol (see Adverse Effects). NMS is characterized by hyperthermia, muscle rigidity, altered consciousness, and signs of autonomic instability including irregular blood pressure, tachycardia, cardiac arrhythmias and diaphoresis. Additional signs may include greatly elevated creatine phosphokinase, myoglobinuria and acute renal failure.

The management of NMS should include immediate discontinuation of all antipsychotic drugs including zuclopenthixol, intensive monitoring of symptoms, and treatment of any associated medical problems. There is no general agreement about specific pharmacological treatment for NMS. If a patient requires antipsychotic drug treatment after recovery from NMS, the reintroduction of therapy should be carefully considered, since recurrence of NMS has been reported.

Tardive Dyskinesia: Tardive dyskinesia is a potentially irreversible neurological syndrome associated with the use of antipsychotic drugs, including zuclopenthixol (see Adverse Effects). It is characterized by stereotypical, repetitive, involuntary movements of the jaw, tongue and in some cases, the extremities. Tardive dyskinesia occurs more frequently in elderly patients. However, patients of any age can be affected. The risk of developing tardive dyskinesia, and the chance of it becoming irreversible, are believed to increase as the duration of treatment and the cumulative dose of antipsychotic drugs increase. However, the syndrome can develop, although less commonly, after relatively brief periods of treatment at low doses. Tardive dyskinesia may remit, partially or completely, if antipsychotic drug treatment is withdrawn. Antipsychotic drug treatment itself, however, may suppress the signs and symptoms of tardive dyskinesia, thereby masking the underlying process.

In view of these considerations, zuclopenthixol should be prescribed in a manner that is most likely to minimize the risk of tardive dyskinesia. The lowest effective dose and the shortest duration of treatment should be used, and treatment should be discontinued at the earliest opportunity, or if a satisfactory response cannot be obtained. If the signs and symptoms of tardive dyskinesia appear during treatment, discontinuation of zuclopenthixol should be considered.

Precautions: Occupational Hazards: Since sedation is known to occur with zuclopenthixol, patients should be cautioned against performing activities requiring a high degree of mental alertness and physical coordination (such as driving a car or operating machinery) until the effect of the drug is determined.

Anticholinergic Effects: Although its anticholinergic effects are weak, zuclopenthixol use should be avoided in patients who are known to have, or suspected of having narrow angle glaucoma. Zuclopenthixol may potentiate anticholinergic effects of concurrent medications.

Endocrine Effects: Antipsychotic drugs elevate prolactin levels with the effect persisting during chronic administration. Since tissue culture experiments indicate that approximately one third of human breast cancers are prolactin dependent, in vitro, zuclopenthixol should only be administered to patients with previously detected breast cancer if the benefits outweigh the potential risks. Caution should also be exercised when considering zuclopenthixol treatment in patients with pituitary tumors. Possible manifestations associated with elevated prolactin levels are amenorrhea, galactorrhea and menorrhagia (see Adverse Effects).

Chronic administration of zuclopenthixol (30 mg/kg/day for 2 years) in rats resulted in small, but significant, increases in the incidence of thyroid parafollicular carcinomas and, in females, of mammary adenocarcinomas and of pancreatic islet cell adenomas and carcinomas. An increase in the incidence of mammary adenocarcinomas is a common finding for D_2 antagonists which increase prolactin secretion when administered to rats. An increase in the incidence of pancreatic islet cell tumors has been observed for some other D_2 antagonists. The physiological differences between rats and humans with regard to prolactin make the clinical significance of these findings unclear.

Antiemetic Effects: An antiemetic effect of zuclopenthixol has been observed in animals. Since this effect may also occur in man, zuclopenthixol may mask signs of toxicity due to overdosage of other drugs, or may mask symptoms of disease such as brain tumor or intestinal obstruction.

Photosensitivity Reactions: Photosensitivity reactions, pigmentary retinopathy and lenticular and corneal deposits have been reported with related drugs. Lens opacity has been reported rarely with zuclopenthixol.

Seizures: Zuclopenthixol should be used with caution in patients with a history of convulsive disorders, as drugs of this class are known to lower seizure threshold.

Cardiovascular Disease: Caution should be used when using zuclopenthixol in patients with advanced cardiovascular disease or in those at risk of developing conduction abnormalities.

Pregnancy: The safe use of zuclopenthixol during pregnancy has not been established. Zuclopenthixol was not teratogenic in either rats or rabbits, however, increases in the number of stillbirths, reduced pup survival and delayed development of pups were seen in rats. The clinical significance of these findings is unclear. It has been shown that zuclopenthixol crosses the placenta of mice. Zuclopenthixol should not be administered during pregnancy unless the expected benefit to the patient outweighs the potential risk to the fetus.

Lactation: Zuclopenthixol is excreted in human milk with an average milk/serum concentration ratio of approximately 0.3. Because the safe use of zuclopenthixol during lactation has not been established, it is recommended that breast-feeding should not be undertaken in women receiving zuclopenthixol.

Children: The safety and efficacy of zuclopenthixol in children under the age of 18 years has not been established; therefore, its use is not recommended.

Geriatrics: The pharmacokinetics, safety, and efficacy of zuclopenthixol in elderly patients with schizophrenia has not been systematically evaluated in clinical trials. Caution should thus be exercised in dose selection for an elderly patient, recognizing the more frequent hepatic, renal and cardiac dysfunction in this population.

Impaired Liver Function: The use of zuclopenthixol in patients with impaired liver function has not been studied. As zuclopenthixol is extensively metabolized by the liver and primarily excreted in the bile (see Pharmacology, Pharmacokinetics), caution should be exercised in dose selection for patients with this condition.

Impaired Renal Function: The use of zuclopenthixol in patients with impaired renal function has not been studied. Caution should thus be exercised in dose selection for patients with this condition.

Drug Interactions: Zuclopenthixol enhances the sedative response to alcohol and the effects of barbiturates and other CNS depressants. It should not be administered with high doses of hypnotics due to the possibility of potentiation.

Zuclopenthixol should not be given concomitantly with guanethidine or similar acting compounds, since antipsychotic drugs such as zuclopenthixol may block the antihypertensive effect of these compounds.

Many antipsychotic and antidepressant drugs may mutually inhibit the metabolism of each other.

Concomitant use of metoclopramide or piperazine increases the risk of extrapyramidal symptoms.

Zuclopenthixol may antagonize the effects of levodopa and dopamine agonists.

Patients with Parkinson's Disease: Zuclopenthixol should be used with caution in patients with Parkinsonism, as it is known that dopamine antagonists such as zuclopenthixol, can cause a deterioration of the disease.

Adverse Effects: Adverse events were recorded in controlled and uncontrolled European and Canadian clinical trials in which 1 922 patients were treated with either zuclopenthixol dihydrochloride, zuclopenthixol acetate or zuclopenthixol decanoate.

The most common adverse events reported were drowsiness, fatigue, dizziness and extrapyramidal symptoms.

All adverse events reported in clinical trials at an incidence of greater than 1% are listed in Table I by formulation.

Table I—Clopixol

Treatment Emergent Adverse Events Reported at a Frequency of >1% from the Combined European and Canadian Clinical Trial Database

	Number of Patients (Percentage of Patients)		
Adverse Event[a]	**Tablet (n=523)**	**Acuphase (n=588)**	**Depot (n=811)**
Body as a Whole			
Asthenia/Fatigue	79 (15.1)	46 (7.8)[b]	111 (13.7)[b]
Malaise	12 (2.3)	—	—
Pain	9 (1.7)	—	—
Paleness	6 (1.1)	—	—
Syncope	6 (1.2)	—	5 (0.6)
Psychiatric			
Somnolence/ Drowsiness	169 (32.3)[b]	95 (16.2)[b,c]	159 (19.6)[b]
Anxiety/Nervousness	88 (16.9)	24 (4.1)	70 (8.6)
Insomnia	85 (16.2)	27 (4.6)[b]	84 (10.4)[b]
Agitation	52 (9.9)	7 (1.2)[b]	11 (1.4)
Depression	41 (7.8)	18 (3.1)	59 (7.3)
Concentration Impaired	40 (7.6)	15 (2.6)	32 (3.9)[b]
Anorexia	20 (3.8)	—	12 (1.5)
Hallucination	18 (3.4)	—	—
Apathy	17 (3.2)	14 (2.4)	7 (0.9)
Confusion	14 (2.7)	1 (0.2)	3 (0.4)
Amnesia	13 (2.5)	12 (2.0)	13 (1.6)
Dreaming Abnormal	12 (2.3)	12 (2.0)	12 (1.5)
Appetite Increased	5 (1.0)	1 (0.2)	18 (2.2)
Neurological			
Hypertonia	98 (18.7)	150 (25.5)	37 (4.6)
Tremor	98 (18.7)	122 (20.7)[b]	68 (8.4)
Hyperkinesia (Akathisia)	71 (13.6)[b]	94 (16.0)[b]	107 (13.2)
Extrapyramidal Disorder	68 (13.0)	3 (0.5)	97 (12.0)
Dizziness	59 (11.3)	121 (20.6)	55 (6.8)[b]
Hypokinesia	39 (7.4)[b]	122 (20.7)[b]	82 (10.1)
Vertigo	27 (5.2)	6 (1.0)	16 (2.0)
Headache	26 (5.0)	8 (1.4)	43 (5.3)[b]
Dystonia	25 (4.8)	83 (14.1)	56 (6.9)
Dyskinesia Tardive	15 (2.9)	1 (0.2)	7 (0.9)
Gait Abnormal	11 (2.1)	—	6 (0.7)

Clopixol (cont'd)

Table I—Clopixol (cont'd)

Neurological Disorder NOS	9 (1.7)	—	1 (0.1)
Paresthesia	6 (1.1)	18 (3.1)	15 (1.8)
Dyskinesia	—	1 (0.2)	10 (1.2)
Gastrointestinal			
Mouth Dry	79 (15.1)	148 (25.2)	106 (13.1)[b]
Constipation	41 (7.8)	4 (0.7)[b]	51 (6.3)[b]
Salivation Increased	40 (7.6)	58 (9.9)	52 (6.4)
Vomiting	17 (3.2)	6 (1.0)	17 (2.1)
Gastrointestinal Disorder NOS	15 (2.9)	1 (0.2)	10 (1.2)
Nausea	10 (1.9)	4 (0.7)	11 (1.4)
Diarrhea	4 (0.8)	4 (0.7)	9 (1.1)
Dyspepsia	—	—	10 (1.2)
Cardiovascular			
Tachycardia	19 (3.6)	58 (9.9)	21 (2.6)
Postural Hypotension	13 (2.5)	2 (0.2)	—
Arterial Hypotension	9 (1.7)	—	—
Palpitation	7 (1.3)	—	15 (1.8)
Musculoskeletal System			
Myalgia	—	—	10 (1.2)
Skin and Appendages			
Sweating Increased	16 (3.0)	7 (1.2)	47 (5.8)[b]
Pruritus	—	1 (0.2)	17 (2.1)
Seborrhea	8 (1.5)	—	2 (0.2)
Skin Disorder	7 (1.3)	—	
Metabolic and Nutritional			
Weight Increase	20 (3.8)	—	17 (2.1)
Weight Decrease	17 (3.2)	—	14 (1.7)
Thirst	5 (1.0)	—	17 (2.1)[b]
Vision			
Accommodation Abnormal	29 (5.5)	65 (11.0)	33 (4.1)
Vision Abnormal	19 (3.6)	—	17 (2.1)[b]
Urinary			
Micturition Disorder	16 (3.0)	3 (0.5)	26 (3.2)
Reproductive			
Libido Decreased	17 (3.2)	1 (0.2)	11 (1.4)
Menstrual Disorder	5 (2.2)	—	12 (4.3)[b]
Ejaculation Failure	1 (0.4)	1 (0.3)	8 (1.8)[b]
Anorgasmia Female	1 (0.4)	—	3 (1.1)

[a] The incidence of adverse events is not directly comparable across formulations, as distinct clinical trials were conducted for each dosage form. Trial duration varied considerably between formulations (i.e., 2 to 12 weeks for Tablets; 3 to 9 days for Acuphase; and 4 to 52 weeks for Depot).
[b] Incidence in Canadian studies at least 10 percentage points higher than the combined European and Canadian incidence.
[c] Somnolence was not rated as an adverse event in many European Acuphase trials, as sedation was considered a therapeutic effect. Therefore, the incidence of this event is considered under-represented for the Acuphase formulation.

Adverse events reported in clinical trials, occurring at rates of 1% or less are summarized below for all three formulations together: Body as a Whole: allergic reaction, application site disorder, arthritis, back pain, chest pain, precordial chest pain, conjunctivitis, faintness, fever, hot flushes and toothache.
Psychiatric: drug dependence, excitability, irritability, increased libido, melancholia and paroniria.
Neurological: acute dyskinesia, ataxia, convulsions, hyperreflexia, hypotonia, migraine, oculogyric crisis, and speech disorder.
Gastrointestinal: abdominal pain, dysphagia, gastric ulcer, glossitis and meteorism.
Cardiovascular: hypotension.
Respiratory: dyspnea, nasal congestion, pharyngitis and rhinitis.
Hematological: purpura.
Special Senses: mydriasis, hyperacusis and tinnitus.
Skin and Appendages: dermatitis, photosensitivity reaction, abnormal pigmentation, rash, erythematous rash and psoriasiform rash.
Urinary: polyuria, urinary incontinence, urinary infection and urinary retention.
Reproductive: erectile dysfunction, galactorrhea, gynecomastia and dry vagina.

In the worldwide postmarketing surveillance database (1964 to 1993; >1 000 000 treated; >80% of the database from Scandinavia, Netherlands, Switzerland and the UK) the following additional serious adverse events have been rarely reported: Neuroleptic Malignant Syndrome (57 cases) (see Warnings); apnea and respiratory depression (13 cases); sudden death (5 cases), agranulocytosis (5 cases).

Alterations in liver function, particularly increased bilirubin levels have occasionally been reported. Transient increases in ALT and ALP values may also occur. Transient, benign leukopenia has been reported rarely. Peripheral edema has occasionally been reported.

Overdose: Symptoms and Treatment: Although there have not been any cases of overdosage reported, the symptoms are likely to be somnolence, coma, extrapyramidal symptoms, convulsions, hypotension, shock, or hyper- or hypothermia.

There is no specific antidote for zuclopenthixol. Treatment should be symptomatic and supportive. Gastric lavage (after intubation, if the patient is unconscious) and administration of activated charcoal should be considered. Measures aimed at supporting the respiratory and cardiovascular systems should be instituted. Hypotension and circulatory collapse may be counteracted by use of i.v fluids. **Epinephrine must not be used as a further lowering of blood pressure may result.** In cases of severe extrapyramidal reactions, antiparkinsonian medication should be administered. Close monitoring and medical supervision should continue until the patient recovers.

In managing overdose, the physician should consider the possibility of multiple drug involvement.

Dosage: Clopixol: Dosage should be individualized according to the patient's condition. In general, small doses should be used initially and increased until an optimal response is obtained.

When initiating treatment with zuclopenthixol tablets, it is recommended that the drug be given in divided doses (b.i.d. or t.i.d.). During the maintenance phase of treatment, tablets may be given as a single nighttime dose.

For acute psychosis, the usual starting dose is 10 to 50 mg/day, which may be increased by 10 to 20 mg every 2 to 3 days, according to the patient's response. The usual therapeutic range is 20 to 60 mg daily. However, as with other antipsychotic drugs, some patients may require lower, while others may require higher dosage in order to obtain optimal benefit. Daily dosage higher than 100 mg is not recommended. For maintenance therapy, dosage should be reduced to the lowest level compatible with symptom control. The usual maintenance dose is 20 to 40 mg/day.

Clopixol-Acuphase: Zuclopenthixol acetate is intended for use during acute psychotic episodes or exacerbation of psychosis associated with schizophrenia, when compliance with oral medication may be unreliable. Zuclopenthixol acetate has an onset of action within 2 to 4 hours, and a duration of action of 2 to 3 days following a single i.m. injection. Significant dose-dependent sedation occurs within 2 hours of injection, usually reaching a maximum after 8 hours. Tolerance to the sedative effect may develop with repeated injection. Maximum serum concentration of zuclopenthixol are reached, on average, 24 to 36 hours after injection.

Dosage should be individually adjusted according to the patient's condition. The usual dose is 50 to 150 mg (1 to 3 mL) administered i.m. and repeated if necessary, at intervals of 2 to 3 days. Some patients may need an additional injection 1 or 2 days after the **first** injection.

Due to the delay in reaching peak zuclopenthixol blood levels and maximum pharmacologic effect, close supervision is required in order to minimize the risk of over-medication or insufficient suppression of psychotic symptoms.

Zuclopenthixol acetate is not intended for long-term use, and the duration of treatment should not exceed 2 weeks. The maximum cumulative dosage should not exceed 400 mg, and the number of injections should not exceed 4.

Following treatment with zuclopenthixol acetate, antipsychotic therapy, when indicated, should be continued with either oral or long-acting injectable antipsychotic medications such as zuclopenthixol dihydrochloride or zuclopenthixol decanoate, respectively. Tables II and III provide guidelines for dosage form conversion. The tablets should usually be started 2 to 3 days after the last injection of Clopixol-Acuphase. If Clopixol Depot is used for maintenance, it can be given concomitantly with the last injection of Clopixol-Acuphase (see Co-injection of Clopixol-Acuphase and Clopixol Depot).

Table II—Clopixol

Suggested Dose to be Used When Transferring Patients from Clopixol-Acuphase to Clopixol Tablets

Clopixol-Acuphase Dose	Clopixol Tablet Dose*
50 mg	20 mg daily
100 mg	40 mg daily
150 mg	60 mg daily

*Initial total daily dose usually given in divided dosages (see Dosage).

Table III—Clopixol

Suggested Dose to be Used When Transferring Patients from Clopixol-Acuphase to Clopixol Depot

Clopixol-Acuphase Dose	Clopixol Depot Dose*
50 mg	100 mg Q2 weekly
100 mg	200 mg Q2 weekly
150 mg	300 mg Q2 weekly

*See Dosage.

Clopixol Depot: Zuclopenthixol decanoate is intended for maintenance treatment of chronic schizophrenia in patients who have been stabilized with oral or other short-acting medication, and who might benefit from transfer to longer-acting injectable therapy.

Close supervision is required during the period following initiation of Depot treatment, in order to minimize the risk of over-medication or insufficient suppression of psychotic symptoms. Supplemental oral antipsychotic medication may be required in diminishing dosage during this period.

The usual maintenance dose is 150 to 300 mg i.m., every 2 to 4 weeks. Some patients may require higher or lower doses, or shorter intervals between doses.

During treatment with zuclopenthixol decanoate, the patient should be maintained at the lowest dose level compatible with adequate symptom control.

Table IV provides guidelines for conversion from oral Clopixol to Clopixol Depot.

Table IV—Clopixol

Suggested Dose to be Used When Transferring Patients from Clopixol Tablets to Clopixol Depot

Clopixol Tablet Dose	Clopixol Depot Dose*
up to 20 mg daily	100 mg Q2 weekly
25 mg to 40 mg daily	200 mg Q2 weekly
50 mg to 75 mg daily	300 mg Q2 weekly
more than 75 mg daily	400 mg Q2 weekly

*See Dosage.

Co-injection of Clopixol-Acuphase and Clopixol Depot: For patients with exacerbation of chronic psychoses, Clopixol-Acuphase and Clopixol Depot can be mixed in a syringe and given as one injection (co-injection). Since Clopixol-Acuphase and Clopixol Depot are dissolved in the same vehicle, mixing will not affect the pharmacokinetics of either formulation and will allow the administration of an acute and maintenance dose with one injection. Subsequent doses of Clopixol Depot and the interval between injections should be adjusted according to the patient's response. **Clopixol-Acuphase cannot be mixed with other antipsychotic depot formulations.**

Geriatrics: The use of zuclopenthixol in elderly patients with schizophrenia has not been systematically evaluated. Caution should thus be exercised in dose selection for an elderly patient, recognizing the more frequent hepatic, renal and cardiac dysfunctions in this population.

Impaired Liver Function: The use of zuclopenthixol in patients with impaired liver function has not been studied. As zuclopenthixol is extensively metabolized by the liver and primarily excreted in the bile (see Pharmacology, Pharmacokinetics), caution should be exercised in dose selection for patients with this condition.

Impaired Renal Function: The use of zuclopenthixol in patients with impaired renal function has not been studied. Caution should be exercised in dose selection for patients with this condition.

Information for the Patient: See Blue Section—Information for the Patient "Clopixol/Clopixol-Acuphase/Clopixol Depot".

Supplied: Clopixol: 10 mg: Each light red-brown, round, biconvex, film-coated tablet contains: zuclopenthixol 10 mg as zuclopenthixol dihydrochloride. Nonmedicinal ingredients: castor oil, ferric oxide, glycerol, hydroxypropyl methylcellulose, lactose, Macrogol 6 000, magnesium stearate, microcrystalline cellulose, polyvidone acetate, potato starch, talc and titanium dioxide. Amber glass bottles of 100. Store between 15 and 25°C.

25 mg: Each red-brown, round, biconvex, film-coated tablet contains: zuclopenthixol 25 mg as zuclopenthixol dihydrochloride. Nonmedicinal ingredients: castor oil, ferric oxide, glycerol, hydroxypropyl methylcellulose, lactose, Macrogol 6 000, magnesium stearate, microcrystalline cellulose, polyvidone acetate, potato starch, talc and titanium dioxide. Amber glass bottles of 100. Store between 15 and 25°C.

40 mg: Each dark red-brown, round, biconvex, film-coated tablet contains: zuclopenthixol 40 mg as zuclopenthixol dihydrochloride. Nonmedicinal ingredients: castor oil, ferric oxide, glycerol, hydroxypropyl methylcellulose, lactose, Macrogol 6 000, magnesium stearate, microcrystalline cellulose, polyvidone acetate, potato starch, talc and titanium dioxide. Amber glass bottles of 100. Store between 15 and 25°C.

Clopixol-Acuphase: Each mL contains: zuclopenthixol acetate 50 mg (equivalent to zuclopenthixol 45.25 mg/mL) in fractionated coconut oil. Colorless glass ampuls of 1 and 2 mL. Packages of 5. Store between 15 and 25°C. Protect from light.

Clopixol Depot: Each mL contains: zuclopenthixol decanoate 200 mg (equivalent to zuclopenthixol 144.4 mg/mL) in fractionated coconut oil. Colorless vials of 10 mL. Store between 15 and 25°C. Protect from light.

(Shown in Product Recognition Section)

Reviewed 1998

CLORAZEPATE

General Monograph, CPhA

see BENZODIAZEPINES

CLOTRIMADERM

Taro

Clotrimazole

Antifungal

Supplied: Topical Cream 1%: Each g contains: clotrimazole 10 mg in a vanishing cream base consisting of sorbitan monostearate, polysorbate 60, cetyl esters wax, cetostearyl alcohol, 2-octyldodecanol, purified water and, as preservative, benzyl alcohol (1%). Tubes of 20, 30 and 50 g. Jars of 500 g.

Vaginal Cream: 1%: Each g contains: clotrimazole 10 mg in a vanishing cream base consisting of sorbitan monostearate, polysorbate 60, cetyl esters wax, cetostearyl alcohol, 2-octyldodecanol, purified water and, as preservative, benzyl alcohol (1%). Each carton contains: one 50 g tube of cream with 6 disposable plastic applicators and patient instructions. 50 g of vaginal cream is sufficient for 6 intravaginal applications with additional cream for extravaginal use if required.

2%: Each g contains: clotrimazole 20 mg in a vanishing cream base consisting of sorbitan monostearate, polysorbate 60, cetyl esters wax, cetostearyl alcohol, 2-octyldodecanol, purified water and, as preservative, benzyl alcohol (1%). Each carton contains: one 25 g tube of cream with 3 disposable plastic applicators and patient instructions. 25 g of vaginal cream is sufficient for 3 intravaginal applications with additional cream for extravaginal use if required.

Store below 30°C. Avoid freezing.

CLOZARIL®

Novartis Pharmaceuticals

Clozapine

Antipsychotic Agent

Pharmacology: Clozapine, a dibenzodiazepine derivative, is an atypical antipsychotic drug because its profile of binding to dopamine receptors and its effects on various dopamine-mediated behaviors differ from those exhibited by conventional antipsychotics. In contrast to conventional antipsychotics, clozapine produces little or no prolactin elevation. Clozapine exerts potent anticholinergic, adrenolytic, antihistaminic and antiserotoninergic activity.

Controlled clinical trials indicate that clozapine improves both positive and negative symptoms.

Patients on rare occasions may report an intensification of dream activity during clozapine therapy. Rapid eye movement (REM) sleep was found to be increased to 85% of the total sleep time. In these patients, the onset of REM sleep occurred almost immediately after falling asleep.

As is true of more typical antipsychotic drugs, clinical EEG studies have shown that clozapine increases delta and theta activity and slows dominant alpha frequencies. Enhanced synchronization occurs, and sharp wave activity and spike and wave complexes may also develop.

Pharmacokinetics: The absorption of orally administered clozapine is 90 to 95%. Food does not affect either the rate or the extent of absorption. Clozapine is subject to first-pass metabolism, resulting in an absolute bioavailability of 50 to 60%.

Plasma concentrations show large inter-individual differences, with peak concentrations occurring approximately 2.5 hours (range: 1 to 6 hours) after dosing. In a dose range of 37.5 mg b.i.d. to 150 mg b.i.d., the area under the curve (AUC) and the peak plasma concentration (C_{max}) increase linearly in a dose-related fashion.

Clozapine is approximately 95% bound to plasma proteins. The elimination of clozapine is biphasic with a mean terminal half-life of 12 hours (range: 6 to 30 hours, calculated from 3 steady-state in vivo studies). After single doses of 75 mg, the mean terminal half-life was 7.9 hours; it increased to 14.2 hours when steady-state conditions were reached by administering daily doses of 75 mg for at least 7 days. Clozapine is almost completely metabolized prior to excretion. Only trace amounts of unchanged drug are detected in the urine and feces. Approximately 50% of the administered dose is excreted in the urine and 30% in the feces.

Recent studies suggest that there is a significant correlation between clozapine plasma levels and clinical response. The concentrations of clozapine, and its major metabolite norclozapine, were significantly higher in responders than in nonresponders although the mean doses of clozapine did not differ between the 2 groups. Of the main metabolites, only norclozapine was found to be active. In patients who responded to treatment, plasma clozapine levels reached at least 350 to 370 ng/mL.

Indications: The management of symptoms of treatment-resistant schizophrenia. In controlled clinical trials, clozapine was found to improve both positive and negative symptoms.

Due to the significant risk of agranulocytosis and seizure associated with its use, clozapine should be limited to treatment-resistant schizophrenic patients who are non-responsive to, or intolerant of, conventional antipsychotic drugs. Nonresponsiveness is defined as the lack of satisfactory clinical response, despite treatment with appropriate courses of at least 2 marketed chemically-unrelated antipsychotic drugs. Intolerance is defined as the inability to achieve adequate benefit with conventional antipsychotic drugs because of dose-limiting, intolerable adverse effects.

Because of the significant risk of agranulocytosis and seizure, events which both present a continuing risk over time, the extended treatment of patients failing to show an acceptable level of clinical response to clozapine should ordinarily be avoided. In addition, the need for continuing treatment in patients exhibiting beneficial clinical responses should be periodically re-evaluated.

Clozapine can be used only if regular hematological examinations can be guaranteed, as specified under Warnings and Dosage.

Clozapine is available only through a distribution system that ensures: weekly or every-2-week hematological testing prior to the delivery of the next period's supply of medication (see Warnings); maintenance of a central national database that monitors the hematological results of all patients on clozapine and provides timely feedback to the treating physician; registration of the patient, treating physician, laboratory and dispensing pharmacist with the system.

Contraindications: Patients with myeloproliferative disorders, a history of toxic or idiosyncratic agranulocytosis or severe granulocytopenia (with the exception of granulocytopenia/agranulocytosis from previous chemotherapy). Clozapine should not be used simultaneously with other agents known to suppress bone marrow function.

Clozapine is also contraindicated in patients with active liver disease associated with nausea, anorexia, or jaundice; progressive liver disease; hepatic failure.

Other contraindications include severe CNS depression or comatose states, severe renal or cardiac disease, uncontrolled epilepsy, and previous hypersensitivity to clozapine or any other components of Clozaril.

Warnings: Agranulocytosis: Because of the significant risk of granulocytopenia and agranulocytosis, a potentially life-threatening adverse event (see below), clozapine should be reserved for use in the treatment of schizophrenic patients who fail to show an acceptable response to adequate courses of conventional antipsychotic drug treatment, either because of insufficient effectiveness or the inability to achieve an effective dose due to intolerable adverse effects.

Patients must have a normal white blood cell (WBC) count and differential count prior to starting clozapine therapy. Subsequently, a WBC count and differential count must be carried out at least weekly for the first 26 weeks of treatment and at least at 2-week intervals thereafter*. Monitoring must continue for as long as the patient is on the drug, as well as for at least 4 weeks after the discontinuation of treatment. *The change from a weekly to a "once every 2 weeks" schedule should be evaluated on an individual patient basis after 26 weeks of treatment. This decision should be made based upon the clinical judgment of the treating physician, and if he/she deems it appropriate, a consulting hematologist, as well as the patient's willingness to pursue a given frequency of blood monitoring. In turn, the clinical evaluation should take into consideration possible factors that would place the patient in a higher risk group, as well as the hematological profile of the patient during the first 26 weeks of treatment.

Clozapine is available only through a distribution system that requires weekly or every-2-week hematological testing prior to the delivery of the next period's supply of medication (see Indications).

Granulocytopenia (defined as a granulocyte count of less than 1.5×10^9/L) and agranulocytosis (defined as a granulocyte count of less than 0.5×10^9/L, including polys+bands) have been estimated to occur in association with clozapine use at an incidence of 3% and 0.7%, respectively. These incidences are derived from post-marketing data as per June 1993, covering over 60 000 patients treated with clozapine for up to 3 years in the U.S., Canada and U.K. Approximately 88% of the cases of agranulocytosis have occurred during the first 26 weeks of therapy.

A fatality rate of 32% for clozapine-induced agranulocytosis had been reported in association with clozapine use as of December 31, 1989. However, more than half of these deaths occurred before 1977, prior to the recognition of the risk of agranulocytosis and the need for routine blood monitoring. From February 1990 to August 21, 1997, among approximately 150 409 patients treated with clozapine in the U.S., 585 new cases of agranulocytosis have been reported, of which 19 (3.2%) had a fatal outcome.

Fatalities occurring in association with clozapine-induced granulocytopenia/agranulocytosis have generally resulted from infections due to compromised immune system responses. Therefore, patients should be advised to report immediately the appearance of lethargy, weakness, fever, sore throat, flu-like complaints or any other signs of infection.

Clozapine treatment should be initiated and carried out according to the following guidelines: Treatment should not be initiated if the WBC count is less than 3.5×10^9/L and/or the absolute neutrophil count (ANC) is less than 2.0×10^9/L, or if the patient has a history of a myeloproliferative disorder, or toxic or idiosyncratic agranulocytosis or severe granulocytopenia (with the exception of granulocytopenia/agranulocytosis from previous chemotherapy).

Independently of their blood monitoring regimen (weekly or at 2-week intervals), patients should be evaluated immediately and WBC and differential counts checked at least **twice weekly** if after the initiation of treatment: i) the total WBC count falls to between 2.0×10^9/L and 3.5×10^9/L, ii) the ANC falls to between 1.5×10^9/L and 2.0×10^9/L, iii) a single fall or sum of falls in WBC count of 3.0×10^9/L or more is measured in the last 4 weeks, reaching a value below 4.0×10^9/L, iv) a single fall or sum of falls in ANC of 1.5×10^9/L or more is measured in the last 4 weeks, reaching a value below 2.5×10^9/L, and/or v) flu-like complaints or other symptoms appear which might suggest infection.

In the event of a fall in total WBC to below 2.0×10^9/L or in ANC to below 1.5×10^9/L, clozapine therapy must be discontinued immediately and the patient closely monitored. **Clozapine therapy must not be resumed.** Particular attention should be paid to any flu-like complaints or other symptoms which might suggest infection. If the patient should develop a further fall in the WBC count to below 1.0×10^9/L, or a decrease in ANC to below 0.5×10^9/L, it is recommended that patients be placed in protective isolation with close observation and be watched for signs of infection by their physician. Should evidence of infection develop, the appropriate cultures should be performed and an appropriate antibiotic regimen instituted.

The development of granulocytopenia and agranulocytosis does not appear to be dose dependent, nor is duration of treatment a reliable predictor. Approximately 88% of the cases have occurred in the first 26 weeks of treatment, but some cases have developed after years of clozapine use. The incidence of neutropenia and agranulocytosis associated with the use of clozapine increases as a function of age. Experience in the U.S. (approximately 58 000 patients, as of June 1993)

Clozaril (cont'd)

reveals that patients over 50 years old would present an approximately 2 to 3 times higher incidence of agranulocytosis when compared with the overall incidence in patients treated with clozapine.

Patients who have shown hematopoietic reactions to other medications may also be more likely to demonstrate such reactions with clozapine. A disproportionate number of the U.S. cases of agranulocytosis occurred in patients of Jewish origin compared to the overall proportion of such patients exposed to the drug in pre-marketing clinical experience in the U.S.

Agranulocytosis associated with other antipsychotic drugs has been reported to occur with a greater frequency in patients who are cachectic or have a serious underlying medical illness.

Seizures: Caution should be used in administering clozapine to patients having a history of seizures or other predisposing factors.

Seizures have been estimated to occur in association with clozapine use at a cumulative incidence at 1 year of approximately 5%, based on the occurrence of 1 or more seizures in the patients exposed to clozapine during clinical trials in the U.S. Dose appears to be an important predictor of seizure. At doses below 300 mg/day, seizure risk is comparable to that of other antipsychotic drugs (about 1 to 2%). At higher doses, seizure risk rises accordingly, reaching 5% at doses of 600 to 900 mg/day. Because of the risk of seizure associated with clozapine use, patients should be advised not to engage in any activity where sudden loss of consciousness could cause serious risk to themselves or others (e.g., driving, operating machinery, swimming, climbing, etc.).

Adverse Cardiovascular Effects: Clozapine should be used with caution in patients with known cardiovascular and/or pulmonary disease, particularly in those with cardiac arrhythmias and conduction disturbances.

Orthostatic hypotension, with or without syncope, can occur with Clozaril and may represent a continuing risk in some patients. Rarely (approximately 1 case per 3 000 patients in the U.S.), collapse can be profound and can be accompanied by respiratory and/or cardiac arrest. Orthostatic hypotension is more likely to occur during initial titration in association with rapid dose escalation and may even occur on the first or second day of initial dosing. Therefore, upon initiation of clozapine therapy or re-initiation of treatment in patients who have had even a brief interval off clozapine, i.e., 2 days or more since the last dose, it is recommended that treatment be re-initiated with only 12.5 mg (one half of a 25 mg tablet) once or twice daily (see Dosage).

Tachycardia, which may be sustained, has been observed in approximately 25% of patients taking clozapine with patients having an average increase in pulse rate of 10 to 15 bpm. The sustained tachycardia is not simply a reflex response to hypotension and is present in all positions monitored. Tachycardia may be due to the anticholinergic effect of clozapine and its ability to elevate plasma norepinephrine. Either tachycardia or hypotension may pose a serious risk for an individual with compromised cardiovascular function.

A minority of clozapine-treated patients experience ECG repolarization changes similar to those seen with other antipsychotic drugs, including S-T segment depression and flattening or inversion of T waves. There have also been reports of ischemic changes, myocardial infarction, nonfatal arrhythmias, sudden unexplained deaths and congestive heart failure in association with clozapine use. Causality assessment was difficult in many of these cases due to serious pre-existing cardiac disease and plausible alternative causes. Rare instances of sudden, unexplained death have been reported in psychiatric patients, with or without associated antipsychotic drug treatment, and the relationship of these events to antipsychotic drug use is unknown.

Isolated cases of cardiac arrhythmias, pericarditis and myocarditis (with or without eosinophilia) have been reported, some of which have been fatal. Therefore, in patients on clozapine who develop non-specific cardiac disorders, the diagnosis of myocarditis should be considered.

Neuroleptic Malignant Syndrome: A potentially fatal symptom complex sometimes referred to as neuroleptic malignant syndrome (NMS) has been reported in association with antipsychotic drugs. There have been several reported cases of NMS in patients treated with clozapine, most of which have included the concomitant use of lithium or other CNS-active agents.

Clinical manifestations of NMS are hyperpyrexia, muscle rigidity, altered mental status (including catatonic signs) and evidence of autonomic instability (irregular pulse or blood pressure, tachycardia, diaphoresis and cardiac dysrhythmias). Additional signs may include elevated creatine phosphokinase, myoglobinuria (rhabdomyolysis), and acute renal failure.

The diagnostic evaluation of patients with this syndrome is complicated. In arriving at a diagnosis, it is important to identify cases where the clinical presentation includes both serious medical illness (e.g., pneumonia, systemic infection, etc.) and untreated or inadequately treated extrapyramidal signs and symptoms (EPS). Other important considerations in the differential diagnosis include central anticholinergic toxicity, heat stroke, drug fever and primary CNS pathology.

The management of NMS should include: 1) immediate discontinuation of antipsychotic drugs and other drugs not essential to concurrent therapy; 2) intensive symptomatic treatment and medical monitoring; and 3) treatment of any concomitant serious medical problems for which specific treatments are available. There is no general agreement about specific pharmacological treatment regimens for uncomplicated NMS.

If a patient requires antipsychotic drug treatment after recovery from NMS, the potential reintroduction of drug therapy should be carefully considered. The patient should be carefully monitored, since recurrences of NMS have been reported.

Tardive Dyskinesia: A syndrome consisting of potentially irreversible, involuntary, dyskinetic movements may develop in patients treated with conventional antipsychotic drugs. Although the prevalence of tardive dyskinesia with conventional antipsychotics appears to be highest among the elderly, especially elderly women, it is impossible to rely upon prevalence estimates to predict, at the beginning of treatment, which patients are likely to develop the syndrome.

Both the risk of developing tardive dyskinesia and the likelihood that it will become irreversible are believed to increase as the duration of treatment and the total cumulative dose of antipsychotic drugs administered to the patient increase. However, the syndrome can develop, although much less commonly, after relatively brief treatment periods at low doses. There is no known treatment for established cases of tardive dyskinesia, although the syndrome may remit, partially or completely, if antipsychotic drug treatment is withdrawn. Antipsychotic drug treatment itself, however, may suppress (or partially suppress) the signs and symptoms of tardive dyskinesia and thereby may possibly mask the underlying process. The effect that symptom suppression has upon the long-term course of the syndrome is unknown.

There are several reasons for predicting that clozapine may be different from other antipsychotic drugs in its potential for inducing tardive dyskinesia. These include the preclinical finding that it has a relatively weak dopamine receptor blocking effect and the clinical finding that it is associated with a low incidence of extrapyramidal symptoms. Very rarely tardive dyskinesia has been reported in patients on clozapine who had been previously treated with other antipsychotic agents, so that a causal relationship cannot be established. Nevertheless, it cannot be concluded, without more extended experience, that clozapine will not induce this syndrome.

Given this consideration, clozapine should be prescribed in a manner that is most likely to minimize the risk of the occurrence of tardive dyskinesia. As with any antipsychotic drug, chronic clozapine use should be reserved for patients who appear to be obtaining substantial benefit from the drug. In such patients, the smallest dose and the shortest duration of treatment should be sought. The need for continued treatment should be reassessed periodically.

Patients in whom tardive dyskinesia developed with other neuroleptics have improved on clozapine.

If signs and symptoms of tardive dyskinesia appear in a patient on clozapine, drug discontinuation should be considered. However, some patients may require treatment with clozapine despite the presence of the syndrome.

Precautions: Because of the significant risk of agranulocytosis and seizure, events which both present a continuing risk over time, the extended treatment of patients failing to show an acceptable level of clinical response to clozapine should ordinarily be avoided. In addition, the need for continuing treatment in patients exhibiting beneficial clinical responses should be reassessed periodically.

Patients with a history of primary bone marrow disorders may be treated only if the benefit outweighs the risk. They should be carefully evaluated by a hematologist prior to starting clozapine.

Patients who have low WBC counts because of benign ethnic neutropenia should be given special consideration and may be started on clozapine after agreement of a hematologist.

Fever: During clozapine therapy, patients may experience transient temperature elevations above 38°C with the peak incidence within the first 3 weeks of treatment. This fever is generally benign and self-limiting; however, on occasion there may be an associated increase or decrease in the white blood cell count. Patients should be carefully evaluated to rule out the possibility of an underlying infectious process or the development of blood dyscrasia. In the presence of high fever, the possibility of neuroleptic malignant syndrome must be considered (see Warnings).

Occupational Hazards: Interference with Cognitive and Motor Performance: Because of the potential for initial sedation, clozapine may impair mental and/or physical abilities especially during the first few days of therapy. The recommendation for gradual dose escalation should be carefully adhered to and patients should be cautioned about activities requiring alertness (e.g., driving, operating machinery, swimming, climbing, etc.) (see Dosage).

Drug Interactions: Clozapine may enhance the central effects of alcohol, MAO inhibitors, CNS depressants including narcotics, antihistamines and benzodiazepines, as well as the effects of anticholinergic and antihypertensive agents.

Caution is advised with patients who are receiving (or have recently received) benzodiazepines or other psychotropic drugs, as these patients may have an increased risk of circulatory collapse accompanied by respiratory and/or cardiac arrest.

Owing to its noradrenolytic action, clozapine may reduce the blood pressure increasing effect of norepinephrine or other predominantly α-adrenergic agents and reverse the pressure effect of epinephrine.

Clozapine should not be used with other agents, such as carbamazepine, having a known potential to suppress bone marrow function. In particular, the concomitant use of long-acting depot antipsychotic drugs should be avoided because these medications, which may have the potential to be myelosuppressive, cannot be rapidly removed from the body.

Concomitant use of valproic acid with clozapine may alter the plasma levels of clozapine.

Clozapine is highly bound to serum protein and should not be administered to a patient taking other drug(s) which are highly bound to protein (e.g., warfarin, digitoxin). Adverse effects may result from the displacement of protein-bound clozapine and/or the displacement of the other highly protein-bound drug(s).

Since the metabolism of clozapine is mainly mediated by cytochrome P450 1A2 and, probably to a minor extent, by cytochrome P450 2D6, the concomitant administration of drugs which possess affinity to 1 or both of these enzymes may result in an increase in the plasma levels of clozapine and/or the co-administered drug. However, with tricyclic antidepressants, phenothiazines and type I_c antiarrhythmics, which are known to bind to cytochrome P450 2D6, no clinically relevant interactions have been observed thus far. On theoretical grounds, however, it is possible that the plasma levels of such drugs are increased by clozapine.

Administration of cimetidine or erythromycin concomitantly with high-dose clozapine therapy was associated with increased plasma clozapine levels (of approximately 63%) and the occurrence of adverse effects.

Elevated serum levels of clozapine have been reported in patients receiving the drug in combination with fluvoxamine (up to 10-fold) or other selective serotonin re-uptake inhibitors such as paroxetine, sertraline or fluoxetine (up to 2-fold).

Conversely, drugs known to increase the activities of cytochrome P450 enzymes may decrease the plasma levels of clozapine. Discontinuation of the concomitant administration of carbamazepine resulted in an increase (up to 58%) of the clozapine plasma levels. The concomitant use of phenytoin has been found to decrease the clozapine plasma concentration (by 65 to 85%), resulting in reduced effectiveness of a previously effective clozapine dose.

Other Precautions: Clozapine has potent anticholinergic effects and great care should be exercised in using the drug in the presence of prostatic enlargement, narrow-angle glaucoma or paralytic ileus. Since clozapine may cause sedation and weight gain, thereby increasing the risk of thromboembolism, immobilization of patients should be avoided.

In the event of eosinophilia, it is recommended to discontinue clozapine if the eosinophil count rises above 3.0×10^9/L, and to re-start therapy only after the eosinophil count has fallen below 1.0×10^9/L.

In the event of thrombocytopenia, it is recommended to discontinue clozapine therapy if the patient falls below 50.0 $\times 10^9$/L.

Patients with stable pre-existing liver disorders may receive clozapine, but need regular liver function test monitoring. In patients in whom, during clozapine treatment, symptoms of possible liver dysfunction such as nausea, vomiting and/or anorexia develop, liver function tests should be performed immediately. If the elevation of these values is clinically relevant or if symptoms of jaundice occur, treatment with clozapine must be discontinued. It may be resumed only when the liver function tests have returned to normal values. In such cases, liver function should be closely monitored after the re-introduction of the drug.

Patients with Concomitant Illness: Clinical experience with clozapine in patients with concomitant systemic diseases is limited. Nevertheless, caution is advised when using clozapine in patients with hepatic, renal or cardiac disease. For severe cases, see Contraindications.

Pregnancy: Reproduction studies, performed in rats and rabbits at doses of approximately 2 to 4 times the human dose, have revealed no evidence of impaired fertility or harm to the fetus due to clozapine. However, there have not been any adequate and well-controlled studies in pregnant women. Because animal reproduction studies are not always predictive of human response and in view of the desirability of keeping the administration of all drugs to a minimum during pregnancy, clozapine should be used only if the benefits clearly outweigh the risks.

Lactation: Animal studies suggest that clozapine may be excreted in breast milk and have an effect on the nursing infant. Therefore, women receiving clozapine should not breast-feed.

Children: Safety and efficacy in children below age 16 have not been established.

Information for the Patient: Physicians are advised to discuss the following issues with patients (and/or their guardians) for whom they prescribe clozapine:

• Patients who are to receive clozapine should be warned about the significant risk of developing agranulocytosis, a potentially life-threatening adverse event. They should be informed that regular blood tests are required to monitor for the occurrence of agranulocytosis, and that clozapine tablets will be made available only through a special program designed to ensure the required blood monitoring. They should also be informed that weekly blood tests will be required for the first 26 weeks of their treatment with clozapine and that, following this initial higher risk period, they could be allowed to change to a "once every 2 weeks" schedule, provided that their clinical condition is permitting such a change in monitoring regimen. Patients should be advised to report immediately the appearance of lethargy, weakness, fever, sore throat, malaise, mucous membrane ulceration or other possible signs of infection. Particular attention should be paid to any flu-like complaints or other symptoms that might suggest infection.

• Patients should be informed of the significant risk of seizure during clozapine treatment and should be advised to avoid activities that require alertness (e.g., driving, operating machinery, swimming, climbing, etc.).

• Patients should be advised of the risk of orthostatic hypotension, especially during the period of initial dose titration.

• Patients should be informed that if they stop taking clozapine for 2 days or more, they should not restart their medication at the same dosage, but should contact their physician for dosage instructions.

• Patients should notify their physician if they are taking, or plan to take, any prescription or over-the-counter drugs or alcohol.

• Patients should notify their physician if they become pregnant or intend to become pregnant during therapy.

• Patients should not breast-feed an infant if they are taking clozapine.

Adverse Effects: The most serious adverse reactions experienced with clozapine are agranulocytosis, seizure, cardiovascular effects and fever (see Warnings and Precautions). The most common side effects are drowsiness, hypersalivation, tachycardia and sedation. See Table I.

CNS: Initially, drowsiness and sedation may be encountered, especially where relatively large doses of clozapine are given. Generally, this effect tends to subside with continued therapy or dose reduction. Clozapine may cause EEG changes, including the occurrence of spike and wave complexes and may lower the seizure threshold and may include myoclonic jerks or generalized seizures. On rare occasions it may induce episodes of delirium.

Extrapyramidal symptoms are limited mainly to tremor, akathisia and rigidity and if such effects occur, they tend to be mild and transient.

Autonomic Nervous System: Hypersalivation is a pharmacologically unexpected but common adverse reaction associated with clozapine therapy which may be profuse, especially during sleep, but may be diminished by dose reduction or the use of peripherally-acting anticholinergic medication. Dry mouth, blurred vision and an increase in body temperature may occur.

Cardiovascular: Rare cases of thromboembolism have been reported.

Endocrine: In contrast to conventional antipsychotics, clozapine produces little or no prolactin response in humans. Consequently, prolactin-dependent effects such as decreased libido, impotence, galactorrhea and amenorrhea are seldom associated with clozapine therapy. With continued treatment, considerable weight gain has been seen in some patients. Therapeutic doses of clozapine, to date, even on long-term treatment, have not been associated with symptoms of thyroid dysfunction. On rare occasions, hyperglycemia has been reported in patients on clozapine treatment.

Gastrointestinal: Constipation and nausea have been reported occasionally. Very rarely, ileus has been reported. Transient, asymptomatic elevations of liver enzymes and, rarely hepatitis and cholestatic jaundice may occur. Very rarely, fulminant hepatic necrosis has been reported. If jaundice develops, clozapine should be discontinued (see Precautions). As a rare event, clozapine treatment may be associated with dysphagia, a possible cause of aspiration. In rare cases, acute pancreatitis has been reported.

Genital: In a few cases, priapism has been reported. Isolated cases of acute interstitial nephritis have been reported in association with clozapine therapy.

Hemic/Lymphatic: Isolated cases of various types of leukemia have been reported in patients treated with clozapine. However, there is no evidence to suggest a causal relationship between the drug and any type of leukemia: the reported occurrence rate is in the range of the background incidence of these diseases in the general population.

Unexplained leukocytosis may occur, especially in the initial weeks of treatment.

Very rarely, clozapine may cause thrombocytopenia.

Respiratory: Rarely, aspiration of ingested food may occur in patients presenting with dysphagia or as a consequence of acute overdosage.

Musculoskeletal: Rarely, increases in CPK values have occurred.

Overdose: Symptoms: The signs and symptoms associated with clozapine overdose are: drowsiness, lethargy, coma, areflexia, confusion, agitation, delirium, hyper-reflexia, convulsions, hypersalivation, mydriasis, blurred vision, thermolability, tachycardia, hypotension, collapse, cardiac arrhythmias, heart block, respiratory depression or failure, hallucinations, extrapyramidal symptoms, aspiration pneumonia and dyspnea.

In cases of acute intentional or accidental clozapine overdosage, for which information on the outcome is available, to date the mortality is about 12%. Most of the fatalities were associated with cardiac failure or pneumonia caused by aspiration and occurred at doses above 2 000 mg. There have been reports of patients recovering from an overdose in excess of 10 000 mg. However, in a few adult individuals, primarily those not previously exposed to clozapine, the ingestion of doses as low as 400 mg led to life-threatening comatose conditions and, in 1 case, to death. In young children, the intake of 50 to 200 mg resulted in strong sedation or coma without being lethal.

Treatment: Establish and maintain an airway; ensure adequate oxygenation and ventilation. Perform gastric lavage and/or the administration of activated charcoal within the first 6 hours after the ingestion of the drug. Activated charcoal, which may be used with sorbitol, may be as or more effective than emesis or lavage, and should be considered in treating overdosage. Cardiac and vital signs monitoring is recommended along with general symptomatic and supportive measures. Surveillance should be continued for several days because of the risk of delayed effects. Avoid epinephrine when treating hypotension, and quinidine and procainamide when treating cardiac arrhythmia.

There are no specific antidotes for clozapine. Forced diuresis, dialysis, hemoperfusion and exchange transfusion are unlikely to be of benefit.

In managing overdosage, the physician should consider the possibility of multiple drug involvement.

Dosage: Clozapine treatment must be initiated on an in-patient basis or in an out patient setting where medical supervision is available and vital signs can be monitored for a minimum of 6 to 8 hours after the initial 2 to 3 doses.

When treatment is initiated in out-patients, special caution is advised in patients who are receiving benzodiazepines or other psychotropic drugs as these patients may have an increased risk of circulatory collapse accompanied by respiratory and/or cardiac arrest (see Precautions, Drug Interactions). Extra caution is advised in patients with cardiovascular disease or a history of seizures (see Warnings).

Table I—Clozaril

Percent of Patients Reporting Adverse Reactions (≥ 1%) During Clozaril Therapy (N=842)

Organ System	Adverse Reaction	
CNS	Drowsiness	39
	Dizziness	19
	Headache	7
	Tremor	6
	Syncope	6
	Agitation	4
	Restlessness	4
	Hypokinesia	4
	Disturbed Sleep	4
	Seizures	4[a]
	Akathisia	3
	Confusion	3
	Rigidity	3
	Fatigue	2
	Insomnia	2
	Hyperkinesia	1
	Weakness	1
	Lethargy	1
Autonomic Nervous System	Hypersalivation	31
	Hyperhidrosis (Sweating)	6
	Dry Mouth	6
	Visual Disturbance	5
Cardiovascular	Tachycardia	25[a]
	Hypotension	9
	Hypertension	4
	Chest Pain (Angina)	1
	ECG Changes	1
Gastrointestinal	Constipation	14
	Nausea	5
	Abdominal Discomfort	4
	Nausea/Vomiting	3
	Vomiting	3
	Diarrhea	2
	Liver Test Abnormality	1
Urogenital	Urinary Abnormalities	2
	Urinary Urgency/ Frequency	1
	Urinary Incontinence	1
	Urinary Retention	1
Respiratory	Nasal Congestion	1
	Throat Discomfort	1
Integumentary (Skin)	Rash	2
Musculoskeletal	Muscle Weakness	1
Hemic/Lymphatic	Decreased WBC	3
	Agranulocytosis	1[c]
	Eosinophilia	1
Miscellaneous	Fever (Pyrexia)	5
	Weight Gain	4[b]

[a] Rate based on population of approximately 1 700 exposed during the premarket clinical evaluation of Clozaril.

[b] Recently published literature suggests that the incidence of weight gain may be higher than 4%.

[c] Rate based on premarket clinical evaluation of Clozaril: post-market data on population of approximately 60 000 patients exposed, indicate an incidence of 0.7%.

Clozapine is restricted to patients who have a normal white blood cell (WBC) count and differential cell (DC) count and in whom a WBC count and DC count can be carried out at least weekly for the first 26 weeks of treatment and at least at 2-week intervals thereafter*. Monitoring must continue for as long as the patient is on the drug, as well as for at least 4 weeks after discontinuation of treatment.

*The change from a weekly to a "once every 2 weeks" schedule should be evaluated on an individual patient basis after 26 weeks of treatment. This decision should be made based upon the clinical judgment of the treating physician, and if he/she deems it appropriate, a consulting hematologist, as well as the patient's willingness to pursue a given frequency of blood monitoring. In turn, the clinical evaluation should take into consideration possible factors that would place the patient in a higher risk group, as well as the hematological profile of the patient during the first 26 weeks of treatment. Weekly hematological testing should be resumed for an additional 6 weeks if therapy is disrupted for more than 3 days. If clozapine is interrupted for 4 weeks or longer, weekly monitoring is required for an additional 26 weeks.

Clozaril (cont'd)

Clozapine is available only through a distribution system that requires weekly or every-2-week hematological testing prior to the delivery of the next period's supply of medication (see Indications).

The dosage of clozapine must be adjusted individually. For each patient the lowest effective dose should be used.

Initial Dose: On the first day, clozapine should be given at a 12.5 mg dose (one-half of a 25 mg tablet) once or twice, followed by one or two 25 mg tablets on the second day. If well tolerated, the dosage may be increased in daily increments of 25 to 50 mg, achieving a target dose of 300 to 450 mg/day by the end of 2 weeks. Subsequent dosage increases should be made no more than once or twice weekly, in increments not to exceed 100 mg. Cautious titration and a divided dosage schedule are necessary to minimize the risks of hypotension, seizure and sedation.

Switching from previous neuroleptics: When clozapine therapy is initiated in a patient undergoing oral neuroleptic therapy, it is generally recommended that the other neuroleptic should first be discontinued by tapering the dosage downwards. Once the neuroleptic is completely discontinued for at least 24 hours, clozapine treatment can be started as described above. It is generally recommended that clozapine should not be used in combination with other neuroleptics.

Therapeutic Dose Range: In most patients, antipsychotic efficacy can be expected within the therapeutic range of 300 to 600 mg/day in divided doses. The total daily dose may be divided unevenly, with the larger portion at bedtime.

Since improvement may be gradual, continued therapeutic response can be expected beyond the first month of treatment.

Maximum Dose: Occasionally, patients may require doses higher than 600 mg/day to obtain an acceptable therapeutic response. Because of the possibility of increased adverse reactions (particularly seizures) at daily doses of 600 mg and higher, the decision to treat in the range of 600 to 900 mg/day must be taken prudently. Patients must be given adequate time to respond to a given dose level before escalation to a higher dose is contemplated. **The maximum dose of 900 mg/day should not be exceeded.**

Maintenance Dose: After achieving maximum therapeutic benefit, many patients can be maintained effectively at lower doses. Careful downward titration is recommended to the level of 150 to 300 mg/day in divided doses. At daily doses not exceeding 200 mg, a single administration in the evening may be appropriate.

Discontinuation of Therapy: In the event of planned termination of clozapine therapy, gradual reduction in dose is recommended over a 1 to 2 week period. However, should a patient's medical condition require abrupt discontinuation (e.g., severe leukopenia), the patient should be carefully observed for the recurrence of psychotic symptoms.

Re-initiation of Treatment in Patients Previously Discontinued: When restarting patients who have had even a brief interval off clozapine, i.e., 2 days or more since the last dose, it is recommended that treatment be re-initiated with 12.5 mg (one half of a 25 mg tablet) once or twice on the first day. If that dose is well tolerated, it may be feasible to titrate patients back to a therapeutic dose more quickly than is recommended for initial treatment.

Certain additional precautions seem prudent when re-initiating treatment. The mechanisms underlying some of the clozapine-induced adverse reactions are unknown. It is conceivable that re-exposure of a patient might enhance the risk of an untoward event's occurrence and increase its severity. Such phenomena, for example, occur when immune mediated mechanisms are responsible. Therefore, any patient who has previously experienced respiratory or cardiac arrest with initial dosing, but was then able to be successfully titrated to a therapeutic dose, should be re-titrated with extreme caution after even 24 hours of discontinuation.

Clozapine therapy must not be resumed in patients who have been discontinued from treatment due to neutropenia (ANC $<1.5\times10^9$/L) or severe leukopenia (WBC $<2.0\times10^9$/L).

Information for the Patient: See Blue Section—Information for the Patient "Clozaril".

Supplied: 25 mg: Each round, pale yellow, uncoated, easy to break, scored tablet, embossed "CLOZARIL" on one side and "25 mg" on the other, contains: clozapine 25 mg. Nonmedicinal ingredients: colloidal silicon dioxide, lactose, magnesium stearate, povidone, starch and talc. Bottles of 100. Store below 30°C.

100 mg: Each round, pale yellow, uncoated, easy to break, scored tablet, embossed "CLOZARIL" on one side and "100 mg" on the other, contains: clozapine 100 mg. Nonmedicinal ingredients: colloidal silicon dioxide, lactose, magnesium stearate, povidone, starch and talc. Bottles of 100. Store below 30°C.

Clozaril is available only through a distribution system that requires weekly or every-2-week hematological testing prior to the delivery of the next period's supply of medication (see Indications).

(Shown in Product Recognition Section)

Reviewed 1999

CoACTIFED® Preparations Ⓝ

Glaxo Wellcome

Triprolidine HCl—Codeine Phosphate—Pseudoephedrine HCl

Antihistamine—Antitussive—Decongestant

Indications: CoActifed Expectorant: To facilitate expectoration and control cough associated with inflamed mucosa and tenacious sputum.

CoActifed Syrup and Tablets: The treatment of cough associated with inflamed mucosa.

Contraindications: This drug should not be used in newborn or premature infants. Hypersensitivity to codeine phosphate or other narcotics, triprolidine hydrochloride, or other antihistamines of similar chemical structure or sympathomimetic amines including pseudoephedrine. Should not be administered to patients receiving MAO inhibitors or who have taken it within the preceding 2 weeks. Patients with severe hypertension or severe coronary artery disease.

Antihistamines should not be used to treat lower respiratory tract symptoms, including asthma.

Warnings: CoActifed should be used with considerable caution in patients with increased intraocular pressure (narrow angle glaucoma), stenosing peptic ulcer, pyloroduodenal obstruction, symptomatic prostatic hypertrophy, bladder neck obstruction, hypertension, diabetes mellitus, ischemic heart disease and hyperthyroidism. In the presence of head injury or other intracranial lesions, the respiratory depressant effects of codeine and other narcotics may be markedly enhanced, as well as their capacity for elevating cerebrospinal fluid pressure. Narcotics also produce other CNS effects, such as drowsiness, that may further obscure the clinical course of patients with head injuries. Codeine or other narcotics may obscure signs on which to judge the diagnosis or clinical course of patients with acute abdominal conditions.

Precautions: Before prescribing medication to suppress or modify cough, it is important to ascertain that the underlying cause of the cough is identified, that modification of the cough does not increase the risk of clinical or physiologic complications, and that appropriate therapy for the primary disease is provided.

In young children the respiratory centre is especially susceptible to the depressant action of narcotic cough suppressants. Benefit to risk ratio should be carefully considered especially in children with respiratory embarrassment, e.g., croup. Estimation of dosage relative to the child's age and weight is of great importance.

CoActifed should be prescribed with caution for certain special risk patients such as the elderly and debilitated, for those with severe impairment of hepatic or renal function, gallbladder disease or gallstones, respiratory impairment, cardiac arrhythmias, history of bronchial asthma, prostate hypertrophy or urethral stricture, and in patients known to be taking other antitussive, antihistamine or decongestant medications. Patients' self-medication habits should be looked into. CoActifed should not be used by patients intolerant to sympathomimetics used for the relief of nasal or sinus congestion. Such drugs include ephedrine, epinephrine, phenylpropanolamine and phenylephrine. Symptoms of intolerance include drowsiness, dizziness, weakness, difficulty in breathing, tenseness, muscle tremors or palpitations. Codeine may be habit forming when used over long periods or in high doses. Patients should take the drug only for as long, in the amounts, and as frequently as prescribed.

The dependence liability of codeine has been found to be too small to permit a full definition of its characteristics. Studies indicate that addiction to codeine is extremely uncommon and requires very high parenteral doses.

Occupational Hazards: Patients should be warned about engaging in activities requiring mental alertness such as driving a car, operating dangerous machinery or hazardous appliances.

Pregnancy: CoActifed should be given to a pregnant woman only if clearly needed.

Lactation: The components of CoActifed are excreted in breast milk in small amounts, but the significance of their effects on the nursing infant is unknown. A decision should be made whether to discontinue nursing or to discontinue the drug, taking into account the importance of the drug to the mother.

Geriatrics: CoActifed is more likely to cause adverse reactions in the elderly (approximately 60 years and older).

Children: CoActifed may elicit either mild stimulation or mild sedation. In infants and children, the ingredients, in overdosage, may produce hallucinations, convulsions and death. Symptoms of toxicity in children may include fixed dilated pupils, flushed face, dry mouth, fever, excitation, hallucinations, ataxia, incoordination, athetosis, tonic clonic convulsions, and postictal depression.

Drug Interactions: Precautions: CoActifed may enhance the effects of MAO inhibitors, other narcotic analgesics, tranquilizers, alcohol, general anesthetics, sedative-hypnotics, surgical skeletal muscle relaxants, or other CNS depressants. It may diminish the antihypertensive effects of guanethidine, bethanidine, methyldopa and reserpine.

Adverse Effects: In some patients, drowsiness, dizziness, dry mouth, nausea and vomiting or mild stimulation may occur.

Overdose: Symptoms: Overdosage with codeine can cause transient euphoria, drowsiness, dizziness, weariness, diminution of sensibility, loss of sensation, vomiting, transient excitement in children and occasionally in adult women, miosis progressing to nonreactive pinpoint pupils, itching sometimes with skin rashes and urticaria, and clammy skin with mottled cyanosis. In more severe cases, muscular relaxation with depressed or absent superficial and deep reflexes and a positive Babinski sign may appear. Marked slowing of the respiratory rate with inadequate pulmonary ventilation and consequent cyanosis may occur. Terminal signs include shock, pulmonary edema, hypostatic or aspiration pneumonia and respiratory arrest, with death occurring within 6 to 12 hours following ingestion.

Overdoses of antihistamines may cause hallucinations, convulsions, or possibly death, especially in infants and children. Antihistamines are more likely to cause dizziness, sedation and hypotension in elderly patients. Overdosage with triprolidine may produce reactions varying from depression to stimulation of the CNS; the latter is particularly likely in children. Atropine-like signs and symptoms (dry mouth, fixed dilated pupils, flushing, tachycardia, hallucinations, convulsions, urinary retention, cardiac arrhythmias and coma) may occur.

Overdosage with pseudoephedrine can cause excessive CNS stimulation resulting in excitement, nervousness, anxiety, tremor, restlessness and insomnia. Other effects include tachycardia, hypertension, pallor, mydriasis, hyperglycemia and urinary retention. Severe overdosage may cause tachypnea or hyperpnea, hallucinations, convulsions or delirium, but in some individuals there may be CNS depression with somnolence, stupor or respiratory depression. Arrhythmias (including ventricular fibrillation) may lead to hypotension and circulatory collapse. Severe hypokalemia can occur, probably due to compartmental shift rather than depletion of potassium. No organ damage or significant metabolic derangement is associated with pseudoephedrine overdosage.

Treatment: Therapy, if instituted within 4 hours of overdosage, is aimed at reducing further absorption of the drug. In the conscious patient, vomiting should be induced even though it may have occurred spontaneously. If vomiting cannot be induced, gastric lavage is indicated. Adequate precautions must be taken to protect against aspiration, especially in infants and children. Charcoal slurry or other suitable agents should be instilled into the stomach after vomiting or lavage. Saline cathartics or milk of magnesia may be of additional benefit.

In the unconscious patient, the airway should be secured with a cuffed endotracheal tube before attempting to evacuate the gastric contents. Intensive supportive and nursing care is indicated, as for any comatose patient. If breathing is significantly impaired, maintenance of an adequate airway and mechanical support of respiration is the most effective means of providing adequate oxygenation.

Hypotension is an early sign of impending cardiovascular collapse and should be treated vigorously.

Do not use CNS stimulants. Convulsions should be controlled by careful administration of diazepam or short-acting barbiturate, repeated as necessary. Physostigmine may be also considered for use in controlling centrally mediated convulsions.

Ice packs and cooling sponge baths, not alcohol, can aid in reducing the fever commonly seen in children.

For codeine, continuous stimulation that arouses, but does not exhaust, the patient is useful in preventing coma. Continuous or intermittent oxygen therapy is usually indicated, while naloxone is useful as a codeine antidote. Close nursing care is essential.

Saline cathartics, such as milk of magnesia, help to dilute the concentration of the drugs in the bowel by draining water into the gut, thereby hastening drug elimination.

Adrenergic receptor blocking agents are antidotes to pseudoephedrine. In practice, the most useful is the betablocker propranolol, which is indicated when there are signs of cardiac toxicity.

There are no specific antidotes to triprolidine. Histamine should not be given.

Pseudoephedrine and codeine are theoretically dialyzable, but the procedures have not been clinically established.

In severe cases of overdosage, it is essential to monitor both the heart (by ECG) and plasma electrolytes and to give i.v. potassium as indicated by these continuous controls. Vasopressors may be used to treat hypotension, and excessive CNS stimulation may be counteracted with parenteral diazepam. Stimulants should not be used.

Dosage: Dosage should be individualized according to the needs and response of the patient.

Usual Dose: To be given every 4 to 6 hours. Do not exceed 4 doses in 24 hours. Adults and children 12 years of age and older: 1 tablet or 10 mL. Children 6 to under 12 years of age: ½ tablet or 5 mL. Children 2 to under 6 years of age: 2.5 mL.

Supplied: Expectorant: Each 5 mL of clear, orange, syrupy liquid with a mixed fruit odor contains: triprolidine HCl 2 mg, pseudoephedrine HCl 30 mg, guaifenesin 100 mg and codeine phosphate 10 mg. Nonmedicinal ingredients: fruit flavor, glycerin, methylparaben, sodium benzoate, sucrose and sunset yellow FCF. Alcohol-free. Bottles of 100 mL and 2 L. Store between 15 to 30°C and protect from light. Do not refrigerate.

Syrup: Each 5 mL of clear, dark red syrupy liquid contains: tripolidine HCl 2 mg, pseudoephedrine HCl 30 mg and codeine phosphate 10 mg. Nonmedicinal ingredients: amaranth, fruit flavor, glycerin, methylparaben, sodium benzoate and sucrose. Alcohol-free. Bottles of 100 mL and 2 L. Store between 15 to 30°C and protect from light.

Tablets: Each white to off white, biconvex tablet, code number WELLCOME P4B on same side as score mark, contains: triprolidine HCl 4 mg, pseudoephedrine HCl 60 mg and codeine phosphate 20 mg. Nonmedicinal ingredients: cornstarch, lactose, gelatin, magnesium stearate and quinoline yellow WS. Each tablet is equivalent to 10 mL of syrup. If tablet is broken in half, it reveals a yellow core. Tartrazine-free. Bottles of 50. Store between 15 to 30°C. Protect from light and keep dry.

(Shown in Product Recognition Section)

COATED ASPIRIN®
Bayer Consumer

ASA

Analgesic—Anti-inflammatory—Antipyretic

Indications: 80 mg: For use in children only for rheumatic and arthritic pain under the supervision of a physician. Do not use to treat fever.

325 mg/500 mg/650 mg: For the temporary relief of arthritic and rheumatic pain, muscle aches, joint pain and back pain.

Coated Aspirin has a special enteric coating recommended by doctors to help prevent stomach upset. Coated Aspirin takes extra time to dissolve. The special enteric coating allows the caplet to pass through the stomach to the intestine before it dissolves, to help prevent stomach irritation.

Precautions: A physician or pharmacist should be consulted prior to taking this medication in case of: allergy to salicylates, asthma, pregnancy and breast-feeding; stomach problems, peptic ulcer, severe liver disease or gout; history of blood coagulation defects, or receiving anticoagulant drugs, or 5 to 7 days prior to surgery, or with severe anemia; intake of other medications containing salicylates or acetaminophen, anti-inflammatory drugs, anticonvulsants, antidiabetic or gout medicine.

Caution: This package contains enough drug to seriously harm a child. Keep out of children's reach. Children and teenagers should not use this medicine for chickenpox or flu symptoms before a physician is consulted about Reye's syndrome, a rare but serious illness reported to be associated with ASA.

Pregnancy and *Lactation:* It is especially important not to use this drug during the last 3 months of pregnancy unless specifically directed to do so by a physician because it may cause problems in the unborn child or complications during delivery. Consult a physician before taking this drug when nursing.

Adverse Effects: Like all medicines, ASA may occasionally produce unwanted side effects. Contact your physician if any of the following side effects develop during treatment: ringing or buzzing in the ears, skin rashes, hives or itching and breathing difficulties, nausea, vomiting, bleeding or irritation of stomach, pain, and any loss of hearing.

Overdose: Symptoms: Usually occur within a few hours after ingestion. They include: stomach upset, convulsions, (seizures), hearing loss, mental confusion, ringing or buzzing in the ears, severe drowsiness or tiredness, severe excitement or nervousness and unusually fast or deep breathing, hallucinations or changes in behavior (especially in children).

Treatment: In case of accidental overdose, call a physician, Poison Control Centre or hospital immediately; if emergency help is not available, induce vomiting at once (within 30 minutes).

Note: Vomiting should never be induced in unconscious individuals or in children younger than 1 year without medical help.

Dosage: The caplets must be swallowed whole. Do not crush or break the caplets before taking them.

80 mg: Under 2 years: as directed by a physician; 2 to 3 years: 2 tablets; 4 to 5 years: 3 tablets; 6 to 8 years: 4 tablets; 9 to 10 years: 5 tablets; 11 years: 6 tablets. May be repeated every 4 hours, not more than 5 times daily.

325 mg: Adults: 1 or 2 caplets with a glass of water. May be repeated every 4 hours, not to exceed 12 caplets/day.

Extra Strength, 500 mg: Adults: 1 or 2 caplets with a glass of water. May be repeated every 4 hours, not to exceed 8 caplets/day. Because each caplet exceeds the standard 325 mg dosage, take only on the advise of a physician.

Super Extra Strength, 650 mg: Adults: 1 caplet with a glass of water. May be repeated every 4 hours, not to exceed 6 caplets per day. Each caplet contains 2 adult standard dosage units.

It is hazardous to exceed the maximum recommended dose unless advised by a physician. Consult a physician if the underlying condition requires continued use for more than 5 days.

Supplied: 80 mg: Each pale blue, enteric coated tablet, with '80' in dark blue ink on one side contains: ASA 80 mg. Nonmedicinal ingredients: carnauba wax, cornstarch, croscarmellose sodium, eudragit, FD&C Blue #1, FD&C Blue #2, hydroxypropyl methylcellulose, lactose, microcrystalline cellulose, propylene glycol, titanium dioxide and triacetin. Bottles of 24 and 120.

325 mg: Each pale yellow, enteric coated caplet, with BAYER 325 in brown ink on one side contains: ASA 325 mg. Nonmedicinal ingredients: carnauba wax, cornstarch, D&C Yellow #10, FD&C Yellow #6, hydroxypropyl methylcellulose, methacrylic acid copolymer, polysorbate 80, potassium hydroxide, sodium lauryl sulfate, synthetic black & brown iron oxides, titanium dioxide and triacetin. Suitable for low-sodium diet. Bottles of 50, 100 and 200.

Extra Strength, 500 mg: Each pale yellow, enteric coated caplet, with BAYER 500 in brown ink, contains: ASA 500 mg. Nonmedicinal ingredients: carnauba wax, cornstarch, D&C Yellow #10, FD&C Yellow #6, hydroxypropyl methylcellulose, methacrylic acid copolymer, polysorbate 80, potassium hydroxide, sodium lauryl sulfate, synthetic black & brown iron oxides, titanium dioxide and triacetin. Suitable for low-sodium diet. Bottles of 50 and 100.

Super Extra Strength, 650 mg: Each orange, enteric coated caplet, with "B" embossed on one side, contains: ASA 650 mg. Nonmedicinal ingredients: colloidal silicon dioxide, cornstarch, FD&C Yellow #6, gelatin, lactose, maltodextrin, metacrylic acid copolymer, polyethylene glycol, sodium hydroxide, sodium lauryl sulfate, talc, titanium dioxide and triethyl citrate. Bottles of 100.

(Shown in Product Recognition Section)

Unfamiliar capsule? Check the color-coded photographs in the PRODUCT RECOGNITION SECTION.

COCAINE HCl Ⓝ
BDH

Local Anesthetic—Vasoconstrictor

Supplied: 4%: Each mL of aqueous solution contains: cocaine HCl 40 mg. Nonmedicinal ingredients: citric acid, D and C Yellow No. 10, FD and C Green No. 3, sodium benzoate and water. Also contains sodium benzoate as a preservative. Unit of use glass bottles of 4 mL, cartons of 5.

10%: Each mL of aqueous solution contains: cocaine HCl 100 mg. Nonmedicinal ingredients: citric acid, D and C Yellow No. 10, FD and C Green No. 3, sodium benzoate and water. Also contains sodium benzoate as a preservative. Unit of use glass bottles of 4 mL, cartons of 5.

Note: External surface of unopened bottle may be sterilized by ethylene oxide only. **Do not steam autoclave.**

Store at controlled room temperature 15 to 30°C.

(Shown in Product Recognition Section)

CODEINE Ⓝ
General Monograph, CPhA

see OPIOID ANALGESICS

CODÉINE Ⓝ
Trianon

Analgesic—Antitussive

Supplied: 15 mg: Each white tablet, scored on one side and engraved with "CT15" on the other side, contains: codeine phosphate 15 mg. Nonmedicinal ingredients: cellulose, colloidal silicon dioxide, croscarmellose, lactose and magnesium stearate. Alcohol-, gluten-, sulfite- and tartrazine-free. Bottles of 100 and 500.

30 mg: Each white tablet, scored on one side and engraved with "CT30" on the other side, contains: codeine phosphate 30 mg. Nonmedicinal ingredients: cellulose, colloidal silicon dioxide, croscarmellose, lactose and magnesium stearate. Alcohol-, gluten-, sulfite- and tartrazine-free. Bottles of 100 and 500.

New Product 1998

CODEINE CONTIN® Ⓝ
Purdue Frederick

Codeine Monohydrate—Codeine Sulfate Trihydrate

Opioid Analgesic

Pharmacology: Codeine is an opioid analgesic which exerts an agonist effect at specific, saturable opioid receptors in the CNS and other tissues. In man, codeine produces a variety of effects including analgesia, constipation from decreased gastrointestinal motility, suppression of the cough reflex, respiratory depression from reduced responsiveness of the respiratory centre to CO_2, nausea and vomiting via stimulation of the CTZ, changes in mood including euphoria and dysphoria, sedation, mental clouding, miosis and alterations of the endocrine and autonomic nervous systems.

Orally administered codeine is approximately 60% as potent as i.m. codeine in terms of total analgesia. The relative potency of i.m. codeine phosphate is approximately 1/12 that of i.m. morphine sulfate and orally, 200 mg of codeine phosphate is equivalent to 20 to 30 mg of morphine sulfate during chronic dosing.

The analgesic efficacy of codeine controlled release has been evaluated in multiple dose studies in patients with cancer pain and chronic nonmalignant pain. In a dose-response study in cancer patients, Codeine Contin 150 mg every 12 hours provided approximately equivalent analgesia to 600 mg acetaminophen plus 60 mg codeine every 6 hours. In patients with cancer pain and chronic nonmalignant pain receiving q4h prn acetaminophen plus codeine, Codeine Contin (100, 150 or 200 mg every 12 hours) produced improved pain control and reduced consumption of supplementary acetaminophen plus codeine. In patients with chronic low back pain, Codeine Contin (100 mg every 12 hours), supplemented with prn plain

Codeine Contin (cont'd)

acetaminophen, produced lower pain scores and less fluctuation in pain throughout the day than prn acetaminophen plus codeine.

Pharmacokinetics: Codeine is readily absorbed from the gastrointestinal tract and has an oral bioavailability of 53%, relative to the i.m. route. Codeine is rapidly distributed from blood to body tissues, passes the blood-brain barrier and is found in fetal tissue and breast milk. Codeine is metabolized in the liver to morphine and norcodeine, each representing about 10% of the administered dose of codeine. Urinary excretion products are free and glucuronide-conjugated codeine (about 70%), free and conjugated morphine (about 10%), normorphine (under 4%) and hydrocodone (<1%). The remainder of the dose appears in the feces.

Codeine controlled release is absorbed to an equivalent extent as immediate-release tablet or liquid formulations of codeine. In single dose studies in fasting, healthy volunteers, the maximum plasma codeine concentration (C_{max}) is approximately 56% of that from immediate-release formulations and is achieved approximately 2.6 times later—at 3.3 hours postdosing. In steady-state studies in healthy volunteers, both the extent of absorption and maximum plasma codeine concentrations are equivalent to those from immediate-release formulations at the same total daily dose. In the presence of food, the extent of absorption of codeine controlled release is not significantly increased, but peak concentrations are somewhat delayed, occurring at 3.9 to 4.5 hours postdose.

Indications: For the relief of mild to moderate pain requiring the prolonged use of an opioid analgesic preparation.

Contraindications: Patients with hypersensitivity to opioid analgesics; acute asthma or other obstructive airway disease and acute respiratory depression; cor pulmonale; acute alcoholism; delirium tremens; severe CNS depression; convulsive disorders; increased cerebrospinal or intracranial pressure; head injury; suspected surgical abdomen; concomitant MAO inhibitors (or within 14 days of such therapy).

Warnings: Drug Dependence: As with other opioids, tolerance and physical dependence may develop upon repeated administration of codeine, and there is potential for development of psychological dependence. Codeine controlled release should therefore be prescribed and handled with the degree of caution appropriate to the use of a drug with abuse potential. Drug abuse is not a problem in patients with pain in whom codeine is appropriately indicated. Withdrawal symptoms may occur following abrupt discontinuation of codeine therapy or upon administration of an opioid antagonist. Therefore, patients on prolonged therapy should be withdrawn gradually from the drug if it is no longer required for pain control.

CNS Depression: Codeine should be used only with caution and in reduced dosage during concomitant administration of other opioid analgesics, general anesthetics, phenothiazines and other tranquilizers, sedative-hypnotics, tricyclic antidepressants and other CNS depressants (including alcohol). Respiratory depression, hypotension and profound sedation or coma may result.

Severe pain antagonizes the subjective and respiratory depressant actions of opioid analgesics. Should pain suddenly subside, these effects may rapidly become manifest. Patients who are scheduled for cordotomy or other interruption of pain transmission pathways should not receive codeine controlled release within 24 hours of the procedure.

Pregnancy: Animal studies with a number of opioids, including codeine, have indicated the possibility of teratogenic effects. In humans, it is not known whether codeine can cause fetal harm when administered during pregnancy or can affect reproductive capacity. Since codeine crosses the placental barrier, codeine controlled release should be given to pregnant patients only when the anticipated benefits outweigh the risks to the fetus.

Precautions: General: The respiratory depressant effects of codeine, and the capacity to elevate cerebrospinal fluid pressure, may be greatly increased in the presence of an already elevated intracranial pressure produced by trauma. Also, codeine may produce confusion, miosis, vomiting and other side effects which obscure the clinical course of patients with head injury. In such patients, codeine must be used with extreme caution and only if it is judged essential.

Codeine should be used with extreme caution in patients with substantially decreased respiratory reserve, pre-existing respiratory depression, hypoxia or hypercapnia. Such patients are often less sensitive to the stimulatory effects of carbon dioxide on the respiratory centre, and the respiratory depressant effects of codeine may reduce respiratory drive to the point of apnea.

Codeine administration may result in severe hypotension in patients whose ability to maintain adequate blood pressure is compromised by reduced blood volume, or concurrent administration of such drugs as phenothiazines or certain anesthetics.

Codeine may obscure the diagnosis or clinical course of patients with acute abdominal conditions.

Special Risk Groups: Codeine should be administered with caution, and in reduced dosages, to elderly or debilitated patients, to patients with severely reduced hepatic or renal function, and in patients with Addison's disease, hypothyroidism, prostatic hypertrophy or urethral stricture.

Labor/Delivery and *Lactation:* Codeine crosses the placental barrier and its administration during labor can produce respiratory depression in the neonate. Codeine has been detected in human breast milk. Caution should be exercised if codeine is administered to a nursing mother.

Occupational Hazards: Driving and Operating Dangerous Machinery: Codeine may impair the mental and/or physical abilities needed for certain potentially hazardous activities such as driving a car or operating machinery. Patients should be cautioned accordingly.

Drug Interactions: Patients should also be cautioned about the combined effects of codeine with other CNS depressants, including other opioids, phenothiazines, sedative/hypnotics and alcohol. The analgesic effect of codeine is potentiated by amphetamines, chlorpromazine and methocarbamol. CNS depressants, such as other opioids, anesthetics, sedatives, hypnotics, barbiturates, phenothiazines, chloral hydrate and glutethimide may enhance the depressant effects of codeine. MAO inhibitors (including procarbazine HCl), pyrazolidone antihistamines, beta-blockers and alcohol may also enhance the depressant effect of codeine. When combined therapy is contemplated, the dose of one or both agents should be reduced.

Adverse Effects: Adverse effects of codeine controlled release are similar to those of other opioid analgesics and represent an extension of pharmacological effects of the drug class. The major hazards associated with codeine, are respiratory and CNS depression and, to a lesser degree, circulatory depression.

Most Common Adverse Effects Requiring Medical Attention: The most frequently observed side effects of opioid analgesics such as codeine are sedation, nausea and vomiting, constipation, lightheadedness, dizziness, and sweating.

Sedation: Sedation is a common side effect of opioid analgesics, especially in opioid naive individuals. Sedation may also occur partly because patients often recuperate from prolonged fatigue after the relief of persistent pain. Most patients develop tolerance to the sedative effects of opioids within 3 to 5 days and, if the sedation is not severe, will not require any treatment except reassurance. If excessive sedation persists beyond a few days, the dose of the opioid should be reduced and alternate causes investigated. Some of these are: concurrent CNS depressant medication, hepatic or renal dysfunction, brain metastases, hypercalcemia and respiratory failure. If it is necessary to reduce the dose, it can be carefully increased again after 3 or 4 days if it is obvious that the pain is not being well controlled. Dizziness and unsteadiness may be caused by postural hypotension, particularly in elderly or debilitated patients, and may be alleviated if the patient lies down.

Nausea and Vomiting: Nausea is a common side effect on initiation of therapy with opioid analgesics and is thought to occur by activation of the chemoreceptor trigger zone, stimulation of the vestibular apparatus and through delayed gastric emptying. The prevalence of nausea declines following continued treatment with opioid analgesics. When instituting therapy with an opioid for chronic pain, the routine prescription of an antiemetic should be considered. In the cancer patient, investigation of nausea should include such causes as constipation, bowel obstruction, uremia, hypercalcemia, hepatomegaly, tumor invasion of celiac plexus and concurrent use of drugs with emetogenic properties. Persistent nausea which does not respond to dosage reduction may be caused by opioid-induced gastric stasis and may be accompanied by other symptoms including anorexia, early satiety, vomiting and abdominal fullness. These symptoms respond to chronic treatment with gastrointestinal prokinetic agents.

Constipation: Practically all patients become constipated while taking opioids on a chronic basis. In some patients, particularly the elderly or bedridden, fecal impaction may result. It is essential to caution the patients in this regard and to institute an appropriate regimen of bowel management at the start of prolonged opioid therapy. Stimulant laxatives, stool softeners and other appropriate measures should be used as required.

Less Frequently Observed with Opioid Analgesics: General and CNS: Dysphoria, euphoria, weakness, headache, agitation, tremor, uncoordinated muscle movements, alterations of mood (nervousness, apprehension, depression, floating feelings, dreams), muscle rigidity, paresthesia, muscle tremor, blurred vision, nystagmus, diplopia and miosis, transient hallucinations and disorientation, visual disturbances, insomnia and increased intracranial pressure may occur.

Cardiovascular: flushing of the face, chills, tachycardia, bradycardia, palpitation, faintness, syncope, hypotension and hypertension.

Respiratory: bronchospasm and laryngospasm.

Gastrointestinal: dry mouth, biliary tract spasm, anorexia, diarrhea, cramps and taste alterations.

Genitourinary: urinary retention or hesitancy and antidiuretic effects.

Dermatologic: pruritus, urticaria, other skin rashes and diaphoresis.

Withdrawal (Abstinence) Syndrome: Physical dependence with or without psychological dependence tends to occur on chronic administration of opioids. An abstinence syndrome may be precipitated when opioid administration is discontinued or opioid antagonists administered. The following withdrawal symptoms may be observed after opioids are discontinued: body aches, diarrhea, gooseflesh, loss of appetite, nervousness or restlessness, runny nose, sneezing, tremors or shivering, stomach cramps, nausea, trouble with sleeping, unusual increase in sweating and yawning, weakness, tachycardia and unexplained fever. In patients who are appropriately treated with opioid analgesics and who undergo gradual withdrawal from the drug, these symptoms are usually mild.

Overdose: Symptoms: Serious overdosage with opioids may be characterized by respiratory depression (a decrease in respiratory rate and/or tidal volume, Cheyne-Stokes respiration, cyanosis), extreme somnolence progressing to stupor or coma, skeletal muscle flaccidity, cold and clammy skin, and sometimes bradycardia and hypotension. In severe overdosage, apnea, circulatory collapse, cardiac arrest and death may occur.

Treatment: Primary attention should be given to the establishment of adequate respiratory exchange through the provision of a patent airway and controlled or assisted ventilation. The opioid antagonist naloxone HCl is a specific antidote against respiratory depression due to overdosage or as a result of unusual sensitivity to opioids. An appropriate dose of the antagonist should therefore be administered, preferably by the i.v. route. The usual initial i.v. adult dose of naloxone is 0.4 mg or higher. Concomitant efforts at respiratory resuscitation should be carried out. Since the duration of action of opioids, particularly sustained release formulations, may exceed that of the antagonist, the patient should be under continued surveillance and doses of the antagonist should be repeated as needed to maintain adequate respiration.

An antagonist should not be administered in the absence of clinically significant respiratory or cardiovascular depression. Oxygen, i.v. fluids, vasopressors and other supportive measures should be used as indicated.

In individuals physically dependent on opioids, the administration of the usual dose of opioid antagonist will precipitate an acute withdrawal syndrome. The severity of this syndrome will depend on the degree of physical dependence and the dose of antagonist administered. The use of opioid antagonists in such individuals should be avoided if possible. If an opioid antagonist must be used to treat serious respiratory depression in the physically dependent patient, the antagonist should be administered with extreme care by using dosage titration, commencing with 10 to 20% of the usual recommended initial dose.

Evacuation of gastric contents may be useful in removing unabsorbed drug, particularly when a sustained release formulation has been taken.

Dosage: Adults: Individual dosing requirements vary considerably based on each patient's age, weight, severity and cause of pain, and medical and analgesic history.

Doses of Codeine Contin are expressed as codeine base. Codeine phosphate formulations contain approximately 75% codeine base. Patients currently receiving oral immediate release formulations of plain codeine phosphate may be transferred to Codeine Contin at an approximately 25% lower total daily codeine dosage, equally divided into two 12 hourly Codeine Contin doses.

For patients who are receiving analgesic combinations of codeine phosphate and acetaminophen or ASA, Table I provides a guide to the recommended initial and maintenance doses of Codeine Contin.

Table I—Codeine Contin

Conversion from Acetaminophen (or ASA) Plus Codeine Phosphate Combinations

Number of 30 mg Codeine Combination Tablets Per Day	Initial Dose of Codeine Contin	Maintenance Dose of Codeine Contin
4-6	50 mg q12h	100 mg q12h
7-9	100 mg q12h	150 mg q12h
10-12	150 mg q12h	200 mg q12h
>12	200 mg q12h	as needed (maximum 300 mg q12h)

Patients with pain who are not currently receiving other opioid analgesics, or who are receiving fewer than 4 tablets/day of a codeine combination preparation, should be initiated at a dose of 50 mg Codeine Contin every 12 hours and the dose titrated as needed.

For patients who are receiving an alternate opioid, the "oral codeine phosphate equivalent" of the analgesic presently being used should be determined. Having determined the total daily dosage of the present analgesic, Table II can be used to calculate the approximate daily oral codeine phosphate dosage that should provide equivalent analgesia. An approximately 25% lower dose of Codeine Contin should then be prescribed, equally divided into two 12 hourly doses.

Codeine Contin tablets should not be chewed or crushed but may be halved.

Dose Titration: Dose titration is the key to success with opioid analgesic therapy. **Proper optimization of doses scaled to the relief of the patient's pain should aim at the regular administration of the lowest dose which will maintain the patient free of pain at all times.** Dosage adjustments should be based on the patient's clinical response. In patients receiving codeine controlled release chronically, the dose should be titrated at intervals of 48 hours to that which provides satisfactory pain relief without unmanageable side effects. Doses of codeine controlled release above 300 mg every 12 hours have not been extensively studied, and above these levels it is preferable that patients be transferred to an opioid such as morphine, which is recommended for severe pain. Codeine controlled release is designed to allow 12 hourly dosing. **If breakthrough pain repeatedly occurs at the end of the dosing interval it is generally an indication for a dosage increase rather than more frequent administration.**

Adjustment or Reduction of Dosage: Following successful relief of pain, periodic attempts to reduce the opioid dose should be made. Smaller doses or complete discontinuation may become feasible due to a change in the patient's condition or mental state.

Opioid analgesics may only be partially effective in relieving dysesthetic pain, postherpetic neuralgia, stabbing pains, activity-related pain and some forms of headache. That is not to say that patients suffering from some of these forms of chronic pain should not be given an adequate trial of opioid analgesics, but it may be necessary to refer such patients at an early time to other forms of pain therapy.

Management of Breakthrough Pain: For patients whose dose has been titrated to the recommended maintenance dose, without attainment of adequate analgesia, the total daily dose may be increased, unless precluded by side effects. If breakthrough pain persists despite appropriate adjustments of codeine controlled release dose, plain acetaminophen may be given (325 to 650 mg every 4 to 6 hours prn to a maximum of 4 000 mg/24 hours). If immediate release codeine phosphate preparations or acetaminophen plus codeine phosphate combination analgesics (every 4 to 6 hours prn) are used for breakthrough pain, the doses of codeine phosphate (based on a rescue dose of codeine base which should not exceed ⅛ of the daily dose of Codeine Contin) are 15, 30, 45, 60, 90 mg for patients receiving Codeine Contin 100, 200, 300, 400, 600 mg/day, respectively.

Table II—Codeine Contin

Opioid Analgesics: Approximate Analgesic Equivalences[a]

Drug	Equivalent Dose (mg)[b] (compared to morphine 10 mg i.m.) Parenteral	Oral	Duration of Action (hours)
Strong Opioid Agonists			
Morphine	10	60[c]	3-4
Oxycodone[f]	15	30	2-4
Hydromorphone	1.5	7.5	2-4
Anileridine	25	75	2-3
Levorphanol	2	4	4-8
Meperidine[d]	75	300	1-3
Oxymorphone	1.5	5 (rectal)	3-4
Methadone[e]	—	—	—
Heroin	5-8	10-15	3-4
Weak Opioid Agonists			
Codeine	120	200	3-4
Propoxyphene	50	100	2-4
Mixed Agonist-Antagonists[g]			
Pentazocine[d]	60	180	3-4
Nalbuphine	10	—	3-6
Butorphanol	2	—	3-4

[a]References:
Cancer Pain: A Monograph on the Management of Cancer Pain, Health and Welfare Canada 1984.
Foley, K.M., New Engl. J. Med. 313: 84-95, 1985.
Aronoff, G.M. and Evans, W.O., In Evaluation and Treatment of Chronic Pain, 2nd Ed, G.M. Aronoff (Ed.), Williams and Wilkins, Baltimore, pp. 359-368, 1992.
Cherny, N.I. and Portenoy, R.K., In: Textbook of Pain, 3rd Ed., P.D. Wall and R. Melzack (Eds.), Churchill Livingstone, London, pp. 1437-1467, 1994.

[b]**Most of this data was derived from single-dose, acute pain studies and should be considered an approximation for selection of doses when treating chronic pain.**

[c]**For acute pain, the oral or rectal dose of morphine is six times the injectable dose. However, for chronic dosing, clinical experience indicates that this ratio is 2 to 3:1 (i.e., 20 to 30 mg of oral or rectal morphine is equivalent to 10 mg of parenteral morphine).**

[d]These drugs are not recommended for the management of chronic pain.

[e]Extremely variable equianalgesic dose. Patients should undergo individualized titration starting at an equivalent to 1/10 of the morphine dose.

[f]Based on single entity oral oxycodone in acute pain.

[g]Mixed agonist-antagonists can precipitate withdrawal in patients on pure opioid agonists.

Information for the Patient: See Blue Section—Information for the Patient "Codeine Contin".

Supplied: 50 mg: Each blue, round, film-coated tablet, with PF printed on one side and CC 50 on the other side, contains: codeine monohydrate 26.5 mg and codeine sulfate trihydrate 31.35 mg (each equivalent to codeine anhydrous 25 mg). Nonmedicinal ingredients: FD&C Blue #2 aluminum lake, hydroxyethyl cellulose, hydroxypropyl cellulose, hydroxypropyl methylcellulose, lactose, magnesium stearate, propylene glycol, stearyl alcohol, talc and titanium dioxide. Opaque, high density polyethylene bottles of 50.

100 mg: Each yellow, round, scored, film-coated tablet, with PF imprinted on one side and CC 100 on the other side, contains: codeine monohydrate 53 mg and codeine sulfate trihydrate 62.7 mg (each equivalent to codeine anhydrous 50 mg). Nonmedicinal ingredients: D&C Yellow #10 aluminum lake, FD&C Yellow #5 aluminum lake, hydroxyethyl cellulose, hydroxypropyl cellulose, hydroxypropyl methylcellulose, lactose, magnesium stearate, propylene glycol, stearyl alcohol, talc and titanium dioxide. Opaque, high density polyethylene bottles of 50.

150 mg: Each red, round, scored, film-coated tablet, with PF imprinted on one side and CC 150 on the other side, contains: codeine monohydrate 79.5 mg and codeine sulfate trihydrate 94.1 mg (each equivalent to codeine anhydrous 75 mg). Nonmedicinal ingredients: FD&C Yellow #6 aluminum lake, FD&C Red #40 aluminum lake, hydroxyethyl cellulose, hydroxypropyl cellulose, hydroxypropyl methylcellulose, lactose, magnesium stearate, propylene glycol, stearyl alcohol, talc and titanium dioxide. Opaque, high density polyethylene bottles of 50.

200 mg: Each orange, caplet-shaped, scored, film-coated tablet, with PF imprinted on one side and CC 200 on the other side, contains: codeine monohydrate 106 mg and codeine sulfate trihydrate 125.4 mg (each equivalent to codeine anhydrous 100 mg). Nonmedicinal ingredients: FD&C Yellow #6 aluminum lake, hydroxyethyl cellulose, hydroxypropyl cellulose, hydroxypropyl methylcellulose, lactose, magnesium stearate, propylene glycol, stearyl alcohol, talc and titanium dioxide. Opaque, high density polyethylene bottles of 50.

Store at 15 to 25°C.

(Shown in Product Recognition Section)

Reviewed 1997

CODEINE PHOSPHATE Ⓝ

Abbott

Analgesic—Antitussive

Supplied: Each mL contains: codeine phosphate 30 mg or 60 mg 0.1%. Nonmedicinal ingredients: phosphoric acid, sodium hydroxide, sodium metabisulfiate and water for injection. Ampuls of 1 mL, boxes of 100.

CODEINE PHOSPHATE Ⓝ

Rougier

Analgesic—Antitussive

Supplied: Syrup: Each 5 mL of colorless, limpid liquid contains: codeine phosphate 25 mg. Also contains alcohol, sucrose and sulfite. Energy: 69.93 kJ (16.65 kcal). Gluten- and paraben-free. Bottles of 500 mL and 2 L.

Tablets: 15 mg: Each white, scored tablet, monographed "N 15", contains: codeine phosphate 15 mg. Also contains lactose, sucrose and sulfite. Energy: 1.11 kJ (0.26 kcal). Gluten- and paraben-free. Bottles of 100 and 500.

30 mg: Each white, scored tablet, monographed "N 30" contains: codeine phosphate 30 mg. Also contains lactose, sucrose and sulfite. Energy: 1.11 kJ (0.26 kcal). Gluten- and paraben-free. Bottles of 100 and 500.

CODEINE PHOSPHATE Ⓝ

Technilab

Opioid Analgesic—Antitussive

Supplied: 15 mg: Each white tablet contains: codeine phosphate 15 mg. Nonmedicinal ingredients: colloidal silicon dioxide, lactose, magnesium stearate, microcrystalline cellulose and stearic acid. Gluten-, paraben-, sodium- and sulfite-free. Bottles of 100 and 500.

30 mg: Each white tablet contains: codeine phosphate 30 mg. Nonmedicinal ingredients: colloidal silicon dioxide, lactose, magnesium stearate, microcrystalline cellulose and stearic acid. Gluten-, paraben-, sodium- and sulfite-free. Bottles of 100 and 500.

COGENTIN® Ⓟ

MSD

Benztropine Mesylate

Antiparkinsonian Agent

Pharmacology: Benztropine is a synthetic compound resulting from the combination of the active portions of atropine and diphenhydramine. Benztropine possesses both anticholinergic and antihistaminic effects, although only the former have been established as therapeutically significant in the management of parkinsonism.

Benztropine antagonizes the effect of acetylcholine. This decreases the imbalance between the neurotransmitters, acetylcholine and dopamine, which may improve the symptoms of early Parkinson's disease.

In a clinical study measuring serum levels of neuroleptics and anticholinergics via radioreceptor assay, the correlation between total daily dose of benztropine and serum concentration was extremely poor (r=0.281). Serum concentrations varied nearly 100-fold with given doses between 2 and 6 mg/day. A markedly nonlinear relationship between daily dose and serum anticholinergic drug levels was observed with an increasing oral dosage of benztropine. In most cases, 2 mg

Cogentin (cont'd)

increments in oral dose were associated with several-fold increases in the serum level of anticholinergic activity.

It has been reported that the duration of action for benztropine may persist for up to 24 to 48 hours following a single 2 mg i.m. injection. Benztropine binds extensively, approximately 95%, with serum proteins. Benztropine crosses the blood-brain barrier.

Indications: Recommended for all etiologic groups of parkinsonism: arteriosclerotic, postencephalitic, idiopathic, and drug-induced.

It can be effective at any stage of the disease, even when a patient has become bedridden. Often it is helpful in patients who have become unresponsive to other agents.

Though parkinsonism is chronic and usually progressive, its symptoms often can be controlled by suitable treatment. Therapy is directed toward control of disturbing symptoms to permit maximum integration of function and minimum discomfort.

In non-drug-induced parkinsonism, partial control of symptoms is the usual therapeutic accomplishment.

Benztropine is a powerful anticholinergic agent, mainly effective in relieving tremor and rigidity. Many other troublesome signs and symptoms, including sialorrhea, drooling, mask-like facies, oculogyric crises, speech and writing difficulties, dysphagia, gait disturbances, and pain and insomnia due to cramps and muscle spasm are also ameliorated.

Extensive muscle rigidity and spasm, often more disturbing than tremor, may be alleviated.

Improvement in muscle function relieves many stigmata of parkinsonism. During therapy with benztropine, the characteristic frozen facies, gait, and posture return toward normal; speech becomes freer; and sustained rigidity, discomfort, and restlessness during sleep usually are relieved.

Physiotherapy can be applied more easily and may be more effective.

Drug-induced Parkinsonism: Benztropine relieves manifestations of parkinsonism that may appear during treatment with phenothiazine derivatives and reserpine. Usually it is helpful in combatting tremulousness; restlessness; feelings of tension; ptyalism; urinary frequency, "lockjaw"; and acute dystonic reactions such as torticollis, oculogyric crises, and dysphagia.

Contraindications: Because of the atropine-like side effects, this drug is contraindicated in children under 3 years of age, and should be used with caution in older children.

The use of the drug is contraindicated in the presence of glaucoma.

Benztropine is contraindicated in patients who are hypersensitive to any component of this product.

Warnings: *Pregnancy:* The safe use of this drug in pregnancy has not been established.

Occupational Hazards: Benztropine may impair mental and/or physical abilities required for performance of hazardous tasks, such as operating machinery or driving a motor vehicle.

Precautions: General: Since benztropine has cumulative action, continued supervision is advisable.

Patients with a tendency to tachycardia, and patients with prostatic hypertrophy, should be closely observed during treatment. Dysuria may occur, but rarely becomes a problem.

The physician should be aware of the possible occurrence of glaucoma. Although the drug does not appear to have any adverse effect on simple glaucoma, it should not be used in narrow-angle glaucoma (see Contraindications).

In large doses, benztropine may cause complaints of weakness and inability to move particular muscle groups. For example, if the neck has been rigid and suddenly relaxes, it may feel weak, causing some concern. In this event, dosage adjustment is required.

Mental confusion and excitement may occur with large doses, or in susceptible patients. Visual hallucinations have been reported occasionally. Furthermore, in the treatment of extrapyramidal symptoms due to CNS drugs, such as phenothiazines, and reserpine in patients with a mental disorder, occasionally there may be intensification of mental disorders. Although benztropine need not be discontinued when this occurs, the psychotogenic potential of antiparkinsonian drugs should be considered when planning the management of patients with mental disorders. Also, when using benztropine in these patients, they should be kept under careful observation especially at the beginning of treatment or if dosage is increased. In such cases, at times, increased doses of antiparkinsonian drugs can precipitate a toxic psychosis.

Tardive dyskinesia may appear in some patients on long-term therapy with phenothiazines and related agents, or may occur after therapy with these drugs has been discontinued. Antiparkinsonism agents usually do not alleviate the symptoms of tardive dyskinesia, and in some instances may aggravate or unmask such symptoms. Benztropine is not recommended in tardive dyskinesia.

Benztropine contains structural features of atropine and may produce anhidrosis. For this reason, it should be given with caution during hot weather, especially when given concomitantly with other atropine like drugs to the chronically ill, the alcoholic, those who have central nervous system disease and those who do manual labor in a hot environment. Anhidrosis may be anticipated to occur more readily when some disturbance of sweating already exists. If there is evidence of anhidrosis, the possibility of hyperthermia should be considered. Dosage should be decreased at the discretion of the physician so that the ability to maintain body heat equilibrium by perspiration is not impaired. Severe anhidrosis and fatal hyperthermia have occurred.

Obstetrics: See Warnings.

Lactation: It is not known whether this drug is excreted in human milk. Because many drugs are excreted in human milk, caution should be exercised when benztropine is administered to a nursing mother.

Children: See Contraindications.

Drug Interactions: When benztropine is given concomitantly with phenothiazines, haloperidol or other drugs with anticholinergic or antidopaminergic activity, patients should be advised to report gastrointestinal complaints, fever or heat intolerance promptly. Paralytic ileus, sometimes fatal, has occurred in patients taking anticholinergic-type antiparkinsonism drugs, including benztropine, in combination with phenothiazines and/or tricyclic antidepressants.

Adverse Effects: Adverse reactions most of which are anticholinergic or antihistaminic in nature, are listed below by body system in order of decreasing severity: Cardiovascular: tachycardia.

Digestive: constipation, dry mouth, nausea, vomiting.

Adjustment of dosage or time of administration sometimes helps to control these reactions. If dry mouth is so severe that there is difficulty in swallowing or speaking, or loss of appetite and weight, reduce dosage, or discontinue the drug temporarily.

Nausea unaccompanied by vomiting usually can be disregarded. Slight reduction in dosage may control the nausea and still give sufficient relief of symptoms. Vomiting may be controlled by temporary discontinuation, followed by resumption at a lower dosage.

Nervous System: Toxic psychosis including confusion, disorientation, memory impairment, visual hallucinations; exacerbation of pre-existing psychotic symptoms; nervousness; depression; listlessness; numbness of fingers.

Special Senses: blurred vision, dilated pupils.

Urogenital: urinary retention, dysuria.

Metabolic/Immune and Skin: Occasionally, an allergic reaction, e.g., skin rash, develops. Sometimes this can be controlled by reducing dosage, but occasionally benztropine has to be discontinued.

Other: heart stroke, hyperthermia, fever.

Overdose: Symptoms: Manifestations: May be any of those seen in atropine poisoning or antihistamine overdosage: CNS depression, preceded or followed by stimulation; confusion; nervousness; listlessness; intensification of mental symptoms or toxic psychosis in patients with mental illness being treated with phenothiazine derivatives or reserpine; hallucinations (especially visual); dizziness; muscle weakness; ataxia; dry mouth; mydriasis; blurred vision; palpitations; nausea; vomiting; dysuria; numbness of fingers; dysphagia; allergic reactions, e.g., skin rash; headache; hot, dry, flushed skin; delirium; coma; shock; convulsions; respiratory arrest; anhidrosis; hyperthermia; glaucoma; constipation.

Treatment: Physostigmine 1 to 2 mg, s.c. or. i.v., reportedly will reverse symptoms of anticholinergic intoxication. A second injection may be given after 2 hours if required. Otherwise treatment is symptomatic and supportive. Induce emesis or perform gastric lavage (contraindicated in precomatose, convulsive, or psychotic states). Maintain respiration. A short-acting barbiturate may be used for CNS excitement, but with caution to avoid subsequent depression; supportive care for depression (avoid convulsant stimulants such as picrotoxin, pentylenetetrazol, or bemegride); artificial respiration for severe respiratory depression; a local miotic for mydriasis and cycloplegia; ice bags or other cold applications and alcohol sponges for hyperpyrexia, a vasopressor and fluids for circulatory collapse. Darken room for photophobia.

Dosage: The tablets should be used when patients are able to take oral medication.

The injection is especially useful for psychotic patients with acute, dystonic reactions or other reactions that make oral medication difficult or impossible. It is also recommended when a more rapid response is desired than can be obtained with the tablets.

Since there is no significant difference in onset of effect after i.v. and i.m. injection, usually there is no need to give benztropine i.v. It is quickly effective after either route, with improvement sometimes noticeable a few minutes after injection. In emergency situations, when the condition of the patient is alarming, 1 to 2 mL i.v. normally will provide quick relief. If the signs of parkinsonism begin to return, the dose can be repeated.

Because benztropine has cumulative action, therapy should be initiated with a low dose which is increased gradually at 5- or 6-day intervals to the smallest amount necessary for optimal relief. Increases should be made in increments of 0.5 mg to a maximum of 6 mg, or until optimal results are obtained without excessive side effects.

Arteriosclerotic, Idiopathic and Postencephalitic Parkinsonism: The usual daily dosage is 1 to 2 mg, with a range of 0.5 to 6 mg orally or parenterally.

As with any agent used in parkinsonism, dosage must be individualized according to age and weight, and the type of parkinsonism being treated. Generally, older patients, thin patients, and patients with arteriosclerotic parkinsonism cannot tolerate large doses. However, most patients with post-encephalitic parkinsonism require fairly large doses and tolerate them well. Patients with a poor mental outlook are usually poor candidates for therapy.

In arteriosclerotic and idiopathic parkinsonism, therapy may be initiated with a single daily dose of 0.5 to 1 mg at bedtime. In some patients, this will be adequate; in others 4 to 6 mg/day may be required.

In postencephalitic parkinsonism, therapy may be initiated in most patients with 2 mg a day in one or more doses. In highly sensitive patients, therapy may be initiated with 0.5 mg at bedtime, and increased as necessary.

Some patients experience greatest relief by taking the entire dose at bedtime; others react more favorably to divided doses, 2 to 4 times a day. Frequently, 1 dose a day is sufficient, and divided doses may be unnecessary or undesirable.

The long duration of action of benztropine makes it particularly suitable for bedtime medication when its effects may last throughout the night. With benztropine patients are better able to turn in bed during the night and to rise in the morning.

When benztropine is started, do not terminate therapy with other antiparkinsonian agents abruptly; rather, reduce or discontinue them gradually. Many patients obtain greatest relief with a combination of benztropine and other drugs.

Benztropine may be used concomitantly with levodopa, in which case the dose of each may need to be adjusted. However, if benztropine is continued when Sinemet is introduced, the dosage of benztropine may need to be adjusted.

Drug-induced Parkinsonism: When treating extrapyramidal disorders due to CNS drugs such as phenothiazine derivatives or reserpine, the recommended dosage is 1 to 4 mg once or twice a day orally or parenterally. Dosage must be individualized according to the need of the patient. Some patients require more than recommended; others do not need as much.

In acute dystonic reactions, 1 to 2 mg i.v. quickly relieves the condition. After that, 1 to 2 mg twice a day orally, usually prevent recurrence.

Extrapyramidal disorders that develop soon after initiation of treatment with phenothiazines or reserpine, are likely to be transient. One to 2 mg of benztropine orally, 2 or 3 times a day, usually provides relief within 1 or 2 days. After 1 or 2 weeks of administration, benztropine should be withdrawn to determine the continued need for it. If parkinsonism recurs, benztropine can be reinstituted.

Certain extrapyramidal disorders which develop slowly, such as tardive dyskinesia, usually do not respond to benztropine.

Patients must be closely observed for severe reactions and benztropine discontinued temporarily if they appear (see Precautions and Adverse Effects).

Benztropine should not be used beyond the period necessary to counteract the extrapyramidal manifestations. Although medication with the drug causing parkinsonism can frequently be continued without change of dosage when adjunct therapy with benztropine is used, a reduction in dosage of the psychotropic drug might be indicated.

Supplied: Injection: Each mL of clear, colorless solution contains: benztropine mesylate 1 mg, sodium chloride and water for injection q.s. Ampuls of 2 mL, boxes of 6.

Tablets: Each white, flat, discoid-shaped, compressed tablet, with a beveled edge, bisected on one side with MSD 60 on the other, contains: benztropine mesylate 2 mg. Nonmedicinal ingredients: calcium phosphate, cellulose, lactose, magnesium stearate and starch. Gluten- and tartrazine-free. Bottles of 100 and 1 000.

(Shown in Product Recognition Section)

Reviewed 1999

COLACE®
Roberts

Docusate Sodium
Stool Softener

Indications: The management of constipation due to hard stools, in painful anorectal conditions, in cardiac and other conditions in which maximum ease of passage is desirable to avoid difficult or painful defecation, and when peristaltic stimulants are contraindicated.

Contraindications: Presence of abdominal pain, nausea or vomiting.

Precautions: Do not administer concomitantly with mineral oil: increased absorption of the oil may result. Do not use in the presence of abdominal pain, nausea, fever or vomiting. Frequent or prolonged use may result in dependence on laxatives. Do not administer docusate within 2 hours of another medicine, to avoid reduction of its effect.

Dosage: Adults and older children: 100 to 200 mg; 0 to 3 years: 10 to 40 mg; 3 to 6 years: 20 to 60 mg; 6 to 12 years: 40 to 120 mg. May be given in divided dosage with water. Retention enema: 5 mL of drops (50 mg) to 90 mL enema fluid. Flushing enema: 1 mL of drops (10 mg) to 100 mL enema fluid. To counteract barium constipation: add 10 to 20 mL (100 to 200 mg) to the barium mixture before administration. Or prescribe 100 to 200 mg as capsules after fluoroscopy. Give syrup or drops in 120 mL of milk or fruit juice or in infant formula, to mask bitter taste.

Supplied: Capsules: Each maroon capsule contains: docusate sodium USP 100 mg. Sodium: <1 mmol (5.17 mg). Bottles of 60 and 100.

Drops: Each mL of solution contains: docusate sodium USP 10 mg (1%). Sodium: <1 mmol (0.65 mg)/mL. Dropper bottles of 25 mL.

Syrup: Each 5 mL of syrup contains: docusate sodium USP 20 mg. Also contains ethyl alcohol 0.03 mL/5 mL. Energy: 50 kJ (12 kcal)/5 mL. Sodium: <1 mmol (3.7 mg)/5 mL. Bottles of 250 mL.

Reviewed 1997

COLCHICINE (ORAL)
General Monograph, CPhA

Gout Therapy

This monograph has been compiled by CPhA. It may contain information different from that approved by Therapeutic Products Programme, Health Canada, and the pharmaceutical manufacturers' approval has not been requested.

Pharmacology: Although its exact mode of action in the relief of gout is not completely understood, colchicine is known to decrease the inflammatory response to urate crystal deposition by inhibiting migration of leukocytes, to interfere with urate deposition by decreasing lactic acid production by leukocytes, to interfere with kinin formation and to diminish phagocytosis and the subsequent anti-inflammatory response. The anti-inflammatory effect of colchicine is relatively selective for acute gouty arthritis. However, other types of arthritis occasionally respond. It is neither an analgesic nor a uricosuric and will not prevent progression to chronic gouty arthritis. It does have a prophylactic, suppressive effect that helps to reduce the incidence of acute attacks and to relieve the residual pain and mild discomfort that patients with gout occasionally experience.

Pharmacokinetics: Colchicine is rapidly absorbed from the gastrointestinal tract. Peak concentrations occur in 0.5 to 2 hours. The drug and its metabolites are distributed in leukocytes, kidneys, liver, spleen and the intestinal tract. The plasma half-life is about 20 minutes while the half-life in leukocytes is approximately 60 hours. Colchicine is metabolized in the liver and excreted primarily in the feces with 10 to 20% eliminated unchanged in the urine.

Indications: The treatment of acute gout. Colchicine is effective in relieving the pain of acute attacks, especially if therapy is begun early in the attack and in adequate dosage. Because of the toxicity of colchicine in high doses, the use of NSAIDs is preferred for acute gout. However, colchicine is very effective in preventing recurrent attacks of gout and is not toxic in the lower doses used for prophylaxis.

Contraindications: Patients with serious gastrointestinal, renal and cardiac disease; known hypersensitivity to colchicine.

Warnings: *Pregnancy:* Cell division in animals and plants can be arrested by colchicine. In mice and hamsters it has produced teratogenic effects and has adversely affected spermatogenesis in animals and humans. The benefit of colchicine therapy in a pregnant woman must be weighed against the possible risk to the fetus.

Precautions: Use with care in geriatric or debilitated patients and those with cardiac, renal or gastrointestinal disease. Dosage reduction is indicated if weakness, anorexia, nausea, vomiting or diarrhea appears.

Drug Interactions: Colchicine has been shown to induce reversible malabsorption of Vitamin B_{12}, apparently by altering the function of ileal mucosa.

Pregnancy: See Warnings.

Lactation: It is not known if colchicine is distributed into human milk.

Children: Safety and effectiveness in this age group have not been established.

Adverse Effects: Reactions to colchicine appear to be dose-related. The most prominent symptoms are related to the gastrointestinal tract (e.g., nausea, vomiting, abdominal pain, diarrhea) and may be particularly troublesome in the presence of peptic ulcer or spastic colon. If these symptoms appear, colchicine should be discontinued as they are early signs of toxicity.

Hypersensitivity to colchicine is a very rare but possible occurrence.

When given for a prolonged period, colchicine may cause bone marrow depression and aplastic anemia. Periodic blood counts should be performed during long-term therapy. Peripheral neuritis or neuropathy, myopathy, hair loss, vesicular dermatitis, anuria, renal damage and hematuria have also been reported with prolonged administration.

Overdose: There is usually a latent period between overdosage and the onset of symptoms, regardless of the route of administration. Deaths have been reported with as little as 7 mg, although higher doses have been taken without fatal results.

Symptoms: The first symptoms to appear are gastrointestinal—nausea, vomiting, abdominal pain and diarrhea. The diarrhea may be severe and bloody owing to hemorrhagic gastroenteritis. Burning sensations in the throat, stomach and skin may also occur. Extensive vascular damage may result in shock. Renal dysfunction may occur. Hematuria and oliguria are common manifestations. Muscular weakness is marked and an ascending CNS paralysis may develop. The patient usually remains conscious. However, delirium and convulsions may occur. Death usually is the result of respiratory depression.

Treatment: Induce emesis or perform gastric lavage followed by the administration of activated charcoal. Symptomatic and supportive treatment. Analgesics may relieve the abdominal pain, but monitor carefully for possible paralytic ileus. Respiratory assistance may be needed to insure proper oxygenation and ventilation.

Dosage: Acute Gouty Arthritis: Colchicine therapy must be initated at the first warning of an acute attack; a delay of a few hours impairs its effectiveness. The usual oral adult dose is 1 or 1.2 mg initially, followed by subsequent doses of 0.5 or 0.6 mg every 2 hours until pain is relieved or toxic symptoms appear. The total amount of colchicine required to alleviate an acute attack is usually 4 to 8 mg. However, as there may be a delay in the effect of colchicine of up to 12 to 48 hours, some clinicians recommend a schedule of 1.2 mg orally every 12 hours, for a maximum of 3 doses. This results in a total dose of up to 3.6 mg for an acute attack and minimizes adverse effects.

To prevent cumulative toxicity, a second course of therapy should not be initiated before 3 days have elapsed since treating the previous attack.

For prophylaxis of recurrent gouty arthritis, the dose of colchicine may range from 0.5 mg 1 to 4 times weekly to 1.8 mg daily, depending on the frequency of attacks. The usual dose is 1 mg daily.

Reviewed 1997

COLCHICINE
Abbott

Gout Therapy

Supplied: Each yellow tablet contains: colchicine 0.6 mg (600 μg). Also contains acacia, cornstarch, D&C yellow #10, lactose, stearic acid and talc. Alcohol-, gluten-, paraben-, sucrose-, sulfite- and tartrazine-free. Bottles of 100.

COLCHICINE
Odan

Gout Therapy

Supplied: 0.6 mg: Each yellow scored tablet, engraved O/0.6, contains: colchicine USP 0.6 mg (600 μg). Nonmedicinal ingredients: D&C Yellow no. 10, FD&C Yellow no. 6, magnesium stearate, polyvinyl pyrrolidine, sodium starch glycolate and sucrose. Alcohol-, gluten-, paraben-, lactose-, sulfite- and tartrazine-free. Amber glass bottles of 100, 500 and 1 000.

1 mg: Each pink, scored tablet, engraved O/1.0, contains: colchicine USP 1 mg. Nonmedicinal ingredients: FD&C red #2, FD&C red #3, FD&C yellow #6, magnesium stearate, polyvinyl pyrrolidine, sodium starch glycolate and sucrose. Alcohol-, gluten-, paraben-, lactose-, sulfite- and tartrazine-free. Amber glass bottles of 100 and 500.

COLCHICINE
Welcker-Lyster

Gout Therapy

Supplied: 0.6 mg: Each yellow, scored tablet, engraved with WL logo, contains: colchicine USP 600 μg (0.6 mg). Energy: 1.29 kJ (0.31 kcal). Plastic bottles of 100 and 500.

1 mg: Each pink, scored tablet, engraved with WL logo, contains: colchicine USP 1 mg. Energy: 1.29 kJ (0.31 kcal). Plastic bottles of 50 and 500.

COLESTID® Ⓟ
Pharmacia & Upjohn

Colestipol HCl
Oral Antihypercholesterolemic

Pharmacology: Colestipol is hygroscopic, water insoluble, and it is neither hydrolyzed by digestive enzymes nor is it absorbed. Colestipol binds with bile acids in the intestine forming a complex that is excreted in the feces. This nonsystemic action results in a continuous, partial removal of bile acids from the enterohepatic circulation preventing their reabsorption. This increased fecal loss of bile acids due to colestipol administration leads to an increased oxidation of cholesterol to bile acids. This results in an increase in the number of hepatic low density lipoprotein (LDL) receptors, and consequently an increased uptake of LDL and a decrease in serum/plasma beta lipoprotein or total and LDL cholesterol levels. Although colestipol produces an increase in the hepatic synthesis of cholesterol in man, serum cholesterol levels fall.

Pharmacokinetics: Following oral ingestion of ^{14}C-labelled colestipol by humans, at a dosage level of 0.07 g/kg body weight, 0.0214% of the radioactive drug was excreted in urine over a 7-day period. Eighty percent of the material excreted in urine was voided during the first day. Recovery of radioactivity in the feces accounted for an additional 93.4% of the administered dose. No drug-related radioactivity was found in plasma samples taken at intervals during the 4-day period following drug administration. In this case, the sensitivity of the plasma level measurements was such that 0.01% of the administered dose, distributed in total body plasma, would have been detected.

Indications: As adjunctive therapy to diet and exercise for the reduction of elevated serum cholesterol in patients with primary hypercholesterolemia (elevated low density lipoproteins). Such a reduction of serum cholesterol may reduce the risks of atherosclerotic coronary artery disease and myocardial infarction. In patients with combined hypercholesterolemia and hypertriglyceridemia, colestipol may be useful in lowering elevated cholesterol but is not indicated where hypertriglyceridemia is the abnormality of most concern.

Colestid (cont'd)

Patients should be placed on a standard cholesterol-lowering diet at least equivalent to the American Heart Association (AHA) Step 1 Diet, which should be continued during treatment. If appropriate, a programme of weight control and physical exercise should be implemented.

Contraindications: In patients with complete biliary obstruction where bile is not secreted into the intestine.

In individuals who have shown hypersensitivity to any of the components of the products.

In addition, the orange granules are contraindicated in phenylketonurics as each 7.5 g contains 18.2 mg phenylalanine.

Warnings: The granules and orange granules should never be taken in its dry form. Esophageal spasm or respiratory distress can result from attempting to swallow the granules dry. The granules and orange granules should always be mixed with water, beverages, cereals, soups or other foods with sufficient fluid for mixing.

Precautions: Studies have suggested that control of elevated cholesterol and triglycerides may not lessen the danger of cardiovascular related mortality, although the incidence of nonfatal myocardial infarctions is decreased.

Before instituting therapy with colestipol, diseases contributing to increased serum cholesterol such as hypothyroidism, diabetes mellitus, nephrotic syndrome, dysproteinemias and obstructive liver disease should be ruled out or specifically treated. In addition, the current medications of the patient should be reviewed for their potential to increase serum LDL-C or total cholesterol.

It should be verified that an elevated LDL-C is responsible for the high total cholesterol level, especially in those patients with marked elevations of HDL-C and elevations of triglyceride over 4.5 mmol/L (400 mg/100 mL). An LDL-C level may be estimated using the following formula:

$$\text{LDL-C} = \text{total cholesterol} - \text{HDL-C} - \frac{\text{triglyceride}}{2.19}$$

All units are in mmol/L. The accuracy of this approximation falls when triglycerides are greater than 4.5 mmol/L. Patients with triglyceride levels above 4.5 mmol/L should not be considered for initial therapy with colestipol alone. Instead, the use of colestipol given in combination with another lipid lowering agent like a fibrate or niacin would be more beneficial.

When used as the sole therapy, colestipol does not improve hypertriglyceridemia and in fact may elevate serum triglycerides. This elevation is generally transient, but may sometimes persist. If a significant rise in triglyceride level occurs consideration should be given to dose reduction, drug discontinuation or combination therapy with another lipid lowering agent.

Appropriate use of serum lipid profiles (with LDL-C and triglyceride levels) at regular intervals is advised so that therapeutic effect can be determined.

Colestipol may produce or worsen pre-existing constipation. In patients with pre-existing constipation, the starting dose should be 5 g colestipol granules, or 2 g colestipol tablets, given once or twice daily. Increased fluid and fiber intake is encouraged to alleviate the constipation. A stool softener may be added if needed. If the initial dose is well tolerated, the dosage may be increased (by daily increments of 5 g colestipol granules or 2 to 4 g colestipol tablets) at monthly intervals. If the constipation worsens or the desired therapeutic response is not achieved at the maximum recommended dose, then combination lipid-lowering therapy or alternate therapy should be considered. Particular effort should be made to avoid constipation in patients with symptomatic coronary artery disease. Constipation may aggravate hemorrhoids.

Since colestipol is a chloride form of an anion exchange resin, there is a possibility that prolonged use may lead to the development of hyperchloremic acidosis.

Carcinogenesis and Mutagenesis: In studies conducted in rats in which cholestyramine resin (a bile acid sequestering agent similar to colestipol) was used as a tool to investigate the role of various intestinal factors, such as fat, bile salts and microbial flora, in the development of intestinal tumors induced by potent carcinogens, the incidence of such tumors was observed to be greater in cholestyramine resin treated rats than in control rats. The relevance of this laboratory observation from studies in rats with cholestyramine resin to the clinical use of colestipol is not known. When colestipol was administered in the diet to rats for 18 months, there was no evidence of any drug related intestinal tumor formation. In the Ames assay, colestipol was not mutagenic.

Pregnancy and *Lactation:* The use of colestipol in pregnancy or lactation or by women of childbearing potential requires that the benefits of drug therapy be weighed against the possible hazards to the mother and the child. Safety for use in pregnant women has not been established.

Children: The use of colestipol in children is limited. Clinical trials conducted in children with the granules have usually employed doses of 5 to 20 g/day. The National Cholesterol Education Program (NCEP) Expert Panel recommends drug therapy be considered in children 10 years or older, who have previously undergone an adequate trial of diet therapy but still have unacceptably high serum cholesterol levels. In certain situations where a young child has extremely high serum cholesterol levels, drug treatment may even be initiated before 10 years of age. If the child is started on drug therapy, a carefully assessed diet therapy should also be continued in order to obtain optimal results.

However, the safety of using the tablets in patients under the age of 18 years has not been established.

Because bile acid sequestrants may interfere with the absorption of fat-soluble vitamins, appropriate monitoring of growth and development is essential if colestipol is used in children.

Geriatrics: Appropriate studies on the relationship of age to the effects of colestipol have not been performed in the geriatric population. However, patients over 60 years of age may be more likely to experience gastrointestinal side effects, as well as adverse nutritional effects.

Effect on Vitamin Absorption: Due to the action of colestipol in sequestering bile acids, colestipol may theoretically interfere with normal fat absorption and thus may reduce the absorption of folic acid and fat soluble vitamins A, D and K. In general, supplementation of vitamins A, D and K is not needed unless a deficiency is shown to exist.

Chronic use of colestipol has been rarely associated with an increased bleeding tendency due to hypoprothrombinemia resulting from vitamin K deficiency. This deficiency can be corrected with oral vitamin K.

Drug Interactions: Since colestipol is an anion-exchange resin, it may have a strong affinity for anions other than the bile acids. Colestipol does not bind in vivo with an affinity and to an extent that results in clinically significant drug-drug interactions with all anionic compounds or weak acids. Clinically relevant reductions in bioavailability have been found for several weakly acid drugs (summarized below). However, other weakly acid (anionic) drugs have been studied and found not to be affected by colestipol co-administration. The drugs that are affected by co-administration of colestipol vary widely in pharmacologic effect and mechanisms, in magnitude of doses, and in physicochemical characteristics. Therefore, it is not possible to predict a priori whether or not co-administration with colestipol will interfere with absorption. Unless a particular drug has been studied, it should be assumed that concomitantly administered drugs have the potential for interacting with colestipol. **Since colestipol may bind other drugs given concurrently, patients should take other drugs at least 1 hour before or 4 hours after colestipol (or at as great an interval as possible) to avoid impeding their absorption.**

Interactions between colestipol and drugs can be divided into 2 major categories: substantially decreased bioavailability (defined as a decrease of >20%), and little or no effect on bioavailability (defined as a decrease of <20%).

Drug Interactions with Other Lipid-Lowering Drugs: Fibric acid derivatives: Based upon the definitions above, colestipol reduced the bioavailability of gemfibrozil (Cmax reduced 27%, AUC reduced 30%) when both drugs were administered together; this interaction was avoided by dosing gemfibrozil either 2 hours before or after colestipol. Colestipol had little or no effect on the bioavailability of clofibrate and fenofibrate.

Niacin (nicotinic acid): Niacin plasma concentrations were highly variable among subjects due in part to rapid absorption and elimination of niacin. The median Cmax and AUC were 35 and 48% lower when niacin was given with colestipol, but were not statistically significantly different from a niacin alone treatment. Concomitant multiple dosing of colestipol and niacin had minimal effect on niacin absorption. The interaction between colestipol and niacin does not appear to be clinically significant as evidenced by the additive efficacy of combination colestipol and niacin.

Other classes of lipid-lowering drugs: Colestipol drug interaction studies have not been conducted with HMG-CoA reductase inhibitors (i.e. lovastatin, simvastatin, etc.) or with probucol. However, clinical studies indicate that the cholesterol-lowering effects of colestipol and HMG-CoA reductase inhibitors are additive; therefore a clinically significant drug interaction is unlikely. Other drug interaction studies have been conducted with cholestyramine (another bile acid sequestrant) and various HMG-CoA reductase inhibitors. Cholestyramine significantly reduced the bioavailability of fluvastatin and pravastatin when the HMG-CoA reductase inhibitor was given 1 hour before and up to 4 hours after the cholestyramine dose. However, in clinical studies cholestyramine and HMG-CoA reductase inhibitors had additive cholesterol-lowering effects. The relevance of these cholestyramine drug interaction findings to colestipol is unknown.

Drug Interactions with Other Drugs: Antibiotics: When co-administered, colestipol significantly reduced the bioavailability of penicillin G (Cmax reduced 79%, AUC reduced 84%) and tetracycline (Cmax reduced 52% and AUC reduced 59%). Colestipol had little effect on clindamycin bioavailability.

Anticoagulants: Colestipol had little effect on the bioavailability of warfarin sodium or phenprocoumon.

Anticonvulsants: Colestipol had little or no effect on the bioavailability of phenytoin or carbamazepine.

Antihypertensives: Repeated doses of colestipol given prior to a single dose of propranolol have been reported to decrease propranolol absorption. However, in a follow-up study involving healthy volunteers, single dose administration of colestipol and propranolol, twice-a-day administration for 5 doses of both agents, did not affect the extent of propranolol absorption, but had a small yet statistically significant effect on its rate of absorption. The time to reach maximum concentration was delayed approximately 30 minutes. Therefore, patients on propranolol should be observed when colestipol is either added or deleted from a therapeutic regimen. The effects on the absorption of other beta-blockers have not been determined. Colestipol had little effect on the bioavailability of methyldopa.

Anti-inflammatory Agents: Colestipol had little effect on the bioavailability of ASA.

Cardiac Glycosides: Particular caution should be exercised with digitalis preparations because there are conflicting results about the effects of colestipol on the bioavailability of digoxin and digitoxin in clinical and animal studies. In a single-dose, crossover study in healthy volunteers, the Cmax and AUC of digoxin did not differ when digoxin was co-administered with colestipol vs. when digoxin was given alone (Cmax was 118% and AUC was 97% of the values determined with digoxin alone). Since the potential for binding of digoxin and digitoxin to colestipol may exist, the serum digoxin and digitoxin levels should be monitored during periods of administration or discontinuation of colestipol products.

Diuretics: Colestipol significantly lowered the bioavailability of hydrochlorothiazide (Cmax reduced 14%, 24-hour urinary excretion reduced 31%), chlorothiazide (urinary excretion reduced 58%) and furosemide (Cmax reduced 86%, AUC reduced 79%).

Hypoglycemic Agents: Colestipol had little effect on the bioavailability of tolbutamide.

Nonmedicinal Ingredients: 1) Silicon Dioxide: The granules and the tablets contain silicon dioxide that can adversely influence patients with irritable bowel syndrome, diverticulosis and diverticulitis. 2) Aspartame: The orange granules contain aspartame. Phenylketonurics are sensitive to the phenylalanine in aspartame.

Adverse Effects: The most frequently encountered adverse effects in clinical trials with colestipol products are gastrointestinal. Constipation is the major single complaint and at times is severe and occasionally accompanied by fecal impaction. Hemorrhoids may be aggravated. Most instances of constipation are mild, transient and controlled with standard treatment. See Precautions for recommendation on how to minimize constipation side effect. Predisposing factors for most complaints of constipation are high dose and increasing age (more than 60 years of age).

Less frequent gastrointestinal complaints are abdominal discomfort (abdominal pain and cramping), bloating, flatulence, indigestion, heartburn, nausea, vomiting, diarrhea and loose stools.

Peptic ulceration, gastrointestinal irritation and bleeding, cholecystitis and cholelithiasis have been rarely reported and are not necessarily drug related. Bleeding hemorrhoids and blood in the stool have been infrequently reported.

Other rarely reported adverse reactions include rash, urticaria, dermatitis, muscle and joint pains, arthritis, headache, dizziness, anxiety, vertigo, drowsiness, anorexia, fatigue, weakness, and shortness of breath.

Transient and modest elevations of AST, ALT and serum alkaline phosphatase were infrequently observed in patients treated with colestipol.

During initial registration studies for the granules, adverse reactions occurring at a frequency of 0.1% or more are listed by body system as follows:

Gastrointestinal: (10%): constipation; (1 to 5%): abdominal pain and distension, belching, flatulence, nausea, vomiting,

diarrhea; (0.1 to 1%): peptic ulceration, gastrointestinal irritation and bleeding, cholecystitis, cholelithiasis.
Hypersensitivity: (0.1 to 1%): urticaria, dermatitis.
Musculoskeletal: (0.1 to 1%): muscle and joint pains, arthritis.
Neurologic: (0.1 to 1%): headache, dizziness, anxiety, vertigo, drowsiness.
Miscellaneous: (0.1 to 1%): anorexia, fatigue, weakness, shortness of breath.

Overdose: Symptoms and Treatment: Overdosage with colestipol has not been reported. Should overdosage occur, the chief potential harm would be obstruction of the gastrointestinal tract. The location of such potential obstruction, the degree of obstruction and the presence or absence of normal gut motility would determine treatment.

Dosage: Treatment for elevated serum cholesterol levels should begin with dietary therapy. Patients should be placed on a standard cholesterol-lowering diet at least equivalent to the American Heart Association (AHA) Step 1 Diet, which should be continued during treatment. If appropriate, a programme of weight control and physical exercise should be implemented. A minimum of 6 months of dietary therapy and counselling should usually be undertaken before initiating drug therapy. Shorter periods can be considered in patients with severe elevations of LDL-C (greater than 225 mg/100 mL or 5.85 mmol/L) or with definite coronary heart disease. Drug therapy should be added to dietary therapy and not substituted for it.

Granules and Orange Granules: Adults: Recommended in doses of 5 to 30 g/day of colestipol given once or in divided doses. Initiation of therapy is recommended at 5 g either once or twice a day, with daily increments of 5 g no more frequently than at 1 month intervals.

Tablets: Adults: Recommended in doses of 2 to 16 g/day given once or in divided doses. Initiation of therapy is recommended at 2 g either once or twice a day. Dosage increments of 2 g once or twice daily may be instituted no more frequently than at 1 month intervals.

Serum cholesterol (total, fractionated and triglyceride levels) should be monitored periodically. Consideration should be given to reducing the dosage of colestipol if serum cholesterol levels fall below the targeted range, such as that recommended by the Second Report of the U.S. National Cholesterol Education Program (NCEP). If the desired serum cholesterol levels are not obtained at maximal colestipol doses with good compliance and acceptable side effects, combination lipid lowering therapy or alternate treatment should be considered.

According to the U.S. NCEP Expert Panel, children 10 years and older can be considered for drug therapy after an adequate trial of diet therapy alone is unsuccessful. If drug therapy is initiated, diet therapy should be continued in order to make the entire treatment regimen as effective as possible. The dose of colestipol used is not related to the body weight of the child but to the levels of total and LDL cholesterol after an adequate trial of diet therapy. Initially start the child on the lowest dose of the granules or orange granules. If needed, this dose is increased gradually over time in order to achieve the required total and LDL cholesterol levels. Breakfast and dinner are preferred times for the administration of this medication to children (see Precautions, Children).

Preparation: The granules and orange granules should always be taken mixed in a liquid such as water or a beverage; or in foods such as cereals, soups, yogurt, pudding, cottage cheese or pulpy fruits.

To avoid accidental inhalation or esophageal distress, the granules and orange granules should not be taken in their dry form.

With beverages: 1. Add the prescribed amount of granules or orange granules to a glass (100 mL or more) of water, milk, flavored drink, juice (orange, tomato, pineapple, etc.), or carbonated beverage. A heavy or pulpy juice may minimize complaints relative to consistency. An unsweetened juice may improve palatability. 2. Stir the mixture until the medication is completely suspended. The granules and orange granules **will not** dissolve in the liquid. 3. After drinking the mixture, rinse the glass with a small amount of additional beverage to make sure all the medication is taken.

With cereals, soups and fruits: The granules or orange granules may be taken with milk in hot or regular breakfast cereals, or in soups with a high fluid content. It may also be added to fruits that are pulpy such as crushed pineapple, pears, peaches, or fruit cocktail.

The tablets should be swallowed whole. Do not cut, chew or crush the tablets. The prescribed amount of tablets can be taken with water or any other appropriate fluid based on patient preference. The tablets should be taken with meals.

Information for the Patient: See Blue Section—Information for the Patient "Colestid Preparations".

Supplied: Granules: Each packet contains: colestipol HCl 5 g. Nonmedicinal ingredients: silicon dioxide. Cartons of 30 foil packets.

Orange Granules: Each level scoop or packet contains: 7.5 g orange granules equivalent to 5 g colestipol HCl. Nonmedicinal ingredients: aspartame (phenylalanine 18.2 mg/7.5 g granules), artificial flavor, beta carotene, citric acid, glycerin, maltol, mannitol, methylcellulose, natural flavor. Bottles of 450 g (equivalent to approximately 60 doses) with a scoop. Cartons of 30 foil packets.

Tablets: Each light yellow, film-coated tablet contains: colestipol HCl 1 g. Nonmedicinal ingredients: carnauba wax, cellulose acetate phthalate, colloidal silicon dioxide, magnesium stearate, methylhydroxypropylcellulose, povidone and triacetin. The tablets contain no calories. Bottles of 120.

Store at controlled room temperature (15 to 30°C). Protect from moisture and humidity.

COLPERMIN™
R & C

Peppermint Oil

Symptomatic Relief of Irritable Bowel Syndrome

Pharmacology: The mechanism of action of peppermint oil or its major component, menthol, in reducing lower bowel motility has not been completely elucidated. It has been postulated that peppermint oil exerts its gastrointestinal smooth muscle inhibitory effect by altering calcium ion transport.

Using intraluminal pressure recordings and ultrasound measurements of colonic activity it has been shown that topical rectally instilled peppermint oil inhibited distal colon motility, causing colonic relaxation and a fall in the intracolonic pressure.

Duthie compared the effect of 0.2 mL of peppermint oil suspension and vehicle alone on colonic motility in volunteers using a perfused tube with the tip placed in the sigmoid colon and rectum 20 cm from the anus. A statistically significant reduction in motility and motility index occurred in all 6 subjects after administration of peppermint oil. This inhibition began within 2 minutes and lasted for 7 to 23 minutes with a mean duration of 12 minutes.

Enteric coated capsules containing the carminative to be tested were prepared and their dissolution monitored by an in vivo radiographic technique. Average dissolution time in patients was 143±14.8 minutes, and dissolution occurred in the small bowel.

The urinary excretion of menthol following administration of Colpermin was significantly delayed compared to that after ingesting peppermint oil in soft gelatin capsules, suggesting that with Colpermin an appreciable amount of menthol came in contact with colonic mucosa. Total 24 hour recoveries of menthol were similar, being 35% and 40% for Colpermin and peppermint oil, respectively.

In a similar study, the pharmacokinetic parameters of Colpermin capsules measured over 24 hours in 7 patients following a single dose of 3 capsules were as follows: lag time (h) 1.07±0.39, T_{max} (h) 5±2, absorption T½ (h) 1.2±0.9, terminal elimination T½ (h) 3.6±0.8, Auc (0–19 h) (mg) 79.5±41.3, Auc (0–inf) (mg) 84.0±42.9.

Indications: For the symptomatic relief of abdominal pain, distension, flatulence and gas associated with the irritable bowel syndrome (IBS).

Contraindications: Do not administer with meals or to patients with achlorhydria.

Warnings: Do not administer to patients allergic to peppermint, menthol, arachis (peanut) oil, or similar essential oils. Do not chew or break the capsules as local irritation of the mouth, esophagus and stomach may occur.

Precautions: Peppermint oil should not be administered to patients with heartburn or active gastric ulcers as symptoms may be exacerbated.

Patients should be administered peppermint oil only after examination has definitely diagnosed the presence of IBS with no associated organic lesions.

The safety of peppermint oil for long-term use has not been established. Until chronic dosing studies have been completed, only occasional use is recommended.

Adverse Effects: Reactions may include heartburn and hypersensitivity to peppermint oil or menthol, which is rare and includes erythematous skin rash, headache, bradycardia, muscle tremor and ataxia.

Overdose: Symptoms: Symptoms include mild respiratory tract symptoms (choking, coughing, dyspnea) transient excitement, ataxia and occasional convulsions and occasional painful urination.

Treatment: No specific antidote is known and thus conventional management of symptoms should be instituted. Gastric lavage with tap water or weak sodium bicarbonate solution may be performed.

Dosage: Adults: 1 capsule 3 times a day swallowed whole with a small quantity of water. Increase dosage to 2 capsules 3 times a day if required. Take 30 to 60 minutes before meals. Do not chew. Do not take immediately after meals or with food.

Do not use for more than 14 days, except on the advice of a physician. The safety of peppermint oil for long-term use has not been established. Until chronic dosing studies have been completed, only occasional use is recommended.

Supplied: Each enteric-coated capsule contains: peppermint oil 187 mg. Nonmedicinal ingredients: arachis oil. Lactose-, gluten- and sucrose-free. Light-resistant blister strips of 10, boxes of 2 strips (20 capsules) and 5 strips (50 capsules). Capsules packaged in blister packs have been shown to be stable for 3 years when stored at 20°C. Store in a cool, dark place.

COLPRONE® Ⓟ
Wyeth-Ayerst

Medrogestone

Progestogen

Supplied: Each white, scored compressed tablet, inscribed Ayerst, contains: medrogestone 5 mg. Nonmedicinal ingredients: cornstarch, lactose, magnesium stearate and polyethylene glycol. Energy: 1.76 kJ (0.42 kcal). Alcohol-, gluten-, parabens-, sulfites- and tartrazine-free. Bottles of 50.

COLY-MYCIN® M PARENTERAL Ⓟ
Parke-Davis

Sodium Colistimethate

Antibiotic

Pharmacology: Sodium colistimethate is the pentasodium salt of the penta (methanesulfonic acid) derivative of colistin. Colistin is a basic polypeptide antibiotic substance produced by the growth of Bacillus polymyxa var. colistinus.

Colistin derivatives appear to alter the permeability of the bacterial cytoplasmic membrane, causing leakage of intracellular nucleosides. The drugs are bactericidal in action.

I.M. administration of sodium colistimethate with activity equivalent to that of 150 mg of colistin produces peak serum levels of approximately 5 to 7.5 µg/mL within 2 hours. Peak serum levels after i.v. administration occur within 10 minutes and are higher but decline more rapidly than those achieved after i.m. administration. The serum half-life is approximately 1.5 hours following i.v. and 2.75 to 3 hours following i.m. administration. Blood levels appear to decline more rapidly in children than in adults.

Hydrolysis of sodium colistimethate is required for antibacterial activity. Sodium colistimethate and its metabolites are excreted primarily by the kidneys; urine levels of the active antibiotic are considerably higher than serum levels. In 24 hours, approximately 66% after i.m. administration and 75% after i.v. administration is excreted.

Indications: The treatment of acute or chronic infections due to sensitive strains of certain gram-negative bacilli. Particularly indicated when the infection is caused by sensitive strains of P. aeruginosa. This antibiotic is not indicated for infections due to proteus or neisseria. Sodium colistimethate has proven clinically effective in treatment of infections due to the following gram-negative organisms: A. aerogenes, E. coli, K. pneumoniae and P. aeruginosa.

Pending results of appropriate bacteriologic cultures and sensitivity tests, sodium colistimethate may be used to initiate therapy in serious infections that are suspected to be due to gram-negative organisms.

Contraindications: Patients with a history of sensitivity to the drug.

Precautions: Maximum daily dose should not exceed 5 mg/kg/day with normal renal function.

Coly-Mycin M Parenteral (cont'd)

Occupational Hazards: Transient neurological disturbances may occur. These include circumoral paresthesias or numbness, tingling or formication of the extremities, generalized pruritus, vertigo, dizziness, and slurring of speech. For these reasons, patients should be warned not to drive vehicles or use hazardous machinery while on therapy.

Reduction of dosage may alleviate symptoms. Therapy need not be discontinued, but such patients should be observed with particular care. Overdosage can result in renal insufficiency, muscle weakness and apnea.

Pregnancy: The safety of sodium colistimethate during human pregnancy has not been established.

Since sodium colistimethate is eliminated mainly by renal excretion, it should be used with caution when the possibility of impaired renal function exists. The decline in renal function with advanced age should be considered.

When actual renal impairment is present, sodium colistimethate may be used, but the greatest caution should be exercised and the dosage should be reduced in proportion to the extent of the impairment. Administration of amounts of sodium colistimethate in excess of renal excretory capacity will lead to high serum levels and can result in further impairment of renal function, initiating a cycle which, if not recognized, can lead to acute renal insufficiency, renal shutdown and further concentration of the antibiotic to toxic levels in the body. At this point, interference of nerve transmission at neuromuscular junctions may occur and result in muscle weakness and apnea.

Easily recognized signs indicating the development of impaired renal function are diminishing urine output, rising BUN and serum creatinine. If present, therapy with sodium colistimethate should be discontinued immediately.

If a life-threatening situation exists, therapy may be reinstated at a lower dosage after blood levels have fallen.

Certain other antibiotics (kanamycin, streptomycin, dihydrostreptomycin, polymyxin, neomycin) have also been reported to interfere with the nerve transmission at the neuromuscular junction and thus should not be given concomitantly with sodium colistimethate except with the greatest caution. The antibiotics with a gram positive antimicrobial spectrum, e.g. penicillin, tetracycline, sodium cephalothin, have not been reported to interfere with nerve transmission and, accordingly, would not be expected to potentiate this activity of sodium colistimethate.

Other drugs, including curariform muscle relaxants (ether, tubocurarine, succinylcholine, gallamine, decamethonium and sodium citrate), potentiate the neuromuscular blocking effect and should be used with extreme caution in patients being treated with sodium colistimethate.

If apnea occurs it may be treated with assisted respiration, oxygen, and calcium chloride injections.

Adverse Effects: Respiratory arrest has been reported following i.m. administration of sodium colistimethate. Impaired renal function increases the possibility of apnea and neuromuscular blockade following administration of sodium colistimethate. This has generally been due to failure to follow recommended guidelines, usually overdosage, failure to reduce dose commensurate with degree of renal impairment, and/or concomitant use of other antibiotics or drugs with neuromuscular blocking potential.

A decrease in urine output or increase in BUN or serum creatinine can be interpreted as signs of nephrotoxicity, which is probably a dose dependent effect of sodium colistimethate. These manifestations of nephrotoxicity are reversible following discontinuation of the antibiotic.

Increases of BUN have been reported for patients receiving sodium colistimethate at dose levels of 1.6 to 5 mg/kg per day. The BUN values returned to normal following cessation of sodium colistimethate administration.

Paresthesia, tingling of the extremities or tingling of the tongue and generalized itching or urticaria have been reported by patients who received sodium colistimethate by i.m. or i.v. injection. In addition, the following adverse reactions have been reported for sodium colistimethate: drug fever and gastrointestinal upset, vertigo, and slurring of speech. The subjective symptoms reported by the adult may not be manifest in infants or young children, thus requiring close attention to renal function.

Overdose: Symptoms: Dizziness, ataxia, speech disturbances, generalized muscular weakness, apnea and elevated BUN.

Treatment: Usual medical regimen for treatment of oliguria or anuria. Consider dialysis, particularly if a massive overdosage is discovered shortly after administration.

Dosage: For i.v. or i.m. use: Average dose is 2.5 mg/kg/day given in 2 to 4 divided doses. In the presence of bacteremia, septicemia or other serious infections, greater than average doses may be required. Maximal dose of 5 mg/kg/day should not be exceeded in patients with normal renal function.

Aerosol use: Dissolve vial contents in 1 to 2 mL sterile saline or 5% dextrose in water. May be administered in a standard nebulizing apparatus or with an IPPB device. Adults: 25 to 50 mg 2 to 3 times daily. Children: 2 to 15 mg 2 to 4 times daily. Discard unused portions after 24 hours.

Supplied: Each vial contains: colistin base activity (as sodium colistimethate) 150 mg as a fluffy, spongy, white to slightly yellow lyophilized cake which forms a clear, aqueous solution when reconstituted with 2.0 mL of sterile water for injection USP. Each mL of reconstituted sterile solution contains: sodium colistimethate equivalent to 75 mg colistin base. Energy: nil. Sodium: <1 mmol (16.6 mg)/vial.

COLYTE™

R & C

PEG-3350—Electrolytes

Colon Electrolyte Lavage Preparation

Pharmacology: Colyte cleanses the bowel by induction of diarrhea. The osmotic activity of polyethylene glycol 3350, in combination with the electrolyte concentration, results in virtually no net absorption or secretion of ions or water. Accordingly, large volumes may be administered without significant changes in fluid and electrolyte balance.

Indications: For bowel cleansing prior to colonoscopy or barium enema x-ray examination or surgical procedures requiring a clean colon. PEG lavage solution is also indicated for the treatment of constipation and impaction in the elderly and has been used occasionally in children.

Contraindications: Patients with ileus, gastric retention, bowel perforation, gastrointestinal obstruction, toxic colitis and toxic megacolon.

Warnings: No additional flavorings or ingredients may be added to the solution. Colyte should be used with caution in patients with severe ulcerative colitis.

Precautions: Patients with impaired gag reflex, unconscious or semiconscious patients and patients prone to regurgitation or aspiration should be observed during the administration of Colyte, especially if it is administered via nasogastric tube.

If gastrointestinal obstruction or perforation is suspected, appropriate studies should be performed to rule out those conditions before administration of Colyte.

When it is used in children, caution should be exercised to avoid dehydration.

Drug Interactions: Oral medications administered within 1 hour of the start of administration of Colyte may be flushed from the gastrointestinal tract and not absorbed.

Carcinogenesis, Mutagenesis, Impairment of Fertility: Long-term carcinogenic and reproductive studies with animals have not been performed.

Pregnancy: Animal reproduction studies have not been conducted with Colyte, and it is not known whether Colyte can affect reproductive capacity or harm the fetus when administered to a pregnant patient. Colyte should be given to a pregnant patient only if clearly needed.

Children: PEG lavage solution has been used for bowel cleansing and the treatment of constipation and fecal impaction in children. Treatment and dosage should be monitored by a physician.

Adverse Effects: Nausea, abdominal fullness, and bloating are the most frequent adverse effects, occurring in up to 50% of patients. Abdominal cramps, vomiting and anal irritation occur less frequently. These adverse effects are transient.

Isolated cases of urticaria, rhinorrhea and dermatitis have been reported which may represent allergic reactions.

Dosage: Prior to gastrointestinal examination or procedure: Colyte can be administered orally or by nasogastric tube. Patients should fast at least 3 hours prior to administration. A 1-hour waiting period after the appearance of clear liquid stools should be allowed prior to examination to complete bowel evacuation. No foods except clear liquids should be permitted prior to examination after Colyte administration.

Oral: The recommended adult oral dose is 240 mL every 10 minutes (see Information for Patients). **Lavage is complete when fecal discharge is clear.** Lavage is usually complete after the ingestion of 3 to 4 L.

Nasogastric Tube: Colyte is administered at a rate of 20 to 30 mL/minute (1.2 to 1.8 L/hour).

Preparation of Solution: Add tap water to **fill** line. Replace cap tightly and mix or shake well until all ingredients have dissolved. (No additional flavorings or ingredients may be added to the solution.)

Information for the Patient: Colyte produces a watery stool which cleanses the bowel prior to examination.

For best results, no solid food should be consumed during the 3 to 4 hour period before Colyte consumption. In no case should solid foods be ingested 3 hours before Colyte administration.

The rate of administration is 240 mL (8 oz) every 10 minutes. Rapid drinking of each portion is preferred rather than drinking small amounts continuously.

The first bowel movement should occur approximately 1 hour after the start of Colyte administration. Administration of Colyte should be continued until the watery stool is clear and free of solid matter. This normally requires the consumption of approximately 3 to 4 L, although more or less may be required in some patients. The unused portion should be discarded.

Chronic Constipation: 240 to 480 mL/day orally or as recommended by a physician.

Fecal Impaction: Fecal impaction should only be treated by a physician. Recommended adult dose is 2 to 3 L orally, over a 3 to 4 hour period.

Children: Dosage should be adjusted bearing in mind the weight of the child.

Supplied: Each disposable 4 L jug contains: 240 g polyethylene glycol 3350, sodium chloride 5.84 g, potassium chloride 2.98 g, sodium bicarbonate 6.72 g, sodium sulfate 22.72 g.

After reconstitution of water-soluble components each Colyte preparation delivers the following, in g/L: polyethylene glycol 3350 60.00, sodium chloride 1.46, potassium chloride 0.745, sodium bicarbonate 1.68, sodium sulfate (anhydrous) 5.68. The reconstituted solution is isosmotic and has a mild fruit flavor.

Reconstituted solution should be used within 48 hours after mixing if stored at room temperature. Refrigerated solution must be used within 30 days. Discard unused portion.

Note: Flavoring for Colyte is premixed with powder inside jug.

COMBANTRIN®

Pfizer Consumer

Pyrantel Pamoate

Anthelmintic

Pharmacology: Pyrantel exerts its anthelmintic effect by interfering with the neuromuscular function of the parasite. It is also a cholinesterase inhibitor and a ganglionic stimulant.

The anthelmintic activity of pyrantel has been demonstrated in several animal models. These tests carried out in mice and dogs showed the compound to be effective against intestinal nematodes representative of those found in humans, such as pinworms, large roundworms and hookworms. It is poorly absorbed by the intestinal mucosa so that its activity is confined to the lumen of the bowel. In the dog, the peak plasma levels were low and similarly the tissue levels were low. Less than 15% is excreted via the urine, the major proportion of the dose being excreted in the feces.

Indications: For the treatment of infection with any of the following gastrointestinal parasites when these are present either alone or as a mixed infection. Enterobius vermicularis (threadworm, pinworm) Ascaris lumbricoides (roundworm), Ancylostoma duodenale (hookworm), Necator americanus (hookworm), Trichostrongylus colubriformis and T. orientalis.

Pyrantel should be used for the treatment of infection with one or more of these parasites in both adults and children. It is well tolerated and will not stain the oral mucosa upon ingestion or the clothing by fecal contamination. The presence of an infection with any of the 5 parasites in one member of a family or group of persons in close proximity may indicate unidentified infection in other members. In these circumstances, pyrantel administration to all the family or group members is recommended. (Rigorous cleaning of living quarters and clothing to destroy helminthic ova will help prevent reinfection.)

Contraindications: In patients who are hypersensitive to the drug or to any of the components of the product.

Warnings: *Pregnancy:* Animal reproductive studies have not resulted in any teratogenic effects, but pyrantel has not been studied in the pregnant patient. It should not be used in pregnant women, unless in the judgment of the physician it is deemed essential for the welfare of the patient.

Lactation: It is not known whether pyrantel is excreted in breast milk; nursing should be discontinued if use of this drug is deemed essential.
Children: Pyrantel should not be used in children under the age of 1 year because safety in this age group has not been established.

Precautions: Should be used with caution in patients with pre-existing hepatic dysfunction, as minor transient elevations of AST have occurred in a small percentage of patients.
Occupational Hazards: The effect of pyrantel on the ability to drive and operate heavy machinery has not been studied. There is no evidence to suggest that pyrantel pamoate may affect these abilities.

Adverse Effects: Pyrantel is well tolerated. The infrequent side effects consist for the most part of vomiting and diarrhea. Headache, insomnia, irritability, drowsiness, dizziness, anorexia, abdominal cramps, nausea and rash have seldom been reported. While adverse reactions have been few at the recommended, therapeutic dose of 11 mg/kg, they become considerably more frequent at higher dose concentrations without significant gain in therapeutic effect. No significant changes in total blood count, urinalysis, AST, ALT, alkaline phosphatase and BUN have been observed.

Overdose: Symptoms: Because of its low rate of absorption, plasma concentrations are low. The probable effects of overdosage would include autonomic dysfunction, muscle spasm, twitches and weakness, prostration and ultimately asphyxia due to muscular paralysis.

Treatment: No specific antidote is known. Early gastric lavage and measures to support respiration and blood pressure may be advisable.

Dosage: Pyrantel should be administered in a single oral dose determined on the basis of body weight, i.e., 11 mg/kg. Treatment of pinworm and roundworm: See Table I.

Table I—Combantrin

Treatment of Pinworm and Roundworm

Patient Weight	Oral Suspension	Tablets
11 kg or less	2.5 mL	125 mg
12–23 kg	5 mL	250 mg
24–45 kg	10 mL	500 mg
46–68 kg	15 mL	750 mg
Over 68 kg	20 mL	1 000 mg

Treatment of Hookworm: The same dosage as in Table I given once daily for 3 days.

Pyrantel may be administered without regard to ingestion of food or time of day, and purging is not necessary prior to or during therapy. On rare occasions a second dose has been necessary to eradicate pinworm or roundworm infection. Pyrantel may be taken with milk or fruit juice. The presence of an infection of Enterobius in one patient may indicate unidentified infections in other members of the family. Pyrantel pamoate treatment for all family members is recommended. Rigorous cleaning of living quarters and clothing to destroy helmintic ova and strict attention to personal hygiene will help prevent reinfection. It will not stain the oral mucosa upon ingestion or the clothing by fecal contamination.
Children: Use in infants under 1 year is not recommended because safety in this age group has not been established.

Information for the Patient: See Blue Section—Information for the Patient "Combantrin".

Supplied: Suspension: Each mL of caramel-flavored suspension contains: pyrantel pamoate equivalent to 50 mg of pyrantel base. Nonmedicinal ingredients: antifoam, citric acid, imitation caramel flavor, glycerin, lecithin, polysorbate 80, povidone, sodium benzoate, sorbitol, veegum and water. Tartrazine-free. Amber glass bottles of 50 mL. The suspension must be kept in the amber glass container to protect from light.

Tablets: Each round, pale orange, scored tablet, contains: pyrantel pamoate equivalent to 125 mg of pyrantel base. Nonmedicinal ingredients: alginic acid, cornstarch, FD&C Yellow #6, magnesium stearate, sodium lauryl sulfate and water. Tartrazine-free. Amber plastic blister packages of 12. Tablets must be kept in the amber blister package to protect from light.

Store between 15 and 30°C.

(Shown in Product Recognition Section)

...Canada's Poison Control Centres are listed in the CLIN-INFO SECTION.

COMBIVENT® Inhalation Aerosol Ⓟ

Boehringer Ingelheim

Ipratropium Bromide—Salbutamol Sulfate

Bronchodilator

Pharmacology: Combivent Inhalation Aerosol is a combination of the anticholinergic bronchodilator, ipratropium bromide, and the β_2-adrenergic bronchodilator, salbutamol sulfate. Each actuation from the valve delivers 20 μg ipratropium bromide and 120 μg salbutamol sulfate (equivalent to 100 μg salbutamol base).

Ipratropium bromide is a quaternary ammonium derivative of atropine and is an anticholinergic with bronchodilator properties. On inhalation of ipratropium bromide the onset of action is noted within 5 to 15 minutes with a peak response between 1 and 2 hours, lasting about 2 additional hours with subsequent decline. An inhaled dose of 40 μg of ipratropium bromide inhalation aerosol induced bronchodilatation lasting for some 6 hours.

Salbutamol produces bronchodilation through stimulation of β_2-adrenergic receptors in bronchial smooth muscle, thereby causing relaxation of bronchial muscle fibres. This action is manifested by an improvement in pulmonary function as demonstrated by spirometric measurements.

In a crossover pharmacokinetic study in 12 healthy male volunteers comparing the pattern of absorption and excretion of 2 inhalations of Combivent Inhalation Aerosol to the 2 active components individually, the coadministration of ipratropium bromide and salbutamol sulfate in a single canister did not potentiate the systemic absorption of either component. From a pharmacokinetic perspective, the synergistic efficacy of Combivent Inhalation Aerosol is due to a local effect on the muscarinic and β_2-adrenergic receptors in the lung.

In two 12-week controlled clinical trials, 1 067 patients with chronic obstructive pulmonary disease (COPD) were evaluated for the bronchodilator efficacy of Combivent Inhalation Aerosol (358 patients) in comparison to its components, ipratropium bromide (362 patients) and salbutamol sulfate (347 patients). In these studies Combivent Inhalation Aerosol produced significant improvements in pulmonary function as demonstrated by increases in FEV_1 of 15% or more compared with baseline. The median time to onset of a 15% increase was 15 minutes and the median time to peak was 1 hour for Combivent Inhalation Aerosol and its components. The median duration of effect was 4 to 5 hours for Combivent Inhalation Aerosol compared to 4 hours for ipratropium bromide and 3 hours for salbutamol sulfate. These studies demonstrated that each component of Combivent Inhalation Aerosol contributed to the efficacy of the combination, especially during the first 4 to 5 hours after dosing, and that Combivent Inhalation Aerosol was significantly more effective than ipratropium bromide or salbutamol sulfate administered alone.

Indications: Treatment of bronchospasm associated with chronic obstructive pulmonary disease (COPD).

Contraindications: In patients with cardiac tachyarrhythmias, hypertrophic obstructive cardiomyopathy and in patients with a history of hypersensitivity to soya lecithin or related food products such as soybean and peanut. Combivent should also not be taken by patients hypersensitive to salbutamol sulfate, ipratropium bromide, atropinics or any other aerosol components.

Warnings: *Pregnancy:* The safety of Combivent Inhalation Aerosol in pregnancy has not been established. The benefits of using Combivent when pregnancy is present or suspected must be weighed against possible hazards caused to the fetus.

Salbutamol, a component of Combivent Inhalation Aerosol, has been shown to be teratogenic in mice when given in doses corresponding to 14 times the human aerosol dose; 5 times the human inhalation dose, 0.2 times the maximum human (child weighing 21 kg) oral dose; and 0.4 times the maximum human oral dose and at doses corresponding to the human nebulization dose.

Lactation: It is not known whether the components of Combivent Inhalation Aerosol are excreted in human milk. As salbutamol is probably secreted in breast milk and because of the potential for tumorigenicity shown for salbutamol in animal studies, a decision should be made whether to discontinue nursing or to discontinue the drug, taking into account the importance of the drug to the mother. It is not known whether salbutamol in breast milk has a harmful effect on the neonate. No specific studies have been conducted on the excretion of ipratropium in breast milk. The benefits of Combivent Inhalation Aerosol use during lactation should therefore be weighed against possible effects on the infant.

Children: The efficacy and safety in children younger than 12 years has not been established.

General: Care should be taken to ensure that Combivent Inhalation Aerosol does not reach the eye. There have been isolated reports of ocular complications (i.e., mydriasis, increased intraocular pressure, glaucoma and eye pain) when aerosolized ipratropium has been released into the eyes. Ocular events have occurred when ipratropium aerosol was used with the standard mouthpiece or with a spacing device. In the event that glaucoma is precipitated or worsened, treatment should include standard measures for this condition.

Special care and supervision are required in patients with idiopathic hypertrophic subvalvular aortic stenosis, in whom an increase in the pressure gradient between the left ventricle and the aorta may occur, causing increased strain on the left ventricle.

Care should be taken with patients suffering from cardiovascular disorders, especially coronary insufficiency, cardiac arrhythmias and hypertension; in patients with convulsive disorders, diabetes mellitus, hyperthyroidism and in patients who are usually responsive to sympathomimetic amines. Fatalities have been reported following excessive use of inhaled sympathomimetic, the exact cause of which is unknown.

Immediate hypersensitivity reactions may occur after administration of salbutamol, as demonstrated by rare cases of urticaria, angioedema, rash, bronchospasm, anaphylaxis, and oropharyngeal edema.

In common with other beta-adrenergic agents, salbutamol can induce reversible metabolic changes; these are more pronounced during infusions of the drug and include hyperglycemia and hypokalemia.

Potentially serious hypokalemia may result from β_2-agonist therapy, mainly from parenteral and nebulized administration. Hypokalemia will increase the susceptibility of digitalis-treated patients to cardiac arrhythmias. It is recommended that serum potassium levels be monitored in such situations. Large doses of i.v. salbutamol have been reported to aggravate pre-existing diabetes mellitus and may precipitate ketoacidosis. The relevance of these observations to the use of Combivent is unknown.

Some patients receiving β_2-adrenergic agonist have been reported to have developed severe paradoxical bronchospasm which has been life threatening. The cause of this refractory state is unknown. In this event, the use of the preparation should be discontinued immediately and alternate therapy instituted, since in the reported cases the patients did not respond to other forms of therapy until the drug was withdrawn.

Combivent Inhalation Aerosol inhaler should be administered with extreme caution to patients being treated with MAO inhibitors or tricyclic antidepressants since the action of salbutamol on the cardiovascular system may be potentiated.

Beta-adrenergic blocking drugs, especially the non-cardioselective ones, may effectively antagonize the action of salbutamol and therefore salbutamol and non-selective beta-blocking drugs, such as propranolol, should not usually be prescribed together.

Precautions: General: To ensure optimal delivery of Combivent Inhalation Aerosol to the bronchial tree, the patient should be properly instructed by the physician or other health professional in the use of the inhaler.

In patients with glaucoma, prostatic hypertrophy or urinary retention Combivent should be used with caution. In patients with glaucoma or narrow anterior chambers, care should be taken to ensure that aerosol does not reach the eye. Due care should be taken when a spacing device is employed. There have been isolated reports of ocular complications (i.e., mydriasis, increased intraocular pressure, angle closure glaucoma) when ipratropium bromide either alone or in combination with an adrenergic β_2-agonist has been released into the eyes. In the event that glaucoma is precipitated or worsened, treatment should include standard measure for this condition.

Like other pressurized aerosol formulations, Combivent Inhalation Aerosol contains fluorocarbon propellants dichlorodifluoromethane, dichlorotetrafluoroethane, trichloromonofluoromethane. Such propellants may be hazardous if they are deliberately abused. Inhalation of high concentrations of aerosol sprays has brought about toxic cardiovascular effects and even death, especially under conditions of hypoxia. **However, evidence attests to the relative safety of aerosols when used properly and with adequate ventilation.** The recommended dose of Combivent Inhalation Aerosol should not be exceeded and the patient should be so informed.

Combivent Inhalation Aerosol (cont'd)

The concomitant use of Combivent with other sympathomimetic agents is not recommended since such combined use may lead to deleterious cardiovascular effects.

Drug Interactions: In patients receiving other anticholinergic drugs, Combivent should be used with caution because of possible additive effects.

Xanthine derivatives and β_2-adrenergic agents may enhance the effect of Combivent Inhalation Aerosol.

Other sympathomimetic aerosol bronchodilators or epinephrine should not be used concomitantly with Combivent Inhalation Aerosol. If additional adrenergic drugs are to be administered by any route, they should be used with caution to avoid deleterious cardiovascular effects. Such concomitant use must be individualized and not given on a routine basis. If regular coadministration is required then alternative therapy must be considered.

Combivent Inhalation Aerosol should be administered with extreme caution to patients being treated with MAO inhibitors or tricyclic antidepressants because the action of salbutamol on the vascular system may be potentiated.

Beta-receptor blocking agents and salbutamol inhibit the effect of each other.

Labor and Delivery: It has been reported that high doses of salbutamol, administered i.v., inhibits uterine contractions. Although this effect is extremely unlikely as a consequence of the use of inhaled formulations, it should be kept in mind.

Oral salbutamol has been shown to delay preterm labor in some reports. There are presently no well-controlled studies which demonstrated that it will stop preterm labor or prevent labor at term. Therefore, cautious use of Combivent Inhalation Aerosol is required in pregnant patients when it is given for relief of bronchospasm so as to avoid interference with uterine contractility.

Adverse Effects: Adverse reaction information concerning Combivent Inhalation Aerosol is derived from two 12-week controlled clinical trials (N=358 for Combivent Inhalation Aerosol).

Adverse reactions, judged by the investigator to be possibly related to drug treatment, occurring in 1% or more of patients in any group in the two 12-week controlled clinical trials, appear in Table I.

Table I—Combivent Inhalation Aerosol

Two Double-Blind, Parallel, 12-Week Studies of Patients with COPD
Adverse Reactions Possibly Related to the Drug Treatment Occurring in 1% or More of Patients in Any Group

	Percentage of Patients		
Total Treated	**Combivent N=358**	**Ipratropium Bromide N=362**	**Salbutamol Sulfate N=347**
Body as a Whole—General			
Headache	1.1	1.7	2.0
Gastrointestinal			
Mouth Dry	0.8	1.4	1.2
Respiratory (Lower)			
Coughing	1.4	1.7	1.2
Bronchitis	1.1	1.9	1.2
Dyspnea	1.1	1.4	1.2
Sputum Increased	0.3	0.0	1.2
Respiratory (Upper)			
Pharyngitis	0.8	1.1	0.3
Special Senses—Other			
Taste Perversion	1.1	1.1	0.0

Additional adverse reactions reported in less than 1% of the patients considered possibly due to Combivent include fatigue, enlarged abdomen, hypertension, nervousness, paresthesia, tremor, dyspepsia, nausea, tachycardia, palpitation, abscess, sinusitis, dysuria and urinary retention.

Additional information is derived from the literature on the use of ipratropium or salbutamol inhalation aerosol singly or in combination. Cases of precipitation or worsening of narrow-angle glaucoma, acute eye pain, blurred vision, nasal congestion, hoarseness, voice changes, drying of secretions, unusual taste, mucosal ulcers, irritation from aerosol, paradoxical bronchospasm, wheezing, exacerbation of COPD symptoms, angina, arrhythmia, heartburn, lightheadedness, drowsiness, insomnia, dizziness, vertigo, CNS stimulation, coordination difficulty, weakness, itching, rash, hives, giant urticaria, angioedema, flushing, alopecia, hypotension, increased blood pressure, indigestion, gastrointestinal distress, burning in stomach, vomiting, diarrhea, constipation and urinary difficulty have been reported.

Overdose: Symptoms and Treatment: The effects of overdosage are expected to be related primarily to salbutamol because acute overdosage with ipratropium is unlikely since ipratropium is not well absorbed systemically after aerosol or oral administration. However, should signs of serious anticholinergic toxicity appear, cholinesterase inhibitors may be considered.

Salbutamol overdosage may cause tachycardia, cardiac arrhythmia, hypokalemia, hypertension and, in extreme cases, sudden death. To antagonize the effect of salbutamol, the judicious use of a cardioselective beta-adrenergic blocking agent, (e.g., metoprolol, atenolol), may be considered, bearing in mind the danger of inducing an asthmatic attack. Serum potassium levels should be monitored.

Dosage: Dosage should be individualized, and patient response should be monitored to determine the requirement for more than a single bronchodilator by the prescribing physician on an ongoing basis.

Counselling on smoking cessation should be the first step in treating patients with chronic bronchitis who smoke. Smoking cessation produces symptomatic benefits and has been shown to confer a survival advantage by slowing or stopping the progression of chronic bronchitis and emphysema.

The recommended dosage is 2 inhalations 4 times/day. The maximum daily dose should not exceed 12 inhalations.

Information for the Patient: See Blue Section—Information for the Patient "Combivent Inhalation Aerosol".

Supplied: Each actuation delivers from the valve: ipratropium bromide 20 µg and salbutamol sulfate 120 µg (equivalent to 100 µg salbutamol base). Nonmedicinal ingredients: propellants (dichlorodifluoromethane, dichlorotetrafluoroethane and trichloromonofluoromethane) and soya lecithin. Metal canisters containing 100 or 200 doses of Combivent with mouthpiece (oral adaptor).

The aerosol canisters should be stored at room temperature (15 to 30°C). Avoid excessive humidity. Caution. Contents under pressure. Container may explode if heated. Do not place in hot water or near radiators, stoves or other sources of heat. Do not puncture or incinerate container or store at temperatures over 30°C.

(Shown in Product Recognition Section)

Reviewed 1997

COMBIVENT® Inhalation Solution Ⓟ

Boehringer Ingelheim

Ipratropium Bromide—Salbutamol Sulfate

Bronchodilator

Pharmacology: Combivent Inhalation Solution is a combination of the anticholinergic bronchodilator, ipratropium bromide, and the beta$_2$-adrenergic bronchodilator, salbutamol sulfate.

Ipratropium bromide is a quaternary ammonium derivative of atropine and is an anticholinergic drug which has bronchodilator properties. On inhalation, the onset of action is noted within 5 to 15 minutes, with a peak response between 1 and 2 hours, lasting about 2 additional hours, with subsequent decline from the peak. Bronchodilation is still evident 8 hours after inhalation.

Salbutamol produces bronchodilation through stimulation of beta$_2$-adrenergic receptors in bronchial smooth muscle, thereby causing relaxation of muscle fibres. This action is manifested by an increase in pulmonary function as demonstrated by spirometric measurements. A measurable decrease in airway resistance is typically observed 5 to 15 minutes after inhalation of salbutamol. The maximum improvement in pulmonary function usually occurs after 60 to 90 minutes, and significant bronchodilator activity has been observed to persist from 3 to 6 hours.

In a crossover pharmacokinetic study in 12 healthy male volunteers comparing the pattern of absorption and excretion of a single-dose of Combivent Inhalation Solution to the 2 active components individually, the co-nebulization of ipratropium bromide and salbutamol sulfate does not potentiate the systemic absorptions of either component.

In another 85 day multi-center, randomized, double-blind, parallel trial, 652 patients with chronic obstructive pulmonary disease (COPD) were evaluated for the bronchodilator efficacy of Combivent Inhalation Solution (222 patients) in comparison to its components, ipratropium bromide (214 patients) and salbutamol sulfate (216 patients). In this study, Combivent Inhalation Solution produced significant improvements in pulmonary function as demonstrated by increases in FEV_1 of 15% or more compared with baseline. The median time to onset of a 15% increase in FEV_1 was 15 minutes for each treatment group. The median time to peak was 1 hour for Combivent, and ranged from 1 to 2 hours for the ipratropium group and 30 minutes to 1 hour for the salbutamol group. The median duration of effect was 3 to 5 hours for Combivent Inhalation Solution compared to 4 hours for ipratropium bromide and 2 to 3 hours for salbutamol sulfate.

These studies demonstrated that each component of Combivent Inhalation Solution contributed to the efficacy of the combination, especially during the first 4 hours after administration, and that Combivent Inhalation Solution was significantly more effective than ipratropium or salbutamol administered alone.

Indications: For the management of bronchospasm in patients suffering from chronic obstructive pulmonary disease (COPD) who require regular treatment with both ipratropium and salbutamol.

Contraindications: Patients with cardiac tachyarrhythmias, hypertrophic obstructive cardiomyopathy and patients with a history of hypersensitivity to any of its components or to atropine or its derivatives.

Warnings: *Pregnancy:* The safety in pregnancy has not been established. The benefits of using Combivent when pregnancy is present or suspected must be weighed against possible hazards caused to the fetus.

Salbutamol, a component of Combivent Inhalation Solution, has been shown to be teratogenic in mice when given in doses corresponding to 14 times the human aerosol dose; 5 times the human inhalation dose, 0.2 times the maximum human (child weighing 21 kg) oral dose; and 0.4 times the maximum human oral dose and at doses corresponding to the human nebulization dose.

Lactation: It is not known whether the components of Combivent Inhalation Solution are excreted in human milk. As salbutamol is probably secreted in breast milk and because of the potential for tumorigenicity shown for salbutamol in animal studies, a decision should be made whether to discontinue nursing or to discontinue the drug, taking into account the importance of the drug to the mother. It is not known whether salbutamol in breast milk has a harmful effect on the neonate. No specific studies have been conducted on the excretion of ipratropium in breast milk. The benefits of Combivent Inhalation Solution use during lactation should therefore be weighed against possible effects on the infant.

Children: The efficacy and safety in children under 12 years has not been established.

General: Care should be taken to ensure that the nebulizer mask fits the patient's face properly and that nebulized solution does not escape into the eyes. In patients with glaucoma or narrow anterior chambers, the administration by nebulizer of a combined ipratropium/beta$_2$-agonist solution should be avoided unless measures (e.g., use of swimming goggles or use of a nebulizer with a mouthpiece) are taken to ensure that nebulized solution does not reach the eye. There have been isolated reports of ocular complications (i.e., mydriasis, increased intraocular pressure, angle closure glaucoma) when nebulized ipratropium either alone or in combination with an adrenergic beta$_2$-agonist solution has escaped into the eyes. In the event that glaucoma is precipitated or worsened, treatment should include standard measures for this condition.

Special care and supervision are required in patients with idiopathic hypertrophic subvalvular aortic stenosis, in whom an increase in the pressure gradient between the left ventricle and the aorta may occur, causing increased strain on the left ventricle.

Care should be taken with patients suffering from cardiovascular disorders, especially coronary insufficiency, cardiac arrhythmias and hypertension; in patients with convulsive disorders, diabetes mellitus, hyperthyroidism and in patients who are usually responsive to sympathomimetic amines. Fatalities have been reported following excessive use of inhaled sympathomimetic amines, the exact cause of which is unknown.

Patients with cystic fibrosis may be more prone to gastrointestinal motility disturbances.

Immediate hypersensitivity reactions may occur after administration of salbutamol, as demonstrated by rare cases of urticaria, angioedema, rash, bronchospasm, anaphylaxis and oropharyngeal edema.

In common with other beta-adrenergic agents, salbutamol can induce reversible metabolic changes; these are more pronounced during infusions of the drug and include hyperglycemia and hypokalemia.

Potentially serious hypokalemia may result from beta$_2$-agonist therapy, mainly from parenteral and nebulized administration.

Particular caution is advised in acute severe asthma as hypokalemia may be potentiated by concomitant treatment with xanthine derivatives, steroids and diuretics: the adverse effects of hypokalemia may be exacerbated by hypoxia.

Hypokalemia will increase the susceptibility of digitalis-treated patients to cardiac arrhythmias. It is recommended that serum potassium levels be monitored in such situations. Large doses of i.v. salbutamol have been reported to aggravate pre-existing diabetes mellitus and may precipitate ketoacidosis. The relevance of these observations to the use of Combivent is unknown.

Some patients receiving beta$_2$-adrenergic agonist have been reported to have developed severe paradoxical bronchospasm which has been life threatening.

Precautions: General: Patients must be instructed in the correct use of Combivent Inhalation Solution and warned not to allow the solution or mist to enter the eyes. Acute angle glaucoma has been reported rarely when nebulized solutions of ipratropium have been used in conjunction with beta$_2$-agonist bronchodilators. Protection of the eyes appears to prevent any increase in intraocular pressure and patients who may be susceptible to glaucoma should be warned specifically on the need for ocular protection.

In the following conditions Combivent Inhalation Solution should only be used after careful risk/benefit assessment: hypertrophic obstructive cardiomyopathy, tachyarrhythmia, inadequately controlled diabetes mellitus, recent myocardial infarction and/or severe organic heart or vascular disorders, hyperthyroidism, prostatic hypertrophy, urinary retention, or bladder-neck obstruction.

The patient should be instructed to consult a doctor immediately in the event of acute, rapidly worsening dyspnea. In addition, the patient should be warned to seek medical advice should a reduced response become apparent.

The concomitant use of Combivent with other sympathomimetic agents is not recommended since such combined use may lead to deleterious cardiovascular effects.

Eye pain or discomfort, blurred vision, visual halos or colored images in association with red eyes from conjunctival and corneal congestion may be signs of acute narrow-angle glaucoma. Should any combination of these symptoms develop, treatment with miotic drops should be initiated and specialist advice sought immediately.

Drug Interactions: In patients receiving other anticholinergic drugs, Combivent should be used with caution because of possible additive effects.

Xanthine derivatives and beta$_2$-adrenergic agents may enhance the effect of Combivent Inhalation Solution.

Other sympathomimetic bronchodilators or epinephrine should not be used concomitantly with Combivent Inhalation Solution. If additional adrenergic drugs are to be administered by any route, they should be used with caution to avoid deleterious cardiovascular effects. Such concomitant use must be individualized and not given on a routine basis. If regular co-administration is required then alternative therapy must be considered.

Combivent Inhalation Solution should be administered with extreme caution to patients being treated with MAO inhibitors or tricyclic antidepressants because the action of salbutamol on the vascular system may be potentiated.

Beta-receptor blocking agents and salbutamol inhibit the effect of each other.

Inhalation of halogenated hydrocarbon anesthetics such as halothane, trichloroethylene and enflurane may increase the susceptibility to the cardiovascular effects of beta-agonists.

Labor and Delivery: It has been reported that high doses of salbutamol, administered i.v., inhibits uterine contractions. Although this effect is extremely unlikely as a consequence of the use of inhaled formulations, it should be kept in mind.

Oral salbutamol has been shown to delay preterm labor in some reports. There are presently no well-controlled studies which demonstrated that it will stop preterm labor or prevent labor at term. Therefore, cautious use of Combivent Inhalation Solution is required in pregnant patients when it is given for relief of bronchospasm so as to avoid interference with uterine contractility.

Adverse Effects: COPD: Adverse reaction information concerning Combivent Inhalation Solution is derived from a total of 1 068 COPD patients randomized and treated with either Combivent (222 patients); ipratropium bromide+salbutamol

Table I—Combivent Inhalation Solution

Number (Percent) of Patients with Adverse Events Thought to be Possibly or Probably Treatment Related by Treatment Group, Body System and Preferred Term

	No. (%) of Patients			
	Combivent	**I+S**	**Ipratropium**	**Salbutamol**
Total Treated	**222**	**100**	**327**	**421**
Total with any possible related event	**24(10.8)**	**15(15.0)**	**34(10.4)**	**47(11.2)**
Body as a Whole (General)				
Rigors*	0	0	1(0.3)	1(0.2)
Headache	2(0.9)	4(4.0)	3(0.9)	7(1.7)
Body odor*	0	0	0	1(0.2)
Fatigue*	0	0	1(0.3)	2(0.5)
Hot flushes*	1(0.5)	0	0	0
Edema (legs*)	1(0.5)	0	0	0
Back pain*	0	0	0	1(0.2)
Influenza-like symptoms*	0	0	1(0.3)	0
Chest pain*	0	0	1(0.3)	0
Pain*	0	0	1(0.3)	0
Cardiovascular				
Hypertension	0	1(1.0)	0	1(0.2)
Cardiac failure*	0	0	0	1(0.2)
ECG abnormal specific	0	0	0	1(0.2)
Syncope*	0	0	0	1(0.2)
Central and Peripheral Nervous System				
Dizziness	1(0.5)	2(2.0)	0	3(0.7)
Dysphonia	3(1.4)	0	1(0.3)	1(0.2)
Somnolence*	1(0.5)	0	2(0.6)	0
Confusion*				1(0.2)
Nervousness	1(0.5)	1(1.0)	0	8(1.9)
Tremor	1(0.5)	0	2(0.6)	3(0.7)
Paresthesia*	0	0	1(0.3)	1(0.2)
Hypoesthesia*	0	0	1(0.3)	1(0.2)
Insomnia*	0	0	0	1(0.2)
Gastrointestinal				
Mouth (dry)	4(1.8)	3(3.0)	7(2.1)	9(2.1)
Nausea	0	0	3(0.9)	5(1.2)
Diarrhea*	0	0	0	1(0.2)
Anorexia*	0	0	0	1(0.2)
Flatulence*	0	0	0	1(0.2)
Stomatitis ulcerative*	0	0	0	1(0.2)
Saliva (increased*)	0	0	1(0.3)	0
Heart Rate and Rhythm				
Arrhythmia	1(0.5)	0	0	0
Palpitation	2(0.9)	0	2(0.6)	0
Tachycardia	0	0	1(0.3)	0
Psychiatric				
Agitation*	1(0.5)	0	0	0
Amnesia*	0	0	0	1(0.2)
Anxiety*	0	0	0	1(0.2)
Depression*	0	0	1(0.3)	0
Resistance Mechanism				
Moniliasis*	1(0.5)	0	0	0
Infection (fungal)	0	0	0	1(0.2)
Respiratory System (Lower)				
Dyspnea*	2(0.9)	0	6(1.8)	8(1.9)
Coughing	2(0.9)	2(2.0)	6(1.8)	1(0.2)
Bronchitis*	0	0	1(0.3)	7(1.7)
Sputum (increased*)	1(0.5)	0	2(0.6)	3(0.7)
Bronchospasm	0	0	1(0.3)	1(0.2)
Hemoptysis*	0	0	0	1(0.2)
Respiratory System (Upper)				
Rhinitis*	0	0	3(0.9)	0
Pharyngitis*	2(0.9)	0	4(1.2)	3(0.7)
Skin and Appendages				
Rash	0	1(1.0)	0	2(0.5)
Sweating (increased)	0	0	0	1(0.2)
Pruritus	0	0	0	1(0.2)
Urticaria	0	0	1(0.3)	0
Special Senses (Other)				
Taste perversion*	1(0.5)	2(2.0)	0	2(0.5)
Urinary				
Micturition frequency	0	0	0	1(0.2)
Dysuria	0	0	0	1(0.2)
Urinary retention	0	0	1(0.3)	0
Vision Disorders				
Conjunctivitis	1(0.5)	0	0	0
Vision (abnormal)	1(0.5)	0	0	2(0.5)
Eye pain	0	0	2(0.6)	0
Musculoskeletal				
Myalgia	0	0	0	1(0.2)

*These adverse events are considered to have no reasonable causal relationship to the treatment.

Combivent Inhalation Solution (cont'd)

sulfate (100 patients); ipratropium bromide (327 patients) or salbutamol sulfate (421 patients).

Adverse reactions, judged by the investigator to be possibly related to drug treatment, occurring in 1 or more patients in any group in the controlled clinical trials, appear in Table I (on previous page).

Additional adverse reactions reported and considered possibly due to Combivent include fatigue, abdominal pain, hypertension, dyspepsia, tachycardia, sinusitis, dysuria, and urinary retention.

Additional information is derived from the literature on the use of ipratropium or salbutamol inhalation solution singly or in combination. Cases of blurred vision, taste perversion, dry mouth, paradoxical bronchospasm, bronchitis, angina, arrhythmia, lightheadedness, drowsiness, insomnia, dizziness, vertigo, CNS stimulation, weakness, itching, rash, flushing, alopecia, hypotension, increased blood pressure, gastrointestinal distress, vomiting, diarrhea, edema, constipation and urinary difficulty have been reported.

Overdose: Symptoms and Treatment: The effects of overdosage are expected to be related primarily to salbutamol because acute overdosage with ipratropium is unlikely since ipratropium is not well absorbed systemically after aerosol or oral administration. However, should signs of serious anticholinergic toxicity appear, cholinesterase inhibitors may be considered.

Salbutamol overdosage may cause tachycardia, cardiac arrhythmia, hypokalemia, hypertension and, in extreme cases, sudden death. To antagonize the effect of salbutamol, the judicious use of a cardioselective beta-adrenergic blocking agent, (e.g., metoprolol, atenolol), may be considered, bearing in mind the danger of inducing an asthmatic attack. Serum potassium levels should be monitored.

Dosage: Dosage should be individualized, and patient response should be monitored to determine the requirement for more than a single bronchodilator by the prescribing physician on an ongoing basis.

Counseling on smoking cessation should be the first step in treating patients with chronic bronchitis who smoke. Smoking cessation produces symptomatic benefits and has been shown to confer a survival advantage by slowing or stopping the progression of chronic bronchitis and emphysema.

Adults and Children over 12 years: COPD: Combivent Inhalation solution in unit dose vials (UDVs) may be administered from a suitable nebulizer or an intermittent positive pressure ventilator. The recommended dosage is 1 UDV vial 3 or 4 times daily.

Dilution Instructions: If necessary, before use, doses may be diluted to a total nebulization volume of 3 to 5 mL with preservative-free 0.9% sterile sodium chloride solution and used immediately. Discard any unused solution. Nebulize over 10 to 15 minutes at gas flow of 6 to 10 L/min. Repeat every 6 hours as necessary.

Supplied: Each unit dose vial contains: ipratropium bromide anhydrous (as monohydrate) 0.5 mg and salbutamol sulfate 3 mg (equivalent to salbutamol base 2.5 mg). Nonmedicinal ingredients: hydrochloric acid, purified water and sodium chloride. Plastic, single dose units in strips of 10, 20 unit dose vials per box. Unopened unit dose vials should be stored at controlled room temperature (between 15 and 25°C) and protected from light and heat. Do not use if solution is discolored. Keep out of reach of children.

Reviewed 1998

COMPLEAT™ MODIFIED
Novartis Nutrition

Therapeutic Nutrient

Indications: A blenderized tube feeding formulated from traditional foods including meat, vegetables and fruit for patients with normal gastrointestinal function.

Recommended for both short-term and long-term tube feeding.

Not recommended when a low residue tube feeding is required.

Precautions: Not for parenteral administration.

Dosage: 6 cans [1 500 mL or 6 700 kJ (1 600 kcal)] provides at least 100% of the Canadian RNI (adult males, 25 to 49) for protein and essential vitamins and minerals.

Ready-to-use: Feed at room temperature. Follow a physician's or dietitian's directions. When initiating feedings, the flow rate, volume and dilution are dependent on the patient's condition and tolerance. Care should be taken to avoid contamination of the product during preparation and administration. Additional fluid requirements should be met by giving water orally with or after feedings or when flushing the feeding tube.

Feeding should be initiated at a slow rate. Rate and volume of feeding can be increased gradually over 48 hours if well tolerated. If intolerance develops, return to previously tolerated rate, or dilute formula to half strength until desired rate is achieved, then switch to full strength. Do not alter strength and volume at the same time. Rinse the tube with 20 to 30 mL water after each intermittent feeding or every 3 to 4 hours during continuous feeding to avoid clogging and provide additional water.

Supplied: Each 250 mL ready-to-use can contains: water, maltodextrin, beef puree, pea puree, green bean puree, corn oil, peach puree, calcium caseinate, orange juice, mono- and diglycerides, disodium phosphate, calcium carbonate, dipotassium phosphate, potassium citrate, potassium chloride, carrageenan, salt, magnesium oxide, choline bitartrate, ascorbic acid, molybdenum yeast, ferric ammonium citrate, selenium yeast, chromium yeast, alpha tocopheryl acetate, zinc sulfate, niacinamide, D-calcium pantothenate, copper gluconate, manganese sulfate, thiamine hydrochloride, pyridoxine hydrochloride, vitamin A palmitate, riboflavin, folic acid, biotin, potassium iodide, vitamin K_1, vitamin D_3, vitamin B_{12}. See Table I.

Energy Distribution: protein 16%, fat 31%, carbohydrate 53%; 446 kJ (107 kcal)/100 mL.

Table I—Compleat Modified

Analysis	100 mL	
Energy	440 (105)	kJ (kcal)
Protein	4.2	g
Carbohydrate	14	g
Fat	3.6	g
Crude Fibre	0.2	g
Linoleic Acid	1.4	g
Sodium	85	mg
Potassium	140	mg
Vitamin A	330	IU
Vitamin C	6	mg
Thiamine	0.15	mg
Riboflavin	0.17	mg
Niacin	2	mg
Calcium	73	mg
Iron	1.2	mg
Vitamin D	27	IU
Vitamin E	3	IU
Vitamin B_6	0.2	mg
Folic Acid	0.026	mg
Vitamin B_{12}	0.0006	mg
Phosphorus	80	mg
Iodine	0.01	mg
Magnesium	27	mg
Zinc	1.5	mg
Copper	0.13	mg
Biotin	0.02	mg
Pantothenic Acid	0.66	mg
Vitamin K	0.0067	mg
Choline	20	mg
Chloride	87	mg
Manganese	0.27	mg
Selenium	0.0067	mg
Chromium	0.01	mg
Molybdenum	0.02	mg
Osmolality	300	mOsm/kg water

Ready-to-use cans of 250 mL, cases of 24. Store unopened at room temperature. Once opened, store covered in refrigerator and use within 24 hours.

COMPLEX 15®
Schering

Dimethicone—Lecithin

Emollient

Indications: To soothe and relieve dry, sensitive skin. Phospholipid lecithin is a water-binding agent which occurs naturally in the deepest layers of the skin. Each phospholipid molecule forms a complex of 15 water molecules creating a moisture reservoir which restores the skin's moisture balance.

Dosage: Apply as often as needed to the hands, body and face.

Supplied: Face Cream: Each 100 mL tube contains: 0.5% dimethicone, 0.1% lecithin.

Hand Cream: Each 50 mL tube contains: 1.5% dimethicone, 0.3% lecithin.

Lotion: Each 275 mL bottle contains: 1% dimethicone, 0.3% lecithin.

Nonmedicinal ingredients: Products are unscented and contain no parabens. Products contain water, caprylic/capric triglyceride, glycerin, glyceryl stearate, dimethicone, PEG-50 stearate, squalene, cetyl alcohol, glycol stearate, myristyl myristate, stearic acid, lecithin, C 10-30 carboxylic acid sterol ester, diazolidinyl urea, carbomer 934, magnesium aluminum silicate, propylene glycol, sodium hydroxide, BHT, tetrasodium EDTA.

CONDYLINE™ Ⓟ
Canderm Pharma

Podofilox

Antimitotic Agent

Pharmacology: Necrosis of visible tissue is observed following treatment of genital warts with podofilox. The exact mechanism of action is unknown.

Podofilox is believed to exert its antimitotic effect by binding to tubulin, at a site close to but not identical to the binding site of colchicine; it is thought that this antimitotic effect causes necrosis of wart tissue, the observed clinical effect. In addition, podofilox is known to interfere with nucleoside transport which may also contribute to its action. Crude podophyllum resin, from which podofilox is extracted, has been shown to produce mitotic arrest and necrosis of wart tissue.

Indications: For the topical treatment of external genital warts (Condylomata acuminata) confined to the penile and vulvar regions. The effectiveness of podofilox in the treatment of perianal or mucous membrane warts has not been established.

Contraindications: Patients who develop hypersensitivity to podofilox or intolerance to any component of the formulation. Podofilox **should not** be applied to open wounds. The consumption of alcoholic beverages for several hours after treatment is to be avoided.

Warnings: Podofilox is intended for topical use only.

Podofilox is a potent vesicant and is to be used only as directed by a physician. Extreme care should be taken to avoid contact with the eye, tongue or any mucosal tissue of the genital area (including vagina, cervix, anus or perianus). If contact with the eyes occurs, flush immediately with copious amounts of water and see a doctor immediately.

Precautions: Diagnosis: Although Condylomata (genital warts) have a characteristic appearance, histopathologic confirmatory tests should be obtained if there is any question of the diagnosis. Differential diagnosis from squamous cell carcinoma (so called "Bowenoid papulosis") is of particular concern. Squamous cell carcinoma may also be associated with human papillomavirus but **should not** be treated with podofilox.

General: Podofilox may not prevent either the recurrence of previously resolved warts or the development of new warts at sites remote from the treatment site. The recommended method of application, frequency of application and duration of usage should not be exceeded (see Dosage).

The use of large volumes, greater than 0.25 mL per application or 0.5 mL/day, should be avoided. This can best be accomplished by limiting the treatment area to less than 10 cm² and instructing the patient in the proper application of the product.

Genital warts may be contagious and the patient should be instructed to abstain from sexual intercourse. If this is not possible, a latex condom must be used until the infected partner is declared cured by the physician.

The patient should be instructed that if the product is accidentally spilled on undiseased skin, it should be wiped off at once and the exposed skin washed vigorously with warm soapy water and rinsed thoroughly. This product should not be used if growth or surrounding tissue is inflamed or irritated. Self-treatment of genital warts with surface areas greater than 10 cm² should not be permitted. The patient should be cautioned against applying the drug to lesions other than warts.

Information for the Patient: The patient should be provided with a Patient Information leaflet when a Condyline prescription is filled.

Long-Term Safety: Reports of lifetime carcinogenicity studies in rodents with podofilox, the drug substance, are not available. In general, podofilox was not shown to be carcinogenic in published animal studies. There are published reports that, in the mouse studies, crude podophyllin resin (containing podofilox) applied topically to the cervix produced changes resembling carcinoma in situ. These changes were reversible at 5 weeks after cessation of treatment. In another published study, epidermal carcinoma of the vagina and cervix was found in 1 out of 18 mice following 120 applications of podophyllin, applied twice weekly over a 15-month treatment period.

Podofilox was not mutagenic in the Ames plate reverse mutation assay, either with or without metabolic activation, at concentrations up to 5 mg/plate. There was no evidence of potential oncogenicity in the BALB/3T3 cell transformation assay. Results from the mouse micronucleus in vivo assay using podofilox 0.5% solution in concentrations up to 25 mg/kg indicate that podofilox should be considered a potential clastogen (a chemical that induces disruption and breakage of chromosomes).

Daily topical application of podofilox at doses up to the equivalent of 0.2 mg/kg (5 times the recommended maximum human dose) to rats throughout gametogenesis, mating, gestation, parturition and lactation for 2 generations demonstrated no impairment of fertility.

Pregnancy: There are no adequate and well-controlled studies in pregnant women. Podofilox should be used in pregnancy only if the potential benefit justifies the potential risk to the fetus.

Lactation: It is not known whether this drug is excreted in human milk. Because of the potential for serious adverse reactions in nursing infants from podofilox, a decision should be made whether to discontinue nursing or to discontinue the drug, taking into account the importance of the drug to the mother.

Children: Safety and effectiveness in children have not been established.

Patients with Special Diseases and Conditions: Podofilox should not be used in diabetics or people with poor blood circulation. Podofilox should not be applied on moles, birthmarks or unusual warts with hair growing from them. Podofilox should not be used on tissue which was recently exposed to laser surgery or cryosurgery.

Adverse Effects: In clinical trials the following have been shown to be the most common local adverse events which were reported at some time during treatment: inflammation 67%, burning 62%, erosion 59%, pain 49%, other, e.g., bleeding, itching, dizziness, insomnia 21%.

These reactions may be greater in the occluded prepuce of the uncircumcised male patient.

Overdose: Symptoms and Treatment: Topical: In cases of tingling, burning or extreme tenderness, soak the area in cold water for 10 minutes; repeat as required for the relief of pain. A mild analgesic, e.g. ASA with codeine or acetaminophen with codeine may be beneficial for pain management in some cases. Adjuvant topical anti-inflammatory therapy e.g. hydrocortisone acetate, can be advantageous for alleviation of local discomfort.

Systemic: Topically applied podofilox may be absorbed systemically. It may cause systemic toxicity after oral ingestion. Neurotoxic reactions are observed after oral doses exceeding 0.5 mg podofilox per kg body weight. For an adult this dose corresponds to the equivalent of the content of 2 bottles of 3.5 mL Condyline.

Systemic toxicity may lead to prolonged peripheral neuropathy. Initial symptoms are weakness, drowsiness, dizziness, diarrhea and general indisposition. A later symptom may be coma with the risk of respiratory failure, ileus, vascular crisis and death.

Treatment of overdosage is principally symptomatic and supportive therapy.

Hemoperfusion through coal filter and symptomatic treatment may prevent a fatal outcome. Possible toxic effects of the bone marrow (e.g. leukocytosis, pancytosis) are generally transitory.

Dosage: Apply twice daily, morning and evening (every 12 hours) for 3 consecutive days followed by 4 days without treatment. The use of podofilox twice a day for 3 days constitutes a treatment cycle. Treatment cycles should be repeated up to 4 times until there is no visible wart tissue. **If there is incomplete response after 4 treatment cycles, alternative treatment should be considered.**

Podofilox is applied to the warts with a cotton tipped applicator supplied with the drug. The wetted applicator should be touched to the wart to be treated, applying the minimum amount of solution necessary to cover the lesion. **Treatment should be limited to less than 10 cm² of wart tissue and to no more than 500 μg of the solution per day.**

To ensure that only the genital warts are treated and properly applied, the physician performs the first application for the patient as an office procedure. The patient is shown how to minimize contact with the surrounding healthy tissue and the use of a hand mirror which may help, when he/she applies the solution at home. There is no evidence to suggest that more frequent application will increase efficacy, but this would be expected to increase the rate of local adverse reactions and systemic absorption.

Before applying the medication, the area to be treated should be gently washed with soap and water and gently patted dry. If an area in the occluded prepuce (under the foreskin) is being treated, care should be taken to allow the solution to dry before letting the foreskin return to its normal position. Avoid contact with clothing until the solution has dried. After each treatment, the used applicator should be properly and safely disposed of in a garbage can, out of reach of children, and the patient should wash his/her hands. It is recommended that the **area not be washed following application** of podofilox as is the practice with traditional podophyllum resin preparations.

Information for the Patient: See Blue Section—Information for the Patient "Condyline".

Supplied: Each mL of topical solution contains: podofilox 0.5%. Amber glass bottles of 3.5 mL with plastic child-resistant cap. Package includes cotton-tipped applicators. Store at controlled room temperature (15 to 30°C), away from light and heat, in a tightly-closed container.

CONGEST Ⓟ

Trianon

Conjugated Estrogens

Estrogen

Supplied: 0.3 mg: Each oval, green, sugar-coated tablet contains: conjugated estrogens CSD 0.3 mg. Nonmedicinal ingredients: calcium phosphate tribasic, carnauba wax, cellulose, colloidal silicon dioxide, gum acacia, lactose, lake, magnesium carbonate, opalux green dye (D&C yellow 10 aluminum lake, FD&C yellow 6 aluminum lake, FD&C blue 1 aluminum lake, methylparaben, polyvinylpyrrolidone, propylparaben, sodium benzoate, sucrose syrup), starch, stearic acid, sucrose syrup, sugar and talc. Alcohol-, gluten-, sulfite- and tartrazine-free. Bottles of 100 and 500.

0.625 mg: Each oval, maroon, sugar-coated tablet contains: conjugated estrogens CSD 0.625 mg. Nonmedicinal ingredients: calcium carbonate, calcium phosphate tribasic, carnauba wax, cellulose, colloidal silicon dioxide, gum acacia, lactose, lake, magnesium carbonate, opalux maroon dye (erythrosine aluminum lake, FD&C blue 2 aluminum lake, FD&C yellow 6 aluminum lake, gum acacia, povidone, sodium benzoate, sucrose syrup, titanium dioxide), starch, stearic acid, sucrose syrup, sugar and talc. Alcohol-, gluten-, sulfite- and tartrazine-free. Bottles of 100 and 500.

0.9 mg: Each oval, pink, sugar-coated tablet contains: conjugated estrogens CSD 0.9 mg. Nonmedicinal ingredients: calcium carbonate, calcium phosphate tribasic, carnauba wax, cellulose, colloidal silicon dioxide, gum acacia, lactose, lake, magnesium carbonate, opalux pink dye (D&C red 27 aluminum lake, FD&C blue 2 aluminum lake, FD&C yellow 6 aluminum lake, methylparaben, polyvinylpyrrolidone, propylparaben, sodium benzoate, sucrose syrup, titanium dioxide), starch, stearic acid, sucrose syrup, sugar and talc. Alcohol-, gluten-, sulfite- and tartrazine-free. Bottles of 100 and 500.

1.25 mg: Each oval, yellow, sugar-coated tablet contains: conjugated estrogens CSD 1.25 mg. Nonmedicinal ingredients: calcium phosphate tribasic, carnauba wax, cellulose, colloidal silicon dioxide, gum acacia, lactose, lake, magnesium carbonate, opalux yellow dye (FD&C yellow 5 aluminum lake, sodium benzoate, sucrose syrup, titanium dioxide), starch, stearic acid, sucrose syrup, sugar and talc. Alcohol-, gluten-, sulfite- and tartrazine-free. Bottles of 100 and 500.

Geriatric patients may experience unique drug-induced effects. Be aware of potential side effects and drug interactions. For more information, refer to the CLIN-INFO SECTION.

CONRAY® 30
CONRAY® 43
CONRAY® 60

Mallinckrodt

Iothalamate Meglumine

Radiopaque Medium

Pharmacology: Following intravascular injection, Conray is rapidly transported through the circulatory system to the kidneys and is excreted unchanged in the urine by glomerular filtration. Renal accumulation is sufficiently rapid that maximum radiographic density in the calyces and pelves occurs in most instances about 3 to 8 minutes after injection. In patients with impaired renal function, diagnostic opacification frequently is achieved only after prolonged periods.

Angiography may be performed following intravascular injection of Conray which will permit visualization until significant hemodilution occurs.

The biliary system, pancreatic duct or joint spaces may be visualized by injecting the contrast medium directly into the region to be studied.

Injectable iodinated contrast agents are excreted either through the kidneys or through the liver. These 2 excretory pathways are not mutually exclusive, but the main route of excretion seems to be related to the affinity of the contrast medium for serum albumin. Iothalamate salts are poorly bound to serum albumin, and are excreted mainly through the kidneys.

The liver and small intestine provide the major alternate route of excretion. In patients with severe renal impairment, the excretion of this contrast medium through the gallbladder and into the small intestine sharply increases.

Pregnancy and *Lactation:* Iothalamate salts cross the placental barrier in humans; and are excreted unchanged in human milk.

Computerized Tomography of the Head: When Conray 30, Conray 43 or Conray 60 is used for contrast enhancement in computed tomographic brain scanning, the degree of enhancement is directly related to the amount of iodine administered. Rapid infusion of the entire dose amount yields peak blood iodine concentrations immediately following the infusion, which fall rapidly over the next 5 to 10 minutes. This can be accounted for by the dilution in the vascular and extracellular fluid compartments which causes an initial sharp fall in plasma concentration. Equilibration with the extracellular compartments is reached by about 10 minutes; thereafter, the fall becomes exponential. With respect to tumors, maximum contrast enhancement frequently occurs at a time following peak blood iodine concentration. This delay in maximum contrast enhancement can range from 5 to 40 minutes, depending on the peak iodine levels achieved and the cell type and vascularity of the tumor. This lag suggests that the contrast enhancement of the image is at least in part dependent on the passage of iodine through the defective blood-brain barrier and on its accumulation within the lesion and outside the blood pool. The image enhancement of nontumoral lesions, such as arteriovenous malformations and aneurysms, is probably dependent on the iodine content of the circulating blood pool. Studies indicate that equilibrated blood iodine levels of 100 mg% are required in most cases to achieve adequate contrast enhancement. This can be accomplished by the infusion of approximately 30 to 40 g of iodine (100 to 150 mL of Conray 60 or 200 to 300 mL of Conray 30).

In brain scanning, the contrast medium does not accumulate in normal brain tissue due to the presence of the "blood brain barrier". The increase in X-ray absorption in the normal brain is due to the presence of the contrast agent within the blood pool. A break in the blood brain barrier, such as occurs in malignant tumors of the brain, allows accumulation of the contrast medium within the interstitial tumor tissue; adjacent normal brain tissue does not contain the contrast medium. When used for cranial computerized angiotomography, rapid bolus injection and/or infusion combined with rapid CT scanning will provide clear delineation of the cerebral vessels.

Computerized Tomography of the Body: In non-neural tissues (during CT of the body), Conray diffuses rapidly from the vascular to the extravascular space. Increase in X-ray absorption is related to blood flow, concentration of the contrast medium and extraction of the contrast medium by interstitial tissue since no barrier exists; contrast enhancement is thus due to the relative differences in extravascular diffusion between normal and abnormal tissue, quite different from that in the brain.

Enhancement of CT with Conray 60 may be of benefit in establishing diagnoses of certain lesions in some sites with

Conray (cont'd)

greater assurance than is possible with unenhanced CT and in supplying additional features of the lesions. In other cases, the contrast medium may allow visualization of lesions not seen with CT alone or may help to define suspicious lesions seen with unenhanced CT.

The pharmacokinetics of Conray in normal and abnormal tissue has been shown to be variable. Contrast enhancement appears to be greatest within 30 to 90 seconds after bolus administration, thus greatest enhancement can be detected by a series of consecutive 2- to 3-second scans ("Dynamic CT Scanning") during this time period. Dynamic scanning may improve enhancement and diagnostic assessment of tumors and other lesions such as an abscess, occasionally revealing more extensive disease. A cyst, or similar nonvascularized lesions may be distinguished from vascularized solid lesions by comparing enhanced and unenhanced scans; the vascularized lesions would show an increase. The latter might be benign, malignant or normal, but it is unlikely that it would be a cyst, hematoma or other nonvascularized lesion.

Venography: Venography may be performed with Conray 43 or Conray 60 following injection into an appropriate vein and will permit visualization until sufficient hemodilution occurs.

Indications: Conray 30: For use in i.v. infusion urography and for contrast enhancement in computerized tomography of the brain.

Conray 43: For use in lower extremity venography, i.v. infusion urography and for the i.v. contrast enhancement in computerized tomography of the brain.

Conray 60: For use in excretory urography, cerebral angiography, peripheral arteriography, venography, arthrography, direct cholangiography, endoscopic retrograde cholangiopancreatography, i.v. contrast enhancement in computed tomography and digital subtraction angiography.

Contraindications: Known hypersensitivity to salts of iothalamic acid and in patients with anuria or severe oliguria. Arthrography should not be performed if infection is present in or near the joint.

Percutaneous transhepatic cholangiography is contraindicated in patients with coagulation defects and prolonged prothrombin times until normal, or near normal, coagulation is achieved.

Endoscopic retrograde cholangiography is contraindicated during an acute attack of pancreatitis or during clinically evident cholangitis. The procedure is also contraindicated in patients in whom endoscopic examination is prohibited.

Conray must not be used for myelography or for injection into cysts and sinuses that might communicate with the subarachnoid space.

Conray should not be used for the enhancement of CT brain images in patients suspected of having cranial subarachnoid hemorrhage.

Warnings: Ionic iodinated contrast media inhibit blood coagulation more than nonionic contrast media. Nonetheless, it is necessary to avoid prolonged contact of blood with syringes containing all contrast media.

Serious, rarely fatal, thromboembolic events causing myocardial infarction and stroke have been reported during angiographic procedures with both ionic and nonionic contrast media. Therefore, meticulous intravascular administration technique is necessary, particularly during angiographic procedures, to minimize thromboembolic events. Numerous factors, including length of procedure, number of injections, catheter and syringe material, underlying disease state, and concomitant medications may contribute to the development of thromboembolic events. For these reasons meticulous angiographic techniques are recommended including close attention to keeping guidewires, catheters and all angiographic equipment free of blood, use of manifold systems and/or 3-way stopcocks, frequent catheter flushing and heparinized saline solutions, and minimizing the length of the procedure. The use of plastic syringes in place of glass syringes has been reported to decrease but not eliminate the likelihood of in vitro clotting.

Serious or fatal reactions have been associated with the administration of iodine containing radiopaque media. It is of utmost importance to be completely prepared to treat any contrast medium reaction.

A definite risk exists in the use of intravascular contrast agents in patients who are known to have multiple myeloma. In some instances anuria has developed resulting in progressive uremia, renal failure and eventually death. Although neither the contrast agent nor dehydration has separately proved to be the cause of anuria in myeloma, it has been speculated that the combination of both may be causative factors. The risk in myelomatous patients is not an absolute contraindication to the procedure; however, partial dehydration in the preparation of these patients for the examination is not recommended since this may predispose to precipitation of myeloma protein in the renal tubules. No form of therapy, including dialysis, has been successful in reversing the effect. Myeloma, which occurs most commonly in persons over 40, should be considered before instituting intravascular administration of contrast agents.

Administration of radiopaque materials to patients known or suspected to have pheochromocytoma should be performed with extreme caution. If, in the opinion of the physician, the possible benefits of such procedures outweigh the considered risks, the procedures may be performed; however, the amount of radiopaque medium injected should be kept to an absolute minimum. The blood pressure should be assessed throughout the procedure, and measures for treatment of a hypertensive crisis should be available.

Contrast media have been shown to promote the phenomenon of sickling in individuals who are homozygous for sickle cell disease when the material is injected i.v. or intra-arterially.

Conray must not be used for myelography or for injection into cysts and sinuses that might communicate with the subarachnoid space.

In computed tomography of the brain, it has been reported that in low density lesions false negative results may be produced following contrast media administration, i.e., contrast media may obscure low density lesions. Steps should be taken to insure that patients undergoing computed tomography have received no injections of water-soluble contrast media at least 24 hours prior to examination. It is recommended that a computed tomographic brain scan always be obtained prior to the administration of Conray.

Precautions: General: All procedures utilizing contrast media carry a definite risk of producing adverse reactions. While most reactions may be minor, life-threatening and fatal reactions may occur without warning. The risk-benefit factor should always be carefully evaluated before such a procedure is undertaken. At all times a fully equipped emergency cart, or equivalent supplies and equipment, and personnel competent in recognizing and treating adverse reactions of all severity or situations which may arise as a result of the procedure, should be immediately available. Since severe delayed reactions have been known to occur, emergency facilities and competent personnel should be available for at least 30 to 60 minutes after administration.

Diagnostic procedures which involve the use of iodinated intravascular contrast agents should be carried out under the direction of personnel skilled and experienced in the particular procedure to be performed.

The possibility of an idiosyncratic reaction in patients who have previously received a contrast medium without ill effect should always be considered. Prior to the injection of any contrast medium, the patient should be questioned to obtain a medical history with emphasis on allergy and hypersensitivity. A positive history of bronchial asthma or allergy, a family history of allergy, or a previous reaction or hypersensitivity to a contrast agent may imply a greater than usual risk. Such a history, by suggesting histamine sensitivity and consequently proneness to reactions, may be more accurate than pretesting in predicting the potential for reaction, although not necessarily the severity or type of reaction in the individual case. A positive history of this type does not arbitrarily contraindicate the use of a contrast agent, when a diagnostic procedure is thought essential, but does call for caution. Premedication with antihistamines or corticosteroids to avoid or minimize the possible allergic reactions in such patients should be considered. Under no circumstance should the antihistamine or the corticosteroid be mixed in the same syringe with the contrast medium because of chemical incompatibility.

In order to screen patients for allergy potential, various pretesting procedures have been developed; however, specific literature reports indicate that none of these provocative test procedures can be relied upon to predict severe or fatal reactions. The pretest most often performed is the slow i.v. injection of 0.5 to 1.0 mL of the radiopaque medium prior to the injection of the full dose. The absence of a reaction to the test dose does not preclude the possibility of a reaction to the full dose. In some instances, reactions to the test dose itself may be extremely severe; therefore, close observation of the patient and facilities for emergency treatment are indicated.

Partial dehydration prior to the examination should be avoided in patients with chronic renal disease, multiple myeloma, diabetes and in infants and small children.

In patients with advanced renal disease, iodinated contrast media should be used with caution, and only when the need for the examination dictates, since excretion of the medium may be impaired. Patients with combined renal and hepatic disease and those with severe hypertension or congestive heart failure may present an additional risk. Renal failure has been reported in patients with liver dysfunction who were given an oral cholecystographic agent, followed by an intravascular iodinated radiopaque agent and also in patients with occult renal disease, notably diabetics and hypertensives.

Administration of Conray should, therefore, be postponed in any patient with a known or suspected hepatic or biliary disorder who has recently taken cholecystographic contrast agent.

Caution should be exercised in performing contrast medium studies in patients with endotoxemia and/or those with elevated body temperatures.

Reports of thyroid storm occurring following the intravascular use of iodinated radiopaque agents in patients with hyperthyroidism or with an autonomously functioning thyroid nodule, suggest that this additional risk be evaluated in such patients before use of this drug.

Iodine-containing contrast agents may alter the results of thyroid function tests which depend on iodine estimation, e.g., PBI and radioactive iodine uptake studies. Such tests, if indicated, should be performed prior to the administration of this preparation.

Pregnancy: Reproduction studies with various concentrations of iothalamate sodium, iothalamate meglumine or a combination of both have been performed in mice, rats, and rabbits, and have revealed no evidence of impaired fertility or harm to the fetus.

There are no well controlled studies in pregnant women, but marketing experience does not include any positive evidence of adverse effects on the fetus. Although there is no clearly defined risk, such experience cannot exclude the possibility of infrequent or subtle damage to the fetus. Conray should be used in pregnant women only when clearly needed.

Lactation: It is not known whether this drug is excreted in human milk. As a general rule, nursing should not be undertaken or continued following administration of this drug since many drugs are excreted in human milk.

Precautions for specific procedures receive comment under that procedure in the Dosage section.

Adverse Effects: General: Adverse reactions accompanying the use of iodine-containing intravascular contrast agents are usually mild and transient, although severe and life-threatening reactions, including fatalities, have occurred. Because of the possibility of severe reactions to both the procedure and radiopaque medium, appropriate emergency facilities and well trained personnel should be available to treat both types. These emergency facilities and personnel should remain available for 30 to 60 minutes following the procedure since severe delayed reactions have been reported.

The following adverse reactions have been observed in conjunction with the use of iodine-containing intravascular contrast agents.

The most frequent reactions are nausea, vomiting, facial flush and a feeling of body warmth. These are usually of brief duration. Other reactions include the following:

Allergic-type: dermal manifestations of urticaria with or without pruritus, erythema and maculopapular rash, dry mouth, sweating, conjunctival symptoms, facial, peripheral and angioneurotic edema. Symptoms relating to the respiratory system include sneezing, nasal stuffiness, coughing, choking, dyspnea, chest tightness and wheezing, which may be initial manifestations of more severe and infrequent reactions including asthmatic attack, laryngospasm and bronchospasm with or without edema, pulmonary edema, apnea and cyanosis. Rarely, these allergic type reactions can progress into anaphylactic shock with loss of consciousness and coma and severe cardiovascular disturbances.

Cardiovascular: generalized vasodilatation, flushing and venospasm. Occasionally, thrombosis or, rarely, thrombophlebitis. Red blood cell clumping and agglutination, crenation and interference in clot formation. Extremely rare cases of disseminated intravascular coagulation resulting in death have been reported. Severe cardiovascular responses include rare cases of hypotensive shock, coronary insufficiency, cardiac arrhythmia, fibrillation and arrest. These severe reactions are usually reversible with prompt and appropriate management; however, fatalities have occurred.

Technique: extravasation with burning pain, hematomas, ecchymosis and tissue necrosis, paresthesia or numbness, vascular constriction due to injection rate, thrombosis and thrombophlebitis, perforation and dissection of blood vessels, dislodgement of atheromatous plaques, injury to neighboring organs.

Neurological: spasm, convulsions, aphasia, syncope, paresis, paralysis resulting from spinal cord injury and pathology associated with the syndrome of transverse myelitis, visual field losses which are usually transient, but may be permanent, coma and death.

Other: headache, trembling, shaking, chills without fever and lightheadedness. Temporary renal shutdown or other nephropathy. (Adverse reactions to specific procedures receive comment under that procedure in the Dosage section.)

Treatment of Adverse Effects to Contrast Media: Contrast media should be administered only by physicians thoroughly familiar with the emergency treatment of all adverse reactions to contrast media. The assistance of other trained personnel such as cardiologists, internists and anesthetists is required in the management of severe reactions.

A guideline for the treatment of adverse reactions is presented below. This outline is not intended to be a complete manual on the treatment of adverse reactions to contrast media or on cardiopulmonary resuscitation. The physician should refer to the appropriate texts on the subject.

It is also realized that institutions or individual practitioners will already have appropriate systems in effect and that circumstances may dictate the use of additional or different measures.

Minor Allergic Reactions: (if considered necessary) The i.v. or i.m. administration of an antihistamine such as diphenhydramine HCl 25 to 50 mg is generally sufficient (contraindicated in epileptics). The resulting drowsiness makes it imperative to ensure that out-patients do not drive or go home unaccompanied.

Major or Life threatening Reactions: A major reaction may be manifested by signs and symptoms of cardiovascular collapse, severe respiratory difficulty and nervous system dysfunction. Convulsions, coma and cardiorespiratory arrest may ensue.

The following measures should be considered: Start emergency therapy immediately—carefully monitoring vital signs. Have emergency resuscitation team summoned—do not leave patient unattended. Ensure patent airway—guard against aspiration. Commence artificial respiration if patient is not breathing. Administer oxygen if necessary. Start external cardiac massage in the event of cardiac arrest. Establish route for i.v. medication by starting infusion of appropriate solution (5% dextrose in water). Judiciously administer specific drug therapy as indicated by the type and severity of the reaction. Careful monitoring is mandatory to detect adverse reactions of all drugs administered: a) soluble hydrocortisone 500 to 1 000 mg i.v. for all acute allergic-anaphylactic reactions. b) epinephrine 1:1 000 solution (in the presence of anoxia it may cause ventricular fibrillation): i) 0.2 to 0.4 mL s.c. for severe allergic reactions. ii) in extreme emergency 0.1 mL/min, appropriately diluted, may be given i.v. until desired effect is obtained. Do not exceed 0.4 mL. iii) in case of cardiac arrest 0.1 to 0.2 mL appropriately diluted may be given intracardially. c) in hypotension (carefully monitoring blood pressure): i) phenylephrine HCl 0.1 to 0.5 mg appropriately diluted slowly i.v. or by slow infusion or ii) levarterenol bitartrate 4 mL of 0.2% solution in 1 000 mL of 5% dextrose by slow drip infusion. d) sodium bicarbonate 5%; 50 mL i.v. every 10 minutes as needed to combat post-arrest acidosis. e) Atropine 0.4 to 0.6 mg i.v. to increase heart rate in sinus bradycardia. May reverse 2nd or 3rd degree block. f) to control convulsions: i) pentobarbital sodium 50 mg in fractional doses slowly i.v. (contraindicated if cyanosis is present) or ii) Diazepam 5 to 10 mg slowly i.v. titrating the dose to the response of the patient. Defibrillation, administration of antiarrhythmics and additional emergency measures and drugs may be required. Transfer patient to intensive care unit when feasible for further monitoring and treatment.

Overdose: Symptoms: Overdosage may occur. The adverse effects of overdosage are life-threatening and affect mainly the pulmonary and cardiovascular system. The symptoms may include cyanosis, bradycardia, acidosis, pulmonary hemorrhage, convulsions, coma and cardiac arrest.

Treatment: Treatment of an overdose is directed toward the support of all vital functions and prompt institution of specific therapy. Iothalamate salts are dialyzable.

Dosage: I.V. Infusion Urography: (Conray 30, Conray 43): I.V. infusion urography enhances the potential for more diagnostic information in those patients in whom the usual i.v. pyelography technique has not provided satisfactory visualization, or in those patients in whom there is reason to believe the usual i.v. pyelography technique will not provide satisfactory visualization. If renal function is not seriously impaired, the infusion urography technique usually provides satisfactory visualization of an unobstructed urinary tract, including nephrogram and cystogram. Additional advantages are the lack of necessity for dehydration of the patients and compression techniques.

Patient Preparation: For urography study, appropriate preparation of the patient is important for optimal visualization. A low residue diet is recommended on the day preceding the examination. Dehydration is not indicated for the performance of infusion urography. Patients should be maintained in an optimal state of hydration prior to the procedure. Unless contraindicated, a laxative may be given the evening before examination.

A preliminary radiograph usually is made prior to infusion of the contrast agent.

Precautions: A definite risk is involved in i.v. infusion urography in patients known to have chronic renal disease or multiple myeloma. This risk is not a contraindication to the procedure. However, partial dehydration in preparation of these patients is not recommended.

In addition to the general precautions previously described, infants and small children should not have any fluid restrictions prior to i.v. infusion urography. Injections of Conray represent an osmotic load which, if superimposed on increased serum osmolality due to partial dehydration, may magnify hypertonic dehydration. I.V. infusion urography in diabetic patients may involve increased risks and partial dehydration in these patients is not recommended (see also Precaution, General).

Patients with severely impaired renal function should be maintained in an appropriate state of hydration before the procedure. The increased osmotic load associated with i.v. infusion urography should be considered in patients with congestive heart failure.

Adverse Reactions: (see Adverse Effects, General).

Dosage: It is advisable that Conray be at or close to body temperature when infused.

Conray 30: The recommended dose for adults, older children and infants is 2 to 4 mL/kg with a maximum not exceeding 300 mL in adults and a proportionally smaller amount in children according to age and weight.

The solution is injected through an appropriate i.v. needle at a rate of approximately 50 mL/min. Any appropriate i.v. administration set may be used observing the usual precautions for maintaining sterility and safety in administration. Films are usually taken at 5-minute intervals following the initiation of the infusion for a total of 20 minutes.

In patients with impaired renal function, diagnostic opacification frequently is achieved only after prolonged periods. In these individuals, periodic film obtained up to 24 hours after infusion might yield useful information.

Special procedures such as nephrotomography and cystography are best accomplished within 30 minutes of the conclusion of the infusion.

Conray 43: The usual dose in adults and children is 2 to 3 mL/kg by i.v. administration, not to exceed a total dose of 200 mL in adults and a proportionally smaller amount in children according to age and weight.

The solution is infused at a rate of approximately 40 to 50 mL/min. Other infusion details are as for Conray 30.

Contrast Enhancement of Computed Tomographic (CT) Brain Imaging: Tumors: Conray may be useful to enhance the demonstration of the presence and extent of certain malignancies such as: gliomas including malignant gliomas, glioblastomas, astrocytomas, oligodendrogliomas and gangliomas; ependymomas, medulloblastomas; meningiomas; neuromas, pinealomas; pituitary adenomas; craniopharyngiomas; germinomas; and metastatic lesions.

The usefulness of contrast enhancement for the investigation of the retrobulbar space and in cases of low grade or infiltrative glioma has not been demonstrated.

Maximum contrast enhancement frequently occurs at a time following peak blood iodine concentration. This delay in maximum contrast enhancement can range from 5 to 40 minutes, depending on the peak blood iodine concentration achieved (total dose and rate of administration) and the cell type of the tumor.

In cases where lesions have calcified, there is less likelihood of enhancement. Following therapy, tumors may show decreased or no enhancement.

Non-neoplastic Conditions: The use of Conray may be beneficial in the image enhancement of non-neoplastic lesions. Cerebral infarctions of recent onset may be better visualized with the contrast enhancement while some infarctions are obscured if contrast media are used. The use of Conray resulted in contrast enhancement in 60% of cerebral infarctions studied from 1 to 4 weeks from the onset of symptoms.

Sites of active infection may also be enhanced following contrast medium administration.

Arteriovenous malformations and aneurysms usually show contrast enhancement. In the case of these vascular lesions, the enhancement is probably dependent on the iodine content of the circulating blood pool.

Hematomas and intraparenchymal bleeders seldom demonstrate any contrast enhancement. However, in case of intraparenchymal clot, for which there is no obvious clinical explanation, contrast medium administration may be helpful in ruling out the possibility of associated arteriovenous malformation.

The opacification of the inferior vermis following contrast medium administration has resulted in false positive diagnosis in a number of normal studies.

Patient Preparation: No special patient preparation is required for contrast enhancement of CT brain scanning. However, it is advisable to ensure that patients are well hydrated prior to examination.

Warning: Convulsions have occurred in patients with primary or metastatic cerebral lesions following the administration of iodine containing radiopaque media for the contrast enhancement of CT brain images.

Dosage: Conray 60: Usual Dose: Computed Tomography of the Brain: The recommended dose of Conray 60 for adults and children is 1 to 2 mL/kg of body weight, not exceeding 150 mL in adults and proportionally smaller amount in children according to age and weight. In most cases, scanning may be performed immediately after completion of administration; however when fast scanning equipment (less than 1 minute) is used consideration should be given to waiting approximately 5 minutes to allow for maximum contrast enhancement of the neoplasm (tumor).

Conray 43: Usual Dose: The usual dose in adults and children is 2 to 3 mL/kg by i.v. administration, not to exceed a total dose of 200 mL in adults and a proportionally smaller amount in children according to age and weight. In most cases, scanning may be performed immediately after completion of administration; however when fast scanning equipment (less than 1 minute) is used consideration should be given to waiting approximately 5 minutes to allow for maximum contrast enhancement.

Conray 30: Usual Dose: The recommended dose for adults and children is 2 to 4 mL/kg, not exceeding 300 mL in adults and proportionately smaller amount in children according to age and weight. The dose should be infused as rapidly as possible through any well vented i.v. administration set and needle, observing the usual precautions for maintaining sterility.

Cranial Computed Angiotomography: Conray 60 may be administered by i.v. bolus injection, or by bolus injection followed by rapid infusion.

For bolus injection, the usual dose in adults and children is 1 mL/kg at an injection rate of 2 mL/s with scanning begun immediately after administration.

This dose may be repeated as necessary. The total dose per procedure should not exceed 200 mL in adults and in children the total dose is reduced in approximate proportion to age and body weight.

In adults, when the rapid, high dose combination bolus and infusion technique is used, a 50 mL bolus injection followed by a rapid infusion of 150 mL may be given or a 100 mL bolus injection followed by a rapid infusion of 100 mL may be used. Scanning is begun immediately after the bolus administration. In children, the dose is reduced in approximate proportion to age and body weight.

Computed Tomography of the Body: Conray 60 may be administered when necessary to visualize vessels and organs in patients undergoing CT of the chest, abdomen and pelvis.

Because unenhanced scanning may provide adequate information in the individual patient, the decision to employ contrast enhancement, which may be associated with additional risk and increased radiation exposure, should be based upon a careful evaluation of clinical, other radiological and unenhanced CT findings.

Continuous or multiple scans separated by intervals of 1 to 3 seconds during the first 30 to 90 seconds postinjection of the contrast medium (dynamic CT scanning) provide enhancement of diagnostic significance. Subsets of patients in whom delayed body CT scans might be helpful have not been identified. Inconsistent results have been reported and abnormal and normal tissues are usually isodense during the time frame used for delayed CT scanning. The risks of such indiscriminate use of contrast media are well known and such use is not recommended. At present, consistent results have been documented using dynamic CT techniques only.

Precautions: In addition to the general precautions previously described, it should be noted that patient motion, including respiration, can markedly effect image quality, therefore,

Conray (cont'd)

patient cooperation is essential. The use of an intravascular contrast medium can obscure tumors in patients undergoing CT evaluation of the liver resulting in a false negative diagnosis (see Pharmacology).

Patient Preparation: No special patient preparation is required for contrast enhancement in computerized tomography. However, it is advisable to insure that patients are well hydrated prior to examination.

In patients undergoing abdominal or pelvic examination, opacification of the bowel may be valuable in scan interpretation.

Usual Dosage: Conray 60 may be administered by bolus injection, by rapid infusion or by a combination of both.

For vascular opacification, a bolus injection of 25 to 50 mL may be used, repeated as necessary. When prolonged arterial or venous phase enhancement is required and for the enhancement of specific lesions, a rapid infusion of 150 mL may be used. In some instances, a 100 to 150 mL infusion may be employed to define the area of interest followed by bolus injections of 20 to 50 mL to clarify selected scans.

Excretory Urography: (Conray 60): Following i.v. injection, Conray is rapidly excreted by the kidneys. Conray may be visualized in the renal parenchyma 30 seconds following bolus injection. Maximum radiographic density of the calyces and pelves occurs in most instances about 3 to 8 minutes after injection. In patients with severe renal impairment, contrast visualization may be substantially delayed, or opacification may not occur at all.

Patient Preparation: Appropriate preparation of the patient is important for optimal visualization. A low residue diet is recommended for the day preceding the examination and a laxative is given the evening before the examination, unless contraindicated. A preliminary radiograph is usually made prior to the injection of the contrast agent.

Precautions: In addition to the general precautions previously described, infants and small children should not have any fluid restrictions prior to excretory urography. Injections of Conray represent an osmotic load which, if superimposed on increased serum osmolality due to partial dehydration, may magnify hypertonic dehydration. Therefore, patients' state of dehydration should be evaluated prior to and following this procedure and adjusted if necessary.

A definite risk is involved in excretory urography in patients known to have chronic renal disease, multiple myeloma or diabetes. This risk is not a contraindication to the procedure (see Warnings and Precautions, General Concerning Preparatory Dehydration).

Adverse Reactions: see Adverse Effects, General.

Usual Dosage: (Conray 60): Adults: The usual dose is 30 to 60 mL. Children 14 years of age and over, of average weight, may receive the adult dose.

The total dose is normally injected within 30 to 90 seconds. The higher dosage may be indicated to achieve optimum results in instances where poor visualization may be anticipated. When nephrograms and/or sequential urograms are desired, the total dose should be rapidly injected, normally within 15 to 30 seconds. The dosage for children is reduced in proportion to age and body weight. The following approximate schedule is recommended for infants and children based on a dosage of about 0.5 mL/kg of body weight: Under 6 months of age: 5 mL, 6 to 12 months: 8 mL, 1 to 2 years: 10 mL, 2 to 5 years: 12 mL, 5 to 8 years: 15 mL, 8 to 12 years: 18 mL, 12 to 14 years: 20 to 30 mL.

Cerebral Angiography: Conray 60 may be used to visualize the cerebral vasculature by any of the accepted techniques, including digital subtraction angiography.

Patient Preparation: Cerebral angiography is normally performed with local or general anesthesia (see Precautions, General). Premedication may be employed as indicated.

A preliminary radiograph is usually made prior to injection of the contrast agent.

Precautions: In addition to the general precautions previously described, cerebral angiography should be performed with special caution in patients with advanced arteriosclerosis, severe hypertension, cardiac decompensation, senility, recent cerebral thrombosis or embolism and migraine.

Adverse Reactions: In addition to the general adverse reactions previously described, the major sources of cerebral arteriographic adverse reactions appear to be related to repeated injections of the contrast material, administration of doses higher than those recommended, the presence of occlusive atherosclerotic vascular disease and the method and technique of injection.

Adverse reactions are normally mild and transient. A feeling of warmth in the face and neck is frequently experienced. Infrequently, a more severe burning discomfort is observed.

Serious neurological reactions that have been associated with cerebral angiography include stroke, amnesia, respiratory difficulties, hemiparesis, visual field loss, aphasia, convulsions, hypotension, bradycardia, coma and death.

Usual Dosage: The usual dosage employed varies with the site and method of injection and the age, condition and weight of the patient. In adults carotid and vertebral angiography, by either the percutaneous needle or catheter methods, is usually performed with a single rapid injection of 6 to 10 mL. Additional injections are made as indicated. Retrograde brachial cerebral angiography, in adults, is usually performed with a single rapid injection of 35 to 50 mL into the right brachial artery. Other dosages may be employed depending upon the vessel injected and the procedure followed. The dose for children is reduced in approximate proportion to age and body weight.

The use of an arterial digital subtraction technique allows the dose (concentration and/or volume) of the contrast material to be reduced by approximately 50% and permits less selective arterial catheterization.

Peripheral Arteriography and Venography: (Conray 60): Conray may be injected to visualize the arterial and venous peripheral circulation. Arteriograms of the upper and lower extremities may be obtained by any of the established techniques. Most frequently a percutaneous injection is made into the brachial artery in the arm or the femoral artery in the leg. Venograms are obtained by injection into an appropriate vein in the upper and lower extremity.

Patient Preparation: The procedure is normally performed with local or general anesthesia (see Precautions, General). Premedication may be employed as indicated. A preliminary radiograph is usually made prior to the injection of the contrast agent.

Precautions: In addition to the general precautions previously described, moderate decreases in blood pressure occur frequently with intra-arterial (brachial) injections. This change is usually transient and requires no treatment; however, the blood pressure should be monitored for approximately 10 minutes following injection. Special care is required when venography is performed in patients with suspected thrombosis, phlebitis, severe ischemic disease, local infection or a totally obstructed venous system. In the presence of venous stasis, vein irrigation with normal saline should be considered following the procedure.

Adverse Reactions: In addition to the general adverse reactions previously described, hemorrhage and thrombosis have occurred at the puncture site of the percutaneous injection.

Brachial plexus injury has been reported following axillary artery injection. Thrombophlebitis, syncope and very rare cases of gangrene have been reported following venography.

Usual Dosage: Peripheral Arteriography: In adults a single rapid injection of 20 to 40 mL is normally sufficient to visualize the entire extremity. The dose for children is reduced in proportion to body weight.

The use of an arterial digital subtraction technique allows the dose (concentration and/or volume) of the contrast material to be reduced by approximately 50% and permits less selective arterial catheterization.

Venography: The usual dose of Conray 60 for adults is a single rapid injection of 20 to 40 mL. The dose for children is reduced in proportion to body weight.

The usual dose of Conray 43 is 30 mL single dose up to a cumulative total dose of 125 mL per lower extremity, depending on the technique used. The dose for children is reduced in proportion to body weight. Following the procedure the venous system should be flushed with either 5% dextrose in water (D5W) or normal saline (Sodium Chloride Injection U.S.P.), or the contrast medium should be removed by leg massage and/or leg elevation.

Arthrography: (Conray 60): Precautions: In addition to the general precautions previously described, strict aseptic technique is required to prevent the introduction of infection. Fluoroscopic control should be used to ensure proper introduction of the needle into the synovial space and prevent extracapsular injection. Aspiration of excessive synovial fluid will reduce the pain on injection and prevent the rapid dilution of the contrast agent. It is important that undue pressures not be exerted during the injection.

Adverse Reactions: In addition to the general adverse reactions previously described, arthrography may induce joint pain or discomfort which is usually mild and transient but occasionally may be severe and persist for 24 to 48 hours following the procedure. Effusion requiring aspiration may occur in patients with rheumatoid arthritis.

Usual Dosage: Arthrography is usually performed under local anesthesia. The amount of contrast agent required is solely dependent on the size of the joint to be injected and the technique employed.

The following dosage schedule for normal adult joints should serve only as a guide since joints may require more or less contrast medium for optimal visualization. Dosage should be reduced for children in proportion to body weight. Knee, hip: 5 to 15 mL. Shoulder, ankle: 5 to 10 mL. Other: 1 to 4 mL.

Passive or active manipulation is used to disperse the medium throughout the joint space.

The lower volumes of contrast medium are usually employed for double contrast examinations. Following the injection of the contrast medium 50 to 100 mL of either filtered room air or carbon dioxide is introduced for examination of the knee and lesser volumes for other joints.

Direct Cholangiography: (Conray 60): Precautions: In addition to the general precautions previously described, percutaneous transhepatic cholangiography should only be attempted when compatible blood for potential transfusions is in readiness and emergency surgical facilities are available.

The patient should be carefully monitored for at least 24 hours to ensure prompt detection of bile leakage and hemorrhage. Appropriate premedication of the patient is recommended and drugs which are cholespastic, such as morphine, should be avoided. Respiratory movements should be controlled during introduction of the needle.

Adverse Reactions: In addition to the general adverse reactions previously described, adverse reactions may often be attributed to injection pressure or excessive volume of the medium resulting in overdistention of the ducts and producing local pain.

Some of the medium may enter the pancreatic duct which may result in pancreatic irritation. Occasionally, nausea, vomiting, fever, and tachycardia have been observed. Pancholangitis resulting in liver abscess or septicemia has been reported.

In percutaneous transhepatic cholangiography, some discomfort is common, but severe pain is unusual. Complications of the procedure are often serious and have been reported in 4 to 5% of patients. These reactions have included bile leakage and biliary peritonitis, gallbladder perforation, internal bleeding (sometimes massive), blood-bile fistula resulting in septicemia involving gram-negative organisms, and tension pneumothorax from inadvertent puncture of the diaphragm or lung. Bile leakage is more likely to occur in patients with obstructions that cause unrelieved high biliary pressure.

Dosage: It is advisable that Conray 60 be at or close to body temperature when injected. The injection is made slowly without undue pressure, taking the necessary precautions to avoid the introduction of bubbles.

Operative Cholangiography: The usual dose is 10 mL but as much as 25 mL may be needed depending upon the caliber of the ducts. If desired, the contrast agent may be diluted 1:1 with Sodium Chloride Injection U.S.P. using strict aseptic procedures. Following surgical exploration of the ductal system, repeat studies may be performed before closure of the abdomen, using the same dose as before.

Postoperative Cholangiography: Postoperatively, under fluoroscopic control, the ductal system may be examined by injection of the contrast agent through an in-place T-tube. These delayed cholangiograms are usually made from the fifth to the tenth postoperative day prior to removal of the T-tube. The usual dose is the same as for operative cholangiography.

Percutaneous Transhepatic Cholangiography: This procedure is recommended for carefully selected patients only for the diagnosis of jaundice in suspected extrahepatic biliary obstruction. The procedure is only employed where oral or i.v. cholangiography and other procedures have failed to provide the necessary information. In obstructed cases, percutaneous transhepatic cholangiography is used to determine the cause and site of obstruction to help plan surgery. The technique may also be of value in avoiding laparotomy in poor risk jaundice patients since failure to enter a duct by an experienced physician is considered to be suggestive evidence against obstructive jaundice. Careful attention to technique is essential for the success and safety of the procedure. The procedure is performed under fluoroscopic control; local anesthesia following analgesic premedication is usually employed.

Depending upon the caliber of the biliary tree, a dose of 10 to 40 mL is generally sufficient to opacify the entire ductal system. If desired, the contrast agent may be diluted 1:1 with Sodium Chloride Injection U.S.P. using strict aseptic procedures.

As the needle is advanced or withdrawn, a bile duct may be located by frequent aspiration for bile or mucus. Before the dose is administered, as much bile as possible is aspirated. The injection may be repeated for exposures in different planes and repositioning of the patient, if necessary, should be done with care. If a duct is not readily located by aspiration, successive small doses of 1 to 2 mL of the medium are injected into the liver as the needle is gradually withdrawn, until a duct is visualized by X-ray. If no duct can be located after 3 or 4 attempts, the procedure should be terminated. Inability to enter a duct by a person experienced in the technique is generally considered to be suggestive evidence against obstructive disease.

Endoscopic Retrograde Cholangiopancreatography: (Conray 60): Endoscopic retrograde cholangiopancreatography (ERCP) is indicated in carefully selected patients with known or suspected pancreatic or biliary tract disease when other diagnostic procedures have failed to provide the necessary diagnostic information. Prior to the development of ERCP, X-ray examination of the pancreatic ducts could only be obtained at laparotomy.

Precautions: In addition to the general precautions previously described, endoscopic retrograde cholangiopancreatography should only be performed by personnel skilled and experienced with the procedure, and careful attention to technique is essential for the success and safety of the procedure. Fluoroscopy is mandatory during injection to prevent over distention of the duct systems.

Filling of the pancreatic parenchyma must be avoided. Retrograde injection of contrast media beyond a significant stenosis or obstruction is not recommended, since this is considered to increase the risk of ascending infection. ERCP should not be performed in patients with a positive test for Hepatitis Associated Antigen, since fiberscopes cannot be sterilized and there is a real possibility of transmitting viral hepatitis to successive patients.

Adverse Reactions: In addition to the general adverse reactions previously described, adverse reactions that have occurred and attributable to either the procedure or contrast agent include nausea, vomiting, fever, severe abdominal pain, duodenal wall intravasation, septicemia, pancreatitis, and perforation of the common bile duct associated with pathology. Frequently, elevation of serum amylase is observed following an ERCP procedure.

Dosage: The procedure is usually performed following pharyngeal anesthesia and analgesic or sedative premedication. Duodenal motility may be controlled in patients with active duodenal peristalsis with an appropriate antiperistaltic agent.

The contrast medium should be injected slowly without undue pressure under fluoroscopic control employing the minimal dose that is adequate to visualize the common bile duct, the pancreatic duct, or both duct systems. When both systems are filled simultaneously, overfilling of the pancreas is a potential risk. The dosage will vary greatly depending on the pathological findings and can range from 10 to 40 mL for visualization of the common bile duct, and from 2 to 10 mL for visualization of the pancreatic duct. Following the procedure, the patient should be kept under close observation for 24 hours.

Intravenous Digital Subtraction Angiography: (Conray 60): I.V. digital subtraction angiography (IV DSA) is a radiographic modality which allows dynamic imaging of the arterial system following i.v. injection of iodinated X-ray contrast media through the use of image intensification, enhancement of the iodine signal and digital processing of the image data. Temporal subtraction of the images obtained during the "first arterial pass" of the injected contrast medium injection yield images which are devoid of bone and soft tissue.

Areas that have been examined by i.v. DSA are the heart, including coronary by-pass grafts; the pulmonary arteries; the arteries of the brachiophalic circulation; the aortic arch; the abdominal aorta and its major branches including the celiac, mesenterics and renal arteries; the iliac arteries; and the arteries of the extremities.

Patient Preparation: No special patient preparation is required for i.v. digital subtraction angiography. However, it is advisable to ensure that patients are well hydrated prior to examination.

Warnings: Convulsions have occurred in patients with primary or metastatic cerebral lesions following the administration of iodine containing radiopaque media for the contrast enhancement of CT brain images.

Patients with diabetes mellitus and impaired renal function are considered to be at greater risk to develop acute renal failure following the injection of large doses of contrast media for contrast enhancement in CT scanning.

Precautions: In addition to the general precautions previously described, the risks associated with IV DSA are those usually attendant with catheter procedures and include intramural injections, vessel dissection or rupture and tissue extravasation. Small test injections of contrast medium made under fluoroscopic observation to ensure the catheter tip is properly positioned, and in the case of peripheral placement that the vein is of adequate size, will reduce the potential for intramural injections, vessel dissection or tissue extravasation occurring.

Patient motion, including respiration and swallowing, can result in marked image degradation yielding nondiagnostic studies. Therefore, patient cooperation is essential.

Adverse Reactions: see section on Adverse Effects, General.

Usual Dosage: Conray 60 may be injected either centrally, into the superior or inferior vena cava, or peripherally into an appropriate arm vein. For central injections, catheters may be introduced at the antecubital fossa into either the basilic or cephalic vein or at the leg into the femoral vein and advanced to the distal segment of the corresponding vena cava. For peripheral injections, the catheter is introduced at the antecubital fossa into an appropriate size arm vein. In order to reduce the potential for extravasation during peripheral injection, a catheter of approximately 20 cm in length should be employed.

Depending on the area to be imaged, the usual adult dose range is 20 to 60 mL. Injections may be repeated as necessary.

Central catheter injections are usually made with a power injection rate of between 10 and 30 mL/s. When making peripheral injections, rates of 12 to 20 mL/s should be used, depending on the size of the vein. Also, since contrast medium may remain in the arm vein for an extended period following injection, it may be advisable to flush the vein, immediately following injection, with an appropriate volume (20 to 25 mL) or 5% Dextrose in water or normal saline.

Administration: It is advisable that sterile Conray product in vials, bottles or in Ultraject syringes be at or close to body temperature when infused.

Supplied: Conray 30: Each mL of sterile aqueous solution contains: iothalamate meglumine 300 mg (organically bound iodine 14.15%–141 mg/mL). Nonmedicinal ingredients: edetate calcium disodium and monobasic sodium phosphate. Conray 30 has an osmolarity of approximately 750 mOsm/L (0.75 mOsm/mL) and is, therefore, hypertonic under conditions of use and is supplied in containers from which the air has been displaced by nitrogen. Bottles of 150 mL containing 100 mL (partial fill), boxes of 12. Bottles of 150 mL, boxes of 12. Infusion bottles of 300 mL, packages of 12.

Conray 43: Each mL of sterile aqueous solution contains: iothalamate meglumine 430 mg (organically bound iodine 20.2%–202 mg/mL). Nonmedicinal ingredients: edetate calcium disodium and monobasic sodium phosphate. Conray 43 has an osmolarity of approximately 800 mOsm/L (0.80 mOsm/mL) and is, therefore, hypertonic under conditions of use and is supplied in containers from which the air has been displaced by nitrogen. Conray 43 has a specific gravity of 1,22 at 25°C and a viscosity of 3 cps at 25°C and 2 cps at 37°C. Vials of 50 mL, packages of 50. Bottles of 150 mL containing 100 mL (partial fill), boxes of 12. Bottles of 200 mL and 250 mL, packages of 12.

Conray 60: Each mL of sterile aqueous solution contains: iothalamate meglumine 600 mg (organically bound iodine 28.2%–282 mg/mL). Nonmedicinal ingredients: edetate calcium disodium and monobasic sodium phosphate. Conray 60 has an osmolarity of approximately 1 000 mOsm/L (1.0 mOsm/mL) and is, therefore, hypertonic under conditions of use and is supplied in containers from which the air has been displaced by nitrogen. Conray 60 has a specific gravity of 1,32 at 25°C and a viscosity of 6 cps at 25°C and 4 cps at 37°C. Vials of 20, 30 and 50 mL, packages of 50. Bottles of 150 and 200 mL, packages of 12. Bottles of 150 mL containing 100 mL (partial fill), packages of 12. Ultraject prefilled syringes of 50 mL (hand held), boxes of 20.

Store between 15 and 30°C. Protect from light. Protect from freezing. Crystallization does not occur at normal room temperatures. Discard unused portion.

Reviewed 1999

CONTAC® COLD 12 HOUR RELIEF EXTRA STRENGTH

SmithKline Beecham Consumer Healthcare

Chlorpheniramine Maleate—Phenylpropanolamine HCl

Antihistamine—Decongestant

Supplied: Each gelatin capsule of red, grey and white sustained-release pellets, with clear cap and body, a red gelatin band, printed CONTAC in blue ink on both body and cap, contains: chlorpheniramine maleate 12 mg and phenylpropanolamine HCl 75 mg. Also contains gluten. Lactose- and tartrazine-free. Cartons of 8.

CONTAC® COLD 12 HOUR RELIEF NON DROWSY

SmithKline Beecham Consumer Healthcare

Pseudoephedrine HCl

Decongestant

Supplied: Each gelatin capsule of white and grey sustained-release pellets, with blue cap and clear body, printed CONTAC-C in black ink on both body and cap, contains: pseudoephedrine HCl 120 mg. Gluten-, lactose- and tartrazine-free. Cartons of 10.

CONTAC® COLD 12 HOUR RELIEF REGULAR STRENGTH

SmithKline Beecham Consumer Healthcare

Chlorpheniramine Maleate—Phenylpropanolamine HCl

Antihistamine—Decongestant

Supplied: Each size No. 1 gelatin regular strength capsule, with clear cap and body sealed with a red gelatin band, printed CONTAC in black ink on both body and cap, containing red, yellow and white sustained-release pellets, contains: chlorpheniramine maleate 8 mg and phenylpropanolamine HCl 75 mg. Also contains gluten. Energy: 7.2 kJ (1.7 kcal). Sodium: <1 mmol (0.001 mg). Lactose- and tartrazine-free. Cartons of 10, 20 and 30.

CONTAC® COUGH, COLD AND FLU DAY & NIGHT™

SmithKline Beecham Consumer Healthcare

Acetaminophen—Pseudoephedrine HCl—Dextromethorphan HBr

Acetaminophen—Pseudoephedrine HCl—Diphenhydramine

Analgesic—Decongestant—Antitussive

Analgesic—Decongestant—Antihistamine

Supplied: Each yellow, capsule-shaped, biconvex, film-coated, daytime caplet, engraved with "C-DAY", contains: acetaminophen 650 mg, pseudoephedrine HCl 60 mg and dextromethorphan HBr 30 mg. Each blue, capsule-shaped, biconvex, film-coated, night-time caplet, engraved with "C-NIGHT", contains: acetaminophen 650 mg, pseudoephedrine HCl 60 mg and diphenhydramine HCl 50 mg. Booklets of 20 (15 daytime caplets and 5 night-time caplets).

...The health care professional should carefully weigh the anticipated therapeutic benefit from any drug against all potential adverse effects.

COPHYLAC® Ⓝ
Hoechst Marion Roussel

Normethadone—p-Hydroxyephedrine HCl Compound

Antitussive

Indications: The treatment of cough associated with inflamed mucosa, which does not respond to products of lesser potency.

Cophylac Expectorant is indicated to facilitate expectoration and control cough associated with inflamed mucosa and tenacious sputum which does not respond to products of lesser potency.

Contraindications: Do not administer to patients receiving MAO inhibitors. Cophylac Expectorant is contraindicated in pertussis and other conditions predisposing to nausea and vomiting.

Precautions: Before prescribing medication to suppress or modify cough, it is important to ascertain that the underlying cause of the cough is identified, that modification of the cough does not increase the risk of clinical or physiologic complications, and that appropriate therapy for the primary disease is provided.

In young children the respiratory centre is especially susceptible to the depressant action of narcotic cough suppressants. Benefit to risk ratio should be carefully considered especially in children with respiratory embarrassment, e.g., croup. Estimation of dosage relative to the child's age and weight is of great importance.

Pregnancy: Since normethadone crosses the placental barrier, its use in pregnancy is not recommended.

As normethadone may inhibit peristalsis, patients with chronic constipation should be given Cophylac only after weighing the potential therapeutic benefit against the hazards involved.

Contains normethadone. May be habit forming.

Overdose: Symptoms: An overdose of 4 mL taken within 4 to 5 hours has produced transient nausea, cold sweat, and tachycardia in one reported case. Should 33% or more of one bottle be ingested, paralysis of the respiratory centre may result.

Treatment: Naloxone HCl.

Dosage: Adults and children over 14 years, 15 drops twice daily; children 3 to 14 years, 5 to 10 drops twice daily; children under 3 years, 2 to 5 drops twice daily.

Drops are dispensed by inverting the drop dispensing bottle. May be taken plain, with sugar or in any beverage, preferably after breakfast and at bedtime. Cophylac Expectorant should not be taken more than twice a day and never on an empty stomach.

Supplied: Cophylac: Each mL of sugar-free solution contains: normethadone HCl 10 mg (1%) and p-hydroxyephedrine HCl 20 mg (2%). Nonmedicinal ingredients: citric acid anhydrous granular, glycerin, lemon oil, methylparaben and purified water. Energy: 3.3 kJ (0.8 kcal). Tartrazine-free. Dispensing bottles of 15 mL.

Cophylac Expectorant: Each mL of sugar-free solution contains: normethadone HCl 10 mg (1%), p-hydroxyephedrine HCl 20 mg (2%) and emetine HCl 1.3 mg (0.13%). Nonmedicinal ingredients: citric acid anhydrous granular, glycerin, lemon oil, methylparaben and purified water. Energy: 3.3 kJ (0.8 kcal). Tartrazine-free. Dispensing bottles of 15 mL.

COPTIN® Ⓟ
Axcan Pharma

Sulfadiazine—Trimethoprim

Antibacterial

Pharmacology: Tetrahydrofolic acid is an essential metabolic co-factor in the biosynthesis of purines and thymine compounds which are ultimately utilized in the synthesis of DNA and RNA. The amino acids, serine and methionine, also require tetrahydrofolic acid for their biosynthesis.

Cotrimazine exerts its antibacterial effect by interfering with 2 consecutive steps in the biosynthesis of tetrahydrofolic acid. Sulfadiazine inhibits bacterial production of dihydrofolic acid by competing with para-aminobenzoic acid. Trimethoprim inhibits the production of tetrahydrofolic acid from dihydrofolic acid by binding to and reversibly inhibiting the enzyme, dihydrofolate reductase. Trimethoprim has only a very weak affinity for the human enzyme in comparison to bacterial forms.

Indications: Treatment of acute, chronic and recurrent urinary tract infections, including asymptomatic bacteriuria, cystitis and pyelonephritis, when these are caused by susceptible strains of bacteria including E. coli, P. mirabilis, P. vulgaris and Klebsiella-Enterobacter species.

Contraindications: Patients known to have hypersensitivity to sulfonamides or trimethoprim; marked parenchymal liver damage or blood dyscrasias and also in patients with marked renal impairment when repeated measurements of the plasma drug concentration cannot be performed.

Children, *Pregnancy* and *Lactation:* Cotrimazine should not be given to women who are pregnant or breast-feeding, nor to premature infants or neonates during the first 12 weeks of life.

Warnings: With the administration of sulfonamides, hypersensitivity reactions, agranulocytosis, aplastic anemia and other blood dyscrasias have been reported. In some instances, these complications have been fatal.

Experience with the use of trimethoprim alone is not extensive but the drug has been reported to interfere with hematopoiesis in some patients. In elderly patients concurrently receiving certain diuretics, primarily thiazides, an increased incidence of thrombocytopenia with purpura has been reported.

During therapy with cotrimazine, patients should be carefully evaluated for clinical evidence of serious blood disorders. If signs such as unexplained infection, fever, pallor, bleeding or jaundice appear, cotrimazine administration should be discontinued immediately and appropriate hematological investigations should be conducted.

Hematological changes related to impairment of folic acid metabolism have been reported in a few patients taking other combinations of a sulfonamide and trimethoprim. When these have occurred, they have been reversible with folinic acid therapy. Blood counts should be performed at appropriate intervals in patients on long-term therapy, in those predisposed to folate deficiency (i.e., the elderly, chronic alcoholics and rheumatoid arthritics), in malabsorption syndromes, malnutrition states, or during the treatment of epilepsy with anticonvulsant drugs such as phenytoin, primidone or barbiturates. If significant hematological abnormalities are noted, cotrimazine administration should be discontinued immediately and appropriate hematological investigations should be conducted.

Precautions: Cotrimazine should be given with caution to patients having impaired renal or hepatic function, to those with possible folate deficiency and to those with severe allergy or bronchial asthma. Therapy should be discontinued when rash or allergy develops.

In glucose-6-phosphate dehydrogenase deficiency, hemolysis may be exacerbated by cotrimazine owing to the sulfonamide component and this effect is frequently dose related.

When cotrimazine therapy is undertaken, it is recommended, as with all sulfonamide-containing agents, that adequate fluid intake be maintained in order to minimize the risk of crystalluria and stone formation.

Urinalysis with careful microscopic examination and renal function tests should be performed during therapy, particularly for those patients with impaired renal function. In individuals with renal impairment, a reduced dosage of cotrimazine is indicated to avoid accumulation of its components. In these patients, measurements of the plasma concentrations of the drugs are advisable. Cotrimazine should not be used when the serum creatinine concentration exceeds 2 mg/100 mL.

The sulfonamides are chemically similar to some goitrogens, diuretics such as acetazolamide and the thiazides, and oral hypoglycemics. Goiter, diuresis, and hypoglycemia may occur occasionally. Cross-sensitivity may exist with these agents.

Drug Interactions: No drug interactions with cotrimazine have been reported to date. However, as is the case with all sulfonamide-containing compounds, cotrimazine should be used with caution in patients receiving coumarin anticoagulants and oral sulfonylurea hypoglycemic agents, as sulfonamides have been reported to enhance the activity of these drugs.

Trimethoprim may possibly potentiate the action of other agents such as methotrexate and pyrimethamine, that interfere with folate metabolism.

Sulfonamides are known to interfere with the plasma protein binding of numerous other drugs. These agents, in turn, may compete with the sulfonamides for available binding sites. The net result depends on the relative concentrations of the agents involved and their binding affinities but, in theory, the plasma level of free sulfonamide or other drug may be altered with enhancement of its action or toxicity, whenever a sulfonamide is used concurrently with another agent that is markedly protein bound. Among the most widely recognized interactions of this type are the displacement of the coumarin anticoagulants, penicillin and phenytoin by sulfonamides and the displacement of sulfonamides by salicylates, sulfinpyrazone, phenylbutazone and certain other nonsteroidal antiarthritic agents. These interactions would seem unlikely to be of clinical significance with the administration of Coptin owing to the relatively small dose of sulfadiazine involved.

Para-aminobenzoic acid antagonizes the antibacterial action of sulfonamides and should not be administered concurrently with cotrimazine.

Adverse Effects: Cotrimazine is usually well tolerated at the recommended dosage. However, gastrointestinal and allergic reactions can occur. The most common adverse reactions to sulfonamides and trimethoprim are listed below though they may not have all been reported with Coptin.

Gastrointestinal: nausea, abdominal pain, emesis, diarrhea, glossitis, somatitis and pancreatitis.

Allergic: erythema multiforme, the Stevens-Johnson syndrome, generalized skin eruptions, epidermal necrolysis, urticaria, serum sickness, pruritus, exfoliative dermatitis, anaphylactoid reactions, periorbital edema, conjunctival and scleral infection, photosensitization arthralgia, allergic myocarditis, drug fever, chills, lupus erythematous phenomena and periarteritis nodosa.

CNS: headache, peripheral neuritis, mental depression, convulsions, ataxia, hallucinations, tinnitus, vertigo, insomnia, apathy, fatigue, muscle weakness and nervousness.

Renal: toxic nephrosis with oligurion, anuria and crystaluria, functional kidney changes resulting in elevated serum urea, creatinine and protein levels.

Hepatic: hepatitis as seen by elevated serum conjugated bilirubin levels. Liver changes such as increase in alkaline phosphatase and serum transaminase levels.

Blood Dyscrasias: agranulocytosis, aplastic anemia, megaloblastic anemia, thrombocytopenia, leukopenia, hemolytic anemia, purpura, hypoprothrombinemia and methemoglobinemia.

Overdose: Symptoms and Treatment: Symptomatic. It may include gastric lavage and forced diuresis. Alkalinization of the urine may help to minimize the risk of sulfadiazine crystal formation. In patients with impaired renal function, both trimethoprim and sulfadiazine may be removed from the blood by dialysis. Calcium folinate (3 to 6 mg i.m. for 5 to 7 days) can be a useful antidote for the adverse hematological effects of trimethoprim.

Dosage: Adults (see Table I) and children over 12 years: 2 Coptin tablets or 20 mL of oral suspension as a single dose administered every 24 hours.

Children 12 years and under: 14 mg sulfadiazine/kg/day + 3 mg trimethoprim/kg/day divided in 2 equal doses administered every 12 hours (see Table II).

Table I—Coptin

Dosage for Adults with Renal Impairment

Creatinine Clearance mL/min	Coptin Tablets (500 mg)
>30	2 tablets once a day
15-30	1 tablet once a day
<15	Not recommended

Table II—Coptin

Dosage for Children 12 Years and Under

Age	Approximate Body weight (kg)	Daily Dose (mg) Sulfadiazine	Trimethoprim	Approximate Dosing with Suspension Twice Daily
3 months	5	70	15	1 mL
3 years	15	210	45	2.5 mL
5 years	20	280	60	3.75 mL
10 years	30	420	90	5 mL
12 years	40	560	120	7.5 mL

Cotrimazine is not recommended for children less than 3 months of age.

Supplied: Oral Suspension: Each 5 mL teaspoonful of banana-flavored oral suspension contains: sulfadiazine 205 mg and trimethoprim 45 mg. Nonmedicinal ingredients: colloidal silicone dioxide, essence of banana, Keltrol, methylparaben, propylparaben, sodium citrate, sodium hydroxide and sorbitol solution. Bottles of 50 and 100 mL.

Tablets: Each white, scored tablet identified with monogram "C 500" on the scored side and "J" on the reverse side, contains: sulfadiazine 410 mg and trimethoprim 90 mg. Nonmedicinal ingredients: cornstarch, magnesium stearate and povidone. Bottles of 100.

(Shown in Product Recognition Section)

CORDARONE® ℞
CORDARONE® I.V. ℞

Wyeth-Ayerst

Amiodarone HCl

Antiarrhythmic Agent

Pharmacology: Amiodarone is generally considered a class III antiarrhythmic drug, but it possesses electrophysiologic characteristics of all 4 Vaughan Williams classes. Like Class I drugs, amiodarone blocks sodium channels at rapid pacing frequencies, and like class II drugs, it exerts antisympathetic activity. One of its main effects, with prolonged administration, is to lengthen the cardiac action potential, a class III effect. The negative chronotropic effect of amiodarone in nodal tissues is similar to the effect of class IV drugs. In addition to blocking sodium channels, amiodarone blocks myocardial potassium channels, which contributes to slowing of conduction and prolongation of refractoriness. The antisympathetic action and block of calcium and potassium channels are responsible for the negative dromotropic effects on the sinus node and for the slowing of conduction and prolongation of refractoriness in the atrioventricular (AV) node.

Additionally, amiodarone has vasodilatory action that can decrease cardiac workload and consequently myocardial oxygen consumption.

A comparison of the electrophysiologic effects of oral amiodarone and amiodarone i.v. is shown in Table I.

At higher doses (>10 mg/kg) of amiodarone i.v., prolongation of the ERP RV and modest prolongation of the QRS have been seen. These differences between oral and i.v. administration suggest that the initial acute effects of amiodarone i.v. may be predominantly focused on the AV node, causing an intranodal conduction delay and increased nodal refractoriness due to calcium channel blockade (Class IV activity) and β-adrenoreceptor antagonism (Class II activity).

Pharmacodynamics: Amiodarone has been reported to produce negative inotropic and vasodilating effects in animals and humans. After long-term treatment with oral amiodarone in a dose range of 200 to 600 mg/day, patients with decreased left ventricular ejection fraction (LVEF) show no significant change in mean LVEF. Hypotension is uncommon (<1%) during chronic oral amiodarone therapy. In clinical studies of patients with refractory ventricular fibrillation (VF) or hemodynamically unstable ventricular tachycardia (VT), drug-related hypotension occurred in 15.6% of 1 836 patients treated with amiodarone i.v. No correlations were seen between the baseline ejection fraction and the occurrence of clinically significant hypotension during infusion of amiodarone i.v.

Clinical Trials: I.V.: A placebo-controlled study of i.v. amiodarone in patients with supraventricular arrhythmias and 2- to 3-consecutive beat ventricular arrhythmias, and a pharmacokinetic/pharmacodynamic study evaluating rapid i.v. loading in patients with recurrent, refractory VT/VF have shown rapid onset of antiarrhythmic activity well before significant blood levels of DEA were present; approximately 1 500 mg/day of i.v. amiodarone were administered using 2- and 3-stage infusion regimens. In the patients with complex ventricular arrhythmias, including sustained and nonsustained VT, amiodarone therapy reduced episodes of VT by 85%.

The acute effectiveness of amiodarone i.v. in suppressing recurrent VF or hemodynamically unstable VT is supported by 2 randomized, parallel, dose-response studies of approximately 300 patients each. In these studies, patients with at least 2 episodes of VF or hemodynamically unstable VT in the preceding 24 hours were randomly assigned to receive doses of approximately 125 or 1 000 mg over the first 24 hours, an 8-fold difference. In one study, a middle dose of approximately 500 mg was evaluated. The dose regimen consisted of an initial rapid loading infusion, followed by a slower 6-hour loading infusion, and then an 18-hour maintenance infusion. The maintenance infusion was continued up to hour 48. Additional supplemental infusions of 150 mg were given for "breakthrough" VT/VF more frequently to the 125-mg dose group, thereby considerably reducing the planned 8-fold differences in total dose to 1.8- and 2.6-fold, respectively, in the 2 studies.

The prospectively defined primary efficacy end point was the rate of VT/VF episodes/hour. For both studies, the median rate was 0.02 episodes/hour in patients receiving the high dose and 0.07 episodes/hour in patients receiving the low dose, or approximately 0.5 versus 1.7 episodes per day (p=0.07, 2-sided, in both studies). In one study, the time to first episode of VT/VF was significantly prolonged (approximately 10 hours in patients receiving the low dose and 14 hours in patients receiving the high dose). In both studies, significantly fewer supplemental infusions were given to patients in the high-dose group. Mortality was not affected in these studies; at the end of double-blind therapy or after 48 hours, all patients were given open access to whatever treatment (including amiodarone i.v.) was deemed necessary.

Pharmacokinetics: The absorption of oral amiodarone is slow and variable, with peak serum amiodarone concentrations being attained at 3 to 12 hours after administration. Absorption may continue for up to 15 hours after oral ingestion. There is extensive intersubject variation: mean oral bioavailability is approximately 50% (mean range, 33% to 65%). First-pass metabolism in the gut wall and liver appears to be an important factor in determining the systemic availability of the drug. The mean terminal half-life after steady-state administration is approximately 50 days and has been found in one study (n=8) to range from 26 to 107 days. Since at least 3 to 4 half-lives are needed to approach steady-state concentrations, loading doses must be administered at the onset of oral amiodarone therapy.

Amiodarone has a very high apparent volume of distribution (approximately 5 000 L) with an extensive accumulation in tissues, especially adipose tissues, and in highly perfused organs such as liver, lung, spleen, heart and kidney. One major metabolite of amiodarone, desethylamiodarone, has been identified but the pharmacological activity of this metabolite is not known. During chronic treatment, the plasma ratio of metabolite to parent compound approximates 1.

In patients on long-term oral therapy, amiodarone has a biphasic elimination pattern, with an initial decline in plasma levels observed from 2.5 to 10 days after discontinuation of therapy. This initial phase is followed by a marked rebound in plasma levels at 12 to 20 days post-dosing, before settling into a slower terminal elimination phase. In one study (n=8), the plasma elimination half-life of the parent compound ranged from 26 to 107 days (mean: 53 days).

Amiodarone exhibits complex disposition characteristics after i.v. administration. Peak serum concentrations after single 5 mg/kg 15-minute i.v. infusions in healthy subjects range between 5 and 41 mg/L. Peak concentrations after 150 mg supplemental infusions in patients with VF or hemodynamically unstable VT range between 7 and 26 mg/L. Due to rapid disposition, serum concentrations decline to 10% of peak values within 30 to 45 minutes after the end of the infusion. In clinical trials, after 48 hours of continued infusions (125, 500, or 1 000 mg/day) plus supplemental (150 mg) infusions (for recurrent arrhythmias), amiodarone mean serum concentrations between 0.7 to 1.4 mg/L were observed (n=260).

Amiodarone is eliminated primarily by hepatic metabolism and biliary excretion. Desethylamiodarone (DEA) is the major active metabolite of amiodarone. At the usual amiodarone daily maintenance dose of 400 mg, mean steady-state DEA/amiodarone ratios ranged from 0.61 to 0.93. High-dose oral amiodarone loading in patients yielded 24-hour DEA/amiodarone ratios of 0.083 to 0.19. High-dose i.v. loading yielded a mean 24-hour DEA/amiodarone ratio of 0.041. No data are presently available on the activity of DEA in humans, but animal studies have shown that it has significant electrophysiologic and antiarrhythmic properties. The major enzyme responsible for the N-deethylation to DEA is believed to be cytochrome P-450 3A4. Large interindividual variability in CYP-450 3A4 activity may explain the variable systemic availability of amiodarone. DEA is highly lipophilic and has a very large apparent volume of distribution, showing a higher concentration than amiodarone in all tissue except fat at steady state. Myocardial concentrations of DEA are approximately 3- to 4.5-fold greater than those of amiodarone during long-term oral amiodarone therapy. However, after either acute oral or acute i.v. administration, both mean serum and mean myocardial DEA concentrations are quite low compared to those of amiodarone.

There is negligible excretion of amiodarone or DEA in urine. Neither amiodarone nor DEA is dialyzable. Amiodarone and DEA cross the placenta and both appear in breast milk.

Table II summarizes the mean ranges of pharmacokinetic parameters of amiodarone reported in single dose i.v. (5 mg/kg over 15 min) and oral (400 or 600 mg) studies of healthy subjects and in in vitro studies. Pharmacokinetics were similar in males and females.

During chronic treatment with oral amiodarone, close monitoring may be prudent for elderly patients and those with severe left ventricular dysfunction. However, during short-term i.v. use, age, sex, renal disease, and hepatic disease (cirrhosis) do not have clinically significant effects on the disposition of amiodarone and DEA. No dosage adjustment is necessary for patients in any of these populations.

There is no well-established relationship between drug concentration and therapeutic response for long-term oral or short-term i.v. use. Steady-state amiodarone concentrations of 1 to 2.5 mg/L, however, have been effective with minimal toxicity following chronic oral amiodarone.

Indications:

No antiarrhythmic drug has been shown to reduce the incidence of sudden death in patients with asymptomatic ventricular arrhythmias. Most antiarrhythmic drugs have the potential to cause dangerous arrhythmias; some have been shown to be associated with an increased incidence of sudden death. In light of the above, physicians should carefully consider the risks and benefits of antiarrhythmic therapy for all patients with ventricular arrhythmias.

Table I—Cordarone/Cordarone I.V.

Effects of Oral and I.V. Cordarone on Electrophysiologic Parameters

Formulation	SCL	QRS	QTc	AH	HV	ERP RA	ERP RV	ERP AVN
Oral	↑	⇆	↑	↑	⇆	↑	↑	↑
I.V.	⇆	⇆	⇆	↑	⇆	⇆	⇆	↑

⇆ No change.

Legend: SCL=sinus cycle length; QRS=a measure of intraventricular conduction; QTc=corrected QT, a measure of repolarization; AH=atrial His, a measure of intranodal conduction; HV=His ventricular, a measure of intranodal conduction; ERP=effective refractory period; RA=right atrium; RV=right ventricle; AVN=atrioventricular node.

Table II—Cordarone/Cordarone I.V.

Amiodarone Pharmacokinetic Profile

Drug	Clearance (mL/h/kg)	V_c (L/kg)	V_{ss} (L/kg)	$t_{1/2}$ (days)	Protein binding	F_{oral} (%)
Amiodarone	90-158	0.2	40-84	20-47	>0.96	33-65
Desethylamiodarone	197-290	–	68-168	≥AMI $t_{1/2}$	–	–

Notes: V_c and V_{ss} denote the central and steady-state volumes of distribution from i.v. studies; F_{oral} is systemic availability of Cordarone. "–" denotes not available. AMI is Amiodarone. $t_{1/2}$=terminal phase elimination half-life. Desethylamiodarone clearance and volume involve an unknown biotransformation factor.

Cordarone (cont'd)

Amiodarone therapy should be initiated in hospital and continued in a monitored environment until adequate control of the arrhythmia has occurred.

Patients treated with amiodarone should be under the supervision of a cardiologist or a physician with equivalent experience in cardiology.

Oral: Because of its potential for serious toxicity and the substantial management difficulties associated with its oral use, amiodarone is indicated only for the treatment of patients with the following documented, life-threatening, recurrent ventricular arrhythmias refractory to all other treatment or when alternative agents could not be tolerated: hemodynamically unstable ventricular tachycardia (VT); recurrent ventricular fibrillation (VF).

I.V.: For initiation of treatment of documented, life-threatening, frequently recurring ventricular fibrillation and hemodynamically unstable ventricular tachycardia in patients refractory to all other treatment. Additionally, amiodarone i.v: can be used to treat patients with VT/VF for whom oral amiodarone is indicated, but who are unable to take oral medication. During or after treatment with amiodarone i.v., patients may be transferred to oral amiodarone therapy (see Dosage).

Amiodarone i.v. should be used for acute treatment until the patient's ventricular arrhythmias are stabilized. Most patients will require this therapy for 48 to 96 hours, but amiodarone i.v. may be administered for longer periods if necessary.

Contraindications: In patients with known hypersensitivity to any of the components of oral amiodarone (tablets) or amiodarone i.v., and in patients with cardiogenic shock, marked sinus bradycardia, and second- or third-degree AV block unless a functioning pacemaker is available. In addition, oral amiodarone is contraindicated in patients with evidence of acute hepatitis (see Precautions), thyroid dysfunction (see Warnings), or pulmonary interstitial abnormalities (see Warnings).

Warnings: Oral: Mortality: The results of the Cardiac Arrhythmia Suppression Trial (CAST) in postmyocardial infarction patients with asymptomatic ventricular arrhythmias showed a significant increase in mortality and in nonfatal cardiac arrest rate in patients treated with encainide or flecainide compared with a matched placebo-treated group. CAST was continued using a revised protocol with the moricizine and placebo treatment groups only. The trial was prematurely terminated because of a trend towards an increase in mortality in the moricizine-treated group.

The applicability of these results to other populations or other antiarrhythmic agents is uncertain, but at present, it is prudent to consider these results when using any antiarrhythmic agent.

Thyroid Dysfunction: Both hyper- and hypothyroidism may occur during, or soon after treatment with oral amiodarone; its occurrence during i.v. therapy is negligible. Thyroid function should be monitored before, and at regular intervals (e.g., every 3 months) during long-term oral amiodarone therapy.

Since amiodarone disturbs the classical thyroid function tests, (PBI, I^{131}) specific measurement of plasma thyroxine levels, as well as those of T_3 and of TSH must be used.

In most of the patients who developed thyroid dysfunction while taking oral amiodarone, this drug was discontinued. A few patients with clinical manifestations of hyper- or hypothyroidism have been maintained on amiodarone concurrent with therapy for control of thyroid function, but the risk of such treatment must be weighed carefully against the apparent benefit of oral amiodarone therapy.

In a rat carcinogenicity study, at doses of 5, 16 and 50 mg/kg/day, amiodarone produced statistically significant dose-related changes in the thyroid gland, including follicular adenomas and carcinomas. The significance of these changes for the long-term use of amiodarone in humans is unknown.

I.V. and Oral: Pulmonary Toxicity: One of the most serious complications resulting from oral amiodarone therapy is pulmonary toxicity, characterized by pneumonitis. Clinical symptoms include cough, dyspnea, weight loss, and weakness.

On chest x-ray, there is a diffuse interstitial pattern of lung involvement frequently with patchy alveolar infiltrates, particularly in the upper lobe. Predicting which patient will develop pulmonary toxicity has been difficult (see Contraindications). Pulmonary toxicity can appear abruptly either early or late during therapy and it commonly mimics viral or bacterial infection or worsening congestive heart failure. The relationship of pulmonary toxicity to duration of therapy, maintenance dose, and total dose is unclear. Besides an immediate cessation of amiodarone administration, steroid therapy may be beneficial. The majority of patients have recovered with this management, although some fatalities have occurred. Chest x-rays and pulmonary function tests are recommended prior to, and periodically during, the chronic administration of oral amiodarone.

Only 1 of more than 1 000 patients treated with amiodarone i.v. in clinical studies developed pulmonary fibrosis. For that patient, the condition was diagnosed 3 months after treatment with amiodarone i.v., during which time she had received oral amiodarone. Amiodarone i.v. therapy should be discontinued if a diagnosis of pulmonary fibrosis is made.

During clinical studies of amiodarone i.v., 2% of patients were reported to have adult respiratory distress syndrome (ARDS). ARDS is a disorder characterized by bilateral, diffuse pulmonary infiltrates with pulmonary edema and varying degrees of respiratory insufficiency. The clinical and radiographic picture can arise after a variety of lung injuries, such as those resulting from trauma, shock, prolonged cardiopulmonary resuscitation, and aspiration pneumonia, conditions present in many of the patients enrolled in the clinical studies. It is not possible to determine what role, if any, amiodarone i.v. played in causing or exacerbating the pulmonary disorder in those patients.

Proarrhythmia/QT Interval Prolongation: Amiodarone may cause a worsening of the existing arrhythmias or precipitate a new arrhythmia. Amiodarone causes prolongation of the QT interval. Proarrhythmia, primarily torsades de pointes, has been associated with prolongation of the QTc interval to 500 ms or greater. Proarrhythmia has been reported (2 to 5%) with oral amiodarone, especially in the presence of concomitant antiarrhythmic therapy and has included new-onset VF, incessant VT, increased resistance to cardioversion, and paroxysmal polymorphic VT associated with QT prolongation (torsades de pointes). Although QTc prolongation occurred frequently in patients receiving amiodarone i.v., torsades de pointes or new-onset VF occurred infrequently (less than 2% of all patients treated with amiodarone i.v. in controlled clinical trials). Patients should be monitored carefully for QTc prolongation during amiodarone therapy.

Bradycardia and AV Block: In patients treated with oral amiodarone, symptomatic bradycardia or sinus arrest with suppression of escape foci occurred in approximately 2 to 4% of patients. Bradycardia was reported as an adverse drug reaction in 4.9% of patients receiving amiodarone i.v. for life-threatening VT/VF in clinical trials. AV block was reported as an adverse drug reaction in 1.4% of patients receiving amiodarone i.v. There was no dose-related increase in bradycardia or AV block in these studies.

In patients who develop symptomatic bradycardia while taking oral amiodarone, dose reduction or discontinuation, and possibly pacing, may be considered. Due to the large body load of amiodarone that accumulates with chronic dose administration, and the long half-life of the drug, levels may drop slowly after dose reduction or discontinuation.

During amiodarone i.v. therapy, bradycardia should be treated by slowing the infusion rate or discontinuing therapy. In some patients inserting a pacemaker is required. Despite such measures, bradycardia was progressive and terminal in 1 (<1%) patient during controlled clinical trials. Patients with a known predisposition to bradycardia or AV block should be treated with amiodarone i.v. in a setting where a temporary pacemaker is available.

I.V.: Hypotension: Hypotension is the most common adverse event seen with amiodarone i.v. therapy: it is uncommon (<1%) during oral amiodarone therapy. In double-blind controlled clinical trials, hypotension was reported as an adverse event in 316 (39%) of 814 patients treated with amiodarone i.v. Clinically significant hypotension during infusions was seen most often in the first several hours of treatment and was not dose related, but appeared to be related to the rate of infusion. Hypotension necessitating temporary discontinuation of amiodarone i.v. therapy was reported in 3% of the 814 patients, with permanent discontinuation required in an additional 2% of the 814 patients. Hypotension should be treated initially by slowing the infusion: additionally standard therapy may be needed including vasopressor drugs, positive inotropic agents and volume expansion. **The initial rate of infusion should be monitored closely and should not exceed that recommended in the Dosage section.**

Precautions: General: Patients with life-threatening arrhythmias may experience serious adverse events during their treatment and therefore should be properly monitored. Amiodarone should be administered only by physicians who are experienced in the treatment of life-threatening arrhythmias, who are thoroughly familiar with the risks and benefits of amiodarone therapy, and who have access to facilities adequate for monitoring the effectiveness and adverse events of treatment (see Indications).

Loading Phase: The higher doses of oral amiodarone used in the loading phase may sometimes be associated with adverse effects such as nausea or tremor. The nausea may respond to dividing the total dose into 2 or 3 fractions taken with meals, or by decreasing the total daily dose. The tremor may respond to dose reduction as well.

Oral: Cardiac Disorders: Oral amiodarone should be used with caution in patients with latent or manifest heart failure because this condition may be worsened by its administration. In these cases, oral amiodarone should be given with appropriate concurrent therapy.

Oral amiodarone therapy may be considered in the treatment of patients with Wolff-Parkinson-White (WPW) syndrome, atrial flutter, or atrial fibrillation, when these conditions are complicated by life-threatening ventricular tachyarrhythmias. In such cases, care is required since the effect of oral amiodarone in these conditions does not appear to be uniform. Electrophysiologic studies may be of value in the selection of these patients who may respond to oral amiodarone, particularly in WPW syndrome.

Nervous System Disorders: Chronic administration of oral amiodarone in rare instances may lead to the development of peripheral neuropathy that may resolve when amiodarone is discontinued, but this resolution has been slow and incomplete.

Dermatologic Disorders: Oral amiodarone may induce photosensitization in some patients. Sunscreen preparations or protective clothing may afford some protection to individual patients experiencing photosensitization. Blue-grey discoloration of exposed skin has been reported during long-term treatment. With discontinuation of therapy, the pigmentation regresses slowly over a period of up to several years. The risk of this phenomenon apppears to be related to dose and duration of therapy.

Ocular Abnormalities: Microdeposits appear in the cornea in the majority of patients treated with oral amiodarone. The deposits are usually discernible only by slit-lamp examination and occasionally give rise to symptoms such as visual halos, which are experienced in as many as 10% of patients. Corneal microdeposits are reversible with reduction of dose or termination of treatment.

Cases of optical neuropathy, usually resulting in visual impairment, have been reported in patients treated with oral amiodarone. A causal relationship to the drug has not been clearly established. If such symptoms appear, prompt ophthalmological examination is recommended. Appearance of optic neuropathy calls for re-evaluation of oral amiodarone therapy. The risk of complications of treatment must be weighed against the benefit of therapy in patients whose lives are threatened by cardiac arrhythmias. Regular ophthalmological examination, including fundoscopy and slit-lamp examination, is recommended during administration of oral amiodarone.

Postsurgical Disorders: Occurrences of adult respiratory syndrome (ARDS) and low cardiac output syndrome have been reported postoperatively in patients receiving oral amiodarone therapy who have undergone either cardiac or noncardiac surgery. An intra-aortic balloon pump augmentation has been required in some patients with the low cardiac output syndrome at discontinuation of cardiopulmonary bypass. In the case of ARDS, although patients usually respond well to vigorous respiratory therapy, in rare instances the outcome has been fatal. A number of patients who developed ARDS were subjected to a high concentration of oxygen in the inspired air; this could have been a factor in the respiratory complications. Therefore, the operative FiO_2 should be kept as close to room air as possible. Caution should also be exercised in considering amiodarone patients for surgery in the presence of preoperative pulmonary dysfunction.

However, as amiodarone has a very long half-life, withdrawal before surgery implies delaying operations by several weeks and putting patients at increased risk of malignant dysrhythmias. The ARDS in these cases has rarely been fatal. Caution should be used in considering amiodarone patients for surgery in the presence of preoperative pulmonary dysfunction.

Hypotension independent of, or associated with, discontinuation of cardiopulmonary bypass following open-heart surgery has been reported. Blood vessels may respond poorly to adrenoreceptor agonists. Atropine-resistant bradycardia and complete heart block have also been reported in patients being weaned from cardiopulmonary bypass.

Urogenital System Disorders: Oral amiodarone-induced epididymitis has been observed in some patients. This form of epididymitis is rare, benign, self-limited, and requires no treatment. Physicians should be aware of it to protect their patients from unnecessary invasive urologic examinations and antibiotic therapy.

Oral and I.V.: Liver Enzyme Elevations: In patients with life-threatening arrhythmias, the potential risk of hepatic injury should be weighed against the potential benefit of amiodarone therapy. However, patients receiving oral or i.v. amiodarone should be monitored carefully for evidence of progressive hepatic injury.

Elevations of blood hepatic enzyme values, ALT, AST and GGT are seen commonly in patients with immediately life-threatening VT/VF. Interpreting elevated AST activity can be difficult because the values may be elevated in patients with recent myocardial infarction, congestive heart failure, and in those who have received multiple electrical defibrillations.

Asymptomatic elevations of liver enzymes (AST and ALT) are frequently associated with the use of oral amiodarone. The mechanism whereby this hepatic effect occurs has not been defined. Phospholipidosis and fibrosis of the liver resembling alcoholic hepatitis or cirrhosis, accompanied by only a mild elevation of hepatic enzymes, have been reported in association with the use of oral amiodarone. Rises in hepatic enzymes, especially when associated with clinical signs and symptoms of hepatitis, or with asymptomatic hepatomegaly, may indicate a liver scan and, if needed, a liver biopsy with ultrastructural study. If serum enzyme levels increase significantly, or persist over time, consideration should be given to discontinuation or reducing the dose of amiodarone. Hepatic failure has been a rare cause of death in patients treated with oral amiodarone.

Approximately 54% of patients receiving amiodarone i.v. in clinical studies had baseline elevations in liver enzyme values, and 13% had clinically significant elevations. In 81% of patients with baseline and on-therapy data available, the liver enzyme elevations either improved during therapy or remained at baseline levels. Baseline abnormalities in hepatic enzymes are not a contraindication to treatment.

Two cases of fatal hepatocellular necrosis after treatment with amiodarone i.v. have been reported. The patients, one 28 years of age and the other 60 years of age, were treated for atrial arrhythmias with an initial infusion of 1 500 mg over 5 hours, a rate much higher than recommended. Both patients developed hepatic and renal failure within 24 hours after the start of amiodarone i.v. treatment and died on day 14 and day 4, respectively. Because these episodes of hepatic necrosis may have been due to the rapid rate of infusion and hypotension is related to the rate of infusion, **the initial rate of infusion should be monitored closely and should not exceed that recommended in the Dosage section.**

Electrolyte Disturbances: Patients with hypokalemia or hypomagnesemia should have the condition corrected whenever possible before being treated with amiodarone, since these disorders can exaggerate the degree of QTc prolongation and increase the potential for torsades de pointes. Special attention should be given to electrolyte and acid-base balance in patients experiencing severe or prolonged diarrhea in patients receiving concomitant diuretics.

Children: The safety and efficacy of amiodarone in children have not been established; therefore, its use in children is not recommended. Experience with the use of oral amiodarone in children is very limited. The following information is provided in order to help the physician who considers that critical and treatment-resistant disease in a pediatric patient makes the use of amiodarone necessary. In a study of 26 patients aged 6 weeks to 29 years (mean 13 years), an amiodarone dose of 5 mg/kg/day, b.i.d. (10 mg/kg/day) was administered for 10 days; the subsequent mean maintenance dose of oral amiodarone was 7.5 mg/kg/day (range 2.5 to 21.5 mg/kg/day).

Pregnancy: Amiodarone has been shown to be embryotoxic in some animal species. In 3 different human case reports, both the parent drug and its DEA metabolite have been shown to pass through the placenta, quantitatively ranging between 10 and 50% of human maternal serum concentrations. Although amiodarone use during pregnancy is uncommon, there have been a small number of published reports of congenital goiter/hypothyroidism and hyperthyroidism. Therefore, amiodarone should be used during pregnancy only if the potential benefit to the mother justifies the risk to the fetus.

Labor and Delivery: It is not known whether the use of amiodarone during labor or delivery has any immediate or delayed adverse effects. Preclinical studies in rodents have not shown any effect on the duration of gestation or on parturition.

Lactation: Amiodarone and its DEA metabolite are excreted in human milk, suggesting that breast-feeding could expose the nursing infant to a significant dose of the drug. Nursing offspring of lactating rats administered amiodarone have demonstrated reduced viability and reduced body weight gains. The risk of exposing the infant to amiodarone should be weighed against the potential benefit of arrhythmia suppression in the mother. The mother should be advised to discontinue nursing.

Drug Interactions: Amiodarone can inhibit the metabolism mediated by cytochrome P-450 enzymes, probably accounting for the significant effects of oral amiodarone (and presumably amiodarone i.v.) on the pharmacokinetics of various therapeutic agents including digoxin, quinidine, procainamide, warfarin, dextromethorphan, and cyclosporine. Hemodynamic and electrophysiologic interactions have also been observed after concomitant administration with propranolol, diltiazem, and verapamil. Conversely, agents producing a significant effect on amiodarone pharmacokinetics include phenytoin, cimetidine, and cholestyramine. The potential for drug interactions may persist long after discontinuation of amiodarone administration because of its long half-life. Few data are available on drug interactions with amiodarone i.v. Except as noted, Tables III and IV summarize the key interactions between oral amiodarone and other therapeutic agents.

having occurred in approximately 75% of patients taking 400 mg or more/day; these adverse events have led to the discontinuation of amiodarone treatment in 7 to 18% of patients. The adverse reactions most frequently requiring discontinuation of amiodarone have included pulmonary infiltrates or fibrosis, paroxysmal ventricular tachycardia, congestive heart failure, and elevation of liver enzymes. Other symptoms causing discontinuations less often have included visual disturbances, solar dermatitis, blue skin discoloration, hyperthyroidism, and hypothyroidism.

Ophthalmological Abnormalities: Corneal microdeposits are apparent upon slit-lamp examination in virtually all adult patients who have taken amiodarone for longer than 6 months. These deposits may give rise to symptoms such as visual halos or blurred vision (see Precautions). Other reported amiodarone-associated abnormalities have included corneal degeneration, photosensitivity, eye discomfort, dry eyes, scotoma, lens opacities, and macular degeneration.

Neurological Abnormalities: Occurring in 20 to 40% of patients, these common disorders have included ataxia, tremor, fatigue, dizziness, weakness, sleep disorders, headaches, cognitive disorders, disturbances of alertness, peripheral motor and sensory neuropathies, proximal muscle weakness, and impotence (see Precautions).

Table III—Cordarone/Cordarone I.V.

Summary of Drug Interactions with Cordarone

Concomitant Drug	**Drugs Whose Effects May Be Increased By Cordarone** **Interaction**
Warfarin	Increases prothrombin time.
Digoxin	Increases serum concentration.
Quinidine	Increases serum concentration.
Procainamide	Increases serum concentration, NAPA concentration.
Disopyramide	Increases QT prolongation which could cause arrhythmia.
Fentanyl	May cause hypotension, bradycardia, decreased cardiac output.
Flecainide	Reduces the dose of flecainide needed to maintain therapeutic plasma concentrations.
Lidocaine	**Oral:** Sinus bradycardia was observed in a patient receiving oral Cordarone who was given lidocaine for local anesthesia. **I.V.:** Seizure associated with increased lidocaine concentrations was observed in one patient.
Cyclosporine	Produces persistently elevated plasma concentrations of cyclosporine resulting in elevated creatinine, despite reduction in dose of cyclosporine.

Table IV—Cordarone/Cordarone I.V.

Summary of Drug Interactions with Cordarone

Concomitant Drug	**Drugs That May Interfere With the Actions of Cordarone** **Interaction**
Cholestyramine	Increases enterohepatic recirculation of amiodarone and may reduce serum levels and $t_{1/2}$.
Cimetidine	Increases serum amiodarone levels.
Phenytoin	Decreases serum amiodarone levels.

Beta-Blockers: Since amiodarone has weak beta-blocking activity, use with beta-blocking agents could increase risk of hypotension and bradycardia.

Calcium Channel Blockers: Amiodarone may have additive effects on atrioventricular conduction or myocardial contractility, increasing the risk of hypotension.

In addition to the interactions noted above, chronic (>2 weeks) oral amiodarone administration impairs metabolism of phenytoin, dextromethorphan, and methotrexate.

Adverse Effects: Oral: Because of the extensive distribution of amiodarone in body tissues, and the prolonged time required for its elimination from the body following discontinuation of long-term therapy, the relationship between adverse reactions and dosage and duration of therapy, has not been fully established. For some adverse reactions—for example, corneal microdeposits—a relationship to dosage and duration of therapy has been established, so that corneal deposits are reversible with dose reduction or with discontinuation of therapy. However, for other adverse reactions—for example, fibrosing alveolitis or peripheral neuropathy—the dose relationship and the reversibility of the adverse reaction have not been established. Certain gastrointestinal reactions (e.g., nausea, vomiting, constipation, and bad taste) and CNS reactions (e.g., fatigue, headaches, vertigo, nightmares, and sleeplessness) occur frequently at the initiation of therapy when high doses are used. These may disappear on reduction of the dose. The time and dose relationship of adverse events are under continued study.

The most serious and potentially life-threatening adverse effects associated with the use of amiodarone are pulmonary fibrosis, the aggravation of arrhythmias, and cirrhotic hepatitis.

Published data reflecting the North American experience with chronic oral amiodarone therapy suggest that amiodarone-associated adverse drug reactions are very common,

Pulmonary Abnormalities: In some studies symptomatic pulmonary disease has been detected at rates as high as 10 to 15%, whereas asymptomatic abnormalities of pulmonary diffusion capacity have been demonstrated at greater than twice that incidence. Pulmonary toxicity has been fatal about 10% of the time (see Warnings).

Cardiovascular Abnormalities: Exacerbation of arrhythmia has had a reported incidence of about 2 to 5% in most series (new ventricular fibrillation, incessant ventricular tachycardia, increased resistance to cardioversion, and paroxysmal polymorphic ventricular tachycardia (torsades de pointes). In addition, symptomatic bradycardia or sinus arrest with suppression of escape foci have occurred in 2 to 4% of patients. Congestive heart failure has occurred in approximately 3% of patients. Second degree AV block and left bundle branch block (LBBB) have occurred in less than 1% of patients. Hypotension independent of—as well as associated with—discontinuation of cardiopulmonary bypass following open-heart surgery has also been reported (see Warnings and Precautions).

Gastrointestinal Abnormalities: Complaints of this nature have occurred in about 25% of patients and have included nausea, vomiting, constipation, anorexia, abnormal taste, dyspepsia, abdominal pain, and diarrhea (see Precautions).

Hepatic Abnormalities: Abnormal elevations of serum levels of enzymes associated with hepatic dysfunction have occurred in approximately 15% of patients. Symptomatic hepatitis has occurred in less than 1% of patients (see Precautions).

Dermatologic Abnormalities: These have occurred in approximately 15% of patients, with photosensitivity (10% of patients) being the most common. Blue-grey skin pigmentation has been reported in 2 to 3% of patients. Hair loss (alopecia) has been observed in up to 4% of patients. Other

Cordarone (cont'd)

amiodarone-associated phenomena reported with less than 1% incidence have included nonspecific skin eruptions, pruritus, acquired keratoderma, hyperhidrosis, onycholysis, generalized pustular psoriasis, vasculitis and polyserositis, and toxic epidermal necrolysis (see Precautions).

Thyroid Abnormalities: Amiodarone-associated hypothyroidism has been reported in 2 to 4% of patients in most series but in 8 to 10% of patients with other series: hyperthyroidism has been reported in 1 to 3% of patients (see Warnings).

The following adverse events are based upon retrospective multicentre analysis of 241 patients treated at various doses of amiodarone for 2 to 1 515 days (mean duration: 441.3 days) (see Table V).

I.V.: In a total of 1 836 patients in controlled and uncontrolled clinical trials, 14% of patients received amiodarone i.v. for up to 1 week, 5% received it for up to 2 weeks, 2% received it for up to 3 weeks, and 1% received it for more than 3 weeks, without an increased incidence of serious adverse events. The mean duration of therapy in these studies was 5.6 days.

Overall, treatment was discontinued in 9% of the patients because of adverse events. The most common serious adverse events leading to discontinuation of amiodarone i.v. therapy were ventricular tachycardia (2%), hypotension (2%), cardiac arrest (asystole/cardiac arrest/electromechanical dissociation) (1%), and cardiogenic shock (1%).

Table VI lists the most common (incidence ≥1%) adverse drug reactions during amiodarone i.v. therapy that were collected from controlled and open-label clinical trials involving 1 836 patients with hemodynamically unstable VT or VF.

Overdose: Symptoms and Treatment: Oral: Overdose may lead to severe bradycardia and to conduction disturbances with the appearance of an idioventricular rhythm, particularly in elderly patients or patients on digitalis therapy.

One report of the acute ingestion of a single 8 g dose of oral amiodarone by a healthy 20-year-old female has been reported. At first assessment, the patient was conscious and profuse perspiration and a slight tachycardia were the only abnormal findings on clinical observation. Slight bradycardia was observed during the second and third day; thereafter, QT interval and heart rate returned to normal. No clinical adverse events were documented over the subsequent 3-month monitoring period.

If an overdose should occur, gastric lavage or induced emesis should be employed to reduce absorption, in addition to general supportive measures. The patient's cardiac rhythm and blood pressure should be monitored, and if clinically significant bradycardia ensues, a temporary pacemaker should be used.

I.V.: The most likely effects of an inadvertent overdose of amiodarone i.v. are hypotension, cardiogenic shock, bradycardia, AV block, and hepatotoxicity. Hypotension and cardiogenic shock should be treated by slowing the infusion rate or with standard therapy: vasopressor drugs, positive inotropic agents and volume expansion. Bradycardia and AV block may require temporary pacing. Hepatic enzyme concentrations should be monitored closely.

Neither amiodarone nor DEA is dialyzable.

Dosage: Oral: General Considerations: **Amiodarone therapy should be initiated in hospital and continued in a monitored environment until adequate control of the arrhythmia has occurred. Patients treated with amiodarone should be under the supervision of a cardiologist or a physician with equivalent experience in cardiology. Dose administration must be individualized, particularly taking into account concomitant antiarrhythmic therapy.**

The dosage schedule for amiodarone is still somewhat controversial, probably in part due to its poor absorption, unusually long elimination half-life, and huge volume of distribution. Extensive tissue stores of amiodarone must be established before the effects on the heart of oral dose administration are apparent. Intersubject variability as well as differences in dosage regimens and methods of assessment have made it difficult to precisely define the time of onset of initial and maximal antiarrhythmic effect in an individual patient. In order to ensure that an antiarrhythmic effect will be observed without waiting several months, loading doses are required. Amiodarone's antiarrhythmic effect after oral administration may be noted in as early as 3 days (72 hours) but more often takes 1 to 3 weeks.

Because of the slow rate of elimination of amiodarone, its antiarrhythmic effects may persist for weeks or months after its discontinuation, but the time of arrhythmia recurrence is variable and unpredictable. In general, when the drug is resumed after recurrence of the arrhythmia, control is established more rapidly relative to the initial response, possibly because tissue stores were not wholly depleted at the time of recurrence.

Table V—Cordarone/Cordarone I.V.

Incidence of Adverse Events in Patients Receiving Oral Cordarone

Body System	Incidence, % n=241	Adverse Event
Gastrointestinal	10-33	Nausea, vomiting
	4-9	Constipation, anorexia
	1-3	Abdominal pain, dyspepsia, diarrhea, abnormal taste, dry mouth
Dermatologic	4-9	Solar dermatitis/photosensitivity
	1-3	Blue skin discoloration, rash
	<1	Alopecia, onycholysis
Neurologic	4-9	Malaise/fatigue, tremor/abnormal involuntary movements, lack of coordination, abnormal gait/ataxia, dizziness, paresthesias
	1-3	Decreased libido/impotence, insomnia and other sleep disturbances, headache, cognitive disturbances and disorders of alertness, general weakness, peripheral motor and sensory neuropathies
	<1	Tinnitus
Ophthalmologic	10-33	Corneal microdeposits
	4-9	Visual disturbances
	up to 2	Optic neuropathy with visual impairment/decreased acuity
Hepatic	4-9	Hepatomegaly, abnormal liver function test results
	1-3	Nonspecific hepatic disorders
Respiratory	4-9	Pulmonary inflammation or fibrosis
Cardiovascular	1-3	Congestive heart failure, cardiac arrhythmias, SA node dysfunction
	<1	Hypotension, cardiac conduction abnormalities
Thyroid	1-3	Hyperthyroidism, hypothyroidism
	<1	Goiter
Other	1-3	Flushing, coagulation abnormalities
	<1	Spontaneous ecchymosis, epididymitis

Table VI—Cordarone/Cordarone I.V.

Summary Tabulation of Adverse Drug Reactions in Patients Receiving Cordarone I.V. in Controlled and Open-label Studies (≥1% Incidence)

Study Event	Controlled Trials (N=814)	Open-label Trials (N=1 022)	Total Incidence (N=1 836)
Any Adverse Reactions	412 (50.6%)	384 (37.5%)	796 (43.3%)
Body as a Whole	54 (6.6%)	32 (3.1%)	86 (4.6%)
Fever	24 (2.9%)	13 (1.2%)	37 (2.0%)
Cardiovascular System	308 (37.8%)	264 (25.8%)	572 (31.1%)
Atrial Fibrillation	15 (1.8%)	9 (<1%)	24 (1.3%)
AV Block	14 (1.5%)	12 (1.2%)	26 (1.4%)
Bradycardia	49 (6.0%)	41 (4.0%)	90 (4.9%)
Congestive Heart Failure	18 (2.2%)	21 (2.0%)	39 (2.1%)
Heart Arrest	29 (3.5%)	26 (2.5%)	55 (2.9%)
Hypotension	165 (20.2%)	123 (12.0%)	288 (15.6%)
Nodal Arrhythmia	15 (1.8%)	15 (1.4%)	30 (1.6%)
QT Interval Prolonged	15 (1.8%)	4 (<1%)	19 (1.0%)
Shock	13 (1.5%)	12 (1.1%)	25 (1.3%)
Ventricular Fibrillation	12 (1.4%)	13 (1.2%)	25 (1.3%)
Ventricular Tachycardia	15 (1.8%)	30 (2.9%)	45 (2.4%)
Digestive System	102 (12.5%)	97 (9.4%)	199 (10.8%)
Diarrhea	8 (<1%)	12 (1.1%)	20 (1.0%)
Liver Function Tests Abnormal	35 (4.2%)	29 (2.8%)	64 (3.4%)
Nausea	29 (3.5%)	43 (4.2%)	72 (3.9%)
Vomiting	16 (1.9%)	17 (1.6%)	33 (1.7%)
Hemic and Lymphatic System	34 (4.1%)	34 (3.3%)	68 (3.7%)
Thrombocytopenia	14 (1.7%)	16 (1.5%)	30 (1.6%)
Metabolic and Nutritional	56 (6.8%)	49 (4.7%)	105 (5.7%)
AST increased	14 (1.7%)	6 (<1%)	20 (1.0%)
ALT increased	14 (1.7%)	5 (<1%)	19 (1.0%)
Nervous System	46 (5.6%)	38 (3.7%)	84 (4.5%)
Respiratory System	54 (6.6%)	61 (5.9%)	115 (6.2%)
Lung Edema	6 (<1%)	15 (1.4%)	21 (1.1%)
Respiratory Disorder	11 (1.3%)	8 (<1%)	19 (1.0%)
Urogenital System	27 (3.3%)	30 (2.9%)	57 (3.1%)
Kidney Function Abnormal	8 (<1%)	16 (1.5%)	24 (1.3%)

The combination of amiodarone with other antiarrhythmic therapy should be reserved for patients with life-threatening arrhythmias who are unresponsive to adequate doses of a single agent (see Precautions, Drug Interactions).

Adults: Ventricular Arrhythmias: Loading Dose: Loading doses of 800 to 1 600 mg/day are required for 1 to 3 weeks (occasionally longer) until therapeutic response occurs. (Administration of amiodarone in divided doses at meals is suggested for total daily doses of 1 000 mg or higher, when gastrointestinal intolerance occurs).

Maintenance Dose: When adequate arrhythmia control has been achieved, or if adverse drug reactions become prominent, the amiodarone dose should be reduced to 600 to 800 mg/day for 1 month and then to the maintenance dose, usually 200 to 400 mg/day (occasionally 600 mg/day). Amiodarone may be administered as a single daily dose, or in patients with severe gastrointestinal intolerance, as a b.i.d. dose. In each patient, the chronic maintenance dose should be determined according to antiarrhythmic effect as assessed by symptoms, Holter recordings, and/or programmed electrical stimulation, and by patient tolerance. Plasma concentrations may be helpful in evaluating nonresponsiveness or unexpectedly severe toxicity.

The lowest effective dose should be used to prevent the occurrence of adverse drug reactions. In all instances, the physician must be guided by the severity of the individual patient's arrhythmia and response to therapy. When dose adjustments are necessary, the patient should be closely monitored for an extended period of time because of the long and variable half-life of amiodarone and the difficulty in predicting the time required to attain a new steady-state level of drug. Dosage suggestions are summarized in Table VII.

Table VII—Cordarone/Cordarone I.V.

Oral Cordarone Dosages for Ventricular Arrhythmia Suppression

Loading Dose (Daily)	Adjustment and Maintenance Dose (Daily)	
1-3 weeks	1 month	usual maintenance
800-1 600 mg	600-800 mg	200-400 mg (some 600 mg)

I.V.: See Table VIII. **Amiodarone i.v. must be delivered by a volumetric infusion pump. The surface properties of solutions containing injectable amiodarone are altered such that the drop size may be reduced. This reduction may lead to underdosage of the patient by up to 30% if drop counter infusion sets are used.**

Amiodarone i.v. should, whenever possible, be administered through a central venous catheter dedicated to that purpose. An in-line filter should be used during administration.

Amiodarone i.v. concentrations greater than 3 mg/mL in D_5W have been associated with a high incidence of peripheral vein phlebitis; however, concentrations of 2.5 mg/mL or less appear to be less irritating. Therefore, for infusions longer than 1 hour, amiodarone i.v. concentrations should not exceed 2 mg/mL unless a central venous catheter is used.

Amiodarone i.v. infusions exceeding 2 hours must be administered in glass or polyolefin bottles containing D_5W.

It is well known that amiodarone adsorbs to polyvinyl chloride (PVC) tubing and the clinical trial dose administration schedule was designed to account for this adsorption. All of the clinical trials were conducted using PVC tubing and its use is therefore recommended. The concentrations and rates of infusion provided in Dosage reflect doses identified in these studies.

Amiodarone i.v. does not need to be protected from light during administration.

Admixture Incompatibility: Amiodarone i.v. in D_5W is physically incompatible with the drugs shown in Table IX.

Table X—Cordarone/Cordarone I.V.

Cordarone I.V. Dose Recommendations—First 24 Hours

Loading Infusions	**Rapid: 150 mg over 10 minutes (15 mg/min).** Add 3 mL of Cordarone I.V. (150 mg) to 100 mL D_5W (concentration=1.5 mg/mL). Infuse 100 mL over 10 minutes.
	Slow: 360 mg over 6 hours (1 mg/min). Add 18 mL of Cordarone I.V. (900 mg) to 500 mL D_5W (concentration=1.8 mg/mL).
Maintenance infusion	**540 mg over 18 hours (0.5 mg/min).** Decrease the rate of the slow loading infusion to 0.5 mg/min.

After the first 24 hours, the maintenance infusion rate of 0.5 mg/min (720 mg/24 hours) should be continued utilizing a concentration of 1 to 6 mg/mL (amiodarone i.v. concentrations greater than 2 mg/mL should be administered via a central venous catheter). In the event of breakthrough episodes of VF or hemodynamically unstable VT, 150 mg supplemental infusions of amiodarone i.v. mixed in 100 mL of D_5W may be administered. Such infusions should be administered over 10 minutes to minimize the potential for hypotension. The rate of the maintenance infusion may be increased to achieve effective arrhythmia suppression.

The first 24-hour dose may be individualized for each patient; however, in controlled clinical trials, mean daily doses above 2 100 mg were associated with an increased risk of hypotension. The initial rate of infusion should not exceed 30 mg/min.

Based on the experience from clinical studies of amiodarone i.v., a maintenance infusion of up to 0.5 mg/min can be cautiously continued for 2 to 3 weeks regardless of the patient's age, renal function, or left ventricular function. There has been limited experience in patients receiving amiodarone i.v. for longer than 3 weeks.

I.V. to Oral Transition: Patients whose arrhythmias have been suppressed by amiodarone i.v. may be switched to oral amiodarone. The optimal dose for changing from i.v. to oral administration of amiodarone will depend on the dose of amiodarone i.v. already administered as well as the bioavailability of oral amiodarone. When changing to oral amiodarone therapy, clinical monitoring is recommended, particularly for elderly patients.

Table VIII—Cordarone/Cordarone I.V.

Stability of Diluted Amiodarone HCl Solutions

Solution	Concentration (mg/mL)	Container	Comments
5% Dextrose in Water (D_5W)	1.0-6.0	PVC	Physically compatible, with amiodarone loss <10% at 2 hours at room temperature.
5% Dextrose in Water (D_5W)	1.0-6.0	Polyolefin, Glass	Physically compatible, with no amiodarone loss at 24 hours at room temperature.

Table IX—Cordarone/Cordarone I.V.

Y-Site Injection Incompatibility

Drug	Vehicle	Amiodarone Concentration mg/mL	Comments
Aminophylline	D_5W	4	Precipitate
Cefamandole Nafate	D_5W	4	Precipitate
Cefazolin Sodium	D_5W	4	Precipitate
Mezlocillin Sodium	D_5W	4	Precipitate
Heparin Sodium	D_5W	–	Precipitate
Sodium Bicarbonate	D_5W	3	Precipitate

Amiodarone shows considerable interindividual variation in response. Thus, although a starting dose adequate to suppress life-threatening arrhythmias is needed, close monitoring with adjustment of dose is essential. The recommended starting dose of amiodarone i.v. is about 1 000 mg over the first 24 hours of therapy, delivered by the infusion regimen in Table X. It is important that the recommended infusion regimen be followed closely.

Table XI provides suggested doses of oral amiodarone to be initiated after varying durations of amiodarone i.v. administration. These recommendations are made on the basis of a comparable total body amount of amiodarone delivered by the i.v. and oral routes, based on a 50% bioavailability of oral amiodarone.

Table XI—Cordarone/Cordarone I.V.

Recommendations for Oral Dosage After I.V. Infusion

Duration of Cordarone I.V. Infusion[a]	Initial Daily Dose of Oral Cordarone (mg)
<1 week	800-1 600
1-3 weeks	600-800
>3 weeks[b]	400

[a]Assuming a 720 mg/day infusion (0.5 mg/min).
[b]Cordarone I.V. is not intended for maintenance treatment.

Supplied: Oral: Each round, flat, pink tablet with a raised "C" and marked "200" on one side with the reverse side scored contains: amiodarone HCl 200 mg. Nonmedicinal ingredients: colloidal silicon dioxide, cornstarch, lactose, magnesium stearate and povidone. Keep bottle tightly closed. Store at room temperature, 15 to 30°C. Protect from light.

I.V.: Each mL of clear, pale yellow solution contains: amiodarone HCl 50 mg. Nonmedicinal ingredients: benzyl alcohol (20.2 mg), polysorbate 80 (100 mg) and water for injection. Clear type 1 flint glass ampuls of 5 mL containing 3 mL of solution. Store at controlled room temperature, 15 to 25°C. Protect from light and excessive heat. Use carton to protect contents from light until use.

(Shown in Product Recognition Section)

Reviewed 1997

COREG™ 🄿

SmithKline Beecham

Carvedilol

Congestive Heart Failure Agent

Pharmacology: Carvedilol is a cardiovascular agent for the treatment of CHF that combines beta-adrenoceptor blockade and vasodilation in a single racemic mixture. Nonselective beta-adrenoceptor blocking activity is present in the S(-) enantiomer and alpha 1-adrenoceptor blocking activity is present at equal potency in both the R(+) and S(-) enantiomers. Carvedilol has no intrinsic sympathomimetic activity. Its action on beta-receptors is 10 times stronger than on alpha 1-receptors.

Carvedilol reduces peripheral vascular resistance by vasodilation, thereby causing a fall in systemic blood pressure after acute administration, predominantly mediated through selective alpha 1-antagonism. Beta-blockade prevents reflex tachycardia with the net result that heart rate is unchanged or decreased. Carvedilol reduces renin release through beta-blockade.

In 2 studies that compared the acute hemodynamic effects of carvedilol to baseline measurements in patients with congestive heart failure, there were significant reductions in systemic blood pressure, pulmonary artery pressure, pulmonary capillary wedge pressure, and heart rate. Initial effects on cardiac output, stroke volume index and systemic vascular resistance were small and variable.

In terms of chronic hemodynamic effects (12 to 14 weeks), carvedilol significantly reduced systemic blood pressure, pulmonary artery pressure, right atrial pressure, systemic vascular resistance and heart rate while stroke volume index was increased.

The mechanism for the beneficial effects of carvedilol in congestive heart failure has not been established.

In a US multicenter program, 1 197 patients with stable symptomatic congestive heart failure, NYHA class II to IV, were challenged with a low dose of carvedilol (3.125 or 6.25 mg twice daily) for 2 to 4 weeks to determine tolerability. Of these patients, 1 094 were then randomized to double-blind treatment with carvedilol (n=696) or placebo (n=398) and stratified to 1 of 4 studies based on baseline exercise performance, with the prestated objective to evaluate total mortality. The average duration of therapy on carvedilol was 6.5 months in this program. Patients entering the program had symptomatic CHF due to ischemic or nonischemic cardiomyopathy with an ejection fraction ≤35%. All patients received conventional therapy, i.e. diuretics, angiotensin-converting enzyme (ACE) inhibitors, if tolerated, with or without digoxin.

On an intent-to-treat basis, total mortality in this program was 3.2% in the carevedilol group and 7.8% in the placebo group. Thus a relative risk reduction of 65% (95% confidence limits 39 and 80%, p=0.001) was observed. Treatment with carvedilol was associated with a significant decrease in the relative risk of death from progressive pump failure (81%, p=0.001) and the relative risk of sudden death (56%, p=0.033). The incidence of cardiovascular hospitalizations was 13% in the carvedilol group and 21% in the placebo group, with a relative risk reduction of 36% (95% confidence limits 14 and 53%, p=0.004).

Improved patient well being was observed with carvedilol treatment in the US multicenter program, as indicated by a change in the NYHA class from baseline to endpoint for the 4 US phase III placebo-controlled studies. The overall between-group difference in distributions, stratified by protocol and baseline classification, was significant (p<0.001) and as also indicated by patient and physician global assessments during US Phase III trials, 78% of patients in the carvedilol group rated their condition as improved compared to 63% in the placebo group (p values over 4 studies from 0.001 to 0.032). However, exercise tolerance was not improved.

In a large multicenter trial of carvedilol, performed in Australia and New Zealand, 443 patients with stable symptomatic congestive heart failure NYHA Class I to III, were challenged with a low dose of carvedilol (3.125 mg or 6.25 mg twice daily) for 2 to 4 weeks to determine tolerability. Of these

Coreg (cont'd)

patients 415 were then randomized to double-blind treatment with carvedilol (n=207) or placebo (n=208). The average duration of therapy on carvedilol was 16.1 months in this study. Patients entering the program had symptomatic CHF due to ischemic cardiomyopathy with an ejection fraction ≤45%. All patients received conventional therapy, i.e. diuretics, angiotensin-converting enzyme (ACE) inhibitors, if tolerated, with or without digoxin.

On an intent-to-treat basis, total mortality in this Australia and New Zealand trial was 10.1% in the carvedilol group and 13.9% in the placebo group, a nonstatistically significant relative risk reduction of 29% (confidence limits 24 and 59%, p=0.231). Cardiovascular hospitalizations were 31% in the carvedilol group and 40% in the placebo group, a relative risk reduction of 28% (95% confidence limits: 1 and 48%, p=0.044). Patient well-being as judged by NYHA class or Specific Activity Scale rating, as well as exercise tolerance were no different in the carvedilol group compared to the placebo group.

Pharmacokinetics: Carvedilol is rapidly absorbed following oral administration, with peak plasma concentrations of carvedilol observed at 1 hour post-dose in fasting subjects. Despite being well-absorbed, absolute bioavailability is approximately 25 to 35% due to a significant degree of first-pass metabolism.

Plasma concentrations achieved are proportional to the oral dose administered. When administered with food, the rate of absorption is slowed, as evidenced by a delay in time to reach peak plasma concentrations (about 2.3 hours post-dose), with no significant difference in extent of bioavailability.

Carvedilol is highly bound to plasma proteins, (greater than 98%) primarily to albumin. The plasma-protein binding is independent of concentration over the therapeutic range. Carvedilol is a basic, lipophilic compound with a steady-state volume of distribution of approximately 115 L.

Following oral administration, the apparent mean terminal elimination half-life of carvedilol ranges from 7 to 10 hours. Plasma clearance ranges from 500 to 700 mL/min. Carvedilol is extensively metabolized with less than 2% of the dose excreted unchanged in the urine. Carvedilol is metabolized mainly by glucuronidation and aromatic ring oxidation by the cytochrome P450 system (primarily 2D6 and 2C9 isozymes). The metabolites of carvedilol are excreted mainly via the bile into the feces. Elimination is mainly biliary. The primary route of excretion is via the feces. A minor part is eliminated via the kidneys in the form of various metabolites.

Carvedilol undergoes stereoselective first-pass metabolism with plasma levels of R(+)-carvedilol approximately 2- to 3-fold higher than S(-)-carvedilol following oral administration in healthy subjects. The mean apparent terminal elimination half-lives for R(+)-carvedilol ranges from 5 to 9 hours compared with 7 to 11 hours for the S(-) enantiomer.

Carvedilol is subject to genetic polymorphism with poor metabolizers of debrisoquin (deficient in cytochrome P450 2D6) exhibiting 2- to 3-fold higher plasma concentrations of the R(+)-carvedilol compared to extensive metabolizers. In contrast, plasma levels of S(-)-carvedilol are increased only about 20 to 25% in poor metabolizers, indicating that the metabolism of this enantiomer is affected to a lesser extent by cytochrome P450 2D6 than R(+)-carvedilol. The pharmacokinetics of carvedilol enantiomers do not appear to be different in poor metabolizers of S-mephenytoin, i.e. deficient in cytochrome P450 CPY 2C19.

There are at least 5 pharmacologically active metabolites of carvedilol: desmethyl, 4'-hydroxyphenyl, 5'-hydroxyphenyl, 1-hydroxycarbazolyl and 8-hydroxycabazolyl metabolites. Each of these metabolites has 2 enantiomeric forms and each metabolite possesses different relative potencies with regard to α- and β-receptor blocking activities. Plasma concentrations of these metabolites are 10- to 50-fold lower than those observed for the parent compound. Therefore, even for metabolites that are more active or at least as active as carvedilol itself, they are present at such low concentrations that they would produce effects less than, or at least not greater than, the parent compound.

In patients with cirrhotic liver disease, the absolute bioavailability of carvedilol was 4 times greater as compared to healthy subjects with median C_{max} and AUC values for carvedilol 4 to 7 times higher in patients with liver disease following oral administration (see Contraindications, Warnings and Precautions).

Although carvedilol is metabolized primarily by the liver, plasma concentrations of carvedilol have been reported to be increased in patients with renal impairment. Based on AUC data, approximately 40 to 50% higher plasma concentrations of carvedilol were observed in hypertensive patients with moderate to severe renal impairment compared to a control group of hypertensive patients with normal renal function. However, the ranges of AUC values were similar for both groups. Changes in C_{max} data were less pronounced, approximately 12 to 26% higher in patients with impaired renal function.

The pharmacokinetics of carvedilol are not altered by hemodialysis.

Steady-state plasma concentrations of carvedilol and its enantiomers increased proportionally over the 6.25 to 50 mg b.i.d. dose range in patients with congestive heart failure. Compared to healthy subjects, patients with Class IV congestive heart failure had increased mean AUC and C_{max} values for carvedilol and its enantiomers with up to 50 to 100% higher values than normal volunteers. The mean apparent terminal elimination half-life for carvedilol was similar to that observed in healthy subjects.

Compared to young subjects (18 to 43 years old), AUC values for carvedilol were, on average, 38% higher in elderly (65 to 76 years old) subjects. Moreover, AUC values were 50% higher for S(-)-carvedilol and 23% for R(+)-carvedilol in the elderly compared to the young subjects. Changes in C_{max} values for carvedilol and its enantiomers were less pronounced, approximately 8 to 17% higher in elderly subjects with no apparent change in T_{max}. Although the terminal elimination half-lives of carvedilol were similar in both young and elderly subjects, the initial decline in plasma concentrations in the elderly appeared to be slower than in the young subjects suggesting a decrease in systemic clearance of carvedilol in the elderly (see Precautions and Dosage).

Indications: For treatment of stable symptomatic congestive heart failure (CHF) in patients with NYHA Class II and III, taking diuretics and with angiotensin converting enzyme inhibitors, with or without digoxin.

Data are limited in NYHA Class IV patients, and therefore, carvedilol is not recommended in these patients.

Carvedilol should be prescribed by a physician experienced in the treatment of heart failure.

> Beta-blockers can cause worsening heart failure. Since carvedilol has beta-blocking properties, care must be taken during initiation and up-titration of the drug in heart failure patients, since worsening heart failure has been observed during this phase of treatment. In order to minimize the risk of these events, it is critical to carefully follow the recommended dosing for carvedilol in patients with congestive heart failure (see Dosage).

Contraindications: In patients with: decompensated cardiac failure requiring i.v. inotropic therapy with sympathomimetic agents; bronchial asthma or related bronchospastic conditions (see Pharmacology and Precautions); second- or third-degree AV block, or sick sinus syndrome (unless a permanent pacemaker is in place); cardiogenic shock; severe hypotension (see Warnings); severe bradycardia (see Warnings); primary obstructive valvular heart disease; clinically manifest hepatic impairment (jaundice, ascites, spider angiomata, esophageal varices, etc.); mental incapacity (e.g., severe Alzheimer's, alcoholism, drug abuse), unless closely supervised by an appropriate caregiver; hypersensitivity to carvedilol or any component of the drug.

Warnings: Hypotension: Hypotension and postural hypotension in congestive heart failure patients occurred with a higher incidence in carvedilol-treated than in placebo-treated patients (see Adverse Effects). The risk of these events was highest during initiation of therapy and during the first 30 days of dosing corresponding to the up-titration period. Therefore, it is of critical importance that the dosing recommendation be followed (see Dosage).

Sinus Bradycardia: Severe sinus bradycardia may occur with the use of carvedilol. In such cases, dosage should be discontinued.

In clinical trials, patients with a resting heart rate of less than or equal to 68 beats/min prior to initiation of carvedilol were not studied.

Hepatic Injury: Hepatocellular injury, confirmed by rechallenge, has occurred rarely with carvedilol therapy.

Hepatic injury has been reversible and has occurred after short-and/or long-term therapy with minimal clinical symptomatology. No deaths due to liver function abnormalities have been reported.

At the first symptom/sign of liver dysfunction (e.g., pruritus, dark urine, persistent anorexia, jaundice, right upper quadrant tenderness or unexplained "flu-like" symptoms), laboratory testing should be performed. If the patient has laboratory evidence of liver injury or jaundice, carvedilol should be stopped and not restarted.

Abrupt Cessation of Therapy: In patients with heart failure treated chronically with carvedilol, abrupt cessation of therapy may lead to deterioration. Therefore discontinuation of carvedilol should be done gradually, if possible.

Patients with ischemic heart disease should be warned against abrupt discontinuation of beta-adrenergic blocking agents. There have been reports of severe exacerbation of angina, and of myocardial infarction or ventricular arrhythmias occurring in patients with angina pectoris, following abrupt discontinuation of beta-blocker therapy.

The last 2 complications may occur with or without preceding exacerbation of angina pectoris. Therefore, when discontinuing carvedilol in patients with angina pectoris, the dosage should be gradually reduced over a period of about 2 weeks and the patient should be carefully observed. The same frequency of administration should be maintained. In situations of greater urgency, carvedilol therapy should be discontinued stepwise and under conditions of closer observation. If angina markedly worsens or acute coronary insufficiency develops, it is recommended that treatment with the drug be re-instituted promptly, at least temporarily.

Oculomucocutaneous Syndrome: Various skin rashes and conjunctival xerosis have been reported with beta-blockers. A severe syndrome (oculomucocutaneous syndrome) whose signs include conjunctivitis sicca and psoriasiform rashes, otitis, and sclerosing serositis has occurred with the chronic use of one beta-adrenergic blocking agent (practolol). This syndrome has not been observed in association with carvedilol or any other such agent. However, physicians should be alert to the possibility of such reactions and should discontinue treatment in the event that they occur.

Uveal Binding: Animal studies have shown that carvedilol binds to the melanin of the uveal tract. The significance of this in humans is not known but periodic ophthalmic examinations are advisable while the patient is taking carvedilol.

Hyperthyroidism: In patients with thyrotoxicosis, possible deleterious effects from long-term use of carvedilol have not been appraised. Beta-blockade, in general, may mask the clinical signs of continuing hyperthyroidism or complications, and give a false impression of improvement. Therefore, abrupt withdrawal of carvedilol may be followed by an exacerbation of the symptoms of hyperthyroidism, including thyroid storm.

Pheochromocytoma: The effect of carvedilol in patients with pheochromocytoma has not been studied. Since paradoxical hypertensive responses have been reported in a few patients with this tumor when treated with β-blockers, physicians should use caution when administering carvedilol to patients with pheochromocytoma.

Precautions: Cardiac Failure: Worsening cardiac failure may occur during initiation and up-titration of carvedilol. Sympathetic stimulation is a vital component supporting circulatory function in CHF, and inhibition with beta-blockade may further depress myocardial contractility.

Cardiac failure should be controlled for at least 4 weeks before carvedilol treatment is initiated. In clinical trials, patients were required to be on stable doses of diuretics and ACE inhibitors (if tolerated) prior to the initiation of carvedilol. Despite these steps to ensure stability, a small number of patients developed worsening heart failure. During the initiation of therapy (doses of 3.125 to 6.25 mg b.i.d. over 2 to 4 weeks) 6% of patients developed worsening CHF. During up-titration (12.5 to 50 mg b.i.d. over 2 to 6 weeks), worsening heart failure was reported in 5.1% of carvedilol-treated patients and in 4.1% of placebo patients. Therefore, administration of carvedilol to patients with controlled heart failure must be carried out under careful supervision. If symptoms occur, diuretics should be increased and the carvedilol dose not advanced or even lowered until clinical stability resumes (see Dosage). However it may be necessary to discontinue carvedilol. Such episodes may not preclude subsequent successful titration of the drug.

Renal Function: Rarely, use of carvedilol in patients with congestive heart failure has resulted in acute renal failure and deterioration of renal function, likely on a pre-renal basis. Patients at risk appear to be those with low blood pressure (systolic BP < 100 mmHg), ischemic heart disease and diffuse vascular disease, and/or underlying renal insufficiency. Renal function has returned to baseline when carvedilol was stopped. In patients with these risk factors it is recommended that renal function be monitored during up-titration of carvedilol and the drug discontinued or dosage reduced if worsening of renal function occurs (see Dosage).

Hepatic Impairment: Since carvedilol undergoes first-pass metabolism in the liver, reduced hepatic metabolism could lead to greater systemic bioavailability of carvedilol in patients with hepatic impairment. Care should be taken in selecting an appropriate dosage regimen for these patients (see Contraindications and Dosage). Physicians should be aware of the potential for increased manifestations of vasodilation (dizziness, postural hypotension, hypotension, syncope) or beta-blockade (bradycardia, AV block) in patients with mild hepatic impairment receiving carvedilol (see Dosage).

Bronchospasm (e.g., Chronic Bronchitis and Emphysema): Patients with bronchospastic disease should, in general, not receive β-blockers (see Contraindications).

In clinical trials of patients with congestive heart failure, patients with bronchospastic disease were enrolled if they did not require oral or inhaled medication to treat their bronchospastic disease. In such patients, it is recommended that carvedilol be used with caution. The dosing recommendations should be followed closely and the dose should be lowered if any evidence of bronchospasm is observed during up-titration.

Allergic Reaction: There may be increased difficulty in treating an allergic-type reaction in patients on beta-blockers. In these patients, the reaction may be more severe due to pharmacological effects of beta-blockers and problems with fluid changes. Epinephrine should be administered with caution since it may not have its usual effects in the treatment of anaphylaxis.

On the one hand, larger doses of epinephrine may be needed to overcome the bronchospasm, while on the other, these doses can be associated with excessive alpha-adrenergic stimulation with consequent hypertension, reflex bradycardia and heart block and possible potentiation of bronchospasm. Alternatives to the use of large doses of epinephrine include vigorous supportive care such as fluids and the use of beta-agonists including parenteral salbutamol or isoproterenol to overcome bronchospasm and norepinephrine to overcome hypotension.

Prinzmetal's Angina: Beta-blocking agents may provoke chest pain in patients with Prinzmetal's angina. There has been no clinical experience with carvedilol in these patients. Caution should be taken in the administration of carvedilol to patients suspected of having Prinzmetal's variant angina.

Primary Regurgitative Valvular Heart Disease: Carvedilol should be used with caution in patients with primary regurgitative valvular disease as experience in this patient population is limited.

Patients with Diabetes: Carvedilol should be administered with caution to patients subject to spontaneous hypoglycemia, or to diabetic patients (especially those with labile diabetes) who are receiving insulin or oral hypoglycemic agents. Beta-adrenergic blocking drugs may enhance hypoglycemia in patients prone to this condition. Also, diabetics on insulin or oral hypoglycemic medication may have an increased tendency towards hypoglycemia when treated with these drugs. It may also be necessary to adjust the dosage of oral hypoglycemics or insulin. Early signs of acute hypoglycemia, especially tachycardia, may be masked or attenuated. Regular monitoring of blood glucose is therefore recommended when carvedilol is initiated, adjusted or discontinued.

Peripheral Vascular Disease: Beta-blockers can precipitate or aggravate symptoms of arterial insufficiency in patients with peripheral vascular disease. Caution should be exercised in such individuals.

Patients and General Surgery: Because of the synergistic negative inotropic and vasodilating effects of carvedilol and anesthetic drugs, the potential for pronounced hypotension during anesthesia exists. If carvedilol treatment is to be continued perioperatively, particular care should be taken when anesthetic agents which depress myocardial function are used.

Contact Lens Use: Wearers of contact lenses should bear in mind the possibility of reduced lacrimation.

Geriatrics: Pharmacokinetic studies indicate that AUC and T_{max} values are increased in elderly patients. Plasma levels of carvedilol averaged about 38% higher in elderly compared to young subjects. Therefore, dosage adjustments should be made with particular caution (see Dosage).

Pregnancy: There have been no clinical studies carried out to specifically examine the use of carvedilol in pregnant women. Beta-blockers reduce placental perfusion, which may result in intrauterine fetal death, immature and premature deliveries. In addition, adverse effects (especially hypoglycemia and bradycardia) may occur in the fetus and neonate. There is an increased risk of cardiac and pulmonary complications in the neonate in the postnatal period.

Animal reproduction studies have revealed no teratogenic potential for carvedilol. Embryotoxicity was observed only after large doses in rabbits. The relevance of these findings for humans is uncertain.

Carvedilol should be used during pregnancy only if the potential benefit justifies the potential risk to the fetus.

Lactation: Carvedilol and/or its metabolites are excreted in breast milk. Therefore, breast-feeding is not recommended during administration of carvedilol.

Children: Safety and efficacy in children have not been established.

Drug Interactions: Antihypertensive Agents: When administered concomitantly with other drugs that are antihypertensive in action or have hypotension as part of their adverse effect profile, carvedilol may have additive effects to excessively lower blood pressure.

Catecholamine-Depleting Agents: Patients taking both agents with β-blocking properties and a drug that can deplete catecholamines (e.g., reserpine and MAO inhibitors) should be observed closely for evidence of hypotension and/or marked bradycardia.

Antiarrhythmics and Calcium Channel Blockers: Isolated cases of conduction disturbance (rarely with hemodynamic compromise) have been observed when carvedilol is coadministered with antiarrhythmic agents or calcium channel blockers such as diltiazem and verapamil that can slow cardiac conduction. As with other agents with β-blocking properties, if carvedilol is to be administered orally with antiarrhythmics that slow conduction or calcium channel blockers of the verapamil or diltiazem type, it is recommended that ECG and blood pressure be monitored.

Digoxin: Following concomitant administration of carvedilol and digoxin, peak concentration of digoxin increased by approximately 30% and steady-state trough concentrations of digoxin were increased by about 15%. Both digoxin and carvedilol slow AV conduction. Therefore, increased monitoring of digoxin levels is recommended when initiating, adjusting or discontinuing carvedilol.

Clonidine: Concomitant administration of clonidine with agents with beta-blocking properties may potentiate blood pressure and heart rate lowering effects. When concomitant treatment with agents with beta-blocking properties and clonidine is to be terminated, the beta-blocking agent should be discontinued first. Clonidine therapy can then be discontinued several days later by gradually decreasing the dosage.

Inducers and Inhibitors of Cytochrome P450: Since carvedilol undergoes substantial oxidative metabolism, care may be required in patients receiving inducers or inhibitors of cytochrome P450, as plasma concentrations may be altered. Pretreatment with rifampin (600 mg daily for 12 days) decreased the AUC and C_{max} for carvedilol approximately 70% following a single oral dose of carvedilol. Coadministration of carvedilol and cimetidine (1 000 mg/day) resulted in a 30% increase in median AUC for carvedilol. Despite the reduction in oral clearance, peak plasma concentrations of carvedilol were unchanged due to an apparent decrease in rate of absorption.

Nitroglycerin: The effect of carvedilol coadministration with nitroglycerin has not been studied. Carvedilol could blunt the reflex tachycardia produced by nitroglycerin through its beta-adrenergic blocking activity. When it is used with nitroglycerin in patients with angina pectoris, additional decreases in blood pressure may occur.

Insulin or Oral Hypoglycemics: Agents with beta-blocking properties may enhance the blood-sugar reducing effect of insulin and oral hypoglycemics. Therefore, in patients taking insulin or oral hypoglycemics, regular monitoring of blood glucose is recommended.

Tricyclic Antidepressants: The effect of carvedilol coadministration with tricyclic antidepressants has not been studied. As an increased incidence of tremor has been observed with other drugs of this class upon coadministration of tricyclic antidepressants, the possibility of a drug interaction cannot be excluded.

Grapefruit Juice: Following simultaneous administration of a single dose of 25 mg of carvedilol with 300 mL of grapefruit juice (an inhibitor of CYP3A4 and CYP1A2), AUC for carvedilol was approximately 16% higher than following administration of carvedilol with 300 mL of water.

Warfarin: Carvedilol (12.5 mg twice daily for 7 days) did not have an effect on warfarin-induced increase in steady-state prothrombin time ratios and did not alter the pharmacokinetics of both enantiomers of warfarin following concomitant administration with warfarin in healthy volunteers.

Adverse Effects: In 6 US placebo controlled trials, 1 313 patients were challenged with carvedilol over a 2 to 4 week period. Of these patients, 1 202 were randomized to double-blind treatment with carvedilol (n=765) or placebo (n=437) and 92.5% of those treated with carvedilol reported at least 1 adverse experience.

During the double-blind phase of these trials, adverse experiences rated as serious were reported in 22.4% of patients treated with carvedilol and 31.8% in the placebo group. The most serious adverse experiences reported with carvedilol were cardiac failure (5.6%), syncope (1.8%), bradycardia (1.6%), hypotension (1.3%), myocardial infarction (0.9%), acute renal failure (0.8%) and AV block (0.7%).

Adverse experiences rated as severe in intensity during the double-blind phase of these trials were reported in 24.3% of patients treated with carvedilol. The most frequent severe adverse experiences were cardiac failure (2.9%), fatigue (2.2%), dizziness (2.0%), dyspnea (1.8%) and syncope (1.7%).

The most common adverse experiences reported in the double-blind phase of the US clinical trial experience (see Table I) with carvedilol were dizziness (32.4%), fatigue (23.9%), dyspnea (21.3%), upper respiratory infection (18.3%), cardiac failure (15.3%) and chest pain (14.4%).

Of the 1 202 patients who received randomized treatment in these trials, 5.4% of carvedilol patients withdrew because of adverse experiences compared with 8.0% of placebo patients. Bradycardia, fatigue, hypotension, dizziness and dyspnea were the most commonly reported adverse experiences leading to discontinuation in carvedilol treated patients (see Table I).

Six deaths occurred in 1 319 patients enrolled in the screening phase (3 to 4 weeks), 11 deaths occurred in 1 313 patients challenged with carvedilol (2 to 4 weeks). There were 8 deaths (3/765 carvedilol; 5/437 placebo) during up-titration phase (2 to 6 weeks) and 47 deaths (20/765 carvedilol; 27/437 placebo) during the maintenance phase (up to 12 months) of the studies.

Withdrawals due to worsening heart failure in US placebo controlled CHF trials were as follows: during challenge 1.4% of patients (18/1 313 for 2 to 4 weeks); during up-titration 0.9% (7/765) of carvedilol patients and 0% (0/437) of placebo patients (2 to 6 weeks); during the maintenance phase 0.7% (5/765) of carvedilol patients and 2.3% (10/437) of placebo patients (up to 12 months).

Worsening renal function, including acute renal failure (see Table I on following page), has been seen in some patients (carvedilol 9.5% and placebo 7.6%). Patients at greatest risk include those with pre-existing renal insufficiency, hypotension and ischemic cardiomyopathy, previous renal insufficiency due to ACE inhibitors, diffuse vascular disease or evidence of renal artery stenosis.

Table I (on following page) shows adverse events in US placebo-controlled clinical trials of congestive heart failure patients that occurred with an incidence of greater than 1% regardless of causality and were more frequent in drug-treated patients than placebo-treated patients. Median study medication exposure was 6.3 months for carvedilol and placebo patients.

In addition to the events in Table I (on following page), the following events occurred in more than 1% of carvedilol-treated patients but rates were equal to, or more common in, placebo-treated patients: asthenia, cardiac failure, flatulence, anorexia, dyspepsia, palpitation, ventricular tachycardia, atrial fibrillation, extrasystoles, bilirubinemia, hyperkalemia, arthritis, angina pectoris, insomnia, depression, amnesia, anemia, viral infection, dyspnea, coughing, respiratory disorder, pneumonia, rhinitis, rash, pruritus and leg cramps.

Adverse experiences related to laboratory parameters reported in greater than 1% of patients are in Table I. Adverse experiences related to laboratory parameters reported in $\leq 1\%$ but more than 0.1% of patients included increased hepatic enzymes (0.4% of congestive heart failure patients were discontinued from therapy because of increases in hepatic enzymes; see Precautions, Hepatic Injury), hypokalemia, hypertriglyceridemia, anemia, leukopenia.

The following adverse events were reported as possibly or probably related in worldwide open or controlled trials with carvedilol in patients with hypertension or congestive heart failure at an incidence of $>0.1\%$ to $\leq 1\%$: Cardiovascular: peripheral ischemia, tachycardia.

Central and Peripheral Nervous System: hypokinesia.

General: substernal chest pain, edema.

Psychiatric: sleep disorder, aggravated depression, impaired concentration, abnormal thinking, paroniria, emotional lability.

Respiratory System: asthma

Reproductive, Male: decreased libido.

Skin and Appendages: pruritus, rash erythematous, rash maculopapular, rash psoriaform, photosensitivity reaction.

Special Senses: tinnitus.

Urinary System: micturition frequency.

Autonomic Nervous System: dry mouth, sweating increased.

Metabolic and Nutritional: diabetes mellitus.

The following adverse events were reported as possibly or probably related in worldwide open or controlled trials with carvedilol in patients with hypertension or congestive heart

Coreg (cont'd)

failure at an incidence of ≤0.1%, and are potentially important: complete AV block, bundle branch block, myocardial ischemia, cerebrovascular disorder, convulsions, migraine, neuralgia, paresis, anaphylactoid reaction, alopecia, exfoliative dermatitis, amnesia, gastrointestinal hemorrhage, bronchospasm, pulmonary edema, decreased hearing, respiratory alkalosis, decreased HDL, pancytopenia and atypical lymphocytes.

Overdose: Symptoms: Cases of overdosage with carvedilol alone or in combination with other drugs have been reported. Quantities ingested in some cases exceeded 1 000 mg. Clinical signs experienced included low blood pressure and heart rate. Standard supportive treatment was provided and individuals recovered.

In the event of inadvertent or intentional overdosage with carvedilol, there may be severe hypotension, excessive bradycardia, heart failure, cardiogenic shock and cardiac arrest due to its pharmacologic activities. There may also be respiratory distress, bronchospasm, vomiting, disturbed consciousness and generalized seizures.

Treatment: Patients who have taken an overdose of carvedilol should be placed supine, with their legs raised. For removal of the drug shortly after ingestion, gastric lavage or pharmacologically induced emesis may be useful. Carvedilol is not removed by hemodialysis. In addition to these general procedures, the patient's vital signs should be monitored under intensive care conditions with continuous monitoring, if necessary.

The following additional supportive therapies can be used: If excessive hypotension occurs, vasopressor, norepinephrine should be administered with continuous monitoring of the circulatory system. Digitalis, diuretics, and if necessary, dopamine or dobutamine should be administered if cardiac failure occurs.

For excessive bradycardia, atropine 0.5 to 2 mg should be given i.v. In addition, glucagon initially 1 to 10 mg i.v., then 2 to 2.5 mg/h for long-term infusion, has been shown to be effective when severe overdosage of beta-blockers causes hypotension and/or bradycardia. For therapy-resistant bradycardia, pacemaker therapy may be necessary.

For bronchospasm, beta-sympathomimetics (as aerosol or i.v.) or i.v. aminophylline should be given.

In the event of seizures, slow i.v. injection of diazepam or clonazepam is recommended.

Note: In the event of severe intoxication where there are symptoms of shock, treatment must be continued for a sufficiently long period of time consistent with the 7 to 10 hour elimination half-life of carvedilol.

Dosage: Dosage must be individualized and patients closely monitored during initiation and up-titration by a physician experienced in the treatment of heart failure.

All patients in whom carvedilol therapy is to be considered must be clinically stable for 4 weeks prior to initiation of carvedilol.

Prior to initiation of carvedilol therapy, patients should be on stable doses of diuretics and angiotensin converting enzyme inhibitors, with or without digitalis. In clinical trials, all patients shown to have benefit were on the above regimen unless they were intolerant to an ACE inhibitor.

The recommended starting dose of carvedilol is 3.125 mg twice daily for 2 weeks. If this dose is tolerated, it can then be increased to 6.25 mg twice daily. Dosing should then be doubled every 2 weeks to the highest level tolerated by the patient. At initiation of each new dose, patients should be observed for signs of dizziness or lightheadedness for 1 to 2 hours. The maximum recommended dose is 25 mg twice daily.

The risk/benefit of carvedilol therapy in clinically stable heart failure patients with a heart rate lower than 68 beats/min should be carefully considered prior to initiation of carvedilol since it has not been studied in these patients (see Warnings).

Carvedilol should be taken with food to slow the rate of absorption and reduce the incidence of orthostatic effects, especially during up-titration.

Before each dose increase the patient should be seen in the office and evaluated for symptoms of worsening heart failure, vasodilation (dizziness, lightheadedness, symptomatic hypotension) or bradycardia, in order to determine tolerability of carvedilol. Transient worsening of heart failure may be treated with increased doses of diuretics, lowering the dose of carvedilol or, if necessary, discontinuation of carvedilol. Symptoms of vasodilation such as dizziness, lightheadedness or decreasing blood pressure may respond to a reduction in

Table I—Coreg

Adverse Events in US Placebo-Controlled Congestive Heart Failure Trials (Incidence >1%, Regardless of Causality; Withdrawal Rates due to Adverse Events)

	Adverse Reactions		Withdrawals	
	Coreg (n=765) % occurrence	**Placebo (n=437) % occurrence**	**Coreg (n=765) % withdrawals**	**Placebo (n=437) % withdrawals**
Autonomic Nervous System				
Sweating Increased	2.9	2.1	–	–
Body as a Whole				
Fatigue	23.9	22.4	0.7	0.7
Chest Pain	14.4	14.2	0.1	–
Pain	8.6	7.6	–	0.2
Injury	5.9	5.5	–	–
Drug Level Increased	5.1	3.7	–	0.2
Edema Generalized	5.1	2.5	–	–
Edema Dependent	3.7	1.8	–	–
Fever	3.1	2.3	–	–
Edema Legs	2.2	0.2	0.1	0.2
Edema Peripheral	1.6	0.7	–	–
Allergy	1.4	0.2	–	–
Sudden Death	1.3	1.1	–	–
Malaise	1.3	0.7	—	–
Hypovolemia	1.2	0.2	–	–
Cardiovascular				
Bradycardia	8.8	0.9	0.8	–
Hypotension	8.5	3.4	0.4	0.2
Syncope	3.4	2.5	0.3	0.2
Hypertension	2.9	2.5	0.1	–
AV Block	2.9	0.5	–	–
Angina Pectoris Aggravated	2.0	1.1	–	–
Fluid Overload	1.7	1.6	–	–
Postural Hypotension	1.2	0.2	–	–
CNS				
Dizziness	32.4	19.2	0.4	–
Headache	8.1	7.1	0.3	–
Paresthesia	2.0	1.8	0.1	–
Hypesthesia	1.7	1.1	–	–
Vertigo	1.4	1.1	–	–
Confusion	1.3	0.9	–	–
Somnolence	1.2	0.9	–	0.2
Gastrointestinal				
Diarrhea	11.8	5.9	0.3	–
Nausea	8.5	4.8	–	–
Abdominal Pain	7.2	7.1	0.3	–
Vomiting	6.3	4.3	0.1	–
Melena	1.4	1.1	–	–
Periodontitis	1.3	0.7	–	–
Hematologic				
Thrombocytopenia	2.0	0.5	0.1	–
Prothrombin Decreased	1.3	1.1	–	–
Purpura	1.3	0.2	–	–
Metabolic				
Hyperglycemia	12.2	7.8	0.1	–
Weight Increase	9.7	6.9	0.1	0.5
Gout	6.3	6.2	–	–
BUN Increased	6.0	4.6	0.3	0.2
NPN Increased	5.8	4.6	0.3	0.2
Hypercholesterolemia	4.1	2.5	–	–
Dehydration	2.1	1.6	–	–
Hypervolemia	2.0	0.9	–	–
Hyperuricemia	1.8	1.6	–	–
Hypoglycemia	1.6	1.4	0.1	–
ALT Increased	1.4	0.9	–	–
Hyponatremia	1.3	1.1	–	–
Phosphatase Alkaline Increase	1.2	1.1	–	–
AST Increased	1.2	0.9	–	–
Glycosuria	1.2	0.7	–	–
Musculoskeletal				
Back Pain	6.9	6.6	–	–
Arthralgia	6.4	4.8	0.1	0.2
Myalgia	3.4	2.7	–	–
Resistance Mechanism				
Upper Respiratory Tract Infection	18.3	17.6	–	–
Infection	2.2	0.9	–	–
Reproductive Male				
Impotence	1.7	0.9	–	–
Respiratory				
Sinusitis	5.4	4.3	–	–
Bronchitis	5.4	3.4	–	0.2
Pharyngitis	3.1	2.7	–	–

Table I—Coreg *(cont'd)*

Adverse Events in US Placebo-Controlled Congestive Heart Failure Trials (Incidence >1%, Regardless of Causality; Withdrawal Rates due to Adverse Events)

	Adverse Reactions		Withdrawals	
	Coreg (n=765) % occurrence	**Placebo (n=437) % occurrence**	**Coreg (n=765) % withdrawals**	**Placebo (n=437) % withdrawals**
Urinary/Renal				
Urinary Tract Infection	3.1	2.7	–	–
Hematuria	2.9	2.1	–	–
Renal Function Abnormal	1.7	1.4	0.3	–
Albuminuria	1.6	1.1	–	–
Acute Renal Failure	1.2	0.5	0.3	–
Vision				
Vision Abnormal	5.0	1.8	0.1	–

Legend: BUN=blood urea nitrogen; NPN=nonprotein nitrogen.

the dose of diuretics. If these changes do not relieve symptoms, the dose of carvedilol should be decreased. If the dose nwas decreased, it should not be increased again until symptoms of worsening heart failure or vasodilation have been stabilized for 2 weeks. Initial difficulty with titration may not preclude later attempts to re-introduce or resume titration of carvedilol, however caution is required in these circumstances. If congestive heart failure patients experience bradycardia (pulse rate below 55 beats/min), the dose should be reduced, or may require discontinuation.

Geriatrics: The frequency and pattern of adverse reactions in patients ≥65 years was similar to that in younger patients. However, plasma levels of carvedilol are higher in older patients compared to younger patients (see Precautions). Therefore, after initiating carvedilol at the same dose in the elderly as in younger patients, up-titration should be done more cautiously in the elderly. A lower total daily dose may be reached at the end of up-titration in such patients compared to younger patients.

Hepatic Impairment: Carvedilol is contraindicated in patients with clinically manifest liver disease (see Contraindications). In patients with milder hepatic impairment, there is a potential for increased manifestations of vasodilation and beta-blockade (see Pharmacology, Pharmacokinetics and Precautions). Therefore, after initiating carvedilol at the same dose in patients with hepatic impairment as in other patients, up-titration should be done more cautiously in patients with hepatic impairment. A lower total daily dose may be reached at the end of up-titration in such patients compared to other patients.

Renal Impairment: Acute, reversible renal failure has been seen in some patients treated with carvedilol, particularly those with underlying renal impairment (see Precautions). Therefore, after initiating carvedilol at the same dose in patients with renal impairment as in other patients, up-titration should be done more cautiously in patients with renal impairment. Renal function (BUN and creatinine) should be checked in such patients as appropriate. If renal function has deteriorated, the dose may need to be reduced or discontinued.

Discontinuation: Should be gradually reduced over a period of about 2 weeks if possible and the patient should be carefully observed (see Warnings, Abrupt Cessation of Therapy).

Information for the Patient: See Blue Section—Information for the Patient "Coreg".

Supplied: 3.125 mg: Each white, oval, film-coated tablet, imprinted with 39 and SB, contains: carvedilol 3.125 mg. Nonmedicinal ingredients: colloidal silicone dioxide, crospovidone, lactose, magnesium stearate, opadry white YS-1-7003 and opadry clear YS-2-7013, povidone and sucrose. HDPE bottles with plastic caps of 100.

6.25 mg: Each white, oval, film-coated, Tiltab tablet, imprinted with 4140 and SB, contains: carvedilol 6.25 mg. Nonmedicinal ingredients: colloidal silicone dioxide, crospovidone, lactose, magnesium stearate, opadry white YS-1-7003 and opadry clear YS-2-7013, povidone and sucrose. HDPE bottles with plastic caps of 100.

12.5 mg: Each white, oval, film-coated, Tiltab tablet, imprinted with 4141 and SB, contains: carvedilol 12.5 mg. Nonmedicinal ingredients: colloidal silicone dioxide, crospovidone, lactose, magnesium stearate, opadry white YS-1-7003 and opadry clear YS-2-7013, povidone and sucrose. HDPE bottles with plastic caps of 100.

25 mg: Each white, oval, film-coated, Tiltab tablet, imprinted with 4142 and SB, contains: carvedilol 25 mg. Nonmedicinal ingredients: colloidal silicone dioxide, crospovidone, lactose, magnesium stearate, opadry white YS-1-7003 and opadry clear YS-2-7013, povidone and sucrose. HDPE bottles with plastic caps of 100.

Store at room temperature, between 15 to 30°C, in tightly closed containers or dispense in a tight, light-resistant container. Protect from high humidity. Since the tablets discolor when exposed to light, they should be kept in a light-resistant container.

(Shown in Product Recognition Section)

Reviewed 1998

CORGARD® Ⓟ

Squibb

Nadolol

Antianginal—Antihypertensive Agent

Pharmacology: Nadolol is a noncardioselective beta-adrenergic blocking agent. It does not possess membrane stabilizing or intrinsic sympathomimetic (partial agonist) activities.

The exact mechanism by which the drug exercises its antianginal effect is not certain. An important factor may be the reduction of myocardial oxygen requirements by blocking catecholamine-induced increases in heart rate, systolic blood pressure and the velocity and extent of myocardial contraction. However, oxygen requirements may be increased by such actions as increases in left ventricular fiber length, end diastolic pressure and the systolic ejection period. When the net physiological effect is advantageous in anginal patients, it manifests itself during exercise or stress by delaying the onset of pain and reducing the incidence and severity of anginal attacks. Nadolol can therefore increase the capacity for work and exercise in such patients.

The mechanism of nadolol's antihypertensive effect has not yet been established. Among the factors that may be involved are: (a) competitive ability to antagonize catecholamine-induced tachycardia at the beta-receptor sites in the heart, thus decreasing cardiac output; (b) inhibition of renin release by the kidneys; (c) inhibition of vasomotor centers.

In humans, approximately 37% of orally administered nadolol is slowly absorbed. Approximately 30% of the nadolol present in serum is reversibly bound to plasma proteins and the drug is extensively distributed to extravascular tissues. Maximum serum concentrations are reached 2 to 4 hours after oral administration, while steady state serum concentrations are reached after 6 to 9 days. The serum half-life is 20 to 24 hours at therapeutic dose levels.

Nadolol is not detectably metabolized by man. Urinary and fecal excretion of nadolol after oral administration to humans averaged approximately 20% and 70% respectively. The latter fraction would include both unabsorbed drug and that fraction of the absorbed drug which is excreted by the liver. Nadolol elimination was found to be proportional to creatinine clearance in patients with renal impairment. In the presence of severe renal impairment (creatinine clearance <5 ml /min.), nadolol's average serum half-life was 45 hours and most of the drug was excreted by nonrenal routes. Nadolol can be removed from the circulation by hemodialysis.

Indications: Prophylaxis of angina pectoris.

In mild or moderate hypertension. Nadolol is usually used in combination with other drugs, particularly a thiazide diuretic. However, it may be tried alone as an initial agent in those patients in whom, in the judgment of the physician, treatment should be started with a beta-blocker rather than a diuretic.

The combination of nadolol with a diuretic has been found to be compatible and generally more effective than nadolol alone. In a few cases where peripheral vasodilators were used with nadolol, no evidence of incompatibility was seen.

Not recommended for the emergency treatment of hypertensive crises.

Contraindications: Allergic rhinitis, bronchospasm (including bronchial asthma), or severe chronic obstructive pulmonary disease (see Precautions); sinus bradycardia; second and third degree AV block; right ventricular failure secondary to pulmonary hypertension; congestive heart failure (see Warnings); cardiogenic shock; anesthesia with agents that produce myocardial depression, e.g., ether.

Warnings: Cardiac Failure: Special caution should be exercised when administering nadolol to patients with a history of heart failure. Sympathetic stimulation is a vital component supporting circulatory function in congestive heart failure, and inhibition with beta-blockade always carries a potential hazard of further depressing myocardial contractility and precipitating cardiac failure. In patients without a history of cardiac failure, continued depression of the myocardium over a period of time can, in some cases, lead to cardiac failure. Therefore, at the first sign or symptom of impending cardiac failure during nadolol therapy, patients should be fully digitalized, and/or given a diuretic, and the response observed closely.

Nadolol acts selectively without blocking the inotropic action of digitalis on the heart muscle. However, the positive inotropic action of digitalis may be reduced by nadolol's negative inotropic effect when the two drugs are used concomitantly. The effects of beta-blockers and digitalis are additive in depressing AV conduction. If cardiac failure continues, despite adequate digitalization and diuretic therapy, discontinue nadolol (see Warning below).

Abrupt Cessation of Therapy: Patients with angina should be warned against abrupt discontinuation of nadolol. There have been reports of severe exacerbation of angina, and of myocardial infarction or ventricular arrhythmias occurring in patients with angina pectoris, following abrupt discontinuation of beta-blocker therapy. The last 2 complications may occur with or without preceding exacerbation of angina pectoris. Therefore, when discontinuation of nadolol is planned in patients with angina pectoris, reduce the dosage gradually over a period of about 2 weeks and observe the patient carefully. Maintain the same frequency of administration. In situations of greater urgency, discontinue nadolol therapy stepwise and under conditions of closer observance. If angina markedly worsens or acute coronary insufficiency develops, reinstitute nadolol treatment promptly, at least temporarily.

Oculomucocutaneous Syndrome: Various skin rashes and conjunctival xerosis have been reported with beta-blockers, including nadolol. A severe syndrome (oculomucocutaneous syndrome) whose signs include conjunctivitis sicca and psoriasiform rashes, otitis and sclerosing serositis has occurred with the chronic use of one beta-adrenergic blocking agent (practolol). This syndrome has not been observed with nadolol or any other such agent. However, physicians should be alert to the possibility of such reactions and should discontinue treatment in the event that they occur.

Sinus Bradycardia: Severe sinus bradycardia due to unopposed vagal activity occurs in approximately 3% of patients following nadolol administration. In such cases, reduce dosage or consider the use of i.v. atropine; if no improvement is seen, consider i.v. isoproterenol.

Thyrotoxicosis: In patients with thyrotoxicosis, nadolol may give a false impression of improvement by diminishing peripheral manifestations of hyperthyroidism without improving thyroid function; therefore, abrupt withdrawal may be followed by an exacerbation of the symptoms of hyperthyroidism, including thyroid storm.

Precautions: Nadolol should be administered with caution to patients prone to nonallergic bronchospasm (e.g., chronic bronchitis, emphysema) since it may block bronchodilation produced by endogenous and exogenous catecholamine stimulation of beta receptors.

Epinephrine and Beta-blockers: There may be increased difficulty in treating an allergic type reaction in patients on beta-blockers. In these patients, the reaction may be more severe due to pharmacologic effects of the beta-blockers and problems with fluid changes. Epinephrine should be administered with caution since it may not have its usual effects in the treatment of anaphylaxis. On the one hand, larger doses of epinephrine may be needed to overcome the bronchospasm, while on the other hand, these doses can be associated with excessive alpha adrenergic stimulation with consequent hypertension, reflex bradycardia and heart block and possible potentiation of bronchospasm. Alternatives to the use of large doses of epinephrine include vigorous supportive care such as fluids and the use of beta agonists including parenteral salbutamol or isoproterenol to overcome bronchospasm and norepinephrine to overcome hypotension.

Administer nadolol with caution to patients subject to spontaneous hypoglycemia, or to diabetic patients (especially those

Corgard (cont'd)

with labile diabetes) who are receiving insulin or oral hypoglycemic agents. Beta-adrenergic blockers may mask the premonitory signs and symptoms of acute hypoglycemia. As beta-blockade also reduces insulin release in response to hyperglycemia, it may be necessary to adjust the dosage of antidiabetic drugs.

Nadolol dosage should be individually adjusted when used concomitantly with other antihypertensive agents (see Dosage).

Patients receiving catecholamine depleting drugs, such as reserpine or guanethidine, should be closely monitored if nadolol is administered concomitantly. The added catecholamine blocking action of nadolol may produce an excessive reduction of the resting sympathetic nervous activity.

Suitable laboratory tests should be carried out at appropriate intervals and caution should be observed in patients with impaired renal or hepatic function. Since nadolol is excreted mainly by the kidneys, dosage reduction may be necessary when renal insufficiency is present.

Patients Undergoing Surgery: The management of patients being treated with beta-blockers and undergoing elective or emergency surgery is controversial. Although beta-adrenergic receptor blockade impairs the heart's ability to respond to beta-adrenergically mediated reflex stimuli, abrupt discontinuation of nadolol therapy may be followed by severe complications (see Warnings). Some patients receiving beta-adrenergic blocking agents have been subject to protracted severe hypotension during anesthesia. Difficulty in restarting and maintaining the heartbeat has also been reported.

For these reasons, in patients with angina undergoing elective surgery, withdraw nadolol gradually following the recommendation given under Abrupt cessation of therapy (see Warnings). Available evidence suggests that the clinical and physiologic effects of beta-blockade induced by nadolol are essentially absent 5 days after cessation of therapy.

In emergency surgery, since nadolol is a competitive inhibitor of beta-adrenergic receptor agonists, its effects may be reversed, if necessary, by sufficient doses of such agonists as isoproterenol or norepinephrine.

Pregnancy: Nadolol has been shown to produce embryo/fetal toxicity in rabbits, but not in rats or hamsters, at doses of 100 to 300 mg/kg. No teratogenic potential was observed in any of these species. Nadolol, when given to pregnant rats, readily crossed the placental barrier.

There is no adequate information on the use of nadolol in pregnant women. Nadolol should be used during pregnancy only if the potential benefit justifies the potential risk to the fetus. Neonates whose mothers were receiving nadolol at parturition have exhibited bradycardia, hypoglycemia and associated symptoms.

Lactation: Nadolol is excreted in human milk. Therefore, use of this drug in lactating women is not recommended.

Children: There is no experience with nadolol in the treatment of pediatric age groups.

Adverse Effects: The most serious adverse reactions encountered are congestive heart failure, AV block and bronchospasm.

The most common adverse reactions reported in clinical trials are severe bradycardia (3%), dizziness (3%), fatigue (2%), hypotension (1%), congestive heart failure (1%) and cold sensations (1%).

Adverse reactions, grouped by system, are as follows:

Cardiovascular: congestive heart failure, pulmonary edema, cardiac enlargement; rhythm or conduction disturbances including AV block, bigeminy and Adams-Stokes syndrome; chest pain; severe bradycardia; hypotension, orthostatic hypotension, syncope; peripheral vascular insufficiency including intermittent claudication and cold extremities; edema.

Respiratory: bronchospasm, dyspnea, cough.

CNS: dizziness; depression, anxiety, nervousness, irritability, hallucinations; lethargy, fatigue; sleep disturbances including insomnia and nightmares; paresthesia; headache; tinnitus; slurred speech.

Gastrointestinal: abdominal pain or pressure; nausea, vomiting, diarrhea, constipation, flatulence; gastritis; anorexia.

Dermatological (see Warnings): rash, pruritus, dry skin.

Ophthalmologic: conjunctivitis, blurred vision, dry eyes.

Miscellaneous: impotence, decreased libido; enlarged thyroid; nasal stuffiness, dry mouth, sweating; weight gain.

Clinical Laboratory: The following parameters have most frequently been found to be outside the normal range: serum triglycerides, blood glucose, serum potassium, AST, ALT, LDH, BUN.

Overdose: Symptoms: The most common signs to be expected with overdosage of a beta-adrenergic blocking agent are bradycardia, congestive heart failure, hypotension, bronchospasm, and hypoglycemia.

Treatment: If overdosage occurs, in all cases, discontinue nadolol therapy and observe the patient closely. In addition, if required, the following therapeutic measures are suggested: 1. Bradycardia: Atropine or another anticholinergic drug. 2. Heart block (second or third degree): Isoproterenol or transvenous cardiac pacemaker. 3. Congestive heart failure: Conventional therapy. 4. Hypotension (depending on associated factors): Epinephrine rather than isoproterenol or levarterenol may be useful in addition to atropine and digitalis (see Precautions). 5. Bronchospasm: Aminophylline or isoproterenol. 6. Hypoglycemia: I.V. glucose.

It should be remembered that nadolol is a competitive antagonist of isoproterenol and hence, large doses of isoproterenol can be expected to reverse many of the effects of excessive doses of nadolol. However, the complications of excess isoproterenol should not be overlooked.

Dosage: Nadolol should be administered as a single daily dose without regard to meals since the presence of food in the gastrointestinal tract does not affect the rate or extent of nadolol's absorption.

Adjust the dosage to the patient's individual needs in accordance with the following guidelines:

Angina Pectoris: Initially, 80 mg daily. If an adequate response is not observed after 1 week, dosage may be increased by 80 mg increments at weekly intervals, until a satisfactory response is achieved. The maximum recommended daily dose is 240 mg. Patients stabilized on 80 mg daily might be tried on 40 mg daily as this dose has been found to be effective in some cases.

The value and safety of doses above 240 mg daily in angina pectoris have not been established.

Hypertension: Initially, 80 mg daily. If an adequate response is not observed after 1 week, dosage may be increased by 80 mg increments at weekly intervals, until a satisfactory response is achieved. The maximum recommended daily dose is 320 mg, although most patients respond to 240 mg or less.

The value and safety of doses above 320 mg daily have not been established.

Supplied: 40 mg: Each off-white round, biconvex tablet, scored on one side and engraved "CORGARD 40" on the other contains: nadolol 40 mg. Nonmedicinal ingredients: citric acid, cornstarch, magnesium stearate, microcrystalline cellulose and povidone. Bottles of 100 and 500.

80 mg: Each off-white, round, biconvex tablet, engraved with "SQUIBB" and a partial bisect bar on one side and "CORGARD 80" on the other contains: nadolol 80 mg. Nonmedicinal ingredients: citric acid, cornstarch, magnesium stearate, microcrystalline cellulose and povidone. Bottles of 100.

160 mg: Each blue, flat, capsule-shaped tablet, scored on both sides with a partial bisect bar and engraved "SQUIBB" on one side and "Corgard 160" on the other contains: nadolol 160 mg. Nonmedicinal ingredients: citric acid, cornstarch, FD&C No. 2 and blue No. 2 aluminum lake, magnesium stearate, microcrystalline cellulose and povidone. Bottles of 100 and 1 000.

Store in tightly closed containers at room temperature (15 to 30°C). Protect from heat, light and moisture.

(Shown in Product Recognition Section)

CORICIDIN® Cold Tablets
Schering

Chlorpheniramine—ASA Compound

Antihistaminic—Antipyretic—Analgesic

Indications: For relief of cold and flu symptoms, fever, aches and pains, accompanying a cold, relief of simple headache.

Contraindications: Sensitivity to any of the components.

Precautions: Since the depressant effects of antihistamines are additive to those of other drugs affecting the CNS, patients should be cautioned against drinking alcoholic beverages or taking hypnotics, sedatives, psychotherapeutic agents or other drugs with CNS depressant effects during antihistaminic therapy.

Persons with chronic lung disease, glaucoma or difficulty in urination due to enlargement of the prostate gland should only take this product under the advice and supervision of a physician. Should not be used by persons who are allergic or sensitive to any of the components of the product.

Occupational Hazards: Patients should be cautioned not to operate vehicles or hazardous machinery until their response to the drug has been determined.

Pregnancy and *Lactation:* The safe use of this product during pregnancy and lactation has not been established and therefore the compound should be used only if the potential benefit justifies the potential risk to the fetus or infant.

Antihistamines should be discontinued approximately 48 hours prior to skin testing procedures since these may prevent or diminish otherwise positive reactions to dermal reactivity indicators.

Children and teenagers should not use this medicine before a physician is consulted about Reye's syndrome, a rare serious illness. Administer with care to patients with hyperthyroidism.

Adverse Effects: Slight to moderate drowsiness occurs relatively infrequently with chlorpheniramine maleate. Other untoward effects include restlessness, dry mouth, dizziness, weakness, anorexia, nausea, headache, nervousness, polyuria, heartburn, diplopia, sweating, dysuria, and very rarely dermatitis.

Overdose: Symptoms and Treatment: If accidental overdose occurs, seek medical assistance immediately.

Dosage: Cold and flu symptoms: Adults, 2 tablets every 4 hours for 3 or 4 days. For minor pains, such as headaches, neuralgia, muscular aches and pains: 2 tablets as required. Not to exceed 12 tablets/day.

Supplied: Each red tablet contains: chlorpheniramine maleate USP 2 mg and ASA 325 mg. Nonmedicinal ingredients: calcium phosphate, cornstarch; cellulose and talc; coating: acacia, carnauba wax, cornstarch, dye-Opalux Red, sucrose, terra alba, tribasic calcium phosphate and white wax. Tartrazine-free. Boxes of 20 in push-through blisters and bottles of 40 in a child's protective package.

(Shown in Product Recognition Section)

CORICIDIN "D"®
Schering

Chlorpheniramine Maleate—Phenylpropanolamine Compound

Antihistaminic—Decongestant—Antipyretic—Analgesic

Indications: Coricidin "D": Symptomatic relief of nasal congestion and other discomforts associated with sinusitis, colds and allergic or vasomotor rhinitis.

Coricidin "D" Long Acting: For up to 12-hour relief of congestion and sneezing due to colds.

Contraindications: Sensitivity to any of the components, patients receiving MAO inhibitors in the preceding 3 weeks.

Precautions: Although phenylpropanolamine causes practically no pressor effect in normotensive individuals, it should be used with caution in patients with hypertension, diabetes, chronic lung disease, latent or clinically recognized angle closure glaucoma, coronary artery disease, congestive heart failure, urinary retention, prostatic hypertrophy and hyperthyroidism.

Occupational Hazards: Patients should be cautioned not to operate vehicles or hazardous machinery until their response to the drug has been determined. Since the depressant effects of antihistamines are additive to those of other drugs affecting the CNS, patients should be cautioned against drinking alcoholic beverages or taking hypnotics, sedatives, psychotherapeutic agents or other drugs with CNS depressant effects during antihistaminic therapy.

Should not be used by persons who are allergic or sensitive to the components of the product. May cause excitability in children; children should be observed by parents.

Pregnancy and *Lactation:* The safe use of this product during pregnancy and lactation has not been established and therefore the compound should be used only if the potential benefit justifies the potential risk to the fetus or infant.

Antihistamines should be discontinued approximately 48 hours prior to skin testing procedures since these may prevent or diminish otherwise positive reactions to dermal reactivity indicators.

Children and teenagers should not use Coricidin "D" tablets before a physician is consulted about Reye's syndrome, a rare serious illness.

Adverse Effects: Drowsiness, dizziness, nausea, increased irritability or excitement may be encountered.

Overdose: Symptoms and Treatment: If accidental overdose occurs, seek medical assistance immediately.

Dosage: Coricidin "D": Adults: 2 tablets every 4 hours, not to exceed 8 tablets in 24 hours. Children 10 to 14 years: ½ adult dose; under 10 years: at discretion of physician. Coricidin "D" Long Acting: Adults and Children 12 years and over: 1 tablet every 12 hours or as directed by physician. Do not exceed recommended dosage or use for a prolonged period of time without consulting a physician.

Supplied: Coricidin "D": Each white, coated tablet contains: chlorpheniramine maleate 2 mg, ASA 325 mg and phenylpropanolamine 12.5 mg. Nonmedicinal ingredients: calcium phosphate, monobasic; cornstarch; cellulose and talc; coating: acacia, carnauba wax, cornstarch, dye-Opalux White, gum rosin, kaolin, cellulose, oleic acid, stearic acid, sucrose, superfloss, terra alba, white wax and zein. Tartrazine-free. Boxes of 20 in push-through blisters and bottles of 40 in a child's protective package.

Coricidin "D" Long Acting: Each blue coated tablet contains: chlorpheniramine maleate USP 8 mg and phenylpropanolamine HCl USP 50 mg. Nonmedicinal ingredients: cornstarch, dye, FD & C Blue No. 1, gelatin, lactose, magnesium stearate and talc; coating: acacia, cornstarch, dye-Opalux Blue, gum rosin, kaolin, oleic acid, soap powder (white, neutral), stearic acid, sucrose, super floss, terra alba, white wax and zein F-200. Tartrazine-free. Boxes of 12 in push-through blisters.

(Shown in Product Recognition Section)

CORICIDIN® NON-DROWSY

Schering

ASA—Phenylpropanolamine

Analgesic—Antipyretic—Decongestant

Indications: Symptomatic relief of sinus pain and congestion.

Contraindications: Sensitivity to any of the components, patients receiving MAO inhibitors in the preceding 3 weeks.

Precautions: Although phenylpropanolamine causes practically no pressor effect in normotensive individuals, it should be used with caution in patients with hypertension, diabetes, chronic lung disease, latent or clinically recognized angle closure glaucoma, coronary artery disease, congestive heart failure, urinary retention, prostatic hypertrophy and hyperthyroidism.

Occupational Hazards: Patients should be cautioned not to operate vehicles or hazardous machinery until their response to the drug has been determined.

Should not be used by persons who are allergic or sensitive to the components of the product.

Pregnancy and *Lactation:* The safe use of this product during pregnancy and lactation has not been established and therefore the compound should be used only if the potential benefit justifies the potential risk to the fetus or infant.

Children and teenagers should not use this medicine before a physician is consulted about Reye's syndrome, a rare serious illness.

Adverse Effects: Drowsiness, dizziness, nausea, increased irritability or excitement may be encountered.

Overdose: Symptoms and Treatment: If accidental overdose occurs, seek medical assistance immediately.

Dosage: Adults: 2 tablets every 4 hours, not to exceed 8 tablets in 24 hours.

Supplied: Each pink-coated tablet contains: phenylpropanolamine HCl USP 12.5 mg and ASA 325 mg. Nonmedicinal ingredients: calcium phosphate, monobasic, cellulose, cornstarch and talc; coating: acacia, cellulose, cornstarch, dye-Opalux Pink, gum rosin, oleic acid, sodium benzoate, sucrose, terra alba and zein. Tartrazine-free. Boxes of 10 in push-through blisters and bottles of 40 in a child's protective package.

(Shown in Product Recognition Section)

CORISTEX®-DH Ⓝ

Technilab

Phenylephrine HCl—Hydrocodone Bitartrate

Antitussive—Decongestant

Supplied: Each 5 mL contains: hydrocodone bitartrate 5 mg and phenylephrine HCl 20 mg. Nonmedicinal ingredients: alcohol, artificial coloring and flavoring, eucalyptol, menthol, methylparaben, propylparaben, purified water, simethicone and sucrose. Energy: 33.1 kJ (7.9 kcal)/5 mL. Bottles of 500 mL. Store between 15 and 30°C. Protect from light and freezing.

CORISTINE®-DH Ⓝ

Technilab

Phenylephrine HCl—Hydrocodone Bitartrate

Antitussive—Decongestant

Supplied: Each 5 mL contains: hydrocodone bitartrate 1.7 mg and phenylephrine HCl 10 mg. Nonmedicinal ingredients: alcohol, artificial coloring and flavoring, glycerin, menthol, methylparaben, propylparaben, purified water, simethicone and sucrose. Energy: 37.1 kJ (8.87 kcal)/5 mL. Bottles of 500 mL. Store between 15 and 30°C. Protect from light and freezing.

CORTAMED® Ⓟ

Sabex

Hydrocortisone Acetate

Corticosteroid

Supplied: Each g of ophthalmic ointment contains: hydrocortisone acetate 25 mg (2.5%). Nonmedicinal ingredients: methylparaben, mineral oil, petrolatum and propylparaben. Tubes of 3.5 g. Store at room temperature.

CORTATE® 0.5 %
CORTATE® 1 % Ⓟ

Schering

Hydrocortisone

Topical Corticosteroid

Indications: For temporary relief of minor skin irritations, itching and rashes due to eczema, dermatitis, insect bites, poison ivy, poison oak, poison sumac, soaps, detergents, cosmetics and jewellery.

Warnings: For external use only. Do not use in or around the eyes. Do not apply to large areas of the body. Do not use to treat vulvar itching associated with vaginal discharge. Use only for 7 days maximum. If symptoms persist beyond 7 days or return after discontinuing use of the product, consult a physician.

Children: Do not use in children 2 years of age or younger, unless directed by a physician.

Dosage: Apply to the affected area not more than 3 or 4 times daily.

Supplied: Cream: 0.5 %: Each g of cream contains: hydrocortisone USP 5 mg (0.5%) in a water miscible emollient base. Nonmedicinal ingredients: cetostearyl alcohol, chlorocresol, mineral oil, phosphoric acid, propylene glycol, sodium phosphate, water and white petrolatum. Tubes of 15 g and jars of 450 g.

1 %: Each g of cream contains: hydrocortisone USP 10 mg (1 %) in a water miscible emollient base. Nonmedicinal ingredients: cetostearyl alcohol, chlorocresol, citric acid, mineral oil, polyethylene glycol 1 000 monocetyl ether, sodium citrate, sodium hydroxide, water and white petrolatum. Tubes of 15 g and jars of 450 g.

Ointment: 0.5 %: Each g of ointment contains: hydrocortisone USP 5 mg (0.5%) in a lanolin-free petrolatum base. Nonmedicinal ingredients: white petrolatum. Tubes of 15 g and jars of 450 g.

1 %: Each g of ointment contains: hydrocortisone USP 10 mg (1 %) in a lanolin-free petrolatum base. Nonmedicinal ingredients: white petrolatum. Tubes of 15 g and jars of 450 g.

Lotion: Each mL of lotion contains: hydrocortisone USP 5 mg (0.5%). Nonmedicinal ingredients: carbomer, isopropyl alcohol, water and sodium hydroxide. Squeeze bottles of 30 mL.

CORTEF® Ⓟ

Pharmacia & Upjohn

Hydrocortisone

Corticosteroid

Pharmacology: Hydrocortisone (cortisol) is a corticosteroid secreted by the adrenal cortex. In physiologic doses, it is administered to replace deficient endogenous hormones. In larger (pharmacologic) doses, hydrocortisone decreases inflammation and suppresses the immune response. It stimulates erythroid cells of the bone marrow, prolongs survival time of erythrocytes and platelets, and produces neutrophilia and eosinopenia. Hydrocortisone promotes protein catabolism, gluconeogenesis, and redistribution of fat from peripheral to central areas of the body. It reduces intestinal absorption and increases renal excretion of calcium.

In pharmacologic doses, systemically administered glucocorticoids suppress release of corticotropin from the pituitary. The degree and duration of hypothalamic-pituitary-adrenal (HPA) axis suppression produced is highly variable among patients and depends on the dose, frequency and time of administration, and duration of therapy. If suppressive doses are administered for prolonged periods, the adrenal cortex atrophies and patients develop cushingoid features and respond to stress like patients with primary adrenocortical insufficiency. The duration of anti-inflammatory activity approximately equals the duration of HPA-axis suppression. In one study, the duration of HPA-axis suppression after a single oral dose of hydrocortisone 250 mg was 1.25 to 1.5 days.

Hydrocortisone is extensively bound to the plasma proteins, corticosteroid binding globulin (transcortin) and albumin. With physiologic concentrations, it is bound primarily to transcortin and only 5 to 10% of cortisol in plasma is unbound.

Hydrocortisone is metabolized in most tissues, but primarily in the liver to biologically inactive compounds. The half-life of hydrocortisone may be prolonged in patients with hypothyroidism. Inactive metabolites are excreted by the kidneys, primarily as glucuronides and sulfates, but also as unconjugated products. Negligible amounts are excreted in bile.

Indications: Endocrine Disorders: Primary or secondary adrenocortical insufficiency (hydrocortisone or cortisone is the first choice; synthetic analogs may be used in conjunction with mineralocorticoids where applicable; in infancy, mineralocorticoid supplementation is of particular importance); congenital adrenal hyperplasia; nonsuppurative thyroiditis; hypercalcemia associated with cancer.

Nonendocrine Disorders: Rheumatic Disorders: As adjunctive therapy for short-term administration (to tide the patient over an acute episode or exacerbation) in: psoriatic arthritis, rheumatoid arthritis, including juvenile rheumatoid arthritis (selected cases may require low dose maintenance therapy), ankylosing spondylitis, acute and subacute bursitis, acute nonspecific tenosynovitis, acute gouty arthritis, post-traumatic osteoarthritis, synovitis of osteoarthritis, epicondylitis.

Collagen Diseases: During an exacerbation or as maintenance therapy in selected cases of systemic lupus erythematosus, acute rheumatic carditis, systemic dermatomyositis (polymyositis).

Dermatologic Diseases: pemphigus, bullous dermatitis herpetiformis, severe erythema multiforme (Stevens-Johnson syndrome), exfoliative dermatitis, mycosis fungoides, severe psoriasis and severe seborrheic dermatitis.

Allergic States: Control of severe or incapacitating allergic conditions intractable to adequate trials of conventional treatment: seasonal or perennial allergic rhinitis, bronchial asthma, contact dermatitis, atopic dermatitis, serum sickness and drug hypersensitivity reactions.

Ophthalmic Diseases: Severe acute and chronic allergic and inflammatory processes involving the eye and its adnexa such as: allergic conjunctivitis, keratitis, allergic corneal marginal ulcers, herpes zoster ophthalmicus, iritis and iridocyclitis, chorioretinitis, anterior segment inflammation, diffuse posterior uveitis and choroiditis, optic neuritis, sympathetic ophthalmia.

Respiratory Diseases: Symptomatic sarcoidosis, Löffler's syndrome not manageable by other means, berylliosis, fulminating or disseminated pulmonary tuberculosis when used concurrently with appropriate antituberculous chemotherapy, aspiration pneumonitis.

Hematologic Disorders: Idiopathic thrombocytopenic purpura in adults, secondary thrombocytopenia in adults, acquired (autoimmune) hemolytic anemia, erythroblastopenia (RBC anemia), congenital (erythroid) hypoplastic anemia.

Neoplastic Diseases: For palliative management of: leukemias and lymphomas in adults, acute leukemia of childhood.

Cortef (cont'd)

Edematous States: To induce a diuresis or remission of proteinuria in the nephrotic syndrome, without uremia, of the idiopathic type or that due to lupus erythematosus.

Gastrointestinal Diseases: To tide the patient over a critical period of the disease in: ulcerative colitis, regional enteritis.

CNS: Acute exacerbations of multiple sclerosis.

Miscellaneous: Tuberculous meningitis with subarachnoid block or impending block when used concurrently with appropriate antituberculous chemotherapy, trichinosis with neurologic or myocardial involvement.

Contraindications: Systemic fungal infections and known hypersensitivity to hydrocortisone or components of the tablet.

Warnings: In patients on corticosteroid therapy subjected to unusual stress, increased dosage of rapidly acting corticosteroids before, during and after the stressful situation is indicated.

Corticosteroids may mask some signs of infection, and new infections may appear during their use. There may be decreased resistance and inability to localize infection when corticosteroids are used. Infections with any pathogen including viral, bacterial, fungal, protozoan or helminthic infections, in any location in the body, may be associated with the use of corticosteroids alone or in combination with other immunosuppressive agents that affect cellular immunity, humoral immunity, or neutrophil function. These infections may be mild, but can be severe and at times fatal. With increasing doses of corticosteroids, the rate of occurrence of infectious complications increases.

Persons who are on drugs which suppress the immune system are more susceptible to infections than healthy individuals. Chickenpox and measles, for example, can have a more serious or even fatal course in nonimmune children or adults on corticosteroids. In such children or adults who have not had these diseases, particular care should be taken to avoid exposure. How the dose, route and duration of corticosteroid administration affects the risk of developing a disseminated infection is not known. The contribution of the underlying disease and/or prior corticosteroid treatment to the risk is also not known. If exposed to chickenpox, prophylaxis with varicella zoster immune globulin (VZIG) may be indicated. If exposed to measles, prophylaxis with pooled i.m. immunoglobulin (IG) may be indicated. If chickenpox develops, treatment with antiviral agents may be considered. Similarly, corticosteroids should be used with great care in patients with known or suspected Strongyloides (threadworm) infestation. In such patients, corticosteroid-induced immunosuppresion may lead to Strongyloides hyperinfection and dissemination with widespread larval migration often accompanied by severe enterocolitis and potentially fatal gram-negative septicemia.

Prolonged use of corticosteroids may produce posterior subcapsular cataracts, glaucoma with possible damage to the optic nerves, and may enhance the establishment of secondary ocular infections due to fungi or viruses.

Allergic reactions (e.g., angioedema) may occur.

Average and large doses of hydrocortisone or cortisone can cause elevation of blood pressure, salt and water retention, and increased excretion of potassium. These effects are less likely to occur with the synthetic derivatives except when used in large doses. Dietary salt restriction and potassium supplementation may be necessary. All corticosteroids increase calcium excretion.

Administration of live or live, attenuated vaccines is contraindicated in patients receiving immunosuppressive doses of corticosteroids. Killed or inactivated vaccines may be administered to patients receiving immunosuppressive doses of corticosteroids. However the response to such vaccines may be diminished. Indicated immunization procedures may be undertaken in patients receiving non-immunosuppressive doses of corticosteroids.

The use of hydrocortisone in active tuberculosis should be restricted to those cases of fulminating or disseminated tuberculosis in which the corticosteroid is used for the management of the disease in conjunction with an appropriate antituberculous regimen.

If corticosteroids are indicated in patients with latent tuberculosis or tuberculin reactivity, close observation is necessary as reactivation of the disease may occur. During prolonged corticosteroid therapy, these patients should receive chemoprophylaxis.

There is no universal agreement on whether corticosteroids per se are responsible for peptic ulcers encountered during therapy; however, glucocorticoid therapy may mask the symptoms of peptic ulcer so that perforation or hemorrhage may occur without significant pain.

Osteoporosis is a common but infrequently recognized adverse effect associated with a long-term use of large doses of glucocorticoid.

Growth may be suppressed in children receiving long-term daily, divided dose glucocorticoid therapy and use of such regimen should be restricted to the most urgent indications. Alternate day glucocorticoid therapy usually avoids or minimizes this side effect.

Host defenses are impaired in patients receiving large doses of glucocorticoids and this effect increases susceptibility to fungus infections as well as bacterial and viral infections.

Pregnancy and *Lactation:* Some animal studies have shown that corticosteroids, when administered to the mother at high doses, may cause fetal malformations. Adequate human reproduction studies have not been done with corticosteroids. Therefore, the use of this drug in pregnancy, nursing mothers or women of childbearing potential requires that the benefits of the drug be carefully weighed against the potential risk to the mother and embryo or fetus. Since there is inadequate evidence of safety in human pregnancy, this drug should be used in pregnancy only if clearly needed.

Corticosteroids readily cross the placenta. Infants born of mothers who have received substantial doses of corticosteroids during pregnancy must be carefully observed and evaluated for signs of adrenal insufficiency. There are no known effects of corticosteroids on labour and delivery. Corticosteroids are excreted in breast milk.

Precautions: Drug induced secondary adrenocortical insufficiency may be minimized by gradual reduction of dosage. This type of relative insufficiency may persist for months after discontinuation of therapy; therefore, in any situation of stress occurring during that period, hormone therapy should be reinstituted. Since mineralocorticoid secretion may be impaired, salt and/or a mineralocorticoid should be administered concurrently.

There is an enhanced effect of corticosteroids on patients with hypothyroidism and in those with cirrhosis.

Corticosteroids should be used cautiously in patients with ocular herpes simplex because of possible corneal perforation.

The lowest possible dose of corticosteroid should be used to control the condition under treatment and when reduction in dosage is possible, the reduction should be gradual.

Psychic derangements may appear when corticosteroids are used, ranging from euphoria, insomnia, mood swings, personality changes and severe depression to frank psychotic manifestations. Also, existing emotional instability or psychotic tendencies may be aggravated by corticosteroids.

ASA and nonsteroidal anti-inflammatory agents should be used cautiously in conjunction with corticosteroids in patients with hypoprothrombinemia.

Corticosteroids should be used with caution in nonspecific ulcerative colitis, if there is a probability of impending perforation, abscess or other pyogenic infection; diverticulitis; fresh intestinal anastomoses; active or latent peptic ulcer; renal insufficiency; hypertension; osteoporosis; or myasthenia gravis.

Because complications of treatment with glucocorticoids are dependent on the size of the dose and the duration of treatment, a risk/benefit decision must be made in each individual case as to dose and duration of treatment and as to whether daily or intermittent therapy should be used.

Convulsions have been reported with concurrent use of methylprednisolone and cyclosporine. Since concurrent administration of these agents results in a mutual inhibition of metabolism, it is possible that convulsions and other adverse events associated with the individual use of either drug may be more apt to occur.

Drug Interactions: The pharmacokinetic interactions listed below are potentially clinically important. Drugs that induce hepatic enzymes such as phenobarbital, phenytoin and rifampin may increase the clearance of corticosteroids and may require increases in corticosteroid dose to achieve the desired response. Drugs such as troleandomycin and ketoconazole may inhibit the metabolism of corticosteroids and thus decrease their clearance. Therefore, the dose of corticosteroid should be titrated to avoid steroid toxicity. Corticosteroids may increase the clearance of chronic high dose ASA. This could lead to decreased salicylate serum levels or increase the risk of salicylate toxicity when the corticosteroid is withdrawn. ASA should be used cautiously in conjunction with corticosteroids in patients suffering from hypothrombinemia. The effect of corticosteroids on oral anticoagulants is variable. There are reports of enhanced as well as diminished effects of anticoagulants when given concurrently with corticosteroids. Therefore, coagulation indices should be monitored to maintain the desired anticoagulant effect.

Information for the Patient: Persons who are on immunosuppressant doses of corticosteroids should be warned to avoid exposure to chickenpox or measles. Patients should also be advised that if they are exposed medical advice should be sought without delay.

Adverse Effects: Note: The following are typical for all systemic corticosteroids. Their inclusion in this list does not necessarily indicate that the specific event has been observed with this particular formulation.

Fluid and Electrolyte Disturbances: sodium retention; fluid retention; congestive heart failure in susceptible patients; potassium loss, hypokalemic alkalosis; hypertension.

Musculoskeletal: steroid myopathy; muscle weakness; osteoporosis; pathologic fractures; vertebral compression fractures, aseptic necrosis of femoral and humeral heads, loss of muscle mass, tendon rupture, particular of the Achilles.

Gastrointestinal: peptic ulcer with possible perforation and hemorrhage; pancreatitis; abdominal distention; ulcerative esophagitis; increases in AST, ALT and alkaline phosphatase have been observed following corticosteroid treatment. These changes are usually small, not associated with any clinical significance.

Dermatologic: impaired wound healing; petechiae and ecchymoses; thin fragile skin; increased sweating, facial erythema may suppress reactions to skin tests.

Metabolic: negative nitrogen balance due to protein catabolism.

Neurological: increased intracranial pressure; pseudotumor cerebri; psychic derangements and seizures; convulsions, vertigo and headache.

Endocrine: menstrual irregularities; development of cushingoid state; suppression of pituitary-adrenal axis particularly at times of stress as in trauma, surgery or illness; decreased carbohydrate tolerance; manifestations of latent diabetes mellitus; increased requirements for insulin or oral hypoglycemic agents in diabetes; suppression of growth in children.

Ophthalmic: posterior subcapsular cataracts; increased intraocular pressure; exophthalmos glaucoma.

Immune System: masking of infections; latent infections becoming active; opportunistic infections; hypersensitivity reactions including anaphylaxis; may suppress reactions to skin tests.

Dosage: The initial dosage may vary from 20 to 240 mg of hydrocortisone per day depending on the specific disease entity being treated. In situations of less severity, lower doses will generally suffice, while in selected patients higher initial doses may be required. The initial dosage should be maintained or adjusted until a satisfactory response is noted. If after a reasonable period of time there is a lack of satisfactory clinical response, hydrocortisone should be discontinued and the patient transferred to another appropriate therapy.

It should be emphasized that dosage requirements are variable and must be individualized on the basis of the disease under treatment and the response of the patient.

After a favorable response is noted, the proper maintenance dosage should be determined by decreasing the initial drug dosage in small decrements at appropriate time intervals until the lowest dosage which will maintain an adequate clinical response is reached. It should be kept in mind that constant monitoring is needed in regard to drug dosage. Included in the situations which may make dosage adjustments necessary are changes in clinical status secondary to remissions or exacerbations in the disease process, the patient's individual drug responsiveness, and the effect of patient exposure to stressful situations not directly related to the disease entity under treatment; in this latter situation it may be necessary to increase the dosage of hydrocortisone for a period of time consistent with the patient's condition.

Supplied: 10 mg: Each white, round, scored, compressed tablet, engraved "Cortef 10", contains: hydrocortisone 10 mg. Nonmedicinal ingredients: calcium stearate, cornstarch, lactose, mineral oil, sorbic acid, sucrose. Sodium: <1 mmol. Gluten- and tartrazine-free. Bottles of 100.

20 mg: Each white, round, scored, compressed tablet, engraved "Cortef 20", contains: hydrocortisone 20 mg. Nonmedicinal ingredients: calcium stearate, cornstarch, lactose, mineral oil, sorbic acid, sucrose. Sodium: <1 mmol. Gluten- and tartrazine-free. Bottles of 100.

(Shown in Product Recognition Section)

Reviewed 1997

CORTENEMA® ℞
Axcan Pharma
Hydrocortisone
Glucocorticoid

Indications: An adjunct in the treatment of nonspecific inflammatory diseases involving the rectum, sigmoid and left colon such as idiopathic ulcerative colitis, ulcerative proctitis, regional enteritis (granulomatous colitis) with left side involvement, proctitis, proctocolitis, and radiation proctitis.

Contraindications: Local contraindications to the use of intrarectal steroids include obstruction, abscess, perforation, peritonitis, fresh intestinal anastomoses, extensive fistulas and sinus tracts.

Active tuberculosis (active, latent or nonpositively healed), ocular herpes simplex, and acute psychosis are usually considered absolute contraindications to the use of corticosteroids.

Relative contraindications include active peptic ulcer, acute glomerulonephritis, myasthenia gravis, osteoporosis, diverticulitis, thrombophlebitis, psychic disturbances, pregnancy, diabetes, hyperthyroidism, acute coronary disease, hypertension, limited cardiac reserve, and local or systemic infections, including fungal, viral or exanthematous diseases. Where these conditions exist, the expected benefits from hydrocortisone retention enema must be weighed against the risks involved in its use.

If there is no evidence of clinical or proctologic improvement within 2 or 3 weeks after starting hydrocortisone retention enema therapy, discontinue the drug.

Precautions: Hydrocortisone retention enema should be administered with caution in patients with severe ulcerative disease because these patients are predisposed to perforation of the bowel wall. In the advanced stages of chronic ulcerative colitis, where there is loss of mucosa, and thickening and fibrosis of the bowel wall, steroid therapy theoretically might hasten deterioration, although this has not been proved with steroids in actual practice.

In severe cases, such as acute fulminating ulcerative colitis, where surgery is imminent, in the absence of marked clinical improvement, it is hazardous to wait more than a few days for a satisfactory response to medical treatment.

Of particular importance is the complication of adrenal insufficiency caused by suppression of the adrenal cortex by glucocorticoids, especially after prolonged therapy. It is therefore important that therapy be withdrawn gradually. If the patient is subjected to unusual stress, while on therapy or up to a year after discontinuation of steroids, adequate supportive measures and increased or reinstated systemic steroid therapy are indicated.

In the case of surgery, these measures should be continued throughout the pre- and the postoperative recovery periods, bearing in mind the possible deleterious effects of corticosteroids on fresh intestinal anastomoses. Steroid therapy might impair the prognosis in surgery by increasing the hazard of infection. If infection is suspected, appropriate antibiotic therapy must be administered, usually in doses larger than those customarily employed.

General precautions common to all corticosteroids therapy should be observed during treatment with hydrocortisone retention enema, including those pertaining to growth suppression in children during prolonged use.

Patients should be kept under close observation, for, as with all drugs, rare individuals may react unfavorably under certain conditions.

If severe reactions or idiosyncrasies occur, steroids should be discontinued immediately and appropriate measures instituted.

Pregnancy: If it is necessary to use hydrocortisone retention enema in pregnant patients, the infants of these mothers should be closely observed following delivery for signs of hypoadrenalism and appropriate measures, including administration of corticosteroids, should be instituted if such signs are seen.

Corticosteroid therapy may cause hyperacidity or peptic ulcer, and may aggravate diabetes mellitus or precipitate manifestations of latent diabetes mellitus.

When hydrocortisone retention enema is used in the presence of glaucoma, intraocular pressure should be measured frequently and optic nerve heads and visual fields observed.

Patients should be advised to inform subsequent physicians of the prior use of corticosteroids.

Adverse Effects: Hydrocortisone retention enema may produce adverse effects known to occur with other forms of hydrocortisone therapy. These include moon face, buffalo hump, fluid retention, excessive appetite and weight gain, abnormal fat deposits, mental symptoms, hypertrichosis, acne, striae, ecchymosis, increased sweating, pigmentation, dry scaly skin, thinning scalp hair, thrombophlebitis, decreased resistance to infection, negative nitrogen balance with delayed bone and wound healing, menstrual disorders, neuropathy, peptic ulcer, decreased glucose tolerance, hypopotassemia, adrenal insufficiency, necrotizing angiitis, hypertension, pancreatitis and increased intraocular pressure.

In children, suppression of growth may occur. Increased intracranial pressure may occur and possibly account for headache, insomnia and fatigue. Subcapsular cataracts may result from prolonged usage. Long-term use of all corticosteroids results in catabolic effects characterized by negative protein and calcium balance. Osteoporosis, spontaneous fractures and aseptic necrosis of the hip and humerus may occur as part of this catabolic phenomenon.

Where hypokalemia and the other symptoms associated with fluid and electrolyte imbalance call for potassium supplementation and salt-poor or salt-free diets, these may be instituted and are compatible with the diet requirements for ulcerative colitis.

Overdose: Symptoms and Treatment: No known antidote but gastric lavage should be performed.

Dosage: The usual dose is one 60 mL enema (100 mg hydrocortisone) daily for 2 or 3 weeks, and every second day thereafter, administered intrarectally in the evening before retiring. Every effort should be made to retain the medication at least 1 hour, and preferably all night. This may be facilitated by prior sedation and/or antidiarrheal medication. Certain cases may require 2 doses a day (30 or 60 mL) until alleviation of symptoms allows better retention. If clinical or proctologic improvement fail to occur within 2 or 3 weeks, hydrocortisone retention enema therapy should be discontinued.

For administration by retention enema, instruct the patient to lie on his left side during instillation of the medication. Shake the bottle vigorously to resuspend the insoluble portion of hydrocortisone. Expose the lubricated tip by removal of the protective sheath, grasping the bottle at the neck where it is most rigid. Carefully, insert the lubricated tip into the rectum in the direction of the sacrum. Slowly express the contents by compressing the container. After instillation, the patient should remain in the same position (on left side) for at least 30 minutes, to allow distribution of the medication in the colon. The 60 mL hydrocortisone retention enema may be expected to distribute throughout the descending colon and rectum.

The duration of treatment is dependent on the degree of response. If a satisfactory response is to be obtained, it usually occurs within 5 to 7 days, as evidenced by a marked reduction of clinical symptoms. Improvement in the appearance of the mucosa, gauged by barium enemas and sigmoidoscopic examinations, may lag somewhat behind clinical improvement.

The usual duration of therapy is 2 weeks.

Minimal control of symptoms is an insufficient basis for the prolonged use of Cortenema. If there is no clinical or proctologic response within 2 or 3 weeks, or if the patient's condition worsens, discontinue the drug.

Because of hydrocortisone absorption, proper precautions against unwanted systemic reactions or side effects should be observed. Symptomatic improvement, evidenced by decreased diarrhea, weight gain, improved appetite, lessened fever, and decrease in leukocytosis, may be misleading and should not be used as the sole criterion in judging efficacy. Actual sigmoidoscopic examination and x-ray visualization are most reliable. Since steroids can inhibit wound healing, enema or drip therapy should not be employed in the immediate or early postoperative period following ileorectostomy.

Supplied: Each single-dose unit contains: hydrocortisone USP 100 mg in 60 mL of an aqueous suspension. Nonmedicinal ingredients: carboxypolymethylene, polysorbate 80, methylparaben, purified water and sodium hydroxide. Lactose-, sulfite- and tartrazine-free. Boxes of 7.

Does a pregnant woman require additional vitamin A and D? To answer this and other recommended nutrient intake questions, see the CLIN-INFO SECTION.

CORTICOSTEROIDS: EYE EAR NOSE ℞
General Monograph, CPhA

Beclomethasone
Betamethasone
Budesonide
Dexamethasone
Flunisolide
Fluorometholone
Fluticasone
Hydrocortisone
Mometasone
Prednisolone
Triamcinolone

This monograph has been compiled by CPhA. It may contain information different from that approved by Therapeutic Products Programme, Health Canada, and the pharmaceutical manufacturers' approval has not been requested.

Pharmacology: Corticosteroids are used to inhibit the inflammatory response of the eye, nasal mucosa, or external ear canal to irritating agents of a mechanical, chemical or immunological nature. Modifications to the chemical structure such as introducing a fluorine atom, an acetonide group or omission or esterification of a hydroxyl group may increase the anti-inflammatory potency of the molecule; however, other properties of the molecule may be affected. For example, adding fluorine to topical ophthalmic drops reduces their corneal penetration which decreases their clinical efficacy in anterior chamber inflammations.

Corticosteroids reduce edema, fibrin deposition, capillary dilation, leukocyte migration, capillary proliferation, deposition of collagen and scar formation. Used intranasally, they inhibit IgE and mast cell-mediated early phase allergic reactions and migration of inflammatory cells into the nasal tissue. Corticosteroids complex with specific cytoplasmic receptors. These complexes stimulate transcription of mRNA and protein synthesis of enzymes responsible for the anti-inflammatory effect. Topical ophthalmic corticosteroids may cause a rise in intraocular pressure in susceptible individuals.

Pharmacokinetics: Corticosteroids applied to the eye are absorbed into the cornea, aqueous humor, iris, choroid, ciliary body and retina. Dosages used ophthalmically are less than those used systemically. As a result, clinical evidence of systemic absorption usually does not occur at recommended doses.

When administered intranasally, beclomethasone, fluticasone, flunisolide, budesonide and triamcinolone may be absorbed and produce systemic effects; however, adrenal suppression has not been observed with these drugs even when used at recommended doses for prolonged periods of time.

The relative potency of corticosteroids depends on the molecular structure, concentration and release of the drug from the vehicle.

Indications: Eye: May be used in the treatment of corticosteroid responsive inflammatory conditions of the anterior segment of the eye and its adnexa such as: iridocyclitis, lid allergy, nonpurulent conjunctivitis including vernal, allergic or catarrhal, herpes zoster ophthalmicus (not to be used in herpes simplex infections), corneal injury caused by foreign body penetration, surgery or aseptic burns (thermal, radiation or chemical), superficial keratitis including punctate epithelial lesions (Thygeson type) and phlyctenular keratoconjunctivitis, deep keratitis including interstitial and parenchymatous keratitis, acne rosacea, sclerosing keratitis, mild acute iritis, recurrent marginal ulceration whether endogenous or allergic, nonpurulent blepharitis including catarrhal and allergic.

Also used in corneal, conjunctival, and scleral injuries from chemical, radiation or thermal burns or penetration of foreign bodies.

Corticosteroids are also used in conjunction with antimicrobials in some cases where bacterial infection or a risk of ocular bacterial infection exists.

Dexamethasone, fluorometholone, medrysone and prednisolone are available as single entity products. Hydrocortisone is commercially available only in combination with anti-infectives.

Corticosteroids: Eye Ear Nose (cont'd)

Acute disorders respond more favorably than chronic disorders. In stubborn cases of anterior segment eye disease, systemic adrenocortical therapy may be required. When the deeper ocular structures are involved, systemic therapy is necessary.

Ear: Dexamethasone is indicated for use in the management of certain diseases of the external ear canal such as localized neurodermatitis, seborrheic dermatitis, eczema and diffuse otitis externa. It is not to be used if the drum is perforated.

Other products are found in combination with antimicrobials and can, in addition, be used in some cases of bacterial otitis externa.

Nasal: Beclomethasone, flunisolide, fluticasone and triamcinolone are used for the treatment of perennial and seasonal rhinitis unresponsive to conventional treatment. Budesonide is used in the above conditions as well as for non-allergic and vasomotor rhinitis. Beclomethasone and budesonide are also indicated for the treatment of nasal polyps to prevent their return after surgery or to prevent their increase in size.

Contraindications: Patients with a history of hypersensitivity to any of the ingredients of these preparations.

Cross-allergenicity among corticosteroids has been demonstrated.

Eye: In epithelial herpes simplex keratitis, vaccinia, varicella and most other viral diseases of the cornea and conjunctiva. In infectious tuberculous lesions of the eye and fungal diseases of ocular structures. After uncomplicated removal of a corneal foreign body. In acute purulent untreated infections of the conjunctiva and lids which like other diseases caused by microorganisms may be masked or enhanced by the presence of a steroid.

Ear: In tuberculous, fungal or viral lesions. In absence of or perforation of the ear drum.

Nasal: In active or quiescent tuberculosis of the respiratory tract or untreated bacterial, fungal or viral infections. Use in children under 6 years of age is contraindicated for budesonide and flunisolide.

Warnings: Corticosteroids may mask some signs of infection and new infections may appear during their use.

Eye: Prolonged ophthalmic use may result in increased intraocular pressure in some individuals. If these products are used for 10 days or longer, intraocular pressure should be monitored. In diseases causing thinning of the cornea or sclera, perforation has been known to occur with the use of topical preparations containing corticosteroids. Protracted use of topical corticosteroids in the eye may result in the development of posterior subcapsular cataracts.

Although corticosteroids are contraindicated in acute viral infection of the cornea caused by herpes simplex, there may be occasion to employ steroids in the healing stage to prevent scarring; however, this must only be done with great caution and close observation, usually under the care of an ophthalmologist. In patients with a history of herpetic infection of the cornea, reactivation of the disease may occur with use of topical ophthalmic corticosteroids. Use of steroids after cataract surgery may delay healing and increase the incidence of filtering blebs.

Nasal: Adrenal insufficiency (even death) may occur when patients are transferred from long-term oral corticosteroid therapy to orally or nasally inhaled preparations. Withdrawal of the oral corticosteroid should be achieved very gradually, after the initiation of inhaled therapy. Symptoms of adrenal insufficiency include weakness, hyperpigmentation of skin and mucous membranes, weight loss, anorexia, nausea, vomiting and hypotension.

Flunisolide is not recommended for those patients with a history of recurrent nasal bleeding.

Pregnancy: Glucocorticoids are known teratogens in rodent species. Adverse effects typical of potent corticosteroids are only seen at high systemic exposure levels; direct ophthalmic, otic or intranasal application ensures minimal systemic exposure; however, the safety of intensive or protracted use of topical steroids during pregnancy has not been established. Use should be avoided during pregnancy unless necessary.

Infants born of mothers who have received substantial dosages of corticosteroids during pregnancy should be carefully observed for hypoadrenalism.

Lactation: Corticosteroids are secreted into human milk; however, the minimal systemic absorption following ophthalmic, otic or intranasal administration reduces the amount of corticosteroid that could possibly be secreted into the milk. The use of corticosteroids by these routes of administration in nursing mothers requires that the possible benefits of the drug be weighed against the potential hazards to the infant.

Precautions: Patients should be advised to inform their physician of any prior use of corticosteroids. Under most circumstances, treatment with corticosteroids should not be stopped abruptly but tapered off gradually.

There may be an enhanced effect of corticosteroids in patients with hypothyroidism and in those with cirrhosis.

ASA should be used cautiously in conjunction with corticosteroids in patients with hypoprothrombinemia.

Eye: During long-term use of preparations containing corticosteroids, the possibility of fungal infection must be considered, especially in the presence of a persistent corneal ulceration that fails to respond to conventional therapy.

If irritation occurs, hypersensitivity to a component of the preparation is a possibility, and use of the product should be discontinued.

If redness, irritation, swelling or pain persists, the product should be discontinued and the physician notified. Patients should be advised regarding the use of contact lenses while on therapy. Use of ophthalmic corticosteroids with contact lenses will increase the risk of infection.

Nasal: Replacement of systemic corticosteroids with intranasal steroids should be gradual and monitored carefully since withdrawal symptoms may occur in spite of maintenance or improvement of respiratory function (see Warnings).

An abnormally heavy challenge of summer allergens may in certain instances, necessitate appropriate additional therapy, particularly to control eye symptoms. Treatment of seasonal rhinitis should, if possible, start before the exposure to allergens.

Patients should be informed that the full effect of triamcinolone acetate and fluticasone is not achieved until after 2 or 3 days of treatment have been completed.

Studies in asthmatic patients have shown that the combined administration of alternate-day prednisone systemic treatment and orally inhaled beclomethasone dipropionate increases the likelihood of HPA axis suppression compared to a therapeutic dose of either drug alone. Patients on alternate-day prednisone therapy should use beclomethasone nasal spray with caution due to the increased likelihood of HPA axis suppression.

Long-term Effects: During long-term therapy, HPA axis function and hematological status should be assessed. Patients using a nasal spray over several months or longer should be examined for possible changes in nasal mucosa. The possibility of atrophic rhinitis and/or pharyngeal candidiasis should be kept in mind.

Inhibitory Effect on Wound Healing: Because of inhibitory effect of corticosteroids on wound healing, patients who have experienced recent nasal septal ulcer, nasal surgery or trauma should use a nasal corticosteroid with caution until healing has occurred. Rare instances of nasal septum perforation have been spontaneously reported.

Effect on Infections: Corticosteroids may mask some signs of infection and new infections may appear. A decreased resistance to localized infections has been observed during corticosteroid therapy; this may require treatment with appropriate therapy or stopping the administration of the intranasal corticosteroid.

Fluorocarbon Propellants: May be hazardous if deliberately abused. Inhalation of high concentrations of aerosol sprays has brought about cardiovascular toxic effects and even death, especially under conditions of hypoxia. Aerosols are safe when used properly and with adequate ventilation, but excessive use should be avoided.

Children: Due to limited clinical data in this age group, the use of intranasal corticosteroids in children under 6 years of age is not recommended.

Adverse Effects: Eye: Increased intraocular pressure may occur. The extent is dependent upon the frequency and duration of use as well as the type and concentration of the corticosteroid. Ocular hypertension may occur after 1 to 6 weeks of therapy. This can be reversed in a few weeks by discontinuing the medication.

Glaucomatous optic nerve damage, posterior subcapsular cataract formation and delayed wound healing have been reported, as well as mydriasis, defects in visual acuity and visual fields, loss of accommodation and ptosis. Topical application may cause discomfort, burning, stinging of the eye and lacrimation in some patients.

Fungal infections of the cornea are particulary prone to develop with long-term application of steroids.

In those diseases causing thinning of the cornea, perforation has occurred with the use of topical steroids.

Ear: Stinging and burning have been reported rarely when the medication has gained access to the middle ear.

Nasal: In general, side effects have been primarily associated with the nasal mucosa and are consistent with what one would expect from applying a topical medication to an already inflamed membrane. Most commonly reported adverse effects are irritation and dryness. Less common are headache, nasal bleeding, nasal stinging, crusting, sore throat, cough, fatigue, nausea, dizziness, loss of sense of taste or smell, stuffy nose, and stomach pains. In rare cases skin reactions such as urticaria, rash or dermatitis occur. Rarely ulcerations of the mucous membranes and nasal septal perforation have been reported.

When patients are transferred to nasal preparations from a systemic steroid, allergic conditions such as asthma or eczema may be unmasked. With beclomethasone, sneezing attacks directly after use occur in about 10% of aerosol users and 4% of those using aqueous suspension. After the sneezing has stopped, the patient should clear their nose and repeat the dose.

Overdose: Symptoms and Treatment: Eye: Overdosage in the use of topical ophthalmic corticosteroids is a remote possibility. Discontinue medication when heavy or protracted use is suspected. Excessive prolonged use may suppress HPA axis function resulting in secondary adrenal insufficiency.

Nasal: Acute overdosing is unlikely in view of the total amount of active ingredient present. However, when used chronically in excessive doses or in conjunction with other corticosteroid formulations, systemic corticosteroid effects such as hypercorticism and adrenal suppression may appear. If such changes occur, the dosage should be discontinued slowly consistent with accepted procedures for discontinuation of chronic steroid therapy.

The restoration of HPA axis function may be slow during periods of pronounced physical stress. Supplementation with systemic steroids may be advisable.

Dosage: For proper dosage and administration of the drug and to attain maximum improvement, the patient must be instructed by the physician or other health care professional in the correct use of these preparations. The patient should contact the physician if the symptoms do not improve, or if the condition worsens or if sneezing or nasal irritation occurs with the use of intranasal preparations.

Eye: For use in the eye corticosteroids are available as sterile solutions, suspensions and ointments. To decrease the likelihood of hampering vision, solutions and suspensions are usually utilized during the day. For inflammatory conditions of the eyelid and for nighttime use ointments are preferred.

To avoid possible contamination, do not touch the tip of the dropper to any surface. Do not allow dispenser tip to touch the surface of the eye. Shake eye suspensions well before use.

Ear: For use in the ear, steroids are available as solutions and suspensions. To decrease the buildup of debris in the ear canal, suspensions should be used sparingly. For administration of solutions or suspensions, the patient should lie with the affected ear upward and then the drops should be instilled. This position should be maintained for 5 minutes to facilitate penetration of the drops into the ear canal. This procedure may be repeated if necessary for the opposite ear.

Patients should avoid contamination of the dropper with material from the eye, ear, fingers or other sources in order to maintain the sterility of the product.

Nasal: For intranasal use corticosteroids are available as nasal aerosols, solutions or suspensions. The therapeutic effects of corticosteroids, unlike those of decongestants, are not immediate. Since the therapeutic effect depends on regular use, patients must be instructed to take the nasal inhalations at regular intervals as prescribed and not, as with other nasal sprays, as they feel necessary.

Careful attention must be given to patients previously treated for prolonged periods with systemic corticosteroids when those patients are transferred to a nasal spray (see Warnings). Initially, the corticosteroid nasal spray and the systemic corticosteroid must be given concomitantly, while the dose of the latter is gradually decreased. Many withdrawal or tapering regimens have been described. Factors such as the dose and duration of systemic therapy and the underlying health of the patient should be considered when determining the withdrawal schedule.

In the presence of excessive nasal mucous secretion or edema of the nasal mucosa, the drug may fail to reach the site of action. In such cases, use a nasal vasoconstrictor for 2 to 3 days prior to treatment.

The reader is referred to individual product monographs for more specific dosing information.

Reviewed 1998

CORTICOSTEROIDS: INHALED ℞

General Monograph, CPhA

Beclomethasone
Budesonide
Flunisolide
Fluticasone
Triamcinolone

> This monograph has been compiled by CPhA. It may contain information different from that approved by Therapeutic Products Programme, Health Canada, and the pharmaceutical manufacturers' approval has not been requested.

Pharmacology: The most important action of inhaled corticosteroids is thought to be inhibition of gene transcription of the cytokines implicated in asthmatic inflammation. Gene transcription is interrupted through the formation of glucocorticoid-receptor complexes, which occurs after the lipophilic drug rapidly enters the airway cell. At the cellular level, corticosteroids may have direct inhibitory effects on cells involved in airway inflammation, including mast cells, macrophages, T-lymphocytes, eosinophils and epithelial cells. They may also inhibit plasma exudation and mucus secretion in inflamed airways.

Long-term treatment with inhaled steroids in children and adults with asthma lessens airway hyper-responsiveness to histamine, cholinergic agonists and allergens, reduces responsiveness to exercise, cold air, fog, adenosine, bradykinin and irritants such as sulfur dioxide and metabisulfites, and lowers the sensitivity and maximal narrowing of the airway in response to spasmogens. Although treatment suppresses inflammation, it may not reverse the persistent structural changes underlying the disease.

Pharmacokinetics: An ideal inhaled corticosteroid should have high topical potency, low oral bioavailability and rapid inactivation after systemic absorption. These properties render maximal topical efficacy with minimal systemic side effects. When inhaled properly from a metered dose inhaler, 10 to 20% of the dose enters the respiratory tract. The remaining 80 to 90% of the dose is then deposited in the oropharynx and swallowed. Table I displays the varying properties of the different corticosteroids. Factors such as age of the patient, degree of airway obstruction, use of spacer devices, severity of airway disease and concurrent therapy may also influence the disposition of inhaled doses.

Indications: Prophylactic management of steroid-responsive bronchial asthma. May be used in asthmatic patients who have not been on steroid therapy in the past or for whom a reduction of systemic steroid dose is desirable.

Inhaled corticosteroids may have a role as adjunctive therapy in the management of COPD in a small percentage of patients with this disease who respond to steroid therapy. Inhaled corticosteroids should be reserved for COPD patients who clearly demonstrate a significant response following a carefully monitored trial of oral prednisone.

Contraindications: Inhaled corticosteroids should not be used in primary treatment of status asthmaticus or other acute episodes of asthma, or in patients with moderate to severe bronchiectasis. They are contraindicated in patients with active or quiescent pulmonary tuberculosis, untreated fungal, bacterial or viral infections of the respiratory system, or patients with a history of hypersensitivity to any ingredients in the preparations.

Warnings: The replacement of systemic steroids with inhaled steroid therapy in asthmatic patients must be gradual and carefully supervised by the physician. Several months are required for recovery of hypothalamic-pituitary-adrenocortical (HPA) function after prolonged systemic corticosteroid therapy is withdrawn. During this transition period, patients may exhibit symptoms of adrenal insufficiency when exposed to trauma, surgery or infections, particularly gastroenteritis. Although inhaled corticosteroid may control asthmatic symptoms during these emergencies they do not provide sufficient systemic steroid. Deaths due to adrenal insufficiency have occurred in asthmatic patients during and after transfer from systemic to inhaled corticosteroids. Systemic withdrawal symptoms such as joint or muscular pain, weakness, nausea, vomiting, diarrhea, weight loss and hyperpigmentation of skin and mucous membranes may occur upon withdrawal of oral steroids. Allergic conditions previously suppressed (e.g., rhinitis, conjunctivitis, eczema) may be unmasked during the transfer and require alternative therapy. Physicians should consider resuming or adding oral steroids during these episodes, periods of stress or severe asthma attacks. Patients who had been steroid-dependent in the past should be advised to resume systemic corticosteroid immediately during these periods and contact their physician. The patient should carry a warning card indicating that they may need supplementary systemic steroids during these situations. In the absence of previous or concomitant treatment with oral corticosteroids, inhaled corticosteroids in doses of 1 500 µg/day or less in adults and 400 µg/day or less in children, have little if any effect on pituitary-adrenal function.

Localized fungal infections with Candida albicans or Aspergillus niger have occurred in the mouth, pharynx and occasionally in the larynx. Rinsing the mouth with water, cleansing dentures after inhalation, as well as the use of a large-volume spacer during inhalation should be helpful in preventing this complication. Some infections may require discontinuation of inhaled steroid therapy and institution of antifungal therapy.

Inhaled corticosteroids are preventive agents and have no role in the acute treatment of an asthmatic attack. Patients should be instructed to contact their physician immediately when their bronchodilator therapy does not provide rapid relief of bronchospasm.

Precautions: Coughing and wheezing have occurred with inhaled corticosteroids. Pretreatment with an aerosol bronchodilator is effective in reducing these symptoms in some patients. These symptoms could be due to the surfactants, therefore, changing from pressurized aerosols to unpressurized dry-powder inhalers may effectively alleviate these symptoms.

Paradoxical bronchospasm, characterized by an immediate increase in wheezing after dosing, may occur. This should be treated immediately with a fast-acting inhaled bronchodilator.

Pulmonary infiltrates with eosinophilia may occur in patients on inhaled corticosteroid therapy. Although it is possible that in some patients this state may become manifest because of systemic steroid withdrawal when inhaled steroid is administered, a causative role of inhaled corticosteroid and/or its vehicle cannot be ruled out.

There is no definitive information about the long-term systemic effects of the agents. Systemic side effects are usually observed when daily doses of >800 µg are inhaled, and whether effects on very sensitive biochemical indices are relevant to long-term deleterious effects is not yet certain. The risk of systemic side effects (such as effects on HPA axis, skin thinning or bruising, cataracts, osteoporosis, growth, glucose and lipid metabolism) are being extensively studied. However, further clinical studies are needed to determine whether and to what extent the changes in laboratory indices actually signify clinically important risks.

Patients should be advised to inform all treating physicians of their present or past use of corticosteroids.

Treatment with inhaled corticosteroids should not be stopped abruptly, but tapered off gradually.

Drug Interactions: Because of the very low plasma drug concentrations achieved after inhaled administration, there are no reports of suspected drug interactions of clinical significance.

Pregnancy: Well-controlled studies relating the safety of inhaled corticosteroids in pregnant women are not available. Yet, it is important to recognize that poorly controlled asthma may retard intrauterine growth and increase the incidence of perinatal mortality. The expected benefit should be weighed against the potential risk to the fetus when these agents are to be used during pregnancy. Infants born of mothers who have received substantial doses during pregnancy should be followed closely for hypoadrenalism.

Lactation: It is not clearly established whether inhaled corticosteroids are excreted in breast milk. Use in nursing mothers requires that the benefit of the drug be weighed against the potential risk to the infant.

Children: In general, inhaled corticosteroids are not recommended for children younger than 6 years of age due to limited clinical data and inability to learn the correct use of inhalers in this age group. Nebulized corticosteroids (available as budesonide only) can be used in younger asthmatic children when inhaled corticosteroids are warranted.

High doses of inhaled corticosteroids may cause a decreased short-term growth rate. Monitoring of growth is advised in children who regularly require higher doses of inhaled corticosteroids.

Although unlikely with usual doses, children receiving higher doses of inhaled corticosteroids may be more susceptible to infectious diseases, especially chickenpox and measles. Care should be taken to avoid exposure in patients who have not had these diseases.

Abuse and Dependence: Fluorocarbon propellants may be hazardous if deliberately abused. Inhalation of high concentrations of aerosol sprays has caused cardiovascular toxicity and even death, especially under conditions of hypoxia. However, evidence attests to the safety of aerosols when used properly with adequate ventilation.

Special Diseases and Conditions: Systemic effects of corticosteroids may be enhanced in patients with advanced liver cirrhosis, and in those with hypothyroidism. In hypoprothrombinemia, ASA should be used cautiously in conjunction with corticosteroids.

Adverse Effects: Local: fungal infections of the mouth, pharynx, larynx; dysphonia; sore throat; throat irritation; coughing; wheezing; dry mouth; rash; facial edema; headache; nausea; unpleasant taste.

Systemic: See Precautions. Psychiatric symptoms including nervousness, restlessness, depression and behavioral changes have been reported with budesonide. For complete information on the systemic effects of corticosteroids, readers are referred to the general monograph, Corticosteroids: Systemic.

Rare cases of immediate and delayed reactions including urticaria, angioedema, rash and bronchospasm have been reported. Usual management of acute hypersensitivity reactions should be instituted in these situations.

Overdose: Symptoms and Treatment: The acute toxicity of inhaled corticosteroids is low. Suppression of adrenal function may occur after inhalation of large amounts of the drug over a short period of time. In most cases, no obvious symptoms are observed, and no emergency action is required. Recovery of HPA function can be verified by measuring plasma cortisol. Chronic use of excessive amounts of inhaled corticosteroid may also cause some degree of adrenal suppression, and gradual dose reduction may be required.

Dosage: Inhaled corticosteroids are available in many different dosage forms including metered dose inhalers which may be used with or without a spacer device, dry powder inhalers, or solutions for use with nebulizers. Each method of administration offers certain advantages and disadvantages which may influence the choice of delivery system for a particular patient. There have been very few studies comparing efficacy among the various inhaled corticosteroids. It is difficult to draw definitive conclusions from these studies, due to the use of different inhalation devices and different study populations. Dosages of inhaled corticosteroid are subdivided arbitrarily into low dose (up to 400 µg/day), moderate dose (400 to 1 600 µg/day) and high dose (>1 600 µg/day). Adverse effects are often dose-related and are uncommon at doses <800 µg/day. Interpatient dosage requirements vary over a wide range, therefore dose adjustment must be flexible. The minimum dose that

Table I—Corticosteroids: Inhaled

Pharmacokinetics

	Relative Binding Affinity[a]	Blanching Potency[b]	Plasma Half-life (h)	Volume of Distribution (L/kg)	Clearance (L/min)	Systemic Availability (%)	Metabolism in Liver
Beclomethasone			NA[c]	NA	NA		BDP metabolized to
dipropionate (BDP)	0.4	600				<5 (BDP)	more active BMP,
monopropionate(BMP)	13.5	450					which then undergoes rapid transformation
Budesonide	9.4	980	2.8	4.3	1.4	10	Extensive first-pass
Flunisolide	1.8	330	1.6	1.8	1.0	20	Extensive first-pass
Fluticasone dipropionate	18.0	1200	3.1	3.7	0.87	<1	Complete first-pass
Triamcinolone acetonide	3.6	300	1.5	2.1	1.2	NA	NA

[a] To human glucocorticoid receptors in vitro; Dexamethasone=1.
[b] Effect on human skin indicating relative topical potency; Dexamethasone=1.
[c] Published data inconsistent.

Corticosteroids: Inhaled (cont'd)

adequately controls symptoms and maintains lung function should be targeted. The reader is referred to individual product monographs, or other specialized references, for more specific information on inhaled corticosteroid dosage in the management of asthma or COPD.

The transfer of steroid-dependent asthmatic patients from oral to inhaled steroid requires special care because of the slow recovery of HPA function. Asthma should be stable before considering the transfer. Initially, the maintenance dose of systemic steroid and the inhaled steroid should be given concurrently. After 1 week, the dose of systemic steroid should be very gradually decreased. Many withdrawal or tapering regimens have been described. Factors such as dose and duration of oral therapy and overall health of the patient should be considered when determining the withdrawal schedule. During dose tapering, some patients may experience symptoms of steroid withdrawal despite maintenance or even improvement of respiratory function. These patients should be encouraged to continue with the inhaler and be monitored closely for signs of adrenal insufficiency (see Warnings). If such signs occur, the systemic steroid dose should be increased temporarily; further withdrawal will have to be done more slowly. In patients being transferred, consideration must be given to supplementation with systemic steroids during periods of stress or severe asthmatic attack. Some patients cannot completely discontinue oral steroids. In these cases, a minimum maintenance oral dose should be given concurrently with the inhaled steroid.

Once asthma is under control, inhaled steroids should be given twice daily in order to improve compliance. The schedule should be increased to 4 times/day for patients with more severe asthma. Once daily dosing may be sufficient for patients with mild asthma.

Patients must be instructed regarding the correct method of using the inhalers to ensure that the drug reaches the target areas within the lung. A spacer device should be encouraged in patients who have difficulty coordinating the use of metered dose inhalers and in patients who require high doses to minimize local side effects. Rinsing the mouth and gargling with water after each inhalation may be helpful in preventing oral candidiasis.

It must be stressed to patients that inhaled corticosteroids are to be used at regular intervals as prescribed and are not intended for treatment of an acute asthamtic attack.

Patients receiving bronchodilators by inhalation should be instructed to use the bronchodilator prior to the steroid therapy. Ideally, several minutes should elapse between the use of the two inhalers to reduce the potential toxicity from the inhaled fluorocarbon propellants and to allow for some bronchodilation to occur. However, because this practice may lead to decreased compliance with corticosteroid therapy, some clinicians do not recommend this waiting period.

Reviewed 1998

CORTICOSTEROIDS: SYSTEMIC ℞

General Monograph, CPhA

Betamethasone
Cortisone
Dexamethasone
Fludrocortisone
Hydrocortisone
Methylprednisolone
Prednisolone
Prednisone
Triamcinolone

This monograph has been compiled by CPhA. It may contain information different from that approved by Therapeutic Products Programme, Health Canada, and the pharmaceutical manufacturers' approval has not been requested.

Pharmacology: Corticosteroids are synthetic analogues of hormones secreted by the adrenal cortex. They possess anti-inflammatory (glucocorticoid) and/or salt-retaining (mineralocorticoid) properties to varying degrees (see Table I). Glucocorticoids affect almost all body systems and cause varied metabolic effects. They promote protein catabolism, gluconeogenesis, and redistribution of fat from peripheral to central areas of the body. They reduce intestinal absorption and increase renal excretion of calcium. Mineralocorticoids affect electrolyte and fluid balance by acting on the distal renal tubule to promote sodium reabsorption and potassium and hydrogen excretion.

The mechanism of action of corticosteroids is not fully understood. Glucocorticoids decrease inflammation through multiple mechanisms, including stabilization of leukocyte lysosomal membranes, inhibition of macrophage accumulation in inflamed areas, and reduction of capillary permeability. They suppress the body's immune responses through mechanisms such as reduction of activity and volume of the lymphatic system, decreased immunoglobulin and complement concentrations as well as decreased passage of immune complexes through basement membranes. They also stimulate the erythroid cells of bone marrow and lengthen the survival time of erythrocytes and platelets. The mechanism of action for the antiemetic effect of corticosteroids is not well established.

Pharmacokinetics: Most glucocorticoids in the form of free alcohols, ketones or acetates are readily absorbed when administered orally. With i.m. administration, the rate of absorption of the lipid soluble acetate and acetonide esters is much slower than that of the water soluble sodium phosphate and sodium succinate salts. A water soluble corticosteroid salt should be administered i.v. to achieve a rapid onset of action.

In animal studies, most glucocorticoids have been shown to be removed rapidly from blood and distributed to muscles, liver, skin, intestine and kidneys. They bind to plasma proteins to varying extents. Because only unbound drug is pharmacologically active, patients with low serum albumin concentrations may be more susceptible to the effects of glucocorticoids than patients with normal serum albumin concentrations. Glucocorticoids cross the placenta and may be distributed into breast milk.

Cortisone and prednisone are reduced to their pharmacologically active forms, hydrocortisone and prednisolone respectively. Pharmacologically active compounds are then metabolized primarily in the liver to biologically inactive compounds. Inactive metabolites, primarily glucuronides and sulfates, are excreted by the kidneys. Small amounts of unmetabolized drug are excreted in urine and bile.

Table I—Corticosteroids: Systemic

Corticosteroid Comparison Chart

Drug	Biologic Half-Life (hours)	Equivalent Anti-inflammatory Dose (mg)*	Relative Mineralo-corticoid Potency
Glucocorticoids:			
Short-acting	8-12		
Cortisone		25	2
Hydrocortisone		20	2
Intermediate-acting	18-36		
Methylprednisolone		4	0
Prednisolone		5	1
Prednisone		5	1
Triamcinolone		4	0
Long-acting	36-54		
Betamethasone		0.6	0
Dexamethasone		0.75	0
Mineralocorticoid:			
Fludrocortisone	12-24	10	125

*Equivalent doses are general approximations and may not apply to all diseases or routes of administration. Duration of HPA axis suppression and degree of mineralocorticoid activities must be considered separately.

Indications: Endocrine Disorders: Primary or secondary adrenocortical insufficiency (hydrocortisone or cortisone is the first choice; synthetic analogues may be used in conjunction with mineralocorticoids where applicable; in infancy, mineralocorticoid supplementation is of particular importance), congenital adrenal hyperplasia, nonsuppurative thyroiditis, hypercalcemia associated with cancer. Used parenterally in acute adrenal cortical insufficiency (hydrocortisone or cortisone is the drug of choice), preoperatively or in the event of serious trauma or illness with known adrenal insufficiency or when adrenal cortical reserve is doubtful, shock unresponsive to conventional therapy if adrenal cortical insufficiency exists or is suspected.

Rheumatic Disorders and Collagen Diseases: As adjunctive therapy for short-term administration (for acute episode or exacerbation) in: psoriatic and rheumatoid arthritis (selected cases may require low dose maintenance therapy), ankylosing spondylitis, acute and subacute bursitis, acute nonspecific tenosynovitis, acute gouty arthritis; for exacerbation or maintenance therapy in selected cases of systemic lupus erythematosus, acute rheumatic carditis, systemic dermatomyositis, polymyositis, polymyalgia rheumatica, giant cell arteritis.

Dermatologic Diseases: pemphigus, bullous dermatitis herpetiformis, severe erythema multiforme (Stevens-Johnson syndrome), exfoliative dermatitis, mycosis fungoides, severe psoriasis, severe seborrheic dermatitis.

Allergic Conditions: control of severe or incapacitating allergic conditions intractable to adequate trials of conventional treatment such as seasonal or perennial allergic rhinitis, bronchial asthma, contact dermatitis, atopic dermatitis, serum sickness and drug hypersensitivity reactions. Parenteral therapy is indicated for urticarial transfusion reactions, angioedema and anaphylaxis (epinephrine is the drug of choice).

Ophthalmic Diseases: severe acute and chronic allergic and inflammatory processes involving the eye and its adnexa such as allergic conjunctivitis, keratitis, allergic corneal marginal ulcers, herpes zoster ophthalmicus (but not herpes simplex), iritis and iridocyclitis, chorioretinitis, anterior segment inflammation, diffuse posterior uveitis and choroiditis, optic neuritis, retrobulbar neuritis, sympathetic ophthalmia.

Respiratory Diseases: symptomatic sarcoidosis, Löffler's syndrome not manageable by other means, berylliosis, fulminating or disseminated pulmonary tuberculosis when concurrently accompanied by appropriate antituberculous chemotherapy, aspiration pneumonitis, pulmonary emphysema where bronchospasm or bronchial edema plays a significant role, diffuse interstitial pulmonary fibrosis (Hamman-Rich syndrome).

Hematological Disorders: idiopathic thrombocytopenia purpura and secondary thrombocytopenia in adults, acquired (autoimmune) hemolytic anemia, aplastic crisis, congenital (erythroid) hypoplastic anemia.

Neoplastic Diseases: for palliative management of leukemias and lymphomas in adults, acute leukemia of childhood.

Edematous States: to induce diuresis or remission of proteinuria in the nephrotic syndrome (without uremia) of the idiopathic type or that due to lupus erythematosus.

Gastrointestinal Diseases: as adjunctive therapy in the treatment of ulcerative colitis and regional enteritis.

Nervous System: acute exacerbations of multiple sclerosis. Methylprednisolone may be used as an adjunct in the management of cerebral edema and acute spinal cord injury. Dexamethasone may be used to treat patients with cerebral edema associated with primary or metastatic brain tumors, neurosurgery, head injury, pseudotumor cerebri and cerebral vascular accident (acute stroke) excluding intracerebral hemorrhage. Dexamethasone may also be used in the preoperative preparation of patients with increased intracranial pressure secondary to brain tumors or for palliation of patients with inoperable or recurrent brain neoplasms.

Organ Transplants: used in high dose concurrently with other immunosuppressive drugs to prevent rejection of transplanted organs.

Miscellaneous: tuberculosis meningitis with subarachnoid block or impending block when concurrently accompanied by appropriate antituberculous chemotherapy; trichinosis with neurologic or myocardial involvement; postoperative dental inflammatory reactions. Dexamethasone is also used in the diagnostic testing of adrenocortical hyperfunction and antenatal prophylaxis of neonatal respiratory distress.

Contraindications: Hypersensitivity to the product and its constituents; systemic fungal infections; administration of live virus vaccines in patients receiving immunosuppressive corticosteroid doses.

Warnings: Adrenal Suppression: Following prolonged therapy, abrupt discontinuation may result in withdrawal syndrome and secondary adrenocortical insufficiency. Symptoms of adrenal insufficiency resulting from rapid withdrawal include: nausea, fatigue, anorexia, dyspnea, hypotension, hypoglycemia, myalgia, fever, malaise, arthralgia, dizziness, desquamation of skin and fainting. This type of relative insufficiency may persist for months after discontinuation of therapy; therefore, in any stressful situation occurring during that period, reinstitute hormone therapy. If the patient is receiving corticosteroids already, the dosage may have to be increased. Since mineralocorticoid secretion may be impaired, salt and/or a mineralocorticoid may need to be used.

Fluid and Electrolyte Balance: Average and large doses of hydrocortisone or cortisone can cause elevation of blood pressure, salt and water retention and increased potassium excretion. These effects are less likely to occur with the synthetic derivatives except when used in large doses. Dietary salt restriction and potassium supplementation may be necessary. All corticosteroids increase calcium excretion.

Gastrointestinal Effects: The association between peptic ulceration and corticosteroid therapy remains controversial. However, corticosteroid therapy may mask the symptoms of peptic ulcer. Perforation or hemorrhage may occur without significant pain.

Corticosteroids should be used with caution in patients with diverticulitis, fresh intestinal anastomoses, active or latent peptic ulcer and in nonspecific ulcerative colitis, if there is a probability of impending perforation, abscess or other pyogenic infection.

Hypersensitivity: Rare instances of anaphylactoid reactions have occurred in patients receiving parenteral corticosteroid therapy. Appropriate precautionary measures should be taken prior to administration, especially when the patient has a history of allergy to any drug. Some corticosteroid products contain tartrazine and sodium bisulfite, both of which may cause severe allergic reactions in susceptible individuals.

Immunosuppression: Patients being treated with corticosteroids should not be vaccinated against smallpox. Other immunization procedures should generally not be undertaken in these patients, especially those on high doses, because of possible neurological complications and a lack of antibody response. Immunization procedures may be undertaken in patients who are receiving corticosteroids as replacement therapy. Corticosteroids may suppress reactions to skin tests.

Infections: In patients on corticosteroid therapy subjected to unusual stress, increased dosage of rapidly acting corticosteroids before, during and after the stressful situation is indicated.

The use of corticosteroids in active tuberculosis should be restricted to those cases of fulminating disseminated tuberculosis in which the corticosteroid is used for the management of the disease in conjunction with an appropriate antituberculous regimen. If corticosteroids are indicated in patients with latent tuberculosis or tuberculin reactivity, close observation is necessary as reactivation of the disease may occur. During prolonged corticosteroid therapy, these patients should receive chemoprophylaxis.

Corticosteroids may mask some signs of infection, and new infections may appear during their use. There may be decreased resistance and inability to localize infection when corticosteroids are used. If corticosteroids have to be used in the presence of bacterial infections, institute appropriate anti-infective therapy. Patients exposed to certain infections (e.g., measles, chickenpox) should seek medical advice.

Corticosteroids may activate latent amebiasis. Amebiasis should be ruled out before giving corticosteroids to a patient who has spent time in the tropics or has unexplained diarrhea.

Ocular Effects: Corticosteroids should be used cautiously in patients with ocular herpes simplex because of possible corneal ulceration and perforation. Prolonged use of corticosteroids may produce posterior subcapsular cataracts, glaucoma with possible damage to the optic nerves and may enhance the establishment of secondary ocular infections due to fungi or viruses.

Renal Function Impairment: Edema may occur in the presence of renal disease with a fixed or decreased glomerular filtration rate. A degree of caution is advised when corticosteroids are used in patients with renal insufficiency, acute glomerulonephritis and chronic nephritis.

Precautions: Because complications of treatment with corticosteroids are dependent on the dosage regimen, a risk/benefit decision must be made in each individual case with respect to dose and duration of treatment and whether daily or intermittent therapy should be used. The lowest effective corticosteroid dose should be used to control the condition under treatment.

When used in myasthenia gravis, hospitalization with careful observation is recommended because a transient worsening of symptoms, possibly leading to respiratory distress, may precede clinical improvement.

Corticosteroid therapy can cause mental or mood disturbances including hypomania, mania, depression and psychosis. These reactions appear to be dose-related and more commonly seen in the first few weeks of therapy, but are sometimes seen following sharp decreases in corticosteroid dosage or during pulse therapy. Existing mood instability or psychotic tendencies may be aggravated by corticosteroids.

Avascular or aseptic necrosis of the femoral or humeral head has been associated with long-term corticosteroid treatment; however, it has also occurred in patients receiving high dose, short-term therapy. This adverse effect is more likely to occur in patients with a predisposing illness such as rheumatoid arthritis or systemic lupus erythematosis.

It has been recommended that patients taking oral corticosteroids maintain an intake of at least 1 500 mg of calcium and 800 IU of vitamin D daily, either through diet or supplementation, to prevent corticosteroid-induced osteoporosis.

There is an enhanced effect of corticosteroids on patients with hypothyroidism and in those with cirrhosis.

ASA and nonsteroidal anti-inflammatory agents should be used cautiously in conjunction with corticosteroids in patients with hypoprothrombinemia.

To minimize the likelihood and severity of dermal atrophy, corticosteroids should not be injected s.c. Injections into the deltoid area or repeat injections into any one site should also be avoided.

Pregnancy: Some animal studies have shown that corticosteroids, when administered to the mother at high doses, may cause fetal malformations. Since adequate human reproduction studies have not been done with corticosteroids, the use of these drugs in pregnancy, nursing mothers or women of child-bearing potential requires that the benefits of the drug be carefully weighed against the potential risk to both mother and fetus. Corticosteroids cross the placenta. Infants born of mothers who have received substantial doses of corticosteroids during pregnancy should be carefully observed for signs of hypoadrenalism.

Lactation: Corticosteroids appear in breast milk and could suppress growth, interfere with endogenous corticosteroid production or cause other unwanted effects. Mothers taking pharmacologic doses of corticosteroids should be advised not to nurse.

Children: Prolonged therapy with corticosteroids in infants and children should be avoided if possible since corticosteroids may suppress growth. If deemed essential to institute corticosteroid therapy alternate day therapy should be considered to minimize this side effect. Growth and development should be closely monitored.

Drug Interactions: See Table II.

Drug-Laboratory Test Interactions: Corticosteroids may decrease I^{131} uptake and produce false negative results in the nitroblue tetrazolium test for systemic bacterial infection.

Adverse Effects: Cardiovascular: thromboembolism; fat embolism; hypercholesterolemia; accelerated atherosclerosis; cardiac arrhythmias or ECG changes due to potassium deficiency; syncope; aggravation of hypertension; myocardial rupture following recent MI; reports of cardiac arrhythmias, fatal arrest or circulatory collapse following rapid administration of i.v. methylprednisolone greater than 0.5 g given over a period of less than 10 minutes.

Dermatologic: impaired wound healing; thin fragile skin; petechiae and ecchymoses; facial erythema; striae; hirsutism; acneiform eruptions; suppressed reactions to skin tests; hypersensitivity reactions such as allergic dermatitis, urticaria, angioneurotic edema.

Endocrine: decreased carbohydrate tolerance; hyperglycemia; glycosuria; increased requirements for oral hypoglycemics or insulin in diabetes; manifestations of latent diabetes mellitus; menstrual irregularities; development of cushingoid state; suppression of growth in children; secondary adrenocortical and pituitary unresponsiveness, particularly in times of stress, as in trauma, surgery or illness; increased sweating.

Fluid and Electrolyte Disturbances: sodium retention; fluid retention; congestive heart failure in susceptible patients; potassium loss; hypokalemic alkalosis; hypertension; hypocalcemia.

Gastrointestinal: nausea, vomiting, anorexia which may result in weight loss; increased appetite which may result in weight gain; diarrhea or constipation, abdominal distention, pancreatitis, gastric irritation and ulcerative esophagitis; peptic ulcer with possible perforation and hemorrhage; perforation of the small and large bowel particularly in inflammatory bowel disease.

Hematologic: leukocytosis, thrombocytopenia, lymphopenia.

Metabolic: negative nitrogen balance due to protein catabolism.

Musculoskeletal: aseptic necrosis of femoral and humeral heads; muscle weakness; steroid myopathy; loss of muscle mass; osteoporosis; spontaneous fractures including vertebral compression fractures and pathologic fractures of long bones.

Neurological: seizures; increased intracranial pressure with papilledema (pseudotumor cerebri) in association with withdrawal of corticosteroid therapy; neuritis; paresthesias.

Ophthalmic: increased intraocular pressure; glaucoma; exophthalmos; posterior subcapsular cataracts.

Psychologic: hallucinations; psychosis; euphoria; mood changes.

Table II—Corticosteroids: Systemic

Corticosteroid Drug Interactions

Drug(s) Involved	Description of Interaction	Action Required
Anticholinesterase agents (e.g., neostigmine, pyridostigmine)	Corticosteroids antagonize the effect of anticholinesterase agents, resulting in severe weakness in patients with myasthenia gravis.	Withdraw anticholinesterase medication if possible at least 24 hours prior to initiation of corticosteroid therapy.
Cyclosporine	Corticosteroid clearance may be decreased and plasma concentrations of cyclosporine may be increased through mutual inhibition of metabolism. Seizures have been reported in patients receiving high dose corticosteroid and cyclosporine concurrently.	Monitor cyclosporine levels closely; adjust dose of both medications if required.
Digoxin	Corticosteroid induced potassium loss may potentiate digoxin toxicity.	Monitor serum potassium.
Estrogens	Corticosteroid clearance may be decreased.	Decrease corticosteroid dose if required.
Hepatic microsomal enzyme inducers (e.g., barbiturates, phenytoin, rifampin)	Corticosteroid clearance may be increased through enzyme induction.	Increase corticosteroid dose if required.
Hepatic microsomal enzyme inhibitors (e.g., erythromycin, ketoconazole)	Corticosteroid clearance may be decreased through enzyme inhibition.	Decrease corticosteroid dose if required.
Isoniazid	Corticosteroids may increase hepatic metabolism and/or excretion of isoniazid.	Increase isoniazid dose if required.
Oral anticoagulants	Corticosteroids may increase or decrease anticoagulant action.	Monitor INR and adjust anticoagulant dose if required.
Potassium-depleting diuretics (e.g., thiazides, furosemide, ethacrynic acid)	Corticosteroid potassium wasting effect is enhanced.	Monitor serum potassium and add supplement if required.
Nonsteroidal anti-inflammatory drugs (NSAIDs)	ASA: Corticosteroids may increase renal clearance of salicylate, resulting in either a decrease in salicylate efficacy, or salicylate toxicity when corticosteroid dose is decreased or discontinued. All NSAIDs: Concomitant use may increase the risk of peptic ulceration.	Monitor salicylate level. Avoid concurrent administration. If deemed necessary, monitor closely for gastrointestinal side effects.
Vaccines or toxoids	Corticosteroids inhibit antibody response resulting in enhanced toxicity from or diminished response to vaccines or toxoids.	Avoid use of vaccines or toxoids in patients receiving immunosuppressive doses of corticosteroids (see Warnings).

Corticosteroids: Systemic (cont'd)

Other: necrotizing angiitis, thrombophlebitis; aggravation or masking of infections; insomnia; anaphylactoid reactions. Burning or tingling of the perineal area may occur after i.v. injection of corticosteroids. Parenteral corticosteroid therapy has also produced hypo or hyperpigmentation, scarring, induration, delayed pain or soreness, subcutaneous and cutaneous atrophy and sterile abscesses.

Overdose: Symptoms and Treatment: Acute overdose even after ingestion of large doses is rarely a clinical problem. Continuous overdosage requires careful reduction of dosage in order to prevent the occurrence of acute adrenal insufficiency.

Anaphylactic and hypersensitivity reactions depending on their severity, may be treated with antihistamines with or without epinephrine. General supportive measures should also be employed.

Dosage: Corticosteroids in appropriate forms may be administered orally, by oral inhalation and by i.v., i.m., s.c., intra-articular, intrabursal, intradermal, intrasynovial, intralesional, or soft tissue injection. Because injections of slightly soluble corticosteroids may produce atrophy at the site of injection, i.m. injections of these products should be made deeply into gluteal muscle; repeated i.m. injections at the same site should be avoided and these products should not be administered s.c.

Dosage ranges for corticosteroids are extremely wide and patient responses are quite variable. Dosage should be individualized according to the diagnosis, severity, prognosis, probable duration of disease, patient response and tolerance. For infants and children, the recommended dosage should be governed by the same considerations rather than by strict adherence to the ratio indicated by age or body weight.

Dosages used in various conditions are considered either physiologic (amount of corticosteroid normally secreted by the adrenal cortex daily) or pharmacologic (anything greater). See Table III. Refer to Table I (on previous page) for equivalent doses for other corticosteroids.

Table III—Corticosteroids: Systemic

Oral Prednisone Dosage

Type of Dosage Range	Approximate Daily Dose
Physiologic	5 mg
Pharmacologic	
Maintenance or Low Dose	5 to 15 mg
Moderate Dose	0.5 mg/kg
High Dose	1 to 3 mg/kg
Massive Dose	15 to 30 mg/kg

Dosage should be decreased or discontinued gradually when the drug has been administered for more than a few weeks to minimize the risk of adrenal insufficiency, as adrenal suppression has occurred after as little as 2 weeks of corticosteroid therapy. A number of different regimens for tapering corticosteroid therapy have been described. It has been suggested that the dosage be reduced by the equivalent of 2.5 to 5 mg of prednisone every 3 days to 2 weeks. An increase in dose followed by a more gradual withdrawal may be necessary if the disease flares up during tapering.

In the management of acute disorders, corticosteroid dosage should be sufficient to ensure that symptoms are controlled quickly, and treatment should be discontinued as soon as possible. In acute conditions where prompt relief is imperative, large doses are permissible and may be mandatory for a short period.

In chronic conditions requiring long-term therapy, use the lowest dosage that provides adequate but not necessarily complete relief. If a high dosage for prolonged periods is considered essential, observe patients closely for signs that might necessitate reduction in dosage or discontinuance of the drug. Chronic conditions are subject to periods of remission. When such periods occur, consider discontinuing corticosteroids gradually. Continued supervision of the patient after cessation of corticosteroids is essential since there may be a reappearance of severe manifestations of the disease.

Alternate day therapy in which a single dose is administered every other morning is considered by many clinicians to be the dosage regimen of choice for long-term corticosteroid treatment of most conditions; however, this remains controversial. Morning administration of the drug simulates the natural circadian rhythm of corticosteroid secretion which is high in the morning and low in the evening. This regimen provides relief of symptoms while minimizing adrenal suppression, cushingoid state, withdrawal symptoms and growth suppression in children. Intermediate-acting agents should be used for alternate day therapy (see Table I).

The reader is referred to individual product monographs for more specific dosing information.

Reviewed 1998

CORTICOSTEROIDS: TOPICAL ℞*

General Monograph, CPhA

Amcinonide
Betamethasone
Clobetasol
Clobetasone
Desonide
Desoximetasone
Diflucortolone
Flumethasone
Fluocinolone
Fluocinonide
Flurandrenolide
Halcinonide
Halobetasol
Hydrocortisone
Methylprednisolone
Mometasone
Triamcinolone

> This monograph has been compiled by CPhA. It may contain information different from that approved by Therapeutic Products Programme, Health Canada, and the pharmaceutical manufacturers' approval has not been requested.

Pharmacology: Topical corticosteroids are synthetic derivatives of cortisone which are effective when applied locally to control many types of inflammatory, allergic and pruritic dermatoses. Certain modifications to the chemical structure of hydrocortisone increase the anti-inflammatory potency of the molecule (see Table I). For example, introduction of fluorine atoms into the molecule enhances anti-inflammatory activity. The more potent topical corticosteroids are generally more effective and more likely to cause adverse effects than less potent preparations.

Topically applied corticosteroids are thought to act by controlling the rate of synthesis of proteins. The overall effect of corticosteroids is a catabolic one. With repeated administration to the same site, 3 times daily for 4 to 5 days, tolerance to the anti-inflammatory effects of the drug may occur. Withdrawal of the drug for 2 to 4 days should restore the response; however, tolerance will recur once application is restarted. Many dermatological disorders respond equally well to low potency corticosteroids such as hydrocortisone, although for severe acute dermatoses a more potent preparation may be preferred initially. Some dermatoses may require occlusion of the drug under a plastic film or intralesional administration.

Pharmacokinetics: Following topical application to normal skin, corticosteroids are minimally absorbed. Only small amounts of drug reach the dermis and are then absorbed into the systemic circulation. Absorption is greater when corticosteroids are applied to certain areas of the body, including the scalp, face, eyelid, axilla and scrotum. Absorption will also be increased by different vehicles, use of an occlusive dressing or if the epidermis is damaged by disease or inflammation. Continued absorption of corticosteroids may occur, even after washing, due to retention of the drug in the stratum corneum.

Following rectal administration or application of corticosteroids to the mucosa of the genitourinary tract, significant systemic absorption may occur. As much as 30 to 90% of hydrocortisone when administered as a retention enema may be absorbed. Absorption will be further increased if the mucosa is inflamed. HPA axis suppression may occur.

Indications: Topical therapy of corticosteroid responsive acute and chronic skin eruptions, where an anti-inflammatory, antiallergenic and antipruritic activity is required in the topical management of these conditions.

Corticosteroid enemas are used as adjunctive therapy in the management of certain inflammatory diseases involving the rectum, or sigmoid and left colon.

Table I—Corticosteroids: Topical

Corticosteroids Potency Comparison Chart
Weak
Hydrocortisone
Hydrocortisone acetate
Methylprednisolone
Methylprednisolone acetate
Moderately Potent
Clobetasone 17-butyrate
Desonide
Flumethasone pivalate
Flurandrenolide
Hydrocortisone valerate
Triamcinolone acetonide
Potent
Amcinonide
Betamethasone benzoate
Betamethasone valerate
Desoximetasone
Diflucortolone diacetate
Fluocinolone acetonide
Fluocinonide
Halcinonide
Mometasone furoate
Very Potent
Betamethasone dipropionate
Clobetasol 17-propionate
Halobetasol propionate

Contraindications: Untreated tubercular, bacterial and fungal infections involving the skin, and in certain viral diseases such as herpes simplex, chickenpox, and vaccinia; hypersensitivity to any of the components of the product.

Warnings: If used under an occlusive dressing, particularly over extensive areas, or on the face, scalp, axilla(e), scrotum or when applied to the genitourinary tract or when administered rectally, sufficient absorption may take place to give rise to adrenal suppression and other systemic effects.

Precautions: Topical corticosteroids (particularly the potent ones) should be used with caution on lesions close to the eye because systemic absorption may cause increased intraocular pressure, glaucoma or cataracts.

Tolerance to the vasoconstrictive effects of topical corticosteroids may occur with repeated administration (see Pharmacology).

Although hypersensitivity reactions have been rare with topically applied steroid products, the drug should be discontinued and appropriate therapy initiated if there are signs of reaction.

Prolonged use of topical corticosteroid products may produce atrophy of the skin and of subcutaneous tissues particularly on flexor surfaces and on the face. If this is noted, discontinue the use of the product.

In cases of infections of the skin, appropriate anti-infective agents should be used in primary therapy. In selected cases, the topical corticosteroid product may be used as an adjunct to control inflammation, erythema, and itching.

Topical corticosteroids should be used with caution in patients with stasis dermatitis and other skin diseases associated with impaired circulation.

If a symptomatic response is not noted within a few days to a week, the local applications of corticosteroid should be discontinued and the patient re-evaluated. During the use of topical corticosteroids secondary infections may occur.

Under certain circumstances such as prolonged use, application over a large area of the body, use of an occlusive dressing, administration by retention enema, use in children or infants or use of a potent agent, adverse systemic corticosteroid effects may occur. If long-term therapy is anticipated, measures such as interrupting treatment periodically or treating one body area at a time may help to minimize the risk of adverse systemic effects. When long-term rectal use is discontinued, it must be tapered gradually.

Patients should be advised to inform current and subsequent physicians of the prior use of corticosteroids.

Occlusive dressings should not be applied if there is an elevation of body temperature.

Pregnancy and *Lactation:* The safety of topical corticosteroids during pregnancy or lactation has not been established. The potential benefit of topical corticosteroids, if used during pregnancy or lactation, should be weighed against possible hazard to the fetus or the nursing infant.

Children: Pediatric patients have a higher skin surface to body weight ratio than do adults and may absorb a higher percentage of topically applied corticosteroids. This may translate into a greater susceptibility to topical corticosteroid-induced HPA axis suppression and to exogenous corticosteroid effects.

HPA axis suppression, Cushing's syndrome, linear growth retardation, delayed weight gain, and intracranial hypertension have been reported in children receiving topical corticosteroids. Manifestations of adrenal suppression in children include low plasma cortisol levels and absence of response to ACTH stimulation. Manifestations of intracranial hypertension include bulging fontanelle, headaches and bilateral papilledema.

Adverse Effects: The following local adverse reactions have been reported with the use of topical corticosteroids: dryness, itching, burning, local irritation, striae, skin atrophy, atrophy of subcutaneous tissues, telangiectasia, hypertrichosis, change in pigmentation and secondary infection. If applied to the face, acne rosacea or perioral dermatitis can occur. When occlusive dressings are used, pustules, miliaria, folliculitis and pyoderma may occur. Contact sensitivity to a particular dressing material or adhesive may occur occasionally.

In rare instances, treatment of psoriasis with systemic or very potent topical corticosteroids (or their withdrawal) is thought to have provoked the pustular form of the disease.

Adrenal suppression has also been reported following topical corticosteroid therapy. Conditions that may increase systemic adsorption include use of the more potent steroids, use over a prolonged period of time, use over large surface area and an occlusive dressing.

Overdose: Symptoms and Treatment: Overdosage is very unlikely to occur. However, in the case of chronic overdosage or misuse, the features of hypercorticism may appear. Recovery of the HPA axis is usually prompt and complete following discontinuation of the topical steroid; however, if symptoms of adrenal insufficiency occur, supplemental oral steroid therapy may be initiated and tapered off gradually.

Dosage: Generally, the least potent effective agent should be used. Ointments may be preferred for dry, scaly lesions. Creams, which are more acceptable cosmetically, are used for most inflammatory lesions. In hairy areas, a lotion or a liquefying vehicle such as a gel may permit better skin contact than creams or ointments. Some, but not all, topical corticosteroids are formulated in bases free of sensitizing agents.

Apply the corticosteroid preparation sparingly to the clean affected skin area(s) either with gentle massage or use under occlusive dressings, as prescribed. Once control is achieved, reduce frequency of application.

Areas of increased permeability (scrotum, axilla, eyelids, scalp and face) respond better than areas such as the forearm, knee, elbow, palm and sole.

Frequency of application has traditionally been 3 to 4 times daily. Because of the repository effect of topical corticosteroids, less frequent applications (1 to 2 times per day) are equally effective.

For instillation of retention enemas, the patient should lie on his left side during administration and for 30 minutes after. The enema should be retained for at least 1 hour and preferably overnight. Various dosage regimens are used, depending on the indication, severity of symptoms and individual response.

*Hydrocortisone single-entity products of strengths less than or equal to 0.5% are available without a prescription.

Reviewed 1998

CORTIFOAM™ Ⓟ
R & C

Hydrocortisone Acetate
Rectal Anti-inflammatory

Pharmacology: Action appears to be due to a local anti-inflammatory effect of hydrocortisone on the mucosa rather than as a result of a systemic effect.

Indications: As adjunctive therapy in the treatment of ulcerative colitis of the sigmoid colon, proctosigmoiditis, granular proctitis and ulcerative proctitis.

Contraindications: To the use of intrarectal steroids include, obstruction, abscess, perforation, peritonitis, fresh intestinal anastomoses, extensive fistulas and sinus tracts. Tuberculosis (active, latent or questionably healed), ocular herpes simplex, varicella, vaccinia, and acute psychosis are usually considered contraindications to the use of corticosteroids.

Other contraindications include peptic ulcer, acute glomerulonephritis, myasthenia gravis, osteoporosis, diverticulitis, thrombophlebitis, psychic disturbances, pregnancy, diabetes, hyperthyroidism, acute coronary disease, hypertension, limited cardiac reserve, and local or systemic infections, including fungal or exanthematous diseases. Where these conditions exist, the expected benefits from steroid therapy must be weighed against the risks involved in its use.

In systemic fungal infection and in the presence of hypersensitivity to any of its components.

Warnings: Caution: Contents are flammable and the aerosol container may explode if heated.

Do not insert any part of the aerosol container into the anus. Do not use in presence of open flame or spark. Contents under pressure. Do not place in hot water or near radiators, stoves or other sources of heat. Do not puncture or incinerate container or store at temperatures over 50°C. Because the drug is not expelled, systemic hydrocortisone absorption may be greater from the foam than from corticosteroid enema formulations. If there is no evidence of clinical or proctologic improvement within 2 or 3 weeks after starting therapy, or if the patient's condition worsens, discontinue the drug.

Signs and symptoms of intestinal perforation and peritonitis may be difficult to detect during corticosteroid treatment.

Precautions: A complete rectal examination to rule out serious pathology and extension of the disease process should be completed before instituting therapy.

Do not use on infected lesions unless accompanied with anti-infective agents.

Steroid therapy should be administered with caution in patients with severe ulcerative disease because these patients are predisposed to perforation of the bowel wall. Where surgery is imminent, it is hazardous to wait more than a few days for a satisfactory response to medical treatment. General precautions common to all corticosteroid therapy should be observed during treatment. These include gradual withdrawal of therapy to allow for possible adrenal insufficiency and awareness of possible growth suppression in children. Patients should be kept under close observation, for as with all drugs, rare individuals may react unfavorably under certain conditions. If severe reactions or idiosyncrasies occur, steroids should be discontinued immediately and appropriate measures instituted. Do not employ in immediate or early postoperative period following ileorectostomy.

Patients should be advised to inform subsequent physicians of the prior use of corticosteroids.

Pregnancy: Steroids should not be used during pregnancy since safety during pregnancy has not been fully established.

If corticosteroids must be administered during pregnancy, particularly during the third trimester, the newborn infant must be observed closely for signs of hypoadrenalism, and the appropriate therapy administered if needed.

Lactation: Mothers using hydrocortisone should be advised not to nurse.

Adverse Effects: Corticosteroid therapy may produce side effects which include moon face, fluid retention, excessive appetite and weight gain, abnormal fat deposits, mental symptoms, hypertrichosis, acne, ecchymosis, increased sweating, pigmentation, dry scaly skin, thinning scalp hair, thrombophlebitis, decreased resistance to infection, negative nitrogen balance with delayed bone and wound healing, menstrual disorders, neuropathy, peptic ulcer, decreased glucose tolerance, hypokalemia, adrenal insufficiency, necrotizing angiitis, hypertension, pancreatitis and increased intraocular pressure. In children, suppression of growth may occur. Increased intracranial pressure may occur and possibly account for headache, insomnia and fatigue. Subcapsular cataracts may result from prolonged usage. Long-term use of all corticosteroids results in catabolic effects characterized by negative protein and calcium balance. Osteoporosis, spontaneous fractures and aseptic necrosis of the hip and humerus may occur as part of this catabolic phenomenon. Where hypokalemia and other symptoms associated with fluid and electrolyte imbalance call for potassium supplementation and salt poor or salt-free diets, these may be instituted and are compatible with diet requirements for ulcerative proctitis.

Local effects of itching and burning have been reported following rectal use.

Overdose: Symptoms: Acute toxicity, even with massive doses is not a clinical problem. Chronic toxicity involves manifestations of the physiologic effects described above and include Cushingoid appearance, muscle weakness, osteoporosis, posterior subcapsular cataracts, peptic ulcers, hypertension, psychosis, and growth suppression in children. Glaucoma, pancreatitis, reactivation of tuberculosis and poor wound healing may occur. Sodium and fluid retention with potassium loss occur to varying degrees, depending upon the mineralocorticoid effects of the particular corticosteroid.

Treatment: Acute overdosage probably requires no treatment. Acute overdosage requires no tapering as in withdrawal of patients on long-term administration. If there is any question that other drugs have been ingested simultaneously, then standard measures for those drugs should be followed as per instructions for their management. Avoid chronic dosage for durations greater than 3 weeks when possible.

When chronic dosage for periods greater than 3 weeks is essential, attempts should be made to manage the underlying disease if possible with alternate day dosage using single daily doses on alternate mornings of shorter acting preparations such as prednisone, prednisolone or methylprednisolone.

Even with alternate day dosage of appropriate agents, continued attempts should be made to minimize dosage compatible with maintained control of the underlying disease.

The diet should have adequate protein content but caloric restrictions should be considered because of the apparent appetite stimulating properties of the corticosteroids.

The ultimate treatment of toxicity should be avoidance of inappropriate usage or if toxicity is already present, withdrawal of the corticosteroids and conventional management of those effects which are treatable such as peptic ulcers, cataracts and hypertension.

Dosage: Usual dose is 1 applicatorful once or twice daily for 2 or 3 weeks, and every second day thereafter, administered rectally. The patient direction insert describes how to use the aerosol container and applicator. Satisfactory response usually occurs within 5 to 7 days marked by a decrease in symptoms. Symptomatic improvement should not be used as the sole criterion for evaluating efficacy. Sigmoidoscopy is also recommended to judge dosage adjustment, duration of therapy and rate of improvement.

Supplied: Each applicatorful delivers approximately 900 mg of foam containing approximately 80 mg of hydrocortisone (as hydrocortisone acetate 90 mg). Nonmedicinal ingredients: cetyl alcohol, ethoxylated stearyl alcohol, methylparaben, polyoxyethylene-10 stearyl ether, propylene glycol, propylparaben, triethanolamine, water and inert propellants, isobutane and propane. Aerosol containers of 15 g with a special rectal applicator will deliver approximately 14 applications.

Contents are flammable and are under pressure. Do not use in presence of open flame or spark. Do not place in hot water or near radiators, stoves or other sources of heat. Do not puncture or incinerate container or store at temperatures over 50°C.

Reviewed 1998

CORTIMYXIN® Ⓟ
Sabex

Hydrocortisone—Neomycin Sulfate—Polymyxin B Sulfate
Anti-inflammatory—Antibacterial

Supplied: Each mL of otic solution contains: polymyxin B sulfate 10 000 units, neomycin sulfate equivalent to 3.5 mg neomycin base and hydrocortisone 10 mg (1%). Nonmedicinal ingredients: copper sulfate pentahydrate, glycerin, polysorbate 80, potassium metabisulfite, propylene glycol, sulfuric acid and/or potassium hydroxide to adjust pH and water for injection. Dropper bottles of 10 mL. Store between 15 and 30°C.

CORTISONE Ⓟ
General Monograph, CPhA

see CORTICOSTEROIDS: SYSTEMIC

CORTISONE ACETATE—ICN Ⓟ
ICN

Cortisone Acetate
Corticosteroid

Supplied: Each white, scored, compressed tablet, imprinted ICN C23, contains: cortisone acetate, USP 25 mg. Nonmedicinal ingredients: cornstarch croscarmellose sodium and lactose. Bottles of 100.

CORTISPORIN® ℞

Glaxo Wellcome

Hydrocortisone—Neomycin—Polymyxin B Compound

Anti-inflammatory—Antibacterial

Pharmacology: Corticosteroids suppress the inflammatory response to a variety of agents and they may delay healing. Since corticosteroids may inhibit the body's defense mechanism against infection, a concomitant antimicrobial drug may be used when this inhibition is considered to be clinically significant in a particular case.

The anti-infective components in the combination are included to provide action against specific organisms susceptible to them. Polymyxin B sulfate, bacitracin and neomycin sulfate together are considered active against the following microorganisms: S. aureus, E. coli, H. influenzae, Klebsiella-Enterobacter species, Neisseria species and P. aeruginosa. This product does not provide adequate coverage against S. marcescens and Streptococci, including S. pneumoniae.

When used topically, polymyxin B, bacitracin and neomycin are rarely irritating and absorption from the intact skin or mucous membrane is insignificant. The incidence of skin sensitization to this combination has been shown to be low on normal skin. Since these antibiotics are seldom used systemically, the patient is spared sensitization to those antibiotics which might later be required systemically.

The relative potency of corticosteroids depends on the molecular structure, concentration, and release from the vehicle.

Indications: Eye/Ear Suspension: For the treatment of nonpurulent bacterial, allergic, vernal and phlyctenular conjunctivitis; nonpurulent blepharitis and episcleritis; interstitial, sclerosing, postoperative or acne rosacea keratitis; chemical and thermal burns of the cornea; superficial bacterial infections of the external auditory canal; infections of mastoidectomy and fenestration cavities caused by organisms susceptible to the antibiotics.

Ointment: Inflammation of anterior segment of eye; skin infections and inflammation.

Ophthalmic Ointment: For the treatment of nonpurulent bacterial, allergic, vernal and phlyctenular conjunctivitis; nonpurulent blepharitis and episcleritis; interstitial, sclerosing, postoperative or acne rosacea keratitis, chemical and thermal burns of the cornea.

Otic Solution: For the treatment of superficial bacterial infections of the external auditory canal caused by organisms susceptible to the action of the antibiotics.

Children: Caution: Safety of corticosteroid in children of the age group 2 years or below has not been established.

Contraindications: Eye/Ear Suspension and Ophthalmic Ointment: In acute purulent conjunctivitis and blepharitis; mycobacterial, fungal or viral lesions of the skin or eye, including herpes simplex, vaccinia, varicella and dendritic keratitis; and in conditions involving the posterior segment of the eye.

For otic use this product is contraindicated in tuberculous, fungal or viral lesions.

This product is contraindicated in those individuals who have shown hypersensitivity to any of its components.

The use of these combinations is always contraindicated after uncomplicated removal of a corneal foreign body.

Only the ophthalmic 3.5 g tube is for use in the eyes and not the regular topical ointment.

Ointment not for use in the external ear canal if the eardrum is perforated.

A possibility of increased neomycin absorption exists in neonates and infants, thus Cortisporin is not recommended for use in neonates, and should be used at reduced dosages in infants.

Warnings: When using neomycin-containing products to control secondary infection in the chronic dermatoses, such as chronic otitis externa or stasis dermatitis, it should be borne in mind that the skin in these conditions is more liable than is normal skin to become sensitized to many substances including neomycin.

The manifestation of sensitization to neomycin is usually a low-grade reddening with swelling, dry scaling and itching. It may be manifested simply as a failure to heal. Periodic examination for such signs is advisable, and the patient should be told to discontinue the product if they are observed. These symptoms regress quickly on withdrawing the medication. Neomycin-containing applications should be avoided for the patient thereafter.

Neomycin may cause cutaneous sensitization. A precise incidence of hypersensitivity reactions (primarily skin rash) due to topical neomycin is not known.

In neonates and infants, absorption by immature skin may be enhanced. Immaturity of renal function may predispose these patients to decreased elimination and increased blood levels.

Ophthalmic Ointment: Use of steroid medication in the treatment of herpes simplex requires great caution.

Acute purulent untreated infections of the eye may be masked or enhanced by the presence of a steroid.

Because of the concern of nephrotoxicity and ototoxicity associated with neomycin, the ointment should not be used over a wide area or for extended periods of time.

Prolonged ophthalmic use may result in glaucoma, with damage to the optic nerve, defects in visual acuity and fields of vision and posterior subcapsular cataract formation.

Prolonged use may suppress the host response and thus increase the hazard of secondary ocular infections. In those diseases causing thinning of the cornea or sclera, perforations have been known to occur with the use of topical steroids. In acute purulent conditions of the eye, steroids may mask infection or enhance existing infection. If these products are used for 10 days or longer, intraocular pressure should be routinely monitored even though it may be difficult in children and uncooperative patients.

Eye/Ear Suspension: The eye/ear suspension should be used with caution in cases of perforated ear drum and in long-standing cases of chronic otitis media, because of the possibility of ototoxicity. In otic use, ototoxicity has been reported (see Adverse Effects).

Prolonged ophthalmic use may result in glaucoma, with damage to the optic nerve, defects in visual acuity and fields of vision and posterior subcapsular cataract formation.

Prolonged use may suppress the host response and thus increase the hazard of secondary ocular infections. In those diseases causing thinning of the cornea or sclera, perforations have been known to occur with the use of topical steroids. In acute purulent conditions of the eye, steroids may mask infection or enhance existing infection. If these products are used for 10 days or longer, intraocular pressure should be routinely monitored even though it may be difficult in children and uncooperative patients.

Otic Solution: The otic solution should be used with care when the integrity of the tympanic membrane is in question because of the possibility of ototoxicity caused by neomycin. Stinging and burning may occur when this product gains access to the middle ear.

The otic solution contains potassium metabisulfite, a sulfite that may cause allergic-type reactions including anaphylactic symptoms and life-threatening or less severe asthmatic episodes in certain susceptible people. The overall prevalence of sulfite sensitivity in the general population is unknown and probably low. Sulfite sensitivity is seen more frequently in asthmatic than in nonasthmatic people.

Precautions: As with any antibiotic preparation, prolonged use may result in the overgrowth of nonsusceptible organisms, including fungi. The possibility of persistent fungal infections of the cornea and ear should be considered after prolonged steroid dosing. Appropriate measures should be taken if this occurs. If the infection is not improved after 1 week, cultures and susceptibility tests should be repeated to verify the identity of the organism and to determine whether therapy should be changed.

Signs and symptoms of exogenous hyperadrenocorticism can occur with the use of topical corticosteroids, including adrenal suppression. Systemic absorption of topically applied steroids will be increased if extensive body surface areas are treated or if occlusive dressings are used. Under these circumstances, suitable precautions should be taken when long-term use is anticipated.

Treatment with the otic solution should not be continued for longer than 10 days.

Allergic cross-reactions may occur which could prevent the use of any or all of the following antibiotics for the treatment of future infections: kanamycin, paromomycin, streptomycin, and possibly gentamicin.

Laboratory Tests: Systemic effects of excessive levels of hydrocortisone may include a reduction in the number of circulating eosinophils and a decrease in urinary excretion of 17-hydroxycorticosteroids.

Carcinogenicity: Long-term studies in animals (rats, rabbits, mice) showed no evidence of carcinogenicity attributable to oral administration of corticosteroids.

Pregnancy and *Lactation:* There is little information to demonstrate the possible effect of topically applied neomycin in pregnancy and lactation. However, neomycin present in maternal blood can cross the placenta and may give rise to a theoretical risk of fetal toxicity, thus use of Cortisporin is not recommended in pregnancy and lactation.

Children: Safety of corticosteroids in children aged 2 years or younger has not been established. Sufficient absorption of hydrocortisone can occur in infants and children during prolonged use to cause cessation of growth, as well as other systemic signs and symptoms of hyperadrenocorticism.

Use of steroids on infected areas should be supervised with care as anti-inflammatory steroids may encourage spread of infection. If this occurs steroid therapy should be stopped and appropriate antibacterial drugs used. Generalized dermatological conditions may require systemic corticosteroid therapy.

The initial prescription and renewal of the eye/ear suspension order beyond 10 days or of the ophthalmic ointment beyond 7 g should be made by a physician only after examination of the patient; in the case of ophthalmic use, with the aid of magnification, such as slit lamp biomicroscopy and, where appropriate, fluorescein staining.

Information for the Patient: Eye/Ear Suspension and Otic Solution: Avoid contaminating the dropper with material from the ear, fingers, or other source. This caution is necessary if the sterility of the drops is to be preserved. If sensitization or irritation occurs, discontinue use immediately and contact your physician.

Eye/Ear Suspension: **Shake well before using.**

Otic Solution: Do not use in the eyes.

If redness, irritation, swelling or pain persists or increases, discontinue use and notify physician.

Adverse Effects: Neomycin occasionally causes skin sensitization. Adverse reactions have occurred with topical use of antibiotic combinations including neomycin and polymyxin B. Exact incidence figures are not available since no denominator of treated patients is available. The reaction occurring most often is allergic sensitization. In one clinical study, using a 20% neomycin patch, neomycin-induced allergic skin reactions occurred in 2 of 2.175 (0.09%) individuals in the general population. In another study, the incidence was found to be approximately 1%. When steroid preparations are used for long periods of time in intertriginous areas or over extensive body areas, with or without occlusive nonpermeable dressings, striae may occur; also there exists the possibility of systemic adverse effects when steroid preparations are used over larger areas or for a long period of time.

The following local adverse reactions have been reported with topical corticosteroids, especially under occlusive dressings: burning, itching, irritation, dryness, folliculitis, hypertrichosis, acneiform eruptions, hypopigmentation, perioral dermatitis, allergic contact dermatitis, maceration of the skin, secondary infection, skin atrophy, milaria.

Eye/Ear Suspension and Sterile Ophthalmic Ointment: Reactions occurring most often from the presence of the anti-infective ingredient in ophthalmic use are localized hypersensitivity, including itching, swelling and conjunctival erythema. Local irritation on instillation has also been reported.

The reactions due to the steroid component, in decreasing order of frequency, are elevation of intraocular pressure with possible development of glaucoma and infrequent optic nerve damage, posterior subcapsular cataract formation and delayed wound healing.

In otic use, ototoxicity and nephrotoxcity have also been reported (see Warnings).

Stinging and burning have been reported rarely when this product has gained access to the middle ear.

Otic Solution: Stinging and burning have been reported when this product has gained access to the middle ear.

Secondary Infection: The development of secondary infection has occurred after use of combinations containing steroids and antimicrobials. Fungal infections of the cornea are particularly prone to develop coincidentally with long-term applications of steroid. The possibility of fungal invasion must be considered in any persistent corneal ulceration where steroid treatment has been used.

Secondary bacterial infection following suppression of host responses also occurs.

Overdose: Symptoms and Treatment: Treatment is symptomatic.

Dosage: A possibility of increased neomycin absorption exists in neonates and infants, thus Cortisporin is not recommended for use in neonates, and should be used at reduced dosages in infants.

Eye/Ear Suspension: Ophthalmic: 1 or 2 drops in the affected eye every 3 or 4 hours, depending on the severity of the condition.

Otic: The external auditory canal should be thoroughly cleansed and dried with a sterile cotton applicator. Three or

4 drops in the ear 3 to 4 times daily. For infants and children, the dose should be reduced, 3 drops are suggested because of the smaller capacity of the ear canal.

The patient should lie with the affected ear upward and then the drops should be instilled. This position should be maintained for 5 minutes to facilitate penetration of the drops into the ear canal. Repeat, if necessary, for the opposite ear.

If preferred, a cotton wick may be inserted into the canal and then the cotton may be saturated with the solution. This wick should be kept moist by adding further solution every 4 hours. The wick should be replaced at least once every 24 hours.

Not more than a 10-day supply should be prescribed initially and the prescription should not be refilled without further evaluation as outlined in Precautions.

The patient should be instructed to avoid contaminating the dropper with material from the eye, ear, fingers, or other sources. This caution is necessary if the sterility of the suspension is to be preserved.

Shake well before using.

Ointment: Apply thin film 2 to 4 times daily.

Ophthalmic Ointment: Apply in the affected eye every 3 or 4 hours, depending on the severity of the condition.

Otic Solution: Adults: 4 drops of the solution should be instilled into the affected ear 3 or 4 times daily. Infants and Children: 3 drops are suggested because of the smaller capacity of the ear canal.

The patient should lie with the affected ear upward and then the drops should be instilled. This position should be maintained for 5 minutes to facilitate penetration of the drops into the ear canal. Repeat, if necessary for the opposite ear.

If preferred, a cotton wick may be inserted into the canal and then the cotton may be saturated with the solution. This wick should be kept moist by adding further solution every 4 hours. The wick should be replaced at least once every 24 hours.

Supplied: Eye/Ear Suspension: Each mL of sterile eye/ear suspension contains: polymyxin B sulfate 10 000 units, neomycin sulfate equivalent to 3.5 mg neomycin base and hydrocortisone 10 mg (1%). Nonmedicinal ingredients: benzalkonium chloride (preservative), cetyl alcohol, glyceryl monostearate, mineral oil, polyoxyethylene stearate, propylene glycol, sulfuric acid (may be added to adjust pH) and water for injection. Bottles of 10 mL.

Ointment: Each g of ointment contains: polymyxin B sulfate 5 000 units, zinc bacitracin 400 units, neomycin sulfate 5 mg, hydrocortisone 10 mg in a low melting point petrolatum base. Tubes of 15 g.

Ophthalmic Ointment: Each g of sterile ophthalmic ointment contains: polymyxin B sulfate 10 000 units, zinc bacitracin 400 units, neomycin sulfate 5 mg, hydrocortisone 10 mg in a low melting point petrolatum base. Tubes of 3.5 g.

Otic Solution: Each mL of sterile otic solution contains: polymyxin B sulfate 10 000 units, neomycin sulfate equivalent to 3.5 mg neomycin base, and hydrocortisone 10 mg (1%). Nonmedicinal ingredients: cupric sulfate, glycerin, potassium metabisulfite and propylene glycol. Bottles of 10 mL with sterilized dropper.

Store between 15 and 25°C.

Reviewed 1999

CORTODERM
Taro

Hydrocortisone

Topical Corticosteroid

Supplied: Mild: Each g of soft emollient ointment contains: hydrocortisone 0.5% in a petrolatum base with fractionated coconut oil and methylparaben and propylparaben. Tubes of 15 g and jars of 454 g.

Regular ℞: Each g of soft emollient ointment contains: hydrocortisone 1% in a petrolatum base with fractionated coconut oil and methylparaben and propylparaben. Tubes of 15 g and jars of 454 g.

...For assistance in the visual identification of drug dosage forms, refer to the PRODUCT RECOGNITION SECTION.

CORTONE® Suspension ℞
MSD

Cortisone Acetate

Corticosteroid

Pharmacology: Cortisone is a natural product of the adrenal cortex. Cortisone is a synthetic steroid with the basic actions and effects of other glucocorticoids.

Cortisone sterile suspension has a slow onset but long duration of action when compared with more soluble preparations. When daily corticosteroid therapy is required and oral therapy is not feasible, the required daily dosage may be given in a single i.m. injection of this preparation.

Naturally occurring glucocorticoids (hydrocortisone and cortisone), which also have salt-retaining properties, are used as replacement therapy in adrenocortical deficiency states. They are also used for their potent anti-inflammatory effects in disorders of many organ systems.

Glucocorticoids cause profound and varied metabolic effects. In addition, they modify the body's immune responses to diverse stimuli.

Indications: When oral therapy is not feasible:
Endocrine Disorders: Primary or secondary adrenocortical insufficiency (hydrocortisone or cortisone is the drug of choice; synthetic analogs may be used in conjunction with mineralocorticoids where applicable; in infancy, mineralocorticoid supplementation is of particular importance). Acute adrenocortical insufficiency (hydrocortisone or cortisone is the drug of choice; mineralocorticoid supplementation may be necessary, particularly when synthetic analogs are used). Preoperatively, and in the event of serious trauma or illness, in patients with known adrenal insufficiency or when adrenocortical reserve is doubtful. Shock unresponsive to conventional therapy if adrenocortical insufficiency exists or is suspected. Congenital adrenal hyperplasia. Nonsuppurative thyroiditis. Hypercalcemia associated with cancer.
Rheumatic Disorders: As adjunctive therapy for short-term administration (to tide the patient over an acute episode or exacerbation) in: post-traumatic osteoarthritis, synovitis of osteoarthritis, rheumatoid arthritis, including juvenile rheumatoid arthritis (selected cases may require low-dose maintenance therapy), acute and subacute bursitis, epicondylitis, acute nonspecific tenosynovitis, acute gouty arthritis, psoriatic arthritis, ankylosing spondylitis.
Collagen Diseases: During an exacerbation or as maintenance therapy in selected cases of: systemic lupus erythematosus, acute rheumatic carditis, systemic dermatomyositis (polymyositis).
Dermatologic Diseases: pemphigus, severe erythema multiforme (Stevens-Johnson syndrome), exfoliative dermatitis, bullous dermatitis herpetiformis, severe seborrheic dermatitis, severe psoriasis, mycosis fungoides.
Allergic States: Control of severe or incapacitating allergic conditions intractable to adequate trials of conventional treatment in: bronchial asthma, contact dermatitis, atopic dermatitis, serum sickness, seasonal or perennial allergic rhinitis, drug hypersensitivity reactions, urticarial transfusion reactions, acute noninfectious laryngeal edema (epinephrine is the drug of first choice).
Ophthalmic Diseases: Severe acute and chronic allergic and inflammatory processes involving the eye such as: herpes zoster ophthalmicus, iritis, iridocyclitis, chorioretinitis, diffuse posterior uveitis and choroiditis, optic neuritis, sympathetic ophthalmia, anterior segment inflammation, allergic conjunctivitis, keratitis, allergic corneal marginal ulcers.
Gastrointestinal Diseases: To tide the patient over a critical period of the disease in: ulcerative colitis (systemic therapy), regional enteritis (systemic therapy).
Respiratory Diseases: symptomatic sarcoidosis, berylliosis, fulminating or disseminated pulmonary tuberculosis when used concurrently with appropriate antituberculous chemotherapy, Löffler's syndrome not manageable by other means, aspiration pneumonitis.
Hematologic Disorders: acquired (autoimmune) hemolytic anemia, erythroblastopenia (RBC anemia), congenital (erythroid) hypoplastic anemia.
Neoplastic Diseases: For palliative management of: leukemias and lymphomas in adults, acute leukemia of childhood.
Edematous States: To induce diuresis or remission of proteinuria in the nephrotic syndrome without uremia, of the idiopathic type or that due to lupus erythematosus.
Miscellaneous: Tuberculous meningitis with subarachnoid block or impending block when used concurrently with appropriate antituberculous chemotherapy, trichinosis with neurologic or myocardial involvement.

Contraindications: Systemic fungal infections.

Hypersensitivity to any component of this product.

As with all corticosteroids, do not use in infected areas or unstable joints, as in the case of osteoporosis around the joint and/or severe joint destruction.

Tuberculosis, whether active or healed, ocular herpes simplex and acute psychoses are usually absolute contraindications to systemic steroid therapy.

The use of sterile suspension cortisone in active tuberculosis should be restricted to those cases of fulminating or disseminated tuberculosis in which the corticosteroid is used for the management of the disease in conjunction with an appropriate antituberculous regimen.

If corticosteroids are indicated in patients with latent tuberculosis or tuberculin reactivity, close observation is necessary, as reactivation of the disease may occur. During prolonged corticosteroid therapy, these patients should receive chemoprophylaxis.

Warnings: Cortisone sterile suspension is for i.m. use only and is not suitable for i.v. or intrathecal injection.

Because rare instances of anaphylactoid reactions have occurred in patients receiving parenteral corticosteroid therapy, appropriate precautionary measures should be taken prior to administration, especially when the patient has a history of allergy to any drug.

In patients on corticosteroid therapy subjected to any unusual stress, increased dosage of rapidly acting corticosteroids before, during, and after the stressful situation is indicated.

Drug-induced secondary adrenocortical insufficiency may result from too rapid withdrawal of corticosteroids and may be minimized by gradual reduction of dosage. This type of relative insufficiency may persist for months after discontinuation of therapy; therefore, in any situation of stress occurring during that period, corticosteroid therapy should be reinstituted. If the patient is receiving steroids already, dosage may have to be increased. Since mineralocorticoid secretion may be impaired, salt and/or a mineralocorticoid should be administered concurrently.

Corticosteroids may mask some signs of infection, and new infections may appear during their use. There may be decreased resistance and inability to localize infection when corticosteroids are used. Moreover, corticosteroids may affect the nitroblue-tetrazolium test for bacterial infection and produce false-negative results.

Corticosteroids may exacerbate systemic fungal infections and therefore should not be used in the presence of such infections unless they are needed to control drug reactions due to amphotericin B. Moreover, there have been cases reported in which concomitant use of amphotericin B and hydrocortisone was followed by cardiac enlargement and congestive failure.

Literature reports suggest an apparent association between use of corticosteroids and left ventricular free wall rupture after a recent myocardial infarction; therefore, therapy with corticosteroids should be used with great caution in these patients.

In cerebral malaria, the use of corticosteroids is associated with prolongation of coma and higher incidence of pneumonia and gastrointestinal bleeding.

Corticosteroids may activate latent amebiasis. Therefore, it is recommended that latent or active amebiasis be ruled out before initiating corticosteroid therapy in any patient who has spent time in the tropics or any patient with unexplained diarrhea.

Prolonged use of corticosteroids may produce posterior subcapsular cataracts, glaucoma with possible damage to the optic nerves, and may enhance the establishment of secondary ocular infections due to fungi or viruses. Corticosteroids should be used cautiously in patients with ocular herpes simplex for fear of corneal perforation.

Average and large doses of cortisone or hydrocortisone can cause elevation of blood pressure, salt and water retention, and increased excretion of potassium. These effects are less likely to occur with the synthetic derivatives except when used in large doses. Dietary salt restriction and potassium supplementation may be necessary. All corticosteroids increase calcium excretion.

Administration of live virus vaccines, including smallpox, is contraindicated in individuals receiving immunosuppressive doses of corticosteroids. If inactivated viral or bacterial vaccines are administered to individuals receiving immunosuppressive doses of corticosteroids, the expected serum antibody response may not be obtained.

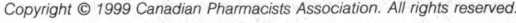

Strict aseptic technique is mandatory. Use of disposable syringes minimizes the possibility of infection. If disposable

Cortone Suspension (cont'd)

syringes are not available, autoclaved syringes should be used.

Pregnancy: Pregnancy is a relative contraindication to corticosteroid therapy, particularly during the first trimester, because fetal abnormalities have been observed in experimental animals. Since adequate human reproduction studies have not been done with corticosteroids, use of these drugs in pregnancy or in women of childbearing potential requires that the anticipated benefits be weighed against the possible hazards to the mother and embryo or fetus. Infants born of mothers who have received substantial doses of corticosteroids during pregnancy should be carefully observed for signs of hypoadrenalism.

Lactation: Corticosteroids appear in breast milk and could suppress growth, interfere with endogenous corticosteroid production, or cause other unwanted effects in the breast-feeding infant. Mothers taking pharmacologic doses of corticosteroids should be advised not to nurse.

Precautions: This product, like many other steroid formulations, is sensitive to heat. Therefore, it should not be autoclaved when it is desirable to sterilize the exterior of the vial.

Protect from freezing.

The preparation should be used only with full cognizance of the characteristic activity of systemic corticosteroid preparations and the varied responses to therapy. Prolonged therapy usually causes a reduction in the activity and size of the adrenal cortex.

The lowest possible effective dose of corticosteroid should be used to control the condition under treatment, and when reduction in dosage is possible, the reduction must be gradual.

Patients should be advised to inform subsequent physicians of the prior use of corticosteroids.

Cortisone causes gluconeogenesis; therefore, hyperglycemia and glycosuria may occur, glucose tolerance may be altered, and diabetes mellitus may be aggravated. Close observation of diabetic patients is recommended.

Following prolonged therapy, withdrawal of corticosteroids may result in symptoms of the corticosteroid withdrawal syndrome including fever, myalgia, arthralgia, and malaise. This may occur in patients even without evidence of adrenal insufficiency.

There is an enhanced effect of corticosteroids in patients with hypothyroidism and in those with cirrhosis.

Psychic derangements may appear when corticosteroids are used, ranging from euphoria, insomnia, mood swings, personality changes, and severe depression to frank psychotic manifestations. Also, existing emotional instability or psychotic tendencies may be aggravated by corticosteroids.

Steroids should be used with caution in nonspecific ulcerative colitis, if there is a probability of impending perforation, abscess, or other pyogenic infection, also in diverticulitis, fresh intestinal anastomoses, active or latent peptic ulcer, renal insufficiency, hypertension, osteoporosis, and myasthenia gravis. Signs of peritoneal irritation following gastrointestinal perforation in patients receiving large doses of corticosteroids may be minimal or absent. Fat embolism has been reported as a possible complication of hypercortisonism.

When large doses are given, some authorities advise that antacids be administered between meals to help prevent peptic ulcer.

Growth and development of infants and children on prolonged corticosteroid therapy should be carefully followed.

Steroids may increase or decrease motility and number of spermatozoa in some patients.

Drug Interactions: ASA should be used cautiously in conjuction with corticosteroids in hypoprothrombinemia.

Phenytoin, phenobarbital, ephedrine, and rifampin may enhance the metabolic clearance of corticosteroids resulting in decreased blood levels and lessened physiologic activity, thus requiring adjustment in corticosteroid dosage.

The prothrombin time should be checked frequently in patients who are receiving corticosteroids and coumarin anticoagulants at the same time because of reports that corticosteroids have altered the response to these anticoagulants. Studies have shown that the usual effect produced by adding corticosteroids is inhibition of response to coumarins, although there have been some conflicting reports of potentiation not substantiated by studies.

When corticosteroids are administered concomitantly with potassium-depleting diuretics, patients should be observed closely for development of hypokalemia.

Injection of a steroid into an infected site is to be avoided.

Adverse Effects: Fluid and Electrolyte Disturbances: sodium retention, fluid retention, congestive heart failure in susceptible patients, potassium loss, hypokalemic alkalosis, hypertension.

Musculoskeletal: muscle weakness, steroid myopathy, loss of muscle mass, osteoporosis, vertebral compression fractures, aseptic necrosis of femoral and humeral heads, pathologic fracture of long bones, tendon rupture.

Gastrointestinal: peptic ulcer with possible subsequent perforation and hemorrhage, perforation of the small and large bowel particularly in patients with inflammatory bowel disease, pancreatitis, abdominal distention, ulcerative esophagitis.

Dermatologic: impaired wound healing, thin fragile skin, petechiae and ecchymoses, erythema, increased sweating, may suppress reactions to skin tests, other cutaneous reactions such as allergic dermatitis, urticaria, angioneurotic edema.

Neurologic: convulsions, increased intracranial pressure with papilledema (pseudotumor cerebri) usually after treatment, vertigo, headache, psychic disturbance.

Endocrine: menstrual irregularities; development of cushingoid state; suppression of growth in children; secondary adrenocortical and pituitary unresponsiveness, particularly in times of stress, as in trauma, surgery, or illness; decreased carbohydrate tolerance; manifestations of latent diabetes mellitus; increased requirements for insulin or oral hypoglycemic agents in diabetics; hirsutism.

Ophthalmic: posterior subcapsular cataracts, increased intraocular pressure, glaucoma, exophthalmos.

Metabolic: negative nitrogen balance due to protein catabolism.

Cardiovascular: myocardial rupture following recent myocardial infarction (see Warnings).

Others: anaphylactoid or hypersensitivity reactions, thromboembolism, weight gain, increased appetite, nausea, malaise.

The following **additional** adverse reactions are related to parenteral corticosteroid therapy: rare instances of blindness associated with intralesional therapy around the face and head, hyperpigmentation or hypopigmentation, s.c. and cutaneous atrophy, sterile abscess.

Overdose: Symptoms and Treatment: Reports of acute toxicity and/or death following overdosage of glucocorticoids are rare. In the event of overdosage, no specific antidote is available; treatment is supportive and symptomatic.

The intraperitoneal LD_{50} of cortisone in female mice was 1 405 mg/kg.

Dosage: For i.m. injection only.

Dosage requirements are variable and must be individualized on the basis of the disease and the response of the patient.

The initial dosage varies from 20 to 300 mg a day depending on the disease being treated. In less severe diseases doses lower than 20 mg may suffice, while in severe disease doses higher than 300 mg may be required. The initial dosage should be maintained or adjusted until the patient's response is satisfactory. If a satisfactory clinical response does not occur after a reasonable period of time, discontinue cortisone sterile suspension and transfer the patient to other therapy.

After a favorable initial response, the proper maintenance dosage should be determined by decreasing the initial dosage in small amounts to the lowest dosage that maintains an adequate clinical response.

Patients should be observed closely for signs that might require dosage adjustment, including changes in clinical status resulting from remissions or exacerbations of the disease, individual drug responsiveness, and the effect of stress (e.g., surgery, infection, trauma). During stress it may be necessary to increase dosage temporarily.

If the drug is to be stopped after more than a few days of treatment, it usually should be withdrawn gradually.

Caution: No attempt should be made to alter the suspension. Diluting it or mixing it with other substances may affect the state of suspension or change the rate of absorption and reduce its effectiveness.

Refrigeration is not desirable as agglomerates may form if stored at low temperature.

Supplied: Each mL of white, mobile, sterile suspension contains: cortisone acetate 50 mg. Nonmedicinal ingredients: benzyl alcohol, polysorbate 80, sodium carboxymethylcellulose, sodium chloride and water for injection. Vials of 10 mL.

Reviewed 1999

CORTONE® Tablets Ⓟ

MSD

Cortisone Acetate

Corticosteroid

Pharmacology: Glucocorticoids are adrenocortical steroids, both naturally occurring and synthetic, which are readily absorbed from the gastrointestinal tract.

Cortisone is a natural product of the adrenal cortex. Cortisone acetate is a synthetic steroid with the basic actions and effects of other glucocorticoids.

Naturally occurring glucocorticoids (hydrocortisone and cortisone), which also have salt-retaining properties, are used as replacement therapy in adrenocortical deficiency states. They are also used for their potent anti-inflammatory effects in disorders of many organ systems.

Glucocorticoids cause profound and varied metabolic effects. In addition, they modify the body's immune responses to diverse stimuli.

Indications: Endocrine Disorders: Primary or secondary adrenocortical insufficiency (hydrocortisone or cortisone is the drug of choice; synthetic analogs may be used in conjunction with mineralocorticoids where applicable; in infancy, mineralocorticoid supplementation is of particular importance), congenital adrenal hyperplasia, nonsuppurative thyroiditis, hypercalcemia associated with cancer.

Rheumatic Disorders: As adjunctive therapy for short-term administration during an acute episode or exacerbation of: psoriatic arthritis, rheumatoid arthritis, including juvenile rheumatoid arthritis (selected cases may require low-dose maintenance therapy), ankylosing spondylitis, acute and subacute bursitis, acute nonspecific tenosynovitis, acute gouty arthritis, post-traumatic osteoarthritis, synovitis of osteoarthritis, epicondylitis.

Collagen Diseases: During an exacerbation or as maintenance therapy in selected cases of: systemic lupus erythematosus, acute rheumatic carditis, systemic dermatomyositis (polymyositis).

Dermatologic Diseases: pemphigus, bullous dermatitis herpetiformis, severe erythema multiforme (Stevens-Johnson syndrome), exfoliative dermatitis, mycosis fungoides, severe psoriasis, severe seborrheic dermatitis.

Allergic States: Control of severe or incapacitating allergic conditions not responsive to adequate trials of conventional treatment in: seasonal or perennial allergic rhinitis, bronchial asthma, contact dermatitis, atopic dermatitis, serum sickness, drug hypersensitivity reactions.

Ophthalmic Diseases: Severe acute and chronic allergic and inflammatory processes involving the eye and its adnexa such as: allergic conjunctivitis, keratitis, allergic corneal marginal ulcers, herpes zoster ophthalmicus, iritis and iridocyclitis, chorioretinitis, anterior segment inflammation, diffuse posterior uveitis and choroiditis, optic neuritis, sympathetic ophthalmia.

Respiratory Diseases: symptomatic sarcoidosis, Löffler's syndrome not manageable by other means, berylliosis, fulminating or disseminated pulmonary tuberculosis when used concurrently with appropriate antituberculous chemotherapy, aspiration pneumonitis.

Hematologic Disorders: idiopathic thrombocytopenic purpura in adults, secondary thrombocytopenia in adults, acquired (autoimmune) hemolytic anemia, erythroblastopenia (RBC anemia), congenital (erythroid) hypoplastic anemia.

Neoplastic Diseases: For palliative management of: leukemias and lymphomas in adults, acute leukemia of childhood.

Edematous States: To induce diuresis or remission of proteinuria in the nephrotic syndrome, without uremia, of the idiopathic type, or that due to lupus erythematosus.

Gastrointestinal Diseases: During a critical period of the disease in: ulcerative colitis, regional enteritis.

Miscellaneous: Tuberculous meningitis with subarachnoid block or impending block when used concurrently with appropriate antituberculous chemotherapy; trichinosis with neurologic or myocardial involvement.

Contraindications: Systemic fungal infections.

Hypersensitivity to any component of this product.

Tuberculosis whether active or healed, ocular herpes simplex and acute psychoses are usually absolute contraindications to systemic steroid therapy.

The use of cortisone acetate tablets in active tuberculosis should be restricted to those cases of fulminating or disseminated tuberculosis in which the corticosteroid is used for the management of the disease in conjunction with an appropriate antituberculous regimen.

If corticosteroids are indicated in patient with latent tuberculosis or tuberculin reactivity, close observation is necessary as reactivation of the disease may occur. During prolonged corticosteroid therapy, these patients should receive chemoprophylaxis.

Warnings: In patients on corticosteroid therapy subjected to any unusual stress, increased dosage of rapidly acting corticosteroids before, during, and after the stressful situation is indicated.

Drug-induced secondary adrenocortical insufficiency may result from too rapid withdrawal of corticosteroids and may be minimized by gradual reduction of dosage. This type of relative insufficiency may persist for months after discontinuation of therapy; therefore, in any situation of stress occurring during that period, corticosteroid therapy should be reinstituted. If the patient is receiving steroids already, dosage may have to be increased. Since mineralocorticoid secretion may be impaired, salt and/or a mineralocorticoid should be administered concurrently.

Corticosteroids may mask some signs of infection, and new infections may appear during their use. There may be decreased resistance and inability to localize infection when corticosteroids are used. Moreover, corticosteroids may affect the nitroblue-tetrazolium test for bacterial infection and produce false-negative results.

Corticosteroids may exacerbate systemic fungal infections and therefore should not be used in the presence of such infections unless they are needed to control drug reactions due to amphotericin B. Moreover, there have been cases reported in which concomitant use of amphotericin B and hydrocortisone was followed by cardiac enlargement and congestive failure.

Literature reports suggest an apparent association between use of corticosteroids and left ventricular free wall rupture after a recent myocardial infarction; therefore, therapy with corticosteroids should be used with great caution in these patients.

In cerebral malaria, the use of corticosteroids is associated with prolongation of coma and higher incidence of pneumonia and gastrointestinal bleeding.

Corticosteroids may activate latent amebiasis. Therefore, it is recommended that latent or active amebiasis be ruled out before initiating corticosteroid therapy in any patient who has spent time in the tropics or any patient with unexplained diarrhea.

Prolonged use of corticosteroids may produce posterior subcapsular cataracts, glaucoma with possible damage to the optic nerves, and may enhance the establishment of secondary ocular infections due to fungi or viruses.

Corticosteroids should be used cautiously in patients with ocular herpes simplex for fear of corneal perforation.

Average and large doses of hydrocortisone or cortisone can cause elevation of blood pressure, salt and water retention, and increased excretion of potassium. These effects are less likely to occur with the synthetic derivatives except when used in large doses. Dietary salt restriction and potassium supplementation may be necessary. All corticosteroids increase calcium excretion.

Administration of live virus vaccines, including smallpox, is contraindicated in individuals receiving immunosuppressive doses of corticosteroids. If inactivated viral or bacterial vaccines are administered to individuals receiving immunosuppressive doses of corticosteroids, the expected serum antibody response may not be obtained. However, immunization procedures may be undertaken in patients who are receiving corticosteroids as replacement therapy, e.g., for Addison's disease.

Pregnancy: Pregnancy is a relative contraindication to corticosteroid therapy, particularly during the first trimester, because fetal abnormalities have been observed in experimental animals. Since adequate human reproduction studies have not been done with corticosteroids, use of these drugs in pregnancy or in women of childbearing potential requires that the anticipated benefits be weighed against possible hazards to mother and embryo or fetus. Infants born of mothers who have received substantial doses of corticosteroids during pregnancy should be carefully observed for signs of hypoadrenalism.

Lactation: Corticosteroids appear in breast milk and could suppress growth, interfere with endogenous corticosteroid production, or cause other unwanted effects in the breast-feeding infant. Mothers taking pharmacologic doses of corticosteroids should be advised not to nurse.

Precautions: The preparation should be used only with full cognizance of the characteristic activity of systemic corticosteroid preparations and the varied responses to therapy. Prolonged corticosteroid therapy usually causes a reduction in the activity and size of the adrenal cortex.

The lowest effective dose of corticosteroid should be used to control the condition under treatment, and when reduction in dosage is possible, the reduction must be gradual.

Patients should be advised to inform subsequent physicians of the prior use of corticosteroids.

Cortisone causes gluconeogenesis; therefore, hyperglycemia and glycosuria may occur, glucose tolerance may be altered, and diabetes mellitus may be aggravated. Close observation of diabetic patients is recommended.

Following prolonged therapy, withdrawal of corticosteroids may result in symptoms of the corticosteroid withdrawal syndrome including fever, myalgia, arthralgia, and malaise. This may occur in patients even without evidence of adrenal insufficiency.

There is an enhanced effect of corticosteroids in patients with hypothyroidism and in those with cirrhosis.

Psychic derangements may appear when corticosteroids are used, ranging from euphoria, insomnia, mood swings, personality changes, and severe depression to frank psychotic manifestations. Also, existing emotional instability or psychotic tendencies may be aggravated by corticosteroids.

Steroids should be used with caution in nonspecific ulcerative colitis, if there is a probability of impending perforation, abscess, or other pyogenic infection, diverticulitis, fresh intestinal anastomoses, active or latent peptic ulcer, renal insufficiency, hypertension, osteoporosis, and myasthenia gravis. Signs of peritoneal irritation following gastrointestinal perforation in patients receiving large doses of corticosteroids may be minimal or absent. Fat embolism has been reported as a possible complication of hypercortisonism.

When large doses are given, some authorities advise that corticosteroids be taken with meals and antacids be taken between meals to help to prevent peptic ulcer.

Growth and development of infants and children on prolonged corticosteroid therapy should be carefully followed.

Steroids may increase or decrease motility and number of spermatozoa in some patients.

Drug Interactions: ASA should be used cautiously in conjunction with corticosteroids in hypoprothrombinemia.

Phenytoin, phenobarbital, ephedrine, and rifampin may enhance the metabolic clearance of corticosteroids resulting in decreased blood levels and lessened physiologic activity, thus requiring adjustment in corticosteroid dosage.

The prothrombin time should be checked frequently in patients who are receiving corticosteroids and coumarin anticoagulants at the same time because of reports that corticosteroids have altered the response to these anticoagulants. Studies have shown that the usual effect produced by adding corticosteroids is inhibition of response to coumarins, although there have been some conflicting reports of potentiation not substantiated by studies.

When corticosteroids are administered concomitantly with potassium-depleting diuretics, patients should be observed closely for development of hypokalemia.

Adverse Effects: Fluid and Electrolyte Disturbances: sodium retention, fluid retention, congestive heart failure in susceptible patients, potassium loss, hypokalemic alkalosis, hypertension.

Musculoskeletal: muscle weakness, steroid myopathy, loss of muscle mass, osteoporosis, vertebral compression fractures, aseptic necrosis of femoral and humeral heads, pathologic fracture of long bones, tendon rupture.

Gastrointestinal: peptic ulcer with possible subsequent perforation and hemorrhage, perforation of the small and large bowel particularly in patients with inflammatory bowel disease, pancreatitis, abdominal distention, ulcerative esophagitis.

Dermatologic: impaired wound healing, thin fragile skin, petechiae and ecchymoses, erythema, increased sweating, may suppress reactions to skin tests, other cutaneous reactions such as allergic dermatitis, urticaria, angioneurotic edema.

Neurologic: convulsions, increased intracranial pressure with papilledema (pseudotumor cerebri) usually after treatment, vertigo, headache, psychic disturbances.

Endocrine: menstrual irregularities; development of cushingoid state; suppression of growth in children; secondary adrenocortical and pituitary unresponsiveness, particularly in times of stress, as in trauma, surgery, or illness; decreased carbohydrate tolerance; manifestations of latent diabetes mellitus; increased requirements for insulin or oral hypoglycemic agents in diabetes; hirsutism.

Ophthalmic: posterior subcapsular cataracts, increased intraocular pressure, glaucoma, exophthalmos.

Metabolic: negative nitrogen balance due to protein catabolism.

Cardiovascular: myocardial rupture following recent myocardial infarction (see Warnings).

Others: hypersensitivity, thromboembolism, weight gain, increased appetite, nausea, malaise.

Overdose: Symptoms and Treatment: Reports of acute toxicity and/or death following overdosage of glucocorticoids are rare. In the event of overdosage, no specific antidote is available; treatment is supportive and symptomatic.

The intraperitoneal LD_{50} of cortisone in female mice was 1 405 mg/kg.

Dosage: Therapy is governed by the following general principles: 1. Dosage must be individualized according to the severity of the disease and the response of the patient. The severity, prognosis, and expected duration of the disease and the reaction of the patient to medication are primary factors in determining dosage. (For infants and children, the recommended doses usually will have to be reduced, but dosage should be dictated by the severity of the condition rather than by age or body weight.)

2. Corticosteroid therapy is an adjunct to, not a replacement of conventional therapy, which should be instituted as indicated.

3. Dosage must be decreased or therapy discontinued gradually when administration has been continued for more than a few days.

4. Continued supervision of the patient after cessation of corticosteroids is essential, since there may be a sudden reappearance of severe manifestations of the disease for which the patient was treated.

In acute conditions where prompt relief is urgent, large doses are permissible and may be mandatory for a short period.

In chronic conditions requiring long term therapy, the lowest dosage that provides adequate, but not necessarily complete, relief should be used. If a high dosage for prolonged periods is considered essential, patients must be observed closely for signs that might necessitate a reduction in dosage or discontinuance of the corticosteroid.

Chronic conditions are subject to periods of spontaneous remission. When such periods occur, corticosteroids should be discontinued gradually.

Routine laboratory studies such as urinalysis, 2-hour postprandial blood sugar, determinations of blood pressure and body weight, and a chest x-ray should be carried out at regular intervals during prolonged therapy. Periodic determinations of serum potassium are advisable if large doses are being used. Upper gastrointestinal x-rays should be taken when treatment is prolonged, in patients with history of ulcer or when there is gastric distress.

The daily requirement should be divided into 4 doses.

Specific Dosage Recommendations: In chronic, usually nonfatal diseases, including endocrine and chronic rheumatic disorders, edematous states, respiratory and gastrointestinal diseases, some dermatologic diseases and hematologic disorders, start with a low dose (25 to 50 mg a day) and gradually increase dosage to the smallest amount that gives the desired degree of symptomatic relief.

When symptoms have been suppressed adequately, dosage should be maintained at the minimum amount capable of providing sufficient relief without excessive hormonal effects.

In chronic adrenocortical insufficiency, 10 to 25 mg a day, or occasionally more, with 4 to 6 g of sodium chloride or 1 to 3 mg of desoxycorticosterone acetate. When immediate support is mandatory, one of the soluble corticosteroid preparations (i.e., dexamethasone sodium phosphate injection) which may be effective within minutes after parenteral administration, can be lifesaving.

In congenital adrenal hyperplasia, the usual daily dose is 15 to 50 mg.

In acute, nonfatal diseases, including allergic states, ophthalmic diseases, acute and subacute rheumatic disorders, dosage ranges between 75 and 150 mg a day; however, higher doses are necessary in some patients. Since the course of these conditions is self-limited, prolonged maintenance therapy is not usually necessary.

In chronic, potentially fatal diseases such as systemic lupus erythematosus, pemphigus, symptomatic sarcoidosis, the recommended initial dosage is 75 to 150 mg a day; higher doses are necessary in some patients.

As soon as adequate relief is obtained, the dosage should be reduced gradually to the minimum amount that will produce the desired therapeutic effect.

When the disease is acute and life-threatening (e.g., acute rheumatic carditis, crisis of systemic lupus erythematosus, severe allergic reactions, pemphigus, neoplastic diseases), the initial dosage is between 125 and 300 mg a day, administered in at least 4 divided doses; this dosage may have to be increased in some patients to establish control. As soon as control is attained, the dosage should be reduced gradually to the minimum amount that will maintain relief.

Cortone Tablets (cont'd)

When an extremely rapid onset of action is desired, one of the soluble corticosteroid preparations (dexamethasone sodium phosphate injection) may be administered i.v. for the first 2 or 3 doses.

Epinephrine is the drug of immediate choice in severe allergic reactions. Cortisone tablets are useful either concurrently or as supplementary therapy.

Supplied: 5 mg: Each white, discoid shaped, flat, compressed tablet, with a beveled edge, unscored with MSD 126 on one side, contains: cortisone acetate 5 mg. Also contains lactose. Gluten- and tartrazine-free. Bottles of 50.

25 mg: Each white, discoid shaped, flat, compressed tablet, with a beveled edge, scored on one side with MSD 219 on the other side, contains: cortisone acetate 25 mg. Also contains lactose. Gluten- and tartrazine-free. Bottles of 100.

(Shown in Product Recognition Section)

Reviewed 1999

CORTROSYN®
Organon

Cosyntropin
Adrenocorticotropic Hormone

Pharmacology: The pharmacologic profile of cosyntropin is similar to that of purified natural ACTH, it has been established that 250 µg of cosyntropin will stimulate the adrenal cortex maximally and to the same extent as 25 units of natural ACTH. These clinical observations confirm earlier animal and assay studies establishing the 1:100 ratio. This dose of cosyntropin will produce maximal secretion of 17-OH corticosteroids, 17-ketosteroids and/or 17-ketogenic steroids. Aldosterone secretion is increased also to some degree.

The extra adrenal effects which natural ACTH and cosyntropin have in common include increased melanotropic activity, increased growth hormone secretion and an adipokinetic effect. These are considered to be without physiological or clinical significance.

Severe hypofunction of the pituitary-adrenal axis is usually associated with subnormal plasma cortisol values but a low basal concentration is not per se evidence of adrenal insufficiency and dose not suffice to make the diagnosis. Many patients with proven insufficiency, will have normal basal concentrations and will develop signs of insufficiency only when stressed. For this reason, the only criterion which should be used in establishing the diagnosis is the failure to respond to adequate corticotropin stimulation as provided by 250 µg of cosyntropin. When presumptive adrenal insufficiency is diagnosed by a negative cosyntropin test, further studies are indicated to determine if it is primary or secondary.

Primary adrenal insufficiency (Addison's disease) is the result of an intrinsic disease process, such as tuberculosis, within the gland. The production of adrenocortical hormones is deficient despite high ACTH concentrations (feedback mechanism). Secondary or relative insufficiency arises as the result of defective production of ACTH leading in turn to disuse atrophy of the adrenal cortex. It is commonly seen, for example, as a result of corticosteroid therapy, Sheehan's syndrome and pituitary tumors or ablation.

The differentiation of both types is based on the premise that a primarily defective gland cannot be stimulated by ACTH whereas a secondarily defective gland is potentially functional and will respond to adequate stimulation with ACTH. Patients selected for further study as the result of a negative cosyntropin test should be given a 3 or 4 day course of treatment with purified cortrophin gel and then retested. Suggested doses are 40 USP units twice daily for 4 days or 60 USP units twice daily for 3 days. Under these conditions little or no increase in plasma cortisol concentrations will be seen in Addison's disease whereas higher or even normal concentrations will be seen in cases with secondary adrenal insufficiency.

Indications: A diagnostic agent in the screening of patients presumed to have adrenocortical insufficiency. Because of its rapid effect on the adrenal cortex it is now possible to perform a 30 minute test of adrenal function (plasma cortisol response) as an office or outpatient procedure, using only 2 venipunctures (see Dosage).

Contraindications: A history of a previous adverse reaction to cosyntropin.

Precautions: *Pregnancy:* When pregnancy is present or suspected, weigh the benefits of using cosyntropin against the possible hazards to the fetus.

It is not advisable to add cosyntropin, a synthetic polypeptide, to blood and plasma transfusions, because prolonged interaction with enzymes present in these fluids may cause breakdown of the polypeptide.

Allergic reactions may occur in response to cosyntropin. Marked redness and pain at the injection site, urticaria, pruritus, severe malaise or dyspnea may occur.

Severe anaphylactic reactions usually can be avoided by discontinuing the use of the drug at the earliest sign of local or systemic hypersensitivity. In the rare event of a serious incident occurring despite these precautions, initiate the following emergency measures as treatment for shock: i.v. injection of epinephrine HCl 100 to 800 µg and high doses of an i.v. corticosteroid, should be administered immediately. Because of the possibility of an allergic reaction occurring the injections should be given under medical supervision and the patient kept under observation for about 1 hour. Self-injection by patients is not recommended. Should prodromal signs occur, further use of cosyntropin should be stopped. Repeat administration may increase the risk of hypersensitivity. Patients should be instructed to inform subsequent physicians of previous use of corticotropic hormones.

Adverse Effects: Cosyntropin is intended for short-term use. Adverse reactions other than a rare hypersensitivity reaction are not anticipated. To date, only 9 such reactions have been reported in the literature and in each instance the patient had a pre-existing allergic disease and/or a previous reaction to natural ACTH.

Dosage: Cosyntropin may be administered i.m. or as a direct i.v. injection when used as a rapid screening test of adrenal function. It may also be given as an i.v. infusion over a 4 to 8 hour period to provide a greater stimulus to the adrenal glands. Doses of 250 to 750 µg have been used in clinical studies and a maximal response noted with the smallest dose.

A suggested method for a rapid screening test of adrenal function is as follows: A control blood sample is taken and 250 µg of cosyntropin, dissolved in sterile saline, is then injected intramuscularly. A second blood sample is collected exactly 30 minutes later and the plasma cortisol response is then determined. In children, aged 2 years or less, a dose of 125 µg will often suffice.

The usual normal response in most cases is an approximate doubling of the basal concentration, provided that this does not exceed the normal range. Patients taking inadvertent doses of hydrocortisone on the test day and women taking estrogen containing drugs may exhibit abnormally high basal plasma cortisol concentrations. A paradoxical response may be noted in the former group as seen in a decrease in plasma cortisol values following a stimulating dose of cosyntropin. In the latter group only a normal incremental response is to be expected. Many patients with normal adrenal function, however, do not respond to the expected degree so that the following criteria have been established to denote a normal response:

1. The control plasma cortisol concentration should exceed 5 µg/100 mL. 2. The 30 minute concentration should show an increment of at least 7 µg/100 mL above the basal concentration. 3. The 30 minute concentration should exceed 18 µg/100 mL.

These criteria also apply when the drug is injected i.v. in 2 to 5 mL of saline over a 2 minute period.

Plasma cortisol concentrations usually peak about 45 to 60 minutes after an injection of cosyntropin and some prefer the 60 minute interval for testing for this reason. While it is true that the 60 minute values are usually higher than the 30 minute values, the difference may not be significant enough in most cases to outweigh the disadvantage of a longer testing period. If the 60 minute test period is used, the criterion for a normal response is an approximate doubling of the basal plasma cortisol value.

When given as an i.v. infusion, 250 µg may be added to glucose or saline solutions and given at the rate of approximately 40 µg/hour over a 6 hour period. It should not be added to blood or plasma as it is apt to be inactivated by enzymes.

Adrenal response may be measured in the usual manner by determining urinary steriod excretion before and after treatment or by measuring plasma cortisol concentrations before and at the end of the infusion. The latter is preferable because urinary steroid excretion does not always accurately reflect the adrenal or plasma cortisol response to ACTH.

Patients receiving hydrocortisone should omit their pretest doses on the day selected for testing. The test may be performed at anytime during the day but, because of the physiological diurnal variation of plasma cortisol, the criteria listed above cannot apply. It has been shown that basal plasma cortisol concentrations and the post-cosyntropin increment exhibit diurnal changes. However, the 30 minute plasma cortisol concentration remains unchanged throughout the day so that only this single criterion should be used.

Supplied: Each vial contains: cosyntropin 250 µg (as a lyophilized powder). Nonmedicinal ingredients: glacial acetic acid, mannitol and sodium chloride. Each ampul of diluent contains: 1 mL of sodium chloride 0.9 % injection. Boxes of 10 vials and 10 ampuls.

COSMEGEN® Ⓟ
MSD

Dactinomycin
Antineoplastic

Pharmacology: Dactinomycin is an antibiotic obtained as the principal component of the mixture of actinomycins produced by S. parvullus. This organism, unlike other species, yields an essentially pure substance that contains only traces of similar compounds differing in the amino acid content of the peptide side chains. It is available for clinical use as a sterile, yellow lyophilized powder which, in aqueous solution, produces a clear gold color.

Generally, the actinomycins exert an inhibitory effect on gram positive and gram negative bacteria and on some fungi. However, the toxic properties of the actinomycins (including dactinomycin) in relation to antibacterial activity are such as to preclude their use as antibiotics in the treatment of infectious diseases.

Because the actinomycins are cytotoxic, they have an antineoplastic effect which has been demonstrated in experimental animals with various types of tumor implant. This cytotoxic action is the basis for their use in the palliative treatment of certain types of cancer.

Pharmacokinetics: Results of a study in patients with malignant melanoma indicate that dactinomycin (^{3}H actinomycin D) is minimally metabolized, is concentrated in nucleated cells, and does not penetrate the blood brain barrier. Approximately 30% of the dose was recovered in urine and feces in one week. The terminal plasma half-life for radioactivity was approximately 36 hours.

Indications: Wilms' Tumor: The neoplasm responding most frequently to dactinomycin is Wilms' tumor. With low doses of both dactinomycin and radiotherapy, temporary objective improvement may be as good as and may last longer than with higher doses of each given alone. In the National Wilms' Tumor study, combination therapy with dactinomycin and vincristine together with surgery and radiotherapy, was shown to have significantly improved the prognosis of patients in groups II and III. Dactinomycin and vincristine were given for a total of seven cycles, so that maintenance therapy continued for approximately 15 months.

Postoperative radiotherapy in group I patients and optimal combination chemotherapy for those in group IV are unsettled issues. About 70% of lung metastases have disappeared with an appropriate combination of radiation, dactinomycin and vincristine.

Rhabdomyosarcoma: Temporary regression of the tumor and beneficial subjective results have occurred with dactinomycin in rhabdomyosarcoma which, like most soft tissue sarcomas, is comparatively radioresistant.

Several groups have reported successful use of cyclophosphamide, vincristine, dactinomycin and doxorubicin hydrochloride in various combinations. Effective combinations have included vincristine and dactinomycin; vincristine, dactinomycin and cyclophosphamide (VAC therapy) and all 4 drugs in sequence. At present, the most effective treatment for children with inoperable or metastatic rhabdomyosarcoma has been VAC chemotherapy. Two-thirds of these children were doing well without evidence of disease at a median time of three years after diagnosis.

Carcinoma of Testis and Uterus: The sequential use of dactinomycin and methotrexate, along with meticulous monitoring of human chorionic gonadotropin levels until normal, has resulted in survival in the majority of women with metastatic choriocarcinoma. Sequential therapy is used if there is: stability in gonadotropin titers following two successive courses of an agent; rising gonadotropin titers during treatment; severe toxicity preventing adequate therapy.

In patients with nonmetastatic choriocarcinoma, dactinomycin or methotrexate or both have been used successfully, with or without surgery.

Dactinomycin has been beneficial as a single agent in the treatment of metastatic non-seminomatour testicular carcinoma when used in cycles of 500 µg/day for 5 consecutive days, every 6 to 8 weeks for periods of four months or longer.
Other Neoplasms: Dactinomycin has been given i.v. or by regional perfusion, either alone or with other antineoplastic compounds or x-ray therapy, in the palliative treatment of Ewing's sarcoma and sarcoma botryoides. For non-metastatic Ewing's sarcoma, promising results were obtained when dactinomycin (45 µg/m²) and cyclophosphamide (1 200 mg/m²) were given sequentially and with radiotherapy, over an 18 month period. Those with metastatic disease remain the subject of continued investigation with a more aggressive chemotherapeutic regimen employed initially.

Temporary objective improvement and relief of pain and discomfort have followed the use of dactinomycin usually in conjunction with radiotherapy for sarcoma botryoides. This palliative effect ranges from transitory inhibition of tumor growth to a considerable but temporary regression in tumor size.

Dactinomycin and Radiation Therapy: Much evidence suggests that dactinomycin potentiates the effects of x-ray therapy. The converse also appears likely; i.e., dactinomycin may be more effective when radiation therapy also is given.

With combined dactinomycin-radiation therapy, the normal skin, as well as the buccal and pharyngeal mucosa, show early erythema. A smaller than usual x-ray dose when given with dactinomycin causes erythema and vesiculation, which progress more rapidly through the stages of tanning and desquamation. Healing may occur in 4 to 6 weeks rather than 2 to 3 months. Erythema from previous x-ray therapy may be reactivated by dactinomycin alone, even when irradiation occurred many months earlier, and especially when the interval between the two forms of therapy is brief. This potentiation of radiation effect represents a special problem when the irradiation treatment area includes the mucous membrane. When irradiation is directed toward the nasopharynx, the combination may produce severe oropharyngeal mucositis. Severe reactions may ensue if high doses of both dactinomycin and radiation therapy are used or if the patient is particularly sensitive to such combined therapy.

Because of this potentiating effect, dactinomycin may be tried in radio-sensitive tumors not responding to doses of x-ray therapy that can be tolerated. Objective improvement in tumor size and activity may be observed when lower, better tolerated doses of both types of therapy are employed.

Dactinomycin and Perfusion Technique: Dactinomycin alone or with other antineoplastic agents has also been given by the isolation-perfusion technique, either as palliative treatment or as an adjunct to resection of a tumor. Some tumors considered resistant to chemotherapy and radiation therapy may respond when the drug is given by the perfusion technique. Neoplasms in which dactinomycin has been tried by this technique include various types of sarcoma, carcinoma, and adenocarcinoma.

In some instances tumors regressed, pain was relieved for variable periods, and surgery made possible. On other occasions, however, the outcome has been less favorable. Nevertheless, in selected cases, the drug by perfusion may provide more effective palliation than when given systemically.

Dactinomycin by the isolation-perfusion technique offers certain advantages, provided leakage of the drug through the general circulation into other areas of the body is minimal. By this technique the drug is in continuous contact with the tumor for the duration of treatment. The dose may be increased well over that used by the systemic route, usually without adding to the danger of toxic effects. If the agent is confined to an isolated part, it should not interfere with the patient's defense mechanism. Systemic absorption of toxic products from neoplastic tissue can be minimized by removing the perfusate when the procedure is finished.

Contraindications: If dactinomycin is given at or about the time of infection with chickenpox or herpes zoster, a severe generalized disease, which may result in death, may occur.

Precautions: General: Dactinomycin should be administered only under the supervision of a physician who is experienced in the use of cancer chemotherapeutic agents.

This drug is highly toxic and both powder and solution must be handled and administered with care. Inhalation of dust or vapors and contact with skin or mucous membranes, especially those of the eyes, must be avoided. Should accidental eye contact occur, copious irrigation with water should be instituted immediately, followed by prompt ophthalmologic consultation. Should accidental skin contact occur, the affected part must be irrigated immediately with copious amounts of water for at least 15 minutes.

As with all antineoplastic agents, dactinomycin is a toxic drug and very careful and frequent observation of the patient for adverse reactions is necessary. These reactions may involve any tissue of the body. The possibility of an anaphylactoid reaction should be borne in mind.

Increased incidence of gastrointestinal toxicity and marrow suppression has been reported when dactinomycin was given with x-ray therapy.

Particular caution is necessary when administering dactinomycin in the first 2 months after irradiation for the treatment of right sided Wilms' tumor, since hepatomegaly and elevated AST levels have been noted.

Nausea and vomiting due to dactinomycin make it necessary to give this drug intermittently. It is extremely important to observe the patient daily for toxic side effects when multiple chemotherapy is employed, since a full course of therapy occasionally is not tolerated. If stomatitis, diarrhea, or severe hemopoietic depression appear during therapy, these drugs should be discontinued until the patient has recovered.

Recent reports indicate an increased incidence of second primary tumors following treatment with radiation and antineoplastic agents, such as dactinomycin. Multi-modal therapy creates the need for careful, long-term observation of cancer survivors.

Laboratory Tests: Many abnormalities of renal, hepatic, and bone marrow function have been reported in patients with neoplastic disease and receiving dactinomycin. It is advisable to check renal, hepatic, and bone marrow functions frequently.

Drug/Laboratory Test Interactions: It has been reported that dactinomycin may interfere with bioassay procedures for the determination of antibacterial drug levels.

Carcinogenesis, Mutagenesis, Impairment of Fertility: The International Agency on Research on Cancer has judged that dactinomycin is a positive carcinogen in animals. Local sarcomas were produced in mice and rats after repeated s.c. or intraperitoneal injection. Mesenchymal tumors occurred in male F344 rats given intraperitoneal injections of 0.05 mg/kg, 2 to 5 times/week for 18 weeks. The first tumor appeared at 23 weeks.

Dactinomycin has been shown to be mutagenic in a number of test systems in vitro and in vivo including human fibroblasts and leucocytes, and HELA cells. DNA damage and cytogenetic effects have been demonstrated in the mouse and the rat.

Adequate fertility studies have not been reported.

Pregnancy: Dactinomycin has been shown to cause malformations and embryotoxicity in the rat, rabbit and hamster when given in doses of 50 to 100 µg/kg i.v. (3 to 7 times the maximum recommended human dose). There are no adequate and well-controlled studies in pregnant women. Dactinomycin should be used during pregnancy only if the potential benefit justifies the potential risk to the fetus.

Lactation: It is not known whether this drug is excreted in human milk. Because many drugs are excreted in human milk and because of the potential for serious adverse reactions in nursing infants from dactinomycin, a decision should be made whether to discontinue nursing or to discontinue the drug, taking into account the importance of the drug to the mother.

Children: The greater frequency of toxic effects of dactinomycin in infants suggests that this drug should be given to infants only over the age of 6 to 12 months.

Adverse Effects: Toxic effects (excepting nausea and vomiting) usually do not become apparent until 2 to 4 days after a course of therapy is stopped, and may not be maximal before 1 to 2 weeks have elapsed. Deaths have been reported. However, adverse effects are usually reversible on discontinuance of therapy. They include the following:

Miscellaneous: malaise, fatigue, lethargy, fever, myalgia, proctitis, hypocalcemia.

Oral: cheilitis, dysphagia, esophagitis, ulcerative stomatitis, pharyngitis.

Gastrointestinal: anorexia, nausea, vomiting, abdominal pain, diarrhea, gastrointestinal ulceration, liver toxicity including ascites, hepatomegaly, hepatitis, and liver function test abnormalities. Nausea and vomiting, which occur early during the first few hours after administration, may be alleviated by giving antiemetics.

Hematologic: anemia, even to the point of aplastic anemia, agranulocytosis, leukopenia, thrombopenia, pancytopenia, reticulopenia. Platelet and white cell counts should be done daily to detect severe hemopoietic depression. If either count markedly decreases, the drug should be withheld until marrow recovery occurs (often up to 3 weeks).

Dermatologic: alopecia, skin eruptions, acne, flare up of erythema or increased pigmentation of previously irradiated skin.

Soft tissues: Dactinomycin is extremely corrosive. If extravasation occurs during i.v. use, severe damage to soft tissues will occur. In at least one instance, this has led to contracture of the arms.

Dosage: Toxic reactions due to dactinomycin are frequent and may be severe (see Adverse Effects), thus limiting in many instances the amount that may be given. However, the severity of toxicity varies markedly and is only partly dependent on the dose employed. The drug must be given in short courses.

I.V.: The dosage of dactinomycin varies depending on the tolerance of the patient, the size and location of the neoplasm, and the use of other forms of therapy. It may be necessary to decrease the usual dosages suggested below when other chemotherapy or x-ray therapy is used concomitantly or has been used previously.

The dosage for adults or children should not exceed 15 µg/kg or 400 to 600 µg/m² of body surface daily i.v. for 5 days. Calculation of the dosage for obese or edematous patients should be on the basis of surface area in an effort to relate dosage to lean body mass.

Adults: The usual adult dosage is 500 µg (0.5 mg) daily i.v. for a maximum of 5 days.

Children: In children 15 µg (0.015 mg)/kg of body weight is given i.v. daily for 5 days. An alternative schedule is a total dosage of 2 500 µg (2.5 mg)/m² of body surface given i.v. over a 1-week period.

In both adults and children, a second course may be given after at least 3 weeks have elapsed, provided all signs of toxicity have disappeared.

Reconstitute dactinomycin by adding 1.1 mL of **Sterile Water for Injection (without preservative)** using aseptic precautions. The resulting solution of dactinomycin will contain approximately 500 µg or 0.5 mg/mL.

Parenteral drug products should be inspected visually for particulate matter and discoloration prior to administration, whenever solution and container permit. When reconstituted, dactinomycin is a clear, gold-colored solution.

Once reconstituted, the solution of dactinomycin can be added to infusion solutions of Dextrose Injection 5% or Sodium Chloride Injection either directly or to the tubing of a running i.v. infusion.

Although reconstituted dactinomycin is chemically stable, the product does not contain a preservative and accidental microbial contamination might result. Any unused portion should be discarded. Use of water containing preservatives (benzyl alcohol or parabens) to reconstitute dactinomycin for injection, results in the formation of a precipitate.

Partial removal of dactinomycin from i.v. solutions by cellulose ester membrane filters used in some i.v. in-line filters has been reported.

Since dactinomycin is extremely corrosive to soft tissue, precautions for materials of this nature should be observed.

If the drug is given directly into the vein without the use of an infusion, the two-needle technique should be used. Reconstitute and withdraw the calculated dose from the vial with one sterile needle. Use another sterile needle for direct injection into the vein.

Discard any unused portion of the dactinomycin solution.

Isolation-Perfusion Technique: The dosage schedules and the technique itself vary from one investigator to another; the published literature, therefore, should be consulted for details. In general, the following doses are suggested: 50 µg (0.05 mg)/kg of body weight for lower extremity or pelvis. 35 µg (0.035 mg)/kg of body weight for upper extremity.

It may be advisable to use lower doses in obese patients, or when previous chemotherapy or radiation therapy has been employed.

Complications of the perfusion technique are related mainly to the amount of drug that escapes into the systemic circulation and may consist of hemopoietic depression, absorption of toxic products from massive destruction of neoplastic tissue, increased susceptibility to infection, impaired wound healing, and superficial ulceration of the gastric mucosa. Other side effects may include edema of the extremity involved, damage to soft tissues of the perfused area, and (potentially) venous thrombosis.

Special Handling: Due to the drug's toxic and mutagenic properties, appropriate precautions including the use of appropriate safety equipment are recommended for the preparation of dactinomycin for parenteral administration. The National Institutes of Health presently recommend that the preparation of

Cosmegen (cont'd)

injectable antineoplastic drugs should be performed in a Class II laminar flow biological safety cabinet and that personnel preparing drugs of this class should wear surgical gloves and a closed front surgical-type gown with knit cuffs.

Supplied: Each vial contains: lyophilized, amorphous yellow dactinomycin powder 500 µg and mannitol 20 mg. Forms a clear gold-colored solution on reconstitution. Protect from light.

COTAZYM®
Organon

Pancrelipase Preparations

Enzymes—Digestant

Indications: Pancreatic enzyme replacement therapy in established pancreatic insufficiency where pancreatic enzymes are absent from or present in insufficient amount in the intestine: pancreatectomy, chronic pancreatitis, cystic fibrosis, steatorrhea and other malabsorption syndromes in which fat digestion is inadequate because of deficiency of pancreatic enzymes.

Contraindications: Allergy to porcine protein.

Warnings: In the event that capsules are opened for sprinkling the powder on food or drink or for any other reason, care should be taken so that powder is not spilled on hands or inhaled since it may prove irritating to the skin or mucous membranes.

These warnings are particularly applicable to allergic persons.

Precautions: A proper balance between fat, protein and starch intake must be maintained to avoid temporary indigestion. Use with caution in patients sensitive to pork protein.

Adverse Effects: As with any pancreatic extract, hyperuricosuria or hyperuricaemia due to the purine content of the product may occur at very high dosage.

Dosage: The capsules should be taken orally with each meal or snack. Average dose: 1 to 3 capsules with each meal and 1 capsule with each snack as directed by physician. They can either be swallowed whole, preferably with some fluid, or can be opened and the contents sprinkled on food or drink.

Supplied: Cotazym: Each clear capsule contains: lipase activity of 8 000 USP units, amylase activity of 30 000 USP units, protease activity of 30 000 USP units. Nonmedicinal ingredients: gelatin, magnesium stearate, opacode S-1-4126 (print ink), precipitated calcium carbonate, pregelatinized starch, silicon dioxide, sodium lauryl sulfate and talc. Tartrazine-free. Bottles of 100 and 1 000.

Cotazym-65 B: Each white capsule contains: lipase activity of 8 000 USP units, amylase activity of 30 000 USP units, protease activity of 30 000 USP units, mixed conjugated bile salts 65 mg, cellulase 2 mg. Nonmedicinal ingredients: colloidal silicon dioxide, gelatin, magnesium stearate, opacode S-1-4126 (print ink), precipitated calcium carbonate, silicon dioxide, sodium lauryl sulfate and titanium dioxide. Tartrazine-free. Bottles of 100.

Cotazym ECS 4: Each clear pink capsule with enteric coated microspheres contains: lipase 4 000 USP units, amylase 11 000 USP units and protease 11 000 USP units. Nonmedicinal ingredients: cellulose acetate phthalate, colloidal silicon dioxide, cornstarch, diethyl phthalate, gelatin, opacode S-1-4126 (print ink), providone, propylene glycol monostearate, silicon dioxide, sodium lauryl sulfate, sucrose and talc. Tartrazine-free. Bottles of 100.

Cotazym ECS 8: Each clear capsule with enteric coated microspheres contains: lipase 8 000 USP units, amylase 30 000 USP units and protease 30 000 USP units. Nonmedicinal ingredients: cellulose acetate phthalate, colloidal silicon dioxide, diethyl phthalate, gelatin, opacode S-1-4126 (print ink), povidone, propylene glycol, propylene glycol monostearate, silicon dioxide, sodium lauryl sulfate, sucrose and talc. Tartrazine-free. Bottles of 100 and 500.

Cotazym ECS 20: Each orange capsule with enteric coated microspheres contains: lipase 20 000 USP units, amylase 55 000 USP units and protease 55 000 USP units. Nonmedicinal ingredients: cellulose acetate phthalate, colloidal silicon dioxide, cornstarch, D&C Yellow No. 10, diethyl phthalate, FD&C Red No. 40, gelatin, opacode S-1-4126 (print ink), povidone, propylene glycol, propylene glycol monostearate, silicon dioxide, sodium lauryl sulfate, sucrose and talc. Tartrazine-free. Bottles of 100.

(Shown in Product Recognition Section)

COTRIDIN Ⓝ
COTRIDIN EXPECTORANT Ⓝ
Technilab

Triprolidine—Pseudoephedrine—Codeine Phosphate

Triprolidine—Pseudoephedrine—Codeine Phosphate—Guaifenesin

Antitussive—Decongestant

Antitussive—Expectorant—Decongestant

Supplied: Cotridin: Each 5 mL contains: triprolidine HCl 2.1 mg, pseudoephedrine HCl 30 mg and codeine phosphate 10 mg. Nonmedicinal ingredients: artificial coloring and flavoring, glycerin, methylparaben, propylparaben, purified water, sorbitol and sucrose. Energy: 69 kJ (16.5 kcal)/5 mL. Bottles of 100 mL and 2 L.

Cotridin Expectorant: Each 5 mL contains: triprolidine HCl 2.1 mg, pseudoephedrine HCl 30 mg, guaifenesin 100 mg and codeine phosphate 10 mg. Nonmedicinal ingredients: artificial flavoring, citric acid, FD&C Yellow #6, maltitol, menthol, methylparaben, polyethylene glycol, propylene glycol, propylparaben, purified water, sodium citrate and sodium cyclamate. Alcohol-free. Energy: 19 kJ (4.5 kcal)/5 mL. Bottles of 500 mL and 2 L.

Protect from light. Store between 15 and 30°C. Do not refrigerate.

COUMADIN® Ⓟ
DuPont Pharma

Warfarin Sodium

Anticoagulant

Pharmacology: Warfarin and other coumarin anticoagulants act by inhibiting the synthesis of vitamin K dependent clotting factors, which include Factors II, VII, IX and X, and the anticoagulant proteins C and S. Half-lives of these clotting factors are as follows: Factor II - 60 hours, VII - 4 to 6 hours, IX - 24 hours, and X - 48 to 72 hours. The half-lives of proteins C and S are approximately 8 hours and 30 hours, respectively. The resultant in vivo effect is a sequential depression of Factors VII, IX, X and II. Vitamin K is an essential cofactor for the post ribosomal synthesis of the vitamin K dependent clotting factors. The vitamin promotes the biosynthesis of g-carboxyglutamic acid residues in the proteins which are essential for biological activity. Warfarin is thought to interfere with clotting factor synthesis by inhibition of the regeneration of vitamin K_1 epoxide. The degree of depression is dependent upon the dosage administered. Therapeutic doses of warfarin decrease the total amount of the active form of each vitamin K dependent clotting factor made by the liver by approximately 30 to 50%.

An anticoagulation effect generally occurs within 24 hours after drug administration. However, peak anticoagulant effect may be delayed 72 to 96 hours. The duration of action of a single dose of racemic warfarin is 2 to 5 days. The effects of warfarin may become more pronounced as effects of daily maintenance doses overlap. Anticoagulants have no direct effect on an established thrombus, nor do they reverse ischemic tissue damage. However, once a thrombus has occurred, the goal of anticoagulant treatment is to prevent further extension of the formed clot and prevent secondary thromboembolic complications which may result in serious and possibly fatal sequelae.

The administration of warfarin via the i.v. route should provide the patient with the same concentration of an equal oral dose, but maximum plasma concentration will be reached earlier. However, the full anticoagulant effect of a dose of warfarin may not be achieved until 72-96 hours after dosing, indicating that the administration of i.v. warfarin should not provide any increased biological effect or earlier onset of action.

There are no differences in the apparent volume of distribution after i.v. and oral administration of single doses of warfarin solution. Warfarin distributes into a relatively small apparent volume of distribution of about 0.14 L/kg. A distribution phase lasting 6 to 12 hours is distinguishable after rapid i.v. or oral administration of an aqueous solution.

Indications: For the prophylaxis and/or treatment of venous thrombosis and its extension, pulmonary embolism, atrial fibrillation with embolization, and as an adjunct in the prophylaxis of systemic embolism after myocardial infarction, including stroke, reinfarction and death.

The following are some of the more common clinical disorders which may be associated with or predispose patients to the above indications: thrombophlebitis, congestive heart failure, surgical procedure or trauma associated with a high risk of thromboembolism, myocardial infarction, cerebral embolism.

It may also be useful as an adjunct in the treatment of transient cerebral ischemic attacks due to intravascular clotting.

Contraindications: Anticoagulation is contraindicated in any localized or general physical condition or personal circumstances in which the hazard of hemorrhage might be greater than the potential clinical benefits of anticoagulation, such as:

Pregnancy: Warfarin passes through the placental barrier and may cause fatal hemorrhage to the fetus in utero. Women of childbearing potential must take precautions not to become pregnant while on warfarin therapy. Furthermore, there have been reports of birth malformations in children born to mothers who have been treated with warfarin during pregnancy.

Embryopathy characterized by nasal hypoplasia with or without stippled epiphyses (chondrodysplasia punctata) has been reported in pregnant women exposed to warfarin during the first trimester. CNS abnormalities also have been reported, including dorsal midline dysplasia characterized by agenesis of the corpus callosum, Dandy-Walker malformation, and midline cerebellar atrophy. Ventral midline dysplasia, characterized by optic atrophy, and eye abnormalities have been observed. Mental retardation, blindness, and other CNS abnormalities have been reported in association with second and third trimester exposure. Although rare, teratogenic reports following in utero exposure to warfarin include urinary tract anomalies such as single kidney, asplenia, anencephaly, spina bifida, cranial nerve palsy, hydrocephalus, cardiac defects and congenital heart disease, polydactyly, deformities of toes, diaphragmatic hernia, corneal leukoma, cleft palate, cleft lip, schizencephaly, and microcephaly.

Spontaneous abortion and still birth are known to occur and a higher risk of fetal mortality is associated with the use of warfarin. Low birth weight and growth retardation have also been reported.

Women of childbearing potential who are candidates for anticoagulant therapy should be carefully evaluated and the indications critically reviewed with the patient. If the patient becomes pregnant while taking this drug, she should be apprised of the potential risks to the fetus, and the possibility of termination of the pregnancy should be discussed in the light of those risks.

Hemorrhagic tendencies or blood dyscrasias.

Recent or contemplated surgery of: CNS, eye, traumatic surgery resulting in large open surfaces.

Bleeding tendencies associated with active ulceration or overt bleeding of gastrointestinal, genitourinary or respiratory tracts; cerebrovascular hemorrhage; aneurysms - cerebral, dissecting aorta; pericarditis and pericardial effusions; bacterial endocarditis.

Threatened abortion, eclampsia and pre-eclampsia.

Inadequate laboratory facilities.

Unsupervised patients with senility, alcoholism, or psychosis or other lack of patient cooperation.

Spinal puncture and other diagnostic or therapeutic procedures with potential for uncontrollable bleeding.

Miscellaneous: major regional, lumbar block anesthesia and malignant hypertension.

Warnings: The most serious risks associated with anticoagulant therapy with warfarin are hemorrhage in any tissue or organ and, less frequently ($<0.1\%$), necrosis and/or gangrene of skin and other tissues. The risk of hemorrhage is related to the level of intensity and the duration of anticoagulant therapy. Hemorrhage and necrosis have in some cases been reported to result in death or permanent disability. Necrosis appears to be associated with local thrombosis and usually appears within a few days of the start of anticoagulant therapy. In severe cases of necrosis, treatment through debridement or amputation of the affected tissue, limb, breast or penis has been reported. Careful diagnosis is required to determine whether necrosis is caused by an underlying disease. Warfarin therapy should be discontinued when warfarin is suspected to be the cause of developing necrosis and heparin therapy may be considered for anticoagulation. Although various treatments have been attempted, no treatment for necrosis has been considered uniformly effective. See below for information on predisposing conditions. These and other risks associated with anticoagulant therapy must be weighed against the risk of thrombosis or embolization in untreated cases.

Warfarin is a potent drug with a half-life of 2.5 days; therefore, its effects may become more pronounced as daily maintenance doses overlap. It cannot be emphasized too strongly that treatment of each patient is a highly individualized matter. Warfarin, a narrow therapeutic range (index) drug, may be affected by factors such as other drugs and dietary Vitamin K. Dosage should be controlled by periodic determinations of prothrombin times (PT) ratio/International Normalized Ratio (INR) or other suitable coagulation tests. Determinations of whole blood clotting and bleeding times are not effective measures for control of therapy. Heparin prolongs the one-stage PT. When heparin and warfarin are administered concomitantly, refer below to Dosage, Conversion from Heparin Therapy for recommendations.

Caution should be observed when warfarin is administered in any situation or in the presence of any predisposing condition where added risk of hemorrhage or necrosis is present.

Anticoagulation therapy with warfarin may enhance the release of atheromatous plaque emboli, thereby increasing the risk of complications from systemic cholesterol microembolization, including the "purple toe syndrome". Discontinuation of warfarin therapy is recommended when such phenomena are observed. While the "purple toe syndrome" is reported to be reversible, other complications of microembolization may not be reversible.

Systemic atheroemboli and cholesterol microemboli can present with a variety of signs and symptoms including purple toes syndrome, livedo reticularis, rash, gangrene, abrupt and intense pain in the leg, foot, or toes, foot ulcers, myalgia, penile gangrene, abdominal pain, flank or back pain, hematuria, renal insufficiency, hypertension, cerebral ischemia, spinal cord infarction, pancreatitis, symptoms simulating polyarteritis, or any other sequelae of vascular compromise due to embolic occlusion. The most commonly involved visceral organs are the kidneys followed by the pancreas, spleen, and liver. Some cases have progressed to necrosis or death.

Purple toes syndrome is a complication of oral anticoagulation characterized by a dark, purplish or mottled color of the toes, usually occurring between 3 to 10 weeks, or later, after the initiation of therapy with warfarin or related compounds. Major features of this syndrome include purple color of plantar surfaces and sides of the toes that blanches on moderate pressure and fades with elevation of the legs; pain and tenderness of the toes; waxing and waning of the color over time. While the purple toes syndrome is reported to be reversible, some cases progress to gangrene or necrosis which may require debridement of the affected area, or may lead to amputation.

A severe elevation (>50 seconds) in activated partial thromboplastin time (aPTT) with a PT ratio/INR in the desired range has been identified as an indication of increased risk of postoperative hemorrhage. This has been noted in patients undergoing elective hip surgery receiving warfarin alone.

Administration of anticoagulants in the following conditions will be based upon clinical judgment in which the risks of anticoagulant therapy are weighed against the risk of thrombosis or embolization in untreated cases. The following may be associated with these increased risks:

Lactation: Warfarin appears in the milk of nursing mothers in an inactive form. Infants nursed by warfarin treated mothers had no change in PT. Effects in premature infants have not been evaluated.

Severe to moderate hepatic or renal insufficiency.

Infectious diseases or disturbances of intestinal flora-sprue, antibiotic therapy.

Trauma which may result in internal bleeding.

Surgery or trauma resulting in large exposed raw surfaces.

Indwelling catheters.

Severe to moderate hypertension.

Known or suspected deficiency in protein C mediated anticoagulant response: Hereditary or acquired deficiencies of protein C or its cofactor, protein S, have been associated with tissue necrosis following warfarin administration. Not all patients with these conditions develop necrosis, and tissue necrosis occurs in patients without these deficiencies. Inherited resistance to activated protein C has been described in many patients with venous thromboembolic disorders but has not yet been evaluated as a risk factor for tissue necrosis. The risk associated with these conditions, both for recurrent thrombosis and for adverse reactions, is difficult to evaluate since it does not appear to be the same for everyone. Decisions about testing and therapy must be made on an individual basis. It has been reported that concurrent anticoagulation therapy with heparin for 5 to 7 days during initiation of therapy with warfarin may minimize the incidence of tissue necrosis. Warfarin therapy should be discontinued when warfarin is suspected to be the cause of developing necrosis and heparin therapy may be considered for anticoagulation.

Miscellaneous: polycythemia vera, vasculitis, and severe diabetes.

Minor and severe allergic/hypersensitivity reactions and anaphylactic reactions have been reported.

In patients with acquired or inherited warfarin resistance, decreased therapeutic responses to warfarin have been reported. Exaggerated therapeutic responses have been reported in other patients.

Patients with congestive heart failure may become more responsive to warfarin, thereby requiring more frequent laboratory monitoring, and reduced doses of warfarin.

Concurrent use of anticoagulants with streptokinase or urokinase is not recommended and may be hazardous. (Please note recommendations accompanying these preparations.)

Precautions: Periodic determination of PT ratio/INR or other suitable coagulation test is essential.

Numerous factors, alone or in combination, including travel, changes in diet, environment, physical state and medication

Table I—Coumadin

The Following Factors, Alone or in Combination, May Be Responsible for Increased PT Ratio or INR Response

Endogenous Factors:

blood dyscrasias–see Contraindications	hyperthyroidism
cancer	poor nutritional state
collagen vascular disease	steatorrhea
congestive heart failure	vitamin K deficiency
diarrhea	
elevated temperature	
hepatic disorders:	
infectious hepatitis	
jaundice	

Exogenous Factors: Potential drug interactions with warfarin are listed below by drug class and by specific drugs.

adrenergic stimulants, central	antineoplastics*	hypnotics*
alcohol abuse reduction preparations	antiparasitic/antimicrobials	hypolipidemics*
analgesics	antiplatelet drugs/effects	MAO inhibitors
anesthetics, inhalation	antithyroid drugs*	narcotics, prolonged
antiarrhythmics*	beta-adrenergic blockers	nonsteroidal anti-inflammatory agents
antibiotics*	bromelains	psychostimulants
aminoglycosides (oral)	cholelitholytic agents	pyrazolones
cephalosporins, parenteral	diabetes agents, oral	salicylates
macrolides	diuretics*	steroids, adrenocortical*
penicillins, i.v., high dose	fungal medications, systemic*	steroids, anabolic (17-alkyl testosterone
quinolones (fluoroquinolones)	gastric acidity and peptic ulcer agents*	derivatives)
sulfonamides,	gastrointestinal, ulcerative colitis agents	thrombolytics
long acting tetracyclines	gout treatment agents	thyroid drugs
anticoagulants	hemorrheologic agents	tuberculosis agents*
anticonvulsants*	hepatotoxic drugs	uricosuric agents
antidepressants*	hyperglycemic agents	vaccines
antimalarial agents	hypertensive emergency agents	vitamins*

Specific Drugs Reported

acetaminophen	fluorouracil	phenylbutazone
alcohol*	glucagon	phenytoin*
allopurinol	halothane	piperacillin
aminosalicylic acid	heparin	piroxicam
amiodarone HCl	ibuprofen	prednisone*
ASA	ifosfamide	propafenone
cefamandole	indomethacin	propoxyphene
cefazolin	influenza virus vaccine	propranolol
cefoperazone	itraconazole	propylthiouracil*
cefotetan	ketoprofen	quinidine
cefoxitin	ketorolac	quinine
ceftriaxone	levamisole	ranitidine*
chenodiol	levothyroxine	sertraline
chloramphenicol	liothyronine	simvastatin
chloral hydrate*	lovastatin	stanozolol
chlorpropamide	mefenamic acid	streptokinase
cholestyramine*	methimazole*	sulfamethizole
cimetidine	methyldopa	sulfamethoxazole
ciprofloxacin	methylphenidate	sulfinpyrazone
clarithromycin	methylsalicylate ointment (topical)	sulfisoxazole
clofibrate	metronidazole	sulindac
cyclophosphamide*	miconazole	tamoxifen
danazol	moricizine HCl*	tetracycline
dextran	nalidixic acid	thyroid
dextrothyroxine	naproxen	ticarcillin
diazoxide	neomycin	ticlopidine
diclofenac	norfloxacin	tissue plasminogen activator (t-PA)
dicumarol	ofloxacin	tolbutamide
diflunisal	olsalazine	trimethoprim/sulfamethoxazole
disulfiram	omeprazole	urokinase
doxycycline	oxaprozin	valproate
erythromycin	oxymetholone	vitamin E
ethacrynic acid	paroxetine	warfarin overdose
fenoprofen	penicillin G, i.v.	
fluconazole	pentoxifylline	

Also: Other medications affecting blood elements which may modify hemostasis dietary deficiencies; prolonged hot weather; unreliable PT determinations.

*Increased and decreased PT ratio/INR responses have been reported.

Coumadin (cont'd)

may influence response of the patient to anticoagulants. It is generally good practice to monitor the patient's response with additional PT ratio/INR determinations in the period immediately after discharge from the hospital, and whenever other medications are initiated, discontinued or taken irregularly. Table I (on previous page) and Table II provide a listing of factors, alone or in combination, which may effect the PT. However, other factors may also affect the anticoagulant response and the tables are provided for your reference only.

Drugs may interact with warfarin through pharmacodynamic or pharmacokinetic mechanisms. Pharmacodynamic mechanisms for drug interactions with warfarin are synergism (impaired hemostasis, reduced clotting factor synthesis), competitive antagonism (vitamin K), and altered physiologic control loop for vitamin K metabolism (hereditary resistance). Pharmacokinetic mechanisms for drug interactions with warfarin are mainly enzyme induction, enzyme inhibition, and reduced plasma protein binding. It is important to note that some drugs may interact by more than one mechanism.

Because a patient may be exposed to a combination of listed factors, the net effect of warfarin on PT ratio/INR responses may be unpredictable. More frequent PT ratio/INR monitoring is therefore advisable.

Medications of unknown interaction with coumarins are best regarded with caution. When these medications are started or stopped, more frequent PT ratio/INR monitoring is advisable. Coumarins may also affect the action of other drugs. Hypoglycemic agents (chlorpropamide and tolbutamide) and anticonvulsants (phenytoin and phenobarbital) may accumulate in the body as a result of interference with either their metabolism or excretion.

It has been reported that concomitant administration of warfarin and ticlopidine may be associated with cholestatic hepatitis.

Special Risk Patients: Warfarin is a narrow therapeutic range (index) drug, and caution should be observed when administered to certain patients such as the elderly or debilitated or when administered in any situation or physical condition where added risk of hemorrhage is present.

I.M. injections of concomitant medications should be confined to the upper extremities which permits easy access for manual compression, inspections for bleeding and use of pressure bandages.

Close monitoring of patients receiving nonsteroidal anti-inflammatory agents (NSAIDs) is recommended to be certain that no change in anticoagulation dosage is required. In addition to specific drug interactions that might affect prothrombin time, NSAIDs can inhibit platelet aggregation, and can cause gastrointestinal bleeding, peptic ulceration and/or perforation.

Acquired or inherited warfarin resistance should be suspected if large daily doses of warfarin are required to maintain a patient's PT ratio/INR within a normal therapeutic range.

Pregnancy: See Contraindications.

Children: Safety and effectiveness in children below 18 years of age have not been established in randomized, controlled clinical trials. However, the use of warfarin in pediatric patients has been documented for the prevention and treatment of thromboembolic events. Difficulty achieving and maintaining therapeutic PT ratio/INR ranges in the pediatric patient has been reported. More frequent PT ratio/INR determinations are recommended because of possible changing warfarin requirements.

Adverse Effects: Potential adverse reactions to warfarin may include:

Fatal or nonfatal hemorrhage from any tissue or organ. This is a consequence of the anticoagulant effect. The signs, and symptoms, and severity will vary according to the location and degree or extent of the bleeding. Hemorrhagic complications may present as paralysis; paresthesia; headache, chest, abdomen, joint, muscle or other pain; dizziness; shortness of breath, difficult breathing or swallowing; unexplained swelling; weakness; hypotension; or unexplained shock. Therefore, the possibility of hemorrhage should be considered in evaluating the condition of any anticoagulated patient with complaints which do not indicate an obvious diagnosis. Bleeding during anticoagulant therapy does not always correlate with PT ratio/INR (see Overdose: Symptoms and Treatment).

Bleeding which occurs when the PT ratio/INR is within the therapeutic range warrants diagnostic investigation, since it may unmask a previously unsuspected lesion, e.g., tumor, ulcer, etc.

Necrosis of skin and other tissues (see Warnings).

Adverse reactions reported infrequently include: hypersensitivity reactions, systemic cholesterol microembolization, purple toes syndrome, vasculitis, hepatitis, cholestatic hepatic injury, jaundice, elevated liver enzymes, fever, dermatitis, including bullous eruptions, urticaria, abdominal pain including cramping, asthenia, nausea, vomiting, diarrhea, headache, pruritus, alopecia, and paresthesia.

Table II—Coumadin

Factors Alone or in Combination, Which May Be Responsible for Decreased PT Ratio or INR Response

Endogenous Factors:		
edema	hyperlipemia	nephrotic syndrome
hereditary coumarin resistance	hypothyroidism	
Exogenous Factors: Potential drug interactions with warfarin are listed below by drug class and by specific drugs.		
adrenal cortical steroid inhibitors	antineoplastics*	hypnotics*
antacids	antipsychotic medications	hypolipidemics*
antianxiety agents	antithyroid drugs*	immunosuppressives
antiarrhythmics*	barbiturates	oral contraceptives, estrogen containing
antibiotics*	diuretics*	
anticonvulsants*	enteral nutritional supplements	steroids, adrenocortical*
antidepressants*	fungal medications, systemic*	tuberculosis agents*
antihistamines	gastric acidity and peptic ulcer agents*	vitamins*
Specific Drugs Reported		
alcohol*	dicloxacillin	primidone
aminoglutethimide	ethchlorvynol	propylthiouracil*
amobarbital	glutethimide	ranitidine*
azathioprine	griseofulvin	rifampin
butabarbital	haloperidol	secobarbital
butalbital	meprobamate	spironolactone
carbamazepine	methimazole*	sucralfate
chloral hydrate*	moricizine HCl*	trazodone
chlordiazepoxide	nafcillin	vitamin C (high dose)
chlorthalidone	paraldehyde	vitamin K
cholestyramine*	pentobarbitalphenobarbital	warfarin underdosage
corticotropin	phenytoin*	
cortisonecyclophosphamide*	prednisone*	
Also: diet high in vitamin K unreliable PT determinations		

*Increased and decreased PT ratio/INR responses have been reported.

Rare events of tracheal or tracheobronchial calcification have been reported in association with long-term warfarin therapy. The clinical significance of this event is unknown.

Priapism has been associated with anticoagulant administration, however, a causal relationship has not been established.

Overdose: Symptoms: Suspected or overt abnormal bleeding (e.g., appearance of blood in stools or urine, hematuria, excessive menstrual bleeding, melena, petechiae, excessive bruising or persistent oozing from superficial injuries) are early manifestations of anticoagulation beyond a safe and satisfactory level.

Treatment: Excessive anticoagulation, with or without bleeding, may be controlled by discontinuing warfarin therapy and if necessary, by administration of oral or parenteral vitamin K_1. (Please see recommendations accompanying vitamin K_1 preparations prior to use.)

Such use of vitamin K_1 reduces responses to subsequent warfarin therapy. Patients may return to a pretreatment thrombotic status following the rapid reversal of a prolonged PT. Resumption of warfarin administration reverses the effect of vitamin K_1, and a therapeutic PT can again be obtained by careful dosage adjustment. If rapid anticoagulation is indicated, heparin may be preferable for initial therapy.

If minor bleeding progresses to major bleeding, give 5 to 25 mg (rarely up to 50 mg) parenteral vitamin K_1. In emergency situations of severe hemorrhage, clotting factors can be returned to normal by administering 200 to 500 mL of whole blood or fresh frozen plasma, or by giving commercial Factor IX complex.

A risk of hepatitis and other viral diseases is associated with the use of these blood products; Factor IX complex is also associated with an increased risk of thrombosis. Therefore, these preparations should be used only in exceptional or life-threatening bleeding episodes secondary to warfarin overdosage.

Purified Factor IX preparations should not be used because they cannot increase the levels of prothrombin, Factor VII and Factor X, which are also depressed along with the levels of Factor IX as a result of warfarin treatment. Packed red blood cells may also be given if significant blood loss has occurred. Infusions of blood or plasma should be monitored carefully to avoid precipitating pulmonary edema in elderly patients or patients with heart disease.

Dosage: Administration: The administration and dosage of warfarin must be individualized according to the patient's responsiveness to the drug. The dosage should be adjusted according to results of the patient's PT ratio/INR. Measurement of warfarin induced effects on PT can vary substantially due to the sensitivity of different thromboplastin reagents.

Early clinical studies of oral anticoagulants, which formed the basis for recommended therapeutic ranges of 1.5 to 2.5 times control PT, used sensitive human brain thromboplastin. When using the less sensitive rabbit brain thromboplastins commonly employed in PT assays today, adjustments must be made to the targeted PT range that reflect this decrease in sensitivity. Available clinical evidence indicates that an INR of 2.0 to 3.0, is sufficient for prophylaxis and treatment of venous thromoboembolism and minimizes the risk of hemorrhage associated with higher INRs. Five recent clincial trials evaluated the effects of warfarin in patients with nonvalvular atrial fibrillation (AF). Findings of these studies revealed that the effects of warfarin in reducing thromboembolic events including stroke were similar at either moderately high INR (2.0 to 4.5) or low INR (1.4 to 3.0). There was a significant reduction in minor bleeds at the low INR. Although clinical studies have used a wide range of warfarin dosing, a more recent study suggests that in patients with atrial fibrillation, anticoagulant prophylaxis is effective at INRs of 2.0 to 3.0. The study also shows that the risk of thromboembolic stroke may increase substantially at INRs less than 2.0. INR value should not exceed 4.0, to reduce the risk of anticoagulant-related bleeding. Similar data from clinical studies in valvular atrial fibrillation patients are not available. The trials in nonvalvular atrial fibrillation support The American College of Chest Physicians'(ACCP) recommendation that an INR of 2.0 to 3.0 be used for long-term warfarin therapy in appropriate AF patients. In cases where the risk of thromboembolism is great, such as in patients with recurrent systemic embolism, a higher INR may be required. An INR ratio of greater than 4.0 appears to provide no additional therapeutic benefit in most patients and is associated with a higher risk of bleeding. In AF patients undergoing elective cardioversion, anticoagulant therapy should be given for 3 weeks before cardioversion and continued until normal sinus rhythm has been maintained for 4 weeks.

Two well-controlled studies in postmyocardial infarction patients demonstrated substantial benefit of long-term oral anticoagulation in reducing the risk of death, recurrent myocardial infarction, and thromboembolic events, such as stroke. Both studies targeted an INR range of 2.8 to 4.8 for evaluating efficacy and safety. Clinical evidence from these two studies suggests that an INR range of 2.0 to 4.0 significantly reduced the risk of thromboembolic events and that INR values greater than 4.0 are associated with an increased risk of bleeding. In postmyocardial patients, warfarin therapy should be initiated early and dosage should be adjusted to maintain an INR of 2.5 to 3.5 long-term. In patients thought to be at increased risk of bleeding complications or on ASA therapy, maintenance of warfarin therapy at the lower end of this INR range is recommended.

The proceedings and recommendations of the 1992 National Conference on Antithrombotic Therapy review and evaluate issues related to oral anticoagulant therapy and the sensitivity of thromboplastin reagents and provide additional guidelines for defining the appropriate therapeutic regimen.

The conversion of the INR to PT ratios for the less-intense (INR 2.0 to 3.0) and more intense (INR 2.5 to 3.5) therapeutic range recommended by the ACCP for thromboplastins over a range of ISI values is shown in Table III.

Table III—Coumadin

Relationship Between INR and PT Ratios for Thromboplastins with Different ISI Values (Sensitivities)
PT Ratios

	ISI				
	1.0	**1.4**	**1.8**	**2.3**	**2.8**
INR=2.0-3.0	2.0-3.0	1.6-2.2	1.5-1.8	1.4-1.6	1.3-1.5
INR=2.5-3.5	2.5-3.5	1.9-2.4	1.7-2.0	1.5-1.7	1.4-1.6

To define the appropriate therapeutic regimen it is important to be familiar with the sensitivity of the thromboplastin reagent used in the laboratory and its relationship to the International Reference Preparation (IRP), a sensitive thromboplastin prepared from human brain.

A system of standardizing the PT in oral anticoagulant control was introduced by the World Health Organization in 1983. It is based upon the determination of an International Normalized Ratio (INR) which provides a common basis for communications of PT results and interpretations of therapeutic ranges. The INR system of reporting is based on a logarithmic relationship between the PT ratios of the test and reference preparation. The INR is the PT ratio that would be obtained if the IRP, which has an International Sensitivity Index (ISI) of 1.0, were used to perform the test. The INR can be calculated as:

$$\text{INR} = (\text{observed PT ratio})^{\text{ISI}}$$
$$\text{observed PT ratio} = (\text{Patient PT/Control PT})$$

where the ISI is the correction factor in the equation that relates local reagent to the reference preparation and is a measure of the sensitivity of a given thromboplastin to reduction of vitamin K-dependent coagulation factors; the lower the ISI, the more "sensitive" the reagent and the closer the derived INR will be to the observed PT ratio.

Initial Dosage: The dosing of warfarin must be individualized according to the patient's response to the drug as indicated by the INR and/or PT ratio. It is recommended that warfarin therapy be initiated with a dose of 2 to 5 mg/day with dosage adjustments based on the results of INR and/or PT ratio determinations. Low initiation doses are recommended for elderly and/or debilitated patients and patients with potential for increased responsiveness to warfarin (see Precautions). Use of a large loading dose may increase the incidence of hemorrhagic and other complications, does not offer more rapid protection against thrombi formation, and is not recommended.

Maintenance: Most patients are satisfactorily maintained at a dose of 2 to 10 mg daily. Flexibility of dosage is provided by breaking scored tablets in half. The individual dose and interval should be gauged by the patient's prothrombin response.

Duration of Therapy: The duration of therapy in each patient should be individualized. In general, anticoagulant therapy should be continued until the danger of thrombosis and embolism has passed.

Missed Dose: The anticoagulant effect of warfarin persists beyond 24 hours. If the patient forgets to take the prescribed dose of warfarin at the scheduled time, the dose should be taken as soon as possible on the same day. The patient should not take the missed dose by doubling the daily dose to make up for missed doses, but should refer back to this or her physician.

I.V. Route of Administration: Warfarin for injection provides an alternate administration route for patients who cannot receive oral drugs. The i.v. dosages would be the same as those that would be used orally if the patient could take the drug by the oral route. Warfarin for injection should be administered as a slow bolus injection over 1 to 2 minutes into a peripheral vein. It is not recommended for i.m. administration. The vial should be reconstituted with 2.7 mL of sterile Water for Injection and inspected for particulate matter and discoloration immediately prior to use. Do not use if either particulate matter and/or discoloration is noted. After reconstitution, warfarin for injection is chemically and physically stable for 4 hours at room temperature. It does not contain any antimicrobial preservative and, thus, care must be taken to assure the sterility of the prepared solution. The vial is not recommended for multiple use and unused solution should be discarded.

Laboratory Control: The INR reflects the depression of vitamin K dependent Factors VII, X and II. The INR should be determined daily after the administration of the initial dose until INR results stabilize in the therapeutic range. Intervals between subsequent INR determinations should be based upon the patient's INR response and the physician's judgment of the patient's reliability. For example, INR may be monitored 2 or 3 times weekly for 1 to 2 weeks, then less often, depending on the stability of the INR results. If the INR response remains stable, the frequency of testing may be reduced with intervals as long as every 4 to 6 weeks for appropriate patients.

To ensure adequate control, it is recommended that additional PT tests are done when other warfarin products are interchanged with Coumadin and also if other medications are coadministered with warfarin (see Precautions).

In switching to another warfarin product, particular emphasis needs to be placed on INR control. INR outside of the therapeutic range may result in serious clinical consequences: lack of efficacy leading to thromboembolic stroke or myocardial infarction, if INR values are low, and intracranial bleeding if they are high.

Treatment during Dentistry and Surgery: The management of patients who undergo dental and surgical procedures requires close liaison between attending physicians, surgeons and dentists. PT ratio/INR determination is recommended just prior to any dental or surgical procedure. In patients undergoing minimal invasive procedures who must be anticoagulated prior to, during, or immediately following these procedures, adjusting the dosage of warfarin to maintain the PT ratio/INR at the low end of the therapeutic range, may safely allow for continued anticoagulation. The operative site should be sufficiently limited and accessible to permit the effective use of local procedures for hemostasis. Under these conditions, dental and surgical procedures may be performed without undue risk of hemorrhage. Some dental or surgical procedures may necessitate the interruption of warfarin therapy. When discontinuing warfarin even for a short period of time, the benefits and risks should be strongly considered.

Conversion from Heparin Therapy: Since the anticoagulant effect of warfarin is delayed, heparin is preferred initially for rapid anticoagulation. Conversion to warfarin may begin concomitantly with heparin therapy or may be delayed 3 to 6 days. To ensure continuous anticoagulation, it is advisable to continue full dose heparin therapy and that warfarin therapy be overlapped with heparin for 4 to 5 days, until warfarin has produced the desired therapeutic response as determined by PT ratio/INR. When warfarin has produced the desired PT ratio/INR or prothrombin activity, heparin may be discontinued.

Warfarin may increase the aPTT test. During initial therapy with warfarin, the interference with heparin anticoagulation is of minimal clinical significance.

As heparin may affect the PT, patients receiving both heparin and warfarin should have blood drawn for PT ratio/INR determination, at least: 5 hours after the last i.v. bolus dose of heparin; or 4 hours after cessation of a continuous i.v. infusion of heparin; or 24 hours after last s.c. heparin injection.

Reconstituted Solutions: Available for i.v. use only. Not recommended for i.m. administration. Reconstitute with 2.7 mL of sterile Water for Injection to yield 2 mg/mL. After reconstitution, store at controlled room temperature (15 to 30°C) and use within 4 hours. Do not refrigerate. Discard any unused solution. The reconstituted solution should be inspected visually for discoloration, haziness, particulate matter and leakage prior to administration.

Information for the Patient: See Blue Section—Information for the Patient "Coumadin".

Supplied: Injection: Each vial contains: warfarin sodium 5.4 mg. Nonmedicinal ingredients: mannitol, sodium chloride, sodium hydroxide (as needed for pH adjustment from 8.1 to 8.3), sodium phosphate, dibasic, heptahydrate and sodium phosphate monobasic, monohydrate. Single use vials, packages of 6. Protect from light. Store in carton until contents have been used. Store at controlled room temperature (15 to 30°C). After reconstitution, store at controlled room temperature (15 to 30°C) and use within 4 hours. Do not refrigerate.

Tablets: 1 mg: Each pink, single scored tablet with $^{\text{COUMADIN}}_{1}$ on one side and DuPont on the other, contains: crystalline warfarin sodium 1 mg. Nonmedicinal ingredients: D&C Red #6, lactose anhydrous, magnesium stearate and pregelatinized tapioca starch. Bottles of 100 and 250.

2 mg: Each lavender, single scored tablet with $^{\text{COUMADIN}}_{2}$ on one side and DuPont on the other, contains: crystalline warfarin sodium 2 mg. Nonmedicinal ingredients: FD&C Blue #2 and FD&C Red #40, lactose anhydrous, magnesium stearate and pregelatinized tapioca starch. Bottles of 100 and 250.

2.5 mg: Each green, single scored tablet with $^{\text{COUMADIN}}_{2\frac{1}{2}}$ on one side and DuPont on the other, contains crystalline warfarin sodium 2.5 mg. Nonmedicinal ingredients: FD&C Blue #1, D&C Yellow #10, lactose anhydrous, magnesium stearate and pregelatinized tapioca starch. Bottles of 100 and 250.

4 mg: Each blue, single scored tablet with $^{\text{COUMADIN}}_{4}$ on one side and DuPont on the other, contains: crystalline warfarin sodium 4 mg. Nonmedicinal ingredients: FD&C Blue #1 Lake, lactose anhydrous, magnesium stearate and pregelatinized tapioca starch. Bottles of 100 and 250.

5 mg: Each peach, single scored tablet with $^{\text{COUMADIN}}_{5}$ on one side and DuPont on the other, contains: crystalline warfarin sodium 5 mg. Nonmedicinal ingredients: FD&C Yellow #6, lactose anhydrous, magnesium stearate and pregelatinized tapioca starch. Bottles of 100 and 250.

10 mg: Each white, single scored tablet with $^{\text{COUMADIN}}_{10}$ on one side and DuPont on the other, contains: crystalline warfarin sodium 10 mg. Nonmedicinal ingredients: lactose anhydrous, magnesium stearate and pregelatinized tapioca starch. Dye-free. Bottles of 100.

Protect from light. Store in carton until contents have been used. Store at controlled room temperature (15 to 30°C). Dispense in a tight, light-resistant container as defined in the USP.

(Shown in Product Recognition Section)

Reviewed 1998

COVERSYL® Ⓟ
Servier

Perindopril Erbumine

Angiotensin Converting Enzyme Inhibitor

Pharmacology: Perindopril is a nonsulphydryl angiotensin-converting enzyme (ACE) inhibitor, which is used in the treatment of hypertension.

Following oral administration, perindopril is rapidly hydrolyzed to perindoprilat, its principal active metabolite.

Angiotensin-converting enzyme catalyzes the conversion of angiotensin I to the vasoconstrictor substance, angiotensin II. Angiotensin II also stimulates aldosterone secretion by the adrenal cortex. Inhibition of ACE activity leads to decreased levels of angiotensin II, thereby resulting in decreased vasoconstriction and decreased aldosterone secretion. The latter change may result in a small increase in serum potassium (see Precautions, Hyperkalemia and Potassium-Sparing Diuretics). Decreased levels of angiotensin II and the accompanying lack of negative feedback on renal renin secretion results in increases in plasma renin activity.

ACE is identical to kininase II. Thus, perindopril administration may interfere with the degradation of the vasodepressor peptide bradykinin. It is not known whether this effect contributes to the therapeutic activity of perindopril.

The mechanism through which perindopril lowers blood pressure appears to result primarily from suppression of the renin-angiotensin-aldosterone system. Although perindopril had an antihypertensive activity in all races studied, black hypertensive patients (usually a low-renin hypertensive population) had a smaller average response to ACE inhibitor therapy than non-black patients.

Pharmacokinetics and Metabolism: After oral administration, perindopril is rapidly absorbed with peak plasma concentrations occurring at about 1 hour, with bioavailability of 65 to 70%.

Following absorption, perindopril is converted into perindoprilat, its active metabolite, with a mean bioavailability of about 20%. Peak plasma concentration of perindoprilat is attained within 4 to 7 hours and corresponding peak pharmacodynamic activity occurs at about 6 hours.

The presence of food in the gastrointestinal tract does not affect the rate or extent of absorption with perindopril. However, the extent of biotransformation of perindopril to perindoprilat is reduced by approximately 35%. Due to the saturable nature of ACE inhibition, pharmacodynamic effect, as measured by area under the plasma ACE inhibition curve, is reduced by approximately 15%.

Perindoprilat is not extensively bound to protein, this being only 10 to 20%, but binding is concentration dependent. The

Coversyl (cont'd)

volume of distribution is approximately 0.2 L/kg for unbound perindoprilat.

Perindoprilat exhibits an apparent mean half-life of 3 to 10 hours for the majority of its elimination from plasma, as well as a prolonged terminal elimination half-life of 30 to 120 hours resulting from slow dissociation of perindoprilat from ACE binding sites. With ongoing administration of perindopril, steady-state plasma levels of perindoprilat are obtained in 3 to 6 days.

Perindopril is extensively metabolized following oral administration, with only 4 to 12% of the dose recovered unchanged in the urine. Six metabolites have been identified. They include perindoprilat, the active form, and 5 others that do not possess appreciable therapeutic activity. These are comprised of perindopril and perindoprilat glucuronides, a perindopril lactam, and two perindoprilat lactams.

The clearance of perindoprilat and other metabolites is primarily by the renal pathway.

In a pharmacokinetic study with single dose administration, mean peak plasma concentrations of perindoprilat were significantly higher in elderly healthy volunteers (32.5 ng/mL) than in younger volunteers (13.5 ng/mL) due to both higher bioavailability and reduced renal clearance in this group.

Single and multiple dose pharmacokinetics of perindopril were evaluated in a study of elderly hypertensive patients (72 to 91 years of age), C_{max} and AUC were found to be approximately 2-fold higher than in healthy younger subjects. The higher concentrations of perindoprilat observed in these patients were reflected in greater ACE inhibition (see Precautions, Geriatrics, and Dosage, Geriatrics).

In patients with renal insufficiency, perindoprilat AUC increases with decreasing renal function. At creatinine clearances of 30 to 80 mL/min, AUC is about double that of 100 mL/min. When creatinine clearance drops below 30 mL/min, AUC increases more markedly.

Patients with heart failure have reduced perindoprilat clearance, which may result in a dose interval AUC that is increased up to 40%.

The bioavailability of perindoprilat is increased in patients with impaired hepatic function. Plasma concentrations in patients with hepatic impairment were about 50% higher than those observed in healthy subjects or hypertensive patients with normal liver function.

Perindopril, and its active metabolite perindoprilat, are dialyzable. In a limited number of patients studied, perindopril hemodialysis clearance ranged from 41.7 to 76.7 mL/min (mean 52.0 mL/min). Perindoprilat hemodialysis clearance ranged from 37.4 to 91.0 mL/min (mean 67.2 mL/min).

Pharmacodynamics: In most patients with mild to moderate essential hypertension, administration of 4 to 8 mg daily of perindopril results in a reduction of both supine and standing blood pressure with little or no effect on heart rate. Antihypertensive activity commences within 1 hour with peak effects usually achieved by 4 to 6 hours after dosing. At recommended doses given once daily, antihypertensive effects persist over 24 hours. The blood pressure reductions observed at trough plasma concentration were 75 to 100% of peak effects. When once and twice daily dosing were compared, the twice daily regimen was slightly superior, but by no more than about 0.5 to 1 mmHg. Abrupt withdrawal of perindopril has not been associated with a rapid increase in blood pressure. In studies carried out in patients with mild to moderate essential hypertension, the reduction in blood pressure was accompanied by a reduction in peripheral resistance with no change in glomerular filtration rate. When perindopril is given together with thiazide-type diuretics, the antihypertensive effects are additive.

In uncontrolled studies in patients with insulin-dependent diabetes, perindopril did not appear to affect glycemic control. In long-term use in this population, no effect on urinary protein excretion was seen.

Indications: In the treatment of mild to moderate essential hypertension. It may be used alone or in association with other drugs, particularly thiazide diuretics.

In using perindopril, consideration should be given to the risk of angioedema (see Warnings).

Perindopril should normally be used in those patients in whom treatment with a diuretic or a beta-blocker was found ineffective or has been associated with unacceptable adverse effects.

Perindopril can also be tried as an initial agent in those patients in whom use of diuretics and/or beta-blockers is contraindicated or in patients with medical conditions in which these drugs frequently cause serious adverse effects.

The safety and efficacy of perindopril in congestive heart failure and renovascular hypertension have not been established and therefore, its use in these conditions is not recommended.

The safety and efficacy of concurrent use of perindopril with antihypertensive agents other than thiazide diuretics have not been established.

Pregnancy: **When used in pregnancy during the second and third trimesters, ACE inhibitors can cause injury or even death of the developing fetus. When pregnancy is detected perindopril should be discontinued as soon as possible (see Warnings, Pregnancy, and Information for the Patient).**

Contraindications: In patients who are hypersensitive to this product and in patients with a history of angioedema related to previous treatment with an angiotensin-converting enzyme inhibitor.

Warnings: Angioedema: Angioedema has been reported in patients treated with ACE inhibitors, including perindopril. Angioedema associated with laryngeal involvement may be fatal. If laryngeal stridor or angioedema of the face, tongue, or glottis occurs, perindopril should be discontinued immediately, the patient treated appropriately in accordance with accepted medical care, and carefully observed until the swelling disappears. In instances where swelling is confined to the face and lips, the condition generally resolves without treatment, although antihistamines may be useful in relieving symptoms. Where there is involvement of the tongue, glottis or larynx, likely to cause airway obstruction, appropriate therapy (including but not limited to 0.3 to 0.5 mL of s.c. epinephrine solution 1:1 000) should be administered promptly (see Adverse Effects).

Patients with a history of angioedema unrelated to ACE inhibitor therapy may be at increased risk of angioedema while receiving an ACE inhibitor (see Contraindications).

Hypotension: Perindopril can cause symptomatic hypotension. It is more likely to occur after the first or second dose or when the dose was increased and in patients who are volume depleted by diuretic therapy, dietary salt restriction, dialysis, diarrhea, or vomiting. In patients with ischemic heart or cerebrovascular disease, an excessive fall in blood pressure could result in a myocardial infarction or cerebrovascular accident (see Adverse Effects). Because of the potential fall in blood pressure in these patients, therapy with perindopril should be started under close medical supervision. Such patients should be followed closely for the first weeks of treatment and whenever the dose of perindopril is increased. In patients with severe congestive heart failure, with or without associated renal insufficiency, excessive hypotension can be associated with oliguria and/or progressive azotemia and, rarely, with acute renal failure and/or progressive death.

If hypotension occurs, the patient should be placed in a supine position and, if necessary, receive an i.v. infusion of 0.9% sodium chloride. A transient hypotensive response is not a contraindication to further doses which usually can be given without difficulty once the blood pressure has increased after volume expansion. However, lower doses of perindopril and/or reduced concomitant diuretic therapy should be considered.

Neutropenia/Agranulocytosis: Agranulocytosis and bone marrow depression have been caused by ACE inhibitors. Several cases of neutropenia have been reported in which a causal relationship to the administration of perindopril cannot be excluded. Periodic monitoring of white blood cell counts should be considered, especially in patients with collagen vascular disease and/or renal disease.

Pregnancy: ACE inhibitors can cause fetal and neonatal morbidity and mortality when administered to pregnant women. Several dozen cases have been reported in the world literature. When pregnancy is detected, perindopril should be discontinued as soon as possible.

In rare cases (probably less than 1 in every 1 000 pregnancies) in which no alternative to ACE inhibitors therapy will be found, the mothers should be apprised of the potential hazards to their fetuses. Serial ultrasound examinations should be performed to assess fetal development and well-being and the volume of amniotic fluid.

If oligohydramnios is observed, perindopril should be discontinued unless it is considered lifesaving to the mother. A nonstress test (NST) and/or a biophysical profiling (BPP) may be appropriate, depending upon the week of pregnancy. If concerns regarding fetal well-being still persist, a contraction stress testing (CST) should be considered. Patients and physicians should be aware, however, that oligohydramnios may not appear until after the fetus has sustained irreversible injury.

Infants with a history of in utero exposure to ACE inhibitors should be closely observed for hypotension, oliguria, and hyperkalemia. If oliguria occurs, attention should be directed toward support of blood pressure and renal perfusion. Exchange transfusion or dialysis may be required as a means of reversing hypotension and/or substituting for impaired renal function; however, limited experience with those procedures has not been associated with significant clinical benefit. Perindopril can be removed from the body by hemodialysis (see Pharmacology, Pharmacokinetics and Metabolism).

Human data: It is not known whether exposure limited to the first trimester of pregnancy can adversely affect fetal outcome. The use of ACE inhibitors during the second and third trimesters of pregnancy has been associated with fetal and neonatal injury including hypotension, neonatal skull hypoplasia, anuria, reversible or irreversible renal failure, and death. Oligohydramnios has also been reported, presumably resulting from decreased fetal renal function; oligohydramnios in this setting has been associated with fetal limb contractures, craniofacial deformation, and hypoplastic lung development. Prematurity and patent ductus arteriosus have also been reported, although it is not clear whether these occurrences were due to the ACE inhibitor exposure.

Animal data: Perindopril was given to mice (1 to 20 mg/kg/day), rats (1 to 16 mg/kg/day), rabbits (0.5 to 5 mg/kg/day) and monkeys (1 to 16 mg/kg/day) during the gestation period. At the highest dose in rats (16 mg/kg/day), maternal toxicity was associated with fetal toxicity but neither embryotoxicity nor teratogenicity was observed. A study in monkeys at high dose (16 mg/kg/day) demonstrated no fetal toxicity although maternal toxicity was slight.

Precautions: Renal Impairment: Renal function should be assessed before initiating therapy with perindopril.

Perindopril should be used with caution in patients with renal insufficiency as they may require reduced or less frequent dosing (see Dosage). Close monitoring of renal function during therapy should be performed as deemed appropriate in those with renal insufficiency. In the majority, renal function will not alter, or may improve.

In patients with severe heart failure, whose renal function may depend on the activity of the renin-angiotensin-aldosterone system, treatment with ACE inhibitors, including perindopril, may be associated with oliguria and/or progressive azotemia and rarely acute renal failure and/or death.

In hypertensive patients with unilateral or bilateral renal artery stenosis, increases in blood urea nitrogen and serum creatinine had been observed in some patients following ACE inhibitor therapy. These increases were almost always reversible upon discontinuation of the ACE inhibitor and/or diuretic therapy. In such patients, renal function should be closely monitored.

Some hypertensive patients, with no apparent pre-existing renal disease, have developed increases in blood urea and creatinine especially when ACE inhibitor has been given concurrently with a diuretic. Dosage reduction and/or discontinuation of the diuretic and/or perindopril may be required.

Anaphylactoid Reactions during Membrane Exposure: Anaphylactoid reactions have been reported in patients dialyzed with high-flux membranes (e.g., polyacrylonitrile [PAN]) and treated concomitantly with an ACE inhibitor. Dialysis should be stopped immediately if symptoms such as nausea, abdominal cramps, burning, angioedema, shortness of breath and severe hypotension occur. Symptoms are not relieved by antihistamines. In these patients, consideration should be given to using a different type of dialysis membrane or a different class of antihypertensive agents.

Anaphylactoid Reactions during Desensitization: There have been isolated reports of patients experiencing sustained, life-threatening anaphylactoid reactions while receiving ACE inhibitors during desensitization treatment with hymenoptera (bees, wasps) venom. In the same patients, these reactions have been avoided when ACE inhibitors were temporarily withheld for at least 24 hours, but they reappeared upon inadvertent rechallenge.

Cough: A dry, persistent cough, which usually disappears only after withdrawal or lowering of the dose of perindopril has been reported. Such possibility should be considered as part of the differential diagnosis of the cough.

Surgery/Anesthesia: ACE inhibitors may augment the hypotensive effects of anesthetics and analgesics. In patients undergoing major surgery or during anesthesia with agents that produce hypotension, perindopril will block the angiotensin II formation that could otherwise occur secondary to compensatory renin release. If hypotension occurs and is considered to be due to this mechanism, it can be corrected by volume expansion.

Hyperkalemia and Potassium-Sparing Diuretics: In clinical trials, hyperkalemia (serum potassium >5.7 mEq/L) occurred in approximately 1.4% of hypertensive patients. In most cases, these were isolated values which resolved despite continued therapy. In controlled studies, no patient discontinued therapy due to hyperkalemia. Risk factors for development of hyperkalemia may include renal insufficiency, diabetes mellitus, and the concomitant use of potassium-sparing diuretics, potassium supplements, potassium-containing salt substitutes or other drugs associated with increases in serum potassium (e.g., heparin) (see Drug Interactions).

Valvular Stenosis: There is concern on theoretical grounds that patients with aortic stenosis might be at particular risk of decreased coronary perfusion when treated with vasodilators because they do not develop as much afterload reduction.

Patients with Impaired Liver Function: Hepatitis (hepatocellular and/or cholestatic), elevations of liver enzymes and/or serum bilirubin have occurred during therapy with ACE inhibitors, in patients with or without pre-existing liver abnormalities. In most cases, the changes were reversed upon discontinuation of the drug.

Elevations of liver enzymes and/or serum bilirubin have been reported with perindopril (see Adverse Effects). Should the patient receiving perindopril experience any unexplained symptoms, particularly during the first weeks or months of treatment, it is recommended that a full set of liver function tests and any other necessary investigation be carried out. Discontinuation of perindopril should be considered when appropriate.

Perindopril should be used with particular caution in patients with pre-existing liver abnormalities. In such patients, baseline liver function tests should be obtained before administration of the drug and close monitoring of response and metabolic effects should apply.

Lactation: Milk of lactating rats contains radioactivity following administration of perindopril. It is not known whether perindopril is secreted in human milk. Because many drugs are secreted in human milk, caution should be exercised when perindopril is given to a nursing mother, and in general, nursing should be interrupted.

Children: The safety and effectiveness of perindopril in children have not been established. Its use in this age group, therefore, is not recommended.

Geriatrics: Although clinical experience has not identified significant differences in response between the elderly (>65 years) and younger patients, greater sensitivity of some older individuals cannot be ruled out.

Drug Interactions: Concomitant Diuretic Therapy: Patients concomitantly taking ACE inhibitors and diuretics, and especially those in whom diuretic therapy was recently instituted, may occasionally experience an excessive reduction of blood pressure after initiation of therapy. The possibility of hypotensive effects after the first dose of perindopril can be minimized by either discontinuing the diuretic or increasing the salt intake prior to initiation of treatment with perindopril. If it is not possible to discontinue the diuretic, the starting dose of perindopril can be reduced, and the patient should be closely observed for several hours following the initial dose and until blood pressure has stabilized (see Warnings and Dosage).

Agents Increasing Serum Potassium: Since perindopril decreases aldosterone production, elevation of serum potassium may occur. Potassium-sparing diuretics such as spironolactone, triamterene or amiloride, or potassium supplements should be given only for documented hypokalemia and with caution and frequent monitoring of serum potassium, since they may lead to significant increase in serum potassium. Salt substitutes that contain potassium should also be used with caution.

Agents Causing Renin Release: The antihypertensive effect of perindopril is augmented by antihypertensive agents that cause renin release (e.g., diuretics).

Lithium: Increased serum lithium levels and symptoms of lithium toxicity have been reported in patients receiving concomitant lithium and ACE inhibitor therapy. These drugs should be coadministered with caution and frequent monitoring of serum lithium levels is recommended. If a diuretic is also used, the risk of lithium toxicity may be further increased.

Agents Affecting Sympathetic Activity: Agents affecting sympathetic activity (e.g., ganglionic blocking agents or adrenergic neuron blocking agents) may be used with caution. Beta-adrenergic blocking drugs add further antihypertensive effect to perindopril.

Digoxin: A pharmacokinetic study has shown no effect on plasma digoxin concentration when coadministered with perindopril.

Information for the Patient: Angioedema: Angioedema, including laryngeal edema, may occur especially following the first dose of perindopril. Patients should be so advised and told to report immediately any signs or symptoms suggesting angioedema (swelling of face, eyes, lips, tongue, difficulty in swallowing or breathing); they should immediately stop taking perindopril and consult with their physician (see Warnings).

Hypotension: Patients should be cautioned to report lightheadedness, especially during the first few days of perindopril therapy. If actual syncope occurs, patients should be told to discontinue the drug and consult with their physician.

All patients should be cautioned that excessive perspiration and dehydration may lead to an excessive fall in blood pressure because of reduction in fluid volume. Other causes of volume depletion such as vomiting or diarrhea may also lead to a fall in blood pressure; patients should be advised to consult with their physician.

Agranulocytosis/Neutropenia: Patients should be advised to report promptly any signs or symptoms of infection (e.g., pharyngitis, fever) since this may be a sign of neutropenia (see Warnings and Adverse Effects).

Impaired Liver Function: Patients should be advised to return to the physician if he/she experiences any symptoms possibly related to liver dysfunction. This would include "viral-like symptoms" in the first weeks to months of therapy (such as fever, malaise, muscle pain, rash or adenopathy which are possible indicators of hypersensitivity reactions), or if abdominal pain, nausea or vomiting, loss of appetite, jaundice, itching or any other unexplained symptoms occur during therapy.

Hyperkalemia: Patients should be advised not to use potassium supplements or salt substitutes containing potassium without consulting their physician (see Precautions and Adverse Effects).

Pregnancy: Since the use of perindopril during pregnancy can cause injury and even death of the developing fetus, patients should be advised to report promptly to their physician if they become pregnant.

Adverse Effects: Perindopril has been evaluated for safety in approximately 3 000 hypertensive patients, of which, 1 216 patients, 181 of which were elderly, participated in controlled clinical trials. Perindopril has been evaluated for long-term safety in approximately 1 000 patients treated for 1 year or more.

The most severe adverse reactions occurring in all patients treated with perindopril in controlled clinical trials were: angioedema (0.1%), orthostatic hypotension (0.4%) and syncope (0.6%). Myocardial infarction and cerebrovascular accident occurred possibly secondary to excessive hypotension in high risk patients (see Warnings).

The most frequent adverse events which occurred in North-American placebo-controlled trials with perindopril monotherapy in hypertension (n=630) were: headache (26.0%), cough (13.0%), asthenia (8.7%), dizziness (8.6%), upper respiratory infection (7.9%), back pain (6.8%), diarrhea (4.6%) and edema (4.3%). Discontinuation of therapy because of adverse events was required in 6.9% of the patients.

Adverse events, irrespective of causal relationship to the drug, which occurred in less than 1% of hypertensive patients treated with perindopril in controlled or uncontrolled trials, and in post-marketing experience are listed as follows:

Body as a Whole: anaphylactic reaction (0.1%), angioedema (0.1%), chest pain, neck pain, edema, facial edema (0.3%), fever, malaise, pain, peripheral edema, thirst

Cardiovascular: arrhythmia, bradycardia, cold extremities, myocardial infarction (0.3%), orthostatic hypotension (0.4%), orthostatic symptoms, syncope, vasodilatation.

Dermatological: alopecia, cutaneous signs, dermatitis, fever blisters, pruritus, purpura (0.1%), rash, sweating, urticaria, toxic erythroderma.

Gastrointestinal: anorexia, constipation, dry mouth, dry mucous membranes, dyspepsia, flatulence, gastrointestinal hemorrhage, increased appetite, mesenteric infarction (1 patient), stomatitis.

Hematological: neutropenia, thrombocytopenia.

Musculoskeletal: arthralgia, arthritis, bone pain, hypertonia/muscle cramps, myalgia, myasthenia.

Neurological/Psychiatric: abnormal dreams, agitation, amnesia, cerebrovascular accident (0.3%), cognitive dysfunction, confusion, depression, hyperkinesia, memory disturbance, mood disturbance, nervousness, perceptual distortion, somnolence, speech difficulties, tremor, vertigo.

Respiratory: bronchitis, dyspnea, pharyngitis, pneumonia, rhinitis, sinusitis, throat disorder, pulmonary fibrosis.

Urogenital: hematuria, kidney stones, menstrual disorder, nocturia, oliguria, polyuria, scrotal edema, urinary frequency, urinary incontinence, urinary retention, renal failure.

Special Senses: abnormal vision, earache, lacrimation, abnormal taste, tinnitus.

Laboratory Test Abnormalities: Serum electrolytes: hyperkalemia (see Precautions).

Blood Urea Nitrogen/Serum Creatinine: Elevations of BUN or serum creatinine (BUN >40 mg/dL; serum creatinine >2.5 mg/dL) have been observed, respectively, in 0.2% and 0.3% of patients treated with perindopril monotherapy. Decreases in serum sodium and increases in serum creatinine occurred more frequently in patients on concomitant diuretics than in those treated with perindopril alone.

Hematology: Small decreases in hemoglobin and hematocrit occurred in hypertensive patients treated with perindopril, but were rarely of clinical importance. In controlled clinical trials, no patient was discontinued from therapy due to the development of anemia.

Liver Function: Elevations of liver enzymes and/or serum bilirubin have been observed (see Precautions).

In an open-labelled European study of about 47 000 patients with essential hypertension, seen in everyday medical practice, and treated for 1 year with perindopril, with or without multiple other medications, the most frequently observed adverse events were: cough 9.7%, digestive symptoms 2.0%, fatigue 1.8%, headache 1.4% and dizziness 1.4%. In total, 5.1% of patients in this study withdrew due to adverse events, 3.2% due to cough.

Overdose: Symptoms and Treatment: Limited data are available regarding overdosage of perindopril in humans. The most likely clinical manifestation would be symptoms attributable to severe hypotension, which should normally be treated by i.v. volume expansion with 0.9% sodium chloride.

However, of the 2 cases reported in the perindopril clinical trials, 1 (dosage unknown) required ventilation assistance and the other developed hypothermia, circulatory arrest, and subsequently died, following ingestion of up to 180 mg of perindopril. Thus, intervention in perindopril overdosage may require vigorous support.

Perindopril can be removed by hemodialysis, with clearances of about 52 mL/min for perindopril, and 67 mL/min for perindoprilat, the active metabolite (see Pharmacology, Pharmacokinetics and Metabolism).

Dosage: Dosage of perindopril must be individualized.

Initiation of therapy requires consideration of recent antihypertensive drug treatment, the extent of blood pressure elevation and salt restriction. The dosage of other antihypertensive agents being used with perindopril may need to be adjusted. The presence of food in the gastrointestinal tract reduces bioavailability of perindoprilat.

Monotherapy: The recommended initial dose of perindopril, in patients not on diuretics, is 4 mg once daily. Dosage should be adjusted according to blood pressure response, generally at intervals of at least 2 weeks. The usual maintenance dose is 4 to 8 mg daily administered in a single daily dose. No additional blood pressure lowering effects were achieved with doses greater than 8 mg daily.

In some patients treated once daily, the antihypertensive effect may diminish towards the end of the dosing interval. This can be evaluated by measuring blood pressure just prior to dosing to determine whether satisfactory control is maintained for 24 hours. If it is not, either twice daily administration with the same total daily dose, or an increase in dose should be considered. If blood pressure is not controlled with perindopril alone, a diuretic may be added. After the addition of a diuretic, it may be possible to reduce the dose of perindopril.

Concomitant Diuretic Therapy: Symptomatic hypotension occasionally may occur following the inital dose of perindopril and is more likely in patients who are currently being treated with a diuretic. The diuretic should, if possible, be discontinued for 2 or 3 days before beginning therapy with perindopril to reduce the likelihood of hypotension (see Warnings). If the diuretic cannot be discontinued, an initial dose of 2 mg perindopril should be used with careful medical supervision for several hours and until blood pressure has stabilized. The

Coversyl (cont'd)

dosage of perindopril should subsequently be titrated to the optimal response.

Geriatrics: In the elderly, treatment should begin with a 2 mg dose in the morning. If necessary, after 1 month of treatment this dose can be increased to 4 mg daily given in 1 or 2 divided doses.

Renal Impairment: In case of renal impairment, the dosage of perindopril must be adjusted. The following dosages are recommended: see Table I.

Table I—Coversyl

Dosage—Renal Impairment

Creatinine Clearance	Recommended Dosage
Between 30 and 60 mL/min	2 mg/day
Between 15 and 30 mL/min	2 mg every other day
<15 mL/min	2 mg on the day of dialysis

In these patients, normal medical follow up includes periodic control of potassium and creatinine.

Supplied: 2 mg: Each white, round, biconvex tablet contains: perindopril erbumine 2 mg. Nonmedicinal ingredients: hydrophobic colloidal silica, lactose, magnesium stearate and microcrystalline cellulose. Boxes containing 1 aluminum/PVC blister strip of 30 tablets.

4 mg: Each white, rod-shaped biconvex, scored tablet contains: perindopril erbumine 4 mg. Nonmedicinal ingredients: hydrophobic colloidal silica, lactose, magnesium stearate and microcrystalline cellulose. Boxes containing 1 aluminum/PVC blister strip of 30 tablets.

Store at room temperature (15 to 30°C).

(Shown in Product Recognition Section)

COZAAR® ℞

MSD

Losartan Potassium

Angiotensin II Receptor Antagonist

Pharmacology: Losartan antagonizes angiotensin II by blocking the angiotensin type 1 (AT_1) receptor.

Angiotensin II is the primary vasoactive hormone of the renin-angiotensin system. Its effects include vasoconstriction and the stimulation of aldosterone secretion by the adrenal cortex.

Losartan and its active metabolite, E-3174, block the vasoconstrictor and aldosterone-secreting effects of angiotensin II by selectively blocking the binding of angiotensin II to AT_1 receptors found in many tissues, including vascular smooth muscle. A second type of angiotensin II receptor has been identified as the AT_2 receptor, but it plays no known role in cardiovascular homeostasis to date. Both losartan and its active metabolite do not exhibit any agonist activity at the AT_1 receptor, and have much greater affinity, in the order of 1 000-fold, for the AT_1 receptor than for the AT_2 receptor. In vitro binding studies indicate that losartan itself is a reversible, competitive antagonist at the AT_1 receptor, while the active metabolite is 10 to 40 times more potent than losartan, and is a reversible, non-competitive antagonist of the AT_1 receptor.

Neither losartan nor its active metabolite inhibits angiotensin converting enzyme (ACE), also known as kininase II, the enzyme that converts angiotensin I to angiotensin II and degrades bradykinin, nor do they bind to or block other hormone receptors or ion channels known to be important in cardiovascular regulation.

Pharmacokinetics: Losartan is an orally active agent that undergoes substantial first-pass metabolism by cytochrome P_{450} enzymes. It is converted, in part, to an active carboxylic acid metabolite, E-3174, that is responsible for most of the angiotensin II receptor antagonism that follows oral losartan administration.

The terminal half-life of losartan itself is about 2 hours, and that of the active metabolite, about 6 to 9 hours. The pharmacokinetics of losartan and this metabolite are linear with oral losartan doses up to 200 mg and do not change over time. Neither losartan nor its metabolite accumulate in plasma upon repeated once-daily administration.

Following oral administration, losartan is well absorbed, with systemic bioavailability of losartan approximately 33%. About 14% of an orally-administered dose of losartan is converted to the active metabolite, although about 1% of subjects did not convert losartan efficiently to the active metabolite.

Mean peak concentrations of losartan occur at about 1 hour, and that of its active metabolite at about 3 to 4 hours. Although maximum plasma concentrations of losartan and its active metabolite are approximately equal, the AUC of the metabolite is about 4 times greater than that of losartan.

Both losartan and its active metabolite are highly bound to plasma proteins, primarily albumin, with plasma free fractions of 1.3% and 0.2% respectively. Plasma protein binding is constant over the concentration range achieved with recommended doses. Studies in rats indicate that losartan crosses the blood-brain barrier poorly, if at all.

Various losartan metabolites have been identified in human plasma and urine. In addition to the active carboxylic acid metabolite, E-3174, several inactive metabolites are formed. In vitro studies indicate that the cytochrome P_{450} isoenzymes 2C9 and 3A4 are involved in the biotransformation of losartan to its metabolites.

The volume of distribution of losartan is about 34 L, and that of the active metabolite is about 12 L.

Total plasma clearance of losartan is about 600 mL/min, with about 75 mL/min accounted for by renal clearance. Total plasma clearance of the active metabolite is about 50 mL/min, with about 25 mL/min accounted for by renal clearance. Both biliary and urinary excretion contribute substantially to the elimination of losartan and its metabolites.

Following oral ^{14}C-labeled losartan, about 35% of radioactivity is recovered in the urine and about 60% in the feces. Following an i.v. dose of ^{14}C-labeled losartan, about 45% of radioactivity is recovered in the urine and 50% in the feces.

Pharmacodynamics: Losartan inhibits the pressor effect of angiotensin II. A dose of 100 mg inhibits this effect by about 85% at peak, with 25 to 40% inhibition persisting for 24 hours. Removal of the negative feedback of angiotensin II causes a 2 to 3 fold rise in plasma renin activity, and a consequent rise in angiotensin II plasma concentration, in hypertensive patients.

Maximum blood pressure lowering, following oral administration of a single dose of losartan, as seen in hypertensive patients, occurs at about 6 hours.

In losartan-treated patients during controlled trials, there was no meaningful change in heart rate.

There is no apparent rebound effect after abrupt withdrawal of losartan therapy.

Black hypertensive patients show a smaller average blood pressure response to losartan monotherapy than other hypertensive patients.

Indications: Treatment of essential hypertension.

Losartan may be used alone or concomitantly with thiazide diuretics.

A great majority of patients with severe hypertension in controlled clinical trials required combination therapy. Losartan has been used concomitantly with beta-blockers and calcium channel blockers, but the data on such use are limited.

Losartan should normally be used in those patients in whom treatment with diuretic or beta-blocker was found ineffective or has been associated with unacceptable adverse effects. Losartan can also be tried as an initial agent in those patients in whom the use of diuretics and/or beta-blockers is contraindicated or in patients with medical conditions in which these drugs frequently cause serious adverse effects.

The safety and efficacy of concurrent use with angiotensin converting enzyme inhibitors have not been established.

Contraindications: In patients who are hypersensitive to any component of this product.

Warnings: *Pregnancy:* Drugs that act directly on the renin-angiotensin system can cause fetal and neonatal morbidity and death when administered to pregnant women. When pregnancy is detected, losartan should be discontinued as soon as possible.

The use of drugs that act directly on the renin-angiotensin system during the second and third trimesters of pregnancy has been associated with fetal and neonatal injury, including hypotension, neonatal skull hypoplasia, anuria, reversible or irreversible renal failure and death. Oligohydramnios has also been reported, presumably resulting from decreased fetal renal function; oligohydramnios in this setting has been associated with fetal limb contractures, craniofacial deformation, and hypoplastic lung development. Prematurity, intrauterine growth retardation, and patent ductus arteriosus have also been reported, although it is not clear whether these occurrences were due to exposure to the drug. These adverse effects do not appear to have resulted from intrauterine drug exposure that has been limited to the first trimester.

Mothers whose embryos and fetuses are exposed to an angiotensin II receptor antagonist only during the first trimester should be so informed. Nonetheless, when patients become pregnant, physicians should have the patient discontinue the use of losartan as soon as possible.

Rarely (probably less often than once in every thousand pregnancies), no alternative to an angiotensin II receptor antagonist will be found. In these rare cases, the mothers should be apprised of the potential hazards to their fetuses, and serial ultrasound examinations should be performed to assess the intra-amniotic environment.

If oligohydramnios is observed, losartan should be discontinued unless it is considered life-saving for the mother. Contraction stress testing (CST), a non-stress test (NST), or biophysical profiling (BPP) may be appropriate, depending upon the week of pregnancy. Patients and physicians should be aware, however, that oligohydramnios may not appear until after the fetus has sustained irreversible injury.

Infants with histories of in utero exposure to an angiotensin II receptor antagonist should be closely observed for hypotension, oliguria, and hyperkalemia. If oliguria occurs, attention should be directed toward support of blood pressure and renal perfusion. Exchange transfusion may be required as means of reversing hypotension and/or substituting for impaired renal function. Neither losartan nor the active metabolite can be removed by hemodialysis.

Animal Data: Losartan has been shown to produce adverse effects in rat fetuses and neonates, which include decreased body weight, mortality and/or renal toxicity. Significant levels of losartan and its active metabolite were shown to be present in rat milk. Based on pharmacokinetic assessments, these findings are attributed to drug exposure in late gestation and during lactation.

Hypotension: Occasionally, symptomatic hypotension has occurred after administration of losartan, in some cases after the first dose. It is more likely to occur in patients who are volume-depleted by diuretic therapy, dietary salt restriction, dialysis, diarrhea or vomiting. In these patients, because of the potential fall in blood pressure, therapy should be started under close medical supervision. Similar considerations apply to patients with ischemic heart or cerebrovascular disease, in whom an excessive fall in blood pressure could result in myocardial infarction or cerebrovascular accident.

Precautions: Renal Impairment: As a consequence of inhibiting the renin-angiotensin-aldosterone system, changes in renal function have been seen in susceptible individuals. In patients whose renal function may depend on the activity of the renin-angiotensin-aldosterone system, such as patients with bilateral renal artery stenosis, unilateral renal artery stenosis to a solitary kidney, or severe congestive heart failure, treatment with agents that inhibit this system has been associated with oliguria, progressive azotemia, and rarely, acute renal failure and/or death. In susceptible patients, concomitant diuretic use may further increase risk.

Use of losartan should include appropriate assessment of renal function.

Impaired Liver Function: Based on pharmacokinetic data which demonstrate significantly increased plasma concentrations of losartan and its active metabolite in cirrhotic patients after administration of Cozaar, a lower dose should be considered for patients with hepatic impairment or a history of hepatic impairment (see Dosage).

Valvular Stenosis: There is concern on theoretical grounds that patients with aortic stenosis might be at particular risk of decreased coronary perfusion when treated with vasodilators because they do not develop as much afterload reduction.

Lactation: It is not known whether losartan or its active metabolite are excreted in human milk, however significant levels of both of these compounds have been shown to be present in the milk of lactating rats. Because many drugs are excreted in human milk, and because of their potential for affecting the nursing infant adversely, a decision should be made whether to discontinue nursing or discontinue the drug, taking into account the importance of the drug to the mother.

Children: Safety and effectiveness have not been established.

Geriatrics: Of the 2 085 patients that received losartan monotherapy in controlled clinical trials, 391 (19%) were 65 years and over. No overall differences in safety were observed between these patients and younger patients, but appropriate caution should nevertheless be used when prescribing to the elderly, as increased vulnerability to drug effect is possible in this patient population.

Drug Interactions: Diuretics: Patients on diuretics, and especially those in whom diuretic therapy was recently instituted, may occasionally experience an excessive reduction of blood pressure after initiation of therapy with losartan. The possibility of symptomatic hypotension with the use of losartan can be minimized by discontinuing the diuretic prior to initiation of treatment and/or lowering the initial dose of losartan (see

Warnings, Hypotension and Dosage). No drug interaction of clinical significance has been identified with thiazide diuretics.
Agents Increasing Serum Potassium: Since losartan decreases the production of aldosterone, potassium-sparing diuretics or potassium supplements should be given only for documented hypokalemia and with frequent monitoring of serum potassium. Potassium-containing salt substitutes should also be used with caution.
Lithium Salts: As with other drugs which eliminate sodium, lithium clearance may be reduced. Therefore, serum lithium levels should be monitored carefully if lithium salts are to be administered.
Digitalis: In 9 healthy volunteers, when a single oral dose of 0.5 mg digoxin was administered to patients receiving losartan for 11 days, digoxin AUC and digoxin C_{max} ratios, relative to placebo, were found to be 1.06 (90% C.I. 0.98 to 1.14) and 1.12 (90% C.I. 0.97 to 1.28), respectively. The effect of losartan on steady-state pharmacokinetics of cardiac glycosides is not known.
Warfarin: Losartan administered for 7 days did not affect the pharmacokinetics or pharmacodynamic activity of a single dose of warfarin. The effect of losartan on steady-state pharmacokinetics of warfarin is not known.
Drugs Affecting Cytochrome P_{450} System: When losartan was administered to 10 healthy male volunteers as a single dose in steady-state conditions of phenobarbital, a cytochrome P_{450} inducer, losartan AUC, relative to baseline, was 0.80 (90% C.I. 0.72 to 0.88), while AUC of the active metabolite, E-3174, was 0.80 (90% C.I. 0.78 to 0.82).

When losartan was administered to 8 healthy male volunteers as a single dose in steady-state conditions of cimetidine, a cytochrome P_{450} inhibitor, losartan AUC, relative to baseline, was 1.18 (90% C.I. 1.10 to 1.27), while AUC of the active metabolite, E-3174, was 1.00 (90% C.I. 0.92 to 1.08).

Adverse Effects: Losartan has been evaluated for safety in more than 3 300 patients treated for essential hypertension. Of these, 2 085 were treated with losartan monotherapy in controlled clinical trials.

In open studies, over 1 200 patients were treated with losartan for more than 6 months, and over 800 for more than 1 year.

In controlled clinical trials, discontinuation of therapy due to clinical adverse experiences occurred in 2.3% and 3.7% of patients treated with losartan and placebo, respectively.

The following potentially serious adverse reactions have been reported rarely with losartan in controlled clinical trials: syncope and hypotension.

In these double-blind controlled clinical trials, the following adverse reactions reported with losartan occurred in ≥1% of patients, regardless of drug relationship: see Table I.

Table I—Cozaar

Adverse Reactions that Occurred in ≥1% of Patients

	Cozaar (n=2 085)	Placebo (n=535)
Body as a Whole		
Asthenia/fatigue	3.8	3.9
Edema/swelling	1.7	1.9
Abdominal pain	1.7	1.7
Chest pain	1.1	2.6
Cardiovascular		
Palpitation	1.0	0.4
Tachycardia	1.0	1.7
Digestive		
Diarrhea	1.9	1.9
Dyspepsia	1.1	1.5
Nausea	1.8	2.8
Musculoskeletal		
Back pain	1.6	1.1
Muscle cramps	1.0	1.1
Nervous/Psychiatric		
Dizziness	4.1	2.4
Headache	14.1	17.2
Insomnia	1.1	0.7
Respiratory		
Cough	3.1	2.6
Nasal congestion	1.3	1.1
Pharyngitis	1.5	2.6
Sinus disorder	1.0	1.3
Upper respiratory infection	6.5	5.6

In these controlled clinical trials, dizziness was the only adverse experience, occurring in more than 1% of cases, that was reported as drug-related, and that occurred at a greater incidence in losartan-treated (2.4%) than placebo-treated (1.3%) patients.

In double-blind, controlled clinical trials, the following adverse reactions were reported with losartan at an occurrence rate of less than 1%, regardless of drug relationship: orthostatic effects, somnolence, vertigo, epistaxis, tinnitus, constipation, malaise and rash.

Other adverse reactions reported rarely in open-label studies or postmarketing use, regardless of drug relationship, include asthenia, diarrhea, migraine, myalgia, pruritus, taste disorder and urticaria.
Laboratory Test Findings: In controlled clinical trials, clinically important changes in standard laboratory parameters were rarely associated with administration of losartan.
Liver Function Tests: In patients treated with losartan monotherapy in double-blind hypertensive trials, elevations of AST 1.1% and ALT 1.9% occurred, compared with placebo values of 0.8% and 1.3% respectively. When AST or ALT elevations ≥2X upper limit of normal were compared, the frequency was similar to that seen in placebo.
Hyperkalemia: In controlled hypertensive trials, a serum potassium >5.5 mEq/L occurred in 1.5% of patients, however, no patient discontinued losartan therapy due to hyperkalemia.
Creatinine, Blood Urea Nitrogen: Minor increases in blood urea nitrogen (BUN) or serum creatinine were observed in less than 0.1 percent of patients with essential hypertension treated with losartan alone. No patient discontinued taking losartan alone due to increased BUN or serum creatinine.
Hemoglobin and Hematocrit: Small decreases in hemoglobin and hematocrit (mean decreases of approximately 0.11 g % and 0.09 volume %, respectively) occurred frequently in patients treated with losartan alone, but were rarely of clinical importance. No patients were discontinued due to anemia.

In clinical trials, the following were noted to occur with an incidence of <1%, regardless of drug relationship: thrombocytopenia, eosinophilia.

Overdose: Symptoms and Treatment: Limited data are available in regard to overdosage with losartan in humans. The most likely manifestation of overdosage would be hypotension and/or tachycardia. If symptomatic hypotension should occur, supportive treatment should be instituted.

Neither losartan nor the active metabolite can be removed by hemodialysis.

Dosage: The dosage of losartan must be individualized.

Initiation of therapy requires consideration of recent antihypertensive drug treatment, the extent of blood pressure elevation, salt restriction, and other pertinent clinical factors. The dosage of other antihypertensive agents used with losartan may need to be adjusted.

Dosing should occur at about the same time each day. Losartan may be administered with or without food, however it should be taken consistently with respect to food intake.
Monotherapy: The usual starting dose of losartan is 50 mg once daily.

Dosage should be adjusted according to blood pressure response. The maximal antihypertensive effect is attained 3 to 6 weeks after initiation of therapy.

The usual dose range for losartan is 50 to 100 mg once daily. A dose of 100 mg daily should not be exceeded, as no additional antihypertensive effect is obtained with higher doses.

In most patients taking losartan 50 mg once daily, the antihypertensive effect is maintained. In some patients treated once daily, the antihypertensive effect may diminish toward the end of the dosing interval. This can be evaluated by measuring the blood pressure just prior to dosing to determine whether satisfactory control is being maintained for 24 hours. If it is not, either twice daily administration with the same total daily dosage, or an increase in the dose should be considered. If blood pressure is not adequately controlled with losartan alone, a non-potassium-sparing diuretic may be administered concomitantly.

For patients with volume depletion, a starting dose of 25 mg once daily should be considered (see Warnings, Hypotension and Precautions, Drug Interactions).
Concomitant Diuretic Therapy: In patients receiving diuretics, losartan therapy should be initiated with caution, since these patients may be volume depleted and thus more likely to experience hypotension following initiation of additional antihypertensive therapy. Whenever possible, all diuretics should be discontinued 2 to 3 days prior to the administration of losartan, to reduce the likelihood of hypotension (see Warnings, Hypotension and Precautions, Drug Interactions). If this is not possible because of the patient's condition, losartan should be administered with caution and the blood pressure monitored closely. Thereafter, the dosage should be adjusted according to the individual response of the patient.
Geriatrics: No initial dosage adjustment is necessary for most elderly patients. However, appropriate monitoring of these patients is recommended.
Renal Impairment: No initial dosage adjustment is usually necessary for patients with renal impairment, including those requiring hemodialysis. However, appropriate monitoring of these patients is recommended.
Hepatic Impairment: An initial dosage of 25 mg should be considered for patients with hepatic impairment or a history of hepatic impairment (see Precautions, Patients with Impaired Liver Function and Pharmacology).

Information for the Patient: See Blue Section—Information for the Patient "Cozaar".

Supplied: 25 mg: Each light green, teardrop shaped, unscored, film-coated tablet, with code 951 on one side and MRK on the other, contains: losartan potassium 25 mg. Nonmedicinal ingredients: coloring agents (D&C Yellow No. 10 aluminum lake, FD&C Blue No. 2 aluminum lake, and titanium dioxide), cornstarch, hydroxypropyl cellulose, hydroxypropyl methylcellulose, lactose, magnesium stearate and microcrystalline cellulose. Blister packages of 30.

50 mg: Each green, teardrop shaped, unscored, film-coated tablet, with code MRK 952 on one side and COZAAR on the other, contains: losartan potassium 50 mg. Nonmedicinal ingredients: coloring agents (D&C Yellow No. 10 aluminum lake, FD&C Blue No. 2 aluminum lake, and titanium dioxide), cornstarch, hydroxypropyl cellulose, hydroxypropyl methylcellulose, lactose, magnesium stearate and microcrystalline cellulose. Blister packages of 30.

100 mg: Each dark green, teardrop shaped, unscored, film-coated tablet, with code 960 on one side and MRK on the other, contains: losartan potassium 100 mg. Nonmedicinal ingredients: coloring agents (D&C Yellow No. 10 aluminum lake, FD&C Blue No. 2 aluminum lake, and titanium dioxide), cornstarch, hydroxypropyl cellulose, hydroxypropyl methylcellulose, lactose, magnesium stearate and microcrystalline cellulose. Blister packages of 30.

Store at room temperature (15 to 30°C). Keep container tightly closed. Protect from light.

(Shown in Product Recognition Section)

Reviewed 1997

CREON® 10

Solvay Pharma

Pancreatic Enzymes

Digestant

Indications: For replacement therapy where digestion is not adequate due to pancreatic exocrine insufficiency as in cystic fibrosis, chronic pancreatitis, steatorrhea, post-pancreatectomy, post-gastrointestinal bypass surgery (e.g., gastroenterostomy) and ductal obstruction from neoplasm.

Contraindications: Patients with known hypersensitivity to porcine proteins or pancreatic enzymes. Do not use during the early stages of acute pancreatitis.

Warnings and Precautions: Rarely, cases of hyperuricosuria and hyperuricemia have been reported with very high doses of pancreatin.

Perianal irritation, and rarely, inflammation, could occur when large doses are used.
Pregnancy and *Lactation:* There is inadequate evidence of safety in use during pregnancy and lactation.
Drug Interactions: None known.

Adverse Effects: Adverse effects from pancreatin products are rare. Diarrhea, constipation, abdominal discomfort and nausea are the most commonly reported reactions, but are also often symptoms of the diseases treated. Also, with high doses, cases of hyperuricosuria, hyperuricemia or perianal irritation/inflammation have been reported.

Overdose: Symptoms and Treatment: Most cases respond to supportive measures, including stopping enzyme therapy and ensuring adequate rehydration.

Dosage: Initially 1 or 2 capsules with each meal and 1 capsule with each snack.

Dosage increases, if required, should be added slowly, with careful monitoring of response and symptomatology.

It is important to ensure adequate hydration of patients at all times during dosing with pancreatic enzymes.

The capsules should be swallowed whole. Where swallowing the capsules is difficult, they may be opened and the minimicrospheres taken with soft food or fluid. Any mixture of the

Creon 10 (cont'd)

minimicrospheres with food or liquids should be used immediately and not stored; otherwise dissolution of the enteric coating may occur.

To protect the enteric coating, the minimicrospheres must not be crushed or chewed.

The product should not be administered after the expiry date printed on the package.

Supplied: Each opaque, brown/colorless-transparent, hard gelatin capsule, imprinted in white with SOLVAY and 1210, contains: buff-colored enteric-coated minimicrospheres of pancreatin 150 mg corresponding to lipase 10 000 USP units, amylase 33 200 USP units and proteases 37 500 USP units. Nonmedicinal ingredients: dibutyl phthalate, dimethicone 1 000, gelatin, iron oxide black, iron oxide red, iron oxide yellow, macrogol 4 000, methylhydroxypropylcellulose phthalate, paraffinum perliquidum and titanium dioxide. Gluten-, lactose- and tartrazine-free. Bottles of 100. Store in a tightly closed, light-resistant container at controlled room temperature (15 to 30°C). Protect from moisture. Do not refrigerate. Keep out of reach of children.

(Shown in Product Recognition Section)

Reviewed 1998

CREON® 25

Solvay Pharma

Pancreatic Enzymes

Digestant

Indications: For replacement therapy where digestion is not adequate due to pancreatic exocrine insufficiency as in cystic fibrosis, chronic pancreatitis, steatorrhea and postpancreatectomy, post gastrointestinal bypass surgery (e.g., gastroenterostomy) and ductal obstruction from neoplasm.

Contraindications: Patients with known hypersensitivity to porcine proteins or pancreatic enzymes. Do not use during the early stages of acute pancreatitis.

Warnings and Precautions: Rarely, cases of hyperuricosuria and hyperuricemia have been reported with very high doses of pancreatin.

Pregnancy and *Lactation:* There is inadequate evidence of safety in use during pregnancy and lactation.

Drug Interactions: None known.

Adverse Effects: Adverse effects from pancreatin products are rare. Diarrhea, constipation, abdominal discomfort and nausea are the most commonly reported reactions, but are also often symptoms of the diseases treated. Also, with high doses, cases of hyperuricosuria, hyperuricemia or perianal irritation/inflammation have been reported.

Overdose: Symptoms and Treatment: Most cases respond to supportive measures, including stopping enzyme therapy and ensuring adequate rehydration.

Dosage: Initially 1 capsule with each meal and 1 capsule with each snack.

Dosage increases, if required, should be added slowly, with careful monitoring of response and symptomatology.

It is important to ensure adequate hydration of patients at all times during dosing with pancreatic enzymes.

The capsules should be swallowed whole. Where swallowing the capsules is difficult, they may be opened and the microspheres taken with soft food or fluid. Any mixture of the microspheres with food or liquids should be used immediately and not stored; otherwise, dissolution of the enteric coating may occur.

To protect the enteric coating, the microspheres must not be crushed or chewed.

The product should not be administered after the expiry date printed on the package.

Supplied: Each opaque, orange/transparent yellow, hard gelatin capsule, imprinted SOLVAY and 1225, contains: enteric-coated microspheres of pancreatin 300 mg corresponding to lipase 25 000 USP units, amylase 74 000 USP units and free proteases 62 500 USP units (corresponding to 62 500 total proteases). Nonmedicinal ingredients: dibutyl phthalate, dimethicone 1 000, gelatin, iron oxide red, iron oxide yellow, macrogol 4 000, methylhydroxypropylcellulose phthalate, paraffinum perliquidum and titanium dioxide. Gluten-, lactose- and tartrazine-free. Bottles of 100. Store in a tightly closed, light-resistant container at controlled room temperature (15 to 30°C). Protect from moisture. Do not refrigerate. Keep out of reach of children.

Reviewed 1998

CREO-RECTAL®

Nadeau

Diphenylpyraline HCl—Camphor—Guaiacol

Expectorant—Antihistaminic

Indications: For the temporary relief of coughs due to colds, bronchitis, bronchial asthma.

Contraindications: Hypersensitivity to any of the components.

Precautions: Since the depressant effects of antihistamines are additive to those of other drugs affecting the CNS, patients should be cautioned against drinking alcoholic beverages or taking hypnotics, sedatives, psychotherapeutic agents or other drugs with CNS depressant effects during antihistaminic therapy.

Guaifenesin may cause a color inteference with certain laboratory determinations of 5-hydroxyindoleacetic acid and vanillylmandelic acid.

Occupational Hazards: Patients should be cautioned not to operate vehicles or hazardous machinery until their response to the drug has been determined.

Adverse Effects: Occasional drowsiness, dizziness, dry mouth, blurred vision, gastrointestinal upset, and nausea may occur.

Overdose: Symptoms and Treatment: Antihistamine effects—if coma and respiratory depression are present, use intubation and artificial respiration. Do not administer stimulants. Maintain blood pressure and control convulsions with diazepam or short acting barbiturates.

Dosage: Adults: 1 adult strength suppository morning and evening. In acute cases, administer 1 or 2 suppositories 3 times daily.

Children, over 1 year: 1 suppository morning, noon and evening.

Infants, up to 3 months: 1 suppository twice daily; 3 months to 1 year: 1 suppository 2 to 4 times daily.

Supplied: Adults: Each white, homogeneous suppository contains: guaiacol 600 mg (as carbonate), diphenylpyraline HCl 1.5 mg and camphor 5 mg. Boxes of 10.

Children: Each white, homogeneous suppository contains: guaiacol 200 mg (as carbonate), diphenylpyraline HCl 0.5 mg and camphor 2 mg. Boxes of 10.

Infants: Each white, homogeneous suppository contains: guaiacol 100 mg (as carbonate), diphenylpyraline HCl 0.25 mg and camphor 1 mg. Boxes of 10.

Keep in refrigerator.

CRIXIVAN® Ⓟ

MSD

Indinavir Sulfate

HIV Protease Inhibitor

Pharmacology: Indinavir is a selective protease inhibitor active against the Human Immunodeficiency Virus (HIV-1).

Mechanism of Action: HIV protease is an enzyme required for the proteolytic cleavage of the viral polyprotein precursors into the individual functional proteins found in infectious HIV. Indinavir binds to the protease active site and inhibits the activity of the enzyme. This inhibition prevents cleavage of the viral polyproteins resulting in the formation of immature noninfectious viral particles.

Antiretroviral Potency: The relationship between in vitro susceptibility of HIV to indinavir and inhibition of HIV replication in humans has not been established. The in vitro activity of indinavir was assessed in cell lines of lymphoblastic and monocytic origin and in peripheral blood lymphocytes. HIV variants used to infect the different cell types include laboratory-adapted variants, primary clinical isolates and clinical isolates resistant to nucleoside analogue and nonnucleoside inhibitors of the HIV reverse transcriptase. The IC_{95} (95% inhibitory concentration) of indinavir in these test systems was in the range of 25 to 100 nM. In drug combination studies with the nucleoside analogues zidovudine and didanosine, as well as with an investigational nonnucleoside (L-697,661), indinavir showed synergistic activity in cell culture.

Virus Mutations: Isolates of HIV with reduced susceptibility to the drug have been recovered from some patients treated with indinavir. Viral resistance was correlated with the accumulation of mutations that resulted in the expression of amino acid substitutions in the viral protease. Eleven amino acid residue positions, at which substitutions are associated with resistance, have been identified. Resistance was mediated by the coexpression of multiple and variable substitutions at these positions. In general, higher levels of resistance were associated with the coexpression of greater numbers of substitutions.

Cross-resistance between indinavir and HIV reverse transcriptase inhibitors is unlikely because the enzyme targets involved are different. Cross-resistance was noted between indinavir and the protease inhibitor ritonavir. Varying degrees of cross-resistance have been observed between indinavir and other HIV-protease inhibitors.

Pharmacokinetics: Absorption of orally administered indinavir is rapid. Peak plasma concentration occurs within 1 hour and is not dose dependent. The oral absorption of a 400 mg dose of indinavir is reduced by 78% when administered with a standard meal high in calories, fat and protein contents. Indinavir has a relatively short half-life of 1.8 hours. There is very little drug accumulation following either an 8- or 6-hour dosing regimen over the clinical dose range.

Indinavir is widely distributed in the body and is approximately 60% bound to human plasma proteins. Less than 20% of indinavir is excreted unchanged in the urine. Following a single 400 mg dose of indinavir, patients with mild to moderate hepatic insufficiency and clinical evidence of cirrhosis had a mean AUC which was found to be higher by approximately 60% compared to that in healthy subjects and the half-life increased to approximately 2.8 hours, a reflection of reduced metabolism.

Therapy with indinavir should be initiated at the full recommended dose to increase suppression of viral replication and therefore inhibit the emergence of resistant virus (see Dosage). No titration is necessary upon initiating therapy.

Nephrolithiasis may occur (see Warnings and Adverse Effects). Adequate hydration (at least 1.5 L/day) is recommended in all patients treated with indinavir.

Indirect hyperbilirubinemia has occurred frequently in both healthy subjects and HIV-1 infected patients at various dosage levels of indinavir (see Precautions and Adverse Effects).

Hyperbilirubinemia and nephrolithiasis occurred more frequently at doses exceeding 2.4 g/day.

Indinavir should not be administered concurrently with terfenadine, astemizole, cisapride, triazolam, and midazolam because competition for P450 (CYP3A4) by indinavir could result in inhibition of the metabolism of these drugs and create the potential for serious and/or life-threatening events (i.e., cardiac arrhythmias, prolonged sedation). The potential exists for interaction between indinavir and other P450 (CYP3A4) substrates which have not been studied (see Warnings).

The combination of indinavir and rifabutin results in an increase in the plasma concentrations of rifabutin and a decrease in the plasma concentrations of indinavir. When indinavir is coadministered with rifabutin, dose reduction of rifabutin to half the standard dose and a dose increase of indinavir are recommended (see Precautions and Dosage, Concomitant Therapy).

Due to an increase in the plasma concentrations of indinavir, a dosage reduction of indinavir should be considered when indinavir and ketoconazole are coadministered (see Dosage, Concomitant Therapy).

Rifampin is a potent inducer of P450 (CYP3A4) which markedly diminishes plasma concentrations of indinavir. Therefore, indinavir and rifampin should not be coadministered.

Other drugs that induce CYP3A4 less potently than rifampin, such as phenobarbital, phenytoin, carbamazepine, and dexamethasone should be used cautiously together with indinavir since they could also diminish plasma concentrations of indinavir.

Indications: For use in combination with reverse transcriptase inhibitor (RTI) nucleoside analogues for the treatment of adults with HIV-1 infection.

This indication is based on analyses of surrogate endpoints obtained at 24 weeks. There are no results from clinical trials confirming clinical benefit in terms of disease progression or survival.

Data from 2 double-blind randomized trials evaluating patients with CD4 counts of 50 to 500 cells/mm³ and mean RNA levels of approximately 20 000 copies/mL who took indinavir alone, or indinavir plus zidovudine, or zidovudine alone demonstrate greater immunologic and virologic responses in groups containing indinavir.

Data from a double-blind randomized trial evaluating patients with CD4 counts of 50 to 400 cells/mm³ and mean RNA levels of approximately 38 000 copies/mL who took indinavir alone, or indinavir plus zidovudine plus lamivudine, or zidovudine plus lamivudine demonstrate greater immunologic and virologic responses in groups containing indinavir.

Data from an open-label randomized trial evaluating patients with CD4 counts of less than 500 cells/mm³ and mean RNA levels of approximately 100 000 copies/mL who took indinavir alone, or indinavir plus zidovudine plus didanosine, or zidovudine plus didanosine suggest greater virologic response in the group containing indinavir and the 2 nucleosides.

No efficacy results are available for combinations involving indinavir and other nucleoside analogue reverse transcriptase inhibitors or other antiretrovirals. Preliminary data from other trials support the safety profile of indinavir when used concomitantly with zalcitabine or stavudine (see Pharmacology).

Contraindications: In patients with clinically significant hypersensitivity to any of its components.

Warnings: Nephrolithiasis may occur with indinavir. If signs and symptoms of nephrolithiasis, including flank pain with or without hematuria (including microscopic hematuria), occur, temporary interruption of therapy (e.g., 1 to 3 days) during the acute episode of nephrolithiasis may be considered. **Adequate hydration is recommended in all patients treated with indinavir (see Adverse Effects, Nephrolithiasis and Dosage, Nephrolithiasis).**

Indinavir should not be administered concurrently with terfenadine, astemizole, cisapride, triazolam, and midazolam because competition for P450 (CYP3A4) by indinavir could result in inhibition of the metabolism of these drugs and create the potential for serious and/or life-threatening events (i.e., cardiac arrhythmias, prolonged sedation). The potential exists for interaction between indinavir and other P450 (CYP3A4) substrates which have not been studied.

Rifampin: Rifampin is a potent inducer of P450 (CYP3A4) which markedly diminishes plasma concentrations of indinavir. Therefore, indinavir and rifampin should not be coadministered.

Other drugs that induce CYP3A4 less potently than rifampin, such as phenobarbital, phenytoin, carbamazepine, and dexamethasone should be used cautiously together with indinavir since they could also diminish plasma concentrations of indinavir.

Hyperglycemia: There have been reports of new onset diabetes mellitus or hyperglycemia, or exacerbation of preexisting diabetes mellitus occurring in HIV-infected patients receiving protease inhibitor therapy. Many of these reports occurred in patients with confounding medical conditions, some of which required therapy with agents that have been associated with the development of diabetes mellitus or hyperglycemia. Some patients required either initiation or dose adjustments of insulin or oral hypoglycemic agents for treatment of these events. In some cases diabetic ketoacidosis has occurred.

In the majority of cases, treatment with protease inhibitors was continued while in some cases treatment was either discontinued or interrupted. In some patients, hyperglycemia persisted after the protease inhibitor was withdrawn, whether or not diabetes was reported at baseline. A causal relationship between protease inhibitor therapy and these events has not been established.

Precautions: General: Indirect hyperbilirubinemia has occurred frequently in both healthy subjects and HIV-1 infected patients at various dosage levels of indinavir and has infrequently been associated with increases in serum transaminases (see Adverse Effects). However, because of the theoretical potential for the compound to exacerbate the physiologic hyperbilirubinemia seen in human neonates, careful consideration must be given to the use of indinavir in pregnant women at the time of delivery (see Pregnancy).

Acute Hemolytic Anemia: Acute hemolytic anemia has been reported. In some cases, it was severe and progressed rapidly. Once a diagnosis is apparent, appropriate measures for the treatment of hemolytic anemia should be instituted which may include discontinuation of indinavir.

Bleeding in Hemophiliacs: There have been reports of increased bleeding including spontaneous skin hematomas and hemarthrosis in patients with Hemophilia Type A and Type B treated with protease inhibitors. In some patients, additional Factor VIII was given. In many of the reported cases, treatment with protease inhibitors was continued or reintroduced. There is no proven relationship between protease inhibitors and such bleeding, however, the frequency of bleeding episodes should be closely monitored in patients on indinavir.

Children: Safety and effectiveness in children have not been established.

Geriatrics: Safety and effectiveness in elderly patients have not been established.

Pregnancy: There are no adequate and well-controlled studies in pregnant women. Indinavir may be used during pregnancy only if the potential benefit justifies potential risk to the fetus.

Hyperbilirubinemia has occurred in patients during treatment with indinavir. It is unknown whether indinavir will exacerbate physiologic hyperbilirubinemia in neonates. The potential risk of this effect is being investigated in an ongoing study in Rhesus monkeys. At present, careful consideration must be given to the use of indinavir in pregnant women at the time of delivery.

Lactation: It is not known whether this drug is excreted in human milk. Because many drugs are excreted in human milk, and because of the potential for adverse reactions from indinavir in nursing infants, mothers should be instructed to discontinue nursing if they are receiving indinavir. In addition, it is advisable for HIV-infected women not to breast-feed to avoid postnatal transmission of HIV to a child who may not be infected.

Patients with Hepatic Insufficiency due to Cirrhosis: In these patients, the dosage of indinavir should be lowered because of decreased metabolism of the drug (see Dosage).

Patients with Renal Insufficiency: Patients with renal insufficiency have not been studied.

CNS Penetration: CNS penetration of indinavir has not been established.

Drug Interactions: See Warnings: Specific drug interaction studies were performed with indinavir and the following drugs: zidovudine, zidovudine/lamivudine, trimethoprim/sulfamethoxazole, fluconazole, isoniazid, clarithromycin, norethindrone/ethinyl estradiol 1/35. No clinically significant interactions were observed with these drugs. However, clinically significant interactions with other drugs are described below.

Rifabutin: Due to an increase in the plasma concentrations of rifabutin and a decrease in the plasma concentrations of indinavir, a dosage reduction of rifabutin and a dosage increase of indinavir are necessary when rifabutin is coadministered with indinavir (see Dosage, Concomitant Therapy).

Ketoconazole: Due to an increase in the plasma concentrations of indinavir, a dosage reduction of indinavir should be considered when indinavir and ketoconazole are coadministered (see Dosage, Concomitant Therapy).

Rifampin: Rifampin is a potent inducer of P450 (CYP3A4) which markedly diminishes plasma concentrations of indinavir. Therefore, indinavir and rifampin should not be coadministered.

Didanosine: When indinavir and didanosine are administered concomitantly, they should be administered at least 1 hour apart on an empty stomach.

Other: See Warnings: Indinavir should not be administered concurrently with terfenadine, astemizole, cisapride, triazolam and midazolam because coadministration with inhibitors of P450 (CYP3A4) may result in inhibition of metabolism of these drugs and create the potential for serious and/or life-threatening events (i.e., cardiac arrhythmias or prolonged sedation).

Other drugs that induce CYP3A4 less potently than rifampin, such as phenobarbital, phenytoin, carbamazepine, and dexamethasone should be used cautiously together with indinavir since they could also diminish plasma concentations of indinavir.

Information for the Patient: Patients should be informed that while indinavir reduces HIV-1 RNA levels, it is not a cure for HIV infection and that they may continue to develop opportunistic infections or other illnesses associated with HIV-1 disease. Indinavir has not been shown to reduce the incidence or frequency of such illnesses.

Patients should be told that the long-term effects of indinavir are unknown at this time. They should be advised that treatment with indinavir has not been shown to reduce the risk of transmission of HIV-1 to others through sexual contact or blood contamination. Studies evaluating the impact of indinavir alone or in combination with approved antiretroviral agents (i.e., nucleoside analogues) on HIV-1 disease progression (such as opportunistic infections and survival) are ongoing.

Capsules of indinavir are sensitive to moisture. Patients should be informed that indinavir should be stored in a tightly closed container at room temperature (15 to 30°C) and protected from moisture.

For optimal absorption, indinavir should be administered without food but with water, 1 hour before or 2 hours after a meal. Alternatively, indinavir may be administered with other liquids such as skim milk, juice, coffee, or tea, or a light meal (e.g., dry toast with jelly, apple juice, and coffee with skim milk and sugar or corn flakes, skim milk and sugar). Ingestion of indinavir with a meal high in calories, fat and protein reduces the absorption of indinavir.

To achieve the best possible antiretroviral activity, indinavir must be taken exactly as prescribed. Patients should be advised to drink at least 1.5 L of liquids during the course of 24 hours. Patients should also be informed that treatment must not be modified or discontinued without first consulting a physician.

Occupational Hazards: Dizziness and blurred vision have been reported with indinavir. Patients should be advised to avoid driving or operating machinery if they experience these reactions.

Adverse Effects: Nephrolithiasis: Nephrolithiasis, including flank pain with or without hematuria (including microscopic hematuria), has been reported in approximately 4% (79/2 205) of patients receiving indinavir). In general these events were not associated with renal dysfunction and resolved with hydration and temporary interruption of therapy (e.g., 1 to 3 days). Following the acute episode, 9.2% (7/76) of patients discontinued therapy (see Warnings and Dosage, Nephrolithiasis).

Hyperbilirubinemia: Asymptomatic hyperbilirubinemia (total bilirubin $\geq$42.75 μmol/L ($\geq$2.5 mg/dL)), reported predominantly as elevated indirect bilirubin, has occurred in approximately 10% of patients treated with indinavir. In $<$1% this was associated with elevations in ALT or AST.

Hyperbilirubinemia and nephrolithiasis occurred more frequently at doses exceeding 2.4 g/day.

Clinical Trial Experience: In controlled clinical trials conducted worldwide, indinavir was administered alone or in combination with other antiretroviral agents (zidovudine, didanosine, and/or lamivudine) and was found to be generally well tolerated. Indinavir did not alter the type, frequency, or severity of known major toxicities associated with the use of zidovudine, didanosine or lamivudine.

Drug-related clinical adverse reactions of moderate or severe intensity in $\geq$ 2% of patients treated with indinavir alone, indinavir in combination with zidovudine, or zidovudine alone are presented in Table I.

Table I—Crixivan

Drug-related Clinical Adverse Reactions of Moderate or Severe Intensity Reported in $\geq$2% of Patients (Study 028 and 033)

Adverse Reactions	Crixivan % (n=196)	Crixivan plus Zidovudine % (n=196)	Zidovudine % (n=195)
Body as a Whole			
Abdominal Pain	8.7	8.2	5.1
Asthenia/Fatigue	3.6	9.2	7.7
Flank Pain	2.6	1.0	0
Malaise	0.5	2.0	1.5
Digestive			
Nausea	11.7	32.1	14.4
Diarrhea	4.6	4.1	2.1
Vomiting	4.1	12.2	4.6
Acid Regurgitation	2.0	2.0	0.5
Anorexia	0.5	2.0	3.1
Dry Mouth	0.5	0	2.1
Musculoskeletal			
Back Pain	2.0	1.0	1.5
Nervous/Psychiatric			
Headache	5.6	11.7	5.1
Insomnia	3.1	1.5	0
Dizziness	1.0	3.6	0.5
Somnolence	1.0	1.5	3.6
Special Senses			
Taste Perversion	2.6	3.6	2.1

In Phase I and II controlled trials, the following adverse reactions were reported significantly more frequently by those randomized to indinavir-containing arms than by those randomized to nucleoside analogues: rash, upper respiratory infection, dry skin, pharyngitis, taste perversion.

Adverse reactions occurring in less than 2% of patients receiving indinavir in all Phase II/Phase III studies and considered at least possibly related or of unknown relationship to treatment and of at least moderate intensity are listed below by body system.

Body as a Whole/Site Unspecified: abdominal distention, chest pain, chills, fever, flank pain, flu-like illness, fungal infection, malaise, pain, syncope.

Cardiovascular: cardiovascular disorder, palpitation.

Digestive: acid regurgitation, anorexia, aphthous stomatitis, cheilitis, cholecystitis, cholestasis, constipation, dry mouth,

Crixivan (cont'd)

dyspepsia, eructation, flatulence, gastritis, gingivitis, glossodynia, gingival hemorrhage, increased appetite, infectious gastroenteritis, jaundice, liver cirrhosis.

Hemic and Lymphatic: anemia, lymphadenopathy, spleen disorder, bleeding in hemophiliacs (see Precautions).

Metabolic/Nutritional/Immune: food allergy.

Musculoskeletal: arthralgia, back pain, leg pain, myalgia, muscle cramps, muscle weakness, musculoskeletal pain, shoulder pain, stiffness.

Nervous and Psychiatric: agitation, anxiety, anxiety disorder, bruxism, decreased mental acuity, depression, dizziness, dream abnormality, dysesthesia, excitement, fasciculation, hypesthesia, nervousness, neuralgia, neurotic disorder, paresthesia, peripheral neuropathy, sleep disorder, somnolence, tremor, vertigo.

Respiratory: cough, dyspnea, halitosis, pharyngeal hyperemia, pharyngitis, pneumonia, rales/rhonchi, respiratory failure, sinus disorder, sinusitis, upper respiratory infection.

Skin and Skin Appendage: body odor, contact dermatitis, dermatitis, dry skin, flushing, folliculitis, herpes simplex, herpes zoster, night sweats, pruritus, seborrhea, skin disorder, skin infection, sweating, urticaria.

Special Senses: accommodation disorder, blurred vision, eye pain, eye swelling, orbital edema, taste disorder.

Urogenital: dysuria, hematuria, hydronephrosis, nocturia, premenstrual syndrome, proteinuria, renal colic, urinary frequency, urinary tract infection, urine abnormality, urine sediment abnormality, urolithiasis.

Laboratory Test Abnormalities: The most frequently occurring selected laboratory adverse experiences (incidence ≥5%) considered to be possibly, probably, or definitely drug-related by the study investigator in the group treated with indinavir alone, were changes in ALT (15.3%), AST (21.4%), indirect serum bilirubin (30.9%), total serum bilirubin (36.2%), and urine protein (20.9%). Only 1% of patients discontinued treatment due to these laboratory adverse experiences, when treated with indinavir alone or in combination with other antiretroviral agents. With the exception of hyperbilirubinemia, the incidences of these adverse events with indinavir monotherapy were lower than in the groups treated with indinavir in combination with other antiretroviral agents. Similar incidences in drug-related laboratory adverse experiences of changes in ALT, AST, and urine protein were observed in the group treated with zidovudine alone.

Presented in Table II are selected laboratory abnormalities reported in patients treated with indinavir alone, indinavir in combination with zidovudine, or zidovudine alone in Phase III clinical trials (Studies 028 and 033).

Postmarketing Experience: The following additional adverse experiences have been reported in postmarketing experience without regard to causality: Digestive: liver function abnormalities, hepatitis including rare reports of hepatic failure.

Endocrine/Metabolic: new onset diabetes mellitus or hyperglycemia, or exacerbation of pre-existing diabetes mellitus (see Warnings).

Hematologic: increased spontaneous bleeding in patients with hemophilia (see Precautions), acute hemolytic anemia.

Hypersensitivity: angioedema, anaphylaxis.

Skin and Skin Appendage: alopecia, hyperpigmentation, urticaria.

Urogenital: nephrolithiasis, generally without renal dysfunction; however, there have been reports of nephrolithiasis with renal dysfunction including acute renal failure, crystalluria.

The following additional laboratory experiences have been reported: increased serum triglycerides.

Overdose: Symptoms and Treatment: It is not known whether indinavir is dialyzable by peritoneal dialysis or hemodialysis. Although no data are available, administration of activated charcoal may be used to aid in removal of unabsorbed drug.

Dosage: The recommended dosage is 800 mg orally every 8 hours. **Therapy must be initiated at the recommended dose of 2.4 g/day.**

For optimal absorption, the drug should be administered without food but with water, 1 hour before or 2 hours after a meal. Alternatively, it may be administered with other liquids such as skim milk, juice, coffee, or tea, or a light meal (e.g., dry toast with jelly, apple juice, and coffee with skim milk and sugar or corn flakes, skim milk and sugar).

To ensure adequate hydration, it is recommended that the patient drink at least 1.5 L of liquids during the course of 24 hours.

Concomitant Therapy: Rifabutin: Dose reduction of rifabutin up to half the standard dose (consult the manufacturers' Product Monograph), and a dose increase of indinavir to 1 000 mg every 8 hours are recommended when rifabutin and indinavir are coadministered (see Precautions and Pharmacology).

Ketoconazole: Dose reduction of indinavir to 600 mg every 8 hours should be considered when administering ketoconazole concurrently (see Pharmacology).

Hepatic Insufficiency Due to Cirrhosis: Dose reduction of indinavir to 600 mg every 8 hours should be considered in patients with mild to moderate hepatic insufficiency due to cirrhosis (see Pharmacology).

Nephrolithiasis: In addition to adequate hydration, medical management in patients who experience nephrolithiasis may include temporary interruption of therapy (e.g., 1 to 3 days) during the acute episode of nephrolithiasis or discontinuation of therapy.

Information for the Patient: See Blue Section—Information for the Patient "Crixivan".

Supplied: 200 mg: Each white, semi-translucent capsule, coded "CRIXIVAN 200 mg" in blue, contains: indinavir 200 mg (as a sulfate salt ethanolate). Nonmedicinal ingredients: anhydrous lactose and magnesium stearate; empty capsule shell: gelatin, silicon dioxide, sodium lauryl sulfate and titanium dioxide. Bottles of 360 (with desiccant).

400 mg: Each white, semi-translucent capsule, coded "CRIXIVAN 400 mg" in green, contains: indinavir 400 mg (as a sulfate salt ethanolate). Nonmedicinal ingredients: anhydrous lactose and magnesium stearate; empty capsule shell: gelatin, silicon dioxide, sodium lauryl sulfate and titanium dioxide. Bottles of 90 and 180 (with desiccant).

Store in a tightly closed container at room temperature (15 to 30°C). Protect from moisture.

(Shown in Product Recognition Section)

Reviewed 1999

Table II—Crixivan

Selected Laboratory Abnormalities Reported in Studies 028 and 033

Adverse Experience	Crixivan % (n=196)	Crixivan plus Zidovudine % (n=196)	Zidovudine % (n=195)
Hematology			
Decreased hemoglobin <8.0 g/dL	0.5	1.1	0.5
Decreased platelet count <50 000/mm³	0.5	0.5	0
Decreased neutrophils <750/mm³	1.1	1.6	3.8
Blood Chemistry			
Increased ALT >500% ULN	3.1	3.2	2.1
Increased AST >500% ULN	2.1	2.1	1.1
Total serum bilirubin >2.5 mg/dL	7.8	7.4	0.5
Increased serum amylase >200% ULN	1.0	2.1	0.5

Legend: ULN: Upper limit of the normal range.

CROMOLYN Nasal Solution
CROMOLYN Ophthalmic Solution
Pharmascience

Cromolyn Sodium

Seasonal Rhinitis Prophylaxis—Antiallergic

Supplied: Nasal Solution: The metered dose pump delivers approximately 0.13 mL of the 2% (w/v) solution or sodium cromoglycate 2.6 mg per spray mist. HDPB bottles of 26 mL with a metered dose pump attached to the bottle.

Ophthalmic Solution: Each drop of sterile ophthalmic solution contains: approximately 0.04 mL of the 2% solution or sodium cromoglycate 0.8 mg. Plastic dropper bottles of 10 mL.

New Product 1998

CROTALID SERUM
Wyeth-Ayerst

see ANTIVENIN

CRYSTAPEN® (Buffered) Ⓟ
Bioniche

Penicillin G Sodium

Antibiotic

Supplied: Each vial contains: penicillin G (as sodium salt) 1 million, 5 million and 10 million IU with 4.5% sodium citrate as a buffer. Trays of 25. Store vials at room temperature (15 to 30°C). Reconstituted solutions may be stored for up to 24 hours at room temperature or for 5 days at a temperature of 4°C or below.

CUPLEX®
TCD

Lactic Acid—Salicylic Acid

Verrucae Therapy

Supplied: Each g of gel contains: salicylic acid USP 11% (w/w) and lactic acid USP 4% (w/w) in a nonmedicinal, colored, viscous gel base containing copper acetate and flexible collodion. Metal tubes of 7 g.

CUPRIMINE® Ⓟ
MSD

Penicillamine

Chelating Agent

Pharmacology: As a chelating agent, penicillamine removes copper and lead from the body. In copper chelation, from in vitro studies which indicate that one atom of copper combines with 2 molecules of penicillamine. It would appear that 1 g of penicillamine should be followed by the excretion of about 200 mg of copper; however, the actual amount excreted is about 1% of this. The manner in which lead is chelated is not known. It may be bound in the same way as copper.

Penicillamine also reduces excess cystine excretion in cystinuria. This is done, at least in part, by disulfide interchange between penicillamine and cystine, resulting in formation of penicillamine-cysteine disulfide, a substance that is much more soluble than cystine and is excreted readily.

Penicillamine interferes with the formation of cross-links between tropocollagen molecules and cleaves them when newly formed.

The mechanism of action of penicillamine in rheumatoid arthritis is unknown although it appears to suppress disease activity. Unlike cytotoxic immunosuppressants, penicillamine markedly lowers IgM rheumatoid factor but produces no significant depression in absolute levels of serum immunoglobulins. Also, unlike cytotoxic immunosuppressants which act on both, penicillamine in vitro depresses T-cell activity but not B-cell activity.

In vitro, penicillamine dissociates macroglobulins (rheumatoid factor) although the relationship of the activity to its effect in rheumatoid arthritis is not known.

Indications: The treatment of Wilson's disease, chronic lead poisoning, cystinuria, and in patients with severe, active rheumatoid arthritis who have failed to respond to an adequate trial of conventional therapy. Available evidence suggests that penicillamine is not of value in ankylosing spondylitis. Because of the severe toxicity of this agent, penicillamine should never be used casually.

Wilson's Disease: Treatment has 2 objectives: to minimize dietary intake and absorption of copper and to promote excretion of copper deposited in tissues.

For the second objective, a copper chelating agent is used. Penicillamine is the only one of these agents that is orally effective.

In symptomatic patients, this treatment usually produces marked neurologic improvement, fading of Kayser-Fleischer rings, and gradual amelioration of hepatic dysfunction and psychic disturbances.

Clinical experience to date suggests that life is prolonged with the above regimen.

Noticeable improvement may not occur for 1 to 3 months. Occasionally, neurologic symptoms become worse during the initiation of therapy with penicillamine. Despite this, the drug should not be discontinued permanently. Although temporary interruption may result in clinical improvement of the neurological symptoms, it carries an increased risk of developing a sensitivity reaction upon resumption of therapy (see Precautions).

Treatment of asymptomatic patients has been carried out for over 10 years. Symptoms and signs of the disease appear to be prevented indefinitely if daily treatment with penicillamine can be continued.

Chronic Lead Poisoning: Penicillamine should be considered adjunctive to rigorous control of environmental exposure to lead.

When used in children with chronic lead poisoning, penicillamine should be used only if the children are asymptomatic, have blood lead levels between 50 and 80 μg/deciliter (1 dL=100 mL) whole blood, and: a) have an erythrocyte protoporphyrin level greater than 400 to 500 μg/dL erythrocytes, as determined by a standard free erythrocyte protoporphyrin method (bearing in mind that values differ according to the method used). b) excrete excessive amounts of δ-aminolevulinic acid (normal=up to 2 mg/m²/day), or of coproporphyrin (normal = 2 μg/kg/day), or both.

When using penicillamine to treat chronic lead poisoning in children, it is essential that whole blood lead levels be determined periodically during treatment.

Penicillamine is recommended for use in adults with chronic lead poisoning.

Cystinuria: Conventional treatment is directed at keeping urinary cystine diluted enough to prevent stone formation, keeping the urine alkaline enough to dissolve as much cystine as possible, and minimizing cystine production by a diet low in methionine (the major dietary precursor of cystine). Patients must drink enough fluid to keep urine specific gravity below 1.010, take enough alkali to keep urinary pH at 7.5 to 8, and maintain a diet low in methionine. This diet is not recommended in growing children and probably is contraindicated in pregnancy because of its low protein content (see Precautions).

When these measures are inadequate to control recurrent stone formation, penicillamine may be used as additional therapy. When patients refuse to adhere to conventional treatment, penicillamine may be a useful substitute. It is capable of keeping cystine excretion to near normal values, thereby hindering stone formation and the serious consequences of pyelonephritis and impaired renal function that develop in some patients.

Bartter and colleagues depict the process by which penicillamine interacts with cystine to form penicillamine-cysteine mixed disulfide as:

$$CSSC + PS' \leftrightarrows CS' + CSSP$$
$$PSSP + CS' \leftrightarrows PS' + CSSP$$
$$CSSC + PSSP \leftrightarrows 2\,CSSP$$

CSSC=cystine. CS′=deprotonated cysteine. PSSP=penicillamine. PS′=deprotonated penicillamine sulfhydryl. CSSP=penicillamine-cysteine mixed disulfide.

In this process, it is assumed that the deprotonated form of penicillamine, PS', is the active factor in bringing about the disulfide interchange.

Rheumatoid Arthritis: Because penicillamine can cause severe adverse reactions, its use in rheumatoid arthritis should be restricted to patients who have severe, active disease and who have failed to respond to an adequate trial of conventional therapy. Even then benefit-to-risk ratio should be carefully considered. Other measures, such as rest, physiotherapy, salicylates, and corticosteroids, may need to be used in conjunction with penicillamine (see Precautions).

Contraindications: *Pregnancy:* Except for the treatment of Wilson's disease or certain cases of cystinuria, use of penicillamine during pregnancy is contraindicated (see Precautions). *Lactation:* Although breast milk studies have not been reported in animals or humans, mothers on therapy with penicillamine should not nurse their infants.

Patients with a history of penicillamine-related aplastic anemia or agranulocytosis should not be restarted on penicillamine (see Precautions and Adverse Effects).

Because of its potential for causing renal damage, penicillamine should not be administered to rheumatoid arthritis patients with a history or other evidence of renal insufficiency.

Penicillamine should not be given to patients with chronic lead poisoning when there is x-ray evidence of lead-containing substances in the gastrointestinal tract. Treatment with the drug may be instituted after the gastrointestinal tract has been cleared of these substances. Studies in animals suggest that penicillamine may be ineffective, and possibly hazardous, if excessive oral ingestion of lead continues during administration of the drug.

Penicillamine should not be used in patients who are receiving gold therapy, antimalarial or cytotoxic drugs, oxyphenbutazone or phenylbutazone because these drugs are also associated with similar serious hematologic and renal adverse reactions. Patients who have had gold salt therapy discontinued due to a major toxic reaction may be at greater risk of serious adverse reactions with penicillamine but not necessarily of the same type.

Warnings: The use of penicillamine has been associated with fatalities due to certain diseases such as aplastic anemia, agranulocytosis, thrombocytopenia, Goodpasture's syndrome, and myasthenia gravis.

Because of the potential for serious hematological and renal adverse reactions occurring at any time, routine urinalysis, white and differential blood cell count, hemoglobin determination, and direct platelet count must be done every 2 weeks for at least the first 6 months of penicillamine therapy and monthly thereafter. Patients should be instructed to report promptly the development of signs and symptoms of granulocytopenia and/or thrombocytopenia such as fever, sore throat, chills, bruising or bleeding. The above laboratory studies should then be promptly repeated.

Leukopenia and thrombocytopenia have been reported to occur in up to 5% of patients during penicillamine therapy. Leukopenia is of the granulocytic series and may or may not be associated with an increase in eosinophils. A confirmed reduction in WBC below 3 500 mandates discontinuance of penicillamine therapy. Thrombocytopenia may be on an idiosyncratic basis, with decreased or absent megakaryocytes in the marrow, when it is part of an aplastic anemia. In other cases the thrombocytopenia is presumably on an immune basis since the number of megakaryocytes in the marrow has been reported to be normal or sometimes increased. The development of a platelet count below 100 000, even in the absence of clinical bleeding, requires at least temporary cessation of penicalamine therapy. A progressive fall in either platelet count or WBC in 3 successive determinations, even though values are still within the normal range, likewise requires at least temporary cessation.

Proteinuria and/or hematuria may develop during therapy and may be warning signs of membranous glomerulopathy which can progress to a nephrotic syndrome. Close observation of these patients is essential. In some patients the proteinuria disappears with continued therapy; in others, penicillamine must be discontinued. When a patient develops proteinuria or hematuria the physician must ascertain whether it is a sign of drug-induced glomerulopathy or is unrelated to penicillamine.

Rheumatoid arthritis patients who develop moderate degrees of proteinuria may be continued cautiously on penicillamine therapy, provided that quantitative 24-hour urinary protein determinations are obtained at intervals of 1 to 2 weeks. Penicillamine dosage should not be increased under these circumstances. Proteinuria which exceeds 1 g/24 hours, or proteinura which is progressively increasing, requires either discontinuance of the drug or a reduction in the dosage. In some patients, proteinuria has been reported to clear following reduction in dosage.

In rheumatoid arthritis patients penicillamine should be discontinued if unexplained gross hematuria or persistent microscopic hematuria develops.

In patients with Wilson's disease or cystinuria the risks of continued penicillamine therapy in patients manifesting potentially serious urinary abnormalities must be weighed against the expected therapeutic benefits.

When penicillamine is used in cystinuria, an annual x-ray for renal stones is advised. Cystine stones form rapidly, sometimes in 6 months.

Up to 1 year or more may be required for any urinary abnormalities to disappear after penicillamine has been discontinued.

Because of rare reports of intrahepatic cholestasis and toxic hepatitis, liver function tests are recommended every 6 months for the duration of therapy.

Goodpasture's syndrome has occurred rarely. The development of abnormal urinary findings associated with hemoptysis and pulmonary infiltrates on x-ray requires immediate cessation of penicillamine.

Obliterative bronchiolitis has been reported rarely. The patient should be cautioned to report immediately pulmonary symptoms such as exertional dyspnea, unexplained cough or wheezing. Pulmonary function studies should be considered at that time.

Myasthenic syndrome, sometimes progressing to myasthenia gravis, has been reported. Ptosis and diplopia, with weakness of the extraocular muscles, are often early signs of myasthenia. In the majority of cases, symptoms of myasthenia have receded after withdrawal of penicillamine.

Most of the various forms of pemphigus have occurred during treatment with penicillamine. Pemphigus vulgaris and pemphigus foliaceus are reported most frequently, usually as a late complication of therapy. The seborrhea-like characteristics of pemphigus foliaceus may obscure an early diagnosis. When pemphigus is suspected, penicillamine should be discontinued. Treatment has consisted of high doses of corticosteroids alone or, in some cases, concomitantly with an immunosuppressant. Treatment may be required for only a few weeks or months, but may need to be continued for more than a year.

Once instituted for Wilson's disease or cystinuria, treatment with penicillamine should, as a rule, be continued on a daily basis. Interruptions for even a few days have been followed by sensitivity reactions after reinstitution of therapy.

Precautions: Some patients may experience drug fever, a marked febrile response to penicillamine, usually in the second to third week following initiation of therapy. Drug fever may sometimes be accompanied by a macular cutaneous eruption.

Should drug fever occur in patients receiving penicillamine, stop the drug. In patients with Wilson's disease, trientine HCl (where available) or zinc compounds such as zinc sulfate may be tried. In patients with cystinuria, in whom these alternative agents are inappropriate, penicillamine should be temporarily discontinued until the reaction subsides. Then penicillamine should be reinstituted with a small dose that is gradually increased until the desired dosage is attained. Systemic steroid therapy may be necessary, and is usually helpful, in such patients in whom toxic reactions develop a second or third time.

In the case of drug fever in rheumatoid arthritis patients, because other treatments are available, penicillamine should be discontinued and another therapeutic alternative tried since experience indicates that the febrile reaction will recur in a very high percentage of patients upon readministration of penicillamine.

The skin and mucous membranes should be observed for allergic reactions. Early and late rashes have occurred. Early rash occurs during the first few months of treatment and is more common. It is usually a generalized pruritic, erythematous, maculopapular or morbilliform rash and resembles the allergic rash seen with other drugs. Early rash usually disappears within days after stopping penicillamine and seldom recurs when the drug is restarted at a lower dosage. Pruritus and early rash may often be controlled by the concomitant administration of antihistamines. Less commonly, a late rash may be seen, usually after 6 months or more of treatment, and requires discontinuation of penicillamine. It is usually on the trunk, is accompanied by intense pruritus, and is usually unresponsive to topical corticosteroid therapy. Late rash may take weeks to disappear after penicillamine is stopped and usually recurs if the drug is restarted.

The appearance of a drug eruption accompanied by fever, arthralgia, lymphadenopathy or other allergic manifestations usually requires discontinuation of penicillamine.

Certain patients will develop a positive antinuclear antibody (ANA) test and some of these may show a lupus erythematosus-like syndrome similar to drug-induced lupus associated with other drugs. The lupus erythematosus-like syndrome is not associated with the hypocomplementemia and may be present without nephropathy. The development of a positive ANA test does not mandate discontinuance of the drug; however, the physician should be alerted to the possibility that a lupus erythematosus-like syndrome may develop in the future.

Some patients may develop oral ulcerations which in some cases have the appearance of aphthous stomatitis. The stomatitis usually recurs on rechallenge but often clears on a lower dosage. Although rare, cheilosis, glossitis and gingivostomatitis have also been reported. These oral lesions are frequently

Cuprimine (cont'd)

dose related and may preclude further increase in penicillamine dosage or require discontinuation of the drug.

Hypogeusia (a blunting or diminution in taste perception) has occurred in some patients. This may last 2 to 3 months or more and develop into a total loss of taste; however, it is usually self limited despite continued penicillamine treatment. Such taste impairment is rare in patients with Wilson's disease.

Patients who are allergic to penicillin may theoretically have cross sensitivity to penicillamine. The possibility of reactions from contamination of penicillamine by trace amounts of penicillin, has been eliminated now that penicillamine is being produced synthetically rather than as a degradation product of penicillin.

Because of their dietary restrictions, patients with Wilson's disease and cystinuria should be given 25 mg/day of pyridoxine during therapy, since penicillamine increases the requirement for this vitamin. Patients also may receive benefit from a multivitamin preparation, although there is no evidence that deficiency of any vitamin other than pyridoxine is associated with penicillamine. In Wilson's disease, multivitamin preparations must be copper free.

Rheumatoid arthritis patients whose nutrition is impaired should also be given a daily supplement of pyridoxine. Mineral supplements should not be given, since they may block the response to penicillamine.

Iron deficiency may develop, especially in children and in menstruating women. In Wilson's disease, this may be a result of adding the effects of the low copper diet, which is probably also low in iron, and the penicillamine to the effects of blood loss or growth. In cystinuria, a low methionine diet may contribute to iron deficiency, since it is necessarily low in protein. If necessary, iron may be given in short courses, but a period of 2 hours should elapse between administration of penicillamine and iron, since orally administered iron has been shown to reduce the effects of penicillamine.

Penicillamine causes an increase in the amount of soluble collagen. In the rat this results in inhibition of normal healing and also a decrease in tensile strength of intact skin. In man this may be the cause of increased skin friability at sites especially subject to pressure or trauma, such as shoulders, elbows, knees, toes, and buttocks. Extravasations of blood may occur and may appear as purpuric areas, with external bleeding if the skin is broken, or as vesicles containing dark blood. Neither type is progressive. There is no apparent association with bleeding elsewhere in the body and no associated coagulation defect has been found. Therapy with penicillamine may be continued in the presence of these lesions. They may not recur if dosage is reduced.

Other reported effects probably due to the action of penicillamine on collagen are excessive wrinkling of the skin and development of small, white papules at venipuncture and surgical sites.

The effects of penicillamine on collagen and elastin make it advisable to consider a reduction in dosage to 250 mg/day, when surgery is contemplated. Reinstitution of full therapy should be delayed until wound healing is complete.

Tumorigenicity: Long-term animal carcinogenicity studies have not been done with penicillamine. There is a report that 5 of 10 autoimmune disease-prone NZB hybrid mice developed lymphocytic leukemia after 6 months intraperitoneal treatment with a dose of 400 mg/kg penicillamine 5 days/week.

Children: The efficacy of penicillamine in juvenile rheumatoid arthritis has not been established.

Pregnancy: Penicillamine has been shown to be teratogenic in rats when given in doses 6 times higher than the highest dose recommended for human use. Skeletal defects, cleft palates and fetal toxicity (resorptions) have been reported.

There are no controlled studies on the use of penicillamine in pregnant women. Although normal outcomes have been reported, characteristic congenital cutis laxa and associated birth defects have been reported in infants born of mothers who received therapy with penicillamine during pregnancy. Penicillamine should be used in women of childbearing potential only when the expected benefits outweigh the possible hazards. Women on therapy with penicillamine who are of childbearing potential should be apprised of this risk and followed closely for early recognition of pregnancy.

Wilson's Disease: Reported experience shows that continued treatment with penicillamine throughout pregnancy protects the mother against relapse of the Wilson's disease, and that discontinuation of penicillamine has deleterious effects on the mother.

If penicillamine is administered during pregnancy to patients with Wilson's disease, it is recommended that the daily dosage be limited to 1 g. If cesarean section is planned, the daily dosage should be limited to 250 mg during the last 6 weeks of pregnancy and postoperatively until wound healing is complete.

Cystinuria: If possible, penicillamine should not be given during pregnancy to women with cystinuria (see Contraindications). There are reports of women with cystinuria on therapy with penicillamine who gave birth to infants with generalized connective tissue defects who died following abdominal surgery. If stones continue to form in these patients, the benefits of therapy to the mothers must be evaluated against the risk of the fetus.

Rheumatoid Arthritis: Penicillamine should not be administered to rheumatoid arthritis patients who are pregnant and should be discontinued promptly in patients in whom pregnancy is suspected or diagnosed.

There is a report that a woman with rheumatoid arthritis treated with less than 1 g a day of penicillamine during pregnancy gave birth (cesarean delivery) to an infant with growth retardation, flattened face with broad nasal bridge, low set ears, short neck with loose skin folds, and unusually lax body skin.

Lactation: See Contraindications.

Adverse Effects: Penicillamine is a drug with a high incidence of untoward reactions, some of which are potentially fatal. Therefore, it is mandatory that patients receiving penicillamine therapy remain under close medical supervision throughout the period of drug administration (see Precautions).

Reported incidences (%) for the most commonly occurring adverse effects in **rheumatoid arthritis** patients are noted, based on 17 representative clinical trials reported in the literature (1 270 patients).

Allergic: Generalized pruritus, early and late rashes (5%), pemphigoid-type reactions, and drug eruptions which may be accompanied by fever, arthralgia, or lymphadenopathy have occurred (see Precautions). Some patients may show a lupus erythematosus-like syndrome similar to drug-induced lupus produced by other pharmacological agents (see Warnings and Precautions).

Urticaria and exfoliative dermatitis have occurred.

Thyroiditis has been reported; hypoglycemia in association with anti-insulin antibodies has been reported. These reactions are extremely rare.

Some patients may develop a migratory polyarthralgia, often with objective synovitis (see Dosage).

Gastrointestinal: Anorexia, epigastric pain, nausea, vomiting, or occasional diarrhea may occur (17%).

Isolated cases of reactivated peptic ulcer have occurred, as have hepatic dysfunction and pancreatitis. Intrahepatic cholestasis and toxic hepatitis have been reported rarely. There have been a few reports of increased serum alkaline phosphatase, lactic dehydrogenase, and positive cephalin flocculation and thymol turbidity tests.

Some patients may report a blunting, diminution, or total loss of taste perception (12%); or may develop oral ulcerations. Although rare, cheilosis, glossitis, and gingivostomatitis have been reported (see Precautions).

Gastrointestinal side effects are usually reversible following cessation of therapy.

Hematologic: Penicillamine can cause bone marrow depression (see Warnings). Leukopenia (2%) and thrombocytopenia (4%) have occurred. Fatalities have been reported as a result of thrombocytopenia, agranulocytosis, aplastic anemia, and sideroblastic anemia.

Thrombotic thrombocytopenic purpura, hemolytic anemia, red cell aplasia, monocytosis, leukocytosis, eosinophilia, and thrombocytosis have also been reported.

Renal: Patients on penicillamine therapy may develop proteinuria (6%) and/or hematuria which, in some, may progress to the development of the nephrotic syndrome as a result of an immune complex membranous glomerulopathy (see Warnings).

CNS: Tinnitus, optic neuritis and peripheral sensory and motor neuropathies (including polyradiculoneuropathy, i.e., Guillain-Barré Syndrome) have been reported. Muscular weakness may or may not occur with the peripheral neuropathies. Visual and psychic disturbances have been reported.

Neuromuscular: Myasthenia gravis: (see Precautions).

Other: Side effects that have been reported rarely include thrombophlebitis; hyperpyrexia (see Precautions); falling hair or alopecia; lichen planus (see Warnings); polymyositis; dermatomyositis; mammary hyperplasia; elastosis perforans serpiginosa; toxic epidermal necrolysis; anetoderma (cutaneous macular atrophy); and Goodpasture's syndrome, a severe and ultimately fatal glomerulonephritis associated with intra-alveolar hemorrhage (see Warnings). Fatal renal vasculitis also reported. Allergic alveolitis and obliterative bronchiolitis, interstitial pneumonitis and pulmonary fibrosis have been reported in patients with severe rheumatoid arthritis, some of whom were receiving penicillamine. Bronchial asthma also reported.

Increased skin friability, excessive wrinkling of skin, and development of small white papules at venipuncture and surgical sites have been reported (see Precautions).

The chelating action of the drug may cause increased excretion of other heavy metals such as zinc and mercury.

Overdose: Symptoms: There are no known instances of acute poisoning with penicillamine. In therapeutic doses, however, it may cause a wide variety of adverse reactions. Penicillamine may cause acute sensitivity reactions early in therapy. Cross sensitivity with penicillin may exist.

Treatment: In general, treatment is symptomatic.

Allergic Reactions: Discontinue penicillamine promptly and treat the patient with glucocorticoids, followed by reinstitution of penicillamine in small doses that are increased gradually to the desired amount.

Iron and Pyridoxine Deficiencies: Administer iron and pyridoxine supplementation.

Impairment of Taste: 5 to 10 mg of copper a day can be administered as 5 to 10 drops of a 4% solution of $CuSO_4\ 5H_2O$ in fruit juice twice a day. (Do not give copper to patients with Wilson's disease.)

Dosage: Physicians planning to use penicillamine should thoroughly familiarize themselves with its toxicity, special dosage considerations, and therapeutic benefits. Penicillamine should never be used casually. Each patient should remain constantly under the close supervision of the physician. Patients should be warned to report promptly any symptoms suggesting toxicity.

In all patients receiving penicillamine, it is important that penicillamine be given on an empty stomach, at least 1 hour before meals or 2 hours after meals, and at least 1 hour apart from any other drug, food, or milk. This permits maximum absorption and reduces the likelihood of inactivation by metal binding.

Wilson's Disease: Optimal dosage can be determined by measurement of urinary copper excretion and the determination of free copper in the serum. The urine must be collected in copper free glassware, and should be quantitatively analyzed for copper before and soon after initiation of therapy with penicillamine.

Determination of 24-hour urinary copper excretion is a greatest value in the first week of therapy with penicillamine. In the absence of any drug reaction, a dose between 0.75 and 1.5 g that results in an initial 24-hour cupruresis of over 2 mg should be continued for about 3 months, by which time the most reliable method of monitoring maintenance treatment is the determination of free copper in the serum. This equals the difference between quantitatively determined total copper and ceruloplasmin-copper. Adequately treated patients will usually have less than 10 µg free copper/dL of serum. It is seldom necessary to exceed a dosage of 2 g/day. If the patient is intolerant to therapy with penicillamine, alternative treatment is trientine HCl (where available) or zinc compounds such as zinc sulfate.

In patients who cannot tolerate as much as 1 g/day initially, initiating dosage with 250 mg/day, and increasing gradually to the requisite amount, gives closer control of the effects of the drug and may help to reduce the incidence of adverse reactions.

Chronic Lead Poisoning: Penicillamine should be given when the gastrointestinal tract is empty of lead-containing substances. It may be given to children by dissolving the contents of the capsules no longer than 5 minutes before administration in a small amount of chilled puréed fruit or fruit juice.

Children: 30 to 40 mg/kg/day, or 600 to 750 mg/m²/day, not to exceed 750 mg/day, as a single dose or in 2 divided doses at least 2 hours before meals. Treatment should be continued until blood lead levels remain below 40 µg/dL whole blood for 2 consecutive months and at least one of the following is achieved: a. erythrocyte protoporphyrin level decreases to less than 3 to 5 times the average normal level. b. excretion of δ-aminolevulinic acid decreases to upper limit of normal. c. excretion of coproporphyrin decreases to upper limit of normal.

Adults: 900 to 1 500 mg a day, in 3 divided doses for 1 to 2 weeks, followed by 750 mg/day in divided doses until blood lead levels are reduced to 60 µg/dL, or until urinary lead excretion remains below 500 µg/L for 2 consecutive months. All doses should be given at least 2 hours before meals.

Cystinuria: It is recommended that penicillamine be used along with conventional therapy. By reducing urinary cystine, it decreases crystalluria and stone formation. In some instances, it has been reported to decrease the size of, and even to dissolve, stones already formed.

The usual dosage of penicillamine in the treatment of cystinuria is 2 g/day for adults, with a range of 1 to 4 g/day. For children, dosage can be based on 30 mg/kg/day. The total daily amount should be divided into 4 doses. If 4 equal doses are not feasible, give the larger portion at bedtime. If adverse reactions necessitate a reduction in dosage, it is important to retain the bedtime dose.

Initiating dosage with 250 mg/day, and increasing gradually to the requisite amount, gives closer control of the effects of the drug and may help to reduce the incidence of adverse reactions.

In addition to taking penicillamine, patients should drink copiously. It is especially important to drink about 0.5 L of fluid at bedtime and another 0.5 L once during the night when urine is more concentrated and more acid than during the day. The greater the fluid intake, the lower the required dose of penicillamine.

Dosage must be individualized to an amount that limits cystine excretion to 100 to 200 mg/day in those with no history of stones, and below 100 mg in those who have had stone formation and/or pain. Thus, in determining dosage, the inherent tubular defect, the patient's size, age, and rate of growth, and his diet and water intake all must be taken into consideration.

The standard nitroprusside cyanide test has been reported useful as a qualitative measure of the effective dose. Add 2 mL of freshly prepared 5% sodium cyanide to 5 mL of a 24-hour aliquot of protein-free urine and let stand 10 minutes. Add 5 drops of freshly prepared 5% sodium nitroprusside and mix. Cystine will turn the mixture magenta. If the result is negative, it can be assumed that cystine excretion is less than 100 mg/g creatinine.

Although penicillamine is rarely excreted unchanged, it also will turn the mixture magenta. If there is any question as to which substance is causing the reaction, a ferric chloride test can be done to eliminate doubt: Add 3% ferric chloride dropwise to the urine. Penicillamine will turn the urine an immediate and quickly fading blue. Cystine will not produce any change in appearance.

Rheumatoid Arthritis: The onset of therapeutic response may not be seen for 2 or 3 months. In those patients who respond, however, the first evidence of suppression of symptoms such as pain, tenderness, and swelling is generally apparent within 3 months. The optimum duration of therapy has not been determined. If remissions occur, they may last from months to years, but usually require continued treatment.

In patients with rheumatoid arthritis, it is important that penicillamine be given on an empty stomach, at least 1 hour before meals and at least 1 hour apart from any other drug, food, or milk. This permits maximum absorption and reduces the likelihood of inactivation by metal binding.

When treatment has been interrupted because of adverse reactions or other reasons, the drug should be reintroduced cautiously by starting with a lower dosage and increasing slowly.

Initial: 125 mg to 250 mg administered as a single daily dose which is thereafter increased at 1 to 3 month intervals, by 125 mg to 250 mg/day, as patient response and tolerance indicates. If a satisfactory remission of symptoms is achieved, the dose associated with the remission should be continued (see Maintenance Therapy). If there is no improvement and there are no signs of potentially serious toxicity after 2 to 3 months of treatment with doses of 500 to 750 mg/day, increases of 125 mg to 250 mg/day at 2 to 3 month intervals may be continued until a satisfactory remission occurs (see Maintenance) or signs of toxicity develop (see Warnings and Precautions). If there is no discernible improvement after 3 to 4 months of treatment with 1 000 to 1 500 mg of penicillamine/day, it may be assumed the patient will not respond and penicillamine should be discontinued.

Maintenance: Must be individualized, and may require adjustment during the course of treatment. Many patients respond satisfactorily to a dosage within the 500 to 750 mg/day range. Some need less.

Changes in maintenance dosage levels may not be reflected clinically or in the erythrocyte sedimentation rate for 2 to 3 months after each dosage adjustment.

Some patients will subsequently require an increase in the maintenance dosage to achieve maximal disease suppression. In those patients who do respond, but who evidence incomplete suppression of their disease after the first 6 to 9 months of treatment, the daily dosage may be increased by 125 mg to 250 mg/day at 3 month intervals. It is unusual in current practice to employ a dosage in excess of 1 g/day, but up to 1.5 g/day has sometimes been required.

Management of Exacerbations: During the course of treatment some patients may experience an exacerbation of disease activity following an initial good response. These may be self limited and can subside within 12 weeks. They are usually controlled by the addition of nonsteroidal anti inflammatory drugs, and only if the patient has demonstrated a true "escape" phenomenon (as evidenced by failure of the flare to subside within this time period) should an increase in the maintenance dose ordinarily be considered.

In the rheumatoid patient, migratory polyarthralgia due to penicillamine is extremely difficult to differentiate from an exacerbation of the rheumatoid arthritis. Discontinuance or a substantial reduction in dosage for up to several weeks will usually determine which of these processes is responsible for the arthralgia.

Duration of Therapy: The optimum duration of therapy in rheumatoid arthritis has not been determined. If the patient has been in remission for 6 months or more, a gradual, stepwise dosage reduction in decrements of 125 mg to 250 mg/day at approximately 3 month intervals may be attempted.

Concomitant Drug Therapy: Penicillamine should not be used in patients who are receiving gold therapy, antimalarial or cytotoxic drugs, oxyphenbutazone, or phenylbutazone (see Contraindications). Other measures, such as salicylates, other nonsteroidal anti-inflammatory drugs, or systemic corticosteroids, may be continued when penicillamine is initiated. After improvement commences, analgesic, and anti-inflammatory drugs may be slowly discontinued as symptoms permit. Steroid withdrawal must be done gradually, and many months of treatment may be required before steroids can be completely eliminated.

Dosage Frequency: Based on clinical experience, dosages up to 500 mg/day can be given as a single daily dose. Dosages in excess of 500 mg/day should be administered in divided doses.

Supplied: 125 mg: Each opaque, yellow and grey capsule marked MSD 672 contains: penicillamine 125 mg, supplied as a white or almost white powder. Nonmedicinal ingredients: D&C Yellow 10, gelatin, iron oxide, lactose, magnesium stearate and titanium dioxide. Gluten- and tartrazine-free. Bottles of 100.

250 mg: Each ivory colored capsule marked MSD 602 contains: penicillamine 250 mg, supplied as a white or almost white powder. Nonmedicinal ingredients: D&C Yellow 10, gelatin, lactose, magnesium stearate and titanium dioxide. Gluten- and tartrazine-free. Bottles of 100.

(Shown in Product Recognition Section)

Reviewed 1997

CYANOCOBALAMIN
General Monograph, CPhA

see VITAMIN B_{12}

CYCLEN® Ⓟ
Janssen-Ortho

Norgestimate—Ethinyl Estradiol

Oral Contraceptive

Pharmacology: The primary mechanism of action is an inhibition of ovulation. Additionally, other effects caused by the treatment (e.g., alteration of the endometrium and the thickening of the cervical mucus), appear to interfere with implantation and conception.

Indications: Conception control.

Contraindications: History of/or actual thrombophlebitis or thromboembolic disorders; history of/or actual cerebrovascular disorders; history of/or actual myocardial infarction or coronary arterial disease; active liver disease or history of/or actual benign or malignant liver tumors; known or suspected carcinoma of the breast; known or suspected estrogen-dependent neoplasia; undiagnosed abnormal vaginal bleeding; any ocular lesion arising from ophthalmic vascular disease, such as partial or complete loss of vision or defect in visual fields; when pregnancy is suspected or diagnosed.

Warnings: Predisposing Factors For Coronary Artery Disease: Cigarette smoking increases the risk of serious cardiovascular side effects and mortality. Birth control pills increase this risk, especially with increasing age. Convincing data are available to support an upper age limit of 35 years for oral contraceptive use by women who smoke.

Other women who are independently at high risk for cardiovascular disease include those with diabetes, hypertension, abnormal lipid profile, or a family history of these. Whether oral contraceptives accentuate this risk is unclear.

In low risk, non-smoking women of any age, the benefits of oral contraceptive use outweigh the possible cardiovascular risks associated with low dose formulations. Consequently, oral contraceptives may be prescribed for these women up to the age of menopause.

> Cigarette smoking increases the risk of serious adverse effects on the heart and blood vessels. This risk increases with age and becomes significant in oral contraceptive users over 35 years of age. Women should be counselled not to smoke.

Discontinue medication at the earliest manifestation of:

A. Thromboembolic and cardiovascular disorders such as: thrombophlebitis, pulmonary embolism, cerebrovascular disorders, myocardial ischemia, mesenteric thrombosis and retinal thrombosis.

B. Conditions which predispose to venous stasis and to vascular thrombosis, (e.g., immobilization after accidents or confinement to bed during long-term illness). Other non-hormonal methods of contraception should be used until regular activities are resumed. For use of oral contraceptives when surgery is contemplated, see Precautions.

C. Visual defects, partial or complete.

D. Papilledema, or ophthalmic vascular lesions.

E. Severe headache of unknown etiology or worsening of pre-existing migraine headache.

Precautions: Physical Examination and Follow-up: Before oral contraceptives are used, a thorough history and physical examination should be performed, including a blood pressure determination. Breasts, liver, extremities and pelvic organs should be examined. A Papanicolaou smear should be taken if the patient has been sexually active.

The first follow-up visit should be 3 months after oral contraceptives are prescribed. Thereafter, examinations should be performed at least once a year or more frequently if indicated. At each annual visit, examination should include those procedures that were done at the initial visit as outlined above or per recommendations of the Canadian Workshop on Screening for Cancer of the Cervix. Their suggestion was that, for women who had 2 consecutive negative Pap smears, screening could be continued every 3 years up to the age of 69.

Pregnancy: Oral contraceptives should not be taken by pregnant women. However, if conception accidentally occurs while taking the pill, there is no conclusive evidence that the estrogen and progestin contained in the oral contraceptive will damage the developing child.

Lactation: In breast-feeding women, the use of oral contraceptives results in the hormonal components being excreted in breast milk and may reduce its quantity and quality. If the use of oral contraceptives is initiated after the establishment of lactation, there does not appear to be any effect on the quantity and quality of the milk. There is no evidence that low dose oral contraceptives are harmful to the nursing infant.

Hepatic Function: Patients who have had jaundice, including a history of cholestatic jaundice during pregnancy, should be given oral contraceptives with great care and under close observation.

The development of severe generalized pruritus or icterus requires that the medication be withdrawn until the problem is resolved.

If a patient develops jaundice that proves to be cholestatic in type, the use of oral contraceptives should not be resumed. In patients taking oral contraceptives, changes in the composition of the bile may occur and an increased incidence of gallstones has been reported.

Hepatic nodules (adenoma and focal nodular hyperplasia) have been reported, particularly in long-term users of oral contraceptives. Although these lesions are extremely rare, they have caused fatal intra-abdominal hemorrhage and should be considered in women with an abdominal mass, acute abdominal pain, or evidence of intra-abdominal bleeding.

Hypertension: Patients with essential hypertension whose blood pressure is well-controlled may be given oral contraceptives but only under close supervision. If a significant elevation of blood pressure in previously normotensive or hypertensive subjects occurs at any time during the administration of the drug, cessation of medication is necessary.

Cyclen (cont'd)

Migraine and Headache: The onset or exacerbation of migraine or the development of headache of a new pattern, that is recurrent, persistent or severe, requires discontinuation of oral contraceptives and evaluation of the cause.

Diabetes: Current low dose oral contraceptives exert minimal impact on glucose metabolism. Diabetic patients, or those with a family history of diabetes, should be observed closely to detect any worsening of carbohydrate metabolism. Patients predisposed to diabetes who can be kept under close supervision may be given oral contraceptives. Young diabetic patients whose disease is of recent origin, well-controlled, and not associated with hypertension or other signs of vascular disease such as ocular fundal changes, should be monitored more frequently while using oral contraceptives.

Ocular Disease: Patients who are pregnant or are taking oral contraceptives may experience corneal edema that may cause visual disturbances and changes in tolerance to contact lenses, especially of the rigid type. Soft contact lenses usually do not cause disturbances. If visual changes or alterations in tolerance to contact lenses occur, temporary or permanent cessation of wear may be advised.

Breasts: Increasing age and a strong family history are the most significant risk factors for the development of breast cancer. Other established risk factors include obesity, nulliparity and late age at first full-term pregnancy. The identified groups of women that may be at increased risk of developing breast cancer before menopause are long-term users of oral contraceptives (more than 8 years) and starters at early age. In a few women, the use of oral contraceptives may accelerate the growth of an existing but undiagnosed breast cancer. Since any potential increased risk related to oral contraceptive use is small, there is no reason to change prescribing habits at present.

Women receiving oral contraceptives should be instructed in self-examination of their breasts. Their physicians should be notified whenever any masses are detected. A yearly clinical breast examination is also recommended because, if a breast cancer should develop, estrogen-containing drugs may cause a rapid progression.

Vaginal Bleeding: Persistent irregular vaginal bleeding requires assessment to exclude underlying pathology.

Fibroids: Patients with fibroids (leiomyomata) should be carefully observed. Sudden enlargement, pain, or tenderness requires discontinuance of the use of oral contraceptives.

Emotional Disorders: Patients with a history of emotional disturbances, especially the depressive type, may be more prone to have a recurrence of depression while taking oral contraceptives. In cases of a serious recurrence, a trial of an alternate method of contraception should be made which may help to clarify the possible relationship. Women with premenstrual syndrome (PMS) may have a varied response to oral contraceptives, ranging from symptomatic improvement to worsening of the condition.

Laboratory Tests: Results of laboratory tests should be interpreted in light of the fact that the patient is on oral contraceptives. The following laboratory tests are modified.

A. Liver Function Tests: Bromsulphthalein Retention Test (BSP): moderate increase; AST and GGT: minor increase; alkaline phosphatase: variable increase; serum bilirubin: increased, particularly in conditions predisposing to or associated with hyperbilirubinemia.

B. Coagulation Tests: Factors II, VII, IX, X, XII and XIII: increased; Factor VIII: mild increase; platelet aggregation and adhesiveness: mild increase in response to common aggregating agents; fibrinogen: increased; plasminogen: mild increase; antithrombin III: mild decrease; prothrombin time: increased.

C. Thyroid Function Tests: Protein-bound Iodine (PBI): increased; Total Serum Thyroxine (T_4): increased; Thyroid Stimulating Hormone (TSH): unchanged.

D. Adrenocortical Function Tests: plasma cortisol: increased.

E. Miscellaneous Tests: serum folate: occasionally decreased; glucose tolerance test: variable increase with return to normal after 6 to 12 months; insulin response: mild to moderate increase; c-Peptide response: mild to moderate increase.

Tissue Specimens: Pathologists should be advised of oral contraceptive therapy when specimens obtained from surgical procedures and Pap smears are submitted for examination.

Return to Fertility: After discontinuing oral contraceptive therapy, the patient should delay pregnancy until at least 1 normal spontaneous menstrual cycle has occurred in order to date the pregnancy. An alternative contraceptive method should be used during this time.

Amenorrhea: Women having a history of oligomenorrhea, secondary amenorrhea, or irregular cycles may remain anovulatory or become amenorrheic following discontinuation of estrogen-progestin combination therapy.

Amenorrhea, especially if associated with breast secretion, that continues for 6 months or more after withdrawal, warrants a careful assessment of hypothalamic-pituitary function.

Thromboembolic Complications—Post-surgery: There is an increased risk of thromboembolic complications in oral contraceptive users after major surgery. If feasible, oral contraceptives should be discontinued and an alternative method substituted at least 1 month prior to **major** elective surgery. Oral contraceptive use should not be resumed until the first menstrual period after hospital discharge following surgery.

Drug Interactions: The concurrent administration of oral contraceptives with other drugs may result in an altered response to either agent (see Table I and Table II on following page). Reduced effectiveness of the oral contraceptive, should it occur, is more likely with the low dose formulations. It is important to ascertain all drugs that a patient is taking, both prescription and nonprescription, before oral contraceptives are prescribed.

Refer to Oral Contraceptives 1994 (Chapter 8), Health Canada, for possible drug interactions with OCs.

Non-contraceptive Benefits of Oral Contraceptives: Several health advantages other than contraception have been reported.

1. Combination oral contraceptives reduce the incidence of cancer of the endometrium and ovaries.
2. Oral contraceptives reduce the likelihood of developing benign breast disease and, as a result, decrease the incidence of breast biopsies.
3. Oral contraceptives reduce the likelihood of development of functional ovarian cysts.
4. Pill-users have less menstrual blood loss and have more regular cycles, thereby reducing the chance of developing iron-deficiency anemia.
5. The use of oral contraceptives may decrease the severity of dysmenorrhea and premenstrual syndrome, and may improve acne vulgaris, hirsutism, and other androgen-mediated disorders.
6. Oral contraceptives decrease the incidence of acute pelvic inflammatory disease and, thereby reduce as well the incidence of ectopic pregnancy.
7. Oral contraceptives have potential beneficial effects on endometriosis.

Oral contraceptives **do not protect** against sexually transmitted diseases (STDs) including HIV/AIDS. For protection against STDs, it is advisable to use latex condoms **in combination with** oral contraceptives.

Adverse Effects: An increased risk of the following serious adverse reactions has been associated with the use of oral contraceptives: thrombophlebitis; pulmonary embolism; mesenteric thrombosis; neuro-ocular lesions, (e.g., retinal thrombosis); myocardial infarction; cerebral thrombosis; cerebral hemorrhage; hypertension; benign hepatic tumors; gallbladder disease.

The following adverse reactions also have been reported in patients receiving oral contraceptives: nausea and vomiting, usually the most common adverse reaction, occurs in approximately 10% or less of patients during the first cycle. Other reactions, as a general rule, are seen less frequently or only occasionally, as follows: gastrointestinal symptoms (such as abdominal cramps and bloating); breakthrough bleeding; spotting; change in menstrual flow; dysmenorrhea; amenorrhea during and after treatment; temporary infertility after discontinuance of treatment; edema; chloasma or melasma which may persist; breast changes: tenderness, enlargement, and secretion; change in weight (increase or decrease); endocervical hyperplasias; possible diminution in lactation when given immediately postpartum; cholestatic jaundice; migraine;

Table I—Cyclen

Drugs Which May Decrease the Efficacy of Oral Contraceptives

Class of Compound	Drug	Proposed Mechanism	Suggested Management
Anticonvulsants	Carbamazepine Ethosuximide Phenobarbital Phenytoin Primidone	Induction of hepatic microsomal enzymes: Rapid metabolism of estrogen and increased binding of progestin and ethinyl estradiol to SHBG.	Use higher dose OCs (50 μg ethinyl estradiol), another drug or another method.
Antibiotics	Ampicillin Cotrimoxazole Penicillin	Enterohepatic circulation disturbance, intestinal hurry.	For short course, use additional method or use another drug. For long course, use another method.
	Rifampin	Increased metabolism of progestins. Suspected acceleration of estrogen metabolism.	Use another method.
	Chloramphenicol Metronidazole Neomycin Nitrofurantoin Sulfonamides Tetracyclines	Induction of hepatic microsomal enzymes. Also disturbance of enterohepatic circulation.	For short course, use additional method or use another drug. For long course, use another method.
	Troleandomycin	May retard metabolism of OCs, increasing the risk of cholestatic jaundice.	
Antifungals	Griseofulvin	Stimulation of hepatic metabolism of contraceptive steroids may occur.	Use another method.
Cholesterol-lowering Agents	Clofibrate	Reduces elevated serum triglycerides and cholesterol; this reduces OC efficacy.	Use another method.
Sedatives and Hypnotics	Benzodiazepines Barbiturates Chloral hydrate Glutethimide Meprobamate	Induction of hepatic microsomal enzymes.	For short course, use additional method or another drug. For long course, use another method or higher dose OCs.
Antacids		Decreased intestinal absorption of progestins.	Dose 2 hours apart.
Other Drugs	Phenylbutazone Antihistamines Analgesics Antimigraine preparations Vitamin E	Reduced OC efficacy has been reported. Remains to be confirmed.	

Table II—Cyclen

Modification of Other Drug Action by Oral Contraceptives

Class of Compound	Drug	Modification of Other Drug Action	Suggested Management
Alcohol		Possible increased levels of ethanol or acetaldehyde.	Use with caution.
Alpha-II Adrenoreceptor Agents	Clonidine	Sedation effect increased.	Use with caution.
Anticoagulants	All	OCs increase clotting factors, decrease efficacy. However, OCs may potentiate action in some patients.	Use another method.
Anticonvulsants	All	Fluid retention may increase risk of seizures.	Use another method.
Antidiabetic Drugs	Oral hypoglycemics and insulin	OCs may impair glucose tolerance and increase blood glucose.	Use low dose estrogen and progestin OC or another method. Monitor blood glucose.
Antihypertensive Agents	Guanethidine and methyldopa	Estrogen component causes sodium retention, progestin has no effect.	Use low estrogen OC or use another method.
	Beta-blockers	Increased drug effect (decreased metabolism).	Adjust dose of drug if necessary. Monitor cardiovascular status.
Antipyretics	Acetaminophen	Increased metabolism and renal clearance.	Dose of drug may have to be increased.
	Antipyrine	Impaired metabolism.	Decrease dose of drug.
	ASA	Effects of ASA may be decreased by the short-term use of OCs.	Patients on chronic ASA therapy may require an increase in ASA dosage.
Aminocaproic Acid		Theoretically, a hypercoagulable state may occur because OCs augment clotting factors.	Avoid concomitant use.
Betamimetic Agents	Isoproterenol	Estrogen causes decreased response to these drugs.	Adjust dose of drug as necessary. Discontinuing OCs can result in excessive drug activity.
Caffeine		The actions of caffeine may be enhanced as OCs may impair the hepatic metabolism of caffeine.	Use with caution.
Cholesterol-lowering Agents	Clofibrate	Their action may be antagonized by OCs. OCs may also increase metabolism of clofibrate.	May need to increase dose of clofibrate.
Corticosteroids	Prednisone	Markedly increased serum levels.	Possible need for decrease in dose.
Cyclosporine		May lead to an increase in cyclosporine levels and hepatotoxicity.	Monitor hepatic function. The cyclosporine dose may have to be decreased.
Folic Acid		OCs have been reported to impair folate metabolism.	May need to increase dietary intake, or supplement.
Meperidine		Possible increased analgesia and CNS depression due to decreased metabolism of meperidine.	Use combination with caution.
Phenothiazine Tranquilizers	All phenothiazines, Reserpine and similar drugs	Estrogen potentiates the hyperprolactinemia effect of these drugs.	Use other drugs or lower dose OCs. If galactorrhea or hyperprolactinemia occurs, use other method.
Sedatives and Hypnotics	Chlordiazepoxide Lorazepam Oxazepam Diazepam	Increased effect (increased metabolism).	Use with caution.
Theophylline	All	Decreased oxidation, leading to possible toxicity.	Use with caution. Monitor theophylline levels.
Tricyclic Antidepressants	Clomipramine (possibly others)	Increased side effects; i.e., depression.	Use with caution.
Vitamin B_{12}		OCs have been reported to reduce serum levels of Vitamin B_{12}.	May need to increase dietary intake, or supplement.

increase in size of uterine leiomyomata; rash (allergic); mental depression; reduced tolerance to carbohydrates; vaginal candidiasis; premenstrual-like syndrome; intolerance to contact lenses; change in corneal curvature (steepening); cataracts; optic neuritis; retinal thrombosis; changes in libido; chorea; changes in appetite; cystitis-like syndrome; rhinitis; headache; nervousness; dizziness; hirsutism; loss of scalp hair; erythema multiforme; erythema nodosum; hemorrhagic eruption; vaginitis; porphyria; impaired renal function; Raynaud's phenomenon; auditory disturbances; hemolytic uremic syndrome; pancreatitis.

Overdose: Symptoms and Treatment: In case of overdosage or accidental ingestion by children, the physician should observe the patient closely although generally no treatment is required. Gastric lavage may be utilized if considered necessary.

Dosage: Information for the Patient on How to Take the Birth Control Pill:

1. **Read these directions:**
   - before you start taking your pills, and
   - any time you are not sure what to do.
2. **Look at your pill pack** to see if it has 21 or 28 pills:
   - 21-Pill Pack: 21 active pills (with hormones) taken daily for 3 weeks, and then take no pills for 1 week

   or
   - 28-Pill Pack: 21 active pills (with hormones) taken daily for 3 weeks, and then 7 "reminder" pills (no hormones) taken daily for 1 week.

Also check the pill pack for instructions on (1) where to start and (2) directions to take pills (see package insert for illustrations).

3. You may wish to use a second method of birth control (e.g., latex condoms and spermicidal foam or gel) for the first 7 days of the first cycle of pill use. This will provide a back-up in case pills are forgotten while you are getting used to taking them.
4. **When receiving any medical treatment, be sure to tell your doctor that you are using birth control pills.**
5. **Many women have spotting or light bleeding or may feel sick to their stomach during the first 3 months on the pill.** If you do feel sick, do not stop taking the pill. The problem will usually go away. If it does not go away, check with your doctor or clinic.
6. **Missing pills also can cause some spotting or light bleeding,** even if you make up the missed pills. You also could feel a little sick to your stomach on the days you take 2 pills to make up for missed pills.
7. **If you miss pills at any time, you could get pregnant. The greatest risks for pregnancy are:**
   - when you start a pack late, or
   - when you miss pills at the beginning or at the very end of the pack.
8. **Always be sure you have ready:**
   - **another kind of birth control** (such as latex condoms and spermicidal foam or gel) to use as a back-up in case you miss pills, and
   - **an extra, full pack of pills.**
9. **If you experience vomiting or diarrhea, or if you take certain medicines,** such as antibiotics, your pills may not work as well. Use a back-up method, such as latex condoms and spermicidal foam or gel, until you can check with your doctor or clinic.
10. **If you forget more than 1 pill 2 months in a row,** talk to your doctor or clinic about how to make pill-taking easier or about using another method of birth control.
11. **If your questions are not answered here, call your doctor or clinic.**

When to start the first pack of pills: Be sure to read these instructions:
- before you start taking your pills, and
- any time you are not sure what to do.

Decide with your doctor or clinic what is the best day for you to start taking your first pack of pills. Your pills may be either a 21-day or a 28-day type.

Directions for 21-Day and 28-Day Pill Packs:

1. **The first day of your menstrual period (bleeding) is Day 1 of your cycle.** The pills may be started up to Day 6 of your cycle. Your starting day will be chosen in discussion with your doctor. You will **always** begin taking your pill on this day of the week. Your doctor may advise you to start taking the pills on Day 1, on Day 5, or on the first Sunday after your period begins. If your period starts on Sunday, start that same day.
2. **If you are using a:**

   21-Day Pill Pack: With this type of birth control pill, you are on pills for 21 days and off pills for 7 days. You must not be off the pills for more than 7 days in a row.

   Take 1 pill at approximately the same time every day for 21 days; **do not take a pill for 7 days.** Start a new pack on the 8th day. You will probably have a period during the 7 days off the pill. (This bleeding may be lighter and shorter than your usual period.)

28-Day Pill Pack: With this type of birth control pill, you take 21 pills that contain hormones and 7 pills that contain no hormones.

Take 1 pill at approximately the same time every day for 28 days. Begin a new pack the next day, **not missing any days on the pills.** Your period should occur during the last 7 days of using that pill pack.

Instructions for Using Your DIALPAK Tablet Dispenser: Follow these instructions carefully (see package insert for illustrations): **21-Day Regimen:** Your starting day will be chosen in discussion with your doctor. You should **always** begin taking your tablets on this day of the week. To set the package to the day you and your physician selected, insert a coin into the middle slot and turn the inner wheel counterclockwise until that day appears in the window. The example shown is for a **Sunday** start. Your first blue tablet is below the "V" notch as shown. Ensure that the tab marked "Lift Out" is set over this tablet. Break off the tab and begin tablet taking. To take your second and all subsequent tablets, turn the clear outer cover clockwise to the next available tablet. Take a tablet a day, for 21 days, completing all blue tablets. After you have taken all of your tablets wait 7 days and begin your next package on your chosen starting day whether you have finished menstruating or not. Always remember to set the starting day of each new package to the day chosen by you and your doctor.

Your first pill of each package is always under the "V" notch.

Cyclen (cont'd)

28-Day Regimen: Always complete the blue tablets before taking the green tablets.

Your starting day will be chosen in discussion with your doctor. You should **always** begin taking your tablets on this day of the week. To set the package to the day you and your physician selected, insert a coin into the middle slot and turn the inner wheel counterclockwise until that day appears in the window. The example shown is for a **Sunday** start. Your first blue tablet is immediately to the right of the green tablets and below the "V" notch as shown. Ensure that the tab marked "Lift Out" is set over this blue tablet. Break off the tab and begin tablet taking. To take your second and all subsequent tablets, turn the clear outer cover clockwise to the next available tablet. Take a tablet a day, every day, first completing all 21 blue tablets, and finally the 7 green tablets. After you have taken all of your tablets, begin your next package the very next day on your chosen starting day, whether you have finished menstruating or not. Always remember to set the starting day of each new package to the day chosen by you and your doctor.

Your first pill of each package is always under the "V" notch.

Instructions for using your Discreet package for both 21-day and 28-day packs. Follow these instructions carefully.

1. **For Day 1 start:** Label the Discreet Package by selecting the day label that starts with Day 1 of your menstrual period (the first day of menstruation is Day 1). For example, if your first day of menstruation is Tuesday, attach the day label that beings with **TUE** in the space provided.

   or

   For Day 5 start: Label the Discreet Package by selecting the day label that starts with the day that is 5 days after your period begins. (Count 5 days **including,** the first day of menstruation.) For example, if your first day of menstruation is Saturday, place the day label that starts with **WED** in the space provided.

   or

   For Sunday start: Label the Discreet Package by selecting the day label that starts with **SUN.** (The first Sunday **after** your period begins, or, if your period starts on Sunday, start that **same day.**)
2. Place the day label in the space where you see the words "Place day label here". Having the Discreet Package labelled with the day of the week will help remind you to take your pill every day.
3. To begin taking your pills, start with the first pill in top row (where you see the word **start**). This pill should correspond to the day of the week that you are taking your first pill. To remove the pill, push through the back of the Discreet Package.
4. On the following day, take the next pill in the same row, always proceeding from left to right (→). Each row will always begin on the same day of the week.

What to do during the month:

1. **Take a pill at approximately the same time every day until the pack is empty.**
   - Try to associate taking your pill with some regular activity like eating a meal or going to bed.
   - Do not skip pills even if you have bleeding between monthly periods or feel sick to your stomach (nausea).
   - Do not skip pills even if you do not have sex very often.
2. **When you finish a pack:**
   - **21 pills: Wait 7 days** to start the next pack. You will have your period during that week.
   - **28 pills:** Start the next pack **on the next day.** Take 1 pill every day. Do not wait any days between packs.

What to do if you miss pills: Table III outlines the actions you should take if you miss 1 or more of your birth control pills. Match the number of pills missed with the appropriate starting time for your type of pill pack.

Note: 28-Day Pack: If you forget any of the 7 "reminder" pills (without hormones) in Week 4, just safely dispose of the pills you missed. Then keep taking 1 pill each day until the pack is empty. You do not need to use a back-up method.

Always be sure you have on hand:

- a back-up method of birth control (such as latex condoms and spermicidal foam or gel) in case you miss pills, and
- an extra full pack of pills.

If you forget more than 1 pill 2 months in a row, talk to your doctor or clinic. Talk about ways to make pill-taking easier or about using another method of birth control.

Information for the Patient: See Blue Section—Information for the Patient "Oral Contraceptives".

Supplied: Each blue tablet, unscored with ORTHO 250 engraved on each side, contains: norgestimate 0.25 mg and ethinyl estradiol 35 µg. In the 28-day regimen, the green tablets, embossed on each side with ORTHO, contain inert ingredients. Nonmedicinal ingredients: Blue tablets: FD&C Blue No. 2 Aluminum lake, lactose, magnesium stearate and starch. Green tablets: D&C Yellow No. 10 Aluminum lake, FD&C Blue No. 2 Aluminum lake, lactose, microcrystalline cellulose and starch. Available in 21-day or 28-day VARIDATE DIALPAK Tablet Dispenser Units and 21-day or 28-day Discreet Packages. Store between 15 and 25°C. Leave contents in protective packaging until time of use.

(Shown in Product Recognition Section)

Reviewed 1999

Table III—Cyclen

What to Do If You Miss Pills

Sunday Start	Other Than Sunday Start
Miss 1 pill	**Miss 1 pill**
Take it as soon as you remember, and take the next pill at the usual time. This means that you might take 2 pills in one day.	Take it as soon as you remember, and take the next pill at the usual time. This means that you might take 2 pills in one day.
Miss 2 pills in a row	**Miss 2 pills in a row**
First 2 Weeks: 1. Take 2 pills the day you remember and 2 pills the next day. 2. Then take 1 pill a day until you finish the pack. 3. Use a back-up method of birth control if you have sex in the 7 days after you miss the pills.	**First 2 Weeks:** 1. Take 2 pills the day you remember and 2 pills the next day. 2. Then take 1 pill a day until you finish the pack. 3. Use a back-up method of birth control if you have sex in the 7 days after you miss the pills.
Third Week: 1. Keep taking 1 pill a day until Sunday. 2. On Sunday, safely discard the rest of the pack and start a new pack that day. 3. Use a back-up method of birth control if you have sex in the 7 days after you miss the pills. 4. You may not have a period this month. **If you miss 2 periods in a row, call your doctor or clinic.**	**Third Week:** 1. Safely dispose of the rest of the pill pack and start a new pack that same day. 2. Use a back-up method of birth control if you have sex in the 7 days after you miss the pills. 3. You may not have a period this month. **If you miss 2 periods in a row, call your doctor or clinic.**
Miss 3 or more pills in a row	**Miss 3 or more pills in a row**
Anytime in the Cycle: 1. Keep taking 1 pill a day until Sunday. 2. On Sunday, safely discard the rest of the pack and start a new pack that day. 3. Use a back-up method of birth control if you have sex in the 7 days after you miss the pills. 4. You may not have a period this month. **If you miss 2 periods in a row, call your doctor or clinic.**	**Anytime in the Cycle:** 1. Safely dispose of the rest of the pill pack and start a new pack that same day. 2. Use a back-up method of birth control if you have sex in the 7 days after you miss the pills. 3. You may not have a period this month. **If you miss 2 periods in a row, call your doctor or clinic.**

CYCLOCORT®

Stiefel

Amcinonide

Topical Corticosteroid

Indications: The relief of inflammatory manifestations of acute and chronic corticosteroid-responsive dermatoses, such as atopic dermatitis, contact and eczematous dermatoses, psoriasis and neurodermatitis.

Topical corticosteroid therapy, although responsible for remissions of dermatoses, especially of allergic origin, cannot be expected to prevent recurrence. In the case of contact or allergic dermatitis, it is important to investigate causal factors and to remove the offending material or allergen.

Contraindications: Fungal diseases of the skin, untreated bacterial infections, tuberculosis of the skin, certain viral diseases such as herpes simplex, vaccinia and varicella. Hypersensitivity to any of the product's components. Not for ophthalmic use.

Precautions: *Pregnancy* and *Lactation:* The safety of topical corticosteroids during pregnancy or lactation has not been established. Weigh the potential benefit of topical corticosteroids, if used during pregnancy or lactation, against possible hazard to the fetus or the infant being nursed.

Significant systemic absorption may occur when corticosteroids are applied over large areas of the body, especially under occlusive dressings. To minimize this possibility, when long-term therapy is anticipated, interrupt treatment periodically, or treat one area of the body at a time. Avoid contact with the eyes.

Although hypersensitivity reactions have been rare with topically applied corticosteroids, discontinue the cream and initiate appropriate therapy if there are signs of sensitivity.

The use of topical corticosteroids on infected areas should be attended with caution and careful observation, bearing in mind the potential spreading of infection and the possible advisability of discontinuing corticosteroid therapy and/or initiating antibacterial measures. If a symptomatic response is not noted within a few days to a week, discontinue the local application until the infection is brought under control.

Advise patients to inform subsequent physicians of the prior use of corticosteroids.

Occlusive dressings should not be applied if there is an elevation of body temperature.

Prolonged use of topical corticosteroids may produce atrophy of the skin and of s.c. tissues, particularly on flexor surfaces and on the face. If this is noted, discontinue the use of topical corticosteroids.

Topical corticosteroids should be used with caution in patients with stasis dermatitis and other skin diseases associated with impaired circulation.

Adverse Effects: When occlusive dressings are used, pustules, miliaria, folliculitis, and pyoderma may occur. The following adverse skin reactions have been reported with the use of topical steroids: dryness, itching, burning, local irritation, striae, skin atrophy, atrophy of s.c. tissues, telangiectasia, hypertrichosis, change in pigmentation, and secondary infection. Adrenal suppression also has been reported following topical corticosteroid therapy. Posterior subcapsular cataracts have been reported following systemic use of corticosteroids.

Dosage: Apply to affected area 2 or 3 times daily and rub in gently. Application twice a day is usually sufficient.

Supplied: Cream: Each tube contains: amcinonide (a fluorinated corticosteroid) 0.1%, compounded with emulsifying wax NF, isopropyl palmitate, glycerin, sorbitol solution, lactic acid, purified water and benzyl alcohol 2.0% as preservative. Lanolin-, paraben-, propylene glycol-, tartrazine- and urea-free. Tubes of 15, 30 and 60 g.

Ointment: Each tube contains: amcinonide 0.1%, emulsifying wax NF, benzyl alcohol 2.0%, TENOX II, and white petrolatum. Tartrazine-free. Tubes of 15, 30 and 60 g.

Lotion: Each bottle contains: amcinonide 0.1%, emulsifying wax NF, isopropyl palmitate, glycerin, sorbitol solution, lactic acid, purified water, and benzyl alcohol 1.0%. Lanolin-, paraben-, propylene glycol-, tartrazine- and urea-free. Bottles of 20 and 60 mL.

...Consult a pharmacist for additional drug information.

CYCLOGYL® ℞

Alcon

Cyclopentolate HCl

Cycloplegic—Mydriatic—Anticholinergic

Supplied: Each dispenser contains: cyclopentolate HCl 1% preserved with benzalkonium chloride. Nonmedicinal ingredients: boric acid, edetate disodium, hydrochloric acid, potassium chloride, purified water and sodium carbonate. Drop-Tainer dispensers of 15 mL.

CYCLOMEN® ℞

Sanofi

Danazol

Pituitary Gonadotropin Inhibitor

Pharmacology: In women of reproductive age, the primary mode of action of danazol is believed to be by suppression of the pituitary-ovarian axis, and inhibition of the output of gonadotropins from the pituitary-gland.

Other mechanisms of action currently postulated to explain its effects are: inhibition of midcycle FSH and LH surges: inhibition of enzymes required for gonadal hormone synthesis: competitive binding of danazol to steroid receptors at target organs.

Danazol may also inhibit cyclic AMP accumulation in granulosa and luteal cells in response to gonadotrophic hormones. A wide range of actions on plasma proteins including increasing prothrombin, plasminogen, antithrombin III, alpha-2-macroglobulin, C1 esterase inhibitor, erythropoietin and reducing fibrinogen, thyroid binding and sex hormone binding globulins has been observed. Danazol increases the proportion and concentration of testosterone carried unbound in the plasma.

In postmenopausal women, danazol suppresses FSH and LH levels. It has a weak dose-related androgenic activity. Danazol is a weak androgen but antiandrogenic, progestogenic, antiprogestogenic, estrogenic and antiestrogenic actions have also been observed. Following oral administration in healthy adult females, danazol displays dose dependent absorption, which approaches linearity over the dosage range 100 to 400 mg twice daily in multiple dosing. Absorption is affected by prandial state, being approximately doubled if danazol is taken just after, compared with 2 hours before, a meal. The principal metabolites of danazol appear to be ethisterone and 17-hydroxymethylethisterone. The mean plasma elimination half-life of danazol is in the order of 24 hours.

Bioavailability studies indicate that blood levels do not increase proportionally with increases in the administered dose. When the dose is doubled, the increase in plasma levels is only about 35 to 40%.

When used for the treatment of endometriosis, danazol alters the endometrium so that it becomes inactive and atrophic. Danazol produces marked regression of ectopic endometrial tissue. Pre- and post-medication laparoscopy was done on 96 subjects. Complete or partial resolution of ectopic endometrial sites was found in 97% of patients receiving 800 mg danazol daily and in 75% of patients receiving 600 mg. This regression is due to the suppression of ovarian function which results in anovulation and associated amenorrhea. Changes in vaginal cytology and cervical mucus reflect danazol's suppressive effect on the gonadal steroid action and were found in 75% of 116 patients.

After institution of therapy with danazol, patients have one additional menstrual period and then become anovulatory and amenorrheic, though some patients have occasional spotting for the duration of treatment. In cases where it has been examined, this bleeding was associated with an atrophic endometrium. On regimens of 200 to 600 mg daily for 3 to 6 months, highly effective relief of the signs and symptoms of endometriosis was obtained. Complete or partial relief of dysmenorrhea occurred in 94% (290/309) of patients, of pelvic pain in 85% (276/322), of dyspareunia in 84% (134/160) and of induration of the cul de sac in 79% (217/274). Dysmenorrhea and pelvic pain are usually relieved within the first few weeks of therapy; relief of dyspareunia and induration of the cul de sac take longer.

Generally danazol's action is reversible. Ovulation and predictable cyclical bleeding usually return within 60 to 90 days when danazol therapy is discontinued. Discontinuation results in a rebound in FSH and LH secretion with consequent increase in fecundity.

In the treatment of fibrocystic breast disease, the mode of action of danazol on the breasts is not known. Therapy with this drug lasting up to 6 months, however, results in relief of pain, tenderness and various degrees of regression of nodularity. An alteration or improvement of the pathological process at the tissue level has not been demonstrated. Oligomenorrhea and amenorrhea occur in a dose-dependent manner in most patients, however, normal menstrual patterns return within 2 months following discontinuation of therapy.

Indications: Endometriosis. The treatment of endometriosis characterized by dysmenorrhea, pelvic pain, infertility, induration of the cul de sac, or dyspareunia.

Primary Menorrhagia: The short-term (up to 6 months) hormonal management of severe primary menorrhagia (excessive menstrual bleeding **at the time of expected menses in a regularly cycling women)**, as determined by history, physical examination, and laboratory studies. Organic pathology (such as polyps, fibroids, and genital neoplasia), abnormalities of blood coagulation (thrombocytopenia, von Willebrand's disease) and endocrine disorders (hypothyroidism), any of which may be the cause of secondary menorrhagia, should be excluded before initiating treatment.

Fibrocystic Breast Disease: The symptomatic relief of pain and tenderness associated with fibrocystic disease of the breast. Danazol should be used in those patients who do not obtain adequate relief through other therapeutic measures or in whom such measures are otherwise inadvisable. Carcinoma of the breast should be excluded prior to commencing treatment.

Contraindications: In patients presenting with undiagnosed abnormal genital bleeding; genital neoplasia; markedly impaired hepatic, renal or cardiac function; pregnancy; lactation (breast-feeding); porphyria—danazol can induce ALA synthetase activity and should not be used in patients with known or suspected acute intermittent porphyria; known hypersensitivity to danazol; androgen-dependent tumor; active thrombosis or thromboembolic disease and history of such events.

Warnings: *Pregnancy:* Danazol may cause fetal harm when administered to a pregnant woman. Exposure to danazol in utero may result in androgenic effects on the female fetus, comprising to date clitoral hypertrophy, labial fusion, urogenital sinus defect, vaginal atresia, and ambiguous genitalia. A sensitive test (e.g., beta subunit test if available) capable of determining early pregnancy is recommended immediately prior to start of therapy. Additionally, denazol should be initiated during menstruation and an effective nonhormonal method of contraception should be used during therapy. If a patient becomes pregnant while taking danazol, administration of the drug should be discontinued and the patient should be apprised of the potential risk to the fetus.

Lactation: Danazol has the theoretical potential for androgenic effects in breast-fed infants and therefore either danazol therapy or breast-feeding should be discontinued. Before initiating therapy of fibrocystic breast disease with danazol, carcinoma of the breast should be excluded.

Nodularity, pain and tenderness due to fibrocystic breast disease may prevent recognition of underlying carcinoma before treatment is begun. As evidenced during clinical trials with danazol, breast pain and tenderness are usually significantly relieved by the first month of treatment and eliminated in 2 to 3 months. Regression of nodularity may require up to 6 months of uninterrupted therapy. Therefore, if any nodule persists or enlarges during treatment, carcinoma should be considered and ruled out.

Attempts should be made to determine the lowest clinically effective dose. In view of the fact that some cases of endometriosis may be resistant to one specific form of hormone therapy and responsive to another, danazol may prove to be of benefit in such cases. There are some limited data in support of the use of danazol in therapy-resistant cases of this type.

Patients should be watched closely for signs of virilization. Some of these, in rare cases (such as deepening of voice, clitoral hypertrophy and more than minimal hirsutism), may not be reversible. In these cases, cessation of therapy should be considered in order to prevent further progression due to the risk of irreversible androgenic effects.

It should be stressed to the patient that danazol treatment involves considerable alterations of hormone levels which may be evidenced by such side effects as the occurrence of acne, weight gain, irregular menstrual patterns or amenorrhea, signs of virilization and that recurrence of the initial symptoms may occur following cessation of therapy.

Experience with danazol greater than 9 months is limited. Therapy with other steroids alkylated at the 17 position has been associated with serious toxicity (cholestatic jaundice, peliosis hepatis). The physician therefore should be alerted to the possibility that similar toxicity may develop during therapy with danazol, especially when administration is continued beyond recommended time periods. Peliosis hepatitis and hepatic adenoma may be silent until complicated by acute potentially life-threatening intra-abdominal hemorrhage.

Extremely rare cases of serious adverse events and death have been reported in individual patients who were taking danazol; however, a causal relationship to the administration of danazol has neither been confirmed nor refuted. These included one case of acute leukemia, one fatal case of primary liver carcinoma, and a few cases of peliosis, hepatomas and the association of danazol with several cases of benign intracranial hypertension (pseudotumor cerebri), thromboembolism, thrombotic and thrombophlebitic events, including sagittal sinus thrombosis and life-threatening or fatal strokes.

Precautions: In view of its pharmacology, known interactions and side effects, particular care should be observed in using danazol in those with hepatic or renal disease; hypertension or other cardiovascular disease; any state which may be exacerbated by fluid retention; diabetes mellitus; polycythemia; epilepsy; lipoprotein disorder; a history of thrombosis or thromboembolic disease; a history of marked or persistent androgenic reaction to previous gonadal steroid therapy; migraine (see below for further precautions on several of these conditions). Danazol may cause erratic results in thyroid function tests. Patients who are taking danazol have shown the uncommon combination of low or low normal serum thyroxine, much reduced thyroxine binding globulin and normal free thyroxine index. In men and women a dose of 600 mg danazol daily for 15 days has been shown to have no significant effect on basal levels of TSH or on its response to thyrotrophin releasing hormone. The finding of normal thyroid stimulating hormone levels and free thyroxine index during danazol therapy indicates that patients are euthyroid. It is believed that the abnormality of thyroid function tests is due to an androgen-like reduction in thyroxine binding globulin rather than a true decrease in thyroid function or interference with the pituitary thyroid axis.

Changes in plasma levels of several other proteins have been observed during danazol administration. Pre-albumin, C_1-esterase inhibitor, haptoglobins, transferrin, antithrombin III, prothrombin and plasminogen were all shown to increase following administration of danazol. The concentrations of T4 binding globulin, pregnancy zone protein and sex hormone binding globulin decreased to one-third or less on administration of danazol. The plasma estradiol content fell correspondingly. The clinical significance of these changes has not yet been determined. A temporary alteration of lipoproteins in the form of decreased high density lipoproteins and possibly increased low density lipoproteins has been reported in some patients during danazol therapy. Prescribers should consider the possible risk of atherosclerosis and coronary artery disease versus the benefit of therapy.

Since hepatic dysfunction has been reported in patients treated with danazol, periodic liver function tests should be performed (see Adverse Effects).

Fatal cases of fulminant hepatitis have been reported in 3 patients while on danazol therapy. One of these patients was shown to have an infection with hepatitis B virus while the symptoms and clinical course of the other 2 patients were consistent with non A—non B hepatitis.

If faced with continuing abnormalities of biochemical tests and/or their corresponding clinical manifestations, the possible risks should be carefully weighed against the potential benefits and discontinuation of danazol treatment should be considered.

It may be prudent to continue nonhormonal contraception after danazol treatment for fibrocystic breast disease until a menstrual period that is normal in amount of flow and duration has occurred.

Drug Interactions: Danazol may potentiate the effects of coumarin-type anticoagulants. In cases where such drugs are given concurrently with danazol, careful attention to and, if necessary, readjustment of, their dosages is recommended.

Danazol can increase the plasma level of carbamazepine and may affect responsiveness to this agent and to phenytoin. A similar interaction with phenobarbital is likely.

Plasma concentrations of cyclosporine and tacrolimus, administered concurrently with danazol may be higher than expected leading to an increase of the renal toxicity of these drugs. Elevated plasma glucagon levels have been reported in a few patients receiving danazol; diabetic patients on insulin or oral hypoglycemic agents may need to have the dosage of those agents increased appropriately in order to maintain euglycemia as danazol can cause insulin resistance.

Danazol can diminish the effectiveness of antihypertensive agents and likely interact with gonadal steroid therapy.

Danazol can increase the calcemic response to alpha calcidol in primary hypoparathyroidism.

Cyclomen (cont'd)

Alteration in values for laboratory tests may occur during danazol therapy including CPK, glucose tolerance, glucagon, thyroid binding globulin, sex hormone binding globulin, other plasma proteins, lipid and lipoproteins and urinary 17-ketosteroids.

Danazol is less likely to be effective in patients who have metrorrhagia in addition to menorrhagia (irregular as well as heavy menses).

Pregnancy: See Contraindications.

Lactation: See Contraindications.

Children: Safety and effectiveness in children have not been established.

Adverse Effects: The lowest dose of 200 mg daily, which is indicated for the treatment of menorrhagia (see Dosage), has clinically demonstrated a significantly lower incidence of side effects than that associated with higher doses used in the treatment of endometriosis. One should however, be aware that any of the following adverse effects can occur: acne, edema, mild hirsutism, decrease in breast size, deepening of the voice, oiliness of the skin or hair, weight gain, and rarely, clitoral hypertrophy. Also hypoestrogenic manifestations such as flushing, sweating, vaginitis including itching, dryness, burning and vaginal bleeding, nervousness, and emotional lability have been reported.

Hepatic dysfunction, as evidenced by reversible elevated serum enzymes has been reported. Jaundice has been reported rarely. It is recommended that patients receiving danazol be monitored for hepatic dysfunction by laboratory tests and clinical observation (see Precautions). Rare occurrences of benign hepatic adenomata, malignant hepatic tumor and peliosis hepatis have also been observed with long-term use. Rare cases of pancreatitis have been reported.

Although the following reactions have also been reported, a causal relationship to the administration of danazol has neither been confirmed nor refuted: Allergic: urticaria, pruritus, rarely nasal congestion.

Skin and Mucous Membranes: rashes (maculopapular, vesicular, papular, purpuric, petechial), acne, hyperpigmentation, hair loss, inflammatory erythematous nodules, altered skin pigmentation, exfoliative dermatitis, erythema multiforme, Stevens-Johnson syndrome and rarely sun sensitivity.

Gastrointestinal: nausea, vomiting, constipation, gastroenteritis and rarely pancreatitis.

Genitourinary: hematuria, prolonged post-therapy amenorrhea, disturbance of the menstrual cycle, intermenstrual spotting and/or prolonged anovulation.

Musculoskeletal: muscle cramps or spasms sometimes with elevation of creatine phosphokinase levels, muscle or joint pain, joint lock-up, joint swelling, pain in back, neck or extremities, fasciculation, limb pain and rarely carpal tunnel syndrome.

Cardiovascular: exacerbation of hypertension, palpitation, tachycardia, thrombotic events have also been observed, including sagittal sinus and cerebrovascular thrombosis as well as arterial thrombosis; cases of myocardial infarction have been reported.

CNS: headache, nervousness and emotional lability, dizziness and fainting, vertigo, depression, fatigue, paresthesias, chills, visual disturbances including visual hallucination followed by seizure, papilledema, retrobulbar neuritis, and rarely benign intracranial hypertension (pseudotumor cerebri), anxiety, sleep disorders, tremor, weakness, changes in appetite, aggravation of epilepsy, provocation of migraine and Guillain-Barré syndrome.

Ophthalmic: visual disturbances such as blurring of vision, difficulty in focusing, difficulty in wearing contact lenses and need for temporary alteration in refractive correction.

Hematologic: an increase in red cell and platelet count, leukopenia, thrombocytopenia and rarely eosinophilia, reversible erythrocytosis, leukocytosis, polycythemia, thrombophlebitis.

Other: hyperglucagonemia, increased insulin requirements in diabetic patients, decreased HDL cholesterol levels, decreased LDL cholesterol levels with variable changes in total cholesterol, decrease in apolipoproteins A1 and A11 (the clinical significance of these changes is not established), induction of aminolevulinic acid (ALA) synthetase, changes in libido, elevation in blood pressure, and rarely nipple discharge, cataracts, bleeding gums, fever, pelvic pain, epigastric and pleuritic pain, interstitial pneumonitis.

Overdose: Symptoms and Treatment: Available evidence suggests that acute overdosage would be unlikely to give rise to immediate serious reaction. Nonetheless, consideration should be given to removal of the drug by emesis or stomach pump and the patient should be kept under observation in case of any delayed reactions.

Dosage: Danazol should be given as a continuous course, dosage being adjusted according to the severity of the condition and the patient's response. A reduction in dosage once a satisfactory response has been achieved may prove possible.

Therapy should begin during menstruation. Otherwise, appropriate tests should be performed to ensure that the patient is not pregnant while on danazol therapy. An effective nonhormonal method of contraception should be used during the complete course of treatment. Regular menstrual patterns, irregular menstrual patterns and amenorrhea each occur in approximately one-third of patients treated with 100 mg danazol. Irregular menstrual patterns and amenorrhea are observed more frequently with higher doses.

Endometriosis: Clinical effectiveness has been achieved with total daily doses of danazol ranging from 200 to 800 mg in 2 to 4 divided doses and administered without interruption for 3 to 6 months. If, at the lower doses, an anovulatory and amenorrheic state is not achieved and if the symptomatology is not relieved in 30 to 60 days, the dose should be increased. In patients with severe presenting symptomatology, the usual starting dose is 800 mg daily. The maximum recommended daily dose is 800 mg. It is essential that therapy continue uninterrupted for 3 to 6 months, but may be extended to 9 months, if necessary. Shorter courses of therapy have been used as adjuncts to surgery. After termination of therapy, if symptoms recur, treatment can be reinstated.

Primary Menorrhagia: A course of 200 to 400 mg of danazol daily in divided doses for up to 6 months. 200 mg is usually sufficient to reduce menstrual blood flow to acceptable limits. If no improvement is observed after 2 or 3 cycles, treatment should be discontinued and the patient should be reassessed for the cause of the excess bleeding.

Fibrocystic Breast Disease: The total daily dose of danazol ranges from 100 to 400 mg in two divided doses depending on patient response. Pain and tenderness usually respond to treatment after 30 to 40 days. Nodularity usually does not begin to regress until 60 to 90 days after initiation of therapy. Treatment should continue uninterrupted until complete disappearance of symptoms or for 6 months, whichever occurs first. Clinical studies have demonstrated that approximately 50% of patients may show evidence of recurrence of symptoms within 1 year. In this event, treatment may be reinstated.

Supplied: 50 mg: Each orange and white capsule contains: danazol 50 mg. Nonmedicinal ingredients: cornstarch, D and C Yellow #10, FD and C Red #3, gelatin, lactose, magnesium stearate, talc and titanium dioxide. Energy: <8 kJ (2 kcal). Bisulfite-, gluten-, sucrose- and tartrazine-free. Bottles of 100.

100 mg: Each yellow capsule contains: danazol 100 mg. Nonmedicinal ingredients: cornstarch, D and C Yellow #10, FD and C Yellow #6, gelatin, lactose, magnesium stearate, talc and titanium dioxide. Energy: <8 kJ (2 kcal). Bisulfite-, gluten-, sucrose- and tartrazine-free. Bottles of 100.

200 mg: Each orange capsule contains: danazol 200 mg. Nonmedicinal ingredients: cornstarch, D and C Yellow #10, FD and C Red #3, gelatin, lactose, magnesium stearate, talc and titanium dioxide. Energy: <8 kJ (2 kcal). Bisulfite-, gluten-, sucrose- and tartrazine-free. Bottles of 100.

(Shown in Product Recognition Section)

Reviewed 1999

CYCLOPENTOLATE HCl Ⓟ

General Monograph, CPhA

Cycloplegic—Mydriatic—Anticholinergic

> This monograph has been compiled by CPhA. It may contain information different from that approved by Therapeutic Products Programme, Health Canada, and the pharmaceutical manufacturers' approval has not been requested.

Pharmacology: Cyclopentolate is an anticholinergic agent that induces relaxation of the sphincter of the iris and the ciliary muscles. When applied topically to the eyes, it causes a rapid, intense cycloplegic and mydriatic effect that is maximal in 15 to 60 minutes; recovery usually occurs within 24 hours. The cycloplegic and mydriatic effects are slower in onset and longer in duration in patients who have dark pigmented irises.

Indications: Cyclopentolate is used mainly to produce mydriasis and cycloplegia for diagnostic purposes.

Contraindications: Cyclopentolate is contraindicated in patients with angle-closure glaucoma or in patients with shallow anterior chambers (see Warnings).

Cyclopentolate should not be used in patients, especially children, who have previously experienced a severe systemic reaction to the drug, or in patients with hypersensitivity to any component of a cyclopentolate formulation.

Warnings: Cyclopentolate may cause increased intraocular pressure. Angle-closure glaucoma may be induced by cyclopentolate in patients with higher susceptibility to increased intraocular pressure including the elderly and individuals with shallow anterior chambers.

Very rarely, some patients with open-angle glaucoma may experience abrupt elevations in intraocular pressure.

The use of cyclopentolate in patients with higher susceptibility to increased intraocular pressure should be preceded by complete ocular examination, including measurement of intraocular pressure.

Precautions: Cyclopentolate may cause an increase in intraocular pressure which if sustained, can potentially lead to irreversible loss of vision (see Warnings). The drug should be discontinued and the physician consulted immediately if eye pain, blurring of vision, rapid pulse or dizziness occurs.

Patients may require the use of dark glasses following the application of cyclopentolate, due to photophobia associated with mydriasis.

Patients should be advised to contact their physician if blurred vision and photophobia continue for more than 48 hours after discontinuing cyclopentolate.

Systemic absorption of topical cyclopentolate from the nasal mucosal surfaces may result in systemic adverse effects. This is particularly the case in children, who are most susceptible to the drug's adverse effects. If signs of systemic toxicity appear, such as dry mouth, tachycardia or dizziness, the dosage schedule should be reduced or the drug discontinued.

Children: Infants and young children and children with blond hair or blue eyes may be especially sensitive to the effects of cyclopentolate, increasing the chance of side effects during treatment. Use of cyclopentolate in children has been associated with psychotic reactions and behavioral disturbances.

Drug Interactions: Cyclopentolate may affect the action of concomitantly administered drugs such as: antihistamines, isoniazid, MAO inhibitors, phenothiazines, procainamide, disopyramide, propranolol, quinidine and tricyclic antidepressants. Anticholinergic agents, such as cyclopentolate, antagonize miosis and ciliary body contraction induced by cholinesterase inhibitors and cholinergic agonists.

Adverse Effects: Blinding acute angle-closure glaucoma and raised intraocular pressure may occur during cyclopentolate therapy. The mydriasis may be reduced by the intraocular application of pilocarpine, physostigmine or isoflurophate.

Transient burning sensation of the eye is more likely with the 1% than the 0.5% solution.

Systemic effects, resulting from excessive absorption from mucosal surfaces or from ingestion of the drug, may include xerostomia, flushing, tachycardia and urinary retention. More severe systemic effects are tachypnea, scarlatiniform rash, delirium, psychosis, fever, stupor, coma, respiratory failure and death.

Overdose: Symptoms: Tachycardia, dizziness, dry mouth, behavioral disturbances, uncoordination or drowsiness.

Treatment: Symptomatic and supportive therapy. In most cases of topical exposure, patients recover without specific therapy. If drops are accidentally ingested, more pronounced anticholinergic effects may occur. Emesis is not advised due to the CNS depression and delirium that may be present. Gastric lavage may be indicated in cases of recent ingestion. Administer activated charcoal and cathartic if no contraindications. Physostigmine should be reserved for severe cases unresponsive to other measures.

Dosage: To produce mydriasis and cycloplegia for diagnostic purposes, in adults and children over 1 year: 1 drop instilled in the eye(s), followed by a second drop 5 minutes later, if necessary. Drops should be administered 40 to 50 minutes prior to the procedure. To minimize systemic absorption, finger pressure should be applied to the lacrimal sac for 2 to 3 minutes following administration. Alternatively, the eyelids should be kept closed for 2 to 5 minutes following instillation.

Patients with heavily pigmented irides may require larger doses.

Complete recovery from mydriasis and cycloplegia should occur within 24 hours.

Reviewed 1998

CYKLOKAPRON® ℞

Pharmacia & Upjohn

Tranexamic Acid

Antifibrinolytic Agent

Pharmacology: Tranexamic acid produces an antifibrinolytic effect by competitively inhibiting the activation of plasminogen to plasmin. It is also a weak noncompetitive inhibitor of plasmin. These properties make possible its clinical use as an antifibrinolytic in the treatment of both general and local fibrinolytic hemorrhages. It has an action mechanism similar to, but about 10 times more potent in vitro than that of epsilon aminocaproic acid (EACA).

Absorption from the human gastrointestinal tract is not complete (40%).

Tranexamic acid binds considerably more strongly than EACA to both the strong and weak sites in the plasminogen molecule in a ratio corresponding to the difference in potency between the compounds. The pharmacological significance of the binding to these different sites has not yet been evaluated.

Tranexamic acid does not bind to serum albumin. The plasma protein binding which seems to be fully accounted for by its binding to plasminogen, appears to be negligible at therapeutic plasma levels of 5 to 10 mg/L.

Possible routes of biotransformation are acetylation or deamination followed by oxidation or reduction. After oral administration approximately 50% of the parent compound, 2% of the deaminated dicarboxylic acid, and 0.5% of the acetylated product are excreted.

Tranexamic acid is eliminated by glomerular filtration, excretion being about 30% at 1 hour, 55% at 3 hours and 90% at 24 hours after i.v. administration of 10 mg/kg. After oral administration of 10 to 15 mg/kg excretion was 1% at 1 hour, 7% at 3 hours and 39% at 24 hours.

I.V. administration of 10 mg/kg gave plasma concentrations of 18.3 μg, 9.6 μg and 5 μg/mL 1, 3 and 5 hours after the injection.

When administered 36 to 48 hours before surgery in 4 doses of 10 to 20 mg/kg an antifibrinolytically active concentration (10 μg/mL) of tranexamic acid remained up to 17 hours in the tissues investigated, and up to 7 to 8 hours in the serum.

Tranexamic acid crosses the placenta. After an i.v. injection of 10 mg/kg the concentration can rise to about 30 μg/mL of fetal serum.

Tranexamic acid also passes over into the breast milk during lactation in concentrations 1/100 of the corresponding serum levels.

After both oral and i.v. administration tranexamic acid passes into the semen and inhibits its fibrinolytic activity, but without affecting the motility of the spermatozoa.

The ability of tranexamic acid to cross the blood-brain barrier has been demonstrated when administered to patients with ruptured intracranial aneurysms.

Tranexamic acid diffuses rapidly to the joint fluid and to the synovial membrane. In the joint fluid the same concentration was obtained as in the serum. The biological half-life in the joint fluid was about 3 hours.

Three hours after a single oral dose of 25 mg/kg, the peak serum level was 15.4 g/L and the aqueous humour level was 1.6 g/L.

Indications: Hereditary angioneurotic edema. Increased local fibrinolysis when the diagnosis is indicative of hyperfibrinolysis, as with conization of the cervix, dental extraction in patients with coagulopathies (in conjunction with antihemophilic factor) epistaxis, hyphema, and menorrhagia (hypermenorrhea).

Contraindications: Patients with a history or risk of thrombosis should not be given tranexamic acid, unless at the same time it is possible to give treatment with anticoagulants. The preparation should not be given to patients with acquired disturbances of color vision. If disturbances of color vision arise during the course of treatment the administration of the preparation should be discontinued.

Warnings: For patients who are to be treated for several weeks with tranexamic acid an ophthalmic checkup is advisable (sharpness of vision, color vision, fundus, field of vision, etc.) if possible, before treatment is initiated and regularly during treatment.

Pregnancy: The safety of tranexamic acid during pregnancy has not yet been established. No harmful effects have been reported.

A woman with fibrinolytic bleeding in the fourth month of pregnancy was treated with tranexamic acid for a total of 64 days. The total dose was 256 g. The delivery occurred spontaneously in the 30th week of pregnancy and was normal in all other respects. The infant was healthy.

In a case of threatened placental abruption that was prevented by giving tranexamic acid, the patient had already lost 2 children in connection with placental abruption. In the 26th week of her third pregnancy bleeding occurred, indicating abruption. Pathological proteolysis with predominant activation of the fibrinolytic system was established. Between the 26th and 33rd week of pregnancy about 250 g of tranexamic acid were given, both i.v. and orally. The bleeding was arrested and a healthy child was delivered by Caesarean section.

Tranexamic acid crosses over to the fetus. After an i.v. injection of 10 mg/kg the concentration can reach a level of about 30 μg/mL fetal serum. Fibrinolytic activity is very high in neonates. It is not known for certain whether a reduction of this activity during the first hours of life is harmful. Kullander and Nilsson who have wide experience with tranexamic acid in connection with childbirth have observed no negative effect on the infants.

Precautions: Care should be taken in cases of renal insufficiency due to the risk of accumulation, and where there is pronounced hematuria from the upper urinary tract, since in isolated cases obstacles to passage have been observed in the tract.

Renal Insufficiency: In patients with serum creatinine concentrations of 120 to 250 μmol/L, 15 mg orally or 10 mg i.v. tranexamic acid/kg body weight twice daily. At serum creatinine levels of 250 to 500 μmol/L the dosage should be 15 mg orally or 10 mg i.v./kg body weight at 24-hour intervals, and at serum creatinine levels of 500 μmol/L or more the same dose should be given at intervals of 48 hours between doses. Tranexamic acid therapy is not indicated in hematuria caused by diseases of the renal parenchyma. Intravascular precipitation of fibrin frequently occurs in these conditions and may aggravate the disease. In addition, in cases of massive renal hemorrhage of any cause, antifibrinolytic therapy carries the risk of clot retention in the renal pelvis.

Lactation: Tranexamic acid is secreted in the mother's milk at a concentration only a hundredth of the corresponding serum levels. The investigators are of the opinion that tranexamic acid can be given during lactation without risk to the child.

Adverse Effects: Gastointestinal symptoms (nausea, vomiting, diarrhea) occur but disappear when the dose is reduced. Isolated cases of dizziness or reduced blood pressure have been reported.

To be observed by reason of experimental findings in animals: In the dog, retinal changes have been observed after long-term administration of large doses of tranexamic acid and in the cat, after i.v. injection of 250 mg/kg/day for 14 days. Such changes have not been obtained in the rat, where the maximum tolerated dose has been administered. No retinal changes have been reported or observed at ophthalmic checkups of patients treated with Cyklokapron for several weeks or months.

Overdose: Symptoms: There is no known case of overdosage of tranexamic acid in humans. Symptoms may be nausea and vomiting, orthostatic symptoms and hypotension.

Treatment: Initiate vomiting, institute gastric lavage and charcoal therapy.

Dosage: Conization of the cervix: 2 to 3 tablets every 8 to 12 hours, 12 days postoperatively.

Epistaxis: 2 to 3 tablets every 8 to 12 hours for 10 days.

Hyphema: 2 to 3 tablets every 8 to 12 hours for 7 days.

Dental surgery in patients with coagulopathies: 2 hours before the operation, Factor VIII and Factor IX should be given as well as Cyklokapron, 25 mg orally or 10 mg i.v/kg body weight. After the operation, 25 mg/kg of tranexamic acid is given orally 3 to 4 times a day for 6 to 8 days. After the operation the patient does not generally require further substitution therapy.

Administer tranexamic acid solution for injection by slow i.v. injection over a period of at least 5 minutes. For i.v. infusion, the tranexamic acid solution for injection may be mixed with electrolyte solutions, carbohydrate solutions, Aminosol and dextran solutions. Heparin may be added to tranexamic acid solution for injection. Cyklokapron solution for injection should not be mixed with blood and infusion solutions containing penicillin.

Menorrhagia (hypermenorrhea): 2 to 3 tablets 3 to 4 times a day for several days. Tranexamic acid treatment should only be started when copious bleeding has begun.

Hereditary Angioneurotic Edema: Some patients can sense the onset of attacks and are best treated intermittently with 2 to 3 tablets 2 to 3 times a day for several days. Others should be treated continuously with this dose.

Children: Dosage should be calculated according to body weight at 25 mg/kg, 2 to 3 times a day.

Supplied: Injection: Each ampul contains: tranexamic acid BP 100 mg/mL. Ampuls of 5 and 10 mL. Packages of 10.

Tablets: Each white, film-coated, capsule-shaped tablet, with CY engraved in arcs, contains: tranexamic acid 500 mg. Tartrazine-free. Bottles of 100.

(Shown in Product Recognition Section)

CYLERT® ℞

Abbott

Pemoline

CNS Stimulant

Pharmacology: Pemoline is a CNS stimulant, which, although structurally different from the amphetamines and methylphenidate, possesses pharmacological activity similar to that of other known stimulants.

Peak serum levels after single doses are reached within 2 to 4 hours and the serum half-life is approximately 12 hours. Multiple dose studies in adults at several dose levels indicate that steady state is reached in approximately 2 to 3 days.

Indications: Attention deficit hyperactivity disorder (ADHD). Because of its association with life-threatening hepatic failure, pemoline should not ordinarily be considered as first-line drug therapy for ADHD (see Warnings).

Pemoline is indicated as an integral part of a total treatment program which typically includes other remedial measures (psychological, educational, social) for a stabilizing effect in children with a behavioral syndrome characterized by the following group of developmentally inappropriate symptoms: moderate to severe distractibility, short attention span, hyperactivity, emotional lability, and impulsivity. The diagnosis of this syndrome should not be made with finality when these symptoms are only of comparatively recent origin. Nonlocalizing (soft) neurological signs, learning disability, and abnormal EEG may or may not be present, and a diagnosis of CNS dysfunction may or may not be warranted.

Attention deficit disorder and hyperkinetic syndrome are among the terms being used to describe the above signs and symptoms. In the past, a variety of terms have been associated with these signs and symptoms including: minimal brain dysfunction, hyperkinetic reaction of childhood, hyperkinetic syndrome, hyperactive child syndrome, minimal brain damage, minimal cerebral dysfunction, and minor cerebral dysfunction.

Contraindications: In patients with known hypersensitivity or idiosyncrasy to the drug (see Adverse Effects).

Pemoline should not be administered to patients with impaired hepatic function (see Warnings and Precautions).

Warnings: Because of its association with life-threatening hepatic failure, pemoline should not ordinarily be considered as first-line drug therapy for ADHD (see Indications).

Since pemoline's marketing in 1975, 13 cases of acute hepatic failure have been reported to the FDA. While the absolute number of reported cases is not large, the rate of reporting ranges from 4 to 17 times the rate expected in the general population. This estimate may be conservative because of under reporting and because the long latency between initiation of pemoline treatment and the occurrence of hepatic failure may limit recognition of the association. If only a portion of actual cases were recognized and reported, the risk could be substantially higher.

Of the 13 cases reported as of May 1996, 11 resulted in death or liver transplantation, usually within 4 weeks of the onset of signs and symptoms of liver failure. The earliest onset of hepatic abnormalities occurred 6 months after initiation of pemoline. Although some reports described dark urine and nonspecific prodromal symptoms (e.g., anorexia, malaise, and gastrointestinal symptoms), in other reports it was not clear if any prodromal symptoms preceded the onset of jaundice. It is also not clear if the recommended baseline and periodic liver function testing are predictive of these instances of acute liver failure. Pemoline should be discontinued if clinically significant hepatic dysfunction is observed during its use (see Precautions).

Pemoline is not recommended for children less than 6 years of age since its safety and efficacy in this age group have not been established.

Clinical experience suggests that in psychotic children, administration of pemoline may exacerbate symptoms of behavior disturbance and thought disorder.

Cylert (cont'd)

Data are inadequate to determine whether chronic administration of pemoline may be associated with growth inhibition; therefore, growth should be monitored during treatment.

Precautions: Drug treatment is not indicated in all cases of the behavioral syndrome characterized by moderate to severe distractibility, short attention span, hyperactivity, emotional lability and impulsivity. It should be considered only in light of the complete history and evaluation of the child. The decision to prescribe pemoline should depend on the physician's assessment of the chronicity and severity of the child's symptoms and their appropriateness for his/her age. Prescription should not depend solely on the presence of one or more of the behavioral characteristics.

When these symptoms are associated with acute stress reactions, treatment with pemoline is usually not indicated.

Since pemoline's market introduction, there have been reports of elevated liver enzymes associated with its use. Many of these patients had this increase detected several months after starting pemoline. Most patients were asymptomatic, with increase in liver enzymes returning to normal after pemoline was discontinued. Liver function tests should be performed prior to and periodically during therapy with pemoline. Treatment with pemoline should be initiated only in individuals without liver disease and with normal baseline liver function tests.

The relationship, if any, between reversible elevations in liver function tests and the occurrence of life-threatening hepatic failure in patients on long-term therapy with pemoline is not known. Liver function testing may not predict the onset of acute liver failure. Nonetheless, pemoline should be discontinued if clinically significant liver function test abnormalities are revealed at any time during therapy with this drug (see Warnings).

Pemoline should be administered with caution to patients with significantly impaired renal function.

Long-term effects of pemoline in children have not been well established.

The interaction of pemoline with other drugs has not been studied in humans. Patients who are receiving pemoline concurrently with other drugs, especially drugs with CNS activity, should be monitored carefully.

Decreased seizure threshold has been reported in patients receiving pemoline concomitantly with antiepileptic medications.

CNS stimulants, including pemoline, have been reported to precipitate motor and phonic tics and Tourette's syndrome. Therefore, clinical evaluation for tics and Tourette's syndrome in children and their families should precede use of stimulant medications.

Pemoline failed to demonstrate a potential for self-administration in primates. However, the pharmacologic similarity of pemoline to other psychostimulants with known dependence liability suggests that psychological and/or physical dependence might also occur with pemoline. There have been isolated reports of transient psychotic symptoms occurring in adults following the long-term misuse of excessive oral doses of pemoline. Pemoline should be given with caution to emotionally unstable patients who may increase the dosage on their own initiative.

Pregnancy and *Lactation:* Safety for use during pregnancy and lactation has not been established. Although CNS stimulants are seldom indicated after puberty, it should be borne in mind that pemoline should not be used during pregnancy or in women who may become pregnant.

Adverse Effects: There have been reports of hepatic dysfunction, ranging from asymptomatic reversible increases in liver enzymes to hepatitis, jaundice and life-threatening hepatic failure, in patients taking pemoline (see Precautions and Warnings).

There have been isolated reports of aplastic anemia.

Insomnia is the most frequently reported side effect; it usually occurs early in therapy, prior to an optimum therapeutic response. In the majority of cases it is transient in nature or responds to a reduction in dosage.

Anorexia with weight loss may occur during the first weeks of therapy. In the majority of cases it is transient in nature; weight gain usually resumes within 3 to 6 months.

Stomach ache, skin rashes, increased irritability, mild depression, nausea, dizziness, headache, drowsiness, and hallucinations have been reported.

A case of elevated acid phosphatase in association with prostatic enlargement has been reported in a 63-year-old male who was treated with pemoline for sleepiness. The acid phosphatase normalized with discontinuation of pemoline and was again elevated with rechallenge.

The following CNS effects have been reported with the use of pemoline: dyskinetic movements of the tongue, lips, face and extremities, nystagmus and nystagmoid eye movements, and convulsive seizures. Literature reports indicate that pemoline may precipitate attacks of Gilles de la Tourette syndrome.

Mild adverse reactions appearing early during the course of treatment with pemoline often remit with continuing therapy. If adverse reactions are of a significant or protracted nature, dosage should be reduced or the drug discontinued.

Overdose: Symptoms and Treatment: Signs and symptoms of acute pemoline overdosage, resulting principally from overstimulation of the CNS and from excessive sympathomimetic effects may include the following: vomiting, agitation, tremors, hyperreflexia, muscle twitching, restlessness, convulsions (may be followed by coma), euphoria, confusion, hallucinations, delirium, sweating, flushing, headache, hyperpyrexia, dyskinetic movements, tachycardia, hypertension and mydriasis. The treatment for an acute overdosage of pemoline is essentially the same as that for an overdosage of any CNS stimulant.

Management is primarily symptomatic and may include induction of emesis or gastric lavage, sedation, and other appropriate supportive measures. The patient must be protected against self-injury and against external stimuli that would aggravate the overstimulation already present. If signs and symptoms are not too severe and the patient is conscious, gastric contents may be evacuated followed by activated charcoal and a cathartic. Chlorpromazine has been reported in the literature to be useful in decreasing CNS stimulation and sympathomimetic effects.

Results of studies in dogs indicate that extracorporeal hemodialysis may be useful in the management of pemoline overdosage; forced diuresis and peritoneal dialysis appear to be of little value.

Dosage: Administer as a single oral dose each morning. The recommended starting dose is 37.5 mg/day. This daily dose should be gradually increased by 18.75 mg at 1-week intervals until the desired clinical response is obtained. The effective daily dose for most patients will range from 56.25 to 75 mg. The maximum recommended daily dose of pemoline is 112.5 mg.

Clinical improvement with pemoline is gradual. Using the recommended schedule of dosage titration, significant benefit may not be evident until the third or fourth week of drug administration.

Where possible, drug administration should be interrupted occasionally to determine if there is a recurrence of behavioral symptoms sufficient to require continued therapy. Hyperactivity diminishes with age to the point where it remains a serious problem in only a minority, although other major handicaps may be present. Usually, by puberty the need for medication has diminished or is no longer required.

Supplied: 37.5 mg: Each orange, monogrammed, grooved tablet contains: pemoline 37.5 mg. Nonmedicinal ingredients: gelatin, lactose monohydrate, magnesium hydroxide, polyethylene glycol 8 000, purified water, starch, talc and yellow FD&C No. 6 aluminum lake. Alcohol-, gluten-, paraben-, sucrose-, sulfite- and tartrazine-free. Bottles of 100.

75 mg: Each tan, monogrammed, grooved tablet contains: pemoline 75 mg. Nonmedicinal ingredients: gelatin, iron oxide brown, lactose monohydrate, magnesium hydroxide, polyethylene glycol 8 000, purified water, starch and talc. Alcohol-, gluten-, paraben-, sucrose-, sulfite- and tartrazine-free. Bottles of 100.

Store at controlled room temperature 15 to 30°C.

(Shown in Product Recognition Section)

Reviewed 1998

CYSTISTAT®
Bioniche

Sodium Hyaluronate
GAG Layer Replacement

Pharmacology: The glycosaminoglycan (GAG) layer on the luminal surface of the bladder wall is believed to provide a protective barrier against microorganisms, carcinogens, crystals and other agents present in the urine and has been identified as the primary defense mechanism in protecting the transitional epithelium from urinary irritants. Deficiencies in this GAG layer of the bladder epithelium may destroy its barrier function and allow the adherence of bacteria, microcrystals, proteins and ions, or the movement of ionic and nonionic solute residues (i.e., urea) across the epithelium. Hyaluronate has been developed to temporarily replenish the deficient GAG layer on the bladder epithelium. The active substance is a specific hyaluronic acid fraction of defined molecular chain length (combined average of 500 000 to 800 000 Daltons) with a high degree of purity.

Indications: Temporary replacement of the glycosaminoglycan (GAG) layer in the bladder.

Contraindications: At the present time there are no known contraindications to the use of sodium hyaluronate when used as recommended.

Precautions: Do not administer to patients with known hypersensitivity reactions.

Dosage: Instill the entire volume of one vial into the bladder after any residual urine has been removed. Discard any unused portion. For best results, Cystistat should be retained in the bladder for as long as possible (a minimum of 30 minutes). There is evidence that the GAG layer is deficient in conditions such as interstitial cystitis. In such situations, it is recommended that hyaluronate be instilled weekly for 4 treatments and then monthly until symptoms resolve.

Supplied: Each vial contains: sodium hyaluronate 40 mg. Single use vials of 50 mL. Discard vial after use. Store at room temperature (15 to 30°C). Do not freeze.

Reviewed 1997

CYSTO-CONRAY®
CYSTO-CONRAY® II
Mallinckrodt

Iothalamate Meglumine
Radiopaque Medium

Description: Retrograde instillation opacifies selected segments of the urinary tract, permitting fluoroscopic and radiographic visualization of structures such as the urethra, bladder, ureters and pelvico-calyceal system.

Indications: Use in retrograde cystography and cystourethrography. Cysto-Conray is also indicated for use in retrograde pyelography.

Contraindications: In patients with a known hypersensitivity to salts of iothalamic acid, the use of this preparation is contraindicated as intravasation may lead to hypersensitivity reactions and anaphylactic shock. However, a history of sensitivity to iodine per se or to other contrast media is not an absolute contraindication to the use of Cysto-Conray or Cysto-Conray II, but calls for extreme caution in administration.

Obstruction and acute or severe infection of the urinary tract are generally regarded as contraindications to instrumentation and to the retrograde instillation of contrast material; do not inject by intravascular, s.c. or i.m. routes.

Warnings: A history of allergy, bronchial asthma, sensitivity to other iodine-containing compounds or a previous reaction to a contrast agent warrant special attention and may predict the likelihood of an allergic reaction.

Anuria may develop following retrograde pyelography, especially in patients with impaired renal function. Retrograde pyelography should not be repeated within 48 hours in patients with impaired renal functions.

Severe irritation of the urinary tract and hemorrhagic cystitis may occur following prolonged exposure to contrast media. It is imperative that the urinary bladder be emptied at the completion of the diagnostic procedures.

Pregnancy: The safe use of these preparations during pregnancy has not been established. Exposures of the abdomen and pelvis to radiation during pregnancy, especially in the first trimester, should be avoided, unless in the judgment of the physician the expected benefits to the mother outweigh the risk to the developing fetus.

Precautions: Diagnostic procedures which involve the use of radiopaque contrast media should be carried out under the direction of appropriately trained personnel. Appropriate facilities should be available for coping with emergencies which may arise.

For sensitivity testing 0.1 mL of the contrast medium may be injected intradermally. The patient should be observed for local and general hypersensitivity reaction for 15 to 30 minutes.

Sensitivity testing cannot be relied upon to predict severe reactions.

An impending reaction is often indicated by apprehension, respiratory difficulty, faintness, sneezing, itching, vomiting or urticaria. In some instances, reactions to the test dose may be delayed.

Since iodine-containing contrast agents may alter the results of thyroid function tests, such tests, if indicated, should be performed prior to the administration of this preparation.

Adverse Effects: Irritation of the bladder or ureter, common to some degree to all contrast media administered for retrograde urographic procedures, may occasionally occur. Hemorrhagic cystitis may result. As with all contrast media, intravasation may lead to hypersensitivity reactions such as a sense of warmth, flushing, sneezing, sweating, chills, fever, urticaria, laryngeal edema, bronchospasm, hypertension, hypotension, cardiac arrhythmias, cardiac arrest and anaphylactic shock. Oliguria or anuria may occur following retrograde pyelography, especially in patients with severe preexisting renal disease. Adverse reactions associated with procedural technique include injury to the urethra, bladder, ureter and introduction of infection.

Treatment of Adverse Effects: Contrast media should be administered only by physicians thoroughly familiar with the emergency treatment of all adverse reactions to contrast media. The assistance of other trained personnel such as cardiologists, internists and anesthetists is required in the management of severe reactions.

Dosage: Cysto-Conray is more concentrated than other currently used retrograde urographic contrast media. The lowest possible concentration giving satisfactory contrast should be employed. The use of undiluted Cysto-Conray should be necessary only in selected adult patients.

Patient Preparation: Unless contraindicated, an appropriate laxative is given the night before the examination. The bladder should be emptied before the contrast agent is instilled.

Radiographic Technique: The radiographic procedure normally employed for cystography, cystourethrography and retrograde pyelography should be employed. A preliminary radiograph is recommended before the contrast agent is administered.

Administration: Sterile catheterization is essential. Cysto-Conray and Cysto-Conray II may be introduced by gravity flow using an appropriate venoclysis set or by syringe. Excessive pressure should be avoided with any method of administration.

Adults: Retrograde Pyelography: Ordinarily about 25 mL of Cysto-Conray are required for bilateral and 15 mL for unilateral pyelograms. About 5 to 6 mL are usually administered for each exposure.

Retrograde Cystography and Cystourethrography: The desired concentration will vary depending on the patient's size and age and also with the technique and equipment used. Sufficient volume of contrast medium is administered to adequately fill the urinary bladder. The volume of solution required will vary depending upon the individual patient. Adults usually require a volume in the range of 200 to 400 mL.

Children: Retrograde Cystography and Cystourethrography: Concentrations of iothalamate meglumine used in children should not exceed 21.5 %. Cysto-Conray II is preferred in this patient population.

Children require a volume in proportion to their body size. The usual dose ranges from 30 to 300 mL. Until further experience has been gained, the use of Cysto-Conray and Cysto-Conray II for retrograde pyelography in children is not recommended.

Supplied: Cysto-Conray: Each mL of sterile aqueous solution contains: iothalamate meglumine 430 mg (iodine 20.2%), edetate calcium disodium 0.110 mg as a stabilizer and sodium biphosphate 0.115 mg as a buffer. Vials of 50, boxes of 50. Bottles of 200 mL fill/250 mL, boxes of 12.

Cysto-Conray II: Each mL of sterile aqueous solution contains: iothalamate meglumine 172 mg (iodine 8.1%), edetate calcium disodium 0.110 mg as a stabilizer and sodium biphosphate 0.115 mg as a buffer. Bottles of 200 mL fill/250 mL, boxes of 12; bottles of 500 mL, boxes of 12.

Cysto-Conray and Cysto-Conray II are hypertonic under conditions of use and are supplied in containers from which the air has been displaced by nitrogen.

Store between 15 to 30°C. Protect from light. Protect from freezing. Discard unused portion.

For comparative information on Barbiturates, see the CPhA General Monograph in the WHITE SECTION.

CYTADREN® Ⓟ

Novartis Pharmaceuticals

Aminoglutethimide

Adrenal Suppressant—Reversible Inhibitor of Peripheral Estrogen Synthesis

Pharmacology: Cushing's Syndrome: Aminoglutethimide is a potent reversible inhibitor of adrenal mineralocorticoid and glucocorticoid synthesis. It partially inhibits the enzymatic conversion of cholesterol to pregnenolone, the reaction that initiates steroidogenesis in the adrenal cortex. As well, aminoglutethimide blocks the C-11, C-18 and C-21 hydroxylation of steroids. In Cushing's syndrome of all etiologies other than drug-induced, the inhibition of cortisol biosynthesis by aminoglutethimide markedly reduces excessive plasma cortisol.

Breast Carcinoma: In addition to the effect on the adrenal cortex, aminoglutethimide also inhibits the aromatization of androgens into estrogens in peripheral tissues. The aromatase mediated conversion of androgens into estrogens is the source of estrogen in the postmenopausal woman. The aromatase enzyme is present in liver, muscle, fat, and breast tissue including breast carcinoma. Aminoglutethimide does not inhibit the formation of testosterone or dehydrotestosterone. Thus, maintenance of androgen levels with relative suppression of estrogens may be of potential benefit.

In vitro studies have shown that the blockade of aromatization occurs at aminoglutethimide concentrations 10 times lower than those required to prevent steroidogenesis. It is believed that this extra-adrenal blockade of aromatization of androgens of adrenal origin into estrogens by aminoglutethimide is of overriding therapeutic importance in the treatment of breast carcinoma in the postmenopausal woman.

Inhibition of adrenal cortisol production by aminoglutethimide leads to a reflex rise in adrenocorticotrophic hormone (ACTH) secretion from the pituitary. The latter overcomes the cortisol-lowering effect of aminoglutethimide leading to the so-called "adrenal escape phenomenon". The compensatory increase in ACTH secretion can be suppressed by the simultaneous administration of a glucocorticoid.

Aminoglutethimide increases the rate of its metabolism and that of certain glucocorticoids including dexamethasone but not of hydrocortisone. Hence, the latter is indicated as the glucocorticoid replacement therapy of choice to maintain a long-lasting adrenal suppressant effect, e.g., to prevent the "adrenal escape phenomenon".

Aminoglutethimide causes a rapid decrease in aldosterone secretion from the adrenal cortex. In some patients, the signs and symptoms of hypoaldosteronemia occur, such as hyponatremia, dizziness, hypotension and weakness. These symptoms may be treated by administration of a mineralocorticoid such as fludrocortisone 0.1 mg orally daily or on alternate days.

Aminoglutethimide inhibits the synthesis of thyroxine by the thyroid gland. There is, however, a compensatory increase in thyroid stimulating hormone (TSH) secretion that is usually of sufficient magnitude to overcome this blockade. Thyroxine replacement therapy is therefore only occasionally required.

In spite of the TSH increase, aminoglutethimide administration, for reasons which are not entirely clear, has not been associated with an increase in prolactin secretion.

Aminoglutethimide only minimally inhibits estrogen production by the ovarian follicle in the premenopausal woman. Hence, it is not feasible to produce a chemical oophorectomy in these women with this drug.

Pharmacokinetics: Aminoglutethimide is completely absorbed from the gastrointestinal tract and its systemic availability is estimated to be 92 to 98%. Absorption is rapid, peak plasma concentrations being reached within 1 to 4 hours after oral administration. The peak concentrations of aminoglutethimide average 5.9 µg/mL (25.4 µmol/L) after ingestion of a 500 mg dose.

Mean steady state plasma concentrations in patients receiving 500 and 1 000 mg aminoglutethimide daily are variable and are approximately 4.5 µg/mL and 9.5 µg/mL respectively, after 3 months of therapy. For doses ranging from 125 to 1 000 mg/day, steady state concentrations are proportional to the dose. The major plasma metabolite, N-acetylaminoglutethimide, reaches steady state concentrations of about 25 to 35% of those of the unchanged drug. The concentration of aminoglutethimide in blood cells is 1.4 to 1.7 times that in plasma. The extent of binding to plasma proteins is 21 to 25%, with the major binding protein being albumin.

Total plasma clearance averages 3.5 L/h following single aminoglutethimide doses. It increases to 4.4 L/h during long-term treatment of patients, owing to hepatic enzyme induction. At the same time the volume of distribution decreases from 76 to 53 L. As a result of these changes, the elimination half-life falls from about 15 hours after a single dose to 9 hours at steady state.

Aminoglutethimide is cleared from the body partly by hepatic metabolism and partly by direct renal excretion. Metabolism primarily involves oxidation and acylation of the aromatic amino group of the drug. The metabolites formed have no inhibitory effect on aromatase and desmolase, or are several times less active than aminoglutethimide.

Excretion of the drug and its metabolites is predominantly renal: 90 to 97% of a dose is recovered in urine, only 3 to 7% in bile. Urinary output of unchanged aminoglutethimide accounts for about 47% of the dose at steady state. N-hydroxylaminoglutethimide is the major urinary metabolite in patients whose liver enzymes have been induced by the drug; it constitutes 20 to 25% of a dose on average.

N-acetylaminoglutethimide is a minor product in urine, accounting for less than 5% of the dose at steady state. The actual yield of this metabolite depends on the phenotype: it is about 4% in fast acetylators and 2% in slow acetylators. Thus, acetylation is an unimportant pathway of drug clearance in either case.

Upon withdrawal of aminoglutethimide, the ability of the adrenal glands to synthesize steroids returned to normal within 36 hours, suggesting that the so-called "chemical adrenalectomy" induced by aminoglutethimide is reversible.

Cushing's Syndrome: Data from various sources indicate that aminoglutethimide is most effective in treating Cushing's syndrome caused by adrenal carcinoma, adrenal adenoma, and ectopic ACTH producing tumors. Clinical and biochemical improvement is manifested in 27 to 55% of these treated patients. Adrenal hyperplasia frequently responds transiently to aminoglutethimide as autonomous, high levels of ACTH reduce the efficacy of the drug.

Treatment with aminoglutethimide has been shown to be useful in reducing the widespread deleterious effects of cortisone excess on body tissues, systems and fluids prior to definitive treatment. Further, aminoglutethimide has been documented to be an effective palliative agent where widespread disease makes definitive treatment impossible.

Metastatic Breast Carcinoma: In data compiled from numerous sources, objective responses (complete response+partial response) to aminoglutethimide were seen in 28 to 37% of patients, lasting for a mean duration of 1.8 years. The responses in general are significantly higher (total 50%) when patients with stabilized disease are included in the final analysis. The remission rate has been shown to be highest in those patients with soft tissue and bone metastases; metastases in liver and lung rarely responded to aminoglutethimide.

The objective response (complete+partial response) was higher in patients with estrogen receptor positive tumors than those with estrogen receptor negative tumors.

The rate and mean duration of objective responses (complete response+partial response) to aminoglutethimide treatment are similar to those seen following surgical ablative procedures.

Aminoglutethimide is as effective as tamoxifen citrate in producing remission of metastatic breast carcinoma. Bone metastases appear to be more responsive to aminoglutethimide than to tamoxifen citrate.

Up to 30% of patients initially refractory to tamoxifen citrate may show an objective response to aminoglutethimide.

After remission and relapse on tamoxifen citrate, up to 48% of these patients may experience an objective response to aminoglutethimide.

Indications: Cushing's Syndrome: For the palliative treatment of Cushing's syndrome of all etiologies other than drug induced. It is effective in reducing elevated plasma cortisol levels to one half or less of pretreatment levels in 30 to 60% of treated patients. A sustained response to aminoglutethimide is most frequently observed in patients with Cushing's syndrome due to adrenal adenoma or carcinoma. However, pituitary-dependent adrenal hyperplasia responds initially to aminoglutethimide in up to 60% of cases. Aminoglutethimide has no effect on the disease processes that underlie Cushing's syndrome. It is useful in the control of hypercortisolism as an interim measure until definitive therapy is instituted or where such therapy is not appropriate. Therapy with aminoglutethimide for longer than 3 months has been studied only in a limited number of patients.

Metastatic Breast Carcinoma: In combination with glucocorticoid replacement for the palliative treatment of metastatic

Cytadren (cont'd)

breast carcinoma in the naturally or artificially induced postmenopausal woman. Patients with estrogen receptor positive tumors are most likely to benefit from aminoglutethimide therapy. The remission rates appear to be the highest in soft tissue and bone metastases; metastases in liver and lung rarely respond to aminoglutethimide.

Up to 30% of patients initially refractory to tamoxifen citrate may show an objective response to aminoglutethimide.

After remission and relapse on tamoxifen citrate, up to 48% of these patients may experience an objective response to aminoglutethimide (see Pharmacology).

Aminoglutethimide treatment should be continued only in those patients who have demonstrated a response to it within the first 3 months.

Contraindications: Severe manifestations of hypersensitivity to glutethimide or aminoglutethimide or its excipients, in premenopausal women with metastatic breast carcinoma and in inducible porphyria.

Warnings: Adrenocortical Insufficiency: Aminoglutethimide may cause adrenocortical insufficiency which will usually present after 24 to 48 hours of treatment. Aminoglutethimide should therefore always be combined with a glucocorticoid, such as hydrocortisone or cortisone acetate. Under conditions of stress such as surgery, trauma, or acute illness, patients should be carefully monitored and the dose of hydrocortisone or cortisone acetate increased. Mineralocorticoid supplements may be indicated. Dexamethasone, prednisone or prednisolone are not recommended because their rates of metabolism are enhanced by aminoglutethimide (see Precautions, Drug Interactions).

Suppression of Aldosterone Production: Aminoglutethimide may suppress aldosterone production by the adrenal cortex and thereby cause orthostatic or persistent hypotension. Blood pressure should be followed in all patients at appropriate intervals. Patients should be advised of the possible occurrence of weakness and dizziness as symptoms of hypotension, and of measures that could be taken should they occur.

CNS Depression: Aminoglutethimide may depress the CNS resulting in lethargy or somnolence. Ataxia has been noted in some cases. These are commonly observed at the beginning of treatment and generally abate after about 6 weeks.

Pregnancy: Aminoglutethimide can cause fetal abnormalities when administered during pregnancy. In the earlier experience with the drug, 2 cases of pseudohermaphroditism in 5 000 pregnancies were reported in female infants whose mothers took aminoglutethimide concomitantly with anticonvulsants. When administered to rats at doses of 0.5 and 1.25 times the maximum human dose, aminoglutethimide caused a decrease in fetal implantation, an increase in fetal deaths and a variety of teratogenic effects. The drug also caused pseudohermaphroditism in rats treated with approximately 3 times the highest recommended human dose. If this drug must be used during pregnancy, or if the patient becomes pregnant while taking the drug, the patient should be advised of the potential hazard to the fetus and the treatment continued only if the benefits outweigh the risks.

The possibility of pregnancy should be excluded before prescribing aminoglutethimide to women of childbearing potential. During treatment such women should employ nonhormonal forms of contraception.

Carcinogenicity Studies: A 2-year carcinogenicity study conducted in rats revealed an increased incidence of benign and malignant neoplasms of the adrenal cortex and thyroid follicular cells with aminoglutethimide at a dose approximately equivalent to the maximum human daily dose, plus a small number of ovarian tubular adenomas at higher doses. These tissues are known sites for the pharmacological action of aminoglutethimide (see Pharmacology).

Precautions: Initiation of Therapy: Aminoglutethimide should be administered only by physicians who are familiar with its use; therapy should be initiated in a hospital setting until a stable dosage regimen is achieved (see Dosage).

Pulmonary Hypersensitivity: Pulmonary hypersensitivity and allergic alveolitis may occur (see Adverse Effects). If these conditions are suspected, aminoglutethimide should be withdrawn immediately.

Hypothyroidism: Hypothyroidism may occur in association with aminoglutethimide; hence, appropriate clinical observations should be undertaken and laboratory evaluations of thyroid function performed when indicated. Supplementary thyroid hormone may be required.

Hematologic Abnormalities: Hematologic abnormalities in patients receiving aminoglutethimide have been reported especially within the first 7 weeks of therapy (see Adverse Effects). Therefore, white blood cell and platelet counts should be performed at weeks 4, 8 and 12 after starting aminoglutethimide. Thereafter, blood counts are indicated in the presence of clinical symptoms. If blood dyscrasias develop, aminoglutethimide should be withdrawn.

Laboratory Abnormalities: Since elevations in AST, GGT, alkaline phosphatase, and bilirubin have been reported, appropriate clinical observations and regular laboratory tests should be performed before and during therapy.

Electrolyte Status: Serum electrolytes should be determined periodically and mineralocorticoids should be administered depending upon the clinical and/or the electrolyte status.

Information for the Patient: Occupational Hazards: Patients should be warned that drowsiness may occur, and when present, they should not drive, operate potentially dangerous machinery, or engage in other activities which require mental alertness. Patients should be warned not to consume alcohol since the effects of aminoglutethimide may be potentiated with this combination.

Patients should also be warned of the possibility of hypotension and its symptoms (see Warnings).

Aminoglutethimide may cause a maculopapular, generalized or urticarial skin rash, often associated with fever which commonly begins on day 10 and subsides by day 15 or 16 of treatment. Forewarning patients of this problem alleviates anxiety should the rash appear (see Dosage).

Drug Interactions: Aminoglutethimide induces hepatic enzymes, increasing its own metabolism and also that of several drugs including synthetic glucocorticoids such as dexamethasone, prednisone and prednisolone; warfarin and other oral anticoagulants; digitoxin; theophylline; medroxyprogesterone and oral antidiabetics. Appropriate laboratory tests must therefore be performed and the dosage adjusted, as necessary.

Concomitant therapy with diuretics may lead to hyponatremia.

The effects of aminoglutethimide may be potentiated if taken in combination with alcohol.

Children: The safety and effectiveness have not been established by adequate and well-controlled studies in children.

Adverse Effects: Adverse reactions reported in patients treated for Cushing's syndrome and metastatic breast cancer include observations in patients who received aminoglutethimide for periods ranging from a few days to several years. Patients concurrently received glucocorticoid and occasionally mineralocorticoid replacement therapy. Approximately 60% of patients reported one or more unwanted effects, most of which disappeared spontaneously with continued administration of aminoglutethimide.

Although some of these symptoms may not be necessarily ascribed to aminoglutethimide therapy, they are listed as alerting information.

CNS: Frequent: drowsiness, lethargy; Occasional: dizziness (vertigo); Rare: ataxia, headache, depression; Isolated cases: insomnia, confusion, anxiety, hallucinations, poor memory, seizures.

Skin and Appendages: Frequent: morbilliform, maculopapular skin rash (sometimes accompanied by fever); Rare: pruritus, urticaria; Isolated cases: exfoliative dermatitis, Stevens-Johnson syndrome, Lyell's syndrome.

Gastrointestinal: Occasional: nausea; Rare: diarrhea, vomiting, constipation, anorexia; Isolated cases: indigestion.

Systemic: Rare: fever, sweating; Isolated cases: chills.

Hepatic: Isolated cases: hepatitis (cholestatic type, associated with itching and skin rash), jaundice.

Endocrine: Rare: adrenal insufficiency (hyponatremia, hypotension, dizziness, hypoglycemia); Isolated cases: hypothyroidism, inappropriate ADH secretion, masculinization and hirsutism in females, precocious sexual development in males in cases where aminoglutethimide has been given without a glucocorticoid.

Genitourinary: Isolated cases: renal function abnormalities, urinary retention.

Cardiovascular: Rare: hypotension; Isolated cases: tachycardia.

Hematology: Rare: agranulocytosis, leukopenia, thrombocytopenia; Isolated cases: pancytopenia, anemia, neutropenia, reduction in hemoglobin and transient decrease in white blood cell counts with chronic administration.

Allergy: Isolated cases: allergic/anaphylactic reaction, allergic alveolitis with interstitial alveolar infiltrates (see Precautions).

Laboratory Abnormalities: Rare: increased GGT (due to the enzyme-inducing effect of aminoglutethimide and usually not a sign of liver damage), hyponatremia, hyperkalemia, hypoglycemia; Isolated cases: hypercholesterolemia, increased bilirubin, elevation of alkaline phosphatase and AST.

Other: Isolated cases: nystagmus, unstable gait, arthralgia.

Adverse Reactions due to Glucocorticoid/Mineralocorticoid Replacement Therapy: Isolated cases: Cushingoid symptoms (moon face, weight gain, edema), hyperadrenalism, hypercalcemia, muscle cramps, hypertension and congestive heart failure due to its marked effect on sodium retention.

Overdose: Symptoms: The most common signs to be expected with overdosage are lethargy, dizziness, respiratory depression, ataxia, sedation, and deep coma with hypoventilation and hypotension.

Extreme weakness has been reported when patients received 3 g/day in divided doses.

Deaths have not been reported following administration of doses up to 7 g.

The signs and symptoms of acute overdosage may be aggravated or modified if alcohol, hypnotics, tranquilizers or tricyclic antidepressants have been taken at the same time.

Treatment: Gastric lavage and supportive treatment have been employed. Full consciousness following deep coma was regained 40 hours or less after ingestion of 3 or 4 g of aminoglutethimide without lavage. No evidence of hematologic, renal, or hepatic effects were subsequently found.

Close monitoring should be provided, and appropriate measures taken to support vital functions, if necessary: a parenteral glucocorticoid, preferably hydrocortisone or cortisone acetate, and/or a mineralocorticoid, such as fludrocortisone, may be indicated in the event of extreme prostration as this may be the result of adrenocortical insufficiency; measures to increase plasma volume; i.v. vasoactive drugs (e.g., norepinephrine); artificial respiration; oxygen administration.

Dialysis may be considered in severe intoxication.

Dosage: Cushing's Syndrome: Adults: Treatment should be instituted in a hospital setting until a stable dosage regimen is achieved. Therapy should be initiated with a daily dose of 1 000 mg in 4 equally divided doses, preferably at 6-hour intervals.

The response of cortisol secreting tissue to aminoglutethimide should be followed by carefully monitoring plasma cortisol levels until the desired level of suppression is achieved. (When glucocorticoid replacement therapy is instituted, monitoring of DHEA-S (dehydroepiandrosterone sulfate) levels will provide a measure of suppression of cortisol secretion.)

If adrenal suppression is inadequate, the daily dose may be increased in increments of 250 mg each week to a **maximum daily dose of 2 000 mg (2 g) in equally divided doses.**

Dose reduction or temporary discontinuation may be required in the event of adverse reactions, including extreme drowsiness or severe skin rash. Incremental increases to maintenance level can then be achieved as the patient's condition allows. If a skin rash persists for longer than 5 to 8 days, or becomes severe, the drug should be discontinued. It may be possible to reinstate therapy at a lower dosage following the disappearance of a mild to moderate rash.

Hydrocortisone: 40 mg/day or cortisone acetate 50 mg/day in equally divided doses orally is suggested as replacement therapy for frank adrenal insufficiency or when cortisol levels drop to a level where increased pituitary ACTH secretion is likely.

Fludrocortisone: If patients show the signs and symptoms of hypoaldosteronemia (e.g., hypotension, dizziness, and/or hyponatremia), fludrocortisone at a daily dose of 0.1 mg orally should be administered daily or on alternate days depending on the severity of symptoms. As fludrocortisone may have a marked effect on sodium retention, physicians should monitor patients closely for signs and symptoms of fluid retention, hypertension, congestive heart failure and related conditions.

Metastatic Breast Cancer: In order to achieve optimal therapeutic effects and to encounter the fewest side effects, aminoglutethimide should be administered orally in escalating doses together with hydrocortisone or cortisone acetate.

Aminoglutethimide: Aminoglutethimide should be administered orally in gradually increasing doses as follows: 125 mg b.i.d. during the first week; 250 mg b.i.d. during the second week; and if needed 250 mg t.i.d. the third week and 250 mg q.i.d. the fourth week. Gradually increasing the dose allows time for aminoglutethimide to induce its own metabolism and for patients to accommodate to the soporific side effects. In exceptional cases the daily dose may be increased to a maximum of 2 000 mg in equally divided doses.

Hydrocortisone: 100 mg/day orally (20 mg a.m.; 20 mg p.m. and 60 mg hs) during the first 2 weeks; thereafter 40 mg daily (20 mg a.m. and 20 mg p.m.).

Cortisone Acetate: 125 mg/day orally (25 mg a.m.; 25 mg p.m. and 75 mg hs) during the first 2 weeks; thereafter 37.5 to 50 mg daily (25 mg a.m. and 12.5 or 25 mg p.m.). The initial high dose of hydrocortisone or cortisone acetate reduces the severity of the skin rash that is highly steroid sensitive and which usually occurs 10 to 15 days after initiation of therapy. If the supplementary glucocorticoid medication gives rise to Cushing-like symptoms, the dosage of the glucocorticoid should be reduced.

Fludrocortisone: If patients show the signs and symptoms of hypoaldosteronemia (e.g., hypotension, dizziness, and/or hyponatremia), fludrocortisone at a daily dose of 0.1 mg orally should be administered daily or on alternate days depending on the severity of symptoms. As fludrocortisone may have a marked effect on sodium retention, physicians should monitor patients closely for signs and symptoms of fluid retention, hypertension, congestive heart failure and related conditions.

Infrequently, patients receiving aminoglutethimide continue to complain of persistent lethargy, somnolence or mild lack of alertness during chronic therapy. If facilities are available to measure plasma levels of aminoglutethimide, allow reduction in dosage to maintain drug concentrations in the therapeutic range of 10 to 15 μg/mL. If unavailable, reduction in dosage to 750 mg daily with 500 mg just before sleep and 250 mg in the morning will often alleviate this problem. It should be remembered that aminoglutethimide is excreted largely unchanged in the urine and patients with compromised renal function may have high blood levels. Five percent of patients cannot tolerate aminoglutethimide in any dosage.

Aminoglutethimide may cause a maculopapular, generalized or urticarial skin rash often associated with fever which commonly begins on day 10 and subsides by day 15 or 16 of treatment. Forewarning patients of this problem alleviates anxiety should the rash appear. The rash is responsive to a daily dose of hydrocortisone or cortisone acetate and improves with concurrent administration of an antihistamine, e.g., diphenhydramine, 25 mg b.i.d. to q.i.d. daily. If the rash persists beyond day 16, the drug should be discontinued until the rash subsides, then restarted at 125 to 250 mg daily with gradual increments to full dosage.

Supplied: Each off-white, round, biconvex tablet, engraved CIBA on one side and GG on the other, fully bisected between G and G, contains: aminoglutethimide 250 mg. Nonmedicinal ingredients: cornstarch, silicon dioxide, stearic acid and talc. Energy: 0.96 kJ (0.23 kcal). Bottles of 100. Protect the tablets from heat (i.e., store between 15 to 30°C), light and humidity. Keep out of reach of children.

(Shown in Product Recognition Section)

Reviewed 1997

CYTARABINE FOR INJECTION USP Ⓟ

Novopharm

Antileukemic

Supplied: Each vial of sterile, lyophilized powder contains: cytarabine 100 mg, 500 mg, 1 000 mg or 2 000 mg and may contain hydrochloric acid and/or sodium hydroxide for pH adjustment. Each vial of sterile, lyophilized powder contains: cytarabine 100 mg (multiple dose 5 mL vials), 500 mg (multiple dose 10 mL vials), 1 000 mg (single dose 20 mL vials) and 2 000 mg (single dose 50 mL vials). Store between 15 and 30°C. Protect from light. **As with all i.v. admixtures, dilution should be made just prior to administration and the resulting, unpreserved solution used within 24 hours.**

CYTARABINE INJECTION Ⓟ

Faulding

Antileukemic

Pharmacology: Cytarabine is converted intracellularly to the nucleotide, cytarabine triphosphate. Although the exact mechanism(s) of action of cytarabine has not been fully elucidated, cytarabine triphosphate appears to inhibit DNA polymerase by competing with the physiologic substrate, deoxycytidine triphosphate, resulting in the inhibition of DNA synthesis. Although limited, incorporation of cytarabine triphosphate into DNA and RNA may also contribute to the cytotoxic effects of the drug.

Cytarabine is a potent immunosuppressant which can suppress humoral and/or cellular immune responses; however, the drug does not decrease pre-existing antibody titres and has no effect on established delayed hypersensitivity reactions.

Cytarabine is ineffective orally; less than 20% of a dose is absorbed from the gastrointestinal tract. Constant i.v. infusions of cytarabine produce relatively constant plasma concentrations of the drug in 8 to 24 hours. Following s.c. administration of cytarabine, peak plasma levels of the drug are attained about 20 to 60 minutes after injection and fall below steady-state infusion levels after about 100 minutes.

Cytarabine is rapidly and widely distributed into tissues. After rapid i.v. injection of cytarabine, approximately 13% of the drug is bound to plasma proteins. Cytarabine crosses the blood-brain barrier to a limited extent. During a continuous i.v. or s.c. infusion, cytarabine concentrations in the cerebrospinal fluid (CSF) are higher than those attained after rapid i.v. injection and are about 40 to 60% of plasma concentrations. Most of an intrathecal dose of cytarabine diffuses into the systemic circulation but is rapidly metabolized and usually only low plasma concentrations of unchanged drug occur. The drug apparently crosses the placenta. It is not known if cytarabine or its metabolites are excreted in breast milk.

Cytarabine disappears rapidly from the plasma following i.v. injection. I.V doses of cytarabine exhibit biphasic elimination with an initial half-life of approximately 10 minutes in which a major fraction of a dose is hepatically metabolized by cytidine deaminase to inactive 1-beta-D-arabinofuranosyluracil (uracil arabinoside). The terminal elimination half-life is about 1 to 3 hours. Reportedly cytarabine undergoes triphasic elimination in some patients. After intrathecal injection, cytarabine concentrations in the CSF decline with a half-life of about 2 hours.

Cytarabine and its metabolite, uracil arabinoside, are excreted in urine. After rapid i.v., s.c. or intrathecal injection or continuous i.v. infusion, about 70 to 80% of the dose is excreted in urine within 24 hours. Approximately 90% of the urinary drug excretion occurs as the metabolite and about 10% as unchanged cytarabine.

Indications: Primarily for induction and maintenance of remission in acute leukemia in both adults and children. It has found use in the treatment of acute myelocytic leukemia (AML), chronic myelocytic leukemia (blast phase), acute lymphocytic leukemia (ALL) and erythroleukemia. It may be used alone or in combination with other antineoplastic agents, superior results being obtained with combination therapy. Cytarabine is often used with daunorubicin, doxorubicin, thioguanine or vincristine.

Good results have been obtained from a combination drug program (LSA_2-L_2), which included cytarabine, in children with nonHodgkin's lymphoma.

Response has been obtained with intrathecal administration of cytarabine in the treatment of meningeal leukemia and other meningeal neoplasms (e.g., lymphoma), as well in children with lymphocytic leukemia with CNS involvement. Intrathecal cytarabine may be useful in patients whose CNS disease does not respond to intrathecal methotrexate or in patients with methotrexate-related neurotoxicity. Focal leukemic involvement of the CNS may not respond to intrathecal cytarabine or intrathecal methotrexate, and may be better treated with radiation therapy.

Cytarabine in high doses (2 to 3 g/m²), given as an i.v. infusion over 1 to 3 hours every 12 hours for 2 to 6 days, with or without additional cancer chemotherapeutic agents, has been shown to be effective in the therapy of poor-risk leukemia, refractory leukemia and relapsed acute leukemia.

Unless followed by maintenance therapy, remissions induced by cytarabine have been brief.

Contraindications: Patients with known hypersensitivity to the drug.

Warnings: Caution: Cytarabine is a potent drug and should only be used by physicians experienced with cancer chemotherapy (see Precautions). Hematologic, hepatic and renal evaluations must be performed at regular intervals.

Cytarabine is a highly toxic drug with a low therapeutic index, and a therapeutic response is not likely to occur without some evidence of toxicity. The drug must be used only under the supervision of physicians experienced with cytotoxic agents.

Cytarabine is a potent myelosuppressive agent capable of producing severe leukopenia, thrombocytopenia and anemia with striking megaloblastic changes. Therapy should be begun with caution in patients with pre-existing drug-induced bone marrow suppression. Treatment of severe hematologic toxicity may consist of supportive therapy, antibiotics for complicating infections resulting from granulocytopenia and other impaired body defences, and blood product transfusions in case of hemorrhage secondary to thrombocytopenia, the consequences of bone marrow suppression.

Some high dosage (2 to 3 g/m²) protocols have incurred severe, sometimes fatal CNS, gastrointestinal and pulmonary toxicities. These have included paraplegia, disseminated necrotizing leukoencephalopathy, blindness, reversible corneal toxicity and hemorrhagic conjunctivitis which may be prevented or diminished by prophylaxis with a local corticosteroid eye drop; cerebral and cerebellar dysfunction including personality changes, somnolence and coma, usually reversible, mucosal alterations and lesions in the gastrointestinal tract with frequent infections complicated by peritonitis, liver abscesses, pneumatosis cystoides intestinalis and sepsis; liver damage with increased hyperbilirubinemia; bowel necrosis; necrotizing colitis and pulmonary edema. Rarely, severe skin rash, leading to desquamation has been reported. Complete alopecia is more commonly seen with high dose therapy than with standard treatment programs (see Adverse Effects).

Pregnancy: Cytarabine is known to be teratogenic in some animal species. The drug should not be used in women who are pregnant (particularly during the first trimester) or who may become pregnant unless the possible benefits outweigh the potential risks.

One infant with upper and lower limb defects and one infant with obvious extremity and ear deformities were delivered by women who had received therapy with cytarabine during the first trimester.

When cytarabine therapy is initiated during the second or third trimester, there is still a considerable risk to the fetus, but it is reduced. A few women have received cytarabine with other antineoplastic drugs during the second and third trimesters (20th to 28th week of gestation) and have delivered apparently normal infants. However, in another report where cytarabine was given together with thioguanine to 4 mothers, beginning at 11, 20, 25 and 26 weeks' gestation, trisomy C was found in a 24-week fetus following a therapeutic abortion, while no abnormalities were detected in the other 3 cases.

Although normal infants have been delivered to patients treated in all 3 trimesters of pregnancy, follow-up of such infants would be advisable.

Precautions: Patients receiving cytarabine must be closely monitored. Leukocyte and platelet counts should be performed frequently during therapy (see Dosage). Periodic determinations of renal and hepatic functions are recommended in patients on cytarabine therapy. Patients who receive myelosuppressive drugs experience an increased frequency of infections as well as possible hemorrhagic complications. Because these complications are potentially fatal, the patient should be told to notify the physician if fever, sore throat, or unusual bleeding or bruising occurs.

Since cytarabine appears to be metabolized to some extent in the liver, the drug should be used cautiously and at a reduced dosage in patients with poor or impaired liver function.

Cytarabine, like other cytotoxic drugs, may induce hyperuricemia secondary to rapid lysis of neoplastic cells. The patient's plasma uric acid level should be monitored and appropriate supportive and pharmacologic measurements should be available. Hyperuricemia may be minimized or prevented by adequate hydration, alkalinization of the urine, and/or administration of allopurinol.

Nausea and vomiting may occur in patients receiving cytarabine and normally occur more frequently and more severely following rapid i.v. injection of large doses than following i.v. infusion of the drug.

Intrathecal administration of cytarabine rarely causes systemic effects; however the hematologic status of the patient must still be monitored. Dosage adjustments of concurrently administered antineoplastic agents may be necessary. The most frequent adverse effects of intrathecal cytarabine are nausea, vomiting, fever, and transient headaches; these effects generally are mild and self-limiting.

Neurotoxicity following intrathecal injection of cytarabine has been associated with diluents containing preservatives. If high dose therapy is given, do **not** use a diluent containing preservative.

Thrombophlebitis has occurred at the site of i.v. drug injection or infusion in some patients. Pain and inflammation at s.c. injection sites are rare. S.C. injection sites should be rotated around the areas of body fat: the abdomen, thighs and flank region. The drug is locally well tolerated in most instances.

Higher total doses are tolerated better when administered by rapid i.v. injection as compared to slow infusion. This may be due to the rapid inactivation of the drug and the brief exposure of susceptible normal and neoplastic cells to significant drug levels after rapid injection.

Clinical experience to date indicates that success with cytarabine therapy depends more on adeptness in modifying day-to-day dosage to obtain maximum leukemic cell kill with tolerable toxicity, than on the fundamental treatment protocol selected

Cytarabine Injection (cont'd)

at the start of therapy. Toxicity necessitating dosage modification almost always occurs.

Remission induction therapy in acute leukemia is usually administered in a short course without adjustment or discontinuation based upon peripheral blood counts. However, depending on the physician's judgment, modifications may be made based on hematologic response. Consider discontinuing the drug if the patient has less than 50 000 platelets or 1 000 polymorphonuclear granulocytes/mm³ in the peripheral blood. These guidelines may be modified depending on signs of toxicity in other systems and on the rapidity of fall in formed blood elements. Restart the drug when there are signs of marrow recovery and the above platelet and granulocyte levels have been attained. **Warning:** Withholding therapy until the patient's blood values are normal may result in escape of the patient's disease from control by cytarabine.

Drug Interactions: The gastrointestinal absorption of oral digoxin tablets has been found to be substantially reduced in patients receiving combination chemotherapy regimens containing cytarabine, possibly as a result of temporary damage to intestinal mucosa caused by cytotoxic agents.

An in vitro study indicated that cytarabine may antagonize the activity of gentamicin against K. pneumoniae. Patients receiving cytarabine and aminoglycoside therapy for the treatment of infections caused by K. pneumoniae should be closely monitored. If therapeutic response is not achieved, re-evaluation of the antibiotic therapy may be necessary.

Limited data suggest that cytarabine may antagonize the antifungal activity of flucytosine, possibly by competitive inhibition of the anti-infective uptake by fungi.

Adverse Effects: The major adverse effect of cytarabine is hematologic toxicity. Myelosuppression is normally manifested by megaloblastosis, leukopenia, anemia, reticulocytopenia and thrombocytopenia. Leukopenia follows mainly from granulocyte depression; lymphocytes are minimally affected. The severity of these adverse effects is dependent on the dose of the drug and schedule of administration. The incidence and severity of hematologic toxicity is minimal after a single i.v. dose of cytarabine, but myelosuppression occurs in almost all patients with daily i.v. injections or continuous i.v. infusions of the drug.

Following 5-day constant i.v. infusions or rapid i.v. injections of cytarabine 50 to 600 mg/m², the white blood cell count follows a biphasic course, regardless of initial white blood cell count, dosage level or schedule. Two distinct nadirs are observed. Initial leukocyte fall occurs within 24 hours of administration, reaching the first nadir at 7 to 9 days. A brief recovery period peaking at about 12 days is again followed by a sharp leukocyte fall to the second nadir (which is greater than the first) occurring between days 15 to 24. Then there is a rapid rise to above baseline levels in the following 10 days. The platelet count starts to fall 5 days after starting cytarabine therapy, reaching the nadir at 12 to 15 days, after which, a rapid rise to above baseline levels occurs in the following 10 days.

Nausea and vomiting may occur in patients on cytarabine therapy, and usually occur more frequently and severely following rapid i.v. administration as opposed to continuous infusion of the drug. Other adverse effects of the gastrointestinal tract include anorexia, diarrhea, oral and anal inflammation or ulceration. Abdominal pain, esophagitis, sore throat, esophageal ulceration and gastrointestinal hemorrhage occur less frequently. In one study, cytarabine induced severe intestinal toxicity when used in several sequential chemotherapeutic protocols. The mucosal alterations induced were characterized by surface and glandular epithelial atypia, immaturity and necrosis. These were associated with diarrhea, ileus, abdominal pain, hematemesis and melena, severe hypokalemia, hypocalcemia, a protein-losing enteropathy, transient weight gains and intestinal infections.

Hepatic dysfunction, characterized by jaundice, elevations in serum bilirubin, transaminases and alkaline phosphates have occurred in patients receiving cytarabine alone or with other antineoplastic agents, but a causal relationship has not been definitely established.

Meningism, paresthesia, paraplegia, spastic paraparesis, and seizures have been reported rarely with the intrathecal administration of cytarabine. Blindness occurred in 2 patients with **all** during remission, who had received systemic combination therapy, prophylactic CNS radiation as well as intrathecal cytarabine. Necrotizing leukoencephalopathy occurred in 5 children who had received triple intrathecal therapy consisting of cytarabine, methotrexate and hydrocortisone, and CNS irradiation.

Other reported adverse effects of cytarabine include fever, rash, conjunctivitis (may occur with rash), alopecia, freckling, skin ulceration, urinary retention, renal dysfunction, chest pain, dizziness, somnolence, neuritis or neural toxicity and reactions at the site of injection such as pain, inflammation, thrombophlebitis or cellulitis.

One patient suffered anaphylaxis with acute cardiopulmonary arrest which required resuscitation, immediately following i.v. administration of the drug.

A cytarabine syndrome, characterized by fever, myalgia, bone pain, malaise, maculopapular rash, conjunctivitis and occasionally chest pain, has been reported. It normally occurs 6 to 12 hours after administration of the drug; corticosteroids have been shown to be of benefit in the treatment and prevention of the syndrome. If treatment of the symptoms of the syndrome is required, administration of corticosteroids should be considered as well as continuation of cytarabine therapy.

Severe and sometimes fatal CNS, gastrointestinal and pulmonary toxicity, which differs from that seen with usual dosages, has been associated with high-dose cytarabine regimens (2 to 3 g/m² given every 12 hours for 12 doses) for refractory or secondary acute leukemia.

Adverse effects of high-dose therapy have included somnolence; cerebral and cerebellar dysfunction which is generally reversible; conjunctivitis and reversible corneal toxicity (keratitis) consisting of ocular pain, tearing, foreign-body sensation, photophobia and blurred vision; pulmonary edema and severe gastrointestinal ulceration including pneumatosis cystoides intestinalis leading to peritonitis; sepsis and liver abscess, liver damage with increased hyperbilirubinemia; pericarditis with tamponade. Rarely severe rash leading to desquamation has occurred. Complete alopecia occurs more frequently with high-dose regimens than with usual dosage regimens of the drug.

A syndrome of sudden respiratory distress, rapidly progressing to pulmonary edema and radiographically pronounced cardiomyopathy with subsequent death, has been reported in patients receiving high-dose cytarabine in combination with cyclophosphamide in preparation for bone marrow transplantation.

Peripheral motor and sensory neuropathies also have occurred occasionally in patients receiving high-dose cytarabine therapy. Diffuse interstitial pneumonitis, possibly related to cytarabine therapy, has been reported occasionally in patients receiving relatively high doses (e.g., 1 g/m²) of cytarabine alone or in combination with other antineoplastic agents.

Pancreatitis has also occurred.

Overdose: Symptoms: Serious myelosuppression may follow chronic overdosage with cytarabine. Nausea and vomiting, severe hemorrhage into the gastrointestinal tract and generalized infection may act as additional warnings of overdosage.

Treatment: Cytarabine should be discontinued and supportive therapy instituted. Platelet transfusions should be given for hemorrhage. Patients should be closely monitored for intercurrent infection. Any infection requires rapid and rigorous treatment with appropriate antibiotic therapy.

Doses exceeding recommended dosage schedules have been used clinically and have been tolerated. The major toxicities with the use of 3 g/m² i.v. infusion over 1 hour every 12 hours for 12 doses and 3 g/m² continuous infusion for 4 days, other than reversible bone marrow suppression has been reversible corneal, cerebral and cerebellar dysfunction. Doses of 4.5 g/m² i.v. infused over 1 hour every 12 hours for 12 doses has caused an unacceptable increase in irreversible toxicity and death.

Dosage: See Special Instructions for Handling Cytotoxic Drugs.

Cytarabine is administered primarily by the i.v. route, by push or by i.v. infusion. Relatively constant plasma levels can be achieved by continuous i.v. infusion. Cytarabine may also be administered s.c. It may be administered intrathecally when unpreserved (see Preparation for Use).

Dosage of cytarabine must be based on the clinical and hematological response and tolerance of the patient so as to obtain optimum therapeutic results with minimum adverse effects. The most effective dosage schedule and method of administration are yet to be established, but it appears that success with cytarabine is dependent more on adeptness in modifying day-to-day dosage to obtain maximum leukemic cell kill with tolerable toxicity than on the basic treatment schedule chosen at the outset of therapy.

Cytarabine used in combination with other cytotoxic drugs, may require dose reduction. Clinicians should consult published protocols for the dosage of cytarabine and other chemotherapeutic agents, and the method as well as the sequence of administration.

Warning on Use of Diluents Containing Preservatives: Preserved diluents are not generally recommended for dilution of cytarabine of Faulding (Canada) Inc. In any case, preserved diluents must not be used for intrathecal administration, and solutions containing benzyl alcohol should not be used for neonates. Because of the potential toxicity of large amounts of benzyl alcohol, diluents containing benzyl alcohol must not be used to dilute cytarabine if high dose regimens are employed.

Suggested I.V. Dosage Regimens: Induction: The usual dosage of cytarabine as a single agent for induction of remissions in patients with acute leukemia is 200 mg/m² daily administered by continuous i.v. infusion for 5 days (120 hours; total dose 1 000 mg/m²) at approximately 2-week intervals. Remission induction therapy in acute leukemia is usually administered in a short course without adjustment or discontinuation based upon peripheral blood counts. However, depending on the physician's judgment, modifications may be made based on hematologic response. Consider discontinuing the drug if the patient has less than 50 000 platelets or 1 000 polymorphonuclear granulocytes/mm³ in the peripheral blood. These guidelines may be modified depending on signs of toxicity in other systems and on the rapidity of fall in formed blood elements. Restart the drug when there are signs of marrow recovery and the above platelet and granulocyte levels have been attained. **Warning:** Withholding therapy until the patient's blood values are normal may result in escape of the patient's disease from control by cytarabine.

Some dosage regimens reported in the literature are described briefly below:

Combination Chemotherapy: Before instituting a program of combination chemotherapy, the physician should be familiar with the literature, adverse reactions, precautions, contraindications and warnings applicable to all the drugs involved in the program.

Cytarabine-Doxorubicin: Cytarabine 100 mg/m²/day, continuous i.v. infusion (days 1 to 10); doxorubicin 30 mg/m²/day, i.v. infusion of 30 minutes (days 1 to 3). Additional (complete or modified) courses as necessary at 2- to 4-week intervals if leukemia is persistent.

Cytarabine-Thioguanine-Daunorubicin: Cytarabine 100 mg/m²/day i.v. infusion over 30 minutes every 12 hours (days 1 to 7); thioguanine 100 mg/m² orally every 12 hours (days 1 to 7); daunorubicin 60 mg/m²/day i.v. infusion (days 5 to 7). Additional (complete or modified) courses as necessary at 2- to 4-week intervals if leukemia is persistent.

Cytarabine-Doxorubicin-Vincristine-Prednisone: Cytarabine 100 mg/m²/day continuous i.v. infusion (days 1 to 7); doxorubicin 30 mg/m²/day i.v. infusion (days 1 to 3); vincristine 1.5 mg/m²/day i.v. infusion (days 1, 5); prednisone 40 mg/m²/day i.v. infusion every 12 hours (days 1 to 5). Additional (complete or modified) courses as necessary at 2- to 4-week intervals if leukemia is persistent.

Cytarabine-Daunorubicin-Thioguanine-Prednisone-Vincristine: Cytarabine 100 mg/m²/day i.v. every 12 hours (days 1 to 7); daunorubicin 70 mg/m²/day i.v. infusion (days 1 to 3); thioguanine 100 mg/m² orally every 12 hours (days 1 to 7); prednisone 40 mg/m²/day orally (days 1 to 7); vincristine 1 mg/m²/day i.v. infusion (days 1 to 7). Additional (complete or modified) courses as necessary at 2- to 4-week intervals if leukemia is persistent.

Cytarabine-Daunorubicin: Cytarabine 100 mg/m²/day continuous i.v. infusion (days 1 to 7); daunorubicin 45 mg/m²/day i.v. push (days 1 to 3). Additional (complete or modified) courses as necessary at 2- to 4-week intervals if leukemia is persistent.

High Dose Chemotherapy: Before instituting a program of high dose and/or combination chemotherapy, the physician should be familiar with the literature, adverse reactions, precautions, contraindications and warnings applicable to high dose regimens of cytarabine and for all the drugs involved in the program.

Cytarabine: 2 mg/m² infused over 3 hours every 12 hours×12 doses (days 1 to 6). 3 g/m² infused over 1 hour every 12 hours×12 doses (days 1 to 6). 3 g/m² infused over 75 minutes every 12 hours×12 doses (days 1 to 6).

Cytarabine-Doxorubicin: Cytarabine 3 g/m² infused over 2 hours every 12 hours×12 doses (days 1 to 6); doxorubicin 30 mg/m² i.v. on days 6 and 7.

Cytarabine-Asparaginase: Cytarabine 3 g/m² infused over 3 hours at 0 hours, 12 hours, 24 hours and 36 hours. At 42 hours, 6 000 units/m² of asparaginase i.m. (days 1 and 2). Repeat the same schedules days 8 and 9.

Maintenance: Appropriate maintenance therapy may be initiated following induction of a complete remission. Maintenance programs are modifications of induction programs and, in general, use similar schedules of drug therapy as were used during induction. Most programs have a greater time spacing between courses of therapy during remission maintenance.

Acute Myelocytic Leukemia (AML): Adults as described above. Children: Childhood AML usually responds better than adult AML given similar regimens. Where the adult dosage is stated in terms of body weight or surface area, the children's dosage may be calculated on the same basis. When specified amounts of a drug are indicated for the adult dosage, these should be adjusted for children on the basis of such factors as age, body weight or body surface area.

Acute Lymphocytic Leukemia: In general, dosage schedules are similar to those used in acute myelocytic leukemia.

NonHodgkin's Lymphoma in Children: Cytarabine has been used as part of a multi-drug program (LSA_2-L_2) to treat Non-Hodgkin's lymphoma in children.

Suggested S.C. Use: S.C. administration of cytarabine has been generally used for maintenance therapy after remission (also see Suggested I.V. Regimens above). A single dose of 1 or 1.5 mg/kg s.c. at intervals of 1 to 4 weeks has been used for maintenance therapy.

S.C. administration of low-dose cytarabine has also been used to treat elderly patients ($\geq$60 years of age), who had underlying disease sufficiently serious to prevent more aggressive therapy. Doses of 10 to 20 mg s.c. have been given by bolus or infusion at 12-hour intervals over periods from 3 to 6 weeks. Cytoreduction usually occurs slowly with these dosage regimens, which are generally well tolerated.

Intrathecal Use: Warning: Do not use preserved diluents for intrathecal administration. See Preparation for use.

Meningeal Leukemia: In the treatment and maintenance therapy of meningeal leukemia and other meningeal neoplasms, cytarabine has been given by intrathecal injection in doses of 5 to 75 mg/m² or 30 to 100 mg once every 2 to 7 days to once daily for 4 or 5 days. The dosage schedule is usually determined by the type and severity of CNS manifestations and the patient's response to prior therapy. A frequently used intrathecal cytarabine dosage has been 30 mg/m² once every 4 days until CSF findings are normal, followed by 1 additional dose. If systemic toxicity occurs with intrathecal cytarabine, modification of other therapy may be necessary.

Renal and Hepatic Impairment: Dosage reduction does not appear to be necessary in cases of renal impairment. Dosage reduction may not be necessary in patients with hepatic impairment; however, these patients should be carefully monitored.

Preparation for Use: S.C. and I.V. Injection: Cytarabine injection is suitable for s.c. or i.v. injection.

I.V. Infusion: Cytarabine injection may be further diluted to 0.1 mg/mL with any of the solutions for i.v. infusion listed: Water for Injection USP, 5% Dextrose Injection USP, 0.9% Sodium Chloride USP and Lactated Ringer's Injection USP.

Intrathecal Injection: Diluents containing preservatives should **not** be used for intrathecal administration. Diluents for intrathecal injection are usually physiologic or isotonic solutions. Cytarabine is usually administered as a 5 mg/mL concentration in 5 to 15 mL of solution, after an equivalent volume of CSF is removed.

Stability of Solutions: Cytarabine injection is supplied in single dose vials. The solution must be used once punctured within 24 hours and the unused portion discarded.

Further diluted solutions should be used within 24 hours from the time of the initial puncture or within 72 hours when refrigerated. Injectable solutions should be inspected visually for particulate matter and discoloration prior to administration.

Further diluted unpreserved solutions for intrathecal injection must be used immediately, since bacterially contaminated intrathecal solutions could pose very grave risks.

Cytarabine injection when admixed with 0.9% Sodium Chloride Injection to a concentration of 32.5 mg/mL of cytarabine, is chemically stable for a period of 6 days at room temperature, protected from light.

Incompatibilities: Cytarabine is known to be incompatible with solutions of heparin, insulin, methotrexate, 5-fluorouracil, nafcillin, oxacillin, penicillin G, hydrocortisone and methylprednisolone.

Special Instructions for Handling Cytotoxic Drugs: The following are precautionary measures recommended in the handling and preparation of cytotoxic agents such as cytarabine:

1. The procedure should be carried out in a vertical laminar flow hood (Biological Safety Cabinet—Class II).
2. PVC gloves, safety glasses, disposable gowns and masks should be worn by personnel.
3. All vials, syringes, needles and other materials which have come in contact with cytarabine should be segregated and destroyed by incineration (sealed containers may explode). If incineration is unavailable, neutralization using 5% sodium hypochlorite or 5% sodium thiosulfate should be carried out instead.
4. Biannual hematologic examinations should be performed on personnel regularly involved in the handling and preparation of cytarabine.

Supplied: Each mL of solution contains: cytarabine 100 mg. Single dose vials of 1, 5, 10 or 20 mL (100 mg, 500 mg, 1 g or 2 g). Intact vials should be stored at controlled room temperatures not exceeding 25°C.

CYTOSAR® Ⓟ

Pharmacia & Upjohn

Cytarabine

Antileukemic

Pharmacology: Cytarabine is metabolized by deoxycytidine kinase and other nucleotide kinases to the nucleotide triphosphate, an effective inhibitor of DNA polymerase; it is inactivated by pyrimidine nucleoside deaminase which converts it to the nontoxic uracil derivative. It appears that the balance of kinase and deaminase levels may be an important factor in determining sensitivity or resistance of the cell to cytarabine.

Cytarabine is rapidly metabolized and is not effective orally; less than 20% of the orally administered dose is absorbed from the gastrointestinal tract.

Following rapid i.v. injection, the disappearance from plasma is biphasic. There is an initial distributive phase with a half-life of about 10 minutes, followed by a second elimination phase with a half-life of about 1 to 3 hours. After the distributive phase, over 80% of plasma radioactivity can be accounted for by the inactive metabolite 1-β-D-arabinofuranosyluracil (ara-U). Within 24 hours about 80% of the administered radioactivity can be recovered in the urine, approximately 90% of which is excreted as ara-U.

After s.c. or i.m. administration, peak plasma levels of radioactivity are achieved about 20 to 60 minutes after injection and are considerably lower than those after i.v. administration.

Cerebrospinal fluid levels of cytarabine are low in comparison to plasma levels after single i.v. injection. However, in one patient in whom cerebrospinal levels were examined after 2 hours of constant i.v. infusion, levels approached 40% of the steady-state plasma level. With intrathecal administration, levels of cytarabine in the cerebrospinal fluid declined with a first order half-life of about 2 hours. Because cerebrospinal fluid levels of deaminase are low, little conversion to ara-U was observed.

Caution: Cytarabine is a potent drug and should be used only by physicians experienced with cancer therapeutic drugs (see Warnings and Precautions). Hematologic, renal and hepatic evaluations must be done at regular intervals.

Indications: Induction and maintenance of remission in acute leukemia in children and adults.

It has been found useful in the treatment of acute myelocytic leukemia, chronic myelocytic leukemia (blast phase), acute lymphocytic leukemia and erythroleukemia. Cytarabine may be used alone or in combination with other antineoplastic agents; the best results are obtained with combination therapy.

Children with nonHodgkin's lymphoma have benefited from a combination drug program (LSA_2L_2) that included cytarabine.

Cytarabine has been used intrathecally in newly diagnosed children with acute lymphocytic leukemia as well as in the treatment of meningeal leukemia.

Cytarabine, in high dose 2 to 3 g/m² as an i.v. infusion over 1 to 3 hours given every 12 hours for 2 to 6 days with or without additional cancer chemotherapeutic agents, has been shown to be effective in the treatment of poor-risk leukemia, refractory leukemia, and relapsed acute leukemia.

Remissions induced by cytarabine not followed by maintenance treatment have been brief.

Table I—Cytosar

Acute Myelocytic Leukemia—Remission Induction: Adults

		No. Patients Evaluated	Complete Remissions	Investigator
Drug Dosage Schedule[a]				
Cytosar Single-Dose Therapy	(Infusion)			
	10 mg/m² 12 h/day	12	2 (17%)	Ellison (1968)
	30 mg/m² 12 h/day	41	10 (24%)	
	10 mg/m² 24 h/day	9	2 (22%)	
	30 mg/m² 24 h/day	36	2 (6%)	
	(Infusion) 200 mg/m² 24 h/5 days	36	9 (25%)	Bodey (1969)
	10 mg/m² i.v. injection initially, then infusions of 30 mg/m²/12 h or 60 mg/m²/day for 4 days	49	21 (43%)	Goodell (1970)
	(Infusion Therapy)			
	800 mg/m²/2 days	53	12 (23%)	Southwest Oncology
	1 000 mg/m²/5 days	60	24 (40%)	Group (1974)
	100 mg/m²/day 1 h infusion	49	7 (14%)	Carey (1975)
	5-12.5 mg/kg/12 h infusion following i.v. synchronizing dose[b]	5	5 (100%)	Lampkin (1976)
Combined Therapy				
Cytosar—doxorubicin		41	30 (73%)	Preisler (1979)
Cytosar—thioguanine daunorubicin		28	22 (79%)	Gale (1977)
Cytosar—doxorubicin vincristine—prednisolone		35	23 (66%)	Weinstein (1980)
Cytosar—daunorubicin thioguanine—prednisone—vincristine		139	84 (60%)	Glucksberg (1981)
Cytosar—daunorubicin		21	14 (67%)	Cassileth (1977)
Cytosar		7	6 (86%)	Lister (1983)
Cytosar		21	12 (57%)	Herzig (1983)
Cytosar		11	8 (73%)	Preisler (1983)
Cytosar—doxorubicin		14	7 (50%)	Willemze (1982)
Cytosar—asparaginase		13	9 (69%)	Capizzi (1983)

[a] Unless otherwise stated, all doses given until drug effect-modifications then based on hematologic reasons. See references available from manufacturer.

[b] Highly experimental—requires ability to study mitotic indices.

Cytosar (cont'd)

Acute Myelocytic Leukemia: Table I (on previous page) and Table II outline the results of treatment with cytarabine alone and in combination with other chemotherapeutic agents, in the treatment of acute myelocytic leukemia in adults and children.

The treatment regimens outlined in the tables should not be compared for efficacy. These were independent studies with a number of variables involved, such as patient population, duration of disease, and previous treatment.

The responsiveness and course of childhood acute myelocytic leukemia (AML) appear to be different from that in adults. Numerous studies show response rates to be higher in children than in adults with similar treatment schedules. Experience indicates that at least with induction and initial drug responsiveness, childhood AML appears to be more similar to childhood acute lymphocytic leukemia (ALL) than to its adult variant.

Acute Lymphocytic Leukemia: Cytarabine has been used in the treatment of acute lymphocytic leukemia in both adults and children. When cytarabine was used with other antineoplastic agents as part of a total therapy program, results were equal to or better than reported with such programs which did not include cytarabine. Used singly, or in combination with other agents, cytarabine has also been effective in treating patients who had relapsed on other therapy. Tables III and IV summarize the results obtained in previously treated patients. Since these are independent studies with such variables as patient population, duration of disease and previous treatment, results shown should not be used for comparing the efficacy of the outlined treatment programs.

Intrathecal Use in Meningeal Leukemia: Cytarabine has been used intrathecally in acute leukemia in doses ranging from 5 to 75 mg/m² of body surface area. The frequency of administration varied from once a day for 4 days to once every 4 days. The most frequently used dose was 30 mg/m² every 4 days until cerebrospinal fluid findings were normal, followed by one additional treatment. The dosage schedule is usually governed by the type and severity of CNS manifestations and the response to previous therapy.

Cytarabine has been used intrathecally with hydrocortisone sodium succinate sterile powder and methotrexate, both as prophylaxis in newly diagnosed children with acute lymphocytic leukemia, as well as in the treatment of meningeal leukemia. Sullivan has reported that prophylactic triple therapy has prevented late CNS disease and given overall cure and survival rates similar to those seen in patients in whom CNS radiation and intrathecal methotrexate was used as initial CNS prophylaxis. The dose of cytarabine was 30 mg/m², hydrocortisone sodium succinate 15 mg/m², and methotrexate 15 mg/m². The physician should be familiar with this report before initiation of the regimen.

Prophylactic triple therapy following the successful treatment of the acute meningeal episode may be useful. The physician should familiarize himself with the current literature before instituting such a program. Focal leukemic involvement of the CNS may not respond to intrathecal cytarabine and may better be treated with radiotherapy.

If used intrathecally, do not use a diluent containing benzyl alcohol. Reconstitute with preservative-free saline and use immediately.

NonHodgkin's Lymphoma in Children: Cytarabine has been used as part of a multidrug program (LSA_2L_2) to treat nonHodgkin's lymphoma in children.

Contraindications: Patients who are hypersensitive to the drug.

Warnings: Cytarabine is a potent bone marrow suppressant. Therapy should be started cautiously in patients with preexisting drug-induced bone marrow suppression. Patients receiving this drug must be under close medical supervision and during induction therapy, should have leukocyte and platelet counts performed daily. Bone marrow examinations should be performed frequently after blasts have disappeared from the peripheral blood. Facilities should be available for management of complications (possibly fatal) of bone marrow suppression (infection resulting from granulocytopenia and other impaired body defences, and hemorrhage secondary to thrombocytopenia).

Severe and at times fatal, CNS, gastrointestinal and pulmonary toxicity (different from that seen with conventional therapy regimens of cytarabine) has been reported following high dose schedules (2 to 3 g/m²) of cytarabine. These reactions include reversible corneal toxicity and hemorrhagic conjunctivitis; which may be prevented or diminished by prophylaxis with a local corticosteroid eye drop; cerebral and cerebellar dysfunction including personality changes, somnolence and coma, usually reversible; severe gastrointestinal ulceration, including pneumatosis cystoides intestinalis, leading to peritonitis; sepsis and liver abscess; pulmonary edema; liver damage with increased bilirubin; bowel necrosis; and necrotizing colitis. Two patients treated with conventional doses of cytarabine sterile powder and daunomycin developed abdominal tenderness (peritonitis) and guaiac positive colitis. Both patients responded to nonoperative medical management. Both patients exhibited neutropenia and thrombocytopenia and were receiving numerous other drugs. The authors recommend careful, conservative management in patients receiving cytarabine who appear to have a surgical abdomen, but in whom a definitive surgical diagnosis cannot be made. Two patients with childhood acute myelogenous leukemia who received intrathecal and i.v. cytarabine at conventional doses, in addition to a number of other concomitantly administered drugs, developed delayed progressive ascending paralysis resulting in death in one of the two patients.

Rarely, severe skin rash, leading to desquamation has been reported. Complete alopecia is more commonly seen with high-dose therapy than with standard treatment programs.

If high-dose therapy is used, do not use a diluent containing benzyl alcohol. Benzyl alcohol is contained in the diluent for this product. Benzyl alcohol has been reported to be associated with a fatal ''Gasping Syndrome'' in premature infants.

An increase in cardiomyopathy with subsequent death has been reported following experimental high dose cytarabine and cyclophosphamide therapy when used for bone marrow transplant preparation.

A syndrome of sudden respiratory distress, rapidly progressing to pulmonary edema and radiographically pronounced cardiomegaly has been reported following experimental high dose cytarabine therapy used for the treatment of relapsed leukemia from one institution in 16/72 patients. In one case, the outcome was fatal.

Acute pancreatitis has been reported to occur in patients being treated with cytarabine in combination with other drugs.

Extensive chromosomal damage, including chromatoid breaks have been produced by cytarabine and malignant transformation of rodent cells in culture has been reported.

Pregnancy: Cytarabine is known to be teratogenic in some animal species. Use of this drug in women who are or who may become pregnant should be undertaken only after due consideration of potential benefit and potential hazard to both mother and child. Women of childbearing potential should be advised to avoid becoming pregnant.

A review of the literature has shown 32 reported cases where cytarabine was given during pregnancy, either alone or in combination with other cytotoxic agents. Eighteen normal infants were delivered. Four of these had first trimester exposure. Five infants were premature or of low birth weight. Twelve of the 18 normal infants were followed up at ages ranging from 6 weeks to 7 years, and showed no abnormalities. One apparently normal infant died at 90 days of gastroenteritis.

Two cases of congenital abnormalities have been reported, one with upper and lower distal limb defects, and the other with extremity and ear deformities. Both of these cases had first trimester exposure.

There were 7 infants with various problems in the neonatal period, including pancytopenia; transient depression of WBC, hematocrit or platelets; electrolyte abnormalities; transient eosinophilia; and one case of increased IgM levels and hyperpyrexia possibly, due to sepsis. Six of the 7 infants were also premature. The child with pancytopenia died at 21 days of sepsis.

Therapeutic abortions were done in 5 cases. Four fetuses were grossly normal, but one had an enlarged spleen and another showed Trisomy C chromosome abnormality in the chorionic tissue.

Because of the potential for abnormalities with cytotoxic therapy, particularly during the first trimester, a patient who is or who becomes pregnant while on cytarabine should be apprised of the potential risk to the fetus and the advisability of pregnancy continuation. There is a definite, but considerably reduced risk if therapy is initiated during the second or third trimester. Although normal infants have been delivered to patients treated in all three trimesters of pregnancy, follow-up of such infants would be advisable.

Lactation: It is not known whether this drug is excreted in human milk. Because many drugs are excreted in human milk and because of the potential for serious adverse reactions in nursing infants from cytarabine, a decision should be made whether to discontinue nursing or to discontinue the drug, taking into account the importance of the drug to the mother.

Table II—Cytosar

Acute Myelocytic Leukemia—Remission Induction: Children (21 and under)

Drug Therapy	No. Patients Evaluated	Complete Remissions	Investigator
Cytosar (5-12.5 mg/kg following i.v. synchronizing dose*)	16	12 (75%)	Lampkin (1976)
Cytosar, vincristine, doxorubicin, prednisolone	48	35 (73%)	Weinstein (1980)
Cytosar, thioguanine, doxorubicin	11	8 (72%)	Hagbin (1975)
Cytosar, thioguanine	47	20 (43%)	Pizzo (1976)
Cytosar, cyclophosphamide	12	7 (58%)	

*Highly experimental—requires ability to study mitotic indices.

Table III—Cytosar

Acute Lymphocytic Leukemia—Remission Induction—Previously Treated Patients, Adults and Children

Drug Therapy	No. Patients Evaluated	Complete Remissions	Response	Investigator
Cytosar 3-5 mg/kg/day (i.v. injection)	43	2 (5%)	15 (35%)	Howard (1968)
Cytosar—asparaginase	9	8 (89%)	8 (89%)	McElwain (1969)
Cytosar—cyclophosphamide	11	7 (64%)	9 (82%)	Bodey (1970)
Cytosar—prednisone	83	–	(49%)	Nesbit (1970)
Cytosar 150-200 mg/m²/5 days (infusion)	34	1 (3%)	4 (12%)	Wang (1970)
Cytosar-L-asparaginase-prednisone-vincristine-doxorubicin	91	72 (79%)	–	Klemperer (1978)
Cytosar-L-asparaginase-prednisone-vincristine-doxorubicin	55	42 (76%)	–	Klemperer (1978)
Cytosar—asparaginase	22	13 (59%)	15 (68%)	Ortega (1972)
Cytosar—thioguanine	19	9 (47%)	9 (47%)	Bryan (1974)

Table IV—Cytosar

Acute Lymphocytic Leukemia—Remission Induction—Previously Treated Patients, Adults and Children

	No. Patients Evaluated	Complete Remissions	Investigator
High-dose Therapy			
Cytosar	8	3 (38%)	Rohatiner (1983)
Cytosar—doxorubicin	3	2 (67%)	Willemze (1982)
Cytosar—asparaginase	10	3 (30%)	Capizzi (1983)

Precautions: Patients receiving cytarabine must be monitored closely. Frequent platelet and leukocyte counts and bone marrow examinations are mandatory. Consider suspending or modifying therapy when drug-induced marrow depression has resulted in a platelet count under 50 000 or a polymorphonuclear granulocyte count under 1 000/mm³. Counts of formed elements in the peripheral blood may continue to fall after the drug is stopped and reach lowest values after drug-free intervals of 12 to 24 days. When indicated, restart therapy when definite signs of marrow recovery appear (on successive bone marrow studies). Patients whose drug is withheld until "normal" peripheral blood values are attained, may escape from control.

When large i.v. doses are given quickly, patients are frequently nauseated and may vomit for several hours post injection. This problem tends to be less severe when the drug is infused.

The human liver apparently detoxifies a substantial fraction of an administered cytarabine dose. Use the drug with caution and at reduced dose in patients whose liver function is poor.

Periodic checks of bone marrow, liver and kidney function should be performed in patients receiving cytarabine.

Children: The safety of the drug for use in infants is not established.

Like other cytotoxic drugs, cytarabine may induce hyperuricemia secondary to rapid lysis of neoplastic cells. The clinician should monitor the patient's blood uric acid level and be prepared to use such supportive and pharmacologic measurements as might be necessary to control this problem.

Adverse Effects: Because cytarabine is a bone marrow suppressant, anemia, leukopenia, thrombocytopenia, megaloblastosis, and reduced reticulocytes can be expected as a result of its administration. The severity of these reactions are dose and schedule dependent. Cellular changes in the morphology of bone marrows and peripheral smears can be expected.

Following 5-day constant infusions or acute injections of 50 mg/m² to 600 mg/m², white cell depression follows a biphasic course. Regardless of initial count, dosage level, or schedule, there is an initial fall starting the first 24 hours with a nadir at days 7 to 9. This is followed by a brief rise which peaks around the twelfth day. A second and deeper fall reaches nadir at days 15 to 24. Then there is a rapid rise to above baseline in the next 10 days. Platelet depression is noticeable at 5 days with a peak depression occurring between days 12 to 15. Thereupon, a rapid rise to above baseline occurs in the next 10 days.

A syndrome has been described which is characterized by fever, myalgia, bone pain, occasionally chest pain, maculopapular rash, conjunctivitis and malaise. It usually occurs 6 to 12 hours following drug administration. Corticosteroids have been shown to be beneficial in treating or preventing this syndrome. If the symptoms of the syndrome are deemed treatable, corticosteroids should be contemplated as well as continuation of therapy with cytarabine.

The following additional adverse reactions have been reported: anorexia, nausea, vomiting, diarrhea, oral and anal inflammation or ulceration, nausea and vomiting following rapid i.v. injection, rash, hepatic dysfunction, fever, thrombophlebitis, bleeding (all sites), sepsis, pneumonia, cellulitis at injection site, skin ulceration, urinary retention, renal dysfunction, neuritis, neural toxicity, sore throat, esophageal ulceration, esophagitis, chest pain, bowel necrosis, abdominal pain, freckling, jaundice, conjunctivitis (may occur with rash), dizziness, alopecia, anaphylaxis, allergic edema, pruritus, shortness of breath, urticaria and headache.

High-Dose Therapy: Severe and at times fatal CNS, gastrointestinal and pulmonary toxicity have been reported following high dose schedules (2 to 3 g/m² every 12 hours for 12 doses). These reactions include reversible corneal toxicity and hemorrhagic conjunctivitis, which may be prevented or diminished by prophylaxis with a local corticosteroid eyedrop; cerebral and cerebellar dysfunction including personality changes, somnolence and coma, usually reversible; severe gastrointestinal ulceration, including pneumatosis cystoides intestinalis leading to peritonitis; sepsis and liver abscess; pulmonary edema; liver damage with increased bilirubin; bowel necrosis; and necrotizing colitis. Two patients with adult acute nonlymphocytic leukemia developed peripheral motor and sensory neuropathies after consolidation with high-dose cytarabine, daunorubicin, and asparaginase. Patients treated with high-dose cytarabine should be observed for neuropathy since dose schedule alterations may be needed to avoid irreversible neurologic disorders.

Ten patients treated with experimental intermediate doses of cytarabine (1 g/m²) with and without other chemotherapeutic agents (meta-AMSA, daunorubicin, VP-16) developed a diffuse interstitial pneumonitis without clear cause that may have been related to the cytarabine.

Rarely, severe skin rash, leading to desquamation has been reported. Complete alopecia is more commonly seen with high dose therapy than with standard treatment programs. If high dose therapy is used, do not use a diluent containing benzyl alcohol.

Cytarabine given intrathecally may cause systemic toxicity and careful monitoring of the hemopoietic system is indicated. Modification of other anti-leukemia therapy may be necessary. Major toxicity is rare. The most frequently reported reactions after intrathecal administration were nausea, vomiting and fever; these reactions are mild and self-limiting. Paraplegia has been reported. Necrotizing leukoencephalopathy occurred in 5 children; these patients had also been treated with intrathecal methotrexate and hydrocortisone, as well as by CNS radiation. Isolated neurotoxicity has been reported. Blindness occurred in 2 patients in remission whose treatment had consisted of combination systemic chemotherapy, prophylactic CNS radiation and intrathecal cytarabine.

Corneal toxicity consisting of ocular pain, tearing, foreign-body sensation, photophobia and blurred vision have been reported.

One case of anaphylaxis that resulted in acute cardiopulmonary arrest and required resuscitation has been reported. This occurred immediately after the i.v. administration of cytarabine.

Overdose: Symptoms and Treatment: There is no antidote for cytarabine overdosage.

Discontinuation of the drug and supportive therapy are of course indicated. Transfusions of platelets should be given if there is any sign of hemorrhage. Patients should be carefully observed for intercurrent infection and if such appears they should be rapidly and rigorously treated with appropriate antibiotic therapy.

Chronic overdosage may cause serious bone marrow suppression. Daily hematological evaluation should be performed to prevent overdosage. Nausea and vomiting, although a general side effect of the drug, may be an additional warning of overdosage. Severe hemorrhage into the gastrointestinal tract may indicate overdosage as may severe generalized infections.

Doses exceeding recommended dosage schedules have been used clinically and have been tolerated. The major toxicity with the use of 3 g/m² i.v. infusion over 1 hour every 12 hours for 12 doses and 3 g/m² continuous infusion for 4 days, other than reversible bone marrow suppression has been reversible corneal, cerebral and cerebellar dysfunction. Doses of 4.5 g/m² i.v. infusion over 1 hour every 12 hours for 12 doses has caused an unacceptable increase in irreversible toxicity and death.

Dosage: Caution: The following precautionary measures are recommended in proceeding with the preparation and handling of cytotoxic agents such as cytarabine:

The procedure should be carried out in a vertical laminar flow hood (Biological Safety Cabinet—Class II).

Personnel should wear: PVC gloves, safety glasses, disposable gowns and masks.

All needles, syringes, vials, and other materials which have come in contact with cytarabine should be segregated and destroyed by incineration (sealed containers may explode). If incineration is not available, neutralization should be carried out using 5% sodium hypochlorite, or 5% sodium thiosulfate.

Personnel regularly involved in the preparation and handling of cytarabine should have biannual hematologic examinations.

Cytarabine is not active orally. The schedule and method of administration varies with the program of therapy to be used. Cytarabine may be given by i.v. infusion, injection/s.c. or intrathecally. Thrombophlebitis has occurred at the site of drug injection or infusion in some patients, and rarely patients have noted pain and inflammation at s.c. injection sites. In most instances, however, the drug has been well tolerated.

Patients can tolerate higher total doses when they receive the drug by rapid i.v. injection as compared with slow infusion. This phenomenon is related to the drug's rapid inactivation and brief exposure of susceptible normal and neoplastic cells to significant levels after rapid injection. Normal and neoplastic cells seem to respond in somewhat parallel fashion to these different modes of administration and no clear-cut clinical advantage has been demonstrated for either.

Clinical experience accumulated to date suggests that success with cytarabine is dependent more on adeptness in modifying day-to-day dosage to obtain maximum leukemic cell kill with tolerable toxicity than on the basic treatment schedule chosen at the outset of therapy. Toxicity necessitating dosage alteration almost always occurs.

Relatively constant plasma levels can be achieved by continuous i.v. infusion.

In many chemotherapeutic programs, cytarabine is used in combination with other cytotoxic drugs. The addition of these cytotoxic drugs has necessitated changes and dose alterations. The dosage schedules for combination therapy outlined below have been reported in the literature.

Acute Myelocytic Leukemia: Induction remission: Adults: 200 mg/m² daily by continuous infusion for 5 days (120 hours). Total dose 1 000 mg/m². This course is repeated approximately every 2 weeks. Modifications must be made based on hematologic response.

Meningeal Leukemia: Intrathecal Use: (see Indications and Warnings).

High-dose Chemotherapy: Before instituting a program of high dose chemotherapy, the physician should be familiar with the literature, adverse reactions, precautions, contraindications, and warnings applicable to all the drugs involved in the program: 2 g/m² infused over 3 hours every 12 hours×12 doses (Days 1 to 6). 3 g/m² infused over 1 hour every 12 hours×12 doses (Days 1 to 6). 3 g/m² infused over 75 minutes every 12 hours×12 doses (Days 1 to 6).

Cytarabine—Doxorubicin: Cytarabine: 3 g/m² infused over 2 hours every 12 hours×12 doses (Days 1 to 6). Doxorubicin: 30 mg/m² i.v. on Days 6 and 7.

Cytarabine—Asparaginase: Cytarabine: 3 g/m² infused over 3 hours at 0 hours, 12 hours, 24 hours, and 36 hours. At 42 hours, 6 000 units/m² of asparaginase i.m. (Days 1 and 2); repeat same schedules Days 8 and 9.

Combined Chemotherapy: Before instituting a program of combined chemotherapy, the physician should be familiar with the literature, adverse reactions, precautions, contraindications, and warnings applicable to all the drugs involved in the program.

Cytarabine—Doxorubicin: Cytarabine 100 mg/m²/day, continuous i.v. infusion (Days 1 to 10). Doxorubicin: 30 mg/m²/day, i.v. infusion of 30 minutes (Days 1 to 3).

Additional (complete or modified) courses as necessary at 2-to 4-week intervals if leukemia is persistent.

Cytarabine—Thioguanine—Daunorubicin: Cytarabine: 100 mg/m², i.v. infusion over 30 minutes every 12 hours (Days 1 to 7). Thioguanine: 100 mg/m², orally every 12 hours (Days 1 to 7). Daunorubicin: 60 mg/m²/day, i.v. infusion (Days 5 to 7).

Additional (complete or modified) courses as necessary at 2-to 4-week intervals if leukemia is persistent.

Cytarabine—Doxorubicin—Vincristine—Prednisone: Cytarabine: 100 mg/m²/day, continuous i.v. infusion (Days 1 to 7). Doxorubicin: 30 mg/m²/day, i.v. infusion (Days 1 to 3). Vincristine: 1.5 mg/m²/day, i.v. infusion (Days 1 and 5). Prednisone: 40 mg/m²/day, i.v. infusion every 12 hours (Days 1 to 5).

Additional (complete or modified) courses as necessary at 2-to 4-week intervals if leukemia is persistent.

Cytarabine—Daunorubicin—Thioguanine—Prednisone—Vincristine: Cytarabine: 100 mg/m²/day, i.v. infusion (Days 1 to 10). Daunorubicin: 70 mg/m²/day, i.v. infusion (Days 1 to 3). Thioguanine: 100 mg/m², orally every 12 hours (Days 1 to 7). Prednisone: 40 mg/m²/day, orally (Days 1 to 7). Vincristine: 1 mg/m²/day, i.v. infusion (Days 1 and 7).

Additional (complete or modified) courses as necessary at 2-to 4-week intervals if leukemia is persistent.

Cytarabine—Daunorubicin: Cytarabine: 100 mg/m²/day, continuous i.v. infusion (Days 1 to 7). Daunorubicin: 45 mg/m²/day, i.v. push (Days 1 to 3).

Additional (complete or modified) courses as necessary at 2-to 4-week intervals if leukemia is persistent.

Acute Myelocytic Leukemia—Maintenance: Adults: Maintenance programs are modifications of induction programs and, in general, use similar schedules of drug therapy as were used during induction. Most programs have a greater time spacing between courses of therapy during remission maintenance.

Acute Myelocytic Leukemia—Induction and Maintenance: Children: Numerous studies have shown that childhood AML responds better than adult AML given similar regimens. Where the adult dosage is stated in terms of body weight or surface area, the children's dosage may be calculated on the same basis. When specified amounts of a drug are indicated for the adult dosage, these should be adjusted for children on the basis of such factors as age, body weight or body surface area.

Acute Lymphocytic Leukemia: In general, dosage schedules are similar to those used in acute myelocytic leukemia with some modifications. Consult the manufacturer for dosage recommendations based on referenced literature.

NonHodgkin's Lymphoma in Children: Cytarabine has been used as part of a multidrug program (LSA_2L_2) to treat non-Hodgkin's lymphoma in children.

Cytosar (cont'd)

LSA_2-L_2 Protocol: Woolner N, Burchenal JH, Lieberman PH, et al: NonHodgkin's Lymphoma in Children—A Comparative Study of Two Modalities of Therapy. Cancer 37:123-134,1976.
Induction Phase: Day 1. Cyclophosphamide 1 200 mg/m² single push injection. Day 3 to 31. Prednisone 60 mg/m² orally divided into 3 daily doses. Day 3, 10, 17, 24. Vincristine 1.5 to 2.25 mg/m² i.v. Day 5, 27, 30. Spinal tap and intrathecal injection of methotrexate 6.25 mg/m². Day 12, 13. Daunomycin 60 mg/m² i.v.

At the end of induction (last dose of intrathecal methotrexate) patient rests for 3 to 5 days before consolidation.

Consolidation Phase: Day 34 or 36, daily i.v. injections of cytosine arabinoside (Ara-C) 150 mg/m² for a total of 15 injections are given. (Injections are given from Monday through Friday.) Thioguanine 75 mg/m² is given orally, 8 to 12 hours after the injection of Ara-C. If the white blood count is 1 500 or more and the platelet count 150 000 or more on the 5th day of Ara-C, the patient continues to receive the same dosage of thioguanine over the weekend. However, both are discontinued temporarily when there is evidence of marrow depression; this usually occurs after the initial seventh to tenth doses of the combination and ordinarily recovers within 7 to 10 days. Hence, the patients may receive more than 15 doses of thioguanine orally, but receive only 15 doses of i.v. cytosine arabinoside (Ara-C). This first phase of the consolidation takes an average of 30 to 35 days. The second phase of the consolidation should be started immediately after completion of the 15 doses of Ara-C; it entails daily i.v. administration of L-asparaginase, 60 000 U/m² for a total of 12 injections, excluding weekends.

Two days after the last injection of the L-asparaginase, 2 more intrathecal injections of methotrexate are given 2 days apart. Three days after the last intrathecal methotrexate, BCNU (1, 3-Bis (2 chloroethyl 1-1-nitrosourea)) 60 mg/m² is given i.v., which completes the consolidation. The average duration of the induction and consolidation is 85 to 120 days.

Maintenance Phase: The maintenance period consists of 5 cycles of 5 days each and is started 3 to 4 days after completion of consolidation.

Cycle I: Oral thioguanine 300 mg/m² for 4 consecutive days: i.v. cyclophosphamide 600 mg/m² on the 5th day. Rest 7 to 10 days.

Cycle II: Oral hydroxyurea 2 400 mg/m² for 4 consecutive days: i.v. daunomycin 45 mg/m² on the 5th day. Rest 7 to 10 days.

Cycle III: Oral methotrexate 10 mg/m² for 4 consecutive days: i.v. BCNU 60 mg/m² on the 5th day. Rest 7 to 10 days.

Cycle IV: I.V. Ara-C 150 mg/m² for 4 consecutive days: i.v. vincristine 1.5 mg/m² on day 5. Rest 7 to 10 days.

Cycle V: Two doses of intrathecal methotrexate 6.25 mg/m² 2 to 3 days apart. Rest 7 to 10 days and restart with Cycle I.

Dosage Modification: The dosage of cytarabine must be modified or suspended when signs of serious hematologic depression appear. In general, consider discontinuing the drug if the patient has less than 50 000 platelets or 1 000 polymorphonuclear granulocytes/mm³ in his peripheral blood. These guidelines may be modified depending on signs of toxicity in other systems and on the rapidity of fall in formed blood elements. Restart the drug when there are signs of marrow recovery and the above platelet and granulocyte levels have been attained. Withholding therapy until the patient's blood values are normal may result in escape of the patient's disease from control by the drug.

Intrathecal Use in Meningeal Leukemia: Cytarabine has been used intrathecally in acute leukemia in doses ranging from 5 mg/m² to 75 mg/m² of body surface area. The frequency of administration varied from once a day for 4 days to once every 4 days. The most frequently used dose was 30 mg/m² every 4 days until cerebrospinal fluid findings were normal, followed by one additional treatment. The dosage schedule is usually governed by the type and severity of CNS manifestations and the response to previous therapy.

Cytarabine has been used intrathecally with hydrocortisone sodium succinate sterile powder and methotrexate, both as prophylaxis in newly diagnosed children with acute lymphocytic leukemia, as well as in the treatment of meningeal leukemia. Sullivan has reported that prophylactic triple therapy has prevented late CNS disease and given overall cure and survival rates similar to those seen in patients in whom CNS radiation and intrathecal methotrexate was used as initial CNS prophylaxis. The dose of cytarabine was 30 mg/m², hydrocortisone 15 mg/m², and methotrexate 15 mg/m². The physician should be familiar with this report before initiation of the regimen.

Prophylactic triple therapy following the successful treatment of the acute meningeal episode may be useful. The physician should familiarize himself with the current literature before instituting such a program.

Cytarabine given intrathecally may cause systemic toxicity and careful monitoring of the hemopoietic system is indicated. Modification of the antileukemia therapy may be necessary. Major toxicity is rare. The most frequently reported reactions after intrathecal administration were nausea, vomiting and fever; these reactions are mild and self-limiting. Paraplegia has been reported. Necrotizing leukoencephalopathy occurred in 5 children; these patients had also been treated with intrathecal methotrexate and hydrocortisone, as well as by CNS radiation. Isolated neurotoxicity has been reported. Blindness occurred in 2 patients in remission whose treatment had consisted of combination systemic chemotherapy, prophylactic CNS radiation and intrathecal cytarabine.

Focal leukemic involvement of the CNS may not respond to intrathecal cytarabine and may better be treated with radiotherapy.

Intrathecal Use: If solutions are used intrathecally, do not use a diluent containing benzyl alcohol. Reconstitute with preservative-free 0.9% Sodium Chloride for Injection. Use immediately.

High-dose Use: Do not use diluent containing benzyl alcohol.

Chemical Stability and Compatibility: Cytosar is compatible for 24 hours at 5°C with Lactated Ringers, Dextrose 5% in Water, 0.9% Sodium Chloride, Dextrose 5% in Water with 0.9% Sodium Chloride.

Cytarabine 0.8 mg/mL and sodium cephalothin 1.0 mg/mL are chemically stable for 8 hours in dextrose 5% in water.

Cytarabine 0.4 mg/mL and prednisolone sodium phosphate 0.2 mg/mL are compatible in dextrose 5% in water for 8 hours.

Cytarabine 16 μg/mL and vincristine sulfate 4 μg/mL are compatible in dextrose 5% in water for 8 hours.

Cytarabine has been known to be physically incompatible with heparin, insulin, methotrexate, 5-fluorouracil, penicillin G, and methylprednisolone sodium succinate.

As with all i.v. admixtures, dilution should be made just prior to administration and the resulting unpreserved solution used within 24 hours.

Reconstitution: Cytarabine sterile powder may be reconstituted with the following diluents: 0.9% Sodium Chloride for injection, Dextrose 5% in Water, Sterile Water for Injection, Bacteriostatic Water for Injection. pH of reconstituted solution is approximately 5. Solutions reconstituted without a preservative should be used immediately. Solutions reconstituted with Bacteriostatic Water for Injection with Benzyl Alcohol 0.9% may be stored at controlled room temperature (15 to 30°C) for 48 hours. Discard any solution in which a slight haze develops.

When reconstituted with a diluent the following concentrations result as shown in Table V.

Table V—Cytosar

Reconstitution

Vial Size	Volume of Diluent to be Added to Vial	Nominal Concentration
100 mg	5 mL	20 mg/mL
500 mg	10 mL	50 mg/mL
1 g	10 mL	100 mg/mL
2 g	20 mL	100 mg/mL

Supplied: 100 mg: Each vial of freeze-dried preparation contains: cytarabine 100 mg. Vials of 5 mL, packs of 5.

500 mg: Each vial of freeze-dried preparation contains: cytarabine 500 mg. Vials of 10 mL, packs of 5.

1 g: Each vial of freeze-dried preparation contains: cytarabine 1 g. Single vials.

2 g: Each vial of freeze-dried preparation contains: cytarabine 2 g. Single vials.

Reviewed 1998

CYTOTEC® Ⓟ

Searle

Misoprostol

Mucosal Protective Agent

Pharmacology: Misoprostol is a synthetic analogue of prostaglandin E_1. In animals and man, it has both gastric antisecretory and mucosal protective effects. Its antisecretory activity is mediated by a direct action on the parietal cells. Misoprostol exerts a mucosal protective effect by enhancing natural mucosal defense mechanisms. Studies conducted in animals and clinical trials in humans have demonstrated that misoprostol can protect the gastric mucosa against various irritants such as alcohol, ASA, naproxen, sodium taurocholate and tolmetin. In addition, misoprostol has been shown to increase mucus production and to increase bicarbonate secretion in the duodenum. Misoprostol has local and systemic activity.

Following administration of a single 200 μg dose of misoprostol to 6 healthy male subjects, the mean C_{max}, AUC (0 to 24) and T_{max} of the primary biologically active acid metabolite were: 309 pg/mL, 355 pg.hr/mL and 0.5 hours respectively. After administration of tritiated misoprostol the elimination half-life of misoprostol acid (the active metabolite of misoprostol) was 20.6 minutes, and the elimination half-life of total organic extractable radioactivity was 1.5 to 1.7 hours. The duration of antisecretory activity is greater than 3 but less than 6 hours.

Pharmacokinetic studies in patients with varying degrees of renal impairment showed an approximate doubling of $T_{1/2}$, C_{max} and AUC compared to normals, but no clear correlation between the degree of impairment and AUC. In subjects over 64 years of age, the AUC for misoprostol acid is increased. No routine dosage adjustment is recommended in older patients or patients with renal impairment, but dosage may need to be reduced if the usual dose is not tolerated.

Indications: For the treatment and prevention of NSAID-induced gastroduodenal ulcers. Also indicated for the treatment of duodenal ulcers caused by Peptic Ulcer Disease (PUD).

Patients at high risk of developing NSAID-induced complications and who may require protection include: patients with a previous history of ulcer disease or a significant gastrointestinal event; patients over 60 years of age; patients judged to be at risk because of general poor health, severe concomitant medical disease, or patients who are poor surgical risks; patients disabled by joint symptoms (e.g., HAQ Disability Index Score >1.5) or those with severe systemic manifestations of arthritis; patients taking other drugs known to damage or exacerbate damage to the gastrointestinal tract such as corticosteroids or anticoagulants; patients taking a high dosage or multiple NSAIDs, including those available over-the-counter.

The risk of NSAID-induced complications may be highest in the first 3 months of NSAID therapy.

Contraindications: Known sensitivity to prostaglandins, prostaglandin analogues or excipients (microcrystalline and hydroxypropyl methylcellulose, sodium starch glycolate and hydrogenated castor oil).

Pregnancy: Contraindicated in pregnancy.

Women should be advised not to become pregnant while taking misoprostol. If pregnancy is suspected, use of the product should be discontinued.

Warnings: *Pregnancy:* Women of childbearing potential should employ adequate contraception (i.e., oral contraceptives or intrauterine devices) while receiving misoprostol (see Contraindications).

Lactation: It is unlikely that misoprostol is excreted in human milk since it is rapidly metabolized throughout the body. However, it is not known if the active metabolite (misoprostol acid) is excreted in human milk. Therefore, misoprostol should not be administered to nursing mothers because the potential excretion of misoprostol acid could cause significant diarrhea in nursing infants.

Children: Safety and effectiveness in patients below the age of 18 have not been established.

Precautions: Selection of Patients: Caution should be used when using symptomatology as the sole diagnostic and follow-up procedure, since misoprostol has not been shown to have an effect on gastrointestinal pain or discomfort.

Before treatment is undertaken, a positive diagnosis of duodenal ulcer or NSAID-induced gastroduodenal ulcer should be made. The general health of the patient should be considered. Misoprostol is rapidly metabolized by most body tissues to inactive metabolites. Nevertheless, caution should be exercised when patients have impairment of renal or hepatic function.

Diarrhea: Rare instances of profound diarrhea leading to severe dehydration have been reported. Patients with an underlying condition such as irritable bowel disease, or those in whom dehydration, were it to occur, would be dangerous, should be monitored carefully if misoprostol is prescribed.

Geriatrics or Renally Impaired: Considerations for Dosage Adjustment: In subjects over 64 years of age or those who are renally impaired the pharmacokinetics may be affected, but not to a clinically significant degree (see Dosage). No routine dosage adjustment is recommended in older patients or those patients with renal impairment. Dosage may need to be reduced if the usual dose is not tolerated. In patients with renal failure, a starting dose in the low range (100 μg q.i.d.) is recommended.

Drug Interactions: The serum protein binding of misoprostol acid (the active metabolite of misoprostol) was not affected by: indomethacin, ranitidine, digoxin, phenylbutazone, warfarin, diazepam, methyldopa, propranolol, triamterene, cimetidine, acetaminophen, ibuprofen, chlorpropamide and hydrochlorothiazide.

Salicylic acid (300 μg/mL) lowered the protein binding of misoprostol from 84 to 52%; this is not considered clinically significant since the binding of misoprostol acid is not extensive and its elimination half-life is very short.

In laboratory studies, misoprostol has shown no significant effect on the cytochrome P450-linked hepatic mixed function oxidase system, and therefore should not affect the metabolism of theophylline, warfarin, benzodiazepines or other drugs normally metabolized by this system.

No clinically significant drug interactions attributable to misoprostol have been observed to date.

Some prostaglandins and prostaglandin analogues have the capacity to produce hypotension through peripheral vasodilation. The results of clinical trials to date indicate that misoprostol has not produced hypotension at dosages effective in promoting the healing of ulcers. Nevertheless, misoprostol should be used with caution in the presence of disease states where hypotension might precipitate severe complications, e.g., cerebral vascular disease or coronary artery disease.

Epileptic seizures have been reported with prostaglandins and prostaglandin analogues administered by routes other than oral. Therefore, misoprostol tablets should be used in known epileptics only when their epilepsy is adequately controlled and then only when expected benefits outweigh potential risks.

Symptomatic responses to misoprostol do not preclude the presence of gastric malignancy.

Adverse Effects: Gastrointestinal: In 18 985 subjects receiving misoprostol daily in clinical trials, the most frequent gastrointestinal adverse events were diarrhea (10.7%), abdominal pain (7.3%), nausea (4.2%), flatulence (3.3%), and dyspepsia (3.2%). The incidence of diarrhea was 7.8% when the total daily dose was 400 μg. In patients receiving placebo, the incidence of diarrhea was 3.6%. The events were usually transient and mild to moderate in severity.

Diarrhea, when it occurred, usually developed early in the course of therapy, was self-limiting and required discontinuation of misoprostol in less than 2% of the patients. The incidence of diarrhea can be minimized by adjusting the dose of misoprostol, by administering after food, and by avoiding coadministration of misoprostol with magnesium-containing antacids.

Gynecological: Women who received misoprostol during clinical trials reported the following gynecological disorders: spotting (0.7%), cramps (0.3%), hypermenorrhea (0.4%), menstrual disorder (0.3%) and dysmenorrhea (0.1%).

Geriatrics: There were no significant differences in the safety profile of misoprostol in approximately 500 ulcer patients who were 65 years of age or older, compared with younger patients.

Confusion has been reported in a small number of patients in postmarketing surveillance of misoprostol.

Incidence greater than 1%: In clinical trials, the following adverse reactions were reported by more than 1% of the subjects receiving misoprostol and may be causally related to the drug: headache (2.5%), vomiting (1.4%) and constipation (1.4%). However, there were no clinically significant differences between the incidences of these events for misoprostol and placebo.

Overdose: Symptoms and Treatment: The toxic dose of misoprostol in human beings has not been determined. Cumulative total daily doses of 1 600 μg have been tolerated with only symptoms of gastrointestinal discomfort being reported. In animals, the acute toxic effects are similar to those reported for other prostaglandins and prostaglandin analogues: relaxation of smooth muscle, respiratory difficulties and depression of the CNS. Possible clinical signs that may indicate an overdose may include: sedation, tremor, fever, convulsions, dyspnea, abdominal pain, diarrhea, palpitations, hypotension or bradycardia. Treatment should be symptomatic and supportive.

It is not known if misoprostol acid is dialyzable. However, because misoprostol is metabolized like a fatty acid, it is unlikely that dialysis would be appropriate treatment for overdosage.

Dosage: Treatment and Prevention of NSAID-Induced Gastroduodenal Ulcers: The recommended adult oral dosage for the prevention and treatment of NSAID-induced gastroduodenal ulcer is 400 to 800 μg a day in divided doses. NSAIDs should be taken according to the schedule prescribed by the physician. When appropriate, misoprostol and NSAIDs are to be taken simultaneously. Misoprostol should be taken after food.

Treatment of Duodenal Ulcer: The recommended adult oral dosage of misoprostol for duodenal ulcer is 800 μg/day for 4 weeks in 2 or 4 equally divided doses (i.e., 200 μg q.i.d. or 400 μg b.i.d.). The last dose should be taken at bedtime with food. Antacids (aluminum based) may be used as needed for relief of pain. Treatment should be continued for a total of 4 weeks unless healing in less time has been documented by endoscopic examination. In the small number of patients who may not have fully healed after 4 weeks, therapy with misoprostol may be continued for a further 4 weeks.

Geriatrics and Renally Impaired: Consideration for Dosage Adjustment: Pharmacokinetic studies in patients with varying degrees of renal impairment showed an approximate doubling of $T_{1/2}$, C_{max} and AUC compared to normals. There was no clear correlation between degree of impairment and AUC. In subjects over 64 years of age the pharmacokinetics may be affected. In both patient groups the pharmacokinetic changes are not clinically significant. No routine dosage adjustment is recommended in older patients or those patients with renal impairment. Dosage may need to be reduced if the usual dose is not tolerated. In patients with renal failure, a starting dose in the low range (100 μg q.i.d.) is recommended.

Information for the Patient: See Blue Section—Information for the Patient "Cytotec".

Supplied: 100 μg: Each white to off-white, round tablet, with SEARLE engraved on one side and CYTOTEC on the other, contains: misoprostol 100 μg. Nonmedicinal ingredients: cellulose, hydrogenated castor oil, hydroxypropyl methylcellulose and sodium starch glycolate. Bottles of 100. Store below 30°C.

200 μg: Each white to off-white, scored, hexagonal tablet, with SEARLE 1461 engraved on one side, contains: misoprostol 200 μg. Nonmedicinal ingredients: cellulose, hydrogenated castor oil, hydroxypropyl methylcellulose and sodium starch glycolate. Bottles of 120 and 500. Store below 30°C.

Pharmacist: Dispense with Patient Insert.

(Shown in Product Recognition Section)

CYTOVENE® Capsules Ⓟ
CYTOVENE® Injection Ⓟ
Roche

Ganciclovir

Ganciclovir Sodium

Antiviral

Pharmacology: Ganciclovir is a synthetic nucleoside analog of guanine which inhibits the replication of herpes viruses both in vitro and in vivo.

Intracellular ganciclovir is phosphorylated to ganciclovir monophosphate by a cellular deoxyguanosine kinase. Further phosphorylation occurs by several cellular kinases to produce ganciclovir triphosphate. It has been shown in vitro that the levels of ganciclovir triphosphate are as much as 100-fold greater in CMV-infected cells than noninfected cells. Thus, there is a preferential phosphorylation of ganciclovir in virus-infected cells. In virus-infected cells, ganciclovir triphosphate is metabolized slowly, with 60 to 70% remaining intracellularly 18 hours after removal of ganciclovir from the extracellular fluid. The antiviral activity of ganciclovir is the result of inhibition of viral DNA synthesis by 2 modes: (1) ganciclovir triphosphate competitively inhibits dGTP incorporation into DNA by DNA polymerase and (2) incorporation of ganciclovir triphosphate into viral DNA causes subsequent termination or very limited viral DNA elongation.

Ganciclovir inhibits mammalian cell proliferation in vitro at concentrations from 10 to 60 μg/mL, with bone marrow colony forming cells being most sensitive (IC_{50} of 10 μg/mL).

Pharmacokinetics: The pharmacokinetics of i.v. ganciclovir have been evaluated in immunocompromised patients with serious CMV disease. In patients with normal renal function, the plasma half-life was 2.9±1.3 hours. Dose independent kinetics were demonstrated over the range of 1.6 to 5.0 mg/kg. Renal excretion through both glomerular filtration and active tubular secretion is the major route of elimination of ganciclovir (see Precautions, Patients with Renal Impairment). At the end of a 1 hour i.v. infusion of 5 mg/kg ganciclovir, total AUC ranged between 22.1±3.2 (n=16) and 26.8±6.1 μg·h/mL (n=16) and C_{max} ranged between 8.27±1.02 (n=16) and 9.0±1.4 μg/mL (n=16).

The absolute bioavailability of ganciclovir following oral administration of ganciclovir capsules under fasting conditions was approximately 5% (n=6) and following food was 6 to 9% (n=32). When ganciclovir was administered orally with food at a total daily dose of 3 g/day (500 mg q3h, 6 times daily and 1 000 mg t.i.d.), the steady-state absorption as measured by area under the serum concentration vs time curve (AUC) over 24 hours and maximum serum concentrations (C_{max}) were similar following both regimens with an AUC_{0-24} of 15.9±4.2 (mean±SD) and 15.4±4.3 μg·h/mL and C_{max} of 1.02±0.24 and 1.18±0.36 μg/mL, respectively (n=16).

Food Effects: When ganciclovir capsules were given with a meal containing 602 calories and 46.5% fat at a dose of 1 000 mg every 8 hours to 20 HIV-positive subjects, the steady-state AUC increased by 22±22% (range: −6% to 68%) and there was a significant prolongation of time to peak serum concentrations (T_{max}) from 1.8±0.8 to 3.0±0.6 hours and a higher C_{max} (0.85±0.25 vs 0.96±0.27 μg/mL) (n=20).

Indications: I.V.: For the treatment of CMV retinitis in immunocompromised patients, including patients with acquired immunodeficiency syndrome (AIDS), iatrogenic suppression secondary to organ transplantation or those administered chemotherapy for neoplasia. Ganciclovir i.v. solution is also indicated for the prevention of CMV disease in transplant recipients at risk for CMV disease.

Oral: For the prevention of CMV disease in solid organ transplant recipients at risk of developing CMV disease.

For the maintenance treatment of CMV retinitis in immunocompromised patients, including patients with AIDS, where the retinitis is stable following at least 3 weeks of therapy with ganciclovir i.v. Oral ganciclovir provides an alternative to continued i.v. therapy following satisfactory induction treatment in patients who have been diagnosed with CMV retinitis, and for whom the risk of more rapid progression is balanced by the benefit associated with avoiding daily i.v. infusions.

Diagnosis of CMV Retinitis: The diagnosis of CMV retinitis is primarily an ophthalmologic one and should be made by indirect ophthalmoscopy. Other conditions in the differential diagnosis of CMV retinitis include candidiasis, toxoplasmosis, histoplasmosis, retinal scars, and cotton wool spots, any of which may produce a retinal appearance similar to CMV. For this reason it is essential that the diagnosis of CMV be established by an ophthalmologist familiar with the retinal presentation of these conditions. The diagnosis of CMV retinitis may be aided by culture of CMV from urine, blood, throat, or other sites, but a negative CMV culture does not rule out CMV retinitis.

Contraindications: In pregnant women and in patients who are hypersensitive to ganciclovir or to acyclovir.

Warnings: The clinical toxicity of ganciclovir includes leukopenia and thrombocytopenia. In animal and in vitro studies ganciclovir caused aspermatogenesis, mutagenicity, teratogenicity and carcinogenicity; therefore it should be considered a potential teratogen and carcinogen in humans. Ganciclovir is indicated for use only in immunocompromised patients, where the potential benefit outweighs the risks stated herein. The safety and efficacy of ganciclovir have not been evaluated for congenital or neonatal CMV disease, nor for treatment of CMV infection in nonimmunocompromised individuals.

Hematologic: Ganciclovir should not be administered if the absolute neutrophil count is less than 0.5×10^9 cells/L or the platelet count is less than 25×10^9 cells/L. Granulocytopenia (neutropenia) and thrombocytopenia have been observed in patients treated with ganciclovir. The frequency and severity of these events vary widely in different patient populations (see Adverse Effects). Ganciclovir should therefore, be used with caution in patients with pre-existing cytopenias, or with a history of cytopenic reactions to other drugs, chemicals, or irradiation.

Neutropenia: Neutropenia typically occurs during the first or second week of induction therapy and prior to administration of a total cumulative dose of 200 mg/kg of ganciclovir i.v. but may occur at any time during treatment. Evidence of recovery of cell counts usually occurs within 3 to 7 days after discontinuing the drug. Colony stimulating factors have been shown to increase neutrophil and white blood cell counts in patients receiving ganciclovir i.v. solution for treatment of CMV retinitis.

Thrombocytopenia: Thrombocytopenia (platelet count of less than 50×10^9/L) was observed in patients treated with ganciclovir. Immunodeficient patients without AIDS were more

Cytovene (cont'd)

likely to develop lowered platelet counts than those with AIDS. Patients with initial platelet counts less than 100×10^9/L were also at increased risk of this toxicity of ganciclovir.

Pregnancy and Reproduction: Animal data indicate that administration of ganciclovir caused inhibition of spermatogenesis and infertility, which were reversible at lower doses and irreversible at higher doses. Although clinical data have not yet been obtained regarding this effect, **it is considered likely that i.v. ganciclovir in the recommended doses will result in temporary or permanent male infertility. Animal data also indicate that permanent suppression of fertility in women may occur.**

Mutagenic tests of ganciclovir have indicated the potential for altering the chromosomes, therefore male and female patients should be advised to practise barrier contraception during treatment with ganciclovir, and males for an additional 90 days following treatment.

Female mice exhibited decreased fertility, decreased mating behavior, and increased embryolethality after daily i.v. doses of 90 mg/kg.

In male mice, fertility was decreased after daily i.v. doses of ≥2 mg/kg and daily oral doses of ≥10 mg/kg. These effects were reversible after daily i.v. doses of 2 mg/kg and daily oral doses of 10 mg/kg, but were irreversible or incompletely reversible after daily i.v. doses of 10 mg/kg and daily oral doses of 100 or 1 000 mg/kg. Ganciclovir has also caused hypospermatogenesis in rats after daily oral doses of ≥100 mg/kg and in dogs after daily i.v. and oral doses of ≥0.4 mg/kg and 0.2 mg/kg, respectively.

Ganciclovir caused maternal/fetal toxicity and embryolethality in mice, at daily doses of 108 mg/kg (see also Lactation).

Ganciclovir caused fetal growth retardation, embryolethality, teratogenicity, and/or maternal toxicity in mice at daily doses of 20 or 60 mg/kg. Teratogenic changes seen included cleft palate, an/microphthalmia, aplastic organs (kidney and pancreas), hydrocephaly, and brachygnathia.

Lactation: It is not known if ganciclovir is excreted in human milk. Since many drugs are, and because carcinogenic and teratogenic effects occurred in animals treated with ganciclovir, the possibility of serious adverse reactions from ganciclovir in nursing infants is considered likely. Ganciclovir should not be given to breast-feeding mothers. The minimum interval before nursing can safely be resumed after the last dose of ganciclovir is unknown.

Daily i.v. doses of 90 mg/kg ganciclovir administered to female mice prior to mating and during gestation and lactation caused hypoplasia of the testes and seminal vesicles in the month-old offspring, as well as pathologic changes in the nonglandular region of the stomach.

Precautions: General: In clinical studies with ganciclovir i.v., the maximum single dose studied has been 6 mg/kg infused i.v. over 1 hour. It is likely that larger doses, or more rapid infusions, could result in increased toxicity. Administration of ganciclovir i.v. solution should be accompanied by adequate hydration.

Solutions of ganciclovir have a high pH (approximately 11) and may cause phlebitis and/or pain at the site of i.v. infusion. Therefore, care must be taken to infuse ganciclovir solutions only into veins with adequate blood flow to afford rapid dilution and distribution.

Information for the Patient: All patients should be informed that the major toxicities of ganciclovir are granulocytopenia (neutropenia), anemia, and thrombocytopenia and that dose modifications may be required, including discontinuation. The importance of close monitoring of blood counts while on therapy should be emphasized.

Patients should be instructed to take ganciclovir capsules with food to maximize bioavailability.

Patients should be advised that ganciclovir has caused decreased sperm production in animals and may cause infertility in humans. Women of childbearing potential should be advised that ganciclovir causes birth defects in animals and should not be used during pregnancy. Women of childbearing potential should be advised to use effective contraception during treatment with ganciclovir. Similarly, men should be advised to practise barrier contraception during and for at least 90 days following treatment with ganciclovir.

Patients should be advised that ganciclovir causes tumors in animals. Although there is no information from human studies, ganciclovir should be considered a potential carcinogen.

Patients with AIDS and CMV Retinitis: Ganciclovir is not a cure for CMV retinitis, and immunocompromised patients may continue to experience progression of retinitis during or following treatment. Patients should be advised to have ophthalmologic followup examinations at a minimum of every 4 to 6 weeks while being treated with ganciclovir. Some patients will require more frequent followup. Patients with AIDS may be receiving zidovudine (ZDV; AZT); patients should be counseled that treatment with both ganciclovir and zidovudine simultaneously may not be tolerated by some patients and may result in severe granulocytopenia (neutropenia). Patients with AIDS may be receiving didanosine (ddI); patients should be counseled that concomitant treatment with both ganciclovir and didanosine can cause didanosine levels to be significantly increased.

Transplant Recipients: Transplant recipients should be counseled regarding the high frequency of impaired renal function in transplant recipients who received ganciclovir i.v. solution in controlled clinical trials, particularly in patients receiving concomitant administration of nephrotoxic agents such as cyclosporine and amphotericin B. Although the specific mechanism of this toxicity, which in most cases was reversible, has not been determined, the higher rate of renal impairment in patients receiving i.v. administered ganciclovir compared with those who received placebo in the same trials may indicate that ganciclovir played a significant role.

Drug Interactions: Probenecid: At a dose of 1 000 mg of ganciclovir oral every 8 hours, ganciclovir serum concentrations increased 45% in the presence of probenecid, 500 mg every 6 hours. Renal clearance of ganciclovir decreased 22%, which is consistent with an interaction involving competition for renal tubular secretion.

Zidovudine: At a dose of 1 000 mg of ganciclovir oral every 8 hours, there was a trend for decreased ganciclovir AUC in the presence of zidovudine, 100 mg every 4 hours (18%), but the decrease was not statistically significant. There was a statistically significant increase in AUC for zidovudine (15%) in the presence of ganciclovir.

Since both zidovudine and ganciclovir have the potential to cause neutropenia and anemia, many patients will not tolerate combination therapy with these two drugs at full dosage strength. However, studies with ganciclovir for the treatment of CMV retinitis in AIDS showed no difference in the rate of severe neutropenia (ANC $<0.5 \times 10^9$ cells/L) nor of severe anemia (hemoglobin <8 g/dL) between those patients taking or not taking concomitant zidovudine.

Didanosine: At a dose of 1 000 mg of ganciclovir oral every 8 hours, the steady-state AUC_{0-12} for didanosine, 200 mg every 12 hours, increased approximately 80% when didanosine was administered 2 hours prior to or concurrently with administration of ganciclovir capsules. Decreased steady-state AUC (23%) was observed for ganciclovir oral in the presence of didanosine when the drug was administered 2 hours prior to administration of ganciclovir capsules, but AUC was not affected by the presence of didanosine when the two drugs were administered simultaneously. There were no significant changes in renal clearance for either drug.

When the standard ganciclovir i.v. induction dose (5 mg/kg infused over 1 hour every 12 hours) was coadministered with didanosine at a dose of 200 mg orally every 12 hours, the steady-state didanosine AUC_{0-12} increased 70±40% (range, 3 to 121%, n=11) and C_{max} increased 49±48% (range, −28 to 125%). In a separate study, when the standard i.v. ganciclovir maintenance dose (5 mg/kg infused over 1 hour every 24 hours) was coadministered with didanosine at a dose of 200 mg orally every 12 hours, didanosine AUC_{0-12} increased 50±26% (range, 22 to 110%, n=11) and C_{max} increased 36±36% (range, −27 to 94%) over the first didanosine dosing interval. Didanosine plasma concentrations (AUC_{12-24}) were unchanged during the dosing intervals when ganciclovir was not coadministered. Ganciclovir pharmacokinetics were not affected by didanosine. In neither study were there significant changes in the renal clearance of either drug.

Didanosine has been associated with pancreatitis. In 3 controlled trials, pancreatitis was reported in 2% of patients taking didanosine and ganciclovir. The rates of pancreatitis were similar in the ganciclovir i.v. solution and capsule groups.

Other than laboratory abnormalities, concomitant treatment with zidovudine, didanosine, or zalcitabine did not appear to affect the type or frequency of reported adverse events, with the exception of moderately increased rate of diarrhea. Among patients taking ganciclovir, the diarrhea rates were 51% and 49% respectively with didanosine versus 39% and 35% respectively, without didanosine.

Imipenem-Cilastatin: Generalized seizures have been reported in patients who received ganciclovir i.v. solution and in patients who received imipenem-cilastatin. These drugs should not be used concomitantly unless the potential benefits outweigh the risks.

Other Medications: It is possible that drugs that inhibit replication of rapidly dividing cell populations such as bone marrow, spermatogonia, and germinal layers of skin and gastrointestinal mucosa may have additive toxicity when administered concomitantly with ganciclovir. Therefore, drugs such as dapsone, pentamidine, flucytosine, vincristine, vinblastine, adriamycin, amphotericin B, trimethoprim/sulfamethoxazole combinations or other nucleoside analogs, should be considered for concomitant use with ganciclovir only if the potential benefits are judged to outweigh the risks.

No formal drug interaction studies of ganciclovir i.v. and drugs commonly used in transplant recipients have been conducted. Allograft recipients treated with ganciclovir i.v. in 3 controlled clinical studies also received a variety of concomitant medications, including amphotericin B, azathioprine, cyclosporine, muromonab-CD3 (OKT3), and/or prednisone. Increases in serum creatinine were observed in patients treated with ganciclovir plus either cyclosporine or amphotericin B, drugs with known potential for nephrotoxicity (see Adverse Effects). In a retrospective analysis of 93 liver allograft recipients receiving ganciclovir (5 mg/kg infused over 1 hour every 12 hours) and oral cyclosporine (at therapeutic doses), there was no evidence of an effect on cyclosporine whole blood concentrations.

Laboratory Testing: Due to the frequency of neutropenia, anemia or thrombocytopenia observed in patients receiving ganciclovir (see Adverse Effects), it is recommended that complete blood counts and platelet counts be performed frequently, especially in patients in whom ganciclovir or other nucleoside analogs have previously resulted in cytopenia, or in whom pretreatment neutrophil counts are less than 1×10^9/L. Because dosing may be modified in patients with renal impairment and because of the incidence of increased serum creatinine levels that have been observed in transplant recipients treated with ganciclovir, patients should have serum creatinine or creatinine clearance monitored carefully (see also sections on renal adverse events under Adverse Effects and Dosage, Patient Monitoring).

Mutagenesis/Carcinogenesis: Ganciclovir caused point mutations and chromosomal damage in mammalian cells in vitro and in vivo, but did not cause point mutations in bacterial or yeast cells, dominant lethality in mice, or morphologically transformed cells in vitro.

In a study conducted over 18 months, ganciclovir was carcinogenic in the mouse after oral doses of 20 and 1 000 mg/kg/day. The principally affected tissues at the dose of 1 000 mg/kg/day were the preputial gland in males, forestomach (nonglandular mucosa) in males and females, and reproductive tissues and liver in females. At dose of 20 mg/kg/day, slightly increased tumor incidences occurred in the preputial and harderian glands in males, forestomach in males and females, and liver in females. All ganciclovir-induced tumors were of epithelial or vascular origin except for histiocytic sarcoma of the liver. No carcinogenic effect occurred at 1 mg/kg/day. The preputial and clitoral glands, forestomach and harderian glands of mice have no human counterpart. Ganciclovir should be considered a potential carcinogen in humans.

Children: **Safety and efficacy of ganciclovir in children have not been established. The use of ganciclovir in children warrants extreme caution due to the probability of long-term carcinogenicity and reproductive toxicity. Administration to children should be undertaken only after careful evaluation and only if the potential benefits of treatment outweigh these considerable risks.**

There has been very limited clinical experience using ganciclovir for the treatment of CMV retinitis in patients under the age of 12 years.

Renal Considerations: Administration of ganciclovir i.v. should be accompanied by adequate hydration, since ganciclovir is excreted by the kidneys and normal clearance depends upon adequate renal function. If renal function is impaired, dosage adjustments are recommended. Such adjustments should be based on creatinine clearance (see Dosage).

It is possible that probenecid, as well as other drugs which inhibit renal tubular secretion or resorption, may reduce renal clearance of ganciclovir and could increase its plasma half-life.

Patients with Renal Impairment: Ganciclovir should be used with caution in patients with impaired renal function. Both the plasma half-life of ganciclovir as well as peak plasma levels are increased in patients with elevated serum creatinine levels. In a small number of patients who were undergoing dialysis, ganciclovir plasma levels were reduced by approximately 50% following dialysis (see Dosage).

Geriatrics: No studies on the efficacy or safety of ganciclovir specifically in elderly patients have been conducted. Since elderly individuals may have reduced renal function, ganciclovir should be administered to the elderly patients with care and with special consideration of their renal status (see Dosage).

Adverse Effects: Adverse events that occurred during clinical trials of ganciclovir are summarized below, according to the participating study subject population.

Subjects with AIDS: Three controlled, randomized, phase 3 trials comparing ganciclovir i.v. and ganciclovir oral for maintenance treatment of CMV retinitis have been completed. During these trials, ganciclovir was prematurely discontinued because of adverse events, new or worsening intercurrent illnesses, or laboratory abnormalities in 9% of the subjects. Laboratory data and adverse events reported during the conduct of these controlled trials are summarized in Table I.

Table I—Cytovene

Laboratory Data: Minimum ANC, Hemoglobin, and Platelets and Maximum Serum Creatinine Values During Treatment With Cytovene In 3 Controlled Clinical Trials[a]

	% of Subjects Capsules[b] (3 000 mg/day) (n=320)	% of Subjects I.V. Solution[c] (5 mg/kg/day) (n=175)
Neutropenia [n(%)]		
ANC/µL		
<500	18	25
500 to <750	17	14
750 to <1 000	19	26
Total ANC ≤1 000	54	66
Anemia [n(%)]		
Hemoglobin g/dL		
<6.5	2	5
6.5 to <8.0	10	16
8.0 to <9.5	25	26
Total Hgb <9.5	36	46
Thrombocytopenia		
Platelets/µL		
<25 000	1	3
25 000 to <50 000	8	5
Total Platelets <50 000	9	8
Serum Creatinine (SeCr)	**(n=320)**	**(n=173)**
SeCr mg/dL		
≥2.5	1	2
≥1.5 to <2.5	12	14
Total SeCr ≥1.5	13	16

[a]Data from Study ICM 1653, Study ICM 1774, and Study AVI034 pooled.
[b]Mean time on therapy=103 days, including allowed reinduction treatment periods.
[c]Mean time on therapy=91 days, including allowed reinduction treatment periods.

Overall, patients treated with ganciclovir i.v. solution experienced lower minimum ANCs and hemoglobin levels, consistent with more neutropenia and anemia, compared with those who received ganciclovir oral (P=0.024 for neutropenia; P=0.027 for anemia).

For the majority of subjects, maximum serum creatinine levels were less than 1.5 mg/dL and no difference was noted between i.v. administered and orally administered ganciclovir for the occurrence of renal impairment. Serum creatinine elevations ≥2.5 mg/dL occurred in <2% of all subjects and no significant differences were noted in the time from the start of maintenance to the occurrence of elevations in serum creatinine values.

Adverse Reactions: Table II shows adverse reactions (possibly or probably related to study drug) reported in ≥1% of the subjects in 3 controlled clinical trials during treatment with either ganciclovir oral (3 000 mg/day) or ganciclovir i.v. (5 mg/kg/day).

Retinal Detachment: Retinal detachment has been observed in subjects with CMV retinitis both before and after initiation of therapy with ganciclovir. The relationship of retinal detachment to therapy with ganciclovir is unknown. Retinal detachment occurred in 11% of patients treated with ganciclovir i.v. solution and in 8% of patients treated with ganciclovir capsules. Patients with CMV retinitis should have frequent ophthalmologic evaluations to monitor the status of their retinitis and to detect any other retinal pathology.

Transplant Recipients: There have been 3 controlled clinical trials of ganciclovir i.v. and 1 controlled clinical trial of ganciclovir oral for the prevention of CMV disease in transplant recipients. Laboratory data and adverse events reported during these trials are summarized below.

Table II—Cytovene

Adverse Reactions (Possibly/Probably Related to Study Drug) Reported in ≥1% of Subjects in 3 Randomized Phase III Studies Comparing Oral to I.V. Ganciclovir Maintenance Treatment

Body System	Adverse Event	Oral (n=326) %	I.V. (n=179) %
Body as a Whole	Fever	2	1
	Asthenia	4	6
	Headache	4	2
	Abdominal Pain	6	2
	Infection	1	1
	Pain	2	<1
	Injection Site Inflammation	0	2
	Injection Site Pain	0	1
	Sepsis	0	3
Digestive System	Diarrhea	13	7
	Nausea	9	7
	Anorexia	3	3
	Vomiting	3	3
	Dyspepsia	2	1
	Nausea & Vomiting	2	0
	Flatulence	3	1
Hemic and Lymphatic System	Leukopenia	22	36
	Anemia	7	14
	Thrombocytopenia	4	3
	Abnormal LFTs	2	1
Nervous System	Paresthesia	1	1
Other	Rash	3	1
	Pruritus	2	<1
	Phlebitis	0	2
Catheter Related*	Total Catheter Events	2	<1
	Catheter Infection	1	0
	Catheter Sepsis	0	2

*Some of these events also appear under other body systems.

Laboratory Data: Table III shows the frequency of granulocytopenia (neutropenia) and thrombocytopenia observed.

Table IV shows the frequency of elevated serum creatinine values in these controlled clinical trials.

In 3 out of 4 trials, patients receiving ganciclovir had elevated serum creatinine levels when compared to those receiving placebo. Most patients in these studies also received cyclosporine. The mechanism of impairment of renal function is not known. However, careful monitoring of renal function during therapy with ganciclovir is essential, especially for those patients receiving concomitant agents that may cause nephrotoxicity.

Adverse Reactions: CNS: In 2 placebo-controlled trials in transplant recipients, headache (17% vs 11%, respectively) and confusion (6% vs 1%, respectively) were noted to occur more frequently in patients treated with ganciclovir i.v. than in placebo-treated patients.

Other: In the same 2 studies, sepsis was observed more frequently in the patients treated with ganciclovir i.v. than in the placebo-treated patients (6% vs 2%, respectively).

Additional Adverse Reactions: General: Adverse events that were thought to be "probably" or "possibly" related to orally administered or i.v. administered ganciclovir in clinical studies in either subjects with AIDS or transplant recipients are listed below. These events all occurred with a frequency of less than 1%.

Body as a Whole: abdomen enlarged, abscess, ascites, back pain, cellulitis, chest pain, chills, chills and fever, drug level increased (ganciclovir), edema, face edema, injection site abscess, injection site edema, injection site hemorrhage, injection site phlebitis, laboratory test abnormality, malaise, photosensitivity reaction, neck pain, neck rigidity.

Digestive: aphthous stomatitis, constipation, dysphagia, eructation, esophagitis, fecal incontinence, gastritis, gastrointestinal moniliasis, gastrointestinal perforation, gingivitis, hemorrhage, hepatitis, jaundice, liver tenderness, melena, mouth ulceration, peptic ulcer, tongue disorder.

Hemic and Lymphatic: eosinophilia, hypochromic anemia, leukocytosis, lymphoma, marrow depression, pancytopenia, splenomegaly.

Respiratory: cough increased, dyspnea, pharyngitis.

Nervous System: abnormal dreams, abnormal gait, agitation, amnesia, anxiety, aphasia, ataxia, coma, confusion, convulsion, depression, dizziness, dry mouth, emotional lability, encephalopathy, euphoria, hyperkinesia, hypertonia, hypesthesia, insomnia, libido decreased, manic reaction, myoclonus, nervousness, psychosis, seizures, somnolence, speech disorder, thinking abnormal, tremor, trismus, vertigo.

Skin and Appendages: acne, alopecia, dry skin, fixed eruption, herpes simplex, maculopapular rash, skin discoloration, sweating, urticaria, vesiculobullous rash.

Special Senses: abnormal vision, amblyopia, blindness, conjunctivitis, deafness, ear disorder, ear pain, eye pain, glaucoma, retinitis, photophobia, taste perversion, tinnitus, vitreous disorder.

Metabolic and Nutritional Disorders: alkaline phosphatase increased, creatinine increased, creatine phosphokinase increased, healing abnormal, hyperglycemia, hypokalemia, lactic dehydrogenase increased, pancreatitis, peripheral edema, AST increased, ALT increased.

Cardiovascular: arrhythmia, deep thrombophlebitis, hypertension, hypotension, migraine, palpitation, vasodilatation.

Table III—Cytovene

Neutropenia and Thrombocytopenia in Trials for the Prevention of CMV Disease in Transplant Recipients

	Cytovene I.V. Heart Allograft[a]		Cytovene I.V. Bone Marrow Allograft[b]		Cytovene Oral Liver Allograft[c]	
	Cytovene n=76 %	Placebo n=73 %	Cytovene n=57 %	Placebo n=55 %	Cytovene n=150 %	Placebo n=154 %
Neutropenia (ANC/µL)						
<500	4	3	12	6	3	1
500–1 000	3	8	29	17	3	2
Thrombocytopenia (platelets/µL)						
<25 000	3	1	32	28	0	3
25 000–50 000	5	3	25	37	5	3

[a]Study ICM 1496: Mean duration of treatment=28 days.
[b]Studies ICM 1570 and ICM 1689: Mean duration of treatment=45 days.
[c]Study GAN040: Mean duration of ganciclovir treatment=82 days.

Table IV—Cytovene

Frequency of Elevated Serum Creatinine Values

Maximum Serum Creatinine Levels	Cytovene I.V. Heart Allograft ICM 1496 Cytovene (N=76) %	Placebo (n=73) %	Cytovene I.V. Bone Marrow Allograft ICM 1570 Cytovene (n=20) %	Control (n=20) %	Bone Marrow Allograft ICM 1689 Cytovene (n=37) %	Placebo (n=35) %	Cytovene Oral Liver Allograft GAN 040 Cytovene (n=150) %	Placebo (n=154) %
Serum Creatinine (≥2.5 mg/dL)	18	4	20	0	0	0	16	10
Serum Creatinine (≥1.5–<2.5 mg/dL)	58	69	50	35	43	44	39	42

Cytovene (cont'd)

Urogenital: breast pain, creatinine clearance decreased, hematuria, impotence, increased blood urea nitrogen (BUN), kidney failure, kidney function abnormal, polyuria, urinary frequency, urinary tract infection.
Laboratory Abnormalities: decreased blood sugar.
Musculoskeletal: arthralgia, bone pain, cyst, leg cramps, myalgia, myasthenia.

The following adverse events reported in patients receiving ganciclovir may be potentially fatal: pancreatitis, sepsis, and multiple organ failure.

Adverse Events Reported in Postmarket Surveillance of Ganciclovir: The following are adverse events reported since the marketing introduction of ganciclovir, and which are not listed under adverse reactions above. Because they are reported voluntarily from a population of unknown size, estimates of frequency cannot be made. These events have been chosen for inclusion due to either the seriousness, frequency of reporting, the apparent causal connection, or a combination of these factors: acidosis, allergic reaction, anaphylactic reaction, arthritis, bronchospasm, cardiac arrest, cardiac conduction abnormality, cataracts, cholelithiasis, cholestasis, congenital anomaly, dry eyes, dysesthesia, dysphasia, elevated triglyceride levels, exfoliative dermatitis, extrapyramidal reaction, facial palsy, hallucinations, hemolytic anemia, hemolytic-uremic syndrome, hepatic failure, hepatitis, hypercalcemia, hyponatremia inappropriate serum ADH, infertility, intestinal ulceration, intracranial hypertension, irritability, ischemia, loss of memory, loss of sense of smell, myelopathy, peripheral oculomotor nerve paralysis, pulmonary fibrosi, renal tubular disorder, rhabdomyolysis, Stevens-Johnson syndrome, stroke, testicular hypotrophy, torsades de pointes, vasculitis, ventricular tachycardia.

Overdose: Symptoms: I.V.: Overdosage with ganciclovir i.v. has been reported in both adults and children below 2 years of age. In 2 cases of overdosage in adults, no adverse events were reported after patients received either one dose of 3 500 mg or 7 doses of 11 mg/kg over a 3 day period. Similarly, the following overdoses in pediatric patients did not result in adverse events: a single dose of 500 mg (72.5 mg/kg) followed by 48 hours of peritoneal dialysis (4-month-old), single dose of approximately 60 mg/kg followed by exchange transfusion (18-month-old), 2 doses of 500 mg instead of 31 mg (21-month-old).

Irreversible pancytopenia developed in 1 adult with AIDS and CMV colitis after receiving 3 000 mg of ganciclovir i.v. on each of 2 consecutive days. He experienced worsening gastrointestinal symptoms and acute renal failure which required short-term dialysis. Pancytopenia developed and persisted until his death from a malignancy several months later. Other adverse events reported following overdosage included: persistent bone marrrow suppression (1 adult with neutropenia and thrombocytopenia after a single dose of 6 000 mg), reversible neutropenia or granulocytopenia (4 adults, overdosages ranging from 8 mg/kg daily for 4 days to a single dose of 25 mg/kg, hepatitis (1 adult receiving 10 mg/kg daily, and one 2 kg infant after a single 40 mg dose), renal toxicity (1 adult with transient worsening of hematuria after a single 500 mg dose, and 1 adult with elevated creatinine [5.2 mg/dL] after a single 5 000 to 7 000 mg dose), and seizure (1 adult with known seizure disorder after 3 days of 9 mg/kg). In addition, 1 adult received 0.4 mL (instead of 0.1 mL) ganciclovir i.v. by intravitreal injection, and experienced temporary loss of vision and central retinal artery occlusion secondary to increased intraocular pressure related to the injected fluid volume.

Oral: There have been no reports of overdosage with orally administered ganciclovir. Doses as high as 6 000 mg/day, given either as 1 000 mg 6 times daily or as 2 000 mg t.i.d., did not result in overt toxicity other than transient neutropenia. Daily doses of more than 6 000 mg have not been studied.

Treatment: Since ganciclovir is dialyzable, dialysis may be useful in reducing serum concentrations. Adequate hydration should be maintained. The use of hematopoietic growth factors should be considered.

Dosage: Caution: Do not administer ganciclovir i.v. by rapid or bolus i.v. Injection. The toxicity of ganciclovir may be increased as a result of excessive plasma levels.

Caution: I.M. or s.c. injection may result in severe tissue irritation due to the high pH (approximately 11) of ganciclovir i.v. solutions.

The recommended dose for ganciclovir i.v. and ganciclovir oral should not be exceeded. The recommended Infusion rate for ganciclovir i.v. should not be exceeded.

Because of individual patient variations in the clinical response of CMV disease and the sensitivity to the myelosuppressive effects of ganciclovir, the treatment of each patient with ganciclovir should be individualized on a case by case basis. Changes in dose should be based on regular clinical evaluations as well as on regular hematologic monitoring.

Treatment of CMV Retinitis: Induction Treatment: The recommended dose for patients with normal renal function is 5 mg/kg every 12 hours for 14 to 21 days, given as a constant i.v. infusion over 1 hour. Ganciclovir capsules should not be used for induction treatment.

Maintenance Treatment: I.V.: Following the induction treatment, the recommended dose is 5 mg/kg given as an i.v. infusion over 1 hour once/day for 7 days each week, or 6 mg/kg once/day for 5 days each week.

Oral: For patients with stable CMV retinitis following at least 3 weeks of treatment with ganciclovir i.v., the recommended maintenance dose is 1 000 mg t.i.d. with food. Alternatively, the dosing regimen of 500 mg 6 times daily with food, during waking hours, may be used.

For patients who experience progression of CMV retinitis while receiving maintenance treatment with either formulation of ganciclovir, reinduction treatment using the twice daily regimen of ganciclovir i.v. is recommended.

The safety and efficacy of ganciclovir oral have not been established for treating any manifestation of CMV disease other than maintenance treatment of CMV retinitis.

Prevention of CMV Disease in Transplant Recipients: I.V.: The recommended initial dose for patients with normal renal function is 5 mg/kg (given i.v. at a constant rate over 1 hour) every 12 hours for 7 to 14 days, followed by either 5 mg/kg once/day if on a 7-day weekly regimen, or 6 mg/kg once/day if on a 5-day weekly regimen.

Oral: The recommended prophylactic dose in patients with normal renal function is 1 000 mg t.i.d. (3 000 mg/day) with food.

The duration of treatment with ganciclovir in transplant recipients is dependent upon the duration and degree of immunosuppression. In controlled clinical trials in bone marrow allograft recipients, treatment with ganciclovir i.v. was continued until day 100 to 120 post-transplantation. CMV disease occurred in several patients who discontinued treatment with ganciclovir i.v. prematurely. In heart allograft recipients, the onset of newly diagnosed CMV disease occurred after treatment with ganciclovir i.v. was stopped at day 28 post-transplant, suggesting that continued dosing may be necessary to prevent late occurrence of CMV disease in this patient population.

In a controlled clinical trial of liver allograft recipients, treatment with ganciclovir oral was continued through Week 14 post-transplantation.

Patient Monitoring: Due to the frequency of granulocytopenia, anemia and thrombocytopenia in patients receiving ganciclovir (see Adverse Effects), it is recommended that complete blood counts and platelet counts be performed frequently, especially in patients in whom ganciclovir or other nucleoside analogs have previously resulted in cytopenia, or in whom neutrophil counts are less than 1 000 cells/μL at the beginning of treatment. Patients should have serum creatinine or creatinine clearance values followed carefully to allow for dosage adjustments in renally impaired patients.

Reduction of Dose: Dosage reductions in renally impaired patients are recommended for ganciclovir i.v. and should be considered for ganciclovir oral (see Renal Impairment). Dosage reductions should also be considered for patients with neutropenia, anemia and/or thrombocytopenia. Ganciclovir should not be administered in patients with severe neutropenia (ANC less than 500/μL) or severe thrombocytopenia (platelets less than 25 000/μL).

Renal Impairment: I.V.: For patients with impairment of renal function (see Precautions), refer to Table V for recommended doses of ganciclovir i.v., and adjust the dosing interval as indicated.

Dosing for patients undergoing hemodialysis should not exceed 1.25 mg/kg 3 times/week, following each hemodialysis session. Ganciclovir i.v. should be given shortly after completion of the hemodialysis session, since hemodialysis has been shown to reduce plasma levels by approximately 50%.

Oral: In patients with renal impairment, consideration should be given to modifying the dose of ganciclovir oral as shown in Table VI.

Table VI—Cytovene Oral

Maintenance Doses of Cytovene Oral in Renal Impairment

Creatinine Clearance* mL/min	Cytovene Oral Dose
≥70	1 000 mg t.i.d. or 500 mg q3h (6x/day)
50 to 69	1 500 mg once a day or 500 mg t.i.d.
25 to 49	1 000 mg once a day or 500 mg b.i.d.
10 to 24	500 mg once a day
<10	500 mg 3 times/week, following hemodialysis

*Creatinine clearance can be related to serum creatinine by the formula below:

$$\text{Males: (mL/min)} = \frac{(140-\text{age [years]})\times(\text{body wt [kg]})}{(72)\times(0.011\times\text{serum creatinine }[\mu\text{mol/L}])}$$

Females: 0.85×the above value

SI units (mL/s) conversion factor=0.01667×value obtained from formula.

I.V. Administration: Infusion concentrations greater than 10 mg/mL are not recommended. Do not administer ganciclovir by rapid or bolus i.v. injection. It should be given by constant i.v. infusion over 1 hour.

Reconstitution of Sterile Lyophilized Powder: Reconstitute by injecting sterile water for injection into the vial (see Table VII).

Table VII—Cytovene I.V.

Reconstitution of Sterile Lyophilized Powder

Vial Size	Diluent to be Added	Approx. Available Volume	Approximate Concentration
500 mg	10 mL	10.29 mL	50 mg/mL

Shake well, until dissolved.

Do not use bacteriostatic water for injection containing parabens, since these are incompatible with ganciclovir sterile powder and may cause precipitation.

The reconstituted solution should be inspected for particulate matter or discoloration prior to proceeding with admixture preparation.

Admixture Preparation: The reconstituted solution is further diluted in one of the solutions listed below for i.v. infusion.

Solutions for I.V. infusion: normal saline, dextrose 5% in water, Ringer's injection, lactated Ringer's injection.

Stability and Storage: Sterile Powder: Store at room temperature (15 to 30°C), avoid excessive heat above 40°C. The reconstituted solution in the vial may be stored at room temperature up to 12 hours and should not be refrigerated.

Ganciclovir, when reconstituted with sterile water for injection, further diluted with 0.9% sodium chloride injection, and stored refrigerated at 5°C in polyvinyl chloride (PVC) bags, remain physically and chemically stable for 14 days. **However, because ganciclovir is reconstituted with nonbacteriostatic sterile water, it is recommended that the infusion solution be used with 24 hours of dilution to reduce the risk of bacterial contamination.** The reconstituted and further diluted solutions should be stored under refrigeration. Freezing is not recommended.

Handling and Disposal: Caution should be exercised in the handling and preparation of ganciclovir solution. Avoid ingestion, inhalation or direct contact with the skin and mucous membranes. Ganciclovir should be considered a potential teratogen and carcinogen in humans. Ganciclovir solutions are

Table V—Cytovene I.V.

Induction and Maintenance Doses of Cytovene I.V. in Renal Impairment

Creatinine Clearance* (mL/min)	I.V. Cytovene Induction Dose (mg/kg)	Dosing Interval (hours)	I.V. Cytovene Maintenance Dose (mg/kg)	Dosing Interval (hours)
≥70	5.0	12	5.0	24
50 to 69	2.5	12	2.5	24
25 to 49	2.5	24	1.25	24
10 to 24	1.25	24	0.625	24
<10	1.25	3 times/week, following hemodialysis	0.625	3 times/week, following hemodialysis

alkaline (pH approximately 11). The use of latex gloves and safety glasses is recommended to avoid exposure in case of breakage of the vial or other accidental spillage. If the solution contacts the skin or mucous membranes, wash thoroughly with soap and water; rinse eyes for at least 15 minutes with plain water. Ganciclovir capsules should not be opened or crushed.

Several guidelines for the handling and disposal of hazardous pharmaceuticals (including cytotoxic drugs) are available (e.g., CSHP, 1991). Disposal of ganciclovir should follow provincial, municipal, and local hospital guidelines or requirements.

Supplied: Capsules: Each opaque, green, hard gelatin capsule, printed in blue with ROCHE logo and CY250 on cap with 2 blue lines partially encircling the capsule body, contains: ganciclovir 250 mg. Nonmedicinal ingredients: croscarmellose sodium, gelatin, indigotine, iron oxide, magnesium stearate, povidone and titanium dioxide. Bottles of 84. Store at controlled room temperature (15 to 30°C).

Sterile Powder: Each 10 mL clear, glass vial of sterile, lyophilized powder contains: ganciclovir sodium equivalent to ganciclovir 500 mg. Sodium: <1 mmol (46 mg). Store at room temperature (15 to 30°C), avoid excessive heat above 40°C.

(Shown in Product Recognition Section)

Reviewed 1999

CYTOXAN® Ⓟ

Bristol

Cyclophosphamide

Antineoplastic Agent

Pharmacology: Cyclophosphamide is activated by metabolism in the liver by the mixed-function oxidase system of the smooth endoplasmic reticulum. The hepatic cytochrome P-450 mixed-function converts cyclophosphamide to 4-hydroxycyclophosphamide, which is in a steady state with the acyclic tautomer, aldophosphamide. The drug and its metabolites are distributed throughout the body including the brain.

Cyclophosphamide, which is biologically relatively inactive, is eliminated from the body very slowly. The activated metabolites alkylate the target sites in susceptible cells in an all-or-none type of reaction or are detoxicated by formation of inactive metabolites that are rapidly excreted by the kidneys.

Cyclophosphamide is absorbed from the gastrointestinal tract and from parenteral sites. It appears to be absorbed also when it is supplied topically to neoplastic tissues, situated on the surface of the body.

Cyclophosphamide is metabolized in the body initially by the mixed function oxidase enzymes of the liver microsomes; several toxic metabolites have been identified.

There is much more variability in the rate of metabolism of cyclophosphamide among different human subjects than there is in non-human species. The plasma half-life of the unchanged drug is apparently independent of age, nationality, sensitivity or resistance to the drug, diagnosis, or dosage. In patients who had received no drug therapy known to affect microsomal metabolic rates, the apparent average half-life of unchanged cyclophosphamide was between 5.0 and 6.5 hours after i.v. administration of C14-labeled cyclophosphamide.

Peak plasma concentrations of metabolites have been found to be almost proportional to the administered dose, but relatively wide individual variations have been reported. Peak plasma alkylating metabolite levels generally are reached at 2 to 3 hours after administration of the drug.

The average plasma alkylating metabolite concentration at 8 hours after i.v. administration of the drug was about 77% of the peak level when studied in 12 patients without prior drug exposure.

Cyclophosphamide does not bind to human plasma proteins in appreciable amounts, but with single i.v. doses about 12 to 14% of the total dose was bound to plasma proteins at plasma cyclophosphamide concentrations of 10 and 200 $m\mu$ moles/mL. Repeated doses increased the amount bound to plasma proteins. Following 5 doses of 40 mg/kg, about 56% of the dose was bound.

The tissue distribution of cyclophosphamide has been examined in cancer patients following i.v. administration. It was found that both unchanged drug and metabolites pass the blood-brain barrier. Cerebral tissue contained drug levels in a concentration range similar to that found in blood.

Biopsies performed 2 hours after administration of the drug revealed that about 30% more drug was present in lymph nodes than in muscle, adipose tissue, or skin, but the relative proportion of unchanged drug metabolites was not established.

In experimental animals, cyclophosphamide inhibits immune phenomena, inflammatory processes, delayed hypersensitivity reactions, experimental allergic inflammatory disease, and body defenses to infectious microorganisms. Although immuno-suppressive and anti-inflammatory actions for cyclophosphamide have not been demonstrated conclusively in humans, they may be associated with the therapeutic use of the drug.

In man, a generally higher proportion of the administered dose is excreted in the urine as metabolites. Recovery of radioactivity after i.v. administered labeled cyclophosphamide ranged from 37% to 82%, with 20% to 45% of that recovered attributable to the unchanged drug. The total urinary excretion of unchanged cyclophosphamide ranged from 3% to 30% of the dose with most cases in the upper half of the range.

Indications: A. Frequently responsive myeloproliferative and lymphoproliferative disorders: malignant lymphomas Stages II to IV: Hodgkin's disease, mixed-cell type lymphoma, lymphocytic lymphoma, histiocytic lymphoma, lymphoblastic lymphosarcoma, Burkitt's lymphoma; multiple myeloma; leukemias: chronic lymphocytic leukemia, chronic granulocytic leukemia (it is ineffective in acute blastic crises), acute myelogenous and monocytic leukemia, acute lymphoblastic (stem-cell) leukemia in children (cyclophosphamide given during remission is effective in prolonging its duration); mycosis fungoides (advanced disease). B. Frequently responsive solid malignancies: neuroblastoma (in patients with disseminated disease), adenocarcinoma of the ovary, retinoblastoma. C. Infrequently responsive malignancies: carcinoma of the breast, malignant neoplasms of the lung.

Contraindications: Sensitivity to cyclophosphamide or to any components of its dosage forms, severe leukopenia, thrombocytopenia, hepatic or renal dysfunction.

Warnings: Caution: Cyclophosphamide is a potent drug and should be used only by physicians experienced with cancer chemotherapeutic drugs (see Precautions). In those patients who develop bacterial, fungal, or viral infections, modification of dosage should be considered. Blood counts should be taken at regular intervals.

Since cyclophosphamide is an inhibitor of serum cholinesterase, patients receiving the drug may exhibit an increased sensitivity to neuromuscular blocking agents such as succinylcholine. If a patient receiving cyclophosphamide is to undergo surgery, advise the anesthesiologist.

The rate of metabolism and the leukopenic activity of cyclophosphamide reportedly are increased by chronic administration of high doses of phenobarbital. The physician should be alert for possible combined drug actions, desirable or undesirable, involving cyclophosphamide even though cyclophosphamide has been used successfully concurrently with other drugs, including other cytotoxic drugs.

Cyclophosphamide has been reported to have oncogenic activity in rats and mice. The possibility that it may have oncogenic potential in man should be considered. Cyclophosphamide may interfere with normal wound healing.

Pregnancy: Cyclophosphamide can be teratogenic or cause fetal resorption in experimental animals. It should not be used in pregnancy, particularly in early pregnancy, unless the potential benefits outweigh the possible risks. Cyclophosphamide is excreted in breast milk and breast-feeding should be terminated prior to institution of cyclophosphamide therapy.

Patients, male or female, capable of conception, ordinarily should be advised of the mutagenic potential of cyclophospha mide. Adequate methods of contraception appear desirable for such patients receiving cyclophosphamide.

Since cyclophosphamide has been reported to be more toxic in adrenalectomized dogs, adjustment of the dose of both replacement steroids and cyclophosphamide may be necessary for the adrenalectomized patient.

Precautions: Administer cautiously to patients with any of the following conditions: leukopenia, thrombocytopenia, tumor cell infiltration of bone marrow, previous x-ray therapy, previous therapy with other cytotoxic agents, impaired hepatic or renal function.

Because cyclophosphamide may exert a suppressive action in immune mechanisms, consider the interruption or modification of dosage for patients who develop bacterial, fungal or viral infections. This is especially true for patients receiving concomitant steroid therapy and perhaps those with a recent history of steroid therapy, since infections in some of these patients have been fatal. Varicella- zoster infections appear to be particularly dangerous under these circumstances.

It is recommended that patients being considered as candidates for long-term therapy have their renal function monitored prior to treatment. Urine should also be examined regularly for red cells which may precede hemorrhagic cystitis.

Adverse Effects: Hematopoietic: Leukopenia is an expected effect and ordinarily is used as a guide to therapy. Thrombocytopenia or anemia may occur in a few patients. These effects are almost always reversible when therapy is interrupted.

Gastrointestinal: Anorexia, nausea, or vomiting are common and related to dose as well as individual susceptibility. There are isolated reports of hemorrhagic colitis, oral mucosal ulceration and jaundice occurring during therapy.

Genitourinary: Sterile hemorrhagic cystitis can result from cyclophosphamide administration. This can be severe, even fatal, and is probably due to metabolites in the urine. Nonhemorrhagic cystitis and/or bladder fibrosis also have been reported to result from cyclophosphamide administration. Atypical epithelial cells may be found in the urinary sediment. Ample fluid intake and frequent voiding help to prevent the development of cystitis, but when it occurs it is ordinarily necessary to interrupt cyclophosphamide therapy. Hematuria usually resolves spontaneously within a few days after cyclophosphamide therapy is discontinued, but may persist for several months. In severe cases, replacement of blood loss may be required. Electrocautery to telangiectatic areas of the bladder and diversion of urine flow has been successfully used in treatment of protracted cases. Cryosurgery has also been used. Nephrotoxicity, including hemorrhage and clot formation in the renal pelvis, has been reported. Hemorrhagic ureteritis and tubular necrosis have been reported in patients treated with cyclophosphamide.

Girls treated with cyclophosphamide during prepubescence generally develop secondary sexual characteristics normally and have regular menses. Ovarian fibrosis with apparently complete loss of germ cells after prolonged cyclophosphamide treatment in late prepubescence has been reported. Girls treated with cyclophosphamide during prepubescence subsequently have conceived.

Men treated with cyclophosphamide may develop oligospermia or azoospermia associated with increased gonadotropin but normal testosterone secretion. Sexual potency and libido are unimpaired in these patients. Boys treated with cyclophosphamide during prepubescence develop secondary sexual characteristics normally but may have oligospermia or azoospermia and increased gonadotropin secretion. Some degree of testicular atrophy may occur. Cyclophosphamide-induced azoospermia is reversible in some patients, though the reversibility may not occur for several years after cessation of therapy. Men temporarily rendered sterile by cyclophosphamide have subsequently fathered normal children.

Integument: It is ordinarily advisable to inform patients in advance of possible alopecia, a frequent complication of cyclophosphamide therapy. Regrowth of hair can be expected although occasionally the new hair may be of a different color or texture. The skin and fingernails may become darker during therapy. Nonspecific dermatitis has been reported to occur with cyclophosphamide.

Pulmonary: Interstitial pulmonary fibrosis has been reported in patients receiving high doses of cyclophosphamide over a prolonged period. There have been reported cases of cyclophosphamide-induced pneumonitis which may continue for one or more months after discontinuation of therapy.

Cardiac Toxicity: Cardiotoxicity has been observed in some patients receiving high doses of cyclophosphamide ranging from 120 to 270 mg/kg administered over a period of a few days, usually as a portion of an intensive antineoplastic multi-drug regimen or in conjunction with transplantation procedures. In a few instances with high doses of cyclophosphamide, severe and sometimes fatal, congestive heart failure has occurred within a few days after the first cyclophosphamide dose. Histopathologic examination has primarily shown hemorrhagic myocarditis.

No residual cardiac abnormalities as evidenced by electrocardiogram or echocardiogram appear to be present in patients surviving episodes of apparent cardiac toxicity associated with high doses of cyclophosphamide.

Cyclophosphamide has been reported to potentiate doxorubicin-induced cardiotoxicity.

Carcinogenesis: Second malignancies have developed in some patients treated with cyclophosphamide used alone or in association with other antineoplastic drugs and/or modalities. Most frequently, they have been urinary bladder, myeloproliferative or lymphoproliferative malignancies. Second malignancies most frequently observed were detected in patients treated for primary myeloproliferative or lymphoproliferative malignancies or nonmalignant disease in which immune processes are believed to be involved pathologically. In some cases, the

Cytoxan (cont'd)

second malignancy developed several years after cyclophosphamide treatment had been discontinued. Urinary bladder malignancies generally have occurred in patients who previously had hemorrhagic cystitis. One case of carcinoma of the renal pelvis was reported in a patient receiving long-term cyclophosphamide therapy for cerebral vasculitis. The possibility of cyclophosphamide-induced malignancy should be considered in any benefit-to-risk assessment for use of the drug.
Adverse reactions in addition to those mentioned have been noted with cyclophosphamide: They include headache, dizziness, hypoprothrombinemia and diabetes mellitus. Also, the possibility of anaphylactic reaction to cyclophosphamide should not be excluded.

Overdose: Symptoms and Treatment: No specific antidote. Institute general supportive measures to sustain the patient through any period of toxicity that might occur.

Concurrent administration of the uroprotective agent Mesna will aid largely in the prevention of bladder toxicity.

Dosage: Chemotherapy with cyclophosphamide, as with other drugs used in cancer chemotherapy, is potentially hazardous and fatal complications can occur. Only physicians aware of the associated risks should administer cyclophosphamide. Therapy may be aimed at either induction or maintenance of remission.
Induction Therapy: The usual initial loading dose for patients with no hematologic deficiency is 40 to 50 mg/kg, usually given i.v. This can be given at the rate of 10 to 20 mg/kg/day for 2 to 5 days depending on patient tolerance.

Patients with any previous treatment that may have compromised the functional capacity of the bone marrow, such as x-ray or cytotoxic drugs, and patients with tumor infiltration of the bone marrow may require reduction of the initial loading dose by one-third to one-half.

A marked leukopenia is usually associated with the above doses, but recovery usually begins after 7 to 10 days. Monitor the white blood cell count closely during induction therapy.

If initial therapy is given orally, a dose of 1 to 5 mg/kg/day can be administered depending on patient tolerance.
Maintenance Therapy: It is frequently necessary to maintain chemotherapy in order to suppress or retard neoplastic growth. A variety of schedules has been used: (1) 1 to 5 mg/kg orally, daily; (2) 10 to 15 mg/kg i.v., every 7 to 10 days; (3) 3 to 5 mg/kg i.v., twice weekly.

Unless the disease is unusually sensitive to cyclophosphamide, the patient should be given the largest maintenance dose that can be reasonably tolerated. The total leukocyte count is a good objective guide for regulating the maintenance dose. Ordinarily, a leukocyte count of 3 000 to 4 000 cells/mm³ can be maintained without undue risk of serious infection or other complications.
Preparation and Handling of Solutions: Prepare Cytoxan for Injection for parenteral use by adding Sterile Water for Injection USP or Bacteriostatic Water for Injection USP (paraben preserved only) to the vial and shaking to dissolve to produce a clear colorless solution. Heating should not be used to facilitate dissolution.
Directions for use: See Table I.

Table I—Cytoxan

Directions for Use

Vial	Diluent Volume	Conc. mg/mL
500 mg	25 mL	20
1 000 mg	50 mL	20
2 000 mg	100 mL	20

Solutions of Cytoxan for Injection may be injected i.v., i.m., intraperitoneally or intrapleurally or they may be infused i.v. in Dextrose Injection USP (5% Dextrose, 5% Dextrose and 0.9% Sodium Chloride) Dextrose 5% and Ringers Injection, Lactated Ringers Injection USP, Sodium Chloride Injection USP (0.45% sodium chloride) and Sodium Lactate Injection USP (1/6 molar sodium lactate). Reconstituted Cytoxan for Injection is chemically and physically stable at room temperature for 24 hours and for 6 days in the refrigerator. For solutions further diluted for i.v. infusion, it is recommended that the solutions be used within 24 hours at room temperature or 72 hours under refrigeration. Solutions prepared with Sterile Water for Injection should be used for single dose administration and any unused solution discarded.

As with all parenteral drug products, i.v. drug admixtures should be inspected visually for clarity, particulate matter, precipitate, discoloration and leakage prior to administration, whenever solution and container permit.

Extemporaneous liquid preparations of Cytoxan for oral administration may be prepared by dissolving Cytoxan for Injection in Aromatic Elixir USP. Store such preparations under refrigeration and use within 14 days.
Handling and Disposal: Preparation of cyclophosphamide should be done in a vertical laminar flow hood (Biological Safety Cabinet—Class II). Personnel preparing cyclophosphamide should wear PVC gloves, safety glasses, disposable gowns and masks. All needles, syringes, vials and other materials which have come in contact with cyclophosphamide should be segregated and incinerated at 1 000°C or more. Sealed containers may explode. Intact vials should be returned to the manufacturer for destruction. Proper precautions should be taken in packaging these materials for transport. Personnel regularly involved in the preparation and handling of cyclophosphamide should have biannual blood examinations.

Supplied: Injection: Each lyophilized vial contains: cyclophosphamide USP 1 000 or 2 000 mg. Nonmedicinal ingredients: mannitol. Cartons of 6.

Tablets: 25 mg: Each white tablet with blue specks contains: cyclophosphamide USP 25 mg. Nonmedicinal ingredients: acacia, cornstarch, D&C yellow No. 10, FD&C blue No. 1, lactose, magnesium stearate, stearic acid and talc. Energy: 4.2 kJ (1 kcal). Bottles of 100.

50 mg: Each white tablet with blue specks contains: cyclophosphamide USP 50 mg. Nonmedicinal ingredients: acacia, cornstarch, D&C yellow No. 10, FD&C blue No. 1, lactose, magnesium stearate, stearic acid and talc. Energy: 8.4 kJ (2 kcal). Bottles of 100.

(Shown in Product Recognition Section)

Suppositories, creams & applicators...

...or the freedom of a single oral dose?

Pr Diflucan-150*

(fluconazole / pfizer)

Simple and preferred for vaginal yeast infections.[1†]

In clinical studies of Diflucan-150, the most common side effects were headache, nausea, abdominal pain and diarrhea. Most side effects were mild-to-moderate in nature. The dosing convenience of oral, single-dose Diflucan-150 should be considered in light of the acceptability of its side effect profile relative to that of topical therapies.

†88% of patients preferred Diflucan-150 over creams and vaginal inserts in an open study of 1017 women.

Reference: 1. Phillips RJM et al. An open multicenter study of the efficacy and safety of a single dose of fluconazole 150 mg in the treatment of vaginal candidiasis in general practice. *Br J Clin Pract* 1990;44:219-222.

PAAB

Pfizer

We're part of the cure

Because
a real test
of any osteoporosis
therapy is
real life.

ON ALL PROVINCIAL FORMULARIES
(EXCEPT ATLANTIC PROVINCES)

Didrocal:*

Proven in clinical trials[1]... experienced in real life.[2]

Significantly decreased vertebral[1†] and non-vertebral fractures.[2]

- 74% of patients remained free of further vertebral fractures through 3 years[1‡]
- Increased vertebral bone mass by 7.6% through 7 years[3†]
- Significantly increased hip bone mass at the trochanter at 3 years[1§]

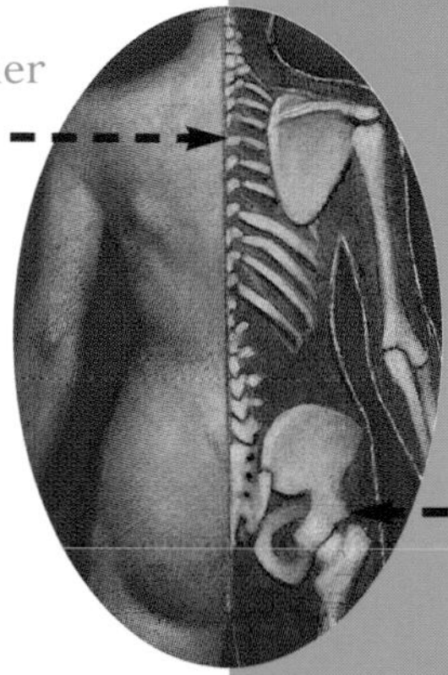

- Epidemiological data based on approximately 16,000 patients have shown a non-vertebral fracture reduction benefit over 3 years[2¶]

24% non-vertebral fracture reduction[2¶]

33% hip fracture reduction[2¶]

Didrocal: tolerability & safety that's been put to the test.

- In clinical trials after 3 years, discontinuation rate due to side effects of 2%[4**]
  – the most common side effects were diarrhea and nausea[1††]
- Over 18 years of world-wide etidronate GI safety data[5]

Patient-friendly: packaged to help promote compliance at less than $0.50/day.[‡‡]

- An alternative therapy for postmenopausal osteoporosis patients who either cannot or prefer not to accept hormone replacement therapy
- Can be taken any time day or night — once daily with water 2 hours before or after eating
- Convenient 90-day kit provides 14 days of the bisphosphonate drug, etidronate disodium to be taken first, and then 76 days of calcium carbonate to complete a full cycle

* Didrocal therapy is indicated for the treatment of established postmenopausal osteoporosis diagnosed by means of objective measuring techniques such as bone densitometry (a bone mineral density of more than 2.67 standard deviations below the young adult mean) or by radiographic evaluation of the spine (≥ 2 vertebral fractures) in women at least 8 years postmenopause. The assessment of vertebral fractures is based upon a minimum 25% reduction in the height of vertebral bodies (anterior, posterior, or central) on lateral radiographs of the spine.

† $p < 0.05$.

‡ In a subpopulation of patients with advanced osteoporosis and at higher risk for vertebral fracture.

§ Increased bone mass by 1-4% at all 3 hip sites with significant difference at the trochanter ($p < 0.05$).

¶ Fracture reduction benefit vs. control in an epidemiological study of ~ 16,000 osteoporotic patients, half of whom received Didrocal.

** In a large, multicentre postmenopausal osteoporosis clinical trial after 3 years, n = 245 (pooled data).

†† In postmenopausal osteoporosis clinical trials, the most common side effects were diarrhea and nausea. In general, side effects in patients who received etidronate were comparable to those in patients who received placebo. Didrocal is contraindicated for patients with clinically overt osteomalacia; appropriate treatment to resolve their osteomalacia should be initiated before prescribing Didrocal therapy. Please see full Prescribing Information for further information on other side effects and patient monitoring.

‡‡ Based on P&G Pharmaceuticals price list 1997, excluding dispensing fee and mark-ups.

IN ESTABLISHED POSTMENOPAUSAL OSTEOPOROSIS

DIDROCAL®

(ETIDRONATE DISODIUM & CALCIUM CARBONATE)

Cyclical Therapy

Easy compliance, reliable efficacy.

Procter&Gamble PHARMACEUTICALS

PAAB MEMBER PMAC

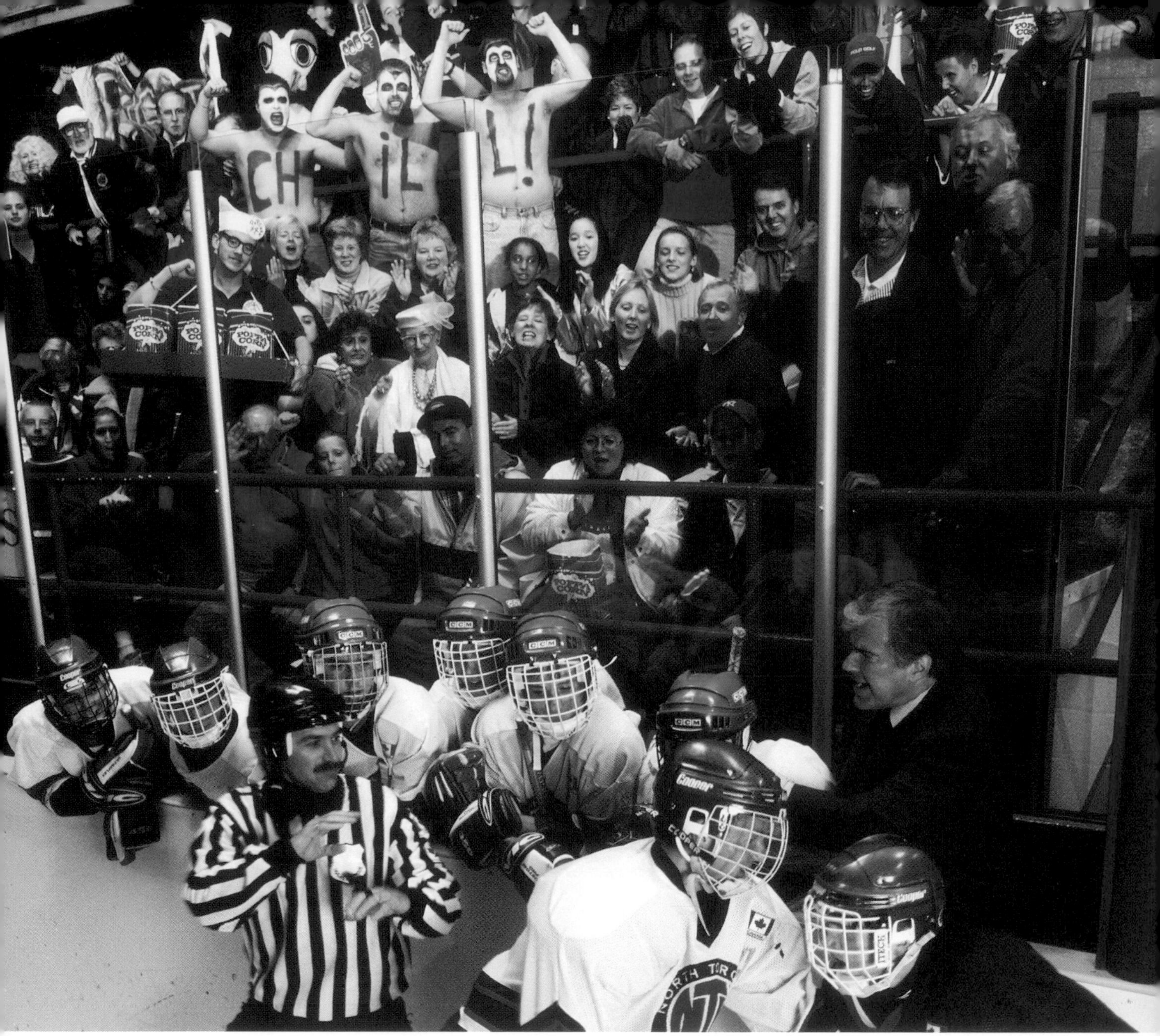

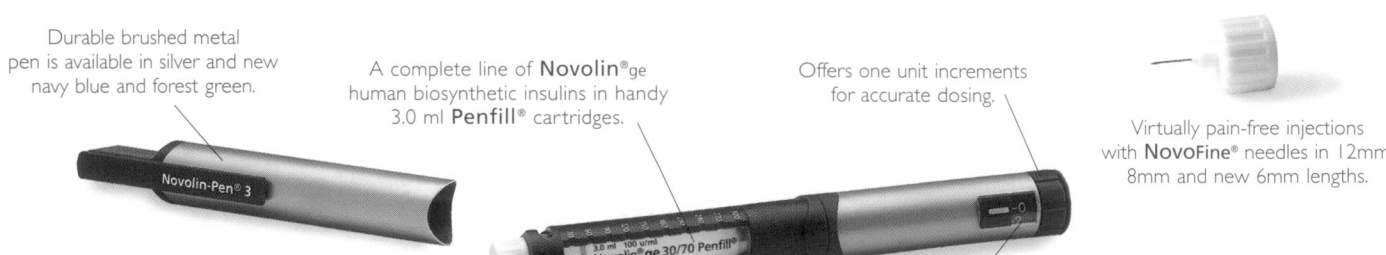

D

DAGENAN® Ⓟ
Rhône-Poulenc Rorer
Sulfapyridine
Antibacterial Sulfonamide

Supplied: Each white, round tablet, marked with logo RPR on one side and Dagenan 500 on the other, contains: sulfapyridine 500 mg. Nonmedicinal ingredients: cornstarch, magnesium stearate, methylcellulose and polacrilin potassium. Sodium- and tartrazine-free. Bottles of 100.

(Shown in Product Recognition Section)

DAIRYAID®
Tanta
Lactase
Lactose Digestant

Supplied: Extra Strength: Each caplet contains: β-D-galactosidase from Aspergillus oryzae 4 500 FCC lactase units. Packs of 80.

Regular Strength: Each white, beveled-edged tablet contains: β-D-galactosidase from Aspergillus oryzae 3 000 FCC lactase units. Packs of 50 and 100.

DALACIN® C Ⓟ
Pharmacia & Upjohn
Clindamycin HCl
Antibiotic

Pharmacology: Clindamycin exerts its antibacterial effect by causing cessation of protein synthesis and also causing a reduction in the rate of synthesis of nucleic acids.

In vitro studies indicate that clindamycin has antibacterial activity against sensitive gram-positive organisms. The spectrum of activity includes staphylococci (including penicillinase-producing and methicillin resistant strains), hemolytic streptococci, S. viridans and S. pneumoniae. In addition, some strains of C. tetani, C. perfringens, C. diphtheriae, P. acnes, A. israelii, H. influenzae, N. gonorrheae and C. trachomatis are sensitive in vitro. Clindamycin is not active against strains of S. faecalis, E. coli, Shigella spp., Salmonella spp., Proteus spp., Pseudomonas spp., and K. pneumoniae.

Clindamycin is rapidly and almost completely absorbed from the gastrointestinal tract in man and peak serum levels are seen in about 45 minutes. The average peak serum level following a single 150 mg dose in adults is 2.74 μg/mL. Therapeutically effective average levels at 6 hours after a 150 mg dose of 0.73 μg/mL are found.

The absorption of clindamycin is not appreciably affected by food intake.

Indications: The treatment of serious infections due to sensitive anaerobic bacteria, such as Bacteroides species, peptostreptococcus, anaerobic streptococci, Clostridium species and microaerophilic streptococci.

Also indicated in serious infections due to sensitive gram-positive organisms (staphylococci, including penicillinase-producing staphylococci, streptococci and pneumococci) when the patient is intolerant of, or the organism resistant to other appropriate antibiotics.

Clindamycin is indicated for prophylaxis against alpha-hemolytic (viridans group) Streptococci before dental, oral and upper respiratory tract surgery.

a) The prophylaxis of bacterial endocarditis in patients allergic to penicillin with any of the following conditions: congenital cardiac malformations, rheumatic and other acquired valvular dysfunction, prosthetic heart valves, previous history of bacterial endocarditis, hypertrophic cardiomyopathy, surgically constructed systemic-pulmonary shunts, mitral valve prolapse with valvular regurgitation or mitral valve prolapse without regurgitation but associated with thickening and/or redundancy of the valve leaflets.

b) Patients taking oral penicillin for prevention or recurrence of rheumatic fever should be given another agent such as clindamycin, for prevention of bacterial endocarditis.

Contraindications: As with all drugs, the use of clindamycin is contraindicated in patients previously found to be hypersensitive to this compound. Although cross-sensitization with lincomycin has not been demonstrated, it is recommended that clindamycin not be used in patients who have demonstrated lincomycin sensitivity.

Until further clinical experience is obtained clindamycin is not indicated in the newborn (infants below 30 days of age), or in pregnant women.

Warnings: Some cases of severe and persistent diarrhea have been reported during or after therapy with clindamycin. This diarrhea has been occasionally associated with blood and mucus in the stools and has at times resulted in acute colitis. When endoscopy has been performed, some of these cases have shown pseudomembrane formation.

If significant diarrhea occurs during therapy, this drug should be discontinued or, if necessary, continued only with close observation. Significant diarrhea occurring up to several weeks post therapy should be managed as if antibiotic-associated.

If colitis is suspected, endoscopy is recommended. Mild cases showing minimal mucosal changes may respond to simple drug discontinuance. Moderate to severe cases, including those showing ulceration or pseudomembrane formation should be managed with fluid, electrolyte and protein supplementation as indicated. Corticoid retention enemas and systemic corticoids may be of help in persistent cases, anticholinergic and antiperistaltic agents may worsen the condition. Other causes of colitis should be considered.

Studies indicate a toxin(s) produced by Clostridia (especially C. difficile) may be a principal cause of clindamycin and other antibiotic-associated colitis. These studies also indicate that this toxigenic Clostridium is usually sensitive in vitro to vancomycin. When 125 mg to 500 mg of vancomycin were administered **orally** 4 times a day for 5 to 10 or more days, there was a rapid observed disappearance of the toxin from fecal samples and a coincidental recovery from the diarrhea.

It should be noted that serious relapses have occurred up to 1 month after apparently successful treatment. A relatively prolonged period of continuing observation is therefore recommended.

Precautions: Clindamycin like any drug, should be prescribed with caution in atopic individuals.

The use of antibiotics occasionally results in overgrowth of nonsusceptible organisms, particularly yeasts. Should superinfections occur, appropriate measures should be taken as dictated by the clinical situation.

As with all antibiotics, perform culture and sensitivity studies in conjunction with drug therapy.

Since abnormalities of liver function tests have been noted occasionally in animals and man, periodic liver function tests should be performed during prolonged therapy. Blood counts should also be monitored during extended therapy.

Clindamycin may be used in anuretic patients. Since the serum half-life of clindamycin in patients with impaired hepatic function is greater than that found in normal patients, the dose of clindamycin should be appropriately decreased. Hemodialysis and peritoneal dialysis are not effective means of removing the compound from the blood. Periodic serum levels should be determined in patients with severe hepatic and renal insufficiency.

Adverse Effects: Only 65 of the 851 patients treated for infections developed side effects representing 7.6% of the total study group or 8% of the 813 patients with follow-up. Only 22 of these patients' symptoms were considered due to clindamycin for an incidence of 2.7% among the 813 cases with follow-up.

Gastrointestinal: Abdominal pain occurred in 12 patients for an overall incidence of 1.4% in 851 patients and was considered drug related in 7 (0.8%).

Diarrhea occurred in 22 cases for an overall incidence of 2.6% and was drug related in 13 (1.5%). Vomiting occurred in 14 cases with an overall incidence of 1.6%. Seven patients (0.8%) had nausea which was drug related in 2 cases (0.2%). Side effects were severe in 10 instances. (see Warnings). Esophagitis, at times severe, has been reported.

Hemopoietic: Transient neutropenia (leukopenia) has been reported. Its relationship to therapy is unknown. No irreversible hematologic toxicity has been reported.

Skin and Mucous Membranes: Skin rashes have been reported in 6 patients (0.7%), none of which could be determined as drug related. One case of urticaria was reported but its relationship to drug therapy could not be determined.

Liver: Although no direct relationship of clindamycin to liver dysfunction has been noted, transient abnormalities in liver function tests (elevations of alkaline phosphatase and serum transaminase) have been observed in a few instances.

Overdose: Symptoms and Treatment: No cases of overdosage have been reported. It would be expected however, that should overdosage occur, gastrointestinal side effects including abdominal pain, nausea, vomiting and diarrhea might be seen. During clinical trials, one 3 year old child was given 100 mg/kg of clindamycin for 5 days and showed mild abdominal pain and diarrhea. One 13 year old patient was given 75 mg/kg for 5 days with no side effects. In both cases laboratory values remained normal.

Overdosage should be treated with simple gastric lavage. No specific antidote is known.

Dosage: Adults: 150 mg every 6 hours; moderately severe infections: 300 mg every 6 hours; severe infections: 450 mg every 6 hours. Children (over 1 month of age): One of the following two dosage ranges should be selected depending on the severity of the infection: 1) 8 to 16 mg/kg/day divided into 3 or 4 equal doses. 2) 16 to 20 mg/kg/day divided into 3 or 4 equal doses.

Absorption of clindamycin is not appreciably modified by ingestion of food and may be taken with meals.

To avoid the possibility of esophageal irritation, clindamycin capsules should be taken with a full glass of water.

For prevention of endocarditis: Adults: 300 mg orally 1 hour before procedure; then 150 mg 6 hours after initial dose.

Children: 10 mg/kg (not to exceed adult dose) orally 1 hour before procedure; then 5 mg/kg 6 hours after initial dose.

Note: With ß-hemolytic streptococcal infections, treatment should continue for at least 10 days to diminish the likelihood of subsequent rheumatic fever or glomerulonephritis.

Supplied: 150 mg: Each hard gelatin capsule with maroon cap and lavender body, branded "Upjohn 225", contains: clindamycin HCl hydrate equivalent to 150 mg of clindamycin base. Nonmedicinal ingredients: cornstarch, lactose, magnesium stearate and talc. Sodium: <1 mmol (0.3 mg). Gluten-free. Bottles of 100 and 500.

300 mg: Each hard gelatin capsule with light blue cap and body branded, "Upjohn 395" contains: clindamycin HCl hydrate equivalent to 300 mg of clindamycin base. Nonmedicinal ingredients: cornstarch, lactose, magnesium stearate and talc. Sodium: <1 mmol. Gluten-free. Bottles of 100 and 500.

(Shown in Product Recognition Section)

DALACIN® C FLAVORED GRANULES Ⓟ
Pharmacia & Upjohn
Clindamycin Palmitate HCl
Antibiotic

Pharmacology: Clindamycin palmitate is a water soluble palmitic acid ester of clindamycin. The intact ester is essentially inactive as an antibacterial agent. Chemical or enzymatic hydrolysis of clindamycin palmitate is necessary to obtain the antibiotic activity of the clindamycin base. Clindamycin base exerts its antibacterial effect by causing cessation of protein synthesis and also be causing a reduction in the rate of synthesis of nucleic acids.

In vitro studies indicate that clindamycin has antibacterial activity against sensitive gram-positive organisms. The spectrum of activity includes staphylococci (including penicillinase-producing and methicillin resistant strains), β hemolytic streptococci, S. viridans and S. pneumoniae. In addition, some strains of C. tetani, C. perfringens, C. diptheriae, P. acnes, A. israelii and M. pneumoniae are sensitive in vitro. Clindamycin is not active against strains of S. faecalis, E. coli, Shigella spp., Salmonella spp., Proteus spp., Pseudomonas spp., and K. pneumoniae.

Indications: The treatment of serious infections due to sensitive anaerobic bacteria, such as Bacteroides species, Peptostreptococcus, anaerobic streptococci, Clostridium species and microaerophilic streptococci.

Also indicated in serious infections due to sensitive gram-positive organisms (staphylococci, including penicillinase-producing staphylococci, streptococci and pneumococci)

Dalacin C Flavored Granules (cont'd)

when the patient is intolerant of, or the organism resistant to other appropriate antibiotics.

Clindamycin palmitate is indicated for prophylaxis against alpha-hemolytic (viridans group) Streptococci before dental, oral and upper respiratory tract surgery.

a) The prophylaxis of bacterial endocarditis in patients allergic to penicillin with any of the following conditions: congenital cardiac malformations, rheumatic and other acquired valvular dysfunction, prosthetic heart valves, previous history of bacterial endocarditis, hypertrophic cardiomyopathy, surgically constructed systemic-pulmonary shunts, mitral valve prolapse with valvular regurgitation or mitral valve prolapse without regurgitation but associated with thickening and/or redundancy of the valve leaflets.

b) Patients taking oral penicillin for prevention or recurrence of rheumatic fever should be given another agent such as clindamycin, for prevention of bacterial endocarditis.

Contraindications: In patients previously found to be hypersensitive to this compound, or any of its salts. Although cross-sensitization with lincomycin has not been demonstrated, it is recommended that clindamycin palmitate not be used in patients who have demonstrated lincomycin sensitivity.

Until further clinical experience is obtained, clindamycin palmitate is not indicated in the newborn (infants below 30 days of age), or in pregnant women.

Warnings: Some cases of severe and persistent diarrhea have been reported during or after therapy with clindamycin palmitate. This diarrhea has been occasionally associated with blood and mucus in the stools and has at times resulted in acute colitis. When endoscopy has been performed, some of these cases have shown pseudomembrane formation.

If significant diarrhea occurs during therapy, this drug should be discontinued, or, if necessary, continued only with close observation. Significant diarrhea occurring up to several weeks post therapy should be managed as if antibiotic-associated.

If colitis is suspected, endoscopy is recommended. Mild cases showing minimal mucosal changes may respond to simple drug discontinuance. Moderate to severe cases, including those showing ulceration or pseudomembrane formation, should be managed with fluid, electrolyte, and protein supplementation as indicated. Corticoid retention enemas and systemic corticoids may be of help in persistent cases. Anticholinergics and antiperistaltic agents may worsen the condition. Other causes of colitis should be considered.

Studies indicate a toxin(s) produced by Clostridia (especially C. difficile) may be a principal cause of clindamycin and other antibiotic-associated colitis. These studies also indicate that this toxigenic Clostridium is usually sensitive in vitro to vancomycin. When 125 to 500 mg of vancomycin were administered **orally** 4 times a day for 5 to 10 or more days, there was a rapid observed disappearance of the toxin from fecal samples and a coincidental recovery from the diarrhea.

It should be noted that serious relapses have occurred up to 1 month after apparently successful treatment. A relatively prolonged period of continuing observation is therefore recommended.

Precautions: Clindamycin palmitate like any other drug, should be prescribed with caution in atopic individuals.

The use of antibiotics occasionally results in overgrowth of non-susceptible organisms, particularly yeasts. Should superinfections occur, appropriate measures should be taken as dictated by the clinical situation.

As with all antibiotics, perform culture and sensitivity studies in conjunction with drug therapy.

Since abnormalities of liver function tests have been noted occasionally in animals and man, periodic liver function tests should be performed during prolonged therapy. Blood counts should also be monitored during extended therapy.

Clindamycin palmitate may be used in anuretic patients. Since the serum half-life of clindamycin in patients with impaired hepatic function is greater than that found in normal patients, the dose should be appropriately decreased. Hemodialysis and peritoneal dialysis are not effective means of removing the compound from the blood. Periodic serum levels should be determined in patients with severe hepatic and renal insufficiency.

Adverse Effects: Only 23 of the 340 patients receiving clindamycin palmitate developed side effects representing 6.8% of the patients with follow-up.

Gastrointestinal: Gastrointestinal side effects were reported by 7 patients (2.05%). Of these 7 patients, 4 reported diarrhea (1.2%) and 3 had other complaints related to the gastrointestinal tract (see Warnings).

Table I—Dalacin C Flavored Granules

Dosage Ranges

Weight (kg)	8-12 mg/kg/day	13-16 mg/kg/day	17-25 mg/kg/day
10–18.2	37.5 mg q 6 h	75 mg q 8 h	75 mg q 6 h
18.2–25	75 mg q 8 h	75 mg q 6 h	150 mg q 8 h
25–34	75 mg q 6 h	150 mg q 8 h	150 mg q 6 h
34–45.4	150 mg q 8 h	150 mg q 6 h	300 mg q 8 h
45.5 and over	150 mg q 6 h	300 mg q 6 h	450 mg q 6 h

Hemopoietic: Transient neutropenia (leukopenia) has been reported with clindamycin but not with clindamycin palmitate. Its relationship to therapy is unknown. No irreversible hematologic toxicity has been reported with either compound.

Skin and Mucous Membranes: Skin rashes have been reported in 9 patients (2.8%) treated with clindamycin palmitate. The rashes were described as maculopapular.

Liver: Although no direct relationship of clindamycin palmitate to liver dysfunction has been noted, transient abnormalities in liver function tests (elevations of alkaline phosphatase and serum transaminase) have been observed in a few instances.

CNS: Two patients in a Canadian series of 143 patients complained of drowsiness and one had a nightmare during therapy with clindamycin palmitate.

Overdose: Symptoms and Treatment: No cases of overdosage have been reported. It would be expected however, that should overdosage occur, gastrointestinal side effects including abdominal pain, nausea, vomiting and diarrhea might be seen. During clinical trials, one 3 year old child was given 100 mg/kg of clindamycin for 5 days and showed mild abdominal pain and diarrhea. One 13 year old patient was given 75 mg/kg of clindamycin for 5 days with no side effects. In both cases laboratory values remained normal. In a study in normal adult volunteers up to 1 800 mg/day for 21 days of clindamycin palmitate was given with only a change in the consistency and frequency of stools reported as well as 3 rashes, 2 cases of nausea and 1 case of dizziness.

Dosage: Children (over 1 month of age): One of the following three dosage ranges should be selected depending on the severity of the infection: 8 to 12 mg/kg/day divided into 3 or 4 equal doses or 13 to 16 mg/kg/day divided into 3 or 4 equal doses or 17 to 25 mg/kg/day divided into 3 or 4 equal doses (see Table I).

Note: In cases of β-hemolytic streptococcal infections, treatment should continue for at least 10 days to diminish the likelihood of subsequent rheumatic fever or glomerulonephritis.

For prevention of endocarditis: Adults: 300 mg orally 1 hour before procedure; then 150 mg 6 hours after initial dose.

Children: 10 mg/kg (not to exceed adult dose) orally 1 hour before procedure; then 5 mg/kg 6 hours after initial dose.

Supplied: After reconstitution with 80 mL demineralized or distilled water, each 5 mL of solution contains: clindamycin palmitate HCl equivalent to 75 mg clindamycin base. Nonmedicinal ingredients: artificial cherry flavor, dextrin, ethyl paraben, methylene chloride, pluronic F68, polymethylsiloxane, sucrose. Energy: 25.1 kJ (6 kcal)/5 mL. Sodium: trace. Gluten-free. Bottles of 100 mL.

Note: Do not refrigerate the reconstituted solution since under conditions of low temperature, the solution may thicken and is difficult to pour. The reconstituted solution is stable at room temperature for 14 days.

DALACIN® C PHOSPHATE STERILE SOLUTION ℞

Pharmacia & Upjohn

Clindamycin Phosphate

Antibiotic

Pharmacology: Following parenteral administration, biologically inactive clindamycin phosphate is rapidly hydrolyzed in plasma to active clindamycin. Clindamycin exerts its antibacterial effect by binding to the 50 S ribosomal subunit of susceptible bacteria, causing a reduction in the rate of synthesis of nucleic acid, and cessation of protein synthesis.

Clindamycin is primarily bacteriostatic, but may be bactericidal at high concentrations. The mechanism of action of clindamycin in combination with primaquine P. carinii is not known.

Pharmacokinetics: See Table I. Clindamycin is distributed into body fluids and tissues including bone, synovial fluid, bile and pleural fluid. Significant levels of clindamycin are not reached in cerebrospinal fluid even in the presence of inflamed meninges. Clindamycin readily crosses the placenta and is distributed into breast milk. The half-life of clindamycin phosphate is 3.5 to 4.5 hours. Approximately 10% of the microbiologically active form is excreted in the urine and about 4% in the feces. The remainder is excreted as biologically inactive metabolites.

Table I—Dalacin C Phosphate Sterile Solution

Average Peak Serum Concentrations After Dosing with Clindamycin Phosphate

Clindamycin Phosphate Dosage Regimen	Clindamycin µg/mL	Clindamycin Phosphate µg/mL
Healthy Adult Male (Post Equilibrium)		
300 mg i.v. in 10 min, q8h	7	15
600 mg i.v. in 20 min, q8h	10	23
900 mg i.v. in 30 min, q12h	11	29
1 200 mg i.v. in 45 min, q12h	14	49
300 mg i.m. q8h	6	3
600 mg i.m. q12h*	9	3
Children (first dose)*		
5-7 mg/kg i.v. in 1 hour	10	
3-5 mg/kg i.m.	4	
5-7 mg/kg i.m.	8	

*Data in this group from patients being treated for infection.

Indications: For the treatment of serious infections due to susceptible anaerobic bacteria, such as Bacteroides species, Peptostreptococcus, anaerobic streptococci, Clostridium species and microaerophilic streptococci.

Also indicated for the treatment of serious infections due to susceptible strains of gram-positive aerobic bacteria (staphylococci, including penicillinase-producing staphylococci, streptococci and pneumococci) as well as in the treatment of C. trachomatis, when the patient is intolerant of, or the organism resistant to other appropriate antibiotics.

Because of the risk of antibiotic-associated pseudomembranous colitis as described in the Warnings section, before selecting clindamycin the physician should consider the nature of the infection and the suitability of alternative therapy.

Clindamycin phosphate is indicated for the treatment of the following serious infections when caused by susceptible strains of the designated organisms in the conditions listed below: Lower respiratory infections including pneumonia, empyema, and lung abscess when caused by anaerobes, S. pneumoniae, other streptococci (except E. faecalis) and S. aureus.

Skin and skin structure infections including cellulitis, abscesses, and wound infections when caused by S. pyogenes. S. aureus and anaerobes.

Gynecological infections including endometritis, pelvic cellulitis, vaginal cuff infections, nongonococcal tubo-ovarian abscess, salpingitis, and pelvic inflammatory disease when caused by susceptible anaerobes or C. trachomatis. Clindamycin should be given in conjunction with an antibiotic of appropriate gram-negative aerobic spectrum.

Intra-abdominal infections including peritonitis and abdominal abscess when caused by susceptible anaerobes. Clindamycin should be given in conjunction with an antibiotic of appropriate gram-negative aerobic spectrum.

Septicemia caused by S. aureus, streptococci (except E. faecalis) and susceptible anaerobes, where the bactericidal efficacy of clindamycin against the infecting organism has been determined in vitro at achievable serum levels.

Bone and joint infections including osteomyelitis and septic arthritis when caused by sensitive strains of S. aureus and anaerobes.

P. carinii pneumonia in patients with AIDS. Clindamycin in combination with primaquine may be used in patients who are intolerant to, or fail to respond to conventional therapy.

Note: Clindamycin phosphate is not indicated in the treatment of meningitis since it penetrates poorly into cerebrospinal fluid, even in the presence of inflamed meninges.

Bacteriologic studies should be performed to determine the causative organisms and their susceptibility to clindamycin.

Indicated surgical procedures and drainage should be performed in conjunction with antibiotic therapy.

Contraindications: In patients with a known hypersensitivity to preparations containing clindamycin or lincomycin.

Warnings: Dalacin C Phosphate contains benzyl alcohol. Benzyl alcohol has been reported to be associated with a fatal "Gasping Syndrome" in premature infants.

Clindamycin has been associated with severe antibiotic-associated colitis. Severe colitis may be fatal if left untreated. If significant diarrhea occurs during therapy, this drug should be discontinued or, if necessary, continued only with close observation. It should be noted that diarrhea, colitis and pseudomembranous colitis have been observed to begin up to 1 month after discontinuation of medication. A relatively prolonged period of continuing observation is therefore recommended.

The diagnosis of colitis is usually made by recognition of the clinical symptoms. Colitis has a clinical spectrum from mild, watery diarrhea to severe, persistent diarrhea, leukocytosis, fever, severe abdominal cramps which may be associated with the passage of blood and mucus, and which, if allowed to progress, may produce peritonitis, shock and toxic megacolon.

If colitis is suspected, endoscopy is recommended. Endoscopic examination may reveal pseudomembranous colitis. Stool culture for C. difficile and stool assay for C. difficile toxin may be helpful diagnostically.

Mild cases showing minimal mucosal changes may respond to simple drug discontinuance. Moderate to severe cases, including those showing ulceration or pseudomembrane formation should be managed with fluid, electrolyte, and protein supplementation as indicated. Corticoid retention enemas and systemic corticoids may be of help in persistent cases. Anticholinergics and antiperistaltic agents may worsen colitis. Other causes of colitis should be considered.

Studies indicate a toxin(s) produced by C. difficile is the primary cause of antibiotic-associated colitis and that toxigenic Clostridium is usually sensitive in vitro to vancomycin. When 125 mg to 500 mg of vancomycin was administered orally 4 times a day for 5 to 10 days, there was a rapid observed disappearance of the toxin from fecal samples and a coincidental recovery from the diarrhea.

In patients with G-6-PD deficiency, the combination of clindamycin with primaquine may cause hemolytic reactions; reference should also be made to the primaquine product monograph for other possible risk groups for other hematologic reactions.

Precautions: General: Clindamycin phosphate should be prescribed with caution in atopic individuals and in individuals with a history of gastrointestinal disease particularly colitis.

Clindamycin phosphate does not diffuse adequately into cerebrospinal fluid and thus should not be used in the treatment of meningitis.

Clindamycin phosphate must be diluted for i.v. administration. It should not be injected undiluted as an i.v. bolus (see Dosage).

The use of antibiotics occasionally results in overgrowth of nonsusceptible organisms, particularly yeasts. Should superinfections occur, appropriate measures should be taken as dictated by the clinical situation.

Periodic liver and kidney function tests and blood counts should be performed during prolonged therapy.

Clindamycin phosphate dose modification is not necessary in patients with renal disease. In patients with moderate to severe liver disease, prolongation of the half-life of clindamycin has been found, but a pharmacokinetic study has shown that, when given every 8 hours, accumulation of clindamycin should rarely occur. Therefore, dosage reduction in liver disease is not generally considered necessary.

Geriatrics: Experience has demonstrated that antibiotic-associated colitis may occur more frequently and with increased severity among elderly (>60 years) and debilitated patients.

Pregnancy: Reproduction studies have been performed in rats and mice using s.c. and oral doses of clindamycin ranging from 20 to 600 mg/kg/day and have revealed no evidence of impaired fertility or harm to the fetus due to clindamycin. In 1 mouse strain, cleft palates were observed in treated fetuses; this response was not produced in other mouse strains or in other species, and therefore may be a strain specific effect.

Safety for use in pregnancy has not been established.

Lactation: Clindamycin has been reported to appear in breast milk in the range of 0.7 to 3.8 μg/mL at doses of 150 mg orally to 600 mg i.v. Because of the potential for adverse reactions in neonates, a decision should be made whether to discontinue nursing or to not administer clindamycin after taking into account the importance of the drug to the mother.

Drug Interactions: Antagonism has been demonstrated between clindamycin and erythromycin in vitro. Because of a possible clinical significance, the two drugs should not be administered concurrently.

Clindamycin has been shown to have neuromuscular blocking properties that may enhance the action of other neuromuscular blocking agents. Therefore, it should be used with caution in patients receiving such agents.

Adverse Effects: Gastrointestinal: abdominal pain, nausea, vomiting and diarrhea, colitis (see Warnings). An unpleasant or metallic taste has occasionally been reported after i.v. administration of higher doses of clindamycin phosphate.

Hypersensitivity Reactions: Maculopapular rash and urticaria have been observed during drug therapy. Generalized mild to moderate morbilliform-like skin rashes are the most frequently reported reactions. Rare instances of erythema multiforme, some resembling Stevens-Johnson syndrome, have been associated with clindamycin. A few cases of anaphylactoid reactions have been reported.

Liver: Jaundice and abnormalities in liver function tests have been observed during clindamycin therapy.

Skin and Mucous Membranes: Pruritus, vaginitis and rare instances of exfoliative and vesiculobullous dermatitis have been reported.

Hematopoietic: Transient neutropenia (leukopenia) and eosinophilia have been reported. Reports of agranulocytosis and thrombocytopenia have been made. No direct etiologic relationship to concurrent clindamycin therapy could be made in any of these instances. However, in clindamycin/primaquine combination studies, serious hematologic toxicities (grade III, grade IV neutropenia or anemia, platelet counts $<50\times10^9$/L, or methemoglobin levels of 15% or greater) have been observed.

Cardiovascular: Rare instances of cardiopulmonary arrest and hypotension have been reported following too rapid i.v. administration (see Dosage).

Renal: Although no direct relationship of clindamycin to renal damage has been established, renal dysfunction as evidenced by azotemia, oliguria and/or proteinuria has been observed in rare instances.

Musculoskeletal: Rare instances of polyarthritis have been reported.

Local Reactions: Local irritation, pain, abscess formation have been seen with i.m. injection. Thrombophlebitis has been reported with i.v. injection. These reactions can be minimized by deep i.m. injection and avoidance of indwelling i.v. catheters.

Overdose: Symptoms and Treatment: Reported cases of overdosage have occurred very infrequently. The majority of these reports have involved infants and young children ranging in age from 1 day to 3 years. In this age group, doses as high as 2.4 g have been used i.v. in 36 hours without observation of adverse reactions. Hemodialysis and peritoneal dialysis are not effective in removing clindamycin from the serum. No specific antidote is known.

Dosage: Note: If diarrhea occurs during treatment, this antibiotic should be discontinued (see Warnings).

Dosage and route of administration should be determined by the severity of the infection, the condition of the patient and the susceptibility of the causative microorganisms.

In cases of β-hemolytic streptococcal infections, treatment should be continued for at least 10 days.

Adults (I.M. or I.V. Administration): The usual daily adult dosage for infections of the intra-abdominal area, female pelvis, and other complicated or serious infections is 2 400 to 2 700 mg given in 2, 3 or 4 equal doses. Less complicated infections may respond to lower doses such as 1 200 to 1 800 mg/day administered in 3 or 4 equal doses.

Doses of up to 4 800 mg daily have been used without adverse effects. Single i.m. doses of greater than 600 mg are not recommended.

Pelvic Inflammatory Disease: 900 mg (i.v.) every 8 hours plus an antibiotic with appropriate gram-negative aerobic spectrum administered i.v. Treatment with i.v. drugs should continue for at least 48 hours after the patient demonstrates significant clinical improvement. Then continue with appropriate oral therapy to complete 10 to 14 days total therapy.

P. carinii pneumonia in patients with AIDS: 600 to 900 mg (i.v.) every 6 hours or 900 mg (i.v.) every 8 hours in combination with oral daily dose of 15 to 30 mg of primaquine. Alternatively, clindamycin HCl 300 to 450 mg may be given orally every 6 hours in combination with 15 to 30 mg of primaquine for 21 days. If patients should develop serious hemotologic adverse effects, reducing the dosage regimen of primaquine and/or clindamycin phosphate should be considered.

Children over 1 month of age (I.M. or I.V. Administration): 20 to 40 mg/kg/day in 3 or 4 equal doses. The higher doses would be used for more severe infections.

Neonates under 1 month of age (I.M. or I.V. Administration): 10 to 20 mg/kg/day in 3 or 4 equal doses. The lower dosage may be adequate for small prematures. See Table II.

Table II—Dalacin C Phosphate Sterile Solution

Dosage—Neonates

Weight	Age	Dose	Route
<2 kg	0–7 days	5 mg/kg q12h	i.v.
<2 kg	8–30 days	5 mg/kg q8h	i.v.
≥2 kg	0–7 days	5 mg/kg q8h	i.v.
≥2 kg	8–30 days	5 mg/kg q6h	i.v.

Note: Clindamycin phosphate injections should be administered with caution to newborn infants less than 30 days of age. This product contains benzyl alcohol which has been associated with a fatal gasping syndrome in infants.

Dilution and Infusion Rates: Clindamycin phosphate must be diluted prior to i.v. administration (see Preparation for I.V. Use for a listing of infusion solutions). The concentration in diluent for infusion should not exceed 18 mg/mL. Infusion rates should **not exceed 30 mg/min** as indicated in Table III.

Table III—Dalacin C Phosphate Sterile Solution

Dilution and Infusion Rates

Dose (mg)	Diluent (mL)	Time (min)
300	50	10
600	50	20
900	100	30
1 200	100	45

Administration of more than 1 200 mg in a single 1-hour infusion is not recommended.

Alternatively, the drug may be administered in the form of a single rapid infusion of the first dose followed by continuous i.v. infusion as in Table IV.

Table IV—Dalacin C Phosphate Sterile Solution

Maintenance of Serum Levels

To Maintain Serum Clindamycin Levels	Rapid Infusion Rate	Maintenance Infusion Rate
Above 4 μg/mL	10 mg/min for 30 min	0.75 mg/min
Above 5 μg/mL	15 mg/min for 30 min	1 mg/min
Above 6 μg/mL	20 mg/min for 30 min	1.25 mg/min

Parenteral Products: All parenteral products should be visually inspected for heaviness, particulate matter, discoloration and leakage prior to administration.

Preparation for I.V. Use: Clindamycin phosphate was found to be compatible over a period of 24 hours when 4 mL (600 mg) of clindamycin phosphate was diluted in 1 000 mL of the following commonly used infusion solutions: Sodium chloride injection, Dextrose 5% in water, Dextrose 5% in saline, Dextrose 5% in Ringer's Solution, Dextrose 5% in half-strength saline plus 40 mEq potassium chloride, Dextrose 2½% in Lactated Ringer's Solution (Hartmann's Solution).

Compatibility with Other Products: Clindamycin phosphate was not stable when added to Dextrose 5% in water plus vitamins. **Although clindamycin phosphate is compatible with Dextrose 5% in water, it is not recommended that clindamycin phosphate be mixed with any infusion solutions containing B vitamins.**

Clindamycin phosphate has been shown to be compatible with gentamicin sulfate, tobramycin sulfate and amikacin sulfate. However, a precipitate has been observed when clindamycin and gentamicin are drawn undiluted into the same syringe before subsequent dilution. This precipitate appears to be a zinc-clindamycin complex which results from the zinc content of some gentamicin products. The particle size of the insoluble material is very small and disappears when the admixture is shaken. To avoid this problem, do not mix clindamycin phosphate and gentamicin sulfate prior to dilution. Rather, dilute one drug or the other, agitate the solution and then add the second antibiotic.

Supplied: Each mL of sterile solution contains: clindamycin phosphate equivalent to 150 mg of clindamycin base, benzyl alcohol 9 mg, disodium edetate 0.5 mg and water for injection q.s. When necessary, the pH is adjusted with sodium hydroxide and/or hydrochloric acid to maintain a pH range of 5.5 to 7.0. Vials of 2, 4 and 6 mL. Pharmacy bulk vials of 60 mL. **The availability of the pharmacy bulk vial is limited**

Dalacin C Phosphate Sterile Solution (cont'd)

to hospitals with a pharmacy based i.v. admixture program. The pharmacy bulk vial is intended for single puncture, multiple dispensing for i.v. use only.

Reviewed 1999

DALACIN® T TOPICAL SOLUTION

Pharmacia & Upjohn

Clindamycin Phosphate

Antibiotic

Pharmacology: Clindamycin phosphate is inactive in vitro but in vivo hydrolysis converts this compound to the antibacterially active clindamycin. Clindamycin has been shown to have in vitro activity against isolates of P. acnes which may account for its usefulness in acne. Clindamycin activity has been demonstrated in serum, urine and in comedonal extracts from acne patients.

The mean concentration of antibiotic activity in extracted comedones after application of clindamycin topical solution for 4 weeks was 597 μg/g of comedonal material (range 60 to 1 490). Clindamycin in vitro inhibits P. acnes cultures tested.

Indications: For the treatment of acne vulgaris.

Contraindications: In individuals with a history of hypersensitivity to preparations containing clindamycin or lincomycin, a history of regional enteritis or ulcerative colitis, or a history of antibiotic-associated colitis.

Pregnancy: Safety in pregnancy has not been established.

Warnings: As with most antibiotics, oral and parenteral clindamycin have been associated with severe diarrhea and pseudomembranous colitis. Diarrhea and colitis including pseudomembranous colitis have been reported infrequently with topical clindamycin. Symptoms can occur after a few days, weeks or months following initiation of clindamycin therapy. They have also been observed to begin up to several weeks after cessation of therapy with clindamycin. Therefore, the physician should be alert to the possible development of antibiotic-associated diarrhea or colitis. If significant or prolonged diarrhea occurs, the drug should be discontinued.

Studies indicate that a toxin produced by C. difficile is the major cause of antibiotic-associated colitis which is characterized by severe persistent diarrhea, severe abdominal cramps and in some cases with passage of blood and mucus in the stool. Endoscopic examination may reveal pseudomembranous colitis. Stool culture for C. difficile and assay for C. difficile toxin may be helpful diagnostically.

Mild cases of colitis may respond to simple drug discontinuance. Vancomycin is effective in the treatment of antibiotic-associated colitis produced by C. difficile. The usual dose is 125 to 500 mg orally, every 6 to 8 hours for 7 to 10 days. Additional supportive medical care may be necessary.

Cholestyramine and colestipol resins have been shown to bind C. difficile toxin in vitro, and cholestyramine has been effective in the treatment of some mild cases of antibiotic-associated colitis. Cholestyramine resins have been shown to bind vancomycin; therefore, when both cholestyramine and vancomycin are used concurrently, their administration should be separated by at least 2 hours.

Anticholinergics and antiperistaltic agents may worsen colitis.

Precautions: Clindamycin contains an alcohol base which will cause burning and irritation of the eye. In the event of accidental contact with sensitive surfaces (eye, abraded skin, mucous membranes), bathe with copious amounts of cool tap water.

The solution has an unpleasant taste and caution should be exercised when applying medication around the mouth.

Clindamycin should be prescribed with caution in atopic individuals.

Pregnancy: Safety for use in pregnancy has not been established.

Lactation: It is not known whether clindamycin when topically applied is excreted in human milk. However, oral and parenteral clindamycin have been reported to appear in breast milk and therefore, nursing should not be undertaken while a patient is on the drug.

Adverse Effects: In a large U.S. postmarketing surveillance study among 1 298 patients treated only with topical clindamycin phosphate solution, skin dryness/irritation, diarrhea or gastrointestinal symptoms were the most commonly reported medical events. Of those, 258 (19.9%) reported 1 or more of the following dermatological events: dry skin, acne worse, rash/redness, peeling, discoloration, irritation, itching, new acne, sunburn and contact dermatitis. Among patients treated with oral antibiotics only, or no antibiotics, the percentage of patients reporting dermatologic event(s) was 20.8% and 25.4% respectively.

The following new gastrointestinal problems were reported in this surveillance study by 18.7% of the clindamycin treated patients, 22.9% of the oral antibiotic treated patients, and 18.4% of the patients with no antibiotic exposure: abdominal pain/cramps, nausea, flu/virus, indigestion, gas/bloating, nervous stomach, ulcers, vomiting and colon problems (not colitis).

Cases of diarrhea, bloody diarrhea and colitis (including pseudomembranous colitis) have been reported as adverse reactions in patients treated with topical formulations of clindamycin. Diarrhea was reported in 5% of clindamycin patients, compared to 3.9% of control patients.

In addition to the above, the following side effects have also been occasionally reported during drug treatment with clindamycin topical solution: oily skin and gram-negative folliculitis.

Dosage: Apply a thin film of topical solution twice daily to the clean and dry skin in the area to be treated. Patients responding to clindamycin topical solution should show improvement in 8 weeks. Treatment beyond 12 weeks may call for evaluation by the physician.

Information for the Patient: See Blue Section—Information for the Patient "Dalacin T Topical Solution".

Supplied: Each mL of topical solution contains: clindamycin phosphate equivalent to clindamycin 10 mg. Nonmedicinal ingredients: isopropyl alcohol 50% v/v, propylene glycol and water. Bottles of 30 and 60 mL. A dab-o-matic applicator and cap is provided external to each bottle for placement into the bottle. To assist the patient, the pharmacist may assemble the bottle upon dispensing as follows: remove cap from bottle and discard, firmly press applicator into bottle, seal firmly by tightening domed-cap. Store in an upright fashion.

DALACIN® VAGINAL CREAM

Pharmacia & Upjohn

Clindamycin Phosphate

Antibacterial

Pharmacology: Although clindamycin phosphate is inactive in vitro, in vivo hydrolysis converts this compound to the antibacterially-active clindamycin. Clindamycin inhibits bacterial protein synthesis by its action at the bacterial ribosome. The antibiotic preferentially binds to the 50S ribosomal subunit, and affects the process of peptide chain initiation. Clindamycin may inhibit the binding of aminoacyl-tRNA or inhibit the translocation reaction following amino acid binding on the ribosome.

Clindamycin has been shown to have in vitro activity against the following organisms: Mobiluncus species. M. hominis, G. vaginalis, Bactercides species and Peptostreptococcus species.

Following once a day dosing of 100 mg of vaginally-administered Dalacin Vaginal Cream in normal volunteers, at a concentration equivalent to 20 mg clindamycin/g of cream, peak serum clindamycin levels average 25 ng/mL (range 6 to 61 ng/mL). Approximately 4% (range 0.6 to 11%) of the administered dose is absorbed systemically. In women with bacterial vaginosis, the amount of clindamycin absorbed systemically following vaginal administration of 5 g of Dalacin Vaginal Cream is also approximately 4% (range 2 to 8%).

Indications: For the treatment of bacterial vaginosis (also known as H. vaginalis vaginitis, G. vaginalis vaginitis, nonspecific vaginitis, Corynebacterium vaginitis, or anaerobic vaginosis).

Diagnosis: The clinical diagnosis of bacterial vaginosis is usually made on the basis of 4 criteria: (1) presence of a milky homogeneous vaginal discharge; (2) an unpleasant, fishy, amine odor accentuated by addition of 10% KOH to the vaginal fluid; (3) vaginal fluid pH greater than 4.5; and (4) presence of clue cells in the vaginal fluid. In general, if 3 or more of the above criteria are present, the patient is considered to have bacterial vaginosis.

An alternate method of diagnosis is a Gram stain of the vaginal fluid. If the Gram stain reveals an absence or marked decrease in Lactobacillus morphotype (large gram-positive rods) and a predominance of G. vaginalis/Bacteroides species morphotypes (small gram variable/gram-negative rods) it is considered compatible with the diagnosis of bacterial vaginosis.

Other pathogens commonly associated with vulvovaginitis (e.g., T. vaginalis and C. albicans) should be ruled out by appropriate laboratory methods.

Contraindications: In individuals with a history of hypersensitivity to preparations containing clindamycin, lincomycin or any components of the cream (see Supplied).

Warnings: The use of antibiotics occasionally results in overgrowth of nonsusceptible organisms, particularly yeasts. Should superinfections occur, take appropriate measures as dictated by the clinical situation.

Oral and parenteral clindamycin have been associated with severe diarrhea and antibiotic-associated colitis. Therefore, the physician should be alert to the possible development of antibiotic-associated diarrhea or colitis. Minimal systemic absorption (approximately 4%) of clindamycin occurs following the use of clindamycin phosphate cream intravaginally; however, if significant or prolonged diarrhea occurs, clindamycin phosphate vaginal cream should be discontinued and appropriate diagnostic procedures and treatment instituted as necessary.

Precautions: General: Clindamycin should be prescribed with caution in atopic individuals.

Cross resistance has been demonstrated between clindamycin and lincomycin.

The effect of concomitant use of clindamycin phosphate vaginal cream with other intravaginal products is not known.

This cream contains mineral oil. Mineral oil may weaken latex or rubber products such as condoms or vaginal contraceptive diaphragms; therefore, use of such products within 72 hours following treatment with the vaginal cream, is not recommended.

In menstruating patients, treatment should be delayed until menstruation is completed.

Pregnancy: Reproduction studies have been performed in rats and mice using s.c. and oral doses of clindamycin ranging from 20 to 600 mg/kg/day and have revealed no evidence of impaired fertility or harm to the fetus due to clindamycin. In one mouse strain, cleft palates were observed in treated fetuses; this response was not produced in other mouse strains or in other species, and therefore may be a strain-specific effect.

In clinical trials, use of vaginally-applied clindamycin phosphate cream in pregnant women in their second trimester, and systemically-administered clindamycin during their second and third trimesters, has not been associated with adverse effects.

There are however, no adequate and well-controlled studies in pregnant women during their first trimester, and because animal reproduction studies are not always predictive of human response, this drug should be used during pregnancy only if clearly needed.

Lactation: It is not known if clindamycin is excreted in breast milk following the use of vaginally-administered clindamycin phosphate. However, orally and parenterally-administered clindamycin have been reported to appear in breast milk. Therefore, a full assessment of benefit-risk should be made when consideration is given to using the vaginal cream in a nursing mother. Approximately 4 mg of an administered dose of 100 mg clindamycin (as clindamycin phosphate) is systemically absorbed following vaginal administration to the mother.

Drug Interactions: The potency of the combination of erythromycin and clindamycin was less than the potency of either drug alone in an in vitro E. coli culture.

Adverse Effects: In clinical trials, involving 764 patients, the following adverse reactions were judged to be associated with the administration of clindamycin phosphate vaginal cream. The most frequently reported adverse reaction was symptomatic vaginitis/cervicitis.

Genital Tract: symptomatic vaginitis/cervicitis (13.6%), symptomatic vaginitis/cervicitis positive for C. albicans (10.2%), symptomatic vaginitis/cervicitis positive for T. vaginalis (1.3%), vulvovaginal irritation (6.2%).

Gastrointestinal: nausea/vomiting, diarrhea/loose stools, abdominal pain, constipation, heartburn.

CNS: dizziness, headache, vertigo.

Dermatological: rash, exanthema.

Hypersensitivity: urticaria, hives.

Note: Unless the percentages are otherwise indicated, the incidence was less than 1%.

Overdose: Symptoms and Treatment: Intravaginal overdosage is unlikely with clindamycin phosphate vaginal cream. Only 4 mg of a total daily dose of 100 mg clindamycin (as clindamycin phosphate) is systemically absorbed when administered vaginally. By comparison, the usual i.v. total daily dose of clindamycin is 2 700 mg. Accidental ingestion could be accompanied by effects related to therapeutic levels of oral clindamycin.

Dosage: The recommended dose is 1 applicatorful (5 g) of vaginal cream intravaginally at bedtime for 7 consecutive nights. This is equivalent to approximately 100 mg of clindamycin (as clindamycin phosphate).

This cream contains mineral oil. Mineral oil may weaken latex or rubber products such as condoms or vaginal contraceptive diaphragms; therefore, use of such products within 72 hours following treatment with the vaginal cream, is not recommended.

In menstruating patients, treatment should be delayed until menstruation is completed.

Information for the Patient: See Blue Section—Information for the Patient "Dalacin Vaginal Cream".

Supplied: Each g of semi-solid white cream contains: clindamycin 20 mg (as clindamycin phosphate). Each full applicator (one dose) contains: clindamycin 100 mg (as clindamycin phosphate) in 5 g of cream. Nonmedicinal ingredients: benzyl alcohol, cetostearyl alcohol, cetyl palmitate, mineral oil, polysorbate 60, propylene glycol, purified water, sorbitan monostearate and stearic acid. Collapsible laminate tubes of 40 g with 7 disposable applicators for intravaginal use. Store at controlled room temperature (15 to 30°C). Protect from freezing.

DALMACOL Ⓝ

Riva

Hydrocodone Bitartrate—Etafedrine HCl

Antihistaminic—Antitussive—Decongestant

Supplied: Each mL contains: hydrocodone bitartrate 0.33 mg, etafedrine HCl 3.33 mg, sodium citrate 40 mg and doxylamine succinate 1.2 mg. Nonmedicinal ingredients: alcohol, aromate, FD&C yellow, glycerin, propylparaben, sorbitol and sucrose. Bottles of 500 mL and 2 L.

DALMANE® Ⓟ

Roche

Flurazepam HCl

Hypnotic

Pharmacology: Flurazepam, a benzodiazepine derivative, is a hypnotic agent which does not appear to decrease dream time as measured by rapid eye movements (REM). Flurazepam decreases sleep latency and number of awakenings for a consequent increase in total sleep time.

The duration of hypnotic effect and the profile of unwanted effects may be influenced by the alpha (distribution) and beta (elimination) half-lives of the administered drug and any active metabolites formed. When half-lives are long, the drug or metabolite may accumulate during periods of nightly administration and be associated with impairments of cognitive and motor performance during waking hours. If half-lives are short, the drug and metabolites will be cleared before the next dose is ingested, and carry-over effects related to sedation or CNS depression should be minimal or absent. However, during nightly use and for an extended period, pharmacodynamic tolerance or adaptation to some effects of benzodiazepine hypnotics may develop. If the drug has a very short elimination half-life, it is possible that a relative deficiency (i.e., in relation to the receptor site) may occur at some point in the interval between each night's use. This sequence of events may account for 2 clinical findings reported to occur after several weeks of nightly use of rapidly eliminated benzodiazepine hypnotics: 1) increased wakefulness during the last third of the night, and 2) the appearance of increased daytime anxiety (see Warnings).

Flurazepam is a benzodiazepine with a long half-life.

Rebound Insomnia: A transient syndrome whereby the symptoms that led to treatment with a benzodiazepine recur in an enhanced form, may occur on withdrawal of hypnotic treatment.

Pharmacokinetics: Following oral administration of 15 mg flurazepam to male and female volunteers, measurable concentrations for the parent compound were not detectable. Flurazepam undergoes rapid and pronounced metabolism to 2 pharmacologically active metabolites, namely hydroxyethyl flurazepam and flurazepam aldehyde. In healthy volunteers, C_{max} values for the 2 metabolites were 8.6 and 2.5 ng/mL, respectively. They were reached in an average of 1.0 and 1.2 hours, respectively. The mean elimination half-lives for these 2 metabolites were less than 2.5 hours.

The final active and principal metabolite, desalkyl flurazepam (DAFLZ), appears in the systemic circulation more slowly, with a mean C_{max} of 14 ng/mL attained an average of 10.6 hours after dosing. The mean elimination half-life of DAFLZ is approximately 75 hours (range 50 to 100 hours). Therefore, multiple-dose therapy with flurazepam leads to the accumulation of DAFLZ.

The half-life of DAFLZ was found to be longer in elderly males than in young males (160 versus 74 hours, $p<0.05$), but was similar in elderly and young females (120 versus 90 hours, p=N.S.). DAFLZ was extensively bound to plasma protein. The unbound fraction increased with age regardless of sex.

Following 15 days of treatment with 15 mg flurazepam once daily, mean steady-state plasma levels of DAFLZ were higher in elderly than in young men (81 and 53 ng/mL, $p<0.05$), but were similar in elderly and young women (86 and 85 ng/mL).

More than 50% of the total dose of flurazepam appears in the urine in 24 hours, with eventual urinary excretion accounting for 80% or more of the total dose. The major urinary metabolite is conjugated hydroxyethyl flurazepam. Less than 1% of the dose is excreted in the urine as DAFLZ. Approximately 10% of the total dose of flurazepam appears in the feces.

Indications: Sleep disturbance may be the presenting manifestation of a physical and/or psychiatric disorder. Consequently, a decision to initiate symptomatic treatment of insomnia should only be made after the patient has been carefully evaluated.

Flurazepam is indicated for the symptomatic relief of transient and short-term insomnia characterized by difficulty in falling asleep, frequent nocturnal awakenings and/or early morning awakening.

Treatment with flurazepam should usually not exceed 7 to 10 consecutive days. Use for more than 2 to 3 consecutive weeks requires complete re-evaluation of the patient. Prescriptions for flurazepam should be written for short-term use (7 to 10 days) and it should not be prescribed in quantities exceeding a one-month supply.

The use of hypnotics should be restricted for insomnia where disturbed sleep results in impaired daytime functioning.

Contraindications: In patients with known hypersensitivity to the drug, any component of its formulation, or to other benzodiazepines; myasthenia gravis; sleep apnea syndrome. Flurazepam is contraindicated in patients who in the past manifested paradoxical reactions to alcohol and/or sedative medications.

Warnings: General: Benzodiazepines should be used with extreme caution in patients with a history of substance or alcohol abuse.

The smallest possible effective dose should be prescribed for elderly patients. Inappropriate, heavy sedation in the elderly, may result in accidental events/falls.

The failure of insomnia to remit after 7 to 10 days of treatment may indicate the presence of a primary psychiatric and/or medical illness or the presence of sleep-state misperception.

Worsening of insomnia or the emergence of new abnormalities of thinking or behavior may be the consequence of an unrecognized psychiatric or physical disorder. These have also been reported to occur in association with the use of drugs that act at the benzodiazepine receptors.

Pregnancy: The use of flurazepam during pregnancy is not recommended. Benzodiazepines may cause fetal damage when administered during pregnancy. During the first trimester of pregnancy, several studies have suggested an increased risk of congenital malformations associated with the use of benzodiazepines. During the last weeks of pregnancy, ingestion of therapeutic doses of a benzodiazepine hypnotic has resulted in neonatal CNS depression due to transplacental distribution. If flurazepam is prescribed to women of childbearing potential, the patient should be warned of the potential risk to a fetus and advised to consult her physician regarding the discontinuation of the drug if she intends to become pregnant or suspects that she might be pregnant.

Memory Disturbance: Anterograde amnesia of varying severity has been reported following therapeutic doses of benzodiazepines. The event is rare with flurazepam. Anterograde amnesia is a dose-related phenomenon and elderly subjects may be at particular risk.

Cases of transient global amnesia and "traveller's amnesia" have also been reported in association with benzodiazepines, the latter in individuals who have taken benzodiazepines, often in the middle of the night, to induce sleep while travelling. Transient global amnesia and traveller's amnesia are unpredictable and not necessarily dose-related phenomena. Patients should be warned not to take flurazepam under circumstances in which a full night's sleep and clearance of the drug from the body are not possible before they need again to resume full activity.

Abnormal thinking and psychotic behavioral changes have been reported to occur in association with the use of benzodiazepines including flurazepam, although rarely. Some of the changes may be characterized by decreased inhibition, e.g., aggressiveness or extroversion that seem excessive, similar to that seen with alcohol and other CNS depressants (e.g., sedative/hypnotics). Particular caution is warranted in patients with a history of violent behavior and a history of unusual reactions to sedatives including alcohol and the benzodiazepines. Psychotic behavioral changes that have been reported with benzodiazepines include bizarre behavior, hallucinations, and depersonalization. Abnormal behaviors associated with the use of benzodiazepines have been reported more with chronic use and/or high doses but they may occur during the acute, maintenance or withdrawal phases of treatment.

It can rarely be determined with certainty whether a particular instance of abnormal behaviors listed above is drug induced, spontaneous in origin, or a result of an underlying psychiatric disorder. Nevertheless, the emergence of any new behavioral sign or symptom of concern requires careful and immediate evaluation.

Confusion: The benzodiazepines affect mental efficency, e.g., concentration, attention and vigilance. The risk of confusion is greater in the elderly and in patients with cerebral impairment.

Anxiety, Restlessness: An increase in daytime anxiety and/or restlessness have been observed during treatment with short half-life benzodiazepines although the syndrome can apply on occasion to drugs with longer elimination half-lives as well. Flurazepam has a long half-life.

Depression: Caution should be exercised if flurazepam is prescribed to patients with signs or symptoms of depression that could be intensified by hypnotic drugs. The potential for self-harm (e.g., intentional overdose) is high in patients with depression and thus, the least amount of drug that is feasible should be available to them at any one time.

Precautions: Drug Interactions: Flurazepam may produce additive CNS depressant effects when coadministered with alcohol, sedative antihistamines, narcotic analgesics, anticonvulsants, or psychotropic medications which themselves can produce CNS depression.

Compounds which inhibit certain hepatic enzymes (particularly cytochrome P450) may enhance the activity of benzodiazepines. Examples include cimetidine or erythromycin.

Drug Abuse, Dependence and Withdrawal: Withdrawal symptoms, similar in character to those noted with barbiturates and alcohol (convulsions, tremor, abdominal and muscle cramps, vomiting, sweating, dysphoria, perceptual disturbances and insomnia) have occurred following abrupt discontinuations of benzodiazepines, and may follow the discontinuation of flurazepam. The more severe symptoms are usually associated with higher dosages and longer usage, although patients given therapeutic dosages for as few as 1 to 2 weeks can also have withdrawal symptoms including daytime anxiety between nightly doses. Consequently, abrupt discontinuation should be avoided and a gradual dosage tapering schedule is recommended in any patient taking more than the lowest dose for more than a few weeks. The recommendation for tapering is particularly important in patients with a history of seizures.

The risk of dependence is increased in patients with a history of alcoholism, drug abuse, or in patients with marked personality disorders. Caution must be exercised in administering flurazepam to these individuals.

As with all hypnotics, repeat prescriptions should be limited to those who are under medical supervision.

Patients with Specific Conditions: Flurazepam should be given with caution to patients with impaired hepatic or renal function, or severe pulmonary insufficiency. Respiratory depression has been reported in patients with compromised respiratory function.

Occupational Hazards: Because of flurazepam's CNS depressant effect, patients receiving the drug should be cautioned against engaging in hazardous occupations requiring complete mental alertness such as operating machinery or driving a motor vehicle. For the same reason, patients should be warned against the concomitant ingestion of flurazepam and alcohol or CNS-depressant drugs.

Pregnancy: For teratogenic effects see Warnings. Nonteratogenic effects: a child born to a mother who is on benzodiazepines may be at risk for withdrawal symptoms from the drug during the postnatal period. Also, neonatal flaccidity has been

Dalmane (cont'd)

reported in an infant born to a mother who had been receiving benzodiazepines.
Lactation: The safety of flurazepam during lactation has not been established. Therefore, its use during nursing is not recommended.
Children: The safety and effectiveness of flurazepam in children below the age of 15 have not been established.
Geriatrics: Elderly patients are especially susceptible to dose-related adverse effects, such as drowsiness, dizziness, or impaired coordination. Inappropriate, heavy sedation may result in accidental events/falls. Therefore, the lowest possible dose (15 mg) should be used in these subjects.
Laboratory Tests: Should flurazepam be used repeatedly, periodic blood counts, liver, and kidney function tests should be performed.

Adverse Effects: The most common adverse effects reported with flurazepam are dizziness, drowsiness, lightheadedness and ataxia. These adverse effects are particularly common in elderly and debilitated patients (see Precautions). Severe sedation, lethargy, disorientation, and coma, probably indicative of drug intolerance or overdosage, have been reported.

Isolated instances of headache, heartburn, upset stomach, nausea, vomiting, amnesia, constipation, diarrhea, gastrointestinal pain, nervousness, apprehension, irritability, weakness, palpitations, chest pains, and genitourinary complaints have been reported. However, in controlled studies, these appeared as often or more often with placebo than with the active drug.

There have also been rare occurrences of leukopenia, granulocytopenia, sweating, flushes, difficulty in focusing, blurred vision, faintness, hypotension, shortness of breath, pruritus, skin rash, dry mouth, bitter taste, excessive salivation, anorexia, euphoria, depression, slurred speech, confusion, restlessness, hallucinations, nightmares, numbed emotions, reduced alertness, changes in libido, inappropriate behavior and elevated AST, ALT, total and direct bilirubins, and alkaline phosphatase. Paradoxical reactions such as excitement, stimulation, agitation, aggressiveness, rages, psychoses and hyperactivity have also been reported in rare instances when using drugs that act at the benzodiazepine receptors.

Overdose: Symptoms: Somnolence, confusion, coma.

Treatment: Respiration, pulse and blood pressure should be monitored as in all cases of drug overdosage. General supportive measures should be employed, along with immediate gastric lavage. I.V. fluids should be administered and an adequate airway maintained. Hypotension and CNS depression may be combated by judicious use of appropriate therapeutic agents. The value of dialysis has not been determined. If excitation occurs in patients following flurazepam overdosage, barbiturates should not be used.

As with the management of intentional overdosage with any drug, it should be borne in mind that multiple agents may have been ingested. The benzodiazepine antagonist, flumazenil is a specific antidote in known or suspected benzodiazepine overdose. (For conditions of use see flumazenil product monograph.)

Dosage: The lowest effective dose should be used. Treatment should be as short as possible, and should usually not exceed 7 to 10 consecutive days. Use for more than 2 to 3 consecutive weeks requires complete re-evaluation of the patient.

Dosage should be individualized for maximal beneficial effects.
Adults: The usual adult dosage is 30 mg before retiring. In some patients, 15 mg may suffice.
Elderly and/or Debilitated Patients: It is recommended that therapy be initiated with 15 mg until individual responses are determined.

Information for the Patient: See Blue Section—Information for the Patient "Dalmane".

Supplied: 15 mg: Each orange and ivory No. 2 hard gelatin capsule imprinted DALMANE 15 ROCHE (black ink) on both body and the cap contains: flurazepam HCl 15 mg. Nonmedicinal ingredients: allura red AC, brilliant blue FCF sodium salt, cornstarch, erythrosine, gelatin, lactose, magnesium stearate, methylparaben, potassium sorbate, propylparaben, quinoline yellow WS, sunset yellow FCF and talc. Also contains lactose 276 mg. Energy: 5.0 kJ (1.2 kcal). Gluten-, sodium-, sulfite- and tartrazine-free. Bottles of 100.

30 mg: Each red and ivory No. 2 hard gelatin capsule imprinted DALMANE 30 ROCHE (black ink) on both body and cap contains: flurazepam HCl 30 mg. Nonmedicinal ingredients: allura red AC, brilliant blue FCF sodium salt, cornstarch, erythrosine, gelatin, lactose, magnesium stearate, methylparaben, quinoline yellow WS, potassium sorbate, propylparaben, sunset yellow FCF and talc. Also contains lactose 263 mg. Energy: 5.0 kJ (1.2 kcal). Gluten-, sodium-, sulfite- and tartrazine-free. Bottles of 100.

Keep in a tightly closed, light-resistant container. Store at 15 to 30°C.

(Shown in Product Recognition Section)

DALTEPARIN

General Monograph, CPhA

see HEPARINS: LOW MOLECULAR WEIGHT

DAN-GARD®

Stiefel

Zinc Pyrithione

Antidandruff Therapy

Supplied: Each mL of shampoo contains: zinc pyrithione 2% plus detergent, foaming and stabilizing agents. Nonmedicinal ingredients: brilliant blue Na 1%, fragrance, isopropylamide oleate, lauryl alcohol ether diglycerol, methyl paraben, monoethanolamide stearate, purified water USP, sodium chloride, sodium lauroyl sarcolinate and stearoylalkanolamide. Plastic finger-grip bottles of 125 and 300 mL.

DAN-TAR PLUS®

Stiefel

Polytar—Pyrithione Disulfide

Antidandruff Therapy

Supplied: Each mL contains: Polytar 1% plus pyrithione disulfide 1%, in a soapless shampoo base with added hair conditioners. Nonmedicinal ingredients: citric acid anhydrous, fragrance, hexylene glycol, modified lauric diethanolamine, oleyl alcohol, polysorbate 80, purified water USP, sodium chloride and triethanolamine lauryl sulfate. pH adjusted to natural hair balance. Plastic finger-grip bottles of 300 mL.

DANTRIUM® CAPSULES

Procter & Gamble Pharmaceuticals

Dantrolene Sodium

Skeletal Muscle Relaxant

Pharmacology: Recordings of muscle tensions and electrical activity in both animal and man suggest that dantrolene has a direct inhibitory effect on the development of contractile tension. Spastic patients receiving dantrolene have shown a 40 to 70% reduction in the skeletal muscle tension induced by direct electrical stimulation of the motor nerve with no alteration of the EMG. This decrease in contractile tension can be attributed to an effect of dantrolene beyond the myoneural junction. Total paralysis does not occur since the dantrolene-induced change in the contractile state of skeletal muscle is limited in magnitude. The reduction in contractile activity accounts for the ability of dantrolene to diminish spasticity resulting from pathological states associated with a hyperative stretch reflex.

Dantrolene also produces CNS effects resulting in such manifestations as drowsiness, dizziness and generalized weakness.

Absorption of dantrolene is slow; dose-related blood levels are obtained which peak in 4 to 6 hours after a single oral dose. The peak pharmacologic effect generally occurs in 1½ to 3 hours at concentrations of 50 to 75% of the peak plasma level. Based on assays of whole blood and plasma, slightly greater amounts of dantrolene are associated with red blood cells than with the plasma fraction of blood. Metabolism is rapid via hepatic microsomal enzymes. The major metabolites in humans are a 5-hydroxy analog and an acetamino analog. Urinary excretion of dantrolene and metabolites occurs in an initially rapid phase ($t_{1/2}$, 2.5 to 3 hours) followed by a slower phase over a 24 hour period. Dantrolene is also removed by biliary excretion.

Dantrolene causes marked, dose-dependent skeletal muscle relaxation in laboratory animals with a long duration of action. The pharmacologic profile of dantrolene in animals is unlike neuromuscular blocking agents in that total muscle paralysis and/or respiratory depression do not occur.

There is a wider margin between doses causing muscle relaxation and doses causing motor incoordination with dantrolene than with centrally acting muscle relaxants. Skeletal muscle relaxation is not associated with anesthetic or analgesic action. Impairment of cornea or pinna reflexes has not been observed in animals treated with dantrolene.

Various studies both in vivo and in vitro demonstrated the apparent selectivity of action of dantrolene for skeletal muscle. There were some non-specific depressant effects seen in several smooth muscle studies and insignificant effects in cardiac muscle in doses which cause skeletal muscle relaxation. Nerve transmission was not affected by dantrolene in severe animal studies.

It has been shown that dantrolene has no effect on the propagated action potential recorded on the muscle membrane, and the total membrane capacitance is not decreased by the drug, indicating that it does not disrupt the function of the transverse tubular system, and acts at a point beyond the electrically excitable surface membrane. Evidence obtained in vitro with muscle preparations exposed to caffeine, an agent known to cause muscle contractions by releasing internal Ca^{++} stores in muscle, suggests that dantrolene acts on skeletal muscle by altering the Ca^{++} release mechanisms. Such an action could explain the apparent specificity of dantrolene for skeletal muscle.

Animal studies have indicated that dantrolene is metabolized by hydrolysis, hydroxylation, nitro-reduction and acetylation of the resulting amine.

Four corresponding metabolites have been identified which probably do not contribute significantly to the activity of dantrolene. Maximal blood levels following oral administration are reached in approximately 1 hour. In dogs approximately 40% of an i.v. dose of dantrolene is excreted as the hydroxylated metabolite in bile whereas only 1% of the dose is excreted in this manner by the rat. High biliary concentrations of this metabolite have also been found in the Rhesus monkey. Total excretion of known metabolites in the urine is estimated at approximately 3% in the dog and approximately 10% in the rat.

Indications: To control the manifestations of chronic spasticity of skeletal muscle resulting from such conditions as spinal cord injury, cerebral palsy, multiple sclerosis, and stroke, whenever such spasticity results in a decrease in functional use of residual motor activity. Dantrolene is not indicated in the relief of skeletal muscle spasms due to rheumatic disorders.

Orally administered dantrolene is also indicated in the preoperative management of malignant hyperthermia-susceptible surgical patients, and for the post-crisis follow-up management of patients stabilized with the i.v. product (for information, consult the Dosage section of Dantrium Intravenous).
Clinical Uses: Dantrolene has been studied in the treatment of selected patients with moderate to severe skeletal muscle spasticity resulting from stroke, spinal cord injury, cerebral palsy, multiple sclerosis, and other neuropathies. It seems to act directly on the skeletal muscle and has been found useful whenever manifestations of spasticity such as increased muscular resistance to stretch, clonus and exaggerated reflex posturing interfere with therapeutic exercise programs, utilization of braces, transfer maneuvers, posture equilibrium, ambulation, and activities of daily living.

Marked reduction or even cessation of spontaneous involuntary movements was observed in many patients receiving dantrolene. The extent to which dantrolene may contribute toward improvement in spasticity and activities in daily living can be tested by withdrawing the drug for 2 to 4 days and observing whether an exacerbation of the patient's condition occurs.

Contraindications: Skeletal muscle spasticity without suitable volitional activity (residual motor activity) may be of value in rehabilitation programs aimed toward sustaining upright posture and balance, and may assist a patient's locomotor pattern. Relief of such spasticity would reduce rather than increase function. Therefore, in cases where spasticity is utilized to obtain or maintain increased function, dantrolene is contraindicated.

Dantrolene is contraindicated in patients with compromised pulmonary function, particularly those with obstructive pulmonary disease and active hepatic disease, such as hepatitis and cirrhosis.

Warnings: Dantrolene has a potential for hepatotoxicity, and should not be used in conditions other than those recommended. Risk of hepatic injury appears to be greater in female patients, in patients over 35 years of age, and in

patients taking other medication(s). Dantrolene may exacerbate pre-existing liver dysfunction. Therefore, dantrolene should not be used without appropriate evaluation and monitoring of hepatic function before and throughout treatment, including frequent determinations of AST and ALT in blood serum. A trial administration of dantrolene is recommended and if after 45 days no observable benefit is evident, dantrolene should be discontinued. The lowest possible effective dose for the individual patient should be prescribed.

Fatal and nonfatal hepatitis have occurred at various dosage levels. The incidences reported in patients taking up to 400 mg/day are much lower than in those taking doses of 800 mg or more/day. Even sporadic short courses of the higher dosage levels markedly increased the risk of serious hepatic injury. Overt hepatitis has been observed most frequently after the second month of therapy. Liver dysfunction, as evidenced by elevated concentrations of liver enzymes in blood serum, has been observed in a number of patients receiving dantrolene for less than 60 days.

Toxicity studies in animals provided evidence of the low grade carcinogenic activity of dantrolene in the rat. In view of the animal findings, potential carcinogenicity in humans cannot be disregarded. Therefore, the potential benefits of the drug should be weighed against the possible risks of drug use for the individual patient. Consideration should be given as to whether the patient has responded to other medication and to the benefits of the trial administration of dantrolene as recommended above. In assessing risk acceptability, the age of the patient, the degree of disability and life expectancy should also be considered. The long-term safety of dantrolene has not yet been established.

Children: In view of the preceding warning, it is particularly important to assess risk acceptability before dantrolene is used in pediatric patients. Since there is insufficient experience with the use of dantrolene in young children (under 5 years of age), the drug is usually not recommended in this age group.

Pregnancy and *Lactation:* The safety of dantrolene in women who are or who may become pregnant has not been established; in such patients it should be given only when the potential benefits have been weighed against possible hazard to mother and child. Dantrolene should not be used in nursing mothers.

Precautions: Although subjective weakness attributable to dantrolene is usually transient, some patients feel excessively weak as long as therapy is continued. Such patients may not be able to manipulate rehabilitation devices such as wheel chairs, crutches, braces, walkers, or canes. Careful attention should be given to patients utilizing these devices. Dantrolene should be discontinued if the weakness persists and interferes with the use of a rehabilitation device.

Use with caution in patients with impaired pulmonary and myocardial function.

Occupational Hazards: Patients should be instructed not to drive a motor vehicle or participate in a hazardous occupation during the first week of therapy. Although the primary pharmacological effect of dantrolene is exerted directly on skeletal muscle, an apparent transient CNS effect also may exist. Therefore, caution should be exercised in the concomitant administration of tranquilizing agents.

Although photosensitization has not been a problem in clinical trials of dantrolene, it is possible that in some subjects the drug might evoke a phototoxic response.

The possibility of cross-sensitivity with compounds of related chemical structure exists; however, no such reactions were reported in extensive clinical trials.

In long-term therapy, perform periodic clinical and laboratory evaluation of organ systems, including hematopoietic, renal and hepatic studies.

Adverse Effects: Side effects most frequently reported were drowsiness, weakness, dizziness, malaise, fatigue and diarrhea. Less commonly reported effects are listed by systems: Cardiovascular: tachycardia, erratic blood pressure, phlebitis.
Gastrointestinal: constipation, anorexia, gastric irritation and bleeding, abdominal cramps, swallowing difficulty, nausea with or without vomiting and liver failure.
CNS: speech and visual disturbances, seizure, headache, lightheadedness, taste alterations, mental depression, confusion, nervousness, diplopia, insomnia.
Urogenital: increased urinary frequency, crystalluria, difficult erection, urinary incontinence and/or nocturia, difficult urination and/or urinary retention.
Musculoskeletal: myalgia, backache.
Integumentary: acne like rash, pruritus, urticaria, eczematoid eruption, abnormal hair growth, sweating.
Hypersensitivity: pleural effusion with pericarditis.
Other: chills, fever, excessive tearing, feeling of suffocation.

Alterations of liver function studies attributable to dantrolene have been observed. It is therefore advisable to perform liver function tests before and during therapy (see Warnings).

Side effects listed as most frequently occurring were generally transient and may be avoided with initial low doses and a gradual increase to optimal doses. Diarrhea may be of sufficient severity to warrant temporary or possibly permanent withdrawal of medication.

Overdose: Symptoms: A single case has been reported of a patient with an 18 year history of multiple sclerosis who consumed 1 600 mg of Dantrium per day for 13 days (a total of 20 800 mg). Other than feeling slightly weaker and "rubbery", the patient appeared to suffer no clinical manifestations of overdosage. Liver function values were transiently elevated although the patient did not become jaundiced.

Treatment: For acute overdosage employ general supportive measures along with immediate gastric lavage. I.V. fluids should be administered in fairly large quantities to avert the possibility of crystalluria. An adequate airway should be maintained and artificial resuscitation equipment made available. ECG monitoring should be instituted, and the patient carefully observed. No experience has been reported with dialysis, hence its value in dantrolene overdosage is not known.

Dosage: Prior to the administration of dantrolene, consideration should be given to the potential response to treatment. A decrease in spasticity sufficient to allow a daily function not otherwise attainable should be the therapeutic goal of treatment with dantrolene. Refer to Indications, Clinical Uses for description of possible areas of response.

It is important to establish a **therapeutic goal** (regain and maintain a specific function such as therapeutic, exercise program, utilization of braces, transfer maneuvers, etc.) before beginning dantrolene therapy. Dosage should be increased until the maximum performance compatible with the dysfunction due to underlying disease is achieved. No further increase in dosage is then indicated.

Usual Dosage: It is important that the dosage be titrated and individualized for maximum effect. The lowest dose compatible with optimal response is recommended.

In view of the potential for liver damage during long-term use, therapy with dantrolene should be discontinued if benefits are not evident within 45 days (see Warnings).

Adults: Begin therapy with 25 mg once daily; increase to 25 mg 2, 3 or 4 times daily and then, by increments of 25 mg, to 100 mg 2, 3 or 4 times daily, if necessary. As most patients will respond to a dose of 400 mg/day or less, rarely should doses higher than 400 mg/day be used. Each dosage level should be maintained for 4 to 7 days, depending on the patient's tolerance, and should be increased only if the therapeutic goal has not been attained.

The dose should not be increased beyond, and may even have to be reduced to the amount at which the patient received maximal benefit without adverse effects.

Children: A similar approach should be utilized starting with 0.5 mg/kg of body weight twice daily; this is increased to 0.5 mg/kg 3 or 4 times daily and then, by increments of 0.5 mg/kg up to as high as 3.0 mg/kg 2, 3 or 4 times daily if necessary. Doses higher than 100 mg 4 times daily should not be used in children.

Supplied: 25 mg: Each opaque orange and brown capsule, coded with 1 black bar and DANTRIUM 25 mg 0149 0030, contains: dantrolene sodium 25 mg. Nonmedicinal ingredients: edible black ink, gelatin, lactose, magnesium stearate, starch, talc, titanium dioxide, carnauba wax, iron oxide red, FD&C Yellow #6, iron oxide yellow, and may contain one or more of the following: FD&C Blue #2, D&C Red #33. Bisulfite-, gluten-, paraben- and tartrazine-free. Bottles of 100 and 500.

100 mg: Each opaque orange and brown capsule, coded with 3 black bars and DANTRIUM 100 mg 0149 0033, contains: dantrolene sodium 100 mg. Nonmedicinal ingredients: edible black ink, gelatin, lactose, magnesium stearate, starch, talc, titanium dioxide, carnauba wax, iron oxide red, FD&C Yellow #6, iron oxide yellow, and may contain one or more of the following: FD&C Blue #2, D&C Red #33. Bisulfite-, gluten-, paraben- and tartrazine-free. Bottles of 100.

Store below 40°C.

Many medications require special consideration when administered to geriatric patients. Refer to Drugs and Older Individuals found within the CLIN-INFO SECTION.

DANTRIUM® INTRAVENOUS

Procter & Gamble Pharmaceuticals

Dantrolene Sodium

Management of Malignant Hyperthermia

Pharmacology: Dantrolene is a muscle relaxant acting specifically on skeletal muscles. In isolated muscle preparations, dantrolene uncouples the excitation and contraction of skeletal muscles, probably by interfering with the release of calcium from the sarcoplasmic reticulum.

In the anesthetic induced malignant hyperthermia syndrome, evidence points to a predisposing intrinsic abnormality of muscle tissue. In affected humans, it has been postulated that "triggering agents" induce a sudden rise in myoplasmic calcium either by preventing the sarcoplasmic reticulum from accumulating calcium adequately, or by accelerating its release. This rise in myoplasmic calcium activates acute catabolic processes common to the malignant hyperthermia crisis.

Dantrolene may prevent the increase in myoplasmic calcium and the acute catabolism within the muscle cell by interfering with the release of calcium from the sarcoplasmic reticulum to the myoplasm. Thus, the physiologic, metabolic and biochemical changes associated with the crisis may be reversed or attenuated.

Based on assays of whole blood and plasma, slightly greater amounts of dantrolene are associated with red blood cells than with the plasma fraction of blood. Significant amounts of dantrolene are bound to plasma proteins, mostly albumin, and this binding is readily reversible. Binding to plasma protein is not significantly altered by diazepam, diphenylhydantoin, or phenylbutazone. Binding to plasma proteins is reduced by warfarin and clofibrate and increased by tolbutamide.

In humans dantrolene metabolism is rapid via hepatic microsomal enzymes. The major metabolites in body fluids are the 5 hydroxy analog and the acetamino analog. Urinary excretion of dantrolene and its metabolites occurs in an initially rapid phase ($t_{1/2}$, 2.5 to 3 hours) followed by a slower phase over a 24-hour period. Dantrolene is also removed by biliary excretion and through the feces. The mean biologic half-life of dantrolene after i.v. administration is about 5 hours. Based on limited information obtained from study patients with malignant hyperthermia, it is estimated that therapeutic efficacy of the drug is obtained at a serum concentration of dantrolene of about 1 μg/mL. No toxic effects have been observed in humans with malignant hyperthermia up to a dose level of 10 mg/kg with serum dantrolene concentrations up to 13.79 μg/mL.

Dantrolene causes marked, dose-dependent skeletal muscle relaxation in laboratory animals with a long duration of action. The pharmacologic profile of dantrolene in animals is unlike neuromuscular blocking agents in that total muscle paralysis and/or respiratory depression do not occur.

Various studies in vivo and in vitro demonstrated the apparent selectivity of action of dantrolene for skeletal muscle. There were some non-specific depressant effects seen in several smooth muscle studies and insignificant effects in cardiac muscle in doses which cause skeletal muscle relaxation. Nerve transmission was not affected by dantrolene in several animal studies.

Dantrolene i.v. has no appreciable effect on the cardiovascular system or on respiratory function. A transient inconsistent effect on smooth muscles has been observed at high doses.

It has been shown that dantrolene has no effect on the propagated action potential recorded on the muscle membrane, and the total membrane capacitance is not decreased by the drug, indicating that it does not disrupt the function of the transverse tubular system, and acts at a point beyond the electrically excitable surface membrane. Evidence obtained in vitro with muscle preparations exposed to caffeine, an agent known to cause muscle contractions by releasing internal Ca^{++} stores in muscle, suggests that dantrolene acts on skeletal muscle by altering the Ca^{++} release mechanisms. Such an action could explain the apparent specificity of dantrolene for skeletal muscle.

In dogs approximately 40% of an i.v. dose of dantrolene is excreted as the hydroxylated metabolite in bile whereas only 1% of the dose is excreted in this manner by the rat. High biliary concentrations of this metabolite have also been found in the Rhesus monkey. Total excretion of known metabolites in the urine is estimated at approximately 3% in the dog and approximately 10% in the rat.

Studies with malignant hyperthermia susceptible swine have shown that in the established syndrome of malignant hyperthermia induced by halothane or succinylcholine dantrolene

Dantrium Intravenous (cont'd)

caused: rapid loss of muscle rigor commencing within 5 minutes and usually complete within 20 minutes; immediate cessation of the increase in deep muscle temperature followed by a rapid decrease; termination of the progressive, inexorable acidosis characteristic of the syndrome rendering easy the buffering of acidosis developed until dantrolene administration.

Survival rates with dantrolene sodium were 100% as contrasted with 40% with procaine administration. Untreated, the developed syndrome had a mortality rate of 100%. Procaine administration was associated with profound cardiovascular effects while dantrolene had no effect on the myocardium, a factor that permitted the drug's use up to the limits of therapeutic effectiveness. Mean doses of dantrolene used to successfully treat these animals were 7 mg/kg.

Indications: The management of malignant hyperthermia crisis. As soon as the crisis is recognized (i.e., tachycardia, tachypnea, central venous desaturation, central venous hypercarbia, metabolic acidosis, fever, skeletal muscle rigidity or cyanosis and mottling of the skin) cooling procedures should be instituted and dantrolene i.v. administered. If anesthetic agents are being administered they should be promptly discontinued. It is also important that appropriate supportive measures be instituted for treatment of the physiologic and metabolic abnormalities. Dantrolene i.v., when given early in the malignant hyperthermia crisis, has caused abrupt lowering of body temperature, correction of the respiratory and/or metabolic acidosis, decrease of the heart rate, stabilization of blood pressure, and disappearance of the rigidity and/or fasiculations. Patients who received dantrolene i.v. during the crisis have less evidence of muscle destruction as shown by serum creatinine phosphokinase measurements than those treated by other measures.

Contraindications: There are no known contraindications when used during an acute malignant hyperthermia crisis.

Warnings: Because of the high pH of the i.v. formulation, care must be taken to prevent extravasation of the i.v. solution into the surrounding tissues.

Precautions: *Pregnancy:* Safety in women who are or who may become pregnant has not been established; it should be given only when the potential benefits have been weighed against the possible risk to mother and child.

Drug Interactions: The combination of therapeutic doses of i.v. dantrolene and verapamil in halothane/-α-chloralose anesthetized swine has resulted in ventricular fibrillation and cardiovascular collapse in association with marked hyperkalemia. It is recommended the combination of i.v. dantrolene and calcium channel blockers, such as verapamil, not be used during the reversal of a malignant hyperthermia crisis until the relevance of these findings to humans is established.

Adverse Effects: The more serious reactions reported with repeated doses of oral dantrolene as a muscle relaxant have been hepatitis, seizures and pleural effusions with pericarditis. Cases of fatal hepatitis have been reported in patients who had received dantrolene for 60 days or longer. Symptomatic hepatitis and laboratory evidence of liver dysfunction have also been reported in a number of patients receiving dantrolene as a muscle relaxant. Acneiform skin reactions have also been infrequently reported. For a list of adverse reactions reported with the use of dantrolene as a muscle relaxant, see Dantrium Capsules monograph.

None of these reactions have been reported during clinical trials in patients treated with short-term dantrolene i.v. therapy for malignant hyperthermia.

Overdose: Symptoms: Drowsiness and generalized muscle weakness have been reported following very large doses of oral dantrolene and would be expected as the major symptoms of overdosage.

Treatment: For acute overdosage general supportive measures should be employed. I.V. fluids should be administered in fairly large quantities to avert the possibility of crystalluria. An adequate airway should be maintained and artificial resuscitation equipment made available. ECG monitoring should be instituted, and the patient carefully observed. No experience has been reported with dialysis, hence its value in dantrolene overdosage is not known.

Dosage: During the crisis: As soon as the malignant hyperthermia reaction is recognized, all anesthetic agents should be discontinued.

Dantrolene i.v. should be administered by continuous rapid i.v. push beginning at a minimum dose of 1 mg/kg, and continuing until symptoms subside or the maximum cumulative dose of 10 mg/kg has been reached.

If the physiologic and metabolic abnormalities reappear, the regimen may be repeated. It is important to note that administration of dantrolene i.v. should be continuous until symptoms subside. The effective dose to reverse the crisis is directly dependent upon the individual's degree of susceptibility to malignant hyperthermia, the amount and time of exposure to the triggering agent, and the time elapsed between onset of the crisis and initiation of treatment.

Children: Experience to date indicates that the dose for children is the same as for adults.

Preoperatively: If after suitable evaluation of the patient, including family history relative to malignant hyperthermia, it is felt that a malignant hyperthermia crisis may develop during anesthesia and surgery, oral dantrolene may be used prophylactically 1 to 2 days prior to surgery. The dantrolene capsules should be given at a dose of 1 to 2 mg/kg 4 times/day up to 3 to 5 hours prior to surgery.

The following criteria may be used as a general guideline in assessing which individuals are likely to be most susceptible to development of a malignant hyperthermia crisis during anesthesia or surgery:

1. Patients who have survived a malignant hyperthermia crisis or have a positive muscle biopsy.
2. A first-degree relative of anyone known to be malignant hyperthermia susceptible or to have a positive muscle biopsy.
3. A member of a suspected family who has a clinically demonstrable muscle abnormality.
4. A member of a suspected family whose plasma CK value has been found elevated in one or more samples (tested on at least 3 occasions).

Post Crisis Follow-up: The dantrolene capsules should also be administered following a malignant hyperthermia crisis in doses of 4 to 8 mg/kg/day in 4 divided doses, for a 1-to 3-day period to prevent recurrence of the manifestations of malignant hyperthermia.

Reconstitution: Each vial should be reconstituted by adding 60 mL of sterile water for injection USP (without a bacteriostatic agent), and the vial shaken until the solution is clear. The contents of the vial must be protected from light and used within 6 hours after reconstitution. Store reconstituted solution at controlled room temperature 15 to 30°C.

Supplied: Each 70 mL vial contains: a sterile lyophilized mixture of 20 mg dantrolene sodium, 3 000 mg mannitol, and sufficient sodium hydroxide to yield a pH of approximately 9.5 when reconstituted. Bisulfite-, gluten-, lactose-, paraben- and tartrazine-free. These are not multiple dose vials. Cartons of 12 vials. Store below 30°C.

Dantrolene i.v. is available only for use in hospitals or in dental clinics that are equipped to provide the necessary supportive measures used in the treatment of the malignant hyperthermia crisis.

Reviewed 1999

DARAPRIM® Ⓟ

Glaxo Wellcome

Pyrimethamine

Antimalarial

Pharmacology: Pyrimethamine is a folic acid antagonist and the rationale for its therapeutic action is based on the differential requirement between host and parasite for nucleic acid precursors involved in growth. This activity is highly selective against plasmodia and Toxoplasma gondii. Pyrimethamine does not destroy gametocytes, but arrests sporogony in the mosquito.

Peak plasma levels are found between 2 and 4 hours after oral administration of 100 mg of pyrimethamine. Plasma concentrations are maintained over a prolonged time with a plasma half-life of approximately 90 hours. Urinary excretion is extended over 30 days or longer. Twenty to 30% of a single 100 mg dose is excreted in the urine. Pyrimethamine is secreted in breast milk and may be of some value in the protection of breast fed infants from malaria.

Indications: The chemoprophylaxis of malaria due to susceptible strains of plasmodia. Fast acting schizonticides (chloroquine, amodiaquin, quinacrine or quinine) are indicated and preferable for the treatment of acute attacks. However, conjoint use of pyrimethamine will initiate transmission control and suppressive cure.

Pyrimethamine is also indicated for the treatment of toxoplasmosis. For this purpose the drug should be used conjointly with a sulfonamide since synergism exists with this combination.

Contraindications: Patients with a history of sensitivity to pyrimethamine.

Precautions: Pyrimethamine should be used with caution in patients with hepatic or renal disorders.

Pyrimethamine may exacerbate folate deficiency due to innate disease or malnutrition.

In areas of known or suspected resistance to pyrimethamine or related compounds, an alternative prophylactic should be used.

When a sulfonamide is given in combination, an adequate fluid intake should be ensured to minimize the risk of crystalluria.

The dosage of pyrimethamine required for the treatment of toxoplasmosis is 10 to 20 times the recommended antimalarial dosage and approaches the toxic level. If signs of folic acid deficiency develop (see Adverse Effects) reduce the dosage or discontinue the drug according to the response of the patient. Folinic acid may be administered in a dosage of 5 to 15 mg orally, i.v. or im. daily for 3 days, or as required to produce a return of depressed platelet or white blood cell counts to safe levels.

Warn patients to keep pyrimethamine out of the reach of children since accidental ingestion has led to fatality.

Pregnancy: Pyrimethamine like other folic acid antagonists, may, in large doses produce teratogenic effects in laboratory animals.

Toxoplasmosis: The risks resulting from the administration of high doses of pyrimethamine must be balanced against the dangers of abortion or fetal malformation due to the infection. Toxoplasmosis is thought not to infect the fetus before the sixth week of pregnancy and only rarely during early placentation.

Treatment is indicated only for women whose serological tests become positive during pregnancy, and women who show rising titres of antibodies against Toxoplasma during pregnancy. Although the eyes are sometimes affected during an acute, acquired attack, most authorities consider that ocular toxoplasmosis is usually a late manifestation of congenital infection. Thus, in the majority of cases, ocular disease does not reflect a danger to the fetus. Pregnant women should be treated only in the presence of rising titres or if the eye lesion threatens maternal vision.

Concurrent administration of folinic acid is recommended when pyrimethamine is used for the treatment of toxoplasmosis during pregnancy.

The recommended dosage for malaria suppression should not be exceeded. In patients receiving high dosage, as for the treatment of toxoplasmosis, semi-weekly blood counts, including platelet counts, should be made. In patients with convulsive disorders a smaller "starting" dose (for toxoplasmosis) is recommended to avoid the potential nervous system toxicity of pyrimethamine.

Drug Interactions: The high protein binding exhibited by pyrimethamine may prevent protein binding by other compound. This will be of relevance when the level of unbound, concomitantly administered drug (e.g. quinine or warfarin) affects its efficacy or toxicity.

The concurrent administration of lorazepam and pyrimethamine may induce hepatotoxicity.

Pyrimethamine, by its mode of action, may further depress folate metabolism in patients receiving treatment with other folate inhibitors. Occasional reports suggest that individuals taking pyrimethamine as malaria prophylaxis at doses in excess of 25 mg weekly may develop megaloblastic anemia if cotrimoxazole is prescribed concurrently.

Pyrimethamine may cause exacerbation of the myelosuppressive effects of cytostatic agents, especially those of the antifolate, methotrexate. Convulsions have occurred after concurrent administration of methotrexate and pyrimethamine to children with central nervous system leukemia and cases of fatal bone marrow aplasia have been associated with the administration of daunorubicin, cytosine arabinoside and pyrimethamine to individuals suffering from acute myeloid leukemia.

Adverse Effects: Malaria Prophylaxis: At the recommended dose, side effects are rare. Occasionally, rashes have been

observed which disappeared when administration of pyrimethamine was stopped.
Malaria Treatment: Nausea, colic, vomiting and diarrhea are seldom recorded. However, the low frequency of reports may reflect the difficulties in distinguishing whether such symptoms are a result of the disease process or attributable to medication. Disorders of cardiac rhythm and hematuria occur infrequently at doses of 75 mg and may be associated to some extent with the nature of the infection.
Toxoplasmosis: Therapeutic doses of pyrimethamine have been shown to depress hematopoiesis in about 25% of patients. The likelihood of anemia or thrombocytopenia developing is reduced by concurrent administration of calcium folinate.

Nausea, colic, vomiting and diarrhea are common during early treatment. They seldom necessitate withholding treatment.

Less common side effects are headache, giddiness, dryness of mouth or throat, fever, malaise, dermatitis, abnormal skin pigmentation and depression.

Hyperphenylalaninemia has occurred in 3 neonates treated for congenital toxoplasmosis. Circulatory collapse and buccal ulceration have been reported in association with pyrimethamine but only in patients treated with doses higher than those recommended. Precipitation of a grand mal attack in one patient predisposed to epilepsy has been reported, but the clinical significance has not been defined.

Overdose: Symptoms: Symptoms reported have included vomiting, cyanosis, respiratory distress, convulsions and tachycardia.

Treatment: Routine supportive treatment, including maintenance of a clear airway and control of convulsions should be given. Adequate fluids should be given to ensure optimal diuresis. Gastric lavage may be of value only if instituted within 2 hours of ingestion, in view of the rapid absorption of pyrimethamine. Fresh blood transfusions to counteract blood dyscrasias should be available.

To counteract possible folate deficiency, calcium folinate 9 to 15 mg daily should be given until the signs of toxicity have subsided. There may be a delay of 7 to 10 days before the leukopenic side effects become evident; therefore, calcium folinate therapy should be continued for the period at risk.

Dosage: Chemoprophylaxis of Malaria: Adults and children over 10 years, 25 mg once weekly; children 5 through 10 years, 12.5 mg once weekly; infants and children under 5 years, 6.25 mg once weekly. Prophylaxis should begin 1 week prior to arrival in endemic area and be continued once weekly. On returning to a nonmalarious area, dosage should be maintained for a further 4 weeks.

Regimens planned to include suppressive cure should be extended through any characteristic periods of early recrudescence and late relapses for at least 10 weeks in each case.
Treatment of acute attacks: Use pyrimethamine in areas where only susceptible plasmodia exist. The drug is not recommended alone in the treatment of acute attacks of malaria in nonimmune persons. Fast acting schizonticides (chloroquine, amodiaquin, quinacrine or quinine) are indicated for treatment of acute attacks. However, conjoint pyrimethamine dosage of 25 mg daily for 2 days will initiate transmission control and suppressive cure.

Should circumstances arise wherein pyrimethamine must be used alone in semi-immune persons, the adult dosage for an acute attack is 50 mg daily for 2 days; children 4 to 10 years old may be given 25 mg daily for 2 days. In any event, clinical cure should be followed by the once-weekly regimen described above.

Pyrimethamine should be given concurrently with sulfalene or sulfadoxine as a single dose. Adults and children over 14 years, 50 to 75 mg pyrimethamine with 1 to 1.5 g sulfalene or sulfadoxine; children 9 to 14 years, 50 mg pyrimethamine with 1 g sulfalene or sulfadoxine; children 4 to 8 years, 25 mg pyrimethamine with 500 mg sulfalene or sulfadoxine; children under 4 years, 12.5 mg pyrimethamine with 250 mg sulfalene or sulfadoxine. A single dose is sufficient to eliminate asexual parasites from the blood of the majority of patients.
Toxoplasmosis: Pyrimethamine should be given concurrently with sulfadiazine or another sulfonamide. Adults and children over 6 years, an initial dose of 50 mg pyrimethamine followed by 25 mg pyrimethamine daily given with 150 mg/kg (maximum 4 g) sulfadiazine daily in 4 divided doses; children 2 to 6 years, an initial dose of 25 mg pyrimethamine followed by 12.5 mg pyrimethamine daily given with 150 mg/kg (maximum 2 g) sulfadiazine daily in 4 divided doses; children 10 months to 2 years, 12.5 mg pyrimethamine daily given with 150 mg/kg (maximum 1.5 g) sulfadiazine daily in 4 divided doses; infants 3 to 9 months: 6.25 mg pyrimethamine daily given with 100 mg/kg (maximum 1 g) sulfadiazine daily in 4 divided doses; infants under 3 months, 6.25 mg pyrimethamine on alternate days given with 100 mg/kg (maximum 750 mg) sulfadiazine given in 4 divided doses on alternate days.

Warning: The risk of administering sulfadiazine or other sulfonamides to neonates should be weighed against their therapeutic benefit.
Treatment: Treatment should be continued for 3 to 6 weeks. If further therapy is indicated a period of 2 weeks should elapse between treatments.

Supplied: Each white, biconvex tablet, with code number DARAPRIM A3A on same side as score mark, contains: pyrimethamine USP 25 mg. Also contains cornstarch, lactose and potato starch. Bottles of 50. Store between 15 to 30°C and keep dry.

(Shown in Product Recognition Section)

DARVON-N® Ⓝ

Lilly

Propoxyphene Napsylate

Analgesic

Indications: For the relief of mild to moderate pain alone or when it is accompanied by fever.

Contraindications: Hypersensitivity to any of the components.

Warnings: Do not prescribe propoxyphene for patients who are suicidal or addiction-prone.

Prescribe propoxyphene with caution for patients taking tranquilizers or antidepressant drugs and patients who use alcohol in excess.

Tell your patients not to exceed the recommended dose and to limit their intake of alcohol.

Propoxyphene products in excessive doses, either alone or in combination with other CNS depressants, including alcohol, are a major cause of drug-related deaths. Fatalities within the first hour of overdosage are not uncommon.

Propoxyphene should not be taken in doses higher than those recommended. The judicious prescribing of propoxyphene is essential to the safe use of this drug. With patients who are depressed or suicidal, consideration should be given to the use of non-narcotic analgesics. Patients should be cautioned about the concomitant use of propoxyphene products and alcohol because of potentially serious CNS-additive effects of these agents. Because of its added depressant effects, propoxyphene should be prescribed with caution for those patients whose medical condition requires the concomitant administration of sedatives, tranquilizers, muscle relaxants, antidepressants, or other CNS-depressant drugs. Patients should be advised of the additive depressant effects of these combinations.

Many of the propoxyphene-related deaths have occurred in patients with previous histories of emotional disturbances or suicidal ideation or attempts, as well as histories of misuse of tranquilizers, alcohol, and other CNS-active drugs. Some deaths have occurred as a consequence of the accidental ingestion of excessive quantities of propoxyphene alone or in combination with other drugs.
Drug dependence: Propoxyphene, when taken in higher-than-recommended doses over long periods of time, can produce drug dependence characterized by psychic dependence and, less frequently, physical dependence and tolerance. Propoxyphene will only partially suppress the withdrawal syndrome in individuals physically dependent on morphine or other narcotics. The abuse liability of propoxyphene is qualitatively similar to that of codeine although quantitatively less, and propoxyphene should be prescribed with the same degree of caution appropriate to the use of codeine.
Occupational Hazards: Ambulatory patients: Propoxyphene may impair the mental and/or physical abilities required for the performance of potentially hazardous tasks, such as driving a car or operating machinery. The patient should be cautioned accordingly.

Precautions: *Drug Interactions:* The CNS-depressant effect of propoxyphene is additive with that of other CNS depressants, including alcohol.
Pregnancy: Safe use in pregnancy has not been established relative to possible adverse effects on fetal development. Instances of withdrawal symptoms in the neonate have been reported following usage during pregnancy. Therefore, propoxyphene should not be used in pregnant women unless, in the judgment of the physician, the potential benefits outweigh the possible hazards.
Lactation: Low levels of propoxyphene have been detected in human milk. In postpartum studies involving nursing mothers who were given propoxyphene, no adverse effects were noted in infants receiving mother's milk.
Children: Propoxyphene is not recommended for use in children, because documented clinical experience has been insufficient to establish safety and a suitable dosage regimen in the pediatric age group.

Confusion, anxiety, and tremors have been reported in a few patients receiving propoxyphene concomitant with orphenadrine.

Adverse Effects: Such adverse effects as dizziness, headache, sedation, somnolence, paradoxical excitement and insomnia, skin rash, and gastrointestinal disturbances (including nausea, vomiting, abdominal pain and constipation) may occur with the recommended doses of propoxyphene napsylate. Euphoria, dysphoria, and minor visual disturbance also have been reported.

The chronic ingestion of propoxyphene in doses exceeding 800 mg per day has caused toxic psychoses and convulsions. A single dose of 1 200 mg of propoxyphene napsylate has caused convulsions.

Overdose: Symptoms: The manifestations of serious overdosage with propoxyphene are similar to those of narcotic overdosage and include respiratory depression (a decrease in respiratory rate and/or tidal volume, Cheyne-Stokes respiration, cyanosis), extreme somnolence progressing to stupor or coma, initial pupillary constriction followed by dilation as hypoxia increases and circulatory collapse. In addition to these characteristics typical of narcotic poisoning, local and generalized convulsions constitute a prominent feature in most cases of severe propoxyphene poisoning, and cardiac arrhythmias and pulmonary edema have occasionally been reported. Apnea, cardiac arrest and death have occurred.

Treatment: Primary attention should be given to the reestablishment of adequate respiratory exchange through provision of a patent airway and institution of assisted or controlled ventilation. The narcotic antagonist naloxone, is a specific antidote against the respiratory depression produced by propoxyphene.

An appropriate dose should be administered, preferably by the i.v. route, simultaneously with efforts at respiratory resuscitation, and should be repeated as necessary, at 20 to 30 minute intervals, until the patient's condition remains satisfactory. The duration of action of the antagonist may be brief. If no response is observed after 10 mg of naloxone have been administered, the diagnosis of propoxyphene toxicity should be questioned. (Nalorphine and levallorphan may be used if naloxone is not available, but these agents are not as satisfactory as naloxone.)

Blood gases, pH, and electrolytes should be monitored in order that acidosis and any electrolytic disturbance present may be promptly corrected. Acidosis, hypoxia, and generalized CNS depression predispose to the development of cardiac arrhythmias. Ventricular fibrillation or cardiac arrest may occur and necessitate the full complement of cardiopulmonary resuscitative (CPR) measures. Respiratory acidosis rapidly subsides as ventilation is restored and hypercapnea eliminated, but residual lactic acidosis may require i.v. bicarbonate for prompt correction.

Electrocardiographic monitoring is essential. Prompt correction of hypoxia, acidosis, and electrolytic disturbance (when present) will help prevent these cardiac complications and will increase the effectiveness of agents administered to restore normal cardiac function. In addition to the use of a narcotic antagonist, the patient may require careful titration with an anticonvulsant to control seizures. Analeptic drugs (e.g., caffeine or amphetamine) should not be used because of their tendency to precipitate convulsions.

General supportive measures, in addition to oxygen, include, when necessary, i.v. fluids, vasopressor-inotropic compounds, and, when infection is likely, anti-infective agents. Gastric lavage may be useful, and activated charcoal can adsorb a significant amount of ingested propoxyphene. Dialysis is of little value in poisoning due to propoxyphene. Efforts should be made to determine whether other agents, such as alcohol, barbiturates, tranquilizers, or other CNS depressants, were also ingested, since these increase CNS depression as well as cause specific toxic effects.

Darvon-N (cont'd)

Dosage: Adults: 1 capsule 3 or 4 times daily. The maximum dose should not exceed 600 mg/day. See Table I.

Table I—Darvon-N

Opioid Analgesics: Approximate Analgesic Equivalences[a]

Drug	Equivalent Dose (mg)[b] (compared to morphine 10 mg i.m.) Parenteral	Oral	Duration of Action (hours)
Strong Opioid Agonists			
Morphine (single dose)	10	60	3–4
(chronic dose)	10	20–30[c]	3 4
Hydromorphone	1.5–2	6–7.5	2–4
Anileridine	25	75	2–3
Levorphanol	2	4	4–8
Meperidine[d]	75	300	1–3
Oxymorphone	1.5	5(rectal)	3–4
Methadone[e]			
Heroin	5–8	10–15	3–4
Weak Opioid Agonists			
Codeine	120	200	3–4
Oxycodone	5–10	10–15	2–4
Propoxyphene	50	100	2–4
Mixed Agonist-Antagonists[f]			
Pentazocine[d]	60	180	3–4
Nalbuphine	10		3–6
Butorphanol	2		3–4

[a] References:
Cancer Pain: A Monograph on the Management of Cancer Pain, Health and Welfare Canada, 1984.
Foley, K. M., New Engl. J. Med. 313: 84-95, 1985.
Aronoff, G. M. and Evans, W. O., In: Evaluation and Treatment of Chronic Pain, 2nd Ed., G.M. Aronoff (Ed.), Williams and Wilkins, Baltimore, pp. 359-368, 1992.
Cherny, N. I. and Portenoy, R. K., In: Textbook of Pain, 3rd Ed., P. D. Wall and R. Melzack (Eds). Churchill Livingstone, London, pp. 1437-1467, 1994.

[b] Most of these data were derived from single-dose, acute pain studies and should be considered an approximation for selection of doses when treating chronic pain.

[c] For acute pain, the oral dose of morphine is 6 times the injectable dose. However, for chronic dosing, this ratio becomes 2 or 3:1, possibly due to the accumulation of active metabolites.

[d] These drugs are not recommended for the management of chronic pain.

[e] Extremely variable equianalgesic dose. Patients should undergo personalized titration starting at an equivalent to 1/10 of the morphine dose.

[f] Mixed agonist-antagonists can precipitate withdrawal in patients on pure opioid agonists.

Supplied: Each No. 3, pink capsule contains: propoxyphene napsylate 100 mg. Identi-Code: H64. Nonmedicinal ingredients: dimethicone and starch. Tartrazine-free. Bottles of 100.

Reviewed 1999

DAUNORUBICIN HYDROCHLORIDE FOR INJECTION, USP ℞

Novopharm

Antimitotic—Antibiotic

Supplied: Each glass vial of sterile lyophilized powder contains: daunorubicin 20 mg as daunorubicin HCl. Nonmedicinal ingredients: mannitol. Packages of 1.

New Product 1998

DAUNOXOME® ℞

NeXstar

Liposomal Daunorubicin

Antineoplastic

Pharmacology: DaunoXome is a liposomal preparation of daunorubicin formulated to selectively target daunorubicin to solid tumors in situ. While in the circulation, this formulation protects the entrapped daunorubicin from chemical and enzymatic degradation, minimizes protein binding, and generally decreases uptake by normal tissues, as well as by the non-reticuloendothelial system. The specific mechanism by which DaunoXome is able to deliver daunorubicin to solid tumors in situ is not known. DaunoXome accumulates in tumor tissue and DaunoXome vesicles enter the tumor cells intact. Daunorubicin is then released over time directly into the cells, where it is able to exert its antineoplastic activity.

DaunoXome has a pharmacokinetic profile different from that of conventional daunorubicin. When administered i.v. over approximately 30 minutes as a single dose of 10, 20, 40, 60 or 80 mg/m², DaunoXome undergoes monoexponential decline, although biexponential or Michaelis-Menton (saturation) kinetics occurred in some instances. Peak plasma levels at 40 mg/m² ranged from 14.8 to 22 µg/mL with a mean peak plasma level of 18 µg/mL. The mean terminal half-life at this dose was 4 hours and mean total body clearance was 10.5 mL/min.

Mean clearance for DaunoXome is 6.6 mL/min versus 223 mL/min for daunorubicin. When combined, these parameters indicate that DaunoXome produces a 36-fold increase in mean area under the plasma curve compared to conventional drug (375.3 vs 10.33 µg·hr/mL).

Indications: For the treatment of advanced HIV-related Kaposi's sarcoma.

Contraindications: DaunoXome should not be given in conjunction with other chemotherapeutic agents that suppress blood counts.

Warnings: DaunoXome is an antineoplastic agent that should be prescribed by clinicians familiar with the use of antineoplastic agents, and having access to facilities for regular monitoring of the clinical, hematological and biochemical parameters, as well as cardiac function, before, during and following therapy.

Daunorubicin has been associated with cardiomyopathy and congestive heart failure. In the clinical experience with DaunoXome, congestive heart failure was observed once, and in this patient the cardiac event was probably not related to DaunoXome therapy. Nevertheless, there must be a presumption that cardiomyopathy and congestive heart failure are possible side effects of DaunoXome. Cardiac function should be evaluated in each patient, including history, physical examination, and appropriate measurements of cardiac ejection fraction as indicated.

DaunoXome should not be given to patients who have had a serious hypersensitivity reaction to previous doses of DaunoXome or to any of its constituents unless the benefit from such treatment warrants the risk.

Daunorubicin has been associated with local tissue necrosis at the site of drug infiltration. Although no such necrosis has been observed with DaunoXome, care should be taken to ensure that there is no extravasation of drug when DaunoXome is administered (see Dosage).

Pregnancy and *Lactation:* Safety for use in pregnant and lactating women has not been established. Therefore, DaunoXome should only be used during pregnancy if the possible benefits outweigh the potential risks. Breast-feeding should be discontinued during treatment.

Fertility/Mutagenicity: Daunorubicin, the active component of DaunoXome, has been shown in experimental animals to impair fertility. Daunorubicin is also teratogenic in experimental animals. For daunorubicin, there is positive evidence of human fetal risk. Daunorubicin is mutagenic both in vitro and in vivo, and a high incidence of mammary tumors was observed in rats treated with daunorubicin. Although no such studies have been conducted with DaunoXome, it is possible that the drug may exhibit a similar profile for carcinogenesis, teratogenesis, mutagenesis and impairments of fertility, as that of daunorubicin.

Children/Geriatrics: The safety and effectiveness in children and the elderly have not been established.

Occupational Hazards: DaunoXome may induce delayed nausea and vomiting; it should not be administered prior to driving, or the use of heavy machinery.

Precautions: All parenteral drug products should be inspected visually for particulate matter prior to administration wherever solution and container permit.

Procedures for proper handling and disposal of anticancer drugs should be followed.

The primary toxicity of DaunoXome is myelosuppression and, as such, close patient observation and frequent monitoring of the blood cell counts is mandated. In patients with malignancies or with HIV infection, the immune system is already compromised, and the use of a cytotoxic agent decreasing the white blood cell count may cause further immunosuppression and make the patient more susceptible to intercurrent or opportunistic infections.

Drug Interactions: No interactions between DaunoXome and other drugs have been observed to date. DaunoXome has been safely administered during antiretroviral therapy with zidovudine (AZT), dideoxycytidine (ddC, zalcitabine) and dideoxyinosine (ddI, didanosine) and with the colony stimulating factor G-CSF (filgrastim). Although interaction of DaunoXome with other drugs has not been observed, patients requiring concomitant drug therapy should be monitored closely.

Adverse Effects: Daunorubicin has been associated with cardiomyopathy and congestive heart failure. Although no such side effects have been attributable to DaunoXome in clinical trials, these side effects may occur. Therefore, cardiac function should be evaluated in each patient, including history, physical examination, and appropriate measures of cardiac ejection fraction, as indicated.

Daunorubicin has also been associated with local tissue necrosis at the site of drug infiltrations. No such local necrosis has been observed with DaunoXome. Nonetheless, care should be taken to ensure that there is no infiltration of drug when DaunoXome is administered i.v.

The primary toxicity of DaunoXome is myelosuppression and, as such, close patient observation and frequent monitoring of the blood cell counts is mandated. In patients with malignancies or with HIV infection, the immune system is already compromised, and the use of a cytotoxic agent decreasing the white blood cell count may cause further immunosuppression and make the patient more susceptible to intercurrent or opportunistic infections.

Back pain, flushing and chest tightness were occasionally reported during the clinical trials. This syndrome may occur during a patient's initial infusion and may also occur in patients who have previously been exposed to DaunoXome without prior side effects. This combination of symptoms does not always appear to be dose related, and generally occurs during the first 10 minutes of the infusion. The etiology is unclear. The symptoms usually subside when the infusion is slowed or halted, and acetaminophen may be used for analgesia. Other allergic or immune reactions have been reported to be associated with hypotension.

Various other reactions, that were manageable and that did not result in patient withdrawal, such as headache, fatigue, chills, mucositis, lightheadedness, nausea and vomiting, mild hair loss, diarrhea have also been reported.

Overdose: Symptoms and Treatment: No experience exists for an overdose with DaunoXome. The primary anticipated toxicity from such an overdose would be myelosuppression, and under these circumstances bone marrow function should be carefully monitored with appropriate therapy for any severe side effects.

Dosage: The dosage must be adjusted individually. Therapy should be instituted at 40 mg/m² every 2 weeks and therapy should be continued as long as disease control can be maintained.

There are no preservative or bacteriostatic agents in DaunoXome or in its diluent. Therefore, aseptic technique must be strictly observed in handling of the drug.

DaunoXome should be diluted with 5% Dextrose Injection (D5W) before administration. The recommended concentration after dilution is between 0.2 mg and 1 mg daunorubicin/mL of solution. DaunoXome should be administered i.v. over a 30 to 60 minute period and within 6 hours of dilution with D5W.

Caution: DaunoXome should not be mixed with saline, bacteriostatic agents such as benzyl alcohol, or any other solution. Saline and bacteriostatics, such as benzyl alcohol, should not be used as diluents for DaunoXome. Use only 5% Dextrose for dilution.

The use of an in-line filter is not recommended for the i.v. infusion of DaunoXome, unless the mean pore diameter of the filter is greater than or equal to 5 µm.

Myelosuppression is a known reaction to DaunoXome therapy. The colony stimulating factor G-CSF (filgrastim) has been used to manage patients whose absolute neutrophil count (ANC) fell below 1 000/mm³.

If any signs or symptoms of extravasation have occurred, immediately terminate the infusion. If it is known or suspected that s.c. extravasation has occurred, the following steps are recommended: elevation of the affected limb; local intermittent application of ice for up to 2 days; consultation with a physician; close observation of the injection site.

Use Aseptic Technique: Aseptic technique must be strictly observed in all handling, since no preservative or bacteriostatic agent is present in DaunoXome or in the materials recommended for dilution. The product should be used within 6 hours of dilution in 5% Dextrose Injection.

Withdraw the calculated volume of DaunoXome into a sterile syringe. Instill the DaunoXome preparation into a sterile container with the correct amount of 5% Dextrose Injection (D5W) and administer within 6 hours. The recommended concentration after dilution is between 0.2 mg and 1 mg daunorubicin/mL of solution. Infuse over a 30 to 60 minute period. As with all parenteral drug products, inspect the solution visually for particulate matter prior to administration.

Caution: The only fluid which may be mixed with DaunoXome is D5W; DaunoXome should not be mixed with saline, bacteriostatic agents such as benzyl alcohol, or any other solution.

An in-line filter is not recommended for the i.v. infusion of DaunoXome. However, if such a filter is used, the mean pore diameter of the filter should not be less than 5 μm.

Procedures for proper handling and disposal of anticancer drugs should be followed.

To date, no incompatibilities of DaunoXome with other drugs have been reported. However, it is known that the active component daunorubicin is physically incompatible with heparin sodium and with dexamethasone phosphate when directly admixed. A precipitate is produced with either drug. Additionally, because of the chemical instability of the glycosidic bond of daunorubicin, admixture into a highly alkaline media (pH >8.0) is not recommended.

DaunoXome should not be mixed with saline; aggregation of the liposomes may result. Admixtures containing bacteriostatic agents such as benzyl alcohol or other detergent-like molecules should be avoided as well because such compounds can rupture the bilayer wall of the liposomes causing premature leakage of the active drug.

Information for the Patient: See Blue Section—Information for the Patient "DaunoXome".

Supplied: Each mL of red and clear to slightly opalescent, sterile, pyrogen-free, preservative-free, liposomal emulsion contains: daunorubicin 2 mg (encapsulated in liposomes). Nonmedicinal ingredients: calcium chloride, cholesterol, citric acid, distearoyl phosphatidylcholine, glycine, sucrose and water for injection. Single dose glass vials of 25 mL (50 mg). Store at 2 to 8°C. Do not freeze. Protect against exposure to light. Do not store partially used vials for future patient use. Vials are for single use only.

Reviewed 1998

DAYPRO™ ℞

Searle

Oxaprozin

Anti-inflammatory—Analgesic

Pharmacology: Oxaprozin is a nonsteroidal anti-inflammatory agent with analgesic and antipyretic properties. The modes of action of oxaprozin, like that of other nonsteroidal anti-inflammatory agents, are not fully established. It is known, however, that it does inhibit prostaglandin synthesis.

Pharmacokinetics: Oxaprozin is almost completely absorbed from the gastrointestinal tract, with peak plasma levels attained 2 to 4 hours after administration. The mean peak plasma concentration (C_{max}) is approximately 120 μg/mL with a single dose of 1 200 mg and approximately 190 μg/mL at steady-state. At therapeutic levels, more than 99% of oxaprozin is bound to plasma proteins, mostly albumin. The mean biological half-life in humans is approximately 50 hours. Total body clearance of oxaprozin rises from 2.5 mL/h/kg after a single 1 200 mg dose to 5 mL/h/kg at steady-state. The apparent volume of distribution rises from 180 to 300 mL/kg from single dose to steady-state. These increases are due to nonlinear protein binding. One study demonstrated that food had no effect on the extent of absorption of oral doses of oxaprozin in healthy subjects, whereas the rate of absorption was slightly slower. No abnormal drug accumulation occurred in patients treated with multiple doses (1 200 mg/day) for up to 6 months.

A dual metabolism has been identified for oxaprozin. Approximately 60% of the drug is oxidized to hydroxyoxaprozin I or II and approximately 30% is glucuronidated to form oxaprozin acyl glucuronide. These inactive metabolic products are excreted in the feces (one third) and in the urine (two thirds). About 30% of an oral dose is recovered as conjugates in urine.

Less than 5% is recovered as oxaprozin. Biliary excretion in cholecystectomized humans accounts for 5% of the drug in 5 days. Oxaprozin does not induce its own metabolism.

Oxaprozin disposition during steady-state conditions is not affected by either subject age or sex. However the volume of distribution declined with increasing age (see Dosage).

The pharmacokinetics of oxaprozin in patients with impaired renal function, patients maintained on hemodialysis, and healthy subjects were evaluated following a single 600 mg oral dose. Total body clearance and elimination half-life did not differ substantially among the 3 groups. In a multiple dose study of subjects and patients with normal albumin levels, who were undergoing hemodialysis, total body clearance and volume of distribution of unbound drug were higher in patients undergoing hemodialysis. Total oxaprozin levels were not affected and there was no evidence of accumulation in subjects or renally impaired patients. Caution should be used when oxaprozin is given to patients with renal impairment (see Dosage).

One study compared the pharmacokinetics of a single dose of oxaprozin in patients with cirrhosis. Elimination half-life, and clearance of unbound drug were unchanged.

The elimination half-life, volume of distribution, and total body clearance of unbound oxaprozin following a single dose were similar for patients with congestive heart failure as compared to healthy subjects.

The effects of therapeutic doses of oxaprozin (1 200 mg) and ASA (3 900 mg) on the gastric mucosa and fecal blood were studied in healthy subjects. Oxaprozin produced significantly less submucosal hemorrhage or bleeding than did ASA in a 10-day crossover study utilizing gastroscopic evaluation of the gastric mucosa. The average amount of fecal blood loss that was induced by oxaprozin during a 2 week study using ^{51}Cr-labelled autologous red blood cells was similar to that caused by placebo during the second week, but was significantly greater during the first week. The fecal blood loss induced by oxaprozin was significantly less than that caused by ASA throughout the 2-week study.

The effects of oxaprozin on renal function were studied in normal subjects and in patients with impaired renal function. In clearance studies of normal subjects during sustained water diuresis, oxaprozin caused no acute reduction in glomerular filtration rate (GFR), had no effect on overall sodium clearance, and had no long-term effect on serum creatinine, blood urea nitrogen, or serum potassium. In renally impaired patients with a GFR below 30 to 40 mL/min and in patients undergoing hemodialysis, oxaprozin was distributed more extensively because of a reduction in binding to plasma proteins. The mean biological half-life was not altered by renal disease, although urinary excretion of both oxaprozin and its conjugates was greatly reduced. A multiple-dose study in patients undergoing hemodialysis demonstrated no impairment of total or unbound clearance in the disease state.

Indications: For acute and chronic use in the relief of the signs and symptoms of rheumatoid arthritis and osteoarthritis.

Contraindications: Active peptic ulcer, a history of recurrent ulceration or active inflammatory disease of the gastrointestinal system. Known or suspected hypersensitivity to oxaprozin, its components, or other NSAIDs. The potential for cross-reactivity between different NSAIDs must be kept in mind. Oxaprozin should not be used in patients with the complete or partial syndrome of nasal polyps, or in whom asthma, anaphylaxis, urticaria, rhinitis, or other allergic manifestations are precipitated by ASA or other nonsteroidal anti-inflammatory agents. Fatal anaphylactoid reactions have occurred in such individuals with other NSAIDs. As well, individuals with the above medical problems are at risk of a severe reaction even if they have taken NSAIDs in the past without any adverse effects. Significant hepatic impairment or active liver disease. Severely impaired or deteriorating renal function (creatinine clearance <30 mL/min), individuals with lesser degrees of renal impairment are at risk of deterioration of their renal function when prescribed NSAIDs and must be monitored. Oxaprozin is not recommended for use with other NSAIDs because of the absence of any evidence demonstrating synergistic benefits and the potential for additive side effects.

Warnings: Serious gastrointestinal toxicity, such as peptic ulceration, perforation and gastrointestinal bleeding, **sometimes severe and occasionally fatal,** can occur at any time, with or without symptoms in patients treated with NSAIDs, including oxaprozin.

Minor upper gastrointestinal problems, such as dyspepsia, are common, usually developing early in therapy. Physicians should remain alert for ulceration and bleeding in patients treated with NSAIDs, even in the absence of previous gastrointestinal tract symptoms.

In patients observed in clinical trials of such agents, symptomatic upper gastrointestinal ulcers, gross bleeding, or perforation appear to occur in approximately 1% of patients treated for 3 to 6 months and in about 2 to 4% of patients treated for 1 year. The risk continues beyond 1 year and possibly increases.

The incidence of these complications increases with increasing dose.

Oxaprozin should be given under close medical supervision to patients prone to gastrointestinal tract irritation, particularly those with a history of peptic ulcer, diverticulosis or other inflammatory disease of the gastrointestinal tract, such as ulcerative colitis and Crohn's disease. In these cases the physician must weigh the benefits of treatment against the possible hazards.

Physicians should inform patients about the signs and/or symptoms of serious gastrointestinal toxicity and instruct them to contact a physician immediately if they experience persistent dyspepsia or other symptoms or signs suggestive of gastrointestinal ulceration or bleeding.

Because serious gastrointestinal tract ulceration and bleeding can occur without warning symptoms, physicians should follow chronically treated patients by checking their hemoglobin periodically and by being vigilant for the signs and symptoms of ulceration and bleeding and should inform the patients of the importance of this follow-up.

If ulceration is suspected or confirmed, or if gastrointestinal bleeding occurs, oxaprozin should be discontinued immediately, appropriate treatment instituted and the patient monitored closely.

No studies, to date, have identified any group of patients **not** at risk of developing ulceration and bleeding. A prior history of serious gastrointestinal events and other factors such as excess alcohol intake, smoking, age, female gender and concomitant oral steroid and anticoagulant use have been associated with increased risk.

Studies to date show that all NSAIDs can cause gastrointestinal tract adverse events. Although existing data does not clearly identify differences in risk between various NSAIDs, this may be shown in the future.

Geriatrics: Patients older than 65 years and frail or debilitated patients are most susceptible to a variety of adverse reactions from NSAIDs; their incidence increases with dose and duration of treatment. In addition, these patients are less tolerant of ulceration and bleeding and most reports of fatal gastrointestinal events are in this population. Older patients are also at risk of lower esophageal ulceration and bleeding.

For such patients, consideration should be given to a starting dose lower than usual, with individual adjustment when necessary, and under close supervision (see Precautions).

Cross-sensitivity: Patients sensitive to any one of the NSAIDs may be sensitive to any of the other NSAIDs also.

Aseptic Meningitis: In occasional cases, with some NSAIDs, the symptoms of aseptic meningitis (stiff neck, severe headaches, nausea and vomiting, fever or clouding of consciousness) have been observed. Patients with autoimmune disorders (systemic lupus erythematosus, mixed connective tissues diseases, etc.) seem to be predisposed. Therefore, in such patients, the physician must weigh the benefits of therapy against the possible hazards before prescribing and must be vigilant to the development of this complication.

Pregnancy and *Lactation*: The use of oxaprozin during pregnancy is not recommended as its safety in this condition has not been established. Oxaprozin should be used during pregnancy only if the benefit justifies the potential risk to the fetus and/or mother.

Oxaprozin is not recommended for use in nursing mothers, since many NSAIDs have been shown to be partially excreted in breast milk. Oxaprozin has been found in the milk of lactating rats.

Children: Oxaprozin is not recommended for use in patients less than 18 years of age.

Precautions: Gastrointestinal System: If gastrointestinal bleeding or perforation is suspected or occurs, oxaprozin should be discontinued, and appropriate treatment instituted and the patient closely monitored.

If gastric ulceration is suspected or confirmed, oxaprozin should be discontinued, and appropriate treatment instituted and the patient closely monitored.

There is no definitive evidence that the concomitant administration of sucralfate, omeprazole, histamine H_2-receptor antagonists and/or antacids will either prevent the occurrence of gastrointestinal side effects or allow continuation of the NSAID therapy when and if these adverse reactions appear.

Renal Function: Long-term administration of some NSAIDs to animals has resulted in renal papillary necrosis and other

Daypro (cont'd)

abnormal renal pathology. In humans, there have been reports of acute interstitial nephritis with hematuria, proteinuria, and occasionally nephrotic syndrome.

A second form of renal toxicity has been seen in patients with prerenal conditions leading to the reduction in renal blood flow or blood volume, where the renal prostaglandins have a supportive role in the maintenance of renal perfusion. In these patients, administration of a NSAID may cause a dose-dependent reduction in prostaglandin formation and may precipitate overt renal decompensation.

Patients at greater risk of this reaction are those with impaired renal function, heart failure, liver dysfunction, those taking diuretics, and the elderly. Discontinuation of nonsteroidal anti-inflammatory therapy is usually followed by recovery to the pretreatment state.

Oxaprozin and its metabolites are eliminated primarily by the kidneys and therefore, the drug should be used with great caution in patients with impaired renal function. In these cases, lower doses of oxaprozin should be anticipated and patients carefully monitored.

During long-term therapy, kidney function should be monitored periodically.

Genitourinary Tract: Some NSAIDs are known to cause persistent urinary symptoms (bladder pain, dysuria, urinary frequency), hematuria or cystitis. The onset of these symptoms may occur at any time after the initiation of therapy with an NSAID. Some cases have become severe on continued treatment. Should urinary symptoms occur, treatment with oxaprozin **must be stopped immediately** to obtain recovery. This should be done before any urological investigations or treatments are carried out.

Hepatic Function: As with other NSAIDs, borderline elevations of one or more liver function tests may occur in up to 15% of patients. These abnormalities may progress, may remain essentially unchanged, or may be transient with continued therapy. A patient with symptoms and/or signs suggesting liver dysfunction, or in whom an abnormal liver test has occurred, should be evaluated for evidence of the development of more severe hepatic reaction while on therapy with oxaprozin. Severe hepatic reactions including jaundice and cases of fatal hepatitis have been reported with oxaprozin as with other NSAIDs.

Although such reactions are rare, if abnormal liver tests persist or worsen, if clinical signs and symptoms consistent with liver disease develop, or if systemic manifestations occur (e.g., eosinophilia, rash, etc.), oxaprozin should be discontinued.

During long-term therapy, liver function tests should be monitored periodically. If oxaprozin needs to be used in the presence of impaired liver function, it must be done under strict observation.

Fluid and Electrolyte Balance: Fluid retention and edema have been observed in patients treated with oxaprozin. Therefore, as with many other NSAIDs, the possibility of precipitating congestive heart failure in elderly patients or those with compromised cardiac function should be born in mind.

Oxaprozin should be used with caution in patients with heart failure, hypertension or other conditions predisposing to fluid retention. With NSAID treatment, there is a potential risk of hyperkalemia particularly in patients with conditions such as diabetes mellitus or renal failure; elderly patients; or in patients receiving concomitant therapy with beta-adrenergic blockers, angiotensin converting enzyme inhibitors or some diuretics.

Serum electrolytes should be monitored periodically during long-term therapy, especially in those patients at risk.

Hematology: Drugs inhibiting prostaglandin biosynthesis do interfere with platelet function to varying degrees, therefore, patients who may be adversely affected by such an action should be carefully observed when oxaprozin is administered.

Blood dyscrasias (such as neutropenia, leukopenia, thrombocytopenia, aplastic anemia and agranulocytosis) associated with the use of NSAIDs are rare, but could occur with severe consequences.

Anemia may occur in patients receiving oxaprozin or other NSAIDs. This may be due to fluid retention, gastrointestinal blood loss, or an incompletely described effect upon erythrogenesis. Patients on long-term treatment with oxaprozin should have their hemoglobin or hematocrit values determined at appropriate intervals as determined by the clinical situation.

Infection: In common with other anti-inflammatory drugs, oxaprozin may mask the usual signs of infection.

Ophthalmology: Blurred and/or diminished vision has been reported with the use of oxaprozin and other NSAIDs. If such symptoms develop, this drug should be discontinued and an ophthalmologic examination performed; ophthalmologic examination should be carried out at periodic intervals in any patient receiving this drug for an extended period of time.

Occupational Hazards: CNS: Some patients may experience drowsiness, dizziness, vertigo, insomnia or depression with the use of oxaprozin. If patients experience these side effects, they should exercise caution in carrying out activities that require alertness.

Drug Interactions: ASA or other NSAIDs: The use of oxaprozin and any other NSAID, including over the counter ones (such as ASA and ibuprofen) is not recommended due to the possibility of additive side effects. Studies in man have shown that such combined administration produces decreased protein-binding of oxaprozin, with a reduced biological half-life, and increased clearance of oxaprozin.

Because of the long biological half-life of oxaprozin (approximately 50 hours), a clinical study of patients with rheumatoid arthritis was conducted to determine its interactions with ASA, naproxen, ibuprofen, and tolmetin sodium after therapy with oxaprozin was discontinued and the other drugs were started. In the same manner, patients with osteoarthritis were studied for interactions between oxaprozin and ASA, naproxen, ibuprofen and indomethacin. No clinically detectable interactions were found.

Anticoagulants: Numerous studies have shown that the concomitant use of NSAIDs and anticoagulants increases the risk of gastrointestinal adverse events such as ulceration and bleeding.

Because prostaglandins play an important role in hemostatis, and NSAIDs affect platelet functions as well, concurrent therapy of oxaprozin with warfarin requires close monitoring to be certain no change in anticoagulant dosage is necessary.

Concomitant warfarin and oxaprozin therapy did not produce further alterations of prothrombin times or a variety of other clotting factors when administered to normal subjects. Patients stabilized on phenprocoumon showed significant potentiation of the anticoagulation effect after 2.5 weeks of oxaprozin therapy. The values returned to pretreatment levels within 1 week after stopping oxaprozin.

Gold Salts, Antimalarial Agents, Corticosteroids: Oxaprozin may be used in combination with gold salts, antimalarial agents, or corticosteroids in the treatment of rheumatoid arthritis in adults.

In patients who received concomitant antimalarial therapy, a significantly higher incidence of muscular cramps/aching/pain, gastrointestinal bleeding, vision disorders and edema of the lower extremities was found. In patients who received concomitant gold therapy, a significantly higher incidence of sedation, skin disorders and E.N.T. disorders or symptoms was found.

Numerous studies have shown that the concomitant use of NSAIDs and oral glucocorticoids increases the risk of gastrointestinal side effects such as ulceration and bleeding. This is especially the case in older (>65 years old) individuals. In patients who received concomitant steroid therapy, significantly higher incidences of constipation, dyspepsia and alteration in taste were found.

Cimetidine/Ranitidine: Concomitant administration of cimetidine or ranitidine results in a clinically insignificant reduction of oxaprozin clearance. This does not require dosage adjustment.

Conjugated Estrogens: No interaction was observed when oxaprozin was administered concomitantly with conjugated estrogens.

Antihypertensives: Some NSAIDs have been reported to reduce the effects of antihypertensive agents. Hypertensive patients treated with the beta-adrenergic blocker, metoprolol, showed a small and transient increase in systolic blood pressure after 2 weeks on oxaprozin, with a return to baseline values at 4 weeks of therapy.

Diuretics: NSAIDs have been shown to interfere with the action of thiazide diuretics and potassium-sparing diuretics.

Lithium: NSAIDs have been reported to increase steady-state plasma lithium concentrations. It is recommended that these concentrations be monitored when initiating, adjusting and discontinuing drug treatment.

Clinical Laboratory Test Interactions: False-positive urine immunoassay screening tests for benzodiazepines have been reported in patients taking oxaprozin. This is due to lack of specificity of the screening tests. False-positive test results may be expected for several days following discontinuation of oxaprozin therapy. Confirmatory tests, such as gas chromatography/mass spectrometry, will distinguish oxaprozin from benzodiazepines.

Adverse Effects: The most common adverse reactions encountered with NSAIDs are gastrointestinal, of which peptic ulcer, with or without bleeding, is the most severe. Fatalities have occurred, particularly in the elderly.

Adverse reaction data were derived from patients who received oxaprozin in multidose, controlled, and open-label clinical trials, and from worldwide marketing experience. Rates for events occurring in more than 1% of patients, and for most of the less common events, are based on 2 253 patients who took 1 200 to 1 800 mg oxaprozin/day in clinical trials. Of these, 1 721 were treated for at least 1 month, 971 for at least 3 months, and 366 for more than 1 year. Rates for rarer events and for events reported from worldwide marketing experience are difficult to estimate accurately and are only listed as less than 1%.

Listed below are the adverse events and their incidences in the first month of use in clinical trials. Most of the events were seen by this time for common adverse reactions. However, the cumulative incidence can be expected to rise with continued therapy, and some events, such as gastrointestinal bleeding seem to occur at a constant or possibly increasing rising rate over time.

The most frequently reported adverse reactions were related to the gastrointestinal tract. They were nausea (8%) and dyspepsia (8%).

Incidence greater than 1%: In clinical trials the following adverse reactions occurred at an incidence greater than 1% and are probably related to treatment. Reactions occurring in 3 to 9% of patients treated with oxaprozin are indicated by an asterisk (*); those reactions occurring in less than 3% of patients are unmarked.

Gastrointestinal: abdominal pain/distress, anorexia, constipation*, diarrhea*, dyspepsia*, flatulence, nausea*, vomiting.

CNS: CNS inhibition (depression, sedation, somnolence, or confusion), disturbance of sleep.

Dermatologic: rash*.

Special Senses: tinnitus.

Urogenital: dysuria or frequency.

Incidence less than 1%: Probable causal relationship: The following adverse reactions were reported in clinical trials or from worldwide marketing experience at an incidence of less than 1%. Those reactions reported only from worldwide marketing experience are in *italics*. The probability of a causal relationship exists between the drug and these adverse reactions.

Gastrointestinal: peptic ulceration and/or gastrointestinal bleeding, liver function abnormalities including hepatitis, stomatitis, hemorrhoidal or rectal bleeding, *pancreatitis*.

Allergic: drug hypersensitivity reactions including anaphylaxis and *serum sickness*.

CNS: weakness, malaise.

Dermatologic: pruritus, urticaria, photosensitivity, *pseudoporphyria, exfoliative dermatitis, erythema multiforme, Stevens-Johnson syndrome, toxic epidermal necrolysis (Lyell's Syndrome)*.

Cardiovascular: edema, blood pressure changes.

Special Senses: blurred vision, conjunctivitis.

Hematologic: anemia, thrombocytopenia, leukopenia, ecchymoses.

Metabolic: weight gain, weight loss.

Respiratory: symptoms of upper respiratory tract infection.

Urogenital: *acute interstitial nephritis*, hematuria, renal insufficiency, *acute renal failure*, decreased menstrual flow.

Causal relationship unknown: The following adverse reactions occurred at an incidence of less than 1% in clinical trials, or were suggested from marketing experience, under circumstances where a causal relationship could not be definitely established. They are listed as alerting information for the physician.

Gastrointestinal: alteration in taste.

Dermatologic: alopecia.

Cardiovascular: palpitations.

Special Senses: hearing decrease.

Respiratory: sinusitis, pulmonary infections.

Urogenital: increase in menstrual flow.

Overdose: Symptoms and Treatment: In the event of overdosage, the stomach should be emptied by inducing vomiting or by gastric lavage. The patient should be carefully observed and given symptomatic and supportive treatment for as long as necessary. The symptoms of overdosage may include: lethargy, drowsiness, nausea, vomiting, and epigastric pain.

Dosage: In a clinical study in which healthy volunteers were administered oxaprozin after a meal, the extent of absorption was unchanged while the rate of absorption was slightly delayed. Oxaprozin may be administered orally once or twice daily with food or milk, and dosage adjusted for optimal response as described below.

Rheumatoid Arthritis: The initial therapy is 1 200 mg once daily. This may be decreased or increased depending on the patient's response. The maximum daily dose should not exceed 1 800 mg, or 26 mg/kg, whichever is less. Doses larger than 1 200 mg/day should be reserved for patients who weigh more than 50 kg, have normal renal and hepatic function, are at low risk of peptic ulcer and whose severity of disease justifies maximal therapy. Physicians should ensure that patients are tolerating lower doses before advancing to the larger doses.

The 1 800 mg dose should be divided into 2 doses (1 200 mg in the morning and 600 mg in the evening).

Osteoarthritis: The initial therapy is 1 200 mg once daily. This may be decreased to 600 mg once daily depending on the patient's response.

For patients of low body weight or with milder disease, an initial dose of 600 mg once daily may be appropriate.

Note: Consideration should be given to reducing the starting dose in elderly patients. In patients with moderate to severe renal impairment, and in those on hemodialysis, a maximum daily dosage of 600 mg administered under careful monitoring is recommended.

Information for the Patient: See Blue Section—Information for the Patient "Daypro".

Supplied: Each white, film-coated, capsule-shaped, scored caplet, with "DAYPRO" debossed on one side and "1381" on the other side, contains: oxaprozin 600 mg. Nonmedicinal ingredients: cellulose, cornstarch, hydroxypropyl methylcellulose, magnesium stearate, methylcellulose, polacrilin potassium, polyethylene glycol and titanium dioxide. HDPE bottles with plastic caps of 100. Store at room temperature at or below 25°C. Protect from light. Keep bottles tightly closed.

(Shown in Product Recognition Section)

Reviewed 1998

DDAVP® INJECTION ℞

Ferring

Desmopressin Acetate

Antidiuretic Hormone Analogue

Pharmacology: Desmopressin is a synthetic structural analogue of the natural human hormone, arginine vasopressin. As such, it exerts its action on the reabsorption of water in the renal tubule.

It also causes a transient increase in all components of the Factor VIII complex and plasminogen activator. These are released very rapidly from their endothelial cell storage sites. Moreover, it may have a direct effect on the vessel wall, with increased platelet spreading and adhesion at injury sites. The duration of action is from 8 to 12 hours. A second dose given before endothelial cell stores are replenished will not have as great an effect as the initial dose. Responses as great as the initial one usually are seen if 48 hours or more have elapsed between doses.

Indications: Antidiuretic hormone replacement therapy in the treatment of central diabetes insipidus, primary and secondary.

For patients with hemophilia A with Factor VIII levels greater than 5%. It will often maintain hemostasis in patients with hemophilia A during surgical procedures and postoperatively, when administered 45 minutes prior to scheduled procedure. It will also stop bleeding in hemophilia A patients with episodes of spontaneous or trauma-induced injuries such as hemarthroses, i.m. hematomas or mucosal bleeding.

In certain clinical situations, it may be justified to try desmopressin in patients with Factor VIII levels between 2 and 5%, however, these patients should be carefully monitored.

Desmopressin is **not indicated for the treatment of hemophilia B** because it has no effect on Factor IX levels.

Desmopressin should not be given to patients with Factor VIII antibodies.

Von Willebrand's Disease (Type 1): For patients with mild to moderate classic von Willebrand's disease (Type 1) with Factor VIII levels greater than 5%. Desmopressin will often maintain hemostasis in patients with mild to moderate von Willebrand's disease during surgical procedures and postoperatively when administered 45 minutes prior to the scheduled procedure.

Desmopressin will usually stop bleeding in mild to moderate von Willebrand's disease patients with episodes of spontaneous or trauma-induced injuries such as hemarthroses, i.m. hematomas or mucosal bleeding.

Those von Willebrand's disease patients who are least likely to respond are those with severe homozygous von Willebrand's disease with Factor VIII coagulant activity, Factor VIII antigen and von Willebrand's factor (ristocetin cofactor) activities less than 1%. Other patients may respond in a variable fashion depending on the type of molecular defect they have.

Bleeding time and Factor VIII coagulant activity, Factor VIII antigen and von Willebrand's factor activities should be checked during administration of desmopressin to ensure that adequate levels are being achieved.

Desmopressin is **not indicated for the treatment of severe classic Type 1 von Willebrand's Disease and Type II B** and when there is evidence of an abnormal molecular form of Factor VIII antigen (see Warnings).

Contraindications: Hypersensitivity to desmopressin.

Warnings: When used for bleeding disorders, desmopressin is for **i.v. use only, by infusion.** Patients who do not have need of antidiuretic hormone for its antidiuretic effect, in particular those who are young or elderly, should be cautioned to ingest only enough fluid to satisfy thirst, in order to decrease potential occurrence of water intoxication and hyponatremia.

Desmopressin should not be used to treat patients with Type II B von Willebrand's Disease, since severe thrombocytopenia may be induced.

Desmopressin must be used with caution in patients prone to vascular headaches, patients with coronary insufficiency and hypertensive cardiovascular diseases, because of possible change in blood pressure and tachycardia. Very occasionally, injection of desmopressin has produced local erythema, swelling or burning pain, along course of vein.

Desmopressin has no therapeutic effect in Glanzmann's thrombasthenia.

Tachyphylaxis may develop with repeated use.

Lack of therapeutic effect has been noted in patients who have been febrile or otherwise stressed' for several days. Whenever possible, therapeutic efficacy (i.e. Factor VIII response in hemophilia and bleeding time correction in other disorders) should be established in individual patients prior to use and followed throughout the course of treatment. The coincident use of anti-fibrinolytic agents to counteract desmopressin-induced plasminogen activator release has been recommended; however, benefit has not been clearly established.

Desmopressin has no therapeutic effect in renal diabetes insipidus.

Precautions: Use desmopressin with caution in patients with coronary arterial insufficiency and/or hypertensive cardiovascular disease because of possible tachycardia, and changes in blood pressure. Severe allergic reactions have not been reported with desmopressin. It is not known whether antibodies to desmopressin acetate are produced after repeated injections.

Hemophilia A: Laboratory tests for assessing patient status include levels of Factor VIII coagulant, Factor VIII antigen and Factor VIII ristocetin cofactor (von Willebrand factor) as well as activated partial thromboplastin time. Factor VIII coagulant activity should be determined before giving desmopressin for hemostasis. If Factor VIII coagulant activity is present at less than 5% of normal, desmopressin should not be relied upon alone.

Hemophilia B: Desmopressin should not be used for these patients, because it has no effect on Factor IX levels.

Von Willebrand's Disease: Laboratory tests for assessing patient status include levels of Factor VIII coagulant, Factor VIII antigen and Factor VIII ristocetin cofactor (von Willebrand factor). The skin bleeding time may be helpful in following these patients and should always be assessed preoperatively.

Diabetes Insipidus: In the control of diabetes insipidus, use the lowest effective dose and assess dosage periodically.

Do not administer desmopressin to dehydrated patients until water balance has been adequately restored.

Laboratory tests for monitoring the patient include urine volume and osmolality. In some cases, plasma osmolality may be required.

Pregnancy: Reproduction studies performed in rats and rabbits with s.c. doses up to 12.5 times the human dose when used for Factor VIII stimulation and 125 times the human dose when used in diabetes insipidus have revealed no evidence of harm to the fetus due to desmopressin. There are several publications of management of diabetes insipidus in pregnant women with no harm to the fetus reported; however, there are no adequate and well controlled studies in pregnant women. Published reports stress that, as opposed to preparations containing the natural hormones, desmopressin in antidiuretic doses has no uterotonic action, but the physician will have to weigh possible therapeutic advantages against possible danger in each case.

Lactation: It is not known whether this drug is excreted in human milk. Because many drugs are excreted in human milk, caution should be exercised when desmopressin is administered to a nursing woman.

Children: Observe children closely for possible hyponatremia and water intoxication due to overingestion of fluids.

Desmopressin should not be used in infants younger than 3 months in the treatment of hemophilia A or von Willebrand's disease.

Adverse Effects: Infrequently, desmopressin has produced transient headache, nausea, mild abdominal cramps and vulvar pain. These symptoms disappear with reduction in dosage. Facial flushing, tachycardia (20 to 40%), mild hypotension (fall in systolic and diastolic blood pressure by approximately 15 torr) have also been reported, and decreased urine output for 6 to 8 hours commonly observed. See Warnings for the possibility of water intoxication and hyponatremia.

Very occasionally, injection of desmopressin has produced local erythema, swelling or burning pain, along course of vein.

<u>*Drug Interactions:*</u> Although the pressor activity of desmopressin is very low compared with the antidiuretic activity, the use of desmopressin doses as large as 0.3 µg/kg with other pressor agents, should be done only with careful patient monitoring.

The coincident use of antifibrinolytic agents to counteract desmopressin-induced plasminogen activator release, has been recommended. Desmopressin has been used with epsilon aminocaproic acid or used with tranexamic acid without adverse effects. However, benefit has not been clearly demonstrated.

Overdose: Symptoms: Headaches, abdominal cramps and nausea (see Adverse Effects).

Treatment: No specific antidote. Reduce dosage and frequency of administration or withdraw the drug according to severity of the condition.

Water intoxication responds rapidly to diuretic therapy (e.g. furosemide) and appropriate replacement fluid support, without interference with hemostatic effects.

Dosage: Hemophilia A and von Willebrand's Disease Type I: Desmopressin is administered as an i.v. infusion. Children: 0.3 µg/kg. Adults: 10.0 µg/m² (maximum dose 20 µg).

Dilution for infusion: Diluted in sterile physiological saline and infused slowly over 20 to 30 minutes. In adults and children weighing more than 10 kg: 50 mL of diluent is used; in children weighing 10 kg or less, 10 mL of diluent is used. Side effects may be decreased by slow infusion. Blood pressure and pulse rate should be monitored during infusion. (If desmopressin is used preoperatively, it should be administered 30 minutes prior to the scheduled procedure.) The peak effect is obtained in 1 hour after administration. Response is immediate for bleeding time reduction.

The necessity for repeat administration of desmopressin or use of any blood products for hemostasis should be determined by laboratory response as well as the clinical condition of the patient. The tendency toward tachyphylaxis (lessening of response) with repeated administration, given more frequently than every 48 hours should be considered in treating each patient.

Parenteral drug products should be inspected visually for particulate matter and discoloration prior to administration whenever solution and container permit.

Diabetes Insipidus: Diagnosis of Central Diabetes Insipidus: Central diabetes insipidus may be demonstrated by the inability to produce urine osmolality above 175 mOsm/kg with dehydration severe enough to cause a loss of greater than 2% of body weight. The patient responding to 5 units of arginine vasopressin given s.c. after dehydration confirms the diagnosis of central diabetes insipidus.

Parenteral application: Desmopressin may be administered s.c., i.m. or i.v. In the majority of adults 1 to 4 µg once daily will provide satisfactory control of the diabetes insipidus. In children a dose of 0.4 µg once a day may be used. The dose should be drawn up from the ampul at a fraction of a mL, using an insulin syringe and not prepared by dilution.

Desmopressin dosage must be determined for each patient and adjusted according to the pattern of response. Response should be estimated by 2 parameters: adequate duration of sleep and adequate, not excessive, water turnover.

To institute desmopressin therapy, patients should be withdrawn from previous medication and allowed to establish a baseline polyuria and polydipsia. The stable polyuria is used as a baseline to determine the magnitude and duration of the response to medication. In less severe cases, prior water loading may be desirable to establish a vigorous flow of urine. When the urine osmolality reaches a plateau at the low level (in most cases, less than 100 mOsm/kg), the first dose of desmopressin is administered intranasally or parenterally. A urine sample is obtained after 2 hours and hourly thereafter following desmopressin administration. Samples are measured for volume and osmolality. When the patient has reached the previous baseline urine osmolality and urine flow, the drug effect has ceased and the next desmopressin dose

DDAVP Injection (cont'd)

is administered. The cycle is then repeated until the patient has reached a stable condition.

I.V., I.M. or S.C.: Children: 0.1 mL (0.4 μg) once daily. Adults: 0.25 to 1 mL (1 to 4 μg) once daily.

One mL (4 μg) of desmopressin solution has an antidiuretic activity of about 16 IU.; 1 μg of desmopressin is equivalent to 4 IU.

For patients who have been controlled on intranasal desmopressin and who must be switched to the injection form, either because of poor intranasal absorption, or because of the need for surgery, the comparable antidiuretic dose of the injection is explained below.

Intranasal administration requires a higher dosage than i.v. administration since only 10% of intranasally administered drug will be absorbed. The intransal dosage that is required is therefore 10 times larger than the i.v. dose, thus an approximate parenteral dosage of 1/10 that of the intranasal, is required and should be adjusted for each patient individually, to obtain an adequate diurnal rhythm of water turnover.

Supplied: Each ampul contains: desmopressin acetate 4 μg (equivalent to 3.6 μg free base) in 1 mL of an isotonic sterile and pyrogen-free water solution, for i.v., i.m. or s.c. administration. Ampuls of 1 mL, cartons of 10. Store at about 4°C in a refrigerator. Do not freeze. Store away from light.

DDAVP® Spray and Rhinyle Nasal Solutions Ⓟ

Ferring

Desmopressin Acetate

Antidiuretic

Pharmacology: Desmopressin is a synthetic structural analogue of the antidiuretic hormone, arginine vasopressin, which alters the permeability of the renal tubule to increase resorption of water. The increase in the permeability of both the distal tubules and collecting ducts appears to be mediated by a stimulation of the adenylcyclase activity in the renal tubules.

Approximately 10 to 20% of the dose of desmopressin solution administered intranasally is absorbed through the nasal mucosa. Antidiuretic effects occur within 1 hour, peak in 1 to 5 hours, persist 8 to 20 hours and then abruptly end over a period of 60 to 90 minutes. Duration of action varies greatly among individuals and is dependent upon the rate of absorption from the nasal mucosa, persistence in plasma, and effect on renal tubules.

Indications: Diabetes Insipidus: Spray and Rhinyle: The management of vasopressin sensitive central diabetes insipidus and the control of temporary polyuria and polydipsia following head trauma, hypophysectomy or surgery in the pituitary region.

Nocturnal Enuresis: Spray only: The short-term management of nocturnal enuresis in patients 5 years of age and older who have normal ability to concentrate urine. Desmopressin should be used in conjunction with nonmedicinal therapy such as motivational counselling and bladder exercises.

Contraindications: Hypersensitivity to desmopressin or to any of the constituents.

Because of the risk of platelet aggregation and thrombocytopenia, desmopressin should not be used in patients with type IIB or platelet-type (pseudo) von Willebrand's disease.

Warnings: For intranasal use only. Desmopressin is not effective in controlling polyuria caused by renal disease, nephrogenic diabetes insipidus, psychogenic diabetes insipidus, hypokalemia or hypercalcemia.

Fluid intake should be adjusted in order to reduce the possibility of water retention and hyponatremia especially in very young and elderly patients (see Dosage). Particular attention should be paid to the risk of an extreme decrease in plasma osmolality and resulting seizures in young children.

Changes in the nasal mucosa resulting from rhinitis, scarring, edema or other disease may cause erratic, unreliable absorption in which case intranasal desmopressin should not be used. In the case of temporary rhinitis, consideration should be given to using an injectable form of desmopressin, until the nasal mucosa returns to normal.

Precautions: General: Desmopressin at high dosage [40 μg (0.4 mL) or more] has very occasionally produced a slight elevation of blood pressure, which disappeared with a reduction in dosage. The drug should be used with caution in patients with coronary artery insufficiency and/or hypertensive cardiovascular disease because of possible tachycardia and changes in blood pressure.

In the control of diabetes insipidus, the lowest effective dose should be used and the effective dosage, as determined by urine volume and osmolality and, in some cases, plasma osmolality, should be assessed periodically.

Desmopressin should not be administered to dehydrated patients until water balance has been adequately restored.

Desmopressin should be used with caution in patients with cystic fibrosis because these patients are prone to hyponatremia.

Children and geriatric patients should be closely observed for possible water retention due to over ingestion of fluids. When fluid intake is not excessive, there is little danger of water intoxication and hyponatremia with the usual intranasal doses of desmopressin used to control diabetes insipidus. Fluid intake should be carefully adjusted to prevent overhydration.

There are reports of changes in response over time, usually when the drug has been administered for periods longer than 6 months. Some patients may show decreased responsiveness, others a shortened duration of effect. There is no evidence that this effect is due to the development of binding antibodies, but may be due to local inactivation of the peptide.

For control of nocturnal enuresis a restricted fluid intake is recommended a few hours before administration.

Drug Interactions: Clofibrate, chlorpropamide and carbamazepine may potentiate the antidiuretic activity of desmopressin while demeclocycline, lithium and norepinephrine may decrease its activity.

Although the pressor activity of desmopressin is very low compared with the antidiuretic activity, use of large doses of desmopressin with other pressor agents should be done only with careful patient monitoring.

Pregnancy: Reproductive studies performed in rats and rabbits have revealed no evidence of harm to the fetus by desmopressin. Use in pregnant women with no harm to the fetus has been reported. However, no controlled studies in pregnant women have been carried out. Unlike preparations containing the natural hormone, desmopressin in antidiuretic doses has no uterotonic action, but the physician should weigh possible therapeutic advantages against potential risks in each case.

Lactation: There have been no controlled studies in nursing mothers. A single study on a postpartum woman demonstrated a marked change in maternal plasma desmopressin level following an intranasal dose of 10 μg (0.1 mL), but little desmopressin was detectable in breast milk.

Children: Desmopressin has been used in children with diabetes insipidus. The dose must be individually adjusted to the patient with attention in the very young to the danger of an extreme decrease of plasma osmolality with resulting convulsions. Dosage in infants younger than 3 months has not been established. Dose should start at 5 μg (0.05 mL) or less. Use of desmopressin in infants and children will require careful fluid intake restriction to prevent possible hyponatremia and water intoxication.

Laboratory Tests: Diagnosis of Central Diabetes Insipidus: Central diabetes insipidus may be demonstrated by the inability to produce urine of osmolality above 175 mOsm/kg with dehydration severe enough to cause a loss of greater than 2% of body weight.

Patients are selected for therapy by establishing a diagnosis by means of a water deprivation test, the hypertonic saline infusion test, and/or response to 5 units arginine vasopressin given s.c. after dehydration. Continued response to desmopressin can be monitored by urine volume and osmolality. In cases of severe dehydration, plasma osmolality determination may be required.

Adverse Effects: Infrequently, high doses of desmopressin have produced transient headache and nausea. Nasal congestion, rhinitis, flushing and mild abdominal cramps have been reported. These symptoms disappeared with reduction in dosage.

Side effects reported from controlled clinical trials involving 638 subjects included headache (2%) and rhinitis (1%), nasal discomfort (1%), epistaxis (1%) and abdominal pain (1%). Other effects, reported at a frequency of less than 1%, included dizziness, chills, wheezing, rash, edema of face and hands, nausea, constipation, anorexia, increased appetite, conjunctivitis and after taste in the mouth. These symptoms disappeared with reduction of dosage or withdrawal of drug. Adverse effects rarely necessitate discontinuance of the drug.

Overdose: Symptoms and Treatment: Overdose symptoms include headaches, abdominal cramps, nausea and facial flushing. There is no known antidote. Dosage and frequency of administration should be reduced, or the drug withdrawn according to the severity of the condition.

Water retention can be controlled by decreasing the dosage of desmopressin; severe water retention caused by overdosage may be treated with a diuretic such as furosemide.

Dosage: Diabetes Insipidus: Central diabetes insipidus may be demonstrated by the inability to produce urine of osmolality above 175 mOsm/kg with dehydration severe enough to cause a loss of greater than 2% of body weight.

Dosage in children up to 3 months of age has not been established.

Dosage must be individualized but clinical experience has shown that the average daily dose for adults is 10 to 40 μg (0.1 to 0.4 mL) desmopressin and for children 3 months to 12 years of age, 5 to 30 μg (0.05 to 0.3 mL). This may be given as a single dose or divided into 2 or 3 doses. About 33% of patients can be treated with a single daily dose. Geriatric patients may be more sensitive to the antidiuretic effect of the usual adult dose of desmopressin.

In those children who require less than 10 μg (0.1 mL), the rhinyle presentation should be used since the spray will only deliver a minimum of 10 μg. In some patients, better control of polyuria is attained with smaller doses given at 6 to 8 hour intervals.

Most adults require 20 μg (0.2 mL) daily, administered in 2 divided doses (in the morning and the evening). Initially, therapy should be directed to control nocturia with a single evening dose. Response to therapy can be measured by the volume and frequency of urination and duration of uninterrupted sleep. The dosage of desmopressin should be adjusted according to the diurnal pattern of response, with the morning and evening doses being adjusted separately. Patients being switched from parenteral to intranasal administration generally require 10 times their maintenance i.v. dose intranasally.

To institute therapy with desmopressin patients should be withdrawn from previous medication and allowed to establish a baseline polyuria to permit determination of the magnitude and duration of the response to medication. In less severe cases, prior water loading may be desirable to establish a vigorous flow of urine. When the urine osmolality reaches a plateau at low level (in most cases, less than 100 mOsm/kg), the first oral dose of desmopressin [10 μg (0.1 mL)] is administered intranasally. A urine sample is obtained after 2 hours and hourly thereafter following desmopressin administration. Urine volume and osmolality is measured. When the patient has reached the previous baseline urine osmolality and urine flow, the drug effect has ceased and the next dose is administered. The cycle is then repeated until the patient has reached a stable condition.

Nocturnal Enuresis: Dosage must be individualized by the physician. The clinically effective intranasal dose varies between patients and ranges between 10 and 40 μg desmopressin daily. A suitable starting dose for adults and children is 20 μg given 1 hour before sleep. A restricted fluid intake is recommended a few hours before administration.

For the method of administering desmopressin by the nasal spray pump refer to Information for the Patient.

Changes in the nasal mucosa resulting from rhinitis, scarring, edema or other disease may cause erratic, unreliable absorption in which case intranasal desmopressin should not be used. In the case of temporary rhinitis, consideration should be given to using an injectable form of desmopressin, until the nasal mucosa returns to normal.

Rarely, patients may develop tolerance to the drug during long-term intranasal use, and require cautious increase in dosage to achieve an adequate therapeutic response.

Information for the Patient: See Blue Section—Information for the Patient "DDAVP Spray and Rhinyle Nasal Solutions".

Supplied: Rhinyle: Each bottle contains: desmopressin acetate 250 μg (equivalent to 225 μg free base) in 2.5 mL of isotonic water, clear, colorless solution, with 1 calibrated rhinyle tube for intranasal administration. Keep in refrigerator at 2 to 8°C but do not freeze. Store out of reach of children.

Spray: Each pre-compression metered dose spray pump contains: desmopressin acetate 0.1 mg/mL in a buffered isotonic aqueous solution. Also contains benzalkonium chloride as a preservative. Each depression delivers desmopressin acetate 10 μg. Spray bottles of 2.5 mL containing 25 doses and 5 mL containing 50 doses. Store at room temperature 15 to 30°C. Do not freeze. Store out of reach of children.

...Your suggestions will help the editors and the *CPS* Editorial Advisory Panel improve the next edition of *CPS*.

DDAVP® Tablets ℞

Ferring

Desmopressin Acetate

Antidiuretic

Pharmacology: Desmopressin is a synthetic structural analogue of the antidiuretic hormone, arginine vasopressin, which alters the permeability of the renal tubule to increase resorption of water. The increase in the permeability of both the distal tubules and collecting ducts appears to be mediated by a stimulation of the adenylcyclase activity in the renal tubules.

Although the bioavailability of orally ingested desmopressin is low, reported as being about 1 to 5%, it is sufficient to induce an antidiuresis (urine osmolality greater than 400 mOsm/kg) lasting 7 to 9 hours in healthy subjects and in patients with diabetes insipidus. Onset of action, as determined by decreased urine volume and increased urine osmolality, is within 1 hour. In both adults and children, there is a log linear relationship between desmopressin doses and maximal urine osmolality and duration of antidiuresis within the dose range 12.5 to 400 µg. Measurements of plasma desmopressin concentrations after peroral desmopressin administration show a linear relationship between amounts of desmopressin absorbed and dose, but with great interindividual differences.

Indications: For the management of vasopressin sensitive central diabetes insipidus, and for the control of temporary polyuria and polydipsia following head trauma, hypophysectomy or surgery in the pituitary region.

Contraindications: Hypersensitivity to desmopressin or any of the tablet's constituents. Because of the risk of platelet aggregation and thrombocytopenia, the drug should not be used in patients with type IIB or platelet-type (pseudo) von Willebrand's disease.

Warnings: Desmopressin is not effective in controlling polyuria caused by renal disease, nephrogenic diabetes insipidus, psychogenic diabetes insipidus, hypokalemia or hypercalcemia.

Fluid intake should be adjusted to reduce the possibility of water intoxication and hyponatremia especially in the very young and elderly patients (see Dosage). Particular attention should be paid to the risk of an extreme decrease in plasma osmolality and resulting seizures in young children.

Keep this medication, as well as all medication out of reach of children.

Precautions: Desmopressin at high dosage (40 µg or more) has occasionally produced a slight elevation of blood pressure, which disappeared with a reduction in dosage. The drug should be used with caution in patients with coronary artery insufficiency and/or hypertensive cardiovascular disease because of possible tachycardia and changes in blood pressure.

Lack of therapeutic response to oral desmopressin may be noted in some patients even at the maximum recommended dosage. These patients should be switched to the intranasal or injectable dosage form of desmopressin.

In the control of diabetes insipidus, the lowest effective dose should be used and the effective dosage, as determined by urine volume and osmolality and in some cases, plasma osmolality, should be assessed periodically.

Desmopressin should not be administered to dehydrated patients until water balance has been adequately restored.

Children and geriatric patients should be closely observed for possible water retention due to over ingestion of fluids. When fluid intake is not excessive, there is little danger of water intoxication and hyponatremia. Fluid intake should be carefully adjusted to prevent overhydration.

There are reports of changes in response over time, usually when the drug has been administered for periods longer than 6 months. Some patients may show decreased responsiveness, others a shortened duration of effect. There is no evidence that this effect is due to the development of binding antibodies, but may be due to local inactivation of the peptide.

Drug Interactions: Clofibrate, chlorpropamide and carbamazepine may potentiate the antidiuretic activity of desmopressin while demeclocycline, lithium and norepinephrine may decrease its activity.

Although the pressor activity of desmopressin is very low compared with the antidiuretic activity, use of large doses of desmopressin with other pressor agents should be done only with careful patient monitoring.

Pregnancy: Reproductive studies performed in rats and rabbits have revealed no evidence of harm to the fetus by desmopressin. The use of desmopressin in pregnant women with no harm to the fetus has been reported.

However, no controlled studies in pregnant women have been carried out. Unlike preparations containing the natural hormone, desmopressin in antidiuretic doses has no uterotonic action, but the physician should weigh possible therapeutic advantages against potential risks in each case.

Lactation: There have been no controlled studies in nursing mothers. A single study on a postpartum woman demonstrated a marked change in maternal plasma desmopressin level following an intranasal dose of 10 µg, but little desmopressin was detectable in breast milk.

Children: Desmopressin has been used in children with diabetes insipidus. The dose must be individually adjusted to the patient with attention in the very young to the danger of an extreme decrease of plasma osmolality with resulting convulsions. Dosage in infants younger than 3 months has not been established. Dose should start at 100 µg or less. Use of desmopressin in infants and children will require careful fluid intake restriction to prevent possible hyponatremia and water intoxication.

Laboratory Tests: Diagnosis of Central Diabetes Insipidus: Central diabetes insipidus may be demonstrated by the inability to produce urine of osmolality above 175 mOsm/kg with dehydration severe enough to cause a loss of greater than 2% of body weight.

Patients are selected for therapy by establishing a diagnosis by means of a water deprivation test, the hypertonic saline infusion test, and/or response to 5 units arginine vasopressin given s.c. after dehydration and by means of Minirin test. Continued response to desmopressin can be monitored by urine volume and osmolality. In cases of severe dehydration, plasma osmolality determination may be required.

Adverse Effects: Infrequently, high doses of desmopressin have produced transient headache and nausea. Nasal congestion, rhinitis, flushing, and mild abdominal cramps have been reported. These symptoms disappeared with reduction in dosage.

Side effects reported from controlled clinical trials involving 638 subjects included headache (2%), and rhinitis (1%), nasal discomfort (1%), epistaxis (1%) and abdominal pain (1%). Other effects, reported at a frequency of less than 1% included dizziness, chills, wheezing, rash, edema of face and hands, nausea, constipation, anorexia, increased appetite, conjunctivitis and after taste in the mouth. These symptoms disappeared with reduction of dosage or withdrawal of drug. Adverse effects rarely necessitate discontinuance of the drug.

Serum AST levels were elevated in 4/16 patients 6 months after commencing oral desmopressin therapy (200 to 600 µg/day). Two of these patients had exhibited baseline levels of AST that were above the normal range and all 4 patients had normal AST levels on repeat test at 9 months, even though desmopressin administration was continued. The possibility that desmopressin has an adverse effect on serum enzymes is therefore remote.

Overdose: Symptoms and Treatment: Overdose symptoms include headaches, abdominal cramps, nausea, and facial flushing. There is no known antidote. Dosage and frequency of administration should be reduced, or the drug withdrawn, according to severity of the condition.

Water retention can be controlled by decreasing the dosage of desmopressin; severe water retention caused by overdosage may be treated with a diuretic such as furosemide.

Dosage: Desmopressin dosage must be determined for each patient and adjusted according to the pattern of response. Response should be estimated by adequate duration of sleep and adequate, not excessive, water turnover and maintenance of urine osmolality at levels of 400 mOsm/kg or greater.

To institute desmopressin therapy, patients should be withdrawn from previous medication and allowed to establish a baseline polyuria and polydipsia. The stable polyuria is used as a baseline to determine the magnitude and duration of the response to medication. In less severe cases, prior water loading may be desirable to establish a vigorous flow of urine. When the urine osmolality reaches a plateau at the low level (in most cases, less than 100 mOsm/kg), the first oral dose (e.g., 100 µg) of desmopressin is administered. A urine sample is obtained after 2 hours and hourly thereafter; urine volume is measured and urine osmolality determined. When the patient has reached the previous baseline urine osmolality and urine flow, the drug effect has ceased and the next desmopressin dose is administered. The cycle is then repeated until the patient has reached a stable condition.

Dosage must be individualized. A suitable starting dose for adults and children is 100 µg (0.1 mg desmopressin) 3 times daily. This dosage regimen should then be adjusted in accordance with the patient's response in order to ensure an optimum dose. For patients who have been controlled on intranasal desmopressin and who are to be switched to the oral form, the oral dose producing comparable antidiuresis is about 10 to 20 times greater than the established intranasal dose. Geriatric patients may be more sensitive to the antidiuretic effect of the usual adult dose of desmopressin.

In children, the evening dose is usually 2x higher than the morning and midday dose to ensure sufficient antidiuresis during sleep. This is generally not a requirement for adult patients, presumably because adults sleep for shorter periods of time.

The maximum recommended dosage for both adults and children is 1.2 mg/day (400 µg t.i.d.). Although there is no evidence that potentially serious adverse reactions would occur at daily doses greater than 1.2 mg, a maximum of 1.2 mg is being recommended at the present time since clinical experiences with daily dosages exceeding 1.2 mg is limited. The lowest effective dosage should be given. Rarely, during long-term use, patients may develop tolerance to the drug and require cautious increase in dosage to achieve adequate therapeutic response.

Supplied: 0.1 mg: Each white, uncoated tablet contains: desmopressin acetate 0.1 mg. Nonmedicinal ingredients: lactose, magnesium stearate, potato starch and povidone. Strip of 30 per carton.

0.2 mg: Each white, uncoated tablet contains: desmopressin acetate 0.2 mg. Nonmedicinal ingredients: lactose, magnesium stearate, potato starch and povidone. Strip of 30 per carton.

Store below 25°C in a dry place.

Reviewed 1997

DECADRON® Phosphate Injection ℞

MSD

Dexamethasone Sodium Phosphate

Corticosteroid

Indications: By i.v. or i.m. injection when oral therapy is not feasible:

Adrenocortical Insufficiency: Dexamethasone sodium phosphate injection has predominantly glucocorticoid activity with low mineralocorticoid activity. Therefore, it does not offer complete replacement therapy, and its use must be supplemented with salt and/or desoxycorticosterone. When so supplemented, dexamethasone sodium phosphate injection is indicated in the impairment of all adrenocortical activity, as in Addison's disease or following bilateral adrenalectomy that requires replacement of both glucocorticoid and mineralocorticoid activity.

Relative Adrenocortical Insufficiency: In the relative adrenocortical insufficiency that may occur following cessation of long-term therapy with suppressive doses of adrenocortical hormones, mineralocorticoid secretion may be unimpaired. Replacement with a hormone that acts predominantly as a glucocorticoid may be sufficient to restore adrenocortical function. When immediate support is mandatory, dexamethasone sodium phosphate injection may be effective within minutes after administration and can be life saving.

Preoperative and postoperative support in patients undergoing bilateral adrenalectomy, or hypophysectomy, or any other surgical procedure when adrenocortical reserve is doubtful, and in postoperative shock unresponsive to conventional therapy.

Nonsuppurative Thyroiditis: By i.v. or i.m. injection when oral therapy is not feasible in thyroid crisis.

Shock: The adjunctive treatment of shock where high (pharmacologic) doses of corticosteroids are needed: e.g., severe shock of hemorrhagic, traumatic, surgical origin. Treatment with dexamethasone sodium phosphate injection is an adjunct to, and not a substitute for, specific or supportive measures that the patient may require, e.g., restoration of circulating blood volume, correction of fluid and electrolyte balance, oxygen, surgical measures and antibiotics.

Rheumatic Disorders: As adjunctive therapy for short-term administration (to support the patient during an acute episode or exacerbation) in: post-traumatic osteoarthritis, synovitis of osteoarthritis, rheumatoid arthritis including juvenile rheumatoid arthritis (selected cases may require low-dose maintenance therapy), acute and subacute bursitis, epicondylitis, acute nonspecific tenosynovitis, acute gouty arthritis, psoriatic arthritis, ankylosing spondylitis.

Decadron Phosphate Injection (cont'd)

Collagen Diseases: During an exacerbation or as maintenance therapy in selected cases of: systemic lupus erythematosus, acute rheumatic carditis.
Dermatologic Diseases: pemphigus, severe erythema multiforme (Stevens-Johnson syndrome), exfoliative dermatitis, bullous dermatitis herpetiformis, severe seborrheic dermatitis, severe psoriasis, mycosis fungoides.
Allergic States: Initial control of severe allergic conditions intractable to adequate trials of conventional treatment in: bronchial asthma, contact dermatitis, atopic dermatitis, serum sickness, seasonal or perennial allergic rhinitis, drug hypersensitivity reactions, urticarial transfusion reactions, acute noninfectious laryngeal edema, anaphylaxis (epinephrine is the drug of first choice).
Ophthalmic Diseases: Severe acute and chronic allergic and inflammatory processes involving the eye and its adnexa, such as: allergic conjunctivitis, keratitis, allergic corneal marginal ulcers, herpes zoster ophthalmicus, iritis, iridocyclitis, chorioretinitis, diffuse posterior uveitis and choroiditis, optic neuritis, sympathetic ophthalmia, anterior segment inflammation.
Gastrointestinal Diseases: To support the patient during a critical period of the disease in: ulcerative colitis (systemic therapy), regional enteritis (systemic therapy).
Respiratory Diseases: Löffler's syndrome not manageable by other means, symptomatic sarcoidosis, berylliosis, fulminating or disseminated pulmonary tuberculosis when concurrently accompanied by appropriate antituberculous chemotherapy, aspiration pneumonitis.
Hematologic Disorders: acquired (autoimmune) hemolytic anemia, idiopathic thrombocytopenic purpura in adults (i.v. only; i.m. administration is contraindicated), secondary thrombocytopenia in adults, erythroblastopenia (RBC anemia), congenital (erythroid) hypoplastic anemia.
Neoplastic Disorders: For palliative management of hypercalcemia associated with cancer, leukemias and lymphomas in adults, acute leukemia of childhood.
Edematous States: To induce diuresis or remission of proteinuria in the nephrotic syndrome without uremia, of the idiopathic type, or that due to lupus erythematosus.
Cerebral Edema: Dexamethasone sodium phosphate injection may be used to treat patients with cerebral edema from various causes: associated with primary or metastatic brain tumors; associated with cerebral vascular accident (acute stroke) excluding intracerebral hemorrhage; associated with neurosurgery; associated with head injury or pseudotumor cerebri.

It may be used also in the preoperative preparation of patients with increased intracranial pressure secondary to brain tumors or for palliation of patients with inoperable or recurrent brain neoplasms.

Use of dexamethasone sodium phosphate injection in cerebral edema is not a substitute for careful neurological evaluation and definitive management such as neurosurgery or other specific therapy.

Miscellaneous: Tuberculous meningitis with subarachnoid block or impending block when concurrently accompanied by appropriate antituberculous chemotherapy.
Trichinosis with neurologic or myocardial involvement.
Diagnostic testing of adrenocortical hyperfunction.
Neonatal Respiratory Distress: antenatal prophylaxis.
In combination with ondansetron for the management of nausea and vomiting associated with cisplatin and noncisplatin emetogenic chemotherapy.
By intra-articular or soft tissue injection. As adjunctive therapy for short-term administration (to support patient during an acute episode or exacerbation) in: synovitis of osteoarthritis, rheumatoid arthritis, acute and subacute bursitis, acute gouty arthritis, epicondylitis, acute nonspecific tenosynovitis, post-traumatic osteoarthritis.
By intralesional injection: keloids, localized hypertrophic, infiltrated, inflammatory lesions of: lichen planus, psoriatic plaques, granuloma annulare, and lichen simplex chronicus (neurodermatitis), discoid lupus erythematosus, necrobiosis lipoidica diabeticorum, alopecia areata, may also be useful in cystic tumors of an aponeurosis or tendon (ganglia).

Contraindications: Systemic fungal infections (see Precautions re: amphotericin B). Hypersensitivity to sulfites or to any component of this medication.

Administration of live virus vaccines (see Warnings).

Warnings: Administration of live virus vaccines is contraindicated in individuals receiving immunosuppressive doses of corticosteroids. If inactivated viral or bacterial vaccines are administered to individuals receiving immunosuppressive doses of corticosteroids, the expected serum antibody response may not be obtained. However, immunization procedures may be undertaken in patients who are receiving corticosteroids as replacement therapy, e.g., for Addison's disease.

Literature reports suggest an apparent association between use of corticosteroids and left ventricular free wall rupture after a recent myocardial infarction; therefore, therapy with corticosteroids should be used with great caution in these patients.

The use of dexamethasone sodium phosphate injection in active tuberculosis should be restricted to those cases of fulminating or disseminated tuberculosis in which the corticosteroid is used for the management of the disease in conjunction with an appropriate antituberculous regimen. If corticosteroids are indicated in patients with latent tuberculosis or tuberculin reactivity, close observation is necessary as reactivation of the disease may occur. During prolonged corticosteroid therapy, these patients should receive chemoprophylaxis.

Corticosteroids may mask some signs of infection and new infections may appear during their use. There may be decreased resistance and inability to localize infection when corticosteroids are used. If corticosteroids have to be used in the presence of bacterial infections, appropriate vigorous anti-infective therapy must be instituted.

Corticosteroids may activate latent amebiasis or strongyloidiasis, or exacerbate active disease. Therefore, it is recommended that latent or active amebiasis and strongyloidiasis be ruled out before initiating corticosteroid therapy in any patient at risk of, or with symptoms suggestive of, either conditon.

Corticosteroids should be used cautiously in patients with ocular herpes simplex because of possible corneal perforation. Prolonged use of corticosteroids may produce posterior subcapsular cataracts, glaucoma with possible damage to the optic nerves, and may enhance the establishment of secondary ocular infections due to fungi or viruses.

Dexamethasone sodium phosphate injection contains sodium bisulfite, a sulfite that may cause allergic-type reactions including anaphylactic symptoms and life-threatening or less severe asthmatic episodes in certain susceptible people. The overall prevalence of sulfite sensitivity in the general population is unknown and probably low. Sulfite sensitivity is seen more frequently in asthmatic than nonasthmatic people.

Pregnancy: Since human reproduction studies have not been done with corticosteroids, the use of these drugs in pregnancy, nursing mothers or women of childbearing potential requires that the possible benefits of the drug be weighed against the possible hazards to the mother and embryo or fetus. Infants born of mothers who have received substantial doses of corticosteroids during pregnancy should be carefully observed for signs of hypoadrenalism.

Lactation: Corticosteroids appear in breast milk and could suppress growth, interfere with endogenous corticosteroid production, or cause other unwanted effects. Mothers taking pharmacologic doses of corticosteroids should be advised not to nurse.

Precautions: Average and large doses of hydrocortisone or cortisone can cause elevation of blood pressure, salt and water retention, and increased excretion of potassium. These effects are less likely to occur with the synthetic derivatives except when used in large doses. Dietary salt restriction and potassium supplementation may be necessary. All corticosteroids increase calcium excretion.

Drug-induced secondary adrenocortical insufficiency may result from too rapid withdrawal of corticosteroids and may be minimized by gradual reduction of dosage. This type of relative insufficiency may persist for months after discontinuation of therapy; therefore, in any situation of stress occurring during that period, corticosteroid therapy should be reinstituted. If the patient is receiving steroids already, the dosage may have to be increased. Since mineralocorticoid secretion may be impaired, salt and/or a mineral corticoid should be administered concurrently.

Following prolonged therapy, withdrawal of corticosteroids may result in symptoms of the corticosteroid withdrawal syndrome including fever, myalgia, arthralgia, and malaise. This may occur in patients even without evidence of adrenal insufficiency.

Because rare instances of anaphylactoid reactions have occurred in patients receiving parenteral corticosteroid therapy, appropriate precautionary measures should be taken prior to administration, especially when the patient has a history of allergy to any drug.

Corticosteroids may suppress reactions to skin tests.

Psychic derangements may appear when corticosteroids are used, ranging from euphoria, insomnia, mood swings, personality changes, and severe depression, to frank psychotic manifestations. Also, existing instability or psychotic tendencies may be aggravated by corticosteroids.

Corticosteroids may exacerbate systemic fungal infections and therefore should not be used in the presence of such infections unless they are needed to control drug reactions due to amphotericin B. Moreover, there have been cases reported in which concomitant use of amphotericin B and hydrocortisone was followed by cardiac enlargement and congestive failure.

Patients should be advised to inform subsequent physicians of the prior use of corticosteroids.

Steroids may increase or decrease motility and number of spermatozoa in some patients.

Intra-articular injection of a corticosteroid may produce systemic as well as local effects.

Appropriate examination of any joint fluid present is necessary to exclude a septic process.

A marked increase in pain accompanied by local swelling, further restriction of joint motion, fever, and malaise are suggestive of septic arthritis. If this complication occurs and the diagnosis of sepsis is confirmed, appropriate antimicrobial therapy should be instituted.

Local injection of a steroid into an infected site is to be avoided.

Corticosteroids should not be injected into unstable joints.

Overdistention of the joint capsule and deposition of steroid along the needle track should be avoided in intra-articular injection, since this may lead to tissue atrophy.

Frequent intra-articular injection may result in damage to joint tissues.

Injection in the deltoid muscle should be avoided because of high incidence of tissue atrophy.

Patients should be impressed strongly with the importance of not overusing joints in which symptomatic benefit has been obtained as long as the inflammatory process remains active.
Children: Growth and development of infants and children on prolonged corticosteroid therapy should be carefully observed.

Steroids should be used with caution in: nonspecific ulcerative colitis if there is a probability of impending perforation, abscess or other pyogenic infection; diverticulitis; fresh intestinal anastomosis; active or latent peptic ulcer; renal insufficiency, hypertension; osteoporosis; and myasthenia gravis. Signs of peritoneal irritation following gastrointestinal perforation in patients receiving large doses of corticosteroids may be minimal or absent. Fat embolism has been reported as a possible complication of hypercortisonism.

There is an enhanced effect of corticosteroids in patients with hypothyroidism and in those with cirrhosis.

Patients who are on drugs which suppress the immune system are more susceptible to infections than healthy individuals. Chickenpox and measles, for example, can have a more serious or even fatal course in nonimmune children or adults on corticosteroids. In such children or adults who have not had these diseases, particular care should be taken to avoid exposure. The risk of developing a disseminated infection varies among individuals and may be related to the dose, route and duration of corticosteroid administration as well as to the underlying disease. Exposed patients should be advised to seek medical advice without delay. If exposed to measles, prophylaxis with i.m. pooled immunoglobulin (IG) may be indicated. If exposed to chickenpox, prophylaxis with varicella zoster immune globulin (VZIG) may be indicated (see the respective product monographs for IG and VZIG for complete prescribing information). If chickenpox develops, treatment with antiviral agents should be considered.

Drug Interactions: Corticosteroids may affect the nitroblue-tetrazolium test for bacterial infection and produce false negative results.

The prothrombin time should be checked frequently in patients who are receiving corticosteroids and coumarin anticoagulants at the same time because of reports that corticosteroids have altered the response to these anticoagulants. Studies have shown that the usual effect produced by adding corticosteroids is inhibition of response to coumarins, although there have been some conflicting reports of potentiation not substantiated by studies.

ASA should be used cautiously in conjunction with corticosteroids in hypoprothrombinemia.

Phenytoin, phenobarbital, ephedrine and rifampin may enhance the metabolic clearance of corticosteroids, resulting in decreased blood levels and lessened physiologic activity, thus requiring adjustment in corticosteroid dosage. These interactions may interfere with the dexamethasone suppression tests which should be interpreted with caution during administration of these drugs.

When corticosteroids are administered concomitantly with potassium-depleting diuretics, patients should be observed closely for development of hypokalemia.

False negative results in the dexamethasone suppression test in patients being treated with indomethacin have been reported.

Adverse Effects: Fluid and electrolyte disturbances: sodium retention; fluid retention; congestive heart failure in susceptible patients; potassium loss; hypokalemic alkalosis; hypertension; hypotension or shock-like reaction.

Musculoskeletal: muscle weakness; steroid myopathy; loss of muscle mass; osteoporosis; vertebral compression fractures; aseptic necrosis of femoral and humeral heads; pathologic fracture of long bones; tendon rupture.

Gastrointestinal: peptic ulcer with possible subsequent perforation and hemorrhage; perforation of the small and large bowel, particularly in patients with inflammatory bowel disease; pancreatitis; abdominal distention; ulcerative esophagitis.

Dermatologic: impaired wound healing; thin fragile skin; petechiae and ecchymoses; erythema; increased sweating; may suppress reactions to skin tests, burning or tingling, especially in the perineal area (after i.v. injection), other cutaneous reactions such as allergic dermatitis, urticaria, angioneurotic edema.

Neurological: convulsions; increased intracranial pressure with papilledema (pseudotumor cerebri) usually after treatment; vertigo; headache; psychic disturbances.

Endocrine: menstrual irregularities; development of cushingoid state; suppression of growth in children; secondary adrenocortical and pituitary unresponsiveness, particularly in times of stress, as in trauma, surgery or illness; decreased carbohydrate tolerance; manifestations of latent diabetes mellitus; increased requirements for insulin or oral hypoglycemic agents in diabetes; hirsutism.

Ophthalmic: posterior subcapsular cataracts; increased intraocular pressure; glaucoma; exophthalmos; retinopathy of prematurity.

Cardiovascular: myocardial rupture following recent myocardial infarction (see Precautions); hypertrophic cardiomyopathy in low birth weight infants.

Metabolic: negative nitrogen balance due to protein catabolism.

Other: anaphylactoid or hypersensitivity reactions, thromboembolism, weight gain, increased appetite, nausea, malaise, hiccups.

The following additional adverse reactions are related to parenteral corticosteroid therapy: rare instances of blindness associated with intralesional therapy around the face and head; hyperpigmentation or hypopigmentation; s.c. and cutaneous atrophy; sterile abscess; postinjection flare (following intra-articular use); Charcot-like arthropathy.

Overdose: Symptoms: hypertension, edema.

Treatment: Anaphylactic and hypersensitivity reactions may be treated with epinephrine, positive-pressure artificial respiration, and aminophylline. The patient should be kept warm and quiet.

Treatment probably is not indicated for reactions due to chronic overdosage.

Reports of acute toxicity and/or death following overdosage of glucocorticoids are rare. There are no specific recommendations for the treatment of overdosage with dexamethasone sodium phosphate injection.

Dosage: I.V. and I.M. injection: The usual initial dosage of dexamethasone sodium phosphate injection may vary from 0.5 mg to 20 mg/day depending on the specific disease entity being treated. Usually the parenteral dosage ranges are 33 to 50% the oral dose given every 12 hours. However, in certain overwhelming, acute, life-threatening situations, administration in dosages exceeding the usual dosages have been used. In these circumstances, the slower rate of absorption by i.m. administration should be recognized.

Dosage requirements are variable and must be individualized on the basis of the disease under treatment and the response of the patient.

If the drug is to be stopped after it has been given for more than a few days, it is recommended that it be withdrawn gradually rather than stopped abruptly.

In emergencies, the usual dose of dexamethasone sodium phosphate injection by i.v. or i.m. injection is 1 to 5 mL (4 to 20 mg) depending on the severity of the condition. In shock, use only the i.v. route (see also Shock). This dose may be repeated until adequate response is noted.

After initial improvement, single doses of 0.5 to 1 mL (2 to 4 mg) repeated as necessary, should be sufficient. The total daily dosage usually need not exceed 20 mL (80 mg) even in severe conditions.

When constant maximal effect is desired, dosage must be repeated at 3- or 4-hour intervals or maintained by slow i.v. drip.

I.V. and i.m. injections are advised in acute illness. When the acute stage has passed, substitute oral steroid therapy as soon as feasible.

Antiemetic Prophylaxis During Emetogenic Chemotherapy: Dexamethasone administered concomitantly with ondansetron has been demonstrated to achieve enhanced efficacy for antiemetic prophylaxis during emetogenic chemotherapy. Various dosing schedules have been used in clinical studies; however, the following is suggested for this combination:

Eight to 20 mg of dexamethasone sodium phosphate injection infused over 5 to 15 minutes just prior to chemotherapy, followed by 4 mg of dexamethasone sodium phosphate orally every 4 to 6 hours, or by 8 mg orally every 8 hours, and tapered in either strength or frequency of administration over 2 to 3 days. In general the total treatment duration for this indication should not exceed 5 days beyond chemotherapy. Alternatively, injectable dexamethasone can be infused i.v. in lieu of an oral formulation of dexamethasone sodium phosphate using various schedules.

For the recommended dosing of ondansetron, see the product monograph for Zofran.

Admixtures containing 8 mg of ondansetron and 20 mg of dexamethasone sodium phosphate in 50 mL of 5% dextrose infusion fluid stored in 50 mL polyvinyl chloride infusion bags, have been shown to be physically and chemically stable for up to 2 days at room temperature or up to 7 days at 2 to 8°C. In addition, these same admixtures have demonstrated compatibility with Continu-Flo administration sets.

Shock (of hemorrhagic, traumatic, surgical origin): The usual dose is 2 to 6 mg/kg body weight given as a single i.v. injection. This may be repeated in 2 to 6 hours, if shock persists. As an alternative, dexamethasone sodium phosphate injection, 2 to 6 mg/kg body weight is given as a single i.v. injection followed immediately by the same dose in an i.v. infusion. Therapy with dexamethasone sodium phosphate injection is an adjunct to, and not a replacement for, conventional therapy (see Precautions).

The dosages of dexamethasone phosphate injection have been suggested by various authors (see Table I).

Table I—Decadron Phosphate Injection

Dosage in Shock Treatment
3 mg/kg of body weight per 24 hours by constant i.v. infusion after an initial i.v. injection of 20 mg.[a]
2 to 6 mg/kg of body weight as a single i.v. injection.[b]
40 mg initially followed by repeat i.v. injection every 4 to 6 hours while shock persists.[c]
40 mg initially followed by repeat i.v. injection every 2 to 6 hours while shock persists.[d]
1 mg/kg of body weight as a single i.v. injection.[e]

[a] Cavanagh D, Singh KB. Endotoxin shock in pregnancy and abortion in: "Corticosteroids in the Treatment of Shock", Schumer W, Nyhus LM, Editors, Urbana, University of Illinois Press 1970:86-96.

[b] Dietzman RH, Ersek RA, Bloch JM, Lillehei RC. High-output, low resistance gram-negative septic shock in man. Angiology 1969;20: 691-700.

[c] Frank E. Clinical observations in shock and management (in: Shields TF, ed.: Symposium on current concepts and management of shock). J Maine Med Ass 1968;59:195-200.

[d] Oaks WW, Cohen HE. Endotoxin shock in the geriatric patient. Geriatrics 1967;22:120-30.

[e] Schumer W. Nyhus LM. Corticosteroid effect on biochemical parameters of human oligemic shock. Arch Surg 1970;100:405-8.

The doses mentioned in Table I are large in comparison with the usual recommended doses of dexamethasone injection but they are for emergency use in acute conditions needing high pharmacologic doses. Administration of high dose corticosteroid therapy should be continued only until the patient's condition has stabilized and usually no longer than 48 to 72 hours.

Cerebral Edema: Associated with primary or metastatic brain tumor, neurosurgery, head injury, pseudotumor cerebri or preoperative preparation of patients with increased intracranial pressure secondary to brain tumor: initially 10 mg (2.5 mL) i.v. followed by 4 mg (1 mL) i.m. every 6 hours until symptoms of cerebral edema subside. Response is usually noted within 12 to 24 hours: dosage may be reduced after 2 to 4 days and gradually discontinued over a period of 5 to 7 days.

High doses of dexamethasone phosphate injection are recommended for initiating short-term intensive therapy for acute life-threatening cerebral edema. Following the high loading dose schedule of the first day of therapy, the dose is scaled down over the 7- to 10-day period of intensive therapy and subsequently reduced to zero over the next 7 to 10 days. When maintenance therapy is required this should be changed to oral dexamethasone as soon as possible.

Suggested high dose schedule in cerebral edema: Adults: Initial dose: 50 mg, i.v.; 1st day: 8 mg, i.v. every 2 hours; 2nd day: 8 mg, i.v. every 2 hours; 3rd day: 8 mg, i.v. every 2 hours; 4th day: 4 mg, i.v. every 2 hours; 5th to 8th day: 4 mg, i.v. every 4 hours; thereafter decrease by daily reduction of 4 mg.

Children (35 kg and over): Initial dose: 25 mg, i.v.; 1st day: 4 mg, i.v. every 2 hours; 2nd day: 4 mg, i.v. every 2 hours; 3rd day: 4 mg, i.v. every 2 hours; 4th day: 4 mg, i.v. every 4 hours; 5th to 8th day: 4 mg, i.v. every 6 hours; thereafter decrease by daily reduction of 2 mg.

Children (below 35 kg): Initial dose: 20 mg, i.v.; 1st day: 4 mg, i.v. every 3 hours; 2nd day: 4 mg, i.v. every 3 hours; 3rd day: 4 mg, i.v. every 3 hours; 4th day: 4 mg, i.v. every 6 hours; 5th to 8th day: 2 mg, i.v. every 6 hours; thereafter, decrease by daily reduction of 1 mg.

Palliative management of patients with recurrent or inoperable brain tumors: Maintenance therapy should be individualized with oral or parenteral dexamethasone.

A dosage of 2 mg 2 or 3 times a day may be effective.

Associated with acute stroke (excluding intracerebral hemorrhage): Initially 10 mg (2.5 mL) i.v. followed by 4 mg (1 mL) i.m. every 6 hours for 10 days. The doses should then be tapered to zero on the ensuing 7 days.

The smallest dosage necessary to control cerebral edema should be utilized.

The usual precautions associated with corticosteroid therapy should be kept in mind. Antacids, anticholinergic drugs, and dietary measures to prevent gastrointestinal ulcer or hemorrhage should be considered.

Neonatal Respiratory Distress: Antenatal Prophylaxis: The recommended dosage of dexamethasone phosphate injection is 5 mg (1.25 mL) administered i.m. to the mother every 12 hours for up to a total of 4 doses. Administration should be initiated preferably between 24 hours and 7 days before estimated delivery.

Dual Therapy: In acute self-limited allergic disorders (e.g., acute allergic rhinitis, acute attacks of seasonal allergic bronchial asthma, urticaria medicamentosus and contact dermatoses), the following dosage schedule combining parenteral and oral therapy is suggested in Table II.

Table II—Decadron Phosphate Injection

Dosage Schedule Combining Parenteral and Oral Therapy

		Total Daily Dosage	Number of Decadron 0.5 mg Tablets
1st day	1 or 2 mL, i.m. of Decadron Phosphate Injection (4 mg/mL) i.m.	4 or 8 mg	
2nd day	2 tablets Decadron (0.5 mg) twice a day	2 mg	4
3rd day	2 tablets Decadron (0.5 mg) twice a day	2 mg	4
4th day	1 tablet Decadron (0.5 mg) twice a day	1 mg	2
5th day	1 tablet Decadron (0.5 mg) twice a day	1 mg	2
6th day	1 tablet Decadron (0.5 mg) per day	0.5 mg	1
7th day	1 tablet Decadron (0.5 mg) per day	0.5 mg	1
8th day	Follow-up visit		

This schedule is designed to provide adequate therapy during acute episodes, with minimizing the risk of overdosage in chronic cases. In some patients, this is all that will be needed to control the condition. Other patients will require further treatment, such as topical steroids, antihistamines, or bronchodilators. A few may require further systemic steroid therapy. By noting the dosage on the day before symptoms

Decadron Phosphate Injection (cont'd)

reappear in the latter group, the physician can decide more easily on any necessary additional therapy.

When acute exacerbations of asthma are accompanied by signs of infection, concomitant administration of antibiotics is recommended.

Intra-articular, Intralesional and Soft-tissue Injection: Intra-articular, intralesional, and soft-tissue injections generally are employed when affected joints or areas are limited to 1 or 2 sites.

Some of the usual single doses are found in Table III.

Table III—Decadron Phosphate Injection

Usual Single Doses for Intra-articular, Intralesional and Soft-tissue Injection

Site of Injection	Volume of Injection (mL)	Amount of Dexamethasone Phosphate (mg)
Large Joints (e.g., knee)	0.5 to 1	2 to 4
Small Joints (e.g., interphalangeal, temporomandibular)	0.2 to 0.25	0.8 to 1
Bursae	0.5 to 0.75	2 to 3
Tendon Sheaths	0.1 to 0.25	0.4 to 1
Soft-tissue Infiltration	0.5 to 1.5	2 to 6
Ganglia	0.25 to 0.5	1 to 2

In the treatment of tendon and tendon sheath inflammations, inject into the tendon sheath rather than into the tendon.

In radiculitis, inject about the involved nerve root near its exit from the spine. Do not inject the steroid directly into the nerve. In intercostal neuritis and neuralgia, pass the needle under the inner edge of the rib, letting it ride over one ridge to a second ridge. Inject the steroid under the rib and infiltrate the painful area. Guard against piercing the pleura. Sudden sharp pain during injection may mean the pleura has been penetrated.

In ganglia, inject directly into the cyst cavity after complete evacuation of its contents with a 16-gauge needle. Seal the puncture wound with a compression bandage for several days.

Repeat injections at appropriate intervals. The frequency of injection varies from patient to patient and ranges from once every 3 to 5 days to once every 2 to 3 weeks.

Stability and Storage Recommendations: This product, like many other steroid formulations, is sensitive to heat. Therefore, it should not be autoclaved when sterilization of the exterior of the vial is desired. Protect from freezing.

Note: Parenteral drug products should be inspected visually for particulate matter and discoloration prior to administration whenever solution and container permit.

Special Instructions: This preparation can be given directly from the vial without mixing or dilution. If preferred, it can be added to Sodium Chloride Injection, or Dextrose Injection, without loss of potency, and administered by i.v. drip.

When dexamethasone sodium phosphate injection is added to an infusion solution, the mixture must be used within 24 hours since infusion solutions do not contain preservatives.

Solutions used for i.v. administration or further dilution of this product should be used preservative-free in the neonate, especially the premature infant.

The usual aseptic techniques governing injections should be observed.

Supplied: Each mL of clear, colorless sterile solution contains: dexamethasone sodium phosphate equivalent to dexamethasone phosphate 4 mg (equal to 3.33 mg of dexamethasone or roughly about 100 mg of hydrocortisone). Nonmedicinal ingredients: creatinine, sodium citrate, sodium hydroxide (to adjust pH) and water for injection with sodium bisulfite, methylparaben, and propylparaben added as preservatives. Vials of 5 mL. Protect from freezing. Do not autoclave.

Look for CPhA general monographs to provide additional drug information. These are shaded gray and listed in the WHITE SECTION of the *CPS*.

DECADRON® Tablets Ⓟ

MSD

Dexamethasone

Corticosteroid

Indications: Allergic States: Control of severe or incapacitating allergic conditions not responsive to adequate trials of conventional treatment: seasonal or perennial allergic rhinitis, bronchial asthma, contact dermatitis, atopic dermatitis, serum sickness, drug hypersensitivity reactions.

Rheumatic Disorders: as adjunctive therapy for short-term administration during an acute episode or exacerbation of: psoriatic arthritis, rheumatoid arthritis including juvenile rheumatoid arthritis (selected cases may require low-dose maintenance therapy), ankylosing spondylitis, acute and subacute bursitis, acute nonspecific tenosynovitis, acute gouty arthritis, post-traumatic osteoarthritis, synovitis of osteoarthritis, epicondylitis.

Dermatologic Diseases: pemphigus, bullous dermatitis herpetiformis, severe erythema multiforme (Stevens-Johnson syndrome), exfoliative dermatitis, mycosis fungoides, severe psoriasis, severe seborrheic dermatitis.

Ophthalmic Diseases: severe acute and chronic allergic and inflammatory processes involving the eye and its adnexa such as allergic conjunctivitis, keratitis, allergic corneal marginal ulcers, herpes zoster ophthalmicus, iritis and iridocyclitis, chorioretinitis, anterior segment inflammation, diffuse posterior uveitis and choroiditis, optic neuritis, sympathetic ophthalmia.

Endocrine Disorders: primary or secondary adrenocortical insufficiency (hydrocortisone or cortisone is the first choice; synthetic analogs may be used in conjunction with mineralocorticoids where applicable; in infancy, mineralocorticoid supplementation is of particular importance); congenital adrenal hyperplasia; nonsuppurative thyroiditis; hypercalcemia associated with cancer.

Respiratory Diseases: symptomatic sarcoidosis, Löffler's syndrome not manageable by other means, berylliosis, fulminating or disseminated pulmonary tuberculosis when concurrently accompanied by appropriate antituberculous chemotherapy, aspiration pneumonitis.

Hematologic Disorders: idiopathic thrombocytopenic purpura in adults, secondary thrombocytopenia in adults, acquired (autoimmune) hemolytic anemia, erythroblastopenia (RBC anemia), congenital (erythroid) hypoplastic anemia.

Neoplastic Diseases: For palliative management of: leukemias and lymphomas in adults, acute leukemia of childhood.

Edematous States: To induce a diuresis or remission of proteinuria in the nephrotic syndrome without uremia, of the idiopathic type or that due to lupus erythematosus.

Cerebral Edema: Dexamethasone may be administered orally to treat patients with cerebral edema from various causes. Patients with cerebral edema associated with primary or metastatic brain tumors may benefit from oral administration of dexamethasone. It may be used also in the preoperative preparation of patients with increased intracranial pressure secondary to brain tumors, and also for palliation of patients with inoperable or recurrent brain neoplasms, and in the management of cerebral edema associated with neurosurgery. Some patients with cerebral edema due to head injury or pseudotumor cerebri also may benefit from therapy with oral dexamethasone. Its use in cerebral edema is not a substitute for careful neurosurgical evaluation and definitive management such as neurosurgery or other specific therapy.

Gastrointestinal Diseases: During a critical period of the disease in: ulcerative colitis, regional enteritis.

Miscellaneous: Tuberculous meningitis with subarachnoid block or impending block when concurrently accompanied by appropriate antituberculous chemotherapy. Trichinosis with neurologic or myocardial involvement. During an exacerbation or as maintenance therapy in selected cases of systemic lupus erythematosus, acute rheumatic carditis. In combination with ondansetron for the management of nausea and vomiting associated with cisplatin and non-cisplatin emetogenic chemotherapy.

Diagnostic testing of adrenocortical hyperfunction.

Contraindications: systemic fungal infections; hypersensitivity to any components of this drug; administration of live virus vaccine (see Warnings).

Warnings: Administration of live virus vaccines is contraindicated in individuals receiving immunosuppressive doses of corticosteroids. If inactivated viral or bacterial vaccines are administered to individuals receiving immunosuppressive doses of corticosteroids, the expected serum antibody response may not be obtained. However, immunization procedures may be undertaken in patients who are receiving corticosteroids as replacement therapy, e.g., for Addison's disease.

The use of dexamethasone in active tuberculosis should be restricted to those cases of fulminating or disseminated tuberculosis in which the corticosteroid is used for the management of the disease in conjunction with an appropriate antituberculous regimen. If corticosteroids are indicated in patients with latent tuberculosis or tuberculin reactivity, close observation is necessary as reactivation of the disease may occur. During prolonged corticosteroid therapy, these patients should receive chemoprophylaxis.

Corticosteroids may mask some signs of infection, and new infections may appear during their use. Corticosteroids may exacerbate systemic fungal infections and therefore should not be used in the presence of such infections unless they are needed to control drug reactions due to amphotericin B. Moreover, there have been cases reported in which concomitant use of amphotericin B and hydrocortisone was followed by cardiac enlargement and congestive failure.

In cerebral malaria, the use of corticosteroids is associated with prolongation of coma and a higher incidence of pneumonia and gastrointestinal bleeding.

Corticosteroids may activate latent amebiasis. Therefore, it is recommended that latent or active amebiasis be ruled out before initiating corticosteroid therapy in any patient who has spent time in the tropics or in any patient with unexplained diarrhea.

Corticosteroids should be used cautiously in patients with ocular herpes simplex because of possible corneal perforation.

Prolonged use of corticosteroids may produce posterior subcapsular cataracts, glaucoma with possible damage to the optic nerves, and may enhance the establishment of secondary ocular infections due to fungi or viruses.

Literature reports suggest an apparent association between use of corticosteroids and left ventricular free wall rupture after a recent myocardial infarction; therefore, therapy with corticosteroids should be used with great caution in these patients.

Pregnancy: Since human reproduction studies have not been done with corticosteroids, the use of these drugs in pregnancy or women of child-bearing potential requires that the anticipated benefits be weighed against the potential hazards to the mother, the embryo or the fetus. Infants born of mothers who have received substantial doses of corticosteroids during pregnancy should be carefully observed for signs of hypoadrenalism.

Lactation: Corticosteroids appear in breast milk and could suppress growth, interfere with endogenous corticosteroid production, or cause other unwanted effects. Mothers taking pharmacologic doses of corticosteroids should be advised not to nurse.

Precautions: The lowest possible dose of corticosteroid should be used to control the condition under treatment, and when reduction in dosage is possible, the reduction should be gradual.

Average and large doses of hydrocortisone or cortisone can cause elevation of blood pressure, salt, and water retention, and increased excretion of potassium. These effects are less likely to occur with the synthetic derivatives except when used in large doses. Dietary salt restriction and potassium supplementation may be necessary. All corticosteroids increase calcium excretion.

Drug-induced secondary adrenocortical insufficiency may result from too rapid withdrawal of corticosteroids and may be minimized by gradual reduction of dosage. This type of relative insufficiency may persist for months after discontinuation of therapy; therefore, in any situation of stress occurring during that period, corticosteroid therapy should be reinstituted or the current dosage may have to be increased. Since mineralocorticoid secretion may be impaired, salt and/or a mineralocorticoid should be administered concurrently.

Following prolonged therapy, withdrawal of corticosteroids may result in symptoms of the corticosteroid withdrawal syndrome including fever, myalgia, arthralgia, and malaise. This may occur in patients even without evidence of adrenal insufficiency.

Steroids should be used with caution in: nonspecific ulcerative colitis if there is a probability of impending perforation, abscess or other pyogenic infection; diverticulitis; fresh intestinal anastomoses; active or latent peptic ulcer, renal insufficiency; hypertension; osteoporosis; and myasthenia gravis. Signs of peritoneal irritation following gastrointestinal perforation in patients receiving large doses of corticosteroids may be minimal or absent. Fat embolism has been reported as a possible complication of hypercortisonism.

There is an enhanced effect of corticosteroids in patients with hypothyroidism and in those with cirrhosis.

Psychic derangements may appear when corticosteroids are used, ranging from euphoria, insomnia, mood swings, personality changes, and severe depression, to frank psychotic manifestations. Also, existing emotional instability of psychotic tendencies may be aggravated by corticosteroids.

Growth and development of infants and children on prolonged corticosteroid therapy should be carefully observed.

Steroids may increase or decrease motility and number of spermatozoa in some patients.

Drug Interactions: ASA should be used cautiously in conjunction with corticosteroids in hypoprothrombinemia.

Phenytoin, phenobarbital, ephedrine and rifampin may enhance the metabolic clearance of corticosteroids, resulting in decreased blood levels and lessened physiologic activity, thus requiring adjustment in corticosteroid dosage. These interactions may interfere with dexamethasone suppression tests which should be interpreted with caution during administration of these drugs.

False-negative results in the dexamethasone suppression test in patients being treated with indomethacin have been reported.

The prothrombin time should be checked frequently in patients who are receiving corticosteroids and coumarin anticoagulants at the same time because of reports that corticosteroids have altered the response to these anticoagulants. Studies have shown that the usual effect produced by adding corticosteroids is inhibition of response to coumarins, although there have been some conflicting reports of potentiation not substantiated by studies.

When corticosteroids are administered concomitantly with potassium-depleting diuretics, patients should be observed closely for development of hypokalemia.

Corticosteroids may affect the nitroblue tetrazolium test for bacterial infection and produce false-negative results.

Patients who are on drugs which suppress the immune system are more susceptible to infections than healthy individuals. Chickenpox and measles, for example, can have a more serious or even fatal course in non-immune children or adults on corticosteroids. In such children or adults who have not had these diseases, particular care should be taken to avoid exposure. The risk of developing a disseminated infection varies among individuals and may be related to the dose, route and duration of corticosteroid administration as well as to the underlying disease. Exposed patients should be advised to seek medical advice without delay. If exposed to measles, prophylaxis with i.m. pooled immunoglobulin (IG) may be indicated. If exposed to chickenpox, prophylaxis with varicella zoster immune globulin (VZIG) may be indicated (see the respective Product Monographs for VZIG and IG for complete prescribing information). If chickenpox develops, treatment with antiviral agents should be considered.

Adverse Effects: Fluid and Electrolyte Disturbances: sodium retention, fluid retention, congestive heart failure in susceptible patients, potassium loss, hypokalemic alkalosis, hypertension.

Musculoskeletal: muscle weakness, steroid myopathy, loss of muscle mass, osteoporosis, vertebral compression fractures, aseptic necrosis of femoral and humeral heads, pathologic fracture of long bones, tendon rupture.

Gastrointestinal: peptic ulcer with possible perforation and hemorrhage, perforation of the small and large bowel, particularly in patients with inflammatory bowel diseases. Pancreatitis; abdominal distention; ulcerative esophagitis.

Dermatologic: impaired wound healing; thin fragile skin; petechiae and ecchymoses; erythema; increased sweating; may suppress reactions to skin tests; other cutaneous reactions, such as allergic dermatitis, urticaria, angioneurotic edema.

Neurologic: convulsions; increased intracranial pressure with papilledema (pseudotumor cerebri) usually after treatment; vertigo; headache; psychic disturbances.

Endocrine: menstrual irregularities; development of cushingoid state; suppression of growth in children; secondary adrenocortical and pituitary unresponsiveness, particularly in times of stress, as in trauma, surgery or illness; decreased carbohydrate tolerance; manifestations of latent diabetes mellitus; increased requirements for insulin or oral hypoglycemic agents in diabetes; hirsutism.

Ophthalmic: posterior subcapsular cataracts; increased intraocular pressure; glaucoma; exophthalmos.

Metabolic: negative nitrogen balance due to protein catabolism.

Cardiovascular: myocardial rupture following recent myocardial infarction (see Precautions).

Other: hypersensitivity; thromboembolism; weight gain; increased appetite; nausea; malaise; hiccups.

Overdose: Symptoms and Treatment: There is no known antidote but gastric lavage should be performed.

Dosage: Dosage requirements are variable and must be individualized according to the severity of the disease and the response of the patient. The usual initial dosage varies from 0.5 to 15 mg a day depending on the disease being treated. (For infants and children, the recommended doses usually will have to be reduced, but dosage should be dictated by the severity of the condition rather than by age or body weight.)

Corticosteroid therapy is an adjunct to, not a replacement of conventional therapy, which should be instituted as indicated.

Dosage must be decreased or therapy discontinued gradually when administration has been continued for more than a few days.

In acute conditions where prompt relief is urgent, large doses are permissible and may be mandatory for a short period. When symptoms have been suppressed adequately, dosage should be maintained at the minimum amount capable of providing sufficient relief without excessive hormonal effects.

Chronic conditions are subject to periods of spontaneous remission. When such periods occur, corticosteroids should be discontinued gradually.

Routine laboratory studies such as urinalysis, 2-hour postprandial blood sugar, determinations of blood pressure and body weight, and a chest x-ray should be carried out at regular intervals during prolonged therapy. Periodic determinations of serum potassium are advisable if large doses are being used.

Patients may be transferred to dexamethasone from any other glucocorticoid with the proper adjustment in dosage.

The following mg equivalents facilitate changing to dexamethasone from other glucocorticoids (see Table I).

Table I—Decadron Tablets

Mg Equivalents

Dexamethasone	Methylprednisolone and Triamcinolone	Prednisolone and Prednisone	Hydrocortisone	Cortisone
0.75 mg	4 mg	5 mg	20 mg	25 mg

Milligram for milligram, dexamethasone is approximately equivalent to betamethasone, 4 to 6 times more potent than methylprednisolone and triamcinolone, 6 to 8 times more potent than prednisone and prednisolone, 25 to 30 times more potent than hydrocortisone, and about 35 times more potent than cortisone. At equipotent anti-inflammatory doses, dexamethasone almost completely lacks the sodium-retaining property of hydrocortisone and closely related derivatives of hydrocortisone.

Specific Dosage Recommendations: In chronic, usually nonfatal diseases including endocrine and chronic rheumatic disorders, edematous states, respiratory and gastrointestinal diseases, some dermatologic diseases and hematologic disorders, start with a low dose (0.5 to 1 mg a day) and gradually increase dosage to the smallest amount that gives the desired degree of symptomatic relief.

Dosage may be administered 2, 3 or 4 times a day.

In congenital adrenal hyperplasia, the usual daily dose is 0.5 to 1.5 mg.

In acute, nonfatal diseases, including allergic states, ophthalmic diseases, acute and subacute rheumatic disorders, dosage ranges between 2 and 3 mg a day, however, higher doses are necessary in some patients. Since the course of these conditions is self-limited, prolonged maintenance therapy is not usually necessary.

Antiemetic Prophylaxis During Emetogenic Chemotherapy, dexamethasone administered concomitantly with ondansetron has been demonstrated to achieve enhanced efficacy for antiemetic prophylaxis during emetogenic chemotherapy. Various dosing schedules have been used in clinical studies; however, the following is suggested for this combination: 8 to 20 mg of dexamethasone infused over 5 to 15 minutes just prior to chemotherapy, followed by 4 mg of dexamethasone orally every 4 to 6 hours, or by 8 mg orally every 8 hours, and tapered in either strength or frequency of administration over 2 to 3 days. In general the total treatment duration for this indication should not exceed 5 days beyond chemotherapy. Alternatively, injectable dexamethasone can be infused i.v. in lieu of an oral formulation of dexamethasone using various schedules.

For the recommended dosing of ondansetron, see the Product Monograph for Zofran.

Admixtures containing 8 mg of ondansetron and 20 mg of dexamethasone phosphate, in 50 mL of 5% dextrose infusion fluid stored in 50 mL polyvinyl chloride infusion bags, have been shown to be physically and chemically stable for up to 2 days at room temperature or up to seven days at 2 to 8°C. In addition, these same admixtures have demonstrated compatibility with Continu-Flo administration sets.

In acute, self-limited allergic disorders or acute exacerbations of chronic allergic disorders (e.g., acute allergic rhinitis, acute attacks of seasonal allergic bronchial asthma, urticaria medicamentosa, and contact dermatoses), the following dosage schedule, combining parenteral and oral therapy, is suggested (see Table II).

Table II—Decadron Tablets

Dosage Schedule

		Total Daily Dosage	Number of 0.5 mg Tablets
1st day	1 or 2 mL, i.m., of Decadron Phosphate Injection (4 mg/mL) i.m.	4 or 8 mg	
2nd day	2 tablets Decadron (0.5 mg) twice a day	2.0 mg	4
3rd day	2 tablets Decadron (0.5 mg) twice a day	2.0 mg	4
4th day	1 tablet Decadron (0.5 mg) twice a day	1.0 mg	2
5th day	1 tablet Decadron (0.5 mg) twice a day	1.0 mg	2
6th day	1 tablet Decadron (0.5 mg)/day	0.5 mg	1
7th day	1 tablet Decadron (0.5 mg)/day	0.5 mg	1
8th day	Follow-up visit		

In chronic, potentially fatal diseases such as systemic lupus erythematosus, pemphigus, symptomatic sarcoidosis, the recommended initial dosage is 2 to 4.5 mg a day; higher doses may be necessary in some patients.

When the disease is acute and life-threatening (e.g., acute rheumatic carditis, crisis of systemic lupus erythematosus, severe allergic reactions, pemphigus, neoplastic diseases), the initial dosage is between 4 and 10 mg a day, administered in at least 4 divided doses.

Epinephrine is the drug of immediate choice in severe allergic reactions. Dexamethasone is useful either concurrently or as supplementary therapy.

In cerebral edema, when maintenance therapy is required. For palliative management of patients with recurrent or inoperable brain tumors, a dosage of 2 mg 2 or 3 times a day may be effective. The smallest dosage necessary to control cerebral edema should be utilized.

In the adrenogenital syndrome, daily dosages of 0.5 to 1.5 mg may keep children in remission and prevent the recurrence of abnormal excretion of 17-ketosteroids.

As massive therapy in certain conditions, such as acute leukemia, the nephrotic syndrome, and pemphigus, the recommended dosage is from 10 to 15 mg a day. Patients receiving such a high dosage must be observed very closely for the appearance of severe reactions.

Dexamethasone Suppression Test: 1. Tests for Cushing's syndrome: Give 1 mg orally at 11:00 p.m. Blood is drawn for plasma cortisol determination at 8:00 a.m. the following morning. For greater accuracy, give 0.5 mg dexamethasone orally every 6 hours for 48 hours. Twenty-four hour urine collections are made for determination of 17-hydroxycorticosteroid excretion.

2. Test to distinguish Cushing's syndrome due to pituitary ACTH excess from Cushing's syndrome due to other causes. Give 2 mg of dexamethasone orally every 6 hours for 48 hours. Twenty-four hour urine collections are made for determination of 17-hydroxycorticosteroid excretion.

Supplied: 0.5 mg: Each white compressed, pentagonal-shaped tablet, scored on one side with MSD 41 on the other, contains: dexamethasone 0.5 mg. Nonmedicinal ingredients: calcium phosphate dibasic, cornstarch, lactose and magnesium stearate. Gluten- and tartrazine-free. Bottles of 100.

4 mg: Each white compressed, pentagonal shaped tablet, scored on one side with MSD 97 on the other, contains: dexamethasone 4 mg. Nonmedicinal ingredients: calcium phosphate dibasic, cornstarch, lactose and magnesium stearate. Gluten- and tartrazine-free. Bottles of 50.

Store at 15 to 30°C.

(Shown in Product Recognition Section)

DECA-DURABOLIN®

Organon

Nandrolone Decanoate

Androgenic—Anabolic Steroid

Indications: As adjunctive therapy in senile and postmenopausal osteoporosis. Anabolic steroids are without value as primary therapy but may be of value in adjunctive therapy. Equal or greater consideration should be given to diet, calcium balance, physiotherapy and good general health promoting measures, in pituitary dwarfism anabolic agents may be used with care until growth hormone is more available.

This product is also useful in treatment of those conditions in which a potent tissue building or protein sparing action is desired. Its principal uses are to induce weight gain and well being by virtue of its anabolic action. Such therapy is most effective when combined with a good dietary regimen. Anabolic effects have been demonstrated in chronic disease and convalescence, debility states, inoperable mammary carcinoma, corticoid induced catabolic states, myopathies, decubitus ulcers, burns and as adjuvant therapy of certain types of anemia (aplastic, sickle cell). It should be used only after diagnosis is established.

Contraindications: Hypersensitivity to nandrolone. Male patients with carcinoma of the prostate, breast.

Pregnancy: Pregnancy, because of possible masculinization of the fetus.

Nephrosis or the nephrotic phase of nephritis. Cardio-renal failure. Liver disease with impaired bilirubin excretion.

Warnings: Caution in patients with cardiac, renal or hepatic disease.

Precautions: If amenorrhea or menstrual irregularities develop the drug should be discontinued until the etiology is determined.

Anabolic steroids may increase sensitivity to oral anticoagulants.

Dosage of the anticoagulant may have to be decreased in order to maintain the prothrombin time at the desired therapeutic level.

Anabolic steroids have been shown to alter glucose tolerance tests. Diabetics should be followed carefully and the insulin or hypoglycemic dosage adjusted accordingly.

Anabolic steroids should be used with caution in patients with benign prostatic hypertrophy.

Serum cholesterol may increase or decrease during therapy. Therefore, caution is required in administering these agents to patients with a history of myocardial infarction or coronary artery disease. Serial determinations of serum cholesterol should be made and therapy adjusted accordingly.

Hypercalcemia may develop both spontaneously and as a result of hormonal therapy in women with disseminated breast carcinoma. If it develops while on this agent, the drug should be stopped.

Signs of masculinization which have been produced by testosterone therapy in women have ranged from mild acne, hoarsening of the voice and an increase in or darkening of the hair of the face. Women and children under seven years of age are more sensitive to androgen therapy. Deca-Durabolin, which is far less androgenic than testosterone, has not produced these signs when given in the recommended doses, save for a few of the milder of these effects. As is common with other steroids of this class, it may be possible with large doses or intensive treatment during the first half of the menstrual cycle to inhibit menses; however, with recommended doses, menses are not apt to be disturbed.

Pregnancy: Should not be used in pregnant women.

Use of anabolic steroids by athletes is not recommended.

Adverse Effects: Note: Included in this listing are a few adverse reactions not reported with this specific drug. However, pharmacological similarities among the anabolic steroids require that each reaction be considered when Deca-Durabolin is prescribed.

Virilization is the most common undesirable effect associated with anabolic steroid therapy.

In males: Prepubertal: phallic enlargement, increased frequency of erections.

Postpubertal: inhibition of testicular function, testicular atrophy, and oligospermia, impotence, chronic priapism, gynecomastia; and epididymitis and bladder irritability.

In females: hirsutism, male pattern baldness, deepening of the voice, and clitoral enlargement. These changes are usually irreversible even after prompt discontinuance of therapy and are not prevented by concomitant use of estrogens. In addition, the following may occur: menstrual irregularities, postmenopausal bleeding, and swelling of breasts.

In both sexes: nausea, increased or decreased libido, leukopenia, symptoms resembling those of peptic ulcer, acne (especially in females and prepubertal males), edema, tolerance, excitation and sleeplessness, chills, bleeding in patients on concomitant anticoagulant therapy, premature closure of epiphyses in children, vomiting, diarrhea, and jaundice rarely with hepatic necrosis and death.

Alterations in clinical laboratory tests: a. Metyrapone test. b. Fasting blood sugar and glucose tolerance test. c. Thyroid function tests: a decrease in the PBI, in thyroxine-binding capacity and RAI uptake, and an increase in T3 uptake by the rbc's or resin may occur. Free thyroxine is usually normal. Altered tests usually persist for 2 to 3 weeks after stopping anabolic therapy. d. Electrolytes: retention of sodium, chlorides, water, potassium, phosphates, and calcium. e. Liver function tests: increased BSP, increased or decreased serum cholesterol, increased AST, increased serum bilirubin, and increased alkaline phosphatase. f. Increase in clotting factors II, V, VII, and X. g. Miscellaneous tests: decreased creatin and creatinine excretion lasting up to 2 weeks after discontinuing therapy, and increased 17-ketosteroid excretion.

There have been rare reports of hepatic tumors, histologically hepatocellular carcinoma, in patients taking 17-alkyl androgenic- anabolic steroids usually for prolonged periods. In some cases, discontinuation of steroids resulted in tumor regression without other therapy.

Following i.m. injection: urticaria at the injection site, post injection induration, furunculosis.

Overdose: Symptoms and Treatment: Large single doses do not give rise to serious side effects. No cases of acute overdosage have been reported.

Dosage: A single i.m. injection every 3 to 4 weeks for continuous periods of up to 12 weeks. If necessary repeat course of therapy following a rest period of 4 weeks. Adults, 50 to 100 mg.

Supplied: Each mL contains: nandrolone decanoate USP 100 mg. Nonmedicinal ingredients: benzyl alcohol and sesame oil. Multidose vials of 2 mL.

DECLOMYCIN®

Wyeth-Ayerst

Demeclocycline HCl

Antibiotic

Indications: Many strains of bacteria have been shown to be resistant to the tetracyclines. These include certain strains of streptococci, staphylococci, pneumococci, gonococci, and many other gram-negative organisms. Therefore, culture and sensitivity testing are advised to determine the susceptibility of the infecting organisms to tetracyclines. Chemotherapy should not be initiated until all the necessary bacteriological investigations have been started.

Microorganisms that have become insensitive to one tetracycline invariably exhibit cross resistance to other tetracyclines.

Some cross resistance between the tetracyclines and chloramphenicol for gram-negative organisms but not for gram-positive ones has been reported. Tetracycline resistant organisms are most likely to be acquired from other individuals in a population where tetracyclines have been widely used.

The tetracyclines are indicated in infections caused by the following microorganisms:

Rickettsiae (Rocky Mountain spotted fever, typhus fever and the typhus group, Q fever, rickettsialpox, tick fevers), M. pneumoniae (PPLO, Eaton agent), agents of psittacosis and ornithosis, agents of L. venereum and G. inguinale, and the spirochetal agent of relapsing fever (B. recurrentis).

The following gram negative organisms: H. ducreyi (chancroid), Y. pestis and F. tularensis, B. bacilliformis, Bacteroides spp., Vibrio comma and V. fetus, and Brucella organisms (in conjunction with streptomycin).

The following gram negative organisms, when bacteriologic testing indicates appropriate susceptibility to the drug: E. coli, E. aerogenes, Shigella spp., Mima spp., Herellea spp., H. influenzae (respiratory infections), and Klebsiella infections (respiratory and urinary).

The following gram positive organisms when bacteriologic testing indicates appropriate susceptibility to the drug: anaerobic streptococci, S. pyogenes (For upper respiratory infections due to Group A beta hemolytic streptococci, penicillin is the drug of choice including prophylaxis of rheumatic fever), S. pneumoniae, and S. aureus. The frequency of resistance to tetracyclines in hemolytic streptococci is highest in strains from infections of the ear, wounds and skin. Tetracyclines should not be prescribed for acute throat infections; also, they are not the drug of choice in any staphylococcal infection.

When penicillin is contraindicated, tetracyclines are alternative drugs in the treatment of infections due to: N. gonorrhoeae, T. pallidum and T. pertenue (syphilis and yaws), L. monocytogenes, Clostridium spp., B. anthracis, Fusobacterium fusiform (Vincent's infection), and Actinomyces.

In acute intestinal amebiasis, the tetracyclines may be a useful adjunct to amebicides. In severe acne the tetracyclines may be useful adjunctive therapy.

Tetracyclines are indicated in the treatment of trachoma, although the infectious agent is not always eliminated, as judged by immunofluorescence.

Inclusion conjunctivitis may be treated with oral tetracyclines or with a combination of oral and topical agents.

Because tetracycline tends to accumulate in certain neoplastic cells and to exhibit a brilliant, yellowish gold fluorescence when exposed to ultraviolet light, it may be useful in experienced hands for the diagnosis of malignancy.

Contraindications: Hypersensitivity to any of the tetracyclines; severe renal or hepatic disease.

Pregnancy and *Lactation:* Pregnant or lactating women unless potential benefit to patient outweighs risk to fetus or child.

Therapy of common infections in children under 12. Any condition in which bactericidal effect is essential (bacterial endocarditis).

Avoid prophylactic administration to surgical cases, if possible.

Precautions: The use of tetracyclines during tooth development (last half of pregnancy, infancy and childhood to the age of 8 years) may cause permanent tooth discoloration (yellow, gray, brown). This reaction is more common during long term use of the tetracyclines, but has been observed following short term courses. Enamel hypoplasia has also been reported. Tetracycline drugs, therefore, should not be used in this age group unless other drugs are not likely to be effective or are contraindicated.

Pregnancy: Results of animal studies indicate that tetracyclines cross the placenta, are found in fetal tissues and can have toxic effects on the developing fetus (often related to retardation of skeletal development). Evidence of embryotoxicity has also been noted in animals treated early in pregnancy.

Lactation: Tetracyclines are present in the milk of lactating women who are taking a drug in this class.

If renal impairment exists, even usual oral or parenteral doses may lead to excessive systemic accumulation of the drug and possible liver toxicity. Under such conditions, lower than usual doses are indicated and, if therapy is prolonged, serum level determinations of the drug may be advisable.

The antianabolic action of the tetracycline may cause an increase in BUN. While this is not a problem in those with normal renal function, in patients with significantly impaired function, higher serum levels of tetracycline may lead to azotemia, hyperphosphatemia, and acidosis. Consequently, increasing levels of BUN may not accurately reflect changes in renal function; the serum creatinine will provide a more reliable index.

Photosensitivity manifested by an exaggerated sunburn reaction has been observed in some individuals taking tetracyclines. Patients should be warned to avoid exposure to direct sunlight and/or ultraviolet light while under treatment with tetracycline drugs, and treatment should be discontinued at the first evidence of skin discomfort.

Tetracycline forms a stable calcium complex in any bone forming tissue. A decrease in the fibula growth rate has been observed in prematures given oral tetracycline in doses of 25 mg/kg every 6 hours. This reaction was shown to be reversible when the drug was discontinued.

Tetracycline administration may result in overgrowth of non-susceptible organisms. Superinfections due to staphylococci and other organisms may occur during oral but rarely during parenteral administration.

C. albicans can produce effects at 3 levels: proliferation in the mouth can cause disturbances ranging from simple soreness to frank and extensive thrush, which may spread to the pharynx and possibly the bronchi; in the bowel, it can be manifested by diarrhea; also, pruritus ani occurs frequently.

Proteus and Pseudomonas species resistant to tetracyclines may become predominant in the bowel and diarrhea is common. Periodic microbiologic examination of materials, such as stool and sputum, during tetracycline therapy may alert one to changes in flora indicating bacteriologic superinfection in time to avert progression to clinical disease.

If superinfections are encountered, tetracyclines should be discontinued and appropriate therapy started. Superinfection of the bowel by staphylococci may be life threatening.

Adhere closely to expiration dates; ingestion of deteriorated tetracyclines has produced kidney damage corresponding clinically to the acute Fanconi syndrome (nausea, vomiting, albuminuria, glycosuria, aminoaciduria, hypophosphatemia, hypokalemia, and acidosis). Such damage is usually reversed slowly after withdrawal of the deteriorated tetracycline, although fatal reactions have been reported.

Before treating gonorrhea, a darkfield examination should be made from any lesion suggesting concurrent syphilis. Serological tests for syphilis should be made for at least 4 months afterwards.

Because the tetracyclines have been shown to depress plasma prothrombin activity, patients who are on anticoagulant therapy may require downward adjustment of their anticoagulant dosage. Interference with vitamin K synthesis by microorganisms in the gut has been reported.

Concurrent use of methoxyflurane and tetracyclines has been reported to impair renal function seriously leading in some cases to death. Such use of these two drugs is therefore not recommended unless the benefits outweigh the risks.

Since bacteriostatic drugs may interfere with the bactericidal action of penicillin, it is advisable to avoid giving demeclocycline in conjunction with penicillin.

Reduced efficacy and increased incidence of breakthrough bleeding has been suggested with concomitant use of tetracycline and oral contraceptive preparations.

During long-term therapy, periodic laboratory evaluation of organ systems, including hematopoietic, renal and hepatic studies should be performed.

All infections due to Group A beta hemolytic streptococci should be treated for at least 10 days.

Since sensitivity reactions are more likely to occur in persons with a history of allergy, asthma, hay fever, or urticaria, the preparations should be used with caution in such individuals. Cross-sensitization among the various tetracyclines is extremely common.

When it is essential to administer any of the tetracyclines i.v., the blood concentration should not be permitted to exceed 15 μg/mL and, if possible, other potentially hepatotoxic drugs should be avoided. Presumably, large doses may be expected to have comparable toxicity by either the i.m. or oral route if renal or hepatic insufficiency is present.

Adverse Effects: Gastrointestinal: anorexia, epigastric distress, nausea, vomiting, diarrhea, bulky loose stools, stomatitis, sore throat, glossitis, black hairy tongue, dysphagia, hoarseness, enterocolitis, pancreatitis, inflammatory lesions (with monilial overgrowth) in the anogenital region, including proctitis, pruritus ani and hepatic toxicity. These reactions have been caused by both the oral and parenteral administration of tetracyclines but are less frequent after parenteral use.
Skin: maculopapular and erythematous rashes. Exfoliative dermatitis has been reported but is uncommon. Onycholysis and discoloration of the nails have been reported rarely. Photosensitivity has occurred (see Precautions). Lesions occurring on the glans penis have caused balanitis.
Renal Toxicity: Rise in BUN has been reported and is apparently dose related (see Precautions). Nephrogenic diabetes insipidus.

Hepatic cholestasis has been reported rarely, and is usually associated with high dosage levels of tetracycline. Hepatic toxicity, associated with pancreatitis in some cases, has been attributed to the long-term use of doses larger than those recommended in patients with renal insufficiency or to the concomitant administration of other potentially hepatotoxic drugs. This serious reaction has occurred most often in pregnant or postpartum patients with pyelonephritis.
CNS: Pseudotumor cerebri (benign intracranial hypertension) in adults has been associated with the use of tetracyclines. The usual clinical manifestations are headache and blurred vision. Bulging fontanels have been associated with the use of tetracyclines in infants. While both of these conditions and related symptoms usually resolve soon after discontinuation of the tetracycline, the possibility for permanent sequelae exists.
Hypersensitivity Reactions: urticaria, angioneurotic edema, anaphylaxis, anaphylactoid purpura, pericarditis, exacerbation of systemic lupus erythematosus, and serum sickness-like reactions such as fever, rash, and arthralgia. When given over prolonged periods, tetracyclines have been reported to produce brownish black microscopic discoloration of thyroid glands. No abnormalities of thyroid function studies are known to occur.

Pseudotumor cerebri (benign intracranial hypertension) in adults has been associated with the use of tetracyclines. The usual clinical manifestations are headache and blurred vision. Bulging fontanels have been associated with the use of tetracyclines in infants. While both of these conditions and related symptoms usually resolve soon after discontinuation of the tetracycline, the possibility for permanent sequelae exists.
Blood: anemia, hemolytic anemia, thrombocytopenia, thrombocytopenic purpura, neutropenia and eosinophilia have been reported.

Dosage: A daily dose of 600 mg of demeclocycline may be considered to be the equivalent of 1 000 mg of tetracycline per day.

The average daily adult dosage is 4 divided doses of 150 mg each or 2 divided doses of 300 mg each. An initial dose of 300 mg may be used in the more severe infections, but a single dose exceeding 300 mg is thought to be unnecessary.

Primary atypical pneumonia (Eaton agent): The average daily adult dosage is 900 mg administered in 3 divided doses for a period of 6 days.

Antacids, containing aluminum, calcium, or magnesium and iron salts impair absorption and should not be given to patients taking demeclocycline. Foods and some dairy products also interfere with absorption. The drug should be given 1 hour before or 2 hours after meals.

Supplied: 150 mg: Each round, red, film-coated tablet, engraved "LL" and "D11", contains: demeclocycline HCl 150 mg. Nonmedicinal ingredients: alginic acid, dye Opadry Red (coating), ethylcellulose, magnesium stearate, mineral oil light (coating), starch and sorbitol. Energy: <4.2 kJ (1 kcal). Sodium- and tartrazine-free. Bottles of 100.

300 mg: Each round, red, film-coated tablet, engraved "LL" and "D12", contains: demeclocycline HCl 300 mg. Nonmedicinal ingredients: alginic acid, ethylcellulose, magnesium stearate, starch and sorbitol. Energy: 4.2 kJ (1 kcal). Sodium- and tartrazine-free. Bottles of 100.

DECONGEST
Technilab

Xylometazoline HCl
Nasal Decongestant

Supplied: Each bottle contains: xylometazoline HCl USP 0.1%. Nonmedicinal ingredients: benzalkonium chloride, dibasic potassium phosphate, EDTA disodium, potassium chloride, purified water, sodium chloride and sodium phosphate monobasic. Plastic squeeze bottles of 20 mL. Cap sealed for protection (security feature). Protect from heat.

New Product 1998

DEHYDRAL®
TCD

Methenamine
Antiperspirant—Antibacterial

Supplied: Each tube contains: methenamine 8% stabilized in a pH balanced, nonstaining, vanishing cream base. Nonmedicinal ingredients: alkasurf S65-0, isopropyl myristate, menthol, purified water, stearic acid and tween 60. Preservative-free. Tubes of 15 g.

DELATESTRYL® ♦
Squibb

Testosterone Enanthate
Androgen

Indications: Androgen therapy in the male (eunuchism, eunuchoidism, impotence of glandular origin, cryptorchidism, climacteric, senile pruritus), and in the female (menorrhagia, frigidity, palliation of premenopausal mammary carcinoma, inhibition of lactation, postpartum breast engorgement, menopausal syndrome), and in males and females (delayed bone healing, spinal paraplegia, senile osteoporosis, dystrophy, cachexia due to wasting illness).

Contraindications: Androgens are contraindicated in male patients with prostatic or breast cancer, in those elderly patients in whom overstimulation is to be avoided, and in those cases of benign prostatic hypertrophy with obstructive symptoms. Androgens are also contraindicated in patients with nephrosis or the nephrotic phase of nephritis.
Pregnancy: Because of the possibility of masculinization of the female fetus, this drug should not be used in the treatment of pregnant women or those who may become pregnant unless in the opinion of the physician the expected benefits outweigh the risks.

Precautions: Premenopausal female patients with breast cancer should receive testosterone enanthate continuously while response is satisfactory to avoid possible acceleration of malignancy. Also, patients must be watched carefully for signs of hypercalcemia, edema, or acceleration of the disease. If any of these signs appear, testosterone therapy should be stopped.

If symptomatic hypercalcemia occurs, discontinue androgen therapy and institute appropriate measures.

Caution is required in administering androgens to patients with cardiac, renal, or hepatic disease. Edema may occur occasionally. Concomitant administration with adrenal steroids or ACTH may add to the edema. Edema may be combatted with a low salt diet and the use of a suitable diuretic; edema of sufficient degree to warrant a reduction of dosage or termination of therapy is rare.

Anabolic steroids may increase sensitivity to anticoagulants. Dosage of the anticoagulant may have to be decreased in order to maintain the prothrombin time at the desired therapeutic level.

Anabolic steroids have been shown to alter glucose tolerance tests. Diabetics should be followed carefully and the insulin or oral hypoglycemic dosage adjusted accordingly.

Serum cholesterol may increase or decrease during therapy. Because of its hypercholesterolemic effects, caution is required when administering this drug to patients with a history of myocardial infarction or coronary artery disease. Serial determinations of serum cholesterol should be made and therapy adjusted accordingly. A cause and effect relationship between myocardial infarction and hypercholesterolemia has not been established.

Inhibition of testicular function and decrease in ejaculatory volume may occur when the drug is administered in doses greater than those used for replacement therapy in hypogonadal males.

Androgens should be used with caution in young boys in order to avoid precocious sexual development and premature closure of the epiphyses.

Use of anabolic steroids by athletes is not recommended. Objective evidence is conflicting and inconclusive as to whether these medications significantly increase athletic performance by increasing muscle strength. Weight gains reported by athletes are due in part to fluid retention, which is a potentially hazardous side effect of anabolic steroid therapy. The risk of other unwanted effects outweigh any possible benefit received from anabolic steroids and make their use in athletes undesirable.

Adverse Effects: In males, the following post pubertal adverse reactions have occurred: inhibition of testicular function, testicular atrophy and oligospermia, impotence, chronic priapism, gynecomastia, epididymitis, and bladder irritability. In addition, the following reactions are known to occur with anabolic steroids: increased or decreased libido, flushing of the skin, acne, habituation, excitation and sleeplessness, chills, leukopenia, and bleeding in patients on concomitant anticoagulant therapy. In addition, females have exhibited hirsutism, deepening or hoarseness of the voice, enlargement of the clitoris and menstrual irregularities; these phenomena in females appear to be reversible, with the occasional exception of voice changes.

I.M. preparations of anabolic steroids have been associated with urticaria at the injection site, post injection induration, and furunculosis.

Alterations may occur in the following clinical laboratory tests: metyrapone test, fasting blood sugar (FBS) and glucose tolerance test, thyroid function tests[decrease in protein bound iodine (PBI), thyroxine binding capacity, and radioactive iodine uptake, and an increase in T3 uptake by the red blood cells or resin; free thyroxine levels remain normal and the altered tests usually persist for 2 to 3 weeks after stopping anabolic therapy], electrolytes (retention of sodium, chloride, water, potassium, calcium, and inorganic phosphates), blood coagulation tests (increase in clotting factors II, V, VII, and X), and miscellaneous laboratory tests (decreased creatinine and creatine excretion lasting up to 2 weeks after discontinuing therapy and increased 17-ketosteroid excretion).

Dosage: Care should be taken to inject the preparation deeply into the gluteal muscle following the usual precautions for i.m. administration.
Note: The use of a wet needle or syringe may cause the solution to become cloudy; however, this does not affect the potency of the material.

The following dosages are suggested. In females: For enhancement of libido (frigidity), 100 mg every 4 weeks; use

Delatestryl (cont'd)

only if uterus is normal in size; not recommended in women with hypertrichosis or acne; discontinue if masculinization occurs.

For mammary cancer (in premenopausal women), 200 to 400 mg every 2 or more weeks; dosage should be adjusted depending upon clinical response; close medical supervision is mandatory; use only in advanced inoperable cases or as an adjunct to surgery or roentgen therapy; hypercalcemia may develop. For dysfunctional uterine bleeding (menorrhagia), 200 to 400 mg to induce endometrial atrophy; 100 to 200 mg every 4 weeks given 1 week before the expected onset of menstruation; a progestogen, then cyclic estrogen-progestogen therapy is generally preferred to androgen. For menopausal syndrome (selected cases), 200 mg every 4 weeks. For prevention of postpartum breast engorgement and inhibition of lactation, 100 to 200 mg at the end of first stage of labor; combining androgen with estrogen therapy is generally preferred.

In males: For hypogonadism, 200 to 400 mg every 4 weeks; androgen therapy is regarded as replacement therapy, being effective only as long as continued; prolonged treatment with chorionic gonadotropin is also recommended. For cryptorchidism, 100 to 200 mg every 4 weeks; chorionic gonadotropin should generally be tried first; use only when no obstructive anatomic lesion exists; if descent has not occurred after 3 or 4 months of therapy, surgical transplantation should be considered. For oligospermia, 100 to 200 mg every 4 to 6 weeks for development and maintenance of testicular tubular function; 200 mg every week for 6 to 12 weeks for suppression of spermatogenesis and rebound stimulation.

In males and females: For anabolic effect, 200 to 400 mg every 4 weeks; combining androgen with estrogen therapy is generally preferred.

In general, total doses of testosterone enanthate above 400 mg per month are not required because of the prolonged action of the preparation. Injections more frequently than every 2 weeks are rarely indicated.

Supplied: Each mL of sterile solution contains: testosterone enanthate 200 mg. Nonmedicinal ingredients: chlorobutanol 0.5% w/v and sesame oil. Vials of 5 mL. Store at room temperature. Low temperatures may result in separation of some crystalline material which redissolves readily on warming.

DELESTROGEN® Ⓟ

Squibb

Estradiol Valerate

Estrogen

Indications: In nonpregnant women, Delestrogen is indicated in the treatment of amenorrhea (primary and secondary); disturbances of the menstrual cycle (hypomenorrhea, oligomenorrhea, irregular cycles, metrorrhagia); deficiency syndromes (castration, primary ovarian failure, menopause); local manifestations of estrogen deficiency (senile vaginitis, pruritus vulvae); abnormal uterine bleeding due to hormonal imbalance in the absence of organic pathology; and for the production of secretory endometrium and desquamation.

Also indicated for the treatment of advanced mammary carcinoma in women 5 years or more postmenopausal and in the relief of postpartum breast engorgement and inhibition of lactation. May also be used in the palliative treatment of inoperable progressing prostatic carcinoma in males.

Contraindications: Estrogens should not be administered to patients with active hepatic dysfunction or disease, especially of the obstructive type; patients with known or suspected endometrial carcinoma or carcinoma of the cervix uteri, carcinoma of the breast except in special circumstances (see Indications); patients with endometrial hyperplasia without accompanying progestogen; hypersensitivity to estrogens.

Estrogens are also contraindicated in the following situations: undiagnosed vaginal bleeding; a history of cerebrovascular accident, coronary thrombosis, or in the presence of classical migraine; thrombophlebitis or thromboembolic disease or a history of these conditions; partial or complete loss of vision or diplopia, from ophthalmic vascular disease; suspected pregnancy.

Steroidal suppression of lactation, in the immediate postpartum period is contraindicated in patients over 35 years of age or in the face of circumstances that predispose to puerperal thromboembolism such as a history of thromboembolism, operative delivery, infection, obesity, multiparity or varicose veins.

Precautions: Before estradiol is administered, the patient should have a complete physical examination including a blood pressure determination. Breasts and pelvic organs should be examined and a Papanicolaou smear should be taken.

The first follow-up examination should be done within 6 months after initiation of treatment. Thereafter, examinations should be made at least once a year. At each annual visit, repeat those procedures outlined above.

If any surgical procedures are performed, advise the pathologist of the patient's therapy when specimens are sent for examination. Liver function tests should be made periodically in subjects who have, or are suspected of having, hepatic disease.

If abnormal vaginal bleeding occurs during therapy, diagnostic aspiration biopsy or curettage should be performed to rule out the possibility of uterine malignancy.

Patients who develop visual disturbances, classical migraine, transient aphasia, proptosis, paralysis, or loss of consciousness should discontinue medication.

If the patient develops any sign of phlebitis or thromboembolic complications, papilledema or retinal vascular lesions, discontinue medication.

Because normal endogenous hormone production varies individually, certain patients may be unusually responsive to estrogenic therapy and may respond with undesirable manifestations of excessive estrogenic stimulation such as abnormal or excessive uterine bleeding, mastodynia, edema.

When large doses of estrogens are used, urinary stress incontinence may occur.

Lactation: Estrogen may be excreted in the mother's milk and an estrogenic effect upon the nursing infant has been described.

In patients with metastatic carcinoma and hypercalcemia, estrogen medication should be used with caution.

Close medical supervision is mandatory when estrogens are used for the treatment of mammary or prostatic carcinoma. Therapy should be immediately discontinued if there is a recurrence or an acceleration of the condition.

Continuous use of estrogens will result in prolonged stimulation of the endometrium and breast. To avoid this in the menopausal or hypogonadal patient, estrogens should be administered cyclically (see Dosage).

Development of sudden enlargement, pain, or tenderness of uterine fibroids requires discontinuation of medication.

Estrogen may cause fluid retention. Particular caution is indicated in cardiac or renal dysfunction, epilepsy, or asthma.

Elevation of blood pressure in previously normotensive or hypertensive patients necessitates cessation of medication.

Diabetic patients or those with a predisposition to diabetes should be observed closely to detect any alterations in carbohydrate metabolism.

When liver or endocrine function tests are indicated, the results should not be considered reliable unless therapy has been discontinued for 2 to 4 months.

Because of the effects of estrogens on epiphyseal closure, they should be used judiciously in young patients in whom bone growth is not complete.

Prolonged high doses of estrogens will inhibit anterior pituitary function. This should be borne in mind when treating patients in whom fertility is desired.

Estrogens should be used with caution in patients with certain metabolic bone diseases that are associated with hypercalcemia or in patients with renal insufficiency.

Discontinue the medication in patients with a history of psychiatric abnormalities if exaggeration of symptoms occur.

Adverse Effects: The following adverse effects have been reported with estrogens generally and may be encountered when giving any estrogen: Gastrointestinal: nausea, anorexia, vomiting, abdominal cramps, bloating, cholestatic jaundice, increase or decrease in body weight.
Genitourinary: sodium and water retention, breakthrough bleeding, spotting and withdrawal bleeding; hypomenorrhea, oligomenorrhea or amenorrhea; increased cervical mucus, reactivation of endometriosis, cystitis like syndrome.
Endocrine: breast swelling and tenderness, increased blood sugar concentrations, and decreased glucose tolerance; In males: gynecomastia, reduced potency and feminization.
CNS: headaches, mental depression, increase or decrease of libido, nervousness, dizziness, fatigue, irritability, malaise.
Dermatologic: hypersensitivity: loss of scalp hair, allergic reactions and rashes, chloasma or melasma; hemorrhagic eruption, itching, erythema nodosum and erythema multiforme.
Musculoskeletal: backache.
Cardiovascular: increase in blood pressure in susceptible individuals, aggravation of migraine headaches.
Hematologic: A statistically significant association between the use of estrogen-progestin preparations and the following serious reactions has been demonstrated: thrombophlebitis, pulmonary embolism and cerebral thrombosis. Coagulation tests may give altered results (increased prothrombin, and Factors VII, VIII, IX and X).

While available evidence suggests an association with the following serious reactions, such a relationship has been neither confirmed nor refuted: coronary thrombosis and neuro-ocular lesions, e.g., retinal thrombosis and optic neuritis.
Miscellaneous: pain at the injection site, sterile abscess, incomplete suppression of breast engorgement, mastodynia, premenstrual like syndrome, precipitation or aggravation of porphyria cutanea tarda in predisposed individuals.

Overdose: Symptoms: Accidental overdosage may result in nausea, vomiting and abdominal cramps, headache, dizziness and general malaise. The transient hyperestrogenic effects may include severe temporary sodium and water retention in some susceptible individuals.

Treatment: Symptomatic. For severe temporary sodium and water retention, administer diuretics.

Dosage: Care should be taken to inject deeply into the upper, outer quadrant of the gluteal muscle following the usual precautions for i.m. administration. By virtue of the low viscosity of the vehicle, Delestrogen may be administered with a small gauge needle. A dry needle and syringe should be used. Use of a wet needle or syringe may cause the solution to become cloudy; however, this does not affect the potency of the material.

In general, estrogens should be given cyclically and in some cases with progestogen or androgen to avoid overstimulation of breast and endometrial tissues. The addition of sufficient progestogen to promote conversion of the endometrium is mandatory in those patients who are receiving sufficient unopposed estrogen to cause vaginal bleeding or endometrial hyperplasia. Obviously, abnormal vaginal bleeding in such patients is an indication for prompt diagnostic measures.

The lowest effective dosage should be used and the requirement for estrogen therapy should be assessed periodically.
Castration, Primary Ovarian Failure, Menopausal Syndrome, Senile Vaginitis, Kraurosis Vulvae With or Without Pruritus: The cyclic therapy schedule should be used, starting anytime and continuing through 4 cycles. Continuous therapy with estrogen alone may induce dysfunctional uterine bleeding.
Inoperable Prostatic Carcinoma: 30 mg or more every 1 to 2 weeks. Close medical supervision is mandatory. Suspend therapy if there is a relapse. Soreness of the breast or gynecomastia may occur; hypercalcemia may develop.
Inhibition of Lactation; Postpartum Breast Engorgement: 10 to 25 mg as a single injection at the end of the first stage of labor.
Amenorrhea, Production of Secretory Endometrium and Desquamation: administer 375 mg of hydroxyprogesterone caproate injection anytime. After 4 days of desquamation or, if there is no bleeding 21 days after hydroxyprogesterone alone, start cyclic therapy schedule. Repeat cyclic therapy every 4 weeks; stop after 4 cycles for amenorrhea, or when cyclic therapy is no longer required for production of secretory endometrium and desquamation. Exclude genital malignancy before hormone therapy is started. To determine onset of normal cyclic function, patient should be observed for 2 to 3 cycles after cessation of therapy.
Disturbances of the Menstrual Cycle (hypomenorrhea, oligomenorrhea, irregular cycles, metrorrhagia): The cyclic therapy schedule should be used, starting at the beginning of the cycle and repeated for 4 cycles. To determine the onset of normal cyclic function, the patient should be observed for 2 to 3 cycles without any hormone therapy.
Advanced Mammary Carcinoma in Women 5 Years or More Postmenopausal: 20 to 40 mg every 2 or 3 weeks. Close medical supervision is mandatory. Suspend therapy if there is a relapse. Therapy may be discontinued briefly after each course of 4 months, to permit the endometrium to regress. Estrogen therapy may induce vaginal bleeding; hypercalcemia may develop.
Cyclic Therapy Schedule: Cyclic therapy is a 28 day cycle which is repeated every 4 weeks. The cyclic therapy schedule is as follows: 20 mg of estradiol valerate injection is administered on Day 1 of each cycle. Two weeks after Day 1, 250 mg of hydroxyprogesterone caproate injection and 5 mg of estradiol valerate injection are administered; 4 weeks after Day 1 is Day 1 of next cycle.

Supplied: Each mL of sterile suspension contains: estradiol valerate 10 mg in sesame oil plus 0.5% chlorobutanol as a preservative. Nonmedicinal ingredients: chlorobutanol 0.5%

w/v and sesame oil. Vials of 5 mL. Delestrogen may be stored at room temperature. Low temperatures may result in separation of some crystalline material which redissolves readily on warming.

DELSYM®
Novartis Consumer Health

Dextromethorphan Polistirex
Antitussive

Pharmacology: Dextromethorphan is a centrally acting antitussive which is comparable to codeine on a mg basis for cough suppression but lacking analgesic or addictive properties.

Antitussive efficacy in adults is seen after 10 to 20 mg doses every 4 hours or 30 mg every 6 to 8 hours. With the usual therapeutic dosage, no effect has been noted on respiratory, cardiovascular or gastrointestinal function. Respiratory depression has been noted following ingestion of very large doses.

Dextromethorphan polistirex is a sustained-release preparation. Clinical bioavailability studies have shown that a single 60 mg dose provides plasma concentrations of dextromethorphan similar to those obtained with two 30 mg doses of dextromethorphan HBr given at 6 hour intervals. After repeated doses at steady state, equivalent plasma concentrations are maintained when Delsym is taken every 12 hours as compared to dextromethorphan HBr every 6 hours.

Indications: For the temporary relief of cough due to minor throat and bronchial irritation as may occur with the common cold or with inhaled irritants.

Warnings: Dextromethorphan should not be taken for persistent or chronic cough such as occurs with smoking, asthma or emphysema, or where cough is accompanied by excessive secretions, except under the advice and supervision of a physician.

Do not give this product to children under 2 years of age except under the advice and supervision of a physician.

Drug Interactions: Two fatalities have been reported following ingestion of dextromethorphan in patients treated with phenelzine. Do not use in patients receiving MAO inhibitors.

Pregnancy and *Lactation:* Do not administer to women who are pregnant or nursing unless, in the opinion of a physician, the potential benefits of the drug outweigh the possible risks.

Precautions: A persistent cough may be a sign of a serious condition. The patient should be advised to consult a physician if cough persists for more than 1 week or if cough tends to recur or is accompanied by high fever, rash or persistent headache.

Dependence Liability: Substitution studies in morphine addicts indicate that dextromethorphan is devoid of dependence liability. Intoxication and bizarre behavior have occurred after ingestion of 300 to 1 500 mg several times daily.

Adverse Effects: Rarely, drowsiness, dizziness, headache, nausea or vomiting may occur.

Overdose: Symptoms and Treatment: Respiratory depression has been noted with very large doses. Ataxia and hyperactivity have also been reported following ingestion of 360 mg of dextromethorphan HBr in a 22-month old child. Administration of 5 μg/kg naloxone HCl i.v. produced rapid resolution of ataxia.

Dosage: Shake well before use.

Adults: 10 mL every 12 hours; do not exceed 20 mL in 24 hours.

Children: 6 to 12 years old: 5 mL every 12 hours; do not exceed 10 mL in 24 hours. 2 to 5 years old: 2.5 mL every 12 hours; do not exceed 5 mL in 24 hours. Under 2 years old: Use only under the advice of a physician.

Supplied: Each 5 mL of controlled release suspension contains: dextromethorphan polistirex equivalent to 30 mg dextromethorphan hydrobromide. Nonmedicinal ingredients: anhydrous citric acid, corn syrup, ethylcellulose, FD&C yellow #6, granulated sugar, gum tragacanth, methylparaben, orange flavor, polyethylene glycol, polysorbate 80, propylene glycol, propylparaben, purified water, vegetable oil, xanthan gum. Energy: 27.6 kJ (6.6 kcal)/5 mL. Sodium: <1 mmol (6.5 mg)/5 mL. Alcohol-, lactose-, gluten- and tartrazine-free. Bottles of 85 and 150 mL. Store at room temperature.

DELTASONE® ℞
Pharmacia & Upjohn

Prednisone
Corticosteroid

Pharmacology: Prednisone is a corticosteroid, which like other steroids, acts by controlling the rate of synthesis of proteins. The corticosteroids react with receptor proteins in the cytoplasm of sensitive cells to form a steroid-receptor complex. The steroid receptor complex moves into the nucleus where it binds to chromatin. Information carried by the steroid or more likely by the receptor protein directs the genetic apparatus to transcribe RNA. Steroid hormones thus stimulate transcription and ultimately the synthesis of specific proteins.

The major physiologic actions of prednisone are: to increase liver glycogen deposition and to decrease the inflammatory response. Prednisone has some effects on sodium and fluid retention.

The mechanism of action is not fully established. It is theorized that the drug's anti-inflammatory effect is due to multiple mechanisms, including the inhibition of leukocyte migration to sites of tissue injury, the impairment of phagocytosis plus reduced capillary permeability. The drug's immunosuppressant effect is attributed to several factors, among them a transient lymphopenia especially of T-lymphocytes, and inhibition of immunoglobulin production of monocytes.

Prednisone is rapidly and completely absorbed from the intestinal tract. After oral administration, maximum plasma concentrations are reached in 1 to 2 hours. Once absorbed, the drug is approximately 75% bound to plasma proteins. The major route of elimination is via the liver ($t_{1/2}$=4 hr.); and the active drug disappears completely in about 12 hours.

Indications: Endocrine Disorders: Primary or secondary adrenocortical insufficiency (hydrocortisone or cortisone is the first choice; synthetic analogs may be used in conjunction with mineralocorticoids where applicable; in infancy, mineralocorticoid supplementation is of particular importance); congenital adrenal hyperplasia; nonsuppurative thyroiditis; hypercalcemia associated with cancer.

Nonendocrine Disorders: Rheumatic disorders: As adjunctive therapy for short-term administration (to tide the patient over an acute episode or exacerbation) in: psoriatic arthritis, rheumatoid arthritis, including juvenile rheumatoid arthritis (selected cases may require low dose maintenance therapy), ankylosing spondylitis, acute and subacute bursitis, acute nonspecific tenosynovitis, acute gouty arthritis, post-traumatic osteoarthritis, synovitis of osteoarthritis, epicondylitis.

Collagen Diseases: During an exacerbation or as maintenance therapy in selected cases of systemic lupus erythematosus, acute rheumatic carditis, systemic dermatomyositis (polymyositis), polymyalgia rheumatica, giant cell arteritis.

Dermatologic Diseases: pemphigus, bullous dermatitis herpetiformis, severe erythema multiforme (Stevens-Johnson syndrome), exfoliative dermatitis, mycosis fungoides, severe psoriasis, severe seborrheic dermatitis.

Allergic States: Control of severe or incapacitating allergic conditions intractable to adequate trials of conventional treatment: seasonal or perennial allergic rhinitis, bronchial asthma, contact dermatitis, atopic dermatitis, serum sickness, drug hypersensitivity reactions.

Ophthalmic Diseases: Severe acute and chronic allergic and inflammatory processes involving the eye and its adnexa such as: allergic conjunctivitis, keratitis, allergic corneal marginal ulcers, herpes zoster ophthalmicus, iritis and iridocyclitis, chorioretinitis, anterior segment inflammation, diffuse posterior uveitis and choroiditis, optic neuritis, sympathetic ophthalmia.

Respiratory Diseases: Symptomatic sarcoidosis, Löffler's syndrome not manageable by other means, berylliosis, fulminating or disseminated pulmonary tuberculosis when used concurrently with appropriate antituberculous chemotherapy, aspiration pneumonitis.

Hematologic Disorders: idiopathic thrombocytopenic purpura in adults, secondary thrombocytopenia in adults, acquired (autoimmune) hemolytic anemia, erythroblastopenia (RBC anemia), congenital (erythroid) hypoplastic anemia.

Neoplastic Diseases: For palliative management of: leukemias and lymphomas in adults, acute leukemia of childhood.

Edematous States: To induce a diuresis or remission of proteinuria in the nephrotic syndrome, without uremia, of the idiopathic type or that due to lupus erythematosus.

Gastrointestinal Diseases: To tide the patient over a critical period of the disease in: ulcerative colitis, regional enteritis.

CNS: Acute exacerbations of multiple sclerosis.

Organ Transplantation.

Miscellaneous: Tuberculous meningitis with subarachnoid block or impending block when used concurrently with appropriate antituberculous chemotherapy, trichinosis with neurologic or myocardial involvement.

Contraindications: Systemic fungal infections and known hypersensitivity to prednisone or to its excipients.

Warnings: In patients on corticosteroid therapy subjected to unusual stress, increased dosage of rapidly acting corticosteroids before, during, and after the stressful situation is indicated.

Corticosteroids may mask some signs of infection, and new infections may appear during their use. There may be decreased resistance and inability to localize infection when corticosteroids are used. Infections with any pathogen including viral, bacterial, fungal, protozoan or helminthic infections, in any location in the body, may be associated with the use of corticosteroids alone or in combination with other immunosuppressive agents that affect cellular immunity, humoral immunity or neutrophil function. These infections may be mild, but can be severe and at times fatal. With increasing doses of corticosteroids, the rate of occurrence of infectious complication increases. Do not use intra-articularly, intrabursally, or for intratendinous administration for local effect in the presence of acute infection.

Prolonged use of corticosteroids may produce posterior subcapsular cataracts, glaucoma with possible damage to the optic nerves, and may enhance the establishment of secondary ocular infections due to fungi or viruses. Allergic reactions (e.g. angioedema) may occur.

Average and large doses of hydrocortisone or cortisone can cause elevation of blood pressure, salt and water retention, and increased excretion of potassium. These effects are less likely to occur with the synthetic derivatives except when used in large doses. Dietary salt restriction and potassium supplementation may be necessary. All corticosteroids increase calcium excretion.

Administration of live or live, attenuated vaccines is contraindicated in patients receiving immunosuppressive doses of corticosteroids. Killed or inactivated vaccines may be administered to patients receiving immunosuppressive doses of corticosteroids. However the response to such vaccines may be diminished. Indicated immunization procedures may be undertaken in patients receiving nonimmunosuppressive doses of corticosteroids.

The use of prednisone in active tuberculosis should be restricted to those cases of fulminating or disseminated tuberculosis in which the corticosteroid is used for the management of the disease in conjunction with an appropriate antituberculous regimen.

If corticosteroids are indicated in patients with latent tuberculosis or tuberculin reactivity, close observation is necessary as reactivation of the disease may occur. During prolonged corticosteroid therapy, these patients should receive chemoprophylaxis.

There is no universal agreement on whether corticosteroids per se are responsible for peptic ulcers encountered during therapy; however, glucocorticoid therapy may mask the symptoms of peptic ulcer so that perforation or hemorrhage may occur without significant pain.

Osteoporosis is a common but infrequently recognized adverse effect associated with a long-term use of large doses of glucocorticoid.

Growth may be suppressed in children receiving long-term daily, divided dose glucocorticoid therapy and use of such regimen should be restricted to the most urgent indications. Alternate day glucocorticoid therapy usually avoids or minimizes this side effect.

Host defenses are impaired in patients receiving large doses of glucocorticoids and this effect increases susceptibility to fungus infections as well as bacterial and viral infections.

Pregnancy and *Lactation:* Some animal studies have shown that corticosteroids, when administered to the mother at high doses, may cause fetal malformations. Adequate human reproductive studies have not been done with corticosteroids. Therefore, the use of this drug in pregnancy, nursing mothers or women of childbearing potential requires that the benefits of the drug be carefully weighed against the potential risk to the mother and embryo or fetus. Since there is inadequate evidence of safety in human pregnancy, this drug should be used in pregnancy only if clearly needed.

Corticosteroids readily cross the placenta. Infants born of mothers who have received substantial doses of corticosteroids during pregnancy must be carefully observed and evaluated for signs of adrenal insufficiency. There are no known effects of corticosteroids on labor and delivery. Corticosteroids are excreted in breast milk.

Deltasone (cont'd)

Precautions: Drug induced secondary adrenocortical insufficiency may be minimized by gradual reduction of dosage. This type of relative insufficiency may persist for months after discontinuation of therapy; therefore, in any situation of stress occurring during that period, hormone therapy should be reinstituted. Since mineralocorticoid secretion may be impaired, salt and/or a mineralocorticoid should be administered concurrently.

There is an enhanced effect of corticosteroids on patients with hypothyroidism and in those with cirrhosis.

Corticosteroids should be used cautiously in patients with ocular herpes simplex because of possible corneal perforation.

The lowest possible dose of corticosteroid should be used to control the condition under treatment and when reduction in dosage, the reduction should be gradual.

Psychic derangements may appear when corticosteroids are used, ranging from euphoria, insomnia, mood swings, personality changes, and severe depression, to frank psychotic manifestations. Also, existing emotional instability or psychotic tendencies may be aggravated by corticosteroids.

ASA and nonsteroidal anti-inflammatory agents should be used cautiously in conjunction with corticosteroids in patients with hypoprothrombinemia.

Corticosteroids should be used with caution in nonspecific ulcerative colitis, if there is a probability of impending perforation, abscess or other pyogenic infection; diverticulitis; fresh intestinal anastomoses; active or latent peptic ulcer; renal insufficiency; hypertension; osteoporosis; or myasthenia gravis.

Because complications of treatment with glucocorticoids are dependent on the size of the dose and the duration of treatment, a risk/benefit decision must be made in each individual case as to dose and duration of treatment and as to whether daily or intermittent therapy should be used.

Convulsions have been reported with concurrent use of methylprednisolone and cyclosporine. SInce concurrent administration of these agents results in a mutual inhibition of metabolism, it is possible that convulsions and other adverse events associated with the individual use of either drug may be more apt to occur.
The possibility of this interaction occurring with prednisone should be considered.

Kaposi's sarcoma has been reported to occur in patients receiving corticosteroid therapy. Discontinuation of corticosteroids may result in clinical remission.
Carcinogenesis, Mutagenesis, Impairment of Fertility: There is no evidence that corticosteroids are carcinogenic, mutagenic, or impair fertility.
Lactation: Some prednisone is excreted in breast milk.
Drug Interactions: The pharmacokinetic interactions listed below are potentially clinically important.

Drugs that induce hepatic enzymes such as phenobarbital, phenytoin and rifampin may increase the clearance of corticosteroids and may require increases in corticosteroid dose to achieve the desired response.

Drugs such as troleandomycin and ketoconazole may inhibit the metabolism of corticosteroids and thus decrease their clearance. Therefore, the dose of corticosteroid should be titrated to avoid steroid toxicity.

Corticosteroids may increase the clearance of chronic high dose ASA. This could lead to decreased salicylate serum levels or increase the risk of salicylate toxicity when the corticosteroid is withdrawn. ASA should be used cautiously in conjunction with corticosteroids in patients suffering from hypothrombinemia.

The effect of corticosteroids on oral anticoagulants is variable. There are reports of enhanced, as well as, diminished effects of anticoagulant when given concurrently with corticosteroids. Therefore, coagulation indices should be monitored to maintain the desired anticoagulant effect.

Adverse Effects: Note: The following are typical for all systemic corticosteroids. Their inclusion in this list does not necessarily indicate that the specific event has been observed with this particular formulation.
Fluid and Electrolyte Disturbances: sodium retention; fluid retention; congestive heart failure in susceptible patients; potassium loss, hypokalemic alkalosis; hypertension.
Musculoskeletal: steroid myopathy; muscle weakness; osteoporosis; pathologic fractures; vertebral compression fractures; aseptic necrosis; loss of muscle mass; tendon rupture—particularly of the Achilles tendon.
Gastrointestinal: peptic ulceration with possible perforation and hemorrhage; gastric hemorrhage; pancreatitis; perforation of the bowel; abdominal distention; ulcerative esophagitis.

Increases in ALT, AST and alkaline phosphatase have been observed following corticosteroid treatment. These changes are usually small, not associated with any clinical syndrome and are reversible upon discontinuation.
Dermatologic: impaired wound healing; petechiae and ecchymoses; thin fragile skin; facial erythema; increased sweating; may suppress reactions to skin tests.
Metabolic: negative nitrogen balance due to protein catabolism.
Neurological: increased intracranial pressure with papilledema (pseudotumor cerebri); vertigo; headache; psychic derangements; seizures.
Endocrine: menstrual irregularities; development of cushingoid state; suppression of pituitary-adrenal axis; decreased carbohydrate tolerance; manifestations of latent diabetes mellitus; increased requirements for insulin or oral hypoglycemic agents in diabetes; suppression of growth in children.
Ophthalmic: posterior subcapsular cataracts; increased intraocular pressure; exophthalmos; glaucoma.
Immune System: masking of infections; latent infections becoming active; opportunistic infections; hypersensitivity reactions including anaphylaxis; may suppress reactions to skin tests.

Dosage: The initial dosage may vary from 5 to 60 mg of prednisone per day depending on the specific disease entity being treated. In situations of less severity, lower doses will generally suffice while in selected patients higher initial doses may be required. The initial dosage should be maintained or adjusted until a satisfactory response is noted. If after a reasonable period of time there is a lack of satisfactory clinical response, prednisone should be discontinued and the patient transferred to other appropriate therapy.

It should be emphasized that dosage requirements are variable and must be individualized on the basis of the disease under treatment and the response of the patient.

After a favorable response is noted, the proper maintenance dosage should be determined by decreasing the initial drug dosage in small decrements at appropriate time intervals until the lowest dosage which will maintain an adequate clinical response is reached. It should be kept in mind that constant monitoring is needed in regard to drug dosage. Included in the situations which may make dosage adjustments necessary are changes in clinical status secondary to remissions or exacerbations in the disease process, the patient's individual drug responsiveness, and the effect of patient exposure to stressful situations not directly related to the disease entity under treatment; in this latter situation it may be necessary to increase the dosage of prednisone for a period of time consistent with the patient's condition.
ADT Alternate Day Therapy: Alternate day therapy is a corticosteroid dosing regimen in which twice the usual daily dose of corticosteroid is administered every other morning. The purpose of this mode of therapy is to provide a patient requiring long-term, pharmacologic dose treatment with the beneficial effects of corticoids while minimizing certain undesirable effects, including pituitary-adrenal suppression, the Cushingoid state, corticoid withdrawal symptoms, and growth suppression in children.

Supplied: 5 mg: Each white tablet, scored on one side and marked with ''Upjohn 45'' on the other, contains: prednisone 5 mg. Nonmedicinal ingredients: calcium stearate, cornstarch, lactose, mineral oil and sucrose. Sodium: $<$1 mmol (5.2 mg)/tablet. Gluten-free. Bottles of 1 000.

50 mg: Each white tablet scored on one side and marked with a ''U'' on the other contains: prednisone 50 mg. Nonmedicinal ingredients: cornstarch, lactose, magnesium stearate, mineral oil, sucrose and talc. Gluten-free. Bottles of 100.

(Shown in Product Recognition Section)

DEMADEX® Ⓟ

Roche

Torsemide

Diuretic—Antihypertensive

Pharmacology: Mechanism of Action: Micropuncture studies in animals have shown that torsemide acts from within the lumen of the thick ascending portion of the loop of Henle, where it inhibits the $Na^+/K^+/2Cl^-$ carrier system. Clinical pharmacology studies have confirmed this site of action in humans, and effects in other segments of the nephron have not been demonstrated. Diuretic activity thus correlates better with the rate of drug excretion in the urine than with the concentration in the blood.

Torsemide increases the urinary excretion of sodium, chloride, and water, but it does not significantly alter glomerular filtration rate, renal plasma flow, or acid-base balance.
Pharmacokinetics: The bioavailability of torsemide tablets is approximately 80%, with little intersubject variation; the 90% confidence interval is 75 to 89%. The drug is absorbed with little first-pass metabolism, and the serum concentration reaches its peak (C_{max}) within 1 hour after oral administration. C_{max} and area under the serum concentration-time curve (AUC) after oral administration are proportional to dose over the range of 2.5 to 200 mg. Simultaneous food intake delays the time to C_{max} by about 30 minutes, but overall bioavailability (AUC) and diuretic activity are unchanged. Absorption is essentially unaffected by renal or hepatic dysfunction.

The volume of distribution of torsemide is 12 to 15 L in normal adults or in patients with mild to moderate renal failure or congestive heart failure. In patients with hepatic cirrhosis, the volume of distribution is approximately doubled.

In normal subjects the elimination half-life of torsemide is approximately 3.5 hours. Torsemide is cleared from the circulation by both hepatic metabolism (approximately 80% of total clearance) and excretion into the urine (approximately 20% of total clearance in patients with normal renal function). The major metabolite in humans is the carboxylic acid derivative, which is biologically inactive. Two of the lesser metabolites possess some diuretic activity, but for practical purposes metabolism terminates the action of the drug.

Because torsemide is extensively bound to plasma protein ($>$99%), very little enters tubular urine via glomerular filtration. Most renal clearance of torsemide occurs via active secretion of the drug by the proximal tubules into tubular urine.

In patients with decompensated congestive heart failure, hepatic and renal clearance are both reduced, probably because of hepatic congestion and decreased renal plasma flow, respectively. The total clearance of torsemide is approximately 50% of that seen in healthy volunteers, and the plasma half-life and AUC are correspondingly increased. Because of reduced renal clearance, a smaller fraction of any given dose is delivered to the intraluminal site of action, so at any given dose there is less natriuresis in patients with congestive heart failure than in normal subjects.

In patients with renal failure, renal clearance of torsemide is markedly decreased but total plasma clearance is not significantly altered. A smaller fraction of the administered dose is delivered to the intraluminal site of action, and the natriuretic response in renal failure may still be achieved if patients are given higher doses. The total plasma clearance and elimination half-life of torsemide remain normal under the conditions of impaired renal function because metabolic elimination by the liver remains intact.

In patients with hepatic cirrhosis, the volume of distribution, plasma half-life, and renal clearance are all increased, but total clearance is unchanged.

The pharmacokinetic profile of torsemide in healthy elderly subjects is similar to that in young subjects except for a decrease in renal clearance related to the decline in renal function that commonly occurs with aging. However, total plasma clearance and elimination half-life remain unchanged.

The pharmacokinetics of torsemide after i.v. administration were studied in normal volunteers at doses of 5, 10 and 20 mg. The pharmacokinetics did not seem to be dependent upon dose, indicating that, over the dose range of 5 to 20 mg, torsemide obeys linear pharmacokinetics. The pharmacokinetic parameters of torsemide following i.v. administration are summarized in Table I.

Table I—Demadex

Pharmacokinetic Parameters of Torsemide after I.V. Administration

Parameter	Range of Mean Values
$t_{1/2}\beta$ (h)	3.6–5.8
CL_r (mL/min)	6.4–12.9
AE (% dose)	15.7–24.3
CL_p (mL/min)	38.3–49.8
Vd (L)	11.4–23.3

Legend: $t_{1/2}\beta$ = elimination half-life.
CL_r = renal clearance.
AE = percent of dose excreted unchanged in the urine.
CL_p = total plasma clearance.
Vd = volume of distribution.

Clinical Effects: The diuretic effects of torsemide begin within 10 minutes of i.v. dosing and peak within the first hour. With oral dosing, the onset of diuresis occurs within 1 hour and the peak effect occurs during the first or second hour. Independent of the route of administration, diuresis lasts about 6 to 8 hours. In healthy subjects given single doses, the dose-response relationship for sodium excretion is linear over the dose range of 2.5 to 20 mg. The increase in potassium excretion is negligible after a single dose of up to 10 mg and only slight (5 to 15 mEq) after a single dose of 20 mg.

Torsemide has been studied in controlled trials in patients with New York Heart Association Class II to Class IV congestive heart failure. Patients who received 10 to 20 mg of daily torsemide in these studies achieved significantly greater reductions in weight and edema than did patients who received placebo.

In single-dose studies in patients with nonanuric renal failure, high doses of torsemide (20 to 200 mg) caused marked increases in water and sodium excretion. In patients with non-anuric renal failure severe enough to require hemodialysis, chronic treatment with up to 200 mg of daily torsemide has not been shown to change steady-state fluid retention. Chronic use of any diuretic in renal disease has not been studied in adequate and well-controlled trials.

When given with aldosterone antagonists, torsemide also caused increases in sodium and fluid excretion in patients with edema or ascites due to hepatic cirrhosis. Urinary sodium excretion rate relative to the urinary excretion rate of torsemide is less in cirrhotic patients than in healthy subjects (possibly because of the hyperaldosteronism and resultant sodium retention that are characteristic of portal hypertension and ascites). However, because of the increased renal clearance of torsemide in patients with hepatic cirrhosis, these factors tend to balance each other, and the result is an overall natriuretic response that is similar to that seen in healthy subjects. Chronic use of any diuretic in hepatic disease has not been studied in adequate and well-controlled trials.

In patients with essential hypertension, torsemide has been shown in controlled studies to lower blood pressure when administered once a day at doses of 5 to 10 mg. The antihypertensive effect is near maximal after 4 to 6 weeks of treatment, but it may continue to increase for up to 12 weeks. Systolic and diastolic supine and standing blood pressures are all reduced. There is no significant orthostatic effect, and there is only a minimal peak-trough difference in blood-pressure reduction.

The antihypertensive effects of torsemide are, like those of other diuretics, on the average greater in black patients (a low-renin population) than in nonblack patients.

When torsemide is first administered, daily urinary sodium excretion increases for at least a week. With chronic administration however, daily sodium loss comes into balance with dietary sodium intake. If the administration of torsemide is suddenly stopped, blood pressure returns to pretreatment levels over several days, without overshoot.

Torsemide has been administered together with β-adrenergic blocking agents, ACE inhibitors, and calcium-channel blockers. Adverse drug interactions have not been observed, and special dosage adjustment has not been necessary.

Indications: For the treatment of edema associated with congestive heart failure, renal disease, or hepatic disease. Chronic use of any diuretic in renal or hepatic disease has not been studied in adequate and well-controlled trials.

Torsemide is indicated for the treatment of mild to moderate essential hypertension alone or in combination with other antihypertensive agents.

Torsemide i.v. injection is indicated when a rapid onset of diuresis is desired or when oral administration is impractical.

Contraindications: In patients with known hypersensitivity to torsemide or to sulfonylureas.

Torsemide is contraindicated in patients who are anuric and in cases of hepatic coma and states of severe electrolyte depletion until the condition is improved or corrected.

> **Warnings:** Torsemide is a potent diuretic which, if given in excessive amounts, can lead to profound diuresis with water and electrolyte depletion. Therefore, careful medical supervision is required and dose and dosage schedule have to be adjusted to the individual patient's needs (see Dosage).

Hepatic Disease with Cirrhosis and Ascites: Torsemide should be used with caution in patients with hepatic disease with cirrhosis and ascites, since sudden alterations of fluid and electrolyte balance may precipitate hepatic coma. In these patients, diuresis with torsemide is best initiated in the hospital. To prevent hypokalemia and metabolic alkalosis, an aldosterone antagonist or potassium-sparing drug should be used concomitantly with torsemide.

Ototoxicity: Tinnitus and hearing loss (usually reversible) have been observed after rapid i.v. injection of other loop diuretics and have also been observed after oral torsemide. Ototoxicity has also been seen in animal studies when very high plasma levels of torsemide were induced. Administered i.v., torsemide should be injected slowly over 2 minutes, and single doses should not exceed 200 mg.

Volume and Electrolyte Depletion: Patients receiving diuretics should be observed for clinical evidence of electrolyte imbalance, hypovolemia, or prerenal azotemia. Symptoms of these disturbances may include one or more of the following: dryness of the mouth, thirst, weakness, lethargy, drowsiness, restlessness, muscle pain or cramps, muscular fatigue, hypotension, oliguria, tachycardia, nausea, and vomiting. Excessive diuresis may cause dehydration, blood-volume reduction, and possibly thrombosis and embolism, especially in elderly patients. In patients who develop fluid and electrolyte imbalances, hypovolemia, or prerenal azotemia, the observed laboratory changes may include hyper- or hyponatremia, hyper- or hypochloremia, hyper- or hypokalemia, acid-base abnormalities, and increased blood urea nitrogen. If any of these occur, torsemide should be discontinued until the situation is corrected; torsemide may be restarted at a lower dose.

In controlled studies in the United States, torsemide was administered to hypertensive patients at doses of 5 or 10 mg daily. After 6 weeks at these doses, the mean decrease in serum potassium was approximately 0.1 mEq/L. In patients with congestive heart failure, hepatic cirrhosis, or renal disease treated with torsemide at doses higher than those studied in U.S. antihypertensive trials (i.e., 10 mg daily), hypokalemia was observed with greater frequency, in a dose-related manner.

In patients with cardiovascular disease, especially those receiving digitalis glycosides, diuretic-induced hypokalemia may be a risk factor for the development of arrhythmias. The risk of hypokalemia is greatest in patients with cirrhosis of the liver, in patients experiencing a brisk diuresis, in patients who are receiving inadequate oral intake of electrolytes, and in patients receiving concomitant therapy with corticosteroids or ACTH.

Periodic monitoring of serum potassium and other electrolytes is advised in patients treated with torsemide.

Torsemide is not removed from circulation by hemodialysis.

Precautions: Laboratory Values: Potassium: See Warnings, Volume and Electrolyte Depletion.

Calcium: Single doses of torsemide increased the urinary excretion of calcium by normal subjects, but serum calcium levels were slightly increased in 4- to 6-week hypertension trials. In long-term hypertension studies, the average 1-year change in serum calcium was a decrease of 0.1 mg/dL (0.02 mmol/L). Among 426 patients treated with torsemide for an average of 11 months, hypocalcemia was not reported as an adverse event.

Magnesium: Single doses of torsemide caused healthy volunteers to increase their urinary excretion of magnesium, but serum magnesium levels were slightly increased in 4- to 6-week hypertension trials. In long-term hypertension studies, the average 1-year change in serum magnesium was an increase of 0.03 mg/dL (0.01 mmol/L). Among 426 patients treated with torsemide for an average of 11 months, 1 case of hypomagnesemia (1.3 mg/dL (0.53 mmol/L)) was reported as an adverse event.

In long-term open clinical study of torsemide in patients with congestive heart failure, who received magnesium supplements, an increase in serum magnesium of 0.2 mg/dL (0.08 mmol/L) was observed. In a 4-week study in which magnesium supplementation was not given, the rate of occurrence of serum magnesium levels below 1.7 mg/dL (0.7 mmol/L) was 6 and 9% in the groups receiving 5 and 10 mg of torsemide, respectively.

Blood Urea Nitrogen (BUN), Creatinine, and Uric Acid: Torsemide produces small dose-related increases in each of these laboratory values. In hypertensive patients who received 10 mg of torsemide daily for 6 weeks, the mean increase in blood urea nitrogen was 1.8 mg/dL (0.6 mmol/L), the mean increase in serum creatinine was 0.05 mg/dL (4 μmol/L), and the mean increase in serum uric acid was 1.2 mg/dL (70 μmol/L).

Little further change occurred with long-term treatment, and all changes reversed when treatment was discontinued.

Symptomatic gout has been reported in patients receiving torsemide.

Glucose: Hypertensive patients who received 10 mg of daily torsemide experienced a mean increase in serum glucose concentration of 5.5 mg/dL (0.3 mmol/L) after 6 weeks of therapy, with a further increase of 1.8 mg/dL (0.1 mmol/L) during the subsequent year. In long-term studies in diabetics, mean fasting glucose values were not significantly changed from baseline. Cases of hyperglycemia have been reported but are uncommon.

Serum Lipids: In controlled hypertension studies of 4 to 6-weeks' duration, daily doses of 5, 10, and 20 mg of torsemide were associated with increases in total plasma cholesterol of 4, 4 and 8 mg/dL (0.1 to 0.2 mmol/L), respectively. The increase with 20 mg of torsemide was statistically significant.

In the same studies, mean increases in plasma triglycerides of 16, 13, and 71 mg/dL (0.15 to 0.8 mmol/L), respectively were observed. The increase with 20 mg was statistically significant.

Other: In long-term studies in hypertensive patients, torsemide has been associated with small mean decreases in hemoglobin, hematocrit, and erythrocyte count and small mean increases in white blood cell count, platelet count, and serum alkaline phosphatase. Although statistically significant, all of these changes were medically inconsequential. No significant trends have been observed in any liver enzyme tests other than alkaline phosphatase.

Drug Interactions: In patients with essential hypertension, torsemide has been administered together with β-blockers, ACE inhibitors, and calcium-channel blockers. In patients with congestive heart failure, torsemide has been administered together with digitalis glycosides, ACE inhibitors, and organic nitrates. None of these combined uses were associated with new or unexpected adverse events.

Glyburide and Warfarin: Torsemide does not affect the protein binding of glyburide or warfarin.

Digoxin: Torsemide does not affect the pharmacokinetics of digoxin. Coadministration of digoxin is reported to increase the area under the curve for torsemide by 50%, but dose adjustment of torsemide is not necessary.

Spironolactone: In healthy subjects, coadministration of torsemide was associated with signficant reduction in the renal clearance of spironolactone, with corresponding increases in the AUC. The pharmacokinetic profile and diuretic activity of torsemide are not altered by spironolactone. Clinical experience indicates that dosage adjustment of either agent is not required.

Cimetidine: The pharmacokinetic profile and diuretic activity of torsemide are not altered by cimetidine.

Salicylates: Because torsemide and salicylates compete for secretion by renal tubules, patients receiving high doses of salicylates may experience salicylate toxicity when torsemide is concomitantly administered. Also, although possible interactions between torsemide and nonsteroidal anti-inflammatory agents (including ASA) have not been studied, coadministration of these agents with another loop diuretic (furosemide) has occasionally been associated with renal dysfunction.

Indomethacin: The natriuretic effect of torsemide is partially inhibited by the concomitant administration of indomethacin. This effect has been demonstrated for torsemide under conditions of dietary sodium restriction (50 mEq/day) but not in the presence of normal sodium intake (150 mEq/day).

Cholestyramine: Concomitant use of torsemide and cholestyramine has not been studied in humans but, in a study in animals, coadministration of cholestyramine decreased the absorption of orally administered torsemide. If torsemide and cholestyramine are used concomitantly, simultaneous administration is not recommended.

Probenecid: Coadministration of probenecid reduces secretion of torsemide into the proximal tubule and thereby decreases the diuretic activity of torsemide.

Lithium: Other diuretics are known to reduce the renal clearance of lithium, inducing a high risk of lithium toxicity, so coadministration of lithium and diuretics should be undertaken with great caution, if at all. Coadministration of lithium and torsemide has not been studied.

Aminoglycoside Antibiotics and Ethacrynic Acid: Other diuretics have been reported to increase the ototoxic potential of aminoglycoside antibiotics and of ethacrynic acid, especially in the presence of impaired renal function. These potential interactions with torsemide have not been studied. In clinical trials tinnitus and hearing loss, usually reversible, have been reported after oral torsemide, therefore, concomitant administration of these products with torsemide is not recommended (see Warnings).

Pregnancy: There was no fetotoxicity or teratogenicity in rats treated with up to 5 mg/kg/day of torsemide or in rabbits treated with 1.6 mg/kg/day. Fetal and maternal toxicity,

Demadex (cont'd)

decrease in average body weight, increase in fetal resorption and delayed fetal ossification, occurred in rabbits and rats given doses 4 (rabbits) and 5 (rats) times larger.

No studies were carried out in pregnant women.

Torsemide should be given to pregnant women only if the potential benefit justifies the potential risk to the fetus.

Labor and Delivery: The effect of torsemide on labor and delivery is unknown.

Lactation: It should be noted that diuretics may partially inhibit lactation. It is not known whether torsemide is excreted in human milk. However, other diuretics do appear in human milk. If the use of torsemide is considered essential the patient should stop nursing.

Children: Safety and effectiveness in children have not been established.

Administration of another loop diuretic to severely premature infants with edema due to patent ductus arteriosus and hyaline membrane disease has occasionally been associated with renal calcifications, sometimes barely visible on x-ray but sometimes in staghorn form, filling the renal pelves. Some of these calculi have been dissolved, and hypercalciuria has been reported to have decreased, when chlorothiazide has been coadministered along with the loop diuretic. In other premature neonates with hyaline membrane disease, another loop diuretic has been reported to increase the risk of persistent patent ductus arteriosus, possibly through a prostaglandin-E-mediated process. The use of torsemide in such patients has not been studied.

Geriatrics: Of the total number of patients who received torsemide in U.S. clinical studies, 24% (198/843) were 65 or older while about 4% (34/843) were 75 or older. Decrease in renal clearance, related to the decline in renal function that commonly occurs with aging, has been observed. However, total plasma clearance and elimination half-life remain unchanged as compared to young healthy subjects (see Pharmacology and Dosage).

Adverse Effects: Torsemide had been evaluated for safety in approximately 3 400 patients. Over 800 of these patients received torsemide for at least 6 months, and over 380 for more than 1 year.

In all North American studies, in which patients were treated for up to one year, 75.6% (536/709) of patients with hypertension, 67.3% (74/110) of patients with congestive heart failure and 54.2% (13/24) of patients with renal disease reported adverse events. Discontinuation of therapy due to adverse events occurred in 9.0% (76/843) of patients treated with torsemide.

In controlled North American studies, in which 564 patients were treated for either hypertension or congestive heart failure, 50.5% (259/513) and 60.8% (31/51) respectively, reported adverse events. Discontinuation of therapy due to adverse events occurred in 3.5% (20/564) of patients treated with torsemide.

In studies conducted in North America and Europe, discontinuations due to adverse events were required in 3% of patients (38/1250) with congestive heart failure, 2% of patients (8/409) with renal disease, and 7.6% of patients (13/170) with liver cirrhosis. Reported adverse events were generally mild to moderate in severity.

The most common reasons for discontinuation of therapy with torsemide were (in descending order of frequency); dizziness, headache, nausea, weakness, vomiting, hyperglycemia, excessive urination, hyperuricemia, hypokalemia, excessive thirst, hypovolemia, impotence, esophageal hemorrhage, and dyspepsia. Discontinuation rates for these adverse events ranged from 0.1% to 0.5%.

Of the nearly 3 400 patients who received torsemide in clinical trials 1.7% experienced at least one serious adverse event. The incidence of these serious adverse events was 1.7% (27/1 595) in patients with hypertension, 1.5% (19/1 250) with congestive heart failure, 1.5% (6/409) with renal insufficiency and 4.1% (7/170) with liver cirrhosis.

Most of these serious adverse events were related to the cardiovascular system. Other frequently affected body systems included the body as a whole and the respiratory and digestive systems. Serious adverse events were atrial fibrillation, chest pain, diarrhea, digitalis intoxication, gastrointestinal hemorrhage, hyperglycemia, hyperuricemia, hypokalemia, hypotension, hypovolemia, shunt thrombosis, rash, rectal bleeding, syncope and ventricular tachycardia.

Table II and Table III (on following page) summarize the most common adverse events (≥ 1%) without regard to causality, occurring in the different patient populations studied in all trials.

Angioedema has been reported in a patient exposed to torsemide who was later found to be allergic to sulfa drugs.

In studies using i.v. administered torsemide, the most frequently reported adverse events were dizziness and dehydration, which were probably associated with volume depletion. Otherwise, i.v. torsemide had an adverse event profile qualitatively similar to that observed for short-term orally administered torsemide.

In studies using orally and i.v. administered torsemide, adverse events which were reported with a frequency less than 1% include: anemia, angina pectoris, anxiety, arrhythmia, AV block, bradycardia, bundle branch block, cerebral ischemia, dry skin, dysuria, excessive thirst, flatulence, hematuria, hyperglycemia, hypovolemia, increased BUN, malaise, postural hypotension, rectal bleeding, somnolence, increased sweating, syncope, tachycardia, and vertigo.

Abnormal Laboratory Findings: Studies in hypertension showed a statistically significant decreasing trend for hemoglobin, hematocrit, erythrocyte count, lymphocytes, sodium, chloride, calcium, potassium and urine specific gravity. Statistically significant increasing trends were detected for platelets, white blood cells, neutrophils, alkaline phosphatase, magnesium glucose and creatinine. Although the trends were statistically significant, the magnitude of the changes were slight (see Warnings and Precautions).

In patients with congestive heart failure, a decreasing trend over time was observed for sodium, potassium, and chloride whereas an increasing trend was observed for magnesium. No significant trends were observed for other electrolytes. Hypomagnesemia was detected in 1 congestive heart failure study in which magnesium supplements were not given.

In studies of patients with renal insufficiency, statistically significant changes were observed for serum calcium and potassium.

In patients with congestive heart failure, renal disease and hepatic cirrhosis, the extent of hypokalemia was dose related and occurred with a greater frequency than in hypertensive patients (see Warnings).

Results of clinical laboratory tests are consistent with the effects anticipated with the use of a diuretic.

Table II—Demadex

Most Common Adverse Events (≥ 1%) in Studies of Orally Administered Torsemide

	Hypertension N=1 226		CHF N=541		Edema due to Renal Disease N=203		Edema due to Liver Disease N=72	
Adverse Events	**N**	**(%)**	**N**	**(%)**	**N**	**(%)**	**N**	**(%)**
Body as a Whole								
Accidental injury	48	(4)						
Abdominal pain	24	(2)						
Asthenia	68	(6)	6	(1)			6	(8)
Back pain	42	(3)						
Flu syndrome	49	(4)						
Neck pain	17	(1)						
Pain	16	(1)						
Pain in extremity	40	(3)						
Cardiovascular								
Chest pain	34	(3)	8	(1)				
Electrocardiogram abnormal	13	(1)						
Palpitation	13	(1)						
Digestive System								
Constipation	15	(1)	9	(2)				
Diarrhea	25	(2)	7	(1)				
Dyspepsia	30	(2)						
Nausea	37	(3)	7	(1)	3	(2)	2	(3)
Sore throat	30	(2)						
Tooth disorder	22	(2)						
Vomiting			7	(1)				
Metabolic and Nutritional Disorder								
Edema	33	(3)						
Hyperuricemia	18	(1)						
Hypomagnesemia			7	(1)				
Musculoskeletal System								
Arthralgia	57	(5)						
Arthritis	23	(2)						
Hypertonia			10	(2)	4	(2)		
Myalgia	39	(3)						
Nervous System								
Depression	17	(1)						
Dizziness	91	(7)	15	(3)				
Headache	123	(10)	9	(2)				
Insomnia	24	(2)						
Nervousness	30	(2)						
Paresthesia	24	(2)						
Respiratory System								
Bronchitis	23	(2)	6	(1)				
Cough Increased	54	(4)						
Dyspnea	16	(1)						
Rhinitis	60	(5)						
Sinusitis	26	(2)						
Upper respiratory infection	125	(10)						
Skin and Appendages								
Rash	20	(2)						
Special Senses								
Blurred vision	13	(1)						
Urogenital System								
Impotence	13	(1)						
Nocturia	18	(1)						
Polyuria	68	(6)						
Urinary tract infection	18	(1)						

Table III—Demadex

Most Common Adverse Events (≥1%) in Studies of I.V. Torsemide

	Edema Due to			
	CHF N=201		Renal Disease N=127	
Adverse Events	N	(%)	N	(%)
Cardiovascular				
Hypotension	3	(1)		
Digestive System				
Diarrhea			2	(2)
Dyspepsia			2	(2)
Metabolic and Nutritional Disorders				
Creatinine increased			2	(2)
Dehydration			3	(2)
Gout			2	(2)
Hypokalemia			2	(2)
Nervous System				
Dizziness			3	(2)
Respiratory System				
Pleural Effusion	5	(1)		

Post Marketing Surveillance: Presently available Post Marketing Surveillance (PMS) data would indicate that the adverse event profile observed during the marketing phase does not significantly differ in type or severity from the adverse event spectrum reported during the clinical development phase of torsemide.

Overdose: Symptoms and Treatment: There is no human experience with overdoses of torsemide, but the signs and symptoms of overdosage can be anticipated to be those of excessive pharmacological effect: dehydration, hypovolemia, hypotension, hyponatremia, hypokalemia, hypochloremic alkalosis, and hemoconcentration. Treatment of overdosage should consist of fluid and electrolyte replacement.

Laboratory determinations of serum levels of torsemide and its metabolites are not widely available.

No data are available to suggest physiological manoeuvres (e.g., manoeuvres to change the pH of the urine) that might accelerate elimination of torsemide and its metabolites. Torsemide is not dialyzable, so hemodialysis will not accelerate elimination.

Dosage: General: Dosage should be individualized with careful monitoring of patients' response.

Simultaneous food intake has no overall effect on bioavailability of torsemide.

Because of the high bioavailability of torsemide, oral and i.v. doses are therapeutically equivalent, so patients may be switched to and from the i.v. form with no change in dose.

Torsemide i.v. injection should be administered slowly over a period of 2 minutes. Before administration, the solution of torsemide should be visually inspected for discoloration and particulate matter. If either is found, the ampul should not be used.

Geriatrics: Decrease in renal clearance related to a decrease in renal function has been observed. However, total plasma clearance and elimination half-life remain unchanged as compared to young healthy subjects. Therefore, special dose adjustment in the elderly with normal renal function is not necessary (see Pharmacology and Precautions).

Congestive Heart Failure: The usual initial dose is 10 or 20 mg of once-daily oral or i.v. torsemide. If the diuretic response is inadequate, the dose should be titrated upward by approximately doubling until the desired diuretic response is obtained. A single dose of 200 mg should not be exceeded.

Chronic Renal Failure: The usual initial dose of torsemide is 20 mg of once-daily oral or i.v. torsemide. If the diuretic response is inadequate, the dose should be titrated upward by approximately doubling until the desired diuretic response is obtained. A single dose of 200 mg should not be exceeded.

Hepatic Cirrhosis: The usual initial dose is 5 or 10 mg of once-daily oral or i.v. torsemide, administered together with an aldosterone antagonist or a potassium-sparing diuretic. If the diuretic response is inadequate, the dose should be titrated upward by approximately doubling until the desired diuretic response is obtained. A single dose of 40 mg should not be exceeded.

Hypertension: The usual initial dose is 5 mg once daily. If the 5 mg dose does not provide adequate reduction in blood pressure within 4 to 6 weeks, the dose may be increased to 10 mg once daily. If the response to 10 mg is insufficient, an additional antihypertensive agent should be added to the treatment regimen.

Reconstitution: For torsemide ampuls for i.v. injection, no dilution or reconstitution is required prior to use.

Information for the Patient: See Blue Section—Information for the Patient "Demadex".

Supplied: Ampuls: Each mL of sterile, colorless, clear liquid contains: torsemide 10 mg. Nonmedicinal ingredients: polyethylene glycol-400, sodium hydroxide (as needed to adjust pH), tromethamine in water for injection. Colorless glass ampuls of 2 and 5 mL, cartons of 10. Store at room temperature (15 to 30°C). Do not freeze.

Tablets: 5 mg: Each white to off-white, oval-shaped biconvex, scored tablet with "5" debossed on one side, and the logo and "102" debossed on the scored, opposite side, contains: torsemide 5 mg. Nonmedicinal ingredients: crospovidone, lactose, magnesium stearate, microcrystalline cellulose and povidone. Unit dose blister packs of 90. Store at room temperature (15 to 30°C).

10 mg: Each white to off-white, oval-shaped biconvex, scored tablet with "10" debossed on one side, and the logo and "103" debossed on the scored, opposite side, contains: torsemide 10 mg. Nonmedicinal ingredients: crospovidone, lactose, magnesium stearate, microcrystalline cellulose and povidone. Unit dose blister packs of 30. Store at room temperature (15 to 30°C).

20 mg: Each white to off-white, oval-shaped biconvex, scored tablet with "20" debossed on one side, and the logo and "104" debossed on the scored, opposite side, contains: torsemide 20 mg. Nonmedicinal ingredients: crospovidone, lactose, magnesium stearate, microcrystalline cellulose and povidone. Unit dose blister packs of 30. Store at room temperature (15 to 30°C).

100 mg: Each white to off-white, oval-shaped biconvex, scored tablet with "100" debossed on one side, and the logo and "105" debossed on the scored, opposite side, contains: torsemide 100 mg. Nonmedicinal ingredients: crospovidone, lactose, magnesium stearate, microcrystalline cellulose and povidone. Unit dose blister packs of 30. Store at room temperature (15 to 30°C).

(Shown in Product Recognition Section)

DEMECLOCYCLINE Ⓟ

General Monograph, CPhA

see TETRACYCLINES

DEMEROL® Ⓝ

Sanofi

Meperidine HCl

Analgesic

Pharmacology: Meperidine is an opioid analgesic which acts predominantly as a mu-agonist.

In its effects on the CNS, meperidine resembles but is not identical to morphine. Analgesic effects are detectable within about 15 minutes following oral administration, reaching a peak within about 2 hours and subsiding gradually over several hours thereafter. Onset of analgesic effect is faster (within 10 minutes) after s.c. or i.m. administration, reaching a peak within about 1 hour that corresponds closely to the peak concentrations in plasma. In clinical use, the duration of effective analgesia is about 3 to 5 hours. Given parenterally, 75 to 100 mg of meperidine is approximately equivalent to 10 mg of morphine in analgesic effectiveness. At equianalgesic dosage, the 2 agents are comparable in the degree of sedation and of respiratory depression they produce. Given parenterally, meperidine is more than twice as effective as given orally in terms of the total analgesic response obtained. This is consistent with an oral bioavailability of about 40 to 60%.

In its effects on the cardiovascular system, meperidine generally resembles morphine, including its ability to release histamine upon parenteral administration. Heart rate is unlikely to be significantly affected with i.m. administration but may increase, with i.v. administration. As with morphine, respiratory depression leads to an accumulation of carbon dioxide which in turn produces cerebrovascular dilatation, increase in cerebral blood flow and elevation of cerebrospinal fluid pressure.

The effects of meperidine on smooth muscle are qualitatively similar, but in relation to analgesic effect less intense than those of other opioids. Meperidine does not cause as much constipation when given over prolonged periods of time. This may be related to its greater facility to enter the CNS, thereby producing analgesia at lower peripheral concentrations. At equianalgesic dosage, the rise in pressure in the common bile duct induced by meperidine is less than that by morphine, but greater than that by codeine. Clinical doses of meperidine nevertheless slow gastric emptying sufficiently to delay absorption of other drugs significantly. The uterus of nonpregnant women is usually mildly stimulated by meperidine. Therapeutic doses given during active labor do not delay the birth process; in fact, the frequency, duration and amplitude of uterine contractions may sometimes be increased. Meperidine does not interfere with normal postpartum contraction or involution of the uterus and does not increase the incidence of postpartum hemorrhage.

Following i.m. injection, peak plasma concentration is usually obtained at about 45 minutes, but the range in time is wide. After oral administration, only about 50% of meperidine escapes first-pass metabolism. Peak concentrations in the plasma are usually observed in 1 to 2 hours. Approximately 60% is bound to plasma proteins. Meperidine is metabolized chiefly in the liver. The plasma elimination half-life is normally 3 to 4 hours, but this may be extended considerably in the presence of significant hepatic disease. In patients with cirrhosis, bioavailability may be increased as much as 80%. Meperidine is hydrolyzed to meperidinic acid, which in turn is partially conjugated. Meperidine also undergoes N-demethylation to normeperidine, which may then be hydrolyzed to normeperidinic acid and subsequently conjugated. Normeperidine has a considerably longer plasma elimination half-life (15 to 20 hours) than its parent molecule. In the presence of renal insufficiency, normeperidine elimination is reduced.

At the usual values of urinary pH, or if the urine is alkaline, excretion of unchanged meperidine is negligible; urinary excretion of meperidine and normeperidine is enhanced by acidification of the urine. Meperidine crosses the placenta and appears in milk.

Indications: The relief of moderate to severe pain in many medical, surgical, obstetrical and dental situations.

Contraindications: Hypersensitivity to meperidine. Contraindicated in patients who are receiving MAO inhibitors or those who have received such agents within 14 days. Therapeutic doses of meperidine have occasionally precipitated unpredictable, severe, and occasionally fatal reactions in patients who have received such agents within 14 days. The mechanism of these reactions is unclear, but may be related to a preexisting hyperphenylalaninemia. Some have been characterized by coma, severe respiratory depression, cyanosis and hypotension, and have resembled the syndrome of acute narcotic overdose. In other reactions the predominant manifestations have been hyperexcitability, convulsions, tachycardia, hyperpyrexia and hypertension. Although it is not known that other narcotics are free of the risk of such reactions, virtually all of the reported reactions have occurred with meperidine. If a narcotic is needed in such patients, a sensitivity test should be performed in which repeated, small, incremental doses of morphine are administered over the course of several hours while the patient's condition and vital signs are under careful observation. (I.V. hydrocortisone or prednisolone have been used to treat severe reactions, with the addition of i.v. chlorpromazine in those cases exhibiting hypertension and hyperpyrexia. The usefulness and safety of narcotic antagonists in the treatment of these reactions is unknown.)

Solutions of meperidine and barbiturates are chemically incompatible.

Warnings: Drug Dependence: Meperidine can produce drug dependence of the morphine type and therefore has the potential for being abused. Psychic dependence, physical dependence, and tolerance may develop upon repeated administration of meperidine, and it should be prescribed and administered with the same degree of caution appropriate to the use of morphine. Like other narcotics, meperidine is subject to the provisions of the Narcotic Control Act.

Drug Interactions: Interactions with Other CNS Depressants: Meperidine should be used with great caution and in reduced dosage in patients who are concurrently receiving other narcotic analgesics, general anesthetics, phenothiazines, other tranquilizers (see Dosage), sedative-hypnotics (including barbiturates), tricyclic antidepressants, and other CNS depressants (including alcohol). Respiratory depression, hypotension, and profound sedation or coma may result.

Head Injury and Increased Intracranial Pressure: The respiratory depressant effects of meperidine and its capacity to elevate cerebrospinal fluid pressure may be markedly exaggerated in the presence of head injury, other intracranial lesions, or a preexisting increase in intracranial pressure. Furthermore, narcotics produce adverse reactions which may

Demerol (cont'd)

obscure the clinical course of patients with head injuries. In such patients, meperidine must be used with extreme caution and only if its use is deemed essential.

I.V.: If necessary, meperidine may be given i.v., but the injection should be given very slowly, preferably in the form of a diluted solution. Rapid i.v. injection of narcotic analgesics, including meperidine, increases the incidence of adverse reactions; severe respiratory depression, apnea, hypotension, peripheral circulatory collapse, and cardiac arrest have occurred. Meperidine should not be administered i.v. unless a narcotic antagonist and the facilities for assisted or controlled respiration are immediately available. When meperidine is given parenterally, especially i.v., the patient should be lying down.

I.M.: Meperidine should be injected well within the body of a large muscle.

Asthma and Other Respiratory Conditions: Meperidine should be used with extreme caution in patients having an acute asthmatic attack, patients with chronic obstructive pulmonary disease or cor pulmonale, patients having a substantially decreased respiratory reserve, and patients with preexisting respiratory depression, hypoxia, or hypercapnia. In such patients, even usual therapeutic doses of narcotics may decrease respiratory drive while simultaneously increasing airway resistance to the point of apnea.

Hypotensive Effect: The administration of meperidine may result in severe hypotension in the postoperative patient or any individual whose ability to maintain blood pressure has already been compromised by a depleted blood volume or the administration of drugs such as the phenothiazines or certain anesthetics.

Occupational Hazards: Ambulatory patients: Meperidine may impair the mental and/or physical abilities required for the performance of potentially hazardous tasks such as driving a car or operating machinery. The patient should be cautioned accordingly.

Meperidine, like other narcotics, may produce orthostatic hypotension in ambulatory patients.

Pregnancy: Meperidine should not be used in pregnant women prior to the labor period, unless the potential benefits outweigh the possible hazards, because safe use in pregnancy prior to labor has not been established relative to possible adverse effects on fetal development.

When used as an obstetrical analgesic, meperidine crosses the placental barrier and can produce respiratory depression or psychophysiologic functions in the newborn; resuscitation may be required (see section on Overdose).

Lactation: Meperidine appears in the milk of nursing mothers receiving the drug.

Precautions: Supraventricular Tachycardias: Meperidine should be used with caution in patients with atrial flutter and other supraventricular tachycardias because of a possible vagolytic action which may produce a significant increase in the ventricular response rate.

Convulsions: Meperidine may aggravate preexisting convulsions in patients with convulsive disorders. If dosage is escalated substantially above recommended levels because of tolerance development, convulsions may occur in individuals without a history of convulsive disorders.

Acute Abdominal Conditions: The administration of meperidine or other narcotics may obscure the diagnosis or clinical course in patients with acute abdominal conditions.

Special Risk Patients: Meperidine should be given with caution and the initial dose should be reduced in certain patients such as the elderly or debilitated, and those with severe impairment of hepatic or renal function, hypothyroidism, Addison's disease and prostatic hypertrophy or urethral stricture.

Adverse Effects: The major hazards of meperidine as with other narcotic analgesics, are respiratory depression and, to a lesser degree, circulatory depression; respiratory arrest, shock, and cardiac arrest have occurred. The most frequently observed adverse reactions include lightheadedness, dizziness, sedation, nausea, vomiting, and sweating. These effects seem to be more prominent in ambulatory patients and in those who are not experiencing severe pain. In such individuals, lower doses are advisable. Some adverse reactions in ambulatory patients may be alleviated if the patient lies down.

Other adverse reactions include: CNS: euphoria, dysphoria, weakness, headache, agitation, tremor, severe convulsions, uncoordinated muscle movements, transient hallucinations and disorientation, visual disturbances. Inadvertent injection about a nerve trunk may result in sensory-motor paralysis which is usually, though not always, transitory.

Gastrointestinal: dry mouth, constipation, biliary tract spasm.

Cardiovascular: flushing of the face, tachycardia, bradycardia, palpitation, hypotension (see Warnings), syncope and phlebitis following i.v. injection.

Genitourinary: urinary retention.

Allergic: pruritus, urticaria, other skin rashes, wheal and flare over the vein with intravenous injection.

Other: pain at injection site; local tissue irritation and induration following subcutaneous injection, particularly when repeated; antidiuretic effect.

Overdose: Symptoms: Serious overdosage with meperidine is characterized by respiratory depression (a decrease in respiratory rate and/or tidal volume, Cheyne-Stokes respiration, cyanosis), extreme somnolence progressing to stupor or coma, skeletal muscle flaccidity, cold and clammy skin, and sometimes bradycardia and hypotension. In severe overdosage, particularly by the i.v. route, apnea, circulatory collapse, cardiac arrest, and death may occur.

Treatment: Primary attention should be given to the reestablishment of adequate respiratory exchange through provision of a patent airway and institution of assisted or controlled ventilation. The narcotic antagonist, naloxone is a specific antidote against respiratory depression which may result from overdosage or unusual sensitivity to narcotics, including meperidine. Therefore, an appropriate dose of this antagonist should be administered, preferably by the i.v. route, simultaneously with efforts at respiratory resuscitation.

An antagonist should not be administered in the absence of clinically significant respiratory or cardiovascular depression.

Oxygen, i.v. fluids, vasopressors, and other supportive measures should be employed as indicated.

In cases of overdosage with oral meperidine, the stomach should be evacuated by emesis or gastric lavage.

Note: In an individual physically dependent on narcotics, the administration of the usual dose of a narcotic antagonist will precipitate an acute withdrawal syndrome. The severity of this syndrome will depend on the degree of physical dependence and the dose of antagonist administered. The use of narcotic antagonists in such individuals should be avoided if possible. If a narcotic antagonist must be used to treat serious respiratory depression in the physically dependent patient, the antagonist should be administered with extreme care and only 10 to 20% of the usual initial dose administered.

Dosage: Pain Relief: Average adult dose is 50 to 150 mg, i.m., s.c. or orally. Repeat at intervals of 3 to 4 hours as required. Children, 1.1 to 1.8 mg/kg orally, i.m. or s.c. at 3 or 4 hour intervals. Do not exceed adult dose.

Dosage should be adjusted according to severity of pain and patient response. While s.c. administration is suitable for occasional use, i.m. is preferred when repeated doses are required. If i.v. administration is required, dosage should be decreased and the injection made very slowly, preferably utilizing a diluted solution. Meperidine is less effective orally than on parenteral administration. When administered concomitantly with phenothiazines and tranquilizers, meperidine dose should be reduced proportionally (usually 25 to 50%) since they potentiate the action of meperidine.

Preoperative Medication: Adults: 50 to 100 mg i.m. or s.c. 30 to 90 minutes prior to anesthesia.

Children: The usual dosage is 1.1 mg/kg to 2.2 mg/kg i.m. or s.c. up to the adult dose, 30 to 90 minutes before the beginning of anesthesia.

Support of Anesthesia: Repeated slow i.v. injections of fractional doses (e.g., 10 mg/mL) or continuous i.v. infusion of a more dilute solution (e.g., 1 mg/mL) should be used. The dose should be titrated to the needs of the patient and will depend on the premedication and type of anesthesia being employed, the characteristics of the particular patient, and the nature and duration of the operative procedure.

Obstetrical Analgesia: 50 to 100 mg i.m. or s.c. when pain becomes regular, may be repeated at 1 to 3 hour intervals.

Supplied: 5% Solution: Each mL of solution contains: meperidine HCl 50 mg in water for injection. Ampuls of 1 mL, boxes of 25—5×5, plastic trays. Multiple dose vials of 30 mL contain metacresol 0.1% as preservative, boxes of 1.

7.5% Solution: Each mL of solution contains: meperidine HCl 75 mg in water for injection. Ampuls of 1 mL, boxes of 25—5×5, plastic trays.

10% Solution: Each mL of solution contains: meperidine HCl 100 mg in water for injection. Ampuls of 1 mL, boxes of 25—5×5, plastic trays. Multiple dose vials of 20 mL contain metacresol 0.1% as preservative, boxes of 1.

Tablets: Each white tablet with stylized W on one side, scored on the other with D above and 35 below, contains: meperidine HCl 50 mg. Nonmedicinal ingredients: calcium phosphate (dibasic, dihydrate), calcium sulfate, (dihydrate), cornstarch, stearic acid and talc. Energy: 0.2 kJ (0.06 kcal). Gluten-, lactose-, sucrose- and tartrazine-free. Bottles of 100 and 1 000.

(Shown in Product Recognition Section)

DEMULEN® 30 Ⓟ
DEMULEN® 50 Ⓟ

Searle

Ethynodiol Diacetate—Ethinyl Estradiol

Oral Contraceptive

Pharmacology: Estrogen-progestogen combinations act primarily through the mechanism of gonadotropin suppression due to the estrogenic and progestational activity of their components. Although the primary mechanism of action is inhibition of ovulation, alterations in the cervical mucus and the endometrium may also contribute to effectiveness.

Indications: Demulen 30: Prevention of pregnancy. Demulen 50: For conception control in circumstances where low-dose estrogen formulations prove to be unacceptable.

Contraindications: History of/or actual thrombophlebitis or thromboembolic disorders; history of/or actual cerebrovascular disorders; history of/or actual myocardial infarction or coronary arterial disease; active liver disease or history of/or actual benign or malignant liver tumors; history of or known or suspected carcinoma of the breast; history of known or suspected estrogen-dependent neoplasia; undiagnosed abnormal vaginal bleeding; any ocular lesion arising from ophthalmic vascular disease, such as partial or complete loss of vision or defect in visual fields; when pregnancy is suspected or diagnosed.

Warnings: Predisposing Factors for Coronary Artery Disease: Cigarette smoking increases the risk of serious cardiovascular side effects and mortality. Birth control pills increase this risk, especially with increasing age. Convincing data are available to support an upper age limit of 35 years for oral contraceptive use in women who smoke.

Other women who are independently at high risk for cardiovascular disease include those with diabetes, hypertension abnormal lipid profile, or a family history of these. Whether oral contraceptives accentuate this risk is unclear.

In low risk, nonsmoking women of any age, the benefits of oral contraceptive use outweigh the possible cardiovascular risks associated with low-dose formulations. Consequently, oral contraceptives may be prescribed for these women up to the age of menopause.

> Cigarette smoking increases the risk of serious adverse effects on the heart and blood vessels. This risk increases with age and becomes significant in oral contraceptive users over 35 years of age. Women should be counselled not to smoke.

Discontinue medication at the earliest manifestation of the following:

A. Thromboembolic and cardiovascular disorders such as: thrombophlebitis, pulmonary embolism, cerebrovascular disorders, myocardial ischemia, mesenteric thrombosis, and retinal thrombosis.

B. Conditions that predispose to venous stasis and to vascular thrombosis, e.g., immobilization after accidents or confinement to bed during long-term illness. Other nonhormonal methods of contraception should be used until regular activities are resumed. For use of oral contraceptives when surgery is contemplated, see Precautions.

C. Visual defects, partial or complete.

D. Papilledema or ophthalmic vascular lesions.

E. Severe headache of unknown etiology or worsening of preexisting migraine headache.

Precautions: Physical Examination and Followup: Before oral contraceptives are used, a thorough history and physical examination should be performed, including a blood pressure determination. Breasts, liver, extremities and pelvic organs should be examined and a Papanicolaou smear should be taken if the patient has been sexually active.

The first follow-up visit should be done 3 months after oral contraceptives are prescribed. Thereafter, examinations should be performed at least once a year or more frequently if indicated. At each annual visit, examination should include those procedures that were done at the initial visit as outlined above or per recommendations of the Canadian Workshop on Screening for Cancer of the Cervix. Their suggestion was that, for women who had 2 consecutive negative Pap smears, screening could be continued every 3 years up to the age of 69.

Pregnancy: Fetal abnormalities have been reported to occur in the offspring of women who have taken estrogen-progestogen combinations in early pregnancy. Rule out pregnancy as soon as it is suspected.

Lactation: The use of oral contraceptives during the period a mother is breast-feeding her infant may not be advisable. The hormonal components are excreted in breast milk and may reduce its quantity and quality. The long-term effects on the developing child are not known.

Hepatic Function: Patients who have had jaundice including a history of cholestatic jaundice during pregnancy should be given oral contraceptives with great care and under close observation.

The development of severe generalized pruritus or icterus requires that the medication be withdrawn until the problem is resolved.

If a patient develops jaundice that proves to be cholestatic in type, the use of oral contraceptives should not be resumed. In patients taking oral contraceptives, changes in the composition of the bile may occur and an increased incidence of gallstones has been reported.

Hepatic nodules have been reported to be associated with use of oral contraceptives, particularly in long-term users of oral contraceptives. These nodules include benign hepatic adenomas, focal nodular hyperplasia and other hepatic lesions. In addition, hepatocellular carcinoma has been reported. Although these lesions are extremely rare, they have caused fatal intra-abdominal hemorrhage and should be considered in women presenting with an abdominal mass, acute abdominal pain, or evidence of intra-abdominal bleeding.

Hypertension: Patients with essential hypertension whose blood pressure is well-controlled may be given oral contraceptives but only under close supervision. If a significant elevation of blood pressure in previously normotensive or hypertensive subjects occurs at any time during the administration of the drug, cessation of medication is necessary.

Migraine and Headache: The onset or exacerbation of migraine or the development of headache of a new pattern which is recurrent, persistent or severe, requires discontinuation of oral contraceptives and evaluation of the cause.

Diabetes: Current low-dose oral contraceptives exert minimal impact on glucose metabolism. Diabetic patients, or those with a family history of diabetes, should be observed closely to detect any worsening of carbohydrate metabolism. Patients predisposed to diabetes who can be kept under close supervision may be given oral contraceptives. Young diabetic patients whose disease is of recent origin, well-controlled, and not associated with hypertension or other signs of vascular disease such as ocular fundal changes, should be monitored more frequently while using oral contraceptives.

Ocular Disease: Patients who are pregnant or are taking oral contraceptives, may experience corneal edema that may cause visual disturbances and changes in tolerance to contact lenses, especially of the rigid type. Soft contact lenses usually do not cause disturbances. If visual changes or alterations in tolerance to contact lenses occur, temporary or permanent cessation of wear may be advised.

Breasts: Increasing age and a strong family history are the most significant risk factors for the development of breast cancer. Other established risk factors include obesity, nulliparity and late age at first full-term pregnancy. The identified groups of women that may be at increased risk of developing breast cancer before menopause are long-term users of oral contraceptives (more than 8 years) and starters at early age. In a few women, the use of oral contraceptives may accelerate the growth of an existing but undiagnosed breast cancer. Since any potential increased risk related to oral contraceptive use is small, there is no reason to change prescribing habits at present.

Women receiving oral contraceptives should be instructed in self-examination of their breasts. Their physicians should be notified whenever any masses are detected. A yearly clinical breast examination is also recommended because, if a breast cancer should develop, drugs that contain estrogen may cause a rapid progression.

Vaginal Bleeding: Persistent irregular vaginal bleeding requires assessment to exclude underlying pathology.

Fibroids: Patients with fibroids (leiomyomata) should be carefully observed. Sudden enlargement, pain, or tenderness requires discontinuance of the use of oral contraceptives.

Emotional Disorders: Patients with a history of emotional disturbances, especially the depressive type, may be more prone to have a recurrence of depression while taking oral contraceptives. In cases of a serious recurrence, a trial of an alternate method of contraception should be made which may help to clarify the possible relationship. Women with premenstrual syndrome (PMS) may have a varied response to oral contraceptives, ranging from symptomatic improvement to worsening of the condition.

Metabolic and Endocrine Diseases: In metabolic or endocrine diseases and when metabolism of calcium and phosphorus is abnormal, careful clinical evaluation should precede medication and a regular follow-up is recommended.

Connective Tissue Disease: The use of oral contraceptives in some women has been associated with positive lupus erythematosus cell tests and with clinical lupus erythematosus. In some instances exacerbation of rheumatoid arthritis and synovitis have been observed.

Laboratory Tests: Results of laboratory tests should be interpreted in the light that the patient is on oral contraceptives. The laboratory tests listed below are modified.

A. Liver function tests: Aspartate serum transaminase (AST): variously reported elevations. Alkaline phosphatase and gamma glutamine transaminase (GGT): slightly elevated.

B. Coagulation tests: Minimal elevation of test values reported for such parameters as Factors VII, VIII, IX and X. Increased platelet aggregation, decreased antithrombin III.

C. Thyroid function tests: Protein binding of thyroxine is increased as indicated by increased total serum thyroxine concentrations and decreased T_3 resin uptake.

D. Lipoproteins: Small changes of unproven clinical significance may occur in lipoprotein cholesterol fractions.

E. Gonadotropins: LH and FSH levels are suppressed by the use of oral contraceptives. Wait 2 weeks after discontinuing the use of oral contraceptives before measurements are made.

Tissue Specimens: Pathologists should be advised of oral contraceptive therapy when specimens obtained from surgical procedures and PAP smears are submitted for examination.

Return to Fertility: After discontinuing oral contraceptive therapy, the patient should delay pregnancy until at least one normal spontaneous cycle has occurred in order to date the pregnancy. An alternate contraceptive method should be used during this time.

Amenorrhea: Women having a history of oligomenorrhea, secondary amenorrhea, or irregular cycles may remain anovulatory or become amenorrheic following discontinuation of estrogen-progestin combination therapy.

Amenorrhea, especially if associated with breast secretion, that continues for 6 months or more after withdrawal, warrants a careful assessment of hypothalamic-pituitary function.

Thromboembolic Complications—Postsurgery: There is an increased risk of postsurgery thromboembolic complications in oral contraceptive users, after major surgery. If feasible, oral contraceptives should be discontinued and an alternative method substituted at least 1 month prior to **major** elective surgery. Oral contraceptives should not be resumed until the first menstrual period after hospital discharge following surgery.

Drug Interactions: The concurrent administration of oral contraceptives with other drugs may result in an altered response to either agent. Reduced effectiveness of the oral contraceptive, should it occur, is more likely with the low dose formulations. It is important to ascertain all drugs that a patient is taking, both prescription and nonprescription, before oral contraceptives are prescribed.

Refer to the revised 1994 Report on Oral Contraceptives, Health Canada.

Noncontraceptive Benefits of Oral Contraceptives: Several health advantages other than contraception have been reported.

Effects on Menses: Increased menstrual cycle regularity, decreased menstrual blood loss; decreased incidence of iron deficiency anemia secondary to reduced menstrual blood loss; decreased incidence of dysmenorrhea.

Effects Related to Ovulation Inhibition: Decreased incidence of functional ovarian cysts; decreased incidence of ectopic pregnancy.

Effects on Other Organs of the Reproductive Tract: Decreased incidence of acute salpingitis; decreased incidence of endometrial cancer (50%); decreased incidence of ovarian cancer (40%); potential beneficial effects on endometriosis; improvement of acne vulgaris, hirsutism, and other androgen-mediated disorders.

Effects on Breasts: Decreased incidence of benign breast disease (fibroadenomas and fibrocystic breast disease); decreased incidence of breast biopsies.

The noncontraceptive benefits or oral contraceptives should be considered in addition to the efficacy of these preparations when counselling patients regarding contraceptive method selection.

Oral contraceptives **do not protect** against sexually transmitted diseases including HIV/AIDS. For protection against STDs, it is advisable to use latex condoms **in combination with** oral contraceptives.

Adverse Effects: An increased risk of the following serious adverse reactions has been associated with the use of oral contraceptives: thrombophlebitis; pulmonary embolism; mesenteric thrombosis; neuro-ocular lesions, e.g., retinal thrombosis; myocardial infarction; cerebral thrombosis; cerebral hemorrhage; hypertension; benign hepatic tumors; gallbladder disease.

The following adverse reactions also have been reported in patients receiving oral contraceptives: nausea and vomiting, usually the most common adverse reaction, occurs in approximately 10% or less of patients during the first cycle. Other reactions, as a general rule, are seen less frequently or only occasionally.

Other adverse reactions: gastrointestinal symptoms (such as abdominal cramps and bloating); breakthrough bleeding; spotting; change in menstrual flow; dysmenorrhea; amenorrhea during and after treatment; infertility after discontinuance of treatment; edema; chloasma or melasma which may persist; breast changes: tenderness, enlargement, and secretion; change in weight (increase or decrease); endocervical hyperplasias; possible diminution in lactation when given immediately post-partum; cholestatic jaundice; migraine; increase in size of uterine leiomyomata; rash (allergic); mental depression; reduced tolerance to carbohydrates; vaginal candidiasis; premenstrual-like syndrome; intolerance to contact lenses; change in corneal curvature (steepening); cataracts; optic neuritis; retinal thrombosis; changes in libido; chorea; changes in appetite; cystitis-like syndrome; rhinitis; headache; nervousness; dizziness; hirsutism; loss of scalp hair; erythema multiforme; erythema nodosum; hemorrhagic eruption; vaginitis; porphyria; impaired renal function; Raynaud's phenomenon; auditory disturbances; hemolytic uremic syndrome; pancreatitis; arterial thromboembolism.

Overdose: Symptoms and Treatment: Numerous cases of the ingestion, by children, of estrogen-progestogen combinations have been reported. Although mild nausea may occur, there appears to be no other reaction. Treatment should be limited to a laxative such as citrate of magnesia with the aim of removing unabsorbed material as rapidly as possible.

Dosage: Information for the Patient on How to Take the Birth Control Pill:

1. **Read these directions:**
   - before you start taking your pills, and
   - any time you are not sure what to do.
2. **Look at your pill pack** to see if it has 21 or 28 pills:
   - 21-Pill Pack: 21 active pills (with hormones) taken daily for 3 weeks, and then no pills taken for 1 week

   or
   - 28-Pill Pack: 21 active pills (with hormones) taken daily for 3 weeks, and then 7 "reminder" pills (no hormones) taken daily for 1 week.

Also check the pill pack for instructions on (1) where to start and (2) directions to take pills (see package insert for illustrations).

3. It is recommended that you use a second method of birth control (e.g., latex condoms and spermicidal foam or gel) for the first 7 days of the first cycle of pill use. This will provide a backup in case pills are forgotten while you are getting used to taking them.
4. **When receiving any medical treatment, be sure to tell your doctor that you are using birth control pills.**
5. **Many women have spotting or light bleeding or may feel sick to their stomach during the first 3 months on the pill.** If you do feel sick, do not stop taking the pill. The problem will usually go away. If it does not go away, check with your doctor or clinic.
6. **Missing pills also can cause some spotting or light bleeding,** even if you make up the missed pills. You also could feel a little sick to your stomach on the days you take 2 pills to make up for missed pills.
7. **If you miss pills at any time, you could get pregnant. The greatest risks for pregnancy are:**
   - when you start a pack late, or

Demulen (cont'd)

- when you miss pills at the beginning or at the very end of the pack.

8. **Always be sure you have ready:**
   - **another kind of birth control** (such as latex condoms and spermicidal foam or gel) to use as a backup in case you miss pills, and
   - **an extra, full pack of pills.**
9. **If you experience vomiting or diarrhea, or if you take certain medicines,** such as antibiotics, your pills may not work as well. Use a backup method, such as latex condoms and spermicidal foam or gel, until you can check with your doctor or clinic.
10. **If you forget more than 1 pill 2 months in a row,** talk to your doctor or clinic about how to make pill-taking easier or about using another method of birth control.
11. **If your questions are not answered here, call your doctor or clinic.**

When to start the first pack of pills: Be sure to read these instructions:

- before you start taking your pills, and
- any time you are not sure what to do.

Decide with your doctor or clinic what is the best day for you to start taking your first pack of pills. Your pills may be either a 21-day or a 28-day type.

A. 21-Day Combination: With this type of birth control pill, you are on pills for 21 days and off pills for 7 days. You must not be off the pills for more than 7 days in a row.

1. **The first day of your menstrual period (bleeding) is Day 1 of your cycle.** Your doctor may advise you to start taking the pills on Day 1, on Day 5, or on the first Sunday after your period begins. If your period starts on Sunday, start that same day.
2. Take 1 pill at approximately the same time every day for 21 days; **then take no pills for 7 days.** Start a new pack on the 8th day. You will probably have a period during the 7 days off the pill. (This bleeding may be lighter and shorter than your usual period.)

B. 28-Day Combination: With this type of birth control pill, you take 21 pills which contain hormones and 7 pills which contain no hormones.

1. **The first day of your menstrual period (bleeding) is Day 1 of your cycle.** Your doctor may advise you to start taking the pills on Day 1, on Day 5, or on the first Sunday after your period begins. If your period starts on Sunday, start that same day.
2. Take 1 pill at approximately the same time every day for 28 days. Begin a new pack the next day, **not missing any days on the pills.** Your period should occur during the last 7 days of using that pill pack.

What to do during the month:

1. **Take a pill at approximately the same time every day until the pack is empty.**
   - Try to associate taking your pill with some regular activity like eating a meal or going to bed.
   - Do not skip pills even if you have bleeding between monthly periods or feel sick to your stomach (nausea).
   - Do not skip pills even if you do not have sex very often.
2. **When you finish a pack:**
   - **21 pills: Wait 7 days** to start the next pack. You will have your period during that week.
   - **28 pills:** Start the next pack **on the next day.** Take 1 pill every day. Do not wait any days between packs.

What to do if you miss pills: Table I outlines the actions you should take if you miss 1 or more of your birth control pills. Match the number of pills missed with the appropriate starting time for your type of pill pack.

Note: 28-Day Pack: If you forget any of the 7 "reminder" pills (without hormones) in Week 4, just safely dispose of the pills you missed. Then keep taking 1 pill each day until the pack is empty. You do not need to use a backup method.

Always be sure you have on hand:

- a backup method of birth control (such as latex condoms and spermicidal foam or gel) in case you miss pills, and
- an extra, full pack of pills.

If you forget more than 1 pill 2 months in a row, talk to your doctor or clinic about ways to make pill-taking easier or about using another method of birth control.

Dosage: A. 21-Day Pack: With this type of birth control pill, the patient is 21 days on pills with 7 days off pills. The patient must not be off the pills for more than 7 days in a row.

1. **The first day of the patient's menstrual period (bleeding) is day 1 of a cycle.** The doctor may advise the patient to start taking the pills on Day 1, on Day 5, or on the first Sunday after a period begins. If a period starts on Sunday, the patient starts that same day.
2. The pack must be labelled correctly before starting. The pack is pre-printed with a Sunday starting day. If the patient is starting on a day other than a Sunday, she should use the Flexi-start sticker labels provided. The patient peels off the label with the chosen starting day and applies it over the pre-printed days on top of the card.
3. The patient takes 1 pill at approximately the same time every day for 21 days; **then she takes no pills for 7 days.** She starts a new pack on the 8th day. She will probably have a period during the 7 days off the pill. (This bleeding may be lighter and shorter than a usual period.)

Table I—Demulen

What to Do if Pills are Missed

Sunday Start	Other than Sunday Start
Miss 1 pill	**Miss 1 pill**
Take it as soon as you remember, and take the next pill at the usual time. This means that you might take 2 pills in 1 day.	Take it as soon as you remember, and take the next pill at the usual time. This means that you might take 2 pills in 1 day.
Miss 2 pills in a row	**Miss 2 pills in a row**
First 2 weeks: 1. Take 2 pills the day you remember and 2 pills the next day. 2. Then take 1 pill a day until you finish the pack. 3. Use a backup method of birth control if you have sex in the 7 days after you miss the pills. **Third week:** 1. Keep taking 1 pill a day until Sunday. 2. On Sunday, safely discard the rest of the pack and start a new pack that day. 3. Use a backup method of birth control if you have sex in the 7 days after you miss the pills. 4. You may not have a period this month. **If you miss 2 periods in a row, call your doctor or clinic.**	**First 2 weeks:** 1. Take 2 pills the day you remember and 2 pills the next day. 2. Then take 1 pill a day until you finish the pack. 3. Use a backup method of birth control if you have sex in the 7 days after you miss the pills. **Third week:** 1. Safely dispose of the rest of the pill pack and start a new pack that same day. 2. Use a backup method of birth control if you have sex in the 7 days after you miss the pills. 3. You may not have a period this month. **If you miss 2 periods in a row, call your doctor or clinic.**
Miss 3 or more pills in a row	**Miss 3 or more pills in a row**
Anytime in the cycle: 1. Keep taking 1 pill a day until Sunday. 2. On Sunday, safely discard the rest of the pack and start a new pack that day. 3. Use a backup method of birth control if you have sex in the 7 days after you miss the pills. 4. You may not have a period this month. **If you miss 2 periods in a row, call your doctor or clinic.**	**Anytime in the cycle:** 1. Safely dispose of the rest of the pill pack and start a new pack that same day. 2. Use a backup method of birth control if you have sex in the 7 days after you miss the pills. 3. You may not have a period this month. **If you miss 2 periods in a row, call your doctor or clinic.**

B. 28-Day Pack: With this type of birth control pill, the patient takes 21 pills which contain hormones and 7 pills which contain no hormones.

1. **The first day of the patient's menstrual period (bleeding) is day 1 of a cycle.** The doctor may advise the patient to start taking the pills on Day 1, on Day 5, or on the first Sunday after a period begins. If a period starts on Sunday, the patient starts that same day.
2. The pack must be labelled correctly before starting. The pack is pre-printed with a Sunday starting day. If the patient is starting on a day other than a Sunday, she should use the Flexi-start sticker labels provided. The patient peels off the label with the chosen starting day and applies it over the pre-printed days on top of the card.
3. The patient takes 1 pill at approximately the same time every day for 28 days. She begins a new pack the next day, **not missing any days on the pills.** The patient's period should occur during the last 7 days of using that pill pack.

What to do during the month:

1. **The patient takes a pill at approximately the same time every day until the pack is empty.**
   - The patient should try to associate taking the pill with some regular activity like eating a meal or going to bed.
   - The patient must not skip pills even if she has bleeding between monthly periods or feels sick to her stomach (nausea).
   - The patient must not skip pills even if she does not have sex very often.
2. **When a pack is finished:**
   - **21 Pills: The patient must wait 7 days** to start the next pack. A period will begin during that week.
   - **28 Pills:** The patient starts the next pack **on the next day.** She takes 1 pill every day. She does not wait any days between packs.

Information for the Patient: See Blue Section—Information for the Patient "Oral Contraceptives".

Supplied: Demulen 30: Each white, circular, biconvex, film-coated tablet, 6 mm in diameter, impressed SEARLE/930 on one side, contains: ethynodiol diacetate 2 mg and ethinyl estradiol 0.03 mg. Energy: 1.4 kJ (0.34 kcal). Sodium: <1 mmol (0.2 mg). Inert peach-colored tablets are impressed "SEARLE" on one side and "P" on the other. Nonmedicinal ingredients: Active tablets: cornstarch, ethylcellulose, hydroxypropylcellulose, lactose, magnesium stearate, opaspray, polyvidone, sodium acide phosphate and sodium phosphate dibasic anhydrous. Placebo tablets: FD&C Yellow No. 6 Lake, lactose, lactose monohydrate, magnesium stearate and microcrystalline cellulose. Dispensers of 21 (21 active tablets) and 28 (21 active and 7 inert tablets) days.

Demulen 50: Each white, round, biconvex tablet, 6.4 mm in diameter, impressed "SEARLE" on one side and "71" on the other, contains: ethynodiol diacetate 1 mg and ethinyl estradiol 0.05 mg. Energy: 0.4 kJ (0.10 kcal). Inert peach-colored tablets are impressed "SEARLE" on one side and "P" on the other. Nonmedicinal ingredients: Active tablets: cornstarch, calcium acetate hydrous, calcium phosphate dibasic anhydrous, hydrogenated castor oil and povidone. Placebo tablets: calcium sulfate dihydrate, cornstarch, FD&C Red No. 3, FD&C Yellow No. 6, magnesium stearate and sugar confectioner's. Dispensers of 21 (21 active tablets) and 28 (21 active and 7 inert tablets) days.

Store below 25°C.

(Shown in Product Recognition Section)

Reviewed 1998

DENOREX®
DENOREX® EXTRA STRENGTH

Whitehall-Robins

Coal Tar—Menthol—Chloroxylenol

Antiseborrheic—Antipruritic

Indications: Denorex: Relieves persistent dandruff flaking and itching.

Denorex Extra Strength: Relieves persistent dandruff flaking, itching, psoriasis and seborrheic dermatitis.

Precautions: Rinse thoroughly to avoid possible discoloration of light-colored hair. Do not use on wounds or abraded skin. Discontinue treatment if irritation develops. Avoid contact with eyes. For external use only.

Dosage: Wet hair thoroughly and briskly massage Denorex in until lathered. Rinse thoroughly and repeat. Scalp may tingle slightly during treatment. Use every other day or daily for difficult scalp conditions.

Supplied: Denorex Regular: Each mL contains: coal tar solution 7.5%, menthol 1.5% and chloroxylenol 0.5%. Nonmedicinal ingredients: alcohol, lauramide DEA, stearic acid, triethanolamine lauryl sulfate and water. Plastic bottles of 200 mL.

Denorex Spring Fresh: Each mL contains: coal tar solution 7.5%, menthol 1.5% and chloroxylenol 0.5%. Nonmedicinal ingredients: alcohol, cellulose, fragrance, lauramide DEA, stearic acid, triethanolamine lauryl sulfate and water. Plastic bottles of 200 mL.

Denorex with Conditioners: Each mL contains: coal tar solution 7.5%, menthol 1.5% and chloroxylenol 0.5%. Nonmedicinal ingredients: alcohol, cellulose, citric acid, fragrance, lanolin, lauramide DEA, polyquaternium, triethanolamine lauryl sulfate and water. Plastic bottles of 100 and 200 mL.

Denorex Extra Strength: Each mL contains: coal tar solution 10.4%, menthol 1.5% and chloroxylenol 0.5%. Nonmedicinal ingredients: alcohol, cellulose, ethylene glycol distearate, FD&C Red No. 40, fragrance, lauramide DEA, triethanolamine lauryl sulfate and water. Plastic bottles of 200 mL.

Denorex Extra Strength with Conditioners: Each mL contains: coal tar solution 10.4%, menthol 1.5% and chloroxylenol 0.5%. Nonmedicinal ingredients: alcohol, cellulose, citric acid, cocoyl quaternized protein, ethylene glycol distearate, FD&C Red No. 40, fragrance, lauramide DEA, lanogel 21, polyquaternium, triethanolamine lauryl sulfate and water. Plastic bottles of 100 and 200 mL.

DEPAKENE® Ⓟ

Abbott

Valproic Acid

Anticonvulsant

Pharmacology: Although valproic acid's mechanism of action has not yet been established, the drug's anticonvulsant activity may be related to increased brain concentrations of gamma-aminobutyric acid (GABA). The effect on the neuronal membrane is unknown.

Valproic acid is rapidly absorbed after oral administration. Peak serum levels occur approximately 1 to 4 hours after a single oral dose. The serum half-life of valproic acid is typically in the range of 6 to 16 hours. Half-lives in the lower part of the above range are usually found in patients taking other antiepileptic drugs. A slight delay in absorption occurs when the drug is administered with meals but this does not affect the total absorption. Valproic acid is rapidly distributed throughout the body and the drug is strongly bound (90%) to human plasma proteins. Increases in dose may result in decreases in the extent of protein binding and variable changes in valproic acid clearance and elimination. The therapeutic plasma concentration range is believed to be from 50 to 100 μg/mL. Occasional patients may be controlled with serum levels lower or higher than this range. A good correlation has not been established between daily dose, serum levels and therapeutic effect.

Valproic acid is primarily metabolized in the liver to the glucuronide conjugate. Very little unmetabolized parent drug is excreted in the urine. Elimination of valproic acid and its metabolites occurs principally in the urine, with minor amounts in the feces and expired air.

See Warnings regarding statement on fatal hepatic dysfunction.

Indications: As sole or adjunctive therapy in the treatment of simple or complex absence seizures, including petit mal, and is useful in primary generalized seizures with tonic-clonic manifestations. Valproic acid may also be used adjunctively in patients with multiple seizure types which include either absence or tonic-clonic seizures.

Simple absence is defined as a very brief clouding of the sensorium or loss of consciousness (lasting usually 2 to 15 seconds) accompanied by certain generalized epileptic discharges without other detectable clinical signs. Complex absence is the term used when other signs are also present.

Contraindications: Patients with hepatic disease or significant dysfunction. Hypersensitivity to valproic acid.

Warnings: Hepatic failure resulting in fatalities has occurred in patients receiving valproic acid. These incidences usually have occurred during the first 6 months of treatment with valproic acid.

A recent survey study of valproate use in the United States in nearly 400 000 patients between 1978 and 1984, has shown that children under 2 years of age who received the drug as part of multiple anticonvulsant therapy were at greatest risk (nearly 20 fold increase) of developing fatal hepatotoxicity. These patients typically had other medical conditions such as congenital metabolic disorders, mental retardation or organic brain disease, in addition to severe seizure disorders. The risk in this age group decreased considerably in patients receiving valproate as monotherapy. Similarly, patients aged 3 to 10 years were at somewhat greater risk if they received multiple anticonvulsants than those who received only valproate. Risk generally declined with increasing age. No deaths have been reported in patients over 10 years of age who received valproate alone.

If valproic acid is to be used in children 2 years old or younger, it should be used with **extreme caution** and as a sole agent. The benefits of seizure control should be weighed against the risk.

Serious or fatal hepatotoxicity may be preceded by nonspecific symptoms such as loss of seizure control, malaise, weakness, lethargy, anorexia and vomiting. Patients and parents should be instructed to report such symptoms. Because of the non-specific nature of some of the early signs, hepatotoxicity should be suspected in patients who become unwell, other than through obvious cause, while taking valproic acid.

Liver function tests should be performed prior to therapy and at frequent intervals thereafter especially during the first 6 months. However, physicians should not rely totally on serum biochemistry since these tests may not be abnormal in all instances, but should also consider the results of careful interim medical history and physical examination. Caution should be observed when administering valproic acid to patients with a prior history of hepatic disease. Patients with various unusual congenital disorders, those with severe seizure disorders accompanied by mental retardation, and those with organic brain disease may be at particular risk.

In high-risk patients, it might also be useful to monitor serum fibrinogen and albumin for decrease in concentrations and serum ammonia for increases in concentration. If changes occur, valproic acid should be discontinued. Dosage should be titrated to and maintained at the lowest dose consistent with optimal seizure control.

The drug should be discontinued immediately in the presence of significant hepatic dysfunction, suspected or apparent. In some cases, hepatic dysfunction has progressed in spite of discontinuation of the drug. The frequency of adverse effects, particularly elevated liver enzymes, may increase with increasing doses. Therefore, the benefit gained by improved seizure control by increasing the dosage must be weighed against the increasing incidence of adverse effects sometimes seen at higher dosages.

Pregnancy: According to recent reports in the medical literature, valproic acid may produce teratogenicity in the offspring of human females receiving the drug during pregnancy. The incidence of neural tube defects in the fetus may be increased in the mothers receiving valproic acid during the first trimester of pregnancy. Based upon a single report, it was estimated that the risk of valproic acid exposed women having children with spina bifida is approximately 1.2%. This risk is similar to that which applies to non-epileptic women who have had children with neural tube defects (anencephaly and spina bifida). Animal studies have demonstrated teratogenicity, and studies in human females have demonstrated placental transfer of the drug.

Multiple reports indicate an association between the use of antiepileptic drugs and an elevated incidence of birth defects in children born to epileptic women taking such medication during pregnancy. The incidence of congenital malformations in the general population is regarded to be approximately 2%, in children of treated epileptic women, this incidence may be increased 2 to 3-fold. The increase is largely due to specific defects, e.g., congenital malformations of the heart, cleft lip and/or palate and neural tube defects. Nevertheless, the great majority of mothers receiving anticonvulsant medications deliver normal infants.

Data are more extensive with respect to phenytoin and phenobarbital, the most commonly prescribed anticonvulsants. Some reports indicate a possible similar association with the use of other antiepileptic drugs, including trimethadione, paramethadione and valproic acid. However, the possibility also exists that other factors, e.g., genetic predisposition or the epileptic condition itself, may contribute to, or may be mainly responsible for the higher incidence of birth defects.

Antiepileptic drugs should not be discontinued in patients to whom the drug is administered to prevent major seizures, because of the strong possibility of precipitating status epilepticus with attendant hypoxia and risks to both the mother and the unborn child. The risks of discontinuing drugs given for minor seizures prior to or during pregnancy should be weighed against the risk of congenital defects in the particular case and with the particular family history.

Epileptic women of childbearing age should be encouraged to seek the counsel of their physician and should report promptly to him the onset of pregnancy. Where the necessity for continued use of antiepileptic medication is in doubt, appropriate consultation might be indicated.

Lactation: Valproic acid is secreted in breast milk. Concentrations in breast milk have been reported to be 1 to 10% of serum concentrations. As a general rule, nursing should not be undertaken while a patient is receiving valproic acid.

Fertility: Chronic toxicity studies in juvenile and adult rats and dogs demonstrated reduced spermatogenesis and testicular atrophy at doses greater than 200 mg/kg/day in rats and 90 mg/kg/day in dogs. Segment I fertility studies in rats have shown that doses up to 350 mg/kg/day for 60 days have no effect on fertility. The effect of valproic acid on the development of the testes and on sperm production and fertility in humans is unknown.

Long-term toxicity studies in rats and mice indicate a potential carcinogenic risk.

Precautions: Hepatic dysfunction: See Contraindications and Warnings.

General: Because of reports of thrombocytopenia and inhibition of platelet aggregation, platelet counts and bleeding time determination are recommended before instituting therapy and at periodic intervals. It is recommended that patients be monitored for platelet count prior to planned surgery. Clinical evidence of hemorrhage, bruising or a disorder of hemostasis/coagulation is an indication for reduction of dosage or withdrawal of therapy pending investigation.

Hyperammonemia with or without lethargy or coma has been reported and may be present in the absence of abnormal liver function tests; if elevation occurs the valproic acid should be discontinued.

Because valproic acid may interact with other antiepileptic drugs, periodic serum level determinations of concurrently administered antiepileptics are recommended during the early part of therapy (see Drug Interactions). There have been reports of breakthrough seizures occurring with the combination of valproic acid and phenytoin.

Valproic acid is partially eliminated in the urine as a ketone-containing metabolite which may lead to a false interpretation of the urine ketone test.

There have been reports of altered thyroid function tests associated with valproic acid: the clinical significance of these is unknown.

Valproic acid may produce CNS depression, especially when combined with another CNS depressant such as alcohol.

Occupational Hazards: Patients should be advised not to engage in potentially hazardous occupations such as driving a car or operating dangerous machinery until it is known that they do not become drowsy from the drug.

Drug Interactions: Valproic acid may potentiate the CNS depressant action of alcohol.

There is evidence that valproic acid may cause an increase in serum phenobarbital levels by impairment of non-renal clearance. This phenomenon can result in severe CNS depression. The combination of valproic acid and phenobarbital has also been reported to produce CNS depression without significant elevations of barbiturate or valproic acid serum levels. Patients receiving concomitant barbiturate therapy should be closely monitored for neurological toxicity. Serum barbiturate drug levels should be obtained, if possible, and the barbiturate dosage decreased, if indicated.

Primidone is metabolized into a barbiturate, and therefore, may also be involved in a similar or identical interaction.

There is conflicting evidence regarding the interaction of valproic acid with phenytoin (see Precautions). It is not known if there is a change in unbound (free) phenytoin serum levels. The dose of phenytoin should be adjusted as required by the clinical situation.

The concomitant use of valproic acid and clonazepam may produce absence status.

Caution is recommended when valproic acid is administered with drugs affecting coagulation, e.g., ASA and warfarin (see Adverse Effects).

Adverse Effects: The most commonly reported adverse reactions are nausea, vomiting and indigestion. Since valproic acid has usually been used with other antiepileptics, in most cases it is not possible to determine whether the adverse reactions mentioned are due to valproic acid alone or to the combination of drugs.

Gastrointestinal: Nausea, vomiting and indigestion are the most commonly reported side effects at the initiation of therapy. These effects are usually transient and rarely require discontinuation of therapy. Diarrhea, abdominal cramps and

Depakene (cont'd)

constipation have also been reported. Anorexia with some weight loss and increased appetite with some weight gain have also been observed.

CNS Effects: Sedative effects have been noted in patients receiving valproic acid alone, but are found most often in patients on combination therapy. Sedation usually disappears upon reduction of other antiepileptic medication. Ataxia, headache, nystagmus, diplopia, asterixis, "spots before the eyes", tremor, dysarthria, dizziness and incoordination have been noted rarely. Rare cases of coma have been reported in patients receiving valproic acid alone or in conjunction with phenobarbital.

Dermatologic: Transient increases in hair loss have been observed. Skin rash and petechiae have rarely been noted.

Endocrine: There have been reports of irregular menses and secondary amenorrhea in patients receiving valproic acid.

Abnormal thyroid function tests have been reported (see Precautions).

Psychiatric: Emotional upset, depression, psychosis, aggression, hyperactivity and behavioural deterioration have been reported.

Musculoskeletal: Weakness has been reported.

Hematopoietic: Thrombocytopenia has been reported. Valproic acid inhibits the second phase of platelet aggregation (see Precautions). This may be reflected in altered bleeding time. Bruising, hematoma formation and frank hemorrhage have been reported. Relative lymphocytosis and hypofibrinogenemia have been noted. Leukopenia and eosinophilia have also been reported. Anemia and bone marrow suppression have been reported.

Hepatic: Minor elevations of transaminases [(e.g. AST and ALT] and LDH are frequent and appear to be dose related. Occasionally, laboratory tests also show increases in serum bilirubin and abnormal changes in other liver function tests. These results may reflect potentially serious hepatotoxicity (see Warnings).

Metabolic: Hyperammonemia (see Precautions). Hyperglycinemia has been reported and associated with a fatal outcome in a patient with pre-existing nonketotic hyperglycinemia.

Pancreatic: There have been reports of acute pancreatitis occurring in association with valproic acid therapy.

Other: Edema of the extremities has been reported.

Overdose: Symptoms: In a reported case of ingestion of 36 g of valproic acid in combination with phenobarbital and phenytoin, the patient presented in deep coma. An EEG recorded diffuse slowing, compatible with the state of consciousness. The patient made an uneventful recovery.

Treatment: Naloxone has been reported to reverse the CNS depressant effects of valproic acid overdose. Because naloxone could theoretically also reverse the antiepileptic effects of valproic acid it should be used with caution.

As valproic acid is absorbed very rapidly, gastric lavage may be of limited value. Apply general supportive measures with particular attention to the prevention of hypovolemia and the maintenance of adequate urinary output.

Dosage: Administered orally. The recommended initial dose is 15 mg/kg/day orally, increasing at 1-week intervals by 5 to 10 mg/kg/day until seizures are controlled or side effects preclude further increases. Maximum recommended dose is 60 mg/kg/day. When the total daily dose exceeds 250 mg, it should be given in a divided regimen (see Table I). A 500 mg enteric-coated capsule may be substituted for two 250 mg capsules. The frequency of adverse effects (particularly elevated liver enzymes) may increase with increasing dose. Therefore, the benefit gained by improved seizure control must be weighed against the increased incidence of adverse effects.

Table I—Depakene

Initial Doses by Weight (based on 15 mg/kg/day)

Weight (kg)	Total daily dose (mg)	Number of 250 mg capsules or teaspoonsful of syrup: Dose 1	Dose 2	Dose 3
10-24.9	250	0	0	1
25-39.9	500	1	0	1
40-59.9	750	1	1	1
60-74.9	1 000	1	1	2
75-89.9	1 250	2	1	2

As the valproic acid dosage is raised, blood levels of phenobarbital and/or phenytoin may be affected (see Precautions).

Patients who experience gastrointestinal irritation may benefit from administration of valproic acid with food or by a progressive dosage increase from an initial low level. The capsules should be swallowed without chewing to avoid local irritation of the mouth and throat.

Supplied: Capsules: 250 mg: Each orange-colored, soft gelatin capsule contains: valproic acid 250 mg. Nonmedicinal ingredients: corn oil, ethyl vanillin, FD&C yellow no. 6, gelatin, glycerin, methylparaben, propylparaben and titanium dioxide. Alcohol-, gluten-, lactose-, sucrose-, sulfite- and tartrazine-free. Bottles of 100 and 500.

500 mg: Each pale yellow, oval, soft gelatin enteric coated capsule contains: valproic acid 500 mg. Nonmedicinal ingredients: cellulose acetate phtalate, dextrose, diethyl phtalate, ethyl acetate, gelatin, glycerin, methylparaben, propylparaben, tartrazine and titanium dioxide. Alcohol-, gluten-, lactose-, sucrose- and sulfite-free. Bottles of 100 and 500.

Syrup: Each 5 mL of red syrup contains: the equivalent of 250 mg valproic acid, as the sodium salt. Nonmedicinal ingredients: artificial flavor, glycerin, hydrochloric acid, methylparaben, propylparaben, Red Amaranth Canadian Certified Food Color, sodium hydroxide, sorbitol, sucrose and vanillin. Energy: 74.08 kJ (17.70 kcal)/5 mL. Alcohol-, gluten-, lactose-, sulfite- and tartrazine-free. Bottles of 450 mL.

(Shown in Product Recognition Section)

DEPEN® ℞

Carter Horner

Penicillamine

Chelating Agent

Pharmacology: As a chelating agent, penicillamine removes copper from the body. In vitro studies indicate that one atom of copper combines with 2 molecules of penicillamine. It would appear that 1 g of penicillamine should be followed by the excretion of about 200 mg of copper; however, the actual amount excreted is about 1% of this.

Penicillamine also reduces excess cystine excretion in cystinuria. This is done, at least in part, by disulfide interchange between penicillamine and cystine, resulting in formation of penicillamine-cysteine disulfide, a substance that is much more soluble than cystine and is excreted readily. Penicillamine interferes with the formation of cross-links between tropocollagen molecules and cleaves them when newly formed.

The mechanism of action of penicillamine in rheumatoid arthritis is unknown although it appears to suppress disease activity. Unlike cytotoxic immunosuppressants, penicillamine markedly lowers IgM rheumatoid factor but produces no significant depression in absolute levels of serum immunoglobulins. Also, unlike cytotoxic immunosuppressants which act on both, penicillamine in vitro depresses T cell activity but not B cell activity.

In vitro, penicillamine dissociates macroglobulins (rheumatoid factor) although the relationship of the activity to its effect in rheumatoid arthritis is not known.

Indications: The treatment of Wilson's disease, cystinuria, and in patients with severe, active rheumatoid arthritis who have failed to respond to an adequate trial of conventional therapy. Available evidence suggests that penicillamine is not of value in ankylosing spondylitis. **Because of the severe toxicity of this agent, penicillamine should never be used casually.**

Contraindications: *Pregnancy:* Patients with rheumatoid arthritis who are or who may become pregnant (see Precautions).

Patients with a history of penicillamine related aplastic anemia or agranulocytosis should not be restarted on penicillamine (see Precautions and Adverse Effects).

Because of its potential for causing renal damage, penicillamine should not be administered to rheumatoid arthritis patients with a history or other evidence of renal insufficiency.

Penicillamine should not be used in patients who are receiving gold therapy, antimalarial or cytotoxic drugs, oxyphenbutazone or phenylbutazone because these drugs are also associated with similar serious hematologic and renal adverse reactions.

Warnings: The use of penicillamine has been associated with fatalities due to certain diseases such as aplastic anemia, agranulocytosis, thrombocytopenia, Goodpasture's syndrome, and myasthenic syndrome.

Because of the potential for serious hematological and renal adverse reactions, routine urinalysis, white and differential blood cell count, hemoglobin determination, and direct platelet count must be done every 2 weeks for the first 6 months of penicillamine therapy and monthly thereafter. Patients should be instructed to report promptly the development of signs and symptoms of granulocytopenia and/or thrombocytopenia such as fever, sore throat, chills, bruising or bleeding. The above laboratory studies then should be promptly repeated.

Leukopenia and thrombocytopenia have been reported to occur in up to 5% of patients during penicillamine therapy. Leukopenia is of the granulocytic series and may or may not be associated with an increase in eosinophils.

A confirmed reduction in WBC below 3 500 mandates discontinuance of penicillamine therapy. Thrombocytopenia may be on an idiosyncratic basis, with decreased or absent megakaryocytes in the marrow, when it is part of an aplastic anemia. In other cases the thrombocytopenia is presumably on an immune basis since the number of megakaryocytes in the marrow has been reported to be normal or sometimes increased. The development of a platelet count below 100 000, even in the absence of clinical bleeding, requires at least temporary cessation of penicillamine therapy. A progressive fall in either platelet count or WBC in three successive determinations, even though values are still within the normal range, likewise requires at least temporary cessation.

Proteinuria and/or hematuria may develop during therapy and these may be warning signs of membranous glomerulopathy which can progress to a nephrotic syndrome. Close observation of these patients is essential. In some patients the proteinuria disappears with continued therapy; in others, penicillamine must be discontinued. When a patient develops proteinuria or hematuria the physician must ascertain whether it is a sign of drug induced glomerulopathy or is unrelated to penicillamine. Rheumatoid arthritis patients who develop moderate degrees of proteinuria may be continued cautiously on penicillamine therapy, provided that quantitative 24 hour urinary protein determinations are obtained at intervals of 1 to 2 weeks. Penicillamine dosage should not be increased under these circumstances. Proteinuria that exceeds 1 g/24 hours, or proteinuria that is progressively increasing, requires either discontinuance of the drug or a reduction in the dosage. In some patients, proteinuria has been reported to clear following reduction in dosage.

In rheumatoid arthritis patients penicillamine should be discontinued if unexplained gross hematuria or persistent microscopic hematuria develops.

In patients with Wilson's disease or cystinuria the risks of continued penicillamine therapy in patients manifesting potentially serious urinary abnormalities must be weighed against the expected therapeutic benefits.

When penicillamine is used in cystinuria, an annual x-ray for renal stones is advised. Cystine stones form rapidly, sometimes in 6 months.

Up to 1 year or more may be required for any urinary abnormalities to disappear after penicillamine has been discontinued.

Because of rare reports of intrahepatic cholestasis and toxic hepatitis, liver function tests are recommended every 6 months during the first 18 months of therapy.

Goodpasture's syndrome has occurred rarely. The development of abnormal urinary findings associated with hemoptysis and pulmonary infiltrates on x-ray requires immediate cessation of penicillamine.

A myasthenic syndrome has been reported. In the majority of cases, symptoms of myasthenia have receded after withdrawal of penicillamine.

Pemphigoid type reactions characterized by bullous lesions clinically indistinguishable from pemphigus have occurred and have required discontinuation of penicillamine and treatment with corticosteroids.

Once instituted for Wilson's disease or cystinuria, treatment with penicillamine should, as a rule, be continued on a daily basis. Interruptions for even a few days have been followed by sensitivity reactions after reinstitution of therapy.

Precautions: Some patients may experience drug fever, a marked febrile response to penicillamine, usually in the second to third week following initiation of therapy. Drug fever may sometimes be accompanied by a macular cutaneous eruption. In the case of drug fever in patients with Wilson's disease or cystinuria, because no alternative treatment is available, penicillamine should be temporarily discontinued until the reaction subsides. Then penicillamine should be reinstituted with a small dose that is gradually increased until the desired dosage is attained. Systemic steroid therapy may be necessary, and is usually helpful, in such patients in whom toxic reactions develop a second or third time.

In the case of drug fever in rheumatoid arthritis patients, because other treatments are available, penicillamine should be discontinued and another therapeutic alternative tried since experience indicates that the febrile reaction will recur in a very high percentage of patients upon readministration of penicillamine.

The skin and mucous membranes should be observed for allergic reactions. Early and late rashes have occurred. Early rash occurs during the first few months of treatment and is more common. It is usually a generalized pruritic, erythematous, maculopapular or morbilliform rash and resembles the allergic rash seen with other drugs. Early rash usually disappears within days after stopping penicillamine and seldom recurs when the drug is restarted at a lower dosage. Pruritus and early rash often may be controlled by the concomitant administration of antihistamines. Less commonly, a late rash may be seen, usually after 6 months or more of treatment, and requires discontinuation of penicillamine. It is usually on the trunk, is accompanied by intense pruritus, and is usually unresponsive to topical corticosteroid therapy. Late rash may take weeks to disappear after penicillamine is stopped and usually recurs if the drug is restarted.

The appearance of a drug eruption accompanied by fever, arthralgia, lymphadenopathy or other allergic manifestations usually requires discontinuation of penicillamine.

Certain patients will develop a positive antinuclear antibody (ANA) test and some of these may show a lupus erythematosus like syndrome similar to drug induced lupus associated with other drugs. The lupus erythematosus like syndrome is not associated with the hypocomplementemia and may be present without nephropathy. The development of a positive ANA test does not mandate discontinuance of the drug; however, the physician should be alerted to the possibility that a lupus erythematosus like syndrome may develop in the future.

Some patients may develop oral ulcerations which in some cases have the appearance of aphthous stomatitis. The stomatitis usually recurs on rechallenge but often clears on a lower dosage. Although rare, cheilosis, glossitis and gingivo-stomatitis have also been reported. These oral lesions are frequently dose related and may preclude further increase in penicillamine dosage or require discontinuation of the drug.

Hypogeusia (a blunting or diminution in taste perception) has occurred in some patients. This may last 2 to 3 months or more and may develop into a total loss of taste; however, it is usually self limited despite continued penicillamine treatment. Such taste impairment is rare in patients with Wilson's disease.

Patients who are allergic to penicillin theoretically may have cross-sensitivity to penicillamine. The possibility of reactions from contamination of penicillamine by trace amounts of penicillin, has been eliminated now that penicillamine is being produced synthetically rather than as a degradation product of penicillin.

Because of their dietary restrictions, patients with Wilson's disease or cystinuria should be given 25 mg/day of pyridoxine during therapy, since penicillamine increases the requirement for this vitamin. Patients also may receive benefit from a multivitamin preparation, although there is no evidence that deficiency of any vitamin other than pyridoxine is associated with penicillamine. In Wilson's disease, multivitamin preparations must be copper free. Rheumatoid arthritis patients whose nutrition is impaired also should be given a daily supplement of pyridoxine. Mineral supplements should not be given, since they may block the response to penicillamine.

Iron deficiency may develop, especially in children and in menstruating women.

In Wilson's disease, this may be a result of adding the effects of the low copper diet, which is probably also low in iron, and the penicillamine to the effects of blood loss or growth. In cystinuria, a low methionine diet may contribute to iron deficiency, since it is necessarily low in protein. If necessary, iron may be given in short courses, but a period of 2 hours should elapse between administration of penicillamine and iron, since orally administered iron has been shown to reduce the effects of penicillamine.

Penicillamine causes an increase in the amount of soluble collagen. In the rat this results in inhibition of normal healing and also a decrease in tensile strength of intact skin. In man this may be the cause of increased skin friability at sites especially subject to pressure or trauma, such as shoulders, elbows, knees, toes, and buttocks. Extravasations of blood may occur and may appear as purpuric areas, with external bleeding if the skin is broken, or as vesicles containing dark blood. Neither type is progressive. There is no apparent association with bleeding elsewhere in the body and no associated coagulation defect has been found. Therapy with penicillamine may be continued in the presence of these lesions. They may not recur if dosage is reduced.

Other reported effects probably due to the action of penicillamine on collagen are excessive wrinkling of the skin and development of small, white papules at venipuncture and surgical sites.

The effects of penicillamine on collagen and elastin make it advisable to consider a reduction in dosage to 250 mg/day when surgery is contemplated. Reinstitution of full therapy should be delayed until wound healing is complete.

Long-term animal carcinogenicity studies have not been done with penicillamine. There is a report that five of ten autoimmune disease-prone NZB hybrid mice developed lymphocytic leukemia after 6 months' intraperitoneal treatment with a dose of 400 mg/kg penicillamine 5 days per week.

Penicillamine has been shown to be teratogenic in rats when given in doses several times higher than the highest dose recommended for human use. Skeletal defects, cleft palates and fetal toxicity (resorptions) have been reported.

Pregnancy: There are no controlled studies in pregnant women with Wilson's disease, but experience does not include any positive evidence of adverse effects on the fetus. Reported experience shows that continued treatment with penicillamine throughout pregnancy protects the mother against relapse of Wilson's disease, and that discontinuation of penicillamine has deleterious effects on the mother. It suggests that the drug may not increase the risks of fetal abnormalities, but it does not exclude the possibility of infrequent or subtle damage to the fetus. If penicillamine is administered during pregnancy to patients with Wilson's disease, it is recommended that the daily dosage be limited to 1 g. If cesarean section is planned, the daily dosage should be limited to 250 mg during the last 6 weeks of pregnancy and postoperatively until wound healing is complete.

If possible, penicillamine should not be given during pregnancy to women with cystinuria. There is a report of a woman with cystinuria treated with 2 g/day of penicillamine during pregnancy who gave birth to a child with a generalized connective tissue defect that may have been caused by penicillamine. If stones continue to form in these patients, the benefits of therapy to the mother must be evaluated against the risk to the fetus.

Penicillamine should not be administered to rheumatoid arthritis patients who are pregnant (see Contraindications) and should be discontinued promptly in patients in whom pregnancy is suspected or diagnosed. Penicillamine should be used in women of childbearing potential only when the expected benefits outweigh possible hazards. Women of child bearing potential should be informed of the possible hazards of penicillamine to the developing fetus and should be advised to discontinue penicillamine if they plan to become pregnant and to report promptly any missed menstrual periods or other indications of possible pregnancy while taking the drug.

There is a report that a woman with rheumatoid arthritis treated with less than 1 g a day of penicillamine during pregnancy gave birth (cesarean delivery) to an infant with growth retardation, flattened face with broad nasal bridge, low set ears, short neck with loose skin folds, and unusually lax body skin.

The efficacy of penicillamine in juvenile rheumatoid arthritis has not been established.

Adverse Effects: Penicillamine is a drug with a high incidence of untoward reactions, some of which are potentially fatal. Therefore, it is mandatory that patients receiving penicillamine therapy remain under close medical supervision throughout the period of drug administration (see Precautions).

Reported incidences (%) for the most commonly occurring adverse reactions in rheumatoid arthritis patients are noted, based on 17 representative clinical trials reported in the literature (1 270 patients).

Allergic: Generalized pruritus, early and late rashes (5%), pemphigoid-type reactions, and drug eruptions that may be accompanied by fever, arthralgia, or lymphadenopathy have occurred (see Warnings and Precautions). Some patients may show a lupus erythematosus-like syndrome similar to that produced by other pharmacological agents (see Precautions).

Urticaria and exfoliative dermatitis have occurred.

Thyroiditis has been reported but is extremely rare.

Some patients may develop a migratory polyarthralgia, often with objective synovitis (see Dosage).

Gastrointestinal: Anorexia, epigastric pain, nausea, vomiting, or occasional diarrhea may occur (17%).

Isolated cases of reactivated peptic ulcer have occurred, as have hepatic dysfunction, cholestatic jaundice, and pancreatitis. There have been a few reports of increased serum alkaline phosphatase, lactic dehydrogenase, and positive cephalin flocculation and thymol turbidity tests.

Some patients may report a blunting, diminution, or total loss of taste perception (12%); or may develop oral ulcerations. Although rare, cheilosis, glossitis, and gingivostomatitis have been reported (see Precautions).

Gastrointestinal side effects are usually reversible following cessation of therapy.

Hematological: Penicillamine can cause bone marrow depression (see Warnings). Leukopenia (2%) and thrombocytopenia (4%) have occurred. Fatalities have been reported as a result of thrombocytopenia, agranulocytosis, and aplastic anemia.

Thrombotic thrombocytopenic purpura, hemolytic anemia, red cell aplasia, monocytosis, leukocytosis, eosinophilia, and thrombocytosis also have been reported.

Renal: Patients on penicillamine therapy may develop proteinuria (6%) and/or hematuria which, in some, may progress to the development of the nephrotic syndrome as a result of an immune complex membranous glomerulopathy (see Warnings).

CNS: Tinnitus has been reported. Reversible optic neuritis has been reported following administration of the racemic penicillamine (dl-form) and may be related to pyridoxine deficiency.

Other: Side effects that have been reported rarely include thrombophlebitis; hyperpyrexia (see Precautions); falling hair or alopecia; myasthenic syndrome (see Warnings); polymyositis; dermatomyositis; mammary hyperplasia; elastosis (cutaneous macular atrophy); and Goodpasture's syndrome, a severe and ultimately fatal glomerulonephritis associated with intraalveolar hemorrhage (see Warnings). Allergic alveolitis and obliterative bronchiolitis have been reported in patients with severe rheumatoid arthritis, some of whom were receiving penicillamine.

Increased skin friability, excessive wrinkling of the skin, and development of small white papules at venipuncture and surgical sites have been reported (see Precautions).

The chelating action of the drug may cause increased excretion of other heavy metals such as zinc and mercury.

Dosage: Physicians planning to use penicillamine should thoroughly familiarize themselves with its toxicity, special dosage considerations, and therapeutic benefits. Penicillamine should never be used casually. Each patient should remain constantly under the close supervision of the physician. Patients should be warned to report promptly any symptoms suggesting toxicity.

Wilson's Disease: Penicillamine should be given on an empty stomach, 4 times a day; ½ to 1 hour before meals, and at bedtime, at least 2 hours after the evening meal.

Optimal dosage can be determined only by measurement of urinary copper excretion. The urine must be collected in copper free glassware, and should be quantitatively analyzed for copper before, and soon after, initiation of therapy with penicillamine. Continued therapy should be monitored by doing a 24 hour urinary copper analysis every 3 months or so for the duration of therapy. Since a low copper diet should keep copper absorption down to less than 1 mg a day, the patient probably will be in negative copper balance if 0.5 to 1 mg of copper is present in a 24 hour collection of urine.

To achieve this, the suggested initial dosage of penicillamine in the treatment of Wilson's disease is 1 g/day for children or adults. This may be increased, as indicated by the urinary copper analyses, but it is seldom necessary to exceed a dosage of 2 g/day.

In patients who cannot tolerate as much as 1 g/day initially, initiating dosage with 250 mg/day, and increasing gradually to the requisite amount, gives closer control of the effects of the drug and may help to reduce the incidence of adverse reactions.

Cystinuria: Penicillamine should be used along with conventional therapy. By reducing urinary cystine, it decreases crystalluria and stone formation. In some instances, it has been reported to decrease the size of, and even to dissolve, stones already formed.

The usual dosage of penicillamine in the treatment of cystinuria is 2 g/day for adults, with a range of 1 to 4 g/day. For children, dosage can be based on 30 mg/kg/day. The total daily amount should be divided into 4 doses. If 4 equal doses are not feasible, give the larger portion at bedtime. If adverse reactions necessitate a reduction in dosage, it is important to retain the bedtime dose.

Initiating dosage with 250 mg/day, and increasing gradually to the requisite amount, gives closer control of the effects of the drug and may help to reduce the incidence of adverse reactions.

In addition to taking penicillamine, patients should drink copiously. It is especially important to drink about a pint of fluid at bedtime and another pint once during the night when urine is more concentrated and more acid than during the day. The greater the fluid intake, the lower the required dosage of penicillamine.

Dosage must be individualized to an amount that limits cystine excretion to 100 to 200 mg/day in those with no history of stones, and below 100 mg in those who have had stone

Depen (cont'd)

formation and/or pain. Thus, in determining dosage, the inherent tubular defect, the patient's size, age and rate of growth, and his diet and water intake all must be taken into consideration.

Rheumatoid Arthritis: In rheumatoid arthritis, the onset of therapeutic response to penicillamine may not be seen for 2 or 3 months. In those patients who respond, however, the first evidence of suppression of symptoms such as pain, tenderness, and swelling is generally apparent within 3 months. The optimum duration of therapy has not been determined. If remissions occur, they may last from months to years, but usually require continued treatment.

In patients with rheumatoid arthritis, it is important that penicillamine be given on an empty stomach, at least 1 hour before meals and at least 1 hour apart from any other drug, food, or milk. This permits maximum absorption and reduces the likelihood of inactivation by metal binding.

When treatment with penicillamine has been interrupted because of adverse reactions or other reasons, the drug should be reintroduced cautiously by starting with a lower dosage and increasing slowly.

Initial: The recommended dosage regimen in rheumatoid arthritis begins with a single daily dose of 125 mg to 250 mg which is thereafter increased at 1 to 3 month intervals, by 125 mg to 250 mg/day, as patient response and tolerance indicates. If a satisfactory remission of symptoms is achieved, the dose associated with the remission should be continued (see Maintenance Therapy). If there is no improvement and there are signs of potentially serious toxicity after 2 to 3 months of treatment with doses of 500 to 750 mg/day, increases of 125 mg to 250 mg/day at 2 to 3 month intervals may be continued until a satisfactory remission occurs (see Maintenance Therapy) or signs of toxicity develop (see Warnings and Precautions). If there is no discernible improvement after 3 to 4 months of treatment with 1 000 to 1 500 mg of penicillamine/day, it may be assumed the patient will not respond and penicillamine should be discontinued.

Maintenance: The maintenance dosage of penicillamine must be individualized, and may require adjustment during the course of treatment. Many patients respond satisfactorily to a dosage within the 500 to 750 mg/day range. Some need less.

Changes in maintenance dosage levels may not be reflected clinically or in the erythrocyte sedimentation rate for 2 to 3 months after each dosage adjustment.

Some patients will subsequently require an increase in the maintenance dosage to achieve maximal disease suppression. In those patients who do respond, but who evidence incomplete suppression of their disease after the first 6 to 9 months of treatment, the daily dosage of penicillamine may be increased by 125 mg to 250 mg/day at 3 month intervals. It is unusual in current practice to employ a dosage in excess of 1 g/day, but up to 1.5 g/day has sometimes been required.

Exacerbations: During the course of treatment some patients may experience an exacerbation of disease activity following an initial good response. These may be self-limited and can subside within 12 weeks. They are usually controlled by the addition of nonsteroidal anti-inflammatory drugs, and only if the patient has demonstrated a true escape phenomenon (as evidenced by failure of the flare to subside within this time period) should an increase in the maintenance dose ordinarily be considered.

In the rheumatoid patient, migratory polyarthralgia due to penicillamine is extremely difficult to differentiate from an exacerbation of the rheumatoid arthritis. Discontinuance or a substantial reduction in dosage of penicillamine therapy for up to several weeks will usually determine which of these processes is responsible for the arthralgia.

The optimum duration of penicillamine therapy in rheumatoid arthritis has not been determined. If the patient has been in remission for 6 months or more, a gradual, stepwise dosage reduction in decrements of 125 mg to 250 mg/day at approximately 3 month intervals may be attempted.

Penicillamine should not be used in patients who are receiving gold therapy, antimalarial or cytotoxic drugs, oxyphenbutazone, or phenylbutazone (see Contraindications). Other measures, such as salicylates, other nonsteroidal anti-inflammatory drugs, or systemic corticosteroids, may be continued when penicillamine is initiated. After improvement commences, analgesic and anti-inflammatory drugs may be slowly discontinued as symptoms permit. Steroid withdrawal must be done gradually, and many months of penicillamine treatment may be required before steroids can be completely eliminated.

Based on clinical experience, dosages up to 500 mg/day can be given as a single daily dose. Dosages in excess of 500 mg/day should be administered in divided doses.

The standard nitroprusside cyanide test has been reported useful as a qualitative measure of the effective dose.

Supplied: Each ellipsoid white, coated tablet, intagliated "37-4401" on one side and "Wallace" on other side, contains: penicillamine 250 mg. Nonmedicinal ingredients: cellulose, edetate disodium, lactose, magnesium stearate, magnesium trisilicate, polyethylene glycol, povidone, simethicone, starch and stearic acid. Energy: 2.9 kJ (0.7 kcal). Sodium: 0.21 mg. Gluten- and tartrazine-free. Bottles of 100.

(Shown in Product Recognition Section)

DEPO-MEDROL® Ⓟ
Pharmacia & Upjohn

Methylprednisolone Acetate
Glucocorticoid

Pharmacology: Depo-Medrol is a sterile aqueous suspension of the **synthetic** glucocorticoid methylprednisolone acetate. It has a strong and prolonged anti-inflammatory, immunosuppressive and antiallergic activity. Depo-Medrol can be administered i.m. for a prolonged systemic activity as well as in situ for a local treatment. The prolonged activity of Depo-Medrol is explained by the slow release of the active substance.

Indications: I.M.: When oral therapy is not feasible and the strength, dosage form, and route of administration of the drug reasonably lend the preparation to the treatment of the condition, the i.m. use of methylprednisolone is indicated as follows:

Endocrine Disorders: Primary or secondary adrenocortical insufficiency (hydrocortisone or cortisone is the drug of choice, synthetic analogs may be used in conjunction with mineralocorticoids where applicable; in infancy, mineralocorticoid supplementation is of particular importance). Acute adrenocortical insufficiency (hydrocortisone or cortisone is the drug of choice; mineralocorticoid supplementation may be necessary, particularly when synthetic analogs are used). Congenital adrenal hyperplasia, hypercalcemia associated with cancer, nonsuppurative thyroiditis.

Rheumatic Disorders: As adjunctive therapy for short-term administration (to tide the patient over an acute episode or exacerbation) in: post traumatic osteoarthritis, synovitis of osteoarthritis, rheumatoid arthritis, including juvenile rheumatoid arthritis (selected cases may require low dose maintenance therapy), acute and subacute bursitis, epicondylitis, acute non-specific tenosynovitis, acute gouty arthritis, psoriatic arthritis, ankylosing spondylitis.

Collagen Diseases: During an exacerbation or as maintenance therapy in selected cases of: systemic lupus erythematosus, systemic dermatomyositis (polymyositis), acute rheumatic carditis.

Dermatologic Diseases: Pemphigus, severe erythema multiforme (Stevens-Johnson syndrome), exfoliative dermatitis, bullous dermatitis herpetiformis, severe seborrheic dermatitis, severe psoriasis, mycosis fungoides.

Allergic States: Control of severe or incapacitating allergic conditions intractable to adequate trials of conventional treatment in: bronchial asthma, contact dermatitis, atopic dermatitis, serum sickness, seasonal or perennial allergic rhinitis, drug hypersensitivity reactions, urticarial transfusion reactions, acute noninfectious laryngeal edema (epinephrine is the drug of first choice).

Ophthalmic Diseases: Severe acute and chronic allergic and inflammatory processes involving the eye, such as: herpes zoster ophthalmicus, iritis, iridocyclitis, chorioretinitis, diffuse posterior uveitis, optic neuritis, drug hypersensitivity reactions, anterior segment inflammation, allergic conjunctivitis, allergic corneal marginal ulcers, keratitis.

Gastrointestinal Diseases: To tide the patient over a critical period of the disease in: ulcerative colitis (systemic therapy), regional enteritis (systemic therapy).

Respiratory Diseases: Symptomatic sarcoidosis, berylliosis, fulminating or disseminated pulmonary tuberculosis when used concurrently with appropriate antituberculous chemotherapy, Lõeffler's syndrome not manageable by other means, aspiration pneumonitis.

Hematologic Disorders: Acquired (autoimmune) hemolytic anemia, secondary thrombocytopenia in adults, erythroblastopenia (RBC anemia), congenital (erythroid) hypoplastic anemia.

Neoplastic Diseases: For palliative management of: leukemias and lymphomas in adults, acute leukemia of childhood.

Edematous states: To induce diuresis or remission of proteinuria in the nephrotic syndrome, without uremia, of the idiopathic type or that due to lupus erythematosus.

CNS: Acute exacerbations of multiple sclerosis.

Miscellaneous: Tuberculous meningitis with subarachnoid block or impending block when used concurrently with appropriate antituberculous chemotherapy, trichinosis with neurologic or myocardial involvement.

Intra-Synovial or Soft Tissue Administration (including periarticular and intrabursal): **See Warnings.** Indicated as adjunctive therapy for short-term administration (to tide the patient over an acute episode or exacerbation) in: synovitis of osteoarthritis, rheumatoid arthritis, acute and subacute bursitis, acute gouty arthritis, epicondylitis, acute nonspecific tenosynovitis, post traumatic osteoarthritis.

Intralesional Administration: Indicated for intralesional use in the following conditions: keloids, localized hypertrophic infiltrated, inflammatory lesions of: lichen planus, psoriatic plaques, granuloma annulare, and lichen simplex chronicus (neurodermatitis), discoid lupus erythematosus, necrobiosis lipoidica diabeticorum, alopecia areata.

May also be useful in cystic tumors of an aponeurosis or tendon (ganglia).

Contraindications: Intrathecal administration.

I.V. administration.

Systemic fungal infections.

Known hypersensitivity to the product and its constituents.

Warnings: Benzyl Alcohol Formulation (20 mg/mL-5 mL vial, 40 mg/mL-2 and 5 mL vial, 80 mg/mL-5 mL vial): Multidose use of methylprednisolone from a single vial requires special care to avoid contamination. Although initially sterile, any multidose use of vials may lead to contamination unless strict aseptic technique is observed. Particular care, such as use of disposable sterile syringes and needles is necessary. Multidose use of methylprednisolone from vials is not recommended for intrasynovial injection.

This product contains benzyl alcohol which is potentially toxic when administered locally to neural tissue.

Depo-Medrol should not be used in premature infants, because the formulation contains benzyl alcohol. Benzyl alcohol has been reported to be associated with fatal "gasping syndrome" in premature infants.

Myristyl Gamma Picolinium Chloride Formulation (40 mg/mL-1 mL vial, 80 mg/mL-1 mL vial): This product is not suitable for multidose use. Following administration of the desired dose, any remaining suspension should be discarded.

General Warnings: While crystals of adrenal steroids in the dermis suppress inflammatory reactions, their presence may cause disintegration of the cellular elements and physiochemical changes in the ground substance of the connective tissue. The resultant infrequently occurring dermal and/or subdermal changes may form depressions in the skin at the injection site. The degree to which this reaction occurs will vary with the amount of adrenal steroid injected. Regeneration is usually complete within a few months or after all crystals of the adrenal steroid have been absorbed.

In order to minimize the incidence of dermal and subdermal atrophy, care must be exercised not to exceed recommended doses in injections. Multiple small injections into the area of the lesion should be made whenever possible. The technique of intrasynovial and i.m. injections should include precautions against injection or leakage into the dermis. Injection into the deltoid muscle should be avoided because of a high incidence of s.c. atrophy.

Methylprednisolone should not be administered by any route other than those listed under Indications. It is critical that, during administration of methylprednisolone, appropriate technique be used and care taken to assure proper placement of drug.

Administration by other than indicated routes has been associated with reports of serious medical events including: arachnoiditis, meningitis, paraparesis/paraplegia, sensory disturbances, bowel/bladder dysfunction, seizures, visual impairment including blindness, ocular and periocular inflammation, and residue or slough at injection site.

In patients on corticosteroid therapy subjected to any unusual stress, increased dosage of rapidly acting corticosteroids before, during, and after the stressful situation is indicated.

Corticosteroids may mask some signs of infection, and new infections may appear during their use. There may be decreased resistance and inability to localize infection when corticosteroids are used. Infections with any pathogen including viral, bacterial, fungal, protozoan or helminthic infections, in any location in the body, may be associated with the use of corticosteroids alone or in combination with other immunosuppressive agents that affect cellular immunity, humoral immunity, or neutrophil function. These infections may be mild, but can be severe and at times fatal. With increasing doses of corticosteroids, the rate of occurrence of infectious complication increases. Do not use intra-articularly, intrabursally, or for intratendinous administration for local effect in the presence of acute infection.

Prolonged use of corticosteroids may produce posterior subcapsular cataracts, glaucoma with possible damage to the optic nerves, and may enhance the establishment of secondary ocular infections due to fungi or viruses.

Growth may be suppressed in children receiving long-term, daily-divided dose glucocorticoid therapy. The use of such a regimen should be restricted to those most serious indications.

Administration of live or live, attenuated vaccines is contraindicated in patients receiving immunosuppressive doses of corticosteroids. Killed or inactivated vaccines may be administered to patients receiving immunosuppressive doses of corticosteroids. However the response to such vaccines may be diminished. Indicated immunization procedures may be undertaken in patients receiving nonimmunosuppressive doses of corticosteroids. While on corticosteroid therapy, patients should not be vaccinated against smallpox. Other immunization procedures should not be undertaken in patients who are on corticosteroids especially in high doses, because of the possible hazards of neurological complications and lack of antibody response.

The use of methylprednisolone in active tuberculosis should be restricted to those cases of fulminating or disseminated tuberculosis in which the corticosteroid is used for the management of the disease in conjunction with appropriate antituberculous regimen.

If corticosteroids are indicated in patients with latent tuberculosis or tuberculin reactivity, close observation is necessary as reactivation of the disease may occur. During prolonged corticosteroid therapy, these patients should receive chemoprophylaxis.

Because rare instances of anaphylactoid reactions have occurred in patients receiving parenteral corticosteroid therapy, appropriate precautionary measures should be taken prior to administration, especially when the patient has a history of allergy to any drug.

Allergic skin reactions have been reported apparently related to the excipients in the formulation. Rarely has skin testing demonstrated a reaction to methylprednisolone acetate, per se.

Average and large doses of cortisone or hydrocortisone can cause elevation of blood pressure, salt and water retention, and increased excretion of potassium. These effects are less likely to occur with the synthetic derivatives except when used in large doses. Dietary salt restriction and potassium supplementation may be necessary. All corticosteroids increase calcium excretion.

Pregnancy and *Lactation:* Some animal studies have shown that corticosteroids, when administered to the mother at high doses, may cause fetal malformations. Adequate human reproduction studies have not been done with corticosteroids. Therefore the use of this drug in pregnancy, nursing mothers, or women of childbearing potential requires that the benefits of the drug be carefully weighed against the potential risk to the mother and embryo or fetus. Since there is inadequate evidence of safety in human pregnancy, this drug should be used in pregnancy only if clearly needed.

Corticosteroids readily cross the placenta. Infants born of mothers who have received substantial doses of corticosteroids during pregnancy must be carefully observed and evaluated for signs of adrenal insufficiency. There are no known effects of corticosteroids on labor and delivery. Corticosteroids are excreted in breast milk.

Precautions: Drug induced secondary adrenocortical insufficiency may be minimized by gradual reduction of dosage. This type of relative insufficiency may persist for months after discontinuation of therapy, therefore, in any situation of stress occurring during that period, hormone therapy should be reinstituted. Since mineralocorticoid secretion may be impaired, salt and/or a mineralocorticoid should be administered concurrently.

There is an enhanced effect of corticosteroids in patients with hypothyroidism and in those with cirrhosis.

ASA should be used cautiously in conjunction with corticosteroids in hypoprothrombinemia.

Growth and development of infants and children on prolonged corticosteroid therapy should be carefully followed.

When multidose vials are used, special care to prevent contamination of the contents is essential. There is some evidence that benzalkonium is not an adequate antiseptic for sterilizing multidose vials. A povidone-iodine solution or similar product is recommended to cleanse the vial top prior to aspiration of contents (see Warnings).

Corticosteroids should be used cautiously in patients with ocular herpes simplex for fear of corneal perforation.

The lowest possible dose of corticosteroid should be used to control the condition under treatment, and when reduction in dosage is possible, the reduction must be gradual.

Psychic derangements may appear when corticosteroids are used, ranging from euphoria, insomnia, mood swings, personality changes, and severe depression to frank psychotic manifestations. Also, existing emotional instability or psychotic tendencies may be aggravated by corticosteroids.

Corticosteroids should be used with caution in nonspecific ulcerative colitis, if there is a probability of impending perforation, abscess or other pyogenic infection. Caution must also be used in diverticulitis, fresh intestinal anastomoses, active or latent peptic ulcer, renal insufficiency, hypertension, osteoporosis, and myasthenia gravis, when steroids are used as direct or adjunctive therapy.

The following additional precautions apply for parenteral corticosteroids: Intra-articular injection of a corticosteroid may produce systemic as well as local effects.

Appropriate examination of any joint fluid present is necessary to exclude a septic process.

A marked increase in pain accompanied by local swelling, further restriction of joint motion, fever, and malaise are suggestive of septic arthritis. If this complication occurs and the diagnosis of sepsis is confirmed, appropriate antimicrobial therapy should be instituted.

Local injection of a steroid into a previously infected joint is to be avoided.

Corticosteroids should not be injected into unstable joints.

Sterile technique is necessary to prevent infections or contamination.

The slower rate of absorption by i.m. administration should be recognized.

Although controlled clinical trials have shown corticosteroids to be effective in speeding the resolution of acute exacerbations of multiple sclerosis, they do not show that corticosteroids affect the ultimate outcome or natural history of the disease. The studies do show that relatively high doses of corticosteroids are necessary to demonstrate a significant effect (see Dosage).

Since complications of treatment with glucocorticoids are dependent on the size of the dose and the duration of treatment, a risk/benefit decision must be made in each individual case as to dose and duration of treatment and as to whether daily or intermittent therapy should be used.

Kaposi's sarcoma has been reported to occur in patients receiving corticosteroid therapy. Discontinuation of corticosteroids may result in clinical remission.

Carcinogenesis, Mutagenesis, Impairment of Fertility: No evidence exists showing that corticosteroids are carcinogenic, mutagenic or impair fertility.

<u>Drug Interactions:</u> The pharmacokinetic interactions listed below are potentially clinically important. Mutual inhibition of metabolism occurs with concurrent use of cyclosporine and methylprednisolone, therefore it is possible that adverse events associated with the individual use of either drug may be more apt to occur. Convulsions have been reported with concurrent use of methylprednisolone and cyclosporine.

Drugs that induce hepatic enzymes such as phenobarbital, phenytoin and rifampin may increase the clearance of methylprednisolone and may require increase in methylprednisolone dose to achieve the desired response.

Drugs such as troleandomycin and ketoconazole may inhibit the metabolism of methylprednisolone and thus decrease its clearance. Therefore the dose of methylprednisolone should be titrated to avoid steroid toxicity.

Methylprednisolone may increase the clearance of chronic high dose ASA. This could lead to a decrease in salicylate serum levels or increase the risk of salicylate toxicity when methylprednisolone is withdrawn. ASA should be used cautiously in conjunction with corticosteroids in patients suffering from hypoprothrombinemia.

The effect of methylprednisolone on oral anticoagulants is variable. There are reports of enhanced as well as diminished effects of anticoagulant when given concurrently with corticosteroids. Therefore coagulation indices should be monitored to maintain the desired anticoagulant effect.

Adverse Effects: Fluid and Electrolyte Disturbances: sodium retention, fluid retention, congestive heart failure in susceptible patients, potassium loss, hypokalemic alkalosis, hypertension.

Musculoskeletal: muscle weakness, steroid myopathy, osteoporosis, vertebral compression fractures, aseptic necrosis of femoral and humeral heads, pathologic fracture of long bones, tendon rupture—particularly of the Achilles tendon.

Gastrointestinal: peptic ulcer with possible subsequent perforation and hemorrhage, pancreatitis, gastric hemorrhage, esophagitis, perforation of the bowel.

Increases in ALT, AST and alkaline phosphatase have been observed following corticosteroid treatment. These changes are usually small, not associated with any clinical syndrome and are reversible upon discontinuation.

Dermatologic: impaired wound healing, thin fragile skin, petechiae and ecchymoses.

Neurological: increased intracranial pressure (pseudotumor cerebri), psychic derangements, seizures.

Endocrine: menstrual irregularities, development of Cushingoid state, suppression of growth in children, decreased carbohydrate tolerance, manifestations of latent diabetes mellitus, increased requirements for insulin or oral hypoglycemic agents in diabetes, suppression of pituitary-adrenal axis.

Ophthalmic: posterior subcapsular cataracts, increased intraocular pressure, glaucoma, exophthalmos.

Metabolic: negative nitrogen balance due to protein catabolism.

Immune System: masking infections, latent infections becoming active, opportunistic infections, hypersensitivity reactions including anaphylaxis, suppressed reactions to skin tests.

The following additional adverse reactions are related to parenteral corticosteroid therapy: rare instances of blindness associated with intralesional therapy around the face and head, anaphylactic reaction or allergic reactions, hyperpigmentation or hypopigmentation, s.c. and cutaneous atrophy, sterile abscess, postinjection flare—following intra-synovial use, Charcot-like arthropathy. Injection site infections can occur following nonsterile technique.

Overdose: Symptoms and Treatment: There is no clinical syndrome of acute overdosage with methylprednisolone.

Repeated frequent doses (daily or several times/week) over a protracted period may result in a Cushingoid state.

Dosage: Because of possible physical incompatibilities, methylprednisolone should not be diluted or mixed with other solutions. Parenteral suspensions should be inspected visually for foreign particulate matter and discoloration prior to administration whenever drug product and container permit.

Administration for Local Effect: Therapy with methylprednisolone does not obviate the need for the conventional measures usually employed. Although this method of treatment will ameliorate symptoms, it is in no sense a cure and the hormone has no effect on the cause of the inflammation.

Rheumatoid and Osteoarthritis: The dose for intra-articular administration depends upon the size of the joint and varies with the severity of the condition in the individual patient. In chronic cases, injections may be repeated at intervals ranging from 1 to 5 or more weeks depending upon the degree of relief obtained from the initial injection. The doses in Table I are given as a general guide.

Table I—Depo-Medrol

Dosage—Rheumatoid and Osteoarthritis

Size of Joint	Examples	Range of Dosage
Large	knees ankles shoulders	20 to 80 mg
Medium	elbows wrists	10 to 40 mg
Small	metacarpophalangeal interphalangeal sternoclavicular acromioclavicular	4 to 10 mg

Procedure: It is recommended that the anatomy of the joint involved be reviewed before attempting intra-articular injection. In order to obtain the full anti-inflammatory effect it is important that the injection be made into the synovial space. Employing the same sterile technique as for a lumbar puncture, a sterile 20 to 24 gauge needle (on a dry syringe) is quickly inserted into the synovial cavity. Procaine infiltration is elective. The aspiration of only a few drops of joint fluid proves the joint space has been entered by the needle. The injection site for each joint is determined by that location where the synovial cavity is most superficial and most free of large vessels and nerves. With the needle in place, the aspirating syringe is removed and replaced by a second syringe containing the desired amount of methylprednisolone. The plunger is then pulled outward slightly to aspirate synovial fluid and to make sure the needle is still in the synovial space.

Depo-Medrol (cont'd)

After the injection, the joint is moved gently a few times to aid mixing of the synovial fluid and the suspension. The site is covered with a small sterile dressing.

Suitable sites for intra-articular injection are the knee, ankle, wrist, elbow, shoulder, phalangeal, and hip joints. Since difficulty is occasionally encountered in entering the hip joint, precautions should be taken to avoid any large blood vessels in the area. Joints not suitable for injection are those that are anatomically inaccessible such as the spinal joints and those like the sacroiliac joints that are devoid of synovial space. Treatment failures are most frequently the result of failure to enter the joint space. Little or no benefit follows injection into surrounding tissue. If failures occur when injections into the synovial spaces are certain, as determined by aspiration of fluid, repeated injections are usually futile. Local therapy does not alter the underlying disease process, and whenever possible comprehensive therapy including physiotherapy and orthopedic correction should be employed.

Following intra-articular steroid therapy, care should be taken to avoid overuse of joints in which symptomatic benefit has been obtained. Negligence in this matter may permit an increase in joint deterioration that will more than offset the beneficial effects of the steroid.

Unstable joints should not be injected. Repeated intra-articular injection may in some cases result in instability of the joint. X-ray follow-up is suggested in selected cases to detect deterioration.

If a local anesthetic is used prior to the injection of methylprednisolone, the anesthetic package insert should be read carefully and all the precautions observed.

Bursitis: The area around the injection site is prepared in a sterile way and a wheal at the site made with 1% procaine HCl solution. A 20 to 24 gauge needle attached to a dry syringe is inserted into the bursa and the fluid aspirated. The needle is left in place and the aspirating syringe changed for a small syringe containing the desired dose. After injection, the needle is withdrawn and a small dressing applied.

Miscellaneous: Ganglion, Tendinitis, Epicondylitis: In the treatment of conditions such as tendinitis or tenosynovitis, care should be taken, following application of a suitable antiseptic to the overlying skin, to inject the suspension into the tendon sheath rather than into the substance of the tendon. The tendon may be readily palpated when placed on a stretch. When treating conditions such as epicondylitis, the area of greatest tenderness should be outlined carefully and the suspension infiltrated into the area. For ganglia of the tendon sheaths, the suspension is injected directly into the cyst. In many cases, a single injection causes a marked decrease in the size of the cystic tumor and may effect disappearance.

The usual sterile precautions should be observed, of course, with each injection.

The dose in the treatment of the various conditions of the tendinous or bursal structures listed above varies with the condition being treated and ranges from 4 to 30 mg. In recurrent or chronic conditions, repeated injections may be necessary.

Injections for Local Effect in Dermatologic Conditions: Following cleansing with an appropriate antiseptic such as 70% alcohol, 20 to 60 mg of the suspension is injected into the lesion. It may be necessary to distribute doses ranging from 20 to 40 mg by repeated local injections in the case of large lesions. Care should be taken to avoid injection of sufficient material to cause blanching since this may be followed by a small slough. One to four injections are usually employed, the intervals between injections varying with the type of lesion being treated and the duration of improvement produced by the initial injection.

When multidose vials are used, special care to prevent contamination of the contents is essential (see Warnings).

Administration for Systemic Effect: The i.m. dosage will vary with the condition being treated. When a prolonged effect is desired, the weekly dose may be calculated by multiplying the daily oral dose by 7 and given as a single i.m. injection.

Dosage must be individualized according to the severity of the disease and response of the patient. For infants and children, the recommended dosage will have to be reduced, but dosage should be governed by the severity of the condition rather than by strict adherence to the ratio indicated by age or body weight.

Hormone therapy is an adjunct to, and not a replacement for, conventional therapy. Dosage must be decreased or discontinued gradually when the drug has been administered for more than a few days. The severity, prognosis and expected duration of the disease and the reaction of the patient to medication are primary factors in determining dosage. If a period of spontaneous remission occurs in a chronic condition, treatment should be discontinued. Routine laboratory studies, such as urinalysis, 2-hour postprandial blood sugar, determination of blood pressure and body weight, and a chest x-ray should be made at regular intervals during prolonged therapy. Upper gastrointestinal x-rays are desirable in patients with an ulcer history or significant dyspepsia.

In patients with the adrenogenital syndrome, a single i.m. injection of 40 mg every 2 weeks may be adequate. For maintenance of patients with rheumatoid arthritis, the weekly i.m. dose will vary from 40 to 120 mg. The usual dosage for patients with dermatologic lesions benefited by systemic corticoid therapy is 40 to 120 mg methylprednisolone administered i.m. at weekly intervals for 1 to 4 weeks. In acute severe dermatitis due to poison ivy, relief may result within 8 to 12 hours following i.m. administration of a single dose of 80 to 120 mg. In chronic contact dermatitis, repeated injections at 5 to 10 day intervals may be necessary. In seborrheic dermatitis, a weekly dose of 80 mg may be adequate to control the condition.

Following i.m. administration of 80 to 120 mg to asthmatic patients, relief may result within 6 to 48 hours and persist for several days to 2 weeks. Similarly in patients with allergic rhinitis (hay fever) an i.m. dose of 80 to 120 mg may be followed by relief of coryzal symptoms within 6 hours persisting for several days to 3 weeks.

If signs of stress are associated with the condition being treated, the dosage of the suspension should be increased. If a rapid hormonal effect of maximum intensity is required, the i.v. administration of highly soluble methylprednisolone sodium succinate is indicated.

Multiple Sclerosis: In treatment of acute exacerbations of multiple sclerosis daily doses of 200 mg of prednisolone for a week followed by 80 mg every other day for 1 month have been shown to be effective (4 mg of methylprednisolone is equivalent to 5 mg of prednisolone).

Supplied: Multidose Vials: 20 mg: Each mL of sterile suspension contains: methylprednisolone acetate 20 mg. Nonmedicinal ingredients: dibasic sodium phosphate, monobasic sodium phosphate, polyethylene glycol, polysorbate 80, sodium chloride to adjust tonicity and benzyl alcohol as a preservative. When necessary, pH was adjusted with sodium hydroxide and/or hydrochloric acid. Vials of 5 mL.

40 mg: Each mL of sterile suspension contains: methylprednisolone acetate 40 mg. Nonmedicinal ingredients: dibasic sodium phosphate, monobasic sodium phosphate, polyethylene glycol, polysorbate 80, sodium chloride to adjust tonicity and benzyl alcohol as a preservative. When necessary, pH was adjusted with sodium hydroxide and/or hydrochloric acid. Vials of 2 and 5 mL.

80 mg: Each mL of sterile suspension contains: methylprednisolone acetate 80 mg. Nonmedicinal ingredients: dibasic sodium phosphate, monobasic sodium phosphate, polyethylene glycol, polysorbate 80, sodium chloride to adjust tonicity and benzyl alcohol as a preservative. When necessary, pH was adjusted with sodium hydroxide and/or hydrochloric acid. Vials of 5 mL.

Single Use Vials: 40 mg: Each mL of sterile suspension contains: methylprednisolone acetate 40 mg. Nonmedicinal ingredients: myristyl gamma picolinium chloride (MGPC), polyethylene glycol and sodium chloride to adjust the tonicity. When necessary, pH was adjusted with sodium hydroxide and/or hydrochloric acid. Vials of 1 mL.

80 mg: Each mL of sterile suspension contains: methylprednisolone acetate 80 mg. Nonmedicinal ingredients: myristyl gamma picolinium chloride (MGPC), polyethylene glycol and sodium chloride to adjust the tonicity. When necessary, pH was adjusted with sodium hydroxide and/or hydrochloric acid. Vials of 1 mL.

Store at room temperature between 15 and 30°C.

DEPO-MEDROL® with Lidocaine ℞

Pharmacia & Upjohn

Methylprednisolone Acetate—Lidocaine HCl

Glucocorticoid with Local Anesthetic

Pharmacology: Methylprednisolone is an anti-inflammatory steroid. Estimates of the relative potencies of methylprednisolone and prednisolone range from 1.13 to 2.1 with an average of 1.5. In general the required daily dose of methylprednisolone can be estimated to be two-thirds (or 0.7) the required daily dose of prednisolone. While the effect of parenterally administered methylprednisolone acetate is prolonged, it has the same metabolic and anti-inflammatory actions as orally administered drug.

Cortisol and its synthetic analogues, such as methylprednisolone acetate, exert their action locally by preventing or suppressing the development of local heat, redness, swelling and tenderness by which inflammation is recognized at the gross level of observation. At the microscopic level, such compounds inhibit not only the early phenomena of the inflammatory process (edema, fibrin deposition, capillary dilatation, migration of phagocytes into the inflamed area and phagocytic activity), but also the later manifestations (capillary proliferation, fibroblast proliferation, deposition of collagen and still later cicatrization). These compounds inhibit inflammatory response whether the inciting agent is mechanical, chemical or immunological.

Lidocaine is a potent local anesthetic agent widely used both for topical and injection anaesthesia. Lidocaine prevents both the generation and the conduction of the nerve impulse. Its main site of action is the cell membrane, and there is seemingly little action of physiological importance on the axoplasm. The exact mechanism whereby a local anesthetic influences the permeability of the membrane is unknown. As a general rule, small nerve fibers are more susceptible to the action of local anesthetics than are large fibers.

Indications: For intra-synovial or soft tissue administration (including periarticular and intrabursal): See Warnings.

Depo-Medrol with Lidocaine is indicated as adjunctive therapy for short-term administration (to tide the patient over an acute episode or exacerbation) in: synovitis of osteoarthritis, rheumatoid arthritis, acute and subacute bursitis, acute gouty arthritis, epicondylitis, acute nonspecific tenosynovitis, post-traumatic osteoarthritis.

Depo-Medrol with Lidocaine may also be useful in cystic tumors of an aponeurosis or tendon (ganglia).

Contraindications: Not for i.v. use or intrathecal administration. Contraindicated in systemic fungal infections and patients with known hypersensitivity to components of the product, lidocaine or other local anesthetics of the amide type.

Warnings: This product contains benzyl alcohol which is potentially toxic when administered locally to neural tissue.

Multidose use of Depo-Medrol with Lidocaine from a single vial requires special care to avoid contamination. Although initially sterile, any multidose use of vials may lead to contamination unless strict aseptic technique is observed. Particular care, such as use of disposable sterile syringes and needles is necessary.

While crystals of adrenal steroids in the dermis suppress inflammatory reactions, their presence may cause disintegration of the cellular elements and physiochemical changes in the ground substance of the connective tissue. The resultant infrequently occurring dermal and/or subdermal changes may form depressions in the skin at the injection site. The degree to which this reaction occurs will vary with the amount of adrenal steroid injected. Regeneration is usually complete within a few months or after all crystals of the adrenal steroid have been absorbed.

In order to minimize the incidence of dermal and subdermal atrophy, care must be exercised not to exceed recommended doses in injections. Multiple small injections into the area of the lesion should be made whenever possible. The technique of intra-articular injection should include precautions against injection or leakage into the dermis.

Depo-Medrol with Lidocaine should not be administered by any route other than those listed under Indications. It is critical that, during administration of this drug appropriate technique be used and care taken to assure proper placement of drug.

Administration by other than indicated routes has been associated with reports of serious medical events including: arachnoiditis, meningitis, paraparesis/paraplegia, sensory disturbances, bowel/bladder dysfunction, seizures, visual impairment including blindness, ocular and periocular inflammation, and residue or slough at injection site. Appropriate measures must be taken to avoid intravascular injection.

In patients on corticosteroid therapy subjected to any unusual stress, increased dosage of rapidly acting corticosteroids before, during, and after the stressful situation is indicated.

Corticosteroids may mask some signs of infection, and new infections may appear during their use. There may be decreased resistance and inability to localize infection when corticosteroids are used. Infections with any pathogen including viral, bacterial, fungal, protozoan or helminthic infections, in any location in the body, may be associated with the use of corticosteroids alone or in combination with other immunosuppressive agents that affect cellular immunity, humoral immunity, or neutrophil function. These infections may be mild, but can be severe and at times fatal. With increasing doses of corticosteroids, the rate of occurrence of infectious complication increases. Do not use intra-articularly, intrabursally, or for intratendinous administration for local effect in the presence of acute infection.

Prolonged use of corticosteroids may produce posterior sub-capsular cataracts, glaucoma with possible damage to the optic nerves, and may enhance the establishment of secondary ocular infections due to fungi or viruses.

If corticosteroids are indicated in patients with latent tuberculosis or tuberculin reactivity, close observation is necessary as reactivation of the disease may occur. During prolonged corticosteroid therapy, these patients should receive chemoprophylaxis.

Because rare instances of anaphylactoid reactions have occurred in patients receiving parenteral corticosteroid therapy, appropriate percautionary measures should be taken prior to administration, especially when the patients have a history of allergy to any drug.

Allergic skin reactions have been reported apparently related to the excipients in the formulation (see Supplied). Rarely has skin testing demonstrated a reaction to methylprednisolone acetate, per se.

Pregnancy: Some animal studies have shown that corticosteroids, when administered to the mother at high doses, may cause fetal malformations. Adequate human reproductive studies have not been done with corticosteroids or with Lidocaine. Therefore the use of this drug in pregnancy, nursing mothers, or women of child bearing potential requires that the benefits of the drug be carefully weighed against the potential risk to the mother and embryo or fetus. Since there is inadequate evidence of safety in human pregnancy, this drug should be used in pregnancy only if clearly needed.

Labor and Delivery: Corticosteroids and lidocaine readily cross the placenta. Infants born of mothers who have received substantial doses of corticosteroids during pregnancy must be carefully observed and evaluated for signs of adrenal insufficiency. There are no known effects of corticosteroids on labor and delivery. The use of local anesthetics such as lidocaine during labor and delivery may be associated with adverse effects on mother and fetus.

Lactation: Corticosteroids are excreted in breast milk. It is not known whether lidocaine is excreted in breast milk.

Children: Growth may be suppressed in children receiving long-term, daily-divided dose glucocorticoid therapy. The use of such a regimen should be restricted to those most serious indications.

Administration of live or live, attenuated vaccines is contraindicated in patients receiving immunosuppressive doses of corticosteroids. Killed or inactivated vaccines may be administered to patients receiving immunosuppressive doses of corticosteroids. However the response to such vaccines may be diminished. Indicated immunization procedures may be undertaken in patients receiving nonimmunosuppressive doses of corticosteroids.

Precautions: When multidose vials are used, special care to prevent contamination of the contents is essential. There is some evidence that benzalkonium chloride is not an adequate antiseptic for sterilizing multidose vials. A povidone-iodine solution or similar product is recommended to cleanse the vial top prior to aspiration of contents (see Warnings).

Corticosteroids should be used cautiously in patients with ocular herpes simplex for fear of corneal perforation.

Psychic derangements may appear when corticosteroids are used, ranging from euphoria, insomnia, mood swings, personality changes, and severe depression to frank psychotic manifestations. Also, existing emotional instability or psychotic tendencies may be aggravated by corticosteroids.

Corticosteroids should be used with caution in nonspecific ulcerative colitis, if there is a probability of impending perforation, abscess or other pyogenic infection. Caution must also be used in diverticulitis, fresh intestinal anastomoses, active or latent peptic ulcer, renal insufficiency, hypertension, osteoporosis, and myasthenia gravis, when steroids are used as direct or adjunctive therapy

The following additional precautions apply for parenteral corticosteroids: Intrasynovial injection of a corticosteroid may produce systemic as well as local effects. No additional benefit derives from the i.m. administration of Depo-Medrol with Lidocaine. Where parenteral corticosteroid therapy for sustained systemic effect is desired, plain Depo-Medrol should be used.

Appropriate examination of any joint fluid present is necessary to exclude a septic process.

A marked increase in pain accompanied by local swelling, further restriction of joint motion, fever, and malaise are suggestive of septic arthritis. If this complication occurs and the diagnosis of sepsis is confirmed, appropriate antimicrobial therapy should be instituted.

Local injection of a steroid into a previously infected joint is to be avoided.

Corticosteroids should not be injected into unstable joints.

Sterile technique is necessary to prevent infections or contamination.

Since complications of treatment with glucocorticoids are dependent on the size of the dose and the duration of treatment, a risk/benefit decision must be made in each individual case as to dose and duration of treatment.

This product contains benzyl alcohol. Benzyl alcohol has been reported to be associated with a fatal "gasping syndrome" in premature infants.

Kaposi's sarcoma has been reported to occur in patients receiving corticosteroid therapy. Discontinuation of corticosteroids may result in clinical remission.

Carcinogenesis, Mutagenesis, Impairment of Fertility: No evidence exists showing that corticosteroids are carcinogenic, mutagenic or impair fertility.

Drug Interactions: The pharmacokinetic interactions listed below are potentially clinically important. Mutual inhibition of metabolism occurs with concurrent use of cyclosporine and methylprednisolone; therefore, it is possible that adverse events associated with the individual use of either drug may be more apt to occur. Convulsions have been reported with concurrent use of methylprednisolone and cyclosporine.

Drugs that induce hepatic enzymes such as phenobarbital, phenytoin and rifampin may increase the clearance of methylprednisolone and may require increase in methylprednisolone dose to achieve the desired response.

Drugs such as troleandomycin and ketoconazole may inhibit the metabolism of methylprednisolone and thus decrease its clearance. Therefore, the dose of methylprednisolone should be titrated to avoid steroid toxicity.

Methylprednisolone may increase the clearance of chronic high dose ASA. This could lead to a decrease in salicylate serum levels or increase the risk of salicylate toxicity when methylprednisolone is withdrawn. ASA should be used cautiously in conjunction with corticosteroids in patients suffering from hypoprothrombinemia.

The effect of methylprednisolone on oral anticoagulants is variable. There are reports of enhanced as well as diminished effects of anticoagulant when given concurrently with corticosteroids. Therefore, coagulation indices should be monitored to maintain the desired anticoagulant effect.

Adverse Effects: Depo-Medrol: Note: The following are typical for all systemic corticosteroids. Their inclusion in this list does not necessarily indicate the specific event has been observed with this particular formulation.

Fluid and electrolyte disturbances: sodium retention, fluid retention, congestive heart failure in susceptible patients, potassium loss, hypokalemic alkalosis, hypertension.

Musculoskeletal: muscle weakness, steroid myopathy, osteoporosis, vertebral compresssion fractures, aseptic necrosis of femoral and humeral heads, pathologic fractures, tendon rupture—particularly of the Achilles tendon.

Gastrointestinal: peptic ulcer with possible subsequent perforation and hemorrhage, pancreatitis, gastrointestinal hemorrhage, esophagitis, perforation of the bowel.

Increases in ALT, AST and alkaline phosphatase have been observed following corticosteroid treatment. These changes are usually small, not associated with any clinical syndrome and are reversible upon discontinuation.

Dermatologic: impaired wound healing, thin fragile skin, petechiae and ecchymoses.

Neurological: increased intracranial pressure, pseudotumor cerebri, psychic derangements, seizures.

Endocrine: menstrual irregularities, development of Cushingoid state, suppression of growth in children, suppression of pituitary-adrenal axis, decreased carbohydrate tolerance, manifestations of latent diabetes mellitus, increased requirements for insulin or oral hypoglycemic agents in diabetics.

Ophthalmic: posterior subcapsular cataracts, increased intraocular pressure, glaucoma, exophthalmos

Metabolic: negative nitrogen balance due to protein catabolism.

Immune System: masking of infections, latent infections becoming active, opportunistic infections, hypersensitivity reactions including anaphylaxis, may suppress reactions to skin tests.

Lidocaine: CNS: lightheadedness, nervousness, apprehension, euphoria, confusion, dizziness, drowsiness, tinnitus, blurred or double vision, vomiting, sensation of heat or cold, numbness, twitching, tremors, convulsions, loss of consciousness, respiratory depression, respiratory arrest.

Cardiovascular: bradycardia, hypotension, cardiovascular collapse, cardiac arrest.

Allergic Reactions: cutaneous lesions, urticaria, edema, anaphylactic reactions.

Overdose: Symptoms and Treatment: There is no clinical syndrome of acute overdosage with Depo-Medrol with Lidocaine.

Repeated frequent doses (daily or several times per week) over a protracted period may result in a Cushingoid state, and other complications of chronic steroid therapy.

Dosage: Because of possible physical incompatibilities, Depo-Medrol with Lidocaine should not be diluted or mixed with other solutions. Parenteral suspensions should be inspected visually for foreign particulate matter and discoloration prior to administration whenever drug product and container permit.

Administration for local effect: Therapy with Depo-Medrol with Lidocaine does not obviate the need for the conventional measures usually employed. Although this method of treatment will ameliorate symptoms, it is in no sense a cure and the hormone has no effect on the cause of the inflammation.

Rheumatoid and Osteoarthritis: The dose for intra-articular administration depends upon the size of the joint and varies with the severity of the condition in the individual patient. In chronic cases, injections may be repeated at intervals ranging from 1 to 5 or more weeks depending upon the degree of relief obtained from the initial injection. The doses in Table I are given as a general guide.

Table I—Depo-Medrol with Lidocaine

Dosage—Rheumatoid and Osteoarthritis

Size of Joint	Examples	Range of Dosage (methylprednisolone acetate)
Large	knees ankles shoulders	20 to 80 mg
Medium	elbows wrists	10 to 40 mg
Small	metacarpophalangeal interphalangeal sternoclavicular acromioclavicular	4 to 10 mg

Procedure: It is recommended that the anatomy of the joint involved be reviewed before attempting intra-articular injection. In order to obtain the full anti-inflammatory effect it is important that the injection be made into the synovial space. Employing the same sterile technique as for a lumbar puncture, a sterile 20 to 24 gauge needle (on a dry syringe) is quickly inserted into the synovial cavity. Procaine infiltration is elective. The aspiration of only a few drops of joint fluid proves the joint space has been entered by the needle. The injection site for each joint is determined by that location where the synovial cavity is most superficial and most free of large vessels and nerves. With the needle in place, the aspirating syringe is removed and replaced by a second syringe containing the desired amount of Depo-Medrol with Lidocaine. The plunger is then pulled outward slightly to aspirate synovial fluid and to make sure the needle is still in the synovial space. After injection, the joint is moved gently a few times to aid mixing of synovial fluid and the suspension. The site is covered with a small sterile dressing.

Suitable sites for intra-articular injection are the knee, ankle, wrist, elbow, shoulder, phalangeal, and hip joints. Since difficulty is not infrequently encountered in entering the hip joint, precautions should be taken to avoid any large blood vessels in the area. Joints not suitable for injection are those that are anatomically inaccessible such as the spinal joints and those like the sacroiliac joints that are devoid of synovial space. Treatment failures are most frequently the result of failure to enter the joint space. Little or no benefit follows injection into surrounding tissue. If failures occur when injections into the synovial spaces are certain, as determined by aspiration of fluid, repeated injections are usually futile. Local therapy does not alter the underlying disease process, and whenever possible comprehensive therapy including physiotherapy and orthopedic correction should be employed.

Following intra-articular steroid therapy, care should be taken to avoid overuse of joints in which symptomatic benefit has been obtained. Negligence in this matter may permit an increase in joint deterioration that will more than offset the beneficial effects of the steroid.

Unstable joints should not be injected. Repeated intra-articular injection may in some cases result in instability of the joint. X-ray follow-up is suggested in selected cases to detect deterioration.

Depo-Medrol with Lidocaine (cont'd)

If a local anesthetic is used prior to injection of Depo-Medrol with Lidocaine, the anesthetic package insert should be read carefully and all the precautions observed.

Bursitis: The area around the injection site is prepared in a sterile way and a wheal at the site made with 1% procaine HCl solution. A 20 to 24 gauge needle attached to a dry syringe is inserted into the bursa and the fluid aspirated. The needle is left in place and the aspirating syringe changed for a small syringe containing the desired dose. After injection, the needle is withdrawn and a small dressing applied.

Miscellaneous: Ganglion, Tendinitis, Epicondylitis: In the treatment of conditions such as tendinitis or tenosynovitis, care should be taken, following application of a suitable antiseptic to the overlying skin, to inject the suspension into the tendon sheath rather than into the substance of the tendon. The tendon may be readily palpated when placed on a stretch. When treating conditions such as epicondylitis, the area of greatest tenderness should be outlined carefully and the suspension infiltrated into the area. For ganglia of the tendon sheaths, the suspension is injected directly into the cyst.

The usual sterile precautions should be observed, of course, with each injection.

The dose in the treatment of the various conditions of the tendinous or bursal structures listed above varies with the condition being treated and ranges from 4 to 30 mg. In recurrent of chronic conditions, repeated injections may be necessary.

When multidose vials are used, special care to prevent contamination of the contents is essential (see Warnings).

Supplied: Each mL contains: methylprednisolone acetate 40 mg and lidocaine HCl 10 mg. Nonmedicinal ingredients: benzyl alcohol, polyethylene glycol, sodium chloride and myristyl-gamma-picolinium chloride in water for injection q.s. When necessary, pH was adjusted with sodium hydroxide and/or hydrochloric acid. Gluten-free. Vials of 1, 2 and 5 mL. Store at room temperature. Protect from freezing.

Reviewed 1998

DEPO-PROVERA® Ⓟ

Pharmacia & Upjohn

Medroxyprogesterone Acetate

Progestogen

Pharmacology: Medroxyprogesterone acetate is a long-acting progestational steroid (progestogen) derived from a natural source (soybeans). Its long duration of action is a result of slow absorption from the injection site. Depo-Provera does not contain estrogen.

For conception control, medroxyprogesterone inhibits the secretion of gonadotropins which, in turn, prevents follicular maturation and ovulation, and results in endometrial thinning. Additional progestational effects that may contribute to the contraceptive effectiveness of medroxyprogesterone include the transformation and maintenance of an endometrium hostile to implantation, and thickening of cervical mucus making sperm penetration of the cervix more difficult.

Medroxyprogesterone administered parenterally to women with adequate endogenous estrogen transforms proliferative endometrium into secretory endometrium.

The anticancer activity of medroxyprogesterone at pharmacologic doses may be dependent on its effect on the hypopituitary/gonadal axis, estrogen receptors and the metabolism of steroids at the tissue level.

Following a single 150 mg i.m. dose of Depo-Provera, medroxyprogesterone acetate (MPA) concentrations, measured by an extracted radioimmunoassay procedure, increase for approximately 3 weeks to reach peak plasma concentrations of 1 to 7 ng/mL. The levels then decrease exponentially until they become undetectable (<100 pg/mL) between 120 to 200 days following injection. Using an unextracted radioimmunoassay procedure for the assay of medroxyprogesterone acetate in serum, the apparent half-life for medroxyprogesterone acetate following i.m. administration of Depo-Provera is approximately 50 days.

The principal metabolite of medroxyprogesterone acetate that has been identified is a 6α-methyl-6β, 17α, 21-trihydroxy-4-pregnene-3, 20-dione-17-acetate, which is excreted in the urine.

Medroxyprogesterone is approximately 90 to 95% protein bound. It crosses the blood-brain barrier and is secreted in breast milk.

The effect of hepatic and/or renal disease on the pharmacokinetics of medroxyprogesterone is unknown.

Indications: Conception control (prevention of pregnancy). Treatment of endometriosis. Adjunctive and/or palliative treatment of recurrent and/or metastatic endometrial or renal cell carcinoma (hypernephroid carcinomas). Adjunctive or palliative treatment of hormonally-dependent, recurrent inoperable, or metastatic carcinoma of the breast in postmenopausal women.

Contraindications: Not for i.v. use.

Medroxyprogesterone is contraindicated in women with: Known or suspected pregnancy or as a diagnostic test for pregnancy. Undiagnosed vaginal and/or urinary tract bleeding. Undiagnosed breast pathology. Thrombophlebitis, thromboembolic disorders, cerebral apoplexy or women with a past history of these conditions. Liver dysfunction or disease. Known hypersensitivity to medroxyprogesterone or any of its other ingredients.

Warnings: Irregular Menstrual Patterns: Disruption of menstrual patterns is common following the administration of medroxyprogesterone. This includes irregular or unpredictable bleeding or spotting, or rarely heavy or continuous bleeding. If undiagnosed vaginal bleeding occurs, or if abnormal bleeding persists or is severe, appropriate investigation should be instituted to rule out the possibility of organic pathology, and appropriate treatment instituted if necessary.

As women continue to use medroxyprogesterone, fewer experience irregular bleeding patterns and more experience amenorrhea. By month 12, amenorrhea was reported by 55% of women, and by month 24 amenorrhea was reported by 68% of women using medroxyprogesterone.

Because of the prolonged effect following i.m. injection of medroxyprogesterone, re-establishment of menstruation may be delayed and difficult to predict. For this reason, medroxyprogesterone is not recommended for treatment of secondary amenorrhea or functional uterine bleeding. For these conditions, oral progestogen therapy is recommended.

Bone Mineral Density Changes: Medroxyprogesterone may be a risk factor for osteoporosis, similar to race, family history, low weight/height ratio, sedentary lifestyle and smoking. Until further information is available, risk factors for osteoporosis should be reviewed, and bone density measurements should be obtained for women with multiple risk factors, especially if the drug is being considered for long-term use. It may be advisable to consider alternate methods for women with bone density measurements in the lower normal range.

Physiologically, although medroxyprogesterone slows the loss of bone density in postmenopausal women due to its anabolic effects, in premenopausal women, it suppresses estrogen production which may lead to a loss of bone density. One study conducted in New Zealand showed a relative decrease in bone density in long-term users of medroxyprogesterone. The level of bone density decrease did not meet the criteria for diagnosis of osteoporosis (>2.5 standard deviations below the mean) and no fractures were reported. The effect appeared to be reversible upon discontinuation. Further prospective study, which is ongoing, is needed to clarify this issue.

Risk of Malignancy: Long-term case-controlled surveillance of users of medroxyprogesterone found slight or no increased overall risk of breast cancer and no overall increased risk of ovarian, liver, or cervical cancer and a prolonged, protective effect of reducing the risk of endometrial cancer in the population of users.

The World Health Organization Study, a component of a pooled analysis, showed an increased RR of 2.19 (95% CI 1.23 to 3.89) of breast cancer associated with use of medroxyprogesterone in women whose first exposure to drug was within the previous 4 years and who were under 35 years of age. However, the overall RR for women who have ever used medroxyprogesterone was only 1.2 (95% CI 0.96 to 1.52). [Note: An RR of 1.0 indicates neither an increased nor a decreased risk of cancer associated with the use of the drug, relative to no use of the drug. In the case of the subpopulation with a RR of 2.19, the 95% CI is fairly wide and does not include the value of 1.0, thus inferring an increased risk of breast cancer in the defined subgroup relative to nonusers. The value of 2.19 means that women whose first exposure to drug was within the previous 4 years and who are under 35 years of age have a 2.19-fold (95% CI 1.23 to 3.89-fold) increased risk of breast cancer relative to nonusers. The National Cancer Institute reports an average annual incidence rate for breast cancer for U.S. women, all races, age 30 to 34 years of 26.7/100 000. An RR of 2.19, thus, increases the possible risk from 26.7 to 58.5 cases/100 000 women. The attributable risk, thus, is 31.8 per 100 000 women/year.]

A statistically insignificant increase in RR estimates of invasive squamous-cell cervical cancer has been associated with the use of medroxyprogesterone in women who were first exposed before the age of 35 years (RR 1.22 to 1.28 and 95% CI 0.93 to 1.70). The overall, nonsignificant relative rate of invasive squamous-cell cervical cancer in women who ever used medroxyprogesterone contraceptive injection was estimated to be 1.11 (95% CI 0.96 to 1.29). No trends in risk with duration of use or times since initial or most recent exposure were observed.

Thromboembolic Disorders: Before prescribing medroxyprogesterone, the physician should be alert to the earliest manifestations of thrombotic disorders (thrombophlebitis, cerebrovascular disorders, pulmonary embolism, and retinal thrombosis). Should any of these occur or be suspected, the drug should be discontinued immediately.

Ocular Disorders: Discontinue medication pending examination, if there is sudden partial or complete loss of vision, or if there is a sudden onset of proptosis, diplopia or migraine. If examination reveals papilledema or retinal vascular lesions, medication should be withdrawn.

Return of Fertility: There is no evidence that medroxyprogesterone causes infertility. A large study of return of fertility, shows that women conceived 9 months on average after the last injection, or 5.5 months after discontinuing (discontinuance is assumed to be 15 weeks after the last injection). In addition, the number of users who had conceived within 2 years of discontinuing their method of contraception (92% of medroxyprogesterone users had conceived within 2 years after discontinuing compared with 93% for users of the IUD and 95% for users of oral contraceptives) were comparable. Discuss this information with women who intend to conceive in the next 1 to 2 years.

In some cases women have not become pregnant after stopping injections of medroxyprogesterone. It is not known whether medroxyprogesterone or other factors resulted in a change in the ability to conceive. Many reasons exist for such changes, including increased age and the onset of menopause. The infertility rate in the normal population is 7%.

Pregnancy: To increase assurance that the woman is not pregnant at the time of the first administration, it is recommended that the first injection be given only within the first 5 days of the onset of a normal menstrual period or, only within the first 5 days postpartum if not breast-feeding. If the woman has chosen to breast-feed, discuss the risk of pregnancy and possible risks of medroxyprogesterone to determine the most appropriate course of action of the individual woman (see Lactation and Dosage).

Infants from unexpected pregnancies that occurred 1 to 2 months after injection of medroxyprogesterone may be at an increased risk of low birth weight, which, in turn, is associated with an increased risk of neonatal death. The attributable risk is low because such pregnancies are uncommon.

A significant increase incidence of polysyndactyly and chromosomal anomalies was observed among infants of users of medroxyprogesterone, the former being most pronounced in women under 30 years of age. The unrelated nature of these defects, the lack of confirmation from other studies, the distant preconceptual exposure to medroxyprogesterone and the chance effects due to multiple statistical comparisons, make a causal association unlikely.

Children exposed to medroxyprogesterone in utero and followed to adolescence, showed no evidence of any adverse effects on their health including their physical, intellectual, sexual, or social development.

Several reports suggest an association between intra-uterine exposure to progestational drugs in the first trimester of pregnancy and genital abnormalities in male and female fetuses. The risk of hypospadias (5 to 8/1 000 male births in the general population) may be approximately doubled with exposure to these drugs. Although there are insufficient data to quantify the risk to exposed female fetuses, some of these drugs induce mild virilization of the external genitalia of the female fetus. Because of these changes, it is prudent to avoid the use of progestogens during the first trimester of pregnancy.

Lactation: Detectable amounts of progestogen have been identified in the milk of mothers receiving medroxyprogesterone. Two studies have indicated that the maximum amount of medroxyprogesterone which might be ingested by a breast-feeding infant whose mother is receiving medroxyprogesterone for contraception would be 1.0 to 1.5 μg/day (or 0.0015 mg/day, 0.045 mg/month, 0.27 mg over 6 months which is about 0.05 mg/kg over 6 months for a 5.5 kg baby). If absorption properties between adult and infant are comparable, this amount would be too low to suppress pituitary function in the infant. No adverse effects related to lactation itself or infant growth were reported in studies where medroxyprogesterone was started 1 to 4 days, 7 days or within 6 weeks postpartum.

In nursing mothers treated with medroxyprogesterone, milk composition, quality and amount are not adversely affected.

To date, no adverse effects have been observed in children whose mothers were using medroxyprogesterone while lactating. A study of children exposed to MPA with median observation periods of 14 to 16 years, indicated no incidence of adverse effects on physical growth, mental growth and development of general health status. However, the long-term effects on the child are not fully understood. The physician and woman should discuss the risks of pregnancy versus the risks to the child, if medroxyprogesterone is used during lactation, to determine the most appropriate course of action for the individual woman.

Ectopic Pregnancy: Physicians should investigate the possibility of an ectopic pregnancy among women using medroxyprogesterone who complain of severe abdominal pain.

Anaphylactic Reactions: Anaphylactic and anaphylactoid reactions have occasionally been reported in women treated with medroxyprogesterone. If an anaphylactic reaction occurs, appropriate therapy should be instituted. Serious anaphylactic reactions require emergency medical treatment.

Adrenocortical Function: Clinical suppression of adrenocortical functions has not been observed at low dose levels used for contraception (ovulation suppression). However, at very high doses (500 mg daily or more) used in the treatment of certain cancers, corticoid-like activity has been reported.

Cushingoid Symptoms: The high doses of medroxyprogesterone used in the treatment of cancer may, in some cases, produce Cushingoid symptoms, e.g., moon faces and blood pressure elevation.

Precautions: General: Pretreatment Examination: Before using medroxyprogesterone, a thorough history and physical examination—including breasts, liver, pelvic organs, blood pressure determination, and Papanicolaou smear—should be performed. Periodic follow-up examinations should be conducted and include all procedures done at the initial visit.

Hepatic Function: Liver function tests should be performed periodically in women who are suspected of, or who are at risk of, having hepatic disease. The physician should be alert to the earliest manifestations of impaired liver function. Should this occur or be suspected, the treatment should not be continued. The woman's status should be re-evaluated at appropriate intervals. If jaundice develops, consideration should be given to discontinue the drug.

Carbohydrate Metabolism: A decrease in glucose tolerance has been observed in some women receiving medroxyprogesterone. The mechanisms of this decrease is obscure. For this reason, diabetic women should be carefully observed while receiving medroxyprogesterone.

Cardiovascular Function: Medroxyprogesterone has not been shown to affect coagulation and has been associated only rarely with cardiovascular incidents (e.g., medullary infarction in a heavy smoker).

Fluid Retention: Since progestogens may cause some degree of fluid retention, conditions that might be influenced by this factor, such as epilepsy, migraine, asthma, or cardiac or renal dysfunction, require careful observation.

CNS Disorders and Convulsions: Women who have a history of mental depression should be carefully observed and this drug discontinued if serious depression reoccurs. Some women may complain of premenstrual-like depression while on medroxyprogesterone therapy. There have been few reported cases of convulsions in patients who were treated with medroxyprogesterone. Association with medroxyprogesterone use or pre-existing conditions is not clear.

Weight Changes: Weight gain may be associated with the use of medroxyprogesterone (see Adverse Effects).

Age: The age of the woman constitutes no absolute limiting factor although treatment with a progestogen may mask the onset of the climacteric.

Laboratory Tests: Certain endocrine and possibly liver function tests may be affected by treatment with medroxyprogesterone. Therefore, if such tests are abnormal in a woman taking medroxyprogesterone, it is recommended that they be repeated 6 to 12 months after the drug has been withdrawn.

The clinical chemist or pathologist should be advised of progestogen therapy when a woman's blood or tissue specimens are submitted for laboratory diagnosis or biochemical analysis.

The following laboratory tests may be affected by the use of medroxyprogesterone: (a) Gonadotropin levels: inhibition of the midcycle LH surge. (b) Plasma progesterone levels: inhibition of ovulation and thus the postovulatory rise of progesterone. (c) Plasma estrogen levels: do not exceed early-to-mid-proliferative phase levels. (d) Plasma cortisol levels: not significantly affected by the dose used for contraception. (e) Glucose tolerance test: occasionally some degree of glucose intolerance may develop. (f) Metyrapone test: modest depression of response to metyrapone test. (g) Plasma lipid concentrations: decrease in high density lipoprotein cholesterol (HDL-C) in some studies. The clinical relevance of this has yet to be determined. (h) Urinary pregnanediol levels. (Note: Medroxyprogesterone does not interfere with the assay of human chorionic gonadotropin (HCG) either chemically or pharmacologically.)

<u>Drug Interactions:</u> Aminoglutethimide: Aminoglutethimide administered concomitantly with medroxyprogesterone may significantly depress the serum concentration of medroxyprogesterone. Users of medroxyprogesterone should be warned of the possibility of decreased efficacy with the use of this or any related drugs.

Rifampin: Rifampin can increase the metabolism of exogenously administered progestational agents. Norethindrone has specifically been affected; a reduction of plasma concentrations has occurred. The extent to which rifampin may alter the metabolism of other progestogens remains to be determined; the possibility of an interaction should be considered.

Conception Control: Counselling: It is very important that adequate explanations of the long-term nature of medroxyprogesterone as a contraceptive be given to each woman prior to her first injection. The possible side effects including changes in menstrual cycle and the relatively slow return of fertility should be emphasized. Every effort should be made to ensure that each woman receives such counselling as to enable her to understand fully these explanations and the possible consequences. A detailed supplementary information booklet that describes the actions, benefits, risks and adverse effects of this contraceptive should be made available to each woman before she makes the decision to use medroxyprogesterone for conception control.

Sexually Transmitted Diseases: Women should be counselled that this product offers no protection from the acquisition of sexually transmitted infections, including HIV and that latex or polyurethane condoms are recommended for this purpose.

Followup Examination: The first followup examination should be made within 6 months after medroxyprogesterone is prescribed and thereafter at least once a year. At each annual visit, the examination should include all procedures done at the initial visit.

The woman must return every 10 to 13 weeks for a repeat injection to maintain contraceptive effectiveness (see Dosage). If an injection is not given within 13 weeks, a pregnancy test should be done before any further treatment with medroxyprogesterone.

Weight Changes: The majority of studies report a mean weight gain of 2.5 kg at the end of 1 year, but only 2% of women discontinued treatment due to excessive weight gain. Many studies indicate that weight gain occurs mainly in the first year of use, however, others do report a slow and continuing increase which may reach a mean of 3.6 kg by the end of 2 years. Some 20 to 40% of medroxyprogesterone users actually lose weight during treatment.

Adverse Effects: The following adverse reactions have been associated with the use of medroxyprogesterone: Irregular Menstrual Patterns: The most common adverse reactions associated with the use of medroxyprogesterone for contraception is the disruption of menstrual patterns. This includes irregular or unpredictable bleeding or spotting, or rarely heavy or continuous bleeding.

In U.S. studies of 3 905 women receiving medroxyprogesterone every 3 months, unpredictable bleeding or spotting were commonly reported during the first few menstrual cycles with frequency, duration and amount of bleeding diminishing gradually. By month 12, amenorrhea was reported by 55% of the women, and by month 24 amenorrhea was reported by 68% of the women using medroxyprogesterone. Bleeding or spotting persisted for more than 10 days of the month in about 12% of the users. And abnormally heavy or prolonged bleeding occurs in about 1 to 2% of users.

Nonmenstrual Adverse Reactions: Other than menstrual changes, weight gain, headache and abdominal discomfort are the most common side effects.

The U.S. studies of 3 905 women receiving medroxyprogesterone every 3 months report a mean weight gain of 2.5 kg at the end of 1 year, but only 2% of women discontinued treatment due to excessive weight gain. Many studies indicate that weight gain occurs mainly in the first year of use, however, others report a slow and continuing increase which may reach a mean of 3.6 kg by the end of 2 years. However, some 20 to 40% of medroxyprogesterone users actually lose weight during treatment.

In a few instances there have been undesirable sequelae at the site of injection, such as a residual lump, change in color of the skin or a sterile abscess.

Anaphylactic and anaphylactoid reactions have been reported on rare occasions.

The occurrence rates for nonmenstrual adverse reactions reported in U.S. studies of 3 905 women receiving medroxyprogesterone every 3 months are listed below; 2 253 women were in the study for 12 months or more; 827 women were in the study for 36 months or more. The total number of patient-months of experience was 82 384. A total of 2 117 of the 3 905 women (54%) reported no side effects.

Allergic: allergic reactions, hives (0.2 to 1.0%).

Cardiovascular: chest pain, tachycardia (0.2 to 1.0%).

CNS: headache (17%), nervousness (12%), dizziness (6%), depression (2%), insomnia, pain, somnolence or drowsiness (0.2 to 1.0%).

Dermatologic: acne, alopecia, rash (1%).

Endocrine: decreased libido (6%), breast swelling/tenderness (3%), hot flashes (1%), galactorrhea, chloasma, hirsutism (0.2 to 1.0%).

Gastrointestinal: abdominal distress (12%), nausea (4%), bloating (2%), anorexia, increased appetite, diarrhea, heartburn, abdominal swelling, vomiting, constipation (0.2 to 1.0%).

Gynecologic/Urologic: vaginal discharge (3%), dysmenorrhea (2%), pruritus vulvae (1%), genitourinary infection, dysuria, bleeding requiring D&C, dyspareunia, urinary frequency (0.2 to 1.0%).

Hepatic: liver disorders with no other symptoms, altered liver function (0.2 to 1.0%).

Metabolic: peripheral edema (2%).

Musculoskeletal: backache (2%).

Neurologic: asthenia (5%), limb pain (4%), pruritus, paresthesia or sensory disturbances (0.2 to 1.0%).

Respiratory: dyspnea (0.2 to 1.0%).

Special Senses: eye discomfort (0.2 to 1.0%).

Overdose: Symptoms and Treatment: Overdosage may result in a period of amenorrhea of a variable length and may be followed by irregular menses for several cycles. There is no known therapy for overdosage.

Dosage: Medroxyprogesterone is intended for **i.m. administration only.** Immediately before use, the sterile aqueous suspension should be vigorously shaken to assure that the dose being administered represents a uniform suspension.

Conception Control (Contraception): The recommended dose for contraception is 150 mg every 3 months, administered by deep i.m. injection. To increase assurance that the woman is not pregnant at the time of the first administration, it is recommended that this injection be given **only** within the first 5 days of the onset of a normal menstrual period or, **only** within the first 5 days postpartum if not breast-feeding. If the woman has chosen to breast-feed, discuss the risks of pregnancy and possible risks of medroxyprogesterone to determine the most appropriate course of action for the individual woman (see Warnings).

If administered within the first 5 days after the onset of a normal menstrual period, medroxyprogesterone is effective from the day of injection. When medroxyprogesterone is given later in the menstrual cycle it may not be effective for the first 3 to 4 weeks after the injection and another method of contraception (nonhormonal) should be used during this time.

After miscarriage or first trimester therapeutic abortion, the injection is normally given within 5 days of the procedure and no extra precautions are required. After a late (second trimester) abortion, some further delay is recommended to reduce the risk of heavy and prolonged bleeding, therefore, the first injection should not be given until 4 weeks after the procedure.

Intervals between injections must not exceed 13 weeks (3 months).

Endometriosis: The recommended dose is 50 mg weekly or 100 mg every 2 weeks i.m. for at least 6 months. It should be noted that return of ovulation may be delayed following this therapy due to the depot properties of the drug (see Warnings).

Endometrial and Renal Carcinoma: Doses of 400 mg to 1 000 mg i.m./week are recommended initially. If improvement is noted within a few weeks or months and the disease appears stabilized, it may be possible to maintain improvement with as little as 400 mg/month. Medroxyprogesterone is not recommended as a primary therapy, but as adjunctive and

Depo-Provera (cont'd)

palliative treatment in advanced, inoperable cases including those with recurrent or metastatic disease.
Breast Cancer: The recommended dosage schedule is 500 mg/day i.m. for 28 days. The woman should then be placed on a maintenance schedule of 500 mg twice weekly as long as she is responding to treatment. A response may not be evident until 8 to 10 weeks of therapy. If a rapid progression of disease occurs at any time during therapy, medroxyprogesterone should be terminated.

Information for the Patient: See Blue Section—Information for the Patient "Depo-Provera".

Supplied: 50 mg/mL: Each mL contains: medroxyprogesterone acetate 50 mg. Nonmedicinal ingredients: methylparaben, polyethylene glycol 3350, polysorbate 80, propylparaben, sodium chloride and water for injection. Vials of 5 mL, boxes of 1.

150 mg/mL: Each mL contains: medroxyprogesterone acetate 150 mg. Nonmedicinal ingredients: methylparaben, polyethylene glycol 3350, polysorbate 80, propylparaben, sodium chloride and water for injection. Vials of 1 mL, boxes of 1 and 5.

Protect from freezing. Store at controlled room temperature 15 to 30°C. Shake well before using.

Reviewed 1998

DEPO-TESTOSTERONE CYPIONATE ◈

Pharmacia & Upjohn

Testosterone Cypionate

Androgen

Pharmacology: Qualitatively similar to testosterone and its esters in physiologic activity, testosterone cypionate has the advantage of prolonged effect. In hypogonadal males, the effect of a single injection of 200 to 400 mg of testosterone cypionate, was observed to be maintained for 2 to 4 weeks, which is 2 to 4 times longer than the effect produced by a comparable dose of testosterone propionate.

Indications: Male: Eunuchism, eunuchoidism, deficiency after castration. Male climacteric symptoms when these are secondary to androgen deficiency. Oligospermia.

Male or Female: Postmenopausal or senile osteoporosis. Androgens are without value as primary therapy, but may be of value as adjunctive therapy. Equal or greater consideration should be given to diet, calcium balance, physiotherapy, and good general health-promoting measures.

Contraindications: In patients with prostatic carcinoma, severe cardiorenal disease and severe persistent hypercalcemia.
Pregnancy: Since it may cause masculinization of the female fetus, testosterone cypionate is also contraindicated during pregnancy.

Precautions: Since androgens, in general, tend to promote retention of sodium and water, patients receiving testosterone cypionate—in particular, elderly patients—should be observed for edema. Hypercalcemia may occur, particularly in immobilized patients; use of testosterone cypionate should be discontinued as soon as hypercalcemia is detected.

Adverse Effects: In the male, excessive doses or prolonged administration of testosterone cypionate may cause inhibition of testicular function resultant oligospermia and decreased ejaculation volume. Gynecomastia has been reported in males treated with testosterone, but this complication usually disappears upon cessation of therapy. In young boys, androgens should be used with caution to avoid precocious sexual development and premature epiphyseal closure.

In the female, large doses of testosterone cypionate may produce masculinization with signs such as hirsutism, deepening of the voice, enlargement of the clitoris, acne, increased libido and menstrual irregularities. WIth the exception of the voice change, these effects tend to disappear following cessation of therapy.

Dosage: Sterile solution of testosterone cypionate is for i.m. use only. Dosage will vary depending upon the individual, the condition being treated, its severity, and prior androgen therapy. Because of the protracted action of testosterone cypionate, injections more frequently than every 2 weeks are seldom required.

Eunuchism, Eunuchoidism: For complete replacement in eunuchs and eunuchoid patients, the usual dose is 200 to 400 mg injected at intervals of 3 to 4 weeks. It is usually preferable to begin treatment with full therapeutic doses, which are later adjusted to individual requirements. Priapism is a sign of excessive dosage and is an indication for temporary withdrawal of androgen therapy.

Impotence due to Testicular Deficiency, Male Climacteric. Testosterone cypionate may be given every 3 to 4 weeks in doses ranging from 200 to 400 mg.

Oligospermia: To stimulate spermatogenesis when trial androgen therapy is indicated in subfertile males with oligospermia, recommended dosage is: (1) 100 to 200 mg every 3 to 6 weeks for development and maintenance of testicular function: or (2) 200 mg each week for 6 to 10 weeks for suppression which may then be followed by rebound spermatogenesis following discontinuance of the injection.

Anabolic Effect, Osteoporosis: The dosage for anabolic effect should be adjusted according to age, sex, and the condition of the individual patient. In the majority of cases, the dose will range from 200 to 400 mg injected every 3 to 4 weeks. In addition, an adequate diet should be provided and prolonged immobilization avoided whenever possible.

Supplied: Each mL contains: testosterone cypionate 100 mg. Nonmedicinal ingredients: benzyl alcohol and benzyl benzoate in cottonseed oil. Vials of 10 mL.

Store at room temperature. Warming and shaking the vial should redissolve any crystals that may have formed during storage at temperatures lower than recommended.

DEPROIC® Ⓟ

Technilab

Valproic Acid

Anticonvulsant

Pharmacology: Valproic acid exhibits anticonvulsant properties. While the exact mechanism of action is unknown, several investigators have proposed that the anticonvulsive effect of valproic acid can be related to increased gamma-amino-butyric acid (GABA) levels in the brain. The effect on the neuronal membrane is unknown. After oral administration, valproic acid is rapidly absorbed, reaching peak serum levels within 1 to 4 hours. Salts of valproate are converted into valproic acid in the digestive tract.

Valproate disappears from the blood in a biexponential manner indicating a 2-compartment pharmacokinetic model. The terminal serum half-life is about 6 to 16 hours. The shorter half-life is usually observed in epileptic patients receiving long-term therapy with some other antiepileptic drugs. A slight delay in the absorption of sodium valproate is observed if it is taken after ingestion of meals, but this does not affect the total absorption. Valproic acid (sodium valproate) is rapidly distributed throughout the body and is strongly bound (90%) to human plasma proteins. Dose increases may result in decreases in the extent of protein binding and variable changes in clearance and elimination of valproic acid. The therapeutic plasma concentration range is about 50 to 100 μg/mL. Occasional patients may be controlled with serum levels lower or higher than this range. A good correlation has not been established between daily dose, serum level and therapeutic effect.

Elimination of valproic acid and its metabolites is principally by urinary excretion, with small amounts expelled in the feces and expired air. Only 1 to 3% of the administered dose is found as unchanged drug in the urine. Valproate is excreted in the urine after glucuronidation or beta oxidation to 2-propylene-2-pentanoic acid and 2-propyl-3-ketopentanoic acid in the liver. The principal metabolite formed in the liver is the glucuronide conjugate.

See Warnings regarding statement on fatal hepatic dysfunction.

Indications: Effective as sole or adjunctive therapy in the treatment of simple or complex absence seizures, including "petit mal", and is useful in primary generalized seizures with tonic-clonic manifestations. Valproic acid may also be used adjunctively in patients with multiple seizure types which include either absence or tonic-clonic seizures.

In accordance with the International Classification of Seizures, simple absence is defined as a very brief clouding of the sensorium or loss of consciousness (lasting usually 2 to 15 seconds), accompanied by certain generalized epileptic discharges without other detectable clinical signs. Complex absence is the term used when other signs are also present.

Contraindications: Patients with hepatic disease or significant dysfunction. It is contraindicated in patients who have shown hypersensitivity to this drug or any of its components.

Warnings: Hepatic failure resulting in fatalities has been reported in patients treated with valproic acid. These incidences usually have occurred during the first 6 months of treatment with valproic acid. A study of valproate use in the US in nearly 400 000 patients from 1978 through 1984, has shown that children under 2 years of age who received the drug as part of a multiple anticonvulsant therapy were at greatest risk (nearly 20 fold increase) of developing fatal hepatotoxicity. These patients typically had other medical conditions such as congenital metabolic disorders, mental retardation or organic brain disease, in addition to severe seizure disorders. The risk in this age group decreased considerably when valproic acid was used as monotherapy.

Similarly, patients aged 3 to 10 years were somewhat at greater risk if they receive multiple anticonvulsant therapy, than those who received valproic acid as monotherapy. Generally, the risk declines with increasing age. No deaths were reported in patients over 10 years old receiving valproic acid alone.

If valproic acid is to be used in children 2 years of age or younger, it should be used with **extreme caution** and as a sole agent. The clinician should watch such patients with particular care, especially in the early months of valproate therapy. The benefits of seizure control should be weighed against the risk.

Serious or fatal hepatotoxicity may be preceded by nonspecific symptoms such as loss of seizure control, vomiting, lethargy, anorexia, malaise and weakness. Patients and parents should be instructed to report such symptoms. Because of the nonspecific nature of some of the early signs, during valproic acid treatment, hepatotoxicity should be suspected in patients who become unwell, other than through obvious causes.

Liver function tests should be performed prior to beginning therapy, 3 to 5 weeks after initiation of therapy, approximately monthly during the first 6 months of use and periodically thereafter. However, physicians should not rely totally on serum biochemistry since liver function tests may not be abnormal in all instances, but should also consider the results of careful interim medical history and physical examination. When administering valproic acid to patients with a prior history of hepatic disease, exercise caution. Patients with various unusual congenital disorders, those with severe seizure disorders accompanied by mental retardation, and those with organic brain disease may be at particular risk.

In high risk patients, it may be useful to monitor serum fibrinogen and albumin for decreases in concentration and serum ammonia for increases in concentration. If changes occur, valproic acid should be discontinued. The dosage should be titrated to and maintained at the lowest dose that produces optimal seizure control.

In presence of significant hepatic dysfunction suspected or apparent, valproic acid should be discontinued immediately. In some cases, hepatic dysfunction has progressed in spite of discontinuation of the drug. The frequency of adverse reactions, particularly elevated liver enzymes, may increase with increasing dose. Therefore, the benefit gained by improved seizure control by increasing dosage must be weighed against the increasing incidence of adverse effects sometimes observed at higher dosages.

Pregnancy: According to recent reports in the medical literature, valproic acid may produce teratogenicity in the offspring of human females receiving the drug during pregnancy. The incidence of neural tube defects in the fetus may be increased in mothers receiving valproic acid during the first trimester of pregnancy. Based upon a single report, it was estimated that the risk of valproic acid exposed women having a child with spina bifida is approximately 1.2%. This risk is similar to that which applies to nonepileptic women who have had children with neural tube defects (anencephaly and spina bifida).

Animal studies have demonstrated that valproic acid produced teratogenic effects. Human studies have demonstrated placental transfer of the drug.

Multiple reports indicate an association between the use of antiepileptic drugs and an elevated incidence of birth defects in children born to epileptic women taking such medication during pregnancy. The incidence of congenital malformations in the general population is approximately 2%, in children of women administered anticonvulsant medication during pregnancy, this incidence may be increased 2- to 3-fold. The increase is largely due to specific defects such as congenital malformations of the heart, cleft lip and/or palate and neural tube defects. Nevertheless, the great majority of mothers receiving anticonvulsant medications during pregnancy deliver normal infants.

Data are more extensive with respect to phenytoin and phenobarbital, but these drugs are also the most commonly prescribed anticonvulsant. Some reports indicate a possible interaction with the use of other antiepileptic drugs, including trimethadione, paramethadione and valproic acid. However, the possibility also exists that other factors such as genetic predisposition or the epileptic condition itself, may contribute to, or may be mainly responsible for the higher incidence of birth defects.

Antiepileptic drugs should not be discontinued in patients to whom the drug is administered to prevent major seizures, because of the strong possibility of precipitating status epilepticus with attendant hypoxia and risks to both the mother and the unborn child. The risks of discontinuing drugs given for minor seizures prior to or during pregnancy should be weighed against the risk of congenital defects in the particular case, taking into account the family history.

Epileptic women of childbearing age should be encouraged to seek the counsel of their physician and should report promptly to him the onset of pregnancy. Where the necessity for continued use of antiepileptic medication is in doubt, appropriate consultation is indicated.

Lactation: Valproic acid is secreted in breast milk. Concentrations in breast milk have been reported to be 1 to 10% of maternal serum concentrations. As a general rule, nursing should not be undertaken while a patient is receiving valproic acid treatment.

Fertility: Chronic toxicity studies performed in juvenile and adult rats and dogs, demonstrated testicular atrophy and reduced spermatogenesis at doses greater than 200 mg/kg/day in rats and 90 mg/kg/day in dogs. Segment I fertility studies in rats have shown that doses up to 350 mg/kg/day for 60 days have no effect on fertility. The effect of valproic acid on the development of the testes and on sperm production and fertility in humans is unknown.

Long-term toxicity studies in rats and mice have demonstrated a possible risk of carcinogenicity.

Precautions: Hepatic Dysfunction: See Contraindications and Warnings.

General: As valproic acid inhibits the secondary phase of platelet aggregation and produced thrombocytopenia, platelet counts and bleeding time determination are recommended before beginning treatment and at periodic intervals. It is recommended that patients receiving valproic acid be monitored for platelet count prior to any surgical intervention. Clinical evidence of hemorrhage, bruising or a disorder of homeostasis/coagulation is an indication for reduction of valproic acid dosage or withdrawal of therapy pending investigation.

Valproic acid should be discontinued if serum ammonia increases. Hyperammonemia with or without lethargy or coma has been reported and may be present in the absence of abnormal liver function tests.

Because valproic acid may interact with other antiepileptic drugs, periodic serum level determinations of concurrently administered antiepileptics are recommended during the early part of therapy (see Drug Interactions). There have been reports of breakthrough seizures occurring with the combination of valproic acid and phenytoin.

Valproic acid is partially eliminated in the urine as a ketone-containing metabolite which may lead to a false interpretation of the urine ketone test.

The alteration of thyroid function tests associated with valproic acid has been reported. The clinical significance of this is unknown.

Valproic acid may potentiate CNS depression, especially when combined with another CNS depressant such as alcohol.

Occupational Hazards: Patients should be advised not to engage in potentially hazardous occupations such as driving a car or operating dangerous machinery until it is known that they do not become drowsy from the drug.

Drug Interactions: **Valproic acid may potentiate the CNS depressant action of alcohol.**

Phenobarbital: **Valproic acid use may result in an increase in serum phenobarbital levels, by impairment of nonrenal clearance. This phenomenon can result in severe CNS depression. The combination of valproic acid and phenobarbital has also been reported to produce CNS depression without significant elevations of barbiturate or valproic acid serum levels. Patients receiving concomitant barbiturate therapy should be closely monitored for neurological toxicity. Serum barbiturate drug levels should be obtained, if possible, and the barbiturate dosage decreased, if indicated.**

Primidone: Primidone is metabolized into a barbiturate, and therefore, may also be involved in a similar or identical interaction.

Phenytoin: **There is conflicting evidence regarding the interaction of valproic acid with phenytoin (see Precautions, General). It is not known if there is a change in unbound (free) phenytoin serum levels. Phenytoin dosage should be adjusted as required by the clinical situation.**

Clonazepam: **Absence status was observed with combination treatment of valproic acid and clonazepam.**

Caution is recommended when valproic acid is administered with drugs affecting coagulation e.g., ASA and warfarin (see Adverse Effects).

Adverse Effects: The most commonly reported adverse reactions are gastrointestinal symptoms; nausea, vomiting and indigestion. Since valproic acid is generally used in conjunction with other antiepileptics, in most cases it is not possible to determine whether the adverse reactions mentioned are due to valproic acid alone or to the combination of drugs.

Gastrointestinal: Nausea, vomiting and indigestion are the most commonly reported side effects at the initiation of therapy. In general, these effects are usually transient, only rarely requiring discontinuation of therapy. Diarrhea, abdominal cramps and constipation have also been reported. Anorexia with some weight loss and increased appetite with some weight gain have also been observed.

CNS: Effects such as sedation have been noted in patients receiving valproic acid alone, but is most often reported during combination therapy. Sedation can generally be corrected upon reduction of other antiepileptic medication. Ataxia, headache, nystagmus, diplopia, asterixis, ''spots before the eyes'', tremor, dysarthria, dizziness and incoordination have been noted rarely. Rare cases of coma have been reported in patients receiving valproic acid alone or in conjunction with phenobarbital.

Dermatological: Transient hair loss has been observed. Skin rash and petechiae have rarely been noted.

Endocrine: There have been reports of irregular menses and secondary amenorrhea in patients receiving valproic acid. Abnormal thyroid function tests have been reported (see Precautions).

Psychiatric: Emotional upset, depression, psychosis, behavioral deterioration, aggression and hyperactivity have been reported.

Musculoskeletal: Weakness has been reported.

Hematopoietic: Thrombocytopenia has been reported. Valproic acid inhibits the second phase of platelet aggregation (see Precautions). This may be reflected in altered bleeding time. Bruising, hematoma formation and frank hemorrhage have been reported. Relative lymphocytosis and hypofibrinogenemia have been noted. Leukopenia and eosinophilia have also been observed. Anemia and bone marrow suppression have been reported.

Hepatic: Minor elevations of transaminases (e.g., AST and ALT) and LDH are frequent and appear to be dose related. Occasionally, laboratory tests also show increases in serum bilirubin and abnormal changes in other liver function tests. These results may reflect potentially serious hepatotoxicity (see Warnings).

Metabolic: Hyperammonemia (see Precautions). Hyperglycinemia has been reported and associated with a fatal outcome in a patient with pre-existing nonketotic hyperglycinemia.

Pancreatic: There have been reports of acute pancreatitis occurring in association with valproic acid therapy.

Other: Adverse reactions such as edema of the extremities have been reported.

Overdose: Symptoms: One overdose case with valproic acid has been reported after ingestion of up to 36 g in combination with phenobarbital and phenytoin. The patient presented in deep coma (responding only to deeply painful stimuli). An EEG recording showed diffused slowing, compatible with the state of consciousness. The patient gradually became more alert and made an uneventful recovery.

Treatment: Naloxone has been reported to reverse the CNS depressant effects in valproic acid overdose. Because naloxone could theoretically reverse the antiepileptic activity of valproic acid it should be used with caution in the treatment of valproic acid overdose.

Valproic acid is absorbed very rapidly, consequently gastric lavage may be of limited value. General supportive measures should be applied with particular attention to the prevention of hypovolemia and the maintenance of adequate urinary output.

Dosage: Administered orally. The recommended initial dosage is 15 mg/kg/day, increasing at 1-week intervals by 5 to 10 mg/kg/day until seizures are controlled or side effects preclude further increases. The maximal recommended dosage is 60 mg/kg/day. When the total daily dose exceeds 250 mg, it should be given in a divided regimen (see Table I). A 500 mg enteric-coated capsule may be substituted for two 250 mg capsules.

The frequency of adverse reactions (particularly elevated liver enzymes) may increase with increasing dose. Therefore, the benefit gained by improved seizure control must be weighed against the increased incidence of adverse reactions.

Table I—Deproic

Initial Doses by Weight (based on 15 mg/kg/day)

Weight kg	Total Daily Dose (mg)	Number of 250 mg Capsules or Teaspoonsful of Syrup: Dose 1	Dose 2	Dose 3
10-24.9	250	0	0	1
25-39.9	500	1	0	1
40-59.9	750	1	1	1
60-74.9	1 000	1	1	2
75-89.9	1 250	2	1	2

As the dosage of valproic acid is raised, blood level concentrations of phenobarbital and/or phenytoin may be affected (see Precautions).

Patients who experience gastrointestinal irritation may benefit from administration of the drug with food or by a progressive increase of the dose from an initial low level. The capsules should be swallowed without chewing to avoid local irritation of the mouth and throat.

Supplied: Capsules: 250 mg: Each orange-colored, soft gelatin capsule, imprinted with black ink, contains: valproic acid 250 mg. Nonmedicinal ingredients: corn oil, FD&C yellow #6, gelatin, glycerin, methylparaben, propylparaben, purified water, sorbitol and titanium dioxide. White, round, HDPE bottles of 100 and 500.

500 mg: Each pale yellow, oval, soft gelatin enteric-coated capsule contains: valproic acid 500 mg. Nonmedicinal ingredients: D&C yellow #10, FD&C yellow #6, gelatin, glycerin, hydroxypropylmethylcellulose, light mineral oil, methacrylic acid copolymer, purified water, simethicone, sodium hydroxide, talc, titanium dioxide and triethyl citrate. White, round, HDPE bottles of 100 and 500.

Syrup: Each 5 mL of red syrup contains: the equivalent of valproic acid 250 mg, as the sodium salt. Nonmedicinal ingredients: artificial flavoring, glycerin, methylparaben, propylparaben, purified water, sorbitol and sucrose. Bottles of 500 mL.

Store between 15 and 30°C. Preserve in tight container.

Reviewed 1998

DEQUADIN® Preparations

Roberts

Dequalinium Chloride

Antibacterial—Antifungal

Indications: For the treatment of mouth and throat infections.

Contraindications: Dequalinium chloride sensitivity.

Precautions: If irritation persists or sensitization occurs, discontinue use and consult a physician.

Adverse Effects: Allergic reactions have been reported rarely.

Dosage: Lozenges: 1 lozenge sucked slowly every 2 or 3 hours. In severe infections, increase frequency of administration.

Oral Paint: Apply freely to infected area, every 2 or 3 hours or as directed by the physician.

Supplied: Lozenges: Each lozenge contains: dequalinium chloride 0.25 mg in a flavored sucrose base. Available in orange, lemon and strawberry flavors. Energy: 18.0 kJ (4.29 kcal). Sodium: <1 mmol (0.273 mg). Strawberry-flavored lozenges contain erythrosine. Gluten- and tartrazine-free. Tubes of 20.

Oral Paint: Each bottle contains: dequalinium chloride 0.5% w/v in a propylene glycol base. Also contains alcohol 3.8% v/v. Cartoned bottles of 25 mL.

DERMASONE® Preparations Ⓟ

Technilab

Clobetasol 17-Propionate

Topical Anti-inflammatory Steroid

Supplied: Cream: Each g contains: clobetasol 17-propionate 0.05% w/w in a cream base. Nonmedicinal ingredients:

Dermasone Preparations (cont'd)

ceteareth-20, chlorocresol, citric acid, glyceryl stearate, polyethylene glycol, propylene glycol, purified water, sodium citrate and stearyl alcohol. Aluminum tubes of 15 and 50 g. Polypropylene jars of 450 g. Store between 15 and 30°C.

Ointment: Each g contains: clobetasol 17-propionate 0.05% w/w in an ointment base. Nonmedicinal ingredients: light mineral oil and petrolatum. Aluminum tubes of 15 and 50 g. Polypropylene jars of 450 g. Store between 15 to 30°C.

Scalp Lotion: Each mL contains: clobetasol 17-propionate 0.05% w/w. Nonmedicinal ingredients: carbomer, isopropyl alcohol, purified water and triethanolamine. Bottles of 20 and 60 mL.

DERMAZIN™ Ⓟ

Pharmascience

Silver Sulfadiazine

Topical Antibacterial

Supplied: Each g of cream contains: silver sulfadiazine 1% in a hydrophilic cream base. Jars of 250 and 400. Tubes of 30 and 50 g. Store in a cool place away from light.

DERMOVATE® Ⓟ

Glaxo Wellcome

Clobetasol 17-Propionate

Topical Corticosteroid

Pharmacology: The corticosteroids are a class of compounds comprising steroid hormones secreted by the adrenal cortex and their synthetic analogs. In pharmacologic doses, corticosteroids are used primarily for their anti-inflammatory and/or immunosuppressive effects. Topical corticosteroids such as clobetasol are effective in the treatment of corticosteroid-responsive dermatoses primarily because of their anti-inflammatory, antipruritic, and vasoconstrictive actions. However, while the physiologic, pharmacologic and clinical effects of the corticosteroids are well known, the exact mechanisms of their actions in each disease are uncertain.

Clobetasol has been shown to have topical and systemic pharmacologic and metabolic effects characteristic of the corticosteroid class of drugs.

Indications: Cream and Ointment: For the topical therapy of recalcitrant corticosteroid-responsive dermatoses, including severe cases of psoriasis (excluding widespread plaque psoriasis) and eczematous dermatitis. Scalp Lotion: application is indicated in the topical therapy of recalcitrant corticosteroid-responsive dermatoses of the scalp, including recalcitrant cases of psoriasis and seborrheic dermatitis.

Contraindications: Rosacea, acne vulgaris, perioral dermatitis or perianal and genital pruritus. These preparations are contraindicated also in primarily infected bacterial or fungal skin lesions if no anti-infective agent is used simultaneously, in primary cutaneous viral infections (i.e., herpes simplex, vaccinia and varicella) and in tuberculous skin lesions. Clobetasol should not be used in patients who are hypersensitive to any of the components of the preparation.

Warnings: Use with caution on lesions close to the eye. Care is needed to ensure that the preparation does not enter the eye as glaucoma may result. Posterior subcapsular cataracts have been reported following systemic use of corticosteroids.

When used over extensive areas for prolonged periods, it is possible that sufficient absorption may take place to give rise to adrenal suppression. Therefore, it is advisable to use clobetasol for brief periods only and to discontinue its use as soon as the lesion has resolved. No more than 50 g of the cream or ointment or 50 mL of the scalp application should be used per week.

Patients should be advised to inform subsequent physicians of their prior use of corticosteroids.

Precautions: Children: Because the safety and effectiveness has not been established in children, its use in this age group is not recommended.

The face, more than other areas of the body, may exhibit atrophic changes after prolonged treatment with potent topical corticosteroids. This must be borne in mind when treating such conditions as psoriasis, discoid lupus erythematosus and severe eczema.

Prolonged use of topical corticosteroids may produce atrophy of the skin and of subcutaneous tissues. If this is noted, the use of the product should be discontinued.

Although hypersensitivity reactions are rare with topically applied steroids, the drug should be discontinued and appropriate therapy initiated if there are signs of hypersensitivity.

Long-term continuous therapy should be avoided where possible as adrenal suppression can occur even without occlusion. Significant systemic absorption may occur when corticosteroids are applied over large areas of the body, especially under occlusive dressings. Because the degree of absorption of clobetasol when applied under occlusive dressing has not been measured, its use in this fashion is not recommended.

Topical steroids may be hazardous in psoriasis for a number of reasons including rebound relapses, development of tolerance, risk of generalized pustular psoriasis and development of local or systemic toxicity due to impaired barrier function of the skin. If used in psoriasis, careful patient supervision is important.

Appropriate antimicrobial therapy should be used whenever treating inflammatory lesions which have become infected. Any spread of infection requires withdrawal of topical corticosteroid therapy and systemic administration of anti-microbial agents.

In cases of bacterial infections of the skin, appropriate antibacterial agents should be used as primary therapy. If it is considered necessary, the topical corticosteroid may be used as an adjunct to control inflammation, erythema and itching. If a symptomatic response is not noted within a few days to a week, the local application of corticosteroid should be discontinued until the infection is brought under control. Bacterial infection is encouraged by the warm, moist conditions induced by occlusive dressings, and the skin should be cleansed before a fresh dressing is applied.

Pregnancy and *Lactation:* Topical administration of corticosteroids to pregnant animals can cause abnormalities of fetal development. The relevance of this finding to human beings has not been established. However, the administration of this drug during pregnancy and lactation should only be considered if the expected benefit to the mother is greater than any possible risk to the fetus. Drugs of this class should not be used extensively in pregnant patients in large amounts or for prolonged periods of time.

Clobetasol scalp applications should not be used near an open flame.

Adverse Effects: As with other topical corticosteroids, prolonged use of large amounts of clobetasol or treatment of extensive areas can result in sufficient systemic absorption to produce the features of hypercorticism.

Provided the weekly dosage is less than 50 g in adults, any suppression of the hypothalamic-pituitary axis (HPA-axis) is likely to be transient with a rapid return to normal values once the short course of steroid therapy has ceased.

Prolonged and extensive treatment with highly active corticosteroid preparations may cause local atrophic changes in the skin such as thinning, striae, and dilatation of the superficial blood vessels, particularly when occlusive dressings are used, or when skin folds are involved. Local burning, irritation, itching, dryness of the skin, telangiectasia, acneform eruptions, change in pigmentation, secondary infection, hypertrichosis and atrophy of skin and s.c. tissue have also been observed following topical corticosteroid therapy. Exacerbation of symptoms may occur.

In rare instances, treatment of psoriasis with corticosteroids (or their withdrawal) is thought to have provoked the pustular form of the disease.

Clobetasol preparations are usually well tolerated, but if signs of hypersensitivity appear, application should be stopped immediately.

Overdose: Symptoms and Treatment: Acute overdosage is very unlikely to occur. However, in the case of chronic overdosage or misuse, the features of hypercorticism may appear. Treatment should be discontinued in this case.

Dosage: Cream and Ointment: Apply sparingly to cover the affected area, and gently rub into the skin. Frequency of application is 2 to 3 times daily according to the severity of the condition. The total dose applied should not exceed 50 g weekly.

Scalp Application: Apply once or twice daily to the affected areas of the scalp and rub in gently. The total dose applied should not exceed 50 mL weekly.

Therapy should be discontinued if no response is noted after a week or as soon as the lesion heals. It is advisable to use clobetasol for brief periods only.

Supplied: Cream: Each g contains: clobetasol 17-propionate 0.05% w/w in a white water miscible cream base. Nonmedicinal ingredients: beeswax substitute, cetostearyl alcohol, chlorocresol, citric acid hydrous, glyceryl monostearate, propylene glycol, purified water and sodium citrate. Paraben- and lanolin-free. Do not dilute the cream. Tubes of 15 and 50 g. Store below 30°C.

Ointment: Each g contains: clobetasol 17-propionate 0.05% w/w in a water repellent ointment base. Nonmedicinal ingredients: propylene glycol, sorbitan sesquiolate and white soft parrafin. Tubes of 15 and 50 g. Store below 30°C.

Scalp Lotion: Each mL of hydroalcoholic solution for application on the scalp contains: clobetasol 17-propionate 0.05% in an aqueous alcohol base. Nonmedicinal ingredients: carbopol 934P, isopropyl alcohol, purified water and sodium hydroxide. Bottles of 20 and 60 mL. Store below 30°C.

DESENEX®

Novartis Consumer Health

Undecylenic Acid—Zinc Undecylenate

Antifungal

Pharmacology: Undecylenic acid is an antifungal agent, effective in the treatment of superficial fungal infections of the skin, such as tinea pedis (athlete's foot), tinea cruris (jock itch) and tina corporis due to T. rubrum, T. mentagrophytes and E. flocossum, exclusive of nails and hair area.

Indications: For the treatment and prevention of superficial fungus infections of the skin, primarily tinea pedis (athlete's foot). Relieves itching, burning and irritation.

Contraindications: Hypersensitivity to any of the components.

Precautions: For external use only. If symptoms do not improve in 2 to 4 weeks or skin irritation occurs, a physician should be consulted. Do not use on children under 2 years of age, except under direction of a physician. Avoid inhaling, and contact with eyes or mucous membranes. Patients with impaired circulation including diabetes should consult a physician before use.

Dosage: Cleanse affected areas with soap and water and dry thoroughly. Apply a thin layer over affected area morning and night for full treatment period of 4 weeks for athlete's foot and 2 weeks for jock itch. For prevention of athlete's foot, cleanse skin with soap and water, dry thoroughly and apply a thin layer to feet, once or twice daily. Pay special attention to spaces between toes. Wear well fitting ventilated shoes and cotton socks.

Supplied: Foot Powder: Each container of powder contains: total undecylenate 25% from zinc undecylenate and undecylenic acid. Nonmedicinal ingredients: fragrance and talc. Containers of 40 and 80 g.

Ointment: Each tube of ointment contains: total undecylenate 22.3% from zinc undecylenate and undecylenic acid. Nonmedicinal ingredients: fragrance, glycolstearate, lanolin, methyl parahydroxybenzoate, petrolatum, polyethyleneglycol monostearate, polyoxyethylene laurate, propyl parahydroxybenzoate, sorbitol, stearic acid, triethanolamine and water. Tubes of 30 g.

Spray-on Powder: Each aerosol of spray-on powder contains: total undecylenate 19% from zinc undecylenate and undecylenic acid. Nonmedicinal ingredients: fragrance, isopropyl myristate, menthol, talc, triethanolamine and isobutane (propellant). Aerosols of 75 g.

Reviewed 1997

DESFERAL® Ⓟ

Novartis Pharmaceuticals

Deferoxamine Mesylate

Iron and Aluminum Chelating Agent

Pharmacology: Deferoxamine is a chelating agent which forms complexes predominantly with trivalent iron and aluminum ions; it is thus of value in the treatment of acute/chronic iron intoxication, and also chronic aluminum overload in dialysis patients with end-stage renal failure (ESRF).

Deferoxamine complexes with iron to form ferrioxamine, a stable chelate, which cannot take part in further chemical reactions. It can also mobilize and chelate tissue-bound aluminum, forming an aluminoxamine complex. Both complexes—ferrioxamine and aluminoxamine—are freely soluble in water and are readily excreted through the kidneys. Excreted ferrioxamine gives the urine a characteristic reddish color. Some of the deferoxamine-metal complexes are also excreted in feces.

Theoretically chelation occurs on a 1:1 molar basis, hence 100 parts by weight of deferoxamine can bind approximately 8.5 and 4.1 parts by weight of trivalent iron and aluminum respectively.

Although primarily effective in raising iron and aluminum excretion, deferoxamine may also cause a slight increase in the excretion of sodium and calcium.

Pharmacokinetics: Deferoxamine is very poorly absorbed orally but well absorbed by the i.m. and s.c. routes. The serum protein-binding rate is less than 10%. It is distributed throughout all body fluids and is excreted through the kidneys by glomerular filtration and tubular secretion. Metabolites were isolated and identified from the urine of patients being treated for iron overload. The metabolism reactions to occur were transamination and oxidation yielding an acid metabolite, beta-oxidation also yielding an acid metabolite, decarboxylation and N-hydroxylation yielding natural metabolites.

In healthy subjects and in patients with transfusion-induced iron overload, plasma concentrations of between 80 and 130 μmol/L were recorded 3 minutes after an i.v. injection of deferoxamine (10 mg/kg), these concentrations falling to one-half within 5 to 10 minutes and thereafter declining more slowly. This rapid fall in the concentration is due not only to distribution and excretion of the active substance but also both to formation of the iron complex ferrioxamine (which commences within a few minutes and the extent of which depends on the individual's iron status) and to metabolic transformation.

During continuous s.c. or i.v. infusion of deferoxamine (100 mg/kg in 24 mL sterile water at a rate of 1 mL/h), the plasma concentrations of deferoxamine and ferrioxamine in healthy subjects rose, depending on the subject's individual iron status (serum ferritin concentration), to a plateau after 6 or, more frequently, after 12 hours, i.e. to maximum levels of 20 μmol/L for deferoxamine and 2.75 μmol/L for ferrioxamine. The corresponding values in patients were 8.3 μmol/L for deferoxamine and 12.9 μmol/L for ferrioxamine. The 48-hour urinary excretion averaged 118 μmol in the healthy subjects and 836 μmol in the patients. In patients with hemochromatosis, the increase in iron excretion occurring in response to deferoxamine was roughly just as high in the feces as in the urine.

Within 12 hours after deferoxamine had been administered to 20 volunteers, 33.1% of the dose was excreted in the urine (the bulk of it in the first 3 hours) in the form of deferoxamine and ferrioxamine and the remainder in the form of metabolites; the corresponding figure in a patient with hemochromatosis was 60.5% of the dose.

There are reported cases where deferoxamine was diluted with water and given by mouth or stomach tube after gastric aspiration and lavage in the treatment of acute iron overload. The aqueous deferoxamine solution was left in the stomach to bind unabsorbed iron in the gastrointestinal tract to prevent further absorption. Note however, that the efficacy of oral deferoxamine for this purpose is not clearly established.

In ESRF dialysis patients who received 40 mg/kg deferoxamine infused i.v. over 1 hour, plasma concentration at the end of infusion was 152 μmol/L (85.2 μg/mL) when the infusion was given between dialysis sessions. Plasma concentrations of deferoxamine were between 13 and 27% lower when the infusion was administered during dialysis. In all cases, concentrations of ferrioxamine were approximately 7 μmol/L (4.3 μg/mL); and for aluminoxamine 2 to 3 μmol/L (1.2 to 1.8 μg/mL). After infusion was discontinued, plasma concentration of deferoxamine decreased rapidly with a half-life of 20 minutes. A smaller fraction of the dose was eliminated with a longer half-life of 14 hours. The plasma concentrations of aluminoxamine continued to increase for up to 48 hours after infusion and reached values of approximately 7 μmol/L (4 μg/mL). Following dialysis, the plasma concentration of aluminoxamine dropped to 2.2 μmol/L (1.3 μg/mL).

During peritoneal dialysis deferoxamine is absorbed if administered in the dialysis fluid.

Indications: Acute iron intoxication; chronic iron overload due to transfusion-dependent anemias; diagnosis of aluminum overload (deferoxamine infusion test); chronic aluminum overload in patients with ESRF under maintenance dialysis.

In cases of acute iron intoxication, deferoxamine is an adjunct to, and not a substitute for, standard therapeutic measures which may include: induction of emesis; gastric lavage; maintenance of clear airways; control of peripheral vascular failure, correction of acidosis.

Contraindications: Patients with a known sensitivity to deferoxamine, except where desensitization is successful.

Warnings: Patients may develop sensitivity reactions (see Contraindications).

In patients with severe renal failure, caution is indicated as the deferoxamine-metal complexes are excreted mainly via the kidneys. Elimination of chelated iron and aluminum can be increased by dialysis.

In patients suffering from iron overload, it has been reported that infections (including septicemia), especially with Y. enterocolitica and Y. pseudotuberculosis, may be promoted by deferoxamine. If a patient under treatment with deferoxamine develops fever accompanied by acute enteritis/enterocolitis, diffuse abdominal pain or pharyngitis the treatment should be temporarily withdrawn, appropriate bacteriological tests performed, and suitable antibiotic therapy instituted at once. **This therapy should include special coverage for Yersinia organisms.** After the infection has cleared, treatment with deferoxamine can be resumed.

In patients undergoing maintenance hemodialysis while receiving deferoxamine for aluminum and/or iron overload, rare cases of mucormycosis have been reported, a severe fungal infection that can be fatal. However, a causal relationship to the drug has not been established. If any of the suspected signs or symptoms are observed, deferoxamine treatment should be discontinued, mycological tests performed and appropriate treatment instituted immediately. Mucormycosis may also occur in dialysis patients who are not receiving deferoxamine therapy, indicating that other factors, e.g. a compromised immune system, may play a role in the development of this infection.

During chronic toxicity tests in dogs, high doses of deferoxamine (>200 mg/kg daily) were associated with cataracts. However, cataracts have rarely been observed in humans who receive deferoxamine over prolonged periods.

There have been reports of visual disturbances, hearing loss and audiometric abnormalities occurring in patients receiving deferoxamine treatment, particularly where the doses used were higher than those recommended and/or where the serum ferritin levels were low. The visual disturbances and hearing loss returned to normal in several cases when the drug was discontinued. However in some cases, a residual effect remained. Renal failure patients receiving maintenance dialysis having low ferritin levels may be particularly prone to adverse reactions.

Visual symptoms have been reported after single doses of deferoxamine. Complete ophthalmological examination, audiological testing and studies of visual evoked potential should be carried out before the start of long-term deferoxamine treatment as well as at regular intervals preferably every 3 months, during the time that deferoxamine treatment is continued.

When low-dose therapy is used the risk of adverse reactions is reduced. If disturbances of vision and/or hearing occur, treatment with deferoxamine should be discontinued in order to further the chances that disturbances of vision and/or hearing will prove reversible. If treatment with deferoxamine is subsequently resumed using a reduced dosage, ophthalmological and auditory examination/testing should be performed at more frequent intervals. It is always important to reconsider the benefit/risk ratio when deferoxamine treatment is resumed after the occurrence of an adverse reaction.

Respiratory distress syndrome has been reported in patients with acute iron intoxication and also in thalassemic patients treated with excessively high doses of i.v. deferoxamine for more than 1 day. The daily dose should not exceed 80 mg/kg up to a maximum of 6 g. Treatment should be terminated at the first signs of respiratory complications (see Dosage).

In patients with aluminum-related encephalopathy, high doses of deferoxamine may exacerbate neurological dysfunction (seizures), probably due to an increase in circulating aluminum. Deferoxamine may also precipitate the onset of dialysis dementia. Pretreatment with clonazepam is reported to provide protection against such neurological deterioration. In addition, aluminum overload treatment may decrease serum calcium and aggravate hyperparathyroidism.

It should be noted that some of the signs and symptoms reported as adverse effects may in fact be manifestations of the underlying disease (iron and/or aluminum overload).

High doses of deferoxamine and concomitant low ferritin levels during the treatment of chronic iron overload in children, have been associated with growth retardation. After reduction of the deferoxamine dose, growth velocity may resume to pretreatment levels in some patients.

Pregnancy: In animal experiments, deferoxamine has proven teratogenic. Women of childbearing potential with chronic iron and/or aluminum overload should not receive deferoxamine unless the use of an effective form of contraception, established before treatment, is continued throughout treatment and for at least the first month after treatment. Those patients reported to have received deferoxamine therapy during pregnancy have born children without any malformations. However, during pregnancy, particularly in the first trimester, deferoxamine should only be used if the hazard of acute iron intoxication is considered to be greater than the potential teratogenic hazard of deferoxamine.

Lactation: It is not known whether deferoxamine passes into the breast milk. Therefore, mothers receiving deferoxamine should not breast-feed their infants.

Precautions: Flushing of the skin, urticaria, hypotension and shock have occurred in a few patients following the rapid i.v. injection of deferoxamine. Treatment by the i.v. route should **not** exceed 15 mg/kg/h.

Pediatric patients receiving deferoxamine should be monitored for body weight and longitudinal growth every 3 months (see Warnings).

Deferoxamine may lower blood sugar, serum calcium and serum sodium and increase blood coagulability. Therefore, these parameters should be monitored during therapy, if possible.

As with all medicines, deferoxamine should be kept out of reach of children.

Drug Interactions: Concurrent treatment with deferoxamine and prochlorperazine, a phenothiazine derivative, may lead to temporary impairment of consciousness.

Where an iron-overload is associated with ascorbic acid deficiency, oral administration of vitamin C in the standard dosage (150 to 250 mg daily) may serve to enhance excretion of the iron complex in response to deferoxamine. Larger doses of vitamin C fail to produce an additional effect.

In patients with severe chronic iron overload receiving combined treatment of deferoxamine with high doses of vitamin C (more than 500 mg daily) impairment of cardiac function may be experienced; the impaired cardiac function proved reversible when the vitamin C was withdrawn. Cardiac impairment results from high doses of vitamin C which increases the labile iron within the tissues to toxic levels.

The following precautions should be taken when deferoxamine and vitamin C are to be used concomitantly: Vitamin C supplements should not be given to patients with cardiac failure. Cardiac function should be monitored before commencing and during the combined therapy of deferoxamine and vitamin C. Vitamin C therapy should be initiated only after an initial month of regular deferoxamine therapy. Vitamin C therapy should be given only if the patient is receiving deferoxamine regularly (ideally soon after setting up the pump). Daily doses of approximately 200 mg of vitamin C in adults, 100 mg of vitamin C in older children and 50 mg of vitamin C in children under 10 years, should not be exceeded.

There is evidence that aluminum intoxication causes reduced erythropoiesis. In dialysis patients with iron and/or aluminum overload receiving deferoxamine and erythropoietin, it is important to adjust the dosage of the latter when necessary. Regular monitoring of iron stores should also be conducted.

Gallium-67-imaging results may be distorted due to rapid urinary excretion of deferoxamine-bound Gallium-67. Discontinuing deferoxamine treatment 48 hours prior to scintigraphy is recommended.

Adverse Effects: Some manifestations mentioned below may also be signs or symptoms of iron and/or aluminum overload.

The following unwanted effects have been observed on rare occasions.

Hypersensitivity/Dermatological: Frequent: pain, swelling, induration, erythema, burning, pruritus, wheals and rash (urticaria) at the infusion or injection site, occasionally accompanied by fever, chills and malaise. Rare: anaphylactic/anaphylactoid reactions with or without shock, angioedema. These reactions occur mainly when the drug is infused s.c. or administered in concentrations higher than those recommended. When signs of local irritation are observed after administration of deferoxamine solution, administration of a lower concentration is recommended.

Cardiovascular: hypotension, shock, tachycardia, arrhythmias.

Respiratory: Isolated cases: adult respiratory distress syndrome with dyspnea, cyanosis and interstitial pulmonary infiltrates (see Warnings).

Neurological: dizziness, convulsions, exacerbation of neurological dysfunction in aluminum-related encephalopathy. Isolated cases: precipitation of dialysis dementia, peripheral sensory neuropathy, paresthesia (see Warnings).

Gastrointestinal: abdominal discomfort, diarrhea, nausea, vomiting.

Desferal (cont'd)

Hematological: Isolated cases: blood dyscrasias (e.g. thrombocytopenia.
Ear: auditory disturbances, hearing loss (including high-frequency sensorineural hearing loss), tinnitus (see Warnings).
Ophthalmological: retinal pigmentary abnormalities (decreased visual acuity, impaired color and night vision, vision loss), blurred vision, visual field defects, opacities of the lenses and cornea, optic neuropathy and neuritis, abnormal visual evoked potentials, scotoma.
Endocrine system: growth retardation (see Warnings).
Other: impairment of hepatic and renal function, dysuria, pyrexia, leg cramps. Isolated cases: malaise, bone pain.

Overdose: Symptoms: Since deferoxamine is available only for parenteral administration, acute intoxication is unlikely to occur.

Rapid i.v. injection of deferoxamine exceeding 15 mg/kg/h has produced flushing of the skin, urticaria, hypotension and shock (see Precautions).

Tachycardia, hypotension and gastrointestinal symptoms have occasionally developed in patients who received overdoses of deferoxamine.

Inadvertent i.v. administration of an overdose of deferoxamine may be associated with acute but transient vision loss, aphasia, agitation, headache, nausea, bradycardia and hypotension.

Respiratory distress syndrome including death has been reported following i.v. administration of excessive doses of deferoxamine (see Warnings).

High doses of deferoxamine for the treatment of chronic iron and/or aluminum overload have resulted in visual disturbances and hearing loss (see Warnings).

Treatment: There is no specific antidote. Signs and symptoms of overdosage may be eliminated by reducing the dosage or interrupting treatment. Deferoxamine is dialyzable.

Dosage: Deferoxamine should only be given parenterally. The dose should not exceed 6 g in a 24-hour period. Although deferoxamine can be given by i.m. injection, in most cases it exerts a considerably greater effect when administered by continuous infusion either i.v. (especially in cases of acute iron intoxication) or s.c. (especially in patients with chronic iron overload).
Acute Iron Intoxication: Deferoxamine is an adjunct to standard measures generally used in treating acute iron intoxication, which may include induction of emesis, gastric lavage, maintenance of clear airways, control of peripheral vascular failure and correction of acidosis.

Treatment should be adapted to the severity of intoxication, with reference to serum iron (SI) and total iron binding capacity (TIBC) which should be regularly monitored. In addition, the total amount of iron ingested and remaining in the gastrointestinal tract should be taken into account.

Deferoxamine should be instituted i.v. or i.m. in: a) All patients with SI > TIBC (> 500 μg/dL or 89.5 μmol/L), b) Any patient with SI > 350 μg/dL or 62.6 μmol/L (if TIBC is unavailable) and evidence of free iron, or c) Any patient where SI is not readily available and the patient demonstrates the signs and symptoms of iron intoxication.
Note: Leukocytosis (WBC > 15 000/mm³), hyperglycemia (blood sugar > 150 mg/dL) or diarrhea strongly suggest SI will be in the toxic range.
I.V. Infusion: The i.v. route should be used when the patient is hypotensive, in shock or major clinical findings are present. In general, provided infusion lines can be readily established and maintained, and SI levels and TIBC can be readily monitored, i.v. infusion is the preferred route of administration. Infusion rates should be adapted to the severity of intoxication. The rate of infusion should not exceed 15 mg/kg/h and should be reduced as soon as the situation permits, usually after 4 to 6 hours such that the total i.v. dose does not exceed 80 mg/kg up to a maximum of 6 g in 24 hours. Respiratory distress syndrome has been reported following i.v. administration of excessive doses of deferoxamine. Treatment should be interrupted if signs of toxicity occur.
I.M. Route: The i.m. route may be used when the patient is normotensive. When administering deferoxamine in children by the i.m. route, initially inject 90 mg/kg. This may be followed by 45 mg/kg every 4 to 12 hours, as necessary, up to a maximum of 6 g/24 hours. **In children, the maximum single injection should not exceed 1 g (2 g in adults).** Attention should be given to volume of solution injected and in small children, 2 injection sites may be required.

Duration of treatment with deferoxamine by either route will depend on the patient's condition and should be based on the SI levels and TIBC.

The effectiveness of treatment is dependent on an adequate output of urine in order to ensure that the iron complex ferrioxamine is excreted from the body. If oliguria or anuria develop, peritoneal dialysis or hemodialysis may become necessary to remove the ferrioxamine.
Chronic Iron Overload: The daily dose of deferoxamine in children and adults should be tailored to the iron burden of the individual patient as reflected by serum ferritin levels and 24-hour urinary iron excretion. These levels should be monitored daily initially and thereafter at longer intervals (but not less than once every 2 weeks).

I.V. infusions usually prove somewhat more effective than s.c. infusions, but the latter are particularly suitable for ambulant patients.

For s.c. infusions, a portable light-weight infusion pump is a practical, effective means of promoting sustained and substantial net urinary iron excretion. The usual needle used is a 25-gauge or 27-gauge, butterfly type, placed in the s.c. tissues of the anterior abdominal wall.

For the purpose of infusion treatment the average daily dose is 1 to 4 g (20 to 60 mg/kg depending upon iron load) administered s.c. or i.v. over a period of approximately 12 hours. In some cases it is possible to achieve a further increase in iron excretion by infusing the same daily dose over a 24-hour period. When administered s.c. by pump, deferoxamine should be given 4 to 7 times/week depending on the severity of the iron overload. Patients with serum ferritin levels less than 2 000 ng/mL require approximately 25 mg/kg/day. Doses of 35 mg/kg/day are required when serum ferritin levels are in the range of 2 000 ng/mL to 3 000 ng/mL. Higher doses should be administered only if the benefits outweigh the risks associated with repeated high daily doses.

For i.m. treatment when more effective s.c. infusions are not feasible, the average initial dose is 0.5 to 1 g daily, given in 1 to 2 injections. The maintenance dose will depend on the patient's iron excretion rate.

Since the iron excretion rates obtained with the above-mentioned modes of administration vary from patient to patient, one should first determine which route and dosage will yield the best results for the individual.
Diagnosis of Aluminum Overload: **Adults with ESRF:** Serum aluminum levels should be determined before and after deferoxamine administration. The deferoxamine infusion test is recommended in patients with serum aluminum levels exceeding 60 ng/mL (2.22 μmol/L) associated with serum ferritin levels above 100 ng/mL. A blood sample is taken just prior to a hemodialysis session to determine the baseline serum aluminum level. A 5 mg/kg dose of deferoxamine is given as a single, slow i.v. infusion at an infusion rate not exceeding 15 mg/kg/h, ideally during post-dialysis to avoid loss of free drug. An acceptable compromise is during the last 60 minutes of the hemodialysis session. A continuous increase in serum aluminum during the 24 to 48 hour period following administration is suggestive of aluminum overload. The test is considered positive if the serum aluminum levels increase above baseline by more than 150 ng/mL (5.55 μmol/L) when a second blood sample is taken at the start of the next hemodialysis session.

The diagnostic capability of the deferoxamine infusion test is greatly enhanced if performed in conjunction with histological and biochemical examination of a bone biopsy.
Children with ESRF: Little clinical experience has been gained to date on the use of deferoxamine in aluminum-overloaded children, the condition being rare in the very young. Dosage should be adapted from the adult dose at the discretion of the physician and adjusted for body-weight (15 to 20 mg/kg).
Chronic Aluminum Overload in Patients with ESRF: The precise dosage should be individually determined and adapted during the course of treatment.

Deferoxamine should be used in the treatment of patients having symptoms or evidence of organ dysfunction due to aluminum overload. In addition, treatment should be considered in symptomatic patients if serum aluminum levels are consistently above 60 ng/mL (2.22 μmol/L) and are associated with a positive deferoxamine infusion test (see above), particularly if bone biopsy findings present evidence of aluminum-related bone disease. Deferoxamine should be given once weekly at a 5 mg/kg dose administered as a slow i.v. infusion not exceeding 15 mg/kg/h infusion rate, ideally during post-dialysis to avoid loss of free drug. An acceptable compromise is during the last 60 minutes of the hemodialysis session.

After completing the first 3-month course of deferoxamine treatment, followed by a 4-week wash out period, the deferoxamine infusion test should be performed. If 2 successive tests performed at 1-month intervals yield an increase in serum aluminum levels of less than 75 ng/mL (2.78 μmol/L) above baseline, further treatment is not recommended.

Patients on continuous ambulatory or cyclic peritoneal dialysis: A 5 mg/kg dose once per week prior to the final daily exchange. The intraperitoneal route is recommended in these patients, however, deferoxamine is equally effective when administered i.m., by slow i.v., or s.c. infusion. The mode of administration should be individually determined and the dosage adapted during the course of therapy.
Reconstitution of Lyophilized Vials: The sterile lyophilized powder in each vial should be reconstituted under aseptic conditions just prior to dilution, only with Sterile Water for Injection as stated in Table I. The solution should appear clear and colorless to slightly yellow.

Table I—Desferal

Reconstitution Table

Vial Size	Diluent Volume to be Added to Vial	Approximate Available Volume	Actual Concentration
500 mg	2 mL	2.38 mL	210 mg/mL
2 g	8 mL	9.52 mL	210 mg/mL

Dilution of Reconstituted Solution for I.V. Infusion: Reconstituted solutions that have been prepared with Sterile Water for Injection can be further diluted with physiological saline (0.9%), glucose in water or Ringer's lactate for infusion prior to infusion. The use of freshly prepared diluted solutions is recommended. Reconstituted solutions and solutions further diluted for infusion should be used or discarded within 24 hours from reconstitution when protected from heat (i.e., store below 23°C) due to the possibility of microbial contamination during preparation. Discard any infusion solution found to have particulate matter or discoloration.
Incompatibilities: Heparin injectable solution or physiological saline (0.9%) should not be used to reconstitute the vials of lyophilized powder.

Supplied: 500 mg: Each vial of white to practically white lyophilized powder contains: deferoxamine mesylate 500 mg. Nonmedicinal ingredients: water. Vials of 7.5 mL, cartons of 10.

2 g: Each vial of white to practically white lyophilized powder contains: deferoxamine mesylate 2 g. Nonmedicinal ingredients: water. Vials of 50 mL, cartons of 4.

Protect vials from heat (store below 25°C).

Reviewed 1997

DESOCORT® Ⓟ

Galderma

Desonide

Topical Corticosteroid

Pharmacology: Desonide, like all topical corticosteroids, exhibits anti-inflammatory, antipruritic and vasoconstrictive actions.

Indications: For the relief of the inflammatory and pruritic manifestations of corticosteroid-responsive dermatoses.

Contraindications: Tuberculous, fungal and most viral lesions of the skin (including herpes simplex, vaccinia and varicella). Hypersensitivity to any of the components. Not for ophthalmic use.

Precautions: General: Systemic absorption of topical corticosteroids has produced reversible hypothalamic-pituitary-adrenal (HPA) axis suppression, manifestations of Cushing's syndrome, hyperglycemia and glucosuria in some patients.

Conditions which augment systemic absorption include the application of the more potent steroids, use over large surface areas, prolonged use, and the addition of occlusive dressings.

Therefore, patients receiving a large dose of a potent topical steroid applied to a large surface area or under an occlusive dressing should be evaluated periodically for evidence of HPA axis suppression by using the urinary free cortisol and ACTH stimulation tests. If HPA axis suppression is noted, an attempt should be made to withdraw the drug, to reduce the frequency of application, or to substitute a less potent steroid.

Recovery of HPA axis function is generally prompt and complete upon discontinuation of the drug. Infrequently, signs and symptoms of steroid withdrawal may occur, requiring supplemental systemic corticosteroids.

Children may absorb proportionally larger amounts of topical corticosteroids and thus be more susceptible to systemic toxicity (see Children).

If irritation develops, topical corticosteroids should be discontinued and appropriate therapy instituted.

In the presence of dermatological infections, the use of an appropriate antifungal or antibacterial agent should be instituted. If a favorable response does not occur promptly, the corticosteroid should be discontinued until the infection has been adequately controlled.
Laboratory Tests: The following tests may be helpful in evaluating the HPA axis suppression: urinary free cortisol test and ACTH stimulation test.
Carcinogenesis, Mutagenesis, and Impairment of Fertility: Long term animal studies have not been performed to evaluate the carcinogenic potential or the effect on fertility of desonide.
Pregnancy: Corticosteroids are generally teratogenic in laboratory animals when administered systemically at relatively low dosage levels. Desonide has been shown to be teratogenic after dermal application in laboratory animals at doses similar to recommended human dose. There are not adequate and well-controlled studies in pregnant women on teratogenic effects from topically applied corticosteroids. Therefore, topical corticosteroids should be used during pregnancy only if the potential benefit justifies the potential risk to the fetus. Drugs of this class should not be used extensively on pregnant patients, in large amounts or for prolonged periods of time.
Lactation: It is not known whether topical administration of corticosteroids could result in sufficient systemic absorption to produce detectable quantities in breast milk. Systemically administered corticosteroids are secreted into breast milk. Caution should be exercised when topical corticosteroids are administered to a nursing woman.
Children: Pediatric patients may demonstrate greater susceptibility to topical corticosteroid-induced HPA axis suppression and Cushing's syndrome than mature patients because of a larger skin surface area to body weight ratio.

Hypothalamic-pituitary-adrenal (HPA) axis suppression, Cushing's syndrome and intracranial hypertension have been reported in children receiving topical corticosteroids. Manifestations of adrenal suppression in children include linear growth retardation, delayed weight gain, low plasma cortisol levels and absence of response to ACTH stimulation. Manifestations of intracranial hypertension include bulging fontanelles, headaches and bilateral papilledema.

Administration of topical corticosteroids to children should be limited to the least amount compatible with an effective therapeutic regimen. Chronic corticosteroid therapy may interfere with the growth and development of children.

Adverse Effects: The following local adverse reactions are reported infrequently with topical corticosteroids, but may occur more frequently with the use of occlusive dressings. These reactions are listed in an approximate decreasing order of occurrence: burning, itching, irritation, dryness, folliculitis, hypertrichosis, acneiform eruptions, hypo-pigmentation, perioral dermatitis, allergic contact dermatitis, maceration of the skin, secondary infection, skin atrophy, striae and miliaria.

Overdose: Symptoms and Treatment: Topically applied corticosteroids can be absorbed in sufficient amounts to produce systemic effects (see Precautions).

Dosage: Cream: Apply a small amount to affected areas 2 or 3 times daily.
Lotion: Shake well before using. Apply a small amount to affected areas 2 or 3 times daily.
Ointment: Apply a small amount to affected areas 2 to 3 times daily.

Occlusive dressings may be used for the management of psoriasis or recalcitrant conditions.

If an infection develops, the use of occlusive dressings should be discontinued and appropriate antimicrobial therapy instituted.

Supplied: Cream: Each tube contains: desonide 0.05% in a water base cream. Nonmedicinal ingredients: emulsifying wax, isopropyl palmitate, polysorbate 60, potassium sorbate, propyl gallate, propylene glycol, purified water, sorbic acid, stearic acid and synthetic beeswax. May contain citric acid and/or sodium hydroxide to adjust pH. Tubes of 15 and 60 g. Store at room temperature (15 to 30°C).

Lotion: Each bottle contains: desonide 0.05% in a water base lotion. Nonmedicinal ingredients: cetyl alcohol, glyceryl stearate SE, methyl paraben, mineral oil, propyl paraben, propylene glycol, purified water, sodium lauryl sulfate, sorbitan monostearate, stearyl alcohol and tetrasodium EDTA. May contain sodium hydroxide and/or citric acid to adjust pH. Bottles of 60 and 120 mL. Store at room temperature (15 to 30°C).

Ointment: Each tube contains: desonide 0.05%. Nonmedicinal ingredients: mineral oil and polyethylene. Tubes of 15 and 60 g. Store at room temperature (15 to 30°C).

DESONIDE ℞
General Monograph, CPhA

see CORTICOSTEROIDS: TOPICAL

DESOXIMETASONE ℞
General Monograph, CPhA

see CORTICOSTEROIDS: TOPICAL

DESQUAM-X® Preparations ℞
Westwood-Squibb

Benzoyl Peroxide

Acne Therapy

Indications: A topical aid for the treatment of acne vulgaris.

Contraindications: Known sensitivity to any of the components.

Precautions: Avoid contact with eyes and mucous membranes. Observe patients carefully for possible local irritation or sensitivity during long-term topical therapy. Apply with caution on neck, circumoral and/or other sensitive areas. If excessive dryness or irritation occurs, discontinue use. May bleach colored fabrics.

Radiation from ultraviolet and cold quartz sources as well as abrasion may add to the desquamating effect produced by benzoyl peroxide and, therefore, should be reduced in intensity and/or frequency.

Dosage: Gel: After washing as indicated, rub Desquam-X into affected areas twice daily. In fair-skinned individuals or under excessively dry atmospheric conditions initiate therapy with 1 application daily. The desired degree of drying and peeling can be obtained by modification of the dosage schedule.
Wash: Wash affected area with Desquam-X twice daily or as directed. Very fair-skinned individuals should begin with one application daily.

Supplied: Gel: Each g of gel contains: benzoyl peroxide 5% (Desquam-X 5%) or 10% (Desquam-X 10% ℞), in a water gel base. Nonmedicinal ingredients: carbomer 940, diisopropanolamine, disodium EDTA, laureth-4 and water. Tubes of 60 g.

Wash: Each g of wash contains: benzoyl peroxide 5% (Desquam-X Wash 5%) or 10% (Desquam-X Wash 10% ℞), in a lathering base of soapless cleansers. Nonmedicinal ingredients: EDTA, magnesium aluminum silicate, methylcellulose, sodium dioctyl sulfosuccinate, sodium lauryl sulfoacetate, sodium octoxynol-2 ethane sulfonate and water. Plastic bottles of 140 g.

DESYREL® ℞
DESYREL® DIVIDOSE ℞
Bristol

Trazodone HCl

Antidepressant

Pharmacology: Trazodone is a psychoactive compound with sedative and antidepressant properties. Its mechanism of action in humans is not clear.

Trazodone is well absorbed after oral administration with peak plasma levels obtained within 0.5 to 2 hours after ingestion. Absorption is somewhat delayed and enhanced by food. The mean plasma elimination half-life is 4.4 hours for the period from 3 to 10 hours after dosing, and 7 to 8 hours for the period from 10 to 34 hours. The drug is extensively metabolized with 3 or 4 major metabolites having been identified in man. Approximately 60 to 70% of C14-labelled trazodone was found to be excreted in the urine within 2 days and 9 to 29% in feces over 60 to 100 hours. Trazodone is 89 to 95% protein bound in vitro at concentrations attained with therapeutic doses.

Indications: For the symptomatic relief of depressive illness.

Contraindications: Known hypersensitivity to trazodone.

Warnings: Trazodone has been associated with the occurrence of priapism. In approximately 33% of the cases reported, surgical intervention was required and, in a portion of these cases, permanent impairment of erectile function or impotence resulted. Male patients with prolonged or inappropriate erections should immediately discontinue the drug and consult their physician. If the condition persists for more than 24 hours, it would be advisable for the treating physician to consult a urologist or appropriate specialist in order to decide on a management approach. Recent clinical studies in patients with pre-existing cardiac disease indicate that trazodone may be arrhythmogenic in some patients in that population. Arrhythmias identified include isolated PVCs, ventricular couplets, and in 2 patients short episodes (3 to 4 beats) of ventricular tachycardia. There have also been several postmarketing reports of arrhythmias in trazodone-treated patients who have pre-existing cardiac disease and in some patients who did not have pre-existing cardiac disease. Until the results of prospective studies are available, patients with pre-existing cardiac disease should be closely monitored, particularly for cardiac arrhythmias. Trazodone is not recommended for use during the initial recovery phase of myocardial infarction.

Precautions: The possibility of suicide in depressed patients remains during treatment and until significant remission occurs. Therefore, the number of tablets prescribed at any one time should take into account this possibility, and patients with suicide ideation should never have access to large quantities of trazodone.

Episodes of grand mal seizures have been reported in a small number of patients. The majority of these patients were already receiving anticonvulsant therapy for a previously diagnosed seizure disorder.
Occupational Hazards: Since trazodone may impair the mental and/or physical abilities required for performance of potentially hazardous tasks, such as operating an automobile or machinery, the patient should be cautioned not to engage in such activities while impaired.
Drug Interactions: Trazodone may enhance the response to alcohol and the effects of barbiturates and other CNS depressants and patients should be cautioned accordingly.

Increased serum digoxin and phenytoin levels have been reported to occur in patients receiving trazodone concurrently with either of those 2 drugs. Little is known about the interaction between trazodone and general anesthetics; therefore, prior to elective surgery, trazodone should be discontinued for as long as clinically feasible.

Because it is not known whether an interaction will occur between trazodone and MAO inhibitors, administration of trazodone should be initiated very cautiously with gradual increase in dosage as required, if an MAO inhibitor is given concomitantly or has been discontinued shortly before medication with trazodone is instituted.

Trazodone may cause hypotension including orthostatic hypotension and syncope; caution is required if it is given to patients receiving antihypertensive drugs and an adjustment in the dose of the antihypertensive medication may be required.

Because of the absence of experience, concurrent administration of electro-shock therapy should be avoided.
Pregnancy and *Lactation:* Since the safety and use of trazodone in pregnant women has not been established, it should not be used in women of childbearing potential unless, in the opinion of the physician, the expected benefits justify the potential risk to the fetus. Since trazodone and/or its metabolites have been detected in the milk of lactating animals, it should not be administered to nursing mothers unless the potential benefits justify the possible risks to the child.
Children: The safety and effectiveness of trazodone in children below the age of 18 have not been established.
Laboratory Tests: It is recommended that white blood cell and differential counts should be performed in patients who develop sore throat, fever, or other signs of infection or blood dyscrasia and trazodone should be discontinued if the white blood cell or absolute neutrophil count falls below normal.
Hyperprolactinemia and Breast Tumors: There is sufficient experimental evidence to conclude that chronic administration of those psychotropic drugs, such as trazodone, which increase prolactin secretion has the potential to induce mammary neoplasms in rodents under appropriate conditions. Tissue culture experiments indicate that approximately 33% of human breast cancers are prolactin dependent in vitro, a factor of potential importance if the prescription of these drugs is contemplated in a patient with a previously detected breast cancer. Although disturbances such as galactorrhea, amenorrhea, gynecomastia and impotence have been reported, the clinical significance of elevated serum prolactin levels or increased secretion and turnover are unknown for most patients. Neither clinical studies nor epidemiological studies conducted to date, however, have shown an association between administration of these drugs and mammary tumorigenesis: available evidence is considered too limited to be conclusive at this time.

Adverse Effects: The most common adverse reactions encountered are drowsiness, nausea/vomiting, headache and

Desyrel (cont'd)

dry mouth. Adverse reactions reported include the following: Behavioral: drowsiness, fatigue, lethargy, retardation, lightheadedness, dizziness, difficulty in concentration, confusion, impaired memory, disorientation, excitement, agitation, anxiety, tension, nervousness, restlessness, insomnia, nightmares, anger, hostility and, rarely, hypomania, visual distortions, hallucinations, delusions and paranoia.
Neurologic: tremor, headache, ataxia, akathisia, muscle stiffness, slurred speech, retarded speech, vertigo, tinnitus, tingling of extremities, paresthesia, weakness, grand mal seizures (see Precautions), and, rarely impaired speech, muscle twitching, numbness, dystonia and involuntary movements.
Autonomic: dry mouth, blurred vision, diplopia, miosis, nasal congestion, constipation, sweating, urinary retention, increased urinary frequency and incontinence.
Cardiovascular: orthostatic hypotension, hypertension, tachycardia, palpitations, shortness of breath, apnea, syncope, arrhythmias, prolonged P-R interval, atrial fibrillation, bradycardia, ventricular ectopic activity (including ventricular tachycardia), myocardial infarction and cardiac arrest.
Gastrointestinal: nausea, vomiting, diarrhea, gastrointestinal discomfort, anorexia, increased appetite.
Endocrine: priapism (see Warnings), decrease and, more rarely, increase in libido, weight gain and loss, and rarely, menstrual irregularities, retrograde ejaculation and inhibition of ejaculation.
Allergic or Toxic: skin rash, itching, edema, and, rarely, hemolytic anemia, methemoglobinemia, liver enzyme alterations, obstructive jaundice, leukocytoblastic vasculitis, purpuric maculopapular eruptions, photosensitivity and fever.
Miscellaneous: aching joints and muscles, peculiar taste, hypersalivation, chest pain, hematuria, red, tired and itchy eyes.

Overdose: Symptoms: Overdosage of trazodone may cause an increase in incidence or severity of any of the reported adverse reactions, e.g. hypotension and excessive sedation. In one known suicide attempt, the patient presented with symptoms of drowsiness and weakness 3 hours after ingesting 7.5 g (12.5 times the maximum daily dose) of trazodone. Recovery was uneventful. Death by deliberate or accidental overdosage has not been reported.

Treatment: There is no specific antidote for trazodone. Management of overdosage should, therefore, be symptomatic and supportive. Any patient suspected of having taken an overdosage should be admitted to hospital as soon as possible and the stomach emptied by gastric lavage. Forced diuresis may be useful in facilitating elimination of the drug.

Dosage: Dosage should be initiated at a low level and increased gradually noting carefully the clinical response and any evidence of intolerance. It should be kept in mind that there may be a lag in the therapeutic response. Increasing the dosage rapidly does not normally shorten this latent period and may increase the incidence of side effects.
Usual Adult Dosage: The recommended initial dose is 150 to 200 mg daily, in 2 or 3 divided doses. Trazodone should be taken shortly after a meal or light snack in order to reduce the incidence of adverse reactions. The initial dose may be increased according to tolerance and response by increments of 50 mg, usually up to 300 mg daily in divided doses. In some patients, doses up to 400 mg daily and rarely up to 600 mg daily in hospitalized patients, may be required. Occurrence of drowsiness may require the administration of a major portion of the daily dose at bedtime or a reduction of dosage. Once an adequate response has been achieved, the dosage may be gradually reduced, with adjustment depending on therapeutic response. During prolonged maintenance therapy the dosage should be kept at the lowest effective level.
Geriatrics: If used in the elderly, doses not exceeding one-half the recommended adult dosage should be used, with adjustments made depending on tolerance and response.

Because safety and effectiveness in children have not been established trazodone is not recommended in the pediatric age group.

Supplied: Desyrel: 50 mg: Each orange, round, scored tablet contains: trazodone hydrochloride 50 mg. Nonmedicinal ingredients: cornstarch, dibasic calcium phosphate, FD&C yellow No. 6 aluminum lake, lactose, magnesium stearate, microcrystalline cellulose, povidone and sodium starch glycolate. May or may not contain castor oil and ethylcellulose. Bottles of 100 and 250.

100 mg: Each white, round, film-sealed, scored tablet contains: trazodone hydrochloride 100 mg. Nonmedicinal ingredients: cornstarch, dibasic calcium phosphate, lactose, magnesium stearate, microcrystalline cellulose, povidone and sodium starch glycolate. May or may not contain castor oil and ethylcellulose. Bottles of 100.

Desyrel Dividose: Each orange rectangular-shaped, trisected and bisected tablet contains: trazodone hydrochloride 150 mg. Nonmedicinal ingredients: FD&C yellow No. 6 aluminum lake, magnesium stearate, microcrystalline cellulose, pregelatinized starch and stearic acid. Each tablet can be broken accurately to provide any of the following dosages: 50 mg (⅓ of a tablet), 75 mg (½ of a tablet), 100 mg (⅔ of a tablet), 150 mg (entire tablet). To break a Dividose tablet accurately and easily, hold the tablet between your thumbs and index fingers, close to the appropriate score (groove). Then with the tablet score facing you, apply pressure and snap the tablet segments apart. Bottles of 100.

(Shown in Product Recognition Section)

DEXAMETHASONE Ⓟ
General Monograph, CPhA

see CORTICOSTEROIDS: EYE EAR NOSE
see CORTICOSTEROIDS: SYSTEMIC

DEXAMETHASONE SODIUM PHOSPHATE Ⓟ
Rivex Ophthalmics

Corticosteroid

Supplied: Each mL of sterile ophthalmic/otic solution contains: dexamethasone sodium phosphate 0.1%. Nonmedicinal ingredients: benzalkonium chloride, creatinine, edetate disodium, hydrochloric acid, phenylethyl alcohol, polysorbate 80, purified water, sodium bisulfite, sodium borate and sodium citrate. Plastic squeeze bottles of 5 mL with controlled tip applicators.

DEXASONE® Ⓟ
ICN

Dexamethasone

Corticosteroid

Supplied: 500 µg: Each oval, yellow, scored tablet, imprinted ICN D11 contains: dexamethasone USP 500 µg. Nonmedicinal ingredients: cornstarch, colloidal silicon dioxide, lactose, magnesium stearate, microcrystalline cellulose and sodium starch glycolate. Bottles of 100.

750 µg: Each oval, pale blue, scored tablet, imprinted ICN D12 contains: dexamethasone USP 750 µg. Nonmedicinal ingredients: cornstarch, colloidal silicon dioxide, lactose, magnesium stearate, microcrystalline cellulose and sodium starch glycolate. Bottles of 100.

4 mg: Each oval, pale green, scored tablet, imprinted ICN D13 contains: dexamethasone USP 4 mg. Nonmedicinal ingredients: cornstarch, colloidal silicon dioxide, lactose, magnesium stearate, microcrystalline cellulose and sodium starch glycolate. Bottles of 100.

DEXEDRINE® ◈
SmithKline Beecham

Dextroamphetamine Sulfate

Sympathomimetic

Pharmacology: Dextroamphetamine (dexamphetamine, d-amphetamine) sulfate is a sympathomimetic agent with indirect effects on adrenergic receptors. It has alpha-and beta-adrenergic activity. It has actions qualitatively similar to those of amphetamine sulfate but is approximately twice as potent. It has a marked stimulant effect on the CNS, particularly the cerebral cortex and the respiratory and vasomotor centers.

Dextroamphetamine sulfate causes a lessening of fatigue, an increase in mental activity, an elevation of mood, and a general feeling of well-being. However, its indiscriminate use in attempts to increase capacity for work or to overcome fatigue is undesirable. At high doses, it produces a euphoria, which upon abrupt withdrawal of the drug reverts to severe depression and lethargy.

The mechanism by which amphetamines produce mental and behavioral effects in children is not conclusively established.

Indications: In the adjunctive treatment of: narcolepsy.
Attention-Deficit Hyperactivity Disorder: Dextroamphetamine may be used as an integral component of a treatment program, typically in combination with psychological, educational, or social measures for a stabilizing effect in children exhibiting the following behavioral syndrome: moderate-to-severe distractibility, short attention span, hyperactivity, emotional lability, and impulsivity. A diagnosis should not be made for symptoms of comparatively recent origin. Nonlocalizing (soft) neurological signs, learning disability, and EEG abnormalities may or may not be present. A diagnosis of CNS dysfunction may be warranted in some, but not all, cases.

Drug treatment is not indicated for all children with Attention-Deficit Hyperactivity Disorder. Stimulants are not appropriate for the treatment of children who are exhibiting symptoms which are secondary to environmental factors and/or primary psychiatric disorders, including psychosis. Suitable educational placement and psychosocial intervention are important. The prescription of stimulant medication will depend upon the physician's evaluation of the chronicity and severity of symptoms in a child whose disorder has proved refractory to remedial measures alone.

Contraindications: Advanced arteriosclerosis, symptomatic cardiovascular disease, moderate to severe hypertension, hyperthyroidism, hypersensitivity or idiosyncrasy to sympathomimetic amines, agitated states, history of drug abuse, glaucoma.

During administration or within 14 days following the withdrawal of MAO, administration of dextroamphetamine may cause hypertensive crises.

Warnings: Amphetamines have been subject to extensive abuse. Tolerance, extreme psychological dependence, and severe social disability can occur. Patients have been reported to increase their dosage to many times the recommended level. The smallest possible amount of the drug should be prescribed or dispensed at one time.

Precautions: Occupational Hazards: Amphetamines may mask extreme fatigue which can impair the ability to perform potentially hazardous activities such as operating machinery or driving motor vehicles; patients should be cautioned accordingly.

Use with caution even in mild hypertension.

Amphetamines may alter insulin requirements in diabetes mellitus, and may decrease the hypotensive effect of guanethidine.

Dextroamphetamine products contain tartrazine (FD&C yellow #5) which can cause allergic type reactions (including bronchial asthma) in susceptible individuals. Cross-sensitivity to salicylates and tartrazine is frequently seen.

The possibility of tolerance and psychological dependence, particularly with excessive use, should be kept in mind. Therefore, care should be used in the selection of candidates for dextroamphetamine therapy. Should psychological dependence occur, discontinue medication. Abrupt cessation following prolonged high dosage administration may result in extreme fatigue and mental depression. Changes have also been noted on the sleep EEG.

Manifestations of chronic intoxication with amphetamines include severe dermatoses, marked insomnia, irritability, hyperactivity, and personality changes. The most severe manifestation of chronic intoxication is psychosis, often clinically indistinguishable from schizophrenia.
Use in Children: Amphetamines are not recommended for use in Attention-Deficit Hyperactivity Disorder in children under 6 years of age.

Long-term effects of amphetamines in children have not been well established.

Chronic administration of amphetamines may be associated with growth inhibition; growth should be monitored during treatment.

Clinical experience suggests that in psychotic children, administration of amphetamines may exacerbate symptoms of behavior disturbance and thought disorder.

The presence of tics or Tourette's syndrome should be ruled out before administering amphetamines to children.
Drug Interactions: Caution should be exercised when coprescribing amphetamines and other drugs since clinically significant interactions with a number of drugs have been reported. In some instances, potentiation of CNS and cardiac effects could be life threatening. Dosages should be closely monitored.

Known interactions with amphetamines are as follows: Synergistic Interactions: tricyclic antidepressants, MAO inhibitors, meperidine, norepinephrine, phenobarbital, phenytoin, propoxyphene, acetazolamide, thiazides, gastrointestinal and urinary alkalinizing agents.

Antagonistic Interactions: adrenergic blockers, antihistamines, antihypertensives, chlorpromazine, ethosuximide, guanethidine, haloperidol, lithium carbonate, methenamine, Veratrum alkaloids, gastrointestinal and urinary acidifying agents.

Pregnancy: Safe use in pregnancy has not been established. Infants born to mothers dependent on amphetamines have an increased risk of premature delivery and low birth weight. Also, these infants may experience symptoms of withdrawal as manifested by dysphoria, agitation and significant lassitude. Reproductive studies in mammals at high multiples of the human dose have suggested an embryotoxic and a teratogenic potential. Use of amphetamines by women who are or who may become pregnant, and especially those in the first trimester of pregnancy, requires that the potential benefit be weighed against the possible hazard to mother and child.

Lactation: Amphetamines are excreted in human milk. Mothers taking dextroamphetamine should be advised to refrain from nursing.

Laboratory Test Interactions: Amphetamines can elevate plasma corticosteroid levels, particularly in the evening, and may interfere with urinary steroid determinations.

Adverse Effects: Cardiovascular: palpitations, tachycardia, elevation of blood pressure. There have been isolated reports of cardiomyopathy associated with chronic amphetamine use.

CNS: overstimulation, restlessness, dizziness, euphoria or dysphoria, dyskinesia, headache, insomnia, exacerbation of motor and phonic tics, Tourette's syndrome, tremor; rarely, psychotic episodes at recommended doses.

Gastrointestinal: dryness of the mouth, unpleasant taste, loss of appetite, diarrhea, constipation. other gastrointestinal disturbances, anorexia and weight loss.

Allergic: Urticaria.

Other: Impotence, changes in libido.

Overdose: The toxic dose of amphetamine varies widely according to the degree of tolerance present. Blood levels are, therefore, of little value in assessing the severity of the overdose; this assessment must depend almost entirely on clinical signs.

Symptoms: Dilated and reactive pupils, shallow rapid respiration, rhabdomyolysis, hyperpyrexia, fever, chills, sweating, hyperactive tendon reflexes. Other symptoms are:

Central effects may include restlessness, tremor, aggressiveness, anxiety, confusion, delirium, hallucinations, panic attacks and even suicidal or homicidal tendencies. The stimulant effect is usually followed by depression, lethargy, exhaustion.

Cardiovascular effects may include anginal pain, extrasystoles and other arrhythmias, flushing, headache, hypertension or hypotension, pallor, palpitations, tachycardia. Circulatory collapse and syncope may occur.

Gastrointestinal effects include nausea, vomiting, diarrhea, abdominal cramps.

Fatal poisoning is usually preceded by convulsions and coma.

Treatment: Treatment is essentially symptomatic and supportive. In addition to the usual measures (including emesis, gastric lavage, catharsis), sedatives should be given when indicated. Oral or parenteral barbiturates are generally used for this purpose. To provide a basal level of sedation, one or more doses of sodium amobarbital may be given by mouth or, if necessary, by i.m. injection. This may be repeated as often as necessary and in quantities sufficient to control the symptoms.

Sedation may also be accomplished with chlorpromazine: in children 1 mg/kg body weight i.m. and in adults 100 mg i.m., repeated at half-hourly intervals if necessary. If the amphetamine has been taken with a barbiturate, as is often the case, the chlorpromazine dosage should be halved.

Note: It has been stated that the effects of amphetamines are best treated with haloperidol (Med Lett 1983 Sep 16;25:87), a dopamine antagonist with minimal anticholinergic side effects. Haloperidol, however, possesses central antiemetic properties; it may prolong the hypnotic action of barbiturates and may potentiate the effects of alcohol and other CNS depressant drugs; it may lower the convulsion threshold.

In general, the hypertension which may result from massive overdose of dextroamphetamine does not require treatment. A gradual drop in blood pressure will usually result when sufficient sedation has been administered. Phentolamine may be used to decrease blood pressure and hyperthermia. In the presence of severe hypotension, the usual procedures employed for shock should be instituted.

Acidification of the urine enhances excretion. Experience with forced diuresis, hemodialysis, peritoneal dialysis or charcoal hemoperfusion is inadequate to permit recommendations in this regard.

Since much of the Spansule capsule medication is coated for gradual release, therapy directed at reversing the effects of the ingested drug and at supporting the patient should be continued for as long as overdosage symptoms remain. Saline cathartics are useful for hastening the evacuation of pellets that have not already released medication.

Dosage: Regardless of indication, amphetamines should be administered at the lowest effective dosage, and dosage should be individually adjusted. Time of administration should receive special attention—particularly with the Spansule capsule form—because of possible insomnia. Late evening medication should be avoided.

Narcolepsy: Daily dosage may range from 5 to 60 mg, depending on individual patient response.

Suggested initial dosage for patients aged 6 to 12: start with 5 mg daily; daily dosage may be raised in increments of 5 mg at weekly intervals until optimal response is obtained.

In patients 12 years of age and older: start with 10 mg daily; daily dosage may be raised in increments of 10 mg at weekly intervals until optimal response is obtained.

If bothersome adverse reactions appear (e.g., insomnia or anorexia), dosage should be reduced. Spansule capsules may be used for once-a-day dosage wherever appropriate. With tablets, give first dose on awakening; additional doses (1 or 2) at intervals of 4 to 6 hours.

Attention-Deficit Hyperactivity Disorder in Children: Daily dosage may range from 2.5 to 40 mg, although some older children may require more than 40 mg daily for optimal response. If bothersome adverse reactions appear (e.g., insomnia or anorexia), dosage should be reduced. Spansule capsules may be used for once-a-day dosage wherever appropriate. With tablets, give first dose on awakening; additional doses (1 or 2) at intervals of 4 to 6 hours.

Not recommended for this use in children under 6 years of age.

In children 6 years of age or older, start with 5 mg once or twice daily; daily dosage may be raised in increments of 5 mg at weekly intervals until optimal response is obtained. Only in rare cases will it be necessary to exceed a total of 40 mg/day.

Most children suffering from Attention-Deficit Hyperactivity Disorder require medication for several years, although once symptoms have been controlled, it may be possible to reduce dosage or to interrupt drug therapy during the summer months and at other times when the child is under less stress. During periods of interrupted drug therapy, behavioral symptoms should be assessed to determine whether their recurrence is sufficient to justify the resumption of treatment.

Supplied: Spansules: 10 mg: Each brown-capped, natural colored body taper-end capsule, with 3 shades of orange pellets, monogrammed "3513" on the cap with "10 mg" and "SB" on the body in white ink, contains: dextroamphetamine sulfate 10 mg, so prepared that a therapeutic dose is released promptly and the remaining dose, delivered gradually and without interruption, sustains the effect for 10 to 12 hours. Nonmedicinal ingredients: acacia, calcium sulfate, cetylpyridinium chloride, FD&C Blue No. 1, FD&C Red No. 40, FD&C Yellow No. 5, FD&C Yellow No. 6, gelatin, glyceryl distearate, glyceryl monostearate, nonpareil seeds, sodium lauryl sulfate, starch and white wax. Energy: 3.72 kJ (0.88 kcal). Bottles of 100.

15 mg: Each brown-capped, natural colored body taper-end capsule, with 3 shades of orange pellets, monogrammed "3514" on the cap with "15 mg" and "SB" on the body in white ink, contains: amphetamine sulfate 15 mg, so prepared that a therapeutic dose is released promptly and the remaining dose, delivered gradually and without interruption, sustains the effect for 10 to 12 hours. Nonmedicinal ingredients: acacia, calcium sulfate, cetylpyridinium chloride, FD&C Blue No. 1, FD&C Red No. 40, FD&C Yellow No. 5, FD&C Yellow No. 6, gelatin, glyceryl distearate, glyceryl monostearate, nonpareil seeds, sodium lauryl sulfate, starch and white wax. Energy: 4.78 kJ (1.14 kcal). Bottles of 100.

Tablets: Each orange, round-cornered, equilaterally triangular shaped, scored, compressed tablet, engraved "SKF E19", contains: dextroamphetamine sulfate 5 mg. Nonmedicinal ingredients: calcium sulfate, confectioners sugar, gelatin, lactose, FD&C Yellow No. 5, FD&C Yellow No. 6, starch, stearic acid and talc. Energy: 1.46 kJ (0.35 kcal). Bottles of 100.

(Shown in Product Recognition Section)

Reviewed 1999

DEXIRON™

Genpharm

Iron Dextran

Hematinic—Iron Supplement

Pharmacology: Iron dextran is absorbed from i.m. injection sites into the capillaries and the lymphatic system. Circulating iron dextran is removed from the plasma by cells of the reticuloendothelial system, which split the complex into its components of iron and dextran. The iron is immediately bound to the available protein moieties to form hemosiderin or ferritin, the physiologic forms of iron, and to a lesser extent transferrin. This iron, which is subject to physiologic control, replenishes hemoglobin and depleted iron stores.

Dextran, a polyglucose, is either metabolized or excreted. Negligible amounts of iron are lost via the urinary or alimentary pathways after administration of iron dextran.

The major portion of iron dextran is absorbed within 72 hours after i.m. injection. Most of the remaining iron dextran is absorbed over the ensuing 3 to 4 weeks.

Studies involving i.v. administered iron dextran to iron deficient subjects who had co-existing end-stage renal disease and other clinical problems, yielded individual plasma half-lives ranging from 9.4 to 87.4 hours. The average half-life was 58.9 hours. These studies measured the total serum iron directly as well as the transferrin-bound iron, non-radioisotopically. It should be understood that these half-life values do not represent clearance of iron from the body. Iron is not easily eliminated from the body, and accumulation of iron can be toxic.

The availability of iron for erythropoiesis and replenishment of iron stores after administration of iron dextran was evaluated in a study of 20 renal dialysis patients. A total dose equivalent to 500 mg of iron, divided into five 100 mg doses was administered i.v. over a period of 10 days. (The dosing schedule varied according to each patient's clinical situation.) Hemoglobin increased from a pretreatment mean of 10.3 g/dL to 11.4 g/dL 2 weeks after completion of the series of injections. Serum ferritin and transferrin saturation peaked in 1 week at 620 ng/mL and 32%, respectively. Total iron binding capacity remained well within the physiological range (245 to 400 µg/dL) for the duration of the 30 day observation period, an indication that free ionic iron is not released from iron dextran. The mean percent utilization of iron from iron dextran was calculated to be $47 \pm 20\%$.

Indications: For the treatment of patients with documented iron deficiency in whom oral iron administration is unsatisfactory or impossible (see Warnings and Dosage).

Contraindications: Hypersensitivity to the drug product. All anemias not associated with iron deficiency.

Warnings: The parenteral use of complexes of iron and carbohydrates has resulted in anaphylactic-type reactions. Deaths associated with such administration have been reported. Therefore, iron dextran should be used only in those patients in whom the indications have been clearly established and laboratory investigations confirm an iron deficient state not amenable to oral iron therapy.

A risk of carcinogenesis may attend the i.m. injection of iron-carbohydrate complexes. Under experimental conditions iron dextran has been found to produce sarcomata when large doses were given to rodents, or when smaller doses were injected repeatedly into the same site in rodents and rabbits.

The long latent period between the injection of a potential carcinogen and the appearance of a tumor makes it impossible to measure accurately the risk in man. There have, however, been several reports in the literature describing tumors at the injection site in humans who had previously received i.m. injections of iron dextran.

Large i.v. doses, such as those used with Total Dose Infusions (TDI), have been associated with an increased incidence of adverse effects. The adverse effects frequently are delayed (1 to 2 days) reactions typified by 1 or more of the following symptoms: arthralgia, backache, chills, dizziness, moderate to high fever, headache, malaise, myalgia, nausea, and vomiting. The onset is usually 24 to 48 hours after administration and symptoms generally subside within 3 to 4 days. These symptoms have also been reported following i.m. injection and generally subside within 3 to 7 days. The etiology of these reactions is unknown. The potential for a delayed reaction must be considered when estimating the risks/benefits of treatment. The TDI method of administration is not currently recommended.

The maximum daily dose should not exceed 2 mL undiluted iron dextran injection.

DexIron (cont'd)

Iron dextran should be used with extreme care in patients with serious impairment of liver function.

Iron dextran should not be used during the acute phase of infectious kidney disease.

Adverse reactions experienced following administration of iron dextran injection may exacerbate cardiovascular complications in patients with pre-existing cardiovascular disease.

Precautions: Unwarranted therapy with parenteral iron will cause excess storage of iron with the consequent possibility of iatrogenic hemosiderosis. Such iron overload is particularly apt to occur in patients with hemoglobinopathies and other refractory anemias that might be erroneously diagnosed as iron deficiency anemias.

Iron dextran should be used with caution in individuals with histories of significant allergies and/or asthma.

Anaphylaxis and other hypersensitivity reactions have been reported after uneventful test doses as well as therapeutic doses of iron dextran injection. Therefore, administration of subsequent test doses during therapy should be considered (see Dosage).

Epinephrine should be immediately available in the event of acute hypersensitivity reactions. The usual adult dose of epinephrine is 0.5 mL of a 1:1 000 solution, by s.c. or i.m. injection. **Note:** Patients using β-blocking agents may not respond adequately to epinephrine. Isoproterenol or similar β-agonist agents may be required in these patients.

Patients with rheumatoid arthritis may have an acute exacerbation of joint pain and swelling following the administration of iron dextran injection.

Reports in the literature from countries outside the United States (in particular, New Zealand) have suggested that the use of i.m. iron dextran in neonates has been associated with an increased incidence of Gram-negative sepsis, primarily due to E. coli.

Drug/Laboratory Test Interactions: Large doses of iron dextran injection (5 mL or more) have been reported to give a brown color to serum when blood samples are drawn 4 hours after administration. Iron dextran injection may cause falsely elevated serum bilirubin values and falsely decreased serum calcium values. Serum iron determinations (especially by colorimetric assays) may not be meaningful for 3 weeks following administration of iron dextran injection. Serum ferritin peaks approximately 7 to 9 days after an i.v. dose and slowly returns to baseline after about 3 weeks. Examination of bone marrow for iron stores may not be meaningful for prolonged periods following therapy with iron dextran injection because residual iron dextran may remain in reticuloendothelial cells. Bone scans involving ^{99m}Tc-diphosphonate have been reported to show a dense, crescentic area of activity in the buttocks, following the contour of the iliac crest, 1 to 6 days after i.m. injections of iron dextran. In the presence of high serum ferritin levels or following iron dextran infusions, bone scans with ^{99m}Tc-labeled bone seeking agents have been reported to show reduction of bony uptake, marked renal activity, and increased blood pool activity and soft tissue accumulation.

Carcinogenesis, Mutagenesis, Impairment of Fertility: See Warnings.

Pregnancy: Iron dextran has been shown to be teratogenic and embryocidal in nonanemic mice, rats, rabbits, dogs and monkeys when given in doses of about 3 times the maximum human dose. No consistent adverse fetal effects were observed in mice, rats, rabbits, dogs, and monkeys at doses of 50 mg iron/kg or less. Fetal and maternal toxicity have been reported in monkeys at a total i.v. dose of 90 mg iron/kg over a 14 day period. Similar effects were observed in mice and rats after administration of a single dose of 125 mg iron/kg. Fetal abnormalities in rats and dogs were observed at doses of 250 mg iron/kg and higher. The animals used in these tests were not iron deficient. There are no adequate and well-controlled studies in pregnant women. **Iron dextran injection should be used in pregnant women only if the potential benefit justifies the potential risk to the fetus.**

Placental Transfer: Various animal studies and studies in pregnant humans have been inconclusive with respect to the placental transfer of iron dextran. It appears that some iron does reach the fetus, but the form in which it crosses the placenta is not clear.

Lactation: Caution should be exercised when iron dextran injection is administered to nursing mothers. Traces of unmetabolized iron dextran are excreted in human milk.

Children: **Not recommended for use in infants under 4 months of age (see Dosage).**

Adverse Effects: Severe/Fatal: Anaphylactic reactions have been reported with the use of iron dextran injection; on occasion these reactions have been fatal. Such reactions, which occur most often within the first several minutes of administration, are generally characterized by sudden onset of respiratory difficulty and/or cardiovascular collapse (see Warnings and Precautions pertaining to the immediate availability of epinephrine).

Cardiovascular: chest pain, chest tightness, shock, hypotension, hypertension, tachycardia, flushing, arrhythmias. (Flushing and hypotension may occur from too rapid injection by the i.v. route.)

Dermatologic: urticaria, pruritus, purpura, rash.

Gastrointestinal: abdominal pain, nausea, vomiting, diarrhea.

Hematologic/Lymphatic: leukocytosis, lymphadenopathy.

Musculoskeletal/Soft Tissue: arthralgia, myalgia, backache, arthritis (may represent reactivation in patients with quiescent rheumatoid arthritis, see Precautions); sterile abscess, atrophy/fibrosis, brown skin or underlying tissue discoloration or staining, soreness or pain at or near i.m. injection sites; cellulitis, swelling, inflammation, local phlebitis at or near i.v. injection sites.

Neurologic: convulsions, seizures, syncope, headache, weakness, unresponsiveness, paresthesia, febrile episodes, chills, dizziness, disorientation, numbness.

Respiratory: respiratory arrest, dyspnea, bronchospasm.

Urologic: hematuria.

Delayed Reactions: arthralgia, backache, chills, dizziness, fever, headache, malaise, myalgia, nausea, vomiting (see Warnings).

Miscellaneous: febrile episodes, sweating, shivering, chills, malaise, altered taste.

The administration of iron dextran injection has been reported to cause fever and exacerbation of joint pain and swelling in patients with rheumatoid arthritis, ankylosing spondylitis, and systemic lupus erythematosus (see Precautions).

Overdose: Symptoms and Treatment: Overdosage with iron dextran injection is unlikely to be associated with any acute manifestations. Excessive doses beyond the requirements for restoration of hemoglobin and replenishment of iron stores may lead to hemosiderosis. Periodic monitoring of serum ferritin levels may be helpful in recognizing a deleterious progressive accumulation of iron. This can occur when uptake of iron from the reticuloendothelial system is impaired, for example, in chronic renal failure, Hodgkin's disease and rheumatoid arthritis.

Dosage: Oral iron should be discontinued prior to administration of iron dextran injection.

Iron Deficiency Anemia: Periodic determination of hemoglobin and hematocrit is a simple and accurate technique for monitoring hematological response, and should be used as a guide to therapy. It should be noted that iron storage may lag behind the appearance of normal blood morphology. Total iron binding capacity (TIBC), transferrin saturation and serum ferritin are other important tests for detecting and monitoring the iron deficient state. Serum ferritin is generally regarded as the most reliable marker of body iron stores; i.e., low serum ferritin correlates closely with low bone marrow iron stores, except in chronic renal dialysis patients who are receiving iron dextran. Serum iron is the least sensitive indicator of the response to iron dextran injection.

After administration of iron dextran injection, evidence of a therapeutic response can be seen in a few days as an increase in the reticulocyte count.

Although there are significant variations in body build and weight distribution among males and females, Table I and the formula below represent a convenient means for estimating the total iron required. This total iron requirement reflects the amount of iron needed to restore hemoglobin concentration to normal or near normal levels plus an additional allowance to provide adequate replenishment of iron stores in most individuals with moderately or severely reduced levels of hemoglobin. It should be remembered that iron deficiency anemia will not appear until essentially all iron stores have been depleted. Thus, therapy should aim at not only the restoration of hemoglobin but also the replenishment of iron stores.

Factors contributing to the formula include:

$$\frac{\text{mg blood iron}}{\text{lb body weight}} = \frac{\text{mL blood}}{\text{lb body weight}} \times \frac{\text{g hemoglobin}}{\text{mL blood}} \times \frac{\text{mg iron}}{\text{g hemoglobin}}$$

a) Blood volume 65 mL/kg of body weight; b) Normal hemoglobin (males and females): over 15 kg (33 lbs) 14.8 g/100 mL, 15 kg (33 lbs) or less 12 g/100 mL; c) Iron content of hemoglobin 0.34%; d) Hemoglobin deficit; e) Weight. Based on these factors, individuals with normal hemoglobin levels will have approximately 33 mg of blood iron per kilogram of body weight (15 mg/lb).

Note: The formula and Table I are applicable for dosage determinations only in patients with iron deficiency anemia; they are not to be used for dosage determinations in patients requiring iron replacement for blood loss.

The total amount of iron dextran in mL required to treat anemia and replenish iron stores may be approximated as follows: Adults and Children over 15 kg (33 lbs): See Table I. Alternatively the total dose may be calculated as follows:

Dose (mL) = 0.0442 (Desired Hb − Observed Hb) × LBW + (0.26 x LBW)

Where, Desired Hb = the target hemoglobin in g/dL. Observed Hb = the patient's current hemoglobin in g/dL. LBW = lean body weight in kg. A patient's lean body weight (or

Table I—DexIron

Total DexIron Requirement for Hemoglobin Restoration and Iron Stores Replacement*

Patient Lean Body Weight		Millilitre Requirement of Iron Dextran Based on Observed Hemoglobin of							
kg	lb	3 g/dL	4 g/dL	5 g/dL	6 g/dL	7 g/dL	8 g/dL	9 g/dL	10 g/dL
5	11	3	3	3	3	2	2	2	2
10	22	7	6	6	5	5	4	4	3
15	33	10	9	9	8	7	7	6	5
20	44	16	15	14	13	12	11	10	9
25	55	20	18	17	16	15	14	13	12
30	66	23	22	21	19	18	17	15	14
35	77	27	26	24	23	21	20	18	17
40	88	31	29	28	26	24	22	21	19
45	99	35	33	31	29	27	25	23	21
50	110	39	37	35	32	30	28	26	24
55	121	43	41	38	36	33	31	28	26
60	132	47	44	42	39	36	34	31	28
65	143	51	48	45	42	39	36	34	31
70	154	55	52	49	45	42	39	36	33
75	165	59	55	52	49	45	42	39	35
80	176	63	59	55	52	48	45	41	38
85	187	66	63	59	55	51	48	44	40
90	198	70	66	62	58	54	50	46	42
95	209	74	70	66	62	57	53	49	45
100	220	78	74	69	65	60	56	52	47
105	231	82	77	73	68	63	59	54	50
110	242	86	81	76	71	67	62	57	52
115	253	90	85	80	75	70	64	59	54
120	264	94	88	83	78	73	67	62	57

* Table values were calculated based on a normal adult hemoglobin of 14.8 g/dL for body weights greater than 15 kg (33 lbs) and a hemoglobin of 12 g/dL for body weights less than or equal to 15 kg (33 lbs).

actual body weight if less than lean body weight) should be used to determine the dose.

To convert the patient's weight from pounds to kg:

$$\frac{\text{patient's weight in pounds}}{2.2} = \text{weight in kg}$$

Males: LBW=50 kg+2.3 kg for each inch of patient's height over 5 feet.

Females: LBW=45.5 kg+2.3 kg for each inch of patient's height over 5 feet.

Children 5 to 15 kg (11 to 33 lbs): Iron dextran should not normally be given in the first 4 months of life (see Precautions). See Table I. Alternatively the total dose may be calculated as follows:

Dose (mL) = 0.0442 (Desired Hb − Observed Hb) × W + (0.26×W)

Where, Desired Hb = the target hemoglobin in g/dL. (Normal hemoglobin for children weighing 15 kg or less is 12 g/dL.) Observed Hb = the patient's current hemoglobin in g/dL. W = weight in kg.

To convert the patient's weight from pounds to kg:

$$\frac{\text{patient's weight in pounds}}{2.2} = \text{weight in kg}$$

Iron Replacement for Blood Loss: Some individuals sustain blood losses on an intermittent or repetitive basis. Such blood losses may occur periodically in patients with hemorrhagic diatheses (familial telangiectasia, hemophilia, gastrointestinal bleeding) and on a repetitive basis from procedures such as renal dialysis.

Iron therapy in these patients should be directed toward replacement of the equivalent amount of iron represented in the blood loss. Table I and formula described under Iron Deficiency Anemia are not applicable for simple iron replacement values.

Quantitative estimates of the individual's periodic blood loss and hematocrit during the bleeding episode provide a convenient method for calculating the required iron dose.

The formula shown below is based on the approximation that 1 mL of normocytic, normochromic red cells contains 1 mg of elemental iron.

Replacement iron (in mg)=Blood loss (in mL) × hematocrit

Example: Blood loss of 500 mL with 20% hematocrit

Replacement iron = 500 × 0.20=100 mg

$$\text{DexIron dose} = \frac{100\text{ mg}}{50\text{ mg/mL}} = 2\text{ mL}$$

Administration: The total amount of iron dextran required for the treatment of iron deficiency anemia or iron replacement for blood loss is determined from Table I or appropriate formula.

I.V. Injection: **Prior to receiving their first iron dextran therapeutic dose, all patients should be given an i.v. test dose of 0.5 mL (see Precautions). The test dose should be administered at a gradual rate over at least 5 minutes.**

Although anaphylactic reactions known to occur following administration of iron dextran injection are usually evident within a few minutes or sooner, it is recommended that a period of 1 hour or longer elapse before the remainder of the initial therapeutic dose is given.

Individual doses of 2 mL or less may be given on a daily basis until the calculated total amount required has been reached. Iron dextran is given undiluted at a **slow gradual rate** not to exceed 50 mg (1 mL)/minute.

I.M. Injection: **Prior to receiving their first iron dextran therapeutic dose, all patients should be given an i.m. test dose of 0.5 mL gradually (see Precautions).** The test dose should be administered in the same recommended test site and by the same technique as described in the last paragraph of this section.

Although anaphylactic reactions known to occur following iron dextran administration are usually evident within a few minutes or sooner, it is recommended that a period of 1 hour or longer elapse before the remainder of the initial therapeutic dose is given.

If no adverse reactions are observed, iron dextran can be given according to the following schedule until the calculated total amount required has been reached. Each day's dose should ordinarily not exceed 0.5 mL (25 mg of iron) for infants under 5 kg; 1 mL (50 mg of iron) for children under 10 kg; and 2 mL (100 mg of iron) for other patients.

Iron dextran should be injected only into the muscle mass of the upper outer quadrant of the buttock—never into the arm or other exposed areas—and should be injected deeply with a 5 cm, 19 or 20 gauge needle. In an obese patient, a longer needle is usually necessary, and in children and frail adults a shorter and smaller needle will suffice. If the patient is standing, he/she should be bearing his/her weight on the leg opposite the injection site. If recumbent, he/she should be in the lateral position with the injection site uppermost. To avoid injection or leakage into the s.c. tissue, a Z-track technique (lateral displacement of the skin prior to injection) is recommended.

The i.m. route of administration is to be used unless there are valid reasons for i.v. administration.

Note: Do not mix DexIron with other medications or add to parenteral nutrition solutions for i.v. infusion. Parenteral drug products should be inspected visually for particulate matter and discoloration prior to administration, whenever the solution and container permit.

Supplied: Each mL of dark brown, slightly viscous, sterile liquid contains: elemental iron as iron dextran 50 mg. Nonmedicinal ingredients: sodium chloride, sodium hydroxide and/or hydrochloric acid and water for injection. Single dose vials of 1 and 2 mL, cartons of 10. Store at controlled room temperature, 15 to 30°C. Protect from excessive heat. Do not freeze. Keep out of reach of children.

New Product 1998

DEXTROSE 50% INJECTION

Bioniche

Caloric Supplement

Supplied: Each mL of sterile, hypertonic solution contains: dextrose 500 mg in water for injection. Energy: 3.4 kcal/g. Osmolarity: 2.52 mOsm/mL. Preservative-free. Single use vials of 50 mL, trays of 25. Store at room temperature (15 to 30°C).

DIAβETA® Ⓟ

Hoechst Marion Roussel

Glyburide

Oral Hypoglycemic

Pharmacology: The principal action of glyburide results in an increased insulin release from the beta cells of the pancreas. Other mechanisms leading to a reduction of blood glucose are also believed to be influenced by glyburide. The insertion of an alkylene chain on the benzene nucleus results in a product of very high potency.

Schulz and Schmidt indicated that the presence of a sulfonamide (sulfaphenazole) decreased the distribution volume of glyburide without influence on the half-life of the oral hypoglycemic agent. As a result, insulin and serum concentrations of glyburide were higher and hypoglycemic attacks could be expected.

Hirn and Konigstein have observed hypoglycemia when phenylbutazone and oxyphenbutazone were added to glyburide. Schulz and Schmidt confirmed that phenylbutazone has an enhancing effect on the blood-sugar-lowering effect of glyburide and found higher insulin levels. The plasma half-life of glyburide did not change with phenylbutazone administration. However, a significant decrease in the renal excretion of the main metabolite of glyburide was observed, suggesting that the elimination in the bile may compensate for the amount not excreted in the urine.

Glyburide micronized powder is well absorbed from the intestinal tract. Glyburide is highly bound to plasma proteins after absorption from the gastrointestinal tract. It is completely metabolized by hydroxylation of the cyclohexyl ring into 3-cis and 4-trans derivatives in the liver and the kidneys play only a minor role in their biotransformation and elimination from plasma. The metabolites have no essential hypoglycemic effect and they are not stored in the body, but they are eliminated via the bile, and in approximately the same amounts in the urine conjugated to glucoronic acid and in the feces.

Maximal plasma levels of insulin, after an oral dose of 5 mg of glyburide in normal subjects were reached 90 minutes after dosing.

Minimal blood levels of glucose, after an oral dose of 5 mg of glyburide in normal subjects were reached 120 minutes after dosing corresponding to a reduction of about 35%.

Raptis et al. found that the effect of an i.v. injection of 1 mg of glyburide on blood glucose and serum insulin levels of healthy subjects was slower in onset and lasted longer than that of 1 g of tolbutamide. Furthermore, when a second injection of glyburide was given 1 hour later, the effects were undiminished. When glyburide was injected at 4 hour intervals in patients with adult-onset diabetes, the effects of glyburide were not diminished.

Indications: To control hyperglycemia in glyburide-responsive diabetes mellitus of stable, mild, nonketosis prone, maturity onset or adult type which cannot be controlled solely by proper dietary management, exercise and weight reduction or when insulin therapy is not appropriate.

Contraindications: Known hypersensitivity or allergy to the active ingredient or any other component of the formulation. Glyburide should not be given to patients with: unstable and/or insulin-dependent diabetes mellitus; ketoacidosis; diabetic precoma; coma; in the presence of pre-existing complications peculiar to diabetes; during stress conditions such as severe infections, trauma or surgery; in the presence of liver disease or renal impairment; or frank jaundice.

Pregnancy: During pregnancy, no oral antidiabetic agent should be given.

Lactation: Due to the possible excretion in human milk, the patient should discontinue nursing or discontinue taking the drug depending on the importance of the drug to the mother. If glyburide is discontinued, the patient should be transferred to insulin therapy.

Warnings: Glyburide will not prevent the development of complications peculiar to diabetes mellitus.

Use of glyburide must be considered as treatment in addition to a proper dietary regimen and not as a substitute for diet. Over a period of time, patients may become progressively less responsive to therapy with oral hypoglycemic agents because of deterioration of their diabetic state. If a loss of adequate blood glucose lowering response to glyburide is detected, the drug should be discontinued.

Precautions: Patient Selection and Followup: Careful selection of patients is important. It is imperative that there be rigid attention to diet, adherence to regular exercise, reduction of body weight in obese patients, careful adjustment of dosage, instruction of the patient on hypoglycemic reactions and their control as well as regular, thorough follow-up examinations.

Since the effects of oral hypoglycemic agents on the vascular changes and other long-term sequelae of diabetes mellitus are not fully known, patients receiving such drugs must be closely observed for both short- and long-term complications.

Periodic assessment of cardiovascular, ophthalmic, hematologic, renal and hepatic status is advisable.

In patients stabilized on glyburide therapy, loss of blood sugar control may occur in cases of acute intercurrent disease or in stressful situations such as trauma or surgery. Under these conditions, discontinuation of glyburide and administration of insulin should be considered.

Oral hypoglycemic agents should be administered with caution to patients with Addison's disease.

Pregnancy: The use of glyburide is not recommended for women planning a pregnancy (see Contraindications); these patients should be changed over to insulin therapy.

Hypoglycemic Reactions: Severe hypoglycemia can be induced by all sulfonylurea drugs. Particularly susceptible are elderly subjects, patients with impaired hepatic or renal function, those who are debilitated or malnourished, and patients with primary or secondary adrenal insufficiency. Hypoglycemia is more likely to occur when the caloric intake is inadequate or after strenuous or prolonged exercise.

Drug Interactions: Patients who receive or discontinue certain medications while undergoing treatment with glyburide may experience changes in blood glucose control.

Hypoglycemia may be potentiated when a sulfonylurea is used concurrently with agents such as: insulin and other oral antidiabetics, anabolic steroids and androgens, azapropazone, chloramphenicol, clofibrate, coumarin derivatives, cyclophosphamide, disopyramide, fenfluramine, fibrates, fluoxetine, ifosfamide, miconazole, monoamine oxidase inhibitors, oxyphenbutazone, para-aminosalicylic acid, phenylbutazone, probenecid, propranolol, quinolones, salicylates, sulfinpyrazone, sulfonamides, sympatholytic agents (e.g., beta-blockers, guanethidine), tetracyclines, tuberculostatics.

Certain drugs tend to produce hyperglycemia and may lead to loss of blood sugar control; these include: acetazolamide, barbiturates, corticosteroids, diazoxide, diuretics (thiazides, furosemide), glucagon, laxatives (after protracted use), nicotinic acid (in pharmacologic doses), oral contraceptives (estrogen plus progestogen), phenothiazines, phenytoin, rifampin, sympathomimetic agents (e.g., epinephrine) and thyroid hormones.

Under the influence of sympatholytic drugs such as beta-blockers, clonidine, guanethidine, and reserpine, the signs of adrenergic counter-regulation to hypoglycemia may be reduced or absent.

Concurrent use of H_2-receptor antagonists, clonidine or reserpine with glyburide may lead to either a potentiation or an attenuation of the blood-glucose-lowering effect.

DiaBeta (cont'd)

Both acute and chronic alcohol intake may potentiate or weaken the blood-glucose-lowering action of glyburide in an unpredictable fashion. Intolerance to alcohol (disulfiram-like reaction: flushing, sensation of warmth, giddiness, nausea, and occasionally tachycardia), may occur in patients treated with oral hypoglycemic drugs. These reactions can be prevented by avoiding the use of alcohol.

Barbiturates should be used cautiously in patients receiving an oral hypoglycemic agent since their action may be prolonged.

Glyburide may potentiate or weaken the effects of coumarin derivatives.

Occupational Hazards: Until optimal control has been achieved, when changing the antidiabetic preparation, or when the tablets have not been taken regularly, alertness and reaction time may be altered to such an extent that the patient cannot safely cope with road traffic or operate machinery.

Adverse Effects: Hypoglycemia (see Precautions): Severe hypoglycemia which may be prolonged and has occasionally been life-threatening, may occur and mimics acute CNS disorders (see Overdose: Symptoms and Treatment). Hepatic and/or renal disease, malnutrition and/or irregular meals, exercise without adequate caloric supplementation, debility, advanced age, patient non-compliance, alcoholism, certain disorders of thyroid function, adrenal or pituitary insufficiency, excessive glyburide dosage, treatment with glyburide in the absence of indication or concurrent use with other agents may be predisposing factors.

Gastrointestinal: Nausea, epigastric fullness and heartburn are common reactions. Vomiting, diarrhea, and abdominal pain have also been reported. These tend to be dose related and may disappear when dosage is reduced.

Dermatologic and Sensitivity Reactions: Allergic and pseudoallergic skin reactions such as pruritus, erythema, urticaria, morbilliform or maculopapular eruptions have been reported in a number of patients. These may subside on continued use of glyburide, but if they persist, the drug should be discontinued. Mild reactions such as urticaria may very rarely develop into serious and life-threatening reactions including dyspnea, hypotension or shock. Porphyria cutanea tarda and photosensitivity reactions have been associated with the use of oral hypoglycemic drugs. Allergic vasculitis have been observed very rarely in patients receiving glyburide and in some circumstances may be life-threatening.

Cross-sensitivity to sulfonamides or their derivatives may occur in patients treated with oral sulfonylurea hypoglycemic agents.

Hematologic: Rare cases of mild to severe thrombocytopenia which can manifest itself as purpura have been reported. Leukopenia, agranulocytosis, pancytopenia (which may be due to myelosuppression), erythrocytopenia, granulocytopenia, hemolytic anemia and aplastic anemia have been observed very rarely with glyburide therapy. These reactions may be reversible following discontinuation of the sulfonylurea antidiabetic agent.

Metabolic: Hepatic porphyria and disulfiram-like reactions have been observed in patients treated with oral hypoglycemic drugs. Elevation of liver enzyme levels has been reported very rarely in patients treated with glyburide. In isolated cases, impairment of liver function (e.g., cholestasis and jaundice) and hepatitis have been observed which can regress after withdrawal of the drug or may lead to life-threatening liver failure.

Endocrine: Reduced radioactive iodine uptake by the thyroid gland has been reported with oral hypoglycemic therapy.

Other: Transient visual disturbances may occur at the commencement of treatment due to fluctuations in blood glucose levels.

In isolated cases, reduction of serum sodium concentrations has been observed in patients receiving glyburide.

Overdose: Symptoms: Overdosage with sulfonylureas may result in hypoglycemia, but it should be noted that the dosage that causes hypoglycemia varies widely, and may be within the accepted therapeutic range in sensitive individuals.

The manifestations of hypoglycemia include: flushing or pallor, chilliness, excessive hunger, trembling, headache, dizziness, nausea, vomiting, restlessness, aggressiveness, depression, speech disorders, sensory and/or visual disturbances, helplessness, lassitude, shallow respiration or bradycardia. In more severe cases, the clinical symptoms of a stroke or coma appear. However, symptoms of hypoglycemia are not necessarily as typical as described above and sulfonylureas may cause insidious development of symptoms mimicking cerebrovascular insufficiency (e.g., disordered sleep, somnolence, impaired alertness and reactions, confusion, delirium, cerebral convulsions, paralytic symptoms or loss of consciousness).

Signs of adrenergic counter-regulation to hypoglycemia include: sweating, damp skin, anxiety, tachycardia, hypertension, palpitations, angina pectoris and cardiac arrhythmias. However, these symptoms may be milder or absent in patients who develop hypoglycemia gradually, patients with autonomic neuropathy, or patients who receive concurrent treatment with sympatholytic agents (e.g., beta-blockers, clonidine, reserpine, guanethidine).

Treatment: Discontinue medication and treat hypoglycemia by giving dextrose promptly and in sufficient quantity.

The symptoms of hypoglycemia nearly always subside when blood glucose control is attained. However, some sulfonylurea-induced hypoglycemias may be refractory to treatment and susceptible to relapse, especially in elderly or malnourished patients. Continuous dextrose infusions for hours to days have been necessary.

Dosage: In diabetic subjects, there is no fixed dosage regimen for management of blood glucose levels. Individual determination of the minimum dose that will lower the blood glucose adequately should be made.

If the maximal recommended dose fails to lower blood glucose adequately in patients on initial trial, glyburide should be discontinued. During the course of therapy a loss of effectiveness may occur. It is advisable to ascertain the contribution of the drug in the control of blood glucose by discontinuing the medication semiannually or at least annually with careful monitoring of the patient. If the need for the drug is not evident, the drug should not be resumed. In some diabetic subjects, short-term administration of the drug may be sufficient during periods of transient loss of blood sugar control.

Adjustment of glyburide dosage should be considered whenever factors predisposing the patient to the development of hypo- or hyperglycemia, such as weight or lifestyle changes, are present (see Contraindications, Warnings, Precautions and Adverse Effects).

Newly Diagnosed Diabetics: The initial dose is 5 mg daily (2.5 mg in patients over 60 years of age) and it should be continued for 5 to 7 days. Depending on the response, the dosage should then be either increased or decreased by steps of 2.5 mg. The maximum daily dose is 20 mg (because higher doses normally have no additional effect on control of metabolic state). Occasionally, control is maintained with 2.5 mg daily. The majority of cases can be controlled by 5 to 10 mg daily given as a single dose during or immediately after breakfast; patients who eat only a light breakfast should defer the first dose of the day until lunch time. If more than 10 mg daily is required, the excess should be taken with the evening meal.

Changeover from Other Oral Hypoglycemic Agents: There is no exact dosage relationship between glyburide and other oral antidiabetic agents. Discontinue previous oral medication and start glyburide 5 mg daily (2.5 mg in patients over 60 years of age). This also applies to patients changed over from the maximum dose of other oral antidiabetic medication. Determine maintenance dosage as in newly diagnosed diabetics.

Consideration must be given to the potency and duration of action of the previous antidiabetic agent. A break from medication may be required to avoid any summation of effects entailing a risk of hypoglycemia.

Changeover from Insulin: If a change from insulin to glyburide is contemplated in a patient with stable, mild, maturity-onset diabetes, treatment with insulin should be discontinued for a period of 2 or 3 days to determine whether any therapy other than dietary regulation and exercise is needed. During this insulin-free interval, the patient's urine should be tested at least 3 times daily for glucose and ketone-bodies and the results monitored carefully by a physician. The appearance of significant ketonuria accompanied by glucosuria within 12 to 24 hours after the withdrawal of insulin strongly suggests that the patient is ketosis-prone, and precludes the change from insulin to glyburide.

Supplied: 2.5 mg: Each white, round, uncoated, beveled tablet, with score-break, and embossed "LB/6" on obverse and Hoechst logo on reverse, contains: glyburide 2.5 mg. Nonmedicinal ingredients: colloidal silicon dioxide, cornstarch, lactose hydrous, magnesium stearate, purified water and talc. Tartrazine-free. Unit pack boxes of 30 (3×10 blister packed) or 300 (10×30).

5 mg: Each white, oblong, uncoated, beveled tablet, with score-break, both faces embossed with "LDI" and the Hoechst logo, contains: glyburide 5 mg. Nonmedicinal ingredients: colloidal silicon dioxide, cornstarch, lactose hydrous, magnesium stearate, purified water and talc. Tartrazine-free. Unit pack boxes of 30 (3×10 blister packed) and 300 (10×30). Plastic bottles of 300.

Store at room temperature, below 25°C, and not beyond the expiry date indicated on the package.

(Shown in Product Recognition Section)

DIABINESE™ Ⓟ

Pfizer

Chlorpropamide

Oral Hypoglycemic

Pharmacology: Chlorpropamide is an orally active hypoglycemic agent which reduces blood sugar concentration without affecting glucose tolerance. It probably acts by stimulating insulin secretion in the presence of functioning pancreatic islet tissue.

Chlorpropamide is absorbed readily from the gastrointestinal tract and is bound to plasma proteins. Within 1 hour after a single oral dose, it is detectable in the blood, and the level reaches a maximum within 2 to 4 hours. It is slowly excreted by the kidneys as unchanged chlorpropamide, 2-hydroxychlorpropamide, p-chlorbenzene- sulfonylurea, and other metabolites. The biological half-life of a single dose of chlorpropamide averages about 36 hours. Within 96 hours, 80 to 90% of a single oral dose is excreted in the urine. When the drug is administered daily in the appropriate therapeutic dose, it accumulates in the body until a steady state equilibrium develops between the amount administered (daily) and the amount eliminated (daily) through metabolism and excretion. This equilibrium is usually reached in about 5 to 7 days and no further accumulation occurs thereafter unless the dosage is excessive.

Chlorpropamide exerts a hypoglycemic effect in normal humans within 1 hour, becoming maximal at 3 to 6 hours and persisting for at least 24 hours.

Indications: In mild, stable diabetes mellitus of the maturity-onset (or adult) variety to control hyperglycemia responsive to the drug. It should not be used in those patients who are prone to ketosis or who can be controlled by dietary management and exercise alone or for whom insulin therapy is more appropriate.

Contraindications: Known hypersensitivity or allergy to chlorpropamide. Unstable and/or insulin dependent diabetes mellitus; ketoacidosis; coma; during stress conditions such as severe infections, trauma or surgery. Pregnancy. In patients with serious impairment of hepatic, renal or thyroid function.

Warnings: Chlorpropamide will not prevent the development of complications peculiar to diabetes mellitus.

Chlorpropamide administration must be considered as treatment in addition to a proper dietary regimen and not as a substitute for diet.

Over a period of time, patients may become progressively less responsive to therapy with oral hypoglycemic agents because of deterioration of their diabetic state. If a loss of adequate blood glucose lowering response to chlorpropamide is detected, discontinue the drug.

Precautions: Patient Selection and Follow-up: Careful selection of patients is important. It is imperative that there be rigid attention to diet, careful adjustment of dosage, instruction of the patient on hypoglycemic reactions and their control as well as regular thorough follow-up examinations.

Since the effects of oral hypoglycemic agents on the vascular changes and other long-term sequelae of diabetes mellitus are not fully known, patients receiving such drugs must be closely observed for both short- and long-term complications. Periodic assessment of cardiovascular, ophthalmic, renal and hepatic status is advisable.

Although chlorpropamide given alone has controlled some patients with mild maturity-onset diabetes of the stable type during the stress of mild infection or minor surgery, insulin therapy is generally essential during intercurrent complications (for example, ketoacidosis, severe trauma, major surgical procedures, severe infections, severe diarrhea, nausea and vomiting). The severity of the diabetes, the nature of the complications, and availability of laboratory facilities determine whether therapy can be continued or should be withdrawn while insulin is being used.

Hypoglycemic Reactions: Severe hypoglycemia can be induced by all sulfonylurea drugs. Particularly susceptible are elderly subjects, patients with impaired hepatic or renal function, those who are debilitated or malnourished and patients with primary or secondary adrenal insufficiency. Hypoglycemia is more likely to occur when the caloric intake is inadequate or after strenuous or prolonged exercise.

Because of the long biological half-life of chlorpropamide, if the patient becomes hypoglycemic during therapy, withdraw the drug and keep the patient under close supervision for 5 to 6 days. Subsequent reinstitution of chlorpropamide at lower dose levels may be considered.

Drug Interactions: As a result of drug interaction, hypoglycemia may be potentiated when a sulfonylurea is used concurrently with agents such as: long-acting sulfonamides, tuberculostatics, phenylbutazone, clofibrate, MAO inhibitors, coumarin derivatives, salicylates, probenecid, or beta-adrenergic blocking agents such as propranolol.

Certain drugs tend to produce hyperglycemia and may lead to loss of blood sugar control; these include diuretics (thiazides, furosemide), corticosteroids, oral contraceptives (estrogen plus progestogen) and nicotinic acid in pharmacologic doses.

Barbiturates should be used cautiously in patients receiving an oral hypoglycemic agent, since their action may be prolonged.

Intolerance to alcohol (disulfiram-like reaction: flushing, sensation of warmth, giddiness, nausea, and occasionally tachycardia) may occur in patients treated with a sulfonylurea. This reaction can be prevented by avoiding alcohol.

Adverse Effects: The majority of the side effects have been dose-related, transient, and have responded to dose reduction or withdrawal of the medication. However, clinical experience thus far has shown that, as with other sulfonylureas, some side effects associated with hypersensitivity may be severe and deaths have been reported in some instances.

Certain untoward reactions associated with idiosyncrasy or hypersensitivity have occurred, including jaundice, skin eruptions rarely progressing to erythema multiforme and exfoliative dermatitis, and probably depression of formed elements of the blood; these reactions show no direct relationship to the size of the dose.

They occur characteristically during the first 6 weeks of therapy. With a few exceptions, these manifestations have been mild and readily reversible on the withdrawal of the drug.

Hypoglycemia (see Precautions): Severe hypoglycemia which mimics acute CNS disorders may occur. Hepatic and/or renal disease, malnutrition, debility, advanced age, alcoholism, adrenal or pituitary insufficiency may be predisposing factors.

Gastrointestinal: Nausea, epigastric fullness and heartburn are common reactions, tend to be dose related and may disappear when dosage is reduced. Cholangiolytic jaundice due to intracanalicular biliary stasis with elevation of serum alkaline phosphatase has been reported rarely. In patients with progressive elevation of serum alkaline phosphatase, chlorpropamide should be discontinued.

Dermatologic: Allergic skin reactions such as pruritus, erythema, urticaria, morbilliform or maculopapular eruptions have been observed. These may subside on continued use of chlorpropamide, but if they persist, discontinue the drug. Porphyria cutanea tarda and photosensitivity reactions have been reported.

Hematologic: leukopenia, agranulocytosis, thrombocytopenia, hemolytic anemia, aplastic anemia.

Metabolic: hepatic porphyria, disulfiram-like reactions.

Endocrine: Reduced RAI uptake by the thyroid gland has been reported.

Chlorpropamide on some occasions has caused a reaction similar to the syndrome of inappropriate antidiuretic hormone (ADH) secretion. This is characterized by excessive water retention and hyponatremia, low serum osmolality and high urine osmolality.

Overdose: Symptoms: Overdosage with sulfonylureas may result in hypoglycemia, but it should be noted that the dosage which causes hypoglycemia varies widely, and may be within the accepted therapeutic range in sensitive individuals.

The manifestations of hypoglycemia include sweating, flushing or pallor, numbness, chilliness, hunger, trembling, headache, dizziness, increased pulse rate, palpitations, increase in blood pressure and apprehensiveness in the mild cases. In more severe cases, coma appears. However, symptoms of hypoglycemia are not necessarily as typical as described above and sulfonylureas may cause insidious development of symptoms mimicking cerebrovascular insufficiency.

Treatment: Discontinue medication and treat hypoglycemia by giving dextrose promptly and in sufficient quantity. Some sulfonylurea-induced hypoglycemias may be refractory to treatment and susceptible to relapse, especially in elderly or malnourished patients. Continuous dextrose infusions for hours to days have been necessary.

Dosage: In diabetic subjects there is no fixed dosage regimen for management of blood glucose levels. Individual determination of the minimum dose that will lower the blood glucose adequately should be made.

If the maximal recommended dose fails to lower blood glucose adequately in patients on initial trial, discontinue chlorpropamide. During the course of therapy a loss of effectiveness may occur. It is advisable to ascertain chlorpropamide's contribution in the control of blood glucose by discontinuing the medication semi-annually or at least annually with careful patient monitoring. If the need for chlorpropamide is not evident, the drug should not be resumed. In some diabetic subjects, short-term chlorpropamide administration may be sufficient during periods of transient loss of blood sugar control.

The total daily dosage is generally taken at a single time each morning with breakfast. Occasionally cases of gastrointestinal intolerance may be relieved by dividing the daily dosage. **A loading or priming dose is not necessary and should not be used.**

Usual Starting Dose: The stable, mild, nonketosis-prone maturity-onset or adult type diabetic should be started on 250 mg daily. Because the geriatric diabetic patient appears to be more sensitive to the hypoglycemic effect of sulfonylurea drugs, older patients should be started on smaller amounts of chlorpropamide in the range of 100 to 125 mg daily.

No transition period is necessary when transferring patients from other oral hypoglycemic agents to chlorpropamide. The other agent may be discontinued abruptly and chlorpropamide started at once in appropriate dosage.

Changeover From Insulin: If a change from insulin to chlorpropamide is desirable in a patient with stable, mild, maturity-onset diabetes, treatment with insulin should be discontinued abruptly or gradually as appropriate. After an insulin-free period of 2 or 3 days it is possible to determine whether any therapy other than dietary regulation and exercise is needed. During this withdrawal and insulin-free interval, the patient's urine should be tested at least 3 times daily for glucose and ketone bodies, and the results monitored carefully. The appearance of significant ketonuria accompanied by glucosuria within 12 to 24 hours after withdrawal of insulin strongly suggests that the patient is ketosis prone and precludes the change from insulin to chlorpropamide.

Five to seven days after the initial therapy, the blood level of chlorpropamide reaches a plateau. Dosage may subsequently be adjusted upward or downward by increments of not more than 50 to 125 mg at intervals of 3 to 5 days to obtain optimal control. More frequent adjustments are usually undesirable.

In most patients the response to chlorpropamide will be evident within an initial trial period of 7 days. Others may require up to 1 month for maximum control. Provided severe loss of control does not intervene, a patient should not be classified as a primary failure unless 4 weeks of therapy have failed to produce a satisfactory response.

Usual Maintenance Dose: Most diabetic patients responsive to chlorpropamide are controlled by approximately 250 mg daily. Many investigators have found that some of these diabetics do well on daily doses of 100 mg or less, but others may require as much as 500 mg daily for adequate control. Patients who do not respond completely to 500 mg daily will usually not respond to higher doses.

Maximal Dose: Maintenance doses above 500 mg daily should be avoided.

Supplied: 100 mg: Each oval, pale yellow, scored tablet with Pfizer impressed on one side, contains: chlorpropamide 100 mg. Nonmedicinal ingredients: alginic acid, aluminum hydroxide, calcium carbonate, cornstarch, D&C Yellow No. 10, FD&C Yellow No. 6, hydroxypropyl cellulose and magnesium stearate/sodium lauryl sulfate. Tartrazine-free. Bottles of 100.

250 mg: Each oval, white, scored tablet with Pfizer impressed on one side, contains: chlorpropamide 250 mg. Nonmedicinal ingredients: alginic acid, calcium carbonate, cornstarch, hydroxypropyl cellulose and magnesium stearate/sodium lauryl sulfate. Tartrazine-free. Bottles of 100 and 500.

Store between 15 and 30°C.

(Shown in Product Recognition Section)

DIAMICRON® Ⓟ

Servier

Gliclazide

Oral Hypoglycemic

Pharmacology: Gliclazide is an hypoglycemic agent of the sulfonylurea group. Its hypoglycemic action is related to an improvement in insulin secretion from the functioning beta cells of the pancreas. It potentiates the insulin release and improves the dynamics of insulin.

Hemobiological properties of gliclazide have been observed in pharmacology studies. These are attributed to gliclazide action on the platelet behavior, prostaglandin equilibrium and fibrinolysis. At normal therapeutic doses gliclazide has been shown in man to reduce abnormal platelet adhesiveness and aggregation.

Gliclazide is rapidly absorbed from the gastrointestinal tract and the plasma peak of gliclazide occurs between 4 and 6 hours. In man it is highly bound to plasma proteins, about 94%. The mean elimination half-life in man approximates 10.4 hours.

Following oral administration the unchanged gliclazide in plasma is extensively metabolized with little of the unchanged compound (<1%) appearing in the urine.

Gliclazide metabolites and conjugates have no hypoglycemic effect. They are primarily eliminated via kidneys 60 to 70% and about 10 to 20% via feces.

Some 5 principal metabolites have been identified in urine, essentially oxidized and hydroxylated derivatives, some as glucuronic acid conjugates.

Indications: Control of hyperglycemia in gliclazide responsive diabetes mellitus of stable, mild, non-ketosis prone, maturity onset or adult type which cannot be controlled by proper dietary management and exercise, or when insulin therapy is not appropriate.

Contraindications: Known hypersensitivity or allergy to gliclazide. Unstable and/or insulin dependent diabetes mellitus, ketoacidosis, coma. During stress conditions such as serious infection, trauma or surgery. In the presence of liver disease or renal impairment. Pregnancy.

Warnings: The use of gliclazide will not prevent the development of complications peculiar to diabetes mellitus.

Use of gliclazide must be considered as treatment in addition to proper dietary regimen and not as substitute for diet.

Patients over a period of time, may become progressively less responsive to therapy with oral hypoglycemic agents because of worsening of their diabetic state. If a loss of adequate blood glucose-lowering response to gliclazide is detected, the drug should be discontinued.

Precautions: Patient Selection and Follow-up: Careful selection of patients is important. It is imperative that there be rigid attention to diet, careful adjustment of dosage and instruction of the patient on hypoglycemic reactions, their recognition, remedies and control as well as regular, thorough medical follow-up.

Since the effects of oral hypoglycemic agents on the vascular changes and other long-term sequelae of diabetes mellitus are not fully known, patients receiving such drugs must be closely observed for both short- and long-term complications. Periodic assessment of cardiovascular, ophthalmic, renal and hepatic status is advisable.

In patients stabilized on gliclazide therapy, loss of blood sugar control may occur in cases of acute intercurrent disease or in stressful situations such as trauma or surgery. Under these conditions, discontinuation of the drug and administration of insulin should be considered.

The metabolism and excretion of sulfonylureas including gliclazide, may be slowed in patients with impaired renal and/or hepatic function. If hypoglycemia should occur in such patients, it may be prolonged and appropriate management should be instituted. In such patients, blood and urine glucose should be regularly monitored.

Hypoglycemic Reactions: As with other sulfonylurea drugs, manifestations of hypoglycemia including dizziness, lack of energy, drowsiness, headache and sweating have been observed and weakness, nervousness, shakiness and paresthesia have also been reported. Severe hypoglycemia can be induced by all sulfonylurea drugs. Particularly susceptible are elderly subjects, patients with impaired hepatic or renal function, those who are debilitated or malnourished and patients with primary or secondary adrenal insufficiency. Hypoglycemia is more likely to occur when caloric intake is inadequate or after strenuous or prolonged physical exercise.

Diamicron (cont'd)

Drug Interactions: As a result of drug interaction, hypoglycemia may be potentiated when a sulfonylurea is used concurrently with agents such as: long-acting sulfonamides, tuberculostatics, phenylbutazone, clofibrate, MAO inhibitors, coumarin derivatives, salicylates, probenecid, propranolol, miconazole, cimetidine, disopyramide and angiotensin converting enzyme inhibitors.

Certain drugs tend to induce hyperglycemia and may lead to loss of control of blood sugar control. These include diuretics (thiazides, furosemide), corticosteroids, oral contraceptives (estrogen plus progestogen) and nicotinic acid in pharmacologic doses.

Barbiturates should be used with caution in patients receiving an oral hypoglycemic agent since they may reduce the hypoglycemic effect.

Intolerance to alcohol (disulfiram-like reaction: flushing, sensation of warmth, giddiness, nausea and occasionally tachycardia) may occur in patients treated with a sulfonylurea. This reaction can be prevented by avoiding the use of alcohol.

Lactation: Some sulfonylurea drugs are excreted in human milk although it is not known whether gliclazide is one of them. Because the potential for hypoglycemia in nursing infants may exist, a decision should be made whether to discontinue nursing or to discontinue the drug, taking into account the importance of the drug to the mother.

Children: Safety and effectiveness in children have not been established.

Adverse Effects: In clinical trials involving about 2 000 patients treated, the overall incidence of adverse reaction was 10.5%, this necessitated the discontinuation of therapy in 1.2% of patients.

Hypoglycemia (see Precautions): As with other sulfonylurea drugs, manifestations of hypoglycemia including dizziness, lack of energy, drowsiness, headache and sweating have been observed. Weakness, nervousness, shakiness and paresthesia have also been reported. Severe hypoglycemia which mimics acute CNS disorders may occur. Hepatic and/or renal disease, malnutrition, debility, advanced age, alcoholism, adrenal or pituitary insufficiency may be predisposing factors.

Gastrointestinal: Nausea, vomiting, diarrhea, epigastric fullness and gastric irritation can be observed. These reactions are generally dose-related and may disappear when the dose is reduced.

Hepatobiliary: Rare cases of jaundice have been reported.

Dermatological: Allergic reactions such as pruritus, erythema, urticaria and morbiliform or maculopapular rash have been reported. These reactions may persist during treatment, which must then be interrupted. Cases of porphyria cutanea tarda and of photosensitivity have also been described with sulfonylurea drugs.

Hematological: As with all hypoglycemic sulfonylurea drugs, a few rare cases have been reported of leukopenia, agranulocytosis, thrombocytopenia and anemia.

Metabolic: Cases of hepatic porphyria and disulfiram-like reactions have been described with sulfonylurea drugs. Clinical experience to date has shown that gliclazide has a low incidence of disulfiram type reactions.

Endocrine: A decrease in the uptake of radioactive iodine by the thyroid gland has been reported with other sulfonylurea drugs. This has not been shown with gliclazide during a study involving 15 patients.

Laboratory Tests: The pattern of laboratory tests abnormalities observed with gliclazide was similar to that for other sulfonylureas. Occasional mild to moderate elevations of AST, LDH and creatinine and decrease in natremia have been observed. These abnormalities frequently encountered with treated or untreated diabetic patients are rarely associated with clinical symptoms and generally not considered to be drug related.

Overdose: Symptoms: Overdosage with sulfonylureas may result in hypoglycemia but it should be noted that the dosage which causes such hypoglycemia varies widely and may be within the accepted therapeutic range in sensitive individuals.

The manifestations of hypoglycemia include sweating, flushing or pallor, numbness, chilliness, hunger, trembling, headache, dizziness, increased pulse rate, palpitations, increased blood pressure and apprehensiveness in mild cases. In more severe cases, coma appears.

However, symptoms of hypoglycemia are not necessarily as typical as those described above and sulfonylureas may cause insidious development of symptoms mimicking cerebrovascular insufficiency.

Treatment: Discontinue medication and treat hypoglycemia by giving dextrose promptly and in sufficient quantity.

Some sulfonylurea-induced hypoglycemias may be refractory to treatment and susceptible to relapse especially in elderly or malnourished patients. Continuous dextrose infusions for hours or days have been necessary.

Dosage: There is no fixed dosage regimen for the management of diabetes mellitus with gliclazide or any other hypoglycemic agent. Determination of the proper dosage for gliclazide for each patient should be made on the basis of frequent determinations of blood glucose during dose titration and throughout maintenance.

The recommended daily dosage is 80 to 320 mg. Dosage of 160 mg and above should be divided into 2 equal parts for twice a day administration. Gliclazide should be taken preferentially with meals.

The recommended starting dose is 160 mg/day taken as 1 tablet twice a day with meals. The total daily dose should not exceed 320 mg.

In patients in whom on initial trial the maximal recommended dose fails to lower blood glucose adequately, the drug should be discontinued. During the course of therapy a loss of effectiveness may occur.

It is advisable to ascertain the contribution of the drug in control of the blood glucose by discontinuing the medication semi-annually or at least annually with careful monitoring of the patient. If the need for the drug is not evident, the drug should not be resumed. In some diabetic subjects, short-term administration periods of the drug may be sufficient during periods of transient loss of blood sugar controls.

Patients Receiving Insulin: Maturity onset diabetics with no ketoacidosis or history of metabolic decompensation and whose insulin requirements are less than 40 units/day may be considered for gliclazide therapy. If a change from insulin to gliclazide is contemplated in such a patient, discontinue insulin for a period of 2 or 3 days to determine whether any therapy other than dietary regulation and exercise is needed. During this insulin-free interval, test the patient's urine at least 3 times daily for glucose and ketone bodies and monitor the results carefully. The appearance of significant ketonuria accompanied by glucosuria within 12 to 24 hours after the withdrawal of insulin, strongly suggests that the patient is ketosis prone, and precludes the change from insulin to sulfonylurea therapy.

Supplied: Each scored, white tablet, breakable into four, contains: gliclazide 80 mg. Tartrazine-free. Boxes of 20 and 60 in blister packs.

(Shown in Product Recognition Section)

DIAMORPHINE Ⓝ

General Monograph, CPhA

see OPIOID ANALGESICS

DIAMOX® Ⓟ

Wyeth-Ayerst

Acetazolamide

Carbonic Anhydrase Inhibitor

Supplied: Sequels: Each orange, soft shell sustained-release capsule, printed "DIAMOX D3", contains: acetazolamide 500 mg. Nonmedicinal ingredients: ink blue (for printing), microcrystalline cellulose, orange H gelatin, sodium lauryl sulfate and soft shell polishing cream. Tartrazine-free. Bottles of 100.

Tablets: Each white, round, quarter-scored tablet, engraved "LLD2" and "DIAMOX 250", contains: acetazolamide 250 mg. Nonmedicinal ingredients: calcium phosphate dibasic dihydrate, magnesium stearate, povidone, sodium starch glycolate and starch. Energy: <4.2 kJ (1 kcal). Tartrazine-free. Bottles of 100.

Injectable: Each vial of sterile, cryodesiccated powder contains: acetazolamide 500 mg. Nonmedicinal ingredients: hydrochloric acid, sodium hydroxide and water for injection. Preservative- and tartrazine-free. Reconstituted solutions retain their physical properties for 3 days under refrigeration at 2 to 8°C or 12 hours at 15 to 30°C.

(Shown in Product Recognition Section)

DIANE®-35 Ⓟ

Berlex Canada

Cyproterone Acetate—Ethinyl Estradiol

Acne Therapy

Pharmacology: Diane-35 is a combination antiandrogen-estrogen for use in the treatment of androgen-dependent dermatological conditions in females.

Cyproterone is a steroid compound with potent antiandrogenic, progestogenic and antigonadotrophic activity. It exerts its antiandrogenic effect by blocking androgen receptors. It also reduces androgen synthesis by a negative feedback effect on the hypothalamo-pituitary-ovarian systems. The estrogen component (ethinyl estradiol) of Diane-35 increases levels of sex hormone binding globulin (SHBG) and thus reduces the free circulating plasma levels of androgens. Cyproterone has no tendency to reduce SHBG levels.

If used alone in women, cyproterone leads to menstrual cycle disturbances which are avoided when combined with ethinyl estradiol. When Diane-35 is administered in a cyclic manner it has the added effect of preventing ovulation and possible conception.

The components of Diane-35 are rapidly absorbed after oral administration. Due to the long terminal half-life of cyproterone, a 4-fold increase in plasma levels occurs after 6 to 12 days of daily dosing. Long-term therapy (36 months) with Diane-35 did not have a significant influence on lipid metabolism. A trend to increased plasma cholesterol and triglyceride levels was observed. There was a slight decrease in low density lipoprotein (LDL) with a simultaneous increase in high density lipoprotein (HDL).

Indications: For the treatment of women with severe acne, unresponsive to oral antibiotic and other available treatments, with associated symptoms of androgenization, including seborrhea and mild hirsutism.

Note: Diane-35 should not be prescribed solely for its contraceptive properties. However, when taken as recommended (see Dosage), Diane-35 will provide reliable contraception in patients treated for the above clinical conditions. If patient compliance is uncertain and contraception is necessary, then a supplementary nonhormonal contraceptive method should be considered.

> Diane-35 has many properties in common with estrogen/progestogen-combination oral contraceptives and the same Contraindications, Warnings and Precautions applicable to this class of drugs should be considered.
>
> Estrogen and/or progestogen should not be taken during treatment with Diane-35.

Contraindications: Thrombophlebitis, thromboembolic disorders, or a history of these conditions; cerebrovascular disorders; myocardial infarction or coronary artery disease; active liver disease or hepatic adenomas or carcinomas; history of cholestatic jaundice; known or suspected carcinoma of the breast; known or suspected estrogen-dependent neoplasia; undiagnosed abnormal vaginal bleeding; any ocular lesion arising from ophthalmic vascular disease, such as partial or complete loss of vision or defect in visual fields; when pregnancy is suspected or diagnosed; previous or existing liver tumors; severe diabetes with vascular changes; a history of otosclerosis with deterioration during pregnancy.

Warnings: Predisposing Factors For Coronary Artery Diseases: In women with predisposing factors for coronary artery disease (such as cigarette smoking, hypertension, hypercholesterolemia, obesity, diabetes and increasing age), the use of estrogen/progestogen combinations have been reported as an additional risk factor.

After the age of 35 years, estrogen/progestogen combinations should be considered only in exceptional circumstances and when the risk/benefit ratio has been carefully weighed by both the patient and the physician.

> Cigarette smoking increases the risk of serious adverse effects on the heart and blood vessels from the use of this class of medication. This risk increases with age and heavy smoking (15 or more cigarettes per day) and is more marked in women over 35 years of age. Women who use such medication should not smoke.

Estrogen/progestogen combinations may cause an increase in plasma lipoproteins and should be administered with caution to women known to have pre-existent hyperlipoproteinemia. Lipid profiles should be determined regularly in these patients.

The combination of obesity, hypertension and diabetes is particularly hazardous to women who are taking this class of medication. Should this triad of conditions develop, the patient should be placed on an alternate form of therapy.

Discontinue medication at the earliest manifestation of:

A. Thromboembolic and cardiovascular disorders such as: thrombophlebitis, pulmonary embolism, cerebrovascular disorders, myocardial ischemia, mesenteric thrombosis and retinal thrombosis.

The use of estrogen/progestogen-combination products should be avoided in conditions which predispose to venous stasis and to vascular thrombosis, e.g., immobilization after accidents or confinement to bed during long-term illness. Under such conditions, other nonhormonal methods of treatment should be considered. For use when surgery is contemplated, see Precautions.

B. Visual defects, partial or complete.

C. Papilledema, or ophthalmic vascular lesions.

D. Severe headache of unknown etiology, or worsening of pre-existing migraine headache.

E. Onset of jaundice or hepatitis.

F. Itching of the whole body.

Pregnancy: Fetal abnormalities have been reported to occur in the offspring of women who have taken estrogen/progestogen combinations in early pregnancy. Rule out pregnancy as soon as it is suspected.

Lactation: The use of estrogen/progestogen combinations during the period a mother is breast-feeding her infant may not be advisable. The hormonal components are excreted in breast milk and may reduce its quantity and quality. The long-term effects on the developing child are not known.

This drug may cause fluid retention. Conditions such as epilepsy, asthma, and cardiac or renal dysfunction require careful observation.

Recognized first-line tests of genotoxicity gave negative results when conducted with cyproterone. However, further tests showed that cyproterone was capable of producing adducts with DNA (and an increase in DNA repair activity) in liver cells from rats and monkeys and also in freshly isolated human hepatocytes. This DNA-adduct formation occurred at exposures that might be expected to occur in the recommended dose regimens for cyproterone. One in vivo consequence of cyproterone treatment was the increased incidence of focal, possibly pre-neoplastic, liver lesions in which cellular enzymes were altered in female rats.

The relevance of these findings does not appear to be clinically significant based on the results of a multicentre international liver tumor case control study which demonstrated that there is no evidence of an increased risk of hepatocellular carcinoma associated with contraceptive steroids containing cyproterone acetate, even after long-term use.

Precautions: Physical Examination and Follow-up: Before estrogen/progestogen combinations are used, a thorough history and physical examination should be made including a blood pressure determination. Breasts, liver, extremities, abdomen and pelvic organs should be examined. A Papanicolaou smear should be taken if the patient has been sexually active and a urinalysis should be done.

The first follow-up examination should be done 3 months after the initial prescription. Thereafter, examinations should be conducted at regular intervals during long-term treatment and more frequently for those patients at greater risk for adverse effects. At each annual visit, examination should include those procedures outlined above that were done at the initial visit.

Hepatic Function: Patients who have had jaundice should be given estrogen/progestogen combinations with great care and under close observation.

If there is a clear-cut history of cholestatic jaundice, especially if it occurred during pregnancy, other methods of treatment should be prescribed. The development of severe generalized pruritus or icterus requires that the medication be withdrawn until the problem is resolved. If the jaundice should prove to be cholestatic in type, therapy should not be resumed. In patients taking estrogen/progestogen combinations, changes in the composition of the bile may occur and an increased incidence of gallstones has been reported. Hepatic nodules (adenoma and focal nodular hyperplasia) have been reported, particularly in long-term users of estrogen/progestogen combinations. Although these lesions are uncommon, they have caused fatal intra-abdominal hemorrhage and should be considered in women presenting with an abdominal mass, acute abdominal pain, or evidence of intra-abdominal bleeding.

Hypertension: Patients with essential hypertension whose blood pressure is well controlled may be given the drug but only under close supervision. If a significant elevation of blood pressure in previously normotensive or hypertensive subjects occurs at any time during the administration of the drug, cessation of medication is necessary.

Migraine and Headache: The onset or exacerbation of migraine or the development of headache of a new pattern which is recurrent, persistent, or severe, requires discontinuation of medication and evaluation of the cause.

Diabetes: Diabetic patients, or those with a family history of diabetes, should be observed closely to detect any alterations in carbohydrate metabolism. Patients predisposed to diabetes who can be kept under close supervision may be given estrogen/progestogen combinations under strict medical supervision. Young diabetic patients whose disease is of recent origin, well-controlled, and not associated with hypertension or other signs of vascular disease such as ocular fundal changes, should be closely observed.

Metabolic and Endocrine Diseases: In metabolic or endocrine diseases and when metabolism of calcium and phosphorus is abnormal, careful clinical evaluation should precede medication and a regular follow-up is recommended.

Ocular Disease: Progressive astigmatic error, possibly leading to keratoconus, has been noted in some myopic women receiving drugs of the estrogen/progestogen class. In women who developed myopia at or near puberty, and in whom myopia stabilized in adult life, estrogen/progestogen combinations after some 6 months of use have increased the refractive error 2- to 3-fold. Women with a family history of myopic astigmatism or keratoconus who are using such therapy may experience rapid advancement of the ocular disorder.

Contact lens wearers who develop visual changes or changes in lens tolerance should be assessed by an ophthalmologist and temporary or permanent cessation of wear considered.

Connective Tissue Disease: The use of estrogen/progestogen combinations in some women has been associated with positive lupus erythematosus cell tests and with clinical lupus erythematosus. In some instances exacerbation of rheumatoid arthritis and synovitis has been observed.

Breasts: Although estrogen/progestogen-combination use has not been shown to increase the risk of developing breast cancer, particular attention should be paid to women who have an immediate family history of this disease and are therefore more prone to its development. Careful monitoring is mandatory because, if a breast cancer should develop, estrogen-containing drugs may cause a rapid progression if the malignancy is hormone-dependent.

Special judgment should be used in prescribing such medications for women with fibrocystic disease of the breast.

Women receiving such medications should be instructed in self-examination of their breasts. Their physicians should be notified whenever any masses are detected.

Vaginal Bleeding: Persistent irregular vaginal bleeding requires special diagnostic judgment to exclude the possibility of pregnancy or neoplasm.

Fibroids: Patients with fibroids (leiomyomata) should be carefully observed. Sudden enlargement, pain or tenderness require discontinuance of medication.

Age: In general, women in the later reproductive years gradually assume an increasing risk of circulatory and metabolic complications which becomes more prominent at 35 years of age. In view of this, closer observation, shorter duration of estrogen/progestogen-combination use and avoidance of cigarette smoking is advisable. Alternatively, adoption of other means of therapy should be considered for this age group.

Estrogen/progestogen combinations may mask the onset of climacteric.

Emotional Disorders: Patients with a history of emotional disturbances, especially the depressive type, are more prone to have a recurrence of depression while taking estrogen/progestogen combinations. In cases of a serious recurrence, a trial of an alternate method of therapy should be made which may help to clarify the possible relationship.

Laboratory Tests: Results of laboratory tests should be interpreted in light of the fact that the patient is taking estrogen/progestogen therapy. The laboratory tests listed below are modified.

A. Liver function tests: Aspartate serum transaminase (AST): variously reported elevations. Alkaline phosphatase and gamma glutamine transaminase (GGT): slightly elevated.

B. Coagulation tests: Minimal elevation of test values reported for such parameters as Factors VII, VIII, IX and X.

C. Thyroid function tests: Protein binding of thyroxine is increased as indicated by increased total serum thyroxine concentrations and decreased T_3 resin uptake.

D. Lipoproteins: Small changes of unproven clinical significance may occur in lipoprotein cholesterol fractions.

E. Gonadotropins: LH and FSH levels are suppressed by the use of estrogen/progestogen therapy. Wait 2 weeks after discontinuing the use of estrogen/progestogen therapy before measurements are made.

Tissue Specimens: Pathologists should be advised of estrogen/progestogen therapy when specimens obtained from surgical procedures are submitted for examination.

Return to Fertility: After discontinuing therapy, the patient should delay pregnancy until at least 1 normal menstrual cycle has occurred. The patient should be instructed to use a nonhormonal method of contraception during this time period.

Amenorrhea: Women having a history of oligomenorrhea, secondary amenorrhea, or irregular cycles may remain anovulatory or become amenorrheic following estrogen/progestogen-combination therapy. Amenorrhea, especially if associated with breast secretion, that continues for 6 months or more after withdrawal, warrants a careful assessment of hypothalamic-pituitary function.

Thromboembolic Complications—Post-surgery: Retrospective studies have reported an increased risk of post-surgery thromboembolic complications in estrogen/progestogen-combination users. If feasible, such drugs should be discontinued at least 1 month prior to elective major surgery. Medication should not be resumed until at least 2 weeks after hospital discharge following surgery.

Drug Interactions: Concurrent use of the following drugs may result in reduced efficacy of Diane-35 and increased incidence of breakthrough bleeding: ampicillin, analgesics, antihistamines, antimigraine preparations, chloramphenicol, griseofulvin, isoniazid, neomycin, nitrofurantoin, penicillin V, phenylbutazone, sulfonamides and tetracycline.

Concurrent use of anticoagulants with estrogen/progestogen combinations may reduce the anticoagulant effect. Effectiveness of the following drugs may be altered when used concurrently: antihypertensives, benzodiazepines (those that undergo oxidative degradation) beta-adrenergic blockers, caffeine, corticosteroids, hypoglycemics, phenothiazines, theophyllines, tricyclic antidepressants and vitamins.

Concurrent use of the following drugs may reduce the efficacy of Diane-35 because of accelerated estrogen metabolism caused by the induction of hepatic enzymes: carbamazepine, phenobarbital, phenytoin, primidone and rifampin.

Diabetics using estrogen/progestogen combinations may require adjustment of their antidiabetic medication.

Concurrent administration of vitamin C (ascorbic acid) with estrogen/progestogen combinations has been reported to result in a significant rise in plasma ethinyl estradiol levels.

Pregnancy: Rule out pregnancy before treatment is begun. Because of the antiandrogenic action of Diane-35, feminization of male fetuses has occurred in animal studies and may possibly occur in humans.

Adverse Effects: General: An increased risk of the following serious adverse reactions has been associated with the use of estrogen/progestogen combinations: thrombophlebitis; arterial thromboembolism; pulmonary embolism; mesenteric thrombosis; neuro-ocular lesions, e.g., retinal thrombosis and optic neuritis; myocardial infarction; cerebral thrombosis; cerebral hemorrhage; hypertension; liver tumors; gallbladder disease and congenital anomalies.

The following adverse reactions also have been reported in patients receiving estrogen/progestogen-combination oral contraceptives: nausea and vomiting, usually the most common adverse reaction occurring in approximately 10% or less of patients during the first cycle. Other reactions, as a general rule, are seen less frequently or only occasionally: gastrointestinal symptoms (such as abdominal cramps and bloating); breakthrough bleeding; spotting; change in menstrual flow; dysmenorrhea; amenorrhea during and after treatment; temporary infertility after discontinuance of treatment; edema; chloasma or melasma which may persist; breast changes: tenderness, enlargement, and secretion; change in weight (increase or decrease); change in cervical erosion and secretion; endocervical hyperplasia; possible diminution in lactation when given immediately postpartum; cholestatic jaundice; migraine; increase in size of uterine leiomyomata; rash (allergic); mental depression; reduced tolerance to carbohydrates; vaginal candidiasis; premenstrual-like syndrome; intolerance to contact lenses; change in corneal curvature (steepening); cataracts; optic neuritis; retinal thrombosis; changes in libido; chorea; changes in appetite; cystitis-like

Diane-35 (cont'd)

syndrome; rhinitis; headache; nervousness; dizziness; hirsutism; loss of scalp hair; erythema multiforme; erythema nodosum; hemorrhagic eruption; vaginitis; porphyria; impaired renal function; Raynaud's phenomenon; auditory disturbances; hemolytic uremic syndrome and pancreatitis.

Product-specific Adverse Reactions: Diane-35 was generally well tolerated in studies involving 1 563 women who were treated for periods of 6 to 36 cycles. The most frequently reported complaint was dysmenorrhea (10.2%) which decreased over time in a manner characteristic of treatment with estrogen/progestogen combinations. Other effects reported were also similar in nature and frequency to those reported with estrogen/progestogen combinations (see Table I).

Table I—Diane-35

Production-Specific Adverse Events	No. of Cycles*	% Frequency (%)
Dysmenorrhea	23 426	10.2
Breast tension/tenderness	23 814	6.5
Headache	23 810	5.2
Nervousness	23 827	4.4
Chloasma	23 112	4.2
Depressed mood	23 829	3.4
Decreased libido	23 821	3.1
Varicosities	23 829	2.9
Nausea	23 822	1.9
Edema	23 118	1.7
Dizziness	23 340	1.1

*Number of cycles evaluated.

Serious postmarketing adverse reactions reported with Diane-35 include deep venous thrombosis, venous thrombosis with pulmonary embolism, arterial emboli involving the extremities and the spleen, cerebral ischemic vascular accident, cerebral venous thrombosis, sinus thrombosis, retinal vein thrombosis, hypertensive crisis, migraine, pancreatitis, focal nodular hyperplasia of the liver, subcapsular liver hematoma, liver adenoma, hepatocellular carcinoma, primary bile duct carcinoma, hepatitis, liver dystrophy, cholangitis, pseudomembranous colitis, cholestasis, abdominal pain, epileptic seizures, cerebral tumor symptoms, acute brachiofacial paresis, acute hydrocephalus, manic syndrome, hyperpathia, anaphylactoid reactions, ascites, diabetes mellitus, acute leukemia and breast cancer.

The following nonserious adverse reactions, listed according to body system, have been reported postmarketing: Cardiovascular: headaches, migraine, superficial phlebitis, palpitations, flushing.

Gastrointestinal: focal nodular hyperplasia, liver tumor, hepatitis, jaundice, hepatomegaly without abnormal liver tests, nausea, diarrhea, flatulence, stomatitis, salivary gland swelling.

Genitourinary: menstrual disorder, ovarian cyst, myoma, cervix dysplasia, vaginitis, urinary tract infection, premature birth, abortion, missed abortion and placenta insufficiency.

Metabolism: abnormal liver enzymes, hyperthyroidism, hyperprolactinemia.

Nervous system: depression, decreased libido, nervousness, insomnia, somnolence, confusion, hypesthesia, paresthesia, seizures (in patients with a history of epilepsy), visual disturbances, symptoms of conjunctival irritation, hearing disorder.

Skin: alopecia, acne, chloasma, exanthema, erythema nodosum, striae, neurodermitis, skin allergy, urticaria, facial edema, pruritus, photosensitivity, pigmentation, dry skin, Herpes zoster, cellulitis, s.c. lumps, eczema, livedo, blue spots.

Overdose: Symptoms and Treatment: There have been no reports of overdose with Diane-35. There are no specific antidotes and treatment should be symptomatic, based on the knowledge of the pharmacological action of the constituents.

Dosage: Diane-35 should not be prescribed solely for its contraceptive properties. If patient compliance is uncertain and contraception is necessary, then a supplementary nonhormonal contraceptive method should be considered.

Diane-35 is supplied in blister pack units consisting of 21 tablets; each tablet containing cyproterone acetate 2 mg and ethinyl estradiol 0.035 mg. Each cycle consists of 21 days on medication and a 7-day interval without medication (3 weeks on, 1 week off).

First Treatment Course: The patient is instructed to take 1 tablet daily for 21 consecutive days beginning on day 1 of her menstrual cycle. (For the first cycle only the first day of menstrual flow is considered Day 1.) The tablets are then discontinued for 7 days (1 week). Withdrawal bleeding should usually occur during the period that the patient is off the tablets. The first cycle will be somewhat shorter than usual, whereas all following cycles will last 4 weeks.

Subsequent Courses: The patient begins her next and all subsequent 21-day course of tablets (following the same 21 days on, 7 days off) on the same day of the week that she began her first course. She begins taking her tablets 7 days after discontinuation, regardless of whether or not withdrawal bleeding is still in progress.

Treatment should be continued for several months, since improvement may not be observed with 4 or 5 cycles. It is recommended to continue treatment with Diane-35 for at least another 3 to 4 cycles after signs have subsided.

Pregnancy should be ruled out before continuing treatment with Diane-35 in patients who have missed a menstrual period. If pregnancy is suspected, medication should be discontinued.

Special Notes on Administration: It is recommended that Diane-35 tablets be taken at the same time each day. Irregular tablet-taking, vomiting or intestinal affections with diarrhea, very rare individual metabolic disturbances or prolonged simultaneous use of certain medical preparations can affect the contraceptive action (see Precautions, Drug Interactions).

If spotting or breakthrough bleeding occurs during the 3 weeks in which Diane-35 is being taken, the patient is instructed to continue taking the medication. This type of bleeding usually is transient and without significance. However, if the bleeding is persistent or prolonged, the patient is advised to consult her physician.

In exceptional cases, menstruation may fail to occur during the 7-day tablet-free interval. The patient is advised not to resume tablet-taking and to consult her physician.

Although the occurrence of pregnancy is highly unlikely if the tablets are taken according to directions, the possibility of pregnancy should be ruled out before continuing treatment with Diane-35 in patients who have missed a period of withdrawal bleeding. The patient should consult her physician and, in the meantime, a supplementary nonhormonal method of contraception should be employed.

If the patient forgets to take a tablet at the usual time, the tablet may be taken within the next 12 hours. If more than 12 hours have elapsed from the time of usual administration, the patient must discard the missed tablet and continue to take the remaining tablets in the pack at the usual time in order to avoid a premature withdrawal bleeding during this cycle. A supplementary nonhormonal method of contraception must be employed until the pack is empty to prevent pregnancy which would necessitate immediate discontinuation of Diane-35 treatment.

Use of the Blister Pack: The patient should be instructed to take the first tablet from the blister pack out of the section marked with the corresponding day of the week (for example "MO" for Monday), and swallow it whole with some liquid. The patient should be instructed to take the tablet at the same time each day.

Information for the Patient: See Blue Section—Information for the Patient "Diane-35".

Supplied: Each beige, round, biconvex, sugar-coated tablet contains: cyproterone acetate 2 mg and ethinyl estradiol 0.035 mg. Nonmedicinal ingredients: cornstarch, lactose, magnesium stearate, povidone and talc; tablet coating: calcium carbonate, ferric oxide yellow, glycerol, polyethylene glycol, povidone, sucrose, talc, titanium dioxide and wax. Blister pack units of 21. Store at room temperature (15 to 25°C).

(Shown in Product Recognition Section)

New Product 1998

DIA-VITE®

R&D Laboratories

Multivitamins

Vitamin Supplement

Supplied: Each film-coated, round, yellow tablet, marked RD12, contains: vitamin C 60 mg, vitamin B_1 1.5 mg, vitamin B_2 1.7 mg, niacinamide 20 mg, vitamin B_6 10 mg, vitamin B_{12} 6 μg, folic acid 1 mg, pantothenic acid 10 mg and biotin 300 μg. Nonmedicinal ingredients: croscarmellose sodium, magnesium stearate, silicon dioxide and stearic acid. Plastic bottles of 100 and 500. For use under medical supervision.

DIAZEMULS® Ⓟ

Pharmacia & Upjohn

Diazepam Injectable Emulsion

Anxiolytic—Sedative

Pharmacology: Diazemuls is an injectable emulsion of diazepam, a drug with known anxiolytic-sedative and muscle relaxant properties. Diazepam has been found useful for short-term symptomatic relief of excessive anxiety and tension in patients with anxiety neurosis, although anxiety and tension associated with the stresses of everyday life usually do not require treatment with anxiolytic drugs.

Diazepam must first be released from the oil phase of the emulsion before it can exert a therapeutic effect. In fact, peak blood levels of diazepam are reached only after 15 minutes following i.v. injection of Diazemuls, and after 2 hours following i.m. administration. Subsequent to a rapid distribution phase, diazepam undergoes a longer elimination phase, which varies with age, from approximately 20 hours at age 20 to approximately 80 hours at age 80.

Diazepam is metabolized in the liver to N-desmethyldiazepam, and to some extent to N-methyl-oxazepam, which in turn is metabolized to oxazepam. Although these metabolites are pharmacologically active, only N-desmethyl-diazepam is formed in sufficient quantity to produce significant clinical effects. The desmethyl metabolite has an elimination half-life of 50 to 120 hours.

Diazepam and its metabolites are excreted mainly in the urine, as glucoronides or sulfates.

Diazepam crosses the placenta and is secreted in breast milk. It is approximately 98% bound to plasma proteins.

Indications: Diazemuls is indicated when an injectable preparation of diazepam is required. It has been found useful: to alleviate the symptoms of acute alcohol withdrawal, such as acute agitation, tremor, impending or acute delirium tremens and hallucinosis; as an adjunct prior to endoscopic procedures if apprehension, anxiety or acute stress reactions are present, and to diminish the patients recall of the procedures (see Warnings); for the relief of muscle spasm in cerebral palsy, athetosis and stiff man syndrome; as premedication for relief of anxiety states prior to surgical procedures (i.m. route) or cardioversion (i.v. route).

Contraindications: Patients with known hypersensitivity to diazepam or the components of the emulsion vehicle (see Supplied); myasthenia gravis; acute narrow angle glaucoma, and open angle glaucoma unless patients are receiving appropriate therapy.

Warnings: Diazemuls should not be administered to patients in shock or coma. There have been rare reports of apnea or cardiac arrest, usually following i.v. administration, especially in elderly or very ill patients and in those with limited pulmonary reserve. Resuscitative equipment including that necessary to support respiration should therefore be readily available. Since lingual obstruction of the airway may occur, particularly in children and in the elderly, caution is required to maintain a free airway in patients receiving Diazemuls injection.

Rapid injection or the use of veins with too small a lumen carries the risk of thrombophlebitis. I.V. injection should therefore be directly into a large lumen vessel, such as an antecubital vein, and the drug should be administered slowly, at the rate of no more than 5 mg (1 mL)/minute. Extreme care should be taken to avoid intra-arterial administration or extravasation.

When used i.v., Diazemuls should be injected directly into the vein without prior dilution or mixing with other products or solutions (see Dosage).

Concomitant use of barbiturates, alcohol or other CNS depressants increases depression with increased risk of apnea. When diazepam is used in a patient taking narcotic analgesics, the dosage of the narcotic should be reduced by at least one-third and administered in small increments. In some instances the use of a narcotic may not be necessary. Diazepam should not be administered to patients with acute alcoholic intoxication with depression of vital signs.

Occupational Hazards: Patients receiving diazepam should be cautioned against engaging in hazardous occupations requiring complete mental alertness, such as operating machinery or driving a motor vehicle.

Physical and Psychological Dependence: Withdrawal symptoms similar to those noted with barbiturates and alcohol may occur following abrupt discontinuance of diazepam (convulsions, tremor, abdominal and muscle cramps, vomiting and sweating). Severe symptoms are usually limited to those patients who have received excessive doses over an extended period of time. Milder withdrawal symptoms have been reported more frequently following abrupt discontinuance of benzodiazepines. Consequently, after extended therapy, abrupt discontinuation should generally be avoided and gradual tapering in dosage followed. Particularly addiction-prone individuals (such as drug addicts or alcoholics) should be under careful surveillance when receiving diazepam or other psychotropic agents because of the predisposition of such patients to habituation and dependence.

Pregnancy: An increased risk of congenital malformations associated with the use of anxiolytic-sedative drugs including diazepam, meprobamate and chlordiazepoxide during the first trimester of pregnancy has been suggested in several studies. Therefore, the use of these drugs during pregnancy should almost always be avoided, unless the expected benefits are considered to outweigh the potential risks. The possibility that a woman of child-bearing potential may be pregnant at the time of institution of therapy should be considered.

Obstetrics: The safety and efficacy of diazepam in obstetrics have not yet been established.

Children: Efficacy and safety of diazepam have not been established in the neonate (30 days or less of age). Prolonged CNS depression has been observed in the neonate, apparently due to inability to biotransform diazepam into inactive metabolites.

In pediatric use, in order to obtain maximal clinical effect with the minimum amount of drug and thus to reduce the risk of hazardous side effects, such as apnea or prolonged periods of somnolence, it is recommended that the drug be given slowly over a 3-minute period in a dosage not to exceed 0.25 mg/kg. After an interval of 15 to 30 minutes the initial dosage can be cautiously repeated. If, however, relief of symptoms is not obtained after a third administration, adjunctive therapy appropriate to the condition being treated should be considered.

Precautions: Geriatrics: Elderly and debilitated patients and those with organic brain disorders have been found to be very prone to CNS depression following even low doses of diazepam. Diazepam should be used in those patients with caution and in low doses to preclude development of ataxia, sedation and other possible adverse effects.

Emotional Disorders: Diazepam is not recommended in the treatment of psychotic or severely depressed patients. Precautions are indicated for severely depressed patients or those who show evidence of impending depression, particularly in the recognition that suicidal tendencies may be present and protective measures may be necessary.

Since excitement and other paradoxical reactions may result from use of the drug in psychotic patients, diazepam should not be used in ambulatory patients suspected of having psychotic tendencies.

Use before Bronchoscopy and Laryngoscopy: Since there are insufficient data available to establish the safety of diazepam prior to bronchoscopy and laryngoscopy, its use is not recommended.

Use before Gastroscopy, Esophagoscopy, Cardioversion and Surgical Procedures: Diazepam should be used only under conditions in which safeguards are available should laryngospasm and circulatory or respiratory depression occur.

Since an increase in cough reflex and laryngospasm may occur with peroral endoscopic procedures, the use of a topical anesthetic agent and the availability of necessary counter measures are recommended.

Concurrent use of narcotics and barbiturates with diazepam may produce a potentiation of effect and, when such combinations are used, appropriate reduction of dosage is required.

Impaired Renal and Hepatic Function: The usual precautions in treating patients with impaired hepatic function should be observed. Since metabolites of diazepam are excreted by the kidney, in order to avoid their excess accumulation, caution should be exercised in the administration of the drug to patients with compromised kidney function.

Potentiation of Drug Effects: Careful consideration should be given if diazepam is to be used concomitantly with other psychotropic agents such as phenothiazines, barbiturates, MAO inhibitors and other antidepressants, since the pharmacological action of these agents may potentiate the action of diazepam.

Due to the possible potentiation of effects and the occurrence of adverse reactions, patients should be advised to abstain from CNS depressant drugs during treatment with diazepam.

The clearance of diazepam and of certain other benzodiazepines can be delayed when used in association of cimetidine.

Parenteral diazepam has produced hypotension or muscular weakness in some patients, particularly when used with barbiturates, narcotics and alcohol.

General: After administration of diazepam, ambulation should be delayed until complete alertness is restored.

Adverse Effects: Evidence suggests that there is a lower incidence of local reactions when Diazemuls is used. Side effects most commonly reported are drowsiness, fatigue and ataxia. Other adverse reactions less frequently reported include:

CNS: confusion, depression, dysarthria, headache, hypoactivity, slurred speech, syncope, tremor, vertigo and floppy infant syndrome.

Gastrointestinal: constipation, nausea.

Urogenital: incontinence, changes in libido, urinary retention.

Cardiovascular: bradycardia, cardiovascular collapse, hypotension, venous thrombosis and phlebitis at site of injection.

Ophthalmological: blurred vision, diplopia, nystagmus.

Dermatological: urticaria, skin rash.

Other: hiccups, changes in salivation, neutropenia, jaundice. Paradoxical reactions such as acute hyperexcited states, anxiety, hallucinations, increased muscle spasticity, insomnia, rage, sleep disturbances and stimulation have been reported; should these occur, use of the drug should be discontinued. Minor changes in EEG patterns, usually low-voltage fast activity, have been observed in patients during and after diazepam therapy and are of no known significance.

In peroral endoscopic procedures, coughing, depressed respiration, dyspnea, hyperventilation, laryngospasm and pain in throat or chest have been reported.

Because of isolated reports of neutropenia and jaundice, periodic blood counts and liver function tests are advisable during long-term therapy.

Overdose: Symptoms and Treatment: Manifestations of diazepam overdosage include somnolence, confusion, coma and diminished reflexes. Respiration, pulse and blood pressure should be monitored, as in all cases of drug overdosage, although, in general, these effects have been minimal unless overdose is extreme. General supportive measures should be employed, along with i.v. fluids, and an adequate airway maintained. Hypotension may be combatted by the use of levarterenol. Dialysis is of limited value.

Dosage: Dosage should be individualized for maximal beneficial effect. The usual recommended dose in older children and adults ranges from 2 to 20 mg i.m. or i.v., depending on the indication and/or the severity of the condition (see Dosage for specific indications). In acute conditions the injection may be repeated within 1 hour, although an interval of 3 to 4 hours is usually satisfactory.

When a continuing drug effect is required, lower doses (usually 2 to 5 mg) with small increments if necessary, should be used in elderly or debilitated patients and when other sedative drugs are administered (see Warnings and Adverse Effects).

For dosage in pediatric use, see Dosage and Warnings.

Because of its delayed action, Diazemuls is not recommended for the management of status epilepticus.

I.V. Use: Diazemuls should be injected slowly, taking at least 1 minute for each 5 mg (1 mL) administered. Extreme care should be taken to avoid intra-arterial administration or extravasation (see Warnings, particularly for use in children).

When i.v. use is indicated, facilities for respiratory assistance should be readily available.

When used i.v., Diazemuls should be injected directly into the vein without prior dilution or mixing with other products or solutions. Diazemuls may, however, be mixed or diluted with Intralipid, but such an admixture should be used within 6 hours. If it is not feasible to administer Diazemuls directly i.v., it may be injected slowly through the infusion tubing as close as possible to the vein insertion.

Diazemuls has been shown to be incompatible with morphine and glycopyrrolate. Mixing or further diluting Diazemuls with products or solutions other than its own emulsion base (Intralipid) may de-stabilize the emulsion. Although such an effect may not be recognizable on visual inspection, it could give rise to potentially serious adverse reactions. Polyethylene-lined or glass infusion sets and polyethylene/polypropylene plastic syringes are recommended for use with Diazemuls. Do not use infusion sets containing polyvinyl chloride.

I.M. Use: Diazemuls should be injected deeply into the muscle.

Dosage: Adults: Acute anxiety or tension states related to stressful conditions or non-psychotic emotional disorders when parenteral administration is required. Depending on severity, 2 to 10 mg, i.m. or i.v. Repeat in 3 to 4 hours, if necessary.

Acute alcohol withdrawal: As an aid in symptomatic relief of acute agitation, tremor, impending or acute delirium tremens and hallucinosis. Initially 10 mg i.m. or i.v., then 5 to 10 mg in 3 to 4 hours, if necessary.

Minor surgical procedures including esophagoscopy and gastroscopy: as an adjunct in relieving anxiety states that may be present before these procedures. Approximately 5 to 10 mg, i.m. or i.v., as required, about 30 minutes prior to procedures.

For the relief of muscle spasm in cerebral palsy, athetosis and stiff man syndrome. Initially, 5 to 10 mg i.m. or i.v., then 5 to 10 mg in 3 to 4 hours, if necessary.

Pre-operative medication for the relief of anxiety states. If premedications other than atropine sulfate, scopolamine hydrobromide, meperidine or fentanyl citrate are desired, they must be administered in separate syringes. Extreme caution must be exercised in patients with chronic lung disease or unstable cardiovascular status. 10 mg i.m. or i.v. 1 to 2 hours before surgery.

Cardioversion: to relieve anxiety and tension and to reduce recall of procedure. 5 to 10 mg, i.v., within 10 to 20 minutes prior to procedure.

Children: See Warnings. Dosage not to exceed 0.25 mg/kg slowly over a 3-minute period.

Geriatrics and Debilitated: See Precautions. 2 to 5 mg, i.m. or i.v.

Once the acute symptomatology has been properly controlled with Diazemuls the patient may be placed on oral therapy with diazepam if further treatment is required.

Supplied: Each mL contains: diazepam 5 mg, dissolved in the oil phase of an oil/water emulsion compounded with purified soybean oil 150 mg, acetylated monoglycerides 50 mg, purified egg phospholipids 12 mg, glycerol anhydrous 22 mg and sodium hydroxide to adjust pH to approximately 8. Diazemuls is a sterile formulation and contains no preservatives. It is intended for i.v. or i.m. use only. Ampuls of 2 mL, packages of 10. Store at controlled temperature below 25°C. Do not freeze.

DIAZEPAM Ⓟ

General Monograph, CPhA

see BENZODIAZEPINES

DIBAN® Ⓝ

Wyeth-Ayerst

Attapulgite—Pectin—Opium—Belladonna Alkaloids Compound

Antidiarrheal

Supplied: Each blue capsule with white "AYERST" monogram contains: activated attapulgite 300 mg, pectin 71.4 mg, powdered opium 12 mg, hyoscyamine sulfate 52 μg, atropine sulfate 10 μg, scopolamine HBr 3 μg. Nonmedicinal ingredients: magnesium stearate and microcrystalline cellulose; empty capsule: FD&C Blue No. 1, FD&C Red No. 3, gelatin, silicon dioxide, sodium lauryl sulfate and titanium dioxide. Energy: <1 kJ (<1 kcal). Bottles of 12.

DICETEL® Ⓟ

Solvay Pharma

Pinaverium Bromide

Gastrointestinal Calcium Antagonist

Pharmacology: Pinaverium is a calcium antagonist which inhibits the calcium influx by blocking the voltage-dependent calcium channel at the smooth muscle cell level. It possesses a high degree of selectivity for the intestinal smooth muscle.

Many studies showed that pinaverium induces a relaxation of the gastrointestinal and the biliary tracts and mainly of the colon, an inhibition of the motor colonic response to food and/or pharmacological stimulations, implying the action of the drug in irritable bowel syndrome.

Indications: For the treatment and relief of symptoms associated with irritable bowel syndrome (IBS): abdominal pain, bowel disturbances and intestinal discomfort.

For the treatment of symptoms related to functional disorders of the biliary tract.

Contraindications: Patients with known hypersensitivity to pinaverium or any of the excipients.

No other contraindications have been identified at this time.

Warnings: Contact of pinaverium with the esophageal mucosa may be irritating. Therefore, it is strongly recommended that the tablet be taken with a glass of water during mealtime. If more than 3 tablets are prescribed per day, the additional

Dicetel (cont'd)

tablet(s) should be taken concurrently with a glass of water and a snack.

Precautions: Pinaverium should not be administered for the relief of motility dysfunction due to underlying organic disease.
Pregnancy: Reproductive studies performed in animals have not revealed the presence of teratogenic effects. However, the safety of pinaverium during pregnancy has not been established. Consequently, in the pregnant patient, this drug should only be administered if, in the judgement of the physician, its use is essential to the welfare of the patient.
Lactation: There have been no controlled studies in nursing women; therefore, the drug should be avoided during lactation.

Adverse Effects: Minor adverse events were reported and listed as mild and moderate. They were mainly minor digestive disorders that may be related to the disease, such as epigastric pain and/or fullness (0.8%), nausea (0.5%), constipation (0.4%), heartburn (0.3%), distension (0.3%) and diarrhea (0.2%).
Other Systems: headache (0.3%), dryness of the mouth (0.3%), drowsiness (0.2%), vertigo (0.2%) and skin allergy (0.2%).

Overdose: Symptoms and Treatment: In man, apart from diarrhea and/or flatulence, pinaverium induced no undesirable effects in daily dosages of up to 1 200 mg.

No cases of overdosage of pinaverium have been reported to date. However, if overdosage occurs, gastric lavage is recommended and symptomatic treatment initiated if deemed necessary.

Dosage: The usual adult dosage is 3 film-coated tablets of 50 mg a day (1 tablet 3 times a day). In exceptional cases, the dosage may be increased up to 6 tablets a day (2 tablets 3 times a day).

It is recommended that the tablet be taken with a glass of water during meals or snacks. The tablet should not be swallowed when in the lying position or just before bedtime.

The duration of treatment depends on the disorders for which pinaverium is given.

Supplied: Each orange-colored, circular-shaped, film-coated tablet, with a slightly convex surface, contains: pinaverium bromide 50 mg. Nonmedicinal ingredients: in the core: hydrophobic anhydrous silica, magnesium stearate, microcrystalline cellulose, modified cornstarch, modified lactose and talc; in the film coating: gastrosoluble acrylic resin, micronized talc, polyoxyethylene glycol 6000 and Sepisperse orange K3020 [titanium dioxide (E 171), sunset yellow lake (E 110), hydroxy propylcellulose (E 463)]; intermediary solvents: acetone, ethanol and isopropanol. Boxes of 100 in blister packs. Store at room temperature (15 to 30°C) in dispensing box.

(Shown in Product Recognition Section)

DICLECTIN® 🅿

Duchesnay

Doxylamine Succinate—Pyridoxine HCl

Antinauseant against Nausea and Vomiting of Pregnancy

Pharmacology: The action of Diclectin is due to 2 unrelated compounds. Doxylamine succinate, an antihistamine, provides the antinauseant and antiemetic activity; pyridoxine HCl provides a supplement of vitamin B_6 to prevent a possible pyridoxine deficiency during pregnancy. Also, studies have shown that pyridoxine itself could have an antinauseant activity. The onset of the antiemetic activity of Diclectin is delayed by a special coating of the tablet; a dose taken at night will be effective in the morning, the time when it is most needed.

Indications: In cases of nausea and vomiting of pregnancy.

Precautions: Occupational Hazards: Due to a risk of drowsiness, Diclectin must be prescribed with caution to automobile drivers and machine operators.

It must also be used with caution in combination with alcohol and other CNS depressing drugs or with epileptic patients.

Adverse Effects: The adverse effects are those produced by the 2 ingredients. Doxylamine succinate may cause drowsiness, vertigo, nervousness, epigastric pain, headache, palpitation, diarrhea, disorientation, irritability, convulsions, urinary retention or insomnia. Pyridoxine is a vitamin that is generally recognized as having no adverse effects.

Overdose: Symptoms: Signs and symptoms of intoxication are restlessness, dryness of mouth, dilated pupils, sleepiness, vertigo, mental confusion and tachycardia.

Treatment: If treatment is needed, it consists of gastric lavage, emetics or activated charcoal and a symptomatic treatment.

Dosage: 2 delayed release tablets at bedtime. Add 1 delayed release tablet in the morning and 1 delayed release tablet in mid-afternoon when nausea or vomiting occurs during the day or in severe cases.

Information for the Patient: See Blue Section—Information for the Patient "Diclectin".

Supplied: Each white, coated, delayed release tablet contains: doxylamine succinate USP 10 mg and pyridoxine HCl 10 mg. Tartrazine-free. Bottles of 100 and 1 000.

DICLOTEC 🅿

Technilab

Diclofenac Sodium

Anti-inflammatory—Analgesic

Pharmacology: Diclofenac sodium is a nonsteroidal anti-inflammatory drug (NSAID) with analgesic and antipyretic properties. The mode of action is not fully known but it does not act through the pituitary-adrenal axis. Diclofenac sodium inhibits prostaglandin synthesis by interfering with the action of prostaglandin synthetase. This inhibitory effect may partially explain its actions.

From a clinical efficacy standpoint, diclofenac sodium 75 mg has activity similar to 3.6 g of ASA.

Diclofenac sodium is similar in activity to equivalent dosages of indomethacin (75 to 150 mg daily) and causes fewer CNS side effects at these doses.

Although diclofenac sodium does not alter the course of the underlying disease, it has been found to relieve pain, reduce fever, swelling and tenderness, and increase mobility in patients with rheumatic disorders of the types listed.
Pharmacokinetics: Absorption: In humans, orally administered diclofenac sodium is rapidly and almost completely absorbed and distributed to blood, liver and kidneys. The plasma concentrations show a linear relationship to the amount of drug administered. No accumulation occurs provided the recommended dosage intervals are observed.

Enteric coating may delay the onset of absorption from 25 and 50 mg tablets. Absorption occurs more rapidly when the drug is administered on an empty stomach (T_{max} 2.5 hours) than with meals (T_{max} 6 hours). The bioavailability remains the same under both conditions. The mean peak plasma concentration of 1.5 μg/mL (5 μmol/L) is attained, on average, 2 hours after ingestion of one 50 mg enteric-coated tablet.

Following administration of the slow-release (SR) diclofenac sodium, C_{max} is reached at approximately 4 hours or later. Significant drug plasma concentrations persist when levels would have dropped almost to baseline values following enteric-coated tablet administration. Mean plasma concentrations of 13 ng/mL (40 nmol/L) were produced 24 hours after diclofenac SR 100 mg, or 16 hours after diclofenac SR 75 mg following administration of a single dose. Trough levels are approximately 22 to 25 ng/mL (70 to 80 nmol/L) during treatment with diclofenac SR 100 mg once daily, or 16 hours after diclofenac SR 75 mg administered twice daily. In pharmacokinetic studies, no accumulation of diclofenac sodium was found following repeated once daily administration of diclofenac SR 100 mg tablets or repeated twice daily administration of diclofenac SR 75 mg tablets.

Suppositories have a more rapid onset, but slower rate of absorption than oral enteric-coated tablets. C_{max} is approximately 2/3 of that produced by an equivalent 50 mg enteric-coated tablet oral dose. T_{max} occurs within 1 hour. The unchanged diclofenac plasma AUC values after rectal administration are within the range of values produced by equivalent oral enteric-coated tablet doses. Since about half the active substance is metabolized during its first passage through the liver ("first pass" effect), the area under the concentration curve (AUC) following oral or rectal administration is about half as large as it is following a parenteral dose of equal size.
Distribution: Diclofenac sodium is extensively bound (99%) to serum albumin. The apparent volume of distribution is 0.12 to 0.17 L/kg. Single-dose (oral or i.m.) studies in rheumatoid patients with joint effusions have shown that diclofenac is distributed to the synovial fluid, where T_{max} occurs 2 to 4 hours after plasma T_{max}. Synovial fluid concentrations exceed plasma levels within 4 to 6 hours of administration. This elevation above plasma concentrations can be maintained for up to 12 hours. The synovial fluid elimination half-life is at least 3 times greater than that for plasma.
Biotransformation: Diclofenac undergoes single and multiple hydroxylation and methoxylation, producing 3'-, 4'-, 5-hydroxy, 4'-5-hydroxy and 3'-hydroxy-4'-methoxy derivatives of diclofenac. These phenolic metabolites are largely inactive and (along with the parent compound) are mostly converted to glucuronide conjugates.
Elimination: Plasma clearance of diclofenac is 263±56 mL/min. The mean terminal drug half-life in plasma is 1.8 hours after oral doses. In humans about 60% of the drug and its metabolites are eliminated in the urine and the balance through bile in the feces. More than 90% of an oral dose is accounted for in elimination products within 72 hours. About 1% of an oral dose is excreted unchanged in urine.
Special Populations: Renal Impairment: A single-dose pharmacokinetic study in patients with varying degrees of renal dysfunction (creatinine clearance rates ranging from 3 mL/min. to 42 mL/min) suggests that moderate renal impairment does not affect the elimination rate of unchanged diclofenac from plasma but that it may reduce the elimination rate of the metabolites of the drug. In 1 patient with a creatinine clearance of <10 mL/min, the theoretical steady-state plasma levels of metabolites (normally devoid of pharmacological activity) were about 4 times higher than those in normal subjects, with metabolites cleared through the bile. Although no accumulation of pharmacologically active substance seems to occur, caution is advised while administering diclofenac sodium to patients with impaired kidney function.
Hepatic Impairment: The kinetics and metabolism of diclofenac, as revealed in a study of 10 patients with impaired hepatic function (chronic hepatitis and nondecompensated cirrhosis) receiving a single oral dose of 100 mg, were the same as in patients without liver disease.
Geriatrics: The ability of elderly subjects to absorb, metabolize and excrete diclofenac sodium does not appear to differ significantly from those of young subjects.

Indications: The symptomatic treatment of rheumatoid arthritis and osteoarthritis, including degenerative joint disease of the hip.

Contraindications: Active peptic ulcer, a history of recurrent ulceration or active inflammatory disease of the gastrointestinal system.

Known or suspected hypersensitivity to the drug or other nonsteroidal anti-inflammatory drugs. The potential for cross-reactivity between different NSAIDs must be kept in mind.

Diclofenac sodium should not be used in patients with the complete or partial syndrome of nasal polyps, or in whom asthma, anaphylaxis, urticaria, rhinitis or other allergic manifestations are precipitated by ASA or other nonsteroidal anti-inflammatory agents. Fatal anaphylactoid reactions have occurred in such individuals. As well, individuals with the above medical problems are at risk of a severe reaction even if they have taken NSAIDs in the past without any adverse effects.

Significant hepatic impairment or active liver disease.

Severely impaired or deteriorating renal function (creatinine clearance <30 mL/min). Individuals with lesser degrees of renal impairment are at risk of deterioration of their renal function when prescribed NSAIDs and must be monitored.

Diclofenac sodium is not recommended for use with other NSAIDs because of the absence of any evidence demonstrating synergistic benefits and the potential for additive side effects.

Suppositories are contraindicated in patients with any inflammatory lesions of the rectum or anus and in patients with a recent history of rectal or anal bleeding.

Warnings: Gastrointestinal (more pertinent to orally administered dosage forms): Serious gastrointestinal toxicity, such as peptic ulceration, perforation and gastrointestinal bleeding, **sometimes severe and occasionally fatal** can occur at any time, with or without symptoms, in patients treated with nonsteroidal anti-inflammatory drugs (NSAIDs) including diclofenac sodium.

Minor upper gastrointestinal problems, such as dyspepsia, are common, usually developing early in therapy. Physicians should remain alert for ulceration and bleeding in patients treated with nonsteroidal anti-inflammatory drugs, even in the absence of previous gastrointestinal tract symptoms.

In patients observed in clinical trials of such agents, symptomatic upper gastrointestinal ulcers, gross bleeding, or perforation appear to occur in approximately 1% of patients treated for 3 to 6 months and in about 2 to 4% of patients treated for one year. The risk continues beyond 1 year and possibly increases.

The incidence of these complications increases with increasing dose.

Diclofenac sodium should be given under close medical supervision to patients prone to gastrointestinal tract irritation, particularly those with a history of peptic ulcer, diverticulosis or other inflammatory disease of the gastrointestinal tract such as ulcerative colitis and Crohn's disease. In these cases, the physician must weigh the benefits of treatment against the possible hazards.

Physicians should inform patients about the signs and/or symptoms of serious gastrointestinal toxicity and instruct them to contact a physician immediately if they experience persistent dyspepsia or other symptoms or signs suggestive of gastrointestinal ulceration or bleeding.

Because serious gastrointestinal tract ulceration and bleeding can occur without warning symptoms, physicians should follow chronically treated patients by checking their hemoglobin periodically and by being vigilant for the signs and symptoms of ulceration and bleeding and should inform the patients of the importance of this follow-up.

If ulceration is suspected or confirmed, or if gastrointestinal bleeding occurs, diclofenac sodium should be discontinued immediately, appropriate treatment instituted and the patient monitored closely.

No studies, to date, have identified any group of patients **not** at risk of developing ulceration and bleeding. A prior history of serious gastrointestinal events and other factors such as excess alcohol intake, smoking, age, female gender and concomitant oral steroid and anticoagulant use have been associated with increased risk.

Studies to date show that all NSAIDs can cause gastrointestinal tract adverse events. Although existing data does not clearly identify differences in risk between various NSAIDs, this may be shown in the future.

Geriatrics: Patients older than 65 years and frail or debilitated patients are most susceptible to a variety of adverse reactions from nonsteroidal anti-inflammatory drugs (NSAIDs): the incidence of these adverse reactions increases with dose and duration of treatment. In addition, these patients are less tolerant to ulceration and bleeding. Most reports of fatal gastrointestinal events are in this population. Older patients are also at risk of lower esophageal ulceration and bleeding.

For such patients, consideration should be given to a starting dose lower than the one usually recommended, with individual adjustment when necessary and under close supervision. See Precautions for further advice.

Cross-sensitivity: Patients sensitive to any one of the nonsteroidal anti-inflammatory drugs may also be sensitive to any of the other NSAIDs.

Aseptic Meningitis: In occasional cases, with some NSAIDs, the symptoms of aseptic meningitis (stiff neck, severe headaches, nausea and vomiting, fever or clouding of consciousness) have been observed. Patients with autoimmune disorders (systemic lupus erythematosus, mixed connective tissues diseases, etc.) seem to be predisposed. Therefore, in such patients, the physician must be vigilant to the development of this complication.

Pregnancy, Labor and *Lactation:* Diclofenac sodium readily crosses the placental barrier. The safety of diclofenac sodium in pregnancy and lactation has not been established, and its use is therefore not recommended. It should only be used during pregnancy for the most compelling reasons, and then only at the lowest effective dose. As with other prostaglandin inhibitors, this applies particularly to the last 3 months of pregnancy, because of the possibility of uterine inertia and/or premature closing of the ductus arteriosus.

The highest diclofenac level observed in the breast milk of 6 patients receiving oral diclofenac sodium doses of 3×50 mg day 1, followed by 2×50 mg day 2, was smaller than 5 ng/g. By extrapolation, an infant of 3 kg consuming 500 g/day (with a maximum concentration of 5 ng/g) of breast milk would receive less than 0.83 μg/kg/day of diclofenac sodium. On the other hand, in 1 patient on long-term treatment with diclofenac sodium 150 mg daily, a level of 100 ng/mL (100 ng/g) was measured in breast milk; by extrapolation, an infant of 3 kg consuming 500 g/day of breast milk would receive less than 17 μg/kg/day of diclofenac sodium.

Children: Diclofenac sodium is not recommended in children under 16 years of age. Safety and dosages for the pediatric age group have not been established.

Occupational Hazards: Headache, dizziness, lightheadedness and mental confusion have been reported following diclofenac sodium therapy. Patients experiencing these symptoms should be made aware that these side effects may occur and be cautioned against operating machinery or motor vehicles should they experience any of these symptoms.

Precautions: General: Diclofenac sodium should not be used concomitantly with diclofenac potassium since both exist in plasma as the same active organic ion.

Gastrointestinal: There is no definitive evidence that the concomitant administration of histamine H_2-receptor antagonists and/or antacids will either prevent the occurrence of gastrointestinal side effects or allow the continuation of diclofenac sodium therapy when and if these adverse reactions appear.

Renal Function: Long-term administration of nonsteroidal anti-inflammatory drugs to animals has resulted in renal papillary necrosis and other abnormal renal pathology. In humans, there have been reports of acute interstitial nephritis with hematuria, proteinuria, and occasionally nephrotic syndrome.

A second form of renal toxicity has been seen in patients with prerenal conditions leading to the reduction in renal blood flow or blood volume, where the renal prostaglandins have a supportive role in the maintenance of renal perfusion. In these patients, administration of a nonsteroidal anti-inflammatory drug (NSAIDs) may cause a dose-dependent reduction in prostaglandin formation and may precipitate overt renal decompensation. Patients at greatest risk of this reaction are those with impaired renal function, heart failure, liver dysfunction, those taking diuretics, and the elderly. Discontinuation of nonsteroidal anti-inflammatory therapy is usually followed by recovery to the pretreatment state.

Diclofenac and its metabolites are eliminated primarily by the kidneys; therefore, the drug should be used with great caution in patients with impaired renal function. In these cases, utilization of lower doses of diclofenac sodium should be considered and patients carefully monitored.

During long-term therapy, kidney function should be monitored periodically.

Genitourinary: Some NSAIDs are known to cause persistent urinary symptoms (bladder pain, dysuria, urinary frequency), hematuria or cystitis. The onset of these symptoms may occur at any time after the initiation of therapy with an NSAID. Some cases have become severe on continued treatment. Should urinary symptoms occur, treatment with diclofenac sodium **must be stopped immediately** to obtain recovery. This should be done before any urological investigations or treatments are carried out.

Hepatic Function: As with other nonsteroidal anti-inflammatory drugs, borderline elevations of one or more liver function tests may occur in up to 15% of patients. These abnormalities may progress, may remain essentially unchanged, or may be transient with continued therapy. A patient with symptoms and/or signs suggesting liver dysfunction, or in whom an abnormal liver test has occurred, should be evaluated for evidence of the development of more severe hepatic reaction while on therapy with this drug. Severe hepatic reactions

Table I—Diclotec

Tabulation of Frequency of Adverse Reactions

Body System	**Frequent (>10%)**	**Occasional (>1-10%)**	**Rare (>0.001%-<1%)**	**Isolated (<0.001%)**
Gastrointestinal		Epigastric, gastric, or abdominal pain, abdominal cramps, nausea, dyspepsia, anorexia, diarrhea, vomiting, flatulence	Gastrointestinal bleeding, gastric and intestinal ulcerations with or without bleeding or perforation	Lower gut disorders (e.g., nonspecific hemorrhagic colitis and exacerbation of ulcerative colitis or Crohn's disease), diaphragm-like intestinal strictures, hyperacidity, stomatitis, glossitis, coated tongue, esophageal lesions, constipation, pancreatitis
Allergic			Hypersensitivity reactions such as asthma in patients sensitive to ASA, e.g., bronchospasm; anaphylactic/anaphylactoid systemic reactions including hypotension.	Vasculitis, pneumonitis
CNS		Dizziness, headache, vertigo	Drowsiness, malaise, impaired concentration, tiredness.	Sensory disturbances including paresthesia, memory disturbance, disorientation, insomnia, irritability, convulsions, depression, anxiety, nightmares, tremor, psychotic reactions, aseptic meningitis
Dermatologic		Rash, pruritus	Urticaria	Bullous eruption, erythema, eczema, erythema multiforme, Stevens-Johnson syndrome, Lyell's syndrome, erythroderma, loss of hair, photosensitivity reactions, purpura
Cardiovascular			Palpitation, angina, arrythmias	Exacerbation of cardiac failure, hypertension
Special Senses				Vision disturbances, impaired hearing, tinnitus, taste alteration disorders
Hematologic				Thrombocytopenia, leukopenia, agranulocytosis, hemolytic anemia, aplastic anemia, anemia secondary to gastrointestinal bleeding
Renal			Edema	Acute renal failure, nephrotic syndrome, urinary abnormalities, interstitial nephritis, papillary necrosis
Hepatic		Elevation of serum amino-transferase enzymes (AST, ALT)	Liver function disorders including hepatitis with or without jaundice	Fulminant hepatitis
Other		Suppository administration may occasionally give rise to local irritation	Local bleeding and exacerbation of hemorrhoids with use of suppositories	

Diclotec (cont'd)

including jaundice and cases of fatal hepatitis have been reported with nonsteroidal anti-inflammatory drugs.

Although such reactions are rare, if abnormal liver tests persist or worsen, if clinical signs and symptoms consistent with liver disease develop, or if systemic manifestations occur (e.g., eosinophilia, rash, etc.), this drug should be discontinued.

During long-term therapy, liver function tests should be monitored periodically. If there is a need to prescribe this drug in the presence of impaired liver function, it must be done under strict observation.

Fluid and Electrolyte Balance: Fluid retention and edema have been observed in patients treated with diclofenac sodium. Therefore, as with many other nonsteroidal anti-inflammatory drugs, the possibility of precipitating congestive heart failure in elderly patients or those with compromised cardiac function should be borne in mind. Diclofenac sodium should be used with caution in patients with heart failure, hypertension or other conditions predisposing to fluid retention.

With nonsteroidal anti-inflammatory treatment there is a potential risk of hyperkalemia, particularly in patients with conditions such as diabetes mellitus or renal failure; elderly patients; or in patients receiving concomitant therapy with β-adrenergic blockers, angiotensin converting enzyme inhibitors or some diuretics. Serum electrolytes should be monitored periodically during long-term therapy, especially in those patients who are at risk.

Hematology: Drugs inhibiting prostaglandin biosynthesis do interfere with platelet function to varying degrees; therefore, patients who may be adversely affected by such an action should be carefully observed when diclofenac sodium is administered.

Blood dyscrasias (such as neutropenia, leukopenia, thrombocytopenia, aplastic anemia and agranulocytosis) associated with the use of nonsteroidal anti-inflammatory drugs are rare, but could occur with severe consequences.

Patients on long-term treatment with diclofenac sodium should have their hemopoietic system evaluated periodically. Bone marrow functional abnormalities, although rare, could have severe consequences. Periodic hematologic examinations (CBC and blood film examination) can detect anemias or blood dyscrasias secondary to possible gastrointestinal tract or bone marrow toxicity.

Infection: In common with other anti-inflammatory drugs, diclofenac sodium may mask the usual signs of infection.

Ophthalmology: Blurred and/or diminished vision has been reported with the use of diclofenac sodium and other nonsteroidal anti-inflammatory drugs. If such symptoms develop, the drug should be discontinued and an ophthalmologic examination performed; ophthalmic examination should be carried out at periodic intervals in any patient receiving this drug for an extended period of time.

CNS: Some patients may experience drowsiness, dizziness, vertigo, insomnia or depression with the use of diclofenac sodium. If patients experience these side effects, they should exercise caution in carrying out activities that require alertness.

Hypersensitivity Reactions: As with other NSAIDs, allergic reactions, including anaphylactic/anaphylactoid reactions, can occur without prior exposure to drug. Careful questioning for patient history of asthma, nasal polyps, urticaria, and hypotension associated with NSAIDs is important before starting therapy.

Drug Interactions: ASA or other NSAIDs: The use of diclofenac sodium in addition to any other NSAID, including those over the counter drugs (such as ASA and ibuprofen) is not recommended due to the possibility of additive side effects.

Serum levels of diclofenac may be reduced when the 2 drugs are taken simultaneously. The bioavailability of ASA is reduced by the presence of diclofenac. Although these pharmacokinetic interactions do not appear to be clinically relevant, there is no proven advantage in using these 2 medications together.

Digoxin: Diclofenac may increase the plasma concentration of digoxin. Dosage adjustment may be required.

Anticoagulants: Numerous studies have shown that the concomitant use of NSAIDs and anticoagulants increases the risk of gastrointestinal adverse events such as ulceration and bleeding.

Because prostaglandins play an important role in hemostasis, and NSAIDs affect platelet function, concurrent therapy of diclofenac sodium with warfarin requires close monitoring to be certain that no change in anticoagulant dosage is necessary.

Oral Hypoglycemics: Pharmacodynamic studies have shown no potentiation of effect with concurrent administration with diclofenac; however, there are isolated reports of both hypoglycemic and hyperglycemic effects in the presence of diclofenac, which necessitated changes in the dosage of hypoglycemic agents.

Diuretics: NSAIDs have been reported to decrease the activity of diuretics. Concomitant treatment with potassium-sparing diuretics may be associated with increased serum potassium, thus making it necessary to monitor levels.

Antihypertensives: Like other NSAIDs, diclofenac can reduce the antihypertensive effects of propranolol and other β-blockers, as well as other antihypertensive agents.

Glucocorticoids: Numerous studies have shown that the concomitant use of NSAIDs and oral glucocorticoids increases the risk of gastrointestinal side effects such as ulceration and bleeding. This is especially the case in older (>65 years of age) individuals.

Methotrexate: Caution should be exercised when NSAIDs are administered less than 24 hours before or after treatment with methotrexate. Elevated blood concentrations of methotrexate may occur, increasing toxicity.

Lithium: Lithium plasma concentrations will increase when administered concomitantly with diclofenac (which affects lithium renal clearance). Dosage adjustment of lithium may be required.

Cyclosporine: Nephrotoxicity of cyclosporine may be increased because of the effect of NSAIDs on renal prostaglandins.

Quinolone antibacterials: There have been isolated reports of convulsions which may have been due to concomitant use of quinolones and NSAIDs.

Clinical Laboratory Tests: Diclofenac increases platelet aggregation time but does not affect bleeding time, plasma thrombin clotting time, plasma fibrinogen, or factors V and VII to XII. Statistically significant changes in prothrombin and partial thromboplastin times have been reported in normal volunteers. The mean changes were observed to be less than 1 second in both instances, and are unlikely to be clinically important.

Persistently abnormal or worsening renal, hepatic or hematological test values should be followed up carefully since they may be related to therapy.

Adverse Effects: The most common adverse reactions encountered with nonsteroidal anti-inflammatory drugs (particularly orally administered formulations) are gastrointestinal, of which peptic ulcer, with or without bleeding, is the most severe. Fatalities have occurred particularly in the elderly.

Adverse reactions reported in clinical trials and spontaneous reports are summarized below. Frequency estimate: frequent >10%, occasional >1 to 10%, rare >0.001 to 1%, isolated cases <0.001%. See Table I (on previous page).

Gastrointestinal (more pertinent to orally administered dosage forms): Occasional: epigastric, gastric, or abdominal pain, abdominal cramps, nausea, dyspepsia, anorexia, diarrhea, vomiting, flatulence. Rare: gastrointestinal bleeding (bloody diarrhea, melena, hematemesis) gastric and intestinal ulcerations with or without bleeding or perforation. Isolated: lower gut disorders (e.g., nonspecific hemorrhagic colitis and exacerbation of ulcerative colitis or Crohn's disease), diaphragm-like intestinal strictures, hyperacidity, stomatitis, glossitis, coated tongue, esophageal lesions, constipation, pancreatitis.

Allergic: Rare: hypersensitivity reactions such as asthma in patients sensitive to ASA, e.g., bronchospasm; anaphylactic/anaphylactoid systemic reactions including hypotension. Isolated: vasculitis, pneumonitis.

CNS: Occasional: dizziness, headache, vertigo. Rare: drowsiness, malaise, impaired concentration, tiredness. Isolated: sensory disturbances including paresthesia, memory disturbance, disorientation, insomnia, irritability, convulsions, depression, anxiety, nightmares, tremor, psychotic reactions, aseptic meningitis.

Dermatologic: Occasional: rash, pruritus. Rare: urticaria. Isolated: bullous eruption, erythema, eczema, erythema multiforme, Stevens-Johnson syndrome, Lyell's syndrome (toxic epidermal necrolysis), erythroderma (exfoliative dermatitis), loss of hair, photosensitivity reactions, purpura including allergic purpura.

Cardiovascular: Rare: palpitation, angina, arrhythmias. Isolated: exacerbation of cardiac failure, hypertension.

Special senses: Isolated: vision disturbances (blurred vision, diplopia), impaired hearing, tinnitus, taste alteration disorders.

Hematologic: Isolated: thrombocytopenia, leukopenia, agranulocytosis, hemolytic anemia, aplastic anemia, anemia secondary to gastrointestinal bleeding.

Renal: Rare: edema (facial, general, peripheral). Isolated: acute renal failure, nephrotic syndrome, urinary abnormalities (e.g., hematuria and proteinuria), interstitial nephritis, papillary necrosis.

Hepatic: Occasional: elevations (≥3 times the upper normal limit) of serum aminotransferase enzymes (AST, ALT). Rare: liver function disorders including hepatitis with or without jaundice. Isolated: fulminant hepatitis.

Other: Administration of suppositories may occasionally give rise to local irritation, rarely local bleeding and exacerbation of hemorrhoids.

Overdose: Symptoms and Treatment: There is no specific antidote. In cases of overdosage with orally administered dosage forms, absorption should be prevented as soon as possible by the induction of vomiting, gastric lavage or treatment with activated charcoal. Supportive and symptomatic treatment should be given for complications such as hypotension, renal failure, convulsions, gastrointestinal irritation and respiratory depression. Measures to accelerate elimination (forced diuresis, hemoperfusion, dialysis) may be considered, but may be of limited use because of the high protein-binding and extensive metabolism.

Dosage: 50 or 100 mg suppositories may be given as substitute for the last of the 3 oral daily doses to a maximum of 150 mg/day.

Use whole suppositories. Do not split or use portions of suppositories.

Not recommended for use in patients under 16 years of age.

Information for the Patient: See Blue Section—Information for the Patient ''Diclotec''.

Supplied: 50 mg: Each yellowish-white, torpedo-shaped suppository contains: diclofenac sodium 50 mg. Nonmedicinal ingredients: semisynthetic glycerides. Boxes of 30.

100 mg: Each yellowish-white, torpedo-shaped suppository contains: diclofenac sodium 100 mg. Nonmedicinal ingredients: semisynthetic glycerides. Boxes of 30.

Protect from light and elevated humidity. Keep away from excessive heat. Store between 15 to 30°C.

New Product 1998

DIDROCAL® Ⓟ

Procter & Gamble Pharmaceuticals

Etidronate Disodium

Calcium Carbonate

Bone Metabolism Regulator

Pharmacology: The Didrocal therapy is a nonhormonal treatment consisting of etidronate disodium administered for 14 days followed by calcium carbonate administered for the next 76 days.

Etidronate Disodium: Etidronate disodium is a bisphosphonate (diphosphonate) that inhibits bone resorption, primarily through the drug's effect on osteoclasts. Etidronate disodium owes its highly selective bone effects to its ability to adsorb to hydroxyapatite on the bone surface.

Two mechanisms of action contribute to increases in bone mass and maintenance of trabecular integrity: 1) etidronate significantly decreases activation frequency of new bone-remodeling cycles, and 2) etidronate significantly decreases resorption cavity depth without reducing the ability of osteoblasts to fill resorption cavities with normal bone.

The therapy has been shown to decrease activation frequency by about 50%. In clinical trials, the reduction in bone turnover was accompanied by a significant decrease in serum alkaline phosphatase after 2 to 4 cycles of treatment. Trends toward a reduced urinary hydroxyproline/creatinine ratio were also observed. These changes remained within normal laboratory limits and were not progressive.

Etidronate disodium is not metabolized. The amount of drug absorbed after an oral dose is approximately 3.5%. Within 24 hours, approximately half the absorbed dose is excreted in the urine; the remainder is distributed to bone compartments from which it is slowly eliminated. In humans, the residence time on bone may vary due to such factors as specific metabolic condition and bone type. The plasma half-life ($t_{1/2}$) of etidronate disodium is between 1 and 6 hours; however, the half-life of the drug on bone is in excess of 90 days. Unabsorbed drug is excreted intact in the feces.

Etidronate does not adversely affect serum levels of parathyroid hormone or calcium. In osteoporotic patients, occasional transient hyperphosphatemia has been observed, apparently due to an etidronate-induced increase in renal tubular reabsorption of phosphate. No adverse effects or clinical findings have been associated with the hyperphosphatemia.

Calcium Carbonate: Absorption of calcium carbonate occurs primarily in the more proximal segments of the small bowel. Approximately 30% of an ingested dose is absorbed, although absorption can be augmented by factors such as intake of vitamin D or a vitamin D metabolite. Calcium excretion in urine is the net result of the quantity filtered and the amount reabsorbed. Unabsorbed calcium is excreted in the feces.

The Didrocal regimen design was intended to suppress the resorptive activity of osteoclasts, while allowing normal bone formation to take place during the rest of the remodeling cycle. Thus a 14-day period of daily etidronate is followed by 76 days of calcium supplementation.

Figure 1 (see company's original product monograph) shows reconstruction of the remodeling cycle in patients after 60 weeks of calcium alone or cyclical etidronate therapy. Several aspects are evident in the etidronate-treated group related to decrease in the **rate** of bone turnover and **depth** of resorption during bone remodeling.

First, the entire remodeling cycle is prolonged, resulting in a slower rate of resorption and formation, which then results in a fewer number of overall skeletal remodeling sites. This produces an increase in overall skeletal bone mass as remodeling spaces are filled in and largely accounts for the clinically relevant increases in bone mass and protection against fracture that have been observed.

Second, there is a decrease in the number of resorptive events ongoing at any one time in the skeleton. With a reduction in the number of resorption cavities, a decreased risk of trabecular perforation or generation of "stress risers" is accomplished, aiding overall bone strength over and above the increases in bone mass, per se.

Finally, there is a reduction in the depth of resorption (resorption depth, rD) in the etidronate-treated patients with maintenance of a normal amount of new bone formation (mean wall thickness, MWT). Consequently, the balance of resorption and formation is moved from negative (−1 micron) to positive (+1.5 micron) so that bone is no longer lost with each remodeling event. This outcome effectively reverses the negative bone balance that occurs with menopause, which is otherwise, part of the pathogenesis of postmenopausal osteoporosis.

Overall, these findings largely explain the clinical outcomes of etidronate cyclical therapy through a salutary modulation of the bone turnover process.

However, it should be noted that in analyses of these and other data, it became apparent that the duration of resorptive and formative processes in these patient populations are in general longer than the etidronate and calcium phases of the Didrocal cyclical therapy. Again referring to Figure 1, the resorptive period was 32 days in duration in the calcium control group, with formation taking 186 days, both periods being longer than the 14 and 76 days used for administration of etidronate and calcium, respectively. It is therefore evident that the intermittent use of this modulator of bone metabolism does not require exact matching of individual remodeling cycles to produce the observed increases in bone mass and maintenance of bone quality.

Indications: For the treatment of established postmenopausal osteoporosis diagnosed by means of objective measuring techniques such as bone densitometry (a bone mineral density of more than 2.67 standard deviations below the young adult mean) or by radiographic evaluation of the spine (≥2 vertebral fractures) in women at least 8 years postmenopause. The assessment of vertebral fractures is based upon a minimum 25% reduction in the height of vertebral bodies (anterior, posterior, or central) on lateral radiographs of the spine.

In a minority of patients bone mineral density measurements of the lumbar spine are falsely elevated by the presence of vascular calcification, osteophytes, scoliosis, or facet joint sclerosis. Such abnormalities may affect only certain vertebrae, in which case appropriate densitometric assessment of the nonaffected vertebrae can be performed, or radiographic criteria (minimum 25% reduction in the height of vertebral bodies) for treatment may be relied upon.

Contraindications: Patients with known hypersensitivity to etidronate disodium. Didrocal is also contraindicated for patients with clinically overt osteomalacia; appropriate treatment to resolve their osteomalacia should be initiated before prescribing Didrocal therapy.

Warnings: The cyclic intermittent, 14-day, etidronate disodium dosage of the Didrocal therapy provides an acceptable therapeutic window. Overdosage of etidronate disodium may result in skeletal bone abnormalities or cause nephrotic syndrome (see Overdose: Symptoms and Treatment).

Precautions: The Didrocal cyclic therapy should be considered only for the patient population described under Indications.

Patients on the Didrocal cyclic therapy require regular clinical follow-ups.

General: There is no experience to specifically guide the use of the Didrocal therapy in patients with impaired renal function or a history of kidney stone formation. Etidronate disodium is not metabolized and is excreted intact via the kidney. In approximately 10% of patients in clinical trials of Didronel I.V. Infusion (etidronate disodium) for hypercalcemia of malignancy, occasional, mild-to-moderate abnormalities in renal function (increases of >0.5 mg/dL serum creatinine) were observed during or immediately after treatment.

Consequently, if patients with impaired renal function or with a history of kidney stone formation are placed on Didrocal therapy, serum and urine calcium and other relevant parameters should be monitored regularly to prevent hypercalcemia or hypercalciuria.

The Didrocal therapy provides intermittent cyclic etidronate disodium 400 mg daily for 14 days followed by elemental calcium for 76 days to support bone formation. Before commencing the therapy, patients' calcium requirements should be adjusted. It is recommended that the appropriately selected postmenopausal women receive at least 1 500 mg calcium/day from all sources, as well as a daily Vitamin D intake of at least 400 IU. The Didrocal therapy provides 500 mg elemental calcium per day.

Patients with a diagnosis of achlorhydria should take calcium carbonate tablets with food to enhance absorption of calcium.

Drug Interactions: Food in the stomach or upper portions of the small intestine, particularly materials with a high calcium content such as milk, may reduce absorption of the etidronate disodium. Vitamins with mineral supplements such as iron, calcium supplements, laxatives containing magnesium, or antacids containing calcium or aluminum should not be taken within 2 hours before or after dosing etidronate disodium, since these also may reduce the absorption of etidronate disodium and could lead to treatment failure (see Dosage).

A small number of patients in the clinical trials received either thiazide diuretics or intravaginal estrogen while on the regimen. The concomitant use of either of these agents did not interfere with the positive effects of the Didrocal therapy on bone.

The concurrent use of etidronate disodium with warfarin has been associated with isolated reports of patients experiencing increases in their prothrombin time. The majority of these reports concerned variable elevations in prothrombin times without clinically significant sequelae. Although the relevance of these reports and any mechanism of coagulation alterations is unclear, patients on warfarin should have their prothrombin time more closely monitored.

Calcium carbonate may interfere with the absorption of tetracycline given concomitantly.

Pregnancy: Didrocal is not intended for administration to pregnant women. In teratology and developmental toxicity studies conducted in rats and rabbits treated with oral dose levels of up to 100 mg/kg (12 times the human dose), no adverse or teratogenic effects have been observed in the offspring. Etidronate disodium has been shown to cause skeletal abnormalities in rat offspring when given to dams in mid-pregnancy at oral dose levels of 300 mg/kg (35 times the human dose); these effects are thought to be the result of the pharmacological effects of the drug on bone. Other effects on the offspring (including decreased live births) have been observed at dose levels that cause significant toxicity in the parent generation and are 60 to 125 times the human dose. There are no adequate and well-controlled studies in pregnant women.

Lactation: Didrocal is not intended for administration during lactation. It is not known whether etidronate is excreted in human milk; it is excreted in the milk of rats. Because many drugs are excreted in human milk and because of the potential for adverse effects on the skeletons of infants, a decision should be made whether to discontinue nursing or to discontinue the drug, taking into account the importance of the drug to the mother.

Children: The safety and effectiveness of Didrocal in children have not been established.

Dependence Liability: Not applicable.

Laboratory Tests: Depending on the time elapsed since the last dose of etidronate, the Didrocal therapy may prevent bone-Imaging diagnostic agents (e.g., technetium-^{99m}-methylene diphosphonate) used in bones scans, from adhering to bone and thus affect the interpretation of imaging results.

Patients: The patient should adhere to the prescribed regimen. The response to therapy is one of slow onset that continues over time.

A patient's risk for developing fractures may also be reduced if, subsequent to health care counseling, she consumes adequate dietary calcium, gets enough weight-bearing exercise, and uses proper lifting and fall-avoidance techniques.

Each etidronate disodium tablet should be taken as a single oral dose on an empty stomach with a full glass of water. The calcium carbonate tablet may be taken with food and this is recommended if the patient has achlorhydria (see Dosage).

Adverse Effects: The overall safety of the Didrocal therapy was evaluated in postmenopausal osteoporotic women enrolled in clinical trials. The 3 pivotal trials were randomized, parallel, double blind, and placebo controlled; 2 of these were multicentre trials conducted in the United States. The most common adverse events reported during the first 2 years of the two U.S. trials are listed in Table I. In general, side effects in patients who received etidronate were comparable to those in patients who received placebo.

Table I—Didrocal

Adverse Events Reported at Least Once by ≥10% of the Patients in Either Treatment Group
U.S. Placebo-Controlled Trials: First 2 Years

Adverse Event	Didrocal (n=105[a]) %Pts	Placebo (n=105[b]) %Pts
Diarrhea	37.1	30.5
Nausea	18.1	14.3
Flatulence	17.1	15.2
Dizziness	16.2	11.4
Constipation	13.3	14.3
Headache	13.3	10.5
Dyspepsia	12.4	10.5
Vomiting	10.5	10.5
Abdominal pain	9.5	10.5
Rash	8.6	12.4

[a] The number of patients who received placebo/etidronate treatment.

[b] The number of patients who received placebo/placebo treatment.

In osteoporosis clinical trials, the most common side effects were diarrhea and nausea.

Reactions reported less frequently include flatulence, dyspepsia, abdominal pain, constipation and vomiting. The incidence of these events was comparable to that with placebo. In addition, 4 events, headache, gastritis, leg cramps and arthralgia, occurred with a significantly greater incidence in patients who received Didrocal cyclical therapy compared with those who received placebo. All episodes of leg cramps were transient in nature, most occurred at night, and most required no treatment. All patients with arthralgia reported joint discomfort or pain that was generally mild and related to underlying osteoarthritis.

The numbers of both deaths and withdrawals due to adverse events were similar in the Didrocal and placebo groups.

Postmarketing Experience: Other adverse events that have been reported in postmarketing studies of a number of indications, and were thought to be possibly related to etidronate disodium include the following: alopecia; arthropathies, including arthralgia and arthritis; bone fracture; esophagitis; glossitis; hypersensitivity reactions, including angioedema, skin rashes (such as follicular eruption, macular rash, maculopapular rash), pruritus, Stevens-Johnson syndrome, and urticaria; osteomalacia; neuropsychiatric events, including amnesia, confusion, depression, and hallucination; paresthesias; burning tongue; erythema multiforme; and exacerbation of asthma.

In patients receiving etidronate disodium, there have been rare reports of leukopenia, agranulocytosis, and pancytopenia. Also, there have been very rare cases of leukemia reported with etidronate use (1/100 000) in ongoing safety surveillance since 1978 encompassing approximately 1.5 million patient-years of treatment. Any causal relationship to either the treatment or to the patients' underlying disease has not been established.

Exacerbation of existing peptic ulcer disease with resulting complications has been reported in a few patients.

Overdose: Symptoms and Treatment: Clinical experience with acute overdosage of etidronate disodium is extremely limited. Decreases in serum calcium following substantial overdosage may be expected in some patients. Signs and symptoms of hypocalcemia may also occur in some of these patients. Some patients may develop vomiting. An 18-year-old female who ingested an estimated single dose of 4 000 to 6 000 mg (67 to 100 mg/kg) of etidronate disodium was reported to be mildly hypocalcemic (7.52 mg/dL) and to have experienced paresthesia of the fingers. Hypocalcemia resolved 6 hours after

Didrocal (cont'd)

lavage and treatment with i.v. calcium gluconate. A 92-year-old female who accidentally received 1 600 mg of etidronate disodium per day for 3.5 days experienced marked diarrhea and required treatment for electrolyte imbalance. Orally administered etidronate disodium may cause hematologic abnormalities in some patients (see Adverse Effects).

Gastric lavage may remove unabsorbed drug. Standard procedures for treating hypocalcemia, including the administration of Ca^{++} i.v., would be expected to restore physiologic amounts of ionized calcium and to relieve signs and symptoms of hypocalcemia. Such treatment has been effective.

Because of its limited intestinal absorption, overdosage with calcium carbonate is not likely. If mild hypercalcemia were to occur, signs and symptoms could include polydipsia, polyuria, nausea, vomiting, constipation, abdominal pain, muscle weakness and confusion.

Treatment of hypercalcemia includes cessation of all calcium and vitamin D. Supportive measures include rehydration with or without loop diuretics.

Prolonged continuous daily etidronate treatment of doses of 10 to 20 mg/kg/day for greater than 6 months (chronic overdosage) has been reported to cause nephrotic syndrome and fractures.

Dosage: The Didrocal therapy is a cyclical regimen administered in 90-day cycles. Each cycle provides 14 white 400 mg etidronate disodium tablets to be taken once daily for 14 days, followed by 76 blue calcium carbonate tablets to be taken once daily for the next 76 days. Patients should maintain an adequate nutritional intake, including calcium and vitamin D. Data from placebo-controlled clinical studies show a significant increase in bone mass of 4 to 5% ($p < 0.05\%$) occurred for up to 12 cycles (3 years) in patients who received Didrocal therapy compared with patients receiving calcium supplementation alone. Safety and tolerance, with maintenance of gains in vertebral bone mass, have been established for 20 cycles (5 years) of therapy. Limited data through 7 years of therapy provide support for maintenance of bone mass benefit with biopsy-proven normal bone quality (no evidence of generalized osteomalacia).

The etidronate disodium tablet portion of the Didrocal therapy should be administered on an empty stomach, 1 tablet/day with a full glass of water. To aid compliance, it is recommended that patients take the therapy at bedtime, at least 2 hours before or after eating. To maximize absorption of etidronate disodium, patients should not take the following within 2 hours of dosing: food, especially food high in calcium, such as milk or milk products; antacids; vitamins with mineral supplements such as iron; calcium supplements; laxatives containing magnesium.

The calcium carbonate tablet portion of the Didrocal therapy may be administered with food and this is recommended for patients with a diagnosis of achlorhydria.

In the clinical studies of Didrocal therapy, serum alkaline phosphatase was shown to decrease 15 to 20% during the first 2 cycles and to maintain the new level with continuing therapy.

The effect of treatment should be assessed by monitoring changes in bone mass. If this is done, then discontinuation of the therapy should be considered if the bone mass does not stabilize or increase after 4 cycles (1 year) of therapy. Patients who attain adequate response to treatment but discontinue treatment for other reasons should be monitored periodically.

Information for the Patient: See Blue Section—Information for the Patient "Didrocal".

Supplied: The Didrocal therapy consists of etidronate disodium administered for 14 days followed by calcium carbonate administered for the next 76 days.

Etidronate Disodium: The first blister card contains a 14-day supply of 14 tablets. Each, white capsule-shaped, unscored tablet, coded "NE1" (engraved on one side and sculptured in an engraved box on the opposite side), contains: etidronate disodium USP 400 mg. Nonmedicinal ingredients: magnesium stearate, microcrystalline cellulose and pregelatinized starch. Lactose-free.

Calcium Carbonate: The remaining 4 blister cards contain a 76-day supply of 76 tablets. Each blue, capsule-shaped, coated tablet, with "NE2" engraved on both sides, contains: elemental calcium 500 mg as calcium carbonate USP 1 250 mg. Nonmedicinal ingredients: edible black ink, FD&C Blue No. 2 Aluminum Lake, hydroxypropyl cellulose, hydroxypropyl methylcellulose 2910, magnesium stearate, polyethylene glycol 3350, polysorbate 80, sodium starch glycolate and titanium dioxide. Lactose-free.

The unit-of-use dispensing system of the Didrocal 90-day therapy consists of patient instructions, a prescription refill reminder card, and the therapy tablets on 5 blister cards. The Didrocal packaging is designed to provide important benefits to patients. The separately blister-packed tablets and the patient instructions help patients to comply with the cyclical regimen. Dispense only in the original packaging to help patients avoid coingestion of calcium carbonate and etidronate disodium, which will interfere with absorption of etidronate. Store at controlled room temperature (15 to 30°C) and protect from light and moisture.

(Shown in Product Recognition Section)

Reviewed 1999

DIDRONEL® Ⓟ

Procter & Gamble Pharmaceuticals

Etidronate Disodium

Bone Metabolism Regulator—Antipagetic Agent—Antihypercalcemic Agent

Pharmacology: Etidronate acts primarily on bone. It can inhibit the formation, growth and dissolution of hydroxyapatite crystals and their amorphous precursors by chemisorption to calcium phosphate surfaces. Inhibition of crystal resorption occurs at lower doses than are required to inhibit crystal growth. Both effects increase as the dose increases.

General: The gastrointestinal absorption of etidronate is approximately 3.5%. The plasma half life ($t_{1/2}$) is between 1 to 6 hours. The drug is not metabolized. It is either rapidly excreted unchanged in the urine or is taken up by bone. About half the dose is deposited in the skeleton, with the subsequent elimination controlled by bone turnover rate, which in turn is influenced by the metabolic conditions and specific bone type.

Paget's Disease: Etidronate acts on bones by slowing the rate of turnover (resorption and accretion) both in Pagetic lesions and to a lesser extent in the normal bone remodeling process. During treatment with etidronate histologic examination of bone from Pagetic lesions shows a decrease in the excessive cellular activity accompanied by a suppression of bone turnover, an improved histologic pattern including lamellar bone formation, a decrease in fibrotic marrow pattern, a decrease in vascularity, and an increase in normal hematopoietic marrow elements.

Etidronate therapy, in patients with Paget's disease, results in lowering of urinary hydroxyproline as well as serum alkaline phosphatase, and radionuclide uptake by Pagetic bone is reduced in many patients. The associated pathophysiological manifestations of increased bone vascularity, increased skin temperature, and increased cardiac output are also improved. These actions are generally accompanied by symptomatic improvement, including reduction of bone pain.

At a dose of 20 mg/kg/day in excess of 3 months and after 6 or more months of therapy at doses of 10 mg/kg/day, unmineralized osteoid can accumulate (see Precautions).

Hypercalcemia of Malignancy: Hypercalcemia of malignancy is usually related to increased bone resorption associated with the presence of neoplastic tissue. It occurs in 8 to 20% of patients with malignant disease. Whereas hypercalcemia is more often seen in patients with demonstrable osteolytic, osteoblastic, or mixed metastatic tumors in bone, discrete skeletal lesions cannot be demonstrated in at least 30% of patients. Etidronate's reduction of abnormal bone resorption is responsible for its therapeutic benefit in hypercalcemia. Following successful treatment with etidronate i.v. infusion, which effectively reduces total and ionized serum calcium, etidronate tablets help maintain clinically acceptable serum calcium levels.

Indications: For the treatment of symptomatic Paget's disease of the bone (osteitis deformans).

For the short-term (30 to 90 days) maintenance of clinically acceptable serum calcium levels **following treatment with etidronate i.v. infusion** (for patients with hypercalcemia of malignancy). The relapse rate without oral etidronate follow-up after about 1 month is high (90%); with such follow-up it is lower (50%). A second course of etidronate i.v. may be effective if hypercalcemia recurs.

Contraindications: Patients with known hypersensitivity to the drug. Also contraindicated for patients with clinically overt osteomalacia; appropriate treatment to resolve their osteomalacia should be initiated before prescribing etidronate.

Warnings: General: Since absorbed etidronate is excreted through the kidneys, periodic renal function assessment should be carried out in patients whose renal function may be deteriorating. While there is no experience to specifically guide treatment in patients with impaired renal function, in such cases renal function should be monitored carefully.

Paget's Disease: The physician should adhere to the recommended dose regimen in order to avoid unnecessary overtreatment with etidronate (see Precautions and Adverse Effects). The response to therapy may be slow onset and may continue even for months after treatment when the drug has been discontinued. Dosage should neither be increased prematurely nor should treatment be resumed before there is clear evidence of reactivation of the disease process.

Retreatment should not be initiated until the patient has had at least a 3-month drug-free interval to determine whether remission has occurred and to promote mineralization of any unmineralized osteoid which may have developed.

The incidence of osteogenic sarcoma is known to be increased in Paget's disease. Pagetic lesions, with or without therapy, may appear by x-ray to progress markedly, possibly with some loss of definition of periosteal margins. Such lesions should be evaluated carefully to differentiate these from osteogenic sarcoma.

Although there is no evidence of impaired fracture healing with etidronate, in case of spontaneous or pathological fractures occurring during etidronate therapy, the drug should be discontinued until complete healing of the fracture takes place (see Adverse Effects).

Precautions: General: To assure optimal absorption of etidronate, the drug should be taken on an empty stomach as a single oral daily dose, at least two hours before or after meals with a full glass of water. It should not be taken with milk.

Etidronate therapy should be approached with caution in patients with gastrointestinal disease, because etidronate may cause diarrhea in some patients at doses above 5 mg/kg/day.

Paget's Disease: Patient Monitoring: During therapy, periodic monitoring of urinary hydroxyproline excretion and/or serum alkaline phosphatase levels to assess disease activity is desirable. Additionally, monitoring of serum phosphate levels may provide indications of patient compliance. A failure of serum phosphate levels to increase at etidronate dose levels of 10 mg/kg/day or above may be suggestive of non-compliance.

Osteoid Mineralization (see Contraindications – osteomalacia): Etidronate may retard mineralization of osteoid laid down during the bone accretion process. This effect is dose and time dependent. There may be an overlap of beneficial and mineralization inhibition effects in some patients at higher doses. Extended periods of continuous medication should be approached cautiously.

When administered at doses of 20 mg/kg/day, etidronate suppresses bone turnover and essentially stops mineralization of new bone in Pagetic lesions and, to a lesser extent, in the uninvolved skeleton. Mineralization of Pagetic lesions has been demonstrated to occur normally after discontinuation of the drug.

Nutrition: Patients with Paget's disease of bone should maintain an adequate nutritional status, and particularly, an adequate intake of calcium and vitamin D. Patients with restricted vitamin D and calcium intake may be particularly sensitive to drugs that affect calcium homeostasis and should be closely followed while under etidronate treatment.

Hyperphosphatemia: Etidronate therapy at daily doses of 10 mg/kg/day and above, and occasionally at doses of 5 mg/kg/day, is associated with serum phosphate elevations, probably due to increased renal tubular reabsorption of phosphate. Serum values of up to 2.26 mmol/L (7 mg%) are seen at the highest doses. The usual increments are approximately 0.32 mmol/L (1 mg%) over the pretreatment levels. Serum phosphate returns to normal within 2 to 4 weeks after the drug is discontinued.

Therapy with etidronate disodium alone is not accompanied by clinically significant changes in serum parathyroid hormone or serum calcium levels.

Bone Pain: Bone pain at the Pagetic site may increase or recur during etidronate therapy even in patients who are experiencing relief of their original symptoms. Continuance of therapy will usually result in resolution of pain. However, on occasion, therapy may have to be discontinued (see Adverse Effects).

Hypercalcemia of Malignancy: Patient Monitoring: Serum calcium levels should be monitored in patients receiving etidronate i.v. infusion therapy and/or oral etidronate maintenance therapy for hypercalcemia of malignancy. The physiologically important component of serum calcium is the ionized portion. In most institutions, this cannot be measured directly. It is important to recognize that factors influencing the ratio of free and bound calcium such as serum proteins, particularly albumin, may complicate the interpretation of total serum calcium measurements. If indicated, a corrected (adjusted) serum calcium value should be calculated using an established algorithm, such as:

$$Ca_{adj} = Ca_T - 0.71\,(A - A_m),$$

where, Ca_{adj} = adjusted calcium concentration (mg/100 mL)

Ca_T = total calcium concentration (mg/100 mL)

A = albumin concentration (g/100 mL)

A_m = mean normal albumin concentration for given laboratory (g/100 mL).

Serum creatinine and blood urea nitrogen should be monitored in patients with known or suspected renal insufficiency.

Drug Interactions: The concurrent use of etidronate with corticosteroid, phosphate, calcitonin, furosemide or mithramycin therapies may result in additive effects.

The concurrent use of etidronate with warfarin has been associated with isolated reports of patients experiencing increases in their prothrombin time. The majority of these reports concerned variable elevations in prothrombin times without clinically significant sequelae. Although the relevance of these reports and any mechanism of coagulation alterations is unclear, patients on warfarin should have their prothrombin time more closely monitored.

Laboratory Tests: Depending on the time elapsed since the last dose of etidronate, the etidronate therapy may prevent bone-imaging diagnostic agents (e.g., technetium-^{99m}-methylene diphosphonate) used in bone scans, from adhering to bone and thus affect the interpretation of imaging results.

Children: The safety and effectiveness of Didronel in children has not been established.

Geriatrics: Special precautions related to the use of etidronate in geriatric patients have not been identified. However, serum creatinine levels should be closely monitored in patients with renal impairment.

Pregnancy: Studies performed in rats and rabbits using orally administered etidronate at doses up to 5 times the maximum human dose have revealed no evidence of impaired fertility or harm to the fetus. At doses of 22 times the maximum human dose, a decrease in live fetuses was observed in rats. Malformations occurred only in rats at exaggerated doses following parenteral administration and were skeletal in nature. These malformations were deemed to be the result of the pharmacologic action of the drug. The relationship of oral and i.v. routes of administration in reproduction/teratology studies is unknown. There are no adequate, well-controlled studies in pregnant women. Because animal reproduction studies are not always predictive of human response, this drug should be used during pregnancy only if clearly needed.

Lactation: Etidronate is not intended for administration during lactation. It is not known whether etidronate is excreted in human milk; it is excreted in the milk of rats. Because many drugs are excreted in human milk and because of the potential for adverse effects on the skeletons of infants, a decision should be made whether to discontinue nursing or to discontinue the drug, taking into account the importance of the drug to the mother.

Osteoporosis: An etidronate 400 mg tablet (see Supplied) is available as part of an intermittent cyclical therapy (ICT) indicated for the treatment of established post menopausal osteoporosis (see Didrocal Product Monograph). The efficacy of solely using etidronate 200 or 400 mg tablets without the ICT regimen has not been established for this indication.

Adverse Effects: General: Diarrhea and loose bowel movement may occur in some patients when etidronate is administered at doses greater than 5 mg/kg/day. The incidence is approximately 20% in patients treated with 20 mg/kg/day of the drug.

Postmarketing Experience: Other adverse events that have been reported in postmarketing studies of a number of indications, and were thought to be possibly related to etidronate include the following: nausea; alopecia; arthropathies, including arthralgia and arthritis; bone fracture; esophagitis; glossitis; hypersensitivity reactions, including angioedema, skin rashes (such as follicular eruption, macular rash, maculopapular rash), pruritus, Stevens-Johnson syndrome, and urticaria; osteomalacia; neuropsychiatric events, including amnesia, confusion, depression, and hallucination; paresthesias; burning tongue; erythema multiforme; and exacerbation of asthma.

In patients receiving etidronate, there have been rare reports of leukopenia, agranulocytosis and pancytopenia. Also, there have been very rare cases of leukemia reported with etidronate use (1/100 000) in ongoing safety surveillance since 1978 encompassing approximately 1.5 million patient-years of treatment. Any causal relationship to either the treatment or to the patients' underlying disease has not been established.

Exacerbation of existing peptic ulcer disease with resulting complications has been reported in a few patients.

Paget's Disease: Increased or recurrent bone pain at existing Pagetic sites and/or the appearance of pain at sites previously asymptomatic may occur even when the patient's overall clinical status is improved. The incidence was about 7% in placebo-treated patients and not substantially higher at the 5 mg/kg/day dose level. At higher doses the figure rose to approximately 20%. In etidronate-treated patients, the pain resolved while therapy was continued in some patients, but persisted for several months in others.

Fractures are recognized as a common feature in patients with Paget's disease. The risk of fracture may be increased when etidronate is taken at a dose level of 20 mg/kg/day in excess of 3 months. This risk may be greater in patients with extensive and severe disease, a history of multiple fractures, and/or rapidly advancing osteolytic lesions. It is recommended that the drug be discontinued when fractures occur and that therapy should not be reinstated until fracture healing is complete.

Hypercalcemia of Malignancy: Continuous oral medication at doses of 20 mg/kg/day for longer than 3 months, or 10 mg/kg/day for longer than 6 months, may result in the accumulation of unmineralized osteoid. Adverse reactions associated with such changes have not been reported in patients treated for hypercalcemia of malignancy.

Overdose: Symptoms and Treatment: Clinical experience with etidronate overdosage is extremely limited. Decreases in serum calcium following substantial overdosage may be expected in some patients. Signs and symptoms of hypocalcemia also may occur in some of these patients. In one event, an 18-year old female who ingested an estimated single dose of 4 000 to 6 000 mg (67 to 100 mg/kg) of etidronate was reported to be mildly hypocalcemic (1.88 mmol/L or 7.52 mg/dL) and experienced paresthesia of the fingers. Hypocalcemia resolved 6 hours after lavage and treatment with i.v. calcium gluconate. A 92-year-old female who accidentally received 1 600 mg of etidronate per day for 3.5 days experienced marked diarrhea and required treatment for electrolyte imbalance. Some patients may develop vomiting and expel the drug.

Gastric lavage may remove unabsorbed drug. Standard procedures for treating hypocalcemia, including the i.v. administration of ionizable calcium salts, would be expected to restore physiologic amounts of ionized calcium and relieve signs and symptoms of hypocalcemia. Such treatment has been effective.

Dosage: General: Etidronate should be taken on an empty stomach as a single oral daily dose, at least 2 hours before or after meals with a full glass of water. However, should gastrointestinal discomfort occur, the dose may be divided. To maximize absorption, patients should avoid taking the following items within 2 hours of dosing: food, especially those high in calcium, such as milk or milk products; vitamins with mineral supplements or antacids which are high in metals such as calcium, iron, magnesium or aluminum.

Paget's Disease: Initial Treatment Guidelines: The recommended initial dose of etidronate for most patients is 5 mg/kg body weight/day, not to exceed a period of 6 months. Doses above 10 mg/kg/day should be reserved for use when there is an overriding requirement for suppression of increased bone turnover associated with Paget's disease or when the patient requires more prompt reduction of elevated cardiac output. Treatment with doses above 10 mg/kg/day should be approached cautiously and should not exceed 3 months' duration. Doses in excess of 20 mg/kg/day are not recommended.

Urinary hydroxyproline excretion and/or serum alkaline phosphatase levels should be monitored periodically during the course of etidronate therapy.

Retreatment Guidelines: Retreatment should be initiated only after 1) an etidronate-free period of at least 90 days and, 2) there is biochemical, symptomatic or other evidence of active disease process.

It is advisable to monitor patients every 3 to 6 months, although some patients may go drug-free for extended periods. Retreatment regimens are the same as for initial treatment. For most patients the original dose will be adequate for retreatment. If not, consideration should be given to increasing the dose within the recommended guidelines.

Hypercalcemia of Malignancy: Etidronate tablets may be started on the day following the last dose of etidronate i.v. infusion. The recommended oral dose of etidronate for patients who have hypercalcemia is 20 mg/kg body weight/day for 30 days. If serum calcium levels remain normal or at clinically acceptable levels, treatment may be extended. Treatment for more than 90 days has not been adequately studied and is not recommended.

Supplied: 200 mg: Each white, rectangular tablet, with "P & G" on one face and "402" on the other face, contains: etidronate disodium USP 200 mg. Nonmedicinal ingredients: magnesium stearate, microcrystalline cellulose and pregelatinized starch. Lactose-free. Bottles of 60. Store at controlled room temperature (15 to 30°C).

400 mg: Each white, unscored capsule shaped tablet, with "NE1" engraved on one face and sculptured on the opposite side in an engraved box, contains: etidronate disodium USP 400 mg. Nonmedicinal ingredients: magnesium stearate, microcrystalline cellulose and pregelatinized starch. Lactose-free. Store at controlled room temperature (15 to 30°C).

Note: 400 mg tablet is only available as part of the Didrocal Intermittent Cyclical Therapy (see Precautions, Osteoporosis).

Reviewed 1999

DIFFERIN®

Galderma

Adapalene

Acne Therapy

Pharmacology: Adapalene is a chemically stable, retinoid-like compound. Biochemical and pharmacological profile studies have demonstrated that adapalene is a potent modulator of cellular differentiation, keratinization and inflammatory processes all of which represent important features in the pathology of acne vulgaris. Although the exact mode of action of adapalene is unknown, current evidence suggests that topical adapalene normalizes the differentiation of follicular epithelial cells resulting in decreased microcomedone formation. Adapalene inhibits the chemotactic (directional) and chemokinetic (random) responses of human polymorphonuclear leucocytes and also inhibits the metabolism of arachidonic acid, by lipoxidation, to inflammatory mediators.

Indications: For the topical treatment of acne vulgaris.

Contraindications: Patients who have demonstrated a hypersensitivity to the drug. Patients with eczema or seborrheic dermatitis.

Warnings: *Pregnancy*: **Topical adapalene should be used by women of childbearing years only after contraceptive counselling. It is recommended that topical adapalene should not be used by pregnant women.**

There have been rare reports of birth defects among babies born to women exposed to topical retinoids during pregnancy. However, there are no well controlled prospective studies of the use of topical retinoids, including adapalene, in pregnant women. A retrospective study of mothers exposed to topical tretinoin during the first trimester of pregnancy found no increase in the incidence of birth defects.

As with retinoids, adapalene administered **orally** at high doses (25 mg/kg/day) is teratogenic. In **topical** adapalene studies with doses of 50 to 200 times the likely clinical dose, no teratogenic effects were observed in rats or rabbits. However, **topical** retinoid teratology studies in rats and rabbits have been inconclusive.

General: For external use only. Avoid contact with the eyes, lips, angles of the nose, mucous membranes and open wounds. Certain cutaneous signs and symptoms such as erythema, dryness, scaling, burning or pruritus are associated with the topical application of retinoids and can also be expected with the use of adapalene. These treatment-related effects generally occur during the first 2 to 4 weeks of therapy and usually resolve as the skin undergoes adjustment with continued use. Depending on the degree of the side effects, patients can be directed to use the medication less frequently or temporarily discontinue use until the symptoms subside (see Dosage).

Differin (cont'd)

Lactation: It is not known whether this drug is excreted in human milk. Because many drugs are excreted in human milk, caution should be exercised when adapalene is administered to a nursing mother.

Children: Safety and effectiveness in children below the age of 12 have not been established.

Precautions: General: For external use only. Patients should be advised to use noncomedogenic cosmetics. Color cosmetics such as blushers and powders are acceptable; however, make-up cosmetics should be water based only. Cosmetics must be removed by thorough cleansing before the area is treated. Exposure to excessive sunlight, including sunlamps, should be avoided while using the preparation, or a suitably effective sunscreen should be employed.

Drug Interactions: There are no known interactions with other medications which are likely to be used topically and concurrently with adapalene. Absorption of adapalene through human skin is low; therefore, interaction with systemic medications is unlikely. As adapalene has the potential for local irritation, it is possible that concomitant use of abrasive cleansers, strong drying agents or irritant products may produce additive irritant effects. Other cutaneous antiacne treatments (e.g., erythromycin topical solution, clindamycin phosphate topical solution 1% or benzoyl peroxide products in concentrations up to 10%) may be used in the morning when adapalene topical cream or gel is used at night.

Adverse Effects: In clinical trials with adapalene topical cream, the total incidence of adverse reactions related to treatment was 5.5% (17 reports from 311 participants). The most frequently reported treatment-related events were skin irritation 1.6% (5/311) and sunburn 1% (3/311). Other dermatologic (treatment-related) events at an incidence rate less than 1% were acne flare 0.6% (2/311), contact dermatitis 0.6% (2/311), eyelid edema 0.6% (2/311), erythema 0.3% (1/311), skin discomfort 0.3% (1/311) and dry skin 0.3% (1/311).

In clinical trials with adapalene topical gel, the total incidence of adverse reactions related to treatment was 4.2% (28 reports from 661 participants). The most frequent adverse reactions reported were erythema (0.9%), dry skin (0.9%), skin irritation (0.6%), burning and stinging (0.6%) and acne flare (0.5%). Other adverse experiences which were attributed to treatment or were possibly related to treatment but occurred less frequently (in less than 0.5% of patients) were pruritus and one instance of sunburn.

Most of the reactions occurred within 2 to 4 weeks of initiation of therapy and were generally observed to resolve with continued use of the product or temporary adjustment of the treatment schedule. Contact allergy to topical adapalene was not reported during clinical trials. To date, all adverse effects of adapalene topical cream or gel, 0.1% have been reversible upon discontinuation of therapy.

Overdose: Symptoms and Treatment: Adapalene topical cream and gel are intended for cutaneous use only. If the medication is applied excessively, no more rapid or better results will be obtained and marked redness, peeling or discomfort may occur. The acute oral toxicity of adapalene topical gel in mice and rats is greater than 10 mL/kg. Inadvertent oral ingestion of adapalene may lead to the same adverse effects as those associated with excessive oral intake of Vitamin A including teratogenesis in women of childbearing years. Therefore, in such cases, pregnancy testing should be carried out in women of childbearing years. In the event of accidental ingestion of the product, an appropriate method of gastric emptying might be considered.

Dosage: Apply to the affected areas of the face, chest and back once a day before retiring and after washing. A small amount should be applied to provide a thin film, avoiding eyes, lips and mucous membranes.

Discontinue treatment if a severe local inflammatory response is experienced. Reinstitute therapy when the reaction has subsided, initially applying the preparation less frequently. Once daily application may be resumed if it is judged that the patient is able to tolerate the treatment.

Clinical improvement is expected to be clearly evident after 4 to 8 weeks of treatment, with further improvement expected with continued use. Cutaneous safety of adapalene topical gel has been demonstrated over a 6-month period of treatment.

Information for the Patient: See Blue Section—Information for the Patient "Differin".

Supplied: Cream: Each g of topical cream contains: adapalene 0.1% (1 mg). Nonmedicinal ingredients: carbomer 934P, cyclomethicone, edetate disodium, glycerin, methyl gluceth-20 sesquistearate, methyl glucose sesquistearate, methylparaben, phenoxyethanol, propylparaben, purified water, squalane and trolamine. Tubes of 15 and 45 g.

Gel: Each g of topical gel contains: adapalene 0.1% (1 mg). Nonmedicinal ingredients: carbomer 940, edetate disodium, methylparaben, poloxamer 182, propylene glycol, purified water and sodium hydroxide and/or hydrochloric acid for pH adjustment. Tubes of 15 and 45 g.

Store between 15 and 30°C. Keep container tightly closed.

Reviewed 1998

DIFLUCAN™ Ⓟ

Pfizer

Fluconazole

Antifungal Agent

Pharmacology: Fluconazole is a highly selective inhibitor of fungal cytochrome P450 sterol C-14-alpha-demethylation. Mammalian cell demethylation is much less sensitive to fluconazole inhibition. The subsequent loss of normal sterols correlates with the accumulation of 14-α-methyl sterols in fungi and may be responsible for the fungistatic activity of fluconazole.

Fluconazole is a polar bis-triazole antifungal drug. Studies have shown that fluconazole exhibits specificity as an inhibitor of the fungal as opposed to mammalian cytochrome P450 mediated reactions, including those involved in steroid biosynthesis and drug metabolism. Many of the clinical advantages of fluconazole are a result of its unique pharmacokinetic properties.

Pharmacokinetics: Adults: Absorption: The pharmacokinetic properties of fluconazole are similar following administration by the i.v. or oral routes and do not appear to be affected by gastric pH. In normal volunteers, the bioavailability of orally administered fluconazole is over 90% compared with i.v. administration. Essentially all of the administered drug reaches systemic circulation; thus, there is no evidence of first-pass metabolism of the drug. In addition, no adjustment in dosage is necessary when changing from p.o. to i.v. or vice versa.

Peak plasma concentrations (C_{max}) in fasted normal volunteers occur rapidly following oral administration, usually between 1 and 2 hours of dosing with a terminal plasma elimination half-life of approximately 30 hours (range 20 to 50 hours) after oral administration. The long plasma elimination half-life provides the basis for once daily dosing with fluconazole in the treatment of fungal infections.

In fasted normal volunteers, administration of a single oral 400 mg dose of fluconazole leads to a mean C_{max} of 6.72 μg/mL (range: 4.12 to 8.08 μg/mL) and after single oral doses of 50 to 400 mg, fluconazole plasma concentrations and AUC (area under the plasma concentration-time curve) are dose proportional.

In normal volunteers, oral bioavailability as measured by C_{max} and AUC was not affected by food when fluconazole was administered as a single 50 mg capsule; however T_{max} was doubled.

Steady-state concentrations are reached within 5 to 10 days following oral doses of 50 to 400 mg given once daily. Administration of a loading dose on the first day of treatment consisting of twice the usual daily dose results in plasma concentrations close to steady state by the second day.

Pharmacokinetics in Children: In children, the following pharmacokinetic data {mean (% cv)} have been reported (see Table I).

Table I—Diflucan

Pharmacokinetics in Children

Age Studied	Dose (mg/kg)	Clearance (mL/min/kg)	Half-life (hours)	C_{max} (μg/mL)	V_{dss} (L/kg)
9 months–13 years	Single—Oral 2 mg/kg	0.40 (38%) n=14	25.0	2.9 (22%) n=16	—
9 months–13 years	Single—Oral 8 mg/kg	0.51 (60%) n=15	19.5	9.8 (20%) n=15	—
5–15 years	Multiple i.v. 2 mg/kg	0.49 (40%) n=4	17.4	5.5 (25%) n=5	0.722 (36%) n=4
5–15 years	Multiple i.v. 4 mg/kg	0.59 (64%) n=5	15.2	11.4 (44%) n=6	0.729 (33%) n=5
5–15 years	Multiple i.v. 8 mg/kg	0.66 (31%) n=7	17.6	14.1 (22%) n=8	1.069 (37%) n=7

Clearance corrected for body weight was not affected by age in these studies. Mean body clearance in adults is reported to be 0.23 mL/min/kg (17%).

In premature newborns (gestation age 26 to 29 weeks), the mean (% cv) clearance within 36 hours of birth was 0.180 (35%, n=7) mL/min/kg, which increased with time to a mean of 0.218 (31%, n=9) mL/min/kg 6 days later and 0.333 (56%, n=4) mL/min/kg 12 days later. Similarly, the half-life was 73.6 hours, which decreased with time to a mean of 53.2 hours 6 days later and 46.6 hours 12 days later.

The dose equivalency scheme (see Table II) should generally provide equivalent exposure in pediatric and adult patients.

Table II—Diflucan

Dose Equivalency

Pediatric Patients	Adults
3 mg/kg	100 mg
6 mg/kg	200 mg
12 mg/kg*	400 mg

* Some older children may have clearances similar to that of adults. Absolute doses exceeding 600 mg/day are not recommended.

Distribution: The apparent volume of distribution of fluconazole approximates that of total body water. Plasma protein binding is low (11 to 12%) and is constant over the concentration range tested (0.1 to 10 mg/L). This degree of protein binding is not clinically meaningful. Following either single- or multiple-oral doses for up to 14 days, fluconazole penetrates into all body tissues and fluids studied (see Table III). In normal volunteers, saliva concentrations of fluconazole were equal to or slightly greater than plasma concentrations regardless of dose, route, or duration of dosing. In patients with bronchiectasis, sputum concentrations of fluconazole following a single 150 mg oral dose were equal to plasma concentrations at both 4 and 24 hours post dose. In patients with fungal meningitis, fluconazole concentrations in the CSF are approximately 80% of the corresponding plasma concentrations. Whole blood concentrations of fluconazole indicated that the drug freely enters erythrocytes and maintains a concentration equivalent to that of plasma.

Table III—Diflucan

Distribution of Fluconazole

Tissue or Fluid	Ratio of Fluconazole Tissue (Fluid)/Plasma Concentration[a]
Cerebrospinal fluid[b]	0.5–0.9
Saliva	1
Sputum	1
Blister fluid	1
Urine	10
Normal skin	10
Nails	1
Blister skin	2

[a] Relative to concurrent concentrations in plasma in subjects with normal renal function.

[b] Independent of degree of meningeal inflammation.

Metabolism and Excretion: Fluconazole is cleared primarily by renal excretion, with approximately 80% of the administered dose appearing in the urine as unchanged drug. Following administration of radiolabeled fluconazole, greater than 90% of the radioactivity is excreted in the urine. Approximately 11% of the radioactivity in urine is due to metabolites. An additional 2% of the total radioactivity is excreted in feces.

The pharmacokinetics of fluconazole do not appear to be affected by age alone but are markedly affected by reduction in renal function. There is an inverse relationship between the elimination half-life and creatinine clearance. The dose of fluconazole may need to be reduced in patients with impaired renal function (see Dosage). A 3-hour hemodialysis session decreases plasma concentrations by approximately 50%.

Pharmacodynamics: The effects of fluconazole on the metabolism of carbohydrates, lipids, adrenal and gonadal hormones were assessed. In normal volunteers, fluconazole administration (doses ranging from 200 to 400 mg once daily for up to 14 days) was associated with small and inconsistent effects on testosterone concentrations, endogenous corticosteroid concentrations, and the ACTH-stimulated cortisol response. In addition, fluconazole appears to have no clinically significant effects on carbohydrate or lipid metabolism in man.

Indications: For the treatment of oropharyngeal and esophageal candidiasis. Fluconazole is also effective for the treatment of serious systemic candidal infections, including urinary tract infection, peritonitis and pneumonia.

Cryptococcal meningitis.

Prevention of the recurrence of cryptococcal meningitis in patients with acquired immunodeficiency syndrome (AIDS).

Specimens for fungal culture and other relevant laboratory studies (serology, histopathology) should be obtained prior to therapy to isolate and identify causative organisms. Therapy may be instituted before the results of the cultures and other laboratory studies are known; however, once these results become available, anti-infective therapy should be adjusted accordingly.

Prophylaxis: Fluconazole is also indicated to decrease the incidence of candidiasis in patients undergoing bone marrow transplantation who receive cytotoxic chemotherapy and/or radiation therapy.

Contraindications: In patients who have shown hypersensitivity to fluconazole or to any of its excipients. There is no information regarding cross hypersensitivity between fluconazole and other azole antifungal agents. Caution should be used in prescribing fluconazole to patients with hypersensitivity to other azoles. Coadministration of terfenadine is contraindicated in patients receiving fluconazole at multiple doses of 400 mg or higher based upon results of a multiple dose interaction study (see Precautions).

Warnings: Hepatic injury: Fluconazole has been associated with rare cases of serious hepatic toxicity, including fatalities primarily in patients with serious underlying medical conditions. In cases of fluconazole associated hepatotoxicity, no obvious relationship to total daily dose, duration of therapy, sex or age of the patient has been observed. Fluconazole hepatotoxicity has usually, but not always been reversible on discontinuation of therapy. Patients who develop abnormal liver function tests during fluconazole therapy should be monitored for the development of more severe hepatic injury. Fluconazole should be discontinued if clinical signs and symptoms consistent with liver disease develop that may be attributable to fluconazole.

Anaphylaxis: In rare cases, anaphylaxis has been reported.

Dermatologic: Patients have rarely developed exfoliative skin disorders during treatment with fluconazole. In patients with serious underlying diseases (predominantly AIDS and malignancy) those have rarely resulted in a fatal outcome. Patients who develop rashes during treatment with fluconazole should be monitored closely and the drug discontinued if lesions progress.

Cisapride: There have been reports of cardiac events including torsades de pointes in patients receiving concomitant administration of fluconazole with cisapride. Patients should be carefully monitored if fluconazole is to be coadministered with cisapride (see Precautions).

Precautions: *Pregnancy:* There are no adequate and well-controlled studies in pregnant women. There have been reports of multiple congenital abnormalities in infants whose mothers were treated with high dose (400 to 800 mg/day) fluconazole therapy for coccidioidomycosis (an unapproved indication). Exposure to fluconazole began during the first trimester in all cases and continued for 3 months or longer. Fluconazole is not recommended in pregnant women unless the potential benefit outweighs the potential risk to mother and fetus.

Fluconazole was administered orally to pregnant rabbits during organogenesis in 2 studies: at 5, 10 and 20 mg/kg, and at 5, 25 and 75 mg/kg respectively. Maternal weight gain was impaired at all dose levels, and abortions occurred at 75 mg/kg (approximately 9.4 × the maximum recommended human dose); no adverse fetal effects were detected. In several studies in which pregnant rats were treated orally with fluconazole during organogenesis, maternal weight gain was impaired and placental weights were increased at the 25 mg/kg dose. There were no fetal effects at 5 or 10 mg/kg; increases in fetal anatomical variants (supernumerary ribs, renal pelvis dilation) and delays in ossification were observed at 25 and 50 mg/kg and higher doses. At doses ranging from 80 mg/kg to 320 mg/kg (approximately 10 to 40 × the maximum recommended human dose), embryolethality in rats was increased and fetal abnormalities included wavy ribs, cleft palate and abnormal cranio-facial ossification. These effects are consistent with the inhibition of estrogen synthesis in rats and may be a result of known effects of lowered estrogen on pregnancy, organogenesis and parturition.

Women of Childbearing Potential: Since the teratologic effects of fluconazole in humans are unknown, women taking fluconazole should consider using adequate contraception (see Pregnancy).

There have been reports of multiple congenital abnormalities in infants whose mothers were treated with high dose (400 to 800 mg/day) fluconazole therapy for coccidioidomycosis (an unapproved indication). Exposure to fluconazole began during the first trimester in all cases and continued for 3 months or longer. Since there are no adequate studies in pregnant women to assess the potential for fetal risk, fluconazole should not be used in pregnant women unless the potential benefit outweighs the potential risk to the fetus.

Lactation: Fluconazole is secreted in human breast milk at concentrations similar to plasma, hence its use in nursing mothers is not recommended.

Children: An open-label, randomized, controlled trial has shown fluconazole to be effective in the treatment of oropharyngeal candidiasis in children 6 months to 13 years of age.

In a noncomparative study of children with serious systemic fungal infections, fluconazole was effective in the treatment of candidemia (10 of 11 patients cured) and disseminated candidiasis (5 of 6 patients cured or improved).

Fluconazole was effective for the suppression of cryptococcal meningitis and/or disseminated cryptococcal infection in a group of 6 children treated in a compassionate study of fluconazole for the treatment of life-threatening or serious mycosis. There is no information regarding the efficacy of fluconazole for primary treatment of cryptococcal meningitis in children.

In addition, the use of fluconazole in children with cryptococcal meningitis, candida esophagitis or systemic candida infections is consistent with the approved use of fluconazole in similar indications for adults and, is supported by pharmacokinetic studies in children (see Pharmacology) establishing dose proportionality between children and adults (see Dosage).

The safety of fluconazole in children has been established in 577 children ages 1 day to 17 years who received doses ranging from 1 to 15 mg/kg/day for 1 to 1 616 days (see Adverse Effects).

Efficacy of fluconazole has not been established in infants less than 6 months of age. A small number of patients (29) ranging in age from 1 day to 6 months have been treated safely with fluconazole.

Geriatrics: Fluconazole was well tolerated by patients aged 65 years and over.

In a small number of elderly patients with bone marrow transplant (BMT) in which fluconazole was administered prophylactically there was a greater incidence of drug discontinuation due to adverse reactions (4.3%) than in younger patients (1.7%).

Superinfections: Development of resistance to fluconazole has not been studied; however, there have been reports of cases of superinfection with candida species other than C. albicans, which are often inherently not susceptible to fluconazole (e.g., Candida krusei). Such cases may require alternative antifungal therapy.

As for other anti-infectives used prophylactically, prudent medical practice dictates that fluconazole be used judiciously in prophylaxis, in view of the theoretical risk of emergence of resistant strains.

Drug Interactions: Clinically or potentially significant drug interactions between fluconazole and the following agents/classes have been observed.

Cimetidine: Absorption of orally administered fluconazole does not appear to be affected by gastric pH. Fluconazole 100 mg was administered as a single oral dose alone and 2 hours after a single dose of cimetidine 400 mg to 6 healthy male volunteers. After the administration of cimetidine, there was a significant decrease in fluconazole AUC (area under the plasma concentration-time curve) and C_{max}. There was a mean±SD decrease in fluconazole AUC of 13%±11% (range −3.4 to −31%) and C_{max} decreased 19%±14% (range: −5 to −40%). However, the administration of cimetidine 600 to 900 mg i.v. over a 4-hour period (from 1 hour before to 3 hours after a single oral dose of fluconazole 200 mg) did not affect the bioavailability or pharmacokinetics of fluconazole in 24 healthy male volunteers.

Antacid: Administration of Maalox (20 mL) to 14 normal male volunteers immediately prior to a single dose of fluconazole 100 mg had no effect on the absorption or elimination of fluconazole.

Cyclosporine: Cyclosporine AUC and C_{max} were determined before and after the administration of fluconazole 200 mg daily for 14 days in 8 renal transplant patients who had been on cyclosporine therapy for at least 6 months and on a stable cyclosporine dose for at least 6 weeks. There was a significant increase in cyclosporine AUC, C_{max}, C_{min} (24-hour concentration), and a significant reduction in apparent oral clearance following the administration of fluconazole. The mean±SD increase in AUC was 92%±43% (range: 18 to 147%). The C_{max} increased 60%±48% range (range: −5 to 133%). The C_{min} increased 157%±96% (range: 33 to 360%). The apparent oral clearance decreased 45%±15% (range: −15 to −60%). Fluconazole administered at 100 mg daily dose does not affect cyclosporine pharmacokinetic levels in patients with bone marrow transplants. Fluconazole may significantly increase cyclosporine levels in renal transplant patients with or without renal impairment. Careful monitoring of cyclosporine concentrations and serum creatinine is recommended in patients receiving fluconazole and cyclosporine.

Warfarin: There was a significant increase in prothrombin time response (area under the prothrombin time-time curve) following a single dosing of warfarin (15 mg) administered to 13 normal male volunteers following oral fluconazole 200 mg administered daily for 14 days as compared to the administration of warfarin alone. There was a mean±SD increase in the prothrombin time response (area under the prothrombin time-time curve) of 7%±4% (range: −2 to 13%). Mean is based on data from 12 subjects as one of 13 subjects experienced a 2-fold increase in his prothrombin time response.

Prothrombin time may be increased in patients receiving concomitant fluconazole and coumarin-type anticoagulants. Careful monitoring of prothrombin time in patients receiving fluconazole and coumarin-type anticoagulants is recommended.

Hydrochlorothiazide: Concomitant oral administration of 100 mg fluconazole and 50 mg hydrochlorothiazide for 10 days in 13 normal volunteers resulted in a significant increase in fluconazole AUC and C_{max} compared to fluconazole given alone. There was a mean±SD increase in fluconazole AUC and C_{max} of 45%±31% (range: 19 to 114%) and 43%±31% (range: 19 to 122%), respectively. These changes are attributed to a mean±SD reduction in renal clearance of 30%±12% (range −10 to −50%).

Oral Hypoglycemics: The effects of fluconazole on the pharmacokinetics of the sulfonylurea oral hypoglycemic agents tolbutamide, glipizide, and glyburide were evaluated in 3 placebo-controlled studies in normal volunteers. All subjects received the sulfonylurea alone as a single dose and again as a single dose following the administration of fluconazole 100 mg daily for 7 days. In these 3 studies, 22/46 (47.8%) of fluconazole-treated patients and 9/22 (40.1%) of placebo-treated patients experienced symptoms consistent with hypoglycemia.

Tolbutamide: In 13 normal male volunteers, there was a significant increase in tolbutamide (500 mg single dose) AUC and C_{max} following the administration of fluconazole. There was a mean±SD increase in tolbutamide AUC of 26%±9% (range: 12 to 39%). Tolbutamide C_{max} increased 11%±9% (range −6 to 27%).

Glipizide: The AUC and C_{max} of glipizide (2.5 mg single dose) were significantly increased following the administration of fluconazole in 13 normal male volunteers. There was a mean±SD increase in AUC of 49%±13% (range: 27 to 73%) and an increase in C_{max} of 19%±23% (range: −11 to 79%).

Glyburide: The AUC and C_{max} of glyburide (5 mg single dose) were significantly increased following the administration of fluconazole in 20 normal male volunteers. There was a mean±SD increase in AUC of 44%±29% (range: −13 to 115%) and C_{max} increased 19%±19% (range: −23 to 62%). Five subjects required oral glucose following the ingestion of glyburide after 7 days of fluconazole administration.

Clinically significant hypoglycemia may be precipitated by the use of fluconazole with oral hypoglycemic agents; 1 fatality has been reported from hypoglycemia in association with combined fluconazole and glyburide use. Fluconazole reduces the metabolism of tolbutamide, glyburide, and glipizide and increases the plasma concentration of these agents. When fluconazole is used concomitantly with these or other sulfonylurea oral hypoglycemic agents, blood glucose concentrations should be carefully monitored and the dose of the sulfonylurea should be adjusted as necessary.

Phenytoin: Phenytoin AUC was determined after 4 days of phenytoin dosing (200 mg daily, orally for 3 days, followed

Diflucan (cont'd)

by 250 mg i.v. for 1 dose) both with and without the administration of fluconazole (oral fluconazole 200 mg daily for 16 days) in 10 normal male volunteers. There was a significant increase in phenytoin AUC. The mean±SD increase in phenytoin AUC was 88%±68% (range: 16 to 247%). The absolute magnitude of this interaction is unknown because of the intrinsically nonlinear disposition of phenytoin.

Fluconazole increases the plasma concentrations of phenytoin. Careful monitoring of phenytoin concentrations in patients receiving fluconazole and phenytoin is recommended.

Rifampin: Administration of a single oral 200 mg dose of fluconazole after 15 days of rifampin administered as 600 mg daily in 8 healthy male volunteers resulted in a significant decrease in fluconazole AUC and a significant increase in apparent oral clearance of fluconazole. There was a mean±SD reduction in fluconazole AUC of 23%±9% (range: −13 to −42%). Apparent oral clearance of fluconazole increased 32%±17% (range: 16 to 72%). Fluconazole half-life decreased from 33.4±4.4 hours to 26.8±3.9 hours.

Rifampin enhances the metabolism of concurrently administered fluconazole. Depending on clinical circumstances, consideration should be given to increasing the dose of fluconazole when it is administered with rifampin.

Zidovudine: Plasma zidovudine concentrations were determined on 2 occasions (before and following fluconazole 200 mg daily for 15 days) in 13 volunteers with AIDS or ARC who were on a stable zidovudine dose for at least 2 weeks. There was a significant increase in zidovudine AUC following the administration of fluconazole. The mean±SD increase in AUC was 20%±32% (range: −27 to 104%). The metabolite, GZDV, to parent drug ratio significantly decreased after the administration of fluconazole, from 7.6±3.6 to 5.7±2.2. Patients receiving this combination should be monitored for the development of zidovudine-related adverse reactions.

Theophylline: The pharmacokinetics of theophylline were determined from a single i.v. dose of aminophylline (6 mg/kg) before and after the oral administration of fluconazole 200 mg daily for 14 days in 16 normal male volunteers. There were significant increases in theophylline AUC, C_{max}, and half-life with a corresponding decrease in clearance. The mean±SD theophylline AUC increased 21%±16% (range: −5 to 48%). The C_{max} increased 13%±17% (range: −13 to 40%). Theophylline clearance decreased 16%±11% (range: −32 to 5%). The half-life of theophylline increased from 6.6±1.7 hours to 7.9±1.5 hours. Patients who are receiving high doses theophylline or who are otherwise at increased risk for theophylline toxicity should be observed for signs of theophylline toxicity while receiving fluconazole, and therapy modified appropriately if signs of toxicity develop.

Oral Contraceptives: In pharmacodynamic studies, single and multiple 50 mg oral doses of fluconazole produced an overall mean increase in ethinyl estradiol or levonorgestrel pharmacokinetics in healthy women taking oral contraceptives. At 200 mg of fluconazole daily, the AUCs of ethinyl estradiol and levonorgestrel were increased, 40% and 24%, respectively.

Twenty-five normal females received daily doses of both 200 mg of fluconazole tablets or placebo for 2, 10-day periods. The treatment cycles were 1 month apart with all subjects receiving fluconazole during one cycle and placebo during the other. The order of study treatment was random. Single doses of an oral contraceptive tablet containing levonorgestrel and ethinyl estradiol were administered on the final treatment day (day 10) of both cycles. Following administration of 200 mg of fluconazole, the mean percentage increase of AUC for levonorgestrel compared to placebo was 25% (range: −12 to 82%) and the mean percentage increase for ethinyl estradiol compared to placebo was 38% (range: −11 to 101%). Both of these increases were statistically significantly different from placebo.

Drugs Prolonging the QTc Interval: The use of fluconazole in patients concurrently taking drugs metabolized by the Cytochrome P450 system may be associated with elevations in the serum levels of these drugs. In the absence of definitive information caution should be used when coadministering fluconazole and such agents. Patients should be carefully monitored.

Terfenadine: Because of the occurrence of serious cardiac dysrhythmias secondary to prolongation of the QTc interval in patients receiving azole antifungals in conjunction with terfenadine, interaction studies have been performed. In one study, 6 healthy volunteers received terfenadine 60 mg b.i.d. for 15 days. Fluconazole 200 mg was administered daily from days 9 through 15. Fluconazole did not affect terfenadine plasma concentrations. Terfenadine acid metabolite AUC increased 36%±36% (range: 7 to 102%) from day 8 to day 15 with the concomitant administration of fluconazole. There was no change in cardiac repolarization as measured by Holter QTc intervals. However, another study at a 400 mg and 800 mg daily dose of fluconazole demonstrated that fluconazole taken in doses of 400 mg/day or greater significantly increases plasma levels of terfenadine when taken concomitantly. Therefore the combined use of fluconazole at doses of 400 mg or higher with terfenadine is contraindicated (see Contraindications). Patients should be carefully monitored if they are being concurrently prescribed fluconazole at multiple doses lower than 400 mg/day with terfenadine.

Astemizole: Definitive interaction studies with fluconazole have not been conducted. The use of fluconazole may be associated with elevations in serum levels of astemizole. Caution should be used when coadministering fluconazole with astemizole. Patients should be carefully monitored.

Cisapride: There have been reports of cardiac events including torsades de pointes in patients to whom fluconazole and cisapride were coadministered. Therefore, caution should be used when coadministering fluconazole with cisapride. Patients should be carefully monitored (see Warnings).

Drug/Drug Interaction: Interaction studies with other medications have not been conducted, but such interactions may occur.

Drug/Laboratory Test Interactions: None known.

Adverse Effects: Adults: Sixteen percent of over 4 000 patients treated with fluconazole in clinical trials of 7 days or more experienced adverse events.

Treatment was discontinued in 1.5% of patients due to adverse clinical events and in 1.3% of patients due to laboratory test abnormalities.

Adverse clinical events were reported more frequently in HIV infected patients (21%) than in non-HIV infected patients (13%). However, the patterns of adverse events in HIV infected and non-HIV infected patients were similar. The proportions of patients discontinuing therapy due to clinical adverse events were similar in the 2 groups (1.5%).

Autonomic Nervous System: dry mouth, increased sweating.
Psychiatric: insomnia, somnolence.
Gastrointestinal: anorexia, constipation, dyspepsia, flatulence.
Liver and Biliary System: cholestasis, hepatocellular damage, jaundice.
Special Senses: taste perversion.
Hematopoietic: anemia.
General: fatigue, malaise, asthenia, fever.
Immunologic: In rare cases, anaphylaxis has been reported.

The following adverse experiences occurred under conditions (e.g., open trials marketing experience) where a causal association is uncertain:
CNS: seizures.
Dermatologic: exfoliative skin disorders including Stevens-Johnson Syndrome and toxic epidermal necrolysis (see Warnings), alopecia.
Hematopoietic and Lymphatic: leukopenia, including neutropenia and agranulocytosis, thrombocytopenia.
Metabolic: hypercholesterolemia, hypertriglyceridemia, hypokalemia.

Laboratory Test Abnormalities: Liver Function: Clinically significant increases were observed in the following proportions of patients: AST 1%, ALT 1.2%, alkaline phosphatase 1.2%, total bilirubin 0.3%. The incidence of elevated serum transaminases was independent of age or route (oral or i.v) of administration but was greater in patients taking fluconazole concomitantly with one or more of the following medications: rifampin, phenytoin, isoniazid, valproic acid or oral hypoglycemic agents. Clinically significant increases also were more frequent in patients who: 1) had AST or ALT elevations greater than 3 times the upper limit of normal (>3×ULN) at the time of entering the study (baseline), 2) had a diagnosis of hepatitis at any time during the study and, 3) were identified as alcohol abusers. The overall rate of serum transaminase elevations of more than 8 times the upper limit of normal was approximately 1% in patients treated with fluconazole during clinical trials (see Table IV).

Table IV—Diflucan

Laboratory Test Abnormalities—Liver Enzymes

Lab Parameter	Number* of Patients	% Abnormal	% Drug-related	Number of Patients	% Abnormal	% Drug-related
		Baseline >3×ULN			Baseline <3×ULN	
AST	53	9.4	3.8	3 007	4.2	0.8
ALT	65	3.1	0.0	2 874	4.8	1.0
		Hepatitis Patients			Non-hepatitis Patients	
AST	160	10.6	1.9	2 900	3.9	0.8
ALT	140	11.4	2.1	2 799	4.4	1.0
		Alcohol Abuse			Non-alcohol Abuse	
AST	42	9.5	2.4	3 018	4.2	0.9
ALT	40	10.0	2.5	2 899	4.7	1.0
		Received I.V. Fluconazole			Never Received I.V. Fluconazole	
AST	144	5.6	1.4	2 916	4.2	0.9
ALT	139	5.0	0.7	2 800	4.7	1.0
		≥65 Years Old			<65 Years Old	
AST	277	4.3	1.1	2 783	4.3	0.9
ALT	258	3.9	1.2	2 681	4.8	1.0

*Note: Only patients who had measurements at baseline and during therapy were included.

The 2 most serious adverse clinical events noted during clinical trials were exfoliative skin disorders and hepatic necrosis.

Because most of these patients had serious underlying disease (predominantly AIDS or malignancy) and were receiving multiple concomitant medications, including many known to be hepatotoxic or associated with exfoliative skin disorders, the causal association of these reactions with fluconazole is uncertain. Two cases of hepatic necrosis and one exfoliative skin disorder (Stevens-Johnson syndrome) were associated with a fatal outcome (see Warnings).

The following treatment-related clinical adverse events occurred at an incidence of 1% or greater in 4 048 patients receiving fluconazole for 7 or more days in clinical trials: nausea 3.7%, headache 1.9%, skin rash 1.8%, vomiting 1.7%, abdominal pain 1.7% and diarrhea 1.5%.

Other treatment-related clinical adverse events which occurred less commonly (0.2 to <1%) are presented by organ system below:
Skin and Appendages: pruritus.
Musculoskeletal: myalgia.
Central and Peripheral Nervous System: convulsions, dizziness, paresthesia, tremor, vertigo.

Renal Function: Clinically significant increases were observed in the following proportions of patients: BUN (0.4%) and creatinine (0.3%).

Hematological Function: Clinically meaningful deviations from baseline in hematologic values which were possibly related to fluconazole were observed in the following proportions of patients: hemoglobin (0.5%), white blood cell count (0.5%) and total platelet count (0.6%).

Children: In Phase II/III clinical trials conducted in the U.S. and in Europe, 577 pediatric patients, ages 1 day to 17 years were treated with fluconazole at doses ranging up to 15 mg/kg/day for up to 1 616 days. Thirteen percent of children experienced treatment related adverse events. The most commonly reported events were vomiting (5.4%), abdominal pain (2.8%), nausea (2.3%) and diarrhea (2.1%). Treatment was discontinued in 2.6% of patients due to adverse clinical events and in 1% of patients due to laboratory test abnormality.

Overdose: Symptoms: There has been 1 reported case of overdosage with fluconazole. A 42-year-old patient infected with human immunodeficiency virus developed hallucinations and exhibited paranoid behavior after reportedly ingesting 8 200 mg of fluconazole. The patient was admitted to the hospital, and his condition resolved within 48 hours.

Treatment: In the event of overdose, symptomatic treatment (with supportive measures and gastric lavage if necessary) may be adequate. Fluconazole is largely excreted in urine. A 3-hour hemodialysis session decreases plasma levels by approximately 50%.

Mice and rats receiving very high doses of fluconazole, whether orally or i.v., displayed a variety of nonspecific, agonal signs such as decreased activity, ataxia, shallow respiration, ptosis, lacrimation, salivation, urinary incontinence and cyanosis. Death was sometimes preceded by clonic convulsions.

Dosage: Oral (Tablets and Oral Suspension) and I.V. Treatment: Fluconazole is well absorbed and excreted predominantly unchanged in urine following oral administration in man. The oral bioavailability is essentially complete (greater than 90%), and is independent of dose. Peak plasma concentrations after oral administration are attained rapidly, usually within 2 hours of dosing. **Since oral absorption is rapid and almost complete, the daily dose of fluconazole is the same for oral tablets and suspension and i.v. administration.** The terminal plasma elimination half-life is approximately 30 hours (range 20 to 50 hours).

The daily dose of fluconazole and the route of administration should be based on the infecting organism, the patient's condition and the response to therapy. Treatment should be continued until clinical parameters and laboratory tests indicate that an active fungal infection has been cured or has subsided. An inadequate period of treatment may lead to recurrence of active infection. Patients with AIDS and cryptococcal meningitis or recurrent oropharyngeal candidiasis usually require maintenance therapy to prevent relapse.

Recommended Dosages in Adults and Children (see also Pharmacology): Loading Dose: **Adults and children: Administration of a loading dose on the first day of treatment, consisting of twice the usual daily dose, results in plasma concentrations close to steady state by the second day. Patients with acute infections should be given a loading dose equal to twice the daily dose, not to exceed a maximum single dose of 400 mg in adults or 12 mg/kg in children, on the first day of treatment.**

Dosage Equivalency Scheme: See Table V.

Table V—Diflucan

Dosage Equivalency Scheme

Pediatric Patients	Adults
3 mg/kg	100 mg
6 mg/kg	200 mg
12 mg/kg*	400 mg

*Some older children may have clearances similar to that of adults. Absolute doses exceeding 600 mg/day are not recommended.

Oropharyngeal Candidiasis: Adults: 100 mg once daily. Treatment should be continued for at least 2 weeks to decrease the likelihood of relapse.

Children: 3 mg/kg once daily. Treatment should be continued for at least 2 weeks to decrease the likelihood of relapse.

Esophageal Candidiasis: Adults: 100 to 200 mg once daily. Patients should be treated for a minimum of 3 weeks and for at least 2 weeks following resolution of symptoms.

Children: 3 mg/kg to 6 mg/kg once daily. Patients should be treated for a minimum of 3 weeks and for at least 2 weeks following resolution of symptoms.

Systemic Candidiasis: (Candidemia and Disseminated Candidal Infections) Adults: 200 to 400 mg once daily. These patients should be treated for a minimum of 4 weeks and for at least 2 weeks following resolution of symptoms.

Children: 6 to 12 mg/kg/day have been used in an open, noncomparative study of a small number of patients.

Cryptococcal Meningitis: Adults: 200 to 400 mg once daily. Although the duration of therapy for cryptococcal meningitis is unknown, it is recommended that the initial therapy should last a minimum of 10 weeks.

Children: 6 to 12 mg/kg once daily. The recommended duration for initial therapy is 10 to 12 weeks after the cerebrospinal fluid becomes culture-negative.

Prevention of Recurrence of Cryptococcal Meningitis in Patients with AIDS: Adults: 200 mg once daily.

Children: 6 mg/kg once daily.

Premature Neonates: Experience with fluconazole in neonates is limited to pharmacokinetic studies in premature newborns (see Pharmacology). Based upon the prolonged half-life seen in premature newborns (gestational age 26 to 29 weeks), these children in the first 2 weeks of life, should receive the same dosage (mg/kg) as in older children, but administered every 72 hours. After the first 2 weeks, these children should be dosed once daily.

Neonates: No information regarding fluconazole pharmacokinetics in full-term newborns is available.

Prophylaxis in Adult Patients: The recommended fluconazole daily dosage for the prevention of candidiasis in adult patients undergoing bone marrow transplantation is 400 mg once daily. Patients who are anticipated to have severe granulocytopenia (less than 500 neutrophils/mm³) should start fluconazole prophylaxis several days before the anticipated onset of neutropenia and continue for 7 days after the neutrophil count rises above 1 000 cells/mm³.

Fluconazole may be administered either orally or by i.v. infusion. The i.v. infusion of fluconazole should be administered at a maximum rate of approximately 200 mg/hour given as a continuous infusion (see Directions for Use).

Impaired Renal Function: Adults: Fluconazole is cleared primarily by renal excretion as unchanged drug. In patients with impaired renal function, an initial loading dose of 50 to 400 mg should be given. After the loading dose, the daily dose (according to indication) should be based on Table VI.

Table VI—Diflucan

Dosage in Adult Patients with Impaired Renal Function

Creatinine Clearance (mL/min)	Percent of Recommended Dose
>50	100%
21-50	50%
11-20	25%
Patients receiving regular hemodialysis	one recommended dose after each dialysis

When serum creatinine is the only measure of renal function available, the following formula (based on sex, weight and age of the patient) should be used to estimate the creatinine clearance:

$$\text{Males: } \frac{\text{weight (kg)} \times (140-\text{age})}{72 \times \text{serum creatinine (mg/100 mL)}}$$

Females: 0.85×the above value

Children: Although the pharmacokinetics of fluconazole has not been studied in children with renal insufficiency, dosage reduction in children with renal insufficiency should parallel that recommended for adults. The following formula may be used to estimate creatinine clearance in children:

$$K \times \frac{\text{linear length or height (cm)}}{\text{serum creatinine (mg/100 mL)}}$$

(Where K=0.55 for children older than 1 year and 0.45 for infants.)

Directions for Use: Mixing Directions: Powder for Oral Suspension: Prepare a suspension at time of dispensing as follows: Tap bottle until all powder flows freely. Add 24 mL of water and shake vigorously to suspend powder and produce 35 mL suspension. Each 5 mL contains 50 mg fluconazole. The concentrations of the recommended suspensions are as follows: See Table VII.

Table VII—Diflucan

Concentrations of the Recommended Suspensions

Fluconazole Content	Concentration of
350 mg	10 mg/mL

Note: Shake oral suspension well before using.

Directions for Use: I.V. Infusion: Inspect visually for particulate matter or discoloration prior to administration. Do not use if cloudiness or precipitation is evident.

Reject the contents as unsterile if the metal seal is broken. **Not intended for multidose use:** discard any portion not used when the seal is first broken.

Connect an i.v. giving set to the bottle of fluconazole i.v. solution and also insert a venting set through the bung. **Infuse the i.v. solution at a maximum rate of 200 mg/hour.** Flush fluconazole i.v. solution remaining in the giving set with sterile normal saline. Because fluconazole is available as a dilute saline solution, consideration should be given to the rate of fluid administration in patients requiring sodium or fluid restriction.

Incompatibility: It is recommended that fluconazole i.v. be infused separately.

Compatibility: Administration Sets (Giving Sets): The i.v. infusion is compatible with (i.e., not susceptible to absorption) sets constructed of a delivery tube (PVC) luer lock (modified phenylene oxide), flash ball (latex) drip chamber (polypropylene) and piercing spike (polypropylene).

Supplied: I.V.: Each mL of sterile aqueous solution for direct infusion contains: fluconazole 2 mg and sodium chloride 9 mg. Clear glass bottles of 100 mL (2×100 mL), affording doses of 200 mg fluconazole, sealed with a rubber bung. Store below 30°C. Do not freeze.

Powder for Oral Suspension: On reconstitution with water (24 mL) each mL of the orange-flavored suspension contains: fluconazole 10 mg (i.e., equivalent to fluconazole 50 mg/5 mL). Nonmedicinal ingredients: citric acid, colloidal silicon dioxide, natural orange flavor, sodium benzoate, sodium citrate, sucrose, titanium dioxide and xanthan gum. Bottles of 350 mg in HDPE bottles of 35 mL.

Before reconstitution (i.e., dry powder): Store below 30°C.

After reconstitution: The reconstituted suspension is stable for 14 days at room temperature between 5 and 30°C. Protect from freezing. Shake well before each use. Discard unused portion after 2 weeks (14 days).

Tablets: 50 mg: Each pink tablet contains: fluconazole 50 mg. Nonmedicinal ingredients: croscarmellose sodium, dibasic calcium phosphate anhydrous, FD&C Red No. 40 aluminum lake dye, magnesium stearate, microcrystalline cellulose and povidone. Opaque polyethylene bottles of 50 and 100. Store below 30°C.

100 mg: Each pink tablet contains: fluconazole 100 mg. Nonmedicinal ingredients: croscarmellose sodium, dibasic calcium phosphate anhydrous, FD&C Red No. 40 aluminum lake dye, magnesium stearate, microcrystalline cellulose and povidone. Opaque polyethylene bottles of 50 and 100. Store below 30°C.

(Shown in Product Recognition Section)

Reviewed 1998

DIFLUCAN-150™ 🄿

Pfizer

Fluconazole

Antifungal Agent

Pharmacology: Fluconazole is a highly selective inhibitor of fungal cytochrome P450 sterol C-14-α-demethylation. Mammalian cell demethylation is much less sensitive to fluconazole inhibition. The subsequent loss of normal sterols correlates with the accumulation of 14-α-methyl sterols in fungi and may be responsible for the fungistatic activity of fluconazole.

Fluconazole is a polar bis-triazole antifungal drug. Studies have shown that fluconazole exhibits specificity as an inhibitor of the fungal as opposed to mammalian cytochrome P450 mediated reactions, including those involved in steroid biosynthesis and drug metabolism. Many of the clinical advantages of fluconazole are a result of its unique pharmacokinetic properties.

Pharmacokinetics: Absorption: The pharmacokinetic properties of fluconazole are similar following administration by the i.v. or oral routes and do not appear to be affected by gastric pH. In normal volunteers, the bioavailability of orally administered fluconazole is over 90% compared with i.v. administration. Essentially all of the administered drug reaches systemic circulation; thus, there is no evidence of first-pass metabolism of the drug. In addition, no adjustment in dosage is necessary when changing from p.o. to i.v. or vice versa.

Peak plasma concentrations (C_{max}) in fasted normal volunteers occur rapidly following oral administration, usually between 1 and 2 hours of dosing with a terminal plasma elimination half-life of approximately 30 hours (range 20 to 50 hours) after oral administration. The long plasma elimination half-life provides the basis for once daily dosing with fluconazole in the treatment of fungal infections.

In fasted normal volunteers, administration of a single oral 150 mg dose of fluconazole produced a mean C_{max} of 2.70 μg/mL (range: 1.91 to 3.70 μg/mL).

In normal volunteers, oral bioavailability as measured by C_{max} and AUC was not affected by food when fluconazole was administered as a single 50 mg capsule; however T_{max} was doubled.

Distribution: The apparent volume of distribution of fluconazole approximates that of total body water. Plasma protein binding is low (11 to 12%) and is constant over the concentration range tested (0.1 to 10 mg/L). This degree of protein binding is not clinically meaningful.

A single oral 150 mg dose of fluconazole administered to 27 patients penetrated into vaginal tissue, resulting in tissue:plasma ratios ranging from 0.94 to 1.14 over the first 48 hours following dosing.

A single oral 150 mg dose of fluconazole administered to 14 patients penetrated into vaginal fluid, resulting in

Diflucan-150 (cont'd)

fluid:plasma ratios ranging from 0.36 to 0.71 over the first 72 hours following dosing.

Metabolism and Excretion: Fluconazole is cleared primarily by renal excretion, with approximately 80% of the administered dose appearing in the urine as unchanged drug. Following administration of radiolabeled fluconazole, greater than 90% of the radioactivity is excreted in the urine. Approximately 11% of the radioactivity in urine is due to metabolites. An additional 2% of the total radioactivity is excreted in feces.

The pharmacokinetics of fluconazole do not appear to be affected by age alone but are markedly affected by reduction in renal function. There is an inverse relationship between the elimination half-life and creatinine clearance. There is no need to adjust single dose therapy for vaginal candidiasis because of impaired renal function.

Pharmacodynamics: The effects of fluconazole on the metabolism of carbohydrates, lipids, adrenal and gonadal hormones were assessed. In normal volunteers, fluconazole administration at doses ranging from 200 to 400 mg once daily for up to 14 days was associated with small and inconsistent effects on testosterone concentrations, endogenous corticosteroid concentrations, and the ACTH-stimulated cortisol response. In addition, fluconazole appears to have no clinically significant effects on carbohydrate or lipid metabolism in man.

Indications: For the oral treatment of: vaginal candidiasis (yeast infections due to Candida).

The diagnosis of vaginal candidiasis should be confirmed by KOH smears and/or cultures before initiating therapy with fluconazole.

Contraindications: In patients who have shown hypersensitivity to fluconazole or to any of its excipients. There is no information regarding cross hypersensitivity between fluconazole and other azole antifungal agents. Caution should be used in prescribing fluconazole to patients with hypersensitivity to other azoles. Coadministration of terfenadine is contraindicated in patients receiving fluconazole at multiple doses of 400 mg or higher based upon results of a multiple dose interaction study (see Precautions).

Warnings: Anaphylaxis: In rare cases, anaphylaxis has been reported.

Hepatic injury: In the treatment of systemic infections multiple doses of fluconazole has been associated with rare cases of serious hepatic toxicity, including fatalities primarily in patients with serious underlying medical conditions. In cases of fluconazole associated hepatotoxicity, no obvious relationship to total daily dose, duration of therapy, sex or age of the patient has been observed. Fluconazole hepatotoxicity has usually, but not always, been reversible on discontinuation of therapy. Patients who develop abnormal liver function tests during fluconazole therapy should be monitored for the development of more severe hepatic injury.

Dermatologic: In rare cases, during the treatment of systemic infections, patients have developed exfoliative skin disorders during treatment with fluconazole.

Cisapride: There have been reports of cardiac events including torsades de pointes in patients receiving concomitant administration of fluconazole with cisapride. Patients should be carefully monitored if fluconazole is to be coadministered with cisapride (see Precautions).

Precautions: General: The convenience of the single oral dose fluconazole regimen for the treatment of vaginal yeast infections **should be weighed against the acceptability of a higher incidence of drug related adverse events** with fluconazole (26%) versus intravaginal agents (16%) in comparative clinical studies where no difference in efficacy was demonstrated (see Adverse Effects).

Fluconazole administered in combination with ethinyl estradiol- and levonorgestrel-containing oral contraceptives produced an overall mean increase in ethinyl estradiol and levonorgestrel levels; however, in some patients there were decreases of up to 47% and 33% of ethinyl estradiol and levonorgestrel levels, respectively (see Precautions, Drug Interactions). The data presently available indicate that the decreases in some individual ethinyl estradiol and levonorgestrel AUC values with fluconazole treatment may be the result of random variation. While there is evidence that fluconazole can inhibit the metabolism of ethinyl estradiol and levonorgestrel, there is no evidence that fluconazole is a net inducer of ethinyl estradiol or levonorgestrel metabolism. The clinical significance of these effects is presently unknown.

Pregnancy: There are no adequate and well-controlled studies in pregnant women. There have been reports of multiple congenital abnormalities in infants whose mothers were treated with high dose (400 to 800 mg/day) fluconazole therapy for coccidioidomycosis (an unapproved indication). Exposure to fluconazole began during the first trimester in all cases and continued for 3 months or longer. Fluconazole should not be used in pregnant women unless the potential benefit outweighs the potential risk to the fetus.

Fluconazole was administered orally to pregnant rabbits during organogenesis in two studies, at 5, 10 and 20 mg/kg and at 5, 25 and 75 mg/kg respectively. Maternal weight gain was impaired at all dose levels, and abortions occurred at 75 mg/kg approximately 9.4 × the maximum recommended human dose); no adverse fetal effects were detected. In several studies in which pregnant rats were treated orally with fluconazole during organogenesis, maternal weight gain was impaired and placental weights were increased at 25 mg/kg. There were no fetal effects at 5 or 10 mg/kg; increases in fetal anatomical variants (supernumerary ribs, renal pelvis dilation) and delays in ossification were observed at 25 and 50 mg/kg and higher doses. At doses ranging from 80 to 320 mg/kg (approximately 10 to 40 × the maximum recommended human dose) embryolethality in rats was increased and fetal abnormalities included wavy ribs, cleft palate and abnormal cranio-facial ossification. These effects are consistent with the inhibition of estrogen synthesis in rats and may be a result of known effects of lowered estrogen on pregnancy, organogenesis and parturition.

Women of Childbearing Potential: Since the teratologic effects of fluconazole in humans are unknown, women taking fluconazole for vaginal candidiasis should consider using adequate contraception (see Pregnancy).

There have been reports of multiple congenital abnormalities in infants whose mothers were treated with high dose (400 to 800 mg/day) fluconazole therapy for coccidioidomycosis (an unapproved indication). Exposure to fluconazole began during the first trimester in all cases and continued for 3 months or longer. Since there are no adequate studies in pregnant women to assess the potential for fetal risk, fluconazole should not be used in pregnant women unless the potential benefit outweighs the potential risk to the fetus.

Lactation: Fluconazole is secreted in human breast milk at concentrations similar to plasma, hence its use in nursing mothers is not recommended.

Children and Adolescents: The safety and effectiveness of fluconazole 150 mg capsules in the treatment of vaginal candidiasis in patients under 18 years of age have not been established.

Drug Interactions: Clinically or potentially significant drug interactions between fluconazole and the following agents/classes have been observed.

Oral Contraceptives: Oral contraceptives were administered as a single dose both before and after the oral administration of fluconazole 50 mg once daily for 10 days in 10 healthy women. There was no significant difference in ethinyl estradiol or levonorgestrel AUC after the administration of fluconazole. The mean increase in ethinyl estradiol AUC was 6% (range: −47 to 108%) and levonorgestrel AUC increased 17% (range: −33 to 141%).

Twenty-five normal females received daily doses of both 200 mg fluconazole or placebo for two, 10-day periods. The treatment cycles were 1 month apart with all subjects receiving fluconazole during one cycle and placebo during the other. The order of study treatment was random. Single doses of an oral contraceptive tablet containing levonorgestrel and ethinyl estradiol were administered on the final treatment day (day 10) of both cycles. Following administration of 200 mg of fluconazole, the mean percentage increase of AUC for levonorgestrel compared to placebo was 25% (range: −12 to 82%) and the mean percentage increase for ethinyl estradiol compared to placebo was 38% (range: −11 to 101%). Both of these increases were statistically significantly different from placebo.

Drugs Prolonging the QTc Interval: The use of fluconazole in patients concurrently taking drugs metabolized by the Cytochrome P450 system may be associated with elevations in the serum levels of these drugs. In the absence of definitive information caution should be used when coadministering fluconazole and such agents. Patients should be carefully monitored.

Terfenadine: Because of the occurrence of serious cardiac dysrhythmias secondary to prolongation of the QTc interval in patients receiving azole antifungals in conjunction with terfenadine, interaction studies have been performed. In 1 study, 6 healthy volunteers received terfenadine 60 mg b.i.d. for 15 days. Fluconazole 200 mg was administered daily from days 9 through 15. Fluconazole did not affect terfenadine plasma concentrations. Terfenadine acid metabolite AUC increased 36%±36% (range: 7 to 102%) from day 8 to day 15 with the concomitant administration of fluconazole. There was no change in cardiac repolarization as measured by Holter QTc intervals. However, another study at a 400 mg and 800 mg daily dose of fluconazole demonstrated that fluconazole taken in doses of 400 mg/day or greater significantly increases plasma levels of terfenadine when taken concomitantly. Therefore the combined use of fluconazole at doses of 400 mg or higher with terfenadine is contraindicated (see Contraindications). Patients should be carefully monitored if they are being concurrently prescribed fluconazole at multiple doses lower than 400 mg/day with terfenadine.

Astemizole: Definitive interaction studies with fluconazole have not been conducted. The use of fluconazole may be associated with elevations in serum levels of astemizole. Caution should be used when coadministering fluconazole with astemizole. Patients should be carefully monitored.

Cisapride: There have been reports of cardiac events including torsades de pointes in patients to whom fluconazole and cisapride were coadministered. Therefore, caution should be used when coadministering fluconazole with cisapride. Patients should be carefully monitored (see Warnings).

Theophylline: The pharmacokinetics of theophylline were determined from a single i.v. dose of aminophylline (6 mg/kg) before and after the oral administration of fluconazole 200 mg daily for 14 days in 16 normal male volunteers. There were significant increases in theophylline AUC, C_{max}, and half-life with a corresponding decrease in clearance. The mean±SD theophylline AUC increased 21%±16% (range: −5 to 48%). The C_{max} increased 13%±17% (range: −13 to 40%). Theophylline clearance decreased 16%±11% (range: −32 to 5%). The half-life of theophylline increased from 6.6±1.7 hours to 7.9±1.5 hours. Patients who are receiving high doses theophylline or who are otherwise at increased risk for theophylline toxicity should be observed for signs of theophylline toxicity while receiving fluconazole, and therapy modified appropriately if signs of toxicity develop.

Cimetidine: Absorption of orally administered fluconazole does not appear to be affected by gastric pH. Fluconazole 100 mg was administered as a single oral dose alone and 2 hours after a single dose of cimetidine 400 mg to 6 healthy male volunteers. After the administration of cimetidine, there was a significant decrease in fluconazole AUC (area under the plasma concentration-time curve) and C_{max}. There was a mean±SD decrease in fluconazole AUC of 13%±11% (range: −3.4 to −31%) and C_{max} decreased 19%±14% (range: −5 to −40%). However, the administration of cimetidine 600 to 900 mg i.v. over a 4-hour period (from 1 hour before to 3 hours after a single oral dose of fluconazole 200 mg) did not affect the bioavailability or pharmacokinetics of fluconazole in 24 healthy male volunteers.

Antacid: Administration of Maalox (20 mL) to 14 normal male volunteers immediately prior to a single dose of fluconazole 100 mg had no effect on the absorption or elimination of fluconazole.

Cyclosporine: Cyclosporine AUC and C_{max} were determined before and after the administration of fluconazole 200 mg daily for 14 days in 8 renal transplant patients who had been on cyclosporine therapy for at least 6 months and on a stable cyclosporine dose for at least 6 weeks. There was a significant increase in cyclosporine AUC, C_{max}, C_{min} (24-hour concentration), and a significant reduction in apparent oral clearance following the administration of fluconazole. The mean±SD increase in AUC was 92%±43% (range: 18 to 147%). The C_{max} increased 60%±48% range (range: −5 to 133%). The C_{min} increased 157%±96% (range: 33 to 360%). The apparent oral clearance decreased 45%±15% (range: −15 to −60%). Fluconazole administered at 100 mg daily dose does not affect cyclosporine pharmacokinetic levels in patients with bone marrow transplants. Fluconazole may significantly increase cyclosporine levels in renal transplant patients with or without renal impairment. Careful monitoring of cyclosporine concentrations and serum creatinine is recommended in patients receiving fluconazole and cyclosporine.

Warfarin: There was a significant increase in prothrombin time response (area under the prothrombin time-time curve) following a single dose of warfarin (15 mg) administered to 13 normal male volunteers following oral fluconazole 200 mg administered daily for 14 days as compared to the administration of warfarin alone. There was a mean±SD increase in the prothrombin time response (area under the prothrombin time-time curve) of 7%±4% (range: −2 to 13%). Mean is based on data from 12 subjects as one of 13 subjects experienced a 2-fold increase in his prothrombin time response.

Prothrombin time may be increased in patients receiving concomitant fluconazole and coumarin-type anticoagulants. Careful monitoring of prothrombin time in patients receiving fluconazole and coumarin-type anticoagulants is recommended.

Hydrochlorothiazide: Concomitant oral administration of 100 mg fluconazole and 50 mg hydrochlorothiazide for 10 days in 13 normal volunteers resulted in a significant increase in fluconazole AUC and C_{max} compared to fluconazole given alone. There was a mean±SD increase in fluconazole AUC and C_{max} of 45%±31% (range: 19 to 114%) and 43%±31% (range: 19 to 122%), respectively. These changes are attributed to a mean±SD reduction in renal clearance of 30%±12% (range −10 to −50%).

Oral Hypoglycemics: The effects of fluconazole on the pharmacokinetics of the sulfonylurea oral hypoglycemic agents tolbutamide, glipizide, and glyburide were evaluated in 3 placebo-controlled studies in normal volunteers. All subjects received the sulfonylurea alone as a single dose and again as a single dose following the administration of fluconazole 100 mg daily for 7 days. In these three studies, 22/46 (47.8%) of fluconazole-treated patients and 9/22 (40.1%) of placebo-treated patients experienced symptoms consistent with hypoglycemia.

Tolbutamide: In 13 normal male volunteers, there was a significant increase in tolbutamide (500 mg single dose) AUC and C_{max} following the administration of fluconazole. There was a mean±SD increase in tolbutamide AUC of 26%±9% (range: 12 to 39%). Tolbutamide C_{max} increased 11%±9% (range −6 to 27%).

Glipizide: The AUC and C_{max} of glipizide (2.5 mg single dose) were significantly increased following the administration of fluconazole in 13 normal male volunteers. There was a mean±SD increase in AUC of 49%±13% (range: 27 to 73%) and an increase in C_{max} of 19%±23% (range: −11 to 79%).

Glyburide: The AUC and C_{max} of glyburide (5 mg single dose) were significantly increased following the administration of fluconazole in 20 normal male volunteers. There was a mean±SD increase in AUC of 44%±29% (range: −13 to 115%) and C_{max} increased 19%±19% (range: −23 to 62%). Five subjects required oral glucose following the ingestion of glyburide after 7 days of fluconazole administration.

Clinically significant hypoglycemia may be precipitated by the use of fluconazole with oral hypoglycemic agents; one fatality has been reported from hypoglycemia in association with combined fluconazole and glyburide use. Fluconazole reduces the metabolism of tolbutamide, glyburide, and glipizide and increases the plasma concentration of these agents. When fluconazole is used concomitantly with these or other sulfonylurea oral hypoglycemic agents, blood glucose concentrations should be carefully monitored and the dose of the sulfonylurea should be adjusted as necessary.

Phenytoin: Phenytoin AUC was determined after 4 days of phenytoin dosing (200 mg daily, orally for 3 days, followed by 250 mg i.v. for 1 dose) both with and without the administration of fluconazole (oral fluconazole 200 mg daily for 16 days) in 10 normal male volunteers. There was a significant increase in phenytoin AUC. The mean±SD increase in phenytoin AUC was 88%±68% (range: 16 to 247%). The absolute magnitude of this interaction is unknown because of the intrinsically nonlinear disposition of phenytoin.

Fluconazole increases the plasma concentrations of phenytoin. Careful monitoring of phenytoin concentrations in patients receiving fluconazole and phenytoin is recommended.

Rifampin: Administration of a single oral 200 mg dose of fluconazole after 15 days of rifampin administered as 600 mg daily in 8 healthy male volunteers resulted in a significant decrease in fluconazole AUC and a significant increase in apparent oral clearance of fluconazole. There was a mean±SD reduction in fluconazole AUC of 23%±9% (range: −13 to −42%). Apparent oral clearance of fluconazole increased 32%±17% (range: 16 to 72%). Fluconazole half-life decreased from 33.4±4.4 hours to 26.8±3.9 hours.

Rifampin enhances the metabolism of concurrently administered fluconazole. Depending on clinical circumstances, consideration should be given to increasing the dose of fluconazole when it is administered with rifampin.

Zidovudine: Plasma zidovudine concentrations were determined on 2 occasions (before and following fluconazole 200 mg daily for 15 days) in 13 volunteers with AIDS or ARC who were on a stable zidovudine dose for at least 2 weeks. There was a significant increase in zidovudine AUC following the administration of fluconazole. The mean±SD increase in AUC was 20%±32% (range: −27 to 104%). The metabolite, GZDV, to parent drug ratio significantly decreased after the administration of fluconazole, from 7.6±3.6 to 5.7±2.2. Patients receiving this combination should be monitored for the development of zidovudine-related adverse reactions.

Drug/Drug Interactions: Interaction studies with other medications have not been conducted, but such interactions may occur.

Drug/Laboratory Test Interactions: None known.

Adverse Effects: In patients with vaginal candidiasis treated with fluconazole as a single oral dose, the adverse events documented in two controlled North American trials were as follows: see Table I.

Table I—Diflucan-150

Adverse Effects

	% of Patients with Side Effects	
	Fluconazole (n=448)	**Intravaginal Products (n=422)**
Drug Related Side Effects	26.1	15.9
Nausea	6.7	0.7
Abdominal Pain	5.6	1.7
Diarrhea	2.7	0.5
Dyspepsia	1.3	0.2
Headache	12.9	6.6
Application Site Reactions	0.0	4.5
Dizziness	1.3	0.0
Taste Perversion	1.3	0.0

Most of the reported side effects were mild to moderate in severity.

Occasional allergic reactions including pruritus and urticaria were reported.

In marketing experience with single dose fluconazole, rare cases of anaphylactic reaction and angioedema have been reported.

Overdose: Symptoms: There has been 1 reported case of overdosage with fluconazole. A 42-year-old patient infected with human immunodeficiency virus developed hallucinations and exhibited paranoid behavior after reportedly ingesting 8 200 mg of fluconazole. The patient was admitted to the hospital, and his condition resolved within 48 hours.

Treatment: In the event of overdose, symptomatic treatment (with supportive measures and gastric lavage if necessary) may be adequate. Fluconazole is largely excreted in urine. A 3-hour hemodialysis session decreases plasma levels by approximately 50%.

Mice and rats receiving very high doses of fluconazole, whether orally or i.v., displayed a variety of nonspecific, agonal signs such as decreased activity, ataxia, shallow respiration, ptosis, lacrimation, salivation, urinary incontinence and cyanosis. Death was sometimes preceded by clonic convulsions.

Dosage: Vaginal Candidiasis: Oral: The recommended dosage for vaginal candidiasis is 150 mg as a single oral dose.

There is no need to adjust single dose therapy for vaginal candidiasis because of impaired renal function.

Information for the Patient: See Blue Section—Information for the Patient "Diflucan-150".

Supplied: Each hard white gelatin capsule, marked with Pfizer logo, contains: fluconazole 150 mg. Nonmedicinal ingredients: colloidal silicon dioxide, lactose, magnesium stearate, maize starch and sodium lauryl sulfate; capsule shell: gelatin and titanium dioxide. Unit dose blister (PVC) pack of 1. Store between 15 and 30°C.

(Shown in Product Recognition Section)

Reviewed 1998

DIFLUCORTOLONE ℞

General Monograph, CPhA

see CORTICOSTEROIDS: TOPICAL

DIGIBIND® ℞

Glaxo Wellcome

Digoxin Immune Fab (Ovine)

Specific Antibody for Digoxin

Pharmacology: Digoxin immune Fab (ovine) is a sterile lyophilized powder of antigen binding fragments (Fab) derived from specific antidigoxin antibodies raised in sheep. It binds molecules of digoxin, making them unavailable for binding at their site of action on cells in the body. The Fab fragment-digoxin complex accumulates in the blood, from which it is excreted by the kidney. The net effect is to shift the equilibrium away from binding of digoxin to its receptors in the body, thereby, reversing its effects.

After i.v. injection of digoxin immune Fab (ovine) in the baboon, digoxin-specific Fab fragments are excreted in the urine with a biological half-life of about 9 to 13 hours. In humans with normal renal function the half-life appears to be 15 to 20 hours. Experimental studies in animals indicate that these antibody fragments have a large volume of distribution in the extracellular space, unlike whole antibody which distributes in a space only about twice that of the plasma volume. Ordinarily, following administration of digoxin immune Fab (ovine), improvement in signs and symptoms of digitalis intoxication begins within one-half hour or less.

The affinity of digoxin for digoxin immune Fab (ovine) is in the range of 10^9 to 10^{11} M^{-1}, which is greater than the affinity of digoxin for (sodium, potassium) ATPase, the presumed receptor for its toxic effects. The affinity of digoxin immune Fab (ovine) for digitoxin is about 10 times less than for digoxin (10^8 to 10^9 M^{-1}).

Indications: For treatment of potentially life-threatening digoxin intoxication. Although designed specifically to treat life-threatening digoxin toxicity, it has also been used successfully to treat life-threatening toxicity due to digitoxin. Since human experience is limited and the consequences of repeated exposures are unknown, this product is not indicated for milder cases of digitalis toxicity.

Manifestations of life-threatening toxicity include severe ventricular arrhythmias such as ventricular tachycardia or ventricular fibrillation, or progressive bradyarrhythmias such as severe sinus bradycardia, or second- or third-degree heart block not responsive to atropine.

Ingestion of more than 10 mg of digoxin in previously healthy adults or 4 mg of digoxin in previously healthy children, or ingestion causing steady-state serum concentrations greater than 10 ng/mL, often results in cardiac arrest. Digitalis-induced progressive elevation of the serum potassium concentration also suggests imminent cardiac arrest. If the potassium concentration exceeds 5 mEq/L in the setting of severe digitalis intoxication, digoxin immune Fab (ovine) therapy is indicated.

Contraindications: There are no known contraindications to the use of digoxin immune Fab (ovine).

Warnings: Suicidal ingestion often involves more than one drug; thus, toxicity from other drugs should not be overlooked.

One should consider the possibility of anaphylactic, hypersensitivity or febrile reactions to digoxin immune Fab (ovine). If an anaphylactoid reaction occurs, the drug infusion should be discontinued and appropriate therapy initiated using aminophylline, oxygen, volume expansion, diphenhydramine, corticosteroids and airway management as indicated. The need for epinephrine should be balanced against its potential risk in the setting of digitalis toxicity.

Since the Fab fragment of the antibody lacks the antigenic determinants of the Fc fragment, it should pose less of an immunogenic threat to patients than does an intact immunoglobulin molecule. Patients with known allergies would be particularly at risk, as would individuals who have previously received antibodies or Fab fragments raised in sheep.

Papain is used to cleave the whole antibody into Fab and Fc fragments, and traces of papain or inactivated papain residues may be present in digoxin immune Fab (ovine). Patients with allergies to papain, chymopapain, or other papaya extracts also may be particularly at risk.

Skin testing for allergy was performed during the clinical investigation of digoxin immune Fab (ovine). Only one patient developed erythema at the site of skin testing, with no accompanying wheal reaction; this individual had no adverse reaction to systemic treatment with digoxin immune Fab (ovine). Since allergy testing can delay urgently needed therapy, it is not

Digibind (cont'd)

routinely required before treatment of life-threatening digitalis toxicity with digoxin immune Fab (ovine).

Skin Testing: Skin testing may be appropriate for high risk individuals, especially patients with known allergies or those previously treated with digoxin immune Fab (ovine). The intradermal skin test can be performed by:

1. Diluting 0.1 mL of reconstituted Digibind (9.5 mg/mL) in 9.9 mL sterile isotonic saline (1:100 dilution, 95 μg/mL).
2. Injecting 0.1 mL of the 1:100 dilution (9.5 μg) intradermally and observing for an urticarial wheal surrounded by a zone of erythema. The test should be read at 20 minutes.

The scratch test procedure is performed by placing 1 drop of a 1:100 dilution of digoxin immune Fab (ovine) on the skin and then making a ¼ inch scratch through the drop with a sterile needle. The scratch site is inspected at 20 minutes for an urticarial wheal surrounded by erythema. If skin testing causes a systemic reaction, a tourniquet should be applied above the site of testing and measures to treat anaphylaxis should be instituted. Further administration should be avoided unless its use is absolutely essential, in which case the patient should be pretreated with corticosteroids and diphenhydramine. The physician should be prepared to treat anaphylaxis.

Precautions: General: Standard therapy for digitalis intoxication includes withdrawal of the drug and correction of factors that may contribute to toxicity, such as electrolyte disturbances, hypoxia, acid-base disturbances and agents such as catecholamines. Also, treatment of arrhythmias may include judicious potassium supplements, lidocaine, phenytoin, procainamide and/or propranolol; treatment of sinus bradycardia or atrioventricular block may involve atropine or pacemaker insertion.

Massive digitalis intoxication can cause hyperkalemia; administration of potassium supplements in the setting of massive intoxication may be hazardous (see Laboratory Tests). After treatment with digoxin immune Fab (ovine), the serum potassium concentration may drop rapidly and must be monitored frequently, especially over the first several hours after digoxin immune Fab (ovine) is given (see Laboratory Tests).

The elimination half-life in the setting of renal failure has not been clearly defined. Patients with renal dysfunction have been successfully treated with digoxin immune Fab (ovine). There is no evidence to suggest the time-course of therapeutic effect is any different in these patients than in patients with normal renal function, but excretion of the Fab fragment-digoxin complex from the body is probably delayed. In patients who are functionally anephric, one would anticipate failure to clear the Fab fragment-digoxin complex from the blood by glomerular filtration and renal excretion. Whether failure to eliminate the Fab fragment-digoxin complex in severe renal failure can lead to reintoxication following release of newly unbound digoxin into the blood is uncertain. Such patients should be monitored for a prolonged period for possible recurrence of digitalis toxicity.

Patients with intrinsically poor cardiac function may deteriorate from withdrawal of the inotropic action of digoxin. Studies in animals have shown that the reversal of inotropic effect is relatively gradual, occurring over hours. When needed, additional support can be provided by use of i.v. inotropes, such as dopamine or dobutamine, or vasodilators. One must be careful in using catecholamines not to aggravate digitalis toxic rhythm disturbances. Clearly, other types of digitalis glycosides should not be used in this setting. Redigitalization should be postponed, if possible, until the Fab fragments have been eliminated from the body, which may require several days. Patients with impaired renal function may require a week or longer.

Laboratory Tests: Digoxin immune Fab (ovine) will interfere with digitalis immunoassay measurements. Thus, the standard serum digoxin concentration measurement can be clinically misleading until the Fab fragment is eliminated from the body.

Serum digoxin or digitoxin concentration should be obtained before digoxin immune Fab (ovine) administration, if at all possible. These measurements may be difficult to interpret if drawn soon after the last digitalis dose, since at least 6 to 8 hours are required for equilibration of digoxin between serum and tissue. Patients should be closely monitored, including temperature, blood pressure, electrocardiogram and potassium concentration, during and after administration of digoxin immune Fab (ovine). The total serum digoxin concentration may rise precipitously following administration of digoxin immune Fab (ovine), but this will be almost entirely bound to the Fab fragment and therefore, not able to react with receptors in the body.

Potassium concentrations should be followed carefully. Severe digitalis intoxication can cause life-threatening elevation in serum potassium concentration by shifting potassium from inside to outside the cell. The elevation in serum potassium concentration can lead to increased renal excretion of potassium. Thus, these patients may have hyperkalemia with total body deficit of potassium. When the effect of digitalis is reversed by digoxin immune Fab (ovine), potassium shifts back inside the cell, with a resulting decline in serum potassium concentration. Hypokalemia may thus develop rapidly. For these reasons, serum potassium concentration should be monitored repeatedly, especially over the first several hours after digoxin immune Fab (ovine) is given, and cautiously treated when necessary.

Carcinogenesis, Mutagenesis, Impairment of Fertility: There have been no long-term studies performed in animals to evaluate carcinogenic potential.

Pregnancy: Animal reproduction studies have not been conducted with digoxin immune Fab (ovine). It is also not known whether digoxin immune Fab (ovine) can cause fetal harm when administered to a pregnant woman, or can affect reproduction capacity. It should be given to a pregnant woman only if clearly needed.

Lactation: It is not known whether this drug is excreted in human milk. Because many drugs are excreted in human milk, caution should be exercised when digoxin immune Fab (ovine) is administered to a nursing woman.

Children: Digoxin immune Fab (ovine) has been successfully used in infants with no apparent adverse sequelae. As in all other circumstances, use of this drug in infants should be based on careful consideration of the benefits of the drug balanced against the potential risks involved.

Adverse Effects: Allergic reactions to digoxin immune Fab (ovine) have been reported rarely. Patients with a history of allergy, especially to antibiotics, appear to be at particular risk (see Warnings). In a few instances, low cardiac output states and congestive heart failure could have been exacerbated by withdrawal of the inotropic effects of digitalis. Hypokalemia may occur from reactivation of (sodium, potassium) ATPase (see Precautions, Laboratory Tests). Patients with atrial fibrillation may develop a rapid ventricular response from withdrawal of the effects of digitalis on the atrioventricular node.

Dosage: General Guidelines: The dosage of digoxin immune Fab (ovine) varies according to the amount of digoxin (digitoxin) to be neutralized. The average dose used during clinical testing was 10 vials.

Dosage for Acute Ingestion of Unknown Amount: Twenty (20) vials (760 mg) is adequate to treat most life-threatening ingestions in both adults and children. However, in children it is important to monitor for volume overload. The physician may consider administering 10 vials, observing the patient's response, and following with an additional 10 vials if indicated.

Dosage for Toxicity During Chronic Therapy: For adults, 6 vials (228 mg) usually is adequate to reverse most cases of toxicity. This dose can be used in patients who are in acute distress or for whom a serum digoxin or digitoxin concentration is not available. In **infants and small children** (≤20 kg) a single vial usually should suffice.

Methods for calculating the dose of digoxin immune Fab (ovine) required to neutralize the known or estimated amount of digoxin or digitoxin in the body are given below (see Dosage Calculation section).

When determining the dose for digoxin immune Fab (ovine), the following guidelines should be considered:

Erroneous calculations may result from inaccurate estimates of the amount of digitalis ingested or absorbed, or from non-steady-state serum digitalis concentrations. Inaccurate serum digitalis concentration measurements are a possible source of error. Most serum digoxin assay kits are designed to measure values less than 5 ng/mL. Dilution of samples is required to obtain accurate measures above 5 ng/mL.

Dosage calculations are based on a steady-state volume of distribution of approximately 5 L/kg for digoxin (0.5 L/kg for digitoxin) to convert serum digitalis concentration to the amount of digitalis in the body. The conversion is based on the principle that body load equals drug steady-state serum concentration multiplied by volume of distribution. These volumes are population averages and vary widely among individuals. Many patients may require higher doses for complete neutralization. Doses should ordinarily be rounded up to the next whole vial.

If toxicity has not adequately reversed after several hours or appears to recur, readministration of digoxin immune Fab (ovine) at a dose guided by clinical judgment may be required.

Failure to respond to digoxin immune Fab (ovine) raises the possibility that the clinical problem is not caused by digitalis intoxication. If there is no response to an adequate dose of digoxin immune Fab (ovine), the diagnosis of digitalis toxicity should be questioned.

Dosage Calculation: Acute Ingestion of Known Amount: Each vial of Digibind contains 38 mg of purified digoxin-specific Fab fragments which will bind approximately 0.5 mg of digoxin (or digitoxin). Thus, one can calculate the total number of vials required by dividing the total digitalis body load in mg by 0.5 mg/vial (see Formula 1).

For toxicity from an acute ingestion, total body load in mg will be approximately equal to the amount ingested in mg multiplied by 0.80 (to account for incomplete absorption) for digoxin tablets. For digitoxin, the total body load will be approximately equal to the amount ingested in mg.

Table I gives dosage estimates in number of vials for **adults and children** who have ingested a single large dose of digoxin and for whom the approximate number of tablets is known. The Digibind dose (in number of vials) represented in Table I can be approximated using the following formula:

Formula 1:

$$\text{Dose (in \# of vials)} = \frac{\text{Total digitalis body load in mg}}{\text{0.5 mg of digitalis bound/vial}}$$

Table I—Digibind

Approximate Digibind Dose for Reversal of a Single Large Digoxin Overdose

Number of Digoxin Tablets*	**Digibind Dose # of Vials**
25	10
50	20
75	30
100	40
150	60
200	80

*0.25 mg tablets with 80% bioavailability.

Calculations Based on Steady-State Serum Digoxin Concentrations: Table II gives dosage estimates in number of vials for **adult patients** for whom a steady-state serum digoxin concentration is known. The Digibind dose (in number of vials) represented in Table II can be approximated using the following formula:

Formula 2: Calculation with digoxin in ng/mL:

$$\text{Dose (in \# of vials)} = \frac{\text{(Serum digoxin concentration in ng/mL)(weight in kg)}}{100}$$

Calculation with digoxin in nmol/L (SI units):

$$\text{Dose (in \# of vials)} = \frac{\text{(Serum digoxin in nmol/L} \times 0.781)\times\text{(weight in kg)}}{100}$$

Table II—Digibind

Adult Dose Estimate of Digibind (in # of Vials) from Steady-State Serum Digoxin Concentration

Patient Weight (kg)	**Serum Digoxin Concentration (nmol/L) 1**	**2**	**4**	**8**	**12**	**16**	**20**	**25**
40	0.5v	1v	2v	3v	4v	5v	7v	8v
60	0.5v	1v	2v	4v	6v	8v	10v	12v
70	1v	2v	3v	5v	7v	9v	11v	14v
80	1v	2v	3v	5v	8v	10v	13v	16v
100	1v	2v	4v	7v	10v	13v	16v	20v

v=vials.

Table III (on following page) gives dosage estimates in mg of digoxin immune Fab (ovine) for infants and small children based on the steady-state serum digoxin concentration. The Digibind dose represented in Table III (on following page) can be estimated by multiplying the dose (in number of vials) calculated from Formula 2 by the amount of Digibind contained in a vial (38 mg/vial) (see Formula 3). Since infants and small children can have much smaller dosage requirements, it is recommended that the 38 mg vial be reconstituted as directed and administered with a tuberculin syringe. For very small doses, a reconstituted vial can be diluted with 34 mL of sterile isotonic saline to achieve a concentration of 1 mg/mL.

Formula 3:

Dose (in mg) = [Dose (in # of vials)][38 mg/vial]

Table III—Digibind

Infants and Small Children Dose Estimates of Digibind (in mg) from Steady-State Serum Digoxin Concentration

	Serum Digoxin Concentration (nmol/L)							
Patient Weight (kg)	**1**	**2**	**4**	**8**	**12**	**16**	**20**	**25**
1	0.3* mg	0.6* mg	1.2* mg	2.5* mg	4 mg	5 mg	6 mg	8 mg
3	1* mg	2* mg	4 mg	8 mg	11 mg	15 mg	18 mg	23 mg
5	1.5* mg	3* mg	6 mg	12 mg	10 mg	24 mg	30 mg	38 mg
10	3* mg	6 mg	12 mg	24 mg	36 mg	48 mg	60 mg	75 mg
20	6 mg	12 mg	24 mg	48 mg	72 mg	95 mg	119 mg	149 mg

*Dilution of reconstituted vial to 1 mg/mL may be desirable.

Calculation Based on Steady-State Digitoxin Concentration: The Digibind dose for digitoxin toxicity can be approximated using the following formula:

Formula 4: Calculation with digitoxin in ng/mL:

$$\text{Dose (in \# of vials)} = \frac{\text{(Serum digitoxin concentration in ng/mL)(weight in kg)}}{1\,000}$$

Calculation with digitoxin in nmol/L (SI units):

$$\text{Dose (in \# of vials)} = \frac{\text{(Serum digitoxin in nmol/L} \times 0.765)\times\text{(weight in kg)}}{1\,000}$$

If the dose based on ingested amount differs substantially from that calculated from the serum digoxin or digitoxin concentration, it may be preferable to use the higher dose.

Administration: Digoxin immune Fab (ovine) is administered by the i.v. route over 30 minutes. It is recommended that it be infused through a 0.22 micron membrane filter to ensure no undissolved particulate matter is administered. If cardiac arrest is imminent, it can be given as a bolus injection.

Reconstituted Solutions: The contents in each vial should be dissolved with 4 mL of Sterile Water for Injection, by gentle mixing, to give clear, colorless, approximately isosmotic solution with a protein concentration of 9.5 mg/mL. Reconstituted product should be used promptly. If it is not used immediately, it may be stored under refrigeration at 2 to 8°C for up to 4 hours. The reconstituted product may be diluted with sterile isotonic saline to a convenient volume. Parenteral drug products should be inspected visually for particulate matter and discoloration prior to administration, whenever solution and container permit.

Supplied: Each vial of sterile, lyophilized powder for injection contains: digoxin-specific Fab fragments 38 mg, sorbitol 75 mg as a stabilizer and sodium chloride 28 mg. Preservative-free. Each vial will bind approximately 0.5 mg digoxin (or digitoxin). Refrigerate at 2 to 8°C. Unreconstituted vials can be stored at up to 30°C for a total of 30 days.

DIHYDROERGOTAMINE (DHE) ℞

Novartis Pharmaceuticals

Dihydroergotamine Mesylate

Vascular Headache Therapy

Pharmacology: Dihydroergotamine displays moderate to high affinity for various serotonergic receptor subtypes (5-HT_{1A}, 5-HT_{1C}, 5-HT_{1D}, 5-HT_2). The compound exerts agonistic activity at the 5-HT_{1D} subtype and antagonistic activity at the 5-HT_2 subtype. Dihydroergotamine also displays blocking actions at alpha adrenergic receptor level, with a direct stimulating effect on the smooth muscle of peripheral blood vessels. Its tonic effect on capacitance vessels (veins) is particularly pronounced, compared to its effects on resistance vessels (arterioles). In comparison to ergotamine, dihydroergotamine is more potent with regard to its adrenergic blocking actions, and less potent with regard to its vasconstrictive actions.

Dihydroergotamine is 93% bound to plasma proteins. Its apparent volume of distribution is about 30 L/kg. The total body clearance is about 1.5 L/min, reflecting mainly the hepatic clearance. Elimination from the plasma is biphasic with an α-phase of 1.5 hours and a β-phase of 15 hours. The major route of excretion is via the bile in the feces. Urinary excretion of parent substance and metabolites amounts to about 10% after i.v. administration.

Indications: As therapy to abort acute attacks of migraine, with and without aura, and related vascular headaches including cluster headaches, where rapid relief is desired.

Contraindications: In patients who have previously shown hypersensitivity to ergot alkaloids.

DHE is contraindicated in patients having conditions predisposing to vasospastic reactions such as peripheral occlusive vascular disease (thromboangiitis obliterans, luetic arteritis, severe arteriosclerosis, thrombophlebitis, Raynaud's disease), coronary artery disease (in particular, unstable or vasospastic angina), angina pectoris, sepsis or other serious infectious states, shock, vascular surgery (especially arterial, recent or contemplated), inadequately controlled hypertension, severely impaired hepatic or renal functions, peptic ulcer, severe pruritus and malnutrition.

Pregnancy: DHE possesses oxytocic properties and, therefore, should not be administered during pregnancy.

Warnings: Intra-arterial injection of dihydroergotamine (DHE) must strictly be avoided. Should this occur by accident, an α-blocker such as phentolamine should be administered.

Caution should be exercised when DHE is administered to patients with severe renal disease, unless they are receiving dialysis. In such cases the dosage should be reduced.

If excessive or prolonged dosage is contemplated, patients should be closely monitored for peripheral vascular complications.

Lactation: It is not known whether dihydroergotamine is excreted in the breast milk. Consequently, DHE should not be used in nursing mothers.

Precautions: Children: Safety and effectiveness of DHE in children have not been established.

Drug Interactions: The concomitant use of erythromycin, troleandomycin or josamycin with DHE should be avoided since these antibiotics may increase the plasma level of dihydroergotamine.

Adverse Effects: Nausea and vomiting (not migraine related) may **occasionally** occur but they are less frequent and less prolonged than with ergotamine tartrate. Numbness and tingling of fingers and toes, muscle pains in the extremities, weakness in the legs, precordial distress and pain, transient tachycardia or bradycardia, localized edema and itching have also been reported.

In a few patients who have taken oral dihydroergotamine continuously over years, development of fibrotic changes, in particular of the pleura and the retroperitoneum, has been observed.

Overdose: Symptoms: Nausea, vomiting; drowsiness; confusion; tachycardia; dizziness; numbness, tingling and pain in the extremities due to ischemia; coma.

Treatment: Symptomatic under close monitoring of the patient.

The treatment includes discontinuation of the drug, local application of warmth to the affected area and nursing care to prevent tissue damage. In case of severe vasospasm, vasodilators such as nitroprusside sodium should be administered.

Dosage: Optimal results are obtained by titrating the dose for several headaches to find the minimal effective dose for each patient and this dose should then be employed at onset of subsequent attacks.

Onset of action occurs in 15 to 30 minutes following i.m. administration and persists for 3 to 4 hours. Repeated dosage at 1 hour intervals up to a total of 3 mL may be required to obtain maximal effect.

The total weekly dosage should not exceed 6 mL (6 mg).

Pretreatment with an antiemetic may be considered when DHE is administered by the i.v. route.

Acute Migraine Attack: 1 mL (1 mg) by i.m. or s.c. injection at the first sign of headache; in refractory cases, a further 1 mL may be administered after 30 to 60 minutes.

Do not exceed a total of 3 mL per attack or per day.

When more rapid effect is desired, the i.v. route may be employed: 1 mL (1 mg) by **slow i.v. injection** at the onset of the attack, followed in an hour by 1 mL (1 mg), if necessary. Do not exceed a total of 2 mL (2 mg) per migraine attack.

Cluster Headache (Horton Syndrome): 0.5 mL (0.5 mg) by slow i.v. injection.

Supplied: Each mL of injectable solution contains: dihydroergotamine mesylate 1 mg. Also contains ethanol 47 mg/mL and glycerol 150 mg. Ampuls of 1 mL, boxes of 5. Protect ampuls from light. Store below 25°C. If the solution becomes discolored, do not use.

(Shown in Product Recognition Section)

DILANTIN® CAPSULES ℞

Parke-Davis

Phenytoin Sodium

Anticonvulsant

Pharmacology: Phenytoin is an anticonvulsant drug which can be useful in the treatment of epilepsy. The primary site of action appears to be the motor cortex where spread of seizure activity is inhibited. Possibly by promoting sodium efflux from neurons, phenytoin tends to stabilize the threshold against hyperexcitability caused by excessive stimulation or environmental changes capable of reducing membrane sodium gradient. This includes the reduction of post-tetanic potentiation at synapses. Loss of post-tetanic potentiation prevents cortical seizure foci from detonating adjacent cortical areas. Phenytoin reduces the maximal activity of brain stem centres responsible for the tonic phase of tonic-clonic (grand mal) seizures.

The plasma half-life in man after oral administration of phenytoin averages 22 hours, with a range of 7 to 42 hours. Steady-state therapeutic levels are achieved at least 7 to 10 days after initiation of therapy with recommended doses of 300 mg/day.

When serum level determinations are necessary, they should be obtained at least 7 to 10 days after treatment initiation, dosage change, or addition or subtraction of another drug to the regimen so that equilibrium or steady-state will have been achieved. Trough levels obtained just prior to the patient's next scheduled dose, provide information about clinically effective serum level range and confirm patient compliance. Peak drug levels, obtained at the time of expected peak concentration, indicate an individual's threshold for emergence of dose-related side effects. For phenytoin, peak serum levels occur 4 to 12 hours after administration.

In most patients maintained at a steady dosage, stable phenytoin serum levels are achieved. There may be wide interpatient variability in phenytoin serum levels with equivalent dosages. Patients with unusually low levels may be noncompliant or hypermetabolizers of phenytoin. Unusually high levels result from liver disease, congenital enzyme deficiency or drug interactions which result in metabolic interference. The patient with large variations in phenytoin serum levels, despite standard doses, presents a difficult clinical problem. Serum level determinations in such patients may be particularly helpful. As phenytoin is highly protein bound, free phenytoin levels may be altered in patients whose protein binding characteristics differ from normal.

Most of the drug is excreted in the bile as inactive metabolites which are then reabsorbed from the intestinal tract and excreted in the urine. Urinary excretion of phenytoin and its metabolites occurs partly with glomerular filtration but more importantly by tubular secretion. Because phenytoin is hydroxylated in the liver by an enzyme system which is saturable at high serum levels small incremental doses may increase the half-life and produce very substantial increases in serum levels, when these are in or above the upper therapeutic range. The steady-state level may be disproportionately increased, with resultant intoxication, from an increase in dosage of 10% or more.

Indications: For the control of generalized tonic-clonic and psychomotor (grand mal and temporal lobe) seizures and prevention and treatment of seizures occurring during or following neurosurgery. Phenytoin serum level determinations may be necessary for optimal dosage adjustments (see Dosage).

Contraindications: In those patients who are hypersensitive to phenytoin or other hydantoins.

Warnings: Abrupt withdrawal of phenytoin in epileptic patients may precipitate status epilepticus. When, in the judgment of the clinician, the need for dosage reduction, discontinuation, or substitution of alternative anticonvulsant medication arises, this should be done gradually. However, in the event of an allergic or hypersensitivity reaction, rapid substitution of alternative therapy may be necessary. In this case, alternative therapy should be an anticonvulsant drug which does not belong to the hydantoin chemical class.

Dilantin Capsules (cont'd)

Cases of acute hepatotoxicity, including infrequent cases of acute hepatic failure, have been reported with phenytoin. These incidents have been associated with a hypersensitivity syndrome characterized by fever, skin eruptions, and lymphadenopathy, and usually occur within the first 2 months of treatment. Other common manifestations include jaundice, hepatomegaly, elevated serum transaminase levels, leukocytosis, and eosinophilia. The clinical course of acute phenytoin hepatotoxicity ranges from prompt recovery to fatal outcomes. In these patients with acute hepatotoxicity, phenytoin should be immediately discontinued and not readministered.

There have been a number of reports suggesting a relationship between phenytoin and the development of lymphadenopathy (local or generalized) including benign lymph node hyperplasia, pseudolymphoma, lymphoma, and Hodgkin's Disease. Although a cause and effect relationship has not been established, the occurrence of lymphadenopathy indicates the need to differentiate such a condition from other types of lymph node pathology. Lymph node involvement may occur with or without symptoms and signs resembling serum sickness, e.g., fever, rash and liver involvement. In all cases of lymphadenopathy, follow-up observation for an extended period is indicated and every effort should be made to achieve seizure control using alternative anticonvulsant drugs.

Acute alcoholic intake may increase phenytoin serum levels while chronic alcoholic use may decrease serum levels.

In view of isolated reports associating phenytoin with exacerbation of porphyria, caution should be exercised in using this medication in patients suffering from this disease.

Pregnancy: A number of reports suggests an association between the use of antiepileptic drugs by women with epilepsy and a higher incidence of birth defects in children born to these women. Data are more extensive with respect to phenytoin and phenobarbital, but these are also the most commonly prescribed antiepileptic drugs; less systematic or anecdotal reports suggest a possible similar association with the use of all known anticonvulsant drugs.

The reports suggesting a higher incidence of birth defects in children of drug-treated epileptic women cannot be regarded as adequate to prove a definite cause and effect relationship. There are intrinsic methodologic problems in obtaining adequate data on drug teratogenicity in humans. Genetic factors or the epileptic condition itself may be more important than drug therapy in leading to birth defects. The great majority of mothers on anticonvulsant medication deliver normal infants. It is important to note that anticonvulsant drugs should not be discontinued in patients in whom the drug is administered to prevent major seizures, because of the strong possibility of precipitating status epilepticus with attendant hypoxia and threat to life. In individual cases where the severity and frequency of the seizure disorder are such that the removal of medication does not pose a serious threat to the patient, discontinuation of the drug may be considered prior to and during pregnancy, although it cannot be said with any confidence that even minor seizures do not pose some hazard to the developing embryo or fetus. The prescribing physician will wish to weigh these considerations in treating or counseling epileptic women of childbearing potential.

In addition to the reports of the increased incidence of congenital malformations, such as cleft lip/palate and heart malformations in children of women receiving phenytoin and other antiepileptic drugs, there have more recently been reports of a fetal hydantoin syndrome. This consists of prenatal growth deficiency, microcephaly and mental deficiency in children born to mothers who have received phenytoin, barbiturates, alcohol, or trimethadione. However, these features are all interrelated and are frequently associated with intrauterine growth retardation from other causes.

There have been isolated reports of malignancies, including neuroblastoma, in children whose mothers received phenytoin during pregnancy.

An increase in seizure frequency during pregnancy occurs in a high proportion of patients, because of altered phenytoin absorption or metabolism. Periodic measurement of serum phenytoin levels is particularly valuable in the management of a pregnant epileptic patient as a guide to an appropriate adjustment of dosage. However, postpartum restoration of the original dosage will probably be indicated.

Neonatal coagulation defects have been reported within the first 24 hours in babies born to epileptic mothers receiving phenobarbital and/or phenytoin. Vitamin K has been shown to prevent or correct this defect and has been recommended to be given to the mother before delivery and to the neonate after birth.

Precautions: General: The liver is the chief site of biotransformation of phenytoin. Patients with impaired liver function, elderly patients, or those who are gravely ill may show early signs of toxicity.

A small percentage of individuals who have been treated with phenytoin have been shown to metabolize the drug slowly. Slow metabolism may be due to limited enzyme availability and lack of induction; it appears to be genetically determined.

Toxic hepatitis, liver damage, and hypersensitivity syndrome have been reported and may, in rare cases, be fatal (See Adverse Effects).

Phenytoin should be discontinued if a skin rash appears (see Warnings section regarding drug discontinuation). If the rash is exfoliative, purpuric, or bullous or if lupus erythematosus or Stevens-Johnson syndrome or toxic epidermal necrolysis is suspected, use of this drug should not be resumed and alternative therapy should be considered (see Adverse Effects). If the rash is of a milder type (measles-like or scarlatiniform), therapy may be resumed after the rash has completely disappeared. If the rash recurs upon reinstitution of therapy, further phenytoin medication is contraindicated.

Literature reports suggest that the combination of phenytoin, cranial irradiation and the gradual reduction of corticosteroids may be associated with the development of erythema multiforme, and/or Stevens-Johnson syndrome, and/or toxic epidermal necrolysis. In any of the above instances, caution should be exercised if using structurally similar compounds (e.g., barbiturates, succinimides, oxazolidinediones and other related compounds) in these same patients.

While macrocytosis and megaloblastic anemia have occurred, these conditions usually respond to folic acid therapy. If folic acid is added to phenytoin therapy, a decrease in seizure control may occur.

Hyperglycemia, resulting from the drug's inhibitory effects on insulin release, has been reported. Phenytoin may also raise the serum glucose level in diabetic patients.

Osteomalacia has been associated with phenytoin therapy and is considered to be due to phenytoin's interference with Vitamin D metabolism.

Phenytoin is not indicated for seizures due to hypoglycemic or other metabolic causes. Appropriate diagnostic procedures should be performed as indicated.

Phenytoin is not effective for absence (petit mal) seizures. If tonic-clonic (grand mal) and absence (petit mal) seizures are present, combined drug therapy is needed.

Serum levels of phenytoin sustained above the optimal range may produce confusional states referred to as delirium, psychosis, or encephalopathy, or rarely irreversible cerebellar dysfunction. Accordingly, at the first sign of acute toxicity, serum drug level determinations are recommended. Dose reduction of phenytoin therapy is indicated if serum levels are excessive; if symptoms persist, termination of phenytoin therapy is recommended (see Warnings).

Information for the Patient: Patients taking phenytoin should be advised of the importance of adhering strictly to the prescribed dosage regimen, and of informing their physician of any clinical condition in which it is not possible to take the drug orally as prescribed, e.g., surgery, etc.

Patients should also be cautioned on the use of other drugs or alcoholic beverages without first seeking their physician's advice.

Patients should be instructed to call their physician if skin rash develops.

The importance of good dental hygiene should be stressed in order to minimize the development of gingival hyperplasia and its complications.

Do not use capsules which are discolored.

Laboratory Tests: Phenytoin serum level determinations may be necessary to achieve optimal dosage adjustments.

Drug Interactions: There are many drugs which may increase or decrease serum phenytoin levels or which phenytoin may affect. Determinations of serum phenytoin concentrations are especially helpful when possible drug interactions are suspected. The **most commonly occurring** drug interactions are listed below:

Drugs which may increase phenytoin serum levels include: acute alcohol intake, cimetidine, dicumarol, disulfiram, ethosuximide, methylphenidate, omeprazole, phenothiazines, ticlopidine and topiramate. Coadministration with topiramate reduces serum topiramate levels by 59%, and has the potential to increase phenytoin levels by 25% in some patients. The addition of topiramate therapy to phenytoin should be guided by clinical outcome. The following drug classes are also included. See Table I.

Table I—Dilantin

Drugs Which May Increase Phenytoin Serum Levels

Drug Classes	**Drugs in Each Class**
Analgesic/Anti-inflammatory Agents	phenylbutazone salicylates
Anesthetics	halothane
Antibacterial Agents	chloramphenicol erythromycin isoniazid sulfonamides
Anticonvulsants	succinimides
Antifungal Agents	amphotericin B fluconazole ketoconazole miconazole itraconazole
Benzodiazepines/Psychotropic Agents	chlordiazepoxide diazepam trazodone
Calcium Channel Blockers/ Cardiovascular Agents	amiodarone diltiazem nifedipine
H_2-antagonists	cimetidine
Hormones	estrogens
Oral Hypoglycemic Agents	tolbutamide
Serotonin Reuptake Inhibitors	fluoxetine

Drugs which may decrease phenytoin serum levels include: antibacterial agents/fluoroquinolones (such as ciprofloxacin and rifampin), carbamazepine, chronic alcohol abuse, diazoxide, reserpine, sucralfate, theophylline and vigabatrin. Coadministration with vigabatrin reduces serum phenytoin levels by 20 to 30%. This may be clinically significant in some patients and may require dosage adjustment.

Molindone HCl contains calcium ions which interfere with the absorption of phenytoin. Ingestion times of phenytoin and calcium preparations, including antacid preparations containing calcium should be staggered to prevent absorption problems.

Drugs which may either increase or decrease phenytoin serum levels are included in Table II.

Table II—Dilantin

Drugs Which May Either Increase or Decrease Phenytoin Serum Levels

Drug Classes	**Drugs in Each Class**
Anticonvulsants	carbamazepine phenobarbital sodium valproate valproic acid
Antineoplastic Agents	
Benzodiazepines	chlordiazepoxide
Phenothiazines	
Psychotropic Agents	diazepam

Similarly, the effect of phenytoin on carbamazepine, phenobarbital, valproic acid and sodium valproate serum levels is unpredictable.

Although not a true drug interaction, tricyclic antidepressants may precipitate seizures in susceptible patients and phenytoin dosage may need to be adjusted.

Drugs whose blood levels and/or effects may be altered by phenytoin include: clozapine, corticosteroids, coumarin anticoagulants, cyclosporine, diazoxide, furosemide, lamotrigine, paroxetine, theophylline, topiramate and vitamin D. Coadministration with topiramate reduces serum topiramate levels by 59%, and has the potential to increase phenytoin levels by 25% in some patients. The addition of topiramate therapy to phenytoin should be guided by clinical outcome. Coadministration with lamotrigine doubles the plasma clearance and reduces the elimination half-life of lamotrigine by 50%. This clinically important interaction requires dosage adjustment. The following drug classes are also included. See Table III (on following page).

Drug-Enteral Feeding/Nutritional Preparations Interaction: Literature reports suggest that patients who have received enteral feeding preparations and/or related nutritional supplements have lower than expected phenytoin plasma levels. It is therefore suggested that phenytoin not be administered concomitantly with an enteral feeding preparation.

Table III—Dilantin

Drugs Whose Blood Levels and/or Effects May Be Altered by Phenytoin

Drug Classes	Drugs in Each Class
Antibacterial Agents	doxycycline praziquantel rifampin tetracycline
Antifungal Agents	
Antineoplastic Agents	
Calcium Channel Blockers/ Cardiovascular Agents	digitoxin nicardipine nimodipine quinidine verapamil
Hormones	estrogens oral contraceptives
Neuromuscular Blocking Agents	pancuronium vecuronium
Opioid Analgesics	methadone
Oral Hypoglycemic Agents	chlorpropamide glyburide tolbutamide

More frequent serum phenytoin level monitoring may be necessary in these patients.

Drug/Laboratory Test Interactions: Phenytoin may cause decreased serum levels of protein-bound iodine (PBI). It may also produce lower than normal values for dexamethasone or metyrapone tests. Phenytoin may cause increased serum levels of glucose, alkaline phosphatase, and gamma glutamyl transpeptidase (GGT). Phenytoin may affect blood calcium and blood sugar metabolism tests.

Carcinogenesis: See Warnings.

Pregnancy: See Warnings.

Lactation: Infant breast-feeding is not recommended for women taking this drug because phenytoin appears to be secreted in low concentrations in human milk.

Children: See Dosage.

Adverse Effects: CNS: The most common manifestations encountered with phenytoin therapy are referable to this system and are usually dose-related. These include nystagmus, ataxia, slurred speech, decreased coordination and mental confusion. Dizziness, insomnia, transient nervousness, motor twitchings, and headaches have also been observed. There have also been rare reports of phenytoin induced dyskinesias, including chorea, dystonia, tremor and asterixis, similar to those induced by phenothiazine and other neuroleptic drugs.

A predominantly sensory peripheral polyneuropathy has been observed in patients receiving long-term phenytoin therapy.

Gastrointestinal: nausea, vomiting, constipation, toxic hepatitis, and liver damage (see Precautions).

Integumentary: Dermatological manifestations sometimes accompanied by fever have included scarlatiniform or morbilliform rashes. A morbilliform rash (measles-like) is the most common; other types of dermatitis are seen more rarely. Other more serious forms which may be fatal have included bullous, exfoliative or purpuric dermatitis, lupus erythematosus, Stevens-Johnson syndrome and toxic epidermal necrolysis (see Precautions).

Hemopoietic: Hemopoietic complications, some fatal, have occasionally been reported in association with administration of phenytoin. These have included thrombocytopenia, leukopenia, granulocytopenia, agranulocytosis, and pancytopenia with or without bone marrow suppression. While macrocytosis and megaloblastic anemia have occurred, these conditions usually respond to folic acid therapy. Lymphadenopathy including benign lymph node hyperplasia, pseudolymphoma, lymphoma, and Hodgkin's Disease have been reported (see Warnings).

Connective Tissue: Coarsening of the facial features, enlargement of the lips, gingival hyperplasia, hypertrichosis and Peyronie's Disease.

Immunologic: Hypersensitivity syndrome (which may include, but is not limited to symptoms such as arthralgias, eosinophilia, fever, liver dysfunction, lymphadenopathy or rash), systemic lupus erythematosus, periarteritis nodosa, and immunoglobulin abnormalities. Several individual case reports have suggested that there may be an increased, although still rare, incidence of hypersensitivity reactions, including skin rash and hepatotoxicity, in black patients.

Overdose: Symptoms: The lethal dose of phenytoin in pediatric patients is not known. The lethal dose in adults is estimated to be 2 to 5 g. The initial symptoms are nystagmus, ataxia, and dysarthria. Other signs are tremor, hyperreflexia, somnolence, drowsiness, lethargy, slurred speech, blurred vision, nausea, vomiting. The patient may become comatose and hypotensive. Death is due to respiratory and circulatory depression.

There are marked variations among individuals with respect to phenytoin plasma levels where toxicity may occur. Nystagmus on lateral gaze, usually appears at 80 µmol/L (20 µg/mL), ataxia at 119 µmol/L (30 µg/mL). Dysarthria and lethargy appear when the serum concentration is >159 µmol/L (40 µg/mL), but a concentration as high as 198 µmol/L (50 µg/mL) has been reported without evidence of toxicity. As much as 25 times the therapeutic dose has been taken to result in a serum concentration over >396 µmol/L (100 µg/mL) with complete recovery.

Treatment: Treatment is nonspecific since there is no known antidote.

The adequacy of the respiratory and circulatory systems should be carefully observed and appropriate supportive measures employed. Hemodialysis can be considered since phenytoin is not completely bound to plasma proteins. Total exchange transfusion has been used in the treatment of severe intoxication in pediatric patients.

In acute overdosage the possibility of other CNS depressants, including alcohol, should be borne in mind.

Dosage: Serum phenytoin concentrations should be monitored when switching a patient from the sodium salt to the free acid form.

Dilantin capsules, are formulated with the sodium salt of phenytoin. The free acid form of phenytoin is used in Dilantin-30 Pediatric and Dilantin-125 Suspensions and Dilantin Infatabs. Because there is approximately an 8% increase in drug content with the free acid form over that of the sodium salt, dosage adjustments and serum level monitoring may be necessary when switching from a product formulated with the free acid to a product formulated with the sodium salt and vice versa.

General: Dosage should be individualized to provide maximum benefit. In some cases, serum blood level determinations may be necessary for optimal dosage adjustments. The clinically effective serum level is usually 40 to 80 µmol/L (10 to 20 µg/mL). Serum blood level determinations are especially helpful when possible drug interactions are suspected. With recommended dosage, a period of 7 to 10 days may be required to achieve therapeutic blood levels with phenytoin and changes in dosage (increase or decrease) should not be carried out at intervals shorter than 7 to 10 days.

Adults: Patients who have received no previous treatment may be started on one 100 mg extended phenytoin sodium capsule 3 times daily, and the dose then adjusted to suit individual requirements. For most adults, the satisfactory maintenance dosage will be 3 to 4 capsules (300 to 400 mg) daily. An increase to 6 capsules daily may be made, if necessary.

Children: Initially, 5 mg/kg/day in 2 or 3 equally divided doses, with subsequent dosage individualized to a maximum of 300 mg daily. A recommended daily maintenance dosage is usually 4 to 8 mg/kg. Children over 6 years old may require the minimum adult dose (300 mg/day). Pediatric dosage forms available include a 30 mg extended phenytoin sodium capsule, a 50 mg palatably flavored Infatab, or an oral suspension form containing 30 mg of phenytoin in each 5 mL.

Alternative Dose: Once-a-day dosage for adults with 300 mg of extended phenytoin sodium capsules may be considered if seizure control is established with divided doses of three 100 mg capsules daily. Studies comparing divided doses of 300 mg with a single daily dose of this quantity indicated that absorption, peak plasma levels, biologic half-life, difference between peak and minimum values, and urinary recovery were equivalent. Once-a-day dosage offers a convenience to the individual patient or to nursing personnel for institutionalized patients, and is intended only to be used for patients requiring this amount of drug daily. A major problem in motivating noncompliant patients may also be lessened when the patient can take all of his medication once-a-day. However, patients should be cautioned not to inadvertently miss a dose. Only extended phenytoin sodium capsules are recommended for once-a-day dosing.

Supplied: 30 mg: Each Coni-Snap white capsule with pink cap, imprinted Parke-Davis and P-D 30 in black ink, contains: extended phenytoin sodium 30 mg. Nonmedicinal ingredients: lactose, magnesium stearate, sugar and talc; capsule shell: D&C Yellow No. 10, FD&C Red No. 3, gelatin and titanium dioxide. Energy: 3.0 kJ (0.7 kcal). Sodium: <1 mmol (2.52 mg). Bottles of 100.

100 mg: Each Coni-Snap white capsule with orange cap, imprinted Parke-Davis and P-D 100 in black ink, contains: extended phenytoin sodium 100 mg. Nonmedicinal ingredients: lactose, magnesium stearate, sugar and talc; capsule shell: FD&C Yellow No. 6, gelatin and titanium dioxide. Energy: 2.6 kJ (0.6 kcal). Sodium: <1 mmol (8.39 mg). Bottles of 100 and 1 000.

Store at controlled room temperature 15 to 30°C. Protect from light and moisture.

(Shown in Product Recognition Section)

Reviewed 1998

DILANTIN® INFATABS
DILANTIN®-30 PEDIATRIC
DILANTIN®-125

Parke-Davis

Phenytoin

Anticonvulsant

Pharmacology: Dilantin Infatabs and Dilantin-30 Pediatric/ Dilantin-125 suspensions are anticonvulsant drugs which can be useful in the treatment of epilepsy. The primary site of action appears to be the motor cortex where spread of seizure activity is inhibited. Possibly by promoting sodium efflux from neurons, phenytoin tends to stabilize the threshold against hyperexcitability caused by excessive stimulation or environmental changes capable of reducing membrane sodium gradient. This includes the reduction of post-tetanic potentiation at synapses. Loss of post-tetanic potentiation prevents cortical seizure foci from detonating adjacent cortical areas. Phenytoin reduces the maximal activity of brain stem centres responsible for the tonic phase of tonic-clonic (grand mal) seizures.

Clinical studies using Dilantin Infatabs have shown an average plasma half-life of 14 hours with a range of 7 to 29 hours. The plasma half-life of phenytoin in man after oral administration of phenytoin oral suspension averages 22 hours, with a range of 7 to 42 hours. Steady-state therapeutic levels are achieved at least 7 to 10 days after initiation of therapy with recommended doses of 300 mg/day.

When serum level determinations are necessary, they should be obtained at least 7 to 10 days after treatment initiation, dosage change, or addition or subtraction of another drug to the regimen so that equilibrium or steady-state will have been achieved. Trough levels obtained just prior to the patient's next scheduled dose, provide information about clinically effective serum level range and confirm patient compliance. Peak drug levels, obtained at the time of expected peak concentration, indicate an individual's threshold for emergence of dose-related side effects. For Dilantin Infatabs, Dilantin-30 Pediatric and Dilantin-125 suspensions, peak serum levels occur 1½ to 3 hours after administration.

In most patients maintained at a steady dosage, stable phenytoin serum levels are achieved. There may be wide interpatient variability in phenytoin serum levels with equivalent dosages. Patients with unusually low levels may be noncompliant or hypermetabolizers of phenytoin. Unusually high levels result from liver disease, congenital enzyme deficiency or drug interactions which result in metabolic interference. The patient with large variations in phenytoin serum levels, despite standard doses, presents a difficult clinical problem. Serum level determinations in such patients may be particularly helpful. As phenytoin is highly protein bound, free phenytoin levels may be altered in patients whose protein binding characteristics differ from normal.

Most of the drug is excreted in the bile as inactive metabolites which are then reabsorbed from the intestinal tract and excreted in the urine. Urinary excretion of phenytoin and its metabolites occurs partly with glomerular filtration but more importantly by tubular secretion. Because phenytoin is hydroxylated in the liver by an enzyme system which is saturable at high serum levels small incremental doses may increase the half-life and produce very substantial increases in serum levels, when these are in or above the upper therapeutic range. The steady-state level may be disproportionately increased, with resultant intoxication, from an increase in dosage of 10% or more.

Clinical studies show that chewed and unchewed Dilantin Infatabs are bioequivalent, yield approximately equivalent plasma levels, and are more rapidly absorbed than Dilantin 100 mg capsules.

Dilantin Infatabs/Dilantin-30 Pediatric/Dilantin-125 (cont'd)

Indications: Dilantin Infatabs and Dilantin-30 Pediatric/Dilantin-125 suspensions are indicated for the control of generalized tonic-clonic (grand mal) and complex partial (psychomotor, temporal lobe) seizures. Phenytoin serum level determinations may be necessary for optimal dosage adjustments (see Pharmacology and Dosage).

Contraindications: Patients who are hypersensitive to phenytoin or other hydantoins.

Warnings: Abrupt withdrawal of Dilantin Infatabs or Dilantin-30 Pediatric/Dilantin-125 suspensions in epileptic patients may precipitate status epilepticus. When, in the judgment of the clinician, the need for dosage reduction, discontinuation, or substitution of alternative anticonvulsant medication arises, this should be done gradually. However, in the event of an allergic or hypersensitivity reaction, rapid substitution of alternative therapy may be necessary. In this case, alternative therapy should be an anticonvulsant drug which does not belong to the hydantoin chemical class.

Cases of acute hepatotoxicity, including infrequent cases of acute hepatic failure, have been reported with phenytoin. These incidents have been associated with a hypersensitivity syndrome characterized by fever, skin eruptions, and lymphadenopathy, and usually occur within the first 2 months of treatment. Other common manifestations include jaundice, hepatomegaly, elevated serum transaminase levels, leukocytosis, and eosinophilia. The clinical course of acute phenytoin hepatotoxicity ranges from prompt recovery to fatal outcomes. In these patients with acute hepatotoxicity, phenytoin should be immediately discontinued and not re-administered.

There have been a number of reports suggesting a relationship between phenytoin and the development of lymphadenopathy (local or generalized) including benign lymph node hyperplasia, pseudolymphoma, lymphoma, and Hodgkin's Disease. Although a cause and effect relationship has not been established, the occurrence of lymphadenopathy indicates the need to differentiate such a condition from other types of lymph node pathology. Lymph node involvement may occur with or without symptoms and signs resembling serum sickness, e.g., fever, rash and liver involvement. In all cases of lymphadenopathy, follow-up observation for an extended period is indicated and every effort should be made to achieve seizure control using alternative anticonvulsant drugs.

Acute alcoholic intake may increase phenytoin serum levels while chronic alcoholic use may decrease serum levels.

In view of isolated reports associating phenytoin with exacerbation of porphyria, caution should be exercised in using this medication in patients suffering from this disease.

Pregnancy: A number of reports suggests an association between the use of anticonvulsant drugs by women with epilepsy and a higher incidence of birth defects in children born to these women. Data are more extensive with respect to phenytoin and phenobarbital, but these are also the most commonly prescribed anticonvulsant drugs; less systematic or anecdotal reports suggest a possible similar association with the use of all known anticonvulsant drugs.

The reports suggesting a higher incidence of birth defects in children of drug-treated epileptic women cannot be regarded as adequate to prove a definite cause and effect relationship. There are intrinsic methodologic problems in obtaining adequate data on drug teratogenicity in humans. Genetic factors or the epileptic condition itself may be more important than drug therapy in leading to birth defects. The great majority of mothers on anticonvulsant medication deliver normal infants. It is important to note that anticonvulsant drugs should not be discontinued in patients in whom the drug is administered to prevent major seizures because of the strong possibility of precipitating status epilepticus with attendant hypoxia and threat to life. In individual cases where the severity and frequency of the seizure disorder are such that the removal of medication does not pose a serious threat to the patient, discontinuation of the drug may be considered prior to and during pregnancy although it cannot be said with any confidence that even minor seizures do not pose some hazard to the developing embryo or fetus. The prescribing physician will wish to weigh these considerations in treating or counseling epileptic women of childbearing potential.

In addition to the reports of the increased incidence of congenital malformations, such as cleft lip/palate and heart malformations in children of women receiving phenytoin and other anticonvulsant drugs, there have more recently been reports of a fetal hydantoin syndrome. This consists of prenatal growth deficiency, microcephaly and mental deficiency in children born to mothers who have received phenytoin, barbiturates, alcohol, or trimethadione. However, these features are all interrelated and are frequently associated with intrauterine growth retardation from other causes.

There have been isolated reports of malignancies, including neuroblastoma, in children whose mothers received phenytoin during pregnancy.

An increase in seizure frequency during pregnancy occurs in a high proportion of patients, because of altered phenytoin absorption or metabolism. Periodic measurement of serum phenytoin levels is particularly valuable in the management of a pregnant epileptic patient as a guide to an appropriate adjustment of dosage. However, postpartum restoration of the original dosage will probably be indicated.

Neonatal coagulation defects have been reported within the first 24 hours in babies born to epileptic mothers receiving phenobarbital and/or phenytoin. Vitamin K has been shown to prevent or correct this defect and has been recommended to be given to the mother before delivery and to the neonate after birth.

Precautions: General: The liver is the chief site of biotransformation of Dilantin Infatabs and Dilantin-30 Pediatric/Dilantin-125 suspensions. Patients with impaired liver function, elderly patients, or those who are gravely ill may show early signs of toxicity.

A small percentage of individuals who have been treated with phenytoin have been shown to metabolize the drug slowly. Slow metabolism may be due to limited enzyme availability and lack of induction; it appears to be genetically determined.

Toxic hepatitis, liver damage, and hypersensitivity syndrome have been reported and may, in rare cases, be fatal (see Adverse Effects).

Phenytoin should be discontinued if a skin rash appears (see Warnings section regarding drug discontinuation). If the rash is exfoliative, purpuric, or bullous or if lupus erythematosus or Stevens-Johnson syndrome or toxic epidermal necrolysis is suspected, use of this drug should not be resumed and alternative therapy should be considered (see Adverse Effects). If the rash is of a milder type (measles-like or scarlatiniform), therapy may be resumed after the rash has completely disappeared. If the rash recurs upon reinstitution of therapy, further phenytoin medication is contraindicated.

Literature reports suggest that the combination of phenytoin, cranial irradiation and the gradual reduction of corticosteroids may be associated with the development of erythema multiforme, and/or Stevens-Johnson syndrome, and/or toxic epidermal necrolysis.

In any of the above instances, caution should be exercised if using structurally similar compounds (e.g., barbiturates, succinimides, oxazolidinediones and other related compounds) in these same patients.

While macrocytosis and megaloblastic anemia have occurred, these conditions usually respond to folic acid therapy. If folic acid is added to phenytoin therapy, a decrease in seizure control may occur.

Hyperglycemia, resulting from the drug's inhibitory effects on insulin release, has been reported. Phenytoin may also raise the serum glucose level in diabetic patients.

Osteomalacia has been associated with phenytoin therapy and is considered to be due to phenytoin's interference with vitamin D metabolism.

Phenytoin is not indicated for seizures due to hypoglycemic or other metabolic causes. Appropriate diagnostic procedures should be performed as indicated.

Phenytoin is not effective for absence (petit mal) seizures. If tonic-clonic (grand mal) and absence (petit mal) seizures are present, combined drug therapy is needed.

Serum levels of phenytoin sustained above the optimal range may produce confusional states referred to as delirium, psychosis, or encephalopathy, or rarely irreversible cerebellar dysfunction. Accordingly, at the first sign of acute toxicity, serum drug level determinations are recommended. Dose reduction of phenytoin therapy is indicated if serum levels are excessive; if symptoms persist, termination of phenytoin therapy is recommended (see Warnings).

Information for the Patient: Patients taking phenytoin should be advised of the importance of adhering strictly to the prescribed dosage regimen, and of informing their physician of any clinical condition in which it is not possible to take the drug orally as prescribed, e.g., surgery, etc.

Patients should also be cautioned on the use of other drugs or alcoholic beverages without first seeking their physician's advice.

Patients should be instructed to call their physician if skin rash develops.

The importance of good dental hygiene should be stressed in order to minimize the development of gingival hyperplasia and its complications.

Laboratory Tests: Phenytoin serum level determinations may be necessary to achieve optimal dosage adjustments.

Drug Interactions: There are many drugs which may increase or decrease serum phenytoin levels or which phenytoin may affect. Determinations of serum phenytoin concentrations are especially helpful when possible drug interactions are suspected. The **most commonly occurring** drug interactions are listed below. See Table I.

Drugs which may increase phenytoin serum levels include: acute alcohol intake, cimetidine, dicumarol, disulfiram, ethosuximide, methylphenidate, omeprazole, phenothiazines, ticlopidine and topiramate. Coadministration with topiramate reduces serum topiramate levels by 59%, and has the potential to increase phenytoin levels by 25% in some patients. The addition of topiramate therapy to phenytoin should be guided by clinical outcome. The following drug classes are also included.

Table I—Dilantin Infatabs/Dilantin-30 Pediatric/Dilantin-125

Drugs Which May Increase Phenytoin Serum Levels

Drug Classes	Drugs in Each Class
Analgesic/Anti-inflammatory Agents	phenylbutazone salicylates
Anesthetics	halothane
Antibacterial Agents	chloramphenicol erythromycin isoniazid sulfonamides
Anticonvulsants	succinimides
Antifungal Agents	amphotericin B fluconazole ketoconazole miconazole itraconazole
Benzodiazepines/Psychotropic Agents	chlordiazepoxide diazepam trazodone
Calcium Channel Blockers/ Cardiovascular Agents	amiodarone diltiazem nifedipine
H_2-antagonists	cimetidine
Hormones	estrogens
Oral Hypoglycemic Agents	tolbutamide
Serotonin Reuptake Inhibitors	fluoxetine

Drugs that may decrease phenytoin serum levels include: antibacterial agents/fluoroquinolones (such as ciprofloxacin and rifampin), carbamazepine, chronic alcohol abuse, diazoxide, reserpine, sucralfate, theophylline and vigabatrin.

Coadministration with vigabatrin reduces serum phenytoin levels by 20 to 30%. This may be clinically significant in some patients and may require dosage adjustment. Molindone HCl contains calcium ions which interfere with the absorption of phenytoin. Ingestion times of phenytoin and calcium preparations, including antacid preparations containing calcium should be staggered to prevent absorption problems.

Drugs which may either increase or decrease phenytoin serum levels are included in Table II.

Table II—Dilantin Infatabs/Dilantin-30 Pediatric/Dilantin-125

Drugs Which May Either Increase or Decrease Phenytoin Serum Levels

Drug Classes	Drugs in Each Class
Anticonvulsants	carbamazepine phenobarbital sodium valproate valproic acid
Antineoplastic Agents	
Benzodiazepines	chlordiazepoxide
Phenothiazines	
Psychotropic Agents	diazepam

Similarly, the effect of phenytoin on carbamazepine, phenobarbital, valproic acid and sodium valproate serum levels is unpredictable.

Although not a true drug interaction, tricyclic antidepressants may precipitate seizures in susceptible patients and phenytoin dosage may need to be adjusted.

Drugs whose blood levels and/or effects may be altered by phenytoin include: clozapine, corticosteroids, coumarin anticoagulants, cyclosporine, diazoxide, furosemide, lamotrigine, paroxetine, theophylline, topiramate and vitamin D. Coadministration with topiramate reduces serum topiramate levels by

59%, and has the potential to increase phenytoin levels by 25% in some patients. The addition of topiramate therapy to phenytoin should be guided by clinical outcome. Coadministration with lamotrigine doubles the plasma clearance and reduces the elimination half-life of lamotrigine by 50%. This clinically important interaction requires dosage adjustment. The following drug classes are also included. See Table III.

Table III—Dilantin Infatabs/Dilantin-30 Pediatric/Dilantin-125

Drugs whose Blood Levels and/or Effects May Be Altered by Phenytoin

Drug Classes	Drugs in Each Class
Antibacterial Agents	doxycycline praziquantel rifampin tetracycline
Antifungal Agents	
Antineoplastic Agents	
Calcium Channel Blockers/ Cardiovascular Agents	digitoxin nicardipine nimodipine quinidine verapamil
Hormones	estrogens oral contraceptives
Neuromuscular Blocking Agents	pancuronium vecuronium
Opioid Analgesics	methadone
Oral Hypoglycemic Agents	chlorpropamide glyburide tolbutamide

Drug-enteral Feeding/Nutritional Preparations Interaction: Literature reports suggest that patients who have received enteral feeding preparations and/or related nutritional supplements have lower than expected phenytoin plasma levels. It is therefore suggested that phenytoin not be administered concomitantly with an enteral feeding preparation.

More frequent serum phenytoin level monitoring may be necessary in these patients.

Drug/Laboratory Test Interactions: Phenytoin may cause decreased serum levels of protein-bound iodine (PBI). It may also produce lower than normal values for dexamethasone or metyrapone tests. Phenytoin may cause increased serum levels of glucose, alkaline phosphatase, and gamma glutamyl transpeptidase (GGT). Phenytoin may affect blood calcium and blood sugar metabolism tests.

Carcinogenesis: See Warnings.

Pregnancy: See Warnings.

Lactation: Infant breast-feeding is not recommended for women taking this drug because phenytoin appears to be secreted in low concentrations in human milk.

Children: See Dosage.

Adverse Effects: CNS: The most common manifestations encountered with Dilantin Infatabs and Dilantin-30 Pediatric/ Dilantin 125 suspensions therapy are referable to this system and are usually dose-related. These include nystagmus, ataxia, slurred speech, decreased coordination and mental confusion. Dizziness, insomnia, transient nervousness, motor twitchings, and headaches have also been observed. There have also been rare reports of phenytoin induced dyskinesias, including chorea, dystonia, tremor and asterixis, similar to those induced by phenothiazine and other neuroleptic drugs.

A predominantly sensory peripheral polyneuropathy has been observed in patients receiving long-term phenytoin therapy.

Gastrointestinal: nausea, vomiting, constipation, toxic hepatitis, and liver damage (see Precautions).

Integumentary System: Dermatological manifestations sometimes accompanied by fever have included scarlatiniform or morbilliform rashes. A morbilliform rash (measles-like) is the most common; other types of dermatitis are seen more rarely. Other more serious forms which may be fatal have included bullous, exfoliative or purpuric dermatitis, lupus erythematosus, Stevens-Johnson syndrome and toxic epidermal necrolysis (see Precautions).

Hemopoietic: Hemopoietic complications, some fatal, have occasionally been reported in association with administration of phenytoin. These have included thrombocytopenia, leukopenia, granulocytopenia, agranulocytosis, and pancytopenia with or without bone marrow suppression. While macrocytosis and megaloblastic anemia have occurred, these conditions usually respond to folic acid therapy. Lymphadenopathy including benign lymph node hyperplasia, pseudolymphoma, lymphoma, and Hodgkin's Disease have been reported (see Warnings).

Connective Tissue: Coarsening of the facial features, enlargement of the lips, gingival hyperplasia, hypertrichosis and Peyronie's Disease.

Immunologic: Hypersensitivity syndrome (which may include, but is not limited to symptoms such as arthralgias, eosinophilia, fever, liver dysfunction, lymphadenopathy or rash), systemic lupus erythematosus, periarteritis nodosa, and immunoglobulin abnormalities. Several individual case reports have suggested that there may be an increased, although still rare, incidence of hypersensitivity reactions, including skin rash and hepatotoxicity, in black patients.

Overdosage: Symptoms: The lethal dose of Dilantin Infatabs and Dilantin-30 Pediatric/Dilantin-125 suspensions in pediatric patients is not known. The lethal dose of phenytoin in adults is estimated to be 2 to 5 g. The initial symptoms are nystagmus, ataxia, and dysarthria. Other signs are tremor, hyperreflexia, somnolence, drowsiness, lethargy, slurred speech, blurred vision, nausea, vomiting. The patient may become comatose and hypotensive. Death is due to respiratory and circulatory depression.

There are marked variations among individuals with respect to phenytoin plasma levels where toxicity may occur. Nystagmus on lateral gaze, usually appears at 80 µmol/L (20 µg/mL), ataxia at 119 µmol/L (30 µg/mL). Dysarthria and lethargy appear when the serum concentration is >159 µmol/L (40 µg/mL), but a concentration as high as 198 µmol/L (50 µg/mL) has been reported without evidence of toxicity. As much as 25 times the therapeutic dose has been taken to result in a serum concentration over >396 µmol/L (100 µg/mL) with complete recovery.

Treatment: Treatment is nonspecific since there is no known antidote.

The adequacy of the respiratory and circulatory systems should be carefully observed and appropriate supportive measures employed. Hemodialysis can be considered since phenytoin is not completely bound to plasma proteins. Total exchange transfusion has been used in the treatment of severe intoxication in pediatric patients.

In acute overdosage the possibility of other CNS depressants, including alcohol, should be borne in mind.

Dosage: Serum phenytoin concentrations should be monitored when switching a patient from the sodium salt to the free acid form.

Dilantin extended release capsules are formulated with the sodium salt of phenytoin. The free acid form of phenytoin is used in Dilantin-30 Pediatric and Dilantin-125 suspensions and Dilantin Infatabs. Because there is approximately an 8% increase in drug content with the free acid form over that of the sodium salt, dosage adjustments and serum level monitoring may be necessary when switching from a product formulated with the free acid to a product formulated with the sodium salt and vice versa.

General: Dilantin Infatabs and Dilantin-30 Pediatric/Dilantin-125 suspensions are not for once-a-day dosing.

Dosage should be individualized to provide maximum benefit. In some cases, serum blood level determinations may be necessary for optimal dosage adjustments. The clinically effective serum level is usually 40 to 80 µmol/L (10 to 20 µg/mL). Serum blood level determinations are especially helpful when possible drug interactions are suspected. With recommended dosage, a period of 7 to 10 days may be required to achieve therapeutic blood levels with phenytoin and changes in dosage (increase or decrease) should not be carried out at intervals shorter than 7 to 10 days.

Adults: Patients who have received no previous treatment may be started on 2 Dilantin Infatabs 3 times daily or on 5 mL of Dilantin-125 Suspension 3 times daily, and the dose then adjusted to suit individual requirements. For some adults, the satisfactory maintenance dosage will be 8 Dilantin Infatabs daily; an increase to 12 Dilantin Infatabs be made, if necessary. With Dilantin-125, an increase to 25 mL daily may be made if necessary.

Children: Initially, 5 mg/kg/day of Dilantin Infatabs, Dilantin-30 or Dilantin-125 suspension may be given in 2 or 3 equally divided doses, with subsequent dosage individualized to a maximum of 300 mg daily. A recommended daily maintenance dosage is usually 4 to 8 mg/kg. Children over 6 years may require the minimum adult dose (300 mg/day). If the daily dosage cannot be divided equally, the larger dose should be given before retiring.

Supplied: Dilantin Infatabs: Each flavored, triangular shaped, grooved tablet contains: phenytoin (free acid form) 50 mg. Nonmedicinal ingredients: alcohol, magnesium stearate, spearmint oil, sugar and talc. Bottles of 100.

Dilantin-30 Pediatric: Each 5 mL of flavored, colored suspension contains: phenytoin (free acid form) 30 mg. Nonmedicinal ingredients: alcohol, banana oil, citric acid, glycerin, magnesium aluminum silicate, orange oil, polysorbate 40, Red #2 FD&C, sodium benzoate, sodium carboxymethylcellulose, sugar, vanillin and yellow #6 FD&C. Bottles of 250 mL.

Dilantin-125: Each 5 mL of flavored, colored suspension contains: phenytoin (free acid form) 125 mg. Nonmedicinal ingredients: alcohol, banana oil, citric acid, glycerin, magnesium aluminum silicate, orange oil, polysorbate 40, sodium benzoate, sodium carboxymethylcellulose, sugar, vanillin and yellow #6 FD&C. Bottles of 250 mL.

Store at controlled room temperature 15 to 30°C. Protect from light and moisture.

(Shown in Product Recognition Section)

Reviewed 1998

DILAUDID® Ⓝ

Knoll

Hydromorphone HCl

Analgesic—Antitussive

Pharmacology: Hydromorphone has a strong analgesic action and antitussive activity. Small doses of hydromorphone produce effective and prompt relief of pain usually with minimal nausea and vomiting. Generally, when given parenterally, hydromorphone's analgesic action is apparent within 15 minutes and remains in effect for more than 5 hours. The onset of action of oral hydromorphone is somewhat slower, with measurable analgesia occurring within 30 minutes. When sleep follows the administration of hydromorphone, it is due to relief of pain, not to hypnosis.

Hydromorphone is approximately 8 times more potent on a milligram basis than morphine. In addition, hydromorphone is better absorbed orally than is morphine; the former is approximately 20 to 25% as active orally as i.m.

Hydromorphone has greater antitussive potency than codeine on a weight basis; however, its dependence liability is also greater than that of codeine.

After absorption hydromorphone is metabolized by the liver to the glucuronide conjugate which is then excreted in the urine.

Indications: Relief of moderate to severe pain.

Contraindications: Intracranial lesion associated with increased intracranial pressure, status asthmaticus, pulmonary edema.

Precautions: May be habit-forming. Hydromorphone is a narcotic with an addiction liability similar to that of morphine and for this reason the same precautions should be taken in administering the drug as with morphine.

Pregnancy: As with all narcotics, hydromorphone should be used in early pregnancy only when expected benefits outweigh risks.

If necessary, hydromorphone may be given i.v. but the injection should be given very slowly. Rapid i.v. injection of narcotic analgesic agents, including hydromorphone, increases the possibility of adverse effects, such as hypotension and respiratory depression.

As with any narcotic analgesic agent, the usual precautions should be observed and the possibility of respiratory depression should be kept in mind. If a patient shows signs of hypersensitivity to hydromorphone the treatment must be stopped.

Dilaudid injection has been reported to be physically or chemically incompatible with solutions containing sodium bicarbonate and thiopental sodium.

Children: Hydromorphone suppositories are not recommended for use in children.

Adverse Effects: Nausea, vomiting, dizziness, somnolence, anorexia and constipation may occur. Pain at injection site; local tissue irritation and induration following s.c. injection, particularly when repeated in the same area.

Overdose: Symptoms: Serious overdose with hydromorphone may be characterized by respiratory depression (a decrease in respiratory rate and/or tidal volume, Cheyne-Stokes respiration, cyanosis), extreme somnolence progressing to stupor or coma, skeletal muscle flaccidity, cold and clammy skin, and sometimes bradycardia and hypotension. In severe overdosage, apnea, circulatory collapse, cardiac arrest and death may occur.

Treatment: If significant respiratory depression occurs, it may be antagonized by naloxone as recommended by the manufacturer. Employ other supportive measures as indicated.

Dilaudid (cont'd)

Dosage: Orally for adults, 2 to 4 mg every 4 to 6 hours as required. The usual adult parenteral dose for pain relief is 2 mg by s.c. or i.m. routes every 4 to 6 hours as necessary. If necessary, hydromorphone may be given i.v., but the injection should be given very slowly. Severe pain can be controlled with 3 to 4 mg every 4 to 6 hours as necessary. Rectal suppositories (3 mg) provide long-lasting relief and are especially useful at night. The oral liquid may be diluted in fruit juice or other beverage, if desired.

Supplied: Ampuls: Each mL of sterile solution contains: hydromorphone HCl 2 mg. Nonmedicinal ingredients: citric acid and sodium citrate. Preservative-free. Ampuls of 1 mL, boxes of 25.

Oral Liquid: Each mL of clear, unflavored, syrupy liquid contains: hydromorphone HCl 1 mg. Nonmedicinal ingredients: glycerin, methylparaben, propylparaben and sucrose. Sucrose: 0.5 g/mL. Energy: 8.4 kJ (2 kcal)/mL. Alcohol-free. Amber glass bottles of 450 mL.

Suppositories: Each suppository contains: hydromorphone HCl 3 mg in a cocoa butter base with 1% colloidal silica. Boxes of 6.

Tablets: Each tablet contains: hydromorphone HCl 1 mg (green), 2 mg (orange), 4 mg (yellow) or 8 mg (white). Nonmedicinal ingredients: lactose anhydrous and magnesium stearate. Tartrazine-free. Bottles of 100. Hospital control packs of 4×25.

(Shown in Product Recognition Section)

DILAUDID-HP® Ⓝ
DILAUDID-HP-PLUS® Ⓝ
DILAUDID-XP® Ⓝ
DILAUDID® STERILE POWDER Ⓝ

Knoll

Hydromorphone HCl

Opioid Analgesic

Pharmacology: Hydromorphone is a hydrogenated ketone of morphine. It is an opioid analgesic with many of the effects common to the class of drugs.

Opioid analgesics have multiple actions but exert their primary effects on the CNS and organs containing smooth muscle. The principal actions of therapeutic value are analgesia and sedation. Opioid analgesics also suppress the cough reflex and cause respiratory depression, mood changes, mental clouding, euphoria, dysphoria, nausea, vomiting, increased cerebrospinal fluid pressure, pinpoint constriction of the pupils, increased biliary tract pressure, increased parasympathetic activity and transient hyperglycemia.

The precise mode of analgesic action of opioid analgesics is unknown. However, specific CNS opiate receptors have been identified. Opioids are believed to express their pharmacological effects by combining with these receptors.

The relationship between plasma concentration of hydromorphone and analgesic effect has not been well established. In patients with chronic pain, hydromorphone should be titrated to the dose required to adequately relieve pain without unmanageable side effects. There is no intrinsic limit to the analgesic effect of hydromorphone; adequate doses will relieve even the most severe pain. Clinically, however, dosage limitations are imposed by the adverse effects, primarily respiratory depression; nausea and vomiting which can result from high doses.

Pharmacokinetics: In normal human volunteers hydromorphone is metabolized primarily in the liver. It is excreted predominantly as the glucuronidated conjugate, with small amounts of parent drug and minor amounts of 6-hydroxy reduction metabolites.

Following i.v. administration of hydromorphone to normal volunteers, the mean half-life of elimination was 2.65 ± 0.88 hours. The mean volume of distribution was 91.5 L, suggesting extensive tissue uptake. Hydromorphone is rapidly removed from the bloodstream and distributed to skeletal muscle, kidneys, liver, intestinal tract, lungs, spleen and brain. It also crosses the placental membranes.

Hydromorphone is approximately 5 to 7 times more potent than morphine (i.e., 1.5 to 2 mg of hydromorphone produces analgesia equal to that produced by 10 mg of morphine). After i.m. administration, hydromorphone has a slightly more rapid onset and slightly shorter duration of action than morphine. The duration of analgesia in the non-tolerant patient with usual doses may be up to 4 to 5 hours. However, in opioid tolerant subjects, duration of analgesia will vary substantially depending on tolerance and dose. Dose should be adjusted so that 3 to 4 hours of pain relief may be achieved.

Indications: Indicated exclusively for the relief of severe pain in patients who require s.c., i.v. or i.m. administered opioids in doses or concentrations higher than those usually needed. Because hydromorphone is highly soluble, a smaller injection volume can be used and discomfort associated with the i.m. or s.c. injection of larger volumes of solution can be minimized.

Contraindications: Patients who are not already receiving high doses or high concentrations of opioids; patients with known hypersensitivity to the drug; patients with respiratory depression in the absence of resuscitative equipment; in patients with severe CNS depression; and in patients with status asthmaticus. High concentrations of hydromorphone preparations are also contraindicated for use in obstetrical analgesia and are not intended for use except in patients with severe pain.

Warnings: Drug Dependence: All opioids, like morphine and hydromorphone can produce drug dependence and therefore have the potential for being abused. As with other opioid drugs, psychic dependence, physical dependence and tolerance are likely to develop upon repeated administration of hydromorphone, and it should be prescribed and administered with the same degree of caution appropriate for the use of morphine. Abrupt discontinuation of the administration of hydromorphone is likely to result in a withdrawal syndrome (see Dependence Liability).

Infants born to mothers physically dependent on hydromorphone will also be physically dependent and may exhibit respiratory difficulties and withdrawal symptoms (see Dependence Liability).

Impaired Respiration: Respiratory depression is the chief hazard of hydromorphone. It occurs most frequently in the elderly, in the debilitated, and in those suffering from conditions accompanied by hypoxia or hypercapnia, when even moderate therapeutic doses may dangerously decrease pulmonary ventilation. This effect may be lessened by careful dose titration as severe pain can antagonize the respiratory depressant action of hydromorphone.

Hydromorphone should be used with extreme caution in patients with chronic obstructive pulmonary disease or cor pulmonale, patients having a substantially decreased respiratory reserve, hypoxia, hypercapnia, or pre-existing respiratory depression. In such patients, even the usual therapeutic doses of opioid analgesics may decrease respiratory drive while simultaneously increasing airway resistance, to the point of apnea.

As mentioned above, severe pain antagonizes the subjective and respiratory depressant actions of hydromorphone. However, should pain suddenly subside, these effects may rapidly become manifest. Patients who are scheduled for cordotomy or other interruptions of pain transmission pathways should not receive hydromorphone within 24 hours of the procedure.

Head Injury and Increased Intracranial Pressure: The respiratory depressant effects of hydromorphone with carbon dioxide retention and secondary elevation of cerebrospinal fluid pressure may be markedly exaggerated in the presence of head injury, other intracranial lesions, or pre-existing increase in intracranial pressure. Opioid analgesics, including hydromorphone, may produce effects which can obscure the clinical course and neurologic signs of further increase in pressure in patients with head injuries.

Hypotensive Effect: Opioid analgesics, including hydromorphone, may cause severe hypotension in individuals whose ability to maintain normal blood pressure has already been compromised by depleted blood volume, or the concurrent administration of drugs such as phenothiazines and other tranquilizers, sedative/hypnotics, tricyclic antidepressants or general anesthetics (see Precautions, Drug Interactions). Hydromorphone may produce orthostatic hypotension in ambulatory patients.

Hydromorphone should be administered with caution to patients in circulatory shock, since vasodilation produced by the drug may further reduce cardiac output and blood pressure.

Pregnancy (see Warnings, Drug Dependence): Animals: Adequate animal studies on reproduction have not been performed to determine whether hydromorphone affects fertility in males or females. However, animal studies with both morphine and hydromorphone have indicated the possibility of teratogenic effects. Humans: There are no well-controlled studies in women. Reports based on marketing experience do not identify any specific teratogenic risks following routine (short-term) clinical use. Although there is no clearly defined risk, such reports do not exclude the possibility of infrequent or subtle damage to the human fetus. Hydromorphone should be used in pregnant women only when clearly needed (see Labor and Delivery and Dependence Liability).

Labor and Delivery: High concentration hydromorphone preparations are contraindicated in labor and delivery (see Contraindications).

Precautions: General:

> When used at high concentrations, the delivery of precise lower doses of hydromorphone may be difficult. Therefore, high concentration hydromorphone preparations should be used only if the amount of hydromorphone required can be delivered accurately.

In general, opioids should be given with caution and the initial dose should be reduced for the elderly or debilitated, and those with severe impairment of hepatic, pulmonary or renal function; myxedema or hypothyroidism; adrenocortical insufficiency (i.e. Addison's disease); CNS depression or coma; elevated intracranial pressure; toxic psychosis; prostatic hypertrophy or urethral stricture; gallbladder disease; acute alcoholism; delirium tremens; or kyphoscoliosis.

Where high concentration hydromorphone preparations are indicated, however, the patient is presumed to be receiving an opioid to which tolerance has developed and the initial dose of hydromorphone selected, should therefore be estimated on the basis of the relative potency of hydromorphone and the opioid previously used by the patient (see Dosage).

The administration of opioid analgesics including hydromorphone may obscure the diagnosis or clinical course in patients with acute abdominal conditions and may aggravate pre-existing convulsions in patients with convulsive disorders.

Opioid analgesics including hydromorphone should also be used with caution in patients about to undergo surgery of the biliary tract, since it may cause spasm of the sphincter of Oddi.

Dependence Liability: Opioid analgesics may cause psychological and physical dependence (see Warnings). Physical dependence results in withdrawal symptoms in patients who abruptly discontinue the drug. Withdrawal symptoms may also be precipitated in the patient with physical dependency by the administration of a drug with opioid antagonist activity, i.e. naloxone or mixed agonist antagonists i.e. pentazocine (see Overdose: Symptoms and Treatment). Physical dependence usually does not occur to a clinically significant degree until after several weeks of continued opioid usage. Tolerance, in which increasingly large doses are required in order to produce the same degree of analgesia, is initially manifested by a shortened duration of analgesic effect and subsequently, by decreases in the intensity of analgesia. The dose required to produce analgesia is, therefore, related to the degree of tolerance.

In chronic pain patients in whom opioid analgesics are abruptly discontinued, a severe abstinence syndrome should be anticipated. This may be similar to the abstinence syndrome noted in patients withdrawing from heroin.

The latter abstinence syndrome may be characterized by restlessness, lacrimation, rhinorrhea, yawning, perspiration, gooseflesh, restless sleep or "yen", and a mydriasis during the first 24 hours. Those symptoms may increase in severity and over the next 72 hours may be accompanied by increasing irritability, anxiety, weakness, twitching and spasms of muscles, kicking movements, severe backache, abdominal and leg pains, abdominal and muscle cramps, hot and cold flashes, insomnia, nausea, anorexia, vomiting, intestinal spasm, diarrhea, coryza and repetitive sneezing, increase in body temperature, blood pressure, respiratory rate and heart rate.

Because of the excessive loss of fluids through sweating, or vomiting and diarrhea, there is usually marked weight loss, dehydration, ketosis, and disturbances in acid-base balance. Cardiovascular collapse can occur. Without treatment, most observable symptoms disappear in 5 to 14 days; however, there appears to be a phase of secondary or chronic abstinence which may last for 2 to 6 months and is characterized by insomnia, irritability, muscular aches, and autonomic instability.

In the treatment of physical dependence on hydromorphone, the patient may be detoxified by gradual reduction of the dosage, although this is unlikely to be necessary in the terminal cancer patient. If abstinence symptoms become severe, the patient may be given methadone. Temporary administration of tranquilizers and sedatives may aid in reducing patient anxiety. Gastrointestinal disturbances or dehydration should be treated accordingly.

Drug Interactions: The concomitant use of other CNS depressants including sedatives or hypnotics, general anesthetics, phenothiazines, tranquilizers and alcohol may produce additive depressant effects. Respiratory depression, hypotension and profound sedation or coma may occur. When such combined therapy is contemplated, the dose of one or both agents should be reduced. Opioid analgesics, including hydromorphone may enhance the action of neuromuscular blocking agents and produce an increased degree of respiratory depression.

Lactation: Low levels of opioid analgesics have been detected in human milk. As a general rule, nursing should not be under taken while a patient is receiving hydromorphone since it and other drugs in this class may be excreted in the milk.

Children: Safety and effectiveness in children have not been established.

Adverse Effects: The adverse effects of hydromorphone are similar to those of other opioid analgesics and represent an extension of pharmacological effects of the drug class. The major hazards include respiratory depression and apnea. To a lesser degree, circulatory depression, respiratory arrest, shock and cardiac arrest have occurred.

The most frequently observed adverse effects are constipation, lightheadedness, dizziness, sedation, nausea, vomiting, and sweating. All of these effects, except constipation seem to be more prominent in ambulatory patients and in those not experiencing severe pain. Some adverse reactions in ambulatory patients may be alleviated if the patient lies down. When instituting prolonged therapy with an opioid for chronic pain, the prescription of antiemetics for nausea and vomiting and an appropriate regimen of bowel management for constipation (stool softeners, laxatives etc.) should be considered.

Sedation: Some degree of sedation is experienced by most patients upon initiation of therapy. This may be at least partly because patients often recuperate from prolonged fatigue after the relief of persistent pain. Most patients develop tolerance to the sedative effects of opioids within 3 to 5 days and, if the sedation is not severe, will not require any treatment except reassurance. If excessive sedation persists beyond a few days, the dose of the opioid should be reduced and alternate causes investigated. Some of these are: concurrent CNS depressant medication, hepatic or renal dysfunction, brain metastases, hypercalcemia and respiratory failure. If it is necessary to reduce the dose, it can be carefully increased again after 3 or 4 days if it is obvious that the pain is not being well controlled. Dizziness and unsteadiness may be caused by postural hypotension particularly in elderly or debilitated patients and may be alleviated if the patient lies down.

Nausea and Vomiting: Nausea is a common side effect on initiation of therapy with opioid analgesics and is thought to occur by activation of the chemoreceptor trigger zone, stimulation of the vestibular apparatus and through delayed gastric emptying. The prevalence of nausea declines following continued treatment with opioid analgesics. When instituting prolonged therapy with an opioid for chronic pain, the routine prescription of an antiemetic should be considered. In the cancer patient, investigation of nausea should include such causes as constipation, bowel obstruction, uremia, hypercalcemia, hepatomegaly, tumor invasion of celiac plexus and concurrent use of drugs with emetogenic properties. Persistent nausea which does not respond to dosage reduction may be caused by opioid-induced gastric stasis and may be accompanied by other symptoms including anorexia, early satiety, vomiting and abdominal fullness. These symptoms respond to chronic treatment with gastrointestinal prokinetic agents.

Constipation: Practically all patients become constipated while taking opioids on a persistent basis. In some patients, particularly the elderly or bedridden, fecal impaction may result. It is essential to caution the patients in this regard and to institute an appropriate regimen of bowel management at the start of prolonged opioid analgesic therapy. Stool softeners, stimulant laxatives and other appropriate measures should be used as required.

Less Frequently Observed with Opioid Analgesics: General and CNS: dysphoria, euphoria, weakness, headache, agitation, tremor, uncoordinated muscle movements, alterations of mood (nervousness, apprehension, depression, floating feelings, dreams), muscle rigidity, paresthesia, muscle tremor, blurred vision, nystagmus, diplopia and miosis, hallucinations and disorientation, visual disturbances, insomnia and increased intracranial pressure may occur.

Cardiovascular: Flushing of the face, chills, tachycardia, bradycardia, palpitation, faintness, syncope, hypotension and hypertension have been reported.

Respiratory: Bronchospasm and laryngospasm have been know to occur.

Gastrointestinal: Dry mouth, constipation, biliary tract spasm, anorexia, diarrhea, cramps and taste alterations have been reported.

Genitourinary: Urinary retention or hesitancy, and antidiuretic effects have been reported.

Dermatologic: Pruritus, urticaria, other skin rashes, wheal and flare over the vein with i.v. injection, and diaphoresis have been reported with narcotic analgesics.

Overdose: Symptoms: Serious overdosage with hydromorphone is characterized by respiratory depression, somnolence progressing to stupor or coma, skeletal muscle flaccidity, cold and clammy skin, constricted pupils and sometimes bradycardia and hypotension. In serious overdosage, particularly following i.v. injection, apnea, circulatory collapse, cardiac arrest and death may occur.

Treatment: In the treatment of overdosage, primary attention should be given to the re-establishment of adequate respiratory exchange through provision of a patent airway and institution of assisted or controlled ventilation. It should be borne in mind that for individuals who are physically dependent on opioids and are receiving large doses of these drugs, the administration of the usual dose of an opioid antagonist will precipitate an acute withdrawal syndrome. The severity will depend on the degree of physical dependence and the dose of the antagonist administered. Use of an opioid antagonist in such persons should be avoided. If necessary to treat serious respiratory depression in the physically dependent patient, the antagonist should be administered with extreme care and by titration, commencing with 10 to 20% of the usual recommended initial dose.

Respiratory depression which may result from overdosage, or unusual sensitivity to hydromorphone, in a nonopioid-tolerant patient, can be managed with the opioid antagonist naloxone. A dose of naloxone (usually 0.4 to 2 mg) should be administered i.v., if possible, simultaneously with respiratory resuscitation. The dose can be repeated in 3 minutes. Naloxone should not be administered in the absence of clinically significant respiratory or circulatory depression. Naloxone should be administered cautiously to persons who are known or suspected to be physically dependent on hydromorphone. In such cases, an abrupt or complete reversal of opioid effects may precipitate an acute abstinence syndrome.

Since the duration of action of hydromorphone may exceed that of the antagonist, the patient should be kept under continued surveillance; repeated doses of the antagonist may be required to maintain adequate respiration. Other supportive measures should be applied when indicated.

Supportive measures, including oxygen and vasopressors, should be employed in the management of circulatory shock and pulmonary edema accompanying overdose, as indicated.

Cardiac arrest or arrhythmias may require cardiac massage or defibrillation.

Dosage:

Dilaudid-HP, Dilaudid-HP-Plus, Dilaudid-XP and Reconstituted Dilaudid Sterile Powder are highly concentrated solutions of hydromorphone HCl. They should be used only in opioid tolerant patients requiring high doses or high concentrations of opioid agonists. Do not confuse Dilaudid-HP, Dilaudid-HP-Plus, Dilaudid-XP and Reconstituted Dilaudid Sterile Powder with the lower concentration of the Dilaudid 2 mg/mL ampuls since overdosage and death could result.

High concentration hydromorphone preparations are indicated for relief of severe pain in opioid-tolerant patients. Thus, these patients will already have received opioid analgesics. If the patient is being changed from one injectable form of hydromophone to higher concentration hydromorphone preparations, similar doses should be used, depending on the patient's clinical response to the drug. If high concentration hydromorphone preparations are substituted for a different opioid analgesic, Table I is provided as a guide to determine the approximate equivalent dose of hydromorphone.

In open clinical trials with hydromorphone in patients with terminal cancer, both s.c. and i.m. injections of hydromorphone were well-tolerated, with minimal pain and/or burning at the injection site. Mild erythema was rarely noted after i.m. injection. S.C. injections of hydromorphone were particularly well tolerated when administered with a short, 30 gauge needle. In addition, continuous s.c. infusions of hydromorphone have been shown to be well tolerated. The most common adverse reaction is local tissue redness which can be relieved with more frequent site changes. Experience with administration of hydromorphone by the i.v. route is limited. Should i.v. administration be necessary, the injection should be given slowly, over at least 2 to 3 minutes. The i.v. route is usually painless.

A gradual increase in dose may be required if analgesia is inadequate, tolerance occurs, or if pain severity increases. The first sign of tolerance is usually a reduced duration of effect.

Reconstitution for Parenteral Products: Dilaudid Sterile Powder is provided sterile as 250 mg of hydromorphone HCl in a 30 mL vial. It can be reconstituted to desired concentration with sterile water for injection, 0.9% sodium chloride or 5% dextrose. Table II (on following page) provides information on

Table I—Dilaudid-HP, Dilaudid-HP-Plus, Dilaudid-XP, Dilaudid Sterile Powder

Opioid Analgesics: Approximate Analgesic Equivalences[a]

Drug	Equivalent Dose (mg)[b] (compared to morphine 10 mg i.m.) Parenteral	Oral	Duration of Action (hours)
Strong Opioid Agonists			
Morphine (single dose)	10	60	3–4
(chronic dose)	10	20–30[c]	3–4
Hydromorphone	1.5–2	6–7.5	2–4
Anileridine	25	75	2–3
Levorphanol	2	4	4–8
Meperidine[d]	75	300	1–3
Oxymorphone	1.5	5 (rectal)	3–4
Methadone[e]			
Heroin	5–8	10–15	3–4
Weak Opioid Agonists			
Codeine	120	200	3–4
Oxycodone	5–10	10–15	2–4
Propoxyphene	50	100	2–4
Mixed Agonist-Antagonists[f]			
Pentazocine[d]	60	180	3–4
Nalbuphine	10		3–6
Butorphanol	2		3–4

[a] References: Cancer Pain: A Monograph on the Management of Cancer Pain, Health and Welfare Canada, 1984. Foley, K.M., New Engl. J. Med. 313: 84-95, 1985. Aronoff, G.M. and Evans, W.O., In: Evaluation and Treatment of Chronic Pain, 2nd Ed., G.M. Aronoff (Ed.), Williams and Wilkins, Baltimore, pp. 359-368, 1992. Cherny, N.I. and Portenoy, R.K., In: Textbook of Pain, 3rd Ed., P.D. Wall and R. Melzack (Eds.), Churchill Livingstone, London, pp. 1437-1467, 1994.

[b] Most of these data were derived from single-dose, acute pain studies and should be considered an approximation for selection of doses when treating chronic pain.

[c] For acute pain, the oral dose of morphine is 6 times the injectable dose. However, for chronic dosing this ratio becomes 2 or 3:1 possibly due to the accumulation of active metabolites.

[d] These drugs are not recommended for the management of chronic pain.

[e] Extremely variable equianalgesic dose. Patients should undergo personalized titration starting at an equivalent to 1/10 of the morphine dose.

[f] Mixed agonist-antagonists can precipitate withdrawal in patients on pure opioid agonists.

Dilaudid (cont'd)

the amount of diluent to be added in order to prepare a variety of concentrations.

Table II—Dilaudid Sterile Powder

Amount of Diluent to be Added to Vial Resulting in a Desired Concentration

Volume of Diluent to be added to Vial	Resulting Volume	Nominal Concentration per mL
24.8 mL	25.0 mL	10 mg/mL
12.4 mL	12.5 mL	20 mg/mL
4.9 mL	5.0 mL	50 mg/mL
2.4 mL	2.5 mL	100 mg/mL
1.6 mL	1.67 mL	150 mg/mL
1.1 mL	1.25 mL	200 mg/mL
0.9 mL	1.0 mL	250 mg/mL

The information provided in Table III is only for physical compatibility and chemical stability of the reconstituted solutions. Continued sterility of the reconstituted solution is dependent on the procedures and equipment used during the preparation of the solution. Each pharmacist must address these factors in determining the duration of use of the solution prepared. The usual recommendation for reconstituted solutions is 24 hours at room temperature or 72 hours under refrigeration.

Dilaudid Sterile Powder for injection is physically compatible and chemically stable in the diluents and containers shown in Table III.

Table III—Dilaudid Sterile Powder

Physical Compatibility and Chemical Stability of the Reconstituted Solutions

Diluent	Final Concentration (mg) Hydromorphone HCl/mL	Storage Condition	Type of Container	*Physical and Chemical Stability (In Days)
Sterile Water for Injection	10, 100, 250	Room Temperature	Amber Glass	42
		Refrigerated (Fridge)	Amber Glass	42
Sterile Water for Injection	10, 100, 250	Room Temperature	Pharmacia Cassettes	42
		Refrigerated (Fridge)	Pharmacia Cassettes	42
Sterile Water for Injection	10, 100, 250	37°C dry heat incubator (after storage in fridge)	Pharmacia Cassettes	10 days after 42 days storage in fridge
0.9% Sodium Chloride Solution	10, 100	Room Temperature	Amber Glass	28
5% Dextrose Solution	10, 100	Room Temperature	Amber Glass	28

* This information does not address sterility. Please see the previous paragraph for further comments.

Solutions made from Dilaudid Sterile Powder (as well as Dilaudid-HP, -HP-Plus and -XP) can be administered by i.v., i.m. or s.c. routes including i.v. and s.c. continuous infusion.

Note: Parenteral drug products should be inspected visually for particulate matter and discoloration prior to administration, whenever solution and container permit. A slight yellowish discoloration may develop in Dilaudid solutions. This yellowish coloration is proportional to hydromorphone concentration and has a tendency to increase over time. The coloration is of an aesthetic nature and not a result of chemical degradation. No loss of potency has been demonstrated.

Supplied: Dilaudid-HP: Each mL of sterile solution contains: hydromorphone HCl 10 mg, citric acid 2 mg and sodium citrate 2 mg, in Water for Injection. No added preservatives. Amber ampuls of 1 and 5 mL, boxes of 10. Vials with white flip-off caps of 50 mL, boxes of 2.

Dilaudid-HP-Plus: Each mL of sterile solution contains: hydromorphone HCl 20 mg, citric acid 2 mg and sodium citrate 2 mg, in Water for Injection. No added preservatives. Amber vials with brown flip-off caps of 50 mL, boxes of 2.

Dilaudid-XP: Each mL of sterile solution contains: hydromorphone HCl 50 mg, citric acid 2 mg and sodium citrate 2 mg, in Water for Injection. No added preservatives. Amber vials with yellow flip-off caps of 50 mL, boxes of 2.

Dilaudid Sterile Powder: Each vial contains: sterile lyophilized hydromorphone HCl 250 mg. No added preservatives. Amber vials of 30 mL with black flip-off caps, boxes of 4.

Store at 15 to 30°C. Protect from light. Do not use beyond the expiry date indicated on the label.

DILTIAZEM HYDROCHLORIDE INJECTION Ⓟ

Novopharm

Antiarrhythmic

Pharmacology: Diltiazem inhibits the influx of calcium ions during membrane depolarization of cardiac and vascular smooth muscle. The therapeutic benefits of diltiazem in supraventricular tachycardias are related to its ability to slow atrioventricular (AV) nodal conduction time and prolong AV nodal refractoriness. Diltiazem exhibits frequency (use) dependent effects on AV nodal conduction such that it may selectively reduce the heart rate during tachycardias involving the AV node with little or no effect on normal AV nodal conduction at normal heart rates.

Diltiazem slows the ventricular rate in patients with a rapid ventricular response during atrial fibrillation or atrial flutter (AF/FL). Diltiazem converts paroxysmal supraventricular tachycardia (PSVT) to normal sinus rhythm by interrupting the reentry circuit in AV nodal reentrant tachycardias and reciprocating tachycardias, e.g., Wolff-Parkinson-White syndrome (WPW).

Diltiazem prolongs the sinus cycle length. It has no effects on the sinus node recovery time or on the sinoatrial (SA) conduction time in patients without SA nodal dysfunction. Diltiazem has no significant electrophysiologic effects on tissues in the heart that are fast sodium channel dependent, e.g., His-Purkinje tissue, atrial and ventricular muscle and extranodal accessory pathways.

Like other calcium channel antagonists, because of its effect on vascular smooth muscle, diltiazem decreases total peripheral resistance resulting in a decrease in both systolic and diastolic blood pressure.

Hemodynamics: In patients with cardiovascular disease, diltiazem administered i.v. in single bolus doses, followed in some cases by a continuous infusion, reduced blood pressure, systemic vascular resistance, the rate-pressure product, and coronary vascular resistance and increased coronary blood flow. Following administration of 1 or 2 i.v. bolus doses of diltiazem, response usually occurs within 3 minutes and maximal heart rate reduction generally occurs in 2 to 7 minutes. Heart rate reduction may last from 1 to 3 hours. Upon discontinuation of infusion, heart rate reduction may last from 0.5 hours to more than 10 hours (median duration=7 hours). Hypotension, if it occurs, may be similarly persistent.

In a limited number of studies of patients with compromised myocardiums (severe congestive heart failure, acute myocardial infarction, hypertrophic cardiomyopathy), administration of i.v. diltiazem produced no significant effect on contractility, left ventricular end diastolic pressure, or pulmonary capillary wedge pressure. The mean ejection fraction and cardiac output/index remained unchanged or increased. Maximal hemodynamic effects usually occurred within 2 to 5 minutes of an injection. However, in rare instances, worsening of congestive heart failure has been reported in patients with preexisting impaired ventricular function.

Pharmacodynamics: The prolongation of PR interval correlated significantly with plasma diltiazem concentration in normal volunteers using the Sigmoidal E_{max} model. Changes in heart rate, systolic blood pressure, and diastolic blood pressure did not correlate with diltiazem plasma concentrations in normal volunteers. Reduction in mean arterial pressure correlated linearly with diltiazem plasma concentration in a group of hypertensive patients.

In patients with atrial fibrillation and atrial flutter, a significant correlation was observed between the percent reduction in HR and plasma diltiazem concentration using the Sigmoidal E_{max} model. Based on this relationship, the mean plasma diltiazem concentration required to produce a 20% decrease in heart rate was determined to be 80 ng/mL. Mean plasma diltiazem concentrations of 130 and 300 ng/mL were determined to produce reductions in heart rate of 30 and 40%.

Pharmacokinetics: Following a single i.v. injection in healthy male volunteers, diltiazem appears to obey linear pharmacokinetics over a dose range of 10.5 to 21.0 mg. The plasma elimination half-life is approximately 3.4 hours. The apparent volume of distribution of diltiazem is approximately 305 L. Diltiazem is extensively metabolized in the liver with a systemic clearance of approximately 65 L/h.

After constant rate i.v. infusion to healthy male volunteers, diltiazem exhibits nonlinear pharmacokinetics over an infusion range of 4.8 to 13.2 mg/h for 24 hours. Over this infusion range, as the dose is increased, systemic clearance decreases from 64 to 48 L/h while the plasma elimination half-life increases from 4.1 to 4.9 hours. The apparent volume of distribution remains unchanged (360 to 391 L).

In patients with AF/FL, diltiazem systemic clearance has been found to be decreased compared to healthy volunteers. In patients administered bolus doses ranging from 2.5 to 38.5 mg, systemic clearance averaged 36 L/h. In patients administered continuous infusions at 10 or 15 mg/h for 24 hours, diltiazem systemic clearance averaged 42 L/h and 31 L/h, respectively.

The metabolic pathways of diltiazem metabolism include N- and O-demethylation (via cytochrome P450), deacetylation (via plasma and tissue esterases), in addition to conjugation (via sulfation and glucuronidation). In vitro studies have demonstrated that CYP 3A4 is the principal CYP isoenzyme involved in N-demethylation. Metabolites N-monodesmethyldiltiazem, and desacetyldiltiazem, desacetyl-N-monodesmethyldiltiazem, desacetyl-O-desmethyldiltiazem, and desacetyl-N, O-desmethyldiltiazem have been identified in human urine following oral administration. With oral administration 2 to 4% of the unchanged diltiazem appears in the urine. Drugs which induce or inhibit hepatic microsomal enzymes may alter diltiazem disposition.

Following single i.v. injection of diltiazem, however, plasma concentrations of N-monodesmethyldiltiazem and desacetyldiltiazem, 2 principal metabolites found in plasma after oral administration, are typically not detected. These metabolites are observed, however, following 24-hour constant rate i.v. infusion.

Total radioactivity measurement following short i.v. administration in healthy volunteers suggests the presence of other unidentified metabolites which attain higher concentrations than those of diltiazem and are more slowly eliminated. Plasma half-life of total radioactivity is about 20 hours compared to 2 to 5 hours for diltiazem.

Diltiazem is 70 to 80% bound to plasma proteins.

Indications: Atrial Fibrillation or Atrial Flutter: Temporary control of rapid ventricular rate in atrial fibrillation or atrial flutter. It should not be used in patients with AF/FL associated with an accessory bypass tract such as in Wolff-Parkinson-White (WPW) syndrome, or short PR syndrome, e.g., Lown-Ganong-Levine syndrome. Diltiazem injection rarely converts atrial fibrillation or atrial flutter to normal sinus rhythm.

Paroxysmal Supraventricular Tachycardia: Rapid conversion of paroxysmal supraventricular tachycardias to sinus rhythm. This includes AV nodal reentrant tachycardias, and reciprocating tachycardias associated with an extranodal accessory pathway, such as the WPW syndrome, or short PR syndrome, e.g., Lown-Ganong-Levine syndrome. Unless otherwise contraindicated, appropriate vagal manoeuvres should be attempted prior to administration of diltiazem injection.

The use of diltiazem injection for control of ventricular response in patients with atrial fibrillation or atrial flutter or conversion to sinus rhythm in patients with paroxysmal supraventricular tachycardia should be undertaken with caution when the patient is compromised hemodynamically or is taking other drugs that decrease any or all of the following:

peripheral resistance, myocardial filling, myocardial contractility, or electrical impulse propagation in the myocardium.

For either indication the setting should include continuous monitoring of the ECG and frequent measurement of blood pressure. A defibrillator and emergency equipment should be readily available.

Contraindications: Patients with sick sinus syndrome except in the presence of a functioning ventricular pacemaker. Patients with second- or third-degree AV block except in the presence of a functioning ventricular pacemaker. Patients with known hypersensitivity to diltiazem. Patients with severe hypotension or cardiogenic shock.

In patients with AF/FL associated with an accessory bypass tract such as in WPW syndrome, or short PR syndrome, e.g., Lown-Ganong-Levine syndrome. As with other agents which slow AV nodal conduction and do not prolong the refractoriness of the accessory pathway (e.g., verapamil, digoxin), in rare instances patients with AF/FL associated with an accessory bypass tract may experience a potentially life-threatening increase in heart rate accompanied by hypotension when treated with diltiazem injection.

In patients with ventricular tachycardia. Administration of other calcium channel blockers to patients with wide complex tachycardia (QRS ≥ 0.12 seconds) has resulted in hemodynamic deterioration and ventricular fibrillation. It is important that an accurate pretreatment diagnosis distinguish wide complex QRS tachycardia of supraventricular origin from that of ventricular origin prior to administration of diltiazem injection.

Pregnancy: In pregnancy and in women of childbearing potential. Fetal malformations and adverse effects on pregnancy have been reported in animals. In repeated dose studies, a high incidence of vertebral column malformations was present in the offspring of mice receiving more than 50 mg/kg of diltiazem orally.

I.V. diltiazem and i.v. beta-blockers should not be administered together or in close proximity (within a few hours).

Warnings: Cardiac Conduction: Diltiazem injection prolongs AV nodal conduction and refractoriness that may rarely result in second-or third-degree AV block in sinus rhythm. Concomitant use of diltiazem with agents known to affect cardiac conduction may result in additive effects (see Precautions, Drug Interactions). If high-degree AV block occurs in sinus rhythm, i.v. diltiazem should be discontinued and appropriate supportive measures instituted (see Overdose: Symptoms and Treatment).

Congestive Heart Failure: Although diltiazem has a negative inotropic effect in isolated animal tissue preparations, hemodynamic studies in humans with normal ventricular function and in patients with a compromised myocardium, such as severe CHF, acute MI, and hypertrophic cardiomyopathy, have not shown a reduction in cardiac index nor consistent negative effects on contractility (dp/dt). Administration of oral diltiazem is contraindicated in myocardial infarction patients who have left ventricular failure manifested by pulmonary congestion. Experience with the use of diltiazem injection in patients with impaired ventricular function is limited. Caution should be exercised when using the drug in such patients.

Hypotension: Decreases in blood pressure associated with diltiazem injection therapy may occasionally result in symptomatic hypotension (see Adverse Effects). In controlled clinical trials, 3.2% of patients required some form of intervention (use of i.v. fluids, or the Trendelenburg position) for blood pressure support following diltiazem injection.

The use of i.v. diltiazem for control of ventricular response in patients with supraventricular arrhythmias should be undertaken with caution when the patient is compromised hemodynamically. In addition, caution should be used in patients taking other drugs that decrease peripheral resistance, intravascular volume, myocardial contractility or conduction.

Acute Hepatic Injury: In rare instances, significant elevations of enzymes such as alkaline phosphatase, LDH, AST, ALT, and symptoms consistent with acute hepatic injury have been noted following oral diltiazem. Although a causal relationship to diltiazem has not been established in all cases, a drug induced hypersensitivity reaction is suspected (see Adverse Effects). Therefore, the potential for acute hepatic injury exists following administration of i.v. diltiazem.

Ventricular Premature Beats (VPBs): VPBs may be present on conversion of PSVT to sinus rhythm with i.v. diltiazem. These VPBs are transient, are typically considered to be benign and appear to have no clinical significance. Similar ventricular complexes have been noted during cardioversion, other pharmacologic therapy, and during spontaneous conversion of PSVT to sinus rhythm.

Precautions: Impaired Hepatic or Renal Function: Diltiazem is extensively metabolized by the liver and excreted by the kidneys and in bile. The drug should be used with caution in patients with impaired renal or hepatic function. Liver cirrhosis was shown to reduce apparent oral diltiazem clearance, prolong the half-life of orally administered diltiazem and increase its bioavailability by 69%.

In subacute and chronic dog and rat studies designed to produce toxicity, high oral doses of diltiazem were associated with hepatic damage. In special subacute hepatic studies, oral doses of 125 mg/kg and higher in rats were associated with histological changes in the liver, which were reversible when the drug was discontinued. In dogs, oral doses of 20 mg/kg were also associated with hepatic changes; however, these changes were reversible with continued dosing.

Dermatologic Disorders: Dermatologic events progressing to erythema multiforme and/or exfoliative dermatitis have been infrequently reported following oral diltiazem (see Adverse Effects). Therefore, the potential for these dermatologic reactions exists following exposure to i.v. diltiazem. Should a dermatologic reaction persist, the drug should be discontinued.

Drug Interactions: Due to potential for additive effects, caution is warranted in patients receiving diltiazem concomitantly with any agent(s) known to affect cardiac contractility and/or SA or AV node conduction (see Warnings).

As with all drugs, care should be exercised when treating patients with multiple medications. Calcium channel blockers undergo biotransformation by the cytochrome P450 system. Coadministration of diltiazem with other drugs which follow the same route of biotransformation may result in altered bioavailability. Dosages of similarly metabolized drugs, particularly those of low therapeutic ratio, and especially in patients with renal and/or hepatic impairment, may require adjustment when starting or stopping concomitantly administered diltiazem to maintain optimum therapeutic blood levels.

Drugs known to be inhibitors of the cytochrome P450 system include: azole antifungals, cimetidine, cyclosporine, erythromycin, quinidine, warfarin.

Drugs known to be inducers of the cytochrome P450 system include: phenobarbital, phenytoin, rifampin.

Drugs known to be biotransformed via P450 include: benzodiazepines, flecainide, imipramine, propafenone, terfenadine, theophylline.

Anesthetics: The depression of cardiac contractility, conductivity, and automaticity as well as the vascular dilation associated with anesthetics may be potentiated by calcium channel blockers. When used concomitantly, anesthetics and calcium blockers should be titrated carefully.

Benzodiazepines: Diltiazem significantly increases peak plasma levels and the elimination half-life of triazolam and midazolam.

Beta-Blockers: I.V. diltiazem has been administered to patients on chronic oral beta-blocker therapy. The combination of the 2 drugs was generally well tolerated without serious adverse effects.

If i.v. diltiazem is administered to patients receiving chronic oral beta-blocker therapy, the possibility for bradycardia, AV block, and/or depression of contractility should be considered (see Contraindications). Oral administration of diltiazem with propranolol in 5 normal volunteers resulted in increased propranolol levels in all subjects and bioavailability of propranolol was increased approximately 50%. In vitro, propranolol appears to be displaced from its binding sites by diltiazem.

Carbamazepine: Concomitant administration of diltiazem with carbamazepine has been reported to result in elevated serum levels of carbamazepine (40 to 72% increase) resulting in toxicity in some cases. Patients receiving these drugs concurrently should be monitored for a potential drug interaction.

Cimetidine: A study in 6 healthy volunteers has shown a significant increase in peak diltiazem plasma levels (58%) and AUC (53%) after a 1-week course of cimetidine at 1 200 mg/day and a single dose of oral diltiazem 60 mg. Ranitidine produced smaller, nonsignificant increases. Patients currently receiving diltiazem therapy should be carefully monitored for a change in pharmacological effect when initiating and discontinuing therapy with cimetidine. An adjustment in the diltiazem dose may be warranted.

Cyclosporine: A pharmacokinetic interaction between diltiazem and cyclosporine has been observed during studies involving renal and cardiac transplant patients. In renal and cardiac transplant recipients, a reduction of cyclosporine dose ranging from 15 to 48% was necessary to maintain cyclosporine trough concentrations similar to those seen prior to the addition of diltiazem. If these agents are to be administered concurrently, cyclosporine concentrations should be monitored, especially when diltiazem therapy is initiated, adjusted or discontinued. The effect of cyclosporine on diltiazem plasma concentrations has not been evaluated.

Digitalis: I.V. diltiazem has been administered to patients receiving either i.v. or oral digitalis therapy. The combination of the 2 drugs was well tolerated without serious adverse effects. However, since both drugs affect AV nodal conduction, patients should be monitored for excessive slowing of the heart rate and/or AV block.

Rifampin: Administration of diltiazem with rifampin markedly reduced plasma diltiazem concentrations and the therapeutic effect of diltiazem.

Short and Long-acting Nitrates: Diltiazem may be safely coadministered with nitrates, but there have been few controlled studies to evaluate the antianginal effectiveness of this combination.

Other Calcium Antagonists: Limited clinical experience suggests that in certain severe conditions not responding adequately to verapamil or to nifedipine, using diltiazem in conjunction with either of these drugs may be beneficial.

Lactation: Diltiazem is excreted in human milk. One report with oral diltiazem suggests that concentrations in breast milk may approximate serum levels. If use of diltiazem is deemed essential, an alternative method of infant feeding should be instituted.

Children: Safety and effectiveness in children have not been established.

Adverse Effects: Adverse reactions were derived from controlled clinical trials in 411 patients with paroxysmal supraventricular tachycardia, atrial fibrillation, or atrial flutter. Adverse reactions were reported in 17.3% of patients with injectable diltiazem, and required discontinuation of treatment in 1.5% of patients.

Worldwide experience in over 1 300 patients was similar. The most common adverse reactions (incidence of at least 1%) were: hypotension 7.5%, symptomatic hypotension 3.2%, injection site reaction (e.g., itching, burning) 3.9%, vasodilation (flushing) 1.7%, and arrhythmia (junctional rhythm or isorhythmic dissociation) 1.0%.

In addition, the following events were reported in less than 1% of cases:

Cardiovascular: atrial flutter, first-degree AV block, second-degree AV block, bradycardia, chest pain, congestive heart failure, sinus pause, sinus node dysfunction, syncope, ventricular arrhythmia, ventricular fibrillation, ventricular tachycardia.

Dermatologic: pruritus, sweating.

Gastrointestinal: constipation, elevated AST or alkaline phosphatase, nausea, vomiting.

Nervous system: dizziness, paresthesia.

Other: amblyopia, asthenia, dry mouth, dyspnea, general edema, headache, hyperuricemia.

Although not observed in clinical trials with injectable diltiazem, other reactions associated with oral diltiazem have been reported:

Cardiovascular: third-degree AV block, bundle branch block, ECG abnormality, palpitations, syncope, tachycardia, ventricular extrasystoles.

Dermatologic: alopecia, erythema multiforme, exfoliative dermatitis, leukocytoclastic vasculitis, petechiae, photosensitivity, purpura, rash, urticaria.

Gastrointestinal: anorexia, diarrhea, dysgeusia, dyspepsia, mild elevations of ALT and LDH, thirst, weight increase.

Nervous system: abnormal dreams, amnesia, depression, extrapyramidal symptoms, gait abnormality, hallucinations, insomnia, nervousness, personality change, somnolence, tremor.

Other: CPK elevation, detached retina, epistaxis, eye irritation, gingival hyperplasia, hemolytic anemia, hyperglycemia, impotence, increased bleeding time, leukopenia, muscle cramps, nasal congestion, nocturia, osteoarticular pain, polyuria, retinopathy, sexual difficulties, thrombocytopenia, tinnitus.

Events such as myocardial infarction have been observed which are not readily distinguishable from the natural history of the disease for the patient.

Overdose: Symptoms and Treatment: Overdosage experience is limited. In the event of overdosage or an exaggerated response, appropriate supportive measures should be employed. The following measures may be considered:

Diltiazem Hydrochloride Injection (cont'd)

Bradycardia: Administer atropine (0.6 to 1 mg). If there is no response to vagal blockade, administer isoproterenol cautiously.

High-degree AV block: Treat as for bradycardia above. Fixed high-degree AV block should be treated with cardiac pacing.

Cardiac failure: Administer inotropic agents (isoproterenol, dopamine, or dobutamine) and diuretics.

Hypotension: Vasopressors (e.g., dopamine or norepinephrine).

The effectiveness of i.v. calcium administration to reverse the pharmacological effects of diltiazem overdose has been inconsistent. In a few reported cases, overdose with calcium channel blockers associated with hypotension and bradycardia that was initially refractory to atropine became more responsive to atropine after the patients received i.v. calcium. In some cases i.v. calcium has been administered (1 g calcium chloride or 3 g calcium gluconate) over 5 minutes, and repeated every 10 to 20 minutes as necessary. Calcium gluconate has also been administered as a continuous infusion at a rate of 2 g/h for 10 hours. Infusions of calcium for 24 hours or more may be required. Patients should be monitored for signs of hypercalcemia.

Actual treatment and dosage should depend on the severity of the clinical situation and the judgment and experience of the treating physician.

The i.v. LD_{50}'s in mice and rats were 58 to 61 and 38 to 39 mg/kg, respectively. The toxic dose in man is not known.

Dosage: Direct I.V. Single Injection (Bolus): The initial dose of diltiazem injection should be 0.25 mg/kg as a bolus administered over 2 minutes. If response is inadequate, a second dose may be administered after 15 minutes. The second bolus dose should be 0.35 mg/kg administered over 2 minutes. Subsequent i.v. bolus doses should be individualized for each patient. Some patients may respond to an initial dose of 0.15 mg/kg, although duration of action may be shorter.

Continuous I.V. Infusion: For continued reduction of the heart rate (up to 24 hours) in patients with AF/FL, an i.v. infusion of diltiazem may be administered. Immediately following bolus administration of 0.25 or 0.35 mg/kg, and reduction in heart rate, begin an i.v. infusion of diltiazem. The recommended initial infusion rate is 10 mg/h. The infusion rate may be increased 5 to 15 mg/h as needed, if further reduction in heart rate is required. Some patients may maintain response to an initial rate of 5 mg/h. The infusion may be maintained for up to 24 hours.

Diltiazem shows dose-dependent, nonlinear pharmacokinetics during continuous i.v. infusion. Duration of infusion longer than 24 hours and infusion rates greater than 15 mg/h have not been studied. Therefore, infusion duration exceeding 24 hours and infusion rates exceeding 15 mg/h are not recommended.

Dilution: To prepare diltiazem for continuous i.v. infusion, aseptically transfer the appropriate quantity (see Table I) of diltiazem i.v. injection to the desired volume of either Normal Saline, D5W, or D5W/0.45% NaCl. Mix thoroughly. Use within 24 hours. Keep refrigerated (2 to 8°C) until use.

Table I—Diltiazem Hydrochloride Injection

Dilution for I.V. Infusion

Diluent Volume	Quantity of Diltiazem Injection	Final Concentration	Administration: Dose	Administration: Infusion Rate
100 mL	125 mg (25 mL)	1.0 mg/mL	5 mg/h*	5 mL/h
			10 mg/h	10 mL/h
			15 mg/h	15 mL/h
250 mL	250 mg (50 mL)	0.83 mg/mL	5 mg/h*	6 mL/h
			10 mg/h	12 mL/h
			15 mg/h	18 mL/h
500 mL	250 mg (50 mL)	0.45 mg/mL	5 mg/h*	11 mL/h
			10 mg/h	22 mL/h
			15 mg/h	33 mL/h

*The recommended initial infusion rate of diltiazem is 10 mg/h. An infusion rate of 5 mg/h may be appropriate for some patients.

Diltiazem injection was tested for compatibility with 3 commonly used i.v. fluids at a maximal concentration of 1 mg diltiazem/mL. Diltiazem injection was found to be physically compatible and chemically stable in the following parenteral solutions for at least 24 hours when stored in glass or in polyvinylchloride (PVC) bags at a controlled room temperature of 15 to 30°C or under refrigeration at 2 to 8°C: Dextrose (5%) Injection, USP; Sodium Chloride (0.9%) Injection, USP; Dextrose (5%) and Sodium Chloride (0.45%) Injection, USP.

Because of potential physical incompatibilities, diltiazem injection should not be mixed with any other drugs in the same container.

Therefore, it is recommended that diltiazem injection not be coinfused in the same i.v. line.

Physical incompatibilities (precipitate formation or cloudiness) were observed when diltiazem injection was infused in the same i.v. line with the following drugs: acetazolamide, acyclovir, aminophylline, ampicillin, ampicillin sodium/sulbactam sodium, cefamandole, cefoperazone, diazepam, furosemide, hydrocortisone sodium succinate, insulin (regular; 100 units/mL), methylprednisolone sodium succinate, mezlocillin, nafcillin, phenytoin, rifampin, and sodium bicarbonate.

Parenteral drug products should be inspected visually for particulate matter and discoloration prior to administration, whenever solution and container permit.

Transition to Further Antiarrhythmic Therapy: Experience in the use of antiarrhythmic agents following diltiazem injection is limited. In controlled clinical trials, therapy with antiarrhythmic agents to maintain reduced heart rate in atrial fibrillation or atrial flutter, or for prophylaxis of paroxysmal supraventricular tachycardia was generally started within 3 hours after bolus administration. Patients should be dosed on an individual basis and reference should be made to the respective manufacturer's product monograph for information relative to dosage and administration of antiarrhythmic agents.

Supplied: Each mL contains: diltiazem HCl 5 mg. Nonmedicinal ingredients: citric acid monohydrate, sodium citrate dihydrate, sorbitol solution and water for injection up to 1 mL. Sodium hydroxide and/or hydrochloric acid may be used for pH adjustment. Preservative-free. Vials of 5 mL, cartons of 10. Vials of 10 mL, cartons of 10.

Store under refrigeration, at 2 to 8°C. Do not freeze. It may be stored at room temperature for up to 1 month. Destroy after 1 month at room temperature.

Dilution for Continuous I.V. Infusion: To prepare diltiazem for continuous i.v. infusion, refer to Dosage section for diluent volumes, compatibility with i.v. fluids and stability of dilutions.

I.V. admixtures should be inspected visually for clarity, particulate matter, precipitate, discoloration and leakage prior to administration whenever solution and container permit.

Reviewed 1998

DILUSOL®

Dermtek

Ethyl Alcohol

Topical Vehicle

Supplied: Each 45 mL polyethylene bottle with a controlled flow applicator filter contains: a transparent unscented liquid formulated with ethyl alcohol 38.7% (w/v), isopropyl alcohol, propylene glycol and laureth-4.

DIMENHYDRINATE INJECTION

Astra

Antiemetic

Pharmacology: While the precise mode of action of dimenhydrinate is not known, it has a depressant action on hyperstimulated labyrinthine functions or associated neural pathways.

Indications: Prevention and relief of motion sickness and the nausea or vomiting incident to these conditions. The treatment or prophylaxis of the nausea and vomiting of radiation sickness, postoperative vomiting, and drug-induced nausea and vomiting; also for the symptomatic treatment of nausea, vomiting and vertigo due to Ménière's disease and other labyrinthine disturbances.

Warnings: Antiemetics must be used with caution since they may mask the presence of underlying organic abnormalities or the toxic effects of certain antibiotics and other drugs, particularly those drugs causing ototoxicity.

Occupational Hazards: Patients receiving dimenhydrinate should be cautioned against operating automobiles or dangerous machinery because of the drowsiness associated with the drug. If drowsiness is excessive, dosage should be reduced.

Precautions: Rarely, prolonged therapy with antihistaminic drugs can produce blood dyscrasia.

Dimenhydrinate should be used with caution in patients in whom anticholinergics may aggravate other clinical conditions.

An additive effect may be produced if alcohol or other CNS depressant drugs are given concomitantly with dimenhydrinate.

Pregnancy: The use of dimenhydrinate by women who are pregnant or may become pregnant requires that the potential benefits be weighed against the potential hazards.

Adverse Effects: Drowsiness may be experienced by some patients, especially at high dosages. Dizziness may also occur. Symptoms of dry mouth, lassitude, excitement and nausea have been reported.

Overdose: Symptoms: Drowsiness is the usual clinical side effect. Convulsions, coma and respiratory depression may occur with massive overdosage.

Children are very susceptible to the convulsant action of antihistamines and doses of 150 to 800 mg of diphenhydramine in children aged 1½ to 3½ have been reported to produce convulsions. A suspected dose of 700 mg of dimenhydrinate produced death in a 22-month-old boy and a dose greater than 800 mg directly caused death in a 2-year-old boy. There has been a report of hallucinations after ingesting 500 mg of diphenhydramine HCl, as well as a few reports of delirium and hallucinations following the ingestion of approximately 750 mg of dimenhydrinate. A single case of severe delirium, closely resembling atropine poisoning and with possible extrapyramidal symptoms, following ingestion of a massive overdose of dimenhydrinate taken by an 18-year-old man has been reported.

Treatment: No specific antidote. Cautiously administer short-acting barbiturates, or other anticonvulsants i.m. or i.v. if convulsions occur. Other treatment is supportive and resuscitative.

Dosage: Adults: Nausea or vomiting may be expected to be controlled for approximately 4 hours with 25 to 50 mg of dimenhydrinate, and prevented by a similar dose every 4 hours. This dosage regimen may cause some degree of drowsiness in some patients and 100 mg every 4 hours may be given in conditions in which drowsiness is not objectionable or is even desirable.

I.M.: 1 to 2 mL (50 to 100 mg) of the 50 mg/mL solution are injected every 4 hours as needed.

I.V.: The 10 mg/mL injection should be given slowly. The preparation designed for i.m. use (50 mg/mL) must not be used i.v. unless it has been diluted at least 1:10 with a compatible i.v. solution, such as Sodium Chloride Injection USP. The maximum daily dose should not exceed 300 mg for adults.

Children: I.M.: 6 to 8 years: 12.5 to 25 mg, 2 or 3 times daily; 8 to 12 years: 25 mg to 50 mg, 2 or 3 times daily; over 12 years: 50 mg, 2 or 3 times daily.

I.V.: The i.v. dose in children has not been established.

Dimenhydrinate should not be given parenterally to neonates.

Supplied: 10 mg/mL Injection: Each mL of solution contains: dimenhydrinate 10 mg in water for injection, ethanol and HCl to adjust to pH 6.4 to 7.2. Polyamp Duofit units of 5 mL for i.v. use.

50 mg/mL Injection: Each mL of solution contains: dimenhydrinate USP 50 mg in a mixture of propylene glycol and water for injection and HCl to adjust to pH 6.4 to 7.2. Polyamp Duofit units of 1 mL for i.m. and, when appropriately diluted, i.v. use.

Substances which are physically incompatible with injectable solutions of dimenhydrinate include: phenothiazine derivatives, aminophylline, ammonium chloride, sodium amobarbital, diphenylhydantoin, heparin, hydrocortisone sodium succinate, pentobarbital, phenobarbital, thiopental and certain antibiotics, e.g. tetracycline HCl.

Do not use if solution is cloudy or contains a precipitate.

Store at controlled room temperature 15 to 30°C. Protect from freezing.

DIMENHYDRINATE INJECTION

Bioniche

Antiemetic

Supplied: Each mL of sterile solution contains: dimenhydrinate 50 mg in a mixture of propylene glycol (50%) and water for injection. Ampuls of 1 mL for i.m. and, when appropriately diluted, i.v. use. Boxes of 10. Store at room temperature (15 to 30°C). Protect from freezing.

DIMETANE®

Whitehall-Robins

Brompheniramine Maleate

Antihistamine

Indications: Prevention and symptomatic relief of manifestations of allergic states such as hay fever, conjunctivitis, angioneurotic edema, pruritus, rhinitis, atopic eczema, urticaria, dermatitis, drug reaction, rhus dermatitis, insect and spider bites.

Contraindications: Hypersensitivity to antihistamines and patients receiving MAO inhibitors.

Precautions: Occupational Hazards: Patients should be cautioned not to operate vehicles or hazardous machinery until their response to the drug has been determined.

Caution recommended for patients with glaucoma, chronic lung disease, prostate enlargement and bladder neck obstruction and in pregnancy or lactation.

Since the depressant effects of antihistamines are additive to those of other drugs affecting the CNS, patients should be cautioned against drinking alcoholic beverages or taking hypnotics, sedatives, psychotherapeutic agents or other drugs with CNS depressant effects during antihistaminic therapy.

Adverse Effects: Hypersensitivity reactions including skin rashes, urticaria, hypotension and thrombocytopenia have been reported on rare occasions. Drowsiness, lassitude, nausea, giddiness, dryness of the mouth, mydriasis, increased irritability or excitement may be encountered.

Overdose: Symptoms and Treatment: No specific therapy. Treatment should be symptomatic and supportive.
Tablets: Gastric lavage may be tried in an effort to remove disintegrated portions of tablets.

Dosage: Adults: 4 mg every 4 to 6 hours. Children 6 to 12 years: 2 mg every 4 to 6 hours. Children under 6 years: Consult a physician.

Supplied: Each compressed, peach-colored tablet, with a bisect line, monogrammed "W-R", contains: brompheniramine maleate 4 mg. Nonmedicinal ingredients: calcium phosphate, cornstarch, D&C Yellow No. 10, FD&C Yellow No. 6, lactose, magnesium stearate and polyethylene glycol. Energy: 3.26 kJ (0.78 kcal). Boxes of 24.

DIMETANE® EXPECTORANT

Whitehall-Robins

Brompheniramine Maleate—Guaifenesin—Phenylephrine HCl—Phenylpropanolamine HCl

Antihistamine—Expectorant—Decongestant

Indications: For the temporary relief of coughing and the complications of allergy states, including perennial and seasonal allergic rhinitis. In addition, indicated for the symptomatic relief of cough, nasal congestion and runny nose accompanying the common cold and other respiratory tract infections.

Contraindications: Hypersensitivity to any of the components; patients receiving MAO inhibitors.

Precautions: Before prescribing medication to suppress or modify cough, it is important to ascertain that the underlying cause of the cough is identified, that modification of the cough does not increase the risk of clinical or physiologic complications, and that appropriate therapy for the primary disease is provided.

Administer with caution to patients with cardiac or peripheral vascular disease, glaucoma, hyperthyroidism, diabetes mellitus or hypertension, chronic lung disease or shortness of breath, prostate enlargement and bladder neck obstruction and in pregnancy or lactation.
Occupational Hazards: Patients should be cautioned not to operate vehicles or hazardous machinery until their response to the drug has been determined. Since the depressant effects of antihistamines are additive to those of other drugs affecting the CNS, patients should be cautioned against drinking alcoholic beverages or taking hypnotics, sedatives, psychotherapeutic agents or other drugs with CNS depressant effects during antihistaminic therapy.

Guaifenesin has been shown to produce a color interference with certain clinical laboratory determinations of 5-hydroxyindoleacetic acid (5-HIAA) and vanillylmandelic acid (VMA).

Adverse Effects: Hypersensitivity reactions to brompheniramine maleate, including skin rashes, urticaria, hypotension and thrombocytopenia may occur rarely. Drowsiness, lassitude, nausea, giddiness, dryness of the mouth, mydriasis, increased irritability or excitement may be encountered.

Overdose: Symptoms and Treatment: No specific therapy. Treatment should be symptomatic and supportive.

Dosage: Adults: 5 to 10 mL 4 times a day. Children 6 to 12 years: 2.5 to 5 mL 3 or 4 times a day. Children under 6 years: Consult a physician.

Supplied: Each 5 mL of pale red liquid, menthol and raspberry taste and odor, contains: brompheniramine maleate 2 mg, guaifenesin 100 mg, phenylephrine HCl 5 mg and phenylpropanolamine HCl 5 mg. Nonmedicinal ingredients: alcohol, caramel color, citric acid, flavors, FD&C Red No. 40, glycerin, invert sugar, sodium benzoate, water. Energy: 15.27 kJ (3.65 kcal). Sodium: <1 mmol (0.8 mg). Bottles of 100 mL and 250 mL.

DIMETANE® EXPECTORANT-C Ⓝ
DIMETANE® EXPECTORANT-DC Ⓝ

Whitehall-Robins

Brompheniramine Maleate—Phenylephrine HCl—Phenylpropanolamine HCl—Guaifenesin—Codeine Phosphate

Brompheniramine Maleate—Phenylephrine HCl—Phenylpropanolamine HCl—Guaifenesin—Hydrocodone Bitartrate

Antihistamine—Decongestant—Expectorant—Antitussive

Indications: The temporary relief of coughing and the complications of allergic states including manifestations such as perennial and seasonal allergic rhinitis. The symptomatic relief of cough, nasal stuffiness and rhinitis accompanying the common cold and other upper respiratory tract infections.

Contraindications: Hypersensitivity to any of the ingredients and patients receiving MAO inhibitors. Should not be used to treat lower respiratory tract symptoms including asthma.

Precautions: Before prescribing medication to suppress or modify cough, it is important to ascertain that the underlying cause of the cough is identified, that modification of the cough does not increase the risk of clinical or physiologic complications, and that appropriate therapy for the primary disease is provided.

Administer with caution to patients with cardiac or peripheral vascular disease, glaucoma, hyperthyroidism, diabetes mellitus or hypertension, chronic lung disease or shortness of breath, prostate enlargement and bladder neck obstruction and in pregnancy or lactation.
Occupational Hazards: Patients should be cautioned not to operate vehicles or hazardous machinery until their response to the drug has been determined. Since the depressant effects of antihistamines are additive to those of other drugs affecting the CNS, patients should be cautioned against drinking alcoholic beverages or taking hypnotics, sedatives, psychotherapeutic agents or other drugs with CNS depressant effects during antihistaminic therapy.

Guaifenesin has been shown to produce a color interference with certain clinical laboratory determinations of 5-hydroxyindoleacetic acid (5-HIAA) and vanillylmandelic acid (VMA).
Dimetane Expectorant-DC: In young children the respiratory centre is especially susceptible to the depressant action of narcotic cough suppressants. Benefit-to-risk ratio should be carefully considered especially in children with respiratory embarrassment, e.g., croup. Estimation of dosage relative to the child's age and weight is of great importance.
Pregnancy: Since hydrocodone crosses the placental barrier, its use in pregnancy is not recommended.

As hydrocodone may inhibit peristalsis, patients with chronic constipation should be given Dimetane Expectorant-DC only after weighing the potential therapeutic benefit against the hazards involved.

Dimetane Expectorant-C contains codeine—may produce drug dependence.

Dimetane Expectorant-DC contains hydrocodone—may be habit forming.

Adverse Effects: Hypersensitivity reactions to brompheniramine maleate, including skin rashes, urticaria, hypotension and thrombocytopenia may occur rarely. Drowsiness, lassitude, nausea, giddiness, dryness of the mouth, mydriasis, increased irritability or excitement may be encountered.

Overdose: Symptoms: May vary from CNS depression to stimulation. Stimulation is particularly likely in children as a result of antihistamine overdosage. Atropine-like signs and symptoms such as dry mouth, fixed, dilated pupils, flushing and gastrointestinal symptoms may also occur.

Treatment: If vomiting has not occurred spontaneously, the patient should be induced to vomit. This is best done by administering syrup of ipecac. Precautions against aspiration must be taken, especially in infants and children. If vomiting is unsuccessful, gastric lavage is indicated within 3 hours after ingestion and even later if large amounts of milk or cream were given beforehand. Emesis or lavage should be followed by the administration of activated charcoal. Stimulants should not be used. Vasopressors may be used to treat hypotension. Naloxone may be used to treat codeine or hydrocodone toxicity.

Dosage: Dimetane Expectorant-C: Adults: 5 to 10 mL every 6 hours. Children 6 to 12 years: 2.5 to 5 mL every 6 to 8 hours.

Dimetane Expectorant-DC: Adults: 5 to 10 mL every 6 hours. Children 6 to 12 years: 2.5 to 5 mL every 6 hours.

Supplied: Dimetane Expectorant-C: Each 5 mL of palatable, cherry-red liquid, menthol and raspberry taste and odor, contains: brompheniramine maleate 2 mg, phenylephrine HCl 5 mg, phenylpropanolamine HCl 5 mg, guaifenesin 100 mg and codeine phosphate 10 mg. Nonmedicinal ingredients: alcohol, citric acid, D&C Red No. 33, FD&C Red No. 40, flavors, glycerin, invert sugar, sodium benzoate and water. Energy: 15.3 kJ (3.65 kcal)/5 mL. Sodium: <1 mmol (0.8 mg). Bottles of 100 and 500 mL and 1 L.

Dimetane Expectorant-DC: Each 5 mL of cherry-red liquid, menthol and raspberry taste and odor, contains: hydrocodone bitartrate 1.8 mg, brompheniramine maleate 2 mg, phenylephrine HCl 5 mg, phenylpropanolamine HCl 5 mg and guaifenesin 100 mg. Nonmedicinal ingredients: alcohol, citric acid, D&C Red No. 33, FD&C Red No. 40, flavors, glycerin, invert sugar, sodium benzoate and water. Energy: 15.3 kJ (3.65 kcal)/5 mL. Sodium: <1 mmol (0.8 mg). Bottles of 100 and 500 mL and 1 L.

DIMETAPP®

Whitehall-Robins

Brompheniramine Maleate—Phenylephrine HCl—Phenylpropanolamine HCl

Antihistamine—Decongestant

Indications: Symptomatic relief of the allergic manifestations of respiratory illnesses such as the common cold, seasonal allergies, etc.

Contraindications: Hypersensitivity to antihistamines or sympathomimetic amines. Patients receiving MAO inhibitors.

Precautions: Administer with caution to patients with cardiac or peripheral vascular diseases, glaucoma, hyperthyroidism, chronic lung disease, diabetes mellitus or hypertension, prostate enlargement and bladder neck obstruction and in pregnancy or lactation.
Occupational Hazards: Patients should be cautioned not to operate vehicles or hazardous machinery until their response to the drug has been determined. Since the depressant effects of antihistamines are additive to those of other drugs affecting the CNS, patients should be cautioned against drinking alcoholic beverages or taking hypnotics, sedatives, psychotherapeutic agents or other drugs with CNS depressant effects during antihistaminic therapy.

Adverse Effects: Hypersensitivity reactions including skin rashes, urticaria, hypotension and thrombocytopenia have been reported on rare occasions. Drowsiness, lassitude, nausea, giddiness, mydriasis, dryness of the mouth, increased irritability or excitement may occur.

Overdose: Symptoms and Treatment: No specific therapy. Treatment should be symptomatic and supportive. **Extentabs** should be purged since they cannot be removed by gastric lavage.

Dosage: Adults and children over 12 years: 1 Extentab every 12 hours; 5 to 10 mL of liquid or 1 or 2 tablets every 6 to 8 hours.
Children: 4 to 12 years: 5 mL of liquid or 1 tablet every 6 to 8 hours; 2 to 4 years: 3.75 mL of liquid or one-half tablet every 6 to 8 hours; 7 months to 2 years: 2.5 mL of liquid every 6 to 8 hours; 1 to 6 months: 1.25 mL of liquid every 6 to 8 hours.

Supplied: Liquid: Each 5 mL of purple-colored, grape-flavored liquid contains: brompheniramine maleate 4 mg, phenylephrine HCl 5 mg, phenylpropanolamine HCl 5 mg. Nonmedicinal

Dimetapp (cont'd)

ingredients: citric acid, D&C Red No. 33, FD&C Blue No. 1, FD&C Red No. 40, flavors, propylene glycol, sodium benzoate, sorbitol and water. Energy: <1 kJ (0.05 kcal). Sodium: <1 mmol (0.8 mg). Alcohol- and sucrose-free. Bottles of 100 and 250 mL.

Extentabs: Each light blue, sugar-coated, extended action tablet, monogrammed "W-R" in black ink, contains: brompheniramine maleate 12 mg, phenylephrine HCl 15 mg and phenylpropanolamine HCl 15 mg. Nonmedicinal ingredients: acacia, calcium carbonate, calcium sulfate, cellulose, FD&C Blue No. 1, FD&C Blue No. 2, FD&C Red No. 40, FD&C Yellow No. 6, gelatin, guar gum, iron oxide, magnesium stearate, monoglycerides, pharmaceutical glaze, polyoxypropylene-polyoxyethylene, polysorbate, povidone, propylene glycol, silicon dioxide, stearic acid, sucrose, titanium dioxide, triacetin, wax, wheat flour and zein. Energy: 0.92 kJ (0.22 kcal). Bottles of 100. Boxes of 12, 20 and 30.

Tablets: Each peach-colored, scored, compressed tablet, engraved "W-R", contains: brompheniramine maleate 4 mg, phenylephrine HCl 5 mg and phenylpropanolamine HCl 5 mg. Nonmedicinal ingredients: cellulose, cornstarch, D&C Yellow No. 10, FD&C Red No. 40, FD&C Yellow No. 6 and magnesium stearate. Energy: <1 kJ (<0.06 kcal). Boxes of 24.

DIMETAPP® CHEWABLES
DIMETAPP® CLEAR
DIMETAPP® LIQUI-GELS®
DIMETAPP® QUICK DISSOLVE

Whitehall-Robins

Brompheniramine Maleate—Phenylpropanolamine HCl

Antihistamine—Decongestant

Indications: Symptomatic relief of the allergic manifestations of respiratory illnesses such as the common cold, seasonal allergies, etc.

Contraindications: Hypersensitivity to antihistamines or sympathomimetic amines. Patients receiving MAO inhibitors.

Precautions: Administer with caution to patients with cardiac or peripheral vascular diseases, glaucoma, hyperthyroidism, chronic lung disease, diabetes mellitus or hypertension, prostate enlargement and bladder neck obstruction and in pregnancy or lactation.

Occupational Hazards: Patients should be cautioned not to operate vehicles or hazardous machinery until their response to the drug has been determined. Since the depressant effects of antihistamines are additive to those of other drugs affecting the CNS, patients should be cautioned against drinking alcoholic beverages or taking hypnotics, sedatives, psychotherapeutic agents or other drugs with CNS depressant effects during antihistaminic therapy.

Adverse Effects: Hypersensitivity reactions including skin rashes, urticaria, hypotension and thrombocytopenia have been reported on rare occasions. Drowsiness, lassitude, nausea, giddiness, mydriasis, dryness of the mouth, increased irritability or excitement may occur.

Overdose: Symptoms and Treatment: No specific therapy. Treatment should be symptomatic and supportive.

Dosage: Dimetapp Chewables: Children 6 to 12 years: 2 chewable tablets every 4 hours. Children 2 to 6 years: 1 chewable tablet every 4 hours. Children under 2 years: Consult a physician.

Dimetapp Clear: Adults and children over 12 years: 10 mL every 4 to 6 hours. Children 6 to 12 years: 5 mL every 4 to 6 hours. Children 2 to 6 years: 2.5 mL every 4 to 6 hours. Children under 2 years: As advised by a physician.

Dimetapp Liqui-Gels: Adults and children over 12 years: 1 liqui-gel every 4 hours. Not recommended for children under 12 years.

Dimetapp Quick Dissolve Tablets: Children 6 to 12 years: 2 quick dissolve tablets every 4 hours. Children 2 to 6 years: 1 quick dissolve tablet every 4 hours. Children under 2 years: Consult a physician.

Supplied: Dimetapp Chewables: Each purple, grape-flavored, scored tablet, engraved "AHR 2290", contains: brompheniramine maleate 1 mg and phenylpropanolamine HCl 6.25 mg. Nonmedicinal ingredients: aspartame, cellulose, citric acid, crospovidone, D&C Red No. 7, D&C Red No. 30, FD&C Blue No. 1, flavor, glycine, magnesium stearate, mannitol, pregelatinized starch, silicone dioxide, sorbitol and stearic acid. Energy: 2.5 kJ (0.60 kcal). Sodium-free. Boxes of 12 and 24.

Dimetapp Clear: Each 5 mL of clear liquid contains: brompheniramine maleate 2 mg and phenylpropanolamine HCl 12.5 mg. Nonmedicinal ingredients: citric acid, sodium benzoate, sorbitol and water. Energy: 0.42 kJ (0.10 kcal)/5 mL. Sodium: <1 mmol (0.8 mg). Bottles of 100 mL.

Dimetapp Liqui-Gels: Each red, transparent, liquid-filled, gelatin capsule, printed "AHR 2255I", contains: brompheniramine maleate 4 mg and phenylpropanolamine HCl 25 mg. Nonmedicinal ingredients: D&C Red No. 33, gelatin, glycerin, pharmaceutical glaze, polyethylene/propylene glycol, povidone, propylene glycol, sorbitol, titanium dioxide and water. Energy: 2.5 kJ (0.6 kcal). Boxes of 12 and 24.

Liqui-Gels is a registered trademark of R.P. Scherer International Corporation.

Dimetapp Quick Dissolve Tablets: Each purple, grape-flavored, freeze-dried, scored tablet, engraved "D", contains: brompheniramine maleate 1 mg and phenylpropanolamine HCl 6.25 mg. Nonmedicinal ingredients: aspartame, FD&C Blue No. 2, FD&C Red No. 40, flavors, gelatin, glycine and mannitol. Energy: 0.42 kJ (0.1 kcal). Boxes of 10 and 20.

Store at room temperature (15 to 30°C).

DIMETAPP® COUGH & COLD LIQUI-GELS®

Whitehall-Robins

Brompheniramine Maleate—Dextromethorphan HBr—Phenylpropanolamine HCl

Antihistamine—Cough Suppressant—Nasal Decongestant

Indications: For the symptomatic relief of runny nose, watery eyes and sneezing, urge to cough and nasal congestion due to colds and allergies.

Contraindications: Hypersensitivity to any of the ingredients and patients receiving MAO inhibitors.

Precautions: Administer with caution to patients with cardiac or peripheral vascular diseases, glaucoma, hyperthyroidism, diabetes mellitus or hypertension, chronic lung disease, shortness of breath or asthma, prostate enlargement, or bladder neck obstruction and in pregnancy and lactation.

Occupational Hazards: Patients should be cautioned not to operate vehicles or hazardous machinery until their response to the drug has been determined. Since the depressant effects of antihistamines are additive to those of other drugs affecting the CNS, patients should be cautioned against drinking alcoholic beverages or taking hypnotics, sedatives, psychotherapeutic agents or other drugs with CNS depressant effects during antihistaminic therapy.

Adverse Effects: Hypersensitivity reactions including skin rashes, urticaria, hypotension, and thrombocytopenia have been reported on rare occasions. Drowsiness, nausea, dryness of the mouth, increased irritability or excitement may occur.

Overdose: Symptoms and Treatment: No specific therapy. Treatment should be symptomatic and supportive.

Dosage: Adults and children over 12 years: Administer 1 Liqui-Gel every 4 hours. Do not exceed 6 Liqui-Gels/day.

Supplied: Each reddish orange, transparent, liquid filled, gelatin capsule, printed "AHR 2279", contains: brompheniramine maleate 4 mg, dextromethorphan HBr 20 mg and phenylpropanolamine HCl 25 mg. Nonmedicinal ingredients: FD&C red No. 40, gelatin, glycerin, pharmaceutical glaze, polyethylene glycol, povidone, propylene glycol, sorbitol, titanium dioxide and water. Energy: 2.5 kJ (0.6 kcal). Sodium-free. Boxes of 24.

Reviewed 1998

DIMETAPP®-A SINUS

Whitehall-Robins

Acetaminophen—Phenylephrine HCl—Phenylpropanolamine HCl

Analgesic—Decongestant

Indications: Control of nasal and sinus congestion, of pain associated with the common cold and sinusitis.

Contraindications: Hypersensitivity to any of the components and patients receiving MAO inhibitors.

Precautions: Do not exceed the recommended dosage. Caution is recommended for patients with hyperthyroidism, heart disease, hypertension, glaucoma, diabetes, prostate enlargement, bladder neck obstruction, liver or kidney disease, chronic alcoholism, or in pregnancy or lactation.

Overdose: Symptoms: Nausea, vomiting, weakness usually occur. Some patients may exhibit few or none of these early symptoms. In case of suspected overdose, antidotal therapy should begin as soon as possible.

Treatment: Supportive measures such as control of respiration, fluid and electrolyte balance. Acetylcysteine, is an antidote for acetaminophen and should be administered.

Dosage: Adults: 1 to 2 tablets every 4 to 6 hours. Not to exceed 8 tablets daily.

Supplied: Each light blue, scored tablet, engraved "W-R" contains: phenylephrine HCl 5 mg, phenylpropanolamine HCl 5 mg and acetaminophen 325 mg. Nonmedicinal ingredients: cellulose, cornstarch, FD&C Blue No. 1, magnesium stearate, povidone and stearic acid. Energy: <1 kJ (0.1 kcal). Blister packages of 24.

DIMETAPP®-C Ⓝ

Whitehall-Robins

Brompheniramine Maleate—Codeine Phosphate—Phenylephrine HCl—Phenylpropanolamine HCl

Antihistamine—Cough Suppressant—Decongestant

Indications: For the symptomatic relief of coughing, nasal congestion, runny nose, sneezing and lacrimation accompanying the common cold and other upper respiratory infections.

Contraindications: Hypersensitivity to any of the ingredients, marked hypertension and in patients receiving MAO inhibitors.

Precautions: Administer with caution to patients with cardiac or peripheral vascular disease, glaucoma, hypertension, hyperthyroidism, bladder neck obstruction, diabetes, chronic lung disease, or shortness of breath and in pregnancy or lactation.

Occupational Hazards: Until the drowsiness potential has been determined, the patient should be cautioned against engaging in operations requiring alertness.

Adverse Effects: Drowsiness, lassitude, nausea, giddiness, dryness of the mouth, mydriasis, increased irritability or excitement may be encountered rarely. Codeine may produce drug dependence and therefore has the potential for being abused.

Dosage: Administer every 4 hours, not to exceed 6 doses in a 24-hour period.

Adults: 2 teaspoonfuls (10 mL).

Supplied: Each 5 mL of light blue-colored, grape-flavored syrup contains: brompheniramine maleate 2 mg, phenylpropanolamine hydrochloride 5 mg, phenylephrine hydrochloride 5 mg and codeine phosphate 10 mg. Nonmedicinal ingredients: citric acid, flavors, FD&C Blue No. 1, FD&C Red No. 40, propylene glycol, sodium benzoate, sodium saccharin, sorbitol and water. Energy: 0.23 kJ (0.054 kcal/5 mL). Sodium: <1 mmol (1.06 mg)/5 mL. Alcohol- and sucrose-free. Bottles of 100 mL, 500 mL and 1 L.

DIMETAPP®-DM

Whitehall-Robins

Brompheniramine Maleate—Dextromethorphan HBr—Phenylephrine HCl—Phenylpropanolamine HCl

Antihistamine—Antitussive—Decongestant

Indications: Symptomatic treatment of allergic manifestations of cough, nasal congestion, runny nose accompanying colds and other upper respiratory infections.

Contraindications: Hypersensitivity to any of the components. Marked hypertension. Do not administer to patients receiving MAO inhibitors.

Pregnancy: Safe use during pregnancy has not been established.

Precautions: Use with care in patients with cardiac or peripheral vascular diseases, hyperthyroidism, glaucoma, diabetes mellitus or hypertension, prostatic enlargement or bladder neck obstruction, chronic lung disease, shortness of breath or asthma, and in pregnancy or lactation.

Occupational Hazards: Patients should be cautioned not to operate vehicles or hazardous machinery until their response to the drug has been determined. Since the depressant effects of antihistamines are additive to those of other drugs affecting the CNS, patients should be cautioned against drinking alcoholic beverages or taking hypnotics, sedatives, psychotherapeutic agents or other drugs with CNS depressant effects during antihistaminic therapy.

Adverse Effects: Hypersensitivity reactions including skin rashes, urticaria, hypotension and thrombocytopenia have been reported as adverse effects to brompheniramine maleate. Drowsiness, lassitude, nausea, giddiness, dryness of the mouth, mydriasis, increased irritability or excitement may be encountered. These occur rarely, however, and are reversible upon reduction of dosage or withdrawal of the drug.

Overdose: Symptoms and Treatment: May vary from CNS depression to stimulation. Stimulation is particularly likely in children as a result of antihistamine overdosage. Atropine like signs and symptoms such as dry mouth; fixed, dilated pupils; flushing and gastrointestinal symptoms may occur. Treatment should be symptomatic and supportive.

Dosage: Tablets: Adults: 1 or 2 tablets every 6 to 8 hours. Children: 6 to 12 years: 1 tablet every 6 to 8 hours; 2 to 6 years: ½ tablet every 6 to 8 hours. Children under 2: as prescribed by a physician.

Liquid: Adults: 1 to 2 teaspoonfuls (5 to 10 mL) every 6 to 8 hours. Children: 6 to 12 years: 1 teaspoonful (5 mL) every 6 to 8 hours; 2 to 6 years: ½ teaspoonful (2.5 mL) every 6 to 8 hours. Children under 2: as prescribed by a physician.

Supplied: Tablets: Each pale green, scored, compressed tablet, engraved "W-R", contains: brompheniramine maleate 4 mg, phenylephrine HCl 5 mg, phenylpropanolamine HCl 5 mg and dextromethorphan HBr 15 mg. Nonmedicinal ingredients: cellulose, cornstarch, D&C Yellow No. 10, FD&C Blue No. 1, magnesium stearate. Energy: 0.42 kJ (0.1 kcal). Boxes of 18.

Liquid: Each 5 mL of red, cherry-vanilla flavored liquid contains: brompheniramine maleate 4 mg, phenylephrine HCl 5 mg, phenylpropanolamine HCl 5 mg and dextromethorphan HBr 15 mg. Nonmedicinal ingredients: citric acid, D&C red No. 33, FD&C red No. 40, flavors, propylene glycol, sodium benzoate, sodium cyclamate, sorbitol and water. Energy: 0.23 kJ (0.06 kcal/5 mL). Alcohol- and sucrose-free. Bottles of 100 and 250 mL.

DIMETAPP® ORAL INFANT DROPS
Whitehall-Robins

Brompheniramine Maleate—Phenylephrine HCl—Phenylpropanolamine HCl

Antihistamine—Decongestant

Indications: For the symptomatic relief of the allergic manifestations of seasonal allergies and the common cold.

Contraindications: Hypersensitivity to any of the ingredients and patients receiving MAO inhibitors.

Precautions: May cause drowsiness or excitability in some children.

Adverse Effects: Hypersensitivity reactions including skin rashes and urticaria have been reported on rare occasions. Dryness of the mouth and increased irritability or excitement may be encountered.

Also, see Dimetapp monograph.

Dosage: Administer every 6 to 8 hours. Infants: As indicated by a physician. 5 kg: 0.5 mL/dose. 7.5 kg: 0.75 mL/dose. 10 kg: 1.0 mL/dose. Children: (2 to 4 years): 1.5 mL/dose.

Supplied: Each mL of grape-flavored, red-colored liquid, with enclosed calibrated dropper (0.5, 0.75, 1 and 1.5 mL), contains: brompheniramine maleate 2 mg, phenylephrine HCl 2.5 mg and phenylpropanolamine HCl 2.5 mg. Nonmedicinal ingredients: citric acid, D&C red No. 33, FD&C red No. 40, flavors, propylene glycol, sodium benzoate, sodium saccharin, sorbitol and water. Energy: 0.23 kJ (0.05 kcal)/5 mL. Sodium: <1 mmol (1.1 mg)/5 mL. Alcohol- and sucrose-free. Bottles of 50 mL.

DIOCAINE
Dioptic

Proparacaine HCl

Ophthalmic Anesthetic

Supplied: Each mL of sterile solution contains: proparacaine HCl 0.5%. Nonmedicinal ingredients: benzalkonium chloride, glycerin and purified water. Plastic dropper bottles of 15 mL. Refrigerate (2 to 8°C) before and after opening. Do not use if solution is colored.

DIOCARPINE Ⓟ
Dioptic

Pilocarpine HCl

Miotic—Cholinergic

Supplied: Each mL of sterile, ophthalmic solution contains: pilocarpine HCl 1%, 2% or 4%. Nonmedicinal ingredients: benzalkonium chloride, boric acid, hydrochloric acid and/or sodium hydroxide to adjust pH, hydroxypropyl methylcellulose, purified water, sodium chloride (present in 1% solution only) and sodium citrate. Plastic dropper bottles of 15 mL. Keep bottle tightly closed when not in use. Store at controlled room temperature (15 to 30°C). Protect from light.

DIOCHLORAM Ⓟ
Dioptic

Chloramphenicol

Ophthalmic Antibiotic

Supplied: Each mL of sterile solution contains: chloramphenicol 0.5%. Nonmedicinal ingredients: chlorobutanol anhydrous, polyethylene glycol 300, polyoxyl 40 stearate and purified water. Plastic dropper bottles of 10 and 15 mL. Refrigerate until dispensed. After dispensing the solution may be kept at room temperature for up to 21 days.

DIODEX Ⓟ
Dioptic

Dexamethasone Sodium Phosphate

Corticosteroid

Supplied: Each mL of sterile ophthalmic solution contains: dexamethasone sodium phosphate 0.1%. Nonmedicinal ingredients: benzalkonium chloride, dibasic sodium phosphate, disodium edetate, monobasic sodium phosphate, sodium chloride and water for injection. Plastic dropper bottles of 5 mL. Store at 15 to 30°C.

DIODOQUIN® Ⓟ
Glenwood

Iodoquinol

Amebicide

Pharmacology: Iodoquinol is amebicidal against E. histolytica, D. fragilis and G. lamblia and is considered effective against the trophozoite and cyst forms.

Indications: In the treatment of intestinal amebiasis.

Contraindications: Hypersensitivity to any 8-hydroxy-quinoline or iodine-containing preparations, hepatic damage and pre-existing optic neuropathy.

Warnings: Optic neuritis, optic atrophy, and peripheral neuropathy have been reported following prolonged high dosage therapy with halogenated 8-hydroxyquinolines. Long-term use of this drug should be avoided.

Pregnancy and *Lactation:* Safety for use in pregnancy or during lactation has not been established.

Precautions: Iodoquinol should be used with caution in patients with thyroid disease.

Protein-bound serum iodine levels may be increased during treatment with iodoquinol and therefore interfere with certain thyroid function tests. These effects may persist for as long as 6 months after discontinuation of therapy. Discontinue the drug if hypersensitivity reactions occur.

Adverse Effects: Skin: various forms of skin eruptions (acneiform papular and pustular; bullae; vegetating or tuberots iododerma), urticaria and pruritus.

Gastrointestinal: nausea, vomiting, abdominal cramps, diarrhea, and pruritus ani.

Fever, chills, headache, vertigo, and enlargement of thyroid have been reported. Optic neuritis, optic atrophy and peripheral neuropathy have been reported in association with prolonged high dosage 0 hydroxyquinoline therapy.

Dosage: 210 mg: Usual adult dose: 3 tablets 3 times daily, after meals for 20 days. Children 6 to 12 years: 2 tablets t.i.d. Children under 6: 1 tablet/6.8 kg of body weight, divided into 3 daily doses for 20 days.

650 mg: Usual adult dose: 1 tablet 3 times a day for 20 days, to be taken after meals. Children: For 20 days, 40 mg/kg of body weight daily divided into 3 doses, not to exceed 1.95 g in 24 hours, for 20 days.

Supplied: Each tablet contains: iodoquinol USP 210 or 650 mg. Nonmedicinal ingredients: colloidal silicon dioxide NF, croscarmellose sodium NF, lactose anhydrous NF, magnesium stearate NF, microcrystalline cellulose NF and povidone USP. Bottles of 60. Store at controlled room temperature 15 to 30°C.

DIOFLUOR® INJECTION
Dioptic

Fluorescein Sodium

Ophthalmic Diagnostic

Supplied: Each mL of sterile, injectable solution contains: fluorescein (as fluorescein sodium) 10% or 25%, sodium hydroxide and/or hydrochloric acid to adjust pH and water for injection. Vials of 2 mL (25%). Vials of 5 mL (10%). Store at controlled room temperature (15 to 30°C).

DIOFLUOR STRIPS®
Dioptic

Fluorescein Sodium

Ophthalmic Diagnostic

Supplied: Each sterile, ophthalmic strip contains: fluorescein sodium 1 mg. Boxes of 200 individually wrapped strips.

DIOGENT Ointment Ⓟ
Dioptic

Gentamicin Sulfate

Topical Antibiotic

Supplied: Each g of ophthalmic ointment contains: gentamicin sulfate 5 mg equivalent to gentamicin 3 mg (0.3%). Nonmedicinal ingredients: methylparaben, mineral oil, propylparaben and white petrolatum. Tubes of 3.5 g with applicator tip. Store at 15 to 30°C.

DIOGENT Solution Ⓟ
Dioptic

Gentamicin Sulfate

Topical Antibiotic

Supplied: Each mL of sterile, buffered, isotonic, ophthalmic solution (0.3%) contains: gentamicin sulfate USP 5 mg (equivalent to gentamicin 3 mg). Nonmedicinal ingredients: benzalkonium chloride, dibasic sodium phosphate, monobasic sodium phosphate and purified water. Plastic dropper bottles of 5 mL. Store at 15 to 30°C.

DIOMYCIN Ⓟ
Dioptic

Erythromycin

Ophthalmic Antibiotic

Supplied: Each g of sterile ointment contains: erythromycin base 5 mg in a petrolatum base. Nonmedicinal ingredients: mineral oil and petrolatum. Collapsible tubes of 3.5 g.

DIONEPHRINE
Dioptic

Phenylephrine HCl

Vasoconstrictor—Mydriatic

Supplied: Each mL of sterile solution contains: phenylephrine HCl 2.5%. Nonmedicinal ingredients: boric acid, benzalkonium chloride, dibasic sodium phosphate anhydrous, monobasic sodium phosphate and purified water. Phosphoric acid or sodium hydroxide may be used to adjust pH. Plastic dropper bottles of 5 and 15 mL. Refrigerate (2 to 8°C). Keep container tightly closed.

DIOPENTOLATE ℞
Dioptic

Cyclopentolate HCl

Mydriatic—Cycloplegic

Supplied: Each mL of sterile ophthalmic solution contains: cyclopentolate HCl 1%. Nonmedicinal ingredients: boric acid, benzalkonium chloride, potassium chloride, povidone, sodium carbonate anhydrous and purified water. Plastic dropper bottles of 15 mL. Store at controlled room temperature (15 to 30°C). Keep container tightly closed.

DIOPHENYL-T ℞
Dioptic

Phenylephrine HCl—Tropicamide

Mydriatic—Cycloplegic

Supplied: Each mL of sterile solution contains: phenylephrine HCl 5.0% and tropicamide 0.8%. Nonmedicinal ingredients: benzalkonium chloride, disodium edetate, purified water and sodium metabisulfite. Plastic dropper bottles of 15 mL. Refrigerate (2 to 8°C). Keep container tightly closed.

DIOPRED ℞
Dioptic

Prednisolone Acetate

Corticosteroid—Anti-inflammatory

Supplied: Each mL of sterile ophthalmic suspension contains: prednisolone acetate 1%. Nonmedicinal ingredients: boric acid, benzalkonium chloride, disodium edetate, hydroxypropyl methylcellulose, purified water, polysorbate 80, sodium bisulfite, sodium chloride and sodium citrate. Plastic dropper bottles of 5 and 10 mL. Store at controlled room temperature (15 to 30°C).

DIOPTIMYD ℞
Dioptic

Sodium Sulfacetamide—Prednisolone Acetate

Ophthalmic Antibacterial—Steroid

Supplied: Each mL of sterile suspension contains: sodium sulfacetamide 10% and prednisolone acetate 0.5%. Nonmedicinal ingredients: benzalkonium chloride, dibasic sodium phosphate, disodium edetate, hydroxypropyl methylcellulose, polysorbate 80, purified water, sodium phosphate monobasic and sodium thiosulfate. Plastic dropper bottles of 5 and 15 mL. Refrigerate (2 to 8°C). Protect from freezing. Keep container tightly closed.

DIOPTROL ℞
Dioptic

Dexamethasone—Neomycin—Polymyxin B

Antibiotic—Anti-inflammatory

Supplied: Each mL of sterile suspension contains: neomycin (as sulfate) 3.5 mg, polymyxin B sulfate 10 000 units and dexamethasone 1 mg. Nonmedicinal ingredients: benzalkonium chloride, hydrochloric acid and/or sodium hydroxide to adjust the pH, hydroxypropyl methylcellulose, polysorbate 20, sodium chloride and water for injection. Plastic dropper bottles of 5 mL. Store at controlled room temperature (15 to 30°C).

DIOSULF ℞
Dioptic

Sulfacetamide Sodium

Ophthalmic Antibacterial

Supplied: Each mL of sterile solution contains: sulfacetamide sodium USP 10% with polyvinyl alcohol. Nonmedicinal ingredients: monobasic sodium phosphate, methylparaben, propylparaben, purified water, polyvinyl alcohol and sodium thiosulfate. Plastic dropper bottles of 15 mL. Refrigerate (2 to 8°C). If the solution discolors on prolonged storage, discard.

DIOTROPE ℞
Dioptic

Tropicamide

Mydriatic—Cycloplegic

Supplied: Each mL of sterile ophthalmic solution contains: tropicamide 0.5% or 1.0%. Nonmedicinal ingredients: benzalkonium chloride, disodium edetate, purified water, sodium chloride and sodium hydroxide and/or hydrochloric acid for pH adjustment. Plastic dropper bottles of 15 mL. Store at controlled room temperature (15 to 30°C). Keep container tightly closed.

DIOVAN® ℞
Novartis Pharmaceuticals

Valsartan

Angiotensin II AT_1 Receptor Blocker

Pharmacology: Valsartan is an orally active angiotensin II AT_1 receptor blocker.

Valsartan acts selectively on AT_1, the receptor subtype that mediates the known cardiovascular actions of angiotensin II, the primary vaso-active hormone of the renin-angiotensin-system. The AT_2 receptor subtype, found in tissues such as brain, endometrium, myometrium and fetal kidney and adrenals, plays no known role in cardiovascular homeostasis to date. Valsartan does not exhibit any partial AT_1 receptor agonist activity and has essentially no activity at the AT_2 receptor. Valsartan does not bind to or block other hormone receptors or ion channels known to be important in cardiovascular regulation. The primary metabolite, valeryl 4-hydroxy valsartan, is essentially inactive.

Angiotensin II has a wide variety of physiological effects; many are either directly or indirectly involved in blood pressure regulation. A potent vasoconstrictor, angiotensin II exerts a direct pressor response. In addition, it promotes sodium retention and aldosterone secretion.

Blockade of angiotensin II AT_1 receptors results in 2- to 3-fold increase in plasma renin and angiotensin II plasma concentrations in hypertensive patients. Long-term effects of increased AT_2 receptor stimulation by angiotensin II are unknown.

Valsartan does not inhibit angiotensin converting enzyme (ACE), also known as kininase II, the enzyme that converts angiotensin I to angiotensin II and degrades bradykinin.

Pharmacokinetics: Since its pharmacokinetics are linear in the 80 to 320 mg dose range, valsartan does not accumulate appreciably in plasma following repeated administration. Plasma concentrations are similar in males and females.

The mean absolute bioavailability of valsartan is about 23%, but with high variability. Peak plasma concentration is reached 2 to 4 hours after dosing.

Giving valsartan with food reduces the area under the valsartan plasma concentration curve (AUC) by 48%. After about 8 hours however, plasma valsartan concentrations are similar in the fed and fasted state.

Valsartan is 94 to 97% bound to serum protein, mainly serum albumin. Steady-state volume of distribution is about 17 L, indicating that valsartan does not distribute into tissues extensively.

Following i.v. administration, valsartan shows biexponential decay kinetics ($t_{1/2}\alpha < 1$ hour and $t_{1/2}\beta$ between 5 to 9 hours). Plasma clearance is relatively slow (about 2 L/h) when compared with hepatic blood flow (about 30 L/h).

Following administration of an oral solution of ^{14}C labelled valsartan, 83% of absorbed valsartan is excreted in the feces and 13% in the urine, mainly as unchanged compound. Valsartan biotransformation does not seem to involve the cytochrome P450 system. The enzyme(s) responsible for valsartan metabolism have not been identified.

On average, patients with mild to moderate chronic liver disease have twice the exposure to valsartan of healthy volunteers as measured by AUC and C_{max} (see Precautions, Impaired Liver Function and Dosage).

Renal clearance accounts for only 30% of total plasma clearance. There is no apparent correlation between renal function and exposure to valsartan, as measured by AUC and C_{max}, in patients with different degrees of renal impairment. In patients with renal failure undergoing hemodialysis, limited information showed that exposure to valsartan is comparable to that in patients with creatinine clearance >10 mL/min.

Valsartan is not removed from plasma by dialysis.

Exposure to valsartan is about 50% higher as measured by AUC and C_{max} and the half life is longer in elderly subjects than in young subjects. However, this difference has not been shown to have any clinical significance.

Pharmacodynamics: Valsartan inhibits the pressor effect of an angiotensin II infusion. An oral dose of 80 mg inhibits the pressor effect by about 80% at peak with approximately 30% inhibition persisting for 24 hours.

After a single oral dose, the antihypertensive activity of valsartan has an onset within approximately 2 hours and peaks within 4 to 6 hours in most patients.

The antihypertensive effect of valsartan persists for 24 hours after dosing. Trough/peak ratio ranges from 0.54 to 0.76. Valsartan reduces blood pressure in hypertensive patients without affecting pulse rate.

During repeated dosing, the maximum blood pressure reduction with any dose is generally attained within 4 weeks, and is sustained during long-term therapy. Combinations with hydrochlorothiazide produce additional reduction in blood pressure.

There is no apparent rebound effect after abrupt withdrawal of valsartan therapy.

Although data available to date indicate a similar pharmacodynamic effect of valsartan in black and white hypertensive patients, this should be viewed with caution since antihypertensive drugs that affect the renin-angiotensin system, such as ACE inhibitors and angiotensin II AT_1 receptor blockers, have generally been found to be less effective in low-renin hypertensives (frequently blacks).

Indications: For the treatment of mild to moderate essential hypertension.

Valsartan may be administered alone, or concomitantly with thiazide diuretics.

Valsartan should normally be used in those patients in whom treatment with diuretic or beta-blocker was found ineffective or has been associated with unacceptable adverse effects. Valsartan can also be tried as an initial agent in those patients in whom the use of diuretics and/or beta-blockers is contraindicated or in patients with medical conditions in which these drugs frequently cause serious adverse effects.

The safety and efficacy of concurrent treatment with Valsartan and angiotensin converting enzyme inhibitors have not been established.

Contraindications: In patients who are hypersensitive to any component of this product (see Supplied).

Warnings: *Pregnancy:* Drugs that act directly on the renin-angiotensin system can cause fetal and neonatal morbidity and death when administered to pregnant women. When pregnancy is detected, valsartan should be discontinued as soon as possible.

The use of drugs that act directly on the renin-angiotensin system during the second and third trimesters of pregnancy has been associated with fetal and neonatal injury, including hypotension, neonatal skull hypoplasia, anuria, reversible or irreversible renal failure and death. Oligohydramnios has also been reported, presumably resulting from decreased fetal renal function; oligohydramnios in this setting has been associated with fetal limb contractures, craniofacial deformation and hypoplastic lung development. Prematurity, intrauterine growth retardation and patent ductus arteriosus have also been reported, although it is not clear whether these occurrences were due to exposure to the drug. These adverse effects do not appear to have resulted from intrauterine drug exposure that has been limited to the first trimester.

Mothers whose embryos and fetuses are exposed to an angiotensin II AT_1 receptor blocker only during the first trimester should be so informed. Nonetheless, when patients become pregnant, physicians should have the patient discontinue the use of valsartan as soon as possible.

Rarely (probably less than 1 in every 1 000 pregnancies), no alternative to angiotensin II AT_1 receptor blocker will be found. In these rare cases, the mothers should be apprised of the potential hazards to their fetuses and serial ultrasound examinations should be performed to assess intra-amniotic environment.

If oligohydramnios is observed, valsartan should be discontinued unless it is considered life-saving for the mother. Contraction stress testing (CST), a nonstress test (NST) or biophysical profiling (BPP) may be appropriate, depending upon the week of pregnancy. Patients and physicians should be aware, however, that oligohydramnios may not appear until after the fetus has sustained irreversible injury.

Infants with histories of in utero exposure to an angiotensin II AT_1 receptor blocker should be closely observed for hypotension, oliguria, and hyperkalemia. If oliguria occurs, attention should be directed toward support of blood pressure and renal perfusion. Exchange transfusion may be required as a means of reversing hypotension and/or substituting for impaired renal function. Valsartan is not removed from plasma by dialysis.

Animal Data: No teratogenic effects were observed when valsartan was administered orally to pregnant mice and rats at doses up to 600 mg/kg/day and to pregnant rabbits at oral doses up to 10 mg/kg/day. However, significant decreases in fetal weight, pup birth weight, pup survival rate and slight delays in developmental milestones were observed in studies in which parental rats were treated orally with valsartan at maternally toxic (reduction in body weight gain and food consumption) doses of 600 mg/kg/day during organogenesis or late gestation and lactation. In rabbits, fetotoxicity associated with maternal toxicity (mortality) was observed at doses of 5 and 10 mg/kg/day.

Hypotension: Occasionally, symptomatic hypotension has occurred after administration of valsartan, in some cases after the first dose. It is more likely to occur in patients who are volume-depleted by diuretic therapy, dietary salt restriction, dialysis, diarrhea, or vomiting. In these patients, because of the potential fall in blood pressure, therapy should be started under close medical supervision. Similar considerations apply to patients with ischemic heart or cerebrovascular disease, in whom an excessive fall in blood pressure could result in myocardial infarction or cerebrovascular accident.

Precautions: Renal Impairment: As a consequence of inhibiting the renin-angiotensin-aldosterone system, changes in renal function have been seen in susceptible individuals. In patients whose renal function may depend on the activity of the renin-angiotensin-aldosterone system, such as patients with bilateral renal artery stenosis, unilateral renal artery stenosis to a solitary kidney, or severe congestive heart failure, treatment with agents that inhibit this system has been associated with oliguria, progressive azotemia, and rarely, acute renal failure and/or death. In susceptible patients, concomitant diuretic use may further increase risk.

Use of valsartan should include appropriate assessment of renal function.

Impaired Liver Function: In general, no dosage adjustment is needed in patients with mild to moderate liver disease. However, care should be exercised in patients with liver disease, especially in those patients with biliary obstructive disorders, as the majority of valsartan is eliminated in the bile. No information is available in patients with severe liver disease (see Pharmacology, Pharmacokinetics).

Valvular Stenosis: There is concern on theoretical grounds that patients with aortic stenosis might be at a particular risk of decreased coronary perfusion, because they do not develop as much afterload reduction.

Lactation: It is not known whether valsartan is excreted in human milk but it was excreted in the milk of lactating rats. Because many drugs are excreted in human milk and because of their potential for affecting the nursing infant adversely, a decision should be made whether to discontinue nursing or discontinue the drug, taking into account the importance of the drug to the mother.

Children: The safety and effectiveness of valsartan in children have not been established.

Geriatrics: Of the 2 542 patients receiving valsartan monotherapy in placebo-controlled clinical trials, 31% were 65 years and older. No overall age-related differences were seen in the adverse effect profile but greater sensitivity in some older individuals cannot be ruled out.

Drug Interactions: Diuretics: Patients on diuretics, and especially those in whom diuretic therapy was recently instituted, may occasionally experience an excessive reduction in blood pressure after initiation of therapy with valsartan. The possibility of symptomatic hypotension with the use of valsartan can be minimized by discontinuing the diuretic prior to initiation of treatment (see Warnings—Hypotension and Dosage). No drug interaction of clinical significance has been identified with thiazide diuretics.

Agents Increasing Serum Potassium: Since valsartan decreases the production of aldosterone, potassium-sparing diuretics or potassium supplements should be given only for documented hypokalemia and with frequent monitoring of serum potassium. Potassium-containing salt substitutes should also be used with caution.

Lithium Salts: As with other drugs which eliminate sodium, lithium clearance may be reduced. Therefore, serum lithium levels should be monitored carefully if lithium salts are to be administered.

Warfarin: Coadministration of valsartan and warfarin over 3 days did not affect the bioavailability of valsartan. Coadministration had no effect on activated partial thromboplastin time (APTT) and resulted in a 12% increase in prothrombin time (PT).

Digoxin: A single dose of digoxin administered with a single dose of valsartan did not result in a clinically significant interaction. No steady-state data are available.

Adverse Effects: Valsartan has been evaluated for safety in over 4 300 patients treated for hypertension, including more than 600 treated for over 6 months and more than 330 for over 1 year. Of these, 3 634 were treated with valsartan monotherapy in controlled clinical trials.

In controlled clinical trials, discontinuation due to adverse effects occurred in 3.1 and 4.0% of patients treated with valsartan monotherapy and placebo, respectively.

The following potentially serious adverse reactions have been reported rarely with valsartan in controlled clinical trials: syncope, hypotension.

Table I is based on double-blind controlled trials in patients treated with valsartan monotherapy at doses of 80 to 160 mg/day. Table I includes all adverse effects with an incidence of 1% or greater in the valsartan treatment group, irrespective of causal relationship to study drug. No adverse effects appeared to have an incidence related to dose. Therefore, adverse effects are grouped irrespective of dose.

Table I—Diovan

Adverse Effects

Systems/Adverse Effects	Diovan N=2 827 (%)	Placebo N=1 007 (%)
CNS		
Headache	8.5	13.6
Dizziness	2.8	3.9
Respiratory		
Upper Respiratory Tract Infection	2.9	2.3
Coughing	2.7	1.3
Rhinitis	1.8	2.0
Sinusitis	1.5	1.7
Pharyngitis	1.3	0.7
Bronchitis	1.1	1.3
Digestive		
Diarrhea	2.5	1.6
Abdominal Pain	1.3	0.9
Nausea	1.5	2.2
Dyspepsia	1.1	1.8
Musculoskeletal		
Arthralgia	1.3	0.9
Back Pain	2.2	1.5
Body as a whole		
Fatigue	1.9	1.3
Other		
Viral Infection	3.1	2.6

In double-blind controlled trials, the following adverse events were reported with valsartan at an occurrence rate of less than 1% regardless of drug relationship: orthostatic effects, chest pain, palpitations, myalgia, asthenia, somnolence, vertigo, impotence, epistaxis, fibrocing alveolitis (1 case), allergic reactions, urticaria, pruritus and rash.

Other adverse reactions reported rarely in postmarketing use include: anaphylaxis (very rarely), angioedema (involving swelling of the face, lips and/or tongue), photosensitivity, increase in blood pressure and taste disorders.

Laboratory Findings: In controlled clinical trials, clinically important changes in standard laboratory parameters were rarely associated with administration of valsartan.

Liver Function Tests: In controlled clinical trials, elevations of AST and ALT occurred in 0.8 and 2% of patients treated with valsartan monotherapy compared to 0.0 and 2.0% of patients receiving placebo.

Serum Potassium: Greater than 20% increases in serum potassium were observed in 5% of valsartan treated patients compared to 3% of placebo treated patients. No patient treated with valsartan discontinued therapy due to hyperkalemia.

Creatinine: Minor elevations in creatinine occurred in 1.1% of patients treated with valsartan and 0.8% of patients given placebo in controlled clinical trials.

Hemoglobin and Hematocrit: In controlled clinical trials, greater than 20% decreases in hemoglobin and hematocrit were observed in 0.4% and 0.8%, respectively, of patients treated with valsartan compared with 0.1 and 0.1% of patients given placebo. One valsartan patient discontinued treatment for microcytic anemia.

Uric Acid: In placebo-controlled trials, elevations of uric acid levels (baseline vs terminal lab) occurred in 2.6% of patients receiving valsartan monotherapy, 8.2% receiving valsartan and hydrochlorothiazide, 6% receiving hydrochlorothiazide alone and 2.3% receiving placebo.

Neutropenia: Neutropenia was observed in 1.9% of patients treated with valsartan and 0.8% of patients treated with placebo.

In controlled clinical trials, thrombocytopenia was observed in 0.1% of patients.

Overdose: Symptoms and Treatment: Limited data are available in regard to overdosage with valsartan in humans. The most likely manifestations of overdosage would be hypotension and/or tachycardia. If symptomatic hypotension should occur, supportive treatment should be instituted.

Valsartan is not removed from the plasma by dialysis.

Dosage: Initiation of therapy requires consideration of recent antihypertensive drug treatment, the extent of blood pressure elevation, salt restriction, and other pertinent clinical factors (see Warnings, Hypotension). The dosage of antihypertensive agents used with valsartan may need to be adjusted.

The recommended dose is 80 mg once daily. The antihypertensive effect is present within 2 weeks and maximal reduction is usually attained within 4 weeks following initiation of therapy. In patients whose blood pressure is not adequately controlled, the daily dose may be increased to 160 mg or a thiazide diuretic added.

Valsartan should be administered consistently with or without food (see Pharmacology, Pharmacokinetics).

Hepatic Impairment: No initial dosage adjustment is required in patients with mild to moderate liver disease. Care should be exercised in patients with liver disease (see Pharmacology—Pharmacokinetics and Precautions—Impaired Liver Function).

Renal Impairment: No initial dosage adjustment is required for patients with renal impairment including those patients requiring hemodialysis. Appropriate monitoring of these patients is however recommended (see Pharmacology—Pharmacokinetics and Precautions—Renal Impairment).

Geriatrics: No dosage adjustment is usually necessary (see Precautions, Geriatrics).

Concomitant Diuretic Therapy: In patients receiving diuretics, valsartan therapy should be initiated with caution, since these patients may be volume-depleted and thus more likely to experience hypotension following initiation of additional antihypertensive therapy. Whenever possible, all diuretics should be discontinued 2 to 3 days prior to the administration of valsartan to reduce the likelihood of hypotension (see Warnings—Hypotension and Precautions—Drug Interactions). If this is not possible because of the patient's condition, valsartan should be administered with caution and the blood pressure monitored closely. Thereafter, the dosage should be adjusted according to the individual response of the patient.

Information for the Patient: See Blue Section—Information for the Patient "Diovan".

Supplied: 80 mg: Each gelatin capsule contains: valsartan 80 mg. Nonmedicinal ingredients: magnesium stearate, microcrystalline cellulose, povidone compounds and sodium lauryl sulfate; capsule shell: black iron oxide, gelatin, red iron oxide and titanium dioxide. Blister strips of 15, cartons of 2.

160 mg: Each gelatin capsule contains: valsartan 160 mg. Nonmedicinal ingredients: magnesium stearate, microcrystalline cellulose, povidone compounds and sodium lauryl sulfate; capsule shell: black iron oxide, gelatin, red iron oxide and titanium dioxide. Blister strips of 15, cartons of 2.

Protect from moisture and heat (store at 15 to 30°C).

(Shown in Product Recognition Section)

New Product 1998

Abbreviations used in the *CPS* are listed in the front of the WHITE SECTION.

DIOVOL®
Carter Horner

Magnesium Hydroxide—Aluminum Hydroxide

Antacid

Indications: Provides fast relief of heartburn and acid indigestion.

Contraindications: Alkalosis, hypermagnesemia, where distention may be due to partial or complete obstruction; not recommended for severely debilitated patients or those with impaired renal function.

Warnings: Do not take more than 16 tablets or 80 mL during a 24-hour period. Do not take for more than 2 weeks or if symptoms recur, unless directed by a physician. Do not take if you suffer from kidney disease except on your physician's advice. Do not take within 2 hours of another medicine, because the effectiveness of the other medicine may be altered. Antacids can interfere with the absorption of iron preparations and/or tetracyclines.

Precautions: Avoid concomitant use with tetracycline antibiotics and/or iron preparations.

Overdose: Symptoms: In the presence of renal insufficiency, accumulation of magnesium in circulation may cause CNS depression. Chronic ingestion may lead to phosphorus deficiency in presence of low phosphorus diet.

Treatment: Symptomatic.

Dosage: Adults: 10 to 20 mL of suspension or 2 to 4 tablets or caplets taken 4 times daily as needed between meals and at bedtime or as directed by the physician.

Supplied: Caplets: Each light blue, oval, convex, beveled edged, opaque, film-coated, mint-flavored caplet, plain on one side, intagliated DIOVOL on the other, contains: dried aluminum hydroxide gel 200 mg and magnesium hydroxide 200 mg. Nonmedicinal ingredients: alumina, cellulose, cornstarch, FD&C Blue No. 2, FD&C Red No. 3, flavor, gelatin, glycerin, magnesium stearate, propylene glycol and titanium dioxide. Energy: 0.83 kJ (<0.2 kcal). Gluten-, sucrose- and tartrazine-free. Boxes of 10 and 50 in push-through format.

Suspension: Each 5 mL of opaque, white suspension with a mint flavor and a peppermint and spearmint odor (pH: 7.3 to 8.5) contains: aluminum hydroxide 165 mg (as aluminum hydroxide compressed gel) and magnesium hydroxide 200 mg. Nonmedicinal ingredients: alcohol (1%), calcium cyclamate, flavors, guar gum, hydrogen peroxide, parabens, simethicone and sorbitol. Energy: 9.6 kJ (2.3 kcal). Sodium: <1 mmol (1 mg)/5 mL. Sucrose- and tartrazine-free. Bottles of 350 mL and 100 mL Hospital Pack. Protect from freezing.

Tablets: Each round, flat, white tablet with beveled edges, intagliated DIOVOL on one side, contains: aluminum hydroxide and magnesium carbonate co-dried gel 300 mg (equivalent to aluminum hyroxide 184 mg) and magnesium hydroxide 100 mg. Nonmedicinal ingredients: calcium cyclamate, cellulose, D&C yellow No. 10 (fruit-flavored tablet), flavor, gelatin, magnesium stearate, mannitol, sorbitol, starch (corn) and talc. Energy: 7.5 kJ (1.8 kcal). Sodium: <1 mmol (1 mg)/tablet. Sucrose- and tartrazine-free. Cartons of 50 in push-through format.

(Shown in Product Recognition Section)

DIOVOL® EX
Carter Horner

Aluminum Hydroxide—Magnesium Hydroxide

Antacid

Indications: Provides fast relief of heartburn, acid indigestion, hyperacidity and acid reflux.

Contraindications: Alkalosis, hypermagnesemia, where distention may be due to partial or complete obstruction; not recommended for severely debilitated patients or those with impaired renal function.

Warnings: Do not take more than 8 tablets or 40 mL during a 24 hour period. Do not take for more than 2 weeks or do not take if you suffer from kidney disease, except under your physician's advice. Antacids can interfere with the absorption of iron preparations and/or tetracyclines.

Precautions: Magnesium salts, in the presence of renal insufficiency may cause CNS depression. Aluminum hydroxide, in the presence of low phosphorus diets, may cause phosphorus deficiency. Aluminum salts tend to cause constipation. Do not administer concomitantly with tetracycline antibiotics or iron preparations.

Overdose: Symptoms and Treatment: Symptomatic.

Dosage: Adults: 5 to 10 mL or 1 to 2 tablets 4 times daily, 20 to 60 minutes after meals and at night or as directed by the physician.

Supplied: Suspension: Each 5 mL of white, peppermint-flavored suspension with a milky appearance contains: aluminum hydroxide wet gel (equivalent to 494 mg aluminum hydroxide) and magnesium hydroxide 300 mg. Nonmedicinal ingredients: alcohol (1%), flavor, guar gum, hydrogen peroxide, parabens and sorbitol. Energy: 20 kJ (4.7 kcal). Sodium: <1 mmol (1 mg)/5 mL. Gluten-, sucrose- and tartrazine-free. Bottles of 350 and 100 mL Hospital Pack.

Tablets: Each round, white, mint-flavored tablet, intagliated DIOVOL EX on one side, contains: aluminum hydroxide dried gel 600 mg (equivalent to 459 mg aluminum hydroxide) and magnesium hydroxide 300 mg. Nonmedicinal ingredients: calcium cyclamate, flavor, gelatin, magnesium stearate, mannitol, sorbitol and starch (contains gluten). Energy: 7.5 kJ (1.8 kcal). Sodium: <1 mmol (1 mg)/tablet. Sucrose- and tartrazine-free. Cartons of 32 in push-through format.

(Shown in Product Recognition Section)

DIOVOL PLUS®
DIOVOL PLUS® AF
Carter Horner

Magnesium Hydroxide—Simethicone Compound

Antacid—Antiflatulent

Indications: Provides fast relief of heartburn, acid indigestion, and gas.

Contraindications: Alkalosis; hypermagnesemia; where distention may be due to partial or complete intestinal obstruction. Not recommended for severely debilitated patients or those with impaired renal function.

Warnings: Do not take more than 16 tablets or 80 mL during a 24-hour period. Do not take for more than 2 weeks or if symptoms recur, unless directed by a physician. Do not take if you suffer from kidney disease, except on your physician's advice. Do not take within 2 hours of another medicine, because the effectiveness of the medicine may be altered. Antacids can interfere with the absorption of iron preparations and/or tetracyclines.

Precautions: Magnesium salts, in the presence of renal insufficiency, may cause CNS depression. Aluminum hydroxide, in the presence of low phosphorus diets, may cause phosphorus deficiency. Aluminum salts tend to cause constipation. Do not administer concomitantly with tetracycline antibiotics or iron preparations.

Overdose: Symptoms and Treatment: Symptomatic.

Dosage: Adults: 10 to 20 mL of suspension, or 2 to 4 tablets taken 4 times a day 20 to 60 minutes after meals and at bedtime or as directed by the physician. Suspension may be taken undiluted or with water. Tablets may be chewed or sucked.

Supplied: Diovol Plus: Suspension: Each 5 mL of white to off-white, peppermint or tropical-fruit-flavored suspension with a milky appearance contains: aluminum hydroxide (as aluminum hydroxide compressed gel) 165 mg, magnesium hydroxide 200 mg and simethicone 25 mg. Nonmedicinal ingredients: alcohol (<1%), calcium cyclamate, D&C Yellow 10 (fruit-flavored suspension), flavor, guar gum, hydrogen peroxide, parabens and sorbitol. Energy: 7.1 kJ (1.7 kcal)/5 mL. Sodium: <1 mmol (<1 mg)/5 mL. Sucrose- and tartrazine-free. pH: 7.5 to 8.5. Bottles of 350 and 100 mL Hospital Pack. Protect from freezing.

Tablets: Each round, flat, beveled edge tablet, monogrammed DIOVOL PLUS on one side, fruit-flavored (yellow, single layer) or peppermint (⅔ white, ⅓ yellow), contains: aluminum hydroxide and magnesium carbonate co-dried gel 300 mg (equivalent to aluminum hydroxide 184 mg), magnesium hydroxide 100 mg and simethicone 25 mg. Nonmedicinal ingredients: calcium cyclamate, cellulose, D&C Yellow 10, FD&C Yellow 6 (mint tablets), flavors, gelatin, magnesium stearate, mannitol, sorbitol, starch (corn) and talc. Energy: 8.4 kJ (2 kcal)/tablet. Sodium: <1 mmol (1 mg). Gluten-, sucrose- and tartrazine-free. Boxes of 10, 50 and 100 in push through format. Boxes of 10 and 50 in push through format. (Diovol Plus fruit-flavored).

Diovol Plus AF: Liquid: Each 5 mL of white to off-white peppermint flavored suspension with a milky appearance contains: calcium carbonate, magnesium hydroxide 200 mg and simethicone 25 mg. Nonmedicinal ingredients: alcohol, benzyl alcohol, edetate calcium disodium, flavors, glycerin, guar gum, hydrogen peroxide, polyethylene glycol, propylene glycol alginate, saccharin sodium and sorbitol. Alcohol: 1%. Energy: 7.1 kJ (1.7 kcal)/5 mL. Sodium: <1 mmol (<2 mg)/5 mL. Bottles of 350 mL.

Tablets: Each round, flat, beveled-edge white tablet, mint flavored, monogrammed DIOVOL PLUS on one side and AF on other side contains: calcium carbonate, magnesium hydroxide 200 mg and simethicone 25 mg. Nonmedicinal ingredients: calcium cyclamate, flavor, gelatin, magnesium stearate and mannitol. Energy: 10.5 kJ (2.5 kcal)/tablet. Sodium: <1 mmol (1 mg)/tablet. Boxes of 50.

(Shown in Product Recognition Section)

DIPENTUM® Ⓟ
Pharmacia & Upjohn

Olsalazine Sodium

Lower Gastrointestinal Anti-inflammatory

Pharmacology: The conversion of olsalazine to 5-aminosalicylic acid (5-ASA) in the colon is similar to that of sulfasalazine, which is converted into sulfapyridine and 5-ASA. On a weight basis olsalazine delivers twice the amount of 5-ASA to the colon compared with sulfasalazine and there is no residual carrier molecule (sulfapyridine) following olsalazine administration. It is thought that the 5-ASA component is therapeutically active in ulcerative colitis. The mechanism of action of 5-ASA (and sulfasalazine) is unknown, but appears to be topical rather than systemic.

After oral administration olsalazine has limited systemic bioavailability. Based on oral and i.v. dosing studies approximately 2.4% of a single 1 g oral dose is absorbed. Less than 1% of olsalazine is recovered in the urine. The remaining 98 to 99% of an oral dose will reach the colon, where each molecule is rapidly converted to 2 molecules of 5-ASA by colonic bacteria. The liberated 5-ASA is absorbed slowly resulting in very high local concentrations in the colon.

Systemically absorbed olsalazine is rapidly cleared from plasma with a half-time of 0.9 hour. The plasma 5-ASA and acetylated-5-aminosalicylic acid (Ac-5-ASA) are rapidly cleared via the kidneys. The elimination half-times are 45 and 80 minutes, respectively. In urine less than 1% is recovered as olsalazine, 20% as Ac-5-ASA and less than 1% as 5-ASA. The remaining 80% is eliminated via the feces as 5-ASA and Ac-5-ASA.

Indications: Long-term maintenance of patients with ulcerative colitis in remission.

Treatment of acute ulcerative colitis of mild to moderate severity, with or without the concomitant use of steroids.

Contraindications: Hypersensitivity to salicylates.

Warnings: All 5-ASA preparations have been reported to cause an exacerbation of colitis symptoms in less than 1% of patients with ulcerative colitis. This reaction may also occur with olsalazine treatment due to the pharmacological similarities among these drugs.

Pregnancy: Animal reproductive studies performed on the rat, rabbit and mouse were negative, thus there is no preclinical evidence of an adverse effect on the parent generation nor on its offspring.

Olsalazine does not pass the rat placental barrier, as shown in an autoradiography study.

Well-controlled studies with olsalazine in pregnant women assessing fetal risk in humans are not available. Because animal reproduction studies are not always predictive of the human response, this drug should be used in pregnancy only if clearly needed.

Lactation: No peri- and postnatal effects have been observed in animal studies. Olsalazine is not appreciably excreted in rat breast milk as shown in a study using radioactively labelled drug.

Well-controlled studies with olsalazine in lactating women are not available. Olsalazine should be used during lactation only if clearly indicated.

Children: For children there are to date no trials to support the use of olsalazine. The benefits of treatment should therefore be weighed against the risks.

Precautions: Dipentum can be used with or without concomitant steroids for treatment of acute ulcerative colitis of mild to moderate severity.

The following definitions may serve as guidelines for selection of patients: **Remission** is defined as 3 or fewer bowel movements a day without macroscopic blood admixture and without sigmoidoscopic evidence of inflammation. **Mild disease** is defined as 3 to 5 bowel movements a day or other symptoms of colitis including rectal bleeding, anorexia or nausea. **Moderate disease** includes patients with at least 6 and up to 10 bowel movements per day, with or without rectal bleeding, anorexia, or nausea. **Severe disease** is indicated by 10 or more bowel movements per day and 1 or more of the following signs: abdominal tenderness, pulse rate greater than 100 beats/minute, body temperature higher than 37.5°C.

Drug Interactions: None known.

Drug/Laboratory Test Interactions: None known.

General: Overall, approximately 15% of patients reported diarrhea when olsalazine was initially administered, resulting in treatment withdrawal in 6%. This diarrhea appears to be dose related although it may be difficult to distinguish it from the underlying symptoms of the disease. The diarrhea is temporary and may depend on the extent of colonic involvement. However, the severity of ulcerative colitis does not appear to influence its occurrence.

Drug-related diarrhea in patients in remission is defined as watery stools 4 or more times a day without blood or sigmoidoscopic signs of inflammation. Withdrawal of the drug results in prompt clinical improvement of the diarrhea.

Disease-induced diarrhea (i.e., relapse of the colitis) is defined as 4 or more bowel movements a day with visible blood in association with sigmoidoscopic evidence of inflammation.

Drug-induced hypersensitivity colitis presents with increasing diarrhea that is frequently bloody. Other signs of hypersensitivity such as fever, skin rash, cramping, abdominal pain, or nausea are often part of this type of acute exacerbation. Sigmoidoscopy reveals the macroscopic changes of an active colitis. Withdrawal of the drug results in prompt improvement of this hypersensitivity reaction.

Information for the Patient: Patients should be made aware that ulcerative colitis rarely remits completely and that the risk of relapse can be substantially reduced by continuous administration of olsalazine. Patients should be instructed to take olsalazine regularly, not to take more than 4 capsules at any one dosing interval and to take the capsules with meals. The drug should be taken in evenly divided doses. Patients should be informed that in approximately 15% of cases loose stools or diarrhea may result on initial administration and that they should contact their physician if severe diarrhea occurs.

Adverse Effects: Olsalazine has been evaluated in ulcerative colitis patients in remission as well as those with acute disease. Both sulfasalazine-tolerant and intolerant patients have been studied in controlled clinical trials. Overall, 10.4% of patients discontinued olsalazine because of an adverse experience as compared with 6.7% of placebo patients (see Table I). In sulfasalazine-controlled trials in which all patients were already known to be sulfasalazine-tolerant, adverse experiences with this drug resulted in a similar rate of discontinuance of treatment (10.0%).

In general, olsalazine is well tolerated; adverse effects appear to be mild and transient, and may be difficult to differentiate from the symptoms of the underlying disease (see Table II). Olsalazine appears to induce loose stools in approximately 15% of patients. This incidence may be reduced if olsalazine is initially titrated and taken with food.

Severe adverse effects commonly attributed to the sulfapyridine moiety of sulfasalazine (agranulocytosis, Stevens-Johnson syndrome, pulmonary oesinophilia, etc.) have not been reported with olsalazine. In addition, there have been no reports of nephrotoxicity.

Over 2 500 patients have also been treated with olsalazine in various uncontrolled, compassionate-use programs. In these studies, olsalazine was administered mainly to patients intolerant to sulfasalazine. The adverse effects related to olsalazine reported in these uncontrolled studies were similar to those seen in the controlled clinical trials. In addition, there were rare reports of the following adverse effects in patients receiving olsalazine. There is currently not enough information to support an estimate of their frequency.

Digestive: pancreatitis, hepatitis, rectal discomfort, flatulence.

CNS: insomnia, mood swings, irritability.

Dermatologic: erythema nodosum, photosensitivity, erythema, hot flashes, alopecia.

Musculoskeletal: muscle cramps.

Cardiovascular: pericarditis, second degree heart block, hypertension, orthostatic hypotension, edema, tightness in chest.

Genitourinary: frequency, dysuria, impotence, heavy menstrual bleeding.

Hematologic: leukopenia, lymphopenia, anemia, reticulocytosis.

Laboratory: elevated liver enzymes.

Special Senses: dry mouth, dry eyes.

Drug Abuse and Dependency: Abuse: None reported.

Dependence: Drug dependence has not been reported with chronic administration of olsalazine.

Table I—Dipentum

Patients Withdrawn from Treatment Due to Adverse Effects in Controlled Studies

	Olsalazine	Placebo
Acute Ulcerative Colitis		
Number of Patients	284	159
Number Withdrawn	24 (8.5%)	14 (8.8%)
Relapse Prevention		
Number of Patients	157	49
Number Withdrawn	22 (14.0%)	0
Total	**441 (10.4%)**	**208 (6.7%)**

Table II—Dipentum

Comparative Incidence (%) of Adverse Effects Reported by 1% or More of Ulcerative Colitis Patients Treated with Olsalazine and Placebo in Double-blind Controlled Trials

Adverse Event	Olsalazine N=441 %	Placebo N=208 %
Digestive System		
Diarrhea	11.1	6.7
Abdominal Pain/Cramps	10.1	7.2
Nausea	5.0	3.9
Dyspepsia	4.0	4.3
Bloating	1.5	1.4
Anorexia	1.3	1.9
Vomiting	1.0	-
Stomatitis	1.0	-
Increased Blood in Stool	-	3.4
CNS/Psychiatric		
Headache	5.0	4.8
Fatigue/Drowsiness/Lethargy	1.8	2.9
Depression	1.5	-
Vertigo/Dizziness	1.0	-
Insomnia	-	2.4
Skin		
Rash	2.3	1.4
Itching	1.3	-
Musculoskeletal		
Arthralgia/Joint Pain	4.0	2.9
Miscellaneous		
URTI/Runny Nose	1.5	-

Dosage: Dosage should be adjusted to the severity of the disease. Increase the dose gradually over a 1-week period, starting with 500 mg (2 capsules)/day. If no response is achieved with 2 g and the drug is well tolerated, the dose may be increased to 3 g daily. A single dose should not exceed 1 g.

The drug should be taken at regular intervals together with meals.

Patients experiencing watery diarrhea associated with increasing dosage can reduce the dose to the previously tolerated dose, for a 2-day period. The dose may then be increased again. Further subdivision of the dose may be necessary.

Usual Adult Dose (including elderly): Acute: 500 mg (2 capsules), 4 times daily.

Prophylaxis: 500 mg (2 capsules), 2 times daily.

Children: No specific dose has been defined for children. Dosage should be adjusted to individual weight and age of the child.

Concomitant therapy with oral or rectal steroids may be used.

Long-term maintenance therapy with olsalazine is recommended in order to avoid relapse and remain free from symptoms.

Supplied: Each opaque, beige, hard gelatin capsule contains: olsalazine sodium 250 mg. Bottles of 100. Store at room temperature (15 to 30°C).

(Shown in Product Recognition Section)

DIPHENYLHYDANTOIN

General Monograph, CPhA

see PHENYTOIN

DIPHTHERIA AND TETANUS TOXOIDS ADSORBED (DT Adsorbed)

Connaught

Active Immunizing Agent

Pharmacology: Immunization against diphtheria and tetanus has been associated with a striking decrease in the incidence of morbidity and mortality from these diseases.

Injection of bacterial proteins such as diphtheria and tetanus toxoids results in the production of protective antibodies. The peak antibody levels achieved with the first dose are usually low, and a primary series is required to prime the immune system and produce a high antibody level. After completion of a primary series, circulating antibodies to tetanus and diphtheria toxoids gradually decline but are thought to persist at protective levels for up to 10 years. Tetanus antitoxin levels of >0.01 IU/mL are generally accepted as good evidence of immunity from tetanus. Diphtheria antitoxin levels of ≥0.01 IU/mL are thought to be the minimal level required for protection. Levels >0.05 IU/mL are considered optimal for protection.

Diphtheria is a serious communicable disease caused by toxigenic strains of C. diphtheriae. The organism may be harbored in the nasopharynx, skin or other sites of asymptomatic carriers, making eradication of the disease difficult. Routine immunization against diphtheria in infancy and childhood has been widely practised in Canada since 1930, resulting in a decline in morbidity and mortality. Fewer than 5 cases are now reported annually in Canada. The case-fatality rate remains 5 to 10%, with the highest death rates in the very young and elderly. The disease occurs most frequently in unimmunized or partially immunized individuals. Diphtheria toxoid is a cell-free preparation of diphtheria toxin detoxified with formaldehyde. The immunity conferred is antitoxic, not antibacterial, and thus protects against the potentially lethal systemic effects of diphtheria toxin but not directly against local infection.

Tetanus is an acute and often fatal disease caused by an extremely potent neurotoxin produced by C. tetani. The organism is ubiquitous and its occurrence in nature cannot be controlled. Immunization is highly effective, provides long-lasting protection, and is recommended for the whole population. Only 2 to 3 cases of tetanus are now reported annually in Canada. Tetanus toxoid is prepared by detoxification of tetanus toxin with formaldehyde.

Indications: For the primary and booster immunization of infants, at or above the age of 2 months, and of children up to their 7th birthday, against diphtheria and tetanus in whom simultaneous immunization against pertussis is not indicated. Age-appropriate immunization always should be started at once if diphtheria is present in the community.

DT Adsorbed may be administered simultaneously with Hib conjugate vaccines, MMR and IPV each at separate sites with separate syringes, and with OPV.

Contraindications: General: Immunization with DT Adsorbed should be deferred in the presence of any acute illness, including febrile illness to avoid superimposing adverse effects from the vaccine on the underlying illness or mistakenly identifying a manifestation of the underlying illness as a complication of vaccine use. A minor afebrile illness such as mild upper respiratory infection is not usually reason to defer immunization.

DT Adsorbed should not be administered to children after their 7th birthday, or to adults because of reactions to diphtheria toxoid.

Absolute: Allergy to any component of DT Adsorbed (see Supplied) an anaphylactic or other allergic reaction to a previous dose of DT Adsorbed or a history of a neurologic reaction following a previous dose are absolute contraindications to vaccination.

Deferral: Elective immunization of persons over 6 months of age should be deferred during an outbreak of poliomyelitis because of the risk of provocation paralysis.

Human Immunodeficiency Virus (HIV) Infected Persons: HIV-infected individuals, both asymptomatic and symptomatic, should be immunized with DT vaccine according to standard schedules (see Warnings).

Diphtheria and Tetanus Toxoids Adsorbed (DT Adsorbed) (cont'd)

Warnings: Arthus-type hypersensitivity reaction, characterized by severe local reactions (generally starting 2 to 8 hours after an injection) may occur, particularly in persons who have received multiple prior boosters. Persons who have experienced Arthus-type hypersensitivity or fever of >39.4°C following a previous dose of tetanus toxoid usually have high serum tetanus antitoxin levels.

I.M. injections should be given with care in patients suffering from coagulation disorders or on anticoagulant therapy because of the risk of hemorrhage.

If DT Adsorbed is used in persons with malignancies, persons receiving immunosuppressive therapies including irradiation, antimetabolites, alkylating agents, cytotoxic drugs, or persons who are otherwise immunocompromised (including HIV infected individuals, transplant recipients, persons suffering from autoimmune disorders), the expected immune response may not be obtained.

Corticosteroid therapy can result in immunosuppression although the exact dose and duration of therapy required to suppress the immune system is not well defined. Persons treated with high doses of systemic steroids, e.g., ≥2 mg/kg/day of prednisone orally for more than 2 weeks, should be considered to have a compromised immune system.

As with any vaccine, immunization with DT Adsorbed may not protect 100% of susceptible individuals.

Precautions: General: The possibility of allergic reactions in individuals sensitive to the components of the product should be evaluated. Epinephrine HCl Solution (1:1 000) and other appropriate agents should be available for immediate use in case an anaphylactic or acute hypersensitivity reaction occurs. Health care providers should be familiar with current recommendations for the initial management of anaphylaxis in non-hospital settings, including proper airway management.

Before administration of any vaccine, all appropriate precautions should be taken to prevent adverse reactions. This includes a review of the patient's history with respect to possible hypersensitivity to the vaccine or similar vaccine, determination of previous immunization history, and the presence of any contraindications to immunization, current health status, and a current knowledge of the literature concerning the use of the vaccine under consideration.

Special care should be taken to ensure that the product is not injected into a blood vessel.

Caution: A separate sterile needle and syringe or a sterile disposable unit must be used for each individual patient to prevent the transmission of infectious agents.

There have been case reports of transmission of HIV and hepatitis by failure to scrupulously observe sterile technique. In particular, the same needle and/or syringe must never be used to re-enter a multidose vial to withdraw vaccine even when it is to be used for inoculation of the same patient. This may lead to contamination of the vial contents and infection of patients who subsequently receive vaccine from the vial.

Needles should not be recapped and should be disposed of properly.

Before administration of DT Adsorbed, health care personnel should inform the parent or guardian or the patient to be immunized of the benefits and risks of immunization, inquire about the recent health status of the patient and comply with any local requirements with respect to information to be provided to the patient before immunization.

Frequent booster doses of tetanus toxoid in the presence of adequate or excessive serum levels of tetanus antitoxin have been associated with increased incidence and severity of reactions and should be avoided. If hypersensitivity to the diphtheria component is suspected, tetanus toxoid should be used for reinforcing doses.

Adverse Effects: Mild local reactions consisting of erythema, pain and tenderness, swelling and induration at the injection site are common, and may be associated with systemic reactions including mild to moderate transient fever and irritability.

Up to 70% of children receiving a booster dose of DPT Adsorbed at 4 to 6 years of age have been reported to develop local redness and/or swelling ≥5 cm in diameter. This is generally self limiting and subsides without treatment.

Persistent nodules at the site of injection have occurred following the use of an adsorbed product, but this complication is unusual, and may be related to s.c. administration. Sterile abscess at the site of injection has been reported following use of adsorbed vaccines (6 to 10 per million doses).

Mild systemic reactions such as fever, drowsiness, fretfulness, anorexia, vomiting, irritability and persistent or unusual crying have been reported. The incidence and severity of fever and irritability can be reduced by administration of acetaminophen (15 mg/kg/dose) at the time of inoculation and again 4 and 8 hours after vaccination.

Rarely, an anaphylactic reaction (i.e., hives, swelling of the mouth, difficulty breathing, hypotension, or shock) have been reported after receiving preparations containing diphtheria and/or tetanus toxoids. Death following anaphylaxis has been reported.

On the basis of a single case report and evidence that a vaccine-induced immunologic response can cause Guillain-Barré Syndrome (GBS), the Institute of Medicine (US) concluded that tetanus toxoid-containing vaccines can trigger GBS in adults. No increased risk for GBS has been observed with the use of DTP in children.

The following neurologic illnesses have been reported as temporally associated with vaccine containing tetanus toxoid: neurological complications including cochlear lesion, brachial plexus neuropathies, paralysis of the radial nerve, paralysis of the recurrent nerve, accommodation paresis, and EEG disturbances with encephalopathy. In the differential diagnosis of polyradiculoneuropathies following administration of a vaccine containing tetanus toxoid, tetanus toxoid should be considered as a possible etiology.

Physicians, nurses, and pharmacists should report any adverse occurrences temporally related to the administration of the product in accordance with local requirements and to the Medical Director, Connaught Laboratories Limited, 1755 Steeles Avenue West, Toronto, Ontario, Canada, M2R 3T4.

Dosage: For primary immunization of infants the following routine DT Adsorbed immunization schedule is recommended: one 0.5 mL dose administered at 2, 4, 6 and 18 months of age.

If for any reason this schedule is delayed, it is recommended that 3 doses of 0.5 mL be administered with an interval 4 to 8 weeks between doses, followed by a 4th dose of 0.5 mL administered approximately 1 year following the 3rd dose.

A booster dose of 0.5 mL should be administered between 4 and 6 years of age (i.e., at the time of school entry). This booster is unnecessary if the 4th primary immunizing dose has been administered after the 4th birthday.

Parenteral biological products should be inspected visually for extraneous particulate matter and/or discoloration before administration. If these conditions exist, the product should not be administered.

Shake the vial or ampul well to distribute uniformly the suspension before withdrawing each dose. Before withdrawing a dose from an ampul, tap the container first to ensure that any vaccine in the ampul neck falls to the lower portion of the ampul. Once the ampul has been opened, any of its contents not used immediately should be discarded. When administering a dose from a rubber-stoppered vial, do not remove either the rubber stopper or the metal seal holding it in place. Aseptic technique must be used for withdrawal of each dose (see Precautions).

Before injection, the skin over the site to be injected should be cleansed with a suitable germicide.

Administer the vaccine **i.m.** The preferred site is into the anterolateral aspect of the mid-thigh (vastus lateralis muscle) or into the deltoid muscle. The former is the site of choice for infants <1 year of age because it provides the largest muscle. In children >1 year of age, the deltoid is the preferred site since use of the anterolateral thigh results in frequent complaints of limping due to muscle pain.

After insertion of the needle, aspirate to ensure that the needle has not entered a blood vessel.

Do not inject i.v.

Each person who is immunized should be given a permanent personal immunization record. In addition, it is essential that the physician or nurse record the immunization history in the permanent medical record of each patient. This permanent office record should contain the name of the vaccine, date given, dose, manufacturer and lot number.

Supplied: Each 0.5 mL dose contains: diphtheria toxoid (25 Lf) tetanus toxoid (5 Lf) and aluminum phosphate 1.5 mg. Thimerosal 0.01% is added as a preservative. Rubber stoppered vials of 5 mL, packages of 1. Glass ampuls of 0.5 mL (single dose), packages of 5. Store between 2 to 8°C. **Do not freeze.** Product exposed to freezing should not be used. Do not use vaccine after expiration date.

Reviewed 1999

For comparative information on Iron Salts, see the CPhA General Monograph in the WHITE SECTION.

DIPHTHERIA AND TETANUS TOXOIDS ADSORBED AND POLIOMYELITIS VACCINE (DT Polio Adsorbed)

Connaught

Vaccine

Indications: For the primary immunization of infants and of children at or above the age of 2 months through 6 years of age (prior to the seventh birthday) against diphtheria, tetanus, and poliomyelitis in whom simultaneous immunization against pertussis is not indicated.

DT Polio Adsorbed may be administered simultaneously with Hib conjugate vaccines and/or MMR at separate sites with separate syringes.

Contraindications: Immunization with DT Polio Adsorbed should be deferred in the presence of any acute illness, including febrile illness.

Elective immunization of individuals over 6 months of age should be deferred during an outbreak of poliomyelitis.

DT Polio Adsorbed should not be administered to children on or after the seventh birthday and to adults because of possible reactions to the pediatric dosage of diphtheria toxoid.

Allergic reaction to any component of DT Polio Adsorbed is a contraindication to vaccination.

Human Immunodeficiency Virus (HIV) Infected Persons: HIV-infected individuals, both asymptomatic and symptomatic, should be immunized with DT Polio Adsorbed according to standard schedules.

Warnings: If DT Polio Adsorbed is used in persons with malignancies, receiving immunosuppressive therapies, including irradiation, antimetabolites, alkylating agents, cytotoxic drugs, or who are otherwise immunocompromised, the expected immune response may not be obtained.

Corticosteroid therapy can result in immunosuppression although the exact dose and duration of therapy required to suppress the immune system is not well defined. Persons treated with high doses of systemic steroids, e.g., ≥2 mg/kg/day of prednisone orally for more than 2 weeks, should be considered to have a compromised immune system.

As with any vaccine, immunization with DT Polio Adsorbed may not protect 100% of susceptible individuals.

Precautions: The possibility of allergic reactions in individuals sensitive to components of the vaccine should be evaluated. Epinephrine HCl solution (1:1 000) and other appropriate agents should be available for immediate use in case an anaphylactic or acute hypersensitivity reaction occurs.

Before an injection of any vaccine, appropriate precautions should be taken to prevent adverse reactions. This includes a review of the patient's history with respect to possible hypersensitivity to the vaccine or similar vaccine, determination of previous immunization history, and the presence of any contraindications to immunization.

Since the vaccine contains 2-phenoxyethanol and may contain trace amounts of polymyxin B and neomycin, the possibility of allergic reactions in individuals sensitive to these substances should be borne in mind when considering the use of this vaccine.

Any febrile illness or acute infection is reason to delay the use of DT Polio Adsorbed.

Special care should be taken to ensure that the product is not injected into a blood vessel.

A separate, sterile syringe and needle, or a sterile disposable unit, must be used for each individual patient to prevent the transmission of infectious agents. There have been case reports of transmission of HIV and hepatitis by failure to scrupulously observe sterile technique.

Do not recap needles.

Frequent booster doses of tetanus toxoid in the presence of adequate or excessive serum levels of tetanus antitoxin have been associated with increased incidence and severity of reactions and should be avoided.

Children with Symptomatic HIV Infection: Available data suggest that routine childhood immunizations are not hazardous to HIV-infected children. Furthermore, there is no evidence that immunization with routine vaccines leads to deterioration of the clinical condition of HIV-infected persons.

Immunization with DPT (Diphtheria, Pertussis and Tetanus), IPV (Inactivated Poliomyelitis Vaccine) and Haemophilus b Conjugate Vaccine is recommended, although immunization may be less effective than it would be for immunocompetent children.

Adverse Effects: Mild local reactions consisting of pain, erythema, tenderness and induration at the injection site are common, usually self-limited and subside without treatment.

Persistent nodules at the site of injection have occurred following the use of an adsorbed vaccine, but this complication is unusual.

Physicians, nurses and pharmacists should report any adverse occurrences temporally related to the administration of the product in accordance with local requirements and report to the Medical Director at Connaught Laboratories Limited, 1755 Steeles Avenue West, Toronto, Ontario, Canada, M2R 3T4.

Dosage: For primary immunization of infants, the following routine DT Polio Adsorbed immunization schedule is recommended: one 0.5 mL dose administered at 2, 4, 6 and 18 months of age.

If for any reason this schedule is delayed, it is recommended that 3 doses of 0.5 mL be administered with an interval of 4 to 8 weeks between doses, followed by a fourth dose of 0.5 mL administered approximately 1 year after the third dose. The same schedule may be used through 6 years of age (prior to the seventh birthday).

A booster dose of 0.5 mL should be administered between 4 and 6 years of age (i.e., at the time of school entry). This booster dose is unnecessary if the fourth primary immunizing dose has been administered after the fourth birthday.

Administration: Parenteral biological products should be inspected visually for extraneous particulate matter and/or discoloration prior to administration. If these conditions exist, the product should not be administered.

Shake ampul well to uniformly distribute the suspension before withdrawing each dose. Before withdrawing a dose from an ampul, tap the container first to ensure that all the vaccine is in the lower portion. Once the ampul has been opened, any of its contents not used immediately should be discarded. Aseptic technique must be used for withdrawal of each dose.

Administer the vaccine i.m. The preferred site is into the anterolateral aspect of the mid-thigh (vastus lateralis muscle) or into the deltoid muscle. The former is the site of choice for infants <1 year of age because it provides the largest muscle. In children >1 year of age, the deltoid is the preferred site since use of the anterolateral thigh results in frequent complaints of limping due to muscle pain.

Before injection, the skin over the site to be injected should be cleansed with a suitable germicide. After insertion of the needle, aspirate to ensure that the needle has not entered a blood vessel.

Do not inject i.v.

Each person who is immunized should be given a permanent personal immunization record. In addition, it is essential that the physician or nurse record the immunization history in the permanent medical record of each patient. This permanent office record should contain the name of the vaccine, date given, dose, manufacturer and lot number.

Supplied: Each single human dose (0.5 mL) of sterile, cloudy, uniform suspension contains: purified poliomyelitis vaccine type 1 (Mahoney), type 2 (M.E.F.1) and type 3 (Saukett), diphtheria toxoid (25 Lf), tetanus toxoid (5 Lf) and aluminum phosphate (1.5 mg). Trace amounts of polymyxin B and neomycin may be present from the cell growth medium. Formaldehyde (27 ppm) and 2-phenoxyethanol (0.5%) are added as a preservative. Ampuls of 0.5 mL, boxes of 5. Store at a temperature between 2 and 8°C. **Do not freeze.** Product which has been exposed to freezing should not be used. Once an ampul is opened, any contents not used immediately should be discarded.

Reviewed 1997

DIPHTHERIA AND TETANUS TOXOIDS ADSORBED AND PERTUSSIS VACCINE AND INACTIVATED POLIOMYELITIS VACCINE (DPT Polio Adsorbed)

Connaught

Vaccine

Pharmacology: Immunization against diphtheria, tetanus, pertussis and poliomyelitis has been associated with a striking decrease in the incidence of morbidity and mortality from these diseases. Simultaneous vaccination with a combination vaccine containing diphtheria and tetanus toxoids and pertussis and poliomyelitis vaccines have been used in Canada since 1958.

Injection of bacterial proteins such as diphtheria and tetanus toxoids results in the production of protective antibodies. The peak antibody levels achieved with the first dose are usually low, and a primary series is required to prime the immune system and produce a high antibody level. After completion of a primary series, circulating antibodies to tetanus and diphtheria toxoids gradually decline but are thought to persist at protective levels for up to 10 years. Tetanus antitoxin levels of >0.01 IU/mL are generally accepted as good evidence of immunity from tetanus. Diphtheria antitoxin levels of ≥0.01 IU/mL are thought to be the minimal level required for protection. Levels >0.05 IU/mL are considered optimal for protection.

Diphtheria is a serious communicable disease caused by toxigenic strains of C. diphtheriae. The organism may be harboured in the nasopharynx, skin or other sites of asymptomatic carriers, making eradication of the disease difficult. Routine immunization against diphtheria in infancy and childhood has been widely practised in Canada since 1930, resulting in a decline in morbidity and mortality. Fewer than 5 cases are now reported annually in Canada. The case-fatality rate remains 5 to 10%, with the highest death rates in the very young and elderly. The disease occurs most frequently in unimmunized or partially immunized individuals. Diphtheria toxoid is a cell-free preparation of diphtheria toxin detoxified with formaldehyde. The immunity conferred is antitoxic, not antibacterial, and thus protects against the potentially lethal systemic effects of diphtheria toxin but not directly against local infection.

Tetanus is an acute and often fatal disease caused by an extremely potent neurotoxin produced by C. tetani. The organism is ubiquitous and its occurrence in nature cannot be controlled. Immunization is highly effective, provides long-lasting protection, and is recommended for the whole population. Only 2 to 3 cases of tetanus are now reported annually in Canada. Tetanus toxoid is prepared by detoxification of tetanus toxin with formaldehyde.

Pertussis (whooping cough) is a highly communicable bacterial disease caused by B. pertussis. Severity and mortality are greatest in infancy, and even infants born to apparently immune mothers are highly susceptible to infection, particularly if maternal immunity was vaccine-induced. During the last 30 years, vaccination has been widely practised in Canada and the incidence and mortality from pertussis have declined remarkably. However, outbreaks of pertussis continue to occur across Canada, with an annual reported rate of 1 000 to 8 000 cases over the past 5 years. Deaths and brain damage from pertussis infections still occur, particularly in young infants who have not been vaccinated. Pertussis vaccine is a suspension of killed B. pertussis organisms. A primary series of 4 doses of vaccine is begun in infancy. Protection from infection is estimated to be 60 to 80%; protection against severe disease is 85% or higher. Protection from disease afforded by the vaccine decreases as the time interval since vaccination increases.

Poliomyelitis is caused by infection with one of the 3 antigenic types of poliovirus. Following introduction of poliovirus vaccine in Canada in 1955, the indigenous disease has been virtually eliminated. The last significant outbreak of poliomyelitis occurred in 1978-79, when there were 11 cases of paralytic disease among unimmunized contacts of imported cases. The last case of poliomyelitis attributed to imported, wild virus occurred in 1988. However, circulation of wild viruses does occur in rare circumstances, and it remains crucial that the highest possible level of vaccine-induced immunity be maintained in the population. Inactivated Poliomyelitis Vaccine (Diploid Cell Origin)—IPV, (sometimes referred to as e-IPV), is an enhanced formalin-inactivated product which has a higher potency than the original IPV.

The 3 poliovirus types are propagated in human diploid cells. A primary series induces protective antibody levels in more than 99% of recipients.

In a clinical trial done in Canada in 1987-88, 120 infants 2 months of age received three 0.5 mL i.m. doses of DPT-P at 2-month intervals. One month following the third dose, 98% had diphtheria antitoxin levels of ≥0.01 IU/mL, 99% had tetanus antitoxin levels of ≥0.01 IU/mL, 99% had pertussis agglutinin levels of ≥1:8. Poliovirus antibody levels of ≥1:4 developed to type 1 in 99%, to type 2 in 100% and to type 3 in 100%.

Indications: For the primary immunization of infants and of children at or above the age of 2 months up to their 7th birthday against diphtheria, tetanus, whooping cough and poliomyelitis.

When both vaccines are indicated, DPT Polio Adsorbed may be used to reconstitute Act-HIB for simultaneous administration of all 5 antigens in a single injection. DPT Polio Adsorbed must **not** be mixed in the same syringe with any other vaccines.

DPT Polio Adsorbed may be administered simultaneously with other Hib conjugate vaccines and with MMR each at separate sites with separate syringes.

Contraindications: General: Immunization with this product should be deferred in the presence of any acute illness, including febrile illness.

DPT Polio Adsorbed should not be administered to children after their 7th birthday or to adults because of reactions to diphtheria toxoid or to pertussis vaccine and because pertussis is less severe in these age groups than in infants and young children.

Absolute Contraindications: Allergy to any component of DPT Polio Adsorbed, or an allergic or anaphylactic reaction to a previous dose of DPT Polio Adsorbed are contraindications to vaccination.

Relative Contraindications: Hypotonic-hyporesponsive episodes: No long-term sequelae have been associated with hypotonic-hyporesponsive episodes; however, it may be prudent in areas of low pertussis incidence to withhold the pertussis component and continue immunization with DT and IPV in children who have experienced a hypotonic-hyporesponsive episode following a previous dose of pertussis-containing vaccine. Immunization of children with DPT Polio can continue if the incidence of disease is high in their area.

Deferral: Deferral of the pertussis component of DPT Polio Adsorbed should be considered in children with a progressive, evolving, or unstable neurologic condition (including seizures) because administration of the pertussis component may coincide with the onset of overt manifestations of such disorders and result in confusion about causation. It is prudent to delay initiation of immunization with pertussis vaccine until further observation and study have clarified the child's neurologic status. In addition, the effect of treatment, if any, can be assessed. Immunization with DPT Polio Adsorbed should be reinstituted when the condition has resolved, been corrected or controlled.

When immunization with pertussis vaccine is contraindicated or deferred, immunization with diphtheria and tetanus toxoids, when necessary, may be continued using DT Adsorbed and Inactivated Poliomyelitis Vaccine (DCO). The use of fractional doses in an attempt to reduce the severity of adverse reactions cannot be recommended because there is insufficient evidence on the safety or efficacy of such smaller doses.

Elective immunization of individuals over 6 months of age should be deferred during an outbreak of poliomyelitis.

Human Immunodeficiency Virus (HIV) Infected Persons: HIV-infected individuals, both asymptomatic and symptomatic, should be immunized with DPT Polio vaccine according to standard schedules.

Warnings: If this product is used in persons with malignancies, receiving immunosuppressive therapies, including irradiation, antimetabolites, alkylating agents, cytotoxic drugs, or who are otherwise immunocompromised, the expected immune response may not be obtained.

Corticosteroid therapy can result in immunosuppression although the exact dose and duration of therapy required to suppress the immune system is not well defined. Persons treated with high doses of systemic steroids, e.g., ≥2 mg/kg/day of prednisone orally for more than 2 weeks, should be considered to have a compromised immune system.

As with any vaccine, immunization with DPT Polio Adsorbed may not protect 100% of susceptible individuals.

Precautions: General: The possibility of allergic reactions in individuals sensitive to components of the vaccine should be evaluated. Epinephrine HCl solution (1:1 000) and other appropriate agents should be available for immediate use in case an anaphylactic or acute hypersensitivity reaction occurs.

Before an injection of any vaccine, appropriate precautions should be taken to prevent adverse reactions. This includes a review of the patient's history with respect to possible hypersensitivity to the vaccine or similar vaccine, determination of previous immunization history, and the presence of any contraindications to immunization.

Special care should be taken to ensure that the product is not injected into a blood vessel.

A separate, sterile syringe and needle, or a sterile disposable unit, must be used for each individual patient to prevent the transmission of infectious agents. There have been case reports of transmission of HIV and hepatitis by failure to scrupulously observe sterile technique. In particular, the same needle and/or syringe must never be used to re-enter a multi-dose vial to withdraw vaccine even when it is to be used for

Diphtheria, Tetanus Toxoids Adsorbed, Pertussis Vaccine and Inactivated Poliomyelitis Vaccine (cont'd)

inoculation of the same patient. This may lead to contamination of the vial contents and infection of patients who subsequently receive vaccine from the vial.

Do not recap needles.

A family history of convulsions in parents and siblings is not a contraindication to pertussis vaccination and children with such family histories should receive Pertussis Vaccine according to the recommended schedule. Parents of infants and children with family histories of convulsions should be informed of their children's increased risk of seizures following DPT vaccination.

Acetaminophen prophylaxis is particularly recommended for children with a personal or family history of convulsions.

Frequent booster doses of tetanus toxoid in the presence of adequate or excessive serum levels of tetanus antitoxin have been associated with increased incidence and severity of reaction and should be avoided.

Adverse Effects: Mild local reactions consisting of erythema, pain and tenderness, swelling and induration at the injection site are common, usually self-limited and subside without treatment.

Up to 70% of children receiving a booster dose at 4 to 6 years of age have been reported to develop local redness and/or swelling ≥5 cm in diameter. This is generally self-limiting and subsides without treatment.

Persistent nodules at the site of injection have occurred following the use of an adsorbed vaccine, but this complication is unusual. Sterile abscess at the site of injection has been reported (6 to 10 per million doses).

Mild to moderate systemic reactions occur frequently following injections of this vaccine. These usually consist of one or more of the following symptoms and signs; temperature elevation ≥38°C, drowsiness, fretfulness, listlessness, anorexia, vomiting, irritability, persistent or unusual crying. These symptoms are most frequent during the first 24 hours following vaccine injection and may persist for 1 to 2 days. The incidence and severity of fever and irritability can be reduced by administration of acetaminophen (15 mg/kg/dose) at the time of inoculation and again 4 and 8 hours after vaccination.

Persistent, inconsolable crying lasting 3 or more hours (1%) and high-pitched, unusual screaming (0.1%) have also been reported after DPT vaccination. Convulsions and a hypotonic-hyporesponsive state have each been reported to occur at a frequency of about 1:1 750 injections of DPT. Most convulsions are brief, generalized and self-limited, and are usually associated with fever. Neither febrile nor afebrile convulsions have been shown to be associated with subsequent seizure disorder. Complete recovery, with no persistent sequelae, has been observed on follow-up of children with hypotonic-hyporesponsive episodes or convulsions. (See also Contraindications and Precautions.)

Although there has been a concern about the possible association of severe neurologic illness (including encephalopathy) occurring within 72 hours of the administration of pertussis-containing vaccines to previously healthy infants, the risk of an association is so small compared to the background rate for these types of events that the question of causation probably cannot be answered.

Reanalysis of the National Childhood Encephalopathy study (NECS) in the United Kingdom has failed to confirm that there was an increased risk of permanent brain damage following acute neurological illness occurring within 7 days of pertussis vaccination. Additional studies have also failed to demonstrate an association between pertussis vaccine and permanent neurologic sequelae.

Sudden infant death syndrome (SIDS) has been reported in temporal relationship to the administration of vaccines containing diphtheria and tetanus toxoids and pertussis vaccine (DPT). Review of the evidence does not indicate a causal relationship between DPT vaccine and SIDS. Studies showing a temporal relation between these events are consistent with the expected occurrence of SIDS over the age range in which DPT immunization usually occurs.

Physicians, nurses, and pharmacists should report any adverse occurrences temporally related to the administration of the product in accordance with local requirements and report to the Medical Director at Connaught Laboratories Limited, 1755 Steeles Avenue West, Toronto, Ontario, Canada, M2R 3T4.

Dosage: For primary immunization of infants the following routine immunization schedule is recommended: one 0.5 mL dose administered at 2, 4, 6 and 18 months of age.

If for any reason this schedule is delayed, it is recommended that 3 doses of 0.5 mL be administered with an interval 4 to 8 weeks between doses, followed by a fourth dose of 0.5 mL administered approximately 1 year after the third dose.

A booster dose of 0.5 mL should be administered between 4 and 6 years of age (i.e., at the time of school entry). This booster dose is unnecessary if the fourth primary immunizing dose has been administered after the fourth birthday.

Administration: Parenteral biological products should be inspected visually for extraneous particulate matter and/or discoloration before administration. If these conditions exist, the product should not be administered.

Shake the vial or ampul well to distribute uniformly the suspension before withdrawing each dose. Before withdrawing a dose from an ampul, tap the container first to ensure that any vaccine in the ampul neck falls to the lower portion of the ampul. Once the ampul has been opened, any of its contents not used immediately should be discarded.

When administering a dose from a rubber-stoppered vial, do not remove either the rubber stopper or the metal seal holding it in place. Aseptic technique must be used for withdrawal of each dose.

Before injection, the skin over the site to be injected should be cleansed with a suitable germicide.

Administer the vaccine **i.m.** The preferred site is into the anterolateral aspect of the mid-thigh (vastus lateralis muscle) or into the deltoid muscle.

The former is the site of choice for infants <1 year of age because it provides the largest muscle. In children >1 year of age, the deltoid is the preferred site since use of the anterolateral thigh results in frequent complaints of limping due to muscle pain.

After insertion of the needle, aspirate to ensure that the needle has not entered a blood vessel.

Do not inject i.v.

Each person who is immunized should be given a permanent personal immunization record. In addition, it is essential that the physician or nurse record the immunization history in the permanent medical record of each patient. This permanent office record should contain the name of the vaccine, date given, dose, manufacturer and lot number.

Storage: Store between 2 and 8°C. **Do not freeze.** Product which has been exposed to freezing should not be used.

Supplied: Each single dose (0.5 mL) contains: diphtheria toxoid (25 Lf), tetanus toxoid (5 Lf), pertussis vaccine (4 to 12 Protective Units [P.U.]), aluminum phosphate (1.5 mg), purified inactivated poliomyelitis vaccine (Type 1 Mahoney, Type 2 M.E.F.1, Type 3 Saukett), 2-phenoxyethanol 0.5% and formaldehyde (27 ppm) added as preservatives. By calculation, the vaccine contains 10 ppm Tween 80, 0.05% albumin (Human) and less than 1 ppm of bovine serum. Trace amounts polymyxin B and neomycin may be present from the cell growth medium. Multiple-dose rubber-stoppered vials of 5 mL and single-dose glass ampuls of 0.5 mL.

DPT Polio Adsorbed is also available in a package containing 5 single dose vials of Act-HIB for reconstitution with 5 single dose ampuls of DPT Polio Adsorbed. This product provides an efficient means of administering routine immunization against diphtheria, tetanus, pertussis, poliomyelitis and H. influenzae type b disease in a single injection at a single visit.

Reviewed 1997

DIPHTHERIA AND TETANUS TOXOIDS ADSORBED AND PERTUSSIS VACCINE (DPT Adsorbed)

Connaught

Vaccine

Pharmacology: Immunization against diphtheria, tetanus, and pertussis has been associated with a striking decrease in the incidence of morbidity and mortality from these diseases. Simultaneous vaccination with a combination vaccine containing diphtheria and tetanus toxoids and pertussis vaccine have been used in Canada since 1958.

Injection of bacterial proteins such as diphtheria and tetanus toxoids results in the production of protective antibodies. The peak antibody levels achieved with the first dose are usually low, and a primary series is required to prime the immune system and produce a high antibody level. After completion of a primary series, circulating antibodies to tetanus and diphtheria toxoids gradually decline but are thought to persist at protective levels for up to 10 years. Tetanus antitoxin levels of >0.01 IU/mL are generally accepted as good evidence of immunity from tetanus. Diphtheria antitoxin levels of ≥0.01 IU/mL are thought to be the minimal level required for protection. Levels >0.05 IU/mL are considered optimal for protection.

Diphtheria is a serious communicable disease caused by toxigenic strains of C. diphtheriae. The organism may be harboured in the nasopharynx, skin or other sites of asymptomatic carriers, making eradication of the disease difficult. Routine immunization against diphtheria in infancy and childhood has been widely practised in Canada since 1930, resulting in a decline in morbidity and mortality. Fewer than 5 cases are now reported annually in Canada. The case-fatality rate remains 5 to 10%, with the highest death rates in the very young and elderly. The disease occurs most frequently in unimmunized or partially immunized individuals. Diphtheria toxoid is a cell-free preparation of diphtheria toxin detoxified with formaldehyde. The immunity conferred is antitoxic, not antibacterial, and thus protects against the potentially lethal systemic effects of diphtheria toxin but not directly against local infection.

Tetanus is an acute and often fatal disease caused by an extremely potent neurotoxin produced by C. tetani. The organism is ubiquitous and its occurrence in nature cannot be controlled. Immunization is highly effective, provides long-lasting protection, and is recommended for the whole population. Only 2 to 3 cases of tetanus are now reported annually in Canada. Tetanus toxoid is prepared by detoxification of tetanus toxin with formaldehyde.

Pertussis (whooping cough) is a highly communicable bacterial disease caused by B. pertussis. Severity and mortality are greatest in infancy, and even infants born to apparently immune mothers are highly susceptible to infection, particularly if maternal immunity was vaccine-induced. During the last 30 years, vaccination has been widely practised in Canada and the incidence and mortality from pertussis have declined remarkably. However, outbreaks of pertussis continue to occur across Canada, with an annual reported rate of 1 000 to 8 000 cases over the past 5 years. Deaths and brain damage from pertussis infections still occur, particularly in young infants who have not been vaccinated. Pertussis vaccine is a suspension of killed B. pertussis organisms. A primary series of 4 doses of vaccine is begun in infancy. Protection from infection is estimated to be 60 to 80%; protection against severe disease is 85% or higher. Protection from disease afforded by the vaccine decreases as the time interval since vaccination increases.

In a clinical trial done in Canada in 1979, 555 infants aged 2 to 6 months received three 0.5 mL i.m. injections of DPT Adsorbed Vaccine with an interval of 4 weeks between doses. High (≥0.11 μg/mL) diphtheria and tetanus antitoxin responses developed in more than 90% and in 100% of recipients respectively, and a pertussis agglutinin titre response of ≥1:64 developed in ≥85% of recipients.

Indications: For the primary and booster immunization of infants, at or above the age of 2 months, and of children up to their 7th birthday against diphtheria, tetanus and whooping cough.

When both vaccines are indicated, DPT Adsorbed may be used to reconstitute Act-HIB for simultaneous administration of all 4 antigens in a single injection. DPT Adsorbed must **not** be mixed in the same syringe with any other vaccines.

DPT Adsorbed may be administered simultaneously with other Hib conjugate vaccines, MMR and IPV each at separate sites with separate syringes, and with OPV.

Contraindications: General: Immunization with this product should be deferred in the presence of any acute illness, including febrile illness.

DPT Adsorbed should not be administered to children after their 7th birthday or to adults because of reactions to diphtheria toxoid or to pertussis vaccine and because pertussis is less severe in these age groups than in infants and young children.

Absolute Contraindications: Allergy to any component of DPT Adsorbed, or an allergic or anaphylactic reaction to a previous dose of DPT Adsorbed are contraindications to vaccination.

Relative Contraindications: Hypotonic-hyporesponsive Episodes: No long-term sequelae have been associated with hypotonic-hyporesponsive episodes; however, it may be prudent in areas of low pertussis incidence to withhold the pertussis component and continue immunization with DT in children who have experienced a hypotonic-hyporesponsive episode following a previous dose of pertussis-containing vaccine. Immunization of children with DPT can continue if the incidence of disease is high in their area.

Deferral: Deferral of the pertussis component of DPT Adsorbed should be considered in children with a progressive, evolving, or unstable neurologic condition (including seizures) because administration of the pertussis component may coincide with the onset of overt manifestations of such disorders and result in confusion about causation. It is prudent to delay initiation of immunization with pertussis vaccine until further observation and study have clarified the child's neurologic status. In addition, the effect of treatment, if any, can be assessed. Immunization with DPT Adsorbed should be reinstituted when the condition has resolved, been corrected or controlled.

When immunization with pertussis vaccine is contraindicated or deferred, immunization with diphtheria and tetanus toxoids, when necessary, may be continued using DT Adsorbed. The use of fractional doses in an attempt to reduce the severity of adverse reactions cannot be recommended because there is insufficient evidence on the safety or efficacy of such smaller doses.

Elective immunization of individuals over 6 months of age should be deferred during an outbreak of poliomyelitis.

Human Immunodeficiency Virus (HIV) Infected Persons: HIV-infected individuals, both asymptomatic and symptomatic, should be immunized with DPT vaccine according to standard schedules.

Warnings: If this product is used in persons with malignancies, receiving immunosuppressive therapies, including irradiation, antimetabolites, alkylating agents, cytotoxic drugs, or who are otherwise immunocompromised, the expected immune response may not be obtained.

Corticosteroid therapy can result in immunosuppression although the exact dose and duration of therapy required to suppress the immune system is not well defined. Persons treated with high doses of systemic steroids, e.g., ≥2 mg/kg/day of prednisone orally for more than 2 weeks, should be considered to have a compromised immune system.

As with any vaccine, immunization with DPT Adsorbed may not protect 100% of susceptible individuals.

Precautions: General: The possibility of allergic reactions in individuals sensitive to components of the vaccine should be evaluated. Epinephrine HCl solution (1:1 000) and other appropriate agents should be available for immediate use in case an anaphylactic or acute hypersensitivity reaction occurs.

Before an injection of any vaccine, appropriate precautions should be taken to prevent adverse reactions. This includes a review of the patient's history with respect to possible hypersensitivity to the vaccine or similar vaccine, determination of previous immunizaton history, and the presence of any contraindications to immunization.

Special care should be taken to ensure that the product is not injected into a blood vessel.

A separate, sterile syringe and needle, or a sterile disposable unit, must be used for each individual patient to prevent the transmission of infectious agents. There have been case reports of transmission of HIV and hepatitis by failure to scrupulously observe sterile technique. In particular, the same needle and/or syringe must never be used to re-enter a multidose vial to withdraw vaccine even when it is to be used for inoculation of the same patient. This may lead to contamination of the vial contents and infection of patients who subsequently receive vaccine from the vial.

Do not recap needles.

A family history of convulsions in parents and siblings is not a contraindication to pertussis vaccination and children with such family histories should receive Pertussis Vaccine according to the recommended schedule. Parents of infants and children with family histories of convulsions should be informed of their children's increased risk of seizures following DPT vaccination. Acetaminophen prophylaxis is particularly recommended for children with a personal or family history of convulsions.

Frequent booster doses of tetanus toxoid in the presence of adequate or excessive serum levels of tetanus antitoxin have been associated with increased incidence and severity of reactions and should be avoided.

Adverse Effects: Mild local reactions consisting of erythema, pain and tenderness, swelling and induration at the injection site are common, usually self-limited and subside without treatment.

Up to 70% of children receiving a booster dose at 4 to 6 years of age have been reported to develop local redness and/or swelling ≥5 cm in diameter. This is generally self-limiting and subsides without treatment.

Persistent nodules at the site of injection have occurred following the use of adsorbed vaccine, but this complication is unusual. Sterile abscess at the site of injection has been reported (6 to 10 per million doses).

Mild to moderate systemic reactions occur frequently following injections of this vaccine. These usually consist of one or more of the following symptoms and signs: temperature elevation ≥38°C, drowsiness, fretfulness, anorexia, vomiting, irritability, persistent or unusual crying. These symptoms are most frequent during the first 24 hours following vaccine injection and may persist for 1 to 2 days.The incidence and severity of fever and irritability can be reduced by administration of acetaminophen (15 mg/kg/dose) at the time of inoculation and again 4 and 8 hours after vaccination.

Persistent, inconsolable crying lasting 3 or more hours (1%) and high-pitched, unusual screaming (0.1%) have also been reported after DPT vaccination. Convulsions and a hypotonic-hyporesponsive state have each been reported to occur at a frequency of about 1:1 750 injections of DPT. Most convulsions are brief, generalized and self-limited, and are usually associated with fever. Neither febrile nor afebrile convulsions have been shown to be associated with subsequent seizure disorder. Complete recovery, with no persistent sequelae, has been observed on follow-up of children with hypotonic-hyporesponsive episodes or convulsions. (See also Contraindications and Precautions.)

Although there has been a concern about the possible association of severe neurologic illness (including encephalopathy) occurring within 72 hours of the administration of pertussis-containing vaccines to previously healthy infants, the risk of an association is so small compared to the background rate for these types of events that the question of causation probably cannot be answered.

Reanalysis of the National Childhood Encephalopathy study (NECS) in the United Kingdom has failed to confirm that there was an increased risk of permanent brain damage following acute neurological illness occurring within 7 days of pertussis vaccination. Additional studies have also failed to demonstrate an association between pertussis vaccine and permanent neurologic sequelae.

Sudden infant death syndrome (SIDS) has been reported in temporal relationship to the administration of vaccines containing diphtheria and tetanus toxoids and pertussis vaccine (DPT). Review of the evidence does not indicate a causal relationship between DPT vaccine and SIDS. Studies showing a temporal relation between these events are consistent with the expected occurrence of SIDS over the age range in which DPT immunization usually occurs.

Physicians, nurses, and pharmacists should report any adverse occurrences temporally related to the administration of the product in accordance with local requirements and report to the Medical Director at Connaught Laboratories Limited, 1755 Steeles Avenue West, Toronto, Ontario, Canada, M2R 3T4.

Dosage: For primary immunization of infants the following routine immunization schedule is recommended: one 0.5 mL dose administered at 2, 4, 6 and 18 months of age.

If for any reason this schedule is delayed, it is recommended that 3 doses of 0.5 mL be administered with an interval 4 to 8 weeks between doses, followed by a fourth dose of 0.5 mL administered approximately 1 year following the third dose.

A booster dose of 0.5 mL should be administered between 4 and 6 years of age (i.e., at the time of school entry). This booster dose is unnecessary if the fourth primary immunizing dose has been administered after the fourth birthday.

Administration: Parenteral biological products should be inspected visually for extraneous particulate matter and/or discoloration before administration. If these conditions exist, the product should not be administered.

Shake the vial or ampul well to distribute uniformly the suspension before withdrawing each dose. Before withdrawing a dose from an ampul, tap the container first to ensure that any vaccine in the ampul neck falls to the lower portion of the ampul. Once the ampul has been opened, any of its contents not used immediately should be discarded. When administering a dose from a rubber-stoppered vial, do not remove either the rubber stopper or the metal seal holding it in place. Aseptic technique must be used for withdrawal of each dose.

Before injection, the skin over the site to be injected should be cleansed with a suitable germicide.

Administer the vaccine **i.m.** The preferred site is into the anterolateral aspect of the mid-thigh (vastus lateralis muscle) or into the deltoid muscle.

The former is the site of choice for infants <1 year of age because it provides the largest muscle. In children >1 year of age, the deltoid is the preferred site since use of the anterolateral thigh results in frequent complaints of limping due to muscle pain.

After insertion of the needle, aspirate to ensure that the needle has not entered a blood vessel.

Do not inject i.v.

Each person who is immunized should be given a permanent personal immunization record. In addition, it is essential that the physician or nurse record the immunization history in the permanent medical record of each patient. This permanent office record should contain the name of the vaccine, date given, dose, manufacturer and lot number.

Supplied: Each 0.5 mL dose contains: diphtheria toxoid (25 Lf), tetanus toxoid (5 Lf), pertussis vaccine (4 to 12 Protective Units) (P.U.) and aluminum phosphate 1.5 mg. Thimerosal 0.01% is added as a preservative. Multidose rubber stoppered vials of 5 mL and single dose glass ampuls of 0.5 mL.

DPT Adsorbed is also available in a package containing 5 single dose vials of Act-Hib for reconstitution with 5 single dose ampuls of DPT Adsorbed. This product provides an efficient means of administering routine immunization against diphtheria, tetanus, pertussis, and H. influenzae type b disease in a single injection at a single visit.

Store between 2 and 8°C. **Do not freeze.** Product which has been exposed to freezing should not be used.

Reviewed 1997

DIPHTHERIA AND TETANUS TOXOIDS (d2T5) ADSORBED

BioChem Vaccines

Vaccine

Indications: Diphtheria and Tetanus Toxoids (d2T5) Adsorbed is the preferred immunizing agent for persons aged 7 years or older. It is recommended for: primary immunization of older children and adults against diphtheria and tetanus; regular booster doses for children at 14 to 16 years of age and every 10 years to adults; and management of wounds when tetanus toxoid is indicated.

Contraindications: Immunization with d2T5 Adsorbed Toxoids should be postponed in the presence of any acute illness, including febrile illness.

It is a contraindication to administer this vaccine to individuals known to be sensitive to thimerosal.

Warnings: If the vaccine is administered to persons receiving immunosuppressive therapy, it should be borne in mind that the expected antigenic response may not be obtained.

Precautions: Individuals who are hypersensitive to the components of the vaccine may develop allergic reactions. Sterile epinephrine HCl solution 1:1 000 should always be readily available in case an acute anaphylactic reaction should occur. If hypersensitivity to the diphtheria component is suspected it is recommended to utilize Diphtheria Toxin for Schick Test and Diphtheria Toxoid for Control as diagnostic aids.

In the case of tetanus, frequent reinforcing (booster) doses of tetanus toxoid in the presence of adequate or excessive serum levels of tetanus antibodies have been associated with increased incidence and severity of reactions and should be avoided.

Caution: A separate **sterile** syringe and needle or a **sterile** disposable unit should always be used for each patient to prevent transmission of hepatitis B virus, HIV virus or other infectious agent from one person to another.

Pregnancy: When there are clear indications for their use, toxoids may be given to pregnant women. It is preferable, however, to defer immunization until after delivery unless immediate risk is involved.

Adverse Effects: Mild local reactions such as pain, erythema, tenderness and induration at the injection site are common, and may be associated with systemic reactions including mild to moderate transient fever, chills, malaise and irritability. Persistent nodules at the injection site have occurred following the use of adsorbed vaccine, but this reaction is unusual.

Systemic reactions may develop and take the form of allergic reactions including urticaria and, less commonly, angioneurotic edema. Influenza-like symptoms have been reported and usually occur within 12 hours of vaccination. Neurological complications such as peripheral neuropathies following tetanus toxoid administration have been reported but are rare.

It has been shown that the incidence of reactions to tetanus toxoid rises according to the number of previously administered doses and occurs mainly in the over-immunized.

Notification of Reactions: It is advisable to report any unusual reactions immediately or shortly following any vaccination to the product manufacturer and the provincial epidemiologist.

Dosage: Primary Immunization: The preferred agent for primary immunization of persons 7 years of age or older is combined adsorbed diphtheria and tetanus toxoids (d2T5) containing less diphtheria toxoid than vaccine preparations given to younger children. This is less likely to cause reactions in older persons. Two doses of 0.5 mL are given at least

Diphtheria and Tetanus Toxoids (d2T5) Adsorbed (cont'd)

8 weeks apart and a further dose 1 year later to complete the course.

Reinforcing (booster) Doses: For children of 14 to 16 years of age who have completed the primary immunization course against diphtheria and tetanus, a single dose of 0.5 mL of combined d2T5 adsorbed toxoids should be administered i.m. as a reinforcing (booster) dose, at 10 year intervals. It is the same for adult persons unless there are contraindications to the administration of tetanus toxoid. When d2T5 adsorbed toxoids are to be used, a prior Schick test or sensitivity test is unnecessary.

Procedure at Time of Injury: No additional dose of d2T5 Adsorbed Toxoids or Tetanus Toxoid is recommended, at the time of injury, for those who, within the previous 5 years, have received a complete primary immunization course or a reinforcing dose against tetanus with either the Combined Toxoids or with Tetanus Toxoid alone.

If more than 5 years have elapsed since the completion of a primary course of immunization or receipt of the last reinforcing dose against tetanus, a single dose of Tetanus Toxoid or an appropriate Combined Vaccine containing tetanus toxoid should be administered.

Should information about previous administration of tetanus toxoid be inadequate or unavailable, a prophylactic dose of 250 U of Tetanus Immune Globulin of human origin (TIG) should be administered in addition to Tetanus Toxoid Adsorbed in cases of clean minor wounds. If the wounds are severe or grossly contaminated, a dose of 500 U of Human Tetanus Immune Globulin (TIG) is recommended along with Tetanus Toxoid Adsorbed.

Should Human Tetanus Immune Globulin (TIG) and Tetanus Toxoid Adsorbed, or a combined vaccine containing tetanus toxoid, be required simultaneously, the 2 preparations should never be mixed in the same syringe. They should be administered in separate syringes and at different sites.

Administration: The skin at the injection site should be cleaned with a suitable antiseptic and dried with a piece of dry sterile cotton. The vaccine should be administered **i.m.** into the deltoid muscle or the mid-lateral aspect of the thigh.

Do not inject i.v. or s.c.

In order to avoid i.v. injection, the plunger of the syringe should be pulled back to ensure that no blood is being withdrawn before injecting the desired dose.

Withdrawal from an Ampul: **Shake** the ampul to disperse the contents thoroughly **immediately before** withdrawing the dose of vaccine.

Tap the ampul to ensure that the contents are in the lower portion rather than in the neck of the ampul.

Using a sterile piece of cotton or a sterile towel, break off the top of the ampul at the colored line (no file is required). Then, using aseptic technique to prevent contamination, and using a **sterile** needle affixed to a **sterile** syringe, withdraw the contents of the ampul into the syringe, holding the ampul in such a way that the tip of the needle is kept immersed throughout the withdrawal.

Once the ampul has been opened, any of its unused contents should immediately be discarded.

Withdrawal from a Vial: **Do not remove the rubber stopper from the vial. Shake** the vial to disperse the contents thoroughly **immediately before** withdrawing each dose of vaccine.

Tear off the central part of the metallic cover-seal. Moisten the exposed surface of the rubber stopper with a sterile piece of cotton soaked with a suitable antiseptic and allow a few minutes for it to take effect. Draw into a sterile syringe a volume of air equal to the amount of vaccine to be withdrawn from the vial, and pierce the center of the rubber stopper with the sterile needle affixed to the syringe. Invert the vial and slowly inject into it the air contained in the syringe. Keeping the tip of the needle immersed, withdraw into the syringe the required amount of vaccine, then, holding the plunger of the syringe steady, withdraw the needle from the vial.

It is desirable that the entire contents of a multidose container be used at the same vaccination session. Only good aseptic technique allows for the sampling of a partially used multidose vial from a previous vaccination session.

Each person who is immunized should be given a permanent personal immunization record. In addition, it is essential that the physician or nurse record the immunization history in the permanent medical record of each patient. This permanent office record should contain the name of the vaccine, date given, dose, manufacturer and lot number.

Disposal: Diphtheria and tetanus toxoids (d2T5) adsorbed and related materials used for vaccination can be disposed of in the same way as other medicines. Because d2T5 is an inactivated product, there is no risk of infection from subsequent handling.

Supplied: The d2T5 adsorbed vaccine is supplied as a sterile, cloudy, uniform suspension of diphtheria and tetanus toxoids adsorbed on aluminum phosphate, in an isotonic sodium chloride solution. Each dose (0.5 mL) contains: diphtheria toxoid 2 Lf, tetanus toxoid 5 Lf, aluminum phosphate 1.5 mg and 0.01% thimerosal as preservative. Scored ampuls of 0.5 mL, boxes of 5. Vials of 5 mL.

Store in the refrigerator between 2 and 8°C. **Do not freeze.** Carefully check the expiry date, and take note that this date applies to unopened containers only. Outdated vaccine should never be used.

Reviewed 1998

DIPHTHERIA ANTITOXIN (EQUINE)

Connaught

Antitoxin

Indications: For the treatment of suspected or confirmed cases of diphtheria.

Precautions: Before administering any serum or antitoxin to a patient, physicians are well advised to ascertain whether the patient has a history of asthma, or hay fever, and particularly, whether the patient suffers distress when in proximity to horses. Patients with such a history may develop serious reactions of an anaphylactic character upon the administration of serum of equine origin either s.c., i.m. or i.v. It should be borne in mind, also, that a patient who has been given a previous injection of serum of equine origin may develop a marked reaction when given a second injection, especially if the previous injection was i.v.

At the time of administering any serum or antitoxin to a patient, it is desirable to have 1 mL of epinephrine HCl solution (1:1 000) immediately available.

Tests for Sensitivity to Serum or Antitoxin: A test for sensitivity to serum or antitoxin should be carried out each time a serum or antitoxin is administered, unless it is being given daily. Sensitivity to any particular serum or antitoxin may be gauged by one of the following methods:

Skin or eye tests for sensitivity should be done before any injection, regardless of whether or not the patient has had the serum previously. The skin test dose is 0.1 mL of a 1:100 saline dilution of the serum to be given intracutaneously. In persons with a history of allergy, the dose is reduced to 0.05 mL of a 1:1 000 dilution, intracutaneously. The reaction is read in 5 to 30 minutes and is positive if a wheal with a hyperemic areola appears.

(In a marked reaction the wheal is likely to have irregular projections.) The extent of the wheal and of its projections, and the dimensions of the hyperemic area provide a rough index of the degree of the patient's sensitivity, and of the resultant likelihood of his reacting unfavorably to the injection of the particular serum or antitoxin concerned.

A negative skin test does not entirely preclude the possibility of the occurrence of serum reactions.

Except in small children, an eye test often is simpler and is less likely to show nonspecific reactions. A drop of a 1:10 dilution of serum in physiologic saline is instilled in one eye, controlled by a drop of physiologic saline solution in the other eye; a positive reaction consists of lacrimation and conjunctivitis appearing in 10 to 30 minutes.

Eye tests have not been known to be fatal, but skin tests have resulted in fatalities. Therefore, a serum should never be injected, nor a skin test performed unless a syringe containing 1 mL of epinephrine HCl solution (1:1 000) is within immediate reach.

Serum Reactions: 1. Anaphylactic Reaction: In the event of a reaction of an anaphylactic character, 0.5 mL of epinephrine HCl solution (1:1 000) should be administered by the s.c. or i.m. route.

2. Thermal Reaction: When this reaction occurs, it usually develops from 20 minutes to 1 hour after the injection of serum or antitoxin. It is characterized by a chilly sensation, slight dyspnea and a rapid rise in temperature.

3. Serum Sickness: The symptoms of serum sickness are fever, skin rashes, edema of the skin, glandular enlargement and pains in the joints. These symptoms may appear individually, or in combination, within 14 days after the administration of a serum or antitoxin. Urticarial reaction is usually relieved by a s.c. or i.m. injection of 0.5 mL of epinephrine HCl solution (1:1 000). In severe cases of serum sickness ACTH or cortisone may be required.

It has been recommended that 0.3 mL of epinephrine HCl solution (1:1 000) be administered not only to every patient who gives a positive reaction to a sensitivity test, or has received serum or antitoxin before, or has a history of allergy, but to every patient before receiving serum irrespective of these factors.

Dosage: Treatment of Diphtheria: Since diphtheria antitoxin injected i.m. is absorbed much more rapidly than when injected s.c., i.m. injections are greatly superior to s.c. injections in the treatment of diphtheria. In the treatment of diphtheria, results are best when very large doses of antitoxin are administered. In an uncomplicated pharyngeal case, the dose should not be less than 20 000 IU for a child or 40 000 IU for an adult. In laryngeal or severe toxic cases, or in cases left untreated for several days much larger doses amounting to 100 000 or even 150 000 units are recommended. Such circumstances call for a combination of i.m. and i.v. injections, and the use of from 10 000 to 20 000 units i.v. is recommended. Diphtheria antitoxin as distributed by the Connaught Laboratories Limited may be quite satisfactorily used i.v., at a 1:10 dilution. It should be at ambient temperature before being injected.

Administration of Antitoxin to Sensitive Persons: Whenever there is a history of allergy, sensitivity to horse serum or manifestations of sensitivity when in proximity to horses, or if the reaction to the skin or eye test is positive, great care must be exercised in the administration of serum (or antitoxin).

No one method can be advised for the administration of serum or antitoxin for sensitive persons as each presents an individual problem. Desensitization of the patient should be carried out by serial injections of diluted antitoxin as indicated below at intervals of 20 minutes, provided no reaction occurs.

Schedule for Desensitization: (a) 0.05 mL of 1:20 dilution s.c., (b) 0.1 mL of 1:10 dilution s.c., (c) 0.3 mL of 1:10 dilution s.c., (d) 0.1 mL undiluted serum s.c., (e) 0.2 mL undiluted serum s.c., (f) 0.5 mL undiluted serum s.c., (g) inject remaining therapeutic doses i.m.

After the patient can properly withstand these doses of serum or antitoxin, it is usually safe to inject larger doses (i.m.) at 20-minute intervals.

If a reaction occurs after a desensitizing dose, injections should be stopped for 1 hour, recommencing the schedule at 20-minute intervals by repeating the last dose which failed to cause a reaction.

If deemed imperative on clinical grounds, i.v. administration of a serum or antitoxin may be commenced after the purpose of the desensitization has been satisfactorily served. The first i.v. dose should be small, however, i.e., 0.1 mL diluted with 10 mL of sterile physiological saline, and it should be injected very slowly, 1 mL/minute. Increasingly larger doses may then be similarly given at half-hourly intervals.

A separate sterilized syringe and needle should be used for each individual patient to prevent transmission of homologous serum hepatitis and other infectious agents from one person to another.

Note: Following the administration of serum (or antitoxin), and particularly in those cases showing a positive skin or eye test, the patient should be kept under close observation for 1 to 2 hours and under reasonably close surveillance for a period of 24 hours.

The site of injection should be prepared with a suitable antiseptic.

If sterile disposable syringes and needles are not used, syringes and needles should be sterilized in an autoclave 121°C for 30 minutes. If this method of sterilization is not available syringes and needles should be boiled for at least 20 minutes. Care should be taken to maintain sterility until used.

Withdrawing the preparation from a rubber-stopped vial: **Do not remove the rubber stopper from the vial.**

Apply a sterile pledget of cotton moistened with a suitable antiseptic to the surface of the rubber stopper and allow it to act for at least 5 minutes. Draw into the sterile syringe a volume of air equal to the amount of the preparation to be withdrawn from the vial. Pierce the centre of the rubber stopper with the sterile needle of the syringe; invert the vial; slowly inject into it the air contained in the syringe; and, keeping the point of the needle immersed, withdraw into the syringe the required amount of the preparation. Then hold the syringe-plunger steady and withdraw the needle from the vial.

The person giving the immunization should record the dose, route of administration, date of immmunization and the antitoxin lot number on the patient's immunization card or medical record.

Supplied: Each vial contains: 20 000 IU of a refined and concentrated preparation of globulins obtained from horse serum modified by enzymatic digestion. Also contains phenol 0.22% as a preservative. Note: The volume of antitoxin in a vial will vary from lot to lot. This is because the potency of the bulk antitoxin varies from lot to lot and it is therefore necessary to adjust the filling volume of each lot so that each vial contains 20 000 IU. As a result, vials from one lot may appear half full while vials from a different lot may appear three-quarters full. Store in a refrigerator between 2 and 8°C.

Reviewed 1998

DIPHTHERIA TOXOID
Connaught

Diphtheria Prophylaxis

Indications: For active immunization against diphtheria.

Dosage: For Infants, Pre-School and School Children: For infants over 6 months of age and children, it is recommended that 3 s.c. doses of 1 mL be administered with an interval of 4 weeks between the first, second and third doses.

Reinforcing Doses: Blood serum of children 2 to 5 years following 3 doses of diphtheria toxoid has shown significant reduction in diphtheria antitoxin content during successive years; and Schick tests made at long intervals following immunization against diphtheria have shown a significant proportion of reversions to the "Schick-positive" state. These findings are not surprising in view of the fact that even among those who recover from diphtheria a considerable number become again susceptible to the disease. Obviously, however, it is desirable that children who were immunized against diphtheria in infancy or during pre-school years should have their immunity reinforced.

It is recommended that a dose of 1 mL of diphtheria toxoid be given s.c. after a period of about 1 year following the initial course of 3 doses and again about 4 years later, at about 5 years of age. At school age an additional reinforcing dose of 0.1 to 0.2 mL is recommended for those who have been immunized according to the above schedule. This small dose can be given without being preceded by a reaction test. For those of school age who have not received reinforcing doses after their primary immunization a full dose of 1 mL, preceded by a reaction test, should be given.

For Older Children and Adults: Under certain circumstances it may be desirable or necessary to immunize older children (over 8 years) or adults who have not been previously immunized or for whom records of previous immunization are lacking. Such a procedure is complicated by the fact that local or general reactions to the toxoid may be encountered. These reactions are due to sensitivity to the diphtheria protein and are seldom encountered in infants or children of pre-school age.

In order to avoid such reactions, a "reaction test" should therefore be carried out before giving a regular course of injections to older children or adults. For this purpose, Diphtheria Toxoid for Reaction Test (diluted toxoid) is supplied in this package. Diphtheria Toxoid for Reaction Test is also available in packages of 5 ampuls, each ampul sufficient for testing up to 5 persons at one time in connection with immunization programs.

Method of Performing the Reaction Test: In making a reaction test, an essential is a suitable 1 mL syringe graduated in tenths and equipped with a fine needle (gauge 26 or 27), both properly sterilized. The test is made by injecting intradermally, in the flexor surface of the forearm, 0.1 mL of the diluted diphtheria toxoid supplied for the test. If, within 48 hours, no redness has developed at the site of injection or if an area of redness less than 13 mm in diameter with no induration has developed, the usual dose of diphtheria toxoid may be given. If, however, redness of more than 13 mm in diameter, or induration is present, it is recommended that use be made of smaller doses, or of the Diphtheria Toxoid Diluted for Immunization of Reactors which is available from the Laboratories.

The diphtheria toxoid supplied for reaction tests is identical with that which is supplied by these Laboratories for use as a control in making Schick tests. Hence, a complete Schick test including this control may be used to determine sensitivity as well as susceptibility, and is desirable prior to giving a series of injections of diphtheria toxoid to an adolescent or an adult, particularly in view of the fact that a significant proportion of adolescents and adults is immune to diphtheria.

Method of Inoculation: The preparation should be administered by s.c. injection. The injection may conveniently be made into s.c. tissue near the insertion of the deltoid muscle. The site of injection should be prepared with a suitable antiseptic.

If sterile disposable syringes and needles are not used, syringes and needles should be sterilized in an autoclave at 121°C for 30 minutes. Failing that they should be boiled for at least 20 minutes. Care should be taken to maintain sterility until used.

In the inoculation of groups of persons, a separate sterilized needle must be used for each injection. Wiping the needle with alcohol is inadequate for its sterilization.

Withdrawing the preparation from a sealed glass ampul: Tap the ampul to ensure that the solution is in the lower portion rather than in the neck of the ampul. Wipe the neck of the ampul with a suitable antiseptic. Using a sterile piece of cotton or a sterile towel, break off the top of the ampul at the colored line (no file is required). Then with the sterile syringe and needle withdraw the contents of the ampul into the syringe, holding the ampul in such a way that the point of the needle is kept immersed throughout the withdrawal.

Once the ampul has been opened, any of its contents not used immediately should be discarded.

Withdrawing the preparation from a rubber-stoppered vial: **Do not remove the rubber stopper from the vial.**

Apply a sterile pledget of cotton moistened with a suitable antiseptic to the surface of the rubber stopper and allow it to act for at least 5 minutes. Draw into the sterile syringe a volume of air equal to the amount of the preparation to be withdrawn from the vial. Pierce the center of the rubber stopper with the sterile needle of the syringe, invert the vial, slowly inject into it the air contained in the syringe, and, keeping the point of the needle immersed, withdraw into the syringe the required amount of the preparation. Then hold the syringe-plunger steady and withdraw the needle from the vial.

Carefully insert the needle into the s.c. tissue. In order to avoid i.v. injection, pull back the plunger of the syringe to make certain that no blood is withdrawn before injecting the desired dose.

Supplied: A toxoid containing 50 Lf purified diphtheria toxoid/mL. Ampuls of 1 mL, boxes of 3 (including 1 ampul of Diphtheria Toxoid for Reaction Test). Vials of 10 mL; 5×1 mL ampuls for "reactors"; 5×0.5 mL ampuls for sensitivity test. Store at 2 to 8°C.

Reviewed 1998

DIPRIVAN® Ⓟ
Zeneca

Propofol

I.V. Emulsion—Anesthetic—Sedative

Pharmacology: Propofol is an i.v. hypnotic agent for use in the induction and maintenance of general anesthesia or sedation. The drug, an alkylphenol formulated in an oil-in-water emulsion, is chemically distinct from currently available i.v. anesthetic agents. I.V. injection of a therapeutic dose of propofol produces hypnosis rapidly and smoothly, usually within 40 seconds from the start of an injection (one arm-brain circulation time), although induction times >60 seconds have been observed.

Pharmacokinetics in Adults: The pharmacokinetic profile of propofol can be described by a 3-compartment open model. After a single bolus dose, there is fast distribution from blood into tissues ($t_{1/2}\alpha$: 1.8 to 8.3 min), high metabolic clearance ($t_{1/2}\beta$: 34 to 66 min) and a terminal slow elimination from poorly perfused tissues ($t_{1/2}\gamma$: 184 to 480 min). With 12- and 24-hour samplings, $t_{1/2}\gamma$ values of 502 and 674 min, respectively, were observed.

Propofol has large volumes of distribution as would be expected with a highly lipophilic anesthetic agent. The volume of central compartment (V_c) is between 21 and 56 L (0.35 to 0.93 L/kg based on a 60 kg patient), and the volume of distribution at steady state (V_{ss}) is between 171 and 364 L (2.85 to 6.07 L/kg). Values for volume of distribution during the terminal phase (V_d) are 2 to 3 times the corresponding V_{ss} values.

The termination of the anesthetic or sedative effects of propofol after a single i.v. bolus or a maintenance infusion is due to extensive redistribution from the CNS to other tissues and high metabolic clearance, both of which will decrease blood concentrations. The mean propofol concentration at time of awakening is 1 μg/mL (range: 0.74 to 2.2 μg/mL). Recovery from anesthesia or sedation is rapid. When propofol is used for both induction (2.0 to 2.5 mg/kg) and maintenance (0.1 to 0.2 mg/kg/min) of anesthesia, the majority of patients are generally awake, responsive to verbal command and oriented in approximately 7 to 8 minutes. Recovery from the effects of propofol occurs due to rapid metabolism and is not dependent on the terminal elimination half-life since the blood levels achieved in this phase are not clinically significant. A study in 6 subjects showed that 72 and 88% of the administered radio-labeled dose was recovered in the urine within 24 hours and 5 days, respectively. Less than 2% was excreted in the feces. Unchanged drug was less than 0.3%. Propofol is chiefly metabolized by conjugation in the liver to inactive metabolites which are excreted by the kidney. Propofol glucuronide accounts for about 50% of the administered dose. The remainder consists of the 1- and 4-glucuronide and 4-sulfate conjugates of 2,6-diisopropyl-1,4-quinol.

The total body clearance (Cl) of propofol ranges from 1.6 L/min to 2.3 L/min (0.026 to 0.038 L/min/kg based on a 60 kg patient). This clearance exceeds estimates of hepatic blood flow, suggesting possible extrahepatic metabolism.

The pharmacokinetics of propofol do not appear to be altered by gender or chronic hepatic cirrhosis. The effects of acute hepatic failure on the pharmacokinetics of propofol have not been studied. In renal failure, the data is based on very limited findings. There was a trend towards longer half-lives, although the differences versus control patients did not reach statistical significance. With increasing age, the dose of propofol needed to achieve a defined anesthetic endpoint (dose-requirement) decreases. Elderly patients had higher propofol blood concentrations at 2 minutes than young ones (6.07 versus 4.15 μg/mL), probably due to a significantly lower initial distribution volume (20 versus 26 L). The relatively high blood concentrations during the first few minutes can predispose elderly patients to cardiorespiratory effects including hypotension, apnea, airway obstruction and/or oxygen desaturation. The clearance of propofol also decreased from a mean±S.D. of 1.8±0.4 L/min in young patients (18 to 35 years) to 1.4±0.4 L/min in elderly patients (65 to 80 years). The reduced clearance could decrease maintenance propofol requirements and prolong recovery if inappropriate infusions are used. Obesity is associated with significantly larger volumes of distribution (399 L versus 153 L) and clearance rates (2.8 L/min versus 1.8 L/min) but there is no change in the elimination half-life.

When given by an infusion for up to 2 hours, the pharmacokinetics of propofol appear to be independent of dose (0.05 to 0.15 mg/kg/min; 3 to 9 mg/kg/hour) and similar to i.v. bolus pharmacokinetics. The steady-state propofol blood concentrations are proportional to the rate of administration.

Propofol is highly protein-bound (97 to 99%); the degree of binding seems to be unrelated to either sex or age.

In the presence of propofol, alfentanil concentrations were higher than expected based upon the rate of infusion. However, alfentanil did not affect the pharmacokinetics of propofol.

Pharmacokinetics in Adult Patients in Intensive Care Unit (ICU): Regarding most parameters, the pharmacokinetics of propofol in these patients are similar to those of patients undergoing anesthesia/sedation for short surgical procedures. However, the terminal half-life ($t_{1/2}\gamma$) is substantially prolonged after long-term infusion, reflecting extensive tissue distribution.

Pharmacokinetics in Children: The results were obtained in ASA I children, ranging in age from 3 to 10 years, who received a single bolus dose of propofol, 2.5 mg/kg. Propofol was rapidly distributed from blood into tissue ($t_{1/2}\alpha$: 1.5 to 4.1 min), metabolic clearance was high ($t_{1/2}\beta$: 9.3 to 56.1 min) and terminal elimination slow ($t_{1/2}\gamma$: 209 to 735 min). The volume of central compartment (V_c) ranged between 0.53 to 0.72 L/kg, the volume of distribution at steady state (V_{ss}) was between 2.1 to 10.9 L/kg and clearance (Cl) ranged between 0.032 to 0.040 L/min/kg. The mean plasma concentration of propofol at awakening was 2.3 μg/mL.

Propofol induces anesthesia in a dose-dependent manner. In unpremedicated, ASA I or II patients, propofol induced anesthesia in 87% and 95% of patients at doses of 2.0 and 2.5 mg/kg, respectively. Elderly patients require lower doses; for unpremedicated patients older than 55 years of age, the mean dose requirement was 1.66 mg/kg. Premedication profoundly alters dose requirements; at 1.75 mg/kg, propofol induced anesthesia in 65% of patients who had no premedication and in 85% and 100% of patients who received diazepam or papaveretum-hyoscine premedication, respectively.

During induction of anesthesia, the hemodynamic effects of propofol vary. If spontaneous ventilation is maintained, the major cardiovascular effects are arterial hypotension (sometimes greater than a 30% decrease) with little or no change in heart rate and no appreciable decrease in cardiac output. If ventilation is assisted or controlled (positive pressure ventilation), the degree and incidence of decrease in cardiac output are accentuated. Maximal fall in blood pressure occurs within the first few minutes of the administration of a bolus dose. The fall in arterial pressure is greater under propofol anesthesia than under anesthesia induced by thiopental or methohexital. Increases in heart rate with propofol are generally

Diprivan (cont'd)

less pronounced or absent after an induction dose, than after equivalent doses of these other 2 agents.

During maintenance of anesthesia with propofol, systolic and diastolic blood pressures generally remain below preanesthetic levels, although the depth of anesthesia, the rate of maintenance infusion as well as stimulation from tracheal intubation and/or surgery may increase or decrease blood pressure. Heart rate may also vary as a function of these factors but will generally remain below preanesthetic levels.

In the presence of a potent opioid (e.g., fentanyl), the blood pressure lowering effect of propofol is substantially increased. Fentanyl also decreases heart rate and this might lead to a significant decrease in cardiac output.

Age is highly correlated with the fall in blood pressure. In elderly subjects, both the incidence and degree of hypotension are greater than in younger subjects. Thus, a lower induction dose and a slower maintenance rate of administration should be used in the elderly (see Dosage). Particular caution should be exercised in elderly patients with severe coronary and/or cerebral arteriosclerosis; reduction in perfusion pressure may impair adequate blood supply to these organs.

Insufficient data are available regarding the cardiovascular effects of propofol when used for induction and/or maintenance of anesthesia or sedation in elderly, hypotensive, debilitated or other ASA III and IV patients. However, limited information suggests that these patients may have more profound cardiovascular responses. It is recommended that if propofol is used in these patients, a lower induction dose and a slower maintenance rate of administration of the drug be used (see Warnings and Dosage).

The first respiratory disturbance after a bolus dose of propofol is a profound fall in tidal volume leading to apnea in many patients. There has been no accompanying cough or hiccough and otherwise anesthesia is smooth. However, there might be some difficulty in uptake of volatile agents if respiration is not assisted.

In unpremedicated, healthy patients, there is a steep dose-response relationship regarding apnea; 0% and 44% of patients had apnea after receiving 2.0 and 2.5 mg/kg of propofol, respectively. Fentanyl enhanced both the incidence and the onset of apnea and the episode lasted for >60 seconds in the majority of patients.

Opioid premedication—in the presence of hyoscine—affected respiratory function (rate of respiration and minute volume) substantially more than atropine premedication. Respiratory function was more depressed when these premedicants were combined with propofol than when they were combined with thiopental. Enhanced respiratory depression with propofol and an opioid have been observed in the postoperative period.

During maintenance, propofol (0.1 to 0.2 mg/kg/min; 6 to 12 mg/kg/hour) caused a decrease in ventilation usually associated with an increase in carbon dioxide tension which may be marked depending upon the rate of administration and other concurrent medication (e.g., narcotics, sedatives, etc.). **Propofol was not evaluated in patients with any respiratory dysfunction.**

During sedation, attention must be given to the cardiorespiratory effects of propofol. Hypotension, apnea, airway obstruction, and/or oxygen desaturation can occur, especially with a rapid bolus injection. During initiation of sedation, slow infusion or slow injection techniques are preferable over rapid bolus administration, and during maintenance of sedation, a variable rate infusion is preferable over intermittent bolus administration in order to minimize undesirable cardiorespiratory effects. In the elderly, debilitated and ASA III or IV patients, rapid (single or repeated) bolus dose administration should not be used for sedation (see Warnings).

Clinical and preclinical studies suggest that propofol is rarely associated with elevation of plasma histamine levels and does not cause signs of histamine release.

Clinical and preclinical studies show that propofol does not suppress the adrenal response to ACTH.

Preliminary findings in patients with normal intraocular pressure indicate that propofol anesthesia produces a decrease in intraocular pressure which may be associated with a concomitant decrease in systemic vascular resistance.

Propofol is devoid of analgesic or antanalgesic activity.

Indications: A short-acting i.v. general anesthetic agent that can be used for both induction and maintenance of anesthesia as part of a balanced anesthesia technique, including total i.v. anesthesia (TIVA), for inpatient and outpatient surgery.

Also indicated for pediatric anesthesia in children 3 years of age and older.

Propofol, when administered i.v. as directed, can be used to initiate and maintain sedation in conjunction with local/regional anesthesia in patients undergoing surgical procedures. Propofol may also be used for sedation during diagnostic procedures (see Warnings and Precautions).

Propofol should only be administered to intubated, mechanically ventilated, adult patients in the Intensive Care Unit (ICU) to provide continuous sedation and control of stress responses. In this setting, propofol should be administered only by persons trained in general anesthesia or critical care medicine.

Propofol is not recommended for **sedation** in children under the age of 18, either during surgical/diagnostic procedures or in the Intensive Care Unit (ICU), as safety and efficacy have not been established.

Contraindications: When general anesthesia or sedation are contraindicated or in patients with a known allergy and/or hypersensitivity to Diprivan or its components.

Warnings: For general anesthesia or sedation for surgical/diagnostic procedures, propofol should be administered only by persons trained in the administration of general anesthesia and not involved in the conduct of surgical/diagnostic procedures. Patients should be continuously monitored and facilities for maintenance of a patent airway, artificial ventilation, and oxygen enrichment and circulatory resuscitation must be immediately available.

For sedation of intubated, mechanically ventilated, adult patients in the Intensive Care Unit (ICU), propofol should be administered only by persons trained in general anesthesia or critical care medicine.

In the elderly, debilitated and ASA III or IV patients, rapid (single or repeated) bolus administration should not be used during general anesthesia or sedation in order to minimize undesirable cardiorespiratory depression including hypotension, apnea, airway obstruction and/or oxygen desaturation.

Propofol should not be coadministered through the same i.v. catheter with blood or plasma because compatibility has not been established. In vitro tests have shown that aggregates of the globular component of the emulsion vehicle have occurred with blood/plasma/serum from humans and animals. The clinical significance is not known.

Propofol should not be used in obstetrics including Cesarean section deliveries, because propofol crosses the placenta and may be associated with neonatal depression.

Propofol should not be used for Intensive Care Unit (ICU) sedation in patients who have severely disordered fat metabolism because the vehicle of propofol is similar to that of Intralipid 10%. The restrictions that apply to Intralipid 10% should also be considered when using propofol in the ICU.

Extreme care should be used in administering propofol in patients with impaired left ventricular function because propofol may produce a negative inotropic effect.

Extreme care should be used in administering propofol in patients who are hypotensive, hypovolemic or in shock because propofol may cause excessive arterial hypotension.

Extreme care should be used in administering propofol in elderly, debilitated or other ASA III or IV patients.

Strict aseptic techniques must always be maintained during handling as propofol is a single-use parenteral product and contains no antimicrobial preservatives. The vehicle is capable of supporting rapid growth of microorganism (see Precautions and Dosage). **Failure to follow aseptic handling procedures may result in microbial contamination causing fever/infection/sepsis which could lead to life-threatening illness.**

Propofol lacks vagolytic activity and has been associated with reports of bradycardia (occasionally profound) and also asystole. The i.v. administration of an anticholinergic agent before induction, or during maintenance of anesthesia should be considered, especially in situations where vagal tone is likely to predominate or when propofol is used in conjunction with other agents likely to cause a bradycardia.

Since various manifestations of seizures have been reported during propofol anesthesia, special care should be taken when giving the drug to epileptic patients.

Occupational Hazards: Patients receiving propofol on an outpatient basis should not engage in hazardous activities requiring complete mental alertness such as driving a motor vehicle or operating machinery until the effects of propofol have completely subsided.

Precautions: General: Patients should be continuously monitored for early signs of significant hypotension and/or bradycardia. Treatment may include increasing the rate of i.v. fluid, elevation of lower extremities, use of pressor agents or administration of anticholinergic agents (e.g., atropine). Apnea often occurs during induction and may persist for more than 60 seconds. Ventilatory support may be required. Because propofol is an emulsion, caution should be exercised in patients with disorders of lipid metabolism such as primary hyperlipoproteinemia, diabetic hyperlipemia and pancreatitis.

When propofol is administered as a sedative for surgical or diagnostic procedures, patients should be continuously monitored by persons not involved in the conduct of the surgical/diagnostic procedure. Oxygen supplementation should be immediately available and provided where clinically indicated; and oxygen saturation should be monitored in all patients. Patients should be continuously monitored for early signs of hypotension, apnea, airway obstruction and/or oxygen desaturation. These cardiorespiratory effects are more likely to occur following rapid initiation (loading) boluses or during supplemental maintenance boluses, especially in the elderly, debilitated and ASA III or IV patients.

Since propofol is rarely used alone, an adequate period of evaluation of the awakened patient is indicated to ensure satisfactory recovery from general anesthesia or sedation prior to discharge of the patient from the recovery room or to home.

Intensive Care Unit (ICU) Sedation: **Strict aseptic techniques must be followed when handling propofol as the vehicle is capable of supporting rapid growth of microorganisms** (see Warnings and Dosage).

The administration of propofol should be initiated as a continuous infusion and changes in the rate of administration made slowly (>5 min) in order to minimize hypotension and avoid acute overdosage.

Patients should be monitored for early signs of significant hypotension and/or cardiovascular depression, which may be profound. These effects are responsive to discontinuation of propofol, i.v. fluid administration, and/or vasopressor therapy.

As with other sedative medications, there is wide interpatient variability in propofol dosage requirements, and these requirements may change with time.

Patients who receive large doses of narcotics during surgery may require very small doses of propofol for appropriate sedation.

Abrupt discontinuation of propofol infusion prior to weaning should be avoided since, due to the rapid clearance of propofol, it may result in rapid awakening with associated anxiety, agitation and resistance to mechanical ventilation. Infusions of propofol should be adjusted to maintain a light level of sedation throughout the weaning process.

Since propofol is formulated in an oil-water emulsion, patients should be monitored for lipemia. Administration of propofol should be adjusted if fat is being inadequately cleared from the body. A reduction in the quantity of concurrently administered lipids is indicated to compensate for the amount of lipid infused as part of the propofol formulation; 1 mL of propofol contains approximately 0.1 g of fat (1.1 kcal).

The long-term administration of propofol to patients with renal failure and/or hepatic insufficiency has not been evaluated.

Pregnancy: Propofol should not be used in pregnancy. Propofol has been used during termination of pregnancy in the first trimester. Teratology studies in rats and rabbits show some evidence of delayed ossification or abnormal cranial ossification; however, such developmental delays are not considered indicative of a teratogenic effect. Reproductive studies in rats suggest that administration of propofol to the dam adversely affects perinatal survival of the offspring.

Lactation: Propofol is not recommended for use in nursing mothers because preliminary findings indicate that it is excreted in human milk and the effects of oral absorption of small amounts of propofol are not known.

Children: General Anesthesia: In the absence of sufficient clinical experience, propofol is not recommended for anesthesia in children less than 3 years of age (see Indications and Dosage).

Sedation: Propofol is not recommended for **sedation** in children under the age of 18, either during surgical/diagnostic procedures or in the Intensive Care Unit (ICU), as safety and efficacy have not been established.

Although no causal relationship has been established, serious adverse events (including fatalities) have been reported in children given propofol for ICU sedation. These events were seen most often in children with respiratory tract infections given doses in excess of those recommended for adults.

Geriatrics: Elderly patients may be more sensitive to the effects of propofol; therefore, the dosage of propofol should be reduced in these patients according to their condition and clinical response (see Pharmacology, Pharmacokinetics and Dosage).

Cardiac Anesthesia: Propofol was evaluated in 328 patients undergoing coronary artery bypass graft (CABG). Of these patients 85% were males (mean age 61, range 32 to 83) and 15% were females (mean age 65, range 42 to 86).

The majority of patients undergoing CABG had good left ventricular function. Experience in patients with poor left ventricular function, as well as, in patients with hemodynamically significant valvular or congenital heart disease is limited.

Slower rates of administration should be utilized in premedicated patients, geriatric patients, patients with recent fluid shift, or patients who are hemodynamically unstable. Any fluid deficits should be corrected prior to administration of propofol. In those patients where additional fluid therapy may be contraindicated, other measures, e.g., elevation of lower extremities, or use of pressor agents, may be useful to offset the hypotension which is associated with the induction of anesthesia with propofol.

Neurosurgical Anesthesia: When using propofol in patients with increased intracranial pressure (ICP) or impaired cerebral circulation, significant decreases in mean arterial pressure should be avoided because of the resultant decreases in cerebral perfusion pressure. When increased ICP is suspected, hyperventilation and hypocarbia should accompany the administration of propofol (see Dosage).

Drug Interactions: Propofol has been used in association with spinal and epidural anesthesia and with a range of premedicants, muscle relaxants, inhalational agents, analgesic agents and with local anesthetic agents; no significant adverse interactions have been observed.

Adverse Effects: Anesthesia and Sedation for Surgical/Diagnostic Procedures: During induction of anesthesia in clinical trials, hypotension and apnea occurred in the majority of patients. The incidence of apnea varied considerably, occurring in between 30 and 100% of patients depending upon premedication, speed of administration and dose (see Pharmacology). Decreases in systolic and diastolic pressures ranged between 10 and 28%, but were more profound in the elderly and in ASA III and IV patients. Excitatory phenomena occurred in up to 14% of adult patients and in 33 to 90% of pediatric patients; they consisted most frequently of spontaneous musculoskeletal movements and twitching and jerking of the hands, arms, feet or legs. Epileptiform movements including convulsions and opisthotonus have occurred rarely, but a causal relationship with propofol has not been established. Flushing and rash have occurred in 10 to 25% of pediatric patients. Local pain occurred during i.v. injection of propofol at an incidence of 28% when veins of the dorsum of the hand were used and 5% when the larger veins of the forearm and the antecubital fossa were used. Propofol increased plasma glucose concentrations significantly, but no other significant changes in hematological or biochemical values were observed.

In the sedation clinical trials, the adverse reaction profile of propofol was similar to that seen during anesthesia. The most common adverse reactions included hypotension, nausea, pain and/or hotness at injection site and headache. Respiratory events included upper airway obstruction, apnea, hypoventilation, dyspnea and cough.

Rarely, clinical features of anaphylaxis, which may include bronchospasm, erythema and hypotension, occur following propofol administration.

There have been reports of fever.

Pulmonary edema may be a potential side effect associated with the use of propofol.

As with other anesthetics, sexual disinhibition may occur during recovery.

Intensive Care Unit (ICU) Sedation: The most frequent adverse reactions during Intensive Care Unit (ICU) sedation were hypotension (31.5%), hypoxia (6.3%), and hyperlipemia (5.5%). In some patients, hypotension was severe. Other reactions considered severe were observed in single patients and included ventricular tachycardia, decreased cardiac output, decrease in vital capacity and negative inspiratory force, increase in triglycerides, and agitation. Two patients with head injury suffered renal failure with severe increases in BUN accompanied in one patient by an increase in creatinine.

Table I compares the overall occurrence rates of adverse reactions in propofol patients from non-ICU and ICU clinical trials where the rate of occurrence was greater than 1%. Major differences include lack of metabolic/nutritional (hyperlipemia) and respiratory events in the non-ICU group and lack of nausea, vomiting, headache, movement and injection site events in the ICU group.

Adverse reactions reported at an incidence of 1% or less during anesthesia and sedation for surgical/diagnostic procedures: Cardiovascular: significant hypotension, premature atrial contractions, premature ventricular contractions, tachycardia, syncope, abnormal ECG, bigeminy, edema.

Table I—Diprivan

Non-ICU vs ICU Adverse Events Occurring in Greater Than 1% of Propofol Patients

Body System	Event	Non-ICU	ICU
Number of patients		2 588	127
Cardiovascular	Hypotension	7.38%	31.50%
	Bradycardia	0.00%	0.94%
	Hypertension	2.82%	1.57%
	Arrhythmia	1.24%	0.79%
	Tachycardia	0.81%	3.15%
	Cardiovascular Disorder	0.23%	2.36%
	Hemorrhage	0.23%	1.57%
	Atrial Fibrillation	0.15%	1.57%
	Cardiac Arrest	0.12%	3.15%
	Ventricular Tachycardia	0.08%	1.57%
Digestive	Nausea	14.57%	0%
	Vomiting	8.31%	0%
	Abdominal Cramping	1.24%	0%
Nervous	Movement	4.44%	0%
	Headache	1.78%	0%
	Dizziness	1.70%	0%
	Twitching	1.47%	0%
	Agitation	0.19%	2.36%
	Intracranial Hypertension	0%	3.94%
Metabolic/ Nutritional	Hyperlipemia	0.08%	5.51%
	Acidosis	0.04%	1.57%
	Creatinine Increased	0%	2.36%
	BUN Increased	0%	1.57%
	Hyperglycemia	0%	1.57%
	Hypernatremia	0%	1.57%
	Hypokalemia	0%	1.57%
Respiratory	Dyspnea	0.43%	1.57%
	Hypoxia	0.08%	6.30%
	Acidosis	0%	1.57%
	Pneumothorax	0%	1.57%
Other	Injection Site:		
	Pain	8.11%	0%
	Burning/Stinging	7.77%	0%
	Fever	1.89%	2.36%
	Hiccough	1.78%	0%
	Cough	1.55%	0%
	Rash	1.20%	1.57%
	Anemia	0.35%	1.57%
	Kidney Failure	0%	1.57%

Respiratory: burning in throat, tachypnea, dyspnea, upper airway obstruction, wheezing, bronchospasm, laryngospasm, hypoventilation, hyperventilation, sneezing.

Excitatory: hypertonia, dystonia, rigidity, tremor.

CNS: confusion, dizziness, paresthesia, somnolence, shivering, abnormal dreams, agitation, delirium, euphoria, fatigue.

Injection Site: phlebitis, hives/itching, redness/discoloration.

Digestive: hypersalivation, dry mouth.

Skin and Appendages: flushing/rash (for incidence in children, see above), urticaria, pruritus.

Special Senses: diplopia, amblyopia, tinnitus.

Musculoskeletal: myalgia.

Urogenital: urine retention.

Adverse reactions reported at an incidence of 1% or less during ICU sedation: Cardiovascular: arrhythmia, extrasystole, heart block, right heart failure, bigeminy, ventricular fibrillation, heart failure, myocardial infarction.

Respiratory: lung function decreased, respiratory arrest.

CNS: seizure, thinking abnormal, akathisia, chills, anxiety, confusion, hallucinations.

Digestive: ileus, hepatomegaly.

Metabolic/Nutritional: osmolality increased.

Urogenital: green urine, urination disorder, oliguria.

Body as a Whole: sepsis, trunk pain, whole body weakness.

Drug Abuse and Dependence: Rare cases of self-administration of propofol by health care professionals have been reported, including some fatalities.

Overdose: Symptoms and Treatment: To date, there is no known case of acute overdosage, and no specific information on emergency treatment of overdosage is available. If accidental overdosage occurs, propofol administration should be discontinued immediately. Overdosage is likely to cause cardiorespiratory depression. Respiratory depression should be treated by artificial ventilation with oxygen. Cardiovascular depression may require repositioning of the patient by raising the patient's legs, increasing the flow rate of i.v. fluids and administering pressor agents.

Dosage: Strict aseptic techniques must always be maintained during handling as propofol is a single-use parenteral product and contains no antimicrobial preservatives. The vehicle is capable of supporting rapid growth of microorganisms. Failure to follow aseptic handling procedures may result in microbial contamination causing fever/infection/sepsis which could lead to life-threatening illness.

Propofol should be shaken well before use.

General: Dosage and rate of administration should be individualized and titrated to the desired effect according to clinically relevant factors including preinduction and concomitant medications, age, ASA status and level of debilitation of the patient. In heavily premedicated patients, both the induction and maintenance doses should be reduced.

Induction of General Anesthesia: Most **adult patients** under 55 years of age and classified ASA I and II are likely to require 2 to 2.5 mg/kg of propofol for induction when unpremedicated or when premedicated with oral benzodiazepines or i.m. narcotics. For induction, it is recommended that propofol should be titrated (approximately 40 mg every 10 seconds) against the response of the patient until the clinical signs show the onset of general anesthesia.

It is important to be familiar and experienced with the appropriate i.v. use of propofol before treating **elderly, debilitated and/or adult patients in ASA Physical Status Classes III and IV.** These patients may be more sensitive to the effects of propofol; therefore, the dosage of propofol should be reduced in these patients by approximately 50% (20 mg every 10 seconds) according to their condition and clinical response. A rapid bolus should not be used as this will increase the likelihood of undesirable cardiorespiratory depression including hypotension, apnea, airway obstruction and/or oxygen desaturation (see Warnings, Precautions and Dosage Guide, Table II).

During **cardiac anesthesia,** a rapid bolus induction should be avoided. A slow rate of approximately 20 mg every 10 seconds until induction onset (0.5 to 1.5 mg/kg) should be used.

Most **children** over 8 years of age require approximately 2.5 mg/kg of propofol for induction of anesthesia. Children 3 to 8 years of age may require somewhat higher doses, however the dose should be titrated by administering propofol slowly until the clinical signs show the onset of anesthesia. Propofol is not recommended for induction of anesthesia in children less than 3 years of age. There is no experience in children in ASA Classes III and IV.

Additionally, as with most anesthetic agents, the effects of propofol may be potentiated in patients who have received i.v. sedative or narcotic premedications shortly prior to induction.

Maintenance of General Anesthesia: Anesthesia can be maintained by administering propofol by infusion or intermittent i.v. bolus injection. The patient's clinical response will determine the infusion rate or the amount and frequency of incremental injections.

When administering propofol by infusion, drop counters, syringe pumps or volumetric pumps must be used to provide controlled infusion rates.

Continuous Infusion: Propofol 0.1 to 0.2 mg/kg/min (6 to 12 mg/kg/h) administered in a variable rate infusion with 60 to 70% nitrous oxide and oxygen provides anesthesia for patients undergoing general surgery. Maintenance by infusion of propofol should immediately follow the induction dose in order to provide satisfactory or continuous anesthesia during the induction phase. During this initial period following the induction injection higher rates of infusion are generally required (0.15 to 0.20 mg/kg/min; 9 to 12 mg/kg/h) for the first 10 to 15 minutes. Infusion rates should subsequently be decreased by 30 to 50% during the first half-hour of maintenance. Changes in vital signs (increases in pulse rate, blood pressure, sweating and/or tearing) that indicate a response to surgical stimulation or lightening of anesthesia may be controlled by the administration of propofol 25 mg (2.5 mL) to 50 mg (5.0 mL) incremental boluses and/or by increasing the infusion rate. If vital sign changes are not controlled after a 5-minute period, other means such as a narcotic, barbiturate, vasodilator or inhalation agent therapy should be initiated to control these responses.

For minor surgical procedures (i.e., body surface) 60 to 70% nitrous oxide can be combined with a variable rate propofol infusion to provide satisfactory anesthesia. With more stimulating surgical procedures (i.e., intra-abdominal) supplementation with i.v. analgesic agents should be considered to provide a satisfactory anesthetic and recovery profile. When supplementation with nitrous oxide is not provided, administration rate(s) of propofol and/or opioids should be increased in order to provide adequate anesthesia.

Diprivan (cont'd)

Infusion rates should always be titrated downward in the absence of clinical signs of light anesthesia until a mild response to surgical stimulation is obtained in order to avoid administration of propofol at rates higher than are clinically necessary. Generally, rates of 0.05 to 0.1 mg/kg/min should be achieved during maintenance in order to optimize recovery times.

During **cardiac anesthesia,** when propofol is used as the primary agent, maintenance infusion rates should not be less than 0.1 mg/kg/min and should be supplemented with analgesic levels of continuous opioid administration. When an opioid is used as the primary agent, propofol maintenance rates should not be less than 0.05 mg/kg/min. Higher doses of propofol will reduce the opioid requirements.

For **children,** the average rate of administration varies considerably, but rates between 0.10 to 0.25 mg/kg/min (6 to 15 mg/kg/h) should achieve satisfactory anesthesia. These infusion rates may be subsequently reduced depending on patient response and concurrent medication.

Intermittent Bolus: Increments of propofol 25 mg (2.5 mL) to 50 mg (5.0 mL) may be administered with nitrous oxide in patients undergoing general surgery. The incremental boluses should be administered when changes in vital signs indicate a response to surgical stimulation or light anesthesia.

Propofol has been used in conjunction with a wide variety of agents commonly used in anesthesia such as atropine, scopolamine, glycopyrrolate, diazepam, depolarizing and nondepolarizing muscle relaxants, and narcotic analgesics, as well as with inhalational and regional anesthetic agents. No pharmacological incompatibilities have been encountered.

Sedation During Surgical or Diagnostic Procedures: When propofol is administered for sedation, rates of administration should be individualized and titrated to clinical response. In most patients, the rates of propofol administration will be approximately 25 to 30% of those used for maintenance of general anesthesia.

During initiation of sedation, slow injection or slow infusion techniques are preferable over rapid bolus administration. During maintenance of sedation, a variable rate infusion is preferable over intermittent bolus dose administration.

Initiation of Sedation: Slow Injection: Most adult patients will generally require 0.5 to 1 mg/kg administered over 3 to 5 minutes and titrated to clinical response.

In the elderly, debilitated, hypovolemic and ASA III or IV patients, the dosage of propofol should be reduced to approximately 70 to 80% of the adult dosage and administered over 3 to 5 minutes.

Infusion: Sedation may be initiated by infusing propofol at 0.066 to 0.100 mg/kg/min (4 to 6 mg/kg/h) and titrating to the desired level of sedation while closely monitoring respiratory function.

Maintenance of Sedation: Patients will generally require maintenance rates of 0.025 to 0.075 mg/kg/min (1.5 to 4.5 mg/kg/h) during the first 10 to 15 minutes of sedation maintenance.

Infusion rates should always be titrated downward in the absence of clinical signs of light sedation until mild responses to stimulation are obtained in order to avoid sedative administration of propofol at rates higher than are clinically necessary.

In addition to the infusion, bolus administration of 10 to 15 mg may be necessary if a rapid increase in sedation depth is required.

In the elderly, debilitated, hypovolemic and ASA III or IV patients, the rate of administration and the dosage of propofol should be reduced to approximately 70 to 80% of the adult dosage according to their condition, responses, and changes in vital signs. Rapid (single or repeated) bolus dose administration should not be used for sedation in these patients (see Warnings).

Intensive Care Unit (ICU) Sedation: Propofol should be individualized according to the patient's condition and response, blood lipid profile, and vital signs.

For intubated, mechanically ventilated, adult patients, Intensive Care Unit (ICU) sedation should be initiated slowly with a continuous infusion in order to titrate to desired clinical effect and minimize hypotension. When indicated, initiation of sedation should begin at 0.005 mg/kg/min (0.3 mg/kg/h). The infusion rate should be increased by increments of 0.005 to 0.010 mg/kg/min (0.3 to 0.6 mg/kg/h) until the desired level of sedation is achieved. A minimum period of 5 minutes between adjustments should be allowed for onset of peak drug effect.

Most adult patients require maintenance rates of 0.005 to 0.050 mg/kg/min (0.3 to 3 mg/kg/h). Dosages of propofol should be reduced in patients who have received large dosages of narcotics. As with other sedative medications, there is interpatient variability in dosage requirements and these requirements may change with time (see Dosage Guide, Table II).

Bolus administration of 10 to 20 mg should only be used to rapidly increase sedation depth in patients where hypotension is not likely to occur. A rapid bolus should not be used as this will increase the likelihood of hypotension. Patients with compromised myocardial function, intravascular volume depletion or abnormally low vascular tone (e.g., sepsis) may be more susceptible to hypotension.

Compatibility and Stability: Propofol injection should not be mixed with other therapeutic agents prior to administration.

Dilution Prior to Administration: When propofol is diluted prior to administration, it should only be diluted with 5% Dextrose Injection, USP, and it should not be diluted to a concentration less than 2 mg/mL because it is an emulsion. Dilutions should be prepared aseptically immediately before administration and should not be used beyond 6 hours of preparation. In diluted form it has been shown to be more stable when in contact with glass than with plastic (95% potency after 2 hours of running infusion in plastic).

Administration into a Running I.V. Catheter: Compatibility of propofol with the coadministration of blood/serum/plasma has not been established (see Warnings). Propofol has been shown to be compatible with the following i.v. fluids when administered into a running i.v. catheter: 5% Dextrose Injection, USP; Lactated Ringers Injection, USP; Lactated Ringers and 5% Dextrose Injection; 5% Dextrose and 0.45% Sodium Chloride Injection, USP; 5% Dextrose and 0.2% Sodium Chloride Injection, USP.

Handling Procedures: Parenteral drug products should be inspected visually for particulate matter and discoloration prior to administration whenever solution and container permit.

Do not freeze.

Do not use if there is evidence of separation of the phases of the emulsion.

Aseptic techniques must be applied to the handling of the drug. Propofol contains no antimicrobial preservatives and the vehicle supports growth of microorganisms. When propofol is to be aspirated it should be drawn into a sterile syringe immediately after breaking the ampul or breaking the vial seal. Administration should commence without delay. Asepsis must be maintained for both propofol and the infusion equipment throughout the infusion period. Any drugs or fluids added to the infusion line must be administered close to the cannula site. Propofol must not be administered via a microbiological filter.

Propofol and any syringe containing propofol are for use in a single patient only. The contents of a propofol ampul must be used within 6 hours of opening or discarded thereafter. If a vial is utilized for infusion, both the reservoir of propofol and the infusion line must be discarded and replaced

Table II—Diprivan

Dosage Guide

Indication	Dosage and Administration
Induction of General Anesthesia	
	Dosage should be individualized.
	Adult Patients less than 55 Years of Age: Are likely to require 2 to 2.5 mg/kg (approximately 40 mg every 10 seconds until induction onset).
	Elderly, Debilitated and/or Adult ASA III or IV Patients: Are likely to require 1 to 1.5 mg/kg (approximately 20 mg every 10 seconds until induction onset) but dose should be carefully titrated to effect.
	Cardiac Anesthesia: Patients are likely to require 0.5 to 1.5 mg/kg (approximately 20 mg every 10 seconds until induction onset).
	Neurosurgical Patients: Are likely to require 1 to 2 mg/kg (approximately 20 mg every 10 seconds until induction onset).
	Pediatric Patients: Children over 8 years of age require approximately 2.5 mg/kg. Children 3 to 8 years of age may require somewhat higher doses but doses should be titrated slowly to the desired effect. In the absence of sufficient clinical experience, propofol is not recommended for anesthesia in children less than 3 years of age (see Indications and Precautions). There is no experience in ASA III or IV children.
Maintenance of General Anesthesia	
Infusion	**Variable rate infusion titrated to the desired clinical effect.**
	Adult Patients less than 55 Years of Age: Generally, 0.1 to 0.2 mg/kg/min (6 to 12 mg/kg/h).
	Elderly, Debilitated and/or Adult ASA III or IV Patients: Generally, 0.05 to 0.1 mg/kg/min (3 to 6 mg/kg/h).
	Cardiac Anesthesia: Most patients require: primary propofol with secondary opioid: 0.1 to 0.15 mg/kg/min (6 to 9 mg/kg/h); low dose propofol with primary opioid: 0.05 to 0.1 mg/kg/min (3 to 6 mg/kg/h).
	Neurosurgical Patients: Generally, 0.1 to 0.2 mg/kg/min (6 to 12 mg/kg/h).
	Pediatric Patients: Generally, 0.10 to 0.25 mg/kg/min (6 to 15 mg/kg/h).
Intermittent Bolus	Increments of 25 to 50 mg, as needed.
Surgical/Diagnostic Sedation	
	Dosage and rate should be individualized and titrated to the desired clinical effect.
	Adult Patients less than 55 Years of Age: Are likely to require 0.5 to 1 mg/kg over 3 to 5 min to initiate sedation, followed by 0.025 to 0.075 mg/kg/min (1.5 to 4.5 mg/kg/h) for continued sedation.
	Elderly, debilitated, hypovolemic and/or ASA III or IV patients: The dosage and rate of administration may need to be reduced in these patients by approximately 20 to 30% (see previous section for details).
	Pediatric Patients: Propofol is not recommended for sedation in children under the age of 18, as safety and efficacy have not been established (see Indications).
Initiation and Maintenance of ICU Sedation in Intubated, Mechanically Ventilated, Adult Patients	
	Dosage and rate of infusion should be individualized.
	For initiation, most patients require an infusion of 0.005 mg/kg/min (0.3 mg/kg/h) for at least 5 minutes. Subsequent increments of 0.005 to 0.010 mg/kg/min (0.3 to 0.6 mg/kg/h) over 5 to 10 minutes may be used until desired level of sedation is achieved.
	For maintenance, most patients require 0.005 to 0.050 mg/kg/min (0.3 to 3 mg/kg/h).
	The long-term administration of propofol to patients with renal failure and/or hepatic insufficiency has not been evaluated.
	Pediatric Patients: Propofol is not recommended for sedation in children under the age of 18, as safety and efficacy have not been established (see Indications).

as appropriate at the end of the procedure or at 12 hours, whichever is sooner (when using **diluted** propofol see Dilution Prior to Administration).

Since propofol contains no preservative or bacteriostatic agents, any unused portions of propofol or solutions containing propofol should be discarded at the end of the surgical procedure.

Supplied: Each mL of white, oil in water emulsion contains: propofol 10 mg for i.v. administration. Nonmedicinal ingredients: egg lecithin, glycerol, soybean oil and water for injection with sodium hydroxide to adjust pH. It is isotonic with a pH of 6.5 to 8.5. Cartons of 5×20 mL ready-to-use ampuls. Glass vials of 50 and 100 mL for single infusion only. Store between 2 and 25°C; do not freeze. The emulsion should be visually inspected for particulate matter, emulsion separation and discoloration prior to use. Any unused portions of propofol or solutions containing propofol should be discarded at the end of the surgical procedure.

DIPROGEN® ℞

Schering

Betamethasone Dipropionate—Gentamicin

Corticosteroid—Antibiotic

Pharmacology: Betamethasone dipropionate with gentamicin combines the anti-inflammatory, antipruritic and vasoconstrictive activity of a synthetic corticosteroid, betamethasone dipropionate, with the broad spectrum anti-bacterial effect of gentamicin.

In secondary skin infections, gentamicin facilitates the treatment of the underlying dermatosis by controlling the infection. Bacteria susceptible to the action of gentamicin include sensitive strains of streptococci (group A beta hemolytic, alpha hemolytic), S. aureus (coagulase positive, coagulase negative, and some penicillinase producing strains), and the gram-negative bacteria P. aeruginosa, E. aerogenes, E. coli, Proteus (both indole positive and indole negative), K. pneumoniae, and S. marcescens.

Diprogen cream is slightly acidic so that it is within the pH range of the normal skin. On application, it leaves minimum residue without stickiness or greasiness. The presence of petrolatum in both cream and ointment offers lubricating qualities and helps to prevent excessive drying.

Indications: The topical treatment of corticosteroid responsive dermatoses when complicated by secondary infection caused by organisms sensitive to gentamicin or when the possibility of such infection is suspected.

The cream is recommended for wet, oozing primary infections, and greasy, secondary infections such as pustular acne or infected seborrheic dermatitis.

The ointment helps retain moisture and has been useful in infection on dry eczematous or psoriatic skin.

Contraindications: Viral diseases including vaccinia, varicella, herpes simplex, fungal infections, tuberculosis of the skin and hypersensitivity to any of the components.

Warnings: *Pregnancy* and *Lactation:* Since safety of topical corticosteroid use in pregnant women has not been established, drugs of this class should be used during pregnancy only if the potential benefit justifies the potential risk to the fetus. Drugs of this class should not be used extensively in large amounts or for prolonged periods of time in pregnant patients. Since it is not known whether topical administration of corticosteroids can result in sufficient systemic absorption to produce detectable quantities in breast milk, a decison should be made to discontinue nursing or to discontinue the drug, taking into account the importance of the drug to the mother. This drug should not be used in or near the eyes since the vehicle is not formulated for ophthalmic use.

Children: Any of the side effects that have been reported following systemic use of corticosteroids, including adrenal suppression, may also occur with topical corticosteroids, especially in infants and children.

Systemic absorption of topical corticosteroids will be increased if extensive body surface areas are treated or if the occlusive technique is used. Suitable precautions should be taken under these conditions or when long-term use is anticipated, particularly in infants and children. Pediatric patients may demonstrate greater susceptibility to topical corticosteroid-induced HPA axis suppression and Cushing's syndrome than mature patients because of a larger skin surface area to body weight ratio. Use of topical corticosteroids in children should be limited to the least amount compatible with an effective therapeutic regimen. Chronic corticosteroid therapy may interfere with growth and development of children.

Precautions: Gentamicin is not effective against fungi, yeasts or viruses. Patients with superficial fungus or yeast infections also must receive specific therapy and the use of the drug may have to be discontinued. The use of such topical preparations may result in an overgrowth of non-susceptible organisms.

Suitable precautions should be taken in using topical corticosteroids in patients with stasis dermatitis and other skin diseases with impaired circulation.

Prolonged use of corticosteroid preparations may produce striae or atrophy of the skin or s.c. tissue. If this occurs, treatment should be discontinued.

Causal factors should be sought and eliminated whenever possible and the sensitivity of an infecting organism to gentamicin should be verified.

Patients should be advised to inform subsequent physicians of the prior use of corticosteroids.

While no systemic effects have been observed following the topical application of gentamicin, toxic systemic concentrations can cause permanent impairment of vestibular function in the presence of renal insufficiency or existing 8th cranial nerve damage.

Caution should be exercised if gentamicin is used in individuals who are known to be sensitive to topically applied antibacterials. If irritation or sensitization develops, treatment should be discontinued.

Application over extensive lesions may result in significant systemic absorption producing hypercortisonism manifesting itself by adrenal suppression, moon face, striae and suppression of growth in children.

Patients should be followed up regularly, and the product should be discontinued when the infection has cleared.

Occlusive dressing should not be used.

Adverse Effects: The following local adverse skin reactions have been reported with the use of topical steroids: dryness, itching, burning, local irritation, striae, skin atrophy, hypertrichosis, change in pigmentation and secondary infection. Adrenal suppression has also been reported following topical corticosteroid therapy. Posterior subcapsular cataracts have been reported following systemic use of corticosteroids.

Overdose: Symptoms: Excessive or prolonged use of topical corticosteroids can suppress pituitary-adrenal function, resulting in secondary adrenal insufficiency, and produce manifestations of hypercorticism, including Cushing's disease.

Treatment: Appropriate symptomatic treatment is indicated. Acute hypercorticoid symptoms are usually reversible. Treat electrolyte imbalance, if necessary. In case of chronic toxicity, slow withdrawal of corticosteroids is advised.

Dosage: A sufficient quantity of the cream or ointment should be applied to cover completely the affected area and should be massaged gently and thoroughly into the skin. The usual frequency of application is twice daily although some patients may be maintained adequately with less frequent application.

Supplied: Cream: Each g of cream contains: betamethasone (as dipropionate USP) 0.5 mg and gentamicin (as sulfate USP) 1 mg in a cream base. Nonmedicinal ingredients: cetostearyl alcohol, chlorocresol, mineral oil, monobasic sodium phosphate, phosphoric acid, polyethylene glycol 1 000 monocetyl ether, sodium hydroxide, white petrolatum and water. Tubes of 30 g.

Ointment: Each g of ointment contains: betamethasone (as dipropionate USP) 0.5 mg and gentamicin (as sulfate USP) 1 mg in an ointment base. Nonmedicinal ingredients: white petrolatum. Tubes of 30 g.

Store under 30°C.

DIPROLENE™ GLYCOL ℞

Schering

Betamethasone Dipropionate

Topical Corticosteroid

Pharmacology: Anti-inflammatory, antipruritic and vasoconstrictive. The propylene glycol components of the vehicle increase penetration and enhance the local effectiveness of betamethasone.

Indications: For the relief of the inflammatory manifestations of resistant or severe psoriasis and corticosteroid-responsive dermatoses.

Contraindications: In viral diseases including vaccinia, varicella, herpes simplex, and fungal infections; also, tuberculosis of the skin. Hypersensitivity to any of its components.

Warnings: *Pregnancy* and *Lactation:* Since safety of topical corticosteroid use in pregnant women has not been established, drugs of this class should be used during pregnancy only if the potential benefit justifies the potential risk to the fetus. Drugs of this class should not be used extensively in large amounts or for prolonged periods of time in pregnant patients.

Since it is not known whether topical administration of corticosteroids can result in sufficient systemic absorption to produce detectable quantities in breast milk, a decision should be made to discontinue nursing or to discontinue the drug, taking into account the importance of the drug to the mother. This drug should not be used in or near the eyes since this product is not formulated for ophthalmic use. This product should not be used under an occlusive dressing.

Children: This product is not recommended for use in children under 12 years of age.

Pediatric patients may demonstrate greater susceptibility to topical corticosteroid-induced HPA axis suppression and to exogenous corticosteroid effects than mature patients because of greater absorption due to a larger skin surface area to body weight ratio.

HPA axis suppression, Cushing's syndrome, linear growth retardation, delayed weight gain, and intracranial hypertension have been reported in children receiving topical corticosteroids. Manifestations of adrenal suppression in children include low plasma cortisol levels and absence of response to ACTH stimulation. Manifestations of intracranial hypertension include a bulging fontanelle, headaches and bilateral papilledema.

The lotion contains isopropyl alcohol and may cause stinging or burning upon application to abraded or sun-burned skin. Do not use in or near the eyes.

Precautions: Suitable precautions should be taken in using topical glucocorticoids in patients with stasis dermatitis and other skin diseases with impaired circulation; hypersensitive subjects and in patients with glaucoma.

Patients should be advised to inform subsequent physicians of the prior use of glucocorticoids.

If irritation, sensitization, excessive dryness develop with its use, treatment should be discontinued.

Application of corticosteroids over extensive lesions, or failure to follow dosage schedule may result in significant systemic absorption producing hypercortisonism manifesting itself by adrenal suppression, moon facies, striae and suppression of growth.

During the use of topical corticosteroids, infections may occur.

If an overt infection is present, appropriate antimicrobial treatment is indicated.

If symptomatic response is not noted within a few days to a week, the local application of corticosteroids should be discontinued and the patient re-evaluated.

Prolonged use of corticosteroid preparations may produce striae or atrophy of the skin or s.c. tissues. It this occurs, treatment should be discontinued.

Diprolene lotion has been shown to suppress the hypothalamic-pituitary adrenal (HPA) axis with repeated application of 7 mL/day.

Therefore, patients receiving large doses of potent topical corticosteroids, applied to a large surface area should be evaluated periodically for evidence of HPA axis suppression. If HPA axis suppression occurs, an attempt should be made to withdraw the drug, to reduce the frequency of application, or to substitute with a less potent corticosteroid agent.

Recovery of HPA axis function is generally prompt and complete upon discontinuation of the drug. Infrequently, signs and symptoms of corticosteroid withdrawal may occur, requiring supplemental systemic corticosteroid therapy.

Adverse Effects: The following adverse reactions were reported with this product: mild to moderate transient folliculitis, increased redness of lesions, increased erythema, itching and vesiculation, perilesional scaling, telangiectasia, dryness, stinging, burning, skin atrophy, local irritation, urticaria. Subnormal plasma cortisol levels were also reported.

The following local adverse skin reactions have been reported with the use of topical steroids: striae, hypertrichosis, change in pigmentation, secondary infection, perioral dermatitis, allergic contact dermatitis, maceration of the skin, acneiform eruptions and miliaria.

Adrenal suppression has also been reported following topical corticosteroid therapy. Posterior subcapsular cataracts have been reported following systemic use of corticosteroids.

Overdose: Symptoms: Excessive prolonged use of topical corticosteroids can suppress pituitary-adrenal function, resulting in secondary-adrenal insufficiency.

Diprolene Glycol (cont'd)

Treatment: Appropriate symptomatic treatment is indicated. Acute hypercorticoid symptoms are virtually reversible. Treat electrolyte imbalance, if necessary, in case of chronic toxicity, slow withdrawal of corticosteroids is advised.

Dosage: Cream and Ointment: A thin film of cream or ointment should be applied to cover completely the affected area once daily, in the morning. It may also be applied twice daily, in the morning and at night or as directed by the physician. Treatment should be discontinued when the dermatologic disorder is controlled. According to clinical response, duration of therapy may vary from a few days to a longer period of time. However, treatment should not be continued for more than 4 weeks without patient re-evaluation.

Lotion: A few drops of lotion should be applied to cover completely the affected area and a gentle massage should be effected until the lotion disappears. Once a day for 3 weeks, is the usual frequency of application.

The cream, lotion and ointment should not be used under an occlusive dressing.

Supplied: Cream: Each g of cream contains: betamethasone 0.5 mg (as dipropionate USP, micronized). Nonmedicinal ingredients: carbomer 940, propylene glycol, sodium hydroxide, titanium dioxide and water. Aluminum tubes of 15 and 50 g.

Lotion: Each g of lotion contains: betamethasone 0.5 mg (as dipropionate USP). Nonmedicinal ingredients: carbomer 940, isopropyl alcohol, propylene glycol, sodium hydroxide and water. Bottles of 30 and 60 mL.

Ointment: Each g of ointment contains: betamethasone 0.5 mg (as dipropionate USP, micronized). Nonmedicinal ingredients: propylene glycol monostearate USP, propylene glycol USP, white wax and white petrolatum. Aluminum tubes of 15 and 50 g.

Store at 2 to 30°C.

DIPROSALIC® Ⓟ

Schering

Betamethasone Dipropionate—Salicylic Acid

Topical Corticosteroid—Keratolytic

Pharmacology: Combines the anti-inflammatory, antipruritic and vasoconstrictive activity of betamethasone dipropionate with the keratolytic effects of salicylic acid.

Indications: Topical management of subacute and chronic hyperkeratotic and dry dermatoses responsive to corticosteroid therapy.

Contraindications: Viral diseases including vaccinia, varicella, herpes simplex, and fungal infections; also tuberculosis of the skin. Hypersensitivity to any one of the components.

Warnings: *Pregnancy* and *Lactation:* Since safety of topical corticosteroid use in pregnant women has not been established, drugs of this class should be used during pregnancy only if the potential benefit justifies the potential risk to the fetus. Drugs of this class should not be used extensively in large amounts or for prolonged periods of time in pregnant patients. Since it is not known whether topical administration of corticosteroids can result in sufficient systemic absorption to produce detectable quantities in breast milk, a decision should be made to discontinue nursing or to discontinue the drug, taking into account the importance of the drug to the mother.

Children: Any of the side effects that have been reported following systemic use of corticosteroids, including adrenal suppression, may also occur with topical corticosteroids, especially in infants and children.

Systemic absorption of topical corticosteroids will be increased if extensive body surface areas are treated or if the occlusive technique is used. Suitable precautions should be taken under these conditions or when long-term use is anticipated, particularly in infants and children. Pediatric patients may demonstrate greater susceptibility to topical corticosteroid-induced HPA axis suppression and Cushing's syndrome than mature patients because of a larger skin surface area to body weight ratio. Use of topical corticosteroids in children should be limited to the least amount compatible with an effective therapeutic regimen. Chronic corticosteroid therapy may interfere with growth and development of children.

The drug should not be used in or near the eyes since the product is not formulated for ophthalmic use: it should also be kept away from the genital area and other orifices.

Precautions: Suitable precautions should be taken in using topical corticosteroids in patients with stasis dermatitis and other skin diseases with impaired circulation. Prolonged use of corticosteroid preparations may produce striae or atrophy of the skin or subcutaneous tissue. If this occurs, treatment should be discontinued. Patients should be advised to inform subsequent physicians of the prior use of corticosteroids. If irritation, sensitization, excessive dryness, or unwanted scaling develop treatment should be discontinued. Application over extensive lesions may result in significant systemic absorption producing hypercortisonism manifesting itself by adrenal suppression, moon facies, striae and suppression of growth. If an overt infection is present, appropriate antimicrobial treatment is indicated. If symptomatic response is not noted within a few days to a week, the local application of corticosteroids should be discontinued and the patient re-evaluated. Occlusive dressings should not be used.

Adverse Effects: The following local adverse reactions have been reported rarely with the use of topical corticosteroids: burning, itching, irritation, dryness, folliculitis, hypertrichosis, acneiform eruptions, hypopigmentation.

The following may occur more frequently with occlusive dressings: maceration of the skin, secondary infection, skin atrophy, striae, miliaria. In addition, the salicylic acid component may cause local reddening of the skin, desquamation, pruritus and smarting. Hypersensitivity to salicylic acid may occur.

Overdose: Symptoms: Excessive or prolonged use of topical corticosteroids can suppress pituitary-adrenal function, resulting in secondary adrenal insufficiency, and produce manifestations of hypercorticism, including Cushing's disease.

Overdosage of salicylates may cause temporary hearing or visual disturbances, drowsiness and nausea. If this occurs, discontinue use until symptoms disappear.

Treatment: Appropriate symptomatic treatment is indicated. Acute hypercorticoid symptoms are usually reversible. Treat electrolyte imbalance, if necessary. In case of chronic toxicity, slow withdrawal of corticosteroids is advised.

Dosage: Lotion: Apply a thin film to cover completely the affected areas of the scalp. The usual frequency of application is twice daily.

Ointment: Apply a sufficient quantity to cover completely the affected area. The ointment should be massaged gently and thoroughly into the skin. The usual frequency of application is twice daily.

For some patients, adequate maintenance may be achieved with less frequent application.

Diprosalic should not be used under occlusive dressing.

Supplied: Lotion: Each g contains: betamethasone 0.5 (as dipropionate USP) and salicylic acid 20 mg. The pH is adjusted to approximately 5. Nonmedicinal ingredients: edetate disodium, hydroxypropyl methylcellulose, isopropyl alcohol, water and sodium hydroxide to adjust pH to approximately 5. Plastic squeeze bottles of 30 mL and 60 mL. Store under 25°C.

Ointment: Each g contains: betamethasone 0.5 mg (as dipropionate USP) and salicylic acid 30 mg in a paraben-free ointment base of white petrolatum and mineral oil. Tubes of 15 and 50 g. Store under 25°C.

DIPROSONE® Ⓟ

Schering

Betamethasone Dipropionate

Topical Corticosteroid

Indications: The topical management of corticosteroid responsive dermatoses including psoriasis, contact dermatitis (dermatitis venenata), atopic dermatitis (infantile eczema, allergic dermatitis), neurodermatitis (lichen simplex chronicus), lichen planus, eczema, eczematous dermatitis, intertrigo, dyshidrosis (pompholyx), seborrheic dermatitis, exfoliative dermatitis, solar dermatitis, stasis dermatitis, anogenital and senile pruritus.

Contraindications: Vaccinia, varicella, acute herpes simplex, tuberculous and fungal conditions. Hypersensitivity to any of the product's components.

Warnings: *Pregnancy* and *Lactation:* Since safety of topical corticosteroid use in pregnant women has not been established, drugs of this class should be used during pregnancy only if the potential benefit justifies the potential risk to the fetus. Drugs of this class should not be used extensively in large amounts or for prolonged periods of time in pregnant patients. Since it is not known whether topical administration of corticosteroids can result in sufficient systemic absorption to produce detectable quantities in breast milk, a decision should be made to discontinue nursing or to discontinue the drug, taking into account the importance of the drug to the mother.

Children: Any of the side effects that have been reported following systemic use of corticosteroids, including adrenal suppression, may also occur with topical corticosteroids, especially in infants and children.

Systemic absorption of topical corticosteroids will be increased if extensive body surface areas are treated or if the occlusive technique is used. Suitable precautions should be taken under these conditions or when long-term use is anticipated, particularly in infants and children. Pediatric patients may demonstrate greater susceptibility to topical corticosteroid-induced HPA axis suppression and Cushing's syndrome than mature patients because of a larger skin surface area to body weight ratio. Use of topical corticosteroids in children should be limited to the least amount compatible with an effective therapeutic regimen. Chronic corticosteroid therapy may interfere with growth and development of children.

The lotion contains isopropyl alcohol and may cause stinging or burning upon application to abraded or sunburned skin.

Precautions: Diprosone should not be used in or near the eyes as the vehicle is not formulated for ophthalmic use.

Although hypersensitivity reactions are rare with topically applied steroids, discontinue the drug and institute appropriate therapy if signs of sensitivity or irritation are noted.

In cases of bacterial or fungal skin infections, use appropriate antimicrobial agents as primary therapy, with betamethasone dipropionate as a topical adjunct to control inflammation, erythema and itching. If a symptomatic response is not noted within a few days to a week, discontinue betamethasone dipropionate until the infection is brought under control.

If extensive areas of the body are treated with topical corticosteroids, particularly under occlusive dressings, sufficient systemic absorption to provide adrenal suppression and systemic corticosteroid effects may occur. To minimize this possibility, when long-term therapy is anticipated, interrupt treatment periodically or treat one area of the body at a time. Occlusive dressings should not be applied if body temperature is elevated.

Take suitable precautions in using topical corticosteroids in patients with stasis dermatitis and other skin diseases with impaired circulation.

Prolonged use of corticosteroid preparations may produce striae or atrophy of the skin or subcutaneous tissue. If this occurs, discontinue treatment.

Adverse Effects: The following local adverse reactions have been reported rarely with the use of topical corticosteroids: burning, itching, irritation, dryness, folliculitis, hypertrichosis, acneiform eruptions, hypopigmentation.

The following may occur more frequently with occlusive dressings: maceration of the skin, secondary infection, skin atrophy, striae, miliaria.

Overdose: Symptoms: Excessive or prolonged use of topical corticosteroids can suppress pituitary-adrenal function, resulting in secondary adrenal insufficiency, and produce manifestations of hypercorticism, including Cushing's disease.

Treatment: Appropriate symptomatic treatment is indicated. Acute hypercorticoid symptoms are usually reversible. Treat electrolyte imbalance, if necessary. In case of chronic toxicity, slow withdrawal of corticosteroids is advised.

Dosage: Apply a sufficient quantity of the cream or ointment to completely cover the affected area. Massage gently and thoroughly into the skin. Although the usual frequency of application is twice daily, some patients on maintenance therapy may require less frequent application.

Supplied: Cream: Each g of cream contains: betamethasone 0.5 mg (as dipropionate USP) in a water miscible base. Nonmedicinal ingredients: cetostearyl alcohol, chlorocresol, mineral oil, monobasic sodium phosphate, phosphoric acid, polyethylene glycol 1000 monocetyl ether, sodium hydroxide, water and white petrolatum. Tubes of 15 and 50 g; jars of 450 g.

Ointment: Each g of ointment contains: betamethasone 0.5 (as dipropionate USP) in a lanolin free base. Nonmedicinal ingredients: white petrolatum USP. Tubes of 15 and 50 g; jars of 450 g.

Lotion: Each mL of lotion contains: betamethasone 0.5 mg (as dipropionate USP). Nonmedicinal ingredients: carbomer 934P, isopropyl alcohol, sodium hydroxide to adjust pH and water. Plastic squeeze bottles of 30 and 75 mL.

Store at 2 to 30°C.

DISALCID™ ℞
3M Pharmaceuticals

Salsalate

Anti-inflammatory—Analgesic

Supplied: 500 mg: Each round, aqua, scored, film-coated tablet, imprinted with "3M" on one side and "Disalcid" on the other, contains: salsalate 500 mg. Nonmedicinal ingredients: ac-di-sol (croscarmellose sodium, type A) NF, avicel (microcrystalline cellulose) NF, hydroxypropyl methylcellulose, magnesium stearate and purified water. Bottles of 100.

750 mg: Each capsule-shaped, aqua, scored, film-coated tablet, imprinted with "3M" on one side and "Disalcid 750" on the other, contains: salsalate 750 mg. Nonmedicinal ingredients: ac-di-sol (croscarmellose sodium, type A) NF, avicel (microcrystalline cellulose) NF, hydroxypropyl methylcellulose, magnesium stearate and purified water. Bottles of 100.

DISIPAL™
3M Pharmaceuticals

Orphenadrine HCl

Antiparkinsonism Agent

Supplied: Each green, film-coated, round tablet, with a white core, '3M' embossed on one face, '161' embossed on the other face, contains: orphenadrine HCl 50 mg. Nonmedicinal ingredients: acetylated monoglycerides, colloidal silicon dioxide, D&C yellow #10, FD&C blue #1, FD&C yellow #6, hydroxypropyl cellulose, hydroxypropyl methylcellulose, lactose, magnesium stearate, microcrystalline cellulose, starch, talc and titanium dioxide. Tartrazine-free. Bottles of 100.

DITROPAN® ℞
Alza

Oxybutynin Chloride

Anticholinergic—Antispasmodic

Pharmacology: Oxybutynin is a tertiary amine anticholinergic agent which exerts antimuscarinic as well as direct antispasmodic action on smooth muscle. In vitro studies have shown that its anticholinergic effects are weaker than those of atropine, but that it possesses greater antispasmodic activity. No blocking effects occur at skeletal neuromuscular junctions or in autonomic ganglia (e.g., no antinicotinic effects).

In addition to its smooth muscle relaxing effects, oxybutynin exerts an analgesic and a local anesthetic effect. In animal studies the CNS and cardiovascular actions of oxybutynin were shown to be similar to but weaker than those of atropine.

Oxybutynin relaxes bladder smooth muscle. In patients with uninhibited neurogenic and reflex neurogenic bladder, cystometric studies have demonstrated that oxybutynin increases bladder (vesical) capacity, diminishes the frequency of uninhibited contractions of the detrusor muscle, and delays the initial desire to void. Oxybutynin thus decreases urgency and the frequency of both incontinent episodes and voluntary urination. These effects are more consistently improved in patients with uninhibited neurogenic bladder.

Oxybutynin is readily absorbed from the gastrointestinal tract. The onset of action is approximately 1 hour after an oral dose and its duration 6 to 10 hours.

Indications: For the relief of symptoms associated with voiding in patients with uninhibited neurogenic and reflex neurogenic bladder (i.e., urgency, frequency, urinary leakage, urge incontinence, dysuria).

Contraindications: Glaucoma, partial or complete obstruction of the gastrointestinal tract, paralytic ileus, intestinal atony of the elderly or debilitated patient, megacolon, toxic megacolon complicating ulcerative colitis, severe colitis, myasthenia gravis, obstructive uropathy, and when the patient has an unstable cardiovascular status in acute hemorrhage. Hypersensitivity to oxybutynin.

Warnings: When oxybutynin is administered in the presence of high environmental temperature, it can cause heat prostration (fever and heat stroke due to decreased sweating).

Diarrhea may be an early symptom of incomplete intestinal obstruction, especially in patients with ileostomy or colostomy. In such cases, treatment with oxybutynin would be inappropriate and possibly harmful.

Occupational Hazards: Oxybutynin may produce drowsiness or blurred vision. The patient should be cautioned regarding activities requiring mental alertness, such as operating a motor vehicle or other machinery or performing hazardous work while taking this drug. Alcohol or other sedative drugs may enhance the drowsiness caused by oxybutynin.

Pretreatment examinations should include cystometry and other appropriate diagnostic procedures. Cystometry should be repeated at appropriate intervals to evaluate response to therapy. The appropriate antimicrobial therapy should be instituted in the presence of infection.

Precautions: Oxybutynin should be used with caution in the elderly and in patients with autonomic neuropathy, hepatic or renal disease. Administration of oxybutynin in large doses to patients with ulcerative colitis may suppress intestinal motility to the point of producing a paralytic ileus and precipitate or aggravate toxic megacolon, a serious complication of the disease.

The symptoms of hyperthyroidism, coronary heart disease, congestive heart failure, cardiac arrhythmias, tachycardia, hypertension and prostatic hypertrophy may be aggravated following administration of oxybutynin. The drug should be administered with caution to patients with hiatal hernia associated with reflux esophagitis, since anticholinergic drugs may aggravate this condition.

Pregnancy: The safety of oxybutynin in pregnancy has not been established. Therefore, oxybutynin should not be used in women of childbearing potential, unless, in the opinion of the physician, the expected benefit to the patient outweighs the possible risk to the fetus.

Lactation: It is not known whether this drug is excreted in human milk. Because many drugs are excreted in human milk, caution should be exercised when oxybutynin is administered to a nursing woman.

Children: Because the safety of oxybutynin in children under the age of 5 has not been established, use of the drug in this age group is not recommended.

Adverse Effects: Dry mouth and throat, difficulty swallowing, decreased sweating, urinary hesitance and retention, blurred vision, dilation of the pupil, cycloplegia, increased ocular tension, palpitations, tachycardia, chest pain, syncope, flushing, nose bleed, drowsiness, weakness, dizziness, headache, insomnia, mood changes, nausea, vomiting, anorexia, metallic taste, constipation, bloated feeling, edema, impotence, suppression of lactation, interference with normal heat regulation, severe allergic reactions or drug idiosyncrasies including urticaria and other dermal manifestations.

Overdose: Symptoms: The symptoms of overdosage with oxybutynin may be any of those seen with other anticholinergic agents. Symptoms may include signs of CNS excitation (e.g., restlessness, tremor, irritability, delirium, hallucinations), flushing, fever, nausea, vomiting, tachycardia, hypotension or hypertension, respiratory failure, paralysis and coma.

Treatment: In the event of an overdose or exaggerated response, treatment should be symptomatic and supportive. Induce emesis or perform gastric lavage (emesis is contraindicated in precomatose, convulsive, or psychotic state) and maintain respiration. Activated charcoal may be administered as well as magnesium sulfate. Physostigmine may be considered to reverse symptoms of anticholinergic intoxication. Hyperpyrexia may be treated symptomatically with ice bags or other cold applications and alcohol sponges.

Dosage: Adults: 5 mg 2 to 3 times a day. Maximum recommended dose: 5 mg 4 times a day.

In elderly and debilitated patients it is advisable to initiate treatment at the lowest recommended dosage and to increase the dosage carefully according to tolerance and response.

Children over 5 years of age: 5 mg 2 times a day. Maximum recommended dose: 5 mg 3 times a day.

Supplied: Tablets: Each scored, biconvex, blue tablet, engraved with Ditropan on one side and 1375 on the other side contains: oxybutynin chloride 5 mg. Nonmedicinal ingredients: calcium stearate, FD&C Blue #1 lake, lactose and microcrystalline cellulose. Bottles of 100 and 500. Store at controlled room temperature of 15 to 30°C in tight, light resistant containers.

Syrup: Each 5 mL of green colored syrup contains: oxybutynin chloride 5 mg. Nonmedicinal ingredients: citric acid, FD&C Green #3, flavor, glycerin, methylparaben, sodium citrate, sorbitol, sucrose and water. Bottles of 473 mL. Store at controlled room temperature of 15 to 30°C.

DIXARIT® ℞
Boehringer Ingelheim

Clonidine HCl

Vascular Stabilizer for the Treatment of Menopausal Flushing

Pharmacology: Clonidine reduces the response of peripheral vessels to either vasoconstrictor or vasodilator stimuli. Clonidine, the active ingredient, is an α-adrenergic agonist which also has some α-adrenergic antagonist effects.

Clonidine therapy has been shown to reduce the frequency, severity, and duration of flushing attacks associated with the menopausal syndrome. There is a gradual onset of therapeutic response, and a gradual return of symptoms on interruption of treatment.

Clonidine will not correct or relieve other menopausal changes that are due to hormonal deficiencies.

Clonidine stimulates α-adrenoreceptors in the brain stem, resulting in reduced sympathetic outflow from the CNS and a decrease in peripheral resistance, renal vascular resistance, heart rate, and blood pressure. Renal blood flow and glomerular filtration rate remain essentially unchanged.

Pharmacokinetics: Clonidine acts relatively rapidly. The patient's blood pressure declines within 30 to 60 minutes after an oral dose, the maximum decrease occurring within 2 to 4 hours. The plasma level of clonidine peaks in approximately 3 to 5 hours and the plasma half-life from 12 to 16 hours. The half-life increases up to 41 hours in patients with severe impairment of renal function. Following oral administration about 40 to 60% of the absorbed dose is recovered in the urine as unchanged drug in 24 hours. About 50% of the absorbed dose is metabolized in the liver.

Acute studies with clonidine in humans have demonstrated a moderate reduction (15 to 20%) of cardiac output in the supine position with no change in the peripheral resistance, at a 45° tilt there is a smaller reduction in cardiac output and a decrease in peripheral resistance. During long-term therapy, cardiac output tends to return to controlled values, while peripheral resistance remains decreased.

Slowing of the pulse rate has been observed in most patients given clonidine, but the drug does not alter normal hemodynamic response to exercise.

Other studies in patients have provided evidence of a reduction in plasma renin activity and in the excretion of aldosterone and catecholamines, but the exact relationship of these pharmacologic actions to the antihypertensive effect has not been fully elucidated.

Clonidine acutely stimulates growth hormone release in both children and adults, but does not produce a chronic elevation of growth hormone with long-term use.

Indications: The relief of menopausal flushing in patients for whom hormonal replacement therapy is either unnecessary or not desirable.

Contraindications: Hypersensitivity to clonidine or to any of the tablet excipients; patients with sinus node function impairment.

Warnings: Clonidine can have a hypotensive effect especially in high doses. In patients whose blood pressure decreases to an intolerable extent when taking clonidine, treatment should be discontinued.

It has been demonstrated that an excessive rise in blood pressure, should it occur on discontinuation of clonidine, can be reversed by resumption of clonidine therapy or by i.v. phentolamine.

An abrupt withdrawal of higher doses of clonidine is followed in some cases by an excess of circulating catecholamines. Therefore, caution should be excercised in concomitant use of drugs which affect the metabolism, tissue uptake or pressor effects of these amines (MAO inhibitors, tricyclic antidepressants and beta-blocking agents).

Precautions: General: Dixarit should not be confused with Catapres. Catapres is a higher dosage form of the same active ingredient, clonidine hydrochloride, and is used for treating hypertension. Catapres is available as white tablets of 0.1 mg and orange tablets containing 0.2 mg of clonidine. Caution should however be exercised in patients receiving antihypertensive therapy because of the possibility of an additive effect.

Because it can lower blood pressure at high doses, clonidine should be used with caution in patients with severe coronary

Dixarit (cont'd)

insufficiency, recent myocardial infarction, cerebral vascular disease, or chronic renal failure.

Depending on the dose given, clonidine can lower the heart and pulse rate. In patients with diseases affecting the rhythmic and AV conduction system of the heart, arrhythmias have been observed after high doses.

Occupational Hazards: Patients who engage in potentially hazardous activities such as operating machinery or driving should be warned of the possible sedative effect of clonidine. Caution should be exercised in the concomitant administration of sedatives, tranquilizing drugs or alcohol.

Patients with a known history of depression should be carefully supervised while under treatment with clonidine as there have been occasional reports of further depressive episodes occurring in such patients.

In several studies clonidine produced a dose-dependent increase in the incidence and severity of spontaneously occurring retinal degeneration in albino rats treated for 6 months or longer. In view of this retinal degeneration, eye examinations were performed in 908 hypertensive patients prior to the start of clonidine therapy, who were then examined periodically thereafter. In 353 of these 908 patients, examinations were performed for periods of 24 months or longer. Except for the dryness of the eyes, no drug-related abnormal ophthalmologic findings were recorded and clonidine did not alter retinal function as shown by specialized tests such as the electroretinogram and macular dazzle.

As with any drug excreted primarily in the urine, smaller doses of the drug are often effective in treating patients with a degree of renal failure. In patients exhibiting renal failure, periodic determination of the BUN is indicated. If, in the physician's opinion, a rising BUN is significant, the drug should be stopped.

A few instances of a condition resembling Raynaud's phenomenon have been reported with the higher doses of clonidine as used in the therapy of hypertension. Caution should be observed if patients with Raynaud's disease or thromboangiitis obliterans are to be treated with clonidine.

Pregnancy: When rats were given clonidine alone in doses as low as one-third the maximum recommended daily human dose, some embryotoxicity was evident. There are, however, no adequate and well-controlled studies in pregnant women. Thus, use of clonidine in pregnancy is not recommended.

Lactation: Since clonidine is distributed into breast milk, the drug should be used with caution in nursing women.

Children: Safety and effectiveness in children has not been established.

Drug Interactions: The doses of clonidine used during clinical trials in menopausal flushing, 0.05 mg b.i.d., did not produce significant changes in blood pressure. Caution should, however, be exercised in patients receiving antihypertensive therapy because of the possibility of an additive effect.

Concomitant use of β-receptor blockers and/or cardiac glycosides can further lower heart rate (bradycardia) or cause dysrhythmia (AV block) in isolated cases.

Withdrawal of higher doses of clonidine may result in an excess of circulating catecholamines (see Warnings). Therefore, caution should be exercised in concomitant use of drugs which affect the metabolism, tissue uptake or pressor effects of these amines (MAO inhibitors, tricyclic antidepressants and beta-blocking agents, respectively).

If combined treatment with a β-blocker necessitates the interim interruption of antihypertensive therapy or even total discontinuation, the β-blocker must always be discontinued slowly first, reducing the dose gradually to avoid sympathetic hyperactivity. Clonidine must then be reduced gradually over several days if previously given in high dosages.

If clonidine and tricyclic antidepressants are administered as concurrent therapy, the effect of clonidine may be reduced, thus necessitating an increase in the dosage of clonidine. Amitriptyline in combination with clonidine enhances the manifestation of corneal lesions in rats.

Clonidine may enhance the CNS-depressive effects of alcohol, barbiturates and other sedatives.

Depending upon the dose administered, tolazoline can reduce or neutralize the effect of clonidine, and therefore, is suitable as an antidote.

Adverse Effects: Clonidine is generally well tolerated. In controlled clinical studies, sedation and other CNS side effects were comparable to those occurring during the placebo period. Dry mouth was encountered in a low proportion of patients treated with the drug. Both dry mouth and fatigue occur particularly during the initial phase of treatment and may be expected to diminish as treatment continues. Muscle or joint pain and cramps of the lower limbs have also been reported during treatment with clonidine. The side effects of treatment with clonidine are to a high degree dose dependent.

When high doses of clonidine were used in treatment of hypertension, the most common reactions observed are dry mouth, drowsiness, dizziness, constipation and sedation. These effects generally tend to diminish with continuation of therapy.

There have been isolated reports of continual dry mouth leading to an accelerated rate of dental caries, in patients receiving higher doses of clonidine.

Overdose: Symptoms: The signs and symptoms of clonidine overdosage include hypotension, bradycardia, lethargy, irritability, weakness, somnolence, diminished or absent reflexes, miosis, vomiting and hypoventilation. With large overdoses, reversible cardiac conduction defects or arrhythmias, apnea, seizures and transient hypertension have been reported. The oral LD_{50} of clonidine in rats was 465 mg/kg, and in mice 206 mg/kg.

In a patient who ingested 100 mg clonidine, plasma clonidine levels were 60 ng/mL (1 hour), 190 ng/mL (1.5 hours), 370 ng/mL (2 hours) and 120 ng/mL (5.5 and 6.5 hours). This patient developed hypertension followed by hypotension, bradycardia, apnea, hallucinations, semicoma, and premature ventricular contractions. The patient fully recovered after intensive treatment.

Treatment: Clonidine overdosage usually responds to symptomatic treatment with careful cardiovascular monitoring. Gastric lavage is only worthwhile if it is guaranteed that part of the dose taken, which has not yet been absorbed, can be removed. Routine hemodialysis is of limited benefit since a maximum of 5% of circulating clonidine is removed.

I.V. tolazoline (an α-antagonist) and naloxone have each been used as antidotes to clonidine poisoning, with inconsistent results. If other efforts fail, these agents may provide some benefit in reversing the effects of clonidine.

Dosage: The recommended dose for the treatment of menopausal flushing is 0.05 mg twice daily. If after 2 to 4 weeks there has been no remission the treatment should be discontinued and the patient reassessed.

Attempts should be made to discontinue treatment at 3- to 6-month intervals for patient re-evaluation of menopausal symptoms.

Supplied: Each blue, sugar-coated, round, biconvex tablet contains: 0.025 mg of clonidine HCl. Nonmedicinal ingredients: Tablet core: $CaHPO_4$, colloidal silica, FD&C Blue #2, lactose (fine), magnesium stearate, maize starch, polyvinylpyrrolidone and soluble starch. Sugar coating: carnauba wax, FD&C Blue #2, gum arabic, polyethylene glycol 6000, polyvinylpyrrolidone, sucrose, talc, titanium dioxide and white wax. Energy: 1.01 kJ (0.24 kcal). Bottles of 100. Store at controlled room temperature (15 to 30°C).

DOAK™ OIL
DOAK™ OIL FORTE
TCD

Mineral Oil—Tar Distillate—Isopropyl Palmitate

Antipruritic Bath Oil

Supplied: Each bottle contains: mineral oil, isopropyl palmitate and "Doak" tar distillate 2% (Doak Oil) or 10% (Doak Oil Forte). Nonmedicinal ingredients: acetulan, amerchol L-101, fragrance A-833, nonoxinol-4, isopropyl palmitate and light mineral oil. Bottles of 250 mL.

DOAN'S® Backache Pills
Novartis Consumer Health

Magnesium Salicylate

Analgesic

Indications: For quick relief of muscular backache pain.

Warnings: *Pregnancy* and *Lactation:* Consult a physician before taking this drug during the last 3 months of pregnancy or if nursing.

Package contains enough drug to seriously harm a child. Keep out of children's reach.

Children and teenagers should not use this medicine for chickenpox or flu symptoms before a physician is consulted about Reye's syndrome, a rare but serious illness.

Not to be administered to children under 2 years of age except on the advice of a physician.

Precautions: If symptoms persist for more than 5 days, consult a physician. It is hazardous to exceed the maximum recommended dose unless advised by a physician.

Dosage: 1 to 2 tablets every 6 hours. Do not exceed 12 tablets in 24 hours.

Supplied: Each dark-green, oval, biconvex, film-coated tablet contains: magnesium salicylate 325 mg. Nonmedicinal ingredients: cellulose, magnesium stearate and stearic acid. Alcohol-, bisulfite-, gluten-, lactose-, parabens-, sodium- and tartrazine-free. Boxes of 24.

DOBUTAMINE HYDROCHLORIDE INJECTION ℞
Abbott

Sympathomimetic

Supplied: Each mL of clear, practically colorless sterile, nonpyrogenic solution, contains: dobutamine HCl 12.5 mg. Nonmedicinal ingredients: sodium metabisulfite and water for injection. Hydrochloric acid and/or sodium hydroxide to adjust pH. Must be diluted prior to i.v. use as directed. Single dose vials of 20 mL. Store at controlled room temperature (15 to 30°C).

DOBUTAMINE HYDROCHLORIDE INJECTION ℞
Novopharm

Inotropic

Pharmacology: Dobutamine is a direct-acting inotropic agent whose primary activity results from stimulation of the β-receptors of the heart while producing less marked chronotropic, hypertensive, arrhythmogenic or vasodilatory effects. Dobutamine, unlike dopamine, does not cause the release of endogenous norepinephrine. No specific effect on the renal vasculature was observed. Dobutamine produces less increase in heart rate and less decrease in peripheral vascular resistance for a given inotropic effect than does isoproterenol as demonstrated in both animal and human studies.

The onset of action occurs within 1 to 2 minutes while the peak effect of a particular infusion may not be reached for 10 minutes. The plasma half-life in humans is 2 minutes.

Indications: In the treatment of adults with cardiac decompensation due to depressed contractility resulting from organic heart disease or following cardiac surgical procedures in which parenteral therapy is necessary for inotropic support.

Most clinical experience with dobutamine is short-term—up to several hours in duration. In the limited number of patients who were studied for 24, 48, and 72 hours, a persistent increase in cardiac output occurred in some, whereas the output of others returned toward base-line values.

Contraindications: Patients with idiopathic hypertrophic subaortic stenosis, in patients with pheochromocytoma, and in those patients with hypersensitivity to dobutamine.

Warnings: Dobutamine may cause a marked increase in blood pressure, especially systolic pressure or in heart rate. About 10% of patients in clinical studies have had rate increases of 30 beats/minute or more, while about 7.5% have had a 50 mmHg or greater increase in systolic pressure. There appears to be an increased risk in patients with pre-existing hypertension of developing an exaggerated pressor response. A reduction of dosage usually results in a prompt reversal of these effects.

Dobutamine may exacerbate or precipitate ventricular ectopic activity but has rarely caused ventricular tachycardia.

Following the administration of dobutamine, reactions suggestive of hypersensitivity including skin rash, fever, eosinophilia, and bronchospasm have been reported occasionally. Dobutamine injection contains sodium bisulfite, a sulfite that may cause allergic-type reactions, including anaphylactic symptoms, in certain susceptible people.

A digitalis preparation should be used prior to instituting therapy with dobutamine in patients who have atrial fibrillation with rapid ventricular response. Patients with atrial fibrillation are at risk of developing rapid ventricular response because dobutamine facilitates atrioventricular conduction.

Dobutamine should not be used in the presence of ventricular fibrillation or uncorrected tachycardia.

There may be no improvement observed following dobutamine administration to patients with marked mechanical obstruction such as severe valvular aortic stenosis.

Minimal vasoconstriction has occasionally been observed, most notably in patients recently treated with a β-blocking drug. The inotropic effect of dobutamine is prevented by β-blocking drugs because the effect stems from stimulation of cardiac β_1 receptors.

Precautions: General: During the administration of dobutamine, ECG, heart rate and blood pressure should be continuously monitored, as with any adrenergic agent. In addition, monitoring of cardiac output and pulmonary wedge pressure should be performed whenever possible to aid in the safe and effective infusion of dobutamine injection.

Caution should be exercised in order to prevent infiltration at the injection site.

Hypovolemia should be corrected with suitable volume expanders prior to the initiation of treatment with dobutamine.

Caution should be exercised when using dobutamine in patients with hyperthyroidism.

Dobutamine should be used with caution in patients receiving anesthetic agents such as halogenated hydrocarbons, or cyclopropane.

Dobutamine should be used with caution in patients taking concomitantly other sympathomimetic amines.

Dobutamine can produce a mild reduction in serum potassium concentration, like other β_2-agonists, but rarely to hypokalemic levels. Accordingly serum potassium levels should be considered for monitoring.

Use Following Acute Myocardial Infarction: Clinical experience with dobutamine following myocardial infarction has been insufficient to establish the safety of this use. There is concern that any agent which increases contractile force and heart rate, such as dobutamine, may increase the size of an infarction by intensifying ischemia, but whether dobutamine does so or not is not known.

Pregnancy: Reproduction studies performed in rats and rabbits that have received dobutamine have revealed no evidence of impaired fertility or harm to the fetus. The drug has not been administered to pregnant women to date and should be used in such patients only when the expected benefits clearly outweigh the potential risks to the mother and fetus.

Children: Both the efficacy and safety of dobutamine for use in children have not been established.

Drug Interactions: Clinical studies indicate that the concomitant use of dobutamine and nitroprusside results in a higher cardiac output and, usually, a lower pulmonary wedge pressure than when either drug is used alone.

No evidence of drug interactions was noted in clinical studies when dobutamine was administered concurrently with other drugs including furosemide and/or digitalis preparations, spironolactone, lidocaine, isosorbide dinitrate, glyceryl trinitrate, atropine, morphine, anticoagulants and potassium chloride supplements.

Adverse Effects: Cardiovascular: The most common adverse reactions relate to the effect of dobutamine on the cardiovascular system.

An increase in heart rate of 5 to 15 beats/minute and a 10 to 20 mmHg increase in systolic blood pressure have been noted in most patients. (see Warnings regarding exaggerated chronotropic and pressor effects). About 5% of patients have had increased premature ventricular beats during infusions. These effects were dose-related.

Hypotension: There have been reports of precipitous decreases in blood pressure associated with dobutamine therapy. A reduction in dose or discontinuation of the drug is necessary to return the blood pressure to baseline levels. In some cases pressor support may be required.

Less commonly occurring effects relating to the cardiovascular system include, cardiac awareness, transient bigeminy, bradycardia, angina, nonspecific chest pain, palpitations, and shortness of breath.

Gastrointestinal: nausea, vomiting and bad taste.

CNS: headache, fatigue, anxiety, and paresthesia.

Hypersensitivity: rash, fever, eosinophilia and bronchospasm have been reported occasionally.

Miscellaneous: dyspnea, thrombocytopenia, pruritus, chill, and sweating were observed rarely. Phlebitis has been occasionally reported. Local inflammatory changes following inadvertent infiltration have also been reported.

Administration of dobutamine, like other catecholamines, has been associated with decreases in serum potassium concentrations, but rarely to hypokalemic values.

Long-Term Safety: Infusions of up to 72 hours have revealed no adverse effects other than those seen with shorter infusions.

Overdose: Symptoms and Treatment: In case of overdosage, as evidenced by tachycardia or excessive blood pressure alteration, reduce the rate of administration, or temporarily discontinue dobutamine until the patient's condition stabilizes. No additional remedial measures are usually necesssary because the duration of action of dobutamine is short.

Dosage: Note: Dobutamine is a potent drug. It is not for direct injection and must be diluted exactly as directed before administration to patients as an i.v. infusion (see Precautions).

The rate of infusion needed to increase cardiac output usually ranges from 2.5 to 10 µg/kg/min (see Table I). Some patients may respond to doses as low as 0.5 µg/kg/min whereas, on rare occasions, infusion rates up to 40 µg/kg/min have been required to obtain the desired effect.

Dobutamine is incompatible with alkaline solutions and should not be mixed with products such as 5% Sodium Bicarbonate Injection. Because of the occurrences of physical incompatibilities with some drugs and the potential for incompatibility with other drugs, it is recommended that dobutamine injection not be mixed with other drugs in the same solution. Dobutámine injection should not be used in conjunction with other agents or diluents containing both sodium bisulfite and ethanol.

Dobutamine injection must be further diluted at the time of administration to at least 50 mL prior to administration in an i.v. container with one of the following i.v. solutions: 5% Dextrose Injection, 0.9% Sodium Chloride Injection, or Sodium Lactate Injection. I.V. solutions should be used within 24 hours of preparation.

Solutions containing dobutamine may exhibit a color that, if present, will increase with time. This color change is due to slight oxidation of the drug, but there is no significant loss of potency during the reconstituted time periods stated above.

The diluted solution should be inspected visually for discoloration and particulate matter prior to administration. Discard unused portion.

Table I—Dobutamine Hydrochloride Injection

Rates of Infusion for Concentrations of 250, 500 and 1 000 mg/L

Drug Delivery Rate (µg/kg/min)	Infusion Delivery Rate 250 mg/L[a] (mL/kg/min)	500 mg/L[b] (mL/kg/min)	1 000 mg/L[c] (mL/kg/min)
2.5	0.01	0.005	0.0025
5	0.02	0.01	0.005
7.5	0.03	0.015	0.0075
10	0.04	0.02	0.01
12.5	0.05	0.025	0.0125
15	0.06	0.03	0.015

[a]One vial/L of admixture.
[b]Two vials/L or 1 vial/500 mL of admixture.
[c]Four vials/L or 1 vial/250 mL of admixture.

The final volume administered should be determined by the fluid requirements of the patient.

The rate of administration and duration of therapy should be adjusted according to the patient's response as determined by heart rate, presence of ectopic activity, blood pressure, urine flow and, whenever possible, measurement of central venous or pulmonary wedge pressure and cardiac output.

Supplied: Each mL contains: dobutamine (as HCl) 12.5 mg. Nonmedicinal ingredients: sodium bisulfite 0.28 mg and water for injection. Sodium hydroxide and/or hydrochloric acid may be used for pH adjustment. Vials of 20 mL, cartons of 10. Store at room temperature (15 to 30°C).

Reviewed 1997

DOBUTREX® Ⓟ

Lilly

Dobutamine HCl

Sympathomimetic

Pharmacology: Dobutamine is a direct acting inotropic agent whose primary activity results from stimulation of the β-receptors of the heart while producing less marked chronotropic, hypertensive, arrhythmogenic or vasodilatory effects. It does not cause the release of endogenous norepinephrine as does dopamine. No specific effect on the renal vasculature has been observed. In both animal and human studies, dobutamine produces less increase in heart rate and less decrease in peripheral vascular resistance for a given inotropic effect than does isoproterenol.

The onset of action is within 1 to 2 minutes, the peak effect of a particular infusion may not be reached for 10 minutes. The plasma half-life in humans is 2 minutes.

Indications: The treatment of adults with cardiac decompensation due to depressed contractility resulting from organic heart disease or following cardiac surgical procedures in which parenteral therapy is necessary for inotropic support.

Most clinical experience with dobutamine is short term up to several hours in duration. In a limited number of patients who were studied for 24, 48 and 72 hours, a persistent increase in cardiac output occurred in some, whereas the output of others returned toward baseline values.

Contraindications: Patients with pheochromocytoma, idiopathic hypertrophic subaortic stenosis and hypersensitivity to dobutamine.

Warnings: Dobutamine may cause a marked increase in heart rate or blood pressure, especially systolic pressure. About 10% of patients in clinical studies have had rate increases of 30 beats/minute or more, while about 7.5% have had a 50 mmHg or greater increase in systolic pressure. Patients with preexisting hypertension appear to have an increased risk of developing an exaggerated pressor response. Reduction of dosage usually reverses these effects promptly.

Dobutamine may precipitate or exacerbate ventricular ectopic activity but has rarely caused ventricular tachycardia.

Reactions suggestive of hypersensitivity associated with administration of dobutamine including skin rash, fever, eosinophilia, and bronchospasm, have been reported occasionally. Dobutamine solution contains sodium bisulfite, a sulfite that may cause allergic-type reactions, including anaphylactic symptoms, in certain susceptible people.

In patients who have atrial fibrillation with rapid ventricular response, a digitalis preparation should be used prior to instituting dobutamine therapy. Because dobutamine facilitates atrioventricular conduction, patients with atrial fibrillation are at risk of developing rapid ventricular response.

Dobutamine should not be used in the presence of uncorrected tachycardia or ventricular fibrillation.

No improvement may be observed in the presence of marked mechanical obstruction such as severe valvular aortic stenosis.

Minimal vasoconstriction has occasionally been observed, most notably in patients recently treated with a β-blocking drug. Because dobutamine's inotropic effects stem from stimulation of cardiac β_1 receptors, this effect is, of course, prevented by β-blocking drugs.

Precautions: During dobutamine administration, monitor EKG, heart rate and blood pressure continuously. In addition, perform monitoring of pulmonary wedge pressure and cardiac output whenever possible to aid in the safe and effective infusion of dobutamine.

Caution should be exercised in order to prevent infiltration at the injection site.

Correct hypovolemia with suitable volume expanders before treatment with dobutamine.

Use with caution in patients with hyperthyroidism.

Use dobutamine with caution in patients receiving anesthetic agents, cyclopropane or halogenated hydrocarbons.

Dobutamine should be used with caution in patients taking concomitantly other sympathomimetic agents.

Dobutamine like other beta-2 agonists can produce a mild reduction in serum potassium concentration (rarely to hypokalemic levels). Accordingly, consideration should be given to monitoring serum potassium.

Usage following acute myocardial infarction: Clinical experience with dobutamine following myocardial infarction has been insufficient to establish the safety of this use. There is concern that any agent which increases contractile force and heart rate may increase the size of an infarction by intensifying ischemia, but whether dobutamine does so is not known.

Pregnancy: Reproduction studies (rats, rabbits) have revealed no evidence of impaired fertility or harm to the fetus due to dobutamine. To date, the drug has not been administered to pregnant women and should be used in such patients only when the expected benefits clearly outweigh the potential risks to the fetus and mother.

Children: Dobutamine's safety and efficacy for use in children have not been established.

Drug Interactions: Clinical studies indicate that the concomitant use of dobutamine and nitroprusside results in a higher cardiac output and, usually, a lower pulmonary wedge pressure than when either drug is used alone.

No evidence of drug interactions were noted in clinical studies when dobutamine was administered concurrently with other drugs including digitalis preparations and/or furosemide, spironolactone, lidocaine, nitroglycerin, isosorbide dinitrate,

Dobutrex (cont'd)

morphine, atropine, anticoagulants and potassium chloride supplements.

Adverse Effects: Cardiovascular: The most common adverse reactions relate to dobutamine's effect on the cardiovascular system.

A 10 to 20 mm Hg increase in systolic blood pressure and an increase in heart rate of 5 to 15 beats/minute have been noted in most patients. (See Warnings regarding exaggerated chronotropic and pressor effects). About 5% of patients have had increased premature ventricular beats during infusions. These effects are dose-related.

Hypotension: Precipitous decreases in blood pressure associated with dobutamine therapy have been reported. A reduction in dose or discontinuation of the drug is necessary to return the blood pressure to baseline levels. In some cases pressor support may be required.

Less common: cardiac awareness, transient bigeminy, bradycardia, angina, palpitations, nonspecific chest pain and shortness of breath.

Gastrointestinal: nausea, vomiting, bad taste.

CNS: headache, anxiety, fatigue, paresthesia.

Hypersensitivity: rash, fever, eosinophilia and bronchospasm have been reported occasionally.

Miscellaneous: rarely—dyspnea, thrombocytopenia, pruritus, chill, sweating. Phlebitis has been occasionally reported. Local inflammatory changes following inadvertent infiltration. Isolated cases of cutaneous necrosis (destruction of skin tissue) have been reported.

Administration of dobutamine, like other β_2-agonists, has been associated with decreases in serum potassium concentrations, rarely to hypokalemic values.

Long-term Safety: Infusion of up to 72 hours have revealed no adverse effects other than those seen with shorter infusions.

Overdose: Symptoms: Excessive blood pressure alteration or tachycardia.

Treatment: Reduce the rate of administration, or temporarily discontinue dobutamine until the patient's condition stabilizes. Because dobutamine's duration of action is short, no additional remedial measures are usually necessary.

Dosage: Dobutrex is a potent drug; it is not for direct injection and must be diluted exactly as directed before administration to patients as an i.v. infusion (see Precautions).

The infusion rate needed to increase cardiac output usually ranges from 2.5 to 10 μg/kg/min (see Table I). Some patients may respond to doses as low as 0.5 μg/kg/min whereas, on rare occasions, infusion rates up to 40 μg/kg/min have been required to obtain the desired effect.

Table I—Dobutrex

Infusion Rates for Concentrations of 250, 500, and 1 000 mg/L

Drug Delivery Rate (μg/kg/min)	Infusion Delivery Rate: 250 mg/L[a] (mL/kg/min)	500 mg/L[b] (mL/kg/min)	1 000 mg/L[c] (mL/kg/min)
2.5	0.01	0.005	0.0025
5	0.02	0.01	0.005
7.5	0.03	0.015	0.0075
10	0.04	0.02	0.01
12.5	0.05	0.025	0.0125
15	0.06	0.03	0.015

[a] 250 mg/L of diluent.
[b] 500 mg/L or 250 mg/500 mL of diluent.
[c] 1 000 mg/L or 250 mg/250 mL of diluent.

The final volume should be determined by the fluid requirements of the patient.

Adjust the administration rate and duration of therapy according to the patient's response as determined by heart rate, presence of ectopic activity, blood pressure, urine flow and, whenever possible, measurement of central venous or pulmonary wedge pressure and cardiac output.

Preparation and Stability: Dobutamine is incompatible with alkaline solutions and it should not be mixed with products such as 5% sodium bicarbonate injection, or to any other strongly alkaline solutions. Because of the occurrences of physical incompatibilities with some drugs and the potential for incompatibility with other drugs, it is recommended that dobutamine not be mixed with other drugs in the same solution. Dobutamine should not be used in conjunction with other agents or diluents containing both sodium bisulfite and ethanol.

At the time of administration dobutamine must be further diluted in an i.v. container to at least 50 mL using one of the following i.v. solutions as a diluent: 5% dextrose injection, 0.9% sodium chloride injection or sodium lactate injection. I.V. solutions should be used within 24 hours of preparation.

Solutions containing dobutamine may exhibit a color that, if present, will increase with time. This color change is due to slight oxidation of the drug, but there is no significant loss of potency during the reconstituted time periods stated above.

Supplied: Each mL of aqueous solution contains: dobutamine (as HCl) 12.5 mg. Nonmedicinal ingredients: sulfur dioxide 0.15 mg and water for injection. Hydrochloric acid and/or sodium hydroxide is used to adjust pH.

DOCUSATE CALCIUM
Taro

Stool Softener

Supplied: Each red, soft gelatin capsule contains: docusate calcium 240 mg in a corn oil base. Sodium- and tartrazine-free. Bottles of 30, 300 and 1 000. Store in a dry place, at room temperature (15 to 25°C).

DOCUSATE CALCIUM
Technilab

Stool Softener

Supplied: Each soft, red, oval-shaped gelatin capsule contains: docusate calcium USP 240 mg. Nonmedicinal ingredients: corn oil, D&C Red #33, FD&C Yellow #6, gelatin, glycerin, methylparaben, propylparaben, purified water and sorbitol. Lactose-, sodium- and tartrazine-free. Unit packs of 30 (3×10 blister packs). Plastic bottles of 1 000.

DOCUSATE SODIUM
Taro

Stool Softener

Supplied: Capsules: Each brown, oval-shaped soft gelatin capsule contains: docusate sodium USP 100 mg in a polyethylene glycol base. Bottles of 100 and 1 000. Store at room temperature.

Syrup: Each 5 mL contains: docusate sodium USP 20 mg in a base consisting of citric acid, ethanol, methylparaben, propylparaben, PEG, pluronic, sodium citrate, sucrose and artificial colors and flavors. Sodium hydroxide may be used to adjust pH. Also contains ethyl alcohol 0.03 mL/5 mL. Energy: 50 kJ (12 kcal)/5 mL. Sodium: <1 mmol/5 mL. Bottles of 250 and 500 mL. Store at room temperature.

DOCUSATE SODIUM
Technilab

Stool Softener

Supplied: Capsules: Each maroon, gelatin, oblong-shaped capsule, contains: docusate sodium USP 100 mg. Nonmedicinal ingredients: FD&C Red #2, FD&C Red #3, FD&C Yellow #6, gelatin, glycerin, methylparaben, polyethylene glycol, propylparaben, purified water and sorbitol. Bottles of 100 and 1 000. Safety sealed cap for protection.

Drops: Each mL of red, vanilla flavored solution, contains: docusate sodium USP 10 mg. Nonmedicinal ingredients: citric acid, D&C Red #33, methylparaben, poloxamer, polyethylene glycol, propylene glycol, propylparaben, purified water, sodium citrate and vanillin. Bottles of 25 mL. Safety sealed bottle for protection.

Syrup: 5 mL of red mint flavored syrup contains: docusate sodium USP 20 mg. Nonmedicinal ingredients: alcohol, artificial flavoring, citric acid, D&C Red #33, FD&C Red #40, menthol, methylparaben, peppermint oil, poloxamer, polyethylene glycol, propylparaben, purified water, sodium citrate and sucrose. Energy: 58.1 kJ (13.9 kcal)/5 mL. Bottles of 250 and 500 mL. Safety sealed bottle for protection.

Unit dose: Each unit dose (25 mL) container contains: docusate sodium USP 100 mg. Nonmedicinal ingredients: alcohol, artificial flavoring, citric acid, D&C Red #33, FD&C Red #40, menthol, methylparaben, peppermint oil, poloxamer, polyethylene glycol, propylparaben, purified water, sodium citrate and sucrose.

Store between 15 and 30°C in a tight, light resistant container in a dry area. Protect from freezing. Do not use the product after the expiration date printed on the container.

DOCUSATE SODIUM
Trianon

Stool Softener

Supplied: Each red, gelatin oblong-shaped capsule contains: docusate sodium USP 100 mg. Nonmedicinal ingredients: FD&C red 40 aluminum lake and polyethylene glycol. Bottles of 100 and 1 000. Safety cap for protection.

New Product 1998

DOLOBID® Ⓟ
Frosst

Diflunisal

Analgesic—Anti-inflammatory

Pharmacology: Diflunisal is a nonsteroidal drug with analgesic, anti-inflammatory and antipyretic properties.

The precise mechanism of the analgesic and anti-inflammatory actions of diflunisal is not known; however, it appears to be a peripherally acting analgesic drug. Diflunisal is a prostaglandin synthetase inhibitor. In animals, prostaglandin sensitize afferent nerves and potentiate the action of bradykinin in inducing pain. Since prostaglandins are known to be among the mediators of pain and inflammation, the mode of action of diflunisal may be due in part to a decrease of prostaglandins in peripheral tissues.

Diflunisal is rapidly and completely absorbed following oral administration with peak plasma concentrations occurring between 2 to 3 hours. The drug is excreted in the urine as 2 soluble glucuronide conjugates accounting for about 90% of the administered dose. Little or no diflunisal is excreted in the feces. Diflunisal appears in human milk in concentrations of 2 to 7% of those in plasma. More than 99% of diflunisal in plasma is bound to proteins.

As is the case with salicylic acid, concentration-dependent pharmacokinetics prevail when diflunisal is administered; a doubling of dosage produces a greater than doubling of drug accumulation.

The effect becomes more apparent with repetitive doses. Following single doses, peak plasma concentrations of 41 ± 11 μg/mL (mean±S.D.) were observed following 250 mg doses, 87 ± 17 μg/mL were observed following 500 mg and 124 ± 11 μg/mL following single 1 000 mg doses. However, following administration of 250 mg twice a day, a mean peak level of 56 ± 14 μg/mL was observed on day 8, while the mean peak level after 500 mg twice a day for 11 days was 190 ± 33 μg/mL. The plasma half-life of diflunisal is 8 to 12 hours. Because of its long half-life and nonlinear pharmacokinetics, several days are required for diflunisal plasma levels to reach steady state following multiple doses. For this reason, an initial loading dose is necessary to shorten the time to reach steady state levels, and 2 to 3 days of observation are necessary for evaluating changes in treatment regimens if a loading dose is not used.

Indications: The relief of mild to moderate pain accompanied by inflammation in conditions such as musculoskeletal trauma, post-dental extraction or post-episiotomy; symptomatic relief of osteoarthritis and rheumatoid arthritis.

Contraindications: Patients who are hypersensitive to any component of this product.

Patients in whom acute asthmatic attacks, urticaria, or rhinitis are precipitated by ASA or other nonsteroidal anti-inflammatory drugs. Fatal anaphylactoid reactions have occurred in such individuals.

Active peptic ulcer or any other active inflammatory disease of the gastrointestinal tract.

Warnings: Gastrointestinal: Peptic ulceration, perforation and gastrointestinal bleeding, sometimes severe and occasionally fatal have been reported during therapy with NSAIDs including diflunisal.

Diflunisal should be given under close medical supervision to patients prone to gastrointestinal tract irritation particularly those with a history of peptic ulcer, diverticulosis or other inflammatory disease of the gastrointestinal tract. In these cases the physician must weigh the benefits of treatment against the possible hazards.

Patients taking any NSAID including this drug should be instructed to contact a physician immediately if they experience symptoms or signs suggestive of peptic ulceration or gastrointestinal bleeding. These reactions can occur without warning symptoms or signs and at any time during the treatment.

Elderly, frail and debilitated patients appear to be at higher risk from a variety of adverse reactions from NSAIDs. For such patients, consideration should be given to a starting dose lower than usual, with individual adjustment when necessary and under close supervision (see Precautions).

Pregnancy: The safety of the drug in pregnancy has not been established, and its use during pregnancy is therefore not recommended.

A dose of 60 mg/kg/day (equivalent to 2 times the maximum human dose) was maternotoxic, embryotoxic, and teratogenic in rabbits. In 3 of six studies in rabbits, evidence of teratogenicity was observed at doses ranging from 40 to 50 mg/kg/day. Teratology studies in mice, at doses up to 50 mg/kg/day, and in rats at doses up to 100 mg/kg/day, revealed no harm to the fetus due to diflunisal. ASA and other salicylates have been shown to be teratogenic in a wide variety of species, including the rat and rabbit, at doses ranging from 50 to 400 mg/kg/day (approximately 1 to 8 times the human dose).

In rats at a dose of 1.5 times the maximum human dose, there was an increase in the average length of gestation. Similar increases in the length of gestation have been observed with ASA, indomethacin, and phenylbutazone, and may be related to inhibition of prostaglandin synthetase. Drugs of this class may cause dystocia and delayed parturition in pregnant animals.

Because of the known effect of drugs of this class on the human fetal cardiovascular system (closure of ductus arteriosus), use during the third trimester of pregnancy is not recommended.

Lactation: Diflunisal is excreted in human milk in concentrations of 2 to 7% of those in plasma. Because of the potential for serious adverse reactions in nursing infants a decision should be made whether to initiate nursing or to administer the drug, taking into account the importance of the drug to the mother.

Children: Safety and effectiveness in infants and children have not been established, and use of the drug in children below the age of 12 years is not recommended.

Precautions: ASA has been associated with Reye's syndrome. Because diflunisal is a derivative of salicylic acid, the possibility of its association with Reye's syndrome cannot be excluded.

Gastrointestinal: If peptic ulceration is suspected or confirmed, or if gastrointestinal bleeding or perforation occurs diflunisal should be discontinued, an appropriate treatment instituted and patient closely monitored.

There is no definitive evidence that the concomitant administration of histamine H_2-receptor antagonists and/or antacids will either prevent the occurrence of gastrointestinal side effects or allow continuation of diflunisal therapy when and if these adverse reactions appear.

When diflunisal was given to normal volunteers at 500 mg twice daily, fecal blood loss was not significantly different from placebo. Diflunisal 1 000 mg twice daily caused a statistically significant increase in fecal blood loss.

Renal: As with other NSAIDs, long-term administration of diflunisal to animals has resulted in renal papillary necrosis and other abnormal renal pathology. In humans, there have been reports of acute interstitial nephritis with hematuria, proteinuria, and occasionally nephrotic syndrome.

A second form of renal toxicity has been seen in patients with prerenal and renal conditions leading to a reduction in renal blood flow or blood volume, where the renal prostaglandins have a supportive role in the maintenance of renal perfusion. In these patients administration of an NSAID may cause a dose dependent reduction in prostaglandin formation and may precipitate overt renal decompensation. Patients at greatest risk of this reaction are those with conditions such as renal or hepatic dysfunction, the elderly, extracellular volume depletion from any cause, congestive heart failure, sepsis, or concomitant use of diuretics or any nephrotoxic drug. Discontinuation of NSAID therapy is typically followed by recovery to the pretreatment state.

Since diflunisal is eliminated primarily by the kidneys, this drug should be used with great caution in patients with impaired renal function and the elderly; a lower daily dosage should be anticipated to avoid excessive drug accumulation, and patients should be carefully monitored. During long term therapy kidney function should be monitored periodically.

Hepatic: As with other NSAIDs, borderline elevations of one or more liver tests may occur in up to 15% of patients. These abnormalities may progress, may remain essentially unchanged, or may be transient with continued therapy. The ALT test is probably the most sensitive indicator of liver dysfunction. Meaningful (3 times the upper limit of normal) elevations of AST or ALT occurred in controlled clinical trials in less than 1% of patients. A patient with symptoms and/or signs suggesting liver dysfunction, or in whom an abnormal liver test has occurred, should be evaluated for evidence of the development of more severe hepatic reaction while on therapy with diflunisal. Severe hepatic reactions, including jaundice and cases of fatal hepatitis, have been reported with nonsteroidal anti-inflammatory drugs. Although such reactions are rare, if abnormal liver tests persist or worsen, if clinical signs and symptoms consistent with liver disease develop, or if systemic manifestations occur (e.g., eosinophilia, rash, etc.). diflunisal should be discontinued since liver reactions can be fatal.

During long-term therapy, liver function tests should be monitored periodically. If this drug is to be used in the presence of impaired liver function, it must be done under strict observation.

Fluid and Electrolyte Balance: Fluid retention and edema have been observed in patients treated with diflunisal. Therefore, as with many other nonsteroidal anti-inflammatory drugs, the possibility of precipitating congestive heart failure in elderly patients or those with compromised cardiac function should be born in mind. Diflunisal should be used with caution in patients with heart failure, hypertension or other conditions predisposing to fluid retention.

Serum electrolytes should be monitored periodically during long-term therapy, especially in those patients at risk.

Hematology: As an inhibitor of prostaglandin synthetase, diflunisal has a dose-related effect on platelet function and bleeding time. In normal volunteers, 250 mg twice daily for 8 days had no effect on platelet function, and 500 mg twice daily had a slight effect. At 1 000 mg twice daily, diflunisal inhibited platelet function. In contrast to acetylsalicylic acid these effects of diflunisal were reversible. Bleeding time was not altered by a dose of 250 mg twice daily, but was slightly increased at 500 mg twice daily. At 1 000 mg twice daily, a greater increase occurred, but was not statistically significantly different from the change in the placebo group. Therefore, patients who may be adversely affected should be carefully observed when diflunisal is administered.

Blood dyscrasias associated with the use of NSAIDs are rare, but could have severe consequences.

Infection: In common with other anti-inflammatory drugs, diflunisal may mask the usual signs of infection.

Ophthalmology: Blurred and/or diminished vision has been reported with the use of diflunisal and other NSAIDs. If such symptoms develop, this drug should be discontinued and an ophthalmologic examination performed; ophthalmic examination should be carried out at periodic intervals in any patients receiving this drug for an extended period of time.

Hypersensitivity Reactions: A potentially life-threatening, apparent hypersensitivity syndrome has been reported. This multisystem syndrome includes constitutional symptoms (fever, chills), and cutaneous findings (see Adverse Effects). It may also include involvement of major organs (changes in liver function, jaundice, leukopenia, thrombocytopenia, eosinophilia, disseminated intravascular coagulation, renal impairment, including renal failure), and less specific findings (adenitis, arthralgia, arthritis, malaise, anorexia, disorientation).

Uricosuric Effect: In normal volunteers, an increase in the renal clearance of uric acid and a decrease in serum uric acid was observed when diflunisal was administered at 500 or 750 mg daily in divided doses. Patients on long-term therapy taking diflunisal at 500 to 1 000 mg daily in divided doses showed a prompt and consistent reduction in mean serum uric acid levels, which were lowered as much as 1.4 mg%. It is not known whether diflunisal interferes with the activity of other uricosuric agents.

Antipyretic Activity: Diflunisal is not recommended for use as an antipyretic agent. In single 250, 500 or 750 mg doses, diflunisal produced measurable but not clinically useful decreases in temperature in patients with fever, however, the possibility that it may mask fever in some patients, particularly with chronic or high doses, should be considered.

Drug Interactions: Nonsteroidal anti-inflammatory drugs: Severe adverse reactions involving the gastrointestinal tract have occurred when diflunisal is administered concomitantly with other NSAIDs. The following information was obtained from studies in normal volunteers.

ASA: In normal volunteers a small decrease in diflunisal levels was observed when multiple doses of diflunisal and ASA were administered concomitantly.

Indomethacin: The administration of diflunisal to normal volunteers receiving indomethacin decreased the renal clearance and significantly increased the plasma levels of indomethacin. Further, the combined use of indomethacin and diflunisal has been associated with fatal gastrointestinal hemorrhage. Therefore, indomethacin and diflunisal should not be used concomitantly.

Sulindac: The concomitant administration of diflunisal and sulindac in normal volunteers resulted in lowering of the plasma levels of the active sulindac sulfide metabolite by approximately one-third.

Naproxen: The concomitant administration of diflunisal and naproxen in normal volunteers had no effect on the plasma levels of naproxen, but significantly decreased the urinary excretion of naproxen and its glucuronide metabolite. Naproxen had no effect on plasma levels of diflunisal.

Oral Anticoagulants: In some normal volunteers, the concomitant administration of diflunisal and warfarin or acenocoumarol resulted in prolongation of prothrombin time. This may occur because diflunisal competitively displaces coumarins from protein binding sites. Accordingly, when diflunisal is administered with oral anticoagulants, the prothombin time should be closely monitored during and for several days after concomitant drug administration. Adjustment of dosage of oral anticoagulants may be required.

Tolbutamide: In diabetic patients receiving diflunisal and tolbutamide, no significant effects were seen on tolbutamide plasma levels or fasting blood glucose.

Furosemide: In normal volunteers, the concomitant administration of diflunisal and furosemide had no effect on the diuretic activity of furosemide. Diflunisal decreased the hyperuricemic effect of furosemide.

Hydrochlorothiazide: In normal volunteers, concomitant administration of diflunisal and hydrochlorothiazide resulted in significantly increased plasma levels of hydrochlorothiazide. Diflunisal decreased the hyperuricemic effect of hydrochlorothiazide.

Antacids: Concomitant administration of antacids may reduce plasma levels of diflunisal. This effect is small with occasional doses of antacids, but may be clinically significant when antacids are used on a continuous schedule.

Coadministration of aluminium hydroxide suspension significantly decreases absorption of diflunisal by approximately 40%.

Methotrexate: Caution should be used if diflunisal is administered concomitantly with methotrexate. NSAIDs have been reported to decrease the tubular secretion of methotrexate and potentiate the toxicity.

Lithium: Concurrent use of NSAIDs with lithium has been reported to increase steady-state plasma lithium concentration. It is recommended to monitor lithium plasma concentration during and following concurrent use.

Acetaminophen: Concomitant administration of diflunisal and acetaminophen to normal volunteers resulted in significantly increased (50%) plasma levels of acetaminophen. Acetaminophen had no effect on plasma levels of diflunisal. Since acetaminophen in high doses has been associated with hepatotoxicity, concomitant administration of diflunisal and acetaminophen should be used cautiously, with careful monitoring of patients.

Adverse Effects: The most common adverse reactions encountered with NSAIDs are gastrointestinal, of which peptic ulcer, with or without bleeding, is the most severe. Fatalities have occurred on occasion, particularly in the elderly.

Dolobid (cont'd)

The adverse reactions (see Table I), listed by body system, have been observed in controlled clinical trials or since the drug was marketed.

Table I—Dolobid

Adverse Reactions		
3-9%	**1-3%**	**<1%**
Gastrointestinal		
nausea	vomiting	peptic ulcer
dyspepsia	constipation	gastrointestinal bleeding
gastrointestinal pain	flatulence	anorexia
		gastrointestinal perforation
diarrhea		gastritis
CNS/Psychiatric		
headache	dizziness	vertigo
	somnolence	light-headedness
	insomnia	paresthesia
		nervousness
		depression
		hallucinations
		confusion
Dermatologic		
rash		erythema multiforme
		Stevens-Johnson syndrome
		toxic epidermal necrolysis
		exfoliative dermatitis
		pruritus
		sweating
		dry mucous membranes
		stomatitis
		photosensitivity
		urticaria
Special Senses	tinnitus	transient visual disturbance (including blurred vision)
Hematologic		
		thrombocytopenia
		leukopenia
		pancytopenia
		agranulocytosis (rarely)
		hemolytic anemia
Renal		
		dysuria
		renal impairment (including renal failure)
		interstitial nephritis
		hematuria
		proteinuria
Hepatic		
		jaundice
		cholestasis
		liver function abnormalities
		hepatitis
Miscellaneous		
	fatigue	asthenia
		edema
Hypersensitivity Reactions		acute anaphylactic reaction with bronchospasm
		angioedema
		hypersensitivity vasculitis
		hypersensitivity syndrome (see Precautions)

Other reactions have been reported in clinical trials or since the drug was marketed abroad, but occurred under circumstances where a causal relationship could not be established. However, in these rarely reported events, that possibility cannot be excluded. Therefore, these observations are listed to serve as alerting information to physicians.

Respiratory: dyspnea.
Cardiovascular: palpitation, syncope.
Miscellaneous: chest pain, muscle cramps.
Renal: nephrotic syndrome.

Overdose: Symptoms: Cases of overdosage have occurred and deaths have been reported. Most patients recovered without evidence of permanent sequelae. The most common signs and symptoms observed with overdosage were drowsiness, vomiting, nausea, diarrhea, hyperventilation, tachycardia, sweating, tinnitus, disorientation, stupor, and coma. Diminished urine output and cardiorespiratory arrest have also been reported. The lowest dosage of diflunisal at which a death has been reported was 15 g without the presence of other drugs. Death has been reported from a mixed drug overdose which included 7.5 g of diflunisal. A dose that is usually fatal has not yet been identified.

Treatment: In the event of overdosage, the stomach should be emptied by inducing vomiting or by gastric lavage, and the patient carefully observed and given symptomatic and supportive treatment. Because of the high degree of protein binding, hemodialysis may not be effective.

Dosage: Diflunisal has slow onset and long duration of action. Diflunisal produces significant analgesia in one hour and maximum analgesia in 2 to 4 hours. Analgesic effect lasts 8 to 12 hours. These characteristics should be considered when prescribing this drug.

Mild to moderate pain: 1 000 mg initially, followed by 500 mg every 12 hours is recommended for most patients.

A lower dosage may be appropriate depending on such factors as pain severity, patient response, weight, or advanced age; for example, 500 mg initially, followed by 250 mg every 12 hours.

For osteoarthritis and rheumatoid arthritis, the dosage range is 500 mg to 1 000 mg daily in 2 divided doses according to patient response.

Maintenance doses higher than 1 000 mg a day are not recommended.

Diflunisal may be administered with water, milk or meals. Tablets should be swallowed whole, not crushed or chewed.

Information for the Patient: See Blue Section—Information for the Patient "Dolobid".

Supplied: Each orange-colored, capsule-shaped, film-coated tablet, coded DOLOBID on one side, contains: diflunisal 500 mg. Nonmedicinal ingredients: cellulose, FD&C Yellow #6 aluminum lake, hydroxypropyl cellulose, hydroxypropyl methylcellulose, magnesium stearate, starch, talc and titanium dioxide. Gluten-, lactose- and tartrazine-free. Bottles of 60.

(Shown in Product Recognition Section)

DONNAGEL®-PG Capsules Ⓝ

Wyeth-Ayerst

Attapulgite—Pectin—Opium

Antidiarrheal

Supplied: Each yellow opaque capsule, monogrammed "W" in black contains: activated attapulgite 300 mg, pectin 71.4 mg and powdered opium 12.0 mg. Nonmedicinal ingredients: magnesium stearate and microcrystalline cellulose. Empty capsule: gelatin, silicon dioxide, sodium lauryl sulfate, titanium dioxide and yellow iron oxide. Energy: <1 kJ (<1 kcal). Bottles of 12.

DONNAGEL®-PG Suspension Ⓝ

Wyeth-Ayerst

Kaolin—Pectin—Opium

Antidiarrheal

Supplied: Each 30 mL of pale yellow, banana-flavored suspension contains: kaolin 6 g, pectin 142.8 mg, powdered opium 24 mg (equivalent to 6 mL of paregoric) and sodium benzoate (preservative) 60 mg. Nonmedicinal ingredients: alcohol, citric acid anhydrous, D&C Yellow No. 10, FD&C Yellow No. 6 sunset, flavor banana imit, glycerin, invert sugar 73% solution, purified water, sodium benzoate, sodium chloride and xanthan gum. Alcohol 5%. Energy: 36.0 kJ (8.6 kcal)/5 mL. Sodium: <1 mmol (2.6 mg)/5 mL. Amber bottles of 140 mL. Shake well.

DONNATAL® ⊕

Wyeth-Ayerst

Belladonna Alkaloids—Phenobarbital

Antispasmodic—Sedative

Supplied: Elixir: Each 5 mL of green, citrus flavored elixir contains: hyoscyamine sulfate 104 μg, atropine sulfate 19 μg, scopolamine HBr 7 μg and phenobarbital 16.2 mg. Nonmedicinal ingredients: D&C Yellow No. 10, FD&C Blue No. 1 Brilliant FCF, FD&C Yellow No. 6 Sunset, flavor (anise oil, coriander oil russian, lemon oil, lime isolate, lime oil imit., orange oil), invert sugar 73% solution and water purified. Alcohol: 23 %. Energy: 41.4 kJ (9.9 kcal)/5 mL. Bottles of 500 mL.

Extentabs: Each pale green, extended action, coated tablet, monogrammed "AHR/Donnatal Extentabs" in black ink, contains: hyoscyamine sulfate 311 μg, atropine sulfate 58 μg, scopolamine HBr 19.5 μg and phenobarbital 48.6 mg. Also contains sugar. Energy: <1 kJ (<1 kcal). Sodium: <1 mmol (2.75 mg). Bottles of 100.

Tablets: Each white, scored, compressed tablet, monogrammed "AYERST" contains: hyoscyamine sulfate 104 μg, atropine sulfate 19 μg, scopolamine HBr 7 μg and phenobarbital 16.2 mg. Nonmedicinal ingredients: magnesium stearate, microcrystalline cellulose, stearic acid and sucrose white. Energy: <1 kJ (<1 kcal). Bottles of 100 and 500 mL.

DOPAMINE HCl and DEXTROSE INJECTION ℞

Abbott

Sympathomimetic Agent

Supplied: Dopamine HCl is a sterile, nonpyrogenic solution in a 250 mL (800 μg) and in a 250 and 500 mL (1 600 μg) single-dose flexible (polyester) container. Each mL contains: dopamine HCl 800 μg, 1 600 μg or 3 200 μg, dextrose monohydrate (or dextrose anhydrous) 50 mg, sodium metabisulfite 0.5 mg as a stabilizer, and hydrochloric acid (may contain sodium hydroxide) for pH adjustment. pH approximately 3.2. Osmolarity approximately 277 mOsm/L (800 μg/mL), 282 mOsm/L (1 600 μg/mL) or 295 mOsm/L (3 200 μg/mL). Store at room temperature (25°C). Protect from light, freezing and extreme heat.

Note: Dopamine HCl as well as other dextrose solutions without electrolytes, should **not** be administered simultaneously with blood through the same infusion set, because of the possibility that pseudoagglutination of red cells may occur.

Parenteral drugs should be visually inspected for particulate matter and discoloration prior to administration, whenever solution and container permit; do not use the solution if it is darker than slightly yellow or discolored in any other way.

DOPAMINE HCl AND 5% DEXTROSE INJECTION ℞

Baxter

Sympathomimetic

Supplied: Each mL of sterile, nonpyrogenic solution contains: dopamine HCl and 5% dextrose in Viaflex Plus plastic (polyvinyl chloride) containers in the following sizes and concentrations: see Table I.

Table I—Dopamine HCl and 5% Dextrose Injection Supplied

Total Volume (mL)	Total Dopamine HCl Content (mg)	Dopamine HCl Concentration (mg/mL)
250	200	0.8
250	400	1.6
250	800	3.2
500	800	1.6

Store below 25°C. Protect from freezing.

DOPRAM®

Wyeth-Ayerst

Doxapram HCl

Respiratory Stimulant

Supplied: Each mL of clear, colorless solution contains: doxapram HCl USP 20 mg. Nonmedicinal ingredients: chlorobutanol (as preservative) and water for injection. pH: 3.5 to 5.0. Rubber stoppered vials of 20 mL.

DOVONEX® ℞

Leo

Calcipotriol

Topical Nonsteroidal Antipsoriatic

Pharmacology: Calcipotriol is a nonsteroidal antipsoriatic agent, derived from the naturally occurring vitamin D. Calcipotriol exhibits a vitamin D-like effect by competing for the 1,25 $(OH)_2D_3$ receptor. Calcipotriol is as potent as 1,25 $(OH)_2D_3$, the naturally occurring active form of vitamin D, in regulating cell proliferation and cell differentiation, but much less active than 1,25 $(OH)_2D_3$ in its effect on calcium metabolism. Calcipotriol induces differentiation and suppresses proliferation (without any evidence of a cytotoxic effect) of keratinocytes, thus reversing the abnormal keratinocyte changes in psoriasis. The therapeutic goal envisaged with calcipotriol is thus a normalization of epidermal growth.

Calcipotriol cream and ointment, applied topically, were found to be efficacious and well-tolerated in the treatment of psoriasis vulgaris. Calcipotriol ointment was used for the treatment of 686 patients with plaque-type psoriasis vulgaris participating in 5 clinical trials lasting from 6 to 8 weeks. The majority of patients had a marked improvement at the end of the treatment. Thickness, erythema and scaling were markedly improved. Only about 1% of the patients were withdrawn because of insufficient therapeutic response. It is characteristic that the improvement occurs rapidly. This data has been repeated in 3 long-term trials involving 334 patients with plaque-type psoriasis vulgaris treated for up to 12 months with calcipotriol ointment. Combination of topical calcipotriol with UVB phototherapy improved the therapeutic response, although to a statistically insignificant degree. Calcipotriol cream was used for the treatment of 159 patients with plaque type psoriasis vulgaris participating in a pivotal clinical trial lasting 8 weeks with efficacy similar to that of calcipotriol ointment.

The safety, efficacy and tolerability of calcipotriol ointment in children (ages 2 to 14 years) has been demonstrated by an 8-week open-label trial as well as an 8-week double-blind vehicle controlled trial. Calcipotriol was significantly more effective than vehicle in reducing the symptoms of redness, thickness and scaliness, and in the overall assessment of efficacy. No significant effects on hematology, serum and urine biochemistry parameters (including calcium levels) and parameters of bone formation or resorption were observed after 8 weeks of treatment (maximum dose 50 g/week/m² body surface area).

Three pivotal trials to evaluate the safety and efficacy of calcipotriol scalp solution in 284 patients with scalp psoriasis were conducted. There was a statistically significant improvement in the scalp psoriasis with a positive effect on total sign score, redness, thickness, scaliness and extent of scalp psoriasis.

Pharmacokinetics: A pharmacokinetic study of calcipotriol ointment has demonstrated that the apparent systemic absorption of the applied dose of calcipotriol over 12 hours is approximately 5.5% of the dose in normal subjects and in psoriatic patients.

Indications: Cream and Ointment: For the topical treatment of mild to moderate psoriasis.

Solution: For the topical treatment of scalp psoriasis.

Contraindications: Hypersensitivity to any constituent of calcipotriol cream, ointment or scalp solution. **Not for ophthalmic use.**

Warnings: Calcipotriol cream, ointment and scalp solution are not generally recommended for severe extensive psoriasis, in view of the risk of hypercalcemia secondary to excessive absorption of calcipotriol when there is extensive skin involvement. If calcipotriol is used for severe extensive psoriasis it is important to monitor the serum calcium levels at regular intervals. If the serum calcium level becomes elevated in such patients, calcipotriol therapy should be discontinued and the serum calcium level monitored in these patients until it returns to normal.

Topical calcipotriol is not recommended for use on the face since this may give rise to itching and erythema of the facial skin. Patients should be instructed to wash their hands after using calcipotriol to avoid inadvertent transfer to the face from other body parts. Should facial dermatitis develop in spite of these precautions, calcipotriol therapy should be discontinued (see Information for the Patient).

Pregnancy and *Lactation:* Safety for use during pregnancy has not yet been established, although studies in experimental animals have not shown teratogenic effects. It is not known whether calcipotriol could be excreted in breast milk. Calcipotriol should be used in women during pregnancy or breast-feeding only if the anticipated benefit clearly outweighs the potential risk.

Infants: There is inadequate experience with the use of calcipotriol in infants under 2 years of age to recommend use in this age group. Use beneath diapers has not been investigated and should be avoided as diapers may be occlusive.

Children: Administration to children should be supervised by a responsible individual to ensure proper administration and dosage.

Precautions: Calcipotriol should be used cautiously in skin folds, where the natural occlusion may give rise to an increase of the irritant effect of calcipotriol.

Treatment with calcipotriol in the recommended amounts (see Dosage) does not generally result in changes in laboratory values. However, it is recommended that base line serum calcium levels be obtained in all patients before starting treatment with calcipotriol, with subsequent monitoring of these serum calcium levels at suitable intervals. The monitoring of serum calcium levels is particularly important if the total dose of calcipotriol exceeds the recommended amount or if calcipotriol is used for severe psoriasis with extensive skin involvement. If the serum calcium becomes elevated, calcipotriol treatment should be discontinued, and the levels of serum calcium should be measured once weekly until the serum calcium levels return to normal values. Patients with marginally elevated serum calcium may be treated with calcipotriol, provided that the serum calcium is monitored at suitable intervals.

Drug Interactions: There is no experience of concomitant therapy with other antipsoriatic drugs applied to the same skin area.

Adverse Effects: In clinical trials reported to-date, the most common adverse reactions have been related to lesional and perilesional irritation. Some patients develop face and scalp irritation which is likely related to the inadvertent transfer of calcipotriol cream or ointment from other body parts. Facial irritation may also occur with the use of calcipotriol scalp solution from inadvertent transfer of the scalp solution to the face. One unconfirmed case of Koebner phenomenon has been reported and 3 unconfirmed cases of hypersensitivity reaction to calcipotriol. Occasionally hypercalcemia has been reported usually related to excessive (greater than the recommended weekly amount—see Dosage) use of the topical calcipotriol or when excessive absorption of calcipotriol has occurred when used for severe psoriasis with extensive skin involvement (see Warnings).

Overdose: Symptoms and Treatment: Hypercalcemia does not occur at the usual dose of calcipotriol (see Dosage). Excessive use, (i.e., more than the recommended weekly amount) may cause elevated serum calcium, which rapidly subsides when treatment is discontinued; in such cases the monitoring of serum calcium levels once weekly until the serum calcium returns to normal levels is recommended.

Dosage: Calcipotriol is available in an ointment or a cream formulation at a concentration of 50 µg/g for use on the body and scalp solution at a concentration of 50 µg/mL for hairy areas. Calcipotriol is indicated **for topical use only** and **not for ophthalmic use.**

Adults: Calcipotriol should be applied topically to the affected area twice daily (i.e., in the morning and in the evening). Less frequent application may be indicated for maintenance treatment. After satisfactory improvement has occurred, the drug can be discontinued. If recurrence takes place after discontinuation, the treatment may be reinstituted.

The maximum recommended weekly dosage of calcipotriol cream and/or ointment is shown in Table I.

Table I—Dovonex

Maximum Weekly Dosage—Cream and/or Ointment

Age (years)	Dose (g/week)
2-5	25
6-10	50
11-14	75
Adults (over 14)	100

The maximum weekly dose of calcipotriol cream and/or ointment for children is based on the adult dose of 100 g/week adjusted for body surface area (maximum 50 g/week/m²). The dosage regimen is based on the following expected body surface area: 2 to 5 years: 0.5 m² (25% of adult); 6 to 10 years: 1.0 m² (50% of adult); 11 to 14 years: 1.5 m² (75% of adult).

The maximum recommended adult weekly dose of calcipotriol scalp solution is 60 mL. There is no clinical trial experience with use of calcipotriol scalp solution in children. When cream, ointment or scalp solution are used together, the total dose of calcipotriol should not exceed the recommended weekly amount for each age group (i.e., 2 to 5 years: 1.25 mg; 6 to 10 years: 2.5 mg; 11 to 14 years: 3.75 mg; adults: 5 mg in any week).

Treatment with calcipotriol can be combined with UVB phototherapy. Treated patients are allowed to expose the skin to sunlight. In such cases, the calcipotriol should be applied after the exposure to UV light.

Information for the Patient: See Blue Section—Information for the Patient "Dovonex".

Supplied: Cream: Each g of white cream contains: calcipotriol 50 µg. Nonmedicinal ingredients: cetomacrogol 1 000, cetostearyl alcohol, chlorallylhexaminium chloride (dowicil 200), disodium edetate, disodium phosphate dihydrate, glycerol 85%, liquid paraffin, purified water and white soft paraffin. Lacquered aluminum tubes (equipped with an aluminum membrane) of 60 and 120 g. Store between 15 and 30°C.

Ointment: Each g of faintly translucent white to yellowish ointment contains: calcipotriol 50 µg. Nonmedicinal ingredients: disodium edetate, disodium phosphate dihydrate, DL-α-tocopherol, liquid paraffin, polyoxyethylene-(2)-stearyl ether, propylene glycol, purified water and white soft paraffin. Lacquered aluminum tubes (equipped with an aluminum membrane) of 60 and 120 g. Store at room temperature between 15 and 25°C.

Scalp Solution: Each mL of colorless, slightly viscous solution contains: calcipotriol 50 µg. Nonmedicinal ingredients: hydroxypropyl cellulose, isopropanol, levomenthol, propylene glycol, purified water and sodium citrate. Polyethylene bottles of 30 and 60 mL. Store below 25°C.

DOXORUBICIN HCl FOR INJECTION USP Ⓟ
Faulding

Antineoplastic Agent

Pharmacology: The precise mechanism(s) of the antineoplastic action of doxorubicin is not fully understood. Experimental evidence indicates that doxorubicin forms a complex with DNA by intercalation between base pairs, causing inhibition of DNA synthesis and DNA-dependent RNA synthesis by the resulting template disordering and steric obstruction. Doxorubicin also inhibits protein synthesis. Doxorubicin is active throughout the cell cycle including interphase.

Of the cell types tested in vitro, cardiac cells are the most sensitive to the effects of doxorubicin, followed by sarcoma and melanoma cells, normal muscle fibroblasts, and normal skin fibroblasts. Normal, rapidly proliferating tissues such as those of bone marrow, gastrointestinal and oral mucosa, and hair follicles are also affected to varying degrees. Doxorubicin also has immunosuppressive activity.

Pharmacokinetics: Absorption: Doxorubicin is not stable in gastric acid, and animal studies indicate that it is not absorbed from the gastrointestinal tract.

Distribution: Doxorubicin is widely distributed in the plasma and in tissues. As early as 30 seconds after i.v. administration, doxorubicin is present in the liver, lungs, heart, and kidneys. Doxorubicin is absorbed by cells and binds to cellular components, particularly to nucleic acids. Doxorubicin does not cross the blood-brain barrier or achieve a measurable concentration in the CSF.

Trace amounts of doxorubicin have been found in fetal mice whose mothers received the drug during pregnancy, and there are limited data which indicate that doxorubicin crosses the human placenta. Limited data indicate that doxorubicin is distributed into milk, achieving concentrations that often exceed those in plasma; doxorubicinol (the major metabolite) also distributes into milk.

Elimination: Plasma concentrations of doxorubicin and its metabolites decline in a triphasic manner. In the first phase, doxorubicin is rapidly metabolized, presumably by a first-pass effect through the liver. It appears that most of this metabolism is completed before the entire dose is administered. Doxorubicin and its metabolites are rapidly distributed into the extravascular compartment with a plasma half-life of approximately 0.6 hours for doxorubicin and 3.3 hours for the metabolites. This is followed by relatively prolonged plasma concentrations of doxorubicin and its metabolites, probably resulting from tissue binding. During the second phase, the plasma half-life of doxorubicin is 16.7 hours and that of its metabolites is 31.7 hours. Patients with impaired hepatic function have prolonged and elevated plasma concentrations of both the drug and its metabolites. Plasma protein binding is approximately 50%.

Doxorubicin is metabolized in the liver and other tissues by an aldo-keto reductase enzyme, yielding doxorubicinol (adriamycinol), the major metabolite which has antineoplastic activity. Other metabolites which are therapeutically inactive include doxorubicinone (adriamycinone), aglycones and conjugates. More than 20% of the total drug in plasma is present as metabolites as soon as 5 minutes after a dose, 70% in 30 minutes, 75% in 4 hours, and 90% in 24 hours.

Doxorubicin is excreted predominantly in bile. Ten to 20% of a single dose is excreted in feces in 24 hours, and 40 to 50% of a dose is excreted in bile or feces within 7 days.

Doxorubicin HCl for Injection USP (cont'd)

About 50% of the drug in bile is unchanged drug, 23% is doxorubicinol, and the remainder is other metabolites including aglycones and conjugates. About 4 to 5% of the administered drug is excreted in urine after 5 days, principally as unchanged doxorubicin. It appears that very little further urinary excretion of the drug occurs after 5 days.

Indications: Doxorubicin has been used successfully both as a single agent and also in combination with other approved cancer chemotherapeutic agents to produce regression in neoplastic conditions such as acute lymphoblastic leukemia, acute myeloblastic leukemia, Wilms' tumor, neuroblastomas, soft tissue sarcomas, bone sarcomas, breast carcinoma, gynecologic carcinomas, testicular carcinomas, bronchogenic carcinoma, lymphomas of both Hodgkin and non-hodgkin types, thyroid carcinoma, bladder carcinomas, squamous cell carcinoma of the head and neck, hepatic and gastric carcinoma. Doxorubicin has also been used by instillation into the bladder for the topical treatment of superficial bladder tumors.

A number of other solid tumors have also shown some responsiveness to doxorubicin alone or in combination with other drugs (see Dosage). Studies to date have shown malignant melanoma, kidney carcinoma, large bowel carcinomas, brain tumors and metastases to the CNS not to be significantly responsive to doxorubicin therapy.

Contraindications: Doxorubicin therapy should not be started in patients who have marked myelosuppression induced by previous treatment with other antiblastic agents or by radiotherapy. Conclusive data are not available on pre-existing heart disease as a cofactor for increased risk of doxorubicin-induced cardiac toxicity. Preliminary data suggest that in such cases cardiac toxicity may occur at doses lower than the recommended cumulative limit. It is therefore not recommended that doxorubicin be started in such cases. Doxorubicin treatment is contraindicated in patients who have received previous treatment with complete cumulative doses of doxorubicin, daunorubicin or other anthracyclines and anthracenes.

Warnings: Caution: Doxorubicin is a potent drug and should be used only by physicians experienced with cancer chemotherapy drugs (see Precautions). Blood counts and hepatic function tests should be performed regularly. Because of the experience with cardiac toxicity, a total dose of doxorubicin exceeding 550 mg/m² with the 21-day regimen and 700 mg/m² with the weekly regimen, is not recommended. Cardiac monitoring is advised in those patients who have received mediastinal radiotherapy, other anthracycline or anthracene therapy, with pre-existing cardiac disease, or who have received prior doxorubicin cumulative doses exceeding 400 mg/m² with the 21-day regimen and 550 mg/m² utilizing the weekly regimen.

Special attention must be given to the cardiac toxicity exhibited by doxorubicin. Although uncommon, acute left ventricular failure has occurred, particularly in patients who have received a total dosage of the drug exceeding the currently recommended limit of 550 mg/m² body surface area for the 21-day regimen or a higher dose limit of the order of 700 mg/m² for the weekly regimen. These limits appear to be lower (400 mg/m² and 500 mg/m², respectively) in patients who received radiotherapy to the mediastinal area or concomitant therapy with other potentially cardiotoxic agents such as cyclophosphamide. The total dose of doxorubicin administered to the patient should also take into account previous or concomitant therapy with related compounds such as daunorubicin or with mitoxantrone. Congestive heart failure and/or cardiomyopathy may be encountered several weeks after discontinuation of doxorubicin therapy.

Cardiac failure is often not favorably affected by presently known medical or physical therapy for cardiac support. Early clinical diagnosis of drug-induced heart failure appears to be essential for successful treatment with digitalis, diuretics, low salt diet, and bed rest. Reduction of afterload with vasodilating agents appears to be beneficial in refractory doxorubicin-induced heart failure. Severe cardiac toxicity may occur precipitously without antecedent ECG changes. Transient ECG changes consisting of T-wave flattening, S-T depression and arrhythmias lasting for up to 2 weeks after a dose or course of doxorubicin are presently not considered indications for suspension of doxorubicin therapy. Doxorubicin cardiomyopathy has been reported to be associated with a persistent reduction in the voltage of the QRS wave, a prolongation of the systolic time interval and a reduction of the ejection fraction as determined by echocardiography or radionuclide angiography. None of these tests have yet been confirmed to consistently identify those individual patients who are approaching their maximally tolerated cumulative dose of doxorubicin. If test results indicate change in cardiac function associated with doxorubicin, the benefit of continued therapy must be carefully evaluated against the risk of producing irreversible cardiac damage.

Because of the experience with cardiac toxicity, a total dose of doxorubicin exceeding 550 mg/m² with the 21-day regimen and 700 mg/m² with the weekly regimen, is not recommended.

Acute life-threatening arrhythmias have been reported to occur during or within a few hours after doxorubicin administration.

There is a high incidence of bone marrow depression, primarily of leukocytes, requiring careful hematologic monitoring. With the recommended dosage schedule, leukopenia is usually transient, reaching its nadir 10 to 14 days after treatment with recovery usually occurring by the 21st day. White blood cell counts as low as 1 000/mm³ are to be expected during treatment with appropriate doses of doxorubicin. Red blood cell and platelet levels should also be monitored since they may also be depressed. Hematologic toxicity may require dose reduction or suspension or delay of doxorubicin therapy. Persistent severe myelosuppression may result in superinfection or hemorrhage.

Doxorubicin may potentiate the toxicity of other anticancer therapies. Exacerbation of cyclophosphamide-induced hemorrhagic cystitis and enhancement of the hepatotoxicity of 6-mercaptopurine have been reported. Radiation-induced toxicity to the myocardium, mucosae, skin and liver has been reported to be increased by the administration of doxorubicin.

Toxicity to recommended doses of doxorubicin is enhanced by hepatic impairment, therefore, prior to the individual dosing, evaluation of hepatic function is recommended using conventional clinical laboratory tests such as AST, ALT, alkaline phosphatase and bilirubin (see Dosage).

Necrotizing colitis manifested by typhlitis (cecal inflammation), bloody stools and severe and sometimes fatal infections have been associated with a combination of doxorubicin given by i.v. push daily for 3 days and cytarabine given by continuous infusion daily for 7 or more days.

On i.v. administration of doxorubicin, extravasation may occur with or without an accompanying stinging or burning sensation, and even if blood returns well on aspiration of the infusion needle (see Dosage). If any signs or symptoms of extravasation have occurred the injection or infusion should be immediately terminated and restarted in another vein.

Doxorubicin and related compounds have also been shown to have mutagenic and carcinogenic properties when tested in experimental models.

Pregnancy and *Lactation:* The safe use of doxorubicin in pregnancy has not been established. Doxorubicin is embryotoxic and teratogenic in rats and embryotoxic and abortifacient in rabbits. Therefore, the benefits to the pregnant patient should be carefully weighed against the potential toxicity to fetus and embryo. The possible adverse effects on fertility in males and females in humans or experimental animals have not been adequately evaluated.

Mothers should be advised not to breast-feed while undergoing chemotherapy with doxorubicin.

Precautions: Initial treatment with doxorubicin requires close observation of the patient and extensive laboratory monitoring.

Like other cytotoxic drugs, doxorubicin may induce hyperuricemia secondary to rapid lysis of neoplastic cells, particularly in patients with leukemia. The clinician should monitor the patient's blood uric acid level and be prepared to use such supportive and pharmacologic measures as might be necessary to control this problem.

Doxorubicin may impart a red coloration to the urine for 1 to 2 days after administration and patients should be advised to expect this during active therapy.

Adverse Effects: Dose limiting toxicities of therapy are myelosuppression and cardiotoxicity (see Warnings). Other reactions reported are: Cutaneous: Reversible complete alopecia occurs in most cases. Hyperpigmentation of nailbeds and dermal creases, primarily in children, have been reported in a few cases. Recall of skin reaction due to prior radiotherapy has occurred with doxorubicin administration.

Gastrointestinal: Acute nausea and vomiting occurs frequently and may be severe. This may be alleviated by antiemetic therapy. Mucositis (stomatitis and esophagitis) may occur 5 to 10 days after administration. The effect may be severe leading to ulceration and represents a site of origin for severe infections. The dose regimen consisting of administration of doxorubicin on 3 successive days results in the greater incidence and severity of mucositis. Ulceration and necrosis of the colon, especially the cecum, may occur leading to bleeding or severe infections which can be fatal. This reaction has been reported in patients with acute nonlymphocytic leukemia treated with a 3-day course of doxorubicin combined with cytarabine. Anorexia and diarrhea have been occasionally reported.

Vascular: Phlebosclerosis has been reported especially when small veins are used or a single vein is used for repeated administration. Facial flushing may occur if the injection is given too rapidly.

Local: Severe cellulitis, vesication and tissue necrosis will occur if doxorubicin is extravasated during administration. Erythematous streaking along the vein proximal to the site of the injection has been reported (see Dosage).

Bladder, local: Instillation of doxorubicin into the bladder may cause pain, hemorrhage and occasionally decreased bladder capacity.

Hypersensitivity: Fever, chills and urticaria have been reported occasionally. Anaphylaxis may occur.

Other: Conjunctivitis and lacrimation occur rarely.

Overdose: Symptoms and Treatment: Acute overdosage with doxorubicin enhances the toxic effects of mucositis, leukopenia and thrombopenia. Treatment of acute overdosage consists of treatment of the severely myelosuppressed patient with hospitalization, antibiotics, platelet and granulocyte transfusions and symptomatic treatment of mucositis.

Chronic overdosage with cumulative doses exceeding 500 mg/m² increases the risk of cardiomyopathy and resultant congestive heart failure. Treatment consists of vigorous management of congestive heart failure with digitalis preparations and diuretics. The use of peripheral vasodilators has been recommended.

Dosage: Refer to Guidelines for Safe Preparation and Handling.

A variety of dose schedules have been used. The following recommendations are for use as a single agent only.

The most commonly used dosage schedule is 60 to 75 mg/m² as a single i.v. injection administered at 21-day intervals. The lower dose should be given to patients with inadequate marrow reserves due to old age, or prior therapy, or neoplastic marrow infiltration. An alternative dose schedule is weekly doses of 20 mg/m² which has been reported to produce a lower incidence of congestive heart failure. Thirty mg/m² on each of 3 successive days repeated every 4 weeks has also been used. Doxorubicin dosage must be reduced if the bilirubin is elevated as follows: Serum bilirubin 1.2 to 3.0 mg/dL – give 1/2 normal dose, >3 mg/dL – give 1/4 normal dose.

When doxorubicin is intravesically instilled for the treatment of superficial bladder carcinomas, the usual dose employed ranges from 50 to 80 mg in 50 to 100 mL of 0.9% Sodium Chloride Injection USP with a contact time of 1 to 2 hours. Care should be taken to ensure that the tip of the catheter is in the bladder lumen before instilling the doxorubicin solution. Instillation is repeated weekly for 4 weeks and subsequently at monthly intervals. Therapy may continue for 1 year or longer as no significant systematic toxicity has been reported. Care should be exercised in the handling and disposal of the voided urine. (Refer to Guidelines for Safe Preparation and Handling.) PVC gloves should be worn and the urine should be inactivated by decolorizing it with 10 mL or more of sodium hypochlorite solution (household bleach).

Other methods of administration have been investigated including intra-arterial administration and also continuous or long-term i.v. infusion utilizing appropriate pumps.

Clinical studies support the efficacy of doxorubicin used concurrently with other chemotherapeutic agents. Listed below are tumor types and drugs used concurrently with doxorubicin: Acute lymphocytic leukemia in adults: doxorubicin with vincristine and prednisone or with cytarabine, vincristine and prednisone.

Acute Lymphocytic Leukemia in Children: doxorubicin with asparaginase, vincristine and prednisone.

Acute Nonlymphocytic Leukemia: doxorubicin with cytarabine or with cytarabine, vincristine and prednisone.

Carcinoma of the Breast: doxorubicin with 5-fluorouracil and/or cyclophosphamide or with vincristine with or without cyclophosphamide.

Bronchogenic Carcinoma, Nonsmall Cell: doxorubicin with cyclophosphamide, methotrexate and procarbazine or with cyclophosphamide and cisplatin. Bronchogenic Carcinoma, Small Cell: doxorubicin with etoposide, vincristine and cyclophosphamide.

Hodgkin's Disease: doxorubicin with bleomycin, vincristine, vinblastine, mechlorethamine and dacarbazine.

non-hodgkin's Lymphoma: doxorubicin with cyclophosphamide, vincristine and prednisone, or bleomycin, cyclophosphamide, vincristine and prednisone, or with etoposide, methotrexate with leucovorin rescue, mechlorethamine or procarbazine.

Carcinoma of the Ovary: doxorubicin with cisplatin.
Soft Tissue Sarcoma: doxorubicin with dacarbazine, or with dacarbazine, cyclophosphamide and vincristine.
Carcinoma of the Bladder: doxorubicin with cisplatin and cyclophosphamide or with 5-fluorouracil, methotrexate and vinblastine.
Carcinoma of the Stomach: doxorubicin with 5-fluorouracil and mitomycin-C.
Administration: Care in the administration of doxorubicin will reduce the chance of perivenous infiltration. It may also decrease the chance of local reactions such as urticaria and erythematous streaking. On i.v. administration of doxorubicin, extravasation may occur with or without an accompanying stinging or burning sensation and even if blood returns well on aspiration of the infusion needle. If any signs or symptoms of extravasation have occurred, the injection or infusion should be immediately terminated and restarted in another vein.

If it is known or suspected that s.c. extravasation has occurred, the injection or infusion of doxorubicin should immediately be terminated. The following subsequent steps are recommended: an attempt should be made to aspirate the infiltrate; intermittent local application of ice for up to 3 days; elevation of affected limb; consultation with a plastic surgeon if local pains persist or skin changes progress after 3 to 4 days. If ulceration begins, early wide excision of the involved area should be considered.

Doxorubicin should be slowly administered into the tubing of a freely running i.v. infusion of Sodium Chloride Injection USP (0.9%) or 5% Dextrose Injection USP. The tubing should be attached to a Butterfly needle, or other suitable device and inserted preferably into a large vein. If possible, avoid veins over joints or in extremities with compromised venous or lymphatic drainage. The rate of administration is dependent on the size of the vein and the dosage; however, the dosage should be administered in not less than 3 to 5 minutes. Local erythematous streaking along the vein as well as facial flushing may be indicative of too rapid administration.
Reconstituted Solutions: Reconstitute doxorubicin for injection USP to approximately 2 mg/mL doxorubicin with Sterile Water for Injection, 5% Dextrose Injection or 0.9% Sodium Chloride Injection, as follows: See Table I.

Table I—Doxorubicin HCl Injection USP

Reconstitution

Amount in Vial	Volume of Solution to be Added
10 mg	5 mL
50 mg	25 mL
150 mg	75 mL

Note: Reconstitution with 0.9% Sodium Chloride Injection will take considerably longer than is seen with other reconstituting solutions.

The reconstituted solutions remain chemically stable for up to 24 hours when stored at room temperature or for 72 hours when stored refrigerated, in glass containers or in plastic disposable syringes, under fluorescent light.

Further diluted solutions of doxorubicin prepared for bladder instillation at a concentration of 0.8 mg/mL in 0.9% sodium chloride in plastic bags, have been determined to be chemically stable for 24 hours when kept at room temperature in the presence of light, or for 72 hours when refrigerated.

Unpreserved reconstituted solutions should not be stored for more than 24 hours at room temperature or 72 hours under refrigeration, due to the possibility of microbial contamination during preparation.
Warning: As with all parenteral drug products, i.v. admixtures should be inspected visually for clarity, particulate matter, precipitate, discoloration and leakage prior to administration, whenever solution and container permit. Solutions showing haziness, particulate matter, precipitate, discoloration or leakage should not be used.
Incompatibilities: Unless specific compatibility data are available, the mixing of doxorubicin solutions with other drugs is not recommended. Precipitation occurs with 5 fluorouracil and heparin.
Guidelines for Safe Preparation and Handling: Preparation and Handling: 1. Preparation of antineoplastic solutions should be done in a vertical laminar flow hood (Biological Safety Cabinet—Class II). 2. Personnel preparing doxorubicin solutions should wear PVC gloves, safety glasses and protective clothing such as disposable gowns and masks. If doxorubicin contacts the skin or mucosa, the area should be washed with soap and water immediately. 3. Personnel regularly involved in the preparation and handling of antineoplastics should have blood examinations on a regular basis.
Disposal: 1. Avoid contact with skin and inhalation of airborne particles by use of PVC gloves and disposable gowns and masks. 2. All needles, syringes, vials and other materials which have come in contact with doxorubicin should be segregated in plastic bags, sealed, and marked as hazardous waste. Incinerate at 1 000°C or higher. Sealed containers may explode if a tight seal exists. 3. If incineration is not available, doxorubicin may be detoxified by adding sodium hypochlorite solution (household bleach) to the vial, in sufficient quantity to decolorize the doxorubicin, care being taken to vent the vial to avoid a pressure build-up of the chlorine gas which is generated. Dispose of detoxified vials in a safe manner.
Needles, Syringes, Disposable and Nondisposable Equipment: Rinse equipment with an appropriate quantity of sodium hypochlorite solution. Discard the solution in the sewer system with running water and discard disposable equipment in a safe manner. Thoroughly wash nondisposable equipment in soap and water.
Spillage/Contamination: Wear gloves, mask, protective clothing. Treat spilled powder or liquid with sodium hypochlorite solution. Carefully absorb solution with gauze pads or towels, wash area with water and absorb with gauze or towels again and place in polyethylene bag; seal, double bag and mark as hazardous waste. Dispose of waste by incineration or by other methods approved for hazardous materials. Pesonnel involved in clean-up should wash with soap and water.

Supplied: Each single dose vial contains: doxorubicin HCl USP 10, 50 or 150 mg as a sterile lyophilized red powder or plug. Also contains lactose (26.3 mg, 32.89 mg and 52.63 mg respectively) in each vial. Store intact vials below 25°C, protected from light.

DOXORUBICIN HYDROCHLORIDE INJECTION USP Ⓟ

Novopharm

Antineoplastic Agent

Pharmacology: Doxorubicin is the hydrochloric acid salt of a glycoside antibiotic produced by S. peucetius var. caesiu. Although not completely elucidated, the mechanism of action of doxorubicin is related mainly to its ability to bind specifically with DNA, by intercalation between adjacent base pairs of the double-helical structure, thereby inhibiting nucleic acid synthesis. Binding to cell membranes as well as to plasma proteins may also be involved. The following have been demonstrated by cell culture studies: rapid cell penetration and perinucleolar chromatin binding, rapid inhibition of mitotic activity and nucleic acid synthesis, mutagenesis and chromosomal aberrations.

Animal studies have shown immunosuppression, activity in a spectrum of experimental tumors, induction of a variety of toxic effects, including delayed and progressive cardiac toxicity, carcinogenic properties in rodents, atrophy of testes in rats and dogs and myelosuppression in all species.

Pharmacokinetic studies show that i.v. administration of doxorubicin has been shown to have a rapid plasma clearance, a large volume of distribution and prolonged tissue binding. Doxorubicin undergoes metabolism in the liver, is eliminated in bile with only minute amounts appearing in the urine. Doxorubicin does not appear to cross the blood-brain barrier.

Indications: Doxorubicin has been used successfully as a single agent and in combination with other chemotherapeutic agents, to produce regression in a variety of tumor types such as acute lymphoblastic and acute myeloblastic leukemia, Wilms' tumor, neuroblastoma, soft tissue and bone sarcomas, breast carcinoma, ovarian carcinoma, testicular carcinoma, transitional cell bladder carcinoma, thyroid carcinoma, squamous cell carcinoma of the head and neck, lymphomas of both Hodgkin's and non-Hodgkin's types, gastric carcinoma and bronchogenic carcinoma.

Doxorubicin has also been used by instillation into the bladder for the topical treatment of superficial bladder tumors.

Studies to date have shown that malignant melanoma, kidney carcinoma, large bowel carcinomas, brain tumors and metastases to the CNS are not significantly responsive to doxorubicin treatment.

Contraindications: Doxorubicin therapy should not be initiated in patients who have marked myelosuppression induced by previous treatment with other antitumor agents or by radiotherapy. Conclusive data are not available on pre-existing heart disease as a cofactor of increased risk of doxorubicin induced cardiotoxicity. Preliminary data suggest that in such cases, cardiotoxicity may occur at doses lower than the recommended cumulative limit. It is therefore not recommended to initiate doxorubicin therapy in such cases. Doxorubicin hydrochloride treatment is contraindicated in patients who have received previous treatment with complete cumulative doses of doxorubicin and/or other anthracyclines and anthracenes.

Warnings: Doxorubicin is a potent drug and should be used only by physicians experienced with cancer chemotherapeutic drugs (see Precautions). Perform blood counts and hepatic function tests regularly. Because of the experience with cardiac toxicity, a total dose of doxorubicin exceeding 550 mg/m² with the 21-day regimen and 700 mg/m² with the weekly regimen is not recommended. Cardiac monitoring is advised in those patients who have received mediastinal radiotherapy, other anthracycline or anthracene therapy, with pre-existing cardiac disease, or those who have received prior doxorubicin cumulative doses exceeding 400 mg/m2 with the 21-day regimen and 550 mg/m² with the weekly regimen.
Cardiac Toxicity: Attention must be given to the cardiac toxicity exhibited by doxorubicin. Although uncommon, left ventricular failure has occurred particularly in patients who have received total dosage of the drug exceeding the current recommended limit of 550 mg/m² for the 21-day regimen or a higher dose limit on the order of 700 mg/m² for the weekly regimen. These limits appear to be lower, 400 mg/m² and 500 mg/m² respectively, in patients who received concomitant therapy with other potentially cardiotoxic agents such as cyclophosphamide or radiotherapy to the mediastinal area. Congestive heart failure and/or cardiomyopathy may occur several weeks after discontinuation of doxorubicin therapy. Children appear to be at particular risk for development of delayed doxorubicin cardiotoxicity in that doxorubicin impairs myocardial growth as they mature, leading to subsequent possible development of congestive heart failure during early adulthood. Dose limitation should be used to prevent doxorubicin cardiomyopathy.

Available evidence appears to indicate that cardiotoxicity is cumulative across members of the anthracycline and anthracene class of drugs. Patients who have previously received other anthracyclines and anthracenes are at particular risk for possible cardiotoxic effects of doxorubicin at a lower total dose than previously untreated patients and, therefore, should be carefully monitored.

Cardiac failure is often unresponsive to presently known medical or physical therapy for cardiac support. Early clinical diagnosis of drug-induced heart failure seems to be essential for successful treatment with diuretics, digitalis, low-salt diet, peripheral vasodilators, and bed rest. Reduction of afterload with vasodilating agents appears to be beneficial in refractory doxorubicin-induced heart failure. Severe cardiac toxicity may occur precipitously without antecedent ECG changes. It is suggested to perform a baseline ECG and ECGs prior to each dose or course after a 300 mg/m2 cumulative dose has been given.

Transient ECG changes consisting of T-wave flattening, S-T depression and arrhythmias lasting for up to 2 weeks after a dose or course of doxorubicin are currently not considered indications for suspension of doxorubicin therapy. Doxorubicin cardiomyopathy has been reported to be associated with a persistent reduction in the voltage of the QRS wave, a prolongation of the systolic time interval, and a reduction of the left ventricular ejection fraction (LVEF) as determined by echocardiography or radionuclide angiography (MUGA scan). None of these tests have yet been confirmed to consistently identify those individual patients who are approaching their maximally tolerated cumulative doses of doxorubicin. If test results indicate change in cardiac function associated with doxorubicin therapy, the benefit of continued therapy must be carefully evaluated against the risk of producing irreversible cardiac damage.

Because of the experience with cardiac toxicity, a total dose of doxorubicin exceeding 550 mg/m² with the 21-day regimen and 700 mg/m² with the weekly regimen is not recommended.

Acute life-threatening arrhythmias have been reported to occur during or within a few hours after administration of doxorubicin.
Bone Marrow Suppression: There is a high incidence of bone marrow depression, primarily of leukocytes, occuring in over 60% of patients requiring careful hematologic monitoring. Leukopenia is usually transient with the recommended dosage schedule, reaching its nadir at 10 to 14 days after treatment, with recovery usually occurring by the 21st day. During treatment with doxorubicin, white blood cell counts as low as 1 000/mm³ are to be expected. Since red blood cell and platelet levels may also be depressed, these should also be

Doxorubicin Hydrochloride Injection USP (cont'd)

monitored. Upon hematologic toxicity, dose reduction or discontinuation or delay of doxorubicin therapy may be required. Persistent severe myelosuppression may result in superinfection or hemorrhage.

Drug Interactions: The toxicity of other anticancer therapies may be potentiated by doxorubicin. There have been reports of exacerbation of cyclophosphamide-induced hemorrhagic cystitis and enhancement of the hepatotoxicity of 6-mercaptopurine. Radiation-induced toxicity to the myocardium, skin, liver and mucosae has been reported to be increased by the administration of doxorubicin.

Since toxicity to recommended doses of doxorubicin is enhanced by hepatic impairment, evaluation of hepatic function using conventional clinical laboratory tests such as AST, ALT, alkaline phosphatase and bilirubin is recommended.

Necrotizing colitis manifested by typhlitis (cecal inflammation), bloody stools and severe and sometimes fatal infections have been associated with a combination of doxorubicin given by i.v. push daily for 3 days and cytarabine given by continuous infusion daily for 7 or more days.

Carcinogenicity: Doxorubicin and related compounds have also been shown to have mutagenic and carcinogenic properties when tested in experimental models.

Local Reactions: Upon i.v. administration of doxorubicin, extravasation may occur with or without an accompanying stinging or burning sensation even if blood returns well upon aspiration of the infusion needle (see Dosage). The injection or infusion should be immediately terminated and restarted in another vein if any signs or symptoms of extravasation occur.

Doxorubicin may impart a red coloration to the urine for 1 to 2 days after administration and patients should be advised to expect this during active therapy.

Pregnancy: There is no conclusive information about doxorubicin adversely affecting human fertility, or causing teratogenesis; however, doxorubicin is embryotoxic and teratogenic in rats and embryotoxic and abortifacient in rabbits. Therefore, women with childbearing potential should be advised to avoid pregnancy. If doxorubicin is to be used during pregnancy, or if the patient becomes pregnant during therapy, the patient should be informed of the potential hazard to the fetus. The benefits to the pregnant patient should be carefully weighed against the potential toxicity to fetus and embryo.

Lactation: Mothers should be advised not to breast-feed while undergoing chemotherapy with doxorubicin.

Precautions: Initial treatment with doxorubicin requires close observation of the patient and extensive laboratory monitoring.

Doxorubicin, like other cytotoxic drugs, may induce hyperuricemia secondary to rapid lysis of neoplastic cells, particularly in patients with leukemia. The clinician should monitor the patient's blood uric acid level and be prepared to use any supportive and pharmacologic measures necessary to control this problem.

Doxorubicin is not an antimicrobial agent.

Adverse Effects: Dose limiting toxicities of doxorubicin are myelosuppression, cardiotoxicity (see Warnings). Other reactions reported are as follows:

Cutaneous: In most cases, reversible partial or complete alopecia occurs. Hair growth usually resumes during treatment or within 2 to 3 months after cessation of drug therapy.

Hyperpigmentation of nailbeds and dermal creases, primarily in children, have been reported in a few cases. Recall of skin reaction associated with prior radiotherapy has occurred with doxorubicin administration.

Gastrointestinal: Acute nausea and vomiting are the immediate effects of doxorubicin therapy, which usually last for 24 to 48 hours. Antiemetic therapy may alleviate these symptoms. Mucositis (stomatitis and esophagitis) may occur 5 to 10 days after administration. This may be severe and in turn may lead to ulceration, representing a site of origin for severe infections. The dose regimen consisting of administration of doxorubicin on 3 successive days results in the greater incidence and severity of mucositis. Ulceration and necrosis of the colon, especially the cecum, may occur leading to bleeding or severe infections which can be fatal. This reaction has been reported in patients with acute nonlymphocytic leukemia treated with a 3-day course of doxorubicin combined with cytarabine. Anorexia and diarrhea have been occasionally reported.

Myelosuppression: Leukopenia is the predominant hematologic toxicity. Thrombocytopenia and anemia may also occur.

The occurrence of secondary acute myeloid leukemia with or without a preleukemic phase has been reported rarely in patients concurrently treated with doxorubicin in association with DNA-damaging antineoplastic agents. Such cases could have a short (1 to 3 years) latency period.

Vascular: When small veins are used or a single vein is used for repeated administration, chemical phlebitis and phlebosclerosis have been reported. If the injection is given too rapidly, facial flushing may occur.

Local: Severe cellulitis, vesication and tissue necrosis may occur if doxorubicin is extravasated during administration. Normal precautions in i.v. administration can prevent this toxicity. Erythematous streaking along the vein proximal to the site of the infection has been reported.

Bladder: Instillation of the doxorubicin compound into the urinary bladder may cause pain, hemorrhage and occasionally decreased bladder capacity.

Hypersensitivity: Fever and chills, facial flushing associated with too rapid drug injection and urticaria have been reported occasionally. Anaphylaxis may occur. A case of apparent cross-sensitivity to lincomycin has been reported.

Other: Conjunctivitis and lacrimation occur rarely.

Overdose: Symptoms and Treatment: Acute overdosage with doxorubicin enhances the toxic effects of mucositis, leukopenia and thrombopenia. The severely myelosuppressed patient (due to acute overdosage) should be hospitalized, and should receive antibiotic therapy, platelet and granulocyte transfusions and symptomatic treatment of mucositis.

Chronic overdosage with cumulative doses exceeding 500 mg/m^2 increases the risk of cardiomyopathy and resultant congestive heart failure. Treatment consists of vigorous management of congestive heart failure with digitalis preparations and diuretics. The use of peripheral vasodilators may be considered in the management of congestive heart failure.

Dosage: A variety of dose schedules have been used. The following recommendations are for the use of doxorubicin as a single agent only.

The most commonly used dosage schedule is 60 to 75 mg/m^2 as a single i.v. injection administered at 21-day intervals. The lower dose should be given to patients with inadequate marrow reserves due to old age or prior therapy, or neoplastic marrow infiltration. An alternative dose schedule consists of weekly doses of 20 mg/m^2 may produce a lower incidence of congestive heart failure. A dose of 30 mg/m^2 on each of 3 successive days repeated every 4 weeks has been used as well. If bilirubin is elevated, doxorubicin hydrochloride dosage must be reduced as follows: serum bilirubin 1.2 to 3 mg/dL: give half of normal dose; >3 mg/dL: give one quarter of normal dose.

When doxorubicin is intravesically instilled for the treatment of superficial bladder carcinomas, the usual dose employed ranges from 50 to 80 mg in 50 to 100 mL of 0.9% Sodium Chloride Injection with a contact time of 1 to 2 hours. Before instilling the doxorubicin solution, care should be taken to ensure that the tip of the catheter is in the bladder lumen. Instillation is repeated weekly for 4 weeks and then at monthly intervals following this period. Therapy may continue for 12 months or for longer, since no significant systematic toxicity has been demonstrated. Care should be exercised in the handling and disposal of the voided urine. PVC gloves should be worn and the urine should be inactivated by decolorizing it with 10 mL or more of sodium hypochlorite solution (household bleach).

Clinical studies support the efficacy of doxorubicin used concurrently with other chemotherapeutic agents. Included below are tumor types and drugs used concurrently with doxorubicin.

Acute Lymphocytic Leukemia in Adults: doxorubicin with vincristine and prednisone or with cytosine arabinoside, vincristine and prednisone.

Acute Lymphocytic Leukemia in Children: doxorubicin with L-asparaginase, vincristine and prednisone.

Acute Nonlymphocytic Leukemia: doxorubicin with arabinosyl cytosine or with arabinosyl cytosine, vincristine and prednisone.

Carcinoma of the Breast: doxorubicin with 5-fluorouracil and/or cyclophosphamide or with vincristine with or without cyclophosphamide.

Bronchogenic Carcinoma, Nonsmall Cell: doxorubicin with cyclophosphamide, methotrexate and procarbazine or with cyclophosphamide and cisplatin.

Bronchogenic Carcinoma, Small Cell: doxorubicin with vincristine or etoposide (VP-16) and cyclophosphamide.

Hodgkin's disease: doxorubicin with bleomycin, vincristine and dacarbazine.

Non-Hodgkin's Lymphoma: doxorubicin with cyclophosphamide, vincristine and prednisone, or bleomycin, cyclophosphamide, vincristine and prednisone.

Carcinoma of the Ovary: doxorubicin with cisplatin.

Soft Tissue Sarcoma: doxorubicin with dacarbazine, or with dacarbazine, cyclophosphamide and vincristine.

Carcinoma of the Bladder: doxorubicin with methotrexate, vinblastine and cisplatin, or cisplatin and cyclophosphamide or with 5-fluorouracil.

Carcinoma of the Stomach: doxorubicin with 5-fluorouracil and mitomycin-C.

Administration: Care in the administration of doxorubicin will reduce the chance of perivenous infiltration. This may decrease the chance of local reactions (such as urticaria and erythematous streaking) as well. Upon i.v. administration of doxorubicin, extravasation may occur with or without an accompanying stinging or burning sensation. This may occur even if blood returns well on aspiration of the infusion needle. If signs or symptoms of extravasation occur, the injection or infusion should be immediately terminated and restarted in another vein.

Once it is known or suspected that s.c. extravasation has occurred, the following steps are recommended: attempt aspiration of the infiltrated doxorubicin solution; local intermittent application of ice for up to 3 days; elevation of the affected limb.

The area of injection should be frequently examined and plastic surgeon consultation should be consulted if local pain persists or skin changes progress after 3 to 4 days. If ulceration begins, early wide excision of the involved area should be considered.

Doxorubicin should be slowly administered into the tubing of a freely running i.v. infusion of 0.9% Sodium Chloride Injection, or 5% Dextrose Injection. The tubing should be attached to a Butterfly needle inserted preferably into a large vein. Where possible, avoid veins over joints or in extremities with compromised venous or lymphatic drainage. The administration rate is dependent on the size of the vein and the dosage, however, the dosage should be administered in not less than 3 to 5 minutes. Facial flushing as well as erythematous streaking along the vein may be indicative of too rapid administration.

Unless specific compatibility data are available, the mixing of doxorubicin solutions with other drugs is not recommended. Precipitation occurs with 5-fluorouracil and heparin.

Parenteral drug products should be inspected visually for particulate matter and discoloration prior to administration, whenever solution and container permit.

Guidelines for Safe Preparation and Handling: Preparation and Handling: Preparation of antineoplastic solutions should be done in a vertical laminar flow hood. (Biological Safety Cabinet-Class II). Personnel preparing doxorubicin solutions should wear PVC gloves, safety glasses and protective clothing such as disposable gowns and masks. If doxorubicin contacts the skin or mucosa, the area should be washed with soap and water immediately. Personnel regularly involved in the preparation and handling of antineoplastics should have blood examinations on a regular basis.

Directions for Dispensing from Pharmacy Bulk Vial: The use of pharmacy bulk vials is restricted to hospitals with a recognized i.v. admixture program. The pharmacy bulk vial is intended for single puncture, multiple dispensing and for i.v. use only.

Entry into the vial must be made with a sterile dispensing device such as the Econo-O-Set Sterile Transfer Systems. Multiple use of a syringe with needle is not recommended since it may cause leakage as well as increasing the potential for microbial and particulate contamination.

In a suitable work area such as a laminar flow hood, swab the vial stopper with an antiseptic solution. Following carefully the manufacturer's instructions, insert the device into the vial. Withdraw contents of vial into syringes, using aseptic technique.

Dispensing from the pharmacy bulk vial should be completed within 8 hours of the **initial entry** because of the potential for microbial contamination. Discard any unused portion. The contents of the syringes filled from the pharmacy bulk vial should be used within 24 hours at room temperature or 48 hours when refrigerated **from the time of the initial entry into the pharmacy bulk vial.**

Disposal: Avoid contact with skin and inhalation of airborne particles by use of PVC gloves and disposable gowns and masks.

All needles, syringes, vials and other materials which have come in contact with doxorubicin should be segregated in plastic bags, sealed, and marked as hazardous waste. Incinerate at 1 000°C or higher. Sealed containers may explode if a tight seal exists.

If incineration is not available, doxorubicin may be detoxified by adding sodium hypochlorite solution (household bleach) to the vial, in sufficient quantity to decolorize the doxorubicin, care being taken to vent the vial to avoid a pressure build-up

of the chlorine gas which is generated. Dispose of detoxified vials in a safe manner.
Needles, Syringes, Disposable and Nondisposable Equipment: Rinse equipment with an appropriate quantity of sodium hypochlorite solution. Discard the solution in the sewer system with running water and discard disposable equipment in a safe manner. Thoroughly wash nondisposable equipment in soap and water.
Spillage/Contamination: Wear gloves, mask, protective clothing. Treat spilled powder or liquid with sodium hypochlorite solution. Carefully absorb solution with gauze pads, or towels. Wash area with water and absorb with gauze or towels again and place in a polyethylene bag; seal, double bag and mark as hazardous waste. Dispose of waste by incineration or by other methods approved for hazardous materials. Personnel involved in a clean-up should wash with soap and water.

Supplied: Vials: 10 mg: Each mL of isotonic, sterile, red-orange solution for i.v. use only, contains: doxorubicin HCl 2 mg. Nonmedicinal ingredients: sodium chloride, water for injection and hydrochloric acid to adjust the pH (3.0). Preservative-free. Single use, flip-top vials of 5 mL, boxes of 10.

50 mg: Each mL of isotonic, sterile, red-orange solution for i.v. use only, contains: doxorubicin HCl 2 mg. Nonmedicinal ingredients: sodium chloride, water for injection and hydrochloric acid to adjust the pH (3.0). Preservative-free. Single use, flip-top vials of 25 mL, boxes of 1.

Pharmacy Bulk Vials: 200 mg: Each mL of isotonic, sterile, red-orange solution for i.v. use only, contains: doxorubicin HCl 2 mg. Nonmedicinal ingredients: sodium chloride, water for injection and hydrochloric acid to adjust the pH (3.0). Preservative-free. Single use, flip-top vials of 100 mL, boxes of 1.

Store at refrigeration (2 to 8°C) and protect form light. Discard any unused solution.

Reviewed 1998

DOXYCIN Ⓟ
Riva

Doxycycline Hyclate
Antibiotic

Supplied: Capsules: Each aqua capsule, imprinted H539 contains: doxycycline hyclate USP equivalent to doxycycline 100 mg. Nonmedicinal ingredients: cellulose, colloidal silicon, lactose, magnesium stearate and stearic acid. Alcohol-, gluten-, paraben-, sucrose- and sulfite-free. Bottles of 100 and 300.

Tablets: Each orange, film-coated tablet, scored on one side and embossed DOXYCIN 100 on the other side, contains: doxycycline hyclate USP equivalent to doxycycline 100 mg. Nonmedicinal ingredients: carnauba wax, cellulose, colloidal silicon, D&C Yellow, FD&C Blue, FD&C Red, FD&C Yellow, hydroxypropyl methylcellulose, magnesium stearate, polyethylene glycol, polysorbate 80, sodium starch glycolate, starch, stearic acid and titanium dioxide. Alcohol-, gluten-, paraben-, sucrose- and sulfite-free. Bottles of 100 and 300. Boxes of 10 and 20 (peel off unit dose blister).

DOXYCYCLINE Ⓟ
General Monograph, CPhA

see TETRACYCLINES

DOXYTEC Ⓟ
Technilab

Doxycycline Hyclate
Antibiotic

Supplied: Capsules: Each blue, hard gelatin capsule contains: doxycycline hyclate equivalent to doxycycline 100 mg. Nonmedicinal ingredients: black iron oxide, D&C yellow #10 aluminum lake, FD&C blue #1 aluminum lake, FD&C blue #2 aluminum lake, FD&C red #40 aluminum lake, gelatin, lactose, magnesium stearate, propylene glycol, shellac, silicone dioxide, sodium croscarmellose, sodium lauryl sulfate, stearic acid and titanium dioxide. Sodium; <1 mmol (0.25 mg). Gluten- and tartrazine-free. Bottles of 100 and 300.

Tablets: Each round, light orange, film-coated tablet contains: doxycycline hyclate equivalent to doxycycline 100 mg. Nonmedicinal ingredients: colloidal silicone dioxide, FD&C yellow #6 aluminum lake, hydroxypropyl methylcellulose, magnesium stearate, microcrystalline cellulose, polyethylene glycol, purified water, sodium croscarmellose and titanium dioxide. Sodium: <1 mmol (0.23 mg). Gluten and tartrazine-free. Bottles of 100 and 300.

DPE™ Ⓟ
Alcon

Dipivefrin HCl
Glaucoma Therapy

Pharmacology: Dipivefrin is converted to epinephrine inside the human eye by enzyme hydrolysis. The liberated epinephrine, an adrenergic agonist, appears to exert its action by decreasing aqueous production and by enhancing outflow facility. The dipivefrin hydrochloride prodrug delivery system is a more efficient way of delivering the therapeutic effects of epinephrine, with fewer side effects than are associated with conventional epinephrine therapy.

Indications: As initial therapy for the control of intraocular pressure in chronic open-angle glaucoma. Patients responding inadequately to other antiglaucoma therapy may respond to the addition of dipivefrin.

Contraindications: Should not be used in patients with narrow angles since any dilation of the pupil may predispose the patient to an attack of angle-closure glaucoma. This product is contraindicated in patients who are hypersensitive to any of its components.

Warnings: Not for injection. For topical ophthalmic use only.
Because the diagnosis of narrow-angle glaucoma is frequently missed during normotensive intervals (between attacks), it is very important that careful slit lamp and gonioscopic study be done before initiating therapy with this drug. Should an elevation of intraocular pressure follow the instillation of dipivefrin, appropriate hypotensive therapy is recommended.

Precautions: General: Aphakic Patients: Macular edema has been shown to occur in up to 30% of aphakic patients treated with epinephrine. Discontinuation of epinephrine generally results in reversal of the maculopathy. Macular edema has been reported rarely with dipivefrin; reversal occurred upon discontinuation of therapy.
Pregnancy: Reproduction studies have been performed in rats and rabbits at daily oral doses up to 10 mg/kg body weight (5 mg/kg in teratogenicity studies) and have revealed no evidence of impaired fertility or harm to the fetus due to dipivefrin. There are, however, no adequate and well controlled studies in pregnant women. Because animal reproduction studies are not always predictive of human response, this drug should be used during pregnancy only if clearly needed.
Lactation: It is not known whether this drug is excreted in human milk. Because many drugs are excreted in human milk, caution should be exercised when dipivefrin is administered to a nursing woman.
Children: Clinical studies to determine safety and efficacy in children have not been done.

Adverse Effects: Cardiovascular: Tachycardia, arrhythmias and hypertension have been reported with ocular administration of epinephrine.
Local Effects: The most frequent side effects reported with dipivefrin alone were injection in 6.5% of patients and burning and stinging in 6%. Follicular conjunctivitis, conjunctivitis, blurred vision, browache, photophobia, mydriasis, hyperemia and hypersensitivity or orbital pain have been reported infrequently.
On rare occasions, systemic adverse effects such as occipital headache, palpitation, paleness, acceleration of the heartbeat, trembling and perspiration have been observed following epinephrine therapy; the slight possibility of their occurrence following therapy with dipivefrin 0.1% should be borne in mind.
Macular edema in aphakic patients has been known to occur with epinephrine therapy. Discontinuation of epinephrine generally results in prompt reversal. Rarely have cases of macular edema in aphakic patients been reported with dipivefrin. Reversal occurred upon discontinuation of therapy.
Epinephrine therapy can lead to adrenochrome deposits in the conjunctiva and cornea. However, these have been reported rarely following the use of dipivefrin.

Overdose: Symptoms and Treatment: Overdosage in the use of topical preparations is a remote possibility. Discontinue medication when heavy or protracted use is suspected and initiate symptomatic treatment if deemed necessary.

Dosage: Initial Glaucoma Therapy: The usual dosage is 1 drop in the eye(s) every 12 hours.
Replacement Therapy: When patients are being transferred to dipivefrin from antiglaucoma agents other than epinephrine, on the first day continue the previous medication and add 1 drop of the dipivefrin ophthalmic solution to each eye(s) every 12 hours. On the following day, discontinue the previously used antiglaucoma agent and continue with dipivefrin.
In transferring patients from conventional epinephrine therapy to dipivefrin, simply discontinue the epinephrine medication and institute the dipivefrin regimen.
Additional Therapy: When patients on other antiglaucoma agents require additional therapy, add 1 drop of dipivefrin every 12 hours.
Concomitant Therapy: For difficult to control patients, the addition of dipivefrin to other agents such as pilocarpine, carbachol, echothiophate iodide or acetazolamide has been shown to be effective.

Information for the Patient: See Blue Section—Information for the Patient "DPE".

Supplied: Each mL of sterile, isotonic, ophthalmic solution contains: dipivefrin hydrochloride 0.1% and benzalkonium chloride 0.005% as preservative. Nonmedicinal ingredients: edetate disodium, purified water, sodium chloride, and hydrochloric acid and/or sodium hydroxide (to adjust pH). Opaque plastic Drop-Tainer dispensers of 5, 10 and 15 mL. Store at controlled room temperature (15 to 25°C). Protect from light and excessive heat.

DRISDOL®
Sanofi

Vitamin D_2
Antirachitic Agent

Supplied: Each mL of solution contains: vitamin D_2 (ergocalciferol solution USP) 8 288 IU in propylene glycol. Approximately, 207 IU per drop, (40 drops=approximately 1 mL). Alcohol-, lactose-, parabens-, starch-, sucrose- and tartrazine-free. Bottles of 60 mL with 1 mL calibrated syringe capable of dropwise delivery.

DRISTAN®
DRISTAN® EXTRA STRENGTH
Whitehall-Robins

Phenylephrine—Chlorpheniramine—Acetaminophen
Decongestant—Antihistamine—Analgesic

Indications: For the symptomatic relief of colds, sinusitis, hay fever or other upper respiratory allergies, nasal congestion, sneezing, runny nose, fever, headache, minor aches and pains.

Contraindications: Hypersensitivity to any of the components. Patients receiving MAO inhibitors.

Precautions: Use with caution on elderly patients or patients with allergy to acetaminophen, chronic alcoholism, serious liver or kidney disease, diabetes, heart or thyroid disease, high blood pressure, chronic lung disease, glaucoma, difficulty in urination due to enlarged prostate, or pregnant or nursing, or taking antidepressants, other antihistamines, tranquilizers, or sedating drugs.
Occupational Hazards: Patients should be cautioned not to operate vehicles or hazardous machinery until their response to the drug has been determined. Since the depressant effects of antihistamines are additive to those of other drugs affecting the CNS, patients should be cautioned against drinking alcoholic beverages or taking hypnotics, sedatives, psychotherapeutic agents or other drugs with CNS depressant effects during antihistamine therapy.
Pregnancy and *Lactation:* Caution should be exercised before giving to women who are pregnant or nursing a baby.

Adverse Effects: Slight to moderate drowsiness may occur. Other possible adverse reactions may include restlessness, dry mouth, nervousness, visual disturbances, dermatitis, weakness and nausea.

Dristan (cont'd)

In therapeutic doses, acetaminophen is relatively non-toxic. Chronic use of large doses of acetaminophen may produce more significant toxicity.

Renal: Nephropathy, including papillary renal failure has been reported following consumption of large amounts of acetaminophen. Renal tubular necrosis has been associated occasionally with hepatic injury produced by acetaminophen overdose.

Hematologic: Neutropenia and thrombocytopenia purpura have been reported and rarely agranulocytosis.

Hypersensitivity: Laryngeal edema, angioedema and anaphylactoid reactions may occur rarely.

Hepatic: Hepatic toxicity has been associated with acetaminophen in overdose. Chronic use of high doses, e.g., ≥5 g daily for several weeks in adults or 150 mg/kg/day for 2 to 4 days in children, has also been associated with hepatotoxicity. Alcoholics, patients with liver disease, the malnourished and patients taking drugs that induce hepatic microsomal enzymes, may be at increased risk for hepatic toxicity.

Respiratory: May aggravate bronchospasm in patients sensitive to ASA or other analgesics.

Dosage: Dristan: Adults: 2 tablets every 4 hours not to exceed 8 tablets daily. Children 6 to 12 years: 1 tablet every 4 hours, not to exceed 4 tablets daily. Children under 6 years: Consult a physician.

Dristan Extra Strength: Adults: 2 caplets every 4 hours not to exceed 8 caplets daily. Use only on the advice of a physician. Children under 12 years: Consult a physician.

Supplied: Dristan: Each yellow and white layered regular strength tablet contains: phenylephrine HCl 5 mg, chlorpheniramine maleate 2 mg and acetaminophen 325 mg. Nonmedicinal ingredients: calcium stearate, cellulose, croscarmellose sodium, crospovidone, D&C yellow No. 10, FD&C yellow No. 6, polyethylene glycol, povidone, pregelatinized starch and stearic acid. Energy: 0.19 kJ (0.05 kcal). Blister packages of 24, 48 and 72.

Dristan Extra Strength: Each yellow and white layered extra strength caplet contains: phenylephrine HCl 5 mg, chlorpheniramine maleate 2 mg and acetaminophen 500 mg. Nonmedicinal ingredients: calcium stearate, cellulose, croscarmellose sodium, crospovidone, D&C yellow No. 10, FD&C yellow no. 6, polyethylene glycol, povidone, pregelatinized starch and stearic acid. Energy: 0.80 kJ (0.19 kcal). Blister packages of 24.

DRISTAN® LONG LASTING NASAL MIST/SPRAY

Whitehall-Robins

Oxymetazoline HCl

Nasal Decongestant

Pharmacology: The sympathomimetic action of oxymetazoline constricts the smaller arterioles of the nasal passages, producing a prolonged (up to 12 hours), gentle and decongesting effect.

Indications: For prompt temporary relief of nasal congestion due to the common cold, sinusitis, hay fever or other upper respiratory allergies for up to 12 hours.

Contraindications: Narrow angle glaucoma, rhinitis sicca. Concurrent therapy with MAO inhibitors. Hypersensitivity to any component. Sensitivity to even small doses of adrenergic substances as manifested by sleeplessness, dizziness, lightheadedness, weakness, tremulousness, or cardiac arrhythmias. Do not use for irrigation or displacement after sinus operations in which the dura may have been entered.

Precautions: For adults only. Do not exceed the recommended dose. Do not use for more than 7 days.

Systemic effects from the use of topical decongestants can occur due to rapid absorption from the nasal mucous membrane, especially when it is inflamed, and from gastrointestinal absorption if given in excess so that the nasally applied solution is swallowed. Such reactions are most likely to occur in infants, young children and the elderly.

Because of the possibility of generalized vasoconstriction and tachycardia, use sympathomimetic amines very cautiously in patients with hypertension, heart disease, including angina, hyperthyroidism, diabetes mellitus, advanced arteriosclerotic conditions and those patients receiving tricyclic antidepressants.

Children: Overdosage in children may produce profound CNS depression, possibly requiring intensive supportive treatment.

Pregnancy: Clinical data are inadequate to establish conditions for safe use in pregnancy or in women of childbearing potential.

To help prevent contamination from nasal secretions, rinse spray tips in hot water after each use. Use of this dispenser by more than one person may spread infection.

Adverse Effects: The following adverse effects may occur with topical nasal decongestants: burning, stinging, dryness of the nasal mucosa, sneezing, palpitations, tachycardia, cardiac arrhythmias, increase in blood pressure, headache, lightheadedness, nervousness, insomnia, blurred vision, drowsiness, CNS depression. Prolonged or excessive use may cause an increase in nasal congestion.

Dosage: With head tilted slightly forward, place nozzle loosely to nostril. Spray firmly 2 to 3 times into each nostril. Breathe deeply. Repeat morning and night. Not to exceed 2 times in 24 hours. Adult use only. Children under 12: Consult a physician.

Supplied: Dristan Long Lasting Nasal Mist: Each bottle contains: oxymetazoline HCl 0.05%. Nonmedicinal ingredients: benzalkonium chloride, cellulose, potassium phosphate, sodium chloride, sodium phosphate, thimerosal and water, purified. Plastic squeeze bottles of 15 and 30 mL.

Dristan Long Lasting Mentholated Nasal Spray: Each bottle contains: oxymetazoline HCl 0.05%. Nonmedicinal ingredients: alcohol, benzalkonium chloride, camphor, cellulose, eucalyptol, menthol, potassium phosphate, sodium chloride, sodium phosphate, thimerosal and water, purified. Plastic spray bottles of 15 and 30 mL.

DRISTAN® NASAL MIST/SPRAY

Whitehall-Robins

Pheniramine—Phenylephrine

Nasal Decongestant

Pharmacology: Phenylephrine is a sympathomimetic agent that constricts the smaller arterioles of the nasal passages producing a gentle and predictable decongesting effect. Pheniramine is an antihistamine that controls rhinorrhea, sneezing and lacrimation associated with elevated histamine levels in disorders of the respiratory tract.

Indications: Prompt temporary relief of nasal congestion due to colds, sinusitis, hay fever or other upper respiratory allergies.

Contraindications: Hypersensitivity to any of the ingredients and patients receiving MAO inhibitors.

Precautions: Do not exceed recommended dosage because symptoms may occur such as burning, stinging, sneezing or increase of nasal discharge. Do not use this product for more than 3 days. If symptoms persist, consult a physician. To help prevent contamination from nasal secretions, rinse spray tip in hot water after each use. Use of this dispenser by more than one person may spread infection. For adult use only. Do not give this product to children under 12 years except under the advice and supervision of a physician. Keep these and all medicines out of children's reach. In case of accidental ingestion, seek professional assistance or contact a Poison Control Centre immediately.

Dosage: With head tilted slightly forward, place nozzle loosely to nostril. Spray firmly 2 to 3 times into each nostril. Breathe deeply. Repeat every 4 hours as needed.

Supplied: Dristan Nasal Mist: Each 15 and 30 mL plastic squeeze bottle contains: phenylephrine HCl 0.5% and pheniramine maleate 0.2%. Nonmedicinal ingredients: alcohol, benzalkonium chloride, cellulose, eucalyptol, menthol, purified water, sodium chloride, sodium phosphate and thimerosal.

Dristan Mentholated Nasal Spray: Each 15 and 30 mL plastic squeeze bottle contains: phenylephrine HCl 0.5% and pheniramine maleate 0.2%. Nonmedicinal ingredients: benzalkonium chloride, camphor, cellulose, eucalyptol, menthol, methylsalicylate, polysorbate, purified water, sodium chloride, sodium phosphate and thimerosal.

The database, reporting form and procedures for monitoring adverse events from vaccines are separate from those of other drug products. See the CLIN-INFO SECTION for a description of the program and a copy of the reporting form.

DRISTAN® N.D.
DRISTAN® N.D. EXTRA STRENGTH

Whitehall-Robins

Acetaminophen—Pseudoephedrine HCl

Analgesic—Decongestant

Indications: For the symptomatic relief of colds, sinusitis, nasal congestion, sneezing, runny nose, fever, headache, minor aches and pains.

Contraindications: Hypersensitivity to any of the components. Patients receiving MAO inhibitors.

Precautions: Use with caution on elderly patients or those with hypertension, diabetes, glaucoma, coronary artery disease, hyperthyroidism, prostatic hypertrophy and patients receiving MAO inhibitors, patients allergic to acetaminophen or pseudoephedrine, serious liver or kidney disease, chronic alcoholism or chronic lung disease.

Pregnancy and *Lactation:* Caution should be exercised before giving to women who are pregnant or nursing a baby.

Adverse Effects: Pseudoephedrine may cause mild stimulation, particularly in patients sensitive to sympathomimetic drugs.

In therapeutic doses, acetaminophen is relatively nontoxic. Chronic use of large doses of acetaminophen may produce more significant toxicity.

Renal: Nephropathy, including papillary renal failure has been reported following consumption of large amounts of acetaminophen. Renal tubular necrosis has been associated occasionally with hepatic injury produced by acetaminophen overdose.

Hematologic: Neutropenia and thrombocytopenia purpura have been reported and rarely agranulocytosis.

Hypersensitivity: Laryngeal edema, angioedema and anaphylactoid reactions may occur rarely.

Hepatic: Hepatic toxicity has been associated with acetaminophen in overdose. Chronic use of high doses, e.g., ≥5 g daily for several weeks in adults or 150 mg/kg/day for 2 to 4 days in children, has also been associated with hepatotoxicity. Alcoholics, patients with liver disease, the malnourished and patients taking drugs that induce hepatic microsomal enzymes, may be at increased risk for hepatic toxicity.

Respiratory: May aggravate bronchospasm in patients sensitive to ASA or other analgesics.

Dosage: Dristan N.D.: Adults: 2 caplets every 4 hours, not to exceed 8 caplets daily. Children 6 to 12 years: 1 caplet every 4 hours, not to exceed 4 caplets daily. Children under 6 years: Consult a physician.

Dristan N.D. Extra Strength: Adults: 2 caplets every 4 hours, not to exceed 8 caplets daily. Children under 12 years: consult a physician.

Supplied: Dristan N.D.: Each yellow caplet contains: d-pseudoephedrine HCl 30 mg and acetaminophen 325 mg. Nonmedicinal ingredients: calcium stearate, cellulose, croscarmellose sodium, crospovidone, D&C yellow No. 10, FD&C yellow No. 6, polyethylene glycol, povidone, pregelatinized starch, stearic acid, titanium dioxide and vegetable oil. Energy: 0.54 kJ (0.13 kcal). Packages of 16.

Dristan N.D. Extra Strength: Each yellow caplet, printed Dristan ND ES/EF, contains: d-pseudoephedrine HCl 30 mg and acetaminophen 500 mg. Nonmedicinal ingredients: calcium stearate, cellulose, cornstarch, croscarmellose sodium, crospovidone, D&C yellow No. 10, FD&C blue No. 2, FD&C red No. 3, FD&C yellow No. 6, pharmaceutical glaze, polyethylene glycol, povidone, pregelatinized starch, propylene glycol, stearic acid, titanium dioxide and vegetable oil. Energy: 0.80 kJ (0.19 kcal). Packages of 16.

DRISTAN® SINUS

Whitehall-Robins

Ibuprofen—Pseudoephedrine HCl

Analgesic—Antipyretic—Nasal Decongestant

Pharmacology: Ibuprofen has exhibited analgesic and antipyretic activity in animal studies designed to specifically demonstrate these effects. Ibuprofen has been shown to have no glucocorticoid-like activity.

Pseudoephedrine is an orally effective nasal decongestant when administered in doses of 60 mg/dose, up to 240 mg/day. In order to comply with the flexible dosing schedule approved for nonprescription ibuprofen, clinical studies were conducted to demonstrate the efficacy of 30 mg pseudoephedrine when administered in the combination product and evidence of dose response between the 30 and 60 mg doses.

A 3-way bioavailability study of ibuprofen, pseudoephedrine and a combination of ibuprofen/pseudoephedrine indicated that the absorption and the disposition of the 2 drugs were **not** different, i.e., there was no pharmacokinetic interaction when the 2 drugs were combined.

In another 3-way bioequivalence comparison of ibuprofen, pseudoephedrine and a combination of the 2 drugs, **no** statistically significant differences were noted among the 3 treatments for any pharmacokinetic variables for ibuprofen or pseudoephedrine.

Indications: For the temporary relief of symptoms associated with the common cold, sinusitis or flu including nasal congestion, headache, fever, body aches and pains.

Contraindications: In patients who have previously exhibited hypersensitivity to it, or to its components (ibuprofen, pseudoephedrine), or in individuals with the angioedema syndrome, nasal polyps or bronchospastic reactivity to ASA or other nonsteroidal anti-inflammatory agents (see Warnings).

In patients with hypertension, coronary artery disease and in patients on MAO inhibitor therapy (see Drug Interactions).

Pregnancy, Lactation and Children: Dristan Sinus should not be used during pregnancy, in nursing mothers or in pediatric patients because its safety under these conditions has not been established.

Aseptic meningitis, fever and rash have been reported in connection with ibuprofen therapy in patients with systemic lupus erythematosus.

Dristan Sinus should not be used by patients with systemic lupus erythematosus except under a physician's supervision.

Dristan Sinus should not be taken by patients with active peptic ulcer disease or gastrointestinal bleeding unless directed by a physician.

Warnings: Anaphylactoid reactions have occurred in patients with known ASA hypersensitivity (see Contraindications).

Peptic ulcerations and gastrointestinal bleeding, sometimes severe, have been reported in patients receiving prescription doses of ibuprofen. Peptic ulcerations, perforation or severe gastrointestinal bleeding can have a fatal outcome, and although few such reports have been received with ibuprofen, a cause and effect relationship has not been established. Patients with a history of upper gastrointestinal tract disease should take Dristan Sinus under the supervision of a physician.

Like other nonsteroidal anti-inflammatory agents, ibuprofen can inhibit platelet aggregation. However, compared to ASA, the effect is quantitatively less, of shorter duration, and reversible upon discontinuation of ibuprofen. Bleeding time has also been prolonged by ibuprofen though within the normal range in normal subjects. Because this effect on bleeding time may be exaggerated in patients with underlying hemostatic defects, Dristan Sinus should be avoided by persons with intrinsic coagulation defects and those on anticoagulant therapy.

Patients with high blood pressure, heart disease, diabetes, narrow-angle glaucoma, thyroid disease or difficulty in urination due to enlargement of the prostate gland should take Dristan Sinus only under the advice and supervision of a physician.

Precautions: Conditions associated with dehydration appear to increase the risk of renal toxicity. Dristan Sinus should therefore be used with caution in patients with chronic renal failure, congestive heart failure or hypertension being treated chronically with diuretics. Caution should be observed in elderly patients, due to increased susceptibility to the effects of sympathomimetic amines and increased risk of toxicity with ibuprofen, and patients with diminished renal function.

Patients on Dristan Sinus should be cautioned to report to their physician any signs or symptoms of gastrointestinal ulceration or bleeding, blurred vision or other eye symptoms, skin rash, weight gain, edema, tinnitus, dizziness or respiratory difficulties.

If Dristan Sinus is taken in conjunction with prolonged corticosteroid therapy and it is decided to discontinue the latter therapy, as under other circumstances, the corticosteroid dosage should be tapered slowly to avoid exacerbation of the disease or adrenal insufficiency.

Pregnancy and *Lactation:* Pregnant women or nursing mothers should seek the advice of a health professional before using Dristan Sinus.

There is a possibility of insomnia if this medicine is taken before bedtime.

If the symptoms do not improve or are accompanied by a high fever, the patient should be advised to report to the physician.

Drug Interactions: Coumarin-type Anticoagulants: Several short-term controlled studies failed to show that ibuprofen significantly affected prothrombin time for a variety of other clotting factors when administered to individuals on coumarin-type anticoagulants. The physician should be cautious when administering Dristan Sinus to patients on anticoagulants.

ASA: Animal studies show that ASA given with nonsteroidal anti-inflammatory agents including ibuprofen yields a net decrease in anti-inflammatory activity with lowered blood levels of the non-ASA drug. Single dose bioavailability studies in normal volunteers have failed to show an effect of ASA on ibuprofen blood levels. Correlative clinical studies have not been conducted.

Other Anti-inflammatory Agents (NSAIDs): The addition of Dristan Sinus to a pre-existent prescribed NSAID regimen in patients with a condition such as rheumatoid arthritis may result in increased risk of adverse effects.

Diuretics: Because of its fluid retention properties, high doses of ibuprofen can decrease the diuretic and antihypertensive effects of diuretics, and increased diuretic dosage may be required. Patients with impaired renal function who are taking potassium-sparing diuretics should not take Dristan Sinus.

Hypoglycemic Agents: Ibuprofen may increase hypoglycemic effects of oral antidiabetic agents and insulin.

Acetaminophen: Although interactions have not been reported, concurrent use with Dristan Sinus is not advisable, as it may increase the risk of adverse renal effect.

Other Drugs: Although ibuprofen binds extensively to plasma proteins, interactions with other protein-bound drugs occur rarely. Nevertheless, caution should be observed when other drugs, also having a high affinity for protein-binding sites, are used concurrently. Some observations have suggested a potential for ibuprofen to interact with furosemide, pindolol, digoxin, phenytoin and lithium salts. However, the mechanisms and clinical significance of these observations are presently not known. No interactions have been reported when ibuprofen has been used in conjunction with hypoglycemic agents, probenecid, digitalis, thyroxine, steroids, antibiotics or benzodiazepines.

Adverse Effects: Ibuprofen: The following adverse reactions have been noted in patients treated with prescription regimens of ibuprofen.

Gastrointestinal: The adverse reactions most frequently seen with prescribed ibuprofen therapy involve the gastrointestinal system: nausea, epigastric pain, heartburn, diarrhea, abdominal distress, vomiting, indigestion, constipation, abdominal cramps, fullness of the gastrointestinal tract (bloating or flatulence).

CNS: dizziness, headache, nervousness.

Dermatologic: rash (including maculopapular type), pruritus.

Special Senses: tinnitus.

Metabolic: decreased appetite, edema, fluid retention. Fluid retention generally responds promptly to drug discontinuation.

Pseudoephedrine: Pseudoephedrine may cause mild CNS stimulation, especially in patients who are hypersensitive to the effects of sympathomimetic drugs. Nervousness, excitability, restlessness, dizziness, weakness and insomnia may occur. Headache and drowsiness have also been reported. Large doses may cause lightheadedness, nausea and/or vomiting. In addition, the possibility of other adverse effects associated with sympathomimetic drugs, including fear, anxiety, tenseness, tremor, hallucinations, seizures, pallor, respiratory difficulty, dysuria and cardiovascular collapse should be considered.

Although oral administration of usual doses of pseudoephedrine to normotensive patients usually produced negligible pressor effects, the drug should be used with caution in hypertensive patients. Pseudoephedrine may increase the irritability of the heart muscle and may alter the rhythmic function of the ventricles, especially in large doses or when administered to patients who are hypersensitive to the myocardial effects of sympathomimetic drugs. Tachycardia or palpitation may occur.

Overdose: Symptoms and Treatment: Due to the rapid absorption of pseudoephedrine and ibuprofen from the gut, emetics and gastric lavage must be instituted within 4 hours of overdosage to be effective. Charcoal is useful only if given within 1 hour. Cardiac status should be monitored and the serum electrolytes measured. If there are signs of cardiac toxicity, propranolol may be administered i.v. A slow infusion of a dilute solution of potassium chloride should be initiated in the event of a drop in the serum potassium levels. Despite hypokalemia, the patient is unlikely to be potassium depleted; therefore, overload must be avoided. Monitoring of the serum potassium is advisable for several hours after administration of the salt. For delirium or convulsions, i.v. administration of diazepam is indicated.

Dosage: Adults and children over 12 years: Take 1 or 2 caplets every 4 hours as needed. Do not exceed 6 caplets in 24 hours, unless directed by a physician.

Children: Do not give to children under 12 years of age, except under the advice and supervision of a physician.

Supplied: Each caplet contains: ibuprofen 200 mg and pseudoephedrine HCl 30 mg. Nonmedicinal ingredients: acetylated monoglyceride, carnauba wax, cellulose, cornstarch, croscarmellose sodium, ethoxyethanol, iron oxide, lecithin, parabens, pharmaceutical glaze, pharmaceutical shellac, povidone, pregelatinized starch, silicon dioxide, simethicone, sodium benzoate, sodium lauryl sulfate, stearic acid, sucrose and titanium dioxide. Packages of 16. Store at room temperature (15 to 30°C).

Reviewed 1998

DRIXORAL®
DRIXTAB®
Schering

Dexbrompheniramine Maleate—Pseudoephedrine Sulfate

Antihistamine—Decongestant

Indications: Symptomatic relief of upper respiratory mucosal congestion in seasonal and perennial nasal allergies, acute rhinitis and rhinosinusitis, acute and subacute sinusitis, eustachian tube blockage and secretory otitis media.

Contraindications: Patients receiving or having received MAO inhibitors in the preceding 2 weeks; known hypersensitivity to pressor amines or antihistamines. Children under 12 years of age (sustained action tablets and capsules only).

Precautions: Although pseudoephedrine causes practically no pressor effect in normotensive individuals, it should be used with caution in elderly persons, patients with hypertension, chronic lung disease, diabetes, latent or clinically recognized angle closure glaucoma, coronary artery disease, congestive heart failure, urinary retention, prostatic hypertrophy and hyperthyroidism.

Pseudoephedrine may cause nervousness, restlessness or insomnia.

Occupational Hazards: Dexbrompheniramine may cause drowsiness which may impair ability to drive or perform other tasks requiring alertness. Since the depressant effects of antihistamines are additive to those of other drugs affecting the CNS, caution patients against drinking alcoholic beverages or taking hypnotics, sedatives, psychotherapeutic agents or other drugs with CNS depressant effects during antihistaminic therapy.

Should not be used by persons who are allergic or sensitive to any of the components of the products. May cause excitability in children; children should be observed by parents.

Pregnancy and *Lactation:* The safe use of this product during pregnancy and lactation has not been established and therefore the compound should be used only if the potential benefit justifies the potential risk to the fetus or infant.

Antihistamines should be discontinued approximately 48 hours prior to skin testing procedures since these may prevent or diminish otherwise positive reactions to dermal reactivity indicators.

Adverse Effects: Mild drowsiness and skin rash have been observed in the occasional patient receiving Drixoral.

Other known possible adverse effects of sympathomimetic (i.e. pseudoephedrine) origin include anxiety, tension, restlessness, nervousness, tremor, weakness, insomnia, headache, palpitation, tachycardia, angina, elevated blood pressure, sweating, mydriasis, anorexia, nausea, vomiting, dizziness, constipation and dysuria due to vesicle sphincter spasm.

Overdose: If accidental overdose occurs, seek medical assistance immediately.

Symptoms: Dexbrompheniramine: sedation, lassitude, muscular weakness, palpitations, dry mouth, gastrointestinal disturbances, dermatitis.

Pseudoephedrine: nervousness, insomnia, headaches, palpitations, nausea, vomiting, precordial pain.

Treatment: No specific antidote. Follow the established principles of treatment of any drug overdosage. Specific therapy will depend on the predominant symptoms observed.

Dosage: Drixoral Sustained Action Tablets: Adults and children 12 years of age and over, 1 tablet in the morning and 1 tablet at bedtime. In exceptional cases, 1 tablet every 8 hours may be required.

Drixoral, Drixtab (cont'd)

Drixtab Tablets: Adults and children 12 years and over, 1 tablet 3 or 4 times daily. Children 6 to 12 years of age, ½ tablet 3 to 4 times daily.

Supplied: Drixoral: Each green, sustained release tablet contains: dexbrompheniramine maleate 6 mg and pseudoephedrine sulfate 120 mg. The two active components are equally distributed between the tablet outer coating and a sustained release inner core. Following ingestion, the content of the outer coating is quickly liberated, and the content of the inner core subsequently becomes available for sustained release. Nonmedicinal ingredients: cornstarch, lactose, magnesium stearate and polyvinylpyrrolidone; coating: acacia, calcium sulfate, carnauba wax, dye, Opalux Green, gelatin, gum rosin, oleic acid, soap powder (white, neutral), sucrose, talc, white wax and zein F-200. Tartrazine-free. Blister packages of 10 and 20; bottles of 250.

Drixtab: Each white tablet contains: dexbrompheniramine maleate USP 2 mg and pseudoephedrine sulfate 60 mg. Nonmedicinal ingredients: cornstarch, lactose, magnesium stearate and povidone. Tartrazine-free (Drixoral Day/Night Cold Relief System).

(Shown in Product Recognition Section)

DRIXORAL® DAY/NIGHT Cold Relief System

Schering

Dexbrompheniramine—Pseudoephedrine Sulfate

Antihistamine—Decongestant

Indications: Symptomatic relief of upper respiratory mucosal congestion in seasonal and perennial nasal allergies, acute rhinitis and rhinosinusitis, acute and subacute sinusitis, eustachian tube blockage and secretory otitis media.

Contraindications: Patients receiving or having received MAO inhibitors in the preceding 2 weeks; known hypersensitivity to pressor amines or antihistamines.

Precautions: Although pseudoephedrine causes practically no pressor effect in normotensive individuals, it should be used with caution in elderly persons, patients with hypertension, chronic lung disease, diabetes, latent or clinically recognized angle closure glaucoma, coronary artery disease, congestive heart failure, urinary retention, prostatic hypertrophy and hyperthyroidism and patients receiving MAO inhibitors. Pseudoephedrine sulfate may cause nervousness, restlessness or insomnia.

Occupational Hazards: Dexbrompheniramine maleate may cause drowsiness which may impair ability to drive or perform other tasks requiring alertness.

Since the depressant effects of antihistamines are additive to those of other drugs affecting the CNS, caution patients against drinking alcoholic beverages or taking hypnotics, sedatives, psychotherapeutic agents or other drugs with CNS depressant effects during antihistaminic therapy.

Should not be used by persons who are allergic or sensitive to any of the components of the product.

Pregnancy and *Lactation:* The safe use of this product during pregnancy and lactation has not been established and therefore the compound should be used only if the potential benefit justifies the potential risk to the fetus or infant.

Antihistamines should be discontinued approximately 48 hours prior to skin testing procedures since these may prevent or diminish otherwise positive reactions to dermal reactivity indicators.

Adverse Effects: Mild drowsiness and skin rash have been observed in occasional patients receiving Drixoral Night.

Other known possible adverse effects of sympathomimetic (i.e. pseudoephedrine) origin include anxiety, tension, restlessness, nervousness, tremor, weakness, insomnia, headache, palpitation, tachycardia, angina, elevated blood pressure, sweating, mydriasis, anorexia, nausea, vomiting, dizziness, constipation and dysuria due to vesicle sphincter spasm.

Overdose: If accidental overdose occurs, seek medical assistance immediately.

Symptoms: Dexbrompheniramine maleate: sedation, lassitude, muscular weakness, palpitations, dry mouth, gastrointestinal disturbances, dermatitis.

Pseudoephedrine: nervousness, insomnia, headaches, palpitations, nausea, vomiting, precordial pain.

Treatment: No specific antidote. Follow the established principles of treatment of any drug overdosage. Specific therapy will depend on the predominant symptoms observed.

Dosage: Drixoral Day (Drixoral N.D. yellow tablet): Adults and children 12 years and over: 1 tablet in morning.

Drixoral Night (Drixtab white tablet): Adults and children 12 years and over: 1 tablet at bedtime.

Supplied: Drixoral Day/Night Cold Relief System: Each daytime yellow sustained action tablet contains: pseudoephedrine sulfate USP 120 mg. Nonmedicinal ingredients: acacia, carnauba wax, calcium sulfate, castor oil hydrogenated flakes, dye Opalux yellow AS-2183, ethyl cellulose, gelatin, gum rosin, magnesium stearate, oleic acid, soap powder (white, neutral), sucrose, talc, white wax and zein F-200.

Each nighttime white tablet contains: dexbrompheniramine maleate USP 2 mg and pseudoephedrine sulfate USP 60 mg. Nonmedicinal ingredients: cornstarch, lactose, magnesium stearate and povidone. Tartrazine-free.

Boxes of 10 and 20.

DRIXORAL® NASAL SOLUTION

Schering

Oxymetazoline HCl

Nasal Decongestant

Indications: The relief of congestion of the nasopharyngeal mucous membranes in a variety of allergic and infectious disorders of the upper respiratory tract, including acute rhinitis and nasopharyngitis; acute and chronic sinusitis; acute and chronic vasomotor rhinitis; perennial allergic rhinitis and seasonal allergic rhinitis (hay fever).

Contraindications: Narrow angle glaucoma, rhinitis sicca. Concurrent therapy with MAO inhibitors. Hypersensitivity to any component. Sensitivity to even small doses of adrenergic substances as manifested by sleeplessness, dizziness, lightheadedness, weakness, tremulousness, or cardiac arrhythmias. Do not use for irrigation or displacement after sinus operations in which the dura may have been entered.

Precautions: To be used only in adults and children over 6 years of age. Do not exceed the recommended dose.

Systemic effects from the use of topical decongestants can occur due to rapid absorption from the nasal mucous membrane, especially when it is inflamed, and from gastrointestinal absorption if given in excess so that the nasally applied solution is swallowed. Such reactions are most likely to occur in infants, young children and the elderly.

Because of the possibility of generalized vasoconstriction and tachycardia, use sympathomimetic amines very cautiously in patients with hypertension, heart disease, including angina, hyperthyroidism, diabetes mellitus, advanced arteriosclerotic conditions and those patients receiving tricyclic antidepressants.

Overdosage in children may produce profound CNS depression, possibly requiring intensive supportive treatment.

Pregnancy: Clinical data are inadequate to establish conditions for safe use in pregnancy or in women of childbearing potential.

To help prevent contamination from nasal secretions, rinse spray tips in hot water after each use. No more than one person should use the same nasal spray or pump.

Adverse Effects: The following adverse effects may occur with topical nasal decongestants: burning, stinging, dryness of the nasal mucosa, sneezing, palpitations, headache, lightheadedness, insomnia. Prolonged or excessive use may cause rebound congestion.

Dosage: Adults or children over 6 years old. Spray 2 or 3 strokes into each nostril 2 times a day every 12 hours.

Supplied: Each spray or pump bottle contains: oxymetazoline HCl 0.05% in aqueous solution. Nonmedicinal ingredients: benzalkonium chloride, edetate disodium, propylene glycol, water and pH adjusted with hydrochloric acid or sodium hydroxide. Conventional spray bottles of 20 mL and metered pump sprays of 25 mL.

For comparative information on Opioid Analgesics, see the CPhA General Monograph in the WHITE SECTION.

DRIXORAL® N.D.

Schering

Pseudoephedrine Sulfate

Decongestant

Indications: Symptomatic relief of upper respiratory mucosal congestion in seasonal and perennial nasal allergies, acute rhinitis and rhinosinusitis, acute and subacute sinusitis, eustachian tube blockage and secretory otitis media.

Contraindications: Patients receiving or having received MAO inhibitors in the preceding 2 weeks; known hypersensitivity to pressor amines or antihistamines.

Precautions: Although pseudoephedrine causes practically no pressor effect in normotensive individuals, it should be used with caution in elderly persons, patients with hypertension, diabetes, latent or clinically recognized angle closure glaucoma, coronary artery disease, congestive heart failure, urinary retention, prostatic hypertrophy and hyperthyroidism and patients receiving MAO inhibitors. Pseudoephedrine sulfate may cause nervousness, restlessness or insomnia.

Should not be used by persons who are allergic or sensitive to any of the components of the product.

Pregnancy and *Lactation:* The safe use of this product during pregnancy and lactation has not been established and therefore the compound should be used only if the potential benefit justifies the potential risk to the fetus or infant.

Adverse Effects: Other known possible adverse effects of sympathomimetic (i.e., pseudoephedrine) origin include anxiety, tension, restlessness, nervousness, tremor, weakness, insomnia, headache, palpitation, tachycardia, angina, elevated blood pressure, sweating, mydriasis, anorexia, nausea, vomiting, dizziness, constipation and dysuria due to vesicle sphincter spasm.

Overdose: If accidental overdose occurs, seek medical assistance immediately.

Symptoms: Nervousness, insomnia, headaches, palpitations, nausea, vomiting, precordial pain.

Treatment: No specific antidote. Follow the established principles of treatment of any drug overdosage. Specific therapy will depend on the predominant symptoms observed.

Dosage: Drixoral N.D.: Adults and children 12 years and over: 1 tablet every 12 hours. Not to exceed 2 tablets in 24 hours. Do not exceed the recommended dosage without consulting a physician. Do not chew tablets, swallow whole.

Supplied: Each yellow, sustained action tablet contains: pseudoephedrine sulfate USP 120 mg. Nonmedicinal ingredients: acacia, carnauba wax, calcium sulfate, castor oil hydrogenated flakes, dye Opalux yellow AS-2183, ethyl cellulose, gelatin, gum rosin, magnesium stearate, oleic acid, soap powder-white neutral, sucrose, talc, white wax and zein F-200. Blister packs of 10.

(Shown in Product Recognition Section)

DRIXTAB®

Schering

see DRIXORAL/DRIXTAB

DROPERIDOL INJECTION, USP Ⓟ

Novopharm

Neuroleptic—Antiemetic

Supplied: Each mL of colorless, sterile, aqueous, injectable solution, contains: droperidol 2.5 mg for i.m. or i.v. injection. Nonmedicinal ingredients: lactic acid and water for injection. Single use vials of 2 mL, packages of 10.

New Product 1998

DTIC® Ⓟ

Bayer

Dacarbazine

Antineoplastic Agent

Pharmacology: Although dacarbazine's exact mechanism of action is not known, 3 hypotheses have been offered: 1. inhibition of DNA synthesis by acting as a purine analog. 2. action as an alkylating agent. 3. interaction with SH groups.

Dacarbazine is only slightly (approximately 5%) protein bound. Its plasma half-life after i.v. administration is approximately 35 minutes. In animals, approximately 46% of a radio labeled dose was recovered from the urine after 6 hours. Of this 46%, almost 50% was unchanged dacarbazine and a like quantity was AIC (amino imidazole carboxamide) a metabolite. Dacarbazine is subject to renal tubular secretion.

Indications: Palliative therapy of metastatic malignant melanoma.

Contraindications: Known hypersensitivity to dacarbazine.

Precautions: Dacarbazine should be administered under the supervision of a qualified physician experienced in the use of cancer chemotherapeutic agents. The drug should be administered to patients who are hospitalized and who can be observed carefully and frequently during and after therapy.

Dacarbazine is toxic to the hemopoietic system and may produce depression of the bone marrow, anemia, leukopenia, thrombocytopenia and bleeding. Leukopenia and thrombocytopenia may be severe enough to cause death. A careful monitoring of hematologic changes is required during and after therapy. Hemopoietic toxicity may warrant temporary suspension or cessation of dacarbazine therapy.

If dacarbazine is used in combination with other cytotoxic agents, the toxic effects may be potentiated.

Studies have demonstrated that dacarbazine has a carcinogenic and teratogenic effect when used in animals.

In the treatment of each patient, the possibility of achieving therapeutic benefit must be weighed carefully against the risk of toxicity.

During i.v. dacarbazine administration, exercise care to avoid s.c. or perivascular extravasation. Extravasation may result in tissue damage necrosis and severe pain.

Adverse Effects: Hemopoietic depression: see Precautions.

Anorexia, nausea and vomiting are experienced in over 90% of patients with the initial doses. Restriction of food and fluid intake for 4 to 6 hours prior to treatment is recommended. Nausea and vomiting may last 1 to 12 hours and may be palliated by antiemetic therapy. After the first few days of treatment, the gastrointestinal symptoms tend to subside. Rarely, intractable nausea and vomiting may necessitate discontinuance of the drug. Diarrhea is uncommon but has been reported.

There have been reports of significant impairment of liver and kidney function. Monitoring of liver and kidney function is recommended.

Less than 10% of patients have experienced an influenza like syndrome of fever to 39°C, myalgia and malaise. These symptoms most frequently occur after large single doses some 7 days after treatment and last for 7 to 21 days. On successive treatment this syndrome may recur. In these cases, supportive management is recommended.

Alopecia has been noted as has facial flushing and facial paresthesia.

Overdose: Symptoms: Accidental dacarbazine overdosage would be expected to intensify hemopoietic depression and gastrointestinal symptomatology.

Treatment should be supportive, with particular attention to fluid balance in the acute phase. Monitor the hemopoietic system and institute appropriate therapy on the basis of these findings.

Dosage: 2 to 4.5 mg/kg/day for 10 days which may be repeated at 3-week intervals. It has been found that dacarbazine may be as efficacious at the lower dosage as at the higher dosage.

Combinations of cancer chemotherapeutic agents have often shown an improved response over the use of single agents.

Administration: The 200 mg/vial is reconstituted with 19.7 mL of Sterile Water for Injection, USP. The resulting solution contains an equivalent of 10 mg/mL of dacarbazine having a pH of 3.0 to 4.0. After the solution has been prepared the calculated dose of the resulting solution is drawn into a syringe and injected i.v. Injection of dacarbazine may be completed in approximately 1 minute. Any solution remaining in the vial may be stored at 4°C for 72 hours. At 20°C the solution is not stable for more than 8 hours.

The reconstituted solution may be further diluted with 5% dextrose injection, USP, or sodium chloride injection, USP and administered as an i.v. infusion. The resulting solution may be stored at 4°C for up to 24 hours or at normal room conditions for up to 8 hours.

Supplied: Each vial contains: sterile dacarbazine 200 mg. Nonmedicinal ingredients: citric acid, mannitol, nitrogen and water for injection. Boxes of 12. Protect from light. Store at 2 to 8°C.

DULCOLAX®
Boehringer Ingelheim Self Medication Division

Bisacodyl

Laxative

Indications: For the treatment of occasional constipation. In the preparation for diagnostic procedures, in pre- and postoperative treatment, and in conditions which require defecation to be facilitated, the use of bisacodyl must be under medical supervision.

Contraindications: In patients with ileus, intestinal obstruction, acute surgical abdominal conditions like acute appendicitis, acute inflammatory bowel diseases, and in severe dehydration.

Bisacodyl is also contraindicated in patients with known hypersensitivity to substances of the triarylmethane group.

Precautions: Do not use bisacodyl in the presence of abdominal pain, nausea, fever or vomiting, or within 2 hours of another medicine since the desired effect of the other medicine may be reduced. Since extended use of any laxative can cause dependence for bowel function, do not take for more than 1 week unless directed by a health professional. If the use of bisacodyl every day for a week does not result in a bowel movement, a doctor should be consulted immediately.

Prolonged excessive use may lead to electrolyte imbalance and hypokalemia, and may precipitate the onset of rebound constipation.

The use of suppositories may lead to painful sensations and local irritation, especially in anal fissures and ulcerative proctitis.

Pregnancy: As with all medications, bisacodyl should only be taken during pregnancy on medical advice.

Children: Children under 6 years old should not take bisacodyl without medical advice.

Adverse Effects: Rarely, abdominal discomfort and diarrhea have been reported.

Drug Interactions: The concomitant use of diuretics or adrenocorticosteroids may increase the risk of electrolyte imbalance if excessive doses of bisacodyl are taken.

Electrolyte imbalance may lead to increased sensitivity to cardiac glycosides.

Overdose: Symptoms: If high doses are taken, watery stools (diarrhea), abdominal cramps, and a clinically significant loss of potassium and other electrolytes can occur.

Treatment: Within a short time after ingestion of oral forms of bisacodyl, absorption can be minimized or prevented by inducing vomiting or gastric lavage. Replacement of fluids and correction of electrolyte imbalance may be required. This is especially important in the elderly and the young.

Dosage: For constipation: Tablets: Adults: 5 to 15 mg. Children 6 to 12 years: 5 mg, taken at bedtime or in the morning before breakfast to produce evacuation approximately 8 hours later. Tablets have a special coating and therefore should not be taken together with milk or antacids. Tablets should be swallowed whole with adequate fluid.

Suppositories: Adults: one 10 mg suppository. Children 6 to 12: one 5 mg pediatric suppository, unwrapped and inserted into the rectum pointed end first. Suppositories are usually effective in about 30 minutes.

Micro-enema: Adults: the contents of 1 micro-enema. Children 6 to 12 years: one half the contents of 1 micro-enema, administered rectally. Micro-enema is usually effective in about 30 minutes.

For diagnostic procedures or pre-operatively: Tablets should be combined with the suppositories or micro-enema in order to achieve complete evacuation of the intestine. Adults: 10 to 20 mg orally (tablets) at bedtime and one 10 mg suppository, or 1 micro-enema, to be inserted rectally the following morning. Children 6 to 12 years: 5 mg orally (tablet) at bedtime and one 5 mg suppository, or one half the contents of 1 micro-enema, inserted rectally the following morning.

Supplied: Micro-Enema: Each 5 mL plastic disposable tube contains: bisacodyl 10 mg. Also contains parabens. Sodium: <1 mmol (0.56 mg). Boxes of 50.

Suppositories: Each rectal suppository contains: bisacodyl 5 mg (children) or 10 mg (adult). Boxes of 3 (5 mg); boxes of 3, 6 and 100 (10 mg). Store at room temperature (less than 30°C).

Tablets: Each yellow, enteric-coated tablet contains: bisacodyl 5 mg. Also contains lactose, polyethylene glycol and tartrazine. Sodium-free. Energy: 1.09 kJ (0.26 kcal). Packages of 10, 30 and 100.

DUO-C.V.P.®
Rhône-Poulenc Rorer

Ascorbic Acid

Antihemorrhagic

Supplied: Each dark brown, hard gelatin capsule, imprinted with "A" in shield, contains: ascorbic acid 200 mg. Nonmedicinal ingredients: citrus bioflavonoids, cornstarch, FD&C Blue No 1, FD&C Red No 3, FD&C Yellow No 6, gelatin, lactose, light mineral oil, magnesium oxide and magnesium stearate. Tartrazine-free. Bottles of 100.

DUOFILM®
Stiefel

Salicylic Acid—Lactic Acid—Collodion

Verrucae Therapy

Supplied: Each mL contains: salicylic acid USP 16.7% and lactic acid USP 16.7% in flexible collodion USP. Bottles of 15 mL with brush applicator.

DUOFORTE® 27
Stiefel

Salicylic Acid

Verrucae Therapy

Indications: For common, plantar and mosaic warts.

Contraindications: Diabetics or patients with impaired blood circulation should not use this product without the advice of a health professional. Do not use on moles, birthmarks or unusual warts with hair growing from them. Do not use near eyes or mucous membranes.

Warnings: Do not use on inflamed and/or infected skin.

Precautions: For external use only. Duoforte 27 gel is highly flammable and should be kept away from fire or flame. Keep tube tightly capped when not in use. Store at controlled room temperature.

If spilled on mucous membranes or in eyes, flush with water, remove precipitated collodion and flush with water for an additional 15 minutes. Contact physician. Keep this and all medication out of reach of children.

Dosage: Thoroughly wash the affected area and soak the wart in warm water for at least 5 minutes. Dry completely with a clean towel. Warts can be contagious, so be sure no one else uses the towel. Remove the soft portion of the wart by gently rubbing with an emery board, pumice stone or coarse washcloth. Apply a thin layer directly to the wart using the pointed applicator tip. Take care to keep away from the skin surrounding the wart.

The gel will dry and form an acrylic barrier, protecting the wart and aiding in the penetration of the medication.

Apply Duoforte 27 gel once each day and continue treatment as directed by physician. If skin irritation develops or if there appears to be no improvement within 10 days or if the condition persists after 14 days of the treatment, contact physician.

Supplied: Each g contains: salicylic acid 27% w/w in a nonmedicinal polyacrylic collodion gel. Nonmedicinal ingredients: polybutylene, ethyl lactate, polymethylmethacrylate, alcohol absolute, flexible collodion and hydroxypropylcellulose. Tubes of 15 g with applicator tips.

DUONALC®
DUONALC-E® MILD
ICN

Isopropyl Alcohol

Ethyl Alcohol

Skin Cleanser

Supplied: Duonalc: Each mL of unscented solution contains: isopropyl alcohol 70%. Nonmedicinal ingredients: polyoxyethylene lauryl ether and propylene glycol. Polyethylene bottles of 50 and 100 mL with controlled flow applicator.

Duonalc (cont'd)

Duonalc-E Mild: Each mL of transparent lotion contains: ethyl alcohol (20%). Nonmedicinal ingredients: isopropyl alcohol, polyoxyethylene lauryl ether and propylene glycol. Bottles of 50 mL with a controlled flow applicator.

DUONALC-E® Solution
ICN

Ethyl Alcohol—Isopropyl Alcohol

Skin Cleanser

Supplied: Each mL of transparent liquid contains: ethyl alcohol 47.5% and isopropyl alcohol 4%. Nonmedicinal ingredients polyoxyethylene lauryl ether and propylene glycol. Bottles of 50 with a controlled flow applicator.

DUOPLANT®
Stiefel

Salicylic Acid—Lactic Acid—Formalin

Plantar Wart Remover

Supplied: Each g contains: salicylic acid USP 25%, lactic acid USP 10%, formalin 5% in a specially formulated base. Nonmedicinal ingredients: lanolin anhydrous, mineral oil light 90, paraffin wax and white soft petrolatum. Plastic tubes of 30 g. Store between 15 and 30°C.

Plantar Wart Removal Kit: Each kit contains: 1 tube of Duoplant 30 g, 1 emery file, 20 self-adhesive bandages, 2 cushion pads and detailed instructions for use.

DUOVENT® UDV Ⓟ
Boehringer Ingelheim

Ipratropium Bromide—Fenoterol Hydrobromide

Bronchodilator

Pharmacology: Duovent UDV inhalation solution is a combination of the anticholinergic bronchodilator ipratropium bromide and the beta$_2$-adrenergic bronchodilator fenoterol hydrobromide. Ipratropium is a quaternary ammonium derivative of atropine and is an anticholinergic drug which has bronchodilator properties. On inhalation of ipratropium the onset of action is noted within 5 to 15 minutes with a peak response between 1 and 2 hours, lasting about 2 additional hours with subsequent decline from the peak. Bronchodilation is still evident 8 hours after inhalation.

The bronchodilating effect of fenoterol is produced primarily by stimulation of β_2 receptors in the bronchial smooth muscles. When administered by inhalation, fenoterol exerts a significant increase in pulmonary function 5 minutes after administration with a maximal effect in 30 to 60 minutes. This effect remains at the same level for 2 to 3 hours before gradually declining. A significant degree of bronchodilation has been reported in some studies for 6 to 8 hours.

The concurrent administration of ipratropium and fenoterol results in dilatation of the bronchi by affecting different pharmacologic sites of action.

Pharmacokinetics: The pharmacokinetics of ipratropium and fenoterol are not altered when the 2 drugs are administered concurrently.

Indications: For the symptomatic relief of bronchospasm associated with acute severe exacerbations of bronchial asthma or chronic obstructive pulmonary disease (COPD).

Duovent UDV inhalaton solution must be administered by means of nebulizer using gas flow (oxygen or compressed air).

Contraindications: Should not be used by patients with tachyarrhythmias, hypertrophic obstructive cardiomyopathy, or by those with a known sensitivity to the component drugs, sympathomimetic amines, atropinics or to any of the product components.

Warnings: Like other inhalation solutions that contain β_2 agonists, Duovent UDV should not be used on a regular basis without appropriate concomitant anti-inflammatory therapy (see Dosage).

Children: Duovent UDV is not currently indicated for use in children under 12 years of age as the dosing regimen and evidence concerning its safety in this age group have not been established.

Pregnancy and *Lactation:* The safety of Duovent UDV in pregnancy and lactation has not been established. It should be used with caution before childbirth in view of the inhibiting effect of β_2 agonists on uterine contractions.

General: Care should be taken in patients suffering from myocardial insufficiency, cardiac arrhythmias, recent myocardial infarction, severe organic heart and/or other vascular disorders, hypertension, hyperthyroidism or diabetes mellitus.

Fatalities, the exact cause of which is unknown, have been reported following excessive use of sympathomimetic amines by inhalation. Cardiac arrest was noticed in several instances.

Some patients receiving inhaled β-adrenergic agonists have developed severe paradoxical bronchospasm, which has been life-threatening. The cause of this refractory state is unknown. If it occurs, the preparation should be discontinued immediately and alternative therapy instituted.

In common with other β-adrenergic agents, fenoterol can induce reversible metabolic changes. These are most pronounced during **infusions** of the drug and include hyperglycemia and hypokalemia.

Potentially serious hypokalemia may result from β_2-agonist therapy, mainly from parenteral and nebulized administration. Particular caution is advised in acute severe asthma as hypokalemia may be potentiated by concomitant treatment with xanthine derivatives, steroids and diuretics; the adverse effects of hypokalemia may be exacerbated by hypoxia. It is recommended that serum potassium levels be monitored in such situations. Hypokalemia will increase the susceptibility of digitalis-treated patients to cardiac arrhythmias.

The bronchodilating action of sympathomimetic drugs may be antagonized by β-adrenergic blocking agents with the result that the respiratory status of patients may worsen when the 2 drugs are used concomitantly. In patients requiring concomitant treatment with Duovent UDV and a β-adrenergic blocking agent, the use of a relatively cardioselective β-blocker (e.g., metoprolol, atenolol, acebutolol) must be considered. During the concomitant treatment, patients should be monitored carefully for possible deterioration in pulmonary function or for the need to adjust the dosage of either drug.

Glaucoma, Angle-Closure: Care should be taken to ensure that the nebulizer mask fits the patient's face properly and that nebulized solution does not escape into the eyes (i.e., use swimming goggles). In patients with glaucoma or narrow anterior chambers, the administration by nebulizer of Duovent UDV should be avoided unless measures (e.g., use of swimming goggles) are taken to ensure that nebulized solution does not reach the eye. Exposure of the eyes of such patients to a nebulized combination of ipratropium and a β_2 agonist solution (i.e., Duovent UDV) has been reported to result in increased intraocular pressure and/or acute angle closure. There have been isolated reports of ocular complications (i.e., mydriasis, increased intraocular pressure, angle closure glaucoma) when nebulized ipratropium either alone or in combination with an adrenergic β_2 agonist solution has escaped into the eyes. In the event that glaucoma is precipitated or worsened, treatment should include standard measures for this condition.

Use of Duovent UDV in Conjunction with IPPV: It has been reported in several cases that the use of intermittent positive-pressure ventilation in acute asthma attacks was related to lethal episodes of hypoxia and pneumothorax. This method of drug administration may be ineffective in patients with severe obstruction and greatly increased airway resistance and it may induce severe hypercapnia and hypoxia. During intermittent positive-pressure ventilation therapy, the monitoring of arterial blood gases is highly desirable.

Precautions: If therapy does not produce a significant improvement or if the patient's condition gets worse, medical advice must be sought in order to determine a new plan of treatment. In the case of acute or rapidly worsening dyspnea, a doctor should be consulted immediately.

Increasing use of β_2 agonists to control symptoms of bronchial obstruction, especially administration on a regular basis or in high amounts, indicates deterioration of asthma control. Under these conditions, the patient's therapy plan has to be revised. It is inadequate simply to increase the use of bronchodilators under these circumstances, in particular over extended periods of time (see Dosage).

Concomitant use of Duovent UDV with other sympathomimetic agents is not recommended since the combined use may lead to deleterious cardiovascular effects. If concomitant use is necessary, this should take place only under strict medical supervision.

Caution is advised against accidental release of the solution into the eyes.

Duovent UDV should be used with caution in patients with glaucoma, prostatic hypertrophy or urinary retention and in asthmatic or emphysematous patients who also have acute and recurring congestive heart failure or in patients sensitive to sympathomimetic amines.

Failure to respond to a **previously effective dose** usually indicates a significant deterioration in the patient's asthmatic condition. The patient should be instructed to contact his/her physician immediately in these circumstances and warned on no account to exceed the recommended dose.

Three retrospective case-control studies, from one group in New Zealand, have suggested that there may be an increased risk of death in those patients using fenoterol whom the studies classified as 'severe' asthmatics. These conclusions have not been confirmed by other studies and are subject to considerable debate and ongoing studies.

To ensure the proper dosage administration, the patient should be instructed by the physician or other health professional on the proper use and maintenance of the nebulizer.

Drug Interactions: Other β-adrenergic agents, anticholinergics, xanthine derivatives and corticosteroids may enhance the effect of Duovent UDV inhalation solution. Avoid concomitant use of Duovent UDV with MAO inhibitors, tricyclic antidepressants or with other sympathomimetic agents since their combined effect on the cardiovascular system may be deleterious to the patient.

Beta-receptor blocking agents and fenoterol inhibit the effect of one another (see Warnings).

In patients receiving other anticholinergic drugs, Duovent UDV should be used with caution because of possible additive effects.

Labor and Delivery: Beta-adrenergic agents have been shown to delay preterm labor in some reports. There are no well-controlled studies which demonstrate that such agents will stop preterm labor or prevent labor at term. Cautious use of β-adrenergics for the relief of bronchospasm is therefore required in pregnant patients to avoid interference with uterine contractility.

Adverse Effects: Frequent undesirable effects of Duovent UDV are fine tremor of skeletal muscles and nervousness, less frequent are tachycardia, dizziness, palpitations or headache, especially in hypersensitive patients.

In isolated cases there may be local reactions such as dryness of the mouth, throat irritation, or allergic reactions. As with other bronchodilators, in some cases cough, in very rare instances paradoxical bronchoconstrictions have been observed.

The adverse reactions noted for the individual components of Duovent UDV inhalation solution are as follows:

Ipratropium: The frequency of adverse reactions recorded in 214 patients receiving ipratropium solution was as follows given by adverse effect (% of patients): dry mouth or throat (9.3); bad taste (5.1); tremor (4.2); exacerbation of symptoms (4.2); burning eyes (0.9); nausea (0.9); sweating (0.9); cough (0.9); headache (0.5); palpitations (0.5).

The adverse effect judged to be most severe was exacerbation of symptoms. This occurred in 8 patients treated with ipratropium solution alone, 6 of whom withdrew from the clinical studies.

Bronchospasm occurred in 3 patients with acute severe asthma who received ipratropium solution alone. In 2 patients, this was reversed after therapy with a β_2 sympathomimetic solution. The third patient received no other therapy.

Table I compares the incidence of adverse effects of the combination of ipratropium and a β_2 agonist solution with that of the β_2 agonist alone.

Table I—Duovent UDV

Comparison of Adverse Effects

Adverse Effect	Atrovent-β_2 agonist (% of 94 patients)	β_2 Agonist (% of 96 patients)
Tremor	31.9	26.0
Dry mouth	16.0	28.1
Bad taste	16.0	13.5
Vomiting	2.1	2.1
Palpitations	2.1	1.0
Headache	1.1	2.1
Cough	1.1	0.0
Flushing	1.1	0.0
Dizziness	0.0	1.0
Numbness in leg	0.0	1.0

There have been isolated reports of ocular effects such as mydriasis, increased intraocular pressure, and acute glaucoma associated with the escape of nebulized ipratropium alone or in combination with a β_2 agonist solution into the eyes.

Fenoterol: At the most frequently used dosage of fenoterol solution of 0.5 to 1 mg, temor occurred in 12% of patients. At higher doses of fenoterol solution (up to 2.5 mg) given for the treatment of severe asthma in a hospital emergency room, mild to moderate tremor occurred in 32% of patients. Other adverse reactions in decreasing order of frequency included nervousness, dizziness, headache, lightheadedness, and palpitations.

In 104 patients who received the highest recommended dosage of 2.5 mg of fenoterol solution, increases in heart rate of 10% or greater within 4 hours after drug administration were observed in 21% of the patients. However, at least an equal number of patients had decreased heart rate of a similar magnitude in the same time period. The remainder showed no significant pulse rate changes.

Local irritation or allergic reactions have been reported rarely. As with other bronchodilators, cough and, very rarely, paradoxical bronchospasm have been observed (see Warnings). Potentially serious hypokalemia may result from β_2 agonist therapy.

Overdose: Symptoms and Treatment: Overdosage resulting in excessive β-adrenergic stimulation may cause tachycardia, arrhythmia, hypertension and in extreme cases, sudden death. If Duovent UDV overdosage occurs, cardiac and respiratory support should be provided as required.

Dosage: COPD: Chronic Bronchitis and Emphysema: Duovent UDV inhalation solution dosage should be individualized, and patient response should be monitored to determine the requirement for more than a single bronchodilator by the prescribing physician on an ongoing basis.

Counselling on smoking cessation should be the first step in treating patients with chronic bronchitis who smoke. Smoking cessation produces symptomatic benefits and has been shown to confer a survival advantage by slowing or stopping the progression of chronic bronchitis and emphysema.

Asthma: Duovent UDV inhalation solution should be used only under medical supervision in patients with severe acute exacerbations of asthma who require more than a single bronchodilator.

In accordance with the present practice for asthma treatment, concomitant anti-inflammatory therapy should be part of the regimen if Duovent UDV needs to be used on a regular daily basis.

If a previous effective dosage regimen fails to provide the usual relief, or the effects of a dose last for less than 3 hours, medical advice should be sought immediately; this is a sign of seriously worsening asthma that requires reassessment of therapy.

Dosage: Adults and children 12 years of age or over: The usual dose is 4 mL of Duovent UDV inhalation solution. Treatment may be repeated after 6 hours when necessary.

Not recommended for children under 12 years of age.

Dilution Instructions: If the full content of Duovent UDV is to be nebulized, squeeze the plastic vial to empty its contents into the nebulizer chamber. If instructions were given to use a dose less than 1 complete vial, use a syringe to transfer the necessary amount to the nebulizer chamber. Any solution left in the plastic vial must be discarded because Duovent UDV does not contain preservatives. Use a syringe to add sterile, preservative-free 0.9% sodium chloride solution to the nebulizer chamber. Sodium chloride solution may be added to fill the nebulizer solution to a maximum of 5 mL.

Information for the Patient: See Blue Section—Information for the Patient "Duovent UDV".

Supplied: Each mL of clear, colorless solution contains: ipratropium bromide 0.125 mg and fenoterol hydrobromide 0.3125 mg. Nonmedicinal ingredients: hydrochloric acid, purified water and sodium chloride. Plastic single use vials of 4 mL, cartons of 20.

Unopened unit dose vials should be stored at controlled room temperature (15 to 25°C) and protected from light. If necessary, the solution may be diluted with preservative-free sterile sodium chloride solution 0.9% and used immediately. Any solution remaining in the vial must be discarded.

Patients should be informed of potential "occupational hazards" which may be induced by medications. Look for this heading under precautions in product monographs.

DUPHALAC®

Solvay Pharma

Lactulose Crystals

Laxative

Pharmacology: Experimental data indicate that lactulose is not significantly absorbed in the small intestine and reaches the colon essentially unchanged. There it is metabolized by bacteria with the formation of low molecular weight acids that acidify the colonic contents. Less than 2% of lactulose is absorbed systemically.

Two mechanisms are believed to be involved in the laxative action of lactulose: 1) Metabolism of lactulose by bacteria results in reduced colonic pH, which stimulates peristalsis and decreases stool transit time. In turn, decreased water reabsorption from the feces further facilitates the passage of soft, well-formed stools. 2) Increased osmotic pressure of fecal material secondary to an increase in colonic organic acids results in accumulation of fluid from surrounding tissues, helping to soften stool mass.

This action takes place gradually, with increased stool volume and frequency normally observed within 24 to 48 hours.

Indications: Relief of constipation, including chronic constipation.

Contraindications: Since lactulose crystals contain galactose and lactose, use is contraindicated in patients who require a low galactose diet.

Lactulose is contraindicated in cases of bowel obstruction.

Precautions: General: As with all laxatives, overuse or extended use may cause dependence for bowel function. No laxative should be taken for more than 1 week without the advice of a physician. No laxative should be used in the presence of abdominal pain, nausea, fever, or vomiting, as such symptoms may signal appendicitis or an inflamed bowel.

Lactulose crystals contain galactose and lactose and should be used with caution in diabetics.

Pregnancy: Animal studies have not revealed significant adverse effects. However, lactulose should not be taken by women who are pregnant, or planning to become pregnant, except on the advice of a physician.

Drug Interactions: No laxative should be taken within 2 hours of another medication, because the desired effect of the other medication may be reduced.

Adverse Effects: Initial dosing may produce flatulence and intestinal cramps, which are usually transient. Excessive dosage can lead to diarrhea. Nausea has been reported.

Overdose: Symptoms and Treatment: Diarrhea and abdominal cramps may be controlled by a dosage reduction.

Dosage: Usual dosage: 10 to 20 g (15 to 30 mL)/day (i.e., 1 to 2 packets/day). After a few days, the dose may be increased up to 40 g (60 mL)/day (i.e., 4 packets/day) if necessary.

A maximum dose of 40 g/day (60 mL, or 4 packets/day) should not be exceeded.

One packet (10 g) of lactulose is equivalent to 15 mL of lactulose crystals. Energy: approximately 2 kcal/packet.

Duphalac should be taken in a single dose at the same time daily, such as breakfast. Crystals can be taken dry from a spoon and washed down with a glass of water or another liquid. The crystals may also be sprinkled on food or mixed with water or fluids before swallowing.

Information for the Patient: See Blue Section—Information for the Patient "Duphalac".

Supplied: Each packet contains: lactulose crystals 10 g (15 mL). Lactulose is a synthetic disaccharide analogue of lactose. Also contains galactose, lactose and other sugars. Energy: 8.4 kJ (2 kcal). Boxes of 10. Store at room temperature (between 10 and 25°C). Keep out of the reach of children.

(Shown in Product Recognition Section)

Reviewed 1998

DURAGESIC® Ⓝ

Janssen-Ortho

Fentanyl

Opioid Analgesic

Pharmacology: Fentanyl is an opioid analgesic which interacts predominantly with the μ-opioid receptor. Fentanyl produces analgesia, sedation, respiratory depression, constipation, and physical dependence but appears to have less emetic activity than other opioid analgesics. Fentanyl may produce muscle rigidity, miosis, cough reflex suppression, alterations in mood, bradycardia and broncho-constriction.

Analgesic blood levels of fentanyl may cause nausea and vomiting directly by stimulating the chemoreceptor trigger zone, but nausea and vomiting are significantly more common in ambulatory than in recumbent patients, as is postural syncope.

Opioids increase the tone and decrease the propulsive contractions of the smooth muscle of the gastrointestinal tract. The resultant prolongation in gastrointestinal transit time may be responsible for the constipating effect of fentanyl. Because opioids may increase biliary tract pressure, some patients with biliary colic may experience worsening rather than relief of pain.

While opioids generally increase the tone of urinary tract smooth muscle, the net effect tends to be variable, in some cases producing urinary urgency, in others, difficulty in urination.

At therapeutic dosages, fentanyl usually does not exert major effects on the cardiovascular system. However, some patients may exhibit orthostatic hypotension and fainting.

Histamine assays and skin wheal testing in man indicate that histamine release rarely occurs with fentanyl. Assays in man show no clinically significant histamine release in dosages up to 50 μg/kg.

Duragesic provides continuous systemic delivery of fentanyl for up to 72 hours. Fentanyl is released along the concentration gradient existing between the saturated solution of the drug in the reservoir of the system and the lower concentration in the skin. While the actual rate of fentanyl delivery to the skin varies over the 72-hour application period, each system is labeled with a nominal flux which represents the average amount of drug delivered to the systemic circulation per hour across average skin.

The total amount of drug released is dependent on the area of the system. The 10, 20, 30 and 40 cm^2 systems are designed to deliver 25, 50, 75 or 100 μg/hour fentanyl to the systemic circulation, representing approximately 0.6, 1.2, 1.8 or 2.4 mg/day. The 50, 75 and 100 μg/hour doses are to be used only in opioid-tolerant patients.

Pharmacokinetics: Following initial Duragesic administration, serum fentanyl concentrations increase gradually, generally leveling off between 12 and 24 hours and remaining relatively constant for the remainder of the 72-hour application period. Peak serum levels of fentanyl generally occur between 24 and 72 hours after the first application.

Serum fentanyl concentrations achieved are proportional to the Duragesic delivery rate. With continuous use, serum fentanyl concentrations continue to rise for the first few system applications. After several sequential 72-hour applications, patients reach and maintain a steady-state serum concentration that is determined by individual variation in skin permeability and body clearance of fentanyl (see Table I).

Table I—Duragesic

Pharmacokinetic Parameters of TTS (Fentanyl)

	Maximal Concentration C_{max} (ng/mL)	Time to Maximal Concentration (h)
Duragesic 25 μg/h	0.3–1.2	26–78
Duragesic 50 μg/h	0.6–1.8*	24–72*
Duragesic 75 μg/h	1.1–2.6	24–48
Duragesic 100 μg/h	1.9–3.8	25–72

*Estimated.

After Duragesic removal, serum fentanyl concentrations decline gradually, falling about 50% in approximately 17 (range 13 to 22) hours. Continued absorption of fentanyl from the skin accounts for a slower disappearance of the drug from the serum than is seen after an i.v. infusion, where the apparent half-life ranges from 3 to 12 hours.

The average volume of distribution for fentanyl is 6 L/kg (range 3 to 8, n=8). The average clearance in patients undergoing various surgical procedures is 46 L/hour (range 27 to 75, n=8).

Elderly, cachectic or debilitated patients may have altered pharmacokinetics due to poor fat stores, muscle wasting or altered clearance. The clearance of fentanyl may be reduced, and the terminal half-life prolonged.

Skin does not appear to metabolize fentanyl delivered transdermally. Fentanyl is metabolized primarily in the liver. In humans, the drug is metabolized primarily by N-dealkylation to norfentanyl and other inactive metabolites. Approximately 75% of an i.v. fentanyl dose is excreted in urine, mostly as metabolites, with less than 10% representing unchanged drug.

Duragesic (cont'd)

Approximately 9% of the dose is recovered in the feces, primarily as metabolites. Mean values for unbound fractions of fentanyl in plasma are estimated to be between 13 and 21%.
Pharmacodynamics: In controlled clinical trials in nonopioid-tolerant patients, 60 mg/day i.m. morphine was considered to provide analgesia approximately equivalent to Duragesic 100 μg/hour in an acute pain model. Minimum effective analgesic serum concentrations of fentanyl in opioid naive patients range from 0.2 to 1.2 ng/mL; side effects increase in frequency at serum levels above 2 ng/mL. Both the minimum effective concentration and the concentration at which toxicity occurs rise with increasing tolerance. The rate of development of tolerance varies widely among individuals.
Clinical Trials: During the premarketing phase, clinical trials were conducted in 153 patients to evaluate the efficacy and safety of Duragesic as therapy for pain due to cancer. The studies were open-labelled with the exception of one trial which incorporated a randomized, double-blind crossover component (Duragesic versus placebo) in 46 patients. Doses in these studies varied between 25 and 600 μg/hour. Patients used Duragesic continuously for up to 866 days; 56% received Duragesic for over 30 days, 28% continued treatment for more than 4 months and 10% used Duragesic for more than 1 year. The results of these studies demonstrated that: 1) satisfactory analgesia was achieved in the majority of patients and, 2) Duragesic was accepted by cancer patients, their caregivers and physicians.

Since the introduction of Duragesic, additional trials have been conducted in approximately 350 chronic cancer pain patients to confirm earlier conclusions. In the largest of these, a Canadian postmarketing surveillance study in 199 patients, a reduction in pain intensity and improved pain relief and well-being were observed in the 127 patients evaluable for efficacy. Patient preference for Duragesic over their previous analgesic therapy was also observed. In these patients, the average treatment duration was 68 days (range: 17 to 118). The mean dose for all study patients increased from 51 μg/hour at baseline to 128 μg/hour at the last dose on therapy.

Indications: In the management of chronic cancer pain in patients requiring continuous opioid analgesia.

Duragesic should not be used in the management of postoperative pain because serious or life-threatening hypoventilation may result.

Contraindications: Because serious or life-threatening hypoventilation could occur, Duragesic is contraindicated in: 1) the management of acute or postoperative pain, including use in out-patient surgeries, 2) the management of mild or intermittent pain that can otherwise be managed, and 3) doses exceeding 25 μg/hour at the initiation of Duragesic therapy in nonopioid-tolerant patients.

Patients with known hypersensitivity to fentanyl or to the adhesives present in the system.

Warnings: Duragesic should not be used in the management of acute or postoperative pain since there is no opportunity for dose titration during short-term use and because serious or life-threatening hypoventilation could result.

As with other CNS depressants, patients who have received Duragesic should be monitored until stabilized.

Since serum fentanyl concentrations decline gradually after system removal, patients who have experienced adverse events should be monitored for at least 12 hours after Duragesic removal or until the adverse reaction has subsided.

Duragesic should only be prescribed by persons knowledgeable in the continuous administration of potent opioids, in the management of patients receiving potent opioids for treatment of pain and in the detection and management of respiratory depression including the use of opioid antagonists.
Patients with Fever/External Heat: Patients who develop fever should be monitored for opioid side effects and the Duragesic dose adjusted if necessary. Serum fentanyl concentrations could theoretically increase by approximately one third for patients with a body temperature of 40°C due to temperature dependent increases in fentanyl release from the system and increased skin permeability. All patients should be advised to avoid exposing the Duragesic application site to direct external heat sources, such as heating pads, electric blankets, heated water beds, heat lamps, hot water bottles, saunas and hot whirlpool spa baths, intensive sunbathing, etc.
Drug Interactions: The concomitant use of other CNS depressants (including other opioids, sedatives or hypnotics, general anesthetics, phenothiazines, tranquilizers), skeletal muscle relaxants, sedating antihistamines and alcoholic beverages may produce additive depressant effects. Hypoventilation, hypotension and profound sedation or coma may occur. When combined therapy is contemplated, the dose of each agent should be reduced by at least 50%.

Severe and unpredictable potentiation by MAO inhibitors has been reported with opioid analgesics. Since the safety of fentanyl in this regard has not been established, the use of fentanyl in patients who have received MAO inhibitors during the previous 14-day period is not recommended.
Children: The use of Duragesic in children under 18 years of age is not recommended as efficacy, safety, and dosage requirements have not been established for this patient population. Life-threatening hypoventilation has been reported in some pediatric patients receiving Duragesic.

Precautions: General: Duragesic doses greater than 25 μg/hour are too high for initiation of therapy in nonopioid-tolerant patients and should not be used to begin Duragesic therapy in these patients (see Dosage).
Occupational Hazards: Psychomotor Impairment: Duragesic may impair mental and/or physical ability required for the performance of potentially hazardous tasks such as driving a car or operating machinery. Patients using Duragesic should not drive or operate dangerous machinery unless they are tolerant to the effects of the drug.
Disposal of Duragesic: Duragesic should be kept out of the reach of children before and after use.

Used systems should be folded so that the adhesive side of the system adheres to itself, then flushed down the toilet immediately upon removal. If the gel from the drug reservoir accidentally contacts the skin, the area should be washed with clear water. Patients should dispose of any systems remaining from a prescription as soon as they are no longer needed. Unused systems should be removed from their pouch and flushed down the toilet.
Respiratory Depression: As with all potent opioids, some patients may experience significant respiratory depression with Duragesic; caution must be exercised and patients carefully observed for untoward reactions. While most patients using Duragesic chronically develop tolerance to fentanyl induced hypoventilation, episodes of slowed respirations may occur at any time during therapy. A small number of patients have experienced clinically significant hypoventilation with Duragesic; medical intervention generally was not required in these instances. The incidence of respiratory depression increases as the Duragesic dose is increased.

Hypoventilation can occur throughout the therapeutic range of fentanyl serum concentrations. However, the risk of hypoventilation increases at serum fentanyl concentrations greater than 2 ng/mL in nonopioid-tolerant patients, especially for patients who have an underlying pulmonary condition or who receive usual doses of opioids or other CNS drugs, associated with hypoventilation, in addition to Duragesic (see Warnings regarding the use of concomitant CNS active drugs). The use of Duragesic should be monitored by clinical evaluation. As with other drug level measurements, serum fentanyl concentrations may be useful clinically, although they do not reflect patients sensitivity to fentanyl and should not be used by physicians as a sole indicator of effectiveness or toxicity.

The duration of the respiratory depressant effect of Duragesic may extend beyond the removal of the system. (See also Overdose concerning respiratory depression).
Drug Dependence: Fentanyl is an opioid substance and can produce drug dependence similar to that produced by morphine. Duragesic therefore has the potential for abuse. Tolerance, physical and psychological dependence may develop upon repeated administration of opioids. Iatrogenic addiction following opioid administration is relatively rare. Physicians should not let concerns of physical dependence deter them from using adequate amounts of opioids in the management of severe pain when such use is indicated.
Patients with Chronic Pulmonary Disease: Fentanyl should be used with caution in patients with chronic pulmonary disease, patients with decreased respiratory reserve and others with potentially compromised respiration. Normal analgesic doses of opioids may further decrease respiratory drive in these patients to the point of respiratory failure.
Head Injuries and Increased Intracranial Pressure: Duragesic should not be used in patients who may be particularly susceptible to the intracranial effects of CO_2 retention such as those with evidence of increased intracranial pressure, impaired consciousness or coma. Opioids may obscure the clinical course of patients with head injury. Duragesic should be used with caution in patients with brain tumors.
Patients with Cardiac Disease: I.V. fentanyl may produce bradycardia. Fentanyl should be administered with caution to patients with bradyarrhythmias.
Patients with Hepatic or Renal Disease: Because of the hepatic metabolism and renal excretion of fentanyl, Duragesic should be used with caution in patients with liver or kidney dysfunction.
Geriatrics and Debilitated Patients: Elderly, cachectic or debilitated patients may have altered pharmacokinetics due to poor fat stores, muscle wasting or altered clearance. These patients should be started on Duragesic 25 μg/hour unless they are taking at least 135 mg of oral morphine a day or an equivalent dose of another opioid (see Dosage).
Pregnancy: Fentanyl has been shown to impair fertility and to have an embryocidal effect in rats when given in i.v. doses 0.3 times the human dose for a period of 12 days. No evidence of teratogenic effects has been observed after the administration of fentanyl to rats.

The safe use of fentanyl has not been established with respect to possible adverse effects upon human fetal development. Therefore, Duragesic should not be used in women of childbearing potential unless, in the judgment of the physician, the potential benefits outweigh the possible hazards.
Labor and Delivery: Duragesic is not recommended for analgesia during labor and delivery.
Lactation: Fentanyl is excreted in human milk; therefore, Duragesic is not recommended for use in nursing women because of the possibility of effects in their infants.
CNS Depressants: When patients are receiving Duragesic, the dose of additional opioids or other CNS depressant drugs (including benzodiazepines) should be reduced by at least 50%. With the concomitant use of CNS depressants, hypotension may occur.
Drug or Alcohol Dependence: Use of Duragesic in combination with alcoholic beverages and/or other CNS depressants can result in increased risk to the patient. Duragesic should be used with caution in individuals who have a history of drug or alcohol abuse, especially those outside a medically controlled environment.

Adverse Effects: In postmarketing experience, deaths from hypoventilation have been reported in cases of inappropriate use of Duragesic.
Premarketing Clinical Trial Experience: The safety of Duragesic has been evaluated in 153 cancer patients and 357 postoperative patients. The duration of use varied in cancer patients; 56% of patients used Duragesic for over 30 days, 28% continued treatment for more than 4 months, and 10% used Duragesic for more than 1 year. In cancer patients, Duragesic was administered in doses of 25 to 600 μg/hour. Patients with acute pain used Duragesic for 1 to 3 days.

Respiratory depression, the most serious adverse reaction, was observed in 3 (2%) of the cancer patients and 13 (4%) of the postoperative patients.

Hypotension and hypertension were observed in 11 (3%) and 4 (1%) of the opioid-naive patients.

A causal relationship of adverse events to Duragesic was not always determined. The frequencies presented here reflect the actual frequency of each adverse effect in patients who received Duragesic. There has been no attempt to correct for a placebo effect, concomitant use of other opioids, or to subtract the frequencies reported by placebo-treated patients in controlled trials.

The adverse reactions in Table II (on following page) were reported in 153 cancer patients at a frequency of 1% or greater; a higher incidence of adverse reactions was seen in the 357 postoperative patients studied.

Overdose: Symptoms: The manifestations of fentanyl overdosage are an extension of its pharmacologic actions with the most serious effect being respiratory depression.

Treatment: For management of respiratory depression, immediate countermeasures include removing the Duragesic and physically or verbally stimulating the patient. These actions can be followed by administration of a specific opioid antagonist such as naloxone. The duration of respiratory depression following an overdose may be longer than the effects of the opioid antagonist's action (the half-life of naloxone ranges from 30 to 81 minutes). The interval between i.v. antagonist doses should be carefully chosen because of the possibility of re-narcotization after system removal; repeated administration of naloxone may be necessary. Reversal of the opioid effect may result in acute onset of pain and release of catecholamines.

If the clinical situation warrants, establish and maintain a patent airway, administer oxygen and assist or control respiration as indicated, and use an oropharyngeal airway or endotracheal tube if necessary. If depressed respiration is associated with muscular rigidity, an i.v. neuromuscular blocking agent may be required to facilitate assisted or controlled respiration. Adequate body temperature and fluid intake should be maintained.

Table II—Duragesic

Adverse Effects

System	Frequency (% of patients)	Adverse Reactions
Body as a Whole	3-10	abdominal pain, headache
Cardiovascular	1-2	arrhythmia, chest pain
Digestive	≥ 10	nausea, vomiting, constipation, dry mouth
	3-10	anorexia, diarrhea, dyspepsia
	1-2	flatulence
Nervous	≥ 10	somnolence, confusion, asthenia
	3-10	dizziness, nervousness, hallucinations, anxiety, depression, euphoria
	1-2	tremor, abnormal coordination, speech disorder, abnormal thinking, abnormal gait, abnormal dreams, agitation, paresthesia, amnesia, syncope, paranoid reaction
Respiratory	3-10	dyspnea, hypoventilation, apnea
	1-2	hemoptysis, pharyngitis, hiccups
Skin and Appendages	≥ 10	sweating
	3-10	pruritus,
	1-2	rash, application site reaction–erythema, papules, itching, edema
Urogenital	3-10	urinary retention

If severe or persistent hypotension occurs, the possibility of hypovolemia should be considered, and managed with appropriate parenteral fluid therapy.

Dosage: Duragesic doses must be individualized based upon the status of each patient and should be assessed at regular intervals after application. Each patient should be maintained at the lowest dose providing acceptable pain control. The most important factor to be considered in determining the appropriate dose is the extent of pre-existing opioid tolerance. Reduced doses of Duragesic are suggested for the elderly and other groups discussed in Precautions.

Duragesic should be applied to nonirritated and nonirradiated skin on a flat surface such as the chest, back, flank, or upper arm. Hair at the application site should be clipped (not shaved) prior to application. If the site of application must be cleansed prior to application of the system, do so with clear water. Do not use soaps, oils, lotions, alcohol or any other agents that might irritate the skin or alter its characteristics. Allow the skin to dry completely prior to system application.

Duragesic should be applied immediately upon removal from the sealed package. The system should not be altered, e.g., cut, in any way prior to its application. The transdermal system should be pressed firmly in place with the palm of the hand for 30 seconds, making sure the contact is complete, especially around the edges.

Each Duragesic may be worn continuously for 72 hours. A new system should be applied on a different skin site after removal of the previous transdermal system.

Initial Dose Selection: **In selecting an initial Duragesic dose, attention should be given to 1) the daily dose, potency, and characteristics of the opioid the patient has been taking previously (e.g., whether it is a pure agonist or mixed agonist-antagonist), 2) the reliability of the relative potency estimates used to calculate the Duragesic dose needed (potency estimates may vary with the route of administration), 3) the degree of opioid tolerance, if any, and 4) the general condition and medical status of the patient.**

There has been no systematic evaluation of Duragesic as an initial opioid analgesic in the management of chronic pain, since most patients in the clinical trials were converted to Duragesic from other opioids. In nonopioid-tolerant patients, the initial dose of Duragesic should not exceed 25 µg/hour.

Elderly, cachectic or debilitated patients may have altered pharmacokinetics due to poor fat stores, muscle wasting or altered clearance. These patients should be started on Duragesic 25 µg/hour unless they are taking at least 135 mg of oral morphine a day or an equivalent dose of another opioid.

To convert **opioid-tolerant patients** from oral or parenteral opioids to Duragesic, the following methodology should be used:

1. Calculate the previous 24-hour analgesic requirement.
2. Convert this amount to the equianalgesic oral morphine dose using Table III.
3. Table IV displays the range of 24-hour oral doses that are recommended for conversion to each Duragesic dose. Use this table to find the calculated 24-hour morphine dose and the corresponding Duragesic dose. This conversion recommendation is intentionally conservative to minimize the potential for Duragesic overdosage.

For delivery rates in excess of 100 µg/hour, multiple systems may be used.

Table III—Duragesic

Opioid Analgesics: Approximate Analgesic Equivalences[a]

Drug	Equivalent Dose (mg)[b] (compared to morphine 10 mg i.m.) Parenteral	Oral	Duration of Action (hours)
Strong Opioid Agonists:			
Morphine (single dose)	10	60	3–4
(chronic dose)	10	20–30[c]	3–4
Hydromorphone	1.5	7.5	2–4
Anileridine	25	75	2–3
Levorphanol	2	4	4–8
Meperidine[d]	75	300	1–3
Oxymorphone	1	10 (rectal)	3–4
Methadone[e]	10	20	
Heroin	5	60	3–4
Weak Opioid Agonists:			
Codeine	130	200	3–4
Oxycodone	15	30	2–4
Propoxyphene	50	100	2–4

[a] References: Foley, K.M., In: Cancer, Principles and Practice of Oncology, 4th Ed., V.T. Devita, Jr., S. Hellman, S.A. Rosenberg (Ed.), J.B. Lippincott Co., Philadelphia, pp. 2417–2448, 1993.
Foley, K.M., New Engl. J. Med. 313: 84–95, 1985.
Aronoff, G.M. and Evans, W.O., In: Evaluation and Treatment of Chronic Pain, 2nd Ed., G.M. Aronoff (Ed.), Williams and Wilkins, Baltimore, pp. 359–368, 1992.
Cherny, N.I., and Portenoy, R.K., In: Textbook of Pain, 3rd Ed., P.D. Wall and R. Melzack (Eds.), Churchill Livingstone, London, pp. 1437–1467, 1994.

[b] Most of these data were derived from single-dose, acute pain studies and should be considered an approximation for selection of doses when treating chronic pain.

[c] For acute pain, the oral dose of morphine is 6 times the injectable dose. However, for chronic dosing, this ratio becomes 2 or 3:1, possibly due to the accumulation of active metabolites.

[d] These drugs are not recommended for the management of chronic pain.

[e] Extremely variable equianalgesic dose. Patients should undergo personalized titration starting at an equivalent to 1/10 of the morphine dose.

Initiate Duragesic treatment using the recommended dose and titrate patients upward (no sooner than 3 days after the initial dose or every 6 days thereafter) until analgesic efficacy is attained. For delivery rates in excess of 100 µg/hour, multiple systems may be used.

The majority of patients are adequately maintained with Duragesic administered every 72 hours. A small number of patients may not achieve adequate analgesia using this dosing interval and may require systems to be applied every 48 hours rather than every 72 hours. An increase in the Duragesic dose should be considered before changing dosing intervals in order to maintain patients on a 72-hour regimen.

Table IV—Duragesic

Recommended Initial Duragesic Dose Based Upon Daily Oral Morphine Dose*

Oral 24-hour Morphine (mg/day)	Duragesic Dose (µg/hour)
45-134	25
135-224	50
225-314	75
315-404	100
405-494	125
495-584	150
585-674	175
675-764	200
765-854	225
855-944	250
945-1 034	275
1 035-1 124	300

* In clinical trials these ranges of daily oral morphine doses were used as a basis for conversion to Duragesic.

Because of the gradual increase in serum fentanyl concentration over the first 24 hours following initial system application, the initial evaluation of the maximum analgesic effect of Duragesic cannot be made before 24 hours of wearing.

Patients should use short-acting analgesics after the initial dose application as needed until analgesic efficacy with Duragesic is attained. Thereafter, some patients still may require periodic supplemental doses of a short-acting analgesic for breakthrough pain.

Dose Titration: The conversion ratio from oral morphine to Duragesic is conservative, and 50% of patients are likely to require a dose increase after initial application of Duragesic. The initial Duragesic dosage may be increased after 3 days, based on the daily dose of supplemental analgesics required by the patient in the second or third day of the initial application.

Physicians are advised that it may take up to 6 days after increasing the dose of Duragesic for the patient to reach equilibrium on the new dose. Therefore, patients should wear a higher dose through 2 applications before any further increase in dosage is made on the basis of the average daily use of a supplemental analgesic.

Appropriate dosage increments should be based on the daily dose of supplementary opioids, using the ratio of 45 to 134 mg/24 hours of oral morphine to a 25 µg/hour increase in Duragesic dose (see Table IV).

Some patients may require additional or alternative methods of opioid administration when the Duragesic dose exceeds 300 µg/hour.

Discontinuation of Duragesic: To convert patients to another opioid, remove Duragesic and titrate the dose of the new analgesic, based upon the patient's report of pain, until adequate analgesia has been attained. It should be noted that it takes 17 hours or more for the fentanyl serum concentration to fall by 50% after system removal. For patients requiring discontinuation of opioids, a gradual downward titration is recommended since it is not known at what dose level the opioid may be discontinued without producing the signs and symptoms of abrupt withdrawal.

Stability and Storage: Store in sealed pouch between 15 and 25°C. Keep out of reach of children before and after use.

Special Instructions: To dispose of Duragesic, fold the system so that the adhesive side of the system adheres to itself. The system should be flushed down the toilet immediately upon removal. If the gel from the drug reservoir accidentally contacts the skin, the area should be washed with clear water. Do not use soap, alcohol or other solvents to remove the gel because they may enhance the drug's ability to penetrate the skin. Patients should dispose of any systems remaining from a prescription as soon as they are no longer needed. Unused systems should be removed from their protective pouch and flushed down the toilet.

Information for the Patient: See Blue Section—Information for the Patient "Duragesic".

Supplied: Each transdermal system provides continuous systemic delivery of fentanyl, a potent opioid analgesic, for 72 hours. Duragesic is a rectangular transparent unit comprising a protective liner and 4 functional layers. Proceeding from the outer surface toward the surface adhering to the skin, these layers are: 1) a backing layer of polyester film, 2) a drug reservoir of fentanyl and alcohol USP gelled with hydroxyethyl cellulose, 3) an ethylene-vinyl acetate copolymer

Duragesic (cont'd)

membrane that controls the rate of fentanyl delivery to the skin surface, and 4) a layer of silicone adhesive. A peelable protective liner covering the adhesive layer must be removed before the system can be applied.

The active component of the system is fentanyl. The amount of fentanyl released from each system per hour is proportional to the surface area (25 μg/hour per 10 cm^2). The remaining components are pharmacologically inactive. Less than 0.2 mL of alcohol is released from the system during a 72-hour use. The composition per unit area of all system sizes is identical.

Information regarding each transparent, rectangular Duragesic is summarized in the accompanying chart (see Table V).

Table V—Duragesic

Availability

System	Nominal Fentanyl Delivery Rate (μg/hour)	Total Fentanyl Content (mg)	System Size (cm^2)
Duragesic 25	25	2.5	10
Duragesic 50	50	5	20
Duragesic 75	75	7.5	30
Duragesic 100	100	10	40

Cartons of 5 individually packaged systems.

(Shown in Product Recognition Section)

Reviewed 1999

DURALITH® Ⓟ

Janssen-Ortho

Lithium Carbonate

Antimanic Agent

Pharmacology: Although lithium is useful for its antimanic effect and in preventing relapses in patients with a clearcut diagnosis of bipolar affective disorder, it has very little, if any, direct effect on moods, normal or abnormal.

Lithium alters sodium transport in nerve and muscle cells, effects a shift toward intraneuronal metabolism of catecholamines and has an inhibitory action on the intracellular formation of cyclic AMP. However, the specific biochemical mechanism of action of lithium in mania is still largely unknown.

Use of a sustained-release lithium preparation can reduce the frequency of absorption-related side effects in selected individuals who are particularly sensitive to rapid increases in serum lithium concentrations. However, reduction of absorption-related side effects should not be the only consideration when prescribing lithium for prolonged maintenance therapy. Clinical evidence suggests that the main long-term toxic effect of lithium on the kidney may not be associated with high peak serum lithium levels (as produced by giving immediate-release lithium in a single daily dose), but rather with the presence of sustained, though lower, serum lithium levels (as produced by giving immediate-release lithium in 2 or 3 divided doses), which allow no opportunity for kidney regeneration in a nearly drug-free environment. Therefore, the long-term maintenance of relatively constant serum lithium levels throughout the day, which tend to result from twice daily administration of sustained-release preparations or from multiple daily doses of immediate-release preparations, may not be desirable.

Two separate studies measuring serum lithium levels were carried out. In Study A, Duralith sustained release lithium carbonate was administered twice daily, and in Study B, a cross over two week study, the serum lithium levels following the once daily administration of Duralith sustained release lithium carbonate and an immediate release formulation of lithium were compared. The results are as follows (see Table I).

As indicated in Table I, although 12-hour plasma levels are similar across studies, the once daily dosing regimen permits reaching lower serum lithium levels, both for Duralith sustained release lithium carbonate and for the immediate release formulation.

Lithium is excreted primarily in the urine, and the elimination half-life is approximately 24 hours. Renal lithium clearance tends to be remarkably constant in the same individual but decreases with age or when sodium intake is lowered. The dose necessary to maintain a given concentration of serum lithium depends on the ability of the kidney to excrete lithium. However, renal lithium excretion may vary greatly between individuals and lithium dosage must, therefore, be adjusted individually. It has been suggested that many patients retain larger amounts of lithium during the active manic phase but recent studies have been unable to confirm a clear difference in excretion patterns; patients in a manic state, however, appear to have increased tolerance to lithium.

Table I—Duralith

Results of Pharmacokinetic Studies

	Study A Twice Daily	Study B Once Daily	
Dose Range:	**900–1 800 mg/day**	**600–1 200 mg/daily**	
Product Used:	**Duralith tablets**	**Duralith tablets**	**Immediate Release tablets**
$C_{max_{ss}}$ (mEq/L)	1.45	N/A	N/A
12-hr plasma levels (mEq/L)	0.75	0.74	0.71
$C_{min_{ss}}$ (mEq/L)*	0.75	0.53	0.51
$T_{max_{ss}}$ (hours)	3–5	N/A	N/A

* In the twice daily regimen, $C_{min_{ss}}$ was measured approximately 12 hours post-dosing, whereas in the once daily regimen it was measured approximately 21 hours post-dose.

Legend: N/A Not available.
$_{ss}$ Steady-state.

Indications: In the lithium treatment of manic episodes of manic-depressive illness. Maintenance therapy has been found useful in preventing or diminishing the frequency of subsequent relapses in bipolar manic-depressive patients (with a history of mania).

Typical symptoms of mania, as an affective disorder, include pressure of speech, motor hyperactivity, reduced need for sleep, flight of ideas, grandiosity, or poor judgment, aggressiveness, and possibly hostility. When given to a patient experiencing a manic episode, lithium may produce a normalization of symptomatology within 1 to 3 weeks.

Contraindications: Sustained-release lithium carbonate should generally not be given to patients with significant brain damage, renal or cardiovascular disease, severe debilitation or dehydration, sodium depletion, or to patients receiving diuretics; the risk of lithium toxicity is very high in such patients. If the psychiatric indication is life-threatening and if such a patient fails to respond to other measures, lithium treatment may be undertaken, in selected cases, with extreme caution, including thorough medical assessment and appropriate consultation for at-risk patients, daily serum lithium determinations and adjustments of the doses to levels tolerated by the individual patients. In such instances, hospitalization is a necessity.

Warnings: Lithium toxicity is closely related to serum lithium levels, and can occur at doses close to the therapeutic levels. Facilities for prompt and accurate serum lithium determinations should be available before initiating therapy.

The ability to tolerate lithium is greater during the acute manic phase and decreases when manic symptoms subside (see Dosage).

Impaired Renal Function: Chronic lithium therapy is frequently associated with a decrease in renal concentrating capacity with development of thirst, polyuria, micturia, weight gain and altered kidney function tests, occasionally presenting as nephrogenic diabetes insipidus. Such patients should be carefully managed to avoid dehydration with resulting lithium retention and toxicity. The evidence suggests that impaired renal function during chronic therapy may be in most instances, only partially reversible when lithium is discontinued.

Prevention of renal toxicity and other toxic effects of long-term therapy requires a firm diagnosis of bipolar manic depressive illness; careful screening for pre-existing renal and other diseases; establishment of standardized 12 hour serum lithium levels which are as low as possible yet clinically effective; maintaining control of treatment by monitoring serum lithium levels and exercising clinical and laboratory surveillance over possible side effects or signs of lithium intoxication; exercising maximum control of at-risk patients; ensuring that long-term lithium therapy is maintained only when clinical response has been clearly established; and adjusting the dosage schedule and preparation used so as to obtain temporarily periods of lithium concentrations as low as possible in the kidney.

Glomerular sclerosis and interstitial fibrosis as well as tubular lesions have been reported in patients on chronic lithium therapy.

When kidney function is assessed for baseline data prior to starting lithium therapy or thereafter, routine urinalysis and other tests may be used to evaluate tubular function (e.g. urine specific gravity or osmolality or 24 hour urine volume) and glomerular function (e.g. serum creatinine or creatinine clearance).

During lithium therapy, progressive or sudden changes in renal function, even within the normal range indicate the need for re-evaluation of treatment including dosage and frequency of lithium administration, and a reassessment of the risk-benefit of long-term lithium therapy.

Pregnancy: Data from lithium birth registries suggest an increase in cardiac and other anomalies, especially Ebstein's anomaly; nephrogenic diabetes insipidus, euthyroid goiter and hypoglycemia have occurred in infants born to women who took lithium during pregnancy. Therefore, lithium should not be used during pregnancy or in women of child-bearing potential unless it cannot be substituted by other appropriate therapy and in the opinion of the physician the expected benefits outweigh the possible hazards to the fetus.

Lactation: Lithium is excreted in human milk. Nursing should not be undertaken during lithium therapy except in rare and unusual circumstances where, in the view of the physician, the potential benefits to the mother outweigh possible hazards to the child.

Children: Since information regarding the safety and effectiveness of lithium in children under 12 years of age is not available, the use of sustained-release lithium carbonate in such patients is not recommended at this time.

Precautions: To maximize benefits, minimize the risks, and reduce as much as possible the adverse effects of lithium therapy, it is essential to provide proper information to patients and relatives about the treatment regimen and control procedures required during treatment, as well as an explanation of the expected benefits and the most commonly experienced immediate and long-term side effects. Appropriate written material should be provided to supplement verbal information.

Out-patients and their families should be warned that the patient must discontinue therapy with sustained-release lithium carbonate and contact the physician if such clinical signs of lithium toxicity such as diarrhea, vomiting, tremor, mild ataxia, drowsiness, or muscular weakness occur.

Occupational Hazards: Further, since lithium may impair mental and/or physical abilities, patients should be cautioned about undertaking activities requiring alertness (e.g. operating vehicles or machinery).

Previously existing underlying thyroid disorders do not necessarily constitute a contraindication to lithium therapy; where hypothyroidism exists, careful monitoring of the thyroid function during lithium stabilization and maintenance allows for correction of changing thyroid parameters, if any. Where hypothyroidism occurs during lithium stabilization and maintenance, supplemental thyroid treatment may be used.

Lithium decreases sodium re-absorption by the renal tubules which would lead to sodium depletion. Therefore, it is essential for the patient to maintain a normal diet, including salt, and an adequate fluid intake (2 500 to 3 000 mL), at least during the initial stabilization period. Decreased tolerance to lithium has been reported to ensue from protracted sweating or diarrhea and, if such occur, supplemental fluid and salt should be administered. In addition to sweating and diarrhea, concomitant infection with elevated temperatures may also necessitate a temporary reduction or cessation of medication.

Drug Interactions: Combined use of haloperidol and lithium: An encephalopathy resembling the malignant neuroleptic syndrome (characterized by weakness, lethargy, fever, tremulousness and confusion, extrapyramidal symptoms, leukocytosis, elevated serum enzymes, BUN and FBS) followed by irreversible brain damage has occurred in a few patients treated with lithium plus haloperidol. A causal relationship between these events and concomitant administration of lithium and haloperidol has not been clearly established; however, patients receiving such combined therapy should be monitored closely for early evidence of neurological toxicity such as rigidity and/or hyperpyrexia and treatment discontinued promptly if such signs appear.

Combined use of phenothiazines and lithium: Both pharmacokinetic interactions and clinical toxicity with the combined use of these agents have been described. Lithium induced reductions in plasma chlorpromazine levels, phenothiazine-induced increases in red cell uptake of lithium and chlorpromazine-induced increases in renal lithium excretion have been reported. Clinically, occasional cases of neurotoxicity have been reported and may be more likely to occur with thioridazine than other phenothiazines, when combined with lithium. Therefore, the clinician should be alert for altered response to either drug when used in combination and when either drug is withdrawn.

The action of neuromuscular blocking agents may be prolonged in patients receiving lithium. Therefore, caution should be exercised when the combination is required. A temporary omission of a few doses of lithium can reduce the risks of this interaction.

Indomethacin has been reported to increase steady state plasma lithium levels by 30 to 59%. There is also evidence that other nonsteroidal anti-inflammatory agents may have a similar effect. When such combinations are used, increased frequency of monitoring plasma lithium levels is recommended.

There are reports that concurrent use of methyldopa or tetracycline may increase the risk of lithium toxicity.

Concurrent use of lithium and carbamazepine or phenytoin might result in an increased risk of CNS toxicity. The administration of aminophylline or theophylline to patients on lithium therapy may require increased lithium doses to maintain the psychotropic effect. Patients stabilized on lithium therapy who receive a thiazide diuretic may require a reduction of lithium dosage to avoid accumulation and toxicity, since there is often a 20 to 40% reduction of renal lithium clearance. Furosemide appears to be less likely to affect lithium clearance.

Adverse Effects: Mild side effects may be encountered even when serum lithium levels remain below 1 mEq/L. The most frequent side effects are the initial post-absorptive symptoms, believed to be associated with rapid rise in serum lithium levels. They include nausea, abdominal pain, vomiting, diarrhea, vertigo, muscle weakness, sleepiness and a dazed feeling, and frequently disappear after stabilization of therapy. The more common and persistent adverse reactions are: fine tremor of the hands which is not responsive to antiparkinson drugs, and at times, fatigue, thirst and polyuria (renal toxicity). These side effects may subside with continued treatment or a temporary reduction or cessation of dosage. If persistent, a lowering or cessation of dosage and reassessment of lithium therapy is indicated.

Mild to moderate toxic reactions may occur at lithium levels from 1.5 to 2 mEq/L, and moderate to severe reactions at levels above 2 mEq/L. Permanent neurological damage has been reported after exposure to toxic levels of lithium.

A number of patients may experience lithium accumulation during initial therapy, increasing to toxic levels and requiring immediate discontinuation of the drug. Some elderly patients with lowered renal clearances for lithium may also experience different degrees of lithium toxicity, requiring reduction or temporary withdrawal of medication. However, in patients with normal renal clearance the toxic manifestations appear to occur in a fairly regular sequence related to serum lithium levels. The usually transient gastrointestinal symptoms are the earliest side effects to occur. A mild degree of fine tremor of the hands may persist throughout therapy. Thirst and polyuria may be followed by increased drowsiness, ataxia, tinnitus, and blurred vision, indicating early intoxication. As intoxication progresses the following manifestations may be encountered: confusion, increasing disorientation, muscle twitching, hyperreflexia, nystagmus, seizures, diarrhea, vomiting and eventually coma and death.

The following toxic reactions have been reported and appear to be related to serum lithium levels, including levels within the therapeutic range.

Neuromuscular: tremor, muscle hyperirritability (fasciculations, twitching, clonic movements of whole limbs), ataxia, choreoathetotic movements, hyperactive deep tendon reflexes.

CNS: blackout spells, epileptiform seizures, slurred speech, dizziness, vertigo, incontinence of urine or feces, somnolence, psychomotor retardation, restlessness, confusion, stupor, coma.

Cardiovascular: cardiac arrhythmia, hypotension, peripheral circulatory collapse.

Gastrointestinal: anorexia, nausea, vomiting, diarrhea.

Genitourinary: albuminuria, oliguria, polyuria, glycosuria.

Dermatologic: drying and thinning of hair, anesthesia of skin, acne, chronic folliculitis, xerosis cutis, alopecia and exacerbation of psoriasis.

Autonomic Nervous System: blurred vision, dry mouth.

Thyroid Abnormalities: euthyroid goiter and/or hypothyroidism (including myxedema) accompanied by lower T_3 and T_4 levels and elevated TSH. Iodine[131] uptake may be elevated. On the average, 5 to 15% of patients on long-term lithium therapy manifest clinical signs or have altered serum hormone levels (see Precautions). Paradoxically, rare cases of hyperthyroidism have been reported.

EEG Changes: diffuse slowing, widening of frequency spectrum, potentiation and disorganization of background rhythm.

ECG Changes: reversible flattening, isoelectricity or inversion of T waves.

Miscellaneous: fatigue, lethargy, transient scotomata, dehydration, weight loss, tendency to sleep.

Miscellaneous reactions frequently unrelated to dosage include: transient EEG and ECG changes, leukocytosis, headache, diffuse non-toxic goiter with or without hypothyroidism, transient hyperglycemia, generalized pruritus with or without rash, cutaneous ulcers, albuminuria, worsening of organic brain syndrome, excessive weight gain, edematous swelling of ankles or wrists, and thirst or polyuria, sometimes resembling diabetes insipidus, and metallic taste.

A single instance has been reported of the development of painful discoloration of fingers and toes and coldness of the extremities within one day of starting treatment with lithium. The mechanism through which these symptoms (resembling Raynaud's syndrome) developed is not known. Recovery followed discontinuance.

Serious reactions to long-term therapy: In addition to other possible adverse reactions, the main concern during chronic lithium therapy centers on the kidney function, the thyroid, parathyroid, the bones and skin.

Overdose: Symptoms: The toxic levels for lithium are close to the therapeutic levels. It is therefore important that patients and their families be cautioned to watch for early symptoms of overdosage and to discontinue lithium tablets and inform the physician should they occur. Early signs of toxicity which may occur at serum lithium levels lower than 2 mEq/L were described under Adverse Effects and usually respond to reduction of dosage. Lithium intoxication has been preceded by the appearance or aggravation of the following symptoms: sluggishness, drowsiness, lethargy, coarse tremors or muscle twitchings, loss of appetite, vomiting and diarrhea. Occurrence of these symptoms requires immediate cessation of medication and careful clinical re-assessment of management. Signs and symptoms of lithium intoxication have already been described under Adverse Effects.

Treatment: No specific antidote for lithium poisoning is known. Early symptoms of lithium toxicity can usually be treated by reduction or cessation of dosage of the drug and resumption of the treatment at a lower dose after 24 to 48 hours. In severe cases of lithium poisoning, the first and foremost goal of treatment consists of elimination of this ion from the patient and supportive care.

Recommended treatment consists of: gastric lavage, correction of fluid and electrolyte imbalance and regulation of kidney function. Urea, mannitol and aminophylline all produce significant increases in lithium excretion. Hemodialysis is an effective and rapid means of removing the ion from the severely toxic patient. Infection prophylaxis, regular chest x-ray, and preservation of adequate respiration are essential.

Dosage: Selection of patients and approach to lithium therapy: The results of lithium therapy depend largely on the nature and course of the illness itself, rather than on the symptoms. The selection of patients for long-term treatment requires a clearcut diagnosis of primary affective disorder, the condition for which the stabilizing effects of lithium have been found useful. The variables that have been more consistently associated with response to lithium therapy in patients with a primary affective disorder are: the good quality of remissions with good function and no significant symptomatology during the free intervals between previous episodes of illness; low frequency of episodes, typically 1 or 2 (and not more than 3 or 4) per year; and symptomatology during the acute episodes that meet strict criteria for a primary affective disorder (DSM-III; Research Diagnostic Criteria).

Screening for lithium candidates should include at least a medical history and physical examination with emphasis on the urinary, cardiovascular, gastrointestinal, endocrine and central nervous systems, and the skin. It should also include: routine 24 hour urine volume, serum creatinine, record of weight, an ECG, possibly electrolytes and TSH, and for long-term treatment, creatinine clearance and a urine concentration test. Other examinations and tests should be used when indicated. Monitoring lithium treatment should include, for each visit, mental status, physical examination, weight, 12 hour serum lithium and a check for lithium side effects and compliance. It should also include serum creatinine every 2 months, plasma thyroid hormone and TSH every 6 to 12 months, particularly in female patients, and attention to renal and thyroid function should be maintained throughout, with tests used for baseline screening repeated as required.

The first objective of treatment is to establish an effective and safe daily dosage of lithium, with the aid of standardized 12 hour serum lithium levels maintained within the therapeutic range, as high as necessary for efficacy, and with the patient as much as possible free of significant side effects. Two daily doses should be used initially, at least until the daily dosage is established. The next aim is to move to an optimal dose, which should be as low as possible, consistent with protection against relapse. During follow-up, an adjustment to lower dosages may be required to minimize adverse effects, and a change in the lithium preparation used and/or the frequency of dosing, either towards multiple doses or towards a single dose, may be necessary to handle absorption-related adverse effects or concern over possible renal toxicity. Intermittent lithium treatment in carefully selected patients has been recommended by some lithium experts, but should not be undertaken without careful planning and great caution. The cooperation of patients and relatives is required throughout.

Before deciding on the institution of long-term treatment, it is essential to establish that the patient has clearly responded to a course of stabilizing lithium therapy and that the risk of such therapy is acceptable. Maintaining a patient with a lithium non-responsive condition on long-term therapy poses an unacceptable risk. A decision with regards to long-term therapy can be made during a time-limited trial of lithium therapy with frequent reassessment of outcome. The following are among the factors to be reassessed before a decision is made: careful reconfirmation of the diagnosis of primary affective disorder; the health status of the patient; the side effects of lithium therapy experienced by the patient; and the response to treatment. Assessment of response to treatment is based strictly on firm evidence of relapse prevention during a reasonable trial period, but can be assisted by consideration of the predictors of response outlined above. Great pains should be taken to exclude false responders and false non-responders. It should also be borne in mind that non-responders are more susceptible to the adverse effects of lithium.

Acute Mania: The therapeutic dose for the treatment of acute mania should be based primarily on the patient's clinical condition. It must be individualized for each patient according to blood levels and clinical response. Manic patients usually require serum lithium levels in excess of 1 mEq/L and the dosage should be adjusted to obtain serum levels between 1 and 1.5 mEq/L (in blood samples drawn before the patient has had the first lithium dose of the day).

In properly screened adult patients with good renal function, the suggested initial dosage for acute mania is 1 200 to 1 800 mg (approximately 50 mEq/L) divided into 2 doses and administered at 12 hour intervals. In view of the large variability of renal lithium excretion between individuals, it is suggested that lithium treatment be started at a dose between 600 and 900 mg/day, reaching a level of 1 200 to 1 800 mg/day, in 2 divided doses, on the second day. Depending on the patient's clinical condition, the initial dosage should be adjusted to produce the desired serum lithium level. The weight of the patient should also influence the choice of the initial dose. Lithium should be used cautiously and in reduced doses in the elderly patient, usually in the range of 600 to 1 200 mg/day or less, starting with smaller doses (see also Warnings and Precautions). Serum lithium levels must always be checked carefully and frequently during initiation of treatment, monitored regularly thereafter and should be kept below 1.5 mEq/L.

Maintenance Therapy: After the acute manic episode subsides, usually within a week, the dosage should be rapidly reduced to achieve serum levels between 0.6 and 1.2 mEq/L, since there is evidence of a decreased tolerance to lithium at this time. The average suggested dosage at this stage is 900 mg/day (approximately 25 mEq) administered in a single dose at bedtime, with a range usually between 600 and 1 200 mg/day. If a satisfactory response is not obtained within 14 days, lithium therapy should be discontinued. When the manic attack is controlled, lithium administration should be maintained for the expected duration of the manic phase, since early withdrawal might lead to relapse. Long-term

Duralith (cont'd)

lithium treatment has been found useful for relapse prevention (see Dosage). It is essential to maintain clinical supervision of the patient and to monitor serum lithium levels as required during treatment (see Warnings and Precautions).

Serum lithium levels in uncomplicated cases receiving maintenance therapy during remission should be monitored at least every 2 months.

Patients abnormally sensitive to lithium may exhibit toxic signs at serum levels of 1.0 to 1.4 mEq/L. Elderly patients often respond to reduced dosage and may exhibit signs of toxicity at serum levels ordinarily tolerated by other patients.

Duralith tablets should be swallowed whole or broken in half. They should not be chewed or crushed.

Note: Blood samples for serum lithium determination should be drawn prior to the next dose and when lithium concentrations are relatively stable (i.e. 10 to 14 hours after the previous dose of lithium). Total reliance must not be placed on serum levels alone. Accurate patient evaluation requires both clinical assessment and laboratory analyses.

Supplied: Each round, off-white, sustained-release tablet, scored one side, imprinted with the McNeil logo on the reverse, contains: lithium carbonate 300 mg (8.12 mmol). Nonmedicinal ingredients: aerosil (colloidal silicon), cherry flavor, magnesium stearate and synchron base. Energy: nil. Gluten-, lactose- and tartrazine-free. Bottles of 100. Store between 15 and 30°C.

(Shown in Product Recognition Section)

Reviewed 1999

DURATEARS® NATURALE

Alcon

Petrolatum Compound

Ocular Lubricant

Supplied: Each tube of sterile ointment contains: white petrolatum 94%, mineral oil 3% and anhydrous liquid lanolin. Tubes of 3.5 g.

DURICEF™ Ⓟ

Bristol

Cefadroxil

Antibiotic

Pharmacology: Cefadroxil is a cephalosporin with bactericidal activity. In vitro studies have shown that the antibacterial activity of the cephalosporins results from their ability to inhibit mucopeptide synthesis in the bacterial cell wall.

Pharmacokinetics: Cefadroxil is well absorbed following oral administration with 93% of a 500 mg dose being recovered unchanged in the urine after 24 hours. Absorption of cefadroxil from the gastrointestinal tract is not inhibited by the presence of food.

Approximately 20% of the dose of cefadroxil is bound to serum proteins. The apparent volume of distribution is 14 to 17% of body weight.

The total urinary excretion following single oral doses of cefadroxil has been determined in a number of experiments and the experimental results are summarized in Table I.

Table I—Duricef

Total Urinary Excretion Following Single Oral Doses of Cefadroxil

Dose of Cefadroxil (mg)	Cumulative Urinary Excretion (mg) 0-3 h	3-6 h	6-12 h	Total 0-12 h
500	290	115	4	449
1 000	455	264	111	830

Table II shows various pharmacokinetic values for 500, 1 000 and 2 000 mg doses.

Lower Respiratory Tissue Levels: Cefadroxil was administered to 7 patients as a 500 mg single dose. At 12 hours, the pleural exudate contained cefadroxil at a level of 2.1 μg/mL compared to 0.8 μg/mL in the serum. Table III shows the pleural fluid concentration after 8 and 12 hours following the administered dose.

Table II—Duricef

Pharmacokinetic Parameters in Normal Human Volunteers

Parameter	Dose of Cefadroxil (mg) 500	1 000	2 000
Time to peak concentration; T_{max} (h)	1.28	2.00	2.00
Peak concentration; C_{max} (μg/mL)	14.8	23.63	32.7
Area under the curve; AUC (μg/h/mL)	45.3	94.20	167.42
Half-life (h)	1.34	1.51	—

Table III—Duricef

Pleural Fluid Concentration Following a Single 500 mg Oral Dose of Cefadroxil

Number of Cases	Time (h) Postdose	Cefadroxil Concentration Pleural Fluid (μg/mL)	Serum (μg/mL)
7	8	3.6	3.4
	12	2.1	0.8

In another study the mean pleural exudate and mean serum levels following a single 1 g dose of cefadroxil exhibited a similar pattern 3 to 5 hours postadministration (i.e., the pleural fluid concentration is higher than the serum concentration, see Table IV).

Table IV—Duricef

Measurement of Cefadroxil in Respiratory Tissues and Fluids Following a Single 1 g Dose

Fluid or Tissue	Number of Cases	Time (h) Postdose	Cefadroxil Concentration Fluids (μg/mL) Tissue (μg/g)	Serum (μg/mL)
Sputum Pleural	9	3-4	1.3	Not done
Exudate	4	3-5	11.4	9.4
Lungs	22	2-4	7.4	11.5

Data from Table III and Table IV indicate that tissue and fluid compartments act as a depot for cefadroxil after serum concentrations have diminished.

Renal Impairment: Single 1 000 mg doses of cefadroxil were administered to 20 fasting patients with varying degrees of renal impairment as determined by creatinine clearance [from anuric to 1.76 mL/s/1.73 m² (105.7 mL/min/1.73 m²)].

Blood and urinary concentrations of cefadroxil were monitored for up to 48 hours postadministration. The results of this study show that as creatinine clearance decreases the elimination rate constant also decreases but the half life increases.

In another study, single 1 000 mg doses of cefadroxil were administered to 8 fasting patients with varying degrees of severe renal impairment. Creatinine clearances varied from 0.004 to 0.54 mL/s/1.73 m², (0.24 to 32.35 mL/min/1.73 m²). Blood and urinary concentrations were monitored for up to 48 hours postadministration. A linear inverse correlation between the half-life of cefadroxil and creatinine clearance was observed.

Indications: The treatment of the following infections when caused by susceptible strains of the organisms indicated:

Acute uncomplicated urinary tract infections caused by E. coli, klebsiella species and some strains of P. mirabilis.

Skin and skin structure infections caused by S. aureus and/or group A beta-hemolytic streptococci.

Acute pharyngitis-tonsillitis when caused by group A beta-hemolytic streptococci.

Lower respiratory tract infections, including pneumonia, caused by S. pneumoniae, S. pyogenes (group A-beta hemolytic streptococci), K. pneumoniae and S. aureus.

Appropriate bacteriological studies should be performed prior to and during therapy in order to identify and determine the susceptibility of the causative organism(s).

Contraindications: Patients with a known hypersensitivity to the cephalosporin group of antibiotics.

Warnings: In patients with known hypersensitivity to the penicillins, cephalosporin antibiotics, including cefadroxil, should be administered with great caution. There is clinical and laboratory evidence of cross allergenicity between the penicillin and the cephalosporin groups of antibiotics. There are instances of patients who have had reactions to both classes of antibiotics (including fatal anaphylactoid reactions after parenteral administration).

Cefadroxil should be administered with caution and then only when absolutely necessary to any patient who has a history of some form of allergy, particularly to drugs.

If an allergic reaction to cefadroxil occurs, discontinue the drug. Serious acute hypersensitivity reactions may require emergency treatment measures.

Treatment with broad spectrum antibiotics alters normal flora of the colon and may permit overgrowth of clostridia. Studies indicate that a toxin produced by C. difficile is one primary cause of antibiotic-associated colitis.

Pseudomembranous colitis has been reported with the use of cephalosporins and other broad spectrum antibiotics. Therefore, it is important to consider its diagnosis in patients who develop diarrhea in association with antibiotic use.

Mild cases of colitis may respond to drug discontinuance alone. Moderate to severe cases should be managed with fluid, electrolyte and protein supplementation as indicated. When the colitis is not relieved by drug discontinuance or when it is severe, oral vancomycin is the treatment of choice for antibiotic-associated pseudomembranous colitis. Other causes of colitis should also be considered.

Precautions: A minimum of 10 days treatment is recommended for infections caused by group A beta-hemolytic streptococci.

Patients should be carefully monitored to detect the development of any adverse effect or other manifestations of drug idiosyncrasy. If an allergic reaction to cefadroxil occurs, its administration should be discontinued and the patient treated with the usual agents (e.g., epinephrine, other pressor amines or corticosteroids).

Prolonged use of cefadroxil can result in the overgrowth of nonsusceptible organisms. Careful observation of the patient is essential. If superinfection occurs during therapy, the administration of cefadroxil should be discontinued and appropriate measures taken. If an organism becomes resistant during treatment with cefadroxil alternate therapy should be instituted.

Cefadroxil should be used with caution in the presence of markedly impaired renal function (i.e., a creatinine clearance rate of less than 0.85 mL/s/1.73 m² (50 mL/min/1.73 m²)—see Dosage. In patients with known or suspected renal impairment careful clinical evaluation and appropriate laboratory studies should be performed prior to and during therapy, since cefadroxil can accumulate in serum and tissues.

If cefadroxil is to be used for long-term therapy, hematologic, renal and hepatic functions should be monitored periodically.

Positive direct Coombs' tests have been reported during treatment with the cephalosporin antibiotics. In hematologic studies or in transfusion cross matching procedures, when antiglobulin tests are performed on the minor side or in Coombs testing of newborns whose mothers have received cephalosporin antibiotics before parturition, it should be recognized that a positive Coombs' test may be due to the drug.

During treatment with cefadroxil, a false positive reaction for glucose in the urine may occur with Benedict's or Fehling's solution or with Clinitest tablets, but not with enzyme based tests such as Clinistix or Tes-Tape.

Pregnancy: The safety of cefadroxil in the treatment of infections during pregnancy has not been established. The administration of cefadroxil is not recommended during pregnancy. If, in the opinion of the attending physician, the administration of cefadroxil is considered to be necessary, its use requires that the anticipated benefits be weighed against the possible hazards to the fetus.

Lactation: Cephalosporin antibiotics are excreted in human breast milk, and therefore, would be ingested by the neonate during breast-feeding. Nursing mothers receiving cefadroxil should discontinue breast-feeding.

Adverse Effects: Adverse effects observed during the use of cefadroxil include: Gastrointestinal: The most frequently observed have been nausea and vomiting. The incidence and severity are dose dependent and the latter has been severe enough to warrant cessation of therapy.

Symptoms of pseudomembranous colitis can appear during or after antibiotic treatment. Other reactions reported were abdominal cramps, gastric upset, heartburn, gas and diarrhea. Rarely dyspepsia has been reported.

Hypersensitivity: fever, pruritus, rash, swollen and running eyes, urticaria, eosinophilia, angioedema and positive direct Coombs' test. These reactions usually subside upon discontinuation of the drug. Erythema multiforme, Stevens-Johnson syndrome, serum sickness and anaphylaxis have been reported rarely.

CNS: dizziness, weakness, drowsiness, vertigo, nervousness and headaches.

Miscellaneous: vaginitis, genital pruritus, genital candidiasis, cramps in side and legs, arthralgia, moderate transient neutropenia and elevations in BUN, alkaline phosphatase and AST.

In common with other cephalosporins, thrombocytopenia and agranulocytosis have been reported rarely.

Overdose: Symptoms and Treatment: Data from a study of children under 6 years of age who had ingested a maximum of 250 mg/kg of penicillin or a cephalosporin derivative suggested that ingestion of less than 250 mg/kg of cephalosporins (i.e., 5 to 10 times recommended dose) is not associated with significant outcomes. No treatment is required other than general support and observation. During the 72-hour evaluation period, most of the children remained asymptomatic. Gastrointestinal disturbances and rash were reported in some children. For amounts greater than 250 mg/kg, induce gastric emptying (emesis induction or gastric lavage).

For information on removal of drug by hemodialysis, see Dosage.

Dosage: Cefadroxil is administered orally and may be taken without regard to meals.

The incidence and severity of gastrointestinal complaints is dose dependent. Administration with food may be helpful to diminish potential intestinal complaints.

A minimum of 10 days treatment is recommended for infections caused by group A beta-hemolytic streptococci.

Adults: Normal Renal Function: The recommended dose is 1 to 2 g/day.

Urinary Tract Infections: The recommended daily dose is 1 or 2 g. This may be given as a single dose at bedtime or divided into 500 mg to 1 g doses for twice a day administration (every 12 hours). The usual duration of therapy is 10 days. While shorter or longer courses may be appropriate for some patients, cefadroxil should be administered for a sufficient period of time to render the urine sterile. The sterility of the urine should be re-evaluated 2 to 4 weeks after cessation of therapy.

Acute Pharyngitis and Tonsillitis: The recommended dose is 1 g/day in single (daily) or divided doses (b.i.d.). Treatment should be for a minimum of 10 days and continued for a minimum of 48 to 72 hours beyond the time that the patient becomes asymptomatic or evidence of bacterial eradication has been obtained.

Lower Respiratory Tract Infections: The recommended dose is 500 mg to 1 g twice daily (every 12 hours).

Skin and Skin Structure Infections: 1 g daily in a single dose.

Impaired Renal Function: The dosage of cefadroxil should be adjusted according to creatinine clearance rates to prevent drug accumulation.

In adults, the dose is 1 g for a patient with normal renal function (see above) and the maintenance dose (based on the creatinine clearance rate) is 500 mg at the time intervals listed in Table V.

Table V—Duricef

Maintenance Dose Interval

Creatinine Clearance (mL/s/1.73 m²)	Creatinine Clearance (mL/min/1.73 m²)	Dose Interval (Hours)
0-0.17	0-10	36
0.17-0.43	10-25	24
0.43-0.85	25-50	12

Patients with creatinine clearance rates greater than 50 mL/min/1.73 m² may be dosed as for those patients with normal renal function.

In 5 adult anuric patients, it was demonstrated that an average of 63% of a 1 g oral dose is extracted from the body during a 6- to 8-hour hemodialysis session.

Children: There is clinical experience for the treatment of urinary tract, and integumentary infections and acute pharyngitis, tonsillitis in children 6 weeks of age and over.

Clinical studies for the treatment of lower respiratory tract infections have been carried out in children 1 year of age and over.

Recommended dose is 30 mg/kg/day in 2 equally divided doses given for 10 days.

Supplied: Each maroon and white hard gelatin capsule contains: cefadroxil USP 500 mg as cefadroxil monohydrate. Nonmedicinal ingredients: magnesium stearate. May contain lactose and silicon dioxide; capsule shell: D&C yellow No. 10 and red No. 33, FD&C blue No. 1 and red No. 3, gelatin, printing ink and titanium dioxide. Bottles of 50 and 100. Store at controlled room temperature (15 to 30°C).

(Shown in Product Recognition Section)

Reviewed 1999

DUVOID® Ⓟ

Roberts

Bethanechol Chloride

Parasympathomimetic Agent

Pharmacology: Bethanechol acts principally by producing the effects of stimulation of the parasympathetic nervous system. It increases the tone of the detrusor urinae muscle, usually producing a contraction sufficiently strong to initiate micturition and empty the bladder. It stimulates gastric motility, increases gastric tone, and often restores rhythmic peristalsis.

Stimulation of the parasympathetic nervous system releases acetylcholine at the nerve endings. When spontaneous stimulation is reduced and therapeutic intervention is required, acetylcholine can be given, but it is rapidly hydrolyzed by cholinesterase, and its effects are transient. Bethanechol is not destroyed by cholinesterase and its effects are more prolonged and predictable than those of acetylcholine.

It has predominant muscarinic action and only feeble nicotinic action. Doses that stimulate micturition and defecation and increase peristalsis do not ordinarily stimulate ganglia or voluntary muscles. Therapeutic test doses in normal human subjects have little effect on heart rate, blood pressure, or peripheral circulation.

Indications: The treatment of acute postoperative and postpartum nonobstructive (functional) urinary retention and for neurogenic atony of the urinary bladder with retention.

Contraindications: Hyperthyroidism, pregnancy, lactation, peptic ulcer, latent or active bronchial asthma, pronounced bradycardia or hypotension, vasomotor instability, coronary artery disease, epilepsy, parkinsonism.

Should not be employed when the strength or integrity of the gastrointestinal or bladder wall is in question, or in the presence of mechanical obstruction; when increased muscular activity of the gastrointestinal tract or urinary bladder might prove harmful, as following recent urinary bladder surgery, gastrointestinal resection and anastomosis, or when there is possible gastrointestinal obstruction; in bladder neck obstruction, spastic gastrointestinal disturbances, acute inflammatory lesions of the gastrointestinal tract, or peritonitis; or in marked vagotonia.

Precautions: Special care and consideration are required when bethanechol is administered to patients being treated concomitantly with other drugs with which pharmacologic interactions may occur. Examples of drugs with potentials for such interactions are: quinidine and procainamide, which may antagonize cholinergic effects; cholinergic drugs, particularly cholinesterase inhibitors, where additive effects may occur. When administered to patients receiving ganglionic blocking compounds a critical fall in blood pressure may occur which usually is preceded by severe abdominal symptoms.

In urinary retention, if the sphincter fails to relax as bethanechol contracts the bladder, urine may be forced up the ureter into the kidney pelvis. If there is bacteriuria, this may cause reflux infection.

Adverse Effects: Abdominal discomfort, salivation, flushing of the skin ("hot feeling"), sweating.

Large doses more commonly result in effects of parasympathetic stimulation, such as malaise, headache, sensation of heat about the face, flushing, colicky pain, diarrhea, nausea and belching, abdominal cramps, borborygmi, asthmatic attacks and fall in blood pressure.

Overdose: Symptoms: Symptoms of an overdose are an extension of the adverse effects. In rare instances violent symptoms of cholinergic over stimulation including fall in blood pressure, circulatory collapse, cardiac arrest, shock, severe abdominal cramps with bloody diarrhea and possibly severe bronchospasm may occur.

Treatment: Atropine is a specific antidote. A syringe containing a dose for adults of 600 µg or more of atropine sulfate should always be available to treat symptoms of toxicity. Use proportionally smaller amounts for children. S.C. injection is preferred except in emergencies; when the i.v. route may be employed. Administer atropine, followed by general supportive and symptomatic treatment.

Dosage: Must be individualized, depending on the type and severity of the condition to be treated. It is preferable to give the drug when the stomach is empty. If taken soon after eating, nausea and vomiting may occur. The usual adult oral dosage is 10 to 50 mg, 3 or 4 times a day. The minimum effective dose is determined by giving 5 to 10 mg initially and repeating the same amount at hourly intervals until a satisfactory response occurs or a maximum of 50 mg has been given. The drug's effects appear within 60 to 90 minutes and persist for up to 6 hours. Individual doses should therefore, be spaced at least 6 hours apart.

Supplied: 10 mg: Each pale orange, flat, beveled, round tablet, bisected and "10" debossed on one side, contains: bethanechol chloride 10 mg. Bisulfite-, gluten-, lactose-, paraben-, sodium- and tartrazine-free. Bottles of 100.

25 mg: Each white, flat, beveled, round tablet, bisected and "25" debossed on one side, contains: bethanechol chloride 25 mg. Bisulfite-, gluten-, lactose-, paraben-, sodium- and tartrazine-free. Bottles of 100.

50 mg: Each tan, flat, beveled, round tablet, bisected and "50" debossed on one side, contains: bethanechol chloride 50 mg. Bisulfite-, gluten-, lactose-, paraben-, sodium- and tartrazine-free. Bottles of 100.

Store below 40°C. Keep container tightly closed.

(Shown in Product Recognition Section)

DYAZIDE® Ⓟ

SmithKline Beecham

Triamterene—Hydrochlorothiazide

Diuretic—Antihypertensive

Pharmacology: Dyazide is a combination of 2 diuretics with different but complementary modes of action.

Diuretic activity following a single dose is evident within the first hour, reaches a peak at 2 to 3 hours, and tapers off during the subsequent 7 to 9 hours.

Because of the potassium-conserving effect of its triamterene component, Dyazide reduces the risk of hypokalemia, seen sometimes with other diuretics. The need for potassium supplements is virtually eliminated with the use of Dyazide. Hypochloremic alkalosis, sometimes a problem with hydrochlorothiazide alone, has not been reported with Dyazide.

Hydrochlorothiazide: The hydrochlorothiazide component blocks reabsorption of sodium (and attendant chloride anions) and thereby increases the quantity of sodium traversing the distal tubule and the volume of water excreted. A portion of the additional sodium presented to the distal tubule is exchanged there for potassium and hydrogen ions. With continued use of hydrochlorothiazide and depletion of sodium, compensatory mechanisms tend to increase this exchange and may produce excessive loss of potassium, hydrogen and chloride ions.

Hydrochlorothiazide also decreases the excretion of calcium and uric acid; it may increase the excretion of iodide and may reduce glomerular filtration rate. The exact mechanism of the antihypertensive effect of hydrochlorothiazide is not known.

Triamterene: The triamterene component of Dyazide exerts its diuretic effect on the distal renal tubule to inhibit the reabsorption of sodium in exchange for potassium and hydrogen ions. This natriuretic activity is limited by the amount of sodium reaching its site of action.

Although triamterene blocks the increase in this exchange, which is stimulated by mineralocorticoids (chiefly aldosterone), its action takes place through a direct effect on the renal tubule and not by competitive antagonism of aldosterone activity. This action of triamterene is not directly related to the level of aldosterone secretion, since it can be demonstrated in adrenalectomized rats and in patients with Addison's disease.

By inhibiting the distal tubular exchange mechanism, triamterene maintains or increases the sodium excretion and reduces the loss of potassium, hydrogen, and chloride ions induced by hydrochlorothiazide. As with hydrochlorothiazide, triamterene may reduce glomerular filtration and renal plasma flow. Via this mechanism it may reduce uric acid excretion although it has no tubular effect on uric acid reabsorption or secretion. Triamterene does not affect calcium secretion. No predictable antihypertensive effect has been demonstrated for triamterene.

Indications: The treatment of edema associated with congestive heart failure, hepatic cirrhosis and the nephrotic syndrome; in corticosteroid edema; and in idiopathic edema. May also be used in patients whose response to other diuretic therapy is inadequate.

The treatment of mild to moderate hypertension in patients who have developed hypokalemia while on thiazide and thiazide-like diuretics alone, and in patients in whom potassium depletion is considered especially dangerous (e.g. digitalized patients). Medical opinion is not unanimous regarding the incidence and/or clinical significance of hypokalemia occurring among hypertensive patients treated with thiazide and thiazide-like diuretics alone, and concerning the use of potassium-sparing combinations as routine therapy in hypertension.

Dyazide (cont'd)

Triamterene alone has little or no antihypertensive effect. The usefulness of Dyazide in hypertension derives from the antihypertensive effect of the hydrochlorothiazide component and the potassium-conserving effect of triamterene.

Contraindications: Combination therapy with other potassium-sparing agents such as spironolactone or amiloride. Severe or progressive renal dysfunction, including oliguria and progressively increasing azotemia, with the possible exception of nephrosis. Severe or progressive hepatic dysfunction. Hypersensitivity to either component or to sulfonamide-derived drugs. Patients who develop hyperkalemia while on the drug. Nursing mothers. Patients with pre-existing elevated serum potassium, as is sometimes seen in patients with impaired renal function or azotemia.

Warnings: Hyperkalemia: Abnormal elevation of serum potassium, though uncommon, is potentially the most severe electrolyte disturbance with Dyazide therapy. Hyperkalemia (>5.4 mEq/L) has been reported ranging in incidence from 4% in patients less than 60 years of age to 12% in patients 60 years and older, with an overall incidence of less than 8%. Hyperkalemia has been reported to be associated with cardiac irregularities. Accordingly, serum potassium determinations should be performed regularly during the course of therapy. This is particularly important in the treatment of patients with suspected or confirmed renal insufficiency such as elderly or diabetic patients. In those patients who develop hyperkalemia, Dyazide should be withdrawn and a thiazide alone substituted.

Potassium supplementation, either in the form of medication or as a potassium-rich diet, should not be used in conjunction with Dyazide since hyperkalemia may result.

Use of Dyazide in patients receiving an angiotensin converting enzyme inhibitor may lead to significant increases in serum potassium. Therefore, such combination of drugs should be given only to patients with documented hypokalemia, and with caution and frequent monitoring of serum potassium.

Hypokalemia: Because of the potassium-conserving effect of triamterene, hypokalemia is a less common occurrence with the use of Dyazide than with thiazides alone but may occur in some cases when the triamterene component is unable to completely compensate for the potassium-wasting effect of the hydrochlorothiazide component or the disease.

Should hypokalemia develop, corrective measures should be taken such as potassium supplementation or increased dietary intake of potassium-rich foods. Institute such measures cautiously with frequent determinations of serum potassium levels. If laboratory determinations reveal an abnormal elevation of serum potassium, discontinue corrective measures immediately, discontinue Dyazide and substitute a thiazide diuretic alone until potassium levels return to normal.

The myocardial effects of digitalis may be exaggerated in patients with hypokalemia. In these patients, signs of digitalis intoxication may be produced by previously tolerated doses of digitalis.

Renal Stones: The triamterene component of Dyazide has been found in renal stones in association with the other usual calculus components. This should be taken into consideration especially in those patients with histories of renal stones.

Precautions: Pertinent laboratory data such as serum potassium, BUN and ECGs should be checked periodically when using Dyazide, especially in elderly patients, in persons with suspected or confirmed renal insufficiency, in diabetics, and in those patients who have developed hyperkalemia during a previous course of therapy with the drug. (Blood samples require careful handling to prevent hemolysis on standing, and resulting false serum potassium readings.)

Patients should be observed regularly for the possible occurrence of electrolyte imbalance, blood dyscrasias, liver damage, or other idiosyncratic reactions. Appropriate laboratory studies should be done as required.

Electrolyte imbalance: Since Dyazide is a combination of 2 potent diuretics, the possibility of electrolyte imbalance should be kept in mind when using high doses for prolonged periods or in patients on a salt-restricted diet.

Electrolyte imbalance, often encountered in such diseases as heart failure, renal disease or cirrhosis of the liver, may be aggravated or caused independently by any diuretic agent, including Dyazide. Signs and symptoms include dryness of the mouth, thirst, weakness, lethargy, drowsiness, restlessness, muscle pain or cramps, muscular fatigue, hypotension, oliguria, tachycardia and gastrointestinal symptoms.

The triamterene component of Dyazide may cause a decrease in alkali reserve, with the possibility of metabolic acidosis.

Blood Dyscrasias: Rare cases of blood dycrasias (agranulocytosis, aplastic anemia, leukopenia, thrombocytopenia) have been reported with both triamterene and the thiazides. Cirrhotics with splenomegaly, by the nature of their illness, may have marked variations in their blood pictures—including thrombocyte and leukocyte levels—which are not related to drug therapy; therefore periodic blood studies are recommended in these patients.

The triamterene component of Dyazide is a weak folic acid antagonist; it may contribute to the appearance of megaloblastosis in cases where folic acid stores are depleted.

Liver: Thiazides should be used with caution in patients with impaired hepatic function. They can precipitate hepatic coma in patients with severe liver disease. Potassium depletion induced by the thiazide may be important in this connection. Administer Dyazide cautiously and be alert for early signs of impending coma such as confusion, drowsiness and tremor; if mental confusion appears discontinue Dyazide for a few days. Attention must be given to other factors that may precipitate hepatic coma, such as blood in the gastrointestinal tract or preexisting potassium depletion.

Blood Chemistry: Dyazide may produce an elevated blood urea nitrogen level, creatinine level, or both. This apparently is secondary to a reversible reduction of glomerular filtration rate or a depletion of intravascular fluid volume (prerenal azotemia) rather than renal toxicity; levels return to normal when Dyazide is discontinued. Elevated levels are seldom seen with every-other-day therapy. If azotemia increases, discontinue Dyazide.

Slight elevations in serum transaminase (AST, ALT), levels sometimes accompany the administration of Dyazide.

Endocrine: Dyazide, because of its hydrochlorothiazide component, may cause hyperglycemia and glycosuria and may alter insulin requirements in diabetes.

Diabetes mellitus which has been latent may become manifest during thiazide administration.

Hyperuricemia may be observed with possible occurrence of gout. Caution is necessary in treating patients with hyperuricemia or a history of gout.

Thiazides may decrease serum PBI levels without signs of thyroid disturbance.

Calcium excretion is decreased by thiazides. Pathological changes in the parathyroid glands with hypercalcemia and hypophosphatemia have been reported in a few patients on prolonged thiazide therapy. The common complications of hyperparathyroidism such as renal lithiasis, bone resorption and peptic ulceration have not been seen. Thiazides should be discontinued before carrying out tests for parathyroid function.

Other Conditions: Sensitivity reactions may occur in patients with or without a history of allergy or bronchial asthma.

Sulfonamide derivatives, including thiazides, have been reported to exacerbate or activate systemic lupus erythematosus.

The antihypertensive effects of Dyazide may be enhanced in the post-sympathectomy patient.

<u>*Drug Interactions:*</u> Dyazide may add to or potentiate the action of other antihypertensive agents. The use of Dyazide with another antihypertensive drug requires reduced dosage of the latter agent. When Dyazide is added to another antihypertensive already being used, the dose of the other antihypertensive drug should be reduced at least by half, particularly if it is a ganglionic blocking agent. Subsequent adjustment of dosage should be made as required.

Thiazides have been shown to decrease arterial responsiveness to norepinephrine (an effect attributed to loss of sodium). This diminution is not sufficient to preclude effectiveness of the pressor agent for therapeutic use.

Thiazides have also been shown to increase the paralyzing effect of non-depolarizing muscle relaxants such as tubocurarine (an effect attributed to loss of potassium); consequently caution should be observed in patients undergoing surgery.

Lithium generally should not be given with diuretics because they reduce its renal clearance and increase the risk of lithium toxicity. Read circulars for lithium preparations before use of such concomitant therapy with Dyazide.

Concurrent use of amphotericin B or corticosteroids or corticotropin (ACTH) with thiazides may intensify electrolyte imbalance, particularly hypokalemia, although the presence of triamterene minimizes the hypokalemic effects.

The effects of oral anticoagulants may be decreased when used concurrently with thiazides; dosage adjustments may be necessary.

Caution is advised in administering nonsteroidal anti-inflammatory agents with Dyazide. A possible interaction resulting in acute renal failure has been reported in a few patients on Dyazide when treated with indomethacin, a nonsteroidal anti-inflammatory agent.

The triamterene component of Dyazide and quinidine have similar fluorescence spectra; thus, Dyazide will interfere with the fluorescent measurement of quinidine.

Concurrent use with chlorpropamide may increase the risk of severe hyponatremia.

Pregnancy: Reproduction studies in animals and clinical use in pregnant patients have produced no evidence of fetal abnormalities due to Dyazide. However, thiazides have been reported to cross the placental barrier and to appear in cord blood. This may result in fetal or neonatal hyperbilirubinemia, thrombocytopenia, altered carbohydrate metabolism and possible other adverse reactions that have occurred in the adult. Therefore, Dyazide should be used in pregnant patients only when, in the judgement of the physician, its use is deemed necessary for the welfare of the patient.

Lactation: Thiazides appear and triamterene may appear in breast milk. If use of Dyazide is deemed essential, the patient should stop nursing (see Contraindications).

Children: Adequate information on the use of Dyazide in children is not available.

Adverse Effects: The following adverse reactions have been associated with the use of thiazide diuretics or triamterene:

Gastrointestinal: dry mouth, anorexia, gastric irritation, nausea, vomiting, diarrhea, constipation, jaundice (intrahepatic cholestatic), pancreatitis, sialadenitis. Nausea can usually be prevented by giving the drug after meals. It should be noted that symptoms of nausea and vomiting can also be indicative of electrolyte imbalance (see Precautions).

CNS: dizziness, vertigo, paresthesias, headache, xanthopsia.

Dermatologic-Hypersensitivity: fever, purpura, anaphylaxis, photosensitivity, rash, urticaria, necrotizing angiitis (vasculitis).

Hematologic: agranulocytosis, aplastic anemia, leukopenia, thrombocytopenia.

Cardiovascular: orthostatic hypotension (which may be potentiated by alcohol, barbiturates, or narcotics), arrhythmia.

Renal: Triamterene has been reported in higher doses to increase the incidence of renal stones. Rare cases of interstitial nephritis have been reported with the use of Dyazide.

Electrolyte imbalance: (see Precautions).

Miscellaneous: glycosuria, hyperglycemia, hyperuricemia; muscle cramps, weakness; restlessness, transient blurred vision; allergic pneumonitis; rare cases of impotence (causal relationship not established).

In rare instances, newborns, whose mothers had received thiazides during pregnancy, have developed thrombocytopenia or pancreatitis.

Overdose: Electrolyte imbalance is the major concern, with particular attention to possible hyperkalemia.

Symptoms: Symptoms reported include polyuria, nausea, vomiting, weakness, lassitude, hypotension, fever, flushed face and hyperactive deep tendon reflexes.

Treatment: There is no specific antidote. Treatment should be symptomatic and supportive. Induce immediate evacuation of the stomach through emesis and gastric lavage. Careful evaluation of the electrolyte pattern and fluid balance should be made. If profound hypotension occurs, pressor agents such as norepinephrine may be used with the usual measures to maintain blood pressure levels.

Dosage: Dyazide should be taken after an adequate meal.

Adults: Edema: The usual starting dosage is 1 tablet twice daily after meals. When dry weight is reached, maintenance dosage of 1 tablet daily will usually suffice. In some patients, 1 tablet every other day may be indicated.

Hypertension: The usual starting dosage is 1 tablet twice daily after meals. Subsequently, dosage may be increased or decreased according to patient's need. If 2 or more tablets per day are needed they should be given in divided doses.

Maximum daily dosage should not exceed 4 tablets, and at this dosage the incidence of adverse effects may increase.

When changing from other diuretics or antihypertensives to Dyazide, stop the previous therapy and start Dyazide at the recommended dosage. Since Dyazide has an antihypertensive effect, its use with another antihypertensive drug requires reduced dosage of the latter agent. When Dyazide is added to another antihypertensive already being used, reduce the dose of the other antihypertensive drug at least by half particularly if it is a ganglionic blocking agent. Make subsequent dosage adjustment as required.

Children: Adequate information on Dyazide's use in children is not available.

Supplied: Each round, flat, bevel-edged, peach-colored, scored, compressed tablet, debossed SKF, contains: triamterene 50 mg and hydrochlorothiazide 25 mg. Nonmedicinal ingredients: FD&C yellow no. 6, magnesium stearate, povidone, sodium lauryl sulfate, sterotex powder and wheat starch. Plastic securitainers of 1 000.

(Shown in Product Recognition Section)

Reviewed 1999

DYCHOLIUM®

Novartis Consumer Health

Dehydrocholic Acid

Hydrocholeretic

Supplied: Each white, scored tablet contains: dehydrocholic acid 300 mg. Nonmedicinal ingredients: cornstarch, magnesium stearate, methylcellulose and water. Tartrazine-free. Boxes of 21 blister packaged tablets and bottles of 500.

DYRENIUM® Ⓟ

SmithKline Beecham

Triamterene

Diuretic

Pharmacology: Triamterene exerts its diuretic effect on the distal renal tubule to inhibit the reabsorption of sodium in exchange for potassium and hydrogen ions. This natriuretic activity is limited by the amount of sodium reaching its site of action.

Although triamterene blocks the increase in this exchange, which is stimulated by mineralocorticoids (chiefly aldosterone), its action takes place through a direct effect on the renal tubule and not by competitive antagonism of aldosterone activity. This action of triamterene is not directly related to the level of aldosterone secretion, since it can be demonstrated in adrenalectomized rats and in patients with Addison's disease.

By inhibiting the distal tubular exchange mechanism, triamterene maintains or increases the sodium excretion and reduces the loss of potassium, hydrogen, and chloride ions. Triamterene may reduce glomerular filtration and renal plasma flow. Via this mechanism it may reduce uric acid excretion although it has no tubular effect on uric acid reabsorption or secretion. Triamterene does not affect calcium secretion.

Diuretic activity following a single dose is evident within the first hour, reaches a peak at 2 to 3 hours, and tapers off during the subsequent 7 to 9 hours.

Indications: The treatment of edema associated with congestive heart failure, hepatic cirrhosis, nephrotic syndrome; also in idiopathic edema, steroid- and estrogen-induced edema and edema due to secondary hyperaldosteronism. May be useful when patients prove resistant or only partially responsive to other diuretics and may be given concurrently with other diuretics either for its added diuretic effect or for its potassium conserving potential. The use of triamterene for potassium conservation is indicated in patients who have developed hypokalemia while on diuretic therapy, or in those patients in whom potassium depletion is considered especially dangerous (e.g., digitalized patients). Triamterene has been used most frequently with thiazides. Triamterene itself has little or no antihypertensive effect.

Contraindications: Severe or progressive renal dysfunction including oliguria and progressively increasing azotemia, with the possible exception of nephrosis. Severe or progressive hepatic dysfunction. Hypersensitivity to triamterene. Nursing mothers.

Triamterene should not be used in patients who develop hyperkalemia while on the drug; or in patients receiving other potassium-sparing agents such as spironolactone, amiloride or angiotensin converting enzyme inhibitors; nor should it be used in patients with preexisting elevated serum potassium, as is sometimes seen in patients with impaired renal function or azotemia.

Warnings: Hyperkalemia: Abnormal elevation of serum potassium, though uncommon is potentially the most severe electrolyte disturbance with Dyrenium therapy. When used in combination with a thiazide diuretic, hyperkalemia (>5.4 mEq/L) has been reported ranging from 4% in patients less than 60 years of age to 12% in patients 60 years and older, with an overall incidence of less than 8%. Hyperkalemia has been reported to be associated with cardiac irregularities. Accordingly, serum potassium determinations should be performed regularly during the course of therapy. This is particularly important in the treatment of patients with suspected or confirmed renal insufficiency such as elderly or diabetic patients. In those patients who develop hyperkalemia, triamterene should be withdrawn.

Potassium supplementation, either in the form of medication or as a potassium-rich diet, should not be used in conjunction with triamterene since hyperkalemia may result.

Hyperkalemia rarely occurs in patients with adequate urinary output, but it is a possibility if large doses of triamterene are administered for prolonged periods or in patients on a salt-restricted diet. The use of full doses of a diuretic when salt intake is restricted can result in a low-salt syndrome. If hyperkalemia is observed, triamterene should be withdrawn.

Because triamterene conserves potassium, it has been theorized that in patients who have received intensive therapy or been given the drug for prolonged periods, a rebound kaliuresis could occur upon abrupt withdrawal. In such patients, withdrawal of triamterene should be gradual.

Hypokalemia: Because of the potassium-conserving effect of triamterene, hypokalemia is a less common occurrence with the use of triamterene than with non-potassium sparing diuretics.

The myocardial effects of digitalis may be exaggerated in patients with hypokalemia. In these patients, signs of digitalis intoxication may be produced by previously tolerated doses of digitalis.

Renal Stones: Triamterene has been found in renal stones in association with the other usual calculus components. This should be taken into consideration especially in those patients with histories of renal stones.

Precautions: Pertinent laboratory data such as serum potassium, BUN and electrocardiograms should be checked periodically when using triamterene, especially in elderly patients, in persons with suspected or confirmed renal insufficiency, in diabetics, and in those patients who have developed hyperkalemia during a previous course of therapy with the drug. (Blood samples require careful handling to prevent hemolysis on standing, and resulting false serum potassium readings).

Patients should be observed regularly for the possible occurrence of electrolyte imbalance, blood dyscrasias, liver damage or other idiosyncratic reactions. Appropriate laboratory studies should be done as required.

Electrolyte imbalance: Often encountered in such diseases as heart failure, renal disease or cirrhosis of the liver, electrolyte imbalance may be aggravated or caused independently by any diuretic agent, including triamterene. Signs and symptoms include dryness of the mouth, thirst, weakness, lethargy, drowsiness, restlessness, muscle pain or cramps, muscular fatigue, hypotension, oliguria, tachycardia and gastrointestinal symptoms.

Triamterene may cause a decrease in alkali reserve, with the possibilty of metabolic acidosis.

Blood Dyscrasias: Rare cases of blood dyscrasias (agranulocytosis, aplastic anemia, leukopenia, thrombocytopenia) have been reported with triamterene. Cirrhotics with splenomegaly, by the nature of their illness, may have marked variations in their blood pictures—including thrombocyte and leukocyte levels—which are not related to drug therapy; therefore, periodic blood studies are recommended in these patients.

Triamterene is a weak folic acid antagonist; it may contribute to the appearance of megaloblastosis in cases where folic acid stores are depleted.

Liver: Hepatic coma may result from electrolyte imbalance in acutely ill cirrhotic patients. As with the use of any diuretic, the physician should proceed cautiously in such patients and be alert for early signs of impending coma such as confusion, drowsiness and tremor.

Blood Chemistry: Triamterene may produce an elevated blood urea nitrogen level, creatinine level, or both. This apparently is secondary to a reversible reduction of glomerular filtration rate or a depletion of intravascular fluid volume (prerenal azotemia) rather than renal toxicity; levels return to normal when Triamterene is discontinued. Elevated levels are seldom seen with every-other-day therapy. If azotemia increases, discontinue triamterene.

Slight elevations in serum transaminase (AST, ALT) levels sometimes accompany the administration of triamterene.

Endocrine: Triamterene appears to have little or no effect on serum uric acid levels or carbohydrate metabolism although some elevation of uric acid was seen in persons predisposed to gouty arthritis. Present experience suggests it is unlikely that triamterene therapy will precipitate either gout or diabetes, but caution is required in susceptible patients.

Other Conditions: Sensitivity reactions may occur in patients with or without a history of allergy or bronchial asthma.

Drug Interactions: Although triamterene has not proved to be a consistent antihypertensive agent, the physician should be aware of a possible lowering of blood pressure. Concomitant use with antihypertensive drugs may result in an additive effect.

Lithium generally should not be given with diuretics because they reduce its renal clearance and increase the risk of lithium toxicity. Read circulars for lithium preparations before use of such concomitant therapy with triamterene.

Caution is advised in administering nonsteroidal anti-inflammatory agents with triamterene. A possible interaction resulting in acute renal failure has been reported in a few subjects when indomethacin, a nonsteroidal anti-inflammatory agent, was given with triamterene.

Triamterene and quinidine have similar fluorescence spectra; thus, triamterene will interfere with the fluorescent measurement of quinidine.

Pregnancy: Reproduction studies in animals have produced no evidence of drug-induced fetal abnormalities. However, as with any drug, care should be observed when prescribing Triamterene for pregnant patients or women of childbearing age. Its safety in pregnancy has not yet been fully established, and therefore it should be used only when, in the judgment of the physician, its use is deemed necessary for the welfare of the patient.

Lactation: Triamterene may appear in breast milk. If its use is deemed essential, the patient should stop nursing (see Contraindications).

Children: Adequate information on the use of triamterene in children is not available.

Adverse Effects: The following adverse reactions have been associated with the use of triamterene:

Gastrointestinal: dry mouth, anorexia, gastric irritation, nausea, vomiting, diarrhea, constipation, jaundice (intrahepatic cholestatic), pancreatitis, sialadenitis. Nausea can usually be prevented by giving the drug after meals. It should be noted that symptoms of nausea and vomiting can also be indicative of electrolyte imbalance (see Precautions).

CNS: dizziness, vertigo, paresthesias, headache, xanthopsia.

Dermatologic-Hypersensitivity: fever, purpura, anaphylaxis, photosensitivity, rash, urticaria, necrotizing angiitis (vasculitis).

Hematologic: agranulocytosis, aplastic anemia, leukopenia, thrombocytopenia.

Cardiovascular: orthostatic hypotension (which may be potentiated by alcohol, barbiturates, or narcotics).

Renal: Triamterene has been found in renal stones in association with the other usual components.

Electrolyte imbalance: (see Precautions).

Miscellaneous: glycosuria, hyperglycemia, hyperuricemia; muscle cramps, weakness, restlessness, transient blurred vision; allergic pneumonitis; rare cases of impotence (causal relationship not established).

Overdose: Electrolyte imbalance is the major concern, with particular attention to possible hyperkalemia.

Symptoms: Symptoms reported include polyuria, nausea, vomiting, weakness, lassitude, hypotension, fever, flushed face and hyperactive deep tendon reflexes.

Treatment: There is no specific antidote. Treatment should be symptomatic and supportive. Immediate evacuation of the stomach should be induced through emesis or gastric lavage. Careful evaluation of the electrolyte pattern and fluid balance should be made. If profound hypotension occurs, pressor agents such as norepinephrine may be used along with the usual measures to maintain blood pressure levels.

Although triamterene is largely protein-bound (approximately 67%), dialysis may be of some benefit in cases of overdosage.

Dosage: It is recommended that triamterene be taken after an adequate meal.

Adults: Adult dosage should be adjusted according to the needs of the individual patient and his response to the drug. When used alone as mild diuretic, the usual starting dosage is 100 mg twice daily after meals. When adequate control of edema has been achieved, the dosage may be reduced, e.g., 100 mg daily; in some patients 100 mg every other day may suffice. Maximum daily dosage should not exceed 300 mg; at this dosage the incidence of side effects may increase.

Most patients will respond to triamterene during the first day of treatment. Maximum therapeutic effect, however, may not be seen for several days. (Triamterene-100 tablets are suitable for use as a mild diuretic.)

When changing from other diuretics to triamterene simply stop the previous therapy and start triamterene at the recommended dosage.

When triamterene is given concomitantly with another diuretic, total dosage of each agent should be lowered initially and then adjusted to the patient's needs. Triamterene has

Dyrenium (cont'd)

been used most frequently with thiazides. (Triamterene-50 tablets are particularly suitable for this use.)

When triamterene is added to existing diuretic therapy, or when patients are switched to triamterene from other diuretics, all potassium supplementation should be discontinued, and serum potassium determinations should be made periodically.

Children: Adequate information on the use of triamterene in children is not available.

Supplied: Dyrenium-50: Each round, flat, beveled-edged, yellow, compressed tablet, debossed SKF H11, contains: triamterene 50 mg. Nonmedicinal ingredients: magnesium stearate, povidone, silica, sodium lauryl sulfate and wheat starch. Bottles of 100.

Dyrenium-100: Each round, flat, beveled-edged, yellow, compressed tablet, debossed SKF H10, contains: triamterene 100 mg. Nonmedicinal ingredients: magnesium stearate, povidone, silica, sodium lauryl sulfate and wheat starch. Bottles of 100.

(Shown in Product Recognition Section)

New IN HIV THERAPY

Pr VIRACEPT™
nelfinavir mesylate

POTENT PROTEASE INHIBITION
that's easy to live with

Potent Protease Inhibition... Indicated for the treatment of HIV infection in combination with reverse transcriptase inhibitor (RTI) nucleoside analogues. VIRACEPT provides potent antiretroviral efficacy for adults and children ≥2. In clinical studies, a 99% (2.28 log_{10}) mean decrease in HIV RNA at 48 weeks was reported in 72 patients receiving VIRACEPT in combination therapy with AZT and 3TC.[1]

Easy to live with... With no strict q8h dosing schedule or difficult mealtime restrictions, VIRACEPT is taken tid with meals or light snacks. This dosing flexibility combined with a generally well tolerated medication help make VIRACEPT easy to live with.[1]

Diarrhea of moderate or greater intensity occurred in 20% of patients receiving VIRACEPT 750 mg in combination with AZT and 3TC[1] - 1.6% of patients discontinued therapy due to diarrhea[2] - 4.0 % due to total adverse events.[2] As with all protease inhibitors, drug interactions must be carefully managed, please see drug interactions in the VIRACEPT Product Monograph.

For more information about VIRACEPT, call 1-888-545-5314.
www.agouron.com

Agouron.
Pharmaceuticals Canada Inc.

PAAB

Pr **estrogel**

17ß-estradiol 0.06%
(as estradiol hemihydrate)
Transdermal gel
Estrogen

ACTIONS AND CLINICAL PHARMACOLOGY

ESTROGEL* (17ß-estradiol [as estradiol hemihydrate] 0.06%) is a transdermal preparation which is comprised of a hydro-alcoholic gel containing 0.06% of the physiological hormone, 17ß-estradiol (E_2). Following application to human skin, ESTROGEL* rapidly penetrates the stratum corneum and then diffuses more slowly into the epidermis, dermis and vascular system over a period of several hours. ESTROGEL* delivers 17ß-estradiol directly to the systemic circulation, thereby avoiding the gastrointestinal tract and first pass hepatic metabolism. Daily percutaneous administration of ESTROGEL* results in increasing plasma estradiol levels which plateau after 3-5 days of treatment, remaining relatively stable thereafter. Mean serum estradiol concentrations of approximately 80 pg/mL (294 pmol/L) and 150 pg/mL (551 pmol/L), respectively, are maintained with daily administration of 2.5 g or 5 g ESTROGEL* (corresponding to 1.5 mg and 3 mg E_2, respectively). Administration of ESTROGEL* also results in increased serum estrone concentrations, producing a physiological estradiol/estrone ratio of approximately one. Therefore, serum concentrations of both estradiol and estrone and the serum estradiol/estrone ratio provided by ESTROGEL* are consistent with physiological levels observed during the follicular phase of the normal menstrual cycle. Long-term administration of ESTROGEL* to postmenopausal women has been shown to provide effective relief from climacteric symptoms such as hot flushes, asthenia, vaginal atrophy and insomnia. Comparative studies have shown ESTROGEL* to be as effective as oral conjugated estrogens in the relief of climacteric symptoms. Co-administration of a progestin does not affect the efficacy of ESTROGEL* to relieve climacteric symptoms and has been shown to be an effective method to prevent estrogen-induced endometrial hyperplasia.

INDICATIONS AND CLINICAL USE

ESTROGEL* (17ß-estradiol [as estradiol hemihydrate] 0.06%) is indicated for replacement therapy in naturally occurring or surgically induced estrogen deficiency states associated with menopausal and postmenopausal symptoms, e.g. hot flushes, sleep disturbances and atrophic vaginitis.

CONTRAINDICATIONS

ESTROGEL* (17ß-estradiol [as estradiol hemihydrate] 0.06%) should not be administered to patients with: • active hepatic dysfunction or disease, especially of the obstructive type; • a personal history of known or suspected estrogen dependent neoplasia such as breast or endometrial cancer; • endometrial hyperplasia; • undiagnosed vaginal bleeding; • a history of cerebrovascular accident; • coronary thrombosis, or in the presence of classical migraine; active thrombophlebitis, thrombosis or thromboembolic disorders, a history of thrombophlebitis, thrombosis or thromboembolic disease associated with previous estrogen use; • partial or complete loss of vision from ophthalmic vascular disease; • known or suspected pregnancy; • known or suspected hypersensitivity to any component of the gel.

WARNINGS

There is evidence from several studies that estrogens, unopposed by progestins, increase the risk of carcinoma of the endometrium in humans. However, administration of a progestin for the last 12 to 14 days of an estrogen treatment cycle protects the endometrium from hyperplasia and reduces the risk of endometrial cancer to that of untreated women. Breast cancer is a multifactorial disease, which increases in frequency in older age. Much of the etiology of breast cancer is unknown. Several published epidemiological studies have documented an association between a modest increase in the risk of developing breast cancer and the use of hormone replacement therapy in menopause when given for periods exceeding 5 years. Information is still lacking to show whether the risks of combination estrogen-progestin therapy differ from those of estrogen used alone. There is a need for caution in prescribing estrogens for women with a strong family history of breast cancer or who present breast nodules, fibrocystic disease of the breast, or abnormal mammograms. Other known risk factors for the development of breast cancer such as nulliparity, obesity, early menarche, late age at first full term pregnancy and at menopause should also be evaluated. It is recommended that a mammography be performed before starting treatment and repeated at regular intervals in patients at high risk for breast cancer. The overall benefits and possible risks of hormone replacement therapy should be fully considered and discussed with patients. Instructions for self-examination of the breasts should be included in this counselling. Contact sensitization is known to occur with topical applications. Although it is extremely rare, patients who develop contact sensitization to any component of the gel should be warned that a severe hypersensitivity reaction may occur with continuing exposure to the causative agent. Benign hepatic adenomas have been associated with the use of combined estrogen and progestin oral contraceptives. Although benign and rare, these tumors may rupture and cause death from intra-abdominal hemorrhage. Such lesions have not yet been reported in association with other estrogen or progestin preparations used in hormone replacement therapy, but they should be considered if abdominal pain and tenderness, abdominal mass, or hypovolemic shock occurs in patients receiving estrogen. Hepatocellular carcinoma has also been reported in women taking estrogen-containing oral contraceptives. The causal relationship of this malignancy to these drugs is not known. The relatively small number of epidemiological studies assessing the relation between hormone replacement therapy and risk of venous thromboembolism has led to conflicting results. While earlier studies have not shown an association, some epidemiological studies have suggested that, for healthy women, there is an increased relative risk of about 2-3.6 for developing deep vein thrombosis or pulmonary embolism for current users of hormone replacement therapy compared to non-users. The physician should be alert to the earliest manifestations of thrombotic disorders (thrombophlebitis, retinal thrombosis, cerebral embolism and pulmonary embolism). If these occur or are suspected, estrogen therapy should be discontinued immediately. Women with a positive family history and women with a history of thromboembolic disorders during pregnancy or in association with estrogen use should be kept under special observation. Women with severe varicose veins, severe obesity (Body Mass Index > 30 kg/m²) or those undergoing immobilization for 3 weeks or more, trauma or surgery requiring bed rest, are generally considered to be at increased risk of venous thromboembolism.

PRECAUTIONS

Physical examination: Patients should have a complete pretreatment physical examination including blood pressure determination, examination of breast and pelvic organs, as well as a Papanicolaou smear and endometrial biopsy. Baseline tests should include those for blood glucose, calcium, triglycerides, cholesterol, and liver function tests. The first follow up examination should be done within six months after initiation of treatment. Thereafter, examinations should be made once a year and should include at least those procedures outlined above. It is important that patients are encouraged to practice frequent self-examination of the breasts. **Addition of a progestin:** Studies have shown that the addition of a progestin for 12 or more days of an estrogen treatment cycle reduces the risk of endometrial cancer to that of untreated women. Morphological and biochemical studies have shown that 12-14 days of progestin treatment provides maximal control of endometrial mitotic activity. There are possible additional risks which may be associated with the inclusion of a progestin in estrogen replacement regimens, therefore the manufacturers' labelling should be consulted. The long-term effects generally depend on the dosage and type of progestin used. **Fluid retention:** Because estrogens may cause some degree of fluid retention, conditions which might be influenced by this factor such as asthma, epilepsy, migraine, and cardiac or renal dysfunction, require careful observation. **Uterine bleeding:** If abnormal vaginal bleeding occurs during therapy, a diagnostic aspiration biopsy or curettage should be performed to rule out the possibility of uterine malignancy. **Uterine Fibroids:** Preexisting uterine leiomyomata may increase in size during prolonged high-dose estrogen use. Growth, pain or tenderness of uterine leiomyoma requires discontinuation of medication. **Endometriosis:** Symptoms and physical findings associated with a previous diagnosis of endometriosis may reappear or become aggravated with estrogen use. **Hepatic Disease:** Liver function tests should be done periodically in subjects who are suspected of having hepatic disease. **Phlebitis and Thromboembolism:** If the patient develops any sign of phlebitis or thromboembolic complications, medication should be discontinued. As estrogens may be associated with an increased risk of thromboembolism, estrogen therapy should be discontinued at least 4 weeks before surgery or during periods of prolonged immobilization. **Hypercalcemia:** Prolonged use of estrogen can alter the metabolism of calcium and phosphorus. Estrogens should be used with caution in patients with metabolic and malignant bone diseases associated with hypercalcemia and in patients with renal insufficiency. **Cerebrovascular Insufficiency:** Patients who develop visual disturbances, classical migraine, transient aphasia, paralysis, or loss of consciousness should discontinue medication. **Jaundice:** In patients with a history of jaundice during pregnancy, there is an increased risk that jaundice will recur with the use of estrogen-containing medications. If jaundice develops, estrogen treatment should be discontinued while the cause is investigated. **Current Medications:** Estrogens may diminish the effectiveness of anticoagulants, antidiabetic and antihypertensive agents. **High Blood Pressure:** Clinical trials have shown that percutaneously administered 17ß-estradiol (0.06%) does not affect renin substrate and has no significant effect on blood pressure in normotensive patients. However, ethinyl estradiol and conjugated estrogens have been shown to increase renin substrate and blood pressure which, in most cases, returns to normal upon discontinuing the drug. This may occur with use of oral estrogens during menopause and blood pressure should be monitored with estrogen use. Therefore, elevation of blood pressure in previously normotensive or hypertensive patients should be evaluated and appropriate action taken. **Glucose Metabolism:** Clinical trials have shown that percutaneously administered 17ß-estradiol (0.06%) does not affect glucose metabolism. However, a worsening of glucose tolerance has been observed in a significant percentage of patients on estrogen-containing oral contraceptives. Therefore, diabetic patients or those with a predisposition to diabetes, should be observed closely to detect any alterations in carbohydrate or lipid metabolism, especially in triglyceride blood levels. **Drugs Inducing Liver Enzymes:** Preparations which induce liver enzymes, such as barbiturates, hydantoins, carbamazepine, meprobamate, phenylbutazone or rifampicin, may interfere with the activity of orally administered estrogens. The effect of these compounds on percutaneously administered 17ß-estradiol (0.06%) is not known. **Hemostatic Factors:** Clinical studies have shown that administration of percutaneous 17ß-estradiol (0.06%) has no effect on hemostatic factors including platelet numbers, factors II, VII, IX, X, prothrombin, fibrinogen, antithrombin III or plasminogen. However, the following changes have been observed with large doses of oral estrogen: increased sulfobromophthalein retention; increased prothrombin time and partial thromboplastin time; increased factors VII, VIII, IX, X; decreased antithrombin III; increased norepinephrine-induced platelet aggregability. **Other Endocrine and Metabolic Tests:** High doses of oral estrogens are also associated with increased thyroxine-binding globulin (TBG), leading to increased circulating total thyroid hormone (T_4) as measured by column or radioimmunoassay; decreased free T_3 resin uptake, reflecting the elevated TBG; free T_4 concentration is unaltered; other binding proteins may be elevated in serum i.e. corticosteroid binding globulin (CBG), sex-hormone binding globulin (SHBG), leading to increased circulating corticosteroids and sex steroids respectively; free or biologically active hormone concentrations are unchanged; reduced response to the metyrapone test; reduced serum folate concentration, increased serum triglyceride and phospholipid concentration and impaired glucose tolerance. Therefore, the results of these tests should not be considered reliable unless therapy has been discontinued for 2-4 months. Advise the pathologist of estrogen therapy when relevant specimens are submitted.

ADVERSE EFFECTS

See Warnings and Precautions regarding potential induction of malignant neoplasms and adverse effects similar to those of oral contraceptives. Itching and redness (allergic contact dermatitis) at the application site have been reported very rarely with ESTROGEL* (17ß-estradiol [as estradiol hemihydrate] 0.06%). The following adverse reactions have been reported with the use of estrogens in general:
Gastrointestinal: Nausea; vomiting; abdominal discomfort (cramps, pressure, pain); bloating, gallbladder disorder; asymptomatic impaired liver function; cholestatic jaundice. **Genitourinary:** Breakthrough bleeding; spotting and vaginal bleeding; change in menstrual flow; dysmenorrhea; vaginal itching/discharge; dyspareunia; dysuria; endometrial hyperplasia; pre-menstrual-like syndrome; reactivation of endometriosis; cystitis; changes in cervical erosion and amount of cervical secretion. **Dermatological/Hypersensitivity:** Allergic contact dermatitis; reversible post-inflammatory pigmentation; general pruritus and exanthema; loss of scalp hair; chloasma; pigmentation of the skin; erythema nodosum; erythema multiforme; hemorrhagic skin eruptions; precipitation or aggravation of porphyria cutanea tarda in predisposed individuals. Isolated cases of anaphylactoid reactions (some of the patients had a history of previous allergy or allergic disorders). **Endocrine:** Breast swelling and tenderness; increased blood sugar levels; decreased glucose tolerance; sodium retention. **Cardiovascular/Hematologic:** Palpitations; isolated cases of thrombophlebitis; pulmonary embolism and cerebral thrombosis; exacerbations of varicose veins; increase in blood pressure (see Precautions); coronary thrombosis; altered coagulation tests. **Central Nervous System:** Aggravation of migraine headaches; headaches; mental depression; nervousness; dizziness; fatigue; irritability; neuro-ocular lesions (e.g., retinal thrombosis, optic neuritis). **Ophthalmic:** Visual disturbances; steepening of the corneal curvature; intolerance to contact lenses; neuro-ocular lesions (see CNS above). **Miscellaneous:** Changes in appetite; changes in body weight; edema; neuritis; change in libido; musculoskeletal pain [including leg pain not related to thromboembolic disease (usually transient, lasting 3-6 weeks). If symptoms persist, the dose of estrogen should be reduced.]

SYMPTOMS AND TREATMENT OF OVERDOSAGE

Numerous reports of the ingestion of large doses of estrogen-containing oral contraceptives by young children indicate that acute serious ill effects do not occur. Overdosage with estrogen may cause nausea, breast discomfort, fluid retention, bloating, abdominal cramps, headache, dizziness or withdrawal bleeding in females. Symptomatic treatment should be given.

DOSAGE AND ADMINISTRATION

Treatment is usually initiated with 2.5 g ESTROGEL* (17ß-estradiol [as estradiol hemihydrate] 0.06%), daily. ESTROGEL* is usually administered on a cyclic schedule from day 1 to day 25 of each calendar month or from day 1 to day 21 of a 28 day cycle. The dose of ESTROGEL* should be adjusted as necessary to control symptoms. Attempts to adjust the necessary dosage should be made after two months of treatment. Breast discomfort and/or breakthrough bleeding are generally signs that the dose is too high and needs to be lowered. However, if the selected dose fails to eliminate the signs and symptoms of estrogen deficiency, a higher dose may be prescribed. For maintenance therapy, the lowest effective dose should be used. Because of the variable absorption of ESTROGEL* between individuals due to the technique of self-administration on the skin, it is recommended to obtain measurement of serum estradiol level after initiation of treatment. This measurement should be done when the patient has developed her technique for ESTROGEL* application when she comes for her regular follow-up visit. This measurement should be similar to the serum estradiol level normally produced by the ovary before menopause during the middle part of the follicular phase of the menstual cycle (150-400 pmol/L). In women who are not currently taking oral estrogens, treatment with ESTROGEL* can be initiated at once. In women who are currently taking oral estrogen, treatment with ESTROGEL* can be initiated 1 week after withdrawal of oral therapy or sooner if symptoms reappear before the week's end. In women with an intact uterus, a progestin should be sequentially co-administered for a minimum of 12-14 days each cycle to prevent endometrial hyperplasia. Continuous, non-cyclic therapy may be indicated in hysterectomized women or in cases where the signs and symptoms of estrogen deficiency become problematic during the treatment-free interval. In women with an intact uterus, a progestin should be sequentially co-administered for a minimum of 12-14 days per cycle to avoid overstimulation of the endometrium. There have been no reported cases of biologically significant estradiol transfer from a patient using ESTROGEL* to their male partner.

ESTROGEL* Metered-Dose Pump:
Two metered actuations will deliver 2.5 g of gel (1.5 mg E^2). All of the gel should be applied with the hands over a large area of skin ($>$ 2000 cm²) in a thin, uniform layer. To measure a 2.5 g dose of ESTROGEL* (1.5 mg E_2), press firmly on the pump once and apply the gel to one arm. Repeat applying the gel to the opposite arm. It is recommended to apply ESTROGEL* to both arms. Alternate sites of application are the abdomen or the inner thighs. It is not necessary to rotate the site of administration. **ESTROGEL* must not be applied to the breasts.** ESTROGEL* must not be applied to the face or to irritated or damaged skin. Allow the gel to dry approximately 2 minutes before covering with clothing. ESTROGEL* does not stain or smell. When a new metered-dose pump is opened, it may be necessary to prime the pump by pressing the pump once or twice. The first metered-dose may not be accurate and should therefore be discarded. The pump contains enough gel for approximately a month's use (i.e. 64 metered-doses). After that, the amount of gel delivered may be lower and thus, it is recommended to change the pump.

PHARMACEUTICAL INFORMATION

DRUG SUBSTANCE

Proper name:	17ß-estradiol (as estradiol hemihydrate)
Chemical name:	estra-1,3,5(10)-triene-3, 17ß-diol hemihydrate

Structural formula:

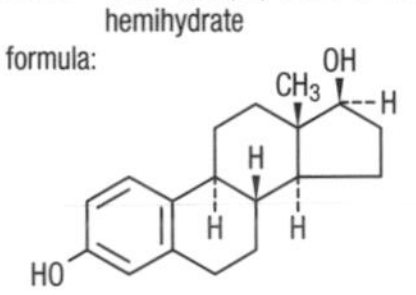

½ H_2O

Molecular formula:	$C_{18}H_{24}O_2$, ½ H_2O
Molecular weight:	281.4
Physical form:	White or creamy white, odorless, crystalline powder
Solubility:	Practically insoluble in water; sparingly soluble in vegetable oils; soluble in alcohol, acetone, dioxane, chloroform and in solutions of fixed alkali hydroxides.
Melting range:	173°C - 179°C

Composition

ESTROGEL* contains 0.06% 17ß-estradiol as the hemihydrate in a specially formulated hydro-alcoholic gel to provide a sustained absorption of the active ingredient. Non-medicinal ingredients include Carbopol 934, triethanolamine, ethanol and purified water.

Stability and Storage Recommendations

Store at controlled room temperature: 15°C - 30°C. Do not freeze.

DOSAGE FORMS

Availability
ESTROGEL* (17ß-estradiol [as estradiol hemihydrate] 0.06%) is packaged in 80 g metered-dose pumps. Each metered actuation delivers 1.25 g of gel (0.75 mg of 17ß-estradiol).

Product monograph available upon request.

SCHERING CANADA INC.
3535 TRANS-CANADA, Pointe-Claire (Québec) H9R 1B4

*Trademark PAAB PMAC MEMBER

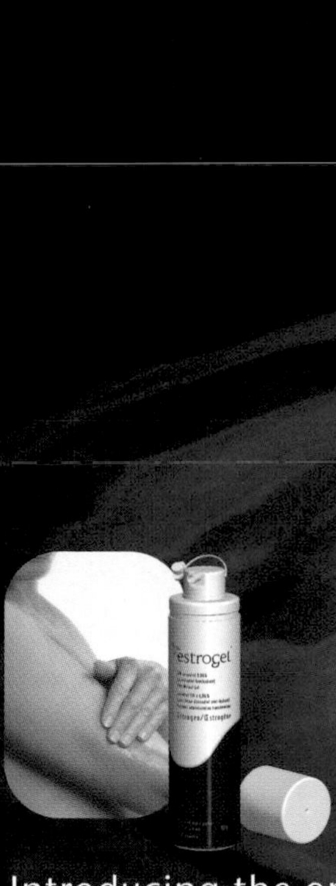
estrogel

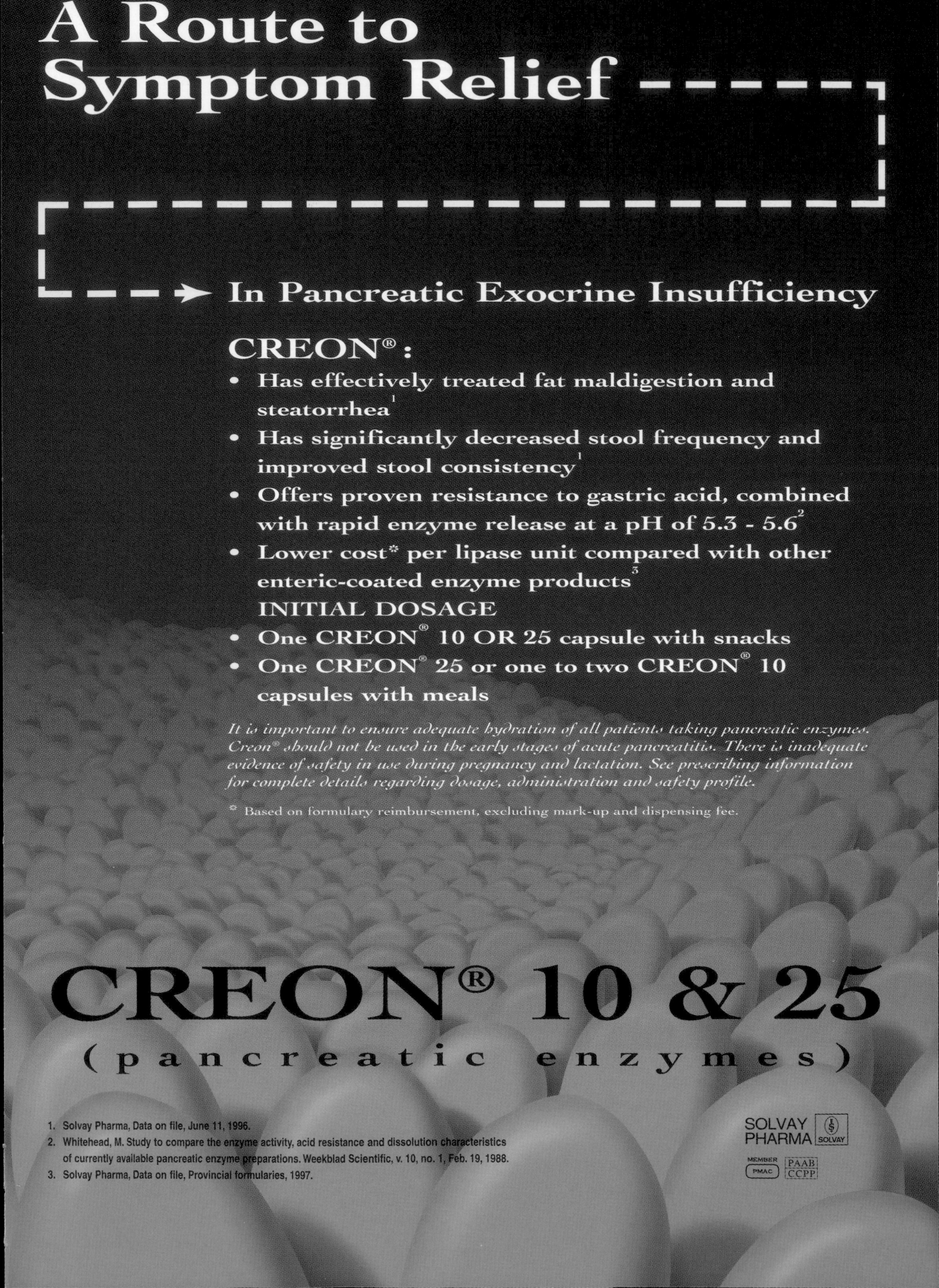
A Route to Symptom Relief
In Pancreatic Exocrine Insufficiency
CREON®:
• Has effectively treated fat maldigestion and steatorrhea[1]
• Has significantly decreased stool frequency and improved stool consistency[1]
• Offers proven resistance to gastric acid, combined with rapid enzyme release at a pH of 5.3 - 5.6[2]
• Lower cost* per lipase unit compared with other enteric-coated enzyme products[3]
INITIAL DOSAGE
• One CREON® 10 OR 25 capsule with snacks
• One CREON® 25 or one to two CREON® 10 capsules with meals
It is important to ensure adequate hydration of all patients taking pancreatic enzymes. Creon® should not be used in the early stages of acute pancreatitis. There is inadequate evidence of safety in use during pregnancy and lactation. See prescribing information for complete details regarding dosage, administration and safety profile.
* Based on formulary reimbursement, excluding mark-up and dispensing fee.
CREON® 10 & 25
(pancreatic enzymes)
1. Solvay Pharma, Data on file, June 11, 1996.
2. Whitehead, M. Study to compare the enzyme activity, acid resistance and dissolution characteristics of currently available pancreatic enzyme preparations. Weekblad Scientific, v. 10, no. 1, Feb. 19, 1988.
3. Solvay Pharma, Data on file, Provincial formularies, 1997.
SOLVAY PHARMA
MEMBER PMAC
PAAB CCPP

E

ECHINACEA ANGUSTIFOLIA
Swiss Herbal

Echinacea Angustifolia Extract
Traditional Herbal Medicine

Indications: For the relief of colds and minor flu symptoms.

Precautions: Contraindicated in autoimmune disease (i.e., multiple sclerosis), individuals with an allergy to plants in the sunflower family should avoid echinacea.

Dosage: Adults: 1 to 2 capsules daily or as directed by a physician or natural health practitioner.

Supplied: Each capsule contains: standardized Echinacea extract 7:1 500 mg, standardized to Echinacosides 4%. Nonmedicinal ingredients: bees wax, glycerin, lecithin in a shell containing gelatin, purified water and soy bean oil. Bottles of 60 and 180.

New Product 1998

ECHOVIST®
Berlex Canada

Galactose
Ultrasound Contrast Agent

Pharmacology: Echovist is an ultrasound contrast agent consisting of a suspension of micron-sized air bubbles, formed upon reconstitution of specially formulated galactose granules with an aqueous galactose solution. Following intrauterine administration of the suspension, the bubbles serve to enhance ultrasound signals from the uterine cavity and fallopian tubes, thus enabling better visualization of these structures.

Upon completion of the ultrasound procedure, most of the administered galactose is discharged from the uterus into the cervix and vagina. The remainder is absorbed into the systemic circulation and rapidly metabolized to glucose by the liver.

Indications: Hysterosalpingo-contrast Sonography (HyCoSy): The product is indicated for contrast enhancement during ultrasound examination of the uterine cavity and fallopian tubes, including evaluation of tubal patency in infertility investigations.

Contraindications: Patients with galactosemia, pelvic inflammatory disease and pregnancy.

Warnings: Aseptic conditions must be maintained during administration to reduce the potential risk of ascending infection.

Precautions: Hypotension: Caution should be exercised in women with autonomic lability or unstable blood pressure, since there is a possible risk of vasovagal reaction, and therefore transient hypotension.

Pregnancy and *Lactation*: If pregnancy is suspected, the product should not be used (see Contraindications). Since galactose is a natural component of breast milk, there is no contraindication for the use of the product during lactation.

Children: The safety and efficacy of the product in children have not been established.

Drug Interactions: The interaction of galactose with drugs or contrast imaging agents has not been fully investigated. In clinical trials, there was no evidence of an interaction between the product and local or general anesthetics.

Adverse Effects: The safety was evaluated in clinical trials involving a total of 1 326 patients undergoing ultrasound examination of the uterus and/or fallopian tubes. Approximately 20% of patients received local or general anesthesia prior to the ultrasound procedure. The most common adverse events reported in the patients who did not receive anesthesia were: pain 54.9%, nausea 2.6%, syncope 2.0%, vasovagal symptoms 2.0% and vomiting 1.2%. In general, pain associated with the product was mild and did not require analgesia. Adverse events rarely prevented the completion of the ultrasound and serious adverse events were uncommon.

The following adverse events were reported in less than 1% of patients: Cardiovascular: bradycardia, hypotension.
Nervous System: dizziness, grand mal seizure.
Body as a Whole: fever, malaise, pain in extremity, discomfort, general weakness, taste perversion, increased sweating, hot flashes.
Respiratory: hyperventilation, respiratory disorder.
Gastrointestinal: diarrhea, vomiting, intestinal perforation.
Genitourinary: salpingitis, vaginal bleeding, vaginal discharge, endometrial injury.

Overdose: Symptoms and Treatment: The risk of accidental overdose with the product is extremely remote. Any overdose should be treated by prompt initiation of symptomatic therapy.

Dosage: Enhancement of the ultrasound signal is dependent on the volume of suspension administered. For examination of the uterine cavity, 2 to 5 mL is usually sufficient. For examination of the fallopian tubes, the addition of further 1 to 2 mL increments should be added under ultrasound control. In general, a total volume of 15 mL is sufficient, with a recommended maximum volume of 30 mL.

A balloon catheter for hysterosalpingo-contrast sonography (HyCoSy) should be used for the administration. The patient should be prepared for the procedure prior to the reconstitution of the granules.

Echovist granules are to be reconstituted with Echovist solution in the following manner: 1. Ensure that the vials of granules and solution are at room temperature. 2. Remove the plastic cap from the vial containing the galactose solution and withdraw the entire contents using a syringe. 3. Remove the plastic cap from the vial containing the granules and insert the mini-spike provided. Transfer the galactose solution in the syringe to the vial of granules through the mini-spike. 4. Shake vigorously by hand for 5 to 10 seconds to produce a homogenous milky-white suspension. Withdraw the suspension through the mini-spike into the syringe and administer immediately.

Take care not to warm the suspension with the hands and avoid using excessive negative pressure when withdrawing the suspension into the syringe.

Once reconstituted, the suspension is stable for approximately 5 minutes without any loss of echogenicity.

Unused portion should be discarded.

Reconstitution: Once reconstituted, Echovist is a suspension of slowly soluble galactose microparticles in a 20% (w/v) aqueous galactose solution with an initial overall microparticle concentration of approximately 200 mg/mL. The median diameter of the galactose microparticles is 2 μm, with 99% of them being less than or equal to 8 μm.

Osmolality of freshly prepared suspension, at 37°C= 1 699 mOsm/kg.

Osmolality upon complete dissolution of the suspension, at 37°C=2 960 mOsm/kg.

Viscosity (rotational viscosimeter) of freshly prepared suspension, at 25°C=approximately 4 mPa.s.

Stability and Storage: The vials of granules and solution should be protected from light and stored between 15 and 30°C.

Once reconstituted, the suspension is stable for approximately 5 minutes without any loss of echogenicity.

Supplied: Each g of granules contains: galactose 1 g. Each mL of sterile aqueous solution contains: galactose 20% (w/v). Cartons containing 1 vial of granules consisting of 3 g of galactose 100%, and 1 vial of solution consisting of 13.5 mL of sterile aqueous galactose 20% (w/v). A mini-spike is also included for reconstitution.

New Product 1998

ECOSTATIN® Preparations Pr
Westwood-Squibb

Econazole Nitrate
Antifungal Agent

Pharmacology: Econazole exhibits antifungal activity against a wide variety of fungi, including dermatophytes, pathogenic yeasts, and moulds. Susceptible pathogenic organisms include C. albicans and other Candida species, T. rubrum, T. mentagrophytes, E. floccosum and M. furfur. It appears to act by altering the internal structure or cell membrane permeability of the fungus.

Indications: Cream: The treatment of infections caused by susceptible dermatophyte and candida species including tinea pedis, tinea cruris, tinea corporis, tinea versicolor and cutaneous candidiasis. It is not indicated for moderate or severe paronychia or onychomycosis.

Ovules: Local treatment of vulvovaginal candidiasis (moniliasis).

Contraindications: Hypersensitivity to econazole or any of the cream's or ovule's components.

Precautions: If marked irritation or sensitization should occur during topical or intravaginal use, discontinue econazole therapy. Cream not for ophthalmic use.

Intractable candidiasis may be the presenting symptom of unrecognized diabetes. Appropriate urine/blood studies may be indicated in patients not responding to the treatment.

During the vaginal treatment period, it may be advisable to instruct the patient to abstain from intercourse or, alternatively, to recommend the use of a condom.

Pregnancy: Since econazole is absorbed in small amounts from the human vagina, it should not be used in the first trimester of pregnancy unless deemed essential for the patient's welfare.

Advise pregnant patients to exercise caution in the use of the vaginal applicator.

Adverse Effects: Econazole nitrate is usually well tolerated. Adverse effects are limited to occasional local skin irritation manifested by erythema, pruritus, and burning or stinging sensation; cessation of therapy is rarely warranted.

Dosage: Cream: Apply twice daily, in the morning and evening. The cream should be massaged gently into the affected and surrounding skin areas.

Clinical improvement usually occurs promptly; however, complete disappearance of the symptoms of the disease may require prolonged treatment. Candida infections should be treated for at least 2 weeks and dermatophyte infections for 1 month to reduce the risk of recurrence. If no improvement has occurred after 1 month of treatment with econazole topical cream, the diagnosis should be reassessed.

Ovules: With the patient in the supine position, insert 1 ovule high into the vagina, by means of the applicator, at bedtime for 3 consecutive days.

Therapy should be continued during menstruation. Continue administration for the complete 3 day period even if the signs and symptoms of the disease disappear.

Although a 3 day course of therapy usually suffices, occasionally it may be necessary to institute a second course of therapy.

Supplied: Cream: Each g of cream contains: econazole nitrate 1.0%. Nonmedicinal ingredients: benzoic acid, butylated hydroxyanisole, fragrance, mineral oil, palm oil, polyethylene glycol, polyethylene glycol stearate and water. Tubes of 15 and 30 g. Store at room temperature (15 to 25°C).

Ovules: Each creamy white to yellowish egg shaped ovule contains: econazole nitrate 150 mg. Nonmedicinal ingredients: hydrogenated vegetable oil. Packages of 3 ovules plus a reusable applicator. Store at room temperature. Avoid prolonged storage at temperatures above 30°C.

ECTOSONE® REGULAR Pr
ECTOSONE® MILD Pr
ECTOSONE® SCALP LOTION Pr
Technilab

Betamethasone Valerate
Topical Corticosteroid

Supplied: Regular Cream: Each g contains: betamethasone 0.1% (as betamethasone valerate USP) in a water-miscible base. Nonmedicinal ingredients: caprylic/capric triglyceride, ceteareth-12, ceteareth-20, cetearyl alcohol, glycerin, methylparaben, propylparaben and purified water. Jars of 450 g. Store at room temperature (15 to 30°C).

Mild Cream: Each g contains: betamethasone 0.05% (as betamethasone valerate USP) in a water-miscible base. Nonmedicinal ingredients: caprylic/capric triglyceride, ceteareth-12, ceteareth-20, cetearyl alcohol, glycerin, methylparaben, propylparaben and purified water. Jars of 450 g. Store at room temperature (15 to 30°C).

Regular Lotion: Each g contains: betamethasone valerate USP 1.22 mg [equivalent to betamethasone 1 mg (0.1%)]. Nonmedicinal ingredients: ceteareth-20, cetearyl alcohol, glycerin, glycol distearate, guar gum, isopropyl alcohol, isopropyl myristate, methylparaben, propylparaben and purified water. Bottles of 60 mL. Store between 15 to 30°C. Protect from freezing.

Ectosone (cont'd)

Mild Lotion: Each g contains: betamethasone valerate USP 0.61 mg [equivalent to betamethasone 0.5 mg (0.05%)]. Nonmedicinal ingredients: ceteareth-20, cetearyl alcohol, glycerin, glycol distearate, guar gum, isopropyl alcohol, isopropyl myristate, methylparaben, propylparaben and purified water. Bottles of 60 mL. Store between 15 to 30°C. Protect from freezing.

Scalp Lotion: Each g contains: betamethasone valerate USP 1.22 mg [equivalent to betamethasone 1 mg (0.1%)]. Nonmedicinal ingredients: carbomer, isopropyl alcohol, purified water and triethanolamine. Plastic squeeze bottles of 30 and 75 mL. Store at room temperature between 15 to 30°C. Protect from freezing.

EDECRIN® Pr
SODIUM EDECRIN® Pr
MSD

Ethacrynic Acid
Ethacrynate Sodium
Diuretic—Saluretic

Pharmacology: Ethacrynic acid is a saluretic-diuretic agent with marked potency and rapid onset of action. It is chemically unrelated to other diuretics. Patients with congestive heart failure (including acute pulmonary edema), renal edema, hepatic cirrhosis with ascites, and other conditions involving fluid retention have responded well to ethacrynic acid.

Ethacrynic acid has the following major characteristics:

Water and electrolyte excretion may be increased several times over that observed with thiazide diuretics. The urinary output is usually dose-dependent and related to the magnitude of fluid accumulation.

Electrolyte excretion pattern differs from that of thiazides. Initially, sodium and chloride excretion is usually substantial, and chloride loss exceeds that of sodium. With prolonged therapy, chloride excretion declines, and potassium and hydrogen ion excretion may increase. In patients with increased diuresis excessive amounts of potassium may be excreted. Ethacrynic acid is effective whether or not there is clinical acidosis or alkalosis.

Rapid onset of action usually is observed within 30 minutes after an oral dose or within 5 minutes after an i.v. injection.

Duration of action is moderate following oral administration (6 to 8 hours). The peak diuretic-saluretic activity occurs in about 2 hours.

Sulfhydryl binding propensity differs in certain respects from that of the organomercurials. Its mode of action is not by carbonic anhydrase inhibition.

Multiple sites of action. Ethacrynic acid acts on the proximal and distal portions of the tubule, and also on the ascending limb of the loop of Henle.

Indications: Especially useful in patients unresponsive to the commonly used diuretics.

It has been found useful in the following conditions: congestive heart failure, acute pulmonary edema, renal edema (nephrotic syndrome), hepatic cirrhosis with ascites.

The majority of patients studied to date have been resistant in some degree to other diuretic agents; the remaining patients received ethacrynic acid as their first diuretic in the treatment of edema or were placed on the drug for comparative evaluations.

Experience to date with the use of ethacrynic acid for oral maintenance therapy has been limited. The duration of studies has varied from short-term investigations to continuous therapy of 1 year or longer.

Patients with chronic **congestive heart failure** many of whom were unresponsive to other diuretics, have responded successfully to short- or long-term therapy. These include patients with arteriosclerotic heart disease, rheumatic heart disease, hypertensive cardiovascular disease, pulmonary heart disease, and congenital heart disease. Long-term studies in patients who have received ethacrynic acid for over 6 months have been in patients with cardiac edema secondary to arteriosclerotic or valvular heart disease. The average duration of these studies has been about 9 months.

Patients with **acute pulmonary edema** have responded rapidly to the i.v. use of ethacrynate sodium. Clinical improvement is coincidental with the large increases in water and electrolyte excretion usually observed to begin within 5 minutes after injection. Ethacrynate sodium offers advantages over other diuretics because of its rapid action and effectiveness.

Ethacrynic acid is indicated for patients with the nephrotic syndrome. The greatest experience with this agent in **renal edema** has been in patients with the nephrotic syndrome. Use of the drug in these patients usually has been of short duration, ranging from 1 to 3 months, with treatment usually being initiated in the hospital.

Saluresis and diuresis may be achieved in patients unresponsive to other diuretics. Patients whose response to other diuretics has been suboptimal may obtain a greater effect from ethacrynic acid.

As with other diuretics, hypoproteinemia may reduce responsiveness to ethacrynic acid and the use of salt-poor albumin should be considered. In some patients, larger doses may be necessary to produce effective diuresis in renal than in cardiac edema. Ethacrynic acid is effective in many patients who have significant degrees of renal insufficiency. It has little or no effect on renal blood flow except following pronounced reduction in plasma volume when associated with rapid diuresis. The extreme sensitivity of patients with chronic renal failure to alterations in fluid or electrolyte balance dictates careful clinical and laboratory observation when diuretics are used, and these agents must be discontinued immediately if further deterioration in renal function occurs.

For reasons given below, initiation of diuretic therapy with ethacrynic acid in the cirrhotic patient with ascites is best carried out in the hospital. When maintenance therapy has been established, the individual can be satisfactorily followed as an outpatient.

Ethacrynic acid is usually effective in patients with cirrhosis who have ascites. Most studies have been of 3 months' duration, or less. Diuresis and saluresis have occurred in previously unresponsive patients. However, cirrhotic patients tolerate poorly acute shifts in electrolyte balance, and potassium excretion is often augmented as a result of associated aldosteronism. Therefore, careful clinical and laboratory observation is essential to avoid serious loss of potassium and chloride ions and the development of metabolic alkalosis, with resultant hepatic encephalopathy. These effects may be minimized by appropriate adjustment of dosage and by the use of supplemental potassium as the chloride with or without a potassium-sparing agent (see Dosage).

A variety of other edematous states have been successfully treated with ethacrynic acid; most of the experience has been of short duration. These include ascites due to malignancy, idiopathic edema, and lymphedema.

Children: Ethacrynic acid has been found useful in patients of the pediatric age group with the nephrotic syndrome. This experience has been mostly of short duration, in hospitalized patients resistant to other therapy. Pediatric patients with congenital heart disease also have responded to this agent. Information in infants is insufficient to recommend therapy with ethacrynic acid.

Contraindications: All diuretics, including ethacrynic acid, are contraindicated in anuria. If increasing azotemia and/or oliguria occur during treatment of severe, progressive renal disease, the diuretic should be discontinued.

Until further experience in infants is accumulated, therapy with oral and parenteral ethacrynic acid is contraindicated.

See also Warnings, Pregnancy and Lactation.

Hypersensitivity to any component of this product.

Warnings: Ethacrynic acid is a potent and rapidly-acting diuretic that may lead to excessive diuresis and natriuresis with water depletion and electrolyte imbalance, which may result in hypokalemia or hypochloremic alkalosis with potassium depletion, hydrogen ion loss and extracellular fluid space contraction. This may occur in patients with marked fluid accumulation or when excessive doses are used but these adverse effects may also be encountered in patients with moderate degrees of edema. The safe use of potent diuretics requires careful understanding of their pharmacologic actions and in particular of the mechanisms of development of electrolyte imbalance. Close attention should be given to the directions of use and to identification of the individual patient response to the drug.

Frequent serum electrolyte, CO_2, and BUN determinations should be performed early in therapy and periodically thereafter during active diuresis. Baseline determination of electrolytes and renal function before therapy is recommended when pre-existing derangements are suspected. Any electrolyte abnormalities should be corrected or the drug temporarily withdrawn.

Ethacrynic acid should be given with caution to patients with advanced cirrhosis of the liver, particularly those with a history of previous episodes of electrolyte imbalance of hepatic encephalopathy. Like other diuretics it may precipitate hepatic coma and death.

Too vigorous a diuresis, as evidenced by rapid and excessive weight loss, may induce an acute hypotensive episode. In elderly cardiac patients, rapid contraction of plasma volume and the resultant hemoconcentration should be avoided to prevent the development of thromboembolic episodes such as cerebrovascular thromboses and pulmonary emboli which may be fatal. In patients receiving digitalis glycosides, excessive loss of potassium may precipitate digitalis toxicity. Care should also be exercised in patients receiving potassium-depleting steroids.

The effects of ethacrynic acid on electrolytes are related to its renal pharmacologic activity and are dose-dependent. The possibility of profound electrolyte and water loss may be avoided by weighing the patient throughout the treatment period, by monitoring electrolyte changes, by careful adjustment of dosage, by initiating treatment with small doses, and by using the drug on an intermittent schedule when possible. When excessive diuresis occurs, the drug should be withdrawn until homeostasis is restored. When excessive electrolyte loss occurs, the dosage should be reduced or the drug temporarily withdrawn, and if necessary judicious repletion of losses should be considered.

Avoidance of potassium depletion may be possible by adequate dietary supplementation, intermittent therapy, and when possible by careful liberalization of salt intake. Supplementary potassium chloride may however be required, particularly in cirrhosis or patients with a pre-existing degree of aldosteronism.

While potassium supplements may be indicated there have been numerous reports, published and unpublished, concerning nonspecific small bowel lesions, consisting of stenosis with or without ulceration, associated with administration of enteric-coated potassium salts alone or with oral diuretics. Surgery was frequently required and deaths have occurred.

Pregnancy: Not recommended for use in pregnant patients. Use of the drug in women of the childbearing age requires that its potential benefits be weighed against the possible hazards to the fetus. The safety and efficacy of the drug in toxemia of pregnancy have not been established.

Lactation: Contraindicated in nursing mothers. If use of the drug is deemed essential, the patient should stop nursing.

Precautions: General: Weakness, muscle cramps, paresthesias, thirst, anorexia, and signs of hyponatremia, hypokalemia, and/or hypochloremic alkalosis may occur following vigorous or excessive diuresis and these may be accentuated by rigid salt restriction. Rarely tetany has been reported following vigorous diuresis. **During therapy with ethacrynic acid, liberalization of salt intake and supplementary potassium chloride are often necessary.**

When metabolic alkalosis may be anticipated, e.g., in cirrhosis with ascites, the use of potassium chloride with or without a potassium-sparing agent before and continuously during therapy with ethacrynic acid may mitigate or prevent the hypokalemia. If a potassium-sparing agent is used, continued monitoring of electrolytes is still required because of the possible occurrence in this case of hyperkalemia.

In a few patients this diuretic has produced severe, watery diarrhea. If this occurs, it should be discontinued and not readministered.

Ethacrynic acid has little or no effect on glomerular filtration or on renal blood flow, except following pronounced reductions in plasma volume when associated with rapid diuresis. A transient increase in serum urea nitrogen may occur. This is usually reversible when the drug is discontinued.

Deafness, tinnitus and vertigo with a sense of fullness in the ears have occurred most frequently in patients with severe impairment of renal function. These symptoms have been associated most often with i.v. administration and with doses in excess of those recommended. The deafness has usually been reversible and of short duration (1 to 24 hours). However, in some critically ill patients the hearing loss has been permanent. A number of these patients were also receiving drugs known to be ototoxic.

Drug Interactions: Antihypertensive Agents: The safety and efficacy of ethacrynic acid in hypertension have not been established. However, the dosage of coadministered antihypertensive agents may require adjustment.

Orthostatic hypotension may occur in patients receiving antihypertensive agents when given ethacrynic acid.

Antibiotics: Ethacrynic acid may increase the ototoxic potential of other drugs such as aminoglycoside antibiotics. Their concurrent use should be avoided.

Warfarin: A number of drugs, including ethacrynic acid, have been shown to displace warfarin from plasma protein; a reduction in the usual anticoagulant dosage may be required in patients receiving both drugs.
Lithium: Lithium should generally not be given to patients receiving diuretics, since diuretics reduce renal clearance of lithium making the risk of lithium toxicity very high in such patients.
Corticosteroids: Ethacrynic acid may increase the risk of gastric hemorrhage associated with corticosteroid treatment.
Patients With Special Diseases and Conditions: Patients with refractory edema or having pre-existing degrees of aldosteronism and those receiving potassium depleting steroids are more likely to develop hypokalemia. This may be responsible for increased digitalis toxicity or result in hepatic coma in patients with advanced liver disease. These patients may therefore require potassium supplementation.
Gastrointestinal: anorexia, malaise, abdominal discomfort or pain, dysphagia, nausea, vomiting, and diarrhea. In a few patients, watery, profuse diarrhea, gastrointestinal bleeding, and acute pancreatitis has been reported.
Metabolic: Reversible hyperuricemia, decreased urinary urate excretion, and hyperglycemia have been reported. Acute gout has been precipitated. Rarely acute symptomatic hypoglycemia with convulsions, jaundice and abnormal tests of hepatocellular function have been reported.
Hematologic: Agranulocytosis, severe neutropenia, thrombocytopenia, and Henoch-Schönlein have been reported rarely.
Special Senses: Vertigo, deafness, and tinnitus, with a sense of fullness in the ears and blurred vision have occurred (see Precautions).
CNS: fatigue, apprehension and confusion.
Other: skin rash, headache, fever, chills and hematuria.

Ethacrynate sodium occasionally has caused local irritation and pain, and a rare instance of local thrombophlebitis has been reported after its use.

A number of possibly drug-related deaths have occurred in critically ill patients refractory to other diuretics. These generally have fallen into two categories: (1) patients with severe myocardial disease who have been receiving digitalis and presumably developed acute hypokalemia with fatal arrhythmia; (2) patients with severely decompensated hepatic cirrhosis with ascites, with or without accompanying encephalopathy, who were in electrolyte imbalance and died because of intensification of the electrolyte defect.

Dosage: Dosage must be regulated carefully to prevent a more rapid or substantial loss of fluid or electrolyte than is indicated or necessary. The magnitude of diuresis and natriuresis is largely dependent on the degree of fluid accumulation present in the patient. Similarly, the extent of potassium excretion is determined in large measure by the presence and magnitude of aldosteronism.

Oral: To Initiate Diuresis: Adults: The smallest dose required to produce gradual weight loss (about 0.5 to 1 kg/day) is recommended.

Onset of diuresis usually occurs at 50 to 100 mg for adults. After diuresis has been achieved, the minimally effective dose (usually from 50 to 200 mg daily) may be given on a continuous or intermittent dosage schedule. Dosage adjustments are usually in 25 to 50 mg increments to avoid derangement of water and electrolyte excretion.

The patient should be weighed under standard conditions before and during the institution of diuretic therapy with this compound. Small alterations in dose might prevent a massive diuretic response.

The following schedule may be helpful in determining the smallest effective dose. Day 1: 50 mg (single dose) after a meal. Day 2: 50 mg twice daily after meals, if necessary. Day 3: 100 mg in the morning and 50 to 100 mg following the afternoon or evening meal, depending upon response to the morning dose.

A few patients may require initial and maintenance doses as high as 200 mg twice daily. These higher doses, which should be achieved gradually, are most often required in patients with severe, refractory edema.
Children: In children, the initial dose should be 25 mg. Careful stepwise increments in dosage of 25 mg should be made to achieve effective maintenance. A dosage for infants has not been established.
Maintenance Therapy: It is usually possible to reduce the dosage and frequency of administration once dry weight has been achieved.

Ethacrynic acid may be given intermittently after an effective diuresis is obtained with the regimen outlined above. Dosage may be on an alternate daily schedule or more prolonged periods of diuretic therapy may be interspersed with rest periods. Such an intermittent dosage schedule allows time for correction of any electrolyte imbalance and may provide a more efficient diuretic response.

The chloruretic effect of this agent may give rise to retention of bicarbonate and metabolic alkalosis. This may be corrected by giving chloride (ammonium chloride or arginine chloride). Ammonium chloride should not be given to cirrhotic patients.

Ethacrynic acid has additive effects when used with other diuretics.

Small doses of ethacrynic acid may be added to existing diuretic regimens to maintain basal weight. This drug may potentiate the action of carbonic anhydrase inhibitors, with augmentation of natriuresis and kaliuresis. Therefore, when adding ethacrynic acid, the initial dose and changes of dose should be in 25 mg increments to avoid electrolyte depletion. Rarely, patients who failed to respond to ethacrynic acid have responded to older established agents.

While many patients do not require supplemental potassium, the use of potassium chloride or potassium-sparing agents or both, during treatment with ethacrynic acid is advisable, especially in cirrhotic or nephrotic patients and in patients receiving digitalis.

Salt liberalization usually prevents the development of hyponatremia and hypochloremia. During treatment with ethacrynic acid, salt may be liberalized to a greater extent than with other diuretics. Cirrhotic patients however, usually require at least moderate salt restriction concomitant with diuretic therapy.

I.V.: For i.v. use when oral intake is impractical or in urgent conditions, such as acute pulmonary edema.
Adults: The usual i.v. dose for the average sized adult is 50 mg, or 0.5 to 1.0 mg/kg of body weight. Usually only 1 dose has been necessary; occasionally a second dose at a new injection site, to avoid possible thrombophlebitis, may be required. A single i.v. dose not exceeding 100 mg has been used in critical situations. Children: Insufficient pediatric experience precludes recommendation for this age group.

The solution may be given slowly through the tubing of a running infusion or by direct i.v. injection over a period of several minutes.

Ethacrynate sodium should not be given s.c. or i.m. because of local pain and irritation.

To reconstitute the dry material, add 50 mL of 5% Dextrose Injection or Sodium Chloride Injection to the vial. Occasionally, some 5% Dextrose Injection solutions may have a low pH (below 5). The resulting solution with such a diluent may be hazy or opalescent. I.V. use of such a solution is not recommended.

Do not mix this solution with whole blood or its derivatives. Because there is no preservative contained in the vial, a fresh solution should be prepared just prior to each administration. Any unused solution should be discarded.

Supplied: Edecrin: Each white, scored tablet, with the MSD symbol on one side, contains: ethacrynic acid 50 mg. Nonmedicinal ingredients: colloidal silicon dioxide, cornstarch, lactose, magnesium stearate and talc. Gluten- and tartrazine-free. Bottles of 50.

Sodium Edecrin: Each vial of dry white material either in a plug form or as a powder, contains: ethacrynate sodium equivalent to ethacrynic acid 50 mg. Nonmedicinal ingredients: mannitol.

(Shown in Product Recognition Section)

Reviewed 1999

EES® 200
EES® 400
EES® 600
Abbott

Erythromycin Ethylsuccinate

Antibiotic

Supplied: Granules: EES 200 (7 days): Each 5 mL of reconstituted banana-flavored suspension contains: erythromycin ethylsuccinate equivalent to 200 mg erythromycin activity. Also contains caramel, flavor, polysorbate 80, sodium citrate, sucrose and xanthan gum. Alcohol-, gluten-, lactose-, paraben-, sulfite- and tartrazine-free. Bottles of 105 mL for 7-day treatment.

EES 200 (10 days): Each 5 mL of reconstituted banana-flavored suspension contains: erythromycin ethylsuccinate equivalent to 200 mg erythromycin activity. Also contains caramel, flavor, polysorbate 80, sodium citrate, sucrose and xanthan gum. Alcohol-, gluten-, lactose-, paraben-, sulfite- and tartrazine-free. Bottles of 150 mL for 10-day treatment.

EES 400 (7 days): Each 5 mL of reconstituted banana-flavored suspension contains: erythromycin ethylsuccinate equivalent to 400 mg erythromycin activity. Also contains caramel, flavor, polysorbate 80, sodium citrate, sucrose and xanthan gum. Alcohol-, gluten-, lactose-, paraben-, sulfite- and tartrazine-free. Bottles of 105 mL for 7-day treatment.

EES 400 (10 days) Each 5 mL of reconstituted banana-flavored suspension contains: erythromycin ethylsuccinate equivalent to 400 mg erythromycin activity. Also contains caramel, flavor, polysorbate 80, sodium citrate, sucrose and xanthan gum. Alcohol-, gluten-, lactose-, paraben-, sulfite- and tartrazine-free. Bottles of 150 mL for 10-day treatment.

Tablets: EES 600: Each ovaloid, yellow Filmtab tablet contains: erythromycin ethylsuccinate USP 600 mg of erythromycin activity. Also contains calcium phosphate dibasic, cornstarch, D&C Yellow #10, hydroxypropyl methylcellulose, magnesium stearate, polyethylene glycol 400, polyethylene glycol 8 000, povidone, sodium starch glycolate, sorbic acid and titanium dioxide. Alcohol-, gluten-, lactose-, paraben-, sucrose-, sulfite- and tartrazine-free. Bottles of 50 and 250.

EFFEXOR®
EFFEXOR® XR
Wyeth-Ayerst

Venlafaxine HCl

Antidepressant

Pharmacology: Venlafaxine is a phenethylamine bicyclic derivative, chemically unrelated to tricyclic, tetracyclic or other available antidepressant agents.

The mechanism of venlafaxine's antidepressant action in humans is believed to be associated with its potentiation of neurotransmitter activity in the CNS. Preclinical studies have shown that venlafaxine and its major metabolite, O-desmethylvenlafaxine (ODV), are potent inhibitors of neuronal serotonin and norepinephrine reuptake and weak inhibitors of dopamine reuptake.

Venlafaxine and ODV have no significant affinity for muscarinic, histaminergic, or α_1-adrenergic receptors in vitro. Pharmacologic activity at these receptors is hypothesized to be associated with the various anticholinergic, sedative, and cardiovascular effects seen with other psychotropic drugs. Venlafaxine and ODV do not possess MAO inhibitory activity.
Pharmacokinetics: Venlafaxine is well absorbed, with peak plasma concentrations with Effexor tablets occurring approximately 2 hours after dosing. Venlafaxine is extensively metabolized, with O-desmethylvenlafaxine, (ODV, the only major active metabolite) peak plasma levels occurring approximately 4 hours after dosing. Following single doses of 25 to 75 mg, mean ($\pm$SD) peak plasma concentrations of venlafaxine range from 37 ± 14 to 102 ± 41 ng/mL, respectively, and are reached in 2 ± 1 hours, and mean peak ODV plasma concentrations range from 61 ± 13 to 168 ± 37 ng/mL and are reached in 4 ± 2 hours. Approximately 87% of a single dose of venlafaxine is recovered in the urine within 48 hours as either unchanged venlafaxine (5%), unconjugated ODV (29%), conjugated ODV (26%), or other minor inactive metabolites (27%), and 92% of the radioactive dose is recovered within 72 hours. Therefore, renal elimination of venlafaxine and its metabolites is the primary route of excretion.

After administration of Effexor XR (extended release capsules), the peak plasma concentrations of venlafaxine and ODV are attained within 6.0 ± 1.5 and 8.8 ± 2.2 hours, respectively. The rate of absorption of venlafaxine from the Effexor XR capsule is slower than its rate of elimination. Therefore, the apparent elimination half-life of venlafaxine following administration of Effexor XR (15 ± 6 hours) is actually the absorption half-life instead of the true disposition half-life (5 ± 2) hours observed following administration of an Effexor immediate release tablet.
Multiple-Dose Pharmacokinetic Profile (Tablets and Extended Release Capsules): Steady-state concentrations of both venlafaxine and ODV in plasma are attained within 3 days of oral multiple-dose therapy. The clearance of venlafaxine is slightly (15%) lower following multiple doses than following a single dose.

Venlafaxine and ODV exhibited approximately linear kinetics over the dose range of 75 to 450 mg/day.

The mean$\pm$SD steady-state plasma clearances of venlafaxine and ODV are 1.3 ± 0.6 and 0.4 ± 0.2 l/h/kg, respectively; apparent elimination half-life is 5 ± 2 and 11 ± 2 hours, respectively; and apparent (steady-state) volume of distribution is 7.5 ± 3.7 and 5.7 ± 1.8 L/kg, respectively.

Effexor (cont'd)

Venlafaxine and ODV renal clearances are 49±27 and 94±56 mL/h/kg, respectively, which correspond to 5±3.0% and 25±13% of an administered venlafaxine dose recovered in urine as venlafaxine and ODV, respectively.

When equal daily doses of venlafaxine were administered as either an immediate release tablet or the extended release capsule, the exposure (AUC, area under the concentration curve) to both venlafaxine and ODV was similar for the 2 treatments, and the fluctuation in plasma concentrations was slightly lower following treatment with the extended release capsule. Therefore, the Effexor XR capsules provide a slower rate of absorption, but the same extent of absorption (i.e., AUC), as the venlafaxine immediate release tablet.

Venlafaxine and ODV are 27 and 30% bound to human plasma proteins, respectively. Therefore, administration of venlafaxine to a patient taking another drug that is highly protein-bound should not cause increased free concentrations of the other drug. Following i.v. administration, the steady-state volume of distribution of venlafaxine is 4.4±1.9 L/kg, indicating that venlafaxine distributes well beyond the total body water.

Following absorption, venlafaxine undergoes extensive presystemic metabolism in the liver. On the basis of mass balance studies, at least 92% of a single dose of venlafaxine is absorbed. The absolute bioavailability of venlafaxine is approximately 45%. The primary metabolite of venlafaxine is ODV, which is an active metabolite. Venlafaxine is also metabolized to N-desmethylvenlafaxine, N,O-didesmethylvenlafaxine, and other minor metabolites. In vitro studies indicate that the formation of ODV is catalysed by CYP2D6 and that the formation of N-desmethylvenlafaxine is catalysed by CYP3A3/4. The results of the in vitro studies have been confirmed in a clinical study with subjects who are CYP2D6 poor and extensive metabolizers. However, despite the metabolic differences between the CYP2D6 poor and extensive metabolizers, the total exposure to the sum of the 2 active species (venlafaxine and ODV, which have comparable activity) was similar in the 2 metabolizer groups.

Food has no significant effect on the absorption of venlafaxine or on the subsequent formation of ODV.

Age and Gender: Population pharmacokinetic analyses of 547 venlafaxine-treated patients from 3 studies involving both venlafaxine immediate release tablets and venlafaxine extended release capsules showed that age and sex do not significantly affect the pharmacokinetics of venlafaxine. A 20% reduction in clearance was noted for ODV in subjects over 60 years old; this was possibly caused by the decrease in renal function that typically occurs with aging. Dosage adjustment based upon age or gender is generally not necessary (see Dosage).

Extensive/Poor Metabolizers: Plasma concentrations of venlafaxine were higher in CYP2D6 poor metabolizers than extensive metabolizers. Because the total exposure (AUC) of venlafaxine and ODV was similar in poor and extensive metabolizer groups, there is no need for different venlafaxine dosing regimens for these 2 groups.

Hepatic Disease: In 9 patients with hepatic cirrhosis, the pharmacokinetic disposition of both venlafaxine and ODV were significantly altered. Venlafaxine elimination half-life was prolonged by about 30%, and clearance was decreased by about 50% in cirrhotic patients compared to normal subjects. ODV elimination half-life was prolonged by about 60% and clearance decreased by about 30% in cirrhotic patients compared to normal subjects.

A large degree of intersubject variability was noted. Three patients with more severe cirrhosis had a more substantial decrease in venlafaxine clearance (about 90%) compared to normal subjects. **Dosage adjustment is necessary in patients with liver disease (see Dosage).**

Renal Disease: In patients with moderate to severe impairment of renal function (GFR=10 to 70 mL/min), venlafaxine elimination half-life was prolonged by 50%, and clearance was decreased by about 24% compared to normal subjects. ODV elimination half-life was prolonged by about 40%, but clearance was unchanged.

In dialysis patients, venlafaxine elimination half-life was prolonged by about 180% and clearance was decreased by about 57%. In dialysis patients, ODV elimination half-life was prolonged by about 142%, and clearance was reduced by about 56% compared to normal subjects. A large degree of intersubject variability was noted.

Dosage adjustment is necessary in patients with renal disease (see Dosage).

Clinical Trials: The efficacy of venlafaxine tablets in the treatment of depression was established in 6-week controlled trials of outpatients whose diagnoses corresponded most closely to the DSM-II or DSM-III-R category of major depressive disorder and in a 4-week controlled trial of inpatients meeting diagnostic criteria for major depressive disorder with melancholia.

The efficacy of venlafaxine extended release capsules as a treatment for depression was established in 2 placebo-controlled, short-term, flexible-dose studies in adult outpatients meeting DSM-III-R or DSM-IV criteria for major depression. An 8-week study utilizing venlafaxine extended release doses in a range 75 to 225 mg/day (mean dose for completers was 177 mg/day) and a 12-week study utilizing venlafaxine extended release doses in a range 75 to 150 mg/day (Mean dose for completers was 136 mg/day) both demonstrated superiority of venlafaxine extended release over placebo on the HAM-D total score, the HAM-D Depressed Mood Item, the MADRS total score, the CGI Severity of illness scale, and the CGI Global Improvement scale. In both studies, venlafaxine extended release was also significantly better than placebo for certain factors of the HAM-D, including the anxiety/somatization factor, the cognitive disturbance factor, and the retardation factor, as well as for the psychic anxiety score.

Indications: For the symptomatic relief of depressive illness.

The effectiveness of venlafaxine in long-term use (i.e., for more than 4 to 6 weeks-immedate release tablets, or 8 to 12 weeks-extended release capsules) has not been systematically evaluated in controlled trials. Therefore, the physician who elects to use venlafaxine for extended periods should periodically re-evaluate the long-term usefulness of the drug for the individual patient.

Contraindications: In patients with known hypersensitivity to venlafaxine or to any of the components of the formulations.

MAO Inhibitors: There have been reports of serious, sometimes fatal reactions in patients receiving antidepressants with pharmacological properties similar to those of venlafaxine in combination with a MAO inhibitor. Therefore, venlafaxine should not be used in combination with MAO inhibitors or within 2 weeks of terminating treatment with MAO inhibitors. Treatment with MAO inhibitors should not be started until 2 weeks after discontinuation of venlafaxine therapy.

Warnings: Sustained Hypertension: Treatment with venlafaxine tablets was associated with modest but sustained increases in blood pressure during premarketing studies. Sustained hypertension, defined as treatment-emergent supine diastolic blood pressure (SDBP) ≥90 mm Hg **and** ≥10 mm Hg above baseline for 3 consecutive visits, showed the following incidence and dose-relationship in Table I.

Table I—Effexor/Effexor XR

Probability of Sustained Elevation in SDBP (Pool of Premarketing Studies with Effexor/Effexor XR)

Treatment Group	**(%) Incidence of Sustained Elevation in SDBP**	
	Immediate Release	**Extended Release**
Venlafaxine		
<100 mg/day	2	3
101-200 mg/day	5	2
201-300 mg/day	6	4
>300 mg/day	13	NE*
Placebo	2	NE*

* Not evaluable.

An analysis of the blood pressure increases in patients with sustained hypertension and in the 19 patients who were discontinued from treatment because of hypertension (<1% of total venlafaxine-treated group) showed that most of the blood pressure increases were in the range of 10 to 15 mm Hg, SDBP.

In placebo-controlled premarketing depression studies with venlafaxine extended release, a final on-therapy mean increase in supine diastolic pressure (SDBP) of <1.2 mm Hg was observed for venlafaxine extended release-treated patients compared with a mean decrease of 0.2 mm Hg for placebo-treated patients.

Less than 3% of venlafaxine extended release patients treated with doses of 75 to 300 mg/day had sustained elevations in blood pressure (defined as treatment-emergent SDBP ≥90 mm Hg and ≥10 mm Hg above baseline for 3 consecutive on-therapy visits). An insufficient number of patients received doses of venlafaxine extended release >300 mg/day to evaluate systematically sustained blood pressure increases. Less than 1% of venlafaxine extended release-treated patients in double-blind, placebo-controlled premarketing depression studies discontinued treatment because of elevated blood pressure compared with 0.4% of placebo-treated patients.

Sustained increases could have adverse consequences. Therefore, it is recommended that patients receiving venlafaxine have their blood pressure monitored regularly. For patients who experience a sustained increase in blood pressure while receiving venlafaxine, either dose reduction or discontinuation should be considered after a benefit-risk assessment is made.

Precautions: General: Suicide: The possibility of a suicide attempt in seriously depressed patients is inherent to the illness and may persist until significant remission occurs. Close supervision of high-risk patients should accompany initial drug therapy, and consideration should be given to the need for hospitalization. In order to reduce the risk of overdose, prescriptions for venlafaxine tablets/capsules should be written for the smallest quantity of tablets/capsules consistent with good patient management.

Seizures: During premarketing testing, seizures were reported in 8 out of 3 082 venlafaxine tablet-treated patients (0.26%). In 5 of the 8 cases with immediate release tablets, patients were receiving doses of 150 mg/day or less. No seizures were seen in 705 venlafaxine extended release capsule-treated patients. However, patients with a history of convulsive disorders were excluded from most of these studies. Venlafaxine should be used cautiously in patients with a history of seizures, and should be promptly discontinued in any patient who develops seizures.

Activation of Mania/Hypomania: During Phase II and III trials, mania or hypomania occurred in 0.5% of venlafaxine tablet-treated patients and in 0.3% of venlafaxine capsule-treated patients. Mania or hypomania occurred in 0.6% of all venlafaxine-treated patients. Mania/hypomania has also been reported in a small proportion of patients with major affective disorder who were treated with other marketed antidepressants. As with all antidepressants, venlafaxine should be used cautiously in patients with a history of mania.

Patients with Concomitant Illness: Clinical experience with venlafaxine in patients with concomitant systemic illness is limited. Caution is advised in administering venlafaxine to patients with diseases or conditions that could affect hemodynamic responses or metabolism. Patients should be questioned about any prescription or "over the counter drugs" that they are taking, or planning to take, since there is a potential for interactions.

Cardiac Disease: Venlafaxine has not been evaluated or used to any appreciable extent in patients with a recent history of myocardial infarction or unstable heart disease. Patients with these diagnoses were systematically excluded from many clinical studies during the product's clinical trials.

Evaluation of the ECG for 769 patients who received venlafaxine immediate release tablets in 4- to 6-week double-blind trials showed that the incidence of trial-emergent conduction abnormalities did not differ from that with placebo.

The electrocardiograms for 357 patients who received venlafaxine extended release and 285 patients who received placebo in 8- to 12-week double-blind, placebo-controlled trials were analyzed. The mean change from baseline in corrected QT interval (QTc) for venlafaxine extended release-treated patients was increased relative to that for placebo-treated patients (increase of 4.7 msec for venlafaxine extended release and decrease of 1.9 msec for placebo). Three of 705 venlafaxine extended release-treated patients in phase III studies experienced QTc prolongation to 500 msec during treatment. Baseline QTc was >450 msec for all 3 patients. No case of sudden unexplained death or serious ventricular arrhythmia, which are possible clinical sequelae of QTc prolongation, was reported in venlafaxine extended release premarketing studies.

The mean heart rate was increased by about 4 beats/minute during treatment with venlafaxine. Venlafaxine treatment has been associated with sustained hypertension (see Warnings).

Hepatic and Renal Disease: In patients with hepatic or renal impairment (GFR=10 to 70 mL/min), the pharmacokinetic disposition of both venlafaxine and ODV are significantly altered. **Dosage adjustment is necessary in these patients (see Dosage).**

Insomnia and Nervousness: Treatment-emergent insomnia and nervousness were more commonly reported for patients treated with venlafaxine than with placebo (see Adverse Effects).

Changes in Appetite and Weight: Treatment-emergent anorexia was more commonly reported for venlafaxine-treated than placebo-treated patients (see Adverse Effects). Significant weight loss, especially in underweight depressed patients, may be an undesirable result of treatment.

Occupational Hazards: Clinical studies were performed to examine the effects of venlafaxine on behavioral performance of healthy individuals. The results revealed no clinically significant impairment of psychomotor, cognitive, or complex behavior performance. However, since any psychoactive drug may impair judgement, thinking or motor skills, patients should be cautioned about operating hazardous machinery, including automobiles, until they are reasonably certain that the drug treatment does not affect them adversely.

Pregnancy, Labor and Delivery: There are no adequate and well controlled studies with venlafaxine in pregnant women. Therefore, venlafaxine should only be used during pregnancy if clearly needed. Patients should be advised to notify their physician if they become pregnant or intend to become pregnant during therapy.

Lactation: It is not known whether venlafaxine or its metabolites are excreted in human milk. Because many drugs are excreted in human milk, lactating women should not nurse their infants while receiving venlafaxine.

Children: Safety and efficacy in children below the age of 18 have not been established.

Geriatrics: Of the 2 897 patients in Phase II and III trials with venlafaxine tablets, 357 (12%) were 65 years of age or older. Forty-three (4%) of the patients in trials with venlafaxine extended release capsules, were 65 years of age or older. No overall differences in effectiveness and safety were observed between these patients and younger patients, and other reported clinical experience has not identified differences in response between the elderly and younger patients. However, greater sensitivity of some older individuals cannot be ruled out.

Discontinuation Symptoms: While the discontinuation effects of venlafaxine have not been systematically evaluated in controlled clinical trials, a retrospective survey of new events occurring during taper or following discontinuation revealed the following 6 events that occurred at an incidence of at least 5%, and for which the incidence for venlafaxine was at least twice the placebo incidence: asthenia, dizziness, headache, insomnia, nausea and nervousness.

With venlafaxine extended release, the following 6 events occurred with an incidence of at least 3% , and for which the incidence of venlafaxine extended release was at least twice the placebo incidence: dizziness, dry mouth, insomnia, nausea, nervousness and sweating.

Therefore, it is recommended that the dosage be tapered gradually and the patient monitored (see Dosage).

Drug Interactions: As with all drugs, the potential for interaction by a variety of mechanisms is a possibility.

Lithium: The steady-state pharmacokinetics of venlafaxine administered as 50 mg every 8 hours was not affected when a single 600 mg oral dose of lithium was administered to 12 healthy male subjects. Venlafaxine had no effect on the pharmacokinetics of lithium.

Diazepam: The steady-state pharmacokinetics of venlafaxine administered as 50 mg every 8 hours was not affected when a single 10 mg oral dose of diazepam was administered to 18 healthy male subjects. Venlafaxine had no effect on the pharmacokinetics of diazepam or its active metabolite, desmethyldiazepam. Additionally, venlafaxine administration did not affect the psychomotor and psychometric effects induced by diazepam.

Cimetidine: Concomitant administration of cimetidine and venlafaxine in a steady-state study for both drugs in 18 healthy male subjects resulted in inhibition of first-pass metabolism of venlafaxine. The oral clearance of venlafaxine was reduced by about 43%, and the exposure (AUC) and maximum concentration (C_{max}) of the drug were increased by about 60%. However, there was no effect on the pharmacokinetics of ODV. The overall pharmacological activity of venlafaxine plus ODV is expected to increase only slightly, and no dosage adjustment should be necessary for most normal adults.

However, for patients with pre existing hypertension, for elderly patients and for patients with hepatic or renal dysfunction, the interaction associated with the concomitant use of cimetidine and venlafaxine is not known and potentially could be more pronounced. Therefore, caution is advised with such patients.

Haloperidol: Venlafaxine administered under steady-state conditions at 150 mg/day in 24 healthy subjects decreased total oral-dose clearance (Cl/F) of a single 2 mg dose of haloperidol by 42%, which resulted in a 70% increase in haloperidol AUC. In addition, the haloperidol C_{max} increased 88% when coadministered with venlafaxine, but the haloperidol elimination half-life ($t_{1/2}$) was unchanged. The mechanism explaining this finding is unknown.

Imipramine: Venlafaxine did not affect the pharmacokinetics of imipramine and 2-OH-imipramine. However, AUC, C_{max} and C_{min} of desipramine (the active metabolite of imipramine) increased by approximately 35% in the presence of venlafaxine. The 2-OH-desipramine AUCs increased by at least 2.5 fold (with venlafaxine 37.5 mg q12h) and by 4.5 fold (with venlafaxine 75 mg q12h). The clinical significance of elevated 2-OH-desipramine levels is unknown.

Imipramine partially inhibited the CYP2D6-mediated formation of ODV. However, the total concentration of active compounds (venlafaxine plus ODV) was not affected by coadministration with imipramine, and no dosage adjustment is required.

Risperidone: Venlafaxine administered under steady-state conditions at 150 mg/day slightly inhibited the CYP2D6-mediated metabolism of risperidone (administered as a single 1 mg oral dose) to its active metabolite, 9-hydroxyrisperidone, resulting in an approximate 32% increase in risperidone AUC. However, venlafaxine coadministration did not significantly alter the pharmacokinetic profile of the total active moiety (risperidone plus 9-hydroxyrisperidone).

Drugs Highly Bound to Plasma Proteins: Venlafaxine is not highly bound to plasma proteins; therefore, administration of venlafaxine to a patient taking another drug that is highly protein bound should not cause increased free concentrations of the other drug.

Drugs that Inhibit Cytochrome P450 Isoenzymes: CYP2D6-Inhibitors: In vitro and in vivo studies indicate that venlafaxine is metabolized to its active metabolite, ODV, by CYP2D6. Therefore, the potential exists for a drug interaction between drugs that inhibit CYP2D6 mediated metabolism and venlafaxine. Drug interactions that reduce the metabolism of venlafaxine to ODV (see Imipramine above) potentially increase the plasma concentrations of venlafaxine and lower the concentrations of the active metabolite. However, the pharmacokinetic profile of venlafaxine in subjects concomitantly receiving a CYP2D6-inhibitor would not be substantially different than the pharmacokinetic profile in subjects who are CYP2D6 poor metabolizers, and no dosage adjustment is required.

CYP3A3/4 Inhibitors: In vitro studies indicate that venlafaxine is likely metabolized to a minor, less active metabolite, N-desmethylvenlafaxine, by CYP3A3/4. Because CYP3A3/4 is typically a minor pathway relative to CYP2D6 in the metabolism of venlafaxine, the potential for a clinically significant drug interaction between drugs that inhibit CYP3A3/4-mediated metabolism and venlafaxine is small. However, because the 2 primary metabolic pathways for venlafaxine are through CYP2D6 and, to a lesser extent, CYP3A3/4, concomitant intake of inhibitors of both of these isoenzymes is not recommended during treatment with venlafaxine. However, interactions between concomitant intake of inhibitors of both CYP2D6 and CYP3A3/4 with venlafaxine has not been studied.

Drugs Metabolized by Cytochrome P450 Isoenzymes: CYP2D6: In vitro studies indicate that venlafaxine is a relatively weak inhibitor of CYP2D6. These findings have been confirmed in vivo by a clinical drug interaction study comparing the effect of venlafaxine with that of fluoxetine on the CYP2D6-mediated metabolism of dextromethorphan to dextrorphan.

CYP3A4: Venlafaxine did not inhibit CYP3A4 in vitro. This finding was confirmed in vivo by clinical drug interaction studies in which venlafaxine did not inhibit the metabolism of several CYP3A4 substrates, including alprazolam, diazepam, and terfenadine.

CYP1A2: Venlafaxine did not inhibit CYP1A2 in vitro. This finding was confirmed in vivo by a clinical drug interaction study in which venlafaxine did not inhibit the metabolism of caffeine, a CYP1A2 substrate.

CYP2C9: Venlafaxine did not inhibit CYP2C9 in vitro. The clinical significance of this finding is unknown.

CYP2C19: Venlafaxine did not inhibit the metabolism of diazepam, which is partially metabolized by CYP2C19 (see Diazepam above).

MAO Inhibitors: See Contraindications.

Other CNS-Active Drugs: The risk of using venlafaxine in combination with other CNS-active drugs (including alcohol) has not been systematically evaluated. Consequently, caution is advised if the concomitant administration of venlafaxine and such drugs is required.

Electroconvulsive Therapy: There are no clinical data on the use of electroconvulsive therapy combined with venlafaxine treatment.

Drug Abuse and Dependence: Physical and Psychological Dependence: In vitro studies revealed that venlafaxine has virtually no affinity for opiate, benzodiazepine, phencyclidine (PCP), or N-methyl-D-aspartic acid (NMDA) receptors. It has no significant CNS stimulant activity in rodents. In primate drug discrimination studies, venlafaxine showed no significant stimulant or depressant abuse liability.

While venlafaxine tablets and capsules have not been systematically studied in clinical trials for their potential for abuse, there was no indication of drug-seeking behavior in the clinical trials. However, it is not possible to predict on the basis of premarketing experience the extent to which a CNS-active drug will be misused, diverted, and/or abused once marketed. Consequently, physicians should carefully evaluate patients for history of drug abuse and follow such patients closely, observing them for signs of misuse or abuse of venlafaxine (e.g., development of tolerance, incrementation of dose, drug-seeking behavior).

Adverse Effects: Commonly Observed Adverse Reactions: The most commonly observed adverse events associated with the use of venlafaxine (incidence of 5% or greater) and not seen at an equivalent incidence among placebo-treated patients (i.e., incidence for venlafaxine at least twice that for placebo), derived from the 2% incidence in Table III, were:

Effexor: asthenia, sweating, nausea, constipation, anorexia, vomiting, somnolence, dry mouth, dizziness, nervousness, anxiety, tremor, blurred vision, and abnormal ejaculation/orgasm and impotence in men.

Effexor XR: abnormal dreams, anorexia, dizziness, dry mouth, nausea, nervousness, somnolence, sweating, and tremor as well as abnormal ejaculation/orgasm in men.

Adverse Reactions Associated with Discontinuation of Treatment: Nineteen percent (537/2 897) of venlafaxine and 12% (88/705) of venlafaxine extended release-treated patients in Phase II and III depression studies discontinued treatment due to an adverse reaction. The more common events (≥ 1%) associated with discontinuation of treatment and considered to be drug-related (i.e., those events associated with dropout at a rate approximately twice or greater for venlafaxine compared to placebo) are shown in Table II.

Table II—Effexor/Effexor XR

Adverse Reactions Associated with Discontinuation of Treatment

	Effexor (n=2 897)	Placebo (n=609)	Effexor XR (n=705)	Placebo (n=285)
CNS				
Somnolence	3%	1%	2%	—
Insomnia	3%	1%	—	—
Dizziness	3%	—	#	@
Nervousness	2%	—	—	@
Dry Mouth	2%	—	—	—
Anxiety	2%	1%	—	—
Gastrointestinal				
Nausea	6%	1%	4%	—
Anorexia	1%	—	1%	—
Urogenital				
Abnormal Ejaculation*	3%	—	—	—
Other				
Headache	3%	1%	#	@
Asthenia	2%	—	—	@
Sweating	2%	—	—	—

* percentages based on the number of males.
— less than 1%.
\# greater than 1% but active drug rate not twice rate for placebo.
@ 1% or greater.

Incidence in Controlled Trials: Table III (on following page) enumerates adverse events that occurred at an incidence of 2% or more, and were more frequent than in the placebo group, among venlafaxine-treated patients.

Effexor: Patients participated in 4- to 8-week placebo-controlled trials in which doses in the range of 75 to 375 mg/day were administered.

Effexor XR: Patients participated in 8- to 12-week placebo-controlled trials in which doses in the range of 75 to 225 mg/day were administered.

Reported adverse events were classified using a standard COSTART-based Dictionary terminology.

The prescriber should be aware that the cited frequencies for venlafaxine extended release cannot be compared with

Effexor (cont'd)

figures obtained from other clinical investigations of venlafaxine which involved different treatments, uses and investigators. The cited figures for venlafaxine extended release, however, do provide the prescribing physician with some basis for estimating the relative contribution of drug and non-drug factors to the side effect incidence rate in the population studied.

Dose Dependency of Adverse Events: A comparison of adverse event rates in a fixed-dose study comparing venlafaxine tablets 75, 225, and 375 mg/day with placebo revealed a dose dependency for some of the more common adverse events associated with venlafaxine use, as shown in Table IV. The rule for including events was to enumerate those that occurred at an incidence of 5% or more for at least one of the venlafaxine groups and for which the incidence was at least twice the placebo incidence for at least 1 venlafaxine group. Tests for potential dose relationships for these events (Cochran-Armitage Test, with a criterion of exact 2-sided p-value ≤ 0.05) suggested a dose-dependency for several adverse events in this list, including chills, hypertension, anorexia, nausea, agitation, dizziness, somnolence, tremor, yawning, sweating and abnormal ejaculation.

Adaptation to Certain Adverse Events: In premarketing experience with venlafaxine tablets over a 6-week period, and venlafaxine extended release capsules over a 12-week period, there was evidence of adaptation to some adverse events with continued therapy (e.g., dizziness and nausea), but less to other effects (e.g., abnormal ejaculation and dry mouth).

Vital Sign Changes: Treatment with venlafaxine tablets (averaged over all dose groups) in clinical trials was associated with a mean increase in pulse rate of approximately 3 beats/minute, compared to no change for placebo. It was associated with mean increases in diastolic blood pressure ranging from 0.7 to 2.5 mm Hg averaged over all dose groups, compared to mean decreases ranging from 0.9 to 3.8 mm Hg for placebo. However, there is a dose dependency for blood pressure increase (see Warnings).

Treatment with venlafaxine extended release capsules for up to 12 weeks in premarketing depression trials was associated with a mean increase in pulse rate of approximately 2 beats/minute, compared with 1 beat/minute for placebo. It was associated with mean increases in diastolic blood pressure ranging from 0.7 to 0.9 mm Hg, compared with mean decreases ranging from 0.5 to 1.4 mm Hg for placebo (see Warnings).

Laboratory Changes: Of the serum chemistry and hematology parameters monitored during clinical trials with venlafaxine, a statistically significant difference with placebo was seen only for serum cholesterol, i.e., patients treated with venlafaxine had mean increases from baseline of 3 mg/dL. In premarketing placebo-controlled depression trials for up to 12 weeks, venlafaxine extended release was associated with a mean final on-therapy increase in serum cholesterol concentration of approximately 1.5 mg/dL. The serum cholesterol changes induced by venlafaxine are of unknown clinical significance.

Table III—Effexor/Effexor XR

Treatment-emergent Adverse Experience Incidence in Placebo-controlled Clinical Trials (Percentage)[a]

Body System	Preferred Term	Effexor (n=1 033)	Placebo (n=609)	Effexor XR (n=357)	Placebo (n=285)
Body as a Whole	Headache	25	24	#	@
	Asthenia	12	6	8	7
	Infection	6	5	#	@
	Chills	3	—	—	—
Cardiovascular	Vasodilation	4	3	4	2
	Increased Blood Pressure/Hypertension	2	—	4	—
	Tachycardia	2	—	—	—
Dermatological	Sweating	12	3	14	3
	Rash	3	2	—	—
Gastrointestinal	Nausea	37	11	31	12
	Constipation	15	7	8	5
	Anorexia	11	2	8	4
	Diarrhea	8	7	#	@
	Vomiting	6	2	4	2
	Dyspepsia	5	4	#	@
	Flatulence	3	2	4	3
Metabolic	Weight Loss	#	—	3	—
Nervous	Somnolence	23	9	17	8
	Dry Mouth	22	11	12	6
	Dizziness	19	7	20	9
	Insomnia	18	10	17	11
	Nervousness	13	6	10	5
	Anxiety	6	3	#	@
	Tremor	5	—	5	2
	Abnormal Dreams	4	3	7	2
	Hypertonia	3	—	—	—
	Paresthesia	3	—	3	—
	Libido Decreased	2	—	3	—
	Agitation	2	—	3	—
	Depression	—	—	3	—
Respiration	Pharyngitis	#	#	7	6
	Yawn	3	—	3	—
Special Senses	Abnormal Vision	6	2	4	—
	Taste Perversion	2	—	—	—
Urogenital	Abnormal Ejaculation/Orgasm	12[b]	—[b]	16[b]	—[b]
	Impotence	6[b]	—[b]	4[b]	—[b]
	Anorgasmia	—[c]	—[c]	3[c]	—[c]
	Urinary Frequency	3	—	—	—
	Urination Impaired	2	—	—	—

[a]Events reported by at least 2% of patients treated with Effexor/Effexor XR are included, and are rounded to the nearest %. Events for which the Effexor/Effexor XR incidence was equal to or less than placebo are not listed in the table, but included the following: abdominal pain, accidental injury, anxiety, back pain, bronchitis, diarrhea, dysmenorrhea[c], dyspepsia, flu syndrome, headache, infection, pain, palpitation, rhinitis and sinusitis.

—Incidence less than 2%.

Incidence greater than 2%, but active drug incidence less than incidence for placebo.

@ Incidence 2% or greater.

[b]Incidence based on number of male patients.

[c]Incidence based on number of female patients.

Table IV—Effexor/Effexor XR

Treatment-emergent Adverse Experience Incidence in a Dose Comparison Trial

Body System/ Preferred Term	Placebo (n=92) %	Effexor Tablets (mg/day) 75 (n=89) %	225 (n=89) %	375 (n=88) %
Body as a Whole				
Abdominal pain	3.3	3.4	2.2	8.0
Asthenia	3.3	16.9	14.6	14.8
Chills	1.1	2.2	5.6	6.8
Infection	2.2	2.2	5.6	2.3
Cardiovascular				
Hypertension	1.1	1.1	2.2	4.5
Vasodilatation	0.0	4.5	5.6	2.3
Digestive				
Anorexia	2.2	14.6	13.5	17.0
Dyspepsia	2.2	6.7	6.7	4.5
Nausea	14.1	32.6	38.2	58.0
Vomiting	1.1	7.9	3.4	6.8
Nervous				
Agitation	0.0	1.1	2.2	4.5
Anxiety	4.3	11.2	4.5	2.3
Dizziness	4.3	19.1	22.5	23.9
Insomnia	9.8	22.5	20.2	13.6
Libido Decreased	1.1	2.2	1.1	5.7
Nervousness	4.3	21.3	13.5	12.5
Somnolence	4.3	16.9	18.0	26.1
Tremor	0.0	1.1	2.2	10.2
Respiratory				
Yawn	0.0	4.5	5.6	8.0
Skin and Appendages				
Sweating	5.4	6.7	12.4	19.3
Special Senses				
Abnormality of Accommodation	0.0	9.1	7.9	5.6
Urogenital				
Abnormal Ejaculation/Orgasm	0.0	4.5	2.2	12.5
Impotence	0.0	5.8	2.1	3.6
(number of men)	(n=63)	(n=52)	(n=48)	(n=56)

ECG Changes: In an analysis of ECGs obtained in 769 patients treated with venlafaxine tablets and 450 patients treated with placebo in controlled clinical trials, the only statistically significant difference observed was for heart rate, i.e., a mean increase from baseline of 4 beats/minute for venlafaxine tablets.

An analysis of ECGs obtained in 357 patients treated with venlafaxine extended release and 285 patients treated with placebo in controlled clinical trials, revealed a mean increase in corrected QT (QTc) interval relative to placebo (see Precautions). A mean increase in heart rate of approximately 4 beats/minute for venlafaxine extended release compared with 1 beat/minute for placebo was observed.

Other Events Observed During the Premarketing Evaluation of Venlafaxine: During its premarketing assessment, multiple doses of venlafaxine extended release were administered to 705 patients in phase III depression studies and venlafaxine tablets were administered to 96 patients. In addition, in premarketing assessment of venlafaxine tablets, multiple doses were administered to 2 897 patients in phase II and III depression studies. The conditions and duration of exposure to venlafaxine in both development programs varied greatly, and included (in overlapping categories) open and double-blind studies, uncontrolled and controlled studies, inpatient (venlafaxine tablets only) and outpatient studies, fixed-dose and titration studies. Untoward events associated with this exposure were recorded by clinical investigators using terminology of their own choosing. Consequently, it is not possible to provide a meaningful estimate of the proportion of individuals experiencing adverse events without first grouping similar types of untoward events into a smaller number of standardized event categories.

In the tabulations that follow, reported adverse events were classified using a standard COSTART-based Dictionary terminology. The frequencies presented, therefore, represent the proportion of the 3 698 patients exposed to multiple doses of either formulation of venlafaxine who experienced an event of the type cited on at least one occasion while receiving venlafaxine. All reported events are included except those already listed in Tables II and III, and those events for which a drug cause was remote. If the COSTART term for an event was so general as to be uninformative, it was replaced with a more informative term. It is important to emphasize that, although the events reported occurred during treatment with venlafaxine, they were not necessarily caused by it.

Events are further categorized by body system and the frequent adverse events are provided below. Frequent adverse events are those occurring on one or more occasions in at least 1/100 patients (only those not already listed in the tabulated results from placebo-controlled trials appear in this listing).
Body as a Whole: chest pain, chills, fever.
Cardiovascular: migraine, postural hypotension, tachycardia.
Digestive: eructation, increased appetite.
Hemic and Lymphatic: ecchymosis.
Musculoskeletal: myalgia.
Nervous: amnesia, emotional lability, hypesthesia, sleep disturbance, thinking abnormal, trismus.
Special Senses: ear pain, taste perversion.
Urogenital: menstrual disorder*, prostatitis*, urinary tract infection, urination impaired, vaginitis*.
*Based on the number of men and women as appropriate.

Overdose: Human Experience: In postmarketing experience, venlafaxine, taken alone, has not been clearly associated with lethal overdose. However, fatal reactions have been reported in patients taking overdoses of venlafaxine in combination with alcohol and/or other drugs.

Symptoms: Effexor: There were 14 reports of acute overdose with venlafaxine, either alone or in combination with other drugs and/or alcohol, among the patients included in the premarketing evaluation. The majority of the reports involved ingestions in which the total dose of venlafaxine taken was estimated to be no more than several-fold higher than the usual therapeutic dose. The 3 patients who took the highest doses were estimated to have ingested approximately 6.75 g, 2.75 g and 2.5 g. The resultant peak plasma levels of venlafaxine for the latter 2 patients were 6.24 and 2.35 μg/mL, respectively, and the peak plasma levels of O-desmethylvenlafaxine were 3.37 and 1.30 μg/mL, respectively. Plasma venlafaxine levels were not obtained for the patient who ingested 6.75 g of venlafaxine. All 14 patients recovered without sequelae. Most patients reported no symptoms. Among the remaining patients, somnolence was the most commonly reported symptom. The patient who ingested 2.75 g of venlafaxine was observed to have 2 generalized convulsions and a prolongation of QTc to 500 msec, compared with 405 msec at baseline. Mild sinus tachycardia was reported in 2 of the other patients.

Effexor XR: Among the patients included in the premarketing evaluation of venlafaxine extended release capsules, there were 2 reports of acute overdosage with venlafaxine extended release, either alone or in combination with other drugs. One patient took a combination of 6 g of venlafaxine extended release and 2.5 mg of lorazepam. This patient was hospitalized, treated symptomatically, and recovered without any untoward effects. The other patient took 2.5 g of venlafaxine extended release. This patient reported paresthesia of all four limbs but recovered without sequelae.

Treatment: Treatment should consist of those general measures employed in the management of overdosage with any antidepressant. Ensure an adequate airway, oxygenation, and ventilation. Monitoring of cardiac rhythm and vital signs is recommended. General supportive and symptomatic measures are also recommended. Use of activated charcoal, induction of emesis, or gastric lavage should be considered. Due to the large volume of distribution of venlafaxine, forced diuresis, dialysis, hemoperfusion and exchange transfusion are unlikely to be of benefit. No specific antidotes for venlafaxine are known.

In managing overdosage, consider the possibility of multiple drug involvement. The physician should consider contacting a poison control centre on the treatment of any overdose.

Dosage: Adults. Effexor: The recommended treatment dose is 75 mg/day, administered in 2 or 3 divided doses, taken with food. If the expected clinical improvement does not occur after a few weeks, a gradual dose increase to 150 mg/day may be considered. If needed, the dose may be further increased up to 225 mg/day. Increments of up to 75 mg/day should be made at intervals of no less than 4 days. In outpatient settings there was no evidence of the usefulness of doses greater than 225 mg/day for moderately depressed patients. More severely depressed inpatients have responded to higher doses, between 350 and 375 mg/day, given in 3 divided doses. Maximum: The maximum dose recommended is 375 mg/day (in an inpatient setting).
Effexor XR: The recommended dose for venlafaxine extended release is 75 mg/day, administered once daily with food, either in the morning or in the evening. Each capsule should be swallowed whole with water. It should not be divided, crushed, chewed, or placed in water. While the relationship between dose and antidepressant response for venlafaxine extended release has not been adequately explored patients not responding to the initial 75 mg may benefit from dose increases. Depending on tolerability and the need for further clinical effect, the dose should be increased by up to 75 mg/day up to a maximum of 225 mg/day for moderately depressed outpatients. Dose increments should be made at intervals of approximately 2 weeks or more, but not less than 4 days. There is very limited experience with venlafaxine extended release at doses higher than 225 mg/day, or in severely depressed inpatients.

It should be noted that, while the maximum recommended dose for moderately depressed outpatients is also 225 mg/day for venlafaxine tablets, more severely depressed inpatients responded to a mean dose of 350 mg/day (range of 150 to 375 mg/day).
Switching Patients from Effexor Tablets: Depressed patients who are currently being treated at a therapeutic dose with venlafaxine tablets may be switched to venlafaxine extended release at the nearest equivalent dose (mg/day), e.g., 37.5 mg venlafaxine 2-times-a-day to 75 mg venlafaxine extended release once daily. However, individual dosage adjustments may be necessary.
Patients with Hepatic Impairment: Given the decrease in clearance and increase in elimination half-life for both venlafaxine and ODV that is observed in patients with hepatic cirrhosis compared with normal subjects (see Pharmacology), it is recommended that the total daily dose be reduced by about 50% in patients with moderate hepatic impairment. For such patients, it may be desirable to start at 37.5 mg/day. Since there was much individual variability in clearance between patients with cirrhosis, it may be necessary to reduce the dose even more than 50%, and individualization of dosing may be desirable in some patients.
Patients with Renal Impairment: Given the decrease in clearance for venlafaxine and increase in elimination half-life for both venlafaxine and ODV that is observed in patients with renal impairment (GFR=10 to 70 mL/min) compared to normal subjects (see Pharmacology), it is recommended that the total daily dose be decreased by 25 to 50%. In patients undergoing hemodialysis, it is recommended that the total daily dose be reduced by 50% and the dose be withheld until the dialysis treatment is completed (4 hours). For such patients, it may be desirable to start at 37.5 mg/day. Since there is so much individual variability in clearance among patients with renal impairment, individualization of dosing may be desirable.
Geriatrics: No dose adjustment is recommended for elderly patients solely on the basis of their age. As with any antidepressant, however, caution should be exercised in treating the elderly. When individualizing the dosage, extra care should be taken when increasing the dose.
Maintenance/Continuation/Extended Treatment: There is no body of evidence available to answer the question of how long a patient should continue to be treated with venlafaxine. It is generally agreed that acute episodes of major depression require several months or longer of sustained pharmacologic therapy. Whether the dose of antidepressant needed to induce remission is identical to the dose needed to maintain and/or sustain euthymia is unknown.
Discontinuing Venlafaxine: When venlafaxine therapy that has been administered for more than 1 week is stopped, it is generally recommended that the dose be tapered gradually to minimize the risk of discontinuation symptoms. Patients who have received venlafaxine for 6 weeks or more should have their dose tapered gradually over a 2-week period. Individualization of tapering may be necessary.
Switching Patients to or from a MAO Inhibitor: At least 14 days should elapse between discontinuation of an MAO inhibitor and initiation of therapy with venlafaxine. In addition, at least 14 days should be allowed after stopping venlafaxine before starting an MAO inhibitor (see Contraindications).

Information for the Patient: See Blue Section—Information for the Patient "Effexor/Effexor XR".

Supplied: Effexor: 37.5 mg: Each shield-shaped, peach-colored, compressed tablet, with a score, with "W" on one side and "37.5" on the other side, contains: venlafaxine HCl equivalent to venlafaxine base 37.5 mg. Nonmedicinal ingredients: cosmetic brown iron oxide, ferric oxide yellow, lactose hydrous, magnesium stearate, microcrystalline cellulose and sodium starch glycolate. Gluten-free. Bottles of 100.

75 mg: Each shield-shaped, peach-colored, compressed tablet, with a score, with "W" on one side and "75" on the other side, contains: venlafaxine HCl equivalent to venlafaxine base 75 mg. Nonmedicinal ingredients: cosmetic brown iron oxide, ferric oxide yellow, lactose hydrous, magnesium stearate, microcrystalline cellulose and sodium starch glycolate. Gluten-free. Bottles of 100.

Effexor XR: 37.5 mg: Each extended release, hard gelatin capsule with gray cap and peach body, with "W" and "Effexor XR" on the cap and "37.5" on the body, in red ink, contains: venlafaxine HCl equivalent to venlafaxine base 37.5 mg. Nonmedicinal ingredients: ethylcellulose, gelatin, hydroxypropyl methylcellulose, iron oxide, microcrystalline cellulose, talc, titanium dioxide and White Tek SB-0007 and/or Opacode Red S-1-15034 ink. Bottles of 100 and 500.

75 mg: Each extended release, hard gelatin capsule, with peach cap and body, with "W" and "Effexor XR" on the cap and "75" on the body, in red ink, contains: venlafaxine HCl equivalent to venlafaxine base 75 mg. Nonmedicinal ingredients: ethylcellulose, gelatin, hydroxypropyl methylcellulose, iron oxide, microcrystalline cellulose, talc, titanium dioxide and White Tek SB-0007 and/or Opacode Red S-1-15034 ink. Bottles of 100 and 500.

150 mg: Each extended release, hard gelatin capsule, with dark orange cap and body, with "W" and "Effexor XR" on the cap and "150" on the body, in white ink, contains: venlafaxine HCl equivalent to venlafaxine base 150 mg. Nonmedicinal ingredients: ethylcellulose, gelatin, hydroxypropyl methylcellulose, iron oxide, microcrystalline cellulose, talc, titanium dioxide and White Tek SB-0007 and/or Opacode Red S-1-15034 ink. Bottles of 100 and 500.

Store at room temperature (15 to 30°C), in a dry place.

(Shown in Product Recognition Section)

Reviewed 1999

EFUDEX® Ⓟ

ICN

Fluorouracil

Topical Antineoplastic

Pharmacology: There is evidence that the metabolism of fluorouracil in the anabolic pathway blocks the methylation reaction of deoxyuridylic acid to thymidylic acid. In this fashion fluorouracil interferes with the synthesis of deoxyribonucleic acid (DNA) and, to a lesser extent, inhibits the formation of ribonucleic acid (RNA). Since DNA and RNA are essential for cell division and growth, the effect of fluorouracil may be to create a thymine deficiency which provokes unbalanced growth and death of the cell. The effects of DNA and RNA deprivation are most marked on those cells which grow more rapidly and which take up fluorouracil at a more rapid pace. The catabolic metabolism of fluorouracil results in degradative products (e.g., CO_2, urea, alpha-fluoro-beta-alanine) which are inactive.

Studies in man with topical application of C^{14}-labelled 'Efudex' demonstrate insignificant absorption as measured by C^{14} content of plasma, urine and respiratory CO_2.

Indications: Recommended for the topical treatment of premalignant keratoses and superficial basal cell carcinoma.

Contraindications: In patients with known hypersensitivity to any of its components.

Warnings: If an occlusive dressing is used, there may be an increase in the incidence of inflammatory reactions in the adjacent normal skin.

Prolonged exposure to ultraviolet light should be avoided while under treatment with fluorouracil because the intensity of the reaction may be increased.
Pregnancy: Since fluorouracil is known to have teratogenic properties, the potential value of its use in women of childbearing potential should be weighed against the risks involved.

Appropriate therapy for pre-existing concomitant inflammatory dermatoses should be instituted before using the drug.

Precautions: The cream is preferably applied with a nonmetal applicator or suitable glove; if it is applied with the fingertips, the hands should be washed immediately afterward. Fluorouracil should be applied with care near the eyes, nose and mouth. To rule out the presence of a frank neoplasm, a biopsy should be made of those lesions failing to respond to treatment or recurring after treatment.

Adverse Effects: The most frequently encountered local reactions are pain, pruritus, hyperpigmentation and burning at the site of application. Other local reactions include dermatitis, scarring, soreness and tenderness. Insomnia, stomatitis, suppuration, scaling, swelling, irritability, medicinal taste, photosensitivity and lacrimation have also been reported.

Efudex (cont'd)

Laboratory abnormalities reported include leukocytosis, thrombocytopenia, toxic granulation and eosinophilia.

Overdose: Symptoms: Since fluorouracil is applied topically, it is highly unlikely that an overdosage would occur. In the event that this preparation is accidentaly ingested, signs of toxicity may include diarrhea, stomatitis, thrombocytopenia (platelets <100 000) and leukopenia (WBC<3 500).

Treatment: These symptoms may be ameliorated by leucovorin.

Dosage: The cream should be applied twice daily with a nonmetal applicator or suitable glove in an amount of the cream sufficient to cover the lesion. When applied to a lesion, a response occurs with the following sequence: erythema, usually followed by vesiculation, erosion, ulceration, necrosis and epithelization. The lower frequency and intensity of activity in adjacent normal skin indicate a selective cytotoxic property. Medication should be continued until the inflammatory reaction reaches the erosion, necrosis, and ulceration stage, at which time use of the drug should be terminated. The usual duration of therapy is from 2 to 4 weeks. Complete healing of the lesion may not be evident for 1 to 2 months following cessation of fluorouracil therapy.

While the patient is undergoing topical fluorouracil therapy, consideration can be given to curettage, wound excision and removal of pathological tissue.

Supplied: Each g of cream contains: fluorouracil 5% (50 mg/g) in a vanishing cream base. Nonmedicinal ingredients: methylparaben, polysorbate 60, propylene glycol, propylparaben, stearyl alcohol and white petrolatum. Sulfite-free. Tubes of 25 g. Store at 15 to 30°C. For external use only.

Reviewed 1999

ELAVIL® ℞

MSD

Amitriptyline HCl

Antidepressant

Indications: In the drug management of depressive illness.

Amitriptyline may be used in depressive illness of psychotic or endogenous nature and in selected patients with neurotic depression. Endogenous depression is more likely to be alleviated than are other depressive states. Amitriptyline, because of its sedative action, is also of value in alleviating the anxiety component of depression.

As with other tricyclic antidepressants, amitriptyline may precipitate hypomanic episodes in patients with bipolar depression. These drugs are not indicated in mild depressive states and depressive reactions.

Contraindications: In patients who have shown prior hypersensitivity to it. It should not be given concomitantly with a MAO inhibiting compound. Hyperpyretic crises, severe convulsions, and deaths have occurred in patients receiving tricyclic antidepressant and MAO inhibiting drugs simultaneously. When it is desired to substitute amitriptyline for a MAO inhibitor, a minimum of 14 days should be allowed to elapse after the latter is discontinued. Amitriptyline should then be initiated cautiously with gradual increase in dosage until optimum response is achieved.

This drug is not recommended for use during the acute recovery phase following myocardial infarction and in the presence of acute congestive heart failure.

See Pregnancy under Warnings.

Warnings: Amitriptyline should be used with caution in patients with a history of seizures, impaired liver function, a history of hepatic damage or blood dyscrasias and, because of its atropine-like action, in patients with a history of urinary retention, or with narrow-angle glaucoma or increased intraocular pressure. In patients with narrow-angle glaucoma, even average doses may precipitate an attack.

There has been a report of fatal dysrhythmia occurring as late as 56 hours after amitriptyline overdose.

Patients with cardiovascular disorders should be watched closely. Tricyclic antidepressant drugs, including amitriptyline, particularly when given in high doses, have been reported to produce arrhythmias, sinus tachycardia, and prolongation of the conduction time.

A few instances of unexpected deaths have been reported in patients with cardiovascular disorders. Myocardial infarction and stroke have also been reported with drugs of this class. Therefore, these drugs should be used with caution in patients with a history of cardiovascular disease, such as myocardial infarction and congestive heart failure.

Concurrent administration of amitriptyline and electroshock therapy may increase the hazards of therapy. Such treatment should be limited to patients for whom it is essential.

Close supervision is required when amitriptyline is given to hyperthyroid patients or those receiving thyroid medication.

Occupational Hazards: May impair mental and/or physical abilities required for performance of hazardous tasks, such as operating machinery or driving a motor vehicle.

Pregnancy: There are no well-controlled studies in pregnant women; therefore, in administering the drug to pregnant patients or women who may become pregnant, the potential benefits must be weighed against the possible hazards to mother and child.

Lactation: Amitriptyline is detectable in breast milk. Because of the potential for serious adverse reactions in infants from amitriptyline, a decision should be made whether to discontinue nursing or discontinue the drug.

Children: In view of the lack of experience with the use of this drug in the treatment of depression in children, amitriptyline is not recommended for depressed patients under 12 years of age.

Precautions: The potency of amitriptyline is such that addition of other antidepressant drugs generally does not result in any additional therapeutic benefit. Untoward reactions have been reported after the combined use of antidepressant agents having varying modes of activity. Accordingly, combined use of amitriptyline and other antidepressant drugs should be undertaken only with due recognition of the possibility of potentiation and with a thorough knowledge of the pharmacology of both drugs. There has been no reports of untoward events when patients receiving amitriptyline were changed immediately to protriptyline or vice versa.

When amitriptyline is used to treat the depressive component of schizophrenia, activation or aggravation of existing psychotic manifestation may occur. Likewise, manic depressive patients may experience hypomanic or manic episodes and hyperactive or agitated patients may become overstimulated. Paranoid delusions, with or without associated hostility, may be exaggerated. A reduction in dose or discontinuation of amitriptyline may be indicated and administration of a neuroleptic such as a phenothiazine, be considered under these circumstances.

Seriously depressed patients should be carefully supervised. The possibility of suicide in depressed patients remains during treatment. Patients should not have access to large quantities of this drug during treatment.

Discontinue the drug several days before elective surgery if possible.

<u>Drug Interactions:</u> Amitriptyline may block the antihypertensive action of guanethidine or similarly acting compounds.

When amitriptyline is given with anticholinergic agents or sympathomimetic drugs, including epinephrine combined with local anesthetics, close supervision and careful adjustment of dosage are required. Paralytic ileus may occur in patients taking tricyclic antidepressants in combination with anticholinergic-type drugs.

Since amitriptyline, in combination with anticholinergic type drugs, may give rise to paralytic ileus, particularly in elderly or hospitalized patients, appropriate measures should be taken if constipation occurs in these patients.

Cimetidine is reported to reduce hepatic metabolism of certain tricyclic antidepressants.

Caution is advised if patients receive large doses of ethchlorvynol concurrently. Transient delirium has been reported in patients who were treated with 1 g of ethchlorvynol and 75 to 150 mg of amitriptyline.

Amitriptyline may enhance the response to alcohol and the effects of barbiturates and other CNS depressants. Delirium has been reported with concurrent administration of amitriptyline and disulfiram.

Hyperpyrexia has been reported when tricyclic antidepressants are administered with anticholinergic agents or with neuroleptic drugs, particularly during hot weather.

Adverse Effects: Note: Included in this listing which follows are a few adverse reactions which have not been reported with this specific drug. However, pharmacological similarities among the tricyclic antidepressant drugs require that each of the reactions be considered when amitriptyline is administered.

Behavioral: drowsiness, fatigue, activation of latent schizophrenia, disorientation, confusional states, hallucinations, delusions, hypomanic reactions, disturbed concentration, nightmares, insomnia, restlessness, agitation, excitement, jitteriness, anxiety, giddiness.

Neurological: epileptiform seizures, coma, dizziness, tremors, numbness, tingling, paresthesias of the extremities, peripheral neuropathy, headache, ataxia, alteration in EEG patterns, extrapyramidal symptoms including abnormal involuntary movements and tardive dyskinesia, dysarthria, tinnitus, incoordination, and slurred speech.

Anticholinergic: urinary retention, dilatation of the urinary tract, constipation, paralytic ileus, especially in the elderly, hyperpyrexia, dry mouth, blurred vision, disturbance of accommodation, increased intraocular pressure, precipitation of latent glaucoma, aggravation of existing glaucoma, and mydriasis.

Cardiovascular: quinidine-like effect and other non-specific ECG changes and changes in AV conduction, prolonged conduction time, asystole, hypotension, syncope, hypertension, palpitation, arrhythmias, heart block, ventricular tachycardia, fibrillation, myocardial infarction, stroke, unexpected death in patients with cardiovascular disorders.

Hematologic: bone marrow depression, including agranulocytosis, leukopenia, eosinophilia, purpura, thrombocytopenia.

Allergic: skin rash, urticaria, photosensitization, edema of the face and tongue, itching.

Gastrointestinal: nausea, epigastric distress, heartburn, vomiting, hepatitis (including altered liver function and jaundice), anorexia, stomatitis, peculiar taste, diarrhea, parotid swelling, black tongue may occur.

Endocrine: testicular swelling, gynecomastia and impotence in the male, breast enlargement and galactorrhea in the female, increased or decreased libido, elevation and lowering of blood sugar levels, syndrome of inappropriate ADH (antidiuretic hormone) secretion.

Miscellaneous: weakness, increased perspiration, edema, urinary frequency, alopecia, increased appetite, weight gain, weight loss.

Withdrawal Symptoms: Abrupt cessation of treatment after prolonged administration may produce nausea, headache, and malaise. Gradual dosage reduction has been reported to produce, within 2 weeks, transient symptoms including irritability, restlessness, and dream and sleep disturbance. These symptoms are not indicative of addiction. Rare instances have been reported of mania or hypomania occurring within 2 to 7 days following cessation of chronic therapy with tricyclic antidepressants.

Overdose: Symptoms: High doses may cause temporary confusion, disturbed concentration, or transient visual hallucinations. Overdosage may cause drowsiness, hypothermia, tachycardia and other arrhythmic abnormalities, such as bundle branch block, ECG evidence of impaired conduction, congestive heart failure, disorders of ocular motility, convulsions, severe hypotension, stupor, coma, polyradiculoneuropathy and constipation. Other symptoms may be agitation, hyperactive reflexes, muscle rigidity, vomiting, hyperpyrexia, or any of those listed under Adverse Effects.

In patients with glaucoma, even average doses may precipitate an attack.

Treatment: Treatment is symptomatic and supportive. Cardiac arrhythmias and CNS involvement pose the greatest threat and may occur suddenly even when initial symptoms appear to be mild. Therefore, patients who may have ingested an overdosage of amitriptyline, particularly children, should be hospitalized and kept under close surveillance. Induced emesis and gastric lavage are recommended in the alert and conscious patient. Following gastric lavage, activated charcoal may be administered. Twenty to 30 g of activated charcoal may be given every 4 to 6 hours during the first 24 to 48 hours after ingestion. It may be helpful to leave the tube in the stomach, with irrigation (with an electrolyte balanced fluid) and continual aspiration of stomach contents possibly promoting more rapid elimination of the drug from the body. If the patient is not alert, a cuffed endotracheal tube should be inserted before lavage is performed, and emesis should not be induced. An open airway should be maintained. Standard measures (oxygen, i.v. fluids, corticosteroids) may be used to manage circulatory shock and metabolic acidosis. Norepinephrine or other pressor agents (but no epinephrine) by i.v. drop infusion under continuous monitoring may be used if necessary. Failing respiration must be maintained by artificial means, but respiratory stimulants should not be used. Regulate body temperature. Hyperpyrexia should be controlled by external measures, such as ice packs and cooling sponge baths. Catheterization should be performed in the unconscious patient. Continuous cardiac monitoring should be instituted in all patients, particularly in the presence of ECG abnormalities and should be maintained for several days after the cardiac rhythm has returned to normal. Because of its effects on cardiac conduction, digitalis should be used only with caution. If rapid digitalization is required for the treatment of congestive heart failure, special care should be exercised in using the drug.

It has been reported that i.v. administration of physostigmine salicylate may reverse some of the CNS and cardiovascular effects of tricyclic antidepressants. The dosage that has been recommended for adults is 1 to 2 mg in **very slow** i.v. injection. In children, the initial dosage should not exceed 0.5 mg and should be adjusted to age and response. Since physostigmine has a short duration of action, administration may have to be repeated at 30 to 60 minute intervals particularly in life-threatening signs such as arrhythmias, convulsions, and deep coma recur or persist after the initial dose of physostigmine. Because physostigmine itself may be toxic, it is not recommended for routine use.

The room should be darkened, with a minimal amount of external stimulation, to reduce the tendency to convulsions. If convulsions occur, they should preferably be controlled by non-barbiturate sedatives, such as chlordiazepoxide or diazepam, or by an inhalation anesthetic (amitriptyline increases the CNS depressant but not the anticonvulsant action of barbiturates). Deaths by deliberate or accidental overdosage have occurred with this class of drugs. Since the propensity for suicide is high in depressed patients, a suicide attempt by other means may occur during the recovery phase. The possibility of simultaneous ingestion of other drugs should also be considered. Dialysis has not been found to be of value for intoxication by amitriptyline alone due to low plasma concentrations of the drug.

Dosage: Dosage should be initiated at a low level and increased gradually, noting carefully the clinical response and any evidence of intolerance.

Outpatient Adults: The recommended initial dose for ambulatory patients is 25 mg 3 times a day. Depending upon tolerance and response, this may be increased to a total of 150 mg a day. Increases are made preferably in the late afternoon and/or bedtime doses. The sedative effect is usually rapidly apparent. The antidepressant activity may be evident within 3 or 4 days or may take up to 30 days to develop adequately.

Hospitalized Patients: Severely ill or hospitalized patients may require 100 mg a day initially. This can be increased gradually to 200 mg a day if necessary. A small number of hospitalized patients may need as much as 300 mg a day.

Adolescent and Elderly Patients: In general, lower dosages are recommended for these patients. In those patients who may not tolerate higher doses, 50 mg daily may be satisfactory. The dose may be administered in divided doses or as a single dose preferably in the evening or at bedtime.

Maintenance: When satisfactory improvement has been reached, dosage should be reduced to the lowest amount that will maintain relief of symptoms. The usual maintenance dose is 50 to 100 mg/day in divided doses; however, in suitable patients, the total daily dosage may be given in a single dose, preferably at bedtime. It is appropriate to continue maintenance therapy throughout the active phase of the depression and for the expected duration of the depressive episode, in order to lessen the possibility of relapse.

Plasma Levels: Because of the wide variation in the absorption and distribution of tricyclic antidepressants in body fluids, it is difficult to directly correlate plasma levels and therapeutic effect. However, determination of plasma levels may be useful in identifying patients who appear to have toxic effects and may have excessively high levels, or those in whom lack of absorption or non-compliance is suspected. Adjustments in dosage should be made according to the patient's clinical response and not on the basis of plasma levels.

Supplied: Suspension: Each 5 mL of light red, oral suspension contains: amitriptyline embonate equivalent to amitriptyline base 10 mg. Nonmedicinal ingredients: carmoisine, indigotine, methyl- and propylparaben, sorbitol, tragacanth and natural and artificial flavors. Bottles of 250 mL.

Tablets: 10 mg: Each blue, biconvex, discoid-shaped, film-coated tablet, engraved MSD 23 on one side, contains: amitriptyline HCl 10 mg. Nonmedicinal ingredients: brilliant blue (sodium and sodium alumina), calcium phosphate dibasic dihydrate, carnauba wax, colloidal silicon dioxide, cornstarch, hydroxypropyl cellulose, hydroxypropyl methylcellulose, lactose, magnesium stearate, powdered cellulose, stearic acid, talc and titanium dioxide. Bottles of 100.

25 mg: Each yellow, biconvex, discoid-shaped, film-coated tablet, engraved MSD 45 on one side, contains: amitriptyline HCl 25 mg. Nonmedicinal ingredients: brilliant blue sodium alumina, calcium phosphate dibasic dihydrate, carnauba wax, colloidal silicon dioxide, cornstarch, hydroxypropyl cellulose, hydroxypropyl methylcellulose, lactose, magnesium stearate, powdered cellulose, quinoline yellow, stearic acid, sunset yellow, talc and titanium dioxide. Bottles of 100 and 500.

50 mg: Each beige, biconvex, discoid-shaped, film-coated tablet, engraved MSD 102 on one side, contains: amitriptyline HCl 50 mg. Nonmedicinal ingredients: calcium phosphate dibasic dihydrate, carnauba wax, colloidal silicon dioxide, cornstarch, hydroxypropyl cellulose, hydroxypropyl methylcellulose, lactose, magnesium stearate, powdered cellulose, quinoline yellow, red and black iron oxides, stearic acid, sunset yellow, talc and titanium dioxide. Bottles of 100.

75 mg: Each orange, biconvex, discoid-shaped, film-coated tablet, engraved MSD 430 on one side, contains: amitriptyline HCl 75 mg. Nonmedicinal ingredients: calcium phosphate dibasic dihydrate, carnauba wax, colloidal silicon dioxide, cornstarch, hydroxypropyl cellulose, hydroxypropyl methylcellulose, lactose, magnesium stearate, powdered cellulose, stearic acid, sunset yellow alumina, talc and titanium dioxide. Bottles of 100.

(Shown in Product Recognition Section)

ELAVIL PLUS® Ⓟ
MSD

Amitriptyline HCl—Perphenazine
Antidepressant—Neuroleptic

Pharmacology: Elavil Plus exerts the actions of its components. Perphenazine is a potent tranquilizer and also a potent antiemetic. Perphenazine has a nonhypnotic depressant activity on the CNS and is capable of relieving anxiety, tension, psychomotor excitement and other psychotic symptoms. Perphenazine has also widespread effects which include central and peripheral adrenergic blocking effects, anticholinergic action and loss of inhibitory control of the basal ganglia, which may result in extrapyramidal symptoms.

In addition it has endocrine, antiemetic, antihistaminic, antiserotonin, metabolic, and other effects. Its central adrenergic blocking action is believed to result from interference with norepinephrine uptake at the nerve cell endings, and appears to act principally in the subcortical area.

Amitriptyline is an antidepressant with sedative properties. Its mechanism of action in man is not known. It is not a MAO inhibitor and it does not act primarily by stimulation of the CNS.

Amitriptyline inhibits the membrane pump mechanism responsible for uptake of norepinephrine and serotonin in adrenergic and serotonergic neurons. Pharmacologically this action may potentiate or prolong neuronal activity since reuptake of these biogenic amines is important physiologically in terminating transmitting activity. This interference with the re-uptake of norepinephrine and/or serotonin is believed by some to underlie the antidepressant activity of amitriptyline. It has also anticholinergic properties.

Indications: In patients with agitated depression. It is particularly indicated in patients with depression associated with marked psychomotor unrest.

It has also been found useful in some schizophrenic patients who have associated symptoms of depression.

Elavil Plus has been used in depressed patients, suffering from marked agitation, anxiety and tension, who may respond to the combination of a phenothiazine with amitriptyline.

Contraindications: In depression of the CNS caused by drugs (barbiturates, alcohol, narcotics, analgesics, antihistamines); in the presence of evidence of bone marrow depression; and in patients known to be hypersensitive to phenothiazines or amitriptyline.

This drug is not recommended for use during the acute recovery phase following myocardial infarction, and in the presence of acute congestive heart failure.

Elavil Plus should not be given concomitantly with guanethidine or similarly acting compounds, since amitriptyline, like other tricyclic antidepressants, is capable of blocking the antihypertensive effect of these compounds.

Monoamine oxidase (MAO) inhibitor drugs may potentiate other drug effects and such potentiation may even cause death. Accordingly, Elavil Plus should not be given to patients who have been receiving an MAO inhibitor, for at least 2 weeks after stopping the MAO inhibitor. In such patients, it is recommended that therapy with Elavil Plus be initiated cautiously with gradual increase in the dosage required to obtain a satisfactory response.

Warnings: Tricyclic antidepressant drugs, including amitriptyline, particularly when given in high doses, have been reported to produce arrhythmias, sinus tachycardia and prolongation of conduction time. A few instances of unexpected death have been reported in patients with cardiovascular disorders. Myocardial infarction and stroke have also been reported with drugs of this class. Therefore, these drugs should be used with caution in patients with a history of cardiovascular disease, such as myocardial infarction and congestive heart failure.

Because of the anticholinergic activity of amitriptyline, Elavil Plus should be used with caution in patients with glaucoma and in those who may be expected to experience problems of urinary retention.

Occupational Hazards: The drug may impair alertness in some patients; operation of automobiles and other activities made hazardous by diminished alertness should be avoided.

Perphenazine can lower the convulsive threshold in susceptible individuals. It should be given with caution to patients with convulsive disorders. Dosage of the anticonvulsive agent may have to be increased.

Tardive Dyskinesia: Tardive dyskinesia, a syndrome consisting of potentially irreversible, involuntary dyskinetic movements may develop in patients treated with neuroleptic (antipsychotic) drugs. Although the prevalence of the syndrome appears to be highest among the elderly, especially elderly women, it is impossible to predict, at the inception of neuroleptic treatment, which patients are likely to develop the syndrome.

If signs and symptoms of tardive dyskinesia appear in a patient on Elavil Plus, drug discontinuation should be considered, as the syndrome may remit, partially or completely. However, some patients may require treatment despite the presence of the syndrome.

Neuroleptic Malignant Syndrome: A potentially fatal syndrome complex, sometimes referred to as neuroleptic malignant syndrome (NMS), has been reported in association with antipsychotic drugs. Clinical manifestations of NMS are muscle rigidity, altered mental status, and evidence of autonomic instability (labile pulse and blood pressure, hyperpyrexia, diaphoresis and cardiac dysrhythmias).

If a patient manifests evidence of NMS, therapy with Elavil Plus should be discontinued immediately. If a patient requires antipsychotic therapy after recovery from NMS, the potential re-introduction of Elavil Plus should be carefully considered. The patient should be carefully monitored, since recurrences of NMS have been reported.

Precautions: General: The possibility of suicide in seriously depressed patients is inherent in the illness and may remain until significant remission occurs. Patients should be closely supervised during the early phase of therapy with Elavil Plus in case they may require hospitalization or concomitant electroshock therapy in addition to therapy with Elavil Plus.

As with any psychotherapeutic agent, patients should be cautioned by the physician against errors of judgment attributable to change in mood.

As with all phenothiazine compounds, perphenazine should not be used indiscriminantly. Caution should be observed in giving it to patients who have previously exhibited severe adverse reactions to other phenothiazines.

Some of the untoward actions of perphenazine tend to appear more frequently when high doses are used. However, as with other phenothiazine compounds, patients receiving perphenazine in any dosage should be kept under close supervision.

The antiemetic effect of perphenazine may obscure signs of toxicity due to overdosage of other drugs, or render more difficult the diagnosis of disorders such as brain tumors or intestinal obstruction.

A significant, not otherwise explained, rise in body temperature may suggest individual intolerance to perphenazine, in which case Elavil Plus should be discontinued.

The tendency for antidepressant medication to provoke mania or hypomania in manic-depressive patients has been reported in the literature. The tranquilizing effect of Elavil Plus has seemed to reduce the likelihood of this effect.

Poor Metabolizers of Debrisoquine/Sparteine: Like other tricyclic antidepressants, Elavil Plus is metabolized by the specific hepatic cytochrome P_{450} isozyme (IID6), which is responsible for the metabolism of debrisoquine and sparteine. Poor metabolizers of debrisoquine/sparteine represent approximately 5 to 10% of the white North American population.

Following usual doses of tricyclic antidepressants, plasma concentrations may be higher than expected in these patients. Cautious dose titration is recommended if Elavil Plus is to be administered to patients known to be poor metabolizers of debrisoquine/sparteine. Monitoring of drug plasma levels should be considered.

Drug Interactions: Phenothiazines may potentiate the action of CNS depressants (opiates, analgesics, antihistamines, barbiturates, alcohol) and atropine. In concurrent therapy with any of these, Elavil Plus should be given in reduced dosage. Patients should be cautioned that the response to alcohol may be

Elavil Plus (cont'd)

increased. Phenothiazines also may potentiate the action of heat and phosphorus insecticides.

If hypotension develops, epinephrine should not be employed, as its action is blocked and partially reversed by perphenazine.

Cimetidine is reported to reduce hepatic metabolism of certain tricyclic antidepressants.

When amitriptyline is given with anticholinergic agents or sympathomimetic drugs, including epinephrine combined with local anesthetics, close supervision and careful adjustment of dosage are required. Paralytic ileus may occur in patients taking tricyclic antidepressants in combination with anticholinergic-type drugs.

Delirium has been reported with concurrent administration of amitriptyline and disulfiram.

Caution is advised if patients receive large doses of ethchlorvynol concurrently. Transient delirium has been reported in patients who were treated with 1 g of ethchlorvynol and 75 to 100 mg of amitriptyline.

Interactions Mediated through Cytochrome P_{450} Isozyme IID6: Like other tricyclic antidepressants, Elavil Plus is metabolized by the hepatic cytochrome P_{450} isozyme, P_{450}IID6, which is responsible for the metabolism of debrisoquine and sparteine. Elevated levels of Elavil Plus may result when the drug is co-administered with agents which compete for metabolism by P_{450}IID6 such as selective serotonin reuptake inhibitors (e.g. paroxetine, fluoxetine, sertraline, and fluvoxamine), phenothiazines (e.g. fluphenazine, thioridazine, perphenazine), and Type 1c antiarrhythmics (e.g. propafenone, flecainide). Agents (e.g., quinidine) which inhibit the isozyme may exert a similar effect. Dosage adjustments and monitoring of drug levels should be considered if Elavil Plus is to be used in combination with these agents.

Children: Since a children's dosage has not been established, Elavil Plus is not recommended for use in children.

Pregnancy: Elavil Plus is not recommended for use in pregnant patients. Reproduction studies in rats have shown no fetal abnormalities; however, clinical experience and follow-up in pregnancy have been limited, and the possibility of adverse effects on fetal development must be considered.

Lactation: Amitriptyline is detectable in breast milk. Because of the potential for serious adverse reactions in infants from amitriptyline, a decision should be made whether to discontinue nursing or discontinue the drug.

Adverse Effects: Clinical evaluation of Elavil Plus has not revealed any adverse reactions peculiar to the combination. The adverse reactions that occurred were limited to those that have been reported previously for perphenazine and amitriptyline.

Perphenazine: Behavioral: oversedation, impaired psychomotor function, paradoxical agitation or excitement and aggravation of psychotic symptoms. Catatonic like states, lassitude, insomnia, bizarre dreams and toxic confusional states have also been described.

Neurological: Extrapyramidal symptoms (opisthotonos, oculogyric crisis, hyperreflexia, dystonia, akathisia, dyskinesia, parkinsonism) have been reported. Their incidence and severity usually increase with an increase in dosage, but there is considerable individual variation in the tendency to develop such symptoms. Extrapyramidal symptoms can usually be controlled by the concomitant use of effective antiparkinsonian drugs, such as benztropine mesylate, and/or by reduction in dosage. In some instances, they may persist after discontinuation of the drug. Paresthesias, slowing of the EEG, disturbed body temperature, muscle weakness and convulsions have also been reported.

Autonomic: Dry mouth, constipation, urinary frequency, blurred vision, and nasal congestion may occur.

Cardiovascular: Severe, acute hypotension has occurred with phenothiazines, and is of particular concern in patients with mitral insufficiency or pheochromocytoma. ECG abnormalities (quinidine-like effect) have also occurred with phenothiazine compounds. Changes in pulse rate and cutaneous vasodilation have been reported.

Toxic and Allergic: The phenothiazine compounds have produced blood dyscrasias (pancytopenia, thrombocytopenic purpura, leukopenia, agranulocytosis, eosinophilia); and liver damage (jaundice, biliary stasis). These have not been observed with perphenazine.

Skin disorders have occurred with phenothiazine compounds (photosensitivity, itching, contact dermatitis, erythema, urticaria, eczema, up to exfoliative dermatitis), as well as other allergic reactions (asthma, laryngeal edema, angioneurotic edema, anaphylactoid reactions).

Endocrine and Metabolic: disturbances in the menstrual cycle, lactation, swollen breasts, failure of ejaculation, reduced sexual urge in the male, increased sexual urge in the female, pseudopregnancy, infertility, and glycosuria. Increased appetite, weight gain, hyperglycemia, altered cerebrospinal fluid proteins, peripheral edema.

Ophthalmological: Centrally located stellate cataracts, corneal opacities, pigmentation of the conjunctiva, cornea or lens, lacrimation, and kerato-conjunctivitis have been reported following the use of phenothiazines. Pigmentary retinopathy has been reported with some phenothiazines with a piperidyl-ethyl side chain.

Miscellaneous: Other adverse reactions reported with various phenothiazine compounds include gastrointestinal effects such as nausea, vomiting and heartburn; potentiation of CNS depressants; headache; and cerebral edema.

Amitriptyline: Behavioral: Confusional states, disturbed concentration, disorientation, delusions, hallucinations, excitement, anxiety, restlessness, drowsiness, insomnia, nightmares.

Neurological: epileptiform seizures, coma, dizziness, tremors, numbness, tingling, paresthesias of the limbs, peripheral neuropathy, headache, ataxia, alteration in EEG patterns, extrapyramidal symptoms including abnormal involuntary movements and tardive dyskinesia, dysarthria, tinnitus, incoordination, and slurred speech.

Anticholinergic: urinary retention, dilatation of the urinary tract, constipation, paralytic ileus, especially in the elderly, hyperpyrexia, dry mouth, blurred vision, disturbance of accommodation, increase intraocular pressure, precipitation of latent glaucoma, aggravation of existing glaucoma, and mydriasis.

Cardiovascular: Quinidine-like effect and other non-specific ECG changes and changes in AV conduction, prolonged conduction time, asystole, hypotension, syncope, hypertension, palpitation, arrhythmias, heart block, ventricular tachycardia, fibrillation, myocardial infarction, stroke, unexpected death in patients with cardiovascular disorders.

Allergic: skin rash, urticaria, photosensitization, edema of face and tongue.

Hematologic: bone marrow depression including agranulocytosis, leukopenia, eosinophilia, purpura, thrombocytopenia.

Gastrointestinal: nausea, epigastric distress, vomiting, anorexia stomatitis, peculiar taste, diarrhea, parotid swelling, black tongue, rarely hepatitis (including altered liver function and jaundice).

Endocrine: testicular swelling and gynecomastia in the male, breast enlargement and galactorrhea in the female, increased or decreased libido, impotence, elevation or lowering of blood sugar levels, syndrome of inappropriate ADH (antidiuretic hormone) secretion.

Miscellaneous: Other adverse reactions that may occur include fainting, weakness, urinary frequency, alopecia and increased perspiration.

Overdose: Symptoms: Deliberate and accidental overdoses with tricyclic antidepressants have been associated with fatalities. Depression of the level of consciousness and marked anticholinergic reactions are the most common manifestations of tricyclic antidepressant overdose. Agitation, confusion, extrapyramidal signs, and hallucinations may also be present. Patients may progress rapidly from lethargy to coma and respiratory failure. Severe hypotension, ventricular arrhythmias, seizures, and respiratory arrest are the major causes of morbidity and mortality. Treatment is essentially supportive.

Treatment: If overdosage with a tricyclic antidepressant is suspected, the patient should be admitted to the Emergency Department without delay. Gastric lavage should be performed promptly. In the obtunded patient, a cuffed endotracheal tube should be used to secure the airway before beginning lavage. Because the anticholinergic effect of these drugs may delay gastric emptying, lavage is recommended for 12 hours or more after the overdose. Activated charcoal with a cathartic such as sorbitol should be given after lavage. Repeated doses of activated charcoal every 6 hours can be given if bowel peristalsis is not suppressed. Persistent unconsciousness (>48 hours) in the absence of hypoxic brain injury should prompt a search for a pill bezoar. The induction of emesis is not indicated as consciousness can be lost precipitously in tricyclic overdose, and aspiration is a frequent complication.

Maintenance of oxygenation and ventilation is crucial. As seizures, coma, and arrhythmias are exacerbated by acidosis, metabolic or respiratory alkalosis should be induced. Intubation should be undertaken early if there is a decreased level of consciousness. Mechanical ventilation can be used to induce an alkalosis. Arrhythmias and seizures may be abolished when the pH has been titrated to a level within a range of 7.45 to 7.55; however, a pH of 7.60 should not be exceeded. An infusion of sodium bicarbonate is often helpful in maintaining the alkalosis.

ICU admission with EKG monitoring is required for all patients with neurological abnormalities, anticholinergic manifestations of overdose, or symptoms of cardiac toxicity (incl. a QRS duration greater than 100 msec). If overdose is suspected, but these abnormalities are not present at admission to the Emergency Department, the patient should be observed for 6 hours. If no such abnormalities develop, the likelihood of significant toxicity is low. EKG monitoring should be continued for a period of 24 hours after full consciousness has been regained and cardiac conduction normalized. Late deaths due to arrhythmias have been reported, but in almost all cases the patients had persistent neurological changes or EKG abnormalities at the time of discharge.

Arrhythmias are usually responsive to aggressive alkalinization. Recalcitrant arrhythmias may respond to lidocaine or phenytoin, but these drugs should be given cautiously since they may induce bradyarrhythmias. Class IA antiarrhythmics (quinidine, procainamide, disopyramide) are contraindicated. Beta-blockers may control tachyarrhythmias, but frequently induce severe hypotension, bradyarrhythmias or third degree atrioventricular block. Overdrive pacing has been used successfully to control tachyarrhythmias. Cardiac pacing is sometimes effective in severe bradycardia or asystole. Potassium replacements should be undertaken cautiously since hyperkalemia may induce or worsen arrhythmias. Because of its effect on cardiac conduction, digitalis should be used only with caution. If rapid digitalization is required for the treatment of congestive heart failure, special care should be exercised in using the drug. Close monitoring of cardiac function of not less than 5 days is advisable.

Hypotension is usually responsive to i.v. fluids. If hypotension persists after 2 to 3 L of normal saline in Ringer's lactate has been infused, right heart catheterization should be considered since the tricyclic antidepressants can cause direct myocardial depression. Inotropes such as dopamine and dobutamine should be used cautiously, since they may induce, or worsen, arrhythmias. Some authorities suggest norepinephrine as the inotrope of choice.

Seizures must be treated aggressively, as they compromise ventilation and induce acidosis. I.V. benzodiazepines are frequently effective, but the control of seizures is often transient. Early intubation should be undertaken and an alkalosis induced. To prevent the recurrence of convulsions, phenytoin (18 mg/kg at 25 to 50 mg/h) should be given to all patients who experience seizures. As bradyarrhythmias and atrioventricular block have been reported with phenytoin administration, continuous EKG monitoring should be performed. Barbiturates may be used to control seizures, but they may produce profound hypotension. Refractory seizures are sometimes responsive to physostigmine. However, the use of physostigmine is controversial and should be reserved for life-threatening situations. Physostigmine is not innocuous and carries a risk of inducing seizures, bronchospasm, increased respiratory secretions, muscle weakness, bradycardia, and asystole. Physostigmine is the only drug of this class which may be used. If symptoms of cholinergic toxicity develop, physostigmine should be discontinued. Atropine should be available for the treatment of toxic cholinergic effects such as bronchoconstriction which may be induced by physostigmine.

Severe hyperthermia has been sporadically reported in association with tricyclic antidepressant overdose. Aggressive treatment with cooling blankets and ice packs is recommended in the event of hyperthermia.

As tricyclic antidepressants exhibit high protein binding and rapid tissue fixation, hemodialysis, peritoneal dialysis, exchange transfusions, and forced diuresis have not proved to be effective in the treatment of overdosage with these drugs.

Dosage: In prescribing Elavil Plus, the recommended indications, management considerations, dosage schedules and attention to tolerance and response that are normal practice in using each of the combined drugs, perphenazine and amitriptyline, should be borne in mind at all times.

Initial dosage: In ambulatory depressed patients with anxiety and/or agitation of such degree as to warrant combined therapy rather than amitriptyline alone, 1 tablet 3 or 4 times a day as an initial dosage, depending on the severity of the agitation and anxiety.

Dosage should be individualized according to the need and response of the patient. Total daily dosage should not exceed 6 tablets.

Children: As a dosage for children has not been established, Elavil Plus is not recommended for use in children.

Maintenance Dosage: Depending on the condition being treated, the onset of therapeutic response may vary from a few days to a few weeks or even longer. The sedative effect of Elavil Plus is more rapidly apparent, while the antidepressant effect is usually delayed. After a satisfactory response is noted, dosage should be reduced to the smallest amount necessary to obtain relief from the symptoms for which Elavil Plus is being administered.

A useful maintenance dosage is 1 tablet 2 to 4 times a day. In some patients, maintenance dosage is required for many months.

Supplied: Each orange, triangular, film-coated tablet, engraved MSD 921 on one side, contains: amitriptyline HCl 25 mg and perphenazine 2 mg. Nonmedicinal ingredients: calcium phosphate dibasic dihydrate, carnauba wax, cornstarch, hydroxypropyl cellulose, hydroxypropyl methylcellulose, lactose, magnesium stearate, powdered cellulose, sunset yellow aluminum lake, talc and titanium dioxide. Gluten- and tartrazine-free. Bottles of 100. Keep container tightly closed. Protect from light.

(Shown in Product Recognition Section)

ELDEPRYL® ℞

Draxis Health

Selegiline HCl

Antiparkinsonian Agent

Pharmacology: Selegiline is an irreversible inhibitor of the enzyme monoamine oxidase (MAO). Because selegiline has greater affinity for type B than type A MAO, it can serve as a selective inhibitor of MAO-B if it is administered at the recommended dose.

Selegiline may have pharmacological effects unrelated to MAO-B inhibition. There is some evidence that it may increase dopaminergic activity by interfering with dopamine re-uptake at the synapse. Effects resulting from selegiline administration may also be mediated through its metabolites. Two of its three principle metabolites, amphetamine and methamphetamine, have pharmacological actions of their own, they interfere with neuronal re-uptake and enhance the release of several neurotransmitters (e.g., norepinephrine, dopamine, serotonin). The extent to which these neurotransmitters contribute to selegiline's effects are unknown.

Rationale for the use of selective MAO-B inhibitors in Parkinson's disease: Many of the prominent symptoms of Parkinson's Disease are due to a deficiency of striatal dopamine that is the consequence of a progressive degeneration and loss of a population of dopaminergic neurons which originate in the substantia nigra and project to the striatum. Early in the course of the disease, the deficit in the capacity of these neurons to synthesize dopamine can be overcome by the administration of exogenous levodopa. After several years of levodopa therapy, the response to a given dose of levodopa is often accompanied by side effects (dyskinesia, on-off phenomena, freezing).

MAO-B inhibitors may be useful under these conditions because by blocking the catabolism of dopamine, they increase the net amount of dopamine available. In patients with advanced Parkinson's Disease, the addition of selegiline to levodopa (usually with a decarboxylase inhibitor) has been shown to improve the therapeutic effect of levodopa.

Recently, in newly diagnosed patients, selegiline was shown to delay the need to implement levodopa therapy.

The mechanisms of action of selegiline, both in newly diagnosed and in severely incapacitated patients, is unknown.

Hypertensive Crisis ("Cheese Reaction"): MAOs are widely distributed throughout the body; their concentration is especially high in liver, kidney, stomach, intestinal wall and brain. In the intestine, type A is the predominant MAO; it is thought to provide vital protection from exogenous amines (e.g., tyramine) that have the capacity to displace norepinephrine from storage sites and thereby cause a hypertensive crisis. MAO-A catabolises the exogenous amines which are found in a variety of foods (fermented cheese, red wine, herring) and drugs (over-the-counter cough/cold medications). Since MAO-A in the gut is not inhibited by therapeutic doses of selegiline, in theory, patients may take medications containing pharmacologically active amines and consume tyramine-containing foods without the risk of uncontrolled hypertension.

To date, clinical experience appears to confirm this prediction: hypertensive crises have not been reported in selegiline treated patients. However, until the pathophysiology of the "cheese reaction" is more completely understood, it seems prudent to assume that selegiline can only be used safely without dietary restrictions at doses where it presumably selectively inhibits MAO-B (e.g., 10 mg/day).

Attention to the dose dependent nature of selegiline's selectivity is critical if it is to be used without restrictions being placed on diet and concomitant drug use (see Warnings and Precautions).

Pharmacokinetics: The extremely short half-life of selegiline (<0.15 hours following a 10 mg i.v. dose) is consistent with the inability to detect unchanged selegiline in the serum and urine following oral administration.

Only preliminary information about the details of the pharmacokinetics of selegiline and its metabolites is available. In a 7-day study undertaken to investigate the effect of selegiline on the kinetics of an oral hypoglycemic agent, subjects were given a 10 mg dose of selegiline for 7 consecutive days. Serum levels of intact selegiline were below the limit of detection (<10 ng/mL). Trough levels of the 3 metabolites were as follows: N-desmethyldeprenyl, the major metabolite, was not detectable; the levels of amphetamine and methamphetamine were 3.5 ng/mL and 8.0 ng/mL, respectively.

The rate of MAO-B regeneration following discontinuation of treatment has not been quantified. It is this rate, dependent upon de novo protein synthesis, which seems likely to determine how fast normal MAO-B activity can be restored.

Indications: May be of value as an adjunct to levodopa (with or without a decarboxylase inhibitor) in the management of the signs and symptoms of Parkinson's disease; in newly diagnosed patients before symptoms begin to affect the patient's social or professional life, at which time more efficacious treatment becomes necessary.

Contraindications: In patients with known hypersensitivity to this drug.

Selegiline should not be used in patients with other extrapyramidal disorders such as excessive tremor or tardive dyskinesia, or in patients with severe psychosis or profound dementia.

Selegiline is contraindicated in combination with meperidine, (see Precautions, Drug Interactions). This contraindication is often extended to other opioids as well.

Selegiline should not be used in patients with active peptic ulcer.

Warnings: Selegiline should not be used at daily doses exceeding those recommended (10 mg/day) because of the risks associated with nonselective inhibition of MAO (see Pharmacology).

The selectivity of selegiline for MAO-B may not be absolute at the recommended daily dose of 10 mg/day, and selectivity is further diminished with increasing daily doses. The precise dose at which selegiline becomes a nonselective inhibitor of all MAO is unknown but may be in the range of 30 to 40 mg/day.

Postmarketing cumulative reports suggest that serious CNS adverse events might occur when selegiline is combined with tricyclic antidepressants (TCAs) and selective serotonin re-uptake inhibitors (SSRIs).

Hyperpyrexia and death have been reported with the combination of tricyclic antidepressants and nonselective MAO inhibitors such as phenelzine and tranylcypromine. Similarly, the combined use of tricyclic antidepressants and selegiline has been associated with hyperpyrexia, tremors, agitation, restlessness, reduced level of consciousness and in rare instances fatalities. Related adverse events also seen after this combination included hypertension, syncope, asystole, diaphoresis, seizure, change in behavioral and mental status, and muscular rigidity.

Serious, sometimes fatal, reactions with signs and symptoms that may include hyperthermia, rigidity, myoclonus, autonomic instability with rapid fluctuations of the vital signs, and mental status changes that include extreme agitation progressing to delirium and coma have been reported with patients receiving a combination of fluoxetine and nonselective MAO inhibitors. Similar signs have been reported in some patients on the combination of selegiline (10 mg a day) and selective serotonin re-uptake inhibitors including fluoxetine, sertraline and paroxetine.

Since the mechanisms of these reactions are not fully understood, it seems prudent, in general, to avoid this combination of selegiline and tricyclic antidepressants as well as selegiline and selective serotonin re-uptake inhibitors. At least 14 days should elapse between discontinuation of selegiline and initiation of treatment with a tricyclic antidepressant or selective serotonin re-uptake inhibitors. Because of the long half-lives of fluoxetine and its active metabolite, at least 5 weeks (perhaps longer, especially if fluoxetine has been prescribed chronically and/or at higher doses) should elapse between discontinuation of fluoxetine and initiation of treatment with selegiline.

Precautions: General: Some patients given selegiline may experience an exacerbation of levodopa-associated side effects, presumably due to the increased amounts of dopamine reacting with supersensitive postsynaptic receptors. These effects may often be mitigated by reducing the dose of levodopa by approximately 10 to 30%.

The decision to prescribe selegiline should take into consideration that the MAO system of enzymes is complex and incompletely understood and there is only a limited amount of carefully documented clinical experience with selegiline. Consequently the full spectrum of possible responses to selegiline may not have been observed in the premarketing evaluation of the drug. It is advisable, therefore, to observe the patients closely for atypical responses.

Information for the Patient: Patients should be advised of the possible need to reduce levodopa dosage after initiation of selegiline therapy. The patients (or their families if the patient is incompetent) should be advised not to exceed the recommended daily dose of 10 mg. The risk of using higher daily doses of selegiline should be explained, and a brief description of the hypertensive crisis ("cheese reaction") provided. While hypertensive reactions with selegiline have not been reported, documented experience is limited. Consequently, it may be useful to inform patients (or their families) about the signs and symptoms associated with MAO inhibitors induced hypertensive reactions. In particular, patients should be urged to report, immediately, any severe headache or other atypical or unusual symptoms not previously experienced.

Laboratory Tests: Transient or continuing abnormalities with a tendency for elevated levels of liver enzymes have been described during long-term therapy. Although serious hepatic toxicity has not been observed, caution is recommended in patients with a history of hepatic dysfunction. Periodic routine evaluation of all patients however, is appropriate.

Drug Interactions: The occurrence of stupor, muscular rigidity, severe agitation and elevated temperature has been reported in a man receiving selegiline and meperidine, as well as other medications. Symptoms resolved over days when the combination was discontinued. This case is typical of the interaction of meperidine and MAO inhibitors.

Other serious reactions (including severe agitation, hallucinations, and death) have been reported in patients receiving this combination. While it cannot be said definitively that all of these reactions were caused by this combination, they are all compatible with this well recognized interaction.

Although the database of documented clinical experience is limited, MAO inhibitors are ordinarily contraindicated for use with meperidine. This warning is often extended to other opioids (see Contraindications).

It is also prudent to avoid the concomitant use of selegiline and selective serotonin re-uptake inhibitors and tricyclic antidepressants (see Warnings).

Other than the possible exacerbation of side effects in patients receiving levodopa therapy, no interactions attributed to the combined use of selegiline and other drugs have been reported. However, because the database of documented clinical experience is limited, the level of reassurance provided by this lack of adverse reporting is uncertain (see Warnings and Precautions).

Carcinogenesis: Studies have not been performed to date to evaluate the carcinogenic potential of selegiline.

Pregnancy: Insufficient animal reproduction studies have been done with selegiline to conclude that selegiline poses no teratogenic potential. However, one rat study carried out at doses as much as 180 fold the recommended human dose revealed no evidence of a teratogenic effect. It is not known whether selegiline can cause fetal harm when administered to a pregnant woman or can affect reproductive capacity. Selegiline should be given to a pregnant woman only if clearly needed.

Lactation: It is not known whether selegiline is excreted in human milk. Because many drugs are excreted in human milk, consideration should be given to discontinuing the use of all but absolutely essential drug treatments in nursing women.

Children: The effects of selegiline in children under 18 have not been evaluated.

Adverse Effects: The side effects of selegiline are usually those associated with excessive dopaminergic stimulation. The drug may potentiate the side effects of levodopa, therefore, adjustment of drug dosages may be required. Some of the most serious adverse reactions reported with the combination of selegiline and levodopa were hallucinations and confusion, particularly visual hallucinations.

Although a cause and effect relationship has not been established, a tendency to a progressive rise in several liver enzymes has been reported after long-term therapy.

In prospective clinical trials, the following adverse effects, (listed in decreasing order of frequency), led to the **discontinuation** of selegiline: nausea, hallucinations, confusion, depression, loss of balance, insomnia, orthostatic hypotension,

Eldepryl (cont'd)

increased akinetic involuntary movements, agitation, arrhythmia, bradykinesia, chorea, delusions, hypertension, new or increased angina pectoris and syncope.

Events reported only rarely as a cause of discontinuation of treatment include anxiety, drowsiness/lethargy, nervousness, dystonia, increased episodes of freezing, increased tremor, weakness, excessive perspiration, constipation, weight loss, burning lips/mouth, ankle edema, gastrointestinal bleeding and hair loss.

In controlled clinical trials involving a very limited number of patients (N=49 receiving Eldepryl; N=50 receiving placebo) the following adverse reactions were reported (incidences are devoid of practical statistical significance) (see Table I).

Table I—Eldepryl

Incidence of Treatment-emergent Adverse Experiences in Placebo-controlled Clinical Trials

A: In Combination with Levodopa

Adverse Event	Number of Patients Reporting Events: Eldepryl N=49	Placebo N=50
Nausea	10	3
Dizziness/lightheaded/fainting	7	1
Abdominal pain	4	2
Confusion	3	0
Hallucinations	3	1
Dry mouth	3	1
Vivid dreams	2	0
Dyskinesia	2	5
Headache	2	1
The following events were reported once in either or both groups:		
Ache, generalized	1	0
Anxiety/tension	1	1
Anemia	0	1
Diarrhea	1	0
Hair loss	0	1
Insomnia	1	1
Lethargy	1	0
Leg pain	1	0
Low back pain	1	0
Malaise	0	1
Palpitations	1	0
Urinary retention	1	0
Weight loss	1	0

B: In Monotherapy

The incidence of adverse reactions occurring in trials using selegiline as monotherapy has not been fully reported to date. Serious adverse reactions were as follows: depression, chest pain, myopathy and diarrhea. Other reported adverse reactions included insomnia, headache, nausea, dizziness and vertigo.

In all prospectively monitored clinical investigations, enrolling approximately 920 patients, the following adverse events, classified by body system, were reported.

CNS: Motor/Coordination/Extrapyramidal: increased tremor, chorea, loss of balance, restlessness, blepharospasm, increased bradykinesia, facial grimace, falling down, heavy leg, muscle twitch, myoclonic jerks, stiff neck, tardive dyskinesia, dystonic symptoms, dyskinesia, involuntary movements, freezing, festination, increased apraxia, muscle cramps.

Mental Status/Behavioral/Psychiatric: hallucinations, dizziness, confusion, anxiety, depression, drowsiness, behavior/mood change, dreams/nightmares, tiredness, delusions, disorientation, lightheadedness, impaired memory, increased energy, transient high, hollow feeling, lethargy/malaise, apathy, overstimulation, vertigo, personality change, sleep disturbance, restlessness, weakness, transient irritability.

Pain/Altered Sensation: headache, back pain, leg pain, tinnitus, migraine, supraorbital pain, throat burning, generalized ache, chills, numbness of toes/fingers, taste disturbance.

Autonomic Nervous System: dry mouth, blurred vision, sexual dysfunction.

Cardiovascular: orthostatic hypotension, hypertension, arrhythmia, palpitations, new or increased angina pectoris, hypotension, tachycardia, peripheral edema, sinus bradycardia, syncope.

Gastrointestinal: nausea/vomiting, constipation, weight loss, anorexia, poor appetite, dysphagia, diarrhea, heartburn, rectal bleeding, bruxism.

Genitourinary/Gynecologic/Endocrine: transient anorgasmia, nocturia, prostatic hypertrophy, urinary hesitancy, urinary retention, decreased penile sensation, urinary frequency.

Skin and Appendages: increased sweating, diaphoresis, facial hair, hair loss, hematoma, rash, photosensitivity.

Miscellaneous: asthma, diplopia, shortness of breath, speech affected.

Toxic delirium has also been reported with selegiline when used as adjunctive therapy to levodopa treatment.

Overdose: Symptoms: No specific information is available about clinically significant overdoses with selegiline. However, experience gained during the development of selegiline reveals that some individuals exposed to doses of 600 mg/day of selegiline suffered severe hypotension and psychomotor agitation.

Since the selective inhibition of MAO-B by selegiline is achieved only at doses recommended for the treatment of Parkinson's Disease (i.e., 10 mg/day), overdoses are likely to cause significant inhibition of both MAO-A and MAO-B. Consequently, the signs and symptoms of overdose may resemble those observed with marketed nonselective MAO inhibitors (e.g., tranylcypromine and phenelzine).

Overdose with Nonselective MAO Inhibitors: Note: This section is provided for reference; it dose not describe events that have actually been observed with selegiline in overdose.

Characteristically, signs and symptoms of nonselective MAO inhibitor overdose may not appear immediately. Delays of up to 12 hours between ingestion of the drug and the appearance of signs may occur. Importantly, the peak intensity of the syndrome may not be reached for upwards of a day following the overdose. Death has been reported following overdose. Therefore, immediate hospitalization, with continuous patient observation and monitoring for a period of at least 2 days following the ingestion of such drugs in overdose is strongly recommended.

The clinical picture of MAO inhibitor overdose varies considerably; its severity may be a function of the amount of drug consumed. The CNS and cardiovascular systems are prominently involved.

Signs and symptoms of overdosage may include, alone or in combination, any of the following: drowsiness, dizziness, faintness, irritability, hyperactivity, agitation, severe headache, hallucinations, trismus, opisthotonos, convulsions and coma; rapid and irregular pulse, hypertension, hypotension and vascular collapse; precordial pain, respiratory depression and failure, hyperpyrexia, diaphoresis, and cool, clammy skin.

Treatment: Because there is no recorded experience with selegiline overdose, the following suggestions, based on the management of nonselective MAO inhibitor poisoning, might be applicable.

Treatment of overdose with nonselective MAO inhibitors is symptomatic and supportive. Induction of emesis or gastric lavage with instillation of charcoal slurry may be helpful in early poisoning, provided the airway has been protected against aspiration. Signs and symptoms of CNS stimulation, including convulsions, should be treated with diazepam, given slowly i.v. Phenothiazine derivatives and CNS stimulants should be avoided. Hypotension and vascular collapse should be treated with i.v. fluids and, if necessary, blood pressure titration with an i.v. infusion of a dilute pressor agent. It should be noted that adrenergic agents may produce a markedly increased pressor response. Respiration should be supported by appropriate measures, including management of the airway, use of supplemental oxygen and mechanically supported ventilatory assistance, as required. Body temperature should be monitored closely. Intensive management of hyperpyrexia may be required. Maintenance of fluid and electrolyte balance is essential.

Dosage: The recommended dosage of selegiline as monotherapy in newly diagnosed patients, or as an adjunct to levodopa (usually with a decarboxylase inhibitor) is 10 mg/day administered as divided doses of 5 mg each taken at breakfast and lunch.

When selegiline adjunctive therapy is added to the existing levodopa therapeutic regime, a reduction, usually of 10 to 30% in the dose of levodopa (in some instances a reduction of the dose of selegiline to 5 mg/day) may be required during the period of adjustment of therapy or in case of exacerbation of adverse effects.

Doses higher than 10 mg/day should not be used. There is no evidence that additional benefit will be obtained from the administration of higher doses. Furthermore, higher doses will result in a loss of selectivity of selegiline towards MAO-B with an increase in the inhibition of type MAO-A. There is an increased risk of adverse reactions with higher doses as well as an increased risk of hypertensive episode (''cheese reaction'').

Supplied: Each almost white, flat tablet, scored on one side with the other face engraved with ''E'', contains: 5 mg of the l-isomer of selegiline HCl (formerly l-deprenyl HCl). Nonmedicinal ingredients: citric acid, lactose, magnesium stearate, microcrystalline cellulose. Bottles of 60. Store between 15 and 30°C.

ELDISINE® INJECTION 🄿

Lilly

Vindesine Sulfate

Antineoplastic

Pharmacology: The mode of action of vindesine is not completely understood. Like the other vinca alkaloids, vinblastine sulfate (Velbe) and vincristine sulfate (Oncovin), vindesine causes arrest of cells in metaphase mitosis. In addition, in vitro investigation has demonstrated that vindesine prevents invasion of normal tissue by malignant cells. Comparative studies with these 3 alkaloids, however, demonstrate differences in their effect at the molecular level. Vindesine has been shown to be 3 times more potent than vincristine and nearly 10 times more potent than vinblastine in effecting mitotic arrest in tissue culture studies designed to arrest from 10% to 15% of the cells in mitosis. At dose levels that arrest 40% to 50% of the cells in mitosis, vindesine and vincristine are approximately equipotent, and both have 3 times the potency of vinblastine. In addition, qualitative differences are noted among the 3 alkaloids. At the lower dose, vinblastine produced a predominance of postmetaphase cells in which the midbody and chromosomes were strikingly apparent. In contrast, cells exposed to vincristine displayed a ball-type metaphase with compact chromosomes within a shrunken spindle.

Unlike vinblastine, vindesine produced very few postmetaphase cells. The spindles in cells exposed to vindesine were swollen with dispersed chromosomes, in distinct contrast to the closely packed chromosomes seen with vincristine.

Vindesine has displayed oncolytic activity in patients who have relapsed while on multiple-agent treatment that included vincristine.

In laboratory animals and man, the biliary system is the major route of excretion of vindesine.

Hematologic Effects: Clinically, temporary leukopenia is an expected effect of vindesine and the level of the leukocyte count is an important guide to therapy with this drug. In general, the larger the dose employed, the more profound and longer-lasting the leukopenia will be. Following administration of vindesine, the nadir in white-blood-cell count may be expected to occur 3 to 6 days after the day of drug therapy. Recovery of the white blood count usually occurs 7 to 10 days after a dose.

Although the thrombocyte count ordinarily is not significantly lowered by therapy with vindesine, patients whose bone marrow has recently been impaired by prior therapy with radiation or with other oncolytic drugs may show thrombocytopenia (fewer than 200 000 platelets/mm^3). Thrombocytopenia is not common when a bolus dose is administered once a week to patients with normal marrow function.

Elevation of platelet count has occurred even when vindesine has produced granulocytopenia.

The pharmacokinetics of vindesine have been studied in patients with advanced cancer. Following a rapid i.v. dose, the kinetics of vindesine were described by a triphasic serum-decay curve. Serum half-lives were 2 minutes, 50 minutes, and 24 hours. The volume of the central compartment approximated the plasma volume in all patients studied. Distribution occurred quickly into a superficial tissue compartment in fairly rapid equilibrium with that in the plasma compartment and also into a deep-tissue compartment with slower redistribution to the central compartment.

Indications: For the treatment of: acute lymphocytic leukemia of childhood which is resistant to vincristine and non-oat-cell lung cancer.

Contraindications: Patients who have drug-induced severe granulocytopenia or severe thrombocytopenia and in those who have serious bacterial infection. Infections must be brought under control prior to initiation of therapy with vindesine. Patients with the demyelinating form of Charcot-Marie-Tooth syndrome.

Warnings: Caution: Vindesine is a potent drug and should be used only by physicians experienced with cancer chemotherapeutic drugs. Blood counts should be taken once or twice weekly. Discontinue or reduce the dosage upon evidence of abnormal depression of the bone marrow.

This preparation is for i.v. use only. It should be administered by individuals experienced in the administration of vindesine. The intrathecal administration of vindesine has resulted in death. Syringes containing this product should be labeled "Warning—For I.V. Use Only".

Extemporaneously prepared syringes containing this product must be packaged in an overwrap which is labeled **"Do not remove covering until moment of injection. Fatal if given intrathecally. For i.v. use only."**

The following treatment successfully arrested progressive paralysis in a single patient mistakenly given the related vinca alkaloid, vincristine, intrathecally. If vindesine is mistakenly administered intrathecally, this treatment is recommended and should be initiated immediately after the intrathecal injection. 1. Remove as much spinal fluid as can be safely done through the lumbar access. 2. Insert a catheter in a lateral cerebral ventricle for the purpose of flushing the subarachnoid space from above with removal through a lumbar access. 3. Initiate flushing through the cerebral catheter with lactated Ringer's solution infused at the rate of 150 mL/hour. 4. As soon as fresh frozen plasma becomes available, infuse the fresh frozen plasma, 25 mL, diluted in 1 L of Lactated Ringer's solution through the cerebral ventricular catheter at the rate of 75 mL/hour with removal through the lumbar access. The rate of infusion should be adjusted to maintain a protein level in the spinal fluid of 150 mg/dL. Repeat this procedure using a second litre of diluted fresh frozen plasma. 5. Administer 10 g of glutamic acid i.v. over 24 hours followed by 500 mg 3 times daily by mouth for 1 month or until neurological dysfunction stabilizes. The role of glutamic acid in this treatment is not certain and may not be essential.

Pregnancy and *Lactation:* Safety for use during pregnancy or lactation has not been established.

Reproduction studies indicated that at toxic levels vindesine was embryotoxic and possibly teratogenic in rats. The benefit-to-risk ratio must be carefully considered before vindesine is used in pregnant or lactating patients. It is not known whether vindesine crosses the placental barrier or is excreted in breast milk.

Doses greater than 4 mg/m^2 should be used only by those skilled in treating children with leukemia.

Precautions: Strict adherence to the recommended dosage is advised. In preliminary assessments, neurotoxicity induced by vindesine is generally less severe and progressive in nature than the effects observed with vincristine. Individual patient variation has been observed with respect to severity of adverse reactions, including neurotoxicity, granulocytopenia, alopecia, and decrease in bowel motility. Prophylactic measures should be taken to prevent constipation that may result from a decrease in bowel motility.

There have been instances in which neurotoxicity has made it necessary to reduce the dosage or temporarily discontinue the use of vindesine.

Particular attention should be given to dosage and neurologic side effects if vindesine is administered to patients with preexisting neuromuscular disease and also when other drugs with neurotoxic potential are being used.

Since the biliary system is the major route of excretion of vindesine, patients with significant hepatic disease should receive an initial dosage that is lower than that recommended, followed by increases based on clinical response (see Dosage).

Extreme care should be exercised to prevent injection of vindesine outside the vein. Extravasation during i.v. injection will cause cellulitis and phlebitis. If the amount of extravasation is great enough, sloughing will occur. Healing of such wounds may require several weeks and may be attended by severe pain. The discomfort may persist after healing of the ulcer.

Acute shortness of breath and severe bronchospasm have been reported following the administration of vinca alkaloids. These reactions have been encountered most frequently when the vinca alkaloid was used in combination with mitomycin-C. The onset may be within minutes or several hours after the vinca is injected.

Care must be taken to avoid contamination of the eye with concentrations of vindesine used clinically. If accidental contamination occurs, severe irritation and/or corneal ulceration may result. The eye should be washed immediately and thoroughly with water or saline.

Neurologic toxicity may appear early in the course of treatment and may be more severe if vindesine is used concomitantly with other drugs having a neurologic potential.

Carcinogenic potential of vindesine has not been detected in the standard tests.

Drug Interactions: The simultaneous oral or i.v. administration of phenytoin and antineoplastic chemotherapy combinations that include vincristine and vinblastine has been reported to reduce blood levels of the anticonvulsant and to increase seizure activity. Dosage adjustment should be based on serial blood level monitoring. The contribution of vincristine and vinblastine to this interaction is not certain. The interaction may result from reduced absorption of phenytoin or an increase in the rate of its metabolism and elimination.

Adverse Effects: Prior to the use of the drug, patients and/or their parents/guardian should be advised of the possibility of untoward symptoms.

In general, the incidence of adverse effects attending the use of vindesine appears to be related to the size of the dose employed. Leukopenia, the most common adverse reaction, is usually the dose-limiting factor. Neurotoxicity and alopecia of varying degree occur.

When alopecia occurs, it may not be total, and hair usually regrows while maintenance therapy continues. Thrombocytopenia has not commonly been observed with the dosage schedule of 1 bolus injection/week, but it has been reported with other dosage schedules and in patients with pre-existing compromised bone-marrow function.

The following adverse reactions have been reported: Gastrointestinal: Constipation, abdominal pain, ileus, nausea, vomiting, vesiculation of the mouth, diarrhea, and anorexia. (Nausea and vomiting usually may be controlled by antiemetic agents.)

Neurologic: Numbness and tingling of digits, (paresthesias), loss of deep-tendon reflexes, jaw pain, mental depression, convulsions, peripheral neuritis, and headache. Cortical blindness has been reported in patients treated with multiple-agent chemotherapy that has included vindesine. The contribution of vindesine to this reaction is uncertain.

Hematologic: Granulocytopenia and thrombocytopenia.

Miscellaneous: Generalized musculoskeletal pain, epilation, chills and fever, malaise, macular skin rash, and pain in tumor site.

Overdose: Symptoms and Treatment: Side effects, following the use of vindesine are dose related. Therefore, following administration of an overdose, patients can be expected to experience side effects in an exaggerated fashion. Supportive care should include the following: 1. Prevention of side effects resulting from the syndrome of inappropriate secretion of antidiuretic hormone (this would include restriction of fluid intake and perhaps the administration of a diuretic affecting the function of the loop of Henle and the distal tubule); 2. administration of anticonvulsant doses of phenobarbital; 3. use of cathartics to prevent ileus; 4. monitoring the cardiovascular system; and 5. determining daily blood counts for guidance in transfusion requirements.

Dosage: This preparation is for i.v. use only. It should be administered by individuals experienced in the administration of vindesine. The intrathecal administration of vindesine has resulted in death. Syringes containing this product should be labeled "Warning—For I.V. Use Only".

Extreme care must be used in calculating and administering the dose of vindesine, since overdosage may have a very serious or fatal outcome.

Since the biliary system is the major route of excretion, patients with significant hepatic disease should receive an initial dosage that is lower than that recommended below, followed by increases based on clinical response.

The drug is administered i.v. according to either of the following 2 protocols. Strict adherence to these regimens is advisable.

1. The dose of vindesine is 4 mg/m^2 for children, and 3 mg/m^2 for adults, administered by i.v. bolus at 7 to 10 day intervals repeated for 8 cycles. The injection should be completed over a 1 to 3 minute period.

2. Alternatively for children with leukemia, a regimen of 2 mg/m^2/day by i.v. bolus injection can be employed for 2 consecutive days, followed by 5 to 7 days without the drug. The cycle is then repeated for 8 cycles.

The optimum dose is that which produces mild to moderate leukopenia. The dose for adults with normal marrow function is 3 mg/m^2 by rapid i.v. injection once a week while that for children is 4 mg/m^2 once a week by bolus injection. The maximum decrease in white-blood-cell count will usually occur 3 to 5 days thereafter, with recovery by the seventh to the tenth day. Sustained white-blood-cell counts lower than 2 500/mm^3 (2.5 times 10^9/m) due to vindesine are to be avoided.

In adult patients with leukemia, it may be necessary to adjust the dosage upward to achieve the desired effect. Adults whose bone marrow function is decreased due to other previous treatment will need lower doses. Those with decreased marrow function induced by disease will require full doses in order to attempt to restore marrow function. This must be done under close supervision.

The use of small amounts of vindesine daily for long periods in the treatment of acute lymphocytic leukemia in children is not advisable, even though the resulting weekly dosage may be similar to the recommended dosage. Little or no added therapeutic advantage has been demonstrated when such regimens have been used, and adverse reactions are increased. Strict adherence to the recommended dosage schedule is very important.

Reconstitution: Reconstitution of the vial with 5 mL Bacteriostatic Sodium Chloride Injection, USP will provide 1 mg/mL.

After reconstitution, Eldisine is stable for 24 hours at room temperature and 14 days under refrigeration (2 to 8°C).

Vindesine should not be mixed with other chemotherapeutic agents or medications in the same vessel.

The solution may be injected either directly into a vein or into the tubing of a running i.v. infusion.

Note: It is extremely important to choose the largest accessible vein and to be certain that the needle is properly positioned in the vein before any vindesine is injected. If leakage into surrounding tissue should occur during i.v. administration, it may cause considerable irritation.

The injection should be discontinued as soon as leakage occurs, and any remaining portion of the dose should then be introduced into another vein. Local injection of hyaluronidase and the application of moderate heat to the area of leakage help disperse the drug and are thought to minimize discomfort and the possibility of cellulitis. After proper injection, the extremity should be elevated so that the site is above the heart level to reduce intravenous pressure to the minimum for a few minutes in order to prevent postinjection leakage.

Supplied: Each 5 mL vial contains: vindesine sulfate 5 mg and mannitol 25 mg. Sodium hydroxide and/or sulfuric acid may have been added during manufacture to adjust the pH. The product is supplied in a lyophilized form. Vindesine is for i.v. administration only. Store at 2 to 8°C.

ELDOPAQUE™
ELDOPAQUE™ FORTE

ICN

Hydroquinone

Depigmenting Agent

Supplied: Eldopaque: Each tube contains: hydroquinone USP 2% in a stabilized, hydrophobic opaque base, inhibiting UVA effect. Tubes of 30 g.

Eldopaque Forte: Each tube contains: hydroquinone USP 4% in a stabilized, hydrophobic opaque base, inhibiting UVA effect. Tubes of 30 g.

ELDOQUIN™
ELDOQUIN™ FORTE

ICN

Hydroquinone

Depigmenting Agent

Supplied: Eldoquin: Each tube contains: hydroquinone USP 2% in a hydrophilic, stabilized, nongreasy base preserved with propylparaben. pH adjusted to 4.8. Sunscreen-free. Tubes of 30 g.

Eldoquin Forte: Each tube contains: hydroquinone USP 4% in a hydrophilic, stabilized, nongreasy base preserved with propylparaben. pH adjusted to 4.8. Sunscreen-free. Tubes of 30 g.

ELECTROPEG

Technilab

Polyethylene Glycol—Electrolytes

Gastrointestinal Lavage Solution

Supplied: Each 277 g container of powder contains: polyethylene glycol 238.8 g, sodium sulfate 22.7 g, sodium bicarbonate 6.7 g, sodium chloride 5.8 g and potassium chloride 3 g. When reconstituted to 4 L with water, each 1 L of solution contains: sodium 125 mEq, potassium 10 mEq, chloride 35 mEq, sulfate 40 mEq and bicarbonate 20 mEq. The reconstituted solution has a mild lemon flavor. Containers of 4 L. Once container is opened, the reconstituted solution must be refrigerated and used within 48 hours.

ELMIRON™ ℞
Alza

Pentosan Polysulfate Sodium
Glycosaminoglycan Substitute

Pharmacology: Pentosan is intended for the treatment of interstitial cystitis. In interstitial cystitis patients, a deficient or defective bladder protective glycosaminoglycan layer allows diffusion of irritating components in urine through to the underlying bladder wall. The resultant inflammatory response in the bladder wall produces the symptoms of interstitial cystitis. Definitive proof for this is not available.

Elmiron is orally bioavailable pentosan polysulfate sodium. Its mechanism of action is thought to be adherence to the bladder surface supplementing the defective natural glycosaminoglycan layer. It is hypothesized that this action ameliorates the symptoms of interstitial cystitis. Orally administered pentosan has a urinary excretion half-life of 4.4 hours for the unchanged drug. A single dose is completely eliminated in 144 hours.

Indications: For the initial and maintenance treatment of interstitial cystitis.

Contraindications: In patients with known hypersensitivity to the drug, and related compounds or excipients.

Warnings and Precautions: General: Pentosan is a weak anticoagulant (only 1/15 the activity of heparin) and has been used in prevention of thrombotic disease. A small number of bleeding complications has been reported (see Adverse Effects). Patients undergoing invasive procedures or having signs/symptoms of underlying coagulopathy or are otherwise at increased risk of bleeding (due to other therapies such as coumarin anticoagulants, heparin, t-PA, streptokinase, high dose ASA) should be evaluated for hemorrhagic risk. Patients at increased hemorrhagic risk due to diseases such as ulcerative gastrointestinal lesions, aneurysms, or diverticulae should also be evaluated carefully if they are to receive pentosan.

Pregnancy: There are no adequate and well-controlled studies in pregnant women. Therefore, this drug should be used during pregnancy only if the potential benefit clearly exceeds the potential risk.

Lactation: It is not known if pentosan is excreted in human milk. Many drugs are excreted in human milk and, therefore, caution should be exercised when pentosan is administered to a nursing mother.

Children: Safety and effectiveness in children and adolescents below the age of 18 years have not been established. This drug should be kept out of the reach of children.

Adverse Effects: Pentosan is usually well tolerated. Reported adverse reactions are infrequent and usually do not require discontinuation of treatment. The most common reactions are gastrointestinal, hematologic or dermatologic (see Precautions).

Low Frequency (≤3%): alopecia, gastrointestinal discomfort, diarrhea, rash, headache, nausea.

Uncommon (≤1%): Digestive: liver function abnormalities, vomiting, mouth ulcer, colitis, esophagitis, gastritis.

Hematologic: anemia, ecchymosis, prothrombin decrease, thrombocytopenia, retinal hemorrhage.

Neurologic: dizziness, paresthesia, insomnia, nervousness.

Metabolic: weight gain, weight loss.

Musculoskeletal: myalgia, arthralgia.

Urogenital: urgency, urinary tract infection, urethritis.

Hypersensitivity Reactions: allergic reaction, photosensitivity.

Other: edema, pelvic pain, malaise, sinusitis, sweating.

Rare Events (single occurrence only in over 1 000 patients with interstitial cystitis): gastritis, leukopenia, depression, rhinitis, lacrimation, angina pectoris, chronic myelogenous leukemia, prostate cancer, loss of appetite, subarachnoid hemorrhage, epistaxis, gum hemorrhage, menorrhagia, hematuria.

Overdose: Symptoms and Treatment: There have been no reported overdosage events and therefore symptoms cannot be described. In human studies, pentosan has been administered i.v. in single bolus doses of 150 mg, in oral doses of 400 mg daily for 3 weeks and orally in total daily doses of 900 mg for up to 3 months without untoward effects. In the event of overdosage, symptomatic treatment is recommended.

Dosage: The recommended dose is 300 mg/day taken as one 100 mg capsule orally 3 times daily. The capsules should be taken with water at least 1 hour before meals or 2 hours after meals.

Some patients with interstitial cystitis may require 6 to 8 weeks of therapy with pentosan to achieve relief of symptoms. Long-term continuation of pentosan therapy is necessary for persistent therapeutic effect.

Supplied: Each white, opaque, hard gelatin capsule, imprinted with "BNP 7600", contains: pentosan polysulfate sodium 100 mg. Nonmedicinal ingredients: magnesium stearate and microcrystalline cellulose. Bottles of 100. Store at controlled room temperature 15 to 30°C.

ELOCOM ℞
Schering

Mometasone Furoate
Corticosteroid

Pharmacology: Mometasone has anti-inflammatory, antipruritic and vasoconstrictive actions. The exact mechanism, however, of corticosteroids in each disease is uncertain. Mometasone has been shown to have topical (dermatologic) and systemic pharmacologic and metabolic effects characteristic of this class of drugs.

Indications: For the relief of the inflammatory and pruritic manifestations of corticosteroid-responsive dermatoses such as psoriasis and atopic dermatitis. The lotion formulation may be applied to scalp lesions.

Contraindications: Hypersensitivity to any one of the components is a contraindication to its use. Topical steroids are contraindicated in untreated fungal, bacterial and viral (i.e. herpes simplex, chickenpox and vaccinia) infections involving the skin.

Warnings: Children: Any of the side effects that have been reported following systemic use of corticosteroids, including adrenal suppression, may also occur with topical corticosteroids, especially in infants and children.

Systemic absorption of topical corticosteroids will be increased if extensive body surface areas are treated or if the occlusive technique is used. Suitable precautions should be taken under these conditions or when long-term use is anticipated, particularly in infants and children. Pediatric patients may demonstrate greater susceptibility to topical corticosteroid-induced HPA axis suppression and Cushing's syndrome than mature patients because of a larger skin surface area to body weight ratio. Use of topical corticosteroids in children should be limited to the least amount compatible with an effective therapeutic regimen. Chronic corticosteroid therapy may interfere with growth and development of children.

The lotion contains isopropyl alcohol and may cause stinging or burning upon application to abraded or sun-burned skin. Do not use in or near the eyes.

Precautions: Geriatrics: Suitable precautions should be taken in using topical glucocorticoids in patients with impaired circulation suffering from stasis dermatitis and other skin diseases.

Pregnancy and *Lactation:* Since safety of topical corticosteroid use in pregnant women has not been established, drugs of this class should be used during pregnancy only if the potential benefit justifies the potential risk to the fetus. Drugs of this class should not be used extensively in large amounts or for prolonged periods of time in pregnant patients.

Since it is not known whether topical administration of corticosteroids can result in sufficient systemic absorption to produce detectable quantities in breast milk, a decision should be made to discontinue nursing or to discontinue the drug, taking into account the importance of the drug to the mother.

Patients should be advised to inform subsequent physicians of the prior use of glucocorticoids.

If irritation, sensitization, excessive dryness develop with the use of mometasone, treatment should be discontinued.

Although mometasone is poorly absorbed, nevertheless, application of corticosteroids over extensive lesions, or exceeding the dosage schedule may result in significant systemic absorption producing hypercortisonism manifesting itself by adrenal suppression, moon facies, striae and suppression of growth.

During the use of topical corticosteroids, infections may occur. If an overt infection is present, appropriate antimicrobial treatment is indicated. If symptomatic response is not noted within a few days to a week, the local application of corticosteroids should be discontinued and the patient re-evaluated.

Prolonged use of corticosteroid preparations may produce striae or atrophy of the skin or s.c. tissues. If this occurs, treatment should be discontinued.

Mometasone is not formulated for ophthalmic use and should not be used in or near the eyes.

Adverse Effects: The following local adverse reactions have been reported: Cream: During clinical studies in 319 patients: burning—1, pruritus—1, skin atrophy—3. Ointment: During clinical studies in 812 patients: burning—13, pruritus—8, skin atrophy—8, tingling/stinging—7, and furunculosis—3. Lotion: During clinical studies in 457 patients: burning—9 (2%), pruritus—4 (1%), skin atrophy—6 (2%) (shininess, thinness, striae, telangiectasia), acneiform reactions—3 (<1%).

The following local adverse reactions have been reported infrequently when other topical dermatologic corticosteroids have been used as recommended. These reactions are listed in an approximate decreasing order of occurrence: burning, itching, irritation, dryness, folliculitis, hypertrichosis, acneiform eruptions, hypopigmentation, perioral dermatitis, allergic contact dermatitis, maceration of the skin, secondary infection, skin atrophy, striae, miliaria.

Adrenal suppression has also been reported following topical corticosteroid therapy. Posterior subcapsular cataracts have been reported following systemic use of corticosteroids.

Cream: The overall incidence of side effects was 1.6%, i.e. 5 of 319 subjects and patients reported treatment-related adverse experiences.

Ointment: The overall incidence of side effects was 4.9%, i.e. 40 of 812 subjects reported treatment-related adverse experiences.

Lotion: The overall incidence of side effects was 5.1%, i.e. 31 of 613 subjects and patients reported treatment-related adverse experiences.

Side effects were mild to moderate and were those typically associated with topical corticosteroid formulations after 7 days of treatment.

No systemic treatment-related adverse experiences were seen.

Overdose: Symptoms and Treatment: No specific antidote is available and treatment should be symptomatic.

Percutaneous absorption of corticosteroids can occur when large amounts of corticosteroids are applied. Toxic effects may include ecchymosis of skin, peptic ulceration, hypertension, aggravation of infection, hirsutism, acne, edema and muscle weakness due to protein depletion. Treatment of a patient with systemic toxic manifestations consists of assuring and maintaining a patent airway and supporting ventilation using oxygen and assisted or controlled respiration as required. This will be sufficient in the management of most reactions. Should circulatory depression occur, vasopressors such as ephedrine or metaraminol and i.v. fluids may be used. Should a convulsion persist despite oxygen therapy, small increments of an ultra-short acting barbiturate (pentobarbital or secobarbital) may be given i.v. Allergic reactions are characterized by cutaneous lesions, urticaria, edema or anaphylactoid reactions.

Dosage: Cream/Ointment: Apply a thin film to the affected skin areas once daily.

Lotion: Apply a few drops of the lotion to the affected skin areas including scalp sites once daily; massage gently and thoroughly until medication disappears.

Do not use occlusive dressings.

Supplied: Cream: Each g of white to off-white uniform cream contains: mometasone furoate 1 mg. Nonmedicinal ingredients: aluminum starch octenylsuccinate, ceteareth-20, hexylene glycol, phosphoric acid, propylene glycol stearate, purified water, stearyl alcohol, titanium dioxide, white petrolatum and white wax. Tubes of 15 and 50 g. Store between 2 and 30°C.

Lotion: Each g of lotion contains: mometasone furoate 1 mg. Nonmedicinal ingredients: hydroxypropylcellulose, isopropyl alcohol, phosphoric acid to adjust pH, propylene glycol, purified water and sodium phosphate monobasic. Plastic bottles of 30 and 75 mL. Store between 2 and 30°C.

Ointment: Each g of ointment contains: mometasone furoate 1 mg. Nonmedicinal ingredients: hexylene glycol, phosphoric acid to adjust pH, propylene glycol stearate, purified water, white petrolatum and white wax. Tubes of 15 and 50 g. Store between 2 and 30°C.

ELTOR® 120
Hoechst Marion Roussel

Pseudoephedrine HCl
Nasal Decongestant

Pharmacology: Pseudoephedrine has been shown to have a similar action on the human nasal mucosa to ephedrine. It is an effective nasal decongestant and bronchodilator. Decongestion of the nasal mucosa occurs through vasoconstriction, and the relief of obstructed air passages by a direct action on the smooth muscle of the bronchi. The vasopressor effect of pseudoephedrine is less than that of ephedrine.

Indications: For conditions of acute coryza, sinusitis, and vasomotor or allergic rhinitis, by providing temporary nasal and sinus decongestion. It may also be used as an adjunct to antibiotics, antihistamines, analgesics and antitussives in the treatment of above conditions.

Contraindications: Patients receiving or having received MAO inhibitors in the preceding 3 weeks; known hypersensitivity to pressor amines.

Precautions: It should be used with caution in hypertensive and diabetic patients; patients with latent or clinically recognized angle closure glaucoma, coronary artery disease, congestive heart failure, prostatic hypertrophy, hyperthyroidism, urinary retention.

Adverse Effects: As with other sympathomimetic amines, headache, dizziness, insomnia, tremor, confusion, CNS stimulation, muscular weakness, dry mouth, nausea, vomiting, difficulty in micturition, palpitations, tightness in the chest and syncope have been encountered.

Overdose: Symptoms: Increase in pulse and respiratory rate, signs of CNS stimulation, disorientation, headache, dry mouth, nausea and vomiting.

Treatment: Gastric lavage, repeated, if necessary. Acidify the urine and institute general supportive measures. If CNS excitement is prominent, a short acting barbiturate may be used.

Dosage: Adults and children over 12 years of age, one 120 mg caplet orally every 12 hours as directed by a physician. Avoid use for prolonged period of time except on the advice of a physician. Do not exceed recommended dosage.

Supplied: Each white caplet, engraved 'ELTOR' on one side contains: pseudoephedrine HCl 120 mg in specially formulated pellets designed to provide a continuous release of the active therapeutic agent over a 12 hour period. Nonmedicinal ingredients: colloidal silicon dioxide, hydroxypropyl methylcellulose, magnesium stearate, methylcellulose, sucrose and water. Packages of 12 and 24.

(Shown In Product Recognition Section)

Reviewed 1999

ELTROXIN® ℞

Glaxo Wellcome

Levothyroxine Sodium

Hypothyroidism Therapy

Pharmacology: Levothyroxine sodium is the monosodium salt of the levorotatory isomer of thyroxine (tetraiodothyronine), the principal hormone secreted by the normal thyroid gland.

Pharmacokinetics: Following oral administration, the absorption of levothyroxine is incomplete and variable (50 to 75%), especially when taken with food. Once absorbed, synthetic levothyroxine is indistinguishable from the endogenous hormone.

Levothyroxine is nearly totally bound to serum proteins and has an elimination half-life of 6 to 7 days in the euthyroid subject. Half-life is shortened in hyperthyroidism and prolonged in hypothyroidism and in pregnancy. Deiodination of levothyroxine (T_4) to 1-triiodothyronine (T_3) occurs in various tissues, particularly liver and kidney. T_3 is approximately 4 times as potent as T_4 on a weight basis.

The mechanism of action of thyroid hormones is not completely understood. The principle effect is to increase the metabolic rate of body tissues. Thyroid hormones have both catabolic and anabolic effects, and are therefore involved in normal metabolism, growth, and development, especially the development of the CNS in infancy.

Indications: Specific hormonal replacement therapy in the presence of hypothyroidism of any etiology.

Contraindications: Patients with hypersensitivity to any ingredient of the tablets and patients with thyrotoxicosis, acute myocardial infarction or uncorrected adrenal insufficiency.

Warnings: *Lactation:* In euthyroid lactating mothers, levothyroxine (endogenous or exogenous) may be secreted into breast milk in amounts sufficient to mask signs of hypothyroidism in the nursing infant.

The use of levothyroxine in the treatment of obesity in patients who are not hypothyroid has been shown to be ineffective and potentially harmful.

Precautions: *Pregnancy:* Levothyroxine does not readily cross the placenta, and when successfully employed to render or maintain the patient in an euthyroid state, therapy is considered to be warranted in pregnant patients. Hypo- or hyperthyroid activity in the mother may unfavorably influence the fetal outcome or well being.

Due to the profound effects of thyroid hormones on energy-requiring metabolic processes, the administration of levothyroxine to a hypothyroid patient may unmask occult cardiovascular, endocrine or metabolic disease.

Long standing hypothyroidism is associated with atherogenesis, which may or may not manifest itself in the hypometabolic state. In such cases levothyroxine should be administered with extreme caution employing low initial dosage increased slowly by small increments, as even a gradual restoration of normal metabolic rate may result in development or exacerbation of myocardial ischemia and angina. In some patients, cardiovascular status may be so compromised that the metabolic demands of the euthyroid state cannot be met, despite the employment of appropriate antianginal therapy. Clinical judgment may then dictate a less-than-complete restoration of thyroid status.

Endocrine disorders such as diabetes mellitus, diabetes insipidus, Addison's disease (adrenal insufficiency) and hypopituitarism are characterized by signs and symptoms which may be diminished in severity or obscured by hypothyroidism.

Treatment with levothyroxine may require that appropriate adjustments in therapy for these concomitant disorders be made. In particular, when hypothyroidism is accompanied by adrenal insufficiency (such as in panhypopituitarism), appropriate adrenocortical replacement therapy should be instituted prior to commencement of treatment with levothyroxine in order to prevent the possible precipitation of Addisonian crisis.

Slightly excessive dosage of thyroid agents were previously recommended for replacement therapy in congenital hypothyroidism (cretinism), since it was thought that slight underdosage was harmful while slightly excessive dosage was not. However, it is currently recommended that excessive dosage be avoided since minimal brain damage has occurred in children with thyrotoxicosis during infancy and excessive dosage may accelerate bone age and cause premature craniosynostosis (see Dosage).

The intestinal absorption of levothyroxine may be impaired in patients with certain malabsorption states, particularly celiac sprue (gluten enteropathy). Higher dosages of levothyroxine may be required in such patients, especially during exacerbations of the enteropathy.

Levothyroxine should be used with caution in elderly patients who may be more sensitive to the effects of thyroid hormones (see Dosage).

Due to potential differences in potency and bioavailability, different levothyroxine products may not be interchangeable. Patients stabilized on a particular brand of levothyroxine should not be unnecessarily switched to another brand. When such a brand change is necessary, the patients must be carefully re-evaluated to assess the potential need for dosage adjustment.

Drug Interactions: Thyroid hormones potentiate the hypoprothrombinemic effects of oral anticoagulant agents such as warfarin. When treatment with levothyroxine is initiated in patients receiving oral anticoagulants, the prothrombin time should be determined frequently and the anticoagulant dosage reduced appropriately.

Administration of levothyroxine to a diabetic patient may result in an increase in the patient's requirements for insulin and/or hypoglycemic medication since thyroxine raises blood sugar levels (see above).

Cholestyramine resin binds levothyroxine in the intestinal tract and substantially impairs its absorption. When the 2 agents must be used concurrently the levothyroxine dose should be taken at least 1 hour before or 4 hours after the dose of cholestyramine, with regular monitoring of thyroid function.

Anticonvulsants such as carbamazepine and phenytoin enhance the metabolism of thyroid hormones and may displace them from plasma proteins.

Phenobarbital induces hepatic enzymes and increases the rate of degradation of thyroid hormones. The dosage of levothyroxine may need to be increased when concurrent therapy with phenobarbital is employed.

Beta-adrenergic blocking agents may decrease peripheral conversion of T_4 to T_3, thereby reducing the efficacy of exogenous levothyroxine.

Estrogens increase serum thyroxine-binding globulin levels, thereby decreasing the unbound fractions of T_3 and T_4. Administration of estrogen-containing preparations (such as oral contraceptives) to hypothyroid patients may cause an increase in their levothyroxine requirements.

Patients receiving thyroid replacement therapy who undergo anesthesia with ketamine should be closely monitored for possible hypertension and tachycardia.

Concurrent use of sympathomimetic agents or tricyclic antidepressants with thyroid hormones may result in enhanced effects of either medication. In patients with coronary artery disease receiving thyroid replacement therapy, administration of sympathomimetic agents increases the risk of coronary insufficiency.

If coadministered with cardiac glycosides, adjustment of dosage of cardiac glycoside may be necessary.

Sucralfate or aluminium-containing antacids may decrease the absorption of levothyroxine. Adjustment of the levothyroxine dose, or cessation of the aluminum-containing medication may be necessary.

Simultaneous ingestion of ferrous sulfate and levothyroxine causes a reduction in thyroxine efficacy. When the two agents must be used concurrently, the levothyroxine and ferrous sulfate doses must be separated by an interval of 2 hours or more, with regular monitoring of thyroid function.

Laboratory Test Interactions: Various physiologic and pathologic conditions or certain drugs can interfere with thyroid function tests and their interpretation. Serum thyroxine-binding globulin (TBG) is increased in pregnancy, on estrogen therapy, or in patients using estrogen-containing oral contraceptives. Infectious hepatitis may also increase serum TBG concentration. Decreased TBG is found in patients on androgen or corticosteroid therapy and also in cases of nephrosis and acromegaly. Some drugs such as phenylbutazone and salicylates bind competitively to TBG or thyroxine-binding prealbumin. Familial hyper-or hypo-thyroxine-binding globulinemias have been reported.

Adverse Effects: Adverse reactions to levothyroxine are confined to hypersensitivity to or intolerance of an ingredient of the tablets, and toxicity due to overdosage of levothyroxine (see Overdose: Symptoms and Treatment).

Overdose: Symptoms and Treatment: Overdosage with levothyroxine can be expected to produce the typical signs and symptoms of thyrotoxicosis. These may include weight loss, increased appetite, palpitations, nervousness, diarrhea, abdominal cramps, sweating, tachycardia, increased pulse and blood pressures, angina pectoris, cardiac dysrhythmias, tremors, headache, insomnia, heat intolerance, fever and dysmenorrhea.

Severe overdosage is equivalent to thyroid storm and may be manifested by coma, cardiac decompensation, and possibly death secondary to cardiac dysrhythmia or failure. The effects of acute overdosage of levothyroxine may take several days to appear.

The manifestations of levothyroxine overdosage should be managed by discontinuation of levothyroxine for 2 to 7 days followed by resumption of treatment with lower doses.

The management of acute severe overdosage should consist principally of reducing absorption of the drug and counteracting central and peripheral effects, mainly those of increased sympathetic nervous activity. Initially, the stomach should be emptied immediately by inducing emesis or by gastric lavage. If the patient is comatose, having seizures, or lacks the gag reflex, gastric lavage may be performed if an endotracheal tube with cuff inflated is in place to prevent aspiration of vomitus. Oxygen may be administered and ventilation maintained. If congestive heart failure develops, cardiac glycosides may be administered. Measures to control fever, hypoglycemia, or fluid loss should be initiated as necessary. A β-adrenergic blocking agent may be useful to counteract many of the effects of increased sympathetic activity. Provided no contraindications for its use exist, propranolol may be administered i.v. in a dosage of 1 to 3 mg every 10 minutes, or orally in a dosage of 80 to 100 mg/day. However, propylthiouracil and other antithyroid agents are **not** effective in the treatment of thyrotoxicosis due to overdosage of exogenous levothyroxine.

Dosage: Dosage of levothyroxine must be carefully adjusted according to individual requirements and response. The age and general physical condition of the patients and the severity and duration of hypothyroid symptoms determine the initial dosage and rate at which dosage may be increased to the eventual maintenance dosage (see Precautions). Adjustment of levothyroxine dosage should be based mainly on the patient's clinical response and confirmed by appropriate laboratory tests. Laboratory tests alone should not be relied upon to guide therapy.

For purposes of conversion, levothyroxine sodium (T_4) 100 μg is usually considered equivalent to desiccated thyroid 60 mg, thyroglobulin 60 mg, or liothyronine sodium (T_3) 25 μg. However, these are rough guidelines only and do not obviate the careful re-evaluation of a patient when switching thyroid

Eltroxin (cont'd)

hormone preparations, including a change from one brand of levothyroxine to another (see Precautions).

Information for the Patient: Patients on thyroid preparations and parents of children on thyroid therapy should be informed that replacement therapy is to be taken essentially for life, with the exception of cases of transient hypothyroidism, usually associated with thyroiditis, and in those patients receiving a therapeutic trial of the drug.

Patients should immediately report to the physician experiences during the course of therapy of any signs or symptoms of thyroid hormone toxicity, e.g., chest pain, increased pulse rate, palpitations, excessive sweating, heat intolerance, nervousness, or any other unusual event.

Patients with concurrent diabetes mellitus or who are on concurrent oral anticoagulant therapy should be warned of the need for close monitoring and possible dosage adjustments.

Parents should be warned that partial loss of hair may be experienced by children in the first few months of thyroid therapy, but this is usually a transient phenomenon and later recovery is normally the rule.

Adults: For the management of mild hypothyroidism, the usual initial dose is 50 μg once daily. Dosage may be increased in increments of 25 to 50 μg/day at intervals of 2 to 4 weeks until the desired response is obtained.

For the management of severe hypothyroidism the usual initial dosage is 12.5 to 25 μg once daily. Dosage may be increased by increments of 25 to 50 μg/day at intervals of 2 to 4 weeks until the desired response is obtained. The usual maintenance dosage for full replacement therapy is 100 to 200 μg/day, although certain patients may require higher dosages. Failure to respond adequately to dosages exceeding 300 to 400 μg/day is rare and should prompt re-evaluation of the diagnosis, or suggest the presence of malabsorption or patient noncompliance.

For geriatric patients with hypothyroidism, the usual initial dosage is 12.5 to 50 μg once daily. Dosage may be increased at intervals of 3 to 8 weeks until the desired response is obtained. Thyroid hormone replacement requirements are about 25% lower in patients over the age of 60 years than in younger adults.

Infants and Children: In infants and children, it is essential to achieve rapid and complete thyroid replacement because of the critical importance of thyroid hormones in sustaining growth and maturation, including the normal development of the CNS. In general, the dosage requirements of children, on a per body weight basis, are higher than those of adults.

The recommended replacement dosages of levothyroxine, to be administered in a single daily dose, are as follows: See Table I.

Table I—Eltroxin

Dosage in Infants and Children

Age	Daily Dose
0-6 months	25-50 μg or 8-10 μg/kg
6-12 months	50-75 μg or 6-8 μg/kg
1-5 years	75-100 μg or 5-6 μg/kg
6-12 years	100-150 μg or 4-5 μg/kg
>12 years	>150 μg or 2-3 μg/kg

Premature neonates weighing less than 2 kg and neonates at risk of cardiac failure may receive an initial dosage of 25 μg once daily; dosage may be increased to 50 μg once daily in 4 to 6 weeks.

Supplied: 50 μg: Each white tablet contains: levothyroxine sodium USP 50 μg. Nonmedicinal ingredients: acacia powder, corstarch, lactose and magnesium stearate. Gluten- and tartrazine-free. Bottles of 100 and 500.

100 μg: Each yellow tablet contains: levothyroxine sodium 100 μg. Nonmedicinal ingredients: acacia powder, Colorcon yellow, cornstarch, lactose and magnesium stearate. Gluten- and tartrazine-free. Bottles of 500.

150 μg: Each blue tablet contains: levothyroxine sodium 150 μg. Nonmedicinal ingredients: acacia powder, Colorcon blue, cornstarch, lactose and magnesium stearate. Gluten- and tartrazine-free. Bottles of 500.

200 μg: Each pink tablet contains: levothyroxine sodium 200 μg. Nonmedicinal ingredients: acacia powder, cornstarch, erythrosine, lactose and magnesium stearate. Gluten- and tartrazine-free. Bottles of 500.

300 μg: Each green tablet contains: levothyroxine sodium 300 μg. Nonmedicinal ingredients: acacia powder, Colorcon green, cornstarch, lactose and magnesium stearate. Gluten- and tartrazine-free. Bottles of 100 and 500.

Protect from light.

(Shown in Product Recognition Section)

Reviewed 1998

EMADINE® Ⓟ

Alcon

Emedastine Difumarate

Antiallergy Agent

Pharmacology: Emedastine is a potent, selective, and topically effective histamine H_1 antagonist with a rapid onset of action. In vitro and in vivo examinations of emedastine's affinity for histamine receptors (H_1, H_2 and H_3) demonstrate 10 000-fold selectivity for the H_1 histamine receptor and concentration-dependent inhibition of histamine-stimulated vascular permeability in the conjunctiva following topical ocular administration. Emedastine is devoid of effects on adrenergic, dopaminergic and serotonin receptors.

As with other topically administered drugs, emedastine is absorbed systemically. In a study involving 10 normal volunteers dosed bilaterally twice daily for 15 days with emedastine ophthalmic solution 0.05%, plasma concentrations of the parent compound were generally below the quantitation limit of the assay (<0.3 ng/mL). Samples in which emedastine was quantifiable ranged from 0.30 to 0.49 ng/mL. These plasma concentrations are at least 10-fold lower than those observed with well-tolerated multiple-dose oral regimens. The human oral bioavailability of emedastine is approximately 50%, and maximum plasma concentrations are achieved within 1 to 2 hours postdose. The elimination half-life of oral emedastine in plasma is 3 to 4 hours. Approximately 44% of the oral dose is recovered in the urine over 24 hours with only 3.6% of the dose excreted as parent drug. Two primary metabolites, 5- and 6-hydroxyemedastine, are excreted in the urine as both free and conjugated forms. The 5'-oxo analogs of 5- and 6-hydroxyemedastine and the N-oxide are also formed as minor metabolites.

Indications: For the relief within minutes of the signs and symptoms of allergic conjunctivitis.

Contraindications: Hypersensitivity to any component of this product.

Warnings: For topical use only. Not for injection. Patients should be instructed not to instill emedastine while wearing contact lenses, but to wait 10 minutes after instillation before inserting contact lenses.

Precautions: Information to be Provided to the Patient: To prevent contaminating the dropper tip and solution, care should be taken not to touch the eyelids or surrounding areas with the dropper tip of the bottle. Keep the bottle tightly closed when not in use.

Carcinogenesis, Mutagenesis, Impairment of Fertility: Emedastine demonstrated no carcinogenicity effects in lifetime studies in mice and rats at dietary doses up to 35 000 and 11 000 times the maximum recommended ocular human dose level, respectively. Higher dose levels were not tested. Emedastine was determined to be nonmutagenic in an in vitro bacterial reverse mutation (Ames) test, an in vitro modification of the Ames test, an in vitro mammalian chromosome aberration test, an in vitro mammalian forward mutation test, an in vitro mammalian DNA repair synthesis test, an in vivo mammalian sister chromatid exchange test and an in vivo mouse micronucleus test. There was no evidence of impaired fertility or reproductive capacity in rats at 6 200 times the maximum recommended ocular human use level.

Pregnancy: Teratology and peri- and postnatal studies have been conducted with emedastine in rats and rabbits. At 6 200 times the maximum recommended ocular human use level, emedastine was shown not to be teratogenic in rats and rabbits and no effects on peri-/postnatal development were observed in rats. There are, however, no adequate and well-controlled studies in pregnant women. Because animal studies are not always predictive of human responses, this drug should be used in pregnant women only if the potential benefit to the mother justifies the potential risk to the embryo or fetus.

Lactation: Emedastine has been identified in breast milk in rats following oral administration. It is not known whether topical ocular administration could result in sufficient systemic absorption to produce detectable quantities in breast milk. Nevertheless, caution should be exercised when emedastine is administered to a nursing mother.

Children: Safety and effectiveness in pediatric patients between the ages of 3 and 16 have been established.

Adverse Effects: In clinical studies of emedastine, mild transient burning or stinging was reported at an incidence of 1.4%. All other ocular and nonocular adverse reactions related to therapy were reported at an incidence equal to or less than 1%.

Ocular: pruritus, hyperemia, dry eye, corneal staining, eye fatigue, foreign body sensation, blurred vision, tearing, infiltrate, irritation.

Nonocular: headache, asthenia, abnormal dreams, dermatitis, taste perversion.

Overdose: Symptoms and Treatment: A topical overdosage may be flushed from the eye(s) with warm tap water.

Dosage: The recommended dose is 1 to 2 drops in each affected eye 4 times daily.

Supplied: Each mL of sterile ophthalmic solution contains: emedastine difumarate equivalent to emedastine 0.5 mg (0.05%) and benzalkonium chloride 0.01% as preservative. Nonmedicinal ingredients: hydrochloric acid and/or sodium hydroxide, hydroxypropyl methylcellulose, purified water, sodium chloride and tromethamine. Drop-Tainer dispensers of 5 mL. Store at 4 to 30°C. Protect from light.

New Product 1998

EMCYT® Ⓟ

Pharmacia & Upjohn

Estramustine Sodium Phosphate

Antineoplastic

Pharmacology: Estramustine has a dual mode of action. The intact molecule acts as an antimitotic agent and after hydrolysis of the carbamate ester bridge the released estrogens exert an antigonadotrophic effect. The low level of clinically manifested side effects may be due to the fact that estramustine binds to a protein present in the tumor tissue, which results in an accumulation of the drug at the target site.

Indications: The treatment of metastatic prostatic carcinoma (stage D) in patients whose disease is refractory to hormonal therapy. Estramustine may produce either a stabilization or regression of the disease process and improvement in ability to function.

Contraindications: In patients with any of the following conditions: known hypersensitivity to either estradiol or to nitrogen mustard, severe hepatic or cardiac disease or active thrombophlebitis or thromboembolic disorders.

Warnings: Caution: Estramustine is a potent drug and should be prescribed only by physicians experienced with cancer chemotherapeutic drugs (see Precautions). Blood counts, as well as renal and hepatic function tests, should be performed regularly. Discontinue the drug if abnormal renal or hepatic function is seen. Capsules should not be opened.

Estramustine should be used with caution in patients with a history of thrombophlebitis, thrombosis or thromboembolic disorders, especially if associated with estrogen therapy. Caution should also be used in patients with cerebral vascular or coronary artery disease.

Angioneurotic edema has been reported in few cases during estramustine therapy, with or without concomitant medication.

Glucose Tolerance: Because glucose tolerance may be decreased, diabetic patients should be carefully observed while receiving the drug.

Elevated Blood Pressure: Because hypertension may occur, blood pressure should be monitored periodically.

Precautions: Estramustine should be administered by individuals experienced in the use of antineoplastic therapy. Professional staff administering estramustine should exercise particular care to prevent spillage and contact with the drug. Should skin contact occur, the area should be vigorously washed with soap and cold water and material used for cleansing disposed of by incineration.

Exacerbation of pre-existing or incipient peripheral edema or congestive heart disease has been seen in some patients receiving estramustine therapy. Other conditions which might be influenced by fluid retention, such as epilepsy, migraine, or renal dysfunction, require careful observation.

Estramustine may be poorly metabolized in patients with impaired liver function and should be administered with caution in such patients.

Because estramustine may influence the metabolism of calcium and phosphorus, it should be used with caution in patients with metabolic bone diseases that are associated with hypercalcemia or in patients with renal insufficiency.

Although testing by the Ames method failed to demonstrate mutagenicity for estramustine, it is known that both estradiol and nitrogen mustard are mutagenic. Patients should therefore be advised to use contraceptive measures during therapy with estramustine.

Laboratory Tests: Certain endocrine and liver function tests may be affected by estrogen-containing drugs. Abnormalities of hepatic enzymes and of bilirubin have occurred in patients receiving estramustine, but have seldom been severe enough to require cessation of therapy. Such tests should be done at appropriate intervals during therapy and repeated 2 months after the drug has been withdrawn.

Food/Drug Interactions: Food like milk, milk products or drugs which contain calcium or other polyvalent ions may impair the absorption of estramustine and must not be taken simultaneously with estramustine.

Angioneurotic edema has been reported in few cases when estramustine was administered concomitantly with ACE-inhibitors.

Adverse Effects: Gastrointestinal disturbances (most commonly transient nausea, but occasionally vomiting, and rarely diarrhea) sometimes occur at the beginning of therapy. In a few cases thrombocytopenia, leukopenia and elevated transaminases/bilirubin have been noted but were completely reversible on reduction of dosage or temporary (1 to 2 weeks) withdrawal of the drug. A few cases of allergic skin rashes, edema and anginal complaints have been reported. A few cases of angioneurotic edema have been reported during estramustine therapy, with or without concomitant medication. As when after conventional estradiol therapy, thromboembolic disorders, gynecomastia, reduced libido and potency may occur.

Overdose: Symptoms and Treatment: There has been no experience, to date, with overdoses of estramustine. In the event of overdosage, treatment should be symptomatic and supportive. Gastric lavage should be performed and measures taken to encourage diuresis. Hematologic and hepatic parameters should be monitored for at least 6 weeks after overdosage of estramustine.

Dosage: The recommended dose of estramustine is 14 mg/kg of body weight/day (i.e., one 140 mg capsule for each 10 kg), given in 3 or 4 divided doses. Most patients have been treated at a dose range of 10 to 16 mg/kg/day.

Treatment for at least 30 days is recommended before assessing the benefits of therapy and may be continued as long as a favorable response lasts. Some patients have been maintained on therapy for more than 2 years at doses ranging from 10 to 16 mg/kg of body weight/day.

The capsules should be taken at not less than 1 hour before or 2 hours after meals.

The capsules should be swallowed with a glass of water. Milk, milk products or calcium containing drugs (such as calcium-containing antacids) must not be used simultaneously with estramustine capsules.

Supplied: Each white, opaque, hard gelatin capsule contains: estramustine sodium phosphate 140 mg. Nonmedicinal ingredients: gelatin capsule, isopropanol, magnesium stearate, silica and sodium laurylsulfate. Bisulfite-, gluten-, lactose- and tartrazine-free. Bottles of 100. Store at 2 to 25°C.

EMINASE® Ⓟ

Roberts

Anistreplase

Fibrinolytic Agent

Pharmacology: Anistreplase is an inactive derivative of a fibrinolytic (thrombolytic) enzyme composed of streptokinase and lys-plasminogen in which the catalytic center of the enzymatic complex is temporarily blocked by a p-anisoyl group.

Anistreplase has high fibrin-binding ability; the lys-plasminogen component of anistreplase has greater fibrin affinity than that of native glu-plasminogen.

Activation of anistreplase to lys-plasminogen-streptokinase occurs by a first order, hydrolytic process, in blood or in the thrombus, with release of the p-anisoyl group by deacylation. The nonenzymatic deacylation process starts immediately after i.v. administration of anistreplase and progresses with a half-life of about 2 hours, as estimated in vitro in human blood.

Anistreplase is a plasminogen activator and, therefore, exerts its fibrinolytic activity by converting plasminogen into its proteolytically active form, plasmin. Plasmin then digests the insoluble fibrin network which stabilizes a thrombus, into smaller, soluble fibrin degradation products which results in thrombolysis.

The hypotensive effect of streptokinase plasminogen was compared with anistreplase in beagle dogs given equivalent doses by rapid i.v. injection. Streptokinase-plasminogen produced a pronounced hypotensive effect within 1 to 3 minutes after administration whereas anistreplase had no hypotensive effect.

After i.v. administration of anistreplase by single injection to patients, the circulating half-life of fibrinolytic activity resulting from anistreplase (mean of 94 minutes; range of 70 to 120 minutes) is longer than that after i.v. infusion of streptokinase (about 20 minutes). The p-anisoyl group in anistreplase permits i.v. administration over 2 to 5 minutes, slows the loss of circulating fibrinolytic activity in the bloodstream and, hence, prolongs the duration of thrombolytic action.

A number of controlled clinical studies have been performed with anistreplase to demonstrate benefit. Heparin anticoagulation was administered to all patients routinely following (about 4 to 6 hours) dosing with anistreplase.

Randomized, controlled studies have demonstrated that anistreplase reduces mortality when administered within 6 hours of the onset of the symptoms of acute myocardial infarction (AMI). The benefit of mortality reduction occurs acutely and is maintained for at least 1 year.

In a randomized, double blind study of 1 258 patients (AIMS trial), at 30 days postinfarction, mortality was decreased (47.2%, $p=0.0001$) in patients receiving anistreplase as compared with placebo. At 1 year, the reduction in mortality was maintained (38%, $p=0.001$). The incidence of heart failure was less in patients treated with anistreplase (17.9%) compared with patients who received placebo (23.3%). In a German multicenter, randomized, controlled trial involving 313 patients (162 received anistreplase, 151 received heparin), reduction in mortality, similar to that obtained in the AIMS trial, was observed (56%, $p=0.032$).

In a double-blind, randomized trial of anistreplase compared with heparin bolus (112 received anistreplase, 119 received heparin), left ventricular function was improved and infarction size reduced. There was significantly ($p<0.01$, 2 sample t-test) higher left ventricular ejection fraction for the anistreplase treatment group (53%) compared with the heparin treatment group (47.5%) when measured 4 days after treatment (intent-to-treat analysis). This difference was maintained when patients were reexamined by radionuclide ventriculography at day 19, even when patients who experienced successful angioplasty were excluded from the analysis ($p=0.04$). About 3 weeks after treatment, mean infarct size was 24% lower in the patients treated with anistreplase compared with those treated with heparin ($n=188$, $p=0.02$). Similarly, if those patients who experienced successful angioplasty were excluded from the analysis, the mean infarct size in patients treated with anistreplase was significantly less than that of heparin-treated patients ($p<0.01$).

In randomized, comparative studies, reperfusion rates of between 50 and 68% have been reported in patients receiving anistreplase within 6 hours of symptom onset. However, for maximum rates of reperfusion, treatment should be initiated as soon as possible after onset of symptoms.

In 2 studies, anistreplase and intracoronary (IC) streptokinase were compared in patients with angiographically proven coronary artery occlusion. Reperfusion occurred about 45 minutes after the start of therapy for both treatment groups. When therapy was initiated within 4 hours of onset of AMI symptoms, reperfusion rates of 59% ($n=87$) and 68% ($n=41$) were observed for anistreplase compared with 59% ($n=85$) and 70% ($n=43$) for IC streptokinase. Of those patients who had coronary artery reperfusion, angiographically demonstrated reocclusion occurred within 24 hours in 3 to 4% of those treated with anistreplase and in 7 to 12% of those treated with streptokinase.

In a multicenter, randomized, comparative study, a patency rate of 72% was obtained with anistreplase compared with 53% for i.v. streptokinase. Patency for 107 patients (54 received anistreplase) was determined by post-treatment angiography.

Anistreplase was also found to have a favorable risk/benefit profile in elderly patients (>65 years, $n=940$) who participated in clinical trials. Use of anistreplase in patients over 75 years old has not been adequately studied.

Indications: For use in the management of AMI in adults for the lysis of thrombi obstructing coronary arteries, the reduction of infarct size, the improvement of ventricular function following AMI, and the reduction of mortality associated with AMI.

Treatment should be initiated as soon as possible after the onset of AMI symptoms.

Contraindications: Because thrombolytic therapy increases the risk of bleeding, anistreplase is contraindicated in the following situations: active internal bleeding; history of cerebrovascular accident (CVA); patients receiving other i.v. thrombolytic agents; recent (within 2 months) intracranial or intraspinal surgery or trauma (see Warnings); intracranial neoplasm, arteriovenous malformation, or aneurysm; known bleeding diathesis; severe, uncontrolled hypertension (see Warnings); recent traumatic cardiopulmonary resuscitation; recent severe trauma (see Warnings).

Anistreplase should not be administered to patients having experienced severe allergic reactions to either this product or streptokinase.

Warnings: Bleeding (see Adverse Effects): The most common complication associated with anistreplase therapy is bleeding. The type of bleeding associated with thrombolytic therapy can be divided into 2 broad categories: Internal bleeding involving the gastrointestinal tract, genitourinary tract, retroperitoneal, ocular, or intracranial sites. Superficial or surface bleeding, observed mainly at invaded or disturbed sites (e.g.,venous cutdowns, arterial punctures, sites of recent surgical intervention).

The concomitant use of heparin anticoagulation may contribute to the bleeding. As fibrin is lysed during anistreplase therapy, bleeding from a recent puncture site may occur. Therefore, thrombolytic therapy requires careful attention to all potential bleeding sites (including catheter insertion sites, arterial and venous puncture sites, cutdown sites and needle puncture sites).

I.M. injections and nonessential handling of the patient should be avoided during treatment with anistreplase. Venipunctures should be performed carefully and only as required. Should an arterial puncture be necessary following administration of anistreplase, it is preferable to use an upper-extremity vessel that is accessible to manual compression. A pressure dressing should be applied, and the puncture site should be checked frequently for evidence of bleeding.

Each patient being considered for therapy with anistreplase should be carefully evaluated and anticipated benefits should be weighed against potential risks associated with the therapy. In the following conditions, the risks of anistreplase therapy may be increased and should be weighed against the anticipated benefits: Recent (within 10 days) major surgery (e.g., coronary artery bypass graft, obstetrical delivery, organ biopsy, previous puncture of noncompressible vessels); cerebrovascular disease; recent gastrointestinal or genitourinary bleeding (within 10 days); recent trauma (within 10 days). Hypertension: systolic BP ≥180 mm Hg and/or diastolic ≥110 mm Hg; high likelihood of left heart thrombus (e.g., mitral stenosis with atrial fibrillation); subacute bacterial endocarditis; hemostatic defects including those secondary to severe hepatic or renal disease; pregnancy; diabetic hemorrhagic retinopathy or other hemorrhagic ophthalmic conditions; septic thrombophlebitis or occluded AV cannula at seriously infected site; advanced age (i.e., over 75 years old); patients currently receiving oral anticoagulants (e.g., warfarin sodium); any other condition in which bleeding constitutes a significant hazard or would be particularly difficult to manage because of its location; acute pericarditis.

Arrhythmias: Coronary thrombolysis may result in arrhythmias associated with reperfusion. These arrhythmias (such as sinus bradycardia, accelerated idioventricular rhythm, ventricular premature depolarization, ventricular tachycardia) are not different from those often seen in the ordinary course of AMI and may be managed with standard antiarrhythmic measures. It is recommended that antiarrhythmic therapy for bradycardia and/or ventricular irritability be available when injections of anistreplase are administered (see Adverse Effects).

Hypotension: Hypotension, sometimes severe, not secondary to bleeding or anaphylaxis, has occasionally been observed soon after i.v. anistreplase administration. Often the hypotension is associated with bradycardia. Patients should be monitored closely and, should symptomatic or alarming hypotension occur, appropriate symptomatic treatment should be administered (see Adverse Effects).

Precautions: General: Standard management of myocardial infarction should be implemented concomitantly with anistreplase treatment. Invasive procedures should be minimized (see Warnings). Anaphylactoid reactions have rarely been reported in patients who received anistreplase. Accordingly, adequate treatment provisions such as epinephrine should be available for immediate use (see Adverse Effects). Anistreplase should be administered in a setting where the appropriate personnel and monitoring techniques are readily available.

Eminase (cont'd)

Readministration: Because of the increased likelihood of resistance due to antistreptokinase antibody, anistreplase may not be effective if administered more than 5 days after prior anistreplase or streptokinase therapy particularly between 5 days and 12 months. Increased antistreptokinase antibody levels after anistreplase or streptokinase may also increase the risk of allergic reactions following readministration.

Repeated administration of anistreplase within 1 week of the initial dose has occurred in 60 patients treated for AMI. The majority of these patients (54/60) received their repeat dosing as part of the early dose-finding studies. Of these, 44 received both doses totaling 30 units of anistreplase or less within 1 hour, 7 received these doses within 24 hours and 3 received these doses between 24 and 72 hours. In addition, there were 6 patients who received a second dose of 30 units of anistreplase. These patients received their second treatment within 24 hours in 4 cases and within 48 hours in the remaining 2 cases.

In the group who received a repeat dose as part of the early dose-ranging studies, there was no evidence that the incidence of any adverse event increased as a consequence of repeat dosing. However, the number of patients in either group was too small to draw definitive conclusions about the safety of readministration within 1 week.

Laboratory Tests: I.V. administration of anistreplase will cause marked decreases in plasminogen and fibrinogen and increases in thrombin time, activated partial thromboplastin, and prothrombin time. Coagulation parameters can be monitored by measurement of thrombin time or prothrombin time. Plasminogen and fibrinogen values have generally returned to normal within 24 to 48 hours of therapy.

Post-dosing coagulation studies are of importance in providing information on which the dose of heparin may be adjusted. Adjustment may be required to maintain the thrombin time or partial thromboplastin time, or similar, at approximately twice the upper limit of laboratory normal range values. These studies may also be of importance in the rare situation in which a patient treated with anistreplase develops severe, uncontrolled bleeding within the first few hours of dosing. In such cases, coagulation monitoring may be helpful in identifying hemostatic deficiencies that may need correction with cryoprecipitate, purified clotting factor concentrates or fresh whole blood. Results of coagulation tests and/or measures of fibrinolytic activity performed during anistreplase therapy may be unreliable unless specific precautions are taken to prevent in vitro artifacts. Anistreplase, when present in blood in pharmacologic concentrations, remains active under in vitro conditions. This can lead to degradation of fibrinogen in blood samples removed for analysis. Collection of blood samples in the presence of aprotinin (2 000 to 3 000 KIU/mL) can, to some extent, mitigate this phenomenon.

Drug Interactions: The use of anistreplase with other cardioactive drugs has not been studied. In addition to bleeding associated with heparin and vitamin K antagonists, drugs that alter platelet function (such as ASA and dipyridamole) may increase the risk of bleeding if administered prior to anistreplase therapy.

Use of Anticoagulants: Anistreplase alone or in combination with antiplatelet agents and anticoagulants may cause bleeding complications. Therefore, careful clinical observation is advised, especially at arterial puncture sites.

Heparin anticoagulation has been routinely administered to all patients after dosing with anistreplase. In all but one of the pivotal studies (a comparator study of anistreplase versus heparin), anticoagulant therapy was initiated 4 to 6 hours after anistreplase treatment (approximately when the thrombin time or activated partial thromboplastin time were less than 2 times the upper limit of normal). The use of antiplatelet agents increased the incidence of bleeding events similarly in patients treated with anistreplase or nonthrombolytic therapy. There was no evidence of a synergistic effect of combined anistreplase and antiplatelet agents on bleeding events. In addition, there was no difference in the incidence of hemorrhagic CVAs in anistreplase-treated patients who did or did not receive ASA.

Carcinogenesis, Mutagenesis, Impairment of Fertility: Long-term studies in animals have not been performed to evaluate the carcinogenic potential of the effect on fertility. Studies to determine mutagenicity and chromosomal aberration assays in human lymphocytes were negative in all concentrations tested.

Pregnancy: Animal reproduction studies have not been conducted with anistreplase. It is also not known whether anistreplase can cause fetal harm when administered to a pregnant woman or can affect reproductive capacity. Anistreplase should be given to a pregnant woman only if clearly needed.

Lactation: It is not known whether anistreplase is excreted in human milk. Because many drugs are excreted in milk, the physician should decide whether the patient should discontinue nursing or not receive anistreplase.

Children: Safety and effectiveness of anistreplase in children have not been established.

Adverse Effects: Bleeding: The incidence of bleeding (major or minor) varied widely from study to study and may depend on the use of arterial catheterization and other invasive procedures, patient population, and concomitant therapy. The overall incidence of bleeding in patients treated with anistreplase in clinical trials (n=5 275) was 14.6%, with nonpuncture-site bleeding occurring in 10.2% and puncture-site bleeding occurring in 5.7%, of these patients. Bleeding at the puncture site occurred more frequently in clinical trials in which the patients underwent immediate coronary catheterization (13.3%, n=637) compared with those who did not (3.0%, n=2 023). The incidence of presumed intracranial bleeding within 7 days postdosing with anistreplase was 0.57% (n=5 275; 0.34%, etiology confirmed hemorrhagic; 0.23%, etiology not confirmed) compared to 0.16% (n=1 249) after nonthrombolytic therapy.

In the AIMS trial the overall incidence of bleeding in patients treated with anistreplase was 14.8% compared with 3.8% for placebo. The incidence of specific bleeding events were as follows: See Table I.

Table I—Eminase

Incidence of Specific Bleeding Events

Type of Bleeding	Eminase (n=500) %	Placebo (n=501) %
Puncture site	4.6	<1
Nonpuncture site hematoma	2.8	<1
Hematuria/Genitourinary	2.4	<1
Hemoptysis	2.2	<1
Gastrointestinal hemorrhage	2	1.4
Intracranial	1	<1
Gum/Mouth hemorrhage	1	0
Epistaxis	<1	<1
Anemia	<1	<1
Eye hemorrhage	<1	<1
Hemorrhage (unspecified)	<1	0

In this study there was no difference between anistreplase and placebo in the incidence of major bleeding events. The incidence of intracranial bleeding, cardiac tamponade, a decrease in hemoglobin greater than 50 g/L, or greater than a 15 point decrease in hematocrit, was 1.6% for anistreplase compared with 1.8% for placebo-treated patients.

Should serious bleeding (not controlled by local pressure) occur in a critical location (intracranial, gastrointestinal, retroperitoneal, pericardial), any concomitant heparin should be terminated immediately and the administration of protamine to reverse heparinization should be considered. If necessary, the bleeding tendency can be reversed with appropriate replacement therapy.

Minor bleeding can be anticipated mainly at invaded or disturbed sites. If such bleeding occurs, local measures should be taken to control the bleeding (see Warnings).

Cardiovascular: The most frequently reported adverse experiences in anistreplase trials (n=5 275) were arrhythmia/conduction disorders which were reported in 38% of patients treated with anistreplase and 46% of nonthrombolytic control patients. Hypotension occurred in 10.4% of the 5 275 patients treated with anistreplase compared to 7.9% for patients who received nonthrombolytic treatment (see Warnings).

Allergic-type Reactions: Anaphylactic and anaphylactoid reactions have been observed rarely (0.2%) in patients treated with anistreplase and are similar in incidence to streptokinase. These included symptoms such as bronchospasm or angioedema.

Other milder or delayed effects such as urticaria, itching, flushing, rashes, eosinophilia have been occasionally observed. A delayed purpuric rash appearing 1 to 2 weeks after treatment has been reported in 0.3% of patients. The rash may also be associated with arthralgia, ankle edema, gastrointestinal symptoms, mild hematuria and mild proteinuria. This syndrome was self-limiting and without long-term sequelae.

Risk of Viral Transmission: Six standard production batches of anistreplase (5 different standard production batches of lys-plasminogen) were used in clinical trials designed specifically to monitor possible hepatitis non-A, non-B transmission. No case of hepatitis was diagnosed in the 48 anistreplase-treated patients that qualified for evaluation. Elevated transaminase levels (at least 2.5 times the upper limit of normal) were used as a marker for non-A, non-B hepatitis.

Lys-plasminogen is derived from human plasma obtained from approved sources and tested for absence of viral contamination, including human immunodeficiency virus type-1 (HIV-1) and hepatitis B surface antigen. The manufacturing process includes a vapor-heat treatment step for inactivation of viruses. The entire manufacturing process has also been validated to yield a cumulative reduction of $\geq 10^{21}$-fold HIV-1 infectious particles, i.e., $\geq 10^{6}$ infectious particles removed by vapor-heat treatment and a cumulative total of $\geq 10^{15}$ infectious particles removed by the various steps in the purification process.

Miscellaneous: Since the following experiences may also be associated with AMI or concomitant AMI therapy, the causal relationship to anistreplase administration is unknown. The following adverse experiences were infrequently (<10%) reported in clinical trials: Body as a Whole: chills, fever, headache, shock.

Cardiovascular: cardiac rupture, chest pain, emboli.

Dermatology: purpura, sweating.

Gastrointestinal: nausea and/or vomiting.

Hemic and Lymphatic: thrombocytopenia.

Metabolic and Nutritional: elevated transaminase levels.

Musculoskeletal: arthralgia.

Nervous: agitation, dizziness, paraesthesia, tremor, vertigo.

Respiratory: dyspnea, lung edema.

Overdose: Symptoms and Treatment: There is no experience with overdosage of anistreplase. Should severe bleeding in a critical location occur, discontinue infusion of anistreplase and any other concomitant anticoagulant therapy immediately. Proteinase inhibitors such as aprotinin (see manufacturer's prescribing information) may be administered to stop the fibrinolytic action of anistreplase. Attention should also be directed to any hemostatic deficiency (see Adverse Effects). If necessary, blood loss can be managed with whole blood or packed red cells.

Dosage: Administer anistreplase as soon as possible after the onset of symptoms. Reduction in mortality was observed when anistreplase was administered within 6 hours of onset of AMI symptoms; reperfusion was greatest when anistreplase was administered within 4 hours of symptom onset. Initiation of treatment beyond 6 hours after onset of symptoms has not been adequately studied.

The recommended dose is 30 units of anistreplase administered only by i.v. injection over 2 to 5 minutes into an i.v. line or vein. If anistreplase is administered via an i.v. line, it should only be injected through the injection port attached to the cannula, not added to the infusion bag or injected into the line further up. As long as the dose is administered through the port, there is no need to flush the line.

There are no incompatibilities of anistreplase with the common neutral infusion fluids such as saline and phosphate/saline solutions. Compatibility with 5% glucose has been investigated because of its low pH (4 to 5). This was considered to possibly cause precipitation or dissociation of the anistreplase complex. However, experiments have shown that anistreplase mixtures with 5% glucose do not precipitate. The compatibility of anistreplase with lidocaine or other common antiarrhythmics has not been studied.

Stability and Storage: Anistreplase should be stored in a refrigerator (2 to 8°C) and must not be used after the expiry date printed on the pack and vial. Vials **must not** be stored at room temperature.

Reconstituted solution should be administered as soon as possible. If unused after 30 minutes the solution must be discarded.

If a vial of anistreplase is removed from the refrigerator but is then not used, the vial can be returned to the refrigerator within 2 to 3 hours, provided the material has not been reconstituted and care has been taken to avoid temperatures greater than 30°C.

Reconstitution: 1. Slowly add 5 mL of Sterile Water for Injection, USP by directing the stream of fluid against the side of the vial. 2. Gently roll the vial, mixing the dry powder and fluid. **Do not shake.** Try to minimize foaming since it makes it difficult to withdraw product. 3. The reconstituted preparation is a colorless to pale yellow transparent solution. Inspect for particulate matter and discoloration before administration. 4. Withdraw the entire contents of the vial. 5. Do not dilute

further, or add to any infusion fluids. 6. Do not add any other medications to the vial or syringe containing anistreplase.
7. If anistreplase is not administered within 30 minutes of reconstitution, it should be discarded.

Supplied: Each unit-dose vial of sterile lyophilized, white to off-white powder contains: anistreplase 30 units, dimethylsulfoxide <3 mg, sodium hydroxide <0.2 mg and the following buffers or stabilizers: p-amidinophenyl-p'-anisate (acylating agent) 150 μg, mannitol 100 mg, L-lysine 46 mg, human serum albumin 30 mg, glycerol <2 mg and ε-aminocaproic acid 1.2 mg. Preservative-free.

Potency is expressed in units of anistreplase using a reference standard which is specific for anistreplase and is not comparable with units used for other fibrinolytics.

(Shown in Product Recognition Section)

Reviewed 1998

EMLA® Cream/Patch

Astra

Lidocaine—Prilocaine

Topical Anesthetic for Dermal Analgesia

Pharmacology: EMLA (Eutectic Mixture of Local Anesthetics) is a 1:1 oil/water emulsion of a eutectic mixture of lidocaine and prilocaine bases. Dermal analgesia is a result of the migration of lidocaine and prilocaine into the epidermal and dermal layers of the skin followed by the accumulation of these agents in the vicinity of dermal pain receptors and nerve endings. Lidocaine and prilocaine are both amide-type local anesthetic agents. They stabilize the neuronal membrane preventing the initiation and conduction of nerve impulses, thereby effecting local anesthetic action. EMLA provides dermal analgesia; the depth of which depends upon the application time and the applied dose. Analgesia may be less for deeper structures.

EMLA may produce a transient biphasic vascular response involving initial vasoconstriction followed by vasodilation at the application site (see Adverse Effects). In patients with atopic dermatitis, a shorter biphasic response involving initial vasoconstriction followed by vasodilation may be seen. Erythema may be observed after 30 to 60 minutes.

Systemic absorption of lidocaine and prilocaine from EMLA is dependent upon the applied dose, application time, the thickness of the skin which varies between different areas of the body, and other conditions of the skin.

It is well known that patients with atopic dermatitis show abnormal vascular reactions to pharmacological stimuli. In patients with atopic dermatitis, percutaneous absorption of EMLA is more rapid and greater than in normal skin. In 2 patients, within 1 hour after application of 4 to 6 g EMLA to a 25 cm² area of the forearm, lidocaine and prilocaine plasma levels were higher than those observed in normal skin. However, in these patients, the systemic plasma levels were 100 times lower than those associated with toxicity. There have been 2 reports of purpura at the application site after 60 minutes. After a repeated application of 30 minutes in 1 of these patients, no reaction was seen. In patients with atopic dermatitis, a shorter application time should be used (see Precautions). It should be noted, however, that dermatological procedures were not performed in the above patients. Clinical data are not available at present to permit dosage recommendations.

Prilocaine has a larger distribution volume than lidocaine which results in lower plasma concentrations of prilocaine when equal amounts of prilocaine and lidocaine are administered. At concentrations produced by application of EMLA, lidocaine is approximately 60 to 80% bound to plasma proteins, primarily alpha-1-acid glycoprotein. At much higher plasma concentrations (1 to 4 μg/mL of free base), the plasma protein binding of lidocaine is concentration dependent. Prilocaine is 55% bound to plasma proteins.

It is not known if lidocaine or prilocaine are metabolized in the skin. Lidocaine is metabolized rapidly by the liver to a number of metabolites including monoethylglycinexylidide (MEGX) and glycinexylidide (GX), both of which have pharmacologic activity similar to, but less potent than that of lidocaine. Prilocaine is metabolized in both the liver and kidneys by amidases to various metabolites including ortho-toluidine and N-n-propylalanine.

Intact Skin: Local analgesia of intact skin is achieved after 60 minutes' application under an occlusive dressing. The analgesic efficacy and the depth of skin analgesia have been shown to increase with application times up to 120 minutes. The duration of analgesia after a 1- to 2-hour application is at least 2 hours. After a longer application time than 5 hours, the analgesia will decrease.

The depth of analgesia, as measured by the insertion of a needle through the skin, is about 3 mm after a 60-minute application, about 4 mm after a 90-minute application and about 5 mm after a 120-minute application.

Both the analgesic efficacy and depth continue to increase after the removal of the cream from the skin surface, i.e., after a 60-minute application time to the dorsum of the hand, the analgesic efficacy continued to increase for 15 minutes, and persisted for a total of 75 minutes after removal of the cream.

After application to the thigh in adults (60 g cream/400 cm² for 3 hours), the extent of absorption was approximately 5% of lidocaine and prilocaine. Maximum plasma concentrations (mean 0.12 and 0.07 μg/mL respectively), were reached approximately 2 to 6 hours after the application.

The extent of systemic absorption was approximately 10% following application to the face (10 g/100 cm² for 2 hours). Maximum plasma levels (mean 0.16 μg/mL lidocaine and 0.06 μg/mL prilocaine) were reached after approximately 1.5 to 3 hours.

In adults, a thick layer of EMLA cream (corresponding to approximately 150 g) has been applied to intact skin areas of up to 1 300 cm² for application times of up to 3 hours. The highest individual plasma levels observed were 1.1 μg/mL lidocaine and 0.2 μg/mL prilocaine. These levels were below those at which symptoms of toxicity would be expected to occur (5 to 10 μg/mL either agent; see also Adverse Effects).

In clinical studies with children, EMLA patch has been shown to be as efficacious and safe as EMLA cream in anesthetizing the skin when applied for 60 to 180 minutes prior to venipuncture. There have been no observed differences in local skin reactions which were of clinical significance.

Genital Mucosa: Absorption from the genital mucosa is more rapid, i.e., maximum plasma concentrations are reached 20 to 45 minutes after application as opposed to 1.5 to 6 hours after application to intact skin. As a result, onset time and duration of action are shorter than after application to intact skin.

After the application of 10 g EMLA cream for 10 minutes to vaginal mucosa, maximum plasma concentrations of lidocaine and prilocaine (mean 0.18 μg/mL and 0.15 μg/mL, respectively) were reached after 20 to 45 minutes.

Leg Ulcers: After application of 5 to 10 g of EMLA to leg ulcers 15 to 64 cm² in size, for 30 minutes, maximum plasma concentrations of lidocaine ranged from 0.05 to 0.25 μg/mL. In one individual, 0.84 μg/mL was reached. Maximum plasma concentrations of prilocaine ranged from 0.02 to 0.08 μg/mL. These maximum concentrations were reached within 1 to 2.5 hours. After prolonged application (24 hours) of 1 g EMLA/10 cm² to leg ulcers 50 to 100 cm², maximum plasma concentrations of lidocaine and prilocaine ranged from 0.18 to 0.7 μg/mL and 0.06 to 0.28 μg/mL, and were observed 2 to 4 hours (in one patient 6 to 8 hours) after administration. With repeated applications, i.e., up to 15 times within a 1-month period, plasma levels of lidocaine and the metabolites, monoglycinexylidide, glycinexylidide and 2,6-xylidine, and prilocaine and the metabolite, o-toluidine, were low with no apparent accumulation.

No negative influence on ulcer healing or bacterial flora has been observed. In studies, EMLA was shown to reduce the number of cleansing sessions required to achieve a clean ulcer compared to placebo cream, and reduced the postcleansing pain up to 4 hours after debridement.

Indications: Cream: Topical analgesia of **intact skin** in connection with needle insertion, e.g., i.v. catheters or prior to blood sampling; superficial surgical procedures, e.g., removal of molluscum contagiosum, split-skin grafting, electrolysis; laser treatment.

Topical analgesia of **genital mucosa** in connection with: local infiltration anesthesia; surgical procedures lasting not longer than 10 minutes on small superficial localized lesions, e.g., removal of condylomata by laser or cautery, and biopsies.

Topical analgesia of **leg ulcers** in connection with: mechanical cleansing/debridement, e.g., the removal of necrotic tissue and debris by curettes, scissors, tweezers, etc.

Patch: Topical analgesia of intact skin in connection with: needle insertion, e.g., i.v. catheters or prior to blood sampling.

Contraindications: Patients who are hypersensitive to local anesthetics of the amide type or to any other component of the product (see Supplied); with congenital or idiopathic methemoglobinemia; who are less than 6 months of age, until further clinical data are available; children between 6 to 12 months requiring treatment with methemoglobin-inducing agents e.g., sulfonamides.

Warnings: EMLA is not recommended in any clinical situation where it can penetrate or migrate into the middle ear. Tests on laboratory animals (guinea pigs) have shown that EMLA has an ototoxic effect when instilled into the middle ear. When the same animals were exposed to EMLA in the external auditory canal, no abnormalities were seen. EMLA causes minor structural damage to the tympanic membrane in rats when applied directly to the membrane. The relevance of this finding to the clinical situation is not known.

Precautions: Due to insufficient data on absorption, EMLA should not be applied to open wounds as a result of trauma. Note: Leg ulcers often follow a slight trauma but are not classified as traumatic wounds.

Care should be taken when applying EMLA to patients with atopic dermatitis. A more rapid and greater absorption through the skin is observed in these patients. A shorter application time should be used (see Pharmacology). Sufficient data regarding absorption and local reactions are not available at present. Clinical data to permit dosage recommendations are also not available.

EMLA should not be applied to or near to the eyes as it causes corneal irritation. This reaction may be reversible. Damage to the eye may also occur from undetected foreign bodies.

Special care should be employed to reduce the risk of rubbing the eye with EMLA. Special care should also be employed to ensure the occlusive bandage or patch is secure. This will avoid accidental dislocation and exposure of EMLA, especially in young children.

Drug Interactions: Prilocaine, a component of EMLA, accentuates the formation of methemoglobin (MetHb) by a mechanism involving metabolism of prilocaine to o-toluidine and subsequent oxidation of hemoglobin to MetHb. The in vivo reduction of MetHb back to O_2Hb is dependent on the presence of MetHb reductase.

In infants below the age of 3 months, the MetHb reductase levels are lower than in older children and in adults. In these infants and in patients treated with other drugs known to induce methemoglobinemia, i.e., sulfonamides, EMLA may induce the formation of methemoglobin and result in overt clinical signs of methemoglobinemia (see Adverse Effects).

With large doses of EMLA, consideration should be given to the risk of systemic toxicity in patients receiving other local anesthetics or agents structurally related to amide type local anesthetics since the toxic effects are additive.

Pregnancy: The safety of EMLA during pregnancy has not been established in humans. Lidocaine and prilocaine cross the placental barrier and may be absorbed by the fetal tissues. It is reasonable to assume that lidocaine and prilocaine have been used in a large number of pregnant women and women of childbearing age. No specific disturbances to the reproductive process have so far been reported, e.g., an increased incidence of malformations. However, care should be given during early pregnancy when maximum organogenesis takes place.

Lactation: Lidocaine and, in all probability, prilocaine, are excreted in human milk, but in such small quantities that there is generally no risk of the infant being affected at therapeutic dose levels due to low systemic absorption.

Children: Until further clinical data are available, EMLA should not be used in children under the age of 6 months, children between 6 and 12 months of age receiving treatment with methemoglobin-inducing agents such as sulfonamides (see Adverse Effects).

Adverse Effects: Intact Skin/Genital Mucosa: Common Events (>1%): Transient local reactions at the application site such as paleness, erythema (redness) and edema. Uncommon Events (>0.1% and <1%): Skin sensations, e.g., an initial mild burning or itching sensation, at the application site. Rare Events (<0.1%): In rare cases, local anesthetics have been associated with allergic reactions; in the most severe instances, anaphylactic shock. Prilocaine in high doses may cause an increase in the methemoglobin level particularly in conjunction with methemoglobin-inducing agents (e.g., sulfonamides) (see Overdose: Symptoms and Treatment).

Leg Ulcer: Common Events (>1%): Transient local reactions at the application site such as paleness, erythema (redness) and edema. Skin sensations, e.g., an initial usually mild burning, itch or warmth at the application site. Uncommon Events (>0.1% and <1%): Skin irritation at the application site. Rare Events (<0.1%): In rare cases, local anesthetics have been associated with allergic reactions; in the most severe instances, anaphylactic shock.

Overdose: Symptoms and Treatment: Rare cases of methemoglobinemia have been reported. In the unlikely event of toxicity following epidermal application of EMLA, signs of systemic toxicity anticipated would be similar in nature to those

EMLA Cream/Patch (cont'd)

observed following other routes of administration of local anesthetics.

Local anesthetic toxicity is manifested by symptoms of nervous system excitation and in severe cases, central nervous and cardiovascular depression.

Severe neurological symptoms (convulsions, CNS depression) must be treated symptomatically by respiratory support and the administration of anticonvulsive drugs. Methemoglobinemia may be treated with methylene blue slowly injected i.v.

Dosage: Cream: Intact Skin: A thick layer of EMLA cream is applied to the skin and covered with an occlusive dressing for at least 1 hour. The occlusive dressing may remain in place for up to 5 hours. No benefit will be derived from application longer than 5 hours.

Minor procedures, e.g., needle insertion and surgical treatment of localized lesions: ½ of a small tube (approximately 2.5 g). Minimum application time: at least 1 hour.

Dermal procedures on larger areas, e.g., split-skin grafting, electrolysis: A thick layer should be applied to the skin (approximately 1.5 to 2 g/10 cm²). Minimum application time: at least 2 hours.

Laser treatment, e.g., removal of warts, tattoos, port-wine stains, dermatofibromata, nevi: A fairly thick layer should be applied to the skin (approximately 1 to 2 g/10 cm²).

Infants between 6 and 12 months of age: At least 1 hour prior to the start of the procedure, a thick layer should be applied to the skin and covered with an occlusive dressing (see also Precautions). The total dose should not exceed 2 g with the total treated skin area not being larger than 16 cm². The application time should not be longer than 4 hours. Pharmacokinetic data for parameters which exceed these recommendations are not available at present.

Infants under the age of 6 months: Not recommended (see Contraindications).

Genital Mucosa: For all procedures, the cream should be left in contact with the mucosa for 5 to 10 minutes. Occlusion is not necessary. The surgical treatment should commence **immediately** after removal of the cream.

Local infiltration anesthesia, ½ of a small tube (approximately 2.5 g) applied to the site selected for infiltration.

Surgical procedures lasting not longer than 10 minutes on localized lesions, e.g., removal of condylomata by laser or cautery, and biopsies: ½ of a small tube (approximately 2.5 g) per lesion.

Infants under the age of 6 months: Not recommended (see Contraindications).

Leg Ulcers: A thick layer of cream is applied to the leg ulcers and covered with an occlusive dressing for at least 30 minutes. An application time of 60 minutes may improve analgesia further, i.e., a longer application time may be required for removal of necrotic tissue compared to fibrinous plaques due to a thicker and more resistant penetration barrier.

Leg ulcers with clinical signs of infection should not be debrided.

The cleansing procedure should start within 10 minutes of removal of the cream. Clinical data from a longer waiting period are not available.

EMLA cream has been used prior to the cleansing of leg ulcers up to 15 times at intervals of 1 to 4 days within a 1- to 2-month period with no apparent loss of effect or increase in local reactions.

Cleansing/Debridement of Leg Ulcers: A thick layer of cream is applied to the leg ulcers (approximately 1 to 2 g/10 cm²). Single-dose Use: a maximum of 10 g/100 cm². Repeated Doses After 24 to 48 hours: a maximum of 10 g/50 cm². Minimum Application Time: at least 30 minutes.

Pharmacokinetic data for doses larger than 10 g are not available.

Infants under the age of 6 months: Not recommended (see Contraindications).

Patch: Minor procedures, e.g., needle insertion. The patch is applied to the skin area selected. Minimum application time: at least 1 hour.

Care should be taken that the patch does not become detached (especially in young children) during the 60-minute wait.

Infants between 6 and 12 months of age: EMLA patch should be applied at least 1 hour prior to the start of the procedure. No more than 2 EMLA patches should be applied at the same time. No increase in methemoglobin levels has been observed following application of 2 g EMLA cream for 4 hours.

Infants under the age of 6 months: Not recommended (see Contraindications).

Information for the Patient: See Blue Section—Information for the Patient "EMLA Cream/Patch".

Supplied: Cream: Each g of cream (5%) contains: lidocaine 25 mg and prilocaine 25 mg as a 1:1 liquid eutectic mixture in a soft, white oil in water cream. Nonmedicinal ingredients: carboxypolymethylene, polyoxyethylene hydrogenated castor oil, sodium hydroxide to adjust pH to 8.7 to 9.7 and purified water. Tubes of 5 g with 2 occlusive dressings and tubes of 30 g without dressings. Store at room temperature (15 to 30°C). Protect from freezing.

Patch: Each single dose unit patch in the form of an occlusive dressing contains: a laminate backing, an absorbent cellulose disc, and an adhesive tape ring. The disc contains 1 g of the EMLA emulsion, the active contact surface area being approximately 10 cm². The surface area of the entire patch is approximately 40 cm². Boxes of 2 and 10 single use patches. Store at room temperature 15 to 30°C. Protect from freezing. Single use. Do not reuse.

(Shown in Product Recognition Section)

Reviewed 1999

EMO-CORT® Ⓟ

TCD

Hydrocortisone

Topical Corticosteroid

Supplied: Cream: A white, odorless, washable cream containing hydrocortisone USP 1% or 2.5%. Nonmedicinal ingredients: ceteareth-20, cetearyl alcohol, germaben II, mineral oil (heavy), purified water and white petrolatum. Amber glass jars of 45 g (1%). Plastic tubes of 45 g (2.5%). Plastic jars of 225 g (2.5%). Protect from excessive heat. Avoid freezing.

Lotion: A white, odorless, washable lotion containing hydrocortisone USP 1% or 2.5%. Nonmedicinal ingredients: ceteareth-20, emulsifying wax, germaben II, isopropyl myristate, purified water and sorbitol solution. Plastic bottles of 60 mL. Protect from excessive heat. Avoid freezing.

Scalp Solution: A clear, odorless hydroalcoholic solution containing hydrocortisone USP 2.5%. Nonmedicinal ingredients: isopropyl alcohol, polyethylene glycol and purified water. Plastic bottles of 60 mL. Store below 30°C.

EMPRACET® -30 Ⓝ
EMPRACET® -60 Ⓝ

Glaxo Wellcome

Acetaminophen—Codeine Phosphate

Analgesic—Antipyretic—Antitussive

Pharmacology: Acetaminophen is in the category of an analgesic and antipyretic, codeine is in the category of analgesic and antitussive. Codeine retains at least one-half of its analgesic activity when administered orally.

Indications: Empract-30: For relief of mild to moderate pain. Empract-60: For relief of moderate to severe pain.

Contraindications: Hypersensitivity to acetaminophen or codeine.

Warnings: Drug dependence: Codeine can produce drug dependence of the morphine type, and therefore, has the potential for being abused. Psychic and physical dependence and tolerance may develop upon repeated administration and it should be prescribed and administered with the same degree of caution appropriate to the use of other oral, narcotic-containing medications.

Occupational Hazards: Acetaminophen with codeine may impair the mental and/or physical abilities required for the performance of potentially hazardous tasks such as driving a car or operating machinery. Patients using this drug should be cautioned accordingly.

Interaction with other CNS depressants: Patients receiving other narcotic analgesics, general anesthetics, phenothiazines, other tranquilizers, sedative-hypnotics, or other CNS depressants (including alcohol) concomitantly with acetaminophen and codeine may exhibit an additive CNS depression. If such combined therapy is contemplated, the dose of 1 or both agents should be reduced. The concurrent use of anticholinergic with codeine may produce paralytic ileus.

Pregnancy: Safety in pregnancy has not been established relative to the possible adverse effects on fetal development. Therefore, acetaminophen with codeine should not be used unless, in the judgment of the physician, the potential benefits outweigh the possible hazards.

Lactation: It is not known whether the components of this drug are excreted in human milk. Because many drugs are excreted in human milk, caution should be exercised when acetaminophen and codeine is administered to a nursing woman.

Precautions: Head Injury and Increased Intracranial Pressure: The respiratory depressant effects of narcotics and their capacity to elevate cerebrospinal fluid pressure may be markedly exaggerated in the presence of head injury or intracranial lesions or pre-existing increase in intracranial pressure. Furthermore, the narcotics produce adverse reactions which may obscure the clinical course of a patient with head injuries.

Acute Abdominal Conditions: The administration of acetaminophen with codeine or other narcotics may obscure the diagnosis or clinical course in patients with acute abdominal conditions.

Special-Risk Patients: Acetaminophen with codeine should be given with caution to certain patients such as the elderly or debilitated, and those with severe impairment of hepatic or renal function, hypothyroidism, Addison's disease, prostatic hypertrophy or urethral stricture. Overdose can cause severe liver toxicity (see Overdose).

Adverse Effects: Being a combination of codeine and acetaminophen, certain problems can be presented due to a large overdose as these compounds produce different types of toxicity.

The adverse effects attributable to therapeutic doses of codeine are seldom serious. These include nausea, vomiting, constipation with repeated doses, epigastric pain, dizziness and occasionally sedation. Allergic reactions may occur but are rare. Overdose of codeine 100 to 500 mg may cause a slow pulse, flush facies, kinetosis and lassitude or excitement. Doses of 800 mg or more have caused prolonged miosis, muscular weakness, semiconsciousness, delirium, convulsions, rapid pulse, and finally circulatory collapse or respiratory paralysis. The human lethal dose for codeine is not known with certainty. Mortalities due to codeine appear to be quite unusual.

Most frequently observed adverse effects referable to acetaminophen include lightheadedness, dizziness, sedation, nausea and vomiting. These effects seem to be more prominent in ambulatory than in nonambulatory patients and some of these adverse reactions may be alleviated if the patient lies down. Other adverse reactions include euphoria, dysphoria, constipation and pruritus. Rare hypersensitivity reactions may occur that require discontinuation of the drug. Hypersensitivity is manifested by rash or urticaria. Regular use of acetaminophen has shown to produce a slight increase in prothrombin time in patients receiving oral anticoagulants, but the clinical significance of this effect is not clear. The incidence of gastrointestinal upset is less than after salicylate administration.

Overdose: Acetaminophen: Serious hepatotoxicity may occur in adults after ingestion of a single dose of 10 g (150 mg/kg or greater) and fatalities have usually been reported after ingestion of a single dose of 15 g or more of acetaminophen.

Symptoms: Patients suffering from an overdose of acetaminophen will progress through 3 stages if untreated. During the first stage, which lasts from 12 to 24 hours, there may be anorexia, nausea, vomiting, diaphoresis and pallor. After 24 hours, earlier symptoms tend to abate and the patient may even feel well for one or a few days. Unfortunately, during this second phase, hepatic enzymes, serum bilirubin and prothrombin time begin to rise as hepatic necrosis progresses and tenderness may develop in the right upper quadrant. Three to 5 days after drug ingestion, the third phase sets in for those patients who develop significant hepatic necrosis. This phase is marked by the sequelae of hepatic necrosis which include jaundice, coagulation effects, hypoglycemia, encephalopathy as well as renal failure and myocardiopathy. Death occurs as a result of hepatic failure.

Treatment: Large overdoses of acetaminophen are potentially fatal, unless an appropriate antidote such as N-acetylcysteine (NAC) is administered early after drug ingestion, usually within 12 to 16 hours. There is some evidence to suggest that NAC may offer some protection even when given up to 24 hours after drug ingestion. The hepatotoxicity of acetaminophen is related to a secondary, reactive metabolite which is detoxified by conjugation with hepatic glutathione. A large overdosage of acetaminophen will result in an increased formation of the reactive metabolite which in turn may deplete stores of glutathione in the liver. Antidotes such as NAC probably act by restoring glutathione levels.

Emergency Procedure: The stomach should be emptied promptly.

Specific Therapy: A careful estimate should be made of the quantity of acetaminophen ingested. Regardless of the quantity ingested, and particularly if it is estimated to be 7.5 g or more, an immediate loading dose of NAC should be administered if 24 hours or less have elapsed since drug ingestion. NAC is available as Mucomyst which contains a 20% solution of N-acetylcysteine in sterile vials of 10 and 30 mL. The 20% solution NAC in Mucomyst should be diluted to a 5% solution for oral administration, by using water, cola, grapefruit juice or orange juice. The diluted mixture should be consumed within 1 hour of preparation. The **loading dose** of NAC is 140 mg/kg of bodyweight. This should be followed by **maintenance doses** of 70 mg of NAC/kg of bodyweight, every 4 hours, for 17 doses. If the patient vomits within 1 hour of administration, the NAC dose should be repeated. If the patient is unable to tolerate oral administration, NAC should be administered i.v. (see the monographs for Mucomyst and Parvolex for detailed instructions). If activated charcoal has been used, lavage must be performed before initiating treatment with NAC.

Cysteamine has also been used previously as an antidote with some success. It must, however, be given i.v., initially as a 2 g loading dose over 10 minutes followed immediately by continuous infusion of 800 mg in 500 mL of dextrose 5% in water over 4 hours, then 800 mg given over 16 hours for a total of 3.6 g in 20 hours. Solutions of cysteamine are unstable and should be prepared immediately before use.

Acetaminophen Plasma Assay: Acetaminophen plasma levels 4 hours post-ingestion of an overdose provide a fairly reliable prognostic indication of potential hepatotoxicity. Values of 200 μg/mL or more at 4 hours postingestion, or 50 μg/mL or more at 12 hours after ingestion, are associated with the possibility of hepatic toxicity. If the plasma levels of acetaminophen are more than 25% below these values, the risk of toxicity is much reduced.

Follow-Up and Supportive Therapy: Monitoring of hepatic and renal function, and supportive measures, should be used as indicated. Hemodialysis or peritoneal dialysis have not been found helpful. Experience indicates that children under 5 years of age are more resistant than adults to the hepatic effects of acetaminophen overdose.

Codeine: Symptoms: The primary symptoms due to overdosage of codeine include euphoria, dysphoria, visual disturbances, hypotension and coma or death due to respiratory depression.

Treatment: Primary attention should be given to the reestablishment of adequate respiratory exchange through provision of a patent airway and the institution of assisted or controlled ventilation. The narcotic antagonists naloxone, nalorphine or levallorphan are specific antidotes against respiratory depression which may result from overdose or unusual sensitivity to narcotics. Therefore, an appropriate dose of one of these antagonists should be administered, preferably by the i.v. route, simultaneously with efforts at respiratory resuscitation. Since the duration of action of acetaminophen with codeine may exceed that of the antagonist, patients should be kept under continued surveillance and repeated doses of antagonists should be administered as needed to maintain adequate respiration. An antagonist should not be administered in the absence of clinically significant respiratory or cardiovascular depression. Oxygen, i.v. fluids, vasopressors and other supportive measures should be employed as indicated.

Dosage: Empracet-30 Adults: 1 to 2 tablets every 4 to 6 hours as required.

Empracet-60: Adults: 1 tablet every 4 to 6 hours as required.

Both strengths of Empracet should not be used in children. Dosage should be adjusted according to the severity of pain and the response of the patient. Acetaminophen with codeine is given orally. It should be kept in mind that tolerance to codeine can develop with continued use and that the incidence of untoward effects is dose related. This product is inappropriate even in high doses for severe or intractable pain. Adult doses of codeine higher than 60 mg fail to give commensurate relief of pain, but merely prolong analgesia and are associated with an appreciably increased incidence of undesirable side effects. Equivalently high doses in children would have similar effects.

Supplied: Empracet-30: Each round, peach-colored tablet, imprinted EMPRACET 30 K9B and scored on the reverse side, contains: acetaminophen 300 mg and codeine phosphate 30 mg. Nonmedicinal ingredients: cornstarch, FD&C yellow No. 6, lactose, magnesium stearate, povidone and stearic acid. Bottles of 500. Store between 15 to 30°C.

Empracet-60: Each round, peach-colored tablet, imprinted EMPRACET 60 L9B, contains: acetaminophen 300 mg and codeine phosphate 60 mg. Nonmedicinal ingredients: cornstarch, FD&C yellow No. 6, lactose, magnesium stearate, povidone and stearic acid. Bottles of 50. Store between 15 to 30°C.

(Shown in Product Recognition Section)

EMTEC®-30 Ⓝ
Technilab

Acetaminophen—Codeine Phosphate

Analgesic—Antipyretic—Antitussive

Supplied: Each round, peach-colored tablet, contains: acetaminophen 300 mg and codeine phosphate 30 mg. Nonmedicinal ingredients: crospovidone, FD&C yellow #6 aluminum lake, magnesium stearate, microcrystalline cellulose, povidone, pregelatinized starch, sodium starch glycolate and stearic acid. Sodium: <1 mmol. Bottles of 500.

ENALAPRIL Ⓟ
General Monograph, CPhA

see ACE INHIBITORS

ENALAPRILAT Ⓟ
General Monograph, CPhA

see ACE INHIBITORS

ENDANTADINE® Ⓟ
Endo

Amantadine HCl

Antiviral—Antiparkinson

Supplied: Each red, soft gelatin capsule contains: amantadine HCl 100 mg. Nonmedicinal ingredients: FD&C Red No. 40, gelatin, glycerin, hydrogenated vegetable oil, lecithin, methylparaben, propylparaben, purified water, soybean oil, titanium dioxide, vegetable shortening and yellow wax. Bottles of 100. Store at controlled room temperature (15 to 30°C) in a tightly closed container.

ENDOCET® Ⓝ
Endo

Oxycodone HCl—Acetaminophen

Opioid Analgesic

Supplied: Each white tablet, scored on one side, with the Endo logo on the other, contains: oxycodone HCl 5 mg and acetaminophen 325 mg. Nonmedicinal ingredients: Cornstarch, microcrystalline cellulose, povidone, pregelatinized starch, silicone dioxide and stearic acid. Lactose-, sodium- and tartrazine-free. Bottles of 100 and 500. Store at room temperature (15 to 30°C).

ENDODAN® Ⓝ
Endo

Oxycodone HCl—ASA

Opioid Analgesic

Supplied: Each yellow tablet, scored on one side, with the Endo logo on the other, contains: oxycodone HCl 5 mg and ASA 325 mg. Nonmedicinal ingredients: cornstarch, FD&C Yellow No. 6, D&C Yellow No. 10 and microcrystalline cellulose. Lactose-, sodium- and tartrazine-free. Bottles of 100 and 500. Store at room temperature (15 to 30°C).

ENDO® LEVODOPA/ CARBIDOPA Ⓟ
Endo

Levodopa Carbidopa

Antiparkinson Agent

Supplied: 100/25: Each yellow, oval, scored, uncoated tablet, engraved Endo on one side and 100/25 on the other, contains: levodopa 100 mg and carbidopa 25 mg, expressed as anhydrous carbidopa. Nonmedicinal ingredients: cornstarch, magnesium stearate, microcrystalline cellulose, pregelatinized starch and quinoline yellow. Bottles of 100 and 500.

100/10: Each dark dapple-blue, oval, uncoated tablet, engraved 100/10 on one side and Endo on the other, contains: levodopa 100 mg and carbidopa 10 mg, expressed as anhydrous carbidopa. Nonmedicinal ingredients: cornstarch, indigotine, magnesium stearate, microcrystalline cellulose and pregelatinized starch. Bottles of 100.

250/25: Each light dapple-blue, oval, scored, uncoated tablet, engraved Endo on one side and 250/25 on the other, contains: levodopa 250 mg and carbidopa 25 mg, expressed as anhydrous carbidopa. Nonmedicinal ingredients: cornstarch, indigotine, magnesium stearate, microcrystalline cellulose and pregelatinized starch. Bottles of 100 and 500.

Store at 15 to 30°C in a tightly closed container. Protect from sunlight.

ENFALAC LYTREN®
Mead Johnson

Oral Electrolyte Solution

Electrolyte Replacement

Indications: Oral administration of electrolyte replacement for infants and children who have experienced electrolyte and fluid loss due to mild or moderate diarrhea and who do not require parenteral therapy.

Contraindications: Do not use in the presence of severe, continuing diarrhea or other critical fluid losses requiring parenteral fluid therapy; in intractable vomiting, adynamic ileus, intestinal obstruction or perforated bowel; when renal function is depressed (anuria, oliguria) or homeostatic mechanisms are impaired.

Dosage: For infants and young children, the requirement should be calculated on the basis of body surface area. Estimated daily water requirements such as the following may be used as a general guide: For maintenance in illness: 1 500 mL/m² of body surface area. For maintenance plus replacement of moderate losses: 2 400 mL/m² of body surface area.

Supplied: Each mL of solution contains: water, dextrose, potassium citrate, sodium chloride, sodium citrate and citric acid. Energy: 10.5 kJ (2.5 kcal)/30 mL. Each L of solution provides: sodium 50 mEq, potassium 25 mEq, citrate 30 mEq, chloride 45 mEq. Available for hospitals in ready-to-use disposable Nursette bottles of 113 mL.

ENFALAC NUTRAMIGEN®
Mead Johnson

Casein Hydrolysate Compound

Infant Food

Indications: Feeding of infants and children allergic or intolerant to ordinary food proteins (intact proteins). Provides a formula with "predigested" protein for infants with diarrhea or other gastrointestinal disturbances. Provides lactose free feedings in galactosemia. May be used for tube feedings in adults with food allergies.

Precautions: Individuals with lengthy episodes of diarrhea and/or receiving antibiotics may require supplemental vitamin K.

In a few instances, premature infants and infants with long-standing malabsorption problems have been reported to have a metabolic acidosis when receiving a casein hydrolysate formula for an extended period of time. The etiology of this acidosis is obscure. The overall incidence is rare and can be satisfactorily controlled by giving the patient 2 to 3 mEq/kg/day of sodium bicarbonate, which may be conveniently added to the formula.

Enfalac Nutramigen (cont'd)

Dosage: Mix with water. Normal dilution—1 packed level measuring scoop of powder to 60 mL of water. This dilution supplies 84 kJ (20 kcal)/30 mL. Initial feedings should be diluted to 42 kJ (10 kcal)/30 mL and gradually increased to 84 kJ (20 kcal)/30 mL over a period of 3 to 5 days.

Supplied: Liquid and Powder: Hypoallergenic formula containing corn syrup solids, palm olein oil, soy oil, coconut oil, high oleic sunflower oil, hydrolyzed casein, modified cornstarch, all known essential vitamins and minerals. Free of intact protein. Ready-to-use liquid available in cans of 945 mL. Powder in tins of 400 g with measure.

Also available for hospitals: presterilized disposable Nursette in bottles of 100 mL—84 kJ (20 kcal)/30 mL.

ENFALAC PREGESTIMIL®

Mead Johnson

Protein Hydrolysate Formula

Pediatric Elemental Diet

Indications: For feeding of infants and children with malabsorption problems which may include: disaccharidase deficiency (relative or absolute), idiopathic defects in digestion or absorption, steatorrhea, cystic fibrosis, food allergies and intestinal resection.

Precautions: Patients with lengthy episodes of diarrhea and/or receiving antibiotics may require supplemental vitamin K. In a few instances, premature infants and infants with long-standing malabsorption problems have been reported to have a metabolic acidosis when receiving a casein hydrolysate formula for an extended period of time. The etiology of this acidosis is obscure. The overall incidence is rare and can be satisfactorily controlled by giving the patient 2 to 3 mEq/kg/day of sodium bicarbonate, which may be conveniently added to the formula.

Dosage: Mix with water: normal dilution—1 packed level measuring scoop (9 g) of powder/60 mL of water. Provides a solution supplying 84 kJ (20 kcal)/30 mL. Initial feedings should be diluted to 10 kcal/30 mL or less and gradually increased to 84 kJ (20 kcal)/30 mL over a period of 3 to 5 days.

Supplied: A hypoallergenic, powdered formula containing: corn syrup solids, hydrolyzed casein, modified cornstarch, medium chain triglycerides, corn oil, high oleic safflower oil, soy oil and essential vitamins and minerals. Cans of 454 g with accompanying measuring scoop. Also available for hospitals: presterilized disposable Nursette bottles of 100 mL, energy: 84 kJ (20 kcal)/30 mL.

ENFALAC PROSOBEE®

Mead Johnson

Soy Protein Isolate

Hypoallergenic Product

Indications: Formula for feeding infants or children with a sensitivity to cow milk protein or a family history of allergies. Symptoms that may require a milk-free source of nutrition include the following: persistent and unexplained eczema, diarrhea, non-specific respiratory disorders, spitting up, and irritability. May be used for adults with food allergies.

Precautions: Opened or prepared formula should be refrigerated or used within 24 to 48 hours. Opened powder formula should be stored in a cool dry place and used within 30 days.

Dosage: Home: Feed as an 84 kJ (20 kcal)/30 mL formula in sufficient quantity to satisfy the hunger and nutritional needs of the infant. Dilution: Equal amounts of ProSobee concentrated liquid and water. 1 scoop of ProSobee powder/60 mL of water.
Hospital: Feedings may be used as an 84 kJ (20 kcal)/30 mL formula, or, if more dilute feedings are desired, they may be prepared as follows: 2 parts liquid to 1 part water, energy: 54.6 kJ (13 kcal)/30 mL. 4 parts liquid to 1 part water, energy: 67.2 (16 kcal)/30 mL.

Either terminal heating or aseptic method of formula preparation may be used in preparing feedings for infants.

Supplied: Liquid: Hypoallergenic formula made from soy protein isolate, palm olein oil, soy oil, coconut oil, sunflower oil, glucose polymers and added vitamins and minerals (including iron).

Powder: Hypoallergenic formula from glucose polymers, soy protein isolate, palm olein oil, soy oil, coconut oil, sunflower oil and added vitamins and minerals (including iron).

Milk-like in appearance and consistency. Each 100 mL supplies 285.6 kJ (68 kcal); each 30 mL supplies 84 kJ (20 kcal). Lactose- and sucrose-free. Available in concentrated liquid in 385 mL cans and in Ready to Use 235 and 945 mL cans and powder in 400 g cans, with measure. Also available, for hospitals: presterilized disposable Nursette bottles, energy: 84 kJ (20 kcal)/30 mL: 100 mL.

ENFLURANE ℞

Abbott

Inhalation Anesthetic

Supplied: Amber-colored bottles of 250 mL. Store at controlled room temperature (15 to 30°C). Enflurane contains no additives and has been demonstrated to be stable at room temperature for periods in excess of 5 years.

ENGERIX®-B

SmithKline Beecham

Hepatitis B Vaccine (Recombinant)

Vaccine

Pharmacology: Hepatitis B vaccine (recombinant) contains purified hepatitis B surface antigen (HBsAg). It is the product of recombinant DNA technology developed by SmithKline Beecham Biologicals, s.a., Belgium. The HBsAg gene from the hepatitis B virus has been cloned by genetic engineering into Saccharomyces cerevisiae.

In vitro experiments have shown that the yeast-derived HBsAg in hepatitis B vaccine (recombinant) contains all the epitopes (antigenic sites) that have been found in the HBsAg in plasma-derived vaccines.

In vivo, the human antibody response to hepatitis B vaccine (recombinant) is similar to the response to plasma-derived vaccines with respect to epitope specificity and avidity. There is no significant modification of the anti-yeast antibody titre after vaccination with hepatitis B vaccine (recombinant).

These studies indicate that hepatitis B vaccine (recombinant) is immunologically similar to the plasma-derived vaccines and provides similar protective efficacy.

In comparative studies commercial plasma-derived vaccines and hepatitis B vaccine (recombinant) exhibited comparable potency in mice and guinea pigs, and comparable protective efficacy in chimpanzees. Hepatitis B vaccine (recombinant) is also highly immunogenic in rabbits, goats and monkeys.

The yeast-derived vaccine hepatitis B vaccine (recombinant) possesses the same immunogenic properties as have been demonstrated by plasma-derived hepatitis B vaccines. Hepatitis B vaccine (recombinant) induces the production of specific antibodies against the surface antigen of hepatitis B virus (anti-HBs).

Since no substances of human origin are used in the production of hepatitis B vaccine (recombinant), the potential for transmission of diseases associated with blood and blood products is eliminated. Potency, safety and sterility are verified for each lot.

It is generally accepted that an anti-HBs titre greater than 10 IU/L correlates with protection against hepatitis B virus infection. More than 90% of healthy adults, children and neonates developed protective anti-HBs titres 1 month after completing a primary vaccination schedule of hepatitis B vaccine (recombinant).

There are data to support 2 schedules of dosing. The 3 dose schedule is 0, 1 and 6 months. The 4 dose schedule is 0, 1, 2 and 12 months. For further details see Dosage.

Females generally seroconvert more quickly than males. As well, anti-HBs titres are higher in females than in males after 3 doses of yeast-derived or plasma-derived vaccine. However, protective anti-HBs titres develop in the same proportion in both sexes.

Anti-HBs titres tend to be slightly lower in older subjects than they are in younger subjects. This influence of age is found for both yeast-derived and plasma-derived vaccines.

The anti-HBs response in children is similar to that in adults.

In ongoing studies, the anti-HBs response in neonates of both carrier and noncarrier mothers to hepatitis B has been shown to be similar to that obtained in adults and children with regard to seroconversion rate and anti-HBs titres attained. Preliminary data indicate that administration of hepatitis B immunoglobulin (HBIG) to the neonate at birth does not appear to affect the immune response to hepatitis B vaccine (recombinant).

The response to hepatitis B vaccine (recombinant) in homosexual males may be slower than it is in heterosexual males. This has also been observed with plasma-derived vaccine. However, the percentages of subjects reaching protective anti-HBs titres 1 month after the third dose of vaccine given at month 6 are similar in the two groups.

The anti-HBs response to the recombinant yeast-derived vaccine is at least as high as that obtained by plasma-derived vaccines in patients affected by thalassemia major.

The anti-HBs response to hepatitis B vaccine (recombinant) in residents of institutions for the mentally retarded is similar to that observed in the general population.

The anti-HBs response of patients on chronic hemodialysis is known to be impaired. However, experience from clinical studies shows that 2 months after 4 double doses i.e., 40 µg (at months 0, 1, 2 and 6), 67% of vaccinees developed protective antibody titres. Anti-HBs titres remained relatively low compared to anti-HBs titres in healthy subjects. These results are similar to those that have been reported with plasma-derived vaccines.

The anti-HBs response in drug addicts does not differ from the response in the general population.

Vaccination against hepatitis B is expected in the long-term to reduce the overall incidence of both hepatitis B and chronic complications such as chronic active hepatitis and cirrhosis.

The hepatitis B virus induces a severe form of viral hepatitis. Other causative agents are hepatitis A virus and the non-A, non-B hepatitis viruses. Hepatitis D virus, a defective virus requiring the keeper function of the hepatitis B virus, occurs either as a coinfection or superinfection in a HBsAg carrier.

There is no specific treatment for hepatitis. The incubation period may be as long as 6 months, followed by a very complex clinical course of an acute or chronic nature, often leading to hospitalization.

Transmission of the virus occurs through percutaneous contact with contaminated blood, serum or plasma. Infection may also occur by the exposure of mucous surfaces, or intact or damaged skin to other body fluids such as saliva, mucosal secretions and semen.

Viral hepatitis caused by hepatitis B virus is a major worldwide health problem, though the incidence and epidemiology vary widely among geographical areas and population subgroups.

In Canada, the United States and Northern Europe, 4 to 6% of the population are infected during their lifetime (mostly young adults); between 5 and 10% of infections lead to persistent viremia (carrier state).

Certain population subgroups in these areas, however, are at high risk (see Indications).

In Asia, infection often occurs early in life, leading to a hepatitis B marker prevalence of more than 70% in the general population and a carrier rate of up to 20%.

It is estimated that the reservoir of persistent hepatitis B surface antigen carriers amounts to 200 million people worldwide. Carriers are at a high risk of developing chronic liver disease which may lead to cirrhosis or primary hepatocellular carcinoma.

Indications: For active immunization against hepatitis B virus infection. The vaccine will not protect against infection caused by hepatitis A and non-A non-B hepatitis viruses. As hepatitis D (caused by the delta agent) does not occur in the absence of hepatitis B infection or carrier state, it can be expected that hepatitis D will also be prevented by vaccination.

The vaccine can be administered at any age from birth onwards. It may be used to start a primary course of vaccination or as a booster dose. It may also be used to complete a primary course of vaccination started with plasma-derived or yeast-derived vaccines or as a booster dose in subjects who have previously received a primary course of vaccination with plasma-derived or yeast-derived vaccines.

In areas of low prevalence of hepatitis B, vaccination is strongly recommended in subjects who are at increased risk of infection. These include the following groups: Health Care Personnel: oral surgeons and dentists; physicians and surgeons, nurses, dental nurses, dental hygienists, podiatrists; i.v. teams and operating room personnel; paramedical personnel in close contact with patients; staff in hemodialysis, nephrology, hepatology, hematology and oncology units; laboratory personnel handling blood and other clinical specimens; blood bank and plasma fractionation workers; pathologists and morgue attendants; cleaning staff who handle waste in hospitals; emergency and first aid workers; ambulance staff; dental, medical and nursing students.

Patients: patients receiving frequent blood transfusions or clotting factor concentrates, such as those in oncology units

and those with thalassemia, sickle-cell anemia, cirrhosis, hemophilia, etc.; patients on hemodialysis.
Personnel and Residents of Institutions: persons with frequent and/or close contacts with high-risk groups; prisoners and prison staff; residents and staff of institutions for the mentally retarded (those who are in contact with aggressive biting residents being at highest risk).
Persons at Increased Risk Due to Their Sexual Practices: sexually promiscuous persons; persons who repeatedly contract sexually transmitted disease; homosexually active males; prostitutes.

Persons who use injectable drugs illicitly.

Travellers to areas of high endemicity and their close contacts.

Household contacts of any of the above groups and of patients with acute or chronic hepatitis B infection.

Infants born of HBsAg-positive mothers.

Others: police; firefighters; armed forces personnel; morticians and embalmers; those who through their work or personal lifestyle may be exposed to the hepatitis B virus.

In areas of both low and high prevalence vaccination should be offered to young children and neonates at risk as well as to adult high risk groups.

Contraindications: Hypersensitivity to any component of the vaccine. As for any vaccine, hepatitis B vaccine (recombinant) should not be administered to subjects with severe febrile infections. Vaccination of a subject with febrile symptoms, with a respiratory infection, or with a contagious or any other disease should be postponed until after recovery. However, the presence of a trivial infection does not contraindicate vaccination.

Warnings: Because hepatitis B has a long incubation period it is possible that there may be latent infection at the time of vaccination. Hepatitis B vaccine (recombinant) may not prevent hepatitis B in such cases.

Patients who develop symptoms suggestive of hypersensitivity after an injection should not receive further injections of hepatitis B vaccine (recombinant) (see Contraindications).

Hepatitis B vaccine (recombinant) should not be administered in the gluteal region or intradermally since these routes of administration may not result in an optimum immune response. Intradermal administration may also result in severe local reactions. The vaccine must never be administered i.v.

In dialysis patients and subjects who have an impairment of the immune system, adequate antibody concentrations may not be maintained after a primary vaccination course of 40 µg doses. Such patients may therefore require repeated administrations of the vaccine.

The immune response to hepatitis B vaccines is related to a number of factors, including older age, male gender, obesity, smoking habits and route of administration. In subjects who may respond less well to the administration of the hepatitis B vaccine (e.g., more than 40 years of age, etc.), additional doses may be considered.

Precautions: A new sterile syringe and a new sterile needle should always be used so as to prevent the transmission from one subject to another of infectious agents, such as the hepatitis B virus, non-A non-B hepatitis virus, or the human immunodeficiency virus (HIV).
Pregnancy: The effect of the antigen on fetal development is unknown and therefore vaccination of pregnant women cannot be recommended. However, vaccination of a pregnant woman may be considered in order to prevent hepatitis B in high-risk situations.

As with all biologicals, a solution of 1 in 1 000 epinephrine should always be readily available for immediate use in case of a rare anaphylactic reaction.

Adverse Effects: Hepatitis B vaccine (recombinant) is generally well tolerated.

The most frequently occurring adverse events, usually mild and transient, are associated with the injection site and include soreness, erythema and induration.

The following adverse events have been reported following widespread use of the vaccine. The frequencies of the adverse events below are calculated taking into account, as the numerator, the total number of spontaneous adverse events reported, and as the denominator, the total number of doses distributed, in those countries with a reliable reporting system for spontaneous adverse events. In many instances, the causal relationship to the vaccine has not been established.
Rare (>1:200 000): Body as a Whole: fatigue, fever, malaise, influenza-like symptoms.
Central and Peripheral Nervous System: dizziness, headache, paresthesia.
Gastrointestinal: nausea, vomiting, diarrhea, abdominal pain.
Liver and Biliary: abnormal liver function tests.
Musculoskeletal: arthralgia, myalgia.
Skin and Appendages: rash, pruritus, urticaria.
Very Rare (1:200 000 to 1:500 000): Cardiovascular: syncope.
Heart Rate and Rhythm: tachycardia.
Musculoskeletal: arthritis.
Respiratory: bronchospasm-like symptoms.
White Cell and Reticulo-Endothelial: lymphadenopathy.
Extremely Rare (< 1:500 000). Body as a Whole: anaphylaxis.
Cardiovascular: hypotension.
Central and Peripheral Nervous System: Bell's Palsy, migraine, paralysis, neuropathy, neuritis (including Guillain-Barré Syndrome, optic neuritis, multiple sclerosis), transverse myelitis, vertigo.
Gastrointestinal: dyspepsia.
Hearing and Vestibular: tinnitus, earache.
Heart Rate and Rhythm: palpitations.
Platelet Bleeding and Clotting: thrombocytopenia, purpura.
Resistance Mechanism: herpes zoster.
Skin and Appendages: angioedema, eczema, erythema multiforme, erythema nodosum.
Vision: conjunctivitis, visual disturbances.

Overdose: Symptoms and Treatment: No information available.

Dosage: See Table I.
Schedule: The recommended schedule is 3 doses administered at 0, 1 and 6 months.

For more rapid protection a 4 dose schedule (0, 1, 2 and 12 months) results in the development of protective anti-HBs titres by 3 months. The fourth dose (at 12 months) is required to maintain prolonged protective anti-HBs titres.

For hemodialysis patients, a 4 dose schedule at 0, 1, 2 and 6 months is recommended.
Dosage: Adults 20 years and over: A dose of 20 µg of antigen protein in 1 mL suspension is recommended for adults.
Neonates, Infants, Children and Adolescents up to 19 years: A dose of 10 µg of antigen protein in 0.5 mL suspension is recommended for neonates, infants, children and adolescents up to 19 years of age inclusive. However, if compliance to the full 0, 1, 6 month schedule cannot be assured in 11- to 19-year-old adolescents, a 20 µg dose should be used to ensure seroprotection. When the pediatric presentation is not available, other presentations may be used for withdrawing the appropriate dose.
Hemodialysis and Immunocompromised Patients: A 2 mL dose (40 µg) is recommended.

Hepatitis B vaccine (recombinant) can effectively boost anti-HBs responses initially elicited by either plasma-derived or yeast-derived vaccines.

For individuals in whom a primary vaccination schedule has been initiated with a plasma-derived vaccine, dosing may be continued with hepatitis B vaccine (recombinant).

Table I—Engerix-B

Dosage

	Recommended Dose	
	Regular Schedule: 0, 1 and 6 months	
Recipients	Rapid Protection Schedule: 0, 1, 2 and 12 months	
	µg	mL
Infants and children ≤19* years of age	10	0.5
Adults	20	1.0
Hemodialysis and immunocompromised patients	40	2.0

* Note: 10 µg for neonates, infants, children and adolescents 0 to 19 years of age. However, for adolescents 11 to 19 years of age, inclusive, the 20 µg dose should be used if compliance to the 3 dose schedule cannot be assured.

Booster Doses: Experience with plasma-derived vaccines has shown that anti-HBs titres gradually decline over time. It is expected that this will also be true for hepatitis B vaccine (recombinant). Hepatitis B vaccine (recombinant) can effectively boost anti-HBs responses initially elicited by either plasma-derived or yeast-derived vaccines.

The timing for a hepatitis B vaccine booster dose will depend upon the anti-HBs titre reached after the completion of the primary immunization schedule. From available data, general guidelines for a booster dose can be made: After the 0, 1, 2 month primary immunization schedule a booster dose is recommended 12 months after the first dose. The next booster will probably not be required for at least another 8 years.

After the 0, 1, 6 month primary immunization schedule a booster dose will probably not be required earlier than 5 years after the primary course.

For hemodialysis and immunocompromised patients, a booster (40 µg) may be required sooner. Regular serological monitoring is recommended to ensure that antibodies are and remain at protective levels.
Administration: Check the expiry date of the vaccine carefully. Do not use vaccine beyond its expiry date.

Shake the vaccine well before use so as to resuspend the sediment of fine white particles of adjuvant (aluminum hydroxide) which settles during storage.

Clean the skin at the site of injection with a suitable antiseptic and dry with a piece of dry sterile cotton. Disinfect the rubber stopper with antiseptic; wipe it dry with a dry sterile cotton swab; then, using a sterile needle, withdraw the vaccine from the vial into a sterile syringe.

Engerix-B should be injected i.m. In adults the injection should be given in the deltoid region. In neonates and infants it may be preferable to inject the vaccine in the anterolateral thigh because of the small size of their deltoid muscle. In special circumstances the vaccine may be administered s.c. in patients with severe bleeding tendencies (e.g., hemophiliacs).

Engerix-B must not be given i.v. or intradermally.

This vaccine may be administered simultaneously with hepatitis B immunoglobulin (HBIG); however, it must be administered at a separate injection site.
Notification of Reactions: It is desirable that all unusual reactions regardless of the vaccine, be reported to the manufacturer as well as to the provincial epidemiologist.

Supplied: 0.5 mL: Each 0.5 mL single pediatric dose vial contains: hepatitis B surface antigen 10 µg adsorbed onto Al^{+++} 0.25 mg as aluminum hydroxide with thimerosal 0.005% as preservative.

1 mL: Each 1 mL single adult dose vial contains: hepatitis B surface antigen 20 µg adsorbed onto Al^{+++} 0.5 mg as aluminum hydroxide with thimerosal 0.005% as preservative.

10 mL: Each 10 mL multidose vial for mass immunization programs contains: hepatitis B surface antigen 200 µg adsorbed onto Al^{+++} 5 mg as aluminum hydroxide with thimerosal 0.005% as preservative.

The vaccine is a slightly opaque, white, sterile suspension. A slow settling of the white, aluminum hydroxide may occur during storage leaving a clear, colorless, supernatant liquid. Cartons of 1 with prescribing information leaflet.

Ship under refrigeration. Store between 2 and 8°C. **Do not freeze.** Vaccine that has been frozen is no longer potent and should be discarded. Potency of unopened vaccine is not significantly affected by short exposure to room temperature (up to 7 days). For multidose vaccine, discard unused portion no longer than 24 hours after first puncture. When stored at 2 to 8°C, Engerix-B is stable until the expiry date shown on the label.

Reviewed 1997

ENLON® Ⓟ
Zeneca

Edrophonium Chloride
Nondepolarizing Neuromuscular Antagonist

Pharmacology: Edrophonium chloride is an anticholinesterase agent which antagonizes the action of nondepolarizing neuromuscular blocking drugs. Edrophonium chloride inactivates the enzyme acetylcholinesterase by combining with it in a reversible manner. The inactivation of the enzyme prevents the hydrolysis of acetylcholine and allows the accumulation of the neurotransmitter. The accumulation of acetylcholine at cholinergic receptor sites leads to the resumption of normal cholinergic transmission at the myoneural junction.

At equiantagonistic doses, the duration of action of edrophonium chloride is comparable to that of neostigmine methylsulfate but shorter than that of pyridostigmine bromide. The onset of action of edrophonium chloride is more rapid than that of either neostigmine methylsulfate or pyridostigmine bromide.

Indications: To reverse the neuromuscular blocking action of nondepolarizing skeletal muscle relaxants such as tubocurarine, atracurium, vecuronium, metocurine, or pancuronium. It is not effective against depolarizing agents such as succinylcholine or decamethonium.

Edrophonium may also be used adjunctively in the treatment of respiratory depression caused by curare overdosage.

Enlon (cont'd)

Contraindications: In patients with known hypersensitivity to anticholinesterase agents, or in patients having intestinal or urinary obstruction of mechanical type.

Warnings: Whenever anticholinesterase drugs are used, atropine sulfate (1 mg) should be available for immediate use to counteract severe cholinergic reactions which may occur in hypersensitive individuals.

Edrophonium should be used with caution in patients with bronchial asthma or cardiac dysrhythmias. Transient bradycardia which sometimes occurs can be relieved by atropine sulfate.

Isolated instances of cardiac and respiratory arrest following administration have been reported. It is postulated that these are vagotonic effects. Special care should be taken in digitalized patients and in jaundiced subjects; cardiac arrest with cholinesterase inhibitors occurred in such subjects.

Precautions: Patients may develop "anticholinesterase insensitivity" for brief or prolonged periods. During these times patients should be carefully monitored and may need respiratory assistance. The dosage of anticholinesterase drugs should be reduced or withheld until subjects again become sensitive to them.

As with any antagonist of nondepolarizing muscle relaxants, adequate recovery of voluntary respiration and neuromuscular transmission must be obtained prior to discontinuation of respiratory assistance.

Edrophonium should not be given prior to the administration of any nondepolarizing muscle relaxant.

Caution should be exercised in anephric patients since a major portion of administered drug is excreted in the urine.

Caution should also be exercised when edrophonium is given to patients with symptoms of myasthenic weakness who are also on anticholinesterase drugs. Since symptoms of anticholinesterase overdose (cholinergic crisis) may mimic underdosage (myasthenic weakness), their condition may be worsened by the use of edrophonium.

Pregnancy and Women of Childbearing Potential: The safety of edrophonium on reproductive capacity and pregnancy has not been established. Thus, edrophonium should be used in women of childbearing potential and during pregnancy only when the potential benefits are expected to outweigh the expected risks.

Lactation: It is not known whether edrophonium is secreted in human milk.

Children: Limited experience suggests that the onset of antagonism of nondepolarizing neuromuscular blocking drugs in children may be different than in adults. Thus, the adequacy of neuromuscular function must be assessed clinically.

Adverse Effects: Awareness of the possibility of severe cholinergic reactions is essential, particularly in hyperreactive individuals.

Reactions common to anticholinesterase agents such as edrophonium are: Cardiovascular: arrhythmias (especially bradycardia), fall in cardiac output leading to hypotension.

Respiratory: increased tracheobronchial secretions, laryngospasm, bronchiolar constriction, respiratory muscle paralysis, and central respiratory paralysis.

CNS: convulsions, dysarthria, dysphonia and dysphagia.

Musculoskeletal: weakness and fasciculations.

Eye: increased lacrimation, pupillary constriction, spasm of accommodation, diplopia and conjuctival hyperemia.

Gastrointestinal: nausea, vomiting, increased peristalsis, increased gastric and intestinal secretions, diarrhea, abdominal cramps.

Miscellaneous: increased urinary frequency and incontinence, diaphoresis.

Overdose: Symptoms and Treatment: With an overdose of cholinesterase inhibitors muscarine-like symptoms (nausea, vomiting, diarrhea, sweating, increased bronchial and salivary secretions, bradycardia) often appear (cholinergic crisis).

Obstruction of the airway by bronchial secretions can be an important complication and may be managed with suction (especially if tracheostomy has been performed) and by the use of atropine. Some experts have advocated a wide range of dosages of atropine for the control of edrophonium induced bronchial secretions. If the secretions are copious, up to 1.2 mg i.v. may be given initially and repeated as required.

An overdose of edrophonium should be counteracted by the following steps: Administration of i.v. atropine sulfate, 0.4 to 0.5 mg, repeated as required. Because of the short duration of action of edrophonium, the atropine requirement seldom exceeds 2 mg; maintenance of adequate respiratory exchange by assuring an open airway and by the use of assisted respiration augmented by oxygen; monitoring of cardiac function until complete stabilization is achieved; pralidoxime chloride (a cholinesterase reactivator) may be given by slow i.v. infusion (50 to 100 mg/minute). The maximal dose should not exceed 2 g. Higher doses of pralidoxime may in themselves cause neuromuscular blockade and inhibit acetylcholinesterase; if convulsions or shock occur, appropriate measures should be instituted.

Dosage: The dose of edrophonium should depend on the expected duration of action of the nondepolarizing neuromuscular blocking agent and on the degree of spontaneous recovery. Edrophonium can be administered at a dose of 0.05 mL/kg body weight (0.5 mg/kg) usually by slow i.v. injection to ensure that the emergence of cholinergic reactions are detected. The maximum recommended dose is 0.1 mL/kg (1 mg/kg). Because edrophonium has a brief duration of action, it should not be administered prior to the nondepolarizing neuromuscular blocking agent. It should be administered at a point of at least 5% spontaneous recovery of twitch height (95% block).

To counteract curare overdosage: The effect of each dose of edrophonium on respiration should be carefully monitored before being repeated. Assisted ventilation should always be employed.

Supplied: Each mL of sterile solution contains: edrophonium chloride 10 mg. Nonmedicinal ingredients: citric acid (anhydrous), phenol, sodium citrate and sodium sulfite. pH adjusted to approximately 5.4. Multiple dose vials of 15 mL, cartons of 5.

Reviewed 1997

ENOXAPARIN Ⓟ

General Monograph, CPhA

see HEPARINS: LOW MOLECULAR WEIGHT

ENTACYL®

Roberts

Piperazine Adipate

Anthelmintic

Indications: Pinworm or roundworm infestations.

Contraindications: Impaired renal or hepatic function, convulsive disorders, or a history of hypersensitivity reactions to piperazine or its salts.

Precautions: In children, avoid prolonged or repeated treatment in excess of that recommended due to potential neurotoxicity.

Pregnancy: Safety of this drug for use during pregnancy has not been established.

If CNS, significant gastrointestinal, or hypersensitivity reactions occur, discontinue the drug. In patients with severe malnutrition, or anemia, exercise appropriate caution.

Adverse Effects: The following reactions have been reported, usually due to excessive dosage:

Gastrointestinal: nausea, vomiting, abdominal cramps, diarrhea.

CNS: rarely, and usually in patients with neurological disturbances or in overdose; headache, vertigo, ataxia, tremors, choreiform movement, muscular weakness, hyporeflexia, paresthesia, blurred vision, paralytic strabismus, convulsion, EEG abnormalities, sense of detachment, memory defect.

Hypersensitivity: urticaria, erythema multiforme, purpura, fever, arthralgia.

Dosage: One day treatment: **Granules:** 2 to 8 years (13.5 to 27.5 kg): 1 packet; 8 to 14 years (27.6 to 41 kg): 1 packet twice in 1 day; over 14 years and adults (over 41 kg): 1 packet 3 times in 1 day. Dissolve contents of 1 packet in 57 mL (2 oz or 1/4 glass) of water, milk or fruit juice. Repeat dosage in 2 weeks' time.

Suspension: Under 2 years: 5 mL (1 teaspoonful) 3 times in 1 day; 2 to 8 years: 10 mL (2 teaspoonfuls) 2 times in 1 day; 8 to 14 years: 10 mL (2 teaspoonfuls) 3 times in 1 day; over 14 years and adults: 15 mL (3 teaspoonfuls) 3 times in 1 day. To be given in divided dosage, as suggested above, over a period of 12 hours. Repeat this dosage in 2 weeks' time.

Supplied: Granules: Each single dose foil packet of orange-flavored granules contains: piperazine adipate 2 g. Energy: 13.8 kJ (3.3 kcal)/2 g. Sodium: <19.2 mg/2 g. Gluten- and tartrazine-free. Cartons of 5 and 10 single dose pouches.

Suspension: Each 5 mL of raspberry-flavored liquid contains: piperazine adipate 600 mg. Energy: 128.9 kJ (30.8 kcal)/5 mL. Sodium: <0.8 mg/5 mL. Gluten- and tartrazine-free. Cartoned bottles of 125 mL.

ENTEX® LA

Purdue Frederick

Phenylpropanolamine HCl—Guaifenesin

Decongestant—Expectorant

Pharmacology: Phenylpropanolamine is an alpha-adrenergic receptor agonist (sympathomimetic) which produces vasoconstriction by stimulating alpha-receptors within the mucosa of the respiratory tract. Clinically, phenylpropanolamine shrinks swollen mucous membranes, reduces tissue hyperemia, edema and nasal congestion, and increases nasal airway patency.

Guaifenesin promotes lower respiratory tract drainage by thinning bronchial secretions, lubricates irritated respiratory tract membranes through increased mucus flow, and facilitates removal of viscous, inspissated mucus. As a result of these combined actions, sinus and bronchial drainage is improved, and dry, nonproductive coughs become more productive.

Indications: Reduces swelling of nasal passages, helps decongest sinus openings and promote nasal and/or sinus drainage. Helps drain bronchial tubes by thinning mucus and relieves irritated membranes in the respiratory passageways by preventing dryness through increased mucus flow.

Contraindications: Known hypersensitivity to sympathomimetics, severe hypertension, or in patients receiving MAO inhibitors.

Warnings: Sympathomimetic amines should be used with caution in patients with hypertension, diabetes mellitus, heart disease, peripheral vascular disease, increased intraocular pressure, hyperthyroidism, or prostatic hypertrophy.

Precautions: Should not be taken by persons who have high blood pressure, heart or thyroid disease, diabetes, persistent/chronic cough; or by pregnant/nursing women; or by persons taking high blood pressure medication or an antidepressant containing a monoamine oxidase inhibitor, except under the advice and supervision of a physician. Consult your physician if symptoms do not improve within 7 days, if cough worsens or is accompanied by high fever, if you have peripheral vascular disease, glaucoma, or prostate disease. Do not exceed recommended dosage. Keep all medicines out of the reach of children. Do not crush or chew tablets.

Drug Interactions: Do not use in patients taking other sympathomimetics or MAO inhibitors.

Drug/Laboratory Test Interactions: Guaifenesin has been reported to interfere with clinical laboratory determinations of urinary 5-hydroxyindole- acetic acid (5-HIAA) and urinary vanillylmandelic acid (VMA).

Pregnancy: It is not known whether Entex LA can cause fetal harm when administered to a pregnant woman or can affect reproduction capacity. Should not be used in pregnancy unless the potential benefits outweigh the possible risks.

Lactation: Not known whether the drugs in Entex LA are excreted in human milk. Because many drugs are excreted in human milk and because of the potential for serious adverse reactions in nursing infants, a decision should be made whether to discontinue nursing or to discontinue the product, taking into account the importance of the drug to the mother.

Children: Not recommended for children under 6 years of age.

Adverse Effects: Possible adverse effects include nervousness, insomnia, restlessness, dizziness, headache, nausea, or gastric irritation. These reactions rarely, if ever, require discontinuation of therapy. Chest tightness has been reported on occasion. Urinary retention may occur in patients with prostatic hypertrophy.

Overdose: Symptoms and Treatment: Provide symptomatic and supportive care. If the amount ingested is considered dangerous or excessive, induce vomiting with ipecac syrup unless the patient is convulsing, comatose, or has lost the gag reflex, in which case perform gastric lavage using a large-bore tube. If indicated, follow with activated charcoal and saline cathartic. Since the effects of Entex LA may last up to 12 hours, continue treatment for at least that length of time.

Dosage: Adults and children 12 years of age and over: 1 tablet twice daily (every 12 hours).

Children 6 to under 12 years of age: ½ a tablet twice daily (every 12 hours). Not recommended for children under 6 years of age.

Tablets may be broken in half for ease of administration without affecting release of medication but should not be crushed or chewed prior to swallowing.

Supplied: Each blue, scored tablet, imprinted "PF", contains: phenylpropanolamine HCl 75 mg and guaifenesin 600 mg, in a special base to provide a prolonged therapeutic effect. Nonmedicinal ingredients: FD&C Blue #1, carbomer 934P, compressible sugar, stearic acid and zinc stearate. Bisulfite-, gluten-, lactose-, paraben-, sodium- and tartrazine-free. Bottles of 100 and boxes of 12 individually foil-packed tablets. Store below 30°C protected from moisture.

(Shown in Product Recognition Section)

ENTOCORT® Capsules ℞

Astra

Budesonide

Glucocorticosteroid for the Treatment of Crohn's Disease Affecting the Ileum and/or Ascending Colon

Pharmacology: The active ingredient of Entocort capsules, budesonide, is a potent nonhalogenated synthetic glucocorticosteroid with high topical potency and weak systemic effects.

The exact mechanism of action of glucocorticosteroids in the treatment of Crohn's disease is not fully understood. Anti-inflammatory actions, such as the inhibition of inflammatory mediator release and inhibition of immunological cellular responses, are probably important.

Data from clinical pharmacology studies and controlled clinical trials indicate that Entocort capsules, at least partly, act topically. Budesonide undergoes an extensive degree (approximately 90%) of biotransformation in the liver to metabolites with low glucocorticosteroid activity. The glucocorticosteroid activity of the major metabolites, 6β-hydroxybudesonide and 16α-hydroxyprednisolone, is less than 1% of that of budesonide.

The favorable separation between topical anti-inflammatory and systemic effect is due to strong glucocorticosteroid receptor affinity and an effective first pass metabolism by the liver with a short half-life. A glucocorticosteroid with such a profile is of particular importance for the local treatment of inflammatory bowel diseases such as Crohn's disease. With regard to treatment of this disease with glucocorticosteroids, it is essential to achieve a high local anti-inflammatory activity in the bowel wall with systemic side effects, e.g., on the hypothalamic pituitary adrenal (HPA) axis function, as low as possible.

Indications: For the induction and maintenance of remission in patients with mild to moderate Crohn's disease affecting the ileum and/or ascending colon.

Contraindications: Systemic or local bacterial, fungal or viral infections. Known hypersensitivity to any of the ingredients. Active tuberculosis.

Warnings: Glucocorticosteroids can reduce the response of the HPA-axis to stress. In situations where patients are subject to surgery or other stress situations, supplementation with a conventional glucocorticosteroid is recommended.

Special care is demanded in treatment of patients transferred from conventional systemic steroids to budesonide capsules, as disturbances in the HPA-axis could be expected in these patients.

Precautions: Glucocorticosteroids may mask some signs of infections and new infections may appear. A decreased resistance to localized infection has been observed during glucocorticosteroid therapy. Viral infections such as chickenpox and measles can have a more serious or fatal course in patients on immunosuppressant glucocorticosteroids. In adults who have not had these diseases, particular care should be taken to avoid exposure. If exposed to chickenpox or measles, therapy with varicella zoster immune globulin (VZIG) or pooled i.v. immunoglobulin (IVIG), as appropriate, may be indicated. If chickenpox develops, treatment with antiviral agents may be considered.

Although treatment with budesonide capsules causes significantly less lowering of plasma cortisol compared to conventional glucocorticosteroids, the knowledge with regard to treatment during the following conditions is limited and therefore cautioned: active peptic ulcer, osteoporosis, acute glomerulonephritis, myasthenia gravis, exanthematous diseases, diverticulitis, thrombophlebitis, psychic disturbances, diabetes, hypertension, hyperthyroidism, acute coronary disease, limited cardiac reserve and pregnancy. In such cases the benefits of an oral glucocorticosteroid must be weighed against the risks.

With the recommended therapeutic doses of budesonide, the risk/benefit ratio seems to be low for the long-term systemic effects. However, as with any other glucocorticosteroid, patients should be carefully followed up for systemic adverse effects. During long-term therapy, adrenal function and hematological status should be periodically assessed.

Particular care is needed in patients who are transferred from systemic glucocorticosteroid treatment with higher systemic effect to budesonide capsules. These patients may have adrenal cortical suppression. Therefore, monitoring of adrenocortical function may be considered in these patients. Some patients feel unwell in a nonspecific way during the withdrawal phase, e.g., pain in muscles and joints. A general insufficient glucocorticosteroid effect should be suspected if, in rare cases, symptoms such as tiredness, headache, nausea and vomiting should occur. In these cases a temporary increase in the dose of systemic glucocorticosteroids is sometimes necessary.

Patients should be advised to inform subsequent physicians of the prior use of glucocorticosteroids.

Glucocorticosteroids should be used with caution in patients if there is a probability of bowel perforation as well as the probability of obstruction, abscess or other pyogenic infection and fresh intestinal anastomoses.

Aggravation of diabetes mellitus or stimulation of manifestations of latent diabetes mellitus may be caused by glucocorticosteroid therapy.

There may be an enhanced systemic effect of budesonide in patients with liver cirrhosis since the metabolism of budesonide may be impaired and, as with other glucocorticosteroids, there may be enhanced effects in those with hypothyroidism. Reduced liver function may affect the elimination of corticosteroids. The i.v. pharmacokinetics of budesonide are, however, similar in cirrhotic patients and in healthy subjects. The pharmacokinetics after oral ingestion of budesonide were affected by compromised liver function as evidenced by increased systemic availability.

Glucocorticosteroid therapy may cause hyperacidity of peptic ulcer.

ASA should be used cautiously in conjunction with glucocorticosteroids in hypoprothrombinemia.

Glucocorticosteroids should be used with caution in patients with cataracts, and may cause elevation of intraocular pressure in glaucoma patients.

Pregnancy: Administration of budesonide during pregnancy should be avoided unless there are compelling reasons. In experimental animal studies, budesonide was found to cross the placental barrier. Like other glucocorticosteroids, budesonide is teratogenic to rodent species. High doses of budesonide administered s.c. produced fetal malformations, primarily skeletal defects, in rabbits, rats, and in mice. The relevance of these findings to humans has not yet been established. In the absence of further studies in humans, budesonide should be used during pregnancy only if the potential benefits clearly outweigh the risk to the fetus. Infants born of mothers who have received substantial doses of glucocorticosteroids during pregnancy should be carefully observed for hypoadrenalism.

Lactation: Glucocorticosteroids are secreted in human milk. It is not known whether budesonide would be secreted in human milk, but it is suspected to be likely. The use of budesonide in nursing mothers requires that the possible benefits of the drug be weighed against the potential hazards to the mother, or infant.

Children: The safety and effectiveness of budesonide in children have not been established, therefore use in this age group is not recommended.

Drug Interactions: To date, budesonide has not been observed to interact with other drugs used for the treatment of intestinal bowel diseases.

Cimetidine: The kinetics of budesonide were investigated in healthy subjects without and with cimetidine, 1 000 mg daily. After a 4 mg oral dose the values of C_{max} (nmol/L) and systemic availability (%) of budesonide without and with cimetidine (3.3 vs 5.1 nmol/L and 10 vs 12%, respectively) indicated a slight inhibitory effect on hepatic metabolism of budesonide, caused by cimetidine. This should be of little clinical importance.

Ketoconazole: Ketoconazole, a potent inhibitor of cytochrome P450 3A, the main metabolic enzyme for corticosteroids, increases plasma levels of orally ingested budesonide.

Omeprazole: At recommended doses, omeprazole has no effect on the pharmacokinetics of oral budesonide.

Adverse Effects: In clinical trials, most adverse events experienced by patients or healthy volunteers receiving budesonide capsules were of mild to moderate intensity and were classified as nonserious. A total of 530 patients with Crohn's disease were treated with budesonide capsules for induction and maintenance of remission, in controlled clinical trials.

Adverse events reported in patients during induction of remission (n=399) with budesonide capsules included dyspepsia (9%), muscle cramps (4%), palpitations (2%), blurred vision (3%), skin reactions including rash and urticaria (6%), and menstrual disorders (2%).

A similar adverse event profile was reported in patients during maintenance treatment (n=131) with budesonide capsules. The incidence of adverse events was the same or less than observed during treatment for induction of remission.

Side effects typical of systemic glucocorticosteroid (such as Cushingoid features) may occur. The systemic effects of budesonide on the HPA-axis were found to be dose-dependent.

Overdose: Symptoms and Treatment: Acute overdosage with budesonide capsules, even in excessive doses, is not expected to be a clinical problem.

Occasional overdosing will not give any obvious symptoms in most cases but it will decrease the plasma cortisol level and increase the number and percentage of circulating neutrophils. The number and percentage of eosinophils will decrease concurrently. Stopping the treatment or decreasing the dose will abolish the induced effects.

Habitual overdosing may cause hypercorticism and HPA-suppression. Decreasing the dose or stopping the therapy, with the accepted procedures for discontinuing prolonged oral therapy with systemic steroids, will abolish these effects, although the restitution of the HPA-axis may be a slow process and during periods with pronounced physical stress (severe infections, trauma, surgical operations, etc.) it may be advisable to supplement with conventional systemic steroids.

Dosage: Active Disease: The recommended daily dose for induction of remission is 9 mg, administered once daily in the morning, for up to 8 weeks. The dose should be taken before meals.

Maintenance of Remission: The recommended daily starting dose for the maintenance of remission is 6 mg, administered once daily in the morning before breakfast. The maintenance dose should be kept as low as necessary for control of disease symptoms.

During prolonged treatment, dosing may have to be adjusted depending on the disease activity.

Treatment with budesonide capsules should be tapered before cessation. It is recommended that the dose be reduced for the last 2 to 4 weeks of therapy. The rate of tapering should be patient-specific and the patient should be monitored by the treating physician during this period.

The capsules should be swallowed whole with water, and not chewed, broken or crushed before being swallowed.

Information for the Patient: See Blue Section—Information for the Patient "Entocort Capsules".

Supplied: Each controlled ileal release, 2-piece hard gelatin capsule, with an opaque light grey body and an opaque pink cap printed $_{3\,mg}^{CIR}$ in radial black ink, contains: micronized budesonide 3 mg. Nonmedicinal ingredients: acetyltributyl citrate, dimethicone, ethylcellulose, gelatin, iron oxide, methacrylic acid copolymer, polysorbate 80, sodium lauryl sulfate, sucrose, talc, titanium dioxide and triethylcitrate. High density polyethylene bottles of 100 with a polypropylene screw cap.

There is a desiccant pellet in the cap. The capsules should be dispensed and stored in the original container. The patient should be advised to keep the bottle tightly capped. Store at controlled room temperature (15 to 30°C).

(Shown in Product Recognition Section)

Reviewed 1999

ENTOCORT® Enema ℞

Astra

Budesonide

Glucocorticosteroid

Pharmacology: Budesonide is a potent nonhalogenated synthetic glucocorticosteroid with strong topical and weak systemic effects.

Entocort Enema (cont'd)

Budesonide has a high topical anti-inflammatory potency. It undergoes an extensive degree (approximately 90%) of biotransformation in the liver to metabolites with low glucocorticosteroid activity. The glucocorticosteroid activity of the major metabolites, 6β-hydroxybudesonide and 16α-hydroxyprednisolone, is less than 1% of that of budesonide.

The favorable separation between topical anti-inflammatory and systemic effect is due to strong glucocorticosteroid receptor affinity and an effective first-pass metabolism with a short half-life.

A glucocorticosteroid with such a profile is of particular importance for the local treatment of inflammatory bowel diseases (IBD) such as ulcerative colitis (UC). With regard to treatment of these diseases with glucocorticosteroids, it is essential to achieve a high local anti-inflammatory activity in the bowel wall with systemic side effects, for example, on the hypothalamic-pituitary-adrenal (HPA) axis function, as low as possible. At the recommended doses, budesonide enema causes no or small suppression of plasma cortisol.

Pharmacokinetics: Absorption in healthy subjects after rectal dosing of 2 mg budesonide low viscosity enema is rapid and essentially complete within 3 hours. The mean maximal plasma concentration after rectal administration is 3 ± 2 nmol/L, reached within 1.5 hours. Similar results are obtained in patients suffering from distal ulcerative colitis. The mean systemic availability after rectal dosing is 15 ± 12%. The plasma half-life is between 2 and 3 hours in adults.

Indications: In the management of distal ulcerative colitis (rectum, sigmoid and descending colon).

Contraindications: Budesonide is contraindicated for the following: Local contraindications to the use of budesonide include imminent bowel perforation as well as the probability of obstruction, abscess or other pyogenic infection, fresh intestinal anastomoses, extensive fistulas and sinus tracts; systemic or local bacterial, fungal or viral infections; known hypersensitivity to any of the ingredients; active tuberculosis; ocular herpes simplex, and acute psychosis.

Warnings: Special care is demanded in treatment of patients transferred from systemic steroids to budesonide as disturbances in the hypothalamic-pituitary-adrenal axis could be expected in these patients.

Precautions: Glucocorticosteroids may mask some signs of infections and new infections may appear. A decreased resistance to localized infection has been observed during corticosteroid therapy. Viral infections such as chickenpox and measles can have a more serious or fatal course in patients on immunosuppressant corticosteroids. In adults who have not had these diseases, particular care should be taken to avoid exposure. If exposed to chickenpox or measles, therapy with varicella zoster immune globulin (VZIG) or pooled i.v. immunoglobulin (IVIG), as appropriate, may be indicated. If chickenpox develops, treatment with antiviral agents may be considered.

At recommended doses, budesonide enema causes no clinically important changes in basal plasma cortisol levels or in the response to stimulation with ACTH. The effects on morning plasma cortisol and adrenal function are significantly less compared with prednisolone enema 25 mg daily. However, knowledge with regard to treatment of the following conditions is limited and therefore cautioned: active or lateral peptic ulcer, osteoporosis, acute glomerulonephritis, myasthenia gravis, exanthematous diseases, diverticulitis, thrombophlebitis, psychic disturbances, diabetes, hypertension, hyperthyroidism, acute coronary disease, limited cardiac reserve and pregnancy. In such cases the benefits of a corticosteroid enema must be weighed against the risks.

There are still insufficient data on the long-term systemic effect of budesonide. With the recommended therapeutic doses, the risk/benefit ratio seems to be very low. However, as with any other glucocorticosteroid, patients should be carefully followed up for systemic adverse effects. During long-term therapy, pituitary-adrenal function and hematological status should be periodically assessed.

Some patients feel unwell in a nonspecific way during the withdrawal phase, e.g., pain in muscles and joints. A general insufficient glucocorticosteroid effect should be suspected if, in rare cases, symptoms such as tiredness, headache, nausea and vomiting should occur. In these cases a temporary increase in the dose of systemic glucocorticosteroids is sometimes necessary.

Glucocorticosteroid enemas should be administered with caution in patients with severe ulcerative colitis because these patients are predisposed to perforations of the bowel wall.

Patients should be advised to inform subsequent physicians of the prior use of glucocorticosteroids.

Aggravation of diabetes mellitus or stimulation of manifestations of latent diabetes mellitus may be caused by corticosteroid therapy.

There may be an enhanced effect of budesonide in patients with liver cirrhosis and, as with other glucocorticosteroids, there may be enhanced effects in those with hypothyroidism. Reduced liver function may affect the elimination of corticosteroids. The i.v. pharmacokinetics of budesonide are, however, similar in cirrhotic patients and in healthy subjects. The pharmacokinetics after oral ingestion of budesonide were affected by compromised liver function as evidenced by increased systemic availability.

Glucocorticosteroid therapy may cause hyperacidity of peptic ulcer.

ASA should be used cautiously in conjunction with corticosteroids in hypoprothrombinemia.

Glucocorticosteroids may cause elevation of intraocular pressure in glaucoma patients.

Pregnancy: Administration of budesonide during pregnancy should be avoided unless there are compelling reasons. In experimental animal studies, budesonide was found to cross the placental barrier. Like other glucocorticosteroids, budesonide is teratogenic to rodent species. High doses of budesonide administered s.c. produced fetal malformations, primarily skeletal defects, in rabbits, rats, and in mice. The relevance of these findings to humans has not yet been established. In the absence of further studies in humans, budesonide should be used during pregnancy only if the potential benefits clearly outweigh the risk to the fetus. Infants born of mothers who have received substantial doses of corticosteroids during pregnancy should be carefully observed for hypoadrenalism.

Lactation: Glucocorticosteroids are secreted in human milk. It is not known whether budesonide would be secreted in human milk, but it is suspected to be likely. The use of budesonide in nursing mothers requires that the possible benefits of the drug be weighed against the potential hazards to the mother, or infant.

Children: The safety and effectiveness of budesonide in children have not been established; therefore, use in this age group is not recommended.

Drug Interactions: To date, budesonide has not been observed to interact with other drugs used for the treatment of intestinal bowel diseases.

Cimetidine: The kinetics of budesonide were investigated in healthy subjects without and with cimetidine, 1 000 mg daily. After a 4 mg oral dose the values of C_{max} (nmol/L) and systemic availability (%) of budesonide without and with cimetidine (3.3 vs 5.1 nmol/L and 10 vs 12%, respectively) indicated a slight inhibitory effect on hepatic metabolism of budesonide, caused by cimetidine. This should be of little clinical importance.

Ketoconazole: Ketoconazole, a potent inhibitor of cytochrome P450 3A, the main metabolic enzyme for corticosteroids, increases plasma levels of orally ingested budesonide.

Omeprazole: At recommended doses, omeprazole has no effect on the pharmacokinetics of oral budesonide.

Adverse Effects: No major side effects attributable to the use of budesonide have been reported. During clinical trials, the frequency of subjectively reported side effects in a total of 247 patients and healthy volunteers given 2 mg budesonide, once daily in the morning, was low.

The most common adverse reactions are gastrointestinal disturbances, e.g., flatulence, nausea, diarrhea. These symptoms were reported in 23 of the 247 patients (9%) receiving 2 mg of budesonide. Psychiatric symptoms (insomnia, agitation, anxiety, depression, dysphoria, emotional lability, somnolence) were reported in 7 patients (3%) receiving 2 mg budesonide. Skin reactions (rash, urticaria) occurred in 5 patients (2%).

Systemic effects of budesonide on the HPA-axis function were found to be dose-dependent. In rare cases, signs or symptoms of systemic glucocorticosteroid effects, including hypofunction of the adrenal gland, may occur with rectally administered glucocorticosteroids, probably depending on dose, treatment time, concomitant and previous glucocorticosteroid intake, and individual sensitivity. Rectal administration of high concentrations of budesonide (10 mg/dose) resulted in significant suppression of endogenous cortisol concentrations as measured by plasma and urinary cortisol levels.

In patients in whom systemic steroids are reduced or stopped, withdrawal symptoms due to decreased systemic activity may occur.

Overdose: Symptoms and Treatment: Acute overdosage with budesonide, even in excessive doses, is not expected to be a clinical problem. When used chronically at excessive doses, systemic corticosteroid effects such as hypercorticism and adrenal suppression may appear. If such changes occur, the dosage of budesonide should be discontinued consistent with accepted procedures for discontinuing prolonged oral steroid therapy. However, the dosage form, enema, and the route of administration make any prolonged overdosage unlikely.

Occasional overdosing will not give any obvious symptoms in most cases but it will decrease the plasma cortisol level and increase the number and percentage of circulating neutrophils. The number and percentage of eosinophils will decrease concurrently. Stopping the treatment or decreasing the dose will abolish the induced effects.

Habitual overdosing may cause hypercorticism and hypothalamic-pituitary-adrenal suppression. Decreasing the dose or stopping the therapy will abolish these effects, although the restitution of the HPA-axis may be a slow process and during periods with pronounced physical stress (severe infections, trauma, surgical operations, etc.) it may be advisable to supplement with systemic steroids.

Dosage: 1 retention enema is given nightly to the patient for 4 weeks. If the patient is not in remission after 4 weeks, the treatment period may be prolonged to 8 weeks.

The enema is reconstituted by adding 1 dispersible tablet into the enema bottle, whereafter the bottle is vigorously shaken for at least 10 seconds or until the tablet is completely dissolved. The tablet will disintegrate rapidly and the suspension will turn slightly yellowish.

Information for the Patient: See Blue Section—Information for the Patient "Entocort Enema".

Supplied: Each retention enema contains: budesonide 0.02 mg/mL and consists of 2 components, a dispersible tablet and a vehicle. The enema is reconstituted before use. The volume of the reconstituted enema is 115 mL. Since the residual volume is about 15 mL, the dose administered to the patient is about 2 mg budesonide. The tablets are provided in an aluminum blister package and the vehicle is in a polyethylene bottle equipped with a rectular nozzle. Nonmedicinal ingredients: tablet: colloidal silicon dioxide, cross-linked polyvidone, lactose, lactose anhydrous, magnesium stearate and riboflavin-5-phosphate sodium; vehicle: methyl parahydroxybenzoate, propyl parahydroxybenzoate, purified water and sodium chloride. Cartons of 7 dispersible tablets and vehicle solutions. Store at 15 to 30°C. After preparation of the enema, the solution is intended for immediate use.

(Shown in Product Recognition Section)

Reviewed 1999

ENTROPHEN®

Johnson & Johnson • Merck

ASA

Nonsteroidal Anti-inflammatory—Analgesic—Platelet Aggregation Inhibitor

Pharmacology: ASA has analgesic, antipyretic and anti-inflammatory properties.

In rheumatic diseases, although the analgesic and antipyretic effects are useful, the major purpose for which ASA is used is to reduce the intensity of the inflammatory process. Inhibition of prostaglandin synthesis may be involved in the anti-inflammatory action of ASA.

ASA also alters platelet aggregation and release reaction by inhibiting prostaglandin synthesis. Thromboxane A_2 is an essential step in platelet aggregation. ASA prevents thromboxane A_2 formation by acetylation of platelet cyclooxygenase. This inhibition of prostaglandin synthesis is irreversible and affects platelet function for the life of the platelet.

The enteric coating substantially resists disintegration in aqueous fluids having a pH lower than 3.5 for a period of at least 2 hours and is capable of disintegrating in aqueous fluids having a pH of at least 5.5 in 10 to 30 minutes. Thus, enteric coating effectively inhibits the release of ASA in the stomach, while allowing the tablet to dissolve in the upper portion of the small intestine for absorption from the duodenal area.

Clinical experience has shown that enteric-coated ASA diminishes or eliminates gastric distress during long-term treatment with high doses of ASA.

Pharmacokinetics: Since Entrophen tablets are enteric-coated, the pharmacological effects are not immediate. Peak serum salicylate concentrations are reached 6 to 8 hours after single oral administration. This means that Entrophen tablets are more useful for chronic administration as in arthritis, than for providing prompt relief of pain and fever.

The plasma half-life of salicylate concentrations is dose-dependent being 3 to 6 hours at low doses (325 mg to 1.3 g) and 15 to 30 hours at high doses.

Indications: Whenever gastric intolerance to ASA is of concern.

For the relief of signs and symptoms of osteoarthritis, rheumatoid arthritis, spondylitis, bursitis and other forms of rheumatism, musculoskeletal disorders, also of rheumatic fever, however, penicillin and other appropriate therapy should be administered concomitantly.

ASA is generally considered to be the primary therapy for most forms of arthritis.

Based on its platelet inhibitory properties, ASA is also indicated for the following: to reduce the risk of recurrent transient ischemic attacks or stroke in men who have had transient ischemia of the brain due to fibrin platelet emboli.

At present, there is no evidence that ASA is effective in reducing transient ischemic attacks in women, or is of benefit in the treatment of completed strokes in men or women. It is also indicated to reduce the risk of morbidity and death in patients with unstable angina and in those with previous myocardial infarction.

Contraindications: Sensitivity to the ingredients; active peptic ulcer. Patients who had a bronchospastic reaction to ASA or NSAIDs.

Warnings: ASA is one of the most frequent causes of accidental poisoning in toddlers and infants. ASA should, therefore, be kept well out of the reach of all children.

Precautions: Salicylates should be administered with caution to patients with asthma and other allergic conditions, with a history of gastrointestinal ulcerations, with bleeding tendencies, with significant anemia or with hypoprothrombinemia.

Salicylates can produce changes in thyroid function tests.

Acute hepatitis has been reported rarely in patients with systemic lupus erythematosus and juvenile rheumatoid arthritis with plasma salicylate concentrations above 25 mg/100 mL. Patients have recovered upon cessation of therapy.

Pregnancy: ASA does not appear to have any teratogenic effects. ASA has been found to delay parturition in rats. This effect has also been described with nonsteroidal anti-inflammatory agents which inhibit prostaglandin synthesis.

High doses (3 g daily) of ASA during pregnancy may lengthen the gestation and parturition time.

Because of possible adverse effects on the neonate and the potential for increased maternal blood loss, ASA should be avoided during the last 3 months of pregnancy.

Children: Recent studies have suggested that ASA usage may cause the development of Reye's Syndrome in children and teenagers with acute febrile illnesses, especially influenza and varicella. Although a direct causal relationship has not been established, it is recommended that salicylates be avoided when possible, in children and teenagers with influenza or varicella.

Drug Interactions: Caution is necessary when ASA and anticoagulants are prescribed concurrently, as ASA may potentiate the action of anticoagulants.

Salicylates may potentiate sulfonylurea hypoglycemic agents. Large doses of salicylates may have a hypoglycemic action, and thus, affect the insulin requirements of diabetics.

Although salicylates in large doses are uricosuric agents, smaller amounts may depress uric acid clearance, and thus, decrease the uricosuric effects of probenecid, sulfinpyrazone and phenylbutazone.

Sodium excretion produced by spironolactone may be decreased in the presence of salicylates.

Salicylates also retard the renal elimination of methotrexate.

Adverse Effects: Gastrointestinal: nausea, vomiting, diarrhea, gastrointestinal bleeding and/or ulceration.
Ear: tinnitus, vertigo, hearing loss.
Hematologic: leukopenia, thrombocytopenia, purpura.
Dermatologic and Hypersensitivity: urticaria, angioedema, pruritus, various skin eruptions, asthma and anaphylaxis.
Miscellaneous: acute reversible hepatotoxicity, mental confusion, drowsiness, sweating and thirst.

Overdose: Symptoms: In mild overdosage, these may include rapid and deep breathing, nausea, vomiting (leading to alkalosis), hyperpnea, vertigo, tinnitus, flushing, sweating, thirst and tachycardia. (High blood levels of ASA lead to acidosis.) Severe cases may show fever, hemorrhage, excitement, confusion, convulsions or coma and respiratory failure.

Treatment: Treatment is essentially symptomatic and supportive. Administer water, universal antidote and remove by gastric lavage or emesis. Force fluids (e.g., salty broth) to replace sodium loss. If the patient is unable to retain fluids orally, the alkalosis can be treated by hypertonic saline i.v. If salicylism acidosis is present, sodium bicarbonate i.v. is preferred because it increases the renal excretion of salicylates. Vitamin K is indicated if there is evidence of hemorrhage. Hemodialysis has been used with success.

Respiratory depression may require artificial ventilation with oxygen. Convulsions may best be treated by the administration of succinylcholine and artificial ventilation with oxygen. CNS depressant agents should not be used.

Hyperthermia and dehydration are immediate threats to life and initial therapy must be directed to their correction and to the maintenance of adequate renal function. External cooling with cool water or alcohol should be provided quickly to any child who has a rectal temperature over 40°C.

Dosage: Adults: Single dose should not exceed 650 mg, to be repeated every 4 to 6 hours; the total daily dosage should not exceed 4 000 mg ASA unless otherwise advised by a physician, i.e., 12 tablets 325 mg, or 8 tablets 500 mg, or 6 tablets 650 mg. If the underlying condition requires continued use of ASA for more than 5 days, a physician should be consulted.
Children: **Only** as directed by a physician.
Analgesic/Antipyretic: Patients should be advised not to exceed 4 g daily. Single doses should not be administered more frequently than every 4 hours.
Anti-inflammatory: Because the suppression of inflammation increases with the dose of salicylate even beyond the point of toxicity, the therapeutic objective is to employ as large a dose as possible short of toxicity. Most patients will tolerate blood salicylate levels in the range of 20 to 25 mg %. The most common reason for failing to obtain a therapeutic response to ASA is the administration of inadequate doses.

The generally accepted way to achieve effective "anti-inflammatory" salicylate blood levels of 20 to 25 mg % is to titrate the dosage by starting with 2.6 to 3.9 g daily, according to the size, age and sex of patient. If necessary, the dosage is then gradually adjusted by daily increments of 0.65 g. Optimally, salicylate therapy should be monitored by periodic blood salicylate level determinations. If this is not practical, the appearance of auditory symptoms in the form of tinnitus or deafness are acceptable as an indication of the maximum tolerated salicylate dose.

In adults, the median dose at which tinnitus develops is 4.5 g/day, but the range extends from 2.6 to 6 g/day.

Intermittent administration is ineffective. Patients should be advised not to vary the dose from day to day depending on the level of pain because that often fluctuates independently of the intensity of the inflammation. A continuous regimen of 0.65 g 4 times daily is considered to be minimum therapy for adults. ASA should be administered 4 times daily. For night-time and early morning benefits, the last dose should be given at bedtime.

There is an inverse relation between blood salicylate levels at which auditory symptoms appear and the age of the patient. In the young adult, this is usually in the range of 20 to 30 mg %. In children, however, the level may be much higher, or the effect apparently absent. Because salicylate toxicity may appear without such warning in children, the usual practice is to give ASA in a daily dose of 50 to 80 mg/kg of body weight and to follow blood levels aiming for a concentration of about 30 mg %.
Unstable Angina or Previous Myocardial Infarction: The recommended dose is 325 mg every second day.
Rheumatic Fever: A total daily dosage of 80 mg/kg of body weight administered in divided doses to allay the pain, swelling and fever.
Cerebral Ischemic Attacks (Men): The recommended dosage is 1 300 mg/day (650 mg twice a day or 325 mg 4 times a day).

Information for the Patient: See Blue Section—Information for the Patient "Entrophen".

Supplied: Regular Strength: Caplets: Each capsule-shaped, yellow, film-coated, delayed-release caplet, printed ENTROPHEN 325 mg in black on one side, contains: ASA 325 mg (enteric-coated). Bottles of 100 (child-resistant package).

Tablets: Each round, brown, film-coated, delayed-release tablet, printed ENTROPHEN 325 mg in black on one side, contains: ASA 325 mg (enteric-coated). Bottles of 24 (child-resistant package), 100 and 1 000 (for dispensing use only).

Extra Strength: Tablets: Each oval, pink, film-coated, delayed-release tablet, printed ENTROPHEN 500 mg in black on one side, contains: ASA 500 mg (enteric-coated). Bottles of 100 (child-resistant package).

10 Super Extra Strength: Caplets: Each capsule-shaped orange, film-coated, delayed-release caplet, printed ENTROPHEN 650 mg in black on one side, contains: ASA 650 mg (enteric-coated). Bottles of 100 (child-resistant package).

Tablets: Each oval, orange, film-coated, delayed-release tablet, printed ENTROPHEN 650 mg in black on one side, contains: ASA 650 mg (enteric-coated). Bottles of 50 (child-resistant package), 100 and 1 000 (for dispensing use only).

Nonmedicinal ingredients: carnauba wax, cellulose acetate phthalate, cornstarch, diethyl phthalate, guar gum, hydrogenated vegetable oil, hydroxypropyl cellulose, hydroxypropyl methylcellulose, microcrystalline cellulose, polyvinyl acetate phthalate, sodium lauryl sulfate, sucrose, talc and coloring agents (allura red aluminum lake, black ferric oxide, red ferric oxide, sunset yellow aluminum lake, titanium dioxide, yellow ferric oxide).

Store at 15 to 30°C. Protect from moisture.

(Shown in Product Recognition Section)

Reviewed 1997

ENUCLENE™
Alcon

Tyloxapol

Cleaning/Lubricating Solution for Artificial Eyes

Supplied: Each mL of sterile, buffered solution contains: tyloxapol 0.25%. Nonmedicinal ingredients: benzalkonium chloride (as preservative), boric acid, dibasic sodium phosphate, hydroxypropyl methylcellulose and purified water. Drop-Tainer dispensers of 15 mL.

EPHEDRINE HCl
Roberts

Decongestant

Pharmacology: Ephedrine is an adrenergic drug which exerts peripheral effects resembling those of epinephrine and central effects resembling those of the amphetamines. Ephedrine produces a more sustained action but is less potent than epinephrine. It stimulates both alpha and beta receptors and its peripheral actions are due partly to norepinephrine release and partly to direct effects on receptors. Ephedrine stimulates the heart, elevating the systolic and usually the diastolic blood pressure. Its vasopressor effect results largely from increased cardiac output and to a lesser extent from peripheral vasoconstriction. Ephedrine produces relaxation of bronchial muscle which is more sustained but less pronounced than that produced by epinephrine. It also stimulates the CNS to a greater extent than epinephrine, but its central action is less potent than that of the amphetamines. The central effects of ephedrine are overshadowed to a large extent by its peripheral actions. It produces sympathomimetic effects when administered orally, parenterally or topically.

Indications: Symptomatic relief of nasal congestion associated with a variety of upper respiratory tract illnesses.

Contraindications: Known hypersensitivity to pressor amines.

Warnings: Do not exceed recommended dosage or take for more than 7 days except on the advice of a physician. Consult a physician prior to use if you have heart or thyroid diseases, high blood pressure, diabetes, glaucoma, difficulty in urination due to an enlargement of the prostate gland or if you are taking any prescription drugs. Do not take if you are currently taking or have recently taken MAO inhibitor drugs. Use only on the advice of a physician.

Precautions: Use with caution in hypersensitive and diabetic patients; patients with latent or clinically recognized angle closure glaucoma, coronary artery disease, congestive heart failure, prostatic hypertrophy, hyperthyroidism, urinary retention.
Pregnancy and *Lactation:* Safety for use in pregnancy and lactation has not been established.
Geriatrics: The elderly (60 years and older) are more likely to have adverse reactions to sympathomimetics. Overdosage of sympathomimetics in this age group may cause hallucinations, convulsions, CNS depression and death.

Adverse Effects: Acute toxic reactions are usually extensions of the therapeutic actions of the drug and are most often due to overdosage. Administration of ephedrine may be followed by headache, restlessness, insomnia, anxiety, tension, tremor, weakness, dizziness, confusion, delirium, hallucinations, pallor, respiratory difficulty, palpitation, precordial pain (occasional), sweating, nausea or vomiting. These effects are

Ephedrine HCl (cont'd)

usually transient and can be minimized by rest and recumbency.

Dosage: The usual adult oral dose is 15 to 30 mg daily or as directed by a physician.

Supplied: 15 mg: Each white, round, flat tablet contains: l-ephedrine 12.29 mg (ephedrine HCl 15 mg). Bottles of 100.

30 mg: Each white, round, flat tablet contains: l-ephedrine 24.58 mg (ephedrine HCl 30 mg). Bottles of 100.

Reviewed 1997

EPHEDRINE SULFATE
Abbott

Sympathomimetic

Supplied: Each mL of sterile, nonpyrogenic solution contains: ephedrine sulfate 50 mg. pH 4.5 to 7.0; the 5% solution has a concentration of 0.35 mOsm/mL (approx.) Nonmedicinal ingredients: water for injection. Single dose ampuls of 1 mL, boxes of 50. Store at room temperature. Protect from light. Discard unused portion.

E-PILO® ℞
CIBA Vision

Pilocarpine—Epinephrine

Glaucoma Therapy

Supplied: Each 10 mL plastic squeeze bottle with dropper tip contains: epinephrine bitartrate 1% (w/v) and pilocarpine HCl, either 1%, 2%, 4% or 6% (w/v). Nonmedicinal ingredients: benzalkonium chloride, dibasic sodium phosphate, disodium edetate, mannitol, monobasic sodium and phosphate, purified water and sodium bisulfite. Store at 15 to 30°C. Protect from light. Keep bottle tightly closed when not in use.

EPI-LYT® AHA MEDICATED LOTION
Stiefel

Glycerin—Lactic Acid

Emollient

Supplied: Each mL of medicated lotion contains: glycerin 25% w/w and lactic acid 5% w/w (an alpha-hydroxy acid) in an exclusive moisturizing lotion base. Nonmedicinal ingredients: butylated hydroxytoluene, oleic acid, propylene glycol and quaternium-26. Plastic bottles of 100 mL.

EPINEPHRINE
Abbott

Sympathomimetic

Pharmacology: The actions of epinephrine resemble the effects of stimulation of adrenergic nerves. It acts on both alpha and beta receptor sites of sympathetic effector cells. Its most prominent actions are on the beta receptors of the heart, vascular and other smooth muscle. When given by rapid i.v. injection, it produces a rapid rise in blood pressure, mainly systolic, by direct stimulation of cardiac muscle which increases the strength of ventricular contraction, increasing the heart rate and constriction of the arterioles in the skin, mucosa and splanchnic areas of the circulation.

When given by slow i.v. injection, epinephrine usually produces only a moderate rise in systolic and a fall in diastolic pressure. Although some increase in pulse pressure occurs, there is usually no great elevation in mean blood pressure. Accordingly, the compensatory reflex mechanisms that come into play with a pronounced increase in blood pressure do not antagonize the direct cardiac actions of epinephrine as much as with catecholamines that have a predominant action on alpha receptors.

Total peripheral resistance decreases by action of epinephrine on beta receptors of the skeletal muscle vasculature and blood flow is thereby enhanced. Usually this vasodilator effect of the drug on the circulation predominates so that the modest rise in systolic pressure which follows slow injection or absorption is mainly the result of direct cardiac stimulation and increase in cardiac output. In some instances, peripheral resistance is not altered or may even rise owing to a greater ratio of alpha to beta activity in different vascular areas.

Epinephrine relaxes the smooth muscles of the bronchi and iris and is a physiologic antagonist of histamine. The drug also produces an increase in blood sugar and glycogenolysis in the liver.

Pharmacokinetics: I.V. injection produces an immediate and intensified response. Following i.v. injection, epinephrine disappears rapidly from the blood stream.

Epinephrine is rapidly inactivated in the body and is degraded by enzymes in the liver and other tissues. The larger portion of injected doses is excreted in the urine as inactivated compounds and the remainder either partly unchanged or conjugated.

The drug becomes fixed in the tissues and is inactivated chiefly by enzymatic transformation to metanephrine or normetanephrine, either of which is subsequently conjugated and excreted in the urine in the form of sulfates and glucuronides. Either sequence results in the formation of 3-methoxy-4-hydroxy-mandelic acid (vanillyl-mandelic acid; VMA) which also is detectable in the urine.

Sodium chloride added to render the solution isotonic for injection of the active ingredient is present in amounts insufficient to affect serum electrolyte balance of sodium (Na+) and chloride (Cl-) ions.

Indications: In general, the most common uses of parenteral epinephrine are to relieve respiratory distress due to bronchospasm, to provide rapid relief of hypersensitivity (anaphylactic or anaphylactoid) reactions to drugs, animal serums and other allergens, and to prolong the action of infiltration anesthetics. Its cardiac effects may be of use in restoring cardiac rhythm in cardiac arrest due to various causes, and attacks of transitory atrioventricular (AV) heart block and syncopal seizures (Stokes-Adams syndrome), but it is not used in cardiac failure or in hemorrhagic, traumatic, or cardiogenic shock.

In acute attacks of ventricular standstill, physical measures should be applied first. When external cardiac compression and attempts to restore the circulation by electrical defibrillation or use of a pacemaker fail, intracardiac puncture and intramyocardial injection of epinephrine may be effective.

Epinephrine is used as a hemostatic agent.

It is also used in treating mucosal congestion of hay fever, rhinitis, and acute sinusitis; to relieve bronchial asthmatic paroxysms; in syncope due to complete heart block or carotid sinus hypersensitivity; for symptomatic relief of serum sickness, urticaria, angioneurotic edema; for resuscitation in cardiac arrest following anesthetic accidents; in simple (open angle) glaucoma; for relaxation of uterine musculature and to inhibit uterine contractions. Epinephrine injection can be utilized to prolong the action of intraspinal and local anesthetics (see Contraindications).

Contraindications: In patients with known hypersensitivity to sympathomimetic amines, in patients with angle closure glaucoma, and patients in shock (nonanaphylactic). It should not be used in patients anesthetized with agents such as cyclopropane or halothane as these may sensitize the heart to arrhythmic action of sympathomimetic drugs.

Epinephrine should not ordinarily be used in cases where vasopressor drugs may be contraindicated, e.g., in thyrotoxicosis, diabetes, patients receiving MAO inhibitors, in obstetrics when maternal blood pressure is in excess of 130/80 or during labor, and in hypertension and other cardiovascular disorders.

Warnings: Inadvertently induced high arterial blood pressure may result in angina pectoris, aortic rupture or cerebral hemorrhage.

Epinephrine may induce potentially serious cardiac arrhythmias in patients not suffering from heart disease and patients with organic heart disease or who are receiving drugs that sensitize the myocardium.

Parenterally administered epinephrine initially may produce constriction of renal blood vessels and decrease urine formation, and large doses may cause complete renal shutdown.

Epinephrine and Beta-Blockers: There may be increased difficulty in treating an allergic-type reaction in patients on beta-blockers. In these patients, the reaction may be more severe due to pharmacologic effects of the beta-blockers and problems with fluid changes (see Precautions, Drug Interactions).

Epinephrine is the preferred treatment for serious allergic or other emergency situations even though this product contains sodium metabisulfite, a sulfite that may cause allergic-type reactions including anaphylactic symptoms or life-threatening or less severe asthmatic episodes in certain susceptible persons. The alternatives to using epinephrine in a life-threatening situation may not be satisfactory. The presence of a sulfite in this product should not deter administration of the drug for treatment of serious allergic or other emergency situations.

Precautions: Although epinephrine can produce ventricular fibrillation, its actions in restoring electrical activity in asystole and in enhancing defibrillation of the fibrillating ventricle are well documented. The drug, however, should be used with caution in patients with ventricular fibrillation.

In patients with prefibrillatory rhythm, i.v. epinephrine must be used judiciously, with extreme caution, because of its excitatory action on the heart. Since the myocardium is sensitized to this action of the drug by many anesthetic agents, epinephrine may convert asystole to ventricular fibrillation if used in the treatment of anesthetic cardiac accidents.

Epinephrine should be used cautiously in the elderly and in patients with hyperthyroidism, hypertension, diabetes and cardiac diseases/arrhythmias. Patients with long-standing bronchial asthma and emphysema, who have developed degenerative heart disease, should be administered the drug with extreme caution.

Fatalities may also result from pulmonary edema because of the peripheral constriction and cardiac stimulation produced. Rapidly acting vasodilators such as nitrites, or alpha-blocking agents may counteract the marked pressor effects of epinephrine.

Drug Interactions: Beta-blockers: There may be increased difficulty in treating an allergic-type reaction in patients on beta-blockers. In these patients, the reaction may be more severe due to pharmacologic effects of the beta-blockers and problems with fluid changes. Epinephrine should be administered with caution, since it may not have its usual effects in the treatment of anaphylaxis. On the one hand, larger doses of epinephrine may be needed to overcome the bronchospasm, while on the other, these doses can be associated with excessive alpha adrenergic stimulation with consequent hypertension, reflex bradycardia and heart-block and possible potentiation of bronchospasm. Alternatives to the use of large doses of epinephrine include vigorous supportive care such as fluids and the use of beta agonists including parenteral salbutamol or isoproterenol to overcome bronchospasm and norepinephrine to overcome hypotension.

Sympathomimetic Drugs: Epinephrine should not be administered concomitantly with other sympathomimetic drugs (such as isoproterenol) because of possible additive effects and increased toxicity. Combined effects may induce serious cardiac arrhythmias. They may be administered alternately when the preceding effect of another such drug has subsided.

Cyclopropane or Halogenated Hydrocarbons: Administration of epinephrine to patients receiving cyclopropane or halogenated hydrocarbon general anesthetics such as halothane, which sensitize the myocardium, may induce cardiac arrhythmias (see Contraindications). When encountered, such arrhythmias may respond to administration of a beta-adrenergic blocking drug.

Diuretics: Diuretic agents may decrease vascular response to pressor drugs such as epinephrine.

Guanethidine: Epinephrine may antagonize the neuron blockade produced by guanethidine, resulting in decreased antihypertensive effect and requiring increased dosage of the latter.

MAO Inhibitors: All vasopressors should be used cautiously in patients taking MAO inhibitors (see Contraindications).

Others: The effects of epinephrine may be potentiated by tricyclic antidepressants; certain antihistamines, e.g., diphenhydramine, tripelennamine, chlorpheniramine and sodium levothyroxine.

Epinephrine also should be used cautiously with other drugs (e.g., digitalis glycosides) that sensitize the myocardium to the actions of sympathomimetic drugs.

Pregnancy: Epinephrine has been shown to be teratogenic in rats when given in doses about 25 times the human doses. It is not known whether epinephrine can cause fetal harm when administered to a pregnant woman or can affect reproduction capacity. Epinephrine should be given to a pregnant woman only if clearly needed.

Labor and Delivery: Parenteral administration of epinephrine, if used to support blood pressure during low or other spinal anesthesia for delivery, can cause acceleration of fetal heart rate and should not be used in obstetrics when maternal blood pressure exceeds 130/80 (see Contraindications). Epinephrine may delay the second stage of labor.

Adverse Effects: Transient and minor side effects of anxiety, headache, fear and palpitations may occur with systemic therapeutic doses, especially in hyperthyroid individuals. Adverse effects, such as cardiac arrhythmias and excessive rise in blood pressure, may also occur with systemic therapeutic doses or inadvertent overdosage. Other adverse reactions include: cerebral hemorrhage, hemiplegia, subarachnoid hemorrhage, anginal pain in patients with angina pectoris, anxiety, restlessness, throbbing headache, tremor, weakness, dizziness, pallor and respiratory difficulty.

Overdose: Symptoms and Treatment: Erroneous administration of large doses of epinephrine may lead to precordial distress, vomiting, headache, dyspnea, as well as unusually elevated blood pressure (see Warnings). Toxic effects of overdosage can be counteracted by injection of an alpha-adrenergic blocker and a beta-adrenergic blocker. In the event of a sharp rise in blood pressure, rapid-acting vasodilators such as the nitrites, or alpha-adrenergic blocking agents can be given to counteract the marked pressor effect of large doses of epinephrine.

Dosage: Epinephrine injection is administered by the following routes: i.v., intracardiac (left ventricular chamber), s.c. or i.m., and via endotracheal tube in the bronchial tree.

Note: The s.c. is the preferred route of administration. If given i.m., injection into the buttocks should be avoided, due to the possibility of poor absorption.

Hypersensitivity Reaction: Adults: For bronchial asthma and certain allergic manifestations, e.g., angioedema, urticaria, serum sickness, anaphylactic shock, use epinephrine 0.2 to 1 mg [0.2 to 1 mL of a 1 mg/mL solution (1:1 000)] s.c. or i.m. S.C. doses may be repeated at 10- to 15-minute intervals in patients with anaphylactic shock. In patients with asthma, s.c. doses may be given at 20-minute to 4-hour intervals, depending on the severity of the condition and the response of the patient. In severe anaphylactic shock, i.v. administration may be necessary since absorption of the drug may be impaired with s.c. or i.m. administration. If necessary, 0.1 to 0.25 mg of epinephrine [1 to 2.5 mL of a 0.1 mg/mL solution (1:10 000)] may be administered i.v. slowly (over 5 to 10 minutes) and repeated every 5 to 15 minutes as necessary. Start with small doses and increase if required.

Children: For bronchial asthma and other allergic manifestations in pediatric patients, administer 0.01 mg/kg [0.01 mL/kg of 1 mg/mL solution (1:1 000)] or 0.3 mg/m^2 [0.3 mL/m^2 of a 1 mg/mL solution (1:1 000)] to a maximum of 0.5 mg [0.5 mL of a 1 mg/mL solution (1:1 000)] s.c. Doses may be repeated at 20-minute to 4-hour intervals, depending on the severity of the condition and the response of the patient. In severe anaphylactic shock, i.v. administration may be necessary since absorption of the drug may be impaired with s.c. administration. If necessary, some clinicians recommend an initial i.v. epinephrine dose of 0.1 mg [10 mL of a 1:100 000 dilution prepared by diluting 0.1 mL of a 1 mg/mL solution (1:1 000)] with 10 mL of 0.9% sodium chloride injection given over 5 to 10 minutes (the initial dose may have to be reduced in young children), followed by a continuous infusion at an initial rate of 0.1 μg/kg/min (to a maximum of 1.5 μg/kg/min).

Cardiac Resuscitation: Adults: A dose of 0.5 mg i.v. [range 0.1 to 1 mg, usually as 1 to 10 mL of a 0.1 mg/mL solution (1:10 000)]. I.V. doses may be repeated every 5 minutes if needed. Adult intracardiac doses of 0.1 to 1 mg [usually as 1 to 10 mL of a 0.1 mg/mL solution (1:10 000)] have been recommended. External cardiac massage should follow intracardiac administration to permit the drug to enter coronary circulation.

Children: The usual **pediatric** i.v. dose is 0.01 mg/kg [0.1 mL/kg of 0.1 mg/mL solution (1:10 000)]. I.V. doses may be repeated every 5 minutes if needed.

The usual **neonatal** i.v. dose is 0.01 to 0.03 mg/kg [0.1 to 0.3 mL/kg of a 0.1 mg/mL solution (1:10 000)]. I.V. doses may be repeated every 5 minutes if necessary.

Endotracheal Dosage: Alternatively, as a means for advanced cardiac life support, when vascular access is hampered and patients intubated, epinephrine can be administered via the endotracheal tube directly into the bronchial tree. To aid delivery of the drug via an endotracheal tube, the dose may be diluted with 0.9% sodium chloride. Adults: 1 mg [10 mL of a 0.1 mg/mL solution (1:10 000)]. Children: 0.01 mg/kg [0.1 mL/kg of a 0.1 mg/mL solution (1:10 000)]. Neonates: 0.01 to 0.03 mg/kg [0.1 to 0.3 mL/kg of a 0.1 mg/mL solution (1:10 000)].

Regional Anesthesia: A final concentration of 1:100 000 to 1:200 000 of epinephrine injection is recommended for infiltration injection, nerve block, caudal or other epidural blocks. From 0.2 to 0.4 mg of epinephrine [0.2 to 0.4 mL of a 1 mg/mL solution (1:1 000)] may be mixed with spinal anesthetic agents.

Supplied: 1:1 000: Each mL of sterile, nonpyrogenic solution contains: epinephrine 1 mg, sodium chloride added to adjust tonicity, sodium metabisulfite 0.90 mg as an antioxidant and hydrochloric acid for pH adjustment. Ampuls of 1 mL, boxes of 5×10.

1:10 000: Each mL of sterile, nonpyrogenic solution contains: epinephrine 0.1 mg, sodium chloride 8.16 mg, sodium metabisulfite 0.46 mg as an antioxidant, citric acid, anhydrous 2 mg, sodium citrate, dihydrate 0.6 mg (as buffers). May contain additional citric acid and/or sodium citrate for pH adjustment - pH 3.3 (2.2 to 5.0). Abboject syringes of 10 mL, boxes of 10.

The solution contains no bacteriostatic or antimicrobial agent and is intended for use as a single-dose injection. When smaller doses are required, the unused portion should be discarded.

Note: This product contains sodium metabisulfite: use with caution (see Warnings).

Parenteral drug products should be inspected visually for particulate matter and discoloration prior to administration, whenever solution and container permit.

Protect from freezing and extreme heat. Store at controlled room temperature (15 to 30°C).

Protect from light by retaining product in carton until ready for use.

Note: Do not use the injection if its color is pinkish or darker than slightly yellow or if it contains a precipitate. Do not administer unless solution is clear and seal is intact. Discard unused portion.

Reviewed 1998

EPINEPHRINE INJECTION

Bioniche

Sympathomimetic

Supplied: Each mL of sterile solution contains: epinephrine 1 mg, sodium metabisulfite (as antioxidant) 1 mg, sodium chloride (for isotonicity) and hydrochloric acid (to adjust pH). Ampuls of 1 mL, boxes of 10. Store at room temperature (15 to 30°C). Protect from light.

EPIPEN®
EPIPEN® JR.

Allerex

Epinephrine

Allergy Therapy Auto-Injector

Pharmacology: Epinephrine is a sympathomimetic drug, acting on both alpha and beta receptors. It is the drug of choice for the emergency treatment of severe allergic reactions to insect bites, insect stings, food, medication and other allergens. It is also indicated for the temporary emergency treatment of severe, life-threatening asthma attacks. The strong vasoconstrictor action of epinephrine acts quickly to counter vasodilation and resulting increased capillary permeability. By its effect on smooth muscle, epinephrine relaxes the bronchioles, relieving wheezing and dyspnea. Its action also relieves angioedema or hives.

Indications: In the emergency treatment of anaphylactic reactions. The auto-injectors are intended for immediate self-administration by individuals with a history of hypersensitivity to insect stings or bites, foods, drugs and other allergens as well as idiopathic or exercise-induced anaphylaxis. They are also intended for self-administration of asthmatics presenting a risk of severe, life-threatening asthma attacks. They are designed as emergency supportive therapy only and not as a replacement or substitute for subsequent medical or hospital care, nor are they intended to supplant insect venom hyposensitization.

Contraindications: In individuals with organic brain damage.

Warnings: Epinephrine is light sensitive and should be stored in the tube provided. Store at room temperature (15 to 30°C). Do not refrigerate. Before using, check to make sure solution in auto-injector is not brown in color. If it is discolored or contains a precipitate, do not use.

Accidental injection into the hands or feet may result in loss of blood flow to the affected areas and should be avoided. If there is an accidental injection into these areas, go immediately to the nearest emergency room for treatment. Epinephrine should only be injected into the thigh. Every effort should be made to avoid possible inadvertent intravascular administration through appropriate selection of an injection site such as the thigh. Do not inject into buttock. Large doses or accidental i.v. injection of epinephrine may result in cerebral hemorrhage due to sharp rise in blood pressure. Rapidly acting vasodilators can counteract the marked pressor effects of epinephrine. Epinephrine should be administered with extreme caution to patients who have developed degenerative heart disease. Use of epinephrine with drugs that sensitize the heart to arrhythmias is not recommended. Anginal pain may be induced by epinephrine in patients with coronary insufficiency.

Precautions: The effects of epinephrine may be potentiated by tricyclic antidepressants; certain antihistamines, e.g., diphenhydramine, tripelennamine, d-chlorpheniramine, and sodium levothyroxine. Administer with caution to hyperthyroid individuals, individuals with cardiovascular disease, hypertension, or diabetes, elderly individuals, psychoneurotic individuals, pregnant women, and children under 30 kg body weight.

Adverse Effects: Transient and minor side effects of epinephrine include palpitation, respiratory difficulty, pallor, dizziness, weakness, tremor, headache, throbbing, restlessness, tenseness, anxiety and fear. Ventricular arrhythmias may follow administration of epinephrine.

Dosage: Dosage in any specific patient should be based on body weight in addition to the patient's risk of anaphylaxis and ability to tolerate epinephrine. Usual epinephrine adult dose for allergic adult emergencies is 0.3 mg. Usual pediatric dose is 0.01 mg/kg body weight. A physician who prescribes EpiPen or EpiPen Jr. should take appropriate steps to insure that the patient understands the indications and use of the device thoroughly. The physician should review with the patient, in detail, the package insert and operation of the auto-injector. Inject the delivered dose of the auto-injector i.m. into the anteriolateral aspect of the thigh. See package insert.

EpiPen and EpiPen Jr. contain 2 mL but deliver a single dose of 0.3 mL **only**, with 1.7 mL remaining in the unit **after use**.

Supplied: The EpiPen device provides epinephrine for i.m. auto-injection in a sterile solution prepared from epinephrine with the aid of hydrochloric acid in pyrogen-free water.

EpiPen: Each auto-injector contains: 2 mL epinephrine injection 1:1 000 and is designed to deliver a single dose of epinephrine 0.3 mg. Each mL contains: epinephrine 1 mg. Also contains sodium chloride 6 mg, sodium metabisulfite 1.67 mg and hydrochloric acid to adjust pH.

EpiPen Jr.: Each auto-injector contains: 2 mL epinephrine injection 1: 2 000 and is designed to deliver a single dose of epinephrine 0.15 mg. Each mL contains: epinephrine 0.5 mg. Also contains sodium chloride 6 mg, sodium metabisulfite 1.67 mg and hydrochloric acid to adjust pH.

Packages of 1 auto-injector and packages of 6 units. Training device for patient instruction purposes also available.

(Shown in Product Recognition Section)

EPIVAL® ℞
EPIJECT® I.V. ℞

Abbott

Divalproex Sodium

Valproic Acid

Anticonvulsant

Pharmacology: Divalproex has anticonvulsant properties, and is chemically related to valproic acid. Divalproex dissociates to the valproate ion in the gastrointestinal tract. Although its mechanism of action has not yet been established, it has been suggested that its activity in epilepsy is related to increased brain concentrations of gamma-aminobutyric acid (GABA). The effect on the neuronal membrane is unknown.

Pharmacokinetics: Epival: Peak serum levels of valproic acid occur in 3 to 4 hours. The serum half-life ($t_{1/2}$) of valproic acid is typically in the range of 6 to 16 hours. Half-lives in the lower part of the above range are usually found in patients taking other drugs capable of enzyme induction. Enzyme induction may result in enhanced clearance of valproic acid by glucuronidation and microsomal oxidation. Because of these changes in valproic acid clearance, monitoring of valproate and concomitant drug concentrations should be intensified whenever enzyme-inducing drugs are introduced or withdrawn. A slight delay in absorption occurs when the drug is administered with meals but this does not affect the total absorption. Valproic acid is rapidly distributed throughout the body and the drug is strongly bound (90%) to human plasma proteins. Increases in doses may result in decreases in the extent of protein binding and variable changes in valproic acid clearance and elimination.

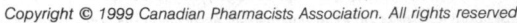

A good correlation has not been established between daily dose, serum level and therapeutic effect. In epilepsy, the therapeutic plasma concentration range is believed to be from

Epival/Epiject I.V. (cont'd)

50 to 100 μg/mL (350 to 700 μmol/L) of total valproate. Occasional patients may be controlled with serum levels lower or higher than this range (see Dosage).

In placebo-controlled clinical studies in acute mania, 79% of patients were dosed to a plasma concentration between 50 and 125 μg/mL. Protein binding of valproate is saturable ranging from 90% at 50 μg/mL to 82% at 125 μg/mL.

Valproate is primarily metabolized in the liver. The principal metabolite formed in the liver is the glucuronide conjugate. Other metabolites in the urine are products of C-3, C-4 and C-5 oxidation. The major oxidative metabolite in the urine is 2-propyl-3-keto-pentanoic acid; minor metabolites are 2-propyl-glutaric acid, 2-propyl-5-hydroxy-pentanoic acid, 2-propyl-3-hydroxy-pentanoic acid and 2-propyl-4-hydroxy-pentanoic acid. Elimination of valproic acid and its metabolites occurs principally in the urine, with minor amounts in the feces and expired air. Very little un-metabolized parent drug is excreted in the urine.

See Warnings for statement regarding fatal hepatic dysfunction.

Epiject I.V.: Valproic acid injection, present as the sodium salt exists as the valproate ion in the blood.

Valproic acid injection has not been studied in children under 2 years of age.

No unique safety concerns were identified in either the 24 patients of 2 to 17 years of age or the 19 patients over 65 years of age who received valproic acid injection in clinical trials.

Mean terminal half-life for valproate monotherapy after a 60-minute i.v. infusion of 1 000 mg was 16±3.0 hours.

Equivalent doses of i.v. valproate and oral valproate products are expected to result in equivalent C_{max}, C_{min}, and total systemic exposure to the valproate ion. However, the rate of valproate ion absorption may vary with the formulation used. These differences should be of minor clinical importance under the steady-state conditions achieved in chronic use in the treatment of epilepsy.

Administration of divalproex sodium tablets and i.v. valproate (given as a 1-hour infusion), 250 mg every 6 hours for 4 days to healthy male volunteers resulted in equivalent AUC, C_{max}, C_{min} at steady state, as well as after the first dose. The T_{max} after i.v. valproate sodium occurs at the end of the 1-hour infusion, while the T_{max} after oral dosing with valproate sodium occurs at approximately 4 hours. Because the kinetics of unbound valproate are linear, bioequivalence between valproate sodium and divalproex sodium up to the maximum recommended dose of 60 mg/kg/day can be assumed. The AUC and C_{max} resulting from administration of i.v. valproate 500 mg as a single 1-hour infusion and a single 500 mg dose of valproic acid syrup to 17 healthy male volunteers were also equivalent.

Patients maintained on valproic acid doses between 750 mg and 4 250 mg daily (average daily dose was 1 961 mg given in divided doses every 6 hours) as oral divalproex sodium alone (n=24) or with another stabilized antiepileptic drug [carbamazepine (n=15), phenytoin (n=11), or phenobarbital (n=1)], showed comparable plasma levels for valproic acid when switching from oral divalproex sodium to i.v. valproate (1-hour infusion).

Indications: Epilepsy: Divalproex is indicated for use as sole or adjunctive therapy in the treatment of simple or complex absence seizures, including petit mal and is useful in primary generalized seizures with tonic-clonic manifestations. Divalproex may also be used adjunctively in patients with multiple seizure types which include either absence or tonic-clonic seizures.

Valproic acid injection is indicated as an i.v. alternative in patients already stabilized on oral valproate products, and for whom oral administration is temporarily not feasible.

There is insufficient information on safety in patients requiring daily doses of i.v. valproate greater than 2 000 mg, or more than 48 hours of i.v. dosing.

Valproic acid injection has not been studied in children under 2 years of age.

Acute Mania: Divalproex is indicated in the treatment of the manic episodes associated with bipolar disorder (DSM-III-R).

The effectiveness of divalproex in long-term use, that is for more than 3 weeks, has not been systematically evaluated in controlled trials.

Divalproex is not indicated for use as a mood stabilizer in patients under 18 years of age.

Contraindications: Divalproex and valproic acid injection should not be administered to patients with hepatic disease or significant hepatic dysfunction.

They are also contraindicated in patients with known hypersensitivity to the drugs.

Warnings: Hepatic failure resulting in fatalities has occurred in patients receiving valproic acid and its derivatives. These incidences usually occurred during the first 6 months of treatment with valproic acid. Experience has indicated that children under the age of 2 years are at a considerably increased risk of developing fatal hepatotoxicity, especially those on multiple anticonvulsants, those with congenital metabolic disorders, those with severe seizure disorders accompanied by mental retardation, and those with organic brain disease.

The risk in this age group decreased considerably in patients receiving valproate as monotherapy. Similarly, patients aged 3 to 10 years were at somewhat greater risk if they received multiple anticonvulsants than those who received only valproate. Risk generally declined with increasing age. No deaths have been reported in patients over 10 years of age who received valproate alone.

If divalproex is to be used for the control of seizures in children 2 years old or younger, it should be used with **extreme caution** and as a sole agent. The benefits of therapy should be weighed against the risks.

Serious or fatal hepatotoxicity may be preceded by non-specific symptoms such as malaise, weakness, lethargy, facial edema, anorexia, and vomiting. In patients with epilepsy, a loss of seizure control may also occur. Patients should be monitored closely for appearance of these symptoms. Patients and parents should be instructed to report such symptoms. Because of the nonspecific nature of some of the early signs, hepatotoxicity should be suspected in patients who become unwell, other than through obvious cause, while taking divalproex.

Liver function tests should be performed prior to therapy and at frequent intervals thereafter especially during the first 6 months. However, physicians should not rely totally on serum biochemistry since these tests may not be abnormal in all instances, but should also consider the results of careful interim medical history and physical examination. Caution should be observed when administering divalproex products to patients with a prior history of hepatic disease. Patients with various unusual congenital disorders, those with severe seizure disorders accompanied by mental retardation, and those with organic brain disease may be at particular risk.

In high-risk patients, it might also be useful to monitor serum fibrinogen and albumin for decreases in concentration and serum ammonia for increases in concentration. If changes occur, divalproex should be discontinued. Dosage should be titrated to and maintained at the lowest dose consistent with optimal seizure control.

The drug should be discontinued immediately in the presence of significant hepatic dysfunction, suspected or apparent. In some cases, hepatic dysfunction has progressed in spite of discontinuation of drug. The frequency of adverse effects (particularly elevated liver enzymes and thrombocytopenia) may increase with increasing dose. The therapeutic benefit which may accompany the higher doses should therefore be weighed against the possibility of a greater incidence of adverse effects.

Pregnancy: According to recent reports in the medical literature, valproic acid may produce teratogenic effects, such as neural tube defects (e.g., spina bifida) in the offspring of human females receiving the drug during pregnancy. The incidence of neural tube defects in the fetus may be increased in mothers receiving valproic acid during the first trimester of pregnancy. Based upon a single report, it was estimated that the risk of valproic acid-exposed women having children with spinal bifida is approximately **1 to 2%**. This risk is similar to that which applies to nonepileptic women who have had children with neural tube defects (anencephaly and spina bifida).

Animal studies have demonstrated valproic acid induced teratogenicity, and studies in human females have demonstrated placental transfer of the drug.

Multiple reports in the clinical literature indicate an association between the use of antiepileptic drugs and an elevated incidence of birth defects in children born to epileptic women taking such medication during pregnancy. The incidence of congenital malformations in the general population is regarded to be approximately 2%; in children of treated epileptic women, this incidence may be increased 2- to 3-fold. The increase is largely due to specific defects, e.g., congenital malformations of the heart, cleft lip and/or palate, craniofacial abnormalities and neural tube defects. Nevertheless, the great majority of mothers receiving antiepileptic medications deliver normal infants.

Data are more extensive with respect to phenytoin and phenobarbital, but these drugs are also the most commonly prescribed antiepileptics. Some reports indicate a possible similar association with the use of other antiepileptic drugs, including trimethadione, paramethadione, and valproic acid. However, the possibility also exists that other factors, e.g., genetic predisposition or the epileptic condition itself may contribute to or may be mainly responsible for the higher incidence of birth defects.

Other congenital anomalies (e.g., craniofacial defects, cardiovascular malformations and anomalies involving various body systems), compatible and incompatible with life, have been reported. Sufficient data to determine the incidence of these congenital anomalies are not available.

Patients taking valproate may develop clotting abnormalities. A patient who had low fibrinogen when taking multiple anticonvulsants including valproate gave birth to an infant with afibrinogenemia who subsequently died of hemorrhage. If valproic acid is used in pregnancy, the clotting parameters should be monitored carefully.

Hepatic failure, resulting in the death of a newborn and of an infant have been reported following the use of valproate during pregnancy.

Antiepileptic drugs should not be abruptly discontinued in patients to whom the drug is administered to prevent major seizures, because of the strong possibility of precipitating status epilepticus with attendant hypoxia and risks to both the mother and the unborn child. With regard to drugs given for minor seizures, the risks of discontinuing medication prior to or during pregnancy should be weighed against the risk of congenital defects in the particular case and with the particular family history.

Epileptic women of childbearing age should be encouraged to seek the counsel of their physician and should report the onset of pregnancy promptly to him. Where the necessity for continued use of antiepileptic medication is in doubt, appropriate consultation is indicated.

Risk-benefit must be carefully considered when treating or counselling women of childbearing age for bipolar disorder.

If divalproex or valproic acid injection is used during pregnancy, or if the patient becomes pregnant while taking this drug, the patient should be made aware of the potential hazard to the fetus.

Tests to detect neural tube and other defects using current accepted procedures should be considered a part of routine prenatal care in childbearing women receiving valproate.

Lactation: Valproic acid is excreted in breast milk. Concentrations in breast milk have been reported to be 1 to 10% of serum concentrations. As a general rule, nursing should not be undertaken while a patient is receiving divalproex or valproic acid injection. It is not known what effect this may have on a nursing infant.

Fertility: The effect of valproate on testicular development and on sperm production and fertility in humans is unknown.

Dose-related Adverse Reactions: The frequency of adverse effects (particularly elevated liver enzymes and thrombocytopenia [see Precautions]) may be dose-related. In a clinical trial of divalproex as monotherapy in patients with epilepsy, 34/126 patients (27%) receiving approximately 50 mg/kg/day on average, had at least 1 value of platelets $\leq 75 \times 10^9$/L. Approximately half of these patients had treatment discontinued with return of platelet counts to normal. In the remaining patients, platelet counts normalized with continued treatment. In this study, the probability of thrombocytopenia appeared to increase significantly at total valproate concentrations of ≥110 μg/mL (females) or ≥135 μg/mL (males). The therapeutic benefit which may accompany the higher doses should therefore be weighed against the possibility of a greater incidence of adverse effects.

Acute Head Injuries: A study was conducted to evaluate the effect of i.v. valproate in the prevention of post-traumatic seizures in patients with acute head injuries. Patients were randomly assigned to receive either i.v. valproate given for 1 week (followed by oral valproate products for either 1 or 6 months per random treatment assignment) or i.v. phenytoin given for 1 week (followed by placebo). In this study, the incidence of death was found to be higher in the two groups assigned to valproate treatment compared to the rate in those assigned to the i.v. phenytoin treatment group (13% vs 8.5%, respectively). Many of these patients were critically ill with multiple and/or severe injuries, and evaluation of the causes of death did not suggest any specific drug-related causation.

Further, in the absence of a concurrent placebo control during the initial week of i.v. therapy, it is impossible to determine if the mortality rate in the patients treated with valproate was greater or less than that expected in a similar group not treated with valproate, or whether the rate seen in the i.v. phenytoin treated patients was lower than would be expected.

Nonetheless, until further information is available, i.v. valproate sodium is not recommended in patients with acute head trauma for the prophylaxis of post-traumatic seizures.

Carcinogenicity: Long-term animal toxicity studies indicate that valproic acid is a weak carcinogen or promoter in rats and mice. The significance of these findings for humans is unknown at present.

Precautions: General: Because of reports of thrombocytopenia, inhibition of the second phase of platelet aggregation, and abnormal coagulation parameters (e.g., low fibrinogen), platelet counts and coagulation tests are recommended before instituting therapy and at periodic intervals. It is recommended that patients receiving divalproex be monitored for platelet count and coagulation parameters prior to planned surgery. Clinical evidence of hemorrhage, bruising or a disorder of hemostasis/coagulation is an indication for reduction of divalproex dosage or withdrawal of therapy pending investigation.

Hyperammonemia with or without lethargy or coma has been reported and may be present in the absence of abnormal liver function tests. Asymptomatic elevations of ammonia are more common than symptomatic elevations and when present require more frequent monitoring. If clinically significant symptoms occur, valproate therapy should be modified or discontinued.

Divalproex is partially eliminated in the urine as a ketone-containing metabolite which may lead to a false interpretation of the urine ketone test.

There have been reports of altered thyroid function tests associated with valproic acid; the clinical significance of these is unknown.

Suicidal ideation may be a manifestation of pre-existing psychiatric disorders, and close supervision of high risk patients should accompany initial drug therapy.

Hepatic Dysfunction: See Contraindications and Warnings.

Renal Impairment: Renal impairment is associated with an increase in the unbound fraction of valproate. In several studies, the unbound fraction of valproate in plasma from renally impaired patients was approximately double that for subjects with normal renal function. Hemodialysis in renally impaired patients may remove up to 20% of the circulating valproate.

Children: Experience has indicated that children under the age of 2 years are at a considerably increased risk of developing fatal hepatotoxicity, especially those with the aforementioned conditions (see Warnings). When divalproex is used in this patient group, it should be used with extreme caution and as a sole agent. The benefits of therapy should be weighed against the risks.

Valproic acid injection has not been studied in children under the age of 2 years. Above the age of 2 years, experience in epilepsy has indicated that the incidence of fatal hepatotoxicity decreases considerably in progressively older patient groups.

Younger children, especially those receiving enzyme-inducing drugs, will require larger maintenance doses to attain targeted total and unbound valproic acid concentrations. The variability in free fraction limits the clinical usefulness of monitoring total serum valproic concentrations. Interpretation of valproic acid concentrations in children should include consideration of factors that affect hepatic metabolism and protein binding.

The safety and effectiveness of divalproex for the treatment of acute mania has not been studied in individuals below the age of 18 years.

Geriatrics: The capacity of elderly patients (age range: 68 to 89 years) to eliminate valproate has been shown to be reduced compared to younger adults (age range: 22 to 26 years). Intrinsic clearance is reduced by 39%; the free fraction is increased by 44%. Accordingly, the initial dosage should be reduced in the elderly (see Dosage).

The safety and efficacy of divalproex in elderly patients with epilepsy and mania has not been systematically evaluated in clinical trials. Caution should thus be exercised in dose selection for an elderly patient, recognizing the more frequent hepatic and renal dysfunctions, and limited experience with divalproex in this population.

Pregnancy: See Warnings.

Occupational Hazards: Divalproex may produce CNS depression, especially when combined with another CNS depressant, such as alcohol. Therefore, patients should be advised not to engage in hazardous occupations, such as driving a car or operating dangerous machinery, until it is known that they do not become drowsy from the drug.

Drug Interactions: Effects of Coadministered Drugs on Valproate: Drugs that affect the level of expression of hepatic enzymes, particularly those that elevate levels of glucuronyl transferases, may increase the clearance of valproate. For example, phenytoin, carbamazepine, and phenobarbital (or primidone) can double the clearance of valproate. Thus, patients on valproate monotherapy will generally have longer half-lives and higher concentrations than patients receiving polytherapy with antiepilepsy drugs.

In contrast, drugs that are inhibitors of cytochrome P_{450} isozymes, e.g., antidepressants, may be expected to have little effect on valproate clearance because cytochrome P_{450} microsomal mediated oxidation is a relatively minor secondary metabolic pathway compared to glucuronidation and beta-oxidation.

The concomitant administration of valproic acid with drugs that exhibit extensive protein binding (e.g., ASA, carbamazepine, dicumarol, warfarin, tolbutamide and phenytoin) may result in alteration of serum drug levels.

Since valproate may interact with concurrently administered drugs which are capable of enzyme induction, periodic plasma concentration determinations of valproate and concomitant drugs are recommended during the early course of therapy and whenever enzyme-inducing drugs are introduced or withdrawn.

The following list provides information about the potential for an influence of several commonly prescribed medications on valproate pharmacokinetics. The list is not exhaustive nor could it be, since new interactions are continuously being reported. Please note that drugs may be listed under specific name, family or pharmacologic class. Reading the entire section is recommended.

Drugs for Which a Potentially Important Interaction Has Been Observed: ASA: A study involving the coadministration of ASA at antipyretic doses (11 to 16 mg/kg) with valproate to pediatric patients (n=6) revealed a decrease in protein binding and an inhibition of metabolism of valproate. Valproate free fraction was increased 4-fold in the presence of ASA compared to valproate alone. The β-oxidation pathway consisting of 2-E-valproic acid, 3-OH-valproic acid was decreased from 25% of total metabolics excreted on valproate alone to 8.3% in the presence of ASA. Caution should be observed when valproate is administered with drugs affecting coagulation, (e.g., ASA and warfarin). (see also Effects of Valproate on Other Drugs and Adverse Effects.)

Carbamazepine/Carbamazepine-10,11-Epoxide: Concomitant use of carbamazepine with valproic acid may result in decreased serum concentrations and half-life of valproate due to increased metabolism induced by hepatic microsomal enzyme activity. Monitoring of serum concentrations is recommended when either medication is added to or withdrawn from an existing regimen (see also Effects of Valproate on Other Drugs).

Cimetidine: Cimetidine may decrease the clearance and increase the half-life of valproic acid by altering its metabolism. In patients receiving valproic acid, serum valproic acid levels should be monitored when treatment with cimetidine is instituted, increased, decreased, or discontinued. The valproic acid dose should be adjusted accordingly.

Felbamate: A study involving the coadministration of 1 200 mg/day of felbamate with valproate to patients with epilepsy (n=10) revealed an increase in mean valproate peak concentration by 35% (from 86 to 115 μg/mL) compared to valproate alone. Increasing the felbamate dose to 2 400 mg/day increased the mean valproate peak concentration to 133 μg/mL (another 16% increase). A decrease in valproate dosage may be necessary when felbamate therapy is initiated. Lower doses of valproate may be necessary when used concomitantly with felbamate.

Rifampin: A study involving the administration of a single dose of valproate (7 mg/kg) 36 hours after 5 nights of daily dosing with rifampin (600 mg) revealed a 40% increase in the oral clearance of valproate. Valproate dosage adjustment may be necessary when it is coadministered with rifampin.

Selective Serotonin Re-uptake Inhibitors (SSRI's): Some evidence suggests that SSRI's inhibit the metabolism of valproate, resulting in higher than expected levels of valproate.

Antipsychotics, MAO Inhibitors and Tricyclic Antidepressants: In addition to enhancing CNS depression when used concurrently with valproic acid, antipsychotics, tricyclic antidepressants and MAO inhibitors may lower the seizure threshold. Dosage adjustments may be necessary to control seizures.

Drugs for Which Either No Interaction or a Likely Clinically Unimportant Interaction Has Been Observed: Antacids: A study involving the coadministration of valproate 500 mg with commonly administered antacids (Maalox, Trisogel, and Titralac - 160 mEq doses) did not reveal any effect on the extent of absorption of valproate.

Chlorpromazine: A study involving the administration of 100 to 300 mg/day of chlorpromazine to schizophrenic patients already receiving valproate (200 mg b.i.d.) revealed a 15% increase in trough plasma levels of valproate.

Haloperidol: A study involving the administration of 6 to 10 mg/day of haloperidol to schizophrenic patients already receiving valproate (200 mg b.i.d.) revealed no significant changes in valproate trough plasma levels.

Lithium: In a double-blind placebo-controlled multiple dose crossover study in 16 healthy male volunteers, pharmacokinetic parameters of lithium were not altered by the presence or absence of divalproex. The presence of lithium, however, resulted in an 11 to 12% increase in the AUC and C_{max} of valproate. T_{max} was also reduced. Although these changes were statistically significant, they are not likely to have clinical importance (see also Effects of Valproate on Other Drugs).

Effects of Valproate on Other Drugs: Valproate has been found to be a weak inhibitor of some P_{450} isozymes, epoxide hydrase, and glucuronyl transferases.

The concomitant administration of valproic acid with drugs that exhibit extensive protein binding (e.g., ASA, carbamazepine, dicumarol, warfarin, tolbutamide and phenytoin) may result in alteration of serum drug levels.

Since valproate may interact with concurrently administered drugs which are capable of enzyme induction, periodic plasma concentration determinations of valproate and concomitant drugs are recommended during the early course of therapy and whenever enzyme-inducing drugs are introduced or withdrawn.

The following list provides information about the potential for an influence of valproate coadministration on the pharmacokinetics or pharmacodynamics of several commonly prescribed medications. The list is not exhaustive nor could it be, since new interactions are continuously being reported. Please note that drugs may be listed under specific name, family or pharmacologic class. Reading the entire section is recommended.

Drugs for Which a Potentially Important Interaction Has Been Observed: Alcohol: Valproate potentiate the CNS depressant action of alcohol.

ASA: Caution is recommended when valproate is administered with drugs affecting coagulation (see Adverse Effects and Precaution, Effects of Coadministered Drugs on Valproate).

Benzodiazepines: Valproic acid may decrease oxidative liver metabolism of some benzodiazepines, resulting in increased serum concentrations (see also Diazepam and Lorazepam).

Carbamazepine/Carbamazepine-10,11-Epoxide: Serum levels of carbamazepine (CBZ) decreased 17% while that of carbamazepine-10,11-epoxide (CBZ-E) increased by 45% upon coadministration of valproate and CBZ to epileptic patients. Monitoring of serum concentrations is recommended when either medication is added to or withdrawn from an existing regimen. Changes in the serum concentration of the 10,11-epoxide metabolite of carbamazepine, however, will not be detected by routine serum carbamazepine assay (see also Effects of Coadministered Drugs on Valproate).

Clonazepam: The concomitant use of valproic acid and clonazepam may induce absence status in patients with a history of absence type seizures.

Diazepam: Valproate displaces diazepam from its plasma albumin binding sites and inhibits its metabolism. Coadministration of valproate (1 500 mg daily) increased the free fraction of diazepam (10 mg) by 90% in healthy volunteers (n=6). Plasma clearance and volume of distribution for free diazepam were reduced by 25% and 20%, respectively, in the presence of valproate. The elimination half-life of diazepam remained unchanged upon addition of valproate.

Ethosuximide: Valproate inhibits the metabolism of ethosuximide. Administration of a single ethosuximide dose of 500 mg with valproate (800 to 1 600 mg/day) to healthy volunteers (n=6) was accompanied by a 25% increase in elimination half-life of ethosuximide and a 15% decrease in its total clearance as compared to ethosuximide alone. Patients receiving valproate and ethosuximide, especially along with other anticonvulsants, should be monitored for alterations in serum concentrations of both drugs.

Lamotrigine: The effects of sodium valproate on lamotrigine were investigated in 6 healthy male subjects. Each subject received a single oral dose of lamotrigine alone and with valproic acid 200 mg every 8 hours for 6 doses starting 1 hour before the lamotrigine dose was given. Valproic acid administration reduced the total clearance of lamotrigine by 21% and increased the plasma elimination half-life from 37.4 hours to 48.3 hours ($p < 0.005$). Renal clearance of lamotrigine was unchanged. In a study involving 16 epileptic patients, valproic acid doubled the elimination half-life of lamotrigine. In an open-labelled study, patients receiving enzyme inducing antiepileptic drugs (e.g., carbamazepine, phenytoin, phenobarbital, or primidone) demonstrated a mean lamotrigine plasma elimination half-life of 14 hours while the elimination half-life was 30 hours in patients taking sodium valproate plus an

Epival/Epiject I.V. (cont'd)

enzyme inducing antiepileptic agent. The latter value is similar to the lamotrigine half-life during monotherapy indicating that valproic acid may counteract the effect of the enzyme inducer. If valproic acid is discontinued in a patient receiving lamotrigine and an enzyme inducing antiepileptic serum lamotrigine concentrations may decrease. Patients receiving combined antiepileptic therapy require careful monitoring when another agent is started, stopped or when the dose is altered.

Phenobarbital: Valproate was found to inhibit the metabolism of phenobarbital. Coadministration of valproate (250 mg b.i.d. for 14 days) with phenobarbital to normal subjects (n=6) resulted in a 50% increase in half-life and a 30% decrease in plasma clearance of phenobarbital (60 mg single-dose). The fraction of phenobarbital dose excreted unchanged increased by 50% in the presence of valproate.

There is evidence for severe CNS depression, with or without significant elevations of barbiturate or valproate serum concentrations. All patients receiving concomitant barbiturate therapy should be closely monitored for neurological toxicity. Serum barbiturate concentrations should be obtained, if possible, and the barbiturate dosage decreased, if appropriate.

Phenytoin: Valproate displaces phenytoin from its plasma albumin binding sites and inhibits its hepatic metabolism. Coadministration of valproate (400 mg t.i.d.) with phenytoin (250 mg) in normal volunteers (n=7) was associated with a 60% increase in the free fraction of phenytoin. Total plasma clearance and apparent volume of distribution of phenytoin increased 30% in the presence of valproate. Both the clearance and apparent volume of distribution of free phenytoin were reduced by 25%.

In patients with epilepsy, there have been reports of breakthrough seizures occurring with the combination of valproate and phenytoin. The dosage of phenytoin should be adjusted as required by the clinical situation.

Primidone: Primidone is metabolized into a barbiturate, and therefore, may also be involved in a similar or identical interaction with valproate as phenobarbital.

Tolbutamide: From in vitro experiments, the unbound fraction of tolbutamide was increased from 20 to 50% when added to plasma samples taken from patients treated with valproate. The clinical relevance of this displacement is unknown.

Warfarin: In an in vitro study, valproate increased the unbound fraction of warfarin by up to 32.6%. The therapeutic relevance of this is unknown, however, coagulation tests should be monitored if valproate therapy is instituted in patients taking anticoagulants.

Caution is recommended when valproate is administered with drugs affecting coagulation (see Adverse Effects).

Zidovudine: In 6 patients who were seropositive for HIV, the clearance of zidovudine (100 mg q8h) was decreased by 38% after administration of valproate (250 or 500 mg q8h); the half-life of zidovudine was unaffected.

Drugs for Which Either No Interaction or a Likely Clinically Unimportant Interaction Has Been Observed: Acetaminophen: Valproate had no effect on any of the pharmacokinetic parameters of acetaminophen when it was concurrently administered to 3 epileptic patients.

Amitriptyline/Nortriptyline: Administration of a single oral 50 mg dose of amitriptyline to 15 normal volunteers (10 males and 5 females) who received valproate (500 mg b.i.d.) resulted in a 21% decrease in plasma clearance of amitriptyline and a 34% decrease in the net clearance of nortriptyline.

Clozapine: In psychotic patients (n=11), no interaction was observed when valproate was coadministered with clozapine.

Lithium: Coadministration of valproate (500 mg b.i.d.) and lithium carbonate (300 mg t.i.d.) to normal male volunteers (n=16) had no effect on the steady-state kinetics of lithium (see also Effects of Coadministered Drugs on Valproate).

Lorazepam: Concomitant administration of valproate (500 mg b.i.d.) and lorazepam (1 mg b.i.d.) in normal male volunteers (n=9) was accompanied by a 17% decrease in the plasma clearance of lorazepam.

Oral Contraceptive Steroids: Evidence suggests that there is an association between the use of certain antiepileptic drugs capable of enzyme induction and failure of oral contraceptives. One explanation for this interaction is that enzyme-inducing drugs effectively lower plasma concentrations of the relevant steroid hormones, resulting in unimpaired ovulation. However, other mechanisms, not related to enzyme induction, may contribute to the failure of oral contraceptives. Valproic acid is not a significant enzyme inducer and would not be expected to decrease concentrations of steroid hormones. However, clinical data about the interaction of valproic acid with oral contraceptives are minimal.

Administration of a single-dose of ethinyloestradiol (50 μg)/levonorgestrel (250 μg) to 6 women on valproate (200 mg b.i.d.) therapy for 2 months did not reveal any pharmacokinetic interaction.

Adverse Effects: Oral Administration: Epilepsy: Adverse events that have been reported with valproate from epilepsy trials, spontaneous reports, and other sources are listed below by body system.

The most commonly reported adverse reactions are nausea, vomiting and indigestion. Since divalproex has usually been used with other antiepilepsy drugs in the treatment of epilepsy, it is not possible in most cases to determine whether the adverse reactions mentioned in this section are due to divalproex alone or to the combination of drugs.

Gastrointestinal: The most commonly reported side effects at the initiation of therapy are nausea, vomiting and indigestion. These effects are usually transient and rarely require discontinuation of therapy. Diarrhea, abdominal cramps and constipation have also been reported. Anorexia with some weight loss and increased appetite with some weight gain have also been reported. The administration of delayed-release divalproex may result in reduction of gastrointestinal side effects in some patients.

CNS: Sedative effects have been noted in patients receiving valproic acid alone but occur most often in patients on combination therapy. Sedation usually disappears upon reduction of other antiepileptic medication. Hallucination, ataxia, headache, nystagmus, diplopia, asterixis, "spots before the eyes", tremor (may be dose-related), confusion, dysarthria, dizziness, hypesthesia, vertigo and incoordination have rarely been noted. Rare cases of coma have been reported in patients receiving valproic acid alone or in conjunction with phenobarbital. Encephalopathy, with or without fever or hyperammonemia, has been reported without evidence of hepatic dysfunction or inappropriate valproate plasma levels. Most patients recovered, with noted improvement of symptoms, upon discontinuation of the drug.

Reversible cerebral atrophy and dementia have been reported in association with valproate therapy.

Dermatologic: Transient increases in hair loss have been observed. Skin rash, photosensitivity, generalized pruritus, erythema multiforme, Stevens-Johnson syndrome, toxic epidermal necrolysis (TEN), and petechiae have rarely been noted.

Endocrine: There have been reports of irregular menses and secondary amenorrhea, breast enlargement, galactorrhea and parotid gland swelling in patients receiving valproic acid. Abnormal thyroid function tests have been reported (see Precautions).

Psychiatric: Emotional upset, depression, psychosis, aggression, hyperactivity and behavioral deterioration have been reported.

Musculoskeletal: Weakness has been reported.

Hematopoietic: Thrombocytopenia has been reported. Valproic acid inhibits the second phase of platelet aggregation (see Precautions, General). This may be reflected in altered bleeding time. Petechiae, bruising, hematoma formation and frank hemorrhage have been reported. Relative lymphocytosis, macrocytosis and hypofibrinogenemia have been noted. Leukopenia and eosinophilia have also been reported. Anemia, including macrocytic with or without folate deficiency, bone marrow suppression and acute intermittent porphyria have been reported.

Hepatic: Minor elevations of transaminases (e.g., AST and ALT) and LDH are frequent and appear to be dose-related. Occasionally, laboratory tests also show increases in serum bilirubin and abnormal changes in other liver function tests. These results may reflect potentially serious hepatotoxicity (see Warnings).

Metabolic: Hyperammonemia (see Precautions), hyponatremia and inappropriate ADH secretion. There have been rare reports of Fanconi's syndrome occurring primarily in children. Hyperglycinemia has been reported and associated with a fatal outcome in a patient with pre-existing nonketotic hyperglycinemia.

Genitourinary: enuresis.

Pancreatic: There have been reports of acute pancreatitis, including rare fatal cases, occurring in patients receiving valproate therapy.

Special Senses: Hearing loss, either reversible or irreversible, has been reported; however, a cause and effect relationship has not been established.

Other: Edema of the extremities has been reported. A lupus erythematosus-like syndrome has been reported rarely.

Bipolar Disorder: The incidence of adverse events has been ascertained based on data from 2 short-term (21 day) placebo-controlled clinical trials of divalproex in the treatment of acute mania, and from 2 long-term (up to 3 years) retrospective open trials.

Most Commonly Observed: During the short-term placebo-controlled trials, the 6 most commonly reported adverse events in patients (N=89) exposed to divalproex were nausea (22%), headache (21%), somnolence (19%), pain (15%), vomiting (12%), and dizziness (12%).

In the long-term retrospective trials (634 patients exposed to divalproex), the 6 most commonly reported adverse events were somnolence (31%), tremor (29%), headache (24%), asthenia (23%), diarrhea (22%), and nausea (20%).

Associated With Discontinuation of Treatment: In the placebo-controlled trials, adverse events which resulted in valproate discontinuation in at least 1% of patients were nausea (4%), abdominal pain (3%), somnolence (2%), and rash (2%).

In the long-term retrospective trials, adverse events which resulted in valproate discontinuation in at least 1% of patients were alopecia (2.4%), somnolence (1.9%), nausea (1.7%), and tremor (1.4%). The time to onset of these events was generally within the first 2 months of initial exposure to valproate. A notable exception was alopecia, which was first experienced after 3 to 6 months of exposure by 8 of the 15 patients who discontinued valproate in response to the event.

Controlled Trials: Table I summarizes those treatment emergent adverse events reported for patients in the placebo-controlled trials when the incidence rate in the divalproex group was at least 5%. (Maximum treatment duration was 21 days; maximum dose in 83% of patients was between 1 000 mg to 2 500 mg/day).

Table I—Epival

Treatment-Emergent Adverse Event Incidence (≥5%) in Short-Term Placebo-Controlled Trials (Oral Administration)

	Percentage of Patients	
Body System/Event	**divalproex (N=89)**	**placebo (N=97)**
Body as a Whole		
Headache	21.3	30.9
Pain	14.6	15.5
Accidental injury	11.2	5.2
Asthenia	10.1	7.2
Abdominal Pain	9.0	8.2
Back Pain	5.6	6.2
Digestive		
Nausea	22.5	15.5
Vomiting	12.4*	3.1
Diarrhea	10.1	13.4
Dyspepsia	9.0	8.2
Constipation	7.9	8.2
Nervous System		
Somnolence	19.1	12.4
Dizziness	12.4	4.1
Tremor	5.6	6.2
Respiratory		
Pharyngitis	6.7	9.3
Skin and Appendages		
Rash	5.6	3.1

*Statistically significant at $P \leq 0.05$ level.

Geriatrics: In elderly patients (above 65 years of age), there were more frequent reports of accidental injury, infection, pain, and to a lesser degree, somnolence and tremor, when compared to patients 18 to 65 years of age. Somnolence and tremor tended to be associated with the discontinuation of valproate.

I.V. Administration: The adverse events that can result from use of valproic acid injection include all of those associated with oral forms of valproate. The following describes experience specifically with valproic acid injection.

Valproic acid injection has been generally well tolerated in clinical trials involving 111 healthy adult male volunteers and 352 patients with epilepsy, given at doses of 125 to 6 000 mg (total daily dose). A total of 2% of patients discontinued treatment with valproic acid injection due to adverse events. The most common adverse events leading to discontinuation were 2 cases each of nausea/vomiting and elevated amylase. Other adverse events leading to discontinuation were hallucinations, pneumonia, headache, injection site reaction, and abnormal gait.

Adverse events reported by at least 0.5% of all those exposed to valproic acid injection during clinical trials are summarized in Table II.

Table II—Epiject I.V.

Adverse Events Reported During Studies of Epiject I.V.

Body System/Event	N=463 (%)
Body as a Whole	
Chest Pain	1.7
Headache	4.3
Injection Site Inflammation	0.6
Injection Site Pain	2.6
Injection Site Reaction	2.4
Pain (unspecified)	1.3
Cardiovascular	
Vasodilation	0.9
Dermatologic	
Sweating	0.9
Digestive	
Abdominal Pain	1.1
Diarrhea	0.9
Nausea	3.2
Vomiting	1.3
CNS	
Dizziness	5.2
Euphoria	0.9
Hypesthesia	0.6
Nervousness	0.9
Paresthesia	0.9
Somnolence	1.7
Tremor	0.6
Respiratory	
Pharyngitis	0.6
Special Senses	
Taste Perversion	1.9

Adverse Events in Pediatric and Elderly Patients: No unique safety concerns were identified in either of the 24 patients 2 to 17 years of age or the 19 patients over 65 years of age who received valproic acid injection in clinical trials.

Overdose: Symptoms and Treatment: Overdosage with valproate may result in somnolence, heart block, and deep coma. Fatalities have been reported, however, patients have recovered from valproate levels as high as 2120 μg/mL.

In a reported case of overdosage with valproic acid after ingesting 36 g in combination with phenobarbital and phenytoin, the patient presented in deep coma. An EEG recorded diffuse slowing, compatible with the state of consciousness. The patient made an uneventful recovery.

In overdose situations, the fraction of drug not bound to protein is high and hemodialysis or tandem hemodialysis plus hemoperfusion may result in significant removal of drug. Since divalproex tablets are enteric-coated, the benefit of gastric lavage or emesis will vary with the time since ingestion. General supportive measures should be applied with particular attention to the prevention of hypovolemia and the maintenance of adequate urinary output.

Naloxone has been reported to reverse the CNS depressant effects of valproic acid overdosage.

Because naloxone could theoretically also reverse the antiepileptic effects of valproate, it should be used with caution in patients with epilepsy.

Dosage: Oral Administration: Epilepsy: Divalproex is administered orally. The recommended initial dosage is 15 mg/kg/day, increasing at one week intervals by 5 to 10 mg/kg/day until seizures are controlled or side effects preclude further increases.

The maximal recommended dosage is 60 mg/kg/day. When the total daily dose exceeds 250 mg, it should be given in a divided regimen (see Table III).

Table III—Epival

Initial Doses by Weight (based on 15 mg/kg/day)

Weight (kg)	Total Daily Dose (mg)	Dosage (mg) equivalent to valproic acid: Dose 1	Dose 2	Dose 3
10–24.9	250	125	0	125
25–39.9	500	250	0	250
40–59.9	750	250	250	250
60–74.9	1 000	250	250	500
75–89.9	1 250	500	250	500

A good correlation has not been established between daily dose, total serum valproate concentration and therapeutic effect. However, therapeutic valproate serum concentrations for most patients with epilepsy will range from 50 to 100 μg/mL (350 to 700 μmol/L). Some patients may be controlled with lower or higher serum concentrations (see Precautions).

Patients receiving combined antiepileptic therapy require careful monitoring when another agent is started, stopped or when the dose is altered (see Precautions, Drug Interactions).

As the dosage of divalproex is titrated upward, blood concentrations of phenobarbital, carbamazepine and/or phenytoin may be affected (see Precautions, Drug Interactions).

Antiepileptic drugs should not be abruptly discontinued in patients in whom the drug is administered to prevent major seizures because of the strong possibility of precipitating status epilepticus with attendant hypoxia and threat to life.

Geriatrics: Due to a decrease in unbound clearance of valproate, the starting dose should be reduced; the ultimate therapeutic dose should be achieved on the basis of clinical response.

Dose-related Adverse Events: The frequency of adverse events (particularly elevated liver enzymes and thrombocytopenia) may be dose related. The probability of thrombocytopenia appears to increase significantly at total valproate concentration of >110 μg/mL (females) or >135 μg/mL (males) (see Precautions). Therefore, the benefit of improved therapeutic effect with higher doses should be weighed against the possibility of a greater incidence of adverse effects.

Gastrointestinal Irritation: Patients who experience gastrointestinal irritation may benefit from administration of the drug with food or by a progressive increase of the dose from the initial low level. The tablets should be swallowed without chewing.

Conversion from Depakene (valproic acid) to Divalproex: Divalproex sodium dissociates to the valproate ion in the gastrointestinal tract. Divalproex sodium tablets are uniformly and reliably absorbed, however, because of the enteric coating, absorption is delayed by an hour when compared to valproic acid. The bioavailability of divalproex sodium tablets is equivalent to that of valproic acid capsules.

In patients previously receiving Depakene (valproic acid) therapy, divalproex sodium should be initiated at the same daily dosing schedule. After the patient is stabilized on divalproex sodium, a dosing schedule of 2 or 3 times a day may be elected in selected patients. Changes in dosage administration of valproate or concomitant medications should be accompanied by increased monitoring of plasma concentrations of valproate and other medications, as well as the patient's clinical status.

Acute Mania: The recommended initial dose is 250 mg 3 times a day. The dose should be increased as rapidly as possible to achieve the lowest therapeutic dose which produces the desired clinical effect or the desired range of plasma concentrations.

In placebo-controlled trials, 84% of patients received and tolerated maximum daily doses of between 1 000 and 2 500 mg/day. The maximum recommended dosage is 60 mg/kg/day.

The relationship of plasma concentration to clinical response has not been established for divalproex. In controlled clinical studies, 79% of patients achieved and tolerated serum valproate concentrations between 50 and 125 μg/mL.

When changing therapy involving drugs known to induce hepatic microsomal enzymes (e.g., carbamazepine) or other drugs with valproate interactions (see Precautions, Drug Interactions), it is advisable to monitor serum valproate concentrations.

I.V. Administration: Valproic acid injection is indicated as an i.v. alternative in patients already stabilized on oral valproate products, and for whom oral administration is temporarily not feasible. The total daily dose of valproic acid injection should be equivalent to the total daily dose of the oral valproate product. There is insufficient information on safety in patients requiring daily doses of I.V. valproate of more than 2 000 mg, or more than 48 hours of i.v. dosing.

Valproic acid injection is for i.v. use only. It should be diluted with at least 50 mL of compatible diluent before administration (see Compatibility of Diluted Solutions) and any unused portion of the vial contents should be discarded.

Valproic acid injection should be administered as a 60 minute infusion, given at the same dosage and frequency as the oral products (every 6 hours), but not more than 10 mg/min. Plasma concentration monitoring and dosage adjustments may be necessary.

A maximum of 48 hours of perfusion, at maximum doses of 2 000 mg/day (500 mg/dose) and a maximum rate of 10 mg/minute should not be exceeded. There are insufficient data to support larger doses and more rapid rates of administration, as well as more than 2 days of infusion.

If the total daily dose exceeds 250 mg, it should be given in a divided regimen. However, the equivalence shown between valproic acid injection and oral valproate products (Depakene) at steady state was only evaluated in an every 6-hour regimen. Whether, when valproic acid injection is given less frequently (i.e., twice or 3 times a day), trough levels fall below those that result from an oral dosage form given via the same regimen, is unknown. For this reason, when valproic acid injection is given twice or 3 times a day, close monitoring of trough plasma levels may be needed.

Rapid infusion of valproic acid injection has been associated with an increase in adverse events. There is limited information on infusion times of less than 60 minutes or rates of infusion >10 mg/min (see Adverse Effects).

Parenteral drug products should be inspected visually for particulate matter and discoloration prior to administration whenever solution and container permit.

Compatibility of Diluted Solutions: Epiject I.V. should be diluted with at least 50 mL of a compatible diluent (2 mg/mL). Epiject I.V. was found to be physically compatible and chemically stable in the following parenteral solutions for at least 24 hours when stored in glass or polyvinyl chloride (PVC) bags at room temperature (15 to 30°C): 5% Dextrose Injection, USP; 0.9% Sodium Chloride Injection, USP; Lactated Ringer's Injection, USP.

Note: Parenteral drug products should be inspected visually for particulate matter and discoloration prior to administration, whenever solution and container permit. Discard unused portion. Use admixture solutions within 24 hours.

Information for the Patient: See Blue Section—Information for the Patient "Epival".

Supplied: Epival: 125 mg: Each enteric-coated, salmon-pink tablet contains: divalproex sodium equivalent to valproic acid 125 mg. Nonmedicinal ingredients: cellulosic polymers, diacetylated monoglycerides, FD&C Blue No. 1, FD&C Red No. 40, povidone, pregelatinized starch (contains cornstarch), silica gel, talc, titanium dioxide and vanillin. Bottles of 100.

250 mg: Each enteric-coated, peach-colored tablet contains: divalproex sodium equivalent to valproic acid 250 mg. Nonmedicinal ingredients: cellulosic polymers, diacetylated monoglycerides, FD&C Yellow No. 6, iron oxide, povidone, pregelatinized starch (contains cornstarch), silica gel, talc, titanium dioxide and vanillin. Bottles of 100 and 500.

500 mg: Each enteric-coated, lavender-colored tablet contains: divalproex sodium equivalent to valproic acid 500 mg. Nonmedicinal ingredients: cellulosic polymers, D&C Red No. 30, diacetylated monoglycerides, FD&C Blue No. 2, iron oxide, povidone, pregelatinized starch (contains cornstarch), silica gel, talc, titanium dioxide and vanillin. Bottles of 100 and 500.

Alcohol-, gluten-, lactose-, paraben-, sucrose-, sulfite- and tartrazine-free. Store between 15 and 30°C.

Epiject I.V.: Each mL of clear, colorless, nonpyrogenic solution for i.v. administration contains: valproate sodium equivalent to valproic acid 100 mg, edetate disodium 0.4 mg and water for injection to volume. The pH is adjusted to a range of 7.0 to 9.0 with sodium hydroxide and/or hydrochloric acid. Preservative-free. Single dose fliptop vials of 10 mL, each containing 5 mL of sterile solution, trays of 5. Store vials bewteen 15 and 25°C. Discard unused portion of container.

(Shown in Product Recognition Section)

Reviewed 1999

EPREX® Ⓟ

Janssen-Ortho

Epoetin Alfa

Erythropoiesis Regulating Hormone

Pharmacology: Erythropoietin is a glycoprotein which stimulates red blood cell production. It is produced in the kidney and stimulates the division and differentiation of committed erythroid progenitors in the bone marrow. Epoetin alfa is a 165 amino acid glycoprotein manufactured by recombinant DNA technology. It has a molecular weight of 30 400 daltons and is produced by mammalian cells into which the human erythropoietin gene has been introduced. The product contains the identical amino acid sequence of isolated natural erythropoietin.

Epoetin alfa is formulated as a sterile, colorless, liquid for i.v. or s.c. administration. The activity of epoetin alfa is determined by comparison of the product to the World Health Organization (WHO) International Reference Standard #2 (10 IU/mL) by both bioassay and radioimmunoassay (RIA).

Eprex (cont'd)

Single-use vials (preservative-free) and single-use prefilled syringes (preservative-free) contain epoetin alfa at a concentration of 2 000, 4 000 or 10 000 IU/mL; multi-use vials (preserved) contain 20 000 IU/mL of epoetin alfa. Multi-use vials also contain 0.9% benzyl alcohol as a preservative.

Chronic Renal Failure (CRF) Patients: Erythropoietin is a glycoprotein which stimulates red blood cell production. Endogenous production of erythropoietin is normally regulated by the level of tissue oxygenation. Hypoxia and anemia generally increase the production of erythropoietin, which in turn stimulates erythropoiesis. In normal subjects, plasma erythropoietin levels range from 0.01 to 0.03 U/mL and increase up to 100 to 1 000 fold during hypoxia or anemia. In contrast, in patients with chronic renal failure (CRF), production of erythropoietin is impaired, and this erythropoietin deficiency is the primary cause of their anemia.

Epoetin alfa has been shown to stimulate erythropoiesis in anemic patients with CRF, including both patients on dialysis and those who do not require regular dialysis. The first evidence of a response to epoetin alfa is an increase in the reticulocyte count within 10 days, followed by increases in the red cell count, hemoglobin and hematocrit, usually within 2 to 6 weeks.

Because several days are required for erythroid progenitors to mature and be released into the circulation, a clinically significant increase in hematocrit is usually not observed in less than 2 weeks and may require up to 6 weeks in some patients. Once the hematocrit reaches the target range (30 to 36%), that level can be sustained by epoetin alfa in the absence of iron deficiency and concurrent illnesses.

The rate of hematocrit increase varies between patients and is dependent upon the dose of epoetin alfa, within a therapeutic range of approximately 50 to 300 IU/kg 3 times/week. Other factors affecting the rate and extent of response include availability of iron stores, the baseline hematocrit, and the presence of concurrent medical problems.

I.V. administered epoetin alfa is eliminated at a rate consistent with first order kinetics with a circulating half-life ranging from approximately 4 to 13 hours in patients with CRF. Within the therapeutic dose range, detectable levels of plasma erythropoietin are maintained for at least 24 hours. After s.c. administration of epoetin alfa to patients with CRF, peak serum levels are achieved within 5 to 24 hours after administration and decline slowly thereafter. In comparison with i.v. administration, s.c. administered epoetin alfa is more slowly absorbed and results in lower serum levels which are maintained for 48 hours. The estimated $AUC_{0\text{-}48}$ for s.c. administration is approximately 15% of the $AUC_{0\text{-}48}$ for the same dose given i.v. Despite these differences, epoetin alfa exhibits a dose-related effect on hematological parameters which is independent of route. There is no apparent difference in half-life between patients not on dialysis whose serum creatinine levels were greater than 264 μmol/L (3 mg/dL), and patients maintained on dialysis. In normal volunteers, the half-life of i.v. administered epoetin alfa is approximately 20% shorter than the half-life in CRF patients.

Zidovudine-treated/HIV-infected Patients: Response to epoetin alfa in zidovudine-treated/HIV-infected patients is manifested by reduced transfusion requirements and increased hematocrit. Responsiveness to epoetin alfa therapy in HIV-infected patients is dependent upon the endogenous serum erythropoietin levels prior to treatment. Zidovudine-treated/HIV-infected patients with endogenous serum erythropoietin levels ≤500 mU/mL respond to epoetin alfa therapy. Patients with endogenous serum erythropoietin levels >500 mU/mL do not appear to respond to epoetin alfa therapy. It appears likely that endogenous serum erythropoietin levels in HIV-infected patients receiving zidovudine are related to the severity of the zidovudine-induced damage to erythroid precursors in the bone marrow.

Maximum benefit from epoetin alfa appears to occur when the hematocrit is maintained in the range of 36 to 40%; however, the target hematocrit for zidovudine-treated/HIV-infected patients must be determined on an individual basis.

Cancer Patients: Anemia in cancer patients may be related to the disease itself or the effect of concomitantly administered chemotherapeutic agents. Epoetin alfa has been shown to increase hematocrit and decrease transfusion requirements (after the first month of therapy) in anemic cancer patients.

In a series of clinical trials enrolling 413 anemic cancer patients who were receiving cyclic chemotherapy (N=289), or not receiving chemotherapy (N=124), approximately 75% of the patients had endogenous serum erythropoietin levels ≤150 mU/mL, and approximately 5% of patients had endogenous serum erythropoietin levels >500 mU/mL. In patients who were not being treated with chemotherapy with endogenous serum erythropoietin levels ≤174 mU/mL, the hematocrit response to epoetin alfa (change in hematocrit from baseline to final evaluation) was significantly greater than the corresponding response in placebo-treated patients. In patients who were being treated with cyclic chemotherapeutic regimens, there was not a statistically significant relationship between response to epoetin alfa therapy and the prestudy endogenous serum erythropoietin level; however, treatment of patients with grossly elevated serum erythropoietin levels (e.g., >200 mU/mL) is not recommended.

Surgery Patients: Use of Epoetin Alfa to Reduce Allogeneic Blood Exposure: Patients undergoing major elective surgery frequently require transfusion of allogeneic blood, both intraoperatively and postoperatively, resulting from blood loss experienced during and after surgery. In patients with a pretreatment hemoglobin of >100 to ≤130 g/L, epoetin alfa has been shown to decrease the risk of receiving allogeneic transfusions and hasten erythroid recovery (i.e., increased hemoglobin levels, hematocrit levels, and reticulocyte counts).

Combined Use of Epoetin Alfa and Autologous Blood Donation (ABD): Epoetin alfa has been shown to stimulate red blood cell production in order to augment autologous blood collection and to limit the decline in hematocrit in adult patients scheduled for major elective surgery who are not expected to predeposit their complete perioperative blood needs. The greatest effects are observed in patients with low hematocrit (≤39%).

Indications: To elevate or maintain the red blood cell level (as manifested by the hematocrit or hemoglobin determinations) and to decrease the need for transfusions. Epoetin alfa is not intended for patients who require immediate correction of severe anemia. Epoetin alfa may obviate the need for maintenance transfusions but is not a substitute for emergency transfusion. Blood pressure should be adequately controlled prior to initiation of epoetin alfa and must be closely monitored and controlled during therapy. Epoetin alfa is not indicated for other specific causes of anemia with established treatments such as iron or folate deficiencies, hemolysis or gastrointestinal bleeding which should be managed appropriately.

Treatment of Anemia of Chronic Renal Failure: In the treatment of anemia associated with chronic renal failure, including patients on dialysis (end-stage renal disease) and patients not on dialysis. Non-dialysis patients with symptomatic anemia considered for therapy should have a hematocrit less than 30%.

Treatment of Anemia in Zidovudine-treated/HIV-infected Patients: For the treatment of transfusion dependent anemia related to therapy with zidovudine in HIV-infected patients. Epoetin alfa is effective in HIV-infected patients treated with zidovudine, when the endogenous serum erythropoietin level is ≤500 mU/mL and when patients are receiving a dose of zidovudine ≤4 200 mg/week.

Treatment of Anemia in Cancer Patients: For the treatment of anemia in patients with nonmyeloid malignancies where anemia is due to the disease itself, or the effect of concomitantly administered chemotherapy after the first month of therapy.

Surgery Patients: In the following elective surgery regimens: Use of Epoetin Alfa to Reduce Allogeneic Blood Exposure: To treat patients who are undergoing major, elective surgery (including patients who do not wish to or are not eligible to participate in an autologous blood donation program) and have a pretreatment hemoglobin of >100 to ≤130 g/L. Epoetin alfa is indicated to reduce allogeneic blood transfusions and hasten erythroid recovery in these patients.

Combined Use of Epoetin Alfa and ABD: To facilitate autologous blood collection within a predeposit program and may decrease the risk of receiving allogeneic blood transfusions in patients with hematocrits of 33 to 39%, who are scheduled for major elective surgery and are expected to require more blood than that which can be obtained through autologous blood collection techniques in the absence of epoetin alfa.

Contraindications: In patients with: uncontrolled hypertension; known hypersensitivity to mammalian cell-derived products, albumin (human) or any component of the product.

In addition, the 20 000 IU/mL formulation, preserved with benzyl alcohol, is contraindicated in premature infants and newborns.

The use of epoetin alfa in patients scheduled for elective surgery and not participating in an autologous blood donation program, is contraindicated in patients with severe coronary, peripheral arterial, carotid, or cerebral vascular disease, including patients with recent myocardial infarction or cerebral vascular accident.

Contraindications defined by the guidelines and methods of practice for ABD programs should be respected in patients receiving epoetin alfa.

Warnings: All Patients: Multi-use Preserved Formulation: The multi-use preserved formulation contains benzyl alcohol. Benzyl alcohol has been reported to be associated with an increased incidence of neurological and other complications in premature infants which are sometimes fatal.

Hypertension: Patients with uncontrolled hypertension should not be treated with epoetin alfa; blood pressure should be controlled adequately before initiation of therapy. Blood pressure may rise during epoetin alfa therapy, often during the early phase of treatment when the hematocrit is increasing, especially in CRF patients.

For patients who respond to epoetin alfa with a rapid increase in hematocrit (e.g., more than 6 percentage points in any 4-week period), the dose of epoetin alfa should be reduced because of the possible association of excessive rate of rise of hematocrit with an exacerbation of hypertension.

Seizures: Epoetin alfa should be used with caution in patients with a history of seizures. Additional close monitoring of all possible risk factors is advisable if the decision is made to treat patients with a history of seizures with epoetin alfa.

Given the potential for an increased risk of seizures in CRF patients during the first 90 days of therapy, blood pressure and the presence of premonitory neurologic symptoms should be monitored closely and CRF patients should be cautioned to avoid potentially hazardous activities such as driving or operating heavy machinery during this period.

It is recommended that the dose of epoetin alfa be decreased if the hematocrit increase exceeds 6 percentage points in any 4-week period.

Thrombotic Events: During hemodialysis, patients treated with epoetin alfa may require increased anticoagulation with heparin to prevent clotting of the artificial kidney. Clotting of the vascular access (AV fistula) has occurred at an annualized rate of about 0.25 events per patient-year on epoetin alfa therapy. Overall, for patients with CRF (whether on dialysis or not), other thrombotic events (e.g., myocardial infarction, cerebrovascular accident, transient ischemic attack) have occurred at an annualized rate of less than 0.04 events per patient-year of epoetin alfa therapy. Patients with pre-existing vascular disease should be monitored closely.

Chronic Renal Failure Patients: In patients with chronic renal failure and clinically evident ischemic heart disease or congestive heart failure, maintenance hematocrit concentration should not exceed the upper limit of the target hematocrit concentration as recommended under Dosage.

Surgery Patients: Combined Use of Epoetin Alfa and ABD: Warnings defined by the guidelines and methods of practice for ABD programs should be respected in patients receiving epoetin alfa.

Precautions: All Patients: General: The parenteral administration of any biologic product should be attended by appropriate precautions in case allergic or other untoward reactions occur. If an anaphylactoid reaction occurs, epoetin alfa should be immediately discontinued and appropriate therapy initiated.

The safety and efficacy of epoetin alfa therapy have not been established in patients with a known history of a seizure disorder or underlying hematologic disease (e.g., sickle cell anemia, myelodysplastic syndromes, or hypercoagulable disorders).

Hypertension: All patients on epoetin alfa should have hematocrit/hemoglobin levels measured at least once a week until a stable level is achieved and periodically thereafter.

Blood pressure should be adequately controlled prior to initiation of epoetin alfa therapy.

In all patients receiving epoetin alfa, blood pressure should be closely monitored and controlled as necessary. Particular attention should be paid to the development of unusual headaches or an increase in headaches as a possible warning signal.

It may be necessary to initiate or increase antihypertensive treatment during epoetin alfa therapy. If blood pressure cannot be controlled, epoetin alfa should be discontinued until blood pressure control is re-established.

Thrombotic/Vascular Events: Patients with conditions associated with thrombotic/vascular events should be closely monitored.

Delayed or Diminished Response: Inadequate response to epoetin alfa should prompt an investigation for causative factors. If the patient fails to respond or to maintain a response, the following etiologies should be considered and evaluated: Iron deficiency: Virtually all patients will eventually require supplemental iron therapy (see Laboratory Monitoring, Iron Evaluation). Underlying infectious, inflammatory, or malignant processes. Occult blood loss. Underlying hematologic diseases (i.e., thalassemia, refractory anemia, or other myelodysplastic disorders). Vitamin deficiencies: folic acid or vitamin B_{12}. Hemolysis. Aluminum intoxication. Osteitis fibrosa cystica. Inflammatory or traumatic episodes.

Laboratory Tests: Hematology: All patients receiving epoetin alfa should have hematocrit/hemoglobin levels measured once a week until hematocrit/hemoglobin has been stabilized, and measured periodically thereafter. (See CRF Patients, Laboratory Monitoring, Hematology for additional laboratory monitoring in CRF patients.)

There may be a moderate dose-dependent rise in the platelet count, within the normal range, during treatment with epoetin alfa. This regresses during the course of continued therapy. Development of thrombocytosis is very rare. The platelet count should be regularly monitored during the first 8 weeks of therapy.

Although reported in dogs and rats, incidence of bone marrow fibrosis was not increased in dialysis patients treated with epoetin alfa for 12 to 19 months.

Iron Evaluation: In most chronic renal failure, cancer, and HIV-infected patients, the serum ferritin concentrations fall concomitantly with the rise in packed cell volume. Therefore, prior to and during epoetin alfa therapy, the patient's iron stores, including transferrin saturation (serum iron divided by iron binding capacity) and serum ferritin, should be evaluated. Transferrin saturation should be at least 20%, and serum ferritin levels should be at least 100 ng/mL. Supplemental iron, e.g., oral elemental iron or i.v. iron, is recommended to increase and maintain transferrin saturation to levels that will adequately support epoetin alfa-stimulated erythropoiesis.

All surgery patients being treated with epoetin alfa should receive adequate iron replacement throughout the course of therapy in order to support erythropoiesis and avoid depletion of iron stores (see Dosage).

Vitamin B_{12} and Folate Evaluation: Prior to starting epoetin alfa therapy, the patient's serum vitamin B_{12} and serum folate should be assessed. A deficiency in vitamin B_{12} and/or folate may blunt the response and should be investigated as per standard clinical practice.

Use in Patients with Known Porphyria: Exacerbation of porphyria has been observed rarely in CRF patients treated with epoetin alfa. However, epoetin alfa has not caused an increased urinary excretion of porphyrin metabolites in normal volunteers, even in the presence of a rapid erythropoietic response. Nevertheless, epoetin alfa should be used with caution in patients with known porphyria.

Use in Patients with History of Gout: Increased serum uric acid (and phosphorus) levels have been observed in normal volunteers and dialysis independent CRF patients treated with epoetin alfa who experienced a rapid rate of rise of hematocrit. This effect may be related to an increased rate of nucleic acid synthesis in the bone marrow. Consequently, epoetin alfa should be administered with caution to patients with a history of gout.

Drug Interactions: No evidence exists that indicates that treatment with epoetin alfa alters the metabolism of other drugs. However, since cyclosporine is bound by red blood cells there is potential for a drug interaction. If epoetin alfa is given concomitantly with cyclosporine, blood levels of cyclosporine should be monitored and the dose of cyclosporine adjusted as necessary.

Hepatic Dysfunction: The safety of epoetin alfa has not been established in patients with hepatic dysfunction.

Pregnancy: Although epoetin alfa has been shown to have adverse effects in rats when given in doses greater than 5 times the human dose it is not known whether it can affect reproduction capacity or cause fetal harm when administered to pregnant women. Epoetin alfa should be given to a pregnant woman only if potential benefit justifies the potential risk to the fetus.

Lactation: It is not known whether epoetin alfa is excreted in human milk. Because many drugs are excreted in human milk, caution should be exercised when epoetin alfa is administered to a nursing woman.

Children: The safety and effectiveness of epoetin alfa in children have not been established.

CRF Patients: In some female chronic renal failure patients, menses have resumed following epoetin alfa therapy; the possibility of potential pregnancy should be discussed and the need for contraception evaluated.

Laboratory Monitoring: Hematology: Sufficient time should be allowed to determine a patient's responsiveness to a dosage of epoetin alfa before adjusting the dose. The hematocrit should be determined weekly until it has stabilized in the target range and the maintenance dose has been established. After any dose adjustment, the hematocrit should also be measured weekly for at least 2 to 6 weeks until it has been determined that the hematocrit has stabilized in response to the dose change. The hematocrit should then be monitored at regular intervals.

A complete blood count with differential and platelet count should be performed regularly. During clinical trials, modest increases were seen in platelets and white blood cell counts. While these changes were statistically significant, they were not clinically significant and the values remained within normal ranges.

In order to avoid reaching the suggested target hematocrit too rapidly, or exceeding the suggested target range (hematocrit of 30 to 36%), the guidelines for dose and frequency of dose adjustments (see Dosage) should be followed.

The elevated bleeding time characteristic of chronic renal failure (CRF) decreases toward normal after correction of anemia in patients treated with epoetin alfa. Reduction of bleeding time also occurs after correction of anemia by transfusion.

Biochemistry: In patients with CRF, serum chemistry values [including blood urea nitrogen (BUN), uric acid, creatinine, phosphorus, and potassium] should be monitored regularly. During clinical trials in patients on dialysis, modest increases were seen in BUN, creatinine, phosphorus, and potassium. In some CRF patients not on dialysis who were treated with epoetin alfa, modest increases in serum uric acid and phosphorus were observed. While changes were statistically significant, the values remained within the ranges normally seen in patients with CRF.

In patients with CRF not on dialysis, renal function and fluid and electrolyte balance should be closely monitored, as an improved sense of well-being may obscure the need to initiate dialysis in some patients. In patients with CRF not on dialysis, placebo-controlled studies of the progression of renal dysfunction over periods of greater than one year have not been completed. In shorter-term trials in patients with CRF not on dialysis, changes in creatinine and creatinine clearance were not significantly different in patients treated with epoetin alfa, compared with placebo-treated patients. Analysis of the slope of 1/serum creatinine vs time plots in these patients indicates no significant change in the slope after the initiation of epoetin alfa therapy.

Dialysis Management: Therapy with epoetin alfa results in an increase in hematocrit and a decrease in plasma volume which could potentially affect dialysis efficiency. In studies to date, the resulting increase in hematocrit did not appear to adversely affect dialyzer function or the efficiency of high flux hemodialysis. During hemodialysis, chronic renal failure patients treated with epoetin alfa may require increased anticoagulation with heparin to prevent clotting of the artificial kidney.

Chronic renal failure patients who are marginally dialyzed may require adjustments in their dialysis prescription. As with all patients on dialysis, the serum chemistry values [including blood urea nitrogen (BUN), creatinine, phosphorus, and potassium] in patients treated with epoetin alfa should be monitored regularly to assure the adequacy of the dialysis prescription.

Diet: As the hematocrit increases and patients experience an improved sense of well-being and quality of life, the importance of compliance with dietary and dialysis prescriptions should be reinforced. In particular, hyperkalemia is not uncommon in patients with CRF.

Predialysis Management: Blood pressure and hematocrit should be monitored in predialysis patients no less frequently than for ESRD patients maintained on dialysis. Renal function and fluid and electrolyte balance should be closely monitored, as an improved sense of well-being may obscure the need to initiate dialysis in some patients.

Based on information to date, the use of epoetin alfa in predialysis patients does not accelerate the rate of progression of renal insufficiency.

Cancer Patients: Growth Factor Potential: Epoetin alfa is a growth factor that primarily stimulates red blood cell production. However, the possibility that epoetin alfa can act as a growth factor for any tumor type, particularly myeloid malignancies, cannot be excluded.

Surgery Patients: Use of Epoetin Alfa to Reduce Allogeneic Blood Exposure: Thrombotic/Vascular Events: Patients scheduled for elective surgery should receive adequate antithrombotic prophylaxis as appropriate for the surgical procedure.

In one study in which epoetin alfa was administered in the perioperative period to patients undergoing coronary artery bypass graft surgery and not participating in an autologous blood donation program, there were 7 deaths in the epoetin alfa-treated groups (n=126) and no deaths in the placebo-treated group (n=56). Among the 7 deaths in the epoetin alfa-treated patients, 3 were related to intercurrent infectious episodes and 4 were at the time of therapy (between study day 2 and 8). The percentage of epoetin alfa-treated patients who died was comparable to the mortality rate reported in the literature for patients undergoing coronary artery bypass graft surgery not treated with epoetin alfa. The 4 deaths at the time of therapy (3%) were associated with thrombotic/vascular event and a causative role of epoetin alfa cannot be excluded.

Hypertension: Rarely blood pressure may rise in the perioperative period in patients being treated with epoetin alfa. Therefore, blood pressure should be monitored.

Combined Use of Epoetin Alfa and ABD: Precautions defined by the guidelines and methods of practice for ABD programs should be respected in patients receiving epoetin alfa.

Independent of epoetin alfa treatment, thrombotic and vascular events may occur in surgical patients with underlying cardiovascular disease following repeated phlebotomy. Therefore, routine volume replacement should be performed in such patients in autologous blood donation programs.

Adverse Effects: All Patients: Hypertension: The most frequent adverse reaction during treatment with epoetin alfa is a dose-dependent increase in blood pressure or aggravation of existing hypertension. This occurred most commonly in chronic renal failure patients. (See Warnings).

Hypertensive crises including malignant hypertension, encephalopathy-like symptoms (e.g., headaches and confused state) and generalized tonic-clonic seizures have occurred in isolated patients, including previously normotensive patients.

Thrombotic/Vascular Events: Thrombotic/vascular events, such as myocardial ischemia, myocardial infarction, cerebrovascular accidents (cerebral hemorrhage and cerebral infarction), transient ischemic attacks, deep venous thrombosis, arterial thrombosis, pulmonary emboli, aneurysms, retinal thrombosis, clotting of vascular access (AV fistula) and clotting of an artificial kidney have been reported in patients receiving epoetin alfa. However, a causal relationship between epoetin alfa therapy and these events has not been established.

In clinical studies conducted in surgery patients with a pretreatment hemoglobin of >100 to ≤ 130 g/L (the recommended population), and not participating in an ABD program, the rate of deep venous thrombosis (DVT) was similar among patients treated with epoetin alfa and placebo. However, in patients with a pretreatment hemoglobin of >130 g/L, the rate of DVTs was higher in the group treated with epoetin alfa than in the placebo-treated group, but within the range of that reported in the literature for orthopedic surgery patients (47 to 74% without anticoagulant therapy and 3 to 37% with use of anticoagulant therapy).

In a study examining the use of epoetin alfa in 182 patients scheduled for coronary artery bypass graft surgery, 23% of patients treated with epoetin alfa and 29% treated with placebo experienced thrombotic/vascular events. There were 4 deaths among the patients treated with epoetin alfa that were associated with a thrombotic/vascular event and a causative role of epoetin alfa cannot be excluded.

Thrombocytosis: Thrombocytosis has been observed but its occurrence is rare.

"Flu-like" Symptoms: "Flu-like" signs and symptoms such as dizziness, drowsiness, fever, headaches, joint and muscle pains, and weakness have occurred, especially at the start of treatment.

Allergic Reactions: Skin rashes, eczema, urticaria, pruritus, eosinophilia, and/or angioedema have been observed with epoetin alfa. The cases have generally been mild to moderate

Eprex (cont'd)

in intensity. There have been rare reports of potentially serious reactions associated with respiratory symptoms and hypotension.

Immune Reactions: The development of immune reactions to epoetin alfa or other components of epoetin alfa is rare. Epoetin alfa appears to have minimal potential for inducing antibody formation.

Reactions at Administration Site: Skin reactions at the injection site have been reported in patients treated with epoetin alfa. These reactions occur more frequently in patients receiving s.c. therapy than in patients receiving i.v. therapy. Patients complain of erythema, burning, and pain, usually mild to moderate, around the site of injection.

Seizures: Seizures have been reported in patients treated with epoetin alfa.

CRF Patients: Studies analyzed to date indicate that epoetin alfa is generally well tolerated irrespective of the route of administration. The adverse events reported are frequent sequelae of CRF and are not necessarily attributable to epoetin alfa therapy. In double-blind, placebo-controlled studies involving 335 patients with CRF (both predialysis and treated with dialysis), the events reported in greater than 5% of patients treated with epoetin alfa (n=200) during the blinded phase were as shown in Table I.

Table I—Eprex

Adverse Events in CRF Patients

Adverse Event	Eprex (n=200)	Placebo (n=135)
Hypertension	24.0%	18.5%
Headache	16.0%	11.9%
Arthralgias	11.0%	5.9%
Nausea	10.5%	8.9%
Edema	9.0%	10.4%
Fatigue	9.0%	14.1%
Diarrhea	8.5%	5.9%
Vomiting	8.0%	5.2%
Chest Pain	7.0%	8.8%
Skin Reaction (Administration Site)	7.0%	11.9%
Asthenia	7.0%	11.9%
Dizziness	7.0%	12.6%
Clotted Access	6.8%	2.3%

Zidovudine-treated/HIV-infected Patients: Adverse experiences reported in clinical trials with epoetin alfa in zidovudine-treated/HIV-infected patients were consistent with the progression of HIV infection. In double-blind, placebo-controlled studies of 3 month duration involving approximately 300 zidovudine-treated/HIV-infected patients, adverse experiences with an incidence of ≥10% in either epoetin alfa-treated patients (n=144) or placebo-treated patients were as shown in Table II.

Table II—Eprex

Adverse Experiences in Zidovudine-treated/HIV-infected Patients

Adverse Experience	Eprex (n=144)	Placebo (n=153)
Pyrexia	38%	29%
Fatigue	25%	31%
Headache	19%	14%
Cough	18%	14%
Diarrhea	16%	18%
Rash	16%	8%
Congestion, Respiratory	15%	10%
Nausea	15%	12%
Shortness of Breath	14%	13%
Asthenia	11%	14%
Skin Reaction (Administration Site)	10%	7%
Dizziness	9%	10%

There were no statistically significant differences between treatment groups in the incidence of above events.

Epoetin alfa does not appear to potentiate progression of HIV disease as measured by: incidence of opportunistic infections; mortality; serum p24 antigen levels; or HIV replication in infected cell lines in vitro.

Cancer Patients: Adverse experiences reported in clinical trials with epoetin alfa in cancer patients were consistent with the underlying disease state. In double-blind, placebo-controlled studies of 3 month duration involving 413 cancer patients, adverse events with an incidence of ≥10% in either patients treated with epoetin alfa or placebo-treated patients were: See Table III.

Table III—Eprex

Adverse Experiences in Cancer Patients

Adverse Experience	Eprex (n=213)	Placebo (n=200)
Nausea	23%	29%
Pyrexia	22%	21%
Asthenia	17%	16%
Fatigue	15%	20%
Vomiting	15%	18%
Diarrhea	15%	9%
Edema	14%	8%
Dizziness	10%	9%
Skin Reaction (Administration Site)	10%	10%
Constipation	10%	9%
Shortness of Breath	8%	15%*
Decreased Appetite	8%	12%
Trunk Pain	8%	12%
Chills	7%	10%

*Significantly higher incidence for placebo patients (p=0.030).

There were no statistically significant differences in the percent of patients treated with epoetin alfa reporting these adverse events compared to the corresponding incidence in placebo-treated patients, except for shortness of breath which occurred in a higher incidence in placebo-treated patients than in patients treated with epoetin alfa.

Surgery Patients: Use of Epoetin Alfa to Reduce Allogeneic Blood Exposure: Adverse events were combined for all groups treated with epoetin alfa and the placebo-treated groups from 4 orthopedic surgery studies where subjects received epoetin alfa at a dose of 300 or 100 IU/kg daily, 600 IU/kg weekly or placebo. Adverse events reported by at least 10% of subjects in any treatment group were as shown in Table IV.

Table IV—Eprex

Adverse Events in Surgery Patients

	Percent of Patients Reporting Event[a]		
Adverse Event	300[b] or 100[c] IU/kg Eprex (Daily) (n=546)	600[d] IU/kg Eprex (Weekly) (n=73)	Placebo (n=250)
Pyrexia	45%	47%	52%
Skin reaction, injection site	42%	26%	40%
Nausea	37%	45%	34%
Constipation	34%	51%	32%
Vomiting	17%	21%	11%
Skin pain	17%	5%	19%
Insomnia	14%	21%	11%
Headache	13%	10%	9%
Pruritus	12%	14%	10%
Dizziness	10%	11%	9%
Diarrhea	9%	10%	9%
Urinary tract infection	8%	11%	10%
Edema	8%	11%	8%
Arthralgia	8%	10%	6%
Urinary retention	7%	11%	7%
Confusion	5%	12%	6%
Flatulence	4%	10%	4%
Anxiety	3%	11%	6%

[a] All patients participating in orthopedic surgery studies regardless of baseline hemoglobin.

[b] 300 IU/kg daily for either 5 or 10 days prior to surgery, on the day of surgery and either 3 or 4 days following surgery (either 9, 14 or 15 daily doses).

[c] 100 IU/kg daily for 10 days prior to surgery, on the day of surgery and 4 days following surgery (15 daily doses).

[d] 600 IU/kg once a week beginning 3 weeks prior to surgery and on the day of surgery (4 weekly doses).

Similar proportions of patients treated with epoetin alfa and placebo-treated subjects reported each adverse event.

Combined Use of Epoetin Alfa and ABD: The incidence of adverse events was calculated across 5 double-blind, placebo-controlled studies, and 1 single-blind study, combining all patients treated with epoetin alfa (n=402), regardless of dose administered, and all placebo patients (n=242). Adverse experiences with an incidence of ≥5% in either patients treated with epoetin alfa or placebo-treated patients were as shown in Table V.

Table V—Eprex

Adverse Events in Surgery Patients

Adverse Event	Eprex (n=402)	Placebo (n=242)
Fatigue	18.41%	19.01%
Dizziness	12.19%	13.64%
Nausea	11.44%	9.09%
Headache	9.20%	11.98%
Asthenia	5.47%	3.72%
Diarrhea	3.48%	7.02%

In general, there were no notable differences between patients treated with epoetin alfa and placebo-treated patients in the incidence of any adverse event.

Overdose: Symptoms and Treatment: The maximum amount of epoetin alfa that can be safely administered in single or multiple doses has not been determined. Doses of up to 1 500 IU/kg 3 times/week for 3 to 4 weeks have been administered without any direct toxic effects of epoetin alfa itself. Humans have received epoetin alfa doses as high as 3 000 IU/kg in a single day without acute toxic effects.

Therapy with epoetin alfa can result in polycythemia if the hematocrit is not carefully monitored and the dose appropriately adjusted. If the target range is exceeded, epoetin alfa may be temporarily withheld until the hematocrit returns to the target range; epoetin alfa therapy may then be resumed using a lower dose (see Dosage). If polycythemia is of concern, phlebotomy may be indicated to decrease the hematocrit to within acceptable ranges. Supportive care should be provided for hypertensive or convulsive events that may be related to overdosing with epoetin alfa.

Dosage: Self-administration and Information to the Patient: In those situations in which the physician determines that a patient can safely and effectively self-administer epoetin alfa, the patient should be instructed as to the proper dosage and administration. The first few doses should be administered under supervision. Following the initial laboratory and clinical assessment, all patients, including those deemed capable of self-administration should be monitored for their response to epoetin alfa, their blood pressure and serum levels, as indicated in the Precautions section. Patients should be referred to the full Information for self-administration section. It is not a disclosure of all possible effects. Patients should be informed of the signs and symptoms of allergic drug reaction and advised of appropriate actions.

If home use is prescribed, the patient should be thoroughly instructed in the importance of proper disposal and cautioned against the reuse of needles, syringes, or drug product. A puncture-resistant container for the disposal of used syringes and needles should be available to the patient. The full container should be disposed of according to the directions provided by the physician.

CRF Patients: The recommended dose to initiate therapy of epoetin alfa is 50 to 100 IU/kg 3 times/week.

The dosage of epoetin alfa must be individualized to maintain the hematocrit within the suggested target range (30 to 36%). At the physician's discretion, the suggested target hematocrit range may be expanded to achieve maximal patient benefit.

Epoetin alfa may be given either as an i.v. or s.c. injection. When used i.v., epoetin alfa usually has been administered as a slow i.v. bolus 3 times/week. While the administration of epoetin alfa is independent of the dialysis procedure, epoetin alfa solution may be administered into the venous line at the end of the dialysis procedure to obviate the need for additional venous access. Generally the s.c. maintenance dose is approximately 20 to 35% lower than the i.v. maintenance dose. Following the change from i.v. to s.c. route of administration the patient should be monitored carefully to ensure that the hematocrit response is appropriate.

During therapy, hematological parameters should be monitored regularly.

Virtually all patients will eventually require supplemental iron to increase or maintain transferrin saturation to levels that will adequately support epoetin alfa-stimulated erythropoiesis.

Table VI (on following page) provides general therapeutic guidelines.

In patients with chronic renal failure and clinically evident ischemic heart disease or congestive heart failure, maintenance hematocrit concentration should not exceed the upper limit of the target hematocrit.

Dose Adjustment: Following epoetin alfa therapy, a period of time is required for erythroid progenitors to mature and be

Table VI—Eprex

General Therapeutic Guidelines

Starting Dose	Reduce Dose When (Starting with 25 IU/kg/dose decrement)	Increase Dose If (Starting with 25 IU/kg/dose increment)	Maintenance Dose	Suggested Target Hct Range
50-100 IU/kg 3 times/week i.v. or s.c.	1) Hct approaches 36%, or 2) Hct increases >6 percentage points in any 4-week period.	Hct does not increase by 5-6 pecentage points after 8-12 weeks of therapy, and Hct is below target range.	Individually titrate.	30-36%

released into circulation resulting in an eventual increase in hematocrit. Additionally, red blood cell survival time affects hematocrit and may vary due to uremia. As a result, the time required to elicit a clinically significant change in hematocrit (increase or decrease) following any dose adjustment may be 2 to 6 weeks.

Dose adjustment should not be made more frequently than once a month, unless clinically indicated. After any dose adjustment, the hematocrit should be determined weekly for at least 2 to 6 weeks (see Precautions, CRF Patients, Laboratory Monitoring).

If the hematocrit is increasing and approaching 36%, the dose should be decreased by approximately 25 IU/kg 3 times/week to maintain the suggested target hematocrit range. If the reduced dose does not stop the rise in hematocrit, and it exceeds 36%, doses should be temporarily withheld until the hematocrit begins to decrease, at which point therapy should be re-initiated at a lower dose.

At any time, if the hematocrit increases by more than 6 percentage points in a 4-week period, the dose should be immediately decreased. After the dose reduction, the hematocrit should be monitored weekly for 2 to 6 weeks, and further dose adjustments should be made (see Maintenance Dose).

If a hematocrit increase of 5 to 6 percentage points is not achieved after an 8-week period and iron stores are adequate (see Delayed or Diminished Response in this section), the dose of epoetin alfa may be increased in increments of 25 IU/kg 3 times/week. Further increases of 25 IU/kg 3 times/week may be added at 4- to 6-week intervals until the desired response is attained.

Maintenance Dose: The maintenance dose must be individualized for each chronic renal failure patient.

If the hematocrit remains below, or falls below, the target range, iron stores should be re-evaluated. If the transferrin saturation is less than 20%, supplemental iron should be administered. If the transferrin saturation is greater than 20%, the dose of epoetin alfa may be increased by 25 IU/kg 3 times/week. Such dose increases should not be made more frequently than once a month, unless clinically indicated, as the response time of the hematocrit to a dose increase can be 2 to 6 weeks. Hematocrit should be measured for 2 to 6 weeks following dose increases.

Delayed or Diminished Response: Over 95% of patients with chronic renal failure responded with clinically significant increases in hematocrit, virtually all patients were transfusion-independent within approximately 2 months of initiation of epoetin alfa therapy.

If a patient fails to respond or maintain a response, other etiologies should be considered and evaluated as clinically indicated (see Precautions).

Zidovudine-treated/HIV-infected Patients: Prior to beginning epoetin alfa therapy, it is recommended that the endogenous serum erythropoietin level be determined (prior to transfusion). Available evidence suggests that patients receiving zidovudine with levels >500 mU/mL are unlikely to respond to therapy with epoetin alfa unless the dose of zidovudine is reduced or temporarily stopped.

Starting Dose: For patients with serum erythropoietin levels ≤500 mU/mL, the recommended starting dose of epoetin alfa is 100 IU/kg as an i.v. or s.c. injection 3 times weekly for 8 weeks.

Increase Dose: During the dose adjustment phase of therapy, the hematocrit should be monitored weekly. If the response is not satisfactory in terms of reducing transfusion requirements or increasing hematocrit after 8 weeks of therapy, the dose of epoetin alfa can be increased by 50 to 100 IU/kg 3 times/week. Response should be evaluated every 4 to 8 weeks thereafter and the dose adjusted accordingly by 50 to 100 IU/kg increments 3 times/week. If patients have not responded satisfactorily to an epoetin alfa dose of 300 IU/kg 3 times/week up to month 12 of therapy, further continuation of treatment is not warranted as it is unlikely that they will respond to higher doses of epoetin alfa.

Maintenance Dose: After attainment of the desired response (i.e., reduced transfusion requirements or increased hematocrit), the dose of epoetin alfa should be titrated to maintain the response based on factors such as variations in zidovudine dose and the presence of intercurrent infectious or inflammatory episodes. If the hematocrit exceeds 40%, the dose should be discontinued until the hematocrit drops to 36%. Resume dosing at 25% less than the previous dose and titrate the dose to maintain the desired hematocrit.

Target Hematocrit Range: Maximum benefit from epoetin alfa therapy appears to occur when the hematocrit is maintained in the range of 36 to 40%; however, the target hematocrit for zidovudine-treated/HIV-infected patients must be determined on an individual basis.

Cancer Patients: Epoetin alfa is recommended for the treatment of patients with symptomatic anemia.

Starting Dose: The initial epoetin alfa dose for the treatment of anemia is 150 IU/kg s.c. 3 times/week.

Iron Evaluation: Iron status should be evaluated for all patients prior to and during treatment and iron supplementation should be administered if necessary. Other causes of anemia should also be excluded before instituting therapy with epoetin alfa.

Dose Adjustment: If after 4 weeks of treatment, either the hemoglobin increase is ≥10 g/L, or the reticulocyte count increase is ≥40 000 cells/μL above baseline, continue dosing until target hemoglobin is achieved.

If the response is not satisfactory, (i.e., if after 4 weeks of treatment, the hemoglobin increases by <10 g/L and the increase in reticulocyte count is <40 000 cells/μL above baseline), the dose of epoetin alfa should be increased to 300 IU/kg for 4 weeks.

If after 4 weeks of therapy at 300 IU/kg, the hemoglobin increase is <10 g/L and the reticulocyte count increase is <40 000 cells/μL above baseline, response is unlikely and treatment should be discontinued.

The recommended epoetin alfa dosing regimen is described in Figure I.

Figure I—Eprex

Dosing Regimen—Cancer Patients

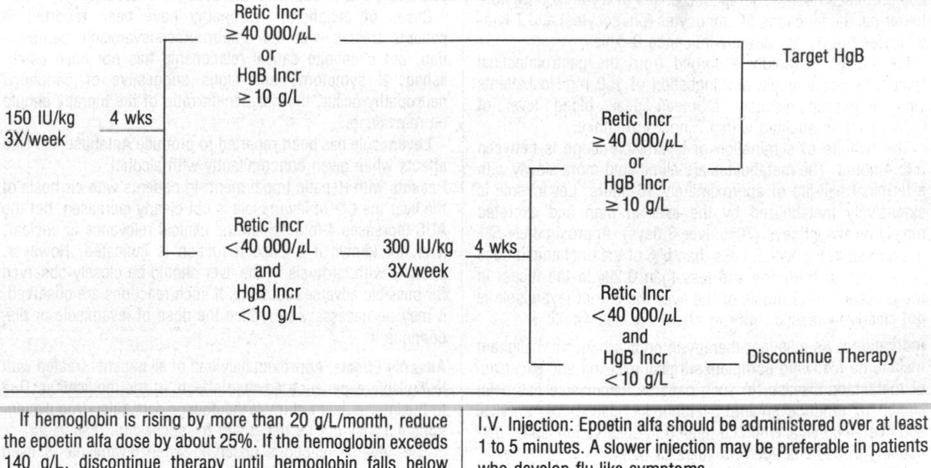

If hemoglobin is rising by more than 20 g/L/month, reduce the epoetin alfa dose by about 25%. If the hemoglobin exceeds 140 g/L, discontinue therapy until hemoglobin falls below 120 g/L and then reinstitute epoetin alfa at a dose 25% below the previous dose.

The need to continue epoetin alfa therapy should be re-evaluated periodically, e.g., after completion of chemotherapy.

Endogenous Serum Erythropoietin Levels: In patients not receiving chemotherapy, available evidence suggests that the hemoglobin response in patients treated with epoetin alfa is significantly greater than the corresponding response in placebo-treated patients when the endogenous serum erythropoietin level is ≤174 mU/mL.

In patients being treated with cyclic chemotherapy, there does not appear to be a significant relationship between the endogenous serum erythropoietin level and response to epoetin alfa therapy. Use of epoetin alfa is not recommended in patients with grossly elevated serum erythropoietin levels (e.g., >200 mU/mL).

Surgery Patients: Use of Epoetin Alfa to Reduce Allogeneic Blood Exposure: The recommended dose regimen is 600 IU/kg s.c. given once weekly for 3 weeks (Days -21, -14, and -7) prior to surgery and on the day of surgery.

If the period prior to surgery is less than 3 weeks, 300 IU/kg s.c. may be given as an alternative dosing regimen for 10 consecutive days prior to surgery, on the day of surgery, and for 4 consecutive days immediately thereafter.

All patients should receive adequate iron replacement. Iron replacement should be initiated no later than the beginning of treatment with epoetin alfa and should continue throughout the course of therapy.

Combined Use of Epoetin Alfa and ABD: Epoetin alfa should be administered twice weekly for 3 weeks prior to surgery if the presurgical predonation interval permits. At each patient visit, a unit of blood is collected and stored for autologous transfusion if the patient has an acceptable hematocrit or hemoglobin for predonation.

The recommended dosage regimen is 600 IU/kg i.v. twice weekly.

Iron status should be evaluated for all patients prior to treatment with epoetin alfa. Iron deficiency, if present, should be corrected. To maintain erythropoiesis, adequate iron supplementation is required beginning as soon as possible and should continue throughout the course of therapy. In anemic patients, the cause of anemia should be explored before starting therapy with epoetin alfa.

Method of Administration: **Do not shake.** Shaking may denature the glycoprotein, rendering it biologically inactive.

Parenteral drug products should be inspected visually for particulate matter and discoloration prior to administration. Do not use any vials or prefilled syringes exhibiting particulate matter or discoloration.

Using aseptic techniques, attach a sterile needle to a sterile syringe. Remove the flip top from the vial containing epoetin alfa, and wipe the septum with a disinfectant. Insert the needle into the vial, and withdraw into the syringe an appropriate volume of solution.

S.C. Injection: The maximum volume per injection site should be 1 mL. In case of larger volumes, more than 1 injection site should be used. The injections should be given in the limbs or the anterior abdominal wall. The patient should always alternate the site for each injection.

I.V. Injection: Epoetin alfa should be administered over at least 1 to 5 minutes. A slower injection may be preferable in patients who develop flu-like symptoms.

Multi-use Vial: Contains benzyl alcohol as a preservative and can be re-entered. The date of first entry into the vial should be recorded on the inside flap of the box. Discard 30 days after first entry.

Single-use Vial and Prefilled Syringe: Do not re-enter the vial. Contains no preservative. Discard unused portions.

Do not administer in conjunction with other drug solutions. The multi-use vial contains 0.9% benzyl alcohol which acts as a local anesthetic and may ameliorate s.c. injection site discomfort.

Eprex (cont'd)

The phosphate-buffered formulation has been found to mitigate injection site discomfort.

Information for the Patient: See Blue Section—Information for the Patient "Eprex".

Supplied: Single-use Vials: Phosphate-buffered: Each mL of sterile solution contains: epoetin alfa 4 000 IU. Nonmedicinal ingredients: albumin (human), citric acid, sodium chloride, sodium citrate and water for injection.

Multi-use Vials: Each mL of sterile citrate-buffered solution contains: epoetin alfa 20 000 IU. Nonmedicinal ingredients: albumin (human), benzyl alcohol, citric acid, sodium chloride, sodium citrate and water for injection.

Single-use Syringes: Each mL of sterile phosphate-buffered solution contains: epoetin alfa 2 000, 3 000, 4 000 or 10 000 IU. Nonmedicinal ingredients: albumin (human), sodium chloride, sodium phosphate dibasic dihydrate, sodium phosphate monobasic dihydrate and water for injection. Syringes fill sizes: 1 000 IU/0.5 mL, 2 000 IU/0.5 mL, 3 000 IU /0.3 mL, 4 000 IU/0.4 mL and 10 000 IU/1.0 mL.

Store at 2 to 8°C. **Do not freeze or shake.** Protect from exposure to light. Multi-use vials should be discarded 30 days after first entry.

(Shown in Product Recognition Section)

Reviewed 1999

EQUANIL® Pr
Wyeth-Ayerst

Meprobamate
Antianxiety Agent

Supplied: Each white tablet, imprinted with "Equanil 400" on one face and scored on the other, contains: meprobamate 400 mg. Nonmedicinal ingredients: lactose hydrous, methylcellulose, polacrilin potassium, stearic acid and syloid. Energy: 1.42 kJ (0.34 kcal). Gluten- and tartrazine-free. Bottles of 50.

ERGAMISOL® Pr
Janssen-Ortho

Levamisole HCl
Immunomodulator

Pharmacology: Levamisole is capable of restoring impaired immune responses preferentially of the cell mediated type in compromised hosts. Therapeutic doses of levamisole restore to normal the functions of monocytes (phagocytes) and T lymphocytes but do not directly influence B cells.

Levamisole is rapidly absorbed from the gastrointestinal tract following a single oral ingestion of 150 mg. In patients with neoplastic disease, a mean peak blood level of 0.86 µg/mL is attained within 2 hours of intake.

The half-life of elimination of levamisole alone is between 3 to 4 hours. The metabolites are eliminated more slowly with a terminal half-life of approximately 16 hours. Levamisole is extensively metabolized by the liver in man and excreted mainly by the kidneys (70% over 3 days). Approximately 5% is excreted in the feces. Less than 5% of the unchanged dose is excreted in the urine and less than 0.2% in the feces. In the presence of cirrhosis of the liver the C^{max} of levamisole is not clearly increased, but the AUC increases 4-fold.

Indications: As adjuvant therapy in poor prognosis malignant melanoma following complete surgical excision and exclusion of metastatic disease. In such patients, levamisole has been shown to produce an improvement in relapse-free survival and overall survival when compared to observation alone, particularly in patients aged 55 years or older.

Also indicated as adjuvant therapy, in combination with 5-fluorouracil, in patients with completely resected Dukes' stage C colon cancer. Evidence of metastatic disease must be excluded before initiating therapy. In patients with Dukes' stage C carcinoma of the colon, a regimen of levamisole plus 5-fluorouracil has been shown to produce significant reductions in both cancer recurrence and overall death rate.

Children: Levamisole is recommended for use in high-dose steroid-dependent nephrotic syndrome in children: as adjuvant therapy following relapse on corticosteroids such as prednisone; or as an alternative to the use of an alkylating agent or cyclosporin. In these patients, levamisole has been shown to induce a significant number of complete remissions, reduce the steroid requirements necessary to induce such a remission and decrease the incidence of relapse of the disease.

Contraindications: Known hypersensitivity to the drug or its excipients.

Warnings: Levamisole has been associated with reversible leukopenia and agranulocytosis; therefore, it is essential that appropriate hematological monitoring be done routinely during therapy with levamisole.

Patients should be instructed to report immediately any sudden change in their state of health which may be manifested by influenza-like symptoms (fever, lassitude, sore throat, shivering or sweating) so that appropriate hematological testing can be done.

Leukopenia (total WBC below 3 000/mm³) is not necessarily a sign of impending agranulocytosis; recovery is possible without withdrawal of the drug. However, with a reduced neutrophil count (less than 20% of the total white blood cell count) levamisole should be discontinued permanently. (Agranulocytosis is attributed to antibody formation and absorption of immune complexes. This process initiates complement activation and cell lysis; levamisole itself does not directly damage granulopoiesis.)

The HLA genotype B27 predisposes to the development of agranulocytosis, particularly in females with concomitant rheumatoid arthritis. The onset is frequently sudden and may be asymptomatic. Following discontinuation of levamisole, neutrophil counts normalize within a week to 10 days. There is no evidence that steroids or WBC transfusions are of significant therapeutic value; prophylaxis of infection during the acute phase of agranulocytosis should be an important consideration.

Precautions: Children (age 1 to 15 years) with Nephrotic Syndrome: It is essential that hematological monitoring be done routinely during therapy with levamisole. In the presence of a reduced neutrophil count (<2 000/mm³) or in the presence of other evidence of agranulocytosis levamisole should be discontinued permanently.

Drug Interactions: In patients with malignant melanoma and colonic carcinoma the therapeutic effect of levamisole may be antagonized by concomitant administration of corticosteroids.

Additional caution is necessary when levamisole is used in combination with other drugs potentially affecting hemopoiesis.

Because of reports of prolongation of prothrombin time beyond the therapeutic range in patients taking concurrent levamisole and coumarin, it is suggested that the prothrombin time be monitored carefully, and the dose of coumarin adjusted accordingly, in patients taking both drugs.

Concomitant administration of phenytoin and levamisole plus fluorouracil has led to increased plasma levels of phenytoin. The physician is advised to monitor plasma levels of phenytoin and to decrease the dose if necessary.

Cases of peripheral neuropathy have been reported in patients treated with the 5-fluorouracil-levamisole combination, but a definite causal relationship has not been established. If symptoms and signs suggestive of peripheral neuropathy occur, the risk-benefit ratio of the therapy should be re-evaluated.

Levamisole has been reported to produce Antabuse-like side effects when given concomitantly with alcohol.

Patients with Hepatic Impairment: In patients with cirrhosis of the liver the C^{max} of levamisole is not clearly increased, but the AUC increases 4-fold. Since the clinical relevance is unclear, it is not known if a dose reduction is indicated. However, patients with cirrhosis of the liver should be closely observed for possible adverse reactions. If such reactions are observed, it may be necessary to reduce the dose of levamisole or discontinue it.

Adverse Effects: Approximately half of all patients treated with levamisole experience adverse effects of the medication. Due to the intermittent nature of the dosage schedule, drug discontinuation may not be necessary for successful resolution.

The adverse reactions observed when levamisole is used in combination with 5-fluorouracil are consistent with those anticipated if 5-fluorouracil is given alone in a comparable dose and schedule. Cases of peripheral neuropathy have been reported in patients treated with the 5-fluorouracil-levamisole combination, but a causal relationship has not been established.

Mild and asymptomatic abnormalities (e.g., a doubling) in the results of liver-function tests (transaminase, alkaline phosphatase and/or bilirubinemia) have been reported more frequently with the 5-fluorouracil plus levamisole combination, than with levamisole alone, and with untreated controls (11.2% vs 4.0% and 2.8%, respectively). In some instances hepatosteatosis was found. These liver abnormalities were reversible upon discontinuation.

The incidence of adverse reactions for levamisole alone in malignant melanoma patients and for levamisole plus 5-fluorouracil in colonic cancer patients is presented in Table I.

An encephalopathy-like syndrome has been reported. Worldwide postmarketing experience with the combination therapy of levamisole and fluorouracil has also included several reports of neurological changes associated with demyelination. The onset of symptoms and clinical presentation in these cases are quite varied. Symptoms may include: memory loss, confusion, paresthesia, lethargy, muscle weakness, speech disturbances, coma and seizures. Cerebrospinal fluid examination may show a mild pleiocytosis, and CT and MRI scans often disclose lesions in the white matter suggestive of demyelination. This picture is known in the literature as MILE (multifocal inflammatory leukoencephalopathy). The occurrence of this syndrome necessitates the discontinuation of treatment. As a rule, the condition is at least partially reversible upon discontinuation and treatment with a corticosteroid.

In some patients an increase in serum triglyceride levels, sometimes associated with a cholesterol rise, may occur during levamisole treatment. These increases are reversible after cessation of levamisole therapy. Occasional cases of acute pancreatitis have been reported, not uncommonly in association with hypertriglyceridemia.

Few adverse experiences have been reported with levamisole during the treatment of frequently relapsing steroid-responsive nephrotic syndrome in children. The most common side effects are mild and include: skin rash, vomiting, nausea, transient hematuria and decreased neutrophil levels. However, a few cases of neutropenia (neutrophil count <2 000/mm³) have also been observed.

In addition, rare cases of fixed drug eruption have also been observed during levamisole therapy.

Table I—Ergamisol

Incidence of Adverse Reactions in Patients Treated with Levamisole for Malignant Melanoma or Colonic Cancer

	Incidence (%)		
	Levamisol	Levamisol Plus 5-FU	
		Colonic Cancer	
Adverse Reactions	**Melanoma**	**Induction**	**Maintenance**
Gastrointestinal			
Nausea	24	37	56
Vomiting	6	8	17
Diarrhea		25	47
Taste Change	10	2	7
Anorexia	1		
Mucocutaneous			
Stomatitis	1	27	28
Dermatitis	4	8	22
Severe		1	1
Alopecia		4	22
Conjunctivitis		1	7
Hyperpigmentation			2
Hematological			
Leukopenia	10		
2 000 to 4 000/mm³		38	38
less than 2 000/mm³		7	2
Thrombocytopenia			
50 000 to 130 000/mm³		4	18
less than 50 000/mm³		2	4
Agranulocytosis	1.4		
Musculoskeletal			
Arthralgia/Myalgia	8	2	4
Neurologic			
Visual Change			2
Smell Change		1	2
Headache		1	5
Dizziness/Vertigo		1	4
Ataxia			3
Anxiety/Irritability		2	2
Depression		1	2
Insomnia			1
Somnolence			1
Impaired Thinking		1	2
Other			
Fatigue/Weakness		5	11
Fever	8		
Impaired Liver Function		1	2

Overdose: Symptoms: According to animal data, levamisole may have minor anticholinesterase activity, and, on i.v. administration, some positive inotropic and chronotropic cardiac effects. Levamisole exhibits convulsant properties at high doses.

A fatality occurred in a 3-year-old child who ingested 15 mg/kg of levamisole. However, a 7-year-old boy survived a 10 mg/kg overdose, and an 8-year-old girl tolerated a single 1 250 mg dose rather well apart from vomiting. Five adults (ages 13 to 28 years) who took an overdose of 12 to 26 mg/kg survived, but one who ingested 32 mg/kg died.

Adverse experiences reported in acute adult high dose trials (600 mg/day and higher) included: nausea, lethargy, cramps, diarrhea, headache, emesis, dizziness, and confusion.

Treatment: In cases of overdosage, gastric lavage with monitoring of vital signs and general supportive measures are recommended. When symptoms of anticholinesterase activity are present, the use of atropine may be considered.

Dosage: Malignant Melanoma: Levamisole should be administered at a dose of 2.5 mg/kg given as a single daily dose, preferably at night, on 2 consecutive days every week. Higher doses are not recommended as they are associated with increased toxicity and have not been shown to provide any additional therapeutic benefit.

Dukes' Stage C Carcinoma of the Colon: Levamisole plus 5-fluorouracil should be administered only by or under the supervision of qualified physicians, experienced in cancer chemotherapy, and well versed in the use of potent antimetabolites.

Therapy with levamisole may be initiated as soon after resection as patients are able to tolerate oral medication, but no sooner than 1 week and no later than 5 weeks after surgery.

Levamisole should be administered orally at a dose of 50 mg t.i.d., for 3 consecutive days, every 2 weeks. This therapy should be continued for at least 1 year.

Administration of 5-fluorouracil should be timed to begin concomitantly with the second 3-day course of levamisole. The initial dosage of 5-fluorouracil should be 450 mg/m^2/day, given i.v., for 5 consecutive days.

Four weeks following the initial 5-day course of 5-fluorouracil, patients should begin maintenance therapy on a once weekly basis with an i.v. injection of 5-fluorouracil at a dose of 450 mg/m^2. Treatment should continue for as long as levamisole is administered.

If the patient experiences stomatitis, diarrhea or leukopenia, the weekly 5-fluorouracil administrations should be deferred until these side effects have subsided. If these side effects are moderate to severe in intensity, 5-fluorouracil should be resumed with a 20% reduction in the dose.

Children (age 1 to 15 years) with Frequently Relapsing Steroid-responsive Nephrotic Syndrome: Levamisole should be administered as a single dose of 2.5 mg/kg/day at least twice/week or on alternate days. Hematological monitoring should be done routinely (see Precautions and Warnings).

Supplied: Each white, film-coated biconvex tablet, with L_{50} inscription on one side and JANSSEN on the other side, contains: levamisole 50 mg as levamisole HCl. Nonmedicinal ingredients: colloidal silicon dioxide, hydrogenated vegetable oil, hydroxypropyl methylcellulose, microcrystalline cellulose, polyethylene glycol, polysorbate and talc. Lactose: 7 mg. Bisulfite-, gluten- and tartrazine-free. Blister packages of 36. Store at 15 to 30°C and protect from moisture and light.

Reviewed 1999

ERGOCALCIFEROL
General Monograph, CPhA

see VITAMIN D

ERGODRYL® Ⓟ
Parke-Davis

Caffeine Citrate—Diphenhydramine HCl—Ergotamine Tartrate

Migraine Therapy

Supplied: Each No. 3, hard, pink capsule with green top contains: ergotamine tartrate 1 mg, caffeine citrate 100 mg, and diphenhydramine HCl 25 mg. Nonmedicinal ingredients: citric acid, hydrogenated vegetable oil, lactose and talc. Energy: 3.0 kJ (0.72 kcal). Gluten-, paraben-, sodium-, sulfite- and tartrazine-free. Bottles of 100.

(Shown in Product Recognition Section)

ERGOMAR® Ⓟ
Rhône-Poulenc Rorer

Ergotamine Tartrate

Migraine Therapy

Pharmacology: The pharmacological properties of ergotamine are extremely complex; some of its actions are unrelated to each other, and even mutually antagonistic. Ergotamine: Has partial agonist and/or antagonist activity against tryptaminergic, dopaminergic and alpha adrenergic receptors depending upon their site; is a highly active uterine stimulant; it causes constriction of peripheral and cranial blood vessels and produces depression of central vasomotor centres. The pain of a migraine attack is believed to be due to greatly increased amplitude of pulsations in the cranial arteries, especially the meningeal branches of the external carotid artery. Ergotamine reduces extracranial blood flow, causes a decline in the amplitude of pulsation in the cranial arteries, and decreases hyperperfusion in the territory of the basilar artery. It does not reduce cerebral hemispheric blood flow. Long-term usage has established the fact that ergotamine tartrate is effective in controlling up to 70% of acute migraine attacks. Ergotamine produces constriction of both arteries and veins. In doses used in the treatment of vascular headaches, ergotamine usually produces only small increases in blood pressure but it does increase peripheral resistance and decreased blood flow in various organs. Small doses of the drug increase the force and frequency of uterine contraction; larger doses also increase the resting tone of the uterine muscle. The gravid uterus is particularly sensitive to these effects of ergotamine. Although specific teratogenic effects attributable to ergotamine have not been found, the fetus may suffer if ergotamine is given during pregnancy. Retarded fetal growth and an increased incidence of intrauterine death and resorption have been seen in animals. These are thought to result from ergotamine induced increases in uterine motility and vasoconstriction in the placental vascular bed.

Indications: Acute migraine and related types of vascular headache.

Contraindications: In peripheral vascular disease (thromboangiitis obliterans, luetic arteritis, severe arteriosclerosis, thrombophlebitis, Raynaud's disease), coronary heart disease, hypertension, angina pectoris, cardiac arrhythmias, heart blocks, impaired hepatic or renal function, severe pruritus, sepsis, peptic ulcer, infectious states, malnutrition. It is also contraindicated in patients who are hypersensitive to any of its components.

Pregnancy and *Lactation:* Ergotamine is contraindicated in women who are pregnant, who may become pregnant or who are breast-feeding.

Warnings: Undesirable reactions to ergotamine may best be prevented by avoidance of excessive dosage and careful supervision of the patient so that they will not use the drug in larger dosage, more frequently, or for a longer time than prescribed by the physician.

Because of the possible cumulative effects of ergotamine tartrate, the dosage must not exceed 3 tablets in any 24 hour period; and, not more than 5 tablets in 1 week. Patients should be cautioned to use the minimal effective dose to control their symptoms.

Individual sensitivity to the vascular effects of ergotamine varies considerably and symptoms of arterial insufficiency have been reported after as little as 2 mg taken orally. This is a rare occurrence, but if such symptoms develop the use of ergotamine should be discontinued. Failure to recognise the early symptoms of arterial insufficiency has on rare occasions led to irreversible vascular change with therapeutic doses of ergotamine.

Precautions: Ergotamine is not recommended as a prophylactic agent in migraine. Prolonged use should be avoided because of risk of potential serious adverse effects.

Patients who have prolonged specific neurological phenomena (visual, sensory, motor) require great caution and careful follow-up.

Like all drugs, ergotamine should be kept out of reach of children.

Children: The safety and efficacy of ergotamine in children has not been established. It is not recommended for use in children.

Pregnancy: Ergotamine may cause fetal harm when administered to a pregnant woman by virtue of its powerful uterine stimulant actions. It is contraindicated in women who are, or may become pregnant.

Lactation: Ergotamine is secreted into human milk. It can reach the breast-fed infant and exert pharmacological effects, therefore ergotamine is contraindicated in nursing women.

Drug Dependence: Patients who take ergotamine for extended periods of time may become dependent upon it and require progressively increasing doses for relief of vascular headaches or to prevent the increasing dysphoric effects which may follow withdrawal of the drug.

Drug Interactions: The concomitant use of ergotamine alkaloids and beta-blocking agents increases the risks of peripheral vasoconstriction. Among patients treated concomitantly with ergotamine and propranolol a few cases of vasospastic reactions have been reported.

There is some evidence that the concomitant use of triacetyloleandomycin (TAO/Troleandomycin), erythromycin or josamycin and ergotamine can result in an elevated concentration of ergotamine in the plasma, thereby increasing the risk of adverse effects.

Adverse Effects: The following adverse reactions were reported after therapeutic doses of ergotamine tartrate: nausea, vomiting, diarrhea, polydipsia, tingling of the hands and feet, muscle pains and cramps, thrombophlebitis, vascular spasm, transient tachycardia or bradycardia, rare cases of gangrene, sleepiness, exhaustion, ECG changes, precordial pain, angina and myocardial infarction.

Overdose: Symptoms: Some cases of ergotamine poisoning have been reported in patients who have taken less than 5 mg of the drug. Usually, however, toxicity is seen in doses of ergotamine tartrate in excess of about 15 mg in 24 hours or 40 mg in a few days.

The symptoms of ergotamine poisoning include cold, pale and numb extremities, muscle pain both with and without activity, decreased or even obliterated peripheral pulses and gangrene of the fingers and toes. Other symptoms of ergotism may occur including anginal pain, tachycardia, bradycardia, hypotension or hypertension, headache, nausea, vomiting, diarrhea, itching, formication, anal burning, weakness, miosis, confusion, depression, drowsiness and possible unconsciousness, increase in muscle tone with pain and trismus, and rarely convulsions and hemiplegia. Respiratory depression can also occur.

Overdosage is particularly likely to occur in patients with sepsis or impaired renal or hepatic function. Patients with peripheral vascular disease are specially at risk of developing peripheral ischemia following treatment with ergotamine.

Treatment: Includes withdrawal and elimination of the offending drug and symptomatic therapy. 1) Emesis: If the patient is conscious, induce vomiting with syrup of ipecac (15 to 30 mL). 2) Perform gastric lavage followed by the administration of activated charcoal if the pharyngeal and laryngeal reflexes are present and if less than 4 hours have elapsed since ingestion. Do not attempt gastric lavage on an unconscious patient unless cuffed endotracheal intubation has been performed to prevent aspiration and pulmonary complications. 3) Catharsis: Following gastric lavage, a saline cathartic (sodium or magnesium sulfate 30 g in 250 mL of water) may be introduced and left in the stomach. 4) Diuresis: There is no evidence that forced diuresis accelerates elimination of ergotamine.

Maintenance of adequate pulmonary ventilation: Perform pharyngeal and tracheal suction to remove mucous secretions. Judicious administration of oxygen is also indicated. However, oxygen without assisted respiration must be used with caution, as its use in hypoventilation-hypoxia may result in further respiratory depression and hypercapnia. In more critical cases, endotracheal intubation and tracheostomy, with or without assisted respiration, may be necessary.

Correction of hypotension: Hypertension may occur in the early stages of acute intoxication. However, in severe cases this is usually followed by hypotension. 1) Mild to moderate cases: Most cases of hypotension can be managed with simple measures such as placing the patient in the Trendelenburg position, or administering i.v. fluids, e.g., physiological saline. 2) Severe cases: If satisfactory relief of hypotension cannot be achieved using the above measures, vasopressors should be considered.

Control of convulsions: Convulsions are always a possibility in acute ergotamine intoxication, and may be controlled with diazepam.

Treatment of peripheral vasospasm: Marked peripheral vasospasm with coldness and poor or absent pulses in the hands and feet are commonly associated with acute ergotamine poisoning. Warmth, but not heat, and protection must be

Ergomar (cont'd)

afforded the ischemic limbs. Vasodilators, such as sodium nitroprusside or tolazoline, may be used with benefit.
General supportive measures for unconscious patients: 1) Good nursing care is of prime importance and should include regular observation and accurate recording of the vital signs and depth of coma, maintenance of the airway, frequent turning and other routine measures usually adopted with unconscious patients. 2) Careful supervision and recording of fluid intake and output is essential. 3) Prophylactic anticoagulant therapy in the patient with evidence of ischemia should be considered.

Dosage: Adults: Initiate therapy as soon as possible after the first symptoms of the attack are noted, since success is proportional to rapidity of treatment, and lower dosages will be effective. At the first sign of an attack, or to relieve the symptoms of the full blown attack, place 1 tablet beneath the tongue. An additional tablet may be taken at half-hourly intervals thereafter, if necessary; but dosage must not exceed 6 mg (3 tablets) in any 24-hour period. Limit dosage to not more than 10 mg (5 tablets) in any 1 week.

Information for the Patient: See Blue Section—Information for the Patient "Ergomar".

Supplied: Each light green sublingual tablet contains: ergotamine tartrate USP 2 mg. Nonmedicinal ingredients: cornstarch, D&C Yellow No. 10, FD&C Blue No. 1, lactose, magnesium stearate, peppermint oil and sodium cyclamate. Tartrazine-free. Packages of 12, sealed in unit dose foil strip. Protect from light and heat.

(Shown in Product Recognition Section)

ERGOMETRINE ℞
General Monograph, CPhA

see ERGONOVINE MALEATE

ERGONOVINE MALEATE ℞
General Monograph, CPhA

Ergometrine Maleate

Oxytocic

> This monograph has been compiled by CPhA. It may contain information different from that approved by Therapeutic Products Programme, Health Canada, and the pharmaceutical manufacturers' approval has not been requested.

Pharmacology: Ergonovine directly stimulates contractions of uterine and vascular smooth muscle. The effect on the uterus is more pronounced than that of most other ergot alkaloids, the difference being more marked on the puerperal uterus than on the normal nonpregnant uterus. The drug has only slight α-adrenergic blocking activity and its vasoconstrictor effects are less than those of ergotamine. Ergonovine's main action is the production of rhythmic contractions, usually followed by periods of relaxation. Within 6 to 15 minutes, oral ergonovine maleate produces a firm tetanic contraction of the postpartum uterus which, in the course of about 90 minutes, gradually changes to a series of clonic contractions that persist for another 90 minutes or more. Parenteral administration causes uterine contractions to begin more rapidly, in 2 or 3 minutes if given i.m. or 1 minute or less if given i.v.
Ergonovine also produces vasoconstriction of coronary arteries and has been used by experienced cardiologists to diagnose coronary artery spasm in patients with variant angina and no major coronary obstruction.

Indications: Prevention or treatment of postpartum or postabortal hemorrhage due to uterine atony.

Contraindications: Previous idiosyncrasy or allergic reactions to ergot preparations; toxemia; hypertension; threatened spontaneous abortion; induction or augmentation of labor.

Precautions: Because nausea and vomiting may occur, ergonovine should be administered with care to patients under general anesthesia.
Ergonovine must be used with caution in patients with heart disease; coronary vasoconstriction may occur. Careful monitoring is required if ergonovine is used during cardiac catheterization to diagnose variant angina, as myocardial infarction and death have occurred.
Prolonged therapy may lead to gangrene and other signs of ergotism.
Drug Interactions: A significant increase in blood pressure may occur, especially when a regional anesthetic containing a vasopressor drug has been used. Avoid prolonged administration or concomitant use of other vasoconstrictors.
Pregnancy: Before ergonovine is administered, the possibility of twin pregnancy should be ruled out and the placenta delivered, to avoid captivation of the placenta.
Lactation: Ergonovine enters breast milk in such quantities that may produce ergotism in breast-fed infants. It is therefore contraindicated.
Note: Ergot preparations are frequently given as a single dose postpartum to control hemorrhage. A single dose of ergonovine should not prevent the mother from breast-feeding.

Adverse Effects: Because ergonovine maleate is usually indicated for a short duration, many of the side effects seen with the other ergot alkaloids do not occur.
CNS: headache, dizziness, vertigo, hallucinations.
Cardiovascular: palpitations, dyspnea, transient chest pain, bradycardia, hypertension that is generally due to an undiluted or too rapid i.v. administration.
Gastrointestinal: nausea and vomiting (usually more common with i.v. administration), diarrhea, abdominal pain.

Overdose: Symptoms: Acute overdose may cause chest pain, increase or decrease in heart rate or blood pressure, confusion, drowsiness, miosis, peripheral vasoconstriction, respiratory depression, seizures, nausea and vomiting, loss of consciousness, numbness and coldness of the extremities, tingling, hypercoagulability, gangrene of the fingers and toes.
Treatment: Empty stomach and follow with activated charcoal and a cathartic. Management consists of supportive measures and close supervision including monitoring of vital signs, electrolytes and ECG. Seizures should be treated with anticonvulsants. Heparin may be used to manage hypercoagulability. A vasodilator may be useful to counteract the peripheral vasoconstriction, with adjustment of dosage according to heart rate and blood pressure.

Dosage: The immediate postpartum dose of ergonovine maleate is 200 μg usually administered i.m. In emergency situations when excessive uterine bleeding has occurred, ergonovine may be administered i.v. over at least 1 minute. Severe uterine bleeding may require repeated parenteral doses; however, injections will rarely be required more often than every 2 to 4 hours, up to 5 doses. To minimize late postpartum bleeding, 200 or 400 μg may be given orally 2 to 4 times daily, every 6 to 12 hours, until the danger of uterine atony has passed, usually 48 hours.

Reviewed 1997

ERGONOVINE MALEATE ℞
Abbott

Oxytocic

Supplied: Each mL contains: ergonovine maleate 0.25 mg. Also contains maleic acid. Ampuls of 1 mL, boxes of 10.

ERGONOVINE MALEATE INJECTION ℞
Bioniche

Oxytocic

Supplied: Each mL of sterile solution contains: ergonovine maleate 0.25 mg and malic acid 5 mg. Ampuls of 1 mL, boxes of 10. Must be refrigerated (2 to 8°C). Protect from light.

ERYBID™ ℞
Abbott

Erythromycin

Antibiotic

Supplied: Each ovaloid, white, particle-coated, dispertab tablet contains: erythromycin base 500 mg. Nonmedicinal ingredients: cellulose microcrystalline, colloidal silicon dioxide, crospovidone, hydrogenated vegetable oil, hydroxypropyl cellulose, hydroxypropyl methylcellulose, polyethylene glycol 400, povidone, propylene glycol, stearic acid, talc powder, titanium dioxide, vanillin and wax. Alcohol-, gluten-, paraben-, sucrose-, sulfite- and tartrazine-free. Bottles of 100 and 250.

ERYC® ℞
Parke-Davis

Erythromycin

Antibiotic

Pharmacology: Erythromycin exerts its antibacterial action by binding with the 50S ribosomal subunit of the organism, inhibiting peptide bond formation and protein synthesis within the cell. The activity is bacteriostatic or bactericidal depending on concentration.

Indications: For the treatment of the following infections caused by susceptible strains of the designated microorganisms.
Upper Respiratory Tract Infections: Those of mild to moderate severity caused by S. pyogenes (group A beta hemolytic streptococci); S. pneumoniae (D. pneumoniae) and H. influenzae. Not all strains of H. influenzae are susceptible to erythromycin with usual therapeutic doses.
Lower Respiratory Tract Infections: Those of mild to moderate severity when caused by S. pyogenes (group A beta hemolytic streptococci); S. pneumoniae (D. pneumoniae) and M. pneumoniae (Eaton's agent).
Pertussis (Whooping Cough): Caused by B. pertussis. Erythromycin is effective in eliminating the organism from the nasopharynx of infected individuals, rendering them noninfectious. Clinical studies suggest that erythromycin may be helpful in the prophylaxis of pertussis in exposed susceptible individuals.
Diphtheria: As an adjunct to antitoxin in infections due to C. diphtheriae, to prevent establishment of carriers and to eradicate the organism in carriers.
Legionnaires' Disease: Caused by L. pneumophila. Controlled clinical efficacy studies have not been conducted. In vitro and limited preliminary clinical data suggest that erythromycin can be effective in the treatment of Legionnaires' disease.
Skin and Soft Tissue Infections: Those of mild to moderate severity when caused by S. pyogenes and S. aureus (resistance of staphylococci may emerge during treatment).
Erythrasma: In the treatment of infections due to C. minutissimum.
The treatment of acne vulgaris.
Sexually Transmitted Diseases: Primary Syphilis: Caused by T. pallidum. Erythromycin is an alternative choice of treatment for primary syphilis in patients allergic to the penicillins. Spinal fluid should be examined before treatment and as part of the follow-up after therapy.
Chlamydia Trachomatis Infection: The 1992 "Canadian Guidelines for the Treatment of Sexually Transmitted Diseases in Neonates, Children, Adolescents and Adults" recommends erythromycin for the treatment of the following infections when caused by Chlamydia trachomatis: In newborns and infants for conjunctivitis and pneumonia. Note: Topical therapy alone for conjunctivitis is **not** adequate. In pregnant women, nursing mothers, and in children under 9 years of age, for uncomplicated urethral, endocervical or rectal infection. In adolescents and adults, when tetracycline or doxycycline is contraindicated or not tolerated, for uncomplicated urethral, endocervical or rectal infection.
Specimens for bacteriologic culture should be obtained prior to therapy in order to isolate and identify the causative organisms and to determine their susceptibility to erythromycin. Therapy may be instituted before results of susceptibility studies are known; however, antibiotic treatment should be reevaluated when the results become available or if the clinical response is not adequate.
Prophylaxis (Alpha-hemolytic Streptococci): For prophylaxis against bacterial endocarditis in patients hypersensitive to penicillin who have congenital heart disease or rheumatic or other acquired valvular heart disease when they undergo dental procedures and surgical procedures of the upper respiratory tract.

Contraindications: In patients with known hypersensitivity to erythromycin or with infections caused by microorganisms that are resistant to the drug.
Concurrent therapy with astemizole, terfenadine or cisapride (see Precautions, Drug Interactions).

Warnings: Erythromycin should be administered with caution to any patient who has demonstrated some form of allergy to drugs. If an allergic reaction to erythromycin occurs, administration of the drug should be discontinued. Serious hypersensitivity reactions may require epinephrine, antihistamines or corticosteroids.
There have been reports of hepatic dysfunction, with or without jaundice, occurring in patients receiving erythromycin products, particularly erythromycin estolate. If findings suggestive of significant hepatic dysfunction occur, therapy should be discontinued.

Pseudomembranous colitis has been occasionally reported to occur in association with erythromycin therapy. Therefore, it is important to consider its diagnosis in patients who develop diarrhea during treatment with erythromycin. Mild cases of colitis may respond to drug discontinuation alone. Moderate to severe cases should be managed with fluid, electrolyte and protein supplementation as indicated. If the colitis is not relieved by discontinuation of erythromycin administration or when it is severe, consideration should be given to the administration of vancomycin or other suitable therapy. Other possible causes of the colitis should also be considered.

Precautions: Prolonged or repeated use of erythromycin may result in an overgrowth of nonsusceptible bacteria or fungi and organisms initially sensitive to erythromycin. If superinfection occurs, erythromycin should be discontinued and appropriate therapy instituted.

Since erythromycin is principally excreted by the liver, caution should be exercised when administering the drug to patients with impaired hepatic function.

Drug Interactions: Theophylline: The concomitant administration of erythromycin and high doses of theophylline may be associated with increased serum theophylline levels and possible theophylline toxicity. The dose of theophylline may require reduction while patients are receiving erythromycin.

Carbamazepine: Erythromycin administration in patients receiving carbamazepine has been reported to cause increased serum levels of carbamazepine with subsequent development of signs of carbamazepine toxicity.

Digoxin/Phenytoin: Concomitant administration of erythromycin and digoxin or phenytoin has been reported to result in elevated serum levels of these agents, leading to toxicity in some patients.

Oral Anticoagulants: There have been reports of increased prothrombin time when erythromycin and oral anticoagulants were used concomitantly.

Ergotamine: There are reports that ischemic reactions may occur when erythromycin is given concurrently with ergotamine-containing drugs.

Cyclosporin: A rise in plasma cyclosporin levels has been reported during concomitant administration of erythromycin.

Lincomycin/Clindamycin/Chloramphenicol: Erythromycin should be used with caution if administered concomitantly with lincomycin, clindamycin, or chloramphenicol. In vitro experiments have demonstrated that binding sites for erythromycin, lincomycin, clindamycin and chloramphenicol overlap and competitive inhibition may occur.

Triazolam: Erythromycin has been reported to decrease the clearance of triazolam and thus may increase the pharmacologic effect of triazolam.

Alfentanil: The concomitant use of erythromycin with alfentanil can significantly inhibit the clearance of alfentanil and may increase the risk of prolonged or delayed respiratory depression.

Terfenadine: Terfenadine undergoes metabolism in the liver by a specific cytochrome P450 isoenzyme. This metabolic pathway may be impaired in patients who are taking erythromycin, an inhibitor of this isoenzyme. Interference with this enzyme can lead to elevated terfenadine plasma levels which may be associated with QT prolongation, and increased risk of ventricular tachyarrhythmias (such as torsades de pointes, ventricular tachycardia, and ventricular fibrillation) (see Contraindications).

Astemizole: Concomitant administration of astemizole with erythromycin is contraindicated because erythromycin is known to impair the Cytochrome P450 enzyme system which also influences astemizole metabolism. There have been two reports to date of syncope with torsades de pointes requiring hospitalization in patients taking astemizole with erythromycin. In each case the QT intervals were prolonged beyond 650 milliseconds at the time of the event; one patient also received ketoconazole and the other patient also had hypokalemia (see Contraindications).

Lovastatin: Patients receiving concomitant lovastatin and erythromycin should be carefully monitored; cases of rhabdomyolysis have been reported in seriously ill patients.

Cisapride: Rare cases of serious cardiovascular adverse events, including death, cardiac arrest, torsades de pointes, and other ventricular arrhythmias have been observed in patients taking cisapride concomitantly with macrolide antibiotics including erythromycin (see Contraindications).

The use of erythromycin in patients taking concurrent drugs which are metabolized by P450 (3A4) system may be associated with elevations in serum levels of these other drugs. There have been reports of interactions of erythromycin with cyclosporine, tacrolimus, hexobarbital and phenytoin. Serum concentrations of drug metabolized by the cytochrome P450 system should be monitored closely in patients concurrently receiving erythromycin.

Pregnancy: The safety of erythromycin for use during pregnancy has not been established. Erythromycin crosses the placental barrier.

Lactation: The safety of erythromycin for use during breast-feeding has not been established. Erythromycin is excreted in breast milk.

Children: The safety of erythromycin for use in neonates has not been established.

Information for the Patient: Eryc 250 and 333 mg capsules are not recommended for sprinkling, since the capsules are very full and some of the medication may be lost through spillage. If, however, the capsule is to be opened, care must be taken to open the capsule over food so as not to lose any of the pellets.

The pellets can be sprinkled on a small amount of pleasant tasting semi-solid foods such as applesauce, fruit jellies, ice cream, etc.

Hold the capsule with the clear end down. Gently twist off the cap to open. Sprinkle the **entire** contents of the capsule on a spoonful of applesauce, fruit jellies or ice cream, etc. The pellets should not be chewed or crushed. Patient should swallow the spoonful of applesauce, fruit jellies or ice cream. Patient should drink some water to make sure all the pellets are swallowed. If the pellets are accidentally spilled, start over with a new capsule.

Adverse Effects: Gastrointestinal: abdominal cramping and discomfort. Nausea, vomiting and diarrhea are also observed, but less frequently. Pseudomembranous colitis has been occasionally reported to occur in association with erythromycin therapy (see Warnings).

Pancreatitis: Recently there has been a report of a case of erythromycin-induced pancreatitis following erythromycin overdose.

Allergic Reactions: Urticaria, mild skin eruptions and anaphylaxis have been reported.

Hepatotoxicity: There have been reports of hepatic dysfunction, with or without jaundice, occurring in patients receiving erythromycin products.

Miscellaneous: During prolonged or repeated therapy, there is a possibility of overgrowth of nonsusceptible bacteria or fungi and organisms initially sensitive to erythromycin (e.g., S. aureus, H. influenzae). If such infections occur, erythromycin should be discontinued and appropriate therapy instituted.

Occasionally there have been reports of reversible hearing loss occurring chiefly in patients with renal insufficiency and in patients receiving high doses of erythromycin.

There have been isolated reports of transient CNS side effects including confusion, hallucinations, seizures and vertigo; however, a cause and effect relationship has not been established.

Overdose: Symptoms and Treatment: With doses of over 2 g per day, abdominal discomfort, nausea or diarrhea may occur. There has been a report of a case of erythromycin-induced pancreatitis following erythromycin overdose. There is no specific treatment for accidental overdosage. Erythromycin should be discontinued and gastric lavage should be considered; otherwise, treatment should be symptomatic. Erythromycin is not removed by peritoneal dialysis or hemodialysis.

Dosage: Blood levels obtained upon administration of enteric-coated erythromycin pellets in the presence of food are above minimum inhibitory concentrations (MICs) of most organisms for which erythromycin is indicated. However, maximum blood levels are obtained in the fasting state (at least 30 minutes and preferably 2 hours before or after a meal).

Adults: The usual dose is 250 mg every 6 hours or 333 mg every 8 hours. If twice-a-day dosage is desired, the recommended dose is 500 mg every 12 hours. Dosage may be increased up to 4 g/day, depending on the severity of infection. Twice-a-day dosing is not recommended when doses larger than 1 g daily are administered.

Children: Age, weight, and severity of the infection are important factors in determining the proper dosage. The usual dosage is 30 to 50 mg/kg/day in equally divided doses. For the treatment of more severe infections, this dosage may be doubled.

Upper and Lower Respiratory Tract and Skin and Soft Tissue Infections: A therapeutic dosage of oral erythromycin should be administered for at least 10 days. The recommended dosage is 1 g/day given in divided doses (2, 3 or 4 times a day), depending on the erythromycin preparation chosen. Depending on the severity of infection, doses up to 4 g may be considered; however, a single dose should not exceed 1 g.

Pertussis: Although optimal dosage and duration of therapy have not been established, doses of erythromycin utilized in reported clinical studies were 40 to 50 mg/kg/day, given in divided doses for 5 to 14 days.

Legionnaires' Disease: Large doses of up to 4 g daily in divided doses are necessary for the treatment of known or suspected Legionella Infections.

Acne Vulgaris: Initially, up to 1 g/day in divided doses. Depending on clinical response this may then be reduced to 333 to 500 mg/day as a maintenance dose. Extended administration of erythromycin requires regular evaluation, particularly of liver function.

Chlamydial Infections: The "Canadian Guidelines for the Treatment of Sexually Transmitted Diseases in Neonates, Children, Adolescents and Adults" recommends the following doses of erythromycin.

1. Conjunctivitis and pneumonia in newborns and infants: 40 mg/kg/day in 4 divided doses for at least 14 days. Note: Topical therapy alone for conjunctivitis is **not** adequate.
2. Uncomplicated urethral, endocervical or rectal infection: Children under 9 years of age; 40 mg/kg/day orally in 4 divided doses (up to a maximum of 500 mg q.i.d. for 7 days). Children over 9 years of age when tetracycline or doxycycline is contraindicated or not tolerated: 40 mg/kg/day orally in 4 divided doses (up to maximum of 500 mg q.i.d. for 7 days). Pregnant women and nursing mothers: 2 g orally/day in 3 or 4 equally divided doses for 7 days; or 1 g orally/day in 3 or 4 equally divided doses for 14 days if the larger dose is not tolerated. Adolescents and adults when tetracycline or doxycycline is contraindicated or not tolerated: 2 g/day in 3 or 4 equally divided doses for 7 days.
3. Complicated infection: The duration of treatment should be for at least 10 days.

As with all sexually transmitted diseases, follow-up cultures after termination of therapy are recommended in order to assess the microbiological response.

Primary Syphilis: 2 to 4 g/day given in divided doses either 2, 3 or 4 times-a-day depending on the erythromycin preparation chosen, over a period of 10 to 15 days.

Prophylaxis: For continuous prophylaxis against recurrence of streptococcal infections in adults with a history of rheumatic heart disease, the recommended dose is 250 mg twice a day.

For the prevention of bacterial endocarditis due to alpha-hemolytic streptococci in penicillin-allergic patients with valvular heart disease who are to undergo dental procedures or surgical procedures of the upper respiratory tract, the adult dose is 1 g 1 hour prior to the procedure and 500 mg 6 hours later. The pediatric prophylactic dose is 20 mg/kg (maximum 1 g) 1 hour before surgery, followed by 10 mg/kg (maximum 500 mg) 6 hours later.

See Precautions regarding alfentanil.

Supplied: Eryc 250: Each 2-tone clear and orange opaque capsule, imprinted Eryc and P-D 696, contains: erythromycin base 250 mg as enteric-coated pellets. Nonmedicinal ingredients: cellulose acetate phthalate, diethyl phthalate, FD&C Yellow No. 6, lactose, methanol, methylene chloride, potassium phosphate monobasic and povidone; capsule shell: FD&C Yellow No. 6, gelatin and titanium dioxide. Energy: 0 kJ (0 kcal). Gluten-, lactose-, paraben-, sodium-, sulfite- and tartrazine-free. Bottles of 100 and 500.

Eryc 333: Each 2-tone clear and opaque yellow capsule, inscription ERYC 333 mg on one end and Parke-Davis on the other, contains: erythromycin base 333 mg as enteric-coated pellets. Nonmedicinal ingredients: cellulose acetate phthalate, diethyl phthalate, FD&C Yellow No. 6, lactose, methanol, methylene chloride, potassium phosphate monobasic and povidone; capsule shell: D&C Yellow No. 10, D&C Red No. 33, gelatin and titanium dioxide. Energy: 0.5 kJ (0.13 kcal). Sodium 0.11 mg. Gluten-, paraben-, sulfite- and tartrazine-free. Bottles of 100 and 500.

Store at room temperature below 30°C. Protect from moisture and light.

(Shown in Product Recognition Section)

ERYSOL® Ⓟ

Stiefel

Erythromycin—Ethyl Alcohol

Topical Acne Therapy

Pharmacology: Erythromycin exerts its antibacterial action by binding to the 50s ribosomal subunit of susceptible bacteria and suppressing protein synthesis. Erythromycin is usually bacteriostatic but may be bactericidal in high concentrations or against highly susceptible organisms. The precise mechanism of action of erythromycin in the treatment of acne has not been established.

Erysol (cont'd)

Ethyl alcohol is a drying and peeling agent.

Indications: In the treatment of inflammatory papular and pustular lesions of acne vulgaris.

Erysol is not indicated for the treatment of cysts or nodules. It is not indicated for use in Grade IV acne.

Contraindications: In persons who have shown hypersensitivity to erythromycin or any of the other ingredients.

Warnings: Erysol is intended for external use only and should be kept away from the eyes, nostrils, mouth and other mucous membranes because of its irritant effects. Concomitant topical anti-acne therapy should be used with caution because a cumulative irritancy effect may occur, especially with preparations having peeling, desquamating or abrasive properties.

Precautions: The use of preparations containing antibiotics such as Erysol may be associated with overgrowth of antibiotic resistant organisms, including those initially sensitive to the drug. Cross-resistance between erythromycin and macrolide antibiotics can occur. If this should occur, therapy should be discontinued and appropriate measures taken. A cross-resistance between erythromycin and clindamycin has rarely been reported.

Pregnancy: The safety of Erysol during pregnancy has not been established. Erythromycin crosses the placental barrier.

Lactation: Erythromycin is excreted in human milk. Caution should be exercised whenever Erysol is given to a nursing mother.

Adverse Effects: Adverse reactions reported with topical erythromycin preparations such as Erysol include mild to severe skin irritation symptoms including dryness, tenderness, pruritus, desquamation, scaling, coriaceousness, fissuring around the mouth, erythema, urticaria, oiliness and burning sensation.

Overdose: Symptoms and Treatment: Accidental ingestion of Erysol could cause alcoholic intoxication and/or intestinal tract irritation (manifested by abdominal discomfort, cramping, diarrhea or vomiting). Treat with a demulcent.

If Erysol comes into contact with the eye, irrigate with copious amounts of water or irrigation solutions for at least 5 minutes. If discomfort persists, consult a physician.

Excessive frequency of application may result in excessive dryness and scaling, pruritus, tenderness, erythema, desquamation and burning sensation. Discontinue use until condition subsides. Appropriate anti-inflammatory measures may be employed.

Dosage: Apply twice a day to areas affected by acne. These areas should be washed first with a mild soap, rinsed well, and patted dry, followed by application of the gel in a gentle rubbing motion, using fingertips to apply the medication. Wash hands thoroughly after application. Care should be taken to avoid eyes, nostrils, mouth and other mucous membranes.

Ethyl alcohol contributes significantly to the efficacy of Erysol due to its drying and peeling properties. Because ethyl alcohol is potentially irritating, the frequency of application may require adjustment to once a day.

Information for the Patient: See Blue Section—Information for the Patient "Erysol".

Supplied: Each g of clear, colorless gel with characteristic odor contains: erythromycin USP 2% (20 mg/g), ethyl alcohol (75%), Parsol MCX 7.5% and Parsol 1789 2%. Sunscreens: SPF15. Nonmedicinal ingredients: cyclomethicone NF, dioctyl maleate, hydroxypropyl cellulose NF and isoarachidyl neopentanoate. Tubes of 25 g. Store at 15 to 30°C.

ERYTHROCIN® ℞

Abbott

Erythromycin Stearate

Antibiotic

Supplied: 125 mg: Each 5 mL of white to off-white opaque, cherry-flavored suspension contains: erythromycin stearate equivalent to 125 mg of erythromycin activity. Energy: 41.04 kJ (9.80 kcal)/5 mL. Sodium: 5.15 mmol (117.8 mg)/5 mL. Nonmedicinal ingredients: artificial flavor, methylparaben, propylparaben, sodium citrate, sodium lauryl sulfate, sorbitol, sucrose and xanthan gum. Alcohol-, gluten-, lactose-, sulfite- and tartrazine-free. Bottles of 500 mL.

250 mg: Each 5 mL of opaque red, cherry-flavored suspension contains: erythromycin stearate equivalent to 250 mg of erythromycin activity. Energy: 38.50 kJ (9.20 kcal)/5 mL. Sodium: 7.7 mmol (176.45 mg)/5 mL. Nonmedicinal ingredients: artificial flavor, methylparaben, propylparaben, red amaranth, sodium citrate, sodium lauryl sulfate, sorbitol, sucrose and xanthan gum. Alcohol-, gluten-, lactose-, sulfite- and tartrazine-free. Bottles of 500 mL.

ERYTHROCIN™ I.V. ℞

Abbott

Erythromycin Lactobionate

Antibiotic

Supplied: ADD-Vantage Vials: Each vial of sterile, lyophilized powder for injection contains: erythromycin base 500 mg or 1 g in the form of erythromycin lactobionate USP. Also contains lactobionic acid. Packages of 10.

Fliptop Vials: Each vial of sterile, lyophilized powder for injection contains: erythromycin base 500 mg or 1 g in the form of erythromycin lactobionate USP. Also contains lactobionic acid. Packages of 10.

Store at room temperature and protect from heat.

ERYTHROMID® ℞

Abbott

Erythromycin

Antibiotic

Supplied: Each ovaloid, opaque, pink Filmtab tablet contains: erythromycin base 250 mg. Nonmedicinal ingredients: castor oil, cellulose acetate phthalate, cellulose microcrystalline, D&C Red Lake #30, magnesium stearate, methyl ethyl ketone, monobasic potassium phosphate, polacrilin potassium, polyethylene glycol 8000, povidone, propylene glycol, sodium citrate, sodium hydroxide, sorbitan monooleate, titanium dioxide and water for injection. Sodium: 3.07 mmol (70.39 mg). Alcohol-, gluten-, lactose-, paraben-, sucrose-, sulfite- and tartrazine-free. Bottles of 100 and 1 000.

ERYTHROMYCIN ℞

General Monograph, CPhA

Antibiotic

> This monograph has been compiled by CPhA. It may contain information different from that approved by Therapeutic Products Programme, Health Canada, and the pharmaceutical manufacturers' approval has not been requested.

Pharmacology: Erythromycin, a macrolide antibiotic, inhibits protein synthesis by binding reversibly to the 50S ribosomal subunits of susceptible microorganisms. Its action may be either bacteriostatic or bactericidal depending on the sensitivity of the microorganism and the concentration of the drug. Erythromycin is most effective in vitro against streptococci and staphylococci. Most gram-positive bacilli are also sensitive, including B. anthracis, Clostridium, Corynebacterium, Erysipelothrix, L. monocytogenes and some Mycobacterium species. Erythromycin is also active in vitro against some gram-negative cocci such as Neisseria, some gram-negative bacilli including H. influenza, Legionella, Pasteurella and Brucella, and gram-negative coccobacilli such as C. jejuni and B. pertussis.

Erythromycin inhibits some Chlamydia, Actinomyces, M. pneumoniae, U. urealyticum, Rickettsia, E. histolytica and spirochetes (T. pallidum and B. burgdorferi). Enterobacteriaceae and Pseudomonas are usually resistant.

Erythromycin probably binds to motilin receptors in the gut, acting as an agonist. This results in accelerated gastric emptying, an effect which is utilized in the treatment of diabetic gastroparesis.

Pharmacokinetics: Absorption of orally administered erythromycins occurs mainly in the duodenum. The bioavailability of the drug is variable and depends on several factors including the formulation of the dosage form administered, acid stability of the derivative, presence of food in the gastrointestinal tract and gastric emptying time. Peak levels are generally reached within 1 to 4 hours following oral administration.

Erythromycin is widely distributed into most body tissues and fluids including the middle ear exudate in patients with otitis media, and prostatic fluid and semen. It does not cross the blood brain barrier.

The extent of binding to plasma proteins varies among the different forms, ranging from 75 to 95%. The half-life ranges from 0.8 to 3 hours. Erythromycin is partly metabolized in the liver and mainly excreted unchanged via bile; small amounts are also excreted in urine.

Only small amounts of erythromycin are removed by hemodialysis.

Indications: Erythromycin is usually the drug of choice for the treatment of infections caused by Legionella species and M. pneumoniae as well as for genital ulcers caused by H. ducreyi (chancroid).

Erythromycin is indicated for the treatment of the following infections when caused by susceptible organisms: bronchitis, acute otitis media, sinusitis, skin and soft tissue infections, chlamydial pneumonia, conjuntivitis, endocervical and urethral infections; diptheria (prophylaxis and treatment); erythrasma caused by Corynebacterium; gonorrhea (not first-line); listeriosis; pertussis; streptococcal pharyngitis in patients allergic to penicillin; pneumonia caused by M. pneumoniae or S. pneumoniae; syphilis (less effective than other regimens); acne vulgaris; actinomycosis; anthrax; chancroid; lymphogranuloma venereum; relapsing fever; enteritis caused by Campylobacter; early Lyme disease (less effective than amoxicillin or doxycycline).

Erythromycin is used in the long-term prophylaxis of rheumatic fever as an alternative to penicillin. Other macrolides (clarithromycin and azithromycin) have replaced erythromycin for use in penicillin-allergic patients in the 1997 Recommendations by the AHA for Prevention of Bacterial Endocarditis.

Erythromycin is used in the treatment of diabetic gastroparesis (i.v. more effective than oral).

Erythromycin base is used with oral neomycin for preoperative bowel preparation.

Ophthalmic Ointment: For the treatment of superficial ocular infections involving the conjunctiva and/or cornea caused by organisms susceptible to erythromycin. For prophylaxis of ophthalmia neonatorum due to N. gonorrhoeae or C. trachomatis.

Topical Solution: Topical treatment of acne vulgaris, primarily in the treatment of the inflammatory papular lesions; superficial infections of the skin.

Contraindications: Erythromycin and its derivatives should not be used in patients with known hypersensitivity to these drugs or any ingredient in the formulations. Erythromycin estolate is contraindicated in persons with pre-existing liver disease or dysfunction and during pregnancy.

Erythromycin is contraindicated in patients taking astemizole, terfenadine or cisapride (see Precautions). Concurrent use with clozapine or ergot alkaloids should also be avoided.

Precautions: The possibility of suprainfection caused by overgrowth of nonsusceptible bacteria or fungi should be considered during prolonged or repeated therapy, especially when other antibacterial agents are given concurrently. In such instances the drug should be withdrawn and appropriate treatment instituted.

Use with caution in patients with impaired hepatic function or impaired biliary excretion.

Use high doses of erythromycin with caution in patients with a history of cardiac arrhythmias or QT prolongation.

Pseudomembranous colitis associated with erythromycin therapy has been reported.

Erythromycin, particularly the estolate, may cause a reversible cholestatic hepatitis. A prodromal syndrome consisting of abdominal cramps, nausea and vomiting may precede the onset of biliary colic, fever, anorexia and hepatic enlargement with or without jaundice. Leukocytosis and eosinophilia may occur, as well as changes in hepatic enzymes, bilirubin and hepatic function tests.

Hepatotoxicity is most likely to occur in adults who have received erythromycin estolate for longer than 10 days, or with repeated courses. Although the hepatotoxic effects are reversible, symptoms may take several weeks to subside after discontinuation of the drug.

Drug Interactions: Erythromycin may, through inhibition of microsomal enzyme systems, decrease the clearance of drugs such as alfentanil, bromocriptine, carbamazepine, chloramphenicol, cisapride, clozapine, cyclosporine, ergot alkaloids, loratadine, lovastatin, midazolam, phenytoin, pimozide, theophylline, triazolam and valproic acid. This may lead to substantially higher serum concentrations of these drugs which could increase the risk of toxicity. Concomitant use of erythromycin with drugs metabolized by the cytochrome P-450 microsomal enzyme system requires close monitoring including serum level determinations and dosage adjustment if necessary.

Antihistamines: Erythromycin should **not** be administered to patients taking astemizole or terfenadine. Erythromycin may inhibit the metabolism of these antihistamines and increase

the risk for potentially life threatening cardiac effects such as prolongation of the QT interval or torsades de pointes.
Clozapine: Concurrent use with erythromycin should be avoided because of an increased risk of seizures.
Digoxin: In a small population of patients (<10%) in which digoxin is metabolized by gastrointestinal bacteria, the concomitant administration of erythromycin may cause increased serum digoxin levels by altering the gastrointestinal flora. Increase in serum digoxin concentration may occur up to several weeks after the discontinuation of erythromycin. If both drugs are used together, it is recommended that patients be monitored for potential increases in the response to digoxin; a lower dose of digoxin may be needed in certain patients.
Ergot Alkaloids: Concurrent use with erythromycin should be avoided because of an increased risk of ergotism.
Oral Anticoagulants: There have been reports of increased anticoagulant effects when erythromycin is used concurrently with warfarin. Close monitoring of INR or prothrombin time is indicated when erythromycin is added or deleted from a drug regimen which includes warfarin. Adjustment of warfarin dosage may be necessary.
Pregnancy: Erythromycin crosses the placenta, reaching fetal serum concentrations of 5 to 20% of maternal serum levels. Safety for use in pregnancy has not been established. However, erythromycin is used for the treatment of chlamydial infections during pregnancy. Erythromycin estolate is not recommended because it has been associated with an increased risk of reversible, subclinical hepatotoxicity in 10% of pregnant women taking the drug.
Lactation: Erythromycin is excreted into breast milk. Safety for use in breast feeding mothers has not been established.
Neonates: Safety for use in neonates has not been established.
Topical Solution: For external use only. Avoid contact with the eyes, nostrils, mouth and other mucous membranes. Contains drying and peeling agents that are potential irritants, therefore reduction in frequency of application may be necessary to avoid excessive irritation. The use of preparations containing antibiotics may be associated with overgrowth of nonsusceptible organisms. If this should occur, therapy should be discontinued and appropriate measures taken. Concomitant topical antiacne therapy should be avoided because a cumulative irritancy effect may occur, particularly with those preparations containing peeling, desquamating or abrasive agents.

Adverse Effects: Gastrointestinal: The most frequent adverse effects are gastrointestinal (such as abdominal pain and cramping) and are dose-related. Nausea, vomiting and diarrhea also occur, especially after large doses.
Hepatic: Elevated transaminase levels (AST, ALT), (<10%), cholestatic jaundice, cholestatic hepatitis (2 to 4%). Risk of hepatotoxicity is thought to be greater with the estolate and ethylsuccinate salts and with increased duration and dose of therapy.
Otic: Reversible ototoxicity, tinnitus and vertigo have been reported rarely. Ototoxicity is more likely in the elderly or in patients receiving large doses who have impaired renal or hepatic function.
Neurological: CNS side effects including seizures, hallucinations, confusion and vertigo have been reported occasionally; however, a cause and effect relationship has not been established.
Local: I.V. administration may cause venous irritation and thrombophlebitis. These effects may be minimized by using a more dilute solution and infusing slowly.
Hypersensitivity: Serious allergic reactions to erythromycin have been extremely infrequent. Mild allergic reactions, such as urticaria and morbilliform skin rashes have occurred. Should a patient demonstrate signs of hypersensitivity, administer appropriate measures such as epinephrine, corticosteroid and antihistamines, and withdraw the antibiotic.
Topical Solution: Symptoms of irritation: erythema, desquamation, tenderness and excessive dryness. Mild to moderate symptoms of irritation were observed in 70% of erythromycin topical solution treated patients, while severe irritation was seen in 12%. Others: pruritus, urticaria, oiliness, leathery skin and fissuring around the mouth.

Overdose: Symptoms: With oral doses of over 2 g per day, abdominal discomfort, nausea or diarrhea may occur.
Topical Solution: Accidental ingestion could result in alcoholic intoxication and/or intestinal tract irritation manifested by vomiting, cramping, diarrhea.

Treatment: No specific treatment for accidental overdosage has been proposed. Treatment should be symptomatic and supportive. Patients should be monitored for several days for signs of possible hepatotoxicity.
Topical Solution: Treat with a demulcent. If eye contact with erythromycin topical solution should occur, wash with copious amounts of water for a least 5 minutes. If discomfort persists,a physician should be contacted.

Excessive frequency of application can cause erythema, excessive scaling and sensations of burning and tenderness. Appropriate anti-inflammatory measures (e.g., compresses or topical corticosteroids) may be employed.

Dosage: Oral erythromycin is available as the base or as the estolate, ethylsuccinate or stearate salt. Two parenteral erythromycin salts are available (gluceptate and lactobionate). Erythromycin base is also available as an ophthalmic ointment and as a topical solution.

Oral: When given orally, erythromycin and its derivatives, with the exception of erythromycin estolate, are variably susceptible to inactivation by acid in the stomach. This can be reduced by administering film-coated preparations at least 1 hour before meals. Enteric-coated erythromycin base and estolate may be taken without regard to meals. Erythromycin ethylsuccinate is optimally absorbed when taken immediately following meals.

The following dosages are expressed in terms of erythromycin base. Individual product monographs should be consulted for specific information on dosage and administration of the available erythromycin formulations. Unless otherwise specified, the adult dose is given.
Antibacterial: 250 mg every 6 hours; 333 mg every 8 hours; 500 mg every 12 hours. Children: 7.5 to 25 mg/kg every 6 hours; 15 to 25 mg every 12 hours.
Acne: 250 mg every 6 hours; 333 mg every 8 hours; 500 mg every 12 hours. After 4 weeks, maintenance of 333 to 500 mg once daily.
Chlamydial Infections of Endocervix or Urethra: 333 mg every 8 hours or 500 mg every 6 hours for 7 days; 250 mg every 6 hours for 14 days. Children <45 kg: 10 mg/kg every 6 hours for 10 to 14 days.
Chlamydial Conjunctivitis: 12.5 mg/kg every 6 hours for at least 10 to 14 days.
Chlamydial Pneumonia: 12.5 mg/kg every 6 hours for 14 days.
Chancroid: 500 mg every 6 hours for 7 days.
Diphtheria: 10 to 12.5 mg/kg every 6 hours for 14 days.
Endocarditis Prophylaxis: 1 g 2 hours prior to procedure followed by 500 mg 6 hours after first dose. Children: 20 mg/kg 2 hours prior to procedure followed by 10 mg/kg 6 hours after first dose.
Enteritis, Campylobacter: 250 mg 4 times daily for 5 days. Children: 10 mg/kg every 6 hours for 5 days.
Gastroparesis: 250 mg 3 times daily, 30 minutes before meals.
Legionnaires' Disease: 500 mg to 1 g every 6 hours.
Lyme Disease: 250 mg 4 times daily for 10 to 21 days. Children: 7.5 mg/kg every 6 hours for 10 to 21 days.
Lymphogranuloma venereum: 500 mg every 6 hours for 21 days.
Pelvic Inflammatory Disease, N. gonnorhoeae: 250 mg every 6 hours for 7 days (following 500 mg i.v. every 6 hours for 3 days.
Pertussis: 10 to 12.5 mg/kg every 6 hours for 10 days.
Streptococcal Pharyngitis: 5 to 7.5 mg/kg every 6 hours or 10 to 15 mg/kg every 12 hours for at least 10 days.
Streptococcus Prophylaxis: 250 mg every 12 hours continuously.
Syphilis, Primary: 30 to 40 g over 10 to 15 days.
Urethritis, Nongonococcal, U. urealyticum: 500 mg every 6 hours for 7 days or 250 mg every 6 hours for 14 days.
Renal Failure: No dosage adjustment is necessary for patients with mild to moderate renal failure. Patients with severe renal failure (ClCr<0.17 mL/s) may receive half of the usual dosage.

Parenteral (I.V.): For use when large doses of erythromycin are needed but not tolerated orally. Oral therapy should replace i.v. administration as soon as possible.

Erythromycin must be adequately and properly diluted and administered slowly to avoid local venous irritation.
Adults: Usual dose is 250 to 500 mg every 6 hours. Up to 4 g daily in more severe infections.
Children: 15 to 20 mg/kg daily divided into 4 doses.

Topical: Ophthalmic Ointment: In the treatment of external ocular infections, apply the ointment directly to the infected structure 1 or more times daily, depending on the severity of the infection.

For prophylaxis of neonatal gonococcal or chlamydial conjunctivitis, a ribbon of ointment approximately 0.5 to 1 cm in length should be instilled into each conjunctival sac. The ointment should not be flushed from the eye following instillation. A new tube should be used for each infant. Infants born by cesarean section as well as those delivered by the vaginal route should receive prophylaxis.

Topical Solution: Apply each morning and evening to the areas affected by acne. Before applying, areas should be washed with mild soap, rinsed well, and patted dry. Use fingertips to apply medication. Wash hands after use. Because the drying and peeling agents in erythromycin topical solution are potentially irritating, the frequency of application may require adjustment to once a day or less.

Reviewed 1999

ERYTHROMYCIN ℞

Rivex Ophthalmics

Antibiotic

Supplied: Each g of sterile ophthalmic ointment contains: crystalline erythromycin base USP 5 mg in mineral oil and white petrolatum. Unit doses of 1 g. Tubes of 3.5 g.

ESTAR®

Westwood-Squibb

Coal Tar

Psoriasis Therapy

Supplied: Each g contains: coal tar extract 2% (biologically equivalent to coal tar 5% USP) contained in a hydroalcoholic gel. Nonmedicinal ingredients: β-alanine, benzyl alcohol, carbomer 940, glycereth-7 coconate, polysorbate 80, SD alcohol 40, simethicone, sorbitol and water. Plastic tubes of 85 g.

ESTINYL® ℞

Schering

Ethinyl Estradiol

Estrogen

Pharmacology: Ethinyl estradiol promotes growth of the endometrium; promotes thickening, stratification and cornification of the vagina. It causes enlargement of the ducts of the mammary glands and promotes the development of secondary female sex characteristics. Ethinyl estradiol inhibits pituitary gonadotropin secretion probably via action on the hypothalamus. Similar to other estrogens it influences calcium and phosphorus metabolism, possesses some anabolic action on protein metabolism and induces retention of sodium and water. In cases of advanced mammary carcinoma in postmenopausal women and in cases of prostatic carcinoma, the metastatic growth may be inhibited by high doses of estrogens.

Indications: Menopausal syndrome; abnormal uterine bleeding due to hormonal imbalance in absence of organic pathology; palliative treatment of progressing inoperable or roentgen resistant mammary carcinoma in women who are at least 5 years postmenopausal; palliative treatment of inoperable prostatic carcinoma.

Contraindications: Patients with active hepatic dysfunction or disease, especially of the obstructive type; or a personal history of breast or endometrial cancer, except in special circumstances.

Endometrial hyperplasia is also a contraindication for estrogen therapy without accompanying progestogen.

The drug is also contraindicated in undiagnosed vaginal bleeding; a history of cerebrovascular accident, coronary thrombosis, or the presence of classical migraine; a history of thrombophlebitis or thromboembolic disease; partial or complete loss of vision or diplopia, from ophthalmic vascular disease; suspected pregnancy.

Warnings: Induction of Malignant Neoplasms: At the present time the effect of replacement hormones on the risk of breast or ovarian cancer is unknown. Most studies suggest a small but significant increased risk of breast cancer after long-term use. There is a need for caution in prescribing estrogens for women with a strong family history of breast cancer or who have breast nodules, fibrocystic disease, or abnormal mammograms. Women on this therapy should have regular breast examinations and should be instructed in breast self-examination.

Independent studies have shown an increased risk of endometrial cancer in postmenopausal women treated with estrogens for prolonged periods. However, administration of a progestogen for the last 10 to 14 days of an estrogen cycle

Estinyl (cont'd)

protects the endometrium from hyperplasia and reduces the risk of endometrial cancer to that of untreated women.

Thromboembolic Disease: It is now well established that users of oral contraceptives have an increased risk of various thromboembolic and thrombotic vascular diseases such as thrombophlebitis, pulmonary embolism, stroke, and myocardial infarction. Cases of retinal thrombosis, mesenteric thrombosis, and optic neuritis have been reported in oral contraceptive users. There is evidence that the risk of several of these adverse reactions is related to the dose of the drug. An increased risk of postsurgery thromboembolic complications has also been reported in users of oral contraceptives. If feasible, estrogen should be discontinued at least 4 weeks before surgery of the type associated with an increased risk of thromboembolism, or during periods of immobilization.

Estrogens should not be used in persons with active thrombophlebitis or thromboembolic disorders, and they should not be used (except in treatment of malignancy) in persons with a history of such disorders in association with estrogen use. They should be used with caution in patients with cerebral vascular or coronary artery disease and only for those in whom estrogens are clearly needed.

Hepatic Adenoma: Benign hepatic adenomas appear to be associated with the use of oral contraceptives. Although benign and rare, these may rupture and may cause death through intra-abdominal hemorrhage. Such lesions have not yet been reported in association with other estrogen or progestogen preparations, but should be considered in estrogen users having abdominal pain and tenderness, abdominal mass, or hypovolemic shock. Hepatocellular carcinoma has also been reported in women taking estrogen-containing oral contraceptives. The relationship of this malignancy to these drugs is not known at this time.

Elevated Blood Pressure: Increased blood pressure is not uncommon in women using oral contraceptives. Blood pressure should be monitored with estrogen use, especially if high doses are used.

Glucose Tolerance: A worsening of glucose tolerance has been observed in a significant percentage of patients on estrogen-containing oral contraceptives. For this reason, diabetic patients should be carefully observed while receiving estrogen.

Hypercalcemia: Administration of estrogens may lead to severe hypercalcemia in patients with breast cancer and bone metastases. If this occurs, the drug should be stopped and appropriate measures taken to reduce the serum calcium level.

Precautions: A complete medical and family history should be taken prior to the initiation of any estrogen therapy. The pretreatment and periodic physical examinations should include special reference to blood pressure, breasts, abdomen and pelvic organs, and should include a Papanicolaou smear. The first follow-up examination should be done within 6 months after initiation of treatment. Thereafter, examinations should be made once a year. At each examination, repeat those procedures outlined above.

If any surgical procedures are performed, advise the pathologist of the patient's therapy when specimens are sent for examination.

Conduct periodic liver function tests in subjects who have, or are suspected of having, hepatic disease.

If abnormal vaginal bleeding occurs during therapy, perform diagnostic aspiration biopsy or curettage to rule out the possibility of uterine malignancy.

Patients who develop visual disturbances, classical migraine, transient aphasia, paralysis, or loss of consciousness should discontinue medication.

If the patient develops any sign of phlebitis or thromboembolic complications, discontinue medication.

Because estrogens influence the metabolism of calcium and phosphorus, they should be used with caution in patients with metastatic breast carcinoma or metabolic bone diseases that are associated with hypercalcemia or in patients with renal insufficiency.

Gallbladder Disease: A recent study has reported a 2 to 3 fold increase in the risk of surgically confirmed gallbladder disease in women receiving postmenopausal estrogens similar to the 2 fold increase previously noted in users of oral contraceptives. In the case of oral contraceptives, the increased risk appeared after 2 years of use.

Development of sudden enlargement, pain or tenderness of uterine fibroids requires discontinuation of medication.

Estrogen may cause fluid retention. Therefore, particular caution is indicated in cardiac or renal dysfunction, epilepsy, or asthma.

Elevation of blood pressure in previously normotensive or hypertensive patients necessitates cessation of medication.

Diabetic patients or those with a predisposition to diabetes should be observed closely to detect any alterations in carbohydrate metabolism.

Because of the effects of estrogens on epiphyseal closure, they should be used judiciously in young patients in whom bone growth is not complete.

Drug/Laboratory Test Interactions: Certain endocrine and liver function tests may be affected by estrogen-containing oral contraceptives. The following similar changes may be expected with larger doses of estrogen: increased sulfobromophthalein retention; increased prothrombin and factors VII, VIII, IX and X; decreased antithrombin 3; increased norepinephrine-induced platelet aggregation; increased thyroid binding globulin (TGB) leading to increased circulating total thyroid hormone, as measured by PBI, T4 by column, or T4 by radioimmunoassay. Free T3 resin uptake is decreased, reflecting the elevated TBG; free T4 concentration is unaltered; impaired glucose tolerance; decreased pregnanediol excretion; reduced response to metyrapone test; reduced serum folate concentration; increased serum triglyceride and phospholipid concentration.

Pregnancy: The use of estrogens during early pregnancy may seriously damage the offspring.

Lactation: Because of the potential for tumorigenicity shown for ethinyl estradiol in animal and human studies, a decision should be made whether to discontinue nursing or to discontinue the drug, taking into account the importance of the drug to the mother.

Children: Safety and effectiveness in children have not been established.

Adverse Effects: Although not all of the following reactions have been specifically associated with ethinyl estradiol, they have been reported with estrogens generally, including oral contraceptives, and may be encountered when giving any estrogen.

Gastrointestinal: nausea, anorexia, vomiting, abdominal cramps, bloating, cholestatic jaundice.

Genitourinary: sodium and water retention, breakthrough bleeding, spotting, and withdrawal bleeding, increased cervical mucus, reactivation of endometriosis, and cystitis like syndrome.

Endocrine: breast swelling and tenderness, possible diminution of lactation when given immediately post partum, increased blood sugar levels, and decreased glucose tolerance.

CNS: headaches, migraine, mental depression, increase or decrease of libido, nervousness, dizziness, fatigue, irritability, and malaise.

Dermatologic Hypersensitivity: chloasma or melasma which may persist when drug is discontinued; loss of scalp hair, allergic reactions and rashes, hemorrhagic eruption, itching, erythema nodosum, erythema multiforme.

Musculoskeletal: backache.

Cardiovascular: an increase in blood pressure in susceptible individuals and aggravation of migraine headaches.

Hematologic: A statistically significant association has been demonstrated between the use of estrogen containing drugs and the following reactions: thrombophlebitis, pulmonary embolism, cerebral thrombosis. Although available evidence is suggestive of an association, such a relationship has been neither confirmed nor refuted for the following serious reactions: coronary thrombosis and neuro-ocular lesions (e.g., retinal thrombosis and optic neuritis).

Ophthalmic: steepening of corneal curvature; intolerance to contact lenses.

Miscellaneous: Premenstrual like syndrome, precipitation or aggravation of porphyria cutanea tarda in predisposed individuals, increase or decrease in body weight.

Overdose: Symptoms: Other than possible nausea, no signs or symptoms are anticipated from a single excessive dose, except maybe abnormal uterine bleeding which usually is self limited and does not require any specific treatment.

Treatment: In case of accidental ingestion by a child, gastric emptying is suggested.

Dosage: In general, estrogen should be given cyclically and in some cases with progestogen or androgen to avoid overstimulation of breast and endometrial tissues. The addition of sufficient progestogen to promote conversion of the endometrium is mandatory in those patients who are receiving sufficient unopposed estrogen to cause vaginal bleeding or endometrial hyperplasia. Obviously, abnormal vaginal bleeding in such patients is an indication for prompt diagnostic measures.

For the relief of menopausal symptoms, administer 5 or 10 μg of ethinyl estradiol daily for 21 days, followed by a 7 day period without medication.

Dosage may require adjustment as therapy progresses. Use the lowest effective dosage and assess the requirement for estrogen therapy periodically.

Functional Uterine Bleeding: 500 μg once or twice daily until hemostasis is secured, then cyclic administration of 50 μg 1 to 3 times daily during the first 2 weeks of the menstrual cycle, followed by progesterone for 5 days. Three such cycles of therapy may be given.

Carcinoma of the Breast in Postmenopausal Women (Palliative): 100 μg 3 times daily.

Prostatic Carcinoma (Palliative): 0.15 to 3 mg daily taken at bedtime. Therapy may be continued with dose adjustment depending on the patient's response.

Supplied: 20 μg: Each buff, coated tablet contains: ethinyl estradiol USP 20 μg. Nonmedicinal ingredients: cornstarch; dye, FD & C Yellow No. 6; lactose; magnesium stearate and povidone; coating: acacia; carnauba wax; cornstarch; dye, Opalux Off-White; gelatin; tribasic calcium phosphate; sucrose and white wax. Tartrazine-free. Bottles of 100.

50 μg: Each pink, coated tablet contains: ethinyl estradiol USP 50 μg. Nonmedicinal ingredients: cornstarch, lactose, magnesium stearate and povidone; coating: acacia; carnauba wax; cornstarch; dye, Opalux Pink; gelatin; tribasic calcium phosphate; sucrose and white wax. Tartrazine-free. Bottles of 100.

500 μg: Each peach, scored tablet contains: ethinyl estradiol USP 500 μg. Nonmedicinal ingredients: cornstarch; dye, FD & C Yellow No. 6; lactose; magnesium stearate and povidone. Tartrazine-free. Bottles of 100.

Store between 2 and 30°C.

(Shown in Product Recognition Section)

ESTRACE® ℞

Roberts

Estradiol-17β (micronized)

Estrogen

Pharmacology: Estrogens are secreted mainly by the gonads and, to a very small amount, by the adrenals. In addition, they are formed, to an important degree, from peripheral conversion of adrenal and gonadal androgens to estrogens. They circulate in both unconjugated and conjugated forms in the blood, with the unconjugated estrogens, either free or bound to proteins, mainly albumin, or to the specific sex-hormone binding globulin (SHBG) which shows a great affinity for estradiol.

Estrogens are metabolized mainly in the liver, with the metabolites being conjugated with glucuronic acid or sulfuric acid and even double conjugates such as estriol-3-sulfate-16α-glucuronide are formed. About ⅓ to ½ of the circulating estrogens are secreted in the bile and of this fraction 20% is reabsorbed after hydrolysis in the intestinal tract. The exact site of the hydrolysis is not known, but it probably takes place in the intestinal lumen and is catalyzed by enzymes secreted into the intestinal tract or present in the microflora. Estradiol is the most potent of the known naturally occurring estrogens in stimulating the growth of the reproductive tissues. Estradiol promotes uterine growth in the rat without undergoing chemical transformation and responsive tissues, such as the uterus and vagina, show a characteristic affinity for estradiol.

When administered to humans about 65% of the dose is excreted in the urine, almost entirely in the water soluble form as β-glucuronides or sulfate esters. Estrone, estradiol and estriol account for about ½ of the excreted products. A number of steroids with 3 oxygen functions have been identified such as 16-epiestriol, 16-ketoestradiol, 16-hydroxyestrone and 2-methoxyestrone with estradiol being a precursor to these compounds.

Estradiol is the most potent physiologic estrogen and, in fact, is the major estrogenic hormone secreted by the human. Estradiol controls the development and maintenance of the female sex organs, the secondary sex characteristics and the mammary glands as well as certain functions of the human uterus and accessory organs, particularly the proliferation of the endometrium, the development of the decidua, and the cyclic changes in the cervix and vagina. The production of estradiol by the ovaries is under the control of pituitary gonadotropins, follicle stimulating hormone (FSH) and luteinizing hormone (LH). In menopausal women, the depletion of ovarian follicles leads to lower plasma estradiol and elevated plasma FSH and LH.

Estrogen deficiency is manifested by hot flushes, sweating, insomnia, paresthesia, irritability, and urogenital atrophy. As replacement therapy in estrogen deficiency states (such as the menopause), low doses of estradiol in cyclic regimens have been found to relieve such deficiency.

Estrogen deficiency is the main cause of postmenopausal bone loss and contributes to age-associated losses leading to osteoporosis. Numerous clinical studies have demonstrated that estrogen therapy prevents bone loss and reduces the incidence of vertebral, hip, and Colles' fractures.

Although the mechanism of action of estrogen on bone metabolism is still not completely elucidated, estrogens have been shown to have several effects: increase in renal tubular absorption of calcium, thus reducing urinary calcium; decrease in the sensitivity of bone to the parathyroid hormone (PTH); increase in the intestinal absorption of calcium and increase in circulating levels of active 1-25-dihydroxy-vitamin D. Recent research has shown that osteoblasts also possess receptors for estrogens.

Indications: For the symptomatic relief of menopausal symptoms. Estradiol-17β may also contribute to the prevention of osteoporosis in naturally occurring or surgically induced estrogen-deficiency states when combined with other important therapeutics such as diet, calcium and exercises. In patients with intact uteruses, estradiol-17β should always be supplemented by sequential administration of progestogen.

Contraindications: Should not be administered to patients with any of the following conditions: active hepatic dysfunction or disease especially of the obstructive type, a history of breast or endometrial cancer except in special circumstances, endometrial hyperplasia, known or suspected estrogen-dependent neoplasia, known or suspected pregnancy, undiagnosed vaginal bleeding, a history of cerebrovascular accident, coronary thrombosis, or in the presence of classical migraine, active thrombophlebitis or thromboembolic disorders, partial or complete loss of vision or diplopia, from ophthalmic vascular disease, a history of thrombophlebitis, thrombosis or thromboembolic disorders associated with previous estrogen use, endometriosis and leiomyoma of the uterus, lactation.

Warnings: Malignant Neoplasm: Long-term continuous administration of natural and synthetic estrogens in certain animal species increases the frequency of carcinomas of the breast, cervix, vagina, and liver. There is now evidence that unopposed estrogens increase the risk of carcinoma of the endometrium in humans.

Three independent case control studies have shown an increased risk of endometrial cancer in postmenopausal women exposed to unopposed exogenous estrogens for prolonged periods. This risk was independent of the other known risk factors for endometrial cancer. The 3 case control studies reported that the risk of endometrial cancer in estrogen users was about 4.5 to 13.9 times greater than in nonusers. The risk appears to depend on both duration of treatment and on estrogen dose. In view of these findings, when estrogens are used for the treatment of menopausal symptoms, the lowest dose that will control symptoms should be utilized and medication should be discontinued as soon as possible. When prolonged treatment is medically indicated, sequential administration of progestogen is indicated for women with intact uteruses.

Studies of the addition of a progestogen for 7 or more days of a cycle of estrogen administration have reported a lowered incidence of endometrial hyperplasia. Morphological and biochemical studies of endometrium suggest that 10 to 13 days of progestogen are needed to provide maximal maturation of the endometrium and to eliminate any hyperplastic changes. Whether this will provide protection from endometrial carcinoma has not been clearly established. There are possible additional risks which may be associated with the inclusion of progestogen in estrogen replacement regimens. The potential risks include adverse effects on carbohydrate and lipid metabolism. The choice of progestogen and dosage may be important in minimizing these adverse effects.

Close clinical surveillance of all women taking estrogens is important. In all cases of undiagnosed abdominal vaginal bleeding, adequate diagnostic measures should be undertaken to rule out malignancy.

At the present time there is no satisfactory evidence that estrogens given to postmenopausal women increase the risk of cancer of the breast. There is a need for caution in prescribing estrogens for women with a strong family history of breast cancer or who have breast nodules, fibrocystic disease, or abnormal mammograms.

Thromboembolic Disease: Although the estrogen content of oral contraceptive therapy has been associated with an increased risk of various thromboembolic, thrombotic and vascular disease, to date no such increased risk in postmenopausal users of estrogens has been detected. Nevertheless, the physician should be alert to earliest manifestations of thrombotic disorders (thrombophlebitis, retinal thrombosis, cerebral embolism and pulmonary embolism). If these occur or are suspected, estrogen therapy should be discontinued immediately.

Precautions: Before estradiol-17β is administered, the patient should have a complete physical examination including a blood pressure determination. Breasts and pelvic organs should be examined and a Papanicolaou smear and endometrial biopsy should be taken. The first follow-up visit should be done 3 months after estradiol-17β tablets are prescribed. Thereafter, examinations should be performed at least once a year or more frequently if indicated. Baseline tests should include blood sugar, calcium, triglyceride, cholesterol and liver function tests.

If any surgical procedures are performed, the pathologist should be advised of the patient's therapy when specimens are sent for examination. If feasible, estrogens should also be discontinued at least 4 weeks before surgery which may be associated with an increased risk of thromboembolism, or during periods of prolonged immobilization. Liver function tests should be made periodically in subjects who have, or are suspected of having, hepatic disease.

Patients who develop visual disturbances, classical migraine, transient aphasia, paralysis, or loss of consciousness should discontinue medication.

Patients taking estrogens may experience corneal edema, that may cause visual disturbances and/or changes in tolerance to contact lenses, especially the rigid type of contact lenses. Soft contact lenses usually do not cause disturbances. If visual changes or alterations in tolerance to contact lenses occur, temporary or permament cessation of wear is advised.

Patients with essential hypertension whose blood pressure is well controlled may be given estradiol-17β tablets but only under close supervision. If a significant elevation of blood pressure in previously normotensive or hypertensive subjects occurs at any time during the administration of the drug, cessation of medication is necessary.

Development of sudden enlargement, pain, or tenderness of uterine fibroids requires discontinuation of medication. Preexisting uterine leiomyoma may increase in size during estrogen use.

Estrogens may cause fluid retention. Where this may be undesirable such as in cardiac or renal dysfunction, epilepsy, asthma or migraine, particular caution is indicated.

Elevation of blood pressure in previously normotensive or hypertensive patients necessitates cessation of medication.

Diabetic patients or those with a predisposition to diabetes should be observed closely to detect any alterations in carbohydrate metabolism.

In patients with metastatic carcinoma and hypercalcemia, estrogen medication should be used with caution. It should also be used with caution in patients with metabolic disease and in patients with renal insufficiency.

When liver or endocrine functions tests are indicated, the results should not be considered reliable unless therapy has been discontinued for 2 to 4 months.

Certain patients may develop undesirable manifestations of excessive estrogenic stimulation, such as abnormal or excessive uterine bleeding and mastodynia.

Prolonged administration of unopposed estrogen therapy has been reported to increase the risk of endometrial hyperplasia in some patients.

A recent study has reported a 2- to 3-fold increase in the risk of surgically confirmed gallbladder disease in women receiving postmenopausal estrogens similar to the 2-fold increase previously noted in users of oral contraceptives.

Estrace 2 mg tablets contain tartrazine which may cause allergic-type reactions in susceptible individuals.

Benign hepatic adenomas have been reported with the use of combined estrogen and progestogen oral contraceptives. Although rare, these tumors may rupture and cause death from intra-abdominal hemorrhage. Such lesions have not yet been reported in association with other estrogen or progestogen preparations, but they should be considered if abdominal pain and tenderness, abnormal mass or hypovolemic shock occurs in patients receiving estrogen. Hepatocellular carcinoma has also been reported in women taking estrogen-containing oral contraceptives. The causal relationship of this malignancy to these drugs is not known.

In patients with history of jaundice during pregnancy, there is an increased risk that jaundice will recur with the use of estrogen-containing oral contraceptives. If jaundice develops, with the use of estrogens, the drug should be discontinued while the cause is investigated.

Estrogens may diminish the effectiveness of anticoagulants and antidiabetic agents.

Preparations inducing liver enzymes, e.g., barbiturates, hydantoins, carbamazepine, meprobamate, phenylbutazone or rifampicin may interfere with the activity of orally administered estrogens.

The results of certain endocrine and liver function tests may be affected by estrogen-containing oral contraceptives. The following changes have been observed with large doses of oral estrogen: increased sulfobromophthalein retention; increased prothrombin time; increased factors VII, VIII, IX, X; decreased antithrombin III; following administration of estradiol-17β tablets for 28 days no effect on antithrombin III levels was seen; increased norepinephrine-induced platelet aggregability; increased thyroxine-binding globulin (TBG), leading to increased circulating total thyroid hormone (T_4) as measured by column or radioimmunoassay; free T_3 resin unptake is decreased, reflecting the elevated TBG, free T_4 concentration is unaltered; TBG was not affected in clinical trials with estradiol-17β; reduced response to the metyrapone test; reduced serum folate concentration; increased serum triglyceride and phospholipid concentration.

The results of these tests should not be considered reliable unless therapy has been discontinued for 2 to 4 months. The pathologist should be informed that the patient is receiving estrogen therapy when relevant specimens are submitted.

Adverse Effects: The following adverse reactions have been reported with the use of estrogens.

Genitourinary: breakthrough bleeding, spotting and withdrawal bleeding, dysmenorrhea, increased cervical mucus, endometrial hyperplasia, reactivation of endometriosis, sodium and water retention, premenstrual like syndrome, increase in size of uterine leiomyoma, vaginal candidiasis, and change in cervical eversion and in degree of cervical secretion.

Breast: breast swelling, tenderness and secretion.

Gastrointestinal: nausea, anorexia, vomiting, abdominal cramps, bloating and cholestatic jaundice.

Skin: loss of scalp hair, allergic reactions and rashes, hemorrhagic eruption, itching, erythema nodosum, erythema multiforme, pigmentation of skin, melasma.

CNS: headaches, mental depression, increase or decrease in libido, nervousness, dizziness, fatigue, and irritability.

Cardiovascular: change in blood pressure in susceptible individuals and aggravation of migraine headaches.

Thromboembolic Effects: A statistically significant association has been demonstrated between the use of estrogen-progestin preparations and the following serious reactions: thrombophlebitis, pulmonary embolism and cerebral thrombosis. Although available evidence is suggestive of an association, such a relationship has been neither confirmed nor refuted for the following serious reactions: coronary thrombosis and neuro-ocular lesions (e.g., retinal thrombosis and optic neuritis). Altered coagulation tests (increase in prothrombin time and Factors VII, VIII, IX, X).

Miscellaneous: increase or decrease in weight, reduced carbohydrate tolerance, precipitation or aggravation of porphyria cutanea tarda in predisposed individuals, edema and increased blood sugar levels.

Overdose: Symptoms and Treatment: Numerous reports of ingestion of large doses of estrogen-containing oral contraceptives by young children indicate that serious ill effects do not occur. Overdosage of estrogen may cause nausea, and withdrawal bleeding may occur in females. Remove ingested drug by gastric lavage and give symptomatic treatment.

Dosage: The lowest dose of estrogen required to prevent menopausal symptoms and to prevent development of osteoporosis should be used.

In general, estrogen is usually administered cyclically for the first 21 to 25 days of each month. In patients with intact uteruses a progestin should be sequentially administered for the last 12 to 14 days of estrogen administration in order to prevent development of endometrial hyperplasia as a result of estrogen stimulation.

In hysterectomized patients estrogen alone should be given continuously.

Menopausal Symptoms: Treatment of menopausal symptoms is usually initiated with a 1 mg tablet/day. Thereafter, the dosage should be adjusted to the needs of the individual. Attempts to taper or discontinue the medication should be made at 3- to 6-month intervals.

For Prevention of Osteoporosis: Prophylactic therapy with estradiol-17β to prevent postmenopausal bone loss should be initiated with 0.5 mg/day as soon as possible after menopause. The dose may be titrated upward and downward based on the patient's clinical status and plasma estradiol levels.

Estrace (cont'd)

Ideally, plasma estradiol levels should be maintained around 50 pg/mL.

Supplied: 0.5 mg: Each white, scored, compressed tablet contains: estradiol-17β micronized 0.5 mg. Nonmedicinal ingredients: acacia, dibasic calcium phosphate, cornstarch, lactose, magnesium stearate, silicon dioxide and talc.

1 mg: Each lavender, scored, compressed tablet contains: estradiol-17β micronized 1 mg. Nonmedicinal ingredients: acacia, dibasic calcium phosphate, cornstarch, D&C red No. 27 aluminum lake, FD&C blue No. 1 aluminum lake, lactose, magnesium stearate, silicon dioxide and talc. Bottles of 100.

2 mg: Each turquoise, scored, compressed tablet contains: estradiol-17β micronized 2 mg. Nonmedicinal ingredients: acacia, dibasic calcium phosphate, cornstarch, FD&C blue No. 1 and yellow No. 5 aluminum lake, lactose, magnesium stearate, silicon dioxide and talc. Bottles of 100.

(Shown in Product Recognition Section)

ESTRACOMB® ℞

Novartis Pharmaceuticals

Estradiol-17β—Norethindrone Acetate—Estradiol-17β

Estrogen—Progestin

Pharmacology: Estracomb is designed to provide continuous estrogen and sequential progestin therapy, in a 28-day treatment cycle, for women with an intact uterus.

Estracomb contains 2 types of transdermal therapeutic systems, Estraderm 50 (10 cm²) and Estragest 250/50 (20 cm²). Estraderm 50 contains estradiol-17β and Estragest 250/50 contains norethindrone acetate (NETA) and estradiol-17β, respectively.

Both transdermal therapeutic systems included in Estracomb are designed to deliver daily about 50 μg estradiol-17β, a physiologic hormone, transdermally into the systemic circulation. Due to the transdermal route of administration, the estradiol-17β does not undergo first-pass liver metabolism. Resultant estradiol-17β plasma levels, which are between 30 and 40 pg/mL above baseline (typically 10 pg/mL), are comparable to those seen in premenopausal women in the early follicular phase of the menstrual cycle. Estradiol-17β stimulates target tissues such as the uterus, breast and vagina.

NETA is administered only when the transdermal therapeutic system Estragest 250/50 is correctly used. NETA, after hydrolysis to the active form, NET (norethindrone), shares some of the biological effects of the endogenously produced progestin, progesterone. Like progesterone, NET induces protein synthesis thereby limiting excessive growth stimulation of the endometrium by estrogen. NET induces the enzyme 17β-hydroxysteroid-dehydroxygenase, which locally oxidizes estradiol to estrone. After application of an Estragest 250/50 patch, plasma NET levels range between 0.5 and 1.0 ng/mL.

The tissue effects of NET are dependent on prior estrogen stimulation. One of the major target organs for NET is the uterus, where it acts by inducing secretory transformation of the estrogen-primed endometrium. Once transformation of the endometrium is completed, the estrogen-primed endometrium is shed resulting in a regular cyclical bleeding. However, amenorrhea has also been reported to occur during treatment with Estracomb.

Estrogen replacement therapy decreases the rate of bone loss in menopausal women; evidence of estrogen receptors on bone cells suggests there is a direct effect of estrogen on bone.

Description: The first type of transdermal system to be applied on the skin to initiate a 28-day treatment cycle is Estraderm 50. Estraderm 50 is a thin, round, multilayer, transparent transdermal therapeutic system, i.e., an adhesive patch, containing estradiol-17β that is designed for application to an area of intact skin.

The Estraderm 50 patch comprises 5 layers. Proceeding from the visible surface toward the surface attached to the skin, these layers are: 1. a transparent polyester **backing film**; 2. a drug **reservoir** of estradiol-17β and ethanol gelled with hydroxypropyl cellulose; 3. an ethylene vinyl acetate copolymer **release-controlling membrane**; 4. an **adhesive** formulation of light mineral oil and polyisobutylene; 5. a **protective liner** of siliconized polyethylene terephthalate film that is attached to the adhesive surface and must be removed before the patch can be used.

The active component of the patch is estradiol-17β. The drug reservoir provides a source for continuous delivery of drug for up to 4 days.

The second type of transdermal therapeutic system to be applied on the skin during the last 14 days of a 28-day treatment cycle is Estragest 250/50. Estragest 250/50 is a thin, twin-shaped, multilayer, transparent patch, with 2 separate drug reservoir chambers and an adhesive surface for application to an area of intact skin. Estragest 250/50 is comprised of the same 5 layers as Estraderm 50. The active substances are released from the drug reservoirs, penetrate the skin and pass directly into the bloodstream (see Supplied).

Estragest 250/50 contains a fixed combination of norethindrone acetate (NETA) and estradiol-17β. Estragest 250/50 releases controlled amounts of NETA and estradiol-17β simultaneously through the skin for up to 4 days.

Indications: The relief of menopausal and postmenopausal symptoms occurring in naturally or surgically induced estrogen deficiency states.

Estracomb is also indicated for the prevention of osteoporosis in naturally occurring or surgically induced estrogen-deficiency states in addition to other important therapeutic measures such as adequate diet and regular exercise.

Estracomb is recommended for the above indications only in patients with an intact uterus since the regimen includes a progestin whose role is to prevent endometrial hyperplasia.

Contraindications: Estracomb should not be administered to patients with any of the following conditions: active hepatic dysfunction or disease, especially of the obstructive type; known or suspected breast cancer; known or suspected estrogen-dependent neoplasia; endometrial hyperplasia; undiagnosed abnormal vaginal bleeding; porphyria; known or suspected pregnancy; a history of cerebrovascular accident, coronary thrombosis, or in the presence of classical migraine; active thrombophlebitis, thrombosis or thromboembolic disorders; partial or complete loss of vision from ophthalmic vascular disease; known or suspected hypersensitivity to any component of the patch.

Warnings: There is evidence from several studies that estrogens, unopposed by progestins, increase the risk of carcinoma of the endometrium in humans. Estracomb provides plasma norethindrone (NET) levels within the therapeutic range to counteract the effects of estradiol-17β on the endometrium. However, the overall impact on health from progestin administration to postmenopausal women is not completely known.

Breast cancer is a multifactorial disease, which increases in frequency in older age. Much of the etiology of breast cancer is unknown. Several published epidemiological studies have documented an association between a modest increase in the risk of developing breast cancer and the use of hormone replacement therapy in menopause when given for periods exceeding 5 years. Information is still lacking to show whether the risks of combination estrogen-progestin therapy differ from those of estrogen used alone. It is recommended to avoid giving estrogens to women previously treated for breast cancer. There is a need for caution in prescribing estrogens for women with a strong family history of breast cancer or who present breast nodules, fibrocystic disease of the breast, or abnormal mammograms. Other known risk factors for the development of breast cancer such as nulliparity, obesity, early menarche, late age at first full term pregnancy and at menopause should also be evaluated. It is recommended that a mammography be performed before starting treatment and repeated at regular intervals in patients at high risk for breast cancer.

The overall benefits and possible risks of hormone replacement therapy should be fully considered and discussed with patients. Instructors for self-examination of the breasts should be included in this counselling.

Contact sensitization is known to occur with topical applications. Although it is extremely rare, patients who develop contact sensitization to any component of the patch should be warned that a severe hypersensitivity reaction may occur with continuing exposure to the causative agent.

Benign hepatic adenomas have been associated with the use of combined estrogen and progestin oral contraceptives. Although benign and rare, these tumors may rupture and cause death from intra-abdominal hemorrhage. Such lesions have not yet been reported in association with other estrogen or progestin preparations, but they should be considered if abdominal pain and tenderness, abdominal mass, or hypovolemic shock occurs in patients receiving estrogen. Hepatocellular carcinoma has also been reported in women taking estrogen-containing oral contraceptives. The causal relationship of this malignancy to these drugs is not known.

The relatively small number of epidemiological studies assessing the relation between hormone replacement therapy and risk of venous thromboembolism has led to conflicting results. While earlier studies have not shown an association, some epidemiological studies have suggested that, for healthy women, there is an increased relative risk of about 2 to 3.6 for developing deep vein thrombosis or pulmonary embolism for current users of hormone replacement therapy compared to nonusers.

The physician should be alert to the earliest manifestations of thrombotic disorders (thrombophlebitis, retinal thrombosis, cerebral embolism and pulmonary embolism). If these occur or are suspected, hormone therapy should be discontinued immediately. Women with severe varicose veins, severe obesity (body mass index >30 kg/m²), or those undergoing immobilization for 3 weeks or more, trauma or surgery requiring bed rest, are generally considered to be at increased risk of venous thromboembolism. These women, and those with a past history of thromboembolic disorders during pregnancy or in association with estrogen use should be kept under special observation while using hormone replacement therapy.

Precautions: Before Estracomb is administered, the patient should have a complete physical examination including a blood pressure determination. Breasts and pelvic organs should be appropriately examined and a Papanicolaou smear and endometrial biopsy should be performed. Baseline tests should include measurements of blood glucose, calcium, triglycerides and cholesterol, and liver function tests.

The first follow-up examination should be done within 6 months after initiation of treatment to assess response to treatment. Thereafter, examinations should be made once a year and should include at least those procedures outlined above. It is important that patients are encouraged to practice frequent self-examination of the breasts.

Abnormal vaginal bleeding due to its prolongation, irregularity or heaviness occurring during therapy should prompt diagnostic measures like endometrial biopsy or curettage to rule out the possibility of uterine malignancy and the treatment should be re-evaluated.

Pre-existing uterine leiomyoma may increase in size during estrogen use. Growth, pain or tenderness of uterine leiomyoma requires discontinuation of medication.

Symptoms and physical findings associated with a previous diagnosis of endometriosis may reappear or become aggravated with estrogen use.

Patients who develop visual disturbances, classical migraine, transient aphasia, paralysis, or loss of consciousness should discontinue medication.

If feasible, estrogens should also be discontinued at least 4 weeks before surgery which may be associated with an increased risk of thromboembolism, or during periods of prolonged immobilization.

Women using oral estrogen and progestin contraceptives sometimes experience increased blood pressure which, in most cases, returns to normal upon discontinuing the drug. This may occur with use of oral estrogens during menopause and blood pressure should be monitored with estrogen use. Elevation of blood pressure in previously normotensive or hypertensive patients should be evaluated and estrogen therapy may have to be discontinued.

Estrogens may cause fluid retention. Therefore, particular caution is indicated in cardiac or renal dysfunction, epilepsy or asthma. Treatment should be stopped if there is an increase in epileptic seizures. If, in any of the above-mentioned conditions, a worsening of the underlying disease is diagnosed or suspected during treatment, the benefits and risks of treatment should be reassessed based on the individual case.

Because the prolonged use of estrogens influences the metabolism of calcium and phosphorus, estrogens should be used with caution in patients with metabolic and malignant bone diseases associated with hypercalcemia and in patients with renal insufficiency.

A worsening of glucose tolerance has been observed in a significant percentage of patients on estrogen-containing oral contraceptives. Therefore, diabetic patients or those with a predisposition to diabetes should be observed closely to detect any alterations in carbohydrate or lipid metabolism, especially in triglyceride blood levels.

A 2- to 4-fold increase in the risk of surgically confirmed gallbladder disease has been reported in postmenopausal women receiving oral estrogens.

Caution is advised in patients with a history of estrogen-related jaundice and pruritus. If cholestatic jaundice develops during treatment, the treatment should be discontinued and appropriate investigations carried out.

Women with familial hypertriglyceridemia need special surveillance. Lipid-lowering measures are recommended additionally, before treatment is started.

Liver function tests should be done periodically in subjects who are suspected of having hepatic disease. For information on endocrine and liver function tests, see the section under Laboratory Tests.

Drug Interactions: Estrogens may diminish the effectiveness of anticoagulants, antidiabetic and antihypertensive agents.

Preparations inducing liver enzymes, (e.g., barbiturates, hydantoins, carbamazepine, meprobamate, phenylbutazone or rifampin) may interfere with the activity of orally administered estrogens. The extent of interference with transdermally administered estradiol-17β and NETA is not known.

Laboratory Tests: The results of certain endocrine and liver function tests may be affected by estrogen-containing products: increased sulfobromophthalein retention; increased prothrombin time and partial thromboplastin time; increased levels of fibrinogen and fibrinogen activity; increased coagulation factors VII, VIII, IX, X; increased norepinephrine-induced platelet aggregability; decreased antithrombin III; increased thyroxine-binding globulin (TBG), leading to increased circulating total thyroid hormone (T_4) as measured by column or radioimmunoassay; free T_3 resin uptake is decreased, reflecting the elevated TBG; free T_4 concentration is unaltered; other binding proteins may be elevated in serum, i.e., corticosteroid binding protein (CBG), sex-hormone binding globulin (SHBG), leading to increased circulating corticosteroids and sex steroids respectively; free or biologically active hormone concentrations are unchanged; reduced response to the metopirone test; reduced serum folate concentration; increased serum triglyceride and phospholipid concentration.

In clinical trials with Estraderm, no effect on fibrinogen, antithrombin III, TBG, CBG or SHBG was seen.

The results of the above laboratory tests should not be considered reliable unless therapy has been discontinued for 2 to 4 months. The pathologist should be informed that the patient is receiving estrogen therapy when relevant specimens are submitted.

Information to be Provided to the Patient: See Information for the Patient.

Adverse Effects: See Warnings and Precautions regarding potential induction of malignant neoplasms and adverse effects similar to those of oral contraceptives.

The most commonly reported adverse reaction to Estracomb in clinical trials was redness and irritation at the application site. This occurred in about 7% of the women treated and caused approximately 6% to discontinue therapy.

The following adverse reactions have been reported with estrogens in general. Gastrointestinal: nausea; vomiting; abdominal discomfort (cramps, pressure, pain); bloating; gallbladder disorder; asymptomatic impaired liver function; cholestatic jaundice.

Genitourinary: The incidence of adverse reactions reported with Estracomb are indicated in brackets.

Breakthrough bleeding (>10%); spotting (>10%); change in menstrual flow (1 to 10%); dysmenorrhea (1 to 10%); vaginal itching/discharge; dyspareunia (<5%); dysuria; endometrial hyperplasia (1.5%); premenstrual-like syndrome (1 to 10%); reactivation of endometriosis; cystitis; changes in cervical erosion and amount of cervical secretion.

Dermatological/Hypersensitivity: allergic contact dermatitis; reversible post-inflammatory pigmentation; general pruritus and exanthema; loss of scalp hair; chloasma; pigmentation of the skin; erythema nodosum; erythema multiforme; hemorrhagic skin eruptions; precipitation or aggravation of porphyria cutanea tarda in predisposed individuals.

Isolated cases of anaphylactoid reactions (some of the patients had a history of previous allergy or allergic disorders).

Endocrine: breast swelling and tenderness; increased blood sugar levels; decreased glucose tolerance; sodium retention.

Cardiovascular/Hematologic: palpitations; isolated cases of: thrombophlebitis, thromboembolic disorders, exacerbations of varicose veins, increase in blood pressure (see Precautions). Coronary thrombosis; altered coagulation tests (see Precautions, Laboratory Tests).

CNS: aggravation of migraine headaches; headaches; mental depression; nervousness; dizziness; fatigue; irritability, neuro-ocular lesions (e.g., retinal thrombosis, optic neuritis).

Ophthalmic: visual disturbances; steepening of the corneal curvature; intolerance to contact lenses; neuro-ocular lesions (see CNS above).

Miscellaneous: Changes in appetite; changes in body weight; edema; neuritis; change in libido; musculoskeletal pain [including leg pain not related to thromboembolic disease (usually transient, lasting 3 to 6 weeks). If symptoms persist, the dose of estrogen should be reduced].

Overdose: Symptoms: Numerous reports of ingestion of large doses of estrogen products and estrogen-containing oral contraceptives by young children have not revealed acute serious ill effects. Overdosage with estrogen may cause nausea, breast discomfort, fluid retention, bloating or vaginal bleeding in women.

Progestin (norethindrone acetate) overdosage has been characterized by depressed mood, tiredness, acne and hirsutism.

Treatment: Owing to the mode of administration (transdermal), plasma levels of estradiol-17β and norethindrone acetate can be rapidly reduced by removal of the patch. Symptomatic treatment should be given.

Dosage: In women who are not currently taking oral estrogens, treatment with Estracomb can be initiated at once. In women who are currently taking oral estrogens, treatment with Estracomb can be initiated on reappearance of menopausal symptoms, following discontinuation of oral therapy.

One 28-day treatment cycle with Estracomb consists of 8 patches, 4 patches of Estraderm 50 and 4 patches of Estragest 250/50. Therapy is started with Estraderm 50. For 2 weeks, 1 Estraderm 50 patch is applied twice weekly i.e., the patch should be changed every 3 to 4 days. For the following 2 weeks, 1 Estragest 250/50 patch is applied twice weekly, i.e., the patch should be changed every 3 to 4 days. Once the 8 patches of Estracomb have been used in the recommended sequence over a 28-day period, the subsequent treatment cycle is again started with Estraderm 50 **immediately** after removal of the last Estragest 250/50 patch.

Estracomb provides, therefore, 14 days of progestin per cycle. The addition of sufficient NETA to induce secretory transformation of the endometrium during estrogen replacement therapy is mandatory.

As observed in the normal menstrual cycle, cyclical administration of NETA from Estragest 250/50 should induce **regular cyclical** bleeding with mean onset toward the end of Estragest 250/50 application phase. The normal duration of vaginal bleeding associated with Estracomb is around 6 days. This cyclical bleeding is expected to be of light intensity or spotting for 60 to 70% of this time. There are individual variations in these parameters. Once all 8 patches of Estracomb have been used as recommended, the first Estraderm 50 patch of the new cycle is applied even if some vaginal bleeding still persists. Vaginal bleeding should stop early in the new cycle.

Abnormal vaginal bleeding due to its prolongation, irregularity or heaviness, in any patient receiving hormone replacement therapy requires institution of prompt diagnostic measures like endometrial biopsy or curettage to rule out the possibility of uterine malignancy.

The short-term effects of NETA coadministration may include vaginal bleeding during or after NETA treatment, breast tenderness, and mood and weight changes. The long-term effects generally depend on the dosage and type of progestin used. The lowest effective dose of estrogen and progestin should be prescribed.

See the Precautions section on the examination of the patient before Estracomb administration.

Dose Adjustment: Menopausal Symptoms: Treatment of menopausal symptoms is usually initiated with a patch that releases 50 μg estradiol-17β/day. Therefore, therapy can be initiated with Estracomb in women with an intact uterus. Thereafter the dosage should be adapted to the needs of the individual.

Breast discomfort, breakthrough or heavy vaginal bleeding, water retention, bloating or nausea (if persisting for more than 6 weeks), are generally signs that the estrogen dose is too high and needs to be lowered. If on the other hand, the selected dose fails to eliminate the signs and symptoms of estrogen deficiency, a higher dose of estrogen may be considered. Women with an intact uterus whose menopausal symptoms require Estraderm 25 or Estraderm 100 should receive appropriate treatment with oral progestins in order to prevent endometrial hyperplasia (details provided in the Estraderm Product Monograph).

For maintenance therapy one should always use the lowest dose that still proves effective. The requirement for hormone replacement therapy for menopausal symptoms should be reassessed periodically. Attempts to taper or discontinue the medication should be made at 3- to 6-month intervals.

Prevention of Osteoporosis: For optimal prevention of postmenopausal bone loss in women for whom the drug is indicated, therapy should be initiated as soon as possible after diagnosis of menopause. The dosage of estradiol-17β may require adjustment according to the patient's clinical status, the plasma estradiol-17β levels and the results of bone mineral density studies.

Women with an intact uterus whose conditions require Estraderm 25 or Estraderm 100 should receive appropriate treatment with oral progestins in order to prevent endometrial hyperplasia (details provided in the Estraderm Product Monograph).

Discontinuation of hormone replacement therapy may reestablish the natural rate of bone loss.

Patch Application: The physician should discuss the most appropriate placement of the patch with the patient. Immediately after removal of a patch from the pouch and removal of the protective liner, the adhesive side of the Estraderm 50 or Estragest 250/50 patch should be placed on a clean, dry area of intact skin. The area selected should not be oily, damaged or irritated, and not exposed to the sun. The site selected should also be one at which little wrinkling of the skin occurs during movement of the body, preferably the buttocks, lower abdomen or hip. The patch may also be placed on the side or lower back. Experience to date has shown that less irritation of the skin occurs on the buttocks than on other sites of application. Therefore it is advisable to apply Estraderm 50 or Estragest 250/50 to the buttocks. The waistline should be avoided, since tight clothing may dislodge the patch. The patch should be pressed firmly in place with the palm of the hand, making sure there is good contact, especially around the edges. In the event that a patch should fall off, it can be reapplied. If it fails to adhere then a new patch may be applied. In either case, the original treatment schedule should be continued. Patches should not be applied to the same skin site twice in succession.

Estraderm 50 and Estragest 250/50 must not be applied to the breasts to avoid potentially harmful effects on the breast tissue.

Information for the Patient: See Blue Section—Information for the Patient "Estracomb".

Supplied: A package consists of the following systems: See Table I. Nonmedicinal ingredients: polyester backing film, hydroxypropyl cellulose and ethanol (drug reservoir), ethylene vinyl acetate copolymer (release-controlling membrane), light mineral oil and polyisobutylene (adhesive) and siliconized polyethylene terephthalate [protective liner (removed before patch is used)].

Table I—Estracomb

Estracomb Composition

	Estraderm 50	**Estragest 250/50**
Estradiol-17β Dosage (Nominal in vivo delivery)	50 μg/day	50 μg/day
NETA Dosage (Nominal in vivo delivery)	—	250 μg/day
Total Estradiol-17β Content	4 mg	10 mg*
Total NETA Content	—	30 mg
Drug-Releasing Area	10 cm^2	20 cm^2
Shape of patch	Round	Twin
Printed (backing side)	—	CG FNF

*In order to achieve the same delivery rate of estradiol-17β for the Estragest 250/50 patch as the Estraderm 50 patch, the content of estradiol-17β had to be increased.

Each Estracomb package contains 4 Estraderm 50 patches (2 patches/week) and 4 Estragest 250/50 patches (2 patches/week) for a 28-day treatment cycle.

Store patches below 25°C. Do not freeze. Each patch is individually sealed in a separate pouch. Do not store out of the pouch. Apply immediately upon removal from the protective pouch.

Keep Estraderm 50 and Estragest 250/50 out of the reach of children and pets both before use and when disposing of used patches.

(Shown in Product Recognition Section)

Reviewed 1999

ESTRADERM®

Novartis Pharmaceuticals

Estradiol-17β

Estrogen

Description: Estraderm is a thin, round, multilayer, transparent transdermal therapeutic system, i.e., an adhesive patch, containing estradiol-17β that is designed for application to an area of intact skin.

Estraderm (cont'd)

The Estraderm patch comprises 5 layers. Proceeding from the visible surface toward the surface attached to the skin, these layers are: 1. a transparent polyester **backing film;** 2. a drug **reservoir** of estradiol-17β and ethanol gelled with hydroxypropyl cellulose; 3. an ethylene vinyl acetate copolymer **release-controlling membrane;** 4. an **adhesive** formulation of light mineral oil and polyisobutylene; 5. a **protective liner** of siliconized polyethylene terephthalate film that is attached to the adhesive surface and must be removed before the patch can be used.

The active component of the patch is estradiol-17β. The drug reservoir provides a source for continuous delivery of drug for up to 4 days. Estraderm is available in 3 strengths; the composition per unit area is identical.

Pharmacology: Estraderm is designed to deliver daily estradiol-17β, a physiologic hormone, transdermally into the systemic circulation. Due to the transdermal route of administration, the estradiol-17β does not undergo first-pass liver metabolism. Resultant estradiol-17β plasma levels are comparable to those seen in premenopausal women in the early follicular phase of the menstrual cycle. Estradiol-17β stimulates target tissues such as the uterus, breast and vagina.

Estrogen replacement therapy decreases the rate of bone loss in menopausal women; evidence of estrogen receptors on bone cells suggests there is a direct effect of estrogen on bone.

Indications: For the relief of menopausal and postmenopausal symptoms occurring in naturally or surgically induced estrogen deficiency states.

Estradiol-17β is also indicated for the prevention of osteoporosis in naturally occurring or surgically induced estrogen deficiency states in addition to other important therapeutic measures such as adequate diet and regular exercise. In postmenopausal women already diagnosed as having osteoporosis and vertebral fractures, treatment with estradiol-17β may retard further bone loss.

In patients with an intact uterus, estradiol-17β should always be supplemented by sequential administration of a progestin whose role is to prevent endometrial hyperplasia.

Contraindications: Should not be administered to patients with any of the following conditions: active hepatic dysfunction or disease, especially of the obstructive type; known or suspected breast cancer; known or suspected estrogen-dependent neoplasia; endometrial hyperplasia; undiagnosed abnormal vaginal bleeding; porphyria; known or suspected pregnancy; a history of cerebrovascular accident, coronary thrombosis, or in the presence of classical migraine; active thrombophlebitis, thrombosis or thromboembolic disorders; partial or complete loss of vision from ophthalmic vascular disease; known or suspected hypersensitivity to any component of the patch.

Warnings: There is evidence from several studies that estrogens, unopposed by progestins, increase the risk of carcinoma of the endometrium in humans. The incidence of endometrial hyperplasia is reported to be lowered with sequential coadministration of a progestin (see Dosage, Coadministration of Progestins).

Breast cancer is a multifactorial disease, which increases in frequency in older age. Much of the etiology of breast cancer is unknown. Several published epidemiological studies have documented an association between a modest increase in the risk of developing breast cancer and the use of hormone replacement therapy in menopause when given for periods exceeding 5 years. Information is still lacking to show whether the risks of combination estrogen-progestin therapy differ from those of estrogen used alone. It is recommended to avoid giving estrogens to women previously treated for breast cancer. There is a need for caution in prescribing estrogens for women with a strong family history of breast cancer or who present breast nodules, fibrocystic disease of the breast, or abnormal mammograms. Other known risk factors for the development of breast cancer such as nulliparity, obesity, early menarche, late age at first full-term pregnancy and at menopause should also be evaluated. It is recommended that a mammography be performed before starting treatment and repeated at regular intervals in patients at high risk for breast cancer.

The overall benefits and possible risks of hormone replacement therapy should be fully considered and discussed with patients. Instructions for self-examination of the breasts should be included in this counselling.

Contact sensitization is known to occur with topical applications. Although it is extremely rare, patients who develop contact sensitization to any component of the patch should be warned that a severe hypersensitivity reaction may occur with continuing exposure to the causative agent.

Benign hepatic adenomas have been associated with the use of combined estrogen and progestin oral contraceptives. Although benign and rare, these tumors may rupture and cause death from intra-abdominal hemorrhage. Such lesions have not yet been reported in association with other estrogen or progestin preparations, but they should be considered if abdominal pain and tenderness, abdominal mass, or hypovolemic shock occurs in patients receiving estrogen. Hepatocellular carcinoma has also been reported in women taking estrogen-containing oral contraceptives. The causal relationship of this malignancy to these drugs is not known.

The relatively small number of epidemiological studies assessing the relation between hormone replacement therapy and risk of venous thromboembolism has led to conflicting results. While earlier studies have not shown an association, some epidemiological studies have suggested that, for healthy women, there is an increased relative risk of about 2 to 3.6 for developing deep vein thrombosis or pulmonary embolism for current users of hormone replacement therapy compared to nonusers.

The physician should be alert to the earliest manifestations of thrombotic disorders (thrombophlebitis, retinal thrombosis, cerebral embolism and pulmonary embolism). If these occur or are suspected, hormone therapy should be discontinued immediately.

Women with severe varicose veins, severe obesity (Body Mass Index >30 kg/m²), or those undergoing immobilization for 3 weeks or more, trauma or surgery requiring bed rest, are generally considered to be at increased risk of venous thromboembolism. These women, and those with a past history of thromboembolic disorders during pregnancy or in association with estrogen use, should be kept under special observation while using hormone replacement therapy.

Precautions: Before estradiol-17β is administered, the patient should have a complete physical examination including a blood pressure determination. Breasts and pelvic organs should be appropriately examined and a Papanicolaou smear and endometrial biopsy should be performed. Baseline tests should include measurements of blood glucose, calcium, triglycerides and cholesterol, and liver function tests.

The first follow-up examination should be done within 6 months after initiation of treatment to assess response to treatment. Thereafter, examinations should be made once a year and should include at least those procedures outlined above. It is important that patients are encouraged to practice frequent self-examination of the breasts.

Abnormal vaginal bleeding due to its prolongation, irregularity or heaviness occurring during therapy should prompt diagnostic measures like endometrial biopsy or curettage to rule out the possibility of uterine malignancy and the treatment should be re-evaluated.

Pre-existing uterine leiomyoma may increase in size during estrogen use. Growth, pain or tenderness of uterine leiomyoma requires discontinuation of medication.

Symptoms and physical findings associated with a previous diagnosis of endometriosis may reappear or become aggravated with estrogen use.

Patients who develop visual disturbances, classical migraine, transient aphasia, paralysis, or loss of consciousness should discontinue medication.

If feasible, estrogens should also be discontinued at least 4 weeks before surgery which may be associated with an increased risk of thromboembolism or during periods of prolonged immobilization.

Women using oral estrogen and progestin contraceptives sometimes experience increased blood pressure which, in most cases, returns to normal upon discontinuing the drug. This may occur with use of oral estrogens during menopause and blood pressure should be monitored with estrogen use. Elevation of blood pressure in previously normotensive or hypertensive patients should be evaluated and estrogen therapy may have to be discontinued.

Estrogens may cause fluid retention. Therefore, particular caution is indicated in cardiac or renal dysfunction, epilepsy or asthma. Treatment should be stopped if there is an increase in epileptic seizures. If, in any of the above-mentioned conditions, a worsening of the underlying disease is diagnosed or suspected during treatment, the benefits and risks of treatment should be reassessed based on the individual case.

Because the prolonged use of estrogens influences the metabolism of calcium and phosphorus, estrogens should be used with caution in patients with metabolic and malignant bone diseases associated with hypercalcemia and in patients with renal insufficiency.

A worsening of glucose tolerance has been observed in a significant percentage of patients on estrogen-containing oral contraceptives. Therefore, diabetic patients or those with a predisposition to diabetes should be observed closely to detect any alterations in carbohydrate or lipid metabolism, especially in triglyceride blood levels.

A 2- to 4-fold increase in the risk of surgically confirmed gallbladder disease has been reported in postmenopausal women receiving oral estrogens.

Caution is advised in patients with a history of estrogen-related jaundice and pruritus. If cholestatic jaundice develops during treatment, the treatment should be discontinued and appropriate investigations carried out.

Women with familial hypertriglyceridemia need special surveillance. Lipid-lowering measures are recommended additionally, before treatment is started.

Liver function tests should be done periodically in subjects who are suspected of having hepatic disease. For information on endocrine and liver function tests, see the section under Laboratory Tests.

<u>Drug Interactions:</u> Estrogens may diminish the effectiveness of anticoagulants and antidiabetic and antihypertensive agents.

Preparations inducing liver enzymes, (e.g., barbiturates, hydantoins, carbamazepine, meprobamate, phenylbutazone or rifampicin) may interfere with the activity of orally administered estrogens. The extent of interference with transdermally administered estradiol-17β is not known.

Laborataory Tests: The results of certain endocrine and liver function tests may be affected by estrogen-containing products: increased sulfobromophthalein retention; increased prothrombin time and partial thromboplastin time; increased levels of fibrinogen and fibrinogen activity; increased coagulation factors VII, VIII, IX, X; increased norepinephrine-induced platelet aggregability; decreased antithrombin III; increased thyroxine-binding globulin (TBG), leading to increased circulating total thyroid hormone (T_4) as measured by column or radioimmunoassay; free T_3 resin uptake is decreased, reflecting the elevated TBG; free T_4 concentration is unaltered; other binding proteins may be elevated in serum i.e., corticosteroid binding protein (CBG), sex-hormone binding globulin (SHBG), leading to increased circulating corticosteroids and sex steroids respectively; free or biologically active hormone concentrations are unchanged; reduced response to Metopirone test; reduced serum folate concentration; increased serum triglyceride and phospholipid concentration.

In clinical trials with Estraderm, no effect on fibrinogen, antithrombin III, TBG, CBG or SHBG and decreases in serum triglycerides were seen.

The results of the above laboratory tests should not be considered reliable unless therapy has been discontinued for 2 to 4 months. The pathologist should be informed that the patient is receiving estrogen therapy when relevant specimens are submitted.

Adverse Effects: See Warnings and Precautions regarding potential induction of malignant neoplasms and adverse effects similar to those of oral contraceptives.

The most commonly reported adverse reaction to Estraderm in clinical trials was redness and irritation at the application site. This occurred in about 17% of the women treated and caused approximately 2% to discontinue therapy.

The following adverse reactions have been reported with estrogens in general.

Gastrointestinal: nausea, vomiting; abdominal discomfort (cramps, pressure, pain); bloating; gallbladder disorder; asymptomatic impaired liver function; cholestatic jaundice.

Genitourinary: breakthrough bleeding, spotting and vaginal bleeding; change in menstrual flow, dysmenorrhea; vaginal itching/discharge, dyspareunia, dysuria, endometrial hyperplasia, premenstrual-like syndrome; reactivation of endometriosis; cystitis; changes in cervical erosion and amount of cervical secretion.

Dermatological/Hypersensitivity: allergic contact dermatitis; reversible post-inflammatory pigmentation; general pruritus and exanthema; loss of scalp hair; chloasma; pigmentation of the skin; erythema nodosum; erythema multiforme; hemorrhagic skin eruptions; precipitation or aggravation of porphyria cutanea tarda in predisposed individuals. Isolated cases of anaphylactoid reactions (some of the patients had a history of previous allergy or allergic disorders).

Endocrine: breast swelling and tenderness; increased blood sugar levels, decreased glucose tolerance, sodium retention.

Cardiovascular/Hematologic: palpitations; isolated cases of: thrombophlebitis, thromboembolic disorders; exacerbations of varicose veins, increase in blood pressure (see Precautions).

Coronary thrombosis; altered coagulation tests (see Precautions, Laboratory Tests).
CNS: aggravation of migraine headaches; headaches; mental depression; nervousness; dizziness; fatigue; irritability, neuro-ocular lesions (e.g., retinal thrombosis, optic neuritis).
Ophthalmic: visual disturbances; steepening of the corneal curvature; intolerance to contact lenses; neuro-ocular lesions (see CNS above).
Miscellaneous: changes in appetite; changes in body weight; edema; neuritis; change in libido; musculoskeletal pain [including leg pain not related to thromboembolic disease (usually transient, lasting 3 to 6 weeks). If symptoms persist, the dose of estrogen should be reduced].

Overdose: Symptoms: Numerous reports of ingestion of large doses of estrogen products and estrogen-containing oral contraceptives by young children have not revealed acute serious ill effects. Overdosage with estrogen may cause nausea, breast discomfort, fluid retention, bloating or vaginal bleeding in women.

Treatment: Owing to the mode of administration (transdermal), plasma levels of estradiol-17β can be rapidly reduced by removal of the patch.

Symptomatic treatment should be given.

Dosage: In women who are not currently taking oral estrogens, treatment with estradiol-17β can be initiated at once. In women who are currently taking oral estrogens, treatment with estradiol-17β can be initiated on reappearance of menopausal symptoms, following discontinuation of oral therapy.

Estraderm should be applied twice weekly i.e., the patch should be changed once every 3 to 4 days.

Cyclical administration is recommended (21 to 25 days of therapy followed by 5 to 7 days without). Continuous non-cyclic therapy may be indicated in hysterectomized women or in cases where the signs and symptoms of estrogen deficiency become problematic during the treatment-free interval. In women with an intact uterus, a progestin should be sequentially coadministered for a **minimum** of 10, but preferably 12 to 14 days per cycle to avoid overstimulation of the endometrium. The addition of sufficient progestin to induce secretory transformation of the endometrium during estrogen replacement therapy is mandatory.

Abnormal vaginal bleeding due to its prolongation, irregularity or heaviness in any patient receiving hormone replacement therapy requires institution of prompt diagnostic measures like endometrial biopsy or curettage to rule out the possibility of uterine malignancy.

The short-term effects of progestin coadministration may include vaginal bleeding during or after progestin treatment, breast tenderness, and mood and weight changes. The long-term effects generally depend on the dosage and type of progestin used. The lowest effective dose of estrogen and progestin should be prescribed (see Coadministration of Progestins).

See the Precautions section on the examination of the patient before estradiol-17β administration.

Dose Adjustment: Menopausal Symptoms: Treatment of menopausal symptoms is usually initiated with a patch that releases 50 μg estradiol-17β/day i.e., Estraderm 50. Thereafter the dosage should be adapted to the needs of the individual.

Breast discomfort, breakthrough or heavy vaginal bleeding, water retention, bloating or nausea (if persisting for more than 6 weeks), are generally signs that the estrogen dose is too high and needs to be lowered. If on the other hand, the selected dose fails to eliminate the signs and symptoms of estrogen deficiency, a higher dose may be considered.

For maintenance therapy one should always use the lowest dose that still proves effective. The requirement for hormone replacement therapy for menopausal symptoms should be reassessed periodically. Attempts to taper or discontinue the medication should be made at 3- to 6-month intervals.

The doses of Estraderm and Premarin which have been shown to produce the same clinical effect on postmenopausal symptomatology are: Estraderm 25: Premarin 0.3 mg; Estraderm 50: Premarin 0.625 mg; Estraderm 100: Premarin 1.25 mg.

Prevention of Osteoporosis: For optimal prevention of postmenopausal bone loss in women for whom the drug is indicated, therapy should be initiated as soon as possible after diagnosis of menopause. The dosage of estradiol-17β may require adjustment according to the patient's clinical status, the plasma estradiol-17β levels and the results of bone mineral density studies. Ideally, plasma estradiol-17β levels should be maintained at 50 pg/mL. To treat patients with established osteoporosis, therapy should be initiated with Estraderm 100.

Discontinuation of hormone replacement therapy may re-establish the natural rate of bone loss.

Patch Application: The physician should discuss the most appropriate placement of the patch with the patient. Immediately after removal of a patch from the pouch and removal of the protective liner, the adhesive side of the Estraderm patch should be placed on a clean, dry area of intact skin. The area selected should not be oily, damaged or irritated, and not exposed to the sun. The site selected should also be one at which little wrinkling of the skin occurs during movement of the body, preferably the buttocks, lower abdomen or hip. The patch may also be placed on the side or lower back. Experience to date has shown that less irritation of the skin occurs on the buttocks than on other sites of application. Therefore, it is advisable to apply Estraderm to the buttocks. The waistline should be avoided, since tight clothing may dislodge the patch. The patch should be pressed firmly in place with the palm of the hand, making sure there is good contact, especially around the edges. In the event that a patch should fall off, it can be reapplied. If it fails to adhere then a new patch may be applied. In either case, the original treatment schedule should be continued. Patches should not be applied to the same skin site twice in succession.

Estraderm must not be applied to the breasts to avoid potentially harmful effects on the breast tissue.

Coadministration of Progestins: Studies have reported that the addition of a progestin for 10 or more days of a cycle of estrogen administration greatly lowers the incidence of endometrial hyperplasia and thereby irregular bleeding and endometrial carcinoma, compared to estrogen treatment alone.

Wide interpatient variation in absorption occurs with progestins.

The following regimens have been shown, in general, to produce histological and biochemical changes consistent with a uniform secretory pattern in the endometrium: norethindrone 0.7 mg/day orally administered sequentially for 12 days each cycle; medroxyprogesterone acetate (MPA) 10 mg/day orally administered sequentially for 12 days each cycle; transdermal norethindrone acetate (NETA) 0.25 mg/day administered sequentially for 14 days each cycle.

There are possible additional risks that may be associated with the inclusion of a progestin in estrogen replacement regimens. The potential risks include adverse effects on carbohydrate and lipid metabolism, mood changes and edema. The choice and dose of progestin may be important in minimizing these adverse effects and may differ among women.

Information for the Patient: See Blue Section—Information for the Patient "Estraderm".

Supplied: See Table I. Nonmedicinal ingredients: polyester backing film, hydroxypropyl cellulose and ethanol (drug reservoir), ethylene vinyl acetate copolymer (release-controlling membrane), light mineral oil and polyisobutylene (adhesive), siliconized polyethylene terephthalate [protective liner (removed before patch is used)]. Bisulfite-, gluten-, lactose-, parabens-, sodium- and tartrazine-free. Patient packs of 8 patches.

Table I—Estraderm

Estraderm Composition

	Estraderm 25	Estraderm 50	Estraderm 100
Estradiol-17β Dosage nominal in vivo delivery	25 μg/day	50 μg/day	100 μg/day
Total Estradiol-17β content	2 mg	4 mg	8 mg
Drug-Releasing Area	5 cm²	10 cm²	20 cm²
Shape of Patch	Round	Round	Oblong
Printed (backing side)	CG DND	—	—

Store below 25°C. Do not freeze. Each patch is individually sealed in a separate pouch. Do not store out of the pouch. Apply immediately upon removal from the protective pouch. Keep out of the reach of children and pets both before use and when disposing of used patches.

(Shown in Product Recognition Section)

Reviewed 1999

Looking for information on drugs in dentistry? Consult the CLIN-INFO SECTION.

ESTRING® Pr

Pharmacia & Upjohn

Estradiol

Estrogen

Pharmacology: Estring is a slightly opaque ring with a whitish core containing a drug reservoir of 2 mg estradiol. Estradiol, silicone polymers and barium sulfate are combined to form the ring. When placed in the vagina, Estring releases estradiol, approximately 7.5 μg/24 hours, in a consistent stable manner over 90 days. Estring has the following dimensions: outer diameter 55 mm; cross-sectional diameter 9 mm; core diameter 2 mm. One Estring should be inserted into the upper third of the vaginal vault, to be worn continuously for 3 months.

At menopause the ovaries cease to secrete estradiol (E_2), leading to symptoms of estrogen deficiency such as sweating, hot flushes and sleep disturbance. A couple of years after the actual menopause, increasing numbers of women also report symptoms of urogenital estrogen deficiency such as vaginal dryness, genital pruritus, dyspareunia, dysuria and urinary urgency. These latter symptoms respond well to vaginal estrogen replacement therapy.

Pharmacokinetics: After a brief initial peak (~50 μg), estradiol vaginal ring releases a low and consistent amount of estradiol, approximately 7.5 μg/24 hours, during 90 days. Average in vitro release rates (in μg/24 hours) over 7 batches were: day 1: 47.6±6.4; day 9: 7.3±0.4; day 16: 7.7±0.4; day 45: 7.3±0.2; day 90: 7.3±0.5. The average in vivo release rate over an 88.4 day period was 9.0±0.06 μg/24 hours (n=215), calculated by subtracting the amount of estradiol in the ring at the end of the treatment period from the amount of estradiol measured in the ring before treatment, and averaging the amount over the treatment period. This gives a slightly higher value than is actually released, since it does not take the initial burst of estradiol into account.

Estrogens used in therapeutics are well absorbed through the skin, mucous membranes, and the gastrointestinal tract. The vaginal delivery of estrogens circumvents first-pass metabolism possibly reducing the induction of several other hepatic proteins.

In a Phase I study of 14 postmenopausal women, the insertion of Estring rapidly increased serum estradiol (E_2) levels attesting to the rapid absorption of estradiol via the vaginal mucosa. The time to attain peak serum estradiol levels (T_{max}) was 0.5 to 1 hour. Peak serum estradiol concentrations post-initial burst declined rapidly over the next 24 hours and were virtually indistinguishable from the baseline mean (range: 5 to 22 pg/mL). Serum levels of estradiol and estrone (E_1) over the following 12 weeks during which the ring was maintained in the vaginal vault remained relatively unchanged (see Table I on following page). The initial estradiol peak postapplication of the second ring in the same women resulted in −38% lower C_{max}, apparently due to reduced systemic absorption via the revitalized vaginal epithelium. The relative systemic exposure from the initial peak of Estring accounted for approximately 4% of the total estradiol exposure over the 12-week period.

The constant and stable release of estradiol from Estring was demonstrated in a Phase II study of 166-222 postmenopausal women who inserted up to 4 rings consecutively at 3-month intervals. Low dose systemic delivery of estradiol from Estring resulted in mean steady-state serum estradiol estimates of 7.8, 7.0, 7.0, 8.1 pg/mL at weeks 12, 24, 36, and 48, respectively. Similar reproducibility is also seen in levels of estrone. Lower systemic exposure to estradiol and estrone is further supported by serum levels measured during a pivotal Phase III study.

In postmenopausal women, mean dose of estradiol systemically absorbed unchanged from Estring is ~8% [95% CI: 2.8-12.8%] of the daily amount released locally. Low systemic exposure to estradiol and estrone resulting from Estring should elicit lower estrogen-dependent effects.

Circulating, unbound estrogens are known to modulate pharmacological response. Estrogens circulate in blood bound to sex-hormone binding globulin (SHBG) and albumin. A dynamic equilibrium exists between the conjugated and the unconjugated forms of estradiol and estrone, which undergo rapid interconversion.

Exogenously delivered or endogenously derived estrogens are primarily metabolized in the liver to estrone and estriol, which are also found in the systemic circulation. Estrogen metabolites are primarily excreted in the urine as glucuronides and sulfates. Of the several estrogen metabolites, urinary estrone and estrone sulfate (E_1S), post-Estring use, are in the normal postmenopausal range.

Estring (cont'd)

Mean percent dose excreted in the 24-hour urine as estradiol, 4 and 12 weeks postapplication of Estring in a Phase I study was 5 and 8%, respectively, of the daily released amount.

No formal drug-drug interactions studies have been done with Estring. It is anticipated that lower exposure to systemic estrogens may reduce the potential for drug interactions thus maintaining the benefit to risk ratio of concomitant drugs.

Table I—Estring

Pharmacokinetic Means Estimates Following Estring Application

Estrogen	C_{max} (pg/mL)	$C_{ss\text{-}48\ h}$ (pg/mL)	$C_{ss\text{-}4w}$ (pg/mL)	$C_{ss\text{-}12w}$ (pg/mL)
Estradiol (E_2)	63.2[a]	11.2	9.5	8.0
Baseline-adjusted E_2[b]	55.6	3.6	2.0	0.4
Estrone (E_1)	66.3	52.5	43.8	47.0
Baseline-adjusted E_1	20.0	6.2	−2.4	0.8

[a] n=14.
[b] Based on means.

The estradiol from the vaginal ring replaces the missing or decreasing endogenous estrogen production in the postmenopausal woman and eliminates or reduces urogenital estrogen deficiency signs and symptoms. Substitution therapy with estradiol vaginal ring restores vaginal pH to premenopausal values and restores the histology and physiology of the vaginal and urethral epithelium to the premenopausal state.

In vivo, estrogens diffuse through cell membranes, distribute throughout the cell, bind to and activate the estrogen receptors, thereby eliciting their biological effects. Estrogen receptors have been identified in tissues of the reproductive tract, breast, pituitary, hypothalamus, liver and bone of women. Estring delivers estradiol constantly at a mean rate of 7.5 μg/24 hours for a period of up to 90 days. Its use in postmenopausal patients in Phase I and II studies showed no apparent effects on systemic levels of hepatic protein SHBG, or FSH. Lowering of the pretreatment vaginal pH from a mean of 6.0 to a mean of 4.6 (as found in fertile women) over the 12- to 48-week treatment period, and improvements evident in the vaginal mucosal epithelium seen in all studies attest to the local dynamic effects of estrogens.

Indications: Postmenopausal urogenital complaints due to estrogen deficiency such as feeling of dryness in the vagina (atrophic vaginitis) with or without pruritus vulvae, dyspareunia, dysuria and urinary urgency (atrophic mucosa in the urethra and trigonum).

Clinical Use: Two pivotal controlled studies have demonstrated the efficacy of Estring in the treatment of postmenopausal urogenital symptoms due to estrogen deficiency.

In a U.S. study where Estring was compared with conjugated estrogens vaginal cream, no difference in efficacy between the treatment groups was found with respect to improvement in the physician's global assessment of vaginal symptoms (83% and 82% of patients receiving Estring and cream, respectively) and in the patient's global assessment of vaginal symptoms (83% and 82% of patients receiving Estring and cream, respectively) after 12 weeks of treatment. In an Australian study, Estring was also compared with conjugated estrogens vaginal cream and no difference in the physician's assessment of improvement of vaginal mucosal atrophy (79% and 75% for Estring and cream, respectively) or in the patient's assessment of improvement in vaginal dryness (82% and 76% for Estring and cream, respectively) after 12 weeks of treatment.

In the U.S. study, symptoms of dysuria and urinary urgency improved in 74% and 65%, respectively, of patients receiving Estring as assessed by the patient. In the Australian study, symptoms of dysuria and urinary urgency improved in 90% and 71%, respectively, of patients receiving Estring as assessed by the patient.

In both studies, Estring and conjugated estrogens vaginal cream had a similar ability to reduce vaginal pH levels and to mature the vaginal mucosa (as measured cytologically using the maturation index and/or the maturation value) after 12 weeks of treatment. In supportive studies, Estring was also shown to have a similar significant treatment effect on the maturation of the urethral mucosa.

Endometrial overstimulation, as evaluated in nonhysterectomized patients participating in the U.S. study by the progestogen challenge test and pelvic sonogram, was reported for none of the 58 (0%) patients receiving Estring and 4 of the 35 patients (11%) receiving conjugated estrogens vaginal cream.

Of the U.S. women who completed 12 weeks of treatment, 95% rated product comfort for Estring as excellent or very good compared with 65% of patients receiving conjugated estrogens vaginal cream, 95% of Estring patients judged the product to be very easy or easy to use compared with 88% of cream patients, and 82% gave Estring an overall rating of excellent or very good compared with 58% for the cream.

Contraindications: Patients with the following conditions: known or suspected estrogen-dependent malignancy; undiagnosed vaginal bleeding; known or suspected pregnancy; patients hypersensitive to any of its ingredients.

Other higher dose estrogen replacement therapies are contraindicated in patients with the following additional conditions: active hepatic dysfunction or disease, particularly of the obstructive type; history of cerebrovascular accident, coronary thrombosis, or presence of classical migraine; history of thrombophlebitis or thromboembolic disease; partial or complete loss of vision or diplopia due to ophthalmic vascular disease.

Warnings: Before estrogens are administered the patient should have a complete physical examination, including examination of breasts and pelvic organs. Unless done recently, a Papanicolaou smear should be taken.

In addition, any woman with symptoms/signs of abnormal vaginal discharge, vaginal discomfort, or any undiagnosed persistent or recurring abnormal vaginal bleeding should be examined fully, to exclude malignancy, ulceration, infection, or unresponsive atrophic vaginitis. Minor signs of irritation are often transient.

For patients with signs of ulceration or severe inflammation due to unresponsive atrophic vaginitis, withdrawal from treatment should be considered.

One of the well documented adverse effects of estrogen replacement therapy is its stimulation of cell growth, with resultant endometrial proliferation. Endometrial biopsy results in postmenopausal women treated for 3 months with Estring showed the incidence of proliferation to be no higher than in untreated peri- and postmenopausal women. The potential risk of endometrial carcinoma still has to be considered if vaginal bleeding occurs. Data currently available on long-term unopposed treatment with Estring, although limited, do not indicate a proliferative effect on the endometrium. Long-term studies on the effect of Estring on the endometrium are ongoing.

Although the estrogen content of oral contraceptive therapy has been associated with an increased risk of various thromboembolic, thrombotic and vascular diseases, to date no such increased risk in postmenopausal users of estrogens has been detected. Nevertheless, the physician should be alert to the earliest manifestations of thrombotic disorders. If these occur or are suspected, estrogen therapy should be discontinued immediately.

Although there is no clear association between the postmenopausal use of estrogens and breast cancer, there is a need for caution in prescribing estrogens of any kind to women with a strong family history of breast cancer or patients who have breast nodules, fibrocystic disease or abnormal mammograms.

Precautions: General: Some women may be unsuitable for treatment with Estring, in particular those with short narrow vaginas due to previous surgery or the effect of atrophy, or those with a degree of uterovaginal prolapse severe enough to prevent retention of the ring.

A potential problem related to the vaginal ring is a tendency in a limited number of patients for the ring to slide down, move or fall out. This was noticed primarily during the first 3 weeks of treatment and was the reason for withdrawal from treatment for 3% of the patients on their first ring (see Information for the Patient).

If any medical procedures are performed, the pathologist should be advised of the patient's therapy when specimens are sent for examination.

Patients should be advised to inform their physician if irritation, pain, discharge or bleeding occur.

X-Ray Procedures: If any x-ray procedures of the lower abdominal tract take place, the vaginal ring should be removed since the barium sulfate containing core is visible on x-ray and could disturb the procedure or evaluation of x-rays.

Liver Disease: Liver function tests should be made periodically in subjects who have, or are suspected of having, hepatic disease. It is advisable that patients with acute intermittent porphyria be treated with caution and that periodic medical examinations be performed.

Other Endocrine or Metabolic Effects: Although no effect of low dose vaginal estradiol supplementation has been seen on glucose tolerance, fluid retention, elevation of blood pressure or other liver or endocrine functions, patients with predisposition to or signs indicating an effect on those variables could indicate caution.

Pregnancy: Estring is indicated for postmenopausal treatment. Women of childbearing potential should, therefore, not be prescribed this product.

Drug Interactions: Enzyme inducers, for example barbiturates, hydantoins, carbamazepine and rifampin can enhance estrogen metabolism, resulting in breakthrough bleeding or vaginal spotting. However, due to the low dose released, and since the estrogen is administered vaginally, thereby circumventing the first pass metabolism of the liver, it is unlikely that this interaction is relevant for Estring.

Uterine Bleeding and Mastodynia: Although uncommon with Estring, certain patients may develop undesirable manifestations of estrogenic stimulation, such as abnormal uterine bleeding and mastodynia.

Location of Estring: Some women have experienced moving or gliding of Estring within the vagina. Instances of Estring being expelled from the vagina in connection with moving the bowels, strain, or constipation have been reported. If this occurs, Estring can be rinsed in lukewarm water and reinserted into the vagina by the patient.

Vaginal Irritation: Estring may not be suitable for women with narrow, short, or stenosed vaginas. Narrow vagina, vaginal stenosis, prolapse, and vaginal infections are conditions that make the vagina more susceptible to Estring-caused irritation or ulceration. Women with signs or symptoms of vaginal irritation should alert their physician.

Vaginal Infection: Vaginal infection is generally more common in postmenopausal women due to the lack of the normal flora of fertile women, especially lactobacillus, and the subsequent higher pH. Vaginal infections should be treated with appropriate antimicrobial therapy before initiation of Estring. If a vaginal infection develops during use of Estring, then Estring should be removed and reinserted only after the infection has been appropriately treated.

Other: Hypercoagulability and hyperlipidemia have been reported in women on other types of estrogen replacement therapy, but these have not been seen with Estring patients.

Fluid retention is another known risk factor with estrogen therapy and may be harmful to patients with asthma, epilepsy, migraine and cardiac or renal dysfunction. Estring treatment has not been associated with any indication of increase in body weight up to 48 weeks of treatment.

Adverse Effects: The biological safety of the silicone elastomer has been studied in various in vitro and in vivo test models. The results show that the silicone elastomer is nontoxic, nonpyrogenic, nonirritating, and nonsensitizing. Long-term implantation induced encapsulation equal to or less than the negative control (polyethylene) used in the USP test. No toxic reaction or tumor formation was observed with the silicone elastomer.

In general, Estring was well tolerated. In the 2 pivotal controlled studies, discontinuation of treatment due to an adverse event was required by 5.4% of patients receiving Estring and 3.9% of patients receiving conjugated estrogens vaginal cream. The most common reason for withdrawal from Estring treatment due to an adverse event were vaginal discomfort and gastrointestinal symptoms.

The adverse events reported with a frequency of 3% or greater in the 2 pivotal controlled studies by patients receiving Estring or conjugated estrogens vaginal cream are listed in Table II (on following page).

Other adverse events (listed alphabetically) occurring at a frequency of 1 to 3% in the 2 pivotal controlled studies by patients receiving Estring include: anxiety, bronchitis, chest pain, cystitis, dermatitis, diarrhea, dyspepsia, dysuria, flatulence, gastritis, genital eruption, genital pruritus, hemorrhoids, leg edema, migraine, otitis media, skin hypertrophy, syncope, toothache, tooth disorder, urinary incontinence.

The following additional adverse events were reported at least once by patients receiving Estring in the worldwide clinical program, which includes controlled and uncontrolled studies. A causal relationship with Estring has not been established.

Body as a Whole: allergic reaction.
CNS/Peripheral Nervous System: dizziness.
Gastrointestinal: enlarged abdomen, vomiting.
Metabolic/Nutritional Disorders: weight decrease or increase.
Psychiatric: depression, decreased libido, nervousness.
Reproductive: breast engorgement, breast enlargement, intermenstrual bleeding, genital edema, vulval disorder.
Skin/Appendages: pruritus, pruritus ani.
Urinary: micturition frequency, urethral disorder.
Vascular: thrombophlebitis.
Vision: abnormal vision.

Table II—Estring

Adverse Events Reported by 3% or More of Patients Receiving Either Estring or Conjugated Estrogens Vaginal Cream in 2 Pivotal Controlled Studies

Adverse Events	Estring (n=257) %	Conjugated Estrogens Vaginal Cream (n=129) %
Musculoskeletal		
Back Pain	6	8
Arthritis	4	2
Arthralgia	3	5
Skeletal Pain	2	4
CNS/Peripheral Nervous System		
Headache	13	16
Psychiatric		
Insomnia	4	0
Gastrointestinal		
Abdominal Pain	4	2
Nausea	3	2
Respiratory		
Upper Respiratory Tract Infection	5	6
Sinusitis	4	3
Pharyngitis	1	3
Urinary		
Urinary Tract Infection	2	7
Female Reproductive		
Leukorrhea	7	3
Vaginitis	5	2
Vaginal Discomfort/Pain	5	5
Vaginal Hemorrhage	4	5
Asymptomatic Genital Bacterial Growth	4	6
Breast Pain	1	7
Resistance Mechanisms		
Genital Moniliasis	6	7
Body as a Whole		
Flu-like Symptoms	3	2
Hot Flushes	2	3
Allergy	1	4
Miscellaneous		
Family Stress	2	3

Overdose: Symptoms and Treatment: The following symptoms and treatment of overdose are for estrogens in general: excessive doses of estrogens may result in nausea, vomiting, abdominal cramps, headache, dizziness and general malaise. Treatment should be discontinued and symptomatic treatment administered.

It is highly unlikely that overdosage would occur with Estring, as the principle of its release mechanism prevents overdose.

Dosage: One Estring is to be inserted as deeply as possible into the upper one-third of the vaginal vault. The ring is to remain in place continuously for 3 months, after which it is to be removed and, if continuation of therapy is deemed appropriate, replaced by a new ring. The need to continue treatment should be assessed at 3- or 6-month intervals.

Should the ring be removed or fall out at any time during the 90-day treatment period, the ring should be rinsed in lukewarm water and re-inserted by the patient, or, if necessary, by a physician or nurse.

Retention of the ring for greater than 90 days does not represent overdosage but will result in progressively greater underdosage with the attendant risk of loss of efficacy and increasing risk of vaginal infections and/or erosions.

Instructions for Insertion: Estring insertion: The ring should be pressed into an oval and inserted into the upper third of the vaginal vault. The exact position is not critical. When Estring is in place, the patient should not feel anything. If the patient feels discomfort, Estring is probably not far enough inside. Gently push Estring further into the vagina.

Estring use: Estring should be left in place continuously for 90 days and then, if continuation of therapy is deemed appropriate, replaced by a new Estring. The patient should not feel Estring when it is in place and it should not interfere with sexual intercourse. Straining at defecation may make Estring move down in the lower part of the vagina. If so, it may be pushed up again with a finger. If Estring is expelled totally from the vagina, it should be rinsed in lukewarm water and reinserted by the patient (or doctor/nurse if necessary).

Estring removal: Estring may be removed by hooking a finger through the ring and pulling it out. For patient instructions, see Information for the Patient.

Information for the Patient: See Blue Section—Information for the Patient "Estring".

Supplied: Each slightly opaque vaginal ring, made of a silicone elastomer sheath surrounding a whitish silicone elastomer core, contains: estradiol 2 mg, barium sulfate as a marker and silicone fluid as a dispersing agent. The estradiol is released slowly, 7.5 μg/24 hours. Individually packed in a heat-sealed rectangular pouch consisting of, from outside to inside: polyester/aluminum foil/low density polyethylene. The pouch is provided with a tear-off notch on one side. Each pouch is packed into a cardboard carton containing a patient information leaflet. Store at room temperature (15 to 30°C).

Reviewed 1998

ETHAMBUTOL HCl ℞

General Monograph, CPhA

Antimycobacterial

This monograph has been compiled by CPhA. It may contain information different from that approved by Therapeutic Products Programme, Health Canada, and the pharmaceutical manufacturers' approval has not been requested.

Pharmacology: Ethambutol is a bacteriostatic agent which diffuses into actively growing mycobacterium cells such as tubercle bacilli, where it inhibits the synthesis of one or more essential metabolites, causing impairment of cell metabolism, arrest of multiplication, and cell death.

It is active in vitro against strains of M. tuberculosis and other Mycobacterium species, but not other bacteria, fungi or viruses.

Resistance develops rapidly if ethambutol is used alone. It seems to develop in a step-wise manner and may be delayed or prevented by using ethambutol in combination with other antituberculosis agents. Cross-resistance has not been reported with other antituberculosis agents.

The minimum inhibitory concentration for susceptible strains is 1 to 8 μg/mL, depending on the culture medium used.

Pharmacokinetics: Ethambutol is about 75 to 80% absorbed after an oral dose. Absorption is rapid and does not seem to be affected by food.

Following a single oral dose of 25 mg/kg of body weight, ethambutol attains a peak serum level of 2 to 5 μg/mL 2 to 4 hours after administration. No drug accumulation has been observed with consecutive single daily doses of 25 mg/kg in patients with normal kidney function, although marked accumulation has been demonstrated in patients with renal insufficiency. Serum concentrations are undetectable 24 hours after the last dose except in some patients with abnormal renal function.

Ethambutol distributes widely into body fluids and tissues. Concentrations in erythrocytes may reach 2 to 3 times the plasma concentrations. It also appears in the lungs, kidneys, urine, and saliva, and to lesser extents in pleural and ascitic fluids. Ethambutol crosses the placenta. CSF concentrations reaching 10 to 50% of serum concentrations may occur with inflamed meninges. Ethambutol is not highly bound to plasma proteins. Its volume of distribution is about 1.6 L/kg.

The half-life of ethambutol is about 3 to 4 hours in patients with normal renal function; it may be as long as 7 to 8 hours in patients with renal insufficiency and 18 to 20 hours in the anephric patient.

Within 24 hours after oral administration, approximately 50% of the initial dose is excreted unchanged in the urine, while an additional 8 to 15% appears as inactive metabolites. The main metabolic path appears to be an initial oxidation of the alcohol to an aldehydic intermediate, followed by conversion to a dicarboxylic acid. From 20 to 22% of the initial dose is excreted in the feces as unchanged drug.

Indications: For the treatment of pulmonary tuberculosis. Ethambutol should only be used in conjunction with at least one other antituberculosis agent.

A 4 drug regimen including ethambutol may be used for initial treatment in persons with known exposure to isoniazid-resistant organisms, those who have previously received antitubercular drugs (i.e., retreatment of relapse cases) and in persons from parts of the world where drug-resistant tuberculosis is prevalent. Isoniazid resistance is common in Latin America, Africa, Southeast Asia, and other areas. Other factors to consider in the selection of antituberculosis therapy are results of in vitro susceptibility testing, considerations of comparative safety, local resistance patterns and severity of the disease.

In the treatment of relapse cases (i.e., retreatment) mycobacterial resistance to other drugs used in initial therapy is frequent. In these patients, ethambutol should be combined with at least one drug not previously administered to the patient and to which in vitro bacterial susceptibility has been indicated.

Ethambutol is also used in conjunction with other agents in the treatment of infections caused by M. avium complex and other mycobacteria.

Contraindications: Known hypersensitivity to the drug; known optic neuritis unless considerations of risk versus benefit (clinical judgment) determine that it may be used.

Warnings: Ethambutol may cause optic neuritis with decreased visual acuity, visual field constriction, loss of red-green color vision, or scotomata. Ocular toxicity may be related to dose and duration of treatment; however, it has occurred rarely after only a few days of therapy. Approximately 6% of patients receiving the drug have exhibited decreases in visual acuity. The effects are generally reversible when detected early and the drug discontinued promptly. Recovery of visual acuity generally occurs over a period of weeks to months after the drug has been discontinued. Some patients have then received ethambutol again, without recurrent loss of visual acuity. In rare cases, recovery may be delayed for up to 1 year or more, and the effects may be irreversible in some cases.

Visual acuity and color vision should be thoroughly tested before beginning treatment with ethambutol and periodically during drug therapy. Monthly examination is recommended for patients receiving doses greater than 15 mg/kg.

The changes in visual acuity may be unilateral or bilateral; hence, each eye must be tested separately and both eyes tested together. Snellen eye charts are recommended for testing of visual acuity. Ophthalmoscopy, finger perimetry and color discrimination should also be included in the baseline evaluation. If corrective lenses are used prior to treatment, they must be worn during visual acuity testing. During 1 to 2 years of ethambutol therapy, a refractive error may develop which must be corrected (by testing visual acuity through a pinhole) in order to obtain accurate results.

In patients with pre-existing visual defects such as cataracts, recurrent inflammatory conditions of the eye, optic neuritis and diabetic retinopathy, the evaluation of changes in visual acuity is more difficult, and care should be taken to ensure that the variations in vision are not due to the underlying disease condition. In such patients, consideration should be given to the expected benefits of ethambutol therapy and the possibility of visual deterioration.

Patients developing ocular toxicities during treatment may show subjective symptoms before, or at the same time as, decreases in visual acuity. All patients receiving ethambutol should be questioned periodically about blurred vision and other subjective eye symptoms. Progressive decreases in visual acuity during therapy must be considered to be due to ethambutol.

Patients should be advised to promptly report any changes in visual acuity to their physician.

Precautions: Use with caution in patients with decreased renal function due to the risk of drug accumulation; ethambutol dosage should be reduced.

Ethambutol may inhibit the response to BCG vaccine.

Periodic assessment of systemic functions, including renal, hepatic and hematopoietic should be made during long-term therapy.

Pregnancy: Reproductive studies in mice or rabbits have shown slight increases in fetal mortality when ethambutol was given at doses 10 times greater than the maximum human use dose. A low incidence of fetal abnormality was seen among animals receiving 4 to 10 times the maximum human use dose. The possibility that these findings are drug-related cannot be ruled out. Clinical experience has not shown an increase in the risk of abnormalities when the drug was administered throughout pregnancy. Although it appears that the possibility of fetal harm is remote, because of the findings in animals, ethambutol should be used during pregnancy only if clearly needed. Loss of fertility and testicular regression among male rats administered ethambutol has been reported. No effects on the testes were seen in other rat studies, or among other species treated with very high doses, for extended periods of time. There have been no reports of an antifertility effect in humans.

Ethambutol HCl (cont'd)

Lactation: Ethambutol is excreted in the milk of nursing mothers.
Children: Ethambutol is not recommended for use in children under 13 years of age, although it has been used in children older than 6 years of age. It should only be used in children whose visual acuity and color vision can be accurately determined and monitored.

Adverse Effects: Ophthalmologic: optic neuritis, decreased visual acuity, constriction of visual fields, central and peripheral scotomata, color vision defects (especially red-green color discrimination).
Dermatologic: dermatitis, pruritus.
Hypersensitivity: anaphylactoid reactions, fever, malaise. Rarely, Stevens-Johnson syndrome, toxic epidermal necrolysis.
Renal: rarely, interstitial nephritis, nephrotoxicity (may be related to other antituberculous therapy).
Hematologic: rare case reports of thrombocytopenia, and neutropenia.
Gastrointestinal: anorexia, nausea, vomiting, abdominal pain, metallic taste.
CNS: headache, dizziness, mental confusion, possible hallucinations. Peripheral neuritis has been reported infrequently.
Hepatic: rarely, jaundice. Since ethambutol is recommended for therapy in conjunction with one or more other antituberculous drugs, these changes may be related to concurrent therapy.
Other: Elevated serum uric acid levels and precipitation of gout have been reported. Joint pain has also been reported.

Overdose: Symptoms: anorexia, nausea, vomiting, gastrointestinal upset, abdominal pain, fever, malaise, headache, dizziness, mental confusion, disorientation and possible hallucinations.

Treatment: No specific antidote. Stop ethambutol administration. Remove drug by emesis or gastric lavage. Anaphylactoid reactions may necessitate emergency treatment.

Dosage: M. tuberculosis: Ethambutol should not be used alone in initial treatment or in retreatment. The drug should be administered on a once every 24 hour basis only. In general, therapy should be continued until bacteriological conversion has become permanent and maximal clinical improvement has occurred.

The duration of therapy should be a minimum of 6 to 9 months for initial treatment cases. Cases of drug-resistant tuberculosis, immunocompromised patients and retreatment cases may require 12 to 18 months or longer of therapy.
Initial Treatment: As part of a multi-drug regimen in adult patients who have not received previous antituberculous therapy, administer ethambutol 15 mg/kg as a single oral dose every 24 hours. The maximum recommended daily dose is 2.5 g.
Retreatment: In adult patients who have received previous antituberculous therapy, administer ethambutol 25 mg/kg as a single oral dose once every 24 hours. Concurrently administer at least one other antituberculosis agent not previously used and to which the organisms have been demonstrated to be susceptible by appropriate in vitro tests. After 60 days of therapy, or when bacteriologic cultures become negative, decrease the dose to 15 mg/kg once every 24 hours. During the period when a patient is on a daily dose of 25 mg/kg, monthly eye examinations are advised.
Twice Weekly Therapy: After an initial period of daily therapy, ethambutol may be given as part of a multiple-drug regimen at an adult dose of 50 mg/kg (up to 2.5 g) twice a week for the remainder of the chosen treatment period. The duration of the initial daily therapy period will depend on the number and combination of antituberculosis agents used as well as the patient's clinical status. Alternatively, ethambutol has been used in combination with other agents at a dose of 25 to 30 mg/kg 3 times weekly.
Children (see Precautions, Children): In children whose visual acuity can be accurately monitored, 10 to 15 mg/kg is given once daily in conjunction with other antituberculosis agents. Specialized pediatric references should be consulted for detailed dosing information.
M. avium complex (M. avium and M. intracellulare): In combination with other agents, the adult dose is 15 to 25 mg/kg/day, continued until patient has been culture-negative for 1 year.
M. kansasii: In combination with rifampin plus isoniazid, the adult dose is 15 to 25 mg/kg/day for a minimum of 12 months.
M. marinum: In combination with rifampin, the adult dose is 15 to 25 mg/kg/day for a minimum of 3 months.
Ethambutol may be used in a dosage of 15 mg/kg/day in combination with other antimycobacterial agents for the treatment of other nontuberculous mycobacterial infections such as those caused by M. xenopi and M. genavense.
Dosage in Renal Failure: If creatinine clearance is 0.17 to 0.83 mL/s, give 50% of the normal dose once daily. Alternately, extend the dosing interval to once every 24 to 36 hours. If creatinine clearance is less than 0.17 mL/s, reduce the dose to 25% of the normal dose once daily, or extend the interval to once every 48 hours.

Reviewed 1999

ETHRANE® Ⓟ
Zeneca

Enflurane

Inhalation Anesthetic

Pharmacology: Enflurane is an inhalation anesthetic. Induction and recovery from anesthesia with enflurane are rapid. Enflurane does not appear to stimulate excessive salivation or tracheabronchial secretions, or affect bronchomotor tone. Pharyngeal and laryngeal reflexes are readily obtunded. The level of anesthesia changes rapidly, which would be predicted based upon its Oswald partition coefficients.

Enflurane reduces ventilation as depth of anesthesia increases. This is a result of a decrease in tidal volume with rate of respiration remaining essentially constant. Enflurane provokes a sigh response reminiscent of diethyl ether.

There is a decrease in blood pressure with induction of anesthesia, followed by a return to near normal with surgical stimulation. A slight fall in cardiac output, stroke volume, and peripheral resistance, and an increase in central venous pressure may occur. Progressive increases in depth of anesthesia produce corresponding increases in hypotension. ECG monitoring and recording indicate that the cardiac rhythm remains remarkably stable. Elevation of CO_2 level in arterial blood does not alter cardiac rhythm.

While enflurane has been shown to sensitize the myocardial conduction system to epinephrine in the dog and may produce serious arrhythmias, studies in cats and man indicate that there is a certain margin of safety in the administration of epinephrine-containing solutions during enflurane anesthesia. Enflurane anesthesia has been used in medical conditions involving high levels of endogenous catecholamines, as well as surgical procedures involving carefully administered quantities of epinephrine-containing solutions. On the basis of this experience, up to 10 mL of 1:100 000 or 1:200 000 epinephrine-containing solution alone or in conjunction with lidocaine 0.5 to 2.0% may be injected s.c. at a rate of not more than 10 mL/10-minute period and no more than 30 mL/h. The concomitant administration of lidocaine enhances the safety of the use of epinephrine during enflurane anesthesia. This effect of lidocaine is dose related. More dilute solutions and reduced dosages should be used in highly vascular areas. All customary precautions in the use of vasoconstrictor substances should be observed, including monitoring of respiration, blood pressure and pulse. Epinephrine should be used in association with enflurane only in patients who have adequate pulmonary function to ensure optimal pulmonary ventilation and should not be used in patients with pre-existing cardiac disease who cannot tolerate the tachycardia or hypertension which may result from the administration of exogenous catecholamines, or in patients with hyperthyroidism.

Muscle relaxation in man may in certain cases be adequate for intra-abdominal operations at normal levels of anesthesia. Should greater relaxation be necessary, minimal doses of muscle relaxants may be used. Nondepolarizing muscle relaxants are markedly potentiated by enflurane. All commonly used muscle relaxants are compatible with enflurane. Neostigmine does not reverse the direct relaxant effect of enflurane.

Enflurane 0.25 to 1.0% (average 0.5%) provides analgesia equal to that produced by 30 to 60% (average 40%) nitrous oxide for vaginal delivery. With either agent, patients remain awake, cooperative and oriented. These anesthetic approaches produce normal Apgar scores and comparable maternal blood losses. Neither enflurane nor nitrous oxide when used for obstetrical analgesia alters BUN, creatinine, uric acid or osmolality. The only difference in the use of these two agents for obstetrical analgesia appears to be higher inspired oxygen concentration that may be used with enflurane.

Analgetic doses of enflurane (e.g. 0.5 to 0.8%) do not significantly depress the frequency of contraction of human uterine muscle. Force of contraction remains at more than 80% of normal. Higher concentrations (1.5 to 3.0%) depress both rate and contractility. Intrauterine manipulations for versions and extractions are easily done at higher concentrations because of the profound uterine relaxation. Blood loss in patients anesthetized for therapeutic abortion with 1.0% enflurane in 70% nitrous oxide is 24 mL greater than blood loss in patients receiving paracervical block anesthesia. Uterine bleeding may be increased when enflurane is used in anesthetizing concentrations for vaginal delivery or delivery by Cesarean section. However, unless the enflurane concentration exceeds 2 to 3%, the uterine muscle remains responsive to oxytocic administration. Babies delivered per vagina or by Cesarean section under nitrous oxide-enflurane anesthesia usually have normal Apgar scores.

The systemic metabolism of enflurane in humans was measured in healthy female patients anesthetized with enflurane and undergoing routine gynecological procedures. In 7 patients, 85.1% of the administered enflurane was recovered; 82.7% as unchanged enflurane and 2.4% as nonvolatile fluorine-containing urinary metabolites. Of the urinary fluorine-containing metabolites, 0.5% was inorganic fluoride and 1.9% organic fluoride. Maximum inorganic fluoride excretion was attained in 7 hours, while maximum urinary organic fluoride excretion was attained on the second day. Although metabolism to the extent of at least 2.4% is attained, the degree is much less than that reported with halothane, methoxyflurane, fluroxene and trichloroethylene.

Serum inorganic fluoride was determined in 66 patients receiving enflurane. The patient population consisted of 23 males, 43 females, with a mean age of 53, age spread of 19 to 88, and a mean duration of anesthesia of 212 minutes. The mean serum inorganic fluoride levels in μmol/L are as follows (the standard error of the mean was 0.03 to 2.6): before anesthesia (control) 1.54; 1 hour anesthesia 11.1; end of anesthesia 15.6; 24 hours postoperatively 7.6; 48 hours postoperatively 3.5.

These levels are well below the 50 μmol/L threshold level which can produce minimal renal damage in normal subjects. However, patients chronically ingesting isoniazid or other hydrazine-containing compounds may metabolize greater amounts of enflurane. Although no significant renal dysfunction has been found thus far in such patients, peak serum fluoride levels can exceed 50 μmol/L, particularly when anesthesia goes beyond 2 MAC hours. Depression of lymphocyte transformation does not follow prolonged enflurane anesthesia in man in the absence of surgery. Thus enflurane does not depress this aspect of the immune response.

Indications: May be used for induction and maintenance of general anesthesia. Enflurane may be used for analgesia in vaginal delivery. Enflurane may also be used for anesthesia during operative vaginal delivery or delivery by Caesarean section. However, as noted above, higher concentrations of enflurane may produce uterine bleeding.

Contraindications: Seizure disorders (see Warnings). Known sensitivity to enflurane or other halogenated anesthetics.

Warnings: With increasing depth of enflurane anesthesia, CNS excitation occurs, manifested by a change in the EEG characterized by high voltage, fast frequency, progressing through spike-dome complexes alternating with periods of electrical silence to frank seizure activity. The latter may or may not be associated with motor movement. Motor activity, when encountered, generally consists of twitching or "jerks" of various muscle groups; it is self-limiting and can be terminated by lowering the anesthetic concentration. This EEG pattern associated with deep anesthesia is exacerbated by hyperventilation producing low arterial CO_2 tension. The pattern serves as a warning that depth of anesthesia is excessive.

Cerebral blood flow and metabolism studies in normal volunteers during seizure patterns show no evidence of cerebral hypoxia, and recovery appears to be uncomplicated. Nevertheless, enflurane should not be used in patients with convulsive disorders.

Since levels of anesthesia may be altered easily and rapidly, only vaporizers producing predictable concentrations should be used. Hypotension and respiratory exchange can serve as a guide to anesthesia depth. With deep levels of anesthesia, more marked hypotension and respiratory depression are encountered.

The action of nondepolarizing relaxants is augmented by enflurane, so less than the usual amounts of those drugs should be used. The time for recovery from the myoneural effect of these relaxants is greater in the presence of enflurane than for other commonly used anesthetics.

Safety of repeat anesthesia with enflurane has not been established.

Epinephrine-containing solutions should be used in association with enflurane only in patients with adequate pulmonary function and should not be used in patients with pre-existing cardiac disease who cannot tolerate the tachycardia or hypertension which may result from the administration of exogenous catecholamines, or patients with hyperthyroidism.

Pregnancy: Safe use in pregnancy other than for analgesia for vaginal delivery or anesthesia during operative vaginal delivery or Cesarean section has not been established. Reproduction studies performed in rabbits and rats reveal no evidence of harm to the animal fetus. The relevance of these studies to the human is not known. There is no adequate experience in pregnant women who have received enflurane during the course of pregnancy (other than at term). Thus, safety to the fetus or pregnant mother has not been established.

Precautions: Bromsulfalein (BSP) retention is mildly elevated postoperatively in some cases. There is some elevation of glucose and WBC count intraoperatively. Glucose elevation should be considered in diabetic patients.

In susceptible individuals, enflurane anesthesia may trigger a skeletal muscle hypermetabolic state leading to high oxygen demand and the clinical syndrome known as malignant hyperthermia. The syndrome includes nonspecific features such as muscle rigidity, tachycardia, tachypnea, cyanosis, arrhythmias, and unstable blood pressure. (It should also be noted that many of these nonspecific signs may appear with light anesthesia, acute hypoxia, etc. The syndrome of malignant hyperthermia secondary to enflurane appears to be rare; by March 1980, 35 cases had been reported in North America for an approximate incidence of 1/725 000 enflurane anesthesias.) An increase in overall metabolism may be reflected in an elevated temperature (which may rise rapidly early or late in the case, but usually is not the first sign of augmented metabolism) and an increased usage of the CO_2 absorption system (hot canister). PaO_2 and pH may decrease, and hyperkalemia and a base deficit may appear. Treatment includes discontinuance of triggering agents (e.g. enflurane), administration of i.v. dantrolene sodium, and application of supportive therapy. Such therapy includes vigorous efforts to restore body temperature to normal, respiratory and circulatory support as indicated, and management of electrolyte-fluid-acid-base derangements. (Consult prescribing information for dantrolene sodium i.v. for additional information on patient management.) Renal failure may appear later, and urine flow should be sustained if possible.

Adverse Effects: Motor activity exemplified by movement of various muscle groups and/or seizures may be encountered with deep levels of enflurane anesthesia.

Hypotension, respiratory depression, arrhythmias, shivering, hyperthermia, nausea and vomiting have been reported.

Elevation of the WBC count has been observed. It has not been determined whether this is related to enflurane or to surgical stress.

Elevation of AST, LDH, alkaline phosphatase, and bilirubin, with or without frank jaundice, have been reported in the postoperative period following enflurane anesthesia in some patients. Hepatitis has been reported very rarely.

Delirium, hallucinations and hiccup occur rarely.

Overdose: Symptoms: Overdosage will generally produce marked hypotension and apnea in the absence of muscle relaxants.

Treatment: In the event of overdosage, or what may appear to be overdosage, the following action should be taken: Stop drug administration. Establish that the airway is clear. Instigate assisted or controlled ventilation with pure oxygen as the circumstances dictate.

Similarly, motor activity and increased electrical and seizure-like activity in the EEG may be indicative of excessive levels of anesthesia. In the event that this occurs, it is recommended that the level of anesthesia be lowered. If motor activity does not cease, the administration of enflurane should be discontinued.

Dosage: The concentration of enflurane being delivered during anesthesia from a vaporizer should be known. This may be accomplished by using: (a) vaporizers calibrated specifically for enflurane; (b) vaporizers from which delivered flows can easily and readily be calculated.

Nothing is present in the agent to alter calibration or affect the operation characteristics of the vaporizer.

Preanesthetic Medication: Preanesthetic medication should be selected according to the needs of the individual patient, taking into account that secretions are weakly stimulated by enflurane and the heart rate remains constant. The use of anticholinergic drugs is a matter of choice.

Surgical Anesthesia: Induction may be achieved using enflurane alone with oxygen or in combination with oxygen-nitrous oxide mixtures. Under these conditions some excitement may be encountered. If excitement is to be avoided, a hypnotic dose of a short-acting barbiturate should be used to induce unconsciousness, followed by the enflurane mixture. In general, inspired concentrations of 2.0 to 4.5% enflurane produce surgical anesthesia in 7 to 10 minutes.

Maintenance: Surgical levels of anesthesia may be maintained with 0.5 to 3.0% enflurane. Maintenance concentrations should not exceed 3.0%. If added relaxation is required, supplemental doses of muscle relaxants may be used. Ventilation to maintain the tension of CO_2 in arterial blood in the 35 to 45 mm Hg range is preferred. Hyperventilation should be avoided in order to minimize possible CNS excitation.

The level of blood pressure during maintenance is an inverse function of enflurane concentration in the absence of other complicating problems. Excessive decreases (unless related to hypovolemia) may be due to depth of anesthesia and in such instances should be corrected by lightening the level of anesthesia.

Analgesia: Enflurane 0.25 to 1.0% provides analgesia for vaginal delivery equal to that produced by 30 to 60% nitrous oxide. These concentrations normally do not produce amnesia.

Enflurane, like some other inhalational anesthetics, can react with desiccated carbon dioxide (CO_2) absorbents to produce carbon monoxide which may result in elevated levels of carboxyhemoglobin in some patients. Case reports suggest that barium hydroxide lime and sodalime become desiccated when fresh gases are passed through the CO_2 absorber cannister at high flow rates over many hours or days. When a clinician suspects that CO_2 absorbent may be desiccated, it should be replaced before the administration of enflurane.

Administration Equipment: Enflurane may be administered from a flow-through type vaporizer manufactured and specifically calibrated for enflurane. Vaporizers which deliver saturated vapor at reasonable flows but are not specifically calibrated for enflurane may be used.

The actual concentration can also be calculaled by the following formula (1) where:

$$(1)\quad F_v\ \%\ \text{Conc}\ \left(\frac{V}{V}\right) = \left(\frac{\dfrac{P_v}{760-P_v}}{F_T}\right)$$

Legend: P_v=Vapor pressure of agent.
F_v=Flow through vaporizer.
F_T=Total flow.

For all practical purposes, Diluent Flow and Total Flow can be considered the same. However, if Diluent Flow is accurately desired, it can be calculated by formula (2).

$$(2)\quad F_D=F_T-\left(\frac{760}{760-P_v}\right)F_v$$

where F_D=Diluent flow.
F_v=Flow through vaporizer.
P_v=Vapor pressure of agent.
F_T=Total flow.

Enflurane contains no stabilizer. Nothing is present in the agent to alter calibration or affect the operation characteristics of the vaporizer.

Keyed Bottle Collar (for use with key-fil vaporizer): Directions for Use: To attach a keyed bottle adaptor, remove cap and seal from anesthetic bottle. Check that the anesthetic bottle neck is not chipped or damaged. Match keyed bottle adaptor to keyed bottle collar and screw together until tight. Now connect the bottle to the vaporizer filler receptable.

Note that color of keyed bottle collar will match the color of the adpator.

(Refer to package insert for calculation of delivered enflurane concentration.)

Supplied: Amber-colored bottles of 250 mL. No additives or stabilizers are present.

Reviewed 1999

ETHYOL® Ⓟ

Lilly

Amifostine

Cytoprotective Agent

Pharmacology: Amifostine is a prodrug that is dephosphorylated to a pharmacologically active metabolite, the free thiol (WR-1065), at the tissue site by membrane-bound alkaline phosphatase. The ability of amifostine to selectively protect normal tissues is based upon the differential metabolism and uptake of the free thiol into normal versus malignant tissues. This differential effect is attributed to the higher capillary alkaline phosphatase activity, as well as higher pH and better vascularity of normal tissues relative to tumor tissue. This results in a more rapid generation of the active free thiol metabolite as well as a higher rate constant for uptake into normal tissues. In addition, cell culture studies have shown that amifostine uptake by normal tissues occurs through facilitated uptake against a concentration gradient, whereas tumor tissue relies on passive, non-facilitated uptake. The higher concentration of free thiol in normal tissues is available to bind to, and thereby detoxify the reactive species of alkylating and platinum agents, as well as act as a scavenger of oxygen free radicals.

Clinical pharmacokinetic studies show that amifostine is rapidly cleared from the plasma with an $t_{1/2\alpha}$ of <1 minute and a $t_{1/2\beta}$ of approximately 8 minutes. Less than 10% of amifostine remains in the plasma 6 minutes after drug administration. Amifostine is rapidly metabolized, especially in normal tissues, to the active free thiol metabolite WR-1065. The disulfide metabolite (WR-33278), which is subsequently produced, is less active than WR-1065. After a 15-minute infusion of a dose of 740 to 910 mg/m², renal excretion of amifostine and its 2 metabolites, WR-1065 (free thiol) and WR-33278 (disulfide), during the hour following drug administration was low, averaging 0.69%, 2.64% and 2.22% of the administered dose, respectively. Concentrations of 82 to 227 μmole/L of the free thiol metabolite, WR-1065, are detectable in aspirated bone marrow cells at 5 to 8 minutes after i.v. infusion of 910 mg/m² of amifostine. This observation, taken together with its rapid clearance from plasma, its very small volume of distribution and the low percentage of amifostine and metabolites excreted in the urine is consistent with the rapid dephosphorylation and entry into normal tissues that is suggested by animal model studies. Pretreatment with dexamethasone or metoclopramide has no effect on amifostine pharmacokinetics. Likewise, studies in 6 patients showed no apparent effect of amifostine on the pharmacokinetics of cisplatin administered 15 minutes after the completion of the amifostine infusion.

Indications: As a cytoprotective agent against the cumulative renal toxicities associated with cisplatin and the hematologic toxicities associated with cyclophosphamide as well as platinum anticancer agents in patients with advanced solid tumors of non-germ cell origin.

This indication is based on the results of a randomized controlled trial of 6 cycles of cyclophosphamide 1 000 mg/m² and cisplatin 100 mg/m² with or without amifostine pretreatment at 910 mg/m² which was conducted in 2 successive cohorts of 121 patients with advanced ovarian cancer. The results of this trial demonstrate that pretreatment with amifostine can protect against both acute and cumulative hematologic and renal toxicity associated with cyclophosphamide and cisplatin (CP), which should allow better adherence to chemotherapy regimens. The protection of bone marrow and kidney was achieved with no reduction in the antitumor efficacy of the CP regimen. Results of the combined analysis of all 242 patients are displayed in Tables I, II and III (on following page).

Contraindications: Patients with known sensitivity to aminothiol compounds.

Warnings: Patients who are hypotensive or in a state of dehydration should not receive amifostine. Patients receiving antihypertensive therapy which cannot be stopped for 24 hours preceding amifostine treatment should not receive amifostine.

Patients should be adequately hydrated prior to amifostine infusion and kept in a supine position during the infusion. Blood pressure should be monitored every 5 minutes during the infusion. It is important that the infusion of the recommended dose range (740 to 910 mg/m²) be given over 15 minutes. The administration of amifostine as a longer infusion is associated with a higher incidence of side effects. If hypotension occurs, patients should be placed in the Trendelenburg position and be given an additional infusion of normal saline using a separate i.v. line. Guidelines for interrupting and re-starting amifostine infusion if a decrease in systolic blood pressure should occur are provided in the Dosage section.

Antiemetic medication should be administered prior to and in conjunction with amifostine. When amifostine is administered with highly emetogenic chemotherapy, the fluid balance of the patient should be carefully monitored.

Reports of clinically relevant hypocalcemia are rare; however, serum calcium levels should be monitored in patients at risk of hypocalcemia, such as those with nephrotic syndrome. If necessary, calcium supplements can be administered as needed.

Precautions: General: Patients should be adequately hydrated prior to amifostine infusion, and blood pressure should be monitored during the infusion. The recommended dose range of amifostine, 740 to 910 mg/m², should be administered as a 15-minute infusion (see Dosage).

Ethyol (cont'd)

Table I—Ethyol

Effect of Ethyol Pretreatment on the Toxicities Associated with the CP Regimen—Protection of Bone Marrow

	Ethyol+CP (N=122)	CP (N=120)	p-value 2-sided
Incidence of neutropenia with fever and/or infection requiring antibiotic therapy	8/122 (7%)	26/120 (22%)	0.001
Days in hospital	71	258	0.003
Days on antibiotics	78	304	0.002
Incidence of withdrawals for hematologic toxicity	1/122 (1%)	8/120 (7%)	0.016
Percent of patients with Grade 4 neutropenia following the last cycle of chemotherapy	27/122 (22%)	51/120 (43%)	0.001
Percent of patients with Grade 4 neutropenia whose neutrophil count failed to recover to ≥1 500/mm³ by day 22±3 days	43/98 (44%)	64/99 (65%)	0.004

Table II—Ethyol

Renal Protection

	Ethyol+CP (N=122)	CP (N=120)	p-value 2-sided
Protracted elevation in serum creatinine levels >1.5 mg/dL at Day 22*	(3%)	(17%)	0.004
Proportion of patients with ≥40% reduction from baseline in creatinine clearance*	(10%)	(32%)	<0.001
Incidence of Grade 2 or worse hypomagnesemia	(2%)	(11%)	0.001

*Assessments based on last cycle of chemotherapy for patients who received at least 4 cycles of cisplatin.

Table III—Ethyol

Lack of Protection by Ethyol on the Antitumor Efficacy of the CP Regimen—Pathologic Tumor Response Rates

Patient Cohort/ Response Rate	Ethyol+CP	CP	% Difference (E+CP→CP)	95% Confidence Interval
Intent to Treat Analysis				
Pathologic complete response rate	26/122 (21.3%)	19/120 (15.8%)	5.5%	(−4.3 to 15.2)
Pathologic complete + partial response rate	45/122 (36.9%)	34/120 (28.3%)	8.6%	(−3.2 to 20.3)
Analysis of Patients Who Underwent Second-Look Surgery				
Pathologic complete response rate	26/60 (43.3%)	19/52 (36.5%)	6.8%	(−11.3 to 24.9)
Pathologic complete + partial response rate	45/60 (75.0%)	34/52 (65.4%)	9.6%	(−7.3 to 26.6)

Drug Interactions: There are no known drug interactions with amifostine. The rapid clearance of amifostine from the plasma minimizes the risk of interaction between amifostine and other drugs. However, special consideration should be given to the concurrent administration of amifostine with antihypertensive medication or other drugs that could potentiate hypotension.

Carcinogenesis, Mutagenesis and Impairment of Fertility: No long-term animal studies have been performed to evaluate the carcinogenic potential of amifostine. The Ames Salmonella typhimurium test revealed no mutagenic activity. Data from both in vitro and in vivo studies demonstrate that amifostine protects against the mutagenicity and genotoxicity of chemotherapeutic agents such as cisplatin, bleomycin and nitrogen mustard and against the carcinogenicity associated with radiation therapy.

Pregnancy: Pregnancy Category C: While amifostine has been shown to have dose-related embryotoxicity in rats at doses greater than 200 mg/kg, it is not teratogenic. There are no adequate and well-controlled studies in pregnant women. If this drug is used during pregnancy or if the patient becomes pregnant while taking this drug, the patient should be apprised of the potential hazard to the fetus.

Lactation: No information is available on the excretion of amifostine or its metabolites into human milk. Because many drugs are excreted in human milk and because of the potential for adverse reactions in nursing infants, it is recommended that breast-feeding be discontinued if the mother is treated with amifostine.

Adverse Effects: The safety profile of amifostine was examined in detail in the randomized trial of cyclophosphamide and cisplatin±amifostine in patients with ovarian cancer. The principal side effects of amifostine were hypotension, characterized as a transient decrease in blood pressure with no long-term CNS or cardiovascular sequelae, and nausea and vomiting. Of the 122 patients treated with amifostine, 75 patients (61%) had reductions in systolic blood pressure which met the protocol definition of hypotension. Seventeen patients required discontinuation of an amifostine infusion prior to receiving the full protocol dose (this includes 5 patients who had terminated their infusion prior to the protocol amendment allowing the infusion to be restarted); 27 patients had an infusion temporarily interrupted but went on to receive the full protocol dose, and 31 patients received the full protocol dose with no interruption at each infusion. Over the course of the study, 145/581 (25%) of the amifostine infusions were associated with reductions in blood pressure which met the protocol definition of hypotension. Reductions were generally noted towards the end of the infusion. The mean time to onset was 14 minutes, and the mean duration was 6 minutes. Hypotension was readily managed by placing the patient into a supine, or if already in a supine position, into the Trendelenburg position and infusing normal saline. Overall, hypotension did not result in lasting medical sequelae in any of the 122 patients treated with amifostine in this study.

The overall frequency of nausea and vomiting was 96% in the amifostine+CP arm versus 88% in the CP arm though the difference was not statistically significant, p=0.08 (2-sided). This increased incidence was restricted to the day of chemotherapy; the incidence of delayed nausea/vomiting, which is commonly associated with cisplatin, was comparable in both arms: 66% in the amifostine+CP arm and 69% in the CP arm. Nausea and vomiting are amenable to treatment with standard antiemetics.

The only other side effects or laboratory abnormalities which occurred more frequently in the amifostine arm were flushing/feeling of warmth, chills/feeling of coldness, dizziness, somnolence, hiccups and sneezing (see Table IV). These effects were transient and did not interfere with the administration of therapy.

Decreased serum calcium concentrations is a known pharmacological effect of amifostine. At the recommended doses, clinical hypocalcemia has occurred rarely.

Allergic reactions, ranging from mild skin rashes to rigors, have occurred in some patients. There has been no reported occurrence of anaphylaxis with amifostine.

Table IV—Ethyol

Incidence of Side Effects Commonly Associated With Amifostine

Side Effect	Ethyol+CP (N=122)	CP (N=120)
Nausea/Vomiting	108 (89%)	80 (67%)
Hypotension[a]	75 (61%)	—[b]
Flushing	49 (40%)	2 (2%)
Sneezing	30 (25%)	2 (2%)
Dizziness	14 (11%)	2 (2%)
Sleepiness	5 (4%)	1 (1%)
Hiccups	5 (4%)	1 (1%)
Chills	5 (4%)	0

[a]Based on blood pressure analysis.
[b]Blood pressures were not measured in patients in the CP arm.

The side effect profile of amifostine observed in Phase I/II clinical trials of 256 patients (139 receiving amifostine prior to chemotherapy and 117 receiving amifostine prior to radiation) was comparable to that observed in the ovarian cancer trials.

Overdose: Symptoms and Treatment: In Phase I trials, the maximum single dose of amifostine administered was 1 330 mg/m². No information is available on single doses higher than this in adults. In the setting of a clinical trial, children have received single doses of amifostine up to 2.7 g/m² with no untoward effects. Multiple doses (up to 3 times the recommended single dose of 740 to 910 mg/m²) have been safely administered within a 24-hour period under study conditions. Following the repeated administration of amifostine at 2 and 4 hours after the initial dose, there has not been any evidence of increased or cumulative side effects, especially nausea and vomiting or hypotension. The most likely symptom of overdosage would be hypotension which should be managed by infusion of normal saline or other appropriate symptomatic treatment.

Dosage: Amifostine for injection is supplied as a sterile lyophilized powder requiring reconstitution for i.v. infusion. Each vial contains 500 mg of amifostine (anhydrous basis). It is reconstituted with 9.7 mL of sterile Sodium Chloride Injection, USP.

In adults, the recommended starting dose is 910 mg/m² administered once daily as a 15-minute i.v. infusion starting within 30 minutes prior to chemotherapy.

The 15-minute infusion is reportedly better tolerated than infusions of more extended duration. Further reduced infusion times have not been systematically investigated.

The infusion of amifostine should be interrupted if the systolic blood pressure decreases significantly from the baseline value as listed in Table V (on following page).

If the blood pressure returns to normal within 5 minutes and the patient is asymptomatic, the infusion may be restarted so that the full dose of amifostine may be administered. If the full dose of amifostine cannot be administered, the dose of amifostine for subsequent cycles should be 740 mg/m².

Children and Geriatrics: Only limited experience is available for the usage of amifostine in children as well as elderly patients (more than 70 years of age).

It is recommended that antiemetic medication be administered prior to and in conjunction with amifostine especially when used with strongly emetogenic chemotherapy such as cisplatin.

Reconstituted Solutions: Each 10 mL vial of amifostine for injection should be reconstituted with 9.7 mL of sterile Sodium Chloride Injection, USP. The solution is chemically stable for up to 6 hours at room temperature (15 to 25°C) or up to 24 hours under refrigeration (2 to 8°C). Amifostine is administered as an i.v. infusion.

I.V. Infusion (Diluent: Sterile Sodium Chloride Injection, USP): When reconstituted with 9.7 mL of sterile Sodium Chloride Injection, USP, each mL contains 50 mg of amifostine at a pH of 6.0 to 8.0. Reconstituted solutions may be further diluted with sterile Sodium Chloride Injection, USP for dosage adjustment. See Table VI (on following page).

Amifostine prepared in polyvinylchloride (PVC) bags at concentration ranges from 5 to 40 mg/mL is chemically stable for up to 6 hours when stored at room temperature (15 to 25°C) or up to 24 hours when stored under refrigerated conditions (2 to 8°C). All unused solutions should be discarded.

Special Instructions: Parenteral products should be inspected visually for particulate matter and discoloration prior to administration whenever solution and container permit. Do not use if cloudiness or precipitate is observed. There are no known incompatibilities.

Table V—Ethyol

Guideline for Interrupting Ethyol Infusion Due to Decrease in Systolic Blood Pressure

	Baseline Systolic Blood Pressure (mm Hg)				
	<100	100-119	120-139	140-179	≥180
Decrease in systolic blood pressure during infusion of Ethyol (mm Hg)	20	25	30	40	50

Table VI—Ethyol

Reconstitution Table

Vial Size	Volume of Sterile Sodium Chloride Injection, USP to be Added to Vial	Approximate Available Volume	Nominal Concentration per mL
10 mL	9.7 mL	10 mL	50 mg

Supplied: Each vial of sterile lyophilized powder contains: amifostine (anhydrous basis) 500 mg. Nonmedicinal ingredients: ethyl alcohol (remvoed during lyophilization), nitrogen (manufacturing auxiliary) and water for injection (removed during lyophilization). Single-use vials of 10 mL, cartons of 3 . Store lyophilized powder at room temperature (15 to 25°C).

Reviewed 1999

ETIBI® ℞
ICN

Ethambutol HCl

Tuberculostatic Agent

Supplied: 100 mg: Each blue, scored, film-coated tablet contains: ethambutol HCl, USP 100 mg. Nonmedicinal ingredients: alcohol, cornstarch, hydroxypropyl cellulose, lactose and magnesium stearate. Bottles of 100.

400 mg: Each blue, scored, film-coated tablet, imprinted ICN E12, contains: ethambutol HCl, USP 400 mg. Nonmedicinal ingredients: alcohol, cornstarch, hydroxypropyl cellulose, lactose and magnesium stearate. Bottles of 100.

ETOPOSIDE INJECTION ℞
BDH

Antineoplastic

Supplied: Each mL contains: etoposide 20 mg. Nonmedicinal ingredients: alcohol, benzyl alcohol, citric acid, polyethylene glycol and polysorbate 80. Clear glass vials of 5 and 25 mL. Store at controlled room temperature 15 to 30°C. Protect from light.

ETOPOSIDE INJECTION ℞
Novopharm

Antineoplastic

Pharmacology: Etoposide is a semisynthetic derivative of podophyllotoxin. Etoposide exhibits cytostatic activity in vitro by preventing cells from entering mitosis or by destroying them at a premitotic stage. Etoposide interferes with the synthesis of DNA and appears to arrest human lymphoblastic cells in the late S-G_2 phases of the cell cycle.

The effects of etoposide on the human hematopoietic system are substantial. The effects evoked included leukopenia and thrombocytopenia. The toxic effects elicited by etoposide are described under Adverse Effects. Experiments using animals have revealed teratogenic and embryotoxic properties to etoposide.

Pharmacokinetics: In humans, administration of higher doses of etoposide resulted in higher levels of the drug in the plasma. Peak levels of etoposide in plasma were reached immediately following administration. Etoposide decayed from plasma in a biphasic manner. The values for $t_{1/2\alpha}$ and $t_{1/2\beta}$ ranged from 0.31 to 0.8 hours and 4.1 to 8.05 hours, respectively. The mean volume of distribution at steady state (VD_{ss}) was 25.2 L/m², the mean plasma clearance rate was 28.0 mL/min/m² and the mean renal clearance rate was 10.0 mL/min/m².

In patients who had previously received cisplatin, higher values were observed for the area under the concentration versus time curve. Slightly lower values were observed for the steady-state volume of distribution and systemic clearance. However, changes in the pharmacokinetic parameters of etoposide when administered concurrently with cyclophosphamide/doxorubicin or carboplatin were not substantial.

Approximately 98% of etoposide was bound to proteins in plasma when incubated in vitro at 37°C. Protein binding was not affected by the concomitant administration of cisplatin. Analysis of biological fluids and tissues suggested that etoposide was present in nonsignificant amount in cerebrospinal fluid (CSF), pleural fluid, saliva and also in the tumors.

Of a dose of 220 to 290 mg/m² of radioactive etoposide infused during 1 hour, 43.5% was recovered in the urine, of which 67% was unchanged etoposide. Recovery in the feces was inconsistent and ranged from <1.5 to 16.31% of the administered dose in 1 study. The levels of etoposide in bile were low and represented 1 to <3% of the original dose administered. The rest of the dose was not accounted for.

When etoposide was administered to children, the peak levels of the drug in plasma also coincided with the first time point after the beginning of the infusion. The decay of etoposide from plasma was biphasic. In a study of 8 children and adolescents receiving 200 mg/m²/day as 30- to 60-minute i.v. infusions during 3 consecutive days, the mean values for $t_{1/2\alpha}$ and $t_{1/2\beta}$ were 0.82 hours and 6.5 hours, respectively. The mean systemic serum clearance rate was 20.9 mL/min/m² and the mean VD_{ss} was 7.2 L/m².

Significantly lower values were seen for systemic clearance, mean residence time and $t_{1/2\beta}$ in patients who previously received cisplatin. No accumulation of the drug occurred after repeated administration. The clearance rate was slower for patients with elevated liver function parameters ALT or AST.

The metabolites of etoposide detected in urine included the glucuronate/sulfate conjugates, aglycone, cis-etoposide, trans isomer of the open ring lactone, cis/trans hydroxy acids and the picrolactones. Cis-etoposide was also detected in cerebrospinal fluid. The metabolites of etoposide observed in bile included the trans-hydroxy acid, glucuronide conjugate and cis-etoposide.

Indications: Small-cell Carcinoma of the Lung: As first-line therapy in combination with other antineoplastics. As second-line therapy or as a single agent in patients who have not relapsed or failed to respond to after treatment with other chemotherapeutic protocols.

Non-small Cell Carcinoma of the Lung: In combination with cisplatin for patients who cannot be surgically treated. For patients requiring chemotherapy following surgery.

Malignant Lymphoma (histiocytic type): As first-line therapy in combination with other antineoplastics.

Testicular Malignancies (notably germ cell tumors including seminomas): In conjunction with other antineoplastics in patients who have received appropriate therapy.

Contraindications: Patients exhibiting previous hypersensitivity to etoposide; or severe leukopenia, thrombocytopenia, severe liver- and/or kidney-related impairment should not be treated with etoposide.

Warnings: Caution: Etoposide is a potent antineoplastic agent. It should only be used by or under the direct supervision of qualified physicians who are experienced in using chemotherapeutic agents. Patients should be routinely tested for myelosuppression and for the toxic effects incurred to the renal and hepatic systems. If these tests indicate unacceptable levels of toxicity, therapy with etoposide should be discontinued.

Etoposide is a potent drug and should be used only by physicians experienced with cancer chemotherapeutic drugs (see Precautions). Etoposide should be administered with caution to patients exhibiting hepatic and/or renal dysfunctions. Appropriate laboratory tests should be performed regularly. Due to the risk of septicemia, bacterial infection should be adequately controlled prior to administration of etoposide. If the number of neutrophils falls below 500/µL, administration of etoposide should be discontinued until the numbers of neutrophils in plasma have returned to normal levels.

Anaphylactic reactions to etoposide may be characterized by chills, fever, tachycardia, bronchospasm, dyspnea and hypotension. Should anaphylaxis be diagnosed, administration of etoposide should cease immediately and symptoms treated appropriately. Physicians may administer vasopressors, corticosteroids, antihistamines, or expanders of plasma volume at their discretion.

Pregnancy and the Use of Birth Control: Etoposide displayed teratogenicity and embryotoxicity when administered to pregnant rats. Etoposide also caused reduced spermatogenesis in monkeys and a reduction in the weights of testes in rats and monkeys. Thus, administration of etoposide during pregnancy is not recommended. Patients receiving etoposide who are able to conceive or bear children are advised to use appropriate methods of birth control. Ovarian dysfunction was experienced after treatment with etoposide, therefore etoposide should be administered with caution to postpubertal women.

Chronic administration to rats showed that etoposide has oncogenic potential. In addition, etoposide has also been shown in vitro to be potentially mutagenic. Thus, the benefit to the patient should be considered in relation to the toxic effects of this drug.

Precautions: Etoposide should only be administered by those experienced in the use of chemotherapeutic antineoplastics. Blood counts and renal and hepatic function should be evaluated frequently. The count of white blood cells, platelets, and granulocytes, will alter the recommended dose (see Table II on following page).

Administration of etoposide should be terminated if the absolute granulocytic count falls below 1 000; or the number of platelets fall below 50 000 cells/µL. The number of neutrophils and platelets reach their lowest levels at 7 to 14 days and 9 to 16 days respectively, after initial treatment with etoposide. Approximately 20 days are required for recovery of the bone marrow.

As hypotension has been reported after bolus administration, etoposide should be mixed with normal saline or 5% dextrose and administered over a period of at least 30 minutes. Vital signs should be monitored during this period.

Interaction of vincristine and etoposide have resulted in severe neuropathies in 0.7% of the patients.

Children: Inadequate use of etoposide in children, currently, does not permit the recommendation of dosages to be used for children.

Lactation: As etoposide may be secreted in human milk, mothers should be advised not to breast-feed while undergoing chemotherapy with etoposide.

See Dosage section; Special Instructions for handling precautions.

Adverse Effects: The following section summarizes the toxic side effects of etoposide. The numbers quoted in Table I (on following page) refer to commonly observed percentages of patients experiencing such side effects.

The major dose-limiting toxic side effect was myelosuppression, manifested mainly as leukopenia, thrombocytopenia and anemia. The nadirs of granulocytes and platelets occurred at 7 to 14 days and 9 to 16 days after treatment, respectively. Recovery of the bone marrow generally occurred by 20 days after treatment. The occasional deaths observed after treatment with combinations containing etoposide were usually associated with myelosuppression.

Nausea and emesis were the main gastrointestinal toxic effects. These effects were usually prevented by antinausea/antiemetic regimens. When etoposide was administered at high doses, stomatitis was often the dose-limiting toxicity.

Anaphylactic reactions were reported after infusion of etoposide. A fatality due to respiratory distress syndrome was also reported. The reactions were controlled by terminating the infusion and administering vasopressors, corticosteroids, antihistamines and plasma volume expanders are required. In one case, a longer period of infusion resolved the reactions.

Overdose: Symptoms and Treatment: There are currently no known antidotes for the adverse effects experienced after administration of etoposide. In the event of overdosage, treatment should be directed at alleviating the symptoms presented and ensuring the survival of the patient through the period of toxicity. The symptoms of overdosage are expected to be associated with hematopoietic toxicity. The functions of the renal and hepatic systems should be monitored for at least 3 to 4 weeks, in case of delayed or persistent toxicity of etoposide.

Dosage: A dose of 50 to 100 mg/m²/day may be administered by i.v. infusion (over at least 30 minutes) for 5 days. The dose should be adjusted depending on the toxic effects experienced by each patient; whether etoposide is used as a single agent or in combination with other antineoplastics; and the specific protocol used to treat the patient.

Etoposide Injection (cont'd)

Table I—Etoposide Injection

Side Effects

Type of Effects	Percent of Patients Experiencing Effects
Hematologic	
Leukopenia	60-91
Severe leukopenia (<1 000/μL)	3-17
Thrombocytopenia	22-41
Severe thrombocytopenia (<50 000/μL)	1-20
Anemia	up to 33
Gastrointestinal	
Nausea/emesis	30-40
Nausea/emesis requiring termination of dose	1-2
Abdominal pain	2
Anorexia	10-13
Diarrhea	1-13
Stomatitis	1-6
Aftertaste, constipation	Rare
Cardiovascular	
Transient hypotension	1-2
Transient hypertension	Rare
Myocardial infarction/congestive heart failure	Rare
Hypersensitivity	
Anaphylactoid reactions (chills, fever, bronchospasm, dyspnea, tachycardia, hypotension, hypertension, flushing, lacrimation, sneezing, coryza, sweating)	0.7-2
Dermatologic/Local	
Reversible alopecia (with occasional baldness)	8-66
Rash, pigmentation, severe pruritus	Rare
Nervous	
Peripheral neuropathy	1-2
Somnolence, fatigue and ototoxicity	≤3

Infection, dysphagia, pancytopenia (3%), oral ulcer (2%), neutropenia, dyspepsia, hyperuricemia, numbness/tingling, dizziness, depression, substernal chest pain, throat pain, back pain, generalized body pain, abdominal cramps and tingling were also reported.

Due to reports of leukopenia and thrombocytopenia after treatment with etoposide, blood counts should be performed to determine the platelets and white blood cells prior to each new administration of etoposide. In the absence of acceptable modification, the following guideline is suggested (see Table II).

Table II—Etoposide Injection

Schedule for Reduction of Dose

Platelet Count	WBC Count >3 000	Absolute Granulocytic Count (% of Usual Dose Given) ≥1 800	1 500-1 800	1 000-1 500	<1 000
≥100 000	100%	100%	75%	50%	0%
70 000-100 000	75%	75%	75%	50%	0%
50 000-70 000	50%	50%	50%	50%	0%
<50 000	0%*	0%	0%	0%	0%

Legend: WBC = white blood cells.
Absolute Granulocytic Count = WBC X (% polys + % stabs).
0%* = indicates that treatment should be postponed for at least a week. Treatment may be resumed when the counts return to an acceptable level, e.g., for a case with a platelet count of 135 000 and an absolute granulocytic count of 1 325, 50% of the total dose of all chemotherapeutic drugs should be administered. This should be 50% of the 100% dose determined originally and not the previously administered dose.

Functions of the liver and kidneys should be monitored regularly. In patients with renal failure, modifications are suggested at doses ≥125 mg/m². In patients with hepatic failure, the following modifications are suggested (see Table III).

Table III—Etoposide Injection

Dosage—Hepatic Failure

Bilirubin (μmol/L)	% of Usual Dose Given
25-50	50%
>50	25%

Administration: Etoposide should not be administered by i.v. push. It should be mixed with normal saline or 5% dextrose injection and should be administered immediately by the i.v. route over a period of not less than 30 minutes.
Etoposide should be diluted as follows: See Table IV.

Table IV—Etoposide Injection

Dilution

Dose Size	Diluent	Volume of Diluent to be Added
50-60 mg/m²	Normal saline	250 mL
	Dextrose 5% in water	250 mL
100-120 mg/m²	Normal saline	500 mL
	Dextrose 5% in water	500 mL

Diluted solutions of etoposide should **not** exceed a concentration of 0.4 mg/mL.

The diluted solution should be inspected visually for discoloration and particulate matter prior to administration. Discard unused portion.

Diluted etoposide is a clear colorless solution.

Diluted etoposide should be administered immediately after dilution.

Special Instructions: A vertical laminar flow hood (Biological Safety Cabinet - Class II) should be used to handle and prepare etoposide. During the handling and dilution, PVC gloves, safety glasses, disposable gowns and masks should be worn. Spillage and self-contact with the drug should be avoided. Spills on the skin should be washed thoroughly with soap and cold water. Materials used to clean spills should be incinerated. Bi-annual blood examinations should be performed on those who are involved in handling etoposide.

All materials including needles, syringes, vials and other materials that have come into contact with etoposide should be separated and incinerated at 1 000°C or higher. Heating may result in the explosion of sealed canisters. Unused/unopened vials may be returned to the manufacturer for disposal. These materials should be appropriately packaged prior to their transport.

Etoposide should not be mixed with other antineoplastics; or come into contact with aqueous buffers, whose pH is above 8.

Supplied: Each mL contains: etoposide 20 mg. Nonmedicinal ingredients: absolute ethanol, citric acid (anhydrous), polyethylene glycol 300 and polysorbate 80. Preservative-free. Clear glass vials of 5, 10, 25 and 50 mL. Store at controlled room temperature, 15 to 25°C. Protect from light.

ETRAFON® Preparations Ⓟ

Schering

Amitriptyline HCl—Perphenazine

Antidepressant—Antipsychotic

Indications: The treatment of patients with anxious or agitated depression. Particularly indicated in patients with depression associated with marked psychomotor unrest and anxiety. Etrafon has also been used in some schizophrenic patients who have associated symptoms of depression and in depressed patients suffering from marked agitation, anxiety and tension, which may respond to a phenothiazine agent.

Contraindications, Precautions and Adverse Effects: See Trilafon and amitriptyline. Known hypersensitivity to any of its components. Discontinue therapy several days before elective surgery if possible.

Dosage: In prescribing Etrafon, the recommended indications, management considerations, dosage schedules and attention to tolerance and response that are normal practice in using each of the combined drugs, perphenazine and amitriptyline, should be borne in mind.

Initial Dosage: In ambulatory depressed patients, when anxiety and/or agitation are of such degree as to warrant combined therapy, 1 tablet of Etrafon-D (2-25) or Etrafon-F (4-25) 3 or 4 times daily, depending on the severity of the agitation and anxiety. In the more severely ill patients with schizophrenia and associated symptoms of depression that may benefit from amitriptyline, Etrafon-F (4-25) may be administered in an initial dose of 2 tablets 3 times a day. If necessary, a fourth dose may be given at bedtime. The total daily dose should not exceed 9 tablets.

In elderly patients and adolescents, and other patients as indicated, 1 tablet of Etrafon-A (4-10) or Etrafon 2-10 may be administered 3 or 4 times daily for the initial dosage and then adjusted if required to produce an adequate response.

Maintenance Dosage: Depending on the condition being treated, the onset of therapeutic response may vary from a few days to a few weeks or even longer.

After a satisfactory response is noted, dosage should be reduced to the smallest amount necessary to obtain relief from the symptoms for which Etrafon is being administered.

A useful maintenance dosage is 1 tablet of Etrafon-D (2-25) or Etrafon-F (4-25) 2 to 4 times daily. In some patients, maintenance dosage is required for many months.

Etrafon 2-10 and Etrafon-A (4-10) can be used to increase flexibility in adjusting maintenance dosage to the lowest amount consistent with relief of symptoms.

Supplied: Etrafon (2-10): Each yellow coated tablet imprinted with a black Schering trade mark on one side and the designation 2-10 on the other side contains: perphenazine USP 2 mg and amitriptyline HCl USP 10 mg. Nonmedicinal ingredients: cornstarch; dye, FD & C Yellow No. 6; lactose; magnesium stearate and povidone; coating: carnauba wax; dye, Opalux Yellow; gelatin; sucrose; talc; terra alba; titanium dioxide and white wax. Tartrazine-free. Bottles of 100.

Etrafon-A (4-10): Each orange coated tablet imprinted with a black Schering trade mark on one side and a black letter A on the other side contains: perphenazine USP 4 mg and amitriptyline HCl USP 10 mg. Nonmedicinal ingredients: cornstarch, lactose, magnesium stearate and povidone; coating: acacia, calcium phosphate, carnauba wax; FD & C Yellow No. 6; gelatin; sucrose; terra alba; titanium dioxide and white wax. Tartrazine-free. Bottles of 100.

Etrafon-D (2-25): Each pink coated tablet imprinted with a black Schering trade mark on one side and a black letter D on the other side contains: perphenazine USP 2 mg and amitriptyline HCl USP 25 mg. Nonmedicinal ingredients: cornstarch; dye, D & C Yellow No. 10; lactose; magnesium stearate and povidone; coating: calcium sulfate, carnauba wax; dye, Opalux Pink; gelatin; sucrose; talc; titanium dioxide and white wax. Tartrazine-free. Bottles of 100 and 500.

Etrafon-F (4-25): Each red coated tablet imprinted with a black Schering trade mark on one side and a black letter F on the other side contains: perphenazine USP 4 mg and amitriptyline HCl USP 25 mg. Nonmedicinal ingredients: calcium sulfate, charcoal, cornstarch, lactose, magnesium stearate and povidone; coating: carnauba wax; dye, Opalux Red; gelatin; sucrose; talc; titanium dioxide and white wax. Tartrazine-free. Bottles of 100.

(Shown in Product Recognition Section)

EUFLEX® Ⓟ

Schering

Flutamide

Nonsteroidal Antiandrogen

Pharmacology: Flutamide demonstrates potent antiandrogenic effects by inhibiting androgen uptake and/or inhibiting nuclear binding of androgen in target tissues. In adult male rats, ventral prostate weights and seminal vesicle weights were markedly reduced by daily administration of flutamide.

Indications: For use in combination with LHRH agonistic analogues (such as leuprolide acetate) for the treatment of metastatic prostatic carcinoma (Stage D_2). To achieve the benefit of the adjunctive therapy with flutamide, treatment must be started simultaneously using both drugs. Also as an adjunctive therapy to orchiectomy, in order to achieve complete androgen blockade.

Flutamide in combination with LHRH agonists are also indicated prior to and during definitive external beam radiotherapy for patients with bulky locally advanced Stage B_2 and Stage C prostatic carcinoma (see Dosage).

Contraindications: Patients who have shown hypersensitivity to flutamide or any component of this preparation.

Warnings: Gynecomastia occurred in 9% of patients receiving flutamide together with medical castration. Physicians must familiarize themselves with the proper use of LHRH before combination medication is contemplated.

Pregnancy and *Lactation:* Flutamide is indicated only for use in male patients. No studies have been conducted in pregnant or lactating women. Therefore, the possibility that flutamide may cause fetal harm if administered to a pregnant woman, or may be present in the breast milk of lactating women must be considered.

There was decreased 24-hour survival in the offspring of rats treated with flutamide at doses of 30, 100, or 200 mg/kg/day (approximately 3, 9, and 19 times the human dose) during pregnancy. A slight increase in minor variations in the development of the sternebra and vertebra was seen in fetuses of rats at the two higher doses. Feminization of the males also occurred at the two higher dose levels. There was a decreased survival rate in the offspring of rabbits receiving the highest dose (15 mg/kg/day; equal to 1.4 times the human dose).

Precautions: Periodic liver function tests and sperm count determinations must be performed in patients on long-term treatment with flutamide. After long-term administration in rats, flutamide produced testicular interstitial cell adenomas and dose-related increases in mammary gland adenomas or carcinomas. The relevance of these findings to humans is unknown. It should be noted that few cases of malignant breast neoplasms have been reported in male patients receiving flutamide; causality has not been established.

Since flutamide tends to elevate plasma testosterone and estradiol levels, fluid retention may occur. Accordingly, flutamide should be used with caution in those patients with cardiac disease.

Hepatic Injury: Since transaminase abnormalities, cholestatic jaundice, hepatic necrosis and hepatic encephalopathy have been reported with the use of flutamide, periodic liver function tests should be considered. Appropriate laboratory testing should be done at the first symptom/sign of liver dysfunction (e.g., pruritus, dark urine, persistent anorexia, jaundice, right upper quadrant tenderness or unexplained "flu-like" symptoms). If the patient has laboratory evidence of liver injury or jaundice, in the absence of biopsy-confirmed liver metastases, flutamide therapy should be discontinued or the dosage reduced. The hepatic injury is usually reversible after discontinuation of therapy and in some patients, after dosage reduction. However, there have been reports of death following severe hepatic injury associated with the use of flutamide.

Drug Interactions: Interactions between flutamide and leuprolide have not occurred. In patients receiving long-term warfarin therapy, increases in prothrombin time have been reported after flutamide monotherapy was initiated. Therefore, close monitoring of prothrombin time is recommended and adjustment of the anticoagulant dose may be necessary when flutamide is administered concomitantly with warfarin.

Information for the Patient: Patients should be informed that flutamide and the drug used for medical castration should be administered concomitantly, and that they should not interrupt their dosing or stop taking these medications without consulting their physician.

Adverse Effects: The most frequently reported adverse reactions to flutamide **monotherapy** are gynecomastia and/or breast tenderness, sometimes accompanied by galactorrhea. These reactions disappear upon discontinuation of treatment or reduction in dosage. The incidence of gynecomastia is reduced greatly when flutamide is administered concomitantly with an LHRH agonist.

The most frequently reported (greater than 5%) adverse experiences during treatment with flutamide in combination with a LHRH agonist are listed in Table I. For comparison, adverse experiences seen with a LHRH agonist and placebo are also listed in Table I.

Table I—Euflex

Adverse Effects

	(n=294) Flutamide + LHRH-agonist % All	(n=285) Placebo + LHRH-agonist % All
Hot Flashes	61	57
Loss of Libido	36	31
Impotence	33	29
Diarrhea	12	4
Nausea/Vomiting	11	10
Gynecomastia	9	11
Other	7	9
Other GI	6	4

As shown in Table I, for both treatment groups, the most frequently occurring adverse experiences (hot flashes, loss of libido, impotence) were those known to be associated with low serum androgen levels and known to occur with LHRH-agonists alone.

The only notable difference between these treatment groups was the higher incidence of diarrhea in the flutamide + LHRH-agonist group (12%) as compared to the placebo + LHRH-agonist group (4%). The cases of diarrhea reported were severe in less than 1% of the patients. In addition, the following adverse reactions were reported during treatment with flutamide + LHRH-agonist. No causal relatedness of these reactions to drug treatment has been made, and some of the adverse experiences reported are those that commonly occur in elderly patients.

Cardiovascular: hypertension in 1% of patients. Rarely thrombophlebitis, pulmonary embolism, myocardial infarction.

CNS: CNS (drowsiness/confusion/depression/anxiety/nervousness) reactions occurred in 1% of patients. Rarely insomnia, tiredness, headache, dizziness, weakness, malaise, blurred vision and decreased libido have been reported.

Endocrine: gynecomastia in 9% of patients. Rarely breast tenderness sometimes accompanied by galactorrhea.

Gastrointestinal: Nausea/vomiting occurred in 11%; diarrhea 12%, anorexia 4%, and other GI disorders occurred in 6% of patients. Increased appetite, indigestion and constipation have also been reported.

Hematopoietic: Anemia occurred in 6% of patients, leukopenia 3%, thrombocytopenia 1%.

Liver and Biliary: Clinically evident hepatitis and jaundice occurred in <1% of patients.

Skin: Irritation at the injection site and rash occurred in 3% of patients. Photosensitivity reactions have been reported.

Other: Pruritus, ecchymosis, herpes zoster, thirst, lymphedema, lupus-like syndrome, hematuria, reduced sperm counts have been reported rarely in long-term treatment. Edema occurred in 4% of patients; neuromuscular, genitourinary symptoms occurred in 2% of patients. Pulmonary symptoms occurred in <1% of patients.

Additional Adverse Experiences: In addition, the following adverse experiences have been reported during worldwide marketing of flutamide: hemolytic anemia, macrocytic anemia, methemoglobinemia, photosensitivity reactions including erythema, ulcerations, bullous eruptions, and epidermal necrolysis and change in urine color to an amber or yellow-green appearance, which can be attributed to flutamide and/or its metabolites. Also observed were cholestatic jaundice, hepatic encephalopathy and hepatic necrosis. The hepatic conditions were usually reversible after discontinuing therapy; however, there have been reports of death following severe hepatic injury associated with use of flutamide.

Two reports of malignant male breast neoplasms in patients being dosed with flutamide have been reported. One involved aggravation of a preexisting nodule which was first detected 3 to 4 months before initiation of flutamide monotherapy in a patient with benign prostatic hypertrophy. After excision, this was diagnosed as a poorly differentiated ductal carcinoma. The other report involved gynecomastia and a nodule noted 2 and 6 months respectively, after initiation of flutamide monotherapy for treatment of advanced prostatic carcinoma. Nine months after the initiation of therapy, the nodule was excised and diagnosed as a moderately differentiated invasive ductal tumor staged T4N0M0, G3, no metastases had advanced.

Laboratory Values: Reported abnormal laboratory test results include elevated AST, ALT; elevated blood urea nitrogen (BUN) and bilirubin levels; less frequently, elevated serum creatinine levels and elevated gamma-glutamyl transferase levels have been reported.

Overdose: Symptoms and Treatment: In animal studies with flutamide alone, signs of overdose included hypoactivity, piloerection, slow respiration, ataxia, and/or lacrimation, anorexia, tranquillization, emesis and methemoglobinemia.

Clinical trials have been conducted with flutamide in doses up to 1 500 mg/day for periods up to 36 weeks with no serious effects reported. Those adverse reactions reported included gynecomastia, breast tenderness and some increases in AST. The single dose of flutamide ordinarily associated with symptoms of overdose or considered to be life-threatening has not been established.

Since flutamide is highly protein bound, dialysis may not be of any use as treatment for overdose. As in the management of overdosage with any drug, it should be borne in mind that multiple agents may have been taken. If vomiting does not occur spontaneously, it should be induced if the patient is alert. General supportive care, including frequent monitoring of the vital signs and close observation of the patient, is indicated.

Dosage: The recommended dosage of flutamide in combination with orchiectomy or in combination with an LHRH agonist is one 250 mg tablet 3 times a day at 8-hour intervals. In combination with an LHRH agonist, either the 2 agents may be initiated simultaneously, or flutamide therapy may be started 24 hours prior to initiation of the LHRH agonist.

In the management of bulky locally advanced Stage B_2 and Stage C prostatic carcinoma, the recommended dosage is one 250 mg tablet, 3 times a day at 8-hour intervals. Flutamide should be started simultaneously or 24 hours prior to initiation of the LHRH agonist. Administration of flutamide should begin 8 weeks prior to external beam radiation therapy and continue through the course of radiation therapy.

Supplied: Each round, biconvex, pale yellow, compressed tablet, engraved with "EUFLEX" on one face, and a single score on the other with the "SP" logo engraved on each side of the score line, contains: flutamide 250 mg. Nonmedicinal ingredients: cellulose, lactose, magnesium stearate, pregelatinized starch, silica gel and sodium lauryl sulfate. Tartrazine-free. Bottles of 100. Store at 2 to 30°C.

(Shown in Product Recognition Section)

Reviewed 1997

EUGLUCON® Ⓟ

Pharmascience

Glyburide

Oral Hypoglycemic

Indications: To control hyperglycemia in glyburide responsive diabetes mellitus of stable, mild, nonketosis prone, maturity-onset or adult type which cannot be controlled by proper dietary management and exercise, or when insulin therapy is not appropriate.

Contraindications: Known hypersensitivity or allergy to glyburide; unstable and/or insulin-dependent diabetes mellitus; ketoacidosis; coma; stress conditions such as severe infections, trauma or surgery; the presence of jaundice, liver disease, or renal disease or impairment; during pregnancy; the presence of important pre-existing complications peculiar to diabetes, such as retinopathy or neuropathy, for which no oral antidiabetic drugs should be given.

Precautions: The use of glyburide will not prevent the development of complications peculiar to diabetes mellitus.

Use of glyburide must be considered as treatment in addition to a proper dietary regimen, and not as a substitute for diet. Patients may, over a period of time, become progressively less responsive to oral hypoglycemic therapy because of a deterioration of their diabetic state. If a loss of adequate blood glucose lowering response to glyburide is detected, discontinue the drug.

Careful selection of patients is important. There must be rigid attention to diet, careful adjustment of dosage, patient instruction on hypoglycemic reactions and their control, as well as regular, thorough follow-up examinations.

Since the effects of oral hypoglycemic agents on the vascular changes and other long-term sequelae of diabetes mellitus are not fully known, patients receiving such drugs must be closely observed for both short- and long-term complications. Periodic assessment of cardiovascular, ophthalmic, renal and hepatic status is advisable.

In patients stabilized on glyburide therapy, loss of blood sugar control may occur in cases of acute intercurrent disease or in stressful situations such as trauma or surgery. Under these conditions, discontinuation of glyburide and insulin administration should be considered.

Hypoglycemic Reactions: Severe hypoglycemia can be induced by all sulfonylureas. Particularly susceptible are elderly subjects, patients with impaired hepatic or renal function, those who are debilitated or malnourished, and patients with primary or secondary adrenal insufficiency. Hypoglycemia is more likely to occur when the caloric intake is inadequate or after strenuous or prolonged exercise.

Drug Interactions: As a result of drug interaction, hypoglycemia may be potentiated when a sulfonylurea is used concurrently with agents such as: long-acting sulfonamides, tuberculostatics, phenylbutazone, clofibrate, MAO inhibitors, coumarin derivatives, salicylates, probenecid or propranolol and other β-adrenergic receptor blockers.

Certain drugs tend to produce hyperglycemia and may lead to loss of blood sugar control; these include diuretics (thiazides, furosemide), corticosteroids, oral contraceptives (estrogen plus progestogen), phenothiazines, calcium channel blocking drugs and nicotinic acid in pharmacological doses.

Barbiturates and other sedatives and hypnotics should be used cautiously in patients receiving an oral hypoglycemic agent, since their action may be prolonged.

Euglucon (cont'd)

Intolerance to alcohol (disulfiram-like reaction: flushing, sensation of warmth, giddiness, nausea, and occasionally tachycardia) may occur in patients treated with a sulfonylurea, including glyburide. This reaction can be prevented by avoiding alcohol.

Adverse Effects: Hypoglycemia: Severe hypoglycemia which mimics acute CNS disorders may occur (see Precautions). Hepatic and/or renal disease, malnutrition, debility, advanced age, alcoholism, adrenal or pituitary insufficiency may be predisposing factors.

Gastrointestinal: Nausea, epigastric fullness, heartburn, are common reactions to sulfonylurea therapy, tend to be dose related and may disappear when dosage is reduced. Jaundice has been reported rarely in conjunction with some sulfonylureas.

Dermatological: Allergic skin reactions such as pruritus, erythema, urticaria, morbilliform or maculopapular eruptions have been observed following sulfonylurea therapy. These may subside on continued use of the drug, but if they persist, discontinue the drug. Porphyria cutanea tarda and photosensitivity reactions have also been reported. In 1 patient, a severe skin reaction occurred as a result of a generalized hypersensitivity to glyburide; hepatic, splanchnic and renal complications, followed by bronchopneumonia and renal failure, resulted in a fatal outcome.

Hematological: Thrombocytopenia has occasionally been observed in patients receiving glyburide. Leukopenia, agranulocytosis, hemolytic anemia and aplastic anemia have been noted as a result of therapy with other sulfonylureas.

Metabolic: hepatic porphyria, disulfiram-like reactions.

Endocrinological: reduced RAI uptake by the thyroid gland.

Miscellaneous: Headache, tinnitus, fatigue, malaise, weakness and dizziness have been reported in a small number of patients.

Overdose: Sulfonylurea overdosage may result in hypoglycemia, but the dosage which causes hypoglycemia varies widely, and may be within the accepted therapeutic range in sensitive individuals.

Symptoms: Manifestations of hypoglycemia include sweating, flushing or pallor, numbness, chilliness, hunger, trembling, headache, dizziness, increased pulse rate, palpitations, increased blood pressure and apprehensiveness in mild cases. In more severe cases, coma occurs. However, symptoms of hypoglycemia are not necessarily as typical as described above and sulfonylureas may cause insidious development of symptoms which mimic cerebrovascular insufficiency.

Treatment: Discontinue medication and treat the hypoglycemia by giving dextrose promptly and in sufficient quantity. Some sulfonylurea-induced hypoglycemias may be refractory to treatment and susceptible to relapse, and may be fatal, especially in elderly or malnourished patients. Continuous dextrose infusions for hours to days have been necessary.

Dosage: In diabetic subjects, there is no fixed dosage regimen for the management of blood glucose concentrations. Individual determination of the minimum dose that will lower the blood glucose adequately should be made.

In patients where, on initial trial, the maximal recommended dose fails to lower blood glucose adequately, the drug should be discontinued. During the course of therapy a loss of effectiveness may occur. The contribution of the drug in the control of blood glucose should be ascertained by discontinuing the medication semi-annually or at least annually with careful patient monitoring. If the need for the drug is not evident, do not resume therapy. In some diabetic subjects, short-term administration of the drug may be sufficient during periods of transient loss of blood sugar control.

Usual Starting Dose: In newly diagnosed diabetics, the initial dose is 5 mg daily (2.5 mg in patients over 60 years of age) for 5 to 7 days. Depending on the response, increase or decrease the dosage in steps of 2.5 mg. Maximum daily dosage is 20 mg.

Usual Maintenance Dose: Occasionally, control is maintained with 2.5 mg daily. The majority of cases can be controlled by 5 to 10 mg daily given as a single dose during or immediately after breakfast; patients who eat only a light breakfast should defer the first dose of the day until lunchtime. If more than 10 mg daily is required, take the excess with the evening meal.

Changeover from Other Oral Hypoglycemic Agents: Discontinue previous oral medication and start glyburide 5 mg daily (2.5 mg in patients over 60 years of age). Determine maintenance dosage as in newly diagnosed diabetics.

Changeover from Insulin: If a change from insulin to glyburide is contemplated in a patient with stable, mild, maturity onset diabetes, discontinue insulin treatment for a period of 2- or 3- test days, to determine whether any therapy other than dietary regulation and exercise is needed. During this insulin-free interval, test the patient's urine at least 3 times daily for glucose and ketone bodies and monitored carefully by a physician. The appearance of significant ketonuria accompanied by glucosuria within 12 to 24 hours after the withdrawal of insulin, strongly suggests that the patient is ketosis prone, and precludes the change from insulin to sulfonylurea therapy.

Supplied: 2.5 mg: Each white, cylindrical, biplane tablet with a "T" superimposed on a smaller "O" printed on one face, and single scored on the other with "A1" printed above and below the score line, contains: glyburide 2.5 mg. Nonmedicinal ingredients: lactose, magnesium stearate, maize starch, silicon dioxide and talc. Tartrazine-free. Blister packs of 30. Bottles of 100 and 500.

5 mg: Each white, oblong, scored tablet, coded BM/EU on both faces, contains: glyburide 5 mg. Nonmedicinal ingredients: lactose, magnesium stearate, maize starch, silicon dioxide and talc. Tartrazine-free. Blister packs of 30. Bottles of 100 and 500.

Store at room temperature.

EUMOVATE® Ⓟ

Glaxo Wellcome

Clobetasone 17-butyrate

Topical Corticosteroid

Pharmacology: The corticosteroids are a class of compounds comprising steroid hormones secreted by the adrenal cortex and their synthetic analogs. In pharmacologic doses, corticosteroids are used primarily for their anti-inflammatory and/or immunosuppressive effects. Topical corticosteroids such as clobetasone are effective in the treatment of corticosteroid-responsive dermatoses primarily because of their anti-inflammatory, anti-puritic, and vasoconstrictive actions. However while the physiologic, pharmacologic and clinical effects of the corticosteroids are well known, the exact mechanism of their actions in each disease are uncertain. Clobetasone has been shown to have topical and systemic pharmacologic and metabolic effects characteristic of the corticosteroid class of drugs.

Indications: Clobetasone, a fluorinated topical corticosteroid, is indicated for the treatment of milder forms of eczema, seborrheic dermatitis, and other corticosteroid responsive skin conditions, which do not require the use of a more potent topical corticosteroid.

Contraindications: Primarily infected skin lesions caused by infection with fungi or bacteria if no anti-infective agent is used simultaneously; primary cutaneous viral infections, including herpes simplex, vaccinia and varicella; tuberculous skin lesions; hypersensitivity to any of the components.

Warnings: This product should not be used in the eye and should be used with caution in lesions close to the eye as glaucoma may result. Posterior subcapsular cataracts have been reported following systemic use of corticosteroids. When used under occlusive dressing, over extensive areas for prolonged periods, it is possible that sufficient absorption may take place to give rise to transient adrenal suppression. Long-term continuous topical corticosteroid therapy should be avoided where possible as adrenal suppression can occur even without occlusion.

Patients should be advised to inform subsequent physicians of the prior use of corticosteroids.

Precautions: Significant systemic absorption may result when corticosteroids are applied over large areas of the body. To minimize this possibility, treatment should be interrupted periodically or one area of the body should be treated at a time when long-term therapy is anticipated. In infants, the diaper may act as an occlusive dressing and increase absorption.

As with all corticosteroids, prolonged application to the face is undesirable.

Prolonged or extensive use of topical corticosteriod products may produce atrophy of the skin and s.c. tissue, particularly on flexor surfaces and on the face. If this is noted, the use of the drug should be discontinued.

Use with caution in patients with stasis dermatitis and other skin diseases associated with impaired circulation.

If a symptomatic response is not noted within a few days to a week, the local application should be discontinued and the patient re-evaluated.

In cases of bacterial infections of the skin, appropriate antibacterial agents should be used as primary therapy. If it is considered necessary, the topical corticosteroid may be used as an adjunct to control inflammation, erythema and itching. If a symptomatic response is not noted within a few days to a week, the local application of corticosteroid should be discontinued until the infection is brought under control.

During the use of topical corticosteroids, secondary infections may occur. Appropriate antimicrobial therapy should be used whenever treating inflammatory lesions which have become infected. Any spread of infection requires withdrawal of topical corticosteroid therapy, and systemic administration of antimicrobial agents. Bacterial infection is encouraged by the warm, moist conditions induced by occlusive dressings, and so the skin should be cleansed before a fresh dressing is applied.

The safety and effectiveness of clobetasone when used under occlusive dressings has not been determined.

Although hypersensitivity reactions are rare with topically applied corticosteroids, the drug should be discontinued and appropriate therapy initiated if there are signs of hypersensitivity.

Pregnancy and *Lactation:* Topical administration of corticosteroids to pregnant animals can cause abnormalities of fetal development. The relevance of this finding to human beings has not been established. However, the administration of clobetasone topical preparations during pregnancy and lactation should only be considered if the expected benefit to the mother is greater than any possible risk to the fetus. Drugs of this class should not be used extensively in pregnant patients in large amounts or for prolonged periods of time.

Adverse Effects: When large areas of the body are being treated with clobetasone, it is possible that some patients will absorb sufficient steroid to cause transient adrenal suppression despite the low degree of systemic activity associated with clobetasone.

Local burning, irritation, itching, skin atrophy, dryness of the skin, atrophy of s.c. tissues, telangiectasia, striae, change in pigmentation, secondary infection, and hypertrichosis have been observed following topical corticosteroid therapy. Exacerbation of symptoms may occur.

Local atrophic changes could possibly occur in situations where moisture increases absorption of clobetasone, but only after prolonged use.

In the unlikely event of signs of hypersensitivity appearing, application should stop immediately.

Overdose: Symptoms and Treatment: Acute overdosage is very unlikely to occur. However, in the case of chronic overdose or misuse, the features of hypercorticism may appear. As with any corticosteroid, discontinue therapy if the typical signs of hypercorticism appear.

Dosage: Apply thinly 2 or 3 times a day (according to the severity of the condition) to the affected area and rub gently into the skin. Maximum adult dosage should not exceed 100 g/week.

Supplied: Cream: Each tube contains: clobetasone butyrate 0.05%. Nonmedicinal ingredients: beeswax substitute, cetostearyl alcohol, chlorocresol, citric acid anhydrous, dimethicone 20, glycerin, glyceryl monostearate, purified water and sodium citrate. Tubes of 15 and 30 g. Store below 30°C.

Ointment: Each tube contains: clobetasone butyrate 0.05%. Nonmedicinal ingredients: mineral oil and white petrolatum. Tubes of 15 and 30 g. Store below 30°C.

EURAX®

Novartis Consumer Health

Crotamiton

Antipruritic

Indications: To relieve itching in most types of dermatosis, notably: atopic dermatitis, chickenpox, contact dermatitis, creeping eruption, dermatitis herpetiformis, dermatitis medicamentosa, dermatophytosis, eczema, insect bites, intertrigo, lichen planus, neurodermatitis, neurotic excoriation, pityriasis rosea, poison ivy dermatitis, pruritus ani, scroti and vulvae, psoriasis, seborrheic dermatitis, senile pruritus, sunburn, urticaria, varicose eczema.

Contraindications: Acutely inflamed skin or raw, weeping areas. Hypersensitivity to crotamiton.

Precautions: For external use only. Crotamiton should not be allowed to come into contact with the eyes. Keep out of reach of children.

Pregnancy: There is no experience to judge the safety of crotamiton in human pregnancy, especially in the first 3 months. *Lactation:* It is not known whether crotamiton passes into the breastmilk when the preparation is applied topically. Nursing mothers should avoid applying crotamiton in the area of the nipples.

Adverse Effects: Allergic sensitivity or primary irritation reactions may occur in some patients. In such instances, treatment should be discontinued.

Overdose: Symptoms and Treatment: In cases of acute intoxication by accidental ingestion, nausea, vomiting and irritation of the buccal, esophagal and gastric mucosa have been reported.

Moreover risk of methemoglobinemia exists in case of accidental ingestion as well as in case of excessive cutaneous absorption.

Dosage: Local application as frequently as required, usually 2 to 3 times daily. Note: The cream should be massaged into skin until dry.

Supplied: Each tube contains: crotamiton USP 10%. Nonmedicinal ingredients: beeswax, fragrance, glycerin, glyceryl monostearate, lanolin, methylparaben, oxyquinoline sulfate, paraffin, polyethylene glycol, polysorbate and propylparaben. Alcohol- and bisulfite-free. Tubes of 20 and 50 g. Protect from heat and light.

Reviewed 1999

EVENING PRIMROSE OIL
Swiss Herbal

Evening Primrose Oil
Essential Fatty Acid Supplement

Supplied: Each capsule contains oil of evening primrose 500 mg (as linoleic acid 345 mg, gamma linolenic acid 47.5 mg and oleic acid 47.5 mg) and mixed tocopherols 4 mg. No artificial preservatives, color, corn, milk, soya, starch, sugar, wheat or yeast. Nonmedicinal ingredients: gelatin, glycerin and purified water. Bottles of 90, 180 and 360.

EVISTA™ Ⓟ
Lilly

Raloxifene HCl
Selective Estrogen Receptor Modulator

Pharmacology: Raloxifene is a selective estrogen receptor modulator (SERM) that belongs to the benzothiophene class of compounds. The SERM profile of raloxifene includes estrogen agonist effects on bone and lipid metabolism but not in uterine or breast tissues.

Pharmacokinetics: The disposition of raloxifene has been evaluated in 276 postmenopausal women in conventional clinical pharmacology studies and in more than 1 300 postmenopausal women in selected raloxifene trials. Raloxifene exhibits high within-subject variability (approximately 30%) of most pharmacokinetic parameters. Table I summarizes the pharmacokinetic parameters of raloxifene.

Absorption: Raloxifene is absorbed rapidly after oral administration. Approximately 60% of an oral dose is absorbed, but presystemic glucuronide conjugation is extensive. Absolute bioavailability of raloxifene is 2%. The time to reach average maximum plasma concentration and bioavailability are functions of systemic interconversion and enterohepatic cycling of raloxifene and its glucuronide metabolites.

Administration of raloxifene with a standardized, high-fat meal increases the absorption of raloxifene slightly, but does not lead to clinically meaningful changes in systemic exposure. Raloxifene can be administered without regard to meals.

Distribution: Following oral administration of single doses ranging from 30 to 150 mg of raloxifene, the apparent volume of distribution is 2 348 L/kg and is not dose dependent.

Raloxifene and the monoglucuronide conjugates are highly bound to plasma proteins. Raloxifene binds to both albumin and α1-acid glycoprotein, but not to sex steroid binding globulin. In vitro, raloxifene did not interact with the binding of warfarin, phenytoin, or tamoxifen.

Metabolism: Biotransformation and disposition of raloxifene in humans have been determined following oral administration of ^{14}C-labeled raloxifene. Raloxifene undergoes extensive first-pass metabolism to the glucuronide conjugates: raloxifene-4'-glucuronide, raloxifene-6-glucuronide, and raloxifene-6, 4'-diglucuronide. No other metabolites have been detected, providing strong evidence that raloxifene is not metabolized by cytochrome P450 pathways. Unconjugated raloxifene comprises less than 1% of the total radiolabeled material in plasma. The terminal log-linear portion of the plasma concentration curve for raloxifene and the glucuronides are generally parallel. This is consistent with interconversion of raloxifene and the glucuronide metabolites.

Following i.v. administration, raloxifene is cleared at a rate approximating hepatic blood flow. Apparent oral clearance is 44.1 L/kg·h. Raloxifene and its glucuronide conjugates are interconverted by reversible systemic metabolism and enterohepatic cycling, thereby prolonging its plasma elimination half-life to 27.7 hours after oral dosing.

Results from single oral doses of raloxifene predict multiple-dose pharmacokinetics. Following chronic dosing, clearance ranges from 40 to 60 L/kg•h. Increasing doses of raloxifene (ranging from 30 to 150 mg) result in slightly less than a proportional increase in the area under the plasma time concentration curve (AUC).

Excretion: Raloxifene is primarily excreted in feces; negligible amounts are excreted unchanged in urine. Less than 6% of the raloxifene dose is eliminated in urine as glucuronide conjugates. In the osteoporosis prevention trials, raloxifene and metabolite concentrations are similar for women with estimated creatinine clearance as low as 23 mL/min.

Special Populations: Geriatrics: The pharmacokinetics of raloxifene are independent of age (42 to 83 years).

Children: The pharmacokinetics of raloxifene have not been evaluated in a pediatric population.

Gender: Total extent of exposure and oral clearance, normalized for lean body weight, are not significantly different between age-matched male and female volunteers.

Race: Pharmacokinetic differences due to race have been studied on a limited basis in 1 053 women consisting of 93.5% Caucasian, 4.3% Hispanic, 1.2% Asian and 0.5% Black in the osteoporosis prevention trials. There were no discernible differences in raloxifene plasma concentrations among these groups.

Renal Insufficiency: Since negligible amounts of raloxifene are eliminated in urine, a study in patients with renal insufficiency was not conducted.

Hepatic Dysfunction: Raloxifene was studied, as a single dose, in Child-Pugh Class A patients with cirrhosis and total serum bilirubin ranging from 0.6 to 2 mg/dL. Plasma raloxifene concentrations were approximately 2.5 times higher than in controls and correlated with bilirubin concentrations. Safety and efficacy have not been evaluated further in patients with hepatic insufficiency (see Precautions).

Drug Interactions: Clinically significant drug-interactions are discussed in Precautions.

Table I—Evista

Summary of Raloxifene Pharmacokinetic Parameters in the Healthy Postmenopausal Woman

	C_{max}[a] (mg/mL)/(mg/kg)	t½ (h)	$AUC_{0-\infty}$[a] (ng•hr/mL)/(mg/kg)	CL/F (L/kg•h)	V/F (L/kg)
Single Dose					
Mean	0.50	27.7	27.2	44.1	2 348
CV(%)	52	10.7 to 273[b]	44	46	52
Multiple Dose					
Mean	1.36	32.5	24.2	47.4	2 853
CV(%)	37	15.8 to 86.6[b]	36	41	56

Abbreviations: C_{max}=maximum plasma concentration, t½=half-life, AUC=area under the curve, CL=clearance, V=volume of distribution, F=bioavailability, CV=coefficient of variation.
[a] data normalized based on dose in mg and body weight in kg.
[b] range of observed half-life.

Ampicillin: Peak concentrations of raloxifene are reduced with coadministration of ampicillin. The reduction in peak concentrations is consistent with reduced enterohepatic cycling associated with antibiotic reduction of enteric bacteria. Since the overall extent of absorption and the elimination rate of raloxifene are not affected, raloxifene can be concurrently administered with ampicillin.

Antacids: Concurrent administration of calcium carbonate or aluminum and magnesium hydroxide-containing antacids does not affect the systemic exposure of raloxifene.

Digoxin: Raloxifene has no effect on the pharmacokinetics of digoxin.

The influence of concomitant medication on raloxifene plasma concentrations was evaluated in the osteoporosis prevention trials. Frequently coadministered drugs included: acetaminophen, nonsteroidal anti-inflammatory drugs (such as ASA, ibuprofen and naproxen), oral antibiotics, H_1 antagonists, H_2 antagonists and benzodiazepines. No clinically relevant effects of the coadministration of the agents on raloxifene disposition were identified.

Pharmacodynamics: General: Postmenopausal women have an increased risk of chronic illnesses such as osteoporosis and atherosclerotic cardiovascular disease resulting from estrogen deficiency. Estrogen replacement reduces the risk of osteoporosis and coronary artery disease, but it also increases the risk of endometrial carcinoma and possibly breast cancer. The selective estrogen receptor modulator (SERM) profile of raloxifene includes estrogen agonist effects on bone and lipid metabolism, and estrogen antagonist effects in uterine and breast tissues. Thus, raloxifene provides an alternative to estrogen replacement therapy for prevention of postmenopausal osteoporosis.

Raloxifene's biological actions, like those of estrogen, are mediated through high-affinity binding to estrogen receptors and regulation of gene expression. This binding results in differential expression of multiple estrogen-regulated genes in different tissues. Recent data suggest that the estrogen receptor can regulate gene expression by at least 2 distinct pathways which are ligand-, tissue- and/or gene-specific.

Effects on the Skeleton: During early to middle adult life, bone undergoes continuous remodeling. In this process, local areas of bone resorption are refilled completely by ensuing bone formation; that is, resorption and formation are in balance. The result is that bone mass remains relatively constant. Ovarian estrogen is important for maintenance of this balance in bone turnover. Marked decreases in estrogen availability, such as after oophorectomy or menopause, lead to marked increases in bone resorption. After menopause, bone is initially lost rapidly because the compensatory increase in bone formation is inadequate to offset resorptive losses.

This imbalance between resorption and formation may be related to loss of estrogen, or to age-related impairment of osteoblasts or their precursors. Estrogen replacement therapy reduces resorption of bone by inhibiting the formation and action of osteoclasts and decreases overall bone turnover. These effects on bone are manifested as reductions in the serum and urine levels of bone turnover markers, histologic evidence of decreased bone resorption and formation, and increased bone mineral density (BMD). Although raloxifene increases BMD to a lesser extent than estrogen, the effects of raloxifene on bone turnover in postmenopausal women parallel those of estrogen, as shown by studies of bone mineral densitometry, radiocalcium kinetics, bone markers and bone histomorphometry.

Effects on Total Body and Regional Bone Mineral Density: The effects of raloxifene on BMD in postmenopausal women were examined in 3 large randomized, placebo-controlled, double-blind osteoporosis prevention trials: (1) a North American trial enrolled 544 women; (2) a European trial, 601 women; and (3) an international trial, 619 women who had undergone hysterectomy. In these trials, all women received calcium supplementation (400 to 600 mg/day). Raloxifene, 60 mg administered once daily, produced significant increases in bone mass versus calcium supplementation alone, as reflected by dual-energy x-ray absorptiometric (DXA) measurements of hip, spine and total body BMD. The increases in BMD were statistically significant at 12 months and were maintained at 24 months (see Table II on following page). In contrast, the calcium-supplemented placebo groups lost approximately 1% of BMD over 24 months.

Raloxifene also increased BMD compared with placebo in the total body by 1.3% to 2% and in Ward's Triangle (hip) by 3.1% to 4%. In the international trial, conjugated equine estrogen 0.625 mg/day (ERT) was used as an active comparator. The mean increases in BMD at 24 months for estrogen compared with placebo were: lumbar spine, 5.4%; total hip, 2.9%.

Evista (cont'd)

Table II—Evista

Raloxifene Increases in BMD For the Three Osteoporosis Prevention Studies Expressed as Percentage Increase Versus Calcium-Supplemented Placebo at 24 Months

	Study		
Site	NA %	EU %	INT[a] %
Total Hip	2.0	2.4	1.3
Femoral Neck	2.1	2.5	1.6
Trochanter	2.2	2.7	1.3
Intertrochanter	2.3	2.4	1.3
Lumbar Spine	2.0	2.4	1.8

Abbreviations: NA=North American, EU=European, INT=international.
[a]Women status post-hysterectomy.

Thus, in postmenopausal women, raloxifene preserves bone mass and increases BMD significantly relative to calcium alone at 24 months. The effect on hip bone mass is similar to that for the spine.

In an interim analysis of a study on 7 705 postmenopausal women with osteoporosis (mean age 66.5 years), raloxifene therapy for 2 years reduced the incidence of vertebral fractures by 34% (95% confidence interval, 15% to 48% reduction) in women with prevalent fractures and by 52% (95% confidence interval, 16% to 72% reduction) in women without prevalent fractures. The effect of raloxifene in reducing the incidence of nonvertebral fracture is not yet known.

Assessments of Bone Turnover: In a 31-week radiocalcium kinetics study, raloxifene was associated with reduced bone resorption and a positive shift in calcium balance (+60 mg Ca/day), due primarily to decreased urinary calcium losses. These findings were similar to those observed with hormone replacement therapy.

In the osteoporosis prevention trials, raloxifene therapy resulted in consistent, statistically significant suppression of bone resorption, bone formation and overall bone turnover, as reflected by changes in serum and urine markers of bone turnover (e.g., bone-specific alkaline phosphatase, osteocalcin and collagen breakdown products). The suppression of bone turnover markers was evident by 3 months and persisted throughout the 24-month observation period.

Bone Histomorphometry: The tissue- and cellular-level effects of raloxifene were assessed by quantitative measurements (bone histomorphometry) on animal bones and human iliac crest bone biopsies taken after administration of a fluorochrome substance to label areas of mineralizing bone. The effects of raloxifene on bone histomorphometry were determined by pre-and post-treatment biopsies in a 6-month study of postmenopausal women. Bone in raloxifene-treated women was histologically normal, showing no evidence of mineralization defects, woven bone, or marrow fibrosis. The patterns of change were consistent with reduced bone turnover, although most changes were not statistically significant. In another bone histomorphometry study, postmenopausal women were treated for 6 months with raloxifene at a higher dose (150 mg/day). Bone was also histologically normal, with no woven bone, marrow fibrosis, or mineralization defects.

In rats, raloxifene prevented increased bone resorption and bone loss after ovariectomy and preserved bone strength in biomechanical studies. Ovariectomized cynomolgus monkeys were treated with raloxifene for 2 years, equivalent at the bone level to 6 years in humans. The biomechanical properties of bone from the raloxifene-treated monkeys were normal. Histologic examination of bone from rats and monkeys treated with raloxifene showed normal cancellous bone morphology and no evidence of woven bone, marrow fibrosis, or mineralization defects.

The animal and human bone histomorphometric results are consistent with data from studies of radiocalcium kinetics and markers of bone metabolism and demonstrate that raloxifene is a skeletal antiresorptive agent.

Effects on Lipid Metabolism: In numerous epidemiologic studies, estrogen use after menopause is associated with reduced risk of atherosclerotic cardiovascular disease. The cardiovascular protective effects of estrogen are believed to be mediated by its effects on lipids and nonlipid risk factors. In animal studies, the effects of raloxifene on cholesterol metabolism were mediated through the estrogen receptor.

The effects of raloxifene on cardiovascular intermediate endpoints were evaluated in a 6-month study of 390 postmenopausal women. Raloxifene was compared with continuous combined estrogen/progestin (0.625 mg conjugated equine estrogen plus 2.5 mg medroxyprogesterone acetate, [HRT]) and placebo (see Table III). Raloxifene decreased serum total and LDL cholesterol without significant effects on serum total HDL cholesterol or triglycerides. Raloxifene significantly increased HDL-2 cholesterol subfraction. In addition, raloxifene significantly decreased serum fibrinogen and lipoprotein (a).

Table III—Evista

Raloxifene and HRT Effects on Cardiovascular Intermediate Endpoints in a 6-Month Study — Median Percentage Change from Baseline

	Treatment Group		
Endpoint	Placebo (N=98) %	Raloxifene (N=95) %	HRT (N=96) %
Total Cholesterol	0.9	-6.6	-4.4
LDL Cholesterol	1.0	-10.9	-12.7
HDL Cholesterol	0.9	0.7	10.6
HDL-2 Cholesterol	0.0	15.4	33.3
Fibrinogen	-2.1	-12.2	-2.8
Lipoprotein (a)	3.3	-4.1	-16.3
Triglycerides	-0.3	-4.1	20.0

Abbreviations: HRT = continuous combined estrogen/progestin (0.625 mg conjugated equine estrogen plus 2.5 mg medroxyprogesterone acetate).

In the osteoporosis prevention studies (N=1 764), 24-month data were consistent with results from the 6-month cardiovascular study. Compared with placebo, raloxifene significantly decreased serum total and LDL cholesterol, but did not increase HDL cholesterol or triglycerides.

Effects on the Uterus: Postmenopausal estrogen deficiency leads to endometrial atrophy. Estrogen replacement therapy is associated with endometrial proliferation and hyperplasia and increased risk of endometrial carcinoma. All forms of hormone replacement therapy are often accompanied by spotting and bleeding. In contrast, raloxifene has no endometrial stimulatory effect and does not induce spotting or bleeding.

In placebo-controlled osteoporosis prevention trials, endometrial thickness was evaluated every 6 months (for 24 months) by transvaginal ultrasonography (TVU), a noninvasive method of visualizing the uterus. A total of 2 978 TVU measurements were collected from 831 women in all dose groups. Raloxifene-treated women consistently had endometrial thickness measurements indistinguishable from placebo. Furthermore, there were no differences between the raloxifene and placebo groups with respect to the incidence of reported vaginal bleeding.

In a 6-month study comparing raloxifene to conjugated equine estrogens (0.625 mg/day [ERT]), endpoint endometrial biopsies demonstrated stimulatory effects of ERT which were not observed for raloxifene (see Table IV). All samples from raloxifene-treated women showed nonproliferative endometrium.

Table IV—Evista

Raloxifene and ERT Effects on Endometrial Histology After 6 Months of Therapy

	Treatment Group	
Endpoint Biopsy Result	Raloxifene (n=10)	ERT (n=8)
Nonproliferative Endometrium[a]	10	2
Proliferative Tissue	0	4
Simple Hyperplasia	0	2

Abbreviations: ERT=conjugated equine estrogens (0.625 mg/day).
[a]The term, nonproliferative endometrium, includes endometrial atrophy, surface endometrium and inadequate sample.

A 12-month study of uterine effects compared a higher dose of raloxifene (150 mg/day) with HRT. At baseline, 43 raloxifene-treated women and 37 HRT-treated women had a nonproliferative endometrium. At study completion, endometrium in all of the raloxifene-treated women remained nonproliferative whereas 13 HRT-treated women had developed proliferative changes. Also, HRT significantly increased uterine volume; raloxifene did not increase uterine volume. Thus, no stimulatory effect of raloxifene on the endometrium was detected at more than twice the recommended dose.

The postmenopausal endometrium is atrophic due to the lack of endogenous estrogen. Consequently, the estrogen antagonist effects of raloxifene on this tissue could not be demonstrated in the clinical trials. However, raloxifene is a potent estrogen antagonist in the rat uterus, where it completely blocks the stimulatory effects of estrogen. In the absence of estrogen stimulation, raloxifene did not have any stimulatory effects on the endometrium in any animal models tested.

Effects on the Breast: Estrogen replacement therapy and hormone replacement therapy stimulate glandular and stromal components of breast tissue, resulting in symptoms of breast pain and tenderness in some postmenopausal women. In contrast, raloxifene does not stimulate breast tissue. Across all placebo-controlled trials, raloxifene was indistinguishable from placebo with regard to frequency and severity of breast symptoms. Raloxifene was associated with significantly fewer breast symptoms than reported by women receiving estrogens with or without added progestin (see Adverse Effects).

The estrogen antagonist aspects of raloxifene's SERM profile were examined in a variety of preclinical breast cancer models. Raloxifene inhibited the growth of MCF-7 human breast cancer cells in vitro and of MCF-7 xenograft tumors in mice. In animal models of carcinogen-induced breast cancer (nitrosomethylurea [NMU] and dimethylbenzanthracene [DMBA]), raloxifene decreased tumor burden.

In clinical trials with raloxifene involving 12 802 patients, approximately 8 300 women were exposed to raloxifene for up to 39 months. There was a statistically significant reduction in the frequency of newly diagnosed breast cancers in raloxifene-treated women compared with placebo (see Adverse Effects, Additional Safety Information). These observations are consistent with the preclinical pharmacologic profile of raloxifene (selective estrogen receptor modulator) and support the conclusion that raloxifene has no intrinsic estrogen agonist activity in mammary tissue. The long-term (beyond 39 months) effects of raloxifene on the incidence of breast cancer are not yet known.

Indications: For the prevention of osteoporosis in postmenopausal women.

Supplemental calcium should be added to the diet if daily intake is inadequate.

No single clinical finding or test result can quantify risk of postmenopausal osteoporosis with certainty. However, clinical assessment can help to identify women at increased risk. Widely accepted risk factors include Caucasian or Asian descent, slender body build, early estrogen deficiency, smoking, alcohol consumption, low calcium diet, sedentary lifestyle and family history of osteoporosis. Evidence of increased bone turnover from serum and urine markers and low bone mass (e.g., at least 1 standard deviation below the mean for healthy, young adult women) as determined by densitometric techniques are also predictive. The greater the number of clinical risk factors, the greater the probability of developing postmenopausal osteoporosis.

Contraindications: Women of childbearing potential. Raloxifene therapy during pregnancy may be associated with an increased risk of congenital defects in the fetus.

Raloxifene is contraindicated in women with active or past history of venous thromboembolic events, including deep vein thrombosis, pulmonary embolism and retinal vein thrombosis.

Raloxifene is contraindicated in women known to be hypersensitive to raloxifene or other constituents of the tablets.

Warnings: Venous Thromboembolic Events: An analysis of raloxifene-treated women across all placebo-controlled clinical trials showed an increased risk of venous thromboembolic events defined as deep vein thrombosis, pulmonary embolism and retinal vein thrombosis. The magnitude of risk is similar to that associated with current use of hormone replacement therapy. Raloxifene should be discontinued at least 72 hours prior to and during prolonged immobilization (e.g., post-surgical recovery, prolonged bed rest) and raloxifene therapy should be resumed only after the patient is fully ambulatory. The risk-benefit balance should be considered in women at risk of thromboembolic disease for other reasons.

Premenopausal Use: There is no indication for premenopausal use of raloxifene. Safety of raloxifene in premenopausal women has not been established and its use is not recommended (see Contraindications).

Hepatic Dysfunction: Raloxifene was studied, as a single dose, in Child-Pugh Class A patients with cirrhosis and serum total bilirubin ranging from 0.6 to 2 mg/dL. Plasma raloxifene concentrations were approximately 2.5 times higher than in controls and correlated with total bilirubin concentrations. Safety and efficacy have not been evaluated further in patients with hepatic insufficiency.

Precautions: General: Concurrent Estrogen Therapy: The concurrent use of raloxifene and systemic estrogen or hormone replacement therapy (ERT or HRT) has not been studied in prospective clinical trials.

Lipid Metabolism: Raloxifene lowers serum total and LDL cholesterol by 6 to 11%, but does not affect serum concentrations of total HDL cholesterol or triglycerides. HDL-2 cholesterol subfraction is increased by raloxifene. These effects should be taken into account in therapeutic decisions for patients who may require therapy for hyperlipidemia. Concurrent use of raloxifene and lipid lowering agents has not been studied.
Endometrium: Raloxifene does not cause endometrial proliferation (see Pharmacology and Adverse Effects). Unexplained uterine bleeding should be investigated as clinically indicated.
Breast: Raloxifene is not associated with breast enlargement, breast pain, or increased risk of breast cancer (see Pharmacology and Adverse Effects). Any unexplained breast abnormality occurring during raloxifene therapy should be investigated.
History of Breast Cancer: Raloxifene has not been studied in women with a prior history of breast cancer.
Use in Men: There is no indication for use of raloxifene in men.
Children: Raloxifene should not be used in pediatric patients.
Information to be Provided to the Patient: For safe and effective use of raloxifene, the physician should inform patients about the following: Patient Immobilization: Raloxifene should be discontinued at least 72 hours prior to and during prolonged immobilization (e.g., postsurgical recovery, prolonged bed rest) and raloxifene therapy should be resumed only after the patient is fully ambulatory because of the increased risk of venous thromboembolic events.
Vasodilatation: Raloxifene is not effective in reducing vasodilatation (hot flashes or flushes) associated with estrogen deficiency. In some patients, vasodilatation may occur on beginning raloxifene therapy.
Other Preventive Measures: Patients should be instructed to take supplemental calcium and vitamin D if daily dietary intake is inadequate. Weight-bearing exercise should be considered along with the modification of certain behavioral factors, such as cigarette smoking and/or alcohol consumption, if these factors exist.
Drug Interactions: Cholestyramine: Cholestyramine significantly reduces the absorption and enterohepatic cycling of raloxifene and should not be coadministered with raloxifene.
Warfarin: Coadministration of raloxifene and warfarin does not alter the pharmacokinetics of either compound. However, modest decreases in prothrombin time have been observed in single-dose studies. If raloxifene is given concurrently with warfarin, prothrombin time should be monitored.
Other Highly Protein-Bound Drugs: Raloxifene is more than 95% bound to plasma proteins, but is found at 2 to 5 nM concentration in human plasma. In vitro, raloxifene did not affect the binding of warfarin, phenytoin or tamoxifen. Nevertheless, caution should be used when raloxifene is coadministered with other highly protein-bound drugs.
Laboratory Test Interactions: Raloxifene is not known to interfere with any common laboratory assays (see Adverse Effects for additional laboratory safety information).
Pregnancy: Raloxifene should not be used in women who are or may become pregnant (see Contraindications).
Labor and Delivery: Raloxifene has no recognized use during labor or delivery.
Lactation: Raloxifene should not be used by lactating women (see Contraindications). It is not known whether raloxifene is excreted in human milk.

Adverse Effects: The safety of raloxifene has been established in Phase 2 and Phase 3 placebo-controlled, estrogen-controlled and HRT-controlled studies. Twelve studies comprise the primary safety database for the prevention indication. The duration of treatment ranged from 2 to 30 months and 2 036 women were exposed to raloxifene. All events were reported irrespective of causality.
Commonly Observed Adverse Events: The most commonly observed treatment-emergent adverse events associated with the use of raloxifene in double-blind, placebo-controlled clinical trials that occurred at an incidence ≥2% are shown in Table V. These events occurred in postmenopausal women who took raloxifene for up to 30 months. The differences between raloxifene and placebo treatments were significant at $p<0.05$.

Table V—Evista

Adverse Events Associated with Use of Raloxifene Occurring at a Frequency Greater than in Placebo-Treated Patients and at an Incidence ≥2% in Either Group

Adverse Event	Raloxifene (N=581) %	Placebo (N=584) %
Vasodilatation	24.6	18.3
Leg Cramps	5.9	1.9

Vasodilatation events (hot flashes or flushes) were common in placebo-treated women and the frequency was modestly increased in raloxifene-treated women. The first occurrence of this event was most commonly reported during the first 6 months of treatment and infrequently was reported de novo after that time. Discontinuation rates due to vasodilatation did not differ significantly between raloxifene and placebo groups (1.7% and 2.2%, respectively).
Adverse Events Associated with Discontinuation of Therapy: The majority of adverse events occurring during clinical trials have been mild and have not required discontinuation of therapy. Discontinuation of therapy due to any clinical adverse experience occurred in 11.4% of 581 raloxifene-treated women and 12.2% of 584 placebo-treated women.
Comparison of Raloxifene and Hormone Replacement Therapy Adverse Events: Raloxifene was compared with estrogen-progestin replacement therapy (HRT) in 3 clinical trials. Table VI shows adverse events occurring at an incidence ≥2% in any group.

Table VI—Evista

Adverse Events Reported In Clinical Trials With Raloxifene and Continuous Combined or Cyclic Estrogen Plus Progestin (HRT) at an Incidence ≥2% In Any Treatment Group

Adverse Event	Raloxifene (N=317) %	HRT-Continuous Combined (N=96) %	HRT-Cyclic (N=219) %
Urogenital			
Breast Pain	4.4	37.5[a]	29.7[a]
Vaginal Bleeding[c]	6.2	64.2[a]	88.5[a]
Digestive			
Flatulence	1.6	12.5[a]	6.4[a]
Cardiovascular			
Vasodilatation	28.7[b]	3.1	5.9
Body as a Whole			
Infection	11.0[b]	0	6.8
Abdominal Pain	6.6	10.4[a]	18.7[a]
Chest Pain	2.8[b]	0	0.5

[a]Significantly greater in specific HRT group than raloxifene ($p<0.05$).
[b]Significantly greater in raloxifene than in HRT ($p<0.05$).
[c]Treatment-emergent uterine-related adverse events, excluding patients who had a hysterectomy. (raloxifene, n=290; HRT-Continuous Combined, n=67; HRT-Cyclic, n=217). Continuous Combined HRT = 0.625 mg conjugated equine estrogen plus 2.5 mg medroxyprogesterone acetate. Cyclic HRT = 0.625 mg conjugated equine estrogen for 28 days with concomitant 5 mg medroxyprogesterone acetate or 0.15 mg norgestrel on Days 1 through 14 or 17 through 28.

Adverse Events in Placebo-controlled Clinical Trials: Table VII lists adverse events occurring in all placebo-controlled clinical trials with raloxifene at a frequency ≥2% in either group and at rates in raloxifene-treated women numerically greater than in placebo-treated women. Events previously discussed are not included in this table. None of the differences shown in the table were statistically significant and no causal inferences can be made.
Additional Safety Information: Incidences of estrogen-dependent carcinoma of the endometrium and breast are being evaluated across all completed and ongoing clinical trials involving 12 802 patients. Approximately 8 300 women have been exposed to raloxifene for up to 39 months.
Endometrium: All cases of endometrial carcinoma are reviewed without knowledge of treatment status (blinded) by an independent Adjudication Review Board. Raloxifene does not increase the risk of endometrial cancer when compared to placebo.
Breast: All cases of breast cancer in women enrolled in clinical trials are reviewed without knowledge of treatment status (blinded) by an independent Adjudication Review Board. A statistically significant 54% reduction (95% confidence interval, 23% to 72% reduction) has been observed in the incidence of newly-diagnosed breast cancer in raloxifene-treated women compared with placebo. The incidence rate of breast cancer was 3.83 per 1 000 subject-years for the women receiving placebo and 1.78 per 1 000 subject-years for those receiving raloxifene. The long-term (beyond 39 months) effects of raloxifene on the incidence of breast cancer are not yet known.

Table VII—Evista

Adverse Events Occurring in Placebo-Controlled Clinical Trials at a Frequency ≥2% in Either Group and at Rates in Raloxifene-Treated Women Numerically Greater Than in Placebo-Treated Women

Body System	Raloxifene N=581 %	Placebo N=584 %
Body as a Whole		
Infection	15.1	14.6
Flu Syndrome	14.6	13.5
Chest Pain	4.0	3.6
Fever	3.1	2.6
Cardiovascular		
Migraine	2.4	2.1
Digestive		
Nausea	8.8	8.6
Dyspepsia	5.9	5.8
Vomiting	3.4	3.3
Flatulence	3.1	2.4
Gastrointestinal Disorder	3.3	2.1
Gastroenteritis	2.6	2.1
Metabolic and Nutritional		
Weight Gain	8.8	6.8
Peripheral Edema	3.3[a]	1.9
Musculoskeletal		
Arthralgia	10.7	10.1
Myalgia	7.7	6.2
Arthritis	4.0	3.6
Nervous		
Depression	6.4	6.0
Insomnia	5.5	4.3
Respiratory		
Sinusitis	10.3	6.5
Pharyngitis	7.6	7.2
Cough Increased	6.0	5.7
Pneumonia	2.6	1.5
Laryngitis	2.2	1.4
Skin and Appendages		
Rash	5.5	3.8
Sweating	3.1	1.7
Urogenital		
Vaginitis	4.3	3.6
Urinary Tract Infection	4.0	3.9
Cystitis	3.3	3.1
Leukorrhea	3.3	1.7
Endometrial Disorder[b]	3.1	1.9

[a]Significant dose trends at $p<0.05$.
[b]Treatment-emergent uterine-related adverse event, including only patients with an intact uterus: Raloxifene, n=354; Placebo, n=364.

Laboratory Changes: The following changes in analyte concentrations are commonly observed during raloxifene therapy: increased serum HDL-2 cholesterol subfraction and apolipoprotein A1; and reduced serum total cholesterol, LDL cholesterol, fibrinogen, apolipoprotein B and lipoprotein (a). Raloxifene modestly increases hormone-binding globulin concentrations, including sex steroid binding globulin, thyroxine binding globulin, and corticosteroid binding globulin with corresponding increases in measured total hormone concentrations. There is no evidence that these changes in hormone binding globulin concentrations affect concentrations of the corresponding free hormones.

Overdose: Symptoms and Treatment: Incidents of overdose in humans have not been reported. In an 8-week study of 63 postmenopausal women, a dose of raloxifene HCl 600 mg/day was safely tolerated. No mortality was seen after a single oral dose in rats or mice at 5 000 mg/kg or in monkeys at 1 000 mg/kg. There is no specific antidote for raloxifene.

Dosage: The recommended dosage is 1 tablet daily which may be administered any time of day without regard to meals.

Supplied: Each white, elliptical, film-coated tablet, imprinted on one side with the tablet code 4165 in blue ink, contains: raloxifene HCl 60 mg. Nonmedicinal ingredients: anhydrous lactose, crospovidone, FD&C Blue No. 2 aluminum lake, hydroxypropyl methylcellulose, lactose monohydrate, macrogol 400, magnesium stearate, polysorbate 80, povidone and titanium dioxide E171. Blister packages of 28. Store at room temperature, 15 to 30°C.
New Product 1998

EX-LAX® Chocolated Pieces
EX-LAX® Sugar Coated Pills
EX-LAX® Extra Strength Sugar Coated Pills

Novartis Consumer Health

Sennosides

Laxative

Pharmacology: Sennosides are a natural source complex of anthraquinone glycosides found in senna. They exert a stimulant laxative effect that increases peristalsis by direct action on the smooth muscle of the intestine. They generally produce bowel movement in 6 to 12 hours.

Indications: For the overnight relief of occasional constipation.

Precautions: Do not take for more than 1 week, without consulting your physician, as overuse or extended use may cause dependence for bowel function. Do not use when abdominal pain, nausea, fever or vomiting are present. Do not take within 2 hours of other medicines since the desired effect of the other medicine may be reduced. Do not exceed the recommended dose. Keep out of reach of children.

Pregnancy and *Lactation:* Do not use if you are pregnant or nursing, unless on the advice of a physician.

Dosage: Chocolated Pieces: Take once or twice daily, preferably at bedtime. Adults and children 12 years of age or over: 1 to 2 pieces. Children 6 to 12 years: 1 piece. Children 2 to 6 years: ½ piece. Children under 2 years: Consult a physician. Pieces should be chewed before swallowing.

Sugar Coated Pills: Take once or twice daily with a glass of water, preferably at bedtime. Adults and children 12 years of age and over: 1 to 2 pills. Children 6 to 12 years: 1 pill. Children under 6 years: Consult a physician.

Extra Strength Sugar Coated Pills: Adults: Take 1 or 2 pills once or twice daily with a glass of water, preferably at bedtime.

Supplied: Chocolated Pieces: Each chocolate piece contains: sennosides USP 15 mg. Nonmedicinal ingredients: cocoa, hydrogenated palm kernel oil, lecithin, milk solids, sugar and vanillin. Boxes of 6, 18, 48 and 72.

Sugar Coated Pills: Each sugar coated pill contains: sennosides USP 15 mg. Nonmedicinal ingredients: acacia, alginic acid, calcium phosphate, carnauba wax, cellulose, iron oxide, magnesium stearate, sodium benzoate, sodium lauryl sulfate, starch, stearic acid, sucrose, talc and titanium dioxide. Blister packs, boxes of 10, 30 and 60.

Extra Strength Sugar Coated Pills: Each sugar coated pill contains: sennosides USP 25 mg. Nonmedicinal ingredients: acacia, alginic acid, calcium phosphate, carnauba wax, cellulose, FD&C blue No. 1, magnesium stearate, polyvinylpyrrolidone, silicon dioxide, sodium benzoate, sodium lauryl sulfate, starch, stearic acid, sucrose, talc and titanium dioxide. Blister packs, boxes of 24 and 48.

New Product 1998

EX-LAX® Stool Softener

Novartis Consumer Health

Docusate Sodium

Laxative

Supplied: Each caplet contains: docusate sodium 100 mg. Nonmedicinal ingredients: alginic acid, calcium phosphate, D&C yellow No. 10, FD&C blue No. 1, hydroxypropyl methylcellulose, magnesium stearate, methylparaben, microcrystalline cellulose, polydextrose, polyethylene glycol, silicon dioxide, sodium croscarmellose, stearic acid, talc, titanium dioxide and triacetin. Blister packs, boxes of 30.

EXOSURF® NEONATAL Ⓟ

Glaxo Wellcome

Colfosceril Palmitate

Synthetic Lung Surfactant

Pharmacology: Surfactant deficiency is an important factor in the development of the neonatal respiratory distress syndrome (RDS). Natural surfactant, a combination of lipids and apoproteins, exhibits not only surface tension reducing properties (conferred by the lipids), but also rapid spreading and adsorption (conferred by the apoproteins). The major fraction of the lipid component of natural surfactant is colfosceril palmitate (also known as dipalmitoylphosphatidylcholine or DPPC), which comprises up to 70% of natural surfactant by weight.

Although DPPC reduces surface tension, DPPC alone is ineffective in RDS because DPPC spreads and adsorbs poorly. In Exosurf Neonatal, which is protein-free, cetyl alcohol acts as a spreading agent for the DPPC on the air-fluid interface. Tyloxapol, a polymeric long-chain repeating alcohol, is a nonionic surfactant, which acts to disperse both DPPC and cetyl alcohol. Sodium chloride is added to adjust osmolality.

Clinical Studies: Exosurf Neonatal has been studied in the U.S. and Canada in controlled clinical trials involving more than 4 400 infants.

Prophylactic Treatment: The efficacy of a single dose of colfosceril in prophylactic treatment of infants at risk of developing respiratory distress syndrome (RDS) was examined in 3 double-blind, placebo-controlled studies (see Table I). The infants were intubated and placed on mechanical ventilation, and received 5 mL/kg colfosceril or placebo (air) within 30 minutes of birth.

An additional study compared the efficacy of 1 versus 3 doses of colfosceril (see Table I). Infants were intubated and placed on mechanical ventilation and received a first 5 mL/kg dose of colfosceril within 30 minutes. Repeat 5 mL/kg doses of colfosceril or placebo (air) were given to all infants who remained on mechanical ventilation at approximately 12 and 24 hours of age.

Rescue Treatment: The efficacy of colfosceril in the rescue treatment of infants with RDS was examined in 2 double-blind, placebo-controlled studies and is presented in Table II. In these rescue treatment studies, infants received an initial dose (5 mL/kg) of colfosceril or placebo (air) between 2 and 24 hours of life followed by a second dose (5 mL/kg) approximately 12 hours later to infants who remained on mechanical ventilation.

Clinical Results: In controlled prophylactic and rescue studies, infants in the colfosceril group showed significant improvements in FiO_2 and ventilator settings which persisted for at least 7 days. Pulmonary air leaks were significantly reduced in each study. Four of these studies also showed a significant reduction in death from RDS. The 1 versus 3-dose prophylactic treatment study in 700 to 1 100 g infants showed a further reduction in overall mortality with 2 additional doses.

Follow-up data at 1 year adjusted age are available on 1 094 of 2 470 surviving infants. Growth and development of infants who received colfosceril in this sample were comparable to infants who received placebo.

Pharmacokinetics: Colfosceril is administered directly into the trachea. Human pharmacokinetic studies of the absorption, biotransformation, and excretion of the components of Exosurf Neonatal have not been performed. Nonclinical studies, however, have shown that DPPC can be absorbed from the alveolus into lung tissue where it can be catabolized extensively and reutilized for further phospholipid synthesis and secretion.

Indications: 1. For prophylactic treatment of infants who are at risk of developing RDS or who have evidence of pulmonary immaturity.

Clinicians should carefully evaluate the potential risks and benefits of colfosceril administration in infants weighing 500 to 700 g. A single prophylactic dose in these infants significantly improved FiO_2 and ventilator settings, reduced pneumothorax, and reduced death from RDS, but increased pulmonary hemorrhage (see Warnings). In this study, overall mortality did not differ significantly between the placebo and colfosceril groups.

For prophylactic treatment, the first dose of colfosceril should be administered as soon as possible after birth (see Dosage, General Guidelines for Administration).

2. Rescue treatment of infants who have developed RDS.

Infants considered as candidates for rescue treatment with colfosceril should be on mechanical ventilation and have a diagnosis of RDS by both of the following criteria: respiratory distress not attributable to causes other than RDS based on

Table I—Exosurf Neonatal

Efficacy Assessments—Prophylactic Treatment

Number of Doses:	**Single Dose**		**Single Dose**		**Single Dose**		**1 Versus 3 Doses[e]**	
Birth Weight Range:	**500 to 700 g**		**700 to 1 350 g**		**700 to 1 100 g**		**700 to 1 100 g**	
Treatment Group:	**Placebo (Air)**	**Exosurf**	**Placebo (Air)**	**Exosurf**	**Placebo (Air)**	**Exosurf**	**1 Exosurf Dose**	**3 Exosurf Doses**
Number of Infants:	**n=106**	**n=109**	**n=185**	**n=176**	**n=222**	**n=224**	**n=356**	**n=360**
	% of Infants		**% of Infants**		**% of Infants**		**% of Infants**	
Death ≤Day 28[a]	53	50	11	6	21	15	16	9[f]
Death through 1 Year[a]	59	60	14	11	30	20[g]	17	12[f]
Death from ARDS[b]	25	13[f]	4	3	10	5[h]	3	2
Intact Cardiopulmonary Survival[a,c]	29	25	69	78[f]	65	68	74	78
Bronchopulmonary Dysplasia (BPD)[a,d]	43	44	23	18	19	21	8	12
RDS Incidence[b]	73	81	46	42	55	55	63	68

[a] "Intent-to-treat" analyses (as randomized) except for the 700 to 1 350 g, single-dose study in which infants' congenital infections and anomalies were excluded.
[b] "As-treated" analyses.
[c] Defined by survival through 28 days of life without bronchopulmonary dysplasia.
[d] Defined by a combination of clinical and radiographic criteria.
[e] Preliminary report.
[f] $p<0.05$.
[g] $p<0.01$.
[h] $p=0.051$.

Table II—Exosurf Neonatal

Efficacy Assessments—Rescue Treatment

Number of Doses:	**2 Doses**		**2 Doses**	
Birth Weight Range:	**700 to 1 350 g**		**1 250 g and above**	
Treatment Group:	**Placebo (Air)**	**Exosurf**	**Placebo (Air)**	**Exosurf**
Number of Infants:	**n=213**	**n=206**	**n=623**	**n=614**
	% of Infants		**% of Infants**	
Death ≤Day 28[a]	23	11[g]	7	4[e]
Death through 1 year[a]	27	15[g]	9	6[h]
Death from ARDS[b]	10	3[f]	3	1[e]
Intact Cardiopulmonary Survival[a,c]	62	75[f]	88	93[f]
Bronchopulmonary Dysplasia (BPD)[a,d]	18	15	6	3[e]

[a] "Intent-to-treat" analyses (as randomized).
[b] "As-treated" analyses.
[c] Defined by survival through 28 days of life without bronchopulmonary dysplasia.
[d] Defined by a combination of clinical and radiographic criteria.
[e] $p<0.05$.
[f] $p<0.01$.
[g] $p<0.001$.
[h] $p=0.067$.

clinical and laboratory assessments and chest radiographic findings consistent with the diagnosis of RDS.

Contraindications: There are no known contraindications to treatment with colfosceril.

Warnings: Intratracheal Administration Only: Colfosceril should be administered only by instillation into the trachea (see Dosage).

General: The use of colfosceril requires expert clinical care by experienced neonatologists and other clinicians who are accomplished at neonatal intubation and ventilatory management. Adequate personnel, facilities, equipment and medications are required to optimize perinatal outcome in premature infants.

Instillation of colfosceril should be performed **only** by trained medical personnel experienced in airway and clinical management of unstable premature infants. Vigilant clinical attention should be given to all infants prior to, during and after administration of colfosceril.

Possible Immediate Effects: Colfosceril can rapidly affect oxygenation and lung compliance. Therefore, when indicated, the following parameters should be adjusted as follows: Lung Compliance: If chest expansion improves substantially after dosing, peak ventilator inspiratory pressures should be reduced immediately, without waiting for confirmation of respiratory improvement by blood gas assessment. Failure to reduce inspiratory ventilator pressures rapidly in such instances can result in lung overdistention and fatal pulmonary air leak.

Hyperoxia: If the infant becomes pink and transcutaneous oxygen saturation is in excess of 95%, FiO_2 should be reduced in small but repeated steps (until saturation is 90 to 95%) without waiting for confirmation of elevated arterial pO_2 by blood gas assessment. Failure to reduce FiO_2 in such instances can result in hyperoxia.

Hypocarbia: If arterial or transcutaneous CO_2 measurements are <30 torr, the ventilator rate should be reduced at once. Failure to reduce ventilator rates in such instances can result in marked hypocarbia, which is known to reduce brain blood flow.

Pulmonary Hemorrhage: In the single study conducted in infants weighing <700 g at birth, the incidence of pulmonary hemorrhage (10% vs 2% in the placebo group) was significantly increased in the colfosceril group. In a cross-study analysis of 5 studies involving infants with birth weights >700 g, pulmonary hemorrhage was reported for 1% (14/1 420) of infants in the placebo group and 2% (27/1 411) of infants in the colfosceril group. Fatal pulmonary hemorrhage occurred in 3 infants; 2 in the colfosceril group and 1 in the placebo group. Mortality from all causes among infants who developed pulmonary hemorrhage was 43% in the placebo group and 37% in the colfosceril group.

Pulmonary hemorrhage in both colfosceril and placebo infants was more frequent in infants who were younger, smaller, male, or who had a patent ductus arteriosus. Pulmonary hemorrhage generally occurred in the first 2 days of life in both treatment groups.

In more than 7 700 infants in an open, uncontrolled study, pulmonary hemorrhage was reported in 4% of colfosceril-treated infants, with a fatality rate of 0.4%.

In the controlled clinical studies, colfosceril-treated infants (birth weights >700 g) who received steroids more than 24 hours prior to delivery or indomethacin postnatally had a lower rate of pulmonary hemorrhage than other colfosceril-treated infants. Attention should be paid to early and aggressive diagnosis and treatment (unless contraindicated) of patent ductus arteriosus during the first 2 days of life (when the ductus arteriosus is often clinically silent). Other potentially protective measures include attempting to decrease FiO_2 preferentially over ventilator pressures during the first 24 to 48 hours after dosing, and attempting to decrease Positive End Expiratory Pressure (PEEP) minimally for at least 48 hours after dosing.

Mucous Plugs: Infants whose ventilation becomes markedly impaired during or shortly after dosing may have mucous plugging of the endotracheal tube, particularly if pulmonary secretions were prominent prior to drug administration. Suctioning of all infants prior to dosing may lessen the chance of mucous plugs obstructing the endotracheal tube. If endotracheal tube obstruction from such plugs is suspected, and suctioning is unsuccessful in removing the obstruction, the blocked endotracheal tube should be replaced immediately.

Precautions: Reflux: Reflux of colfosceril into the endotracheal tube during dosing has been observed and may be associated with rapid drug administration. If reflux occurs, drug administration should be halted and, if necessary, peak inspiratory pressure on the ventilator should be increased by 4 to 5 cm H_2O until the endotracheal tube clears.

>20% Drop in Transcutaneous Oxygen Saturation: If transcutaneous oxygen saturation declines during dosing, drug administration should be halted and, if necessary, peak inspiratory pressure on the ventilator should be increased by 4 to 5 cm H_2O for 1 to 2 minutes. In addition, increases of FiO_2 may be required for 1 to 2 minutes.

Heart Rate Effects: Bradycardia (<60 beats/min) and tachycardia (>200 beats/min) have been reported during dosing.

Apnea: Infants treated with colfosceril in controlled clinical trials have been noted to have a higher incidence of apnea, associated with an increased use of methylxanthine therapy, than have infants in the control groups.

Adverse Effects: In controlled clinical studies evaluating the safety and efficacy of colfosceril, numerous safety assessments were made. In infants receiving colfosceril, pulmonary hemorrhage, apnea and use of methylxanthines were increased. A number of other adverse events were significantly reduced in the colfosceril group, particularly various forms of pulmonary air leaks and use of pancuronium. Table III and Table IV (on following page) summarize the results of the major safety evaluations from the controlled clinical studies.

Abnormal Laboratory Values: Abnormal laboratory values are common in critically ill, mechanically ventilated, premature infants. A higher incidence of abnormal laboratory values in the colfosceril group was not reported.

Overdose: Symptoms and Treatment: There have been no reports of overdose with colfosceril.

Dosage: Prophylactic Treatment: The first dose should be administered as a single 5 mL/kg dose as soon as possible after birth. Second and third doses should be administered approximately 12 and 24 hours later to all infants who remain on mechanical ventilation at those times.

Rescue Treatment: Colfosceril should be administered in two 5 mL/kg doses. The initial dose should be administered as soon as possible after the diagnosis of RDS is confirmed. The second dose should be administered approximately 12 hours following the first dose, provided the infant remains on mechanical ventilation.

Preparation of Suspension: Exosurf is best reconstituted immediately before use because it does not contain antibacterial preservatives. However, the reconstituted suspension is chemically and physically stable and remains sterile (when reconstituted using aseptic techniques) when stored between 2 and 30°C for up to 12 hours following reconstitution.

Solutions containing buffers or preservatives should not be used for reconstitution. **Do not use Bacteriostatic Water for Injection, USP.** Each vial of colfosceril should be reconstituted only with 8 mL of preservative-free Sterile Water for Injection as follows:

1. Fill a 10 mL or 12 mL syringe with 8 mL preservative-free Sterile Water for Injection using an 18- or 19-gauge needle.
2. Allow the vacuum in the vial to draw the sterile water into the vial.
3. Aspirate as much as possible of the reconstituted suspension out of the vial into the syringe (while maintaining the vacuum), then **suddenly** release the syringe plunger. Repeat 3 or 4 times to ensure adequate mixing of the vial contents.

If vacuum is not present, the vial of colfosceril should not be used.

The appropriate dosage volume for the entire dose (5 mL/kg) should then be drawn into the syringe from **below** the froth in the vial (again maintaining the vacuum).

Reconstituted Exosurf Neonatal is a milky white suspension with a total volume of 8 mL/vial. Each mL of reconstituted Exosurf contains colfosceril palmitate 13.5 mg, cetyl alcohol 1.5 mg, tyloxapol 1 mg, and sodium chloride to provide a

Table III—Exosurf Neonatal

Safety Assessments[a]—Prophylactic Treatment

Number of Doses:	**Single Dose**		**Single Dose**		**Single Dose**		**1 Versus 3 Doses**	
Birth Weight Range:	**500 to 700 g**		**700 to 1 350 g**		**700 to 1 100 g**		**700 to 1 100 g**	
Treatment Group:	**Placebo (Air)**	**Exosurf**	**Placebo (Air)**	**Exosurf**	**Placebo (Air)**	**Exosurf**	**1 Exosurf Dose**	**3 Exosurf Doses**
Number of Infants:	**n=108**	**n=107**	**n=193**	**n=192**	**n=222**	**n=224**	**n=356**	**n=360**
	% of Infants		**% of Infants**		**% of Infants**		**% of Infants**	
Intraventricular Hemorrhage (IVH)								
Overall	51	57	31	27	36	36	38	35
Severe IVH	26	25	10	8	13	14	9	9
Pulmonary Air Leak (PAL)								
Overall	52	48	16	11	32	25	29	27
Pneumothorax	23	10[c]	5	6	19	11[c]	14	12
Pneumopericardium	1	4	2	0	<1	1	1	1
Pneumomediastinum	2	1	2	3	7	1[d]	3	2
Pulmonary Interstitial Emphysema	43	44	13	7[c]	26	20	23	22
Death from PAL	4	6	<1	<1	2	1	2	1
Patent Ductus Arteriosus	49	53	66	70	50	55	59	57
Necrotizing Enterocolitis	2	4	11	13	3	4	6	2[c]
Pulmonary Hemorrhage	2	10[d]	2	4	1	4	4	6
Congenital Pneumonia	4	4	2	4	2	2	1	1
Nosocomial Pneumonia	10	10	2	4	4	7	14	15
Non-Pulmonary infections	33	35	34	39	28	29	35	34
Sepsis	30	34	30	34	23	24	30	27
Death from Sepsis	4	4	3	3	1	2	3	2
Meningitis	4	6	3	1	2	3	1	2
Other infections	7	4	5	3	6	10	10	11
Major Anomalies	3	1	2	4	7	4	4	4
Hypotension	70	77	52	47	59	62	54	50
Hyperbilirubinemia	22	21	63	61	27	31	20	21
Exchange Transfusion	4	3	1	2	2	2	3	1
Thrombocytopenia[b]	21	25	not available		9	8	12	10
Persistent Fetal Circulation	0	1	1	1	0	2[c]	1	<1
Seizures	11	8	2	2	11	0	6	5
Apnea	34	33	76	73	55	65[c]	62	68
Drug Therapy								
Antibiotics	96	99	98	96	98	99	>99	99
Diuretics	55	60	39	37	59	63	64	65
Anticonvulsants	14	18	23	24	20	16	9	8
Inotropes	46	40	20	20	26	20	28	27
Sedatives	62	71	65	64	63	57	52	52
Pancuronium	19	11	22	14[c]	19	13[c]	15	11
Methylxanthines	38	43	77	77	61	72[c]	75	82[c]

[a] All parameters were examined with "as-treated" analyses.
[b] Thrombocytopenia requiring platelet transfusion.
[c] $p<0.05$.
[d] $p<0.01$.

Exosurf Neonatal (cont'd)

0.1 N concentration. If the suspension appears to separate, gently shake or swirl the vial to resuspend the preparation. **The reconstituted product should be inspected visually for homogeneity immediately before administration; if persistent large flakes or particulates are present, the vial should not be used.**

Use of Special Endotracheal Tube Adapter: Endotracheal tube adapters equipped with a special right-angle Luer-lock sideport should be used. The adapters provided as part of the Exosurf kit are clean but not sterile. The adapters should be used as follows:

1. Select an adapter size which corresponds to the inside diameter of the endotracheal tube.
2. Insert the adapter into the endotracheal tube with a firm push-twist motion.
3. Connect the breathing circuit ''Y'' to the adapter.
4. Remove the cap from the sideport on the adapter. Attach the syringe containing drug to the sideport.
5. After completion of dosing, remove the syringe and **recap the sideport.**

Administration: **The infant should be suctioned prior to administration of colfosceril.**

Colfosceril suspension is administered via the sideport on the special endotracheal tube adaptor **without interrupting mechanical ventilation.**

Each colfosceril dose is administered in two 2.5 mL/kg half-doses. Each half-dose is instilled slowly over a minimum of 1 to 2 minutes (30 to 50 mechanical breaths) in small bursts timed with inspiration. After the first 2.5 mL/kg half-dose is administered in the midline position, the infant's head and torso are turned 45° to the **right** for 30 seconds while mechanical ventilation is continued. After the infant is returned to the midline position, the second 2.5 mL/kg half-dose is given in an identical fashion over a minimum of 1 to 2 minutes. The infant's head and torso are then turned 45° to the **left** for 30 seconds while mechanical ventilation is continued, and the infant is then turned back to the midline position. These manoeuvres allow gravity to assist in the distribution of colfosceril in the lungs.

Heart rate, color, chest expansion, facial expressions, the oximeter and the endotracheal tube patency and position should all be monitored during dosing. If heart rate slows, the infant becomes dusky or agitated, transcutaneous oxygen saturation falls more than 15%, or colfosceril backs up in the endotracheal tube, dosing should be slowed or halted and, if necessary, the peak inspiratory pressure, ventilator rate and/or FiO_2 turned up. On the other hand, rapid improvements in lung function may require immediate reductions in peak inspiratory pressure, ventilator rate, and/or FiO_2 (see Warnings and see below for additional information concerning administration).

Suctioning should not be performed for 2 hours after colfosceril is administered, except when dictated by clinical necessity.

General Guidelines for Administration: Administration of colfosceril should not take precedence over clinical assessment and stabilization of critically ill infants.

Intubation: Prior to dosing with colfosceril, it is important to ensure that the endotracheal tube tip is in the trachea and not in the esophagus or right or left mainstem bronchus. Brisk and symmetrical chest movement with each mechanical inspiration should be confirmed prior to dosing, as should equal breath sounds in the 2 axillae. In prophylactic treatment, dosing with colfosceril need not be delayed for radiographic confirmation of the endotracheal tube tip position. In rescue treatment, bedside confirmation of endotracheal tube tip position is usually sufficient, if at least one chest radiograph subsequent to the last intubation confirmed proper position of the endotracheal tube tip. Some lung areas will remain undosed if the endotracheal tube tip is too low.

Monitoring: Continuous ECG and transcutaneous oxygen saturation monitoring during dosing are essential. In most infants treated prophylactically, it should be possible to initiate such monitoring prior to administration of the first dose of colfosceril. For subsequent prophylactic and all rescue doses, arterial blood pressure monitoring during dosing is also highly desirable. After both prophylactic and rescue dosing, frequent arterial blood gas sampling is required to prevent post-dosing hyperoxia and hypocarbia (see Warnings).

Ventilatory Support During Dosing: The 5 mL/kg dosage volume may cause transient impairment of gas exchange by physical blockage of the airway, particularly in infants on low ventilator settings. As a result, infants may exhibit a drop in oxygen saturation during dosing, especially if they are on low ventilator settings prior to dosing. These transient effects are easily overcome by increasing peak inspiratory pressure on the ventilator by 4 to 5 cm H_2O for 1 to 2 minutes during dosing. FiO_2 can also be increased if necessary. In infants who are particularly fragile or reactive to external stimuli, increasing peak inspiratory pressure by 4 to 5 cm H_2O and/or FiO_2 20% just prior to dosing may minimize any transient deterioration in oxygenation. However, in virtually all cases it should be possible to return the infant to pre-dosing settings within a very short time of dose completion.

Post-Dosing: At the end of dosing, position of the endotracheal tube should be confirmed by listening for equal breath sounds in the 2 axillae. Attention should be paid to chest expansion, color, transcutaneous oxygen saturation, and arterial blood gases. Some infants who receive colfosceril and other surfactants respond with rapid improvements in pulmonary compliance, minute ventilation, and gas exchange (see Warnings). Constant bedside attention of an experienced clinician for at least 30 minutes after dosing is essential. Frequent blood gas sampling also is absolutely essential. Rapid changes in lung function require immediate changes in peak inspiratory pressure, ventilator rate and/or FiO_2.

Table IV—Exosurf Neonatal

Safety Assessments[a]—Rescue Treatment

Number of Doses:	**2 Doses**		**2 Doses**	
Birth Weight Range:	**700 to 1 350 g**		**1 250 g and above**	
Treatment Group:	**Placebo (Air)**	**Exosurf**	**Placebo (Air)**	**Exosurf**
Number of Infants:	**n=213**	**n=206**	**n=622**	**n=615**
	% of Infants		**% of Infants**	
Intraventricular Hemorrhage (IVH)				
Overall	48	52	23	18[c]
Severe IVH	13	9	5	4
Pulmonary Air Leak (PAL)				
Overall	54	34[e]	30	18[e]
Pneumothorax	29	20[c]	20	10[e]
Pneumopericardium	4	1	1	2
Pneumomediastinum	8	4	5	2[d]
Pulmonary Interstitial Emphysema	48	25[e]	24	13[e]
Death from PAL	7	3	<1	1
Patent Ductus Arteriosus	66	57	54	45[c]
Necrotizing Enterocolitis	3	3	1	2
Pulmonary Hemorrhage	3	1	<1	1
Congenital Pneumonia	2	3	2	2
Nosocomial Pneumonia	5	7	2	2
Non-Pulmonary Infections	19	22	13	13
Sepsis	15	17	8	8
Death from Sepsis	<1	<1	1	<1
Meningitis	1	<1	1	<1[c]
Other Infections	5	8	5	6
Major Anomalies	3	3	4	4
Hypotension	62	57	50	39[d]
Hyperbilirubinemia	17	19	12	10
Exchange Transfusion	3	4	1	2
Thrombocytopenia[b]	10	11	4	<1[d]
Persistent Fetal Circulation	1	1	6	2[d]
Seizures	10	10	6	3[c]
Apnea	48	65[d]	37	44[c]
Drug Therapy				
Antibiotics	100	99	98	98
Diuretics	60	65	45	34[e]
Anticonvulsants	17	17	10	5[d]
Inotropes	36	31	27	16[e]
Sedatives	72	68	76	64[e]
Pancuronium	34	17[d]	33	15[e]
Methylxanthines	62	74[d]	49	53

[a] All parameters were examined with ''as-treated'' analyses.
[b] Thrombocytopenia requiring platelet transfusion.
[c] $p<0.05$.
[d] $p<0.01$.
[e] $p<0.001$.

Supplied: Each vial contains: colfosceril palmitate 108 mg in a powder form. Kits of one 10 mL vial of Exosurf Neonatal (8 mL Fill Vial), one 10 mL vial of Sterile Water for Injection and 5 endotracheal tube adapters (2.5, 3.0, 3.5, 4.0 and 4.5 mm I.D.). Store between 15 and 30°C in a dry place.

EXTRA STRENGTH ACETAMINOPHEN
EXTRA STRENGTH ACETAMINOPHEN with Codeine Ⓝ

WestCan

Acetaminophen

Acetaminophen—Caffeine—Codeine Phosphate

Analgesic—Antipyretic

Supplied: Extra Strength Acetaminophen: Each tablet contains: acetaminophen USP 500 mg. Bottles of 30, 50, 100, 125 and 200. Child resistant caps supplied for bottles of 100, 125 and 200.

Extra Strength Acetaminophen with Codeine: Each tablet contains: acetaminophen USP 500 mg, caffeine 15 mg and codeine phosphate 8 mg. Bottles of 30, 50 and 60 with child resistant caps.

EYE DROPS

Rivex Ophthalmics

Tetrahydrozoline HCl

Vasoconstrictor

Supplied: Each mL of sterile ophthalmic solution contains: tetrahydrozoline HCl 0.05%. Nonmedicinal ingredients: benzalkonium chloride, boric acid, edetate disodium, purified water, sodium borate and sodium chloride. Plastic squeeze bottles of 15 mL with controlled tip applicators.

EYESTIL

Ophtapharma

Sodium Hyaluronate

Eye Lubricant

Supplied: Each bottle contains: sodium hyaluronate 0.15% p/v. Nonmedicinal ingredients: dibasic sodium phosphate, distilled water, monobasic sodium phosphate and sodium chloride. Amber glass bottles of 10 mL. Boxes of 25 disposable unit-dose containers of 0.4 mL.

EYE-STREAM®

Alcon

Balanced Salt Solution

Extraocular Irrigation

Supplied: Each 30 or 118 mL plastic dispenser bottle contains: a balanced salt solution of sodium chloride 0.64%, potassium chloride 0.075%, magnesium chloride 0.03%, calcium chloride 0.048%. Buffered with sodium acetate and sodium citrate. Preserved with benzalkonium chloride.

EYEWASH

Rivex Ophthalmics

Boric Acid

Isotonic Buffered Ophthalmic Solution

Supplied: Each mL of sterile ophthalmic solution contains: boric acid 1.2%. Nonmedicinal ingredients: benzalkonium chloride, boric acid, edetate disodium, hydrochloric acid, potassium chloride, purified water, sodium carbonate and sodium hydroxide. Plastic containers of 120 mL with nozzle applicators.

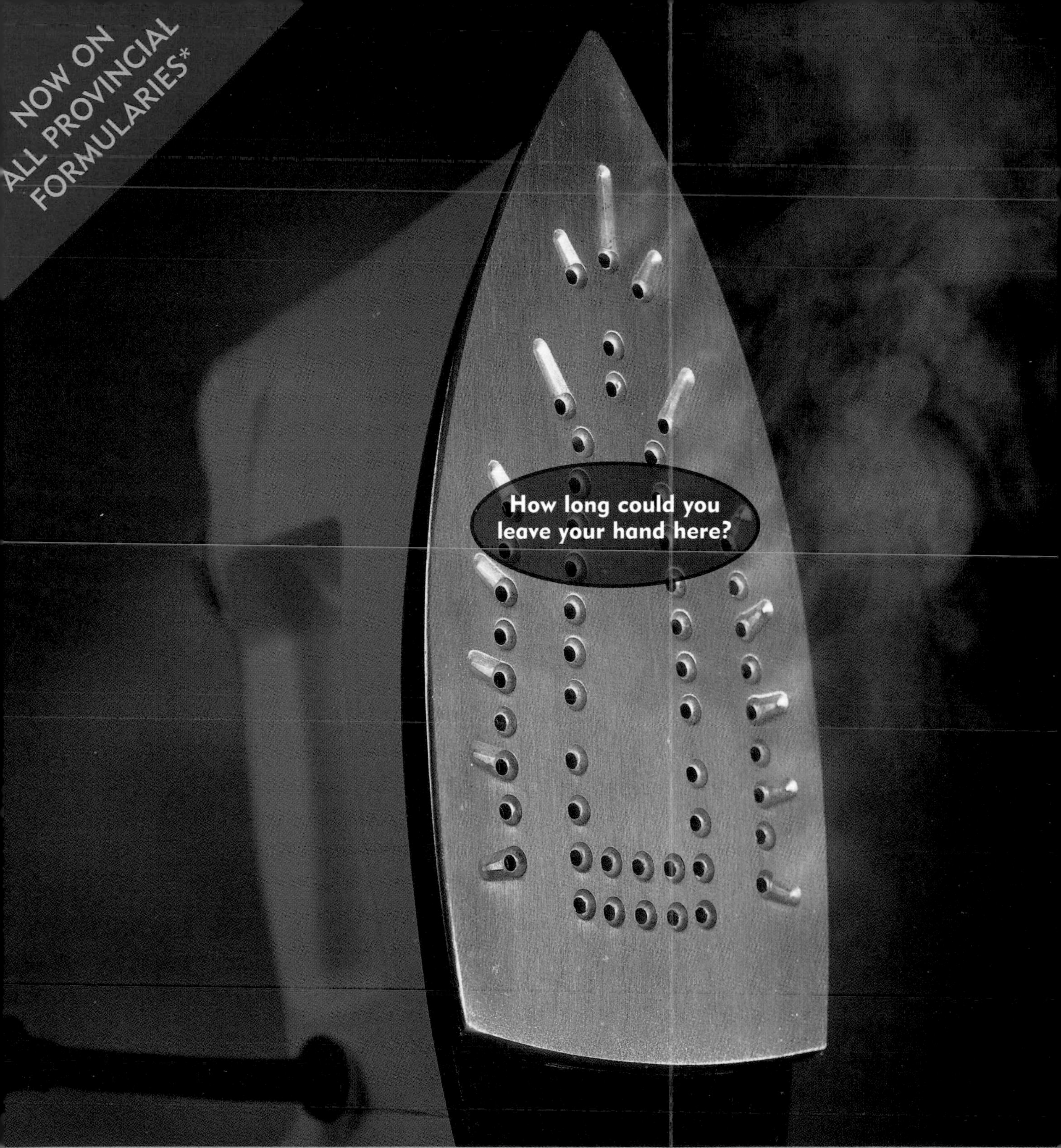

How long could a person with PHN suffer? 3.3 months less with Famvir.[1,Δ]

The burning pain of Post Herpetic Neuralgia (PHN) can leave sufferers in agony.[2] With Famvir they can experience relief sooner.[1,3,†,Δ]

Chronic unrelenting pain is the most common complication of herpes zoster.[2,3] Famvir is the only antiviral indicated to reduce the duration of PHN when used to treat shingles.[3,4]

In fact, in patients with PHN over 50 years of age, Famvir reduced the time spent suffering by 3.3 months versus placebo (n=72; p=0.004).[1,3]

Famvir. Relief from the searing pain of PHN sooner.[Δ]

†Therapy should be initiated within 72 hours of rash onset.[Δ]In patients over 50 years, PHN lasted 63 days versus 163 days in Famvir and placebo groups respectively (n=72; p=0.004). Most common adverse reactions reported with Famvir in clinical trials were headache and nausea. In patients with moderately or severely reduced renal function, dosage reduction is recommended.

SHORTENS THE DURATION OF PHN

FAMVIR®
famciclovir 500 MG TID for 7 DAYS

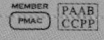

SmithKline Beecham Pharma

MEMBER PMAC PAAB CCPP

*Please see individual formularies for special/exceptional/limited use drug status.

Nasonex*

Mometasone Furoate Monohydrate
Aqueous Nasal Spray

PRESCRIBING INFORMATION

NAME OF DRUG: NASONEX* Mometasone Furoate Monohydrate Aqueous Nasal Spray 50 µg/metered spray (as mometasone furoate)

THERAPEUTIC CLASSIFICATION: Corticosteroid

CLINICAL PHARMACOLOGY: Mometasone furoate is a topical glucocorticosteroid with local anti-inflammatory properties at doses that are minimally systemically active. Mometasone furoate, administered as a nasal spray, has negligible (≤ 0.1%) systemic bioavailability and is generally undetectable in plasma, despite the use of a sensitive assay with a lower quantitation limit of 50 pg/ml; thus, there are no relevant pharmacokinetic data for this dosage form. Mometasone furoate suspension is very poorly absorbed from the gastrointestinal tract, and the small amount that may be swallowed and absorbed undergoes extensive first-pass metabolism prior to excretion in urine and bile.

In two clinical studies utilizing nasal antigen challenge, **NASONEX*** (mometasone furoate monohydrate) Aqueous Nasal Spray has shown anti-inflammatory activity in both the early- and late-phase allergic responses. This has been demonstrated by decreases (vs placebo) in histamine and eosinophil activity and reductions (vs baseline) in eosinophils, neutrophils, and epithelial cell adhesion proteins. The clinical significance of these findings is not known.

INDICATIONS AND CLINICAL USE: NASONEX* (mometasone furoate monohydrate) Aqueous Nasal Spray is indicated for use in adults and children 12 years of age and older to treat the symptoms of seasonal or perennial allergic rhinitis.

CONTRAINDICATIONS: Hypersensitivity to any ingredients of **NASONEX*** (mometasone furoate monohydrate) Aqueous Nasal Spray.

NASONEX* Aqueous Nasal Spray should be used with caution, if at all, in patients with active or quiescent tuberculous infections of the respiratory tract, or in untreated fungal, bacterial, systemic viral infections or ocular herpes simplex.

PRECAUTIONS: General: **NASONEX*** (mometasone furoate monohydrate) Aqueous Nasal Spray should not be used in the presence of untreated localized infection involving the nasal mucosa.

Because of the inhibitory effect of corticosteroids on wound healing, patients who have experienced recent nasal surgery or trauma should not use a nasal corticosteroid until healing has occurred.

Following 12 months of treatment with **NASONEX*** Aqueous Nasal Spray, there was no evidence of atrophy of the nasal mucosa; also, mometasone furoate tended to reverse the nasal mucosa closer to a normal histologic phenotype. As with any long-term treatment, patients using **NASONEX*** Aqueous Nasal Spray over several months or longer should be examined periodically for possible changes in the nasal mucosa. If localized fungal infection of the nose or pharynx develops, discontinuance of **NASONEX*** Aqueous Nasal Spray therapy or appropriate treatment may be required. Persistence of nasopharyngeal irritation may be an indication for discontinuing **NASONEX*** Aqueous Nasal Spray.

There is no evidence of hypothalamic-pituitary-adrenal (HPA) axis suppression following prolonged (12 months) treatment with **NASONEX*** Aqueous Nasal Spray. However, patients who are transferred from long-term administration of systemically active corticosteroids to **NASONEX*** Aqueous Nasal Spray require careful attention. Systemic corticosteroid withdrawal in such patients may result in adrenal insufficiency for a number of months until recovery of HPA axis function. If these patients exhibit signs and symptoms of adrenal insufficiency, systemic corticosteroid administration should be resumed and other modes of therapy and appropriate measures instituted.

During transfer from systemic corticosteroid to **NASONEX*** Aqueous Nasal Spray, some patients may experience symptoms of withdrawal from systemically active corticosteroids (e.g., joint and/or muscular pain, lassitude, and depression initially) despite relief from nasal symptoms and will require encouragement to continue **NASONEX*** Aqueous Nasal Spray therapy. Such transfer may also unmask pre-existing allergic conditions such as allergic conjunctivitis and eczema, previously suppressed by systemic corticosteroid therapy.

Patients receiving corticosteroids who are potentially immunosuppressed should be warned of the risk of exposure to certain infections (e.g., chickenpox, measles) and of the importance of obtaining medical advice if such exposure occurs.

Following the use of intranasal aerosolized corticosteroids, instances of nasal septum perforation or increased intraocular pressure have been reported very rarely.

Pregnancy and Nursing Mothers: There are no adequate or well controlled studies in pregnant or nursing women. Following intranasal administration of the maximal recommended clinical dose to patients, mometasone plasma concentrations are not measurable; thus fetal or breast milk exposure is expected to be negligible and the potential for reproductive or nursing toxicity, very low.

As with other nasal corticosteroid preparations, **NASONEX*** Aqueous Nasal Spray should be used in pregnant women, nursing mothers or women of childbearing age only if the potential benefit justifies the potential risk to the mother, fetus or infant. Infants born of mothers who received corticosteroids during pregnancy should be observed carefully for hypoadrenalism.

Children under 12 years of age: NASONEX* (mometasone furoate monohydrate) Aqueous Nasal Spray is not presently recommended for children younger than 12 years of age due to limited clinical data in this age group.

Drug Interactions: NASONEX* Aqueous Nasal Spray has been administered concomitantly with loratadine with no apparent effect on plasma concentrations of loratadine or its major metabolite. Mometasone furoate plasma concentrations were not detectable. The combination therapy was well tolerated.

ADVERSE REACTIONS: Treatment-related local adverse events reported in clinical studies include epistaxis (e.g., frank bleeding, blood-tinged mucus, and blood flecks) (8%), pharyngitis (4%), nasal burning (2%), and nasal irritation (2%), which are typically observed with use of a corticosteroid nasal spray.

Epistaxis was generally self-limiting and mild in severity, and occurred at a higher incidence compared to placebo (5%), but at a comparable or lower incidence compared to the active control nasal corticoids studied (up to 15%). The incidence of all other effects was comparable with that of placebo.

SYMPTOMS AND TREATMENT OF OVERDOSAGE: Because of the negligible (≤ 0.1%) systemic bioavailability of **NASONEX*** (mometasone furoate monohydrate), overdose is unlikely to require any therapy other than observation, followed by initiation of the appropriate prescribed dosage.

DOSAGE AND ADMINISTRATION: The therapeutic effects of corticosteroids, unlike those of decongestants, are not immediate. Since the effect of **NASONEX*** (mometasone furoate monohydrate) Aqueous Nasal Spray depends on its regular use, patients should be instructed to take the nasal inhalation at regular intervals and not, as with other nasal sprays, as they feel necessary.

After initial priming of the **NASONEX*** Aqueous Nasal pump (usually 6 or 7 actuations, until a uniform spray is observed), each actuation delivers approximately 100 mg of mometasone furoate suspension, containing mometasone furoate monohydrate equivalent up to 50 µg mometasone furoate. If the spray pump has not been used for 14 days or longer, it should be reprimed before next use.

Shake container well before each use.

Adults (including geriatric patients) and children 12 years of age and older: The usual recommended dose is two sprays (50 µg/spray) in each nostril once daily (total dose 200 µg). Once symptoms are controlled, dose reduction to one spray in each nostril (total dose 100 µg) may be effective for maintenance.

If symptoms are inadequately controlled, the dose may be increased to four sprays in each nostril (total 400 µg). Dose reduction is recommended following control of symptoms.

In the presence of excessive nasal mucous secretion or edema of the nasal mucosa, the drug may fail to reach the site of action. In such cases, it is advisable to use a nasal vasoconstrictor for 2 to 3 days prior to starting treatment with **NASONEX*** Aqueous Nasal Spray. Patients should be instructed on the correct method of use, which is to blow the nose, then insert the nozzle carefully into the nostril, compress the opposite nostril and actuate the spray while inspiring through the nose, with the mouth closed.

Clinically significant onset of action occurs as early as 12 hours after the first dose.

PHARMACEUTICAL INFORMATION

Drug Substance

Proper Name:	Mometasone furoate monohydrate
Chemical Name:	9,21-dichloro-17-[(2-furanylcarbonyl)oxy]-11β-hydroxy-16α-methylpregna-1,4-diene-3,20-dione monohydrate
Structural Formula:	

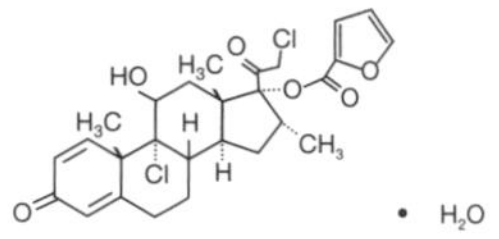

Molecular Formula:	$C_{27}H_{30}Cl_2O_6 \cdot H_2O$
Molecular Weight:	539.45
Description:	
Physical form:	White to off-white powder
Solubility:	Mometasone furoate monohydrate is practically insoluble in water (0.02 mg/mL). It is slightly soluble (4-8 mg/mL) in methanol, ethanol, and isopropanol. It is soluble (59-74 mg/mL) in acetone and chloroform, and freely soluble (>100 mg/mL) in tetrahydrofuran.
pKa and pH values:	Mometasone furoate monohydrate contains no functional group that can protonate/deprotonate, and hence, has no dissociation constant (pKa).
Partition co-efficient:	The partition coefficient for n-octanol/water is greater than 1×10^4.
Melting point:	*ca.* 220°C with decomposition

Composition: Each actuation delivers approximately 100 mg of mometasone furoate suspension, containing mometasone furoate monohydrate equivalent to 50 µg mometasone furoate. Inactive ingredients include: benzalkonium chloride, citric acid, dispersable cellulose BP 65 cps, glycerol, phenylethyl alcohol, Polysorbate 80, purified water, sodium citrate dihydrate.

Stability and Storage Recommendations: NASONEX* should be stored between 2° and 25°C and protected from light.

AVAILABILITY OF DOSAGE FORMS: NASONEX* (mometasone furoate monohydrate) Aqueous Nasal Spray is formulated as an aqueous nasal suspension for nasal administration via a metered-dose manual pump spray delivering 120 doses. Each actuation delivers approximately 100 mg of mometasone furoate suspension, containing mometasone furoate monohydrate equivalent to 50 µg mometasone furoate.

Reference:

1. Nasonex* Product Monograph. Schering Canada Inc.

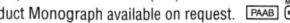

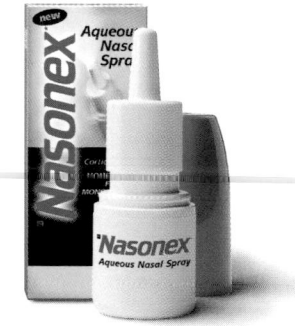

Landmark Study in Postmenopausal Women with Osteoporosis Proves PrFOSAMAX® Significantly Reduces the Risk of Fractures[1,†]

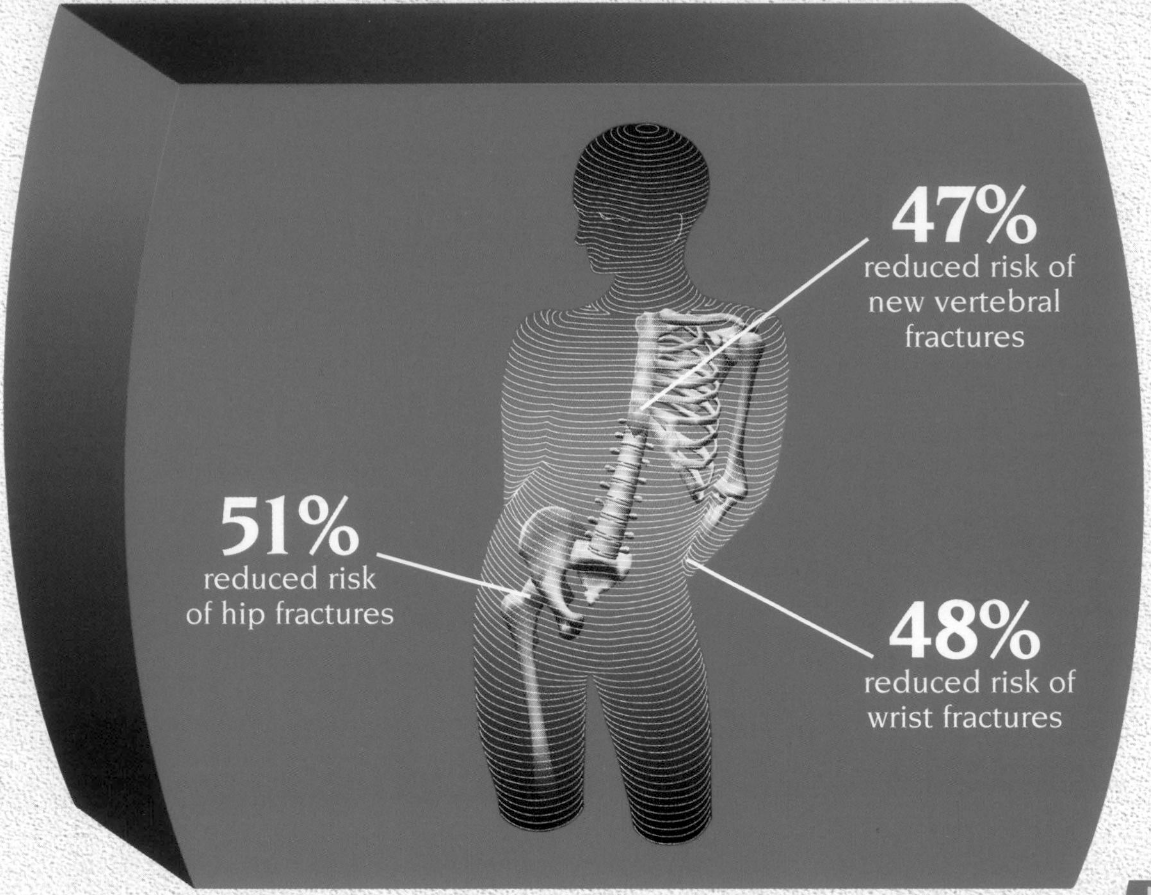

- The vertebral fracture arm of the Fracture Intervention Trial (FIT), a landmark study in osteoporosis involved 2,027 community-dwelling, postmenopausal women with osteoporosis and existing vertebral fractures.[1]
- The results of FIT showed that FOSAMAX® significantly reduced the risk of hip, vertebral, and wrist fractures.[1]
- In FIT, FOSAMAX® was generally well tolerated and the side effects associated with FOSAMAX® did not differ significantly from placebo.[1,*]

* Please refer to the enclosed prescribing information for contraindications and precautions with respect to upper gastrointestinal adverse events.

† hip, vertebral, and wrist fractures.

1. Black DM et al for the Fracture Intervention Trial Research Group. Randomised trial of effect of alendronate on risk of fracture in women with existing vertebral fractures. Lancet 1996;348:1535-41.

FOSAMAX®
alendronate sodium

Please visit our Web site at:
http://www.merckfrosst.ca

MERCK FROSST

BEFORE PRESCRIBING, PLEASE CONSULT THE ENCLOSED PRESCRIBING INFORMATION.

MERCK SHARP & DOHME CANADA
DIV. OF MERCK FROSST CANADA INC.
KIRKLAND, QUEBEC

PAAB

FSM-97-CDN-1508a-JA

F

FACTREL® ℞

Wyeth-Ayerst

Gonadorelin HCl

Synthetic Luteinizing Hormone/ Releasing Hormones (LH-RH)

Supplied: Each single-dose vial contains: gonadorelin 100 or 500 μg. Nonmedicinal ingredients: lactose. Each vial is also accompanied by 1 ampul of Bacteriostatic Water for Injection, benzyl alcohol 2% w/v.

FAMVIR™ ℞

SmithKline Beecham

Famciclovir

Antiviral Agent

Pharmacology: Famciclovir is the orally administered pro-drug of the antiviral agent penciclovir. Famciclovir itself has no antiviral activity until it is biotransformed to penciclovir. Following oral administration little or no famciclovir is detected in plasma or urine since famciclovir is rapidly converted via deacetylation and oxidation to penciclovir. Studies in volunteers have shown that famciclovir is well absorbed and produces plasma penciclovir concentrations superior to those obtained following oral administration of penciclovir alone.

The mean bioavailability of penciclovir after administration of oral famciclovir is 77%. The mean peak plasma concentration of penciclovir, following a 500 mg oral dose of famciclovir was 3.3 μg/mL and occurred at a mean time of 0.89 hours postdose. Plasma concentration time curves of penciclovir are similar following single and repeat dosing. The terminal plasma elimination half-life of penciclovir after both single and repeat oral dosing with famciclovir is 2.3 hours. The elimination of famciclovir is by metabolism, principally to penciclovir and its 6-deoxy precursor, which are subsequently excreted in urine.

Penciclovir is a substituted guanine analogue with potent and selective antiviral activity against varicella zoster virus and other human herpes viruses. Penciclovir is in the same class of antiviral drugs as acyclovir, and both are phosphorylated by viral thymidine kinase and then by cellular enzymes to the active triphosphate form in virus-infected cells. Penciclovir triphosphate inhibits viral DNA polymerase competitively with deoxyguanosine triphosphate and is incorporated into the extending DNA chain, preventing significant chain elongation. Consequently, viral DNA synthesis and, therefore, viral replication are inhibited. Inhibition of the virus reduces the period of viral shedding, limits the degree of spread and level of pathology, and thereby facilitates healing.

Penciclovir is not readily phosphorylated in uninfected cells and does not inhibit cellular DNA synthesis even at concentrations ≥20 times those achieved in clinical usage.

Clinical Trials: Herpes Zoster and Postherpetic Neuralgia: In patients with uncomplicated herpes zoster, famciclovir has been shown to significantly reduce the duration of virus shedding and to relieve the signs and symptoms of the disease.

A 7-day, double-blind, placebo-controlled trial was conducted in 419 patients with uncomplicated herpes zoster treated within 72 hours of initial lesion appearance. According to the randomization scheme, 138 patients were given famciclovir 500 mg t.i.d., 135 patients famciclovir 750 mg t.i.d. and 146 patients given placebo. No additional efficacy was demonstrated with the higher dose of famciclovir (750 mg t.i.d.), when compared to famciclovir 500 mg t.i.d. In the total population, 65.2% of patients had a positive viral culture at some time during their acute infection. Patients treated with famciclovir 500 mg had a shorter median duration of viral shedding (time to last positive viral culture) than did placebo-treated patients (1 day and 2 days, respectively; p=0.0001).

The times to loss of vesicles (p=0.01), loss of ulcers (p=0.01), and loss of crusts (p=0.05), were shorter for famciclovir 500 mg-treated patients than for placebo-treated patients in the overall study population.

The follow-up phase of this trial was designed to monitor the progression of postherpetic neuralgia (PHN) after treatment with either famciclovir or placebo for 7 days during acute infection. There was no difference in the incidence of postherpetic neuralgia between the treatment groups at the time of rash resolution. In the 186 patients (44.4% of total study population) who did develop postherpetic neuralgia, the median duration of postherpetic neuralgia was shorter in patients treated with famciclovir 500 mg than in those treated with placebo (63 days and 119 days, respectively; p=0.02).

A second 7-day, double-blind, controlled trial involved 545 patients with uncomplicated herpes zoster treated within 72 hours of initial lesion appearance. According to the randomization scheme, 134 patients received 250 mg t.i.d. of famciclovir, 134 patients received 500 mg t.i.d. of famciclovir, 138 patients received 750 mg t.i.d. of famciclovir and 139 patients received 800 mg of acyclovir given 5 times a day. Famciclovir was found to be as effective as acyclovir at all dose levels for cutaneous lesion healing parameters, time to loss of pain and viral shedding.

Genital Herpes Infections: Treatment of Recurrent Episodes: Famciclovir was studied in two placebo-controlled trials of 626 otherwise healthy patients with a recurrence of genital herpes who were treated with famciclovir 125 mg b.i.d. (n=160), famciclovir 250 mg b.i.d. (n=169), famciclovir 500 mg b.i.d. (n=154) or placebo (n=143) for 5 days. In the two studies combined, the median time to healing in famciclovir 125 mg-treated patients was 4 days compared to 5 days in placebo treated patients (p= 0.0001) and the median time to cessation of viral shedding was 1.8 vs 3.4 days in famciclovir 125 mg and placebo recipients, respectively (p= 0.0001). The median time to loss of all symptoms was 3.2 days in famciclovir 125 mg-treated patients vs 3.8 days in placebo treated patients (p= 0.0001). Pretreatment, self-obtained viral cultures were positive in 31%, 25%, 30% and 24% for the famciclovir 125 mg, 250 mg, 500 mg and placebo recipients respectively in the patient-initiated study. Of those patients whose pretreatment culture was negative, significantly fewer patients self-initiating famciclovir treatment went on to become viral culture positive compared to placebo. Patients initiating treatment early (during the prodrome) were half as likely to commence viral shedding compared to placebo patients. Additionally, in the clinic-initiated study, famciclovir reduced the number of patients who developed new lesions.

Famciclovir was also studied in three acyclovir-controlled, double-blind trials in 951 otherwise healthy patients with first episode genital herpes.

Famciclovir for 5 or 10 days provided comparable efficacy to acyclovir although the studies were not powered to show statistical equivalence.

Suppression of Recurrent Episodes: A total of 934 otherwise healthy adults with frequently recurring genital herpes, were enrolled in two 12-month, placebo-controlled studies. Patients either had at least six recurrences 12 months prior to study entry or a history of at least 6 recurrences per year while not receiving other suppressive therapies. Sixty-two percent of patients had experienced at least 12 genital herpes recurrences in the previous 24 months. Treatment arms consisted of famciclovir 125 mg t.i.d. (n=233), 250 mg b.i.d. (n=236), 250 mg t.i.d. (n=232) and placebo (n=233). Compared to placebo, famciclovir 250 mg b.i.d. significantly delayed the time to developing the first clinically confirmed recurrence by 10 months in one study (medians: >365 days for famciclovir vs. 67 days for placebo; p=0.0001) and 9.5 months in another study (medians: 336 days for famciclovir vs. 47 days for placebo; p=0.0001). Approximately 80% of famciclovir-treated patients in both studies remained free from HSV recurrences documented by viral culture for up to 6 months compared with approximately 25% of patients treated with placebo (<0.001). Treatment effects were sustained for 12 months.

Indications: For the treatment of acute herpes zoster (shingles). Early treatment of acute herpes zoster (shingles) in immune-competent individuals with oral famciclovir resulted in decreased time to loss of vesicles; decreased time to loss of crusts; and decreased viral shedding.

The results of clinical studies indicate that early treatment of acute herpes zoster with oral famciclovir resulted in decreased duration of postherpetic neuralgia. Those most likely to benefit are patients who initiate treatment within 48 hours of onset of rash or are greater than 50 years of age or those patients with severe pain at the time of treatment initiation.

Famciclovir is indicated to treat or suppress recurrent episodes of genital herpes in immunocompetent adults.

In clinical studies of immunocompetent patients with recurrent genital herpes (typically ≥6 episodes in a 12 month period) famciclovir suppressed lesional episodes, slowed the rate to first recurrence and patients were more likely to remain free from recurrences for a 12-month period. Suppressive therapy in patients with fewer than 6 episodes of genital herpes in a 12 month period was not evaluated in these clinical studies.

Initiation of famciclovir treatment of recurrent genital herpes during the prodrome or as soon as possible after the onset of lesions resulted in decreased duration of viral shedding, decreased time to lesion healing and decreased time to resolution of symptoms (including pain, tenderness, itching and burning).

Contraindications: Patients with known hypersensitivity to the product.

Precautions: General: The efficacy of famciclovir has not been established for first episode genital herpes infections, ophthalmic zoster, disseminated zoster or in immunocompromised patients (see Pharmacology). Dosage adjustment may be required when administering famciclovir to patients with moderate or severe renal dysfunction (see Dosage).

Genital herpes is a sexually transmitted disease with an increased risk of transmission during acute episodes. There are no data evaluating whether famciclovir will prevent transmission of infection to others. Patients should be advised to avoid intercourse when lesions and/or symptoms are present (even if treatment with an antiviral has been initiated) in order to avoid infecting partners. Genital herpes can also be transmitted in the absence of symptoms through asymptomatic viral shedding.

Pregnancy: Although animal studies have not shown any embryotoxic or teratogenic effects with famciclovir or penciclovir, the safety of famciclovir in human pregnancy has not been established. Because animal reproductive studies are not always predictive of human response, famciclovir should, therefore, not be used in pregnancy unless the potential benefits are considered to outweigh the potential risks associated with treatment.

Lactation: Following oral administration of famciclovir to lactating rats, penciclovir is excreted in milk. It is not known whether it (penciclovir) is excreted in human milk, thus, a decision should be made whether to discontinue nursing or to discontinue the drug, taking into account the importance of the drug to the mother.

Children: Safety and efficacy in children under the age of 18 years has not been established.

Geriatrics: Of 816 patients with herpes zoster in clinical studies who were treated with famciclovir, 248 (30.4%) were ≥65 years of age and 103 (13%) were ≥75 years of age. No overall differences were observed in safety between younger and older patients (see Adverse Effects).

Drug Interactions: No clinically significant alterations in penciclovir pharmacokinetics were observed following single dose administration of 500 mg famciclovir after pretreatment with multiple doses of cimetidine, allopurinol, theophylline or zidovudine. Furthermore, no clinically significant effect on penciclovir pharmacokinetics was observed following multiple-dose (t.i.d.) administration of famciclovir (500 mg) with multiple doses of digoxin. After single dose administration of 0.375 mg digoxin and 500 mg famciclovir in 12 healthy male volunteers, the C_{max} of digoxin increased 19±18% as compared to digoxin administered alone. There was no change in digoxin AUC 0-t where t ranged from 10 to 72 hours. The pharmacokinetics of penciclovir or digoxin were not altered by concomitant administration of multiple doses of famciclovir (500 mg t.i.d.) and digoxin to 22 healthy volunteers for 14 days. Probenecid and other drugs that affect renal physiology could affect plasma levels of penciclovir. The conversion of 6-deoxy penciclovir to penciclovir is catalyzed by aldehyde oxidase. No clinically relevant drug interactions mediated via this enzyme are reported in the literature. Interactions with other drugs metabolized by aldehyde oxidase could potentially occur.

Impairment of Fertility: As with other drugs of this class, testicular toxicity has been observed in animals receiving both famciclovir and penciclovir. Two placebo-controlled studies in a total of 130 otherwise healthy men with normal sperm profile over an 8 week baseline period and recurrent genital herpes receiving oral famciclovir (250 mg bid) (n=66) or placebo

Famvir (cont'd)

(n=64) therapy for 18 weeks showed no evidence of significant effects on sperm count, motility or morphology during treatment or during an 8 week follow-up. Preliminary results of another placebo-controlled trial in a total of 117 otherwise healthy men with recurrent genital herpes and a normal sperm profile over an 8 week baseline period receiving famciclovir (250 mg bid, n=59) and placebo (n=58) therapy for 52 weeks showed no evidence of significant effects in sperm concentration, total sperm count, percent motility, percent abnormal morphology and percent dead sperm during treatment or during a 12 week follow-up.

Adverse Effects: The most frequent adverse reactions reported during herpes zoster clinical trials with oral famciclovir 3 times daily were as shown in Table I.

Table I—Famvir

Patients (%) Reporting Adverse Events Related* to Study Medication by Preferred Term in Famciclovir Zoster Trials within 30 Days of the Last Dose

Patients Receiving Study Medication	Famciclovir 816	Placebo 146
Event	**%**	**%**
Body as a Whole		
Headache	7.1	6.8
Fatigue	1.6	0.7
Fever	1.1	0.0
Rigors	0.6	1.4
Herpes Zoster Symptoms	0.5	1.4
CNS		
Dizziness	1.5	0.7
Somnolence	1.2	2.7
Gastrointestinal		
Nausea	4.3	8.2
Diarrhea	1.8	2.1
Abdominal Pain	1.5	0.0
Constipation	1.0	0.0
Vomiting	1.2	0.7
Anorexia	0.5	1.4
Dermatologic		
Pruritus	1.2	0.7
Sweating Increased	1.0	0.0
Hepatic		
ALT Increased	0.6	1.4
Gamma GT Increased	0.6	1.4
Hepatic Enzymes Increased	0.2	1.4
Special Senses		
Tinnitus	0.0	1.4

* Includes events assessed by the investigator as related, probably related, possibly related and adverse events where the relationship was unassessable or missing.

The most frequent adverse reactions reported within 30 days of the last dose, during genital herpes clinical trials with oral famciclovir were as shown in Table II.

Table II—Famvir

Patients (%) Reporting Adverse Events Related* to Study Medication by Preferred Term in Famciclovir Genital Herpes Trials

Patients Receiving Study Medication	Famciclovir 1 500	Placebo 255
Event	**%**	**%**
Body as a Whole		
Headache	5.5	3.9
Fatigue	1.5	1.6
CNS		
Dizziness	2.3	3.1
Gastrointestinal		
Nausea	4.9	3.9
Diarrhea	1.8	1.6
Dyspepsia	1.3	1.2
Abdominal Pain	0.9	1.6
Autonomic Nervous System		
Mouth Dry	0.3	1.2

* Includes events assessed by the investigator as related, probably related, possibly related or where relationship was unaccessible or not given.

The most frequent adverse events (incidence of ≥1%) are listed in Table III for patients receiving double-blind famciclovir or placebo for at least 10 months in the two 12-month-long trials.

Table III—Famvir

Patients (%) Reporting A/Es Related[a] to Study Medication by Preferred Term in Famciclovir Genital Herpes Suppression Trials

	Famciclovir	Placebo
Patients Receiving Study Medication	**458**	**63**
Event	**%**	**%**
Body as a Whole		
Headache	8.7	9.5
CNS		
Dizziness	1.5	0
Gastrointestinal		
Abdominal Pain	2.4	4.8
Dyspepsia	2.0	3.2
Nausea	1.5	3.2
Diarrhea	1.3	0
Flatulence	1.1	0
Enzyme Abnormality[b]	2.2	3.2
Bilirubinemia	1.3	1.6
Leukopenia	1.3	0

[a] Includes events assessed by the investigator as related, probably related, possibly related and AEs where the relationship was unassessable or missing.

[b] Reports of elevated lipase.

Market Experience: During clinical practice, confusion (including delirium, disorientation, confusional state) has been reported. While infrequent, most of these spontaneous reports have occurred in the elderly.

Overdose: Symptoms and Treatment: No acute overdosage has been reported. Appropriate symptomatic and supportive therapy should be given. Penciclovir is dialyzable; plasma concentrations are reduced by approximately 75% following 4 hours hemodialysis.

Dosage: Herpes Zoster Infections: The recommended dose is 500 mg 3 times/day for 7 days. Therapy should be initiated within 72 hours of the onset of rash.

Genital Herpes Infections: Recurrent Episodes: The recommended dosage is 125 mg tablet twice a day for 5 days. Initiation of treatment is recommended during the prodromal period or as soon as possible after onset of lesions.

Suppression of Recurrent Episodes: The recommended dosage is 250 mg twice daily for up to 1 year. The safety and efficacy of Famvir therapy beyond 1 year of treatment has not been established.

Tablets should be swallowed whole and may be taken with or without food.

In patients with moderately or severely reduced renal function, dosage reduction is recommended (see Table IV).

Table IV—Famvir

Dosage in Reduced Renal Function

Indication	Creatinine Clearance (mL/min/1.73 m²)	Dosage
Herpes Zoster	≥60	500 mg every 8 hours
	40-59	500 mg every 12 hours
	20-39	500 mg every 24 hours
	<20	250 mg every 48 hours
Recurrent	≥40	125 mg every 12 hours
Genital Herpes	20-39	125 mg every 24 hours
	<20	125 mg every 48 hours
Suppression of	≥40	250 mg every 12 hours
Recurrent	20-39	125 mg every 12 hours
Genital Herpes	<20	125 mg every 24 hours

Hemodialysis Patients: The recommended dose of famciclovir is 250 mg (herpes zoster) or 125 mg (genital herpes) administered following each dialysis treatment.

Information for the Patient: See Blue Section—Information for the Patient "Famvir".

Supplied: 125 mg: Each white, round, film-coated tablet, with a raised hexagonal shaped area on both faces, debossed with FAMVIR on one side and 125 on the other, contains: famciclovir 125 mg. Nonmedicinal ingredients: hydroxypropyl cellulose, hydroxypropyl methylcellulose, lactose, magnesium stearate, polyethylene glycol, sodium starch glycolate and titanium dioxide. Blister packages of 10.

250 mg: Each white, round, film-coated tablet, with a raised hexagonal shaped area on both faces, debossed with FAMVIR on one side and 250 on the other, contains: famciclovir 250 mg. Nonmedicinal ingredients: hydroxypropyl cellulose, hydroxypropyl methylcellulose, lactose, magnesium stearate, polyethylene glycol, sodium starch glycolate and titanium dioxide. Bottles of 30 and 60.

500 mg: Each white, oval, film-coated tablet, debossed with FAMVIR on one side and 500 on the other, contains: famciclovir 500 mg. Nonmedicinal ingredients: hydroxypropyl cellulose, hydroxypropyl methylcellulose, lactose, magnesium stearate, polyethylene glycol, sodium starch glycolate and titanium dioxide. Bottles of 21.

Store at controlled room temperature (15 to 30°C).

(Shown in Product Recognition Section)

Reviewed 1999

FANSIDAR® Ⓟ

Roche

Sulfadoxine—Pyrimethamine

Antimalarial

Pharmacology: Fansidar is a combination of sulfadoxine and pyrimethamine, which inhibits sequential steps involved in the biosynthesis of tetrahydrofolic acid. This depletes folic acid, an essential cofactor in the biosynthesis of nucleic acids, resulting in interference with protozoal nucleic acid and protein production. Sulfadoxine is a structural analogue of para-aminobenzoic acid (PABA) and competitively inhibits the enzyme dihydropteroate synthetase. Pyrimethamine is a competitive inhibitor of the enzyme dihydrofolate reductase. The effect of the dual sequential action is to reduce the minimum effective dose of each agent (synergism).

Indications: Treatment (Single Administration): For the treatment of patients with P. falciparum malaria when chloroquine resistance is suspected and oral treatment is appropriate.

Prophylaxis (Repeated Administration): Fansidar is not routinely recommended for malaria prophylaxis. Prophylaxis with Fansidar can only be considered for areas where P. falciparum malaria is endemic and sensitive to Fansidar, and when alternative drugs are not available or are contraindicated.

Strains of P. falciparum may be encountered which have developed resistance to Fansidar.

Contraindications: Treatment and Prophylaxis: Known hypersensitivity to sulfonamides or to pyrimethamine. If skin reactions are observed, Fansidar must be withdrawn immediately, as these may be indicative of a life-threatening reaction to the drug. Premature or newborn infants during the first 2 months of life, due to immaturity of the glucuronide-forming enzyme system. Patients with acute intermittent porphyria and variegate porphyria, because sulfonamides are reported to precipitate acute attacks of porphyria.

Prophylaxis (Repeated Administration): In the prophylactic treatment of: patients with severe renal insufficiency, marked liver parenchymal disease or blood dyscrasias; patients with megaloblastic anemia due to folate deficiency because of the antifolate action of the sulfonamide component; pregnant women at term because sulfonamides cross the placenta and may cause kernicterus (see Warnings); and women who are nursing because sulfonamides are excreted in breast milk and may cause kernicterus (see Warnings).

Warnings: Fatalities associated with the administration of Fansidar have occurred due to severe hypersensitivity reactions including Stevens-Johnson syndrome and toxic epidermal necrolysis. Fansidar prophylaxis must be discontinued at the first appearance of skin rash, if a significant reduction in the count of any formed blood elements is noted, or upon the occurrence of active bacterial or fungal infections.

Fatalities associated with the administration of Fansidar have occurred due to severe reactions including fulminant hepatic necrosis, agranulocytosis, aplastic anemia and other blood dyscrasias.

Excessive exposure to the sun must be strictly avoided, since sulfonamides may induce photosensitivity reactions. Such exposure (especially when sunburn ensues), may also play a decisive role in the occurrence of severe cutaneous adverse reactions to Fansidar.

Leukopenia has been reported in patients treated with Fansidar.

Fansidar used prophylactically (repeated administration) has been associated with lower white blood cell counts and reduced serum folate concentrations. It should not be used in conjunction with other antifolate agents.

Hemolysis may occur in individuals administered Fansidar who are deficient in glucose-6-phosphate dehydrogenase.

An increased incidence of severe adverse reactions may occur in elderly patients receiving sulfonamides, particularly when complicating conditions exist; for example, impaired kidney and/or liver function or concomitant use of other drugs. Similar effects could be anticipated with Fansidar.

Compared with the general population, the incidence of side effects (rash, fever and leukopenia) with trimethoprim-sulfamethoxazole therapy in patients with Acquired Immunodeficiency Syndrome (AIDS) has been reported to be increased. AIDS patients treated with Fansidar may have a similar increased risk, especially if they have previously reacted to cotrimoxazole.

Pregnancy and *Lactation* (see also Contraindications): The safety of Fansidar (treatment or prophylaxis) during human pregnancy has not been established. It should not be used by pregnant women at term. The potential benefit of the use of Fansidar for malaria treatment or prophylaxis during earlier stages of pregnancy must be carefully weighed against the potential risk to the embryo or fetus. Both pyrimidine and sulfadoxine cross the placental barrier and pass into breast milk.

Malaria is associated with increased maternal and fetal mortality. Fansidar is teratogenic in rats at low multiples of the human dose and is embryolethal at higher doses. Women who are travelling to areas where malaria is endemic should be warned of the risks associated with malaria and with Fansidar during pregnancy.

Precautions: The changing patterns and degree of parasite resistance to antimalarial drugs in various parts of the world and the resultant changes in recommended antimalarial therapy should be reviewed prior to the prescription of Fansidar.

Fansidar should be given only with caution to patients with impaired renal or hepatic function, to those with severe allergy or bronchial asthma, and to those with possible folate deficiency. Subclinical folate deficiency may be anticipated if one or more of the following occur: improper nutrition, excessive alcohol intake, advanced age, pregnancy, and use of antifolate agents. When patients are administered Fansidar prophylactically, urinalysis with microscopic examination, renal function tests and complete blood counts should be performed periodically.

Travellers using Fansidar for prophylactic therapy should be cautioned that the appearance of skin rash, sore throat, fever, pallor, purpura, jaundice or glossitis may be early indications of serious disorders. They should be instructed to discontinue the use of the drug and seek medical advice immediately.

During treatment, adequate fluid intake must be maintained in order to prevent crystalluria and stone formation.

Severe orthostatic hypotension has been associated with the administration of a single 3 tablet dose of Fansidar for the treatment of malaria. Orthostatic hypotension is also a common and prominent clinical feature of malaria, and may be exacerbated by the administration of Fansidar. Patients should be advised that they may become faint following the ingestion of Fansidar for the treatment of malaria.

Drug Interactions: Limited data exist regarding potential interactions between Fansidar and other antimalarial drugs. The concurrent or sequential use of Fansidar and quinine is not known to produce increased adverse drug reactions or interactions.

There have been reports which may indicate an increase in incidence and severity of adverse reactions when chloroquine is used with Fansidar.

Fansidar should not be taken with antibiotics having antifolic acid activity.

Folic acid supplements (folinic acid; leucovorin) may antagonize the action of Fansidar. Consequently, the effectiveness of Fansidar may be reduced by the concomitant administration of folic acid.

The combined use of Fansidar with other drugs having antifolate activity may produce megaloblastic anemia. Thus, pyrimethamine, trimethoprim, sulfonamides or trimethoprim-sulfamethoxazole combinations should not be used while the patient is receiving Fansidar prophylactically.

If signs of folic acid deficiency develop, discontinue the administration of Fansidar. The administration of folic acid supplements (folinic acid; leucovorin) may be considered for cases in which depressed platelets or white blood cell counts may be due to drug induced folate deficiency.

Plasma protein binding displacement and/or inhibition of hepatic metabolism may account for a number of interactions between sulfonamides and other drugs (e.g. phenylbutazone, oxyphenbutazone, salicylates and sulfinpyrazone). Sulfonamides have been reported to increase the half-life and inhibit the hepatic metabolism of phenytoin.

The sulfonamide in Fansidar may displace orally administered anticoagulants from their carrier proteins which may result in an increased anticoagulant effect.

Diuresis and hypoglycemia have occurred in patients receiving sulfonamides. Similar effects could be anticipated with Fansidar. Since the sulfonamide component bears chemical similarities to some goitrogens, diuretics (acetazolamide and the thiazides) and oral hypoglycemic agents, the possibility of an interaction exists. The blood glucose-lowering effect of sulfonamides should be borne in mind when prescribing Fansidar to patients with diabetes.

Para-aminobenzoic acid (PABA) or its derivatives antagonize the action of sulfonamides. It has been reported that the percutaneous absorption of PABA from sunscreen preparations is 1.6 to 9.6% of the applied dose. Therefore, the possibility of an interaction between PABA and the sulfadoxine component of Fansidar should be considered in patients using sunscreens concomitantly with this drug.

Mutagenicity, Carcinogenicity and Impairment of Fertility: The significance to humans of the following laboratory observations has not been determined. Pyrimethamine was found to be mutagenic to mouse and human bone marrow cells in addition to rat embryo. A carcinogenicity study in mouse suggested a dose related increase in pulmonary tumors but was inconclusive due to reduced survival. Although the fertility of male rats was unaffected, a delay in sperm maturation was noted. Fertility was, however, significantly affected in female rats and teratogenic effects were observed.

Adverse Effects: Fansidar use has been associated with severe cutaneous adverse reactions (erythema multiforme, Stevens-Johnson syndrome or toxic epidermal necrolysis). The incidence of such reactions during prophylactic use in U.S. patients administered concomitant chloroquine has been estimated as 1:5 000 to 1:8 000 with a risk of fatality of 1:11 000 to 1:25 000. Similar incidences of severe cutaneous reactions (1:10 000) and fatalities (1:35 000) following Fansidar monoprophylaxis have been reported in Sweden. Amongst Swiss travellers, however, the estimated incidence of reactions is lower (1:150 000), with no fatalities reported.

For completeness, major reactions to sulfonamides or to pyrimethamine are included below. Most of these reactions have been reported with Fansidar.

Allergic: erythema multiforme, Stevens-Johnson syndrome, generalized skin eruptions, toxic epidermal necrolysis, urticaria, Sézary syndrome-like erythroderma, angioedema, serum sickness, pruritus, exfoliative dermatitis, bruising, petechia, anaphylactoid reactions, periorbital edema, conjunctival and scleral injection, photosensitization, photodermatitis, arthralgia, myalgia, allergic myocarditis, drug fever, vasculitis, allergic pericarditis. Pulmonary hypersensitivity reactions and a fatal reaction involving the skin (toxic epidermal necrolysis), liver and kidneys have also been reported.

Blood Dyscrasias: agranulocytosis, aplastic anemia, megaloblastic anemia, thrombocytopenia, leukopenia, neutropenia, hemolytic anemia, purpura, hypoprothrombinemia, methemoglobinemia, and eosinophilia.

Gastrointestinal: glossitis, stomatitis, gastritis, dyspepsia, dry mouth, black tongue, gastroenteritis, anorexia, nausea, vomiting, abdominal pains, diarrhea, pancreatitis, and pseudomembranous enterocolitis.

Mild, transient gastrointestinal reactions (nausea,vomiting, abdominal pain, diarrhea) occurred in 30% of 50 male patients with symptomatic falciparum malaria administered a 3-tablet treatment dose of Fansidar.

Hepatic: abnormal liver function test results (e.g. elevated serum ALT, AST, alkaline phosphatase and bilirubin concentrations), jaundice, hepatitis, hepatocellular necrosis and hepatic granulomas.

CNS: headache, peripheral neuritis, mental depression, convulsions, ataxia, hallucinations, tinnitus, vertigo, dizziness, insomnia, apathy, fatigue, muscle weakness and nervousness.

Mild, transient dizziness and tinnitus occurred in 6% of 50 male patients.

Respiratory: pulmonary infiltrates, pneumonitis, dyspnea.

Miscellaneous: chills, alopecia, epistaxis, toxic nephrosis with oliguria, anuria, dysuria, crystalluria, hematuria, bloody stool, jaundice, renal failure. Orthostatic hypotension and sinus bradycardia. Orthostatic hypotension and sinus bradycardia occurred in 20% and 32% respectively, of 50 male patients with symptomatic falciparum malaria administered a 3-tablet treatment dose of Fansidar. Four of the patients with sinus bradycardia had abnormal heartbeat prior to treatment. Periarteritis nodosa and lupus erythematosus and Jarisch-Herxheimer-like phenomenon have also occurred.

Canadian data provided by physicians or their patients who received Fansidar alone or in combination with chloroquine for prophylactic use were analyzed retrospectively. Out of a total of 5 089 individuals, 1 632 or 32% of these patients experienced approximately 3 840 adverse reactions (2.4/individual), judged to be possibly drug related. The reaction(s) reported for 33 patients were rated as serious. Seventeen of these 33 patients, 15 of whom received concomitant chloroquine, reported skin reactions, including one case of a Stevens-Johnson-like syndrome. One case of disseminated intravascular coagulation and a severe hematological reaction were also reported in 2 elderly women. The 96 individuals who received Fansidar alone reported 180 possible adverse reactions. The most frequently occurring reactions were those of the gastrointestinal tract (n=68) and CNS (n=31). Effects observed included diarrhea (n=23), stomach/abdominal pain or discomfort (n=23), nausea (n=10), headache (n=13), depression, anxiety, nervousness (n=8), tiredness, fatigue, drowsiness (n=6) and dizziness and fainting (n=3). Other reactions included: skin rash (n=7), sensitivity to sunlight (n=7), itchiness (n=4), sore throat (n=4), itchy or sore eyes, visual disturbances (n=7), fever (n=10), nonspecific malaise (n=4), and flu-like symptoms (n=3).

Overdose: Symptoms: Symptoms of overdosage may include anorexia, vomiting and CNS stimulation, including convulsions. These symptoms may be followed by megaloblastic anemia, leukopenia, thrombocytopenia, glossitis and crystalluria.

Treatment: The treatment of overdosage should consist of general supportive measures. If drug ingestion is discovered within a relatively short time, induction of emesis and gastric lavage may be of benefit. If the drug has passed through the stomach, the administration of mineral oil may promote fecal elimination.

Because of the possibility of crystalluria and stone formation, the patient should be adequately hydrated to prevent renal damage. Since Fansidar is excreted from the body over a prolonged period of time ($t_{1/2}$: sulfadoxine=184 hours; pyrimethamine=95 hours), urine should be checked regularly for crystalluria; renal and hepatic function as well as hematopoietic systems should also be monitored for at least 1 month after an overdosage. For depressed platelet or white blood cell counts, folinic acid (leucovorin) should be administered.

If the patient experiences convulsions, appropriate anticonvulsive measures should be taken.

Dosage: Fansidar should be taken with water and, when appropriate, with food.

Treatment (Single Administration): Adults: >45 kg, a single dose of 3 tablets. Children (Fansidar should not be administered to infants less than 2 months of age): 30 to 45 kg, a single dose of 2 tablets; 11 to 29 kg, a single dose of 1 tablet; 5 to 10 kg, a single dose of ½ tablet.

If aparasitemia and clearance of symptoms are not achieved within 2 to 4 days, the patient should be re-evaluated.

In cases of severe infection requiring rapid emergency measures, the use of faster acting antimalarial agents may be required.

Prophylaxis (Repeated Administration): The malaria risk must be carefully weighed against the risk of serious adverse drug reactions. If Fansidar is prescribed for prophylaxis, it is important that the physician inquires about any history of sulfonamide intolerance and points out the risk and the need for immediate drug withdrawal if skin reactions occur. The first dose of Fansidar should be taken 2 weeks prior to arrival at an endemic area. Treatment should be continued on a weekly basis throughout the stay in the malarious region, and for 6 weeks subsequent to leaving the area.

Adults: >45 kg, 1 tablet once weekly. Children (Fansidar should not be administered to infants less than 2 months of age): 30 to 45 kg, ¾ tablet once weekly; 11 to 29 kg, ½ tablet once weekly; 5 to 10 kg, ¼ tablet once weekly.

Prophylaxis with Fansidar should not be continued for more than 2 years since no experience of more prolonged administration is currently available.

Impaired Renal and Hepatic Function: At the present time there is insufficient data to recommend a special dosage regimen (see Precautions).

Information for the Patient: See Blue Section—Information for the Patient "Fansidar".

Supplied: Each white tablet, cross-scored on one face, "ROCHE" and hexagon imprint on the other face, contains sulfadoxine 500 mg and pyrimethamine 25 mg. Also contains: starch, gelatin, lactose, magnesium stearate and talc. Energy: 2.8 kJ (0.7 kcal). Packages of 3. Stable for 5 years from the date of manufacture when stored at 15 to 30°C.

(Shown in Product Recognition Section)

Reviewed 1999

FASTIN® ⊕

SmithKline Beecham

Phentermine HCl

Anorexiant

Pharmacology: Phentermine is a sympathomimetic amine with pharmacologic activity similar to the prototype drugs of this class used in obesity, the amphetamines. Actions include CNS stimulation and elevation of blood pressure. Tachyphylaxis and tolerance have been demonstrated with all drugs of this class in which these phenomena have been looked for.

Drugs of this class used in obesity are commonly known as anorectics or anorexigenics . It has not been established, however, that the action of such drugs in treating obesity is primarily one of appetite suppression. Other CNS actions, or metabolic effects may be involved, for example.

Indications: As a short-term (i.e., a few weeks) adjunct to continued dietary treatment in the medical management of obesity in patients not responding to an appropriate weight reducing diet alone. Phentermine is recommended only for obese patients with an initial body mass index (BMI) ≥ 30 kg/m², or a BMI ≥ 27 kg/m² in the presence of other risk factors (e.g., hypertension, diabetes, hyperlipidemia). See Table I.

When prescribing anorectic agents it should be borne in mind that the role of these drugs in the management of obesity is strictly limited, since patients treated with anorectics lose only a fraction of a pound per week more than those who are on a weight-reducing diet alone. Prolonged administration of these agents must also be avoided since it can lead to drug dependence and abuse (see Warnings).

Table I—Fastin

Body Mass Index (BMI), kg/m²

Weight (pounds)	Height (feet, inches) 5′0″	5′3″	5′6″	5′9″	6′0″	6′3″
140	**27**	25	23	21	19	18
150	**29**	**27**	24	22	20	19
160	31	**28**	26	24	22	20
170	33	30	**28**	25	23	21
180	35	32	**29**	**27**	25	23
190	37	34	31	**28**	26	24
200	39	36	32	30	**27**	25
210	41	37	34	31	**29**	26
220	43	39	36	33	30	**28**
230	45	41	37	34	31	**29**
240	47	43	39	36	33	30
250	49	44	40	37	34	31

Patients with BMI values ≥ 30 kg/m² may be candidate for phentermine therapy.

Patients with BMI values of 27 to 29 kg/m² may be candidates for phentermine therapy if they also have a concomitant risk factor (e.g., hypertension, diabetes, hyperlipidemia).

Contraindications: In advanced arteriosclerosis, cardiovascular disease, moderate to severe hypertension, hyperthyroidism, known hypersensitivity or idiosyncrasy to the sympathomimetic amines, glaucoma. Phentermine is also contraindicated in agitated states, patients with a history of drug abuse, and during or within 14 days following the administration of MAO inhibitors (hypertensive crisis may result).

Warnings: Risk of Primary Pulmonary Hypertension (PPH): **Anorexigens increase the risk of developing primary pulmonary hypertension, an often fatal disorder.**

Although phentermine was not identified, an epidemiological study has indicated that use of other anorexigens for longer than 3 months was associated with a 23-fold increase in the risk of developing PPH. There was no significant increase in risk for persons who had used these agents for 3 months or less.

Obesity itself (BMI ≥ 30 kg/m²) was also independently associated with an increase of about 2-fold in the risk of developing PPH. In the general population, the yearly occurrence of PPH is estimated to be about 1 to 2 cases per 1 000 000 persons. Therefore, the estimated risk associated with the long-term use of anorexigen drugs is about 23 to 46 cases per million persons exposed per year. The study further suggested that the risk of PPH rises with increasing duration of use of these drugs. The effect of intermittent compared to continuous use of anorexigens on the risk of PPH has not been determined.

The onset or aggravation of exertional dyspnea, or unexplained symptoms of angina pectoris, syncope, or lower extremity edema suggest the possibility of occurrence of pulmonary hypertension. Under these circumstances, treatment should be immediately discontinued, and the patient should be evaluated for the possible presence of PPH.

Valvular Heart Disease: Serious regurgitant cardiac valvular disease, primarily affecting the mitral, aortic and/or tricuspid valves, has been reported in otherwise healthy persons who had taken a combination of phentermine with fenfluramine or dexfenfluramine for weight loss. The etiology of these valvulopathies has not been established and their course in individuals after the drugs are stopped is not known. There have been no reported cases to date of this valvular condition occurring with the use of phentermine alone.

Tolerance: Tolerance to the anorectic effect usually develops within a few weeks. When this occurs, the recommended dose should not be exceeded in an attempt to increase the effect; rather, the drug should be discontinued.

Occupational Hazards: Phentermine may impair the ability of the patient to engage in potentially hazardous activities such as operating machinery or driving a motor vehicle; the patient should, therefore, be cautioned accordingly.

Drug Dependence: Experience with anorectic drugs with amphetamine-like properties such as phentermine has established that prolonged use of these drugs can produced tolerance, severe psychological dependence and has led to extensive abuse. This should be kept in mind when assessing the desirability of using the drug and caution should be exercised not to use the drug in individuals whose histories suggest they may increase the dosage on their own initiative. If psychological dependence occurs, gradual withdrawal of the medication is recommended. Abrupt cessation following prolonged high dosage may result in extreme fatigue and mental depression. Abuse of these drugs may lead to moderate to severe manifestations of chronic intoxication including marked insomnia, irritability, hyperactivity, personality changes and even psychosis.

Pregnancy: Phentermine should not be administered to women who are or who are likely to become pregnant unless in the opinion of the prescribing physician the potential benefits of drug therapy outweigh the possible risk to mother and fetus.

Children: Phentermine is not recommended for use in children under 12 years of age.

Adverse Effects: The most frequently encountered side effects have been dry mouth, insomnia, constipation. Other side effects are: Cardiovascular: palpitation, tachycardia, elevation of blood pressure, primary pulmonary hypertension and/or regurgitant cardiac valvular disease (see Warnings).

CNS: overstimulation, restlessness, dizziness, euphoria, dysphoria, tremor, headache, insomnia ; rarely psychotic episodes at recommended doses.

Gastrointestinal: unpleasant taste, dryness of mouth, diarrhea, constipation, other gastrointestinal disturbances.

Allergic: urticaria.

Endocrine: impotence, changes in libido.

Overdose: Symptoms: Manifestations of acute overdosage with phentermine include restlessness, tremor, hyperreflexia, rapid respiration, confusion, assaultiveness, hallucinations, panic states. Fatigue and depression usually follow the central stimulation. Cardiovascular effects include arrhythmias, hypertension or hypotension, and circulatory collapse. Gastrointestinal symptoms include nausea, vomiting, diarrhea, and abdominal cramps. Fatal poisoning usually terminates in convulsions and coma.

Treatment: Management of acute phentermine intoxication is largely symptomatic and includes lavage and sedation with a barbiturate. Experience with hemodialysis or peritoneal dialysis is inadequate to permit recommendations in this regard. Acidification of the urine increases phentermine excretion. I.V. phentolamine has been suggested for possible acute, severe hypertension, if this complicates phentermine overdosage.

Dosage: Exogenous Obesity: One capsule approximately 2 hours after breakfast for appetite control. Late evening medication should be avoided because of the possibility of resulting insomnia.

Administration of 1 capsule (30 mg) daily has been found to be adequate in depression of the appetite for 12 to 14 hours.

Phentermine is not recommended for use in children under 12 years of age.

Phentermine should be used for a duration of no more than a few weeks (see Warnings).

Supplied: Each blue and white capsule contains: phentermine HCl 30 mg (equivalent to phentermine 24 mg). Nonmedicinal ingredients: FD&C Blue No. 1, invert sugar, methylcellulose, polyethylene glycol, starch, sucrose and titanium dioxide. The branding ink used on the gelatin capsules contains: ethyl alcohol, FD&C Blue No. 1 aluminum lake, isopropyl alcohol, n-butyl alcohol, propylene glycol and shellac. Gluten-, lactose- and tartrazine-free. Bottles of 100.

Reviewed 1999

FEIBA® VH IMMUNO

Baxter

Human Plasma Factor VIII Inhibitor

Coagulant Complex Anti-inhibitor

Description: Feiba VH Immuno, is a freeze-dried sterile human plasma fraction with Factor VIII inhibitor bypassing activity. In vitro, Feiba VH Immuno shortens the activated partial thromboplastin time (APTT) of plasma containing Factor VIII inhibitor. Factor VIII inhibitor bypassing activity is expressed in arbitrary units. One Immuno Unit of activity is defined as that amount of Feiba VH Immuno which shortens the APTT of a high titer Factor VIII inhibitor reference plasma to 50% of the blank value. The product is intended for i.v. administration.

It contains Factors II, IX, and X, mainly non-activated, and Factor VII mainly in the activated form. The product contains approximately equal unitages of Factor VIII inhibitor bypassing activity and Prothrombin Complex Factors. In addition, 1 to 6 units of Factor VIII coagulant antigen (F VIII C: Ag)/mL are present. The preparation contains only traces of factors of the kinin generating system. It contains no heparin.

Feiba VH Immuno has been prepared from Source Plasma and/or Fresh Frozen Plasma. All units of plasma used in the manufacture have been tested for hepatitis surface antigen (HB_sAg) and for anti-HIV-III by FDA approved methods and found nonreactive.

The product has been subjected to in-process virus inactivation where vapor is first applied for 10 hours at 60°C and an excess pressure of 190±20 mbar followed by 1 hour at 80°C and an excess pressure of 370±30 mbar (see Warnings).

Indications: For the control of spontaneous bleeding episodes or to cover surgical interventions in hemophilia A and B patients with inhibitors.

In addition, its use has been described in a few nonhemophiliacs with acquired inhibitors to Factors VIII, XI, and XII. It has been reported to be effective in a patient with von Willebrand's disease with an inhibitor.

Clinical experience suggests that patients with a Factor VIII inhibitor titer of less than 5 B.U. may be successfully treated with Antihemophilic Factor. Patients with titers ranging between 5 and 10 B.U. may either be treated with Antihemophilic Factor or with this product. Cases with Factor VIII inhibitor titers greater than 10 B.U. have generally been refractory to treatment with Antihemophilic Factor.

Contraindications: In patients who are known to have a normal coagulation mechanism.

Warnings: This product must be used only in patients with circulating inhibitors to 1 or more coagulation factors and should not be used for the treatment of bleeding episodes resulting from coagulation factor deficiencies. It should not be given to patients with significant signs of disseminated intravascular coagulation (DIC) or fibrinolysis.

It is prepared from large pools of human plasma. Each unit of plasma used in the manufacture of this product has been tested and found nonreactive for HB_sAg and HIV antibody by FDA approved tests. In addition, this product has been subjected to a vapor heat treatment during the manufacturing process to reduce the risk of transmitting viral infections. It must be emphasized that no procedure has been shown to be totally effective in eliminating viral infectivity from this product.

It has been reported that Feiba VH Immuno and antifibrinolytics have been given simultaneously without complications. It is, however, recommended not to use antifibrinolytics until 12 hours after the administration of Feiba VH Immuno.

Anamnestic responses with rise in Factor VIII inhibitor titer have been observed in 20% of the cases.

Precautions: If clinical signs of intravascular coagulation occur, which include changes in blood pressure, pulse rate, respiratory distress, chest pain and cough, the infusion should be stopped promptly and the patient monitored for DIC by appropriate laboratory tests. Laboratory indications of DIC are decreased fibrinogen, decreased platelet count, and/or presence of fibrin-fibrinogen degradation products (FDP). Other indications of DIC include significantly prolonged thrombin time, prothrombin time, or partial thromboplastin time.

Tests used to control efficacy such as APTT, WBCT, and TEG do not correlate with clinical improvement. For this reason, attempts at normalizing these values by increasing the dose of Feiba VH Immuno may not be successful and are strongly discouraged because of the potential hazard of producing DIC by overdosage.

Pregnancy: Animal reproduction studies have not been conducted with this product. It is also not known whether it can cause fetal harm when administered to a pregnant woman or can affect reproduction capacity. It should be given to a pregnant woman only if clearly needed.

Children: No data are available regarding its use in newborns.

Adverse Effects: After application of high doses (single infusion of more than 100 units/kg body weight and daily doses of 200 units/kg) of Feiba VH, laboratory and/or clinical signs of DIC have occasionally been observed. For this reason, patients receiving more than 100 units/kg must be monitored continually for signs of accelerated coagulation.

As with all human plasma products, any kind of allergic reaction may be seen, ranging from mild, short-term urticarial rashes to severe anaphylactoid reactions.

Administration should be discontinued immediately, if such signs appear. Allergic reactions should be treated with antihistamines and glucocorticoids. Shock should be treated in the usual way.

Dosage: Parenteral drug products should be inspected visually for particulate matter and discoloration prior to administration, whenever solution and container permit.

Clinical trials have demonstrated that the response to treatment with Feiba may differ from patient to patient with no correlation to the patient's inhibitor titer. Response may also vary between different types of hemorrhage (e.g., joint hemorrhage vs CNS hemorrhage).

As a general guideline a dosage range of 50 to 100 units/kg is recommended. However, care should be taken to distinguish between the following 4 indications, all of which have undergone careful clinical evaluation:

Joint Hemorrhage: 50 units/kg is recommended at 12-hour intervals, which may be increased to doses of 100 units/kg at 12-hour intervals.

Treatment should be continued until clear signs of clinical improvement appear, such as relief of pain, reduction of swelling or mobilization of the joint.

Mucous Membrane Bleeding: 50 units/kg is recommended to be given at 6-hour intervals under careful monitoring (visible bleeding site, repeated measurements of the patient's hematocrit). Again, if hemorrhage does not stop, the dose may be increased to 100 units/kg at 6-hour intervals. However, 2 such administrations or 200 units/kg a day should not be exceeded.

Soft Tissue Hemorrhage: For serious soft tissue bleeding, such as retroperitoneal bleeding, doses of 100 units/kg at 12-hour intervals are recommended. A daily dosage of 200 units/kg should not be exceeded.

Other Severe Hemorrhages: Severe hemorrhages, such as CNS bleedings, have been effectively treated with doses of 100 units/kg at 12-hour intervals. Sometimes, Feiba VH may be indicated at 6-hour intervals until clear clinical improvement is achieved.

Do not refrigerate after reconstitution.

After complete reconstitution the injection or infusion should be commenced as promptly as practicable, but must be completed within 3 hours following reconstitution.

The solution must be given by i.v. injection or i.v. drip infusion and the **maximum injection or infusion rate must not exceed 2 units/kg/minute.** In a patient with a body weight of 75 kg, this corresponds to an infusion rate of 2.5 to 7.5 mL/minute depending on the number of units/vial (see label on vial).

Supplied: Freeze-dried powder, accompanied by a suitable volume of sterile water for injection, USP, a sterile double-ended needle, and a sterile filter needle. The number of Immuno Units of human plasma factor VIII inhibitor bypassing activity is stated on the label of each bottle. Store at refrigerator temperature (2 to 8°C). **Avoid freezing, which may damage the diluent bottle.**

FELDENE™ Ⓟ

Pfizer

Piroxicam

Anti-inflammatory—Analgesic

Pharmacology: Piroxicam is a nonsteroidal anti-inflammatory agent with analgesic and antipyretic properties. Its mechanism of action is incompletely known. Piroxicam inhibits the activity of prostaglandin synthetase. The resulting decrease in prostaglandin biosynthesis may partially explain its anti-inflammatory action. Piroxicam does not act by pituitary-adrenal stimulation.

In rheumatoid arthritis the efficacy of piroxicam 20 mg daily has been found to be similar to 4.5 g daily of ASA.

Piroxicam is well absorbed following oral or rectal administration. After a single oral dose of 20 mg, peak plasma levels are achieved in about 4 hours. When the drug is administered daily, plasma concentrations increase for 7 to 12 days during which a steady state is reached. Concentrations attained are not exceeded following further constant daily drug intake. The plasma half-life is approximately 50 hours in man. The extent and rate of absorption are not influenced by administration with food or antacids.

After a single rectal dose of 20 mg, the pharmacokinetics are similar to that obtained after oral administration except for peak plasma levels which are achieved at about 10 hours.

Piroxicam is extensively metabolized and less than 5% of the daily dose is excreted unchanged in urine and feces. The main metabolic pathway is hydroxylation of the pyridyl ring, followed by conjugation with glucuronic acid and urinary elimination. Approximately 5% of the dose is metabolized to and excreted as saccharin.

Over a 4-day period of observation, 20 healthy men, taking piroxicam 20 mg daily in single or divided doses, showed significantly less mean daily fecal blood loss than did 10 healthy male controls taking 3.9 g of ASA daily.

The effects of age and sex on the pharmacokinetics of piroxicam have been examined in 3 single-dose, 3 multiple-dose, and 5 therapeutic drug-monitoring studies. Although not consistent across all studies, some indicated a tendency towards a modest decrease in total body clearances and an increase in elimination half-life and steady-state plasma concentrations in the elderly, particularly elderly females. Irrespective of age, some patients had plasma concentration levels that are substantially greater than the mean.

Indications: The symptomatic treatment of rheumatoid arthritis, osteoarthritis (degenerative joint disease) and ankylosing spondylitis and primary dysmenorrhea.

Contraindications: Peptic ulcer or active inflammatory disease of the gastrointestinal system, or patients with a recent or recurrent history of these conditions.

Known or suspected hypersensitivity to the drug. Piroxicam should not be used in patients in whom acute asthmatic attacks or symptoms of asthma, urticaria, rhinitis (nasal polyps), angioedema or other allergic manifestations are precipitated by ASA or other nonsteroidal anti-inflammatory agents since cross-sensitivity exists. Fatal anaphylactoid reactions have occurred in such individuals.

Piroxicam suppositories should not be used in patients with any inflammatory lesions of the rectum or anus, or in patients with a recent history of rectal or anal bleeding.

Warnings: Peptic ulceration, perforation and gastrointestinal bleeding, sometimes severe, and occasionally fatal, have been reported during therapy with nonsteroidal anti-inflammatory drugs (NSAIDs) including piroxicam.

Piroxicam should be given under close medical supervision to patients prone to gastrointestinal tract irritation particularly those with a history of peptic ulcer, diverticulosis or other inflammatory disease of the gastrointestinal tract. In these cases the physician must weigh the benefits of treatment against the possible hazards.

Patients taking any NSAID including this drug should be instructed to contact a physician immediately if they experience symptoms or signs suggestive of peptic ulceration or gastrointestinal bleeding. These reactions can occur without warning symptoms or signs and at any time during the treatment.

Elderly, frail and debilitated patients appear to be at higher risk from a variety of adverse reactions from nonsteroidal anti-inflammatory drugs. For such patients, consideration should be given to a starting dose lower than usual, with individual adjustment when necessary and under close supervision (see Precautions for further advice).

Gastrointestinal side effects are dose-related and doses greater than 20 mg daily should not be used. The minimum maintenance dose needed to control symptoms is recommended.

Pregnancy and *Lactation:* The use of piroxicam during pregnancy or lactation is not recommended as its safety in these conditions has not been established. The presence of piroxicam in breast milk has been determined during initial and long-term dosing conditions (52 days). Piroxicam appeared in breast milk at about 1 to 3% of the maternal plasma concentration. No accumulation of piroxicam occurred in milk relative to that in plasma during treatment.

No teratogenic effects have been observed in animal reproductive studies. Rats and rabbits receiving piroxicam during pregnancy have shown an increased frequency of dystocia and delayed parturition. Rats have exhibited suppression of lactation.

Precautions: Gastrointestinal System: If peptic ulceration is suspected or confirmed, or if gastrointestinal bleeding or perforation occurs piroxicam should be discontinued, an appropriate treatment instituted and patient closely monitored.

There is no definitive evidence that the concomitant administration of histamine H_2-receptor antagonists and/or antacids will either prevent the occurrence of gastrointestinal side effects or allow continuation of therapy when and if these adverse reactions appear (see Drug Interactions).

Renal Function: As with other nonsteroidal anti-inflammatory drugs, long-term administration of piroxicam to animals has resulted in renal papillary necrosis and other abnormal renal pathology. In humans, there have been reports of acute interstitial nephritis with hematuria, proteinuria and occasionally nephrotic syndrome.

Acute renal failure and hyperkalemia as well as reversible elevations of BUN and serum creatinine have been reported with piroxicam. The effect is thought to result from inhibition of renal prostaglandin synthesis resulting in a change in medullary and deep cortical blood flow with an attendant effect on renal function. Patients with impaired renal function or on diuretics, as well as elderly patients and those with congestive heart failure or liver cirrhosis with ascites are more at risk. Because of the extensive renal excretion of piroxicam and its biotransformation products (less than 5% of the daily dose excreted unchanged), lower doses of piroxicam should be anticipated in patients with impaired renal function and they should be carefully monitored.

During long-term therapy kidney function should be monitored periodically.

Hepatic Function: As with other nonsteroidal anti-inflammatory drugs, borderline elevations of one or more liver test may occur. These abnormalities may progress, may remain essentially unchanged, or may be transient with continued therapy. The ALT test is probably the most sensitive indicator of liver dysfunction. Meaningful (3 times the upper limit of normal) elevations of ALT or AST occurred in controlled clinical trials in less than 1% of patients. A patient with symptoms and/or signs suggesting liver dysfunction, or in whom an abnormal liver test has occurred, should be evaluated for evidence of the development of more severe hepatic reaction while on therapy with this drug. Severe hepatic reactions, including jaundice and cases of fatal hepatitis, have been reported with this drug as with other nonsteroidal anti-inflammatory drugs. Although such reactions are rare, if abnormal liver tests persist or worsen, if clinical signs and symptoms consistent with liver disease develop, or if systemic manifestations occur (e.g., eosinophilia, rash, etc.), this drug should be discontinued (see Adverse Effects).

During long-term therapy, liver function tests should be monitored periodically. If this drug is to be used in the presence of impaired liver function, it must be done under strict observation.

Fluid and Electrolyte Balance: Fluid retention and edema have been observed in patients treated with piroxicam. Therefore, as with many other nonsteroidal anti-inflammatory drugs, the possibility of precipitating congestive heart failure in elderly patients or those with compromised cardiac function should be borne in mind. The drug should be used with caution in patients with heart failure, hypertension or other conditions predisposing to fluid retention since its use may be associated with worsening of these conditions.

Serum electrolytes should be monitored periodically during long-term therapy, especially in those patients at risk.

Hematology: Drugs inhibiting prostaglandin biosynthesis do interfere with platelet function to some degree; therefore, patients who may be adversely affected by such an action should be carefully observed when piroxicam is administered.

At the recommended dose of 20 mg/day increased fecal blood loss due to gastrointestinal irritation did not occur, but in about 4% of the patients treated with piroxicam alone or concomitantly with ASA, reductions in hemoglobin and hematocrit values were observed. Therefore, these values should be determined periodically.

Blood dyscrasias associated with the use of nonsteroidal anti-inflammatory drugs are rare, but could be with severe consequences.

Infection: In common with other anti-inflammatory drugs, piroxicam may mask the usual signs of infection.

Dermatological and/or Allergic: A combination of dermatological and/or allergic signs and symptoms suggestive of serum sickness have occasionally occurred in conjunction with the

Feldene (cont'd)

use of piroxicam. These include arthralgias, pruritus, fever, fatigue and rash including vesiculo bullous reactions and exfoliative dermatitis.
Ophthalmology: Blurred and/or diminished vision has been reported with the use of piroxicam and other nonsteroidal anti-inflammatory drugs. If such symptoms develop this drug should be discontinued and an ophthalmologic examination performed; ophthalmic examination should be performed at periodic intervals in any patient receiving this drug for an extended period of time.
Children: Piroxicam is not recommended for use in children under 16 years of age as the dose and indications have not been established.
Drug Interactions: ASA or other NSAIDs: Plasma concentrations of piroxicam are reduced to approximately 80% of their normal concentrations when piroxicam is administered in conjunction with ASA (3.9 g/day). The use of piroxicam in conjunction with ASA or another nonsteroidal anti-inflammatory agent is not recommended since data are not available demonstrating that the combination produces greater improvement than that achieved with either drug alone and the potential for adverse reactions is increased.
Anticoagulants: Piroxicam is highly protein bound, and therefore, might be expected to displace other protein bound drugs. The physician should closely monitor dosage requirements of coumarin anticoagulants and other drugs that are highly protein bound when these are administered concomitantly with piroxicam.
Lithium: Nonsteroidal anti-inflammatory agents, including piroxicam, have been reported to increase steady-state plasma lithium concentrations. It is recommended that these concentrations are monitored when initiating, adjusting and discontinuing drug treatment.
Cimetidine: Results of 2 separate studies indicate a slight increase in absorption of piroxicam following cimetidine administration but no significant changes in elimination parameters. Cimetidine increases the area under the curve (AUC 0 to 120 hours) and C_{max} of piroxicam by approximately 13 to 15%. Elimination rate constants and half-life show no significant differences. The clinical significance of this small but significant increase in absorption is yet unknown.
Digoxin or Digitoxin: Concurrent therapy with piroxicam and digoxin and/or piroxicam and digitoxin did not affect the plasma levels of either drug.
Antacids: Concomitant administration of antacids had no effect on piroxicam plasma levels.
Diuretics: Nonsteroidal anti-inflammatory drugs, including piroxicam may cause sodium and fluid retention, and may interfere with the natriuretic action of diuretic agents. These properties should be kept in mind when treating patients with compromised cardiac function or hypertension since they may be responsible for a worsening of those conditions.
Methotrexate: Although up to date there have been no reports of an interaction with piroxicam, isolated cases indicate that the concomitant use of some NSAIDs in patients receiving methotrexate may be associated with severe or sometimes fatal methotrexate toxicity.

Until more information is available on this interaction, caution should be used if piroxicam as well as other NSAIDs, are administered concomitantly with methotrexate, particularly in patients with pre-existing renal impairment, who may be more susceptible.
Beta-adrenergic Blockers: As with other nonsteroidal anti-inflammatory drugs, concomitant administration of piroxicam with propranolol can reduce the hypotensive effect. Patients should be monitored for altered antihypertensive or antianginal response to beta-blockers when piroxicam is initiated or discontinued.
Cholestyramine: Preliminary study indicates that in healthy subjects coadministration of cholestyramine to piroxicam results in enhanced elimination of piroxicam (i.e., reduction in half-life by 40% and increase in clearance by 52%). Although the magnitude of these changes in piroxicam disposition appear sufficient to inhibit its therapeutic effects, studies in patients are needed to confirm this. It is suggested that the doses of piroxicam and cholestyramine be separated as much as possible, and that the patients be monitored for inadequate response to therapy. If an inadequate anti-inflammatory response appears to be related to the concomitant use of cholestyramine, consideration should be given to the use of alternative hypolipidemic therapy.

Adverse Effects: The most common adverse reactions encountered with nonsteroidal anti-inflammatory drugs are gastrointestinal, of which peptic ulcer, with or without bleeding is the most severe. Fatalities have occurred on occasion, particularly in the elderly.

In approximately 2 300 patients receiving a daily dose of 20 mg or less of piroxicam in clinical trials, the most frequent side effects observed have been gastrointestinal (approximately 20% of patients). Of the patients experiencing gastrointestinal side effects, approximately 5% discontinued therapy with an overall incidence of peptic ulceration of about 1% and gastrointestinal bleeding of approximately 0.1%. The incidence of adverse reactions is summarized below.
Gastrointestinal (17.4%): epigastric distress (6.4%), nausea (4.1%), constipation (2.4%), abdominal discomfort (2.2%), flatulence (2.1%), diarrhea (1.8%), abdominal pain (1.5%), indigestion (1.3%), anorexia (1.2%), peptic ulceration (about 1%); stomatitis, vomiting, hematemesis, melena, perforation, dry mouth, pancreatitis, each in less than 1% of patients.

Ano-rectal reaction presenting as local pain, burning, pruritus, tenesmus and rare instances of rectal bleeding have been reported in 2.9% of patients with the use of piroxicam suppositories.
Allergic (<1%): anaphylaxis, bronchospasm, urticaria/angioedema, vasculitis, serum sickness (see Precautions), each in less than 1% of patients.
CNS (5%): headache (1.8%), malaise (1%); dizziness, drowsiness/sedation (somnolence), vertigo, depression, hallucinations, insomnia, nervousness, paresthesia, personality change, dream abnormalities, mental confusion, each in less than 1% of patients.
Dermatologic (2%): rash (2%); pruritus, erythema, bruising, desquamation, exfoliative dermatitis, erythema multiforme, toxic epidermal necrolysis (Lyell's Disease), vesiculo bullous reaction, onycholysis, Stevens-Johnson syndrome, photoallergic skin reactions, each in less than 1% of patients.
Cardiovascular (<1%): hypertension, palpitations, worsening of congestive heart failure (see Precautions), exacerbation of angina, each in less than 1% of patients.
Special Senses: Eyes, ears, nose and throat reactions (<1%): tinnitus (about 1%); blurred vision, eye irritation/swelling, each in less than 1% of patients.
Hematologic (15%): decreases in hemoglobin (4.6%) and hematocrit (4.2%) (see Precautions), thrombocytopenia (2.4%), eosinophilia (1.8%), leukocytosis (1.7%), basophilia (1.7%), leukopenia (1.4%); petechial rash, ecchymosis, bone marrow depression including aplastic anemia, epistaxis, each in less than 1% of patients.
Renal (1%): edema (1.6%) (see Precautions); dysuria, hematuria, proteinuria, interstitial nephritis, renal failure, hyperkalemia, glomerulitis, nephrotic syndrome (see Precautions), each in less than 1% of patients.
Hepatic (<1%): jaundice, hepatitis (see Precautions), each in less than 1% of patients.
Respiratory (<1%): dyspnea.
Metabolic (<1%): hypoglycemia, hyperglycemia, weight increase/decrease, each in less than 1% of patients.
Miscellaneous (<1%): sweating, pain (colic), fever, flu-like syndrome (see Precautions), weakness, each in less than 1% of patients.
Primary Dysmenorrhea: In primary dysmenorrhea the side effect profile of piroxicam is similar in nature to that observed in rheumatic diseases.
Laboratory Parameters: Changes in laboratory parameters observed during piroxicam therapy have included an elevation of BUN, creatinine (see Precautions), uric acid and liver enzymes LDH, AST, ALT and alkaline phosphatase.
Other: Since market introduction, isolated reports have included delayed wound healing, thrombophlebitis, pemphigus, alopecia, mastodynia, reduction or loss of libido, impotence, urinary frequency, oliguria, menorrhagia, amnesia, anxiety, tremor, hearing impairment, deafness, thirst, chills, increased appetite, akathisia, tachycardia, flushing, tooth discoloration, glossitis, chest pain, anemia, hemolytic anemia, pancreatitis, and positive antinuclear factor (ANA); a causal relationship has not been established for those rarely reported events.

Overdose: Symptoms and Treatment: In the event treatment for overdosage is required, the long plasma half-life (see Pharmacology) of piroxicam should be considered. The absence of experience with acute overdosage precludes characterization of sequelae and recommendation of specific antidotal efficacy at this time. It is reasonable to assume, however, that the standard measures of gastric evacuation and general supportive therapy would apply. In addition to supportive measure, the use of activated charcoal may effectively reduce the absorption and reabsorption of piroxicam. Experiments in dogs have demonstrated that the use of multiple-dose treatments with activated charcoal could reduce the half-life of piroxicam elimination from 27 hours (without charcoal) to 11 hours and reduce the systemic bioavailability of piroxicam by as much as 37% when activated charcoal is given as late as 6 hours after administration of piroxicam.

Dosage: Oral: In rheumatoid arthritis and ankylosing spondylitis it is recommended that therapy with piroxicam be initiated as a single daily dose of 20 mg. If desired, this dose may be given as 10 mg twice a day. Most patients will be maintained on 20 mg daily. A relatively small number of patients may be maintained on 10 mg daily.

In osteoarthritis the recommended starting dosage of piroxicam is 20 mg once daily. If desired, this dose may be given as 10 mg twice a day. The usual maintenance dose is 10 to 20 mg daily.

Piroxicam should not be given in doses greater than 20 mg daily owing to an increased incidence of gastrointestinal side effects.
Geriatrics and Debilitated: As elderly patients appear to be at higher risk from a variety of adverse reactions from nonsteroidal anti-inflammatory drugs and as elderly, frail or debilitated patients tolerate gastrointestinal side effects less well, consideration should be given to a starting dose that is lower than usual and to an increase of the dose only if symptoms remain uncontrolled. Such patients must be very carefully supervised.

In primary dysmenorrhea the treatment is initiated at the earliest onset of symptoms with a recommended starting dose of 40 mg given as a single daily dose on the first day. For the remainder of the treatment period (usually 2 to 4 days), the dose should be reduced to 20 mg daily.
Rectal: For each indication, the dosage of piroxicam suppositories, when used alone, is identical with the dosage of piroxicam capsules.

Suppositories offer an alternative route of administration for those physicians who may wish to prescribe them in certain patients, or for those patients who prefer them.
Combined Administration: The total daily dose administered as capsules and/or suppositories should not exceed 20 mg/day.

Information for the Patient: See Blue Section—Information for the Patient "Feldene".

Supplied: Capsules: 10 mg: Each No. 2 maroon/blue opaque hard gelatin capsule, printed with Feldene and Pfizer, contains: piroxicam 10 mg. Nonmedicinal ingredients: cornstarch, lactose and magnesium stearate/sodium lauryl sulfate; capsule shell: gelatin, silicon dioxide, titanium dioxide and dyes FD&C Red No. 3 and FD&C Blue No 1. Tartrazine-free. Bottles of 100.

20 mg: Each No. 2 maroon/opaque hard gelatin capsule, printed with Feldene and Pfizer, contains: piroxican 20 mg. Nonmedicinal ingredients: cornstarch, lactose and magnesium stearate/sodium lauryl sulfate; capsule shell: gelatin, silicon dioxide, titanium dioxide and dyes FD&C Red No. 3 and FD&C Blue No 1. Tartrazine-free. Bottles of 100.

Suppositories: 10 mg: Each white to off-white torpedo-shaped suppository contains: piroxicam 10 mg. Nonmedicinal ingredients: semisynthetic glycerides, microcrystalline wax and propyl gallate. Packages of 30.

20 mg: Each white to off-white torpedo-shaped suppository contains: piroxicam 20 mg. Nonmedicinal ingredients: semisynthetic glycerides, microcrystalline wax and propyl gallate. Packages of 30.

Store at 15 to 30°C.

(Shown in Product Recognition Section)

FEMARA® Ⓟ

Novartis Pharmaceuticals

Letrozole

Nonsteroidal Aromatase Inhibitor—Inhibitor of Estrogen Biosynthesis—Antitumor Agent

Pharmacology: Letrozole is a potent and highly specific nonsteroidal aromatase inhibitor. It inhibits the aromatase enzyme by competitively binding to the heme of the cytochrome P450 subunit of the enzyme, resulting in a reduction of estrogen biosynthesis in all tissues.

Letrozole exerts its antitumor effect by depriving estrogen-dependent breast cancer cells of their growth stimulus. In postmenopausal women, estrogens are derived mainly from the action of the aromatase enzyme, which converts adrenal androgens—primarily androstenedione and testosterone—to estrone (E1) and estradiol (E2). The suppression of estrogen biosynthesis in peripheral tissues and the malignant tissue can be achieved by specifically inhibiting the aromatase enzyme.

In healthy postmenopausal women, single oral doses of 0.1, 0.5 and 2.5 mg letrozole suppressed serum estrone by 75 to 78% and estradiol by 78% from baseline. Maximum suppression is achieved in 48 to 78 hours.

In postmenopausal women with advanced breast cancer, daily letrozole doses of 0.1 to 5 mg suppress estradiol, estrone and estrone sulfate plasma levels by 75 to 95% from baseline in all patients treated. With 0.5 mg doses and higher, many plasma levels of estrone and estrone sulfate are below the limit of detection of the assays, indicating that higher estrogen suppression is achieved with these doses. Estrogen suppression was maintained throughout treatment in all patients.

Letrozole is highly specific in inhibiting aromatase activity. Impairment of adrenal steroidogenesis has not been observed. No clinically relevant changes in the plasma levels of cortisol, aldosterone, 11-deoxycortisol, 17-hydroxy-progesterone, ACTH (adrenocorticotropic hormone) or in plasma renin activity were found in postmenopausal patients treated with 0.1 to 5 mg letrozole daily. The ACTH stimulation test performed after 6 and 12 weeks of treatment with daily doses of 0.1 to 5 mg letrozole did not indicate any attenuation of aldosterone or cortisol production. Thus, glucocorticoid or mineralocorticoid supplementation is not required.

Letrozole had no effect on plasma androgen concentrations (androstenedione and testosterone) among healthy postmenopausal women after single doses of 0.1, 0.5 and 2.5 mg, or on plasma androstenedione concentrations among postmenopausal patients treated with daily doses of 0.1 to 5 mg. These results indicate that accumulation of androgenic precursors does not occur. Plasma levels of LH and FSH are not affected by letrozole in patients, nor is thyroid function as evaluated by TSH, T_4 and T_3 uptake.

In a controlled double-blind clinical trial, the overall objective tumor response rate (complete and partial response) was 23.6% in letrozole-treated patients compared to 16.4% in patients on 160 mg megestrol acetate. Treatment comparison of the response rate showed a statistically significant difference in favor of 2.5 mg letrozole (p=0.04).

Pharmacokinetics: Absorption: Letrozole is rapidly and completely absorbed from the gastrointestinal tract (absolute bioavailability=99.9%). Food slightly decreases the rate of absorption (median t_{max} 1 hour fasted vs 2 hours fed and mean C_{max} 129±20.3 nmol/L fasted vs 98.7±18.6 nmol/L fed), but the extent of absorption (area under the curve (AUC)) remains unchanged. This minor effect on absorption rate is not considered to be of clinical relevance and therefore letrozole may be taken with or without food.

Distribution: Letrozole is rapidly and extensively distributed into tissues (Vd_{ss}=1.87±0.47 L/kg). Plasma protein binding is approximately 60%, mainly to albumin. The letrozole concentration in erythrocytes is about 80% of that in plasma. After administration of 2.5 mg ^{14}C-labeled letrozole, approximately 82% of the radioactivity in plasma was unchanged compound. Systemic exposure to metabolites is therefore low.

Biotransformation and Elimination: Metabolic clearance to a pharmacologically inactive carbinol metabolite, CGP 44645, is the major elimination pathway of letrozole (Cl_m=2.1 L/h), but it is relatively slow when compared to hepatic blood flow (about 90 L/h). The cytochrome P450 isoenzymes 3A4 and 2A6 were found to be capable of converting letrozole to this metabolite. Formation of minor unidentified metabolites and direct renal and fecal excretion play only a minor role in the overall elimination of letrozole. Within 2 weeks after administration of 2.5 mg ^{14}C-labeled letrozole to healthy postmenopausal volunteers, 88.2±7.6% of the radioactivity was recovered in urine and 3.8±0.9% in feces. At least 75% of the radioactivity recovered in urine up to 216 hours (84.7±7.8% of the dose) was attributed to the glucuronide of the carbinol metabolite, about 9% to 2 unidentified metabolites, and 6% to unchanged letrozole.

The apparent terminal elimination half-life in plasma is about 2 days. After daily administration of 2.5 mg steady-state levels are reached within 2 to 6 weeks. Plasma concentrations at steady-state are approximately 7 times higher than concentrations measured after a single dose of 2.5 mg, while they are 1.5 to 2 times higher than steady-state values predicted from the concentrations measured after a single dose, indicating a slight non-linearity in the pharmacokinetics of letrozole upon daily administration of 2.5 mg. Since steady-state levels are maintained over time, it can be concluded that no continuous accumulation of letrozole occurs.

Indications: For the hormonal treatment of advanced/metastatic breast cancer in women with natural or artificially induced postmenopausal status, who have disease progression following antiestrogen therapy.

Contraindications: Premenopausal endocrine status, pregnancy, lactation.

Known or suspected hypersensitivity to letrozole, other aromatase inhibitors, or to the nonmedicinal ingredients (see Supplied).

Warnings: Occupational Hazards: Letrozole is unlikely to impair the ability of patients to drive or to operate machinery. However, in some cases, fatigue and dizziness have been observed with use. Patients should be advised that their physical and/or mental abilities required for operating machinery or driving a car may be impaired.

Use with Other Anticancer Agents: There is no clinical experience to date on the use of letrozole in combination with other anticancer agents.

Reproductive Toxicology: Letrozole was evaluated for maternal toxicity as well as embryotoxic, fetotoxic and teratogenic potential in female rats following oral administration of daily doses of 0.003, 0.01 or 0.03 mg/kg on gestation days 6 through 17. Oral administration of letrozole to pregnant rats resulted in teratogenicity and maternal toxicity at 0.03 mg/kg. Embryotoxicity and fetotoxicity were seen at doses ≥0.003 mg/kg, and there was an increase in the incidence of fetal malformation among the animals treated. However it is not known whether this was an indirect consequence of the pharmacological activity of letrozole (inhibition of estrogen biosynthesis) or a direct drug effect.

Precautions: Special Populations: Hepatic Impairment: In a single dose trial with 2.5 mg letrozole in volunteers with hepatic impairment, mean AUC values of the volunteers with moderate hepatic impairment was 37% higher than in normal subjects, but still within the range seen in subjects with normal hepatic function. These results indicate that no dosage adjustment is necessary for breast cancer patients with hepatic dysfunction. However, since letrozole elimination depends mainly on intrinsic metabolic clearance, caution is recommended.

Renal Impairment: Pharmacokinetics of a single 2.5 mg letrozole dose were unchanged in a study in postmenopausal women with varying degrees of renal function (24-hour creatinine clearance=9 to 116 mL/min). In a study in 364 patients with advanced breast cancer there was no significant association between letrozole plasma levels and calculated CL_{cr} (range 22.9 to 211.9 mL/min). No dosage adjustment is required in patients with CL_{cr} ≥10 mL/min. No data are available for patients with CL_{cr} ≤9 mL/min.

Letrozole is weakly bound to plasma proteins; it is anticipated that it could be removed from blood by dialysis. The potential risks and benefits to such patients should be considered carefully before prescribing letrozole.

Geriatrics: There have been no age-related effects observed on the pharmacokinetics of letrozole.

Drug Interactions: Clinical trials of interaction with letrozole and cimetidine or warfarin indicate that coadministration does not result in clinically significant drug interactions.

In a large clinical trial there was no evidence of clinically relevant interactions in patients treated with letrozole receiving other commonly prescribed drugs (e.g., benzodiazepines; barbiturates; furosemide; NSAIDs such as diclofenac sodium, ibuprofen; omeprazole).

In vitro, letrozole inhibits the cytochrome P450 isoenzymes 2A6 and 2C19. Thus, caution should be used in the concomitant administration of drugs whose disposition is mainly dependent on the isoenzymes and whose therapeutic index is narrow.

Food Interactions: Food slightly decreases the rate of absorption (median t_{max} 1 hour fasted vs 2 hours fed and mean C_{max} 129±20.3 nmol/L fasted vs 98.7±18.6 nmol/L fed), but the extent of absorption (area under the curve (AUC)) remains unchanged. This minor effect on absorption rate is not considered to be of clinical relevance, and therefore, letrozole may be taken with or without food.

Drug/Laboratory Test Interactions: No clinically significant changes in the results of clinical laboratory tests have been observed.

Adverse Effects: In clinical trials, adverse experiences (AEs) were generally mild to moderate and rarely severe enough to require discontinuation of treatment. Many AEs were attributed either to the underlying disease or to the normal physiological consequences of estrogen deprivation (e.g., hot flushes, hair thinning).

Table I shows in decreasing order of frequency the AEs—considered possibly related to trial drug according to the investigator—that have been reported with an incidence of more than 2.0% (whether for letrozole or for megestrol acetate) in a controlled clinical trial with letrozole (2.5 mg daily) and megestrol acetate (160 mg daily) for up to 33 months.

Table I—Femara

Frequency of Adverse Experiences (Experience >2%)

Adverse Experience	Femara % (N=174)	Megestrol Acetate % (N=189)
Headache	6.9	4.8
Nausea	6.3	4.2
Peripheral edema	6.3	3.7
Fatigue	5.2	6.3
Hot flushes	5.2	3.7
Hair thinning	3.4	1.1
Rash[a]	3.4	0.5
Vomiting	2.9	1.6
Dyspepsia	2.9	1.6
Weight increase	2.3	8.5
Musculoskeletal pain[b]	2.3	1.1
Anorexia	2.3	1.1
Vaginal bleeding	1.7	3.2
Leukorrhea	1.7	2.6
Constipation	1.7	2.1
Dizziness	1.1	3.7
Increased appetite	1.1	3.7
Increased sweating	1.1	2.1
Dyspnea	0.6	5.8
Thrombophlebitis[c]	0.6	3.7
Vaginal spotting	0.6	2.1
Hypertension	0	2.6
Pruritus	0	2.6

[a] Including: erythematous rash, maculopapular rash.
[b] Including: arm pain, back pain, leg pain, skeletal pain.
[c] Including: superficial and deep thrombophlebitis.

Other adverse experiences considered to be possibly drug related and reported in at least 3 patients treated with letrozole, with a frequency below 2%, included weight loss and generalized edema.

There were no differences in the incidence and severity of adverse reactions in patients ≤55 years, 55 to 69 years, and ≥70 years.

Overdose: Symptoms and Treatment: There is no experience with letrozole overdosage. No specific treatment for overdosage is known; treatment should be symptomatic and supportive.

Dosage: Adults and Geriatrics: The recommended dose is one 2.5 mg tablet once daily. Treatment should continue until further tumor progression is evident. No dose adjustment is required for elderly patients.

Patients with Hepatic and/or Renal Impairment: No dosage adjustment is required for patients with hepatic impairment or renal impairment (creatinine clearance ≥ 10 mL/min).

Information for the Patient: See Blue Section—Information for the Patient "Femara".

Supplied: Each dark yellow, round, slightly biconvex tablet with beveled-edge, bearing the imprint "FV" on one side and "CG" on the other, contains: letrozole 2.5 mg. Nonmedicinal ingredients: cellulose compounds, cornstarch, iron oxide, lactose, magnesium stearate, polyethylene glycol, sodium starch glycolate, silicon dioxide, talc and titanium dioxide. Blister packages of 30. Protect from heat (store below 30°C).

(Shown in Product Recognition Section)

Reviewed 1998

FENTANYL ®

General Monograph, CPhA

see OPIOID ANALGESICS

FENTANYL CITRATE ®

Abbott

Narcotic Analgesic

Supplied: Each mL of sterile, nonpyrogenic solution contains: fentanyl 50 μg as the citrate in water for injection. The solution may contain sodium hydroxide or hydrochloric acid for pH adjustment. Ampuls of 2, 5, 10 and 20 mL and flip-top vials of 10 and 20 mL.

FENTANYL CITRATE INJECTION USP Ⓝ

Faulding

Narcotic Analgesic—Adjunct to Anesthesia

Supplied: Each mL of sterile, unpreserved solution contains: fentanyl 50 μg (provided by 0.0785 mg of fentanyl citrate USP) in sterile water for injection. Single dose ampuls of 2, 5, 10 and 20 mL, packages of 5. Discard any unused portion in an appropriate manner. Store at 15 to 30°C, protected from light.

FER-IN-SOL®

Mead Johnson

Ferrous Sulfate

Hematinic

Indications: Prevention and treatment of iron deficiency anemia.

Contraindications: Hemosiderosis, hemochromatosis, hemolytic anemia.

Precautions: Oral iron preparations may aggravate existing peptic ulcer, regional enteritis and ulcerative colitis.

Iron compounds taken orally can impair the absorption of tetracycline antibiotics. Antacids given concomitantly with iron compounds decrease iron absorption. When iron drops are given to babies some darkening of the gum tissue directly surrounding the teeth may occur. This is not serious and may be removed by rubbing the teeth with baking soda. Discoloring will fade with discontinued use.

Adverse Effects: Mild gastrointestinal upsets may rarely occur in iron-sensitive patients.

Dosage: Drops: Prophylactic Dosage: up to 6 years, 0.5 mL daily; older children 1 mL daily. Therapeutic Dosage: Give 3 times a day. Up to 2 years, 1 to 2 mL; 2 to 6 years, 2 mL; older children, 2 to 3 mL. Give in water or fruit juice (not milk) and preferably between meals.

Syrup: Prophylactic Dosage: Give once daily. Children up to 6 years, 1.25 mL; older children, 2.5 mL. Therapeutic Dosage: Give 3 times a day. Up to 2 years, 2.5 to 5 mL; 2 to 6 years, 5 mL; older children, 5 to 10 mL; adults, 10 to 15 mL.

Supplied: Drops: Each mL of liquid contains: ferrous sulfate 75 mg (equivalent to 15 mg elemental iron). Nonmedicinal ingredients: artificial flavoring, citric acid anhydrous, ethyl alcohol, purified water, sodium bisulfite, sorbitol solution and sucrose. Alcohol: 1.6%. Energy: 6.93 kJ (1.65 kcal). Sodium: <1 mmol (0.1 mg). Bottles of 50 mL with calibrated dropper.

Syrup: Each 5 mL of syrup contains: ferrous sulfate 150 mg (equivalent to 30 mg elemental iron). Nonmedicinal ingredients: artificial flavoring, citric acid anhydrous, purified water, sodium bisulfite, sodium chloride, sorbitol solution, sucrose and sulfuric acid. Energy: 50.82 kJ (12.1 kcal)/5 mL. Sodium: <1 mmol (7.5 mg)/5 mL. Alcohol-free. Bottles of 250 mL.

All bottles have child-resistant closures and are safety sealed.

FERMALAC®

Rougier

Lactobacillus Acidophilus Compound

Flora Modifier

Indications: The treatment of mild diarrhea and intestinal upset, particularly when associated with antibiotic therapy.

Precautions: Store under refrigeration. Should not be used to prepare yogurt or acidophilus milk.

Dosage: Adults: 1 to 2 capsules 3 times/day.

Supplied: Each No. 0 enteric coated capsule with opaque blue top and opaque white bottom contains: 1 billion fully viable bacilli (lyophilized mixed cultures)—Lactobacillus acidophilus, Lactobacillus bulgaricus, Streptococcus lactis (var. thermophilus). Energy: 6.19 kJ (1.47 kcal). Sealed bottles of 40.

FERMALAC® VAGINAL

Rougier

Lactobacillus Acidophilus Compound

Vaginitis Therapy

Indications: Adjunctive treatment of specific vaginal infections to restore and maintain normal vaginal flora.

Dosage: One capsule inserted into the vagina once daily at bedtime for 10 consecutive days or as prescribed.

Supplied: Each opaque white No. 000 capsule contains: more than 2 billion fully viable bacilli (lyophilized cultures)—Lactobacillus acidophilus, Lactobacillus bulgaricus and Streptococcus lactis (var. thermophilus). Boxes of 10 with applicator. Store in refrigerator.

FERMENTOL®

Carter Horner

Pepsin

Digestant

Indications: For the relief of mild, acute and chronic dyspepsia without hyperacidity, and as a vehicle for the administration of medicinals compatible with alcohol.

Dosage: 5 mL after meals for chronic indigestion; 30 mL for acute indigestion. As a vehicle, the mixture should contain at least 50% Fermentol, 80% is recommended.

Supplied: Each 30 mL of green-colored, transparent liquid contains: pepsin 100 mg. Nonmedicinal ingredients: alcohol, D&C Green No. 5 and Yellow No. 10, FD&C Yellow No. 6, flavor, glycerin, hydrochloric acid and sodium hydroxide to adjust pH, lactose and sodium cyclamate. Energy: 96 kJ (23 kcal). Sodium: <1 mmol (3 mg). Gluten- and tartrazine-free. pH is 4.4 to 4.6. Bottles of 250 and 500 mL.

FERODAN™ Infant Drops
FERODAN™ Syrup

Odan

Ferrous Sulfate USP

Hematinic

Supplied: Infant Drops: Each mL of light amber to green/gold solution with an aromatic fruity flavor contains: ferrous sulfate USP 75 mg (equivalent to elemental iron 15 mg). Nonmedicinal ingredients: citric acid, glycerin, lemon flavor, pineapple flavor, purified water, sodium bisulfite, sorbitol, strawberry flavor and sucrose. Alcohol-free. Plastic amber bottles of 50 mL with child resistant closures and calibrated dropper.

Syrup: Each 5 mL of light amber solution with an aromatic fruity flavor contains: ferrous sulfate $7H_2O$ USP 150 mg (equivalent to elemental iron 30 mg). Nonmedicinal ingredients: citric acid, glycerin, lemon flavor, pineapple flavor, purified water, sodium benzoate, sodium bisulfite, sorbitol, strawberry flavor and sucrose. Alcohol-, gluten- and tartrazine-free. Plastic amber bottles of 250 and 500 mL with child-resistant closures and safety seals.

FERO-GRAD®

Abbott

Ferrous Sulfate

Hematinic

Supplied: Each round, convex, cherry red, Filmtab tablet contains: ferrous sulfate 525 mg (105 mg elemental iron) in delayed release form. Nonmedicinal ingredients: alcohol, castor oil, ethylcellulose, FD&C Red #40, FD&C Yellow #6, hydroxypropylcellulose, hydroxypropyl methylcellulose, polyethylene glycol 400, purified water and titanium dioxide. Gluten-, lactose-, paraben-, sodium-, sucrose-, sulfite- and tartrazine-free. Bottles of 100.

FERTINORM® HP Ⓟ

Serono

Urofollitropin

Gonadotropin

Pharmacology: Fertinorm HP is a highly purified preparation of the gonadotropin, Follicle Stimulating Hormone (FSH) extracted from the urine of postmenopausal women. The principal action of Fertinorm HP is the induction of follicular growth in infertile women who do not have primary ovarian failure. Treatment in most instances results only in follicular growth and maturation. In order to effect ovulation in the absence of an endogenous LH surge, human Chorionic Gonadotropin (hCG) must be given following the administration of Fertinorm HP once follicular maturation has occurred.

Pharmacokinetics: Following a single s.c. or i.m. administration of Fertinorm HP 150 IU, to male volunteers: Peak serum FSH levels were reached 15±7 (s.c.) and 10±4 (i.m.) hours later with an increase of 4.0±2 IU/L of FSH over baseline values, for both the s.c. and i.m. routes; 72 hours after administration, serum FSH levels were still significantly higher than baseline values. The elimination half-life of FSH was estimated to be between 30 to 40 hours.

Indications: Fertinorm HP followed by chorionic gonadotrophin (hCG), stimulates follicular development and ovulation in women with hypothalamic-pituitary dysfunction who present with either oligomenorrhea or amenorrhea. These women are classified as WHO Group II patients and usually receive clomiphene citrate as primary therapy. They have evidence of endogenous estrogen production and thus will either spontaneously menstruate or experience withdrawal bleeding after progesterone administration. Polycystic ovarian disease is part of the WHO II classification and is present in the majority of these patients.

Contraindications: Women who exhibit: high levels of FSH indicating primary ovarian failure, uncontrolled thyroid or adrenal dysfunction, an organic intracranial lesion such as a pituitary tumor, the presence of any cause of infertility other than anovulation as stated in the Indications, abnormal uterine bleeding (see Precautions), ovarian cyst or enlargement of undetermined origin, a prior hypersensitivity to menotropins/urofollitropin, or any excipients used in the formulation, sex hormone dependent tumors of the reproductive tract and accessory organs.

Pregnancy and *Lactation:* Fertinorm HP should not be administered in case of pregnancy and lactation.

Warnings: Caution: Fertinorm HP should only be used by physicians who are thoroughly familiar with infertility problems and their management. It is a potent gonadotropic substance capable of causing mild to severe adverse reactions. Gonadotropin therapy requires a certain time commitment by physicians and supportive health professionals, and requires the availability of appropriate monitoring facilities (see Precautions, Laboratory Tests). In female patients it must be used with a great deal of care.

Overstimulation of the Ovary During Fertinorm HP Therapy: Ovarian Enlargement: Mild to moderate uncomplicated ovarian enlargement which may be accompanied by abdominal distension and/or abdominal pain occurs in approximately 20% of those treated with urofollitropin and hCG, and generally regresses without treatment within 2 or 3 weeks.

The Ovarian Hyperstimulation Syndrome (OHSS): OHSS is a medical event distinct from uncomplicated ovarian enlargement. OHSS may progress rapidly (within 24 hours to several days) to become a serious medical event. It is characterized by an apparent dramatic increase in vascular permeability which can result in an accumulation of fluid in the peritoneal cavity, thorax and rarely in the pericardial cavities. The early warning signs of development of OHSS are severe pelvic pain, nausea, vomiting and weight gain. The following symptomatology has been seen with cases of OHSS: abdominal pain, abdominal distension, gastrointestinal symptoms including nausea, vomiting and diarrhea, severe ovarian enlargement, weight gain, dyspnea and oliguria. Clinical evaluation may reveal hypovolemia, hemoconcentration, electrolyte imbalances, ascites, hemoperitoneum, pleural effusions, hydrothorax, acute pulmonary distress and thromboembolic events (see Thromboembolic Events).

OHSS occurred in approximately 6% of patients treated with urofollitropin therapy in the initial clinical trials, in patients treated for anovulation due to polycystic ovarian syndrome. OHSS develops rapidly and most often after treatment with urofollitropin or hCG has been discontinued, reaching its maximum at about 7 to 10 days following treatment. Patients, therefore, should be followed for at least 2 weeks after urofollitropin or hCG administration. Cases of OHSS are more common, more severe, and more protracted if pregnancy occurs. Usually, OHSS resolves spontaneously with the onset of menses. If there is evidence that OHSS may be developing prior to hCG administration (see Precautions, Laboratory Tests), the hCG should be withheld.

If OHSS occurs, treatment should be stopped and the patient hospitalized. Treatment is primarily symptomatic, consisting of bed rest, fluid and electrolyte management, and analgesics if needed. The phenomenon of hemoconcentration associated with fluid loss into the peritoneal cavity, pleural cavity, and pericardial cavity has been seen to occur and should be thoroughly assessed in the following manner: 1) fluid intake and output, 2) weight, 3) hematocrit, 4) serum and urinary electrolytes, 5) urine specific gravity, 6) BUN and creatinine and 7) abdominal girth. These determinations are to be performed daily or more often if the need arises.

With OHSS there is an increased risk of injury to the ovary. The ascitic, pleural, and pericardial fluids should not be removed unless absolutely necessary to relieve symptoms such as pulmonary distress or cardiac tamponade. Pelvic examination may cause rupture of an ovarian cyst, which may result in hemoperitoneum, and should therefore be avoided. If this does occur, and if bleeding becomes such that surgery is required, the surgical treatment should be designed to control bleeding and to retain as much ovarian tissue as possible. Intercourse should be prohibited in those patients in whom significant ovarian enlargement occurs after ovulation because of the danger of hemoperitoneum resulting from ruptured ovarian cysts.

The management of OHSS may be divided into three phases: the acute, the chronic and the resolution phases. Because the use of diuretics can accentuate the diminished intravascular volume, diuretics should be avoided except in the late phase of resolution.

Acute Phase: Management during the acute phase should be designed to prevent hemoconcentration due to loss of intravascular volume to the third space and to minimize the risk of thromboembolic phenomena and kidney damage. Treatment is designed to normalize electrolytes while maintaining an acceptable but somewhat reduced intravascular volume. Full correction of the intravascular volume deficit may lead to an unacceptable increase in the amount of third space fluid accumulation. Management includes administration of limited i.v. fluids, electrolytes and human serum albumin. Monitoring for the development of hyperkalemia is recommended.

Chronic Phase: After stabilizing the patient during the acute phase, excessive fluid accumulation in the third space should be limited by instituting severe potassium, sodium and fluid restriction.

Resolution Phase: A fall in hematocrit and an increasing urinary output without an increased intake are observed due to the return of third space fluid to the intravascular compartment. Peripheral and/or pulmonary edema may result if the kidneys are unable to excrete third space fluid as rapidly as it is mobilized. Diuretics may be indicated during the resolution phase if necessary to combat pulmonary edema.

Thromboembolic Events: Thromboembolic events, both in association with, and separate from Ovarian Hyperstimulation Syndrome have been reported following gonadotropin therapy. These included thrombophlebitis, pulmonary embolism, stroke and arterial occlusion resulting in the loss of a limb. In rare cases, thromboembolic events have resulted in death.

Multiple Births: Multiple births have been associated with Fertinorm HP therapy, as with other agents used to stimulate ovulation; however, the majority of multiple conceptions are twins. The patient and her husband should be advised of the potential risk of multiple births before starting therapy.

Precautions: General: Careful attention should be given to diagnosis in the selection of candidates for Fertinorm HP therapy.

Before treatment with Fertinorm HP is instituted, a thorough gynecologic and endocrinologic evaluation must be performed. This should include a hysterosalpingogram (to rule out uterine and tubal pathology) and documentation of anovulation by means of basal body temperature, serial vaginal smears, examination of cervical mucus, determination of serum (or urinary) progesterone, and endometrial biopsy.

Primary ovarian failure should be excluded by the determination of gonadotropin levels.

Careful examination should be made to rule out the presence of an early pregnancy.

Patients in late reproductive life have a greater predisposition to endometrial carcinoma as well as a higher incidence of anovulatory disorders. A thorough diagnostic evaluation should always be performed in patients who demonstrate abnormal uterine bleeding or other signs of endometrial abnormalities.

Evaluation of the husband's fertility potential should also be performed before starting Fertinorm HP therapy.

In order to minimize the hazard associated with the occasional abnormal ovarian enlargement which may occur with Fertinorm HP hCG therapy, the lowest dose consistent with expectation of good results should be used. Careful monitoring of ovarian response can further minimize risk of overstimulation.

If the ovaries are abnormally enlarged on the last day of Fertinorm HP therapy, hCG should not be administered in this course of therapy; this will reduce the chances of development of the Ovarian Hyperstimulation Syndrome.

Information for the Patient: Prior to therapy with Fertinorm HP, patients should be informed of the duration of treatment and the monitoring of their condition that will be required. Possible adverse reactions (see Adverse Effects) and the risk of multiple births should be discussed.

Laboratory Tests: In most instances, treatment with Fertinorm HP results only in follicular growth and maturation. In order to effect ovulation in the absence of an endogenous LH surge, hCG must be given following the administration of Fertinorm HP when clinical assessment of the patient indicates that sufficient follicular maturation has occurred.

This may be estimated by measuring serum (or urinary) estrogen levels and sonographic visualization of the ovaries. The combination of both estradiol levels and ultrasonography is useful for monitoring the growth and development of follicles, timing hCG administration, as well as for detecting ovarian enlargement and minimizing the risk of OHSS and multiple gestation.

Urinary and/or plasma estrogen determinations provide an indirect index of follicular maturity since as the follicles grow and develop, they secrete estrogens in increasing amounts. However, plasma and/or urinary estrogen levels represent the sum of ovarian activity. It is recommended that the number of growing follicles be confirmed using ultrasonography because plasma and/or urinary estrogens do not give an indication of the number of follicles.

Other clinical parameters which may have potential use for monitoring Fertinorm HP therapy include: changes in the vaginal cytology, appearance and volume of the cervical mucus, spinnbarkeit and ferning of the cervical mucus.

The above clinical indices provide an indirect estimate of the estrogenic effect upon the target organs and, therefore, should only be used adjunctively with more direct estimates of follicular development, i.e., serum estradiol and ultrasonography.

The clinical confirmation of ovulation, with the exception of pregnancy, is obtained by direct and indirect indices of progesterone production. The indices most generally used are as follows: a rise in basal body temperature, increase in serum progesterone and menstruation following the shift in basal body temperature.

When used in conjunction with indices of progesterone production, sonographic visualization of the ovaries will assist in determining if ovulation has occurred. Sonographic evidence of ovulation may include the following: fluid in the cul-de-sac, ovarian stigmata, collapsed follicle and secretory endometrium.

Because of the subjectivity of the various tests for the determination of follicular maturation and ovulation, it cannot be overemphasized that the physician should choose tests with which he/she is thoroughly familiar.

Drug Interactions: No clinically significant drug/drug or drug/food interactions have been reported during Fertinorm HP therapy.

Carcinogenesis and Mutagenesis: Carcinogenicity studies have not been performed. Fertinorm HP exhibited no mutagenic activity in a range of mutagenicity studies.

Pregnancy: Contraindicated in pregnancy.

Lactation: Fertinorm HP should not be administered during lactation.

Dependence Liability: There have been no reports of abuse or dependence with Fertinorm HP.

Adverse Effects: The following adverse reactions, reported during urofollitropin and menotropin therapy, are listed in decreasing order of potential severity: thromboembolic events (see Warnings), Ovarian Hyperstimulation Syndrome (see Warnings), mild to moderate ovarian enlargement, abdominal pain; sensitivity to Fertinorm HP (Febrile reactions which may be accompanied by chills, musculoskeletal aches, joint pains, malaise, headache and fatigue have occurred after the administration of urofollitropin/menotropin. It is not clear whether or not these were pyrogenic responses or possible allergic reactions); ovarian cysts; gastrointestinal symptoms (nausea, vomiting, diarrhea, abdominal cramps, bloating); pain, rash, swelling, and/or irritation at the site of the injection; breast tenderness; headache; dermatological symptoms (dry skin, body rash, hair loss, hives), and hemoperitoneum has been reported during menotropins therapy and, therefore, may also occur during Fertinorm HP therapy.

The following medical events have been reported subsequent to pregnancies resulting from urofollitropin therapy: Ectopic pregnancy, congenital malformations have been reported in pregnancies after the use of urofollitropin for ovulation induction or ovarian stimulation prior to IVF. The prevalence of these malformations does not exceed the prevalence in spontaneous pregnancies. Pregnancy loss is higher than that in the normal population, but comparable with the rates found in women with other fertility problems.

Ovarian cancer has been reported in a very small number of infertile women who have been treated with fertility drugs. A causal relationship between treatment with fertility drugs and ovarian cancer has not been established.

Overdosage: Symptoms and Treatment: Aside from possible OHSS and possible multiple gestations (see Warnings), little is known concerning the consequences of acute overdosage with Fertinorm HP.

Dosage: The dose to produce follicular maturation must be individualized. To minimize the hazard associated with the occasional abnormal ovarian enlargement which may occur with Fertinorm HP therapy, the lowest dose consistent with the expectation of good results should be used. An initial dose of 75 IU/day, administered s.c. or i.m. for 7 to 12 days, is generally recommended. In the absence of an endogenous LH surge, the ovulating dose of hCG (5 000 to 10 000 U) should be administered 1 day after the last day of Fertinorm HP therapy.

In the ovaries of patients with polycystic ovarian syndrome, follicles are found in all stages of development and atresia. The reaction of these ovaries to Fertinorm HP stimulation depends on the stage of development of the follicle at the time Fertinorm HP stimulation is begun. The duration of treatment to induce follicular maturation may vary. The importance of careful and prospective monitoring cannot be overemphasized.

The patient should be treated until indices of estrogenic activity, as indicated under Precautions, are equivalent to or greater than those of the normal individual. If the ovaries are abnormally enlarged or significant abdominal pain occurs, Fertinorm HP treatment should be discontinued, hCG should not be administered and the patient should be advised to refrain from intercourse until resolution of the cycle. This will reduce the chances of development of the Ovarian Hyperstimulation Syndrome.

If there is evidence of ovulation but not pregnancy, repeat this dosage regimen for at least 2 more courses before increasing the dose of Fertinorm HP to 150 IU/day for 7 to 12 days or longer. As before, this dose should be followed by 5 000 to 10 000 U of hCG on the day after the last dose of Fertinorm HP. If evidence of ovulation is present but pregnancy does not ensue, repeat the same dose for 2 or more courses. Doses larger than this are not routinely recommended.

During treatment with both Fertinorm HP and hCG and during the 2-week post-treatment period, patients should be examined at least every other day for signs of excessive ovarian stimulation (see Warnings). In most cases, OHSS occurs after treatment has been completed and reaches its maximum on the 7th to 10th day after hCG administration.

Patients should be followed for at least 2 weeks after hCG administration. The couple should be encouraged to have intercourse daily, beginning on the day prior to the administration of hCG until ovulation becomes apparent from the indices employed for the determination of progestational activity.

Preparation of Solution: Open the diluent ampul. Withdraw diluent (0.5 or 1.0 mL depending on dosage prescribed). Open Fertinorm HP ampul and inject syringe containing diluent into the ampul of powder. The powder will dissolve very quickly to form a clear solution. Do not shake the solution, as this may cause air bubbles.

Withdraw the Fertinorm HP solution from the ampul. Repeat procedure with other powder ampuls, until you have the prescribed number of powder ampuls dissolved in the solution. See Table I for further instructions.

To minimize the possibility of irritation, change to a new 1 mL needle before injection. Administer immediately by s.c. or i.m. injection.

Although the reconstituted Fertinorm HP has been shown to be stable for at least 24 hours, the solution should be used immediately after reconstitution and any unused material should be discarded after use.

Fertinorm HP (cont'd)

Parenteral drug products should be inspected visually for particulate matter and discoloration prior to administration. Do not use the reconstituted solution if it appears cloudy, lumpy or discolored.

Reconstitution: Up to 5 ampuls of Fertinorm HP (75 IU) or up to 2 ampuls of Fertinorm HP (150 IU) can be reconstituted in 1 mL of diluent (Sodium Chloride Injection, USP). A smaller volume of diluent can be used for the reconstitution of 1 or 2 ampuls of Fertinorm HP (75 IU). See Table I.

Table I—Fertinorm HP

Reconstitution Table

Ampul Size	Number of Ampuls	Diluent to be Added to Ampul	Approximate Available Volume	Approximate Concentration (IU/mL)
75 IU	1	0.5 mL	0.5 mL	150
	2	0.5 mL	0.5 mL	300
	3	1.0 mL	1.0 mL	225
	4	1.0 mL	1.0 mL	300
	5	1.0 mL	1.0 mL	375
150 IU	1	1 mL	1 mL	150
	2	1 mL	1 mL	300

See Preparation of Solution above for further instructions.

Stability and Storage of Parenteral Solutions: To minimize potential losses of FSH due to adsorption onto the syringe, Fertinorm HP should preferably be administered immediately after reconstitution. The degree of adsorption which may occur has been shown to have no significant effect on the dose required for clinical efficacy. Any unused solution should be discarded.

Parenteral drug products should be inspected visually for particulate matter and discoloration prior to administration. Do not use the reconstituted solution if it appears cloudy, lumpy or discolored.

Supplied: Each 3 mL ampul of sterile lyophilized powder contains: urofollitropin 75 or 150 IU and lactose 10 mg as excipient. Supplied with a 2 mL ampul of Sodium Chloride Injection, USP, for reconstitution. One IU of human urinary FSH is equivalent to the activity contained in 0.11388 mg of the First International Standard. Single dose ampuls of 3 mL, cartons of 1 and 10 with diluent. Lyophilized powder in unopened ampuls is stable up to the expiry date shown on the label. Store refrigerated or at room temperature (3 to 25°C). Protect from light.

FEXICAM ℞

Technilab

Piroxicam

Nonsteroidal Anti-inflammatory—Analgesic—Antipyretic

Pharmacology: Piroxicam is a nonsteroidal anti-inflammatory agent with analgesic and antipyretic properties. Its mechanism of action is incompletely known. Piroxicam inhibits the activity of prostaglandin synthetase. Its anti-inflammatory action may be partially explained by the resulting decrease in prostaglandin biosynthesis. Its therapeutic action is not due to pituitary-adrenal stimulation.

In rheumatoid arthritis the efficacy of piroxicam 20 mg daily has been found to be similar to 4.5 g daily of ASA.

Piroxicam is well absorbed following oral or rectal administration. After a single oral dose of 20 mg, peak plasma levels of piroxicam are achieved in about 4 hours. When the drug is administered daily, the plasma concentrations increase for 7 to 12 days during which a steady state is reached. Concentrations attained are not exceeded following further constant daily drug intake. The plasma half-life is approximately 50 hours in man. The extent and rate of absorption are not influenced by administration with food or antacids.

After a single rectal dose of 20 mg, the pharmacokinetics are similar to that obtained after oral administration except for peak plasma levels which are achieved at about 10 hours.

Piroxicam is extensively metabolized and less than 5% of the daily dose is excreted unchanged in urine and feces. The main metabolic pathway is hydroxylation of the pyridyl ring, followed by conjugation with glucuronic acid and urinary elimination. Approximately 5% of the dose is metabolized to and excreted as saccharin.

Over an observation period of 4 days, 20 healthy men taking piroxicam 20 mg daily in single or divided doses showed significantly less mean daily fecal blood loss than did 10 healthy male controls taking 3.9 g of ASA daily.

The effects of age and sex on the pharmacokinetics of piroxicam have been examined in 3 single-dose, 3 multiple-dose, and five therapeutic drug-monitoring studies. Although not consistent across all studies, some indicated a tendency towards a modest decrease in total body clearances and an increase in elimination half-life and steady-state plasma concentrations in the elderly, particularly elderly females. Irrespective of age, some patients had plasma concentration levels that were substantially greater than the mean.

Indications: For the symptomatic treatment of rheumatoid arthritis, osteoarthritis (degenerative joint disease) and ankylosing spondylitis and primary dysmenorrhea.

Contraindications: Active peptic ulcer, a history of recurrent ulceration or active inflammatory disease of the gastrointestinal system.

Known or suspected hypersensitivity to the drug or other nonsteroidal anti-inflammatory drugs. The potential for cross-reactivity between different NSAIDs must be kept in mind.

Piroxicam should not be used in patients with the complete or partial syndrome of nasal polyps, or in whom asthma, anaphylaxis, urticaria, rhinitis or other allergic manifestations are precipitated by ASA or other nonsteroidal anti-inflammatory agents. Fatal anaphylactoid reactions have occurred in such individuals. As well, individuals with the above medical problems are at risk of a severe reaction even if they have taken NSAIDs in the past without any adverse effects.

Significant hepatic impairment or active liver disease.

Severely impaired or deteriorating renal function (creatinine clearance <30 mL/min). Individuals with lesser degrees of renal impairment are at risk of deterioration of their renal function when prescribed NSAIDs and must be monitored.

Piroxicam is not recommended for use with other NSAIDs because of the absence of any evidence demonstrating synergistic benefits and the potential for additive side effects.

Piroxicam suppositories should not be used in patients with any inflammatory lesions of the rectum or anus, or in patients with a recent history of rectal or anal bleeding.

Warnings: Gastrointestinal: Serious gastrointestinal toxicity, such as peptic ulceration, perforation and gastrointestinal bleeding, **sometimes severe and occasionally fatal** can occur at any time, with or without symptoms in patients treated with nonsteroidal anti-inflammatory drugs (NSAIDs) including piroxicam.

Minor upper gastrointestinal problems, such as dyspepsia, are common, usually developing early in therapy. Physicians should remain alert for ulceration and bleeding in patients treated with nonsteroidal anti-inflammatory drugs, even in the absence of previous gastrointestinal tract symptoms.

In patients observed in clinical trials of such agents, symptomatic upper gastrointestinal ulcers, gross bleeding, or perforation appear to occur in approximately 1% of patients treated for 3 to 6 months and in about 2 to 4% of patients treated for 1 year. The risk continues beyond 1 year and possibly increases.

The incidence of these complications increases with increasing dose.

Piroxicam should be given under close medical supervision to patients prone to gastrointestinal tract irritation, particularly those with a history of peptic ulcer, diverticulosis or other inflammatory disease of the gastrointestinal tract such as ulcerative colitis and Crohn's disease. In these cases, the physician must weigh the benefits of treatment against the possible hazards.

Physicians should inform patients about the signs and/or symptoms of serious gastrointestinal toxicity and instruct them to contact a physician immediately if they experience persistent dyspepsia or other symptoms or signs suggestive of gastrointestinal ulceration or bleeding.

Because serious gastrointestinal tract ulceration and bleeding can occur without warning symptoms, physicians should follow chronically treated patients by checking their hemoglobin periodically and by being vigilant for the signs and symptoms of ulceration and bleeding and should inform the patients of the importance of this follow-up.

If ulceration is suspected or confirmed, or if gastrointestinal bleeding occurs, piroxicam should be discontinued immediately, appropriate treatment instituted and the patient monitored closely.

No studies, to date, have identified any group of patients **not** at risk of developing ulceration and bleeding. A prior history of serious gastrointestinal events and other factors such as excess alcohol intake, smoking, age, female gender and concomitant oral steroid and anticoagulant use have been associated with increased risk.

Studies to date show that all NSAIDs can cause gastrointestinal tract adverse events. Although existing data does not clearly identify differences in risk between various NSAIDs, this may be shown in the future.

Geriatrics: Patients older than 65 years and frail or debilitated patients are most susceptible to a variety of adverse reactions from nonsteroidal anti-inflammatory drugs: the incidence of these adverse reactions increases with dose and duration of treatment. In addition, these patients are less tolerant to ulceration and bleeding. Most reports of fatal gastrointestinal events are in this population. Older patients are also at risk of lower esophageal ulceration and bleeding.

For such patients, consideration should be given to a starting dose lower than the one usually recommended, with individual adjustment when necessary and under close supervision. See Precautions for further advice.

Cross-sensitivity: Patients sensitive to any one of the nonsteroidal anti-inflammatory drugs may also be sensitive to any of the other NSAIDs.

Aseptic Meningitis: In occasional cases, with some NSAIDs, the symptoms of aseptic meningitis (stiff neck, severe headaches, nausea and vomiting, fever or clouding of consciousness) have been observed. Patients with autoimmune disorders (systemic lupus erythematosus, mixed connective tissues diseases, etc.) seem to be predisposed. Therefore, in such patients, the physician must be vigilant to the development of this complication.

Pregnancy, Labor and *Lactation:* The use of piroxicam during pregnancy or lactation is not recommended as its safety in these conditions has not been established. The presence of piroxicam in breast milk has been determined during initial and long-term dosing conditions (52 days). Piroxicam appeared in breast milk at about 1 to 3% of the maternal plasma concentration. No accumulation of piroxicam occurred in milk relative to that in plasma during treatment.

No teratogenic effects have been observed in animal reproductive studies. Rats and rabbits receiving piroxicam during pregnancy have shown an increased frequency of dystocia and delayed parturition. Rats have exhibited suppression of lactation.

Children: The administration of piroxicam is not recommended in children under 16 years of age as the dose and indications have not been established.

Doses of piroxicam greater than 20 mg daily should not be used. The minimum maintenance dose needed to control symptoms is recommended.

Precautions: Gastrointestinal: There is no definitive evidence that the concomitant administration of histamine H_2-receptor antagonists and/or antacids will either prevent the occurrence of gastrointestinal side effects or allow the continuation of piroxicam therapy when and if these adverse reactions appear.

Renal Function: Long-term administration of nonsteroidal anti-inflammatory drugs to animals has resulted in renal papillary necrosis and other abnormal renal pathology. In humans, there have been reports of acute interstitial nephritis with hematuria, proteinuria and occasionally nephrotic syndrome.

A second form of renal toxicity has been seen in patients with prerenal conditions leading to the reduction in renal blood flow or blood volume, where the renal prostaglandins have a supportive role in the maintenance of renal perfusion. In these patients, administration of a nonsteroidal anti-inflammatory drug may cause a dose-dependent reduction in prostaglandin formation and may precipitate overt renal decompensation. Patients at greatest risk of this reaction are those with impaired renal function, heart failure, liver dysfunction, those taking diuretics, and the elderly. Discontinuation of nonsteroidal anti-inflammatory therapy is usually followed by recovery to the pretreatment state.

Piroxicam and its metabolites are eliminated primarily by the kidneys; therefore, the drug should be used with great caution in patients with impaired renal function. In these cases, utilization of lower doses of piroxicam should be considered and patients carefully monitored.

During long-term therapy, kidney function should be monitored periodically.

Acute renal failure and hyperkalemia as well as reversible elevations of BUN and serum creatinine have been reported with piroxicam. The effect is thought to result from inhibition of renal prostaglandin synthesis resulting in a change in medullary and deep cortical blood flow with an attendant effect on renal function. Patients with impaired renal function or on diuretics, as well as elderly patients and those with congestive heart failure or liver cirrhosis with ascites, are more at risk.

Genitourinary: Some NSAIDs are known to cause persistent urinary symptoms (bladder pain, dysuria, urinary frequency), hematuria or cystitis. The onset of these symptoms may occur at any time after the initiation of therapy with an NSAID. Some cases have become severe on continued treatment. Should urinary symptoms occur, treatment with piroxicam **must be stopped immediately** to obtain recovery. This should be done before any urological investigations or treatments are carried out.

Hepatic Function: As with other nonsteroidal anti-inflammatory drugs, borderline elevations of one or more liver function tests may occur in up to 15% of patients. The ALT test is probably the most sensitive indication of liver dysfunction. Meaningful (3 times the upper limit of normal) elevations of ALT or AST occurred in controlled clinical trials in less than 1% of patients. These abnormalities may progress, may remain essentially unchanged, or may be transient with continued therapy. A patient with symptoms and/or signs suggesting liver dysfunction, or in whom an abnormal liver test has occurred, should be evaluated for evidence of the development of more severe hepatic reaction while on therapy with this drug. Severe hepatic reactions including jaundice and cases of fatal hepatitis have been reported with NSAIDs.

Although such reactions are rare, if abnormal liver tests persist or worsen, if clinical signs and symptoms consistent with liver disease develop, or if systemic manifestations occur (e.g., eosinophilia, rash, etc.), this drug should be discontinued.

During long-term therapy, liver function tests should be monitored periodically. If there is a need to prescribe this drug in the presence of impaired liver function, it must be done under strict observation.

Fluid and Electrolyte Balance: Fluid retention and edema have been observed in patients treated with piroxicam. Therefore, as with many other nonsteroidal anti-inflammatory drugs, the possibility of precipitating congestive heart failure in elderly patients or those with compromised cardiac function should be borne in mind. Piroxicam should be used with caution in patients with heart failure, hypertension or other conditions predisposing to fluid retention.

With nonsteroidal anti-inflammatory treatment there is a potential risk of hyperkalemia, particularly in patients with conditions such as diabetes mellitus or renal failure; elderly patients; or in patients receiving concomitant therapy with β-adrenergic blockers, angiotensin-converting enzyme inhibitors or some diuretics. Serum electrolytes should be monitored periodically during long-term therapy, especially in those patients who are at risk.

Hematology: Drugs inhibiting prostaglandin biosynthesis do interfere with platelet function to varying degrees; therefore, patients who may be adversely affected by such an action should be carefully observed when piroxicam is administered.

Blood dyscrasias (such as neutropenia, leukopenia, thrombocytopenia, aplastic anemia and agranulocytosis) associated with the use of nonsteroidal anti-inflammatory drugs are rare, but could occur with severe consequences.

At the recommended dose of 20 mg/day of piroxicam, increased fecal blood loss due to gastrointestinal irritation did not occur, but in about 4% of the patients treated with piroxicam alone or concomitantly with ASA, reductions in hemoglobin and hematocrit values were observed. Therefore, these values should be determined periodically.

Infection: In common with other anti-inflammatory drugs, piroxicam may mask the usual signs of infection.

Ophthalmology: Blurred and/or diminished vision has been reported with the use of piroxicam and other nonsteroidal anti-inflammatory drugs. If such symptoms develop, this drug should be discontinued and an ophthalmologic examination performed; ophthalmic examination should be performed at periodic intervals in any patient receiving this drug for an extended period of time.

CNS: Some patients may experience drowsiness, dizziness, vertigo, insomnia or depression with the use of piroxicam. If patients experience these side effects, they should exercise caution in carrying out activities that require alertness.

Hypersensitivity Reactions: A combination of dermatological and/or allergic signs and symptoms suggestive of serum sickness have occasionally occurred in conjunction with the use of piroxicam. These include arthralgia, pruritus, fever, fatigue and rash including vesiculo bullous reactions and exfoliative dermatitis.

<u>*Drug Interactions:*</u> ASA or other NSAIDs: The use of piroxicam in addition to any other NSAID, including those over-the-counter drugs (such as ASA and ibuprofen), is not recommended due to the possibility of additive side effects.

Plasma concentrations of piroxicam are reduced to approximately 80% of their normal concentrations when piroxicam is administered in conjunction with ASA (3 900 mg/day).

The use of piroxicam in conjunction with ASA or another nonsteroidal anti-inflammatory agent is not recommended since data are not available demonstrating that the combination produces greater improvement than that achieved with either drug alone and the potential for adverse reactions is increased.

Digoxin or Digitoxin: Concurrent therapy with piroxicam and digoxin and/or piroxicam and digitoxin did not affect the plasma levels of either drug.

Anticoagulants: Numerous studies have shown that the concomitant use of NSAIDs and anticoagulants increases the risk of gastrointestinal adverse events such as ulceration and bleeding.

Because prostaglandins play an important role in hemostasis, and NSAIDs affect platelet function, concurrent therapy of piroxicam with warfarin requires close monitoring to be certain that no change in anticoagulant dosage is necessary.

Piroxicam is highly protein bound and, therefore, might be expected to displace other protein-bound drugs. The physician should closely monitor dosage requirements of coumarin anticoagulants and other drugs that are highly protein-bound when these are administered concomitantly with piroxicam.

Diuretics: As with other nonsteroidal anti-inflammatory drugs, piroxicam may cause sodium and fluid retention and may interfere with the natriuretic action of diuretic agents. These properties should be kept in mind when treating patients with compromised cardiac function or hypertension since they may be responsible for a worsening of those conditions.

Antihypertensives: As with other nonsteroidal anti-inflammatory drugs, concomitant administration of piroxicam with propranolol can reduce the hypotensive effect. Patients should be monitored for altered antihypertensive or antianginal response to beta-blockers when piroxicam is initiated or discontinued.

Glucocorticoids: Numerous studies have shown that the concomitant use of NSAIDs and oral glucocorticoids increases the risk of gastrointestinal side effects such as ulceration and bleeding. This is especially the case in older (>65 years of age) individuals.

Antacids: Concomitant administration of antacids had no effect on piroxicam plasma levels.

Methotrexate: Although to date there have been no reports of an interaction with piroxicam, isolated cases indicate that the concomitant use of some NSAIDs in patients receiving methotrexate may be associated with severe or sometimes fatal methotrexate toxicity.

Until more information is available on this interaction, caution should be used if piroxicam, as well as other NSAIDs, are administered concomitantly with methotrexate, particularly in patients with pre-existing renal impairment, who may be more susceptible.

Lithium: As with other nonsteroidal anti-inflammatory drugs, piroxicam has been reported to increase steady-state plasma lithium concentrations. It is recommended that these concentrations are monitored when initiating, adjusting and discontinuing piroxicam treatment.

Other Drug Interactions: Cimetidine: Results of 2 separate studies indicate a slight increase in absorption of piroxicam following cimetidine administration but no significant changes in elimination parameters. Cimetidine increases the area under the curve (AUC 0 to 120 hours) and C_{max} of piroxicam by approximately 13 to 15%. Elimination rate constants and half-life show no significant differences. The clinical significance of this small but significant increase in absorption is yet unknown.

Cholestyramine: Preliminary study indicates that in healthy subjects co-administration of cholestyramine to piroxicam results in enhanced elimination of piroxicam (i.e., reduction in half-life by 40% and increase in clearance by 52%). Although the magnitude of these changes in piroxicam disposition appears sufficient to inhibit its therapeutic effects, studies in patients are needed to confirm this. It is suggested that the doses of piroxicam and cholestyramine be separated as much as possible, and that the patients be monitored for inadequate response to piroxicam therapy. If an inadequate anti inflammatory response appears to be related to the concomitant use of cholestyramine, consideration should be given to the use of alternative hypolipidemic therapy.

Adverse Effects: The most common adverse reactions encountered with nonsteroidal anti-inflammatory drugs are gastrointestinal, of which peptic ulcer, with or without bleeding, is the most severe. Fatalities have occurred, particularly in the elderly.

In approximately 2 300 patients receiving a daily dose of 20 mg or less of piroxicam in clinical trials, the most frequent side effects observed have been gastrointestinal (approximately 20% of the patients). Of the patients experiencing gastrointestinal side effects, approximately 5% discontinued therapy with an overall incidence of peptic ulceration of about 1% and gastrointestinal bleeding of approximately 0.1%. The incidence of adverse reactions is summarized below.

Gastrointestinal (17.4%): epigastric distress (6.4%), nausea (4.1%), constipation (2.4%), abdominal discomfort (2.2%), flatulence (2.1%), diarrhea (1.8%), abdominal pain (1.5%), indigestion (1.3%), anorexia (1.2%), peptic ulceration (about 1%), stomatitis, vomiting, hematemesis, melena, perforation, dry mouth, pancreatitis, each in less than 1% of patients.

Anorectal reaction presenting as local pain, burning, pruritus, tenesmus and rare instances of rectal bleeding have been reported in 2.9% of patients with the use of piroxicam suppositories.

Allergic (<1%): anaphylaxis, bronchospasm, urticaria/angioedema, vasculitis, serum sickness (see Precautions), each in less than 1% of patients.

CNS (5%): headache (1.8%), malaise (1%); dizziness, drowsiness/sedation (somnolence), vertigo, depression, hallucinations, insomnia, nervousness, paresthesia, personality change, dream abnormalities, mental confusion, each in less than 1% of patients.

Dermatologic (2%): rash (2%); pruritus, erythema, bruising, desquamation, exfoliative dermatitis, erythema multiforme, toxic epidermal necrolysis (Lyell's disease), vesiculo bullous reaction, onycholysis, Stevens-Johnson syndrome, photoallergic skin reactions, each in less than 1% of patients.

Cardiovascular (<1%): hypertension, palpitations, worsening of congestive heart failure (see Precautions), exacerbation of angina, each in less than 1% of patients.

Special Senses: Eyes, ears, nose and throat reactions (<1%); tinnitus (about 1%); blurred vision, eye irritation/swelling, each in less than 1% of patients.

Hematologic (15%): decreases in hemoglobin (4.6%) and hematocrit (4.2%) (see Precautions), thrombocytopenia (2.4%), eosinophilia (1.8%), leukocytosis (1.7%), basophilia (1.7%), leukopenia (1.4%); petechial rash, ecchymosis, bone marrow depression including aplastic anemia, epistaxis, each in less than 1% of patients.

Renal (1%): edema (1.6%) (see Precautions); dysuria, hematuria, proteinuria, interstitial nephritis, renal failure, hyperkalemia, glomerulitis, nephrotic syndrome (see Precautions), each in less than 1% of patients.

Hepatic (<1%): jaundice, hepatitis (see Precautions), each in less than 1% of patients.

Respiratory (<1%): dyspnea.

Metabolic (<1%): hypoglycemia, hyperglycemia, weight increase/decrease, each in less than 1% of patients.

Miscellaneous (<1%): sweating, pain (colic), fever, flu-like syndrome (see Precautions), weakness, each in less than 1% of patients.

Tabulated Adverse Reactions: See Table I (on following page).

Primary Dysmenorrhea: In primary dysmenorrhea the side effect profile of piroxicam is similar in nature to that observed in rheumatic diseases.

Laboratory Parameters: Changes in laboratory parameters observed during piroxicam therapy have included an elevation of BUN, creatinine (see Precautions), uric acid and liver enzymes LDH, ALT, AST and alkaline phosphatase.

Other: Since market introduction, isolated reports have included delayed wound healing, thrombophlebitis, pemphigus, alopecia, mastodynia, reduction or loss of libido, impotence, urinary frequency, oliguria, menorrhagia, amnesia, anxiety, tremor, hearing impairment, deafness, thirst, chills,

Fexicam (cont'd)

Table I—Fexicam

Tabulated Adverse Reactions

Frequency >1%	**Frequency <1%**
Gastrointestinal Epigastric distress (6.4%), nausea (4.1%), constipation (2.4%), abdominal discomfort (2.2%), flatulence (2.1%), diarrhea (1.8%), abdominal pain (1.5%), indigestion (1.3%), anorexia (1.2%), peptic ulceration (about 1%) and local pain, burning, pruritus, tenesmus and bleeding of the rectum/anus (2.9%).	Stomatitis, vomiting, hematemesis, melena, perforation, dry mouth, pancreatitis.
Allergic	Anaphylaxis, bronchospasm, urticaria/angioedema, serum sickness.
CNS Headache (1.8%), malaise (1%).	Dizziness, drowsiness/sedation (somnolence), vertigo, depression, hallucinations, insomnia, nervousness, parasthesia, personality change, dream abnormalities, mental confusion.
Dermatologic Rash (2%).	Pruritus, erythema, bruising, desquamation, exfoliative dermatitis, erythema multiforme, toxic epidermal necrolysis (Lyell's Disease), vesiculo bullous reaction, onycholysis, Stevens-Johnson syndrome, photoallergic skin reactions.
Cardiovascular	hypertension, palpitations, worsening of congestive heart failure, exacerbation of angina.
Special Senses Tinnitus (about 1%).	Eyes, ears, nose and throat reactions, blurred vision, eye irritation/swelling.
Hematologic Decreases in hemoglobin (4.6%), hematocrit (4.2%), thrombocytopenia (2.4%), eosinophilia (1.8%), leukocytosis (1.7%), basophilia (1.7%), leukopenia (1.4%).	Petechial rash, ecchymosis, bone marrow depression including aplastic anemia, epistaxis.
Renal Edema (1.6%).	Dysuria, hematuria, proteinuria, interstitial nephritis, renal failure, hyperkalemia, glomerulitis, nephrotic syndrome.
Hepatic	Jaundice, hepatitis.
Respiratory	Dyspnea.
Metabolic	Hypoglycemia, hyperglycemia, weight increase/decrease.
Miscellaneous	Sweating, pain (colic), fever, flu-like syndrome, weakness.

increased appetite, akathisia, tachycardia, flushing, tooth discoloration, glossitis, chest pain, anemia, hemolytic anemia, pancreatitis and positive antinuclear factor (ANA); a causal relationship has not been established for those rarely reported events.

Overdose: Symptoms and Treatment: In the event that treatment for overdosage is required, the long plasma half-life (see Pharmacology) of piroxicam should be considered. The absence of experience with acute overdosage precludes characterization of sequelae and recommendation of specific antidotal efficacy at this time. It is reasonable to assume, however, that the standard measures of gastric evacuation and general supportive therapy would apply. In addition to supportive measures, the use of activated charcoal may effectively reduce the absorption and reabsorption of piroxicam. Experiments in dogs have demonstrated that the use of multiple-dose treatments with activated charcoal could reduce the half-life of piroxicam elimination from 27 hours (without charcoal) to 11 hours and reduce the systemic bioavailability of piroxicam by as much as 37% when activated charcoal is given as late as 6 hours after administration of piroxicam.

Dosage: Adults: Oral: In rheumatoid arthritis and ankylosing spondylitis it is recommended that therapy with piroxicam capsules be initiated as a single daily dose of 20 mg. If desired, this dose may be given as 10 mg b.i.d. Most patients will be maintained on 20 mg daily. A relatively small number of patients may be maintained on 10 mg daily.

In osteoarthritis the recommended starting dosage of piroxicam is 20 mg once daily. If desired, this dose may be given as 10 mg b.i.d. The usual maintenance dose is 10 to 20 mg daily.

Piroxicam should not be given in doses greater than 20 mg daily owing to an increased incidence of gastrointestinal side effects.

Geriatrics: As elderly patients appear to be at higher risk from a variety of adverse reactions from nonsteroidal anti-inflammatory drugs and as elderly, frail or debilitated patients tolerate gastrointestinal side effects less well, consideration should be given to a starting dose that is lower than usual and to an increase of the dose only if symptoms remain uncontrolled. Such patients must be very carefully supervised.

In primary dysmenorrhea the treatment is initiated at the earliest onset of symptoms with a recommended starting dose of 40 mg given as a single daily dose on the first day. For the remainder of the treatment period (usually 2 to 4 days), the dose should be reduced to 20 mg daily.

Rectal: For each indication, the dosage of Fexicam suppositories, when used alone, is identical with the dosage of piroxicam capsules.

Fexicam suppositories offer an alternative route of administration for those physicians who may wish to prescribe them in certain patients, or for those patients who prefer them.

Use whole suppositories. Do not split or use portions of suppositories.

Combined Administration: The total daily dose of piroxicam administered as capsule and/or suppositories should not exceed 20 mg/day.

Fexicam is available only as a 20 mg suppository.

Information for the Patient: See Blue Section—Information for the Patient "Fexicam".

Supplied: Each white to yellowish, smooth torpedo-shaped suppository contains: piroxicam USP 20 mg. Nonmedicinal ingredients: semisynthetic glycerides. Boxes of 30. Store between 15 and 30°C.

New Product 1998

FIORINAL® ◈
Novartis Pharmaceuticals

ASA—Caffeine—Butalbital
Analgesic—Sedative

Indications: For tension (or muscle contraction) headache and conditions where a simultaneous sedative and analgesic action is required, such as mixed migraine headaches, menstrual and postpartum tension and pain.

Contraindications, Precautions and Adverse Effects: See Fiorinal-C monograph.

A possible association between Reye's syndrome and the use of salicylates has been suggested but not established. Reye's syndrome has also occurred in many patients not exposed to salicylates. However, caution is advised when prescribing salicylate-containing medications for children, teenagers and young adults with influenza or chickenpox.

Note: Fiorinal products have the potential for being abused and should be avoided in chronic pain states leading to continuous daily use.

Overdose: Symptoms and Treatment: See Fiorinal-C monograph.

Dosage: Adults: 2 tablets or capsules at once, followed if necessary, by 1 tablet or capsule every 3 to 4 hours; up to 6 capsules or tablets daily, or as prescribed.

Children: 1 to 3 tablets or capsules a day, according to age.

Supplied: Capsules: Each hard gelatin, oblong capsule, purple opaque with blue opaque cap, printed with FIORINAL and △ in white ink contains: butalbital, USP 50 mg, caffeine, USP 40 mg and ASA, USP 330 mg. Nonmedicinal ingredients: cornstarch, microcrystalline cellulose, stearic acid and talc. Bottles of 100 and 500.

Tablets: Each white compressed tablet embossed FIORINAL on one side and △ on the other contains: butalbital, USP 50 mg, caffeine, USP 40 mg, ASA, USP 330 mg. Nonmedicinal ingredients: cornstarch, microcrystalline cellulose, silicon dioxide, sodium lauryl sulfate and stearic acid. Bottles of 100 and 500.

(Shown in Product Recognition Section)

FIORINAL®-C ¼, ½ Ⓝ
Novartis Pharmaceuticals

ASA—Caffeine—Codeine—Butalbital
Analgesic—Sedative

Indications: The relief of acute and chronic pain of mild, moderate, or severe degree, which is accompanied by tension or anxiety and in all indications where a simultaneous sedative and analgesic action is required, such as: tension headache, musculoskeletal pain, including low back pain, postoperative, post partum pain, dysmenorrhea, pain associated with dental procedures, neoplastic disease or trauma.

Contraindications: Porphyria, gastrointestinal ulceration and hypersensitivity to any of the components. Overdosage of, or intoxication due to alcohol, hypnotics, analgesics and psychotropic drugs.

Precautions: Because of its ASA content, Fiorinal-C should be used with caution in patients with a history of bleeding tendencies or peptic ulceration.

A possible association between Reye's syndrome and the use of salicylates has been suggested but not established. Reye's syndrome has also occurred in many patients not exposed to salicylates. However, caution is advised when prescribing salicylate-containing medications for children, teenagers and young adults with influenza or chickenpox.

Long-term use of preparations containing barbiturates and/or codeine may lead to habituation and physical dependence. Fiorinal-C, because of its codeine and butalbital content, should be avoided in patients with head injury, in whom a depressed CNS is suspected. Similarly, it should not be used in patients with actual or a predisposition towards respiratory depression.

Occupational Hazards: Barbiturate containing preparations may impair the mental and/or physical alertness required for the efficient performance of hazardous tasks such as driving a vehicle or operating machinery.

Should be used with caution in patients with impaired liver and renal functions or in osteomalacia and osteoporosis.

Pregnancy and *Lactation:* During pregnancy and lactation, Fiorinal-C should be taken only as prescribed.

Drug Interactions: The concomitant use of alcohol or other CNS depressants may have and additive effect, and patients should be warned accordingly.

The prolonged ingestion of barbiturates gives rise to enzyme induction. This increases the rate of metabolism of certain drugs, including oral anticoagulants and oral contraceptives, thus reducing their effectiveness.

Note: Fiorinal products have the potential for being abused and should be avoided in chronic pain states leading to continuous daily use.

Adverse Effects: Drowsiness, dizziness, nausea, vomiting, constipation, skin rash and miosis are possible adverse effects.

Overdose: Symptoms: 1) Acute barbiturate poisoning: drowsiness, confusion and coma, with reduced or absent reflexes; prominent, persistent respiratory depression; hypotension, followed by circulatory collapse and a typical shock like state in severe intoxication; respiratory complications, renal failure, and, possibly, death. 2) Acute ASA poisoning: principal toxic effects include hypercapnia; acid-base disturbances with the development of metabolic acidosis, especially in children; and gastrointestinal irritation with vomiting and abdominal pain. Also, acetone odor in breath, tinnitus, sweating, hyperthermia, dehydration, hypoprothrombinemia with spontaneous bleeding, restlessness, delirium, convulsions and coma may occur. 3) Acute caffeine poisoning: insomnia, restlessness, tinnitus and flashes of light; tachycardia and extrasystoles; tremor, delirium and coma, following high doses in the region of 10 g. Death has not been reported with caffeine overdosage. 4) Acute codeine poisoning: symptoms will be more pronounced with the capsules containing the higher doses. These include the triad of: pinpoint pupils, marked depression of respiration, and loss of consciousness.

Note: Because large doses of barbiturate alone may cause marked respiratory and CNS depression, an even more profound depressant effect may be expected after an overdosage of Fiorinal-C.

The dangers of Fiorinal-C overdosage are increased when the drug is ingested in the presence of alcohol, phenothiazines, minor tranquilizers and/or narcotics.

Treatment: The management of acute Fiorinal-C overdosage may involve the treatment of the toxic effects of all its constituents, with the possible exception of caffeine, which is toxic in very high doses only. Generally, it is the management of the barbiturate intoxication, the correction of the acid-base imbalance due to salicylism, and the reversal of the effects of codeine which demand most attention. The therapeutic procedures most commonly employed are:

Elimination of the offending drug: 1) Emesis: If the patient is conscious, induce vomiting with syrup of ipecac (15 to 30 mL). 2) Perform gastric lavage followed by the administration of activated charcoal if the pharyngeal and laryngeal reflexes are present and if less than 4 hours have elapsed since ingestion. Do not attempt gastric lavage on the unconscious patient unless cuffed endotracheal intubation has been performed to prevent aspiration and pulmonary complications. 3) Catharsis: Following gastric lavage, a saline cathartic (sodium or magnesium sulfate 30 g in 250 mL of water) may be introduced and left in the stomach. 4) Encourage diuresis by administration of i.v. fluids assisted, if necessary, by 100 to 150 mL 25% mannitol solution given slowly i.v. Note: Mannitol should not be mixed with blood in a transfusion set, as red cell crenation and agglutination may occur. 5) Alkalinization of the urine (see caution): I.V. isotonic sodium bicarbonate solution accelerates urinary excretion of barbiturates. Maximum alkalinization may be more successfully attained if the sodium bicarbonate infusion is accompanied by acetazolamide 250 mg given as a single i.v. injection every 6 hours. (Caution: Perform urinary alkalinization with care in children.) 6) Peritoneal dialysis and hemodialysis have been used with success in acute barbiturate intoxication and may be life saving. However, before embarking on either method, weigh the risks inherent to these procedures against the risk of not using them at all.

Maintenance of adequate pulmonary ventilation: Respiratory depression is an early and often profound manifestation of acute barbiturate poisoning. Meticulous attention to this aspect of treatment is essential. Perform pharyngeal and tracheal suction diligently to remove excess mucous secretions. Judicious administration of oxygen is also indicated. However, oxygen without assisted respiration must be used with caution, as its use in hypoventilation hypoxia may result in further respiratory depression and hypercapnia. In more critical cases, endotracheal intubation or tracheotomy, with or without assisted respiration, may be necessary.

Correction of hypotension: Vigorous treatment is essential, as circulatory collapse and renal failure are frequent causes of death. 1) Mild cases: The usual head down position and other supportive measures may be adequate. 2) Severe cases: Vasopressors (dopamine, levarterenol) may be given i.v. with the usual precautions and serial blood pressure monitoring.

Narcotic antagonism: naloxone injection may reverse the respiratory depression caused by codeine and should be used until respiration improves.

Note: Respiratory depression caused by barbiturates will **not** respond to narcotic antagonists. Unwitting overdosage with narcotic antagonists may occur in an attempt to reverse respiratory depression caused by mixed barbiturate-codeine intoxication.

Special features due to salicylate overdosage: 1) The prominent features of salicylate intoxication are metabolic acidosis and electrolyte disturbance, and these require evaluation and correction. Sodium bicarbonate 400 mg (5 mEq)/kg as a 1% solution in 5% dextrose water is not only effective in correcting acidosis, but effectively and rapidly accelerates salicylate excretion by the kidneys. The administration of sodium bicarbonate must be carefully monitored with frequent blood pH and plasma CO_2 content determinations, as large amounts of sodium bicarbonate may result in severe alkalosis, particularly in children. THAM, an osmotic alkalinizing diuretic, also greatly increases the excretion of salicylate. This is given as a 0.3 molar solution at a rate not exceeding 5 mL/kg/hour. Potassium deficiency may occur and should be corrected. 2) Treat hyperthermia and dehydration with ice packs and i.v. fluids. 3) Treat hypoprothrombinemia with vitamin K_1 50 mg given daily i.v. 4) Hemodialysis, peritoneal dialysis or exchange transfusion are indicated in very severe salicylate intoxication. However, in Fiorinal-C overdosage, these measures are indicated mainly for barbiturate intoxication but would be effective for both.

General supportive measures: 1) Good nursing care is of prime importance, particularly in the comatose patient, and should include regular observation and accurate recording of the vital signs and depth of coma, maintenance of a free airway, frequent turning, and other routine measures usually adopted with unconscious patients. 2) Careful supervision and recording of fluid intake and output is essential. 3) Take blood samples to determine barbiturate blood concentrations and for electrolyte and other pertinent blood studies.

Dosage: Adults: 1 or 2 capsules at once, followed if necessary, by 1 capsule every 3 to 4 hours, up to 6 capsules daily, or as prescribed.

Supplied: Fiorinal-C ¼ Capsules: Each hard gelatin oblong capsule, white opaque body with blue opaque cap, printed with FIORINAL C 1/4 and [logo] in black ink contains: butalbital, USP 50 mg, caffeine, USP 40 mg, ASA, USP 330 mg, codeine phosphate, USP 15 mg. Nonmedicinal ingredients: cornstarch, microcrystalline cellulose, stearic acid and talc. Bottles of 100 and 500.

Fiorinal-C ½ Capsules: Each hard gelatin oblong capsule, light blue opaque with blue opaque cap, printed with FIORINAL C 1/2 and [logo] in black ink contains: butalbital, USP 50 mg, caffeine, USP 40 mg, ASA, USP 330 mg and codeine phosphate, USP 30 mg. Nonmedicinal ingredients: cornstarch, microcrystalline cellulose, stearic acid and talc. Bottles of 100 and 500.

(Shown in Product Recognition Section)

FLAGYL® Ⓟ
Rhône-Poulenc Rorer
Metronidazole
Antibacterial—Antiprotozoal

Pharmacology: Metronidazole is bactericidal against anaerobic bacteria, it exerts trichomonacidal activity and is also active against Giardia lamblia and Entamoeba histolytica. Its exact mechanism of action has not been entirely determined as yet. It has been proposed that an intermediate in the reduction of metronidazole, produced only in anaerobic bacteria and protozoa is bound to deoxyribonucleic acid and electron-transport proteins, inhibits subsequent nucleic acid synthesis.

Following oral administration, metronidazole is completely absorbed with plasma concentration usually reaching a peak within 1 to 2 hours. After single oral 500 mg doses, peak plasma levels of approximately 13 mg/L were obtained. On a regimen of 500 mg t.i.d. administered by the i.v. route, a steady state was achieved after approximately 3 days. The mean peak and trough concentrations measured at that time were 26 and 12 mg/L respectively, and the elimination half-life was approximately 7 to 8 hours. Comparison of the pharmacokinetics of oral and i.v. metronidazole revealed that the area under the plasma metronidazole concentration against time curves were essentially identical.

The major route of elimination of metronidazole and its metabolites is via the urine (60 to 80% of the dose) with fecal excretion accounting for 6 to 15% of the dose. The metabolites that appear in the urine result primarily from side chain oxidation (i.e. 1-(β-hydroxyethyl)- 2-hydroxymethyl 5-nitroimidazole and 2-methyl-5-nitroimidazole-1-yl-acetic acid) and glucuronide conjugation, with unchanged metronidazole accounting for approximately 20% of the total.

Metronidazole is the major component appearing in the plasma with lesser quantities of the 2-hydroxymethyl metabolite also being present. The ratio of these components varies with time but the maximum concentration of the metabolite (C_{max}) is approximately 20% of the C_{max} of metronidazole for the oral route of administration.

Less than 20% of the circulating metronidazole is bound to plasma proteins.

Decreased renal function does not appear to alter the single dose pharmacokinetics of metronidazole although the elimination half-life of the metabolites is prolonged.

During hemodialysis, the hydroxy metabolite is removed from the plasma about 3 times more rapidly than in normal subjects. Therefore, no accumulation should occur in anuric patients undergoing regular dialysis.

In patients with impaired liver function, the plasma clearance of metronidazole is decreased and accumulation can therefore result.

Indications: Bacterial Infections: I.V. metronidazole is indicated in the treatment of serious anaerobic intra-abdominal infections due to susceptible anaerobic bacteria, such as B. fragilis (and other species of Bacteroides), Clostridium, Fusobacterium, Peptococcus, and Peptostreptococcus species.

Culture and susceptibility studies should be performed to determine the causative organisms and their susceptibility to metronidazole. Based on clinical judgment and anticipated bacteriological findings, therapy may be started while awaiting the results of these tests. However, modification of the treatment may be necessary once these results become available.

In mixed aerobic and anaerobic infections, consideration should be given to the concomitant administration of an antibiotic appropriate for the treatment of the aerobic component of the infection (see Warnings).

Metronidazole has also been used in the treatment of a small number of cases of brain or lung infections (some with abscesses) caused by anaerobic bacteria.

Bacterial Vaginosis: The 1988 Canadian Guidelines for the Treatment of Sexually Transmitted Diseases in Neonates, Children, Adolescents and Adults recommends metronidazole for the treatment of this condition.

Protozoal Infections: Trichomonal infections in men as well as in women. Hepatic and intestinal amebiasis. Giardiasis.

Contraindications: Hypersensitivity to metronidazole or other nitroimidazole derivatives.

Metronidazole should not be administered to patients with active neurological disorders or a history of blood dyscrasia, hypothyroidism and hypoadrenalism.

Warnings: Metronidazole has no direct activity against aerobic or facultative anaerobic bacteria. In patients with mixed aerobic-anaerobic infections, appropriate concomitant antibiotics active against the aerobic component should be considered.

Known or previously unrecognized moniliasis may present more prominent symptoms after treatment with metronidazole.

Studies in rats and mice have provided some evidence that metronidazole may cause tumors in these species when administered orally for a long period at high doses. The relevance of these findings in humans is not known. However, it is therefore recommended that in the treatment of trichomoniasis, the use of metronidazole should be confined to those patients in whom significant T. vaginalis infection has been confirmed by appropriate diagnostic techniques.

Severe neurological disturbances (i.e. convulsive seizures and peripheral neuropathy) have been reported in patients treated with metronidazole. These have been observed very infrequently.

Precautions: Where there is clinical evidence of a trichomonal infection in the sexual partner, he should be treated concomitantly to avoid reinfection.

A rare case of reversible but profound neurological deterioration has been reported following a single oral dose of metronidazole; it is therefore advisable that a patient taking this drug for the first time not be left unattended for a period of 2 hours. The appearance of abnormal neurologic signs demands prompt discontinuation of metronidazole therapy and, when severe, immediate medical attention. Gastric lavage may be considered if no more than 2 or 3 hours have elapsed since administration of the drug.

Treatment with metronidazole should be discontinued if ataxia or any other symptom of CNS involvement occurs.

Patients with severe hepatic disease metabolize metronidazole slowly with resultant accumulation of metronidazole and its metabolites in the plasma. Accordingly, for such patients, doses of metronidazole below those usually recommended should be administered and with caution.

Treatment with metronidazole should be discontinued should pancreatitis occur once other causes of this disease are excluded.

Flagyl (cont'd)

Administration of solutions containing sodium ions may result in sodium retention. Care should be taken when administering metronidazole injection to patients receiving corticosteroids or to those predisposed to edema.

Hematologic: Transient eosinophilia and leukopenia have been observed during treatment with metronidazole. Regular total and differential leukocyte counts are advised if administration for more than 10 days or a second course of therapy is considered to be necessary.

Pregnancy: Metronidazole crosses the placental barrier and enters the fetal circulation rapidly. Although it has been given to pregnant women without apparent complication, it is advisable that oral administration be avoided in pregnant patients and metronidazole be withheld during the first trimester of pregnancy. In serious anaerobic infections, if the administration of metronidazole to pregnant patients is considered to be necessary, its use requires that the potential benefits be weighed against the possible risks to the fetus.

Lactation: Metronidazole is secreted in breast milk in concentrations similar to those found in plasma. Administration of metronidazole should be avoided in the nursing mother.

Children: Clinical experience in children is very limited. The monitoring of this group of patients is particularly important. The safety and effectiveness of i.v. metronidazole in children has not been established.

Laboratory Test Interferences: Metronidazole interferes with serum AST, ALT, LDH, triglycerides and hexokinase glucose determinations which are based on the decrease in ultraviolet absorbance which occurs when NADH is oxidized to NAD. Metronidazole causes an increase in absorbance at the peak of NADH (340 nm) resulting in falsely decreased values.

Drug Interactions: Patients taking metronidazole should be warned against consuming alcohol during therapy and for at least 1 day afterwards, because of a possible disulfiram-like reaction. This reaction appears to be due to the inhibition of the oxidation of acetaldehyde, the primary metabolite of alcohol.

Administration of disulfiram and metronidazole has been associated with acute psychoses and confusion in some patients; therefore, these drugs should not be used concomitantly.

Metronidazole has been reported to potentiate the anticoagulant effect of warfarin resulting in a prolongation of prothrombin time. This possible drug interaction should be considered when metronidazole is prescribed for patients on this type of anticoagulant therapy.

In single dose studies, metronidazole injection did not interfere with the biotransformation of diazepam, antipyrine or phenytoin in man.

However, patients maintained on phenytoin were found to have toxic blood levels after oral metronidazole administration. Phenytoin concentration returned to therapeutic blood level after discontinuance of metronidazole.

The metabolism of metronidazole has been reported to be increased by concurrent administration of phenobarbital. It is recommended that increased doses of metronidazole injection be considered in such cases.

A slight potentiation of the neuromuscular blocking activity of vecuronium has been reported in patients administered metronidazole at a dose of 15 mg/kg.

Concomitant use of lithium and metronidazole may result in lithium intoxication due to decreased renal clearance of lithium. Persistent renal damage may develop. When metronidazole must be administered to patients on lithium therapy, it may be prudent to consider tapering or discontinuing lithium temporarily when feasible. Otherwise frequent monitoring of lithium, creatinine and electrolyte levels and urine osmolality should be done.

Adverse Effects: Gastrointestinal: diarrhea, nausea, vomiting, anorexia, epigastric distress, dyspepsia, constipation and rare cases of pseudomembranous colitis. Reversible cases of pancreatitis have been reported infrequently.

Mouth: furred tongue, dry mouth, unpleasant metallic taste.

Hematopoietic: transient eosinophilia or leukopenia.

Dermatologic: rash and pruritus.

Cardiovascular: palpitation and chest pain.

CNS: convulsive seizures, peripheral neuropathy, transient ataxia, dizziness, drowsiness, insomnia, headache and psychiatric disorders, such as confusion and hallucinations.

Peripheral neuropathies have been reported in a few patients on moderately high to high dose prolonged oral treatment with metronidazole. It would appear that the occurrence is not directly related to the daily dosage and that an important predisposing factor is the continuation of oral and/or i.v. medication for several weeks or months.

Profound neurological deterioration, within 2 hours after metronidazole administration has been reported. The occurrence is not directly related to the dosage level.

Metabolic: An antithyroid effect has been reported by some investigators but three different clinical studies failed to confirm this.

Local Reactions: Thrombophlebitis has occurred with i.v. administration.

Other: Proliferation of C. albicans in the vagina, vaginal dryness and burning; dysuria; occasional flushing and headaches, especially with concomitant ingestion of alcohol; altered taste of alcoholic beverages.

Darkening of the urine has been reported. This is probably due to a metabolite of metronidazole and seems to have no clinical significance. Reversible lowering of serum lipids has been reported.

A single case of gynecomastia has been reported which resolved on discontinuing metronidazole administration.

Overdose: Symptoms: Massive ingestion may produce vomiting, ataxia and slight disorientation. Neurotoxic effects, including seizures and peripheral neuropathy have been reported after 5 to 7 days of oral doses of 6 to 10.4 g every other day.

Treatment: There is no specific antidote. Early gastric lavage may remove a large amount of the drug; otherwise, symptomatic treatment.

Dosage: Anaerobic Infections: Treatment should be initiated by the i.v. route. Oral medication may be substituted when it is feasible and/or practical.

Duration of therapy depends upon clinical and bacteriological assessment. Treatment for 7 days should be satisfactory for most patients. However, in cases where infection sites cannot be drained or which are liable to endogenous recontamination by anaerobic pathogens, a longer treatment may be required.

Adults: Oral: 500 mg every 8 hours.

I.V.: 100 mL (500 mg) by slow i.v. infusion (i.e. at the rate of 5 mL/min) every 8 hours.

Children: The safety and effectiveness of metronidazole in children is not known. Due to lack of pharmacokinetic data, no dosage recommendations can be made (see Precautions).

Bacterial Vaginosis: Adults: 500 mg orally twice a day for 7 days. Concurrent treatment of sexual partners is not usually indicated.

Trichomoniasis: Consideration should be given to use metronidazole therapy (oral or vaginal) in female patients, only when trichomonal infection has been confirmed by appropriate diagnostic techniques. In the male patient, oral metronidazole is recommended in those who are evidently the source of reinfection in female consorts and those with demonstrated urogenital trichomoniasis (see Warnings).

Oral: Single Dose Treatment: For both women and men, 2 g administered as a single dose after a meal.

Standard 10 Day Treatment: Women: 250 mg twice a day, morning and night for 10 consecutive days.

Men: 250 mg twice a day for 10 consecutive days. For both men and women, it may be occasionally necessary to give a second 10 day course after 4 to 6 weeks.

Vaginal Insert: One vaginal insert of 500 mg inserted deep into the vagina every night for 10 or 20 consecutive days, even during menstruation. In order to facilitate disintegration, the vaginal insert may be immersed in water for a few seconds just before introduction into the vagina.

Vaginal Cream: One applicatorful of metronidazole cream once or twice a day into the vagina for 10 or 20 consecutive days even during menstruation.

Amebiasis: Adults: Intestinal Amebiasis: 750 mg 3 times daily for 5 to 7 days. Amebic Abscesses of the Liver: 500 to 750 mg 3 times daily for 5 to 7 days. Children: 35 to 50 mg/kg/day in 3 divided doses for 5 to 7 days.

Giardiasis: Adults: 250 mg 2 times daily for 5 to 7 days. Children: 25 to 35 mg/kg/day in 2 divided doses for 5 to 7 days.

Note: Although efficacy of recommended doses for the treatment of amebiasis and giardiasis has been demonstrated, the optimal dose, duration of treatment and risk of recurrence have not been established.

Supplied: Oral Capsules: Each pale green and light grey capsule, printed (logo) and 500, contains: metronidazole 500 mg. Nonmedicinal ingredients: colloidal silicon dioxide, D&C Red No. 33, D&C Yellow No. 10, FD&C Blue No. 1, FD&C Green No. 3, gelatin, lactose, magnesium stearate, polacrilin potassium, sodium lauryl sulfate and titanium dioxide. Sodium: <1 mmol (5.47 mg). Tartrazine-free. S-Pak of 4 capsules. Boxes of 12 S-Pak; bottles of 100.

Vaginal Cream: Each tube contains: metronidazole 10% w/w in a cream base. Nonmedicinal ingredients: glycerin, glyceryl monostearate, methylparaben, propylparaben, purified water, stearic acid and triethanolamine. Tartrazine-free. Tubes of 60 g with applicator.

Vaginal Inserts: Each white capsule-shaped insert contains: metronidazole 500 mg. Nonmedicinal ingredients: alginic acid, calcium phosphate, colloidal silicon dioxide, cornstarch, dextrin, magnesium stearate, sodium bicarbonate, sodium oleate and talc. Tartrazine-free. Boxes of 10 with applicator.

(Shown in Product Recognition Section)

FLAGYL® 500 INJECTION

Baxter

Metronidazole

Antibacterial—Antiprotozoal

Supplied: Each mL of sterile, nonpyrogenic solution contains: metronidazole 5 mg in water for injection isotonic with sodium chloride and buffers. Viaflex Plus plastic (polyvinyl chloride) containers of 100 mL. Store at room temperature. Protect from light.

FLAGYSTATIN®

Rhône-Poulenc Rorer

Metronidazole—Nystatin

Trichomonacide—Moniliacide

Indications: Mixed vaginal infection due to Trichomonas vaginalis and C. albicans.

Contraindications: Hypersensitivity to either of the components. Combined treatment with oral Flagyl should be avoided in cases of active neurological disorders or a history of blood dyscrasia, hypothyroidism or hypoadrenalism unless in the opinion of the physician the benefits outweigh the possible hazard to the patient. See also Flagyl monograph.

Warnings: Nystatin possesses little or no antibacterial activity while metronidazole is selective against certain anaerobic bacteria; therefore, Flagystatin may not be effective in bacterial vaginal infections and should not be prescribed unless there is direct evidence of trichomonal infestation. See also Flagyl monograph.

Precautions: Where there is evidence of trichomonal infestation in the sexual partner, he should be treated concomitantly with oral Flagyl to avoid reinfestation.

It is possible that adverse effects normally associated with oral administration of metronidazole may occur following the vaginal administration of Flagystatin.

See also Flagyl monograph.

Adverse Effects: Infrequent and minor adverse reactions reported to date include: vaginal burning and granular sensation; bitter taste, nausea and vomiting, already known to occur with metronidazole were mainly seen when oral metronidazole was administered concomitantly with Flagystatin local treatment.

In the course of clinical trials, reactions, not necessarily related to the product, were observed: spots on the skin around the knees, welts all over the body, aching and swelling of wrists and ankles, pruritus, headache, coated tongue and fatigue.

Overdose: Symptoms: No case of accidental massive ingestion of Flagystatin has been reported yet. However, should this occur, symptoms such as nausea, vomiting, diarrhea and slight disorientation may be observed.

Treatment: No specific antidote. Treatment should be symptomatic after gastric lavage.

Dosage: One vaginal insert or ovule, or 1 applicatorful of cream daily, inserted deep into the vagina, before retiring, for 10 consecutive days. In order to facilitate disintegration, moisten the vaginal tablet under water for a second or two just before introduction in the vagina.

If after 10 days of treatment a cure has not been achieved a second 10 day course of treatment should be given. If Trichomonas vaginalis has not been completely eliminated, oral metronidazole 250 mg should be administered twice daily for 10 days.

Supplied: Vaginal Cream: Each applicatorful of cream delivers: metronidazole 500 mg and nystatin 100 000 units.

Nonmedicinal ingredients: glycerin, glyceryl monostearate, methylparaben, propylparaben, purified water, stearic acid and triethanolamine. Tartrazine-free. Tubes of 55 g with applicator.

Vaginal Inserts: Each vaginal insert contains: metronidazole 500 mg and nystatin 100 000 units. Nonmedicinal ingredients: cellulose, colloidal silicon dioxide, dicalcium phosphate, magnesium stearate, polacrilin potassium, sodium oleate and talc. Tartrazine-free. Boxes of 10 with applicator.

Vaginal Ovules: Each ovule contains: metronidazole 500 mg and nystatin 100 000 units. Nonmedicinal ingredients: hydrogenated vegetable glycerides. Tartrazine-free. Boxes of 10 with applicator.

(Shown in Product Recognition Section)

FLAMAZINE® Ⓟ
Smith & Nephew
Silver Sulfadiazine
Topical Antibacterial

Pharmacology: Silver sulfadiazine is released slowly from the cream, and thus rapid depletion of chloride and associated electrolyte disturbances are minimized. Silver sulfadiazine is not inhibited by PABA.

In burned pigs, the absorption of silver was less than 1% of the applied dose, however 5 to 8% of the sulfadiazine was absorbed. There is very little penetration of the silver below the outer layers of the wound surface, and the largest amount of the absorbed silver is found in the liver. In addition, high concentrations of silver have been measured in the bile, which suggest a hepatobiliary excretion of the silver moiety. The sulfadiazine moiety is excreted via the kidneys.

After a 500 to 1 000 g application of 1% silver sulfadiazine, (corresponding to 5 to 10 g of silver sulfadiazine), to burn patients, serum levels of sulfadiazine were 2 to 5 mg/L, and the urine levels were 60 to 1 000 mg/L. The daily urinary excretion of sulfadiazine was 100 to 200 mg, corresponding to less than 5% of the applied amount of silver sulfadiazine.

The sulfadiazine concentration in burn wound exudates, was 900 to 1 000 mg/L 24 hours after application, which is approximately 20 times the MIC of sensitive bacteria (50 mg/L).

In one study of 23 patients, mean silver serum levels were moderately higher than the normal range however the urinary excretion of silver, was markedly elevated (0.402 mg/24h). The 6 patients with 60% or greater B.S.A. burns had a mean peak excretion of 1.100 mg/24 hours (approximately 1 000 times the normal level). None of the patients had silver toxicity.

Indications: For the treatment of leg ulcers, burns, skin grafts, incisions and other clean lesions, abrasions, minor cuts and wounds.

Silver sulfadiazine is especially indicated in the treatment and prophylaxis of infection in serious burn victims.

Contraindications: Sulfonamide therapy is known to increase the possibility of kernicterus. Silver sulfadiazine should not be used in pregnant females at term, in premature infants, or in newborn infants during the first month of life.

The product should not be used on patients with a known sensitivity to any of its components.

Warnings: Sensitization to topically applied silver sulfadiazine is rarely predicted or proven by patch testing. Caution should be exercised in the use of silver sulfadiazine in individuals who have previously shown sensitization reactions to sulfonamides.

Silver sulfadiazine should be used with caution on patients with a history of G-6-PD deficiency as hemolysis may occur.

When treatment with silver sulfadiazine involves prolonged administration and/or large burned surfaces, considerable amounts of silver sulfadiazine are absorbed. Serum concentration of silver sulfadiazine may approach adult therapeutic levels (8 to 12 mg%).

Precautions: Silver sulfadiazine should be used with caution in patients with significant hepatic or renal impairment.

Leukopenia has been reported following the use of silver sulfadiazine, especially on patients with large area burns. This may be a drug-related effect, and often occurs 2 to 3 days after treatment has commenced. It is usually self-limiting and therapy with silver sulfadiazine does not normally need to be discontinued, as the WBC count usually returns to the normal range in a few days. WBC counts should be closely monitored.

Pregnancy: The safe use of silver sulfadiazine has not been established in pregnancy. Silver sulfadiazine should only be used in badly burned pregnant women if the benefit to the patient outweighs the risk to the fetus. Silver sulfadiazine should not be used when the patient is near term (see Contraindications).

Drug Interactions: Enzymatic Debriding Agents: Silver sulfadiazine may inactivate enzymatic debriding agents, thus the concomitant use of these compounds may be inappropriate.

Oral Hypoglycemic Agents and Phenytoin: In patients with large area burns where serum sulfadiazine levels may approach therapeutic levels, the action of oral hypoglycemic agents and phenytoin may be potentiated and it is recommended that blood levels be monitored.

Cimetidine: In patients with large area burns, it has been reported that co-administration of cimetidine may increase the incidence of leukopenia.

Adverse Effects: Leukopenia: In patients with large area burns, silver sulfadiazine treatment has been reported to have caused a rash in 2 to 5% of patients. Moderate, and usually transient leukopenia has been reported in up to 3 to 5% of patients and occurs within 48 to 72 hours after therapy has commenced, and generally occurs in patients with at least 30% burns. It is usually self-limiting and the leukocyte count is normalized within 2 to 3 days regardless of whether treatment with silver sulfadiazine is continued or terminated.

Caution should be exercised in individuals who have previously shown a sensitization to sulfonamides, however sensitization to topically applied silver sulfadiazine is rarely predicted or proven by patch testing.

Sulfonamide: During the treatment of burns over large body surfaces (greater than 20% body surface area), significant amounts of SSD are systematically absorbed. Therefore, it is possible that any adverse reactions associated with sulfonamides may occur.

Overdose: Symptoms and Treatment: In extensively burned patients or in patients suspected of showing symptoms of excessive absorption, it is important to optimally maintain fluid balance not only to prevent dehydration but also to avoid the possibility of renal impairment.

Dosage: Burns: The burn wounds should be cleaned and silver sulfadiazine applied over all the affected areas to a depth of 3 to 5 mm.

One technique is to apply the cream with a sterile gloved hand and/or sterile non metallic spatula. Where necessary, the cream should be re-applied to any area from which it has been removed by patient activity.

The cream should be re-applied at least every 24 hours.

Hand burns and finger injuries: One recommended method which has been found successful is to apply silver sulfadiazine to the burn and the whole hand is then enclosed in a clear plastic bag or glove, which is then closed at the wrist. The patient should be encouraged to move the hand and fingers. The dressing should be changed every 3 days or when an excessive amount of exudate has accumulated in the bag.

Leg Ulcers: One acceptable method involves filling the cavity of the ulcer with silver sulfadiazine to a depth of at least 3 to 5 mm. Care should be taken to prevent the spread of the cream onto non-ulcerated areas. The cream should be followed by an absorbent pad or gauze dressing, with further application of pressure bandaging as appropriate for the ulcer. The dressing should be changed every 2 or 3 days, with cleaning and debriding being performed before application of silver sulfadiazine.

It is not recommended that silver sulfadiazine be used in leg ulcers that are very exudative.

A container of silver sulfadiazine should be reserved for use for a specific patient and should be discarded when no longer required.

Supplied: Each g of cream contains: silver sulfadiazine 1% w/w. Sterile jars of 500 g and sterile tubes of 50 and 30 g. Store at 15 to 20°C. Discard cream which has darkened.

FLAMAZINE® C Ⓟ
Smith & Nephew
Silver Sulfadiazine—Chlorhexidine Digluconate
Topical Antibacterial

Pharmacology: The mechanism of silver sulfadiazine's antibacterial action has not been fully elucidated. After exposure to the drug, structural changes in the bacterial cell membrane occur, including distortion and enlargement of the cell and a weakening of the cell wall membrane. This is accompanied by reduced viability in sensitive strains.

The silver sulfadiazine molecule dissociates and the silver moiety is bound to the bacterial cells. It is believed that, after penetrating the cell wall, the silver moiety is attached to deoxyribonucleic acid (DNA) and prevents bacterial cell proliferation. There is approximately 100 times more DNA in mammalian cells than in bacterial cells. It is thought that the ratio of silver sulfadiazine to bacterial DNA is sufficiently high to prevent bacterial division but the corresponding ratio to epithelial DNA is low enough not to block epithelial cell regeneration.

The sulfadiazine moiety also provides a bacteriostatic action against sensitive organisms.

It has been suggested that the presence of chlorhexidine in subminimal inhibitory concentrations does not alter the cell membrane sufficiently to permit the efflux of nitrogen bases, nucleotides and nucleosides, but the alteration is sufficient to permit the entry of sulfadiazine molecules. The combination of these drugs may be bactericidal.

In adults, up to 10% of the sulfadiazine may be absorbed and 60 to 85% of the absorbed amount is excreted in the urine. In children with 13% body surface area burns, the urinary sulfadiazine concentration was 31.8 mg/L.

Percutaneous absorption studies in rats and man with radiolabelled chlorhexidine, have shown that less than 1% of the applied quantity was absorbed across the skin. Oral and i.v. studies indicate that over 90% of the drug is excreted in the feces.

Indications: For the treatment of leg ulcers, burns, skin grafts, incisions and other clean lesions, abrasions, minor cuts and wounds.

Contraindications: *Pregnancy* and Children: Sulfonamide therapy is known to increase the possibility of kernicterus. Flamazine C should not be used in pregnant females at term, in premature infants, or in newborn infants during the first month of life.

Flamazine C should not be used in patients with a known sensitivity to any of its components.

Warnings: Sensitization to topically applied silver sulfadiazine is rarely predicted or proven by patch testing. Caution should be exercised in the use of Flamazine C in individuals who have previously shown sensitization reactions to sulfonamides.

Silver sulfadiazine cream should be used with caution on patients with a history of G-6-PD deficiency as hemolysis may occur.

When treatment with silver sulfadiazine cream involves prolonged administration and/or large burned surfaces, considerable amounts of silver sulfadiazine are absorbed. Serum concentration of silver sulfadiazine may approach adult therapeutic levels (8 to 12 mg%).

Precautions: Flamazine C should be used with caution in patients with significant hepatic or renal impairment.

Leukopenia has been reported following the use of silver sulfadiazine, especially in patients with large area burns. This may be a drug-related effect, and often occurs 2 to 3 days after treatment has commenced. It is usually self-limiting and therapy with Flamazine C does not normally need to be discontinued, as the WBC count usually returns to the normal range in a few days. WBC counts should be closely monitored.

Pregnancy: The safe use of Flamazine C has not been established in pregnancy. Flamazine C should only be used in badly burned pregnant women if the benefit to the patient outweighs the risk to the fetus. Flamazine C should not be used when the patient is near term (see Contraindications).

Drug Interactions: Anionic surfactants: Due to the cationic properties of chlorhexidine, Flamazine C should not be used in conjunction with anionic surfactants.

Enzymatic debriding agents: Flamazine C may inactivate enzymatic debriding agents, thus the concomitant use of these compounds may be inappropriate.

Oral hypoglycemic agents and Phenytoin: In patients with large area burns where serum sulfadiazine levels may approach therapeutic levels, the action of oral hypoglycemic agents and phenytoin may be potentiated and it is recommended that blood levels be monitored.

Cimetidine: In patients with large area burns, it has been reported that co-administration of cimetidine may increase the incidence of leukopenia.

Adverse Effects: In patients with large area burns, silver sulfadiazine treatment has been reported to have caused a rash in 2 to 5% of patients. Moderate, and usually transient leukopenia has been reported in up to 3 to 5% of patients and occurs within 48 to 72 hours after therapy has commenced, and generally occurs in patients with at least 30% burns. It is usually self-limiting and the leukocyte count is normalized within 2 to 3 days regardless of whether treatment with Flamazine C is continued or terminated.

A very low incidence of photosensitivity, hypersensitivity, and contact eczema reactions have been observed with the use of chlorhexidine preparations.

Flamazine C (cont'd)

Caution should be exercised in individuals who have previously shown a sensitization to sulfonamides, however sensitization to topically applied silver sulfadiazine is rarely predicated or proven by patch testing.

Sulfonamide: During the treatment of burns over large body surfaces (greater than 20% body surface area), significant amounts of silver sulfadiazine are systemically absorbed. Therefore, it is possible that any adverse reactions associated with sulfonamides may occur.

Overdose: Symptoms and Treatment: In extensively burned patients or in patients suspected of showing symptoms of excessive absorption, it is important to optimally maintain fluid balance not only to prevent dehydration but also to avoid the possibility of renal impairment.

Dosage: Burns: The burn wounds should be cleaned and Flamazine C applied over all the affected areas to a depth of 3 to 5 mm.

One technique is to apply the cream with a sterile gloved hand and/or sterile non metallic spatula. Where necessary, the cream should be re-applied to any area from which it has been removed by patient activity.

Flamazine C should be re-applied at least every 24 hours. The wounds may be dressed or left open.

Duration of administration can be from a few days to several months, depending upon the nature and severity of the wound. Treatment should be continued until satisfactory healing has occurred or until the burn site is ready for grafting. The drug should not be withdrawn from the therapeutic regimen while there remains the possibility of infection except if a significant adverse reaction occurs.

A container of Flamazine C should be reserved for use for a specific patient and should be discarded when no longer required.

Supplied: Each g of white cream contains: silver sulfadiazine 1% w/w and chlorhexidine digluconate 0.2% w/w in a water soluble base. Sterile jars of 500 g and sterile tubes of 50 g. Store at 15 to 20°C and protect from light. Discard cream which has darkened.

FLAREX® Ⓟ

Alcon

Fluorometholone Acetate

Corticosteroid

Pharmacology: Adrenocorticoids suppress the inflammatory response (edema, fibrin deposition, capillary dilation, leukocyte migration, capillary proliferation, deposition of collagen and scar formation) to chemical, immunological or mechanical irritants. Adrenocorticoids may cause a rise in intraocular pressure in susceptible individuals. They are absorbed into aqueous humor, cornea, iris, choroid, ciliary body, and retina. Systemic absorption occurs but may be significant only at higher doses than recommended.

Indications: For use in the treatment of allergic and other steroid-responsive inflammatory conditions of the palpebral and bulbar conjunctiva, cornea, and anterior segment of the eye.

Contraindications: In acute superficial herpes simplex keratitis, vaccinia, varicella, and most viral diseases of the cornea and conjunctiva; tuberculosis of the eye; fungal diseases of the eye, acute purulent untreated infections of the eye, which, like other diseases caused by microorganisms, may be masked or enhanced by the presence of the steroid; and in those persons who have a known hypersensitivity to any component of this preparation.

Warnings: Fluorometholone acetate ophthalmic suspension is not for injection.

Use of topical corticosteroid may cause increased intraocular pressure in certain individuals. It is necessary that the intraocular pressure be checked frequently and particularly in patients with a history of glaucoma or with a family history of glaucoma. Prolonged use may result in glaucoma, damage to the optic nerve, defects in visual acuity and visual field, posterior subcapsular cataract formation, and/or may aid in the establishment of secondary ocular infections from pathogens due to suppression of host response. Acute purulent infections of the eye may be masked or exacerbated by the presence of steroid medications. In those diseases causing thinning of the cornea or sclera, perforation has been known to occur with the chronic use of topical steroids.

If sensitivity or other untoward reactions occur, discontinue the medication.

Pregnancy: Animal reproduction studies have not been conducted with this product. However, it has been reported that studies with fluorometholone (alcohol) applied ocularly to pregnant rabbits at approximate human doses and above resulted in a significant dose-related increase in fetal abnormalities and in fetal loss. It is not known whether Flarex ophthalmic suspension can cause fetal harm when administered to a pregnant woman. It should be used in pregnancy only if the potential benefit outweighs the potential risk to the fetus.

Precautions: Fungal infections of the cornea are particularly prone to develop coincidentally with long-term local steroid application; fungus invasion must be considered in any persistent corneal ulceration where a steroid has been used or is in use.

It is advisable to check intraocular pressure in some individuals (see Warnings). In diseases due to microorganisms, the infection may be masked, enhanced or activated by corticosteroids. Whenever there is a possibility of infection, supplemental therapy with suitable antibiotic agents should be considered.

Patients should be advised to inform their physicians of any prior use of corticosteroids.

Lactation: It is not known whether this drug is excreted in human milk. Because many drugs are excreted in human milk, caution should be exercised when it is administered to a nursing woman.

Children: Safety and effectiveness in children have not been established.

Adverse Effects: Glaucoma with optic nerve damage, visual acuity and field defects, cataract formation and secondary ocular infection following suppression of host response may occur.

Extended ophthalmic use of corticosteroid drugs may cause increased intraocular pressure in certain individuals and in those diseases causing thinning of the cornea, perforation has been known to occur.

Rarely, filtering blebs have been reported when topical steroids have been used following cataract surgery.

Occasionally, stinging or burning may occur.

Overdose: Symptoms and Treatment: Overdosage in the use of topical ophthalmic corticosteroids is a remote possibility. Discontinue medication when heavy or protracted use is suspected.

Dosage: 1 or 2 drops instilled into the conjunctival sac 2 to 4 times daily. During the initial 24 to 48 hours the dosage may be safely increased to 2 drops every 2 hours. Care should be taken not to discontinue therapy prematurely.

Special Instructions: Patients should be advised to shake well before using and to avoid contamination of the dropper tip.

Supplied: Each 5 mL Drop-Tainer dispenser of sterile ophthalmic suspension contains: fluorometholone acetate 0.1%. Nonmedicinal ingredients: benzalkonium chloride 0.01% (as preservative), edetate disodium, hydrochloric acid and/or sodium hydroxide (to adjust pH), hydroxyethyl cellulose, monobasic sodium phosphate, purified water, sodium chloride and tyloxapol. Plastic Drop-Tainer dispensers of 5 mL. Protect from freezing. Store upright at room temperature.

FLAXEDIL® Ⓟ

Rhône-Poulenc Rorer

Gallamine Triethiodide

Muscle Relaxant

Pharmacology: Gallamine is a competitive neuromuscular blocking agent. It acts by combining with the cholinergic receptor sites in muscle and competitively blocking the transmitter action of acetylcholine. Gallamine has a parasympatholytic effect on the cardiac vagus nerve which causes tachycardia and occasionally hypertension. Very high doses cause histamine release.

Following usual i.v. doses muscle relaxation occurs rapidly and reaches a maximum within 3 minutes. The duration of action averages about 15 to 20 minutes. Redistribution of the drug is primarily responsible for termination of action after a single dose. Gallamine is excreted unchanged in the urine. Gallamine will cross the placenta and may produce significant serum levels in the infant.

Indications: Adjunctive medication: in general anesthesia to provide more complete muscular relaxation during minor and major surgical, manipulative orthopedic, endoscopic and intubation procedures; in obstetrics for delivery when the cervix is fully dilated.

May also be used to prevent accidents during electroshock therapy, to decrease severity of muscular spasms in tetanus, spastic paraplegia and other convulsive states.

Contraindications: Respiratory depression or deficiency, severe renal impairment, myasthenia gravis, iodine sensitivity.

Precautions: Use with caution in patients with hypertension or cardiac insufficiency when tachycardia would be undesirable; it should preferably be avoided in obstetric surgery.

If used with cyclopropane anesthesia, gallamine may provoke ventricular arrhythmias.

May be added to or mixed with Pentothal but not vice versa. Do not use syringes previously used for Pentothal. Do not use yellow colored solutions of the drug.

Gallamine should be administered by, or under the supervision of, an experienced anesthesiologist. Facilities for intubation, artificial respiration, and oxygen therapy should be available, as well as edrophonium or neostigmine and atropine as antidotes.

Adverse Effects: Moderate increase in blood pressure. Ventricular rhythm changes may occur, which may be prevented by the administration of an association of halothane-nitrous oxide-oxygen. Respiratory muscle paresis may cause respiratory depression.

Dosage: After induction of light (second plane) anesthesia, administer as follows:

Surgery: Adults: about 1 mg/kg (40 to 80 mg). If necessary, repeated doses of 0.5 to 1 mg/kg or less, at intervals of 50 to 60 minutes or longer, may be given.

Children: up to 2 mg/kg. Since in children, the duration of action is shorter than in adults, additional doses should be repeated more frequently.

Obstetrics: 20 to 40 mg i.v. when the cervix is fully dilated.

Electroconvulsive Therapy: Average adult dose: 40 to 60 mg.

Supplied: Each mL of injectable solution contains: 20 mg of gallamine triethiodide. Nonmedicinal ingredients: potassium metabisulfite, sodium sulfite and water for injection. Ampuls of 2 and 5 mL, boxes of 10. Protect from light.

FLEET ENEMA®
FLEET ENEMA® Mineral Oil

Johnson & Johnson • Merck

Sodium Phosphates
Mineral Oil

Laxative

Pharmacology: Fleet Enema: Useful as a laxative in the relief of constipation, and as a bowel evacuant for a variety of diagnostic, surgical and therapeutic indications. Dibasic sodium phosphate and monobasic sodium phosphate are poorly absorbed from the gastrointestinal tract and retain water in the lumen of the intestine. When administered rectally as an enema, they produce a watery evacuation of the bowel. Fleet Enema provides cleansing action and induces complete emptying of the left colon usually in 2 to 5 minutes.

Fleet Enema Mineral Oil: Serves to soften and lubricate the contents of the intestinal tract, easing their passage without irritating the mucosa. Results approximate a normal bowel movement in that only the rectum, sigmoid and part or all of the descending colon are evacuated. Results are usually obtained in 2 to 15 minutes.

Indications: Fleet Enema: Useful as a laxative in the relief of constipation. As a routine enema, when bowel evacuation is needed for proctoscopy and sigmoidoscopy, preoperative cleansing and general postoperative care, to help relieve fecal or barium impaction, collecting stool specimens, during pregnancy and pre- and postnatally.

Fleet Enema Mineral Oil: Lubricant laxative. For the relief of occasional constipation. Especially suitable for bowel cleansing when straining might be dangerous, painful, or unproductive, as in: hypertension, cardiovascular syndromes, pelvic hernia, hemorrhoids, care of many postoperative conditions, gastrointestinal irritations, atonic colon, impaction in the paralyzed patient, chronic pelvic inflammatory disease and abdominal aneurysm; to obtain the laxative benefits of mineral oil when oral cathartics are contraindicated.

Contraindications: Fleet Enema: Should **not** be used when the following medical problems exist: appendicitis (or symptoms of), intestinal blockage, ulcerative colitis, ileitis, heart disease, rectal bleeding, high blood pressure, kidney disease.

Fleet Enema: Children: Not recommended for infants under 6 months of age.
Fleet Enema Mineral Oil: Should **not** be used when the following medical problems exist: appendicitis (or symptoms of), intestinal blockage, ulcerative colitis, ileitis, rectal bleeding, kidney disease.

Warnings: Fleet Enema: Do **not** use in the presence of abdominal pain, nausea, fever or vomiting, (this could refer to signs of appendicitis or inflamed bowel), cardiac disease, severe dehydration or debility.

Frequent or prolonged use of enemas may result in dependence for bowel function. Use only when needed or when prescribed by a physician.
Children and Geriatrics: Children and elderly persons are more sensitive to the effects of enemas.
Fleet Enema Mineral Oil: Do **not** use in the presence of abdominal pain, nausea, fever or vomiting (this could refer to signs of appendicitis or inflamed bowel).

Frequent or prolonged use of enemas may result in dependence for bowel function.
Children and Geriatrics: Give to children only on the advice of, and as directed by a physician. Children and elderly persons are more sensitive to the effects of enemas.

Precautions: Fleet Enema: **Do not administer to children under 2 years of age except on the advice of a physician.** In dehydrated or debilitated patients, volume of solution administered must be carefully determined since the solution is hypertonic and may cause further dehydration. Care should be taken to ensure that the contents of the bowel are expelled after administration. Repeated usage at short intervals should be avoided. Laxative products should not be used longer than 1 week unless directed by a physician.
Fleet Enema Mineral Oil: **Do not administer to children under 2 years of age except on the advice of a physician.** Care should be taken to ensure that the contents of the bowel are expelled after administration. Laxative products should not be used longer than 1 week unless directed by a physician.

Dosage: For rectal use only.
Fleet Enema: Adults: 120 mL. Children 2 to 12 years: 60 mL as a single dose or as directed by a physician. Children under 2 years: consult a physician.

The enema does not require warming. May be used at room temperature.
Preferred Position: Lying on left side with knees flexed, or in the knee-chest position. Remove protective cap from the prelubricated rectal tube before using. Insert tube gently, pointing it in the direction of the navel. Slowly squeeze bottle to empty contents into rectum. Rubber diaphragm at base of tube prevents accidental leakage and assures controlled flow of the enema solution. Withdraw the tube from rectum. (An extra amount of solution is provided to allow for the quantity normally remaining in bottle after squeezing.) Maintain position until defecation impulse is felt, usually within 2 to 5 minutes.
Fleet Enema Mineral Oil: Adults and children 12 years and older: 120 mL as a single dose. Children 2 to 12 years: 60 mL as a single dose. Children under 2 years: Consult a physician.

The enema should first be warmed by placing bottle in water at body temperature.
Preferred Position: Lying on left side with knees flexed, or in the knee-chest position. Remove protective cap from the prelubricated rectal tube before using. Insert the tube gently pointing it in the direction of the navel and squeeze bottle to empty contents into rectum. Rubber diaphragm at base of tube prevents accidental leakage and assures controlled flow of the enema solution. Withdraw the tube from rectum. (An extra amount of oil solution is provided to allow for the quantity normally remaining in bottle after squeezing.) The body position should be maintained until a strong urge to have a bowel movement is felt or the enema should be retained for length of time indicated by physician. Results are usually felt within 2 to 15 minutes. Contents of the bowel should then be expelled.

Supplied: Fleet Enema: Each 100 mL of solution contains: monobasic sodium phosphate 16 g and dibasic sodium phosphate 6 g in single dose disposable unit. Nonmedicinal ingredients: sodium methylhydroxybenzoate. Ready-to-use, hand size plastic squeeze bottles of 130 mL, with a 5 cm prelubricated rectal tube and protective cap.

Fleet Enema Mineral Oil: Each single dose disposable unit of solution contains: mineral oil USP 130 mL. Ready-to-use hand-size plastic squeeze bottle, with a 5 cm prelubricated rectal tube and protective cap.

Also available: Fleet Enema Pediatric (sodium phosphates enema) (65 mL).

FLEET® PHOSPHO®-SODA
Johnson & Johnson • Merck

Sodium Phosphates
Laxative

Pharmacology: Depending on dosage, sodium phosphates oral solution is useful as a laxative in the relief of constipation, or as a bowel evacuant for a variety of diagnostic, surgical and therapeutic indications. Dibasic sodium phosphate and monobasic sodium phosphate are poorly absorbed from the gastrointestinal tract and retain water in the lumen of the intestine. When administered orally, they produce a bowel movement in 0.5 to 6 hours, depending on dosage.

Indications: As a laxative, for the relief of occasional constipation. As a purgative, for use as part of a bowel cleansing regimen in preparing the patient for surgery or for preparing the colon for x-ray or endoscopic examination.

Contraindications: Do not use this product in patients who have kidney disease or are on a sodium-restricted diet, unless directed by a physician.

Warnings: Do not exceed recommended dose unless directed by a physician. Serious side effects may occur from excessive dosage.

Do not use in patients with congenital megacolon or congestive heart failure, as hypernatremic dehydration may occur. Use with caution in patients with impaired renal function as hypocalcemia, hyperphosphatemia, hypernatremia and acidosis may occur.

Since Fleet Phospho-Soda contains dibasic sodium phosphate and monobasic sodium phosphate, there is a risk of acute elevation of sodium concentration in the serum and consequent dehydration, particularly in children with megacolon. Additional fluids by mouth are recommended where appropriate.

In addition, elevated levels of serum phosphates and decreased levels of serum calcium have been reported in patients with renal disease (and with prolonged use).

Do not use a laxative product when nausea, vomiting, or abdominal pain is present unless directed by a physician. Patients who have noticed a sudden change in bowel habits that persists over a period of 2 weeks should consult a physician before using a laxative. Rectal bleeding or failure to have a bowel movement may indicate a serious condition. Laxative products should not be used longer than 1 week unless directed by a physician.

Precautions: Fleet Phospho-Soda is not recommended for pregnant or nursing women, or children under 5 years old, except on the advice of a physician.

Overdose: Symptoms: Overdosage with Fleet Phospho-Soda may cause hypocalcemia, hyperphosphatemia, hypernatremia, hypernatremic dehydration and acidosis.

Treatment: Hypocalcemia, Hyperphosphatemia, Hypernatremia and Acidosis: Calcium, phosphate, chloride and sodium levels should be carefully monitored. Immediate corrective action should be taken to restore electrolyte balance with appropriate fluid replacements.
Hypernatremic Dehydration: Calcium, phosphate, chloride and sodium levels should be carefully monitored. Promptly administer parenteral fluids with lower concentrations of sodium and chloride than extracellular fluid (40 to 50 mEq/L) and moderate concentration of potassium (20 to 30 mEq/L) administered at a rate of 3 000 to 4 000 mL/m² of body surface during the first 12 to 24 hours dependent on the severity of dehydration and the clinical response.

Dosage: Do not exceed single daily dosage (see Table I).

Table I—Fleet Phospho-Soda

Dosage Table		
Single Daily Dosage (Do Not Exceed)		
Laxative	Adults and children 12 years and over	20 mL
	Children 10 to under 12 years	10 mL
	Children 5 to under 10 years	5 mL
Purgative	Adults Only	45 mL

Directions for Use: Best if taken on an empty stomach; upon rising, 30 minutes before a meal, or at bedtime for overnight action. **Dilute recommended dosage with ½ glass (120 mL) cool water. Drink, then follow with 1 glass (240 mL) cool water.**

Supplied: Unflavored: Each 5 mL contains: monobasic sodium phosphate 2.4 g and dibasic sodium phosphate 0.9 g in a stable, buffered, aqueous solution. Nonmedicinal ingredients: sodium benzoate. Plastic bottles of 45 mL.

Ginger-lemon Flavor: Each 5 mL contains: monobasic sodium phosphate 2.4 g and dibasic sodium phosphate 0.9 g in a stable, buffered, aqueous solution. Nonmedicinal ingredients: ginger-lemon flavor, glycerin, saccharin sodium and sodium benzoate. Plastic bottles of 45 mL.

Reviewed 1999

FLEXALL®
Chattem

Menthol
Topical Analgesic

Indications: For temporary relief from minor arthritis pain, bursitis, tendonitis, backache, strains and sprains.

Warnings: For external use only. Keep out of the reach of children. Keep away from eyes, mucous membranes, broken or irritated skin. If rash occurs, discontinue use. Do not bandage tightly or use heating pad.

Dosage: Apply generously to muscles and joints and gently massage until gel disappears. Use after exercise. Repeat as needed up to 4 times/day.

Supplied: Ice Formula: Each g of gel contains: menthol 6%. Bottles of 170 g.

Original Strength Formula: Each g of gel contains: menthol 7% in a vitamin E, aloe vera base. Bottles of 55 and 110 g.

Ultra-Extra Strength Formula: Each g of gel contains: menthol 10% in a vitamin E, aloe vera base. Bottles of 55 and 110 g.

Reviewed 1998

FLEXALL® STICK
Chattem

Menthol—Methyl Salicylate
Topical Analgesic

Indications: For temporary relief from minor arthritis pain, bursitis, tendonitis, backache, strains and sprains.

Warnings: For external use only. Keep out of the reach of children. Keep away from eyes, mucous membranes, broken or irritated skin. If rash or excessive irritation occurs, discontinue use. If condition worsens or persists for more than 7 days, or clears and reoccurs within a few days, discontinue use and consult a physician. Do not bandage tightly or use heating pad. **Do not use if allergic to salicylate or if taking anticoagulants.**

Overdose: Symptoms and Treatment: If swallowed, call a physician.

Dosage: Apply generously to muscles and joints and gently massage until medication disappears. Use after exercise. Repeat as necessary up to 4 times/day.

Supplied: Each g of stick contains: menthol 10% and methyl salicylate 30%. Sticks of 49 g.

Reviewed 1998

FLEXERIL® Ⓟ
Frosst

Cyclobenzaprine HCl
Skeletal Muscle Relaxant

Pharmacology: Cyclobenzaprine relieves skeletal muscle spasm of local origin without interfering with muscle function. It is ineffective in muscle spasm due to CNS disease.

Controlled clinical studies show that cyclobenzaprine improves the signs and the symptoms of skeletal muscle spasm.

Pharmacokinetics: Cyclobenzaprine is well absorbed in man. After oral or i.v. doses (10 mg) of ^{14}C-labeled cyclobenzaprine to human subjects, plasma levels of radioactivity were comparable. In addition, the excretion of radioactivity was similar after both routes (38 to 51% in the urine; 14 to 15% in the feces), suggesting that oral absorption is almost complete. The half-life varies from 1 to 3 days. No effect on plasma levels or bioavailability was noted in 14 human subjects, when cyclobenzaprine and multiple doses of ASA was coadministered.

Cyclobenzaprine is extensively metabolized in man. In the study with ^{14}C-labeled drug, about 4% of the dose was excreted in the urine as unchanged cyclobenzaprine. The

Flexeril (cont'd)

metabolites (probably glucuronides) were excreted as water-soluble conjugates. After oral or i.v. administration of 40 mg of unlabeled cyclobenzaprine to 2 subjects, only 0.2 to 1.5% of the dose was excreted as unchanged drug in the urine within 24 hours.

Indications: An adjunct to rest and physical therapy for relief of muscle spasm associated with acute, painful musculoskeletal conditions.

Cyclobenzaprine should be used only for short periods (up to 2 or 3 weeks), because adequate evidence of effectiveness for more prolonged use is not available, and because muscle spasm associated with acute, painful musculoskeletal conditions is generally of short duration and specific therapy for longer periods is seldom warranted.

Cyclobenzaprine has not been found effective in the treatment of spasticity associated with cerebral or spinal cord disease, or in children with cerebral palsy.

Contraindications: Hypersensitivity to cyclobenzaprine. Concomitant use of MAO inhibitors or within 14 days after their discontinuation. Acute recovery phase of myocardial infarction, and patients with arrhythmias, heart block or conduction disturbances, or congestive heart failure. Hyperthyroidism.

Warnings: Use of cyclobenzaprine for periods longer than 2 or 3 weeks is not recommended (see Indications).

Cyclobenzaprine is closely related to the tricyclic antidepressants, e.g., amitriptyline and imipramine. In short-term studies for indications other than muscle spasm associated with acute musculoskeletal conditions, and usually at doses somewhat greater than those recommended for skeletal muscle spasm, some of the more serious CNS reactions noted with tricyclic antidepressants have occurred (see Warnings below and Adverse Effects).

Cyclobenzaprine may interact with MAO inhibitors. Hyperpyretic crises, severe convulsions and deaths have occurred in patients receiving tricyclic antidepressants and MAO inhibitors.

Tricyclic antidepressants have been reported to produce arrhythmias, sinus tachycardia, prolongation of the conduction time leading to myocardial infarction and stroke.

Cyclobenzaprine may enhance the effects of alcohol, barbiturates, and other CNS depressants.

Precautions: Occupational Hazards: Cyclobenzaprine may impair the mental and/or physical abilities required for performance of hazardous tasks, such as operating machinery or driving a motor vehicle.

Because of its atropine-like action, cyclobenzaprine should be used with caution in patients with a history of urinary retention, angle-closure glaucoma, increased intraocular pressure, and in patients taking anticholinergic medication.

Tricyclic antidepressants may block the antihypertensive action of guanethidine and similarly acting compounds.

Pregnancy: The safe use of cyclobenzaprine in pregnant women has not been established. Therefore, it should not be administered to women of childbearing potential unless, in the opinion of the treating physician, the anticipated benefits outweigh the possible hazards to the fetus.

Lactation: Because it is likely that cyclobenzaprine is excreted in milk, it should not be given to nursing mothers.

Children: Safety and effectiveness of cyclobenzaprine in children below the age of 15 have not been established.

Adverse Effects: The following adverse reactions have been reported with cyclobenzaprine.

Most frequent: drowsiness (40%), dry mouth (28%), dizziness (11%).

Less frequent: increased heart rate (and several cases of tachycardia), weakness, fatigue, dyspepsia, nausea, paresthesia, unpleasant taste, blurred vision, insomnia, convulsions and abnormal liver function: hepatitis, jaundice and cholestasis.

Rare: sweating, myalgia, dyspnea, abdominal pain, constipation, coated tongue, tremors, dysarthria, euphoria, nervousness, disorientation, confusion, headache, urinary retention, decreased bladder tonus, ataxia, depressed mood, hallucinations and allergic reactions including rash, urticaria and edema of the face and tongue.

The listing which follows includes other adverse reactions which have been reported with tricyclic compounds, but not with cyclobenzaprine when used in short term studies in muscle spasm of peripheral origin. Some of these reactions were noted, however, when cyclobenzaprine was studied for other indications, usually in higher dosage. Pharmacologic similarities among the tricyclic drugs require that each of the reactions be considered when cyclobenzaprine is administered.

Cardiovascular: hypotension, hypertension, palpitation, myocardial infarction, arrhythmias, heart block, stroke.

CNS and Neuromuscular: confusional states, disturbed concentration, delusions, excitement, anxiety, restlessness, nightmares, numbness and tingling of the extremities, peripheral neuropathy, incoordination, seizures, alteration in EEG patterns, extrapyramidal symptoms, tinnitus, syndrome of inappropriate ADH (antidiuretic hormone) secretion.

Anticholinergic: disturbance of accommodation, paralytic ileus, dilatation of urinary tract.

Allergic: photosensitization.

Hematologic: bone marrow depression including agranulocytosis, leukopenia, eosinophilia, purpura, thrombocytopenia.

Gastrointestinal: epigastric distress, vomiting, anorexia, stomatitis, diarrhea, parotid swelling, black tongue.

Endocrine: testicular swelling and gynecomastia in the male, breast enlargement and galactorrhea in the female. Increased or decreased libido, elevation and lowering of blood sugar levels.

Other: weight gain or loss, urinary frequency, mydriasis, alopecia.

Withdrawal Symptoms: Abrupt cessation of treatment after prolonged administration may produce nausea, headache and malaise. These are not indicative of addiction.

Overdose: Symptoms: High doses may cause temporary confusion, disturbed concentration, transient visual hallucinations, agitation, hyperactive reflexes, muscle rigidity, vomiting, or hyperpyrexia, in addition to anything listed under Adverse Effects. Based on known pharmacologic actions of the drug, overdosage may cause drowsiness, hypothermia, tachycardia and other cardiac rhythm abnormalities such as bundle branch block, ECG evidence of impaired conduction, and congestive heart failure. Other manifestations may be dilated pupils, convulsions, severe hypotension, stupor and coma.

Treatment: Symptomatic and supportive. Empty the stomach as quickly as possible by emesis, followed by gastric lavage. After gastric lavage, activated charcoal may be administered. Twenty to 30 g of the activated charcoal may be given every 4 to 6 hours during the first 24 to 48 hours after ingestion. An ECG should be taken and close monitoring of cardiac function must be instituted if there is any evidence of dysrhythmia. Maintenance of an open airway, adequate fluid intake, and regulation of body temperature are necessary.

The slow i.v. administration of 1 to 3 mg of physostigmine salicylate is reported to reverse symptoms of poisoning by atropine and other drugs with anticholinergic activity. Physostigmine may be helpful in the treatment of cyclobenzaprine overdose. Because physostigmine is rapidly metabolized, its dosage should be repeated as often as required when life-threatening signs such as arrhythmias, convulsions, and deep coma recur or persist.

Use standard medical measures to manage circulatory shock and metabolic acidosis. Cardiac arrhythmias may be treated with neostigmine, pyridostigmine, or propranolol. When signs of cardiac failure occur, the use of a short-acting digitalis preparation should be considered. Close monitoring of cardiac function for not less than 5 days is advisable.

Anticonvulsants may be given to control seizures.

Dialysis is probably of no value because of low plasma concentrations of the drug.

Since overdosage is often deliberate, patients may attempt suicide by other means during the recovery phase. Deaths by deliberate or accidental overdosage have occurred with this class of drugs.

Dosage: 10 mg 3 times/day, with a range of 20 to 40 mg/day in divided doses. Dosage should not exceed 60 mg/day. Use of cyclobenzaprine is not indicated or recommended for periods longer than 2 or 3 weeks.

Supplied: Each butterscotch yellow, film-coated, D-shaped tablet, coded 931, contains: cyclobenzaprine HCl 10 mg. Also contains lactose. Gluten- and tartrazine-free. Bottles of 100 and 500.

(Shown in Product Recognition Section)

FLEXITEC Ⓟ

Technilab

Cyclobenzaprine HCl

Skeletal Muscle Relaxant

Supplied: Each butterscotch yellow, film-coated tablet contains: cyclobenzaprine HCl USP 10 mg. Nonmedicinal ingredients: colloidal silicon dioxide, hydroxypropyl cellulose, hydroxypropyl methylcellulose, lactose, magnesium stearate, polyethylene glycol, polysorbate, starch, synthetic yellow iron oxide and titanium dioxide. Bottles of 100 and 500. Store between 15 and 30°C in tightly sealed containers. Protect from heat.

New Product 1998

FLINTSTONES®

Bayer Consumer

Vitamins—Minerals

Supplied: Multiple Vitamins: Each flavored, chewable, shaped tablet contains: vitamin A 5 000 IU, vitamin B_1 1.5 mg, vitamin B_2 1.5 mg, niacinamide 15 mg, vitamin B_6 1 mg, vitamin B_{12} 3 μg, folic acid 0.1 mg, vitamin C 50 mg and vitamin D 400 IU. Nonmedicinal ingredients: citric acid, erythrosine, FD&C Blue #2, FD&C Yellow #6, flavors (grape, orange, strawberry, tangerine), magnesium stearate, malic acid, microcrystalline cellulose, Red #3 and sugar. Bottles of 90.

Multiple Vitamins Complete: Each flavored, chewable, shaped tablet contains: vitamin A 5 000 IU, vitamin B_1 1.5 mg, vitamin B_2, 1.5 mg, niacinamide 15 mg, pantothenic acid 10 mg, vitamin B_6 1 mg, vitamin B_{12} 3 μg, folic acid 0.1 mg, vitamin C 50 mg, vitamin D 400 IU, vitamin E (as acetate) 10 IU, biotin 30 μg, elemental iron (as ferrous fumarate) 4 mg, calcium (as dicalcium phosphate) 160 mg, phosphorus (as dicalcium phosphate) 125 mg and copper (as cupric oxide) 1 mg. Nonmedicinal ingredients: aspartame, carrageenan, citric acid, cornstarch, erythrosine, FD&C Blue #2, FD&C Yellow #6, flavors (cherry, grape, lemon, orange, raspberry, tutti-fruitti), gelatin, magnesium stearate, malic acid, monoammonium glycyrrhizinate, silica gel and sorbitol. Bottles of 60.

Multiple Vitamins Plus Iron: Each flavored, chewable, shaped tablet contains: vitamin A 5 000 IU, vitamin B_1 1.5 mg, vitamin B_2 1.5 mg, niacinamide 15 mg, vitamin B_6 1 mg, vitamin B_{12} 3 μg, folic acid 0.1 mg, vitamin C 50 mg, vitamin D 400 IU and elemental iron (as ferrous fumarate 12 mg) 4 mg. Nonmedicinal ingredients: citric acid, erythrosine, FD&C Blue #2, FD&C Yellow #6, flavors (grape, orange, strawberry, tangerine), magnesium stearate, malic acid, microcrystalline cellulose, Red #3 and sugar. Bottles of 90.

Multiple Vitamins with Extra C: Each flavored, chewable, shaped tablet contains: vitamin A 5 000 IU, vitamin B_1 1.5 mg, vitamin B_2 1.5 mg, niacinamide 15 mg, vitamin B_6 1 mg, vitamin B_{12} 3 μg, folic acid 0.1 mg, vitamin C 250 mg and vitamin D 400 IU. Nonmedicinal ingredients: citric acid, erythrosine, FD&C Blue #2, FD&C Yellow #6, flavors (grape, orange, strawberry, tangerine), fructose, magnesium stearate, malic acid, microcrystalline cellulose, Red #3, sodium ascorbate and sugar. Bottles of 60.

(Shown in Product Recognition Section)

FLOLAN® Ⓟ

Glaxo Wellcome

Epoprostenol Sodium

Vasodilator

Pharmacology: Epoprostenol, also known as prostacyclin, PGI_2 or PGX, a metabolite of arachidonic acid, is a naturally occurring prostaglandin. Epoprostenol has two major pharmacological actions: (1) direct vasodilation of pulmonary and systemic arterial vascular beds, and (2) inhibition of platelet aggregation. In animals, the vasodilatory effects of epoprostenol reduce right and left ventricular afterload and increase cardiac output and stroke volume. The effect of epoprostenol on heart rate in animals varies with dose. At low doses, there is vagally mediated bradycardia, but at higher doses, epoprostenol causes reflex tachycardia in response to direct vasodilation and hypotension. No major effects on cardiac conduction have been observed. Additional pharmacologic effects of epoprostenol in animals include bronchodilation, inhibition of gastric acid secretion and decreased gastric emptying.

Pharmacokinetics: Epoprostenol is rapidly hydrolyzed at neutral blood pH and is also subject to enzymatic degradation. Animal studies using tritium-labeled epoprostenol have indicated a high clearance (93 mL/min/kg), small volume of distribution (357 mL/kg) and a short half-life (2.7 minutes). During infusions in animals, steady-state plasma concentrations of tritium-labeled epoprostenol were reached within 15 minutes and were proportional to infusion rates.

No available chemical assay is sufficiently sensitive and specific to assess the in vivo human pharmacokinetics of epoprostenol. The in vitro half-life of epoprostenol in human blood at 37°C and pH 7.4 is approximately 6 minutes; the in vivo half-life of epoprostenol in man is therefore expected to be no greater than 6 minutes. The in vitro pharmacologic half-life of epoprostenol in human plasma, based on inhibition of platelet aggregation, is 10.6 minutes in males (n=954) and 10.8 minutes in females (n=1 024).

Tritium-labeled epoprostenol has been administered to humans in order to identify the metabolic products of epoprostenol. Epoprostenol is metabolized to 6-keto-$PGF_{1\alpha}$ (formed by spontaneous degradation) and 6,15-diketo-13,14-dihydro-$PGF_{1\alpha}$ (enzymatically formed), both of which have pharmacological activity at orders of magnitude less than epoprostenol in animal test systems. The recovery of radioactivity in urine and feces over a 1-week period was 82% and 4% of the administered dose, respectively. Fourteen additional minor metabolites have been isolated from urine, indicating that epoprostenol is extensively metabolized in man.

Pharmacodynamics: Acute i.v. infusions of epoprostenol for up to 15 minutes in patients with primary pulmonary hypertension (PPH) produced dose-related increases in cardiac index (CI) and stroke volume (SV), and dose-related decreases in pulmonary vascular resistance (PVR), total pulmonary resistance (TPR), and mean systemic arterial pressure (SAPm). The effects of epoprostenol on mean pulmonary artery pressure (PAPm) in patients with PPH were variable and minor.

Chronic hemodynamic effects were generally similar to acute effects. CI, SV, and arterial oxygen saturation were increased, and PAPm, right atrial pressure (RAP), TPR, and systemic vascular resistance (SVR) were decreased in patients who received epoprostenol chronically, compared to those who did not.

Survival was improved in NYHA functional Class III and Class IV PPH patients treated with epoprostenol for 12 weeks in a multicenter, open, randomized, parallel, controlled study. At the end of the treatment period, 8 of 40 patients receiving standard therapy alone had died, whereas none of the 41 patients receiving epoprostenol had died (p=0.003).

Indications: For the long-term i.v. treatment of primary pulmonary hypertension (PPH) in NYHA functional Class III and Class IV patients.

Prior to initiation of therapy, the potential benefit of epoprostenol should be weighed against the risks associated with use of the drug and the presence of an indwelling central venous catheter.

Epoprostenol should be used only by clinicians experienced in the diagnosis and treatment of PPH. The diagnosis of PPH should be carefully established by standard clinical tests to exclude secondary causes of pulmonary hypertension.

Contraindications: The chronic use of epoprostenol in patients with congestive heart failure (CHF) due to severe left ventricular systolic dysfunction is contraindicated. A large study evaluating the effect of epoprostenol on survival in NYHA Class III and IV patients with CHF due to severe left ventricular systolic dysfunction was terminated after an interim analysis of 471 patients revealed a higher mortality in patients receiving epoprostenol plus standard therapy than in those receiving standard therapy alone.

Epoprostenol is also contraindicated in patients with known or suspected hypersensitivity to the drug or any of its excipients, or to structurally related compounds.

Warnings: Epoprostenol must be reconstituted only as directed using specific sterile diluent. Epoprostenol must not be reconstituted or mixed with any other parenteral medications or solutions prior to or during administration.

Epoprostenol is not to be used for bolus administration (see Adverse Effects, Adverse Events During Acute Dose-Ranging).

Abrupt Withdrawal: Abrupt withdrawal (including interruptions in drug delivery) or sudden large reductions in dosage of epoprostenol may result in symptoms associated with rebound pulmonary hypertension, including dyspnea, dizziness, and asthenia. In clinical trials, there were rare reports of deaths considered attributable to the interruption of epoprostenol. Abrupt withdrawal should be avoided.

Pulmonary Edema: A minority of patients have PPH associated with pulmonary veno-occlusive disease. Some of these patients develop pulmonary edema during dose-ranging. Where pulmonary edema arises within hours to days of starting epoprostenol infusion, a diagnosis of veno-occlusive disease should be considered. In such cases consideration should be given to discontinuation of epoprostenol.

Epoprostenol should not be used chronically in patients who develop pulmonary edema during dose-ranging.

Sepsis: Sepsis is a known risk associated with the presence of an indwelling central venous catheter and requires immediate access to expert medical care (see Adverse Effects, Adverse Events Attributable to the Drug Delivery System).

Precautions: Epoprostenol is a potent pulmonary and systemic vasodilator. Acute dose-ranging with epoprostenol must be performed in a hospital setting with adequate personnel and equipment for physiologic monitoring and emergency care.

During the early phase of chronic administration, intense patient education is required.

Due to the potential for problems associated with the drug delivery system, immediate access to medical care should be available during chronic treatment.

Epoprostenol is infused continuously through a permanent indwelling central venous catheter via a small, portable infusion pump. Thus, therapy with epoprostenol requires commitment by the patient to drug reconstitution, drug administration, care of the permanent central venous catheter, and access to intense and ongoing patient education. Sterile technique must be adhered to in preparing the drug and in the care of the catheter, and even brief interruptions in the delivery of epoprostenol may result in rapid symptomatic deterioration. The decision to receive epoprostenol for PPH should be based upon the understanding that there is a high likelihood that therapy with epoprostenol will be needed for prolonged periods, possibly years, and the patient's ability to accept and care for a permanent i.v. catheter and infusion pump should be carefully considered.

Based on clinical trials, the acute hemodynamic response to epoprostenol did not correlate well with survival during chronic use of epoprostenol. Dosage of epoprostenol during chronic use should be adjusted at the first sign of recurrence or worsening of symptoms attributable to PPH, or the occurrence of adverse events associated with epoprostenol (see Dosage). Following dosage adjustments, standing and supine blood pressure and heart rate should be monitored closely for several hours.

During ongoing treatment, patients should avoid situations which promote vasodilation such as saunas, hot baths and sunbathing. Severe hypotension has been seen in patients treated with chronic epoprostenol infusions under such circumstances.

Epoprostenol use has been associated with an increased incidence of bradycardia in patients with PPH and with episodes of severe hypotension, including fatalities.

Risk of Bleeding: Prothrombin times should be monitored because anticoagulant therapy is generally recommended in these patients. Platelet counts should also be monitored.

Drug Interactions: Additional reductions in blood pressure may occur when epoprostenol is administered with diuretics, antihypertensive agents or other vasodilators. When NSAIDs or other drugs affecting platelet aggregation are used concomitantly, there is the potential for epoprostenol to increase the risk of bleeding. In clinical trials, epoprostenol was used with digoxin, diuretics, anticoagulants, oral vasodilators and supplemental oxygen.

Pregnancy: There are no adequate and well-controlled studies in pregnant women.

Labor and Delivery: The use of epoprostenol during labor, vaginal delivery or caesarean section has not been adequately studied in humans.

Lactation: It is not known whether this drug is excreted in human milk. Because many drugs are excreted in human milk, consideration should be given to discontinuation of breast feeding when epoprostenol is to be administered to a nursing woman.

Children: The safety and effectiveness of epoprostenol in children have not been established.

Geriatrics: Clinical studies of epoprostenol did not include sufficient numbers of patients aged 65 and over to determine whether they respond differently from younger patients. In general, dose selection for an elderly patient should be made carefully, reflecting the greater frequency of decreased hepatic, renal, or cardiac function and of concomitant disease or other drug therapy.

Adverse Effects: During clinical trials, adverse events were classified as follows: (1) adverse events during acute dose-ranging, (2) adverse events during chronic dosing, and (3) adverse events associated with the drug delivery system.

Adverse Events During Acute Dose-Ranging: During acute dose-ranging in clinical trials, epoprostenol was administered in 2 ng/kg/min increments until the patients developed symptomatic intolerance. The most common adverse events and those that limited further increases in dose were generally related to the major pharmacologic effect of epoprostenol, i.e., vasodilation. Table I lists the adverse events reported during acute dose-ranging in decreasing order of frequency as well as the % of cases where the event was dose limiting. Age-related differences (>16 vs ≤16 years) in the incidence of adverse events are shown in Table II.

Table I—Flolan

Adverse Events During Acute Dose-Ranging

Adverse Events Occurring in ≥1% of patients	Flolan (n=391) % of patients where event was reported	Flolan (n=391) % of patients where event was dose limiting
Flushing	58	14
Headache	49	18
Nausea/Vomiting	32	19
Hypotension	16	15
Anxiety, nervousness, agitation	11	7
Chest pain	11	7
Dizziness	8	4
Bradycardia	5	4
Abdominal pain	5	2
Musculoskeletal pain	3	2
Dyspnea	2	2
Back pain	2	—
Sweating	1	≤1
Dyspepsia	1	≤1
Hypesthesia/Paresthesia	1	≤1
Tachycardia	1	≤1

Table II—Flolan

Age-Related Adverse Events During Acute Dose-Ranging

Adverse Events	<16 years (n=63) % of patients reporting event	≥16 years (n=328) % of patients reporting event
Flushing	14	66
Headache	8	57
Nausea/Vomiting	40	30
Hypotension	14	16
Anxiety, nervousness, agitation	21	9
Chest pain	0	13
Dizziness	2	9
Bradycardia	6	5
Abdominal pain	6	5

Adverse Events During Chronic Administration: Interpretation of adverse events is complicated by the clinical features of PPH, which may be similar to some of the pharmacologic effects of epoprostenol (e.g., dizziness, syncope). Adverse events probably related to the underlying disease include dyspnea, fatigue, chest pain, right ventricular failure and pallor. Several adverse events, on the other hand, can clearly be attributed to epoprostenol. These include jaw pain, flushing, headache, diarrhea, nausea and vomiting, flu-like symptoms and anxiety/nervousness. In an effort to separate the adverse effects of the drug from the adverse effects of the underlying

Flolan (cont'd)

disease, Table III lists adverse events that occurred at a rate at least 10% different in the 2 groups in controlled trials.

Table III—Flolan

Adverse Events Regardless of Attribution Occurring During Chronic Administration in Controlled Trials with ≥10% Difference between Flolan and Standard Therapy Alone

Adverse Event	Flolan (n=52) % of patients	Standard Therapy (n=54) % of patients
Occurrence More Common with Flolan		
General		
Chills/Fever/Sepsis/Flu-Like Symptoms	25	11
Cardiovascular		
Tachycardia	35	24
Flushing	42	2
Gastrointestinal		
Diarrhea	37	6
Nausea/Vomiting	67	48
Musculoskeletal		
Jaw pain	54	0
Myalgia	44	31
Nonspecific musculoskeletal pain	35	15
Neurological		
Anxiety/Nervousness/Tremor	21	9
Dizziness	83	70
Headache	83	33
Hypesthesia, hyperesthesia, paresthesia	12	2
Occurrence More Common with Standard Therapy		
Cardiovascular		
Heart failure	31	52
Syncope	13	24
Shock	0	13
Respiratory		
Hypoxia	25	37

Thrombocytopenia has been reported during uncontrolled clinical trials in patients receiving epoprostenol.

Table IV lists those additional adverse events reported in PPH patients receiving epoprostenol plus standard therapy vs standard therapy alone during controlled clinical trials where the difference in incidence of the event between treatment groups was <10%.

Although the number of patients was small, in controlled trials there was a trend towards increased incidence of bradycardia associated with chronic treatment in patients <16 vs those ≥16 years of age.

Adverse Events Attributable to the Drug Delivery System: Chronic infusions of epoprostenol are delivered using a small, portable infusion pump through an indwelling central venous catheter. During controlled trials of up to 12 weeks duration, 21% of patients reported a local infection and 13% of patients reported pain at the injection site. During subsequent long-term follow-up, sepsis was reported at least once in 14% of patients and occurred at a rate of 0.32 infections per patient per year in patients treated with epoprostenol. When suspected, sepsis should be diagnosed and treated quickly. It is therefore important that these patients have immediate access to expert medical care. Malfunctions in the delivery system resulting in an inadvertent bolus of, or a reduction in, epoprostenol were associated with symptoms related to excess or insufficient epoprostenol respectively, that may lead to serious consequences including death (see Warnings, Adverse Effects, Adverse Events During Chronic Administration and Overdose: Symptoms and Treatment).

Overdose: Symptoms and Treatment: Signs and symptoms of excessive doses of epoprostenol are the expected dose-limiting pharmacologic effects of epoprostenol including flushing, headache, hypotension, tachycardia, nausea, vomiting and diarrhea. Treatment will ordinarily require dose reduction of epoprostenol.

One patient with secondary pulmonary hypertension accidentally received 50 mL of an unspecified concentration of epoprostenol. The patient vomited and became unconscious with an initially unobtainable blood pressure. Epoprostenol was discontinued, and the patient regained consciousness within seconds.

Table IV—Flolan

Adverse Events Regardless of Attribution Occurring During Chronic Administration in Controlled Trials with <10% Difference between Flolan and Standard Therapy Alone

Adverse Event	Flolan (n=52) % of patients	Standard Therapy (n=54) % of patients
General		
Asthenia	87	81
Cardiovascular		
Angina pectoris	19	20
Arrhythmia	27	20
Bradycardia	15	9
Supraventricular tachycardia	8	0
Pallor	21	30
Cyanosis	31	39
Palpitation	63	61
Cerebrovascular accident	4	0
Hypotension	27	31
Myocardial ischemia	2	6
Gastrointestinal		
Abdominal pain	27	31
Anorexia	25	30
Ascites	12	17
Constipation	6	2
Metabolic		
Edema	60	63
Hypokalemia	6	4
Weight reduction	27	24
Weight gain	6	4
Musculoskeletal		
Arthralgia	6	0
Bone pain	0	4
Chest pain	67	65
Neurological		
Confusion	6	11
Convulsion	4	0
Depression	37	44
Insomnia	4	4
Respiratory		
Cough increase	38	46
Dyspnea	90	85
Epistaxis	4	2
Pleural effusion	4	2
Dermatologic		
Pruritus	4	0
Rash	10	13
Sweating	15	20
Special Senses		
Amblyopia	8	4
Vision abnormality	4	0
Other		
Hemorrhage	19	11

Dosage: Epoprostenol must be reconstituted only with specific sterile diluent. Reconstituted solutions of epoprostenol must not be diluted or administered with other parenteral solutions or medications (see Warnings).

Epoprostenol is not to be used for bolus administration.

During acute dose-ranging, asymptomatic increases in pulmonary artery pressure coincident with increases in cardiac output occurred rarely. In such cases, dose reduction should be considered, but such an increase does not imply that chronic treatment is contraindicated. However, in the rare occurrence of pulmonary edema, chronic treatment is contraindicated.

During chronic use, epoprostenol is delivered continuously on an ambulatory basis through a permanent indwelling central venous catheter. Unless contraindicated, anticoagulant therapy should be administered to PPH patients receiving epoprostenol to reduce the risk of pulmonary thromboembolism or systemic embolism through a patent foramen ovale. In order to reduce the risk of infection, aseptic technique must be used in the reconstitution and administration of epoprostenol as well as in routine catheter care. Because epoprostenol is metabolized rapidly, even brief interruptions in the delivery of epoprostenol may result in symptoms associated with rebound pulmonary hypertension including dyspnea, dizziness, and asthenia. The decision to initiate therapy with epoprostenol should be based upon the understanding that there is a high likelihood that i.v. therapy with epoprostenol will be needed for prolonged periods, possibly years, and the patient's ability to accept and care for a permanent i.v. catheter and infusion pump should be carefully considered.

Acute Dose-Ranging: The initial chronic infusion rate of epoprostenol is determined by an acute dose-ranging procedure. During controlled clinical trials, this procedure was performed during cardiac catheterization. The infusion rate is initiated at 2 ng/kg/min and increased in increments of 2 ng/kg/min every 15 minutes or longer until dose-limiting pharmacologic effects are elicited. The most common dose-limiting pharmacologic effects during dose-ranging are flushing, nausea, vomiting, headache, hypotension, chest pain, dizziness and bradycardia (see Adverse Effects, Adverse Events During Dose-Ranging). During acute dose-ranging in clinical trials, the mean maximum dose that did not elicit dose-limiting pharmacologic effects was 8.6±0.3 ng/kg/min.

Continuous Chronic Infusion: Chronic continuous infusion of epoprostenol should be administered through a central venous catheter. Temporary peripheral i.v. infusions may be used until central access is established. Chronic infusions of epoprostenol should be initiated at 4 ng/kg/min less than the maximum-tolerated infusion rate determined during acute dose-ranging. If the maximum-tolerated infusion rate is less than 5 ng/kg/min, the chronic infusion should be started at one-half the maximum-tolerated infusion rate. During clinical trials, the mean initial chronic infusion rate was 5 ng/kg/min.

Dosage Adjustments: Changes in the chronic infusion rate should be based on persistence, recurrence or worsening of the patient's symptoms of PPH and the occurrence of adverse events due to excessive doses of epoprostenol. In general, the need for increases in dose from the initial chronic dose should be expected over time. In the controlled 12-week trial, for example, the dose increased from a mean starting dose of 5.2 ng/kg/min (4 ng/kg/min less than the new tolerated dose) to 9.2 ng/kg/min by the end of week 12, just 1.6 ng/kg/min less than the mean nontolerated dose in acute dose-ranging.

Increments in dose should be considered if symptoms of PPH persist or recur after improving. The infusion should be increased by 1 to 2 ng/kg/min increments at intervals sufficient to allow assessment of clinical response and tolerability; these intervals should be of at least 15 minutes. Following establishment of a new chronic infusion rate, the patient should be observed, and standing and supine blood pressure and heart rate monitored for several hours to ensure that the new dose is tolerated.

During chronic infusion, the occurrence of dose-related pharmacologic events similar to those observed during acute dose-ranging may necessitate a decrease in infusion rate, but the adverse event may occasionally resolve without dosage

Table V—Flolan

Preparation of Reconstituted Solutions

Directions	To Make 100 mL of Solution with Final Concentration of:
Dissolve contents of one 0.5 mg vial with 5 mL of **sterile diluent**. Withdraw 3 mL and add to sufficient **sterile diluent** to make a total of 100 mL.	3 000 ng/mL
Dissolve contents of one 0.5 mg vial with 5 mL of **sterile diluent**. Withdraw entire vial contents and add sufficient **sterile diluent** to make a total of 100 mL.	5 000 ng/mL
Dissolve contents of two 0.5 mg vials each with 5 mL of **sterile diluent**. Withdraw entire vial contents and add sufficient **sterile diluent** to make a total of 100 mL.	10 000 ng/mL
Dissolve contents of one 1.5 mg vial with 5 mL of **sterile diluent**. Withdraw entire vial contents and add sufficient **sterile diluent** to make a total of 100 mL.	15 000 ng/mL

adjustment. Dosage decreases should generally be made gradually in 2 ng/kg/min decrements every 15 minutes or longer until the dose-limiting effects resolve. Abrupt withdrawal of epoprostenol or sudden large reductions in infusion rates should be avoided. Except in life-threatening situations (e.g., unconsciousness, collapse, etc.), infusion rates of epoprostenol should be adjusted only under the direction of a physician.

In patients receiving lung transplants, doses of epoprostenol were tapered after the initiation of cardiopulmonary bypass.

Administration: Epoprostenol is administered by continuous i.v. infusion via a central venous catheter using an ambulatory infusion pump as recommended by the physician. During dose-ranging, epoprostenol may be administered peripherally.

The ambulatory infusion pump used to administer epoprostenol should: (1) be small and lightweight, (2) be able to adjust infusion rates in 2 ng/kg/min increments, (3) have occlusion, end of infusion, and low battery alarms, (4) be accurate to ±6% of the programmed rate, (5) be positive pressure driven (continuous or pulsatile) with intervals between pulses not exceeding 3 minutes at infusion rates used to deliver epoprostenol, and (6) have design characteristics that minimize the likelihood of accidental bolus administration. The reservoir should be made of polyvinyl chloride, polypropylene, or glass.

To avoid potential interruptions in drug delivery, the patient should have access to a back-up infusion pump and additional i.v. infusion sets. A multilumen catheter should be considered if other i.v. therapies are routinely administered.

Preliminary data suggest that peristaltic pumps may have advantages over syringe pumps.

Prior to use, reconstituted solutions of epoprostenol must be protected from light and must be refrigerated at 2 to 8°C if not used immediately. Under these conditions, reconstituted epoprostenol solution may be stored for up to 24 hours before being transferred to the infusion pump. Reconstituted epoprostenol solution that has not been transferred to the infusion pump within 24 hours (i.e., that has been stored for more than 24 hours) is to be discarded. Do not freeze reconstituted solutions of epoprostenol.

Once placed in the pump, a single reservoir of reconstituted epoprostenol solution can be administered for up to 24 hours by maintaining the temperature between 2 to 8°C with the use of 2 frozen 170 mL gel packs in a cold pouch. The gel packs should be changed every 12 hours or every 8 hours if the ambient temperature approaches 30°C. **When stored or in use, reconstituted epoprostenol must not be exposed to direct sunlight.**

Reconstitution: Parenteral drug products should be inspected visually for particulate matter and discoloration prior to administration whenever solution and container permit.

Eporostenol is only stable when reconstituted with specific sterile diluent. Epoprostenol must not be reconstituted or mixed with any other parenteral medications or solutions prior to or during administration.

A concentration for the solution of epoprostenol for acute dose-ranging or chronic therapy should be selected that is compatible with the infusion pump being used with respect to minimum and maximum flow rates, reservoir capacity and the infusion pump criteria listed above. Epoprostenol, when administered chronically, should be prepared in a drug delivery reservoir appropriate for the infusion pump with a total reservoir volume of at least 100 mL. Epoprostenol should be prepared using 2 vials of the specific **sterile diluent for epoprostenol** for use during a 24-hour period. Table V (on previous page) gives directions for preparing several different concentrations of epoprostenol.

Infusion Rates During Acute Dose-Ranging: More than one solution strength may be required to accommodate the range of infusions anticipated during acute dose-ranging. Generally, 3 000 and 10 000 ng/mL are satisfactory concentrations to deliver between 2 to 16 ng/kg/min in adults. Infusion rates may be calculated using the following formula:

$$\text{Infusion Rate (mL/h)} = \frac{[\text{Dose (ng/kg/min)} \times \text{Weight (kg)} \times 60 \text{ min/h}]}{\text{Final Concentration (ng/mL)}}$$

Tables VI through IX provide infusion rates for doses up to 16 ng/kg/min based upon patient weight, drug delivery rate, and concentration of the solution of epoprostenol to be used. These tables may be used to select the most appropriate concentration of epoprostenol that will result in an infusion rate between the minimum and maximum flow rates of the infusion pump and which will allow the desired duration of infusion from a given reservoir volume.

Table VI—Flolan

Infusion Rates for Flolan at a Concentration of 3 000 ng/mL

Patient Weight (kg)	Dose or Drug Delivery Rate (ng/kg/min)							
	2	4	6	8	10	12	14	16
	Infusion Delivery Rate (mL/h)							
10	—	—	1.2	1.6	2.0	2.4	2.8	3.2
20	—	1.6	2.4	3.2	4.0	4.8	5.6	6.4
30	1.2	2.4	3.6	4.8	6.0	7.2	8.4	9.6
40	1.6	3.2	4.8	6.4	8.0	9.6	11.2	12.8
50	2.0	4.0	6.0	8.0	10.0	12.0	14.0	16.0
60	2.4	4.8	7.2	9.6	12.0	14.4	16.8	19.2
70	2.8	5.6	8.4	11.2	14.0	16.8	19.6	22.4
80	3.2	6.4	9.6	12.8	16.0	19.2	22.4	25.6
90	3.6	7.2	10.8	14.4	18.0	21.6	25.2	28.8
100	4.0	8.0	12.0	16.0	20.0	24.0	28.0	32.0

Table VII—Flolan

Infusion Rates for Flolan at a Concentration of 5 000 ng/mL

Patient Weight (kg)	Dose or Drug Delivery Rate (ng/kg/min)							
	2	4	6	8	10	12	14	16
	Infusion Delivery Rate (mL/h)							
10	—	—	—	1.0	1.2	1.4	1.7	1.9
20	—	1.0	1.4	1.9	2.4	2.9	3.4	3.8
30	—	1.4	2.2	2.9	3.6	4.3	5.0	5.8
40	1.0	1.9	2.9	3.8	4.8	5.8	6.7	7.7
50	1.2	2.4	3.6	4.8	6.0	7.2	8.4	9.6
60	1.4	2.9	4.3	5.8	7.2	8.6	10.1	11.5
70	1.7	3.4	5.0	6.7	8.4	10.1	11.8	13.4
80	1.9	3.8	5.8	7.7	9.6	11.5	13.4	15.4
90	2.2	4.3	6.5	8.6	10.8	13.0	15.1	17.3
100	2.4	4.8	7.2	9.6	12.0	14.4	16.8	19.2

Table VIII—Flolan

Infusion Rates for Flolan at a Concentration of 10 000 ng/mL

Patient Weight (kg)	Dose or Drug Delivery Rate (ng/kg/min)						
	4	6	8	10	12	14	16
	Infusion Delivery Rate (mL/h)						
20	—	—	1.0	1.2	1.4	1.7	1.9
30	—	1.1	1.4	1.8	2.2	2.5	2.9
40	1.0	1.4	1.9	2.4	2.9	3.4	3.8
50	1.2	1.8	2.4	3.0	3.6	4.2	4.8
60	1.4	2.2	2.9	3.6	4.3	5.0	5.8
70	1.7	2.5	3.4	4.2	5.0	5.9	6.7
80	1.9	2.9	3.8	4.8	5.8	6.7	7.7
90	2.2	3.2	4.3	5.4	6.5	7.6	8.6
100	2.4	3.6	4.8	6.0	7.2	8.4	9.6

Table IX—Flolan

Infusion Rates for Flolan at a Concentration of 15 000 ng/mL

Patient Weight (kg)	Dose or Drug Delivery Rate (ng/kg/min)						
	4	6	8	10	12	14	16
	Infusion Delivery Rate (mL/h)						
30	—	—	1.0	1.2	1.4	1.7	1.9
40	—	1.0	1.3	1.6	1.9	2.2	2.6
50	—	1.2	1.6	2.0	2.4	2.8	3.2
60	1.0	1.4	1.9	2.4	2.9	3.4	3.8
70	1.1	1.7	2.2	2.8	3.4	3.9	4.5
80	1.3	1.9	2.6	3.2	3.8	4.5	5.1
90	1.4	2.2	2.9	3.6	4.3	5.0	5.8
100	1.6	2.4	3.2	4.0	4.8	5.6	6.4

Infusion Rates During Chronic Infusion: More concentrated solutions than those described in Tables VI to IX may be necessary in some cases where higher drug delivery rates are indicated. Generally, over time the daily dose of epoprostenol requires up-titration.

Information for the Patient: See Blue Section—Information for the Patient "Flolan".

Supplied: Each vial of sterile, freeze-dried powder contains: epoprostenol sodium equivalent to epoprostenol 0.5 mg (500 000 ng) or 1.5 mg (1 500 000 ng). Nonmedicinal ingredients: glycine, mannitol, sodium chloride and sodium hydroxide (added to adjust pH). Flint glass vials, individually packaged in a carton. Store at 15 to 25°C. Protect from light.

Each vial of sterile diluent contains: glycine 94 mg, sodium chloride 73.3 mg, sodium hydroxide (added to adjust pH) and water for injection USP q.s. to 50 mL. Glass vials of 50 mL, trays of 2. Store at 15 to 25°C. Do not freeze.

Reviewed 1998

FLOMAX® Ⓟ

Boehringer Ingelheim

Tamsulosin HCl

Selective Antagonist of Alpha$_{1A}$-adrenoceptor Subtype in the Prostate

Pharmacology: Tamsulosin, an alpha$_1$-adrenoceptor blocking agent, exhibits selectivity for alpha$_1$ receptors in the human prostate. At least 3 discrete alpha$_1$-adrenoreceptor subtypes have been identified: alpha$_{1A}$, alpha$_{1B}$ and alpha$_{1D}$; their

Flomax (cont'd)

distribution differs between human organs and tissue. Approximately 70% of the $alpha_1$-receptor in human prostate is of the $alpha_{1A}$ subtype.

The symptoms associated with benign prostatic hyperplasia (BPH) are related to bladder outlet obstruction, which is comprised of two underlying components: The static and dynamic. The static component is related to an increase in prostate size caused, in part, by a proliferation of smooth muscle cells in the prostatic stroma. However, the severity of BPH symptoms and the degree of urethral obstruction do not correlate well with the size of the prostate. The dynamic component is a function of an increase in smooth muscle tone in the prostate and bladder neck leading to constriction of the bladder outlet. Smooth muscle tone is mediated by the sympathetic nervous stimulation of $alpha_1$ adrenoceptors, which are abundant in the prostate, prostatic capsule, prostatic urethra, and bladder neck. Blockade of these adrenoreceptors can cause smooth muscles in the bladder neck and prostate to relax, resulting in an improvement in urine flow rate and a reduction in symptoms of BPH.

Tamsulosin is not intended for use as an antihypertensive drug.

The pharmacokinetics of tamsulosin have been evaluated in adult healthy volunteers and patients with BPH with doses ranging from 0.1 to 1 mg.

Absorption: Absorption of tamsulosin from the Flomax sustained-release formulation is essentially complete (>90%) following oral administration under fasted conditions. Time to maximum concentration (T_{max}) is reached by 4 to 5 hours under fasted conditions and by 6 to 7 hours when tamsulosin is administered with food. The delay in T_{max} when tamsulosin is administered with food has the desirable effect of smoothing the tamsulosin plasma concentration profile, thereby reducing fluctuation of the plasma peak and trough concentrations with multiple dosing. Taking tamsulosin under fasted conditions results in a 30% increase in bioavailability (AUC) and 40 to 70% increase in peak concentration (C_{max}) compared to fed conditions. The effects of food on the pharmacokinetics of tamsulosin are consistent regardless of whether tamsulosin is taken with a light breakfast or a high-fat breakfast (see Table I).

Likewise, tamsulosin had no effect on the extent of binding of these drugs.

Metabolism/Excretion: Tamsulosin is extensively metabolized by cytochrome P450 enzymes (CYP3A) in the liver, followed by extensive glucuronide or sulfate conjugation of metabolites. On administration of a radiolabeled dose of tamsulosin to 4 healthy volunteers, 97% of the administered radioactivity was recovered, with urine (76%) representing the primary route of excretion compared to feces (21%) over 168 hours. Less than 10% of the dose was recovered as unchanged (parent) compound in the urine.

Metabolites of tamsulosin do not contribute significantly to tamsulosin adrenoceptor antagonist activity. Furthermore, there is no enantiomeric bioconversion from tamsulosin [R(−) isomer] to the S(+) isomer in studies with mice, rats, dogs, and humans.

Tamsulosin undergoes restrictive clearance in humans, with a relatively low systemic clearance (2.88 L/h). Tamsulosin exhibits linear pharmacokinetics following single or multiple dosing resulting in a proportional increase in C_{max} and AUC at therapeutic doses. Intrinsic clearance is independent of tamsulosin binding to AAG, but diminishes with age, resulting in a 40% overall higher exposure (AUC) in subjects of age 55 to 75 years compared to subjects of age 20 to 32 years.

Following i.v. or oral administration of an immediate-release formulation, the elimination half-life of tamsulosin in plasma ranged from 5 to 7 hours. Because of absorption rate-controlled pharmacokinetics with the tamsulosin sustained-release formulation, the apparent half-life of tamsulosin increases to approximately 9 to 13 hours in healthy volunteers and to 14 to 15 hours in the target population.

Incubations with human liver microsomes showed no evidence of clinically significant interactions between tamsulosin and drugs which are known to interact or be metabolized by hepatic enzymes, such as amitriptyline, diclofenac, albuterol (beta-agonist), glyburide (glibenclamide), finasteride (5 alpha-reductase inhibitor for treatment of BPH), and warfarin.

Indications: For the treatment of the signs and symptoms of benign prostatic hyperplasia (BPH). Tamsulosin is not indicated for the treatment of hypertension.

Contraindications: Patients known to be hypersensitive to tamsulosin or any component of the sustained-release formulation.

Table I—Flomax

Mean Pharmacokinetic Parameters Following Daily Dosing with Flomax 0.4 mg Once Daily or 0.8 mg Once Daily with a Light Breakfast, High-fat Breakfast or Fasted

Pharmacokinetic Parameter	0.4 mg Once Daily to Healthy Volunteers (Age Range 18-32 Years)		0.8 mg Once Daily to Healthy Volunteers (Age Range 55-75 Years)		
	Light Breakfast	Fasted	Light Breakfast	High-fat Breakfast	Fasted
AUC (ng·h/mL)	151	199	440	449	557
T_{max} (h)*	6.0	4.0	7.0	6.5	5.0
C_{max} (ng/mL)	10.1	17.1	29.8	29.1	41.6
C_{min} (ng/mL)	3.8	4.0	12.3	13.5	13.3
C_{max}/C_{min} Ratio	3.1	5.3	2.7	2.5	3.6

*Median.

Legend: AUC: Area under the tamsulosin plasma time curve over the dosing interval.
T_{max}: Median time-to-maximum concentration.
C_{max}: Observed maximum tamsulosin plasma concentration.
C_{min}: Observed minimum concentration. Coefficients of variation (%CV) for C_{max} and AUC generally ranged from 35 to 53%, collectively.

Distribution: The mean steady-state apparent volume of distribution of tamsulosin after i.v. administration to 10 healthy male adults was 16 L, which is suggestive of distribution into extracellular fluids in the body. Additionally, whole body autoradiographic studies in mice, rats and dogs indicate that tamsulosin is widely distributed to most tissues including kidney, prostate, liver, gallbladder, heart, aorta, and brown fat, and minimally distributed to the brain, spinal cord, and testes. Tamsulosin is extensively bound to human plasma proteins (94 to 99%), primarily alpha-1-acid glycoprotein (AAG) in humans, with linear binding over a wide concentration range (20 to 600 ng/mL). The results of 2-way in vitro studies indicate that the binding of tamsulosin to human plasma proteins is not affected by amitriptyline, diclofenac, glyburide, simvastatin plus simvastatin-hydroxy acid metabolite, warfarin, diazepam, propranolol, trichlormethiazide, or chlormadinone.

Warnings: The signs and symptoms of orthostasis (postural hypotension, dizziness and vertigo) were detected more frequently in tamsulosin-treated patients than in placebo recipients. As with other alpha-adrenergic blocking agents, there is a potential risk of syncope (see Adverse Effects).

Patients beginning treatment with tamsulosin should be cautioned to avoid situations where injury could result should syncope occur (see Adverse Effects).

Precautions: General: Carcinoma of the Prostate: Carcinoma of the prostate and BPH cause many of the same symptoms. These two diseases frequently coexist. Patients should be evaluated prior to the start of tamsulosin therapy to rule out the presence of carcinoma of the prostate.

Orthostatic Hypotension: While syncope is the most severe orthostatic symptom of tamsulosin, other symptoms can occur (dizziness and postural hypotension). In the two U.S. double-blind, placebo-controlled studies (studies 1 and 2), orthostatic testing was conducted at each visit. Postural hypotension was reported in three patients (0.6%) receiving tamsulosin.

In 2 102 patients included in U.S., European, and Japanese placebo-controlled clinical studies, 0.3% of patients receiving tamsulosin experienced postural hypotension, 10.2% experienced dizziness, and 0.7% experienced vertigo; patients receiving placebo experienced postural hypotension, dizziness, and vertigo at rates of 0.1%, 7.2%, and 0.4%, respectively.

Occupational Hazards: Patients in occupations in which orthostatic hypotension could be dangerous should be treated with particular caution.

If hypotension occurs, the patient should be placed in the supine position and, if this measure is inadequate, volume expansion with i.v. fluids or vasopressor therapy may be used. A transient hypotensive response is not a contraindication to further therapy with tamsulosin.

Special Populations: Geriatrics: Cross-study comparisons of tamsulosin overall exposure (AUC) and half-life indicate that the pharmacokinetic disposition of tamsulosin may be slightly prolonged in geriatric males compared to young healthy male volunteers. However, tamsulosin has been found to be a safe and effective $alpha_1$-adrenoceptor antagonist when administered at therapeutic doses (0.4 and 0.8 mg once daily) to patients over the age of 65 years.

Children: Tamsulosin is not indicated for use in children.

Gender Effects: Tamsulosin is not indicated for use in women. Safety, effectiveness, and pharmacokinetics have not been evaluated in women.

Drug Interactions: No clinically significant drug-drug interactions were observed in the 8 controlled clinical studies conducted to determine if a clinically significant interaction would occur when tamsulosin 0.4 or 0.8 mg was administered with one of the following therapeutic agents: nifedipine, atenolol, enalapril, warfarin, digoxin, furosemide, cimetidine, or theophylline.

Nifedipine, Atenolol, Enalapril: No dosage adjustments are necessary when tamsulosin is administered concomitantly with Procardia XL (nifedipine), atenolol, or enalapril. In 3 studies in hypertensive subjects (age range 47 to 79 years) whose blood pressure was controlled with stable doses of Procardia XL (nifedipine), atenolol or enalapril for at least 3 months, tamsulosin 0.4 mg for 7 days followed by tamsulosin 0.8 mg for another 7 days (n=8 per study) resulted in no clinically significant effects on blood pressure and pulse rate compared to placebo (n=4 per study).

Warfarin: No dosage adjustments are recommended when tamsulosin is administered concomitantly with warfarin. In healthy volunteers (age range 20 to 43 years) receiving warfarin, treatment with tamsulosin (0.4 or 0.8 mg) had no significant effect on the anticoagulant activity of warfarin compared to placebo. While definitive conclusions cannot be drawn as only 6 subjects completed the study (3 subjects on tamsulosin and three subjects on placebo), the results suggest that coadministration of tamsulosin with warfarin does not alter the pharmacodynamic activity of warfarin.

Digoxin and Theophylline: No dosage adjustments are necessary when tamsulosin is administered concomitantly with digoxin or theophylline. In 2 studies in healthy volunteers (n=10 per study; age range 19 to 39 years), receiving tamsulosin 0.4 mg/day for 2 days, followed by tamsulosin 0.8 mg/day for 5 to 8 days, single i.v. doses of digoxin 0.5 mg or theophylline 5mg/kg resulted in no change in the pharmacokinetics of digoxin or theophylline. Furthermore, the safety profiles for the 2 drugs in combination with tamsulosin were acceptable.

Furosemide: No dosage adjustments are necessary when tamsulosin is administered concomitantly with furosemide. The pharmacokinetic and pharmacodynamic interaction between tamsulosin 0.8 mg/day (steady-state) and furosemide 20 mg i.v. (single dose) was evaluated in 10 healthy volunteers (age range 21 to 40 years). Tamsulosin had no effect on the pharmacodynamics (excretion of electrolytes) of furosemide. While furosemide produced an 11 to 12% reduction in tamsulosin C_{max} and AUC, these changes are expected to be clinically insignificant and do not require adjustment of the tamsulosin dosage.

Cimetidine: No dosage adjustments are necessary when tamsulosin is administered concomitantly with cimetidine. The effects of cimetidine at the highest recommended dose (400 mg every 6 hours for 6 days) on the pharmacokinetics of a single tamsulosin 0.4 mg dose was investigated in 10 healthy volunteers (age range 21 to 38 years). Treatment with cimetidine resulted in a significant decrease (26%) in the clearance of tamsulosin which resulted in a moderate increase in tamsulosin AUC (44%). However, the effects by cimetidine are of questionable clinical significance and no adjustment in the tamsulosin dosage is recommended.

Information to be Provided to the Patient (see Patient Package Insert): Patients should be told that dizziness can occur with tamsulosin, requiring caution in people who must drive, operate machinery, or perform hazardous tasks. Patients should be advised not to crush, chew, or open the capsules of tamsulosin sustained-release formulation. These capsules are specially formulated to control the delivery of tamsulosin HCl to the blood stream.

Laboratory Tests: No laboratory test interactions with tamsulosin are known. Treatment with tamsulosin for up to 12 months had no significant effect on prostate specific antigen (PSA).

Table II—Flomax

Treatment Emergent Adverse Events Occurring in ≥1% of Tamsulosin or Placebo Patients During Short-term (U.S. and European) Placebo-controlled Trials*

Body System/ Adverse Event	Tamsulosin (N=1 783) (%)	Placebo (N=798) (%)
Body as a Whole		
Headache	14.7	15.5
Infection	7.9	6.8
Pain	7.6	7.3
Asthenia	6.1	5.0
Back Pain	6.2	4.5
Abdominal Pain	3.4	4.3
Chest Pain	3.3	3.1
Accidental Injury	2.1	3.0
Flu Syndrome	2.1	2.9
Neck Pain	1.0	1.1
Fever	1.0	1.0
Chills	0.7	1.0
Malaise	0.4	1.1
Cardiovascular		
Hypertension	0.9	1.1
Digestive		
Diarrhea	4.4	4.4
Dyspepsia	3.8	5.4
Nausea	2.6	2.9
Constipation	1.3	1.4
Tooth Disorder	1.1	0.9
Metabolic and Nutritional Disorders		
Peripheral Edema	0.8	1.0
Musculoskeletal		
Arthralgia	3.0	3.3
Myalgia	1.7	2.1
Arthritis	1.1	1.0
Nervous		
Dizziness	11.8	8.9
Somnolence	2.5	1.5
Insomnia	1.7	0.6
Hypertonia	1.1	1.5
Libido Decreased	1.2	0.9
Paresthesia	0.4	1.1
Respiratory		
Rhinitis	11.6	6.9
Pharyngitis	4.3	3.9
Cough Increased	3.1	2.4
Sinusitis	2.1	1.3
Dyspnea	1.1	1.1
Lung Disorder	1.1	0.9
Skin and Appendages		
Rash	1.8	1.8
Pruritus	1.0	1.0
Sweating	1.1	0.8
Urogenital		
Abnormal Ejaculation	8.7	0.5
Urinary Tract Infection	1.5	0.4
Dysuria	1.2	1.3
Impotence	1.2	1.5

*Adverse events from patients given 0.1 to 0.8 mg tamsulosin daily were pooled.

Pregnancy: Studies in pregnant rats and rabbits at daily doses of 300 and 50 mg/kg, respectively (30 000 and 5 000 times the anticipated human dose), revealed no evidence of harm to the fetus. Tamsulosin is neither indicated nor recommended for use in women.

Lactation: Tamsulosin is not indicated for use in women.

Children: Tamsulosin is not indicated for use in children.

Adverse Effects: The incidence of treatment emergent adverse events has been ascertained from 6 short-term U.S. and European placebo-controlled clinical trials in which daily doses of 0.1 to 0.8 mg tamsulosin were used. These studies evaluated safety in 1 783 patients treated with tamsulosin and 798 patients administered placebo. The data suggest that tamsulosin is generally well tolerated at daily dose levels ranging from 0.1 to 0.8 mg. Adverse events seen were generally mild, transient, and self-limiting. Table II summarizes the treatment emergent adverse events occurring in ≥1% of patients receiving either tamsulosin or placebo during these 6 short-term, (U.S. and European) placebo-controlled trials.

No new types of adverse events were apparent after long-term treatment with tamsulosin. Those adverse events reported with the higher incidence by patients receiving tamsulosin compared to those receiving placebo in the short-term studies were reported with a similar pattern in the long-term studies.

Tamsulosin has not been associated with any clinically significant changes in the urinalysis or the routine biochemical and hematologic tests.

Table III shows the treatment emergent adverse events from which ≥0.5% of the patients administered tamsulosin (N=1 783) placebo (N=798) discontinued U.S. and European short-term, placebo-controlled clinical studies. The most frequent adverse events resulting in discontinuation of tamsulosin treatment were dizziness, asthenia, abnormal ejaculation, and chest pain.

Table III—Flomax

Description of Discontinuations Occurring in ≥0.5% of Tamsulosin or Placebo Patients in U.S. and European Short-term Placebo-controlled Clinical Studies[a]

Body System/ Adverse Event	Tamsulosin (N=1 783) (%)	Placebo (N=798) (%)
Body as a Whole		
Asthenia	0.7	0.6
Headache	0.4	0.6
Chest Pain	0.5	0.3
Nervous System		
Dizziness	1.4	0.9
Urogenital		
Abnormal Ejaculation[b]	0.6	0

[a] Adverse events from patients given 0.1 to 0.8 mg tamsulosin daily were pooled.

[b] Abnormal ejaculation includes ejaculation failure, ejaculation disorder, retrograde ejaculation and ejaculation decrease. Abnormal ejaculation was dose related in U.S. studies: 8.4% in 0.4 mg group, 18.1% in 0.8 mg group. Withdrawal from these clinical studies of Flomax because of abnormal ejaculation was also dose dependent: 1.6% in the 0.8 mg group, and no patients in the 0.4 mg or placebo groups.

Overdose: Symptoms and Treatment: Should overdosage of tamsulosin lead to hypotension (see Precautions), support of the cardiovascular system is of first importance. Restoration of blood pressure and normalization of heart rate may be accomplished by keeping the patient in the supine position. If this measure is inadequate, then administration of i.v. fluids should be considered. If necessary, vasopressors should then be used and renal function should be monitored and supported as needed. Laboratory data indicate that tamsulosin is 94 to 99% protein bound; therefore, dialysis is unlikely to be of benefit.

One patient reported an overdose of 30 capsules of tamsulosin 0.4 mg. Following the ingestion of the capsules, the patient reported a headache judged to be severe and probably drug-related that resolved the same day.

Dosage: 0.4 mg once daily is recommended as the dose for the treatment of the signs and symptoms of BPH. It should be administered approximately one-half hour following the same meal each day.

Depending on individual patient symptomatology and/or flow rates, the dose may be adjusted to 0.8 mg once daily. If tamsulosin administration is discontinued or interrupted for several days at either the 0.4 or 0.8 mg dose, therapy should be reinstituted, beginning with the 0.4 mg once daily dose.

Information for the Patient: See Blue Section—Information for the Patient "Flomax".

Supplied: Each sustained-release capsule contains: tamsulosin HCl 0.4 mg. Nonmedicinal ingredients: calcium stearate, Eudragit L30D-55 (methacrylic acid copolymer, polysorbate 80, and sodium lauryl sulfate), FD&C Blue No. 2, ferric oxide (red and yellow), gelatin, microcrystalline cellulose, talc, titanium dioxide and triacetin, printing ink: black iron oxide, dimethylpolysiloxane, 2-ethoxyethanol, industrial methylated spirit, purified water, shellac and soya lecithin. HDPE bottles of 100. Store at room temperature (15 to 30°C).

(Shown in Product Recognition Section)

New Product 1998

FLONASE® Ⓟ

Glaxo Wellcome

Fluticasone Propionate

Corticosteroid for Nasal Use

Pharmacology: Fluticasone is a potent anti-inflammatory steroid with strong topical and weak systemic activity. When administered intranasally in therapeutic doses, it has a direct anti-inflammatory action on the nasal mucosa, the mechanism of which is not yet completely defined.

The onset of action is not immediate, and 2 to 3 days treatment may be required before maximum relief is obtained. This is because the anti-inflammatory activities of glucocorticoids are related to specific steroid effects, which involve several biochemical events, including protein synthesis.

A portion of an intranasally administered dose will be swallowed. However, oral bioavailability of fluticasone approaches zero due to poor absorption and extensive first-pass metabolism. In clinical trials, no hypothalamic-pituitary-adrenal (HPA) axis effects have been observed.

Indications: For the treatment of seasonal allergic rhinitis including hay fever, and perennial rhinitis poorly responsive to conventional treatment.

Regular usage is essential for full therapeutic benefit since maximum relief may not be obtained until after 2 to 3 days of treatment.

Contraindications: In patients with a history of hypersensitivity to any of its ingredients, and in patients with active or quiescent tuberculosis, or untreated fungal, bacterial and viral infection.

Warnings: In patients previously on systemic steroids, either over prolonged periods or in high doses, the replacement with a topical corticosteroid can be accompanied by symptoms of withdrawal e.g. joint and/or muscular pain, lassitude, and depression and, in severe cases, adrenal insufficiency may occur, necessitating the temporary resumption of systemic steroid therapy.

Careful attention must be given to patients with asthma or other clinical conditions in whom a rapid decrease in systemic steroids may cause a severe exacerbation of their symptoms.

Precautions: Patients should be informed that the full effect of fluticasone therapy is not achieved until 2 to 3 days of treatment have been completed. Treatment of seasonal rhinitis should, if possible, start before the exposure to allergens. Although fluticasone will control seasonal allergic rhinitis in most cases, an abnormally heavy challenge of summer allergens may in certain instances necessitate appropriate additional therapy, particularly to control eye symptoms. Under most circumstances, treatment with corticosteroids should not be stopped abruptly but tapered off gradually.

The replacement of a systemic steroid with fluticasone must be gradual and carefully supervised by the physician. The guidelines under Dosage should be followed in all such cases.

Corticosteroids may mask some signs of infection and new infections may appear. A decreased resistance to localized infections has been observed during corticosteroid therapy; this may require treatment with appropriate therapy or stopping the administration of fluticasone.

During long-term therapy, HPA axis function and hematological status should be assessed.

The long-term effects of fluticasone in humans are still unknown, in particular, its local effects; the possibility of atrophic rhinitis and/or pharyngeal candidiasis should be kept in mind.

There is an enhanced effect of corticosteroids on patients with hypothyroidism and in those with cirrhosis. ASA should be used cautiously in conjunction with corticosteroids in hypothrombinemia.

Flonase (cont'd)

In patients who have had recent nasal surgery or trauma, a nasal corticosteroid should be used with caution until healing has occurred, because of the inhibitory effect of corticosteroids on wound healing.

Patients should be advised to inform subsequent physicians of prior use of corticosteroids.

To ensure proper dosage and administration of the drug, the patient should be instructed by a physician or other health professional in the use of fluticasone (see Information for the Patient).

Pregnancy: The safety of fluticasone in pregnancy has not been established. If used, the expected benefits should be weighed against the potential hazard to the fetus, particularly during the first trimester of pregnancy.

Like other glucocorticosteroids, fluticasone is teratogenic to rodent species. Adverse effects typical of potent corticosteroids are only seen at high systemic exposure levels; direct intranasal application ensures minimal systemic exposure. The relevance of these findings to humans has not yet been established. Infants born of mothers who have received substantial doses of glucocorticosteroids during pregnancy should be carefully observed for hypoadrenalism.

Lactation: Glucocorticosteroids are excreted in human milk. It is not known whether fluticasone is excreted in human milk. When measurable plasma levels were obtained in lactating laboratory rats following s.c. administration there was evidence of fluticasone in the breast milk. However, following intranasal administration to primates, no drug was detected in the plasma, and it is therefore unlikely that the drug would be detectable in milk. The use of fluticasone in nursing mothers, requires that the possible benefits of the drug be weighed against the potential hazards to the infant.

Children: Fluticasone is not presently recommended for children younger than 4 years of age due to limited clinical data in this age group.

Until greater clinical experience has been gained, the continuous, long-term treatment of children under age 12 is not recommended.

Adverse Effects: Adverse reactions in controlled clinical studies with fluticasone have been primarily associated with irritation of the nasal mucous membranes, and are consistent with those expected from application of a topical medication to an already inflamed membrane. The adverse reactions reported by patients treated with fluticasone were similar to those reported by patients receiving placebo.

The most frequently reported adverse reactions (≥1% in any treatment group) considered by the investigator to be potentially related to fluticasone or placebo in trials of seasonal allergic rhinitis are listed in Table I. These studies conducted in 948 adults and in 499 children evaluated 14 to 28 days of treatment with recommended doses of fluticasone compared with placebo.

In two 6 month trials involving 831 patients aged 12 to 75 years with perennial allergic rhinitis, the adverse reactions reported by patients treated with fluticasone were similar in type and incidence to those reported in seasonal trials, with the exception of epistaxis (≤13.3%) and blood in nasal mucous (≤8.3%). In addition to the events reported most frequently in the seasonal trials, patients receiving fluticasone in the 6 month trials reported nasal soreness (≤2.5%), nasal excoriation (≤2.0%), sinusitis (≤1.6%), and nasal dryness (≤1.3%).

Infrequent adverse reactions (incidence of 0.1% to 1% and greater than placebo) reported by patients receiving fluticasone at the recommended daily dose of 200 µg (or 100 µg/day for children 4 to 11 years of age) in the aforementioned clinical trials included pharyngeal irritation, nasal stinging, nausea and vomiting, unpleasant smell and taste, and sinus headache (0.3%); lacrimation, eye irritation, xerostomia, cough, urticaria, and rash (0.2%); and nasal septum perforation (0.1%). Hypersensitivity reactions including skin rash, edema of the face or tongue and, rarely, bronchospasm and anaphylaxis/anaphylactic reactions have been reported.

Overdose: Symptoms and Treatment: Like any other nasally administered corticosteroid, acute overdosing is unlikely in view of the total amount of active ingredient present. However, when used chronically in excessive doses or in conjunction with other corticosteroid formulations, systemic corticosteroid effects such as hypercorticism and adrenal suppression may appear. If such changes occur, the dosage of fluticasone should be discontinued slowly, consistent with accepted procedures for discontinuation of chronic steroid therapy (see Dosage).

The restoration of HPA axis function may be slow. During periods of pronounced physical stress (i.e. severe infections, trauma, surgery) a supplement with systemic steroids may be advisable.

Dosage: See Warnings.

The therapeutic effects of corticosteroids, unlike those of decongestants, are not immediate. Since the effect of fluticasone depends on its regular use, patients must be instructed to take the nasal inhalation at regular intervals and not, as with other nasal sprays, as they feel necessary.

Adults and Children 12 years of age and older: The usual dosage is 2 sprays (50 µg each) in each nostril once a day (total daily dosage, 200 µg). Some patients with severe rhinitis may benefit from 2 sprays in each nostril every 12 hours. The recommended maximum daily dose is 400 µg (4 sprays in each nostril).

Children 4 to 11 years of age: The usual dosage is 1 or 2 (50 µg/actuation) sprays in each nostril in the morning (100 or 200 µg/day). The recommended maximum daily dose is 200 µg (2 sprays in each nostril).

The safety and efficacy of fluticasone in children below 4 years of age have not been established and therefore, fluticasone is not recommended in this patient population.

Until greater clinical experience has been gained, the continuous, long-term treatment of children under age 12 is not recommended.

An improvement of symptoms usually becomes apparent within a few days after the start of therapy. However, symptomatic relief may not occur in some patients for as long as 2 weeks. Fluticasone should not be continued beyond three weeks in the absence of significant symptomatic improvement.

In the presence of excessive nasal mucous secretion or edema of the nasal mucosa, the drug may fail to reach the site of action. In such cases it is advisable to use a nasal vasoconstrictor for 2 to 3 days prior to starting treatment with fluticasone. Patients should be instructed on the correct method of use, which is to blow the nose, then insert the nozzle carefully into the nostril, compress the opposite nostril and actuate the spray while inspiring through the nose, with the mouth closed (see Information for the Patient).

Careful attention must be given to patients previously treated for prolonged periods with systemic corticosteroids when transferred to fluticasone. Initially, fluticasone and the systemic corticosteroid must be given concomitantly, while the dose of the latter is gradually decreased. The usual rate of withdrawal of the systemic steroid is the equivalent of 1 mg of prednisone every 4 days if the patient is under close supervision. If continuous supervision is not feasible, the withdrawal of the systemic steroid should be slower, approximately 1 mg of prednisone (or equivalent) every 10 days. If withdrawal symptoms appear, the previous dose of the systemic steroid should be resumed for a week before further decrease is attempted.

Information for the Patient: See Blue Section—Information for the Patient ''Flonase''.

Supplied: Each 100 mg of spray delivered by the nasal adaptor (1 actuation), contains: fluticasone propionate 50 µg. Nonmedicinal ingredients: benzalkonium chloride, dextrose, microcrystalline cellulose and carboxymethylcellulose sodium, phenylethyl alcohol, Polysorbate 80 and purified water. Amber glass bottles containing sufficient formulation for either 120 metered sprays (16 g net weight) or 60 metered sprays (9 g net weight). Store between 4 and 30°C. Shake gently before use.

(Shown in Product Recognition Section)

Table I—Flonase

Adverse Reactions Reported Most Frequently in Clinical Trials of Seasonal Allergic Rhinitis

	Adults (age ≥ 12 years)			Children (age 4–11 years)		
	Fluticasone 100 µg bid (n=312) %	Fluticasone 200 µg od (n=322) %	placebo (n=314) %	Fluticasone 100 µg od (n=167) %	Fluticasone 200 µg od (n=164) %	placebo (n=168) %
Nasal burning	2.2	3.4	2.5	1.8	2.4	1.2
Pharyngitis	1.3	1.6	<1	<1	0	0
Runny nose	<1	1.6	<1	<1	<1	<1
Blood in nasal mucus	0	1.6	<1	0	<1	0
Epistaxis	1.6	2.8	2.2	3.0	3.7	3.6
Sneezing	<1	1.2	2.2	0	<1	0
Crusting in nostrils	0	0	0	1.2	0	0
Nasal congestion	0	0	0	0	1.2	0
Nasal ulcer	<1	0	0	1.2	1.2	1.2
Headache	1.3	2.5	1.9	1.2	1.2	1.2

FLORINEF® Ⓟ

Roberts

Fludrocortisone Acetate

Addison's Disease Therapy

Pharmacology: The physiologic action of fludrocortisone is similar to that of hydrocortisone. However, the effects of fludrocortisone, particularly on electrolyte balance, but also on carbohydrate metabolism, are considerably heightened and prolonged. In small oral doses, fludrocortisone produces marked sodium retention and increased urinary potassium excretion. It also causes a rise in blood pressure, apparently because of these effects on electrolyte levels. In larger doses, fludrocortisone inhibits endogenous adrenal cortical secretion, thymic activity, and pituitary corticotropin excretion: promotes the deposition of liver glycogen; and, unless protein intake is adequate, induces negative nitrogen balance.

Indications: Partial replacement therapy for primary and secondary adrenocortical insufficiency in Addison's disease and for the treatment of salt losing adrenogenital syndrome.

Contraindications: Corticosteroids are contraindicated in patients with systemic fungal infections.

Precautions: Because of its marked effect on sodium retention, the use of fludrocortisone in the treatment of conditions other than those indicated herein is not advised.

Corticosteroids may mask some signs of infection, and new infections may appear during their use. There may be decreased resistance and inability to localize infection when corticosteroids are used. If an infection occurs during fludrocortisone therapy, it should be promptly controlled by suitable antimicrobial therapy.

Prolonged use of corticosteroids may produce posterior subcapsular cataracts, glaucoma with possible damage to the optic nerves, and may enhance the establishment of secondary ocular infections due to fungi or viruses.

Average and large doses of hydrocortisone or cortisone can cause elevation of blood pressure, salt and water retention, and increased excretion of potassium. These effects are less likely to occur with the synthetic derivatives except when used in large doses. However, since fludrocortisone is a potent mineralocorticoid, both the dosage and salt intake should be carefully monitored in order to avoid the development of hypertension, edema, or weight gain. Periodic checking of serum electrolyte levels is advisable during prolonged therapy; dietary salt restriction and potassium supplementation may be necessary. All corticosteroids increase calcium excretion.

Patients should not be vaccinated against smallpox while on corticosteroid therapy. Other immunization procedures should not be undertaken in patients who are on corticosteroids, especially on high dose, because of possible hazards of neurological complications and a lack of antibody response.

The use of fludrocortisone in patients with active tuberculosis should be restricted to those cases of fulminating or disseminated tuberculosis in which the corticosteroid is used for the management of the disease in conjunction with an appropriate antituberculous regimen. If corticosteroids are indicated in patients with latent tuberculosis or tuberculin reactivity, close observation is necessary since reactivation of the disease may occur. During prolonged corticosteroid therapy these patients should receive chemoprophylaxis.

Pregnancy and *Lactation:* Since adequate human reproduction studies have not been done with corticosteroids, the use of these drugs in pregnancy, nursing mothers, or women of childbearing potential requires that the possible benefits of the drug be weighed against the potential hazards to the mother, embryo, fetus or nursing infant. Infants born of mothers who have received substantial doses of corticosteroids during pregnancy should be carefully observed for signs of hypoadrenalism.

Adverse reactions to corticosteroids may be produced by too rapid withdrawal or by continued use of large doses.

To avoid drug induced adrenal insufficiency, supportive dosage may be required in times of stress (such as trauma, surgery, or severe illness) both during treatment with fludrocortisone and for a year afterwards.

There is an enhanced corticosteroid effect in patients with hypothyroidism and in those with cirrhosis.

Corticosteroids should be used cautiously in patients with ocular herpes simplex because of possible corneal perforation.

The lowest possible dose of corticosteroid should be used to control the condition being treated. A gradual reduction in dosage should be made when possible.

Psychic derangements may appear when corticosteroids are used. These may range from euphoria, insomnia, mood swings, personality changes, and severe depression, to frank psychotic manifestations. Existing emotional instability or psychotic tendencies may also be aggravated by corticosteroids.

ASA should be used cautiously in conjunction with corticosteroids in patients with hypoprothrombinemia.

Corticosteroids should be used with caution in patients with nonspecific ulcerative colitis if there is a probability of impending perforation, abscess, or other pyogenic infection.

Corticosteroids should also be used cautiously in patients with diverticulitis, fresh intestinal anastomoses, active or latent peptic ulcer, renal insufficiency, hypertension, osteoporosis, acute glomerulonephritis, vaccinia, varicella, exanthema, Cushing's syndrome, antibiotic resistant infections, diabetes mellitus, congestive heart failure, chronic nephritis, thromboembolitic tendencies, thrombophlebitis, convulsive disorders, metastatic carcinoma, and myasthenia gravis.

Growth and development of infants and children on prolonged corticosteroid therapy should be carefully observed.

Adverse Effects: In the recommended small dosages, the side effects seen with cortisone and its derivatives are not usually a problem with fludrocortisone. However, the following untoward effects should be kept in mind, particularly when this agent is used over a prolonged period of time or in conjunction with cortisone or a similar glucocorticoid:

Fluid and electrolyte disturbances: sodium retention, fluid retention, congestive heart failure in susceptible patients, potassium loss, hypokalemic alkalosis, and hypertension.

Musculoskeletal: muscle weakness, steroid myopathy, loss of muscle mass, osteoporosis, vertebral compression fractures, aseptic necrosis of femoral and humeral heads, pathologic fracture of long bones, and spontaneous fractures.

Gastrointestinal: peptic ulcer with possible perforation and hemorrhage, pancreatitis, abdominal distention, and ulcerative esophagitis.

Dermatologic: impaired wound healing, thin fragile skin, bruising, petechiae and ecchymoses, facial erythema, increased sweating, subcutaneous fat atrophy, purpura, striae, hyperpigmentation of the skin and nails, hirsutism, and acneiform eruptions; reactions to skin tests may be suppressed.

Neurological: convulsions, increased intracranial pressure with papilledema (pseudotumor cerebri) usually after treatment, vertigo, headache, and severe mental disturbances.

Endocrine: menstrual irregularities; development of the Cushingoid state; suppression of growth in children; secondary adrenocortical and pituitary unresponsiveness, particularly in times of stress (e.g. trauma, surgery, or illness); decreased carbohydrate tolerance; manifestations of latent diabetes mellitus; and increased requirements for insulin or oral hypoglycemic agents in diabetics.

Ophthalmic: posterior subcapsular cataracts, increased intraocular pressure, glaucoma, and exophthalmos.

Metabolic: hyperglycemia, glycosuria, and negative nitrogen balance due to protein catabolism.

Other adverse reactions that may occur following the administration of a corticosteroid are necrotizing angiitis, thrombophlebitis, aggravation or masking of infections, insomnia, syncopal episodes, and anaphylactoid reactions.

Dosage: Addison's disease: Usual dose is 0.1 mg daily, although dosage ranging from 0.1 mg 3 times a week to 0.2 mg daily has been employed. In the event transient hypertension develops as a consequence of therapy, the dose should be reduced to 0.05 mg daily. Fludrocortisone is preferably administered in conjunction with cortisone (10 to 37.5 mg daily in divided doses) or hydrocortisone (10 to 20 mg daily in divided doses).

Salt losing adrenogenital syndrome: 0.1 to 0.2 mg daily.

Supplied: Each light pink, scored tablet contains: fludrocortisone acetate 0.1 mg. Bottles of 100.

(Shown in Product Recognition Section)

FLOVENT® ℞

Glaxo Wellcome

Fluticasone Propionate

Corticosteroid

Pharmacology: Fluticasone is a highly potent glucocorticoid anti-inflammatory steroid with strong topical and negligible systemic activity. When administered by inhalation at therapeutic dosages, it has a direct potent anti-inflammatory action within the lungs, resulting in reduced symptoms and exacerbations of asthma without the adverse effects observed when corticosteroids are administered systemically.

In comparisons with beclomethasone dipropionate, fluticasone propionate has demonstrated greater topical potency.

Pharmacokinetics: Following i.v. administration, the pharmacokinetics of fluticasone are proportional to the dose. Fluticasone is extensively distributed within the body. The volume of distribution at steady state is approximately 300 L and has a very high clearance which is estimated to be 1.1 L/min indicating extensive hepatic extraction. Peak plasma fluticasone concentrations are reduced by approximately 98% within 3 to 4 hours and only low plasma concentrations are associated with the terminal half-life, which is approximately 8 hours. Following oral administration of fluticasone, 87 to 100% of the dose is excreted in the feces. Following doses of either 1 or 16 mg, up to 20% and 75% respectively, is excreted in the feces as the parent compound. Absolute oral bioavailability is negligible (<1%) due to a combination of incomplete absorption from the gastrointestinal tract and extensive first-pass metabolism.

Following inhaled dosing, systemic absolute bioavailability of fluticasone is estimated as 12 to 26%, dependent on presentation. Systemic absorption of fluticasone occurs mainly through the lungs, and is initially rapid, then prolonged.

The plasma protein binding of fluticasone propionate is 91%. Fluticasone is extensively metabolised by CYP3A4 enzyme to an inactive carboxylic acid derivative. As fluticasone is given at very low doses, any effect on coadministered drugs is unlikely. In clinical programmes, there were no reports of suspected drug interactions while patients were on inhaled fluticasone therapy.

The limited data available for pediatric pharmacokinetics show consistency with adult findings.

In most but not all patients, the daily output of adrenocortical hormones remain within the normal range during chronic treatment with inhaled fluticasone, even at the highest recommended doses in children (200 μg/day) and adults (2 000 μg/day). After transfer from other inhaled steroids to fluticasone propionate, the daily output gradually improves despite past and present intermittent use of oral steroids, thus demonstrating return of normal adrenal function on inhaled fluticasone. The adrenal reserve also remains normal during chronic treatment with inhaled fluticasone, as measured by a normal increment on a stimulation test. However, any residual impairment of adrenal reserve from previous treatments may persist for a considerable time and should be kept in mind (see Warnings and Precautions).

Indications: For the prophylactic management of steroid-responsive bronchial asthma in adults and children over 4 years of age.

Adults and Adolescents above 16 Years of Age: Mild Asthma: PEF values greater than 80% of predicted at baseline with less than 20% variability. Patients requiring intermittent symptomatic bronchodilator asthma medication on more than an occasional basis.

Moderate Asthma: PEF values 60 to 80% of predicted at baseline with 20 to 30% variability. Patients requiring regular asthma medication and patients with unstable or worsening asthma on currently available prophylactic therapy or bronchodilator alone.

Severe Asthma: PEF values less than 60% of predicted at baseline with greater than 30% variability. Patients with severe, chronic asthma. On introduction of inhaled fluticasone, many patients who are dependent on systemic corticosteroids for adequate control of symptoms may be able to reduce significantly or to eliminate their requirements for oral corticosteroids.

Severe asthma requires regular medical assessment as death may occur. Patients with severe asthma have constant symptoms and frequent exacerbations, with limited physical capacity. These patients will require high dose inhaled (see Dosage) or oral corticosteroid therapy. Sudden worsening of symptoms may require increased corticosteroid dosage which should be administered under urgent medical supervision.

Children above 4 Years of Age: For any child above 4 years of age who requires prophylactic medication, including patients not controlled on currently available prophylactic medication.

Contraindications: Patients with a history of hypersensitivity to any of its ingredients and in patients with active or quiescent pulmonary tuberculosis, or untreated fungal, bacterial or viral infections of the respiratory tract.

Not to be used in the primary treatment of status asthmaticus or other acute episodes of asthma, or in patients with moderate to severe bronchiectasis.

Warnings: Systemic Steroid Replacement by Inhaled Steroid: Particular care is needed in asthmatic patients who are transferred from systemically active corticosteroids to inhaled corticosteroids because deaths due to adrenal insufficiency have occurred during and after transfer. For the transfer of patients being treated with oral corticosteroids, inhaled fluticasone should first be added to the existing oral steroid therapy, which is then gradually withdrawn.

Patients with adrenocortical suppression should be monitored regularly and the oral steroid reduced cautiously. Some depression of plasma cortisol may occur in a small number of adult patients on higher doses (e.g., >1 mg/day). However, in most but not all patients, adrenal function and adrenal reserve remain within normal range on inhaled fluticasone therapy. Some patients transferred from other inhaled steroids or oral steroids remain at risk of impaired adrenal reserve for a considerable time after transferring to inhaled fluticasone.

After withdrawal from systemic corticosteroids, a number of months are required for recovery of hypothalamic-pituitary-adrenal (HPA) function. During this period of HPA suppression, patients may exhibit signs and symptoms of adrenal insufficiency when exposed to trauma, surgery or infections, particularly gastroenteritis. Although fluticasone may provide control of asthmatic symptoms during these episodes, it does not provide the systemic steroid which is necessary for coping with these emergencies. The physician may consider supplying oral steroids for use in times of stress (e.g., worsening asthma attacks, chest infections, surgery).

During periods of stress or a severe asthmatic attack, patients who have been withdrawn from systemic corticosteroids should be instructed to resume systemic steroids immediately and to contact their physician for further instruction. These patients should also be instructed to carry a warning card indicating that they may need supplementary systemic steroids during periods of stress or a severe asthma attack. To assess the risk of adrenal insufficiency in emergency situations, routine tests of adrenal cortical function, including measurements of early morning and evening cortisol levels, should be performed periodically in all patients. An early morning resting cortisol level may be accepted as normal only if it falls at or near the normal mean level.

Transfer of patients from systemic steroid therapy to inhaled fluticasone may unmask allergic conditions outside the pulmonary tract that were previously suppressed by the systemic steroid therapy, e.g., rhinitis, conjunctivitis and eczema. These allergies should be symptomatically treated with antihistamine and/or topical preparations, including topical steroids.

Candidiasis: Therapeutic dosages frequently cause the appearance of C. albicans (thrush) in the mouth and throat. The development of pharyngeal and laryngeal candidiasis is a cause for concern because the extent of its penetration into the respiratory tract is unknown. Patients may find it helpful to rinse out their mouths with water after using the inhaler. Symptomatic candidiasis can be treated with topical antifungal therapy while still continuing to use fluticasone.

Paradoxical Bronchospasm: As with other inhalation therapy, paradoxical bronchospasm may occur characterized by an immediate increase in wheezing after dosing. This should be treated immediately with a fast-acting inhaled bronchodilator (e.g., salbutamol) to relieve acute asthmatic symptoms. Fluticasone should be discontinued immediately, the patient assessed, and if necessary, alternative therapy instituted.

Monitoring Asthma Control: Increasing use of short-acting inhaled bronchodilators to control symptoms indicates deterioration of asthma control. Sudden and progressive deterioration

Flovent (cont'd)

in asthma control is potentially life-threatening and consideration should be given to increasing corticosteroid dosage. Patients should be instructed to contact their physicians if they find that relief with short-acting bronchodilator treatment becomes less effective or they need more inhalations than usual. During such episodes, patients may require therapy with systemic corticosteroids.

Fluticasone is not indicated for rapid relief of bronchospasm but for regular daily treatment of the underlying inflammation. There is no evidence that control of bronchial asthma can be achieved by the administration of fluticasone in amounts greater than the recommended dosages.

Lack of response or severe exacerbations of asthma should be treated by increasing the dose of fluticasone and, if necessary, by giving a systemic steroid and/or an antibiotic if there is an infection.

Precautions: General: It is essential that the patients be instructed that fluticasone is a preventative agent which must be taken daily at the intervals recommended by their doctors and is not to be used as acute treatment for an asthmatic attack.

Patients should be advised to inform subsequent physicians of the prior use of corticosteroids.

Systemic Steroid Replacement by Inhaled Steroid: The replacement of a systemic steroid with inhaled steroid must be gradual and carefully supervised by the physician since upon withdrawal systemic symptoms (e.g., joint and/or muscular pain, lassitude, depression) may occur despite maintenance or improvement of respiratory function. The guidelines under Dosage should be followed in all such cases.

Long-term Effects: The long-term effects of fluticasone in human subjects are still unknown. In particular, the local effects of the drug on developmental or immunologic processes in the mouth, pharynx, trachea and lungs are unknown. There is also no information about the possible long-term systemic effects of the agent. During long-term therapy, HPA axis function and hematological status should be assessed periodically.

Discontinuance: Treatment with fluticasone should not be stopped abruptly, but tapered off gradually.

Pulmonary Infiltration by Eosinophils: As with other glucocorticoids, pulmonary infiltration by eosinophils may occur in patients on fluticasone therapy. Although it is possible that in some patients this state may become manifest because of systemic steroid withdrawal when inhaled steroids are administered, a causative role for fluticasone and/or its vehicle cannot be ruled out.

Pregnancy: The safety of fluticasone in pregnancy has not been established. If used, the expected benefits should be weighed against the potential risk to the fetus, particularly during the first trimester of pregnancy.

Like other glucocorticoids, fluticasone is teratogenic to rodent species. Adverse effects typical of potent corticosteroids are only seen at high systemic exposure levels; administration by inhalation ensures minimal systemic exposure. The relevance of these findings to humans has not yet been established since well-controlled trials relating to fetal risk in humans are not available. Infants born of mothers who have received substantial doses of glucocorticoids during pregnancy should be carefully observed for hypoadrenalism.

Lactation: Glucocorticoids are excreted in human milk. The excretion of fluticasone into human breast milk has not been investigated. When measurable plasma levels were obtained in lactating laboratory rats following s.c. administration there was evidence of fluticasone in the breast milk. However, plasma levels in patients following inhaled fluticasone at recommended doses are likely to be low. The use of fluticasone in nursing mothers requires that the possible benefits of the drug be weighed against the potential risk to the infant.

Children: Fluticasone is not presently recommended for children younger than 4 years of age due to limited clinical data in this age group.

Effect on Infection: Corticosteroids may mask some signs of infections and new infections may appear. A decreased resistance to localized infection has been observed during corticosteroid therapy. This may require treatment with appropriate therapy or stopping the administration of fluticasone until the infection is eradicated.

Abuse of Fluorocarbon Propellants: Fluorocarbon propellants may be hazardous if they are deliberately abused. Inhalation of high concentrations of aerosol sprays has brought about cardiovascular toxic effects and even death, especially under conditions of hypoxia. However, evidence attests to the safety of aerosols when used properly with adequate ventilation.

Hypothyroidism and Cirrhosis: There is an enhanced effect of corticosteroids on patients with hypothyroidism and in those with cirrhosis.

Corticosteroids and ASA: ASA should be used cautiously in conjunction with corticosteroids in hypoprothrombinemia.

Proper Use of the Inhaler: To ensure the proper dosage and administration of the drug, the patient must be instructed by a physician or other health professional in the use of the Inhaler or Diskus (see Information for the Patient). Inhaler actuation should be synchronized with inspiration to ensure optimum delivery of the drug to the lungs.

Oral Hygiene: In some patients, corticosteroids may cause hoarseness or candidiasis of the mouth and throat (thrush). Adequate oral hygiene is of primary importance in minimizing overgrowth of microorganisms such as C. albicans. Patients may find it helpful to rinse out their mouth with water after using the inhaler (see Dosage). Symptomatic candidiasis can be treated with topical antifungal therapy while still continuing treatment with fluticasone.

Drug Interactions: No specific drug interaction studies have been performed; however, because of the very low plasma drug concentrations achieved after inhaled dosing, there are unlikely to be any implications for displacement drug interactions. There were no reports of suspected drug interactions in clinical trials with fluticasone.

Adverse Effects: In general, inhaled corticosteroid therapy may be associated with dose dependent increases in the incidence of ocular complications, reduced bone density, suppression of HPA axis responsiveness to stress, and inhibition of growth velocity in children. Such events have been reported rarely in clinical trials with fluticasone.

Glaucoma may be exacerbated by inhaled corticosteroid treatment for asthma or rhinitis. In patients with established glaucoma who require long-term inhaled corticosteroid treatment, it is prudent to measure intraocular pressure before commencing the inhaled corticosteroid and to monitor it subsequently. In patients without established glaucoma, but with a potential for developing intraocular hypertension (e.g., the elderly), intraocular pressure should be monitored at appropriate intervals.

In elderly patients treated with inhaled corticosteroids, the prevalence of posterior subcapsular and nuclear cataracts is probably low but increases in relation to the daily and cumulative lifetime dose. Cofactors such as smoking, ultraviolet B exposure, or diabetes may increase the risk. Children may be less susceptible.

A reduction of growth velocity in children or teenagers may occur as a result of inadequate control of chronic diseases such as asthma or from use of corticosteroids for treatment. Physicians should closely follow the growth of adolescents taking corticosteroids by any route and weigh the benefits of corticosteroid therapy and asthma control against the possibility of growth suppression if any adolescent's growth appears slowed.

Osteoporosis and fracture are the major complications of long-term asthma treatment with parenteral or oral steroids. Inhaled corticosteroid therapy is also associated with dose-dependent bone loss although the degree of risk is very much less than with oral steroid. This risk may be offset by estrogen replacement in postmenopausal women, and by titrating the daily dose of inhaled steroid to the minimum required to maintain optimal asthma control. It is not yet known whether the peak bone density achieved during youth is adversely affected if substantial amount of inhaled corticosteroid are administered prior to 30 years of age. Failure to achieve maximal bone density during youth could increase the risk of osteoporotic fracture when those individuals reach 60 years of age and older.

No major side effects attributable to the use of fluticasone have been reported. Adverse reactions in controlled clinical studies with fluticasone have been primarily those normally associated with asthma. Apart from asthma and related events and pharmacologically predicted events (candidiasis and hoarseness), there were no dose-related trends. Cutaneous hypersensitivity reactions have been observed. The adverse reactions reported by patients treated with fluticasone were similar to those reported by patients treated with beclomethasone dipropionate.

The most frequently reported adverse reactions (≥1%) considered by the investigator to be potentially drug-related during controlled clinical trials with fluticasone in over 4 400 adults and 1 100 children are presented in Table I.

Table I—Flovent

Most Frequently Reported Adverse Reactions

	Percentage of Patients Reporting Adverse Reactions	
	Adults (≥16 Years) (n=3 640)	**Children (4–16 Years) (n=778)**
Asthma & related events	2	3
Oral candidiasis	3	<1
Hoarseness	2	<1
Sore throat	1	<1
Cough	1	

Infrequent adverse reactions (incidence of 0.1 to 1%) reported by patients receiving recommended dosages of inhaled fluticasone (200 to 2 000 μg/day for adults; 100 to 200 μg/day for children) in these clinical trials included headache, musculoskeletal pain, diabetes, hypertension, weight gain, viral infection, respiratory tract infection, nausea, gastric pain, allergy, depression and oral ulcer.

Adrenal Suppression: Studies in which adrenal reserve has been investigated have shown that even at daily dosages of fluticasone Inhaler greater than 1 mg, adrenal reserve is maintained in the majority of patients.

Overdose: Symptoms and Treatment: The acute toxicity of fluticasone is low. The only harmful effect that follows inhalation of large amounts of the drug over a short period of time is suppression of adrenal function. No special emergency action need be taken. In such cases, treatment with inhaled fluticasone should be continued at a dose sufficient to control asthma; adrenal function recovers in a few days and can be verified by measuring plasma cortisol.

Chronic use of inhaled fluticasone in daily doses in excess of 2 mg may lead to some degree of adrenal suppression. Monitoring of adrenal reserve may be indicated. Gradual reduction of the inhaled dose may be required. Treatment with inhaled fluticasone should be continued at a dose sufficient to control asthma.

Dosage: General: **The lowest dose of fluticasone required to maintain good asthma control should be used. When the patient's asthma is well controlled, a reduction in the dose of fluticasone should be attempted in order to identify the lowest possible dose required to maintain control. Such an attempt at dose reduction should be carried out on a regular basis.**

Fluticasone Inhaler and Diskus are to be administered by oral inhalation only.

Since the effect of fluticasone depends on its regular use and on the proper technique of inhalation, the patient should be made aware of the prophylactic nature of therapy with inhaled fluticasone, and that for optimum benefit fluticasone should be taken regularly, even when the patient is asymptomatic. The onset of therapeutic effect is within 4 to 7 days.

If patients find that relief with short-acting bronchodilator treatment becomes less effective or they need more inhalations than usual, medical attention should be sought.

Patients using inhaled bronchodilators should be advised to use the bronchodilator before the fluticasone inhaler in order to enhance the penetration of fluticasone into the bronchial tree. Several minutes should lapse between the use of the 2 inhalers to reduce the potential toxicity from the inhaled fluorocarbon propellants and to allow for some bronchodilation to occur.

In the presence of excessive mucus secretion, the drug may fail to reach the bronchioles. Therefore, if an obvious response is not obtained after 10 days, attempts should be made to remove the mucus with expectorants and/or with a short course of systemic corticosteroid treatment. Continuation of treatment with inhaled fluticasone usually maintains the improvement achieved, the systemic steroid being gradually withdrawn.

As a general rule, rinsing the mouth and gargling after each inhalation with water can help in preventing the occurrence of candidiasis. Cleansing dentures has the same effect.

Treatment with fluticasone should not be stopped abruptly, but tapered off gradually.

Administration: Patients must be instructed, as described in Information for the Patient, in the correct method of using the Inhaler or Diskus to ensure that the drug reaches the target areas within the lungs.

Inhalers: When using the inhaler, each prescribed dose should be given by a minimum of 2 inhalations. Before the first use, and after a long period without use, the inhaler should be primed before treatment by actuating the inhaler 4 times.

Inhaler actuation should be synchronized with inspiration to ensure optimum delivery of drug to the lungs. In patients who find coordination of a pressurized metered dose inhaler difficult, a spacer device such as Vent-A-Haler may be used with the fluticasone inhaler.

Diskus: Flovent Diskus is a device for delivering the dry powder formulation of fluticasone. When using the Diskus, the usual prescribed dose is 1 blister (inhalation) twice a day.

The dosage of fluticasone should be adjusted according to individual response.

Adults: Usual dosage is 100 to 500 μg twice daily.

Patients should be given a starting dose of inhaled fluticasone which is appropriate for the severity of their disease (see Indications) as follows: mild asthma: 100 to 250 μg twice daily; moderate asthma: 250 to 500 μg twice daily; severe asthma: 500 μg twice daily. Very severe patients requiring higher doses of corticosteroids such as those patients currently requiring oral steroids may use doses up to 1 000 μg twice daily.

The dose may then be adjusted until control is achieved or reduced to the minimum effective dose according to the individual response.

Alternatively, the starting dose of fluticasone may be gauged at half the total daily dose of beclomethasone dipropionate or equivalent as administered by metered-dose inhaler. Onset of effect occurs within 4 to 7 days of the start of treatment with fluticasone. If no improvement is noted in this time frame, an increase in dose should be considered.

Adolescents: Above 16 years of age, the adult dosage applies.

Children (over 4 years of age): Children should be given a starting dose of inhaled fluticasone which is appropriate for the severity of their disease. This may be 50 or 100 μg twice daily. The dose may then be adjusted until control is achieved or reduced to the minimum effective dose according to the individual response.

Special Patient Groups: There is no need to adjust the dose in elderly patients or those with hepatic or renal impairment.

Patients Receiving Systemic Steroids: The transfer of steroid-dependent patients to inhaled fluticasone and their subsequent management needs special care mainly because recovery from impaired adrenocortical function, caused by prolonged systemic therapy, is slow. Patients' bronchial asthma should be stable before being given inhaled fluticasone in addition to the usual maintenance dose of systemic steroid. After about a week, gradual withdrawal of the systemic steroid is started by reducing the daily dose by 1 mg of prednisone, or its equivalent of other corticosteroid, at not less than weekly intervals, if the patient is under close observation. In children, the usual rate of withdrawal is 1 mg of the daily dose of prednisone every 8 days when under close supervision. **If continuous supervision is not feasible, the withdrawal of the systemic steroid should be slower,** approximately 1 mg of the daily dose of prednisone (or equivalent) every 10 and every 20 days in adults and in children, respectively. A slow rate of withdrawal cannot be over-emphasized.

If withdrawal symptoms appear, the previous dose of the systemic drug should be resumed for a week before any further decrease is attempted. Patients who have been treated with systemic steroids for long periods of time or at a high dose may have adrenocortical suppression. In these patients adrenocortical function should be monitored regularly and their dose of systemic steroid reduced cautiously.

Some patients feel unwell during the withdrawal phase experiencing symptoms such as joint and/or muscular pain, lassitude and depression, despite maintenance or even improvement of respiratory function. Such patients should be encouraged to persevere with fluticasone but should be watched carefully for objective signs of adrenal insufficiency such as hypotension and weight loss. If evidence of adrenal insufficiency occurs, the systemic steroid dosage should be boosted temporarily and thereafter further withdrawal should be continued more slowly.

Transferred patients whose adrenocortical function is impaired should carry a warning card indicating that they need supplementary treatment with systemic steroids during periods of stress, e.g., surgery, chest infection, or severe asthma attack. Consideration should be given to supplying such patients with oral steroids to use in an emergency. The dose of inhaled fluticasone should be increased at this time and then reduced to the maintenance level after the systemic steroid has been discontinued.

Exacerbations of bronchial asthma which occur during the course of treatment with fluticasone should be treated with a short course of systemic steroid which is gradually tapered as these symptoms subside. Under stressful conditions or when the patient has a severe exacerbation of bronchial asthma, after complete withdrawal of the systemic steroid, use of the latter must be resumed in order to avoid relative adrenocortical insufficiency.

There are some patients who cannot completely discontinue the oral corticosteroid. In these cases, a minimum maintenance dosage should be given in addition to fluticasone.

Information for the Patient. See Blue Section—Information for the Patient "Flovent".

Supplied: Inhaler: Each actuation of metered-dose aerosol contains: fluticasone propionate (micronized) 25, 50, 125 or 250 μg. Nonmedicinal ingredients: dichlorodifluoromethane, lecithin and trichlorofluoromethane. Aluminum canisters fitted with a metering valve of 60 and 120 doses. Each unit is housed in a suitable actuator/adaptor. Store between 2 and 30°C. Protect from frost and direct sunlight. Contents under pressure. Container may explode if heated. Do not place in hot water or near radiators, stoves, or other sources of heat. Even when apparently empty, do not puncture or incinerate container or store at temperatures over 30°C. As with most inhaled medications in pressurized canisters, the therapeutic effect of this medication may decrease when the canister is cold.

Diskus: Each plastic inhaler device contains a foil strip with 60 blisters. Each blister contains: fluticasone propionate 50, 100, 250 or 500 μg. Nonmedicinal ingredients: lactose, which acts as a "carrier". Store between 2 and 30°C. Protect from frost and direct sunlight.

(Shown in Product Recognition Section)

Reviewed 1999

FLOXIN® Ⓟ

Janssen-Ortho

Ofloxacin

Antibacterial

Pharmacology: Ofloxacin is a broad-spectrum, synthetic fluoroquinolone antibacterial agent for oral administration.

Ofloxacin is thought to exert a bactericidal effect on susceptible bacterial cells by inhibiting the essential bacterial enzyme, DNA gyrase, a critical catalyst in the duplication, transcription and repair of bacteria.

Pharmacokinetics: The pharmacokinetic profile of ofloxacin tablets is comparable to the profile of ofloxacin administered i.v. The bioavailability of ofloxacin in the tablet formulation is approximately 98%. Ofloxacin is rapidly and completely absorbed from the upper small bowel following oral administration.

The pharmacokinetic parameters of oral ofloxacin following single doses of 200, 300 and 400 mg and multiple doses of 400 mg to healthy 70 to 80 kg males are summarized in Table I.

The following are mean peak serum concentrations in healthy 49 to 102 kg male volunteers after single and multiple doses of 200 and 400 mg of i.v. ofloxacin (see Table II).

Elimination is mainly by renal excretion. Ofloxacin undergoes minimal biotransformation.

Indications: The treatment of adults with the following infections caused by susceptible strains of the designated microorganisms:

Lower Respiratory Tract Infections: **Pneumonia** and **acute exacerbation of chronic bronchitis** due to H. influenzae or S. pneumoniae, M. catarrhalis.

Urinary Tract Infections: **Uncomplicated cystitis** due to E. coli, K. pneumoniae or P. mirabilis. **Complicated urinary tract infections** due to E. coli, K. pneumoniae or P. mirabilis.

Prostatitis: due to E. coli.

Sexually Transmitted Diseases: Acute, uncomplicated urethral and cervical gonorrhea due to N. gonorrheae. Urethritis/cervicitis due to C. trachomatis, or mixed infections due to N. gonorrheae and C. trachomatis.

Note: Ofloxacin is not effective in the treatment of syphilis. All patients with gonorrhea should have an initial serologic test for syphilis and a follow-up serologic test after 3 months (see Warnings).

Acute pelvic inflammatory disease of mild to moderate severity appropriate for outpatient management when due to N. gonorrhea and/or C. trachomatis.

Note: Empiric therapy for pelvic inflammatory disease must provide broad spectrum coverage of likely pathogens such as N. gonorrhea, C. trachomatis, anaerobes, G. vaginalis, H. influenzae, enteric gram-negative rods and S. agalactae. Ofloxacin has demonstrated clinical effectiveness only against N. gonorrhea and C. trachomatis, therefore, consideration should be given to inclusion of additional agents if ofloxacin is used empirically for the treatment of pelvic inflammatory infection.

Note: Clinical trials with ofloxacin therapy have not provided information regarding intermediate and long-term outcomes.

Skin and Skin Structure Infections: **Uncomplicated skin and skin structure infections** due to S. aureus or S. pyogenes.

Appropriate culture and susceptibility tests should be performed before treatment in order to isolate and identify organisms causing the infection and to determine their susceptibility to ofloxacin. Therapy with ofloxacin may be initiated before results of these tests are known; once the results of bacteriological testing become known, therapy should be adjusted if required.

As with other drugs in this class, some strains of P. aeruginosa may develop resistance fairly rapidly during treatment with ofloxacin. Culture and susceptibility testing performed periodically during therapy will provide information not only on the therapeutic effect of the antimicrobial agent but also on the possible emergence of bacterial resistance.

If anaerobic organisms are suspected of or known to be contributing to the infection, appropriate therapy for anaerobic pathogens should be considered.

Contraindications: Persons with a history of hypersensitivity to ofloxacin or members of the quinolone group of antibacterial agents.

Warnings: The safety and efficacy of ofloxacin in children, adolescents (under the age of 18 years), pregnant women, and lactating women has not been established (see Precautions, Children, Pregnancy, Lactation).

The oral administration of ofloxacin has produced lesions in weight-bearing articular cartilage and lameness in several species of immature animals. Consequently, ofloxacin should not be used in prepubertal patients.

Syphilis: **Ofloxacin is not effective in the treatment of syphilis.** Antimicrobial agents used in high doses for short periods of time to treat gonorrhea may mask or delay the symptoms of incubating syphilis. All patients with gonorrhea should have a serologic test for syphilis at the time of diagnosis. Patients

Table I—Floxin

Pharmacokinetic Parameters

Dose	C_{max} μg/mL ±S.D.	$AUC_{0\text{-last pt.}}$ μg×h/mL ±S.D.	T_{max} ±S.D.	$t_{1/2}$
200 mg -single dose	1.7±0.3	14.1±2.3	1.5±0.3	4.9
300 mg -single dose	2.6±0.4	21.2±2.5	1.7±0.5	4.6
400 mg -single dose	3.7±0.7	31.4±4.7	1.8±0.6	3.8
400 mg -steady state	5.0±1.0	62.9±14.5	1.7±0.5	5.2

Table II—Floxin

Mean Peak Serum Concentrations

Dose	C_{max}μg/mL ±S.D.	$AUC_{0\text{-last pt.}}$ μg×h/mL ±S.D.	T_{max}	$t_{1/2}$
200 mg -single dose	2.29±0.5	12.20±1.8	1.0	5.29
200 mg -steady state*	2.89±0.5	12.96±1.6	—	5.15
400 mg -single dose	4.49+0.8	25.28+3.30	1.0	5.50
400 mg -steady state*	5.47	64.55	1.1	6.05

*at 7th day of therapy.

Floxin (cont'd)

treated with ofloxacin should have a follow-up serologic test for syphilis after 3 months.

Hypersensitivity Reactions: Serious and occasionally fatal hypersensitivity (anaphylactic/anaphylactoid) reactions, have been reported in patients receiving therapy with quinolones, including ofloxacin. These reactions often occur following the first dose. Some reactions were accompanied by cardiovascular collapse, hypotension/shock, seizure, loss of consciousness, tingling, angioedema (including tongue, laryngeal, throat or facial edema/swelling, etc.), airway obstruction (including bronchospasm, shortness of breath and acute respiratory distress), dyspnea, urticaria/hives, itching and other serious skin reactions. A few patients had a history of hypersensitivity reactions. The drug should be discontinued immediately at the first appearance of a skin rash or any other sign of hypersensitivity. Serious acute hypersensitivity reactions may require treatment with epinephrine and other resuscitative measures, including oxygen, i.v. fluids, antihistamines, corticosteroids, pressor amines and airway management, as clinically indicated (see Precautions and Adverse Effects).

Serious and sometimes fatal events of uncertain etiology have been reported in patients receiving therapy with quinolones including, extremely rarely, ofloxacin. These events may be severe and generally occur following the administration of multiple doses. Clinical manifestations may include one or more of the following: fever, rash or severe dermatologic reactions (e.g., toxic epidermal necrolysis, Stevens-Johnson syndrome, etc.); vasculitis, arthralgia, myalgia, serum sickness; allergic pneumonitis; interstitial nephritis, acute renal insufficiency/failure; hepatitis, jaundice, acute hepatic necrosis/failure; anemia including hemolytic and aplastic, thrombocytopenia including thrombotic thrombocytopenic purpura, leukopenia, agranulocytosis, pancytopenia, and/or other hematologic abnormalities. The administration of ofloxacin should be discontinued immediately after appearance of a skin rash or any other sign of hypersensitivity and supportive measures instituted (see Precautions and Adverse Effects).

CNS Effects: Convulsions, increased intracranial pressure and toxic psychosis have been reported in patients receiving quinolones, including ofloxacin. Quinolones, including ofloxacin, may also cause CNS stimulation, which may lead to: tremors, restlessness/agitation, nervousness/anxiety, lightheadedness, confusion, hallucinations, paranoia and depression, nightmares, insomnia, and rarely, suicidal thoughts or acts. These reactions may occur following the first dose. If these reactions occur in patients receiving ofloxacin, the drug should be discontinued and appropriate measures instituted. As with all quinolones, ofloxacin should be used with caution in patients with a known or suspected CNS disorder that may predispose to seizures or lower the seizure threshold (e.g., severe cerebral arteriosclerosis, epilepsy, etc.) or in the presence of other risk factors that may predispose to seizures or lower the seizure threshold (e.g., certain drug therapy, renal dysfunction, etc.) (see Precautions and Adverse Effects).

Gastrointestinal Effects: Pseudomembranous colitis has been reported with nearly all antibacterial agents, including ofloxacin, and may range in severity from mild to life-threatening. Therefore, it is important to consider this diagnosis in patients who present with diarrhea subsequent to the administration of antibacterial agents.

Treatment with antibacterial agents alters the normal flora of the colon and may permit overgrowth of clostridia. Studies indicate that a toxin produced by C. difficile is one primary cause of "antibiotic-associated colitis". After the diagnosis of pseudomembranous colitis has been established, therapeutic measures should be initiated. Mild cases of pseudomembranous colitis usually respond to drug discontinuation alone. In moderate to severe cases, consideration should be given to management with fluids and electrolytes, protein supplementation and treatment with an oral antibacterial drug effective against C. difficile (see Adverse Effects).

Precautions: General: Periodic assessment of organ system functions, including renal, hepatic and hematopoietic, is advisable during prolonged therapy (see Warnings and Adverse Effects).

Adequate hydration of patients receiving ofloxacin should be maintained to prevent the formation of a highly concentrated urine.

Renal/Hepatic: Administer ofloxacin with caution in the presence of renal or hepatic insufficiency/impairment. In patients with known or suspected renal or hepatic insufficiency/impairment, careful clinical observation and appropriate laboratory studies should be performed prior to and during therapy since elimination of ofloxacin may be reduced. Alteration of the dosage regimen is necessary for patients with impairment of renal function (creatinine clearance $\leq$50 mL/min) (see Pharmacology and Dosage).

Allergic Reactions: Moderate to severe phototoxicity reactions have been observed in patients who are exposed to direct sunlight while receiving some drugs in this class including ofloxacin. Excessive sunlight should be avoided. Therapy should be discontinued if phototoxicity (e.g., a skin eruption, etc.) occurs.

Pregnancy: Doses equivalent to 50 and 10 times the maximum therapeutic dose of ofloxacin (based on mg/kg) were fetotoxic (i.e., decreased fetal body weight and increased fetal mortality) in rats and rabbits, respectively. Minor skeletal variations were reported in rats receiving doses of 810 mg/kg/day, which is more than 10 times higher than the maximum intended human dose (based on mg/m²).

Safety and efficacy have not been established in pregnant women. Ofloxacin should not be used during pregnancy unless the potential benefit justifies the potential risk to the fetus (see Warnings).

Lactation: In nursing females, a single 200 mg oral dose resulted in concentrations of ofloxacin in milk which were similar to those found in plasma. Because of the potential for serious adverse reactions from ofloxacin in nursing infants, a decision should be made whether to discontinue nursing or to discontinue the drug, taking into account the importance of the drug to the mother (see Warnings and Adverse Effects).

Children: Safety and effectiveness in children and adolescents below the age of 18 years have not been established. Ofloxacin causes arthropathy (arthrosis) and osteochondrosis in juvenile animals of several species (see Warnings).

Patients with Special Diseases and Conditions: CNS Disorders: As with all quinolones, ofloxacin should be used with caution in any patient with a known or suspected CNS disorder that may predispose to seizures or lower the seizure threshold (e.g., severe cerebral arteriosclerosis, epilepsy, etc.) or in the presence of other risk factors that may predispose to seizures or lower the seizure threshold (e.g., certain drug therapy, renal dysfunction, etc.) (see Warnings and Drug Interactions).

Disturbances of Blood Glucose: As with other quinolones, disturbances of blood glucose, including symptomatic hyper- and hypoglycemia, have been reported, usually in diabetic patients receiving concomitant treatment with an oral hypoglycemic agent (e.g., glyburide/glibenclamide, etc.) or with insulin. In these patients careful monitoring of blood glucose is recommended. If a hypoglycemic reaction occurs in a patient being treated with ofloxacin, the patient should discontinue ofloxacin immediately and appropriate ancillary measures should be instituted (see Drug Interactions and Adverse Effects).

Drug Interactions: Antacids, Sucralfate, Metal Cations, Multivitamins, etc.: Quinolones have the potential to form stable complexes with many metal ions. Administration of oral quinolones with antacids containing calcium, magnesium or aluminum; sucralfate; divalent or trivalent cations such as iron; or multivitamins containing zinc may substantially interfere with the absorption of oral quinolones resulting in systemic levels considerably lower than desired. These agents should not be taken within the 2-hour period before or within the 2-hour period after oral ofloxacin administration.

Cimetidine: Cimetidine has demonstrated interference with the elimination of some quinolones. This interference has resulted in significant increases in half-life and AUC of some quinolones. The potential for interaction between ofloxacin and cimetidine has not been studied.

Cyclosporine: Elevated serum levels of cyclosporine have been reported with concomitant use with some other quinolones. The potential for interaction between ofloxacin and cyclosporine has not been studied.

Drugs Metabolized by Cytochrome P450 Enzymes: Most quinolone antimicrobial drugs inhibit cytochrome P450 enzyme activity. This may result in a prolonged half-life for some drugs that are also metabolized by this system (e.g., cyclosporine, theophylline/methylxanthines, warfarin, etc.) when coadministered with quinolones. The extent of this inhibition varies among different quinolones (see other Drug Interactions).

Nonsteroidal Anti-inflammatory Drugs (NSAIDs): The concomitant administration of an NSAID with a quinolone, including ofloxacin, may increase the risk of CNS stimulation and convulsive seizures (see Warnings).

Probenecid: The concomitant use of probenecid with certain other quinolones has been reported to affect renal tubular secretion. The effect of probenecid on the elimination of ofloxacin has not been studied.

Theophylline: Steady-state theophylline levels may increase when ofloxacin and theophylline are given concurrently. As with other quinolones, concomitant administration of ofloxacin may prolong the half-life of theophylline, elevate serum theophylline levels, and increase the risk of theophylline-related adverse reactions. Theophylline levels should be closely monitored and theophylline dosage adjustments made when ofloxacin and theophylline are coadministered. Adverse reactions (including seizures, etc.) may occur with or without an elevation in the serum theophylline level (see Warnings and Precautions, General).

Warfarin: Some quinolones have been reported to enhance the effects of the oral anticoagulant warfarin or its derivatives. Therefore, if a quinolone antibiotic is administered concomitantly with warfarin or its derivatives, the prothrombin time (PT) (or other appropriate test(s) of coagulation) should be monitored and the dose of warfarin modified as appropriate.

Antidiabetic Agents (e.g., insulin, glyburide/glibenclamide, etc.): Since disturbances of blood glucose, including hyperglycemia and hypoglycemia, have been reported in patients treated concurrently with quinolones and an antidiabetic agent,

Table III—Floxin

Adverse Events

	Adverse Event Without Regard to Relationship to Drug or Route of Administration	
Body System	**<1%**	**1 to 3%**
Body as a Whole	asthenia, chills, extremity pain, malaise, pain, epistaxis	chest pain, fatigue, abdominal pain and cramps, trunk pain and pharyngitis
Nutritional/Metabolic	thirst, weight loss	decreased appetite, dry mouth, dysgeusia
Special Senses	decreased hearing acuity, photophobia, tinnitus	visual disturbances
Nervous System	anxiety, cognitive change, confusion, depression, dream abnormality, euphoria, hallucinations, paresthesia, seizures, syncope, vertigo, tremor	nervousness, sleep disorders, somnolence
Cardiovascular	cardiac arrest, edema, hypertension, hypotension, palpitations, vasodilation	
Respiratory	cough, respiratory arrest, rhinorrhea	—
Gastrointestinal	dyspepsia	flatulence, gastrointestinal distress, constipation
Genital/Reproductive	burning, irritation, pain and rash of the female genitalia, dysmenorrhea, menorrhagia, metrorrhagia	vaginal discharge
Urinary	dysuria, urinary frequency, urinary retention	—
Skin/Hypersensitivity	angioedema, diaphoresis, urticaria, vasculitis	pruritus, fever, rash
Musculoskeletal	arthralgia, myalgia	

Table IV—Floxin

Adverse Events

Body System	Adverse Event
Special Senses	diplopia, nystagmus, blurred vision, disturbances of: taste, smell, hearing and equilibrium, usually reversible following discontinuation
Nervous System	nightmares; suicidal thoughts or acts, disorientation, psychotic reactions, paranoia; phobia, agitation, restlessness, aggressiveness/hostility, manic reaction, emotional lability; peripheral neuropathy, ataxia, incoordination; possible exacerbation of: myasthenia gravis and extrapyramidal disorders; dysphasia, lightheadedness (see Warnings and Precautions)
Cardiovascular	cerebral thrombosis, pulmonary edema, tachycardia, hypotension/shock, syncope
Respiratory	bronchospasm, dyspnea, allergic pneumonitis, stridor
Gastrointestinal	hepatic dysfunction including: hepatic necrosis, hepatitis, jaundice (cholestatic or hepatocellular); intestinal perforation; pseudomembranous colitis, gastrointestinal hemorrhage; hiccough, painful oral mucosa, pyrosis (see Warnings)
Genital/Reproductive	vaginal candidiasis
Urinary	anuria, polyuria, renal failure, renal calculi, urinary retention, interstitial nephritis, hematuria (see Warnings and Precautions)
Skin/Hypersensitivity	anaphylactic/anaphylactoid reactions/shock; purpura, serum sickness, erythema multiforme/Stevens-Johnson syndrome, exfoliative dermatitis, photosensitivity, toxic epidermal necrolysis, erythema nodosum, hyperpigmentation, conjunctivitis, vesiculobullous eruption (see Warnings and Precautions)
Endocrine/Metabolic	hyper- or hypoglycemia, especially in diabetic patients on insulin or oral hypoglycemic agents (see Precautions, General and Drug Interactions)
Hematopoietic	anemia, including hemolytic and aplastic; hemorrhage, pancytopenia, agranulocytosis, leukopenia, reversible bone marrow depression, thrombocytopenia, thrombotic thrombocytopenic purpura, petechiae, ecchymosis/bruising (see Warnings)
Musculoskeletal	tendonitis/rupture; weakness
Laboratory Abnormalities	Hematopoietic: prolongation of prothrombin time Serum Chemistry: acidosis, elevation of: serum triglycerides, serum cholesterol, serum potassium, liver function tests including: GGTP, LDH, bilirubin Urinary: albuminuria, candiduria

careful monitoring of blood glucose is recommended when these agents are used concomitantly.

Adverse Effects: Clinical Trials Experience: The following is a compilation of the data for ofloxacin based on clinical experience with both the oral and i.v. formulations. The incidence of drug-related adverse reactions in patients during phase 2 and 3 clinical trials was 11%. Among patients receiving multiple-dose therapy, 4% discontinued ofloxacin due to adverse experiences.

In clinical trials, the following events were considered likely to be drug-related in patients receiving multiple doses of ofloxacin: nausea 3%, insomnia 3%, rash 1%, external genital pruritus in women 1%, diarrhea 1%, vomiting 1%, dizziness 3%, pruritus 1%, vaginitis 1%, headache 3%, dysgeusia 1%.

In clinical trials, the most frequently reported adverse events, regardless of relationship to drug, were: nausea 10%, vomiting 4%, diarrhea 4%, external genital pruritus in women 6%, insomnia 7%, headache 9%, vaginitis 5%, dizziness 5%.

Additional events occurring in clinical trials at a rate of 1 to 3% and less than 1% regardless of relationship to drug or route of administration were shown in Table III (on previous page).

The following laboratory abnormalities appeared in ≥1% of patients receiving multiple doses of ofloxacin. It is not known whether these abnormalities were caused by the drug or the underlying conditions being treated.

Hematopoietic: anemia, leukopenia, leukocytosis, neutropenia, neutrophilia, increased band forms, lymphocytopenia, eosinophilia, lymphocytosis, thrombocytopenia, thrombocytosis, elevated ESR.

Hepatic: elevated: alkaline phosphatase, AST, ALT.

Serum Chemistry: hyperglycemia, hypoglycemia, elevated creatinine, elevated BUN.

Urinary: glucosuria, proteinuria, alkalinuria, hyposthenuria, hematuria, pyuria.

Worldwide Marketing Experience: Additional adverse events regardless of relationship to drug were reported from worldwide marketing experience with quinolones, including ofloxacin (see Table IV).

In clinical trials using multiple-dose therapy, ophthalmologic abnormalities including cataracts and multiple punctate lenticular opacities have been noted in patients undergoing treatment with other quinolones. The relationship of the drugs to these events is not presently established.

Table V—Floxin

Dosage Chart (Patients with Normal Renal Function)

Infection	Description	Unit Dose	Frequency	Duration	Daily Dose
Lower Respiratory Tract Infections	Exacerbation of chronic bronchitis or pneumonia	400 mg	q12h	10 days	800 mg
Sexually Transmitted Diseases	Acute, uncomplicated gonorrhea	400 mg	single dose	1 day	400 mg
	Cervicitic/urethritic due to C. trachomatis or mixed infections due to C. trachomatis and N. gonorrheae	300 mg	q12h	7 days	600 mg
	Acute Pelvic Inflammatory Disease	400 mg	q12h	10–14 days	800 mg
Skin and Skin Structure Infections	Uncomplicated Complicated	400 mg 400 mg	q12h q12h	10 days 10 days	800 mg 800 mg
Urinary Tract	Acute cystitis Uncomplicated UTI Complicated UTIs	200 mg 200 mg 200 mg	q12h q12h q12h	3 days 7 days 10 days	400 mg 400 mg 400 mg
Prostatitis	—	300 mg	q12h	6 weeks	600 mg

Overdose: Symptoms: Information on overdosage with ofloxacin is limited. One incident of accidental overdosage has been reported. In this case, an adult female received 3 g of ofloxacin i.v. over 45 minutes. A blood sample obtained 15 minutes after the completion of the infusion revealed an ofloxacin level of 39.3 μg/mL. In 7 hours, the level had fallen to 16.2 μg/mL, and by 24 hours to 2.7 μg/mL. During the infusion, the patient developed drowsiness, nausea, dizziness, hot and cold flushes, subjective facial swelling and numbness, slurring of speech, and mild to moderate disorientation. All complaints except the dizziness subsided within 1 hour after discontinuation of the infusion. The dizziness, most bothersome while standing, resolved in approximately 9 hours. Laboratory testing reportedly revealed no clinically significant changes in routine parameters in this patient.

Treatment: In the event of acute overdose, the patient should be observed and appropriate hydration maintained. Ofloxacin is not efficiently removed by hemodialysis or peritoneal dialysis.

Dosage: General: The dosing recommendations apply to patients with normal renal function (i.e., creatinine clearance >50 mL/min). For patients with altered renal function (i.e., creatinine clearance ≤50 mL/min) see Dosage Adjustment for Renal Impairment. The usual dose of ofloxacin is 200 to 400 mg orally every 12 hours as described in Table V.

Antacids containing calcium, magnesium or aluminum; sucralfate; divalent or trivalent cations such as iron; or multivitamins containing zinc should not be taken within the 2-hour period before or within the 2-hour period after oral administration of ofloxacin (see Precautions).

Dosage Adjustment for Renal Impairment: Dosage should be adjusted in patients with a creatinine clearance value of ≤50 mL/min. After a normal initial dose, the dosing interval should be adjusted as shown in Table VI.

Table VI—Floxin

Dosage Adjustment for Renal Impairment

Creatinine Clearance	Maintenance Unit Dose	Frequency
20–50 mL/min	as recommended in Dosage Chart	q24h
<20 mL/min	1/2 recommended dose in Dosage Chart	q24h

When only the serum creatinine is known, the following formula may be used to estimate creatinine clearance. The serum creatinine should represent steady-state of renal function:

Men:

$$\text{Creatinine clearance (mL/min)} = \frac{\text{Weight (kg)} \times (140 - \text{age})}{72 \times \text{serum creatinine (mg/dL)}}$$

Women: 0.85×the value calculated for men.

Patients with Cirrhosis: The excretion of ofloxacin may be reduced in patients with severe liver function disorders (e.g., cirrhosis with or without ascites). A maximum dose of 400 mg of ofloxacin per day should therefore not be exceeded.

Supplied: 200 mg: Each light yellow, film-coated tablet, engraved with FLOXIN and 200 mg, contains: ofloxacin 200 mg. Nonmedicinal ingredients: anhydrous lactose, cornstarch, hydroxypropyl cellulose, hydroxypropyl methylcellulose, magnesium stearate, polyethylene glycol, polysorbate 80, sodium starch glycolate, synthetic yellow iron oxide and titanium dioxide. Bottles of 50.

300 mg: Each white, film-coated tablet, engraved with FLOXIN and 300 mg, contains: ofloxacin 300 mg. Nonmedicinal ingredients: anhydrous lactose, cornstarch, hydroxypropyl cellulose, hydroxypropyl methylcellulose, magnesium stearate, polyethylene glycol, polysorbate 80, sodium starch glycolate and titanium dioxide. Bottles of 50.

400 mg: Each pale gold, film-coated tablet, engraved with FLOXIN and 400 mg, contains: ofloxacin 400 mg. Nonmedicinal ingredients: anhydrous lactose, cornstarch, hydroxypropyl cellulose, hydroxypropyl methylcellulose, magnesium stearate, polyethylene glycol, polysorbate 80, sodium starch glycolate, synthetic yellow iron oxide and titanium dioxide. Bottles of 50.

Store in well-closed containers. Store at controlled room temperature (15 to 30°C).

Reviewed 1999

...Drug identification problem? Consult the PRODUCT RECOGNITION SECTION.

FLUANXOL® DEPOT INJECTION Ⓟ
FLUANXOL® TABLETS Ⓟ

Lundbeck

Flupenthixol Decanoate
Flupenthixol Dihydrochloride

Antipsychotic

Pharmacology: Flupenthixol is the decanoate ester of a thioxanthene derivative with antipsychotic properties. The esterification of flupenthixol results in the slow release of the drug from the injection site with consequent prolongation of duration of action. The onset of action usually occurs in the range of 24 to 72 hours after injection and the improvement of symptoms continues for 2 to 4 weeks. However, there is considerable variation in the individual response of patients to flupenthixol and its use for maintenance therapy requires careful supervision.

The exact mechanism of action of flupenthixol has not been established. Its effects resemble those of the phenothiazine, fluphenazine, in that it belongs among the antipsychotic drugs which are less likely to cause sedation and hypotension, but have greater propensity for producing extrapyramidal reactions.

In pharmacokinetic studies measuring flupenthixol blood levels, peak concentrations of the drug were found between days 4 and 7, following i.m. injections of 40 mg of flupenthixol 2% or 10%. It could still be detected in the blood 3 weeks after injection. The metabolites of flupenthixol appear to be inactive.

Flupenthixol dihydrochloride is well absorbed from the gastrointestinal tract reaching maximum serum concentrations within 3 to 8 hours. Flupenthixol is excreted mainly in the feces, with some excretion also occurring in the urine.

Indications: The maintenance therapy of chronic schizophrenic patients whose main manifestations do not include excitement, agitation or hyperactivity.

Contraindications: In patients with known hypersensitivity to the thioxanthenes. The possibility of cross-sensitivity between the thioxanthenes and phenothiazine derivatives should be considered.

Flupenthixol is also contraindicated in the presence of CNS depression due to any cause, comatose states, suspected or established subcortical brain damage, blood dyscrasias, pheochromocytoma, liver damage, cerebrovascular or renal insufficiency, and severe cardiovascular disorders. It is not indicated for the management of severely agitated psychotic patients, psychoneurotic patients or geriatric patients with confusion and/or agitation. As with phenothiazines, flupenthixol should not be used concomitantly with large doses of hypnotics due to the possibility of potentiation.

Pregnancy and *Lactation:* Safety in pregnancy has not been established. Therefore, it should not be administered to women of childbearing potential or during lactation, unless, in the opinion of the physician, the expected benefit to the patient outweighs the potential risk to the fetus or child.

Children: Safety and efficacy in children have not been established, and its use is not recommended in the pediatric age group.

Warnings and Precautions: Severe adverse reactions requiring immediate medical attention may occur and are difficult to predict. Therefore, the evaluation of tolerance and response, and establishment of adequate maintenance therapy require careful stabilization of each patient under continuous, close medical observation and supervision.

Flupenthixol is not recommended for excitable, overactive or manic patients, and the relative lack of sedating effect may cause restlessness and insomnia. The drug should be used with caution in patients with parkinsonism or severe arteriosclerosis.

Occupational Hazards: Although flupenthixol is a relatively non-sedating drug, sedation may occur in some patients. Therefore, ambulatory patients should be warned about engaging in activities such as driving a car or operating machinery and about the concomitant use of alcohol and other CNS depressant drugs, since potentiation of their effects may occur.

Flupenthixol should be used with caution in patients with a history of convulsive disorders since it may lower the convulsive threshold.

The possibility of the development of irreversible dyskinesia should be borne in mind when patients are on prolonged therapy.

The antiemetic effect observed with flupenthixol in animal studies may also occur in man; therefore, the drug may mask signs of toxicity due to overdosage of other drugs, or it may mask the symptoms of disease, such as brain tumor or intestinal obstruction.

Although its anticholinergic properties are relatively weak, flupenthixol should be used with caution in patients who are known or are suspected to have glaucoma, and in those patients who might be exposed to extreme heat, or organophosphorus insecticides or who are receiving atropine or related drugs. Paralytic ileus has occasionally been reported, particularly in the elderly, when several drugs with anticholinergic effects have been used simultaneously.

Blood dyscrasias and liver damage have been reported with this class of drugs, but only eosinophilia has been reported to date with flupenthixol. Therefore, routine blood counts and hepatic function tests are advisable, particularly during the first months of therapy. Should either of these disorders occur, supportive treatment should be instituted and the drug discontinued.

Photosensitivity reactions, pigmentary retinopathy, and lenticular and corneal deposits, although not reported to date with flupenthixol, have been reported with related drugs.

Caution should be observed when using a drug of this category in patients who may have a propensity for development of defects in cardiac conduction.

Patients on large doses of flupenthixol who are undergoing surgery should be watched carefully for possible hypotensive phenomena, and anesthetic or CNS depressant drug dosages may have to be reduced.

To lessen the likelihood of adverse reactions related to drug accumulation, patients on long-term therapy, particularly on high doses, should be evaluated periodically to decide whether the maintenance dosage can be lowered or drug therapy discontinued.

Neuroleptic drugs elevate prolactin levels; the elevation persists during chronic administration. Tissue culture experiments indicate that approximately one-third of human breast cancers are prolactin-dependent in vitro, a factor of potential importance if the prescription of these drugs is contemplated in a patient with a previously detected breast cancer. Although disturbances such as galactorrhea, amenorrhea, gynecomastia and impotence have been reported, the clinical significance of elevated serum prolactin levels is unknown for most patients. An increase in mammary neoplasms has been found in rodents after chronic administration of neuroleptic drugs. Neither clinical studies, nor epidemiologic studies conducted to date, however, have shown an association between chronic administration of these drugs and mammary tumorogenesis; the available evidence is considered too limited to be conclusive at this time.

Withdrawal Emergent Neurological Signs: Abrupt withdrawal after short-term administration of antipsychotic drugs does not generally pose problems. However, transient dyskinetic signs are experienced by some patients on maintenance therapy after abrupt withdrawal. The signs are very similar to those described under Tardive Dyskinesia, except for duration. Although it is not known whether gradual withdrawal of antipsychotic drugs will decrease the incidence of withdrawal emergent neurological signs, gradual withdrawal would appear to be advisable.

Adverse Effects: Extrapyramidal symptoms have occurred in up to 30% of patients.

Flupenthixol shares many of the pharmacologic properties of other thioxanthenes and phenothiazines. Therefore, the known adverse reactions of these drugs should be borne in mind when flupenthixol is used.

CNS: Extrapyramidal symptoms, including hypo- and hyperkinetic states, tremors, pseudoparkinsonism, dystonia, hypertonia, akathisia, oculogyric crises, opisthotonos, hyperreflexia and tardive dyskinesia (see below). The symptoms, if they are to occur, usually appear within the first few days of drug administration and can usually be controlled or totally curtailed by reduction in dosage and/or standard anticholinergic antiparkinsonian medication. The incidence of extrapyramidal symptoms appears to be more frequent with the first few injections of flupenthixol, and diminish thereafter. The routine prophylactic use of antiparkinsonian medication is not recommended. Extrapyramidal reactions may be alarming, and patients should be forewarned and reassured.

Other CNS effects reported with flupenthixol include restlessness, insomnia, overactivity, psychomotor agitation, hypomania, epileptiform convulsions, headache, drowsiness, somnolence, depression, fatigue, and anergia.

Persistent Tardive Dyskinesia: As with other antipsychotic agents, tardive dyskinesia may appear in some patients on long-term therapy or may occur after drug therapy has been discontinued. The risk seems to be greater in elderly patients on high dose therapy, especially females. The symptoms are persistent and in some patients appear to be irreversible. The syndrome is characterized by rhythmical involuntary movements of the tongue, face, mouth, or jaw (e.g. protrusion of tongue, puffing of cheeks, puckering of mouth, chewing movements). Sometimes these may be accompanied by involuntary movements of the extremities.

There is no known effective treatment for tardive dyskinesia; antiparkinsonian agents usually do not alleviate the symptoms of this syndrome. It is suggested that all antipsychotic agents be discontinued if these symptoms appear. Should it be necessary to reinstitute treatment, or increase the dosage of the agent, or switch to a different antipsychotic agent, the syndrome may be masked. The physician may be able to reduce the risk of this syndrome by minimizing the unnecessary use of neuroleptic drugs and reducing the dose or discontinuing the drug, if possible, when manifestations of this syndrome are recognized, particularly in patients over the age of fifty. It has been reported that fine vermicular movements of the tongue may be an early sign of the syndrome and if the medication is stopped at that time, the syndrome may not develop.

Autonomic Nervous System: Dry mouth, blurred vision, constipation, excessive salivation, excessive perspiration, nausea, difficulty in micturition, dizziness, palpitations and fainting have been observed with flupenthixol but are uncommon. Miosis, mydriasis, paralytic ileus, polyuria, nasal congestion, glaucoma, tachycardia, hypotension, hypertension, fluctuations in blood pressure, non specific ECG changes and cardiac arrhythmias have been reported with related drugs. If hypotension occurs, **epinephrine should not be used** as a pressor agent since a paradoxical further lowering of blood pressure may result.

Metabolic and Endocrine: Weight change, galactorrhea, elevation in serum prolactin levels, impotence, loss of libido, and sexual excitement have been reported with flupenthixol. Related drugs have been also associated with breast enlargement, menstrual irregularities, false positive pregnancy tests, peripheral edema, gynecomastia, hypo- and hyperglycemia and glycosuria.

Toxic and Allergic: Eosinophilia, jaundice and increased levels of AST, ALT and alkaline phosphatase have been reported with flupenthixol. Other antipsychotic drugs have been associated with leukopenia, agranulocytosis, thrombocytopenic or nonthrombocytopenic purpura, hemolytic anemia and pancytopenia. If any soreness of the mouth, gums or throat or any symptoms of upper respiratory infection occur and confirmatory leukocyte count indicates cellular depression, therapy should be discontinued and other appropriate measures instituted immediately.

Skin reactions, such as pruritus, rash, urticaria, erythema, seborrhea, eczema, exfoliative dermatitis, and contact dermatitis have been reported with flupenthixol or related drugs. The possibility of anaphylactoid reactions occurring in some patients should be borne in mind.

Miscellaneous: Sudden, unexpected and unexplained deaths have occasionally been reported in patients who have received certain phenothiazine derivatives. Previous brain damage or seizures may be predisposing factors; high doses should be avoided in known seizure patients. Several patients have shown flare ups of psychotic behavior patterns shortly before death. Autopsy findings have usually revealed acute fulminating pneumonia or pneumonitis, aspiration of gastric contents or intramyocardial lesions.

The following adverse reactions have also occurred with phenothiazine derivatives: photosensitivity, systemic lupus erythematosus-like syndrome, hypotension severe enough to cause fatal cardiac arrest, altered ECG and EEG tracings, altered CSF proteins, cerebral edema, asthma, laryngeal edema, and angioneurotic edema. Skin pigmentation, and lenticular and corneal opacities have been seen with long-term use of phenothiazines.

Overdose: Symptoms: Sedation, frequently preceded by extreme agitation, excitement and confusion. Extrapyramidal symptoms may develop, and respiratory and circulatory collapse may occur.

Treatment: Symptomatic. In cases of oral overdosing, gastric lavage should be carried out immediately and measures aimed at supporting the respiratory and cardiovascular systems instituted. If overdosing with parenteral flupenthixol occurs, no further injections should be given until the patient shows signs of relapse and the dosage should then be decreased. An airway should be maintained. Severe hypotension calls for the immediate use of an i.v. vasopressor drug, such as levarterenol. Epinephrine should **not** be used, as a further lowering of blood pressure may result. Antiparkinsonian medication should be administered only if extrapyramidal symptoms develop.

Dosage: Injection: Flupenthixol is administered by deep i.m. injection, preferably in the gluteus maximus. Flupenthixol is NOT for i.v. use.

As a long acting depot preparation, flupenthixol has been found useful in the maintenance treatment of non agitated chronic schizophrenic patients who have been stabilized with short acting neuroleptics and might benefit from transfer to a longer acting injectable medication. The changeover of medication should aim at maintaining a clinical outcome similar to or better than that obtained with the previous therapy. To achieve and maintain the optimum dose, the changeover from other neuroleptic medication should proceed gradually and constant supervision is required during the period of dosage adjustment in order to minimize the risk of overdosage or insufficient suppression of psychotic symptoms before the next injection.

Patients not previously treated with long acting depot neuroleptics should be given an initial test dose of 5 mg (0.25 mL) to 20 mg (1.0 mL). An initial dose of 20 mg (1.0 mL) is usually well tolerated; however, a 5 mg (0.25 mL) test dose is recommended in elderly, frail and cachectic patients, and in patients whose individual or family history suggests a predisposition to extrapyramidal reactions. In the subsequent 5 to 10 days, the therapeutic response and the appearance of extrapyramidal symptoms should be carefully monitored. Oral neuroleptic drugs may be continued, but in diminishing dosage, during this period.

In patients previously treated with long acting depot neuroleptics who displayed good tolerance to these drugs, an initial dose of 20 to 40 mg (1.0 to 2.0 mL) may be adequate.

Subsequent doses and the frequency of administration must be determined for each patient. There is no reliable dosage comparability between a shorter acting neuroleptic and depot flupenthixol, and, therefore, the dosage of the long acting drug must be individualized.

Except in particularly sensitive patients, a second dose of 20 (1.0 mL) to 40 mg (2.0 mL) can be given 4 to 10 days after the initial injection. Subsequent dosage adjustments are made in accordance with the response of the patient, but the majority of patients can be adequately controlled by 20 to 40 mg (1.0 to 2.0 mL) of flupenthixol 2% every 2 to 3 weeks. The optimal amount of the drug has been found to vary with the clinical circumstances and individual response. Doses greater than 80 mg (4.0 mL) are usually not deemed necessary, although higher doses have been used occasionally in some patients.

Although the response to a single injection usually lasts for 2 to 3 weeks, it may last for 4 weeks or more, particularly when higher doses are used. Since higher doses increase the incidence of extrapyramidal reactions and other adverse effects, the amount of drug used should not be increased merely in order to prolong the intervals between injections. With higher doses there may also be more variability in the action of flupenthixol and, therefore, unit dose increments should not exceed 20 mg (1.0 mL). After an appropriate dosage adjustment is achieved, regular and continuous supervision and reassessment is considered essential in order to permit any further dosage adjustments that might be required to ensure use of the lowest effective individual dose and avoid troublesome side effects.

Patients who require higher doses of flupenthixol to control symptoms of schizophrenia and/or those who complain of discomfort with a large injection volume may be administered flupenthixol 10% (100 mg/mL) in preference to flupenthixol 2% (20 mg/mL).

As with all oily injections it is important to ensure, by aspiration before injection, that inadvertent intravascular injection does not occur.

Tablets: The dosage should be individualized and adjusted according to the severity of symptoms and tolerance to the drug. The initial recommended dose is 1 mg, 3 times daily. This may be increased, if necessary by 1 mg every 2 to 3 days until there is effective control of psychotic symptoms. The usual maintenance dosage is 3 to 6 mg daily in divided doses, although doses of up to 12 mg daily or more have been used in some patients.

During the initial therapeutic period, disturbance of sleep may occur, especially in those patients who have previously received neuroleptics possessing a marked sedative effect. In this event, the evening dose may be reduced.

Until further clinical evidence is available, it is not recommended for use in children.

Following stabilization on flupenthixol dihydrochloride tablets, patients may be treated with flupenthixol decanoate administered by the i.m. route.

Supplied: Depot Injection: 2% Solution: Each mL contains: flupenthixol decanoate 20 mg. Vials of 10 mL.

10% Solution: Each mL contains: flupenthixol decanoate 100 mg. Vials of 2 mL.

Solutions are yellowish and oil based. Store at room temperature. Protect from light.

Tablets: 0.5 mg: Each ochre-yellow, sugar-coated, biconvex tablet contains: flupenthixol dihydrochloride 0.5 mg. Also contains sucrose. Bottles of 100.

3 mg: Each ochre-yellow, sugar-coated, biconvex tablet contains: flupenthixol dihydrochloride 3 mg. Also contains sucrose. Bottles of 100.

(Shown in Product Recognition Section)

FLUDARA® Ⓟ

Berlex Canada

Fludarabine Phosphate

Antineoplastic

Pharmacology: Fludarabine is a fluorinated analog of adenine that is relatively resistant to deamination by adenosine deaminase.

Fludarabine (2F-ara-AMP) is rapidly dephosphorylated to 2-fluoro-ara-A (2F-ara-A) and then phosphorylated intracellularly by deoxycytidine kinase to the active 2-fluoro-ara-ATP (2F-ara-ATP). The antitumor activity of this metabolite is the result of inhibition of DNA synthesis via inhibition of ribonucleotide reductase and DNA polymerase α. Maximum 2F-ara-ATP levels in leukemic lymphocytes of chronic lymphocytic leukemia (CLL) patients were observed at a median of 4 hours and exhibited a considerable variation. 2F-ara-ATP levels in leukemic cells were always considerably higher than maximum 2F-ara-A levels in the plasma, indicating an accumulation at the target sites. 2F-ara-ATP elimination from CLL target cells likewise showed a considerable scattering with a median half-life of approximately 23 hours.

Clinical pharmacology studies have focused on 2F-ara-A pharmacokinetics in plasma. After doses of fludarabine phosphate of 80 to 260 mg/m², and with sampling continuing for 30 hours, elimination of 2F-ara-A was characterized as triphasic with calculations of an initial half-life ($t_{1/2\alpha}$) of 5.4 minutes, an intermediate half-life ($t_{1/2\beta}$) of 1.4 hours and a terminal half-life ($t_{1/2\gamma}$) of 10.2 hours. Other studies, in which sampling was performed for up to 72 hours, gave comparable initial and intermediate half-lives, but revealed a 2F-ara-A terminal half-life of up to 31 hours.

In patients receiving 20 to 125 mg/m² of fludarabine as an i.v. infusion the area under the concentration-time curve for 2F-ara-A was directly related to the dose of fludarabine given. In addition, the terminal half-life was approximately the same (8 hours) for all dose levels, indicating dose-independent elimination in this dose range.

The mean steady-state volume of distribution (Vd_{ss}) of 2F-ara-A in one study was 96 L/m² suggesting a significant degree of tissue binding. Another study, in which Vd_{ss} for patients was determined to be 44 L/m², supports the suggestion of tissue binding.

Based upon compartmental analysis of pharmacokinetic data, the rate-limiting step for excretion of 2F-ara-A from the body appears to be release from tissue binding sites. Total body clearance of 2F-ara-A has been shown to be inversely correlated with serum creatinine, suggesting renal elimination of the compound.

Two open-label studies of fludarabine have been conducted in patients with CLL refractory to at least one prior standard alkylating-agent containing regimen. Overall objective response rates were 32% in one study, and 48% in the other, with median time to response at 21 and 7 weeks respectively.

Indications: The use of fludarabine should be restricted to second line therapy in patients with CLL who have failed other conventional therapies. Such patients should be treated by well-trained oncologists skilled in the use of chemotherapeutic agents.

Contraindications: In those patients who are hypersensitive to this drug or its components.

Warnings: Fludarabine should be administered under the supervision of a qualified physician experienced in the use of antineoplastic therapy. Fludarabine can severely suppress bone marrow function. When used at high doses in dose-ranging studies in patients with acute leukemia, fludarabine was associated with severe irreversible neurologic effects, including blindness, coma and death. This severe CNS toxicity occurred in 36% of patients treated with doses approximately 4 times greater (96 mg/m²/day for 5 to 7 days) than the recommended dose. Similar severe CNS toxicity has been rarely (<0.2%) reported in patients treated at doses in the range of the dose recommended for CLL.

Instances of life-threatening and sometimes fatal autoimmune hemolytic anemia have been reported to occur during or after treatment with fludarabine. The causality of the development of this complication has not been identified. Patients undergoing treatment with fludarabine should be evaluated and closely monitored for signs of autoimmune hemolytic anemia (decline in hemoglobin linked with hemolysis and a positive Coombs' test). Discontinuation of therapy with fludarabine is recommended in the event of hemolysis. The transfusion of irradiated blood and the administration of adrenocorticoid preparations are the most common treatment measures for autoimmune hemolytic anemia.

In a clinical investigation using fludarabine in combination with pentostatin (deoxycoformycin) for the treatment of refractory CLL, there was an unacceptably high incidence of fatal pulmonary toxicity. Therefore, the use of fludarabine in combination with pentostatin is not recommended.

When high doses of fludarabine were administered in dose-ranging studies in acute leukemia patients, a syndrome with delayed onset, characterized by blindness, coma, and death was identified. Symptoms appeared from 21 to 60 days post dosing. Demyelination, especially of the occipital cortex of the brain was noted. The majority of these cases occurred in patients treated with doses approximately four times greater (96 mg/m²/day for 5 to 7 days) than the recommended dose. Thirteen of 36 patients (36.1%) who received fludarabine at high doses (≥96 mg/m²/day for 5 to 7 days/course) developed severe neurotoxicity, while only one of 443 patients (0.2%) who received the drug at low doses (≤40 mg/m²/day for 5 days/course) developed the toxicity. The effect of chronic administration of fludarabine on the central nervous system is unknown. Periodic neurological assessments are recommended.

Bone marrow suppression, notably thrombocytopenia, anemia, leukopenia and neutropenia, may occur with administration of fludarabine and requires careful hematologic monitoring. In a Phase I study in solid tumor patients, the median time to nadir counts was 13 days (range, 3 to 25 days) for granulocytes and 16 days (range, 2 to 32 days) for platelets. Most patients had hematologic impairment at baseline either as a result of disease or as a result of prior myelosuppressive therapy. Cumulative myelosuppression may be seen. While chemotherapy-induced myelosuppression is often reversible, administration of fludarabine requires careful hematologic monitoring.

Instances of life-threatening and sometimes fatal autoimmune hemolytic anemia have been reported to occur during or after treatment with fludarabine in patients with or without a previous history of autoimmune hemolytic anemia or a positive Coombs' test and who may or may not be in remission from their disease. Steroids may or may not be effective in controlling these hemolytic episodes. One study was performed with 31 patients with hemolytic anemia related to the administration of fludarabine. Since the majority (90%) of these patients rechallenged with fludarabine developed a recurrence in the hemolytic process, rechallenge with fludarabine should be avoided. The mechanism(s) which predispose patients to the development of this complication has not been identified. Patients undergoing treatment with fludarabine should be evaluated and closely monitored for signs of autoimmune hemolytic anemia (decline in hemoglobin linked with hemolysis and a positive Coombs' test). Discontinuation of therapy with fludarabine is recommended in the event of hemolysis. The transfusion of irradiated blood and the administration of adrenocorticoid preparations are the most common treatment measures for autoimmune hemolytic anemia.

Tumor lysis syndrome associated with fludarabine treatment has been reported in CLL patients with large tumor burdens. Since fludarabine can induce a response as early as the first week of treatment, precautions should be taken in those patients at risk of developing this complication.

Transfusion-associated graft-versus-host disease has been observed rarely after transfusion of nonirradiated blood in patients treated with fludarabine. Fatal outcome as a consequence of this disease has been reported with a high frequency. Therefore, patients who require blood transfusion and who are undergoing, or who have received treatment with fludarabine should receive irradiated blood only.

Fludara (cont'd)

There are inadequate data on dosing of patients with renal insufficiency. Fludarabine must be administered cautiously in patients with renal insufficiency. It is recommended that the fludarabine dose should be reduced by up to 50% for patients with a creatinine clearance between 30 and 70 mL/min, and close hematologic monitoring should be used to assess toxicity. In addition, fludarabine therapy is not recommended in renally impaired patients with creatinine clearance <30 mL/min (see Dosage).

Pregnancy: Safe use of fludarabine in pregnancy has not been established. Fludarabine has been shown to be teratogenic in rats and in rabbits. A study in rats demonstrated a transfer of fludarabine and/or metabolites across the placental barrier. Therefore, the benefits to the pregnant patient should be carefully weighed against the potential toxicity to the fetus.

Precautions: General: Fludarabine is a potent antineoplastic agent with potentially significant toxic side effects. Patients undergoing therapy should be closely observed for signs of hematologic and nonhematologic toxicity. Periodic assessment of peripheral blood counts is recommended to detect the development of neutropenia, thrombocytopenia, anemia and leukopenia.

Laboratory Tests: During treatment, the patient's hematologic (particularly neutrophils and platelets) and serum chemistry profiles should be monitored regularly.

Drug Interactions: In a clinical investigation using fludarabine in combination with pentostatin (deoxycoformycin) for the treatment of refractory CLL, there was an unacceptably high incidence of fatal pulmonary toxicity. Therefore, the use of fludarabine in combination with pentostatin is not recommended.

Impairment of Fertility: Preclinical toxicology studies in mice, rats and dogs have demonstrated dose-related adverse effects on the male reproductive system. Observations consisted of a decrease in mean testicular weights in dogs and degeneration and necrosis of spermatogenic epithelium of the testes in mice, rats and dogs. The possible adverse effects on fertility in males and females in humans have not been adequately evaluated. Therefore, it is recommended that females of childbearing potential and males take contraceptive measures during fludarabine therapy, and for at least 6 months after the cessation of fludarabine therapy.

Lactation: It is not known whether fludarabine is excreted in human milk. However, there is evidence from animal data that fludarabine and/or metabolites transfer from maternal blood to milk. Therefore, breast-feeding is not recommended during fludarabine therapy.

Children: The safety and effectiveness of fludarabine in children have not been established.

Geriatrics: Since there are limited data for the use of fludarabine in elderly persons (>75 years), caution should be exercised with the administration of fludarabine in these patients. The total body clearance of the principal plasma metabolite 2F-ara-A shows a correlation with creatinine clearance, indicating the importance of the renal excretion pathway for the elimination of the compound. Patients with reduced kidney function demonstrated an increased total body exposure (AUC of 2F-ara-A). Limited clinical data are available in patients with impairment of renal function (creatinine clearance below 70 mL/min). Since renal impairment is frequently present in patients over the age of 70 years, creatinine clearance should be measured. If creatinine clearance is between 30 and 70 mL/min, the dose should be reduced by up to 50%, and close hematologic monitoring should be used to assess toxicity (see Warnings and Dosage).

Adverse Effects: The most common adverse events occurring with fludarabine use include myelosuppression (anemia, leukopenia, neutropenia and thrombocytopenia), fever and chills, decreased resistance to infection, and nausea and vomiting. Other events reported include malaise, fatigue, anorexia, weakness and edema.

Hematopoietic: Myelosuppression and anemia have been reported in patients treated with fludarabine. Myelosuppression may be severe and cumulative. Life-threatening and sometimes fatal autoimmune hemolytic anemia have been reported to occur in patients receiving fludarabine. The majority of patients rechallenged with fludarabine developed a recurrence in the hemolytic process. (See Warnings for information on autoimmune hemolytic anemia associated with fludarabine).

Nervous System: Following administration of fludarabine at doses of 20 to 30 mg/m²/day in 133 patients with CLL, reported events included weakness, visual disturbances, loss of hearing, numbness, agitation, confusion and coma. There was one case of peripheral neuropathy and one case of wrist drop. (See Warnings for the information on neurotoxicity associated with high doses of fludarabine).

Pulmonary: Pneumonia, cough and shortness of breath have all been reported. Pneumonia, a frequent manifestation of infection in CLL patients occurred in 16 and 22% of those treated with fludarabine in the MDACC and SWOG studies, respectively. Pulmonary hypersensitivity reactions to fludarabine characterized by dyspnea, cough and interstitial pulmonary infiltrate have been observed.

Gastrointestinal: Gastrointestinal disturbances such as nausea and vomiting, anorexia, diarrhea, stomatitis and gastrointestinal bleeding have been reported in patients treated with fludarabine.

Skin: Skin toxicity, consisting primarily of skin rashes, has been reported in patients treated with fludarabine. Additionally, in rare cases, a toxic epidermal necrolysis (Lyell's disease) may develop.

Cardiovascular: Edema has been frequently reported. One patient developed a pericardial effusion possibly related to treatment with fludarabine. No other severe cardiovascular events were considered to be drug related.

Genitourinary: Rare cases of hemorrhagic cystitis.

Metabolic: Tumor lysis syndrome has been reported in CLL patients treated with fludarabine. This complication may include hyperuricaemia, hyperphosphatemia, hypocalcemia, metabolic acidosis, hyperkalemia, hematuria, urate crystalluria and renal failure. The onset of this syndrome may be heralded by flank pain and hematuria. Changes of hepatic and pancreatic enzymes are possible.

The spectrum of adverse reactions reported in patients (n=3 000) receiving fludarabine in studies of lymphomas and other leukemias and solid tumors is consistent with the above data.

Overdose: Symptoms and Treatment: High doses of fludarabine have been associated with an irreversible CNS toxicity characterized by delayed blindness, coma and death. High doses are also associated with bone marrow suppression manifested by thrombocytopenia and neutropenia. There is no known specific antidote for fludarabine overdosage. Treatment consists of drug discontinuation and supportive therapy.

Dosage: Usual Dose: The usual starting dose is 25 mg/m² administered i.v. over a period of approximately 30 minutes, daily for 5 days every 28 days. Dosage may be decreased based on evidence of hematologic or nonhematologic toxicity.

Fludarabine should be prepared for parenteral use by aseptically adding Sterile Water for Injection USP. When reconstituted with 2 mL of Sterile Water for Injection USP, each mL of the resulting solution will contain 25 mg of fludarabine phosphate. The product may be further diluted for i.v. administration to a concentration of 1 mg/mL in 5% Dextrose Injection USP, or in 0.9% Sodium Chloride Injection USP.

Note that in patients with decreased renal function (creatinine clearance between 30 and 70 mL/min), the dose should be reduced by up to 50% (see Warnings).

The optimal duration of treatment has not been clearly established. It is recommended that 3 additional cycles of fludarabine be administered following the achievement of a maximal response and then the drug should be discontinued.

Stability and Storage: Store under refrigeration at 2 to 8°C. Fludara contains no antimicrobial preservative and thus care must be taken to assure the sterility of prepared solutions. It is recommended to discard unused solutions 8 hours after reconstitution.

Parenteral drug products should be inspected visually for particulate matter and discoloration prior to administration.

Reconstitution: See Table I.

Table I—Fludara

Reconstituted Solutions

Vial Size	Volume of Diluent to be Added to Vial	Approximate Available Volume	Nominal Concentration Per Vial
6 mL	2 mL	2 mL	50 mg

Fludarabine should be prepared for parenteral use by aseptically adding Sterile Water for Injection USP. When reconstituted with 2 mL of Sterile Water for Injection USP, each mL of the resulting solution will contain 25 mg of fludarabine, 25 mg of mannitol and 3 mg of sodium. The pH range of the final solution is 7.2 to 8.2.

The product may be further diluted for i.v. administration to a concentration of 1 mg/mL in 5% Dextrose Injection USP, or in 0.9% Sodium Chloride Injection USP.

Incompatibilities: There are no known incompatibilities.

Handling and Disposal: Fludarabine should not be handled by pregnant staff. Proper handling and disposal procedures should be observed, with consideration given to the guidelines used for cytotoxic drugs. Any spillage or waste material may be disposed of by incineration.

Caution should be exercised in the preparation of the fludarabine solution. The use of latex gloves and safety glasses is recommended to avoid exposure in case of breakage of the vial or other accidental spillage. If the solution comes into contact with the skin or mucous membranes, the area should be washed thoroughly with soap and water. In the event of contact with the eyes, rinse them thoroughly with copious amounts of water. Exposure by inhalation should be avoided.

Supplied: Each 6 mL vial of sterile lyophilized solid cake or powder contains: fludarabine phosphate sodium equivalent to fludarabine phosphate 50 mg. Nonmedicinal ingredients: mannitol and sodium. For i.v. administration. Single vial carton, packs of 5.

(Shown in Product Recognition Section)

Reviewed 1999

FLUDROCORTISONE Ⓟ
General Monograph, CPhA

see CORTICOSTEROIDS: SYSTEMIC

FLUMETHASONE Ⓟ
General Monograph, CPhA

see CORTICOSTEROIDS: TOPICAL

FLUNISOLIDE Ⓟ
General Monograph, CPhA

see CORTICOSTEROIDS: EYE EAR NOSE
see CORTICOSTEROIDS: INHALED

FLUOCINOLONE Ⓟ
General Monograph, CPhA

see CORTICOSTEROIDS: TOPICAL

FLUOCINONIDE Ⓟ
General Monograph, CPhA

see CORTICOSTEROIDS: TOPICAL

FLUODERM Ⓟ
Taro

Fluocinolone Acetonide

Topical Corticosteroid

Supplied: Cream: Each g contains: fluocinolone acetonide 0.025% (regular) or 0.01% (mild) in a water-washable base consisting of cetostearyl alcohol, propylene glycol, isopropyl myristate, ceteareth 12, anoxid and purified water with methylparaben and propylparaben as preservatives. Tubes of 15 g and jars of 500 g.

Ointment: Each g contains: fluocinolone acetonide 0.025% (regular) or 0.01% (mild) in a petrolatum base with fractionated coconut oil, with methylparaben and propylparaben as preservatives. Tubes of 15 g and jars of 454 g.

FLUORACAINE™
Dioptic

Fluorescein Sodium—Proparacaine HCl

Ophthalmic Diagnostic—Anesthetic

Supplied: Each mL of sterile, ophthalmic solution contains: fluorescein sodium 0.25% and proparacaine HCl 0.5%. Nonmedicinal ingredients: acetic acid to adjust pH, glycerin, povidone, purified water and thimerosal. Bottles of 5 mL with dropper tips. Refrigerate at 2 to 8°C before and after opening.

FLUOR-A-DAY®
Pharmascience
Sodium Fluoride
Dental Caries Prophylaxis

Supplied: Tablets: 1 mg: Each chewable, airplane-shaped, white, raspberry flavored, compressed tablet contains: sodium fluoride USP 2.21 mg (equivalent to 1 mg fluoride ion) in a specially formulated anticaries vehicle containing xylitol. Bottles of 120 and 1 000.

0.5 mg: Each chewable, car-shaped, white, raspberry flavored, compressed tablet contains: sodium fluoride USP 1.10 mg (equivalent to 0.5 mg fluoride ion) in a specially formulated anticaries vehicle containing xylitol. Bottles of 120 and 1 000.

0.25 mg: Each chewable, train-shaped, white, raspberry flavored, compressed tablet contains: sodium fluoride USP 0.56 mg (equivalent to 0.25 mg fluoride ion) in a specially formulated anticaries vehicle containing xylitol. Bottles of 120 and 1 000.

Drops: Each mL of clear, colorless and odorless liquid contains: sodium fluoride USP 5.56 mg (equivalent to 1 mg fluoride ion per 8 drops). Bottles of 60 mL.

FLUORESCITE®
Alcon
Fluorescein Sodium
Ophthalmic Diagnostic Aid

Supplied: Each ampul contains: a sterile aqueous solution of fluorescein sodium (equivalent to fluorescein) 10% (5 mL ampuls), or 25% (2 mL ampuls). Sodium hydroxide and/or hydrochloric acid to adjust pH, and water for injection. Store at 8 to 27°C; do not freeze.

FLUORETS™
Ophtapharma
Fluorescein Sodium
Ophthalmic Diagnostic

Supplied: Each sterile, ophthalmic strip contains: fluorescein sodium 1 mg. Individually wrapped strips of 100. Store between 15 and 30°C.

FLUOROMETHOLONE Ⓟ
General Monograph, CPhA
see CORTICOSTEROIDS: EYE EAR NOSE

FLUOROPLEX® Ⓟ
Allergan
Fluorouracil
Antineoplastic—Antimetabolite

Supplied: Each g of cream contains: fluorouracil USP 1%. Nonmedicinal ingredients: benzyl alcohol 0.5% (as preservative), emulsifying wax, isopropyl myristate, mineral oil, purified water and sodium hydroxide. Collapsible aluminum tubes of 30 g. Avoid freezing. Store at 15 to 30°C.

FLUOROURACIL ROCHE® Ⓟ
Roche
5-Fluorouracil
Antineoplastic

> Caution: 5-fluorouracil is a potent drug and should be prescribed only by physicians experienced with cancer chemotherapeutic drugs (see Precautions). Blood counts as well as renal and hepatic function tests should be performed regularly. Discontinue the drug if there is significant leukopenia (under 3 000/mm³) or granulocytopenia (under 1 500/mm³).

Pharmacology: 5-Fluorouracil is a fluorinated pyrimidine antimetabolite which is structurally similar to uracil, one of the necessary building blocks in cellular division and growth.

Its usefulness is based on uracil being utilized preferentially for nucleic acid biosynthesis in some tumors. 5-fluorouracil is metabolized to 5-fluorouridine triphosphate (F-UTP), 2-deoxyfluorouridine monophosphate (Fd-UMP), and 2-deoxyfluorouridine triphosphate (Fd-UTP) in cells to concentrations that result in both DNA-directed and RNA-directed cytotoxicities. Fd-UMP is the intracellular cytotoxic form of 5-fluorouracil. It competes with the natural substrate d-UMP (deoxyuridine monophosphate) for the catalytic site on thymidylate synthetase (a key enzyme in DNA synthesis), forming a covalent complex with the enzyme that is unable to undergo the normal catalytic reaction of converting d-UMP to d-TMP. The presence of a reduced folate cofactor is required for tight binding of Fd-UMP to thymidylate synthetase. Folinic acid (leucovorin), which is metabolized to 5,10-methylenetetrahydropteroylglutamine (a reduced folate), is able to modulate the antineoplastic effect of 5-fluorouracil by promoting the formation and stabilization of the ternary complex formed between Fd-UMP and thymidylate synthetase. In this way, leucovorin produces a synergistic effect on 5-fluorouracil therapy.

At the same time, 5-fluorouracil interferes with the mechanism of action of RNA, resulting from the formation of "fraudulent" RNA by the incorporation of F-UTP in the ribonucleotides. Incorporation into RNA has been associated with toxicity and has major effects on both the processing and functions of RNA.

By interference with the formation of DNA and RNA, 5-fluorouracil provokes unbalanced growth and death of cells. The effects of DNA and RNA deprivation are most marked on those cells which grow rapidly and which take up 5-fluorouracil rapidly.

While there is no evidence that 5-fluorouracil prolongs survival time generally, the usefulness of the drug has been demonstrated by the relief of pain and other symptoms in certain types of human malignances. There have also occasionally been regressions of tumors.

Pharmacokinetics: The steady-state plasma concentrations of 5-fluorouracil following bolus i.v. doses of 400 to 600 mg/m² (10 to 15 mg/kg) range from 0.1 to 1.0 mM. Following continuous infusion of 1 100 mg/m²/day, plasma concentrations of 0.5 to 2.5 μM are observed. 5-Fluorouracil readily penetrates the blood-brain barrier and CSF concentrations of about 7 μM are reached within 30 minutes after i.v. administration. The volume of distribution of 5-fluorouracil ranges from 0.1 to 0.4 L/kg. The elimination half-life is 6 to 20 minutes and is dose-dependent. Following an i.v. injection, no intact drug can be detected in the plasma after 3 hours. For bolus doses, 5-fluorouracil plasma clearance is 0.5 to 1.4 L/min. Clearance values are 10- to 60-fold higher following i.v. infusion. This non-linearity likely represents saturation of a metabolic or transport process at higher drug concentrations. Plasma protein binding of 5-fluorouracil is 10%.

The metabolism of 5-fluorouracil occurs mainly in the liver and results in degradation products (e.g., carbon dioxide, urea, α-fluoro-β-alanine) which are inactive. Approximately 15% of the dose is excreted intact in the urine in 6 hours and over 90% of this is excreted in the first hour; 60 to 80% is excreted as respiratory carbon dioxide in 8 to 12 hours.

Indications: The palliative management of carcinoma of the breast, colon, rectum, stomach and pancreas. In clinical practice, 5-fluorouracil is often combined with other cytotoxic agents such as methotrexate, cyclophosphamide, cisplatin, vincristine, mitomycin, adriamycin, levamisole and interferon alpha-2a; or drugs which may enhance its effect on killing tumor cells such as calcium leucovorin.

Various combinations of 5-fluorouracil/interferon and 5-fluorouracil/leucovorin/interferon are also used in clinical practice.

5-fluorouracil does not replace surgery or other recognized forms of therapy and should be used only when these measures are not possible or have been tried and have failed.

Contraindications: In pregnant women, in patients in a poor nutritional state, those with severely depressed bone marrow, with potentially serious infections or with known hypersensitivity to 5-fluorouracil.

Warnings: The drug should be given only by or under the supervision of a qualified physician who is experienced in cancer chemotherapy and well-versed in the use of potent antimetabolites.

5-fluorouracil should be used with extreme caution in patients who have undergone recent major surgery; those with a history of high-dose irradiation to bone marrow-bearing areas (pelvis, spine, ribs, etc.) or previous use of myelosuppressive chemotherapeutic agents; those with a widespread involvement of bone marrow by metastatic tumors; or those with renal or liver impairment. Although severe toxicity is more likely in debilitated patients, fatalities may be encountered occasionally even in patients in relatively good conditions.

5-Fluorouracil should be used with great care in patients who are known or suspected to have a dihydropyrimidine dehydrogenase deficiency, as these patients are at a greater risk of experiencing symptoms of toxicity.

Pregnancy: Although it is not known whether 5-fluorouracil crosses the human placenta, it has been shown to cross the rat placenta and enter into the fetal circulation of this rodent. Positive teratologic findings have been observed in animals. Therefore, this drug should not be used during pregnancy.

Lactation: It is not known whether 5-fluorouracil is excreted in human milk. Because 5-fluorouracil inhibits DNA, RNA and protein synthesis, mothers should not nurse while receiving this drug.

Mutagenesis: Positive mutagenic findings have been observed in the usual mutagenicity screening tests.

Drug Interactions: Combined Therapy: Leucovorin (folinic acid) and 5-fluorouracil are routinely used together in the treatment of colorectal cancer. There is biochemical rationale for the synergism produced by the combination of 5-fluorouracil and leucovorin. Leucovorin is metabolized to a reduced folate cofactor that is necessary for maximal inhibition of thymidylate synthetase by Fd-UMP, the active metabolite of 5-fluorouracil. Studies with tumor lines in vitro have confirmed this effect and several clinical studies have shown evidence that there may be some increased therapeutic benefit from providing a source of reduced folate.

Clinical trials have been reported using sequenced methotrexate/fluorouracil in head and neck, breast and colorectal cancers. Methotrexate has been shown to improve the effectiveness of 5-fluorouracil against tumor cells in vitro and in vivo. The sequence of administration is of importance. Administration of methotrexate followed by 5-fluorouracil leads to a synergistic interaction. Biochemical modulation might occur both through effects on RNA and DNA synthesis and enhancement of 5-fluorouracil uptake. The importance of the time interval between methotrexate and 5-fluorouracil exposure in the treatment of metastatic colon cancer has been demonstrated. When these 2 agents are separated by 24 hours as compared with 1 hour, the response rate, time to progression and survival are significantly improved. However, different tumors may respond differently to changes in the time interval between methotrexate and 5-fluorouracil.

Any form of therapy which adds to the stress of the patient, interferes with nutrition, or depresses bone marrow function, may increase the toxicity of 5-fluorouracil.

When combining 5-fluorouracil with other anticancer agents (such as methotrexate, cyclophosphamide, cisplatin, vincristine, mitomycin, adriamycin, levamisole or interferon alpha-2a) and leucovorin, drug interactions increasing both the efficacy and/or toxicity have been reported. A hemolytic-uremic syndrome has been reported to occur after long-term use of 5-fluorouracil in combination with mitomycin.

Precautions: 5-fluorouracil should be administered by individuals experienced in the use of antineoplastic therapy. Fluorouracil Roche is both an irritant and a highly toxic drug. Professional staff administering 5-fluorouracil should exercise particular care to prevent spillage and contact with the drug. Should skin contact occur, the area should be vigorously washed with soap and cold water and the material used for cleansing disposed by incineration. In the case of contact with the eyes, irrigate immediately with water and contact a physician. If inhaled or ingested, seek immediate medical attention (see Dosage, Special Instructions).

5-fluorouracil is a highly toxic drug with a narrow margin of safety. Therefore, patients should be carefully supervised. Therapy should be properly adjusted or discontinued if: significant stomatitis, mucositis or esophagitis, severe diarrhea or vomiting, or gastrointestinal ulcers or bleeding occurs; leukopenia (WBC count under 3 000/mm³), thrombocytopenia (platelet count under 80 000/mm³), or granulocytopenia (under 1 500/mm³); central or peripheral nervous system toxicity, including ataxia, tremor; cardiac toxicity.

Therapeutic response is unlikely to occur without some evidence of toxicity. Patients should be informed of expected toxic effects, particularly oral manifestations (see Adverse Effects).

Because of the possibility of leukopenia, frequent blood counts (every 2 to 3 days) are essential during initial therapy. If the count falls, it is advisable to obtain differentials with each count. If the count is less than 1 500/mm³ with marked granulocytopenia (less than 1 000/mm³), it is recommended

Fluorouracil Roche (cont'd)

that the patient be carefully followed and considered for prophylactic antibiotics. During maintenance therapy, counts before each course are sufficient.

In the case of severe gastrointestinal, cardiac or neurological toxicity, continued treatment with 5-fluorouracil is not recommended.

Severe hematological effects, gastrointestinal hemorrhage and even death may result from the use of 5-fluorouracil despite meticulous selection of patients and careful adjustment of dosage; but severe toxicity is more frequent in poor-risk patients.

Laboratory Test Interactions: The results of tests for bilirubin (icteric index), and for 5-hydroxyindole acetic acid in the urine, may be increased or false positive.

Adverse Effects: Stomatitis, mucositis and esophagopharyngitis (which may lead to sloughing and ulceration), diarrhea, anorexia, nausea and emesis are commonly seen during therapy. Allergic reactions including anaphylaxis, bronchospasm, urticaria and pruritus have also been reported. If anaphylactic shock occurs, the usual countermeasures should be employed. Diarrhea usually reponds to antidiarrheal agents. Uncontrolled nausea and vomiting can be treated with antiemetic agents.

Leukopenia with neutropenia usually follows each course of adequate therapy. The lowest white blood cell counts are commonly observed between the 9th and 14th days after the first dose, although the maximal depression may occasionally be delayed for as long as 20 days. By the 30th day the count usually returns to the normal range. Pancytopenia, agranulocytosis, anemia, hemolytic anemia and thrombocytopenia have also been reported. Due to immunosuppression, infections (sometimes serious), may develop in patients treated with 5-fluorouracil.

Alopecia and dermatitis may be seen in a substantial number of cases. Patients should be alerted to the possibility of alopecia, but, since the alopecia is reported to be reversible, special measures do not seem to be indicated. The dermatitis seen most often is a pruritic maculopapular rash appearing usually on the extremities and sometimes on the trunk. It is generally reversible and responsive to symptomatic treatment.

Other adverse reactions are:

Cardiovascular: myocardial ischemia, angina, precordial pain, cardiac arrhythmias, ischemia and heart failure resulting rarely in death.

Gastrointestinal: gastrointestinal ulceration and bleeding.

CNS: ataxia, dysarthria, nystagmus, disorientation, headache, confusion, euphoria, acute cerebellar syndrome (which may persist following discontinuation of treatment). Extrapyramidal or cortical dysfunction (usually reversible). Isolated cases of leucoencephalopathy have also been reported.

Dermatologic: dry skin; fissuring; photosensitivity as manifested by erythema or increased pigmentation of the skin; palmar-plantar erythrodysesthesia syndrome (hand-foot syndrome), as manifested by tingling of the hands and feet followed by pain, erythema and swelling. Palmar-plantar erythrodysesthesia syndrome gradually resolves 5 to 7 days after interruption of therapy. This syndrome may be treated with the concomitant oral administration of pyridoxine at doses of 100 to 150 mg/day.

Ophthalmic: visual changes; photophobia; oculomotor disturbances and lacrimation, optic neuritis. Lacrimal duct stenosis (canalicular fibrosis) associated with prolonged administration of fluorouracil has been reported as rare. This condition is reversible upon reduction or temporary cessation of 5-fluorouracil therapy, but on occasion may necessitate surgical intervention.

Miscellaneous: thrombophlebitis, epistaxis, nail changes (including loss of nails), chest pain, vein pigmentation. Hepatocellular damage and, in very rare cases, fatal hepatic necrosis have been observed.

Overdose: Symptoms and Treatment: The main symptoms of overdose are nausea, vomiting, diarrhea, stomatitis, esophagopharyngitis, gastrointestinal ulceration and bleeding, hemorrhage from any site and bone marrow depression (including thrombocytopenia, leukopenia and agranulocytosis). No specific antidotal therapy exists. Patients who have been exposed to an overdose of 5-fluorouracil should be monitored hematologically with regular white cell counts, differentials and platelet counts. Should abnormalities appear, appropriate symptomatic therapy should be utilized. Suitable counter measures are withdrawal of medication or dosage reduction and, depending on the symptoms, blood transfusions, leukocyte or platelet infusions or anti-infective therapy. Nausea, vomiting and diarrhea may be controlled by appropriate therapy.

Dosage: Criteria for the selection of patients: In order to be considered for 5-fluorouracil therapy, a prospective patient must meet the following: 1) No history of high irradiation to major bone marrow-bearing areas. Adequate bone marrow functions, i.e., a white blood cell count of 3 000/mm³ or over, a granulocyte count of 1 500/mm³ or over and a platelet count of 80 000/mm³ or over. 2) Adequate hepatic and renal functions.

5-fluorouracil should only be administered i.v., and care should be taken to avoid extravasation. No dilution of the solution is required when 5-fluorouracil is given by direct i.v. injection.

In most cases, dosage should be based on the patient's actual weight or actual body surface area. However, if the patient is obese or if there has been a spurious weight gain due to edema, ascites or other forms of abnormal fluid retention, the ideal weight or ideal body surface area should be used. Following major weight loss, the dose of 5-fluorouracil should be reduced.

It is recommended that each patient be carefully evaluated prior to treatment, in order to estimate as accurately as possible the optimum initial dosage of 5-fluorouracil. Likewise, the duration of therapy must be determined by a specialist, based on the type and course of the disease.

The following dosage schedules may be used.

General Recommendations: I.V. Injection: 1) 800 mg/m² (19 mg/kg) single dose. 2) 480 mg/m² (12 mg/kg)/day on days 1, 2, 3, 4 followed by 240 mg/m² (6 mg/kg)/day on days 6, 8, 10 and 12. Repeat course every 30 days. 3) 300 to 450 mg/m² (7 to 11 mg/kg)/day for 5 days. Repeat every 4 weeks. 4) 400 to 480 mg/m² (10 to 12 mg/kg) or 500 to 600 mg/m² (12 to 15 mg/kg)/week.

I.V. Infusion: Administration by infusion may result in slightly less toxicity. 5-fluorouracil may be diluted with 300 to 500 mL of 5% dextrose solution. 1) 480 mg/m² (12 mg/kg) over a period of 4 hours daily until signs of toxicity are observed, usually within 8 to 15 days. 2) 1 000 to 2 000 mg/m² (24 to 49 mg/kg) over a period of 24 hours daily for 5 days. Repeat course every 4 weeks.

Combination Therapy with Folinic Acid: I.V. injection 370 to 400 mg/m² (9 to 10 mg/kg) for 5 days plus folinic acid 200 to 500 mg/m² (5 to 12 mg/kg) for 5 days. Repeat course every 4 weeks.

The patient must be monitored for toxic signs. Drug therapy should be appropriately adjusted or discontinued should toxic signs such as gastrointestinal bleeding become manifested.

Recommendations for Poor Risk Patients: For poor risk patients, the following dosage schedules may be used: I.V. Injection: 240 mg/m² (6 mg/kg)/day on days 1, 2, 3 followed by 120 mg/m² (3 mg/kg)/day on days 5, 7, 9. Repeat course every 30 days.

I.V. Infusion: 240 mg/m² (6 mg/kg) over a period of 4 hours daily until signs of toxicity are observed, usually within 8 to 15 days.

Renal Impairment: Due to the impairment of bone marrow function in azotemia, secondary to kidney failure, a dose adjustment appropriate to the degree of renal failure and to the reaction of the individual patient to 5-fluorouracil is recommended.

Liver Impairment: Since 5-fluorouracil is metabolized mainly in the liver, a dosage reduction should be considered when liver function is impaired.

Note: The patient's reaction to the previous course should be taken into account when determining the dosage. Some patients have received from 9 to 45 courses of treatment over periods ranging from 12 to 60 months.

Frequent blood counts (every 2 or 3 days) are essential during initial therapy. During maintenance therapy, counts before each course are sufficient.

Therapy should be properly adjusted or discontinued whenever any of the following signs of toxicity appear: significant stomatitis, mucositis or esophagitis, severe diarrhea or vomiting, or gastrointestinal ulcers or bleeding occurs; leukopenia (WBC count under 3 000/mm³), thrombocytopenia (platelet count under 80 000/mm³), or granulocytopenia (under 1 500/mm³); central or peripheral nervous system toxicity, including ataxia, tremor; cardiac toxicity.

Dosage Reduction in Combination Therapy: When 5-fluorouracil is combined with other cytostatics of similar toxicity profile or with radiotherapy, the recommended dosage should be reduced accordingly.

Dilution: No dilution of the solution is required when Fluorouracil Roche is given by direct i.v. injection.

Fluorouracil Roche may be diluted with 300 to 500 mL of 5% dextrose and administered by infusion over a period of 4 or 24 hours (see Dosage). Infusions prepared with 5% dextrose solution should be used within 24 hours.

Special Instructions: 1. As for all antineoplastic agents, personnel handling these agents should wear polyvinylchloride gloves, safety glasses, disposable gowns and masks and should work in a vertical laminar flow hood.

2. Fluorouracil Roche is both an irritant and a highly toxic drug. Professional staff administering antineoplastic agents should exercise particular care to prevent spillage and contact with the drug. Should skin contact occur, the area should be vigorously washed with soap and water. In the case of contact with the eyes, irrigate immediately with water and contact a physician. If inhaled or ingested, seek immediate medical attention.

3. As 5-fluorouracil is frequently adsorbed by regular glass surfaces, silanized glass should be used when 5-fluorouracil is given.

All materials which have come in contact with cytotoxic agents including needles, syringes, open ampuls or vials, polyvinylchloride gloves, gowns, masks and materials used for cleansing, should be segregated and incinerated at 1 000°C or more. If incineration is not possible, add household bleach (sodium hypochlorite solution) or 0.1 molar sodium hydroxide solution and place the sealed container in a landfill site.

4. Personnel regularly involved in the preparation and handling of cytotoxic agents should have bi-annual blood examinations.

Supplied: Each mL contains: 5-fluorouracil 50 mg (as the sodium salt); sodium hydroxide is added to solubilize the compound and to adjust the pH to approximately 9.2. Sodium: <1 mmol (7.6 mg)/mL. Alcohol-, paraben- and sulfite-free. Single-dose vials of 10 mL, boxes of 10.

Store at room temperature (15 to 30°C). Protect from light. Although the solution may discolor slightly during storage, the potency and safety are not adversely affected and are maintained until the expiry date. If a precipitate occurs during storage, resolubilize by heating to 60°C with vigorous shaking; allow to cool to body temperature before using.

Reviewed 1999

FLUOTIC® Ⓟ

Hoechst Marion Roussel

Sodium Fluoride

Otospongiosis Therapy

Pharmacology: Sodium fluoride acts partly by reducing bone resorption in the bone remodeling cycle and partly by increasing bone deposition. In organ culture of otospongiotic bone removed at operation, sodium fluoride increased radioactive calcium uptake. Analysis of the fluoride content of otospongiotic bone showed a higher fluoride content in untreated patients, than in the endochrondral bone of the noninvolved stapes, or the skeletal bone of the meatus. This is explained by the increased vascularity and bone remodeling activity, with increased opportunity of trace amounts of fluoride normally present in food and water, to contact the active focus. Following moderate dosage of sodium fluoride treatment for 6 months, the fluoride content of meatal bone and stapedial crura is barely perceptibly increased, but that of otospongiotic bone is increased nearly threefold compared to untreated conditions. Thus, otospongiotic bone has an affinity for circulating fluoride.

The most convincing evidence of the effectiveness of sodium fluoride in reducing the activity of otospongiotic bone has been provided by enzyme studies in organ cultures of mature and immature specimens removed at surgery from treated and untreated patients. These investigations indicate a marked reduction in the enzyme activity of otospongiotic bone after treatment and during cultivation when fluoride is added to the culture medium.

Of great significance has been the finding that cytotoxic enzymes, found in the majority of patients undergoing stapedectomy who had shown progression in sensorineural loss before operation, were very rarely found in similar patients after sodium fluoride treatment for 6 months. The toxic enzymes liberated by the active focus appear to be the mechanism of the sensorineural deterioration. Sodium fluoride acts partly as an enzyme inhibitor and partly to decrease osteoclastic resorption and to increase calcification of the focus, thus arresting its activity.

Over 9 000 cases of otospongiotic patients treated with sodium fluoride have been reported in the medical literature since 1964. In most cases, between 40 to 60 mg of sodium fluoride a day was administered. The duration of treatment in these studies varied between 6 months to more than 7 years in certain cases with no ill effects to the patients.

The drug was generally well tolerated, especially in patients who received concomitantly a supplement of calcium and of vitamin D. The side effects most frequently reported were gastrointestinal complaints and musculoskeletal pain. There seems to be a relationship between therapeutic results and serum blood levels of fluoride and the optimum serum level appears to be from 8 to 12 μmol/L.

The overall clinical results indicate a stabilization of the sensorineural loss of hearing in 80% of cases. Other symptoms such as tinnitus, vertigo and postural imbalance associated with otospongiosis may be improved in 50 to 80% of cases depending on the symptoms involved and the severity of the condition.

Sodium fluoride is rapidly and almost completely absorbed from the gastrointestinal tract.

Certain cations such as calcium, magnesium, aluminum and iron retard the absorption of fluoride ion by forming low solubility complexes in the gastrointestinal tract.

Fluoride can be detected in all organs and tissues and especially in bones, thyroid, aorta and kidney. Fluoride is predominantly deposited in the skeleton and teeth and the degree of skeletal storage is related to age and intake. 50% of a given dose is excreted in the urine while the rest forms a chemical bond with bone.

Indications: Nonsurgical cases: In patients with diagnosed neurosensorial hearing loss or tinnitus due to otospongiosis, especially if accompanied by a positive Schwartze sign indicating a vascular active focus.

In patients with postural imbalance and/or vertigo caused by a lesion of the posterior labyrinth consecutive to otospongiosis and in patients with radiologically demonstrated demineralization of the cochlear capsule.

Postsurgical cases: In patients where, following surgery, a soft vascular focus is encountered at the oval window or when the patient begins to experience progressive neurosensorial deterioration after successful stapedectomy.

Contraindications: *Pregnancy*, Children and Adolescents: Since the safety of sodium fluoride has not been established in pregnant women, in children and adolescents up to 18 years old, the drug should not be used in these patients.

The drug is also contraindicated in severe renal insufficiency and in patients with an active peptic ulcer.

Warnings: Fluotic is not intended for dental use. The drug should preferably be prescribed with a daily supplement of calcium and vitamin D.

Adverse Effects: Sodium fluoride, at the recommended dosage, is usually well tolerated. Mild reactions consisting of gastrointestinal complaints, musculoskeletal pain and skin rash may occur.

Overdose: Symptoms: Initial symptoms are secondary to the local action of sodium fluoride on the mucosa of the gastrointestinal tract. Salivation, nausea, abdominal pain, vomiting, and diarrhea are frequent. Systemic symptoms are varied and severe. The patient shows signs of increasing irritability of the nervous system, including paresthesias, a positive Chvostek sign, hyperactive reflexes, and tonic and clonic convulsions.

These signs are related to the calcium binding effect of sodium fluoride. Hypocalcemia and hypoglycemia are frequent laboratory findings. The signs may be delayed for several hours. Pain in various muscle groups may occur. The blood pressure falls, presumably due to central vasomotor depression as well as a direct toxic action on cardiac muscle. The respiratory center is first stimulated and later depressed. Death usually results from either respiratory paralysis or cardiac failure. It is stated that the lethal dose of sodium fluoride for man is about 5 g; however, recovery has been reported in patients ingesting much larger doses, whereas a dose as low as 2 g has been fatal. In children as little as 500 mg of sodium fluoride may be fatal.

Treatment: 1) Act quickly; 2) Start i.v. therapy with glucose in isotonic saline solution to maintain blood sugar and to have a venous channel available for transfusion in the event of shock; 3) Wash the stomach with limewater (0.15% calcium hydroxide solution) and then give limewater at frequent intervals; 4) Have calcium gluconate available for i.v. administration and watch closely for signs of tetany; 5) Maintain high urine volumes with parenteral fluid.

Dosage: The average dose of Fluotic is 20 mg 3 times a day with meals. Clinical experience with sodium fluoride in osteoporosis, multiple myeloma and otospongiosis has shown that best results can be achieved by the addition of a calcium salt and of vitamin D.

The addition of calcium, preferably calcium carbonate, 2 to 3 g a day, is of prime importance since the use of sodium fluoride alone has been associated with a fall of serum calcium and hyper-parathyroidism. The net result is osteomalacia and increased bone resorption which may negate any beneficial effect that fluoride may have on bone formation. The effect of fluoride alone on bone is well known. Stimulation of osteoblastic bone formation occurs but in the absence of additional calcium, the bone is incompletely mineralized.

Recalcification of the focus is the indication to reduce the dosage to a maintenance level, while continued or increased activity as shown by polytomography, positive Schwartze sign and neurosensorial loss progression are the indications to continue treatment or to increase the dosage.

Control of patients: It is important to make periodic examinations of patients as follows:

Clinical examination of patients should be made every 6 to 12 months along with a renal function test and a serum fluoride determination.

Radiological examination to exclude the possibility of fluorosis should be made every 2 years.

Clinical experience has shown that the optimum fluoride serum level should be between 8 to 12 μmol/L.

Supplied: Each red, enteric film-coated tablet contains: sodium fluoride 20 mg. Nonmedicinal ingredients: cellulose acetate phthalate, colloidal silicon dioxide, diethyl phthalate, FD&C red #40 aluminum lake, FD&C yellow #6 aluminum lake, hydroxypropyl methylcellulose, lactose, microcrystalline cellulose, polyethylene glycol, polysorbate, stearic acid and titanium dioxide. Gluten-free. Bottles of 100.

FLUOXETINE Ⓟ

General Monograph, CPhA

see SELECTIVE SEROTONIN REUPTAKE INHIBITORS

FLUPHENAZINE Ⓟ

General Monograph, CPhA

Antipsychotic

This monograph has been compiled by CPhA. It may contain information different from that approved by Therapeutic Products Programme, Health Canada, and the pharmaceutical manufacturers' approval has not been requested.

Pharmacology: Fluphenazine is a short-acting piperazine phenothiazine. Phenothiazines are thought to elicit their antipsychotic effects via interference with central dopaminergic pathways in the mesolimbic zone of the brain. Extrapyramidal side effects are a result of interaction with dopaminergic pathways in the basal ganglia.

Fluphenazine has alpha adrenergic blocking activity and can cause orthostatic hypotension.

Compared to other phenothiazines, fluphenazine has weak anticholinergic, sedative and hypotensive activity, weak antiemetic effects and strong extrapyramidal effects. It is the most potent of the phenothiazine antipsychotics.

Pharmacokinetics: Rapid absorption occurs following oral or i.m. administration. Fluphenazine is distributed into most body tissues. It is highly bound to plasma proteins. Onset of action is within 1 hour; duration of action is 6 to 8 hours. The reported half-life ranges from 13 to 33 hours or more. Extensive hepatic metabolism does occur but the exact metabolic fate of fluphenazine is unclear. Metabolites and unchanged drug are excreted in urine and feces.

Esterification of fluphenazine slows its release from fatty tissue. I.M. or s.c. injection of the esters in a sesame oil base also slows their release. The clinical result is a longer duration of action. Two fluphenazine esters are commercially available in a sesame oil vehicle, fluphenazine decanoate and fluphenazine enanthate. Their onset of action is 24 to 72 hours with an average duration of action of 2 to 3 weeks.

Indications: The symptomatic management of psychotic disorders. The long-acting (depot) injectable forms of fluphenazine are most commonly used as maintenance therapy in patients who are unreliable in taking daily oral medications.

Contraindications: Fluphenazine is contraindicated in patients who have a known hypersensitivity to the drug. Cross-sensitivity between fluphenazine and other phenothiazine drugs may occur.

Fluphenazine should not be used in patients who are comatose, in patients with severe CNS depression secondary to use of CNS depressant medications and in patients with blood dyscrasias or bone marrow depression.

Phenothiazines are contraindicated in patients with suspected or established subcortical brain damage with or without hypothalamic damage, since a hyperthermic reaction with temperatures in excess of 40° C may occur in such patients, sometimes not until 14 to 16 hours after drug administration.

Warnings: The antiemetic effect of phenothiazines may mask vomiting as a sign of toxicity due to overdosage of other drugs, or may obscure the cause of vomiting in various disorders such as brain tumor, intestinal obstruction, or Reye's syndrome.

Precautions: During the first month of therapy, routine blood counts, renal and hepatic function tests are advised as blood dyscrasias and cholestatic jaundice may occur. Renal function should be monitored in patients on long-term therapy.

Fluphenazine may cause agranulocytosis. Most reported cases of agranulocytosis associated with the administration of phenothiazine derivatives have occurred between the fourth and tenth week of treatment. Therefore, observe patients on prolonged therapy with particular care during that time for the appearance of such signs as sore throat, fever and weakness. If these symptoms appear, discontinue the drug and perform WBC and differential counts.

Fluphenazine may cause hypotension. It should be used with caution in the elderly, alcoholics and in patients with cardiovascular disease or in patients undergoing surgery. The dosage of anesthetic and CNS depressants may have to be reduced in the perioperative period. Epinephrine should not be used to treat fluphenazine-induced hypotension (see Drug Interactions).

ECG changes have been associated with the administration of phenothiazines. These changes appear to be reversible and related to a disturbance in repolarization. Use fluphenazine with caution in patients with cardiovascular disease.

Fluphenazine should be used with caution in patients who have impaired liver function or alcoholic liver disease. CNS depression may be potentiated. If bilirubinemia or icterus occurs, discontinue the drug and perform liver function tests.

Use cautiously in patients with respiratory difficulties as CNS depression may cause some respiratory failure in these patients.

Paralytic ileus resulting from the anticholinergic action of fluphenazine may occur, especially in the elderly. Administer with caution also in those patients with glaucoma or prostatic hypertrophy.

Fluphenazine may lower the seizure threshold and should be used cautiously in patients with a history of seizures.

Phenothiazines affect thermoregulation. Use fluphenazine with caution in those patients who may be exposed to extreme heat or cold.

Photosensitivity may occur. Patients should utilize sunscreens when exposed to sunlight for significant lengths of time.

Administer fluphenazine with caution to patients exposed to organophosphate insecticides.

Use with caution in patients with hypocalcemia. These individuals are more susceptible to dystonic reactions.

Phenothiazines have been associated with retinopathy. Discontinue fluphenazine if retinal changes are observed.

Phenothiazines do not produce psychogenic dependence; however, gastritis, nausea and vomiting, dizziness and tremulousness have been reported following abrupt cessation of high-dose therapy; therefore, therapy should be tapered slowly over a period of 1 to 2 weeks. Reports suggest that these symptoms can be reduced if concomitant antiparkinsonian agents are continued for several weeks after the phenothiazine is withdrawn.

Neuroleptic drugs elevate prolactin levels; the elevation persists during chronic administration. Although disturbances such as galactorrhea, amenorrhea, gynecomastia, and impotence have been reported, the clinical significance of elevated serum prolactin levels is unknown for most patients.

Occupational Hazards: Mental and physical abilities required for driving a car or operating heavy machinery may be impaired. Potentiation of the effects of alcohol may also occur.

Drug Interactions: Anticonvulsants: Fluphenazine may lower the seizure threshold. Dosage adjustment of anticonvulsants may be necessary.

Anticholinergics: Anticholinergic drugs such as antihistamines, antiparkinsonian drugs, atropine, MAO inhibitors and tricyclic antidepressants may have additive anticholinergic effects when administered with fluphenazine. Concomitant use of these drugs may increase the predisposition of patients treated with phenothiazines to heat stroke and paralytic ileus.

Antidepressants, Tricyclic: Concomitant use of fluphenazine and tricyclic antidepressants may result in increased plasma concentrations of both drugs, with additive anticholinergic,

Fluphenazine (cont'd)

sedative and hypotensive effects. The risk of neuroleptic malignant syndrome may also be increased.

Antihypertensives: Concomitant use of fluphenazine and antihypertensives may result in additive hypotensive effects and an increase risk of orthostatic hypotension or syncope.

Antithyroid Agents: Concomitant use of fluphenazine and antithyroid agents such as methimazole and propylthiouracil may increase the risk of agranulocytosis.

CNS Depressants: Fluphenazine may enhance the CNS depressant effects of drugs including alcohol, anticonvulsants, antihistamines, barbiturates, benzodiazepines, MAO inhibitors, narcotic analgesics and tricyclic antidepressants. Monitor to avoid excessive sedation or respiratory depression.

Epinephrine: Epinephrine should not be used to treat fluphenazine-induced hypotension. Fluphenazine blocks peripheral alpha-adrenergic receptors, thereby inhibiting alpha-agonist effects of epinephrine such as vasoconstriction and increased blood pressure. The beta-agonist effects of epinephrine (vasodilation) may be left unopposed and a further fall in blood pressure may result. Agents such as phenylephrine, methoxamine or norepinephrine may be suitable alternatives to raise blood pressure.

Haloperidol: Concomitant use of fluphenazine and haloperidol may increase the risk of extrapyramidal reactions.

Levodopa: Fluphenazine may inhibit the antiparkinsonian effects of levodopa as a result of its dopamine blocking effects in the CNS.

Lithium: Patients receiving lithium and fluphenazine for treatment of acute mania should be monitored closely for signs of adverse neurologic effects, especially if serum concentrations of lithium are in the upper range. Rare cases of severe neurotoxicity have been reported.

Metoclopramide: Concomitant use of fluphenazine and metoclopramide may increase the risk of extrapyramidal reactions.

Metrizamide: Fluphenazine should not be used in patients receiving the radiopaque contrast agent metrizamide. Concomitant use increases the risk of seizures.

Pregnancy: Safe use of phenothiazines in pregnancy has not been established. Most studies indicate these agents are not teratogenic but there are reports of defects in infants exposed to these drugs during the first trimester. Toxic effects observed after high doses near term include: hypotonia, lethargy, depressed reflexes, paralytic ileus, jaundice, and persistent extrapyramidal syndrome. Therefore, they should be administered cautiously to women of childbearing potential particularly during the first trimester of pregnancy and near term.

Lactation: Phenothiazines are distributed into breast milk. Use with caution during lactation because of the possible sedative and anticholinergic side effects to the infant.

Children: Safety and efficacy of fluphenazine hydrochloride in children has not been established. It is not recommended for use in pediatric patients.

Geriatrics: Use reduced dosages. Fluphenazine may adversely affect many of the conditions commonly occurring in the aged, including cardiovascular problems (especially orthostatic hypotension). The elderly may be at greater risk for developing extrapyramidal or parkinsonian symptoms, and may be more susceptible to sedation or to the anticholinergic effects (e.g., constipation, blurred vision, urinary retention, mental confusion).

Adverse Effects: Adverse effects with different phenothiazines vary in type, frequency and mechanism of occurrence, i.e., some are dose-related, while others involve individual patient sensitivity. Some adverse effects may be more likely to occur or occur with greater intensity, in patients with special medical problems, i.e., hypotension may be a particular problem in patients with pheochromocytoma or mitral insufficiency. Severe hypotension has occurred with usual dosages of phenothiazines in these patients.

In general, members of the piperazine group of phenothiazines have more marked stimulating effects, are more likely to cause motor disorders associated with extrapyramidal reactions, particularly in children, but are less likely to cause blood dyscrasias, hypotension, tachycardia, and drowsiness than the members of the other phenothiazine groups.

Not all of the following adverse reactions have been observed with every phenothiazine derivative, but they have been reported with one or more and should be borne in mind when drugs of this class are administered.

Autonomic Nervous System: dry mouth, fainting, stuffy nose, photophobia, blurred vision, miosis, constipation, ileus, salivation, impaired temperature regulation, headache.

Behavioral Reactions: oversedation; impaired psychomotor function; paradoxical effects, such as agitation, excitement, insomnia, bizarre dreams, aggravation of psychotic symptoms; toxic confusional states.

Cardiovascular: hypotension, tachycardia, ECG changes (see Precautions).

CNS: extrapyramidal reactions, including pseudoparkinsonism (with motor retardation, rigidity, mask-like facies, pill rolling and other tremors, drooling, shuffling gait,); dystonic reactions (including perioral spasms, and trismus, tics, torticollis, oculogyric crises, protrusion of the tongue, difficulty swallowing, carpopedal spasm and opisthotonos of the back muscles); and akathisia. Persistent dyskinesias resistant to treatment have been reported, particularly in elderly patients with previous brain damage. In addition, altered EEG tracings, disturbed body temperature and lowering of the convulsive threshold have occurred. Dizziness has been reported.

Tardive dyskinesia may appear in some patients on long-term antipsychotic therapy or may appear after drug therapy has been discontinued. The risk appears to be greater in elderly patients on high-dose therapy, especially females; it appears that longer durations of therapy and the cumulative dose received may also increase risk. Anticholinergic drugs tend to worsen the symptoms. The symptoms are persistent and in some patients appear to be irreversible. The syndrome is characterized by rhythmical involuntary movements of the tongue, face, mouth or jaw (e.g., protrusion of tongue, puffing of cheeks, puckering of mouth, chewing movements). Sometimes these may be accompanied by involuntary movements of extremities.

There is no known effective treatment for tardive dyskinesia; antiparkinsonian agents usually do not alleviate the symptoms of this syndrome. All antipsychotic agents should be discontinued if these symptoms appear. Should it be necessary to reinstitute treatment, or increase the dosage of the agent, or switch to a different antipsychotic agent, tardive dyskinesia may be masked. The effect that masking of the symptoms may have on the long-term course of the syndrome is unknown. The physician may be able to reduce the risk of this syndrome by minimizing the unnecessary use of neuroleptics and reducing the dose or discontinuing the drug, if possible, when manifestations of this syndrome are recognized, particularly in patients over the age of 50. Fine vermicular movements of the tongue may be an early sign of the syndrome. If the medication is stopped at that time, the syndrome may not develop. Periodic assessment (e.g., every 3 months) for signs and symptoms of tardive dyskinesia and the need for continued phenothiazine and/or anticholinergic therapy is recommended.

Dermatologic: itching, rash, hypertrophic papillae of the tongue, angioneurotic edema, erythema, allergic purpura, exfoliative dermatitis, contact dermatitis, skin-eye syndrome (see Ophthalmologic).

Endocrine: increased prolactin secretion; altered libido, menstrual irregularities, lactation, false positive pregnancy tests, gynecomastia, weight gain.

Gastrointestinal: anorexia, increased appetite, gastric irritation, nausea, vomiting, constipation, paralytic ileus.

Genitourinary: retention, incontinence, inhibition of ejaculation, priapism.

Hematologic: agranulocytosis, leukopenia, granulocytopenia, eosinophilia, thrombocytopenia, anemia, aplastic anemia, pancytopenia.

Hepatic: cholestatic jaundice; symptoms generally subside following discontinuance of the drug, but cholestasis may be prolonged.

Neuroleptic Malignant Syndrome: As with other neuroleptic drugs, a symptom complex sometimes referred to as neuroleptic malignant syndrome (NMS) has been reported. Cardinal features of NMS are hyperpyrexia, muscle rigidity, altered mental status (including catatonic signs), and evidence of autonomic instability (irregular pulse or blood pressure). Additional signs may include elevated CPK, myoglobinuria (rhabdomyolysis), and acute renal failure. NMS is potentially fatal, requires intensive symptomatic treatment and immediate discontinuation of neuroleptic treatment.

Ophthalmologic: A skin-eye syndrome has been described following long-term treatment with phenothiazines. This reaction is marked by progressive pigmentation of areas of skin or conjunctiva and/or discoloration of the exposed sclera and cornea. Opacities of the anterior lens and cornea described as irregular or stellate in shape have been reported. Patients expected to receive higher doses of phenothiazines for prolonged periods should have complete eye examinations at baseline and every 6 to 12 months.

Miscellaneous: Sudden unexpected and unexplained deaths have been reported in patients receiving phenothiazines, especially during long-term administration of the drugs. In some cases, the death was apparently due to cardiac arrest; in others, the cause appeared to be asphyxia due to failure of the cough reflex. In some patients, the cause could not be determined nor could it be established that the death was due to the phenothiazine.

Overdose: Symptoms: Symptoms of fluphenazine overdosage are related to an extension of its pharmacologic action. The primary symptoms observed are severe extrapyramidal reactions, hypotension and sedation. Mild or early intoxication may cause restlessness, confusion and excitement. CNS sedation may progress to coma. Other symptoms may include: tachycardia, cardiac arrhythmias, seizures, miosis, hypothermia and respiratory and/or vasomotor collapse.

Treatment: Empty stomach using gastric lavage. Administer one dose of activated charcoal and a saline cathartic. Support respiratory and cardiac functions as needed. Maintain fluid and electrolyte balance. Treat hypotension with i.v. fluids and by placing the patient in the Trendelenburg position. If unresponsive, dopamine or norepinephrine may be required. Do not use epinephrine (see Precautions, Drug Interactions). Seizures may be treated with i.v. diazepam or lorazepam. If seizures are uncontrolled or recur, use i.v. phenobarbital or phenytoin. Treat arrhythmias with phenytoin. Extrapyramidal reactions may be treated with i.v. diphenhydramine or benztropine followed by maintenance therapy for 48 hours. Manage hypothermia with external warming. Hemodialysis is of little value in enhancing elimination of phenothiazines.

Dosage: Oral: Dosage should be initiated at a low level and increased gradually, noting carefully the clinical response. Patients on long-term therapy should be evaluated periodically to evaluate the need for continued therapy.

Initial Dose for Adults: 2.5 to 10 mg daily in divided doses every 6 to 8 hours. Doses greater than 20 mg should be used with caution. Dosages up to 40 mg have been used in severe cases.

Maintenance: When satisfactory improvement has been achieved, dosage should be gradually reduced to the lowest dose that will maintain relief of symptoms. The usual maintenance dose is 1 to 5 mg daily as a single dose.

Geriatrics: In general, lower dosages are recommended: 1 to 2.5 mg as an initial dose.

Parenteral: Fluphenazine hydrochloride may be given i.m. or s.c. It is not for i.v. use. The i.m. dose of fluphenazine is approximately one-half to one-third the oral dose. The patient should be switched to oral therapy once symptoms are controlled.

Initial Dose for Adults: 1.25 mg. Doses may range from 2.5 mg to 10 mg in divided doses every 6 to 8 hours. Doses greater than 10 mg should be used with caution.

Depot: For maintenance therapy, in patients who have been stabilized on oral fluphenazine therapy and may benefit from switching to long-acting injections because of poor compliance or other reasons. A precise formula for converting patients from oral to depot therapy has not been established. It has been proposed that fluphenazine decanoate 12.5 mg every 3 weeks is approximately equivalent to an oral fluphenazine dosage of 10 mg daily.

The usual adult dose of fluphenazine decanoate in the management of chronic schizophrenia is 12.5 to 25 mg i.m. or s.c. every 2 to 3 weeks. The duration of effect may be longer in some patients.

The usual adult dose of fluphenazine enanthate is 25 mg i.m. or s.c. every 2 weeks.

Reviewed 1999

FLURANDRENOLIDE Ⓟ

General Monograph, CPhA

see CORTICOSTEROIDS: TOPICAL

FLURAZEPAM Ⓟ

General Monograph, CPhA

see BENZODIAZEPINES

FLUTICASONE

General Monograph, CPhA

see CORTICOSTEROIDS: EYE EAR NOSE
see CORTICOSTEROIDS: INHALED

FLUVIRAL®

BioChem Vaccines

Influenza Virus Vaccine Trivalent, Inactivated Whole-Virion

Active Immunizing Agent

Pharmacology: Fluviral whole virion influenza vaccine, promotes an active immunization against influenza. Within 7 days after injection of the vaccine there is an increase in circulating antibody to the viral hemagglutination, and peripheral blood lymphocytes are primed to respond to in vitro stimulation by vaccine antigens. I.M. injection of inactivated vaccine leads to the presence of local IgG antibody in the upper and lower respiratory tract.

Cytotoxic T lymphocyte response occurs after administration of either killed or live virus vaccines and is detectable in the absence of demonstrable antibody response.

Indications: Annual vaccination is recommended for the following groups:

Adults and children over 13 years with: a) chronic cardiac or pulmonary disorders (including bronchopulmonary dysplasia, cystic fibrosis and asthma) severe enough to require regular medical follow-up or hospital care; b) other chronic conditions such as diabetes and other metabolic diseases, cancer, immunodeficiency (including HIV infection) or immunosuppression, renal disease, or hemoglobinopathy and anemia.

Chronic cardiac and pulmonary disorders in persons over the age of 45 are by far the most important risk factors for influenza-related mortality.

Residents of nursing homes and other chronic care facilities: Such residents generally have one or more of the medical conditions outlined in above group. In addition, their institutional environment may promote spread of the disease.

Recent studies have shown that the use of vaccine in this setting will decrease occurrence of illness, and has an even greater impact on reducing the rates of hospitalization, pneumonia and death.

Geriatrics: Persons ≥65 years of age: The risk of severe morbidity and mortality related to influenza is moderately increased in healthy persons over 65 years of age but is not nearly as great as in persons with chronic underlying disease.

Children and adolescents (aged 6 months to 18 years) treated for long periods with ASA: Treatment with ASA for long periods might increase the risk of Reye's syndrome after influenza infection.

Persons infected with human immunodeficiency virus (HIV): Limited information exists regarding the frequency and severity of influenza illness among HIV-infected persons, but reports suggest that symptoms may be prolonged and the risk of complications increased for some HIV-infected persons. Because influenza can result in serious illness and complications, vaccination is a prudent precaution and will result in protective antibody levels in many recipients. However, the antibody response to vaccine may be low in persons with advanced HIV-related illnesses; giving a second dose of vaccine 4 or more weeks after the first does not improve the immune response for these persons. Further studies are also required to determine whether influenza immunization can adversely affect patients infected with HIV. To date, some studies indicate that influenza immunization can be associated with transient increases in plasma HIV concentration, but no study has demonstrated an adverse effect of this temporary change on HIV disease progression.

People capable of transmitting influenza to those at high risk should receive annual vaccination.

Health-care personnel who have extensive contact with individuals in the high-risk groups previously described: The potential for introducing influenza to persons in the high-risk groups outlined above, particularly those in institutions, should be reduced through vaccination programs targeted to health-care personnel.

Household contacts (including children) of individuals at risk: Because low antibody responses to influenza vaccine may occur in some individuals at high risk (e.g., the elderly, people with immunodeficiency), annual vaccination of their household contacts may reduce the risk of influenza exposures.

Other people: People who provide essential community services may be considered for vaccination programs to minimize the disruption of routine activities in epidemics. Influenza vaccine may also be administered to those persons who wish to reduce their chances of acquiring infection.

Pregnancy: Vaccination is recommended for pregnant women in high risk groups (see above section). Vaccine is considered safe for pregnant women regardless of their stage of pregnancy. Although excess morbidity and mortality were observed among pregnant women during the pandemic outbreaks in 1918-1919 and 1957-1958, further studies are needed to determine whether pregnancy per se is a risk factor that warrants routine influenza immunization.

People at high risk of influenza complications embarking on foreign travel to destinations where influenza is likely to be circulating should be vaccinated with the most current available vaccine. In the tropics, influenza can occur throughout the year. In the southern hemisphere, peak activity occurs from April through September. In the northern hemisphere, peak activity occurs from November through March.

Contraindications: Not recommended for children, but only for persons 13 years of age and older.

Fluviral vaccine should not be given to subjects with an acute respiratory infection or with any other active infection or serious febrile illness. On the other hand, a minor indisposition such as a mild infection of the upper respiratory tract is not necessarily a contraindication to vaccinations.

Allergic reactions are extremely rare and usually attributable to extreme sensitivity to certain components of the vaccine, probably to trace amounts of residual egg protein. Vaccination is not recommended for subjects who develop anaphylactic type reactions when they eat eggs [urticaria (hives), edema of the mouth and throat, difficulty in breathing, hypotension and shock]. Subjects whose allergy to eggs is not of the anaphylactic type, as well as those who are allergic to chicken and to feathers may be vaccinated.

Do not administer this vaccine to individuals known to be sensitive to thimerosal.

Warnings: It is possible that the normal immune response following influenza vaccination may not develop in subjects undergoing immunosuppressive therapy.

Precautions: Sterile epinephrine HCl solution 1:1 000 should always be readily available in case an acute anaphylactic reaction should occur. Increase of serum theophylline to toxic levels following the administration of influenza vaccine has been recorded in individuals who take oral theophylline as a maintenance therapy. Some doctors recommended a cessation of theophylline or a reduction in dose for 24 hours following vaccination.

The administration of influenza vaccination may also delay the hepatic metabolism of other medicaments such as oral anticoagulants.

False-positive HIV antibody tests were reported after immunization with the 1991-1992 influenza vaccines. The incidence of false-positive tests declined with the development of different tests so that such false-positive HIV antibody tests are not likely to be a problem now.

Pregnancy: The National Advisory Council on Immunization considers influenza vaccine safe in pregnancy.

Children: In infants <6 months of age, influenza vaccine is less immunogenic than in infants and children aged 6 to 18 months. Therefore, immunization with currently available influenza vaccine is not recommended for infants <6 months.

Simultaneous Administration of Other Vaccines: The target groups for influenza and pneumococcal vaccination overlap considerably. Health care providers should take the opportunity to vaccinate eligible persons against pneumococcal disease during the same visit at which influenza vaccine is given. The concurrent administration of the 2 vaccines at different sites does not increase the risk of side effects. Pneumococcal vaccine, however, is given only once, whereas influenza vaccine is given annually. Children at high risk may receive influenza vaccine at the same time but at a different site from that used for routine pediatric vaccines.

Adverse Effects: Local reactions such as redness, soreness and induration at the site of injection lasting for 1 or 2 days are common. Several kinds of systemic reactions associated with influenza vaccine have been described: Fever, malaise, and myalgia may occur within 6 to 12 hours after vaccination and last 1 to 2 days, especially in young adults who have received the whole-virus vaccine and those receiving vaccine for the first time. Prophylactic acetaminophen may decrease the frequency of some side effects in adults.

Immediate, allergic-type responses, such as hives, angioedema, allergic asthma, or systemic anaphylaxis occur extremely rarely. These reactions probably result from sensitivity to some vaccine component, most likely residual egg protein (see Contraindications).

Other neurological illnesses, including facial paralysis, encephalitis, encephalopathy, demyelinating disease and labyrinthitis have been reported. Any relationship, other than temporal, to vaccine has not been established.

Unlike the 1976 to 1977 swine influenza vaccine, subsequent vaccines prepared from other virus strains have not been clearly associated with an increased frequency of Guillain-Barre syndrome. Influenza vaccine is not known to predispose to Reye's syndrome.

Notification of Reactions: It is desirable that all unusual reactions, arising from any vaccination whatsoever, or following shortly thereafter, be reported to the manufacturer of the product and to the provincial epidemiologist.

Dosage: Adults (13 years and older): a **single** dose of 0.5 mL. In children less than 13 years of age, only a split virus vaccine should be used.

Check carefully the expiry date of the vaccine. Any vaccine beyond its expiry date should not be used.

Caution: A separate sterile syringe and needle should be used for each injection to prevent transmission of hepatitis B, HIV, or other infectious agents from one person to another.

Shake the container vigorously each time before withdrawing vaccine.

Never remove the rubber stopper from the container. Moisten the surface of the rubber stopper with a tampon of sterile cotton wool soaked in a suitable antiseptic and allow the antiseptic to act for a few moments, then wipe dry with a sterile dry swab. Draw into the syringe a volume of air equal to the amount of vaccine to be withdrawn from the container. Shake the container vigorously then pierce the center of the rubber stopper with the sterile needle attached to the syringe. Turn the vial upside down and inject into it the air from the syringe. Keeping the point of the needle immersed in the vaccine, withdraw immediately (into the syringe) the desired volume.

Disinfect the skin at the site of injection with a suitable antiseptic and wipe dry with a tampon of sterile cotton wool. The injection of 0.5 mL of Fluviral **should be given i.m.**, usually in the detoid muscle. **Do not inject Fluviral i.v.** To avoid injection into a vein, it is necessary, before injecting the dose of vaccine, to withdraw the piston of the syringe sufficiently to ensure that the needle has not entered a blood vessel.

All vaccinees should be observed for about 15 minutes after vaccination. If an anaphylactic reaction develops, sterile epinephrine HCl (1:1 000) should be administered.

It is desirable that the entire contents of a multidose container be utilized at the same vaccination session. Only good aseptic technique allows for sampling of a partially used multidose vial from a previous vaccination session.

Each person who is immunized should be given a permanent personal immunization record. In addition, it is essential that the physician or nurse record the immunization history in the permanent medical record of each patient. This permanent office record should contain the name of the vaccine, date given, dose, manufacturer and lot number.

Disposal: Fluviral vaccine and materials used during vaccination may be disposed of in the same way as other medicaments. Since Fluviral is an inactivated vaccine, it presents no risk of contaminating the work area during manipulation.

Supplied: Fluviral vaccine **for i.m. injection,** is a trivalent, whole virus, influenza vaccine prepared from viruses grown in the allantoic cavity of embryonated hens' eggs. The viruses are inactivated with formaldehyde and purified by centrifugation. The vaccine is a whitish, slightly opalescent liquid. The composition of Fluviral for the 1998-1999 season has been established in agreement with the recommendations of the Canadian National Advisory Committee on Immunization (N.A.C.I.) Each dose of 0.5 mL contains: hemagglutinin of strain A/Beijing/262/95 (H1N1) 15 μg; hemagglutinin of strain A/Sydney/5/97 (H3N2) 15 μg and hemagglutinin of strain B/Harbin/7/94 15 μg. The vaccine also contains 0.01% thimerosal. Containers of 5 mL (holding 10× 0.5 mL doses). Store in the refrigerator between 2 and 8°C. **Do not freeze.** Freezing destroys activity. Do not use vaccine which has been frozen.

Reviewed 1999

FLUVIRAL S/F®

BioChem Vaccines

Whole-Virion and Split-Virion Influenza Virus Vaccine, Inactivated

Active Immunizing Agent

Pharmacology: Fluviral S/F, split-virion influenza vaccine, promotes an active immunization against influenza. Within 7 days after injection of the vaccine there is an increase in circulating antibody to the viral hemagglutination, and peripheral blood lymphocytes are primed to respond to in vitro stimulation by vaccine antigens. I.M. injection of inactivated vaccine leads to the presence of local IgG antibody in the upper and lower respiratory tract.

Cytotoxic T lymphocyte response occurs after administration of either killed or live virus vaccines and is detectable in the absence of demonstrable antibody response.

Indications: For the active immunization of people in the following groups: Adults and children with: a) chronic cardiac or pulmonary disorders (including bronchopulmonary dysplasia, cystic fibrosis and asthma) severe enough to require regular medical follow-up or hospital care; b) other chronic conditions such as diabetes and other metabolic diseases, cancer, immunodeficiency (including HIV infection) or immunosuppression, renal disease, or hemoglobinopathy and anemia.

Chronic cardiac and pulmonary disorders in persons over the age of 45 are by far the most important risk factors for influenza-related mortality.

Residents of nursing homes and other chronic care facilities: Such residents generally have one or more medical conditions outlined in above group. In addition, their institutional environment may promote spread of the disease. Recent studies have shown that the use of vaccine in this setting will decrease occurrence of illness, and has an even greater impact on reducing the rates of hospitalization, pneumonia and death.

Geriatrics: Persons ≥65 years of age: The risk of severe morbidity and mortality related to influenza is moderately increased in healthy persons over 65 years of age but is not nearly as great as in persons with chronic underlying disease.

Children and adolescents (aged 6 months to 18 years) treated for long periods with ASA: Treatment with ASA for long periods might increase the risk of Reye's syndrome after influenza infection.

Persons infected with human immunodeficiency virus (HIV): Limited information exists regarding the frequency and severity of influenza illness among HIV-infected persons, but reports suggest that symptoms may be prolonged and the risk for complications increased for some HIV-infected persons. Because influenza can result in serious illness and complications, vaccination is a prudent precaution and will result in protective antibody levels in many recipients. However, the antibody response to vaccine may be low in persons with advanced HIV-related illnesses; giving a second dose of vaccine 4 or more weeks after the first does not improve the immune response for these persons. Further studies are also required to determine whether influenza immunization can adversely affect patients infected with HIV. To date, some studies indicate that influenza immunization can be associated with transient increases in plasma HIV concentration, but no study has demonstrated an adverse effect of this temporary change on HIV disease progression.

People capable of transmitting influenza to those at high risk should receive annual vaccination.

Health-care personnel who have extensive contact with individuals in the high-risk groups previously described: The potential for introducing influenza to persons in the high-risk groups outlined above, particularly those in institutions, should be reduced through vaccination programs targeted to health-care personnel.

Household contacts (including children) of individuals at risk: Because low antibody responses to influenza vaccine may occur in some individuals at high risk (e.g., the elderly, people with immunodeficiency), annual vaccination of their household contacts may reduce the risk of influenza exposures.

Other people: People who provide essential community services may be considered for vaccination programs to minimize the disruption of routine activities in epidemics. Influenza vaccine may also be administered to those persons who wish to reduce their chances of acquiring infection.

Pregnancy: Vaccination is recommended for pregnant women in high risk groups (see above section). Vaccine is considered safe for pregnant women—regardless of their stage of pregnancy. Although excess morbidity and mortality were observed among pregnant women during the pandemic outbreaks in 1918-1919 and 1957-1958, further studies are needed to determine whether pregnancy per se is a risk factor that warrants routine influenza immunization.

People at high risk of influenza complications embarking on foreign travel to destinations where influenza is likely to be circulating should be vaccinated with the most current available vaccine. In the tropics, influenza can occur throughout the year. In the southern hemisphere, peak activity occurs from April through September. In the northern hemisphere, peak activity occurs from November through March.

Contraindications: Fluviral S/F should not be given to subjects with an acute respiratory infection or with any other active infection or serious febrile illness. On the other hand, a minor indisposition such as a mild infection of the upper respiratory tract is not necessarily a contraindication to vaccination.

Allergic reactions are extremely rare and usually attributable to extreme sensitivity to certain components of the vaccine, probably to trace amounts of residual egg protein. Vaccination is not recommended for subjects who develop anaphylactic type reactions when they eat eggs [urticaria (hives), edema of the mouth and throat, difficulty in breathing, hypotension and shock]. Subjects whose allergy to eggs is not of the anaphylactic type, as well as those who are allergic to chicken and to feathers may be vaccinated.

Do not administer this vaccine to individuals known to be sensitive to thimerosal.

Warnings: It is possible that the normal immune response following influenza vaccination may not develop in subjects undergoing immunosuppressive therapy.

Precautions: Sterile epinephrine HCl solution 1:1 000 should always be readily available in case an acute anaphylactic reaction should occur.

Increase of serum theophylline to toxic levels following the administration of influenza vaccine has been recorded in individuals who take oral theophylline as a maintenance therapy. Some doctors recommended a cessation of theophylline or a reduction in dose for 24 hours following vaccination.

The administration of influenza vaccine may also delay the hepatic metabolism of other medications such as oral anticoagulants.

False-positive HIV antibody tests were reported after immunization with the 1991-1992 influenza vaccines. The incidence of false-positive tests declined with the development of different tests so that such false-positive HIV antibody tests are not likely to be a problem now.

Pregnancy: The National Advisory Council on Immunization considers influenza vaccine safe in pregnancy.

Children: In infants <6 months of age, influenza vaccine is less immunogenic than in infants and children aged 6 to 18 months. Therefore, immunization with currently available influenza vaccine is not recommended for infants <6 months.

Simultaneous Administration of Other Vaccines: The target groups for influenza and pneumococcal vaccination overlap considerably. Health care providers should take the opportunity to vaccinate eligible persons against pneumococcal disease during the same visit at which influenza vaccine is given. The concurrent administration of the 2 vaccines at different sites does not increase the risk of side effects. Pneumococcal vaccine, however, is given only once, whereas influenza vaccine is given annually. Children at high risk may receive influenza vaccine at the same time but at a different site from that used for routine pediatric vaccines.

Information for the Patient: Patients should be informed of the most common side effects:

Local Reactions: Soreness and redness at the injection site that may last for up to 2 days.

Systemic Reactions: fever, headache, myalgia. These reactions begin 6 to 12 hours after vaccination and can persist for 1 or 2 days.

Note: Should these symptoms persist or worsen, patients should be instructed to see a physician.

Adverse Effects: Subvirion, or split-virion vaccines contain purified portions of the virus rather than the entire virus. Generally, these have been shown to be associated with fewer adverse effects in children and young adults, while maintaining an immunogenicity similar to that of whole virus preparations. Because of their lower rates of side effects, only split virus preparations are recommended for children under 13 years of age.

Local and systemic reactions are reported after vaccination with a split-virion influenza vaccine.

The data in Table I and Table II have been derived from three studies with 3 lots of BioChem Vaccines Inc. split-virion vaccine (A, B, C) compared to another subvirion vaccine (D) and to a whole virion vaccine (E) from BioChem Vaccines Inc.

There were very few reports of fever as defined by temperature over 38°C.

Soreness at the injection site was the most frequently reported symptom, and was generally rated as mild and resolved the day after vaccination.

For systemic symptoms, headache and muscle aches were the most common. As with local symptoms, these were generally reported as mild and of limited duration.

Immediate, allergic-type responses, such as hives, angioedema, allergic asthma, or systemic anaphylaxis occur extremely rarely. These reactions probably result from sensitivity to some vaccine component—most likely residual egg proteins (see Contraindications).

There have been reports of other neurological illnesses, including facial paralysis, encephalitis, encephalopathy, demyelinating disease and labyrinthitis, associated with other influenza vaccines. Any relationship, other than temporal, to the vaccine has not been established.

Unlike the 1976-1977 swine influenza vaccine, subsequent vaccines prepared from other virus strains have not been clearly associated with an increased frequency of Guillain-Barre syndrome. Influenza vaccine is not known to predispose to Reye's syndrome.

Notification of Reactions: It is desirable that all unusual reactions, arising from any vaccination whatsoever, or following shortly thereafter, be reported to the manufacturer of the product and to the provincial epidemiologist.

Dosage: See Table III (on following page).

Table I—Fluviral S/F

Percentage of Subjects in Each Group Reporting Symptoms

	Young Adults (19–45 years)					Children (3–12 years)		Elderly (over 65 years)		
Lots	**A**	**B**	**C**	**D**	**E**	**A**	**D**	**B**	**D**	**E**
No (of patients)	54	56	54	56	56	65	65	58	57	57
Local Reactions(%)										
Soreness	72	71	68	75	95	57	58	24	21	25
Redness	22	27	26	18	27	12	14	3	3	5
Swelling	15	4	13	10	23	15	22	7	5	5
Limitation of movement	22	16	13	21	30	12	14	3	3	4

Table II—Fluviral S/F

Percentage of Subjects in Each Group Reporting Symptoms

	Young Adults (19–45 years)					Children (3–12 years)		Elderly (over 65 years)		
Lots	**A**	**B**	**C**	**D**	**E**	**A**	**D**	**B**	**D**	**E**
Systemic Reactions(%)										
Headache	37	20	24	20	34	15	17	29	14	9
Loss of appetite	11	5	5	2	11	12	8	7	5	5
Muscle aches	26	20	22	19	30	14	11	19	9	12
Chills	15	14	7	0	12	3	6	21	16	5
Nausea	13	3	2	7	14	3	3	9	9	5
Vomiting	2	0	0	0	2	1	0	3	0	0
Diarrhea	13	3	5	2	11	6	6	3	5	2
Redness/Rash	15	0	0	3	5	3	3	2	2	2

Table III—Fluviral S/F

Influenza Vaccine Dosage, by Age Group

Age Group	Product	Dosage (mL)	No. of Doses	Route[a]
6–35 months	Split virus only	0.25	1 or 2[b]	i.m.
3–8 years	Split virus only	0.50	1 or 2[b]	i.m.
9–12 years	Split virus only	0.50	1	i.m.
13 years and older	Whole or split virus	0.50	1	i.m.

[a] The recommended site of vaccination is the deltoid muscle for adults and older childen. The preferred site for infants and young children is the anterolateral aspect of the thigh.

[b] Two doses administered at least 1 month apart are recommended for children younger than 9 years of age who are receiving influenza vaccine for the first time.

Since the likelihood of febrile convulsions is greater in children aged 6 to 35 months, special care should be taken in weighing relative risks and benefits in this group.

Administration: **Caution:** A separate **sterile** syringe and needle or a **sterile** disposable unit should be used for each injection to prevent transmission of hepatitis B virus, HIV virus, or other infectious agents from one person to another.

Check carefully the expiry date of the vaccine. Any vaccine beyond its expiry date should not be used.

Shake the container vigorously each time before withdrawing vaccine.

Never remove the rubber stopper from the container. Moisten the surface of the rubber stopper with a tampon of sterile cotton wool soaked in a suitable antiseptic and allow the antiseptic to act for a few moments, then wipe dry with a sterile dry swab. Draw into the syringe a volume of air equal to the amount of vaccine to be withdrawn from the container. Shake the container vigorously then pierce the center of the rubber stopper with the sterile needle attached to the syringe. Turn the vial upside down and inject into it the air from the syringe. Keeping the point of the needle immersed in the vaccine, withdraw immediately (into the syringe) the desired volume.

Disinfect the skin at the site of injection with a suitable antiseptic and wipe dry with a tampon of sterile cotton wool. The injection of 0.5 mL of Fluviral S/F, **should be given i.m.,** usually in the deltoid muscle.

Do not inject split-virion influenza vaccine i.v.

To avoid injection into a vein, it is necessary, before injecting the dose of vaccine, to withdraw the piston of the syringe sufficiently to ensure that the needle has not entered a blood vessel.

All vaccinees should be observed for about 15 minutes after vaccination. If an anaphylactic reaction develops, sterile epinephrine HCl (1:1 000) should be administered.

It is desirable that the entire contents of a multidose vial be used at the same vaccination session.

Each person who is immunized should be given a permanent personal immunization record. In addition, it is essential that the physician or nurse record the immunization history in the permanent medical record of each patient. This permanent office record should contain the name of the vaccine, date given, dose, manufacturer and lot number.

Disposal: Fluviral S/F vaccine and materials used during vaccination may be disposed of in the same way as other drugs. Since Fluviral S/F is an inactivated vaccine, it presents no risk of contaminating the work area during manipulation.

Supplied: Fluviral S/F for i.m. injection is a trivalent, split-virion influenza vaccine prepared from virus grown in the allantoic cavity of embryonated hens' eggs. The virus is inactivated with formaldehyde purified by centrifugation and disrupted with sodium deoxycholate in Triton X-100. Each dose of 0.5 mL of a whitish, slightly opalescent liquid, contains: hemagglutinin 15 µg of each of the following strains: A/Beijing/262/95 (H1N1), A/Sydney/5/97 H3N2, B/Harbin/7/94. The composition of Fluviral S/F is established in agreement with the recommendations of the Canadian National Advisory Committee on Immunization (N.A.C.I.). Thimerosal 0.01% is present in both whole and split-virion preparations as a preservative. Split-virion vaccine also contains trace residual amounts of egg proteins and deoxycholate. Vials of 5 mL (10 doses). Store in the refrigerator between 2 and 8°C. **Do not freeze.** Freezing destroys activity. Do not use vaccine which has been frozen.

Reviewed 1999

FLUVOXAMINE

General Monograph, CPhA

see SELECTIVE SEROTONIN REUPTAKE INHIBITORS

FLUZONE®

Connaught

Influenza Virus Vaccine Trivalent Types A and B (Zonal Purified, Subvirion)

Active Immunizing Agent

Pharmacology: The inoculation of antigen prepared from inactivated influenza virus stimulates the production of specific antibodies. Protection is afforded only against those strains of virus from which the vaccine is prepared or closely related strains.

Influenza A viruses are classified into subtypes on the basis of 2 surface antigens: hemagglutinin (H) and neuraminidase (N). Three subtypes of hemagglutinin (H1, H2, H3) and 2 subtypes of neuraminidase (N1, N2) are recognized among influenza A viruses that have caused widespread human disease. Immunity to these antigens—especially to the hemagglutinin—reduces the likelihood of infection and lessens the severity of disease if infection occurs. Infection with a virus of one subtype confers little or no protection against viruses of other subtypes. Furthermore, over time, antigenic variation (antigenic drift) within a subtype may be so marked that infection or vaccination with one strain may not induce immunity to distantly related strains of the same subtype. Although influenza B viruses have shown more antigenic stability than influenza A viruses, antigenic variation does occur. For these reasons, major epidemics of respiratory disease caused by new variants of influenza continue to occur. The antigenic characteristics of circulating strains provide the basis for selecting the virus strains included in each year's vaccine.

Each year's influenza vaccine contains 3 virus strains (usually 2 type A and 1 type B) representing the influenza viruses that are likely to circulate in Canada in the coming winter.

Most vaccinated children and young adults develop high postvaccination hemagglutination-inhibition antibody titres. These antibody titres are protective against illness caused by strains similar to those in the vaccine or the related variants that may emerge during outbreak periods. Elderly persons and persons with certain chronic diseases may develop lower postvaccination antibody titres than healthy young adults and thus may remain susceptible to influenza-related upper-respiratory-tract infection.

However, even if such persons develop influenza illness despite vaccination, the vaccine can be effective in preventing lower-respiratory-tract involvement or other secondary complications, thereby reducing the risk for hospitalization and death.

The effectiveness of influenza vaccine in preventing or attenuating illness varies, depending primarily on the age and immunocompetence of the vaccine recipient and the degree of similarity between the virus strains included in the vaccine and those that circulate during the influenza season. When a good match exists between vaccine and circulating viruses, influenza vaccine has been shown to prevent illness in approximately 70 to 90% of healthy persons less than 65 years of age. In these circumstances, studies also have indicated that the effectiveness of influenza vaccine in preventing hospitalization for pneumonia and influenza among elderly persons living in settings other than nursing homes or similar chronic-care facilities ranges from 30 to 70%.

Among elderly persons residing in nursing homes, influenza vaccine is most effective in preventing severe illness, secondary complications, and death. Studies of this population have indicated that the vaccine can be 50 to 60% effective in preventing hospitalization and pneumonia and 80% effective in preventing death, even though efficacy in preventing influenza illness may often be in the range of 30 to 40% among the frail elderly. Achieving a high rate of vaccination among nursing home residents and staff can reduce the spread of infection in a facility, thus preventing disease through herd immunity. Vaccination of health care workers in nursing homes also has been demonstrated to reduce the impact of influenza among residents.

Although the current influenza vaccine can contain 1 or more of the antigens administered in previous years, annual vaccination using the current vaccine is necessary because immunity declines in the year following vaccination.

Indications: For adults and children 6 months of age and older when influenza vaccine is recommended.

The National Advisory Committee on Immunization recommends annual vaccination for individuals in the following categories: People at High Risk: Vaccination of people at high risk is the single most important measure for reducing the impact of influenza. Priority should be given to ensure annual vaccination of people in the following groups: Adults and children with chronic cardiac or pulmonary disorders (including bronchopulmonary dysplasia, cystic fibrosis, and asthma) severe enough to require regular medical follow-up or hospital care: Chronic cardiac and pulmonary disorders are by far the most important risk factors for influenza-related death.

People of any age who are residents of nursing homes and other chronic care facilities: Such residents often have one or more of the medical conditions outlined in the first group. In addition, their institutional environment may promote spread of the disease. Studies have shown that the use of vaccine in this setting will decrease occurrence of illness and has an even greater impact in reducing the rates of hospitalization, pneumonia and death.

People 65 years of age and over: The risk of severe illness and death related to influenza is moderately increased in healthy people in this age group, but is not as great as in people with chronic underlying disease. Vaccination is effective in preventing hospitalization and death.

Adults and children with chronic conditions such as diabetes mellitus and other metabolic diseases, cancer, immunodeficiency, immunosuppression, renal disease, anemia and hemoglobinopathy: The degree of risk associated with chronic renal and metabolic diseases in children is uncertain but this uncertainty should not preclude consideration of vaccination.

Children and adolescents (age 6 months to 18 years) with conditions treated for long periods with ASA: ASA might increase the risk of Reye's syndrome after influenza.

Persons infected with Human Immunodeficiency Virus (HIV): Limited information exists regarding the frequency and severity of influenza illness among HIV-infected persons, but reports suggest that symptoms may be prolonged and the risk for complications increased for some HIV-infected persons. Because influenza can result in serious illness and complications, vaccination is a prudent precaution and will result in protective antibody levels in many recipients. However, the antibody response to vaccine may be low in persons with advanced HIV-related illnesses; giving a second dose of vaccine 4 or more weeks after the first does not improve the immune response for these persons.

HIV load does not increase with influenza immunization according to a randomized, placebo-controlled trial.

Because influenza can result in serious illness and complications and because influenza vaccination may result in protective antibody titres, vaccination will benefit many HIV-infected patients.

People capable of transmitting influenza to those at high risk: People who are potentially capable of transmitting influenza to those at high risk should receive annual vaccination.

Health care and other personnel who have significant contact with people in the high risk groups previously described: The potential for infecting people at high risk outlined above, particularly those in institutions, may be reduced through vaccination programs for health care personnel. Such personnel include: physicians, nurses and other personnel in both hospital and outpatient-care settings; employees of nursing homes and chronic-care facilities who have contact with patients or residents; providers of home care to persons at high risk (e.g., visiting nurses and volunteer workers).

Household contacts (including children) of people at high risk who either cannot be vaccinated or may respond inadequately to vaccination: Because low antibody responses to influenza vaccine may occur in some people at high risk (e.g., the elderly, people with immunodeficiency), annual vaccination of their household contacts may reduce the risk of influenza exposure.

Other People: People who provide essential community services should be considered for vaccination to minimize disruption of routine activities in epidemics. Employers and their employees should consider yearly influenza immunization for healthy working adults as this has been shown to decrease work absenteeism because of respiratory and other illnesses.

Fluzone (cont'd)

Pregnant Women: Vaccination is recommended for pregnant women in high-risk groups (see above), regardless of their stage of pregnancy (see Precautions, Pregnancy).
Foreign Travellers: Predeparture influenza immunization for prevention of the disease in travellers should be considered for anyone leaving Canada during the local influenza transmission season and should be offered to anyone leaving Canada who will be exposed during the influenza transmission season at the destination.
General Population: Health care providers should administer influenza vaccine to any person who wishes to reduce the likelihood of becoming ill with influenza.

Students or other persons in institutional settings (e.g., those who reside in dormitories) should be encouraged to receive vaccine to minimize disruption of routine activities during epidemics.

Vaccine should be offered to both children and adults up to and even after influenza virus activity is documented in a community.

Contraindications: General: The influenza virus for Fluzone is propagated in eggs, therefore, this vaccine should not be administered to anyone with a history of hypersensitivity (allergy) and especially anaphylactic reactions, to eggs or egg products. It is also a contraindication to administer this vaccine to individuals known to be sensitive to thimerosal. In any case, epinephrine HCl solution (1:1 000) must be immediately available should an acute anaphylactic reaction occur due to any component of the vaccine.
Absolute Contraindication: Allergy to any component of Fluzone (see Supplied) or an allergic or anaphylactic reaction to a previous dose of influenza vaccine are contraindications to vaccination.
Children: The use of Fluzone in infants less than 6 months of age is not recommended.

Immunization with Fluzone should be deferred in the presence of any acute illness, including febrile illness, or active infection to avoid superimposing adverse effects from the vaccine on the underlying illness or mistakenly identifying a manifestation of the underlying illness as a complication of vaccine use. A minor afebrile illness such as mild upper respiratory infection is not usually reason to defer immunization.

Immunization should be delayed in a patient with an active neurologic disorder, but should be considered when the disease process has been stabilized.

Warnings: I.M. injections should be given with care in persons suffering from coagulation disorders or on anticoagulant therapy because of the risk of hemorrhage.

During recent decades, data on influenza vaccine immunogenicity and side effects have been obtained for i.m. administered vaccine. Because recent influenza vaccines have not been adequately evaluated when administered by other routes, the i.m. route is recommended.

This product contains dry natural rubber as follows: The stopper to the vial contains dry natural rubber. In the case of the syringe, the needle cover contains dry natural rubber, but the plunger for the syringe contains no rubber of any kind.

If Fluzone is used in persons with malignancies, persons receiving immunosuppressive therapies, including irradiation, antimetabolites, alkylating agents, cytotoxic drugs, or who are otherwise immunocompromised (including HIV-infected individuals, transplant recipients, persons suffering from autoimmune disorders), the expected immune response may not be obtained.

Corticosteroid therapy can result in immunosuppression although the exact dose and duration of therapy required to suppress the immune system is not well defined. Persons treated with high doses of systemic steroids, e.g., ≥2 mg/kg/day of prednisone orally for more than 2 weeks, should be considered to have a compromised immune system.

Although influenza vaccination can inhibit the clearance of warfarin, theophylline, and phenytoin, clinical studies have consistently failed to show any adverse effects attributable to these drugs in people receiving influenza virus vaccine.

Influenza virus is remarkably capricious in that significant antigenic changes may occur from time to time. It is known definitely that Fluzone, as now constituted, is not effective against all possible strains of influenza virus. Protection is afforded most people only against those strains of virus from which the vaccine is prepared or against closely related strains.

As with any vaccine, immunization with influenza vaccine may not protect 100% of susceptible individuals.

Precautions: General: The possibility of allergic reactions in individuals sensitive to the components of the vaccine should be evaluated. Epinephrine HCl solution (1:1 000) and other appropriate agents should be available for immediate use in case an anaphylactic or acute hypersensitivity reaction occurs. Health care providers should be familiar with current recommendations for the initial management of anaphylaxis in non-hospital settings including proper airway management.

Before administration of any vaccine, all appropriate precautions should be taken to prevent adverse reactions. This includes a review of the patient's history with respect to possible hypersensitivity to the vaccine or similar vaccine, determination of previous immunization history, and the presence of any contraindications to immunization, current health status, and a current knowledge of the literature concerning the use of the vaccine under consideration.

Special care should be taken to ensure that the product is not injected into a blood vessel.

A separate, sterile needle and syringe, or a sterile disposable unit, must be used for each individual patient to prevent the transmission of infectious agents.

There have been case reports of transmission of HIV and hepatitis by failure to scrupulously observe sterile technique. In particular, the same needle and/or syringe must never be used to re-enter a multidose vial to withdraw vaccine even when it is to be used for inoculation of the same patient. This may lead to contamination of the vial contents and infection of patients who subsequently receive vaccine from the vial.

Needles should not be recapped and should be disposed of properly.

Before administration of Fluzone, health care personnel should inform the parent or guardian or the patient to be immunized of the benefits and risks of immunization, inquire about the recent health status of the patient and comply with any local requirements with respect to information to be provided to the patient before immunization.

Pregnancy: Reproduction studies have not been conducted with Fluzone. Fluzone should be given to a pregnant woman only if clearly needed (see Indications).

Simultaneous Administration of Other Vaccines: Pneumococcal vaccine and influenza vaccine can be given at the same visit at different sites with separate sterile needles and syringes without an increase in side effects, but it should be emphasized that, whereas influenza vaccine is given annually, pneumococcal vaccine should be given only once to adults. Detailed immunization records should be provided to each patient to help ensure that additional doses of pneumococcal vaccine are not given. Children at high risk may receive influenza vaccine at the same time as routine pediatric vaccines but at separate sites with separate sterile needles and syringes.

Adverse Effects: Split-virus vaccines, produced by chemically disrupting the influenza virus, are generally associated with somewhat fewer side effects in children and young adults than are whole-virus vaccines; consequently, only split-virus vaccines are recommended for persons under 13 years of age.

Because Fluzone contains only noninfectious viruses, it cannot cause influenza. Respiratory disease after vaccination represents coincidental illness unrelated to influenza vaccination. The most frequent side effect of vaccination is soreness at the vaccination site that lasts for up to 2 days; this is reported by fewer than one-third of vaccinees. In addition, 2 types of systemic reactions have occurred: 1. Fever, malaise, myalgia, and other systemic symptoms occur infrequently and most often affect persons who have had no exposure to the influenza virus antigens in the vaccine (e.g., young children). These reactions begin 6 to 12 hours after vaccination and can persist for 1 to 2 days. Recent placebo-controlled trials suggest that in elderly persons and healthy young adults, split-virus influenza vaccine is not associated with higher rates of systemic symptoms (e.g., fever, malaise, myalgia, and headache) when compared with placebo injections.
2. Immediate—presumably allergic—reactions (such as hives, angioedema, allergic asthma, or systemic anaphylaxis), occur rarely after influenza vaccination. These reactions probably result from hypersensitivity to some vaccine component—the majority are most likely related to residual egg protein. Although current influenza vaccines contain only a small quantity of egg protein, this protein may induce immediate hypersensitivity reactions among persons with severe egg allergy. Persons who have developed hives, have had swelling of the lips or tongue, or have experienced acute respiratory distress or collapse after eating eggs should consult a physician for appropriate evaluation to help determine if vaccine should be administered. Persons who have documented immunoglobulin E(IgE)–mediated hypersensitivity to eggs–including those who have had occupational asthma or other allergic responses due to exposure to egg protein–also might be at increased risk for reactions from influenza vaccine, and similar consultation should be considered.

The protocol for influenza vaccination developed by Murphy and Strunk may be considered for patients who have egg allergies and medical conditions that place them at increased risk for influenza-associated complications.

Prophylactic acetaminophen may decrease the frequency of some side effects in adults.

Unlike the 1976 swine influenza vaccine, subsequent vaccines prepared from other virus strains have not been clearly associated with an increased frequency of Guillain-Barré Syndrome (GBS). However, it is difficult to obtain strong evidence for a possible small increase in risk for a rare condition such as GBS, which has an annual background incidence of only 10 to 20 cases per million in the adult population. During 3 of 4 seasons studied between 1977 and 1991 in the USA, the point estimates of the overall relative risks of GBS after influenza vaccination were slightly elevated; but were not statistically significant in any of these studies. However, a recent U.S. study of the 1992-93 and 1993-94 seasons found an elevation in the overall relative risk of 1.83 (95% Confidence Interval 1.12 to 3.00) during the 6 weeks following vaccination, representing an excess of an estimated 1 to 2 cases per million persons vaccinated; the combined number of GBS cases peaked 2 weeks after vaccination. The increase in the relative risks and the increased number of cases in the second week after vaccination may be the result of vaccination but also could be due to other factors (e.g., confounding or diagnostic bias) rather than a true vaccine-related risk.

Among persons who received the swine influenza vaccine in 1976, the rate of GBS that exceeded the background rate was slightly less than 10 cases per million vaccinations. Even if GBS were a true side effect in subsequent years, the estimated risk for GBS of 1 to 2 cases per million vaccinations is substantially less than that for severe influenza, which could be prevented by vaccination among all age groups, especially for persons 65 years of age or more and those who have medical indications for influenza vaccination. Estimates of excess hospitalization rates during different influenza epidemics have ranged from approximately 200 to 300 hospitalizations per million previously healthy persons age 5 to 44 years to 2 000 to greater than 10 000 hospitalizations per million persons aged 65 and older. Estimates of influenza-associated death rates have ranged from approximately 300 to 1 500 per million persons aged 65 and older, which account for more than 90% of all influenza-associated deaths. The average case-fatality ratio for GBS is approximately 6% and increases with age. There is no indication that the case-fatality ratio for GBS differs by influenza vaccination status. The potential benefits of influenza vaccination clearly outweigh the possible risks for vaccine-associated GBS.

Whereas the incidence of GBS in the general population is very low, persons with a history of GBS have a substantially greater likelihood of subsequently developing GBS than persons without such a history. Thus, the likelihood of coincidentally developing GBS after influenza vaccination is expected to be greater among persons with a history of GBS than among persons with no history of this syndrome. Whether influenza vaccination might be causally associated with this risk for recurrence is not known. Avoiding subsequent influenza vaccination of persons known to have developed GBS within 6 weeks of a previous influenza vaccination seems prudent. However, for most persons with a history of GBS who are at high risk for severe complications from influenza, many experts believe the established benefits of influenza vaccination justify yearly vaccination.

Influenza vaccine is not known to predispose to Reye's syndrome.

Neurological disorders temporally associated with influenza vaccination such as encephalopathy, optic neuritis, facial paralysis, labyrinthitis, and brachial plexus neuropathy have been reported. However, no cause and effect has been established. Almost all persons affected were adults, and the described clinical reactions began as soon as a few hours and as late as 2 weeks after vaccination. Full recovery was almost always reported.

Fatalities from a variety of other causes have been reported in the high-risk population following influenza vaccination without the establishment of a definite causal relationship.

Physicians, nurses and pharmacists should report any adverse occurrences temporally related to the administration of the product in accordance with local requirements and to the Medical Director, Connaught Laboratories Limited, 1755 Steeles Avenue West, Toronto, Ontario, Canada, M2R 3T4.

Dosage: Parenteral biological products should be inspected visually for extraneous particulate matter and/or discoloration before administration. If these conditions exist, the product should not be administered.

Shake the vial well to distribute uniformly the suspension before withdrawing each dose. When administering a dose from a rubber-stoppered vial, do not remove either the rubber stopper or the metal seal holding it in place. Aseptic technique must be used for withdrawal of each dose (see Precautions).

Shake the prefilled syringe well before administering dose.

Before injection, the skin over the site to be injected should be cleansed with a suitable germicide.

Administer the vaccine **i.m.**, preferably in the region of the deltoid muscle, in adults and older children. The preferred site for infants and young children (<1 year of age) is the anterolateral aspect of the thigh.

After insertion of the needle, aspirate to insure the needle has not entered a blood vessel.

Do not inject i.v.

Fluzone may be used for all age groups. **It is not recommended for infants under 6 months of age.** The dosage is as follows: See Table I.

Table I—Fluzone

Recommended Influenza Vaccine Dosage by Age 1998-1999

Age Group	Vaccine Type	Dose	Number of Doses
13 years and older	Whole-virus or split-virus	0.5 mL	1
9-12 years	Split-virus	0.5 mL	1
3-8 years	Split-virus	0.5 mL	1 or 2*
6-35 months	Split-virus	0.25 mL	1 or 2*

*Children under age 9 require 2 doses with an interval of 4 weeks; the second dose is not needed if the child received 1 or more doses of influenza virus vaccine prepared for a previous season.

Each person who is immunized should be given a permanent personal immunization record. In addition, it is essential that the physician or nurse record the immunization history in the permanent medical record of each patient. This permanent office record should contain the name of the vaccine, date given, dose, manufacturer and lot number.

Supplied: Fluzone Influenza Virus Vaccine Trivalent Types A and B (Zonal Purified, Subvirion) is prepared from the allantoic fluids of chicken embryos infected with a specific type of influenza virus. The virus containing fluids are harvested and the virus inactivated with formaldehyde. Influenza virus is concentrated and purified in a linear sucrose density gradient solution using a continuous flow centrifuge. The virus is then chemically disrupted using glycol p-isooctylphenyl ether (Triton X-100) producing a "split-antigen". The split antigen is then further purified by chemical means and suspended in sodium phosphate buffered, isotonic sodium chloride solution. This product has been standardized according to USPHS requirements.

For the 1998-99 season, the vaccine contains not less than 45 μg hemagglutinin (HA). Each dose (0.5 mL) contains the following 3 strains: A/Beijing/262/95 (H1N1) 15 μg HA, A/Sydney/5/97 (H3N2) 15 μg HA, B/Harbin/07/94 (a B/Beijing/184/93-like strain) 15 μg HA. Gelatin 0.05% is added as a stabilizer and thimerosal 0.01% is added as a preservative. After shaking syringe/vial well, Fluzone is essentially clear and slightly opalescent in color. **Antibiotics are not used in the manufacture of this vaccine.**

Vials of 5 mL (10 doses), boxes of 1. Prefilled syringes of 0.5 mL (single dose), boxes of 1 and 10. Store between 2 and 8°C. **Do not freeze.** Product which has been exposed to freezing should not be used. Do not use after expiration.

Reviewed 1999

FML FORTE® ℞

Allergan

Fluorometholone

Corticosteroid—Anti-inflammatory

Supplied: Each mL of sterile ophthalmic suspension contains: fluorometholone 0.25%. Nonmedicinal ingredients: benzalkonium chloride 0.005% (as preservative), edetate disodium, polysorbate 80, polyvinyl alcohol, sodium biphosphate, sodium chloride and sodium phosphate. Plastic dropper bottles of 5 and 10 mL. Protect from freezing. Shake well before using.

FML® LIQUIFILM® ℞

Allergan

Fluorometholone

Corticosteroid

Supplied: Each mL of sterile ophthalmic suspension contains: fluorometholone 0.1%. Nonmedicinal ingredients: benzalkonium chloride 0.004% (as preservative), edetate disodium, Liquifilm (polyvinyl alcohol), polysorbate 80, sodium chloride, sodium phosphate dibasic and sodium phosphate monobasic. Plastic dropper bottles of 5 and 10 mL.

FOLIC ACID ℞*

General Monograph, CPhA

Pteroylglutamic Acid
Folate Sodium

Anemia Therapy

This monograph has been compiled by CPhA. It may contain information different from that approved by Therapeutic Products Programme, Health Canada, and the pharmaceutical manufacturers' approval has not been requested.

Pharmacology: Folic acid is a B complex vitamin. After absorption from the gastrointestinal tract, folic acid is hepatically converted to tetrahydrofolic acid which is a cofactor in the biosynthesis of purines and thymidylates of nucleic acids. An exogenous source of folic acid is necessary for the maintenance of normal erythropoiesis.

Folic acid deficiency can lead to meagloblastic and macrocytic anemias, as a result of impairment of thymidylate synthesis.

Folic acid occurs in a variety of foods in the form of polyglutamate conjugates. Folic acid found in oral or injectable pharmaceutical preparations is synthetically derived.

Studies have provided strong scientific support for periconceptual prophylaxis with folic acid in reducing the risk of neural tube defects.

Folic acid supplementation has been shown to reduce elevated fasting plasma homocysteine levels, one of the known risk factors for atherosclerotic disease. Studies measuring clinical outcomes are in progress and will establish whether such therapy will result in a reduction of cardiovascular risk.

Pharmacokinetics: Folic acid polyglutamates from food sources are enzymatically hydrolyzed in the gastrointestinal tract to monoglutamates prior to absorption, which occurs mainly in the proximal small intestine. In the presence of malabsorption syndrome, folic acid from oral supplements will still be absorbed, whereas absorption of folic acid from food sources may be impaired.

Following absorption of 1 mg or less, folic acid is converted in the liver and plasma to its metabolically active form tetrahydrofolic acid, which is then distributed into all body tissues. Normal serum folate concentrations range from 0.016 to 0.021 μg/mL. The liver contains about 50% of total body folate stores. Larger doses of folic acid may escape metabolism by liver and appear in the blood mainly as folic acid. Following oral administration of single 0.1 to 0.2 mg doses of folic acid in healthy adults, only a trace amount of the drug appears in urine. Following administration of large doses, the renal tubular reabsorption maximum is exceeded, and excess folate is excreted unchanged in urine. After doses of about 2.5 to 5 mg, about 50% of a dose is excreted in urine and after a 15 mg dose, up to 90% may be recovered in urine. Small amounts of orally administered folic acid have been recovered from feces.

Indications: Folic acid is used in the treatment of megaloblastic and macrocytic anemias caused by folate deficiency. It is also used in the treatment of megaloblastic anemias of pregnancy, infancy and childhood, as well as megaloblastic anemias associated with primary liver disease, alcoholic cirrhosis, intestinal strictures, anastomoses or sprue. In large doses, folic acid is used in the treatment of tropical sprue.

There is strong evidence that prophylactic therapy with folic acid, prior to and during pregnancy, can reduce the risk of fetal neural tube defects. Expert groups recommend that all women of child bearing potential, whether planning pregnancy or not, should maintain an adequate daily intake of folic acid (see Dosage).

Folic acid is not effective in reversing the effects of folic acid reductase inhibitors such as methotrexate, for which leucovorin calcium (folinic acid) must be used.

Precautions: Use only as an adjunct to treatment with vitamin B_{12} whenever pernicious anemia is present or suspected. The use of folic acid in pernicious anemia without adequate vitamin B_{12} therapy may result in hematologic improvement, while neurologic manifestations continue to progress.

Folic acid is not effective as an antidote or in the rescue treatment of overdosage of folic acid antagonists such as methotrexate.

Drug Interactions: Folic acid therapy in folate deficient individuals may decrease serum levels of phenytoin.

Drugs which may cause folate deficiency include phenytoin, isoniazid, primidone, barbiturates, oral contraceptives, ethanol, sulfasalazine, cycloserine, glutethamide, methotrexate, pyrimethamine, trimethoprim and triamterene.

When cholestyramine and folic acid are administered together, there may be a reduction or delay in folic acid absorption. If concomitant therapy is required, folic acid should be administered at least 1 hour before or 4 to 6 hours after cholestyramine.

Pregnancy: Pregnant women are more prone to develop folate deficiency which can lead to complications and fetal abnormalities (see Pharmacology).

Lactation: Folic acid is actively excreted in human breast milk. Adverse effects in breast-fed infants have not been documented with intake of normal daily requirements of folic acid during lactation.

Adverse Effects: Folic acid is relatively nontoxic but has rarely caused allergic reactions including erythema, pruritus and/or urticaria. High doses (e.g. 15 mg/day) have rarely been associated with seizures, psychosis and gastrointestinal symptoms.

Dosage: To prevent deficiency, adequate dietary intake of folic acid is preferred over supplementation whenever possible. For a listing of food sources of folic acid, see Vitamin Food Sources in the Clin-Info section. For information on the daily requirements of folic acid, see Recommended Nutrient Intake in the Clin-Info section.

Treatment of Deficiency: Oral: The usual therapeutic dose of folic acid for adults and children is 0.25 to 1 mg daily; however, some patients may require higher doses. Within the first 48 hours of treatment, the bone marrow begins to become normoblastic. Reticulocytosis begins within 2 to 5 days. To maintain a normoblastic marrow, lower daily maintenance doses of folic acid are used: adults and children 4 years and over, 0.4 mg; children up to 4 years, 0.3 mg; infants, 0.1 mg. Higher maintenance doses may be required in alcoholics, patients with hemolytic anemia or chronic infections, or in patients taking anticonvulsants.

Higher doses have been recommended for the treatment of tropical sprue: 3 to 15 mg daily.

Parenteral: When the oral route is not feasible, an equivalent dose of folic acid may be given by i.v., s.c. or deep i.m. injection. However, most patients with malabsorption syndrome are still able to absorb oral folic acid supplements.

Prophylaxis vs Neural Tube Defects (NTD): The Society of Obstetricians and Gynaecologists of Canada, in its 1993 Policy Statement, recommended that all women of child bearing potential, whether planning pregnancy or not, should consider maintaining a folic acid intake of at least 0.4 mg daily, either in the diet or as a supplement. Pregnant women with no previous history of fetal NTD and no other predisposing factors are advised to maintain an intake of at least 0.4 mg daily until 10 to 12 weeks after last menstrual period.

Women with a history of pregnancy complicated by NTD are considered at high risk for recurrence and are advised to consider taking 4 mg folic acid daily when not using reliable birth control (or at least 2 to 4 weeks prior to conception), continuing until 10 to 12 weeks after last menstrual period.

Women with no previous history of NTD-affected pregnancy but who may be at increased risk due to 1st degree relative (child, sibling or parent) with NTD, or for medical reasons such as type I diabetes or therapy with valproic acid or carbamazepine, are advised to consider taking 1 to 4 mg folic acid daily while not using reliable birth control, continuing for 10 to 12 weeks after last menstrual period.

*Products with strengths less than 1 mg are available without a prescription.

Reviewed 1998

FOLLOW-UP®
Nestlé, Carnation

Infant Formula

Indications: A cow's milk based, iron fortified formula designed to meet the nutritional needs of babies from 6 to 12 months of age who are already eating baby foods.

Follow-Up Formula is designed to be the liquid portion of a 6 to 12 month old baby's diet. It is a nutritionally superior alternative to cow's milk for the older baby.

Follow-Up Formula will help assure that a 6 to 12 month old baby receives the necessary nutrients, including iron, for healthy growth and development.

Contraindications: Not intended for feeding infants younger than 6 months of age. Follow-Up Formula is a milk-based formula which contains whole milk proteins and is therefore not suitable for infants with confirmed milk allergy.

Dosage: As determined by the individual infant's needs, based on solid food consumption along with the liquid diet. Consult the physician for specific feeding recommendations.

Preparation: Concentrated Liquid: Clean can top. Shake well, and open. After opening, can may be covered and stored in refrigerator to be used within 48 hours. Mix equal amounts of formula and previously boiled water in a clean container and stir. Pour prepared formula directly into a clean bottle, cup, or mix with cereal or other solid foods. Feed immediately, or cover and refrigerate to be used within 48 hours. Discard unused formula left in bottle, cup or bowl after feeding.

Powder: Pour desired amount of previously boiled water into a clean container. Add 1 unpacked level scoop (9.4 g), enclosed, of powder for each 60 mL of water in the container. Stir well until powder is completely dissolved. Pour prepared formula directly into a clean bottle, cup, or mix with cereal or other solid foods. Feed immediately, or cover and store in refrigerator to be used within 24 hours. Discard unused formula left in bottle, cup or bowl after feeding.

One can will make approximately 2.4 L of formula.

Ready-To-Feed: Clean can top. Shake well, and open. After opening, can may be covered and stored in refrigerator to be used within 48 hours. Pour formula directly into clean bottle, cup, or mix with cereal or other solid foods. Feed immediately, or cover and refrigerate to be used within 48 hours. Discard unused formula left in bottle, cup or bowl after feeding.

Supplied: Concentrated Liquid: Each can contains: water, skim milk powder, corn syrup, palm olein, maltodextrin, soybean oil, coconut oil, high monounsaturate safflower oil, minerals (tricalcium phosphate, calcium citrate, potassium chloride, ferrous sulfate, zinc sulfate, copper sulfate, manganese sulfate, potassium iodide), soy lecithin, vitamins (sodium ascorbate, inositol, choline chloride, alpha-tocopheryl acetate, niacinamide, vitamin A acetate, vitamin D_3, calcium pantothenate, thiamine mononitrate, riboflavin, pyridoxine HCl, folic acid, phylloquinone, biotin, vitamin B_{12}). See Table I.

Cans of 385 mL, cases of 12. Store unopened cans at room temperature. Avoid excessive temperatures. Use before date shown on top of can.

Powder: Each can contains: skim milk powder, corn syrup solids, palm olein, maltodextrin, soybean oil, coconut oil, high monounsaturate safflower oil, minerals (tricalcium phosphate, calcium citrate, potassium chloride, sodium citrate, potassium citrate, ferrous sulfate, zinc sulfate, copper sulfate, manganese sulfate, potassium iodide), soy lecithin, vitamins (sodium ascorbate, inositol, choline chloride, alpha-tocopheryl acetate, niacinamide, vitamin A acetate, vitamin D_3, calcium pantothenate, thiamine mononitrate, riboflavin, pyridoxine HCl, folic acid, phylloquinone, biotin, vitamin B_{12}). See Table II.

Cans of 340 g, cases of 6. Cover opened can and store in a cool dry place. Use within 1 month after opening. Use before date shown on bottom of can.

The safety of immunization programs is in part maximized through monitoring vaccine-associated adverse events. To report a vaccine-associated adverse event, complete the form "Report of Vaccine-associated Adverse Event" found in the CLIN-INFO SECTION.

Table I—Follow-Up, Concentrated Liquid

Dilution Analysis

Average Composition	Concentrate/ 100 mL	Units	Standard Dilution/ 100 mL
Energy	560 (134)	kJ (kcal)	280 (67)
Carbohydrate	16.8	g	8.9
Fat	5.6	g	2.8
Protein	3.4	g	1.7
Ash	1	g	0.5
Linoleic Acid	0.98	g	0.49
Linolenic Acid	0.10	g	0.049
Vitamin A	340	IU	170
Vitamin D	88	IU	44
Vitamin E	2.6	IU	1.3
Vitamin K	0.011	mg	0.0055
Vitamin C	10.8	mg	5.4
Thiamine	0.108	mg	0.054
Riboflavin	0.13	mg	0.065
Vitamin B_6	0.088	mg	0.044
Vitamin B_{12}	0.0004	mg	0.0002
Niacin	1.76	mg	0.88
Folacin	0.022	mg	0.011
Pantothenic Acid	0.64	mg	0.32
Biotin	0.0026	mg	0.0013
Choline	16.2	mg	8.1
Inositol	24	mg	12
Calcium	180	mg	90
Phosphorus	120	mg	60
Magnesium	11.2	mg	5.6
Iron	2.6	mg	1.3
Zinc	0.84	mg	0.42
Manganese	0.0094	mg	0.0047
Copper	0.094	mg	0.047
Iodine	0.008	mg	0.004
Sodium	52	mg	26
Potassium	180	mg	90
Chloride	120	mg	60

Table II—Follow-Up, Powder

Dilution Analysis

Average Composition	Powder/ 100 g	Units	Standard Dilution/ 100 mL
Energy	2 140 (471)	kJ (kcal)	280 (67)
Carbohydrate	62	g	8.9
Fat	19.3	g	2.8
Protein	12.2	g	1.7
Ash	3.3	g	0.5
Linoleic Acid	3.2	g	0.49
Linolenic Acid	0.32	g	0.049
Vitamin A	1 177	IU	170
Vitamin D	306	IU	44
Vitamin E	9.4	IU	1.3
Vitamin K	0.038	mg	0.0055
Vitamin C	38	mg	5.4
Thiamine	0.38	mg	0.054
Riboflavin	0.45	mg	0.065
Vitamin B_6	0.31	mg	0.044
Vitamin B_{12}	0.0015	mg	0.0002
Niacin	6	mg	0.88
Folacin	0.075	mg	0.011
Pantothenic Acid	2.3	mg	0.32
Biotin	0.0094	mg	0.0013
Choline	56	mg	8.1
Inositol	85	mg	12
Calcium	635	mg	90
Phosphorus	423	mg	60
Magnesium	39	mg	5.6
Iron	8.9	mg	1.3
Zinc	3	mg	0.42
Manganese	0.033	mg	0.0047
Copper	0.36	mg	0.047
Iodine	0.027	mg	0.004
Sodium	184	mg	26
Potassium	635	mg	90
Chloride	424	mg	60

Ready-To-Feed: Each can contains: water, skim milk powder, corn syrup, palm olein, maltodextrin, soybean oil, coconut oil, high monounsaturate safflower oil, minerals (tricalcium phosphate, calcium citrate, potassium chloride, sodium citrate, potassium citrate, ferrous sulfate, zinc sulfate, copper sulfate, manganese sulfate, potassium iodide), soy lecithin, vitamins (sodium ascorbate, inositol, choline chloride, alpha-tocopheryl acetate, niacinamide, vitamin A acetate, vitamin D_3, calcium pantothenate, thiamine mononitrate, riboflavin, pyridoxine HCl, folic acid, phylloquinone, biotin, vitamin B_{12}). See Table III.

Cans of 945 mL, cases of 6. Store unopened cans at room temperature. Avoid excessive temperatures. Use before date shown on top of can.

Table III—Follow-Up, Ready-To-Feed

Average Composition	Per 100 mL	Units
Energy	280 (67)	kJ (kcal)
Carbohydrate	8.9	g
Fat	2.8	g
Protein	1.7	g
Ash	0.5	g
Linoleic Acid	0.49	g
Linolenic Acid	0.049	g
Inositol	12	mg
Choline	8.1	mg
Vitamin A	170	IU
Vitamin D	44	IU
Vitamin E	1.3	IU
Vitamin C	5.4	mg
Niacin	0.88	mg
Pantothenic Acid	0.32	mg
Riboflavin	0.065	mg
Thiamine	0.054	mg
Vitamin B_6	0.044	mg
Folacin	0.011	mg
Vitamin K	0.0055	mg
Biotin	0.0013	mg
Vitamin B_{12}	0.0002	mg
Potassium	90	mg
Calcium	90	mg
Phosphorus	60	mg
Chloride	60	mg
Sodium	26	mg
Magnesium	5.6	mg
Iron	1.3	mg
Zinc	0.42	mg
Copper	0.047	mg
Manganese	0.0047	mg
Iodine	0.004	mg

Reviewed 1998

FOLLOW-UP SOY®
Nestlé, Carnation

Soy Infant Formula

Indications: A soy based, iron fortified formula designed to meet the nutritional needs of babies from 6 to 12 months of age who are already eating baby foods.

Follow-Up soy formula is designed to be the liquid portion of a 6 to 12 month old baby's diet. It is a nutritionally superior formula for milk-free feeding for babies 6 to 12 months.

Follow-Up soy formula will help assure that a 6 to 12 month old baby receives the necessary nutrients, including iron, for healthy growth and development.

Dosage: As determined by the individual infant's needs, based on solid food consumption along with the liquid diet. Consult the physician for specific feeding recommendations.

Preparation: Pour desired amount of previously boiled water into a clean container. Add 1 unpacked level scoop (9.3 g), enclosed, of powder for each 60 mL of water in the container. Stir well until powder is completely dissolved. Pour prepared formula directly into a clean bottle, cup, or mix with cereal or other solid foods. Feed immediately, or cover and store in refrigerator to be used within 24 hours. Discard unused formula left in bottle, cup or bowl after feeding.

One can (396 g) will make approximately 2.8 L of formula.

Supplied: Each can contains: corn maltodextrin, soy protein isolate, sucrose, palm olein, soybean oil, coconut oil, minerals (calcium citrate, tricalcium phosphate, potassium chloride, potassium citrate, magnesium phosphate, sodium chloride, ferrous sulfate, zinc sulfate, copper sulfate, potassium iodide, sodium selenate), high monosaturate safflower oil, soy lecithin, vitamins (sodium ascorbate, choline bitartrate, inositol, alpha-tocopheryl acetate, niacinamide, calcium pantothenate, thiamine HCl, vitamin A acetate, riboflavin, pyridoxine HCl, folic acid, phylloquinone, beta-carotene, biotin, vitamin D_3, vitamin B_{12}), l-methionine, taurine, l-carnitine. See Table I.

Table I—Follow-Up Soy

Dilution Analysis

Average Composition	Powder/ 100 g	Units	Standard Dilution/ 100 mL
Energy	2 010 (481)	kJ (kcal)	280 (67)
Carbohydrate	58	g	8
Fat	21	g	2.9
Protein	15	g	2
Ash	3.2	g	0.44
Linoleic Acid	4.1	g	0.57
Linolenic Acid	0.41	g	0.057
Vitamin A	1 500	IU	208
Vitamin D	300	IU	42
Vitamin E	11	IU	1.6
Vitamin K	0.039	mg	0.0054
Vitamin C	77	mg	10
Thiamine	0.43	mg	0.06
Riboflavin	0.45	mg	0.06
Vitamin B_6	0.41	mg	0.06
Vitamin B_{12}	0.0015	mg	0.0002
Niacin	6	mg	0.8
Folacin	0.077	mg	0.01
Pantothenic Acid	2.3	mg	0.31
Biotin	0.037	mg	0.005
Choline	58	mg	8
Taurine	32	mg	4.4
Inositol	87	mg	12
L-Carnitine	5.8	mg	0.8
L-Methionine	220	mg	30
Calcium	645	mg	90
Phosphorus	433	mg	60
Magnesium	63	mg	8.7
Iron	8.7	mg	1.2
Zinc	5.8	mg	0.8
Manganese	0.18	mg	0.025
Selenium	0.0096	mg	0.001
Copper	0.58	mg	0.08
Iodine	0.038	mg	0.0054
Sodium	209	mg	29
Potassium	565	mg	79
Chloride	375	mg	53

Cans of 396 g, cases of 6. Cover opened can and store in a cool dry place. Use within 1 month after opening. Use before date shown on bottom of can.

Reviewed 1998

FORADIL® ℞

Novartis Pharmaceuticals

Formoterol Fumarate

Bronchodilator

Pharmacology: Formoterol is a potent selective long-acting (12 hours) β_2-adrenergic stimulant. It exerts a bronchodilator effect in patients with reversible airways obstruction. The effect is seen within 1 to 3 minutes and is still significant 12 hours after inhalation.

Single dose studies have shown that formoterol is effective in preventing bronchospasm induced by allergen, exercise, cold air, histamine or methacholine challenge. The bronchoprotective effect of formoterol against methacholine provocation has been shown to persist for 12 hours.

In vitro, formoterol inhibits the release of histamine and leukotrienes from passively sensitized human lung. In humans, formoterol was more effective than salbutamol at suppressing late phase airway obstruction and increased airway responsiveness to allergen. The clinical significance of these findings is unclear because the long duration of action of formoterol may produce an apparent effect on late phase reactions due to functional antagonism.

Pharmacokinetics: As for other inhaled drugs, it is likely that 90% of formoterol administered from an inhaler is swallowed and absorbed from the gastrointestinal tract. Formoterol acts locally in the lung; plasma levels therefore do not predict therapeutic effect. Systemic levels of formoterol are low or undetectable after inhalation of recommended doses.

Indications: As long-term, twice-daily administration in the maintenance treatment of asthma in patients 12 years of age and older with reversible obstructive airways disease, including patients with symptoms of nocturnal asthma, who are using optimal corticosteroid treatment and experiencing regular or frequent breakthrough symptoms requiring use of a short-acting bronchodilator. Formoterol should not be used in patients whose asthma can be managed by occasional use of short-acting inhaled β_2-agonists.

Corticosteroids should not be stopped because formoterol is prescribed.

Formoterol is a long-acting β_2-agonist and should not be used as a rescue medication. To relieve acute asthmatic symptoms a short-acting inhaled bronchodilator (e.g., salbutamol) should be used.

Contraindications: Patients with cardiac tachyarrhythmias. Formoterol contains lactose (see Supplied) and is contraindicated in patients with an allergy to lactose, milk or in those who have ever had any unusual or allergic reaction to formoterol.

Warnings: Important Information: Formoterol should not be initiated in patients with significantly worsening or acutely deteriorating asthma (see Precautions).

Formoterol should not be used to treat acute symptoms. It is crucial to advise patients accordingly and prescribe a short-acting, inhaled bronchodilator for this purpose. Medical attention should be sought if patients find that short-acting relief bronchodilator treatment becomes less effective or that they need more inhalations than usual (see Precautions).

Formoterol is not a substitute for inhaled or oral corticosteroids. Its use is complementary to them. Corticosteroids should not be stopped when formoterol is initiated. Patients must be warned not to stop or reduce corticosteroid therapy without medical advice (see Precautions).

Formoterol and the Management of Asthma: The management of asthma should normally follow a stepwise program, with patient response monitored clinically and by lung function tests. Current asthma management guidelines recommend the following for long-acting β_2-agonists: Oral or inhaled corticosteroids should not be stopped. Adequate education should be provided to the patient regarding the use of long-acting β_2-agonists and the acute treatment of asthma, with close follow-up to ensure compliance. Long-acting β_2-agonists should not be introduced in unstable asthma. Long-acting β_2-agonists should never be used as rescue medication.

Increasing use of short-acting inhaled β_2-agonists to control symptoms indicates deterioration of asthma control and the need to reassess the patient's therapy.

Sudden or progressive deterioration in asthma control is potentially life-threatening; the treatment plan must be re-evaluated, and consideration given to increasing corticosteroid therapy. In patients at risk, daily peak flow monitoring with precise instructions for acceptable variation limits should be considered.

Cardiovascular and Other Nonpulmonary Effects: Potentially serious ECG changes (such as increased QTc interval) and hypokalemia may result from β_2-agonist therapy. Although clinically not significant, a small increase in QT_c interval and/or decrease in serum potassium has been reported at therapeutic doses of formoterol. The effects of single doses of formoterol at 12 to 96 µg were studied in 22 adult asthmatics, all of whom were receiving inhaled corticosteroids and an inhaled short-acting β_2-agonist prior to entering the trial. The number of patients whose longest measured QT_c in this trial was >440 msec was greater for placebo (3 patients) than it was for formoterol 12 µg (no patient), 24 µg (2 patients), and 48 µg (2 patients). Five patients treated with formoterol 96 µg showed QT_c prolongations >440 msec. Six patients had clinically meaningful (K^+ <3.2 mmol/L) hypokalemia at 96 µg, compared with one each at 12 and 48 µg. It is not known if these effects become clinically significant when concomitant medications causing similar effects are prescribed and/or in the presence of heart diseases, hypokalemia, or hypoxia. Particular caution is advised in severe asthma as these effects may be potentiated by hypoxia and concomitant treatment with xanthine derivatives, steroids and diuretics. Hypokalemia will increase the susceptibility of digitalis patients to cardiac arrhythmias (see Precautions). It is recommended that serum potassium levels be monitored in such situations.

Beta-adrenergic Blockers: Beta-adrenergic blockers, especially noncardioselective agents, should not be administered to asthmatic patients (see Precautions, Drug Interactions) since these antagonize the action of β_2-agonists including formoterol and may produce severe, resistant bronchospasm.

Paradoxical Bronchospasm: As with other inhaled asthma medication, paradoxical bronchospasm (which can be life-threatening) has been reported following the use of formoterol. If it occurs, treatment with formoterol should be discontinued immediately and alternative therapy instituted.

Labor and Delivery: There are no well-controlled human studies that have investigated the effects of formoterol on preterm labor or labor at term. Because of the potential for β-agonist interference with uterine contractility, use of β_2-agonists, such as formoterol, during labour should be restricted to those patients in whom the benefits clearly outweigh the risks.

Postmarketing Experience: Fatalities, the exact cause of which is unknown, have been reported following excessive use of inhaler preparations containing sympathomimetic amines. In individual patients, any β_2-agonist may have a clinically adverse cardiac effect. The incidence of mortality in patients receiving formoterol is consistent with that typically seen in the asthmatic population. In an open-label, uncontrolled study conducted in Europe an overall crude mortality rate of approximately 14/1 000 person years (8 of 1 393 patients followed for 4.8±2.6 months) was reported.

Precautions: Do not introduce formoterol as a treatment for acutely deteriorating asthma. Formoterol is intended for the maintenance treatment of asthma (see Indications) and should not be introduced in acutely deteriorating asthma, which is a potentially life threatening condition. There are no data demonstrating that long-acting β_2-agonists provide greater efficacy than or additional efficacy to short-acting, inhaled β_2-agonists in patients with worsening asthma. As with other long-acting β_2-agonists, serious acute respiratory events, including fatalities, have been reported in patients receiving formoterol, some of which have occurred in patients with severe asthma and/or patients in whom asthma has been acutely deteriorating. Although it is not possible from these reports to determine the causal relationship between long-acting β_2-agonists and these adverse events, the use of a long-acting β_2-agonist in patients with acutely deteriorating asthma is inappropriate (see Warnings, Postmarketing Experience).

Do not use formoterol to treat acute symptoms. Formoterol should not be used to relieve acute asthma symptoms. When prescribing formoterol, the physician must also provide the patient with a short-acting, inhaled β_2-agonist (e.g., salbutamol) for treatment of symptoms that occur acutely, despite regular twice-daily use of formoterol.

When beginning treatment with formoterol, patients who have been taking short-acting, inhaled β_2-agonists on a regular basis (e.g., q.i.d.) should be instructed to discontinue the regular use of these drugs and use them only for symptomatic relief if they develop acute asthma symptoms while using formoterol (see Blue Section—Information for the Patient). Although formoterol has a rapid onset of action (1 to 3 minutes), current asthma management guidelines recommend that long-acting inhaled bronchodilators should be used only as twice-daily maintenance bronchodilator therapy.

Watch for increased need for short-acting, inhaled β_2-agonists. Asthma may deteriorate acutely over a period of hours or chronically over several days or longer. If the patient's short-acting inhaled β_2-agonist becomes less effective or a patient needs more inhalation than usual, this may be a marker of destabilization of asthma. In this setting, the patient requires reassessment of the treatment regimen. Those patients who require increasing doses or inhalations of short-acting β_2-agonists for relief of symptoms should consult a physician for re-evaluation. **Increasing the daily dosage of formoterol in this situation is not appropriate. Formoterol should not be used more frequently than twice daily or at higher doses than recommended.**

Do not use formoterol as a substitute for oral or inhaled corticosteroids. Patients must be warned not to stop or reduce corticosteroid therapy without medical advice, even if they feel better as a result of formoterol treatment.

Do not exceed recommended dosage. As with other inhaled β_2-agonist drugs, formoterol should not be used more often or at higher doses than recommended. Fatalities have been reported in association with excessive use of inhaled sympathomimetic drugs (see below).

Cardiovascular and Other Medical Conditions: Usually no effect on the cardiovascular or CNS is seen after the administration of formoterol at recommended doses, but the cardiovascular and CNS effects seen with all sympathomimetic drugs (e.g., increased heart rate, cardiac contractility, tremor) can occur while using formoterol. Potentially serious ECG changes and hypokalemia were seen at increased doses (96 µg or 4 times the recommended maximum dose) of inhaled formoterol. Therefore, special care and supervision, with particular emphasis on dosage limits, is required in patients receiving formoterol when the following conditions may exist: ischemic heart disease, cardiac arrhythmias, especially third degree

Foradil (cont'd)

AV block, severe cardiac decompensation, idiopathic subvalvular aortic stenosis, hypertrophic obstructive cardiomyopathy, thyrotoxicosis, known or suspected prolongation of the QT-interval (QT_c >0.44 seconds).

Use with caution in patients with idiopathic hypertrophic subvalvular aortic stenosis, in whom an increase in the pressure gradient between the left ventricle and the aorta may occur, causing increased strain on the left ventricle.

Immediate Hypersensitivity Reactions: Immediate hypersensitivity reactions may occur after administration of formoterol. Formoterol contains lactose and is contraindicated in patients with allergy to lactose, milk or in those who have ever had any unusual or allergic reaction for formoterol (see Contraindications).

Metabolic Effects: Due to the hyperglycemic effect of β_2-stimulants, additional blood glucose controls are recommended in diabetic patients.

Pregnancy: The safety of formoterol during pregnancy has not yet been established (see Warnings, Labor and Delivery).

Lactation: Formoterol was found to be excreted in the milk of lactating rats after oral administration. It is not known whether inhaled formoterol passes into the breast milk in humans. Therefore, mothers nursing their infants should refrain from taking formoterol.

Labor and Delivery: See Warnings.

Geriatrics: No special considerations are required in elderly patients.

Children: Formoterol is not recommended for use in children younger than 12 years of age in the absence of further clinical trial experience in this age group.

Adolescent Patients and Asthma Severity Reassessment: In adolescent patients the severity of asthma may be variable with age and periodic reassessment should be considered to determine if continued maintenance therapy with formoterol is still indicated. Compliance, especially neglect of anti-inflammatory therapy and overuse of short-acting β_2-agonists, should be carefully followed in adolescents receiving long-acting β_2-agonists.

Drug Interactions: Short-acting β_2-agonists: Aerosol bronchodilators of the short-acting adrenergic stimulant type may be used for relief of breakthrough symptoms while using formoterol. However, increasing use of such preparations to control symptoms indicates deterioration of asthma control and the need to reassess the patient's therapy.

Concomitant administration of other sympathomimetic agents may potentiate the undesirable effects of formoterol.

MAO Inhibitors and Tricyclic Antidepressants: Formoterol should be administered with extreme caution in patients being treated with MAO inhibitors or tricyclic antidepressants because the action of formoterol on the cardiovascular system may be potentiated by these agents.

Corticosteroids, Methylxanthines and Diuretics: Concomitant treatment with xanthine derivatives, steroids, or diuretics may potentiate a possible hypokalemic effect of β_2-agonists. Hypokalemia may increase susceptibility to cardiac arrhythmias in patients treated with digitalis.

β-adrenergic Blockers: β-adrenergic blockers may weaken or antagonise the effect of formoterol. Therefore formoterol should not be given together with β-adrenergic blockers (including eye drops) unless there are compelling reasons for their use.

Other Drugs: Drugs such as quinidine, disopyramide, procainamide, phenothiazines, antihistamines, and tricyclic antidepressants may be associated with QT-interval prolongation and an increased risk of ventricular arrhythmia (see Warnings).

Information for the Patient: See Blue Section—Information for the Patient and package insert for illustrations. It is important that patients understand how to use formoterol capsules with the supplied Aerolizer inhalation device and how it should be used in relation to other asthma medications they are taking. Patients should be given the following information:

The recommended dosage (1 or 2 capsules twice daily, morning and evening) should not be exceeded.

Formoterol is not meant to relieve acute asthma symptoms and extra doses should not be used for that purpose. Acute symptoms should be treated with a short-acting, inhaled β_2-agonist such as salbutamol (the physician should provide the patient with such medication and instruct the patient in how it should be used).

The physician should be notified immediately if any of the following situations occur, which may be a sign of seriously worsening asthma: decreased effectiveness of short-acting, inhaled β_2-agonists; need for more inhalations than usual of short-acting, inhaled β_2-agonists.

Formoterol should not be used as a substitute for oral or inhaled corticosteroids. The dosage of these medications should not be changed and they should not be stopped without consulting the physician, even if the patient feels better after initiating treatment with formoterol.

Patients should be cautioned regarding potential adverse cardiovascular effects, such as palpitations or chest pain.

In patients receiving formoterol, other inhaled medications should be used only as directed by the physician.

Parents/guardians of adolescent children who have been prescribed formoterol should be alerted to the general concern regarding asthma therapy compliance, especially neglect of anti-inflammatory therapy and overuse of short-acting β_2-agonists.

Adverse Effects: The adverse reactions observed with formoterol in controlled, comparative and noncomparative clinical studies were dose-dependent and corresponded to those known to occur with other β_2-adrenergic agonists. The most common adverse reactions (<10%) were tremor, palpitations, headache, dizziness, and oropharyngeal irritation. Rarely (<1%) muscle cramps, myalgia, tachycardia, agitation, anxiety, nervousness, insomnia, and, very rarely (<0.01%) aggravated bronchospasm.

The clinical trial program conducted with formoterol has involved over 6 000 patients. The profile of adverse events considered to be causally related to treatment from 3 controlled multidose trials of 3-months duration with formoterol dry powder inhaler is presented in Table I.

Table I—Foradil

Adverse Event Profile in Three 3-Month Controlled Trials (≥1%)

	Total Number of Patients Reporting (%)				
	Formoterol			Salbutamol	Placebo
	I: 12 µg b.i.d.	II: 24 µg b.i.d.	I+II	400 µg q.i.d.	
Total Number of Patients	292	197	489	294	101
Cardiovascular System					
Palpitation	2 (0.7)	5 (2.5)	7 (1.4)	10 (3.4)	1 (1.0)
Nervous System					
Tremor	6 (2.1)	10 (5.1)	16 (3.3)	6 (2.0)	1 (1.0)
Headache	9 (3.1)	4 (2.0)	13 (2.7)	10 (3.4)	2 (2.0)
Dizziness	5 (1.7)	2 (1.0)	7 (1.4)	3 (1.0)	0

Based on its worldwide use involving over 6 million of patient-treatment-months since first introduction onto the market in 1990, the adverse events profile of formoterol is in keeping with those observed in controlled clinical trials.

Isolated cases of the following adverse events have been reported through spontaneous reporting from those countries where the product is already marketed: hypersensitivity reactions such as severe hypotension, urticaria, angioedema, pruritus, exanthema. Peripheral edema, taste perversion, nausea.

Overdose: Symptoms: An overdosage of formoterol is likely to lead to effects that are typical of β_2-adrenergic stimulants: nausea, vomiting, headache, tremor, somnolence, palpitations, tachycardia, ventricular arrhythmias, metabolic acidosis, hypokalemia, hyperglycemia.

Treatment: Supportive and symptomatic treatment is indicated. Serious cases should be hospitalized.

Use of cardioselective β-adrenergic blockers may be considered, but only subject to extreme caution since the use of β-adrenergic blocker medication may provoke bronchospasm.

Dosage: Formoterol should not be initiated in patients with significantly worsening or acutely deteriorating asthma, which may be a life-threatening condition (see Precautions).

Formoterol is not a replacement for inhaled or oral corticosteroid therapy; its use is complementary to it. Patients must be warned not to stop or reduce anti-inflammatory therapy without medical advice, even if they feel better on formoterol.

Formoterol should not be used to treat acute symptoms. It is crucial to inform patients of this and prescribe a short-acting, inhaled β_2-agonist for this purpose. The need for additional symptomatic bronchodilator therapy is usually reduced with formoterol. Medical attention should be sought if patients find that short-acting relief bronchodilator treatment becomes less effective or if they need more inhalations than usual.

Bronchodilators should not be the only or main treatment in patients with moderate to severe asthma. Patients with severe asthma require regular medical assessment since death may occur. These patients will require high-dose inhaled or oral corticosteroid therapy. Sudden worsening of symptoms may require increased corticosteroids dosage which should be administered under medical supervision (see Precautions).

Long-term Maintenance Therapy: Adults: 1 capsule (12 µg) is inhaled using the Aerolizer inhaler twice daily, in the morning and evening. In severe cases, adults may require 2 capsules (2×12 µg) twice daily, in the morning and evening. In adults, the maximum recommended daily dose of formoterol is 48 µg.

Adolescent Children (12 to 16 years): 1 capsule (12 µg) is inhaled using the Aerolizer inhaler twice daily, in the morning and evening. A daily dose of 24 µg should not be exceeded. In adolescent patients the severity of asthma may be variable with age and periodic reassessment should be considered to determine if continued maintenance therapy with formoterol is still indicated (see Precautions).

If a previously effective dosage fails to provide the usual relief, medical advice should be sought immediately; this is a sign of seriously worsening asthma that requires reassessment of therapy. **Formoterol should not be used more than twice daily with a 12-hour interval between doses.**

Special Instructions: Only use formoterol capsules with the Aerolizer inhaler that is provided with each prescription refill. Do not use another type of inhaler with the capsules. Do not use other capsules in the Aerolizer inhaler.

Always use the new Aerolizer inhaler that is supplied with each prescription refill. To ensure proper administration of the drug, the physician or other health professional should show the patient how to operate the Aerolizer inhaler. Remove the capsules from the blister pack only immediately before use.

The emitted dose from 1 capsule when inhaled by the Aerolizer inhaler is 9.6 µg.

Information for the Patient: See Blue Section—Information for the Patient "Foradil".

Supplied: Each clear, hard gelatin capsule of white free flowing powder for inhalation only, contains: formoterol fumarate 12 µg. Use capsules only with the supplied Aerolizer inhalation device. Nonmedicinal ingredients: lactose. Cartons of 60 along with 1 Aerolizer inhalation device. Protect from heat (i.e., store between 15 to 25°C) and humidity.

(Shown in Product Recognition Section)

Reviewed 1999

FORANE® Ⓟ

Zeneca

Isoflurane

Inhalation Anesthetic

Pharmacology: Isoflurane is an inhalation anesthetic whose low solubility (blood/gas partition coefficient equals 1.4), permits a rapid induction of and recovery from anesthesia. The mild pungency of isoflurane may limit the rate of induction, although excessive salivation or tracheobronchial secretions do not appear to be stimulated. The level of anesthesia may be changed rapidly with isoflurane. Pharyngeal and laryngeal reflexes are readily and easily obtunded. Isoflurane is a profound respiratory depressant. An increase in anesthetic dose will decrease tidal volume without changing respiratory rate. This depression is partially reversed by surgical stimulation, even at deeper levels of anesthesia. Isoflurane evokes a sigh response reminiscent of that seen with diethyl ether and enflurane.

Blood pressure decreases with induction of anesthesia but returns toward normal with surgical stimulation. Progressive increases in depth of anesthesia correspondingly decrease blood pressure. Nitrous oxide diminishes the inspired concentration of isoflurane required to reach a desired level of anesthesia and has a favorable effect on the parameters of the anesthetic process. With controlled ventilation and normal $PaCO_2$, cardiac output is maintained despite increasing depth of anesthesia primarily through an increase in heart rate which compensates for a reduction in stroke volume. The hypercapnia which attends spontaneous ventilation during isoflurane anesthesia further increases heart rate and raises cardiac output above awake levels.

The cardiac rhythm during isoflurane anesthesia is stable. In dog studies, isoflurane has not been found to sensitize the myocardium to exogenously administered epinephrine. Limited data indicate that s.c. injection of 0.25 mg of epinephrine (50 mL of 1:200 000 solution) does not cause ventricular arrhythmias in patients anesthetized with isoflurane. Doubling this dose will produce ventricular extrasystoles in about half of patients anesthetized with 1.25 MAC isoflurane.

Muscle relaxation usually is adequate for intra-abdominal operations at normal levels of anesthesia. All commonly used muscle relaxants are compatible with isoflurane. Complete paralysis can be attained with small doses of muscle relaxants. Isoflurane potentiates all commonly used muscle relaxants, the effect being most profound with nondepolarizing relaxants. Neostigmine reverses the effect of nondepolarizing muscle relaxants in the presence of isoflurane but does not reverse the direct neuromuscular depression of isoflurane.

The metabolism of isoflurane is low in miniature swine, black C-57 mice and Fischer 344 rats. Less than 0.5% of isoflurane taken up in humans can be recovered as metabolites.

Indications: Induction and maintenance of general anesthesia. Adequate data have not been developed to establish its application in obstetrical anesthesia.

Contraindications: Known sensitivity to isoflurane or to other halogenated agents.

Warnings: Levels of anesthesia may be altered easily and rapidly; therefore, only vaporizers producing predictable concentrations should be used. Hypotension and respiratory depression increase as anesthesia is deepened.

Respiration must be monitored closely and supported when necessary.

Isoflurane potentiates all commonly used muscle relaxants, the effect being most profound with the nondepolarizing type. Therefore, less than the usual amounts of such agents should be used. Neostigmine reverses the effects of nondepolarizing muscle relaxants, but does not reverse the direct neuromuscular depression of isoflurane.

Blood loss during abortion is increased when halogenated agents such as isoflurane are used for anesthesia.

Isoflurane may increase cerebral blood flow and hence cerebral spinal fluid pressure, and therefore should be used with special care in patients with pre-existing increases in cerebrospinal fluid pressure. This effect on flow and pressure is reversed by hyperventilation.

The safety of repeated anesthesia with isoflurane has not been established.

Pregnancy: The safety of isoflurane anesthesia to mother and fetus has not been established. Reproduction studies in rats and mice reveal no evidence of harm to the fetus. The relevance of these studies to the human is not known. There are no data on the use of isoflurane in pregnant women.

Precautions: Bromsulfalein (BSP) retention is mildly elevated postoperatively in some cases. There is some elevation of glucose and white blood count intraoperatively. Glucose elevation should be considered in diabetic patients.

Malignant Hyperthermia: In susceptible individuals, isoflurane anesthesia may trigger a skeletal muscle hypermetabolic state leading to high oxygen demand and the clinical syndrome known as malignant hyperthermia. The syndrome includes nonspecific features such as muscle rigidity, tachycardia, tachypnea, cyanosis, arrhythmias, and unstable blood pressure. (It should also be noted that many of these nonspecific signs may appear with light anesthesia, acute hypoxia, etc.) An increase in overall metabolism may be reflected in an elevated temperature (which may rise rapidly early or late in the case, but usually is not the first sign of augmented metabolism) and an increased usage of the CO_2 absorption system (hot canister). PaO_2 and pH may decrease, and hyperkalemia and a base deficit may appear. Treatment includes discontinuance of triggering agents (e.g., isoflurane), administration of i.v. dantrolene sodium, and application of supportive therapy. Such therapy includes vigorous efforts to restore body temperature to normal, respiratory and circulatory support as indicated, and management of electrolyte-fluid-acid-base derangements. (Consult prescribing information for dantrolene sodium i.v. for additional information on patient management.) Renal failure may appear later, and urine flow should be sustained if possible.

Adverse Effects: Hypotension, respiratory depression, arrhythmias, shivering, nausea, vomiting, and postoperative ileus have been reported. As with all other anesthetics, elevation of the white blood count has been observed following anesthesia even in the absence of surgical stress.

Elevation of AST, LDH, alkaline phosphatase and bilirubin with or without frank jaundice, have been reported in the postoperative period following isoflurane anesthesia in some patients. Hepatitis has been reported very rarely.

Delirium, hallucinations and hiccup occur rarely.

Overdose: Symptoms: Overdosage with isoflurane produces marked hypotension and may cause apnea.

Treatment: In the event of overdosage, or what appears to be overdosage, the following should be done: Stop drug administration. Establish that the airway is clear. Instigate assisted or controlled ventilation with pure oxygen as the circumstances dictate.

Dosage: Preanesthetic Medication: Premedication should be selected according to the need of the individual patient, taking into account that secretions are weakly stimulated by isoflurane and that the heart rate tends to be increased. The use of anticholinergic drugs is a matter of choice.

Induction: Induction with isoflurane in oxygen or in combination with oxygen-nitrous oxide mixtures may produce coughing, breath-holding, or laryngospasm. These difficulties may be avoided by use of a hypnotic dose of a short acting barbiturate preceding the isoflurane mixture. Inspired concentrations of 1.5 to 3.0% isoflurane with a background of 50 to 70% nitrous oxide usually produce surgical anesthesia in 7 to 10 minutes. If nitrous oxide is not used, an additional 1.0 to 1.5% isoflurane may be required for induction of anesthesia.

Maintenance: Surgical levels of anesthesia may be sustained with a 1.0 to 2.5% concentration when 50 to 70% nitrous oxide is used concomitantly. An additional 0.5 to 1.0% may be required when isoflurane is given in oxygen alone. Additional relaxation may be produced with supplemental doses of muscle relaxants.

In the absence of other complicating problems, blood pressure during maintenance varies inversely with isoflurane concentration. Excessive decreases may be due to depth of anesthesia and in such instances may be corrected by lightening anesthesia.

MAC (minimum alveolar concentration) in man: see Table I.

Table I—Forane

MAC (Minimum Alveolar Concentration) in Man

Age	With 100% Oxygen	With 70% N_2O
26±4	1.28%	0.56%
44±7	1.15%	0.50%
64±5	1.05%	0.37%

Isoflurane, like some other inhalational anesthetics, can react with desiccated carbon dioxide (CO_2) absorbents to produce carbon monoxide which may result in elevated levels of carboxyhemoglobin in some patients. Case reports suggest that barium hydroxide lime and sodalime become desiccated when fresh gases are passed through the CO_2 absorber cannister at high flow rates over many hours or days. When a clinician suspects that CO_2 absorbent may be desiccated, it should be replaced before the administration of isoflurane.

Administration Equipment: The delivered concentration of isoflurane should be known. Isoflurane may be vaporized from a flow-through vaporizer specifically calibrated for isoflurane. Vaporizers which deliver saturated vapor at reasonable flows but are not specifically calibrated for isoflurane may be used. The delivered concentration from such a vaporizer may be calculated using the formula:

$$\% \text{ isoflurane} = \frac{100\, P_V F_V}{F_T(P_A - P_V)}$$

Legend: P_A=Pressure of atmosphere.
P_V=Vapor pressure of isoflurane.
F_V=Flow of gas through vaporizer (mL/min).
F_T=Total flow gas used (mL/min).

Isoflurane contains no stabilizer and vaporization of isoflurane does not leave a residual material which might alter the calibration or operation of a vaporizer.

Keyed Bottle Collar (for use with key-fil Vaporizer) Directions for Use: To attach a keyed bottle adaptor, remove cap and seal from anesthetic bottle. Check that the anesthetic bottle neck is not chipped or damaged. Match keyed bottle adaptor to keyed bottle collar and screw together until tight. Now connect the bottle to the vaporizer filler receptacle.

Note that color of keyed bottle collar will match the color of the adaptor.

(Refer to package insert for calculation of delivered isoflurane concentration.)

Supplied: Amber bottles of 100 mL.

Reviewed 1999

FORMULEX®
ICN
Dicyclomine HCl
Antispasmodic

Supplied: Each blue, #4 capsule printed ICN F11, contains: dicyclomine HCl, USP 10 mg. Nonmedicinal ingredients: lactose, magnesium stearate and starch. Bottles of 100 and 500.

FORTAZ® ℞
Glaxo Wellcome
Ceftazidime Pentahydrate
Antibiotic

Pharmacology: In vitro studies indicate that the bactericidal action of ceftazidime, a semisynthetic cephalosporin antibiotic, results from inhibition of bacterial cell wall synthesis.

Ceftazidime has a high affinity for the Penicillin-Binding Protein-3 (PBP-3) and moderate affinity for the PBP-1a of certain gram-negative organisms such as E. coli and P. aeruginosa. The affinity for PBP-1b is much less than that for either PBP-3 or PBP-1a. PBP-3 is involved in the process of cross-wall formation (septation). Binding to this protein results in formation of filaments and eventual death of the bacterium. PBP-1a and PBP-1b are involved in longitudinal wall synthesis (elongation) prior to septation. Binding to these proteins results in spheroplast formation followed by rapid lysis.

Ceftazidime has high affinity for PBP-1 and PBP-2 of S. aureus. However, the drug's affinity for PBP-3 is very much less in this organism.

Ceftazidime is poorly absorbed when given orally (e.g. following a 250 mg dose the average urinary recovery was less than 1% of the dose). Doses of 250, 500 and 1 000 mg administered as a single bolus injection over 1minute resulted in peak serum concentrations within 20 minutes of about 20, 46 and 88 mg/L respectively. Mean urinary recovery of unchanged drug over 24 hours ranged from 77.4 to 85.5% with over 50% being excreted in the first 2 to 4 hours. Single i.v. infusions of 500, 1 000 and 2 000 mg administered over 20 to 30 minutes to normal adult volunteers resulted in peak serum concentrations within 30 minutes of about 41, 68 and 169 mg/L respectively. Mean urinary recovery of unchanged drug over 24 hours ranged from 83.7 to 87.1% with over 50% being excreted in the first 2 to 4 hours. In both routes, serum concentration-time curves follow a biexponential decay.

Peak serum concentrations following i.m. injections of 500 or 1 000 mg occurred at 1 hour and were about 17.4 and 38.8 mg/L respectively. Mean urinary recovery of ceftazidime over 24 hours ranged from 78.9 to 84.6%.

No accumulation of drug was noted during repeated i.m. doses of ceftazidime (1 g, t.i.d., 10 days).

In vitro studies with human serum revealed that 5 to 23% of ceftazidime is protein bound and is independent of drug concentration.

Ceftazidime is not metabolized. Metabolites were not detected either in the serum by HPLC or in the urine by chromatography or bioautography.

Hepatic clearance (i.e. biliary excretion) accounts for less than 1% of the total clearance of ceftazidime in the presence of normally functioning kidneys.

The mean renal clearance of ceftazidime was 97.6 mL/min (range 76 to 110 mL/min). The calculated plasma clearance of 116.4 mL/min (range 97 to 139 mL/min) indicated nearly complete elimination of ceftazidime by the renal route. Administration of probenecid prior to dosing had no effect on the elimination kinetics of ceftazidime. This suggested that ceftazidime is eliminated by glomerular filtration and is not actively secreted by renal tubular mechanisms.

Indications: For the treatment of patients with infections caused by susceptible strains of the designated organisms in the following diseases:

Lower Respiratory Tract Infections: Pneumonia caused by P. aeruginosa; H. influenzae including ampicillin-resistant

Fortaz (cont'd)

strains; Klebsiella species; Enterobacter species; P. mirabilis; E. coli; Serratia species; S. pneumoniae; and S. aureus including ampicillin-resistant (but not methicillin-resistant) strains.

Urinary Tract Infections: caused by P. aeruginosa; Enterobacter species; Proteus species (indole positive and negative); Klebsiella species, and E. coli.

Due to the nature of the underlying conditions which usually predispose patients to Pseudomonas infections of the lower respiratory and urinary tracts, a good clinical response accompanied by bacterial eradication may not be achieved despite evidence of in vitro sensitivity.

Skin Structure Infections: caused by P. aeruginosa; Klebsiella species; E. coli; P. mirabilis; Enterobacter species; S. aureus, including ampicillin-resistant (but not methicillin-resistant) strains; and S. pyogenes.

Bacteremia/Septicemia: caused by P. aeruginosa; Klebsiella species; E. coli; Serratia species; S. pneumoniae; S. aureus, including ampicillin-resistant (but not methicillin-resistant) strains; and S. epidermidis.

Bone Infections: caused by P. aeruginosa; P. mirabilis; Enterobacter species; and S. aureus, including ampicillin-resistant (but not methicillin-resistant) strains.

Peritonitis: caused by E. coli; Klebsiella species; and Peptostreptococcus species. Patients infected with Bacteroides species have also responded.

Meningitis: caused by H. influenzae and N. meningitidis. Ceftazidime has also been used successfully in a limited number of cases of meningitis due to P. aeruginosa.

Specimens for bacteriologic culture should be obtained prior to therapy in order to identify the causative organisms and to determine their susceptibilities to ceftazidime. Therapy may be instituted before results of susceptibility testing are known. However, modification of the treatment may be required once these results become available.

Contraindications: Patients who have shown hypersensitivity to ceftazidime or the cephalosporin group of antibiotics.

Warnings: Before therapy with ceftazidime is instituted, careful enquiry should be made to determine whether the patient has had previous hypersensitivity reactions to ceftazidime, cephalosporins, penicillins, or other drugs. Ceftazidime should be administered with caution to any patient who has demonstrated some form of allergy, particularly to drugs. It should be given with caution to patients with Type 1 hypersensitivity reactions to penicillin. If an allergic reaction to ceftazidime occurs, treatment should be discontinued and standard agents (e.g. epinephrine, antihistamines, corticosteroids) administered as necessary.

Pseudomembranous colitis has been reported to be associated with treatment with ceftazidime (and other broad-spectrum antibiotics). Therefore, it is important to consider its diagnosis in patients administered ceftazidime who develop diarrhea. Treatment with broad-spectrum antibiotics, including ceftazidime, alters the normal flora of the colon and may permit overgrowth of Clostridia. Studies indicate that a toxin produced by C. difficile is one primary cause of antibiotic-associated colitis. Mild cases of colitis may respond to drug discontinuance alone. Moderate to severe cases should be managed with fluid, electrolyte, and protein supplementation as indicated. When the colitis is not relieved by discontinuance of ceftazidime administration or when it is severe, consideration should be given to the administration of vancomycin or other suitable therapy. Other possible causes of colitis should also be considered.

Precautions: Ceftazidime should be administered with caution to individuals with a history of gastrointestinal disease, particularly colitis.

Patients with impaired renal function (i.e. creatinine clearance of 50 mL/min/1.73 m² or less) should be placed on the special dosage schedule for ceftazidime. (see Dosage). Normal dosages in these individuals are likely to produce excessive serum concentrations of ceftazidime. Elevated levels of ceftazidime in these patients could lead to convulsions.

The concomitant administration of aminoglycosides and some cephalosporins has caused nephrotoxicity. Although transient elevations of BUN and serum creatinine have been observed in clinical studies, there is no evidence that ceftazidime, when administered alone, is significantly nephrotoxic. However, the effect of administering it concomitantly with aminoglycosides is not known. Studies suggest that the concomitant use of potent diuretics, such as furosemide and ethacrynic acid, may increase the risk of renal toxicity with cephalosporins.

Ceftazidime is eliminated via the kidneys, therefore the dosage should be reduced according to the degree of renal impairment. Neurological sequelae have occasionally been reported when the dose has not been reduced appropriately (see Dosage in Impaired Renal Function).

Prolonged treatment may result in the overgrowth of nonsusceptible organisms, including species originally sensitive to the drug. Repeated evaluation of the patient's condition is essential. If superinfection occurs during therapy, appropriate measures should be taken.

Development of resistance during the administration of ceftazidime has been observed for S. aureus, members of the Enterobacteriaceae family, Acinetobacter species, and Pseudomonas species.

Chloramphenicol is antagonistic in vitro with ceftazidime and other cephalosporins. The clinical relevance of this finding is unknown, but if concurrent administration of ceftazidime with chloramphenicol is proposed, the possibility of antagonism should be considered.

Pregnancy: Safety in pregnancy has not been established. The use of ceftazidime in pregnant women requires that the likely benefit from the drug be weighed against the possible risk to the mother and fetus.

Reproduction studies have been performed in mice and rats employing ceftazidime doses of up to 25 times those usually administered to humans. These studies have revealed no evidence of impaired fertility or harm to the fetus caused by ceftazidime. Animal reproduction studies, however, are not always predictive of human response.

Lactation: Ceftazidime is excreted in human milk in low concentrations (3.8 to 5.2 mg/L). The clinical significance of this is unknown, therefore, caution should be exercised when ceftazidime is administered to a nursing mother.

Geriatrics: The elimination of ceftazidime may be reduced due to impairment of renal function.

Drug-laboratory Test Interactions: Ceftazidime may cause a false-positive reaction for glucose in the urine with copper reduction tests (Benedict's or Fehling's solution). As a false-negative result may occur in the ferricynaide test, it is recommended that either glucose oxidase or hexokinase method be used to determine blood plasma glucose levels in patients receiving ceftazidime. Ceftazidime does not interfere in the alkaline picrate assay for creatinine. A positive Coombs' test has been reported during treatment with cephalosporins. This phenomenon can interfere with cross matching of blood.

Adverse Effects: The most common adverse effects have been local reactions following i.v. injection, allergic reactions, and gastrointestinal reactions. Other adverse effects have been encountered less frequently.

Local (2.8% of patients): thrombophlebitis or phlebitis and pain with i.v. administration. Pain after i.m. injection.

Hypersensitivity (2.7% of patients): pruritus, urticaria, allergic exanthema, and fever. There have been rare reports of toxic epidermal necrolysis. Angioderma and anaphylaxis (including bronchospasm and/or hypotension) have been reported very rarely.

Gastrointestinal (<4% of patients): diarrhea, nausea, vomiting, colitis and abdominal pain. Pseudomembranous colitis has been reported (see Warnings). Oral thrush has been reported very rarely.

CNS (<1% of patients): headache, dizziness, hallucinations, and lethargy. There have been reports of neurological sequelae including tremor, myoclonia, convulsions and encephalopathy occurring in patients with renal impairment in whom the dose of ceftazidime has not been appropriately reduced.

Renal (<1% of patients): transient elevations of blood urea, BUN and serum creatinine.

Hepatic (<4% of patients): transient elevations of serum bilirubin, alkaline phosphatase, LDH, AST, ALT and GGT.

Hematopoietic: eosinophilia (3.4%), positive direct Coombs' test (5.1%), and with an incidence of <1%: thrombocytosis, transient leukopenia, neutropenia, agranulocytosis, thrombocytopenia, lymphocytosis and very rarely hemolytic anemia.

Miscellaneous (<1% of patients): paresthesia, blurred vision, bad taste, flushing, candidiasis, and vaginitis.

Overdose: Symptoms and Treatment: Overdosage of cephalosporins can lead to neurological sequelae including encephalopathy, convulsions and coma. Excessive serum levels of ceftazidime can be reduced by hemodialysis or peritoneal dialysis.

Dosage: Ceftazidime may be administered either i.v. or i.m. after reconstitution.

Dosage and route of administration should be determined by severity of infection, susceptibility of the causative organism(s), and condition of the patient. The i.v. route is preferable for patients with septicemia, peritonitis or other severe or life-threatening infections, or for patients who may be poor risks because of lowered resistance resulting from such debilitating conditions as malnutrition, trauma, surgery, diabetes, heart failure, or malignancy, particularly if shock is present or pending.

The usual duration of treatment is 7 to 14 days. For Streptococcal infections, therapy should be continued for at least 10 days.

Adults: 0.5 to 6 g daily administered in equally divided doses every 8 to 12 hours (see Table I).

Table I—Fortaz

Dosage in Adults

Type of Infection	Daily Dose (g)	Frequency and Route
uncomplicated pneumonia or skin structure infection	1.5–3.0	0.5–1.0 g i.m. or i.v. q8h
uncomplicated urinary tract infections	0.5	250 mg i.m. or i.v. q12h
complicated urinary tract infections	1.0–1.5	500 mg i.m. or i.v. q8h or q12h
bone infections	4.0	2 g i.v. q12h
peritonitis or septicemia	6.0	2 g i.v. q8h
meningitis	6.0	2 g i.v. q8h

For the treatment of infections caused by Staphylococcus species, a dosage of 1 or 2 g administered every 8 hours is recommended. For the treatment of infections (except those confined to the urinary tract) caused by Enterobacter species, a dosage of at least 1 g administered every 8 hours is recommended.

Children: (see Table II).

Table II—Fortaz

Dosage in Children

Type of Infection	Age Group* Dosage	Dosage
Infections other than meningitis	1 month-2 months	25-50 mg/kg i.v. q 12h to a maximum of 6 g/day
	2 months-12 years	30-50 mg/kg i.v. q 8h to a maximum of 6 g/day
Meningitis	1 month-12 years	50 mg/kg i.v. q8h to a maximum of 6 g/day

Children: The maximum daily dose in children is 6 g.

Neonates (aged 0 to 28 days): In children aged 1 month or less the recommended dose is 25 to 50 mg/kg given twice daily.

Data indicate that half-life of ceftazidime in neonates increases with decreasing gestational age and can be 3 to 4 times that in adults. An adjustment in dosing interval may be necessary with an increasing degree of prematurity. Additionally, clearance may increase rapidly in the first 2 to 3 weeks of life necessitating a readjustment of dose and/or dosing interval.

Geriatrics: In acutely ill elderly patients with reduced renal clearance of ceftazidime, the daily dosage should not exceed 3 g.

Impaired Hepatic Function: No adjustment in dosage is required for patients with hepatic dysfunction provided renal function is not impaired.

Adults With Impaired Renal Function: Ceftazidime is excreted almost exclusively by glomerular filtration. In patients in whom the glomerular filtration rate (GFR) is less than or equal to 50 mL/min (0.83 mL/s), the dosage must be reduced to compensate for its slower excretion. After an initial loading dose of 1 g, a maintenance dosage schedule should be followed (see Table III).

Table III—Fortaz

Recommended Maintenance Doses in Renal Insufficiency

Creatinine Clearance		Recommended Unit Dose		
mL/min/1.73 m²	mL/s/1.73 m²	Moderate Infections	Severe Infections	Frequency* of Dosing
31–50	0.51–0.83	1 g	1.5 g	q12h
16–30	0.26–0.50	1 g	1.5 g	q24h
6–15	0.10–0.25	500 mg	750 mg	q24h
≤5	≤0.09	500 mg	750 mg	q48h

* If the severity of the infection necessitates an increase in the dosing frequency, serum concentrations of ceftazidime should be used as guidelines.

When only serum creatinine levels are known, the following formulas may be used to estimate creatinine clearance. The serum creatinine must represent a steady state of renal function.

Males:

$$\text{Creatinine clearance (mL/s)} = \frac{\text{Weight (kg)} \times (140-\text{age})}{49 \times \text{serum creatinine } (\mu\text{mol/L})}$$

or

$$\text{Creatinine clearance (mL/min)} = \frac{\text{Weight (kg)} \times (140-\text{age})}{72 \times \text{serum creatinine (mg/dL)}}$$

Females: 0.85×above value

Mean serum half-life of ceftazidime in patients with no kidney function was reduced from a range of 24.0 to 35.4 hours between dialysis sessions to a range of 2.8 to 4.6 hours during hemodialysis. Therefore a loading dose of 1 g is recommended followed by 0.5 to 1.0 g after each hemodialysis period. Serum concentrations of ceftazidime should be carefully monitored and used as a basis to adjust the dosage.

Ceftazidime can also be used in patients undergoing peritoneal dialysis and continuous ambulatory peritoneal dialysis. In such patients, a loading dose of 1 g is suggested, followed by 500 mg every 24 hours. Serum concentrations of ceftazidime should be carefully monitored and used as a basis to adjust the dosage.

I.M.: Ceftazidime may be administered by deep i.m. injection into a large muscle mass such as the upper outer quadrant of the gluteus maximus or vastus lateralis. The maximum dose should be 1 g for a single i.m. injection.

I.V.: Intermittent i.v. administration: The reconstituted solution may be slowly injected into the vein over a period of 3 to 5 minutes or given through the tubing of an administration set. During the infusion of the solution containing ceftazidime, the administration of other solutions should be discontinued temporarily.

Continuous i.v. infusion: Ceftazidime may also be administered over a longer period of time.

Note: If therapy is carried out in combination with an aminoglycoside antibiotic, each should be administered at different sites because of a physical incompatibility. An aminoglycoside should not be mixed with this product in the same container.

Reconstitution: Caution: Ensure adequate venting. Addition of diluent generates a positive pressure.

I.M.: Solutions for reconstitution are sterile water for injection or, if required bacteriostatic water for injection with benzyl alcohol or parabens (not for use in neonates) and 0.5 to 1.0% lignocaine hydrochloride injection. See Table IV.

Table IV—Fortaz

Reconstitution Table for I.M. Use

Vial Size	Diluent to be added to Vial	Approximate Available Volume	Approximate Average Concentration
500 mg	1.5 mL	1.8 mL	280 mg/mL
1 g	3.0 mL	3.6 mL	280 mg/mL

Shake well until dissolved.

I.V.: Solutions for reconstitution are sterile water for injection. See Table V.

Table V—Fortaz

Reconstitution Table for I.V. Use

Vial Size	Diluent to be added to Vial	Approximate Available Volume	Approximate Average Concentration
500 mg	5 mL	5.3 mL	100 mg/mL
1 g	10 mL	10.6 mL	100 mg/mL
2 g	10 mL	11.2 mL	180 mg/mL

Shake well until dissolved. The prepared solution may be further diluted to the desired volume with any of the solutions listed under Solutions for I.V. Infusion.

Direct I.v. Injection: Reconstitute as directed above.

Intermittent i.v. infusion: Reconstitute as directed above for 1 g or 2 g vials.

Continuous i.v. infusion: Vials: Reconstitute 1 g or 2 g vials with 10 mL Sterile Water for Injection. The appropriate quantity of the reconstituted solution may be added to any of the solutions listed under Solutions for I.V. Infusion.

Pharmacy Bulk Vial 6 g: **The availability of the pharmacy bulk vial is restricted to hospitals with a recognized i.v. admixture program.**

This product does not contain any preservatives. The Pharmacy Bulk Vial is intended for multiple dispensing for i.v. use only, employing a single puncture. Reconstitute with 26 mL Sterile Water for Injection. See Table VI.

Table VI—Fortaz

Reconstitution Table

Vial Size	Diluent to be added to Vial	Approximate Available Volume	Approximate Average Concentration
6 g	26 mL	30 mL	200 mg/mL

Shake well until dissolved. Following reconstitution with Sterile Water for Injection, the solution should be dispensed and diluted for use within 8 hours at room temperature (not exceeding 25°C). Any unused reconstituted solution should be discarded after 8 hours. The appropriate quantity of the reconstituted solution may be added to an i.v. bottle containing any of the solutions listed below.

Solutions for I.V. Infusion and Infusion Bottles: 0.9 % sodium chloride injection, M/6 sodium lactate injection, Ringers injection USP, lactated Ringers injection USP, 5% dextrose injection, 5% dextrose and 0.225% sodium chloride injection, 5% dextrose and 0.45% sodium chloride injection, 5% dextrose and 0.9% sodium chloride injection, 10% dextrose injection, 10% invert sugar in water for injection and Normosol-M in 5% dextrose injection.

Stability: Reconstituted solutions should be administered within 12 hours when stored at room temperature (not exceeding 25°C), and within 48 hours when refrigerated, from the time of reconstitution, both when prepared as bolus injections, i.m. or i.v., and as infusion admixtures with the recommended i.v. diluents.

Incompatibility: Ceftazidime should not be added to blood products, protein hydrolysates or amino acids. It should not be mixed together with an aminoglycoside. Ceftazidime is less stable in Sodium Bicarbonate Injection than in other i.v. fluids; therefore it is not recommended as a diluent.

Precipitation has been reported when vancomycin has been added to ceftazidime in solution. Therefore, it would be prudent to flush giving sets and the i.v. lines between administration of these two agents.

Supplied: I.M. or direct i.v. injection: Each vial contains: the equivalent of 500 mg and 1 g ceftazidime. Nonmedicinal ingredients: sodium carbonate. Packs of 10. **I.V. injection or infusion:** Each vial contains: the equivalent of 1 g and 2 g ceftazidime. Packs of 10. Vials contain: the equivalent of 6 g ceftazidime. Packs of 6. Vials contain a mixture of ceftazidime pentahydrate and sodium carbonate. Sodium carbonate at a concentration of 118 mg/g of ceftazidime activity has been admixed to facilitate dissolution. Total sodium content of the mixture is approximately 2.3 mEq/g (54 mg of ceftazidime activity). Gluten- and tartrazine-free.

Ceftazidime pentahydrate is a white to cream-colored powder. Solutions range in color from light yellow to amber, depending upon the diluent and volume used. The pH of freshly reconstituted solutions ranges from 5.0 to 7.5.

Store the dry powder between 15 and 30°C. Protect from light.

FOSAMAX® Ⓟ

MSD

Alendronate Sodium

Bone Metabolism Regulator

Pharmacology: Alendronate is an aminobisphosphonate that acts as a potent, specific inhibitor of osteoclast-mediated bone resorption. Bisphosphonates are synthetic analogs of pyrophosphate that bind to the hydroxyapatite found in bone.

Pharmacokinetics: Absorption: Relative to an i.v. reference dose, the mean oral bioavailability of alendronate in women was 0.7% for doses ranging from 5 to 40 mg when administered after an overnight fast and 2 hours before a standardized breakfast. Oral bioavailability of the 10 mg tablet in men (0.59%) was similar to that in women (0.78%) when administered after an overnight fast and 2 hours before breakfast. See Table I.

A study examining the effect of timing of a meal on the bioavailability of alendronate was performed in 49 postmenopausal women. Bioavailability was decreased (by approximately 40%) when 10 mg alendronate was administered either 0.5 or 1 hour before a standardized breakfast, when compared to dosing 2 hours before eating. In studies of treatment and prevention of osteoporosis, alendronate was effective when administered at least 30 minutes before breakfast.

Bioavailability was negligible whether alendronate was administered with or up to 2 hours after a standardized breakfast. Concomitant administration of alendronate with coffee or orange juice reduced bioavailability by approximately 60%.

Distribution: Preclinical studies (in male rats) show that alendronate transiently distributes to soft tissues following 1 mg/kg i.v. administration but is then rapidly redistributed to bone or excreted in the urine. The mean steady-state volume of distribution, exclusive of bone, is at least 28 L in humans. Concentrations of drug in plasma following therapeutic oral doses are too low (less than 5 ng/mL) for analytical detection. Protein binding in human plasma is approximately 78%.

Metabolism: There is no evidence that alendronate is metabolized in animals or humans.

Excretion: Following a single i.v. dose of ^{14}C alendronate, approximately 50% of the radioactivity was excreted in the urine within 72 hours and little or no radioactivity was recovered in the feces. Following a single 10 mg i.v. dose, the renal clearance of alendronate was 71 mL/min, and systemic clearance did not exceed 200 mL/min. Plasma concentrations fell by more than 95% within 6 hours following i.v. administration. The terminal half-life in humans is estimated to exceed 10 years, probably reflecting release of alendronate from the skeleton. Based on the above, it is estimated that after 10 years of oral treatment with alendronate (10 mg daily) the amount of alendronate released daily from the skeleton is approximately 25% of that absorbed from the gastrointestinal tract.

Special Populations: Children: Alendronate pharmacokinetics have not been investigated in patients <18 years of age.

Gender: Bioavailability and the fraction of an i.v. dose excreted in urine were similar in men and women.

Geriatrics: Bioavailability and disposition (urinary excretion) were similar in elderly (≥65 years of age) and younger patients. No dosage adjustment is necessary (see Dosage).

Race: Pharmacokinetic differences due to race have not been studied.

Renal Insufficiency: Preclinical studies show that, in rats with kidney failure, increasing amounts of drug are present in plasma, kidney, spleen, and tibia. In healthy controls, drug that is not deposited in bone is rapidly excreted in the urine. No evidence of saturation of bone uptake was found after 3 weeks dosing with cumulative i.v. doses of 35 mg/kg in young male rats. Although no clinical information is available, it is likely that, as in animals, elimination of alendronate via the kidney will be reduced in patients with impaired renal function. Therefore, somewhat greater accumulation of alendronate in bone might be expected in patients with impaired renal function.

No dosage adjustment is necessary for patients with mild-to-moderate renal insufficiency (creatinine clearance 0.58 to 1 mL/s [35 to 60 mL/min]). Alendronate is not recommended for patients with more severe renal insufficiency (creatinine clearance <0.58 mL/s [<35 mL/min]) due to lack of experience.

Hepatic Insufficiency: As there is evidence that alendronate is not metabolized or excreted in the bile, no studies were conducted in patients with hepatic insufficiency. No dosage adjustment is necessary.

<u>*Drug Interactions*</u> (also see Precautions, Drug Interactions): I.V. ranitidine was shown to double the bioavailability of oral alendronate. The clinical significance of this increased bioavailability and whether similar increases will occur in patients given oral H_2-antagonists is unknown; no other specific drug interaction studies were performed.

Products containing calcium and other multivalent cations likely will interfere with absorption of alendronate.

Table I—Fosamax

Summary of Pharmacokinetic Parameters in the Normal Population

	Mean	90% Confidence Interval
Absolute bioavailability of 5 mg tablet, taken 2 hours before first meal of the day	0.63% (females)	(0.48, 0.83)
Absolute bioavailability of 10 mg tablet, taken 2 hours before first meal of the day	0.78% (females)	(0.61, 1.04)
	0.59% (males)	(0.43, 0.81)
Absolute bioavailability of 40 mg tablet, taken 2 hours before first meal of the day	0.60% (females)	(0.46, 0.78)
Renal Clearance mL/s (mL/min) (n=6)	1.18 (71)	(1.07, 1.3) (64,78)

Fosamax (cont'd)

Pharmacodynamics: Osteoporosis in Postmenopausal Women: Osteoporosis is characterized by low bone mass that leads to an increased risk of fracture. The diagnosis can be confirmed by the finding of low bone mass, evidence of fracture on x-ray, a history of osteoporotic fracture, or height loss or kyphosis, indicative of vertebral fracture. Osteoporosis occurs in both males and females but is most common among women following the menopause, when bone turnover increases and the rate of bone resorption exceeds that of bone formation. These changes result in progressive bone loss and lead to osteoporosis in a significant proportion of women over age 50. Fractures, usually of the spine, hip, and wrist, are the common consequences. From age 50 to age 90, the risk of hip fracture in white women increases 50-fold and the risk of vertebral fracture 15- to 30-fold. It is estimated that approximately 40% of 50-year-old women will sustain one or more osteoporosis-related fractures of the spine, hip, or wrist during their remaining lifetimes. Hip fractures, in particular, are associated with substantial morbidity, disability, and mortality.

Alendronate is an aminobisphosphonate that binds to bone hydroxyapatite and specifically inhibits the activity of osteoclasts, the bone-resorbing cells. Alendronate reduces bone resorption with no direct effect on bone formation, although the latter process is ultimately reduced because bone resorption and formation are coupled during bone turnover. Alendronate thus reduces the elevated rate of bone turnover observed in postmenopausal women to approximate more closely that in premenopausal women.

Daily oral doses of alendronate (5, 20 and 40 mg for 6 weeks) in postmenopausal women produced biochemical changes indicative of dose-dependent inhibition of bone resorption, including decreases in urinary calcium and urinary markers of bone collagen degradation (such as deoxypyridinoline and cross-linked N-telopeptides of type I collagen). These biochemical changes tended to return toward baseline values as early as 3 weeks following the discontinuation of therapy with alendronate and did not differ from placebo after 7 months.

In long-term (2- or 3-year) osteoporosis treatment studies, alendronate 10 mg/day reduced urinary excretion of markers of bone resorption, including deoxypyridinoline and cross-linked N-telopeptides of type I collagen, by approximately 50 to 60% to reach levels similar to those seen in healthy premenopausal women. Similar decreases were seen in patients in osteoporosis prevention studies who received alendronate 5 mg/day. The decrease in the rate of bone resorption indicated by these markers was evident as early as 1 month and at 3 to 6 months reached a plateau that was maintained for the entire duration of treatment with alendronate. In osteoporosis treatment studies, alendronate 10 mg/day decreased the markers of bone formation, osteocalcin and total serum alkaline phosphatase, by approximately 50% and 25 to 30%, respectively, to reach a plateau after 6 to 12 months. In osteoporosis prevention studies, alendronate 5 mg/day decreased these markers by approximately 40% and 15%, respectively. These data indicate that the rate of bone turnover reached a new steady-state, despite the progressive increase in the total amount of alendronate deposited within bone.

As a result of inhibition of bone resorption, asymptomatic reductions in serum calcium and phosphate concentrations were also observed following treatment with alendronate. In the long-term studies, reductions from baseline in serum calcium (approximately 2%) and phosphate (approximately 4 to 6%) were evident the first month after the initiation of alendronate 10 mg, but no further decreases were observed for the 3-year duration of the studies. Similar reductions were observed with alendronate 5 mg/day. The reduction in serum phosphate may reflect not only the positive bone mineral balance due to alendronate but also a decrease in renal phosphate reabsorption.

Paget's Disease of Bone: Paget's disease of bone is a chronic, focal skeletal disorder characterized by greatly increased and disorderly bone remodeling. Excessive osteoclastic bone resorption is followed by osteoblastic new bone formation, leading to the replacement of the normal bone architecture by disorganized, enlarged, and weakened bone structure.

Clinical manifestations of Paget's disease range from no symptoms to severe morbidity due to bone pain, bone deformity, pathological fractures, and neurological and other complications. Serum alkaline phosphatase, the most frequently used biochemical index of disease activity, provides an objective measure of disease severity and response to therapy.

Alendronate decreases the rate of bone resorption directly, which leads to an indirect decrease in bone formation. In clinical trials, alendronate 40 mg once daily for 6 months produced highly significant decreases in serum alkaline phosphatase as well as in urinary markers of bone collagen degradation. As a result of the inhibition of bone resorption, alendronate induced generally mild, transient, and asymptomatic decreases in serum calcium and phosphate.

Indications: Osteoporosis: For the treatment and prevention of osteoporosis in postmenopausal women. For the treatment of osteoporosis, alendronate increases bone mass and prevents fractures, including those of the hip, wrist, and spine (vertebral compression fractures).

Osteoporosis may be confirmed by the finding of low bone mass (e.g., at least 2.0 standard deviations below the premenopausal mean) or by the presence or history of osteoporotic fracture.

For the prevention of osteoporosis, alendronate may be considered in postmenopausal women who are at risk of developing osteoporosis and for whom the desired clinical outcome is to maintain bone mass and to reduce the risk of future fracture.

Bone loss is particularly rapid in postmenopausal women younger than age 60. Risk factors often associated with the development of postmenopausal osteoporosis include early menopause; moderately low bone mass; thin body build; Caucasian or Asian race; and family history of osteoporosis. The presence of such risk factors may be important when considering the use of alendronate for prevention of osteoporosis.

Paget's Disease of Bone: For the treatment of Paget's disease of bone. Treatment is indicated in patients having serum alkaline phosphatase at least 2 times the upper limit of normal, or those who are symptomatic, or those at risk for future complications from their disease.

Contraindications: Abnormalities of the esophagus which delay esophageal emptying such as stricture or achalasia; inability to stand or sit upright for at least 30 minutes; hypersensitivity to any component of this product; hypocalcemia (see Precautions); renal insufficiency with creatinine clearance <0.58 mL/s [<35 mL/min] (see Dosage).

Warnings: Alendronate, like other bisphosphonates, may cause local irritation of the upper gastrointestinal mucosa.

Esophageal adverse experiences, such as esophagitis, esophageal ulcers and esophageal erosions have been reported in patients receiving treatment with alendronate. In some cases these have been severe and required hospitalization. Physicians should therefore be alert to any signs or symptoms signalling a possible esophageal reaction and patients should be instructed to discontinue alendronate immediately and seek medical attention if they develop dysphagia, odynophagia or retrosternal pain.

The risk of severe esophageal adverse experiences appears to be greater in patients who lie down after taking alendronate and/or who fail to swallow it with a full glass of water, and/or who continue to take alendronate after developing symptoms suggestive of esophageal irritation. Therefore, it is very important that the full dosing instructions are provided to, and understood by, the patient (see Dosage).

Because of possible irritant effects of alendronate on the upper gastrointestinal mucosa and a potential for worsening of the underlying disease, caution should be used when alendronate is given to patients with active upper gastrointestinal problems, such as dysphagia, esophageal diseases, gastritis, duodenitis, or ulcers.

Precautions: To facilitate delivery to the stomach and thus reduce the potential for esophageal irritation patients should be instructed to swallow alendronate with a **full** glass of water and not to lie down for at least 30 minutes **and** until after their first food of the day. Patients should not chew or suck on the tablet because of a potential for oropharyngeal ulceration. Patients should be specifically instructed not to take alendronate at bedtime or before arising for the day. Patients should be informed that failure to follow these instructions may increase their risk of esophageal problems. Patients should be instructed that if they develop symptoms of esophageal disease (such as difficulty or pain upon swallowing, retrosternal pain or new or worsening heartburn) they should stop taking alendronate immediately and consult their physician.

While no increased risk was observed in extensive clinical trials, there have been rare (postmarketing) reports of gastric and duodenal ulcers, some severe and with complications. However, a causal relationship has not been established.

Causes of osteoporosis other than estrogen deficiency and aging should be considered.

Hypocalcemia must be corrected before initiating therapy with alendronate (see Contraindications). Other disturbances of mineral metabolism (such as vitamin D deficiency) should be treated.

Paget's Disease of Bone: Due to the positive effects of alendronate to increase bone mineral, small, asymptomatic decreases in serum calcium and phosphate may occur, especially in patients with Paget's disease, in whom the pretreatment rate of bone turnover may be greatly elevated. Adequate calcium and vitamin D nutrition must be ensured to provide for these enhanced needs.

Geriatrics: In clinical studies, there was no age-related difference in the efficacy or safety profiles of alendronate.

Children: Alendronate has not been studied in patients <18 years of age and should not be given to them.

Pregnancy: Alendronate has not been studied in pregnant women and should not be given to them.

Lactation: Alendronate has not been studied in nursing mothers and should not be given to them.

Men: Safety and effectiveness in male osteoporosis have not been established.

Drug Interactions: If taken at the same time it is likely that calcium supplements, antacids, and other oral medications will interfere with absorption of alendronate. Therefore, patients must wait at least one-half hour after taking alendronate before taking any other oral medication.

I.V. ranitidine was shown to double the bioavailability of oral alendronate. The clinical significance of this increased bioavailability and whether similar increases will occur in patients given oral H_2-antagonists is unknown.

A number of postmenopausal women in the osteoporosis trials received estrogen (intravaginal, transdermal, or oral) while taking alendronate. No adverse experiences attributable to their concomitant use were identified.

However, the effectiveness of the concomitant use of hormone replacement therapy and alendronate in postmenopausal women has not been established. Specific interaction studies were not performed. Alendronate was used in studies of treatment (10 mg/day) and prevention (5 mg/day) of osteoporosis in postmenopausal women with a wide range of commonly prescribed drugs without evidence of clinical adverse reactions.

In clinical studies, the incidence of upper gastrointestinal adverse events was increased in patients receiving therapy with dosages of alendronate greater than 10 mg/day and ASA-containing compounds.

Alendronate may be administered to patients taking NSAIDs. In a 3-year, controlled, clinical study (n=2 027) during which a majority of patients received concomitant NSAIDs, the incidence of upper gastrointestinal adverse events was similar in patients taking alendronate 5 or 10 mg compared to those taking placebo. However, since NSAID use is associated with gastrointestinal irritation, caution should be used during concomitant use with alendronate.

Animal studies have demonstrated that alendronate is highly concentrated in bone and is retained only minimally in soft tissue. No metabolites have been detected. Although alendronate is bound approximately 78% to plasma protein in humans, its plasma concentration is so low after oral dosing that only a small fraction of plasma-binding sites is occupied, resulting in a minimal potential for interference with the binding of other drugs. Alendronate is not excreted through the acidic or basic transport systems of the kidney in rats, and thus it is not anticipated to interfere with the excretion of other drugs by those systems in humans. In summary, alendronate is not expected to interact with other drugs based on effects on protein binding, renal excretion, or metabolism of other drugs.

Adverse Effects: Clinical Studies: In clinical studies, alendronate was generally well tolerated. Side effects, which usually were mild, generally did not require discontinuation of therapy.

Alendronate has been evaluated for safety in clinical studies in more than 3 800 postmenopausal women.

Treatment of Osteoporosis in Postmenopausal Women: In 2 large, 3-year, placebo-controlled, double-blind, multicenter studies (U.S. and Multinational) of virtually identical design, with a total of 994 postmenopausal women, the overall safety profiles of alendronate 10 mg/day and placebo were similar. Discontinuation of therapy due to any clinical adverse experience occurred in 4.1% of 196 patients treated with alendronate 10 mg/day and 6.0% of 397 patients treated with placebo.

Adverse experiences reported by the investigators as possibly, probably, or definitely drug-related in $\geq 1\%$ of patients treated with either alendronate 10 mg/day or placebo are presented in Table II.

Table II—Fosamax

Drug-Related* Adverse Experiences Reported in ≥1% of Patients Treated for Osteoporosis

	Fosamax 10 mg/day % (n=196)	Placebo % (n=397)
Gastrointestinal		
Abdominal Pain	6.6	4.8
Nausea	3.6	4.0
Dyspepsia	3.6	3.5
Constipation	3.1	1.8
Diarrhea	3.1	1.8
Flatulence	2.6	0.5
Acid Regurgitation	2.0	4.3
Esophageal Ulcer	1.5	0.0
Vomiting	1.0	1.5
Dysphagia	1.0	0.0
Abdominal Distention	1.0	0.8
Gastritis	0.5	1.3
Musculoskeletal		
Musculoskeletal Pain (bone, muscle or joint)	4.1	2.5
Muscle Cramp	0.0	1.0
Nervous System/Psychiatric		
Headache	2.6	1.5
Dizziness	0.0	1.0
Special Senses		
Taste Perversion	0.5	1.0

*Considered possibly, probably or definitely drug-related as assessed by the investigators.

Rarely, rash and erythema have occurred.

One patient treated with alendronate (10 mg/day), who had a history of peptic ulcer disease and gastrectomy and who was taking concomitant ASA developed an anastomotic ulcer with mild hemorrhage, which was considered drug-related. ASA and alendronate were discontinued and the patient recovered.

In the Vertebral Fracture Study of the Fracture Intervention Trial, discontinuation of therapy due to any clinical adverse experience occurred in 7.6% of 1 022 patients treated with alendronate 5 mg/day for 2 years and 10 mg/day for the third year and 9.4% of 1 005 patients treated with placebo. Similarly, discontinuations due to upper gastrointestinal adverse experiences were comparable: alendronate, 2.6%; placebo, 2.6%. The overall adverse experience profile was similar to that seen in other studies with alendronate 5 or 10 mg/day.

Prevention of Osteoporosis in Postmenopausal Women: The safety of alendronate in postmenopausal women 40 to 60 years of age has been evaluated in 3 double-blind, placebo-controlled studies involving over 1 400 patients randomized to receive alendronate for either 2 or 3 years. In these studies the overall safety profiles of alendronate 5 mg/day and placebo were similar. Discontinuation of therapy due to any clinical adverse experience occurred in 7.5% of 642 patients treated with alendronate 5 mg/day and 5.7% of 648 patients treated with placebo. Adverse experiences reported by the investigators as possibly, probably or definitely drug related in ≥1% of patients treated with either alendronate 5 mg/day or placebo are presented in Table III.

Table III—Fosamax

Drug-Related* Adverse Experiences Reported in ≥1% of patients—Prevention of Osteoporosis

	Fosamax 5 mg/day % (n=642)	Placebo % (n=648)
Gastrointestinal		
Abdominal Pain	1.7	3.4
Acid Regurgitation	1.4	2.5
Diarrhea	1.1	1.7
Dyspepsia	1.9	1.7
Nausea	1.4	1.4

*Considered possibly, probably, or definitely drug-related as assessed by the investigators.

Paget's Disease of Bone: In clinical studies (Paget's disease and osteoporosis), adverse experiences reported in 175 patients taking alendronate 40 mg/day for 3 to 12 months were similar to those in postmenopausal women treated with alendronate 10 mg/day. However, there was an apparent increased incidence of upper gastrointestinal adverse experiences in patients taking alendronate 40 mg/day (17.7% alendronate vs 10.2% placebo). Isolated cases of esophagitis and gastritis resulted in discontinuation of treatment.

Additionally, musculoskeletal pain (bone, muscle or joint), which has been described in patients with Paget's disease treated with other bisphosphonates, was reported by the investigators as possibly, probably, or definitely drug-related in approximately 6% of patients treated with alendronate 40 mg/day vs approximately 1% of patients treated with placebo, but rarely resulted in discontinuation of therapy. Discontinuation of therapy due to any clinical adverse experience occurred in 6.4% of patients with Paget's disease treated with alendronate 40 mg/day and 2.4% of patients treated with placebo.

Postmarketing Experience: The following adverse reactions have been reported in postmarketing use:

Body as a Whole: hypersensitivity reactions including urticaria and rarely angioedema.

Gastrointestinal: esophagitis, esophageal erosions, esophageal ulcers, and oropharyngeal ulceration. Some of these have been serious and required hospitalization. Rarely, gastric or duodenal ulcers, some severe and with complications, although a causal relationship has not been established (see Warnings, Precautions and Dosage).

Laboratory Tests: In double-blind, multicenter, controlled studies, asymptomatic, mild, and transient decreases in serum calcium and phosphate were observed in approximately 18 and 10%, respectively, of patients taking alendronate vs approximately 12 and 3% of those taking placebo. However, the incidences of decreases in serum calcium to <8 mg/dL (2 mM) and serum phosphate to ≤2 mg P/dL (0.65 mM) were similar in both treatment groups.

In a small, open label study, at higher doses (80 mg/day) some patients had elevated transaminases. However, this was not observed at 40 mg/day. No clinically significant toxicity was associated with these laboratory abnormalities.

Rare cases of leukemia have been reported following therapy with other bisphosphonates. Any causal relationship to either the treatment or to the patients' underlying disease has not been established.

Overdose: Symptoms and Treatment: No specific information is available on the treatment of overdosage with alendronate. Hypocalcemia, hypophosphatemia, and upper gastrointestinal adverse events, such as upset stomach, heartburn, esophagitis, gastritis, or ulcer, may result from oral overdosage. Milk or antacids should be given to bind alendronate. Due to the risk of esophageal irritation, vomiting should not be induced and the patient should remain fully upright.

Dialysis would not be beneficial.

Dosage: Alendronate must be taken at least one-half hour before the first food, beverage, or medication of the day with plain water only. Other beverages (including mineral water), food, and some medications are known to reduce the absorption of alendronate (see Precautions, Drug Interactions). Waiting less than 30 minutes will lessen the effect of alendronate by decreasing its absorption into the body.

To facilitate delivery to the stomach and thus reduce the potential for esophageal irritation, alendronate should only be swallowed upon arising for the day with a **full** glass of water (200 to 250 mL) and patients should not lie down for at least 30 minutes **and** until after their first food of the day. Alendronate should not be taken at bedtime or before arising for the day. Failure to follow these instructions may increase the risk of esophageal adverse experiences (see Warnings).

All patients must receive supplemental calcium and vitamin D, if dietary intake is inadequate.

Although no specific studies have been conducted on the effects of switching patients on another therapy for osteoporosis or Paget's disease to alendronate, there are no known or theoretical safety concerns related to alendronate in patients who previously received any other antiosteoporotic or antipagetic therapy.

Treatment with alendronate for longer than 4 years has not been studied; extension studies are ongoing.

No dosage adjustment is necessary for the elderly or for patients with mild-to-moderate renal insufficiency (creatinine clearance 0.58 to 1 mL/s [35 to 60 mL/min]). Alendronate is not recommended for patients with more severe renal insufficiency (creatinine clearance <0.58 mL/s [<35 mL/min]) due to lack of experience.

Treatment of Osteoporosis in Postmenopausal Women: The recommended dosage is 10 mg once a day.

Prevention of Osteoporosis in Postmenopausal Women: The recommended dosage is 5 mg once a day.

Paget's Disease of Bone: The recommended treatment regimen is 40 mg once a day for 6 months.

Retreatment of Paget's Disease: In clinical studies in which patients were followed every 6 months, relapses during the 12 months following therapy occurred in 9% (3 out of 32) of patients who responded to treatment with alendronate. Specific retreatment data are not available, although responses to alendronate were similar in patients who had received prior bisphosphonate therapy and those who had not. Retreatment with alendronate may be considered, following a 6-month post-treatment evaluation period, in patients who have relapsed based on increases in serum alkaline phosphatase (which should be measured periodically). Retreatment may also be considered in those who failed to normalize their serum alkaline phosphatase.

Information to be Provided to the Patient: Patients must be instructed that the expected benefits of alendronate may only be obtained when each tablet is swallowed with plain water the first thing upon arising for the day at least 30 minutes before the first food, beverage or medication of the day. Even dosing with orange juice or coffee has been shown to markedly reduce the absorption of alendronate.

To facilitate delivery to the stomach and thus reduce the potential for esophageal irritation patients should be instructed to swallow alendronate with a **full** glass of water and not to lie down for at least 30 minutes **and** until after their first food of the day. Patients should not chew or suck on the tablet because of a potential for oropharyngeal ulceration. Patients should be specifically instructed not to take alendronate at bedtime or before arising for the day. Patients should be informed that failure to follow these instructions may increase their risk of esophageal problems. Patients should be instructed that if they develop symptoms of esophageal disease (such as difficulty or pain upon swallowing, retrosternal pain or new or worsening heartburn) they should stop taking alendronate immediately and consult their physician.

Information for the Patient: See Blue Section—Information for the Patient "Fosamax"

Supplied: 5 mg: Each white, round, uncoated tablet, with an outline of a bone image on one side and MRK 925 on the other, contains: alendronate 5 mg as alendronate sodium. Nonmedicinal ingredients: anhydrous lactose, croscarmellose sodium, magnesium stearate and microcrystalline cellulose. Blister packages of 30.

10 mg: Each white, round, uncoated tablet, with an embossed bone image on each side and FOSAMAX engraved on one side and MRK 936 on the other, contains: alendronate 10 mg as alendronate sodium. Nonmedicinal ingredients: anhydrous lactose, croscarmellose sodium, magnesium stearate and microcrystalline cellulose. Blister packages of 30.

40 mg: Each white, triangle-shaped, uncoated tablet, with FOSAMAX on one side and MRK 212 on the other, contains: alendronate 40 mg as alendronate sodium. Nonmedicinal ingredients: anhydrous lactose, croscarmellose sodium, magnesium stearate and microcrystalline cellulose. Blister packages of 30.

Store at room temperature (15 to 30°C).

(Shown in Product Recognition Section)

Reviewed 1999

FOSINOPRIL

General Monograph, CPhA

see ACE INHIBITORS

FRAGMIN®

Pharmacia & Upjohn

Dalteparin Sodium

Anticoagulant—Antithrombotic

Pharmacology: Dalteparin is an antithrombotic agent. Dalteparin sodium (low molecular weight heparin sodium) has an average molecular weight of 5 000.

Dalteparin is produced through controlled nitrous acid depolymerization of sodium heparin from porcine intestinal mucosa. It is composed of strongly acidic sulfated polysaccharide chains with an average molecular weight of 5 000 and about 90% of the material within the range 2 000 to 9 000. Dalteparin is composed of molecules with and without a specially characterized pentasaccharide, the antithrombin binding

Fragmin (cont'd)

site, that is essential for high affinity binding to the plasma protein antithrombin (ATIII).

Dalteparin acts antithrombotically mainly by accelerating the rate of the neutralization of certain activated coagulation factors by ATIII but other mechanisms may also be involved. Dalteparin potentiates preferentially the inhibition of coagulation factor Xa and only slightly affects other hemostatic mechanisms such as clotting time and the antithrombotic effect of dalteparin is well correlated to the inhibition of factor Xa.

Heparin and dalteparin dosages cannot be measured directly in the blood stream. Rather their effect on clotting mechanisms is a function of the dosage. Heparin dosage is monitored by both prolongation of APTT, and by anti-Xa activity. For dalteparin however, only extremely high doses lead to noticeable increases in the APTT, therefore measurement of APTT can be used only as an indicator of overdosage. In the case of dalteparin, anti-Xa activity of plasma is used both as an estimate of clotting activity, and as a basis to determine dosage. Dalteparin potency is described in international anti-Xa units (IU).

The specific activity of dalteparin on factor Xa (by measurement of anti-factor Xa IU/mg) is 130, and its specific activity on factor IIa (by measurement of anti-factor IIa IU/mg) is 58. The ratio of anti-Xa/anti-IIa activity for dalteparin is 2.2 (for unfractionated heparin the anti-Xa/anti-IIa is equal to 1). The antithrombotic activity is comparable to heparin while the bleeding effect is reduced.

The % inhibition of thrombin generation by dalteparin compared with unfractionated heparin, is 38% in platelet poor plasma and 73% in platelet rich plasma. The % of antithrombotic activity of dalteparin compared with unfractionated heparin is 47%.

Dalteparin has a smaller effect on platelet function and platelet adhesion than heparin, and thus has only a small effect on primary hemostasis. Heparin treatment depletes the pool of platelet factor 4, while dalteparin has much less of an effect.

Heparin administration releases lipoprotein lipase from tissue sites into the circulation, depleting the pool of these enzymes, which leads to increased plasma triglyceride levels and altered lipid metabolism. Dalteparin has been shown to have a substantially reduced effect on lipid metabolism.

Some studies have shown that dalteparin has less of an effect than heparin on platelet function and adhesion and less disturbance on primary hemostasis. Also, at low doses, dalteparin has been found to depress ATIII levels to a lesser extent than does heparin.

Pharmacokinetics: Dalteparin has a much longer half-life than standard heparin. The half-life after i.v. injection is 2 hours and after s.c. injection, 3 to 4 hours. The bioavailability after s.c. injection is approximately 90% and the pharmacokinetics are non-dose dependent. The plasma concentration of dalteparin following s.c. administration is easily predicted since there is a direct relationship between the administered dose and the anti-Xa activity in plasma (measured as area under the activity curve). The volume of distribution is found to be the plasma volume, approximately 3 L, and the AUCs show good dose dependency. Because of the high bioavailability of dalteparin administered s.c., other pharmacokinetic parameters are similar, regardless of route of administration. Depending on the level of anticoagulation required, the therapeutic plasma level of dalteparin used has been 0.2 to 1 anti-Xa units/mL.

Animal studies using radioactively labelled drug have shown that the distribution of dalteparin is similar, whether the dose is administered i.v. or s.c. After 4 hours about 20% is seen in the urine, with the major organs for the remainder being the liver, gastrointestinal tract and kidney. After 72 hours, 70% of a radioactive dalteparin dose has been excreted. Less dalteparin is found in the liver than standard heparin; the kidneys are the major site of dalteparin metabolism. Dalteparin, in contrast to heparin, is not cleared by a saturable mechanism; low doses are expressed in plasma and increasing the dose does not modify its clearance.

Indications: Thromboprophylaxis in conjunction with surgery.

Treatment of acute deep venous thrombosis.

Unstable coronary artery disease (UCAD), i.e., unstable angina and non-Q-wave myocardial infarction.

Prevention of clotting in the extracorporeal system during hemodialysis and hemofiltration in connection with acute renal failure or chronic renal insufficiency.

Contraindications: Dalteparin should not be administered i.m.

Hypersensitivity to dalteparin or other low molecular weight heparins and/or heparins e.g., history of confirmed or suspected immunologically mediated heparin induced thrombocytopenia (delayed onset severe thrombocytopenia); acute gastroduodenal ulcer and cerebral hemorrhage; septic endocarditis (endocarditis lenta, subacute endocarditis); injuries to and operations on the central nervous system, eyes and ears; uncontrollable active bleeding; major blood clotting disorders; severe untreated hypertension; diabetic or hemorrhagic retinopathy; other diseases involving an increased risk of hemorrhage; for the treatment of acute DVT and UCAD where repeated high dosages of dalteparin are required, spinal/epidural anesthesia is contraindicated due to an increased risk of bleeding.

Warnings: Dalteparin should be used with care in patients with hepatic insufficiency, renal insufficiency or a history of gastrointestinal ulceration.

Determination of anti-factor Xa levels in plasma is the only method available for monitoring dalteparin activity. Routine clotting assays are unsuitable for monitoring its anticoagulant activity. Only at very high plasma dalteparin levels is APTT prolongation observed.

Thromboprophylaxis in Conjunction with Surgery Only: There have been cases of intra-spinal hematomas with the concurrent use of low molecular weight heparins and spinal/epidural anesthesia resulting in long-term or permanent paralysis. The risk of these events may be higher with the use of postoperative indwelling epidural catheters or by the concomitant use of drugs affecting hemostasis: nonsteroidal anti-inflammatory drugs (NSAIDs), platelet inhibitors, or other drugs and diseases affecting coagulation. The risk also appears to be increased by traumatic or repeated epidural or spinal procedure. Dalteparin should only be used concurrently with spinal/epidural anesthesia when the therapeutic benefits to the patients outweigh the possible risks. Careful vigilance for neurological signs is recommended with rapid diagnosis and treatment, if signs occur (see also Adverse Effects).

When a higher dose (5 000 IU s.c.) of dalteparin is administered for thromboprophylaxis in conjunction with surgery, no spinal/epidural invasion should be performed for at least 12 hours following the last dose of dalteparin and the next dose should be held until at least 12 hours after the anesthetic procedure. Alternatively, when a lower dose (2 500 IU s.c.) of dalteparin is administered, the dose can be initiated 1 to 2 hours prior to surgery. Dalteparin injection should be given after spinal/epidural anesthesia and only if the anesthesiologist considers the spinal/epidural puncture as uncomplicated. If a second dose is required on the same day (for general surgery associated with other risk factors and elective hip surgery), it should be administered 8 to 12 hours after the surgery. Indwelling catheters should not be removed or manipulated for at least 10 to 12 hours following the last dose of dalteparin.

Dalteparin dosage should be carefully monitored in patients with severely impaired renal function. The main route of elimination is via the kidney. In clinical trials with patients with impaired renal function, the $T_{1/2}$ for anti-Xa activity was 6.3 to 7 hours, much longer than for healthy volunteers.

Except under special circumstances, dalteparin should not be used when abortion is imminent or threatened. It may be used in such cases only when, in the opinion of the physician, the increased risk of bleeding is outweighed by the risk of thrombosis and thromboembolism.

Pregnancy and *Lactation:* Clinical experience of use in pregnant women is limited. No increased incidence of fetal damage has been detected in animal experiments.

The 25 000 IU/mL multidose vial containing benzyl alcohol is not recommended to be used during pregnancy. Benzyl alcohol may cross the placenta.

No information is available as to whether dalteparin passes into breast milk. Mothers receiving dalteparin should avoid breast-feeding.

Children: To date there are no trials in children to support the use of dalteparin. The benefits of treatment should, therefore, be weighed against the risks.

Use in Knee Surgery: The risk of bleeding in knee surgery patients receiving low molecular weight heparins may be greater than in other orthopedic surgical procedures. It should be noted that hemarthrosis is a serious complication of knee surgery. The frequency of bleeding events observed with dalteparin in orthopedic surgery patients is derived from clinical trials in hip replacement surgery patients. The physician should weigh the potential risks with the potential benefits to the patient in determining whether to administer a low molecular weight heparin in this patient population.

Use in Unstable Coronary Artery Disease: When thrombolytic treatment is considered appropriate in patients with unstable angina and non-Q-wave myocardial infarction, concomitant use of an anticoagulant such as dalteparin may increase the risk of bleeding.

Precautions: Dalteparin cannot be used interchangeably (unit for unit) with unfractionated heparin (UFH) or other low molecular weight heparins (LMWHs) as they differ in their manufacturing process, molecular weight distribution, anti-Xa and anti-IIa activities, units and dosages. Special attention and compliance with instructions for use of each specific product is required during any change in treatment.

Biochemical Monitoring: Dalteparin has only a moderate prolonging effect on clotting time assays such as APTT or thrombin time. For laboratory monitoring of effect, anti-Xa methods are recommended. Prolongation of APTT during hemodialysis and treatment of acute deep venous thrombosis should only be used as a criterion of overdose. Dose increases aimed at prolonging APTT could cause overdosing and bleeding.

When dalteparin is administered s.c., the individual patient's antifactor Xa activity level will not remain within the range that would be expected with unfractionated heparin by continuous i.v. infusion throughout the entire dosing interval. The peak plasma antifactor Xa level occurs approximately 4 hours after s.c. administration (see Table I). For the twice daily dosing regimen (100 IU/kg/12 hours), the steady state level is attained after 2 to 4 injections (24 to 48 hours). Dalteparin should be administered as directed in the Dosage section.

Table I—Fragmin

Peak Plasma Anti-Xa Levels

Dosage	Antifactor Xa levels (IU/mL) at peak 3-4 hrs post s.c. injections* Mean ± SD
2 500 IU	0.20±0.08
5 000 IU	0.49±0.13
100 IU/kg	0.61±0.17
120 IU/kg	0.91±0.32
200 IU/kg	1.2±0.43

*For 2 500 IU and 5 000 IU, peak levels were obtained from populations of healthy volunteers; for doses of 100 IU/kg, 120 IU/kg and 200 IU/kg, peak levels were obtained from patient populations treated for acute DVT.

Patient Monitoring: As with all antithrombotic agents, there is a risk of systemic bleeding with dalteparin administration.

Care should be taken with dalteparin use in high dose treatment of newly operated patients. After treatment is initiated patients should be carefully monitored for bleeding complications. This may be done by regular physical examination of the patients, close observation of the surgical drain and periodic measurements of hemoglobin, and antifactor Xa determinations. Bleeding complications may be considered major if hemoglobin is decreased by 2 g/dL or if a transfusion of 2 or more units has been required.

With normal prophylactic doses, dalteparin does not modify global clotting tests of activated partial thromboplastin time (APTT), prothrombin time (PT) and thrombin clotting time (TT). Therefore, treatment can not be monitored with these tests.

Platelets: Platelet counts should be determined prior to the start of treatment with dalteparin and, subsequently, twice weekly for the duration of treatment.

Caution is recommended when administering dalteparin to patients with congenital or drug induced thrombocytopenia, or platelet defects.

In patients who have a history of heparin-induced thrombocytopenia (HIT), the risk of this occurrence for the individual patient in response to the low molecular weight heparins cannot be estimated, but would be expected to be increased relative to the general populations (see also Contraindications).

Prior to instituting dalteparin, an in vitro test for antiplatelet antibody in presence of dalteparin for instance, a platelet aggregation test should be performed. There are limitations to this test. It may, nevertheless, be used as a guide. A positive result contraindicates dalteparin. With a negative result, treatment with dalteparin may be instituted, but patients must be monitored with particular care to include platelet counts at least once daily.

During dalteparin administration, special caution is necessary in rapidly developing thrombocytopenia and severe thrombocytopenia ($<100\ 000/\mu L$). A positive or unknown result of in vitro tests for antiplatelet antibody in the presence of dalteparin or other low molecular weight heparins and/or heparins would contraindicate dalteparin.

Hemodialysis: Patients undergoing chronic hemodialysis with dalteparin normally require only a few dose adjustments and therefore only occasional monitoring of anti-Xa levels is required. Patients undergoing acute hemodialysis have a narrower therapeutic interval and should be subjected to comprehensive monitoring of anti-Xa levels.

Selection of General Surgery Patients: Risk factors associated with postoperative venous thromboembolism following general surgery include history of venous thromboembolism, varicose veins, obesity, heart failure, malignancy, previous long bone fracture of a lower limb, bed rest for more than 5 days prior to surgery, predicted duration of surgery of more than 30 minutes, age 60 years or above.

Cardiovascular: See also Warnings and Contraindications.

Geriatrics: Age is highly correlated to thrombosis risk and as the proportion of patients aged over 65 is high in the dalteparin documentation, there is a large body of clinical experience in the treatment of elderly patients. No dose reduction or increased bleeding has been noted in the clinical studies with dalteparin with respect to elderly patients.

Drug Interactions: As dalteparin can cause a rise in liver transaminases, this should be considered when liver function tests are assessed.

Concomitant medication with effect on hemostasis, such as ASA, NSAIDs, vitamin-K antagonists and dextran may enhance the anticoagulant effect of dalteparin. However, unless specifically contraindicated, patients with UCAD (unstable angina and non-Q-wave myocardial infarction) should receive ASA.

For information concerning the antidote in cases of excess, see Overdose: Symptoms and Treatment.

Adverse Effects: Bleeding: Injection site hematomas are a common side effect with heparin. These occurred less often with dalteparin in the clinical trials, and are of minor clinical importance but are still the most common side effect of the drug, occurring at a frequency of about 5% with lower (prophylaxis) doses to less than 10% with higher (treatment) doses.

Other bleeding side effects are rare. In the clinical trials with dalteparin, bleeding occurred at low frequency which did not differ from that for heparin overall. Dalteparin patients with altered APTT values are at bleeding risk, indicating a plasma anti-Xa activity of about 2 U/mL. Other risk factors associated with bleeding for heparin are: a serious concurrent illness, chronic heavy consumption of alcohol, use of platelet inhibiting drugs, renal failure, age and female sex. These risk factors should be expected to apply for dalteparin, too. Bleeding may range from minor local hematomas to major hemorrhagic events. Often the first sign of bleeding may be epistaxis, hematuria, or melena. Bleeding may be from any site and may be difficult to detect, i.e., retroperitoneal bleeds. Bleeding may also occur from surgical sites. Petechiae or easy bruising may precede frank hemorrhage.

Skeletal: A similar weak osteopenic effect was observed for dalteparin and heparin in a 6-month dog study. Since this symptom has been reported as an adverse effect after long-term treatment with heparin in high doses, the risk of osteoporosis cannot be ruled out. Caution should be used for patients on long-term therapy.

Liver: Transient slight to moderate elevation of liver transaminases (AST, ALT) has been observed for dalteparin. This observation has not been correlated to any long-term effect on liver function.

Hypersensitivity: Mild, nonimmunological thrombocytopenia is common but usually reversible during treatment. Skin necrosis and allergic reactions are rare. Dalteparin therapy should be discontinued in patients showing local or systemic allergic responses. Few cases of anaphylactoid reactions have been observed, as well as a few cases of the severe immunologically mediated thrombocytopenia associated with arterial and/or venous thrombosis or thromboembolism.

Lipid Metabolism: Increases in lipolytic activity and lipoprotein lipase can be expected during dalteparin therapy, although lipid metabolism is disturbed to a much greater extent by heparin than by dalteparin.

Overdose: Symptoms and Treatment: Hemorrhage is the major clinical sign of overdosage. In case of accidental overdosage, the platelet count and other coagulation parameters should be measured. Minor bleeding rarely requires specific therapy, and reducing or delaying subsequent doses of dalteparin is usually sufficient. Dalteparin should be discontinued in cases of major bleeding. Protamine sulfate may be administered in more serious cases with special caution.

The anticoagulant effect induced by dalteparin is inhibited by protamine. Prolongation of the coagulation time can be neutralized by protamine. Anti-Xa is neutralized by protamine to about 25 to 50%.

One mg protamine inhibits the effect of 100 anti-Xa international units of dalteparin sodium. Please refer to the product monograph for protamine sulfate injection for dosage and directions.

One mg protamine inhibits the effect of 100 anti-Xa international units of dalteparin.

Dosage: Dalteparin may be given by s.c. injection or by intermittent or continuous i.v. infusion, depending upon the circumstances. Because of the long half-life, high bioavailability, low incidence of side effects, and ease of administration of dalteparin, s.c. administration may be the route of choice.

Thromboprophylaxis in Conjunction with Surgery: The dose required for adequate prophylaxis without increased bleeding varies depending on the risk factors involved.

General Surgery with Associated Risk of Thromboembolic Complications: 2 500 IU administered s.c. 1 to 2 hours before the operation, and thereafter 2 500 IU s.c. each morning until the patient is mobilized, in general 5 to 7 days or longer.

General Surgery Associated with Other Risk Factors and Elective Hip Surgery: 5 000 IU is given s.c. the evening before the operation and 5 000 IU s.c. the following evenings. Treatment is continued until the patient is mobilized, in general 5 to 7 days or longer. As an alternative 2 500 IU is given s.c. 1 to 2 hours before operation and 2 500 IU s.c. 8 to 12 hours later. On the following days 5 000 IU is given s.c. each morning.

Treatment of Acute Deep Venous Thrombosis: The following dosage is recommended: 200 IU/kg body weight given s.c. once daily. The expected plasma anti-Xa levels during s.c. treatment would be <0.3 IU anti-Xa/mL before injection and <1.7 IU anti-Xa/mL 3 to 4 hours after injection. In order to individualize the dose, a functional anti-Xa assay should be performed 3 to 4 hours post-injection. The single daily dose should not exceed 18 000 IU.

For patients with increased risk of bleeding, a dose of 100 IU/kg body weight given s.c. twice daily or 100 IU/kg body weight administered over a period of 12 hours as continuous i.v. infusion, can be used. The expected plasma anti-Xa levels during s.c. treatment would be >0.1 IU anti-Xa/mL before injection and <1.0 IU anti-Xa/mL 3 to 4 hours after injection.

Normally concomitant treatment with vitamin-K antagonists is started immediately. Treatment with dalteparin should be continued until the levels of the prothrombin complex factors (FII, FVII, FIX, FX) have decreased to a therapeutic level, in general for approximately 5 days.

Unstable Coronary Artery Disease (Unstable Angina and Non-Q-Wave Myocardial Infarction): 120 IU/kg body weight given s.c. twice daily with a maximum dose of 10 000 IU/12 hours. The expected plasma anti-Xa levels during s.c. treatment would be >0.1 IU anti-Xa/mL before injection and <1.6 IU anti-Xa/mL 3 to 4 hours after injection. These levels were obtained from another patient population. Treatment should be continued for up to 6 days. Concomitant therapy with ASA is recommended.

Anticoagulation for Hemodialysis and Hemofiltration: Chronic Renal Failure, Patients with No Known Bleeding Risk: Hemodialysis and hemofiltration for a maximum of 4 hours. Dose as below or only i.v. bolus injection of 5 000 IU. Hemodialysis and hemofiltration for more than 4 hours: i.v. bolus injection of 30 to 40 IU/kg body weight followed by i.v. infusion of 10 to 15 IU/kg body weight per hour. This dose normally produces plasma levels lying within the range of 0.5 to 1.0 IU anti-Xa/mL.

Acute Renal Failure, Patients with High Bleeding Risk: I.V. bolus injection of 5 to 10 IU/kg body weight, followed by i.v. infusion of 4 to 5 IU/kg body weight per hour. Plasma level should lie within the range of 0.2 to 0.4 IU anti-Xa/mL.

Dilution: Dalteparin solution for injection may be mixed with isotonic sodium chloride and isotonic glucose infusion solutions in glass infusion bottles and plastic containers. Post-dilution concentration: 20 IU/mL. See Table II.

As with all parenteral drug products, i.v. admixtures should be inspected visually for clarity, particulate matter, precipitation, discoloration and leakage prior to administration, whenever solution and container permit.

Table II—Fragmin

Dilution

	1 mL 2 500 IU	1 mL 10 000 IU
Isotonic NaCl (9 mg/mL)	125 mL	500 mL
Isotonic Glucose (50 mg/mL)	125 mL	500 mL

The infusion rate is 10 mL/hour. The solution should be used within 24 hours.

Information for the Patient: See Blue Section—Information for the Patient "Fragmin".

Supplied: Potency is described in International anti-Xa units (IU). One unit (anti-Xa) of dalteparin sodium, average molecular weight 5 000, corresponds to the activity of one unit of the 1st International Standard for Low Molecular Weight Heparin with respect to inhibition of coagulation Factor Xa in plasma utilizing the chromogenic peptide substrate S-2765 (N-α-Benzyloxycarbonyl-D-arginyl-glycyl-arginine-pNA·2HCl).

Ampuls: 2 500 IU/mL: Each mL of solution for injection contains: dalteparin sodium 2 500 IU (anti-Xa). Nonmedicinal ingredients: hydrochloric acid, sodium chloride, sodium hydroxide and water for injection. Packages of 10×4 mL ampuls.

10 000 IU/mL: Each mL of solution for injection contains: dalteparin sodium 10 000 IU (anti-Xa). Nonmedicinal ingredients: hydrochloric acid, sodium chloride, sodium hydroxide and water for injection. Packages of 10×1 mL ampuls.

Prefilled Syringes: 2 500 IU: Each single dose syringe contains: dalteparin sodium 2 500 IU (anti-Xa). Nonmedicinal ingredients: hydrochloric acid, sodium chloride, sodium hydroxide and water for injection. Prefilled syringes of 0.2 mL, packages of 10.

5 000 IU: Each single dose syringe contains: dalteparin sodium 5 000 IU (anti-Xa). Nonmedicinal ingredients: hydrochloric acid, sodium chloride, sodium hydroxide and water for injection. Prefilled syringes of 0.2 mL, packages of 10.

Vials: Each mL of solution for injection contains: dalteparin sodium 25 000 IU (anti-Xa). Nonmedicinal ingredients: benzyl alcohol, hydrochloric acid, sodium chloride, sodium hydroxide and water for injection. Multidose vials of 3.8 mL.

Store at room temperature (15 to 30°C). The 25 000 IU/mL multidose vial must be used within 2 weeks after initial penetration.

Reviewed 1999

FRAXIPARINE™ Pr

Sanofi

Nadroparin Calcium

Anticoagulant—Antithrombotic

Pharmacology: Nadroparin is a low molecular weight heparin. It is a heterogeneous mixture of sulfated polysaccharide glycosaminoglycan chains obtained by depolymerisation of porcine mucosal sodium heparin, extraction/purification and conversion to the calcium salt. Of the low molecular weight heparins, nadroparin has the lowest mean molecular weight of approximately 4 300 daltons; 75 to 95% of the molecular masses are in the range of 2 000 to 8 000 daltons. Nadroparin is composed of molecules with and without a specially characterized pentasaccharide, which is the specific site for high affinity binding to the plasma protein antithrombin III (ATIII). This binding leads to an accelerated inhibition of factor Xa, which accounts for the antithrombotic effect of nadroparin.

Nadroparin is an anticoagulant/antithrombotic drug with high anti-Xa activity (95 to 130 IU/mg), but relative to unfractionated heparin has a low inhibitory effect on factor IIa activity. (The ratio of anti-Xa to anti-IIa activity for nadroparin is 2.5 to 4, whereas it is 1 for heparin.) This greater ratio of anti-Xa activity to anti-IIa activity has the potential to provide equivalent antithrombotic efficacy with reduced hemorrhagic complications. It has both immediate and prolonged antithrombotic action.

Following s.c. injection, nadroparin is almost completely absorbed. Peak plasma anti-Xa activity occurs at 2 to 3 hours. Maximal prolongation of APTT and thrombin time occurs at approximately 4 hours. Although anti-Xa activity persists for at least 18 hours after injection, the elimination half-life is approximately 3.5 hours.

After s.c. administration of prophylactic doses (i.e., 0.3 mL) of nadroparin in healthy volunteers, maximum APTT and thrombin time were increased by a negligible 2 seconds at 4 hours, and APTT returned to baseline by 8 hours. After administration of treatment doses, APTT was only slightly prolonged (1.2 times the control value; with unfractionated heparin, APTT values at curative dosage are aimed at obtaining 1.5 to 2.5 times the control value). In the pharmacokinetic studies, a linear relationship between nadroparin dose and plasma anti-Xa activity was observed.

Elimination of nadroparin is prolonged in patients suffering from renal insufficiency. In subjects with severe renal insufficiency, the anti-Xa activity was shown to have an elimination half-life of approximately 6 hours, and time to reach peak activity was approximately 4 hours.

Fraxiparine (cont'd)

Indications: Prophylaxis of thromboembolic disorders (particularly deep vein thrombosis and pulmonary embolism) in general surgery and in orthopedic surgery.

Treatment of deep vein thrombosis.

Prevention of clotting during hemodialysis.

Contraindications: Nadroparin must **not** be administered by the i.m. route. Hypersensitivity to nadroparin. Injuries to and operations on the CNS, eyes and ears. History of thrombocytopenia occurring with nadroparin, or in patients in whom an in vitro platelet aggregation test is positive in the presence of nadroparin. Severe uncontrolled hypertension. Signs of hemorrhage or increased risk of hemorrhage in relation with hemostasis disorders, except for disseminated intravascular coagulation not induced by heparin. Organic lesion which is likely to bleed (such as active peptic ulceration). Acute infective endocarditis. Hemorrhagic cerebrovascular event.

Warnings: Nadroparin should be used with care in patients with a history of gastrointestinal ulceration.

Determination of anti-factor Xa levels in plasma is the only method available for monitoring nadroparin activity. Routine clotting assays are unsuitable for monitoring its anticoagulant activity. Only at very high plasma anti-Xa levels is APTT prolongation observed.

Drug Interactions: ASA and other salicylate drugs, nonsteroidal anti-inflammatory drugs increase the risk of hemorrhage due to the effect on platelets. Similarly, antiplatelet drugs increase the risk of hemorrhage due to the inhibition of the platelet function (see also Precautions).

Pregnancy and *Lactation:* Clinical experience of use in pregnant women is limited. Animals studies have not shown any teratogenic or fetotoxic effects. Clinical data concerning transplacental passage are limited; therefore, use of nadroparin during pregnancy is not advised unless the therapeutic benefits outweigh the possible risks. There are no clinical data concerning excretion in breast milk. Mothers receiving nadroparin should avoid breast-feeding.

Children: There are no trials to support the use of nadroparin in children. Therefore, the use of nadroparin is not advised unless the therapeutic benefits outweigh the possible risks.

Knee Surgery: Knee replacement is a delicate surgery, and may carry a greater risk of both deep vein thrombosis (DVT) and clinically important bleeding than hip replacement surgery. For this reason it is important to ensure appropriate dosing of this drug in this patient population.

Precautions: The various low molecular weight heparins have concentrations expressed in different units systems or in mg. These doses are not identical or interchangeable. Particular attention is therefore required to the doses and units in which the dose is expressed, and the specific instructions for the particular low molecular weight heparin should be strictly observed.

Monitoring: Nadroparin activity is monitored by measuring anti-factor-Xa activity in plasma. Standard global clotting tests, such as APTT, PT and TT cannot be used to monitor the activity of nadroparin. Only at very high plasma anti-Xa levels is APTT prolongation observed.

Because of the possibility of rare heparin-induced thrombocytopenia, platelet counts should be determined prior to the start treatment with nadroparin and, subsequently, twice weekly throughout the course of treatment.

Thrombocytopenia: Rare cases of thrombocytopenia have been reported. In the event of thrombocytopenia treatment should be discontinued immediately. Thrombocytopenia may be associated with arterial or venous thrombosis, exacerbation of the pre-existing thrombosis or disseminated intravascular coagulation; the platelet count should be assessed if these events are suspected. These effects are probably immunological in origin, and in the case of the first course of heparin treatment usually occur between the 5th and 21st day.

When there is a history of thrombocytopenia occurring with another heparin, careful clinical monitoring including assessment of platelet count at least once daily should be undertaken. Treatment should be discontinued immediately if thrombocytopenia occurs.

Reduced doses should be considered in patients with moderate to severe renal insufficiency. Nadroparin dosage should be carefully monitored in patients with severely impaired renal function. The main route of elimination is the kidney. After administration of prophylactic doses of nadroparin in patients with severe renal impairment, maximum plasma anti-Xa activity was reached 4 hours after injection at a mean of 0.64±0.22 IU/mL. The half-life for anti-Xa was 6 hours as compared to 3.5 hours for healthy volunteers and patients with normal kidney function.

Nadroparin should be administered with caution in cases of hepatic insufficiency.

Nadroparin should be used with caution in patients undergoing epidural anesthesia. Clinical studies of nadroparin in surgical patients were carried out primarily in patients undergoing general anesthesia. Nadroparin should be discontinued before administering epidural anesthesia when there are signs of impaired coagulation.

Hemodialysis: In clinical trials, patients undergoing chronic hemodialysis with nadroparin normally required few dose adjustments during the first few weeks of therapy. Thereafter, only occasional monitoring of anti-Xa levels would be required. Nadroparin was not studied in patients undergoing acute hemodialysis, but a narrower therapeutic interval would be anticipated. These patients should be subjected to comprehensive monitoring of anti-Xa levels.

Drug Interactions: Concomitant use of ASA (or other salicylates) or nonsteroidal anti-inflammatory drugs is not recommended, nor is the use of antiplatelet agents (see Warnings) as they may increase the risk of bleeding. Where such combinations cannot be avoided, careful clinical and biological monitoring should be undertaken.

Nadroparin should be administered with caution in patients receiving systemic (gluco-) corticosteroids or dextrans.

As with all other low molecular weight heparin preparations, during transfer to oral anticoagulant therapy increased monitoring is required (the treatment with nadroparin should be continued until the INR is stabilized at the target value).

Adverse Effects: Bleeding: As with other low molecular weight heparin preparations, nadroparin increases the risk of overt or concealed hemorrhage, especially in patients with other risk factors (see Contraindications).

The most common side effect of nadroparin was the development of injection site hematomas, which occurred at a frequency of about 5%. Other bleeding side effects were rare in clinical trials and ranged in severity from minor local hematomas to major hemorrhagic events, including death. Frequently, the first signs of bleeding include epistaxis, hematuria or melena. Petechiae or unexpected bruising may precede overt hemorrhage. Bleeding may be from any site and may be difficult to detect; e.g., retroperitoneal bleeding. In surgical patients, bleeding may occur from the surgical site. Established risk factors for bleeding in response to heparin and low molecular weight heparins include the use of platelet inhibiting medication, chronic heavy alcohol consumption, serious concurrent illness, renal failure, and advanced age. Patients taking low molecular weight heparins who experience noticeable prolongation of APTT, are at risk for bleeding. Frequently this is associated with plasma anti-Xa activity of 2 IU/mL or more.

Thrombocytopenia: Rare cases of thrombocytopenia, sometimes thrombogenic, have been reported (see Precautions).

Other infrequent serious side effects include: cutaneous necrosis, usually occurring at the injection site, which has been reported both with unfractionated heparin and with low molecular weight heparins; it is preceded by purpura or infiltrated or painful erythematous blotches, which may or may not be manifested by systemic upset. In such cases, treatment should be discontinued immediately.

Cutaneous or generalized hypersensitivity reactions requiring discontinuation of treatment.

Other adverse events which occur occasionally at an incidence similar to that of treatment with unfractionated heparin include: elevations in transaminases (AST and ALT) which are transient and has not been correlated to long-term effects on liver function; reversible hypoaldosteronism which may be associated with hyperkalemia and/or hyponatremia.

Overdose: Symptoms and Treatment: Hemorrhage is the major clinical sign of overdosage. In case of accidental overdosage, the platelet count and other coagulation parameters should be measured. Minor bleeding rarely requires specific therapy, and reducing or delaying subsequent doses of nadroparin is usually sufficient.

The use of protamine sulfate should only be considered in more serious cases. It largely neutralizes the anticoagulant activity of nadroparin, but some anti-Xa activity will remain. A dose of 0.6 mL protamine (6 mg, 625 A.H.U.) neutralizes approximately 0.1 mL (950 AXa IU) of nadroparin. The rate of administration of protamine should not exceed 20 mg/min, since too rapid administration can cause severe hypotensive and anaphylactoid-like reactions.

Dosage: Nadroparin is a sterile solution for s.c. injection into the anterolateral abdominal wall, alternatively, on the right and left sides of the abdominal wall. The thigh may be used as an alternative site. The needle should be fully inserted, perpendicularly into a pinched-up fold of skin.

The use of the intravascular route is not necessary except for hemodialysis given the high degree of bioavailability of nadroparin by the s.c. route (approximately 98%). Nadroparin is contraindicated for i.m. administration.

Prophylaxis and Treatment of Thromboembolic Disorders: Prophylaxis in General Surgery: The dose of nadroparin required for adequate prophylaxis without increased bleeding varies depending on the risk factors: single daily s.c. injections of 2 850 anti-Xa IU (0.3 mL). The first dose should be given 2 to 4 hours before surgery. Treatment should continue for at least 7 days. In all cases, prophylaxis should continue throughout the risk period and at least until the patient is actively ambulant or is no longer at risk of deep vein thrombosis.

Prophylaxis in Orthopedic Surgery: Single daily s.c. doses should be adjusted according to the patient bodyweight, as follows: 38 anti-Xa IU/kg administered 12 hours before surgery, 38 anti-Xa IU/kg administered 12 hours after surgery, 38 anti-Xa IU/kg re-administered on a daily basis, up to and including postoperative Day 3, 57 anti-Xa IU/kg administered as of postoperative Day 4.

Treatment should continue for at least 10 days and should continue in all cases throughout the risk period and at least until the patient is actively ambulant.

As an example, the following dosages as a function of patient body weight are recommended (see Table I).

Table I—Fraxiparine

Recommended Dosages—Prophylaxis in Orthopedic Surgery

Body weight	Fraxiparine volume per injection and per day: Preoperatively and until Day 3	as of Day 4
<50 kg	0.2 mL	0.3 mL
50-69 kg	0.3 mL	0.4 mL
≥70 kg	0.4 mL	0.6 mL

Treatment of Deep Vein Thrombosis: Twice daily s.c. doses should be given for 10 days adjusted to body weight. The dose per injection is 86 anti-Xa IU/kg.

As an example, the following dosages as a function of patient body weight are recommended (see Table II).

Table II—Fraxiparine

Recommended Dosages—Treatment of Deep Vein Thrombosis

Body weight	Fraxiparine volume per injection; 2 injections daily
<50 kg	0.4 mL
50-59 kg	0.5 mL
60-69 kg	0.6 mL
70-79 kg	0.7 mL
80-89 kg	0.8 mL
≥90 kg	0.9 mL

Monitoring of the activity of nadroparin is performed as a functional method for anti-Xa. Blood samples drawn 3 to 4 hours postdosing should show anti-Xa levels of 0.5 to 1 IU anti-Xa/mL.

As with other low molecular weight heparins, concomitant therapy with vitamin K antagonists is usually started immediately. Nadroparin therapy should continue until the INR ratio is within the therapeutic range, usually at least 5 days.

Prevention of Clotting During Hemodialysis: All clinical trial patients were patients with chronic renal failure, and the following dosage recommendations are for that patient population, in patients with no risk of hemorrhage.

Optimisation of dosage is required for each individual patient (different clotting stimuli are produced by different dialysis circuits and membranes, and there is inter-patient variability).

Single dose of approximately 65 anti-Xa IU/kg into the arterial line at the start of each session, for a session lasting 4 hours or less in patients with no risk of hemorrhage. This dose normally produces plasma anti-Xa levels in the range 0.5 to 1 IU anti-Xa/mL.

An additional dose may be given during sessions lasting longer than 4 hours.

Doses in subsequent dialysis sessions should be adjusted as required.

As an example, the following dosages as a function of patient body weight are recommended (see Table III).

Table III—Fraxiparine

Recommended Dosages—Prevention of Clotting During Hemodialysis

Body weight	Volume of Fraxiparine
<50 kg	0.3 mL
50-69 kg	0.4 mL
≥70 kg	0.6 mL

In patients with a risk of hemorrhage, dialysis sessions may be carried out using halved doses. An additional smaller dose may be given during dialysis for sessions lasting longer than 4 hours. The dose in subsequent dialysis sessions should be adjusted as necessary to achieve plasma levels within the range of 0.2 to 0.4 IU anti-Xa/mL.

Special Populations: Reduced doses of nadroparin should be considered in patients with moderate to severe renal insufficiency.

As with all other low molecular weight heparins, nadroparin should be administered with caution in cases of hepatic insufficiency, and in those with a history of peptic ulceration or other organic lesion likely to bleed.

Information for the Patient: See Blue Section—Information for the Patient "Fraxiparine".

Supplied: Each mL of aqueous solution contains: nadroparin calcium 9 500 IU anti-Xa. Single dose, disposable prefilled syringes of 0.2 mL (ungraduated syringes) 1 900 IU anti-Xa; 0.3 mL (ungraduated syringes) 2 850 IU anti-Xa; 0.4 mL (ungraduated syringes) 3 800 IU anti-Xa; 0.6 mL (graduated syringes) 5 700 IU anti-Xa; 0.8 mL (graduated syringes) 7 600 IU anti-Xa; and 1 mL (graduated syringes) 9 500 IU anti-Xa. Ungraduated 0.2 mL, 0.3 mL and 0.4 mL syringes are intended for administration of fixed dosages; 0.6 mL, 0.8 mL and 1 mL syringes are graduated so that adjusted dosages can be given. Cartons of 2 and 10. Store between 15 and 30°C. Do not freeze. Do not refrigerate, as cold injections may be painful. Discard unused portion of each syringe. Do not mix with other preparations.

New Product 1998

FRISIUM® Ⓟ

Hoechst Marion Roussel

Clobazam

Anticonvulsant for Adjunctive Therapy

Pharmacology: Clobazam is a 1,5-benzodiazepine with anticonvulsant properties.

In general, the mode of antiepileptic action of clobazam is probably largely analogous to that of the 1,4-benzodiazepines. The differences between clobazam (a 1,5-benzodiazepine) and the 1,4-benzodiazepines in terms of therapeutic efficacy and neurotoxicity are possibly due to the variation in degree of the agonist action at the high affinity benzodiazepine receptor or to differing relative action at the high and low affinity benzodiazepine receptors.

Regarding the mechanism of action it is likely that modifications to the function of gamma-aminobutyric acid (GABA) as an important inhibitory neurotransmitter underlie the pharmacological effects of the benzodiazepines. Electrophysiologic studies have shown that benzodiazepines potentiate GABA-ergic transmission at all levels of the neuroaxis, including the spinal cord, hypothalamus, hippocampus, substantia nigra, cerebellar cortex and cerebral cortex. The changes induced by the interaction of GABA with its receptors is enhanced by benzodiazepines, resulting in a decrease in the firing rate of critical neurons in many regions of the brain.

The oral absorption of clobazam, like that of all benzodiazepines, is fast and complete. The time to peak concentration ranges from 1 to 4 hours. The administration of food with the drug has variable effects on the rate of absorption. The drug is highly lipophilic and is rapidly distributed in fat and cerebral grey matter. Within 1 to 4 hours of administration it has accumulated in white matter and is then redistributed widely. The volume of distribution is large.

Clobazam is extensively metabolized and is not excreted in unchanged form by any species studied. Clobazam forms a number of metabolites with N-desmethylclobazam being the most important. The half-life of N-desmethylclobazam is much longer (mean 42 hours; range 36 to 46 hours) than for clobazam (mean 18 hours; range 10 to 30 hours). N-desmethylclobazam reaches higher serum levels, especially with long-term administration of clobazam. The half-life increases with the patient's age. The drug is about 85% protein-bound; hepatic disease may alter both the metabolism of the drug and its protein binding thus affecting plasma clobazam levels. There have been no studies that have demonstrated a clear-cut correlation between serum levels of clobazam or of N-desmethylclobazam to clobazam efficacy.

Most reports indicate there is no, or only a very weak, correlation between the clobazam dose, or blood levels, and its clinical effects. Therapeutic blood levels for clobazam are in the range of 50 to 300 ng/mL with the corresponding range for N-desmethylclobazam being from 1 000 to 4 000 ng/mL. The serum levels at which anticonvulsant effects can be expected are not yet known but it can be assumed that the therapeutic range lies in the order of the figures given above. Since N-desmethylclobazam blood levels are 10 to 20 times higher than those for clobazam, and this metabolite also has antiepileptic effects, it may be more important to the antiepileptic efficacy of clobazam than the parent compound itself.

After oral administration of ^{14}C-labeled clobazam to man, approximately 90% of the radioactivity was recovered in urine.

Seven double-blind studies have been reported in which clobazam was given as adjunctive therapy versus placebo within an established antiepileptic regimen; clobazam was shown to be significantly superior to placebo.

Indications: Clobazam has been found to be of value as adjunctive therapy in patients with epilepsy who are not adequately stabilized with their current anticonvulsant therapy.

Contraindications: Hypersensitivity to clobazam, severe muscle weakness (myasthenia gravis) and narrow-angle glaucoma.

Warnings: Geriatrics: Clobazam should be used with caution in elderly and debilitated patients, and those with organic brain disorders, with treatment initiated at the lowest possible dose (see Precautions).

Potentiation of Drug Effects: Patients should be cautioned about the possibility of additive effects when clobazam is combined with alcohol or other drugs with CNS depressant effects. Patients should be advised against consumption of alcohol during treatment with clobazam (see Precautions).

Physical and Psychological Dependence: Physical and psychological dependence are known to occur in persons taking benzodiazepines. Caution must be exercised if it is at all necessary to administer clobazam to individuals with a history of drug misuse or those who may increase the dose on their own initiative. Such patients must be placed under careful surveillance. Signs and symptoms of withdrawal may follow discontinuation of use of clobazam; thus it should not be abruptly discontinued after prolonged use (see Precautions).

Pregnancy and *Lactation:* Clobazam should not be used in the first trimester of pregnancy and thereafter only if strictly indicated. Nursing mothers in whom therapy with clobazam is indicated should cease breast-feeding, since clobazam passes into breast milk.

Several studies have suggested an increased risk of congenital malformations associated with the use of minor tranquilizers (chlordiazepoxide, diazepam and meprobamate) during the first trimester of pregnancy. If clobazam is prescribed to a woman of childbearing potential she should be warned to consult her physician regarding the discontinuation of the drug if she intends to become, or suspects she might be, pregnant.

Anterograde Amnesia: Anterograde amnesia is known to occur after administration of benzodiazepines.

Patients with Depression or Psychosis: Clobazam is not recommended for use in patients with depressive disorders or psychosis.

Precautions: Occupational Hazards: Clobazam possesses a mild CNS depressant effect, therefore, patients should be cautioned against driving, operating dangerous machinery or engaging in other hazardous activities, particularly in the dose adjustment period, or until it has been established that they do not become drowsy or dizzy.

Geriatrics: Elderly and debilitated patients, or those with organic brain syndrome, have been found to be prone to the CNS depressant activity of benzodiazepines even after low doses. Manifestations of this CNS depressant activity include ataxia, oversedation and hypotension. Therefore, medication should be administered with caution to these patients, particularly if a drop in blood pressure might lead to cardiac complications. Initial doses should be low and increments should be made gradually, depending on the response of the patient, in order to avoid oversedation, neurological impairment and other possible adverse reactions.

Dependence Liability: Clobazam should not be administered to individuals prone to drug abuse. Caution should be observed in all patients who are considered to have potential for psychological dependence. Withdrawal symptoms have been observed after abrupt discontinuation of benzodiazepines. These include irritability, nervousness, insomnia, agitation, tremors, convulsions, diarrhea, abdominal cramps, vomiting and mental impairment. As with other benzodiazepines, clobazam should be withdrawn gradually.

Tolerance: Loss of part or all of the anticonvulsant effectiveness of clobazam has been described in patients who have been receiving the drug for some time. There is no absolute or universal definition for the phenomenon and reports vary widely on its development. The reported success of clobazam in intermittent therapy in catamenial epilepsy implies that tolerance may be minimized by intermittent treatment, but long-term follow-up is unreported. No studies have identified or predicted which patients are likely to develop tolerance or precisely when this might occur.

Mental and Emotional Disorders: It should be recognized that suicidal tendencies may be present in patients with emotional disorders; particularly those depressed. Protective measures and appropriate treatment may be necessary and should be instituted without delay.

Since excitement and other paradoxical reactions can result from the use of benzodiazepines in psychotic patients, clobazam should not be used in patients suspected of having psychotic tendencies.

Patients with Impaired Renal or Hepatic Function: Clobazam requires dealkylation and hydroxylation before conjugation. Usual precautions should be taken if clobazam is used in patients who may have some impairment of renal or hepatic function. It is suggested that the dose in such cases be carefully titrated. In patients for whom prolonged therapy with clobazam is indicated, blood counts and liver function should be monitored periodically.

Patients with Acute, Severe Respiratory Insufficiency: In patients with acute, severe respiratory insufficiency, respiratory function should be monitored.

Laboratory Tests: If clobazam is administered for repeated cycles of therapy, periodic blood counts and liver and thyroid function tests are advisable.

Drug Interactions: Most studies of the potential interactions of clobazam with other antiepileptic agents have failed to demonstrate significant interactions with phenytoin, phenobarbital or carbamazepine. However, one study noted that the addition of clobazam caused a 25% increase in serum drug levels in 29% of patients taking carbamazepine, 63% of patients taking phenytoin, 13% of those taking valproate and 14% of those on phenobarbital. The contradictory findings in different studies are presumably due to variations in patient susceptibility, and although clinically significant interactions are unusual, they may occur. Alcohol may also significantly increase plasma clobazam levels.

Several of the established antiepileptic agents: carbamazepine, phenytoin, phenobarbital, valproic acid, cause the blood levels of clobazam to decrease slightly. Findings are less consistent with regard to N-desmethylclobazam: serum levels are lower with concurrent valproic acid, but higher with carbamazepine and phenytoin.

Toxicologic Studies: In mouse, clobazam was associated with hepatomas in high-dose males. In rat, an increased incidence of thyroid adenomas was seen in males. There were 3 malignancies: 2 (male and female) in the thyroid and 1 (female) in the liver. The relevance of these findings to man has not been established.

Adverse Effects: From 19 published studies of clobazam use in epileptic patients, the overall incidence of side effects was 33% of which drowsiness, dizziness and fatigue were most frequently reported. Canadian experience provides a similar overall incidence (32%) with drowsiness reported in 17.3% of patients, and 12% of patients terminating treatment because of side effects.

The incidence of side effects was lower in patients under 16 years of age (23.7%) than the incidence in adults (43.1%): $p<0.05$, whereas treatment discontinuation incidences were similar across age groups: 10.6% and 13.8% respectively. The following side effects occurred at incidences of greater than 1% [ataxia (3.9%), weight gain (2.2%), dizziness (1.8%), nervousness (1.6%), behavior disorder (1.4%), hostility and blurred vision (1.3%)] while other effects occurred at a less than 1% incidence.

Symptoms of tiredness may sometimes appear, especially at the beginning of treatment with clobazam and when higher

Frisium (cont'd)

doses are used. Also in rare instances and usually only temporarily, the patient may experience dryness of the mouth, constipation, loss of appetite, nausea, dizziness, muscle weakness, disorientation, tiredness, or a fine tremor of the fingers, but also paradoxical reactions, e.g., restlessness and irritability.

After prolonged use of benzodiazepines, impairment of consciousness combined with respiratory disorders has been reported in very rare cases, particularly in elderly patients; it sometimes persisted for some length of time.

Occupational Hazards: Under experimental conditions, impairment of alertness has been observed to be less pronounced after therapeutic doses of clobazam than after other benzodiazepines. Nevertheless, even when used as directed, the drug may alter reactivity to such an extent as to impair driving performance or the ability to operate machinery, especially when it is taken in conjunction with alcohol.

As with other drugs of this type (benzodiazepines), the therapeutic benefit must be balanced against the risk of habituation and dependence during prolonged use.

Isolated cases of skin reactions such as rashes or urticaria have been observed.

Overdose: Symptoms: The cardinal manifestations are drowsiness, confusion, reduced reflexes, increasing sedation and coma.

Effects on respiration, pulse and blood pressure are noticed with large overdoses. Patients exhibit some jitteriness and overstimulation usually when the effects of the drug begin to wear off.

Treatment: Immediate gastric lavage may be beneficial if performed soon after ingestion of clobazam. Given the route of excretion, (see Pharmacology) forced diuresis by short-acting loop diuretic may be useful some hours post-ingestion. If respiratory depression and/or coma are observed, the presence of other CNS depressants should be suspected. Respirations, pulse and blood pressure should be monitored. General supportive measures aimed at maintaining cardiopulmonary function should be instituted and administration of i.v. fluids started. Hypotension and CNS depression are managed by the usual means.

Dosage: As with other benzodiazepines, the possibility of a decrease in anticonvulsant efficacy in the course of treatment must be borne in mind.

In patients with impaired liver and kidney function, clobazam should be used in reduced dosage.

Adults: Small doses, 5 to 15 mg/day, should be used initially, gradually increasing to a maximum daily dose of 80 mg as necessary.

Children: In infants (<2 years), the initial daily dose is 0.5 to 1 mg/kg/day. The initial dose in children (2 to 16 years) should be 5 mg/day, which may be increased at 5-day intervals to a maximum of 40 mg/day.

As with all benzodiazepines, abrupt withdrawal may precipitate seizures. It is therefore recommended that clobazam be gradually reduced in dose before treatment is discontinued.

If the daily dose is divided, the higher portion should be taken at night. Daily doses up to 30 mg may be taken as a single dose at night.

Supplied: Each white, uncoated, bevelled, round tablet, 7 mm diameter, marked with "BGL" above and below the scorebreak on the obverse and the "Hoechst Tower and Bridge" logo on the reverse, contains: clobazam 10 mg. Nonmedicinal ingredients: colloidal silicon dioxide, cornstarch, lactose, magnesium stearate and talc. Blister packs (PVC film and aluminum foil) of 30 (3×10). Store in original containers at room temperature, below 25°C.

(Shown in Product Recognition Section)

Reviewed 1999

FROBEN® Ⓟ
FROBEN SR® Ⓟ

Knoll

Flurbiprofen

Nonsteroidal Anti-inflammatory Agent

Pharmacology: Flurbiprofen is a nonsteroidal anti-inflammatory drug with analgesic and antipyretic activity. Although its mechanism of action has not been completely elucidated it has been shown to be an inhibitor of prostaglandin synthesis, specifically cyclo-oxygenase, and to some extent lipoxygenase, and is not due to pituitary-adrenal stimulation.

Flurbiprofen is well absorbed and the rate of absorption is not altered with old age. Following a single oral dose of 100 mg, peak plasma levels are achieved in about 2 hours. Absorption may be delayed in some individuals when administered with food but the total amount of drug absorbed is not affected. The elimination half-life is approximately 4 hours. When the drug is administered daily, steady state concentrations are reached with no drug accumulation. Twenty to 25% of flurbiprofen is recovered from the urine as free and conjugated unchanged drug, with 60 to 80% being hydroxylated metabolites. At therapeutic blood levels, flurbiprofen is at least 99% bound to serum proteins. Excretion of flurbiprofen is completed 24 hours after the final dose.

Bioavailability for Froben SR is comparable to that of standard Froben with no evidence of dose dumping or excessive accumulation. Steady state is reached within 2 to 3 days. Froben SR is less rapidly absorbed than the conventional Froben tablet, reaching maximum plasma concentrations in a longer period of time.

Froben: Following a single 100 mg oral dose of flurbiprofen tablets to healthy volunteers, peak serum concentrations of 12.7±2.8 μg/mL were reached in 1.9±0.7 hours. The apparent elimination half-life was 3.8±0.4 hours. Multiple dose studies of 50 mg 3 times a day in volunteers resulted in no drug accumulation and steady state serum concentrations of 5 to 6 μg/mL. Administration of a single 50 mg dose of flurbiprofen to elderly men (age range 66 to 90 years) resulted in peak blood levels of 5 to 6 μg/mL, similar to those seen in young, healthy males.

Elderly females, however, (74 to 94 years) had higher mean peak concentrations of 8.7±0.8 μg/mL as compared to elderly and young males, however, this difference is not significant. These higher concentration levels are not related to a reduction in elimination of flurbiprofen since the half-life of elimination is similar to that found in young, healthy male volunteers. The mean volume of distribution is lower in elderly females than in elderly or young males. The total amount of drug absorbed or the time to reach peak levels does not differ between age groups indicating that the rate of absorption is not altered with old age and thus the onset of action in geriatric patients is not delayed.

Flurbiprofen absorption was delayed up to 2 hours in some individuals when administered with food resulting in lower maximum plasma levels, but the total amount of drug absorbed was not affected by concomitant food intake.

In man, 20 to 25% of a dose of flurbiprofen is recovered from the urine as free and conjugated unchanged drug. Three major urinary metabolites have been identified with the most abundant being hydroxylation products, representing about 60 to 80% of the administered dose. At therapeutic blood levels, flurbiprofen is at least 99% bound to serum proteins. Excretion of flurbiprofen is completed 24 hours after the last dose.

Froben SR: Comparison of the AUC values for the sustained release capsules and conventional tablets show that the capsule has adequate bioavailability in most volunteers with no evidence of dose dumping or excessive accumulation of flurbiprofen. A steady state is reached within 2 to 3 days. The elimination half-life for flurbiprofen is 3 to 4 hours and is not significantly different following long-term administration.

Pharmacokinetic parameters determined in elderly patients have been shown to be comparable with those seen in younger patients. Studies in which young and elderly patients received single daily doses of sustained release capsules resulted in a C_{max}, C_{max}^{ss}, AUC_{0-48} and AUC_{0-48}^{ss} of 7.53 μg/mL, 10.33 μg/mL, 134 μg• h/mL and 192.7 μg• h/mL, respectively in elderly patients compared to 8.56 μg/mL, 10.78 μg/mL, 138.5 μg• h/mL and 195.5 μg• h/mL, respectively in young patients.

The effect of food on Froben SR causes a delay in T_{max} (from 5.5 to 8.3 hours), increases C_{max} significantly (to 10 μg/mL) and increases bioavailability. The AUC for the sustained release capsules increases to a figure close to that of conventional tablets (taken fasting).

Indications: For the symptomatic treatment of rheumatoid arthritis, osteoarthritis and ankylosing spondylitis.

Also indicated for the relief of pain associated with dysmenorrhea.

Contraindications: Peptic ulcer or active inflammatory disease of the gastrointestinal system. Known or suspected hypersensitivity to flurbiprofen. Flurbiprofen should not be used in patients in whom acute asthmatic attacks, urticaria, rhinitis or other allergic manifestations are precipitated by ASA or other nonsteroidal anti-inflammatory agents. Fatal anaphylactoid reactions have occurred in such individuals.

Warnings: Peptic ulceration, perforation and gastrointestinal bleeding, sometimes severe and occasionally fatal have been reported during therapy with nonsteroidal anti-inflammatory drugs (NSAIDs) including flurbiprofen.

Flurbiprofen should be given under close medical supervision to patients prone to gastrointestinal tract irritation particularly those with a history of peptic ulcer, diverticulosis or other inflammatory disease of the gastrointestinal tract. In these cases the physician must weigh the benefits of treatment against the possible hazards.

Patients taking any NSAID including this drug should be instructed to contact a physician immediately if they experience symptoms or signs suggestive of peptic ulceration or gastrointestinal bleeding. These reactions can occur without warning symptoms or signs and at any time during the treatment.

Elderly, frail and debilitated patients appear to be at higher risk from a variety of adverse reactions from NSAIDs. For such patients, consideration should be given to a starting dose lower than usual, with individual adjustment when necessary and under close supervision (see Precautions).

Pregnancy and *Lactation:* Flurbiprofen should not be used during pregnancy, or in nursing mothers as its safety under these conditions has not been established. Although no teratogenic effects were seen in animal studies, parturition was delayed and prolonged and the number of stillbirths was increased. Flurbiprofen has been found to cross the placental barrier, but it is not known if it is secreted in breast milk.

Children: The safety and efficacy of flurbiprofen has not been established in children, and therefore its use in this age group is not recommended.

Precautions: General: Elderly patients, particularly women, should be carefully followed for the appearance of side effects and the dosage decreased accordingly.

Gastrointestinal: If peptic ulceration is suspected or confirmed, or if gastrointestinal bleeding or perforation occurs, flurbiprofen should be discontinued, an appropriate treatment instituted and patient closely monitored.

There is no definitive evidence that the concomitant administration of histamine H_2-receptor antagonists and/or antacids will either prevent the occurrence of gastrointestinal side effects or allow continuation of therapy when and if these adverse reactions appear.

Renal: As with other nonsteroidal anti-inflammatory drugs (NSAIDs), long-term administration of flurbiprofen to animals has resulted in renal papillary necrosis and other abnormal renal pathology. In humans, there have been reports of acute interstitial nephritis with hematuria, proteinuria, and occasionally nephrotic syndrome.

A second form of renal toxicity has been seen in patients with prerenal conditions leading to the reduction in renal blood flow or blood volume, where the renal prostaglandins have a supportive role in the maintenance of renal perfusion. In these patients, administration of a NSAID may cause a dose-dependent reduction in prostaglandin formation and may precipitate overt renal decompensation. Patients at greatest risk of this reaction are those with impaired renal function, heart failure, liver dysfunction, those taking diuretics, and the elderly. Discontinuation of nonsteroidal anti-inflammatory therapy is usually followed by recovery to the pre-treatment state.

Flurbiprofen and its metabolites are eliminated primarily by the kidneys, therefore the drug should be used with great caution in patients with impaired renal function. In these cases lower doses of flurbiprofen should be anticipated and patients carefully monitored.

During long-term therapy kidney function should be monitored periodically.

Hepatic: As with other NSAIDs, borderline elevations of one or more liver tests may occur. These abnormalities may progress, may remain essentially unchanged, or may be transient with continued therapy. A patient with symptoms and/or signs suggesting liver dysfunction, or in whom an abnormal liver test has occurred, should be evaluated for evidence of the development of more severe hepatic reaction while on therapy with this drug. Severe hepatic reactions including jaundice and cases of fatal hepatitis have been reported with this drug as with other NSAIDs. Although such reactions are rare, if abnormal liver tests persist or worsen, if clinical signs and symptoms consistent with liver disease develop, or if systemic manifestations occur (e.g. eosinophilia, rash, etc.), this drug should be discontinued.

During long-term therapy, liver function tests should be monitored periodically. If this drug is to be used in the presence of impaired liver function, it must be done under strict observation.

Fluid and Electrolyte Balance: Fluid retention and edema have been observed in patients treated with flurbiprofen. Therefore, as with many other NSAIDs, the possibility of precipitating congestive heart failure in elderly patients or those with compromised cardiac function should be borne in mind. Flurbiprofen should be used with caution in patients with heart failure, hypertension or other conditions predisposing to fluid retention.

Serum electrolytes should be monitored periodically during long-term therapy, especially in those patients at risk.

Hematology: Drugs inhibiting prostaglandin biosynthesis do interfere with platelet function to some degree; therefore, patients who may be adversely affected by such an action should be carefully observed when flurbiprofen is administered.

Blood dyscrasias associated with the use of NSAIDs are rare, but could be with severe consequences.

Infection: In common with other anti-inflammatory drugs, flurbiprofen may mask the usual signs of infection.

Ophthalmology: Blurred and/or diminished vision has been reported with the use of flurbiprofen and other NSAIDs. If such symptoms develop, this drug should be discontinued and an ophthalmologic examination performed; ophthalmic examination should be carried out at periodic intervals in any patient receiving this drug for an extended period of time.

Drug Interactions: ASA or other NSAIDs: The concomitant administration of ASA with flurbiprofen caused decreased serum levels and peak concentrations of flurbiprofen. The rates of absorption and elimination of flurbiprofen were not affected.

Digoxin: Flurbiprofen does not change the rate of elimination of digoxin and the rate of elimination of flurbiprofen is not altered by co-administration of digoxin. Although, digoxin absorption may be delayed during co-administration of flurbiprofen.

Coumarin Type Anticoagulants: In a short-term study flurbiprofen did not significantly affect prothrombin time but the bleeding time increased slightly, although it remained within the normal range. Flurbiprofen should therefore be administered with caution to patients on concomitant coumarin-type anticoagulant therapy. Such patients should be closely monitored.

Oral Hypoglycemic Drugs: Co-administration of flurbiprofen with glibenclamide, metformin, chlorpropamide or phenformin did not lead to interaction effects of any clinical significance. A tendency towards a reduction in blood sugar levels occurred over a 24 hour period however no hypoglycemic reactions occurred. No interaction in terms of blood sugar or immunoreactive insulin occurred following the co-administration of flurbiprofen and tolbutamide.

Methotrexate: Caution is advised in the concomitant administration of flurbiprofen and methotrexate since nonsteroidal anti-inflammatory agents have been reported to increase the blood concentration of methotrexate, thereby possibly enhancing its toxicity.

Lithium: Nonsteroidal anti-inflammatory agents have been reported to increase the steady state plasma levels of lithium. It is recommended that lithium plasma levels be monitored when co-administering it with flurbiprofen.

Diuretics: Flurbiprofen antagonizes the action of i.v. or oral furosemide.

Antihypertensives: No significant alterations in the pharmacokinetics of either propranolol or atenolol followed pre-treatment with placebo or flurbiprofen. However, pre-treatment with flurbiprofen attenuated the effects of propranolol on blood pressure but not on heart rate. The hypotensive effect caused by atenolol was attenuated to a lesser degree following flurbiprofen pre-treatment.

Antacids: The pharmacokinetics of a single oral dose of flurbiprofen are not altered by the concomitant administration of a magnesium and aluminum hydroxide antacid formulation.

Clinical Laboratory Tests: Flurbiprofen and Thyroid Function Tests: Flurbiprofen does not modify the laboratory parameters of thyroid function. Flurbiprofen is extensively bound to plasma protein and thus patients receiving concomitant drugs such as oral diabetic agents, sulfonamides, anticoagulants, and phenytoin should be monitored closely for side effects and/or clinical effectiveness and dosage adjustments made, if necessary.

Adverse Effects: The most common adverse reactions encountered with NSAIDs are gastrointestinal, of which peptic ulcer, with or without bleeding, is the most severe. Fatalities have occurred on occasion, particularly in the elderly.

Froben: The adverse reaction incidences were those reported during controlled clinical trials and include data from 2 141 patients on the conventional Froben tablets. Gastrointestinal adverse reactions were the most common, with ulceration and bleeding the most severe. The trials included 55 patients who received flurbiprofen for 3 months, 85 for 6 months at doses up to 300 mg daily, and 191 who received it for 3 years at a dose of 200 mg daily. The adverse report figures below represent the percent of treated patients reporting an adverse reaction.

Gastrointestinal (26.4%): dyspepsia (5.9%); nausea (with or without vomiting) (5.4%); gastrointestinal pain (4.5%); gastrointestinal bleeding (0.3%); diarrhea (2.3%); constipation (1.6%); gastritis (0.3%); flatulence (0.3%); anorexia (0.5%); peptic ulceration (0.3%); melena (0.1%); stomatitis (0.3%); others (4.7%). Although not reported in this series of clinical trials, glossitis and eructation have been observed.

CNS (7.2%): headache (2.0%); dizziness (1.6%); depression (0.6%); drowsiness (0.4%); insomnia (0.2%); confusion (0.2%); other (2.2%). Although not reported in this series of clinical trials, vertigo, paresthesia, nervousness, mood alteration, ataxia, and tremor have been observed.

Dermatological (1.8%): rash (0.9%); pruritus (0.6%); urticaria (0.1%) and dryness of skin (0.1%). Two cases of Stevens-Johnson syndrome have been reported.

Renal (0.9%): edema (0.6%); frequency (0.3%) and hematuria (0.1%). Although not reported in this series of trials, dysuria, urinary incontinence and urine abnormalities (decreased osmolality, albuminuria) have been reported.

Hematological (0.3%): epistaxis (0.2%) and anemia (0.1%). Although not seen in this series of clinical trials, aplastic anemia, thrombocytopenia, granulocytopenia, leukopenia, purpura, and petechia have been observed.

Respiratory (1.2%): dry mouth/nose (0.4%); chest pain (0.3%) and dyspnea (0.1%). Although not seen in this series of clinical trials, asthma has been observed.

Cardiovascular (0.3%): cramps (0.1%) and palpitations (0.1%).

Miscellaneous (3.6%): weight gain/loss (0.2%); exhaustion (0.6%); sweating (0.4%); hot flushes (0.3%) and others (2.1%). Although not seen in this series of clinical trials, vaginal hemorrhage has been reported.

Hepatic: Although not reported in this series of clinical trials, increased AST and alkaline phosphatase and hepatitis have been reported.

Special Senses: One case of tinnitus was reported. Although not reported in this series of studies, blurred vision, conjunctivitis, photophobia, abnormal accommodation, corneal opacity and taste alteration have been reported.

Froben SR: Reports from clinical trials involving a total of 2 231 patients on both the conventional tablets and the sustained release capsules (1 787 patients were administered the sustained release capsules) showed similar adverse reactions for both dosage forms.

Overdose: Symptoms: No fatal cases of overdosage have been reported in conjunction with flurbiprofen ingestion and those suffering with overdosage recovered without sequelae.

Treatment: No specific antidote is known. Stomach emptying is advisable and supportive and symptomatic treatment with maintenance of electrolytes and acid balance is recommended.

Dosage: Froben: Rheumatoid Arthritis: The usual recommended initial dose is 150 to 200 mg/day given in 3 or 4 divided doses. Some patients may initially require 250 to 300 mg/day. The dose should be adjusted until the minimum effective maintenance dose is established. During the course of treatment the maximum daily dose of 300 mg should be used only during symptom exacerbations and not for maintenance therapy.

Osteoarthritis: The usual recommended initial dose is 100 to 150 mg/day given in 2 or 3 divided doses. Some patients may initially require 200 to 300 mg/day. The dose should be adjusted until the minimum effective maintenance dose is established. During the course of treatment, the maximum daily dose of 300 mg should be used only during symptom exacerbations and not for maintenance therapy.

Ankylosing Spondylitis: The usual recommended initial dose is 200 mg/day given in 4 divided doses. Some patients may initially require 250 to 300 mg/day. The dose should be adjusted until the minimum effective maintenance dose is established. During the course of treatment, the maximum daily dose of 300 mg should be used only during symptom exacerbations and not for maintenance therapy.

Dysmenorrhea: The usual recommended dosage is 50 mg given 4 times daily, beginning with the onset of dysmenorrhea and ending with the cessation of pain.

Froben SR: This dosage form is recommended for maintenance therapy of patients whose dose has been previously adjusted to 200 mg daily. The recommended daily dose of Froben SR is one 200 mg capsule, taken in the evening after food. The capsule should be swallowed whole.

Children: The safety and efficacy of flurbiprofen has not been established in children and therefore its use in this group is not recommended.

Information for the Patient: See Blue Section—Information for the Patient "Froben/Froben SR".

Supplied: Froben: Each white, sugar coated tablet contains: flurbiprofen 50 mg (overprinted F50 in black) or 100 mg (overprinted F100 in black). Nonmedicinal ingredients: carnauba wax, colloidal silicon dioxide, cornstarch, dimethylpolysiloxane, gum juniper (sandarac), iron oxide black, lactose, liquid glucose, magnesium stearate, povidone, shellac, sodium benzoate, soya lecithin, stearic acid, sucrose, talc and titanium dioxide. Bottles of 100.

Froben SR: Each hard gelatin capsule with a yellow opaque cap and a transparent yellow body containing white to off-white beads, printed FSR in black, contains: flurbiprofen 200 mg in sustained release form. Nonmedicinal ingredients: avicel PH101 microcrystalline cellulose, colloidal silicon dioxide, eudragit RS100, magnesium stearate B.P. and polyethylene glycol 6 000. Capsule shell: Nonmedicinal ingredients: erythrosine, gelatin, glycerin, quinoline yellow, red iron oxide, sodium metabisulfate, titanium dioxide. Printing ink: nonmedicinal ingredients: black iron oxide, polydimethylsiloxane, soya lecithin and shellac. Bottles of 100.

(Shown in Product Recognition Section)

FUCIDIN® Cream Ⓟ
FUCIDIN® Ointment Ⓟ
FUCIDIN® Intertulle Ⓟ

Leo

Fusidic Acid

Sodium Fusidate

Sodium Fusidate

Antibiotic

Pharmacology: Fusidic acid inhibits bacterial protein synthesis by interfering with amino acid transfer from aminoacyl-sRNA to protein on the ribosomes. Fusidic acid may be bacteriostatic or bactericidal depending on inoculum size. Although bacterial cells stop dividing almost within 2 minutes after contact with the antibiotic in vitro, DNA and RNA synthesis continue for 45 minutes and 1 to 2 hours, respectively.

Fusidic acid is virtually inactive against gram-negative bacteria. The differences in activity against gram-negative and gram-positive organisms are believed to be due to a difference in cell wall permeability.

Mammalian cells are much less susceptible to inhibition of protein synthesis by fusidic acid than sensitive bacterial cells. These differences are believed to be due primarily to a difference in cell wall permeability.

Indications: The treatment of primary and secondary skin infections caused by sensitive strains of S. aureus, Streptococcus species and C. minutissimum. Primary skin infections that may be expected to respond to treatment with fusidic acid topical include: impetigo contagiosa, erythrasma and secondary skin infections such as infected wounds and infected burns.

Appropriate culture and susceptibility studies should be performed. However, while waiting results of these studies and, if antibiotic therapy is considered to be necessary, fusidic acid topical may be administered to those patients in whom an infection caused by susceptible bacteria is suspected. This antibiotic treatment may subsequently require modification once these results become available.

In addition, local concentrations of fusidic acid topical are active against other Corynebacteria, Neisseria, Clostridia and Bacteroides species. No cross-resistance has been observed to date between Fucidin and other antibiotics presently in clinical use.

Resistance to fusidic acid has readily been induced in vitro. The development of resistance has also been shown to occur in the clinical setting.

Contraindications: Sensitivity to fusidic acid and its salts, or lanolin in respect of Fucidin ointment or intertulle.

Precautions: Treatment of severe or refractory skin lesions should be supplemented with the administration of a systemic antibacterial agent. Use of topical antibiotics occasionally allows overgrowth of non-susceptible organisms. If this occurs, or irritation or sensitization develop, treatment should be discontinued and appropriate therapy instituted. Fusidic

Fucidin (cont'd)

acid topical preparations should not be used in or near the eye because of the possibility of conjunctival irritation.

Pregnancy and *Lactation:* Safety in the treatment of infections during pregnancy has not been established. If administration to pregnant patients is considered necessary, its potential benefits should be weighed against the possible hazards to the fetus. There is evidence to suggest that the drug can penetrate the placental barrier and is detectable in the milk of nursing mothers. Safety of fusidic acid for the treatment of infections in women who are breast-feeding has not been established.

Adverse Effects: Mild irritation has occasionally been reported in patients with dermatoses treated with fusidic acid. It was not usually necessary to discontinue therapy. The application of fusidic acid to deep leg ulcers has been associated with pain. Reports of hypersensitivity reactions have been rare.

Overdose: Symptoms and Treatment: Overdosage has not been known to occur during topical therapy with fusidic acid ointment or cream.

Dosage: Ointment and Cream: Apply a small amount to the lesion 3 or 4 times daily until favorable results are achieved. Whenever the lesion is to be covered with a gauze dressing, less frequent applications (1 or 2 daily) may be used. In impetigo contagiosa, it has not been shown necessary to remove the crusts before application.

Intertulle: A single layer applied directly to the wound and covered with an appropriate dressing. If exudative, dressings should be changed at least daily. In non-exudative lesions, the dressing may be changed less frequently. The intertulle may be cut to the appropriate size for the lesion.

In some cases of severe exudative lesions, two layers should be applied to prevent adherence of the dressing.

When dressing the face, care should be taken to avoid the eye. The package should not be issued nor the contents used if the wrapper is broken.

When required, incision and drainage of infected skin lesions should be carried out before treatment with fusidic acid.

Supplied: Cream: Each tube contains: fusidic acid 2% in a cream base. Nonmedicinal ingredients: α-tocopherol, butylhydroxyanisole, cetanol, glycerin 85%, paraffin liquid, paraffin white soft, polysorbate 60, potassium sorbate, purified water. Tubes of 15 and 30 g.

Intertulle: Each sterile gauze, impregnated with an ointment, contains: sodium fusidate 2% and lanolin. Nonmedicinal ingredients: cetyl alcohol, liquid paraffin, white soft paraffin, wool fat (lanolin). Cartons of 10 foil packs, each containing one 10 cm×10 cm piece.

Ointment: Each tube contains: sodium fusidate 2% in an ointment base containing lanolin. Nonmedicinal ingredients: α-tocopherol, cetanol, lanolin anhydrous, liquid paraffin, white soft paraffin. Tubes of 15 and 30 g.

FUCIDIN® Tablets Ⓟ
FUCIDIN® I.V. Ⓟ
FUCIDIN® Suspension Ⓟ

Leo

Sodium Fusidate
Sodium Fusidate
Fusidic Acid

Antibiotic

Pharmacology: The antibacterial action of fusidic acid results from the inhibition of bacterial protein synthesis. The drug interferes with amino acid transfer from aminoacyl-sRNA to protein on the ribosomes. Fusidic acid may be bacteriostatic or bactericidal depending on inoculum size. Although bacterial cells stop dividing almost within 2 minutes after contact with the antibiotic in vitro, DNA and RNA synthesis continue for 45 minutes and 1 to 2 hours, respectively. Fucidin is active in vitro against gram-positive bacteria and Neisseria species, but has almost no antibacterial activity against gram-negative organisms.

Fucidin is readily absorbed and peak blood concentrations are reached between 2 and 3 hours following oral administration. Average peak concentrations of 25 to 35 μg/mL following single doses of the tablets and suspension are approximately 55 to 80% of those obtained following i.v. infusion of comparable dose. Fusidic acid suspension is less completely absorbed than sodium fusidate tablets, thus a single administration of 737 mg of fusidic acid is required to produce an effective dose comparable to that produced by 500 mg of sodium fusidate. Following a single dose the average peak concentration is reached after approximately 4 hours with the tablets versus 2 hours with the suspension. Although there is a delay in the absorption of the tablets and a lower peak concentration, similar areas under the curve are obtained with all 3 oral formulations.

The plasma half-life of Fucidin has been found to be between 5 and 6 hours (for all dosage forms and routes), which results in significant accumulation with repeated doses. Steady-state levels, usually between 50 to 100 μg/mL, are normally reached within 3 or 4 days with a dose of 500 mg of sodium fusidate or 737 mg of fusidic acid 3 times daily. Cumulative serum levels in humans have been found to be quite variable from patient to patient.

The concentrations observed in various body tissues and fluids, except for urine and possibly sputum are in excess of those required to inhibit most staphylococci in vitro. The minimum inhibitory concentration of Fucidin against S. aureus ranges from 0.03 to 0.50 μg/mL.

Fucidin has been shown to penetrate into avascular foci of infection, such as bone sequestra in patients with osteomyelitis. Fucidin has been found in synovial fluid, in patients with rheumatoid arthritis and osteoarthritis, in burn crusts, in pus and in aqueous humor of uninflamed eyes.

The drug is 97.2% protein bound in human serum thus only 2 to 3% is available in the active free form. The possibility of synergism between sodium fusidate and other antibiotics has been tested. Synergism was demonstrated with penicillin V, penicillin G, erythromycin and picromycin. Synergism between the penicillins and fusidic acid has only been observed with strains of S. aureus that produce small amounts of penicillinase and not with penicillinase stable penicillins.

The MIC's of combinations of benzylpenicillin or methicillin with fusidic acid were determined by the serial dilution tube titration method. When penicillin was added 2 hours before fusidic acid, the combination was synergistic. However, when penicillin was added at the same time or later than fusidic acid, the two agents acted antagonistically. It has been suggested that these apparently opposing effects occur because fusidic acid rapidly inhibits protein synthesis, but the action of penicillin requires active cell growth. Fucidin and methicillin act antagonistically against staphylococcal strains which are susceptible to methicillin but not in methicillin resistant strains.

Fucidin is excreted almost exclusively in the bile. In individuals with normally functioning gall bladders the Fucidin concentrations were found to be 12 times higher in bile than in serum, but in severely inflamed gall bladders, the concentration fell to only 7% of the serum level. Seven metabolites of Fucidin have been isolated from the bile and only a small amount is excreted unchanged in the feces. The 3 major metabolites have been identified as: 1) a glucuronic acid conjugate, 2) a dicarboxylic ester and 3) a glycol, although the structure of the latter has not been positively confirmed. None of the 3 compounds has significant antibacterial activity as compared to fusidic acid against S. aureus.

Sodium fusidate had no discernible effect on adrenocortical function in investigations of urinary hormone excretion and of eosinophil count.

Fucidin crosses the blood-brain barrier only when the meninges are inflamed.

In one patient given a single dose of 1 g orally, Fucidin crossed the placental barrier.

Fucidin has been given to 40 neonates with spina bifida from the day of birth for up to 1 year. No evidence of liver, renal, blood or ocular toxicity was observed.

Indications: The treatment of the following infections when due to susceptible strains of S. aureus, both penicillinase producing and nonpenicillinase producing: skin and soft tissue infections, osteomyelitis.

For patients with staphylococcal infections where other antibiotics have failed (e.g., patients with staphylococcal septicemia, burns, endocarditis, pneumonia, cystic fibrosis).

Appropriate culture and susceptibility studies should be performed. Fucidin is bound to protein, and a small amount of blood in agar medium renders the sensitivity test invalid. While awaiting results of these studies, if antibiotic therapy is considered to be necessary due to a potentially serious infection, Fucidin may be administered to those patients in whom a staphylococcal infection is suspected. This antibiotic treatment may subsequently require modification once these results become available.

No cross resistance has been observed to date between Fucidin and other antibiotics presently in clinical use.

Resistance to Fucidin has readily been induced in vitro. The development of resistance has also been shown to occur in the clinical setting.

Contraindications: Known hypersensitivity to fusidic acid and its salts.

Warnings: Fucidin must not be administered either i.m. or s.c., since it has been demonstrated that local tissue injury occurs. Fucidin should not be infused with amino acid solutions or with whole blood because of the risk of hemolysis of the erythrocytes.

Extreme caution should be exercised in patients with impaired liver function. Liver function tests should be performed regularly during treatment.

Precautions: Fucidin is excreted mainly in the bile and periodic liver function tests should be carried out when high doses are used or when the drug is given for prolonged periods.

Caution should be exercised if Fucidin is administered with other drugs, including antibiotics (e.g., lincomycin and rifampicin), which have a similar biliary excretion pathway.

Cases of jaundice have rarely developed during therapy usually following a rapid infusion or an excessive i.v. dose. The jaundice is usually accompanied by an elevated serum bilirubin level, and occasionally serum transaminases may also be elevated. Alteration of the administration procedure by lengthening the infusion period or changing to oral therapy may help control this adverse effect. Liver function should continue to be closely monitored until the serum bilirubin concentration has returned to a satisfactory level; if an elevated bilirubin level persists, administration of the drug should be discontinued.

Infusions should only be made into a wide bore vein with a good blood flow and completed over a period of not less than 6 hours.

In patients with hypocalcemia, Fucidin i.v. should be administered with caution and serum calcium monitored since the reconstituted i.v. contains a large amount of phosphate/citrate buffer.

Pregnancy and *Lactation:* Safety during pregnancy has not been established. If administration to pregnant patients is considered to be necessary, its use requires that the potential benefits be weighed against the possible hazards to the fetus. There is evidence to suggest that the drug can penetrate the placental barrier and is detectable in the milk of nursing mothers. Safety in women who are breast-feeding has not been established.

Fusidic acid displaces bilirubin from its albumin binding site in vitro. The clinical significance of this finding is uncertain and kernicterus has not been observed in neonates receiving Fucidin. This observation should be borne in mind when the drug is given to preterm, jaundice, acidotic or seriously ill neonates.

Adverse Effects: Gastrointestinal Reactions: Nausea, vomiting, epigastric pain, anorexia, diarrhea and dyspepsia. Treatment was discontinued in approximately 1.7% of the patients treated because of gastric intolerance. The incidence of these effects can be lessened by taking the medication with food.

In some patients treated either orally or i.v., jaundice has been reported. The jaundice is usually resolved on cessation of therapy (see Precautions).

Venospasm and thrombophlebitis have been observed with i.v. administration. Inflammation and redness at the infusion site have also been observed.

Skin rashes and pruritus have been observed on rare occasions.

Dizziness, blurred vision, decreased white blood cell count, psychic disturbance, swollen legs and headaches have been generally mild and infrequent.

Overdose: Symptoms: I.V. Infusion: I.V. doses of Fucidin Leo in excess of those recommended may result in hypocalcemia due to the large amount of phosphate/citrate buffer administered (i.e., each 50 mL of phosphate/citrate buffer for i.v. infusion contains 980 mg disodium hydrogen phosphate equivalent to 5.5 mmols phosphate). This may require patient monitoring, serum calcium determinations and treatment as appropriate.

Abnormal liver biochemistry or reversible jaundice have been reported. These symptoms can be alleviated by stopping the drug. If the clinical condition allows, changing to the oral formulation has been associated with a lower incidence of jaundice.

Oral Administration: Early symptoms may include epigastric or gastric discomfort and possibly diarrhea. Prolonged ingestion of high doses may produce jaundice and abnormal liver biochemistry.

Treatment: Since there have not been any reports of accidental massive overdosage with Fucidin, there has been no experience with any specific treatment. Treatment should be restricted to symptomatic and supportive measures. Dialysis is of no benefit, since the drug is not significantly dialyzed.

Dosage: Fucidin may be administered orally or by i.v. infusion. Do not administer i.m. or s.c (see Table I).

Table I—Fucidin

Dosage

Dose	Oral	Suspension	I.V. Infusion
Adults:	500 mg sodium fusidate 3 times daily.	15 mL 3 times daily.*	1 vial (500 mg sodium fusidate) 3 times daily.
Children: Up to 1 yr. of age:		1 mL/kg daily, in 3 divided doses	All ages: Calculate daily dose as 20 mg sodium fusidate/kg in 3 divided doses administered over a 6-hr period.
1 to 5 yrs:		5 mL 3 times daily.*	
6 to 12 yrs:		10 mL 3 times daily.*	

* Due to incomplete absorption of fusidic acid hemihydrate, the effective dose is 70% of stated figure. To avoid underdosing, recommendations must be adhered to.

In fulminating infections, the above recommended oral dosages may be doubled. If additional injectable antibacterial therapy is necessary, use separate infusion fluids.

The total duration of therapy should be dictated by the patient's clinical condition and the results of bacteriological monitoring. The following guidelines may be used: the minimum duration of treatment should be 1 to 2 weeks for skin and soft tissue infections; for acute osteomyelitis a minimum of 2 to 4 weeks is recommended; the treatment of chronic osteomyelitis may require several months. For more deep seated infections where other antibiotics have failed, a minimum of 2 to 4 weeks is recommended for septicemia, pneumonia and burns; 1 to 2 months for endocarditis.

The dosage in patients undergoing hemodialysis needs no adjustment, as Fucidin is not significantly dialyzed. Fucidin can be given to patients with renal failure since Fucidin is excreted by the biliary route.

Note: Fucidin is not recommended in infections due to streptococci or N. gonorrhea.

If gastrointestinal upset occurs, the symptoms may be lessened by taking the medication with food.

Fucidin i.v. should be administered only into a wide bore vein with a good blood flow over a period not less than 6 hours.

Preparation of Solution for i.v. Infusion: Dissolve one vial of sodium fusidate (500 mg) with the 10 mL of buffer solution provided.

For adults over 50 kg of body weight dilute to 250 to 500 mL with one of the following: sodium chloride i.v. infusion BP 0.9% (1 to 2 mg/mL); dextrose i.v. infusion BP 5% (1 to 2 mg/mL); compound sodium lactate i.v. infusion BP (Ringer's Lactate solution) (1 mg/mL); potassium chloride 40 mEq (0.3%) and sodium chloride (0.9%) i.v. infusion BP (1 mg/mL); potassium chloride 40 mEq (0.3%) and dextrose (5%), i.v. infusion BP (1 mg/mL).

For **children and adults weighing less than 50 kg,** the required amount of reconstituted drug **should be further diluted at least ten-fold** with the appropriate infusion fluid. If opalescence is encountered, the solution should be discarded (e.g., upon use of acidic dextrose solutions).

Infusion solutions containing Fucidin Leo are incompatible with kanamycin, gentamicin, vancomycin, cephaloridine, carbenicillin, whole blood, amino acid solutions and calcium containing solutions. If additional i.v. therapy is to be concurrently employed, it is recommended that separate infusions be used.

Reconstituted solution should be used within 24 hours (refrigerated).

Note: Opalescence may occur with some dextrose diluents which may be slightly acidic. The solution should be discarded.

Note: Fucidin should not be diluted with amino acid solutions or whole blood.

Supplied: I.V.: Each pack of two 10 mL vials for i.v. infusion contains: 1 vial of sodium fusidate 500 mg as a dry powder; and a second vial containing 10 mL sterile phosphate citrate buffer (pH 7.3 to 7.7).

Suspension: Each 5 mL of banana-flavored, aqueous suspension contains: fusidic acid 246 mg . Nonmedicinal ingredients: banana essence, citric acid monohydrate, hydroxyethylcellulose, liquid glucose, methocel A 15, potassium sorbate, sodium phosphate dibasic dihydrate, sodium saccharinate and water purified. Bottles of 50 mL.

Tablets: Each white, ovoid, film-coated tablet contains: sodium fusidate BP 250 mg (equivalent to 240 mg fusidic acid). Nonmedicinal ingredients: cellulose microcrystalline, colloidal anhydrous silica, crospovidone, gelatine, hydroxypropylmethylcellulose, lactose, magnesium stearate, povidone, talc, titanium dioxide. Bottles of 100. Store below 25°C.

Note: Owing to incomplete absorption the effective dose is 70% of the stated drug weight or approximately 172 mg/5 mL.

FULVICIN® P/G ℞

Schering

Griseofulvin (Ultramicrosize)

Antifungal Antibiotic

Indications: For the treatment of ringworm infections of the skin, hair and nails, namely: tinea corporis, tinea pedis, tinea cruris, tinea barbae, tinea capitis, tinea unguium (onychomycosis) when caused by susceptible strains of the following genera of fungi: T. rubrum, T. tonsurans, T. mentagrophytes, T. interdigitale, T. verrucosum, T. sulphureum, T. schoenleinii, T. megninii, T. gallinae, T. crateriforme, M. audouini, M. canis, M. gypseum and E. floccosum.

Concomitant use of appropriate topical (keratolytic) agents is usually required.

Since other fungal diseases are not affected by Fulvicin P/G, careful mycological study with identification of the responsible organism is the only basis on which therapy can be selected accurately.

Fulvicin P/G is not effective in the following conditions: bacterial infections, candidiasis (moniliasis), histoplasmosis, actinomycosis, sporotrichosis, chromoblastomycosis, coccidioidomycosis, North American blastomycosis, cryptococcosis (torulosis), tinea versicolor, and nacardiosis.

Fulvicin P/G is not indicated in the prophylaxis of fungal infections.

Contraindications: Porphyria, hepatocellular failure, and individuals with a history of hypersensitivity to griseofulvin.

Pregnancy: Griseofulvin may have harmful effects on the genotype. For this reason, it is recommended to male persons who are treated with griseofulvin not to beget a child during the next 6 months after termination of the treatment. Female persons should not become pregnant during the treatment with griseofulvin.

Griseofulvin should not be administered during pregnancy.

Fulvicin P/G therapy is not indicated in minor infections that will respond to topical agents alone.

Warnings: Photosensitivity reactions may be associated with Fulvicin P/G therapy and patients should be warned to avoid exposure to intense, natural or artificial, sunlight. Should a photosensitivity reaction occur, lupus erythematosus may be aggravated.

Alcoholic beverages should be forbidden during treatment with Fulvicin P/G since griseofulvin may augment or potentiate the effects of alcohol which may lead to tachycardia and flush and can be the cause of more serious consequences.

Precautions: Patients on prolonged therapy should be under close observation, and periodic monitoring of organ system functions, including renal, hepatic, and hematopoietic, should be done.

Fulvicin P/G should be discontinued if granulocytopenia occurs.

Griseofulvin can potentiate an increase in hepatic enzymes that metabolize estrogens at an enhanced rate, including the estrogen component of oral contraceptives, thereby causing possible decreased contraceptive effects and menstrual irregularities.

As Fulvicin P/G has been shown to cause induction of liver metabolizing enzymes, the activity of oral anticoagulants may be reduced and dosage adjustment of the anticoagulant may be required during and after treatment.

Similarly, barbiturates, by inducing liver metabolizing enzymes, usually decrease griseofulvin plasma levels, and concomitant administration may require a dosage adjustment of Fulvicin P/G.

The possibility of cross sensitivity with penicillin exists since Fulvicin P/G is derived from species of Penicillium, however, known penicillin-sensitive patients have been treated with Fulvicin P/G without difficulty.

As with all antibiotics, the use of Fulvicin P/G may result in an overgrowth of nonsusceptible organisms, particularly monilia.

Adverse Effects: CNS: headache (sometimes severe and usually disappears as therapy is continued or when drug is taken with meals), paresthesia of hands and feet, peripheral neuritis, lethargy, fever, mental confusion, impairment of performance of routine efforts, fatigue, syncope, vertigo, blurred vision, transient macular edema and augmentation of the effects of alcohol.

Gastrointestinal: Nausea, vomiting, diarrhea, heartburn, flatulence, dry mouth, oral thrush, thirst, angular stomatitis, glossodynia, black and furred tongue.

Hematological (which often disappear despite continuation of therapy): Leukopenia, neutropenia, punctate basophilia, monocytosis, granulocytopenia. Serum sickness syndromes develop rarely.

Renal: Albuminuria and cylinduria without evidence of renal insufficiency are common. Proteinuria is rare.

Allergic: Urticaria, photosensitivity, lichen planus, erythema, erythematous multiform-like rashes, vesicular and morbilliform eruptions, lupus erythematosus, and angioneurotic edema occur rarely.

Estrogen-like effects in children: In children, enlargement of the breast and hyperpigmentation of mammary areolae, nipple and external genitalia have been reported.

Other: Hepatotoxicity has been observed (see Contraindications). A moderate but inconsistent increase of fecal protoporphyrins has been noted when the drug is used for a long period of time.

Overdose: Symptoms and Treatment: No toxicity has been reported even when taken in massive doses. Should toxicity occur, withdrawal of the drug is indicated.

Dosage: Accurate diagnosis of the infecting organism is essential. Identification should be made either by direct microscopic examination of a mounting of infected tissue in a solution of potassium hydroxide or by culture on an appropriate medium.

Adults: Daily administration of 1 x 330 mg. Fulvicin P/G Tablet(s) will provide a satisfactory response in most patients with tinea corporis, tinea cruris and tinea capitis. For those fungal infections that are most difficult to eradicate, such as tinea pedis and tinea unguium, a daily 660 mg dose is recommended.

Children 2 years of age and older: Approximately 5.5 mg/kg/day is an effective dose for most children. Medication must be continued until the infecting organism is completely eradicated. It is advisable to continue therapy for at least 2 weeks after all signs of infection have disappeared. General hygienic measures should be observed to control sources of infection or reinfection. Adjunctive therapy with keratolytic agents generally is indicated in areas of hyperkeratosis.

Duration of Therapy: Tinea capitis: 4 to 6 weeks. Tinea corporis: 2 to 4 weeks. Tinea pedis: 4 to 8 weeks. Tinea unguium: Depending on the rate of growth of: fingernails: at least 4 months; toenails: at least 6 months.

Supplied: Each tablet contains: ultramicrosize griseofulvin 330 mg. Nonmedicinal ingredients: cornstarch, lactose, magnesium stearate, polyethylene glycol 8 000 and sodium lauryl sulfate. Tartrazine-free. Bottles of 100. Store between 2 and 30°C.

(Shown in Product Recognition Section)

FULVICIN® U/F ℞

Schering

Griseofulvin (Microsize)

Antifungal Antibiotic

Indications: Orally effective against superficial infections caused by those fungi responsible for dermatomycoses in man and animals, namely: M. canis, M. gypseum, M. audouini, E. floccosum, T. tonsurans, T. rubrum, T. mentagrophytes, T. megninii, T. gallinae, T. verrucosum, T. sulfureum, T. interdigitale, T. schoenleinii, T. crateriform. Griseofulvin is inactive against: C. albicans (monilia), C. neoformans, B. dermatitidis, A. israeli, H. capsulatum, C. immitis, M. furfur (tinea versicolor) and bacteria. The drug is useful in the treatment of fungal infections of the scalp and those of the glabrous skin. The drug is less effective in chronic infections of the feet, palms, and nails. Since these chronic fungal infections tend to cause hyperkeratosis, concomitant topical keratolytic therapy is almost always necessary.

Fulvicin U/F (cont'd)

Contraindications: Porphyria, hepatocellular failure, and individuals with a history of hypersensitivity to griseofulvin.

Pregnancy: Griseofulvin may have harmful effects on the genotype. For this reason, it is recommended to male persons who are treated with griseofulvin not to beget a child during the next 6 months after termination of the treatment. Female persons should not become pregnant during the treatment with griseofulvin.

Griseofulvin should not be administered during pregnancy.

Warnings: Alcoholic beverages should be forbidden during treatment with Fulvicin U/F since griseofulvin may augment or potentiate the effects of alcohol which may lead to tachycardia and flush and can be the cause of more serious consequences.

Precautions: As with all antibiotics, the use of this drug may result in an overgrowth of nonsusceptible organisms, particularly monilia. Periodic blood cell counts should be done during griseofulvin therapy, and its administration should be discontinued if granulocytopenia occurs. Albuminuria and hyaline casts have been associated with the use of griseofulvin, but renal function tests have revealed no impairment. The urine of patients on prolonged therapy should be examined for porphobilinogen. Since griseofulvin is derived from a species of penicillin, the possibility of cross sensitivity with penicillin exists, however known penicillin sensitive patients have been treated without difficulty.

Griseofulvin can potentiate an increase in hepatic enzymes that metabolize estrogens at an enhanced rate, including the estrogen component of oral contraceptives, thereby causing possible decreased contraceptive effects and menstrual irregularities.

As griseofulvin may alter prothrombin activity in some patients, it is recommended that prothrombin times be determined at least 2 or 3 times a week with patients on anticoagulant therapy if griseofulvin is added to the regimen.

Concomitant administration of phenobarbital and griseofulvin may result in reduced blood levels of griseofulvin due to the enzymatic acceleration of griseofulvin metabolism. During therapy with griseofulvin, patients should be advised to avoid exposure to intense natural or artificial sunlight.

Adverse Effects: Severe reactions occur infrequently. Headache may occur, but usually disappears when the drug is taken with meals. Nausea, epigastric distress, heartburn, abdominal cramps, vomiting or diarrhea have been reported in a few patients. Chest pain, dryness of the mouth, breathlessness, arthralgia, neuritic pains, vertigo, and fever have also been reported. Allergic reactions, occurring rarely, include urticaria and angioneurotic edema, serum sickness, lupus erythematosus. Fatigue, lethargy, vertigo, decreased mental acuity, and secondary monilial skin infections have been reported as well as a few cases of photosensitivity. Proteinuria and leukopenia have been reported rarely. If granulocytopenia occurs, the administration of the drug should be discontinued. In children receiving griseofulvin, enlargement of the breast and hyperpigmentation of mammary areolae, nipples and external genitalia have been reported.

Dosage: Dosage must be individualized. Adults: 500 mg daily (125 mg 4 times a day or 250 mg twice daily). Children: A dosage of 10 mg/kg is usually adequate (children from 14 to 23 kg, 125 to 250 mg daily; children over 23 kg, 250 to 500 mg, in divided doses). Patients with less severe infections may require less, whereas those with widespread lesions may require a starting dose of 0.75 to 1 g per day.

Supplied: Each white, scored tablet contains: ultra fine griseofulvin USP 250 mg or 500 mg. Nonmedicinal ingredients: 250 mg: cornstarch, magnesium stearate and polysorbate 80. 500 mg: colloidal silicon dioxide, cornstarch, magnesium stearate and pluronic F-68. Tartrazine-free. Bottles of 100.

(Shown in Product Recognition Section)

FUNGIZONE® INTRAVENOUS Ⓟ

Squibb

Amphotericin B

Antifungal

Indications: Amphotericin B is specifically intended for the treatment of disseminated mycotic infections, including coccidioidomycosis; cryptococcosis (torulosis); disseminated candidiasis, histoplasmosis, South American leishmaniasis, North and South American blastomycosis; mucormycosis (phycomycosis) caused by species of the genera Mucor, Rhizopus, Absidia, Entomophthora, and Basidiobolus, sporotrichosis (S. schenckii), and aspergillosis (A. fumigatus).

Other Clinical Uses: Limited studies have shown that amphotericin B powder for injection may be useful when administered by routes other than i.v. for the treatment of certain types of fungal infections.

Bladder Irrigation: Successful treatment of fungal infections of the bladder by amphotericin B has been noted in the literature.

The basic method used for bladder irrigation is as follows: 15 mg Fungizone powder is dissolved in 100 to 400 mL of sterile water and injected via catheter after complete emptying of the bladder. The patient is then asked to retain the solution for as long as possible. An alkalizing mixture should be given every 4 hours. The treatment may be repeated until the culture is negative and the symptoms have disappeared.

Aerosol: Amphotericin B has also been administered by aerosol (nebulizer) for the treatment of pulmonary fungal infections. A preparation suitable for administration by aerosol is prepared as follows: Dissolve a 50 mg vial of Fungizone in a bottle of Alevaire or in 10 mL of distilled or sterile water. Administer 1 to 2 mL of this solution (5 to 10 mg amphotericin B) 3 to 4 times daily for a period of 1 to 2 weeks.

Eye Infections: Several studies have been done using topical administration of amphotericin B for fungal infections of the eye. Such use has shown a low degree of efficacy after prolonged therapy and is not recommended unless there is no other alternative. It is unlikely to be of value except in superficial infections.

Reconstitute a 50 mg vial of amphotericin B by adding 10 mL of sterile water, giving a concentration of 5 mg/mL. Shake until the solution is clear. Further dilution of 1 mL of this solution to a concentration of 1 mg/mL using sterile water provides a solution suitable for use in the eye. Dosage varies from 2 drops every hour to 1 drop every 4 to 6 hours. Intervals between administration may be lengthened as improvement occurs. Amphotericin B has been reported in some instances to be toxic to the eye when applied locally and may cause local irritation and discomfort.

Solutions of 1.5 mg/mL up to 4.0 mg/mL have also been used. Normal (isotonic) saline is not recommended for dilution since it may cause precipitation of amphotericin B.

Higher concentrations can lead to serious damage to the eye and must not be used.

Ear infections: There is little evidence to support the efficacy of such use.

Contraindications: In those persons who have shown hypersensitivity to amphotericin B or any other component in the formulation, unless, in the opinion of the physician, the condition requiring treatment is life threatening and amenable only to amphotericin B therapy.

Warnings: Amphotericin B should be administered **primarily** to patients with progressive, potentially fatal infections. This potent drug should not be used to treat the common apparent forms of fungal diseases which show only positive skin or serologic tests.

Amphotericin B is frequently the only available treatment for potentially fatal fungal diseases. In each case, its possible lifesaving benefit must be balanced against its untoward and dangerous side effects.

Precautions: General: Prolonged therapy with amphotericin B is usually necessary. Adverse reactions are quite common when the drug is given parenterally at therapeutic dosage levels. Some of these reactions are potentially dangerous. Hence, amphotericin B should be used only in hospitalized patients or those under close clinical observation by medically trained personnel, and should be reserved for those patients in whom a diagnosis of the progressive, potentially fatal forms of susceptible mycotic infections has been firmly established preferably by positive culture or histologic study.

Rapid i.v. infusion, over less than 1 hour, particularly in patients with renal insufficiency, has been associated with hyperkalemia and arrhythmias, and should, therefore, be avoided (see Dosage).

Leukoencephalopathy has been reported following use of amphotericin B in patients who received total body irradiation.

Urinalysis and BUN determinations should be performed at least weekly during therapy, as should serum creatinine or endogenous creatinine clearance tests. If the BUN level exceeds 40 mg/100 mL or the serum creatinine level exceeds 3 mg/100 mL, administration of amphotericin B should, whenever feasible, be discontinued or dosage markedly reduced, until the level returns to near normal limits (usually in 1 or 2 weeks). Some authorities suggest that the serum creatinine clearance rate permits better evaluation of renal function.

Weekly hemograms and serum potassium and magnesium determinations are also advisable. Low serum magnesium levels have also been noted during treatment with amphotericin B. Therapy should be discontinued if the results of liver function tests are abnormal (elevated BSP, alkaline phosphatase and bilirubin).

Whenever medication is interrupted for a period longer than 7 days, therapy should be resumed by starting with the lowest dosage level, e.g., 0.25 mg/kg/day of body weight and increased gradually to an optimum level as outlined in Dosage.

Drug Interactions: Corticosteroids and corticotropin (ACTH) may potentiate amphotericin B-induced hypokalemia and should not be administered concomitantly unless they are necessary to control drug reactions. Since deep fungal infections sometimes emerge in patients undergoing therapy with antibiotics and antineoplastic agents such as nitrogen mustard, they should not be given concomitantly with amphotericin B if avoidable. Other nephrotoxic agents (e.g., cisplatin, pentamidine, aminoglycosides and cyclosporine) may enhance the potential for renal toxicity and should not be given concomitantly except with great caution.

Concomitant administration of flucytosine may increase the toxicity of flucytosine possibly by increasing its cellular uptake and/or impairing its renal excretion.

Though not observed in all studies, acute pulmonary reactions have been observed in patients given amphotericin B during or shortly after leukocyte transfusions, thus it is advisable to separate these infusions as far as possible and to monitor pulmonary function.

Caution should be observed when agents whose effects or toxicity may be increased by hopokalemia (e.g., digitalis glycosides, skeletal muscle relaxants and antiarrhythmic agents) are administered concomitantly.

Pregnancy: Reproduction studies in animals have revealed no evidence of harm to the fetus due to amphotericin B. Systemic fungal infections have been successfully treated in pregnant women with amphotericin B for injection without obvious effects to the fetus, but the number of cases reported has been small. Because animal reproduction studies are not always predictive of human response, and adequate and well-controlled studies have not been conducted in pregnant women, this drug should be administered during pregnancy with caution and only if the potential benefit to the mother outweighs the potential risk to the fetus.

Lactation: It is not known whether amphotericin B is excreted in human milk. Likewise, data are in conflict as to the extent of oral absorption, if any. Because many drugs are excreted in human milk and considering the potential toxicity of amphotericin B, it is prudent to advise a nursing mother to discontinue nursing.

Children: Safety and effectiveness in pediatric patients have not been established through adequate and well-controlled studies. Systemic fungal infections have been treated in pediatric patients without reports of unusual side effects.

Adverse Effects: While a few patients may tolerate full i.v. doses of amphotericin B without difficulty, most will exhibit some intolerance, often at less than the full therapeutic dosage. The adverse reactions most commonly observed are:

General (Body as a Whole): fever (sometimes accompanied by shaking chills occurring within 15 to 20 minutes after initiation of treatment), malaise and weight loss.

Digestive: anorexia, nausea, vomiting, diarrhea, dyspepsia and cramping epigastric pain.

Hematologic: reversible normochromic and normocytic anemia.

Local: local venous pain at the injection site with or without phlebitis or thrombophlebitis.

Musculoskeletal: generalized pain, including muscle and joint pains.

Neurologic: headache.

Renal: decreased renal function and renal function abnormalities including azotemia, hyposthenuria, renal tubular acidosis and nephrocalcinosis, an increase in the serum creatinine level, a decrease in the serum creatinine clearance rate or a decrease in the phenol-sulfonphthalein (PSP) excretion is commonly observed. Hypokalemia with or without concomitant impairment of renal function has often been observed. Potassium replacement may be considered by oral or parenteral route. Concomitant diuretic therapy may be a predisposition for renal impairment whereas sodium repletion or supplementation may reduce the occurrence of nephrotoxicity.

Renal damage is often accompanied by the appearance of granular and hyaline casts, and sometimes by microhematuria. Renal dysfunction is usually reversible on discontinuation of therapy, but serious and permanent renal damage has been reported in patients given large doses for prolonged periods; especially in those receiving a total dose exceeding 5 g.

The following adverse reactions have also been reported.

General (Body as a Whole): flushing.
Allergic: anaphylactoid and other allergic reactions.
Cardiovascular: cardiovascular toxicity including arrhythmias, ventricular fibrillation, cardiac arrest, hypertension and hypotension.
Dermatologic: maculopapular rash and pruritus (without rash).
Digestive: acute liver failure, jaundice, liver function test abnormalities, melena or hemorrhagic gastroenteritis and hepatotoxicity.
Hematologic: coagulation defects, thrombocytopenia, leukopenia, agranulocytosis, eosinophilia, leukocytosis.
Neurologic: hearing loss, tinnitus, transient vertigo, blurred vision or diplopia, peripheral neuropathy, encephalopathy, convulsions and other neurologic symptoms.
Pulmonary: dyspnea, bronchospasm, noncardiac pulmonary edema and hypersensitivity pneumonitis.
Renal: hypomagnesemia, hyperkalemia, acute renal failure, anuria and oliguria.

Fever, nausea, vomiting, hadache and malaise sometimes subside with continued administration. Reactions to amphotericin B may be made less severe by administration of an antipyretic, e.g., ASA, an antihistaminic and/or an antiemetic prior to and concurrently with amphotericin B, or by modifying the rate of infusion. Addition of a small amount of heparin, rotation of the injection site, the use of a pediatric scalp-vein needle and alternate day therapy may lessen the incidence of thrombophlebitis and anorexia. Supplemental alkali medication may decrease renal tubular acidosis complications. Extravasation may cause chemical irritation.

I.V. or i.m. administration of small doses of adrenal corticosteroids just prior to, or during the amphotericin B infusion may decrease febrile reactions. The dosage and duration of such corticosteroid therapy should be kept to a minimum (see Precautions).

If a severe reaction occurs during the course of an infusion, therapy should be interrupted for about 15 minutes to allow the patient to recover. If the reaction recurs, therapy should be resumed at a lower dosage the next day. Blood transfusions may be required when reversible normocytic, normochromic anemia occurs during prolonged therapy.

Overdose: Symptoms and Treatment: Amphotericin B overdoses can result in cardiorespiratory arrest. If an overdose is suspected, discontinue therapy and monitor the patient's clinical status (e.g., cardiorespiratory, renal, and liver function, hematologic status, serum electrolytes) and administer supportive therapy as required. Amphotericin B is not hemodialyzable. Prior to reinstituting therapy, the patient's condition should be stabilized (including correction of electrolyte deficiencies, etc.).

Dosage: Amphotericin B should be administered by **slow** i.v. infusion, given over a period of approximately 6 hours, observing the usual precautions for i.v. therapy. The recommended concentration for i.v. infusion is 0.1 mg/mL (1 mg/10 mL).

Since tolerance to amphotericin B varies individually, dosage must be adjusted to the specific requirements of each patient. Therapy is usually initiated with a total daily dose of 0.25 mg/kg of body weight and **gradually** increased as tolerance permits. There are insufficient data presently available to define total dosage requirements and duration of treatment necessary for eradication of mycoses such as phycomycoses. The optimal dose is unknown. The total daily dose may range up to a level of 1 mg/kg of body weight. Dosage may range up to 1.5 mg/kg when an alternate day regimen is used.
Caution: Under no circumstances should a total daily dosage of 1.5 mg/kg be exceeded. Amphotericin B overdoses can result in cardiorespiratory arrest (see Overdose: Symptoms and Treatment).

Duration of therapy depends on such factors as the etiologic agent, anatomic locations of the lesions, stage and severity of the infection and ability of the patient to tolerate amphotericin B. Several months of therapy are usually necessary; a shorter period of therapy may produce an inadequate response and lead to a relapse.

Therapy with i.v. amphotericin B for sporotrichosis has ranged up to nine months. The usual dose per injection is 20 mg.

Aspergillosis has been treated with amphotericin B administered i.v. for a period up to 11 months with a total dose of up to 3.6 g.

Rhinocerebral phycomycosis, a fulminating disease, generally occurs in association with diabetic ketoacidosis. Therefore, it is imperative that rapid restoration of diabetic control be instituted before successful treatment can be accomplished. In contradistinction, pulmonary phycomycosis, which is more common in association with hematologic malignancies, is often an incidental finding at autopsy. A cumulative dose of at least 3 g of amphotericin B is recommended. Although a total dose of 3 to 4 g will sometimes cause lasting renal impairment, this would seem a reasonable minimum where there is clinical evidence of invasion of the deep tissues. Since rhinocerebral phycomycosis usually follows a rapidly fatal course, the therapeutic approach must necessarily be more aggressive than that used in indolent mycoses.
Preparation of Solutions: Reconstitute the dry powder as follows: An initial concentrate of 5 mg amphotericin B/mL is first prepared by adding 10 mL Sterile Water for Injection USP **without a bacteriostatic agent** to the vial of dry powder and shaking the vial until the liquid is clear.

The infusion liquid, providing 0.1 mg amphotericin B/mL is then obtained by further dilution (1:50) with 5% Dextrose Injection USP **of pH above 4.2** to a volume of 500 mL. The pH of each container of Dextrose Injection should be ascertained before use. Commercial Dextrose Injection usually has a pH above 4.2; however, if it is below 4.2, 1 or 2 mL of sterile buffer should be added to the Dextrose Injection before it is used to dilute the concentrated solution of amphotericin B. The Dextrose Injection should then be retested to ascertain that the pH has been adjusted to the required range.
The recommended buffer has the following composition: dibasic sodium phosphate (anhydrous) 1.59 g, monobasic sodium phosphate (anhydrous) 0.96 g, water for injection USP q.s. 100 mL.

The buffer should be sterilized before it is added to the Dextrose Injection, either by filtration through a bacterial retentive stone, mat or membrane (maximum pore size of 0.45 microns), or by autoclaving for 30 minutes at 15 pounds pressure (121°C).
Caution: Aseptic technique must be strictly observed in all handling, since no preservative or bacteriostatic agent is present in the antibiotic or in materials used to prepare it for administration. All entries into the vial or into the diluents must be made with a sterile needle. Do not reconstitute with saline solutions.

The use of any diluent other than the ones recommended or the presence of a bacteriostatic agent (e.g., benzyl alcohol) in the diluent may cause precipitation of the antibiotic. Do not use the initial concentrate or the infusion solution if there is any evidence of precipitation or foreign matter in either one.

An in-line membrane filter may be used for i.v. infusion of amphotericin B; however, the mean pore diameter of the filter should not be less than 1.0 micron in order to assure passage of the antibiotic dispersion.
Storage: Store dry powder in the refrigerator (2 to 8°C), protected against exposure to light. The concentrate (5 mg amphotericin B per mL after reconstitution with 10 mL of sterile water for injection USP) may be stored in the dark at room temperature for 24 hours, or in the refrigerator (2 to 8°C) for 1 week with minimal loss of potency and clarity. Any unused material should then be discarded. Solutions prepared for i.v. infusion (0.1 mg or less amphotericin B/mL) should be used promptly after preparation and should be protected from light during administration.

Supplied: A sterile, lyophilized powder in 20 mL vials providing 50 mg amphotericin B. Nonmedicinal ingredients: sodium desoxycholate and sodium phosphate.

FUROSEMIDE INJECTION Ⓟ

Abbott

Furosemide

Diuretic

Supplied: Each mL contains: furosemide 10 mg in sterile isotonic solution. Nonmedicinal ingredients: hydrochloric acid, sodium chloride, sodium hydroxide and water for injection. pH 9.1. Amber ampuls of 2 and 4 mL. Boxes of 50 (2 mL). Boxes of 25 (4 mL). Abboject syringes of 4 mL. Boxes of 10.

New Once-A-Week
AVONEX™
(Interferon beta-1a)
Canadians with MS should plan their treatment around their lives.
Not their lives around their treatment.
CANADA
http://www.biogen.com
1-888-456-2263
PAAB

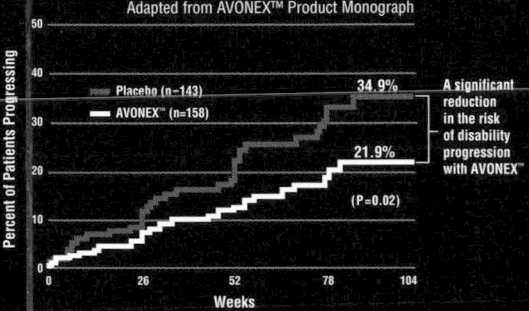

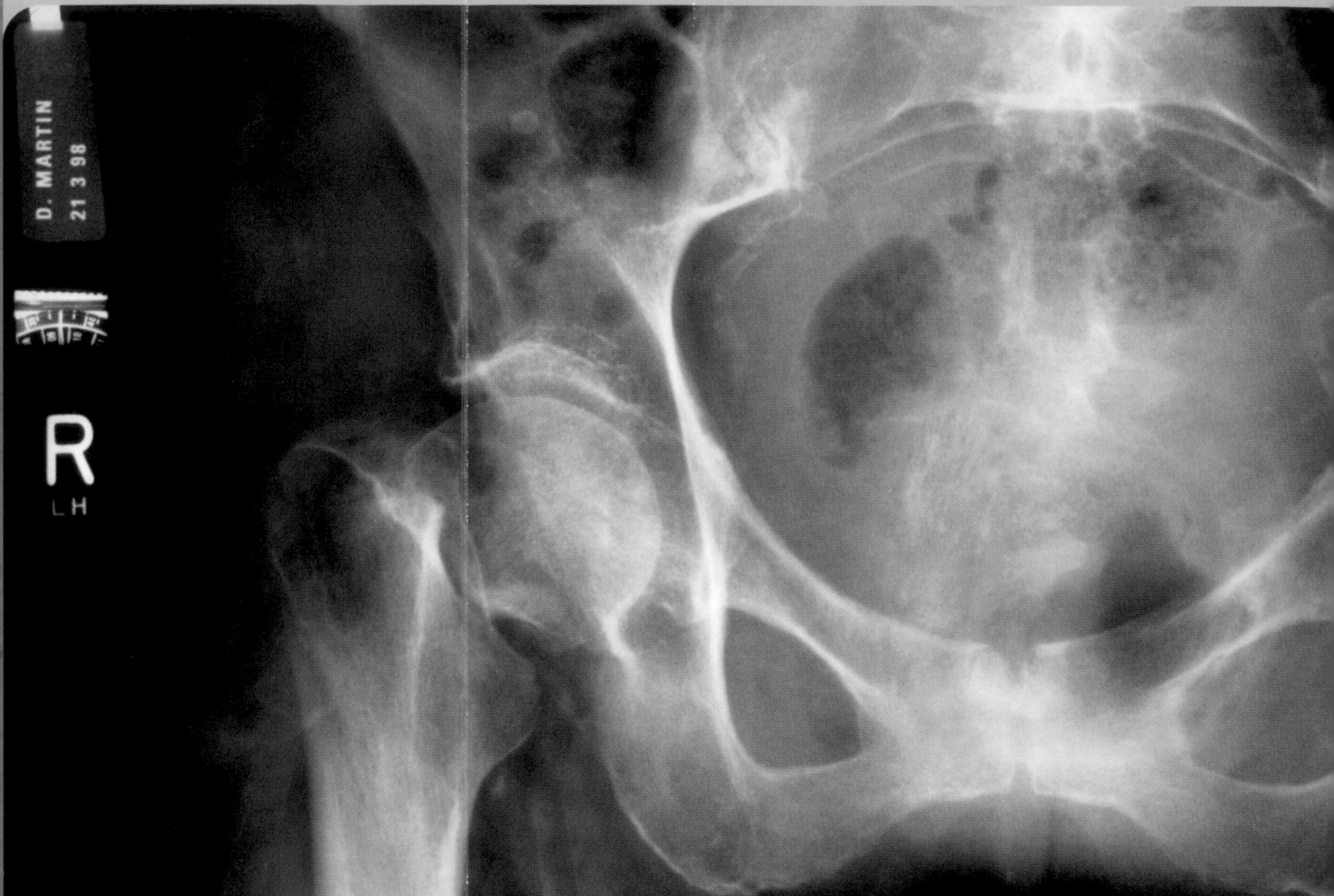
D. MARTIN
21 3 98
R
LH

Osteoporosis affects one in four women over the age of 50 in Canada.[1] Twelve to 20% of Canadian women who sustain a fracture of the hip will die within six months.[2] That's where Premarin can help. When taken long-term, Premarin has been shown to reduce osteoporotic fractures by 50%.*[3] Premarin can also offer relief from hot flushes, night sweats, vaginal dryness, and many other symptoms of menopause.[4] As well, hormone replacement therapy offers direct benefits on quality of life.[1] So when your patients ask about osteoporosis and menopause, tell them you have some very comforting news.

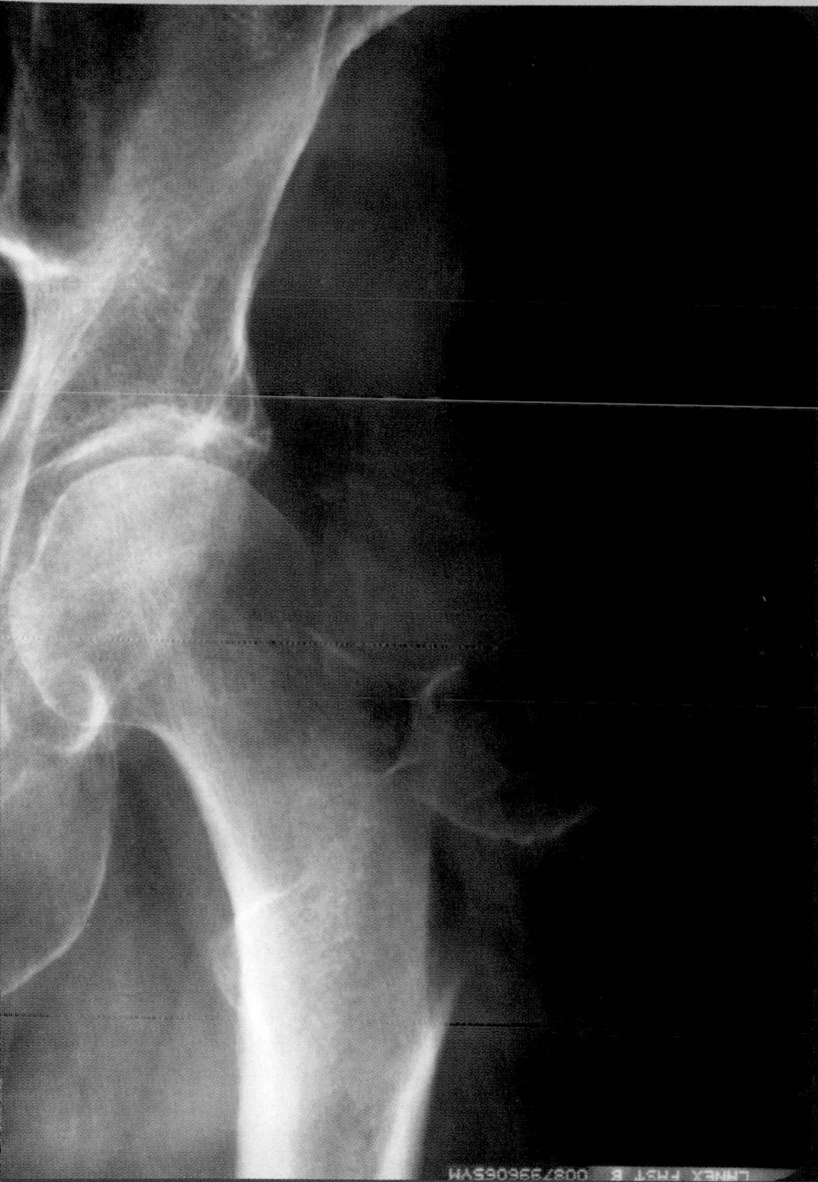

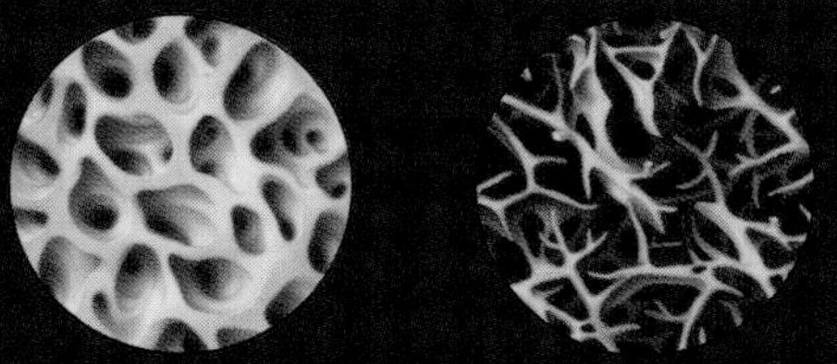

Normal Bone

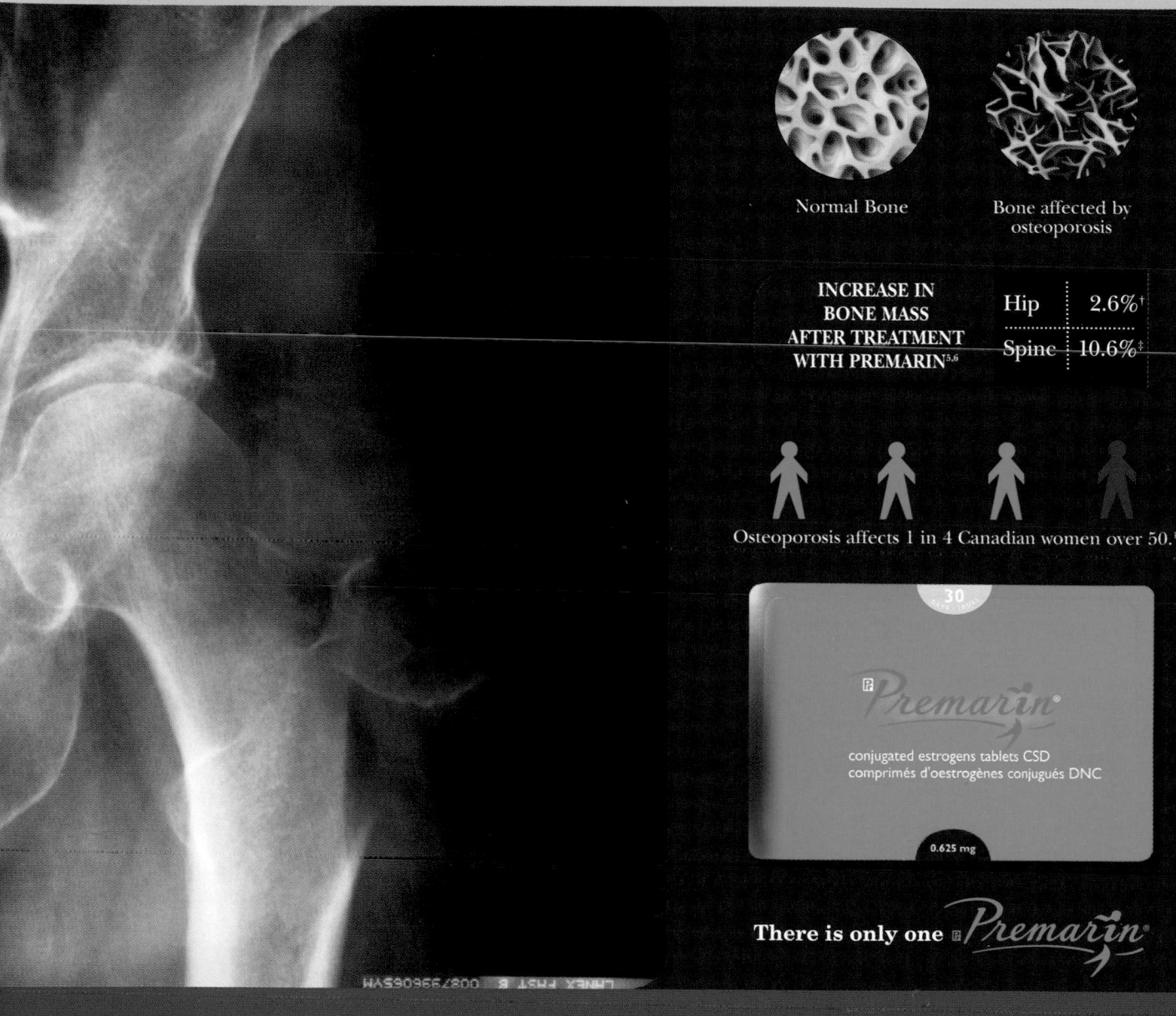

Bone affected by osteoporosis

INCREASE IN BONE MASS AFTER TREATMENT WITH PREMARIN[5,6]

Hip	2.6%†
Spine	10.6%‡

Osteoporosis affects 1 in 4 Canadian women over 50.[1]

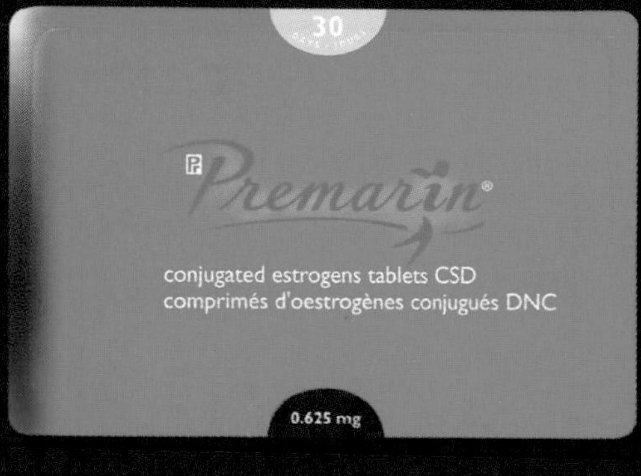

There is only one Premarin®

ve cushioned her fall.

n addition to other therapeutic measures such as diet and exercise.
ncrease from baseline in bone mineral density after 3 yrs. treatment with CEE 0.625 mg/day +/- progesterone, n=630, p=.047

WYETH-AYERST CANADA INC.
Montreal, Canada H4R 1J6

“The primary goal in the treatment of essential hypertension should be the reduction of all end-organ damage in addition to reduction of blood pressure.”[1†]

ALTACE – Bodyguard for hypertensives

- Smooth, reliable ***24-hour plus*** blood pressure control provides protection from early morning BP rise.[2,3]
- Cardioprotection that improves survival in post-AMI patients.[4‡]
- Higher tissue penetration and stronger affinity for ACE than either captopril or enalapril.[5§]

ALTACE®
ramipril
BODYGUARD FOR HYPERTENSIVES

† ALTACE, like all ACE inhibitors, is not indicated to reduce end-organ damage.

‡ Comparative clinical significance has not been established; *in-vitro* results.
§ In NYHA class I-III patients. Treatment initiated between day 3 and day 10 after AMI in stabilized patients with clinically confirmed heart failure. Average follow-up = 15 months.

In the treatment of essential hypertension, ALTACE is indicated normally when beta-blockers and diuretics are inappropriate and following acute myocardial infarction in clinically stable patients with signs of left ventricular dysfunction to improve survival and reduce hospitalization for heart failure. Like other ACE inhibitors, ALTACE is not recommended for pregnant or lactating women and should be used with caution in patients with renal insufficiency.

Product monograph available to physicians and pharmacists upon request.

Hoechst Marion Roussel

Hoechst Marion Roussel Canada Inc.
2150 St. Elzear Blvd.West
Laval, Quebec H7L 4A8

Hoechst

Hoechst Marion Roussel
The Pharmaceutical Company of Hoechst

MEMBER PMAC PAAB 50030221

G

GAMIMUNE® N

Bayer

Immune Globulin (Human), I.V.

Passive Immunizing Agent

Pharmacology: Primary Humoral Immunodeficiency: Gamimune N treated with solvent/detergent supplies a broad spectrum of opsonic and neutralizing IgG antibodies for the prevention or attenuation of a wide variety of infectious diseases. Since Gamimune N is administered i.v., essentially 100% of the infused IgG antibodies are immediately available in the recipient's circulation. Studies using a modified i.v. immunoglobulin at pH 6.8 have shown that approximately 30% of the infused IgG disappeared from the circulation in the first 24 hours due primarily to equilibration of IgG between the plasma and the extravascular space. A further decline of about 40% of the peak level found immediately post-infusion is to be expected during the first week. The in vivo half-life of Gamimune N equals or exceeds the 3-week half-life reported for IgG in the literature, but individual patient variation in half-life has been observed. Thus, this variable as well as the amount of immune globulin administered per dose is important in determining the frequency of administration of the drug for each individual patient.

A comparative study of Gamimune N, 5% treated with solvent/detergent and Gamimune N, 5% in 16 subjects demonstrated bioequivalence. A comparative study of Gamimune N 10% with Gamimune N, 5% (in 10% maltose) in 18 subjects demonstrated equivalent post-infusion recovery for the two preparations. A comparative study of Gamimune N, 10% treated with solvent/detergent and Gamimune N, 10% in 17 subjects demonstrated bioequivalence.

Idiopathic Thrombocytopenic Purpura: While Gamimune N has been shown to be effective in some cases of idiopathic thrombocytopenic purpura (ITP) (see Indications) the mechanism of action has not been fully elucidated.

Allogeneic Bone Marrow Transplantation: Gamimune N has been shown to be effective in allogeneic bone marrow transplant patients ≥20 years of age at increased risk for the following complications in the first 100 days post transplant: prevention of systemic and local infections, interstitial pneumonia of infectious and idiopathic etiologies and acute graft-versus-host disease (GVHD) (see Indications).

Administration of Gamimune N to allogeneic bone marrow transplant patients significantly increased IgG and IgG subclass levels while those seen in the control group fell below predicted levels. The mechanism of action of Gamimune N in reducing the incidence of GVHD is presently unknown.

Pediatric HIV Infection: Children infected with human immunodeficiency virus (HIV) may display defects in both cellular and humoral immunity. As a result, children with AIDS have a markedly increased rate of serious, potentially life-threatening bacterial infections. The types of bacterial and viral infections observed in HIV-infected children are similar to those in children with primary hypogammaglobulinemia. The replacement of opsonic and neutralizing IgG antibodies has been shown to reduce a wide variety of infectious diseases in HIV-infected children.

General: The i.v. administration of solutions of maltose has been studied by several investigators. Healthy subjects tolerated the infusions well, and no adverse effects were observed at a rate of 0.25 g maltose/kg body weight/hour. In safety studies, infusions of 10% maltose administered at 0.27 to 0.62 g maltose/kg/h to normal subjects produced either mild side effects (e.g., headache) or no adverse reaction. Following i.v. administrations of maltose, maltose was detected in the peripheral blood; there was a dose-dependent excretion of maltose and glucose in the urine and a mild diuretic effect. These alterations were well tolerated without significant adverse effects. The highest recommended infusion rate, 0.06 mL/kg body weight/min (see Dosage), is equivalent to 0.36 g maltose/kg body weight/h.

The buffer capacity of Immune Globulin (Human), 5% is 16.5 mEq/L (approximately 0.3 mEq/g protein). A dose of 1 000 mg/kg body weight therefore represents an acid load of 0.33 mEq/kg body weight. The total buffering capacity of whole blood in a normal individual is 45 to 50 mEq/L of blood, or 3.6 mEq/kg body weight. Thus, the acid load delivered with a dose of 1 000 mg/kg of Gamimune N, 5% would be neutralized by the buffering capacity of whole blood alone, even if the dose were infused instantaneously. (An infusion usually lasts several hours.)

In Phase 1 human studies, no change in arterial blood pH measurements was detected following the i.v. administration of Gamimune N, 5% at a dose of 150 mg/kg body weight; following a dose of 400 mg/kg body weight in 37 patients, there were no clinically important differences in mean venous pH or bicarbonate measurements in patients who received Gamimune N, 5% compared with those who received a chemically modified i.v. immunoglobulin preparation with a pH of 6.8.

Glycine (aminoacetic acid) is a non-essential amino acid normally present in the body. Glycine is a major ingredient in amino acid solutions employed in i.v. alimentation. While toxic effects of glycine administration have been reported, the doses and rates of administration were 3 to 4-fold greater than those for Gamimune N, 10%.

The buffer capacity of Gamimune N, 10% is 35 mEq/L (approximately 0.35 mEq/g protein). A dose of 1 000 mg/kg body weight therefore represents an acid load of 0.35 mEq/kg body weight. The total buffering capacity of whole blood in a normal individual is 45 to 50 mEq/L of blood, or 3.6 mEq/kg body weight. Thus, the acid load delivered with a dose of 1 000 mg/kg of Gamimune N, 10% would be neutralized by the buffering capacity of whole blood alone, even if the dose were infused instantaneously.

In Phase I human studies comparing Gamimune N, 10% with Gamimune N, 5% (in 10% maltose) venous blood measurements were taken following the i.v. administration of 400 mg/kg body weight in 18 patients. There were no clinically important changes in mean venous pH, bicarbonate, or base excess measurements in these patients receiving either preparation.

In a similar, earlier Phase I study Gamimune N, 5% (in 10% maltose) was compared with a chemically modified 5% i.v. immunoglobulin preparation with a pH of 6.8. No clinically important changes in mean venous pH and bicarbonate measurements were detected following infusions of either preparation at doses of 400 mg/kg body weight in 37 patients.

In patients with limited or compromised acid-base compensatory mechanisms, consideration should be given to the effect the additional acid and/or protein load Gamimune N might present.

Indications: Primary Humoral Immunodeficiency: Gamimune N is efficacious in the treatment of primary immunodeficiency states in which severe impairment of antibody forming capacity has been shown, such as congenital agammaglobulinemias, common variable immunodeficiency, Wiskott-Aldrich syndrome, x-linked immunodeficiency with hyper IgM, and severe combined immunodeficiencies. It is especially useful when high levels or rapid elevation of circulating antibodies are desired or when i.m. injections are contraindicated.

Idiopathic Thrombocytopenic Purpura (ITP): In clinical situations in which a rapid rise in platelet count is needed to control bleeding or to allow a patient with ITP to undergo surgery, administration of Gamimune N should be considered. Studies with Gamimune N, 5% demonstrate that in patients in whom a response was achieved, the rise of platelets was generally rapid (within 1 to 5 days), transient (most often lasting from several days to several weeks) and were not considered curative. It is presently not possible to predict which patients with ITP will respond to therapy, although the increase in platelet counts in children seems to be better than that of adults. Childhood ITP may, however, respond spontaneously without treatment.

Gamimune N, 10% has been studied in 31 adult and pediatric subjects with ITP using a dosage of 1 000 mg/kg body weight on either 1 day or 2 consecutive days. Fourteen of 16 children (87.5%) and 9 of 10 adults with platelet follow-up (90%) responded to treatment with clinically significant platelet increments of ≥30 000/mm³. In the 12 children with acute ITP, there was an average increase in platelet count above baseline of 274 000/mm³ (range 33 000 to 529 000/mm³).

Two different dosing regimens of Gamimune N, 5% have been studied in clinical investigations: a regimen consisting of 400 mg/kg body weight daily for 5 consecutive days, and a high dose treatment regimen consisting of 1 000 mg/kg body weight administered on either 1 day or 2 consecutive days (these studies are summarized below).

In clinical studies of Gamimune N, 5%, 5 of 6 (83.3%) children and 12 of 16 (75%) adults with acute or chronic ITP treated with 400 mg/kg body weight for 5 consecutive days demonstrated clinically significant platelet increments of ≥30 000 mm³ over baseline. The mean platelet count in children with ITP rose from 27 800/mm³ at baseline to 297 000/mm³ (range 50 000 to 455 000/mm³) and the mean platelet count in adults with ITP rose from 27 900/mm³ at baseline to 124 900/mm³ (range 11 000 to 341 000/mm³). Two of 3 children with acute ITP rapidly went into complete remission.

Thirteen of 14 children (92.9%) and 26 of 29 adults (89.7%) with acute or chronic ITP treated with Gamimune N, 5%, 1 000 mg/kg body weight administered on either 1 day or 2 consecutive days responded to treatment with clinically significant platelet increments of ≥30 000/mm³ over baseline. This included 3 of 3 patients with ITP that were human immunodeficiency virus (HIV) antibody positive and 2 of 2 patients with ITP that were pregnant. The mean platelet count in children with ITP treated with Gamimune N, 5% 1 000 mg/kg body weight on 1 day or 2 consecutive days rose from 44 400/mm³ at baseline to 285 600/mm³ (range 89 000 to 473 000/mm³) and the mean platelet count in adults with ITP treated with the regimen rose from 23 400/mm³ at baseline to 173 100/mm³ (range 28 000 to 709 000/mm³). Two patients, one each with acute adult and chronic childhood ITP, entered complete remission with treatment.

Six of the 29 adult patients with ITP received Gamimune N, 5% 1 000 mg/kg on 1 day or 2 consecutive days to increase the platelet count prior to splenectomy. Mean platelet counts rose from 14 500/mm³ at baseline to 129 300/mm³ (range 51 000 to 242 000/mm³) prior to surgery.

The duration of the platelet rise following treatment of ITP with either treatment regimen of Gamimune N, 5% was variable, ranging from several days to 12 months or more. Some ITP patients have demonstrated continuing responsiveness over many months to intermittent infusions of Gamimune N, 5% at doses of 400 to 1 000 mg/kg body weight, administered as a single maintenance dose, at intervals as indicated by the platelet count.

Allogeneic Bone Marrow Transplantation: Gamimune N could be considered for use in allogeneic bone marrow transplant (BMT) patients ≥20 years of age to decrease the risk of septicemia and other infections, interstitial pneumonia of infectious or idiopathic etiologies and acute graft-versus-host disease (GVHD) in the first 100 days post-transplant.

Gamimune N is not indicated in allogeneic bone marrow transplant patients below 20 years of age.

In a controlled study of 369 evaluable bone marrow transplant patients (185 untreated and 184 treated with Gamimune N, 5% in doses of 500 mg/kg body weight on days −7 and −2 pretransplant then weekly through day 90 post-transplant), post-transplant complications were evaluated. Analysis of the study group as a whole and of those <20 and ≥20 years of age showed significant reductions in post-transplant complications in the first 100 days. This was most evident in patients 20 years of age and over. For patients ≥20 years of age (128 patients in the control group and 119 patients in the treated group), there was a statistically significant reduction in interstitial pneumonia from 21% in the control group to 9% in the treated group (p=0.0032) during the first 100 days post-transplant. Also significantly reduced in this age group were: overall septicemia from 41% in the control group to 22% in the treated group (relative risk [RR] 2.36, p=0.0025); gram-negative septicemia from 19% in the control group to 7% in the treated group (RR 2.53, p=0.015); and Grade II to IV acute GVHD from 53% (58 of 110) in the control group to 35% in the treated group (38 of 108, p=0.0051).

In patients below age 20, there appeared to be no benefit from treatment with Gamimune N, either in reducing the incidence of infections or the incidence of acute GVHD.

Pediatric HIV Infection: Gamimune N, 5%, 400 mg/kg every 28 days, significantly decreases the frequency of serious and minor bacterial infections (laboratory-proven and clinically diagnosed) and the frequency of hospitalization, and increases the time free of serious infection in children with clinical or immunologic evidence of HIV disease with CD4+ counts of ≥200 mm³. Gamimune N, 5% did not have any effect on mortality or on the frequency of opportunistic infection. To

Gamimune N (cont'd)

achieve optional efficacy the CD4+ counts should be determined prior to the onset of therapy. See Table I.

Table I—Gamimune N

No. of Serious Infections				
	None	1	2 to 5	≥5
Gamimune N, 5%	136	30	25	0
Placebo	107	45	40	1

In a randomized, double-blind, placebo-controlled, multicenter study, 383 HIV-infected, nonhemophilic children less than 13 years of age were randomized. Of the children randomized, 369 were included in the efficacy analysis and 376 in the safety analysis. The study population had 1) a mean age of 40 months (range 2.4 to 136.8 months), 2) acquired HIV primarily through vertical transmission (91%), 3) a majority (82%) of CDC Class P-2 (symptomatic), and 4) had a median CD4+ count of 937 cells/mm³ (range 0 to 6 660 cells/mm³). At the time of study entry, 14% (52 of 369) were receiving P. carinii pneumonia (PCP) prophylaxis. During the course of the study, 51% (189 of 369) received PCP prophylaxis and 44% (154 of 359) received zidovudine (ZDV). Children with HIV-1 infection were initially stratified into 2 groups based upon CD4+ count (<200 cells/mm³ versus ≥200 cells/mm³) and CDC classification of pediatric HIV disease (history of opportunistic infections [P-2-D-1] and recurrent serious bacterial infections [P-2-D-2] versus others). Subjects received Gamimune N, 5% (400 mg/kg=8 mL/kg) (n=185) or an equivalent volume of placebo (0.1% Albumin [Human]) (n=184) every 28 days. The mean follow-up for subjects receiving Gamimune N, 5% was 17.9 months and 17.6 months for patients on placebo.

The number of subjects who had at least 1 serious bacterial infection was 86 of 184 (47%) in the placebo group and 55 of 185 (30%) in the Gamimune N, 5% group (p=0.0009). All p-values reported are 2-sided. Treatment with Gamimune N, 5% compared to placebo was also associated with a significant reduction in both the number of subjects with at least 1 laboratory-proven infection (36 of 184 vs. 18 of 185, p=0.0081), and the number of subjects with at least 1 clinically diagnosed infection (71 of 184 vs. 45 of 185, p=0.0036). Efficacy in patients with CD4+ counts <200/mm³ was not established, possibly because of the small number of subjects in this category.

The 2-year treatment period defined in the protocol was truncated for some patients by the DSMB based on data from the interim analysis. Rates of serious bacterial infections per 100 patient years were computed and analyzed to take into account both the unequal duration of treatment and follow-up, as well as recurrent infections in individual subjects.

Children treated with Gamimune N, 5% experienced a 50% lower frequency of laboratory-proven serious bacterial infection compared to the group treated with placebo (9.1 vs. 18.2 infections per 100 patient years, p=0.031), a 36% lower frequency of clinically diagnosed serious infections (24 vs. 37.5 infections per 100 patient years, p=0.003), a 40.6% reduction in total serious infections (laboratory proven and clinically diagnosed) (33.1 vs. 55.7 infections per 100 patients years, p=0.009), a 60% lower frequency of primary bacteremia (5.8 vs. 14.5 infections per 100 patient years, p=0.009), a 75.5% lower frequency of S. pneumoniae bacteremia (1.1 vs. 4.4 bacteremias per 100 patient years, p=0.026), a 54.3% lower frequency of clinically diagnosed pneumonias (12.7 vs. 27.8 infections per 100 patient years, p=0.001), and a 22.5% lower frequency of minor bacterial infections (including otitis media, skin and soft tissue infections, and upper respiratory tract infections) (123.6 vs. 159.5 infections per 100 patient years, p=0.033).

In addition to a reduced frequency of infection, children treated with Gamimune N, 5% had a 36.8% lower number of hospitalizations per 100 patient years (72 vs. 114 per 100 patient years, p=0.002) and a reduced average annual number of hospital days (6.9 vs. 10.5, p=0.030) than patients treated with placebo. In addition, Gamimune N, 5% treated patients had a higher probability of remaining free of laboratory proven infections (p=0.0093) and combined laboratory proven and clinically diagnosed infections (p=0.0015) for 24 months than the group treated with placebo. At 24 months, the estimated probabilities of remaining infection-free for the Immune Globulin I.V. (Human) and placebo arms were 87.8% vs. 76% respectively, for laboratory proven infections and 63.5% vs. 44.5% respectively, for combined laboratory proven and clinically diagnosed infections.

There was no effect of Gamimune N, 5% therapy on mortality, which was low in all study groups, or on frequency of opportunistic infection, regardless of treatment group.

This study was not designed to evaluate possible interactions between Gamimune N, 5% and trimethoprim/sulfamethoxazole (TMP-SMZ) but a study by Spector et al did prospectively stratify patients receiving TMP-SMZ. However, the Bayer study stratified patients based on CD4+ counts <200/mm³ and/or HIV defining infection vs CD4+ counts >200/mm³ and no HIV defining infection. In actuality, these 2 different stratification schemes probably selected for nearly the same subgroups (namely less vs. more ill). In both studies, the effect of Gamimune N, 5% was less apparent in the more ill group (i.e., CD4+ count <200/mm³ group in the Bayer study, TMP-SMZ group in the Spector study). When a statistical correction was applied to the Bayer database to assess the effect of TMP-SMZ on Gamimune N, 5% affect, there was no interaction specifically seen.

Contraindications: In individuals who are known to have had an anaphylactic or severe systemic response to Immune Globulin (Human). Individuals with selective IgA deficiencies who have known antibody against IgA (anti-IgA antibody) should not receive Gamimune N since these patients may experience severe reactions to the IgA which may be present.

Warnings: Gamimune N should be administered i.v. only, since the i.m. and s.c. routes have not been evaluated.

Gamimune N has, on rare occasions, caused a precipitous fall in blood pressure and a clinical picture of anaphylaxis, even when the patient is not known to be sensitive to immune globulin preparations. These reactions may be related to the rate of infusion. Accordingly, the infusion rate given under Dosage should be closely followed, at least until the physician has had sufficient experience with a given patient. The patient's vital signs should be monitored continuously and careful observation made for any symptoms throughout the entire infusion. Epinephrine should be available for the treatment of an acute anaphylactic reaction.

Precautions: General: Any vial that has been entered should be used promptly. Partially used vials should be discarded. Do not use if turbid. Solution which has been frozen should not be used.

An aseptic meningitis syndrome (AMS) has been reported to occur infrequently in association with Immune Globulin I.V. (Human) (IGIV) treatment. The syndrome usually begins within several hours to 2 days following IGIV treatment. It is characterized by symptoms and signs including severe headache, nuchal rigidity, drowsiness, fever, photophobia, painful eye movements, and nausea and vomiting. Cerebrospinal fluid studies are frequently positive with pleocytosis up to several thousand cells per cu.mm, predominantly from the granulocytic series, and elevated protein levels up to several hundred mg/dL. Patients exhibiting such symptoms and signs should receive a thorough neurological examination, including CSF studies, to rule out other causes of meningitis. AMS may occur more frequently in association with high dose (2 g/kg) IGIV treatment. Discontinuation of IGIV treatment has resulted in remission of AMS within several days without sequelae.

Isolated reports have appeared of transient and reversible renal insufficiency following administration of Immune Globulin I.V. therapy. The mechanics involved are uncertain.

Drug Interactions: Antibodies in Gamimune N may interfere with the response to live viral vaccines such as measles, mumps and rubella. Therefore, use of such vaccines should be deferred until approximately 6 months after Gamimune N administration.

Please see Dosage for other drug interactions.

Pregnancy: Animal reproduction studies have not been conducted with Gamimune N. It is not known whether Gamimune N can cause fetal harm when administered to a pregnant woman or can affect reproduction capacity. Gamimune N should be given to a pregnant woman only if benefits outweigh risks.

Adverse Effects: In a study of 37 patients with immunodeficiency syndromes receiving Gamimune N, 5% at a monthly dose of 400 mg/kg body weight, reactions were seen in 5.2% of the infusions. Symptoms reported included malaise, a feeling of faintness, fever, chills, headache, nausea, vomiting, chest tightness, dyspnea and chest, back or hip pain. Mild erythema following infiltration of Gamimune N, 5% at the infusion site was reported in some cases. A safety study has been conducted in 16 adult and adolescent subjects with primary immunodeficiency syndrome, comparing the side effects and bioequivalency of Gamimune N, 5% with those of Gamimune N, 5% treated with solvent/detergent. The incidence, nature and severity of reactions with Gamimune N, 5% treated with solvent/detergent were not different from those observed with Gamimune N, 5%.

A safety study has been conducted in 20 adult and pediatric subjects with primary immunodeficiency syndrome comparing side effects of Gamimune N, 5% with those of Gamimune N, 10%. The incidence, nature, or severity of reactions with Gamimune N, 10% were not different from those observed with Gamimune N, 5%, and were consistent with those observed in previous studies with Gamimune N, 5%. Symptoms related to the infusion of Gamimune N, 10% were observed in 9 (3.5%) of 255 infusions. These symptoms were all mild to moderate in severity and included chills, fever, headache and emesis.

A safety study has been conducted in 17 adult and adolescent subjects with primary immunodeficiency syndrome, comparing side effects and bioequivalency of Gamimune N, 10% with those of Gamimune N, 10% treated with solvent/detergent. The incidence, nature and severity of reactions with Gamimune N, 10% treated with solvent/detergent were not different from those observed with Gamimune N, 10%.

In studies of Gamimune N, 5% administered at a dose of 400 mg/kg body weight in the treatment of adult and pediatric patients with ITP, systemic reactions were noted in 4 of 154 (2.6%) infusions, and all but one occurred at rates of infusions greater than 0.04 mL/kg body weight/minute. The symptoms reported included chest tightness, a sense of tachycardia (pulse was 84 beats/minute), and a burning sensation in the head; these symptoms were all mild and transient.

In studies of Gamimune N, 5% administered at a dose of 1 000 mg/kg body weight either as a single dose or as 2 doses on consecutive days in the treatment of adult and pediatric patients with ITP, adverse reactions were noted in 25 of 251 (10%) infusions. Symptoms reported included headache, nausea, fever, chills, back pain, chest tightness, shortness of breath. In children, the high dose regimen has been well-tolerated at the highest rates of infusion. In adults, however, the frequency of adverse reactions tended to increase with infusion rates in excess of 0.06 mL/kg/min. In general, reactions reported with infusion of Gamimune N, 5% in these studies were reported as mild or moderate.

An investigation of Gamimune N, 10% in 31 adult and pediatric subjects with ITP encountered side effects in 17 of 119 (14.3%) infusions. The dosage in these studies was 1 000 mg/kg body weight for 1 day or 2 consecutive days. However, in the adult study, an induction dosage of 500 mg/kg body weight for 1 day or 2 consecutive days was associated with 17 of these infusions. Of those 17 infusions, three had adverse events. Overall side effects included mild chest pain, mild and moderate emesis, moderate fever, mild or moderate headache (severe on one occasion) and a single incidence of hives, pruritus and rash. At least 17 of the 50 infusions in the pediatric study were given at rates of ≥0.1 mL/kg body weight per minute as part of a rate escalation investigation. Maximum infusion rates obtained were not limited by or interrupted due to adverse effects.

In studies of Gamimune N, 5% administered to 185 bone marrow transplant recipients at doses of 500 mg/kg (10 mL/kg) from day −7 and day −2 pretransplant then weekly through day 90 post-transplant, adverse reactions were noted in 12 (6.5%) of the 185 treated patients and in 14 (0.6%) of 2 176 infusions. All reactions reported were rate-related and classified as mild. Chills were the most common symptom reported, occurring in 9 patients. The other symptoms reported included headache, flushing, fever, pruritus and slight back discomfort. All reactions resolved satisfactorily, usually without treatment or decreasing the infusion rate.

In a study with pediatric HIV infection patients, 376 patients, 187 treated with Gamimune N, 5% 400 mg/kg, and 189 treated with placebo [0.1% Albumin (Human)], were evaluated for safety. Adverse reactions occurred during or within 24 hours of an infusion in 50 of 3 451 (1.4%) infusions of Gamimune N, 5% and 62 of 3 447 (1.8%) infusions of placebo. Fever was the most common symptom reported for both groups treated with placebo and Gamimune N, 5% with 30 of 105 (28.6%) reported symptoms and 19 of 78 (24.4%) reported symptoms, respectively. Irritability was the second most common reported, with 10 (9.5%) reports for the placebo group and 9 (11.5%) for the group treated with Gamimune N, 5%. A large number of diverse symptoms accounted for the remaining symptoms in both groups. In general, the number of adverse events reported was comparable in both the placebo and Gamimune N, 5% treated groups. Three serious adverse reactions were reported. One patient experienced a hypersensitivity reaction and did not receive further Gamimune N, 5% treatment. A second patient developed tachycardia and was admitted to an intensive care unit, but later continued treatment with Gamimune N, 5%. A third patient had skin infiltration during infusion and developed a full thickness skin slough over the dorsum of the hand that required skin grafting.

In the studies undertaken to date, other types of reactions have not been reported with Gamimune N. It may be, however, that adverse effects will be similar to those previously reported with i.v. and i.m. immunoglobulin administration. Potential reactions, therefore, may also include anxiety, flushing, wheezing, abdominal cramps, myalgias, arthralgia, and dizziness; rash has been reported rarely. Reactions to i.v. immunoglobulin tend to be related to the rate of infusion.

True anaphylactic reactions to Gamimune N may occur in recipients with documented prior histories of severe allergic reactions to i.m. immunoglobulin, but some patients may tolerate cautiously administered i.v. immunoglobulin without adverse effects. Very rarely an anaphylactoid reaction may occur in patients with no prior history of severe allergic reactions to either i.m. or i.v. immunoglobulin.

Dosage: General: For i.v. use only. Dosages for specific indications are indicated below, but in general, it is recommended that Gamimune N be infused by itself at a rate of 0.01 to 0.02 mL/kg body weight/min for 30 minutes; if well-tolerated, the rate may be **gradually** increased to a maximum of 0.08 mL/kg body weight/minute. Investigations indicate that Gamimune N is well-tolerated and less likely to produce side effects when infused at the indicated rate. If side effects occur, the rate may be reduced, or the infusion interrupted until symptoms subside. The infusion may then be resumed at the rate which is comfortable for the patient. Parenteral drug products should be inspected visually for particulate matter and discoloration prior to administration, whenever solution and container permit.

It is recommended that infusion of Gamimune N be given by a separate line, by itself, without mixing with other i.v. fluids or medications the patient might be receiving. Gamimune N should not be mixed with Immune Globulin I.V. (Human), from another manufacturer. Gamimune N is not compatible with saline. If dilution is required, Gamimune N, may be diluted with 5% dextrose in water (D5/W). No other drug interactions or compatibilities have been evaluated.

In patients with limited or compromised acid base compensatory mechanisms and in patients in whom there is already an expanded fluid volume (e.g., during pregnancy), consideration should be given to the effect of the additional acid or protein load that i.v. Gamimune N might present.

Primary Humoral Immunodeficiency: The usual dosage of Gamimune N for prophylaxis in primary immunodeficiency syndromes is 100 to 200 mg/kg of body weight administered approximately once a month by i.v. infusion. The dosage may be given more frequently or increased as high as 400 mg/kg body weight, if the clinical response is inadequate, or the level of IgG achieved in the circulation is felt to be insufficient. The minimum level of IgG required for protection has not been determined.

Idiopathic Thrombocytopenic Purpura (ITP): Induction: An increase in platelet count has been observed in children and some adults with acute or chronic ITP receiving Gamimune N, 5% 400 mg/kg body weight daily for 5 days. Alternatively, studies in adults and children with Gamimune N, 5% and Gamimune N, 10% using a dose of 1 000 mg/kg body weight daily for 1 day or 2 consecutive days have also shown increases in platelet count. In the latter treatment regimen, if an adequate increase in the platelet count is observed at 24 hours, the second dose of 1 000 mg/kg body weight may be withheld. The high dose regimen (1 000 mg/kg for 1 to 2 days) is not recommended for individuals with expanded fluid volumes or where fluid volume may be a concern. With both treatment regimens, a response usually occurs within several days and is maintained for a variable period of time. In general, a response is seen less often in adults than in children.

Maintenance: In adults and children with ITP, if after induction therapy the platelet count falls to a level felt to be insufficient for the protection or normal function of the patient and/or the patient manifests clinically significant bleeding, Gamimune N 400 mg/kg body weight may be given as a single infusion. If an adequate response does not result, the dose can be increased to 800 to 1 000 mg/kg of body weight given as a single infusion. Maintenance infusions may be administered intermittently as clinically indicated to maintain an adequate platelet count.

Allogeneic Bone Marrow Transplantation: Gamimune N should be administered in doses of 500 mg/kg body weight beginning on days −7 and −2 pretransplant (or at the time conditioning therapy for transplantation is begun), then weekly through day 90 post-transplant. Gamimune N may be administered by itself through a Hickman line while it is in place, and thereafter through a peripheral vein.

Pediatric HIV Infection: A reduction in the incidence of infections has been observed in children infected with the HIV virus whose CD4+ counts are ≥200 mm³. Gamimune N, 5% should be administered at a dose of 400 mg/kg (8 mL/kg) body weight every 28 days.

Supplied: Gamimune N, 5%: Immune Globulin I.V. (Human), 5% treated with solvent/detergent, is a sterile 4.5 to 5.5% solution of human protein in 9 to 11% maltose; it contains no preservatives. Each mL contains approximately 50 mg of protein, not less than 98% of which has the electrophoretic mobility of gamma globulin and approximately 100 mg maltose. Not less than 90% of the immunoglobulin is monomer. Also present are traces of IgA and of IgM. The distribution of IgG subclasses is similar to that found in normal serum. Gamimune N, 5% has a buffer capacity of 16.5 mEq/L of solution (approximately 0.3 mEq/g of protein). The calculated osmolality is 309 mOsm/kg of solvent (water) and the calculated osmolarity is 278 mOsm/L of solution.

Single use vials of 10, 20, 50, 100, 250 and 500 mL. The 10 mL vial contains 500 mg protein; the 20 mL vial contains 1 g protein; the 50 mL vial contains 2.5 g protein; the 100 mL vial contains 5 g protein; the 250 mL vial contains 12.5 g protein; the 500 mL vial contains 25 g protein.

Gamimune N, 10%: Immune Globulin I.V. (Human), 10% treated with solvent/detergent, is a sterile solution of human protein containing no preservative. Gamimune N, 10% consists of 9 to 11% protein in 0.16 to 0.24 M glycine. Each mL contains approximately 100 mg of protein, not less than 98% of which has the electrophoretic mobility of gamma globulin, and approximately 12 to 18 mg glycine. Not less than 90% of the IgG is monomer. Also present are traces of IgA and of IgM. The distribution of IgG subclasses is similar to that found in normal serum. The measured buffer capacity is 35 mEq/L and the osmolality is 274 mOsmol/kg solvent.

Single use vials of 10, 25, 50, 100 and 200 mL. The 10 mL vial contains 1g protein; the 25 mL vial contains 2.5 g protein; the 50 mL vial contains 5 g protein; the 100 mL vial contains 10 g protein; the 200 mL vial contains 20 g protein.

The products are made by cold ethanol fractionation of large pools of human plasma. Part of the fractionation may be performed by another licensed manufacturer. The immunoglobulin is isolated from Cohn Effluent III by diafiltration and ultrafiltration. The solution is adjusted to 0.3 to 0.4% tri-n-butyl phosphate (TNBP) and 0.2 to 0.3% sodium cholate. After addition of the solvent (TNBP) and the detergent (sodium cholate), the solution is heated at 30° C and maintained at that temperature for not less than 6 hours. After the viral inactivation step the reactants are removed by precipitation, filtration and finally diafiltration and ultrafiltration. The protein has not been chemically modified other than in the adjustment of the pH of the solution to 4.0 to 4.5. Isotonicity is achieved by the addition of maltose, for Gamimune N, 5%, or glycine for Gamimune N, 10%. Gamimune N, 5% and 10% treated with solvent/detergent are then incubated in the final container (at the low pH of 4.25), for a minimum of 21 days at 20° C. The products are intended for i.v. administration.

The removal and inactivation of spiked model enveloped and non-enveloped viruses during the manufacturing process for Gamimune N, 5% and 10% has been validated in laboratory studies. Human Immunodeficiency Virus, Type 1 (HIV-1) was chosen as the relevant virus for blood products; Bovine Viral Diarrhea Virus (BVDV) was chosen to model for Hepatitis C Virus; Pseudorabies Virus (PRV) was chosen to model for Hepatitis B and Herpes viruses; and Reo Virus type 3 (Reo) was chosen to model non-enveloped viruses and for its resistance to physical and chemical inactivation. Significant removal of model enveloped and non-enveloped viruses is seen between the Fraction II + IIIW and the Effluent III steps and between the Effluent III and the Filtrate III steps. Significant reduction of enveloped viruses is achieved at the time of treatment of Filtrate III with TNBP/sodium cholate and also at the time of the low pH incubation in the final container.

Store between 2 and 8°C. Do not freeze. Do not use after expiration date.

Reviewed 1998

...The health care professional should carefully weigh the anticipated therapeutic benefit from any drug against all potential adverse effects.

GARAMYCIN® Ophthalmic/Otic Preparations ℞

Schering

Gentamicin Sulfate

Topical Antibiotic

Pharmacology: Gentamicin, an aminoglycoside antibiotic, is active against the gram-positive bacteria commonly found in eye-ear infections: coagulase-positive and coagulase-negative Staphylococci; Group A beta-hemolytic and non-hemolytic Streptococci; and Diplococcus pneumoniae. Garamicin is also active against gram-negative bacteria including P. aeruginosa, indole-positive and indole-negative Proteus species, E. coli, species of the Klebsiella-Enterobacter-Serratia group, Citrobacter species, Salmonella and Shigella, Moraxella species, Providencia species, H. vaginicoli and Neisseria species, especially the gonococcus.

Indications: Ophthalmic: The treatment of superficial bacterial infections of the conjunctiva, cornea, eyelids, tear ducts, and skin adjacent to the eye. Such infections include conjunctivitis, blepharitis, blepharoconjunctivitis, keratitis, keratoconjunctivitis, episcleritis, dacryocystitis, corneal ulcers, and infected eye sockets. Also for the prevention of ocular infection if injury makes the eye or adjacent area vulnerable to infections: after removal of foreign bodies; after burns or laceration of the lids or conjunctivae; or after damage from chemical or physical agents; and before and after eye surgery.

Otic: May be used for the topical treatment of otitis externa caused by susceptible bacteria.

Contraindications: Sensitivity to any of the components in the preparations. As with all ophthalmic preparations containing benzalkonium chloride, patients are advised not to wear soft contact lenses during treatment with gentamicin ophthalmic preparations. Contraindicated in patients with absent or perforated tympanic membranes.

Precautions: Use of topical antibiotics occasionally allows overgrowth of nonsusceptible microorganisms such as fungi. If this occurs, or if irritation or sensitization to any of the components of this preparation develops, treatment with it should be discontinued and appropriate therapy initiated. To avoid possible contamination of the drops or ointment, do not touch the dropper tip or the ointment tube tip to any surface.

Clinical studies have shown that organisms previously sensitive to gentamicin have become resistant during therapy. Although this has occurred infrequently, the possibility should nevertheless be considered. There is evidence that cross-resistance between gentamicin and the aminoglycoside antibiotics may occur since bacteria made resistant to aminoglycoside antibiotics artificially in the laboratory are also resistant to gentamicin; however, gentamicin may be active against clinical isolates of bacteria resistant to other aminoglycosides. Conversely, organisms resistant to gentamicin may be sensitive to other aminoglycoside antibiotics.

Pregnancy and *Lactation:* The safety during pregnancy has not been established. Since it is not known whether components of gentamicin ophthalmic/otic solution are excreted in human milk, caution should be exercised when administered to a nursing woman.

Children: Safety and effectiveness in children below the age of 6 years have not been established.

Adverse Effects: Eye and ear medications may sting briefly on application, and gentamicin ophthalmic and otic preparations are no exception.

After application of gentamicin ophthalmic or otic drops no sensitization or allergy has been reported to date. The most frequently reported adverse reactions at least possibly related to gentamicin are ocular burning and irritation upon drug instillation, non-specific conjunctivitis, conjunctival epithelial defects and conjunctival hyperemia.

The possibility of ototoxicity following otic application should be kept in mind, and the patient monitored accordingly.

Overdose: Symptoms: A single overdose of gentamicin would not be expected to produce symptoms.

Treatment: Although a single overdose is not expected to require treatment, gentamicin can be removed from the blood by hemodialysis or peritoneal dialysis.

Dosage: Ophthalmic: Drops: Instill 2 drops into the conjunctival sac of the affected eye 3 or 4 times daily. Dosage may be increased in severe infections and reduced at the end of treatment. In the infections that may develop intermittently

Garamycin Ophthalmic/Otic Preparations (cont'd)

in the immature tear ducts of children (dacryocystitis), hot compresses and massage of the area over the tear duct may be useful as adjuncts to the solution.

In the treatment of acute pseudomonal corneal ulcer, 1 or 2 drops every 15 minutes in the daytime hours can be supplemented with the ophthalmic ointment at bedtime. For prophylaxis, such as after removal of a foreign body or following physical or chemical trauma, instill 1 to 2 drops 3 to 4 times daily until signs of inflammation have subsided. For prophylaxis before intraocular surgery, 1 to 2 drops should be instilled 4 to 5 times, preferably within 8 hours prior to surgery. Gentamicin ophthalmic/otic solution may be administered as part of the routine post-operative daily dressing of the eye, until recovery from post-surgical inflammation is evident.

Ointment: Apply ophthalmic ointment to the affected areas in or near the eye 3 or 4 times a day. If the eye/ear drops are used during the day, the ointment can be used at bedtime to continue treatment during the night.

Otic: Drops: Thoroughly clean the ear canal of cerumen or debris. Instill 3 or 4 drops in the infected ear 3 times daily. The patient should lie with the affected ear upward; instill the solution and let the patient remain in this position for several minutes to insure penetration of the medication into the ear canal.

Supplied: Ophthalmic: Drops: Each mL of sterile aqueous solution buffered to approximately pH 7 contains: gentamicin 3 mg (as sulfate USP). Nonmedicinal ingredients: benzalkonium chloride, sodium chloride, sodium phosphate dibasic and sodium phosphate monobasic. Plastic dropper bottles of 5 mL.

Ointment: Each g of sterile ointment contains: gentamicin 3 mg (as sulfate USP). Nonmedicinal ingredients: methylparaben, propylparaben and white petrolatum. Tubes of 3.5 g with applicator tip.

Otic: Drops: Each mL of sterile aqueous solution buffered to approximately pH 7 contains: gentamicin 3 mg (as sulfate USP). Nonmedicinal ingredients: benzalkonium chloride, sodium chloride, sodium phosphate dibasic and sodium phosphate monobasic. Plastic dropper bottles of 7.5 mL.

Store in a cool place away from heat (2 to 30°C).

Reviewed 1997

GARAMYCIN® Parenteral Ⓟ

Schering

Gentamicin Sulfate

Antibiotic

Pharmacology: Gentamicin is a bactericidal antibiotic which affects bacterial growth by specific inhibition of normal protein synthesis in susceptible bacteria.

It is active against a wide variety of pathogenic gram-negative and gram-positive bacteria: P. aeruginosa, Proteus species (both indole-positive and indole-negative), E. coli, K. pneumoniae, E. aerogenes, S. marcescens and Staphylococcus species (including penicillin- and methicillin-resistant strains).

In addition, gentamicin sulfate is active in vitro against certain species of Streptococcus. Only minimal activity has been found against S. faecalis and S. pneumoniae. Most anaerobes (species of Clostridium, Bacteroides, and Diphtheroids) are resistant.

The bactericidal concentration of gentamicin is usually 1 to 4 times the minimal inhibitory concentration. Gentamicin was over 8 times more active in vitro at pH 7.5 than at pH 5.5, against several urinary pathogens.

If susceptibility tests indicate the causative organism is resistant to gentamicin, institute other or additional antimicrobial therapy.

Combined therapy with gentamicin and a penicillin type of drug has been used in suspected sepsis until bacteriological studies have identified the etiological organism.

Gentamicin serum concentrations via the i.m. route: Adults: In patients with normal renal function, peak serum concentrations, bactericidal for susceptible bacteria, occur between 30 and 90 minutes after injection, the peak serum concentration (μg/mL) being 4 times the single dose (mg/kg). The mean serum half-life is approximately 2 hours.

Infants and neonates: Peak serum concentrations of 2.2 to 8.6 μg/mL (mean 4.0 μg/mL) are observed 0.5 to 1 hour after 2.5 mg/kg of gentamicin sulfate are administered i.m. to infants 7 days of age and under.

The mean serum gentamicin half-life is approximately 5 hours in neonates under 72 hours of age. This may be considerably prolonged in infants weighing less than 1 500 g. In low birth weight infants, prolonged half-life values may extend through the second week of life. In contrast, values of 3 to 3.5 hours are usually observed in full term infants who are 7 days of age and older.

Gentamicin concentrations in serum of infants 2 to 24 months of age following i.m. doses of 2 and 2.5 mg/kg were shown to be in the range of 2.5 to 7.5 μg/mL.

Serum concentrations via the i.v. route: Adults: After a 2-hour infusion of a dose of 1 mg/kg to a group of patients, peak gentamicin concentrations were reached at the end of the infusion and averaged 4.5 μg/mL (range 0.5 to 8 μg/mL).

Slow i.v. injection at recommended doses in patients gave serum levels of 5 to 9 μg/mL after 10 minutes.

The mean serum half-life is the same as for the i.m. route of administration.

Infants and neonates: Levels in serum and half-life values after i.v. infusion of gentamicin were similar to those after i.m. administration.

In man, about 25 to 30% of the administered dose of gentamicin is bound by serum protein. Gentamicin is excreted principally in the urine by glomerular filtration. After initial administration to patients with normal renal function, 30 to 100% of the drug is recoverable in the urine in 24 hours. Renal clearance of gentamicin is similar to that of endogenous creatinine.

In patients with impaired renal function, the clearance of gentamicin is decreased; the more severe the impairment, the slower the clearance.

In the newborn, approximately 30% of the administered dose is excreted in 12 hours.

Following parenteral administration gentamicin is detected in tissues and body fluids. Concentrations in bile in general have been low and have suggested minimal biliary excretion. Gentamicin has been found in the cerebrospinal fluid after i.m. injection; however, concentrations have been low and may be inadequate for treatment of certain CNS infections.

Concentrations of gentamicin in CSF of infants with purulent meningitis range from 0.2 to 3.5 μg/mL after a dose of 1.5 to 2.5 mg/kg. Peak values are found 4 to 6 hours after the dose, and are dependent on degree of meningeal inflammation and dosage.

Gentamicin has also been found in the sputum, pleural fluid and peritoneal cavity. Gentamicin crosses the peritoneal as well as the placental membranes.

Gentamicin at considerably higher doses than normally recommended, like other aminoglycoside antibiotics, causes neuromuscular blockade in animals. This phenomenon is antagonized by neostigmine or calcium (see Precautions).

Minimal amounts of gentamicin are absorbed following oral administration; therefore, oral administration is not recommended.

Gentamicin has been shown to affect vestibular and renal functions in animals and man. Chronic administration of 5 mg/kg for 50 days in dogs, 10 mg/kg for 40 days in cats and 20 mg/kg for 24 days in rats resulted in mild toxicity in some animals studied. Higher toxic doses resulted in renal and vestibular function damage which appeared to be dose related. In humans the only serious side effect to date has been damage to the eighth cranial nerve, predominantly the vestibular branch. Proteinuria, a rise in BUN or serum creatinine have also occurred (see Adverse Effects). These findings have usually reverted to normal when the drug was discontinued.

Indications: The parenteral treatment of serious infections caused by laboratory determined susceptible bacteria, with due regard for relative antibiotic toxicity. Therefore, the drug may be considered for treatment of: (1) bacteremia (2) respiratory tract infections (3) urinary tract infections (4) infected wounds: surgical and traumatic (5) bone and soft tissue infections, including peritonitis and burns complicated by sepsis.

In the majority of cases bacteriologic cultures should be obtained initially, to identify the causative organism and to determine its sensitivity to gentamicin. Garamycin sensitivity discs (2 and 10 μg) are available.

In suspected or documented gram-negative septicemia, particularly when shock or hypotension are present, gentamicin injectable may be considered for initial antimicrobial therapy. Gentamicin may also be considered in serious staphylococcal infections when other conventional antimicrobial therapy is inappropriate or when bacterial susceptibility testing and clinical judgment indicate its use. If anaerobic organisms are suspected, additional antimicrobial therapy should be added to the gentamicin regimen.

The decision to continue therapy with gentamicin should be based on results of the sensitivity tests, clinical response of the patient, and consideration of relative antibiotic toxicity.

Clinical studies have shown that organisms previously sensitive to gentamicin have become resistant during therapy. Although this has occurred infrequently, the possibility should nevertheless be considered. There is evidence that cross resistance between gentamicin and aminoglycoside antibiotics may occur since bacteria made resistant to aminoglycoside antibiotics artificially in the laboratory are also resistant to gentamicin; however, gentamicin may be active against clinical isolates of bacteria resistant to other aminoglycosides. Conversely, organisms resistant to gentamicin may be sensitive to other aminoglycoside antibiotics.

Contraindications: A history of hypersensitivity or toxic reactions to gentamicin.

Pregnancy: The safety of gentamicin for use during pregnancy has not been established. Aminoglycoside antibiotics cross the placenta and may cause harm when administered to pregnant women. Irreversible bilateral congenital deafness in children whose mothers received streptomycin during pregnancy has been reported. Serious side effects to mother, fetus, or newborn have not been reported following treatment of pregnant women with other aminoglycosides, however, the potential for fetal toxicity exists. It is not known whether gentamicin can cause fetal harm when administered to pregnant women or can affect reproductive capacity. Gentamicin should be used during pregnancy only in life-threatening situations or severe infections, bearing in mind the possible adverse effects on the fetus.

Lactation: Studies in nursing mothers indicate that small amounts of the drug are excreted in breast milk. Because of the potential for serious adverse reactions from aminoglycosides in nursing infants, a decision should be made whether to discontinue nursing, or to discontinue gentamicin therapy, taking into account the importance of the drug to the mother.

Precautions: Ototoxicity: Gentamicin, in common with the antibiotics streptomycin, neomycin and kanamycin, has produced ototoxicity in experimental animals and man. This adverse reaction which may be delayed in onset, is manifested primarily by damage to vestibular function. The reversibility of this adverse reaction is frequently contingent upon early recognition of potential ototoxicity. In all patients developing tinnitus, dizziness or loss of hearing, the attending physician should strongly consider discontinuing this antibiotic except in those cases where gentamicin appears to be the only proven course of therapy.

Complete damage has occurred mainly in patients who were uremic, had renal dysfunction, had prior therapy with ototoxic drugs or received higher doses and longer courses of therapy than those recommended.

In patients who have previously been treated with drugs likely to affect eighth cranial nerve function (e.g., streptomycin, neomycin, kanamycin, etc.), gentamicin should be used with caution and with the understanding that toxic effects may be cumulative with these agents.

Potent diuretics such as ethacrynic acid and furosemide have been associated with eighth cranial nerve dysfunction, and the concomitant use of either of these drugs with gentamicin should be avoided. It is believed that i.v. diuretics may cause fairly rapid rise in gentamicin serum levels and potentiate ototoxicity.

In patients with impaired renal function, the frequency of gentamicin administration should be reduced (see Dosage), and renal function should be monitored along with evaluation of auditory and vestibular function. Serum concentrations of gentamicin should be monitored whenever feasible; prolonged concentrations above 12 μg/mL should be avoided.

Nephrotoxicity: Nephrotoxicity manifested by an elevated BUN or serum creatinine level or a decrease in the creatinine clearance has been reported with gentamicin. In most cases, these changes have been reversible when the drug has been discontinued.

The administration of other potentially nephrotoxic agents prior to or in conjunction with gentamicin may increase the risk of nephrotoxicity.

As with other antibiotics, treatment with gentamicin may occasionally result in overgrowth of nonsensitive organisms. If superinfection occurs, appropriate measures should be taken.
Neuromuscular Blocking Action: Neuromuscular blockage and respiratory paralysis have been reported in the cat receiving high doses (40 mg/kg) of gentamicin. The possibility of these phenomena occurring in man should be considered if gentamicin is administered to patients receiving general anesthesia and/or neuromuscular blocking agents such as succinylcholine and tubocurarine.

In patients with myasthenia gravis, use of drugs with potential neuromuscular blocking action may be dangerous.

Neuromuscular blocking action produced by gentamicin in animals may be antagonized by neostigmine or calcium.

Adverse Effects: In addition to the ototoxicity and nephrotoxicity discussed under Precautions, other adverse reactions reported infrequently and possibly related to gentamicin include increased serum transaminase (AST, ALT), increased reticulocyte count, and increased serum bilirubin, anemia, rash, granulocytopenia, urticaria, thrombocytopenia, headache, vomiting and muscle twitching.

Adverse reactions reported rarely and possibly related to gentamicin are nausea, increased salivation, lethargy and decreased appetite, weight loss, pulmonary fibrosis, purpura, splenomegaly, transient hepatomegaly, itching, numbness, skin tingling, laryngeal edema and spasm, joint pain, drug fever, convulsions, hypotension, hypertension, decreased reticulocyte count, decreased serum calcium, decreased hemoglobin and hematocrit, fifth nerve paresthesia and gastrointestinal hemorrhage. One case of neuromuscular blocking action has been reported in the literature.

Overdose: Symptoms and Treatment: In the event of overdose or toxic reactions, hemodialysis will aid in the removal of gentamicin from the blood. The rate of gentamicin removal is considerably less by peritoneal dialysis than it is by hemodialysis. In the newborn infant, exchange transfusions may also be considered. These procedures are of particular importance for patients with impaired renal function.

Dosage: Using the recommended doses, considerable variation in the serum concentrations between individual patients has been observed. In order to insure adequate therapeutic concentrations which may be critical, while at the same time avoiding potentially toxic concentrations, it is desirable to measure peak and trough gentamicin serum concentrations. Following i.v. or i.m. administration, 2 or 3 times daily, the peak concentration, measured 30 minutes to 1 hour after administration, is expected to be in the range of 4 to 6 μg/mL. With once daily administration, transient, high peak concentrations can be anticipated. With all regimens, the dosages should be adjusted to avoid prolonged concentrations above 10 to 12 μg/mL. Trough levels above 2 μg/mL, measured just before the next dose, would also be avoided. Determination of the adequacy of a serum level for a particular patient must take into consideration susceptibility of the causative microorganism, severity of infection, and the status of the patient's host-defense mechanisms.

The usual duration of treatment for all patients is 7 to 10 days. In complicated infections, a longer course of therapy may be necessary. In such cases, monitoring of renal, auditory and vestibular functions is recommended, since toxicity is more likely to occur with treatment extended over 10 days. Dosage should be reduced if clinically indicated.

I.M.: Patients with normal renal function: Urinary tract infections: Gentamicin is highly concentrated in urine and renal tissue. In patients with lower urinary tract infection particularly if chronic or recurrent and without evidence of impairment of renal function, gentamicin may be administered i.m. either in a dose of 160 mg once a day or 80 mg twice daily for 7 to 10 days. For adults weighing less than 60 kg, the single dose should be 3 mg/kg.

Upper urinary tract infections, such as pyelonephritis, and more particularly if there are signs of systemic involvement, should be treated according to one of the dosage schedules for systemic infections.

Since gentamicin activity is increased at pH 7.5, it may be advantageous to alkalinize the urine of patients treated for urinary tract infections.
Systemic Infections: Adults with serious infections and normal renal function: 3 mg/kg/day administered i.m. in 3 equal doses. Therefore, for patients weighing over 60 kg, the usual dosage is 80 mg 3 times daily. For patients weighing 60 kg or less, the usual dosage is 60 mg 3 times a day. In severe infections, the recommended dosage is 3 to 6 mg/kg/day administered in 3 equal doses, every 8 hours. If a dosage greater than 3 mg/kg/day is administered initially, it should be reduced to 3 mg/kg/day when clinically indicated.
Life-Threatening Infections: Administer dosages up to 5 mg/kg/day in 3 or 4 equally divided doses. Reduce to 3 mg/kg/day as soon as clinically indicated.
Children: The precautions for the treatment of infection in children are the same as those for adults.
Infants and Neonates (see Contraindications): In premature and full term neonates, 1 week of age or less, a dosage of 6 mg/kg/day may be administered in 2 equal doses every 12 hours. In infants older than 1 week, gentamicin may be administered in 3 equal doses every 8 hours.
Patients with Impaired Renal Function: Dosage must be adjusted in patients with impaired renal function. Since the creatinine clearance rate and serum creatinine concentration have high correlation with the serum half-life of gentamicin, these laboratory tests may provide the guidance necessary for adjustment of the interval between doses. The serum half-life (in hours) of gentamicin may be estimated by multiplying the serum creatinine (mg/100 mL) by 4. The frequency of administration (in hours) may be approximated by doubling the serum half-life.

In patients with renal failure who are undergoing 14-hour hemodialysis twice weekly, administration of gentamicin 1 mg/kg, at the end of each dialysis period has been suggested.

In those instances when only BUN concentration is available, this value may be utilized initially; however, it should be supplemented with a serum creatinine level or creatinine clearance rate whenever possible.

This dosage schedule is not intended as a rigid recommendation but is provided as a guide to dosage when the measurement of gentamicin serum levels is not feasible. It should be used in conjunction with close clinical and laboratory observations of the patients and modified as deemed necessary by the treating physician.

I.V.: For use in those circumstances when the i.m. route is not feasible, e.g., patients in shock, with hemorrhagic disorders, severe burns, or reduced muscle mass.

The usual dose of gentamicin administered i.v. is 3 mg/kg/day in 3 equally divided doses. For i.v. administration, a single dose (1 mg/kg) is diluted in 100 to 200 mL of sterile normal saline or in a sterile solution of dextrose 5% in water. The solution is infused over a period of 1 to 2 hours and repeated every 8 hours if necessary.

A single dose of gentamicin injectable undiluted may also be given directly into the side arm of an i.v. tubing set, slowly over a period of 2 to 3 minutes and repeated every 8 hours, if necessary.

Compatibility: Garamycin Injection should not be physically premixed with other drugs, but should be administered separately in accordance with the recommended route of administration and dosage schedule.

Supplied: 10 mg/mL: Each mL of aqueous parenteral solution contains: gentamicin (as sulfate USP) 10 mg. pH 3.0 to 4.5. Nonmedicinal ingredients: disodium edetate, methylparaben, propylparaben and sodium bisulfite. Multiple dose vials of 2 and 20 mL. Vials of 2 mL.

40 mg/mL: Each mL of aqueous parenteral solution contains: gentamicin (as sulfate USP) 40 mg. pH 3.0 to 4.5. Nonmedicinal ingredients: disodium edetate, methylparaben, propylparaben and sodium bisulfite. Multiple dose vials of 2 and 20 mL.

Solutions are heat stable and do not require refrigeration. Store at 15 and 30°C.

GARAMYCIN® Topical Preparations ℞

Schering

Gentamicin Sulfate

Topical Antibiotic

Indications: For use in the treatment of primary and secondary infections caused by sensitive strains of streptococci (Group A beta-hemolytic, alpha-hemolytic), S. aureus (coagulase positive, coagulase-negative, and some penicillinase producing strains), and the gram-negative bacteria P. aeruginosa, A. aerogenes, E. coli, P. vulgaris, and K. pneumoniae. Primary skin infections that may be expected to respond to treatment with gentamicin include: impetigo contagiosa, superficial folliculitis, ecthyma, furunculosis, sycosis barbae, and pyoderma gangrenosum; also such secondary skin infections as infectious eczematoid dermatitis, pustular acne, pustular psoriasis, infected seborrheic dermatitis, infected contact dermatitis (including poison ivy), infected excoriations, and bacterial superinfections of fungal or viral origin infected burns, insect bites or stings, infected cuts, scrapes and wounds following surgical procedures. Gentamicin has been used successfully in infants over 1 year of age as well as in adults and children.

Contraindications: Sensitivity to any of the components of the preparation.

Precautions: Treatment of severe or refractory skin lesions should be supplemented with the administration of a systemic antibacterial agent. Use of topical antibiotics occasionally allows overgrowth of nonsusceptible organisms such as fungi. If this occurs, or if irritation, sensitization or superinfection develop, treatment with gentamicin should be discontinued and appropriate therapy instituted. Patients sensitive to neomycin can be treated with gentamicin, although regular observation of patients sensitive to topical antibiotics is advisable when such patients are treated with any topical antibiotic.
Pregnancy: The safety of gentamicin for use during pregnancy has not been established.

Adverse Effects: In patients with dermatoses treated with gentamicin, mild irritation (erythema and pruritus) that did not usually require discontinuance of treatment, has been reported in a small percentage of cases. There was no evidence of irritation or sensitization, however, in any of these patients patch tested subsequently with gentamicin on normal skin. Possible photosensitization has been reported in several patients but could not be elicited in these patients by reapplication of gentamicin followed by exposure to ultraviolet radiation.

Overdose: Symptoms: A single overdose of gentamicin would not be expected to produce symptoms. Excessive prolonged use of topical gentamicin may lead to overgrowth of lesions by fungi or nonsusceptible bacteria.

Treatment: Appropriate antifungal or antibacterial therapy is indicated if overgrowth occurs.

Dosage: A small amount of cream or ointment should be applied gently to the lesions 3 or 4 times daily until favorable results are achieved. The area treated can be covered with a gauze dressing if desired. In impetigo contagiosa, the crusts should be removed before application to permit maximum contact between the antibiotic and the infection. Care should be exercised to avoid further contamination of the infected skin. Infected stasis ulcers have responded well to gentamicin under gelatin packing. Concomitant treatment of the skin around the ulcer with a topical corticosteroid helps control inflammation. Treatment of infected skin cysts and certain other skin abscesses must be preceded by incision and drainage to permit adequate contact between the antibiotic and the infecting bacteria.

Supplied: Cream: Each g contains: gentamicin 1 mg (as sulfate USP). The cream is recommended for wet and oozing primary or secondary infections. Nonmedicinal ingredients: cetostearyl alcohol, chlorocresol, mineral oil, monobasic sodium phosphate, polyethylene glycol 1 000 monocetyl ether, water and white petrolatum. Tubes of 15 g and jars of 450 g.

Ointment: Each g contains: gentamicin 1 mg (as sulfate USP). The ointment helps retain moisture and has been useful in infections on dry eczematous or psoriatic skin. Nonmedicinal ingredients: methylparaben, propylparaben and white petrolatum. Tubes of 15 g and jars of 450 g.

Store below 30°C.

GARASONE™ Ophthalmic/Otic Preparations ℞

Schering

Betamethasone Sodium Phosphate—Gentamicin Sulfate

Topical Corticosteroid—Antibiotic

Pharmacology: The anti-inflammatory activity of betamethasone is combined with the broad spectrum bactericidal activity

Garasone Ophthalmic/Otic Preparations (cont'd)

of gentamicin. Betamethasone inhibits the inflammatory response of the eye and ear to irritating agents of a mechanical, chemical or immunological nature, while gentamicin is active in vitro against a wide variety of pathogenic gram-negative and gram-positive bacteria.

Indications: Ophthalmic: In ocular inflammation, when concurrent use of an antimicrobial is judged necessary: e.g., staphylococcal blepharoconjunctivitis. For the treatment of non-purulent bacterial infections of the anterior segment of the eye due to organisms sensitive to gentamicin and when the anti-inflammatory action of betamethasone sodium phosphate is indicated, as in allergic vernal and phlyctenular conjunctivitis; non-purulent blepharitis; interstitial sclerosing post-operative keratitis; superficial chemical and thermal burns of the cornea. In stubborn cases of anterior segment eye disease or in deep-seated ocular diseases, systemic therapy may be required. However, in these diseases Garasone solution may be used as adjunctive therapy.

Otic: For the treatment of lesions in the external ear canal, such as acute otitis externa, eczematoid-dermatitis, seborrheic dermatitis and contact dermatitis secondarily infected with susceptible organisms.

Contraindications: Those individuals who have shown hypersensitivity to any of its components and to other aminoglycosides or to other corticosteroids.

Ophthalmic: In epithelial herpes simplex keratitis (dendritic keratitis), vaccinia, varicella, and many other viral diseases of the cornea and conjunctiva, mycobacterial infections of the eye, trachoma, fungal diseases of ocular structures.

Use of corticosteroid/antibiotic combinations is contraindicated after removal of a corneal foreign body or in the presence of acute local viral lesions, e.g. herpes, and in patients with absent or perforated tympanic membranes. As with all ophthalmic products containing benzalkonium chloride, patients are advised not to wear soft contact lenses during treatment with Garasone ophthalmic/otic solution.

Warnings: Prolonged ophthalmic use of Garasone preparations may result in increased intraocular pressure in some individuals. If these products are used for 10 days or longer, intraocular pressure should be routinely monitored. In diseases causing thinning of the cornea or sclera, perforation has been known to occur with the use of topical preparations containing corticosteroids. Protracted use of topical corticosteroids in the eye may result in the development of posterior subcapsular cataracts. Acute anterior uveitis may occur in susceptible individuals, primarily blacks.

Prolonged use may suppress the host response and thus increase the hazard of secondary ocular infections. In acute purulent conditions of the eye, steroids may mask infection or enhance existing infection.

Although corticosteroids are contraindicated in acute viral infection of the cornea caused by herpes simplex, there may be occasion to employ steroids in the healing stage to prevent scarring; however, this must only be done with great caution and close observation. In patients with a history of herpetic infection of the cornea, reactivation of the disease may occur with the use of topical ophthalmic or otic corticosteroids.

The use of steroids after cataract surgery may delay healing and increase the incidence of filtering blebs.

Precautions: During long-term use of preparations containing corticosteroids, the possibility of fungal infection must be considered, especially in the presence of a persistent corneal ulceration that fails to respond to conventional therapy. By reducing inflammation, steroids may mask the symptoms of serious ocular disease or that due to organisms resistant to gentamicin.

In ophthalmic use, intraocular pressure should be checked frequently (see Warnings). Slit-lamp examination should be done for dendritic keratitis.

If irritation occurs, hypersensitivity to a component of the preparation is a possibility and use of the product should be discontinued. Cross-allergenicity among aminoglycosides and corticosteroids has been demonstrated (see Contraindications).

To avoid possible contamination, do not touch the tip of dropper or tube to any surface. Do not allow dispenser tip to touch the surface of the eye.

It is not advisable to treat bacterial corneal ulcers, which may be due to P. aeruginosa, with a combination antibiotic-anti-inflammatory product as initial therapy. It is prudent to use an anti-infective agent alone initially. For ulcers caused by Pseudomonas, Garamycin ophthalmic ointment would be indicated. If the infection responds to the anti-infective treatment, then the addition of an anti-inflammatory agent to minimize the fibrous reaction and scarring of the cornea is suggested.

Clinical studies have shown that microorganisms previously sensitive to gentamicin have become resistant during therapy. Although this has occurred infrequently, the possibility should nevertheless be considered. There is evidence that cross resistance between gentamicin and other aminoglycoside antibiotics may occur since bacteria made resistant to aminoglycoside antibiotics artificially in the laboratory are also resistant to gentamicin. However, gentamicin may be active against clinical isolates of bacteria resistant to other aminoglycosides. Conversely, organisms resistant to gentamicin may be sensitive to other aminoglycoside antibiotics.

Pregnancy: Safety of topical corticosteroid/antibiotic preparations during pregnancy has not been established.

Lactation: Since it is not known whether the components of Garasone are excreted in the human milk, caution should be exercised when administering to a nursing woman.

Children: Safety and effectiveness in children below the age of 8 years have not been established.

Adverse Effects: Ophthalmic: Adverse reactions reported include: increased ocular pressure; ocular hypersensitivity manifested by increased ocular hyperemia, edema and burning sensation.

Adverse reactions reported with other steroid-anti-infective combinations include: allergic sensitization due to the antibiotic component; elevation of intraocular pressure with possible development of glaucoma and infrequent optic nerve damage, posterior subcapsular cataract formation and delayed wound healing due to the steroid component.

Corticosteroid-containing preparations can also cause anterior uveitis or perforation of the globe. Mydriasis, defects in visual acuity and visual fields, loss of accommodation and ptosis have also been reported.

Otic: The possibility of ototoxicity should be kept in mind and the patient monitored accordingly.

Overdose: Symptoms: Excessive prolonged use of topical corticosteroids can suppress pituitary-adrenal function resulting in secondary adrenal insufficiency. A single overdosage of gentamycin would not be expected to produce symptoms.

Treatment: Appropriate symptomatic treatment of corticosteroid overdosage is indicated. Acute hypercorticoid symptoms are virtually reversible. Treat electrolyte imbalance, if necessary. In cases of chronic toxicity, slow withdrawal of corticosteroids is advised.

Dosage: Ophthalmic/Otic Solution: Ophthalmic: Instill 2 drops into the conjunctival sac of the affected eye 3 or 4 times daily. During the acute stage, 2 drops may be administered every 2 hours.

Otic: Thoroughly clean the ear canal of cerumen and debris. Instill 3 or 4 drops into the affected ear 3 times daily or as directed by the physician. The patient should lie with the affected ear turned upward; instill the solution and let the patient remain in this position for several minutes to insure penetration of the medication into the ear canal. If preferred, a cotton wick may be inserted into the canal and then saturated with the solution. The wick should be kept moist by adding further solution every 4 hours. The wick should be replaced once every 24 hours.

Ophthalmic Ointment: Apply a thin film to the affected area 3 or 4 times per day. When a favorable response is observed, the number of daily applications may be reduced. The ointment form is also indicated for application at bedtime in conjunction with daytime use of the drops.

Improvement usually occurs within 48 hours, with clearing of the signs and symptoms usually within 2 weeks. In chronic conditions, withdrawal of treatment should be carried out by gradually decreasing the frequency of application.

Supplied: Ophthalmic/Otic Solution: Each mL of sterile aqueous solution contains: gentamicin (as sulfate USP) 3 mg and betamethasone 1.0 mg (as sodium phosphate USP). Nonmedicinal ingredients: benzalkonium chloride, edetate disodium, sodium borate, sodium chloride, sodium citrate dihydrate, sodium phosphate dibasic and sodium phosphate monobasic. Dropper bottles of 7.5 mL. Store between 2 and 30°C.

Ophthalmic Ointment: Each g of sterile ointment contains: gentamicin (as sulfate USP) 3 mg and betamethasone 1.0 mg (as sodium phosphate USP). Nonmedicinal ingredients: mineral oil and white petrolatum. Tubes of 3.5 g. Store between 2 and 30°C.

Reviewed 1997

GARATEC Ⓟ
Technilab

Gentamicin Sulfate

Topical Antibiotic

Supplied: Ophthalmic Solution: Each mL of sterile aqueous solution buffered to approximately pH 7 contains: gentamicin sulfate USP 5 mg (equivalent to gentamicin 3 mg). Nonmedicinal ingredients: benzalkonium chloride, dibasic sodium phosphate, disodium EDTA, sodium chloride, sodium phosphate monobasic and water for injection. Plastic dropper bottles of 5 mL.

Otic Solution: Each mL of sterile aqueous solution buffered to approximately pH 7 contains: gentamicin sulfate USP 5 mg (equivalent to gentamicin 3 mg). Nonmedicinal ingredients: benzalkonium chloride, dibasic sodium phosphate, disodium EDTA, sodium chloride, sodium phosphate monobasic and water for injection. Plastic dropper bottles of 5 mL.

Store between 15 and 25°C.

GASTROLYTE®
Rhône-Poulenc Rorer

Electrolytes—Dextrose

Antidiarrheal

Indications: For the management of watery diarrhea of varying types, including gastroenteritis and oral correction of fluid and electrolyte loss in infants, children and adults.

Contraindications: There are no known contraindications to this product.

Warnings: Cow's milk and artificial milk feeds in infants should be stopped for 24 hours and gradually introduced when the diarrhea has lessened. However, breast feeding should be continued.

Precautions: For oral administration only, Gastrolyte should not be reconstituted in diluents other than water. Each sachet should always be dissolved in 200 mL of water. A weaker solution than recommended will not contain the optimal dextrose and electrolyte concentration while a stronger solution than recommended may give rise to electrolyte imbalance. The composition of Gastrolyte stimulates intestinal water absorption.

With intractable vomiting, adynamic ileus, intestinal obstruction or perforated bowel, nothing should be administered orally.

If the diarrhea does not improve promptly, the patient should be reassessed.

Dosage: Reconstitution: The contents of each sachet should be dissolved in sufficient drinking water to make 200 mL. An infant's feeding bottle is a convenient measure of this volume. The solution should be made up immediately prior to feeding and any solution remaining an hour after reconstitution should be discarded. However, the solution may be used for up to 24 hours if stored in a refrigerator immediately after reconstitution. The reconstituted solution must not be boiled.

For oral administration only. A basic principle of treatment of diarrhea is to replace fluid loss and then to maintain sufficient fluid intake to replace further loss from stools.

For toddlers, older children and adults, Gastrolyte solution may be given freely until the thirst is satisfied.

For infants, a number of different regimens are used by different physicians, but the basic principle is to omit milk feeds or solids initially, while maintaining adequate fluid intake. Milk can then be re-introduced to provide calories, but to avoid worsening or prolonging the diarrhea, this should be gradual.

The following dosage and Table I (on following page) are only a general guide and the volume of the product given and

Table I—Gastrolyte

General Dosage Guide

Infant's Age		0–2 months	3–4 months	5–6 months	6 months-2 years
Day 1	No. of sachets during 1st 24 hrs	3	5	7	7 10
	Diet	No milk or solids			
Day 2	No. of sachets during 2nd 24 hrs	2	3	4	4–5
	Diet	Half usual quantities of milk or light solids (cereals, toast, etc.)			
Day 3	No. of sachets during 3rd 24 hrs	1	2	3	3–4
	Diet	Gradual return to full quantities of milk or solids			

the speed of re-introduction of the normal feeds is at the discretion of the physician.

General Dosage Guide: 150 mL of Gastrolyte solution/kg of body weight/day.

In those patients who are vomiting at the start of treatment, it may be advisable to give very small volumes initially until vomiting is under control. Infantile diarrhea is uncommon in breastfed infants. However, if treatment with this product becomes necessary, it is suggested that the infant be breastfed until satisfied followed by the solution if necessary.

Supplied: Each foil/laminate sachet contains: sodium chloride 470 mg, disodium citrate 530 mg, potassium chloride 300 mg and dextrose monohydrate 3 560 mg.

Gastrolyte Fruit: A liter made up of 5 sachets×200 mL contains: sodium 60 mmol, potassium 20 mmol, chloride 60 mmol and dextrose (anhydrous) 90 mmol. Nonmedicinal ingredients: aspartame, colloidal silica, disodium hydrogen citrate, flavor grapefruit, flavor pineapple, glucose, potassium chloride and sodium chloride. Boxes of 10×4.9 g sachets.

Gastrolyte Regular: A liter made up of 5 sachets×200 mL contains: sodium 60 mmol, potassium 20 mmol, chloride 60 mmol and dextrose (anhydrous) 90 mmol. Nonmedicinal ingredients: aspartame, colloidal silica, disodium hydrogen citrate, glucose, potassium chloride and sodium chloride. Boxes of 10×4.9 g sachets.

Store in a cool, dry place.

GAS-X®
GAS-X® EXTRA STRENGTH

Novartis Consumer Health

Simethicone

Antiflatulent

Pharmacology: The active ingredient, simethicone acts in the stomach and intestines to disperse and reduce the formation of mucus-trapped gas bubbles. This defoaming action reduces the surface tension of gas bubbles so that they are more easily eliminated.

Indications: Effective antiflatulent that helps relieve the discomfort caused by excess gas in the stomach and intestinal tract, which occurs 30 minutes to several hours after eating.

Warning: Do not take for more than 2 weeks, or if symptoms recur, unless directed by a physician. **Keep out of reach of children.**

Overdose: Symptoms and Treatment: Symptomatic.

Dosage: Gas-X: Adults and Children 12 Years and Older: Chew 1 or 2 tablets as needed after meals and at bedtime. Children under 12 years: Use only on the advice and under the supervision of a physician. Do not exceed 6 tablets in 24 hours. Do not increase dosage unless recommended by your physician.
Gas-X Extra Strength: Adults: Adults and Children 12 Years and Older: Chew 1 or 2 tablets as needed after meals and at bedtime. Children under 12 years: Use only on the advice and under the supervision of a physician. Do not exceed 4 tablets in 24 hours. Do not increase dosage unless recommended by your physician.

Supplied: Gas-X: Peppermint Creme: Each white, round, flat, beveled-edge, uncoated tablet, with "Gas-X" embossed on one side and single score on the other, contains: simethicone 80 mg. Nonmedicinal ingredients: calcium carbonate, dextrose, flavor, maltodextrin. Security feature: Blister sealed tablets, boxes of 36.

Gas-X Extra Strength: Peppermint Creme: Each yellow, round, flat, beveled-edge, uncoated tablet, with "Gas-X ES" embossed on one side and single score on the other, contains: simethicone 125 mg. Nonmedicinal ingredients: calcium phosphate, D&C Red No. 30, D&C Yellow No. 10, dextrose, flavor, maltodextrin and silicon dioxide. Security feature: Blister sealed tablets, boxes of 18.

Cherry Creme: Each reddish pink, round, flat, beveled-edge, uncoated tablet, with "Gas-X ES" embossed on one side and single score on the other, contains: simethicone 125 mg. Nonmedicinal ingredients: calcium phosphate, D&C Red No. 30, dextrose, flavors, maltodextrin and silicon dioxide. Security feature: Blister sealed tablets, boxes of 18.

Store at room temperature in a dry place.

New Product 1998

GAVISCON® Heartburn Relief Formula

SmithKline Beecham Consumer Healthcare

Alginic Acid Compound

Gastroesophageal Reflux Disease Therapy

Pharmacology: The liquid or tablets, when chewed, produce a viscous, demulcent antacid foam which floats on the stomach contents, serving as a protective barrier for the esophagus against reflux of gastric contents. The alkaline foam readily flows up into the esophagus during reflux, aiding in the neutralization of refluxed gastric acids. Gaviscon also reduces the frequency of the reflux episodes.

Indications: The symptomatic treatment of heartburn and reflux esophagitis associated with gastric acid reflux (stomach acid reflux) and other causes.

Precautions: Each 5 mL of liquid contains approximately 30 mg of Na^+ and each tablet contains approximately 22 mg of Na^+, which should be noted for patients on severely restricted sodium diets.

The cations of magnesium and aluminum interfere with the absorption of tetracycline, iron and phosphate. In addition, oral magnesium may accumulate in the plasma of patients with impaired renal function, thus individuals with kidney ailments should consult a physician prior to taking this product.
Pregnancy: While no formal studies have been conducted to establish the safety of alginate compounds during pregnancy, there have been no reported adverse effects on fetal development.

Adverse Effects: Nausea, vomiting, eructation, flatulence.

Overdose: Symptoms and Treatment: Should overdosage occur, gastric distention may result and is best treated conservatively.

Dosage: Regular Strength Tablets or Liquid: Adults: 2 to 4 tablets chewed thoroughly, or 10 to 20 mL of liquid after meals, at bedtime or as required. Maximum 16 tablets or 80 mL/day.

Extra Strength Tablets: Adults: 2 to 4 tablets chewed thoroughly, after meals, at bedtime or as required. Maximum 10 tablets/day.

Extra Strength Aluminum-Free Tablets: Adults: 2 to 4 tablets chewed thoroughly, after meals, at bedtime, or as required. Maximum 12 tablets/day.

Administration should be followed by a drink of water or milk. **Do not swallow tablets whole.**

Supplied: Liquid: Each 5 mL of a light tan-colored, pleasantly fruit-flavored suspension or cream-colored, mint-flavored suspension contains: sodium alginate 250 mg and aluminum hydroxide 100 mg. Also contains parabens. Sodium: 1.3 mmol (30 mg). Alcohol-, gluten-, lactose-, sucrose- and tartrazine-free. No energy content. Plastic bottles of 50 (fruit only), 340 and 600 mL.

Tablets: Regular Strength (200 mg): Each round, creamy-white, butterscotch or fruit-flavored tablet, debossed "GAVISCON" on one side and "G" on the other, contains: alginic acid 200 mg and aluminum hydroxide 80 mg. Also contains sucrose 1.2 g. Energy: 20 kJ (4.7 kcal). Sodium: <1 mmol (22 mg)/tablet. Gluten-, lactose-, starch- and tartrazine-free. Plastic bottles of 40 and 100. Blisters of 8.

Extra Strength (400 mg): Each round, creamy-white, butterscotch, fruit or strawberry-flavored tablet, debossed "GAVISCON" on one side and EXTRA on the other, contains: alginic acid 400 mg and aluminum hydroxide 160 mg. Also contains sucrose 1.8 g. Gluten-, lactose-, starch- and tartrazine-free. Plastic bottles of 25 and 60. Blister foil samples of 2 are also available.

Aluminum-Free: Regular Strength (200 mg): Each round, creamy-white, peppermint-flavored tablet contains: alginic acid 200 mg and magnesium carbonate 40 mg. Also contains sodium and sucrose. Bottles of 100.

Aluminum-Free: Extra Strength (313 mg): Each round, creamy-white, peppermint-flavored tablet contains: alginic acid 313 mg and magnesium carbonate 63 mg. Also contains sodium and sucrose. Bottles of 60.

Reviewed 1999

GELFILM®

Pharmacia & Upjohn

Absorbable Gelatin Film

Surgical Implant

Description: Gelfilm Sterile Film and Gelfilm Sterile Ophthalmic Film are absorbable gelatin film approximately 0.075 mm in thickness, designed for use as an absorbable gelatin implant in neurosurgery and thoracic and ocular surgery.

In the dry state absorbable gelatin film has the appearance and texture of cellophane of equivalent thickness; when moistened, it assumes a rubbery consistency and can be cut to desired size and shape and fitted to rounded or irregular surfaces.

Pharmacology: Rate of absorption of absorbable gelatin after implantation ranges from 1 to 6 months depending on size of the implant and site of implantation. Pleural and muscle implants have been reported to be completely absorbed in eight to 14 days, whereas dural and ocular implants usually require at least 2 to 5 months for absorption. Absence of undue tissue reaction incident to implantation and absorption of absorbable gelatin film, with consequent decreased likelihood of developing adhesions, has been found to be of particular value in dural and ocular implants.

Indications: Neurosurgery: Nonconducive to undue inflammatory reaction and absorbable at a rate sufficiently slow to permit dural regeneration and healing of the arachnoid layer, absorbable gelatin favorably meets requisites for a dural substitute. Use in patients undergoing craniotomies has been reported to prevent development of meningocerebral adhesions and thereby reduce risk of postoperative sequelae.
Thoracic Surgery: In repair of pleural defects in connection with thoracotomies, thoracoplasties, and extrapleural procedures, implantation of absorbable gelatin film has been observed to be followed by minimal tissue reaction and closure of the defect by ingrowth of regenerating pleural and fibrous tissue across the gradually resorbed gelatin film implant.
Ocular Surgery: Various ocular surgical procedures in which absorbable gelatin sterile ophthalmic film has been used include glaucoma filtration operations (i.e., iridencleisis and trephination), extraocular muscle surgery, and diathermy or scleral "buckling" operations for retinal detachment. Experimental studies in rabbits and clinical trials in patients have shown a remarkable lack of cellular reaction to absorbable gelatin film implanted subconjunctivally or used as a seton into the anterior chamber. Objective evidence that absorbable gelatin implants aid in preventing formation of adhesions between contiguous ocular structures has been reported as follows: in iridencleisis in which absorbable gelatin was employed as a seton, the resultant filtrating areas were large and there was no postoperative rise in intraocular tension; in extraocular muscle surgery and operations for retinal detachment, insertion of absorbable gelatin implants between contiguous tissue layers was found to enhance the ease of secondary operations.

Contraindications: None known.

Precautions: Because the rate of absorption of absorbable gelatin sterile film and absorbable gelatin sterile ophthalmic film is likely to be increased in presence of purulent exudation, it is recommended that absorbable gelatin film not be

Gelfilm (cont'd)

implanted in grossly contaminated or infected surgical wounds.

Dosage: Directions for Use: To prepare for use, immerse absorbable gelatin film in sterile saline solution and allow it to soak until it becomes quite pliable; it may then be cut to desired size and shape without difficulty and applied as follows:

For covering dural defects, absorbable gelatin sterile film is placed over the surface of the brain, the edges of the implant tucked beneath the dura and the wound then closed in the usual manner. If desired, the absorbable gelatin film can be sutured loosely to the dura. Care must be exercised, however, because moist film tears easily. **For covering pleural defects,** absorbable gelatin sterile film is placed over the defect and anchored in place by small interrupted sutures.

For use as a seton in iridencleisis, a small piece of absorbable gelatin sterile ophthalmic film (approximately 4×10 mm) is placed over the prolapsed iris pillar parallel to the limbus; Tenon's capsule and the conjunctiva are then closed with continuous absorbable sutures spaced to insure tight closure. **In diathermy or scleral "buckling" operations,** absorbable gelatin sterile ophthalmic film may be placed over the sclera, the muscle and the conjunctiva then sutured over the underlying absorbable gelatin film. **In extraocular muscle surgery,** absorbable gelatin sterile ophthalmic film may be placed over and beneath the muscle before Tenon's capsule and the conjunctiva are closed in layers.

Supplied: Sterile Film: For use in neurosurgery and thoracic surgery, approximately 0.075 mm in thickness, size 125 sq cm (10×12.5 cm). Sterile envelopes, cartons of one.

Sterile Ophthalmic Film: For use in ocular surgery, approximately 0.075 mm in thickness, size 12.5 sq cm (2.5×5 cm). Sterile envelopes, cartons of 6.

Store at controlled room temperature 15 to 30°C. Once the envelopes have been opened, contents are subject to contamination. To insure sterility, it is recommended that absorbable gelatin film be used immediately after withdrawal from the envelope.

Reviewed 1998

GELFOAM®

Pharmacia & Upjohn

Absorbable Gelatin

Hemostatic

Description: Gelfoam is a medical device, intended for application to bleeding surfaces as a hemostatic. It is a water-insoluble, off-white, nonelastic, porous, pliable product prepared from purified pork Skin Gelatin USP granules and Water for injection, USP and is able to absorb and hold within its interstices, many times its weight of blood and other fluids. Gelfoam sterile powder is a fine, dry, heat-sterilized light powder prepared by milling absorbable gelatin sponge. Gelfoam sterile sponge may be cut without fraying.

Pharmacology: Gelfoam has hemostatic properties. While its mode of action is not fully understood, its effect appears to be more physical than the result of altering the blood clotting mechanism.

When not used in excessive amounts. Gelfoam is absorbed completely, with little tissue reaction. This absorption is dependent on several factors, including the amount used, degree of saturation with blood or other fluids, and the site of use. When placed in soft tissues, Gelfoam is usually absorbed completely in from 4 to 6 weeks, without inducing excessive scar tissue. When applied to bleeding nasal, rectal or vaginal mucosa, it liquefies within 2 to 5 days.

Indications: Hemostasis: Gelfoam sterile sponge, used dry or saturated with sterile sodium chloride solution, and Gelfoam sterile powder, saturated with sterile sodium chloride solution are indicated in surgical procedures as a hemostatic device, when control of capillary, venous, and arteriolar bleeding by pressure, ligature, and other conventional procedures is either ineffective or impractical.

However, in case of brisk arterial bleeding, the pressure of the flow may prevent the sponge from remaining securely anchored, and bleeding is likely to continue.

Contraindications: Gelfoam should not be used in closure of skin incisions because it may interfere with healing of the skin edges. This is due to mechanical interposition of gelatin and is not secondary to intrinsic interference with wound healing.

Gelfoam should not be placed in intravascular compartments, because of the risk of embolization.

Warnings: Gelfoam is not intended as a substitute for meticulous surgical technique and the proper application of ligatures, or other conventional procedures for hemostasis.

Gelfoam sterile sponge should not be resterilized by heat, because heating may change absorption time. Ethylene oxide is not recommended for resterilization because it may be trapped in the interstices of the foam. Although, not reported for Gelfoam, the gas is toxic to tissue, and in trace amounts may cause burns or irritation.

Gelfoam sterile powder is supplied as a sterile product and cannot be resterilized. Unused, opened jars of Gelfoam should be discarded.

Only the minimum amount of Gelfoam necessary to achieve hemostasis should be used. Once hemostasis is attained, excess Gelfoam should be carefully removed.

The use of Gelfoam is not recommended in the presence of infection. Gelfoam should be used with caution in contaminated areas of the body. If signs of infection or abscess develop where Gelfoam has been positioned, reoperation may be necessary in order to remove the infected material and allow drainage.

The safety and efficacy of the combined use of Gelfoam with other agents such as topical thrombin has not been evaluated in controlled clinical trials and therefore cannot be recommended. If in the physician's judgment concurrent use of topical thrombin or other agents are medically advisable, the product literature for that agent should be consulted for complete prescribing information.

While packing a cavity for hemostasis is sometimes surgically indicated, Gelfoam should not be used in this manner unless excess product not needed to maintain hemostasis is removed.

Whenever possible, it should be removed after use in laminectomy procedures and from foramina in bone, once hemostasis is achieved. This is because Gelfoam may swell on absorbing fluids, and produce nerve damage by pressure within confined bony spaces.

The packing of Gelfoam, particularly within bony cavities, should be avoided, since swelling may interfere with normal function and/or possibly result in compression necrosis of surrounding tissues.

Precautions: The minimum amount of Gelfoam needed for hemostasis should be applied together with pressure until the bleeding stops. The excess should then be removed.

Gelfoam should not be used for controlling postpartum hemorrhage or menorrhagia. It has been demonstrated that fragments of another hemostatic agent, microfibrillar collagen, pass through the 40 μ transfusion filters of blood scavenging systems. Gelfoam should not be used in conjunction with autologous blood salvage circuits since the safety of this use has not been evaluated in controlled clinical trials.

Microfibrillar collagen has been reported to reduce the strength of methylmethacrylate adhesives used to attach prosthetic devices to bone surfaces. As a precaution, Gelfoam should not be used to attach prosthetic devices to bone surfaces. As a precaution, Gelfoam should not be used in conjunction with such adhesives.

Gelfoam is not recommended for the primary treatment of coagulation disorders.

It is not recommended that Gelfoam be saturated with an antibiotic solution or dusted with antibiotic powder.

Because Gelfoam absorbs fluid, it may expand and impinge on neighboring structures. Therefore, when placed into cavities or closed tissue spaces, minimal preliminary compression is advised and care should be taken to avoid overpacking.

Adverse Effects: There have been reports of fever associated with the use of Gelfoam, without demonstrable infection. Gelfoam may serve as a nidus for infection and abscess formation, and has been reported to potentiate bacterial growth. Giant-cell granuloma has been reported at the implantation site of absorbable gelatin product in the brain, as has compression of the brain and spinal cord resulting from the accumulation of sterile fluid.

Foreign body reactions, "encapsulation" of fluid and hematoma have also been reported.

When Gelfoam was used in laminectomy operations, multiple neurologic events were reported, including but not limited to cauda equina syndrome, spinal stenosis, meningitis, arachnoiditis, headaches, paresthesias, pain, bladder and bowel dysfunction, and impotence.

Excessive fibrosis and prolonged fixation of a tendon have been reported when absorbable gelatin products were used in severed tendon repair.

Toxic shock syndrome has been reported in association with the use of Gelfoam in nasal surgery.

Fever, failure of absorption, and hearing loss have been reported in association with the use of Gelfoam during tympanoplasty.

Adverse Reactions Reported From Unapproved Uses: Gelfoam is not recommended for use other than as an adjunct for hemostasis.

While some adverse medical events following the unapproved use of Gelfoam have been reported to Pharmacia & Upjohn (see Adverse Effects), other hazards associated with such use may not have been reported.

When Gelfoam has been used during intravascular catheterization for the purpose of producing vessel occlusion, the following adverse events have been reported: fever, duodenal and pancreatic infarct, embolization of lower extremity vessels, pulmonary embolization, splenic abscess, necrosis of specific anatomic areas, asterixis and death.

These adverse medical events have been associated with the use of Gelfoam for repair of dural defects encountered during laminectomy and craniotomy operations: fever, infection, leg paresthesias, neck and back pain, bladder and bowel incontinence, cauda equina syndrome, neurogenic bladder, impotence, and paresis.

Dosage: Sterile technique should always be used. The minimum amount of Gelfoam should be applied to the bleeding site (see Directions For Use) with pressure until hemostasis is observed. Opened packages or jars of unused Gelfoam should always be discarded.

Directions for Use: Sponge: Always use sterile technique when handling Gelfoam sterile sponge.

Gelfoam should be cut to the minimum size required to attain hemostasis. Gelfoam may be applied dry or saturated with a physiologic saline solution.

When applied dry, Gelfoam should be manually compressed before application to the bleeding site. When used with saline, Gelfoam should be soaked in the solution, then withdrawn, squeezed between gloved fingers to expel air bubbles present in the interstices, replaced in saline, and kept there until needed. Gelfoam should immediately return to its original size and shape when returned to the solution. If it does not swell, it should be removed and kneaded vigorously until all air is expelled and it does expand to its original shape when dropped into the solution. Gelfoam can be used wet or blotted to dampness on gauze before application to the bleeding site.

Gelfoam should be applied to the bleeding surface and held in place with moderate pressure until hemostasis is attained. It is not necessary to apply suction to Gelfoam, since Gelfoam will draw up blood into its interstices by capillary action.

Usually, the first application of Gelfoam will control bleeding, but if not, additional applications may be made, using fresh pieces of Gelfoam.

Directions for Use: Powder: Gelfoam sterile powder can be saturated with sterile, isotonic sodium chloride solution (sterile saline), before use as an adjunct to hemostatis. The jar of Gelfoam sterile powder should be opened and the contents (1 g) poured carefully into a sterile beaker, avoiding contamination. Using sterile technique, a putty-like paste is prepared by adding a total of approximately 3 to 4 mL of sterile saline to the Gelfoam. Dispersion of the powder can be avoided by initially compressing it with the gloved fingers into the bottom of the beaker and then kneading it into the desired consistency. The resulting doughy paste may be smeared or pressed against the bleeding surface to control bleeding. When bleeding stops the excess should be removed.

Use only the minimum amount of Gelfoam, necessary to produce hemostasis. The Gelfoam may be left in place at the bleeding site, when necessary. Since Gelfoam causes little more cellular reaction than does the blood clot, the wound may be closed over it. Gelfoam may be left in place when applied to mucosal surfaces until it liquefies.

Supplied: Powder: Each jar contains: absorbable gelatin powder 1 g.

Sponge: Size 12.7 mm: 20 mm×60 mm (12 cm²)×7 mm, boxes of 4 sponges in individual envelopes.

Size 100: 80 mm×125 mm (100 cm²)×10 mm, boxes of 6 sponges in individual envelopes.

Size 2 cm: (approximately 40 cm×2 cm), individual envelopes.

Dental Pack Size 4: 20 mm×20 mm (4 cm²)×7 mm, jars of 15 sponges.

Store at controlled room temperature 15 to 30°C. Once the package or jar is opened, the contents are subject to contamination. It is recommended that Gelfoam be used as soon as the package or jar is opened and the unused contents discarded.

Reviewed 1999

GELUSIL®
GELUSIL® EXTRA STRENGTH
Warner-Lambert Consumer Healthcare

Aluminum Hydroxide—Magnesium Hydroxide

Antacid

Indications: For the temporary relief and treatment of duodenal and stomach ulcers, gastritis, hiatus hernia, esophagitis, heartburn and any similar gastrointestinal disorders in which control of gastric hyperacidity is desirable.

Contraindications: Should not be given to patients who are severely debilitated or suffering from kidney failure, alkalosis or hypermagnesemia.

Precautions: Antacids can interfere with the absorption of iron preparations and/or tetracyclines. Should not be taken for more than 2 weeks, or if symptoms recur, unless otherwise directed by a physician. Should not be taken within 2 hours of another medication, because the effectiveness of other medications may be altered.

Overdose: Symptoms and Treatment: Massive doses are unlikely to produce more than a mild gastrointestinal upset.

Dosage: Gelusil: 10 to 20 mL of liquid or 2 to 4 tablets 4 times daily, between meals and at bedtime as required to relieve symptoms and promote recovery. Tablets should be chewed. May be used diluted with water to make a 25% solution and administered at the rate of 18 drops per minute as a continuous gastric or duodenal drip for hospitalized patients.
Gelusil Extra Strength: 10 mL of liquid or 2 to 4 tablets 4 times a day, between meals and at bedtime as required to relieve symptoms and promote recovery of active peptic ulcer disease.

Supplied: Gelusil: Liquid: Each 5 mL of viscous, white, peppermint-flavored liquid contains: magnesium hydroxide 200 mg and dried aluminum hydroxide gel 200 mg (equivalent to 153 mg aluminum hydroxide). Nonmedicinal ingredients: calcium cyclamate, citric acid, flavor, hydroxypropyl methylcellulose, menthol, parabens, peppermint oil, simethicone, sodium carboxymethylcellulose, sorbitol, water and xanthan gum. Energy: 4.6 kJ (1.1 kcal). Sodium: <1 mmol (0.84 mg)/5 mL. Gluten-, lactose-, sucrose-, sulfite- and tartrazine-free. Bottles of 350 mL.

Tablets: Each white, mint-flavored tablet contains: magnesium hydroxide 200 mg and dried aluminum hydroxide gel 200 mg (equivalent to 153 mg aluminum hydroxide). Nonmedicinal ingredients: flavors, magnesium stearate, mannitol, sorbitol and sugar. Energy: 11.7 kJ (2.8 kcal). Sodium: <1 mmol (1.1 mg). Gluten-, lactose-, paraben-, sulfite- and tartrazine-free. Boxes of 50 and 100.

Gelusil Extra Strength: Liquid: Each 5 mL of white, peppermint-flavored liquid contains: magnesium hydroxide 350 mg and dried aluminum hydroxide gel 650 mg (equivalent to 497 mg aluminum hydroxide). Nonmedicinal ingredients: calcium cyclamate, citric acid, flavor, menthol, parabens, peppermint oil, simethicone, sorbitol and water. Energy: 5.0 kJ (1.2 kcal). Sodium: <1 mmol (1.4 mg)/5 mL. Gluten-, lactose-, sucrose-, sulfite- and tartrazine-free. Bottles of 350 mL.

Tablets: Each white, mint-flavored tablet contains: magnesium hydroxide 400 mg and dried aluminum hydroxide gel 400 mg (equivalent to 306 mg aluminum hydroxide). Nonmedicinal ingredients: flavors, magneisum stearate, sorbitol and sucrose. Energy: 14.7 kJ (3.5 kcal). Sodium: <1 mmol (1.6 mg)/tablet. Gluten-, lactose-, paraben-, sulfite- and tartrazine-free. Boxes of 50 blister packaged.

GEMFIBROZIL 🄿
AltiMed

Antihyperlipidemic Agent

Supplied: 300 mg: Each maroon and white capsule, imprinted "CL 300", contains: gemfibrozil 300 mg. Nonmedicinal ingredients: cornstarch, polysorbate 80 and silica gel; capsule shell: colloidal silicon dioxide, FD&C Blue No. 1, FD&C Red No. 3, gelatin, sodium lauryl sulfate and titanium dioxide. Energy: 3.4 kJ (0.8 kcal). Gluten-, lactose-, paraben-, sodium-, sulfite- and tartrazine-free. Bottles of 100 and 250.

600 mg: Each white, ellipsoidal, film-coated tablet, imprinted "CL 600", contains: gemfibrozil 600 mg. Nonmedicinal ingredients: calcium stearate, candelilla wax, colloidal silicon dioxide, hydroxypropyl methylcellulose, hydroxypropyl cellulose, methylparaben, microcrystalline cellulose, Opacode Black, polyethylene glycol, polysorbate 80, pregelatinized starch, propylparaben and titanium dioxide. Energy: 2.0 kJ (0.47 kcal). Gluten-, lactose-, paraben-, sodium, sulfite and tartrazine-free. Bottles of 100 and 250.

Store below 30°C.

GEMZAR® 🄿
Lilly

Gemcitabine HCl

Antineoplastic Agent

> Caution: Gemcitabine is a cytotoxic drug and should be used only by physicians experienced with cancer chemotherapeutic drugs. Prolongation of the infusion time beyond 60 minutes and more frequent than weekly dosing have been shown to increase toxicity. The dosage should be reduced, omitted, or the drug discontinued upon evidence of abnormal suppression of the bone marrow. Acute shortness of breath with a temporal relationship to gemcitabine administration may occur. Some reports of parenchymal lung toxicity were consistent with drug-induced pneumonitis in association with the use of gemcitabine.
> This preparation is for i.v. administration only.

Pharmacology: Gemcitabine is a cell-cycle dependent oncolytic agent of the antimetabolite class. It is a deoxycytidine analog (difluoro-deoxycytidine; dFdC) that is metabolized intracellularly to the active diphosphate (dFdCDP) and triphosphate (dFdCTP) nucleosides. The cytotoxic effects of gemcitabine are exerted through dFdCDP-assisted incorporation of dFdCTP into DNA, resulting in inhibition of DNA synthesis and induction of apoptosis.
Pharmacokinetics: Gemcitabine disposition was studied in 5 patients who received a single 1 000 mg/m²/30 min infusion of radiolabeled drug. Within 1 week, 92 to 98% of the dose was recovered, almost entirely in the urine. Gemcitabine (<10%) and the inactive uracil metabolite, 2'-deoxy-2', 2'-difluorouridine (dFdU), accounted for 99% of the excreted dose. The metabolite dFdU is also found in plasma. Gemcitabine plasma protein binding is negligible.

The pharmacokinetics of gemcitabine were examined in 353 patients, about 2/3 men, with various solid tumors. Pharmacokinetic parameters were derived using data from patients treated for varying durations of therapy given weekly with periodic rest weeks and using both short infusions (<70 minutes) and long infusions (70 to 285 minutes). The total gemcitabine dose varied from 500 to 3 600 mg/m².

Gemcitabine pharmacokinetics are linear and are described by a 2-compartment model. Population pharmacokinetic analyses of combined single and multiple dose studies showed that the volume of distribution of gemcitabine was significantly influenced by duration of infusion and gender. Clearance was affected by age and gender. Differences in either clearance or volume of distribution based on patient characteristics or the duration of infusion result in changes in half-life and plasma concentrations. Table I shows plasma clearance and half-life of gemcitabine following short infusions for typical patients by age and gender.

Table I—Gemzar

Gemcitabine Clearance and Half-life for the Typical Patient

Age	Clearance Men (L/h/m²)	Clearance Women (L/h/m²)	Half-life* Men (min)	Half-life* Women (min)
29	92.2	69.4	42	49
45	75.7	57.0	48	57
65	55.1	41.5	61	73
79	40.7	30.7	79	94

*Half-life for patients receiving a short infusion (<70 minutes).

Gemcitabine half-life for short infusions ranged from 32 to 94 minutes, and the value for long infusions varied from 245 to 638 minutes, depending on age and gender, reflecting a greatly increased volume of distribution with longer infusions. The lower clearance in women and the elderly results in higher concentrations of gemcitabine for any given dose.

The volume of distribution was increased with infusion length. Volume of distribution of gemcitabine was 50 L/m² following infusions lasting <70 minutes, indicating that gemcitabine, after short infusions, is not extensively distributed into tissues. For long infusions, the volume of distribution rose to 370 L/m², reflecting slow equilibration of gemcitabine within the tissue compartment.

The maximum plasma concentrations of dFdU (inactive metabolite) were achieved up to 30 minutes after discontinuation of the infusions. The metabolite was excreted in urine without undergoing further biotransformation and did not accumulate with weekly dosing. Its elimination is dependent on renal excretion and the metabolite could accumulate with decreased renal function.

The effects of significant renal or hepatic insufficiency on the disposition of gemcitabine have not been assessed.

The active metabolite, gemcitabine triphosphate, can be extracted from peripheral blood mononuclear cells. The half-life of the terminal phase for gemcitabine triphosphate from mononuclear cells ranges from 1.7 to 19.4 hours.

Indications: For the treatment of patients with locally advanced (nonresectable Stage II or Stage III) or metastatic (Stage IV) adenocarcinoma of the pancreas to achieve a Clinical Benefit Response (a composite measure of clinical improvement).

Gemcitabine is also indicated for the palliative treatment of patients with locally advanced or metastatic nonsmall cell lung cancer (NSCLC).

Contraindications: Patients with a known hypersensitivity to the drug (see Adverse Effects, Allergic).

Warnings: Gemcitabine is a cytotoxic drug and should be used only by physicians experienced with cancer chemotherapeutic agents. Blood counts should be taken prior to each dose. Reduce, omit or discontinue the dosage upon evidence of abnormal suppression of the bone marrow (see Dosage).

Prolongation of the infusion time beyond 60 minutes and more frequent than weekly dosing have been shown to increase toxicity (see Dosage).

Acute shortness of breath in association with gemcitabine administration may occur. There have been reports of parenchymal lung toxicity consistent with drug induced pneumonitis in association with the use of gemcitabine (see Adverse Effects, Pulmonary and Dosage).

There have been cases of histologically confirmed Hemolytic Uremic Syndrome (HUS) reported in patients treated with gemcitabine (see Adverse Effects, Renal). Patients with preexisting renal dysfunction should be followed closely while being treated with gemcitabine.
Pregnancy: Gemcitabine has been shown to be embryotoxic and/or fetotoxic in animals. Therefore gemcitabine should be used in pregnancy only following the careful consideration of the benefits vs the risks.
Lactation: It is not known whether the drug is excreted in human milk. Because many drugs are excreted in human milk and because of the potential for serious adverse reactions in nursing infants, it is recommended that nursing be discontinued.
Children: Safety and effectiveness in children have not been established.

Precautions: Selection of Patients: In all instances where the use of gemcitabine is considered for chemotherapy, the physician must evaluate the need and usefulness of the drug against the risk of adverse events. If severe adverse events occur, the drug should be reduced in dosage, omitted, or discontinued and appropriate corrective measures should be taken based on the clinical judgment of the physician (see Dosage).

Gemcitabine should be used with extreme caution in patients whose bone marrow reserve may have been compromised by prior irradiation or chemotherapy, or whose marrow function is recovering from previous chemotherapy.

Most drug-related adverse reactions are reversible.
Hematologic: See Warnings.
Fever and Flu-like Symptoms: Gemcitabine may cause fever, with or without flu-like symptoms, in the absence of clinical infection (see Adverse Effects). The administration of acetaminophen may provide symptomatic relief.
Rash: Gemcitabine administration has been associated with rash (see Adverse Effects). Topical corticosteroids may provide symptomatic relief.
Pulmonary: Acute shortness of breath in association with gemcitabine administration may occur (see Warnings). Bronchodilators, corticosteroids and/or oxygen produce symptomatic relief.
Pregnancy and *Lactation:* See Warnings.
Gender: Gemcitabine clearance is affected by gender (see Pharmacology). There is no evidence, however, that further dose adjustments (i.e., other than those already recommended in Dosage) are necessary in women.

Gemzar (cont'd)

Geriatrics: Gemcitabine has been well tolerated in patients over the age of 65. Although clearance is affected by age (see Pharmacology), there is no evidence that further dose adjustments, (i.e., other than those already recommended in Dosage) are necessary in patients over the age of 65.

Children: See Warnings.

Patients with Renal or Hepatic Impairment: Gemcitabine should be used with caution in patients with renal or hepatic insufficiency. No data are available in patients with significant renal or hepatic impairment (see Adverse Effects).

Radiosensitizing Effect: In a single trial where gemcitabine at a dose of 1 000 mg/m² was administered for up to 6 consecutive weeks concurrently with therapeutic thoracic radiation to patients with NSCLC, significant toxicity was observed in the form of severe, and potentially life-threatening, esophagitis and pneumonitis, particularly in patients receiving large volumes of radiotherapy. No clinical studies have been carried out to date to elucidate the optimum regimen that may be used for the safe administration of gemcitabine with therapeutic doses of radiation.

Drug Interactions: No confirmed interactions have been reported with the use of gemcitabine. No specific drug interaction studies have been conducted.

Information for the Patient: Patients should be informed that the major acute toxicities of gemcitabine are related to bone marrow toxicity, specifically myelosuppression, with increased susceptibility to infection. They should also be advised that shortness of breath may develop or worsen during treatment either due to disease progression or in rare cases, due to a direct effect of the drug. Patients should be instructed to immediately report a developing or worsening of shortness of breath to the treating physician. Gemcitabine should not be used in pregnancy unless the physician feels the potential benefit justifies the risk of potential harm to the fetus.

Adverse Effects: The overall safety database for gemcitabine consists of a total of 979 patients to whom gemcitabine was administered as a single agent, using starting doses in the range of 800 to 1 250 mg/m² administered weekly as a 30-minute infusion for the treatment of a wide variety of malignancies. Of the 979 patients only 10.4% (102) were discontinued due to an adverse event regardless of causality. WHO grade 3 or 4 toxicity of nonlaboratory events, was less than 1% for all parameters except nausea and vomiting, pulmonary toxicity, infection and pain.

All WHO-graded laboratory toxicities for a total of 979 patients are listed in Table II, regardless of causality. Nonlaboratory WHO-toxicities were available for 565 patients. They are listed in Table II (for parameters that occurred in ≥5% of patients), or discussed below. Edema, extravasation and flu-like symptoms were reported regardless of causality as treatment emergent signs and symptoms (TESS*; N=979).

Data are also shown (see Table II) for the subset of patients (N=360) with nonsmall cell lung cancer treated in 4 clinical studies (2 studies WHO laboratory toxicities; 2 studies nonlaboratory WHO-toxicities) and the subset of patients (N=159) with pancreatic cancer treated in 5 clinical studies (WHO laboratory and nonlaboratory toxicities). The frequency of all grades were generally similar for the overall safety database and the subsets of patients with nonsmall cell lung cancer and pancreatic cancer.

*TESS: An event was considered treatment-emergent, if it occurred for the first time or worsened while receiving therapy following baseline evaluation. It is important to emphasize that although the events were reported during therapy, they were not necessarily caused by the therapy.

Hematologic: Myelosuppression is the major dose-limiting toxicity with gemcitabine; it was usually of short duration, reversible and not cumulative over time. Less than 1% of patients discontinued therapy for either anemia, leukopenia, or thrombocytopenia. Red blood cell transfusions were required by 19% of patients and less than 1% of patients required platelet transfusion. The incidence of major infection (WHO grade toxicity of 3) was only 1.1% and only one grade 4 toxicity for infection occurred.

Gastrointestinal: Mild or moderate nausea and vomiting (WHO toxicity grade 1 and 2) was reported in 64% of all patients. WHO grade 3 toxicity, defined as vomiting requiring therapy, was reported in 17.1% of patients. Any patient who received prophylactic antiemetics, was automatically graded ≥WHO grade 3, even if they only developed mild nausea. Diarrhea and stomatitis were usually mild and occurred in less than 13% of patients. WHO toxicity for constipation was mild (WHO grade 1) in the majority of cases and was reported for 7.8% of patients.

Hepatic: Gemcitabine was associated with transient elevations of serum transaminases (predominantly WHO grades 1 and 2) in approximately ⅔ of patients, but there was no evidence of increasing hepatic toxicity with either longer duration of treatment with gemcitabine or with greater total cumulative dose.

Renal: Mild Proteinuria and hematuria were commonly reported. Clinical findings consistent with the hemolytic uremic syndrome (HUS) were reported in 6 out of 2 429 patients (0.25%) receiving gemcitabine in clinical trials (see Warnings). Renal failure associated with HUS, may not be reversible even with discontinuation of therapy and dialysis may be required.

Fever and Infection: Fever of any severity was reported in 37.3% of patients. Fever was frequently associated with other flu-like symptoms and was usually mild and clinically manageable. Less than 1% of patients were discontinued for fever. The incidence of fever contrasts with the incidence of infection (8.7%) and indicates that gemcitabine may cause fever in the absence of clinical infection (see Precautions).

Cutaneous Toxicity: A rash is seen in 24.8% of patients, it is usually mild, not dose limiting and responds to local therapy (see Precautions). The rash was typically a macular or finely granular maculopapular pruritic eruption of mild to moderate severity involving the trunk and extremities.

Pulmonary and Allergic: The administration of gemcitabine has been infrequently associated with shortness of breath (see Warnings, Dyspnea). Dyspnea when graded by WHO-toxicity criteria (see Table II), was reported in 8%, and severe dyspnea (WHO grades 3 and 4) was reported in 1.4% of patients.

Dyspnea, regardless of causality (TESS) was reported in 23% of patients and serious dyspnea was reported in 3% of patients. It should be noted that in both of these analyses, the occurrence of dyspnea may have been due to underlying disease such as lung cancer (40% of study population) or pulmonary manifestations of other malignancies. Dyspnea was occasionally accompanied by bronchospasm (<1% of patients).

Pulmonary effects, sometimes severe (such as pulmonary edema, interstitial pneumonitis, or adult respiratory distress syndrome [ARDS] have been reported rarely in association with gemcitabine therapy. The etiology of these effects is unknown. If such effects develop, consideration should be given to discontinuing gemcitabine. Early use of supportive care measures may help ameliorate the condition.

Edema: The occurrence of edema is reported regardless of causality, as a treatment emergent event (TESS). Edema (13%), peripheral edema (20%) and facial edema (<1%) were reported. Overall, edema was usually mild to moderate and reversible. Less than 1% of patients (N=979) discontinued due to edema.

Table II—Gemzar

WHO-Graded Toxicities Occurring with a ≥5% Frequency in Patients Receiving Gemzar (WHO Grades (in % Frequency) are Rounded to the Closest Integer)

	All Patients (% incidence)			Nonsmall Cell Lung Cancer Patients (N=360)			Pancreatic Cancer Patients (N=244)			Discontinuations (%)
	All Grades	Grade 3	Grade 4	All Grades	Grade 3	Grade 4	All Grades	Grade 3	Grade 4	All Patients
Laboratory	(N=979)			(N=360)			(N=244)			(N=979)
Hematologic										
Anemia	68	7	1	65	5	<1	73	8	3	<1
Leukopenia	62	9	<1	55	7	<1	63	8	1	<1
Neutropenia	63	19	6	61	20	5	61	17	7	
Thrombocytopenia	24	4	1	16	1	1	36	7	<1	<1
Hepatic										
ALT	68	8	2	70	9	3	72	10	1	<1
AST	67	7	2	67	5	1	78	12	5	
Alkaline Phosphatase	55	7	2	48	2	0	77	16	4	
Bilirubin	13	2	<1	8	<1	<1	26	6	3	
Renal										
BUN	16	0	0	16	0	0	15	0	0	<1
Creatinine	7	<1	0	6	<1	0	6	0	0	
Proteinuria	36	<1	0	52	<1	0	15	<1	0	
Hematuria	31	<1	0	43	2	0	14	0	0	
Nonlaboratory	(N=565)			(N=243)			(N=159)			
Nausea and Vomiting	64	17	1	69	19	<1	62	12	2	<1
Fever	37	<1	0	46	<1	0	28	<1	0	<1
Skin Rash	25	<1	0	30	0	0	22	0	0	<1
Alopecia	14	<1	0	14	<1	0	14	0	0	0
Pain	16	1	0	16	1	0	12	2	0	<1
Diarrhea	12	<1	0	6	<1	0	24	2	0	0
Infection	9	1	<1	10	0	0	8	1	0	<1
State of Consciousness/ Somnolence	9	<1	0	6	0	0	10	3	0	<1
Dyspnea	8	1	<1	8	2	0	6	0	0	<1
Constipation	8	<1	0	7	<1	0	13	2	0	0
Stomatitis	8	<1	0	7	<1	0	10	0	0	<1

Grade based on criteria from the World Health Organization (WHO).

Flu-like Symptoms: "Flu-syndrome" was reported regardless of causality (TESS) for 18.9% of patients (N=979). Individual symptoms of headache, fever, chills, myalgia and asthenia were the most commonly reported symptoms. Cough, rhinitis, malaise, sweating and insomnia were also commonly reported. Less than 1% of patients discontinued due to flu-like symptoms.

Alopecia: Hair loss (alopecia), usually minimal, was reported for any WHO grade in only 13.7% of patients. No grade 4 toxicity (nonreversible alopecia) was reported, and only 0.4% of patients reported grade 3 toxicity (complete but reversible alopecia).

Neurotoxicity: WHO grade 1 or 2 peripheral neurotoxicity† was reported for 3.3% of patients. No patient reported WHO grade 3 or 4 toxicity.

State of consciousness toxicity was usually mild to moderate (WHO grades 1 and 2), somnolence was reported for 4.6% of patients.

Extravasation: Gemcitabine is well tolerated during the infusion with only a few cases (4%) of injection site reaction reported. Gemcitabine does not appear to be a vesicant (see Dosage). There have been no reports of injection site necrosis.

Cardiac Toxicity: Less than 2% of patients discontinued therapy with gemcitabine due to cardiovascular events such as myocardial infarction, arrhythmia, chest pain, heart failure, pulmonary edema and hypertension. Many of these patients had a prior history of cardiovascular disease.

†WHO grade 1 peripheral neurotoxicity is defined as paresthesia and/or decreased tendon reflexes and WHO grade 2 toxicity is defined as severe paresthesia and/or mild weakness.

Overdose: Symptoms and Treatment: There is no known antidote for overdoses of gemcitabine. Myelosuppression, and paresthesia were the principal toxicities seen when a single dose as high as 5 700 mg/m² was administered by i.v. infusion over 30 minutes every 2 weeks to several patients in a Phase I study. In the event of a suspected overdose, the patient should be monitored with appropriate blood counts and should receive supportive therapy, as necessary.

Dosage: This preparation is for i.v. use only. It should be administered by individuals experienced in the administration of cancer chemotherapeutic drugs.

Gemcitabine should be used by i.v. infusion at a dose of 1 000 mg/m² over 30 minutes.

In the treatment of patients with locally advanced or metastatic adenocarcinoma of the pancreas, gemcitabine should be administered once weekly for up to 7 weeks (or until toxicity necessitates reducing or holding a dose), followed by a week of rest from treatment. Subsequent cycles should consist of infusions once weekly for 3 consecutive weeks out of every 4 weeks.

In the palliative treatment of patients with locally advanced or metastatic nonsmall cell lung cancer, gemcitabine should be administered once weekly for 3 weeks, followed by a 1-week rest period. This 4-week cycle is repeated.

Dosage escalation or reduction is based upon the degree of toxicities experienced by the patient.

Dosage Reduction and Treatment Discontinuation: Patients receiving gemcitabine should be monitored prior to each dose for granulocyte and platelet counts and, if necessary, the dose of gemcitabine may be either reduced or withheld in the presence of hematological toxicity according to the following scale (see Table III).

Table III—Gemzar

Dose Adjustments Based on Granulocyte and Platelet Counts

Absolute Granulocyte Count (×10⁶/L)		Platelet count (×10⁶/L)	% of Full Dose
>1 000	and	>100 000	100
500–1 000	or	50 000–100 000	75
<500	or	<50 000	hold

Liver and kidney functions including transaminases and serum creatinine should also be followed in patients receiving this drug (see Precautions).

Acute shortness of breath in association with gemcitabine administration may occur. Bronchodilators, corticosteroids and/or oxygen produce symptomatic relief. Some reports of parenchymal lung toxicity were consistent with drug induced pneumonitis in association with the use of gemcitabine (see Adverse Effects, Pulmonary). The mechanism of this toxicity is not known. Patients suspected of experiencing drug-induced pneumonitis should be discontinued and not be rechallenged with the drug.

Administration Precautions: Gemcitabine is well tolerated during the infusion, with only a few cases of injection site reaction reported. There have been no reports of injection site necrosis. The drug also does not appear to act as a vesicant in a case of extravasation. It may be administered on an outpatient basis.

As with other toxic compounds, caution should be exercised in handling and preparing solutions with gemcitabine. The use of gloves is recommended. If the solution of gemcitabine contacts the skin or mucosa, immediately wash the skin or mucosa thoroughly with soap and water or rinse the mucosa with copious amounts of water.

Parenteral drugs should be inspected visually for particulate matter and discoloration, prior to administration, whenever solution and container permit. The reconstituted solution is stable for 24 hours at 15 to 30°C. Any unused solution should be discarded.

Reconstitution: To reconstitute, add at least 5 mL of 0.9% Sodium Chloride Injection to the 200 mg vial or at least 25 mL of 0.9% Sodium Chloride Injection to the 1 g vial. Invert to dissolve. These dilutions each yield a gemcitabine concentration of 38 mg/mL. The appropriate amount of drug may be administered as prepared or further diluted with 0.9% Sodium Chloride Injection to concentrations as low as 0.1 mg/mL.

Reconstitution of concentrations greater than 40 mg/mL may result in incomplete dissolution, and should not be attempted.

Solutions for Reconstitution: Sterile isotonic saline (0.9% Sodium Chloride Injection) without added preservatives.

Handling and Disposal: Procedures for proper handling and disposal of anticancer drugs should be considered. Several guidelines on this subject have been published.

Supplied: 200 mg: Each vial of sterile lyophilized powder contains: gemcitabine HCl equivalent to gemcitabine 200 mg as free base. Nonmedicinal ingredients: mannitol and sodium acetate. Vials of 10 mL.

1 g: Each vial of sterile lyophilized powder contains: gemcitabine HCl equivalent to gemcitabine 1 g as free base. Nonmedicinal ingredients: mannitol and sodium acetate. Vials of 50 mL.

For i.v. use only. Store in glass vials, at 15 to 30°C.

Reviewed 1999

GEN-ALPRAZOLAM Ⓟ

Genpharm

Alprazolam

Anxiolytic—Antipanic

Supplied: 0.25 mg: Each white, oval, biconvex tablet, marked "AL/0.25" on one side and "G" on the other, contains: alprazolam 0.25 mg. Also contains lactose. Bottles of 100 and 1 000.

0.5 mg: Each pale orange, oval, biconvex tablet, marked "AL/0.5" on one side and "G" on the other, contains: alprazolam 0.5 mg. Also contains lactose and FD&C Yellow #6. Bottles of 100 and 1 000.

1 mg: Each mauve, oval, biconvex tablet, marked "AL/1.0" on one side and "G" on the other, contains: alprazolam 1 mg. Also contains lactose. Bottles of 100 and 1 000.

2 mg: Each white, oblong, beveled-edged tablet, marked "/A/L/" on one side and "/G/2/" on the other, contains: alprazolam 2 mg. Also contains lactose. Bottles of 100 and 1 000.

Store at room temperature, between 15 and 30°C.

GEN-AMANTADINE (Antiparkinsonian) Ⓟ

Genpharm

Amantadine HCl

Antiparkinsonian

Supplied: Each red, oblong, soft gelatin capsule, imprinted "A100" in white ink on one side with off-white opaque semi-solid filling, contains: amantadine HCl 100 mg. Nonmedicinal ingredients: beeswax, D&C Red No. 33, gelatin, glycerin, hydrogenated soybean flakes, hydrogenated vegetable oil, lecithin, parabens, refined soybean oil, titanium dioxide and water. Bottles of 100 and 500. Store in a light-resistant container at temperatures between 15 and 30°C.

GEN-AMANTADINE (Antiviral) Ⓟ

Genpharm

Amantadine HCl

Antiviral

Supplied: Each red, oblong, soft gelatin capsule, imprinted "A100" in white ink on one side, with off-white opaque semi-solid filling, contains: amantadine HCl 100 mg. Nonmedicinal ingredients: beeswax, D&C Red No. 33, gelatin, glycerin, hydrogenated soybean flakes, hydrogenated vegetable oil, lecithin, parabens, refined soybean oil, titanium dioxide and water. Bottles of 100 and 500. Store in a light-resistant container at temperatures between 15 and 30°C.

GEN-ATENOLOL Ⓟ

Genpharm

Atenolol

Antihypertensive—Antianginal Agent

Supplied: 50 mg: Each white, round, biconvex tablet, with G/G on one side and AT/50 on the other side, contains: atenolol 50 mg. Bottles of 30, 100 and 500.

100 mg: Each white, round, biconvex tablet, with "G" on one side and AT/100 on the other side, contains: atenolol 100 mg. Bottles of 30, 100 and 500.

Protect from light and moisture. Store between 15 and 30°C.

GEN-AZATHIOPRINE Ⓟ

Genpharm

Azathioprine

Immunosuppressive Agent

Supplied: Each pale yellow biconvex tablet embossed "AE", Breakline "50" on one side and "G" on reverse, contains: azathioprine 50 mg. Nonmedicinal ingredients: lactose, magnesium stearate, potato starch, povidone, purified water and stearic acid. Bottles of 100, blisters of 10. Securitainers of 100.

New Product 1998

GEN-BACLOFEN Ⓟ

Genpharm

Baclofen

Muscle Relaxant—Antispasticity Agent

Supplied: 10 mg: Each round, flat, white, bevelled edge tablet, marked "BN" and "10" on one side and G on the reverse, contains: baclofen 10 mg. Alcohol-, bisulfite-, parabens-, and tartrazine free. Bottles of 100 and 500.

20 mg: Each round, flat, white, bevelled edge tablet, scored and marked BN breakline 20 on one side and G on the reverse, contains: baclofen 20 mg. Alcohol-, bisulfite-, parabens-, and tartrazine free. Bottles of 100.

GEN-BECLO AQ. Ⓟ

Genpharm

Beclomethasone Dipropionate

Corticosteroid

Supplied: Each spray of suspension delivered by the nasal applicator contains: beclomethasone dipropionate 50 µg. Amber glass bottles of 200 doses fitted with a metering pump and a nasal applicator. Nonmedicinal ingredients: benzalkonium chloride, dextrose, microcrystalline cellulose, phenyl ethanol, polysorbate, purified water and sodium carboxymethyl cellulose. Store between 15 and 30°C. Protect from light. Do not refrigerate.

GEN-BROMAZEPAM [P]
Genpharm

Bromazepam

Anxiolytic—Sedative

Supplied: 1.5 mg: Each white, round, flat beveled-edge tablet, with "B" bisect and "1.5" on one side and "G" on the other, contains: bromazepam 1.5 mg. Nonmedicinal ingredients: lactose, magnesium stearate, microcrystalline cellulose, starch and talc. Bottles of 100.

3 mg: Each pink, round, flat beveled-edge tablet, with "B" bisect and "3" on one side and "G" on the other, contains: bromazepam 3 mg. Nonmedicinal ingredients: lactose, lake blend red, magnesium stearate, microcrystalline cellulose, starch and talc. Bottles of 100 and 500.

6 mg: Each pale green, round, flat, 9 mm beveled-edge tablet, with "B" bisect and "6" on one side and "G" on the other, contains: bromazepam 6 mg. Nonmedicinal ingredients: D&C Yellow #10, FD&C Blue #1, iron oxide, lactose, magnesium stearate, microcrystalline cellulose, starch and talc. Bottles of 100 and 500.

Store between 15 and 30°C.

GEN-BUDESONIDE AQ. [P]
Genpharm

Budesonide

Glucocorticosteroid

Supplied: Each metered dose of a white to off-white, thixotropic aqueous suspension contains: budesonide 100 µg. Amber glass bottles of 10 mL (equivalent to 165 doses minimum), provided with a pump spray mechanism, nasal adapter and patient instruction leaflet. Store between 15 and 30°C.

GEN-BUSPIRONE [P]
Genpharm

Buspirone HCl

Anxiolytic

Supplied: Each white, barrel-shaped tablet, imprinted "B" vertical scoreline "10" on one side and no markings on the other side, contains: buspirone HCl 10 mg. Nonmedicinal ingredients: colloidal silicon dioxide, lactose, magnesium stearate, microcrystalline cellulose and sodium starch glycolate. Bottles of 100 and 500.

New Product 1998

GEN-CAPTOPRIL [P]
Genpharm

Captopril

Angiotensin Converting Enzyme Inhibitor

Supplied: 12.5 mg: Each white, capsule-shaped tablet, with partial bisect and "G" on one side and partial bisect and "C 12.5" on the other, contains: captopril 12.5 mg. Bottles of 100 and 500. Unit dose of 100.

25 mg: Each white, square, biconvex tablet, with C/25 on one side and quadrisected on the other, contains: captopril 25 mg. Bottles of 100 and 1 000. Unit dose of 100.

50 mg: Each white, oval, biconvex tablet, with "C 50" on one side and with a partial bisect and "G" on the other, contains: captopril 50 mg. Bottles of 100 and 500. Unit dose of 100.

100 mg: Each white, oval, biconvex tablet, with "C 100" on one side and with a partial bisect and "G" on the other, contains: captopril 100 mg. Bottles of 100.

GEN-CIMETIDINE [P]
Genpharm

Cimetidine

Histamine H_2-Receptor Antagonist

Supplied: 200 mg: Each light green, round, biconvex, film-coated tablet, with "G" on one side and "CM/200" on the other, contains: cimetidine 200 mg. Bottles of 100.

300 mg: Each light green, round, biconvex, film-coated tablet, with "G" on one side and "CM/300" on the other, contains: cimetidine 300 mg. Bottles of 100, 500 and 1 000.

400 mg: Each light green, ellipsoid, biconvex, film-coated tablet, with "G" on one side and "CM 400" on the other, contains: cimetidine 400 mg. Bottles of 100 and 500.

600 mg: Each light green, ellipsoid, biconvex, film-coated tablet, with "G" on one side and "CM 600" on the other, contains: cimetidine 600 mg. Bottles of 100 and 500.

800 mg: Each light green, ellipsoid, biconvex, film-coated tablet, with "G" on one side and "CM 800" on the other, contains: cimetidine 800 mg. Bottles of 100.

GEN-CLOBETASOL [P]
Genpharm

Clobetasol 17-propionate

Topical Corticosteroid

Supplied: Cream: Each g of cream contains: clobetasol 17-propionate 0.05% w/w. Tubes of 15 and 50 g. Store between 15 and 30°C.

Ointment: Each g of ointment contains: clobetasol 17-propionate 0.05% w/w. Tubes of 15 and 50 g. Store between 15 and 30°C.

GEN-CLOBETASOL Scalp Application [P]
Genpharm

Clobetasol 17-Propionate

Topical Corticosteroid

Supplied: Each mL of aqueous, alcohol base scalp application contains: clobetasol 17-propionate 0.05% w/w. White, opaque, plastic bottles of 20 and 60 mL. Store between 15 and 30°C.

GEN-CLOMIPRAMINE [P]
Genpharm

Clomipramine HCl

Antidepressant—Antiobsessional

Supplied: 10 mg: Each yellow, triangular film-coated, biconvex tablet marked with "CI" on one side and "10" on the other side, contains: clomipramine HCl 10 mg. Nonmedicinal ingredients: hydroxypropyl cellulose, hydroxypropyl methylcellulose, iron oxide, lactose, magnesium stearate, maize starch, povidone, propylene glycol, quinoline, sodium starch glycolate and titanium dioxide. Bottles of 100 and 500.

25 mg: Each film-coated, yellow, biconvex tablet, with CI/25 imprinted on one side and G on the other, contains: clomipramine HCl 25 mg. Nonmedicinal ingredients: hydroxypropyl cellulose, hydroxypropyl methylcellulose, iron oxide, lactose, magnesium stearate, maize starch, povidone, propylene glycol, quinoline yellow, sodium starch glycolate and titanium dioxide. Bottles of 100 and 500.

50 mg: Each film-coated, white, biconvex tablet, with CI/50 imprinted on one side and G on the other, contains: clomipramine HCl 50 mg. Nonmedicinal ingredients: hydroxypropyl cellulose, hydroxypropyl methylcellulose, lactose, magnesium stearate, maize starch, povidone, propylene glycol, sodium starch glycolate and titanium dioxide. Bottles of 100 and 500.

Protect from heat and moisture. Store at room temperature between 15 and 30°C. Keep out of the reach of children.

GEN-CLONAZEPAM [P]
Genpharm

Clonazepam

Anticonvulsant

Supplied: 0.5 mg: Each round, flat-faced, beveled edge, peach tablet, engraved with "CN/0.5" on one side and "G" on the other, contains: clonazepam 0.5 mg. Bottles of 100 and 500.

2 mg: Each round, flat-faced, beveled edge, white tablet, engraved with "CN/2" on one side and "G" on the other, contains: clonazepam 2 mg. Bottles of 100 and 500.

Keep in a tightly closed, light-resistant container. Store between 15 and 30°C.

GEN-CROMOGLYCATE Nasal Solution [P]
Genpharm

Sodium Cromoglycate

Seasonal Rhinitis Prophylaxis

Supplied: Each metered dose contains: sodium cromoglycate 2% w/v. Nonmedicinal ingredients: water. benzalkonium chloride, disodium edetate and purified water. HDPB with pump attached. The bottle contains not less than 26 mL of solution. The pump delivers approximately 2.6 mg of sodium cromoglycate (0.13 mL of the 2% w/v solution) per mist.

New Product 1998

GEN-CROMOGLYCATE STERINEBS® [P]
Genpharm

Sodium Cromoglycate

Asthma Prophylaxis

Supplied: Each mL of aqueous solution contains: sodium cromoglycate 1% w/v. Ampuls of 2 mL, cartons of 20 and 50. Store at room temperature, between 15 and 30°C. Do not refrigerate. Protect from direct sunlight.

GEN-CYCLOPRINE [P]
Genpharm

Cyclobenzaprine HCl

Skeletal Muscle Relaxant

Supplied: Each white, shield-shaped, film-coated tablet with "CZ10" on one side and "G" on the other, contains: cyclobenzaprine HCl 10 mg. Nonmedicinal ingredients: lactose, magnesium stearate and pregelatinized starch; coating: hydroxypropyl methylcellulose, polydextrose, polyethylene glycol, synthetic yellow iron oxide, titanium dioxide and triacetin. Bottles of 100 and 500.

New Product 1998

GEN-DILTIAZEM [P]
Genpharm

Diltiazem HCl

Antianginal

Supplied: 30 mg: Each green, round, biconvex tablet, with "DT 30" on one side and "G" on the other, approximately 9 mm in diameter, contains: diltiazem HCl 30 mg. Bottles of 100 and 500.

60 mg: Each yellow, round, biconvex tablet, with "DT/60" on one side and "G" on the other, approximately 10 mm in diameter, contains: diltiazem HCl 60 mg. Bottles of 100 and 500.

GEN-DILTIAZEM SR [P]
Genpharm

Diltiazem HCl

Antihypertensive—Antianginal

Supplied: 60 mg: Each ivory/brown, extended release capsule, imprinted with "G" on one end and "DSR60" on the opposite end, contains: diltiazem HCl 60 mg. Nonmedicinal ingredients: acetone, alcohol, diethyl phthalate, ethylcellulose, gelatin, isopropyl alcohol, methacrylic acid copolymer, povidone, starch and sucrose. Bottles of 100. Blister packs of 100.

90 mg: Each gold/brown, extended release capsule, imprinted with "G" on one end and "DSR90" on the opposite end, contains: diltiazem HCl 90 mg. Nonmedicinal ingredients: acetone, alcohol, diethyl phthalate, ethylcellulose, gelatin, isopropyl alcohol, methacrylic acid copolymer, povidone, starch and sucrose. Bottles of 100 and 300. Blister packs of 100.

120 mg: Each caramel/brown, extended release capsule, imprinted with "G" on one end and "DSR120" on the opposite end, contains: diltiazem HCl 120 mg. Nonmedicinal ingredients: acetone, alcohol, diethyl phthalate, ethylcellulose, gelatin, isopropyl alcohol, methacrylic acid copolymor, povi done, starch and sucrose. Bottles of 100 and 300. Blister packs of 100.

New Product 1998

GEN-FAMOTIDINE ℞

Genpharm

Famotidine

Histamine H_2 Receptor Antagonist

Supplied: 20 mg: Each beige, film-coated, D-shaped, biconvex tablet, imprinted "FM 20" on one side and "G" on the other, contains: famotidine 20 mg. Blister packs of 30 and 100. Bottles of 100 and 500.

40 mg: Each caramel, film-coated, D-shaped, biconvex tablet, imprinted "FM 40" on one side and "G" on the other, contains: famotidine 40 mg. Blister packs of 30 and 100. Bottles of 100 and 500.

GEN-FIBRO ℞

Genpharm

Gemfibrozil

Antihyperlipidemic

Supplied: Capsules: Each white and maroon colored capsule, printed in black with "G" on cap and "G 300" on body, contains: gemfibrozil 300 mg. Nonmedicinal ingredients: cornstarch, FD&C blue #1, FD&C red #40, gelatin, methylparaben, polysorbate 80, propylparaben, silicon dioxide and titanium dioxide. Bottles of 50, 100 and 1 000. Store between 15 and 30°C. Protect from humidity.

Tablets: Each white, oval, film-coated tablet, with "G 600" on one side and plain on the other, contains: gemfibrozil 600 mg. Bottles of 100 and 500. Keep in a tightly closed, light-resistant container. Store between 15 and 30°C.

GEN-GLYBE ℞

Genpharm

Glyburide

Oral Hypoglycemic

Supplied: 2.5 mg: Each white, flat, bevel-edged, round tablet, scored and marked "GE" and "2.5" on one side and "G" on the reverse, contains: glyburide 2.5 mg. Tartrazine-free. Bottles of 300 and unit dose boxes of 30.

5 mg: Each white, oblong, biconvex tablet, scored on one side and marked "GE" and "5" and "GG" on the reverse, contains: glyburide 5 mg. Tartrazine-free. Bottles of 300 and unit dose boxes of 30.

Store at 15 to 30°C.

GEN-INDAPAMIDE ℞

Genpharm

Indapamide Hemihydrate

Diuretic—Antihypertensive Agent

Supplied: Each round, biconvex, pink, film-coated tablet, marked "IE 2.5" on one side and "G" on the other, contains: indapamide hemihydrate 2.5 mg. Tartrazine-free. Blister-packs of 30 and 100. Store below 30°C.

GEN-MEDROXY ℞

Genpharm

Medroxyprogesterone Acetate

Progestational Agent

Supplied: 2.5 mg: Each oval, peach tablet, scored on one side and debossed with "G2.5" on the reverse side, contains: medroxyprogesterone acetate 2.5 mg. Bottles of 100 and 500.

5 mg: Each oval, blue tablet, scored on one side and debossed with "G5" on the reverse side, contains: medroxyprogesterone acetate 5 mg. Bottles of 100 and 500.

10 mg: Each oval, white tablet, scored on one side and debossed with "G10" on the reverse side, contains: medroxyprogesterone acetate 10 mg. Bottles of 100 and 500.

Store at controlled room temperature, between 15 and 30°C.

GEN-METFORMIN ℞

Genpharm

Metformin HCl

Oral Antihyperglycemic Agent

Supplied: 500 mg: Each white, convex tablet, marked "MF/1" on one side and "G" on the other, contains: metformin HCl 500 mg. Nonmedicinal ingredients: magnesium stearate and povidone. Bottles of 100 and 500.

850 mg: Each oblong, normal convex, white, film-coated tablet, marked "MF2" on one side and "G" on the other, contains: metformin HCl 850 mg. Nonmedicinal ingredients: magnesium stearate and povidone. Bottles of 100 and 500.

Store between 15 and 30°C.

GEN-MINOCYCLINE ℞

Genpharm

Minocycline HCl

Antibiotic

Supplied: 50 mg: Each hard gelatin capsule with medium orange body, printed "M 50" in black, and medium orange opaque cap, printed "G" in black, contains: minocycline HCl equivalent to minocycline 50 mg. Bottles of 100 and 500.

100 mg: Each hard gelatin capsule with medium orange body, printed "M 100" in black, and lavender opaque cap, printed "G" in black, contains: minocycline HCl equivalent to minocycline 100 mg. Bottles of 50, 100 and 500.

Store at room temperature (15 to 30°C). Protect from light.

GEN-MINOXIDIL ℞

Genpharm

Minoxidil

Hair Growth Stimulant

Supplied: Each mL of topical solution contains: minoxidil 20 mg (2%). Nonmedicinal ingredients: alcohol, propylene glycol and water. Bottles of 60 mL with a metered disposable pump spray applicator. An extended-spray-tip is also available. For external use only. Keep container tightly closed. Store at controlled room temperature, between 15 to 30°C.

GEN-NIFEDIPINE ℞

Genpharm

Nifedipine

Antianginal Agent

Supplied: Each mustard-colored, opaque soft gelatin capsule, imprinted "G" on one side and "NE 10" on the other, contains: nifedipine 10 mg. Gluten- and tartrazine-free. Bottles of 100 and 500. Blister packs of 10, boxes of 120×3. Store between 15 and 25°C. Avoid freezing. Protect from light.

GEN-NORTRIPTYLINE ℞

Genpharm

Nortriptyline HCl

Antidepressant

Supplied: 10 mg: Each white and yellow #4 capsule, imprinted with "G" and "N10", contains: nortriptyline HCl, USP 11.38 mg (equivalent to nortriptyline base 10 mg). Nonmedicinal ingredients: colloidal silicon dioxide, cornstarch and sodium lauryl sulfate. Bottles of 100 and 500.

25 mg: Each white and yellow #1 capsule, imprinted with "G" and "N25", contains: nortriptyline HCl, USP 28.45 mg (equivalent to nortriptyline base 25 mg). Nonmedicinal ingredients: colloidal silicon dioxide, cornstarch and sodium lauryl sulfate. Bottles of 100 and 500.

New Product 1998

GEN-OXYBUTYNIN ℞

Genpharm

Oxybutynin Chloride

Anticholinergic—Antispasmodic Agent

Supplied: Each blue, round, biconvex tablet, "OX/5" on one side and imprinted with "G" on the other side, contains: oxybutynin chloride 5 mg, USP. Nonmedicinal ingredients: FD&C Blue #1 Aluminum Lake 12%, lactose, magnesium stearate and microcrystalline cellulose. Bottles of 100 and 500.

New Product 1998

GEN-PINDOLOL ℞

Genpharm

Pindolol

Antianginal—Antihypertensive

Supplied: 5 mg: Each white, biconvex, round tablet, with "G" on one side and "P5" on the other side, contains: pindolol 5 mg. Bottles of 100 and 500.

10 mg: Each white, biconvex, round tablet, with "G" on one side and "P10" on the other side, contains: pindolol 10 mg. Bottles of 100 and 500.

15 mg: Each white, biconvex, round tablet, with "G" on one side and "P breakline 15" on the other side, contains: pindolol 15 mg. Bottles of 100.

Store at 15 to 30°C. Protect from light.

GEN-PIROXICAM ℞

Genpharm

Piroxicam

Anti-inflammatory—Analgesic

Supplied: 10 mg: Each hard gelatin capsule, with powder blue opaque bodies imprinted with "026" and maroon opaque caps imprinted with "G", contains: piroxicam 10 mg. Nonmedicinal ingredients: cornstarch, D&C Red #28, FD&C Blue #1, FD&C Red #40, gelatin, lactose, magnesium stearate, sodium lauryl sulfate and titanium dioxide. Bottles of 100 and 500.

20 mg: Each hard gelatin capsule, with maroon opaque bodies imprinted with "027" and maroon opaque caps imprinted with "G", contains: piroxicam 20 mg. Nonmedicinal ingredients: cornstarch, D&C Red #28, FD&C Blue #1, FD&C Red #40, gelatin, lactose, magnesium stearate, sodium lauryl sulfate and titanium dioxide. Bottles of 100 and 500.

Store between 15 and 30°C. Protect from moisture.

GEN-RANITIDINE ℞

Genpharm

Ranitidine HCl

Histamine H_2-Receptor Antagonist

Supplied: 150 mg: Each white to off-white, round, biconvex, film-coated tablet, with "G" on one side and "150" on the other, contains: ranitidine HCl equivalent to ranitidine 150 mg. Bottles of 100 and 500. Blister packs of 30 and 60.

300 mg: Each white to off-white, capsule-shaped, film-coated tablet, with "G" on one side and "300" on the other, contains: ranitidine HCl equivalent to ranitidine 300 mg. Bottles of 100 and 500. Blister packs of 30.

Store in a dry place between 15 and 30°C. Protect from light.

GEN-SALBUTAMOL Respirator Solution Ⓟ

Genpharm

Salbutamol Sulfate

Bronchodilator

Supplied: Each mL of respirator solution contains: salbutamol sulfate equivalent to salbutamol base 5 mg. Nonmedicinal ingredients: benzalkonium chloride and sulfuric acid. Glass containers of 10 mL.

New Product 1998

GEN-SALBUTAMOL STERINEBS™ P.F. Ⓟ

Genpharm

Salbutamol Sulfate

Bronchodilator

Supplied: Each mL of sterile aqueous solution contains: salbutamol sulfate equivalent to salbutamol base 1 or 2 mg. Sodium hydroxide or sulfuric acid may be included to adjust pH. Preservative-free. Plastic sterinebs of 2.5 mL. Cartons of 20 with information leaflets. Store between 2 and 25°C. Protect from light.

GEN-SELEGILINE Ⓟ

Genpharm

Selegiline HCl

Antiparkinsonian Agent

Supplied: Each white, flat, beveled-edged tablet, embossed S/S on one side and "G" on the reverse side, contains: 5 mg of the l-isomer of selegiline HCl (formerly l-deprenyl HCl). Bottles of 60 and 1 000. Store at or below 25°C.

GEN-SOTALOL Ⓟ

Genpharm

Sotalol HCl

Antiarrhythmic

Supplied: 80 mg: Each blue, capsule-shaped tablet, engraved with "G" on one side and "S" scoreline "80" on the other, contains: sotalol HCl 80 mg. Bottles of 100 and 500.

160 mg: Each blue, capsule-shaped tablet, engraved with "G" on one side and "S" scoreline "160" on the other, contains: sotalol HCl 160 mg. Bottles of 100 and 500.

240 mg: Each blue, capsule-shaped tablet, engraved with "G" on one side and "S" scoreline "240" on the other, contains: sotalol HCl 240 mg. Bottles of 100 and 500.

Store between 15 and 30°C.

GENTACIDIN® Ⓟ

CIBA Vision

Gentamicin Sulfate

Ophthalmic Antibiotic

Supplied: Each 5 mL plastic squeeze bottle with dropper tip contains: gentamicin sulfate 5 mg (equivalent to 3 mg gentamicin base). Nonmedicinal ingredients: benzalkonium chloride 0.01% w/v (preservative), dibasic sodium phosphate, hydrochloric acid and/or sodium hydroxide (to adjust pH), monobasic sodium phosphate, purified water and sodium chloride. Store at 2 to 30°C. Keep bottle tightly closed when not in use.

GENTAMICIN SULFATE Ⓟ

Rivex Ophthalmics

Antibiotic

Supplied: Each mL of sterile ophthalmic solution contains: gentamicin sulfate 0.3%. Nonmedicinal ingredients: benzalkonium chloride, hydrochloric acid, purified water, sodium chloride, sodium hydroxide, sodium phosphate dibasic and sodium phosphate monobasic. Plastic squeeze bottles of 5 mL with controlled tip applicators.

GENTAMICIN SULFATE Ⓟ

Technilab

Topical Antibiotic

Supplied: Cream: Each g contains: gentamicin (as sulfate USP) 1 mg (0.1%). Nonmedicinal ingredients: cetyl alcohol, chlorocresol, glyceryl stearate, mineral oil, polysorbate 60, polysorbate 80, propylene glycol and purified water. Tubes of 15 g and jars of 450 g.

Ointment: Each g contains: gentamicin (as sulfate USP) 1 mg (0.1%). Nonmedicinal ingredients: light mineral oil, methylparaben, petrolatum and propylparaben. Tubes of 15 g and jars of 450 g.

Store between 15 and 30°C.

GENTAMICIN SULFATE IN 0.9% SODIUM CHLORIDE INJECTION Ⓟ

Abbott

Antibiotic

Supplied: Each flexible (PVC) container of sterile nonpyrogenic solution contains: gentamicin (as sulfate) 0.8 mg/mL (80 mg/100 mL), 1 mg/mL (100 mg/100 mL) and 1.2 mg/mL (60 mg/50 mL) in 0.9% sodium chloride injection. May contain sulfuric acid and sodium hydroxide for pH adjustment. The pH is approximately 4 and the osmolarity is approximately 284 mOsm/L.

GENTAMICIN SULFATE INJECTION IN 0.9% SODIUM CHLORIDE Ⓟ

Baxter

Antibiotic

Supplied: Each mL of sterile, isotonic solution contains: gentamicin sulfate in 0.9% sodium chloride. Viaflex Plus plastic (polyvinyl chloride) containers in the following sizes and concentrations: see Table I.

Table I—Gentamicin Sulfate Injection in 0.9% Sodium Chloride

Supplied		
Total Volume (mL)	**Total Gentamicin Sulfate Content (mg)**	**Gentamicin Sulfate Concentration (mg/mL)**
50	60	1.2
50	80	1.6
100	100	1
100	120	1.2

pH ranges from 3 to 5.5. Store at controlled room temperature 15 to 30°C.

GENTAMICIN SULFATE INJECTION USP Ⓟ

Novopharm

Antibiotic

Pharmacology: Gentamicin exerts its bactericidal effect by specific inhibition of normal protein synthesis in susceptible bacteria. It binds primarily to the 30S subunit of bacterial ribosomes.

Gentamicin is poorly absorbed following oral administration and must be given parenterally for systemic use. When administered i.m., peak serum concentrations are attained in 0.5 to 1 hour. Peak serum concentrations following i.v. administration occur at the end of the infusion and vary with the rate of infusion. The serum elimination half-life is about 2 hours in patients with normal renal function.

Gentamicin is excreted by the kidney in unchanged form, mostly by glomerular filtration. After initial administration of gentamicin, 30 to 100% of the dose is recoverable in the urine in 24 hours in patients with normal renal function. Approximately 30% is excreted in 12 hours in the newborn.

Gentamicin Serum Levels via the I.M. Route in Adults: Peak bactericidal serum concentrations for susceptible bacteria in patients with normal renal function occur between 30 and 90 minutes after injection. The peak serum level (μg/mL) was found to be 4 times the single dose (mg/kg), and the mean serum half-life is approximately 2 hours.

Gentamicin Serum Levels via the I.M. Route in Infants and Neonates: Gentamicin administered i.m. to infants 7 days of age and under resulted in peak serum concentrations of 2.2 to 8.6 μg/mL (mean 4.0 μg/mL) one-half to 1 hour after a dose of 2.5 mg/kg.

The mean serum gentamicin half-life in neonates under 72 hours of age is approximately 5 hours. The half-life may be considerably prolonged in infants weighing less than 1 500 g. Prolonged half-life values may extend through the second week of life in low birth weight infants.

In contrast, full-term infants 7 days of age and older have half-lives of about 3 to 3.5 hours. I.M. doses of 2 and 2.5 mg/kg administered to infants 2 to 24 months of age resulted in gentamicin serum concentrations in the range of 2.5 to 7.5 μg/mL.

Gentamicin Serum Levels via the I.V. Route in Adults: Peak gentamicin concentrations were reached at the end of a 2-hour infusion of a dose of 1 mg/kg to a group of patients and averaged 4.5 μg/mL (range 0.5 to 8 μg/mL).

Serum levels of 5 to 9 μg/mL were obtained following slow i.v. injection after 10 minutes at recommended doses.

The mean serum half-life is approximately 2 hours which is the same as for the i.m. route of administration.

Gentamicin Serum Levels via the I.V. Route in Infants and Neonates: Half-life values and serum gentamicin levels after i.v. infusion were similar to those after i.m. administration.

Gentamicin Excretion: Following a dose of gentamicin in man, about 25 to 30% is bound by serum protein, and it is released as the drug is excreted.

Gentamicin is excreted principally in the urine in an unchanged form by glomerular filtration thus resulting in high urinary concentration of the antibiotic. After initial administration of gentamicin, 30 to 100% of the dose is recoverable in the urine in 24 hours in patients with normal renal function. Renal clearance of gentamicin is similar to the renal clearance of endogenous creatinine. The clearance of gentamicin is decreased in patients with impaired renal function; the more severe the impairment, the slower the clearance.

Approximately 30% of the administered dose is excreted in 12 hours in the newborn.

Gentamicin Penetration (Distribution): Gentamicin is detected in tissues and body fluids following parenteral administration. In general, gentamicin concentration in the bile has been low suggesting minimal biliary excretion. Following i.m. injection, gentamicin has been found in the cerebrospinal fluid in low concentrations which may be inadequate for treatments of certain CNS infections.

Following a dose of 1.5 to 2.5 mg/kg of gentamicin in infants with purulent meningitis, gentamicin concentrations in CSF range from 0.2 to 3.5 μg/mL. Peak values are dependent on the degree of meningeal inflammation and dosage and are noted 4 to 6 hours after the dose.

Gentamicin has also been found in the peritoneal cavity, sputum and pleural fluid. Gentamicin crosses placental as well as peritoneal membranes. Oral administration is not recommended since minimal amounts of gentamicin are absorbed orally.

Indications: In the treatment of serious infections caused by susceptible strains of the following microorganisms: P. aeruginosa, Proteus species (indole negative and indole positive), E. coli, K. pneumoniae, E. aerogenes, S. marcescens, Staphylococcus species (including penicillin and methicillin-resistant strains).

Gentamicin may be considered for the treatment of the following: (1) bacteremia (2) respiratory tract infections (3) urinary tract infections (4) infected wounds: surgical and traumatic (5) soft tissue infections, including peritonitis and burns complicated by sepsis (6) bone infections.

Gentamicin injection should be considered for initial antimicrobial therapy in suspected or documented gram-negative septicemia, particularly when shock or hypotension are present. Gentamicin should also be considered when bacterial susceptibility testing and clinical judgment indicate its use or in serious Staphylococcus infections when other conventional antimicrobial therapy is inappropriate. Additional antimicrobial therapy should be added to the gentamicin regimen if anaerobic organisms are suspected.

Susceptibility: In the majority of cases, appropriate cultures and susceptibility studies should be obtained initially to identify the causative organism and to determine its sensitivity to gentamicin.

The decision to continue therapy with gentamicin injection should be based on consideration of relative antibiotic toxicity, results of the sensitivity tests and the clinical response of the patient.

Additional or other antimicrobial therapy should be instituted if susceptibility tests indicate that the causative organism is resistant to gentamicin. In suspected sepsis, combined therapy with gentamicin and a penicillin type of drug has been used until bacteriological studies have identified the etiological organism.

Clinical studies have revealed that organisms previously sensitive to gentamicin have become resistant during therapy. Although this is an infrequent occurrence, the possibility should always be considered. There is evidence that cross resistance may occur between gentamicin and aminoglycoside antibiotics since bacteria made artificially resistant to aminoglycoside antibiotics in the laboratory are also resistant to gentamicin; however, gentamicin may be active against clinical isolates of bacteria resistant to other aminoglycosides. Conversely, gentamicin-resistant organisms may be sensitive to other aminoglycoside antibiotics.

Contraindications: Individuals with a history of hypersensitivity or toxic reactions to its use. A history of hypersensitivity or serious toxic reactions to other aminoglycosides may contraindicate use of gentamicin because of the known cross-sensitivity of patients to drugs in this class. Aminoglycosides, including gentamicin, are not indicated in uncomplicated initial episodes of urinary tract infections unless the causative organisms are susceptible to these antibiotics and are not susceptible to antibiotics having less potential for toxicity.

Warnings: Patients treated with aminoglycosides should be under close clinical observation because of the potential toxicity associated with their use.

Neurotoxicity: Neurotoxicity manifested by ototoxicity, both vestibular and auditory can occur in patients treated with gentamicin, primarily in those with preexisting renal damage and in patients with normal renal function treated with higher doses and/or for longer periods than recommended. Aminoglycoside-induced ototoxicity is usually irreversible.

The onset of ototoxicity may be delayed and is primarily manifested by damage to vestibular function. Physicians should strongly consider discontinuing gentamicin in patients developing tinnitus, dizziness or hearing loss, except in cases where gentamicin appears to be the only proven course of therapy.

Irreversible damage has occurred mainly in patients who had prior therapy with ototoxic drugs, received higher doses and longer courses of therapy than recommended, had renal dysfunction or were uremic.

Gentamicin injection should be used with caution in patients who have previously been treated with drugs likely to affect eighth cranial nerve function (e.g., streptomycin, neomycin, kanamycin, etc.) and with the understanding that toxic effects may be cumulative with these agents.

Nephrotoxicity: As with other aminoglycosides, gentamicin is potentially nephrotoxic. Nephrotoxicity may be manifested by elevated serum creatinine or blood urea nitrogen levels or by a decrease in the creatinine clearance. These changes have been reversible in most cases when the drug has been discontinued. The risk of nephrotoxicity is greater in patients with impaired renal function and in those who receive high dosage or prolonged therapy.

The risk of nephrotoxicity may be increased with the administration of other potentially nephrotoxic agents prior to or in conjunction with gentamicin.

Note: Gentamicin injection contains sodium bisulfite, a sulfite that may cause allergic-type reactions including anaphylactic symptoms and life-threatening or less severe asthmatic episodes in certain susceptible people. The overall prevalence of sulfite sensitivity in the general population is unknown and probably low. Sulfite sensitivity is seen more frequently in asthmatic than in nonasthmatic people.

Precautions: The frequency of administration of gentamicin should be reduced in patients with impaired renal function (see Dosage). In addition, renal function should be monitored and auditory and vestibular function evaluated in patients with impaired renal function.

Whenever feasible, serum concentrations of gentamicin should be monitored and prolonged concentrations above 12 μg/mL should be avoided.

Superinfection: Overgrowth of nonsensitive organisms may occasionally result with gentamicin treatment.

Neuromuscular Blocking Action: The administration of high doses (40 mg/kg) of gentamicin in the cat has resulted in neuromuscular blocking and respiratory paralysis. These phenomena may occur in man with the concomitant administration of gentamicin with general anesthetics and/or neuromuscular blocking agents such as succinylcholine and tubocurarine, or massive transfusions of citrate anticoagulated blood. Neuromuscular blocking action produced by gentamicin may be antagonized by neostigmine or calcium salts.

The use of drugs with potential neuromuscular blocking action may be dangerous in patients with myasthenia gravis.

Drug Interactions: The concomitant use of potent diuretics such as ethacrynic acid and furosemide with gentamicin has been associated with eighth cranial nerve dysfunction and should therefore be avoided. In addition, when administered i.v., diuretics may enhance aminoglycoside toxicity by altering the antibiotic concentration in serum and tissue. It is believed that i.v. diuretics may potentiate ototoxicity and cause a fairly rapid rise in gentamicin serum levels.

Concurrent and/or sequential systemic or topical use of other potentially neurotoxic and/or nephrotoxic drugs, such as cisplatin, cephaloridine, kanamycin, amikacin, neomycin, polymyxin B, colistin, paromomycin, streptomycin, tobramycin, vancomycin and viomycin should be avoided.

Although the in vitro mixing of gentamicin and carbenicillin results in a rapid and significant inactivation of gentamicin, this interaction has not been demonstrated in patients with normal renal function who received both drugs by different routes of administration. A reduction in gentamicin serum half-life has been reported in patients with severe renal impairment receiving carbenicillin concomitantly with gentamicin.

Cross-allergenicity among aminoglycosides has been demonstrated.

Geriatrics: Elderly patients may have reduced renal function which may not be evident in the results of routine screening tests, such as BUN or serum creatinine. A creatinine clearance determination may be more useful. Monitoring of renal function during treatment with gentamicin, as with other aminoglycosides, is particularly important in such patients. A Fanconi-like syndrome, with aminoaciduria and metabolic acidosis, has been reported in some adults and infants being given gentamicin injections.

Pregnancy: Gentamicin injection is not recommended during pregnancy except in life-threatening situations, even though studies in expectant animals have not revealed teratogenic effects. Aminoglycoside antibiotics cross the placenta, and there have been several reports of total irreversible bilateral congenital deafness in children whose mothers received streptomycin during pregnancy. Serious side effects to mother, fetus, or newborn have not been reported in the treatment of pregnant women with other aminoglycosides.

Newborns: Except for life-threatening infections, gentamicin injection should be used with caution in premature and neonatal infants because of their renal immaturity and the resultant prolongation of serum half-life of the drug. No adverse reactions have been revealed in these cases although follow-up has been limited.

Adverse Effects: Adverse reactions reported infrequently and possibly related to gentamicin, in addition to the ototoxicity and nephrotoxicity discussed under Precautions, include the following grouped by system: Hypersensitivity: rash, urticaria, itching, drug fever, anaphylactoid reactions.

Gastrointestinal: vomiting, nausea, decreased appetite, weight loss, gastrointestinal hemorrhage, stomatitis.

Blood: increased and decreased reticulocyte counts, anemia, granulocytopenia, thrombocytopenia, leukopenia, eosinophilia, transient agranulocytosis, hypotension, hypertension, decreased hemoglobin and hematocrit, increased serum LDH, purpura, splenomegaly, decreased serum calcium, magnesium, sodium and potassium.

Hepatic: increased serum transaminase (AST, ALT), increased serum bilirubin, transient hepatomegaly.

Local Reactions: pain at the injection site, s.c. atrophy or fat necrosis, joint pain.

CNS: headache, muscle twitching, convulsions, fifth nerve paresthesia, confusion, depression, pseudotumor cerebri, acute organic brain syndrome, numbness, skin tingling.

Respiratory: respiratory depression, neuromuscular blockade, pulmonary fibrosis.

Miscellaneous: increased salivation, lethargy, laryngeal edema and spasm, visual disturbances, generalized burning, alopecia.

Overdose: Symptoms and Treatment: Peritoneal dialysis or hemodialysis will aid in the removal of gentamicin from the blood in the event of overdosage or toxic reactions. These procedures are particularly important in patients with impaired renal function. The rate of removal of gentamicin is considerably less by peritoneal dialysis than it is by hemodialysis.

Dosage: I.M. injection is the usual route of administration for gentamicin injection. Administration via the i.v. route is generally reserved for special indications (see I.V. Administration). Treatment usually lasts from 7 to 10 days. A longer course of therapy may be necessary, however, in difficult and complicated infections. Monitoring of vestibular, auditory and renal functions is advisable in such cases.

The patient's pretreatment body weight should be obtained for calculation of correct dosage. The dosage of aminoglycosides in obese patients should be based on an estimate of the lean body mass.

Serum concentrations of aminoglycosides should be monitored when feasible to assure adequate levels and to avoid potentially toxic levels. When monitoring gentamicin peak concentrations, dosage should be adjusted so that prolonged levels above 12 μg/mL are avoided. When monitoring gentamicin trough concentrations, dosage should be adjusted so that levels above 2 μg/mL are avoided. Excessive peak and/or trough serum concentrations of aminoglycosides may increase the risk of renal and eighth cranial nerve toxicity.

I.M. Administration: Patients with Normal Renal Function: Urinary Tract Infections: Gentamicin is highly concentrated in renal tissue and urine. Gentamicin may be administered i.m. either in a dose of 160 mg once a day or 80 mg b.i.d. for 7 to 10 days in patients with lower urinary tract infections particularly if chronic or recurrent and without evidence of impairment of renal function. The single daily dose should be 3 mg/kg of body weight for adults weighing less than 60 kg.

Dosage schedules for systemic infections should be followed for patients with upper urinary tract infections, such as pyelonephritis, and more particularly, if there are signs of systemic involvement.

It may be advantageous to alkalinize the urine of patients treated for urinary tract infections since gentamicin activity is increased at pH 7.5.

Systemic Infections: Adults: For adult patients with serious infection and normal renal function: 3 mg/kg/day administered i.m. in 3 equal doses (every 8 hours). Therefore, the usual dosage is 80 mg 3 times daily for patients weighing over 60 kg. The usual dosage is 60 mg 3 times daily for patients weighing 60 kg or less.

Life-Threatening Infections: Dosages up to 5 mg/kg/day should be administered in 3 or 4 equally divided doses in patients with life-threatening infections. As soon as clinically indicated, this dosage should be reduced to 3 mg/kg/day.

Table I is a dosage schedule guide for adults with normal renal function.

Table I—Gentamicin Sulfate Injection USP

Dosage Schedule Guide for Adults with Normal Renal Function (Dosage at 8-Hour Intervals) 40 mg/mL

Patient's Weight[a] kg	Usual Dose for Serious Infections 1 mg/kg q8h (3 mg/kg/day) mg/Dose	mL/Dose q8h	Dose for Life-Threatening Infections[b] 1.7 mg/kg q8h[c] (5 mg/kg/day) mg/Dose	mL/Dose q8h
40	40	1.0	66	1.6
45	45	1.1	75	1.9
50	50	1.25	83	2.1
55	55	1.4	91	2.25
60	60	1.5	100	2.5
65	65	1.6	108	2.7
70	70	1.75	116	2.9
75	75	1.9	125	3.1
80	80	2.0	133	3.3
85	85	2.1	141	3.5
90	90	2.25	150	3.75
95	95	2.4	158	4.0
100	100	2.5	166	4.2

[a] The dosage of aminoglycosides in obese patients should be based on an estimate of the lean body mass.
[b] Reduce as soon as clinically indicated.
[c] For q6h schedules, dosage should be recalculated.

Children: The precautions for the treatment of infection in children are the same as those for adults.

The recommended dosage for children 1 to 12 years of age is 3 to 6 mg/kg/day in 3 equal doses every 8 hours for severe infections. If a dosage greater than 3 mg/kg/day is initially administered, it should be reduced to 3 mg/kg/day when clinically indicated.

Infants and Neonates (see Precautions): A dosage of 6 mg/kg/day in 2 equal doses every 12 hours may be administered to premature and full-term neonates, 1 week of age or less. Gentamicin may be administered at 6 mg/kg/day in

Gentamicin Sulfate Injection USP (cont'd)

3 equal doses every 8 hours in infants older than 1 week to approximately 1 year of age.

Considerable variation in the serum levels between individual patients has been observed with these recommended doses. Serum levels should be monitored in order to insure adequate therapeutic levels which may be critical, while at the same time avoiding potentially toxic concentrations. Following i.m. administration, a serum level in excess of 10 to 12 μg/mL should be considered potentially toxic.

Patients with Impaired Renal Function: Dosage adjustments must be made in patients with impaired renal function to assure therapeutically adequate, but not excessive, blood levels. Serum concentrations of gentamicin must be monitored in these patients.

One method of dosage adjustment is to increase the interval between administration of the usual dosage.

Since the serum half-life of gentamicin is highly correlated with the creatinine clearance rate and serum creatinine concentration, these laboratory tests may provide the guidance necessary for adjustment of the interval between doses of gentamicin injection. To estimate the serum half-life of gentamicin (in hours), multiply the serum creatinine (μmol/L) by 0.045. The frequency of administration (in hours) may be approximated by doubling the serum half-life.

A second method of dosage adjustment is to administer the antibiotic at the usual interval but in reduced dose (see Table II).

Table II—Gentamicin Sulfate Injection USP

Dosage Adjustment Guide for Patients with Renal Impairment (Dosage at 8-Hour Intervals After the Usual Initial Dose)

Serum Creatinine (μmol/L)	Approximate Creatinine Clearance Rate (mL/s/1.73 m²)	Percent of Usual Doses Shown in Table I	Approximate Creatinine Clearance Rate (mL/min/ 1.73 m²)
≤90	≥1.67	100	≥100
100–118	1.17–1.67	80	70–100
127–145	0.92–1.17	65	55–70
154–172	0.75–0.92	55	45–55
181–200	0.67–0.75	50	40–45
209–227	0.58–0.67	40	35–40
236–272	0.50–0.58	35	30–45
281–318	0.42–0.50	30	25–30
327–363	0.33–0.42	25	20–25
372–463	0.25–0.33	20	15–10
472–600	0.17–0.25	15	10–15
609–727	≤0.17	10	≥10

When only serum creatinine levels are available, the following formula (based on sex, weight, and the age of the patient) may be used to convert this value into estimated creatinine clearance. The serum creatinine should represent a steady-state of renal function.

$$\text{Males: Creatinine Clearance (mL/s)} = \frac{\text{Weight (kg)} \times (140 - \text{age})}{49 \times \text{serum creatinine } (\mu\text{mol/L})}$$

$$\text{Females:} = 0.85 \times \text{above value.}$$

In patients with renal failure who are undergoing 14-hour hemodialysis twice weekly, administration of gentamicin injection in a dose of 1 mg/kg at the end of each dialysis period has been suggested.

This dosage schedule is not intended as a rigid recommendation but is a guide to dosage when the measurement of gentamicin serum levels is not feasible. This schedule should be used in conjunction with laboratory and close clinical observations of patients and should be modified as deemed necessary by the treating physician.

I.V. Injection: In those circumstances when the i.m. route is not feasible, e.g., patients in shock, with hemorrhagic disorders, severe burns, or reduced muscle mass, the i.v. administration of gentamicin injection is recommended.

The recommended dosage for i.v. administration is identical to that recommended for i.m. use.

Administration: For i.v. administration, a single dose of gentamicin injection is diluted in 100 to 200 mL of sterile normal saline or in a sterile solution of dextrose 5% in water. The solution is infused over a period of 1 to 2 hours and repeated every 8 hours, if necessary.

A single dose of gentamicin injection undiluted may also be given directly into the side-arm of an i.v. tubing set, slowly over a period of 2 to 3 minutes and repeated every 8 hours, if necessary.

I.V. Administration: The appropriate dose of gentamicin injection may be added to either of the solutions for i.v. infusion listed below: Normal Saline, Dextrose 5% in water.

The diluted infusion mixture should be prepared immediately before use and any unused portion must be discarded. Store at room temperature (15 to 30°C).

Incompatibility: Gentamicin injection should be administered separately in accordance with the recommended route of administration and dosage schedule and should not be physically premixed with other drugs.

Supplied: Each mL of sterile, aqueous solution contains: gentamicin (as sulfate) 10 mg or gentamicin (as sulfate) 40 mg. Nonmedicinal ingredients: edetate disodium 0.1 mg, sodium metabisulfite 0.8 mg and water for injection. Sodium hydroxide and/or sulfuric acid may be added to adjust pH to a range of 3.0 to 5.5. Vials of 2 mL. Store at room temperature (15 to 30°C).

Reviewed 1997

GEN-TAMOXIFEN Ⓟ

Genpharm

Tamoxifen Citrate

Antineoplastic

Supplied: 10 mg: Each white, round, biconvex tablet, marked with TN 10 on one side and "G" on the other, contains: tamoxifen citrate 15.2 mg (equivalent to tamoxifen 10 mg). Tartrazine-free. Plastic containers of 250 or boxes of 30 and 60 in aluminum blister packs. Store at room temperature protected from light.

20 mg: Each white, octagonal-shaped biconvex tablet, marked with TN breakline 20 on one side and "G" on the other, contains: tamoxifen citrate 30.4 mg (equivalent to tamoxifen 20 mg). Tartrazine-free. Plastic containers of 250 or boxes of 30 and 60 in aluminum blister packs. Store at room temperature protected from light.

GENTEAL®

CIBA Vision

Hydroxypropyl Methylcellulose

Artificial Tears

Supplied: Each bottle contains: hydroxypropyl methylcellulose 3 mg/g. Nonmedicinal ingredients: boric acid, phosphonic acid, potassium chloride, purified water, sodium chloride, sodium hydroxide and/or sulfuric acid (to adjust pH) and sodium perborate (preservative). Dropper-tipped, plastic squeeze bottles of 15 mL. Store at controlled room temperature (15 to 30°C).

New Product 1998

GEN-TEMAZEPAM Ⓟ

Genpharm

Temazepam

Hypnotic

Supplied: 15 mg: Each pink and maroon, size 3 hard gelatin capsule, printed "0046" and "G" in black, contains: temazepam 15 mg. Nonmedicinal ingredients: D&C Red #28, D&C Yellow #10 Aluminum Lake, FD&C Red #40, FD&C Blue #1, FD&C Blue #2 Aluminum Lake, FD&C Red #40 Aluminum Lake, FD&C Blue #1 Aluminum Lake, gelatin, lactose, magnesium stearate, red iron oxide T3469, silicon dioxide, sodium lauryl sulfate, synthetic black iron oxide and titanium dioxide. Bottles of 100.

30 mg: Each deep powder blue and maroon, size 3 hard gelatin capsule, printed "0047" and "G" in black, contains: temazepam 30 mg. Nonmedicinal ingredients: D&C Red #28, D&C Yellow #10 Aluminum Lake, FD&C Red #40, FD&C Blue #1, FD&C Blue #2 Aluminum Lake, FD&C Red #40 Aluminum Lake, FD&C Blue #1 Aluminum Lake, gelatin, lactose, magnesium stearate, silicon dioxide, sodium lauryl sulfate, synthetic black iron oxide and titanium dioxide. Bottles of 100.

New Product 1998

GEN-TIMOLOL Ⓟ

Genpharm

Timolol Maleate

Glaucoma Therapy

Supplied: Each mL of clear, colorless ophthalmic solution contains: timolol maleate equivalent to 2.5 mg (0.25%) or 5 mg (0.5%) timolol. Also contains benzalkonium chloride. White opaque plastic ophthalmic dispensers of 5 and 10 mL with controlled drop tip. Store between 15 and 30°C in a tight, light resistant container. Protect from freezing.

GENT-L-TIP®

Baxter

Sodium Phosphate—Sodium Biphosphate

Cleansing Enema

Supplied: Each 100 mL of solution contains: sodium biphosphate 16 g and sodium phosphate 6 g. Containers of 133 mL. Cases of 48 individually boxed units and 48 bulk packed units. Store at room temperature.

GENTRAN® 40
GENTRAN® 70

Baxter

Dextran

Plasma Volume Expander

Supplied: Gentran 40: Each mL of sterile, nonpyrogenic solution contains: 10 g dextran 40 in 5% dextrose injection or 0.9% sodium chloride injection. Viaflex Plus plastic (polyvinyl chloride) containers of 500 mL.

Gentran 70: Each mL of sterile, nonpyrogenic solution contains: 6 g dextran 70 in 0.9% sodium chloride injection. Viaflex Plus plastic (polyvinyl chloride) containers of 500 mL. Store between 15 and 30°C.

GEN-TRAZODONE Ⓟ

Genpharm

Trazodone

Antidepressant

Supplied: 50 mg: Each pale orange, round, biconvex tablet, embossed with "G" over "TZ5" on one side and scored on the other, contains: trazodone 50 mg. Nonmedicinal ingredients: alcohol, cellulose, croscarmellose sodium, FD&C Yellow #6 Aluminum Lake 15%, lactose, magnesium stearate and povidone. Plastic bottles of 100, 250 and 500.

100 mg: Each white, round, biconvex tablet, embossed with "G" over "TZ10" on one side and scored on the other, contains: trazodone 100 mg. Nonmedicinal ingredients: alcohol, cellulose, croscarmellose sodium, lactose, magnesium stearate and povidone. Plastic bottles of 100 and 500.

New Product 1998

GEN-TRIAZOLAM Ⓟ

Genpharm

Triazolam

Hypnotic

Supplied: 0.125 mg: Each mauve, oval-shaped, flat, beveled-edged tablet, marked "TZ" on one side and scored on the other side, contains: triazolam USP 0.125 mg. Tartrazine-free. Blister packages of 7 per blister strip, cartons of 70.

0.25 mg: Each blue, oval-shaped, flat, beveled-edged tablet, marked "TZ" on one side and scored on the other side, contains: triazolam USP 0.25 mg. Tartrazine-free. Blister packages of 7 per blister strip, cartons of 70.

Store in a tight, light resistant package between 15 and 30°C.

GEN-VALPROIC ℞

Genpharm

Valproic Acid

Anticonvulsant

Supplied: Each oblong, orange, soft gelatin capsule, with clear fill liquid, imprinted in black ink with "VA250" on one side, contains: valproic acid 250 mg. Bottles of 100 and 500.

GEN-VERAPAMIL SR ℞

Genpharm

Verapamil HCl

Antihypertensive Agent

Supplied: 120 mg: Each off-white, round, biconvex, film-coated tablet, marked with "120/SR" on one side and "KNOLL" on the other, contains: verapamil HCl 120 mg. Nonmedicinal ingredients: cellulose, hydroxypropyl methylcellulose, magnesium stearate, polyethylene glycol, povidone, sodium alginate, talc, titanium dioxide and wax. Bottles of 100.

180 mg: Each light-pink, oval, film-coated tablet marked with "SR" scoreline "180" on one side and "KNOLL" on the other, contains: verapamil HCl 180 mg. Nonmedicinal ingredients: cellulose, hydroxypropyl methylcellulose, magnesium stearate, polyethylene glycol, povidone, red iron oxide, sodium alginate, talc, titanium dioxide and wax. Bottles of 100.

240 mg: Each light-green, oblong, film-coated tablet, scored on both sides, marked with "SR 240" on one side and plain on the other side, contains: verapamil HCl 240 mg. Nonmedicinal ingredients: cellulose, hydroxypropyl methylcellulose, indigotine lake, magnesium stearate, polyethylene glycol, povidone, quinoline yellow lake, sodium alginate, talc, titanium dioxide and wax. Bottles of 100 and 500.

Special Note to Pharmacists: Gen-Verapamil SR 240 mg tablet may be split in half. Crushing Gen-Verapamil SR tablets is not recommended since the sustained-release effect will be altered by damage to the tablet structure. Use of Gen-Verapamil SR 120 mg is recommended.

GLAXAL® BASE

Roberts

Dermatological Base—Moisturizer

Supplied: Cartoned tubes of 50 g, cartoned jars of 100 g; jars of 450 g.

GLICLAZIDE ℞

General Monograph, CPhA

see SULFONYLUREAS

GLUCAGON INJECTION

Lilly

Glucagon HCl

Hyperglycemic Agent

Pharmacology: Glucagon causes an increase in blood glucose concentration. Glucagon acts only on liver glycogen, converting it to glucose.

Parenteral administration of glucagon produces relaxation of the smooth muscle of the stomach, duodenum, small bowel and colon.

The half-life of glucagon in plasma is approximately 3 to 6 minutes.

Indications: Hypoglycemia: Glucagon is useful in counteracting severe hypoglycemic reactions.

The patient with type I diabetes does not have as great a response in blood glucose levels as does the stable type II diabetic. Therefore, supplementary carbohydrate should be given as soon as possible, especially to a child or adolescent patient.

Diagnostic Aid: As a diagnostic aid in the radiologic examination of the stomach, duodenum, small bowel and colon when a hypotonic state would be advantageous.

Contraindications: In patients with known hypersensitivity to glucagon or patients with pheochromocytoma.

Warnings: Glucagon should be administered cautiously to patients with a history suggestive of insulinoma and/or pheochromocytoma. In patients with insulinoma, i.v. administration of glucagon will produce an initial increase in blood glucose however, because of glucagon's insulin releasing effect, it may cause the insulinoma to release its insulin and subsequently cause hypoglycemia. A patient developing symptoms of hypoglycemia after a dose of glucagon should be given glucose orally, i.v., or by gavage, whichever is more appropriate.

Exogenous glucagon also stimulates the release of catecholamines. In the presence of pheochromocytoma, glucagon can cause the tumor to release catecholamines which results in a sudden and marked increase in blood pressure. If a patient suddenly develops a marked increase in blood pressure, 5 to 10 mg of phentolamine mesylate may be administered i.v. in an attempt to control the blood pressure. Generalized allergic reactions, including urticaria, respiratory distress, and hypotension, have been reported in patients who received glucagon by injection.

Precautions: Glucagon is helpful in hypoglycemia only if liver glycogen is available. Because glucagon is of little or no help in states of starvation, adrenal insufficiency, or chronic hypoglycemia, glucose should be considered for the treatment of hypoglycemia.

Laboratory Tests: Blood glucose determinations may be obtained to follow the patient in hypoglycemic shock until he or she is asymptomatic.

Pregnancy: Reproduction studies have been performed in rats at doses up to 2 mg/kg b.i.d., (up to 120 times the human dose), and have revealed no evidence of harm to the fetus due to glucagon. There are, however, no adequate and well-controlled studies in pregnant women. Because animal reproduction studies are not always predictive of human response, this drug should be used during pregnancy only if clearly needed.

Lactation: It is not known whether this drug is excreted in human milk. Glucagon is not active when taken orally because it is destroyed in the gastrointestinal tract before it can be absorbed.

Adverse Effects: Nausea, vomiting, and hypokalemia may occur occasionally. Generalized allergic reactions have been reported.

Overdose: Symptoms: No cases of human overdosage of glucagon have been reported. Glucagon is generally well tolerated. If overdosage occurred, it would not be expected to cause consequential toxicity, but would be expected to be associated with nausea, vomiting, gastric hypotonicity, and diarrhea.

I.V. administration of glucagon has been shown to have a positive inotropic and chronotropic effect. A transient increment in both blood pressure and pulse rate may occur following the administration of glucagon. Patients taking β-blockers might be expected to have a greater increment in both pulse rate and blood pressure. This increase will be transient because of glucagon's short half-life. The increase in blood pressure and pulse rate may require therapy in patients with pheochromocytoma or coronary artery disease.

When glucagon was given in large doses to cardiac patients, investigators reported a positive inotropic effect. These investigators administered glucagon in doses of 0.5 to 16 mg/hour by continuous infusion for periods of 5 to 166 hours. Total doses ranged from 25 to 996 mg, and a 21-month-old child received approximately 8.25 mg in 165 hours. Side effects included nausea, vomiting, and decreasing serum potassium concentration. Serum potassium concentration could be maintained within normal limits with supplemental potassium. The i.v. median lethal dose for glucagon in rats and mice is approximately 300 mg/kg.

Because glucagon is a polypeptide, it would be rapidly destroyed in the gastrointestinal tract if it were to be accidentally ingested.

Treatment: In managing overdosage, consider the possibility of multiple drug overdoses, interaction among drugs, and unusual drug kinetics in your patient.

In view of the extremely short half-life of glucagon and its prompt destruction and excretion, the treatment of overdosage is symptomatic, primarily for nausea, vomiting and possible hypokalemia.

If the patient develops a dramatic increase in blood pressure, 5 to 10 mg of phentolamine has been shown to be effective in lowering blood pressure for the short time that control would be needed.

Forced diuresis, peritoneal dialysis, hemodialysis, or charcoal hemoperfusion have not been established as beneficial for an overdose of glucagon; it is extremely unlikely that one of these procedures would ever be indicated.

Dosage: Hypoglycemia: The diluent is provided for use only in the preparation of glucagon for intermittent parenteral injection and for no other use.

If glucagon is to be given at doses higher than 2 mg, it should be reconstituted with Sterile Water for Injection instead of the supplied diluting solution and used immediately.

Directions for use of Glucagon: 1. Dissolve the lyophilized glucagon in the accompanying diluent.

2. Glucagon should not be used at concentrations greater than 1 mg/mL (1 unit/mL).

3. Glucagon solutions should not be used unless they are clear and of a water-like consistency.

4. For adults and for children weighing more than 20 kg, give 1 mg (1 unit) by s.c., i.m., or i.v. injection.

5. For children weighing less than 20 kg, give 0.5 mg (0.5 unit) or a dose equivalent to 20 to 30 μg/kg.

6. The patient will usually awaken within 15 minutes. If the response is delayed, there is no contraindication to the administration of 1 or 2 additional doses of glucagon; however, in view of the deleterious effects of cerebral hypoglycemia and depending on the duration and depth of coma, the use of parenteral glucose **must** be considered by the physician.

7. I.V. glucose **must** be given if the patient fails to respond to glucagon.

8. When the patient responds, give supplemental carbohydrate to restore the liver glycogen and prevent secondary hypoglycemia.

Instructions to the Family: Instructions describing the method of using glucagon are included in the literature which accompanies the patient's package. It is advisable for the patient and family members to become familiar with the technique of preparing Glucagon for Injection before an emergency arises. Patients are instructed to use 1 mg (1 unit) for adults and, if recommended by a doctor, ½ the adult dose (0.5 mg [0.5 unit]) for children weighing less than 20 kg.

General Management of Hypoglycemia: The following are helpful measures in the prevention of hypoglycemic reactions due to insulin: 1. Reasonable uniformity from day to day with regard to diet, insulin, and exercise.

2. Careful adjustment of the insulin program so that the type (or types) of insulin, dose, and time (or times) of administration are suited to the individual patient.

3. Frequent testing of the urine so that a change in insulin requirements can be foreseen.

4. Routine carrying of sugar, candy, or other readily absorbable carbohydrate by the patient so that it may be taken at the first warning of an oncoming reaction.

If the patient is unaware of the symptoms of hypoglycemia, he may lapse into insulin shock; therefore, the physician should instruct the patient in this regard when feasible.

It is important that the patient be aroused as quickly as possible, because prolonged hypoglycemic reactions may result in cortical damage. Glucagon or i.v. glucose will awaken the patient sufficiently so that oral carbohydrates may be taken.

Caution: Although glucagon may be used for the treatment of hypoglycemia by the patient during an emergency, the physician must still be notified when hypoglycemic reactions occur so that the dose of insulin may be adjusted more accurately.

Diagnostic Aid: Dissolve the lyophilized glucagon in the accompanying diluting solution. Glucagon should not be used at concentrations greater than 1 mg/mL (1 unit/mL).

The doses in Table I may be administered for relaxation of the stomach, duodenum, and small bowel, depending on the time of onset of action and the duration of effect required for the examination. Since the stomach is less sensitive to the effect of glucagon, 0.5 mg (0.5 unit) i.v. or 2 mg (2 units) i.m. are recommended.

Table I—Glucagon Injection

Dosage as a Diagnostic Aid

Dose	Route of Administration	Time of Onset of Action	Approximate Duration of Effect
0.25-0.5 mg[b]	I.V.	1 minute	9–17 minutes
1 mg[b]	I.M.	8–10 minutes	12–27 minutes
2 mg[a,b]	I.V.	1 minute	22–25 minutes
2 mg[a,b]	I.M.	4–7 minutes	21–32 minutes

[a] Administration of 2 mg (2 units) doses produces a higher incidence of nausea and vomiting than do lower doses.
[b] 1 mg equals 1 unit.

Glucagon Injection (cont'd)

For examination of the colon, it is recommended that a 2 mg (2 units) dose be administered i.m. approximately 10 minutes prior to initiation of the procedure. Relaxation of the colon and reduction of discomfort to the patient will allow the radiologist to perform a more satisfactory examination.

Prior to reconstitution, the vials may be stored at controlled room temperature, 15 to 30°C.

Glucagon should be used immediately after reconstitution. **Discard any unused portion.**

Information for the Patient: See Blue Section—Information for the Patient "Glucagon Injection".

Supplied: Each rubber-stoppered vial of lyophilized powder contains: glucagon for injection USP 1 unit (1 mg) (as the hydrochloride). Nonmedicinal ingredients: vial of lyophilized glucagon: lactose 49 mg; diluting solution: glycerin and phenol. May contain sodium hydroxide and/or hydrochloric acid for pH adjustment. Vials of 1 mL.
Glucagon Emergency Kit: Each kit contains: 1 vial of glucagon 1 unit (1 mg) and a prefilled Hyporet of diluting solution.

GLUCODEX®

Rougier

Dextrose

Diagnostic Agent For Diabetes

Indications: Glucose tolerance test.

Contraindications: In patients with the glucose-galactose malabsorption syndrome.

Precautions: Dextrose should be administered with care to patients with diabetes insipidus.
Drug Interactions: Purgatives may inhibit the intestinal absorption of dextrose.

Adverse Effects: Concentrated dextrose solutions given by mouth may cause nausea and vomiting.

Dosage: Glucose tolerance test: Adults (except pregnant women): 75 g. Children: 1.75 g/kg of ideal body weight. Pregnant women: 100 g or according to physician's advice. Serve cold.

Supplied: 50 g: Each mL of orange-flavored, light orange liquid, contains: dextrose USP 166.6 mg. Bottles of 300 mL.

75 g: Each mL of orange-flavored, orange liquid, contains: dextrose USP 250 mg. Bottles of 300 mL.

100 g: Each mL of orange-flavored, dark orange liquid, contains: dextrose USP 333.3 mg. Bottles of 300 mL.

GLUCOPHAGE® Ⓟ

Hoechst Marion Roussel

Metformin HCl

Antihyperglycemic Agent

Pharmacology: Metformin is a biguanide derivative producing an antihyperglycemic effect which can only be observed in man or in the diabetic animal and only when there is insulin secretion. Metformin, at therapeutic doses, does not cause hypoglycemia when used alone in man or in the non-diabetic animal, except when using a near lethal dose. Metformin has no effects on the pancreatic beta cells. The mode of action of metformin is not fully understood. It has been postulated that metformin might potentiate the effect of insulin or that it might enhance the effect of insulin on the peripheral receptor site. This increased sensitivity seems to follow an increase in the number of insulin receptors on cell surface membranes.

Metformin absorption is relatively slow and may extend over about 6 hours. The drug is excreted in urine at high renal clearance rate of about 450 mL/min. The initial elimination of metformin is rapid with a half-life varying between 1.7 and 3 hours. The terminal elimination phase accounting for about 4 to 5 % of the absorbed dose is slow with a half-life between 9 and 17 hours. Metformin is not metabolized. Its main sites of concentration are the intestinal mucosa and the salivary glands. The plasma concentration at steady-state ranges about 1 to 2 μg/mL. Certain drugs may potentiate the effects of metformin (see Precautions).

Indications: To control hyperglycemia in metformin responsive, stable, mild, non-ketosis prone, maturity onset type of diabetes (Type II) which cannot be controlled by proper dietary management, exercise and weight reduction or when insulin therapy is not appropriate.

Metformin can be of value for the treatment of obese diabetic patients.

Contraindications: Unstable and/or insulin-dependent (Type I) diabetes mellitus.

Acute or chronic metabolic acidosis, including diabetic ketoacidosis, with or without coma, history of ketoacidosis with or without coma. Diabetic ketoacidosis should be treated with insulin.

In patients with a history of lactic acidosis, irrespective of precipitating factors.

In the presence of renal impairment or when renal function is not known, and also in patients with serum creatinine levels above the upper limit of normal range. Renal disease or renal dysfunction (e.g., as suggested by serum creatinine levels ≥136 μmol/L (males), ≥124 μmol/L (females) or abnormal creatinine clearance) which may result from conditions such as cardiovascular collapse (shock), acute myocardial infarction, and septicemia (see also Warnings and Precautions).

In excessive alcohol intake, acute or chronic.

In patients suffering from severe hepatic dysfunction, since severe hepatic dysfunction has been associated with some cases of lactic acidosis, metformin should generally be avoided in patients with clinical or laboratory evidence of hepatic disease.

Metformin should be temporarily withheld in patients undergoing radiologic studies involving parenteral administration of iodinated contrast materials, because use of such products may result in acute alteration of renal function (see Warnings and Precautions).

In cases of cardiovascular collapse and in disease states associated with hypoxemia such as cardiorespiratory insufficiency, which are often associated with hyperlactacidemia.

During stress conditions, such as severe infections, trauma or surgery and the recovery phase thereafter.

In patients suffering from severe dehydration.

Known hypersensitivity or allergy to metformin or any of the excipients.

Pregnancy: During pregnancy.

Warnings: Lactic Acidosis: Lactic acidosis is a rare, but serious, metabolic complication that occurs due to metformin accumulation during treatment with metformin; when it occurs, it is fatal in approximately 50% of cases. Lactic acidosis may also occur in association with a number of pathophysiologic conditions, including diabetes mellitus, and whenever there is significant tissue hypoperfusion and hypoxemia. Lactic acidosis is characterized by elevated blood lactate levels (>5 mmol/L), decreased blood pH, electrolyte disturbances with an increased anion gap, and an increased lactate/pyruvate ratio. When metformin is implicated as the cause of lactic acidosis, metformin plasma levels >5 μg/mL are generally found.

The reported incidence of lactic acidosis in patients receiving metformin is very low (approximately 0.03 cases/1 000 patient-years, with approximately 0.015 fatal cases/1 000 patient-years). Reported cases have occurred primarily in diabetic patients with significant renal insufficiency, including both intrinsic renal disease and renal hypoperfusion, often in the setting of multiple concomitant medical/surgical problems and multiple concomitant medications. The risk of lactic acidosis increases with the degree of renal dysfunction and the patient's age. The risk of lactic acidosis may, therefore, be significantly decreased by regular monitoring of renal function in patients taking metformin and by use of the minimum effective dose of metformin. In addition, metformin should be promptly withheld in the presence of any condition associated with hypoxemia or dehydration. Because impaired hepatic function may significantly limit the ability to clear lactate, metformin should generally be avoided in patients with clinical or laboratory evidence of hepatic disease. Patients should be cautioned against excessive alcohol intake, either acute or chronic, when taking metformin, since alcohol intake potentiates the effect of metformin on lactate metabolism. In addition, metformin should be temporarily discontinued prior to any intravascular radiocontrast study and for any surgical procedure (see Precautions). The onset of lactic acidosis often is subtle, and accompanied only by nonspecific symptoms such as malaise, myalgias, respiratory distress, increasing somnolence and non-specific abdominal distress. There may be associated hypothermia, hypotension and resistance bradyarrhythmias with more marked acidosis. The patient and the patient's physician must be aware of the possible importance of such symptoms and the patient should be instructed to notify the physician immediately if they occur (see Precautions). Metformin should be withdrawn until the situation is clarified. Serum electrolytes, ketones, blood glucose and, if indicated, blood pH, lactate levels and even blood metformin levels may be useful. Once a patient is stabilized on any dose level of metformin, gastrointestinal symptoms, which are common during initiation of therapy, are unlikely to be drug related. Later occurrence of gastrointestinal symptoms could be due to lactic acidosis or other serious disease. Levels of fasting venous plasma lactate above the upper limit of normal but less than 5 mmol/L in patients taking metformin do not necessarily indicate impending lactic acidosis and may be explainable by other mechanisms, such as poorly controlled diabetes or obesity, vigorous physical activity or technical problems in sample handling. Lactic acidosis should be suspected in any diabetic patient with metabolic acidosis lacking evidence of ketoacidosis (ketonuria and ketonemia).

Lactic acidosis is a medical emergency that must be treated in a hospital setting. In a patient with lactic acidosis who is taking metformin, the drug should be discontinued immediately and general supportive measures promptly instituted. Because metformin is dialysable (with clearance of up to 170 mL/min under good hemodynamic conditions), prompt hemodialysis is recommended to correct the acidosis and remove the accumulated metformin. Such management often results in prompt reversal of symptoms and recovery (see Contraindications and Precautions).

If acidosis of any kind develops, metformin should be discontinued immediately.

Increased Risk of Cardiovascular Mortality: The administration of oral antidiabetic drugs has been reported to be associated with increased cardiovascular mortality as compared to treatment with diet alone or diet plus insulin. This warning is based on the study conducted by the University Group Diabetes Program (UGDP), a long-term prospective clinical trial designed to evaluate the effectiveness of glucose-lowering drugs in preventing or delaying vascular complications in patients with non-insulin-dependent diabetes. The study involved 1 027 patients who were randomly assigned to one of the five treatment groups.

The UGDP reported that patients treated for 5 to 8 years with diet plus a fixed dose of tolbutamide (1.5 g/day) or diet plus a fixed dose of phenformin (100 mg/day), had a rate of cardiovascular mortality approximately 2.5 times that of patients treated with diet alone, resulting in discontinuation of both these treatments in the UGDP study. Total mortality was increased in both the tolbutamide-and phenformin-treated groups and this increase was statistically significant in the phenformin-treated group. Despite controversy regarding the interpretation of these results, the findings of the UGDP study provide an adequate basis for this warning. The patient should be informed of the potential risks and benefits of metformin and alternative modes of therapy.

Although only one drug in the sulfonylurea category (tolbutamide) and one in the biguanide category (phenformin) were included in this study, it is prudent from a safety standpoint to consider that this warning may also apply to other related antidiabetic drugs, in view of the similarities in mode of action and chemical structure among the drugs in each category.

The use of metformin will not prevent the development of complications peculiar to diabetes mellitus.

Use of metformin must be considered as treatment in addition to proper dietary regimen and not as a substitute for diet.

Care should be taken to ensure that metformin is not given when a contraindication exists.

If during metformin therapy the patient develops acute intercurrent disease such as: clinically significant hepatic dysfunction, cardiovascular collapse, congestive heart failure, acute myocardial infarction, or other conditions complicated by hypoxemia, the drug should be discontinued.

Radiologic studies involving the use of iodinated contrast materials (e.g., i.v. urogram, i.v. cholangiography, angiography and scans with contrast materials): Parenteral contrast studies with iodinated materials can lead to acute renal failure and have been associated with lactic acidosis in patients receiving metformin (see Contraindications). Therefore, in patients in whom any such study is planned, metformin should be withheld for at least 48 hours prior to, and 48 hours subsequent to, the procedure and reinstituted only after renal function has been re-evaluated and found to be normal.

Precautions: Patient Selection and Followup: Careful selection of patients is important. It is imperative that there be rigid attention to diet and careful adjustment of dosage. When metformin is combined with a sulfonylurea, instruct the patient on hypoglycemic reactions and their control. Regular through followup examinations are necessary (see Warnings).

If vomiting occurs, withdraw drug temporarily, exclude lactic acidosis, then resume dosage cautiously (see Adverse Effects).

Particular attention should be paid to short range and long range complications which are peculiar to diabetes. Periodic cardiovascular, ophthalmic, hematological, hepatic and renal assessments are advisable (see Warnings).

Monitoring of Renal Function: Metformin is known to be substantially excreted by the kidney, and the risk of metformin accumulation and lactic acidosis increases with the degree of impairment of renal function. Thus, patients with serum creatinine levels above the upper limit of normal for their age should not receive metformin. In patients with advanced age, metformin should be carefully titrated to establish the minimum dose for adequate glycemic effect, because aging is associated with reduced renal function. In elderly patients, renal function should be monitored regularly and generally, metformin should not be titrated to the maximum dose (see Dosage).

Before initiation of metformin therapy and every 6 months while on metformin therapy, renal function should be assessed and verified as being within normal range.

In patients in whom development of renal dysfunction is anticipated, renal function should be assessed more frequently and metformin discontinued if evidence of renal impairment is present.

Use of Concomitant Medications That May Affect Renal Function or Metformin Disposition: Concomitant medication(s) that may affect renal function or result in significant hemodynamic change or may interfere with disposition of metformin, such as cationic drugs that are eliminated by renal tubular secretion (see Drug Interactions), should be used with caution.

Hypoxic States: Cardiovascular collapse (shock) from whatever cause, acute congestive heart failure, acute myocardial infarction and other conditions characterized by hypoxemia have been associated with lactic acidosis and may also cause prerenal azotemia. When such events occur in patients on metformin therapy, the drug should be promptly discontinued.

Surgical Procedures: Metformin therapy should be temporarily suspended for any surgical procedure (except minor procedures not associated with restricted intake of food and fluids). Metformin should be discontinued 2 days before surgical intervention and should not be restarted until the patient's oral intake has resumed and renal function has been evaluated as normal.

Alcohol Intake: Alcohol is known to potentiate the effect of metformin on lactate metabolism. Patients, therefore, should be warned against excessive alcohol intake, acute or chronic, while receiving metformin.

Impaired Hepatic Function: Since impaired hepatic function has been associated with some cases of lactic acidosis, metformin should generally be avoided in patients with clinical or laboratory evidence of hepatic disease.

Vitamin B_{12} Levels: Impairment of vitamin B_{12} and folic acid absorption has been reported in some patients. Therefore, measurements of serum vitamin B_{12} and folic acid are advisable at least every 1 to 2 years in patients on long-term treatment with metformin.

A decrease to subnormal levels of previously normal serum vitamin B_{12} levels, without clinical manifestations, is observed in approximately 7% of patients receiving metformin in controlled clinical trials of 28 weeks duration. Such decrease, possibly due to interference with B_{12} absorption from B_{12}-intrinsic factor complex is, however, very rarely associated with anemia and appears to be rapidly reversible with discontinuation of metformin or vitamin B_{12} supplementation. Measurement of hematologic parameters on an annual basis is advised in patients on metformin and any apparent abnormalities should be appropriately investigated and managed (see Laboratory Tests). Certain individuals (those with inadequate vitamin B_{12} or calcium intake or absorption) appear to be predisposed to developing subnormal vitamin B_{12} levels.

Change in Clinical Status of Previously Controlled Diabetic: A diabetic patient previously well controlled on metformin who develops laboratory abnormalities or clinical illness (especially vague and poorly defined illness) should be evaluated promptly for evidence of ketoacidosis or lactic acidosis. Evaluation should include serum electrolytes and ketones, blood glucose and, if indicated, blood pH, lactate, pyruvate and metformin levels. If acidosis of either form occurs, metformin must be stopped immediately and appropriate corrective measures initiated (see Warnings).

Hypoglycemia: Hypoglycemia does not occur in patients receiving metformin alone under usual circumstances of use, but could occur when caloric intake is deficient, when strenuous exercise is not compensated by caloric supplementation, or during concomitant use with other glucose lowering agents (such as sulfonylureas) or ethanol.

Elderly, debilitated or malnourished patients, and those with adrenal or pituitary insufficiency or alcohol intoxication are particularly susceptible to hypoglycemic effects. Hypoglycemia may be difficult to recognize in the elderly, and in people who are taking beta-adrenergic blocking drugs.

Loss of control of blood glucose: When a patient stabilized on any diabetic regimen is exposed to stress such as fever, trauma, infection, or surgery, a temporary loss of glycemic control may occur. At such times, it may be necessary to withhold metformin and temporarily administer insulin. Metformin may be reinstituted after the acute episode is resolved.

The effectiveness of oral antidiabetic drugs in lowering blood glucose to a targeted level decreases in many patients over a period of time. This phenomenon, which may be due to progression of the underlying disease or to diminished responsiveness to the drug, is known as secondary failure, to distinguish it from primary failure in which the drug is ineffective during initial therapy. Should secondary failure occur with metformin or sulfonylurea monotherapy, combined therapy with metformin and sulfonylurea may result in a response. Should secondary failure occur with combined metformin/sulfonylurea therapy, it may be necessary to initiate insulin therapy.

Laboratory Tests: Response to all diabetic therapies should be monitored by periodic measurements of fasting blood glucose and glycosylated hemoglobin levels, with a goal of decreasing these levels toward the normal range. During initial dose titration, fasting glucose can be used to determine the therapeutic response. Thereafter, both glucose and glycosylated hemoglobin should be monitored. Measurements of glycosylated hemoglobin may be especially useful for evaluating longterm control (see Dosage).

Initial and periodic monitoring of hematologic parameters (e.g., hemoglobin/hematocrit and red blood cell indices) and renal function (serum creatinine) should be performed, at least on an annual basis. While megaloblastic anemia has rarely been seen with metformin therapy, if this is suspected, vitamin B_{12} deficiency should be excluded.

Pregnancy: Safety in pregnant women has not been established. Metformin was not teratogenic in rats and rabbits at doses up to 600 mg/kg/day, or about 2 times the maximum recommended human daily dose on a body surface area basis. Determination of fetal concentrations demonstrated a partial placental barrier to metformin. Because animal reproduction studies are not always predictive of human response, any decision to use this drug should be balanced against the benefits and risks.

Because recent information suggests that abnormal blood glucose levels during pregnancy are associated with a higher incidence of congenital abnormalities, there is a consensus among experts that insulin be used during pregnancy to maintain blood glucose levels as close to normal as possible.

Lactation: Studies in lactating rats show that metformin is excreted into milk and reaches levels comparable to those in plasma. Similar studies have not been conducted in nursing mothers, but caution should be exercised in such patients, and a decision should be made whether to discontinue nursing or to discontinue the drug, taking into account the importance of the drug to the mother.

Children: Safety and effectiveness in pediatric patients have not been established.

Geriatrics: Controlled clinical studies of metformin did not include sufficient numbers of elderly patients to determine whether they respond differently from younger patients, although other reported clinical experience has not identified differences in responses between the elderly and younger patients. Metformin is known to be substantially excreted by the kidney and because the risk of serious adverse reactions to the drug is greater in patients with impaired renal function, it should only be used in patients with normal renal function (see Contraindications). Because aging is associated with reduced renal function, metformin should be used with caution as age increases. Care should be taken in dose selection and should be based on careful and regular monitoring of renal function. Generally, elderly patients should not be titrated to the maximum dose of metformin.

Drug Interactions: Certain drugs may potentiate the effect of metformin, particularly sulfonylurea type of drugs in the treatment of diabetes. The simultaneous administration of these two types of drugs could produce a hypoglycemic reaction, especially if they are given in patients already receiving other drugs which, themselves, can potentiate the effect of sulfonylureas. These drugs can be: long-acting sulfonamides, tuberculostatics, phenylbutazone, clofibrate, MAO inhibitors, salicylates, probenecid and propranolol.

In healthy volunteers, the pharmacokinetics of propranolol and ibuprofen were not affected by metformin when co-administered in single-dose interaction studies.

Metformin is negligibly bound to plasma proteins and is, therefore, less likely to interact with highly protein-bound drugs such as salicylates, sulfonamides, chloramphenicol, and probenecid, as compared to sulfonylureas, which are extensively bound to serum proteins.

Glyburide: In a single-dose interaction study in NIDDM subjects, coadministration of metformin and glyburide did not result in any changes in either metformin pharmacokinetics or pharmacodynamics. Decreases in glyburide AUC and C_{max} were observed, but were highly variable. The single-dose nature of this study and the lack of correlation between glyburide blood levels and pharmacodynamics effects, makes the clinical significance of this interaction uncertain.

Furosemide: A single-dose, metformin-furosemide drug interaction study in healthy subjects demonstrated that pharmacokinetic parameters of both compounds were affected by coadministration. Furosemide increased the metformin plasma and blood C_{max} by 22% and blood AUC by 15%, without any significant change in metformin renal clearance. When administered with metformin, the C_{max} and AUC of furosemide were 31% and 12% smaller, respectively, than when administered alone, and the terminal half-life was decreased by 32%, without any significant change in furosemide renal clearance. No information is available about the interaction of metformin and furosemide when coadministered chronically.

Nifedipine: A single-dose, metformin-nifedipine drug interaction study in healthy volunteers demonstrated that coadministration of nifedipine increased plasma metformin C_{max} and AUC by 20% and 9%, respectively, and increased the amount excreted in the urine. T_{max} and half-life were unaffected. Nifedipine appears to enhance the absorption of metformin. Metformin had minimal effects on nifedipine.

Cationic Drugs: Cationic drugs (e.g., amiloride, digoxin, morphine, procainamide, quinidine, quinine, ranitidine, triamterene, trimethoprim, and vancomycin) that are eliminated by renal tubular secretion, theoretically have the potential for interaction with metformin by competing for common renal tubular transport systems. Such an interaction has been observed between metformin and oral cimetidine in normal healthy volunteers in both single and multiple-dose, metformin-cimetidine drug interaction studies, with a 60% increase in peak metformin plasma and whole blood concentrations and a 40% increase in plasma and whole blood metformin AUC was observed. There was no change in elimination half-life in the single-dose study. Metformin had no effect on cimetidine pharmacokinetics. Therefore, careful patient monitoring and dose adjustment of metformin or the interfering drug is recommended in patients who are taking cationic medications that are excreted via renal tubular secretion.

Other: Other drugs tend to produce hyperglycemia and may lead to a loss of blood sugar control. These include thiazide and other diuretics, corticosteroids, phenothiazines, thyroid products, estrogens, estrogen plus progestogen, oral contraceptives, phenytoin, nicotinic acid, sympathomimetics, calcium channel blocking drugs, and isoniazid. When such drugs are administered to patients receiving metformin, the patient should be closely observed to maintain adequate glycemic control.

Elimination rate of the anticoagulant phenprocoumon has been reported to be increased by 20% when used concurrently with metformin. Therefore, patients receiving phenprocoumon or other antivitamin K anticoagulants should be monitored carefully when both types of drugs are used simultaneously. In such cases, an important increase of prothrombin time may occur upon cessation of metformin therapy, with an increased risk of hemorrhage.

Note: When used as indicated, there has not been a single case of lactic acidosis in Canada. The reported incidence of lactic acidosis in patients receiving metformin is very low (approximately 0.03 cases/1 000 patient/years with approximately 0.015 fatal cases/1 000 patient/years). Metformin should be immediately discontinued in the presence of acidosis.

Physicians should instruct their patients to recognize the symptoms which could signal the onset of lactic acidosis (see Warnings).

Adverse Effects: Lactic Acidosis: (See Warnings, Precautions, and Overdose).

Gastrointestinal: Gastrointestinal symptoms (diarrhea, nausea, vomiting, abdominal bloating, flatulence, and anorexia) are the most common reactions to metformin and are approximately 30% more frequent in patients on metformin monotherapy than in placebo-treated patients, particularly during initiation of metformin therapy. These symptoms are generally transient and resolve spontaneously during continued treatment. Occasionally, temporary dose reduction may be useful.

Because gastrointestinal symptoms during therapy initiation appear to be dose-related, they may be decreased by gradual

Glucophage (cont'd)

dose escalation and by having patients take metformin with meals (see Dosage).

Because significant diarrhea and/or vomiting can cause dehydration and prerenal azotemia, metformin should be temporarily discontinued, under such circumstances.

For patients who have been stabilized on metformin, nonspecific gastrointestinal symptoms should not be attributed to therapy unless intercurrent illness or lactic acidosis have been excluded.

Special Senses: During initiation of metformin therapy, approximately 3% of patients may complain of an unpleasant or metallic taste, which usually resolves spontaneously.

Dermatologic: The incidence of rash/dermatitis in controlled clinical trials was comparable to placebo for metformin monotherapy and to sulfonylurea for metformin/sulfonylurea therapy.

Hematologic: During controlled clinical trials of 29 weeks duration, approximately 9% of patients on metformin monotherapy and 6% of patients on metformin/sulfonylurea therapy developed asymptomatic subnormal serum vitamin B_{12} levels; serum folic acid levels did not decrease significantly. However, only five cases of megaloblastic anemia have been reported with metformin administration (none during U.S. clinical studies) and no increased incidence of neuropathy has been observed. Therefore, serum vitamin B_{12} levels should be appropriately monitored or periodic parenteral B_{12} supplementation considered (see also Precautions).

Overdose: Symptoms and Treatment: Available information concerning treatment of a massive overdosage of metformin is very limited. It would be expected that adverse reactions of a more intense character including epigastric discomfort, nausea and vomiting followed by diarrhea, drowsiness, weakness, dizziness, malaise and headache might be seen. Should those symptoms persist, lactic acidosis should be excluded. The drug should be discontinued and proper supportive therapy instituted.

Hypoglycemia has not been seen even with ingestion of up to 85 g of metformin, although lactic acidosis has occurred in such circumstances (see Warnings). Metformin is dialysable with a clearance of up to 170 mL/min under good hemodynamic conditions. Therefore, hemodialysis may be useful for removal of accumulated drug from patients in whom metformin overdosage is suspected.

Dosage: In diabetic patients, individual determination of the minimum dose that will lower blood glucose adequately should be made.

In patients where on initial trial the maximal recommended dose fails to lower the blood glucose adequately, the drug should be discontinued. Deterioration of the patient's condition can occur during the treatment of diabetes. It is advisable to ascertain the contribution of the drug in the control of blood glucose by discontinuing the medication semi-annually or at least annually with careful monitoring of the patient. If the need for the drug is not evident, the drug should not be resumed. In some diabetic subjects, short-term administration of the drug may be sufficient during periods of transient loss of blood sugar control.

The usual dose is 500 mg 3 or 4 times a day, or 850 mg two or three times a day. Maximal dose should not exceed 2.55 g a day. To minimize gastric intolerance such as nausea and vomiting, metformin should be taken with food whenever possible.

Supplied: 500 mg: Each white, round, biconvex tablet, scored on one face and debossed with "HMR" on the other, contains: metformin HCl 500 mg. Nonmedicinal ingredients: magnesium stearate and povidone. Bottles of 100 and 500.

850 mg: Each white, oval tablet, debossed with "HMR" on one side and 850 on the other, contains: metformin 850 mg. Nonmedicinal ingredients: magnesium stearate and povidone. Bottles of 100.

Store at room temperature (15 to 30°C) in well closed containers.

(Shown in Product Recognition Section)

Reviewed 1999

GLYBURIDE ℞
General Monograph, CPhA
see SULFONYLUREAS

GLYCERIN Suppositories
Nadeau
Laxative

Supplied: Adults: Each 2.65 g suppository contains: glycerin USP 90%. Boxes of 12, 15, 24, 30, 48 and 100.

Infants/Children: Each 1.8 g suppository contains: glycerin USP 90%. Boxes of 12, 15 and 30.

GLYCERIN Suppositories
Warner-Lambert Consumer Healthcare
Laxative

Supplied: Adult: Each suppository contains: glycerin USP approximately 96% w/w equivalent to 2.6 g/suppository. Nonmedicinal ingredients: sodium bicarbonate, sodium chloride and stearic acid. Boxes of 12, 24 and 48.

Infant/Child: Each suppository contains: glycerin USP approximately 96% w/w equivalent to 1.44 g/suppository. Nonmedicinal ingredients: sodium bicarbonate, sodium chloride and stearic acid. Boxes of 12.

GLYCON ℞
ICN
Metformin HCl
Antihyperglycemic Agent

Supplied: Each white, round biconvex, film-coated tablet, embossed M21 on one side and ICN on the other side, contains: metformin HCl BP 500 mg. Nonmedicinal ingredients: alcohol, croscarmellose sodium, magnesium stearate, microcrystalline cellulose and povidone; coating: carnauba wax, Opaspray white K-1-7000 and yellow #1. Bottles of 100 and 500.

GLYSENNID®
Novartis Consumer Health
Sennosides
Laxative

Pharmacology: Glysennid is a laxative which selectively stimulates the colon 8 to 12 hours after ingestion. Therefore, if Glysennid is taken before retiring, sleep is usually not disturbed.

Indications: Atonic constipation (e.g., in the elderly, after surgery, in the puerperium or due to neurological disorders).

Contraindications: Known hypersensitivity to sennosides or any of the ingredients; appendicitis, intestinal hemorrhage, spastic constipation, intestinal obstruction, ulcerative colitis and abdominal pain or of other acute undiagnosed pathological abdominal conditions; electrolyte imbalance (i.e., hypokalemia); during lactation.

Precautions: Frequent or continued use of the preparation may lead to dependence on laxatives. The lowest effective dosage for the re-establishment of normal bowel function should be employed. Use of Glysennid requires supervision by a physician in the following conditions: use exceeding 1 week; after abdominal surgery; in children below 6 years of age; during pregnancy.

Glysennid should be kept out of the reach of children.

Adverse Effects: Abdominal colic, diarrhea, irritation of the intestinal mucosa and loss of electrolytes may occur, particularly due to overdosage; discoloration of urine.

Overdose: Symptoms: Mainly those related to excessive catharsis: purging, griping abdominal pain, possible blood in the stool, electrolyte disturbances, excessive loss of water, nausea, diarrhea, irritation of the gastrointestinal tract and circulatory collapse.

Treatment: Gastric lavage. Careful observation and recording of vital signs. Relief of griping abdominal pain with antispasmodics. Monitoring of the cardiovascular system as well as the fluid and electrolyte balance. General supportive therapy with i.v. fluid administration for prevention and treatment of circulatory collapse.

Dosage: Adults, 17.2 to 24 mg with fluids before retiring. Children, 6 to 12 years, 8.6 to 12 mg with fluids before retiring; under 6 years, as prescribed.

Supplied: 8.6 mg: Each white coated tablet contains: senna glycosides 8.6 mg derived from purified senna extract 14.33 mg (sennosides USP). Also contains cornstarch and lactose. Energy: 1.42 kJ (0.34 kcal). Sodium: trace. Bottles of 100.

12 mg: Each pink coated tablet contains: senna glycosides 12 mg derived from purified senna extract 20 mg (sennosides USP). Also contains cornstarch, lactose and tartrazine. Energy: 1.51 kJ (0.36 kcal). Sodium: trace. Bottles of 100.

GoLYTELY™
Baxter
Electrolytes
Gastrointestinal Lavage Solution

Supplied: In powdered form, for oral administration as a solution following reconstitution. Each disposable 4 800 mL jug contains in powdered form: 236 g polyethylene glycol 3 350, sodium sulfate 22.74 g, sodium bicarbonate 6.74 g, sodium chloride 5.86 g, potassium chloride 2.97 g. When made up to 4 L volume with water, the solution contains 17.6 mmol/L PEG 3 350, sodium 125 mmol/L, sulfate 40 mmol/L, chloride 35 mmol/L, bicarbonate 20 mmol/L, and potassium 10 mmol/L. pH 5.5 to 7.5. Osmolality 280 mosm/kg. Store in sealed container at 15 to 30°C. When reconstituted, keep solution refrigerated. Use within 48 hours. Discard unused portion.

GONAL-F® ℞
Serono
Follitropin alpha (rDNA origin)
Gonadotropin

Pharmacology: Gonal-F is a gonadotropin preparation of recombinant DNA origin. The active ingredient, recombinant human follicle stimulating hormone (r-hFSH), is a human glycoprotein hormone which consists of 2 noncovalently linked, nonidentical protein components designated as the α- and β-subunits. The physicochemical, immunological, and biological activities of r-hFSH are similar to those of human menopausal urine-derived hFSH, but free of urinary protein and of any LH component.

Gonal-F stimulates ovarian follicular growth in women who do not have primary ovarian failure. FSH is the primary hormone responsible for follicular recruitment and development. To complete follicular maturation and effect ovulation in the absence of an endogenous luteinizing hormone (LH) surge, human chorionic gonadotropin (hCG) is given when monitoring of the patient indicates that sufficient follicular development has occurred. There may be a degree of interpatient variability in response to FSH administration, with lack of response to FSH in some patients.

Pharmacokinetics: Following i.v. administration, follitropin alpha (rDNA origin) is distributed to the extracellular fluid space with an initial half-life around 2 hours and eliminated from the body with a terminal half-life of about 1 day. The steady-state volume of distribution and total clearance are 10 L and 0.6 L/h, respectively. One-eighth of the follitropin alpha (rDNA origin) dose is excreted in the urine.

Following s.c. or i.m. administration, the absolute bioavailability is about 70%. Following repeated administration, Gonal-F accumulates 3-fold at steady-state within 3 to 4 days. In women whose endogenous gonadotropin secretion is suppressed, Gonal-F has nevertheless been shown to effectively stimulate follicular development and steroidogenesis, despite unmeasurable LH levels.

Indications: For the stimulation of multiple follicular development in ovulatory patients undergoing Assisted Reproductive Technologies (ART) such as in vitro fertilization. To complete follicular maturation in the absence of an endogenous LH surge, hCG is given.

Gonal-F is also indicated for the stimulation of follicular development in patients with hypothalamic-pituitary dysfunction who present either oligomenorrhea or amenorrhea (WHO

Group II). To complete follicular maturation and effect ovulation, hCG is given.
Selection of Patients: Before treatment with Gonal-F is instituted, a thorough gynecologic and endocrinologic evaluation must be performed. This should include an assessment of pelvic anatomy.

Primary ovarian failure should be excluded by the determination of gonadotropin levels.

Pregnancy: Appropriate evaluation should be performed to exclude pregnancy.

Patients in late reproductive life have a greater predisposition to endometrial carcinoma as well as a higher incidence of anovulatory disorders. A thorough diagnostic evaluation should always be performed in patients who demonstrate abnormal uterine bleeding or other signs of endometrial abnormalities before starting Gonal-F therapy.

Evaluation of the husband's fertility potential should be included in the initial evaluation.

Contraindications: Women who exhibit: High levels of FSH indicating primary ovarian failure. Uncontrolled thyroid or adrenal dysfunction. An organic intracranial lesion such as a pituitary tumor. The presence of any cause of infertility other than anovulation, as stated in the Indications unless the women are candidates for Assisted Reproductive Technologies. Abnormal uterine bleeding (see Indications, Selection of Patients). Ovarian cyst or enlargement of undetermined origin (see Indications, Selection of Patients). Sex hormone dependent tumors of the reproductive organs and breasts. Pregnancy/lactation. History of previous allergic reaction to any component of Gonal-F.

Warnings: Gonal-F should only be used by physicians who are thoroughly familiar with infertility problems and their management. Gonal-F is a potent gonadotropic substance capable of causing mild to severe adverse reactions. Gonadotropin therapy requires a certain time commitment by physicians and supportive health professionals, and requires the availability of appropriate monitoring facilities (see Precautions, Laboratory Tests). Safe and effective use of Gonal-F requires monitoring of ovarian response with ultrasound, alone or in combination with measurement of serum estradiol levels, on a regular basis.
Overstimulation of the Ovary During FSH Therapy: Ovarian Enlargement: Use of FSH therapy to stimulate follicular development may result in the recruitment of a number of follicles. This may result in mild to moderate uncomplicated ovarian enlargement which may be accompanied by abdominal distention and/or abdominal pain. This degree of enlargement has been reported to occur in approximately 20% of those treated with urofollitropin and hCG, and generally regresses without treatment within 2 or 3 weeks.

To minimize the hazard associated with the occasional abnormal ovarian enlargement which may occur with Gonal-F therapy, the lowest dose consistent with the expectation of good results should be used. Careful monitoring of ovarian response can further minimize the risk of ovarian enlargement.

If there is clinical evidence of excessive ovarian response (see Precautions, Laboratory Tests), treatment should be discontinued and hCG should not be administered. This will reduce the chances of development of the Ovarian Hyperstimulation Syndrome.
Ovarian Hyperstimulation Syndrome (OHSS): OHSS is a medical event distinct from uncomplicated ovarian enlargement. OHSS may progress rapidly (within 24 hours to several days) to become a serious medical event. It is characterized by an apparent dramatic increase in vascular permeability which can result in an accumulation of fluid in the peritoneal, pleural and, rarely, in the pericardial cavities. The early warning signs of development of OHSS are severe pelvic pain, nausea, vomiting and weight gain. The following symptomatology has been seen with cases of OHSS: abdominal pain, abdominal distention, severe ovarian enlargement, weight gain, dyspnea, oliguria and gastrointestinal symptoms including nausea, vomiting and diarrhea. Clinical evaluation may reveal hypovolemia, hemoconcentration, electrolyte imbalances, ascites, hemoperitoneum, pleural effusions, hydrothorax, acute pulmonary distress and thromboembolic events (see Pulmonary and Vascular Complications). Transient liver function test abnormalities suggestive of hepatic dysfunction, which may be accompanied by morphologic changes on liver biopsy, have been reported in association with the OHSS.

Severe OHSS occurred in approximately 6% of patients treated with urofollitropin therapy in the initial clinical trials, in patients treated for anovulation due to polycystic ovarian syndrome. In these studies, prospective monitoring of ovarian response using serum estradiol determination or ultrasonographic visualizations was not routinely employed. In the clinical trials in oligo-anovulatory infertile women treated with Gonal-F in which both estradiol and ultrasound measurements were utilized to monitor follicular development, the incidence of severe OHSS was 1 in 513 treatment cycles (0.2%). In the clinical trials in ovulatory infertile women treated with Gonal-F for induction of multiple follicular induction for IVF/ET in which both estradiol and ultrasound measurements were utilized to monitor follicular development, there was no incident of severe OHSS. OHSS may be more severe and more protracted if pregnancy occurs. OHSS develops rapidly; therefore, patients should be followed for at least 2 weeks after hCG administration. Most often, OHSS occurs after treatment has been discontinued and reaches its maximum at about 7 to 10 days following treatment. Usually, OHSS resolves spontaneously with the onset of menses. If there is evidence that OHSS may be developing prior to hCG administration (see Precautions, Laboratory Tests), the hCG **must** be withheld.

If severe OHSS occurs, treatment should be stopped and the patient should be hospitalized. A physician experienced in the management of this syndrome, or who is experienced in the management of fluid and electrolyte imbalances should be consulted.

Pulmonary and Vascular Complications: The following paragraph describes serious medical events reported following gonadotropin therapy. Serious pulmonary conditions (e.g., atelectasis, acute respiratory distress syndrome and exacerbation of asthma) have been reported. In addition, thromboembolic events both in association with, and separate from Ovarian Hyperstimulation Syndrome have been reported. Intravascular thrombosis and embolism can result in reduced blood flow to critical organs or the extremities. Sequelae of such events have included venous thrombophlebitis, pulmonary embolism, pulmonary infarction, cerebral vascular occlusion (stroke), and arterial occlusion resulting in loss of limb. In rare cases, pulmonary complications and/or thromboembolic events have resulted in death.

Multiple Births: Reports of multiple births have been associated with Gonal-F treatment. The risk of multiple births in patients undergoing ART procedures is related to the number of embryos replaced. In other patients, the incidence of multiple births may be increased by Gonal-F, as has been observed with other gonadotropin preparations. The patient and her husband should be advised of the potential risk of multiple births before starting treatment.

Precautions: General: Careful attention should be given to diagnosis in candidates for Gonal-F therapy (see Indications, Selection of Patients).
Information for the Patient: Prior to therapy with Gonal-F, patients should be informed of the duration of treatment and monitoring of their condition that will be required. Possible adverse reactions (see Adverse Effects) and the risk of multiple births should also be discussed.
Laboratory Tests: In most instances, treatment with Gonal-F results only in follicular recruitment and development. In the absence of an endogenous LH surge, hCG is given when monitoring of the patient indicates that sufficient follicular development has occurred. This may be estimated by ultrasound alone or in combination with measurement of serum estradiol levels. The combination of both ultrasound and serum estradiol measurement are useful for monitoring the development of follicles, for timing of the ovulatory trigger, as well as for detecting ovarian enlargement and minimizing the risk of the Ovarian Hyperstimulation Syndrome and multiple gestation. It is recommended that the number of growing follicles be confirmed using ultrasonography because plasma estrogens do not give an indication of the size or number of follicles.

The clinical confirmation of ovulation, with the exception of pregnancy, is obtained by direct and indirect indices of progesterone production. The indices most generally used are as follows: a rise in basal body temperature; increase in serum progesterone and menstruation following a shift in basal body temperature.

When used in conjunction with the indices of progesterone production, sonographic visualization of the ovaries will assist in determining if ovulation has occurred. Sonographic evidence of ovulation may include the following: fluid in the cul-de-sac; ovarian stigmata; collapsed follicle and secretory endometrium.

Accurate interpretation of the indices of follicle development and maturation require a physician who is experienced in the interpretation of these tests.

For patients undergoing extended cycles of treatment, PTT and liver enzymes should be monitored.

<u>Drug Interactions:</u> Clomiphene citrate used with Gonal-F may enhance follicular response, and caution is indicated when using the two together. No other clinically significant drug/drug or drug/food interactions have been reported during Gonal-F therapy.
Carcinogenesis, Mutagenesis, Impairment of Fertility: Long-term studies in animals have not been performed to evaluate the carcinogenic potential of Gonal-F. However, r-hFSH showed no mutagenic activity in a series of tests performed to evaluate its potential genetic toxicity including, bacterial and mammalian cell mutation tests, a chromosome aberration test and a micronucleus test.

Impaired fertility has been reported in rats exposed to pharmacological doses of r-hFSH (≥40 IU/kg/day) for extended periods through reduced fecondity.

Pregnancy: There are no adequate and well-controlled studies in pregnant women.

Given in high doses (>5 IU/kg/day) Gonal-F caused an increase in deaths, fetal effects and dystocia in pregnant rats and rabbits, but without being a teratogen. However, since Gonal-F is not indicated in pregnancy, these data are of limited clinical relevance.

Lactation: It is not known whether this drug is excreted in human milk, although animal studies have shown that r-hFSH is excreted in milk. Therefore, Gonal-F is contraindicated in lactating mothers.

Adverse Effects: The following adverse reactions reported during gonadotropin therapy are listed in decreasing order of potential severity: pulmonary and vascular complications (see Warnings); Ovarian Hyperstimulation Syndrome (see Warnings); adnexal torsion (as a complication of ovarian enlargement); hemoperitoneum; mild to moderate ovarian enlargement; abdominal pain; ovarian cysts; gastrointestinal symptoms (nausea, vomiting, diarrhea, abdominal cramps, bloating); pain, rash, swelling, and/or irritation at the site of injection; breast tenderness; headache and dermatological symptoms (dry skin, body rash, hair loss, hives).

The following medical events have been reported subsequent to pregnancies resulting from Gonal-F therapy in controlled clinical trials: spontaneous abortion, ectopic pregnancy, premature labor, postpartum fever.
Congenital Abnormalities: Two incidents of congenital cardiac malformations have been reported in children born following pregnancies resulting from treatment with Gonal-F and hCG in clinical studies. In addition, a pregnancy occurring in a study following treatment with Gonal-F and hCG was characterized by apparent failure of intrauterine growth and terminated for a suspected syndrome of congenital abnormalities. No specific diagnosis was made.

Three incidents of chromosomal abnormalities and 4 birth defects have been reported following urofollitropin-hCG or urofollitropin, Pergonal (menotropins for injection)-hCG therapy in clinical trials for stimulation prior to in vitro fertilization. The aborted pregnancies included 1 Trisomy 13, 1 Trisomy 18, and 1 fetus with multiple congenital anomalies (hydrocephaly, omphalocele and meningocele). One meningocele, 1 external ear defect, 1 dislocated hip and ankle and 1 dilated cardiomyopathy in presence of maternal Systemic Lupus Erythematosus were reported. None of these events were thought to be drug-related. The incidence does not exceed that found in the general population.

There have been infrequent reports of ovarian neoplasms, both benign and malignant, in women who have undergone multiple drug regimens for ovulation induction; however, a causal relationship has not been established.
Drug Abuse and Dependence: There have been no reports of abuse or dependence with Gonal-F.

Overdose: Symptoms and Treatment: Aside from possible ovarian hyperstimulation and multiple gestations (see Warnings), little is known concerning the consequences of acute overdosage with Gonal-F. Apart from expected ovarian and endometrial effects, no acute toxicity was seen in animals given doses of r-hFSH up to 1 000-fold the human dose.

Dosage: The dose to stimulate development of the follicle must be individualized for each patient and the particular indication. To minimize the hazard associated with the occasional abnormal ovarian enlargement which may occur with therapy, the lowest dose consistent with the expectation of good results

Gonal-F (cont'd)

should be used. It should be administered s.c. or i.m. until adequate follicular development is indicated by ultrasound alone or in combination with measurement of serum estradiol levels. Over the course of treatment, doses may range between 75 to 450 IU depending on the indication and the individual patient response. To complete follicular development and effect ovulation in the absence of an endogenous LH surge, hCG is given when monitoring of the patient indicates that sufficient follicular development has occurred. If the ovaries are abnormally enlarged or significant abdominal pain occurs, Gonal-F treatment should be discontinued, hCG should not be administered, and the patient should be advised to refrain from intercourse until resolution of the cycle; this will reduce the chances of development of the Ovarian Hyperstimulation Syndrome and, should spontaneous ovulation occur, reduce the chances of multiple gestation. While individual dosing regimens will differ between patients, typical treatment regimens are presented below.

Assisted Reproductive Technologies: In patients undergoing Assisted Reproductive Technologies (ART) whose endogenous gonadotropin levels are not suppressed, Gonal-F should be initiated in the early follicular phase (cycle day 2 or 3) at a dose of 150 IU/day, administered s.c. or i.m. Treatment should be continued until adequate follicular development is indicated as determined by either ultrasound alone or in combination with measurement of serum estradiol levels. Adjustments to dose, based on the patient's response, should only be considered after the first 5 days of treatment; subsequently dosage should be adjusted no more frequently than every 3 to 5 days and by no more than 75 to 150 IU additionally at each adjustment. Treatment should be continued until adequate follicular development is indicated. Once adequate follicular development is evident, hCG (5 000 to 10 000 USP units) should be administered to induce final follicular maturation in preparation for oocyte retrieval.

In patients undergoing ART, whose endogenous gonadotropin levels are suppressed indicating a hypogonadotropic state, Gonal-F should be initiated at a dose of 225 IU/day, administered s.c. or i.m. Treatment should be continued until adequate follicular development is indicated as determined by either ultrasound alone or in combination with measurement of serum estradiol levels. Adjustments to dose may be considered after 5 days based on the patient's response; subsequently dosage should be adjusted no more frequently than every 3 to 5 days and by no more than 75 to 150 IU additionally at each adjustment. Doses greater than 450 IU/day are not generally recommended. As before, once adequate follicular development is evident hCG (5 000 to 10 000 USP units) should be administered to induce final follicular maturation in preparation for oocyte retrieval.

Polycystic Ovarian Syndrome: Patients with Polycystic Ovarian Syndrome (PCO) tend to show a more rapid and exaggerated response to treatment. Therefore, in this patient population, particular care should be employed to ensure that patients are adequately monitored and that the lowest dose consistent with the expectation of good results is employed.

It is recommended that treatment of any patient be initiated at a dose of 75 IU Gonal-F/day, administered s.c. or i.m., for 7 to 12 days. Administration may exceed 12 days if inadequate follicular development is indicated by ultrasound alone or in combination with measurement of serum estradiol levels. Once adequate follicular development is evident, hCG (5 000 to 10 000 USP units) should be administered to induce final follicular maturation and effect ovulation. The patient should attempt to have intercourse at a consistent frequency of at least 3 times/week from the day prior to administration of hCG until ovulation becomes apparent.

If there is evidence of ovulation but pregnancy does not ensue, this regimen should be repeated for at least 2 more courses before increasing the dose to 150 IU/day for 7 to 12 days. As before, this dose should be followed by the administration of 5 000 to 10 000 USP units of hCG when adequate follicular development is evident. If evidence of ovulation is present but pregnancy does not ensue, repeat the same dose for 2 more courses. Doses larger than this are not routinely recommended.

Administration: Gonal-F should be administered s.c. or i.m. immediately after reconstitution with 0.5 to 1 mL Sterile Water for Injection. To avoid the injection of large volumes, up to 3 ampuls may be dissolved in 1 mL Sterile Water for Injection. Any unused reconstituted material should be discarded.

Parenteral drug products should be inspected visually for particulate matter and discoloration prior to administration, whenever solution and container permit.

Reconstituted Solutions: The Sterile Water for Injection provided with the lyophilized material should be used for reconstituting the product. Volumes used for reconstitution should be between 0.5 and 1 mL; up to 3 ampuls may be dissolved in 1 mL of Sterile Water for Injection. Reconstituted ampuls should be used immediately, and any unused solution should be discarded.

Parenteral Products: The reconstituted product may be administered either i.m. or s.c. Reconstituted ampuls should be visually examined for particulate matter prior to administration.

Information for the Patient: See Blue Section—Information for the Patient "Gonal-F".

Supplied: 75 IU: Each single dose ampul of sterile, lyophilized white pellets, intended for s.c. or i.m. injection after reconstitution, contains: FSH activity 75 IU. Diluent provided for reconstitution is Sterile Water for Injection. Nonmedicinal ingredients: dibasic sodium phosphate, monobasic sodium phosphate monohydrate and sucrose. O-phosphoric acid and/or sodium hydroxide may be used for pH adjustment prior to lyophilization. Single dose ampuls of 3 mL. Packages of 1, 10 and 100 ampuls accompanied by 1, 10 and 100 ampuls (1 mL) Sterile Water for Injection, respectively.

150 IU: Each single dose ampul of sterile, lyophilized white pellets, intended for s.c. or i.m. injection after reconstitution, contains: FSH activity 150 IU. Diluent provided for reconstitution is Sterile Water for Injection. Nonmedicinal ingredients: dibasic sodium phosphate, monobasic sodium phosphate monohydrate and sucrose. O-phosphoric acid and/or sodium hydroxide may be used for pH adjustment prior to lyophilization. Single dose ampuls of 3 mL. Packages of 1 and 50 ampuls accompanied by 1 and 50 ampuls (1 mL) Sterile Water for Injection, respectively.

Lyophilized ampuls are stable when stored at or below room temperature (25°C) and protected from light. Do not use the product after the expiry date indicated on the label.

Reviewed 1998

GOOD START®

Nestlé, Carnation

Infant Formula

Indications: A nutritionally complete iron fortified infant formula for routine feeding of infants from birth if breast-feeding is not an option or if a supplement is required.

Good Start has the added benefit of being easier to tolerate than routine cow's milk or soy based formula because the protein has been partially broken down to reduce the possibility of an allergic reaction.

Contraindications: Not suitable for feeding infants with severe cow's milk allergy, with or without gastrointestinal complications where there is risk of anaphylactic shock; severe acute or chronic diarrhea with gastrointestinal damage when a special therapeutic formula would be indicated; the rare condition of galactosemia; low birth weight (less than 2 500 g).

Warnings: After using Good Start, baby's stools may be softer and either a yellowish or dark green color, similar to those of breast-fed infants. This is quite normal.

Dosage: As determined by the individual infant's needs for the first year of life. Consult the physician for specific feeding recommendations.

Preparation: Concentrated Liquid: Bring clean bottles, nipples, rings and preparation utensils to a full boil and cool before using. Do not use a microwave to sterilize utensils or to warm formula. In a separate container, bring water to a boil. Allow water to cool to 40°C or for approximately 20 to 30 minutes before using. Clean can top. Shake well, and open. After opening, can may be covered and stored in refrigerator to be used within 48 hours. Mix equal amounts of formula and warm water in a sterilized bottle, cap and shake well. Bottled formula may be covered and stored in refrigerator to be used within 48 hours. Formula should be at body temperature before feeding. Formula is at the right temperature if you do not feel a temperature difference when placing a drop on your own hand. Discard unused formula left in bottle after feeding.

Powder: Bring clean bottles, nipples, rings and preparation utensils to a full boil and cool before using. Do not use a microwave to sterilize utensils or to warm formula. In a separate container, bring water to a boil. Allow water to cool to 40°C or for approximately 20 to 30 minutes before using. Pour desired amount of water into bottle. Add one unpacked level scoop (8.7 g), enclosed, of powder for each 60 mL of water in bottle. Cap bottle and shake well. Feed immediately or bottled formula may be covered and stored in refrigerator to be used within 24 hours. Formula should be at body temperature before feeding. Formula is at the right temperature if you do not feel a temperature difference when placing a drop on your own hand. Discard unused formula left in bottle after feeding.

One can will make approximately 2.6 L of formula.

Ready-To-Feed: Bring clean bottles, nipples, rings and preparation utensils to a full boil and cool before using. Do not use a microwave to sterilize utensils or to warm formula. Clean can top. Shake well, and open. After opening, can may be covered and stored in refrigerator to be used within 48 hours. Pour formula directly into nursing bottle. Bottled formula may be covered and stored in refrigerator to be used within 48 hours. Formula should be at body temperature before feeding. Formula is at the right temperature if you do not feel a temperature difference when placing a drop on your own hand. Discard unused formula left in bottle after feeding.

Supplied: Concentrated Liquid: Each can contains: water, whey protein concentrate, lactose, maltodextrin, palm olein, soybean oil, coconut oil, safflower oil, minerals (calcium chloride, tricalcium phosphate, magnesium chloride, ferrous sulfate, zinc sulfate, copper sulfate, potassium iodide, manganese sulfate), vitamins, trypsin, taurine, nucleotides, l-carnitine. See Table I.

Cans of 385 mL, cases of 12. Store unopened cans at room temperature. Avoid excessive temperatures. Use before date shown on top of can.

Table I—Good Start, Concentrated Liquid

Dilution Analysis

Average Composition	Concentrate/ 100 mL	Units	Standard Dilution/ 100 mL
Energy	560 (134)	kJ (kcal)	280 (67)
Carbohydrate	14.8	g	7.4
Fat	7	g	3.5
Protein	3.2	g	1.6
Ash	0.6	g	0.3
Linoleic Acid	1.14	g	0.57
Linolenic Acid	0.11	g	0.057
Vitamin A	400	IU	200
Vitamin D	80	IU	40
Vitamin E	2.6	IU	1.3
Vitamin K	0.011	mg	0.0055
Vitamin C	10.8	mg	5.4
Thiamine	0.08	mg	0.04
Riboflavin	0.18	mg	0.09
Vitamin B_6	0.1	mg	0.05
Vitamin B_{12}	0.0003	mg	0.00015
Niacin	1	mg	0.5
Folacin	0.012	mg	0.006
Pantothenic Acid	0.6	mg	0.3
Biotin	0.003	mg	0.0015
Choline	16.2	mg	8.1
Taurine	10.8	mg	5.4
Inositol	24	mg	12
L-Carnitine	2.2	mg	1.1
Calcium	88	mg	44
Phosphorus	48	mg	24
Magnesium	9	mg	4.5
Iron	2	mg	1
Zinc	1	mg	0.51
Manganese	0.0096	mg	0.0048
Copper	0.11	mg	0.054
Iodine	0.011	mg	0.0054
Sodium	32	mg	16
Potassium	132	mg	66
Chloride	80	mg	40

Powder: Each can contains: whey protein concentrate, lactose, maltodextrin, palm olein, soybean oil, coconut oil, safflower oil, soy lecithin, minerals, vitamins, trypsin, taurine, nucleotides, l-carnitine. See Table II (on following page).

Cans of 340 g, cases of 6. Cover opened can and store in a cool dry place. Use within 1 month after opening. Use before date shown on bottom of can.

Table II—Good Start, Powder

Dilution Analysis

Average Composition	Powder/ 100 g	Units	Standard Dilution/ 100 mL
Energy	2 142 (512)	kJ (kcal)	280 (67)
Carbohydrate	56	g	7.4
Fat	26.4	g	3.5
Protein	12.2	g	1.6
Ash	2.1	g	0.3
Linoleic Acid	4.4	g	0.57
Linolenic Acid	0.44	g	0.057
Vitamin A	1 528	IU	200
Vitamin D	305	IU	40
Vitamin E	9.9	IU	1.3
Vitamin K	0.042	mg	0.0055
Vitamin C	41	mg	5.4
Thiamine	0.3	mg	0.04
Riboflavin	0.7	mg	0.09
Vitamin B_6	0.4	mg	0.05
Vitamin B_{12}	0.0011	mg	0.00015
Niacin	3.8	mg	0.5
Folacin	0.046	mg	0.006
Pantothenic Acid	2.3	mg	0.3
Biotin	0.011	mg	0.0015
Choline	62	mg	8.1
Taurine	41	mg	5.4
Inositol	92	mg	12
L-Carnitine	8	mg	1.1
Calcium	335	mg	44
Phosphorus	183	mg	24
Magnesium	34	mg	4.5
Iron	7.6	mg	1
Zinc	3.8	mg	0.51
Manganese	0.036	mg	0.0048
Copper	0.4	mg	0.054
Iodine	0.041	mg	0.0054
Sodium	120	mg	16
Potassium	500	mg	66
Chloride	305	mg	40

Table III—Good Start, Ready-To-Feed

Average Composition	Standard Dilution/ 100 mL	Units
Energy	280 (67)	kJ (kcal)
Carbohydrate	7.4	g
Fat	3.5	g
Protein	1.6	g
Ash	0.3	g
Linoleic Acid	0.57	g
Linolenic Acid	0.057	g
Vitamin A	200	IU
Vitamin D	40	IU
Vitamin E	1.3	IU
Vitamin C	5.4	mg
Niacin	0.5	mg
Pantothenic Acid	0.3	mg
Riboflavin	0.09	mg
Vitamin B_6	0.05	mg
Thiamine	0.04	mg
Folacin	0.006	mg
Vitamin K	0.0055	mg
Biotin	0.0015	mg
Vitamin B_{12}	0.00015	mg
Potassium	66	mg
Calcium	44	mg
Chloride	40	mg
Phosphorus	24	mg
Sodium	16	mg
Magnesium	4.5	mg
Iron	1	mg
Zinc	0.51	mg
Copper	0.054	mg
Iodine	0.0054	mg
Manganese	0.0048	mg
Choline	8.1	mg
Taurine	5.4	mg
Inositol	12	mg
L-Carnitine	1.1	mg

Ready-To-Feed: Each can contains: water, whey protein concentrate, lactose, maltodextrin, palm olein, soybean oil, coconut oil, safflower oil, minerals, vitamins, trypsin, taurine, nucleotides, l-carnitine. See Table III.

Cans of 945 mL, cases of 6. Store unopened cans at room temperature. Avoid excessive temperatures. Use before date shown on top of can.

Reviewed 1998

GRAMCAL®

Novartis Consumer Health

Calcium Preparation

Calcium Therapy

Indications: Osteoporosis; conditions requiring supplemental calcium.

Contraindications: Hypercalcemia and hypercalciuria (e.g., in hyperparathyroidism, vitamin D overdosage, decalcifying tumors such as plasmocytoma, bone metastases); severe renal disease; and in calcium loss due to immobilization. Gramcal is suitable for patients with sodium or potassium restricted diets. Hypersensitivity to any of the components.

Precautions: In mild hypercalciuria (exceeding 300 mg/ 24 hours) as well as in chronic renal failure, or where there is evidence of stone formation in the urinary tract, adequate checks must be made on urinary calcium excretion. If necessary, the dosage should be reduced or calcium therapy discontinued. In patients prone to formation of calculi in the urinary tract, an increased fluid intake is recommended.

Drug Interactions: Administration of corticosteroids may interfere with calcium absorption.

Calcium compounds should not be taken within 3 hours of oral tetracycline or fluoride administration (possible interference of absorption).

High vitamin D intake should be avoided during calcium therapy, unless especially indicated.

Thiazide diuretics cause calcium retention and this may exacerbate hypercalcemia from $CaCO_3$ (calcium carbonate).

Administration of calcium may reduce the response to verapamil and possibly other calcium channel blockers.

Given in large doses to digitalized patients, calcium may increase the risk of cardiac arrhythmias.

Drug/Food Interactions: Certain dietary substances interfere with the absorption of calcium. These include oxalic acid (found in large quantities in rhubarb and spinach), phytic acid (bran and whole cereals) and phosphorus (milk and other dairy products).

Adverse Effects: Occasional diarrhea has been reported with high doses of calcium. In other patients, high calcium intake is an occasional cause of constipation.

Overdose: Symptoms and Treatment: Acute overdosage has not been reported. It would be expected to cause gastrointestinal disturbances but not to result in hypercalcemia, except in patients treated with an excessive dose of vitamin D.

Dosage: Usual dose in osteoporosis, 1 or 2 effervescent tablets (dissolved in water) daily, or as prescribed.

Supplied: Each whitish, effervescent tablet contains: calcium lactate gluconate 2 327 mg, calcium carbonate 1 750 mg and provides 1 000 mg (25 mmol) of elemental calcium. Nonmedicinal ingredients: aspartame, citric acid, flavor and polyethylene glycol. Energy: 59.3 kJ (14.17 kcal). Potassium: 0.01 mmol (0.382 mg). Sodium: 0.07 mmol (1.69 mg). Tubes of 20, cartons of 10. Protect from heat and humidity.

(Shown in Product Recognition Section)

GRAVERGOL® Ⓟ

Carter Horner

Ergotamine Tartrate—Caffeine—Dimenhydrinate

Migraine Therapy

Indications: For the relief of migraine headaches and other recurrent vascular headaches as well as nausea, vomiting and dizziness that accompany the attacks.

Contraindications: Sepsis, occlusive vascular disease (thromboangiitis obliterans, luetic arteritis, severe arteriosclerosis, coronary artery disease, thrombophlebitis, Raynaud's disease), hepatic disease, renal disease, hypertension, angina pectoris, peptic ulcer, infectious states, malnutrition, severe pruritus, pregnancy, lactation. Hypersensitivity to any of the components.

Precautions: Use cautiously in debilitated or anemic patients and in thyrotoxicosis. Discontinue therapy if patient reports cold, numbness, pain in extremities or muscle cramps.

Occupational Hazards: If medication causes drowsiness, avoid activities requiring alertness.

See also Gravol Preparations monograph.

There is some evidence that the concomitant use of triacetyloleandomycin (TAO/troleandomycin) and ergotamine may give rise to untoward peripheral vasoconstriction.

Overdose: Ergotamine might produce peripheral vascular complications, precordial distress and pain, transient tachycardia or bradycardia. See also Overdose section of Gravol Preparations monograph.

Symptoms: Theoretically, toxicity could be caused by either dimenhydrinate or ergotamine tartrate. These agents could produce vomiting, diarrhea, dizziness, weak pulse, convulsions, dyspnea and coma.

Treatment: No specific or known antidote. Employ general measures and treat convulsions, if necessary.

Dosage: 2 capsules at very first sign of attack, then 1 capsule at 0.5 hour intervals if required. Maximum dose for any single attack: 6 capsules. Maximum weekly dose: 12 capsules. Note: The total number of capsules required to relieve an attack should be noted and taken as a single dose for future attacks.

Supplied: Each dark green, No. 1 hard gelatin capsule of pink powder, contains: ergotamine tartrate 1 mg, caffeine 100 mg and dimenhydrinate 50 mg. Nonmedicinal ingredients: alumina, D&C Yellow No. 10, FD&C Red No. 3 and Green No. 3, gelatin, lactose and magnesium stearate. Energy: 5.7 kJ (1.35 kcal)/capsule. Alcohol-, gluten- and tartrazine-free. Bottles of 20 and 100.

(Shown in Product Recognition Section)

GRAVOL® Preparations

Carter Horner

Dimenhydrinate

Antiemetic—Antivertigo

Indications: Prevention or relief of motion sickness, radiation sickness, postoperative vomiting, and drug induced nausea and vomiting; it has also been used for the symptomatic relief of nausea and vertigo due to Ménière's disease and other labyrinthine disturbances.

Contraindications: Glaucoma, chronic lung disease, difficulty in urination due to prostatic hypertrophy.

Warnings: As dimenhydrinate has a CNS depressant effect, the concomitant use of alcohol should be avoided.

If Gravol I.M. is required for i.v. use, it must be diluted at least 1:10 with a compatible physiological solution such as sterile saline or 5% dextrose in water, to prevent propylene glycol-associated serious adverse reactions, and should be injected slowly over 2 to 3 min.

Occupational Hazards: Patients receiving dimenhydrinate should be cautioned against operating automobiles or dangerous machinery because of drowsiness associated with the drug. If drowsiness is excessive, dosage should be reduced.

It should be borne in mind that antiemetics should be used with caution since they may mask the presence of underlying organic abnormalities or the toxic effects of other drugs.

Patients in whom anticholinergics may aggravate other clinical conditions, should use dimenhydrinate with caution, and preferably on a physician's advice. Patients should not take dimenhydrinate with other antihistamines, tranquilizers or any other sedative drugs without first consulting their physician.

Pregnancy and *Lactation:* The use of dimenhydrinate by women who are pregnant or may become pregnant, or nursing mothers, require that potential benefits be weighed against the potential risks.

Adverse Effects: Drowsiness may be experienced by some patients, especially at high dosages. Dizziness may also occur. Symptoms of dry mouth, lassitude, excitement (especially in children) and nausea have been reported.

Overdose: Children are susceptible to the convulsant action of antihistamines. Cases of convulsions and eventually coma have been reported in children 1.5 to 3 years (especially in the presence of dehydration) having received large doses of 150 to 800 mg diphenhydramine HCl (equivalent to 260 to 1 400 mg dimenhydrinate). There have been reports of hallucinations after the ingestion of 500 and 700 mg dimenhydrinate.

Symptoms: Drowsiness, ataxia, disorientation, nystagmus, convulsions, stupor, coma and respiratory depression.

Treatment: No specific antidote. Gastric lavage. If coma and respiratory depression are present, use resuscitative

Gravol Preparations (cont'd)

measures, not stimulants. Maintain blood pressure with dopamine or levarterenol bitartrate. It has been reported that anticholinergic induced delirium, confusion, hallucinations, agitation, ataxia, dysarthria and somnolence are reversed by i.v. or s.c. administration of 1 to 2 mg physostigmine salicylate.

Dosage: Motion Sickness: Initial dose should be taken at least ½ hour and preferably 1 to 2 hours before departure.
Adults: For the treatment of motion sickness, nausea, vomiting, dizziness and vertigo: 50 to 100 mg every 4 hours if necessary to a maximum of 400 mg in 24 hours. For extended relief: 1 to 2 Gravol 75 mg long acting capsules every 8 hours to a maximum of 5 capsules in 24 hours. Rectal: 50 to 100 mg suppository every 6 to 8 hours as necessary. (For ease and comfort smooth any edges on suppository prior to use.)
Radiation Sickness: 50 to 100 mg administered rectally or parenterally, 30 to 60 minutes before treatment. This dose is repeated as necessary to a maximum of 400 mg in 24 hours. To control postoperative nausea and vomiting: 50 to 100 mg may be administered orally or 50 mg i.m. as a preoperative dose to be followed postoperatively by similar doses as needed to a maximum of 400 mg in 24 hours.
Children: Under 1 year: Not recommended.
Children: Under 2 years: As directed by a physician.
2 to 6 years: Oral: 15 to 25 mg every 6 to 8 hours as necessary to a maximum of 75 mg in 24 hours. Rectal: 12.5 to 25 mg not to be repeated except on the advice of a physician.
6 to 8 years: Oral: 25 to 50 mg every 6 to 8 hours as necessary to a maximum of 150 mg in 24 hours. Rectal: 12.5 to 25 mg every 8 to 12 hours as necessary.
8 to 12 years: Oral: 25 to 50 mg every 6 to 8 hours as necessary to a maximum of 150 mg in 24 hours. Rectal: 25 to 50 mg every 8 to 12 hours as necessary.
12 years and over: Oral: 50 mg every 4 to 6 hours as necessary to a maximum of 300 mg in 24 hours. Rectal: 50 mg every 8 to 12 hours as necessary.

Supplied: I.V. Ampuls: Each single dose ampul of clear solution contains: dimenhydrinate 50 mg and must be administered by slow i.v. injection only. Nonmedicinal ingredients: alcohol 17%. Tartrazine-free. Ampuls of 5 mL, boxes of 10. Store at controlled room temperature (15 to 30°C). Protect from freezing.

I.M. Injection: Each mL contains: dimenhydrinate 50 mg. This dosage form is for i.m use only, unless diluted at least 1:10 with a compatible physiological solution, i.e., sterile saline or 5% dextrose in water. Nonmedicinal ingredients: methylparaben (multidose vials only), propylene glycol and propylparaben (multidose vials only). Tartrazine-free. Multidose vials of 5 mL, boxes of 3 and 25. Unit dose ampuls of 1 mL (preservative-free), boxes of 10. Store at controlled room temperature (15 to 30°C). Protect from freezing.

L/A Capsules: Each No. 1 hard gelatin capsule with blue top and clear bottom holding a white powder with hard, pink coated granules distributed throughout, contains: 25 mg of dimenhydrinate for immediate release and 50 mg of dimenhydrinate for sustained release. Nonmedicinal ingredients: cellulose, FD&C Blue No. 1, FD&C Red No. 2 and No. 3, gelatin, lactose, light mineral oil, magnesium stearate, povidone, shelac, silicon dioxide, sodium lauryl sulfate. starch (corn and wheat) (contains gluten) and talc. Energy: 5 kJ (1.2 kcal)/capsule. Tartrazine-free. Push through packages of 10 and 30; bottles of 100 and 500.

Liquid: Each 5 mL of yellow, transparent, viscous liquid with a bittersweet mixed fruit flavor, contains: dimenhydrinate 15 mg. Nonmedicinal ingredients: citric acid, D&C Yellow No. 10, FD&C Yellow No. 6, flavor, propylene glycol, sodium benzoate, sorbitol and sucrose. Energy: 61.5 kJ (14.7 kcal)/ 5 mL. Sodium: <1 mmol (0.8 mg). Gluten- and tartrazine-free. Bottles of 75 and 250 mL.

Suppositories: Each white, opaque suppository contains: dimenhydrinate 25 mg children or 50 mg junior both with rounded nose or 100 mg (adult) with a pointed nose. Nonmedicinal ingredients: polyethylene glycol, silicon dioxide and titanium dioxide. Gluten- and tartrazine-free. Boxes of 10 and 100. Individually sealed in foil. Store in a cool place.

Filmkote Tablets: 15 mg: Each round, biconvex, yellow lime tablet, intagliated GRAVOL on one side, contains: dimenhydrinate 15 mg. Nonmedicinal ingredients: alumina, cellulose, D&C Yellow No. 10, FD&C Blue No. 2, glycerin, lactose, magnesium stearate, propylene glycol, silicon dioxide, starch (corn), talc and titanium dioxide. Energy: 1 kJ (0.2 kcal). Gluten- and tartrazine-free. Push through packages of 10.

25 mg (Junior Strength): Each round, biconvex, pale yellow tablet, intagliated GRAVOL on one side, contains: dimenhydrinate 25 mg. Nonmedicinal ingredients: alumina, cellulose, D&C Yellow No. 10, FD&C Yellow No. 6 and Blue No. 2, lactose, magnesium stearate, polyethylene glycol, povidone, silicon dioxide, starch (corn), talc and tianium dioxide. Energy: 1.3 kJ (0.3 kcal). Gluten- and tartrazine-free. Push through packages of 10.

50 mg: Each round, biconvex, peach coral tablet, intagliated GRAVOL on one side and quadrisected on the other, contains: dimenhydrinate 50 mg. Nonmedicinal ingredients: alumina, cellulose, FD&C Yellow No. 6, lactose, magnesium stearate, polyethylene glycol, silicon dioxide, starch (corn), talc and titanium dioxide. Energy: 1.3 kJ (0.3 kcal)/tablet. Gluten- and tartrazine-free. Push through packages of 10 and 30; bottles of 100 and 1 000, unit dose cartons of 5×20 and unit dose tins of 1 000.

Chewable Tablets for Children: Each round, flat, light purple, cherry-flavored tablet with bevelled edge intagliated GRAVOL 15 mg on one side, plain on the other side, contains: dimenhydrinate 15 mg. Nonmedicinal ingredients: alumina, aspartame, cellulose, citric acid, FD&C Red No. 40, flavors, magnesium stearate, methacrylic acid copolymer, monoglycerides, polyethylene glycol, sorbitol and starch (corn). Energy: 5.8 kJ (1.4 kcal). Gluten- and tartrazine-free. Push through packages of 12.

Chewable Tablets for Adults: Each round, flat, light pink, orange-flavored tablet with bevelled edge, intagliated GRAVOL 50 on one side, bisected on the other side, contains: dimenhydrinate 50 mg. Nonmedicinal ingredients: alumina, aspartame, cellulose, citric acid, FD&C Yellow No. 6, flavors, magnesium stearate, methacrylic acid copolymer, monoglycerides, polyethylene glycol, sorbitol and starch (corn). Energy: 10.9 kJ (2.6 kcal). Gluten- and tartrazine-free. Push through packages of 8.

(Shown in Product Recognition Section)

GRISOVIN® FP Ⓟ
Roberts

Griseofulvin Microcrystalline

Antifungal Antibiotic

Indications: Orally effective against superficial infections caused by those fungi responsible for dermatomycoses in man and animals, namely: M. canis, M. gypseum, M. audouini, E. floccosum, T. tonsurans, T. rubrum, T. mentagrophytes, T. magnini, T. gallinae, T. verrucosum, T. sulfureum, T. interdigitale, T. schoenleini, T. crateriform. Griseofulvin is inactive against: C. albicans (monilia), C. neoformans, B. dermatitidis, A. israeli, H. capsulatum, C. immitis, M. furfur (tinea versicolor) and bacteria. The drug is useful in the treatment of fungal infections of the scalp and those of the glabrous skin. The drug is less effective in chronic infections of the feet, palms, and nails. Since these chronic fungal infections tend to cause hyperkeratosis, concomitant topical keratolytic therapy is almost always necessary.

Contraindications: Porphyria, hepatocellular failure, and individuals with a history of hypersensitivity to griseofulvin. The exacerbation of systemic lupus erythematosus has been reported in patients treated with griseofulvin. Not recommended in pregnancy or in minor or trivial infections which will respond to topical antifungal agents alone.
Pregnancy: Griseofulvin may have harmful effects on the genotype. For this reason, it is recommended that male persons who are treated with griseofulvin not father children during the next 6 months after termination of the treatment. Female persons should not become pregnant during the treatment with griseofulvin.

Precautions: As with all antibiotics, the use of this drug may result in an overgrowth of nonsusceptible organisms particularly monilia. Periodic blood cell counts should be done during griseofulvin therapy, and its administration should be discontinued if granulocytopenia occurs. Albuminuria and hyaline casts have been associated with the use of griseofulvin, but renal function tests have revealed no impairment. The urine of patients on prolonged therapy should be examined for porphobilinogen. Since griseofulvin is derived from a species of penicillin, the possibility of cross sensitivity with penicillin exists; however, known penicillin sensitive patients have been treated without difficulty.

As griseofulvin may alter prothrombin activity in some patients, it is recommended that prothrombin times be determined at least 2 or 3 times a week with patients on anticoagulant therapy if griseofulvin is added to the regimen.

Concomitant administration of phenobarbital and griseofulvin may result in reduced blood levels of griseofulvin due to the enzymatic acceleration of griseofulvin metabolism. During therapy with griseofulvin, patients should be advised to avoid exposure to intense natural or artificial sunlight. Griseofulvin has also been reported as interfering with the efficacy of oral contraceptives. Patients should be warned that an enhancement of the effects of alcohol by griseofulvin has been reported.
Occupational Hazards: In those rare cases where individuals are affected by drowsiness while taking griseofulvin, they should not drive vehicles or operate machinery.

Long-term administration of high doses of griseofulvin with food has been reported to induce hepatomas in mice and thyroid tumors in rats but not hamsters. The clinical significance of these findings is not known. In view of these data, griseofulvin tablets should not be used prophylactically. There is no doubt that griseofulvin is capable of inducing aneuploidy (abnormal segregation of chromosomes following cell division) in mammalian cells exposed to the compound in vitro. In the absence of the relevant in vivo data, it is prudent to warn men that they should not father children within 6 months of treatment.

Adverse Effects: Severe reactions occur infrequently. Headache may occur, but usually disappears when the drug is taken with meals. Nausea, epigastric distress, heartburn, abdominal cramps, vomiting or diarrhea have been reported in a few patients. Chest pain, dryness of the mouth, breathlessness, arthralgia, neuritic pains, vertigo, and fever have also been reported. Allergic reactions, occurring rarely, include urticaria and angioneurotic edema, skin rashes, serum sickness, lupus erythematosus. Fatigue, lethargy, vertigo, decreased mental acuity, dizziness, confusion, peripheral neuropathy and secondary monilial skin infections have been reported as well as a few cases of photosensitivity. Toxic epidermal necrolysis and erythema multiforme have been reported. Proteinuria and leukopenia have been reported rarely. If granulocytopenia occurs, the administration of the drug should be discontinued. In children receiving griseofulvin, enlargement of the breast and hyperpigmentation of mammary areolae, nipples and external genitalia have been reported.

Dosage: Dosage should be taken after meals, otherwise absorption is likely to be inadequate. Dosage must be individualized. Adults: 500 mg daily. Children: A dosage of 10 mg/kg is usually adequate (children from 14 to 23 kg, 125 to 250 mg daily; children over 23 kg, 250 to 500 mg, in divided doses). Patients with less severe infections may require less, whereas those with widespread lesions may require a starting dose of 0.75 to 1 g/day. Therapy should be continued for at least 2 weeks after all signs of infection have disappeared.

Supplied: Each scored tablet contains: microcrystalline griseofulvin 250 mg. Energy: 0.63 kJ (0.15 kcal). Sodium: <1 mmol (0.48 mg). Tartrazine-free. Bottles of 100.

Reviewed 1997

GUAIFENESIN
General Monograph, CPhA

Glyceryl Guaiacolate

Expectorant

> This monograph has been compiled by CPhA. It may contain information different from that approved by Therapeutic Products Programme, Health Canada, and the pharmaceutical manufacturers' approval has not been requested.

Pharmacology: Guaifenesin is believed to produce its effect through a local or reflex irritant action that activates the vagus nerve to stimulate secretion or respiratory tract fluid. This is thought to increase sputum volume, decrease its viscosity, enhance the flow of less viscid secretions and promote mucociliary clearance.
Pharmacokinetics: The drug is rapidly absorbed from the gastrointestinal tract and excreted in the urine.

Indications: An expectorant agent used in the symptomatic relief of respiratory conditions associated with productive cough, with the presence of mucus in the respiratory tract. May also be useful in the management of dry, unproductive cough by easing expectoration of thick, viscous secretions.

Precautions: Consult a physician if cough persists for longer than 7 days or if high fever, skin rash, persistent headache, or sore throat is present with cough.

Guaifenesin may cause a color interference with certain laboratory determinations of 5-hydroxyindoleacetic acid and vanillylmandelic acid.

Adverse Effects: Nausea, gastrointestinal upset and drowsiness occur infrequently.

Dosage: Table I provides recommendations on dosing for guaifenesin.

Table I—Guaifenesin Dosage

Age (years)	Dose (mg) Every 4-6 Hours	Maximum Daily Dose (mg)
2-6	50-100	600
6-12	100-200	1 200
>12	200-400	2 400

GYNECURE™
Pfizer Consumer

Tioconazole
Antifungal Agent

Pharmacology: Tioconazole is a member of the imidazole class of antifungal agents. Although the mode of action of tioconazole has not as yet been determined, several studies have demonstrated that the imidazoles inhibit ergosterol synthesis in fungi by blocking C-14 demethylation. As a result, there is an accumulation of C-14 methyl sterol intermediates like langosterol, and a decrease in ergosterol. Langosterol cannot support yeast growth in the absence of ergosterol, and the inhibition of ergosterol synthesis or the accumulation of langosterol may be the primary antifungal mechanism of this class of drugs. At high drug concentrations the imidazoles have been postulated to exert a fungicidal effect by rapid membrane damage of the fungi.

Indications: Tioconazole vaginal ointment and ovule are indicated for the local treatment of vulvo-vaginal candidiasis (moniliasis). Cream in the Tandempak may help to relieve the vulvar itching and irritation that is commonly associated with vaginal yeast infection.

The diagnosis of vulvo-vaginal candidiasis should be confirmed by KOH smears and/or cultures before initiating therapy with the vaginal ointment or ovule.

Tioconazole vaginal ointment and ovule may be used in patients taking oral contraceptives.

Contraindications: In those patients who have a history of sensitization to tioconazole or to any of the other components of the vaginal ointment, the ovule, the vulvar cream or to other imidazole antifungal agents.

Warnings: *Pregnancy:* There are no adequate and well controlled studies which establish the safety of tioconazole vaginal ointment, ovule and the Tandempak in pregnant women.

In limited uncontrolled clinical use, the vaginal ointment and ovule applied as a single dose to about 20 patients during various stages of pregnancy did not appear to interfere with the normal progress of the pregnancy and at delivery.

However, local and systemic administration to rats indicate that adverse effects of parturition and/or fetal development were observed.

Accordingly, the vaginal ointment, ovule or Tandempak should be used during pregnancy only if in the opinion of the physician the potential benefit outweighs the potential risk to the fetus.

Lactation: It is not known whether this drug is excreted in human milk. Because many drugs are excreted in human milk, nursing should be temporarily discontinued while tioconazole preparations are administered. Tioconazole should **not** be used by nursing women unless, in the judgment of a physician, the potential benefit outweighs the possible risk.

Children: Safety and effectiveness in children have not been established.

Others: The ointment and the vulvar cream component of the Tandempak are not for ophthalmic use; the vaginal ovules are not for oral use.

Precautions: Constituents of the vaginal ointment, ovule, and Tandempak, may be incompatible with rubber in both contraceptive condoms and diaphragms.

Skin and mucosal sensitization may occur. Use of tioconazole vaginal ointment, ovule or Tandempak should be discontinued should such reaction occur, and appropriate therapy instituted.

The vaginal ointment or ovule is intended for single dose intravaginal administration only.

The safety and effectiveness of repeated application of the vaginal ointment or ovule for the use and suppression of recurrent candidiasis has not been established.

Adverse Effects: Vaginal Ointment: In 1 000 patients treated with tioconazole vaginal ointment, the most frequently observed local side effects were burning (6%) and itching (5%). In most instances these did not interfere with the course of therapy and were not transmitted to the sexual partner.

Isolated local vaginal symptoms such as irritation, discharge, labial swelling, swelling, vaginal pain, dysuria, nocturia, dyspareunia, dryness of vaginal secretions, vulva edema, desquamation and inflamed sensation, were observed. Vaginal Ovules: Out of 173 patients treated with tioconazole vaginal ovule, 3 patients (1.7%) reported burning as a sole side effect, one of which required symptomatic treatment. However, the possibility of occurrence of side effects similar to those reported for tioconazole ointment should be considered. Vulvar Cream Component of the Tandempak: This cream is the same as the dermal cream Trosyd AF and the following reactions are those associated with this cream. Symptoms of local irritation have been reported by some patients (7.2%). They are usually seen during the first week of treatment and are most often transient. The most commonly observed symptoms of local irritation reported in clinical studies were burning sensation (3.2%), itching (2.8%), erythema (1.5%), rash (0.8%) and edema (0.2%).

Treatment was discontinued in 1.9% of the patients. The principal reason for termination of treatment was the development of eczematous reactions or dermatitis.

Vulvar cream component of the Tandempak is well tolerated upon local application and no systemic adverse reactions have been observed with the dermal application of the drug.

Overdose: Symptoms and Treatment: None known.

Dosage: Vaginal Ointment, Vaginal Ovules, Tandempak: The recommended single dose treatment is 1 applicator full of ointment 6.5% w/w or 1 ovule 300 mg inserted intravaginally, preferably at bedtime. Vaginal candidiasis may be accompanied by vulval infection. Therefore, concomitant local treatment with the cream component of the Tandempak applied to the vulva and as far as the anal region once or twice daily is advisable. A small amount of the cream should be gently rubbed onto the irritated area, moving from front to back for up to 7 days as needed. The cream should not be used for vulvar itching or irritation due to causes other than a yeast infection.

In vulvo-vaginal candidiasis concomitant topical treatment of consort(s) is not necessary unless candidal dermatitis of the penis is present. To treat the male partner, a small amount of cream should be applied onto the glans penis once or twice daily for up to 7 days as needed or to help prevent reinfection by the partner.

Information for the Patient: See Blue Section—Information for the Patient "Gynecure".

Supplied: Vaginal Ointment: Each g of vaginal ointment contains: tioconazole 6.5% w/w. Nonmedicinal ingredients: aluminum magnesium silicate, butylated hydroxyanisole and white soft paraffin. Each ready to use prefilled single dose vaginal applicator delivers 4.6 g of ointment containing tioconazole 300 mg.

Vaginal Ovule: Each off-white, opaque soft gelatin ovule containing a cream-colored viscous suspension contains: tioconazole 300 mg. Nonmedicinal ingredients: beeswax, gelatin, glycerin, glycine, hydrogenated vegetable fat, lecithin, liquid paraffin, polysorbate, potassium sorbate, titanium dioxide and water. Single-unit package with 1 disposable applicator.

Tandempak: Vaginal Ointment: Each g of vaginal ointment contains: tioconazole 6.5% w/w. Nonmedicinal ingredients: aluminum magnesium silicate, butylated hydroxyanisole and white soft paraffin. Prefilled single dose vaginal disposable applicator sealed in individual wallet with a vulvar 1% cream 10 g tube in a Tandempak.

Vaginal Ovules: Each off-white, opaque soft gelatin ovule contains: tioconazole 300 mg. Nonmedicinal ingredients: beeswax, gelatin, glycerin, glycine, hydrogenated vegetable fat, lecithin, liquid paraffin, polysorbate, potassium sorbate, titanium dioxide and water. Single dose and 1 disposable applicator with a vulvar 1% cream 10 g tube in a Tandempak.

Store between 15 and 30°C. Avoid freezing.

(Shown in Product Recognition Section)

Reviewed 1997

GYNE-T® Intrauterine Copper Contraceptive
Janssen-Ortho

Intrauterine Copper
Intrauterine Contraceptive

Description: The Gyne-T copper intrauterine consists of a polyethylene support in the shape of a "T" (horizontal arm 32 mm in length and 1.59 mm in diameter. The vertical arm is 36 mm in length and 1.52 mm in diameter. The "T" carries 120 mg of copper wire (0.25 mm in diameter; 265 mm in length) wound around the vertical arm providing a nominal initial copper surface area of 208 mm². The polyethylene support contains 20% barium sulfate to provide x-ray contrast and has high density polyethylene white threads attached to the end of the vertical arm. The insertion tube is equipped with a moveable flange to aid in gauging the depth to which the insertion tube should be inserted through the cervical canal into the uterine cavity. The flange is elongated to allow the plane of the flange to occupy the same plane as the "T" arms. This facilitates insertion by ensuring that the "T" arms, when released, open in the desired direction.

Pharmacology: Available data indicate that the contraceptive effectiveness of the Gyne-T device is enhanced by a minute quantity of copper being released continuously from the copper coil into the uterine cavity. The exact mechanism by which metallic copper enhances the contraceptive effect of an intrauterine device (IUD) has not been conclusively demonstrated. Various hypotheses have been advanced, including that copper placed in the uterus interferes with enzymatic or other processes that regulate blastocyst implantation. In addition, animal studies suggest that copper may play a role in reducing sperm transport within the uterine environment. Long-term effects of the release of copper are unknown.

Indications: Intrauterine contraception. A candidate for use of the Gyne-T device is any gynecologically normal woman of child bearing age who is not pregnant and wishes to minimize the possibility of pregnancy.

Clinical studies with the Gyne-T intrauterine contraceptive device comprise experience with greater than 42 000 known insertions and 106 322 cycles of use. In addition, these investigations have involved clinics world-wide.

Effectiveness: Data are calculated by the life-table method of analysis; pregnancy rates are not expressed by the Pearl formula.

Pregnancy Rate: In a 1-year comparative study with Lippes Loop D, the pregnancy rate for the Gyne-T device was in the range of 1 to 2 per 100 women.

Eleven (68.8%) of the 16 pregnancies in Gyne-T device users occurred in 1 of the clinics which contributed only 13% of the women-months for that device. This disproportionate weighting of pregnancies in one clinic is believed to be due to the device not being placed high enough in the uterus and was accompanied by a high rate of expulsion. The statistical effect can best be illustrated in Table I (per 100 women for 1 year of use).

Table I—Gyne-T Intrauterine Copper Contraceptive

Pregnancy Rate per 100 Women for 1 Year of Use

	All Investigators Excluding Clinic A	All Investigators	Clinic A
Gyne-T Device	0.8	2.2	11.8
Lippes Loop D Device	2.8	3.0	3.9

Thus the pregnancy rate for the Gyne-T device compares very favorably with the pregnancy rates usually quoted for other available intrauterine contraceptive devices.

Effect of Time: There is no evidence of decreasing effectiveness with time up to 2 years. Monthly pregnancy rates have not shown upward trends after at least 24 months of use.

Reversibility: Fertility has been regained immediately after removing copper devices from the uteri of animals, and experience in humans lends support to a recovery of normal fertility, in most cases, after removing the device.

In the Chilean studies 68 of 73 women on whom information is available and who had the Gyne-T device removed because they desired pregnancy, became pregnant within 6 months.

In the North American studies, 13 of 17 patients became pregnant within 6 months after removing the device.

Contraindications: Pregnancy or suspicion of pregnancy, anemia, distortion of uterine cavity, acute pelvic inflammatory disease or a history of repeated pelvic inflammatory disease,

Gyne-T Intrauterine Copper Contraceptive (cont'd)

postpartum endometritis or septic abortion in the past 3 months, previous ectopic pregnancy, endometrial or cervical malignancy, unexplained genital bleeding, acute cervicitis, known or suspected allergy to copper, diagnosed Wilson's disease, valvular heart disease, leukemia, or use of chronic corticosteroid therapy because of the increased susceptibility to infection with certain microorganisms.

Warnings: *Pregnancy:* Septic Abortion: Reports have indicated an increased incidence of septic abortion, associated in some instances with septicemia, septic shock and death in patients becoming pregnant with one of several types of IUDs in place. Most of these reports have been associated with the mid trimester of pregnancy. In some cases the initial symptoms have been insidious and not easily recognized. If pregnancy should occur with an IUD in situ, the IUD should be removed if the string is visible even though removal may increase the chances of miscarriage. If a decision is made not to remove a device, or removal proves to be difficult, interruption of the pregnancy should be considered and offered as an option. If the patient elects to maintain the pregnancy and the IUD remains in situ, she should be warned that there may be an increased risk of abortion or premature labor and/or sepsis and she should be followed with close vigilance.

Ectopic Pregnancy: A pregnancy which occurs with an IUD in situ is more likely to be ectopic than a pregnancy occurring in the absence of an IUD. Therefore patients who become pregnant while using an IUD should be carefully evaluated for the possibility of an ectopic pregnancy.

Special attention should be directed to patients with delayed menses, slight metrorrhagia and/or unilateral pelvic pain, and to those patients who wish to interrupt a pregnancy occurring in the presence of the IUD, to determine whether an ectopic pregnancy has occurred.

Continuation of Pregnancy: If the patient chooses to continue the pregnancy and an IUD remains in situ, she must be warned of the increased risk of spontaneous abortion and the increased risk of sepsis, including death. The patient must be closely observed and she must be advised to report immediately all abnormal symptoms, such as a flu-like syndrome, fever, abdominal cramping and pain, bleeding or vaginal discharge, because generalized symptoms of septicemia may be insidious.

Pelvic Infection: An increased risk of pelvic inflammatory disease associated with the use of IUDs has been reported. This risk appears to be greatest for nulliparous women who have a multiplicity of sexual partners. Salpingitis can result in tubal damage and occlusion, thereby threatening future fertility. Therefore, it is recommended that patients be advised to look for and report symptoms of pelvic inflammatory disease. The decision to use an IUD in a particular case must be made by the physician and patient with consideration of a possible deleterious effect on future fertility if pelvic infection occurs.

Pelvic infection may occur with an IUD in situ and at times result in the development of tubo-ovarian abscesses or general peritonitis. The symptoms of pelvic infection include: new development of menstrual disorders (prolonged or heavy bleeding), abnormal vaginal discharge, abdominal or pelvic pain, dyspareunia, fever. The symptoms are especially significant if they occur following the first few cycles after insertion. Appropriate aerobic and anaerobic bacteriologic studies should be done and antibiotic therapy initiated promptly. If the infection does not show marked clinical improvement within 24 to 48 hours, the IUD should be removed and continuing treatment reassessed on the basis of the results of culture and sensitivity tests.

Genital actinomycosis has been associated primarily with long-term IUD use. It has been reported with copper-bearing IUDs as well. Treatment requires prompt removal of the IUD and appropriate antibiotic therapy.

Embedment: Partial penetration or lodging of the IUD in the endometrium or myometrium can increase the difficulty of removal. This may occur more frequently in smaller uteri.

Perforation: Partial or total perforation of the uterine wall or cervix may occur with the use of an IUD, most commonly during IUD insertion. The possibility of perforation must be kept in mind during insertion and at the time of any subsequent examination. If perforation occurs, laparotomy or laparoscopy should be performed as soon as medically feasible and the IUD removed. Abdominal adhesions, intestinal penetration, intestinal obstruction, and local inflammatory reaction with abscess formation and erosion of adjacent viscera may result if the IUD is left in the peritoneal cavity.

Medical Diathermy: The use of medical diathermy (short-wave and microwave) in a patient with a metal-containing IUD may cause heat injury to surrounding tissue. Therefore, medical diathermy to the abdominal and sacral areas should not be used on patients using a copper-bearing IUD.

Effects of Copper: Additional amounts of copper available to the body from a copper IUD may precipitate symptoms in women with undiagnosed Wilson's disease. The estimated incidence of Wilson's disease is 1 in 200 000.

The long-term effects of intrauterine copper on the offspring are unknown.

Malonaldehyde (MA) is a normal trace by-product of both prostaglandin biosynthesis and the oxidative breakdown of body fat, and occurs naturally in the human body. MA and related fat breakdown products have been reported to be mutagenic in a variety of test systems, and carcinogenic when applied to the skin of mice at higher than naturally occurring levels. A study has reported that levels of MA were detected in the cervical mucus of women using copper-bearing IUDs, but not in controls. The author stated that increased levels of MA within the uterus represent an increased risk of carcinogenesis. The concentrations of MA reported to be mutagenic in bacterial or cell culture systems or carcinogenic in mice are higher than the concentration of MA observed in the cervical mucus of women using copper-bearing IUDs.

Precautions: Patient Counselling: **Prior to insertion, the physician must review with the patient the risks and benefits associated with the use of this contraceptive product. The patient should be given the opportunity to discuss fully any questions she may have concerning the IUD as well as other methods of contraception and she must be fully warned of the risks associated with each method.**

Patient Evaluation and Clinical Considerations: A complete medical history should be obtained to determine conditions that might influence the selection of an IUD as a method of contraception. A physical examination should include a pelvic examination, "Pap smear", gonorrhea culture and, if indicated, appropriate tests for other forms of genital disease, including actinomycosis, which can usually be detected on the Pap test.

The uterus should be carefully sounded prior to insertion to determine the degree of patency of the endocervical canal and the internal os, and the direction and depth of the uterine cavity. Care should be exercised to avoid perforation with the sound. Occasionally, severe cervical stenosis may be encountered. Excessive force should not be used to overcome this resistance.

The uterus usually sounds to a depth of 6 to 8 cm. Insertion of an IUD into a uterine cavity measuring less than 6.5 cm by sounding may result in pain, bleeding, partial or complete expulsion, perforation, and possibly pregnancy.

To reduce the possibility of insertion in the presence of an existing undetermined pregnancy, the optimal time for insertion is the latter part of the menstrual flow or one or two days thereafter.

It is necessary to place the IUD as high as possible within the uterine cavity to help avoid partial or complete expulsion that could result in pregnancy.

Since the Gyne-T device represents a unique design in intrauterine contraception, physicians are cautioned that it is imperative for them to become thoroughly familiar with the instructions for insertion before attempting placement of the Gyne-T device.

IUDs should be used with caution in those patients who have anemia or a history of menorrhagia or hypermenorrhea. Patients experiencing menorrhagia and/or metrorrhagia following IUD insertion may be at risk for the development of anemia. As well, IUDs should be used with caution in patients receiving anticoagulants or in those with a coagulopathy.

Syncope, bradycardia or other neurovascular episodes may occur during insertion or removal of IUDs, especially in patients with a previous disposition to these conditions.

Patients with valvular or congenital heart disease are more prone to develop subacute bacterial endocarditis than patients who do not have valvular or congenital heart disease. Use of an IUD in these patients may represent a potential source of septic emboli.

Use of an IUD in those patients with acute cervicitis should be postponed until proper treatment has cleared up the infection.

Since an IUD may be partially or completely expelled, patients should be re-examined and evaluated shortly after the first post-insertion menses, but definitely within 3 months after insertion. Thereafter annual examination with appropriate medical and laboratory evaluation and a Pap smear, including examination for actinomycosis organisms, should be carried out. The Gyne-T device should be replaced every 24 months.

The patient should be told that some bleeding or cramps may occur during the first few weeks after insertion, and that if these symptoms continue or are severe she should report them to her physician. She should be instructed on how to check after each menstrual period to make certain that the thread still protrudes from the cervix and cautioned that there is no contraceptive protection if an IUD has been expelled. She should also be cautioned not to dislodge the IUD by pulling on the thread. If a partial expulsion occurs, removal is indicated and a new IUD may be inserted. The patient should be told to return within 24 months for removal of the IUD and for replacement if desired.

Rarely a copper-induced urticarial allergic skin reaction may develop in women using a copper-containing IUD. If symptoms of such an allergic response occur, the patient should be instructed to tell the consulting physician if a copper-containing device is being used.

An IUD should be removed for the following medical reasons: menorrhagia and/or metrorrhagia producing significant anemia, uncontrolled pelvic infection, genital actinomycosis, intractable pain often aggravated by intercourse, dyspareunia, pregnancy if the thread is visible, endometrial or cervical malignancy, uterine or cervical perforation, or any indication of partial expulsion.

If the retrieval thread cannot be observed, it may have retracted into the uterus, been broken off, or the IUD may have been expelled. The IUD may be located by feeling with a probe; if not, x-ray or sonography can be used.

If any patient with an IUD suddenly develops overt clinical hepatitis or abnormal liver function tests, appropriate diagnostic procedures should be initiated.

It has been reported that pregnancy rates in copper IUD users may be considerably higher among diabetics than among non diabetics. Other reports, however, indicate similar pregnancy rates in the 2 groups.

Requirements for Continuation and Removal: The Gyne-T device must be replaced before the end of the second year of use. The patient should be informed of the known duration of contraceptive efficacy and be advised to return in 2 years for removal and replacement of the device.

An IUD should be removed for the medical reasons mentioned above.

The usual method for removing the device is to exert traction on the thread. When this method is used, physicians are advised to exert traction on both strings simultaneously.

Continuing Care of Patients Using IUDs: Since an IUD may be partially or completely expelled, patients should be re-examined and evaluated shortly after the first post-insertion menses, but definitely within 3 months after insertion.

Thereafter annual examination with appropriate medical and laboratory evaluation and a Pap smear, including examination for actinomycosis organisms, should be carried out. The Gyne-T device should be replaced every 24 months.

Adverse Effects: Perforations of the uterus and cervix may occur. Perforation into the abdomen may be followed by abdominal adhesions, intestinal penetration, intestinal obstruction, local inflammatory reaction with abscess formation and erosion of adjacent viscera. Pregnancy may occur with an IUD in situ or when an IUD has been partially or completely expelled. When conception occurs with intrauterine devices in situ, the incidence of spontaneous abortion, with or without sepsis, appears to be increased over that in unprotected women. Insertion cramping, usually of no more than a few minutes' duration, may occur; however, some women may experience residual cramping for several hours or even days. Intermenstrual spotting or bleeding or prolonged or increased menstrual flow may occur.

Pelvic infection including salpingitis with tubal damage or occlusion may occur. This may result in future infertility. Complete or partial expulsion of the device may sometimes occur, particularly in those patients with uteri measuring less than 6.5 cm by sounding. Urticarial allergic skin reaction may occur.

The following complaints have also been reported with IUDs: amenorrhea or delayed menses, backaches, cervical erosion, cystic masses in the pelvis, vaginitis, leg pain or soreness, weight loss or gain, nervousness, dyspareunia, cystitis, endometritis, septic abortion, septicemia, leukorrhea, infection of reproductive organs with actinomycosis, ectopic pregnancy, difficult removal, uterine embedment, anemia, pain, neurovascular episodes including bradycardia and syncope associated with insertion or removal, dysmenorrhea, fragmentation of the copper wire on the IUD, breakage of the string.

Dosage: Device Insertion: The Gyne-T device is placed in the uterine cavity. The optimal time of insertion is during the latter part of the menstrual period or 1 or 2 days thereafter. The cervical canal is relatively patent at this time and there is little chance that the patient may then be pregnant.

The Gyne-T device must be removed and a new one inserted within 24 months from the date of insertion.

The Gyne-T represents a unique design in intrauterine contraceptives. Physicians are, therefore, cautioned that they should become thoroughly familiar with the instructions for insertion before attempting its placement. The insertion technique is different in several respects from that employed with other intrauterine contraceptives currently available, and the physician should pay particular attention to the drawings and commentary accompanying these instructions.

Pre-Insertion: It is essential that sterile technique be utilized throughout the insertion procedure. Take a medical history and perform a thorough pelvic examination to determine freedom from overt disease and to determine position and shape of the uterus. Rule out pregnancy and other contraindications to the use of the Gyne-T device. Appropriate microbiological tests, including gonorrhea cultures, should be taken. The endocervix should be cleansed with an antiseptic solution. With a speculum in place, gently insert a sterile sound to determine the depth and direction of the uterine cavity. Be sure to determine the position of the uterus before insertion. The use of a tenaculum to straighten the uterine canal prior to sounding and insertion is recommended. The Gyne-T device should preferably be inserted during or shortly after menstruation to ensure a non-pregnant state. (This approach may not be practical in certain clinical situations.)

Insertion: **Caution: It is generally believed that most perforations occur at the time of insertion, although the perforation may not be detected until some time later. The position of the uterus should be determined during the pre-insertion examination. Great care must be exercised during the pre-insertion sounding and subsequent insertion. No attempt should be made to force the insertion.**

How to Insert: Step 1: To minimize the chance of introducing contamination, do not remove the "T" from the insertion tube prior to placement in the uterus. Do not bend the arms of the "T" earlier than 5 minutes before it is to be introduced into the uterus.

Using the Loading Capsule (consult the drawing in the package insert): Place package on a flat surface with the "clear" side of the package facing upward. Peel back the top layer completely and detach the loading capsule from the insertion tube.

Push the insertion tube against the loading capsule to fold the arms of the "T".

Continue to push until the arms of the "T" are fully enclosed in the narrow end of the loading capsule.

Withdraw the insertion tube slightly until clear of the arms of the "T".

Re-insert the insertion tube while squeezing the flexible walls of the loading capsule to place the arms of the "T" inside the walls of the insertion tube. Insert no further than necessary to ensure retention of the arms.

Twist ¼ turn to free the loaded "T" and insertion tube with the loaded T. The T is now ready for insertion.

Step 2: Adjust the movable flange so that it indicates the depth to which the Gyne-T device should be inserted and the direction in which the arms of the T will open. At this point, make certain that the horizontal arms of T and the long axis of the flange lie in the same horizontal plane. Introduce the loaded inserter through the cervical canal into the uterine cavity until the T lies in contact with the fundus. The movable flange should be at the cervix. **Do not force the insertion.**

Step 3: To release the Gyne-T device from the insertion tube, hold the solid rod stationary and retract the insertion tube. This withdrawal method releases the arms of the T without further upward movement of the T.

Step 4: After the arms are released, the inserter tube should be gently moved upward until the resistance of the fundus is reached. This will assure placement of the T at the highest possible position within the endometrial cavity.

Step 5: Withdraw the solid rod while holding the insertion tube stationary.

Step 6: Withdraw the insertion tube from the cervical os until the strings are visible. Be sure sufficient length of string is visible to facilitate checking for its presence.

Supplied: Individual sterile package units plus insertion tube, solid rod and loading capsule. Boxes of 10 and 50.

Reviewed 1999

GYNE-T® 380 Slimline Intrauterine Copper Contraceptive

Janssen-Ortho

Intrauterine Copper Contraceptive

Intrauterine Contraception

Description: The intrauterine device consists of a polyethylene support in the shape of a "T". The horizontal arm is 32 mm in length and 1.59 mm in diameter. The vertical arm is 36 mm in length and 1.52 mm in diameter. The vertical arm has at its tip a spherical enlargement, 0.3 mm in diameter. The "T" carries 180 mg of copper wire (265 mm in length and 0.25 mm in diameter) wound around the vertical arm providing a nominal initial copper surface area of 320 mm^2 and one collar with 70 mg of pure copper providing an exposed surface area of 30 mm^2 on the distal portion of each transverse arm. The copper collars are continuous with the horizontal arms of the plastic "T". The polyethylene support contains 20% barium sulfate to provide x-ray contrast and has high density polyethylene white threads attached to the end of the vertical arm. The insertion tube is equipped with a moveable flange to aid in gauging the depth to which the insertion tube should be inserted through the cervical canal into the uterine cavity. The flange is elongated to allow the plane of the flange to occupy the same plane as the "T" arms. This facilitates insertion by ensuring that the "T" arms, when released, open in the desired direction.

Rationale for the Design: The theoretical advantage of placing the collars on the horizontal arms of the "T" is that the copper supply is brought closer to the fundus of the uterus. Because implantation tends to occur high in the uterus, fundal placement of the copper is considered to enhance effectiveness.

The Gyne-T 380 Slimline device has been designed so that the copper sleeves are continuous with the horizontal arms of the plastic "T". This facilitates insertion of the device.

Pharmacology: Available data indicate that the contraceptive effectiveness of the Gyne-T 380 Slimline device is enhanced by a minute quantity of copper being released continuously from the copper coil into the uterine cavity. The exact mechanism by which metallic copper enhances the contraceptive effect of an IUD has not been conclusively demonstrated. Various hypotheses have been advanced, including that copper placed in the uterus interferes with enzymatic or other processes that regulate blastocyst implantation. Animal studies suggest that copper may play a role in reducing sperm transport within the uterine environment. Long-term effects of the release of copper are unknown.

Indications: For contraception. A candidate for use of the Gyne-T 380 Slimline device is any gynecologically normal woman of child bearing age who is not pregnant and wishes to minimize the possibility of pregnancy.

Effectiveness: Data are calculated by the life-table method of analysis; pregnancy rates are not expressed by the Pearl formula.

The copper on the horizontal arms of the Gyne-T 380 Slimline device is the same diameter as the plastic "T" and is situated on the distal portion of each transverse arm as compared to the mid-section with the Gyne-T 380 Slimline device (Copper-T Model TCu 380).

The use-effectiveness of the Gyne-T 380 Slimline device is not expected to be significantly different from that seen with the Copper-T Model TCu 380.

In clinical trials conducted in the United States, use-effectiveness of the Copper-T Model TCu 380 as calculated by the Life-Table Method of Analysis was determined. (Rates are expressed as events per hundred women through 12, 24, 36 and 48 months of use.)

This experience is based on 23 126 women months of use, including 679 women who completed 12 months of use, 440 women who completed 2 years of use, 284 women who completed 3 years of use and 153 women who completed 4 years of use. Cumulative rates are shown in Table I.

Table I—Gyne-T 380 Slimline Intrauterine Copper Contraceptive

Cumulative Rates	12 months	24 months	36 months	48 months
Pregnancy	0.9	1.2	1.8	1.9
Expulsion	5.8	8.2	9.2	10.0
Medical Removal	14.6	23.9	29.5	33.7
Continual Rate	75.7	56.9	44.5	35.1

Relevance of Time of Insertion: Data are available to compare event rates for late postpartum insertion (21 to 90 days postpartum), late post abortion (21 to 90 days post abortion), interval (greater than 90 days postpartum or post abortion) and never pregnant (Sivin and Stern). No significant differences were found in two year pregnancy rates for the TCu 300 as a function of time of insertion, although the TCu 200 gave higher rates when inserted late post abortion or late post partum. Expulsion rates were moderately higher for the late postpartum and never pregnant insertion of the TCu 380 than for interval insertion. Time of insertion made little difference to removal rates for bleeding and pain, although the lowest rate among TCu 380 users was observed in last post-abortion insertions.

Age: Age at acceptance had appreciable effects on most aspects of performance. Pregnancy rates and expulsion rates among TCu 380 users at two years were highest in the below 20 age group. Removals for bleeding and pain were similar for women less than 20 years and those 20 to 24 years of age at acceptance, but slightly higher than those TCu 380 users 25 years and older.

Reversibility and Return to Fertility: Tatum (1975) has investigated the return of fertility among 420 women terminating the use of the TCu 380 or TCu 220C for the reason of planned pregnancy.

Of those who were followed subsequent to removal, 319 were reported to have conceived. Life table pregnancy rates show that 20.5% had conceived in the first calendar year month subsequent to removal and 78.1% had conceived by the end of the calendar year. There was no difference in conception rates for these 2 devices.

Effect of Time: There is no evidence of decreasing contraceptive efficacy with time before 4 years, but the contraceptive effectiveness at longer times has yet to be established; therefore, the patient should be informed of the known duration of contraceptive efficacy and be advised to return in 30 months for removal and possible reinsertion.

Contraindications: Pregnancy or suspicion of pregnancy, anemia, distortion of uterine cavity, acute pelvic inflammatory disease or a history of repeated pelvic inflammatory disease, postpartum endometritis or septic abortion in the past 3 months, previous ectopic pregnancy, endometrial or cervical malignancy, unexplained genital bleeding, acute cervicitis, known or suspected allergy to copper, diagnosed Wilson's disease, valvular heart disease, leukemia, or use of chronic corticosteroid therapy because of the increased susceptibility to infection with certain microorganisms.

Warnings: *Pregnancy:* Septic Abortion: Reports have indicated an increased incidence of septic abortion, associated in some instances with septicemia, septic shock and death in patients becoming pregnant with one of several types of IUDs in place. Most of these reports have been associated with the mid trimester of pregnancy. In some cases the initial symptoms have been insidious and not easily recognized. If pregnancy should occur with an IUD in situ, the IUD should be removed if the string is visible even though removal may increase the chances of miscarriage. If a decision is made not to remove a device, or removal proves to be difficult, interruption of the pregnancy should be considered and offered as an option. If the patient elects to maintain the pregnancy and the IUD remains in situ, she should be warned that there may be an increased risk of abortion or premature labor and/or sepsis and she should be followed with close vigilance.

Ectopic Pregnancy: A pregnancy which occurs with an IUD in situ is more likely to be ectopic than a pregnancy occurring in the absence of an IUD. Therefore, patients who become pregnant while using an IUD should be carefully evaluated for the possibility of an ectopic pregnancy.

Special attention should be directed to patients with delayed menses, slight metrorrhagia and/or unilateral pelvic pain, and to those patients who wish to interrupt a pregnancy occurring in the presence of the IUD, to determine whether an ectopic pregnancy has occurred.

Continuation of Pregnancy: If the patient chooses to continue the pregnancy and an IUD remains in situ, she must be warned of spontaneous abortion and the increased risk of sepsis, including death. The patient must be closely observed and she must be advised to report immediately all abnormal symptoms, such as a flu-like syndrome, fever, abdominal cramping and pain, bleeding or vaginal discharge, because generalized symptoms of septicemia may be insidious.

Pelvic Infection: An increased risk of pelvic inflammatory disease associated with the use of IUD's has been reported. This risk appears to be greatest for nulliparous women who have a multiplicity of sexual partners. Salpingitis can result in tubal damage and occlusion, thereby threatening future fertility. Therefore, it is recommended that patients be advised to look

Gyne-T 380 Slimline (cont'd)

for and report symptoms of pelvic inflammatory disease. The decision to use an IUD in a particular case must be made by the physician and patient with the consideration of a possible deleterious effect on future fertility if pelvic infection occurs.

Pelvic infection may occur with an IUD in situ and at times result in the development of tubo-ovarian abscesses or general peritonitis. The symptoms of pelvic infection include: new development of menstrual disorders (prolonged or heavy bleeding), abnormal vaginal discharge, abdominal or pelvic pain, dyspareunia, fever. The symptoms are especially significant if they occur following the first few cycles after insertion. Appropriate aerobic and anaerobic bacteriologic studies should be done and antibiotic therapy initiated promptly. If the infection does not show marked clinical improvement within 24 to 48 hours, the device should be removed and continuing treatment reassessed on the basis of the results of culture and sensitivity tests.

Genital actinomycosis has been associated primarily with long-term IUD use. It has been reported with copper-bearing IUDs as well. Treatment requires prompt removal of the IUD and appropriate antibiotic therapy.

Embedment: Partial penetration or lodging of the IUD in the endometrium or myometrium can increase the difficulty of removal. This may occur more frequently in smaller uteri.

Perforation: Partial or total perforation of the uterine wall or cervix may occur with the use of an IUD, most commonly during IUD insertion. The possibility of perforation must be kept in mind during insertion and at the time of any subsequent examination. If perforation occurs, laparotomy or laparoscopy should be performed as soon as medically feasible and the IUD removed. Abdominal adhesions, intestinal penetration, intestinal obstruction, and local inflammatory reaction with abscess formation and erosion of adjacent viscera may result if the IUD is left in the peritoneal cavity.

Medical Diathermy: The use of medical diathermy (short-wave and microwave) in a patient with a metal-containing IUD may cause heat injury to the surrounding tissue. Therefore, medical diathermy to the abdominal and sacral area should not be used on patients using a copper-bearing IUD.

Effects of Copper: Additional amounts of copper available to the body from a copper IUD may precipitate symptoms in women with undiagnosed Wilson's disease. The estimated incidence of Wilson's disease is 1 in 200 000.

The long-term effects of intrauterine copper on the offspring are unknown.

Malonaldehyde (MA) is a normal trace by-product of both prostaglandin biosynthesis and the oxidative breakdown of body fat, and occurs naturally in the human body. MA and related fat breakdown products have been reported to be mutagenic in a variety of test systems, and carcinogenic when applied to the skin of mice at higher than naturally occuring levels. A study (Bond et al) has reported that levels of MA were detected in the cervical mucus of women using copper-bearing IUDs, but not in controls. The author stated that increased levels of MA within the uterus represent an increased risk of carcinogenesis. The concentrations of MA reported to be mutagenic in bacterial or cell culture systems or carcinogenic in mice are higher than the concentration of MA observed in the cervical mucus of women using copper-bearing IUDs.

Precautions: Patient Counselling: **Warning: Prior to insertion, the physician must review with the patient the risks and benefits associated with the use of this contraceptive product. The patient should be given the opportunity to discuss fully any questions she may have concerning the Gyne-T 380 Slimline device as well as other methods of contraception and she must be fully warned of the risks associated with each method.**

Patient Evaluation and Clinical Considerations: A complete medical history should be obtained to determine conditions that might influence the selection of an IUD as a method of contraception. A physical examination should include a pelvic examination, Pap smear, gonorrhea culture and, if indicated, appropriate tests for other forms of genital disease, including actinomycosis, which can usually be detected on the Pap test.

The uterus should be carefully sounded prior to insertion to determine the degree of patency of the endocervical canal and the internal os, and the direction and depth of the uterine cavity. Care should be exercised to avoid perforation with the sound. Occasionally, severe cervical stenosis may be encountered. Excessive force should not be used to overcome this resistance.

The uterus usually sounds to a depth of 6 to 8 cm. Insertion of an IUD into a uterine cavity measuring less than 6.5 cm by sounding may result in pain, bleeding, partial or complete expulsion, perforation and possibly pregnancy.

To reduce the possibility of insertion in the presence of an existing undetermined pregnancy, the optimal time for insertion is the latter part of the menstrual flow or one or two days thereafter.

It is necessary to place the IUD as high as possible within the uterine cavity to help avoid partial or complete expulsion that could result in pregnancy.

Since the Gyne-T 380 Slimline device represents a unique design in intrauterine contraception, physicians are cautioned that it is imperative for them to become thoroughly familiar with the instructions for insertion before attempting placement of the Gyne-T 380 Slimline device.

IUDs should be used with caution in those patients who have anemia or a history of menorrhagia or hypermenorrhea. Patients experiencing menorrhagia and/or metrorrhagia following IUD insertion may be at risk for the development of anemia. As well, IUDs should be used with caution in patients receiving anticoagulants or in those with a coagulopathy.

Syncope, bradycardia or other neurovascular episodes may occur during insertion or removal of IUDs, especially in patients with a previous disposition to these conditions.

Patients with valvular or congenital heart disease are more prone to develop subacute bacterial endocarditis than patients who do not have valvular or congenital heart disease. Use of an IUD in these patients may represent a potential source of septic emboli.

Use of an IUD in those patients with acute cervicitis should be postponed until proper treatment has cleared up the infection.

Since an IUD may be partially or completely expelled, patients should be re-examined and evaluated shortly after the first post-insertion menses, but definitely within 3 months after insertion. Thereafter, annual examination with appropriate medical and laboratory evaluation and a Pap smear, including examination for actinomycosis organisms, should be carried out. The Gyne-T 380 Slimline device should be replaced every 30 months.

The patient should be told that some bleeding or cramps may occur during the first few weeks after insertion, and that if these symptoms continue or are severe she should report them to her physician. She should be instructed on how to check after each menstrual period to make certain that the thread still protrudes from the cervix and cautioned that there is no contraceptive protection if an IUD has been expelled. She should also be cautioned not to dislodge the IUD by pulling on the thread. If a partial expulsion occurs, removal is indicated and a new IUD may be inserted. The patient should be told to return within 30 months for removal of the IUD and for replacement if desired.

Rarely, a copper-induced urticarial allergic skin reaction may develop in women using a copper-containing IUD. If symptoms of such an allergic response occur, the patient should be instructed to tell the consulting physician that a copper containing device is being used.

An IUD should be removed for the following medical reasons: menorrhagia and/or metrorrhagia producing significant anemia, uncontrolled pelvic infection, genital actinomycosis, intractable pain often aggravated by intercourse, dyspareunia, pregnancy if the thread is visible, endometrial or cervical malignancy, uterine or cervical perforation, or any indication of partial expulsion.

If the retrieval thread cannot be observed, it may have retracted into the uterus, have been broken off, or the IUD may have been expelled. Localization usually may be made by feeling with a probe; if not, x-ray or sonography can be used.

If any patient with an IUD suddenly develops overt clinical hepatitis or abnormal liver function tests, appropriate diagnostic procedures should be initiated.

It has been reported that pregnancy rates in copper IUD users may be considerably higher among diabetics than among non-diabetics. Other reports, however, indicate similar pregnancy rates in the 2 groups.

Requirements for Continuation and Removal: The Gyne-T 380 Slimline device must be replaced before the end of the 30 months of use. The patient should be informed of the known duration of contraceptive efficacy and be advised to return in 30 months for removal and replacement.

An IUD should be removed for the medical reasons referred to in Precautions above.

The usual method for removing the device is by exerting traction on the thread. When this method is used, physicians are advised to exert traction on both strings simultaneously.

Continuing Care of Patients Using IUDs: Since an IUD may be partially or completely expelled, patients should be re-examined and evaluated shortly after the first post-insertion menses, but definitely within 3 months after insertion. Thereafter annual examination with appropriate medical and laboratory evaluation and a Pap smear, including examination for actinomycosis organisms, should be carried out. The Gyne-T 380 Slimline device should be replaced every 30 months.

Adverse Effects: Perforations of the uterus and cervix may occur. Perforation into the abdomen may be followed by abdominal adhesions, intestinal penetration, intestinal obstruction, local inflammatory reaction with abscess formation and erosion of adjacent viscera. Pregnancy may occur with an IUD in situ or when it has been partially or completely expelled. When conception occurs with intrauterine devices in situ, the incidence of spontaneous abortion, with or without sepsis, appears to be increased over that in unprotected women. Insertion cramping, usually of no more than a few minutes duration, may occur; however, some women may experience residual cramping for several hours or even days. Intermenstrual spotting or bleeding or prolonged or increased menstrual flow may occur.

Pelvic infection including salpingitis with tubal damage or occlusion may occur. This may result in future infertility.

Complete or partial expulsion of the device may sometimes occur, particularly in those patients with uteri measuring less than 6.5 cm by sounding. Urticarial allergic skin reactions may occur.

The following complaints have also been reported with IUD's: amenorrhea or delayed menses, backaches, cervical erosion, cystic masses in the pelvis, vaginitis, leg pain or soreness, weight loss or gain, nervousness, dyspareunia, cystitis, endometritis, septic abortion, septicemia, leukorrhea, infection of reproductive organs with actinomycosis, ectopic pregnancy, difficult removal, uterine embedment, anemia, pain, neurovascular episodes including bradycardia and syncope associated with insertion or removal, dysmenorrhea, fragmentation of the copper wire on the IUD and breakage of the string.

Dosage: Device Insertion: The Gyne-T 380 Slimline device is placed in the uterine cavity. The optimal time of insertion is during the latter part of the menstrual period or 1 or 2 days thereafter. The cervical canal is relatively patent at this time and there is little chance that the patient may then be pregnant.

The Gyne-T 380 Slimline device must be removed and a new one inserted within 30 months from the date of insertion.

The physician should become thoroughly familiar with the instructions for insertion before attempting placement of the Gyne-T 380 Slimline device.

Matters to Discuss With Your Patient: (1) What the patient should know about the Gyne-T 380 Slimline IUD.
(2) Use Effectiveness.
(3) Preconditions: (a) What the patient must tell the physician. (b) Adverse reactions. (c) Contraindications.
(4) Post-Insertion Instructions: (a) Ongoing care of the IUD. (b) Side effects. (c) Warnings and need for follow-up: severe or prolonged bleeding; pelvic pain and cramps; venereal disease; allergic reactions–rash; no medical diathermy; pregnancy and IUD; removal; change every 30 months.

This list is to assist the physician in providing information and warning to the patient. Although this list is provided as a matter of convenience, the physician must familiarize himself/herself thoroughly with the detailed information and warnings relating to this product set out in the enclosed prescribing brochure.

Instructions for Insertion: The Gyne-T 380 Slimline Intrauterine Copper Contraceptive represents a unique design in intrauterine contraceptives. Physicians are therefore cautioned that they should become thoroughly familiar with instructions for insertion before attempting placement of the Gyne-T 380 Slimline device. The insertion technique is different in several respects from that employed with other intrauterine contraceptives currently available, and the physician should pay particular attention to the drawings and commentary accompanying these instructions.

Pre-Insertion: It is essential that sterile technique be utilized throughout the insertion procedure. Take a medical history and perform a thorough pelvic examination to determine freedom from overt disease and to determine position and shape of the uterus. **Rule out pregnancy and other contraindications.** Appropriate microbiological tests including, gonorrhea cultures, should be taken. The endocervix should be cleansed with an antiseptic solution. With a speculum in place, gently insert a sterile sound to determine the depth and direction of the uterine cavity. Be sure to determine the position of the uterus before insertion. The use of a tenaculum to straighten the uterine canal prior to sounding and insertion is recommended. The Gyne-T 380 Slimline device should preferably be inserted during or shortly after menstruation to ensure a non-pregnant state. (This approach may not be practical in certain clinical situations.)

Insertion: **Caution: It is generally believed that most perforations occur at the time of insertion, although the perforation may not be detected until some time later. The position of the uterus should be determined during the pre-insertion examination. Great care must be exercised during the pre-insertion sounding and subsequent insertion. No attempt should be made to force the insertion.**

How to Insert (see package insert for illustrations):

Step 1: To minimize the chance of introducing contamination, do not remove the **"T" from the insertion tube prior to placement in the uterus. Do not bend the arms of the "T" earlier than 5 minutes before it is to be introduced into the uterus.**

Using the Loading Capsule: Place package on a flat surface with the "clear" side of the package facing upward. Peel back the top layer completely and detach the loading capsule from the insertion tube.

Push the insertion tube against the loading capsule to fold the arms of the "T".

Continue to push until the arms of the "T" are fully enclosed in the narrow end of the loading capsule.

Withdraw the insertion tube slightly until clear of the arms of the "T".

Reinsert the insertion tube while squeezing the flexible walls of the loading capsule to place the arms of the "T" inside the walls of the insertion tube. Insert no further than necessary to ensure retention of the arms.

Twist a quarter turn to disengage the "T" and the insertion from the capsule. The "T" is now ready for insertion.

Step 2: Adjust the moveable flange so that it indicates the depth to which the Gyne-T 380 Slimline device should be inserted and the direction in which the arms of the "T" will open. At this point, make certain that the horizontal arms of "T" and the long axis of the flange lie in the same horizontal plane. Introduce the loaded inserter through the cervical canal into the uterine cavity (do not take out until the "T" lies in contact with the fundus). The moveable flange should be at the cervix. **Do not force the insertion.**

Step 3: To release the Gyne-T 380 Slimline device from the insertion tube, hold the solid rod stationary and retract the insertion tube. This withdrawal method releases the arms of the "T" without further upward movement of the "T".

Step 4: After the arms are released, the inserter tube should be gently moved upward until the resistance of the fundus is reached. This will assure placement of the "T" at the highest possible position within the endometrial cavity.

Step 5: Withdraw the solid rod while holding the insertion tube stationary.

Step 6: Withdraw the insertion tube from the cervical os until the strings are visible. Be sure sufficient length of string is visible to facilitate checking for its presence.

Supplied: The Gyne-T 380 Slimline Intrauterine Copper Contraceptive is packaged in individual sterile package units plus insertion tube, solid rod and loading capsule. Boxes of 10 and 50.

(Shown in Product Recognition Section)

Reviewed 1999

H

HABITROL®

Novartis Consumer Health

S(-)-Nicotine

Smoking Cessation Aid

Pharmacology: Habitrol delivers S(-)-nicotine, the active component of tobacco smoke, transdermally into the systemic circulation, continuously over 24 hours. Habitrol releases S(-)-nicotine in controlled amounts at a rate sufficient to produce plasma nicotine concentrations comparable to trough levels observed in smokers before smoking a cigarette. Because of the low, continuous delivery of S(-)-nicotine through the skin, Habitrol does not produce the rapid increases in plasma nicotine concentrations that occur with cigarette smoking and which are primarily responsible for smoking's addictive effects. Habitrol has been shown to increase rates of cessation in smokers who are motivated to quit.

Indications: As a temporary aid used to facilitate smoking cessation in smokers who strongly desire to give up their smoking habit. Habitrol is intended to be used as part of a smoking cessation strategy and should, whenever possible, be combined with behavior modification therapy.

Contraindications: In nonsmokers, occasional smokers and children under 18 years of age (see Warnings).

Known hypersensitivity of the skin, allergy to nicotine or Habitrol components; generalized skin disorders; recovery phase of acute myocardial infarction, unstable or worsening angina pectoris, severe cardiac arrhythmias and recent cerebrovascular accident.

Pregnancy and *Lactation:* Any form of nicotine administration is contraindicated in pregnant and breast-feeding women.

Warnings: In view of its pharmacological effects, S(-)-nicotine should not be used in smokers with the following conditions unless there has been careful consideration of the risks and benefits of therapy: hypertension, stable angina pectoris, variant (Prinzmetal's) angina, cerebrovascular disease, occlusive peripheral arterial and vasospastic diseases, heart failure, hyperthyroidism, diabetes mellitus, renal and hepatic insufficiency, peptic ulcer. Use of Habitrol in these smokers should only be considered if tobacco withdrawal with psychological support alone has been unsuccessful. If these smokers continue to smoke while wearing Habitrol, excessive nicotine levels could be produced that can exacerbate pre-existing diseases and can cause serious adverse reactions (see Adverse Effects).

Adult smokers tolerate doses of nicotine that can be poisonous or fatal to children and pets. Both new and used Habitrol systems contain enough nicotine to cause serious harm if applied or ingested. Therefore, it is important that smokers keep both new and used systems out of the reach of children and pets (see Information for the Patient for the recommended disposal procedure).

Treatment with Habitrol should be discontinued in cases of severe or persistent skin reactions.

No experience is available on treatment with Habitrol in smokers under 18 years of age and is limited in ages 65 years and above.

Precautions: Continued Smoking and Adverse Reactions: If the user continues to smoke while wearing Habitrol, adverse reactions consistent with excessive nicotine exposure, including cardiovascular effects, may be more frequent and more pronounced.

Strenuous Exercise: Preliminary evidence suggests that wearing a nicotine transdermal patch during periods of strenuous exercise may lead to nicotine toxicity as a result of increased absorption of nicotine from the depot of nicotine in the skin under the patch, due to increased skin temperature and increased cutaneous vasodilation and perfusion from exercising. Three cases illustrating this phenomenon were described in Health Canada Adverse Reaction Newsletter, Volume 6, No. 1, Jan. 1996. Advice to remove the nicotine patch before engaging in strenuous exercise was recommended by: W. Dafoe and P. Huston, Current Trends in Cardiac Rehabilitation, Canadian Medical Association Journal, Feb 15, 1997; 156 (14): 527-532. Until definitive studies have been undertaken to clarify this hazard, it is advisable to remove the nicotine patch prior to engaging in strenuous activity.

Occupational Hazards: Effects on Ability to Drive or Use Machines: Nicotine acts as a central nervous stimulant agent. While no direct effect on reaction time is to be expected, the smoker should be cautioned that sleep disturbance, irritability and nervousness may occur during smoking cessation, and could affect performance.

Drug Interactions: To date, no information is available on interactions between S(-)-nicotine and any other drugs. Experience with other forms of nicotine replacement therapy has shown that there are no pharmacodynamic or pharmacokinetic interactions of clinical relevance with various concomitant treatments.

Tobacco withdrawal, with or without nicotine substitution, may alter the response to concomitant medication in ex-smokers. Through enzyme induction, smoking is thought to increase the metabolism—and thus lower the blood levels—of drugs such as antipyrine, caffeine, phenacetin, imipramine, lidocaine, pentazocine, warfarin, theophylline, oxazepam, lorazepam, desmethyldiazepam and estrogens. Smoking cessation may result in increased blood levels of these drugs, therefore requiring appropriate adaptation of dose. Smoking reduces the analgesic efficacy of propoxyphene. Absorption of s.c. insulin may be increased upon cessation of smoking.

Although the relevance to transdermal nicotine therapy is unknown, reported drug interactions with smoking which do not involve alteration of pharmacokinetics (e.g., enzyme induction) include: increased cortisol concentrations; increased circulating levels of catecholamines necessitating dose adjustments for adrenergic agonists (e.g., phenylephrine, isoproterenol), adrenergic α and β receptor antagonists, (e.g., prazosin and propranolol, respectively) and calcium channel blockers (e.g., nifedipine); reduced diuretic response to furosemide, and reduced clinical efficacy of H_2-antagonists.

Cessation of smoking may reverse these actions.

Contact Sensitization to Nicotine: Contact sensitization to nicotine has been reported in transdermal nicotine users. Smokers developing this contact sensitization should be cautioned against using nicotine-containing products. Delayed type hypersensitivity reactions (e.g., generalized urticaria, edema) or severe allergic reactions could result.

Adverse Effects: In principle, S(-)-nicotine can cause adverse reactions similar to those associated with nicotine administered by smoking, or those that accompany tobacco withdrawal, especially in the gastrointestinal and CNS systems. However, since the plasma S(-)-nicotine concentrations reached with Habitrol are substantially lower and fluctuate less than those produced by smoking, nicotine related adverse reactions occurring during treatment with Habitrol can be expected to be less marked. If the user continues to smoke while wearing Habitrol, adverse reactions consistent with excessive nicotine exposure may be more frequent and more pronounced. Severe and fatal adverse reactions have occurred in smokers who continued to smoke while using nicotine transdermal systems. Smokers are strongly advised to stop smoking during Habitrol therapy, especially high-risk smokers, as described in Warnings.

The most commonly reported adverse effect associated with Habitrol in clinical trials was skin reaction at the application site. This was responsible for about 6% of premature discontinuations and included symptoms such as erythema, pruritus, edema, burning sensation, blisters, rash and pinching. Most cases were mild in severity, usually resolving within 48 hours, but in more severe cases erythema and infiltration lasted 1 to 3 weeks. The majority of cases with notable symptoms of erythema (severity: well-defined, moderate or severe) and edema (severity: very slight, slight or moderate) occurred within 3 to 8 weeks. There have been isolated reports of skin reactions beyond the application site. The incidence of cutaneous hypersensitivity is 1.5 to 2.0%.

The most commonly reported adverse reactions/withdrawal symptoms reported (considered possibly related to Habitrol) in 3 double-blind trials, irrespective of causal association, were as shown in Table I.

Table I—Habitrol

Adverse Reactions

Body System	Adverse Event	Habitrol (N=401) %	Placebo (N=391) %
CNS	Headache	29.7	29.2
	Dizziness	6.0	5.9
	Insomnia	6.5	5.4
	Anxiety	3.7	4.6
	Emotional lability	2.2	2.8
	Irritability	2.2	2.8
	Abnormal dreaming	2.0	1.0
Respiratory, Ears, Nose and Throat	Cold and flu-like symptoms	12.0	8.4
	Pharyngitis	4.0	3.6
	Sinusitis	3.2	2.8
	Coughing	2.7	1.5
	Rhinitis	2.5	3.1
	Upper respiratory symptoms	2.2	2.3
Gastrointestinal	Nausea	6.2	4.6
	Diarrhea	4.5	5.1
	Dyspepsia	5.2	4.4
	Abdominal pain	3.5	1.5
	Constipation	2.2	3.3
Musculoskeletal	Myalgia	6.1	4.0
	Back pain	4.7	5.6
	Arthralgia	3.5	4.1
	Arthritis	2.0	1.0
Dermatological	Application site reaction	34.9	17.6
Miscellaneous	Dysmenorrhea	6.6	8.8
	Toothache	3.5	3.6
	Allergy	2.7	1.5

Adverse events having an incidence of <2% (causality not established) were also reported as shown in Table II.

Overdose: Symptoms and Treatment: The toxicity of nicotine cannot be directly compared to that of smoking, since tobacco smoke contains additional toxic substances (e.g., carbon monoxide and tar).

Acute Toxic Effects: The acute lethal oral dose of nicotine in nonsmoking adults is about 40 to 60 mg. In children the following signs and symptoms have been reported after ingestion of tobacco products: vomiting, agitation, nausea, diarrhea, pallor, weakness, absence of reaction and twitching of the extremities. In nonsmoking adults the following signs and symptoms have been reported in cases of severe nicotine poisoning: pallor, sweating, nausea, salivation, vomiting, abdominal cramps, diarrhea, headache, dizziness, tremor, mental confusion, hearing and visual disturbances, muscular

Table II—Habitrol

Adverse Reactions

Body System	Incidence Rates: Incidence between 1-2%	Incidence ≤1%
CNS	Somnolence, Impaired concentration	Taste perversion, Abnormal vision, Paresthesia, Memory impairment, Confusion, Agitation, Twitching
Respiratory, Ears, Nose and Throat	Bronchitis, Earache	Dyspnea
Gastrointestinal	Vomiting	Gastric ulcer, Flatulence, Abnormal stool, Dysphagia
Cardiovascular	Chest pain, Blood pressure changes	Hot flushes, Local edema, Extrasystoles, Palpitations, Hypertension
Dermatological	Rash, Herpetic rash	Pruritus, Urticaria, Acne
Oral Cavity		Dry mouth, Gingivitis
Musculoskeletal		Leg cramps
Miscellaneous	Fatigue	Angioneurotic edema, Thyroid disorders, Lymph gland tenderness, Cytosis, Increased appetite, Increased sweating, Migraine

Habitrol (cont'd)

weakness, convulsions, prostration, absence of neurological reaction and respiratory failure. Lethal doses quickly produce convulsions, and death follows as a result of cardiac failure or (more frequently) peripheral or central respiratory paralysis.

Chronic smoking causes the development of tolerance, which means that chronic smokers can tolerate acute, highly toxic doses of nicotine.

The application of several Habitrol systems simultaneously, could result in serious overdosage. The effects of chewing and swallowing Habitrol are unknown.

Chronic Toxic Effects: No experience has been obtained with S(-)-nicotine treatment longer than 3 months' duration.

Management of Excessive Topical Exposure: If the smoker shows signs of overdosage, Habitrol should be removed immediately. The skin may be washed with water only, as soap may facilitate absorption. Owing to a depot of nicotine in the skin, delivery of nicotine to the bloodstream will continue for several hours afterward.

Management of Nicotine Poisoning: In cases of severe poisoning, the following measures are recommended: supportive measures for seizure control, warming the body to normal temperature, artificial respiration in the case of respiratory failure, atropine for excessive bronchial secretions and vigorous fluid support for pronounced hypotension or cardiovascular collapse.

Dosage: When starting treatment with Habitrol, the smoker should stop smoking completely.

One Habitrol system should be applied daily and left on the skin for 24 hours.

If the smoker has been unable to maintain or otherwise re-establish initial abstinence with the aid of Habitrol after 1 month, the treatment should be discontinued.

Prolonged continuous use of Habitrol should not exceed 3 months.

Treatment is divided into 3 components: selection and evaluation of an initial dosage strength, a maintenance phase and a weaning phase. Treatment may be completed in as little as 7 weeks, but more typically lasts 9 to a maximum of 12 weeks. The dosage strengths employed, and the duration of use of each, depend upon the individual smoker's response. Tobacco withdrawal must be accompanied by behavioral support at all times.

Selection and Evaluation: Treatment is initiated with Habitrol 21 mg/day or 14 mg/day, depending on the number of cigarettes smoked per day. Habitrol 21 mg/day is usually recommended for smokers with a consumption of more than 20 cigarettes a day. Habitrol 14 mg/day is usually sufficient for smokers with a consumption of up to 20 cigarettes daily. The dosage strength may be adjusted early in the maintenance phase in response to either the appearance of side effects or difficulty in maintaining abstinence.

Maintenance: The intial dosage strength selected should generally be worn for 3 to 4 weeks, but this period may be extended. Consideration may be given to an extension of this period to 6 to 8 weeks if Habitrol 14 mg/day was selected as the initial dosage strength.

Weaning: The goal of a stepwise reduction from Habitrol 21 mg/day to the lowest dosage strength is accomplished by an intermediate step employing Habitrol 14 mg/day, typically worn for 3 to 4 weeks, whereas Habitrol 7 mg/day is employed directly after maintenance on Habitrol 14 mg/day. Habitrol 7 mg/day, designed to reduce nicotine substitution toward the end of therapy and consolidate abstinence, should typically be worn for 3 to 4 weeks. The weaning phase may be compressed if the maintenance phase has been extended.

After completing treatment with Habitrol it is advisable for behavioral therapy to be continued.

No experience is available on treatment with Habitrol in smokers below the age of 18 and is limited in ages 65 years and above (see Warnings).

Administration: To avoid evaporative loss of nicotine, and as a matter of safety concerning accidental exposure of children and pets, the system should be applied promptly after its removal from the protective pouch. After removing the release liner (first the smaller strip and then the larger portion), the Habitrol system should be applied to a clean, oil-free, nonhairy, dry, intact area of skin on the trunk, or the upper outer arm. A different site of application should be chosen each day, and no site should be re-used within 1 week. The smoker should be advised that the system not be worn for longer than 24 hours, and to dispose of used systems out of the reach of children and pets. For detailed instructions see Information for the Patient.

Note: Dosage adjustment cannot be achieved by cutting a transdermal system. This will cause the nicotine to evaporate rapidly, and render the pieces ineffective.

Safety Note Concerning Children: Nicotine is a highly toxic substance. Doses of nicotine which are tolerated by adults during treatment with Habitrol can produce severe symptoms of poisoning in small children (see Warnings). Even after use, Habitrol contains more than half its initial nicotine content. Therefore smokers must be cautioned that new and used systems must not be handled casually or left where they may be misused (by application) or ingested.

Similarly, care must also be taken when disposing of used systems (for detailed instructions see Information for the Patient).

Information for the Patient: See Blue Section—Information for the Patient "Habitrol".

Supplied: See Table III. Nonmedicinal ingredients: acrylate vinylacetate, copolymers, fractionated coconut oil and methacrylic acid esters copolymers.

Table III—Habitrol

Dosage Forms

	Habitrol 7 mg/day	Habitrol 14 mg/day	Habitrol 21 mg/day
Average dose (mg) of S(-)-nicotine delivered in vivo during 24 hours	7	14	21
Content of S(-)-nicotine (mg)	17.5	35	52.5
Drug releasing area (cm^2)	10	20	30
Printed code (on backing film)	CWC	FEF	EME

The total amount of S(-)-nicotine in the reservoir is needed to maintain the delivery pattern as required while the system is being worn.

Since the amount of S(-)-nicotine released from Habitrol per cm^2 is constant, the dose administered is determined solely by the size of the contact area of the system.

Boxes of 7 patches. Store below 25°C. Do not store unpouched. Apply immediately upon removal from the protective pouch.

(Shown in Product Recognition Section)

Reviewed 1999

HALCINONIDE ℞

General Monograph, CPhA

see CORTICOSTEROIDS: TOPICAL

HALCION® ℞

Pharmacia & Upjohn

Triazolam

Hypnotic

Pharmacology: Triazolam is a benzodiazepine hypnotic with a very short elimination half-life (about 3 hours).

In sleep laboratory studies of 1 to 21 days duration, triazolam significantly decreased sleep latency, increased duration of sleep and decreased the number of nocturnal awakenings. However, after 2 weeks of consecutive nightly administration, the drug's effect on total wake time was decreased, and the values recorded in the last third of the night approached baseline levels. On the first and/or second night after drug discontinuance (first or second post-drug night), total time asleep, and percentage of time spent sleeping frequently were significantly decreased, and sleep latency significantly increased when compared to baseline (predrug) nights. This effect is often called "rebound" insomnia.

The duration of hypnotic effect and the profile of unwanted effects may be influenced by the alpha (distribution) and beta (elimination) half-lives of the administered drug and any active metabolites formed. When half-lives are long, the drug or metabolites may accumulate during periods of nightly administration and be associated with impairments of cognitive and motor performance during waking hours. If half-lives are short, the drug and metabolites will be cleared before the next dose is ingested, and carry-over effects related to sedation or CNS depression should be minimal or absent. However, during nightly use and for an extended period, pharmacodynamic tolerance or adaptation to some effects of benzodiazepine hypnotics may develop. If the drug has a very short elimination half-life, it is possible that a relative deficiency (i.e., in relation to the receptor site) may occur at some point in the interval between each night's use. This sequence of events may account for two clinical findings reported to occur after several weeks of nightly use of rapidly eliminated benzodiazepine hypnotics: 1) increased wakefulness during the last third of the night and 2) the appearance of increased day-time anxiety (see Warnings).

When sedation and psychomotor performance were compared in healthy elderly and young subjects, in response to 0.125 and 0.25 mg doses of triazolam, the degree of sedation was greater and the impairment of psychomotor performance more pronounced in the elderly. The age dependent difference was closely associated with the correspondingly higher plasma triazolam concentrations measured in elderly subjects.

Patients with severe liver disease also demonstrated greater psychomotor impairment than control subjects or patients with minimal liver dysfunction.

Pharmacokinetics: Triazolam is rapidly absorbed and peak plasma levels are reached within 2 hours following oral administration. Peak plasma concentration (C_{max}) and area under the plasma-concentration curve (AUC) increase in proportion to the dose, while the time to peak plasma concentration (T_{max}), elimination half-life ($t\frac{1}{2}\beta$), and clearance are independent of dose. Triazolam has a short half-life; the range is reported to be 1.5 to 5.5 hours.

Triazolam is metabolized via hepatic microsomal oxidation. The hydroxylated metabolites, which are inactive, are excreted primarily in the urine as conjugated glucuronides. The two primary metabolites account for approximately 80% of the urinary excretion.

Repeated administration of triazolam for 7 days does not lead to accumulation and does not alter the rate of elimination.

Pharmacokinetics in the elderly: The kinetics of triazolam are significantly influenced by age (see Table I). Following single oral doses of 0.125 mg and 0.25 mg of triazolam, peak plasma concentrations and area under the curve were significantly higher and clearance significantly lower in elderly subjects (mean age: 69 years) than in younger ones (mean age: 30 years). Age, however, did not influence the time to peak plasma levels and differences in elimination half-life were small.

Pharmacokinetics in Patients With Renal Failure: Following oral administration of triazolam, 0.5 mg, peak plasma triazolam concentrations were lower in 11 patients with renal failure undergoing dialysis (4.04±1.83 ng/mL) than in patients with normal renal function (6.54±1.70 ng/mL). Other pharmacokinetic parameters were not significantly different between patients with impaired and normal renal function.

Pharmacokinetics in Patients With Hepatic Failure: Following oral administration of triazolam, 0.25 mg, triazolam clearance was reduced in 8 subjects with biopsy-proven cirrhosis (4.99±3.14 mL/min/kg) as compared to 7 normal subjects (6.69±2.52 mL/min/kg). Peak plasma levels and time to peak concentration were not different between the groups. The

Table I—Halcion

Mean (± standard deviation) Pharmacokinetic Parameters Following Single Oral Doses of Triazolam in Young and Elderly Volunteers

	Triazolam 0.125 mg		Triazolam 0.25 mg	
Parameter	**Young (n=26)**	**Elderly (n=21)**	**Young (n=26)**	**Elderly (n=21)**
C_{max} (ng/mL)	1.08±0.08	1.67±0.16*	2.02±0.15	3.06±0.22*
T_{max} (hr)	0.88±0.08	0.95±0.11	0.96±0.10	0.88±0.07
AUC (ng/mL.hr)	3.85±0.45	6.24±0.82*	7.01±0.68	12.03±1.11*
$t\frac{1}{2}\beta$ (hr)	2.94±0.4	3.03±0.25	2.43±0.16	3.00±0.24*
Clearance (mL/min/kg)	11.4±2.2	6.8±0.9*	10.5±1.0	5.8±0.4*

*Statistically significant for young versus elderly at indicated dose.

reduction in triazolam clearance in subjects with cirrhosis correlated with the severity of liver dysfunction.

Indications: For the short-term treatment and symptomatic relief of insomnia characterized by difficulty in falling asleep, frequent nocturnal awakenings and/or early morning awakenings.

Treatment with triazolam should usually not exceed 7 to 10 consecutive days. Use for more than 2 to 3 consecutive weeks requires complete re-evaluation of the patient.

The use of hypnotics should be restricted for insomnia where disturbed sleep results in impaired daytime functioning.

Contraindications: In patients with known hypersensitivity to the drug or any component of its formulation, and in those with severe impairment of respiratory function, e.g., significant sleep apnea syndrome.

Pregnancy: Triazolam is contraindicated in pregnant women. Benzodiazepines may cause fetal damage when administered during pregnancy. During the first trimester of pregnancy, several studies have suggested an increased risk of congenital malformations associated with the use of benzodiazepines. During the last weeks of pregnancy, ingestion of therapeutic doses of a benzodiazepine hypnotic has resulted in neonatal CNS depression due to transplacental distribution. If triazolam is prescribed to women of childbearing potential, the patient should be warned of the potential risk to a fetus and advised to consult her physician regarding the discontinuation of the drug if she intends to become pregnant.

Triazolam is contraindicated in patients who have a history of uncorrected narrow-angle glaucoma.

Warnings: General: Sleep disturbance may be the presenting manifestation of a physical and/or psychiatric disorder. Consequently, a decision to initiate symptomatic treatment of insomnia should only be made after the patient has been carefully evaluated.

The failure of insomnia to remit after 7 to 10 days of treatment may indicate the presence of a primary psychiatric and/or medical illness.

Worsening of insomnia or the emergence of new abnormalities of thinking or behavior may be the consequence of an unrecognized psychiatric or physical disorder. These have also been reported to occur in association with the use of triazolam.

Triazolam should be used with caution in patients who in the past manifested paradoxical reactions to alcohol and/or sedative medications.

Triazolam should be used with caution in patients who have myasthenia gravis or severe hepatic insufficiency.

> Memory Disturbance:
>
> • Anterograde amnesia of varying severity has been reported following therapeutic doses of benzodiazepines including triazolam. Anterograde amnesia is a dose-related phenomenon and elderly subjects may be at a particular risk. Data from several sources suggest that anterograde amnesia and next day memory loss may occur at a higher rate with triazolam than with other benzodiazepines.
>
> • Cases of transient global amnesia and "traveler's amnesia" have also been reported in association with triazolam, the latter in individuals who have taken the drug to induce sleep while travelling. Transient global amnesia and traveler's amnesia are unpredictable and not necessarily dose-related phenomena. Patients should be warned not to take triazolam under circumstances in which a full night's sleep and clearance of the drug from the body are not possible before they need again to resume full activity (e.g., an overnight flight of less than 7 to 8 hours).

Abnormal thinking and psychotic behavioral changes have been reported to occur in association with the use of benzodiazepine hypnotics including triazolam. Some of the changes may be characterized by decreased inhibition, e.g., aggressiveness or extroversion that seem excessive, similar to that seen with alcohol and other CNS depressants (e.g., sedative/hypnotics). Particular caution is warranted in patients with a history of violent behavior. Psychotic behavioral changes that have been reported include bizarre behavior, hallucinations, and depersonalization. Abnormal behaviors associated with triazolam have been reported more with chronic use or high doses.

It can rarely be determined with certainty whether a particular instance of the abnormal behaviors listed above is drug induced, spontaneous in origin, or a result of an underlying psychiatric or physical disorder. Nevertheless, the emergence of any new behavioral sign or symptom of concern requires careful and immediate evaluation.

Confusion: The benzodiazepines affect mental efficiency, e.g., concentration, attention and vigilance. The risk of confusion is greater in the elderly and in patients with cerebral impairment.

Anxiety, Restlessness: An increase in daytime anxiety (interdose rebound anxiety) and/or restlessness have been observed during treatment with triazolam. This may be a manifestation of interdose withdrawal, due to the very short elimination half-life of the drug.

Depression: Caution should be exercised if triazolam is prescribed to patients with signs or symptoms of depression that could be intensified by hypnotic drugs. Suicidal tendencies, e.g., intentional overdose, is more common in these patients thus, the least amount of drug that is feasible should be available to them at any one time.

Precautions: *Drug Interactions:* Triazolam produces additive CNS depressant effects when coadministered with alcohol, antihistamines, anticonvulsants, or psychotropic medications which themselves can produce CNS depression.

Pharmacokinetic interactions can occur when triazolam is administered along with drugs that interfere with its metabolism. Examples include cimetidine or erythromycin which when coadministered with triazolam cause an approximate doubling of the plasma levels and elimination half-life of triazolam. Consequently, consideration of dose reduction may be appropriate when patients are treated concomitantly with triazolam and either cimetidine or erythromycin.

When a single oral 0.25 mg dose of triazolam was coadministered with nefazodone (200 mg bid) at steady state, triazolam peak concentrations, half-life, and AUC were increased 1.7-, 3- and 4-fold respectively. The pharmacokinetics of nefazodone were not altered. The concomitant use of triazolam and nefazodone was also associated with an increase in psychomotor impairment presumably due to increased triazolam plasma concentrations. The interactive effects of higher doses of these agents have not been studied. The concomitant use of nefazodone and triazolam should be avoided.

Drug Abuse, Dependence and Withdrawal: Withdrawal symptoms, similar in character to those noted with barbiturates and alcohol (convulsions, tremor, abdominal and muscle cramps, vomiting, sweating, dysphoria, perceptual disturbances and insomnia) have occurred following abrupt discontinuance of benzodiazepines, including triazolam. The more severe symptoms are usually associated with higher dosages and longer usage, although patients given therapeutic dosages for as few as 1 to 2 weeks can also have withdrawal symptoms, including **daytime anxiety,** between nightly doses (see Pharmacology and Warnings). Consequently, abrupt discontinuation should be avoided and a gradual dosage tapering schedule is recommended in any patient taking more than the lowest dose for more than a few weeks. The recommendation for tapering is particularly important in patients with a history of seizures.

The risk of dependence is increased in patients with a history of alcoholism, drug abuse, or in patients with marked personality disorders (see Warnings). Interdose daytime anxiety and rebound anxiety may increase the risk of dependency in triazolam-treated patients.

As with all hypnotics, repeat prescriptions should be limited to those who are under medical supervision.

Patients with Specific Conditions: Triazolam should be given with caution to patients with impaired hepatic or renal function, severe pulmonary insufficiency, or sleep apnea. Respiratory depression and apnea have been reported in patients with compromised respiratory function.

Occupational Hazards: Because of triazolam's CNS depressant effect, patients receiving the drug should be cautioned against engaging in hazardous occupations requiring complete mental alertness such as operating machinery or driving a motor vehicle. For the same reason, patients should be warned against the concomitant ingestion of triazolam and alcohol or CNS depressant drugs.

Pregnancy: For teratogenic effects see Contraindications. Non-teratogenic Effects: A child born to a mother who is on benzodiazepines may be at some risk for withdrawal symptoms from the drug during the postnatal period. Also, neonatal flaccidity has been reported in an infant born to a mother who had been receiving benzodiazepines.

Lactation: Human studies have not been performed but studies in rats have shown that triazolam and its metabolites are secreted in the milk. Therefore, administration of triazolam to nursing mothers is not recommended.

Children: The safety and effectiveness of triazolam in children below the age of 18 have not been established.

Geriatrics: Elderly patients are especially susceptible to dose-related adverse effects, such as drowsiness, dizziness, or impaired coordination. Therefore, the lowest possible dose should be used in these subjects.

Adverse Effects: The most frequent adverse reactions associated with the use of triazolam are extensions of the pharmacological effects of the drug, e.g., sedation (morning drowsiness, somnolence), dizziness, nervousness/irritability and impaired coordination.

The most serious adverse reactions which may occur include memory impairment, abnormal thinking/behavior, confusion, anxiety, and depression (see Warnings).

The incidence of adverse reactions among patients receiving triazolam or placebo is listed in Table II. The figures cannot be used to predict precisely the incidence of untoward events in the course of usual medical practice where patient characteristics and other factors often differ from those in clinical trials. Comparison of the cited figures, however, can provide the prescriber with some basis for estimating the relative contributions of drug and nondrug factors to the untoward event incidence rate in the population studied.

The adverse reaction profile of triazolam observed in controlled clinical trials illustrates the dose-dependency of most of the adverse reactions. **At present, the higher dose range is not recommended** (see Dosage).

Rare (i.e., less than 0.5%) adverse reactions include dysesthesia/paresthesia, dream abnormalities, drug abuse/habituation, drug withdrawal symptoms, hallucinations, muscle tone

Table II—Halcion

Percent of Patients Reporting Adverse Reactions (≥0.5%)

Body System	Adverse Reaction	Triazolam 0.1-0.3 mg N=1002	Triazolam 0.4-0.6 mg N=2370	Placebo N=2036
CNS	drowsiness/sedation	9.5	18.6	14.5
	headache	5.9	8.1	6.2
	dizziness	4.4	9.0	5.8
	nervousness/irritability	3.7	4.6	6.4
	impaired coordination	1.7	4.3	1.2
	insomnia	1.0	1.2	2.8
	confusion	0.7	1.0	0.5
	mood changes	0.7	0.8	0.7
	depression	0.5	1.1	0.7
	memory impairment	0.2	1.0	0
Metabolic/Nutrition	appetite change	0	0.5	0.6
Special Senses	visual disturbance	0.4	0.7	0.2
	taste alteration	0.4	0.6	0.3
Cardiovascular	palpitations	0.5	0.4	0.4
Respiratory	respiratory infection	1.1	1.7	0.9
Gastrointestinal	nausea/vomiting	2.9	3.8	3.5
	dry mouth	0.5	0.9	1.4
	abdominal pain/discomfort	0.4	0.6	0.5
	diarrhea	0.2	0.8	0.1
Musculoskeletal	musculoskeletal/joint pain	0.8	0.9	0.7

Halcion (cont'd)

disorder, tremor, tinnitus, hearing impairment, eye irritation/redness, edema, chest pain, hot/cold flashes, hypertension, syncope, dyspnea, constipation, flatulence, oral irritation, micturition difficulties, dermatitis, diaphoresis, muscular cramps, muscular weakness, malaise, sexual dysfunction. Elevated levels of AST, bilirubin, and alkaline phosphatase have also been noted.

Overdose: Symptoms and Treatment: Manifestations of triazolam overdosage include extensions of its pharmacological effects, namely, somnolence, confusion, impaired coordination, slurred speech, and ultimately, coma. Respiratory depression and apnea have been reported with overdosages of triazolam.

Death has been reported in association with overdoses of triazolam by itself, as it has with other benzodiazepines. In addition, fatalities have been reported in patients who have overdosed with a combination of alcohol and a single benzodiazepine, including triazolam. In some of these cases, blood levels of the benzodiazepine and alcohol were lower than those usually associated with reports of fatalities with either substance alone.

As in all cases of drug overdosage, respiration, pulse and blood pressure should be monitored and supported by general measure when necessary. Immediate gastric lavage should be performed. An adequate airway should be maintained. I.V. fluids may be administered. As with the management of intentional overdosage with any drug, the physician should bear in mind that multiple agents may have been ingested by the patient.

The benzodiazepine antagonist, flumazenil, is a specific antidote in known or suspected benzodiazepine overdose. (For conditions of use, see Anexate product monograph.)

Experiments in animals have indicated that cardiopulmonary collapse can occur with massive i.v. doses of triazolam. This could be reversed with positive mechanical respiration and i.v. infusion of norepinephrine bitartrate or metaraminol bitartrate. Hemodialysis and forced diuresis are probably of little value.

Dosage: The lowest effective dose should be used. Treatment with triazolam should usually not exceed 7 to 10 consecutive days. Use for more than 2 to 3 consecutive weeks requires complete re-evaluation of the patient.

The starting dose in all patients should be 0.125 mg; for many patients this dose immediately before retiring should be sufficient. In most adults, a dose of 0.25 mg should not be exceeded. A dose of 0.5 mg should be used only for exceptional patients who do not respond adequately to a trial of the lower dose since the risk of several adverse reactions increases with the size of the dose administered.

For elderly, or debilitated patients and patients with disturbed liver/kidney function, the dose should not exceed 0.125 mg before retiring. The 0.25 mg dose should be used only for exceptional patients who do not respond to a trial of the lower dose.

Information for the Patient: See Blue Section—Information for the Patient "Halcion".

Supplied: Each powder blue, scored tablet branded "Upjohn 17" contains: triazolam 0.25 mg. Nonmedicinal ingredients: cellulose, cornstarch, docusate sodium, FD&C Blue No. 2, lactose, magnesium stearate and silicon dioxide. Gluten-free. Blister packages of 7, cartons of 10 blister packages. Store at controlled room temperature (15 to 30°C).

(Shown in Product Recognition Section)

Reviewed 1999

HALDOL® Ⓟ

Janssen-Ortho

Haloperidol

Antipsychotic

Pharmacology: Haloperidol is a butyrophenone derivative with antipsychotic properties that has been considered particularly effective in the management of hyperactivity, agitation, and mania. Haloperidol is an effective neuroleptic and also possesses antiemetic properties; it has a marked tendency to provoke extrapyramidal effects and has relatively weak alpha-adrenolytic properties. It may also exhibit hypothermic and anorexiant effects and potentiate the action of barbiturates, general anesthetics, and other CNS depressant drugs.

As with other neuroleptics, the mechanism of action of haloperidol has not been entirely elucidated, but has been attributed to the inhibition of the transport mechanism of cerebral monoamines, particularly by blocking the impulse transmission in dopaminergic neurons.

Pharmacokinetics: Peak plasma levels of haloperidol occur within 2 to 6 hours of oral dosing and about 20 minutes after i.m. administration. The mean plasma (terminal elimination) half-life has been determined as 20.7±4.6 (SD) hours, and although excretion begins rapidly, only 24 to 60% of ingested radioactive drug is excreted (mainly as metabolites in urine, some in feces) by the end of the first week, and very small but detectable levels of radioactivity persist in the blood and are excreted for several weeks after dosing. About 1% of the ingested dose is recovered unchanged in the urine.

Indications: Management of manifestations of acute and chronic psychosis, including schizophrenia and manic states. It may also be of value in the management of aggressive and agitated behavior in patients with chronic brain syndrome and mental retardation and in the symptomatic control of Gilles de la Tourette's syndrome.

Contraindications: In comatose states and in the presence of CNS depression due to alcohol or other depressant drugs. It is also contraindicated in patients with severe depressive states, previous spastic diseases, lesions of the basal ganglia, and in Parkinson's syndrome, except in the case of dyskinesias due to levodopa treatment. It should not be used in patients known to be sensitive to the drug, nor in senile patients with preexisting Parkinson-like symptoms.

Children: Safety and effectiveness in young children have not been established; therefore, haloperidol is contraindicated in this age group.

Pregnancy and *Lactation:* Haloperidol has shown no significant increase in fetal anomalies in large population studies. There have been isolated case reports of birth defects following fetal exposure to haloperidol in combination with other drugs. It should, therefore, not be administered to women of childbearing potential or nursing mothers unless, in the opinion of the physician, the expected benefits of the drug outweigh the potential hazard to the fetus or child. Haloperidol is excreted in breast milk. Extrapyramidal symptoms have been observed in breast-fed infants of haloperidol-treated women.

Warnings: Rare cases of sudden death have been reported in psychiatric patients receiving antipsychotic drugs, including haloperidol. Since QT-prolongation has been observed during haloperidol treatment, it is advisable to be cautious in patients with QT-prolonging conditions (QT-syndrome, hypokalemia, drugs known to prolong QT).

Tardive Dyskinesia: Tardive dyskinesia is known to occur in patients treated with neuroleptics with antipsychotic properties and other drugs with substantial neuroleptic activity.

Although the dyskinetic syndrome may remit partially or completely if the medication is withdrawn, it is irreversible in some patients. At the present time there is uncertainty as to whether neuroleptic drugs differ in their potential to cause tardive dyskinesia.

Since there is a significant prevalence in this syndrome associated with the use of neuroleptic drugs, and since there is no known effective treatment, chronic use of these drugs should generally be restricted to patients for whom neuroleptics are known to be effective and for whom there is no alternative therapy available with better risk acceptability. If manifestations of tardive dyskinesia are detected during the use of a neuroleptic, the drug should be discontinued.

The risk of a patient developing tardive dyskinesia and of the syndrome becoming irreversible appear to increase with the duration of treatment and the total amount of drugs administered, although, in some instances, tardive dyskinesia may develop after relatively short periods of treatment at low doses. The risk of developing tardive dyskinesia may, therefore, be minimized by reducing the dose of the neuroleptic drug used and its duration of administration, consistent with the effective management of the patient's condition. Continued use of neuroleptics should be periodically reassessed.

Withdrawal Emergent Neurological Signs: Generally, patients receiving short-term therapy experience no problems with abrupt discontinuation of antipsychotic drugs. However, some patients on maintenance treatment experience transient dyskinetic signs after abrupt withdrawal. In certain cases the dyskinetic movements are indistinguishable from the syndrome described under Tardive Dyskinesia except for duration.

It is not known whether gradual withdrawal of antipsychotic drugs will reduce the rate of occurrence of withdrawal emergent neurological signs but until further evidence becomes available it seems reasonable to gradually withdraw use of antipsychotic drugs.

In rare cases, the following symptoms were reported during the concomitant use of lithium and haloperidol: encephalopathy, extrapyramidal symptoms, tardive dyskinesia, neuroleptic malignant syndrome, brain stem disorder, acute brain syndrome and coma. Most of these symptoms were reversible; it remains unclear whether this represents a distinct clinical entity. Nonetheless, it is advised that in patients who are treated concomitantly with lithium and haloperidol, therapy should be stopped immediately if such symptoms occur.

Elderly or debilitated patients receiving the drug should be carefully observed for lethargy and a decreased sensation of thirst due to central inhibition which might lead to dehydration and reduced pulmonary ventilation and could result in complications, such as terminal bronchopneumonia.

Occupational Hazards: Although haloperidol is a relatively non-sedating neuroleptic, sedation may occur in some patients. Therefore, physicians should be aware of this possibility and caution patients about the danger of participating in activities requiring complete mental alertness, judgment and physical coordination, such as driving and operating dangerous machinery.

Haloperidol may prolong the hypnotic action of barbiturates and may potentiate the effects of alcohol and other CNS depressant drugs such as anesthetics and narcotics; caution should therefore be exercised when it is used with agents of this type and adjustments in their dosage may be required.

Precautions: Administration to patients with severe cardiac involvement should be guarded, despite the fact that haloperidol is well tolerated by patients with cardiac insufficiency and that it has been used with favorable results to maintain the cardiovascular function of patients with excitive crises. In very rare instances, it has been felt that haloperidol was contributory to the precipitation of attacks in angina-prone patients. Moderate hypotension may occur with parenteral administration or excessive oral doses of haloperidol; however, vertigo and syncope occur only rarely.

It has been reported that seizures can be triggered by haloperidol. Caution is advised in patients suffering from epilepsy and in conditions predisposing to convulsions such as alcohol withdrawal and brain damage.

As with other antipsychotic agents, haloperidol should be administered cautiously to patients with severe impairment of liver or kidney function, and to patients with known allergies, or history of allergies to other neuroleptic drugs.

Haloperidol has lowered the level of cholesterol in the serum and liver of monkeys. An accumulation of desmosterol has been observed in the serum of rats given repeated high doses (10 mg/kg) of haloperidol. In man, mild transient decreases in serum cholesterol were reported in preliminary studies. However, in a study involving a group of schizophrenic patients on extended medication, significant lowering of serum cholesterol was not observed with haloperidol, and there was no accumulation of desmosterol or 7-dehydrocholesterol. A significant lowering of cholesterol together with an accumulation of another sterol (possibly 7-dehydrocholesterol) has been reported in patients receiving a chemically related drug (trifluperidol), and skin and eye changes (ichthyosis and cataracts) have occurred clinically with another butyrophenone derivative. Skin and eye changes have not been observed in patients receiving haloperidol. However, it is advisable that all patients receiving haloperidol for a prolonged period of time should be carefully observed for any changes in the skin and eyes. If such changes are seen, the drug should be discontinued promptly.

Drug Interactions: Haloperidol has been reported to interfere with the anticoagulant properties of phenindione in an isolated case, and the possibility should be kept in mind of a similar effect occurring when haloperidol is used with other anticoagulants.

Haloperidol may antagonize the action of epinephrine and other sympathomimetic agents and reverse the blood-pressure-lowering effects of adrenergic-blocking agents such as guanethidine. Enhanced CNS effects have been reported when haloperidol is used in combination with methyldopa.

As with all antipsychotic agents, haloperidol should not be used alone where depression is predominant. It may be combined with antidepressants to treat those conditions in which depression and psychosis coexist.

If concomitant antiparkinson medication is required, it may have to be continued after stopping haloperidol if its excretion is faster than that of haloperidol in order to avoid the development or aggravation of extrapyramidal symptoms.

Haloperidol inhibits the metabolization of tricyclic antidepressants, thereby increasing plasma levels of these drugs.

In pharmacokinetic studies, mild to moderately increased haloperidol levels have been reported when haloperidol was given concomitantly with the following drugs: quinidine, buspirone, fluoxetine. It may be necessary to reduce the haloperidol dosage.

When prolonged treatment with enzyme-inducing drugs such as carbamazepine, phenobarbital, rifampin is added to haloperidol therapy, this results in a significant reduction of haloperidol plasma levels. Therefore, during combination treatment, the haloperidol dose should be adjusted, when necessary. After stopping such drugs, it will be necessary to reduce the dosage of haloperidol.

Haloperidol may impair the antiparkinson effects of levodopa. If an antiparkinson agent is used concomitantly with haloperidol, both drugs should not be discontinued simultaneously, since extrapyramidal symptoms, previously controlled by antiparkinson agents, may occur due to the slower excretion rate of haloperidol.

The physician should keep in mind the possibility of an increase in intraocular pressure when anticholinergic drugs, including antiparkinson agents, are administered concomitantly with haloperidol.

When haloperidol is used to control mania in cyclic disorders, there may be a rapid mood swing to depression.

The antiemetic action of haloperidol may obscure signs of toxicity due to overdosage of other drugs or mask the symptoms of some organic diseases, such as brain tumor or intestinal obstructions.

Severe neurotoxicity (rigidity, inability to walk or talk) may occur in patients with thyrotoxicosis who are also receiving antipsychotic medication, including haloperidol.

Carcinogenicity studies in mice (18 months) and rats (24 months) showed a significant increase in mammary gland neoplasia and total tumor incidence in female mice at 1.25 and 5 mg/kg/day and in pituitary gland neoplasia in female mice at 5 mg/kg. A significant dose-related increase in pituitary gland hyperplasia was observed in female rats at 1.25 and 5 mg/kg/day. The potential significance of these findings in man is not known. Neuroleptic drugs elevate prolactin levels; the elevation persists during chronic administration. Tissue culture experiments indicate that approximately one-third of human breast cancers are prolactin dependent in vitro, a factor of potential importance if the prescription of these drugs is contemplated in a patient with a previously detected breast cancer. Although disturbances such as galactorrhea, amenorrhea, gynecomastia, and impotence have been reported, which are presumed to be linked to elevated prolactin levels, the clinical significance of elevated serum prolactin levels is unknown for most patients. An increase in mammary neoplasms has been found in rodents after chronic administration of neuroleptic drugs. Neither clinical studies nor epidemiologic studies conducted to date, however, have shown an association between chronic administration of these drugs and mammary tumorigenesis. The available evidence is considered too limited to be conclusive at this time.

Occupational Hazards: Effects on driving ability and use of machinery: Some degree of sedation or impairment of alertness may occur, particularly with higher doses and at the start of treatment and may be potentiated by alcohol. Patients should be advised not to drive or operate machinery during treatment, until their susceptibility is known.

Adverse Effects: Neurological effects are the most common.

Extrapyramidal Symptoms: In common with all neuroleptics, extrapyramidal symptoms may occur, e.g., tremor, rigidity, hypersalivation, bradykinesia, akathisia, acute dystonia. Headache, vertigo and cerebral seizures have also been reported. The extrapyramidal reactions are usually dose-related in occurrence and severity and, as a rule, tend to subside when the dose is reduced or the drug is temporarily discontinued. However, considerable inter-patient variability exists, and, although some individuals may tolerate higher than average doses of haloperidol, severe extrapyramidal reactions, necessitating discontinuation of the drug, may occur at relatively low doses.

Antiparkinson drugs of the anticholinergic type may be prescribed as required, but should not be prescribed routinely as a preventive measure.

Tardive Dyskinesia: As with all antipsychotic agents, tardive dyskinesia may appear in some patients on long-term therapy or may appear after drug therapy has been discontinued. The syndrome is characterized by rhythmical involuntary movements of the tongue, face, mouth or jaw (e.g., protrusion of tongue, puffing of cheeks, puckering of mouth, chewing movements). Sometimes these may be accompanied by involuntary movements of extremities. The manifestations may be permanent in some patients.

The syndrome may be masked when treatment is reinstituted, when the dosage is increased or when a switch is made to a different antipsychotic drug. Treatment should be discontinued as soon as possible.

Tardive dystonia, not associated with the above syndrome, has also been reported. Tardive dystonia is characterized by delayed onset of choreic or dystonic movements, is often persistent, and has the potential of becoming irreversible.

Other CNS Effects: Insomnia, depressive reactions, and toxic confusional states are the more common effects encountered. Drowsiness, lethargy, stupor and catalepsy, confusion, restlessness, agitation, anxiety, euphoria, vertigo, grand mal seizures, and exacerbation of psychotic symptoms, including hallucinations, have also been reported.

Cardiovascular: Tachycardia, hypertension, and ECG changes including ventricular arrhythmias and/or prolongation of the QT-interval and ECG pattern changes compatible with the polymorphous configurations of torsades de pointes have been reported. Hypotension has occurred, but severe orthostatic hypotension has not been reported. However, should it occur, supportive measures, including i.v. vasopressors such as norepinephrine, may be required. **Epinephrine should not be used,** since haloperidol may block the vasoconstrictor effects of this drug.

Autonomic: Dry mouth, blurred vision, urinary retention, incontinence, diaphoresis and priapism, erectile dysfunctions, peripheral edema, excessive perspiration or salivation, heartburn, and body temperature disregulation have been reported.

Allergic and Toxic: The overall incidence of significant hematologic changes in patients on haloperidol has been low. Occasionally there have been reports of mild and usually transient leukopenia and leukocytosis, decreases in blood cell counts, anemia, and a tendency toward lymphomonocytosis. Agranulocytosis and thrombocytopenia have rarely been reported with the use of haloperidol, and then only in association with other medication. Impairment of liver function (jaundice or hepatitis, most often cholestatic) has been reported rarely. One case of photosensitization is known and isolated cases of idiosyncratic cutaneous involvement have been observed.

Endocrine: Hormonal effects of antipsychotic neuroleptic drugs include hyperprolactinemia, which may cause galactorrhea, gynecomastia and oligo- or amenorrhea. Lactation, breast engorgement, mastalgia, menstrual irregularities, gynecomastia, impotence, increased libido and changes in blood sugar levels and very rare cases of Syndrome of Inappropriate ADH Secretion have been reported.

Gastrointestinal: Heartburn, nausea, vomiting, anorexia, weight loss, constipation, diarrhea and hypersalivation have been reported.

Miscellaneous: Other untoward effects encountered include peripheral edema, hypocholesterolemia, alopecia, laryngospasm, bronchospasm and increased depth of respiration and stasis pneumonia. Hyperammonemia has been reported in a 5 ½-year-old child with citrullinemia, an inherited disorder of ammonia excretion, following treatment with haloperidol.

Cases of sudden and unexpected death have been reported in association with the administration of haloperidol. The nature of the evidence makes it impossible to determine definitively what role, if any, haloperidol played in the outcome of the reported cases. The possibility that haloperidol caused death cannot, of course, be excluded, but it is to be kept in mind that sudden and unexpected death may occur in psychotic patients when they go untreated or when they are treated with other neuroleptic drugs.

Neuroleptic Malignant Syndrome: As with other neuroleptic drugs, a symptom complex sometimes referred to as neuroleptic malignant syndrome (NMS) has been reported. Cardinal features of NMS are hyperpyrexia, generalized muscle rigidity, altered mental status (including catatonic signs), and evidence of autonomic instability (irregular pulse or blood pressure). Hyperthermia is often an early sign of this syndrome. Additional signs may include elevated CPK, myoglobinuria (rhabdomyolysis), and acute renal failure. NMS is potentially fatal, requires intensive symptomatic treatment and immediate discontinuation of neuroleptic treatment.

Hyperpyrexia and heat stroke, not associated with the above symptom complex, has also been reported.

Overdosage: Symptoms: In general, the symptoms of overdosage would be an exaggeration of known pharmacologic effects and adverse reactions, the most prominent of which would be 1) severe extrapyramidal reactions, 2) hypotension, or 3) sedation. The patient would appear comatose with respiratory depression and hypotension which could be severe enough to produce a shock-like state. The extrapyramidal reaction would be manifest by muscular weakness or rigidity and a generalized or localized tremor as demonstrated by the akinetic or agitans types respectively.

In extreme cases, the patient would appear comatose with respiratory depression and hypotension that could be severe enough to produce a shock-like state. The risk of ventricular arrhythmias, possibly associated with QT-prolongation, should be considered. (For further information regarding torsades de pointes, see Adverse Effects.)

Treatment: Since there is no specific antidote, treatment is primarily supportive but gastric lavage or induction of emesis is advised (unless the patient is obtunded, comatose or convulsing) followed by administration of activated charcoal. For comatose patients, a patent airway must be established by use of an oropharyngeal airway or endotracheal tube or in prolonged cases of coma, by tracheostomy. Respiratory depression may be counteracted by artificial respiration and mechanical respirators. Hypotension and circulatory collapse may be counteracted by use of i.v. fluids, plasma, or concentrated albumin, and vasopressor agents such as norepinephrine. Epinephrine should not be used since it may cause profound hypotension in the presence of haloperidol. In case of severe extrapyramidal reactions, antiparkinson medication should be administered. ECG and vital signs should be monitored especially for signs of QT-prolongation or dysrhythmias and monitoring should continue until the ECG is normal. Severe arrhythmias should be treated with appropriate antiarrhythmic measures.

Dosage: Initial dosage should be individualized through consideration of severity of symptoms, age, weight, health, previous response to neuroleptic drugs, and concomitant disease states. It is important initially to increase dosage adequately until symptoms are controlled or side effects requiring lowering the dosage or discontinuing the drug are encountered. When a satisfactory therapeutic response is achieved, dosage should then be reduced gradually to the lowest effective maintenance level. Patients with previous adverse responses to other neuroleptic drugs, children, and the elderly or debilitated may require less haloperidol. The optimal response in such patients is best obtained if therapy is initiated at a lower dosage level and titration is more gradual.

Parenteral: When symptoms are severe or rapid control is desired, haloperidol may be administered i.m. Dosages in the range of 2.5 to 5 mg are recommended, and should be employed on a prn basis until the desired effect is achieved. Administration every 4 to 6 hours is sufficient in most cases, although for resistant patients the dosage may be repeated as often as every hour if required. Parenteral administration of high doses may be accompanied by rapid appearance of extrapyramidal effects as control of symptomatology is achieved.

Clinical experience has shown that it is seldom necessary to employ dosages greater than 4 to 6 mg t.i.d. However, 30 to 40 mg daily may be required in severely disturbed patients who remain inadequately controlled by lower doses, and up to 100 mg daily has been used occasionally in particularly resistant patients.

Nevertheless, the safety of prolonged administration of the higher doses has not been established. After a therapeutic response has been achieved, dosages should be gradually adjusted downwards until a schedule providing adequate maintenance is reached. Maintenance dosages are commonly in the range of 2 mg t.i.d. or q.i.d.

Children: The safety and effectiveness of i.m. administration in children have not been established.

Elderly or Debilitated Patients: Lower doses are recommended in these patients since they may be more sensitive to the drug. Initially, daily doses ranging from 0.5 to 1.5 mg (0.25 to 0.5 mg, 2 or 3 times a day) should be employed. Upward adjustment of these doses should be made gradually; maximum and maintenance doses should be individualized and are generally lower in this type of patient.

The oral dosage form should supplant the injectable as soon as practicable. For an initial approximation of the total daily dose required, the parenteral dose administered in the preceding 24 hours may be used.

Since this dose is only an initial estimate, it is recommended that careful monitoring of clinical signs and symptoms, including clinical efficacy, sedation, and adverse effects, be carried out periodically for the first several days following the initiation of switchover. In this way, dosage adjustments, either upward or downward, can be quickly accomplished. Depending on the patient's clinical status, the first oral dose should be given within 12-24 hours following the last parenteral dose.

Supplied: Each mL ampul contains: haloperidol 5 mg (as a lactate). Nonmedicinal ingredients: lactic acid sufficient to adjust the pH within the range of 3.0 to 3.6, methylparaben, propylparaben and water. **Do not dilute with sterile saline.** Ampuls of 1 mL, units of 10. Store at controlled room temperature (15 to 30°C). Protect from light. Do not freeze.

Reviewed 1999

HALDOL® LA ℞

Janssen-Ortho

Haloperidol Decanoate

Antipsychotic

Pharmacology: Haloperidol decanoate, an ester derivative of haloperidol obtained from condensation of haloperidol with decanoic acid possesses the antipsychotic properties of haloperidol. When it is administered as an i.m. depot in sesame oil, esterases present in blood and tissues hydrolyze haloperidol decanoate to provide a slow release of the active neuroleptic haloperidol from the depot into the systemic circulation. The onset of action occurs within a few days after injection and the therapeutic effect continues for 2 to 4 weeks, although adequate control is frequently maintained with 1 injection every 4 weeks. Careful supervision is required throughout treatment due to the variations in individual patient response.

Haloperidol decanoate possesses antiemetic properties; it has a marked tendency to provoke extrapyramidal effects and has relatively weak alpha-adrenolytic properties. It may also exhibit hypothermic and anorexiant effects and potentiate the action of barbiturates, general anesthetics, and other CNS depressant drugs.

As with other neuroleptics, the mechanism of action of haloperidol decanoate has not been entirely elucidated, but has been attributed to the inhibition of the transport mechanism of cerebral monoamines by haloperidol, particularly by blocking the impulse transmission in dopaminergic neurons.

Pharmacokinetics: The pharmacokinetics of haloperidol decanoate were studied in chronic psychotic patients receiving monthly injections for up to 2 years. The initial dose was based on the observation that the bioavailability of oral haloperidol is 60 to 70%, corresponding to a monthly dose of haloperidol decanoate of about 20 times the daily oral dose. Patients were switched abruptly from their previous oral maintenance medication and plasma levels of haloperidol were measured at fixed intervals after injections. At the end of the first 4-week period, plasma haloperidol levels were similar to steady state levels attained with oral administration; however, the levels immediately following injection were considerably higher. Accumulation of plasma levels was observed for the first 3 to 6 months, after which a steady state was reached at levels about 2 to 3 times higher than in the first month of treatment.

Depending on the dose (25 to 400 mg equivalents of haloperidol), at the end of injection period steady state levels ranged from about 1 to 13 ng/mL; this range of blood levels is similar to that found in patients administered oral haloperidol.

Plasma haloperidol levels were also measured in patients who first received haloperidol decanoate in the 50 mg eq/mL concentration and subsequently were given the 100 mg eq/mL concentration. No significant differences in plasma levels were observed.

The half-life has been estimated at about 3 weeks. Haloperidol is metabolized in the liver and excreted in urine and feces.

Indications: Is of value in the management of manifestations of chronic schizophrenia.

Contraindications: In comatose states and in the presence of CNS depression due to alcohol or other depressant drugs. It is also contraindicated in patients with severe depressive states, previous spastic diseases, lesions of the basal ganglia and in Parkinson's syndrome, except in the case of dyskinesias due to levodopa treatment. It should not be used in patients known to be sensitive to the drug, nor in senile patients with preexisting Parkinson-like symptoms.

Children: Safety and effectiveness in children have not been established; therefore, haloperidol decanoate is contraindicated in this age group.

Pregnancy and *Lactation:* Haloperidol decanoate has shown no significant increase in fetal anomalies in large population studies. There have been isolated case reports of birth defects following fetal exposure to haloperidol decanoate in combination with other drugs. It should, therefore, not be administered to women of childbearing potential or nursing mothers unless, in the opinion of the physician, the expected benefits of the drug outweigh the potential hazard to the fetus or child. Haloperidol is excreted in breast milk. Extrapyramidal symptoms have been observed in breast-fed infants of haloperidol decanoate-treated women.

Warnings: Rare cases of sudden death have been reported in psychiatric patients receiving antipsychotic drugs, including haloperidol decanoate. Since QT-prolongation has been observed during haloperidol decanoate treatment, it is advised to be cautious in patients with QT-prolonging conditions (QT-syndrome, hypokalemia, drugs known to prolong QT).

Tardive Dyskinesia: Tardive dyskinesia is known to occur in patients treated with neuroleptics with antipsychotic properties and other drugs with substantial neuroleptic activity. Although the dyskinetic syndrome may remit partially or completely if the medication is withdrawn, it is irreversible in some patients. At the present time there is uncertainty as to whether neuroleptic drugs differ in their potential to cause tardive dyskinesia.

Since there is a significant prevalence in this syndrome associated with the use of neuroleptic drugs, and since there is no known effective treatment, chronic use of these drugs should generally be restricted to patients for whom neuroleptics are known to be effective and for whom there is no alternative therapy available with better risk acceptability. If manifestations of tardive dyskinesia are detected during the use of a neuroleptic, the drug should be discontinued.

The risk of a patient developing tardive dyskinesia and of the syndrome becoming irreversible appear to increase with the duration of treatment and the total amount of drugs administered, although, in some instances, tardive dyskinesia may develop after relatively short periods of treatment at low doses. The risk of developing tardive dyskinesia may, therefore, be minimized by reducing the dose of the neuroleptic drug used and its duration of administration, consistent with the effective management of the patient's condition. Continued use of neuroleptics should be periodically reassessed.

Withdrawal Emergent Neurological Signs: Generally, patients receiving short-term therapy experience no problems with abrupt discontinuation of antipsychotic drugs. However, some patients on maintenance treatment experience transient dyskinetic signs after withdrawal. In certain of these cases the dyskinetic movements are indistinguishable from the syndrome described above under Tardive Dyskinesia, except for duration. It is not known whether gradual withdrawal of antipsychotic drugs will reduce the rate of occurrence of withdrawal emergent neurological signs but, until further evidence becomes available, it seems reasonable to gradually withdraw use of antipsychotic drugs.

In rare cases the following symptoms were reported during the concomitant use of lithium and haloperidol: encephalopathy, extrapyramidal symptoms, tardive dyskinesia, neuroleptic malignant syndrome, brain stem disorder, acute brain syndrome and coma. Most of these symptoms were reversible; it remains unclear whether this represents a distinct clinical entity. Nonetheless, it is advised that in patients who are treated concomitantly with lithium and haloperidol, therapy should be stopped immediately if such symptoms occur.

Elderly or debilitated patients receiving the drug should be carefully observed for lethargy and a decreased sensation of thirst due to central inhibition, which might lead to dehydration and reduced pulmonary ventilation, and could result in complications such as terminal bronchopneumonia.

Occupational Hazards: Although haloperidol is a relatively nonsedating neuroleptic, sedation may occur in some patients. Therefore, physicians should be aware of this possibility and caution patients about the danger of participating in activities requiring complete mental alertness, judgment, and physical coordination, such as driving and operating dangerous machinery.

Haloperidol may prolong the hypnotic action of barbiturates and may potentiate the effects of alcohol and other CNS depressant drugs, such as anesthetics and narcotics; caution should, therefore, be exercised when it is used with agents of this type and adjustments in their dosage may be required.

Precautions: Administration to patients with severe cardiac involvement should be guarded, despite the fact that haloperidol is well tolerated by patients with cardiac insufficiency and that it has been used with favorable results to maintain the cardiovascular function of patients with excitive crises. In very rare instances, it has been felt that haloperidol was contributory to the precipitation of attacks in angina-prone patients. Moderate hypotension may occur with parenteral administration or excessive oral doses of haloperidol; however, vertigo and syncope occur only rarely.

It has been reported that seizures can be triggered by haloperidol decanoate. Caution is advised in patients suffering from epilepsy and in conditions predisposing to convulsions (e.g., alcohol withdrawal and brain damage).

As with other antipsychotic agents, haloperidol should be administered cautiously to patients with severe impairment of liver or kidney function, and to patients with known allergies, or history of allergies to other neuroleptic drugs. Caution is also advised in patients with pheochromocytoma and conditions predisposing to epilepsy, such as alcohol withdrawal and brain damage.

Haloperidol has lowered the level of cholesterol in the serum and liver of monkeys. An accumulation of desmosterol has been observed in the serum of rats given repeated high doses (10 mg/kg) of haloperidol. In man, mild transient decreases in serum cholesterol were reported in preliminary studies. However, in a study involving a group of schizophrenic patients on extended medication, significant lowering of serum cholesterol was not observed with haloperidol, and there was no accumulation of desmosterol or 7-dehydrocholesterol. A significant lowering of cholesterol together with an accumulation of another sterol (possibly 7-dehydrocholesterol) has been reported in patients receiving a chemically related drug (trifluperidol) and skin and eye changes (ichthyosis and cataracts) have occurred clinically with another butyrophenone derivative. Skin and eye changes have not been observed in patients receiving haloperidol. However, it is advisable that all patients receiving haloperidol for a prolonged period of time be carefully observed for any changes in the skin and eyes. If such changes are seen, the drug should be discontinued promptly.

Drug Interactions: Haloperidol has been reported to interfere with the anticoagulant properties of phenindione in an isolated case, and the possibility should be kept in mind of a similar effect occurring when haloperidol is used together with other anticoagulants.

Haloperidol may antagonize the action of epinephrine and other sympathomimetic agents and reverse the blood pressure-lowering effects of adrenergic-blocking agents, such as guanethidine.

Enhanced CNS effects have been reported when haloperidol is used in combination with methyldopa. Haloperidol inhibits the metabolization of tricyclic antidepressants, thereby increasing plasma levels of these drugs.

When prolonged treatment with enzyme-inducing drugs such as carbamazepine, phenobarbital, rifampin is added to haloperidol therapy, this results in a significant reduction of haloperidol plasma levels. Therefore, during combination treatment, the haloperidol dose should be adjusted, when necessary. After stopping such drugs it will be necessary to reduce the dosage of haloperidol.

Haloperidol may impair the antiparkinson effects of levodopa. If concomitant antiparkinson medication is required, it may have to be continued for at least a couple of weeks after the last Haldol LA injection due to the very long half-life of haloperidol decanoate.

The physician should keep in mind the possibility of an increase in intraocular pressure when anticholinergic drugs, including antiparkinson agents, are administered concomitantly with haloperidol.

The antiemetic action of haloperidol may obscure signs of toxicity due to overdosage of other drugs or mask the symptoms of some organic diseases, such as brain tumor or intestinal obstructions.

Severe neurotoxicity (rigidity, inability to walk or talk) may occur in patients with thyrotoxicosis who are also receiving antipsychotic medication, including haloperidol.

Carcinogenicity studies in mice (18 months) and rats (24 months) showed a significant increase in mammary gland neoplasia and total tumor incidence in female mice at 1.25 and 5 mg/kg/day and in pituitary gland neoplasia in female mice at 5 mg/kg. A significant dose-related increase in pituitary gland hyperplasia was observed in female rats at 1.25 and 5 mg/kg/day. The potential significance of these findings to man is not known.

Neuroleptic drugs elevate prolactin levels; the elevation persists during chronic administration. Tissue culture experiments indicate that approximately one-third of human breast cancers are prolactin dependent in vitro, a factor of potential importance if the prescription of these drugs is contemplated in a patient with a previously detected breast cancer. Although disturbances such as galactorrhea, amenorrhea, gynecomastia, and impotence have been reported, which are presumed to be linked to elevated prolactin levels, the clinical significance of elevated serum prolactin levels is unknown for most patients. An increase in mammary neoplasms has been found in rodents after chronic administration of neuroleptic drugs. However, neither clinical studies nor epidemiologic studies conducted to date have shown an association between chronic administration of these drugs and mammary tumorigenesis: the available evidence is considered too limited to be conclusive at this time.

It is recommended that patients being considered for haloperidol decanoate therapy be initially put on oral haloperidol to exclude the possibility of an unexpected adverse sensitivity to haloperidol.

As with all antipsychotic agents, haloperidol decanoate should not be used alone where depression is predominant. It may be combined with antidepressants to treat those conditions in which depression and psychosis coexist.

In pharmacokinetic studies mild to moderately increased haloperidol decanoate levels have been reported when haloperidol was given concomitantly with the following drugs: quinidine, buspirone, fluoxetine. It may be necessary to reduce the haloperidol decanoate dosage.
Occupational Hazards: Some degree of sedation or impairment of alertness may occur, particularly with higher doses and at the start of treatment and may be potentiated by alcohol. Patients should be advised not to drive or operate machinery during treatment, until their susceptibility is known.

Adverse Effects: Neurological effects are the most common.
Extrapyramidal Symptoms: In common with all neuroleptics, extrapyramidal symptoms may occur, e.g. tremor, rigidity, hypersalivation, bradykinesia, akathisia, acute dystonia. Headache, vertigo, and cerebral seizures have also been reported. The extrapyramidal reactions are usually dose-related in occurrence and severity and, as a rule, tend to subside when the dose is reduced or the drug is temporarily discontinued. However, considerable inter-patient variability exists, and, although some individuals may tolerate higher than average doses of haloperidol, severe extrapyramidal reactions, necessitating discontinuation of the drug, may occur at relatively low doses.

Antiparkinson drugs of the anticholinergic type may be prescribed as required, but should not be prescribed routinely as a preventive measure.
Tardive Dyskinesia: As with all antipsychotic agents, tardive dyskinesia may appear in some patients on long-term therapy or may appear after drug therapy has been discontinued. The syndrome is characterized by rhythmical involuntary movements of the tongue, face, mouth or jaw (e.g., protrusion of tongue, puffing of cheeks, puckering of mouth, chewing movements). Sometimes these may be accompanied by involuntary movements of extremities. The manifestations may be permanent in some patients.

The syndrome may be masked when treatment is reinstituted, when the dosage is increased or when a switch is made to a different antipsychotic drug. Treatment should be discontinued as soon as possible.

Tardive dystonia, not associated with the above syndrome, has also been reported. Tardive dystonia is characterized by delayed onset of choreic or dystonic movements, is often persistent, and has the potential of becoming irreversible.
Other CNS Effects: Insomnia, depressive reactions, and toxic confusional states are the more common effects encountered. Drowsiness, lethargy, stupor and catalepsy, confusion, restlessness, agitation, anxiety, euphoria, vertigo, grand mal seizures and exacerbation of psychotic symptoms, including hallucinations, have also been reported.
Cardiovascular: Tachycardia, hypertension and ECG changes including ventricular arrhythmias and/or prolongation of the QT interval and ECG pattern changes compatible with the polymorphous configurations of torsades de pointes have been reported. Hypotension has occurred, but severe orthostatic hypotension has not been reported. However, should it occur, supportive measures, including i.v. vasopressors, such as norepinephrine, may be required. **Epinephrine should not be used;** since haloperidol decanoate may block the vasoconstrictor effects of this drug.
Autonomic: Dry mouth, blurred vision, urinary retention, incontinence, diaphoresis and priapism, erectile dysfunctions, peripheral edema, excessive perspiration or salivation, heartburn, and body temperature disregulation have been reported.
Allergic and Toxic: The overall incidence of significant hematologic changes in patients on haloperidol has been low. Occasionally there have been reports of mild and usually transient leukopenia and leukocytosis, decreases in blood cell counts, anemia, and a tendency toward lymphomonocytosis. Agranulocytosis has rarely been reported with the use of haloperidol, and then only in association with other medication. Impairment of liver function (jaundice or hepatitis) has been reported rarely. One case of photosensitization is known and isolated cases of idiosyncratic cutaneous involvement have been observed.

Agranulocytosis and thrombocytopenia have rarely been reported with the use of haloperidol, and then only in association with other medication.
Endocrine: Hormonal effects of antipsychotic neuroleptic drugs include hyperprolactinemia, which may cause galactorrhea, gynecomastia and oligo- or amenorrhea. Lactation, breast engorgement, mastalgia, menstrual irregularities, gynecomastia, impotence, increased libido, changes in blood sugar levels and very rare cases of Syndrome of Inappropriate ADH secretion have been reported.
Gastrointestinal: Heartburn, nausea, vomiting, anorexia, weight loss, weight gain, constipation, diarrhea and hypersalivation have been reported.
Miscellaneous: Other untoward effects which may be encountered include peripheral edema, hypocholesterolemia, alopecia, laryngospasm, bronchospasm and increased depth of respiration and stasis pneumonia. Hyperammonemia has been reported in a 5½ year old child with citrullinemia, an inherited disorder of ammonia excretion, following treatment with haloperidol.

Cases of sudden and unexpected death have been reported in association with the administration of haloperidol. The nature of the evidence makes it impossible to determine definitively what role, if any, haloperidol played in the outcome of the reported cases. The possibility that haloperidol caused death cannot, of course, be excluded, but it is to be kept in mind that sudden and unexpected death may occur in psychotic patients when they go untreated or when they are treated with other neuroleptic drugs.
Neuroleptic Malignant Syndrome: As with other neuroleptic drugs, a symptom complex sometimes referred to as neuroleptic malignant syndrome (NMS) has been reported. Cardinal features of NMS are hyperpyrexia, generalized muscle rigidity, altered mental status (including catatonic signs), and evidence of autonomic instability (irregular pulse or blood pressure). Hyperthermia is often an early sign of this syndrome. Additional signs may include elevated CPK, myoglobinuria (rhabdomyolysis), and acute renal failure. NMS is potentially fatal, requires intensive symptomatic treatment and immediate discontinuation of neuroleptic treatment.

Hyperpyrexia and heat stroke, not associated with the above symptom complex, have also been reported.

Overdose: Symptoms: In general, the symptoms of overdosage would be an exaggeration of known pharmacologic effects and adverse reactions, the most prominent of which would be: severe extrapyramidal reactions; hypotension; or sedation. The patient would appear comatose with respiratory depression and hypotension which could be severe enough to produce a shock-like state. The extrapyramidal reaction would be manifest by muscular weakness or rigidity and a generalized or localized tremor as demonstrated by the akinetic or agitans types respectively.

In extreme cases the patient would appear comatose with respiratory depression and hypotension that could be severe enough to produce a shock-like state. The risk of ventricular arrhythmias, possibly associated with QT-prolongation should be considered. (For further information regarding torsades de pointes, please refer to Adverse Effects.)

Treatment: Since there is no specific antidote, treatment is, primarily supportive but gastric lavage or induction of emesis is advised (unless the patient is obtunded, comatose, or convulsing) followed by administration of activated charcoal. For comatose patients, a patent airway must be established by use of an oropharyngeal airway or endotracheal tube or, in prolonged cases of coma, by tracheostomy. Respiratory depression may be counteracted by artificial respiration and mechanical respirators. Hypotension and circulatory collapse may be counteracted by use of i.v. fluids or plasma or concentrated albumin and vasopressor agents such as norepinephrine. **Epinephrine should not be used since it may cause profound hypotension in the presence of haloperidol.** In case of severe extrapyramidal reactions, antiparkinson medication should be administered. ECG and vital signs should be monitored especially for signs of QT prolongation or dysrhythmias and monitoring should continue until the ECG is normal. Severe arrhythmias should be treated with appropriate antiarrhythmic measures.

Dosage: Haloperidol decanoate is administered by deep i.m. injection, preferably in the gluteus maximus. This drug is **not** for i.v. use.

As a long-acting, depot neuroleptic, it has been found useful in the maintenance management of chronic schizophrenic patients who have been stabilized with short-acting medication, and who might benefit from transfer to longer acting injectable therapy. The changeover to haloperidol decanoate should aim at maintaining a clinical outcome similar to or better than that obtained with previous therapy in patients who cannot be relied upon to take oral medication regularly.

It is suggested that previous antipsychotic medication be discontinued before instituting therapy with haloperidol decanoate. Continuous supervision is required during the initial period of dosage adjustment in order to minimize the risk of overdosage or insufficient suppression of psychotic symptoms before the next injection. Supplemental oral haloperidol may be required in diminishing dosage during this period.

The selection of the initial dose of haloperidol decanoate should be based on the patient's symptomatology and previous oral neuroleptic dosage. A ratio of 20:1 of haloperidol decanoate to oral haloperidol appears to produce comparable steady state plasma levels of haloperidol with both dosage forms. However, control of psychotic symptoms has also been achieved with doses based on lower ratios (10 to 15 times the daily maintenance dose of oral haloperidol). In order to reduce the possible occurrence of adverse effects, it is advisable to initiate therapy with haloperidol decanoate at lower doses and adjust the dose upwards as needed. There is limited experience with patients transferred to haloperidol decanoate from other oral neuroleptics. If such a transfer is deemed desirable, it is suggested that the patient be converted initially from the previous antipsychotic medication to oral haloperidol in order to exclude the possibility of an unexpected adverse sensitivity to haloperidol.

The average duration of action of haloperidol decanoate is 4 weeks. However, the frequency of administration and the dosage must be individually determined for each patient. The dose should not be increased with the intent of prolonging the interval between injections beyond 4 weeks, since higher doses may increase the incidence of extrapyramidal symptoms and other adverse effects. Occasional patients may require higher dosages and/or shorter injection intervals, such as 3 or even 2 weeks.

Clinical experience with haloperidol decanoate at doses greater than 300 mg has been limited and much lower doses are usually adequate to achieve symptom control. In order to minimize the possible occurrence of serious and potentially irreversible adverse effects, the lowest neuroleptic dosage should be used which is consistent with effective management of the patient.

After appropriate dosage adjustment is achieved, regular reassessment is considered essential to allow additional adjustments which will ensure that the lowest effective individual doses are used.
Geriatrics and Debilitated Patients: Lower initial doses and more gradual titration are recommended in elderly and debilitated patients.

Patients who require higher doses of haloperidol decanoate and/or those who complain of discomfort with a large injection volume may be administered haloperidol decanoate 100 mg eq/mL in preference to haloperidol decanoate 50 mg eq/mL.

As with all oily injections it is important to insure, by aspiration before injection, that inadvertent intravascular injection does not occur.

A dry syringe and a dry 5 cm needle of 21 gauge should be used for patients with a normal amount of body fat. Obese patients should be injected with a 6.5 cm needle in order to ensure that the injection goes into muscle.

Supplied: 50 mg/mL: Each mL of slightly amber, slightly viscous solution contains: haloperidol 50 mg (haloperidol decanoate 70.52 mg). Nonmedicinal ingredients: benzyl alcohol and sesame oil. Ampuls of 1 mL. Multidose vials of 5 mL.
100 mg/mL: Each mL of slightly amber, slightly viscous solution contains: haloperidol 100 mg (haloperidol decanoate 141.04 mg). Nonmedicinal ingredients: benzyl alcohol and sesame oil. Ampuls of 1 mL. Multidose vials of 5 mL.

Store at controlled room temperature (15 to 30°C). Do not refrigerate or freeze. **Protect from light.** Keep in carton until empty.

Reviewed 1999

HALFAN™ ℞

SmithKline Beecham

Halofantrine HCl

Antimalarial

Pharmacology: Halofantrine is schizonticidal and exerts its action at the erythrocytic stage of the life cycle (trophozoite and schizont). It is not effective against exo-erythrocytic (hepatic) schizonts or against the sporozoite, merozoite or gametozoite stages of the life cycle of Plasmodium species investigated.

The precise mechanism of action of halofantrine is not certain. It has been hypothesized that halofantrine interferes with the neutralization of a toxic metabolite involved in the digestion of hemoglobin within the plasmodium. The toxic metabolite accumulates and breaks down internal cell membranes resulting in the death of the parasite.

In addition there is evidence to suggest that halofantrine may inhibit the energy-dependent proton pump on the external surface of the plasmodia in erythrocytes, thereby destroying the membrane integrity of the parasite.
Pharmacokinetics. After administration of single doses of halofantrine, plasma levels of halofantrine reach maximum concentrations at approximately 6 hours after dosing, while those

Halfan (cont'd)

of the equipotent metabolite desbutal halofantrine occur somewhat later, usually between 10 and 18 hours postdose. The maximum concentration of halofantrine after a single dose of 500 mg averages about 270 nmol/L (135 ng/mL) and concentrations of the metabolite reach about one-half this level. The blood profile and area under the curve (AUC) indicate that halofantrine appears in the systemic circulation within 1 hour of administration and that the absorption continues at a relatively low rate for several hours.

The elimination half-life of halofantrine from blood varies with the individual but is generally 2 to 3 days. The desbutyl metabolite has a half-life of about twice the parent compound.

The major route of elimination from the body is via the feces.

The absorption of halofantrine is known to be variable following single doses (250 mg to 2 000 mg) in healthy subjects, hence the rationale for divided dosing to ensure adequate blood concentrations.

The relative bioavailability of halofantrine is increased approximately 6-fold when taken with a fatty meal. This must not be used as a method of enhancing absorption.

Indications: In the treatment of acute uncomplicated malaria due to Plasmodium falciparum and Plasmodium vivax, including those strains resistant to chloroquine. Administration of halofantrine in the treatment of malaria caused by P. vivax should be followed up by treatment with an 8-aminoquinoline derivative to eliminate hepatic forms.

Halofantrine may be given to patients intolerant to chloroquine.

Prophylaxis: Halofantrine should not be used as a prophylactic agent.

Resistance: In vitro sensitivity studies and sentinel cases have suggested that cross resistance between halofantrine and mefloquine can occur.

Note: The safety and efficacy of halofantrine in the treatment of patients with cerebral malaria and other forms of complicated malaria are not known.

Contraindications: In patients with congenital or acquired QTc interval prolongation (see Warnings).

Halofantrine is contraindicated in patients with a known hypersensitivity to the drug.

Warnings: General: **Halofantrine prolongs QTc interval at the recommended therapeutic dose. Risks of prolonged QTc interval include torsades de pointes and ventricular fibrillation. Halofantrine is not recommended in patients with known QTc prolongation, in combination with drugs or in clinical conditions known to prolong QTc interval, or in patients with ventricular dysrhythmias, AV conduction disorders, severe electrolyte abnormalities or unexplained syncopal attacks. Higher than recommended doses of halofantrine have been shown to further prolong QTc interval. The prolongation of the QTc time is reversible within 3 to 4 days.**

An ECG should be performed in all patients who are being considered for treatment with halofantrine to assess whether there are conduction abnormalities or a prolonged QTc interval.

Drug Interactions: An interaction between halofantrine and mefloquine has been reported to lead to further prolongation of the QTc interval.

Pregnancy: The use of halofantrine in pregnant women is not recommended, unless the benefits are considered to outweigh the potential risk. No teratogenicity was seen in rat studies at doses up to 120 mg/kg/day (4 times the recommended human dose based on mg/kg). Studies in rabbits revealed that doses up to 60 mg/kg/day (2 times the recommended human dose based on mg/kg) did not produce harmful effects to the mother or fetus. Severe maternal toxicity was evident in a second rabbit teratology study where a slight increase in the incidence of skeletal malformations was observed in the high dose group only (120 mg/kg which is 4 times the recommended human dose based on mg/kg).

Lactation: The use of halofantrine is not recommended in breast-feeding mothers. Animal data suggest that halofantrine may be secreted in maternal milk, resulting in reduced rate of weight gain of offspring.

Precautions: General: While a phototoxic potential for halofantrine cannot be ruled out on the basis of the chemical structure of the drug and on the results of animal studies, there is no clinical evidence of this effect in humans.

Children: The use of halofantrine in children is not recommended.

Geriatrics: The use of halofantrine in elderly patients has not been studied.

Liver/Kidney Diseases: The use of halofantrine in subjects with liver or kidney diseases has not been investigated.

Adverse Effects: Halofantrine is generally well tolerated. In clinical studies the most frequently reported adverse events were diarrhea (6.7%), vomiting (3.9%), coughing (3.5%), nausea (3.3%), pruritus (3.2%), headache (2.5%) and fever (2.4%), but the causal relationship has not been established.

Skin rash, and very rarely, convulsions, anaphylaxis and angioedema have been reported with halofantrine. Hemolytic reactions which have compromised renal function have been reported in patients with malaria.

There have been rare reports of serious ventricular dysrhythmias sometimes associated with death. These cases have occurred particularly under certain conditions which include use of doses higher than recommended, recent or concomitant treatment with mefloquine or presence of preexisting prolongation of QTc interval. Palpitations and dizziness are often symptoms of malaria but may also be associated with cardiac arrhythmias.

Occasional elevation of serum transaminases have been reported following treatment. Their relation to medication is unclear since such changes are commonly seen in acute malaria. Values have generally returned to normal within 1 week after treatment.

Overdose: Symptoms and Treatment: The absence of experience with acute overdosage with halofantrine precludes characterization of sequela and assessment of antidotal efficacy at this time. However, in case of accidental overdosage, immediate induction of emesis or gastric lavage is recommended, in conjunction with supportive measures which should include ECG monitoring.

Dosage: It is important that halofantrine be given on an empty stomach 1 hour before or 3 hours after meals due to the observation that absorption is increased when taken with a fatty meal. High plasma levels of the parent drug may be associated with significant QT prolongation and therefore increased potential for cardiotoxicity.

Adults: Non-immune Patients: Patients with no previous exposure or minimal exposure to malaria should be considered non-immune. These patients should receive 500 mg (2×250 mg tablets) every 6 hours for 3 doses (total first course dosage 1 500 mg). This course of therapy should be repeated 7 days after the first course.

Semi-immune Patients: Patients with a history of life-long residence in malaria endemic areas and who have a clear history of recent malarial infection with the same species of parasite may be considered semi-immune. These patients should receive 500 mg (2×250 mg tablets) every 6 hours for 3 doses (total dosage 1500 mg).

Children: The use of halofantrine is not recommended in children.

Information for the Patient: See Blue Section—Information for the Patient ''Halfan''.

Supplied: Each white to off-white, capsule-shaped tablet with a breakline on one side and inscribed HALFAN on the other side, contains: halofantrine HCl 250 mg. Nonmedicinal ingredients: magnesium stearate, microcrystalline cellulose, povidone, pregelatinized starch, sodium starch glycollate and talc. Blister packs of 6 and 12. Store at room temperature (below 30°C).

Reviewed 1998

HALOG® Preparations

Westwood-Squibb

Halcinonide

Topical Corticosteroid

Indications: Halcinonide, a synthetic fluorinated corticosteroid, is indicated for topical application for the relief of the inflammatory manifestations of acute or chronic corticosteroid responsive dermatoses; under occlusion, in the management of recalcitrant cases of psoriasis and neurodermatitis.

Contraindications: Tuberculous, fungal and most viral lesions of the skin (including herpes simplex, vaccinia, and varicella). Patients with history of hypersensitivity to any of the components. Not intended for use in the eye nor in the external auditory canal of patients with perforated eardrums.

Precautions: Adrenal suppression and other systemic adverse effects may occur and must be kept in mind, particularly during use over large areas or over an extended period of time. Occasionally, symptoms of steroid withdrawal may develop when the medication is stopped after prolonged use.

Pregnancy and *Lactation:* Safety in pregnancy and lactation has not yet been established. Weigh potential benefit against potential hazard to the fetus or nursing infant.

In cases of bacterial skin infections, use appropriate antibacterial agents as primary therapy. If necessary, halcinonide may be used as an adjunct to control inflammation, erythema and itching. If a symptomatic response is not noted within a few days to a week, discontinue the local application of corticosteroid until the infection is controlled.

If local irritation or sensitization develops, discontinue halcinonide and institute appropriate therapy.

Use topical corticosteroids with caution on lesions close to the eye.

Advise patients to inform subsequent physicians of the prior use of corticosteroids.

Prolonged use of topical corticosteroid products may produce atrophy of the skin and of subcutaneous tissues, particularly on flexor surfaces and on the face. If this is noted, discontinue the use of topical corticosteroids.

Topical corticosteroids should be used with caution in patients with stasis dermatitis and other skin diseases associated with impaired circulation.

Use of occlusive dressings increases the percutaneous absorption of corticosteroids; their extensive use increases the possibility of systemic adverse effects. For patients with extensive lesions, it may be preferable to use a sequential approach. Prolonged occlusive therapy necessitates close observation of the patient. Impairment of thermal homeostasis may occur if large areas of the body are occluded. Discontinue use of the occlusive dressing if elevation of the body temperature occurs.

Plastic films, commonly used as occlusive dressings, are often flammable; warn patients when using such materials. Employ extreme caution when such films are used on children to avoid the possibility of suffocation.

Occasionally, a patient may develop a sensitivity reaction to a particular occlusive dressing material or adhesive. If infection develops, discontinue the use of the occlusive dressings and institute appropriate antimicrobial therapy.

Adverse Effects: Significant local irritation is uncommon; a transient burning sensation may occur in some patients. The use of corticosteroids under occlusive dressings is known to produce miliaria, folliculitis, pyoderma, maceration of the skin or localized cutaneous atrophy. Striae occasionally may develop when used extensively in intertriginous areas or under occlusive dressings. Erythema, dryness, itching, hypertrichosis and change in skin pigmentation have been reported with topical steroids.

Adrenal suppression has also been reported following topical corticosteroid therapy. Posterior subcapsular cataracts have been reported following systemic use of corticosteroids.

Overdose: Symptoms: Mild, reversible suppression of adrenal function, ecchymoses of the skin, peptic ulceration, hypertension, aggravation of infection, hirsutism, acne, edema and muscle weakness due to protein depletion are all toxic symptoms when large amounts of corticosteroids are absorbed. Animal studies suggest that overdosage in females may result in swollen breasts or lactation.

Treatment: No specific antidote available. Treatment should be chiefly symptomatic. Discontinue corticosteroid administration.

Dosage: Apply to the affected area 2 or 3 times daily. Rub in gently.

Occlusive dressing technique: Gently rub a small amount of cream or ointment into the lesion until the cream or ointment disappears. Then re-apply the cream or ointment, leaving a thin coating on the lesion and cover with a pliable nonporous film. Good results have been obtained by applying the cream or ointment under occlusion in the evening and reapplying it without occlusion in the morning (i.e. 12 hour occlusion). Reapplication of the cream or ointment is essential at each dressing change.

Supplied: Cream: Each g contains: halcinonide 0.1%. Nonmedicinal ingredients: cetyl alcohol, dimethicone, glyceryl monostearate, isopropyl palmitate, polysorbate, propylene glycol, titanium dioxide and water. Tubes of 15, 30 and 60 g.

Ointment: Each g contains: halcinonide 0.1%. Nonmedicinal ingredients: butylated hydroxytoluene, mineral oil, polyethylene, polyethylene glycol and polyethylene glycol distearate. Tubes of 30 and 60 g.

Solution: Each mL contains: halcinonide 0.1%. Nonmedicinal ingredients: butylated hydroxytoluene, disodium edetate dihydrate, polyethylene glycol 300 and water. pH adjusted with sodium hydroxide. Plastic bottles of 60 mL.

Store at room temperature. Avoid freezing. Avoid storage at temperatures exceeding 30°C.

HALOPERIDOL LA

Sabex

Haloperidol Decanoate

Antipsychotic

Supplied: 50 mg: Each mL contains: haloperidol 50 mg as the decanoate, benzyl alcohol 1.2% v/v as preservative and sesame oil q.s. Multidose vials of 5 mL, boxes of 1.

100 mg: Each mL contains: haloperidol 100 mg as the decanoate, benzyl alcohol 1.2% v/v as preservative and sesame oil q.s. Ampuls of 1 mL, boxes of 5. Multidose vials of 5 mL, boxes of 1.

Store between 15 and 30°C. Protect from light.

HALOTESTIN®

Pharmacia & Upjohn

Fluoxymesterone

Androgenic—Anabolic Steroid

Pharmacology: Endogenous androgens are responsible for normal growth and development of the male sex organs and for maintenance of secondary sex characteristics. These effects include growth and maturation of the prostate, seminal vesicles, penis, and scrotum; development of male hair distribution, such as beard, pubic, chest, and axillary hair; laryngeal enlargement, vocal cord thickening, and alterations in body musculature and fat distribution. Drugs in this class also cause retention of nitrogen, sodium, potassium, and phosphorus, and decreased urinary excretion of calcium. Androgens have been reported to increase protein anabolism and decrease protein catabolism. Nitrogen balance is improved only when there is sufficient intake of calories and protein.

Androgens are responsible for the growth spurt of adolescence and for eventual termination of linear growth, brought about by fusion of the epiphyseal growth centers. In children, exogenous androgens accelerate linear gowth rates, but may cause disproportionate advancement in bone maturation. Use over long periods may result in fusion of the epiphyseal growth centers and termination of the growth process. Androgens have been reported to stimulate production of red blood cells by enhancing production of erythropoietic stimulation factor.

During exogenous administration of androgens, endogenous testosterone release is inhibited through feedback inhibition of pituitary luteinizing hormone (LH). At large doses of exogenous androgens, spermatogenesis may also be suppressed through feedback inhibition of pituitary follicle stimulating hormone (FSH).

Inactivation of testosterone occurs primarily in the liver.

The half-life of fluoxymesterone after oral administration is approximately 9.2 hours.

Indications: Males: Replacement therapy in conditions associated with symptoms of deficiency or absence of endogenous testosterone such as the male climacteric and/or impotence resulting from: a. Primary hypogonadism (congenital or acquired)—testicular failure due to cryptorchidism, bilateral torsion, orchitis, vanishing testis syndrome; or orchidectomy. b. Hypogonadotropic hypogonadism (congenital or acquired)—idiopathic gonadotropin or LHRH deficiency, or pituitary-hypothalamic injury from tumors, trauma, or radiation.

Delayed puberty, provided it has been definitely established as such, and is not just a familial trait.

Females: For palliation of androgen-responsive recurrent mammary cancer in women who are more than 1 year but less than 5 years postmenopausal, or who have been proven to have a hormone-dependent tumor as shown by previous beneficial response to castration.

Contraindications: Known hypersensitivity to the drug. Males with carcinoma of the breast. Males with known or suspected carcinoma of the prostate gland.

Pregnancy: Women known or suspected to be pregnant.

Patients with serious cardiac, hepatic or renal disease.

Warnings: Hypercalcemia may occur in immobilized patients and in patients with breast cancer. If this occurs, the drug should be discontinued.

Prolonged use of high doses of androgens (principally the 17-alpha-alkyl-androgens) has been associated with development of hepatic adenomas, hepatocellular carcinoma, and peliosis hepatis—all potentially life-threatening complications.

Cholestatic hepatitis and jaundice may occur with 17-alpha-alkyl-androgens. Should this occur, the drug should be discontinued. This is reversible with discontinuation of the drug.

Geriatrics: Geriatric patients treated with androgens may be at an increased risk of developing prostatic hypertrophy and prostatic carcinoma although conclusive evidence to support this concept is lacking.

Edema, with or without congestive heart failure, may be a serious complication in patients with pre-existing cardiac, renal or hepatic disease.

Gynecomastia may develop and occasionally persists in patients being treated for hypogonadism.

Androgen therapy should be used cautiously in males with delayed puberty. Androgens can accelerate bone maturation without producing compensatory gain in linear growth. The effect on bone maturation should be monitored by assessing bone age of the wrist and hand every 6 months.

This drug has not been shown to be safe and effective for the enhancement of athletic performance. Because of the potential risk of serious adverse health effects, this drug should not be used for such purpose.

Precautions: General: Women should be observed for signs of virilization which is usual following androgen use at high doses. Discontinuation of drug therapy at the time of evidence of mild virilism is necessary to prevent irreversible virilization. A decision may be made by the patient and the physician that some virilization will be tolerated during treatment for breast carcinoma.

Patients with benign prostatic hypertrophy may develop acute urethral obstruction. Priapism or excessive sexual stimulation may develop. Oligospermia may occur after prolonged administration or excessive dosage. If any of these effects appear, the androgen should be stopped and if restarted, a lower dosage should be utilized.

This product contains FD&C Yellow No. 5 (tartrazine) which may cause allergic-type reactions (including bronchial asthma) in certain susceptible individuals. Although the overall incidence of FD&C Yellow No. 5 (tartrazine) sensitivity in the general population is low, it is frequently seen in patients who also have ASA hypersensitivity.

Information for the Patient: Patients should be instructed to report any of the following: nausea, vomiting, changes in skin color and ankle swelling. Males should be instructed to report too frequent or persistent erections of the penis and females any hoarseness, acne, changes in menstrual periods or increase in facial hair.

Laboratory Tests: Women with disseminated breast carcinoma should have frequent determination of urine and serum calcium levels during the course of androgen therapy (see Warnings).

Because of the hepatotoxicity associated with the use of 17-alpha-alkylated androgens, liver function tests should be obtained periodically.

Periodic (every 6 months) x-ray examinations of bone age should be made during treatment of prepubertal males to determine the rate of bone maturation and the effects of androgen therapy on the epiphyseal centers.

Hemoglobin and hematocrit levels (to detect polycythemia) should be checked periodically in patients receiving long-term androgen administration. Serum cholesterol may increase during androgen therapy.

Drug Interactions: Androgens may increase sensitivity to oral anticoagulants. Dosage of the anticoagulant may require reduction in order to maintain satisfactory therapeutic hypoprothrombinemia.

Concurrent administration of oxyphenbutazone and androgens may result in elevated serum levels of oxyphenbutazone.

In diabetic patients, the metabolic effects of androgens may decrease blood glucose and, therefore, insulin requirements.

Drug/Laboratory Test Interferences: Androgens may decrease levels of thyroxine-binding globulin, resulting in decreased total T-4 serum levels and increased resin uptake of T-3 and T-4. Free thyroid hormone levels remain unchanged, however, and there is no clinical evidence of thyroid dysfunction.

Carcinogenesis, Mutagenesis, Impairment of Fertility: Animal Data: Testosterone has been tested by s.c. injection and implantation in mice and rats. The implant induced cervical-uterine tumors in mice, which metastasized in some cases. There is suggestive evidence that injection of testosterone into some strains of female mice increases their susceptibility to hepatoma. Testosterone is also known to increase the number of tumors and to decrease the degree of differentiation of chemically-induced carcinomas of the liver in rats.

Human Data: There are rare reports of hepatocellular carcinoma in patients receiving long-term therapy with androgens in high doses. Withdrawal of the drugs did not lead to regression of the tumors in all cases.

Geriatrics: Geriatric patients treated with androgens may be at an increased risk of developing prostatic hypertrophy and prostatic carcinoma although conclusive evidence to support this concept is lacking.

This compound has not been tested for mutagenic potential. However, as noted above, carcinogenic effects have been attributed to treatment with androgenic hormones. The potential carcinogenic effects likely occur through a hormonal mechanism rather than by a direct chemical interaction mechanism.

Impairment of fertility was not tested directly in animal species. However, as noted under Adverse Effects, oligospermia in males and amenorrhea in females are potential adverse effects of treatment with fluoxymesterone tablets. Therefore, impairment of fertility is a possible outcome of treatment with fluoxymesterone.

Lactation: Fluoxymesterone is not recommended for use in nursing mothers.

Children: Androgen therapy should be used very cautiously in children and only by specialists aware of the adverse effects on bone maturation. Skeletal maturation must be monitored every 6 months by an x-ray of the hand and wrist.

Adverse Effects: Endocrine and Urogenital: Female: The most common side effects of androgen therapy are amenorrhea and other menstrual irregularities; inhibition of gonadotropin secretion; and virilization, including deepening of the voice and clitoral enlargement. The latter usually is not reversible after androgens are discontinued. When administered to a pregnant woman, androgens can cause virilization of external genitalia of the female fetus.

Male: gynecomastia and excessive frequency and duration of penile erections. Oligospermia may occur at high dosage.

Skin and Appendages: hirsutism, male pattern of baldness, seborrhea and acne.

Fluid and Electrolyte Disturbances: retention of sodium, chloride, water, potassium, calcium and inorganic phosphates.

Gastrointestinal: nausea, cholestatic jaundice, alterations in liver function tests, rarely, hepatocellular neoplasms and peliosis hepatis.

Hematologic: suppression of clotting factors II, V, VII and X; bleeding in patients on concomitant anticoagulant therapy and polycythemia.

Nervous System: increased or decreased libido, headache, anxiety, depression and generalized paresthesia.

Allergic: hypersensitivity, including skin manifestations and anaphylactoid reactions.

Overdose: Symptoms and Treatment: No specific antidote. Perform gastric lavage.

Dosage: The dosage will vary depending upon the individual, the condition being treated, and its severity. The total daily oral dose may be administered singly or in divided (3 or 4) doses.

Male Hypogonadism: For complete replacement in the hypogonadal male, a daily dose of 5 to 20 mg will suffice in the majority of patients. It is usually preferable to begin treatment with full therapeutic doses which are later adjusted to individual requirements. Priapism is indicative of excessive dosage and is indication for temporary withdrawal of the drug.

Delayed Puberty: Dosage should be carefully titrated utilizing a low dose, appropriate skeletal monitoring, and by limiting the duration of therapy to 4 to 6 months.

Inoperable Carcinoma of the Breast in the Female: The recommended total daily dose for palliative therapy in advanced inoperable carcinoma of the breast is 10 to 40 mg. Because of its short action, fluoxymesterone should be administered to patients in divided, rather than single, daily doses to ensure more stable blood levels. In general, it appears necessary to continue therapy for at least 1 month for a satisfactory subjective response, and for 2 to 3 months for an objective response.

Supplied: Each green, round, scored, compressed tablet, engraved "Upjohn" contains: fluoxymesterone 5 mg. Nonmedicinal ingredients: calcium stearate, cornstarch, FD&C yellow No. 5 (tartrazine), lactose, myrtiline green R. and sucrose. Bottles of 50.

(Shown in Product Recognition Section)

Reviewed 1999

HAVRIX™
SmithKline Beecham
Hepatitis A Vaccine (Inactivated)
Active Immunization Agent against infection by Hepatitis A virus

Pharmacology: Hepatitis A vaccine (inactivated) confers immunity against hepatitis A virus (HAV) infection by inducing the production of specific anti-HAV antibodies.

In clinical studies involving subjects of 18 to 50 years of age, specific humoral antibodies against HAV were detected in more than 88% of vaccinees at day 15 and 99% at month 1 following administration of a single dose of Havrix 1440.

In clinical studies involving subjects of 1 to 18 years of age, specific humoral antibodies against HAV were detected in more than 93% of vaccinees at day 15 and 99% of vaccinees 1 month following administration of Havrix 720 Junior.

Results of a hepatitis A outbreak control program showed a substantial drop in symptomatic cases in 4 930 vaccinees within 3 weeks of receiving 1 dose of hepatitis A vaccine. In villages where more than 70% of estimated susceptible individuals were vaccinated, a dramatic drop in the number of symptomatic cases of disease was observed within 8 weeks of vaccination.

The mean titre of anti-HAV antibodies induced by hepatitis A vaccine (inactivated) is at least 3 times higher than the maximum observed after passive immunization using immune globulin (human). In a randomly selected subset of subjects, vaccine-induced anti-HAV antibodies were shown to be qualitatively indistinguishable from immune globulin (human) anti-HAV antibodies.

To obtain long-term immunity a booster dose is recommended at any time between 6 and 12 months after primary vaccination, to induce long term antibody titres.

Primates exposed to the virulent heterologous hepatitis A strain were vaccinated 2 days after exposure. This post exposure vaccination resulted in total protection of the animals.

Indications: For active immunization against HAV infection in subjects at risk of exposure to HAV.

Hepatitis A vaccine (inactivated) will not prevent hepatitis infection caused by other agents such as hepatitis B virus, hepatitis C virus, hepatitis E virus or other pathogens known to infect the liver.

In areas of low and intermediate prevalence of hepatitis A, immunization is particularly recommended in subjects who are, or will be, at increased risk of infection such as: Travelers: Persons traveling to areas where the prevalence of hepatitis A is high. These areas include Africa, Asia, the Mediterranean basin, the Middle East, Central and South America.

Armed Forces: Armed Forces personnel who travel to higher endemicity areas or to areas where hygiene is poor have an increased risk of HAV infection. Active immunization is indicated for these individuals.

Persons for whom Hepatitis A is an Occupational Hazard: These include employees in day-care centres, nursing, medical and paramedical personnel in hospitals and institutions, especially gastroenterology and pediatric units, sewage workers, and food handlers, among others.

Persons for whom There is an Increased Risk of Transmission of Hepatitis A: e.g., homosexuals, persons with multiple sexual partners, abusers of injectable drugs, hemophiliac patients.

Contacts of Infected Persons: Since virus shedding of infected persons may occur for a prolonged period, active immunization of close contacts is recommended.

Specific Population Groups known to have Higher Incidence of Hepatitis A: e.g., North American Indians, Inuits, recognized community-wide HAV epidemics.

Subjects with chronic liver disease or who are at risk of developing chronic liver disease (e.g., HB and HC chronic carriers and alcohol abusers): Hepatitis A tends to compromise the outcome of chronic liver disease.

In areas of intermediate to high prevalence of hepatitis A (e.g., Africa, Asia, the Mediterranean basin, the Middle East, Central and South America) susceptible individuals may be considered for active immunization.

Contraindications: Hepatitis A vaccine (inactivated) should not be administered to subjects with known hypersensitivity to any component of the vaccine preparation, or to subjects having shown signs of hypersensitivity after previous administration.

As with other vaccines, the administration of hepatitis A vaccine (inactivated) should be postponed in subjects with severe febrile illness. The presence of a minor infection however, is not a contraindication.

Precautions: General: As with other injectable vaccines, appropriate medication (e.g., epinephrine) should be readily available for immediate use in case of anaphylaxis or anaphylactoid reactions following administration of the vaccine. For this reason, the vaccinee should remain under medical supervision for 30 minutes after immunization.

Hepatitis A vaccine (inactivated) should be administered with caution to subjects with thrombocytopenia or a bleeding disorder since bleeding may occur following an i.m. administration to these subjects.

It is possible that subjects may be in the incubation period of a hepatitis A infection at the time of immunization. It is not known whether hepatitis A vaccine (inactivated) will prevent hepatitis A in such cases.

Since there is a possibility that the vaccine may contain trace amounts of neomycin, the possibility of an allergic reaction in individuals sensitive to this substance should be kept in mind when considering the use of this vaccine.

Pregnancy: The effect on fetal development has not been assessed. However, as with all inactivated viral vaccines, the risks to the fetus are considered to be negligible. Hepatitis A vaccine (inactivated) should be used during pregnancy only when clearly needed.

Lactation: It is unknown whether hepatitis A vaccine (inactivated) is excreted in breast milk. Therefore, caution should be exercised if it is to be administered to breast-feeding women.

Patients with Special Diseases and Conditions: As with other vaccines, hemodialysis patients and subjects with an impaired immune system may not obtain adequate antibody titres after the primary immunization course. Such patients may require administration of additional doses of hepatitis A vaccine (inactivated). However, no specific dosing recommendations can be made at this time.

Drug Interactions: The concomitant administration of hepatitis A vaccine (inactivated) and immune globulin (human) does not influence the seroconversion rate, but may result in a relatively lower anti-HAV antibody titre than when the vaccine is given alone. Hepatitis A vaccine (inactivated) and immune globulin (human) should be administered at separate injection sites.

Since hepatitis A vaccine (inactivated) is an inactivated vaccine, its concomitant use with other inactivated vaccines is unlikely to result in interference with immune responses. When concomitant administration of other vaccines is considered necessary, the vaccines must be given with different syringes and at different injection sites.

Clinical experiences with the concomitant administration of hepatitis A vaccine (inactivated) and the recombinant hepatitis B virus vaccine, have been satisfactory. No interference in the respective immune responses to both antigens has been observed.

Concomitant administration of typhoid, yellow fever, cholera (injectable) or tetanus vaccine does not interfere with hepatitis A vaccine (inactivated) immune response.

Hepatitis A vaccine (inactivated) must not be mixed with other vaccines.

Adverse Effects: Hepatitis A vaccine (inactivated) is well tolerated. In controlled clinical studies, signs and symptoms were monitored in all subjects for 4 days following administration of the vaccine. A checklist was used for this purpose. The vaccinees were also requested to report any clinical events occurring during the study period.

The frequency of solicited adverse events was lower following the booster dose of hepatitis A vaccine (inactivated). Most events reported were considered by the subjects as "mild" and did not last for more than 24 hours. The frequency of solicited adverse events reported following administration is not different from the frequency of solicited adverse events reported following the administration of other aluminum adsorbed purified antigen vaccines.

Of the local solicited adverse events the most frequently reported was injection site soreness (less than 0.5% reported as severe) which resolved spontaneously. Other local solicited reactions reported were mild redness and swelling, with a frequency varying between 4 and 7% of all vaccinations.

The systemic adverse events reported by vaccinees were essentially mild, did not last for more than 24 hours and included headache, malaise, fatigue, fever, nausea, and loss of appetite. These events were reported with a frequency varying between 1 and 12.8% of vaccinations.

The nature of the signs and symptoms observed in children is similar to that of adults, however, these have been reported less frequently.

As with other vaccines, rare events, such as anaphylaxis, have been observed in temporal association with the administration of the vaccine (see Precautions).

Dosage: Primary Immunization: Adults 19 years and over: A single dose of Havrix 1440 is used for primary immunization. Children and adolescents: 1 year up to and including 18 years: A single dose of Havrix 720 Junior is used for primary immunization. If a pediatric vial is not available, a pediatric dose of 0.5 mL may be withdrawn from the Havrix 1440 vial.

Booster Dose: A booster dose is recommended at any time between 6 and 12 months after a single dose of Havrix 1440 or Havrix 720 Junior in order to ensure long-term protection.

Concomitant Administration with Immune Globulin (Human): Concomitant administration of hepatitis A vaccine (inactivated) and immune globulin (human) may be considered when a subject is at risk of being exposed to hepatitis A before adequate anti-HAV antibody titres can be reached.

Method of Administration: Hepatitis A vaccine (inactivated) should be injected **i.m.** in the deltoid region in adults and children, and in the anterolateral part of the thigh in children up to 2 years of age. The vaccine **should not** be administered i.m. in the gluteal region or s.c./intradermally since administration by these routes may result in a less than optimal anti-HAV antibody response.

As with all parenterals, vaccine products should be inspected visually for any foreign particulate matter or discoloration prior to administration. Before use of hepatitis A vaccine (inactivated), the vial/syringe should be well shaken to obtain a slightly opaque, white suspension. Discard if the contents of the vial/syringe appear otherwise.

The vaccine must be used as supplied.

Hepatitis A vaccine (inactivated) should never be administered i.v.

Supplied: Each mL of sterile suspension contains: formaldehyde-inactivated hepatitis A virus (HM175 hepatitis A virus strain) adsorbed onto 0.5 mg of aluminum in the form of aluminum hydroxide. The viral antigen content is determined by an Elisa test. Each dose is standardized to ensure a viral antigen content of not less than: Havrix 720 Junior: 720 Elisa Units of viral antigen in a 0.5 mL dose volume. Havrix 1440: 1440 Elisa Units of viral antigen in a 1 mL dose volume. Nonmedicinal ingredients: aluminum hydroxide, amino acids for injection, disodium phosphate, monopotassium phosphate, neomycin sulfate (less than 10 ng), polysorbate 20, potassium chloride, sodium chloride and water for injection.

Havrix meets the World Health Organization requirement for biological substances including those for final vaccine residual bovine serum albumin. Havrix 720 Junior: single dose prefilled syringes of 0.5 mL, packages of 1. Havrix 1440: single dose vials and prefilled syringes of 1 mL, packages of 1.

The vaccine should not be used beyond the expiry date stamped on the vial or syringe. Store at 2 to 8°C. **Do not freeze; discard if vaccine has been frozen.** Stability studies of Havrix show that the potency of unopened vaccine is not significantly affected after exposure at 37°C for up to 3 weeks. However, this is **not** a storage recommendation.

Reviewed 1998

HEALON®
HEALON® GV
Pharmacia & Upjohn
Sodium Hyaluronate
Ophthalmosurgical Aid

Description: Sodium hyaluronate is a sterile, nonpyrogenic, viscoelastic preparation of a highly purified, noninflammatory, high molecular weight fraction of sodium hyaluronate. Healon contains 10 mg/mL of sodium hyaluronate 5 000 and Healon GV contains 14 mg/mL of sodium hyaluronate 7 000 dissolved in physiological sodium chloride-phosphate buffer (pH 7.0 to 7.5). This high molecular weight polymer is made up of repeating disaccharide units of N-acetylglucosamine and sodium glucuronate linked by β 1–3 and β 1–4 glycosidic bonds.

Sodium hyaluronate is a physiological substance that is widely distributed in the extracellular matrix of connective tissues in both animals and man. For example, it is present in the vitreous and aqueous humor of the eye, the synovial fluid, the skin and the umbilical cord. Sodium hyaluronates prepared from various human and animal tissues are not chemically different from each other.

Healon is a specific fraction of sodium hyaluronate developed as an ophthalmosurgical aid for use in surgery. It is specific in that: it has a high molecular weight; it is reported to be nonantigenic; it does not cause inflammatory or foreign body reactions; it has a high viscosity; it is transparent.

Healon GV contains a specific high molecular weight fraction of sodium hyaluronate developed as an ophthalmosurgical aid for use in anterior segment procedures. Healon GV is specific in that it has a high viscosity, it is highly elastic and it does not cause inflammatory or foreign body reactions.

Sodium hyaluronate protects corneal endothelial cells and other ocular structures. It does not interfere with epithelialization and normal wound healing.

Indications: The principle intended use for Healon is as an ophthalmosurgical aid in various anterior segment procedures, such as intra- and extra capsular cataract surgery, intraocular lens (IOL) implantation, keratoplasty, glaucoma surgery and post-trauma surgery. It has also been used successfully as a vitreous replacement after vitrectomy and retinal detachment surgery.

Healon GV is indicated for use as a surgical aid in various anterior segment procedures, such as cataract extraction, (IOL) implantation, corneal transplant surgery, glaucoma filtration and trauma surgery.

In surgical procedures in the anterior segment of the eye, instillation of sodium hyaluronate serves to maintain a deep anterior chamber during surgery, allowing for more efficient manipulation with less trauma to the corneal endothelium and other surrounding tissues.

Due to its viscoelasticity, Healon and Healon GV can be used to manoeuvre and control tissues.

Contraindications: At present, there are no known contraindications to the use of Healon and Healon GV when used as recommended.

Precautions: Those normally associated with the surgical procedure being performed should be observed.

Overfilling of the anterior or posterior segment of the eye with Healon and Healon GV may cause increased intraocular pressure.

Postoperative intraocular pressure may be elevated as a result of pre-existing glaucoma, compromised outflow and by operative procedures and sequelae thereto, including enzymatic zonulysis, absence of an iridectomy, trauma to filtration structures, and by blood and lenticular remnants in the anterior chamber. Since the exact role of these factors is difficult to predict in any individual case, the following precautions are recommended:

1. Do not overfill the eye with sodium hyaluronate (except in glaucoma surgery, see Dosage).
2. Remove some of the sodium hyaluronate by irrigation and/or aspiration at the close of surgery (except in glaucoma surgery, see Dosage).
3. Carefully monitor intraocular pressure, especially during the immediate postoperative period. If significant rises are observed, treat with appropriate therapy.

When air is used in conjunction with sodium hyaluronate, care should be taken to avoid trapping the air behind the iris.

Because sodium hyaluronate is a highly purified fraction extracted from avian tissues and is known to contain minute amounts of protein, the physician should be aware of potential risks of the type that can occur with the injection of any biological material.

Physicians should be aware that the solution may contain minute rubber particles presumably formed when the diaphragm is punctured. Express a small amount of sodium hyaluronate from the syringe prior to use, and carefully examine the solution as it is injected.

Sporadic reports have shown that Healon may become cloudy or form a slight precipitate following instillation into the eye. The clinical significance of the precipitate, if any, is not known since no effect on ocular tissues has been identified. Physicians should be aware of this phenomenon and, should it be observed, the cloudy or precipitated material should be removed by irrigation and/or aspiration. In vitro laboratory studies have shown opalescence of sodium hyaluronate when mixed with solutions containing quarternary ammonium compounds. Therefore, sodium hyaluronate should not be instilled through a cannula used in connection with such solutions. Consequently, reuse of cannulas should be avoided.

Use only if solution is clear.

Adverse Effects: Healon and Healon GV have been extremely well tolerated after injection into human eyes. A transient rise of intraocular pressure postoperatively has been reported in some cases.

Rarely, postoperative, inflammatory reactions (iritis, hypopyon) following the use of sodium hyaluronate, as well as incidents of corneal edema and corneal decompensation have been reported. Their relationship to sodium hyaluronate has not been established.

Dosage: Cataract Surgery, IOL Implantation: A sufficient amount of sodium hyaluronate is slowly and carefully introduced into the anterior chamber to replace the aqueous humor before any instrument is introduced into the eye. Filling the anterior chamber and the capsular bag facilitates in-the-bag implantation.

Additional sodium hyaluronate can be injected during surgery to replace any sodium hyaluronate lost during surgical manipulation (see Precautions).

Glaucoma Filtration Surgery: In trabeculectomy, sodium hyaluronate is injected slowly and carefully through a corneal paracentesis to reconstitute the anterior chamber. Further injection can be continued to allow it to extrude into the subconjunctival filtration site through and around the sutured outer scleral flap.

Corneal Transplant Surgery: During trepanation of the cornea, the anterior chamber is filled with sodium hyaluronate. The donor graft can then be placed on top of the bed of sodium hyaluronate and sutured in place. Additional Healon may be injected to replace any Healon lost as a result of surgical manipulation (see Precautions).

Trauma: Healon GV can be used in the management of various kinds of penetrating eye trauma. It is injected to reform the anterior chamber, to manoeuvre, protect and support ocular tissues and to create space for surgical instruments during reconstructive surgery.

Supplied: 10 mg: Each mL of sterile, nonpyrogenic, viscoelastic preparation contains: sodium hyaluronate 5 000, 10 mg. Nonmedicinal ingredients: disodium hydrogen phosphate dihydrate, sodium chloride, sodium dihydrogen phosphate hydrate and water for injection USP q.s. Disposable glass syringes, delivering 0.55 and 0.85 mL sodium hyaluronate dissolved in physiological sodium chloride phosphate buffer (pH: 7.0 to 7.5).

14 mg: Each mL of sterile, nonpyrogenic, viscoelastic preparation contains: sodium hyaluronate 7 000, 14 mg. Nonmedicinal ingredients: disodium hydrogen phosphate dihydrate, sodium chloride, sodium dihydrogen phosphate hydrate and water for injection USP q.s. Disposable glass syringes, delivering 0.55 and 0.85 mL sodium hyaluronate dissolved in physiological sodium chloride phosphate buffer (pH: 7.0 to 7.5).

A sterile single-use 27G eye cannula is supplied in the box. Syringes are terminally sterilized and aseptically packaged. Prior to use, ensure that the assembled unit functions properly by expressing a small amount of Healon or Healon GV from the syringe. Inspect the expressed solution. Do not use if the solution is cloudy or if rubber particles are present. Refrigerated Healon and Healon GV should be allowed to attain room temperature (approximately 30 minutes) prior to use. Store at 2 to 8°C. Protect from freezing. Protect from light.

Reviewed 1999

HEMAREXIN®
Technilab

Multiple Vitamins—Minerals
Vitamin/Mineral Supplement

Supplied: Each 10 mL of dark, brown liquid with an aromatic odor, contains: sodium (as sodium glycerophosphate) 3.65 mg, thiamine (vitamin B_1) 1 mg, riboflavin (vitamin B_2) (as riboflavin 5′-phosphate sodium) 1 mg and niacinamide 10 mg. Nonmedicinal ingredients: alcohol, caffeine, calcium (as calcium glycerophosphate), caramel, ethyl vanillin, glycerin, kola tincture, magnesium (as magnesium chloride), methylparaben, natural flavoring, phosphoric acid, propylparaben, purified water and sugar. Plastic ampuls of 10 mL, boxes of 20 and 30. Bottles of 250 mL. Protect from light. Store at room temperature 15 to 30°C.

New Product 1998

HEMCORT® HC Ⓟ
Technilab

Hydrocortisone—Zinc Sulfate
Anorectal Therapy

Supplied: Ointment: Each g of ointment contains: hydrocortisone acetate 0.5% and zinc sulfate monohydrate 0.5%. Nonmedicinal ingredients: light mineral oil and petrolatum. Tubes of 15 and 30 g with applicator.

Suppositories: Each suppository contains: hydrocortisone acetate 10 mg and zinc sulfate monohydrate 10 mg. Nonmedicinal ingredients: semisynthetic glycerides. Boxes of 12. Protect from freezing.

Store between 15 and 30°C.

HEPALEAN®
Organon Teknika

Heparin Sodium
Anticoagulant

Indications: Used in the treatment of thrombophlebitis, phlebothrombosis, and cerebral, coronary, and retinal vessel thrombosis to prevent extension of clots and thromboembolic phenomena. Also used prophylactically to prevent the occurrence of thromboembolism, and to prevent clotting during dialysis and other surgical procedures, particularly vascular surgery.

When using in conjuction with dialysis machines or where heparin is added to glucose or saline it is most important that the pH is not less than 5 for heparin to act as an effective anticoagulant. Under pH 5 degradation sets in and with a pH around 4 or less there is very little activity. Likewise, with pH over 8.5 there will be some degradation. Recent work has indicated that early hemodialysis is of value in cases of multiple trauma.

Heparin has also been used as an anticoagulant in blood transfusion samples, particularly when the presence of citrates, oxalates, or fluorides might interfere with laboratory tests, such as electrolyte determination. Anti-inflammatory and diuretic activity have been obtained with heparin. However, these properties have not yet been put to any widespread clinical use.

Low Dose S.C. Heparin: For the prevention of serious venous thromboembolic complications in high risk surgical patients.

Contraindications: Hemophilia and severe clotting disorders; severe liver damage; shock; hypersensitivity to heparin. Active bleeding from a local lesion such as an acute ulcer or ulcerating carcinoma. Recent neurosurgery or spinal surgery.

Warnings: Administration of large doses of heparin should be delayed 4 hours postoperatively.

When any of the conditions mentioned under precautions are present the advantages of heparin therapy must be carefully weighed against the possibility of deleterious results.

Precautions: Purpura, and other blood dyscrasias with bleeding tendencies; active ulcerative diseases of the gastrointestinal tract; jaundice; subacute bacterial endocarditis; increased capillary fragility; threatened abortion; postoperative disease, following brain or spinal cord surgery. Malignant hypertension.

Heparin should be used with caution in the immediate postoperative period. Bleeding may be concealed, as in the case of hemothorax.

Pregnancy: Heparin should be used with caution in pregnancy although it does not cross the placental barrier and is the safest and most useful form of therapy in thromboembolic disorders of pregnancy.

For these reasons strict laboratory control of dosage is necessary. Heparin should be used with caution in patients with allergy. Patients on long term daily administration should be observed for the possible development of osteoporosis and spontaneous fractures of ribs and/or vertebrae.

Care must be taken where large doses of antibiotics and/or drugs containing amino groups are administered along with or prior to heparin administration.

Drugs such as codeine phosphate, pethidine HCl, streptomycin, erythromycin, kanamycin, neomycin, novobiocin, tetracyclines, ampicillin, penicillin G, polymyxin B, vancomycin, hydrocortisone sodium succinate, pentobarbitone, promazine HCl, vitamin B complex and vitamin C may complex with heparin. This complex may be reversible (heparin rebound) and may result in excess bleeding at the surgical site. Extra protamine sulfate may then be indicated.

Please also refer to the pH requirements in hemodialysis under indications.

Heparin has not been reported to interact pharmacologically in vivo with any other drugs. An increased bleeding tendency may be seen when heparin is used in combination with ethacrynic acid, ASA and dextran. Although digitalis, quinine, tetracycline, antihistamines, and nicotine have been stated to interfere with the anticoagulant activity of heparin, there is no substantial literature support for such interactions. The chemical interaction occurring between heparin and protamine

Hepalean (cont'd)

is well known. This interaction is used clinically to antagonize the anticoagulant effect of heparin.

I.V. administered ethacrynic acid can cause gastrointestinal bleeding. However, a significantly higher incidence of gastrointestinal bleeding has been attributed to the concurrent use of i.v. ethacrynic acid and heparin. Furosemide may be a safer alternative when such diuretic therapy is indicated in the patient receiving heparin.

In a review article of heparin therapy, it was advocated that concurrent ASA administration be scrupulously avoided. While documentation to support this interaction is incomplete, it would be prudent to avoid concurrent therapy. ASA impairs the platelet release reaction and this platelet function defect combined with the anti-coagulant effect of heparin may produce a hemorrhagic tendency.

Limited data suggest that dextran and heparin may act synergistically when administered concurrently. Although the data are inadequate to document the clinical significance of this interaction, baseline laboratory measurements of anticoagulant activity should be obtained upon initiation of concurrent therapy as well as at frequent intervals during such therapy.

Adverse Effects: Hemorrhage is the chief complication which may result from heparin therapy (see Overdose).

Hypersensitivity reactions, such as fever, skin eruptions, naso-pharyngeal congestion, bronchial asthma, anaphylactic shock, and osteoporosis, have been reported in some patients following heparin injection. Alopecia, effecting the entire scalp or confined to the temple, has been reported; the mechanism is unknown. Thrombocytopenia has also been described with heparin treatment.

Overdose: Symptoms and Treatment: Bleeding which may occur during therapy with heparin can usually be corrected by withdrawal. Clotting time should then return to normal in 30 to 60 minutes provided venous clotting time is not longer than 15 minutes when the infusion is interrupted. Should withdrawal of heparin fail to control bleeding, fresh, matched blood (not more than 3 days old) may be administered in quantities of 250 to 500 mL.

The most rapid means of counteracting the effects of heparin is i.v. administration of protamine sulfate. However, protamine is by itself an anticoagulant and, therefore, excess must be avoided. The amount of heparin neutralized by protamine varies with the organ from which it is derived, method of manufacture and specific activity of heparin. The amount of protamine required to neutralize 1 000 units of each lot of heparin used in the preparation of Hepalean is therefore accurately determined and is stated on the label as the number of mg of protamine sulfate required to neutralize 1 000 units.

Allowance should be made for the rapid removal of heparin from circulation. The rate of heparin removal from plasma is dose-dependent. However, it may be assumed that about 30 minutes after an i.v. injection, about 50% of the heparin is removed from circulation.

So the amount of protamine sulfate required to neutralize the heparin will be approximately half of that required for the original dose. For example if 1 000 units required 8.4 mg of protamine sulfate for neutralization, half an hour after i.v. administration of a 5 000 unit dose, the amount of protamine sulfate required will only be approximately:

$$5/2 \times 8.4 = 21 \text{ mg}$$

Do not administer more than 50 mg protamine sulfate at any one time.

Dosage: I.M. injection (especially in the arm or thigh) and shallow s.c. injection are not recommended. The duration of effect is shortened and it is more likely to produce pain and hematoma.

Heparin activity is expressed in USP units and should be prescribed in units only.

The route of administration may be i.v. or s.c., depending upon the situation and the choice of the prescriber (see Table I). Adequate heparin-induced anti-coagulant therapy is present when the clotting time is elevated from 2 to 3 times normal as measured by the Lee-White method. Two types of dosage schedule are suggested: heparin may be administered i.v. in a dose of 5 000 USP units every 4 hours or in a dose of 10 000 USP units every 6 hours, depending upon the results of a whole blood clotting time test performed at the bedside just prior to each additional dose. If the clotting time is less than twice normal, the next dose is increased by one-third to one-half. If the clotting time is more than 2 ½ times normal, the next dose is decreased by one-third to one-half. If the clotting time is between 2 and 2½ times normal, the regular dose is repeated.

S.C. Injection Technique: Use of a 1 mL tuberculin syringe with a No. 25 or No. 26, ½ inch needle is recommended.

Disinfect area with alcohol then apply pressure between finger and thumb to the dermal fold until the injection site is blanched; insert the needle into the raised, blanched area. Reduce the pressure on the skin and inject slowly; withdraw the needle quickly and apply alcohol swab with pressure to the site of injection for 5 to 10 seconds to prevent loss of the heparin.

Table I—Hepalean

Dosage

Administration Method	Frequency	Recommended dosage[a]
Low-dose s.c.[b]	Every 8 to 12 hours	5 000 units
S.C.	Every 8 hours	10 000 to 20 000 units initially[c] then 8 000 to 10 000 units 3 times a day.
Intermittent i.v.	Every 4 to 6 hours	10 000 units initially, then 5 000 to 10 000 units 4 to 6 times a day.
I.V. infusion	Continuous or intermittent	20 000 to 40 000 units per L at a rate of 15 to 30 units per minute.
Dialysis	See below	See below
Usual pediatric dose	Every 4 hours	By i.v. infusion 50 units per kg of body weight initially, followed by 100 units per kg or 3 333 units per square meter of body surface, 6 times a day.

[a]Based on 68 kg of body weight.
[b]It is not necessary to monitor low-dose prophylactic heparin.
[c]Following immediately after an initial dose of 5 000 units i.v.

Low Dose S.C. Heparin: There is now good evidence that low dose herapin is effective in preventing serious venous thromboembolic complications in high risk surgical patients. The usually recommended dose is 5 000 units s.c. 2 hours before surgery and then 5 000 units given either 12 hourly or 8 hourly after surgery with the first dose given at approximately 12 hours after surgery. It is not necessary to monitor low dose prophylactic heparin.

Therapeutic Anticoagulant Action (Immediate and Short-term): The dose should be adjusted in keeping with the patient's clotting time which should be determined just prior to the injection during the first day of treatment. It is also recommended that, in order to help regulate dosage, the clotting time be determined on the second and third day of treatment. (The recommended method is the Lee-White whole blood method.)

Anticoagulation is adequate when the clotting time is 2 to 3 times the normal value.

S.C. administration is usually employed for maintenance therapy after initial regulation.

Long-term Protective Anticoagulant Action: S.C. administration of 15 000 units every 12 hours is usually employed. Daily injections of 20 000 to 30 000 units have also been employed with success. After initial regulation the dosage should be adjusted according to weekly to monthly clotting time determinations. Anticoagulant therapy should not be terminated abruptly but should be gradually reduced over 3 to 4 days.

Deep Venous Thrombosis and Pulmonary Emoblism: Dosage of 20 000 units daily for 6 to 10 days has been of value.

Hemodialysis: (a) Multiple trauma: Recent literature has suggested the use of early hemodialysis in multiple trauma. (b) Chronic renal failure: The use of hemodialysis in this area has increased dramatically in recent years and may be in hospital or home dialysis.

It is most important to stress that the instructions for each equipment manufacturer's unit must be followed scrupulously.

The following is merely intended as an overall summary of possible general procedures: 3 000 units of heparin is added to 1 000 mL of sterile saline as a dialyser flush prior to connection. Initial dosage: 5 000 units of heparin into the venous shunt or 2 500 units into the arterial fistula needle. With the shunt type the usual continuing dosage is 2 000 units per hour, with the fistula type, 1 500 units per hour by means of a suitable syringe and a pump to allow continuing infusion. Heparin reversal with protamine will be decided by the individual physician. Usually this is not done unless dialysis is being performed soon after surgery.

Coronary and Vascular Surgery: Patients undergoing total body perfusion for open heart surgery should receive an initial dose of not less than 150 units of heparin/kg. Frequently a dose of 300 units of heparin/kg is used for procedures estimated to last less than 60 minutes; or 400 units/kg for those estimated to last longer than 60 minutes.

Supplied: Aqueous solutions, containing 1.0% benzyl alcohol as preservative, color coded labels: 1 000 USP units/mL in 10 or 30 mL vials; 10 000 USP units/mL in 5 mL vials; 25 000 USP units/mL in 2 mL vials. Cartons of 10 (2, 5, 10 and 30 mL).

Aqueous solution without preservative: 1 000 USP units/mL in 1 mL vial and 10 000 USP units/mL in 1 mL vial. Cartons of 100 (1 mL).

Source: Porcine intestinal mucosa.

HEPALEAN®-LOK

Organon Teknika

Heparin Sodium

Heparin Lock

Indications: Maintenance of patency of i.v. injection devices only. **Not** to be used for anticoagulant therapy.

Dosage: To prevent clot formation in a heparin lock set following its proper insertion, inject dilute heparin solution via the injection hub in a quantity sufficient to fill the entire set to the needle tip. Replace the solution each time the heparin lock is used. If the drug to be administered is incompatible with heparin, flush the entire heparin lock set with normal saline before and after the medication is administered; following the second flush the dilute heparin solution may be re-instilled into the set. Consult the manufacturer's instructions for specifics concerning the heparin lock set in use at a given time.*

Note: Since repeated injections of small doses of heparin can alter tests for activated partial thromboplastin time (APTT), obtain a baseline value for APTT prior to insertion of a heparin lock set.

*Refer to Hepalean monograph for general information.

Supplied: Each mL of solution contains: heparin sodium 10 (purple label) or 100 USP units, benzyl alcohol 1% as preservative, sodium chloride to isotonicity. Vials of 1 mL (without preservatives), cartons of 100. Vials of 10 mL, boxes of 10.

HEPARIN LEO®

Leo

Heparin Sodium

Anticoagulant

Pharmacology: Heparin is an anticoagulant which prevents the formation of thrombin by accelerating the neutralization of activated coagulation factors by naturally occurring inhibitors.

Indications: For the prophylaxis and management of intravascular clotting and embolism in susceptible patients.

It is also used in extra-corporeal circulation, i.e. heart-lung and renal dialysis machines and blood transfusions.

Contraindications: Hemorrhagic disorders and patients with an actual or potential bleeding site, e.g. peptic ulcer.

Low doses of heparin, administered as recommended, do not cause alterations in clotting times in most patients, but occasionally local hematomata may occur at injection sites.

Pregnancy and *Lactation:* Menstruation and pregnancy are not contraindications to heparin therapy since heparin does not cross placenta or appear in breast milk.

Warnings: Patients with hemorrhagic disorders may experience bleeding, especially from surgical wounds. The relative risks and benefits of heparin administration in these patients should be assessed carefully.

Oral anticoagulants or drugs which interfere with platelet function, e.g. ASA and dextran solutions, should be administered with caution.

Overdose: Symptoms and Treatment: If bleeding should occur, the effect of heparin can be reversed immediately by i.v. administration of a 1% protamine sulfate solution (1 mg for every 100 I.U. of heparin to be neutralized). The precise dose of protamine sulfate required for neutralization should be determined accurately by titrating with the patient's plasma.

Dosage: Low dose for prophylaxis (by s.c. injection only): Patients undergoing surgery: 5 000 IU should be given 2 to

6 hours pre-operatively and every 8 to 12 hours post-operatively for 10 to 14 days or until ambulation, whichever is the longer.

Other Patients: 5 000 units every 8 to 12 hours.

Therapeutic dose (by i.v. or s.c. injection): Average daily dose: 20 000 to 40 000 IU daily. However, the dose should be monitored with coagulation tests and varied according to individual response. The treatment period varies and can be as long as 6 weeks in patients with established thrombosis.

Stability in Infusion Fluids: Heparin Leo is stable for 24 hours at room temperature in the following infusion fluids: sodium chloride 0.9%, dextrose solutions (55 and 100 g/L), invertose (100 mg/L), Ringer solution, Ringer glucose, Ringer acetate, sodium bicarbonate 8.4%, Vamin with glucose. Stability tests were carried out using heparin concentrations of 10 and 20 units/mL.

Supplied: 100 IU/mL: Nonmedicinal ingredients: chlorobutanol hemihydrate, sodium chloride, sodium citrate and water for injection. Ampuls of 2 mL, vials of 10 mL.

1 000 IU/mL: Nonmedicinal ingredients: sodium chloride, sodium citrate and water for injection. Ampuls of 1 mL*.

Nonmedicinal ingredients: benzyl alcohol, methyl parahydroxybenzoate, propyl parahydroxybenzoate, sodium chloride, sodium citrate and water for injection. Vials of 10 and 20 mL.

10 000 IU/mL: Nonmedicinal ingredients: water for injection. Ampuls of 1 mL*.

Nonmedicinal ingredients: benzyl alcohol, methyl parahydroxybenzoate, propyl parahydroxybenzoate, sodium chloride, sodium citrate and water for injection. Vials of 5 mL.

25 000 IU/mL: Nonmedicinal ingredients: water for injection. Ampuls of 0.2 mL*.

Nonmedicinal ingredients: benzyl alcohol, methyl parahydroxybenzoate, propyl parahydroxybenzoate, sodium chloride, sodium citrate and water for injection. Vials of 2 mL.

*Preservative-free.

Store below 25°C. Admixture of heparin with solutions of other medicinal products may result in precipitation or loss of potency.

HEPARIN LOCK FLUSH

Abbott

Heparin Sodium

Heparin Lock Flush

Indications: Maintenance of patency of i.v. injection devices. **Not** to be used for anticoagulant therapy.

Supplied: Each mL contains: heparin sodium 10 USP units (derived from porcine intestinal mucosa), sodium chloride and edetate disodium anhydrous 0.01% as a stabilizer. Also contains benzyl alcohol and sodium hydroxide. Syringes of 1 mL. Boxes of 50. Multidose vials of 10 mL. Boxes of 25.

Each mL contains: heparin sodium 100 USP units (derived from porcine intestinal mucosa sodium chloride, edetate disodium anhydrous as a stabilizer. Also contains benzyl alcohol and sodium hydroxide. Multidose vials of 10 mL. Boxes of 25.

HEPARIN SODIUM AND 0.9% SODIUM CHLORIDE INJECTION

Baxter

Anticoagulant

Supplied: Each mL of sterile, nonpyrogenic solution contains: heparin sodium USP in 0.9% sodium chloride injection. Viaflex Plus plastic (polyvinylchloride) containers in the following sizes and concentrations: see Table I.

Table I—Heparin Sodium and 0.9% Sodium Chloride Injection

Supplied		
Total Volume (mL)	**USP Heparin Units**	**Heparin Concentration (U/mL)**
500	1 000	2
1 000	2 000	2

Do not store above 30°C. Protect from freezing.

HEPARIN SODIUM IN 5% DEXTROSE INJECTION

Abbott

Anticoagulant

Supplied: Each mL of sterile, nonpyrogenic fluid for i.v. administration contains: heparin sodium 2 units (1 000 units/500 mL), 40 units (20 000 units/500 mL) or 50 units (25 000 units/500 mL) in 500 mL 5% Dextrose Injection. Nonmedicinal ingredients: citric acid, sodium metabisulfite, sodium phosphate dibasic and water for injection.

HEPARIN SODIUM IN 5% DEXTROSE INJECTION

Baxter

Anticoagulant

Supplied: Each mL of sterile, nonpyrogenic solution contains: heparin sodium USP equivalent to 40, 50 and 100 USP heparin units in 5% dextrose injection. Viaflex Plus plastic (polyvinyl chloride) containers in the following sizes and concentrations: see Table I.

Table I—Heparin Sodium in 5% Dextrose Injection

Supplied		
Total Volume (mL)	**USP Heparin Units**	**Heparin Concentration (U/mL)**
500	20 000	40
500	25 000	50
250	25 000	100

Exposure of pharmaceutical products to heat should be minimized. Avoid excessive heat. It is recommended the products be stored at room temperature (25°C); brief exposure up to 40°C does not adversely affect the product.

HEPARIN: UNFRACTIONATED

General Monograph, CPhA

Heparin Sodium

Anticoagulant

> This monograph has been compiled by CPhA. It may contain information different from that approved by Therapeutic Products Programme, Health Canada, and the pharmaceutical manufacturers' approval has not been requested.

Pharmacology: Heparin is a heterogeneous preparation of sulfated mucopolysaccharide polymers whose molecular weights range from 3 000 to 30 000 daltons, averaging between 12 000 and 15 000 daltons. Heparin exerts its anticoagulant activity by reversibly binding to antithrombin III (AT III), accelerating the ability of AT III to neutralize thrombin and activated coagulation factor X (Xa). The heparin-AT III complex also inactivates activated coagulation factors IX, XI, XII and plasmin. Thrombin and factor Xa are the most sensitive to inactivation by the heparin-AT III complex.

Heparin is not a thrombolytic agent. It does not directly cause clot lysis, but prevents progression of the existing clot by inhibiting any further clotting processes, allowing naturally occurring thrombolytics to slowly effect clot lysis.

At therapeutic doses, heparin prolongs several coagulation tests including activated coagulation time, activated partial thromboplastin time (APTT, used clinically), plasma recalcification time, prothrombin time (minimally), thrombin time and whole blood clotting time.

Pharmacokinetics: Heparin is not absorbed through the gastrointestinal mucosa and must be given parenterally, usually by i.v. infusion or deep s.c. injection. The onset of action is immediate after i.v. injection but can be delayed 20 to 60 minutes following s.c. injection. Heparin is extensively bound to plasma proteins. Heparin does not cross the placental barrier and is not distributed into breast milk. Heparin is not removed by hemodialysis.

The dose-response relationship of heparin is not linear. Anticoagulant effect increases disproportionately in intensity and duration as the dose is increased. The plasma half-life of heparin increases from approximately 60 minutes with a 100 unit/kg dose to about 150 minutes with a 400 unit/kg dose. Clinically a half-life of approximately 90 minutes is used.

Heparin is cleared via a dual mechanism. At low doses, clearance is predominantly through a saturable mechanism by the reticuloendothelial system. At higher doses, renal clearance through a nonsaturable mechanism also occurs. The rapid saturable mechanism predominates at therapeutic heparin concentrations.

The clearance of heparin from plasma is accelerated in patients with pulmonary embolism and may be reduced in patients with cirrhosis or severe renal impairment.

There is no definitive evidence that the pharmacokinetic or anticoagulant properties of the forms of heparin derived from porcine or bovine sources or prepared as sodium or calcium salts are different (see Adverse Effects).

Indications: Heparin is used in the treatment of acute deep venous thrombosis and pulmonary embolism. It is effective when used prophylactically in low doses to prevent the occurrence of venous thromboembolism in moderate risk patients.

Heparin is used to prevent clotting during dialysis and to prevent intravascular coagulation during open heart surgical procedures.

The use of heparin in the treatment of cerebral and coronary thrombosis is controversial. If used during stroke, heparin should only be used if hemorrhage has been ruled out and there are major, progressing neurological deficits. In patients with acute MI who are also receiving thrombolytics, i.v. heparin therapy in conjunction with low dose oral ASA is recommended. In patients with unstable angina, continous i.v. heparin can reduce the incidence of acute MI and recurrent angina, but it is not known if mortality is reduced.

Dilute concentrations of heparin are used to maintain the patency of i.v. injection devices; however, in the case of peripheral devices, heparin is no more effective than 0.9% sodium chloride for injection.

Contraindications: Patients with a generalized hemostatic abnormality such as hemophilia, Christmas disease, idiopathic thrombocytopenic purpura and patients with active bleeding from a local lesion such as an acute ulcer or ulcerating carcinoma; patients who have had recent neurosurgery or spinal surgery; hypersensitivity to heparin, including thrombocytopenia; severe liver damage; shock.

Warnings: Administration of large doses of heparin should be delayed at least 4 hours postoperatively.

Precautions: Anticoagulants are thought to be of no value in completed stroke and may even increase the risk of fatal cerebral bleeding. When considered for use in any of the following conditions, the advantages of heparin therapy must be carefully weighed against the risks:

Cardiovascular: subacute bacterial endocarditis; increased capillary permeability; dissecting aneurysm; severe hypertension; during and immediately following major surgery, especially of the brain, spinal cord and eye.

Hematologic: conditions associated with increased bleeding tendencies such as hemophilia, some purpuras and thrombocytopenia. In patients with a history of heparin-induced thrombocytopenia (HIT), danaparoid and ancrod are considered alternatives.

When used in therapeutic doses, heparin should be regulated by frequent blood coagulation indicators particularly the APTT. If the indicator is unduly prolonged or if hemorrhage occurs, heparin should be at least temporarily discontinued (see Overdose). Monitoring can be effectively performed using a weight-based heparin dose adjustment nomogram (see Table III on following pages).

Heparin can prolong the prothrombin time.

Apparent resistance to heparin may be encountered in patients with acquired or familial AT III deficiency, since adequate levels of AT III are required for heparin's anticoagulant effect. Larger doses of heparin may be required initially in patients with various disease states due to alterations in their physiology, the pharmacokinetics of the drug, or elevations in levels of acute phase heparin binding proteins. Some of these disease states have been reported to be: febrile illness, infections associated with thrombosing tendencies, pulmonary embolism, myocardial infarction, extensive thrombotic disorders especially those associated with neoplastic disease and following surgery.

Gastrointestinal: inaccessible ulcerative lesions; ulcerative colitis; continuous tube drainage of stomach or small intestine.

Obstetric: threatened abortion; menstruation.

Heparin should be used with caution in the presence of severe hepatic or renal disease, or in patients with indwelling catheters. A higher incidence of bleeding may be seen in women over 60 years of age.

Heparin: Unfractionated (cont'd)

Patients on long-term daily administration of heparin should be observed for the possible development of osteoporosis and spontaneous fracture of ribs and/or vertebrae.

Drug Interactions: Oral anticoagulants (i.e., warfarin) can contribute to a small extent to an increase in APTT. Heparin can contribute to an increase in PT. While these two drugs are given together, the fact that each may contribute to an increase in PT and APTT should be taken into account (see Precautions).

Heparin is often started with or several hours after thrombolytic therapy with alteplase or streptokinase, to increase patency of coronary vessels after coronary thrombolysis. The APTT should be monitored closely, starting 4 to 6 hours after initiation of heparin therapy. Close patient monitoring for clinical signs of bleeding is indicated.

Salicylates, other nonsteroidal anti-inflammatory agents, dextran, dipyridamole and ticlopidine interfere with platelet aggregation which increases the risk of bleeding. Use with caution and monitor patients for signs of hemorrhage.

Cefamandole, cefotetan, methimazole, propylthiouracil and valproic acid may cause hypoprothrombinemia and increase the risk of bleeding; monitor patient for signs of bleeding.

Probenecid may increase and prolong the anticoagulant action of heparin.

Nitroglycerin, i.v., may reduce heparin's anticoagulant effect and necessitate higher doses. This interaction has been reported to occur regardless of whether or not propylene glycol is used as a solvent for the nitroglycerin. The mechanism has not been conclusively documented. When i.v. nitroclycerin therapy is initiated, monitor patients closely to ensure anticoagulation remains adequate. Likewise, when nitroglycerin therapy is stopped, a decrease in heparin dosage may be necessary and patients should be monitored for signs of excessive anticoagulation.

Digitalis, quinine, ACTH, insulin, corticosteroids, antihistamines and nicotine have been reported to interfere with the anticoagulant effect of heparin; however, there is no substantial literature support to document these interactions.

I.M. injections of other drugs should be avoided during heparin therapy to reduce the risk of hematoma formation and bleeding from the site. Most drugs can be given by another route (i.v. or s.c.).

Pregnancy: Heparin does not cross the placenta and has not been related to congenital defects. However, its use during pregnancy has been associated with a 13 to 22% risk of fetal mortality or prematurity. While this appears high, it is not clear whether severity of maternal disease or an indirect effect of heparin is responsible. Coumarin anticoagulants have been associated with a 31% unfavorable outcome and a definite drug-induced pattern of malformations has been demonstrated (fetal warfarin syndrome). However, the incidence of warfarin-induced fetopathic effects in the second and third trimesters is very low. In general, heparin is considered to be the anticoagulant of choice in pregnancy. Long-term usage (>3 to 5 months) of therapeutic doses of heparin during pregnancy increases the risk of osteoporosis and warrants careful monitoring of patients on this type of therapy. Like heparin, low molecular weight heparins (LMWHs) do not cross the placenta and may be considered in pregnant patients with osteoporosis (see Adverse Effects). Heparin therapy during the last trimester and immediate postpartum period is associated with a risk of maternal hemorrhage. Changes in pharmacokinetics during pregnancy require caution and close patient monitoring if heparin is used.

Reports of therapeutic failure with adjusted-dose heparin therapy in pregnant patients with prosthetic heart valves may have been due to inadequate dosing or to an inherent limitation in these patients. If used in this group, heparin should be administered in high doses with careful laboratory monitoring.

Lactation: Heparin is not excreted in breast milk because of its high molecular weight.

Adverse Effects: Hematologic: Bleeding is the most common side effect of heparin and is an extension of its pharmacological effect. Occurrence is approximately 10% overall but may increase up to 20% in patients treated with high dose therapy. Risk of bleeding likely increases with APTT ratios above the recommended target range. Other risk factors associated with bleeding are: a serious concurrent illness, chronic heavy consumption of alcohol, use of platelet-inhibiting drugs, renal failure, age and female sex. Bleeding may range from minor local ecchymoses to major hemorrhagic events. Often the first sign of bleeding may be epistaxis, hematuria or melena. Bleeding may be from any site and can be difficult to detect, i.e., retroperitoneal bleeds. Bleeding may also occur from surgical sites. Petechiae or easy bruising may precede frank hemorrhage. A supratherapeutic APTT or minor bleeding during therapy can usually be controlled by adjusting the dosage or withdrawing the drug (see Overdose).

HIT is an allergic reaction. It has been reported to occur in 1 to 30% of patients treated with standard heparin. It has also occurred with the use of LMWHs, both in patients with a history of HIT and patients with no previous exposure to heparin. The risk of developing HIT may be lower with LMWHs but cannot be reliably estimated until more patients have been exposed. It is thought to be more common with heparin derived from bovine lung (5 to 10%) than from porcine gut (2 to 5%). Two types of acute, reversible thrombocytopenia have been described. Mild thrombocytopenia most commonly occurs between 5 and 12 days after initiation of full dose therapy. Platelet count usually remains above 100×10^9/L, and heparin therapy does not necessarily have to be withdrawn. Platelet count may remain stable or even increase despite continued therapy; however, it should still be monitored. The more severe, delayed form of thrombocytopenia (platelets $< 100 \times 10^9$/L), is much less frequent, usually appearing 5 to 12 days after starting heparin therapy and recurs rapidly on rechallenge. It has occurred with low dosages and is not dose related. It is generally reversible, platelet counts usually begin to return to normal within 4 days of stopping heparin. Paradoxically, patients may develop thrombotic complications including arterial thrombosis, gangrene, stroke, myocardial infarction and disseminated intravascular coagulation. Thrombosis is due to "white clots" composed of platelets and fibrin that result from marked in vivo platelet aggregation. Patients receiving heparin acutely should have platelet counts monitored at least every 2 or 3 days.

Bone and Joint: Therapeutic doses of heparin administered for longer than 3 months have been associated with osteoporosis and spontaneous vertebral fractures. Recent reports indicate that osteoporosis may be reversible after discontinuation of heparin.

Hepatic: Heparin has been reported to cause elevations of AST and ALT in approximately 27 and 59% of patients, respectively. Transient increases in serum LDH levels have also occurred. No clinical signs of liver dysfunction have been reported and the significance is not known, except that interpretation of liver enzymes for other purposes (i.e., liver disease) must take into consideration the possible contribution of heparin.

Hypersensitivity: Heparin-induced thrombocytopenia (see Adverse Effects, Hematologic). Other allergic reactions to heparin are rare. The most common manifestations of hypersensitivity are chills, fever and urticaria. Asthma, rhinitis, tearing, headache, nausea, vomiting, shock and anaphylactoid reactions have also occurred. Vasopasm has been reported 6 to 10 days after starting heparin; the etiology is thought to be allergic. Vasospasm often appears in a limb where an artery has recently been catheterized. The affected limb is usually painful, ischemic and cyanotic. Protamine sulfate is of no use in hypersensitivity reactions.

Miscellaneous: Alopecia, affecting the entire scalp or confined to the temple, may occur. Itching and burning of the plantar surfaces of the feet. Suppression of aldosterone production, hyperkalemia (due to aldosterone suppression), priapism and rebound hyperlipidemia have also been reported.

Overdose: Symptoms and Treatment: If the APTT is excessive but bleeding is not apparent or minor, heparin infusion may be stopped temporarily and then restarted if desired, at a reduced rate. The heparin antagonist, protamine sulfate, can be considered for severe bleeding, especially if the APTT is greater than 3 times control.

If immediate reversal of heparinization is desired, 1 mg of protamine sulfate can be used to neutralize approximately 90 units of bovine lung source heparin and 115 units of porcine intestinal mucosa source heparin. The amount of heparin neutralized by protamine not only varies with the organ from which it is derived but also with the method of manufacture and the specific activity of heparin. The amount of protamine required to neutralize 1 000 units of an individual lot of heparin can be determined and may be listed on individual product labels.

Too rapid administration of protamine can cause severe hypotensive and anaphylactoid-like reactions. Facilities to treat shock should be readily available when administering protamine. The rate of protamine administration should not exceed 20 mg/min and no more than 50 mg should be given in any 10-minute period. Doses exceeding 100 mg in a short period of time should be avoided, unless there is certain knowledge of larger protamine requirements. Any excess protamine sulfate, not complexed to heparin, has its own intrinsic anticoagulant effect. However, one study found overdose of protamine up to 600 to 800 mg i.v. to have only minor, transient effects on blood coagulation.

Due to the relatively short half-life of heparin (approximately 90 minutes), decreasing amounts of protamine sulfate are required as time from the last heparin injection increases (see Table I).

Table I—Heparin: Unfractionated

Protamine Dosing in Heparin Overdose

Time from last i.v. heparin injection (minutes)	Protamine dose in mg/100 units of heparin remaining
0–29	1–1.5
30–60	0.5–0.75
>120	0.25–0.375

If heparin is given by continuous infusion, 25 to 50 mg of protamine sulfate may be given slowly after stopping the infusion. If heparin was given by deep s.c. injection, protamine dosage should be determined according to the amount given.

Dosage: Heparin may be given by intermittent or continuous i.v. infusion or by deep (intrafat) s.c. injection, depending upon the situation and the prescriber's choice. Avoid i.m. injection of heparin. Continuous infusion is the preferred method for administration of full-dose heparin therapy, but requires the use of a constant rate infusion pump. Intermittent infusions are not recommended, having been associated with a higher incidence of bleeding, likely due to higher total dosages required. Undesirable fluctuations of over- and under-coagulation also occur with intermittent infusions due to the short half-life of heparin. The s.c. route is usually reserved for prophylactic administration of heparin; however, it can also be given in dosages sufficient to treat thromboembolism. Ideally, the dose of heparin should be adjusted to prolong the APTT to a targeted therapeutic range based on a "gold standard" heparin assay (0.2 to 0.4 units/mL by protamine sulfate titration).

Dosage requirements for full-dose heparin therapy vary widely between individuals. Body weight is a relatively good predictor of heparin dose and initial dosages may be calculated on a unit/kg basis (see Table III on following page).

An initial APTT should be obtained 6 hours after commencement of heparin therapy and after every change in infusion rate. In children, an APTT should be obtained 4 hours after the loading dose and every 4 hours following each change in infusion rate. It is desirable to obtain 2 or 3 APTT determinations in the first 24 hours to stabilize the dose, and then one each day for the remainder of heparin therapy. Further dosage changes should reflect both laboratory and clinical findings.

The duration of heparin therapy ranges from 5 to 14 days. The 5-day course has been reported to be as effective as 7- to 10-day courses for proximal venous thrombosis and submassive pulmonary embolism. For patients with recurrent thrombotic events, massive pulmonary embolism or massive iliofemoral venous thrombosis, a 7- to 10-day course may be more effective.

Treatment of Venous Thrombosis and Pulmonary Embolism (Full-Dose Therapy) (see Table II on following page): The following regimens have been recommended: I.V.: a) Initial bolus of 5 000 units, followed by 30 000 to 40 000 units by continuous infusion over 24 hours. b) Initial bolus of 80 units/kg, followed by continuous infusion of 18 units/kg/h.

Children: Initial bolus of 75 to 100 units/kg followed by continuous infusion of 28 units/kg/h for infants, 20 units/kg/h for children older than 1 year of age and 18 units/kg/h for older children.

S.C.: Initial i.v. bolus of 5 000 units. Starting dose should be 17 500 units s.c. every 12 hours but ranges from 15 000 to 20 000 units s.c. every 12 hours. The APTT should be taken at 6 hours postdose (midpoint of dosing interval) and dosage adjusted to maintain APTT between 1.5 and 2 times control.

Prevention of Venous Thromboembolism (Fixed-Dose Therapy) (see Table II): The usual prophylactic dose for general surgical and medical patients at risk for thromboembolism is 5 000 units s.c. every 12 hours, starting 2 hours preoperatively and continuing for 5 to 7 days or until the patient is fully ambulatory, whichever is longer. The APTT is usually not prolonged by this dose and it is not necessary to monitor the APTT. The patient must still be clinically assessed for signs of thrombotic events (i.e., failure of prophylaxis) and full-dose heparin initiated if this occurs.

Certain groups of patients at high risk for thromboembolic events, i.e., those undergoing major orthopedic surgery or those with a previous history of venous thrombosis, should

Table II—Heparin: Unfractionated

Initial Heparin Dosage Summary

Indication	Route	Dosage
Treatment (Full-Dose Therapy) Adults	Continuous I.V.	Bolus: 5 000 units, then 30 000 to 40 000 units/24 hours. OR Bolus: 80 units/kg then 18 units/kg/hour.
	Subcutaneous	Initial i.v. bolus of 5 000 units then 15 000 to 20 000 units q12h. OR 17 500 units q12h.
Children	Continuous I.V.	Initial bolus of 75 to 100 units/kg then 28 units/kg/h for infants, 20 units/kg/h for children older than 1 year, 18 units/kg/h for older children.
Prophylaxis (Fixed-Dose Therapy)		
Adults General Medical/ Surgical	Low Dose Subcutaneous	5 000 units s.c. q12h starting 2 hours preoperatively.
High Risk	Subcutaneous	5 000 units s.c. q12h, adjust to upper end of APTT range.

Table III—Heparin: Unfractionated

Body Weight-Based Dosing of Intravenous Heparin in Adults[a,b]

APTT (seconds)	Dose Change (units/kg/h)	Additional Action	Next APTT (h)
<35 (<1.2×mean normal)	+4	Rebolus with 80 units/kg	6
35-45 (1.2-1.5×mean normal)	0	Rebolus with 40 units/kg	6
46-70[c] (1.5-2.3×mean normal)	0	0	6[d]
71-90 (2.3-3.0× mean normal)	−2	0	6
>90 (>3×mean normal)	−3	Stop infusion for 1 h	6

[a] Adapted with permission from: Hirsh, J., Guidelines for Antithrombotic Thearpy, 2nd Ed., B.C. Decker Inc. 1995.
[b] Initial dosing: 80 units/kg; maintenance infusion of heparin, at a rate dictated by body weight through an infusion apparatus calibrated for low flow rates: 18 units/kg/h (APTT in 6 hours).
[c] The therapeutic range in seconds should correspond to a plasma heparin level of 0.2 to 0.4 units/mL by protamine sulfate titration. When APTT is checked at 6 hours or longer, steady-state kinetics can be assumed.
[d] During the first 24 hours, repeat APTT every 6 hours. Thereafter, monitor APTT once every morning unless it is outside the therapeutic range.

receive an adjusted low dose of heparin s.c. that maintains the APTT at the upper end of the normal range (see Table III).

Long-term Therapy: Low dose s.c. heparin has been used for prevention of venous thrombosis or for follow-up treatment of deep vein thrombosis in patients in whom the use of oral anticoagulants is not feasible (i.e., pregnancy). Dosages have ranged from 5 000 units every 8 to 12 hours over 6 weeks to 6 months.

Disseminated Intravascular Coagulation: Heparin therapy for the treatment of DIC is controversial. For adults, 50 to 100 units/kg and for children 25 to 50 units/kg by i.v. infusion over 4 hours or by i.v. injection every 4 hours has been recommended. If no improvement is apparent by 4 to 8 hours, heparin should be discontinued.

Hemodialysis: For patients with multiple trauma or chronic renal failure, follow the equipment manufacturers operating instructions carefully.

Coronary Surgery: Heparin (10 000 units as an i.v. bolus) should be commenced immediately prior to angioplasty or coronary stent placement and followed by repeated boluses or continuous infusion of heparin to maintain the activated clotting time greater than 300 seconds with the Hemotec and greater than 300 seconds with the Hemochron. Alternatively, a weight adjusted regimen of 100 to 175 units/kg followed by 10 to 15 units/kg/h may be used. Heparin should be stopped after 2 to 4 hours in uncomplicated cases, but may be continued for up to 24 hours in complicated cases.

Peripheral Arterial Surgery: Heparin in doses of 100 to 150 units/kg i.v. is usually administered prior to cross clamping and supplemented with doses of 50 units/kg i.v. every 40 minutes until flow is restored. Protamine sulfate should be administered at the end of the procedure.

Heparin Lock Flush: Heparin lock flush solution in a concentration of 10 to 100 units/mL can be used to maintain the patency of indwelling venipuncture devices. However, recent literature indicates that the use of heparin-containing solutions to maintain catheter patency of peripheral indwelling infusion devices is not necessary and that normal saline for injection is equally effective.

Reviewed 1997

HEPARINS: LOW MOLECULAR WEIGHT Ⓟ

General Monograph, CPhA

Dalteparin
Enoxaparin
Nadroparin
Tinzaparin

Anticoagulant

This monograph has been compiled by CPhA. It may contain information different from that approved by Therapeutic Products Programme, Health Canada, and the pharmaceutical manufacturers' approval has not been requested.

Pharmacology: Low molecular weight heparins (LMWHs) are fragments of heparin produced by enzymatic or chemical depolymerization. They have an average molecular weight of 4 000 to 5 000 daltons (range 1 000 to 10 000 daltons) which is approximately one-third that of standard heparin.

Most heparin molecules with molecular weights smaller than 5 400 daltons are unable to bind thrombin and antithrombin simultaneously, as can unfractionated heparin. Therefore, LMWHs are less able to accelerate the inactivation of thrombin (factor II) but retain the ability to catalyze the inhibition of factor Xa. The anti-factor Xa to anti-factor IIa ratio of LMWHs ranges from 2:1 to 4:1, compared to 1:1 for unfractionated heparin. These ratios are based on in vitro testing and may not reflect the relative anticoagulant activity in humans (see Table I).

Pharmacokinetics: Unlike heparin, LMWHs do not bind significantly to plasma proteins. This accounts for the different pharmacokinetic properties, dosing regimens and laboratory monitoring requirements of these two classes of heparins. Furthermore, LMWHs do not bind to endothelial cells and macrophages, which is felt, in part, to contribute to their longer plasma half-lives in comparison with unfractionated heparin.

The biological half-life of LMWHs is not dose-dependent and is about 2 to 4 times longer than that of unfractionated heparin at therapeutic doses. In contrast, unfractionated heparin exhibits a dose-dependent biological half-life due to a rapid phase of saturable intracellular elimination followed by nonsaturable renal elimination.

LMWHs are cleared primarily by the renal route. The half-life is extended in patients with renal failure. Consult individual product monographs for recommendations regarding dosage adjustment in renal failure. Table II compares the pharmacokinetics of LMWHs and unfractionated heparin.

Table I—Heparins: Low Molecular Weight

Pharmacologic Comparison, including Unfractionated Heparin

	Anti-Xa to Anti-IIa Activity Ratio	Average Molecular Weight (daltons)
Dalteparin	2.2 : 1.0	5 000
Enoxaparin	>4.0 : 1.0	4 500
Nadroparin	2.5 to 4.0 : 1.0	4 300
Tinzaparin	1.9 : 1.0	4 500
Unfractionated heparin	1.0 : 1.0	15 000

Table II—Heparins: Low Molecular Weight

Pharmacokinetic Comparison of Low Molecular Weight Heparins vs. Unfractionated Heparin

Pharmacokinetic Property	Low Molecular Weight Heparins	Unfractionated Heparin
Plasma protein binding	minimal	significant
Endothelial cell/ macrophage binding	no	yes
Dose-dependent clearance	no	yes
Bioavailability at low-dose (subcutaneous)	>90%	10–30%
Bioavailability at high-dose	>90%	90%
Elimination	renal (nonsaturable)	low-dose cellular uptake (saturable) high-dose renal (nonsaturable)
Half-life	dose-independent (2 to 4 hours)	dose-dependent (0.5 to 4 hours)

Indications: Currently, no data are available which directly compare the efficacy of different LMWHs for a given indication using recommended doses; therefore, the available agents cannot be used interchangeably.

Table III (on following page) lists the current labeled indications for the available LMWHs.

Contraindications: LMWHs should not be used when the following medical problems exist: uncontrolled active bleeding, severe hypertension (because of increased risk of cerebral hemorrhage), hemorrhagic stroke, allergy or hypersensitivity to heparin, pork products or to the LMWH, or a history of thrombocytopenia with the specific LMWH.

LMWHs should be avoided in patients with a history of heparin-induced thrombocytopenia (HIT). Specialists recommend danaparoid or ancrod as alternatives in these patients.

Warnings: LMWHs should not be injected by the i.m. route because of the risk of hematoma.

There have been reports of intraspinal hematoma resulting in long-term or permanent paralysis in patients undergoing spinal or epidural anesthesia while on LMWH therapy. The risk may be higher with repeated or traumatic catheter insertion or with concurrent use of other drugs affecting hemostasis. Caution is advised if concurrent LMWH therapy and spinal or epidural anesthesia is considered.

LMWHs, like other anticoagulants, should be used with extreme caution in any medical procedure or condition in which the risk of bleeding or hemorrhage is present such as: septic endocarditis, major blood clotting disorders, blood dyscrasias, active gastric or duodenal ulceration, injuries to or surgery involving the CNS, eyes or ears, diabetic or hemorrhagic retinopathy, or severe hepatic or renal insufficiency.

Doses of LMWHs recommended for prophylaxis are lower and not appropriate for the treatment of acute thrombosis.

Precautions: Periodic complete blood counts including platelet counts and stool occult blood tests are recommended during the course of treatment. Physical examinations should be performed to monitor for bleeding complications.

Heparins: Low Molecular Weight (cont'd)

Table III—Heparins: Low Molecular Weight

Labeled Indications

Indication	Dalteparin	Enoxaparin	Nadroparin	Tinzaparin
Prophylaxis of deep vein thrombosis in:				
Surgery	Yes		Yes	Yes[a]
Orthopedic surgery			Yes	Yes
Orthopedic surgery, specifically of knee or hip		Yes		
High-risk abdominal, gynecological or urological surgery		Yes		
Colorectal surgery		Yes		
Treatment of venous thrombosis	Yes		Yes	
Prevention of clotting in the extracorporeal system during hemodialysis and hemoperfusion in patients with chronic renal failure	Yes		Yes	
Treatment of unstable angina or non-Q-wave MI, concurrently with ASA	Yes	Yes		

[a]General surgery in patients at high risk for developing postoperative venous thromboembolism.

Table IV—Heparins: Low Molecular Weight

Dosage

Indication	Dalteparin	Enoxaparin	Nadroparin	Tinzaparin
Prophylaxis of Deep Vein Thrombosis in:				
General surgery	2 500 anti-Xa IU s.c. 1 to 2 hours before surgery, then each morning for at least 5 to 7 days.[a]		2 850 anti-Xa IU s.c. 2 to 4 hours before surgery then daily for at least 7 days.	3 500 anti-Xa IU s.c. 2 hours before surgery,[b] then 3 500 anti-Xa IU s.c. daily for 7 to 10 days.
Orthopedic surgery		30 mg s.c. every 12 hours starting 12 to 24 hours after surgery, for 7 to 14 days.	38 anti-Xa IU/kg s.c. 12 hours before surgery, 12 hours after surgery and daily for 3 days, then 57 anti-Xa IU/kg s.c. daily for at least 7 days.	
Orthopedic surgery, specifically of knee or hip	Hip Surgery: 5 000 anti-Xa IU s.c. the evening before surgery, then every evening for at least 5 to 7 days.[c]			Hip Surgery: 50 anti-Xa IU/kg s.c. 2 hours before surgery, then 50 anti-Xa IU/kg daily for 7 to 10 days **OR** 75 anti-Xa IU s.c. daily postoperatively for 7 to 10 days. Knee Surgery: 75 anti-Xa IU/kg s.c. daily postoperatively, for 7 to 10 days.
Colorectal surgery or high-risk abdominal, gynecological or urological surgery		40 mg s.c. 2 hours before surgery, then daily for 7 to 10 days.		
Treatment of venous thrombosis	200 anti-Xa IU/kg s.c. daily. Single daily dose should not exceed 8 000 IU.	1.5 mg/kg s.c. daily **OR** 1 mg/kg s.c. every 12 hours. Single daily dose should not exceed 180 mg.	86 anti-Xa IU/kg s.c. twice daily for 10 days.	175 anti-Xa IU/kg s.c. daily.
Prevention of clotting in the extracorporeal system during hemodialysis and hemoperfusion in patients with chronic renal failure with no known bleeding risk[d]	30 to 40 anti-Xa IU/kg i.v. bolus at start of session then i.v. infusion of 10 to 15 anti-Xa IU/kg/hour. Alternatively, for sessions lasting 4 hours or less, may give one i.v. bolus injection of 5 000 anti-Xa IU.		65 anti-Xa IU/kg into the arterial line at start of each session; if session longer than 4 hours, may give a repeat dose.	
Treatment of unstable angina and non-Q-wave MI, concurrently with ASA	120 anti-Xa IU/kg s.c. twice daily, with a maximum of 10 000 IU/dose, for up to 6 days.[e]	1 mg/kg s.c. every 12 hours, with a maximum of 10 000 IU/dose, for 2 to 8 days.[e]		

[a]Prophylaxis should continue until patient is well-mobilized.
[b]General surgery in patients at high risk for developing postoperative venous thromboembolism.
[c]This dosing regimen may also be used for patients with other bleeding risk factors undergoing general surgery.
[d]Consult individual product monographs for recommendations pertaining to hemodialysis in patients with acute renal failure or high risk of bleeding.
[e]Concomitant therapy with ASA (100 to 325 mg daily) is recommended.

With usual dosing, LMWHs do not consistently modify global clotting tests of activated partial thromboplastin time (APTT), prothrombin time (PT) and thrombin clotting time (TT); therefore, treatment cannot be monitored with these tests. Anti-factor-Xa activity has been used for assessing the activity of LMWHs. However, it does not correlate directly with therapeutic efficacy. The proposed therapeutic range is 0.5 to 1 IU anti-Xa/mL, between 3 and 4 hours after a s.c. injection.

Drug Interactions: Caution should be exercised when using LMWHs together with oral anticoagulants or platelet inhibitors because of an increased risk of bleeding.

Pregnancy: Large and well-controlled studies in humans have not been done. In animal studies LMWHs were shown not to be teratogenic or embryotoxic. LMWHs do not cross the placental barrier, and individual case reports have described the use of LMWH during pregnancy without maternal or fetal complications. Small studies have suggested that LMWH prophylaxis is safe during pregnancy. However, LMWHs should not be used in pregnancy unless the therapeutic benefits to the patient outweigh the possible risks.

Lactation: It is not known if LMWHs are distributed into breast milk. The manufacturers recommend that patients receiving LMWHs should avoid breast-feeding; however, given that these agents have a high molecular weight when compared with many other classes of drugs, it is highly probable that the extent of excretion into breast milk would be negligible.

Children: Safety and efficacy has not been established.

Adverse Effects: The incidence of hemorrhagic complications during treatment with LMWHs has been low. The incidence of bleeding may increase with higher doses.

The most commonly reported side effect is hematoma at the injection site. Mild local irritation, pain and erythema following s.c. injection are reported less frequently.

The following side effects have been reported rarely: allergic reactions (e.g., pruritus, rash, fever, injection site reaction, hives), skin necrosis, anaphylactoid reactions and thrombocytopenia. To date, LMWHs have been associated with a lower risk of thrombocytopenia than standard heparin; however, until a greater number of patients have been exposed, the exact incidence cannot be reliably estimated.

A slight to moderate elevation of liver transaminases (AST, ALT) has been reported but has not correlated to any long-term effect on liver function. Transaminase determinations are important in the differential diagnosis of myocardial infarction, liver disease or pulmonary embolism; elevations should be interpreted carefully.

Bleeding complications associated with overdose may include: hematuria, bloody or black tarry stools, bruising, hemoptysis, hematemesis, ecchymosis, hematoma, hypochromic anemia, nosebleed, persistent bleeding or oozing from mucous membranes or surgical wounds, shortness of breath, vomiting of material that resembles coffee grinds.

Osteoporosis has been reported with prolonged use of LMWHs.

Overdose: Symptoms and Treatment: Accidental overdosage with LMWHs may lead to severe bleeding. This may be reduced by slow i.v. injection of protamine sulfate. A dose of 1 mg of protamine sulfate is administered for every 100 anti-factor Xa IU of dalteparin or tinzaparin, for each 158 anti-factor Xa IU of nadroparin, or for each 1 mg of enoxaparin. If the APTT measured 2 to 4 hours after the first infusion remains prolonged, a second infusion of 0.5 mg protamine sulfate per 100 anti-factor Xa IU of dalteparin or tinzaparin or per mg of enoxaparin may be administered. Even after an additional dose of protamine, the APTT may remain more prolonged following administration of a LMWH than after standard heparin. Protamine sulfate should completely neutralize the anti-factor IIa effect but not the anti-factor Xa effect which is neutralized to a maximum of only 60 to 75%, depending on the particular LMWH.

Protamine sulfate should be administered cautiously to avoid overdosing. Severe hypotension and anaphylactoid reactions, including death, may occur with protamine sulfate. It should be administered only when treatment of anaphylactic shock and resuscitation techniques are readily available.

Dosage: In general, LMWHs are administered by deep s.c. injection once or twice daily as recommended by the manufacturer. They should not be injected by the i.m. route (see Warnings). Dalteparin may also be administered by intermittent or continuous i.v. infusion; however, the manufacturer suggests that s.c. administration may be the route of choice because of the long half-life, high bioavailability, low incidence of side effects and ease of administration.

Depending on the product, injection sites include: a U-shaped area around the navel, the upper outer aspect of the thigh, or upper outer quadrangle of the buttock. The site should be varied daily. The patient should be sitting or lying down during injection. If giving the injection around the navel or the thigh, a fold of skin must be lifted up with thumb and forefinger and the entire length of the needle inserted at a 45 to 90 degree angle.

There has been limited clinical experience with the use of LMWHs in the treatment of deep vein thrombosis in very obese patients. Some experts recommend periodic monitoring of anti Xa levels in such patients.

LMWHs cannot be used interchangeably (unit for unit) with unfractionated heparin or with other LMWHs since they differ in their relative inhibition of factor Xa and factor IIa.

Table IV (on previous page) lists the dosage recommendations for the labeled indications of the available LMWHs. It is not meant to be exhaustive; product monographs should be consulted.

Reviewed 1999

HERACLINE® Ⓟ
Technilab
Hematopoietic

Supplied: Each 10 mL oral ampul contains: glandular extracts corresponding to fresh adrenal cortex 2.5 g, fresh testicular gland 5 g, veal liver extract containing vitamin B_{12} 6 μg and alcohol 95% 1.8 g. Nonmedicinal ingredients: granulated sugar and parabens. Boxes of 12.

HERBAL LAXATIVE
Swiss Herbal
Senna Compound
Laxative

Supplied: Each tablet contains: senna leaves 240 mg, cascara sagrada 150 mg, rhubarb root 8 mg, gentian root 8 mg, liquorice root 30 mg, juniper berries 8 mg, buchu leaves 4 mg, oil of peppermint q.s. Preservative-free. Nonmedicinal ingredients: cellulose, magnesium stearate, silicon dioxide and starch. Bottles of 90, 180 and 500.

HERBAL NERVE
Swiss Herbal
Liquorice Compound

Supplied: Each tablet contains: valerian root 78 mg, scullcap 78 mg, gentian root 52 mg and liquorice powder 130 mg. Nonmedicinal ingredients: dolomite, magnesium stearate and starch. Bottles of 90 and 180.

HERPLEX® Ⓟ
Allergan
Idoxuridine
Antiviral

Supplied: Each mL of sterile ophthalmic solution contains: idoxuridine 0.1%. Nonmedicinal ingredients: benzalkonium chloride (as preservative), disodium edetate, polyvinyl alcohol (Liquifilm) and sodium chloride. Plastic dropper bottles of 15 mL. Store at room temperature. Protect from light.

HERPLEX®-D Ⓟ
Allergan
Idoxuridine
Antiviral Agent

Supplied: Each mL of sterile, topical solution contains: idoxuridine 0.1%. Nonmedicinal ingredients: benzalkonium chloride (as preservative), edetate disodium, polyvinyl alcohol (Liquifilm) and sodium chloride. Plastic dropper bottles of 10 mL. Store at room temperature. Protect from light.

HEXABRIX® 200
HEXABRIX® 320
Mallinckrodt
Ioxaglate Meglumine—Ioxaglate Sodium
Radiopaque Medium

Pharmacology: Following intravascular injection, Hexabrix is rapidly transported through the circulatory system to the kidneys and is excreted unchanged in the urine. The pharmacokinetics of intravascularly administered radiopaque contrast media are usually best described by a two compartment model with a rapid alpha phase for drug distribution and a slower beta phase for drug elimination. In patients with normal renal function, the alpha and beta half-lives of Hexabrix 320 were 12 and 92 minutes, respectively.

Following the i.v. administration of 50 mL of Hexabrix 320 in normal volunteers, the mean peak plasma concentration occurred at 2 minutes, reaching a concentration of 2.13 mg/mL. Fifty percent of the i.v. administered dose was recovered in the urine at 2 hours, and approximately 90% was recovered at 24 hours.

Injectable iodinated contrast agents are excreted either through the kidneys or through the liver. These 2 excretory pathways are not mutually exclusive, but the main route of excretion seems to be related to the affinity of the contrast medium for serum albumin. Ioxaglate salts are poorly bound to serum albumin and are excreted mainly through the kidneys.

The liver and small intestine provide the major alternate route of excretion. Hexabrix appears to be excreted primarily by glomerular filtration but some tubular re-absorption may occur. In the rat, biliary excretion plays a major role (up to 30%). As with iothalamate, in patients, especially with renal impairment, the excretion of this contrast medium through the gallbladder and into the small intestine sharply increases. Occasional visualization of the gallbladder following administration of Hexabrix is suggestive of such a mechanism. Heterogenic excretion to a lesser extent occurs via the saliva, sweat and colon.

Studies in the pregnant mouse have shown that ioxaglate and diatrizoate are capable of crossing the placental barrier and invading fetal tissue.

Angiography: Hexabrix opacifies vessels along the path of injection until such time as hemodilution renders them no longer visible. The digital subtraction technique allows arterial visualization following i.v. injection of Hexabrix 320, or following intra-arterial injection of the lower concentration contrast medium Hexabrix 200. The joint spaces, as well as the uterus and fallopian tubes, may be visualized by direct injection of the contrast medium into those structures.

Computerized Tomography of the Head: When Hexabrix is used for contrast enhancement in computed tomographic brain scanning, the degree of enhancement is related to the amount of iodine administered. Rapid infusion of the entire dose amount yields peak blood iodine concentrations immediately following the infusion, which fall rapidly over the next 5 to 10 minutes. This can be accounted for by the dilution in the vascular and extracellular fluid compartments which causes an initial sharp fall in plasma concentration. Equilibrium with the extracellular compartments is reached by about 10 minutes; thereafter, the fall becomes exponential. With respect to tumors, maximum contrast enhancement frequently occurs at a time following peak blood iodine concentration. This delay in maximum contrast enhancement can range from 5 to 40 minutes, depending on the peak iodine levels achieved and the cell type and vascularity of the tumor. This lag suggests that the contrast enhancement of the image is at least in part dependent on the passage of iodine through the defective blood-brain barrier and on its accumulation within the lesion and outside the blood pool. The image enhancement of nontumoral lesions, such as arteriovenous malformations and aneurysms, is probably dependent on the iodine content of the circulating blood pool. Studies indicate that equilibrated blood iodine levels of 100 mg% are required in most cases to achieve adequate contrast enhancement. This can be accomplished by the rapid infusion of approximately 30 to 40 g of iodine (95 to 125 mL of Hexabrix 320).

In brain scanning, the contrast medium does not accumulate in normal brain tissue due to the presence of the blood-brain barrier. The increase in x-ray absorption in the normal brain is due to the presence of the contrast agent within the blood pool. A break in the blood-brain barrier, such as occurs in malignant tumors of the brain allows accumulation of the contrast medium within the interstitial tumor tissue; adjacent normal brain tissue does not contain the contrast medium.

Computerized Tomography of the Body: In non-neural tissues (during CT of the body), Hexabrix diffuses rapidly from the vascular to the extravascular space. Increase in x-ray absorption is related to blood flow, concentration of the contrast medium and extraction of the contrast medium by interstitial tissue since no barrier exists; contrast enhancement is thus due to the relative differences in extravascular diffusion between normal and abnormal tissue, a situation quite different from that in the brain.

Enhancement of CT with Hexabrix may be of benefit in establishing diagnoses of certain lesions in some sites with greater assurance than is possible with unenhanced CT and in supplying additional features of the lesions. In other cases, the contrast medium may allow visualization of lesions not seen with CT alone or may help to define suspicious lesions seen with unenhanced CT.

The pharmacokinetics of Hexabrix in normal and abnormal tissue has been shown to be variable. Contrast enhancement appears to be greatest within 30 to 90 seconds after bolus administration, thus greatest enhancement can be detected by a series of consecutive 2 to 3 second scans (Dynamic CT Scanning) during this time period. Dynamic scanning may improve enhancement and diagnostic assessment of tumors and other lesions such as an abscess, occasionally revealing more extensive disease. A cyst, or similar nonvascularized lesion may be distinguished from vascularized solid lesions by comparing enhanced and unenhanced scans; the nonvascularized lesions show no change in CT number, the vascularized lesions would show an increase. The latter might be benign, malignant or normal, but it is unlikely that it would be a cyst, hematoma or other nonvascularized lesion.

Due to the low osmolality of Hexabrix, the increase in circulating blood volume is less than that caused by traditional iodinated contrast agents. This was demonstrated by hematocrit determinations in animals and is consistent with mean values for cardiac output observed in controlled clinical studies. In some double blind clinical trials, Hexabrix produced statistically significant reductions in some hemodynamic changes and discomfort (pain) when compared to contrast agents with higher osmolalities, and different iodine content and concentration.

Hexabrix produced significant but transient reductions in respiratory rate, increase or decrease in pulse rate, significant post-injection increases or decreases in systolic and diastolic blood pressure, LVSP, RVSP, LVEDP, RVEDP, and pulmonary artery pressure.

Statistically significant laboratory parameter changes have occurred, such as decreased HB, RBC, HCT, relative lymphopenia, increased ALT, CPK, LDH, bilirubin and decreased serum Na, Cl, K and Ca.

With respect to ECG changes, arrhythmias and ST wave changes, these showed a similar incidence with Hexabrix 320 and Na meglumine diatrizoate 37% I.

Two studies of the action of Hexabrix 320 on the EEG have been carried out. In one, changes were seen in only 1 patient out of 16, who had shown Stage 1 coma and evidence of intracranial hypertension prior to the examination. In the other transient low voltage delta waves were noted 5 times in 38 injections.

Effects of Hexabrix on thyroid function consisted of significant but slight rises in hormonal iodine and T_3 and minor decreases in rT_3. There were no changes in TSH. Both Hexabrix and diatrizoic acid activated both the classical and alternative complement pathways in vitro.

Hexabrix 320 has a viscosity of 8.9 at 37°C, as compared to iothalamate meglumine 52% and iothalamate sodium 26% (40% I) which is approximately 9.0, iothalamate meglumine 60% (28.2% I) which is approximately 4.0, and diatrizoate meglumine 66% and diatrizoate sodium 10% (37% I) which has a viscosity of approximately 7.6 at 37°C.

Indications: Hexabrix 200: For use in phlebography, intra-arterial digital subtraction angiography, and for i.v. contrast enhancement of computed tomography of the body.

Hexabrix 320: For use in cerebral angiography, peripheral arteriography, selective coronary arteriography with or without left ventriculography, pediatric angiocardiography, i.v. digital subtraction angiography and i.v. contrast enhancement of computed tomography of the brain and body. It is also indicated in phlebography, arthrography, excretory urography and hysterosalpingography.

Contraindications: Use in myelography and in any other intrathecal procedure. This preparation must not be used in patients with severe hepatic and renal disease and in patients with hypersensitivity to salts of ioxaglic acid (see Warnings and Precautions concerning hypersensitivity to other agents).

Hexabrix (cont'd)

Warnings: Ionic iodinated contrast media inhibit blood coagulation, in vitro, more than nonionic contrast media. Nonetheless, it is prudent to avoid prolonged contact of blood with syringes containing ionic contrast media.

Serious, rarely fatal, thromboembolic events causing myocardial infarction and stroke have been reported during angiographic procedures with both ionic and nonionic contrast media. Therefore, meticulous intravascular administration technique is necessary, particularly during angiographic procedures, to minimize thromboembolic events.

Numerous factors, including length of procedure, catheter and syringe material, underlying disease state and concomitant medications may contribute to the development of thromboembolic events. For these reasons, meticulous angiographic techniques are recommended including close attention to guidewire and catheter manipulation, use of manifold systems and/or 3-way stopcocks, frequent catheter flushing with heparinized saline solutions and minimizing the length of the procedure. The use of plastic syringes in place of glass syringes has been reported to decrease but not eliminate the likelihood of in vitro clotting.

Serious or fatal reactions have been associated with the administration of all iodine containing radiopaque media. It is of utmost importance to be completely prepared to treat any contrast medium reaction. As with any contrast medium, serious neurologic sequelae, including permanent paralysis, can occur following cerebral arteriography and injection into vessels supplying the spinal cord. The injection of a contrast medium should never be made following the administration of vasopressors since they strongly potentiate neurologic effects.

A previous reaction to a contrast medium of different chemical structure or a history of iodine sensitivity is not an absolute contraindication to the use of Hexabrix if the examination is essential for the welfare of the patient. However, extreme caution should be exercised in injecting these patients and prophylactic therapy should be considered (see Precautions, General).

A definite risk exists in the use of intravascular contrast agents in patients who are known to have multiple myeloma. In such instances anuria has developed resulting in progressive uremia, renal failure and eventually death. Although neither the contrast agent nor dehydration has separately proved to be the cause of anuria in myeloma, it has been speculated that the combination of both may be causative factors. The risk in myelomatous patients is not a contraindication to the procedure; however, partial dehydration in the preparation of these patients for the examination is not recommended since this may predispose to precipitation of myeloma protein in the renal tubules. No form of therapy, including dialysis, has been successful in reversing the effect. Myeloma, which occurs most commonly in persons over 40, should be considered before instituting intravascular administration of contrast agents.

Administration of radiopaque materials to patients known or suspected to have pheochromocytoma should be performed with extreme caution. If, in the opinion of the physician, the possible benefits of such procedures outweigh the considered risks, the amount of radiopaque medium injected should be kept to an absolute minimum. The blood pressure should be assessed throughout the procedure, and measures for treatment of a hypertensive crisis should be available.

Intravascular administration of contrast media may promote sickling in individuals who are homozygous for sickle cell disease. Fluid restriction is not advised. In patients with advanced renal disease, iodinated contrast media should be used with caution, and only when the need for the examination dictates, since excretion of the medium may be impaired. Patients with combined renal and hepatic disease, those with severe hypertension or congestive heart failure and recent renal transplant recipients may present an additional risk.

Precautions: General: Diagnostic procedures which involve the use of iodinated intravascular contrast agents should be carried out under the direction of a physician skilled and experienced in the particular procedure to be performed.

All procedures utilizing contrast media carry a definite risk of producing adverse reactions. While most reactions are minor, life-threatening and fatal reactions may occur without warning. The risk-benefit factor should always be carefully evaluated before such a procedure is undertaken. At all times a fully equipped emergency cart, or equivalent supplies and equipment, and personnel competent in recognizing and treating adverse reactions of all severity, or situations which may arise as a result of the procedure, should be immediately available. If a serious reaction should occur, immediately discontinue administration and institute appropriate treatment. Since severe delayed reactions have been known to occur, emergency facilities and competent personnel should be available for at least 30 to 60 minutes after administration.

Some severe, life-threatening reactions suggest hypersensitivity to the radiopaque agent, which has prompted the use of several provocative pretesting methods, none of which can be relied on to predict severe reactions. No conclusive relationship between severe reactions and antigen-antibody reactions or other manifestations of allergy has been established.

The possibility of an idiosyncratic reaction in patients who have previously received a contrast medium without ill effect should always be considered. A positive history of bronchial asthma or allergy, a family history of allergy, or a previous reaction of hypersensitivity to another contrast agent warrant special attention. Such a history, by suggesting histamine sensitivity and consequently proneness to reactions, may be more accurate than pre-testing in predicting the potential for reaction, although not necessarily the severity or type of reaction in the individual case. A positive history of this type does not arbitrarily contraindicate the use of a contrast agent, when a diagnostic procedure is thought essential, but calls for caution.

Prophylactic therapy including corticosteroids and antihistamines should be considered for patients who present with a strong allergic history, a previous reaction to a contrast medium, or a positive pre-test since in these patients the incidence of reaction is 2 to 3 times that of the general population. Adequate doses of corticosteroids should be started early enough prior to contrast medium injection to be effective and should continue through the time of injection and for 24 hours after injection.

Antihistamines should be administered within 30 minutes prior to the contrast medium injection. A separate syringe should be used for this injection because of chemical incompatibility.

The sensitivity test most often performed is the slow injection of 0.5 to 1.0 mL of the radiopaque medium, administered i.v., prior to injection of the full dose. It should be noted that the absence of a reaction to the test dose does not preclude the possibility of a reaction to the full dose. If the test dose (or subsequent diagnostic injection) causes an untoward response, the examination should be terminated and appropriate measures taken to combat the adverse reaction. In rare instances, reactions to the test dose itself may be extremely severe, therefore, close observation of the patient, and facilities for emergency treatment, are indicated.

Renal failure has been reported in patients with liver dysfunction who were given an oral cholecystographic agent followed by an intravascular iodinated radiopaque agent and also in patients with occult renal disease, notably diabetics and hypertensives. Administration of Hexabrix should be postponed in patients with hepatic or biliary disorder who have recently taken a cholecystographic agent. Especially in these classes of patients there should be no fluid restriction and every attempt made to maintain normal hydration, prior to contrast medium administration, since dehydration is the single most important fact influencing further renal impairment. **Partial dehydration is not necessary; it may be dangerous and is not recommended for uro-angiographic procedures.** Consideration must be given to the functional ability of the kidneys before injecting this preparation because of the possibility of inducing or aggravating renal damage. An interval of at least 48 hours should be allowed between examinations, especially in patients with reduced renal reserve. Caution should be exercised in performing contrast medium studies in patients with homocystinuria, endotoxemia and in those with elevated body temperatures. Acute renal failure has been reported in patients with diabetic nephropathy and in susceptible non-diabetic patients (often elderly with preexisting renal disease) following administration of iodinated contrast agents. Careful consideration of the potential risks should be given before performing these radiographic procedures in these patients.

General anesthesia may be indicated in the performance of some procedures in selected patients; however, a higher incidence of adverse reactions has been reported in these patients, and may be attributable to the inability of the patient to identify untoward symptoms or to the hypotensive effect of anesthesia which can prolong the circulation time and increase the duration of contact of the contrast agent.

Reports of thyroid storm occurring following the intravascular use of iodinated radiopaque agents in patients with hyperthyroidism or with an autonomously functioning thyroid nodule, suggest that this additional risk be evaluated in such patients before use of this drug. Iodine containing contrast agents may alter the results of thyroid function tests. Such tests, if indicated, should be performed prior to the administration of this preparation.

Special precaution is advised in patients with increased intracranial pressure, cerebral thrombosis or embolism, primary or metastatic cerebral lesions, subarachnoid hemorrhage, arterial spasm, transient ischemic attacks, and in any condition when the blood brain barrier is breached or the transit time of the contrast material through the cerebral vasculature is prolonged, since clinical deterioration, convulsions, and serious temporary or permanent neurological complications (including stroke, aphasia, cortical blindness, etc.) may occur following i.v. or intra-arterial injection of relatively large doses of contrast media. Such patients, and patients in clinically unstable or critical condition should undergo examinations with intravascular contrast media only if in the opinion of the physician the expected benefits outweigh the potential risks, and the dose should be kept to the absolute minimum.

There have been reports in the literature indicating that patients on adrenergic beta-blockers may be more prone to severe adverse reactions to contrast media. At the same time, treatment of allergic-anaphylactoid reactions in these patients is more difficult. Epinephrine should be administered with caution since it may not have its usual effects. On the one hand larger doses of epinephrine may be needed to overcome the bronchospasm, while on the other, these doses can be associated with excessive alpha adrenergic stimulation with consequent hypertension, reflex bradycardia and heart-block and possible potentiation of bronchospasm. Alternatives to the use of large doses of adrenaline include vigorous supportive care such as fluids and the use of beta agonists including parenteral salbutamol or isoproterenol to overcome bronchospasm and norepinephrine to overcome hypotension.

Pregnancy: Reproduction studies have been performed in rats and rabbits at doses up to 2 times the maximum adult human dose and have revealed no conclusive evidence of impaired fertility or harm to the fetus due to Hexabrix. It is, however, known that Hexabrix crosses the placenta and reaches fetal organs and tissues. There are, however, no adequate and well controlled studies in pregnant women. Because animal reproduction studies are not always predictive of human response, this drug should be used during pregnancy only if clearly needed.

Lactation: Because contrast media are excreted in human milk and because of the potential for serious adverse reactions in nursing infants from Hexabrix, a decision should be made whether to discontinue nursing and substitute bottle feedings for breast-feeding for a minimum of 24 hours following administration of this drug, or not to administer the drug taking into account the importance of the drug to the mother.

(Precautions for specific procedures receive comment under that procedure.)

Adverse Effects: General: **Note:** Since Hexabrix is an iodinated intravascular contrast agent, all of the side effects and toxicity associated with this class of compound are possible, and this should be borne in mind when it is administered. Adverse reactions accompanying the use of iodine-containing contrast agents are usually mild and transient, although severe and life-threatening reactions, including fatalities, have occurred. Because of the possibility of severe reactions to both the procedure and the radiopaque medium appropriate emergency facilities and well trained personnel should be available to treat both types. Emergency facilities and personnel should remain available for 30 to 60 minutes following the procedure since severe delayed reactions have been reported.

The most frequent adverse reactions are nausea, vomiting, facial flush and a feeling of body warmth. These are usually of brief duration.

Other reactions include the following: Hypersensitivity: dermal manifestations of urticaria with or without pruritus, erythema and maculopapular rash, dry mouth, allergic glossitis, sweating, conjunctival symptoms, facial, peripheral and angioneurotic edema.

Respiratory system: sneezing, nasal stuffiness, coughing, choking, dyspnea, chest tightness and wheezing, which may be initial manifestations of more severe and infrequent reactions including asthmatic attack, laryngospasm and bronchospasm with or without edema, pulmonary edema, apnea and cyanosis. Rarely, these allergic-type reactions can progress into potentially fatal anaphylactic shock with loss of consciousness and coma and severe cardiovascular disturbances.

Cardiovascular: generalized vasodilation, flushing and venospasm. Occasionally, thrombosis or rarely, thrombophlebitis. Extremely rare cases of disseminated intravascular coagulation resulting in death have been reported. Severe cardiovascular responses include rare cases of hypotensive shock, coronary insufficiency, cardiac arrhythmia, fibrillation and arrest. These severe reactions are usually reversible with prompt and appropriate management; however, fatalities have occurred.

Neurological: spasm, convulsions, aphasia, syncope, paresis, paralysis, visual field losses which are usually transient but may be permanent, coma and death.

Other: headache, trembling, shaking, chills without fever, hyperthermia and lightheadedness renal shutdown or other nephropathy. Laboratory parameter changes include decreased lymphocytes, HB, RBC hematocrit, serum Na, Cl, K, Ca. Elevation of liver enzymes and bilirubin have been reported.

Technique: extravasation with burning pain, hematomas, ecchymosis and tissue necrosis, vascular constriction due to injection rate, thrombosis and thrombophlebitis, bleeding, perforation and dissection of blood vessels, dislodgement of atheromatous plaques, and injury to neighboring organs. (Adverse effects to specific procedures receive comment under that procedure).

Treatment of Adverse Effects: Contrast media should be administered only by physicians thoroughly familiar with the emergency treatment of all adverse reactions to contrast media. The assistance of other trained personnel such as cardiologists, internists and anesthetists is required in the management of severe reactions.

A guideline for the treatment of adverse reactions is presented below. This outline is not intended to be a complete manual on the treatment of adverse reactions to contrast media or on cardiopulmonary resuscitation. The physician should refer to the appropriate texts on the subject.

It is also realized that institutions or individual practitioners will already have appropriate systems in effect and that circumstances may dictate the use of additional or different measures.

Minor Allergic Reactions (if considered necessary): The i.v. or i.m. administration of an antihistamine such as diphenhydramine hydrochloride 25 to 50 mg is generally sufficient (contraindicated in epileptics). The resulting drowsiness makes it imperative to ensure that outpatients do not drive or go home unaccompanied.

Major or Life-threatening Reactions: A major reaction may be manifested by signs and symptoms of cardiovascular collapse, severe respiratory difficulty and nervous system dysfunction. Convulsions, coma and cardiorespiratory arrest may ensue.

The following measures should be considered: Start emergency therapy immediately, carefully monitoring vital signs. Have emergency resuscitation team summoned: do not leave patient unattended. Ensure patent airway: guard against aspiration. Commence artificial respiration if patient is not breathing. Administer oxygen, if necessary. Start external cardiac massage in the event of cardiac arrest. Establish route for i.v. medication by starting infusion of appropriate solution (5% dextrose in water). Judiciously administer specific drug therapy as indicated by the type and severity of the reaction. Careful monitoring is mandatory to detect adverse reactions of all drugs administered: a) soluble hydrocortisone 500 to 1 000 mg i.v. for all acute allergic-anaphylactic reactions. b) epinephrine 1:1 000 solution (in the presence of anoxia it may cause ventricular fibrillation; Caution in patients on adrenergic beta blockers. See Precautions): i) 0.2 to 0.4 mL s.c. for severe allergic reactions. ii) in extreme emergency 0.1 mL/minute, appropriately diluted, may be given i.v. until desired effect is obtained. Do not exceed 0.4 mL. iii) in case of cardiac arrest 0.1 to 0.2 mL, appropriately diluted, may be given intracardially. c) in hypotension (carefully monitoring blood pressure): i) phenylephrine hydrochloride 0.1 to 0.5 mg appropriately diluted slowly i.v. or by slow infusion or ii) levarterenol bitartrate 4 mL of 0.2% solution in 1 000 mL of 5% dextrose by slow drip infusion. d) sodium bicarbonate 5%; 50 mL i.v. every 10 minutes as needed to combat post-arrest acidosis. e) atropine 0.4 to 0.6 mg i.v. to increase heart rate in sinus bradycardia. May reverse 2nd or 3rd degree block. f) to control convulsions: i) pentobarbital sodium 50 mg in fractional doses slowly i.v. (contraindicated if cyanosis is present) or ii) diazepam 5 to 10 mg slowly i.v. titrating the dose to the response of the patient. Defibrillation, administration of antiarrhythmics and additional emergency measures and drugs may be required. Transfer patient to intensive care unit when feasible for further monitoring and treatment.

Dosage: It is advisable that Hexabrix be at or close to body temperature when injected. Discard unused portion. The patient should be instructed to omit the meal that precedes the examination, but it should be ensured that the patients are not dehydrated. Appropriate premedication, which may include a barbiturate, tranquilizer or analgesic drug, may be administered prior to the examination.

A preliminary film is recommended to check the position of the patient and the x-ray exposure factors prior to the injection of the contrast medium.

If during administration a minor reaction occurs, the injection should be stopped until the reaction has subsided. If a major reaction occurs, the injection should be discontinued immediately.

Under no circumstances should other drugs be administered concomitantly in the same syringe or i.v. administration set because of a potential for chemical incompatibility.

Sufficient time should be permitted to elapse between injections to allow for the subsidence of hemodynamic disturbances.

Patency of the vessel and the position of the catheter tip or needle should be checked with a small pilot dose before injecting the full dose. The catheter tip should be kept free of aspirated blood.

Parenteral drug products should be inspected visually for particulate matter and discoloration prior to administration. If either is present, the vial should not be used.

Contrast media should not be transferred into other delivery systems except immediately before use.

Cerebral Angiography: Hexabrix 320 may be used to visualize the cerebral vasculature by any of the accepted techniques.

Patient Preparation: Suitable premedication may be given. Introduction of the catheter or needle is normally performed with local anesthesia. General anesthesia is rarely required (see Precautions, General).

Precautions: In addition to the general precautions previously described, cerebral angiography should be performed with special caution in patients with advanced arteriosclerosis, severe hypertension, cardiac decompensation, senility, recent cerebral thrombosis, embolism or subarachnoid hemorrhage, and following a recent attack of migraine.

Adverse Effects: The major sources of cerebral arteriographic adverse reactions appear to be related to repeated injections of the contrast material, administration of doses higher than those recommended, the presence of occlusive atherosclerotic vascular disease and the method and technique of injection.

Adverse reactions are normally mild and transient. A feeling of warmth in the face and neck is frequently experienced. Infrequently, a more severe burning discomfort is observed. Transient visual hallucinations have been reported.

Serious neurological reactions that have been associated with cerebral angiography include stroke, amnesia, hemiparesis, visual field loss, cortical blindness, aphasia, confusion, disorientation, hallucination, convulsions, coma and death.

Cardiovascular reactions that may occur with some frequency are bradycardia and either an increase or decrease in systemic blood pressure. The blood pressure change is transient and usually requires no treatment.

Usual Dosage: The usual dosage of Hexabrix 320 employed varies with the site and method of injection and the age and condition of the patient. The usual adult dose range for common carotid arteriography is 6 to 12 mL; for vertebral arteriography, 5 to 10 mL; for aortic arch injection (4 vessel studies), 30 to 50 mL.

These doses may be repeated if indicated. The total dose per procedure should be limited to the smallest volume necessary to achieve a diagnostic examination.

Intra-arterial Digital Subtraction Angiography: Hexabrix 200 is suitable for intra-arterial digital subtraction angiography (IA-DSA), since with this technique lower iodine concentrations yield diagnostic images. Other advantages of the procedure are the use of less contrast medium and a decreased need for selective arterial catheterization. However, with aortic arch injection visualization of intracranial vasculature may be insufficient.

Patient Preparation: No special patient preparation is required for IA-DSA. However, it is advisable to insure that patients are well hydrated prior to examination.

Precautions: In addition to the general precautions described, the risks associated with IA-DSA are those usually associated with cerebral arteriography and catheter procedures. Following the procedure, gentle pressure hemostasis is required, followed by observation and immobilization of the limb for several hours to prevent hemorrhage from the site of arterial puncture. Patient motion, including respiration and swallowing, can result in misregistration leading to image degradation and non-diagnostic studies.

Usual Adult Dosage: As a general rule, the volume and concentration used for IA-DSA are about 50%, or less, of that used for conventional procedures. The actual dosage and flow rate will vary depending on the selectivity of the injection site and the area being examined.

The following suggested volumes per injection of Hexabrix 200 are intended as a guide. Injections may be repeated if necessary. It is advisable to inject at rates approximately equal to the flow rate of the vessel being injected. Carotid arteries 6 to 10 mL; vertebral arteries 4 to 8 mL; aortic arch (4 vessel study) 25 to 50 mL; subclavian or brachial arteries 2 to 10 mL; femoral arteries 8 to 10 mL.

Peripheral Arteriography: Hexabrix 320 may be injected to visualize the arterial peripheral circulation. Arteriograms of the upper and lower extremities may be obtained by any of the established techniques.

Patient Preparation: The procedure is normally performed with local anesthesia. In rare instances, general anesthesia may be required (see Precautions, General).

A preliminary radiograph is usually made prior to the injection of the contrast agent.

Precautions: In addition to the general precautions previously described, moderate decreases in blood pressure occur frequently with intra-arterial injections. This change is usually transient and requires no treatment; however, the blood pressure should be monitored for approximately 10 minutes following injection.

Extreme caution during injection of the contrast agent is necessary to avoid extravasation and fluoroscopy is recommended. This is especially important in patients with severe arterial disease (e.g. thromboangiitis obliterans, ischemia, thrombosis, obstruction). When injections are being made in the distal aorta for aorto-iliac run-off studies, the possibility of inadvertent injection of a large dose into a branch of the aorta or intramural dissection should be considered.

To prevent these occurrences, the position of the catheter tip or needle should be carefully evaluated. Pulsation must be present in the artery to be injected. A small dose of 1 to 2 mL should be administered to locate the exact site of the needle or catheter tip. Severe pain, paresthesia or peripheral muscle spasm during injection may require discontinuance of the procedure and a re-evaluation of the catheter tip or needle placement.

Great care is necessary to avoid entry of a large bolus into an aortic branch. Mesenteric necrosis, acute pancreatitis, renal shutdown and serious neurologic complications, including paraplegia and quadriplegia have been reported and may be attributable to an excessive dose being injected into an aortic branch or arterial trunks supplying the spinal arteries or to prolonged contact time of the concentrated contrast medium on the CNS tissue. Conditions which can contribute to prolonged contact time include decreased circulation, aortic occlusions distal to the site of injection, abdominal compression, hypotension, general anesthesia or the administration of vasopressors. When these conditions exist or occur, the necessity of performing or continuing the procedure should be carefully evaluated and the dose and number of repeat injections should be maintained at a minimum with appropriate intervals between injections. Following catheter procedures, gentle pressure hemostasis is advised, followed by observation and immobilization of the limb for several hours to prevent hemorrhage from the site of arterial puncture.

Adverse Effects: In addition to the general adverse reactions previously described, extravasation, hematoma, gangrene, hemorrhage and thrombosis have occurred. Brachial plexus injury has been reported following axilliary artery injection. Dissecting aneurysm, arteriovenous fistula are additional complications.

Usual Dosage: The single adult dose of Hexabrix 320 for aorto-iliac run-off studies is 20 to 60 mL; for common iliac, the external iliac and the femoral arteries, 10 to 40 mL; for the upper limb, 10 to 30 mL. These doses may be repeated as indicated. The total procedural dose should be limited to the smallest volume required to obtain a diagnostic examination.

Selective Coronary Arteriography with or without Left Ventriculography: Precautions: In addition to the general precautions previously described, it is recommended that this procedure should not be performed for approximately 4 weeks following the diagnosis of myocardial infarction. Mandatory prerequisites to the procedure are experienced personnel, ECG monitoring apparatus and adequate facilities for immediate resuscitation and cardioversion.

The patient's ECG and vital signs should be monitored continuously throughout the procedure. The injection of large volumes of hypertonic solutions into the heart chambers can cause significant hemodynamic changes.

Special care should be exercised in patients being treated with calcium ion antagonists, since in such circumstances a few instances of serious arrhythmias have been reported.

Adverse Effects: Most patients will have transient ECG changes during the procedure. The following adverse effects have occurred in conjunction with the administration of iodinated intravascular contrast agents for this procedure: hypotension, shock, anginal pain, myocardial infarction, cardiac

Hexabrix (cont'd)

arrhythmias (bradycardia, ventricular tachycardia, ventricular fibrillation) and cardiac arrest. Fatalities have been reported. Complications to the procedures include dissection of coronary arteries, dislodgement of atheromatous plaques, perforation, hemorrhage and thrombosis.

Usual Dosage: The usual adult dose range of Hexabrix 320 for left coronary arteriography is 2 to 10 mL and for right coronary arteriography is 1 to 8 mL. For left ventriculography, the usual single adult dose is 35 to 40 mL. These doses may be repeated if indicated; however, several minutes should be allowed to elapse between injections to allow for subsidence of hemodynamic disturbance, and the total procedural dose should be limited to the smallest volume necessary to obtain a diagnostic examination.

Pediatric Angiocardiography: Angiocardiography with Hexabrix 320 may be performed by any accepted technique.

Patient Preparation: Normal patient hydration should be maintained. Appropriate pre-medication should be given.

Warnings: In addition to general warnings previously described, the inherent risk of angiocardiography in cyanotic infants must be weighed against the necessity for performing this procedure. A dose of 10 to 20 mL may be particularly hazardous in infants weighing less than 7 kg. This risk is probably significantly increased if these infants have preexisting right heart strain, heart failure and effectively decreased or obliterated pulmonary vascular beds.

Apnea, bradycardia and other arrhythmias, cerebral effects, electrolyte and hemodynamic disturbances are more likely to occur in cyanotic infants. Infants are more likely than adults to respond with convulsions, particularly after repeated injections.

Adverse Effects: Injection of contrast media into the cardiac chambers or great vessels causes significant hemodynamic disturbances, especially in right sided injections. Depending on the injection site and the time of recording, significant changes include a drop in cardiac output, elevation or decrease in ventricular pressures (RVSP, LVSP, LVEDP, RVEDP), systemic pressure, peripheral hypotension, brady- or tachycardia, ectopic beats and other arrhythmias. If repeat injections are made in rapid succession, these changes are likely to be more pronounced.

It is suggested that hemodynamic changes be monitored and that pressures considered abnormal under roentgenographic conditions be allowed to return to a pre-angiographic level before continuation of radiopaque injection; this usually takes 15 minutes.

Precautions: Although contrast media of low osmolality, such as Hexabrix are expected to cause less osmolality-related adverse effects, and less subjective discomfort, such as pain, it is desirable that vital signs and laboratory parameters be closely monitored to detect immediate or delayed adverse effects (arrhythmias, electrolyte and hemodynamic disturbances).

Usual Dosage: The suggested average single dose of Hexabrix 320 is 1.0 mL/kg (range 0.5 to 2.0 mL/kg). The dose may be repeated if indicated. The total procedural dose should be limited to the smallest volume necessary to obtain a diagnostic examination and should not normally exceed 4 mL/kg. Sufficient time (approximately 15 minutes) should be allowed to elapse between injections to allow for subsidence of hemodynamic disturbances.

I.V. Digital Subtraction Angiography: I.V. digital subtraction angiography (IV DSA) is a radiographic procedure which allows dynamic imaging of the arterial system following i.v. injection of iodinated x-ray contrast media through the use of image intensification, enhancement of the iodine signal and digital processing of the image data. Temporal subtraction of the images obtained prior to and during the first arterial pass of the injected contrast medium yield images which are devoid of bone and soft tissue.

Areas that have been examined by i.v. DSA are the arteries of the brachiocephalic circulation, the aortic arch, the abdominal aorta and its major branches including the arteries of the extremities.

Patient Preparation: No special patient preparation is required for IV DSA. However, it is advisable to insure that patients are well hydrated prior to examination.

Precautions: In addition to the general precautions previously described, the risks associated with IV DSA include intramural injections, rupture or dissection of venous structures with extravasation into the tissues of extremities or the mediastinum. Small test injections of contrast medium made under fluoroscopic observation to insure the catheter tip is properly positioned, and in the case of peripheral placement that the vein is of adequate size, will reduce this potential. With high pressure injection, however, the catheter tip initially placed in a large venous structure may still recoil into a small tributary causing rupture of a small vein with extravasation into neighboring tissues.

Patient motion, including respiration and swallowing, can result in misregistration leading to image degradation and nondiagnostic studies. Therefore, patient cooperation is essential.

Adverse Effects: Rupture of venous structures with tissue or mediastinal extravasation and severe pain. Thrombophlebitis, hypotension, arrhythmia, neurological complications and renal failure have been reported with IV DSA.

Usual Dosage: Hexabrix 320 may be injected i.v. for digital dynamic imaging of the arterial system following any established technique. The dose is usually administered by a venous catheter threaded into a large vein, the superior or inferior vena cava, using mechanical pressure injection or rapid manual injection.

Depending on the area to be imaged, the usual adult dose range per injection is 30 to 50 mL. Injections may be repeated if necessary. The total procedural dose should be kept to the smallest volume required to achieve a diagnostic examination and should not exceed 200 mL.

Injection rates will vary depending on the site of catheter placement and vessel size. Central catheter injections are usually made at a rate of between 10 and 25 mL/second. Peripheral injections are usually made at a rate of between 10 and 15 mL/second. Since a part of the injected medium can sometimes remain in the arm vein for an extended period, it may be advisable to flush the vein immediately following injection with an appropriate volume (20 to 25 mL) of 5% dextrose in water or normal saline.

I.V. Contrast Enhancement in Computed Tomography (CT): Because unenhanced scanning may provide adequate information in the individual patient, the decision to employ contrast enhancement, which is associated with additional risk, increased radiation exposure and may obscure certain lesions, should be based upon a careful evaluation of clinical, other radiological and unenhanced CT findings.

Computed Tomography of the Brain: Hexabrix 320 may be useful to enhance the demonstration of the presence and extent of certain malignancies such as: gliomas including malignant gliomas, glioblastomas, astrocytomas, oligodendrogliomas and gangliomas; ependymomas; medulloblastomas, meningiomas; neuromas; pinealomas; pituitary adenomas; craniopharyngiomas; germinomas; and metastatic lesions.

The usefulness of contrast enhancement for the investigation of the retrobulbular space and in cases of low grade or infiltrative glioma has not been demonstrated.

In cases where lesions have calcified, there is less likelihood of enhancement. Following therapy, tumors may show decreased or no enhancement. Maximum contrast enhancement of certain tumors may be delayed necessitating delayed scans.

Non-Neoplastic Conditions: The use of Hexabrix 320 may be beneficial in the image enhancement of non-neoplastic lesions. Cerebral infarctions of recent onset may be better visualized with the contrast enhancement, while some infarctions are obscured if contrast media are used. The use of iodinated contrast media results in contrast enhancement in about 60% of cerebral infarctions studied from 1 to 4 weeks from the onset of symptoms. Sites of active infection may also be enhanced following contrast medium administration.

Arteriovenous malformations and aneurysms will show contrast enhancement. In the case of these vascular lesions, the enhancement is probably dependent on the iodine content of the circulating blood pool.

Hematomas and intraparenchymal bleeders seldom demonstrate any contrast enhancement. However, in cases of intraparenchymal clot, for which there is no obvious clinical explanation, contrast medium administration may be helpful in ruling out the possibility of associated arteriovenous malformation (see Precautions).

The opacification of the inferior vermis following contrast medium administration has resulted in false positive diagnoses in a number of normal studies.

Usual Dosage: For adults the usual dosage is 1.0 to 2.0 mL/kg, not exceeding 150 mL.

Body Computed Tomography: Hexabrix 320 or Hexabrix 200 may be administered when necessary for contrast enhancement of the organs, tissues and blood vessels of the chest, abdomen and pelvis.

Continuous or multiple scans separated by intervals of 1 to 3 seconds during the first 30 to 90 seconds post-injection of the contrast medium (dynamic CT scanning) are required to demonstrate enhanceable lesions. Subsets of patients in whom delayed body CT scans might be helpful have not been identified.

Inconsistent results have been reported and abnormal and normal tissues are usually isodense during the time frame used for delayed CT scanning. The risks of such indiscriminate use of contrast media are well known and such use is not recommended. At present, consistent results have been documented using dynamic CT techniques only.

Warnings: Patients with diabetes mellitus and impaired renal function are considered to be at greater risk to develop acute renal failure following the injection of large doses of contrast media required for contrast enhancement in CT scanning.

Convulsions and other serious neurologic complications have occurred in patients with primary or metastatic cerebral lesions or breached blood brain barrier following the administration of iodine-containing radiopaque media for enhancement of CT brain images.

Patient Preparation: No special patient preparation is required for contrast enhancement in computerized tomography. However, it is advisable to insure that patients are well hydrated prior to examination. In patients undergoing abdominal or pelvic examination, opacification of the bowel by dilute oral contrast medium may be valuable in scan interpretation.

Precautions: In addition to the general precautions previously described, it is advisable to insure that patients are adequately hydrated prior to examination. Patient motion, including respiration, can markedly affect image quality, therefore, patient cooperation is essential. The use of an intravascular contrast medium can obscure tumors in patients undergoing CT evaluation resulting in a false negative diagnosis.

Usual Adult Dosage: Hexabrix 320 may be administered by bolus injection, rapid infusion or by a combination of both. Depending on the area to be examined, doses of 30 to 150 mL (0.5 to 2.0 mL/kg) may be administered. When prolonged enhancement is required up to 150 mL can be used, usually with 25 to 50 mL as a rapid bolus and the remainder as an infusion.

Hexabrix 200 has been used in CT of the thorax at single doses of 60 mL. For prolonged enhancement a total dose of up to 200 mL has been used, with 40 to 80 mL as a rapid bolus and the remainder as an infusion.

Phlebography: Hexabrix 320 and Hexabrix 200 may be used to visualize the peripheral venous circulation. Venograms are obtained by injection or infusion into an appropriate vein in the upper or lower extremity.

Precautions: In addition to the general precautions previously described, special caution is advised when venography is required in patients with suspected thrombosis, phlebitis, severe ischemic disease, local infection or a significantly obstructed venous system.

Extreme caution is necessary to avoid extravasation and fluroscopy is recommended. This is especially important in patients with severe arterial or venous disease.

Complications of the procedure include bleeding, thrombosis, thrombophlebitis, gangrene and major systemic adverse reactions.

Usual Dosage: The usual single dose for adults is 40 to 60 mL of full strength (32% iodine) Hexabrix 320 as a single injection for the lower extremity and 10 to 20 mL for an upper extremity.

Hexabrix 200 may also be employed. Opacification of the deep veins may be less than with a more concentrated contrast material. The usual dose of Hexabrix 200 will range from 50 to 100 mL for the lower extremity, and 15 to 30 mL for the upper extremity.

Following the procedure, the venous system should be flushed with normal saline and 5% dextrose in water. Massage and elevation are also helpful for clearing the contrast medium from the extremity.

Excretory Urography: Following i.v. injection, Hexabrix 320 is rapidly excreted by the kidneys. Hexabrix 320 may be visualized in the renal parenchyma 1 minute following bolus injection. Maximum radiographic density in the calyces and pelves occurs in most instances within 7 to 12 minutes after injection. In patients with severe renal impairment, contrast visualization may be substantially delayed, or may not occur at all. With low osmolar contrast media, the collecting system may be less distended and appear more dense. The nephrographic effect may be less pronounced.

Patient Preparation: A low residue diet the day preceding the examination and a laxative the evening before the examination may be given, unless contraindicated. Partial dehydration is not recommended and may be dangerous. Maintenance of normal hydration is desirable.

Precautions: Adequate renal function must be present. Dehydration will not improve contrast quality in patients with impaired renal function and will increase the risk of contrast

induced renal damage (see Warnings and Precautions, General, concerning preparatory dehydration).
Usual Dosage: The usual dose range of Hexabrix 320 is 0.5 to 1.0 mL/kg, amounting to a single dose of 50 mL in the average normal adult. The dose is injected i.v., usually within 30 to 90 seconds.
Arthrography: Preliminary experience with Hexabrix 320 indicates that filling of narrow fissures and tears may be delayed necessitating more massage and delayed films. The rate of contrast medium absorption as well as the production of synovial fluid and consequent dilution of the medium may be reduced.
Precautions: In addition to the general precautions previously described, strict aseptic technique is required to prevent the introduction of infection. Arthrography should not be performed when there is infection in or near the joint. Fluoroscopic control should be used to insure proper introduction of the needle into the synovial space and prevent extracapsular injection, which is painful and may lead to incapacity lasting 24 to 48 hours. Aspiration of excessive synovial fluid will reduce the pain on injection and prevent the dilution of the contrast agent. It is important that undue pressure not be exerted during the injection.
Adverse Effects: In addition to the general adverse reactions previously described, arthrography may induce joint pain or discomfort which is usually mild and transient but occasionally may be severe and persist for 24 to 48 hours following the procedure. Effusion requiring aspiration may occur. Systemic adverse reactions have occurred.
Usual Dosage: Arthrography is usually performed under local anesthesia. The amount of contrast agent required is dependent on the size of the joint to be injected and the technique employed.

The following dosage schedule for normal adult joints should serve only as a guide since joint may require more or less contrast medium for optimal visualization. Knee, hip, shoulder: Hexabrix 320: 5 to 15 mL; temporomandibular: 0.5 to 0.7 mL.

Massage, passive or active manipulation is necessary to disperse the medium throughout the joint space and to insure that small tears are well outlined with the contrast material.

Lower volumes of contrast medium are usually employed for double contrast examinations in which either filtered room air or carbon dioxide may be introduced for examination of the joints.
Hysterosalpingography: Patient Preparation: It is preferable to perform the procedure approximately 8 to 10 days after the onset of menses. The patient should empty the bladder before the examination.
Precautions: Caution should be exercised in patients suspected of having cervical or tubal carcinoma to avoid possible spread of the lesion by the procedure. The procedure is contraindicated in pregnancy. The examination should not be performed during the menstrual period or when infection is present in any portion of the genital tract; its use is not advised for 6 months after termination of pregnancy or 30 days after cervical conization or endometrial curettage. Delayed onset of pain and fever (1 to 2 days) may be indicative of pelvic infection.
Adverse Effects: In addition to the general adverse reactions described previously, fever and pain, cramping and tenderness of the abdomen have been reported. Systemic reactions may occur.
Usual Dosage: The total volume administered will vary depending upon anatomical variations and/or disease processes. The usual dose varies from 5 to 10 mL, administered slowly through a cannula under fluoroscopic control, without undue pressure.
Supplied: Hexabrix is a sterile, nonpyrogenic, aqueous solution intended for intravascular administration as a diagnostic radiopaque medium.

Hexabrix 200: Hexabrix 200 contains 24.6% w/v of the meglumine salt and 12.3% w/v of the sodium salt of ioxaglic acid. Each mL contains: ioxaglate meglumine 246 mg, ioxaglate sodium 123 mg and edetate calcium disodium 0.10 mg as a stabilizer. The solution contains 0.095 mmol (2.2 mg) sodium/mL and provides 20% (200 mg/mL) organically bound iodine. Hexabrix 200 has a viscosity (cps) of 3.5 at 25°C and 2.5 at 37°C. Vials of 20 and 50 mL, packages of 50; bottles of 100 mL fill/150 mL, boxes of 12; bottles of 150 mL, boxes of 12; bottles of 200 mL fill/250 mL, boxes of 12.

Hexabrix 320: Hexabrix 320 contains 39.3% w/v of the meglumine salt and 19.6% w/v of the sodium salt of ioxaglic acid. Each mL contains: ioxaglate meglumine 393 mg, ioxaglate sodium 196 mg and edetate calcium disodium 0.10 mg as a stabilizer. The solution contains 0.15 mmol (3.48 mg) sodium/mL and provides 32% (320 mg/mL) organically bound iodine. Hexabrix 320 has a viscosity (cps) of 14.7 at 25°C and 8.9 at 37°C. Vials of 20, 30 and 50 mL, boxes of 12; bottles of 100 mL fill/150 mL, boxes of 12; bottles of 150 mL, boxes of 12; bottles of 200 mL fill/250 mL, boxes of 12.
Pharmacy Bulk Vial: Multiple dispensing bottles of 500 mL, boxes of 12.

Solutions of ioxaglate (Hexabrix) provide 6 iodine atoms for each 2 dissociated ions. Conventional iodinated contrast agents provide only 3 iodine atoms for each 2 dissociated ions. Since osmolality is related to the number of ions in solution, Hexabrix has an osmolality of about one third the osmolality of traditional iodinated contrast agents at equivalent iodine concentrations. The osmolality of Hexabrix 320 is approximately 600 mOsm/kg; that of Hexabrix 200 is 356 mOsm/kg.

Store between 15 and 30°C. Protect from light. Protect from freezing. Discard unused portion.

HEXADROL® PHOSPHATE INJECTION Ⓟ

Organon Teknika

Dexamethasone Sodium Phosphate

Corticosteroid

Pharmacology: After administration of the injection, dexamethasone sodium phosphate is rapidly converted into dexamethasone. This is a synthetic glucocorticoid which has 7 times the anti-inflammatory potency of prednisolone. Like other glucocorticoids, dexamethasone also has antiallergic, antitoxic, antishock, antipyretic and immunosuppressive properties. Dexamethasone has practically no water and salt-retaining properties and is, therefore, particularly suitable for use in patients with cardiac decompensation or hypertension. Because of the long biological half-life (36 to 54 hours), dexamethasone is especially suitable in conditions where a continuous glucocorticoid action is desired.

Indications: Dexamethasone sodium phosphate may be given by i.v. or i.m. injection when oral therapy is not feasible in the following conditions:
Endocrine Disorders: Primary or secondary adrenocortical insufficiency (hydrocortisone or cortisone is the drug of choice; synthetic analogs may be used in conjunction with mineralocorticoids where applicable; in infancy, mineralocorticoid supplementation is of particular importance).

Acute adrenocortical insufficiency (hydrocortisone or cortisone is the drug of choice: mineralocorticoid supplementation may be necessary, particularly when synthetic analogs are used.)

Preoperatively and in the event of serious trauma or illness, in patients with known adrenal insufficiency or when adrenocortical reserve is doubtful.

Shock unresponsive to conventional therapy if adrenocortical insufficiency exists or is suspected.

Congenital adrenal hyperplasia.

Nonsuppurative thyroiditis.
Rheumatic Disorders: As adjunctive therapy for short-term administration (to support the patient during an acute period of exacerbation) in post traumatic osteoarthritis, synovitis of osteoarthritis, rheumatoid arthritis, acute gouty arthritis, psoriatic arthritis, ankylosing spondylitis, juvenile rheumatoid arthritis.
Collagen Diseases: During an exacerbation or as maintenance therapy in selected cases of systemic lupus erythematosus, acute rheumatic carditis.
Dermatologic Diseases: pemphigus, bullous dermatitis herpetiformis, severe erythema multiforme (Stevens-Johnson syndrome), exfoliative dermatitis, severe seborrheic dermatitis, severe psoriasis. Allergic states: Initial control of severe allergic conditions: seasonal or perennial allergic rhinitis, bronchial asthma (including status asthmaticus), contact dermatitis, atopic dermatitis, serum sickness, drug hypersensitivity reactions, urticarial transfusion reactions, acute noninfectious laryngeal edema (epinephrine is the drug of first choice).
Ophthalmic Diseases: Severe acute and chronic allergic and inflammatory processes involving the eye and its adnexa, such as: herpes zoster ophthalmicus (but **not** herpes simplex), iritis, iridocylitis, chorioretinitis, anterior segment inflammation, diffuse posterior uveitis and choroiditis optic neuritis, retrobulbar neuritis, sympathetic ophthalmia.
Gastrointestinal Diseases: To support the patient during a critical period of the disease in ulcerative colitis (systemic therapy), regional enteritis (systemic therapy).
Respiratory Diseases: Sarcoidosis, berylliosis, fulminating or disseminated pulmonary tuberculosis when concurrently accompanied by appropriate antituberculous chemotherapy, aspiration pneumonitis.
Hematologic Disorders: idiopathic thrombocytopenic purpura in adults (i.v. only; i.m. administration is contraindicated), acquired (autoimmune) hemolytic anemia.
Neoplastic Disorders: For palliative management of leukemias and lymphomas in adults, acute childhood leukemia, hypercalcemia associated with cancer.
Edematous States: To induce diuresis or remission of proteinuria in the nephrotic syndrome without uremia, of the idiopathic type, or that due to lupus erythematosus.
Cerebral Edema: May be used to treat patients with cerebral edema of diverse etiologies in conjunction with adequate neurological evaluation and management.
Miscellaneous: tuberculous meningitis with subarachnoid block or impending block when concurrently accompanied by appropriate antituberculous chemotherapy.

Diagnostic testing of adrenocortical hyperfunction.

When given intrasynovially or locally into soft tissue sites this product may provide relief of symptoms in: traumatic arthritis, ganglia, bursitis, tendinitis, fibrositis, localized myositis, heloma.

Contraindications: Bacteremia and systemic fungal infections, glaucoma, hypersensitivity to any of the product's components, Cushing's syndrome, gastric and duodenal ulcers, certain viral infections, i.e. varicella, herpes genitalis.

Warnings: In patients on corticosteroid therapy subjected to unusual stress, increased dosage of rapidly acting corticosteroids before, during and after the stressful situation is indicated.

While on corticosteroid therapy patients should not be vaccinated against smallpox because of potential complications. Conversely, patients with vaccinia should not receive corticosteroid therapy. Other immunization procedures should not be undertaken in patients who are on corticosteroids, especially on high doses, because of possible hazards of neurological complications and a lack of antibody response. However, immunization procedures may be undertaken in patients who are receiving corticosteroids as replacement therapy, e.g., for Addison's disease.
Pregnancy: Since adequate human reproduction studies have not been done with corticosteroids, the use of these drugs in pregnancy, nursing mothers or women of childbearing potential requires that the possible benefits of the drug be weighed against the potential hazards to the mother and embryo or fetus. Infants born of mothers who have received substantial doses of corticosteroids during pregnancy should be carefully observed for signs of hypoadrenalism.
Lactation: Corticosteroids appear in breast milk and could suppress growth, interfere with endogenous corticosteroid production, or cause other unwanted effects. Mothers taking pharmacological doses of corticosteroids should be advised not to nurse.

The use of corticosteroids in active tuberculosis should be restricted to those cases of fulminating or disseminated tuberculosis in which the corticosteroid is used for the management of the disease in conjunction with an appropriate antituberculous regimen. If corticosteroids are indicated in patients with latent tuberculosis or tuberculin reactivity, close observation is necessary as reactivation of the disease may occur. During prolonged corticosteroid therapy, these patients should receive chemoprophylaxis.

Prolonged use of corticosteroids may produce posterior subcapsular cataracts, glaucoma with possible damage to the optic nerves and may enhance the establishment of secondary ocular infections due to fungi or viruses or tuberculosis.

Corticosteroids should be used cautiously in patients with ocular herpes simplex for fear of corneal ulcerations and perforation.

Corticosteroids may mask some signs of infection and new infections may appear during their use. There may be decreased resistance and inability to localize infection when corticosteroids are used. Moreover, corticosteroids may affect the nitroblue-tetrazolium test for bacterial infection and produce false negative results. If corticosteroids have to be used in the presence of bacterial infections, institute appropriate vigorous anti-infective therapy. Patients with latent or overt cardiac failure, renal dysfunction, hypertension or migraine, certain parasitic infections, particularly amebiasis should be monitored.

Average and large doses of corticosteroids can cause elevation of blood pressure, salt and water retention, and increased excretion of potassium. The effects are less likely to occur with the synthetic derivatives except when used in large doses. Dietary salt restriction and potassium supplementation may be necessary. All corticosteroids increase calcium excretion.

Hexadrol Phosphate Injection (cont'd)

Because rare instances of serious anaphylactoid reactions such as glottis edema and bronchospasm have occurred in patients receiving parenteral corticosteroid therapy, appropriate precautionary measures should be taken prior to administration, especially when the patient has a history of allergy to any drug.

Idiopathic thrombocytopenic purpura in adults should be treated by i.v. injection.

Precautions: When large doses are given, some authorities advise that antacids be administered between meals to help prevent peptic ulcer.

Use the lowest possible dose of corticosteroid to control the condition under treatment, and when dosage reduction is possible, the reduction should be gradual.

When corticosteroids are administered concomitantly with potassium depleting diuretics, patients should be observed closely for development of hypokalemia.

The prothrombin time should be checked frequently in patients receiving corticosteroids and coumarin anticoagulants concomitantly because of reports that corticosteroids alter the response to these anticoagulants. Studies have shown that the usual effect produced by adding corticosteroids is inhibition of response to coumarins, although there have been some conflicting reports of potentiation not substantiated by studies.

Use ASA cautiously in conjunction with corticosteroids in hypoprothrombinemia.

If patients undergoing long-term therapy with glucocorticoids are concomitantly given salicylates, any reduction in glucocorticoid dosage should be made with caution, since salicylate intoxication has been reported in such cases.

Use corticosteroids with caution in: nonspecific ulcerative colitis if there is a probability of impending perforation, abscess or other pyogenic infection; diverticulitis; fresh intestinal anastomoses; active or latent peptic ulcer; renal insufficiency; hypertension; osteoporosis; and myasthenia gravis.

There is an enhanced effect of corticosteroids on patients with hypothyroidism and in those with cirrhosis.

Psychic derangements may appear when corticosteroids are used, ranging from euphoria, insomnia, mood swings, personality changes, and severe depression, to frank psychotic manifestations and convulsions. Also, existing emotional instability or psychotic tendencies may be aggravated by corticosteroids.

Psychological and/or physiological dependency may develop with long term use of corticosteroids. Discontinuance of therapy may lead to the development of withdrawal symptoms, including anorexia, vague pains, weakness and lethargy.

Growth and development of infants and children on prolonged corticosteroid therapy should be carefully observed.

Corticosteroids may increase or decrease motility and number of spermatozoa in some patients.

Phenytoin, phenobarbital, rifampin and ephedrine may enhance the rate of metabolism and clearance of corticosteroids and this may require corticosteroid dosage adjustment. Interpret dexamethasone suppression test results cautiously during concurrent administration of these drugs.

Advise patients to inform subsequent physicians of the prior use of corticosteroids.

Corticosteroids may suppress reactions to skin tests and decrease responsiveness to vaccination.

Intra-articular corticosteroid injection may produce systemic as well as local effects. Frequent intra-articular injection may result in damage to joint tissues. Avoid overdistension of the joint capsule and deposition of steroid along the needle track in intra-articular injection, since this may lead to tissue atrophy.

Intra-articular injections should be given under strictly aseptic conditions as glucocorticoids decrease the resistance to infection. In intercostal neuritis and neuralgia, guard against entering the pleura.

Appropriate examination of any joint fluid present is necessary to exclude a septic process. Avoid local injection of a corticosteroid into an infected site (septic arthritis).

The slower rate of absorption by i.m. administration must be recognized.

A marked increase in pain accompanied by local swelling, further restriction of joint motion, fever, and malaise are suggestive of septic arthritis. If this complication occurs and the diagnosis of sepsis is confirmed, institute appropriate antimicrobial therapy.

Do not inject corticosteroids into unstable joints.

Avoid injection in the deltoid muscle because of high incidence of tissue atrophy.

Patients should be impressed strongly with the importance of not over using joints in which symptomatic benefit has been obtained as long as the inflammatory process remains active.

Patients treated concomitantly with glucocorticoids and 1 of the following drugs should be monitored: diuretics and/or cardiac glucosides, since potassium loss may be enhanced. This is a particular risk in patients using cardiac glucosides, since hypokalemia increases the toxicity of these drugs; antidiabetics, since glucocorticoids may impair glucose tolerance, thereby increasing the need for antidiabetic drugs; nonsteroidal anti-inflammatory drugs, since the incidence and/or severity of gastrointestinal ulceration may increase.

Adverse Effects: Fluid and Electrolyte Disturbances: sodium retention; fluid retention; congestive heart failure in susceptible patients; potassium loss; hypokalemic alkalosis; hypertension; hypotension or shock like reaction.

Musculoskeletal: muscle weakness; steroid myopathy; loss of muscle mass; osteoporosis; vertebral compression fractures; aseptic necrosis of femoral and humeral heads; pathologic fracture of long bones.

Gastrointestinal: nausea; gastric and peptic ulcer and possible subsequent perforation and hemorrhage; pancreatitis; abdominal distention; ulcerative esophagitis.

Dermatologic: impaired wound healing; thin fragile skin; striae; petechiae and ecchymoses; facial erythema; increased sweating; burning or tingling, especially in the perineal area (after large doses of corticosteroid phosphates), acne, other cutaneous reactions.

Neurological: convulsions; increased intracranial pressures with papilledema (pseudotumor cerebri) usually after treatment; vertigo; headache.

Endocrine: menstrual irregularities; development of Cushingoid state; hirsutism suppression of growth in children; secondary adrenocortical and pituitary unresponsiveness, particularly in times of stress, as in trauma, surgery or illness; decreased carbohydrate tolerance; manifestations of latent diabetes mellitus; increased requirements for insulin or oral hypoglycemic agents in diabetes.

Ophthalmic: posterior subcapsular cataracts; increased intraocular pressure; glaucoma; exophthalmos.

Metabolic: negative nitrogen balance due to protein catabolism.

Other: anaphylactoid or hypersensitivity reactions; thromboembolism; malaise; weight gain; increased appetite; psychological or physiological dependence.

The following additional adverse reactions are related to parenteral corticosteroid therapy: rare instances of blindness associated with intralesional therapy around the face and head; hyperpigmentation or hypopigmentation; subcutaneous and cutaneous atrophy; sterile abscess; postinjection flare (following intra-articular use); Charcot like arthropathy.

Compatibility with Infusion Fluids: Stability studies of Hexadrol Phosphate injection diluted in various i.v. solutions such as 5% Dextrose in H_2O, 0.9% Sodium Chloride, 5% Dextrose in Saline, and Lactated Ringers, in glass or plastic containers, have demonstrated that potency is maintained up to 4 weeks at room temperature.

Overdose: Symptoms: Hypertension, edema.

Treatment: Anaphylactic and hypersensitivity reactions may be treated with epinephrine, positive pressure artificial respiration, and aminophylline. Keep the patient warm and quiet. Treatment probably is not indicated for reactions due to chronic overdosage.

Dosage: For general principles governing corticosteroid administration, refer to the introductory paragraphs of the Dosage section of the Hexadrol tablet monograph.

The dose for i.m. or i.v. administration varies from 4 to 20 mg depending on the nature and severity of the disease being treated. Give i.v. doses exceeding 8 mg slowly over a period of several minutes. Repeat the initial dose as necessary until the desired response is noted. Maintenance doses average 2 to 4 mg daily. After achieving satisfactory control, switch the patient to oral therapy as soon as feasible.

In the treatment of unresponsive shock, high pharmacologic doses of glucocorticoids are recommended currently. Various dosage regimens have been suggested in the literature. These include (1) the use of a single i.v. injection of 1 to 6 mg/kg, (2) continuous infusion of 3 mg/kg/24 hours after initial i.v. bolus of 20 mg, and (3) initial i.v. bolus of 40 mg followed by repeat i.v. injections every 2 to 6 hours while the state of shock persists.

Whenever possible use i.v. route for the initial and for as many subsequent doses as are given while the patient is in shock (because of irregular absorption by other routes in such patients). When the blood pressure responds, use the i.m. route until oral therapy can be substituted.

For the treatment of cerebral edema in adults an initial i.v. dose of 10 mg is recommended, followed by 4 mg i.v. or i.m. every 6 hours until maximum response has been noted. This regimen may then be tapered over several days using either parenteral or oral dexamethasone. Non-operative cases of cerebral edema may require continuous therapy to remain free of symptoms of increased intracranial pressure. The smallest effective dose may be used in children, preferably orally. This may approximate 0.2 mg/kg/24 hours in divided doses.

There is a tendency in current medical practice to use high doses of parenteral dexamethasone in the short term therapy of selected cases of lifethreatening cerebral edema. The following dosage regimens have been suggested:

Adults: 48 mg as a single dose then 8 mg every 2 hours on days 1 and 3, 4 mg every 2 hours on days 2 and 4, 4 mg every 4 hours on days 5 through 8. All doses are to be given parenterally.

Alternatively: 100 mg i.v. followed by 100 mg i.m. 6 hours later; then, 4 mg i.m. every 6 hours for 8 days. Thereafter, taper daily by 4 mg.

Children: 10 to 14 years of age: 50% of the adult dose; less than 10 years of age: 25% of the adult dose.

Alternatively: Adults and Children: 1.5 mg/kg as a loading dose followed by 1.5 mg/kg/day for the first 5 days. Then taper slowly over the following 5 days and discontinue. All doses are to be given parenterally.

The dose for intrasynovial administration is usually 4 mg for large joints and 0.8 to 1 mg for small joints. For soft tissue and bursal injections a dose of 2 to 4 mg is recommended. Ganglia require a dose of 1 to 2 mg. A dose of 0.4 to 1 mg is used for injection into tendon sheaths and helomata. Injection into intervertebral joints should not be attempted at any time and hip joint injection cannot be recommended as an office procedure.

Employ intrasynovial and soft tissue injections only when affected areas are limited to 1 or 2 sites. Corticosteroids provide palliation only and other conventional or curative methods of therapy should be employed when indicated.

Patients currently being treated with other glucocorticoids may be conveniently transferred to this agent using the following dosage equivalents: dexamethasone 0.75 mg=methylprednisolone and triamcinolone 4.0 mg=prednisone and prednisolone 5 mg=hydrocortisone 20 mg=cortisone 25 mg.

Supplied: 4 mg/mL: Each mL contains: dexamethasone sodium phosphate USP, equivalent to 4 mg of dexamethasone phosphate. Nonmedicinal ingredients: benzyl alcohol NF 10 mg, citric acid USP or sodium hydroxide USP q.s. to adjust pH 7.9, sodium citrate USP (to isotonicity) q.s., sodium sulfite and water for injection USP q.s. to 1 mL. Multiple dose vials of 5 mL.

10 mg/mL: Each mL contains: dexamethasone sodium phosphate USP equivalent to 10 mg dexamethasone phosphate. Nonmedicinal ingredients: benzyl alcohol NF 10 mg, citric acid USP or sodium hydroxide USP q.s. to pH 7.9, sodium citrate USP (to isotonicity) q.s., sodium sulfite and water for injection USP q.s. to 1 mL. Multiple dose vials of 10 mL.

HEXALEN® Ⓟ

Lilly

Altretamine

Antineoplastic Agent

Pharmacology: Altretamine, better known in the scientific literature as hexamethylmelamine (HMM), is a synthetic cytotoxic antineoplastic s-triazine derivative. While altretamine bears structural similarity to, and cross-reactivity with, triethylenemelamine (TEM), a classical alkylating agent, evidence demonstrating altretamine to be an alkylating agent is not conclusive. Altretamine does not consistently demonstrate cross-resistance with classical alkylating agents used in rodent tumors or in human cancer treatment, but its clinical antitumor spectrum resembles that of an alkylating agent. Additionally, altretamine has been demonstrated to be efficacious for tumors resistant to classical alkylating agents.

The mechanism of action of altretamine is not completely understood. There are no mechanistic studies to suggest antifolate or antimetabolite properties of the molecule, and the parent drug is chemically very stable. Metabolism, specifically N-demethylation, has been shown to be necessary for the antitumor activity of altretamine. It has been proposed that altretamine N-demethylation may produce reactive intermediates which covalently bind to tissue macromolecules, including DNA.

Pharmacokinetics: Radiolabelled studies indicate that altretamine is rapidly absorbed and almost completely absorbed orally: the maximum plasma level of radioactivity is obtained within 1 to 4 hours and the elimination half-life is about 13 hours. Once absorbed, altretamine is extensively metabolized by N-demethylation via hepatic microsomal enzymes, producing variation in altretamine plasma levels.

In man, about 61% of the administered dose is recovered in the urine within 24 hours. In contrast, elimination in the feces is negligible.

Indications: As palliative therapy in ovarian carcinoma as follows: First-line therapy in combination with other established antineoplastic agents: Impressive response rates and median survival times have been reported in advanced ovarian cancer studies of Hexalen in combination with other known chemotherapeutic agents including cyclophosphamide, doxorubicin, cisplatin, 5-fluorouracil and methotrexate. These results are summarized in Tables I to III.

Second-line combination or single-agent therapy in patients who have not responded or who have relapsed on other chemotherapeutic regimens.

Results from Northwestern University Medical School, Hershey Medical Center, and Norwegian Radium Hospital demonstrate the efficacy of altretamine as second-line therapy after failure of first-line, platinum-based combination chemotherapy (see Table IV on following page).

Contraindications: In individuals with known hypersensitivity to the drug.

It is also contraindicated in patients with severe myeloid suppression (leukopenia, thrombocytopenia, anemia).

Therapy with altretamine should be deferred for at least 3 weeks after prior alkylating agent therapy.

Warnings: Altretamine is a potent drug and should be used only by physicians experienced with cancer chemotherapeutic drugs (see Precautions). Toxicity to altretamine is dose-related and cumulative. Blood counts should be monitored weekly and neurological examinations performed regularly.

When used as indicated, the physician must carefully weigh the therapeutic benefit versus risk of toxicity which may occur.

Altretamine should be given cautiously to individuals with pre-existing renal and hepatic impairment.

If altretamine is used in combination with other cytotoxic agents, the toxic effects may be potentiated.

Pregnancy: The safe use of altretamine in pregnant women has not been established. It should not be used in pregnancy, particularly in early pregnancy, unless in the judgement of the physician, the potential benefits outweigh the possible risks.

Lactation: It is not known whether altretamine or its metabolites are excreted in human milk. Nursing should be discontinued in patients receiving altretamine.

Precautions: Altretamine should be administered by physicians experienced in the use of antineoplastic agents.

The toxicities seen with altretamine have been gastrointestinal (nausea and vomiting), hematologic (leukopenia and mild anemia) and, occasionally, neurologic (ataxia, depression and peripheral neuropathy). Since toxicity to altretamine is not only dose-related, but also dose-cumulative, peripheral blood counts should be monitored weekly and neurological examinations performed regularly. Antiemetics may be of help in reducing gastric upset.

Altretamine should be given cautiously to patients with the following: leukopenia, thrombocytopenia and/or anemia; tumor infiltration of bone marrow; previous radiation therapy or treatment with cytotoxic agents.

Adverse Effects: Gastrointestinal: With continuous high-dose daily altretamine, nausea and vomiting of gradual onset occur frequently. Although in most instances these symptoms are controllable with antiemetics, at times the severity requires altretamine dose reduction or, rarely, discontinuation of altretamine therapy. In some instances, a tolerance to these symptoms develops after several weeks of therapy. The incidence and severity of nausea and vomiting are reduced with moderate-dose administration of altretamine. In 2 clinical studies of single-agent altretamine utilizing a moderate, intermittent dose and schedule, only 1 patient (1%) discontinued altretamine due to severe nausea and vomiting.

Neurotoxicity: Peripheral neuropathy and CNS symptoms (mood disorders, disorders of consciousness, ataxia, dizziness, vertigo) have been reported. They are more likely to occur in patients receiving continuous, high-dose daily altretamine than moderate-dose altretamine administered on an intermittent schedule. Neurologic toxicity has been reported to be reversible when therapy is discontinued. Data from a randomized trial of altretamine and cisplatin plus or minus pyridoxine in ovarian cancer indicated that pyridoxine significantly reduced neurotoxicity; however, it adversely affected response duration suggesting that pyridoxine should not be administered with altretamine and/or cisplatin.

Hematologic: Altretamine causes mild to moderate dose-related myelosuppression. Leukopenia below 3 000 WBC/mm³ occurred in < 15% of patients on a variety of intermittent or continuous dose regimens. Less than 1% had leukopenia below 1 000 WBC/mm³. Thrombocytopenia below 50 000 platelets/mm³ was seen in < 10% of patients. When given in doses of 8 to 12 mg/kg/day over a 21-day course, nadirs of leukocyte and platelet counts were reached by 3 to 4 weeks, and normal counts were regained by 6 weeks. With continuous administration at doses of 6 to 8 mg/kg/day, nadirs are reached in 6 to 8 weeks (median).

Table I—Hexalen

Addition of Hexalen to Platinum-Based Combination Regimens in the First-Line Treatment of Advanced Ovarian Cancer

Study Reference	Treatment Regimen	Summary of Results
Vanderbilt Univ.	H-CAP: Hexalen-150 mg/m², p.o., Days 1–14 Cyclophosphamide-350 mg/m², i.v., Days 1,8 Doxorubicin-20 mg/m², i.v., Days 1,8 Cisplatin-60 mg/m², i.v., Day 1	Objective response: HCAP-96% (58% complete remission) CAP-64% (41% complete remission) (p < 0.001)
	CAP: Cyclophosphamide-350 mg/m², i.v., Days 1,8 Doxorubicin-20 mg/m², i.v., Days 1,8 Cisplatin-60 mg/m², i.v., Day 1	Median survival (all patients): HCAP-49.1 months CAP-20.5 months (p = 0.006)
	(Repeated every 4 weeks for 6 courses)	Median survival (residual disease ≤ 3 cm): HCAP-113 months (estimate) CAP-20.7 months (p < 0.001)
NCCTG-Mayo Clinic*	H-CAP: Hexalen-150 mg/m², p.o., Days 2–8 Cyclophosphamide-400 mg/m², i.v., Day 1 Doxorubicin-30 mg/m², i.v., Day 1 Cisplatin-60 mg/m², i.v., Day 1	6-year survival rate: HCAP-32% CP-19% (p = 0.025)
	CP: Cyclophosphamide-1 000 mg/m², i.v., Day 1 Cisplatin-60 mg/m², i.v., Day 1	Median survival (patients with less massive disease): HCAP-48.5 months CP-28.2 months
	(Repeated every month for 12 months)	(p = 0.012)
Mt. Sinai	CHAP-II: Cyclophosphamide-500 mg/m², i.v., Day 3 Hexalen-100 mg/m², p.o., Days 4–15 Doxorubicin-20 mg/m², i.v., Day 3 Cisplatin-50 mg/m², i.v., Day 1	Median survival: CHAP-II-42.5 months CAP-24.6 months (p = 0.034)
	CAP: Cyclophosphamide-500 mg/m², i.v., Day 3 Doxorubicin-20 mg/m², i.v., Day 3 Cisplatin-50 mg/m², i.v., Day 1	
	(Repeated every 4 weeks)	

*Includes results from unpublished data.

Table II—Hexalen

Substitution of Hexalen for Cisplatin in the First-Line Treatment of Advanced Ovarian Cancer

Study Reference	Treatment Regimen	Summary of Results
Milan	HAC: Hexalen-150 mg/m², p.o., Days 1–14 Doxorubicin-50 mg/m², i.v., Day 1 Cyclophosphamide-70 mg/m², p.o., Days 1–14	Median survival: HAC-23 months PAC-24 months
	PAC: Cisplatin-50 mg/m², i.v., Day 1 Doxorubicin-50 mg/m², i.v., Day 1 Cyclophosphamide-70 mg/m², i.v., Day 1, p.o., Days 2–14	7-year survival: HAC-17% PAC-25%
	(Repeated every 4 weeks)	

Table III—Hexalen

Hexalen in Combination Chemotherapy in the First-Line Treatment of Advanced Ovarian Cancer

Study Reference	Treatment Regimen	Summary of Results
NCI	Hexa-CAF: Hexalen-150 mg/m², p.o., Days 1–14 Cyclophosphamide-150 mg/m², p.o., Days 1–14 5-Fluorouracil-600 mg/m², i.v., Days 1,8 Methotrexate-40 mg/m², i.v., Days 1,8	Overall response rate: Hexa-CAF-75% L-PAM-54% (p < 0.05)
	L-PAM: Melphalan-0.2 mg/kg, p.o., Days 1–5	Median survival: Hexa-CAF-29 months L-PAM-17 months
	(Repeated every month for 6 cycles)	(p < 0.02)

Hexalen (cont'd)

Table IV—Hexalen

Single-Agent Hexalen in the Second-Line Treatment of Patients with Advanced Ovarian Cancer[a]

Reference	Treatment Regimen	Summary of Results
Northwestern University	260 mg/m²/day, Days 1-21, repeated every 28 days	Overall response rate: 33% (11/33-7 CR/4 PR) Survival times: Responders at 1 year-100% at 2 years-86% at 3 years-36% Non-Responders at 1 year-14% at 2 years-14% at 3 years-0% (p=0.0001)
Hershey Medical Center	260 mg/m²/day, Days 1-14, repeated every 28 days	9/52 (17%) patients had no evidence of disease[b] Overall median survival: Responders-75.2 months Non-Responders-9.3 months
Norwegian Radium Hospital	260 mg/m²/day, Days 1-14, repeated every 28 days	Tumor response rate: 14% (7/50-3 CR/4 PR) Median survival: Responders-9+ months Non-Responders-5 months

Legend: CR: complete response; PR: partial response.

[a]Over 96% of the patients had received platinum-based therapy as first-line treatment. The cohort of patients treated at the Norwegian Radium Hospital all met the criteria for platinum-resistant disease, i.e., progression or stable disease during platinum therapy, or relapse within 6 months after the end of first-line therapy.

[b]Manetta and Podczaski. Unpublished Meeting Abstract, 1993.

Data in Table V are based on the experience of 76 patients with ovarian cancer previously treated with a cisplatin-based combination regimen who received single-agent altretamine. In 1 study, altretamine (260 mg/m²/day) was administered for 14 days of a 28-day cycle. In another study, altretamine (6 to 8 mg/kg/day) was administered for 21 days of a 28-day cycle.

Additional adverse reaction information is available from 13 single-agent altretamine studies (total of 1 014 patients) conducted under the auspices of the National Cancer Institute. The treated patients had a variety of tumors and many were heavily pretreated with other chemotherapies; most of these trials utilized high, continuous daily doses of altretamine (6 to 12 mg/kg/day). In general, adverse reaction experiences were similar in the 2 trials described above. Additional toxicities, not reported in Table V, included hepatic toxicity, skin rash, pruritus and alopecia, each occurring in <1% of patients.

Overdose: Symptoms and Treatment: Accidental overdosage with altretamine would be expected to intensify the severity of hematopoietic depression, gastrointestinal and neurological symptomatology. In the event of overdosage, general supportive measures should be instituted to sustain the patient through any period of toxicity that might occur.

Dosage: Chemotherapy with altretamine, as with other drugs used in cancer chemotherapy, is potentially hazardous. It is therefore recommended that it be administered by physicians aware of the associated risks.

The usual daily dose of altretamine as a single agent is 260 mg/m² (6 to 8 mg/kg) administered orally in 3 or 4 divided doses in 14- to 21-day cycles. A 7- to 14-day off-drug period between cycles is recommended.

When employed in combination with other antineoplastic agents, the daily dose of altretamine may be appropriately reduced to 150 mg/m² (4 to 6 mg/kg) given in 3 or 4 divided doses in 7- to 14-day cycles. A 14- to 21-day off-drug period between cycles is recommended.

If intolerable side effects occur, a dose reduction or a temporary discontinuation of the drug should be considered.

Table V—Hexalen

Adverse Experiences in 76 Previously Treated Ovarian Cancer Patients Receiving Single-Agent Hexalen

	Incidence	
Gastrointestinal		
Nausea and vomiting	33%	
Mild to moderate		32%
Severe		1%
Increased alkaline phosphatase	9%	
Neurologic		
Peripheral sensory neuropathy	31%	
Mild		22%
Moderate to severe		9%
Anorexia and fatigue	1%	
Seizures	1%	
Hematologic		
Leukopenia	5%	
WBC 2 000–2 999/mm³		4%
WBC <2 000/mm³		1%
Thrombocytopenia	9%	
Platelets 75 000–99 000/mm³		6%
Platelets <75 000/mm³		3%
Anemia	33%	
Mild		20%
Moderate to severe		13%
Renal		
Serum creatinine 1.6-3.75 mg/dL	7%	
BUN	9%	
25-40 mg%		5%
41-60 mg%		3%
>60 mg%		1%

Concomitant antiemetics have been useful in the control of severe nausea and vomiting.

Supplied: Each clear, hard gelatin capsule, imprinted with the following inscription: USB001 HEXALEN 50 mg, contains: altretamine 50 mg. Nonmedicinal ingredients: calcium stearate and lactose, anhydrous; capsule shell: gelatin, silicon dioxide and sodium lauryl sulfate. Bottles of 100. Store at controlled room temperature (15 to 30°C).

HEXIT™

Odan

Lindane

Scabicide—Pediculicide

Supplied: Each mL of shampoo contains: lindane USP (gamma benzene hexachloride) 1% in a nonmedicinally scented, sudsing shampoo base. Nonmedicinal ingredients: acetone, citric acid, cocoamide DEA, glycol distearate and sodium laureth sulfate and cocoamide MEA and laureth-9, Germall II, methylcellulose, methylparaben, perfurme, polysorbate, propylparaben, purified water and sodium lauryl ether sulfate. Amber glass bottles of 50 and 250 mL with child proof safety caps.

HIBIDIL® 1:2000

Zeneca

Chlorhexidine Gluconate

Antiseptic

Pharmacology: Chlorhexidine is effective against a wide range of gram-negative and gram-positive vegetative bacteria, yeasts, dermatophyte fungi and lipophilic viruses. It is inactive against bacterial spores except at elevated temperatures.

Because of its cationic nature, chlorhexidine binds strongly to skin, mucosa and other tissues and is thus very poorly absorbed. No detectable blood levels have been found in man following oral use. Percutaneous absorption, if it occurs at all, is insignificant.

Indications: A potent antibacterial agent active against a wide range of organisms. Recommended for swabbing wounds and burns and in obstetrics.

Contraindications: For patients who have previously shown a hypersensitivity reaction to chlorhexidine. However, such reactions are extremely rare.

Warnings: For external use only. Keep out of the eyes and avoid contact with brain, meninges, or middle ear. Do not inject. Do not use in body cavities.

If chlorhexidine solutions come into contact with eyes, wash out promptly and thoroughly with water.

Discard any surplus solution immediately after use since sterility can no longer be assured.

Do not use the solution in the eyes before or after ophthalmic surgery. If accidental contact is suspected, wash thoroughly with sterile water before starting surgical procedure. Do not use solution with alcohol (e.g. 450 mL) on deep wounds and deep burns or in obstetrics. Do not use solution with alcohol for eye irrigation. On broken skin, use only sterile solutions.

Precautions: Hypochlorite bleaches may cause brown stains to develop in fabrics which have previously been in contact with chlorhexidine solutions. Use a perborate bleach instead. Hibidil is incompatible with anionic agents.

Adverse Effects: Irritative skin reactions can occasionally occur. Generalized allergic reactions to chlorhexidine have also been reported but are extremely rare.

Overdose: Symptoms and Treatment: Accidental or deliberate poisoning: Accidental ingestion: Chlorhexidine taken orally is poorly absorbed. Treat with gastric lavage using milk, raw egg, gelatin or mild soap. Employ supportive measures as appropriate.

Accidental i.v. infusion: Blood transfusion may be necessary to counteract hemolysis.

Dosage: Apply undiluted.

Supplied: Each mL of sterile aqueous solution contains: chlorhexidine gluconate 0.05% w/v. Nonmedicinal ingredients: isopropyl alcohol and water. Parabens-, sulfites- and tartrazine-free. Plastic bottles of 450 mL.

Each mL of sterile solution contains: chlorhexidine gluconate 0.05% w/v. Nonmedicinal ingredients: water. Alcohol-free. Unit-dose packages of 30 mL, boxes of 10.

Store at temperature not exceeding 25°C. Protect from light. Protect from freezing.

HIBITANE® Skin Cleanser

Zeneca

Chlorhexidine Gluconate

Antibacterial Skin Cleanser

Pharmacology: Chlorhexidine is effective against a wide range of gram-negative and gram-positive vegetative bacteria, yeasts, dermatophyte fungi and lipophilic viruses. It is inactive against bacterial spores except at elevated temperatures.

Because of its cationic nature, chlorhexidine binds strongly to skin, mucosa and other tissues and is thus very poorly absorbed. No detectable blood levels have been found in man following oral use. Percutaneous absorption, if it occurs at all, is insignificant.

Indications: An antiseptic preparation for preoperative surgical hand disinfection, for general antiseptic handwashing, for handwashing procedures in food processing facilities and preoperative and post-operative skin antisepsis for patients undergoing elective surgery.

Contraindications: For persons who have previously shown a hypersensitivity reaction to chlorhexidine. However, such reactions are extremely rare.

Warnings: For external use only. Keep out of the eyes and avoid contact with brain, meninges, or middle ear. Do not use Hibitane skin cleanser as a pre-operative skin preparation of the periorbital or eyelid areas. If chlorhexidine solutions come into contact with eyes, wash out promptly and thoroughly with water.

In patients with head or spinal injuries or perforated ear drum, the benefit of use in pre-operative preparation should be evaluated against the risk of contact.

Precautions: Hypochlorite bleaches may cause brown stains to develop in fabrics which have previously been in contact with chlorhexidine solutions. Use a perborate bleach instead. Hibitane Skin Cleanser is incompatible with anionic agents.

Adverse Effects: Irritative skin reactions can occasionally occur. Generalized allergic reactions to chlorhexidine have also been reported, but are extremely rare.

Overdose: Symptoms and Treatment: Accidental or deliberate poisoning: Accidental ingestion: Chlorhexidine taken orally is poorly absorbed. Treat with gastric lavage using milk, raw egg, gelatin or mild soap. Employ supportive measures as appropriate.

Accidental contact with eyes: If Hibitane Skin Cleanser comes into contact with the eyes, wash out promptly and thoroughly with water.

Dosage: For pre-operative surgical scrub: Wet hands and forearms, apply 5 mL of Hibitane Skin Cleanser 4% undiluted and wash for 1 minute cleaning the fingernails with a brush. Rinse, apply a further 5 mL of skin cleanser and continue washing for a further 2 minutes. Rinse thoroughly and dry.
For general antiseptic handwashing: Wet the hands and forearms, apply 5 mL of Hibitane Skin Cleanser 4% and wash for 1 minute. Rinse thoroughly and dry.
Note: In noncritical areas and in food processing facilities, where due to frequent handwashing the product is required only to maintain asepsis, the 2% solution may be used instead.
For pre-operative skin preparation for the patient: The patient washes his whole body in a bath or shower on at least 2 occasions, usually the day before and on the day of the operation as follows: The day before the operation, the patient washes with 25 mL of Hibitane Skin Cleanser 4% beginning with the face and working downwards paying particular attention to areas around the nose, axillae, umbilicus, groin and perineum. The body is then rinsed and the wash repeated with a further 25 mL, this time including the hair. Finally, the patient rinses his entire body thoroughly and dries with a clean towel. This procedure should be repeated the following day. Patients confined to their bed can be washed with Hibitane Skin Cleanser using a standard bed-bath technique.

Conventional disinfection of the operation site will then be performed when the patient is in the operating room with Hibitane 0.5% in 70% isopropyl alcohol.

Supplied: Each mL of red antibacterial solution contains: chlorhexidine gluconate 2 or 4% w/v. Nonmedicinal ingredients: ammonyx, dye (red), fragrance, gluconate delta lactone, isopropyl alcohol, poloxamer, propylene glycol, sodium hydroxide and water. Parabens-, sulfites- and tartrazine-free. Plastic containers of 500 mL and 4.5 L (2% solution) and plastic containers of 110 mL, 500 mL and 4.5 L (4% solution). Store at a temperature not exceeding 25°C. Protect from light. Protect from freezing.

HI POTENCY B-COMPOUND "50"

Swiss Herbal

Vitamin Supplement

Supplied: Each tablet contains: vitamin B_1 50 mg, vitamin B_2 50 mg, vitamin B_3 50 mg, vitamin B_6 50 mg, vitamin B_{12} 50 μg, biotin 50 μg, folic acid 1 mg, D'pantothenic acid 50 mg, choline bitartrate 50 mg and inositol 50 mg. Nonmedicinal ingredients: cellulose, dicalcium phosphate, magnesium stearate, stearic acid and vanilla. Bottles of 50, 90, 180 and 500.

HIP-REX™

3M Pharmaceuticals

Methenamine Hippurate

Urinary Antibacterial

Supplied: Each scored, white tablet contains: methenamine hippurate 1 g. Nonmedicinal ingredients: magnesium stearate, povidone and saccharin. Tartrazine-free. Bottles of 100.

HISMANAL® Ⓟ

Johnson & Johnson • Merck

Astemizole

Histamine H_1-Antagonist

Pharmacology: Astemizole is a potent, long acting, and selective histamine H_1-antagonist. It produces a dose-related inhibition of skin reactions to intradermal histamine. Astemizole inhibits the nose reaction to nasal challenge with histamine and allergens. It inhibits the bronchial reaction to inhaled histamine and allergens in asthmatic patients. Astemizole has extremely weak serotonin antagonism, no anticholinergic properties, antagonism of dopamine and other catecholamines. In clinical studies, astemizole did not cause daytime sedation or evening somnolence.
Pharmacokinetics: Astemizole is rapidly absorbed after a single oral administration with peak plasma levels of approximately 0.5 ng/mL (0.3 to 1.0) being achieved within 1 hour. Astemizole undergoes extensive first pass metabolism in the liver; plasma levels of astemizole remain detectable (0.1 ng/mL) for 4 hours after administration due to rapid tissue distribution and the formation of metabolites. Peak plasma levels of the major active metabolite, desmethylastemizole, are similar to those of the unchanged drug and are reached at 2 hours. The terminal half-lives of astemizole and desmethylastemizole after a single oral administration were 1 to 3 and 11 to 16 days respectively.

Following chronic oral administration, steady-state plasma levels were reached in 7 to 10 days for astemizole (0.4 to 1.2 ng/mL) and within 4 to 5 weeks for desmethylastemizole (2 to 9 ng/mL). Peak plasma levels at steady-state were obtained within 1 hour for astemizole and after 4.2 hours (range 2 to 8) for desmethylastemizole. At steady-state, 90% of the plasma concentrations of astemizole plus its metabolite desmethylastemizole (considered together to represent the pharmacologically active fraction), fall within the range of 1 and 7 ng/mL. The terminal half-life is 1 to 2 days for astemizole and 8 to 18 days for desmethylastemizole. These elimination half-lives are similar to those after a single oral administration, which demonstrate that the pharmacokinetics of both astemizole and desmethylastemizole remain linear.

In human blood, only 2.3% was present as free drug in the plasma water, 61.5% was bound to plasma proteins and 36.2% was distributed to the blood cell fraction. Astemizole or its metabolites did not accumulate in erythrocytes.

Indications: For the treatment of seasonal allergic rhinitis, allergic conjunctivitis, chronic urticaria and other allergic conditions.

Contraindications: Concurrent therapy of astemizole with erythromycin is contraindicated because erythromycin is known to impair the cytochrome P450 enzyme system which also influences astemizole metabolism. Concomitant administration of astemizole with other macrolide antibiotics (e.g., clarithromycin) prone to the formation of inactive cytochrome P450-metabolite complexes is contraindicated. An open-label study of the effects of azithromycin on the steady-state pharmacokinetics and cardiovascular safety of astemizole was conducted in 21 healthy adult males. Azithromycin treatment led to a neglible decrease in the bioavailability of astemizole and did not cause any clinically meaningful further increase in QT or QTc intervals. More data in a wider population would be required to allow for the conclusion that coadministration of azithromycin and astemizole has no negative impact on the QTc.

Concurrent therapy of astemizole with oral ketoconazole is contraindicated because available human pharmacokinetic data indicate that oral ketoconazole significantly inhibits the metabolism of astemizole, resulting in elevated plasma levels of astemizole and desmethylastemizole. Serious cardiac effects and arrhythmias (prolongation of the QT interval, torsades de pointes) can occur when astemizole is used in the daily recommended dose in conjunction with erythromycin and/or ketoconazole.

Due to the chemical similarity of fluconazole, itraconazole and metronidazole to ketoconazole, concomitant use with an oral or parenteral formulation of these products with astemizole is also contraindicated.

Concurrent administration of astemizole with quinine is contraindicated. Therapeutic doses of quinine may decrease the metabolism of astemizole and result in elevated plasma levels.

Concomitant administration of astemizole with drugs known to prolong the QT interval is contraindicated. These include certain class IA and III antiarrhythmic drugs (quinidine, procainamide amiodarone, sotalol, bretylium), certain psychiatric drugs (thioridazine, pimozide, phenothiazines, haloperidol, tricyclic antidepressants, lithium, chloral hydrate), terfenadine, certain antimalarial drugs (quinine, chloroquine, halofantrine, mefloquine) and others such as amantidine, pentamidine, cisapride, probucol, TMP-SMX and tacrolimus.

Concomitant administration of astemizole is contraindicated with drugs or foods that inhibit the metabolism of astemizole at the cytochrome P450 level. This includes serotonin reuptake inhibitors (e.g., fluoxetine, fluvoxamine, nefazodone, paroxetine, sertraline), and HIV protease inhibitors (e.g., indinavir, ritonavir, saquinavir) and grapefruit juice. Certain calcium channel blocking agents that are primarily metabolized by the hepatic CYP 3A4 isoenzyme, such as the dihydropyridines, also have the potential to elevate plasma astemizole levels.

In patients with hepatic dysfunction such as hepatitis, jaundice, or chronic alcoholism, and in patients with electrolyte abnormalities (e.g., hypokalemia, hypomagnesemia) or in patients taking certain diuretics, systemic corticosteroids or liquid protein diets with the potential for inducing electrolyte abnormalities.

In patients with congenital QT-syndrome or have conditions leading to QT-prolongation.

In patients with heart disease unless authorized by a physician.

In patients with a known hypersensitivity to the drug or to its excipients.

Warnings: Rare cases of serious cardiovascular adverse events, including death, cardiac arrest, QT prolongation, torsades de pointes and other ventricular arrhythmias have been reported in patients taking astemizole, particularly in overdosage. Torsades de pointes have rarely occurred at doses 2 to 3 times the recommended dose (20 to 30 mg). It is therefore very important that the recommended dose (10 mg) not be exceeded.

Episodes of syncope, dizziness, chest pain, dyspnea, and/or palpitations in association with the use of astemizole should be carefully investigated. The drug should be discontinued and a full electrocardiographic evaluation for QT prolongation and arrhythmias carried out.
Pregnancy: Experience with astemizole in pregnant women is inadequate to determine whether there exists a potential for harm to the fetus. Therefore, astemizole should be used in pregnant women only when, in the opinion of the physician, the potential benefits outweigh the possible hazards. In view of the prolonged half-life, women of childbearing potential should discontinue the use of astemizole for at least 4 weeks prior to contemplating pregnancy.
Lactation: In nursing dogs, astemizole and its metabolites are excreted in the maternal milk. Therefore, astemizole should not be administered to lactating women unless in the judgment of a physician, the potential benefits outweigh the possible risks.

Precautions: General: A negative skin prick test to allergens immediately following astemizole treatment should be viewed with caution since astemizole can affect skin test results even after cessation of therapy. Therefore further tests should be performed after a drug free period of at least 2 and preferably 4 weeks.
Use with CNS Depressants: Astemizole had no potentiating effects with alcohol or other CNS depressants in clinical and laboratory studies.
Drug Interactions: The main metabolic pathway of astemizole is through the hepatic CYP 3A4 isoenzyme. The concomitant use of drugs that significantly inhibit these enzymes may result in increased plasma levels of astemizole, which could enhance the risk of QT-prolongation. Therefore, the use of such drugs is contraindicated. Examples are: an oral or parenteral formulation of azole antifungals; macrolide antibiotics; serotonin reuptake inhibitors; HIV protease inhibitors such as ritonavir and indinavir; in vitro studies suggest that saquinavir is only a weak inhibitor.

In the absence of clinical studies demonstrating safety, coadministration of astemizole with drugs that have shown significant CYP 3A inhibition is not recommended.

Concomitant administration of astemizole with therapeutic doses of quinine is contraindicated.

Astemizole is contraindicated in patients where conditions or the use of other drugs favor the prolongation of the QT interval.

See Contraindications and Warnings for discussion of information regarding potential drug interactions.
Food Interactions: As the medical literature indicates that there is a potential for grapefruit juice to influence the metabolism of drugs whose metabolism is highly CYP 3A4 dependent and until the clinical significance is fully established, the ingestion of grapefruit juice by patients taking astemizole should be avoided.

In an open study, the influence of the consumption of grapefruit juice on the steady-state pharmacokinetics and cardiovascular safety of astemizole and desmethylastemizole was investigated. Twelve healthy volunteers took 30 mg astemizole for 4 days, followed by 10 mg astemizole daily for 20 days. After reaching steady-state, a total of 4 glasses of 200 mL of grapefruit juice, one every 4 hours, were drunk. The results of the study demonstrate that grapefruit juice does not interact with the kinetics of astemizole. Until confirmation is obtained in a larger, more comprehensive study, a potential food interaction between grapefruit juice and astemizole cannot be excluded.

Adverse Effects: The incidence of adverse experiences during astemizole treatment was comparable to that during placebo control treatment.

During chronic treatment, body weight tended to increase. This is probably due to an increase in appetite.

Rare cases spontaneously reported from postmarketing experience with astemizole include hypersensitivity reactions such as: angioedema, bronchospasm, photosensitivity, pruritus, rash, anaphylactoid reactions and serious, life-threatening cardiovascular adverse events (see Warnings).

Hismanal (cont'd)

There have also been isolated cases of convulsions, benign paresthesias, myalgia/arthralgia, edema, mood disturbance, insomnia, nightmares, liver enzyme elevations and hepatitis. In most cases, a causal relationship with astemizole is unclear.

Overdose: Symptoms and Treatment: Overdoses with astemizole with doses as low as 2 to 3 times the recommended daily dose (20 or 30 mg) have been associated with cardiac adverse effects. In cases of overdose, or when adverse effects are suspected, cardiac monitoring should be instituted and continued until the QT interval has returned to normal. With overdoses, the standard measures to remove any unabsorbed drug (emesis, gastric lavage, charcoal) also should be carried out. Hemodialysis does not increase the clearance of the drug. Consideration should be given to the fact that the half-life of elimination for astemizole and its major active metabolite, desmethylastemizole, is at least 10 to 14 days. Appropriate antiarrhythmic treatment may be needed but treatment with antiarrhythmics known to prolong the QT interval should be avoided.

In some cases, severe arrhythmias have been preceded by or associated with 1 or more episodes of syncope. Therefore, syncope in patients receiving astemizole should lead to immediate discontinuation of treatment and appropriate clinical evaluation, including ECG testing.

In 2 overdose cases (100 to 270 mg), patients experienced seizures that were caused by anoxia and metabolic acidosis secondary to overdose and cardiac arrest.

Dosage: Adults and children 12 years and over: 10 mg once a day.

The following dosage may guide the physician when prescribing astemizole for children under 12 years of age: Children between 6 and 12 years of age: 5 mg once a day. Astemizole tablets are not suited for children below 6 years of age.

Do not exceed the recommended dosage.

Note: Although loading doses are not, and never were, recommended in Canada, other regulatory agencies have approved this practice. Such a dosage regimen can be dangerous and should never be used.

Astemizole should not be taken with grapefruit juice.

Clinical studies indicate that the onset of symptomatic relief with astemizole is comparable to that of other antihistamines. Patients should be instructed that peak symptomatic relief may not be achieved for up to 3 days. It is therefore important that daily therapy be continued for at least this long in order to obtain and maintain this relief. Clinical effects of the medication may be seen for several days following discontinuation of therapy.

Prolonged use should be only as directed by a physician.

Supplied: Each white, round, scored, compressed tablet contains: astemizole 10 mg. Nonmedicinal ingredients: anhydrous silica, cornstarch, lactose, magnesium stearate, microcrystalline cellulose, povidone, pregelatinized potato starch and sodium lauryl sulfate. Bisulfite-, gluten- and tartrazine-free. Blister packs of 6, 12, 18 and 24 (on a seasonal basis).

(Shown in Product Recognition Section)

Reviewed 1999

HISTAMINE
Bioniche

Histamine Phosphate
Diagnostic Aid

Indications: To test the ability of the gastric mucosa to produce hydrochloric acid.

Contraindications: The gastric histamine test is contraindicated in patients with a history of hypersensitivity to histamine products, in patients with hypotension, severe hypertension, vasomotor instability, bronchial asthma (past or present), urticaria (past or present), or severe cardiac, pulmonary or renal disease.

Precautions: Attacks of severe asthma or other serious allergic conditions may be precipitated. The possible benefit that may be derived from the gastric histamine test should be carefully weighed against the serious untoward reactions that may develop in patients with allergic diseases. Small doses by any route of administration may precipitate asthma in patients with bronchial disease. Use the utmost caution in administering histamine to such patients. When histamine phosphate is administered, pull back on the syringe plunger before the injection is made to be sure the end of the needle is not in a blood vessel. Avoid accidental introduction into a vein or artery. Epinephrine HCl 1:1 000 aqueous solution, should be immediately available to counteract the effects of histamine.

Pregnancy and *Lactation:* The safety of histamine phosphate for use during pregnancy or lactation has not been established. However, based on histamine's known ability to contract uterine muscle, exposure or repeated doses should be avoided. Therefore, the benefits must be weighed against its possible hazards to the mother and child.

The risk/benefit ratio must be carefully weighed when considering the use of the gastric histamine test in patients with pheochromocytoma.

Histamine increases the acid of the gastric juice and may cause symptoms of peptic ulcer. A large dose of histamine may cause severe occipital headache, blurred vision, anginal pain, a rapid drop in blood pressure and cyanosis of the face. Overdosage may cause severe symptoms, including circulatory collapse, shock, and even death. Monitor the blood pressure and pulse carefully during injection of histamine.

Use with caution in elderly patients and in patients with any cardiac abnormality.

Adverse Effects: Average or large doses of histamine may include such local reactions as erythema and edema and/or such systemic reactions as flushing, dizziness, headache, bronchial constriction, dyspnea, visual disturbances, faintness, syncope, urticaria, asthma, marked hypertension or hypotension, palpitation, tachycardia, nervousness, abdominal cramps, nausea, diarrhea, vomiting, metallic taste, local or generalized allergic manifestations, or collapse with convulsions. These reactions may be serious and excessive dosage can produce collapse and shock, and may be fatal.

Overdose: Symptoms: See Adverse Effects.

Treatment: If accidental overdosage is discovered early, temporary application of a tourniquet proximally to the injection site may be tried to slow down the absorption of the drug. Antidotes to histamine are the following: epinephrine HCl, 0.1 to 0.5 mL of a 1:1 000 aqueous solution, given s.c. in case of emergency due to severe reactions; an antihistamine preparation, given orally in case of mild allergic reactions caused by the usual dose of the drug.

Dosage: Gastric Acid Test: The patient fasts for 12 hours. A plastic duodenal tube is passed into the stomach, the gastric content withdrawn, and its acidity determined. Care should be taken to prevent the patient from swallowing salivary secretions during administration of the test results. The alkalinity of the saliva may interfere with the test results. Histamine phosphate 500 to 750 μg is injected s.c.

Gastric content is again removed after 5 minutes and at 15-minute intervals thereafter on 3 occasions.

The volume and acidity of each specimen are determined. If no acidity is detected, a maximum histamine stimulation test can be performed using 40 μg/kg histamine phosphate s.c. Pulse rate and blood pressure should be determined immediately after histamine injection.

Supplied: Each mL contains: histamine phosphate USP 1 mg. Nonmedicinal ingredients: sodium chloride. Ampuls of 1 mL, boxes of 10. Store between 15 and 30°C. Protect from light. Do not freeze.

HIVID® Ⓟ
Roche

Zalcitabine
Antiretroviral Agent

Pharmacology: Zalcitabine is a synthetic nucleoside analogue of the naturally occurring nucleoside 2′-deoxycytidine in which the 3′-hydroxyl group is replaced by hydrogen. Within cells, zalcitabine is converted to the active metabolite, dideoxycytidine 5′-triphosphate (ddCTP), by cellular enzymes. ddCTP serves as an alternative substrate to deoxycytidine triphosphate (dCTP) for HIV-reverse transcriptase and inhibits the in vitro replication of HIV-1 by inhibition of viral DNA synthesis. This inhibition has been demonstrated in vitro in human primary cell cultures and in established cell lines. In DNA biosynthesis, DNA chain extension occurs through the formation of a phosphodiester bridge between the 3′-hydroxyl group of the growing end of a DNA chain and the 5′-phosphate group of the incoming deoxynucleotide. Because ddCTP lacks the 3′-hydroxyl group required for chain elongation, its incorporation into a growing DNA chain leads to premature chain termination. ddCTP serves as a competitive inhibitor of the natural substrate, dCTP, for the active site of the viral reverse transcriptase and thus further inhibits viral as well as cellular DNA synthesis.

Cellular mitochondrial DNA polymerase gamma has a high affinity for the active metabolite, ddCTP, which has been reported to be incorporated into the DNA of cells in culture. However, DNA chain termination with cellular DNA polymerases has not been demonstrated. The half-life of ddCTP in established cell lines and in human peripheral blood mononuclear cells in culture has been determined to be in the range of 2.6 to 10 hours.

Indications: Monotherapy for Zidovudine Intolerant or Zidovudine Failures in Advanced HIV Infection: Zalcitabine is indicated for the treatment of adult patients with advanced HIV infection who have demonstrated intolerance or significant clinical or immunologic deterioration during zidovudine therapy.

Combination Therapy with Zidovudine in Advanced HIV Infection: Zalcitabine in combination with zidovudine is indicated for the treatment of selected patients with advanced HIV disease (CD4 cell counts ≤300 cells/mm³).

In zidovudine-naive patients this indication is based on greater increases in CD4 cell counts that were maintained longer for patients treated with combination therapy as compared to zidovudine monotherapy. There have been no studies showing clinical benefit from combination therapy in zidovudine-naive patients. For patients with prior zidovudine exposure, this indication is based on a subgroup analysis of clinical data that showed a clinical benefit only for those patients with a CD4 count ≥150 cells/mm³ at the time of the initiation of therapy. No benefit from combination therapy has been observed from studies of zidovudine-exposed patients with CD4 cell counts <150 cells/mm³, and combination therapy is therefore not currently recommended for these patients.

Contraindications: In patients with clinically significant hypersensitivity to zalcitabine or to any of the components of the formulation.

Warnings: In patients who have shown clinical or immunologic deterioration while receiving zalcitabine as monotherapy or in combination with zidovudine, consideration should be given to the use of alternative antiretroviral therapy.

The major clinical toxicities of zalcitabine are peripheral neuropathy and much less frequently, pancreatitis. Rare occurrences of hepatic toxicity have also been reported with the use of nucleoside analogues, including zidovudine and zalcitabine. Toxicities previously associated with zidovudine monotherapy are likely to occur in patients treated with combined zalcitabine and zidovudine therapy. It is recommended that physicians refer to the product monograph for zidovudine before prescribing combination therapy with zalcitabine and zidovudine.

The decision to use zalcitabine should be made in consultation with a physician experienced in the care of patients with HIV infection.

Peripheral Neuropathy: The major clinical toxicity of zalcitabine, possibly or probably related to drug treatment, is peripheral neuropathy which occurred in 21 to 36% of subjects who received monotherapy zalcitabine in Phase 2 and 3 clinical studies (see Table I). Moderate to severe peripheral neuropathy was noted in 20 to 23% of these subjects. By comparison, neuropathy occurred in as many as 19% of patients treated with monotherapy zidovudine, and in up to 10% of these patients, the neuropathy was moderate to severe. When combined zalcitabine and zidovudine were used, the occurrence of peripheral neuropathy was similar to that which was seen with monotherapy zalcitabine (i.e., 21 to 28%, with 4 to 19% classified as moderate to severe).

Zalcitabine-related peripheral neuropathy is a sensorimotor neuropathy characterized initially by numbness and burning dysesthesia involving the distal extremities. These symptoms may be followed by sharp shooting pains or severe continuous burning pain if the drug is not withdrawn. The neuropathy may progress to severe pain requiring narcotic analgesics and is potentially irreversible, especially if zalcitabine is not stopped promptly. In some patients, symptoms of neuropathy may initially progress despite discontinuation of zalcitabine. With prompt discontinuation of zalcitabine the neuropathy is usually slowly reversible.

There are no data regarding the use of zalcitabine in patients with pre-existing peripheral neuropathy since these patients were excluded from clinical trials; therefore, zalcitabine should be used with extreme caution in these patients. Zalcitabine should also be used with particular caution in individuals with low CD4 cell counts (CD4 <50 cells/mm³) for whom the risk of developing peripheral neuropathy while on zalcitabine therapy is greater. Careful monitoring is strongly recommended for these individuals. Individuals with moderate or severe peripheral neuropathy, as evidenced by symptoms accompanied by objective findings, are advised to avoid zalcitabine.

Zalcitabine should be stopped promptly when moderate discomfort from numbness, tingling, burning or pain of the extremities progresses, or any related symptoms occur that are accompanied by an objective finding. Peripheral neuropathy requiring zalcitabine interruption is defined as moderate discomfort of the lower extremities (requiring non-narcotic analgesics) that is bilateral and persists for ≥3 days, or mild symptoms accompanied by the loss of a previously present Achilles reflex. If symptoms resolve to mild intensity, rechallenge with half-dosage is permitted. Peripheral neuropathy requiring permanent discontinuation of zalcitabine is defined as any severe discomfort of the extremities requiring narcotic analgesics, or moderate discomfort progressing for ≥1 week.

Pancreatitis: Documented fatal pancreatitis has been observed with the administration of zalcitabine alone or the combination of zalcitabine with zidovudine. Pancreatitis is an uncommon complication of zalcitabine monotherapy, occurring in 1.1% of patients. The occurrence of asymptomatic elevated serum amylase of any etiology while on zalcitabine monotherapy was 1.6%. Among patients treated with zalcitabine in the expanded access safety study who had a history of prior pancreatitis or increased amylase, 5.3% developed pancreatitis and an additional 4.4% developed asymptomatic elevated serum amylase. There was no apparent difference in the occurrence of pancreatitis between the 2 doses of zalcitabine (2.25 mg or 1.125 mg daily) used in the Expanded Access trial.

Caution should be exercised when administering zalcitabine to any patient with a history of pancreatitis or a known risk factor for the development of pancreatitis. There have been isolated cases of death from fulminant pancreatitis. In one case, the patient was treated with combination zalcitabine and zidovudine; in a second case, the patient was treated concomitantly with i.v. pentamidine and zalcitabine.

All patients receiving i.v. pentamidine for the treatment of P. carinii pneumonia (PCP) should have zalcitabine treatment interrupted for the period of pentamidine administration. Treatment with zalcitabine should also be interrupted if therapy with another drug known to cause pancreatitis is required (see Precautions, Drug Interactions).

Patients with a history of pancreatitis or a history of elevated serum amylase should be followed more closely while on zalcitabine therapy. The significance of an asymptomatic increase in serum amylase levels in HIV-infected patients prior to starting zalcitabine or while on zalcitabine is unclear. Treatment with zalcitabine should be interrupted in the setting of a rising serum amylase level associated with dysglycemia, rising triglycerides level, decreasing serum calcium or other parameters or symptoms suggestive of impending pancreatitis, until a clinical diagnosis is reached.

Treatment with zalcitabine should be stopped immediately if nausea, vomiting, abdominal pain or other symptoms suggestive of pancreatitis develop, until a definitive diagnosis can be established. Zalcitabine should be restarted only after pancreatitis has been ruled out. If clinical pancreatitis develops during zalcitabine administration, it is recommended that zalcitabine be permanently discontinued.

Hepatic Toxicity: Rare occurrences of lactic acidosis in the absence of hypoxemia and severe hepatomegaly with steatosis have been reported with the use of nucleoside analogues, including zidovudine and zalcitabine, and are potentially fatal. In addition, rare cases of hepatic failure (1 which coincided with renal failure) and death considered possibly related to underlying hepatitis B and zalcitabine monotherapy have been reported.

Treatment with zalcitabine in patients with pre-existing liver disease, liver enzyme abnormalities, a history of ethanol abuse or hepatitis should be interrupted or discontinued in the setting of deterioration of liver function tests, hepatic steatosis, progressive hepatomegaly or unexplained lactic acidosis. In clinical trials, drug interruption was recommended if liver function tests exceeded 5 times the upper limit of normal.

Other Serious Toxicities: Oral Ulcers: Severe oral ulcers occurred in approximately 3% of patients receiving zalcitabine in 2 clinical studies; less severe oral ulcerations have occurred at higher frequencies in other clinical trials.

Esophageal Ulcers: Infrequent cases of esophageal ulcers have been attributed to zalcitabine therapy. Interruption of zalcitabine should be considered in patients who develop esophageal ulcers that do not respond to specific treatment for opportunistic pathogens in order to assess a possible relationship to zalcitabine.

Cardiomyopathy/Congestive Heart Failure: Cardiomyopathy and congestive heart failure in patients with AIDS have been associated with the use of nucleoside antiretroviral agents. Infrequent cases have been reported in patients receiving zalcitabine. In one case, the investigator considered that the exacerbation of preexisting cardiomyopathy was possibly related to zalcitabine. Treatment with zalcitabine in patients with baseline cardiomyopathy or a history of congestive heart failure should be approached with caution.

Anaphylactoid Reaction: There has been one report of an anaphylactoid reaction occurring in a patient receiving both zalcitabine and zidovudine in an alternating regimen. In addition, there have been several reports of urticaria without other signs of anaphylaxis.

Because severe adverse effects may be attributable to either zalcitabine or zidovudine singly or to their combination, the complete prescribing information for zidovudine should be consulted before initiation of combination therapy or reinstitution of monotherapy with zidovudine following an adverse reaction.

Precautions: General: Patients receiving zalcitabine or any other antiretroviral therapy may continue to develop opportunistic infections and other complications of HIV infection, and therefore should remain under close clinical observation by physicians experienced in the treatment of patients with HIV disease.

Lymphoma: High doses of zalcitabine, administered for 3 months to $B_6C_3F_1$ mice (resulting in plasma concentrations over 1 000 times those seen in patients taking the recommended doses of zalcitabine) induced an increased incidence of thymic lymphoma. Although the pathogenesis of the effect is uncertain, a predisposition to chemically induced thymic lymphoma and high rates of spontaneous lymphoreticular neoplasms have previously been noted in this strain of mice.

The incidence of lymphomas was reviewed in 13 comparative and 7 expanded-access studies using zalcitabine. In one study a statistically significant increase in the rate of lymphomas was seen in patients receiving zalcitabine or combination zalcitabine and zidovudine compared to zidovudine alone (rates of 0, 1.3 and 2.3 per 100 person years were recorded for zidovudine, zalcitabine, and combination zalcitabine/zidovudine, respectively. Based on a review of the literature, the expected incidence of lymphomas in HIV infected patients with advanced disease on zidovudine monotherapy would be approximately 1 to 2 per 100 person years of follow-up.

Children: The safety and effectiveness of zalcitabine in combination with zidovudine or as monotherapy in HIV-infected children younger than 13 years of age has not been established.

Pregnancy: There are no adequate and well-controlled studies of zalcitabine use in pregnant women. Zalcitabine should be used during pregnancy only if the potential benefit justifies the potential risk to the fetus. Fertile women should not receive zalcitabine unless they are using effective contraception during therapy.

Zalcitabine has been shown to be teratogenic in mice at calculated exposure levels of 1 365 and 2 730 times of those achieved with the maximum recommended human dose (MRHD) based on AUC measurements. In rats, zalcitabine was teratogenic at a calculated exposure level of 2 142 times the MRHD but not at an exposure level of 485 times the MRHD.

In a perinatal and postnatal study in the rat, a high incidence of hydrocephalus was observed in the F1 offspring derived from the litters of dams treated with 1 071 times the MRHD (based on AUC measurements) but not at an exposure level of 485 times the MRHD.

Increased embryolethality was observed in pregnant mice at doses 2 730 times the MRHD and in rats above 485 times the MRHD (based on AUC measurements). Average fetal body weight was significantly decreased in mice at doses of 1 365 times the MRHD and in rats at 2 142 times the MRHD.

Lactation: It is not known whether zalcitabine is excreted in human milk. Because of uncertainties related to transmission of virus and to excretion of zalcitabine in breast milk, it is advisable to caution mothers against breast-feeding.

Patients with Special Diseases and Conditions: Renal Impairment: Patients with renal impairment (estimated creatinine clearance <55 mL/min) may be at a greater risk of toxicity from zalcitabine due to decreased drug clearance. Zalcitabine dosage reduction should be considered in these patients (see Dosage).

Hepatic Impairment: The use of zalcitabine may be associated with exacerbation of hepatic dysfunction especially in individuals with pre-existing liver disease, liver enzyme abnormalities, a history of ethanol abuse, or hepatitis. In such patients, zalcitabine should be interrupted or discontinued in the setting of deteriorating liver function tests (LFTs), hepatic steatosis, progressive hepatomegaly or unexplained lactic acidosis. Of 85 patients in the expanded access safety study with a prior history of LFT elevation before starting zalcitabine, 10 (12%) developed increases in LFTs greater than 5 times the upper limit of normal while on zalcitabine. In clinical trials, drug interruption was recommended if LFTs exceeded 5 times the upper limit of normal (see Warnings, Hepatic Toxicity).

Drug Interactions: The concomitant use of zalcitabine with drugs that have the potential to cause peripheral neuropathy should be avoided where possible. Drugs which have been associated with peripheral neuropathy include chloramphenicol, cisplatin, dapsone, disulfiram, ethionamide, glutethimide, gold, hydralazine, iodoquinol, isoniazid, metronidazole, nitrofurantoin, phenytoin, ribavirin, and vincristine. Concomitant use of zalcitabine with didanosine is not recommended.

Drugs such as amphotericin, foscarnet, and aminoglycosides may increase the risk of developing peripheral neuropathy or other zalcitabine-associated toxicities by interfering with the renal clearance of zalcitabine (and thereby raising systemic exposure). Patients who require the use of one of these drugs with zalcitabine should have frequent clinical and laboratory monitoring with dosage adjustment for any significant change in renal function.

Treatment with zalcitabine should be interrupted when the use of a drug that has the potential to cause pancreatitis is required. Death due to fulminant pancreatitis possibly related to zalcitabine and i.v. pentamidine was reported. If i.v. pentamidine is required to treat P. carinii pneumonia, treatment with zalcitabine should be interrupted for the period of pentamidine administration (see Warnings).

Concomitant administration of probenecid or cimetidine decreases the elimination of zalcitabine, most likely by inhibition of renal tubular secretion of zalcitabine. This represents an increase in exposure to zalcitabine of approximately 50% and 36% with concomitant administration of probenecid and cimetidine, respectively. Patients receiving these drugs in combination with zalcitabine should be monitored for signs of toxicity and the dose of zalcitabine reduced if warranted.

Absorption of zalcitabine is moderately reduced (approximately 25%) when coadministered with magnesium/aluminum containing products. The clinical significance of this reduction is not known, hence zalcitabine is not recommended to be ingested simultaneously with magnesium/aluminum containing antacids. Bioavailability is mildly reduced (approximately 10%) when zalcitabine and metoclopramide are coadministered.

Administration of single doses of 1.5 mg zalcitabine during loperamide treatment (4 mg, 16 hours before zalcitabine; 2 mg, 10 and 4 hours before zalcitabine; and 2 mg, 2 hours after zalcitabine) to 12 HIV-positive patients with diarrhea resulted in no significant pharmacokinetic interaction between zalcitabine and loperamide.

Information for the Patient: Zalcitabine is not a cure for HIV infection. Illnesses associated with advanced HIV infection including opportunistic infections may still happen and zalcitabine has not been shown to reduce the incidence or frequency of such illnesses. Since it is frequently difficult to determine whether symptoms are a result of drug effect or underlying disease manifestation, all changes in your condition should be reported to your physician. The use of zalcitabine or other antiretroviral drugs do not preclude the ongoing need to maintain practices designed to prevent transmission of HIV.

The major toxicity of zalcitabine is peripheral neuropathy. Pancreatitis is another serious and potentially life-threatening toxicity that has been reported in 1.1% of patients treated with zalcitabine alone. Liver disturbances occur rarely, particularly in patients with a history of liver illness.

Symptoms of peripheral neuropathy include tingling, burning, pain or numbness in the hands or feet. Symptoms of pancreatitis include abdominal pain, and nausea and vomiting. Liver disturbances may not result in any symptoms, but can be recognized by your doctor through regular blood tests. All symptoms should be promptly reported to your physician. Since the development of peripheral neuropathy appears to be dose-related to zalcitabine, you should follow your physician's instructions regarding the precribed dose.

The long-term effects of zalcitabine in combination with zidovudine are presently unknown.

If you are a female of child-bearing age, you should use effective contraception while using zalcitabine.

Adverse Effects: The major toxicities of zalcitabine are peripheral neuropathy and, less frequently, pancreatitis (see Warnings).

The following data on adverse reactions are based primarily on the administration of zalcitabine at the recommended dose, as either monotherapy or in combination with zidovudine, to patients who are intolerant of or who have failed zidovudine

Hivid (cont'd)

and in patients with AIDS or advanced ARC (CD4 cell count ≤200 cells/mm³).

Table I summarizes the occurrence of peripheral neuropathy, possibly or probably related to drug treatment. Table II summarizes clinical adverse events or symptoms considered possibly or probably related to study drug which occurred in ≥3% of all zalcitabine-treated patients with advanced HIV disease who were enrolled in studies comparing monotherapy zalcitabine to monotherapy zidovudine (N3300/ACTG 114, N3492/ACTG 119 and EV14370/ACTG 155). Clinical adverse events that occurred in ≥3% of the patients in the comparative monotherapy trial (CPCRA 002) of zalcitabine vs. didanosine (ddI) are listed in Table IIA. Clinical adverse events considered possibly or probably related to combination treatment with zalcitabine and zidovudine (Protocols N3447/ACTG 106 and EV14370/ACTG 155) are presented in Table III (on following page).

These tables are followed by 2 lists of additional clinical adverse events which are possibly or probably related to study drug: a listing of events that occurred in the above trials at a frequency of <3%, and a listing of any further clinical events which occurred in zalcitabine-treated patients from the expanded access safety study (N3544) which were not previously reported in the controlled clinical trials.

One patient with advanced HIV disease in Protocol N3447/ACTG 106 died of refractory acidosis, mild pancreatitis, hepatomegaly with steatosis, and an unexplained neurological syndrome. The investigator assessed this event as remotely related to zidovudine and/or the combination of zalcitabine and zidovudine. The occurrence of clinical adverse events at each dosage combination of zalcitabine and zidovudine did not vary significantly.

Table I—Hivid[a]

Percentage of Patients with Peripheral Neuropathy Possibly/Probably Related to Drug Treatment

	Phase II/III Clinical Studies					Phase III Clinical Study		
Study	**N3300/ACTG 114**		**N3492/ACTG 119**		**N3447/ACTG 106**	**EV14370/ACTG 155**		
	≤3 months prior ZDV		**≥12 months prior ZDV**		**No prior ZDV**	**Prior ZDV**		
	Hivid 0.750 mg q8h	**ZDV 100 mg q4h**	**Hivid 0.750 mg q8h**	**ZDV 100 mg q4h**	**Hivid + ZDV Pooled concomitant regimens**	**Hivid 0.750 mg q8h**	**ZDV 100 mg q4h**	**Hivid + ZDV**
Severity	**n=320**	**n=318**	**n=60**	**n=55**	**n=47[b]**	**n=285**	**n=284**	**n=425**
All	35.9	18.6	33.3	0	27.7	21.4	10.6	20.9
Moderate/Severe	23.1	6.0	21.7	0	4.3	20.0	9.9	18.6
Severe	11.3	2.2	3.3	0	2.1	3.2	0.7	1.6

[a]Study CPCRA 002 not included here, due to different criteria for recording of Adverse Events (see Table IIA).
[b]Only 8 patients were treated with the recommended combination regimen.

Table II—Hivid

Percentage of Patients with Clinical Adverse Experiences Occurring in ≥3% of Patients Treated with Hivid Monotherapy Considered Possibly or Probably Related to Study Drug in at Least One of These Studies

	N3300/ACTG 114[a] <3 months prior ZDV				**N3492/ACTG 119[a] >12 months prior ZDV**				**EV14370/ACTG 155[d] Prior ZDV**	
	Hivid 0.750 mg q8h n=320		**ZDV[b] 100 mg q4h n=318[c]**		**Hivid 0.750 mg q8h n=60**		**ZDV[b] 100 mg q4h n=55**		**Hivid 0.750 mg q8h n=285**	**ZDV 100 mg q4h n=284**
Body System/ Adverse Event	**mild/ mod/ sev**	**mod/ sev**	**mild/ mod/ sev**	**mod/ sev**	**mild/ mod/ sev**	**mod/ sev**	**mild/ mod/ sev**	**mod/ sev**	**mod/sev**	**mod/sev**
Peripheral Neuropathy					See Table I					
Gastrointestinal										
Oral Ulcers	14.1	8.4	6.9	3.8	16.7	15.0	1.8	1.9	7.0	2.8
Nausea	8.1	3.1	20.1	8.8	1.7	1.7	0.0	0.0	3.5	7.0
Dysphagia	3.4	3.1	0.0	0.0	1.7	1.7	0.0	0.0	4.2	1.1
Anorexia	3.4	2.2	6.3	2.8	0.0	0.0	0.0	0.0	0.0	0.0
Abdominal Pain	3.8	1.9	3.1	2.2	3.3	3.3	0.0	0.0	8.1	7.7
Vomiting	2.5	1.3	5.7	4.1	1.7	1.7	0.0	0.0	3.5	4.6
Diarrhea	3.1	1.3	3.1	3.1	0.0	0.0	0.0	0.0	9.5	10.6
Mouth Lesion	0.0	0.0	0.0	0.0	0.0	0.0	0.0	0.0	3.2	1.4
Skin and Appendages										
Rash	7.8	4.1	3.5	3.1	0.0	0.0	0.0	0.0	11.2	8.8
Pruritus	4.4	2.5	3.5	2.2	0.0	0.0	0.0	0.0	4.9	4.2
Nervous System										
Headache	9.4	5.6	14.2	7.5	0.0	0.0	0.0	0.0	12.3	16.2
Dizziness	3.1	1.3	2.5	0.9	0.0	0.0	0.0	0.0	1.1	1.4
Musculoskeletal										
Myalgia	7.2	3.8	7.2	3.8	1.7	1.7	1.8	1.8	6.0	10.2
Body as a Whole										
Fatigue	8.1	3.8	13.2	9.7	3.3	1.7	5.5	5.5	13.3	17.3
Fever/Febrile	1.3	0.6	0.6	0.3	0.0	0.0	0.0	0.0	16.8	17.6
Respiratory										
Pharyngitis	2.5	2.2	0.0	0.0	5.0	3.3	0.0	0.0	1.8	1.1
Nasal Discharge	0.0	0.0	0.0	0.0	0.0	0.0	0.0	0.0	3.5	6.0
Cough	0.6	0.3	0.6	0.3	0.0	0.0	0.0	0.0	6.3	7.7
Metabolic/Nutrition										
Loss of Appetite	0.0	0.0	0.0	0.0	0.0	0.0	0.0	0.0	3.9	6.7
Abn. Weight Loss	1.9	0.0	1.3	0.0	0.0	0.0	0.0	0.0	4.9	6.3

[a]Median duration of treatment for N3300 was 47 weeks for Hivid, 69 weeks for ZDV; for N3492, treatment was 52 weeks for Hivid, 29 weeks for ZDV.
[b]Reduced to 100 mg q4h ZDV when dose was approved (initially 200 mg q4h ZDV).
[c]315 patients randomized to ZDV arm. Three patients on Hivid inadvertently received ZDV. For safety analyses, the 3 patients were included in the denominators of both Hivid and ZDV arms.
[d]Includes events for which causality was "Unassessable"; laboratory abnormalities which were recorded as clinical events in this study are discussed under Laboratory Test Abnormalities.

Table IIA—Hivid

Percentage of Patients with Clinical Adverse Experiences Considered Unassessable or Possibly Related to Study Drug and ≥Grade III[a] Occurring in ≥3% of Patients in Either Treatment Group of CPCRA 002

	CPCRA 002[b] ZDV Intolerant or Failure N=437	
Body System Adverse Event	**Hivid 0.750 mg q8h[c] N=237**	**ddI 250 mg q12h[c] N=230**
Systemic		
Fatigue	3.8	2.6
Abdominal Pain	3.0	7.0
Gastrointestinal		
Oral lesions/Stomatitis	3.0	0
Vomiting/Nausea	3.4	7.0
Diarrhea	2.5	17.0
Hepatic		
Abnormal Hepatic Function	8.9	7.0
Neurological		
Peripheral Neuropathy	28.3	13.0
Skin		
Rash/Pruritus/Urticaria	3.4	3.9

[a]Event resulting in marked impact on activity usually requiring some assistance and medical intervention/therapy; Grade II Adverse Events (mild to moderate impact on activity, may require some assistance and/or minimal medical intervention) were included if study drug dosage was changed or interrupted.
[b]Median duration of treatment was 34 weeks for both the Hivid and didanosine groups; laboratory abnormalities which were recorded as adverse events in this study are discussed under Laboratory Test Abnormalities.
[c]Hivid and ddI dosed by body weight. Only 1 Hivid patient and 3 ddI patients received 0.375 mg t.i.d. and 167 mg b.i.d. respectively.

Other Adverse Events: Controlled Clinical Trials: Clinical adverse events considered possibly or probably related to study drug which occurred in <3% of patients receiving zalcitabine as either **monotherapy** or in **combination** with zidovudine in all controlled clinical trials are listed below (Note: the data from studies ACTG 155 and CPCRA 002 includes events for which causality was "unassessable"; additionally, only events of Grade III severity or worse [see Table IIA for details] were recorded in CPCRA 002).

Body as a Whole: chest pain/tightness (1.7%), chills (1.0%); asthenia, dry eyes/mouth, general debilitation, stomach/abdominal cramps, hot/cold liquid intolerance, difficulty moving, pain (facial, flank, pelvic/groin, epigastric, extremities and/or generalized), infection (sepsis [H. influenza], herpes, septicemia), cutaneous/allergic reaction (all <1%).

Cardiovascular: hypertension, cold hands/feet, tachycardia/heart racing, atrial fibrillation, cardiac dysrhythmias, ventricular ectopy, abnormal cardiac movement, subarachnoid hemorrhage, cardiomyopathy, thrombus (all <1%).

Gastrointestinal: swallowing painful (1.2%); hemorrhoids, GI tract hemorrhage, anal/rectal pain, sore/inflamed or bleeding gums, ulcers (esophageal/rectal), dyspepsia, heartburn, pancreatitis, glossitis, loose stools, flatulence, abdominal bloating, abdomen enlarged, rectal mass, oral candidiasis, increased saliva, facial swelling, esophagitis, sore throat (all <1%).

Hepatic: abnormal liver function tests (1.1%); hepatitis, jaundice, hepatocellular damage, hepatomegaly (all <1%).

Lymph System: lymphadenopathy, lymphoma, unspecified hematologic toxicity, pancytopenia (all <1%).

Metabolic/Nutrition: edema (unspecified and peripheral), polydipsia (all <1%).

Musculoskeletal: musculoskeletal pain and/or weakness (different locations, each <1%), joint swelling/pain, arthritis, joint inflammation, myopathy, muscle/leg cramps, muscle stiffness, muscle disorder, CPK elevated (all <1%).

Nervous System: confusion, concentration impaired, convulsions/seizures, twitch, tremor, anxiety, amnesia/loss of memory, paranoid state, hypertonia, mood swings, psychotic

Table III—Hivid

Percentage of Patients with Clinical Adverse Experiences Occurring in ≥3% of Patients Treated with Hivid Combination Therapy Considered Possibly or Probably Related to Study Drug in at least One of These Studies

Body System/ Adverse Event	N3447/ACTG 106[a] No prior ZDV Pooled Concomitant Regimens n=47 mild/mod/sev	mod/sev	EV14370/ACTG 155[b] n=428 mod/sev	sev
Peripheral Neuropathy		See Table I		
Gastrointestinal				
Nausea	36.2	8.5	8.2	0.5
Oral Ulcers	27.7	4.3	5.6	0.9
Abdominal Pain	21.3	8.5	7.1	1.9
Diarrhea	14.9	10.6	10.6	1.2
Vomiting	14.9	2.1	6.6	0.7
Anorexia	12.8	6.4	0.0	0.0
Constipation	6.4	2.1	1.4	0.2
Dysphagia	0.0	0.0	3.5	0.7
Skin and Appendages				
Pruritus	14.9	4.3	4.0	0.5
Night Sweats	6.4	2.1	3.8	0.5
Rash	14.9	2.1	9.4	0.7
Erythematous Rash	6.4	2.1	0.2	0.0
Maculopapular Rash	4.3	2.1	0.5	0.0
Follicular Rash	4.3	0.0	0.0	0.0
Nervous System				
Headache	38.3	8.5	15.3	2.6
Insomnia	0.0	0.0	4.2	0.2
Depression	0.0	0.0	4.0	0.7
Musculoskeletal				
Myalgia	14.9	2.1	8.0	0.5
Arthralgia	8.5	2.1	0.0	0.0
Weakness, leg muscle	0.0	0.0	4.2	0.0
Body as a Whole				
Fatigue	34.0	8.5	18.1	3.5
Fever	14.9	2.1	16.2	3.8
Rigors	8.5	2.1	0.0	0.0
Chest Pain	6.4	2.1	2.8	0.2
Weight Decrease	6.4	4.3	9.4	0.5
Respiratory				
Pharyngitis	8.5	2.1	2.4	0.0
Nasal Discharge	0.0	0.0	6.4	0.2
Cough	0.0	0.0	8.2	0.2
Metabolic/Nutrition				
Loss of Appetite	0.0	0.0	7.3	0.9

[a] Median duration of treatment ranged from 22 to 92 weeks among the arms.
[b] Includes events for which causality was "unassessable"; laboratory abnormalities which were recorded as clinical events in this study are discussed under Laboratory Test Abnormalities.

episode, somnolence, stress reaction, hallucinations, neurologic function decreased, facial nerve palsy, vertigo, suicide attempt, decreased motivation/sexual desire (all <1%).

Reproductive: testicular swelling, sore/swollen penis, vaginal ulcer/pain, vaginal/cervical disorder, vaginal itch, genital lesion (all <1%).

Respiratory: dyspnea (1.7%); rales/rhonchi, sinus congestion/pain, acute nasopharyngitis, bacterial pneumonia, hemoptysis, chest congestion, shortness of breath, wheezing, dry nasal mucosa (all <1%).

Skin/Mucous Membranes: dermatitis, exfoliative dermatitis, urticaria, cellulitis, impetigo, alopecia, cold sore, skin disorder, night sweats/chills, excessive sweating, lip blister, skin lesion, onychomycosis, carbuncle/furuncle, rash, epistaxis, skin ulcer, nail disorder, fissure (skin), dry skin, finger inflammation (all <1%).

Special Senses/Vision: eye (pain, irritation, inflammation, hemorrhage), xerophthalmia, dry eyes, photophobia, vision (decrease, loss, blurred), tears increased, yellow sclera, redness of eyes, conjunctivitis, retinitis, ear pain, tinnitus, hearing loss, fluid in ears, taste perversion or decrease, smell dysfunction (all <1%).

Urinary System: dysuria, urination (frequency), nocturia, abnormal renal function, glycosuria, bladder pain, renal cyst (all <1%).

Other Adverse Events: Expanded Access Safety Study: Additional clinical adverse events at least possibly related to zalcitabine reported from 4 030 patients treated with either 0.375 mg or 0.750 mg q8h zalcitabine in expanded-access safety study (Protocol N3544), but not reported in the above controlled clinical trials are listed below by body system:

Body as a Whole: cachexia, rigors, influenza syndrome, sarcoma (all <0.1%).

Cardiovascular: palpitation, cardiac failure, arrhythmia, syncope (all <0.1%).

Gastrointestinal: eructation, left quadrant pain, colitis pseudomembranous, hairy leukoplakia, gastritis, salivary gland enlargement (all <0.1%).

Hematologic: purpura (<0.1%).

Hepatic: cholecystitis (<0.1%).

Metabolic/Nutritional: anemia (0.7%); diabetes mellitus, hot flushes, aplastic anemia, hemolytic anemia (all <0.1%).

Musculoskeletal: myositis, arthrosis, bursitis olecranon (all <0.1%).

Nervous: neuritis (0.3%), nervousness (0.2%), agitation, depersonalization, neuralgia, ataxia, hyperkinesia, emotional lability, thinking abnormal, abnormal coordination, migraine, stupor, paralysis, speech disorder/dysphonia, euphoria, delirium (all <0.1%).

Reproductive: impotence (<0.1%).

Skin/Mucous Membranes: flushing, infection, bullous eruption, acne, photosensitivity reaction, moniliasis (all <0.1%).

Special Senses/Vision: ear blockage, parosmia, burning eyes, eye itching (all <0.1%).

Urinary System: urinary retention, hyperuricemia, polyuria, renal calculus, gout, toxic nephropathy, acute renal failure, albuminuria (all <0.1%).

Laboratory Test Abnormalities: Table IV (on following page) summarizes laboratory test abnormalities which occurred in the 2 comparative monotherapy trials of zalcitabine versus zidovudine (N3300/ACTG 114 and N3492/ACTG 119) and in the monotherapy arms of the comparative combination trial of zalcitabine and zidovudine (EV14370/ACTG 155). Table IVA (on following page) summarizes the laboratory test abnormalities which occurred in the monotherapy trial of zalcitabine versus ddI (CPCRA 002).

Table V (on following page) summarizes laboratory test abnormalities which occurred in patients taking zalcitabine in combination with zidovudine in comparative combination trials (EV14370/ACTG 155 and N3447/ACTG 106).

Overdose: Symptoms and Treatment: Acute Overdosage: There is little experience with acute zalcitabine overdosage and the sequelae are unknown. There is no known antidote for zalcitabine overdosage. It is not known whether zalcitabine is dialyzable by peritoneal dialysis or hemodialysis.

Inadvertent pediatric overdoses have occurred with doses up to 1.5 mg/kg zalcitabine. The children had prompt gastric lavage and treatment with activated charcoal and had no sequelae. Mixed overdoses including zalcitabine and other drugs have led to drowsiness and vomiting (with zalcitabine or placebo, zidovudine and cotrimoxazole), or increased GGT (with 18.75 mg zalcitabine with zidovudine and lormetazam) or increased creatinine phosphokinase (with zalcitabine or placebo, zidovudine, fluconazole, dapsone and wine).

Chronic Overdosage: In an initial dose-finding study in which zalcitabine was administered at doses 25 times (0.25 mg/kg q8h) the currently recommended dose, 1 patient discontinued zalcitabine after one and one-half weeks of treatment subsequent to the development of a rash and fever.

In the early Phase I studies, all patients receiving zalcitabine at approximately 6 times the current total daily recommended dose experienced peripheral neuropathy by week 10. Eighty percent of patients who received approximately 2 times the current total daily recommended dose experienced peripheral neuropathy by week 12.

Dosage: The daily recommended monotherapy regimen is: one 0.75 mg tablet orally, administered every 8 hours, (2.25 mg zalcitabine total daily dose).

The daily recommended combination regimen is: one 0.75 mg tablet orally, administered concomitantly with 200 mg of zidovudine every 8 hours, (2.25 mg zalcitabine total daily dose and 600 mg zidovudine total daily dose).

Based on preliminary data, the following zalcitabine dose reductions are recommended for patients with impaired renal clearance: 0.75 mg zalcitabine every 12 hours (creatinine clearance of 10 to 40 mL/min); or 0.75 mg zalcitabine every 24 hours (creatinine clearance of <10 mL/min).

Monitoring of Patients: Periodic complete blood counts and clinical chemistry tests should be performed. Serum amylase levels should be monitored in those individuals who have a history of elevated amylase, pancreatitis, ethanol abuse, who are on parenteral nutrition or who are otherwise at high risk of pancreatitis. Careful monitoring for signs or symptoms suggestive of peripheral neuropathy is recommended, particularly in individuals with a low CD4 cell count or who are at a greater risk of developing peripheral neuropathy on therapy (see Warnings). All patients, particularly those at high risk, should be watched carefully for signs and symptoms of liver toxicity (see Warnings).

Dose Adjustment for Monotherapy with Zalcitabine and Combination Therapy with Zalcitabine and Zidovudine: For toxicities in patients receiving monotherapy which are likely to be associated with zalcitabine (e.g., peripheral neuropathy, severe oral ulcers) zalcitabine should be interrupted or dose reduced. For severe toxicities or those persisting after dose reduction, zalcitabine should be interrupted.

For recipients of combination therapy with zalcitabine and zidovudine, dose adjustments for either drug should be based on the known toxicity profile of the individual drugs. For toxicities more likely to be associated with zalcitabine (e.g., peripheral neuropathy, severe oral ulcers) zalcitabine should be interrupted or the dose reduced (see Warnings and Precautions).

For patients experiencing toxicities more likely to be associated with zidovudine (e.g., anemia, granulocytopenia), zidovudine should be interrupted or the dose reduced first.

For any interruption of zalcitabine, and especially if zalcitabine is permanently discontinued, the zidovudine dosage schedule should be adjusted from 200 mg q8h to 100 mg q4h as recommended in the product monograph for zidovudine.

For severe toxicities, toxicities in which the causative drug is unclear, or those persisting after dose interruption or reduction of one drug, the other drug should also be interrupted or the dose reduced. Physicians should refer to the product monograph for zidovudine for a description of known zidovudine-associated adverse reactions.

Patients developing moderate discomfort with signs or symptoms of peripheral neuropathy (e.g., numbness, tingling, hypoaesthesias, burning or shooting pains of the lower or upper extremities, or loss of vibratory sense or ankle reflex)

Hivid (cont'd)

Table IV—Hivid

Percentage of Patients with Grade 3/4 Laboratory Abnormalities[a]

	N3300/ACTG 114 ≤3 months prior ZDV		N3492/ACTG 119 ≥12 months prior ZDV		EV14370/ACTG 155[b] Prior ZDV	
	Hivid	ZDV	Hivid	ZDV	Hivid	ZDV
Laboratory Abnormality	0.750 mg q8h n=320	100 mg q4h n=315	0.750 mg q8h n=60	100 mg q4h n=55	0.750 mg q8h n=285	100 mg q4h n=283
Anemia (<7.5 g/dL)	5.6	15.6	3.3	7.3	6.0	4.2
Leukopenia (<1 500 cells/mm³)	10.6	15.9	13.3	14.5	9.1	12.7
Neutropenia (<750 cells/mm³)	17.6	34.6	13.3	20.0	15.1	18.7
Eosinophilia (>1 000 cells/mm³ or 25%)	9.4	5.4	5.0	0	6.3	4.6
Thrombocytopenia (<50 000 cells/mm³)	5.6	4.1	0	7.3	2.8	2.1
ALT (>250 U/L)	10.0	10.5	8.3	7.3	3.2	3.9
AST (>250 U/L)	6.3	7.0	6.7	7.3	3.2	4.2
Alkaline Phosphatase (>625 U/L)	5.0	5.1	0	9.1	1.4	1.1

[a] All percentages based on number of patients tested, not on number of patients in study.
[b] Other laboratory abnormalities reported as moderate/severe adverse events in EV14370/ACTG 155 were:
≥3%: hyperglycemia, hypoglycemia, hyponatremia, increased bilirubin, increased amylase.
<3%: hypomagnesemia, hypocalcemia, hypophosphatemia, hypernatremia, hyperkalemia, hypokalemia, abnormal GGT, creatinine increase, abnormal LDH, abnormal triglycerides, abnormal lipase, increased BUN.

Table IVA—Hivid

Percentage of Patients with Laboratory Abnormalities

	Monotherapy Hivid (ZDV Intolerant, ZDV Failures)	
Laboratory Abnormality[c]	Hivid[a] 0.750 mg q8h[b] N=237	ddI 250 mg q12h[b] N=230
Anemia (<6.5 g/dL)	8.4	7.4
Leukopenia (<1 500 cells/mm³)	13.1	9.6
Eosinophilia (>1 000 cells/mm³ or 25%)	2.5	1.7
Neutropenia (<500 cells/mm³)	16.9	11.7
Thrombocytopenia (<20 000 cells/mm³)	1.3	4.8
AST (>10×ULN)	7.6	5.7

[a] Other laboratory abnormalities reported as adverse events in CPCRA 002 were:
<3%: hyponatremia, pancytopenia, elevated triglycerides, increased bilirubin, increased alkaline phosphatase.
[b] Because of low body weights, 1 Hivid patient (0.375 mg t.i.d.) and 3 ddI patients (167 mg b.i.d.) received lower doses.
[c] Protocol Grade 3-4 Hematological Toxicity/Hepatic Function Toxicity.

Table V—Hivid

Percentage of Patients with Grade 3/4 Laboratory Abnormalities[a]

	N3447/ACTG 106	EV14370/ACTG 155[b]
	No prior ZDV	Prior ZDV
Laboratory Abnormality	Pooled concomitant regimens n=47	Hivid+ZDV n=423
Anemia (<7.5 g/dL)	8.5	5.7
Leukopenia (<1 500 cells/mm³)	2.1	13.9
Neutropenia (<750 cells/mm³)	8.5	22.7
Eosinophilia (>1 000 cells/mm³ or 25%)	4.3	5.0
Thrombocytopenia (<50 000 cells/mm³)	4.3	3.1
ALT (>250 U/L)	8.5	3.1
AST (>250 U/L)	4.3	3.5
Alkaline Phosphatase (>625 U/L)	2.1	1.2

[a] All percentages based on number of patients tested, not on number of patients in study.
[b] Other laboratory abnormalities reported as moderate/severe adverse events in EV14370/ACTG 155 were:
≥3%: hypoglycemia, hyperglycemia, increased bilirubin, increased amylase; <3%: hypomagnesemia, hypocalcemia, hypophosphatemia, hypernatremia, hyponatremia, hyperkalemia, hypokalemia, abnormal GGT, increased creatinine, abnormal LDH, abnormal triglycerides, hemoglobinemia, decreased alkaline phosphatase, decreased hematocrit, increased BUN, granulocytosis, neutrophilia.

should stop zalcitabine, especially if these symptoms are bilateral and progress for >72 hours. Zalcitabine-associated peripheral neuropathy may continue to worsen despite interruption of zalcitabine. Zalcitabine should be re-introduced (at 50% dose -0.375 mg q8h) only if all findings related to peripheral neuropathy have improved to mild symptoms. Zalcitabine should be permanently discontinued when patients experience severe discomfort related to peripheral neuropathy or moderate discomfort progressing for ≥1 week.

If other moderate to severe clinical adverse reactions or laboratory abnormalities (such as increased liver function tests) occur, then zalcitabine in those patients receiving monotherapy, or both zalcitabine and zidovudine should be interrupted until the adverse reactions abate. Zalcitabine or zidovudine monotherapy or zalcitabine and zidovudine combination therapy should then be carefully reintroduced at lower doses if appropriate. If adverse reactions recur at the reduced dose, therapy should be discontinued. The minimum effective dose of zalcitabine in combination with zidovudine for the treatment of adult patients with advanced HIV infection has not been established.

In patients with poor bone marrow reserve, particularly those patients with advanced symptomatic HIV disease, frequent monitoring of hematologic indices is recommended to detect serious anemia or granulocytopenia. Zidovudine-related toxicities such as significant anemia (hemoglobin of <7.5 g/dL or reduction of >25% of baseline) and/or granulocytopenia (granulocyte count of <750 cells/mm³ or reduction of >50% from baseline) may require a treatment interruption of zalcitabine and zidovudine until evidence of marrow recovery is observed. For less severe anemia or granulocytopenia, a reduction in daily dose of zidovudine in those patients receiving combination therapy may be adequate. In patients who experience hematologic toxicity, reduction in hemoglobin may occur as early as 2 to 4 weeks after initiation of therapy, and granulocytopenia usually occurs after 6 to 8 weeks of therapy. In patients who develop significant anemia, dose modification does not necessarily eliminate the need for transfusion. If marrow recovery occurs following dose modification, gradual increases in dose may be appropriate depending on hematologic indices and patient tolerance. For more details refer to the product monograph for zidovudine.

Information for the Patient: See Blue Section—Information for the Patient "Hivid".

Supplied: 0.375 mg: Each oval, beige, film-coated tablet, with Hivid 0.375 imprinted on one side and ROCHE on the other side, contains: zalcitabine 0.375 mg. Gluten-, parabens-, sucrose-, sulfites- and tartrazine-free. Nonmedicinal ingredients: croscarmellose sodium, hydroxypropylmethylcellulose, lactose, magnesium stearate, microcrystalline cellulose, polyethylene glycol and polysorbate 80 along with the following colorant system: brown, black, red and yellow iron oxide and titanium dioxide. Bottles of 100.

0.750 mg: Each oval, grey, film-coated tablet, with Hivid 0.750 imprinted on one side and ROCHE on the other side, contains: zalcitabine 0.750 mg. Gluten-, parabens-, sucrose-, sulfites- and tartrazine-free. Nonmedicinal ingredients: croscarmellose sodium, hydroxypropylmethylcellulose, lactose, magnesium stearate, microcrystalline cellulose, polyethylene glycol and polysorbate 80 along with the following colorant system: black iron oxide and titanium dioxide. Bottles of 100.

Keep in a tightly closed container at 15 to 30°C.

(Shown in Product Recognition Section)

Reviewed 1997

HOMATROPINE

General Monograph, CPhA

Mydriatic—Cycloplegic—Anticholinergic

This monograph has been compiled by CPhA. It may contain information different from that approved by Therapeutic Products Programme, Health Canada, and the pharmaceutical manufacturers' approval has not been requested.

Pharmacology: Homatropine HBr is a tertiary amine anticholinergic agent used topically to produce mydriasis and cycloplegia. It blocks the responses of the iris sphincter and ciliary muscle to cholinergic stimuli. Homatropine is less potent than atropine and has a shorter duration of action. Complete cycloplegia is not usually attainable. The maximum mydriatic effect occurs in about 10 to 30 minutes, and the maximum cycloplegic effect in about 30 to 90 minutes. Mydriasis may last 6 hours to 4 days and cycloplegia may persist 10 to 48 hours.

Indications: To dilate the pupils prior to retinoscopy, in the treatment of uveitis and keratitis and to paralyze accommodation temporarily.

Contraindications: Patients with primary glaucoma or a predisposition to glaucoma; patients whose intraocular pressures are unknown; patients with narrow angle or shallow anterior chambers since they are susceptible to acute angle-closure glaucoma; hypersensitivity to belladonna alkaloids.

Precautions: Measurement of the depth of the angle of the anterior chamber should be obtained prior to administration of homatropine to patients with a predisposition to glaucoma.

Excessive ophthalmic use, especially in children and the elderly, may produce systemic symptoms of atropine poisoning. Do not exceed recommended dosage. Not for frequent or prolonged use. If dryness of the mouth occurs, decrease dosage. Discontinue use if rapid pulse or dizziness occurs. Homatropine may cause an increase in intraocular pressure. If eye pain occurs, discontinue use immediately as this may indicate undiagnosed glaucoma.

Pregnancy: Safety has not been established.

Lactation: Documentation is lacking or conflicting regarding the excretion of anticholinergics (especially atropine) in breast milk and the reduction in breast milk production caused by these drugs. Although there is no documentation of adverse effects in breast-fed infants, it is advisable to closely monitor infants of nursing mothers for anticholinergic side effects.

Children: Young children and infants may be more susceptible to the systemic effects of homatropine.

Adverse Effects: Prolonged use may cause local irritation. Increased intraocular pressure may occur, especially in patients with glaucoma (see Precautions). Excessive use may produce atropine-like systemic effects. Low doses may produce dry mouth, thirst, tachycardia, palpitations, constipation, visual disturbances, flushed dry skin and temperature elevation. Higher doses may produce headache, restlessness, excitement, disorientation, delirium and hallucinations.

Dosage: To produce mydriasis and cycloplegia for diagnostic purposes: Adults: Instill one drop of 2% or 5% solution in the eye(s) immediately prior to procedure; may be repeated at 5- to 10-minute intervals as needed.
Children: 1 drop of 2% solution instilled in the eye(s) immediately prior to procedure; may be repeated at 10-minute intervals as needed.
Treatment of Inflammatory Conditions of the Uveal Tract: Adults: 1 drop of 2% or 5% solution instilled in the eye(s) 2 or 3 times daily.
Children: 1 drop of 2% solution 2 or 3 times daily.

Reviewed 1998

HONVOL® Ⓟ

Carter Horner

Diethylstilbestrol Diphosphate

Prostatic Carcinoma Therapy

Indications: For intensive and selective palliative therapy of inoperable prostatic carcinoma.

Contraindications: Patients with active hepatic dysfunction or disease, especially of the obstructive type; a personal history of breast cancer, except in special circumstances; a history of cerebrovascular accident, coronary thrombosis or the presence of classical migraine; a history of thrombophlebitis or thromboembolic disease; partial or complete loss of vision or diplopia, from ophthalmic vascular disease.

Precautions: Before diethylstilbestrol diphosphate is administered, the patient should have a complete physical examination including a blood pressure determination. Breasts should be examined.

The first followup examination should be done within 6 months after initiation of treatment. Thereafter, examinations should be made once a year. At each annual visit, repeat those procedures outlined above.

If any surgical procedures are performed, advise the pathologist of the patient's therapy when specimens are sent for examination. Liver function tests should be made periodically in subjects who have, or are suspected of having, hepatic disease.

Patients who develop visual disturbances, classical migraine, transient aphasia, paralysis, or loss of consciousness should discontinue medication.

If the patient develops any sign of phlebitis or thromboembolic complications, discontinue the medication.

Estrogen may cause fluid retention. Particular caution is indicated in cardiac or renal dysfunction, epilepsy, or asthma.

Elevation of blood pressure in previously normotensive or hypertensive patients necessitates cessation of medication.

Diabetic patients or those with a predisposition to diabetes should be observed closely to detect any alterations in carbohydrate metabolism.

When liver or endocrine function tests are indicated, the results should not be considered reliable unless therapy has been discontinued for 2 to 4 months.

Adverse Effects: Although not all of the reactions listed below have been specially associated with the use of diethylstilbestrol diphosphate, they have generally been reported following estrogen therapy, and may be encountered in susceptible patients treated with a product containing an estrogen:
Gastrointestinal: nausea, anorexia, vomiting, abdominal cramps, bloating, cholestatic jaundice, increase or decrease in body weight.
Genitourinary: sodium and water retention.
Endocrine and metabolic: breast tenderness, gynecomastia, reduced potency and feminization.
CNS: headaches, mental depression, decrease of libido, nervousness, dizziness, fatigue, irritability.
Dermatologic—hypersensitivity: allergic reactions and rashes, chloasma.
Cardiovascular: an increase in blood pressure in susceptible individuals, aggravation of migraine headaches.
Hematologic: A statistically significant association has been demonstrated between the use of preparations containing estrogens and the following serious reactions: thrombophlebitis, pulmonary embolism and cerebral thrombosis. Although available evidence is suggestive of an association, such a relationship has been neither confirmed nor refuted for the following serious reactions: coronary thrombosis and neuro-ocular lesions (e.g., retinal thrombosis and optic neuritis); altered coagulation tests (increase in prothrombin and Factors VII, VIII, IX, X).
Miscellaneous: precipitation or aggravation of porphyria cutanea tarda in predisposed individuals.

Overdose: Symptoms: Estrogens may produce headache, nausea and vomiting, abdominal cramps, dizziness and general malaise.

Treatment: Symptomatic. Remove orally ingested drug by gastric lavage.

Dosage: Prostatic carcinoma is generally associated with elevated levels of serum acid and alkaline phosphatases, particularly if metastases have occurred. The therapeutic effects of diethylstilbestrol diphosphate can be estimated not only by the clinical picture but also by a return to normal values of the acid, and then the alkaline serum phosphatases. This normalization provides relevant criteria for dosage. Treatment is in 2 distinct stages: intensive initial dosage to induce palliation, followed by maintenance therapy to control further tumor growth.
Active tumor growth: 500 mg daily for 5 to 10 days, then 250 mg daily for 10 to 20 days by slow i.v. injection. Patients may experience mild pain or a sensation of tingling or warmth in the genito-anal area and frequently at metastatic sites during injections. Give the injection slowly in the supine position to avoid this problem as much as possible. Dilute the ampuls either with 5% dextrose in water or saline and administer by i.v. drip.

The total recommended daily dose should be added to 250 mL of 5% dextrose and water or saline. Allow infusion to proceed at a rate of 1 or 2 mL/minute during the first 10 to 15 minutes and then adjust the rate so that the remaining solution is infused within 1 hour.
Maintenance: I.V.: 250 to 500 mg 3 or 4 times weekly for 1 or 2 months, then 250 to 500 mg twice a week for 2 or 4 months, reducing to 250 mg weekly or at longer intervals, depending on clinical condition and/or serum phosphatase levels.
Oral: 83 or 166 mg 3 times daily, gradually reducing to the lowest daily dose that will control serum phosphatase levels.

Supplied: Ampuls: Each ampul of injection contains: diethylstilbestrol diphosphate 250 mg (as diethylstilbestrol diphosphate sodium 300 mg). Nonmedicinal ingredients: none. pH: 7.5 to 9.0. Tartrazine-free. Ampuls of 5 mL, boxes of 10.

Tablets: Each white, round, flat, uncoated tablet, bisected on one side, with bevelled edge contains: diethylstilbestrol diphosphate 83 mg (as diethylstilbestrol diphosphate sodium 100 mg). Nonmedicinal ingredients: lactose, magnesium stearate, povidone and starch (contains gluten). Energy: 1.3 kJ (0.3 kcal). Tartrazine-free. Bottles of 25.

(Shown in Product Recognition Section)

HORMODAUSSE®

Technilab

Vitamin Supplement

Supplied: Each 10 mL oral ampul contains: thiamine 2 mg, niacinamide 6.86 mg, vitamin B_{12} 2.3 µg, iron 5 mg, thick extract of calves' liver 30 mg and proteins from beef serum 50 mg, methylparaben 0.2%. Boxes of 18.

HUMALOG™

Lilly

Insulin Lispro

Antidiabetic Agent

Pharmacology: Insulin lispro is a rapid-acting analogue of human insulin. Due to its quick onset of action, insulin lispro should be given within 15 minutes of a meal. Insulin lispro is created by inverting the natural Pro-Lys sequence in human insulin at positions 28 and 29 in the C terminal portion of the B chain. This change in amino acid sequence slightly modifies the physicochemical properties of the molecule relative to native human insulin in such a manner that insulin lispro self-associates less avidly and dissociates into its monomeric form more rapidly than regular insulin. As a result, insulin lispro is absorbed more rapidly than regular soluble insulin from s.c. sites of injection and also has a shorter duration of action.

S.C. injected regular insulin typically results in serum insulin concentrations that peak later and remain elevated for a longer time than those following normal pancreatic insulin secretion in nondiabetics. When regular insulin is used to control postprandial blood glucose, adequate control is often not achieved because the amount of regular insulin needed to normalize postprandial glucose excursion often leads to late hypoglycemia. By producing more rapid and higher serum insulin concentrations with a shorter duration of activity (2 to 5 hours), insulin lispro decreases glucose excursion during and after meals with less chance for hypoglycemia.

The reversed sequence of lysine and proline in insulin lispro, is identical to that on human IGF-1's B-chain. The incidence of self-association with IGF-1 is known to be lower than observed with human insulin. Incorporating this IGF-1-like feature into the human insulin molecule markedly changes the physicochemical behavior of insulin lispro but does not significantly alter its pharmacodynamic action because the terminal part of the B-chain does not participate in insulin's interaction with the insulin receptor. In vitro experiments showed that insulin lispro interacts with the insulin receptor much like regular human insulin does. Although binding to the IGF-1 receptor is higher than for regular human insulin (×1.5), it is significantly less than that of IGF-1 itself (more than 1 000 times less) and does not promote cell growth in biological assays to any greater extent than human insulin.

A glucose clamp study was performed, in healthy volunteers, in which a 10 U dose of insulin lispro was compared to Humulin R. Doses were given s.c.; an additional 10 U dose of i.v. regular insulin was given as an absolute reference.

Insulin lispro showed statistically higher peak concentrations (C_{max}) which occurred earlier than Humulin R (T_{max}). Total absorption was comparable, with area under the curve (AUC) values of serum concentration vs time which were not statistically different (see Tables I and II).

Table I—Humalog

Pharmacokinetics of Humalog Compared with Humulin R in Healthy Volunteers

Mean±SD	Humalog	Humulin R
T_{max} (min)	53±30	101±40
C_{max} (ng/mL)	3.20±1.33	1.79±0.77
AUC (ng·min/mL)	380±52.2	423±71.8

Table II—Humalog

Pharmacodynamics of Humalog Compared with Humulin R in Healthy Volunteers

Mean±SD	Humalog	Humulin R
Duration of Action (h)*	3.5-4.75 h	5.0-7.5 h
Onset of Action (h)*	0.5-0.75 h	0.5-1.0 h
Time of Maximum Effect (h)*	0.75-2.5 h	0.75-4.5 h

*Results predicted from a pharmacokinetic-pharmacodynamic link model.

Subsequent pharmacokinetic studies in Type I patients confirmed that a significantly faster increase in serum insulin levels and a shorter plasma half-life resulted from an injection of Humalog when compared to Humulin R.

In clinical studies after 1 year, the decrease in glucose excursion during and after meals with insulin lispro was consistent, although not always significant, when compared to Humulin R. However, there was no significant difference in hemoglobin A_{1c} levels between the 2 treatment groups. The frequency of hypoglycemia was not statistically significant in 1 year parallel studies (Humalog, n=543; Humulin R, n=561), but was significantly less with insulin lispro therapy in a 6 month crossover study in Type I patients (n=1 008) which also demonstrated a significant reduction in nocturnal hypoglycemia with insulin lispro.

Indications: For the treatment of patients with diabetes mellitus who require insulin for the maintenance of normal glucose homeostasis. Insulin lispro is also indicated for the initial stabilization of diabetes mellitus. Insulin lispro is a short-acting insulin analogue and is for use in conjunction with a longer acting human insulin.

Contraindications: During episodes of hypoglycemia (see Hypoglycemia in Overdose: Symptoms and Treatment) and in patients sensitive to insulin lispro or one of Humalog's excipients.

Warnings: Due to its quick onset of action, insulin lispro should be given within 15 minutes of a meal.

Any change of insulin or human insulin analogue should be made cautiously and only under medical supervision. Changes in purity, strength, brand (manufacturer), type (insulin lispro, regular, NPH, lente, etc.), species (beef, pork, beef-pork, human), and/or method of manufacture (recombinant DNA vs animal source insulin) may result in the need for a change in dosage.

Humalog (cont'd)

Precautions: General: Insulin lispro had a similar safety profile to Humulin R over the course of the clinical studies although its efficacy has not been studied in clinical trials beyond 1 year. Insulin lispro has been shown to control hemoglobin A_{1c} levels as effectively as human insulin although there is currently no evidence that better control is obtained with long-term use.

Visual disturbances in uncontrolled diabetes due to refractive changes are reversed during the early phase of effective management. However, since alteration in osmotic equilibrium between the lens and ocular fluids may not stabilize for a few weeks after initiating therapy, it is wise to postpone prescribing new corrective lenses for 3 to 6 weeks.

A study in nondiabetic human volunteers with mild to moderate or severe to endstage renal disease showed that the clearance of both insulin lispro and Humulin R did not differ. However, there is no specific information at this time with regard to the use of insulin lispro in diabetes patients with renal impairment.

Additional adjustment of dosage may be required during intercurrent illness and/or emotional disturbances.

Transferring Patients from Other Insulins: Patients taking insulin lispro may require a change in dosage from that used with their usual insulins. If an adjustment is needed, it may occur with the first dose or during the first several weeks or months.

A few patients who have experienced hypoglycemic reactions after transfer from animal-source insulin to human insulin have reported that the early warning symptoms of hypoglycemia were less pronounced or different from those experienced with their previous insulin. However, the counter-regulatory and symptomatic (autonomic and neuroglycopenic) responses to hypoglycemia were studied and found to be superimposable for insulin lispro and regular human insulin.

Patients whose blood glucose is greatly improved, e.g., by intensified insulin therapy, may lose some or all of the warning symptoms of hypoglycemia and should be advised accordingly. Uncorrected hypoglycemic or hyperglycemic reactions can cause loss of consciousness, coma, or death.

Allergic Reaction: Prompt recognition and appropriate management of the allergic complications of insulin therapy are important for the safe and effective control of diabetes mellitus. Antibodies to insulin are frequently cross-reactive. Therefore, patients who have demonstrated an allergic reaction to other insulins may demonstrate an allergic reaction to insulin lispro. Local allergy in patients occasionally occurs as redness, swelling, and itching at the site of insulin injection. This condition usually resolves in a few days to a few weeks. In some instances, this condition may be related to factors other than insulin, such as irritants in the skin cleansing agent or poor injection technique. Systemic allergy may cause rash over the whole body, shortness of breath, wheezing, reduction in blood pressure, fast pulse, or sweating. Severe cases of generalized allergy may be life-threatening (see Contraindications).

Pregnancy: The use of insulin lispro in pregnancy has not been studied. It is essential to maintain good glucose control in both gestational diabetes and throughout pregnancy in Type I and II patients. In insulin dependent diabetes mellitus, insulin requirements usually decrease during the first trimester and increase during the second and third trimesters.

Patients with diabetes should be advised to inform their doctor if they are pregnant or are contemplating pregnancy. Careful monitoring of glucose control, as well as general health is essential in pregnant patients with diabetes.

Lactation: The use of insulin lispro in nursing mothers has not been studied. Diabetic patients who are nursing may require adjustments in insulin dose and/or diet.

Drug Interactions: Drug interactions with insulin formulations including insulin lispro may include the following: Insulin requirements may be reduced in the presence of drugs with hypoglycemic activity, such as oral hypoglycemics, salicylates, sulfa antibiotics, and certain antidepressants.

Hormones that tend to counteract the hypoglycemic effects of insulin include growth hormone, corticotropin, glucocorticoids, thyroid hormone and glucagon. Epinephrine not only inhibits the secretion of insulin, but also stimulates glycogen breakdown to glucose. Thus, the presence of such diseases as acromegaly, Cushing's syndrome, hyperthyroidism, and pheochromocytoma complicate the control of diabetes.

The hypoglycemic action of insulin may also be antagonized by phenytoin. Insulin's hypoglycemic action can be increased in some patients by concomitant administration of anabolic steroids, MAO inhibitors, guanethidine, alcohol, propranolol (masking effect), or other drugs affecting beta-adrenergic receptors, or by daily doses of 1.5 to 6 g of salicylates.

Insulin requirements can be increased, decreased, or unchanged in patients receiving diuretics. Concomitant administration of oral contraceptives can cause a decrease in glucose tolerance in diabetic women possibly resulting in increased daily insulin requirements.

The physician should be consulted when using other medications in addition to insulin lispro.

Adverse Effects: Rarely, administration of insulin s.c. can result in lipoatrophy (depression in the skin) or lipohypertrophy (enlargement or thickening of tissue). If you notice either of these conditions, consult your doctor. A change in your injection technique may help alleviate the problem.

Overdose: Symptoms: With the rapid onset of activity of insulin lispro, it is important that the insulin analogue be given close to mealtime (within 15 minutes of a meal). A significant deviation could put the patient at risk of hypoglycemia.

Insulins have no specific overdose definitions because serum glucose concentrations are a result of complex interactions between insulin levels, glucose availability and other metabolic processes. Hypoglycemia may occur as a result of an excess of insulin or insulin lispro relative to food intake and energy expenditure or in patients who have an infection or become ill (especially with diarrhea or vomiting).

Symptoms are likely to appear anytime when the blood sugar concentration falls below 3 mmol/L (50 mg/100 mL) but may occur with a sudden drop in blood glucose even when the value remains above 3 mmol/L (50 mg/100 mL).

Hypoglycemia may be associated with listlessness, confusion, palpitations, headache, sweating and vomiting.

Treatment: Mild hypoglycemic episodes will respond to oral administration of glucose or sugar-containing foods.

Correction of moderately severe hypoglycemia can be accomplished by i.m. or s.c. administration of glucagon, followed by oral carbohydrate when the patient recovers sufficiently. Patients who fail to respond to glucagon must be given glucose solution i.v.

Patients who are unable to take sugar orally or who are unconscious should be treated with i.v. administration of glucose at a medical facility or should be given an injection of glucagon (either i.m. or s.c.). The patient should be given oral carbohydrates as soon as consciousness is recovered.

Dosage: Although insulin lispro has a quicker onset of action and shorter duration of activity, dosing is comparable to regular human insulin. The dosage of insulin lispro, like all other insulin formulations, is dependent upon the individual patient requirements. The dose and number of insulin injections should be adjusted to maintain blood glucose concentrations as close to normal as possible.

Additional adjustment of dosage may be required in diabetes patients with renal impairment, during intercurrent illness and/or emotional disturbances.

Adjustment of dosage may also be necessary if patients undertake increased physical activity or change their usual diet.

New Patients: Patients receiving insulin for the first time can be started on insulin lispro in the same manner as they would be on animal-source or human insulin.

Patients should be monitored closely during the adjustment period.

Transfer Patients: When transferring patients to insulin lispro, use the same dose and dosage schedule. However, some patients transferring to insulin lispro may require a change in dosage from that used with their previous insulin. Analysis of a database of IDDM patients indicates that basal insulin requirements increase by 0.04 U/kg, while insulin lispro requirements decrease by 0.03 U/kg, after 1 year of treatment. For NIDDM patients both short acting and basal insulin requirements increase slightly after 1 year of treatment with both insulin lispro and Humulin R.

Changes in total daily dosage, the number of injections per day, and/or timing of injections may be necessary to achieve maximum glycemic control.

Administration: Insulin lispro is a clear, colorless solution. It is important to always examine the appearance of the vial or cartridge before withdrawing a dose. Do not use it if it is cloudy, unusually viscous or gelled, precipitated, or even slightly colored; if there are clumps floating in the liquid, or if particles appear to be sticking to the sides or bottom of the vial or cartridge.

Insulin lispro preparations should be given by s.c. injection but may, although not recommended, also be given by i.m. injection. It may also be administered i.v. under conditions where regular human insulin is given i.v.

S.C. administration, preferably by the patient, should be in the upper arms, thighs, buttocks or abdomen. When compared to Humulin R, insulin lispro retains its more rapid onset and shorter duration of action irrespective of the s.c. injection site used. Therefore, injection sites can be rotated so that the same site is not used more than approximately once a month.

Care should be taken to ensure that a blood vessel has not been entered. The injection site should not be massaged.

The effects of mixing insulin lispro with either animal-source insulins or human insulin preparations produced by other manufacturers have not been studied. This practice is not recommended.

If insulin lispro is mixed with a longer-acting insulin, it should be drawn into the syringe first to prevent clouding of the insulin lispro by the longer-acting insulin. Injection should be made immediately after mixing.

Information for the Patient: See Blue Section—Information for the Patient "Humalog".

Supplied: Vials of 10 mL, boxes of 1. Cartridges of 1.5 and 3 mL, boxes of 5. All in a strength of 100 units/mL. Cartridges are designed for use with B-D Pen Cartridge Systems or future Lilly injector systems. Nonmedicinal ingredients: dibasic sodium phosphate, glycerin, m-cresol and zinc. Hydrochloric acid and/or sodium hydroxide may have been added. The cartridge containing insulin lispro is not designed to allow any other insulin to be mixed in the cartridge or for the cartridge to be reused. Preparations should be stored in a refrigerator between 2 and 10°C. They should not be frozen or exposed to excessive heat or sunlight. If refrigeration is not possible, the vial or cartridge being used can be kept at ambient temperature for up to 28 days, below 30°C and away from direct heat and light. Following insertion in a pen, the cartridge and pen should not be refrigerated. Do not use after expiry date on label.

Reviewed 1998

HUMAN INSULIN
Novo Nordisk

see INSULIN HUMAN (Biosynthetic) Preparations

HUMATIN™ ℞
Parke-Davis

Paromomycin Sulfate

Antibiotic

Pharmacology: Paromomycin is a broad spectrum aminoglycoside antibiotic produced by S. rimosus var. paromomycinus. The drug is structurally related to neomycin, streptomycin and kanamycin.

It is poorly absorbed after oral administration with almost 100% of the drug recoverable in the stool.

Paromomycin is considered a luminal or contact amebicide since it acts principally in the intestinal lumen. Unlike tetracyclines, paromomycin is a direct-acting amebicide and is effective either in the presence or absence of bacteria.

Like other aminoglycosides, paromomycin is bactericidal and appears to inhibit protein synthesis in susceptible bacteria at the 30S segment of the ribosome.

Paromomycin has a broad spectrum of activity, including activity against protozoa, bacteria and cestodes. Paromomycin is active against protozoa, especially E. histolytica. The drug is believed to act against both the trophozoite and encysted forms of Entamoeba.

Paromomycin has an antibacterial spectrum quite similar to that of neomycin and is bactericidal to many normal and pathogenic organisms in the gastrointestinal tract. Almost complete cross-resistance exists between paromomycin and kanamycin, neomycin and streptomycin.

Indications: For intestinal amebiasis, acute and chronic. It is not effective in extraintestinal amebiasis.

Contraindications: Individuals with a history of previous hypersensitivity reactions to paromomycin. It is also contraindicated in intestinal obstruction.

Precautions: The use of this antibiotic, as with other antibiotics, may result in an overgrowth of nonsusceptible organisms, including fungi. Constant observation of the patient is essential. If new infections caused by nonsusceptible organisms appear during therapy, appropriate measures should be taken.

The drug should be used with caution in individuals with ulcerative lesions of the bowel to avoid renal toxicity through inadvertent absorption.

Adverse Effects: Nausea, abdominal cramps and diarrhea have been reported in patients on doses over 3 g daily.

Dosage: Adults and Children: Usual dose 25 to 35 mg/kg body weight daily, administered in 3 doses with meals, for 5 to 10 days.

Supplied: Each capsule contains: paromomycin sulfate equivalent to paromomycin 250 mg. Nonmedicinal ingredients: capsule shell: D&C yellow No. 10, FD&C blue No. 1, FD&C red No. 3, FD&C yellow No. 6, gelatin and titanium dioxide. Bottles of 100. Store at controlled room temperature 15 to 30°C. Protect from moisture.

(Shown in Product Recognition Section)

HUMATROPE® ℞
Lilly

Somatropin

Growth Stimulant

Pharmacology: Somatropin is a polypeptide hormone of recombinant DNA origin. The amino acid sequence is identical to that of human growth hormone of pituitary origin. Somatropin is synthesized in a strain of E. coli which has been modified by the addition of the gene for human growth hormone.

Somatropin stimulates linear growth in pediatric patients lacking adequate normal endogenous growth hormone. Treatment of growth hormone-deficient pediatric patients and patients with Turner Syndrome with somatropin produces increased growth rate and IGF-I (Insulin-like Growth Factor-I/Somatomedin C) concentrations similar to those seen in therapy with human growth hormone of pituitary origin. As a result of replacement therapy in growth hormone deficient adults, body composition improved, HDL cholesterol values normalized, and health related quality of life measures concerning physical mobility and social isolation improved in placebo-controlled clinical trials. Exercise capacity improved as compared to placebo.

In addition, the following actions have been demonstrated for somatropin and/or human growth hormone of pituitary origin.

Tissue Growth: 1. Skeletal Growth: Somatropin stimulates skeletal growth in pediatric patients with growth hormone deficiency. The measurable increase in body length after administration of either Humatrope or human growth hormone of pituitary origin results from an effect on the growth plates of long bones. Concentrations of IGF-1, which may play a role in skeletal growth, are low in the serum of growth hormone-deficient pediatric patients but increase during treatment with somatropin. Elevations in mean serum alkaline phosphatase concentrations are also seen.

2. Cell Growth: It has been shown that there are fewer skeletal muscle cells in short-statured pediatric patients who lack endogenous growth hormone as compared to normal pediatric populations. Treatment with human growth hormone of pituitary origin results in an increase in both the number and the size of muscle cells.

Protein Metabolism: Linear growth is facilitated in part by increased cellular protein synthesis. Nitrogen retention as demonstrated by decreased urinary nitrogen excretion and serum urea nitrogen, follows the initiation of therapy with human growth hormone of pituitary origin. Treatment with somatropin results in a similar decrease in serum urea nitrogen.

Carbohydrate Metabolism: Pediatric patients with hypopituitarism sometimes experience fasting hypoglycemia, which is improved by treatment with somatropin. Large doses of human growth hormone may impair glucose tolerance. Untreated patients with Turner syndrome have an increased incidence of glucose intolerance. Administration of human growth hormone to normal adults or patients with Turner syndrome resulted in increases in mean serum fasting and postprandial insulin levels although mean values remained in the normal range. In addition, mean fasting and postprandial glucose and hemoglobin A_{1c} levels remained in the normal range.

Lipid Metabolism: In growth hormone-deficient patients, long-term administration of human growth hormone of pituitary origin has resulted in lipid mobilization, reduction in body fat stores, and an increase in plasma fatty acids.

Mineral Metabolism: Retention of sodium, potassium and phosphorus is induced by human growth hormone of pituitary origin. Serum concentrations of inorganic phosphate increased in patients with growth hormone deficiency after therapy with somatropin or human growth hormone of pituitary origin. Serum calcium is not significantly altered in patients treated with either human growth hormone of pituitary origin or somatropin.

Pharmacokinetics: In vitro, preclinical, and clinical testing have demonstrated that Humatrope is therapeutically equivalent to human growth hormone of pituitary origin with equivalent pharmacokinetics in normal adults.

Absorption: Humatrope has been studied following i.m., s.c. and i.v. administration in adult volunteers. The absolute bioavailability of somatropin is 75% and 63% after s.c. and i.m. administration respectively.

Distribution: The volume of distribution of somatropin after i.v. injection is about 0.07 L/kg.

Metabolism: Extensive metabolism studies have not been conducted. The metabolic fate of somatropin involves classical protein catabolism in both the liver and kidneys. In renal cells, at least a portion of the breakdown products of growth hormone is returned to the systemic circulation. In normal volunteers, mean clearance is 0.14 L/h/kg. The mean half-life of i.v. somatropin is 0.36 hours, whereas s.c. and i.m. administered somatropin have mean half-lives of 3.8 and 4.9 hours, respectively. The longer half-life observed after s.c. or i.m. administration is due to slow absorption from the injection site.

Excretion: Urinary excretion of intact Humatrope has not been measured. Small amounts of somatropin have been detected in the urine of pediatric patients following replacement therapy.

Indications: Children: For the long-term treatment of pediatric patients who have growth failure due to an inadequate secretion of normal endogenous growth hormone and whose epiphyses are not closed.

Adults: For replacement of endogenous growth hormone in adults with growth hormone deficiency who meet both of the following 2 criteria: 1. Biochemical diagnosis of somatotropin deficiency syndrome, by means of a negative response to a standard growth hormone stimulation test [maximum peak <5 ng/mL when measured by RIA (polyclonal antibody) or <2.5 ng/mL when measured by IRMA (monoclonal antibody)] **and** 2. Adult Onset: Patients must have somatotropin deficiency syndrome, either alone or with multiple hormone deficiencies (hypopituitarism), as a result of pituitary disease, hypothalamic disease, surgery, radiation therapy, or trauma; **or** Childhood Onset: Patients who were growth hormone-deficient during childhood who have somatotropin deficiency syndrome confirmed as an adult before replacement therapy with somatropin is started.

Turner Syndrome: For the treatment of short stature associated with Turner Syndrome in patients whose epiphyses are not closed.

Contraindications: Somatropin should not be used for growth promotion in pediatric patients with closed epiphyses.

Somatropin should not be used or should be discontinued when there is any evidence of active malignancy. Antimalignancy treatment must be complete with evidence of remission prior to the institution of therapy.

For patients with a known sensitivity to either m-cresol or glycerin, somatropin should not be reconstituted with the supplied diluent for somatropin.

Warnings: If patients are sensitive to m-cresol or glycerin or if sensitivity to the diluent develops, the vials should be reconstituted with Sterile Water for Injection, USP. Use only 1 somatropin dose per vial and discard unused portion (see Dosage).

Precautions: General: Somatropin therapy should be directed by physicians experienced in the diagnosis and management of patients with growth hormone deficiency, Turner syndrome or adult patients with either childhood-onset or adult-onset growth hormone deficiency.

Patients with pre-existing tumors or with growth hormone deficiency secondary to an intracranial lesion should be examined routinely for progression or recurrence of the underlying disease process. In pediatric patients, clinical literature has demonstrated no relationship between human growth hormone replacement therapy and CNS tumor recurrence. In adults, it is unknown whether there is any relationship between growth hormone replacement therapy and CNS tumor recurrence.

For patients with diabetes mellitus, the dose of insulin might require adjustment when somatropin is instituted. Because human growth hormone may induce a state of insulin resistance, patients should be observed for evidence of glucose intolerance. Patients with diabetes or glucose intolerance should be monitored closely during therapy with human growth hormone.

In patients with hypopituitarism (multiple hormonal deficiencies) standard hormonal replacement therapy should be monitored closely when human growth hormone therapy is administered. Hypothyroidism may develop during treatment with human growth hormono. Inadequate treatment of hypothyroidism may prevent optimal response to human growth hormone.

If injected s.c., the injection site should be rotated to minimize the risk of lipoatrophy occurring.

Children (see General): Patients with endocrine disorders, including growth hormone deficiency, may develop slipped capital epiphyses more frequently. Any pediatric patient with onset of a limp during growth hormone therapy should be evaluated.

Growth hormone has not been shown to increase the incidence of scoliosis. Progression of scoliosis can occur in pediatric patients who experience rapid growth. Because growth hormone increases growth rate, patients with a history of scoliosis who are treated with growth hormone should be monitored for progression of scoliosis.

Intracranial hypertension (IH) with papilledema, visual changes, headache, nausea and/or vomiting has been reported in a small number of patients treated with growth hormone products. Symptoms usually occurred within the first 8 weeks of the initiation of growth hormone therapy. In all reported cases, IH-associated signs and symptoms resolved after termination of therapy or a reduction of the growth hormone dose. Funduscopic examination of patients is recommended at the initiation and periodically during the course of growth hormone therapy.

Adults (see Precautions, General): Patients with epiphyseal closure who were treated with growth hormone replacement therapy in childhood should be re-evaluated according to the criteria in Indications before continuation of growth hormone replacement therapy at the reduced dose level required for growth hormone-deficient adults.

Experience in patients above 60 years is lacking.

Experience with prolonged treatment in adults is limited.

Turner Syndrome (see Precautions, General): Skeletal abnormalities including scoliosis are commonly seen in untreated Turner syndrome patients.

Patients with Turner syndrome may be at increased risk for development of intracranial hypertension.

Patients with Turner syndrome should be evaluated carefully for otitis media and other ear disorders since these patients have an increased risk of ear or hearing disorders (see Adverse Effects).

Patients with Turner syndrome are at risk for cardiovascular disorders (e.g., stroke, aortic aneurysm, hypertension) and these conditions should be monitored closely.

Patients with Turner syndrome have an inherently increased risk of developing autoimmune thyroid disease. Therefore, patients should have periodic thyroid function tests and be treated as indicated (see Precautions, General).

Drug Interactions: Excessive glucocorticoid therapy will inhibit the growth promoting effect of human growth hormone. Patients with coexisting ACTH deficiency should have their glucocorticoid replacement dose carefully adjusted to avoid an inhibitory effect on growth.

Pregnancy: Animal reproduction studies and animal studies for impairment of fertility with somatropin have not been performed. It is not known whether somatropin can cause fetal harm when administered to a pregnant woman or can affect reproduction capacity. Somatropin should be given to a pregnant woman only if clearly needed.

Lactation: There have been no studies conducted with somatropin in nursing mothers. It is not known whether this drug is excreted in human milk. Because many drugs are excreted in human milk, caution should be exercised when somatropin is administered to a nursing woman.

Carcinogenesis/Mutagenesis: Long-term animal studies for carcinogenicity with this human growth hormone (somatropin) have not been performed. There has been no evidence to date of somatropin-induced mutagenicity. Patients developing neoplasia should be reported to the HPB by the treating physician.

Information to be Provided to the Patient: Patients being treated with growth hormone and/or their parents should be informed of the potential benefits and risks associated with treatment. If home use is determined to be desirable by the physician, instructions on appropriate use should be given, including a review of the contents of the patient information insert. This information is intended to aid in the safe and effective administration of the medication. It is not a disclosure of all possible adverse or intended effects.

Humatrope (cont'd)

If home use is prescribed, a puncture resistant container for the disposal of used syringes and needles should be recommended to the patient. Patients and/or their parents should be thoroughly instructed in the importance of proper needle disposal and cautioned against any reuse of needles and syringes.

Adverse Effects: Growth-hormone Deficient Pediatric Patients: As with all protein pharmaceuticals, a small percentage of patients may develop antibodies to the protein. During the first 6 months of somatropin therapy in 314 naive patients, only 1.6% developed specific antibodies to somatropin (binding capacity ≤ 0.02 mg/L). None had antibody concentrations which exceeded 2 mg/L. Throughout 8 years of this same study, 2 patients (0.6%) had binding capacity >2 mg/L. Neither patient demonstrated a decrease in growth velocity at or near the time of increased antibody production. It has been reported that growth attenuation from pituitary-derived growth hormone may occur when antibody concentrations are >1.5 mg/L.

In addition to an evaluation of compliance with the treatment program and of thyroid status, testing for antibodies to human growth hormone should be carried out in any patient who fails to respond to therapy.

In studies with growth hormone-deficient pediatric patients, injection site pain was reported infrequently. Mild and transient edema (either localized or generalized) was observed in 2.5% of patients during the course of treatment.

Leukemia has been reported in a small number of pediatric patients who have been treated with growth hormone, including growth hormone of pituitary origin and recombinant somatrem and somatropin. The relationship, if any, between leukemia and growth hormone therapy is uncertain.

Adult Patients: In clinical studies in which high doses of somatropin were administered to healthy adult volunteers, the following events occurred infrequently: headache, localized muscle pain, weakness, mild hyperglycemia and glucosuria.

In the first 6 months of controlled, blinded trials, adult-onset growth hormone deficient patients experienced a statistically significant increase in edema (somatropin 17.3% vs placebo 4.4%, $p=0.043$) and peripheral edema (11.5% vs. 0% respectively, $p=0.017$).

In patients with adult-onset somatotropin deficiency syndrome, edema, muscle pain and joint pain and disorder, were reported early in therapy and tended to be transient or responsive to dosage titration.

Two out of 113 adult onset patients developed carpal tunnel syndrome after beginning maintenance therapy without a low dose (0.00625 mg/kg/day) lead-in phase. Symptoms abated in these patients after dosage reduction.

In growth hormone deficient adults, treatment-emergent adverse events reported after 18 months of therapy which are possibly related to replacement therapy but were not statistically significant during the first 6 months, include carpal tunnel syndrome, edema, arthralgia, paresthesia, hypesthesia, myalgia, peripheral edema, back pain, headache and joint disorder.

Adult patients treated with growth hormone, following diagnosis of growth hormone deficiency in childhood, reported side effects less frequently than those with adult onset growth hormone deficiency.

Turner Syndrome: Patients with Turner Syndrome should be evaluated carefully for otitis media and other ear disorders since these patients have an increased risk of ear or hearing disorders. In a randomized, concurrent controlled trial, there was a statistically significant increase, as compared to untreated controls, in otitis media (43% vs 26%), ear disorders (18% vs 5%) and surgical procedures (45% vs 27%) in patients receiving somatropin.

Overdose: Symptoms and Treatment: Acute overdosage could lead initially to hypoglycemia and subsequently to hyperglycemia. Long-term overdosage could result in signs and symptoms of gigantism/acromegaly, consistent with the known effects of excess human growth hormone (see recommended and maximal dosage instructions given under Dosage).

Dosage: When injected s.c., the injection sites should be varied in order to avoid lipoatrophy.

Growth Hormone-deficient Pediatric Patients: The recommended weekly dosage is 0.18 mg/kg of body weight (0.54 IU/kg based on a specific activity of 3 IU/mg protein). The maximal replacement weekly dosage is 0.3 mg/kg (0.90 IU/kg) of body weight. It should be divided into equal doses given either on 3 alternate days, 6 times/week or daily. The s.c. route of administration is preferable; i.m. injection is also acceptable. The dosage and administration schedule for somatropin should be individualized for each patient.

Growth Hormone-deficient Adult Patients: The recommended dosage at the start of therapy is not more than 0.006 mg/kg/day (0.018 IU/kg/day) given as a daily s.c. injection. The dose may be increased according to individual patient requirements to a maximum of 0.0125 mg/kg/day (0.0375 IU/kg/day).

During therapy, dosage should be titrated if required by the occurrence of side effects or to maintain the IGF-I response below the upper limit of normal IGF-I levels matched for age and sex. To minimize the occurrence of adverse events in patients with increasing age or excessive body weight, dose reductions may be necessary.

Turner Syndrome: A weekly dosage of up to 0.375 mg/kg (1.125 IU/kg) of body weight administered by s.c. injection is recommended. It should be divided into equal doses given either daily or on 3 alternate days.

Humatrope Vials: Reconstitute each vial of Humatrope with 1.5 to 5 mL of diluent for Humatrope. Inject the diluent for Humatrope (m-cresol and glycerin solution) into the vial of Humatrope aiming the stream of liquid against the glass wall. Following reconstitution, swirl the vial with a **gentle rotary** motion until the contents are completely dissolved. **Do not shake.** The resulting solution should be clear, without particulate matter. If the solution is cloudy or contains particulate matter, the contents **must not** be injected.

Before and after injections, the septum of the vial should be wiped with rubbing alcohol or another alcoholic antiseptic solution to prevent contamination of the contents by repeated needle insertions. Somatropin should be administered using sterile, disposable syringes and needles. The syringes should be of small enough volume that the prescribed dose can be drawn from the vial with reasonable accuracy. The needle should be of sufficient length (usually 2.5 cm or more) to ensure that the injection reaches the muscular layer for i.m. injections.

If sensitivity to the diluent should occur, the vials may be reconstituted with Sterile Water for Injection, USP. When reconstituting with water, use only once and discard the unused portion. The vial should be used immediately after reconstitution. Although not recommended, the solution can be stored refrigerated (2 to 8°C) but must be used within 24 hours.

Humatrope Cartridges: Each Humatrope cartridge (for use with the Humatro-Pen II) should be reconstituted using the accompanying diluent syringe and the diluent connector. Following cartridge attachment to the Humatro-Pen II, attach the diluent connector to the cartridge and then inject the entire contents of the pre-filled diluent syringe into the cartridge. The diluent connector automatically aims the stream of liquid against the glass wall of the cartridge. Following reconstitution, the cartridge should be **gently rocked** back and forth until the contents are completely dissolved. **Do not shake**. The resulting solution should be clear, without particulate matter. If the solution is cloudy or contains particulate matter, the contents **must not** be injected.

If sensitivity to the accompanying diluent occurs, Sterile Water for Injection, USP, may be used for reconstitution. Attach the cartridge to the Humatro-Pen II and inject 3.15 mL of Sterile Water for Injection, USP, into the cartridge through the rubber septum, aiming the stream of liquid against the glass wall of the cartridge. Following reconstitution, the cartridge should be **gently rocked** back and forth until the contents are completely dissolved. **Do not shake**. The resulting solution should be clear, without particulate matter. If the solution is cloudy or contains particulate matter, the contents **must not** be injected.

Before and after injections, the septum of the cartridge should be wiped with rubbing alcohol or another alcoholic antiseptic solution. The Sterile Water for Injection, USP, should be administered using a sterile, disposable syringe and needle. The syringe should be of small enough volume that 3.15 mL can be measured with reasonable accuracy.

Humatrope reconstituted in this manner should be used immediately. Although not recommended, the solution can be stored refrigerated (2 to 8°C) but must be used within 24 hours. Discard any unused portion. However, to minimize waste, the smallest vials of Humatrope rather than cartridges are recommended.

Humatrope cartridges are designed for use only with the Humatro-Pen II. The diluent connector is for single use only. Discard it after use. A sterile needle should be used for each administration of somatropin.

For complete instructions on the use of the Humatro-Pen II, see the Humatro-Pen II Instruction Manual.

Stability and Storage: Before Reconstitution: Vials of Humatrope, Humatrope cartridges for use with the Humatro-Pen II and the supplied diluent for Humatrope are stable when stored at 2 to 8°C. Protect from light. Avoid freezing diluent for Humatrope. Expiration dates are stated on the labels.

After Reconstitution: Vials of Humatrope and Humatrope cartridges for use with the Humatro-Pen II are stable for up to 21 days when reconstituted with the supplied diluent for Humatrope and stored at 2 to 8°C. Avoid freezing the reconstituted vials and cartridges of Humatrope and the diluent for Humatrope.

If Humatrope vials or cartridges are reconstituted with Sterile Water for Injection, USP, they should be used immediately after reconstitution. Although not recommended, the solution can be stored refrigerated (2 to 8°C) but must be used within 24 hours.

Supplied: Vial Combination Package: Each package contains: 1 vial of somatropin 5 mg (15 IU) and 1 vial of diluent. Nonmedicinal ingredients: Vial: dibasic sodium phosphate, glycine and mannitol. Diluent: glycerin and m-cresol.

Cartridge Combination Packages for Use with Humatro-Pen II: Each package contains: 1 cartridge of somatropin 6.7 mg (20 IU) or 13.3 mg (40 IU) with 3.15 mL syringe diluent and diluent connector. Nonmedicinal ingredients: Cartridges: dibasic sodium phosphate, glycine and mannitol. Diluent: glycerin and m-cresol.

All vials and cartridges of Humatrope and accompanying diluent may contain dimethicone, hydrochloric acid, phosphoric acid and sodium hydroxide.

Humatro-Pen II is available separately with a Humatro-Pen II Instruction Manual.

Reviewed 1999

HUMEGON® Ⓟ

Organon

Human Gonadotropin

Human Gonadotropins

Pharmacology: Humegon (human gonadotropin) is a purified preparation of gonadotropins extracted from the urine of post menopausal and pregnant women. It contains follicle-stimulating hormone (FSH) and luteinizing hormone (LH), both of which are necessary for the normal gamete maturation (follicle ripening in the female and spermatogenesis in the male) and for gonadal steroid production. Unlike menotropins, human gonadotropin is standardized with hCG. Human gonadotropin is used to stimulate these processes in selected cases of disturbed gonadal function. It is generally used in combination with a gonadotropin with LH activity, such as human chorionic gonadotropin (hCG). The combined treatment may be either sequential (in the case of ovulation induction) or concomitant (in the case of Leydig cell stimulation).

Indications: Women: Human gonadotropin and human chorionic gonadotropin (hCG) given sequentially are indicated for the induction of ovulation and pregnancy in females infertile due to anovulation where the cause of anovulation is functional and not due to primary ovarian failure.

Men: Human gonadotropin and concomitant hCG is indicated for the stimulation of spermatogenesis in males with primary or secondary hypogonadotropic hypogonadism.

Contraindications: Women: Ovarian tumors. In patients whose blood levels of gonadotropins and/or prolactin are above normal. A high level of urinary gonadotropins—indicating primary ovarian failure. In the presence of overt thyroid and adrenal dysfunction. An organic intracranial lesion such as a pituitary tumor. The presence of any cause of infertility other than anovulation as stated in the indications. In women with abnormal vaginal bleeding of undetermined origin.

Men: Testicular and pituitary tumors. In patients whose blood levels of gonadotropins and/or prolactin are above normal. Normal urinary gonadotropin levels indicating normal pituitary function. Infertility disorders other than hypogonadotropic hypogonadism.

Warnings: Because human gonadotropin is a potent gonadotropic agent that is capable of causing severe adverse effects in women, it should be used only by physicians who are experienced in the management of fertility disorders and only when facilities for appropriate clinical and endocrinologic evaluations are available.

Overstimulation of the Ovary During Human Gonadotropin Therapy: To minimize the risk associated with abnormal ovarian enlargement in women receiving human gonadotropin and chorionic gonadotropin therapy for induction of ovulation and pregnancy, the drugs should be administered at the lowest possible effective dosage. Since human gonadotropin may cause ovarian enlargement and/or hyperstimulation, patients should be examined at least every other day for signs of excessive ovarian stimulation during menotropins/human chorionic gonadotropin (hCG) therapy and for a 2 week post treatment period. Careful monitoring of ovarian response can minimize the risk of overstimulation.

Mild to moderate uncomplicated ovarian enlargement which may be accompanied by abdominal distension and/or abdominal pain occurs in approximately 20% of patients treated with human gonadotropin/menotropins and hCG, and generally regresses without treatment within 2 to 3 weeks.

Ovarian hyperstimulation syndrome is characterized by sudden ovarian enlargement accompanied by ascites with or without pain and/or pleural effusion.

If hyperstimulation occurs, treatment should be stopped and the patient hospitalized. Hyperstimulation syndrome develops rapidly within 3 to 4 days and generally during the 2 week period following treatment.

Hemoconcentration associated with fluid loss into the abdominal cavity has been observed to occur and should be thoroughly assessed as follows: 1) fluid intake and output; 2) weight; 3) hematocrit; 4) serum and urinary electrolytes; and 5) urine specific gravity. These determinations should be performed daily or more often if needed. Treatment consists of primarily bed rest, fluid and electrolyte replacement, and analgesics as needed. Generally, the ascitic fluid should not be removed because of the potential for damage to the ovary.

Hemoperitoneum may occur from ruptured ovarian cysts. This is usually the result of pelvic examination. Should this occur accompanied by bleeding to the extent that surgery is required, partial resection of the enlarged ovary or ovaries is generally adequate.

Intercourse should be prohibited in those patients in whom significant ovarian enlargement occurs after ovulation due to the risk of hemoperitoneum resulting from ruptured ovarian cysts.

Arterial Thromboembolism: Arterial thromboembolism has been reported in patients who have received human gonadotropin/menotropins and hCG, both in association with and separate from ovarian hyperstimulation syndrome. Complications resulting from thromboembolism have included venous thrombophlebitis, pulmonary embolism, pulmonary infarction, stroke, arterial occlusion necessitating limb amputation, and (rarely) death.

Pregnancy: Multiple ovulations with resulting multiple births occur (mostly twins) frequently (~20% of pregnancies) following treatment with human gonadotropin/menotropins and hCG. Prior to human gonadotropin and hCG therapy, the patient and her male sexual partner should be informed of the possibility and potential risks associated with multiple births.

Spontaneous abortion rates have been reported from 10 to 25% of all patients following gonadotropin treatment. Increased abortion rates are more common in women over 35 years of age and are more common in the infertile couple. The increased frequency of multiple pregnancy is also associated with an increased rate of abortion.

Precautions: Prior to treating patients for inadequate endogenous stimulation of the gonads, a physical examination should be performed to exclude anatomical abnormalities of the genital organs or non-gonadal endocrinopathies (e.g. thyroid or adrenal disorders, diabetes).

In pregnancies occurring after induction of ovulation with gonadotropic preparations, there is an increased risk of miscarriages and multiplets.

Adverse Effects: Women (see Warnings for further details): Arterial thromboembolism. Serious respiratory complications. Serious respiratory complications including atelectasis and acute respiratory distress syndrome have occurred with human gonadotropins/menotropins therapy. These events are rare but death has resulted. Hyperstimulation syndrome (~2%). Hemoperitoneum. Abnormal ovarian enlargement (~20%). Ectopic pregnancy (~3%). Sensitivity to human gonadotropin. Fever has been reported rarely in patients receiving human gonadotropins/menotropins; however, it is not clear if this is a pyrogenic response or a possible allergic reaction. Pain, rash, swelling and/or irritation at the site of injection. Defects at birth. Congenital abnormalities including imperforate anus, aplasia of the sigmoid colon, hypospadias, cecovesical fistula, bifid scrotum, meningocele, bilateral internal tibial torsion, right metatarsus adductus, cardiac lesions, supernumerary digit, exstrophy of the bladder, and Down's syndrome have been reported in infants conceived following human gonadotropin/menotropins and human chorionic gonadotropin (hCG) therapy; however, these effects have not been directly attributed to gonadotropin therapy.

Men: Gynecomastia may occur occasionally during human gonadotropin and hCG therapy. This effect is known to occur in patients receiving hCG alone. Erythrocytosis has been reported in one patient.

Overdose: Symptoms and Treatment: The acute toxicity of human gonadotropin has been shown to be very low. However, too high a dosage for more than 1 day may lead to hyperstimulation of the ovaries (see Warnings).

Dosage: Selection of Patients. Women. A thorough gynecologic and endocrinologic evaluation must be performed prior to treatment with human gonadotropin. The evaluation may include hysterosalpingogaphy to detect uterine and tubal pathology. Anovulation should be confirmed by observation of the basal body temperature pattern, examination of serial vaginal smears and cervical mucus, determination of urinary pregnanediol excretion, and endometrial biopsy. Tumors of the thyroid, adrenals, pituitary, and ovary may cause anovulation and patients with such tumors should be excluded from human gonadotropin therapy.

Determination of urinary gonadotropin concentrations should be obtained to rule out primary ovarian failure.

The presence of early pregnancy should be ruled out by thorough examination and biochemical pregnancy test.

Cervical dilation and curettage should be performed prior to starting human gonadotropin treatment in the following patients: a) in late reproductive life in order to diagnose endometrial carcinoma and anovulatory disorders; b) with abnormal uterine bleeding.

Evaluation of the fertility of the male sexual partner should also be performed.

Men: The presence of functional reproductive organs, absence of mechanical causes for sperm defects, the absence of interfering endocrinopathies and the documented lack of pituitary function should be the criteria for patient selection. Prior to treatment, patients with pituitary insufficiency will have low serum testosterone concentrations and low or absent serum gonadotropin levels. Those patients with primary hypogonadotropic hypogonadism will exhibit a less than normal development of masculinization and patients with secondary hypogonadotropic hypogonadism will have decreased masculinization.

Women: The dosage of human gonadotropin required to produce follicular maturation must be individualized for each patient.

Measurement of serum estradiol concentrations is recommended starting 1 week after the beginning of each course of human gonadotropin and continuing through the day of human chorionic gonadotropin (hCG) administration. This is necessary to determine the optimal dose and to detect ovarian hyperstimulation. Ultrasound examination is recommended during human gonadotropin therapy and prior to administration of hCG to provide information on the number and size of mature follicles, to follow development, and to minimize the risk of ovarian hyperstimulation syndrome and multiple gestation.

The usual initial dosage of human gonadotropin to produce follicular maturation is 75 IU of FSH/LH daily, administered i.m., for 9 to 12 days until evidence of follicular maturation occurs. Follicles of 17 mm or more in diameter, as revealed by ultrasound, can be considered mature. Human gonadotropin should not be administered for longer than 12 days in a single course of therapy. A single dose of chorionic gonadotropin of 5 000 to 10 000 USP units should be given 1 day after the last dose of human gonadotropin if the following criteria are met: total urinary estrogens or estrone-1-glucuronide reach levels of 150 to 250 ng/24 hours; or serum concentrations of 300 to 600 pg/mL estradiol are achieved; and between 1 and 3 follicles are 17 mm or more in diameter.

Following administration of chorionic gonadotropin, the couple should be encouraged to have daily sexual intercourse beginning on the day prior to administration of chorionic gonadotropin until ovulation occurs.

Clinical confirmation of ovulation is obtained through the indices of progesterone production. Increasing progesterone secretion by the corpus luteum and a concomitant increase in basal body temperature are indirect signs of ovulation. Urinary pregnanediol levels higher than 2 mg/24 hours, indicate that ovulation has occurred. A serum progesterone level of over 10 ng/mL (30 nmol/L) also provides adequate proof of a functional corpus luteum. Lower concentrations of serum progesterone may be supplemented by luteal phase injections of up to 5 000 IU hCG.

If there is evidence of ovulation but no pregnancy, repeat this dosage regimen for at least 2 more courses.

If necessary, on the basis of serum estradiol determinations, the dose of human gonadotropin may be increased to 150 Units FSH/LH/day for 9 to 12 days. Again follow this dose with 5 000 to 10 000 Units of hCG 1 day after the last dose of human gonadotropin. Generally, a dose of 150 IU of FSH/LH/day is the most effective dose. If evidence of ovulation is present, but pregnancy does not ensue, repeat the same dose for 2 more courses. Doses larger than 150 IU FSH/LH/day are not routinely recommended.

Human chorionic gonadotropin (hCG) should not be administered under the following circumstances: a) if the ovaries are abnormally enlarged following the last dose of human gonadotropin because the hyperstimulation syndrome is more likely to occur; b) if the total daily urinary estrogen excretion is greater than 100 µg daily; c) urinary estriol excretion is greater than 50 µg daily; or d) if 4 or more follicles over 17 mm in diameter are detected using ultrasonography. The couple should be advised not to have sexual intercourse for 1 week.

Patients should be closely monitored for 2 weeks following human gonadotropin and chorionic gonadotropin treatment to ensure that hyperstimulation does not occur. If the ovaries become abnormally enlarged or abdominal pain occurs, administration of human gonadotropin should be stopped. Most ovarian hyperstimulation occurs after treatment has been discontinued and reaches its maximum at about 7 to 10 days post-ovulation.

Men: Prior to treatment with human gonadotropin and hCG, hCG alone is required to stimulate spermatogenesis in males with primary or secondary hypogonadotropic hypogonadism.

The recommended dose of human gonadotropin is 1 ampul 3 times a week, administered i.m., and 2 000 IU hCG twice a week. To insure detecting spermatozoa in the ejaculate, treatment should continue for a minimum of 4 months, as it takes 74 ± 4 days in the human male for germ cells to reach the spermatozoa stage.

If evidence of increased spermatogenesis does not occur following 4 months of human gonadotropin and hCG therapy, treatment can be continued at the same dosage or human gonadotropin may be increased to 150 IU FSH/LH 3 times weekly. The dosage of hCG, however, must not be changed.

Reconstitution: Reconstitute each ampul with 1 mL of sodium chloride injection 0.9% to obtain a solution containing 75 IU of FSH activity/mL and 75 IU of LH activity/mL. Use immediately after reconstitution.

Supplied: Each box contains: 1 ampul of freeze-dried human gonadotropin and 1 ampul of sodium chloride injection USP 0.9%. Each ampul contains: 75 IU of FSH activity and 75 IU of LH activity. Nonmedicinal ingredients: disodium hydrogen phosphate (anhydrous), mannitol, sodium dihydrogen phosphate (anhydrous). LH activity is standardized by the addition of hCG. Each ampul of diluent contains: 1 mL of sodium chloride injection USP 0.9%. Store at 2 to 25°C. Protect from light.

HUMULIN®

Lilly

Insulin, Human Biosynthetic

Antidiabetic Agent

Pharmacology: Humulin is a polypeptide hormone consisting of a 21 amino acid A-chain and a 30 amino acid B-chain linked by two disulfide bonds.

Humulin is found to be chemically, physically, biologically and immunologically equivalent to pancreatic human insulin which differs slightly from porcine or bovine insulin in amino acid composition.

Studies indicate immunogenicity problems with biosynthetic human insulin (BHI) produced by recombinant DNA technology are less likely than with insulin derived from animal origin. Biosynthetic human insulin is devoid of all protein contaminants of pancreatic origin normally present in trace amounts in all insulins of pancreatic origin. The purification procedures used in the manufacture of biosynthetic human insulin result in a product which contains an insufficient quantity of E. coli polypeptides to be antigenic in deliberately sensitized animals. No antibodies to E. coli polypeptides have been detected in specifically designed radioimmunoassay methods examining patient serum samples.

The administration of suitable doses of insulin to patients with diabetes mellitus, along with controlled diet and exercise, temporarily restores their ability to metabolize carbohydrates, fats and proteins; to store glycogen in the liver; and to convert glucose to fat. When given in suitable doses at regular intervals to a patient with diabetes mellitus, the blood sugar is maintained within a reasonable range, the urine remains relatively free of sugar and ketone bodies, and diabetic acidosis and coma are prevented.

Insulin preparations differ in onset, peak and duration of action. The addition of protamine to insulin, in the presence

Humulin (cont'd)

of zinc, produces a stable complex with less intense and more prolonged action, due to its slow dissolution.

Humulin-R, Regular, Insulin Injection, Human Biosynthetic, is a rapidly acting insulin with a relatively short duration of activity (6 to 8 hours).

Humulin-N, NPH, Insulin Isophane, Human Biosynthetic, is an intermediate-acting insulin with a slower onset of action than Regular insulin and a longer duration of activity of up to 24 hours.

Humulin-L, Lente, Insulin Zinc Suspension Medium, Human Biosynthetic, is an intermediate-acting insulin with a slower onset of action than Regular insulin and a longer duration of activity of up to 24 hours.

Humulin-U, Ultralente, Insulin Zinc Suspension Prolonged, Human Biosynthetic, is a long-acting insulin with a slower onset of action than Regular insulin and a longer duration of activity (of at least 24 hours or more).

Humulin Mixtures (10/90, 20/80, 30/70, 40/60 and 50/50 Insulin Injection, Human Biosynthetic and Insulin Isophane, Human Biosynthetic) are intermediate-acting insulins with a more rapid onset of action than NPH alone and a duration of activity of up to 24 hours.

Humulin-N, Humulin-L or Humulin-U may be mixed with Humulin-R to meet individual metabolic requirements of the patient as determined by the physician.

Indications: For the treatment of insulin-requiring diabetic patients.

Humulin-R **only** should be used for the treatment of emergencies such as diabetic coma and pre-coma, in diabetics undergoing surgery, but **not** Humulin-N, Humulin-L, Humulin-U or Humulin Mixtures.

In switching patients from animal source insulins to Humulin, it is possible that the patients will require a change in dosage; the adjustment may be made with the first dose or over a period of several weeks. Any change of insulin should be made cautiously and only under medical supervision.

Changes in refinement, purity, strength, brand, type and/or method of manufacture (recombinant DNA versus animal source insulin) may result in the need of a change in dosage.

Contraindications: Hypoglycemia (see Hypoglycemia in Overdose).

Humulin-N, Humulin Mixtures, Humulin-L and Humulin-U should not be given i.v. or used for treatment of diabetic coma.

Warnings: A few patients who experienced hypoglycemic reactions after being transferred to Humulin have reported that these early warning symptoms were less pronounced than they were with animal-source insulin.

Under no circumstances should any Humulin Mixture be given i.v.

Do not use the Humulin-N, Humulin-L, Humulin-U or Humulin Mixtures if you see lumps that float or that stick to the sides of the vial, or if the contents of the vial are clear and remain clear after the bottle is shaken or rotated. Note: The contents of the vial of Humulin-R should be clear. Do not use if cloudy.

Precautions: Visual disturbances in uncontrolled diabetes due to refractive changes are reversed during the early phase of effective management. However, since alteration in osmotic equilibrium between the lens and ocular fluids may not stabilize for a few weeks after initiating therapy, it is wise to postpone prescribing new corrective lenses for 3 to 6 weeks.

Insulin requirements may be increased during illness or emotional disturbances or if the patient is receiving concurrent administration of drugs with hyperglycemic activity, e.g. oral contraceptives, corticosteroids or thyroid replacement therapy.

Insulin requirements may be reduced in the presence of renal or hepatic impairment or if the patient is receiving concurrent administration of drugs with hypoglycemic activity, e.g. monoamine oxidase inhibitors and beta-adrenergic blockers.

The number and size of daily doses and the time of administration, as well as diet and exercise, are problems that require direct and continuous medical supervision. Usually, the most satisfactory injection time is before breakfast.

Prompt recognition and appropriate management of the allergic complications of insulin therapy are essential for the safe and effective control of diabetes mellitus.

Transferring from Other Insulins: A small number of patients transferring from insulins of animal source to insulins of recombinant DNA origin may require a reduced dosage, especially if they are tightly controlled and bordering on hypoglycemia. The dosage reduction may occur with the first dose or over a period of several weeks. There is a risk of hypoglycemia if the insulin requirement is decreased, and both the physician and the patient should be aware of this possibility. The risk can be considered to be minimal if the daily dose is less than 40 units.

Pregnancy: It is essential to maintain good control of the insulin-diabetic patient throughout pregnancy. Insulin requirements usually decrease during the first trimester and increase during the second and third trimesters.

Lactation: Diabetic patients who are nursing may require adjustments in insulin dose and/or diet.

Drug Interactions: Hormones that tend to counteract the hypoglycemic effects of insulin include growth hormone, corticotropin, glucocorticoids, thyroid hormone and glucagon. Epinephrine not only inhibits the secretion of insulin, but also stimulates glycogen breakdown to glucose. Thus, the presence of such diseases as acromegaly, Cushing's syndrome, hyperthyroidism, and pheochromocytoma complicate the control of diabetes.

The hypoglycemic action of insulin may also be antagonized by phenytoin. Insulin's hypoglycemic action can be increased in some patients by concomitant administration of anabolic steroids, MAO inhibitors, guanethidine, alcohol, propranolol (masking effect) or other drugs affecting beta-adrenergic receptors, or by daily doses of 1.5 to 6 g of salicylates.

Insulin requirements can be increased, decreased, or unchanged in patients receiving diuretics. Concomitant administration of oral contraceptives can cause a decrease in glucose tolerance in diabetic women possibly resulting in increased daily insulin requirements.

Adverse Effects: Since Humulin has been available worldwide, reports of local and systemic allergic reactions in patients receiving it have been received. As with all insulins, local inflammatory responses may result from improper cleansing of the skin, contamination of the injection site with alcohol, use of an antiseptic containing impurities or accidental intracutaneous rather than s.c. injection. Local reactions that result in skin sensitivity phenomena usually subside spontaneously.

Insulin lipohypertrophy has been reported with Humulin. This complication has been ascribed to the local pharmacologic effects of the s.c. injection of insulin. A few cases of lipoatrophy and serum sickness have also been reported.

Overdose: Hypoglycemia: Cause: Hypoglycemia (low blood glucose, also called "insulin reaction") can occur if the patient takes too much insulin, misses meals, exercises or works too hard just before a meal, or has an infection or becomes ill (especially with diarrhea or vomiting) or if his/her body's need for insulin changes for other reasons.

Symptoms: Hypoglycemia may occur in any patient receiving insulin and is most commonly manifested by hunger, nervousness, warmth and sweating, and palpitations. Patients also may experience headache, confusion, drowsiness, fatigue, anxiety, blurred vision, diplopia, or numbness of the lips, nose or fingers. The clinical manifestations of hypoglycemia can be masked by the concomitant administration of propranolol or other beta-adrenergic blockers.

Symptoms are likely to appear anytime when the blood sugar concentration falls below 2.2 mmol/L (40 mg/100 mL) but may occur with a sudden drop in blood glucose even when the value remains above 2.2 mmol/L (40 mg/100 mL).

Treatment: If a patient is unable to take soluble carbohydrate or fruit juice orally, hypoglycemia is treated with 10 to 20 g of dextrose i.v. or glucagon may be given s.c. or i.m.

Dosage: The dosage should be determined by the physician, according to the requirements of the patient.

New Patients: Patients receiving insulin for the first time can be started on Humulin in the same manner as they would be on animal-source insulin.

Patients should be monitored closely during the adjustment period.

Transfer Patients: When transferring patients from animal-source insulin to Humulin, use the same dose and dosage schedule.

Some patients transferring to Humulin will require a change in dosage from that used with animal-source insulin. If an adjustment is needed, it may be made with the first dose or over a period of several weeks.

Changes in total daily dosage, the number of injections per day, and/or timing of injections may be necessary to achieve maximum glycemic control.

When a patient on high doses of animal insulin is switched to Humulin, it may be appropriate to reduce the starting dosage and monitor the patient carefully.

Patients who have systemic allergy to pork or beef insulin may also react to human insulin. In such patients, appropriate procedures (intradermal testing and, if necessary, desensitization) should be undertaken before therapeutic doses of human insulin are administered.

A few patients who experienced hypoglycemic reactions after being transferred to Humulin have reported that the early warning symptoms, i.e., nervousness, sweating and palpitations, were less pronounced than they were with animal-source insulin.

Formulations of Humulin appear to produce a slightly faster onset and slightly shorter duration of action than the corresponding forms of animal-source insulins.

Humulin-R is a clear, colorless solution. It may be administered by s.c., i.m. or i.v. injection.

Humulin-N, Humulin Mixtures, Humulin-L and Humulin-U are suspensions. They should be administered by s.c. injection only.

S.C. administration, preferably by the patient, should be in the upper arms, thighs, buttocks or abdomen. Injection sites should be rotated so that the same site is not used more than approximately once a month.

Care should be taken to ensure that a blood vessel has not been entered. The injection site should not be massaged.

Mixing Instructions: The rapid action of Humulin-R is preserved when mixed with Humulin-N; independent of the time lag between mixing and administration, and independent of the proportion of regular insulin incorporated in the mixture.

Humulin-L and Humulin-R bind immediately after mixing resulting in a delay in the onset of the regular insulin action, reduction in peak activity magnitude, and prolonged total duration of activity.

Mixing Humulin-R and Humulin-U results in reduction of the quick-acting effect of regular insulin.

The effects of mixing Humulin with animal-source insulins have not been studied. This practice is not recommended.

Stability and Storage: Insulin should be stored in a cold place (2 to 10°C), preferably in a refrigerator, but not in a freezer. Do not let it freeze or leave it in direct sunlight. Expiration dates are stated on the labels.

When in use, vials and cartridges may be kept at room temperatue for up to 28 days.

Information for the Patient: See Blue Section—Information for the Patient "Humulin".

Supplied: Humulin-R: Each mL contains 100 units of Regular insulin. Nonmedicinal ingredients: glycerol and m-cresol. May contain: dimethicone, hydrochloric acid and sodium hydroxide. Cartridges of 1.5 and 3 mL, boxes of 5. Vials of 10 mL.

Humulin-N: Each mL contains 100 units of NPH insulin. Nonmedicinal ingredients: dibasic sodium phosphate, glycerol, m-cresol, phenol, protamine sulfate and zinc. May contain: dimethicone, hydrochloric acid and sodium hydroxide. Cartridges of 1.5 and 3 mL, boxes of 5. Vials of 10 mL.

Humulin-L: Each mL contains 100 units of Lente insulin. Nonmedicinal ingredients: methyl paraben, sodium acetate, sodium chloride and zinc. May contain dimethicone, hydrochloric acid and sodium hydroxide. Vials of 10 mL.

Humulin-U: Each mL contains 100 units of Ultralente insulin. Nonmedicinal ingredients: methyl paraben, sodium acetate, sodium chloride and zinc. May contain: dimethicone, hydrochloric acid and sodium hydroxide. Vials of 10 mL.

Humulin 10/90: Each mL contains 10 units of Regular insulin and 90 units of NPH insulin. Nonmedicinal ingredients: dibasic sodium phosphate, glycerol, m-cresol, phenol, protamine sulfate and zinc. May contain: dimethicone, hydrochloric acid and sodium hydroxide. Cartridges of 1.5 and 3 mL, boxes of 5. Vials of 10 mL.

Humulin 20/80: Each mL contains 20 units of Regular insulin and 80 units of NPH insulin. Nonmedicinal ingredients: dibasic sodium phosphate, glycerol, m-cresol, phenol, protamine sulfate and zinc. May contain: dimethicone, hydrochloric acid and sodium hydroxide. Cartridges of 1.5 and 3 mL, boxes of 5. Vials of 10 mL.

Humulin 30/70: Each mL contains 30 units Regular insulin and 70 units of NPH insulin. Nonmedicinal ingredients: dibasic sodium phosphate, glycerol, m-cresol, phenol, protamine sulfate and zinc. May contain: dimethicone, hydrochloric acid and sodium hydroxide. Cartridges of 1.5 and 3 mL, boxes of 5. Vials of 10 mL.

Humulin 40/60: Each mL contains 40 units of Regular insulin and 60 units of NPH insulin. Nonmedicinal ingredients: dibasic sodium phosphate, glycerol, m-cresol, phenol, protamine sulfate and zinc. May contain: dimethicone, hydrochloric acid and sodium hydroxide. Cartridges of 1.5 and 3 mL, boxes of 5. Vials of 10 mL.

Humulin 50/50: Each mL contains 50 units of Regular insulin and 50 units of NPH Insulin. Nonmedicinal ingredients: dibasic sodium phosphate, glycerol, m-cresol, phenol, protamine sulfate and zinc. May contain: dimethicone, hydrochloric acid and sodium hydroxide. Cartridges of 1.5 and 3 mL, boxes of 5. Vials of 10 mL.

Humulin cartridges are designed for use with the B-D Pen, B-D Pen Ultra Cartridge System, or future Lilly injector systems.

HYCAMTIN™ Ⓟ

SmithKline Beecham

Topotecan HCl

Antineoplastic

Pharmacology: Topotecan inhibits topoisomerase-I, an enzyme that functions in DNA replication to relieve the torsional strain introduced ahead of the moving replication fork. Topotecan inhibits topoisomerase-I by stabilizing the covalent complex of enzyme and strand-cleaved DNA which is an intermediate of the catalytic mechanism, thereby inducing breaks in the protein-associated DNA single-strands, resulting in cell death.

Pharmacokinetics: Following i.v. administration of topotecan at doses of 0.5 to 1.5 mg/m² as a 30-minute infusion daily for 5 days, topotecan demonstrated a clearance of 1 030 mL/min with a plasma half-life of 2 to 3 hours.

Comparison of pharmacokinetic parameters did not suggest any change in pharmacokinetics over the dosing period. AUC increased approximately in proportion to the increase in dose.

Distribution: Topotecan has a volume of distribution of 130 L. The binding of topotecan to plasma proteins is 35%. Topotecan is evenly distributed between blood cells and plasma.

Metabolism: Topotecan undergoes pH dependent hydrolysis, with the equilibrium favoring the ring-opened hydroxy-acid form at physiologic pH.

Excretion: The renal clearance of topotecan could not be measured in humans due to the effect of urine pH on interconversion, although measurement of total topotecan (the lactone ring and the ring-opened hydroxy acid) in urine suggests that a variable fraction of the dose (generally 20 to 60%) is excreted in urine. Topotecan has also been measured in human bile samples indicating that topotecan is excreted by both biliary and urinary routes in humans.

Pharmacodynamics: The dose-limiting toxicity for topotecan is leukopenia. The relationship between decreased white blood count and either topotecan or total topotecan AUC can be described by a sigmoid E_{max} model.

Pharmacokinetics in Special Populations: Renal Impairment: Plasma clearance of topotecan in patients with mild renal impairment (creatinine clearance [Cl_{cr}] of 40 to 60 mL/min) decreased to about 67% compared with control patients. Volume of distribution was slightly decreased and thus half-life only increased by 14%.

In patients with moderate renal impairment (Cl_{cr} of 20 to 39 mL/min), topotecan plasma clearance was reduced to 34% of the value in control patients. Volume of distribution also decreased by about 25%, which resulted in an increase in mean half-life from 1.9 to 4.9 hours. Total topotecan clearance also decreased by 57% in patients with moderate renal impairment and by 17% in patients with mild renal impairment. Based on clinical data and on total topotecan pharmacokinetics, no dosage adjustment is required for patients with mild renal impairment (Cl_{cr} 40 to 60 mL/min). Dosage adjustment to 0.75 mg/m² is recommended for patients with moderate renal impairment. Topotecan is not recommended for patients with a creatinine clearance of <20 mL/min.

Hepatic Impairment: Based on clinical data and total topotecan pharmacokinetics, no dosage adjustment is required in patients with hepatic impairment (serum bilirubin <10 mg/dL). Plasma clearance in patients with hepatic impairment decreased to about 67% when compared with a control group of patients. Topotecan half-life was increased by about 30%, but no change in volume of distribution was observed. Total topotecan clearance in patients with hepatic impairment only decreased by about 10% compared with the control group of patients.

Children: The pharmacokinetics of topotecan were studied in 12 pediatric patients treated with topotecan at doses between 2 and 7.5 mg/m² as a 24-hour continuous infusion. Mean plasma clearance was 28.3 L/h/m² with a range of 18.1 to 44.2 L/h/m². These values are similar to plasma clearance values seen in adults (approximately 36 L/h/m²) who received 24-hour topotecan infusions.

Gender: At this time, topotecan is indicated for the treatment of ovarian cancer, therefore the gender specific effects of topotecan have not been elucidated.

Geriatrics: Topotecan pharmacokinetics have not been specifically investigated in elderly patients. However, a population pharmacokinetic analysis in female patients did not identify age as a significant factor. Renal clearance is likely to be a more important determinant of topotecan clearance than age in this patient population.

Race: The effect of race on topotecan pharmacokinetics has not been determined.

Clinical Studies: Topotecan was studied in 4 clinical trials of 452 patients with metastatic ovarian carcinoma.

Patients in these 4 studies received an initial dose of 1.5 mg/m² given by i.v. infusion over 30 minutes for the first 5 consecutive days of a 21-day course.

In a randomized Phase III study, topotecan was compared with paclitaxel. This study treated 112 patients with topotecan (1.5 mg/m²/day for the first 5 consecutive days of a 21-day course) and 114 patients with paclitaxel (175 mg/m² over 3 hours on day 1 of a 21-day course).

Response rates, response duration (measured from the time of documented response), time to progression, time to response and survival for the comparative study are provided in Table I.

Patients receiving topotecan achieved a higher response rate (21 vs 14%, p=0.196) than those receiving paclitaxel; a longer duration of response (median of 26 vs 22 weeks, hazard ratio=0.778, p=0.476); a longer time to progression [median of 19 vs 15 weeks (hazard ratio=0.764, p=0.0718)]; and a longer estimated median survival (63 vs 53 weeks, hazard ratio=0.986, p=0.9315).

However, the median time to response was longer with topotecan compared to paclitaxel: median of 8 vs 6 weeks (hazard ratio=0.615, p=0.1465). Consequently there is a risk of underestimating the expected efficacy of topotecan if patients are withdrawn from treatment prematurely (see Dosage).

Table I—Hycamtin

Comparative Efficacy Parameters of Hycamtin vs Paclitaxel in Ovarian Cancer

Parameter	Hycamtin (n=112)	Paclitaxel (n=114)
Complete Response Rate (%)	4.5	2.6
Partial Response Rate (%)	16.1	11.4
Overall Response Rate (%)	20.5	14.0
95% CI	(13.1 - 28.0)	(7.7 - 20.4)
(p-value)	(0.196)	
Response Duration (Weeks)		
Median	26*	22*
95% CI	(22.1 - 32.9)	(16.0 - 34.6)
Hazard-ratio (p-value)	0.778 (0.476)	
Time to Progression (Weeks)		
Median	19	15
95% CI	(12.1 - 23.6)	(11.9 - 18.3)
Hazard-ratio (p-value)	0.764 (0.0718)	
Time to Response (Weeks)		
Median	8.0*	6.0*
Range	3.1 - 19.0	2.4 - 12.3
Hazard-ratio (p-value)	0.615 (0.1465)	
Survival (Weeks)		
Median	63	53
Range	0.7 - 122.1	0.6 - 129.9
Hazard-ratio (p-value)	0.986 (0.9315)	

*Topotecan (n=23), paclitaxel (n=16).

Patients who failed on the initial arm of this study were allowed to switch to the alternate treatment. Eight of 61 (13.1%) patients who received topotecan after paclitaxel responded. Five of 49 (10.2%) patients who received paclitaxel after topotecan responded.

Topotecan was active in patients who had developed resistance to platinum-containing therapy, defined as tumor progression while on, or tumor relapse within 6 months after completion of, a platinum-containing regimen. One complete and 7 partial responses were seen in 60 patients, for a response rate of 13%. In the same study, there were no complete responders and only 4 partial responders on the paclitaxel arm, for a response rate of 7%.

Topotecan remained active in patients who did not respond to or eventually failed paclitaxel, as shown by the responders in this trial and the trial in platinum and paclitaxel failures (see below).

The safety profile for paclitaxel in this study was consistent with the product's monograph; the safety profile for topotecan in this study was consistent with that observed in all 452 patients from the 4 ovarian clinical trials (see Adverse Effects).

The 3 additional studies were open-labeled and noncomparative in design. The first of these enrolled 111 patients who had failed 1 prior platinum-containing regimen. The response rate was 14% (95% CI:=7.9 to 20.9%). The median duration of response was 16 weeks (range: 4.6 to 41.9 weeks). The time to progression was 11 weeks (range: 0.7 to 72.1 weeks). The median survival was 52 weeks (range: 1.4 to 72.3 weeks).

A second open study enrolled 139 patients who had failed 1 (62 patients) or 2 (77 patients) prior regimens containing platinum and paclitaxel. The response rates in this study for evaluable patients were 12.9% and 16.9%, respectively. Median response duration was 18.1 weeks. Median time to progression was 12 weeks (range: 0.6 to 52.7 weeks). Median survival was 51.3 weeks for patients failing first-line therapy.

The third open study enrolled 30 patients who had failed 1 or 2 prior platinum-containing regimens. The response rate was 13% (95% CI:=3.8 to 30.7%). The median duration of response was 28 weeks (range: 16 to 59 weeks).

Indications: For the treatment of patients with metastatic carcinoma of the ovary after failure of initial or subsequent therapy.

Contraindications: Patients who have a history of hypersensitivity reactions to topotecan or to any of its other ingredients.

Pregnancy and *Lactation:* Should not be used in patients who are pregnant or breast-feeding.

Topotecan is contraindicated in patients who already have severe bone marrow depression prior to starting first course, as evidenced by baseline neutrophils <1 500 cells/mm³ and/or a platelet count of <100 000/mm³.

Topotecan is contraindicated in patients with severe renal impairment (creatinine clearance of <20 mL/min).

Warnings: Topotecan should be administered under the supervision of a physician experienced in the use of cancer chemotherapeutic agents. Bone marrow suppression, primarily neutropenia, is the dose-limiting toxicity. Therapy with topotecan should not be given to patients with baseline neutrophil counts of 1 500 cells/mm³ or less. In order to monitor the occurrence of bone marrow suppression, frequent peripheral blood cell counts should be performed on all patients receiving topotecan.

Hematology: Bone marrow suppression (primarily neutropenia) is the dose-limiting toxicity. The nadir for neutrophil count occurred at a median of 11 days, and the nadir for platelet and hemoglobin counts occurred at a median of 15 days. The median duration of Grade 4 neutropenia was 7 days, and of thrombocytopenia was 5 days. The median duration of Grade 3/4 anemia was 7 days. (All grading scales reported are based on National Cancer Institute criteria.) Topotecan should only be administered in patients with adequate bone marrow reserves including baseline neutrophil counts of at least 1 500 cells/mm³ and platelet count at least 100 000/mm³. Frequent monitoring of blood counts should be instituted during treatment with topotecan.

There are no adequate data to define a safe and effective regimen for topotecan and cisplatin in combination. See Precautions.

Pregnancy: Topotecan may cause fetal harm when administered to a pregnant woman. Topotecan was shown to cause embryonic and fetal lethality when given to rats and rabbits at doses less than the human clinical i.v. dose (1.5 mg/m²). If this drug is used during pregnancy, or if the patient becomes pregnant while taking this drug, the patient should be apprised of the potential hazard to the fetus. Women of childbearing potential should be advised to avoid becoming pregnant during therapy with topotecan.

Lactation: It is not known whether the drug is excreted in human milk. Breast-feeding should be discontinued when women are receiving topotecan (see Contraindications).

Children: Safety and effectiveness in pediatric patients have not been established.

Precautions: General: Inadvertent extravasation with topotecan has been associated only with mild local reactions such as erythema (and bruising).

Drug Interactions: Myelosuppression was more severe when topotecan was given in combination with cisplatin in Phase I studies. There are no adequate data to define a safe and effective regimen for topotecan and cisplatin in combination.

Hycamtin (cont'd)

Concomitant administration of G-CSF can prolong the duration of neutropenia. If G-CSF is to be used, it should not be initiated until day 6 of the course of therapy (the day after completion of treatment with topotecan).

Hematology: Topotecan should not be administered to patients with baseline neutrophil counts of less than 1 500 cells/mm³. To monitor the occurrence of myelotoxicity, it is recommended that frequent peripheral blood cell counts be performed on all patients receiving topotecan. Patients should not be retreated with subsequent courses of topotecan until neutrophils recover to a level >1 000 cells/mm³; platelets recover to a level >100 000 cells/mm³ and hemoglobin recovers to 9 g/dL, using transfusion if necessary.

In the case of severe neutropenia (<500 cells/mm³ for 7 days or more) during a course of topotecan, a reduction in dose of 0.25 mg/m² for subsequent courses of therapy is recommended.

Carcinogenesis, Mutagenesis, Impairment of Fertility: The carcinogenic potential of topotecan has not been studied (see Warnings, Pregnancy).

Topotecan has been shown to be genotoxic to mammalian cells (mouse lymphoma cells and human lymphocytes) in vitro, and mouse bone marrow cells in vivo, but is not mutagenic in bacterial cells (S. typhimurium and E. coli).

Pregnancy: (See Warnings.) Topotecan was shown to cause embryo-fetal lethality when given to rats (0.59 mg/m²) and rabbits (1.25 mg/m²). At maternally toxic doses (0.59 mg/m²), topotecan caused malformations, primarily of the eye, brain, skull and vertebrae.

Adverse Effects: Data in the following section (see Tables II and III) are based on the experience of 452 patients with metastatic ovarian carcinoma treated with topotecan in Phase II/III studies.

Table II—Hycamtin

Summary of Hematologic Adverse Events in 452 Patients Receiving Hycamtin

Hematologic Adverse Events	Patients n=452 % Incidence	Courses n=2 375 % Incidence
Neutropenia		
<1 500 cells/mm³	98	78
<500 cells/mm³	81	40
Leukopenia		
<3 000 cells/mm³	98	77
<1 000 cells/mm³	32	11
Thrombocytopenia		
<75 000 mm³	63	39
<25 000 mm³	26	9
Anemia		
<10 g/dL	95	76
<8 g/dL	40	16
Sepsis and Fever/Infection with Grade 4 Neutropenia	26	7
Platelet Transfusions	13	4
RBC Transfusions	56	23

Hematologic: Neutropenia (reversible and noncumulative over time) was the major dose-limiting toxicity. Severe (<500 cells/mm³) neutropenia was most common during course 1 of treatment (60% of patients). It occurred in 40% of total courses and generally resolved within 1 week. Neutrophil nadirs occurred at a median of 11 days. Prophylactic G-CSF was administered in 27% of courses.

Therapy-related sepsis associated with death occurred in 0.7% of patients. There were no episodes of serious bleeding. Severe anemia (Grade 3/4) occurred in 16% of courses. Median platelet and hemoglobin nadirs occurred on day 15 of treatment.

Gastrointestinal: (See Table III.) Prophylactic antiemetic use was not routine in patients treated with topotecan. Gastrointestinal effects were usually mild at the recommended dose level. Severe (Grade 3 or 4) nausea, vomiting, diarrhea and stomatitis incidence was 6, 4.5, 3.4 and 2% respectively. A small incidence (approximately 8%) of mild abdominal pain was also reported among patients.

Skin/Appendages: Total alopecia (Grade 2) occurred in 42% of patients.

Central and Peripheral Nervous Systems: Headache (19%) was the most frequently reported neurologic toxicity. Paresthesia were generally Grade 1 (8%).

Liver/Biliary: Grade 1 transient elevations in liver enzymes (5%); Grade 3/4 elevations (<1%).

Respiratory: Dyspnea (19%); Grade 3/4 dyspnea (3%).

Note: **All grading scales are based on National Cancer Institute criteria.**

Overdose: Symptoms and Treatment: There is no known antidote for overdosage with topotecan. The primary anticipated complication of overdosage would consist of bone marrow suppression. In a phase I study, one patient was incorrectly dosed at 35 mg/m² during course 9 of therapy and experienced hematologic toxicity associated with this increased dose.

The LD_{10} Rate in mice receiving single i.v. infusions of topotecan was 74.85 mg/m² (95% CI: 47.22 to 97.41).

Dosage: Prior to administration of the first course of topotecan, patients must have a baseline neutrophil count of >1 500 cells/mm³ and a platelet count of >100 000 cells/mm³.

The recommended dose is 1.5 mg/m² by i.v. infusion over 30 minutes daily for 5 consecutive days, starting on day 1 of a 21-day course. A minimum of 4 courses is recommended because median time to response in three clinical trials was 9 to 12 weeks. In the event of severe neutropenia, the dose should be reduced by 0.25 mg/m² for subsequent courses. As an alternative, G-CSF may be administered before reducing the dose, starting from day 6 of the course (the day after completion of topotecan administration). Routine premedication for the prevention of nonhematological adverse events is not required.

Hepatic Impairment: No dosage adjustment is required for treating patients with hepatic impairment (plasma bilirubin >1.5 to <10 mg/dL).

Renally Impaired Patients: No dosage adjustment is required for patients with mild renal impairment (Cl_{cr} 40 to 60 mL/min). Dosage adjustment to 0.75 mg/m² is recommended for patients with moderate renal impairment (Cl_{cr} 20 to 39 mL/min). Treatment in patients with severe renal impairment (Cl_{cr} <20 mL/min) is not recommended (see Contraindications).

Table III—Hycamtin

Summary of Nonhematologic Adverse Events in 452 Patients Receiving Hycamtin

Nonhematologic Adverse Events	All Grades % Incidence		Grade 3 % Incidence		Grade 4 % Incidence	
	n=452 Patients	n=2 375 Courses	n=452 Patients	n=2 375 Courses	n=452 Patients	n=2 375 Courses
Gastrointestinal						
Nausea	77	50	10	3	<1	<1
Vomiting	58	26	6	3	3	<1
Diarrhea	42	19	4	1	<1	<1
Constipation	39	18	2	<1	1	<1
Abdominal Pain	33	13	4	<1	2	<1
Stomatitis	24	9	2	<1	<1	<1
Anorexia	19	8	2	<1	0	0
Body as a Whole						
Fatigue	37	25	6	2	0	0
Fever	34	13	1	<1	<1	<1
Asthenia	21	10	3	<1	1	<1
Skin/Appendages						
Alopecia	59	62	NA	NA	NA	NA

Legend: NA: Not applicable.

Children: Insufficient data are available in pediatric patients to provide a dosage recommendation.

Preparation for Administration: Precautions: Topotecan is a cytotoxic anticancer drug. As with other potentially toxic compounds, it should be prepared under a vertical laminar flow hood while wearing gloves and protective clothing. If the solution contacts the skin, wash the skin immediately and thoroughly with soap and water. If the drug contacts mucous membranes, flush thoroughly with water.

Preparation for I.V. Administration: Each 4 mg vial is reconstituted with 4 mL Sterile Water for Injection, giving a final concentration of 1 mg/mL. Then the appropriate volume of the reconstituted solution is further diluted to an infusion concentration of 20 to 500 µg/mL in 50 to 100 mL of either 0.9% Sodium Chloride i.v. infusion or 5% Dextrose i.v. infusion prior to administration.

Reconstituted Vials: Vials which have been reconstituted with Water for Injection are stable for up to 24 hours when refrigerated at 5°C or stored at 30°C.

The reconstituted solution ranges in color from yellow to yellow-green and is intended for administration by i.v. infusion. However, since the vials contain no preservative, it is recommended that the product should be used immediately after reconstitution. If not used immediately, the reconstituted solution should be stored in a refrigerator and discarded after 24 hours.

Diluted Solutions: Reconstituted vials diluted for infusion are stable for up to 24 hours at approximately 20 to 25°C and ambient lighting conditions. If not used immediately, the diluted solution should be stored in a refrigerator in line with good pharmaceutical practice.

As with all parenteral drug products, i.v. admixtures should be inspected visually for clarity and particulate matter, discoloration and leakage prior to administration, whenever solution and container permit.

Handling and Disposal: Procedures for proper handling and disposal of anticancer drugs should be used. Several guidelines on this subject have been published.

Supplied: Each single dose vial of a sterile lyophilized, buffered, light yellow to greenish powder contains: topotecan HCl equivalent to 4 mg of topotecan as free base. Nonmedicinal ingredients: mannitol and tartaric acid. Hydrochloric acid and sodium hydroxide may be used to adjust to a pH of 3. The solution pH ranges from 2.5 to 3.5. Single dose vials. Packages of 5. Unopened vials are stable until the date indicated on the package when stored between 15 and 30°C and protected from light in the original package.

Reviewed 1998

HYCODAN® Ⓝ

DuPont Pharma

Hydrocodone Bitartrate

Antitussive

Pharmacology: Clinical trials have proven hydrocodone bitartrate to be an effective antitussive agent which is pharmacologically 2 to 8 times as potent as codeine. At equi-effective doses, its sedative action is greater than that of codeine. The precise mechanisms of action of hydrocodone and other opiates are not known; however, hydrocodone is believed to act by directly depressing the cough centre. In excessive doses, hydrocodone, like other opium derivatives, can depress respiration. The effects of therapeutic doses of hydrocodone on the cardiovascular system are insignificant. The constipating effects of hydrocodone are much weaker than those of morphine and no stronger than those of codeine. Hydrocodone can produce miosis, euphoria, physical and psychological dependence. At therapeutic antitussive doses, it does exert analgesic effects. Following a 10 mg oral dose of hydrocodone administered to 5 male human subjects, the mean peak serum concentration was 23.6±5.2 ng/mL. Maximum serum levels were achieved at approximately 1.3±0.3 hours and the half-life was determined to be approximately 3.8±0.3 hours. Hydrocodone exhibits a complex pattern of metabolism including O-demethylation, N-demethylation and 6-keto reduction to the corresponding 6-α- and 6-β-hydroxymetabolites.

Indications: The control of exhausting, nonproductive cough.

Contraindications: Hypersensitivity to any component of the drug. Patients known to be hypersensitive to other opioids may exhibit cross-sensitivity to hydrocodone. Hydrocodone is contraindicated in the presence of an intracranial lesion associated with increased intracranial pressure, and whenever ventilatory function is depressed.

Warnings: Hydrocodone can produce drug dependence and, therefore, has the potential for being abused. Psychic dependence, physical dependence and tolerance may develop upon repeated administration. Prescribe and administer with the same degree of caution appropriate to the use of other narcotic drugs (see Drug Abuse and Dependence).

Hydrocodone produces dose-related respiratory depression by directly acting on the brain stem respiratory centres. If respiratory depression occurs, it may be antagonized by the use of naloxone HCl and other supportive measures when indicated.

Occupational Hazards: Hydrocodone may impair the mental and/or physical abilities required for the performance of potentially hazardous tasks such as driving a car or operating machinery. Caution patients accordingly.

The respiratory depressant effects of narcotics and their capacity to elevate cerebrospinal fluid pressure may be markedly exaggerated in the presence of head injury, other intracranial lesions or a pre-existing elevated intracranial pressure. Furthermore, narcotics may produce adverse reactions which can obscure the clinical course of patients with head injuries.

The administration of hydrocodone or other opioids may obscure the diagnosis or clinical course in patients with acute abdominal conditions.

Patients receiving other narcotic analgesics, general anesthetics, phenothiazines or other tranquilizers, tricyclic antidepressants, sedative-hypnotics or other CNS depressants (including alcohol) concomitantly with hydrocodone may exhibit an additive CNS depression. When such combined therapy is contemplated, reduce the dose of one or both agents.

Precautions: Before prescribing medication to suppress or modify cough, it is important to ascertain that the underlying cause of the cough is identified, that modification of the cough does not increase the risk of clinical or physiologic complications, and that appropriate therapy for the primary disease is provided.

In young children the respiratory centre is especially susceptible to the depressant action of narcotic cough suppressants. Benefit to risk ratio should be carefully considered, especially in children with respiratory embarrassment, e.g., croup. Estimation of dosage relative to the child's age and weight is of great importance.

As hydrocodone may inhibit peristalsis, patients with chronic constipation should be given the drug only after weighing the potential therapeutic benefit against the hazards involved.

In patients with asthma or pulmonary emphysema, indiscriminate use may precipitate respiratory insufficiency resulting from increased viscosity of bronchial secretions and suppression of the cough reflex.

Use with caution in sedated or debilitated patients, in patients who have undergone thoracotomies or laparotomies, since suppression of the cough reflex may lead to retention of secretions postoperatively in these patients.

The CNS-depressant effect of hydrocodone may be additive with that of other drugs which depress the CNS (see Warnings).

Carcinogenicity, mutagenicity and reproduction studies have not been conducted.

Pregnancy: Animal reproduction studies have not been conducted. It is not known if hydrocodone can cause fetal harm when administered to a pregnant woman or can affect reproductive capacity. Hydrocodone crosses the placental barrier. Give to pregnant women only if clearly needed.

Babies born to mothers who have been taking opioids regularly prior to delivery will be physically dependent. Withdrawal signs include: irritability and excessive crying, tremors, hyperactive reflexes, increased respiratory rate, increased stools, sneezing, yawning, vomiting, and fever. Intensity of the syndrome does not always correlate with the duration of maternal opioids use or dose. There is no consensus on the best method of managing withdrawal. Chlorpromazine (0.7 to 1.0 mg/kg q6h), phenobarbital (2 mg/kg q6h), and paregoric (2 to 4 drops/kg q4h) have been used to treat withdrawal symptoms in infants. Duration of therapy is 4 to 28 days, with dosages decreased as tolerated.

Lactation: It is not known if this drug is excreted in human milk. Because many drugs are excreted in human milk and because there is potential for serious adverse reactions in nursing infants, a decision should be made whether to discontinue nursing or discontinue the drug. Take into account the importance of the drug to the mother.

Drug Interactions: The CNS depressant effect of hydrocodone may be additive with that of other CNS depressants (see Warnings).

Adverse Effects: Respiratory: Hydrocodone produces dose-related respiratory depression by acting directly on brain stem respiratory centres.

Cardiovascular: Hypertension, postural hypotension and palpitations.

Genitourinary: Ureteral spasm, spasm of vesical sphincters and urinary retention have been reported with opiates.

CNS: Sedation, drowsiness, mental clouding, lethargy, impairment of mental and physical performance, anxiety, fear, dysphoria, dizziness, psychic dependence, mood changes and blurred vision.

Gastrointestinal: Nausea and vomiting occur more frequently in ambulatory than in recumbent patients. Constipation may also occur.

Drug Abuse and Dependence: Exercise special care in prescribing hydrocodone for emotionally unstable patients and for those with a history of drug misuse. Supervise such patients closely when long-term therapy is contemplated.

Psychic dependence, physical dependence, and tolerance may develop upon repeated administration of narcotics; prescribe and administer hydrocodone with caution. Physical dependence is the condition in which continued administration of the drug is required to prevent the appearance of a withdrawal syndrome.

Patients physically dependent on opioids will develop an abstinence syndrome upon abrupt discontinuation of the opioid or following administration of a narcotic antagonist. The character and severity of the withdrawal symptoms are related to the degree of physical dependence. Manifestations of opioid withdrawal are similar to, but milder than that of morphine and include: lacrimation, rhinorrhea, yawning, sweating, restlessness, dilated pupils, anorexia, gooseflesh, irritability, and tremor. In more severe forms, nausea, vomiting, intestinal spasm and diarrhea, increased heart rate and blood pressure, chills, and pains in bones and muscles of the back and extremities may occur. Peak effects will usually be apparent at 48 to 72 hours.

Treatment of withdrawal is usually managed by providing sufficient quantities of an opioid to suppress severe withdrawal symptoms and then gradually reducing the dose of opioid over a period of several days.

Overdose: Symptoms: Respiratory depression (a decrease in respiratory rate and/or tidal volume, Cheyne-Stokes respiration, cyanosis), extreme somnolence progressing to stupor or coma, skeletal muscle flaccidity, cold, clammy skin, and sometimes bradycardia and hypotension. In severe overdosage, apnea, circulatory collapse, cardiac arrest and death may occur.

Treatment: Give primary attention to the re-establishment of adequate respiratory exchange by providing a patent airway and instituting assisted or controlled ventilation. The narcotic antagonist naloxone HCl is a specific antidote against respiratory depression which may result from overdosage or unusual sensitivity to narcotics, including hydrocodone. Administer an appropriate dose of naloxone, preferably by the i.v. route, simultaneously with efforts at respiratory resuscitation. Since the duration of action of hydrocodone may exceed that of the antagonist, keep the patient under continued surveillance and administer repeated doses of the antagonist as needed to maintain adequate respiration. Observe carefully the manufacturer's package insert instructions. Employ oxygen, i.v. fluids, vasopressors, and other supportive measures as indicated.

Gastric emptying may be useful in removing unabsorbed drug. Activated charcoal may be of benefit.

Dosage: Adults: 5 mg (1 tablet or 5 mL) not less than 4 hours apart, after meals and at bedtime with food or a glass of milk, not to exceed 30 mg (6 tablets or 30 mL) in a 24-hour period. Maximum single dose 15 mg (3 tablets or 15 mL).

Children over 12 yrs: 5 mg (1 tablet or 5 mL) not less than 4 hours apart, after meals and at bedtime with food or a glass of milk, not to exceed 30 mg (6 tablets or 30 mL) in a 24-hour period. Maximum single dose 10 mg (2 tablets or 10 mL).

Age 2 to 12 yrs: 2.5 mg (one half tablet or 2.5 mL) not less than 4 hours apart, after meals and at bedtime with food or a glass of milk, not to exceed a total of 15 mg (3 tablets or 15 mL) in a 24-hour period. Maximum single dose 5 mg (1 tablet or 5 mL).

Age less than 2 yrs: 1.25 mg (one quarter tablet or 1.25 mL) not less than 4 hours apart, after meals and at bedtime with food or a glass of milk, not to exceed a total of 7.5 mg (1.5 tablets or 7.5 mL) in a 24-hour period. Maximum single dose 1.25 mg (one quarter tablet or 1.25 mL).

Supplied: Syrup: Each 5 mL of red, wild-cherry-flavored syrup contains: hydrocodone bitartrate 5 mg. Nonmedicinal ingredients: artificial cherry flavor, caramel syrup, FD&C RED No. 2, hydrochloric acid, methylparaben, propylparaben, purified water, sorbitol solution 70% and sucrose. Alcohol-, lactose-, sodium-, sulfite- and tartrazine-free. Bottles of 100 and 500 mL.

Tablets: Each white, scored tablet contains: hydrocodone bitartrate 5 mg. Nonmedicinal ingredients: cornstarch, lactose, pregelatinized tapioca starch, stearic acid, talc and zinc stearate. Sodium- and tartrazine-free. Bottles of 100.

Store at room temperature (15 to 30°C) in a tightly closed container. Protect from light. Dispense syrup in a tight, light resistant container.

(Shown in Product Recognition Section)

HYCOMINE® Ⓝ
HYCOMINE®-S Ⓝ

DuPont Pharma

Hydrocodone Compound

Antitussive—Antihistaminic—Decongestant

Pharmacology: See Hycodan for pharmacology of hydrocodone.

Pyrilamine maleate is a competitive H_1-receptor histamine-blocking drug, thereby counteracting the effects of histamine release associated with allergic manifestations of upper respiratory tract inflammatory disorders. H_1-blocking drugs inhibit the actions of histamine on smooth muscle, capillary permeability, and can both stimulate and depress the CNS.

Phenylephrine HCl effects its vasoconstrictor activity by releasing norepinephrine from sympathetic nerve endings, and from direct stimulation of α-adreno-receptors in blood vessels.

Ammonium chloride exerts an expectorant effect by virtue of a local action on the gastric mucosa.

Indications: To control cough, and to provide symptomatic relief of congestion in the upper respiratory tract due to the common cold, nasopharyngitis, tracheitis, and bronchitis, which do not respond to products of lesser potency.

Contraindications: Hypersensitivity to any of the components. Patients known to be hypersensitive to other opioids, antihistamines or sympathomimetic amines may exhibit cross-sensitivity to hydrocodone, pyrilamine or phenylephrine. Do not use in patients using monoamine oxidase inhibitors. Hydrocodone is contraindicated in the presence of an intracranial lesion associated with increased intracranial pressure, and whenever ventilatory function is depressed.

Phenylephrine is contraindicated in patients with heart disease, hypertension, diabetes or hyperthyroidism.

Warnings: See Hycodan.

Hypersensitive crises can occur with concurrent use of phenylephrine and MAO inhibitors, indomethacin or with beta-blockers and methyldopa. If a hypertensive crisis occurs, discontinue these drugs immediately and institute therapy to lower blood pressure. Manage fever by external cooling.

Pyrilamine may produce drowsiness or excitation, particularly in children and elderly patients.

Precautions: Before prescribing medication to suppress or modify cough, it is important to ascertain that the underlying cause of cough is identified, that modification of cough does not increase the risk of physiological complications, and that appropriate therapy for the primary disease is provided.

In young children the respiratory centre is especially susceptible to the depressant action of narcotic cough suppressants. Benefit-to-risk ratio should be carefully considered, especially in children with respiratory embarrassment, e.g., croup. Estimation of dosage relative to the child's age and weight is of great importance.

As hydrocodone may inhibit peristalsis, patients with chronic constipation should be given these preparations only after weighing the potential therapeutic benefit against the hazards involved.

In patients with asthma or pulmonary emphysema, indiscriminate use may precipitate respiratory insufficiency resulting from increased viscosity of bronchial secretions and suppression of the cough reflex.

Use with caution in sedated or debilitated patients, in patients who have undergone thoracotomies or laparotomies, since suppression of the cough reflex may lead to retention of secretions postoperatively in these patients.

Use with caution in glaucoma, prostatic hypertrophy, urinary retention, and in the aged.

The CNS-depressant effect of hydrocodone may be additive with that of other CNS depressants (see Warnings).

Hycomine (cont'd)

Carcinogenicity, mutagenicity and reproduction studies have not been conducted.

Pregnancy: Animal reproduction studies have not been conducted. It is also not known whether Hycomine syrup or Hycomine-S pediatric syrup can cause fetal harm when administered to a pregnant woman or can affect reproductive capacity. Since hydrocodone crosses the placental barrier, give the hydrocodone formulations to pregnant women only if clearly needed.

Babies born to mothers who have been taking opioids regularly prior to delivery will be physically dependent. The withdrawal signs include: irritability and excessive crying, tremors, hyperactive reflexes, increased respiratory rate, increased stools, sneezing, yawning, vomiting and fever. The intensity of the syndrome does not always correlate with the duration of maternal opioids use or dose. There is no consensus on the best method of managing withdrawal. Chlorpromazine (0.7 to 1.0 mg/kg q6h), phenobarbital (2 mg/kg q6h), and paregoric (2 to 4 drops/kg q4h), have been used to treat withdrawal symptoms in infants. The duration of therapy is 4 to 28 days, with the dosages decreased as tolerated.

Lactation: It is not known whether hydrocodone is excreted in human milk. Because many drugs are excreted in human milk and because of the potential for serious adverse reactions in nursing infants from Hycomine syrup, a decision should be made whether to discontinue nursing or discontinue the drug, taking into account the importance of the drug to the mother. Only Hycomine-S pediatric syrup is recommended for pediatric use.

Drug Interactions: The CNS-depressant effect of Hycomine syrup and Hycomine-S pediatric syrup may be additive with that of other CNS depressants (see Warnings).

Adverse Effects: See Hycodan.

Overdose: Symptoms: The signs and symptoms of overdosage of the individual components of Hycomine syrup or Hycomine-S pediatric syrup may be modified in varying degrees by the presence of other active ingredients.

Serious overdosage with hydrocodone may be characterized by: respiratory depression (a decrease in respiratory rate and/or tidal volume, Cheyne-Stokes respiration, cyanosis), extreme somnolence progressing to stupor or coma, skeletal muscle flaccidity, cold and clammy skin, and sometimes bradycardia and hypotension. In severe overdosage, apnea, circulatory collapse, cardiac arrest, and death may occur.

Treatment: Give primary attention to re-establishing adequate respiratory exchange by providing a patent airway and instituting assisted or controlled ventilation. The narcotic antagonist naloxone is a specific antidote against respiratory depression which may result from overdosage or unusual sensitivity to narcotics, including hydrocodone. Administer an appropriate dose of naloxone, preferably by the i.v. route, simultaneously with efforts at respiratory resuscitation. Since the duration of action of hydrocodone hydrochloride may exceed that of the antagonist, keep the patient under continued surveillance and repeat doses of the antagonist as needed to maintain adequate respiration. Observe carefully the manufacturer's package insert instructions.

Employ oxygen, i.v. fluids, vasopressors, and other supportive measures as indicated.

Gastric emptying may be useful in removing unabsorbed drug. Activated charcoal may be of benefit.

Dosage: Hycomine: Adults, 5 mL after meals and at bedtime with food or a glass of milk at intervals of not less than 4 hours not to exceed 30 mL in a 24-hour period. Maximum single dose 15 mL.

Hycomine-S: Children over 12 years: 10 mL after meals and at bedtime with food or a glass of milk at intervals of not less than 4 hours, not to exceed a total of 60 mL in a 24-hour period. Maximum single dose 20 mL.

Children 6 to 12 years: 5 mL after meals and at bedtime with food or a glass of milk at intervals of not less than 4 hours: not to exceed a total of 30 mL in a 24-hour period. Maximum single dose 10 mL.

Children 3 to 6 years: 2.5 mL after meals and at bedtime with food or a glass of milk, at intervals of not less than 4 hours, not to exceed a total of 15 mL in a 24-hour period. Maximum single dose 5 mL.

Children less than 2 years: According to weight on the basis of 300 μg (0.3 mg) hydrocodone bitartrate/kg body weight/day, divided into 4 equal doses taken after meals and at bedtime.

Supplied: Hycomine: Each 5 mL of orange, cherry-flavored syrup contains: hydrocodone bitartrate 5 mg, pyrilamine maleate 12.5 mg, phenylephrine HCl 10 mg and ammonium chloride 60 mg. Nonmedicinal ingredients: casiline orange, cherry flavor, hydrochloric acid, methylparaben, propylparaben, purified water, sorbitol solution and sucrose. Alcohol-, lactose-, sodium-, sulfite- and tartrazine-free. Bottles of 100 and 500 mL.

Hycomine-S: Each 5 mL of green, cherry-flavored pediatric syrup contains: hydrocodone bitartrate 2.5 mg, pyrilamine maleate 6.25 mg, phenylephrine HCl 5 mg and ammonium chloride 30 mg. Nonmedicinal ingredients: cherry flavor, hydrochloric acid, methylparaben, minoline green, propylparaben, purified water, sorbitol solution and sucrose. Alcohol-, lactose-, sodium-, sulfite- and tartrazine-free. Bottles of 100 and 500 mL.

Store at room temperature (15 to 30°C) in a tightly closed container. Protect from light.

(Shown in Product Recognition Section)

HYCORT™ Ⓟ

ICN

Hydrocortisone

Glucocorticoid

Supplied: Each retention enema contains: hydrocortisone, USP 100 mg. Nonmedicinal ingredients: carboxypolymethylene carbomer, methylparaben, polysorbate 80 and sodium hydroxide. Bottles of 60 mL. Store away from heat and direct light. Keep from freezing.

HYDERGINE® Ⓟ

Novartis Pharmaceuticals

Ergoloid Mesylates

Adjunctive Management of Idiopathic Dementia

Pharmacology: The possible mechanism of action of ergoloid mesylates has not been determined. There is no evidence that ergoloid mesylates affect cerebrovascular insufficiency or cerebral arteriosclerosis.

Ergoloid mesylates do not have the vasoconstrictor effects of the natural ergot alkaloids.

Indications: May be of some value in the adjunctive management of selective symptoms of elderly patients with cognitive decline and a moderate impairment of self care, when used as part of a comprehensive therapeutic program, including medical and psychosocial support.

Clinical trials with Hydergine have described a modest improvement in symptoms that reflect on the level of self care in some of these patients.

Contraindications: Hypersensitivity to the drug, severe bradycardia, and severe hypotension. It is also contraindicated in patients who have acute or chronic psychosis regardless of its etiology.

Warnings: Before using ergoloid mesylates, a careful diagnosis should be made to exclude treatable causes of dementia, including affective disorders, which may respond to specific therapy. Particular care should be taken to exclude delirium and dementiform illness secondary to systemic disease, primary neurological disease, or primary disturbance of mood.

Hydergine is not indicated in aged individuals with normal cognitive function.

Precautions: Hydergine should be kept out of the reach of children.

Adverse Effects: Nausea and vomiting, headaches, dizziness, flushing, blurring of vision, rash, anorexia, nasal stuffiness, abdominal cramps, bradycardia and tachycardia have been noted.

Overdose: Symptoms: The symptoms of overdosage with Hydergine are nasal stuffiness, flushing of the face, headache, nausea and vomiting, tremulousness, spasticity, hypotension, circulatory collapse and coma.

Treatment: Symptomatic and supportive. Empty the stomach by emesis or lavage depending upon the level of consciousness of the patient, ensuring maintenance of an adequate airway. I.V. fluids should be administered with careful supervision of intake and output, but there is no evidence that forced diuresis accelerates the elimination of the drug. Circulatory collapse should be prevented by appropriate positioning of the patient, fluids and, if necessary, vasopressor agents.

Dosage: 1 tablet 3 to 4 times daily with food.

Since alleviation of symptoms is usually gradual, improvement may not be observed before several weeks. If no clinical improvement is seen at 3 to 4 weeks it is advisable to discontinue the drug. Full expression of the beneficial effects of Hydergine may take several weeks. In patients who have responded with clinical improvement, it is advisable to discontinue the drug from time to time, in order to assess the need for its continued administration.

Supplied: Each round, white, compressed, 8 mm diameter, flat, beveled tablet, scored with "VJ" on one side and "SANDOZ" insignia on the other contains: ergoloid mesylates 1 mg. Nonmedicinal ingredients: alcohol anhydrous, cornstarch, lactose anhydrous, povidone, purified water, stearic acid and talc. Bottles of 100.

(Shown in Product Recognition Section)

HYDERM

Taro

Hydrocortisone Acetate

Topical Corticosteroid

Supplied: Each g contains: hydrocortisone acetate 1% Ⓟ or 0.5% in a water-washable cream base of cetostearyl alcohol, purified water, propylene glycol, sodium lauryl sulfate and white petrolatum. Paraben-free. Tubes of 15 g and jars of 500 g.

HYDRASENSE® NASAL CARE

Schering

Sea Water

Nasal Cleanser

Indications: Cleanses and relieves excessive mucus accumulation by clearing nasal cavities congested by colds, allergies, sinusitis and rhinitis. It is a simple and effective solution to relieve dry nasal conditions commonly associated with heating or air conditioning systems in homes or airplanes.

Precautions: Safe for infants, Hydrasense Baby Mist can be used with confidence without fear of harming delicate, sensitive nasal tissues when used as directed. Hydrasense Gentle Mist or Medium Stream can be used safely and with confidence by children (age 2 and over) and adults. Hydrasense Full Stream can be used by all adults. No rebound congestion and no side effects have been reported.

Dosage: Baby Mist: Remove the protective cap and insert nasal applicator into the top of the bottle. The patented applicator has been specially designed to fit comfortably into nostrils. Lay baby on his/her back with head turned towards the right. Insert into baby's left nostril and press down gently on applicator. Follow the same procedure for the right nostril, turning baby's head to the left.

Gentle Mist, Medium Stream and Full Stream: Remove the protective cap and insert nasal applicator into the top of the bottle. The patented applicator has been specially designed to fit comfortably into nostrils. Bend the head forward slightly over the sink, tilting horizontally towards the left. Insert into right nostril and press down gently on applicator. Let the water flow through nasal passages to cleanse, lubricate and remove impurities. Tilt head horizontally towards the right and repeat procedure in the left nostril.

Remove and wash the nasal applicator after use and replace the protective cap. Repeat the procedure as often as required during the day. Recommended use: 4 daily applications.

Supplied: Each mL contains: isotonic, sterile, desalinated, 100% natural-source sea water. Nondiluted and ozone friendly. Contains no preservatives or propellant gases. Hypoallergenic. Hydrasense Nasal Care is extracted from the mineral-rich ocean tides off the shores of Saint-Malo, France. Bottles of 135 mL with 4 different jet applicators using SteriFlo dispensing system: Baby Mist, Gentle Mist, Medium Stream and Full Stream.

New Product 1998

HYDREA®

Squibb

Hydroxyurea

Antineoplastic Agent

Pharmacology: Neoplastic Disease: The precise mechanism by which hydroxyurea produces its antineoplastic effects cannot, at present, be described. However, the reports of various studies in rat and human tissue cultures lend support to the hypothesis that hydroxyurea causes an immediate inhibition of DNA synthesis, by acting as a ribonucleotide reductase inhibitor, without interfering with the synthesis of ribonucleic acid or of protein. Hydroxyurea probably acts by decreasing the rate of conversion of ribonucleotides and deoxyribonucleotides. This effect is particularly apparent in cells with a high rate of proliferation.

Potentiation of Irradiation Therapy: Three mechanisms have been postulated for the potentiation of the therapeutic effects of irradiation by hydroxyurea on squamous cell (epidermoid) carcinomas of the head and neck. In vitro studies utilizing Chinese hamster cells suggest that hydroxyurea is lethal to normally radioresistant S-stage cells and holds other cells of the cell cycle in the G1 or pre-DNA synthesis stage where they are most susceptible to the effects of irradiation. The third mechanism of action has been theorized on the basis of in vitro studies of HeLa cells: it appears that hydroxyurea, by inhibition of DNA synthesis, hinders the normal repair process of cells damaged but not killed by irradiation, thereby decreasing their survival rate; there is no alteration of RNA and protein syntheses.

Pharmacokinetics: After oral administration in humans, hydroxyurea is readily absorbed from the gastrointestinal tract. The drug reaches peak serum concentrations within 2 hours; by 24 hours the concentration in the serum is essentially undetectable. Approximately 80% of an oral or i.v. dose of 7 to 30 mg/kg may be recovered in the urine within 12 hours. Hydroxyurea crosses the blood-brain barrier.

Indications: For concomitant use with irradiation therapy in the treatment of primary squamous cell (epidermoid) carcinomas of the head and neck, excluding the lip.

Tumor responses to hydroxyurea have been reported in melanoma and resistant chronic myelocytic leukemia.

Contraindications: In patients with marked bone marrow depression, i.e., leukopenia (<2 500 WBC/mm³) or thrombocytopenia (<100 000/mm³), or severe anemia.

Warnings: Hydroxyurea should be administered under the supervision of a physician experienced in the use of cancer chemotherapeutic agents.

Treatment with hydroxyurea should not be initiated if bone marrow function is depressed (see Contraindications). Hydroxyurea may produce bone marrow suppression; leukopenia is generally its first and most common manifestation. Thrombocytopenia and anemia occur less often and are seldom seen without a preceding leukopenia. The recovery from myelosuppression is rapid when hydroxyurea therapy is interrupted. Bone marrow depression is more likely in patients who have previously received radiotherapy or cytotoxic cancer chemotherapeutic agents; hydroxyurea should be used cautiously in such patients.

Patients who have received irradiation therapy in the past may have an exacerbation of post-irradiation erythema when hydroxyurea is given.

Severe anemia must be corrected before initiating therapy with hydroxyurea.

Erythrocytic Abnormalities: Megaloblastic erythropoiesis, which is self-limiting, is often seen early in the course of hydroxyurea therapy. The morphologic change resembles that seen in pernicious anemia, but is not related to vitamin B_{12} or folic acid deficiency. Hydroxyurea may also delay plasma iron clearance and reduce the rate of iron utilization by erythrocytes, but it does not appear to alter the red blood cell survival time.

Hydroxyurea should be used with caution in patients with marked renal dysfunction.

Geriatrics: Elderly patients may be more sensitive to the effects of hydroxyurea and may require a lower dose regimen.

In patients receiving long-term therapy with hydroxyurea for myeloproliferative disorders, such as polycythemia vera and thrombocytopenia, secondary leukemia has been reported. It is unknown whether this leukemogenic effect is secondary to hydroxyurea or is associated with the patients' underlying disease.

Pregnancy: Hydroxyurea is a known teratogen in animals. Malformations have been observed in the offspring of rabbits given doses equivalent to that of the maximum human dose, and in rats given doses equivalent to 3 times the maximum human dose. There are no adequate and well-controlled studies in pregnant women. If hydroxyurea is used during pregnancy or if the patient becomes pregnant while on hydroxyurea therapy, the patient should be apprised of the potential hazard to the fetus. Women of childbearing potential should be advised to avoid becoming pregnant.

Hydroxyurea should not be used to treat males contemplating conception.

Precautions: General: Secondary leukemia has been reported in patients receiving long-term hydroxyurea for myeloproliferative disorders (see Warnings).

Carcinogenesis, Mutagenesis, Impairment of Fertility: No long-term animal studies have been performed to evaluate carcinogenic potential. Drugs which affect DNA synthesis, such as hydroxyurea, may be potentially mutagenic, and this possibility should be considered before administering the drug to male or female patients who may contemplate conception. In rats, hydroxyurea at high dosage levels produced aspermatogenesis. In dogs, reversible spermatogenic arrest was noted at high dose levels.

Children: Safety and effectiveness in children have not been established.

Pregnancy: Hydroxyurea is a known teratogen in animals. Malformations have been observed in the offspring of rabbits given doses equivalent to that of the maximum human dose, and in rats given doses equivalent to 3 times that of the maximum human dose. There are no adequate and well-controlled studies in pregnant women. If hydroxyurea is used during pregnancy or if the patient becomes pregnant while on hydroxyurea therapy, the patient should be apprised of the potential hazard to the fetus. Women of childbearing potential should be advised to avoid becoming pregnant.

Lactation: Hydroxyurea is excreted in human milk. Because of the potential for serious adverse reactions in nursing infants from hydroxyurea, breast-feeding should be discontinued.

Drug Interactions: Concurrent use of hydroxyurea and other myelosuppressive agents or radiation therapy may increase the likelihood of bone marrow depression or other adverse events (see Warnings and Adverse Effects).

Since hydroxyurea may raise the serum uric acid level, dosage adjustment of uricosuric medication may be necessary.

In vitro studies have shown a significant increase in cytarabine cytotoxic activity in hydroxyurea-treated cells. Whether this interaction will lead to synergistic toxicity in the clinical setting or the need to modify cytarabine doses has not been established.

Occupational Hazards: The effect of hydroxyurea on driving and operating machinery has not been studied. Since hydroxyurea may cause drowsiness and other neurologic effects (see Adverse Effects, Neurologic), alertness may be impaired.

Information for the Patient: Patients should be informed to maintain adequate fluid intake. The physician should be consulted regarding missed doses.

Adverse Effects: Hematologic: bone marrow depression (leukopenia, anemia, and occasionally thrombocytopenia) (see Warnings).

Gastrointestinal: Stomatitis, anorexia, nausea, vomiting, diarrhea, and constipation.

Dermatologic: Maculopapular rash, facial erythema, peripheral erythema, and skin ulceration. Alopecia occurs rarely. Hyperpigmentation, erythema, atrophy of skin and nails, scaling, violet papules, and alopecia have been observed in some patients after several years of long-term daily maintenance therapy with hydroxyurea. Skin cancer has also been reported rarely.

Neurologic: Drowsiness, rare instances of headache, dizziness, disorientation, hallucinations, and convulsions. Their relationship to hydroxyurea administration is questionable because cerebral metastatic disease was not excluded.

Renal: Elevated serum uric acid, BUN, and creatinine levels; rare instances of dysuria. Abnormal BSP retention has been reported.

Other: Fever, chills, malaise, asthenia, and elevation of hepatic enzymes; rare instances of acute pulmonary reactions (diffuse pulmonary infiltrates/fibrosis, and dyspnea).

Combined Hydroxyurea and Irradiation Therapy: Adverse reactions observed with combined hydroxyurea and irradiation therapy were similar to those reported with the use of hydroxyurea alone, primarily bone marrow depression (leukopenia and anemia), and gastric irritation. Nearly all patients receiving an adequate course of combined hydroxyurea and irradiation therapy will develop leukopenia. Decreased platelet counts (<100 000 cells/mm³) have occurred rarely and usually in the presence of marked leukopenia. Hydroxyurea may potentiate some adverse reactions usually seen with irradiation alone, such as gastric distress and mucositis.

Overdose: Symptoms and Treatment: Acute mucocutaneous toxicity has been reported in patients receiving hydroxyurea at a dosage several times the therapeutic dose. Soreness, violet erythema, edema on palms and foot soles followed by scaling of hands and feet, severe generalized hyperpigmentation of skin, and stomatitis have also been observed.

Dosage: Because of the rarity of carcinomas of the head and neck in children, dosage regimens have not been established.

Dosage regimens in the treatment of the neoplastic diseases should be based on the patient's actual or ideal weight, whichever is less.

Dosage Adjustment: Concurrent use of hydroxyurea with other myelosuppressive agents may require adjustments of dosages.

Solid Tumors: Intermittent Therapy: 80 mg/kg administered orally as a **single** dose every **third** day.

This intermittent dosage schedule may offer the advantage over daily therapy of reduced toxicity (e.g., bone marrow depression).

Concomitant Therapy with Irradiation (Carcinoma of the head and neck): 80 mg/kg administered orally as a **single** dose every **third** day.

Administration of hydroxyurea should be started at least 7 days before initiation of irradiation, and continued during radiotherapy and continue indefinitely thereafter, provided the patient is kept under adequate observation and exhibits no unusual or severe toxicity.

Resistant Chronic Myelocytic Leukemia: 20 to 30 mg/kg administered orally as a single daily dose.

An adequate trial period for determining the effectiveness of hydroxyurea is 6 weeks. When there is regression in tumor size or arrest in tumor growth, therapy should be continued indefinitely. Therapy should be interrupted if the white blood cell count drops below 2 500/mm³, or the platelet count below 100 000/mm³. In these cases, the counts should be re-evaluated after 3 days, and therapy resumed when the counts return to acceptable levels. Hematopoietic rebound is usually rapid. If rapid rebound has not occurred during combined hydroxyurea and irradiation therapy, irradiation may also be interrupted. Anemia, even if severe can be managed without interrupting hydroxyurea therapy.

Hydroxyurea should be administered cautiously to patients who have recently received extensive radiation therapy or chemotherapy with other cytotoxic drugs.

Pain or discomfort from inflammation of the mucous membranes at the irradiated site (mucositis) is usually controlled by measures such as topical anesthetics and orally administered analgesics. If the reaction is severe, hydroxyurea therapy may be temporarily interrupted; if it is extremely severe, irradiation dosage may, in addition, be temporarily postponed.

Severe gastric distress, such as nausea, vomiting, and anorexia, resulting from combined therapy may usually be controlled by temporary interruption of hydroxyurea administration.

Instructions for Handling: If the patient prefers, or is unable to swallow capsules, the contents of the capsules may be emptied into a glass of water and taken immediately (see Precautions, Information for Patients). Some inert material used as a vehicle in the capsule may not dissolve, and float on the surface.

Patients who take the drug by emptying the contents of the capsule into water should be reminded that this is a potent medication that must be handled with care. Patients must be cautioned not to allow the powder to come in contact with the skin and mucous membranes, including avoidance of inhaling the powder when opening the capsules. If the powder is spilled, it should be immediately wiped up with a damp towel and disposed of, as should the empty capsules. The medication, particularly the open capsules, should be kept away from children and pets.

Procedures for proper handling and disposal of anticancer drugs should be considered. Several guidelines on this subject have been published. There is no general agreement that all of the procedures recommended in the guidelines are necessary or appropriate.

Supplied: Each capsule contains: hydroxyurea 500 mg. Nonmedicinal ingredients: citric acid, dibasic sodium phosphate, lactose and magnesium stearate; capsule shell: FD&C blue No. 2 and red No. 3, gelatin, sodium lauryl sulfate, titanium dioxide and yellow iron oxide. Bottles of 100. Store at room temperature. Protect from excessive heat and moisture.

(Shown in Product Recognition Section)

Reviewed 1999

HYDROCHLOROTHIAZIDE Ⓟ

General Monograph, CPhA

Diuretic—Antihypertensive

This monograph has been compiled by CPhA. It may contain information different from that approved by Therapeutic Products Programme, Health Canada, and the pharmaceutical manufacturers' approval has not been requested.

Pharmacology: Hydrochlorothiazide inhibits reabsorption of sodium and chloride in the distal tubule thus promoting water loss. The higher urine volume increases potassium loss; this loss can often be decreased by restricting sodium intake. Oral doses are well absorbed and reach peak effect in about 4 hours, with a 6 to 12 hour duration. It is excreted unchanged in the urine with a half-life of 3 to 5 hours.

The mild blood pressure reducing effects are initially due to volume reduction but the persisting effect includes other undetermined mechanisms that reduce peripheral resistance. A high salt intake reverses its antihypertensive effect.

Indications: Adjunctive therapy in edema associated with congestive heart failure, hepatic cirrhosis with ascites, in drug induced edema (corticosteroid and estrogen therapy) and in edema of renal origin (i.e., nephrotic syndrome, acute glomerulonephritis, chronic renal disease).

In the management of hypertension, hydrochlorothiazide may be used alone or as an adjunct to other antihypertensive drugs. Since it enhances the action of these agents, the dosage of either or both agents must be reduced to avoid an excessive drop in blood pressure.

Contraindications: Anuria; discontinue if increasing azotemia and oliguria occur during treatment of severe progressive renal disease. Do not use in patients known to be sensitive to thiazides or other sulfonamide derived drugs.

Precautions: May precipitate or increase azotemia; cumulative effects may develop in presence of impaired renal function; discontinue if increasing azotemia and oliguria occur during treatment of severe progressive renal disease. Use with caution in impaired hepatic function or progressive liver disease since minor alterations of fluid and electrolyte balance or of serum ammonia may precipitate hepatic coma.

The possibility of sensitivity reactions should be considered in patients with or without a history of allergy or bronchial asthma.

The possibility that hydrochlorothiazide may exacerbation or activate systemic lupus erythematosus has been reported.

Patients should be carefully monitored for signs of fluid and electrolyte imbalance, namely hyponatremia, hypochloremic alkalosis and hypokalemia. Hypomagnesemia may also occur. Serum and urine electrolyte determinations are particularly important when the patient has other disorders that predispose to fluid and electrolyte imbalance such as vomiting, diarrhea, heart failure, liver or renal disease, is on a salt-restricted diet, or is receiving parenteral fluids. The elderly may be at greater risk for developing electrolyte abnormalities, including hypomagnesemia, due to age-related changes in renal function. Warning signs of fluid and electrolyte imbalance include: dry mouth, thirst, weakness, lethargy, drowsiness, restlessness, muscle pains or cramps, muscular fatigue, hypotension, oliguria, tachycardia, and gastrointestinal disturbances (nausea, vomiting), seizures or confusion.

Hypokalemia may be prevented or treated with potassium-rich foods, a potassium-sparing diuretic or potassium supplements.

Dilutional hyponatremia most commonly occurs during hot weather in patients with chronic congestive heart failure or hepatic disease. It may also be aggravated during chronic thiazide therapy. Treatment includes withdrawal of the diuretic, fluid restriction, and potassium and/or magnesium supplementation. Administration of sodium chloride is usually not required except in rare instances when the hyponatremia is life-threatening.

Although any chloride deficit is generally mild and usually does not require specific treatment except under extraordinary circumstances (as in liver disease or renal disease), chloride replacement may be required in the treatment of metabolic or hypochloremic alkalosis.

Because thiazides decrease calciuresis and increase serum calcium levels, use of thiazides may unmask subclinical hyperparathyroidism with hypercalcemia and hypophosphatemia. The common complications of hyperparathyroidism such as renal lithiasis, bone resorption, and peptic ulceration have not been reported. Thiazides should be discontinued before carrying out parathyroid function tests.

Caution is necessary in patients with hyperuricemia or a history of gout.

Low doses of thiazides for treatment of hypertension usually do not cause alterations in lipid levels; however, thiazides are not recommended in patients with severe hyperlipidemia which requires drug therapy.

The antihypertensive effect of the drug may be enhanced in the post sympathectomy patient.

Drug Interactions: Hypokalemia may develop (especially with brisk diuresis) in severe cirrhosis; with concomitant steroid or ACTH therapy; or with inadequate electrolyte intake. Principally hypokalemia, but also hypomagnesemia and hypercalcemia, can sensitize or exaggerate the response of the heart to toxic effects of digitalis.

Thiazides may cause prolonged neuromuscular blockade in patients receiving nondepolarizing neuromuscular blocking agents (e.g., tubocurarine).

The hyperglycemic effect of hydrochlorothiazide may exacerbate diabetes mellitus resulting in increased dosage requirements of insulin or sulfonylureas and may worsen glycemic control in some patients. This effect may occur after several days to many months of thiazide therapy.

Hydrochlorothiazide may add to or potentiate the action of other antihypertensive drugs, and decrease responsiveness to norepinephrine.

Hydrochlorothiazide may enhance the cardiotoxic (e.g., ECG changes) and neurotoxic (e.g., ataxia, confusion and mental disorientation) effects of lithium. If possible, an alternative agent should be used. In those rare instances when these drugs must be given together, dosage should be reduced, and patients should be observed closely for signs and symptoms of lithium toxicity. Close monitoring of serum electrolytes and lithium concentrations and maintenance of adequate fluid, potassium and sodium intake also are recommended.

NSAIDs: Concomitant use may increase the risk of renal failure and reverse the antihypertensive effect. This combination should be avoided if possible. If these drugs must be given together, close monitoring of serum creatinine, potassium concentrations and patient's weight is recommended.

Pregnancy: The routine use of thiazide diuretics in an otherwise healthy pregnant woman with or without edema is not appropriate. Edema in pregnancy, resulting from restriction of venous return by the expanded uterus, is treated through elevation of the lower extremities and use of support hose. A short course of diuretics may be appropriate in patients with severe hypervolemia not relieved by rest or these measures. Pathological edema such as cardiac, nephrotic or hepatic edema may be an indication for use of thiazide diuretics. Thiazides do not prevent toxemia of pregnancy, nor are they useful in its treatment.

Thiazides cross the placental barrier. Possible risks include fetal or neonatal jaundice, thrombocytopenia, and possibly other adverse reactions that have occurred in the adult.

Lactation: Thiazides are excreted into the milk of nursing women, although apparently not in significant amounts. The potential for idiosyncratic or allergic reactions in the infant should be considered. It should be noted that thiazides may partially suppress lactation.

Adverse Effects: Cardiovascular: Orthostatic hypotension may occur, especially in elderly patients with reduced plasma volume and may be potentiated by alcohol, barbiturates or narcotics.

CNS: dizziness, vertigo, paresthesias, headache, xanthopsia.

Gastrointestinal: anorexia, gastric irritation, nausea, vomiting, cramping, diarrhea, constipation, jaundice (intrahepatic cholestatic), pancreatitis, sialadenitis.

Hematologic: leukopenia, thrombocytopenia, agranulocytosis, aplastic anemia, hemolytic anemia.

Hypersensitivity: purpura, photosensitivity, rash, urticaria, necrotizing angiitis, fever, respiratory distress including pneumonitis, anaphylactic reactions.

Miscellaneous: muscle spasm, weakness, restlessness, hyperglycemia, glycosuria, transient hyperlipidemia, hyperuricemia, transient blurred vision.

Whenever adverse reactions are moderate or severe, thiazide dosage should be reduced or therapy withdrawn.

Overdose: Symptoms: Overdosage may lead to excessive diuresis with electrolyte depletion (hypokalemia, hypochloremia, hyponatremia) and dehydration. If digitalis has also been administered, hypokalemia may accentuate myocardial abnormalities (e.g., cardiac arrhythmias).

Signs are dry mouth, thirst, weakness, lethargy, drowsiness, restlessness, muscle pains or cramps, muscular fatigue, hypotension, oliguria, tachycardia, gastrointestinal disturbances, mental confusion, delirium, convulsions, shock, coma.

Treatment: There is no specific antidote. If ingestion is recent, gastric lavage or emesis may reduce absorption; activated charcoal may be given. Otherwise, management includes symptomatic treatment with special attention to cardiac rate and output, blood volume, electrolyte balance, dehydration, paralytic ileus, urinary function, hepatic coma, and cerebral activity. Administration of sympathomimetic drugs (e.g., dopamine) may be indicated. Administer oxygen or artificial respiration for respiratory impairment.

Dosage: Diuresis: the usual adult dose is 25 to 100 mg per day, depending on patient response. Some patients may respond to intermittent therapy (alternate days or 3 to 5 days per week). The usual oral dosage for children is 2 mg/kg per day, given in 2 divided doses. Infants under 6 months of age may require up to 3 mg/kg per day, in 2 divided doses.

Hypertension: Doses as low as 12.5 mg daily may be effective, especially in the elderly. Some clinicians advocate the use of 6.25 mg as a starting dose. Usual adult dose is 25 to 50 mg daily, adjusted as necessary every 2 to 4 weeks. Doses above this level may offer only a limited increase in effectiveness while increasing the severity of side effects. In hypertension associated with volume overload in renal failure, more potent agents such as loop diuretics may be required.

Reviewed 1997

HYDROCODONE Ⓝ

General Monograph, CPhA

see OPIOID ANALGESICS

HYDROCORTISONE Ⓟ

General Monograph, CPhA

see CORTICOSTEROIDS: EYE EAR NOSE
see CORTICOSTEROIDS: SYSTEMIC
see CORTICOSTEROIDS: TOPICAL

HydroDIURIL® Ⓟ

MSD

Hydrochlorothiazide

Diuretic—Antihypertensive

Pharmacology: Hydrochlorothiazide is a diuretic and antihypertensive. Hydrochlorothiazide interferes with the renal tubular mechanism of electrolyte reabsorption. It increases excretion of sodium and chloride in approximately equivalent amounts. Natriuresis may be accompanied by some loss of potassium, magnesium and bicarbonate. Urinary calcium excretion may be decreased. While this compound is predominantly a saluretic agent, in vitro studies have shown that it has a carbonic anhydrase inhibitory action which seems to be relatively specific for the renal tubular mechanism. It does not appear to be concentrated in erythrocytes or the brain in sufficient amounts to influence the activity of carbonic anhydrase in those tissues.

Hydrochlorothiazide is useful in the treatment of hypertension. It may be used alone or as an adjunct to other antihypertensive drugs. Hydrochlorothiazide does not usually affect normal blood pressure. The mechanism of its antihypertensive action is not known.

Indications: Edema associated with congestive heart failure, hepatic cirrhosis, in drug-induced edema (corticosteroid and estrogen therapy), nephrotic syndrome, acute glomerulonephritis, and chronic renal failure.

Hypertension may be used alone or in combination with other antihypertensive drugs. Since it enhances the action of these agents, their dosage must be reduced to avoid an excessive drop in pressure and other unwanted side effects.

Contraindications: Anuria. If increasing azotemia and oliguria occur during treatment of severe progressive renal disease, the diuretic should be discontinued. Hydrochlorothiazide is contraindicated in persons known to be sensitive to any component of this product or to other sulfonamide-derived drugs. See Warnings, Pregnancy and Lactation.

Warnings: Impaired Renal Function and/or Azotemia: When creatinine clearance falls below 30 mL/min thiazide diuretics are ineffective.

Azotemia may be precipitated or increased by hydrochlorothiazide. Cumulative effects of the drug may develop in

patients with impaired renal function. If increasing azotemia and oliguria occur during treatment of renal disease the diuretic should be discontinued.
Hepatic Disease: Thiazides should be used with caution in patients with impaired hepatic function or progressive liver disease, since minor alterations of fluid and electrolyte balance, may precipitate hepatic coma.
Metabolic: Hyperuricemia may occur or gout may be precipitated in certain patients receiving thiazide therapy.

Thiazide therapy may impair glucose tolerance. Dosage adjustment of antidiabetic agents, including insulin, may be required.

Increases in cholesterol and triglyceride levels may be associated with thiazide diuretic therapy.

Nonspecific small bowel lesions consisting of stenosis with or without ulceration, may occur in association with the administration of enteric-coated potassium salts, alone or with oral diuretics. These small bowel lesions have caused obstruction, hemorrhage and perforation. Surgery was frequently required and deaths have occurred. Available information tends to implicate enteric-coated potassium salts, although lesions of this type also occur spontaneously. Such preparations should be used only when adequate dietary supplementation is not practical, and should be discontinued immediately if abdominal pain, distention, nausea, vomiting or gastrointestinal bleeding occur.
Other: Sensitivity reactions may occur in patients with or without a history of allergy or bronchial asthma.

The possibility of exacerbation or activation of systemic lupus erythematosus has been reported.
Pregnancy: The routine use of diuretics in otherwise healthy pregnant women with or without mild edema is not recommended and exposes mother and fetus to unnecessary hazard. Diuretics do not prevent development of toxemia of pregnancy and there is no satisfactory evidence that they are useful in the treatment of toxemia.

Thiazides cross the placental barrier and appear in cord blood. When hydrochlorothiazide is used in pregnancy or in women of childbearing age, the potential benefits of the drug should be weighed against the possible hazards to the fetus. These hazards include fetal or neonatal jaundice, thrombocytopenia, and possibly other adverse reactions which have occurred in the adult.
Lactation: Thiazides appear in breast milk. If use of the drug is deemed essential, the patient should stop nursing.

Precautions: Electrolyte Imbalance: Careful check should be kept for signs of fluid and electrolyte imbalance namely, hyponatremia, hypochloremic alkalosis, hypokalemia, and hypomagnesemia. Serum and urine electrolyte determinations are particularly important when the patient is vomiting excessively or receiving parenteral fluids. Warning signs or symptoms of fluid and electrolyte imbalance include: dryness of mouth, thirst, weakness, lethargy, drowsiness, restlessness, seizures, confusion, muscle pains or cramps, muscular fatigue, hypotension, oliguria, tachycardia, and gastrointestinal disturbances such as nausea and vomiting.

Hypokalemia may develop with hydrochlorothiazide as with any other potent diuretic, especially with brisk diuresis, after prolonged therapy or when severe cirrhosis is present. Hypokalemia can sensitize or exaggerate the response of the heart to the toxic effects of digitalis (e.g., increased ventricular irritability).

Although any chloride deficit is generally mild and usually does not require specific treatment except under extraordinary circumstances (as in liver disease or renal disease), chloride replacement may be required in the treatment of metabolic alkalosis.

Diuretic induced hyponatremia is usually mild and asymptomatic. In a few patients, hyponatremia may become severe and symptomatic. Such patients require immediate attention and appropriate treatment.

Dilutional hyponatremia may occur in edematous patients in hot weather; appropriate therapy is water restriction, rather than administration of salt except in rare instances when the hyponatremia is life threatening. In actual salt depletion, appropriate replacement is the therapy of choice.

The antihypertensive effect of the drug may be enhanced in the postsympathectomy patient.

Thiazides may decrease serum PBI levels without signs of thyroid disturbance.

Thiazides may decrease urinary calcium excretion. Thiazides may cause intermittent and slight elevation of serum calcium in the absence of known disorders of calcium metabolism. Thiazides should be discontinued before carrying out tests for parathyroid function.
Drug Interactions: When given concurrently, the following drugs may interact with thiazide diuretics.

Alcohol, barbiturates or narcotics: Potentiation of orthostatic hypotension may occur.
Antidiabetic drugs (oral agents and insulin): Dosage adjustment of the antidiabetic drug may be required.
Other antihypertensive drugs: Additive effect. Diuretic therapy should be discontinued for 2 to 3 days prior to initiation of therapy with an ACE inhibitor to reduce the likelihood of first dose hypotension.
Cholestyramine and colestipol resins: Absorption of hydrochlorothiazide is impaired in the presence of anionic exchange resins. Single doses of either cholestyramine or colestipol resins bind the hydrochlorothiazide and reduce its absorption from the gastrointestinal tract by up to 85% and 43% respectively.
Corticosteroids, ACTH: intensified electrolyte depletion, particularly hypokalemia.
Pressor amines (e.g., adrenaline): Possible decreased response to pressor amines but not sufficient to preclude their use.
Skeletal muscle relaxants, nondepolarizing (e.g., tubocurarine): Possible increased responsiveness to the muscle relaxant.
Lithium: Diuretic agents reduce the renal clearance of lithium and add a high risk of lithium toxicity; concomitant use is not recommended. Refer to the Product Monographs for lithium preparations before use of such preparations.
NSAIDs: In some patients, the administration of a NSAIDs can reduce the diuretic, natriuretic, and antihypertensive effects of diuretics.
Drug/Laboratory Test Interactions: Because of their effects on calcium metabolism, thiazides may interfere with tests for parathyroid function (see Precautions).

Adverse Effects: Gastrointestinal: anorexia, gastric irritation, nausea, vomiting, cramping, diarrhea, constipation, jaundice (intrahepatic cholestatic jaundice), pancreatitis, sialoadenitis.
CNS: dizziness, vertigo, paresthesias, headache, xanthopsia.
Hematologic: leukopenia, agranulocytosis, thrombocytopenia, aplastic anemia, hemolytic anemia.
Cardiovascular: hypotension, including orthostatic hypotension.
Hypersensitivity: purpura, photosensitivity, rash, urticaria, necrotizing angiitis (vasculitis, cutaneous vasculitis), fever, respiratory distress, including pneumonitis and pulmonary edema, anaphylactic reactions, toxic epidermal necrolysis.
Metabolic: hyperglycemia, glycosuria, hyperuricemia, electrolyte imbalance, including hyponatremia and hypokalemia.
Renal: renal dysfunction, interstitial nephritis, renal failure.
Other: muscle spasm, weakness, restlessness, transient blurred vision.

Overdose: Symptoms and Treatment: The most common signs and symptoms observed are those caused by electrolyte depletion (hypokalemia, hypochloremia, hyponatremia) and dehydration resulting from excessive diuresis. If digitalis has also been administered, hypokalemia may accentuate cardiac arrhythmias.

In the event of overdosage, symptomatic and supportive measures should be employed. If ingestion is recent, emesis should be induced or gastric lavage performed. Dehydration, electrolyte imbalance, hepatic coma and hypotension should be corrected by established procedures. If required, give oxygen or artificial respiration for respiratory impairment.

Dosage: Therapy should be individualized according to patient response. Use the smallest dosage necessary to achieve the required response.
Adults: Edema: The usual starting dosage is 25 to 100 mg a day given in a single dose or in 2 divided doses. Many patients respond to intermittent therapy (administration on alternate days or on 3 to 5 days each week) which may avoid an excessive response and undesirable electrolyte imbalance.

The maximum recommended daily dosage is 100 mg.
Hypertension: The usual starting dosage is 25 mg a day as a single or divided dose.

In some patients, when hydrochlorothiazide is given as a single entity or in combination with other antihypertensive agents, a starting dose of 12.5 mg daily may be sufficient. Dosage should be adjusted according to blood pressure response.

The maximum recommended daily dosage is 50 mg.

When thiazides are used with other antihypertensives, the dose of the latter may need to be reduced to avoid excessive decrease in blood pressure.
Infants and Children: The usual pediatric dosage is 2.5 mg/kg of body weight/day in 2 doses. Infants under 6 months of age may require up to 3.5 mg/kg/day in 2 doses.

On this basis, infants up to 2 years of age may be given 12.5 to 37.5 mg daily in 2 doses. Children from 2 to 12 years of age may be given 37.5 to 100 mg daily in 2 doses. Dosage in both age groups should be based on body weight.

Supplied: 25 mg: Each flat, peach, compressed tablet, with bevelled edge, scored on one side and coded MSD 42 on the other, contains: hydrochlorothiazide 25 mg. Nonmedicinal ingredients: calcium phosphate dibasic, cornstarch, lactose, magnesium stearate and sunset yellow. Gluten- and tartrazine-free. Bottles of 100.

50 mg: Each flat, peach, compressed tablet, with bevelled edge, scored on one side and coded MSD 105 on the other, contains: hydrochlorothiazide 50 mg. Nonmedicinal ingredients: calcium phosphate dibasic, cornstarch, lactose, magnesium stearate and sunset yellow. Gluten- and tartrazine-free. Bottles of 100.

Store at 15 to 30°C.

(Shown in Product Recognition Section)

HYDROMORPH CONTIN® Ⓝ

Purdue Frederick

Hydromorphone HCl

Opioid Analgesic

Pharmacology: Hydromorphone, a semi-synthetic μ opioid agonist, is a hydrogenated ketone of morphine and shares the pharmacologic properties typical of opioid analgesics. Hydromorphone and related opioids produce their major effects on the CNS and gastrointestinal tract. These include analgesia, drowsiness, mental clouding, changes in mood, euphoria or dysphoria, respiratory depression, cough suppression, decreased gastrointestinal motility, nausea, vomiting, increased cerebrospinal fluid pressure, increased biliary pressure, pinpoint constriction of the pupils, increased parasympathetic activity and transient hyperglycemia.

Estimates of the relative analgesic potency of parenterally administered hydromorphone to morphine in acute pain studies in man range from approximately 7:1 to 11:1.

The relationship between plasma concentration of hydromorphone and analgesic effect has not been well established. In patients with chronic pain, hydromorphone should be titrated to the dose required to adequately relieve pain without unmanageable side effects.

There is no intrinsic limit to the analgesic effect of hydromorphone; like morphine, adequate doses will relieve even the most severe pain. Clinically however, dosage limitations are imposed by the adverse effects, primarily respiratory depression, nausea and vomiting, which can result from high doses.
Pharmacokinetics: After oral administration of conventional release hydromorphone tablets, the drug is rapidly absorbed and, like morphine, undergoes presystemic elimination (approximately 50%), presumably as a result of metabolism in the liver. The terminal elimination half-life after i.v. administration is approximately 2.5 to 3 hours. The pharmacokinetics of hydromorphone have been shown to be linear over a range of i.v. doses from 10 to 40 μg/kg. The principal mode of elimination is by excretion in the urine as hydromorphone-3-glucuronide, which, at steady-state is present in plasma at concentrations approximately 26 times those of the parent drug. The pharmacologic activity of this and other hydromorphone metabolites in humans is not known.

Hydromorphone controlled release capsules administered 12 hourly provides equivalent analgesia to conventional hydromorphone tablets (Dilaudid) administered every 4 hours in patients with cancer pain. Steady-state pharmacokinetic studies demonstrate that maximum plasma concentrations (C_{max}) of hydromorphone are achieved at a mean of 4.8 hours after administration of Hydromorph Contin, with maximum and minimum concentrations equivalent to those obtained with 4 hourly administration of the conventional release tablets. The extent of absorption of hydromorphone from Hydromorph Contin is equivalent to that from conventional tablets (Dilaudid) and is not significantly influenced when administered in the presence of food. In patients with chronic cancer pain receiving doses of Hydromorph Contin ranging from 6 mg to 216 mg/day there was a linear relationship between area under the plasma concentration-time curve (AUC) and dose.

Indications: For the relief of severe pain requiring the prolonged use of an oral opioid preparation.

Contraindications: Should not be given to patients with: hypersensitivity to opioid analgesics; acute asthma or other obstructive airway disease and acute respiratory depression; cor pulmonale; acute alcoholism; delirium tremens; severe CNS depression; convulsive disorders; increased cerebrospinal or intracranial pressure; head injury; suspected surgical

Hydromorph Contin (cont'd)

abdomen; concomitant MAO inhibitors (or within 14 days of such therapy).

Warnings: Drug Dependence: As with other opioids, tolerance and physical dependence tend to develop upon repeated administration of hydromorphone and there is a potential for abuse of the drug and for development of psychological dependence. Hydromorphone should therefore be prescribed and handled with the high degree of caution appropriate to the use of a drug with strong abuse potential. Drug abuse is not a problem in patients with severe pain in which hydromorphone is appropriately indicated. However, in the absence of a clear indication for a strong opioid analgesic, drug-seeking behavior must be suspected and resisted, particularly in individuals with a history of, or propensity for drug abuse. Withdrawal symptoms may occur following abrupt discontinuation of therapy or upon administration of an opioid antagonist. Therefore, patients on prolonged therapy should be withdrawn gradually from the drug if it is no longer required for pain control.

CNS Depression: Hydromorphone should be used only with caution and in reduced dosage during concomitant administration of other opioid analgesics, general anesthetics, phenothiazines and other tranquilizers, sedative-hypnotics, tricyclic antidepressants and other CNS depressants, including alcohol. Respiratory depression, hypotension and profound sedation or coma may result.

Severe pain antagonizes the subjective and respiratory depressant actions of hydromorphone. Should pain suddenly subside, these effects may rapidly become manifest. Patients who are scheduled for cordotomy or other interruption of pain transmission pathways should not receive hydromorphone within 24 hours of the procedure.

Pregnancy: Animal studies with both morphine and hydromorphone have indicated the possibility of teratogenic effects. While experience in humans has not identified this as a risk, hydromorphone should be given to pregnant patients only when the anticipated benefits outweigh the potential risks to the fetus.

Precautions: General: The respiratory depressant effects of hydromorphone, and the capacity to elevate cerebrospinal fluid pressure, may be greatly increased in the presence of an already elevated intracranial pressure produced by trauma. Also, hydromorphone may produce confusion, miosis, vomiting and other side effects which obscure the clinical course of patients with head injury. In such patients, hydromorphone must be used with extreme caution and only if it is judged essential.

Hydromorphone should be used with extreme caution in patients with substantially decreased respiratory reserve, pre-existing respiratory depression, hypoxia or hypercapnia. Such patients are often less sensitive to the stimulatory effects of carbon monoxide on the respiratory centre and the respiratory depressant effects of hydromorphone may reduce respiratory drive to the point of apnea.

Hydromorphone administration may result in severe hypotension in patients whose ability to maintain adequate blood pressure is compromised by reduced blood volume, or concurrent administration of such drugs as phenothiazines or certain anesthetics.

Hydromorphone may obscure the diagnosis or clinical course of patients with acute abdominal conditions.

Special Risk Groups: Hydromorphone should be administered with caution, and in reduced dosages, to elderly or debilitated patients, to patients with severely reduced hepatic or renal function, and in patients with Addison's disease, hypothyroidism, prostatic hypertrophy or urethral stricture.

Labor/Delivery and *Lactation:* In view of the potential for opioids to cross the placental barrier and to be excreted in breast milk, hydromorphone should be used with caution during labor or in nursing mothers. Physical dependence or respiratory depression may occur in the infant.

Occupational Hazards: Hydromorphone may impair the mental and/or physical abilities needed for certain potentially hazardous activities such as driving a car or operating machinery. Patients should be cautioned accordingly.

Drug Interactions: CNS depressants, such as other opioids, anesthetics, sedatives, hypnotics, barbiturates, phenothiazines, chloral hydrate and glutethimide may enhance the depressant effects of hydromorphone. MAO inhibitors (including procarbazine HCl), pyrazolidone antihistamines, beta-blockers and alcohol may also enhance the depressant effect of hydromorphone. When combined therapy is contemplated, the dose of one or both agents should be reduced.

Hydromorphone may increase the anticoagulant activity of coumarin and other anticoagulants.

Adverse Effects: Adverse effects of hydromorphone are similar to those of other opioid analgesics, and represent an extension of pharmacological effects of the drug class. The major hazards of hydromorphone include respiratory and CNS depression. To a lesser degree, circulatory depression, respiratory arrest, shock and cardiac arrest have occurred.

The most frequently observed adverse effects are sedation, nausea, vomiting, constipation, lightheadedness, dizziness and sweating.

Sedation: Some degree of sedation is experienced by most patients upon initiation of therapy. This may be at least partly because patients often recuperate from prolonged fatigue after the relief of persistent pain. Most patients develop tolerance to the sedative effects of opioids within 3 to 5 days and, if the sedation is not severe, will not require any treatment except reassurance. If excessive sedation persists beyond a few days, the dose of the opioid should be reduced and alternate causes investigated. Some of these are: concurrent CNS depressant medication, hepatic or renal dysfunction, brain metastases, hypercalcemia and respiratory failure. If it is necessary to reduce the dose, it can be carefully increased again after 3 or 4 days if it is obvious that the pain is not being well controlled. Dizziness and unsteadiness may be caused by postural hypotension particularly in elderly or debilitated patients and may be alleviated if the patient lies down.

Nausea and Vomiting: Nausea is a common side effect on initiation of therapy with opioid analgesics and is thought to occur by activation of the chemoreceptor trigger zone, stimulation of the vestibular apparatus and through delayed gastric emptying. The prevalence of nausea declines following continued treatment with opioid analgesics. When instituting prolonged therapy with an opioid for chronic pain, the routine prescription of an antiemetic should be considered. In the cancer patient, investigation of nausea should include such causes as constipation, bowel obstruction, uremia, hypercalcemia, hepatomegaly, tumor invasion of celiac plexus and concurrent use of drugs with emetogenic properties. Persistent nausea which does not respond to dosage reduction may be caused by opioid-induced gastric stasis and may be accompanied by other symptoms including anorexia, early satiety, vomiting and abdominal fullness. These symptoms respond to chronic treatment with gastrointestinal prokinetic agents.

Constipation: Practically all patients become constipated while taking opioids on a persisent basis. In some patients, particularly the elderly or bedridden, fecal impaction may result. It is essential to caution the patients in this regard and to institute an appropriate regimen of bowel management at the start of prolonged opioid analgesic therapy. Stool softeners, stimulant laxatives and other appropriate measures should be used as required.

Less Frequently Observed with Opioid Analgesics: General and CNS: dysphoria, euphoria, weakness, headache, agitation, tremor, uncoordinated muscle movements, alterations of mood (nervousness, apprehension, depression, floating feelings, dreams), muscle rigidity, paresthesia, muscle tremor, blurred vision, nystagmus, diplopia and miosis, transient hallucinations and disorientation, visual disturbances, insomnia and increased intracranial pressure may occur.

Cardiovascular; flushing of the face, chills, tachycardia, bradycardia, palpitation, faintness, syncope, hypotension and hypertension.

Respiratory: bronchospasm and laryngospasm.

Gastrointestinal: dry mouth, biliary tract spasm, anorexia, diarrhea, cramps and taste alterations.

Genitourinary: urinary retention or hesitancy and antidiuretic effects.

Dermatologic: pruritus, urticaria, other skin rashes and diaphoresis.

Withdrawal (Abstinence) Syndrome: Physical dependence with or without psychological dependence tend to occur on chronic administration. An abstinence syndrome may be precipitated when opioid administration is discontinued or opioid antagonists administered. The following withdrawal symptoms may be observed after opioids are discontinued: body aches, diarrhea, gooseflesh, loss of appetite, nervousness or restlessness, runny nose, sneezing, tremors or shivering, stomach cramps, nausea, trouble with sleeping, unusual increase in sweating and yawning, weakness, tachycardia and unexplained fever. In patients who are appropriately treated with opioid analgesics and who undergo gradual withdrawal from the drug, these symptoms are usually mild.

Overdose: Symptoms: Serious overdosage with hydromorphone may be characterized by respiratory depression (a decrease in respiratory rate and/or tidal volume, Cheyne-Stokes respiration, cyanosis), extreme somnolence progressing to stupor or coma, skeletal muscle flaccidity, cold and clammy skin, and sometimes bradycardia and hypotension. In severe overdosage, apnea, circulatory collapse, cardiac arrest and death may occur.

Treatment: Primary attention should be given to the establishment of adequate respiratory exchange through the provision of a patent airway and controlled or assisted ventilation. The opioid antagonist naloxone hydrochloride is a specific antidote against respiratory depression due to overdosage or as a result of unusual sensitivity to hydromorphone. An appropriate dose of the antagonist should therefore be administered, preferably by the i.v. route. The usual initial i.v. adult dose of naloxone is 0.4 mg or higher. Concomitant efforts at respiratory resuscitation should be carried out. Since the duration of action of hydromorphone, particularly sustained release formulations, may exceed that of the antagonist, the patient should be under continued surveillance and doses of the antagonist should be repeated as needed to maintain adequate respiration.

An antagonist should not be administered in the absence of clinically significant respiratory or cardiovascular depression. Oxygen, i.v. fluids, vasopressors and other supportive measures should be used as indicated.

In individuals physically dependent on opioids, the administration of the usual dose of opioid antagonist will precipitate an acute withdrawal syndrome. The severity of this syndrome will depend on the degree of physical dependence and the dose of antagonist administered. The use of opioid antagonists in such individuals should be avoided if possible. If an opioid antagonist must be used to treat serious respiratory depression in the physically dependent patient, the antagonist should be administered with extreme care by using dosage titration, commencing with 10 to 20% of the usual recommended initial dose.

Evacuation of gastric contents may be useful in removing unabsorbed drug, particularly when a sustained release formulation has been taken.

Dosage: Adults: Individual dosing requirements vary considerably based on each patient's age, weight, severity and cause of pain, and medical and analgesic history.

Patients currently receiving other oral hydromorphone formulations may be transferred to Hydromorph Contin at the same total daily hydromorphone dosage, equally divided into two 12-hourly Hydromorph Contin doses.

For patients who are receiving an alternate opioid, the "oral hydromorphone equivalent" of the analgesic presently being used should be determined. Having determined the total daily dosage of the present analgesic, Table I can be used to calculate the approximate daily oral hydromorphone dosage that should provide equivalent analgesia. This total daily oral hydromorphone dose should then be equally divided into two 12-hourly Hydromorph Contin doses.

Patients who are opioid naive or receiving low, intermittent doses of weak opioid analgesics may be initiated on Hydromorph Contin 3 mg every 12 hours.

Dose Titration: Dose titration is the key to success with opioid analgesic therapy. Proper optimization of doses scaled to the relief of the individual's pain should aim at the regular administration of the lowest dose which will maintain the patient free of pain at all times. Dosage adjustments should be based on the patient's clinical response.

In patients receiving hydromorphone chronically the dose should be titrated at intervals of 48 hours to that which provides satisfactory pain relief without unmanageable side effects. Hydromorph Contin is designed to allow 12 hourly dosing. If breakthrough pain repeatedly occurs at the end of the dosing interval it is generally an indication for a dosage increase rather than more frequent administration.

Adjustment or Reduction of Dosage: Following successful relief of severe pain, periodic attempts to reduce the opioid dose should be made. Smaller doses or complete discontinuation may become feasible due to a change in the patient's condition or mental state.

Capsules should be swallowed intact. They may be sprinkled on soft food but neither the capsules nor the beads should be crushed or chewed.

Opioid analgesics may only be partially effective in relieving dysesthetic pain, postherpetic neuralgia, stabbing pains, activity-related pain and some forms of headache. That is not to say that patients with advanced cancer suffering from some of these forms of pain should not be given an adequate trial of opioid analgesics, but it may be necessary to refer such patients at an early time to other forms of pain therapy.

Table I—Hydromorph Contin

Opioid Analgesics: Approximate Analgesic Equivalences[a]

Drug	Equivalent Dose (mg)[b] (compared to morphine 10 mg i.m.)		Duration of Action (hours)
	Parenteral	Oral	
Strong Opioid Agonists			
Morphine	10	60[c]	3–4
Hydromorphone	1.5	7.5[d]	2–4
Anileridine	25	75	2–3
Levorphanol	2	4	4–8
Meperidine[e]	75	300	1–3
Oxymorphone	1.5	5 (rectal)	3–4
Methadone[f]			
Heroin	5–8	10–15	3–4
Weak Opioid Agonists			
Codeine	120	200	3–4
Oxycodone		10–15[g]	2–4
Propoxyphene	50	100	2–4
Mixed Agonist-Antagonists[h]			
Pentazocine[e]	60	180	3–4
Nalbuphine	10		3–6
Butorphanol	2		3–4

[a] References: Cancer Pain: A Monograph on the Management of Cancer Pain, Health and Welfare Canada 1984. Foley, K.M., New Engl. J. Med. 313: 84-95, 1985. Aronoff, G.M. and Evans, W.O., In Evaluation and Treatment of Chronic Pain, 2nd Ed, G.M. Aronoff (Ed.), Williams and Wilkins, Baltimore, pp. 359-368, 1992. Cherny, N.I. and Portenoy, R.K., In: Textbook, of Pain, 3rd Ed., P.D. Wall and R. Melzack (Eds.), Churchill Livingstone, London, pp. 1437-1467, 1994.

[b] Most of this data was derived from single-dose, acute pain studies and should be considered an approximation for selection of doses when treating chronic pain.

[c] For acute pain, the oral or rectal dose of morphine is six times the injectable dose. However, for chronic dosing, clinical experience indicates that this ratio is 2-3:1 (i.e., 20-30 mg of oral or rectal morphine is equivalent to 10 mg of parenteral morphine).

[d] Clinical experience indicates that during chronic dosing the oral morphine/oral hydromorphone dose ratio is 5-7.5:1.

[e] These drugs are not recommended for the management of chronic pain.

[f] Extremely variable equianalgesic dose. Patients should undergo individualized titration starting at an equivalent to 1/10 of the morphine dose.

[g] In combination with acetaminophen or ASA. For acute pain, single entity oral oxycodone is twice as potent as oral morphine.

[h] Mixed agonist-antagonists can precipitate withdrawal in patients on pure opioid agonists.

Information for the Patient: See Blue Section—Information for the Patient "Hydromorph Contin".

Supplied: 3 mg: Each green, controlled release capsule, imprinted with the letters PF and HYDROMORPH CONTIN, and the strength 3 mg, contains: hydromorphone HCl 3 mg. Nonmedicinal ingredients: colloidal silicon dioxide, dibutyl sebacate, ethyl cellulose, hydroxypropylmethyl cellulose, magnesium stearate and microcrystalline cellulose. Polypropylene bottles of 50.

6 mg: Each pink, controlled release capsule, imprinted with the letters PF and HYDROMORPH CONTIN, and the strength 6 mg, contains: hydromorphone HCl 6 mg. Nonmedicinal ingredients: colloidal silicon dioxide, dibutyl sebacate, ethyl cellulose, hydroxypropylmethyl cellulose, magnesium stearate and microcrystalline cellulose. Polypropylene bottles of 50.

12 mg: Each orange, controlled release capsule, imprinted with the letters PF and HYDROMORPH CONTIN, and the strength 12 mg, contains: hydromorphone HCl 12 mg. Nonmedicinal ingredients: colloidal silicon dioxide, dibutyl sebacate, ethyl cellulose, hydroxypropylmethyl cellulose, magnesium stearate and microcrystalline cellulose. Polypropylene bottles of 50.

24 mg: Each grey, controlled release capsule, imprinted with the letters PF and HYDROMORPH CONTIN, and the strength 24 mg, contains: hydromorphone HCl 24 mg. Nonmedicinal ingredients: colloidal silicon dioxide, dibutyl sebacate, ethyl cellulose, hydroxypropylmethyl cellulose, magnesium stearate and microcrystalline cellulose. Polypropylene bottles of 50.

30 mg: Each red, controlled release capsule, imprinted with the letters PF and HYDROMORPH CONTIN, and the strength 30 mg, contains: hydromorphone HCl 30 mg. Nonmedicinal ingredients: colloidal silicon dioxide, dibutyl sebacate, ethyl cellulose, hydroxypropylmethyl cellulose, magnesium stearate and microcrystalline cellulose.

Store at 15 to 25°C.

(Shown in Product Recognition Section)

HYDROMORPHONE Ⓝ
General Monograph, CPhA

see OPIOID ANALGESICS

HYDROMORPHONE HYDROCHLORIDE Ⓝ
Sabex

Opioid Analgesic

Supplied: Injection: 2 mg/mL: Each mL of isotonic solution contains: hydromorphone HCl 2 mg. Nonmedicinal ingredients: citric acid, sodium citrate, sodium chloride, hydrochloric acid or sodium hydroxide to adjust pH and water for injection. Preservative-free. Single use vials of 1 mL, boxes of 10.

10 mg/mL (Hydromorphone HP 10): Each mL of isotonic solution contains: hydromorphone HCl 10 mg. Nonmedicinal ingredients: citric acid, disodium edetate, sodium citrate, sodium chloride, hydrochloric acid or sodium hydroxide to adjust pH and water for injection. Preservative-free. Single use vials of 1 mL, boxes of 10. Single use vials of 5 mL, boxes of 5. Single use vials of 50 mL, boxes of 1.

20 mg/mL (Hydromorphone HP 20): Each mL of isotonic solution contains: hydromorphone HCl 20 mg. Nonmedicinal ingredients: citric acid, disodium edetate, sodium citrate, sodium chloride, hydrochloric acid or sodium hydroxide to adjust pH and water for injection. Preservative-free. Single use vials of 50 mL, boxes of 1.

50 mg/mL (Hydromorphone HP 50): Each mL of isotonic solution contains: hydromorphone HCl 50 mg. Nonmedicinal ingredients: citric acid, disodium edetate, sodium citrate, sodium chloride, hydrochloric acid or sodium hydroxide to adjust pH and water for injection. Preservative-free. Single use vials of 50 mL, boxes of 1.

Store between 15 and 30°C. Protect from light. Discard unused portion.

Suppositories: Each suppository contains: hydromorphone HCl 3 mg. Boxes of 6. Store between 15 and 30°C.

HYDROPRES®-25 Ⓟ
MSD

Hydrochlorothiazide—Reserpine

Diuretic—Antihypertensive

Indications: Fixed-dose combination drugs are not indicated for initial therapy. Patients should be titrated on the individual drugs. If the fixed combination represents the dosage so determined, its use may be more convenient in patient management. If during maintenance therapy dosage adjustment is necessary it is advisable to use the individual drugs.

In many cases of hypertension, Hydropres-25 alone may control the blood pressure. If a greater antihypertensive effect is required, more potent drugs can be added in comparatively small dosage and with smoother control.

Contraindications: All diuretics, including hydrochlorothiazide, are contraindicated in anuria. If increasing azotemia and oliguria occur during treatment of severe progressive renal disease, Hydropres-25 should be discontinued. Electroshock therapy should not be given to patients while on reserpine, as severe and even fatal reactions have been reported with minimal convulsive electroshock dosage. At least 7 days should elapse between discontinuance of reserpine and initiation of electroshock therapy. Hydropres-25 is contraindicated in persons known to be sensitive to hydrochlorothiazide or to other sulfonamide-derived drugs or to reserpine. This combination is contraindicated, because of its reserpine content, in active peptic ulcer, in ulcerative colitis, and in active mental depression, especially with suicidal tendencies. See also Pregnancy and Lactation under Warnings.

Warnings: Azotemia may be precipitated or increased by hydrochlorothiazide. Cumulative effects of the drug may develop in patients with impaired renal function. If increasing azotemia and oliguria occur during treatment of severe progressive renal disease Hydropres-25 should be discontinued.

Thiazides should be used with caution in patients with impaired hepatic function or progressive liver disease, since minor alterations of fluid and electrolyte balance, or of serum ammonia, may precipitate hepatic coma.

Sensitivity reactions may occur in patients with or without a history of allergy or bronchial asthma.

Hydrochlorothiazide adds to or potentiates the action of other antihypertensive drugs. Potentiation occurs with ganglionic or peripheral adrenergic blocking drugs.

The possibility of exacerbation or activation of systemic lupus erythematosus has been reported for sulfonamide derivatives (including thiazides), and reserpine.

The occurrence of mental depression due to reserpine in doses of 0.25 mg daily or less is unusual. In any event, Hydropres-25 should be discontinued at the first sign of depression.

Nonspecific small bowel lesions consisting of stenosis with or without ulceration, may occur in association with the administration of enteric coated potassium salts, alone or with oral diuretics. These small bowel lesions have caused obstruction, hemorrhage and perforation. Surgery was frequently required and deaths have occurred. Available information tends to implicate enteric coated potassium salts, although lesions of this type also occur spontaneously. Such preparations should be used only when adequate dietary supplementation is not practical, and should be discontinued immediately if abdominal pain, distension, nausea, vomiting or gastrointestinal bleeding occur.

Pregnancy: Reserpine has been demonstrated to cross the placental barrier in guinea pigs with depression of adrenal catecholamine stores in the newborn. There is some evidence that side effects such as nasal congestion, lethargy, depressed Moro reflex, and bradycardia may appear in infants born of reserpine-treated mothers. Thiazides cross the placental barrier and appear in cord blood. When Hydropres-25 is used in pregnancy or in women of childbearing age, the potential benefits of the drug should be weighed against the possible hazards to the fetus. These hazards include fetal or neonatal jaundice, thrombocytopenia, and possibly other adverse reactions which have occurred in the adult.

Lactation: Since thiazides and reserpine appear in breast milk, Hydropres-25 is contraindicated in nursing mothers. If use of the drug is deemed essential, the patient should stop nursing.

Precautions: Since reserpine may increase gastric secretion and motility, it should be used cautiously in patients with a history of peptic ulcer, ulcerative colitis, or other gastrointestinal disorders. This compound may precipitate biliary colic in patients with gallstones, or bronchial asthma in susceptible persons.

Reserpine may cause hypotension including orthostatic hypotension. In hypertensive patients on reserpine therapy significant hypotension and bradycardia may develop during surgical anesthesia.

Therefore, Hydropres-25 should be discontinued two weeks before giving anesthesia. For emergency surgical procedures, it may be necessary to give vagal blocking agents parenterally to prevent or reverse hypotension and/or bradycardia.

Anxiety or depression, as well as psychosis, may develop during reserpine therapy. If depression is present when therapy is begun, it may be aggravated. Mental depression is unusual with reserpine doses of 0.25 mg daily or less. In any case, Hydropres-25 should be discontinued at the first sign of depression. Extreme caution should be used in treating patients with a history of mental depression, and the possibility of suicide should be kept in mind.

As with most antihypertensive therapy, caution should be exercised when treating hypertensive patients with renal insufficiency, since they adjust poorly to lowered blood pressure levels. Use reserpine cautiously with digitalis and quinidine; cardiac arrhythmias have occurred with reserpine preparations.

Careful check should be kept for signs of fluid and electrolyte imbalance, namely, hyponatremia, hypochloremic alkalosis, hypokalemia and hypomagnesemia. Serum and urine electrolyte determinations are particularly important when the patient is vomiting excessively or receiving parenteral fluids. Warning signs, irrespective of cause, are: dryness of mouth, thirst, weakness, lethargy, drowsiness, restlessness, muscle pains or cramps, muscular fatigue, hypotension, oliguria, tachycardia and gastrointestinal disturbances.

Hypokalemia may develop with hydrochlorothiazide as with any other potent diuretic, especially with brisk diuresis, when severe cirrhosis is present, or during concomitant steroid or ACTH administration. Interference with adequate electrolyte

Hydropres-25 (cont'd)

intake will contribute to hypokalemia. Hypokalemia can sensitize or exaggerate the response of the heart to the toxic effects of digitalis (e.g., increased ventricular irritability). Hypokalemia may be avoided or treated by giving foods with a high potassium content of if necessary by the use of potassium chloride.

Any chloride deficit is generally mild and usually does not require specific treatment except under extraordinary circumstances (as in liver disease or renal disease). Dilutional hyponatremia may occur in edematous patients in hot weather; appropriate therapy is water restriction, rather than administration of salt except in rare instances when the hyponatremia is life threatening. In actual salt depletion, appropriate replacement is the therapy of choice.

Thiazides may decrease serum PBI levels without signs of thyroid disturbance.

Calcium excretion is decreased by hydrochlorothiazide and magnesium excretion is increased.

Pathological changes in the parathyroid glands with hypercalcemia and hypophosphatemia have been observed in a few patients on prolonged thiazide therapy. The common complications of hyperparathyroidism such as renal lithiasis, bone resorption, and peptic ulceration have not been seen. Thiazides should be discontinued before carrying out tests for parathyroid function.

Hyperuricemia may occur or gout may be precipitated.

Patients should be observed regularly for the possible occurrence of liver dysfunction, idiosyncratic reactions, or blood dyscrasias.

Sensitivity reactions to thiazides may occur in patients with or without a history of allergy or bronchial asthma.

The possibility of exacerbation or activation of systemic lupus erythematosus has been reported with the thiazides.

Insulin requirements in diabetic patients may be increased, decreased or unchanged. Diabetes mellitus which has been latent may become manifest during thiazide administration.

Drug Interactions: Hydrochlorothiazide potentiates the action of other antihypertensive drugs. Therefore, the dosage of these agents, especially the ganglion blockers, may need to be reduced when Hydropres-25 is added to the regimen.

Lithium should generally not be given to patients receiving diuretics, since the risk of lithium toxicity is very high in such patients.

Thiazide-containing drugs may increase the responsiveness to tubocurarine. The antihypertensive effect of the drug may be enhanced in the postsympathectomy patient.

Hydrochlorothiazide may decrease arterial responsiveness to norepinephrine. This diminution is not sufficient to preclude the effectiveness of the pressor agent for therapeutic use.

Orthostatic hypotension may occur and may be potentiated by alcohol, barbiturates, or narcotics.

Adverse Effects: Reserpine: The reactions most often reported include: excessive sedation, nightmares, nasal congestion, conjunctival injection, enhanced susceptibility to colds, muscular aches, headache, dizziness, dyspnea, anorexia, nausea, increased intestinal motility, diarrhea, weight gain, dryness of the mouth, blurred vision, flushing of the skin and pruritus. Skin rash, dysuria, syncope, nonpuerperal lactation, impotence or decreased libido, increased salivation, vomiting, bradycardia, mental depression, nervousness, paradoxical anxiety, epistaxis, excessive bleeding following prostatic surgery, purpura due to thrombocytopenia, angina pectoris and other direct cardiac effects (e.g., premature ventricular contractions, fluid retention, congestive failure), and CNS sensitization, manifested by dull sensorium, deafness, glaucoma, uveitis, and optic atrophy also have been noted. In some patients reserpine has produced a syndrome similar to Parkinson's Disease, though this effect usually is reversible with decreased dosage or discontinuance of therapy. Hydropres-25 should be given with caution to hypertensive patients who have also coronary artery disease to avoid a precipitous drop in blood pressure. Side effects due to reserpine may disappear with continued use and in many cases can be controlled by reducing the dosage. Rarely, it may be necessary to discontinue therapy.

Hydrochlorothiazide: Gastrointestinal: anorexia, gastric irritation, nausea, vomiting, cramping, diarrhea, constipation, jaundice (intrahepatic cholestatic jaundice), pancreatitis, sialadenitis.

CNS: dizziness, vertigo, paresthesias, headache, xanthopsia.

Hematologic: leukopenia, agranulocytosis, thrombocytopenia, aplastic anemia, hemolytic anemia.

Cardiovascular: orthostatic hypotension (may be aggravated by alcohol, barbiturates or narcotics).

Hypersensitivity: purpura, photosensitivity, rash, urticaria, necrotizing angiitis (vasculitis) (cutaneous vasculitis), fever, respiratory distress, including pneumonitis, anaphylactic reactions.

Other: hyperglycemia, glycosuria, hyperuricemia, muscle spasm, weakness, restlessness, transient blurred vision.

Whenever adverse reactions are moderate or severe, thiazide dosage should be reduced or therapy withdrawn.

Overdose: Symptoms: Reserpine: Impairment of consciousness may occur and may range from drowsiness to coma, depending upon the severity of overdosage. Flushing of the skin, conjunctival injection, and pupillary constriction are to be expected. Hypotension, hypothermia, central respiratory depression and bradycardia may develop in cases of severe overdosage. Diarrhea may also occur.

Hydrochlorothiazide: Overdosage may lead to excessive diuresis with electrolyte depletion (hypokalemia, hypochloremia, hyponatremia) and dehydration.

Signs are dryness of mouth, thirst, weakness, lethargy, drowsiness, restlessness, muscle pains or cramps, muscular fatigue, hypotension, oliguria, tachycardia, gastrointestinal disturbances, mental confusion, delirium, convulsions, shock, coma.

If digitalis has also been administered, hypokalemia may accentuate myocardial abnormalities (e.g., cardiac arrhythmias).

Hydrochlorothiazide may precipitate hepatic coma in cirrhotics, potentiate other antihypertensive agents, and decrease responsiveness to norepinephrine.

Treatment: There is no specific antidote. Treatment is symptomatic and supportive.

Evacuate stomach contents, taking adequate precautions against aspiration and for the protection of the airway, instill activated charcoal slurry.

Correct dehydration, electrolyte imbalance, hepatic coma, by established procedures. Administer oxygen or artificial respiration for respiratory impairment.

If hypotension is severe enough to require treatment with a vasopressor, use one having a direct action upon vascular smooth muscle (e.g., phenylephrine, levarterenol). If bradycardia becomes marked, especially with cardiac arrhythmias, consider the use of vagal blocking agents along with other appropriate measures. Since reserpine is long acting, watch the patient carefully for at least 72 hours, administering treatment as required.

Dosage: Adults: 1 tablet 1 to 4 times a day; Within this range, the dosage is increased or decreased according to the blood pressure response of the patient.

Supplied: Each green, flat, compressed tablet with a beveled edge, scored on one side with MSD symbol on the other contains: hydrochlorothiazide 25 mg and reserpine 125 μg. Also contains lactose. Gluten- and tartrazine-free. Bottles of 100.

(Shown in Product Recognition Section)

HYDROXOCOBALAMIN
General Monograph, CPhA
see VITAMIN B$_{12}$

HYGROTON®
Novartis Pharmaceuticals
Chlorthalidone
Diuretic—Antihypertensive

Pharmacology: Chlorthalidone inhibits reabsorption of sodium and chloride in the distal renal tubule thus promoting water loss. The higher urine volume increases potassium loss. Little information is available on the absorption of the drug. Its long elimination half-life and clinical experience place it as a long-acting thiazide derivative. This may not be important clinically because the biological effects of thiazides particularly as antihypertensives may be prolonged compared to their elimination rate. The longer acting agents appear to cause increased potassium loss.

Although a mild diuretic, its combination with loop diuretics is particularly potent because the latter presents much more sodium chloride to the distal tubule.

The blood pressure lowering effects are initially due to volume reduction but the persisting effect includes other undetermined mechanisms that reduce peripheral resistance. A high salt intake reverses its antihypertensive effect.

The major portion of an absorbed dose of chlorthalidone is excreted by the kidneys with an elimination half-life averaging 50 hours. Metabolism and hepatic excretion into the bile constitute a minor way of elimination. Within 120 hours, about 70% of the dose is excreted in the urine and in the feces, mainly in an unchanged form.

Indications: For the treatment of hypertension. It may be used alone or in association with other antihypertensive agents.

Chlorthalidone is also indicated for adjunctive therapy of edema associated with: renal disease; congestive heart failure of mild to moderate degree (functional class II, III), when glomerular filtration rate is greater than 30 mL/min; ascites due to cirrhosis of the liver in stable patients; estrogen therapy; corticosteroid therapy.

Contraindications: Anuria, severe renal failure (creatinine clearance lower than 30 mL/min), severe hepatic failure, refractory hypokalemia or conditions involving enhanced potassium loss, hyponatremia, hypercalcemia, symptomatic hyperuricemia (history of gout or uric acid calculi).

Pregnancy: See Precautions, Pregnancy.

Hypersensitivity or suspected hypersensitivity to chlorthalidone and other sulfonamide derivatives or their excipients.

Warnings: Should be used with caution in patients with renal disease or with impaired hepatic function (see Contraindications and Precautions). Because of the possibility of progression of renal damage, periodic determination of the BUN and serum creatinine are indicated. Should there be an elevation of either parameter, treatment should be discontinued. Like thiazides, chlorthalidone may lose its diuretic efficacy when glomerular filtration rate drops below 30 mL/min, a point at which treatment with loop diuretics may be more appropriate.

Precautions: Electrolytes: As with thiazide diuretics, kaluresis induced by chlorthalidone is dose dependent, and there is inter-individual variability in magnitude. With 25 mg/day, serum potassium concentration decreases average 0.5 mmol/L. If chronic treatment is contemplated, serum potassium concentrations should be determined initially, and then 3 to 4 weeks later. If, thereafter, potassium balance is not disturbed further, concentrations should be assessed every 4 to 6 months. Conditions that may alter potassium balance (especially in the presence of brisk diuresis) include: vomiting, diarrhea, malnutrition, change in renal function (e.g., nephrosis), liver cirrhosis, hyperaldosteronism, or concomitant use of corticosteroids or ACTH.

Titrated co-administration of an oral potassium salt (e.g., KCl) may be considered in patients: receiving digitalis; exhibiting signs of coronary heart disease, unless they are also receiving an ACE inhibitor; on high doses of a beta-adrenergic agonist; whose plasma potassium concentrations are less than 3.0 mmol/L.

If oral potassium preparations are not tolerated, chlorthalidone may be combined with a potassium-sparing diuretic (e.g., triamterene).

Patients receiving thiazides and their analogues should be carefully observed for clinical signs of fluid or electrolyte imbalance. Warning signs or symptoms of fluid and electrolyte imbalance include dryness of mouth, thirst, weakness, lethargy, drowsiness, restlessness, muscle pains or cramps, muscular fatigue, gastrointestinal disturbances, hypotension, oliguria, tachycardia, and cardiac arrhythmias or corresponding ECG changes.

In all combination treatment regimens, maintenance or normalization of the potassium balance should be closely checked. If hypokalemia is accompanied by clinical signs (e.g., muscular weakness, paresis and ECG alteration), chlorthalidone should be discontinued.

Combined treatment consisting of chlorthalidone and a potassium salt or a potassium-sparing diuretic must be avoided in patients also receiving ACE inhibitors.

Close monitoring of serum electrolytes is indicated particularly in the elderly, in digitalized patients, in patients vomiting excessively or receiving parenteral fluids, patients with ascites due to liver cirrhosis, and in patients with edema due to nephrotic syndrome. For the latter condition, chlorthalidone should be used only under close control in normokalemic patients with no signs of volume depletion or severe hypoalbuminemia.

Excessively strict low-salt diets should be avoided. Hyponatremia, accompanied by neurological symptoms (nausea, debility, progressive disorientation, apathy), has been observed in isolated cases.

Should hypochloremic alkalosis or hyponatremia occur, consider appropriate therapy. Water restriction rather than actual salt replacement may be considered appropriate treatment of any chloride deficit except in rare instances when hyponatremia is life threatening, then appropriate salt replacement is the therapy of choice.

Patients receiving relatively high doses of thiazides or their analogues may develop hypomagnesemia accompanied by such signs and symptoms as nervousness, muscle spasm, and cardiac arrhythmias.

Thiazides may decrease protein bound iodine levels without signs of thyroid disturbance.

Pathological changes in the parathyroid glands, with hypercalcemia and hypophosphatemia, have been observed in a few patients on prolonged thiazide therapy. The common complications of hyperparathyroidism such as renal lithiasis, bone resorption, and peptic ulceration have not been seen. Discontinue thiazides and their analogues before carrying out tests for parathyroid function.

Calcium excretion is decreased by thiazide diuretics.

Metabolic Effects: Chlorthalidone may raise the serum uric acid level, but attacks of gout (in predisposed patients) are rarely observed during chronic treatment. In cases where prolonged and significant elevation of blood uric acid concentrations is considered potentially deleterious, concomitant use of a uricosuric agent is effective in reversing hyperuricemia without loss of diuretic and/or antihypertensive activity.

Small and partially reversible increases in plasma concentrations of total cholesterol, triglycerides, or low-density lipoprotein cholesterol were reported in patients during long-term treatment with thiazides and thiazide-like diuretics. The clinical relevance of these findings is equivocal.

Chlorthalidone should not be used as a first-line drug for long-term treatment in patients with overt diabetes mellitus or in patients with hypercholesterolemia. If chlorthalidone must be used, serum lipids should be regularly monitored. If there is a rise in lipid levels, withdrawal of chlorthalidone should be considered.

Although glucose tolerance may be adversely affected, diabetes mellitus very seldom occurs under treatment.

Patients with Special Diseases and Conditions: In patients with impaired hepatic function or progressive liver disease, caution should be exercised since even minor alterations in fluid and electrolyte balance or of serum ammonia may precipitate hepatic coma.

Treatment with thiazide diuretics should be initiated cautiously in postsympathectomy patients since the antihypertensive effects may be enhanced.

A cautious dosage schedule should be adopted in patients with severe coronary or cerebral atериosclerosis.

General: The antihypertensive effect of ACE inhibitors is potentiated in the presence of agents that increase plasma renin activity (diuretics). A cautious dosage schedule should therefore be adopted when an ACE inhibitor is added to a diuretic agent.

Occupational Hazards: Because dizziness and impaired patient reaction time are possible side effects of chlorthalidone, especially at the start of therapy, patients should be warned about the possible hazards of operating machines or driving motor vehicles.

Pregnancy: Chlorthalidone, like other diuretics, can cause placental hypoperfusion. Since they do not prevent or alter the course of EPH (edema, proteinuria, hypertension)-gestosis (pre-eclampsia), these drugs must not be used to treat hypertension in pregnant women. The use of chlorthalidone for other indications (e.g., heart disease) in pregnancy should be avoided, particularly in the first trimester, unless the potential benefits outweigh the possible risks (e.g., when there are no safer alternatives).

As thiazides increase blood uric acid concentration, levels should be taken before and during pregnancy but their value in assessing the onset of toxemia may still be lost.

Chlorthalidone crosses the placental barrier. Levels in fetal whole blood were about 15% of those found in the maternal blood of mothers receiving 50 mg chlorthalidone daily pre- and postpartum. Concentration in amniotic fluid is approximately 4% of maternal blood levels.

Lactation: Chlorthalidone appears in breast milk, attaining concentrations of approximately 4% of maternal blood levels. Therefore use in nursing mothers should be avoided.

Drug Interactions: Antihypertensive Agents: Diuretics potentiate the action of curare derivatives and antihypertensive agents (e.g., guanethidine, methyldopa, beta-blockers, vasodilators, calcium antagonists, ACE inhibitors).

Postural hypotension may occur and may be potentiated by alcohol, anesthetics, sedatives, barbiturates or narcotics.

Digitalis: Thiazide-induced hypokalemia or hypomagnesemia may increase the likelihood of digitalis-induced cardiac arrhythmias (see also Precautions).

Corticosteroids: The hypokalemic effects of diuretics may be increased by corticosteroids, ACTH and amphotericin.

Insulin and Oral Antidiabetic Agents: It may be necessary to adjust the dosage of insulin or oral antidiabetic agents in response to changes in glucose tolerance that chlorthalidone may produce (see Precautions, Metabolic Effects).

NSAIDs: Concomitant administration of certain NSAIDs (e.g., indomethacin) may weaken the diuretic and antihypertensive activity of thiazides, and there have been isolated reports of a deterioration of renal function in predisposed patients.

Curare Derivatives and Ganglionic Blocking Agents: Thiazides may increase responsiveness to curare derivatives and ganglionic blocking agents.

Allopurinol: Co-administration of thiazide diuretics may increase the incidence of hypersensitivity reactions to allopurinol.

Amantadine: Co-administration of thiazide diuretics may increase the risk of adverse effects from amantadine.

Antineoplastic Agents (e.g., cyclophosphamide, methotrexate): Concomitant use of thiazide diuretics may reduce renal excretion of cytotoxic agents and enhance the myelosuppressive effects.

Anticholinergics (e.g., atropine, biperiden): The bioavailability of thiazide-type diuretics may be increased by anticholinergic agents, apparently due to a decrease in gastrointestinal motility and rate of gastric emptying.

Lithium: Diuretics enhance the cardiotoxic (manifested in ECG changes) and neurotoxic (manifested by ataxia, confusion, and mental disorientation) effects of lithium and these drugs should not be administered concurrently. In those rare instances when these drugs must be given together, patients should be observed closely for signs and symptoms of lithium toxicity. Close monitoring of serum electrolytes and lithium concentrations and maintenance of adequate fluid, potassium and sodium intake are also necessary.

Cholestyramine: Absorption of thiazide diuretics is decreased by cholestyramine, therefore a decrease in pharmacological effect may be expected.

Vitamin D: Concomitant use of thiazide diuretics may decrease urinary excretion of calcium, and co-administration of Vitamin D may potentiate the increase in serum calcium.

Cyclosporin: Concomitant treatment with diuretics may increase the risk of hyperuricemia and gout-type complications.

Calcium Salts: Concomitant use of thiazide-type diuretics may cause hypercalcemia by increasing tubular calcium reabsorption.

Diazoxide: Thiazide diuretics may enhance the hyperglycemic effect of diazoxide.

Adverse Effects: Frequency estimates are as follows: Frequent: >10%, Occasional: 1 to 10%, Rare: 0.001 to 1% and Isolated Cases: <0.001%.

Electrolytes and Metabolic Disorders: Frequent: mainly at higher doses, hypokalemia, hyperuricemia, and rise in blood lipids. Occasional: hyponatremia, hypomagnesemia, and hyperglycemia. Rare: hypercalcemia, glycosuria, worsening of diabetic metabolic state, and gout. Isolated cases: hypochloremic alkalosis.

Dermatology: Occasional: urticaria and other forms of skin rash. Rare: photosensitization.

Liver: Rare: Intrahepatic cholestasis or jaundice.

Cardiovascular: Occasional: postural hypotension, which may be aggravated by alcohol, anesthetics or sedatives. Rare: cardiac arrhythmias.

CNS: Occasional: dizziness, slow mentation and decreased reaction time (see Precautions). Rare: paresthesia, headache.

Gastrointestinal: Occasional: loss of appetite and minor gastrointestinal distress. Rare: mild nausea and vomiting, gastric pain, constipation, and diarrhea. Isolated cases: pancreatitis.

Hematology: Rare: thrombocytopenia, leukopenia, agranulocytosis and eosinophilia, aplastic anemia.

Miscellaneous: Occasional: impotence. Rare: disturbances of vision. Isolated cases: idiosyncratic pulmonary edema (respiratory disorders). Allergic interstitial nephritis and vasculitis.

Overdose: Symptoms: Symptoms of chlorthalidone overdosage may include nausea, weakness, dizziness, somnolence, hypovolemia, hypotension, and electrolyte disturbances associated with cardiac arrhythmias and muscle spasm.

Treatment: There is no specific antidote. To reduce absorption, induce vomiting or gastric lavage and administer activated charcoal. Intravenous dextrose-saline and potassium chloride may be given, if necessary, with due caution.

Dosage: Therapy should be initiated with the lowest possible dose, and be titrated thereafter to gain maximum therapeutic benefit while keeping side effects to a minimum (e.g., determine the minimum effective maintenance dose for each patient). A single dose daily or every other day given in the morning with food is recommended.

Hypertension: Usual adult dose is 25 to 50 mg daily. The clinically useful dosage range is 12.5 to 50 mg daily. Doses greater than 50 mg per day increase metabolic complications and are rarely of therapeutic benefit. For a given dose, the full effect is reached after 3 to 4 weeks. If the decrease in blood pressure obtained using doses of 25 or 50 mg/day proves inadequate, combined treatment with other antihypertensive drugs (such as beta-blockers and ACE inhibitors) is recommended. When adding an ACE inhibitor, chlorthalidone is to be reduced or discontinued.

Edema of Specific Origin (see Indications): The lowest effective dose is to be identified by titration. Maintenance doses should not exceed 50 mg/day and should be administered over limited periods only. The dosage should be individually adapted to the clinical picture and patient's response. For long-term therapy, the lowest possible dosage sufficient to maintain an optimal effect should be employed; this applies particularly to elderly patients.

The therapeutic effect of chlorthalidone occurs even without salt restriction and is well sustained during continued use.

Supplied: Each yellow-beige, round, scored, flat-faced, beveled-edge tablet, engraved GEIGY on one side and ZA on the other, fully bisected between the Z and A, contains: chlorthalidone 50 mg. Nonmedicinal ingredients: cellulose compounds, cornstarch, iron oxides, magnesium stearate and silicone dioxide. Energy: 0.2 kJ (0.05 kcal). Alcohol-, bisulfite-, gluten-, lactose-, parabens-, sodium- and tartrazine-free. Bottles of 100. Protect from heat (store between 2 and 30°C) and humidity.

(Shown in Product Recognition Section)

Reviewed 1997

HYOSCINE

General Monograph, CPhA

see SCOPOLAMINE

HYPAQUE® PARENTERAL

Nycomed Imaging A.S.

Diatrizoate Sodium—Diatrizoate Meglumine

Contrast Media

Pharmacology: When injected into the chambers of the heart or into blood vessels, diatrizoate sodium and diatrizoate meglumine opacify their lumina, then they are rapidly carried via the bloodstream to the kidneys, where they are excreted unchanged mainly by glomerular filtration, permitting radiographic visualization of opacified heart chambers, blood vessels and the urinary tract. Administration into the urinary bladder, ureter, uterus, biliary system or joint cavities opacifies these structures.

When diatrizoate sodium and/or diatrizoate meglumine are employed for contrast enhancement of computed tomography, the degree of enhancement is reported to be directly related to the amount of iodine administered. In adults the amount of iodine usually required for contrast enhancement ranges from 28 to 42 g.

Peak iodine blood levels occur immediately following rapid injection of the dose and fall rapidly within 5 to 10 minutes. With respect to tumors, maximum contrast enhancement frequently occurs after peak blood iodine levels are reached. The delay in maximum contrast enhancement can range from 5 to 40 minutes, depending on the peak iodine levels achieved and the cell type and vascularity of the tumor. The radiographic enhancement of intracranial lesions other than tumors, e.g., aneurysms and arteriovenous malformations is probably dependent on the iodine content of the circulating blood pool.

Indications: Hypaque-M 18%: I.V. drip infusion pyelography, retrograde cystography and voiding urethrocystography and retrograde pyelography.

Hypaque-M 30%: I.V. drip infusion pyelography, retrograde cystography and voiding urethrocystography, retrograde pyelography and i.v. contrast enhancement in computerized tomography.

Hypaque Sodium 50%: Excretory urography, i.v. drip infusion pyelography, retrograde pyelography, operative and postoperative cholangiography, intraosseous venography, hysterosalpingography and i.v. contrast enhancement in computerized tomography.

Hypaque-M 60%: Excretory urography, i.v. drip infusion pyelography, retrograde pyelography, retrograde cystography

Hypaque Parenteral (cont'd)

and voiding urethrocystography, hysterosalpingography, aortography, angiography (peripheral arteriography and venography), cerebral arteriography, operative and postoperative cholangiography, arthrography and i.v. contrast enhancement in computerized tomography.

Hypaque-M 76%: Excretory urography, aortography, peripheral arteriography, angiocardiography, selective coronary arteriography, combined coronary arteriography and left ventriculography, i.v. contrast enhancement in computerized tomography and i.v. digital subtraction arteriography.

Contraindications: General: Patients with a hypersensitivity to salts of diatrizoic acid. A history of sensitivity to iodine or to contrast media of different chemical formulae is not an absolute contraindication to the use of Hypaque. The presence of hypersensitivity does however, call for extreme caution in the administration of these media.

Patients with a significant degree of renal failure. Urography and large dose vascular procedures are contraindicated in dehydrated, azotemic patients.

Do not use these solutions for myelography or for examination of dorsal cysts or sinuses which might communicate with the subarachnoid space. Injection of even a small amount into the subarachnoid space may produce convulsions and result in fatality. Epidural injection is also contraindicated.

Warnings: Serious or fatal reactions have been associated with the administration of radiopaque media. It is important that a course of action be planned in advance for the immediate treatment of serious reactions, and that adequate and appropriate facilities and personnel be readily available in the event that a severe reaction occurs.

Ionic iodinated contrast media inhibit blood coagulation more than nonionic contrast media. Nonetheless, it is necessary to avoid prolonged contact of blood with syringes containing all contrast media. Serious, rarely fatal, thromboembolic events causing myocardial infarction and stroke have been reported during angiographic procedures with nonionic and also with ionic contrast media. Therefore, meticulous intravascular administration technique is necessary, particularly, during angiographic procedures, to minimize thromboembolic events. Numerous factors, including length of procedure, number of injections, catheter and syringe material, underlying disease state and concomitant medications may contribute to the development of thromboembolic events. For these reasons, meticulous angiographic techniques are recommended including close attention to keeping guidewires, catheters and all angiographic equipment free of blood, use of manifold systems and/or 3-way stopcocks, frequent catheter flushing with heparinized saline solutions, and minimizing the length of the procedure. Although ionic contrast media have been used as flush solutions, the safety of this procedure has not been studied systematically. The use of plastic syringes in place of glass syringes has been reported to decrease but not eliminate the likelihood of clotting.

Administration of radiopaque materials to patients known or suspected to have pheochromocytoma should be performed with extreme caution. If, in the opinion of the physician, the possible benefits of such procedures outweigh the considered risk, the amount of radiopaque material injected should be kept to an absolute minimum. The blood pressure should be assessed throughout the procedure, and measures for treatment of a hypertensive crisis should be available.

Contrast media have been shown to promote the phenomenon of sickling in individuals who are homozygous for sickle cell disease when the material is injected i.v. or intraarterially. Fluid restriction is not advised in these patients.

Some clinicians consider multiple myeloma a contraindication to the use of contrast media because of the possibility of producing transient to fatal renal failure. If contrast media are used in the presence of multiple myeloma, dehydration should be avoided since it favors protein precipitation in renal tubules.

Caution is advised in patients with severe cardiovascular disease, hyperthyroidism, concomitant severe renal and hepatic disease and in patients with a history of bronchial asthma or other allergic manifestations, or of sensitivity to iodine.

Pregnancy: Safety for use in pregnancy has not been determined. Before administration of the solution to women of childbearing potential, the benefit to the patient should be carefully weighed against the possible risk to the fetus.

Lactation: Since diatrizoate contrast media are known to be excreted in breast milk, nursing should be stopped and alternate feeding substituted for 24 to 48 hours following administration of this product.

Precautions: Diagnostic procedures which involve the use of radiopaque contrast agents should be carried out under the direction of personnel with the prerequisite training and with a thorough knowledge of the particular procedure to be performed.

Prior to injection, the patient should be questioned for a history of allergy. Although a history of allergy may imply a greater than usual risk, it does not arbitrarily contraindicate the use of the medium. Premedication to avoid or minimize possible allergic reactions may be considered. Antihistamines should be given by a separate injection because precipitation may occur when mixed in the same syringe with these radiopaque media.

Do not prefill plastic syringes or other delivery systems with diatrizoate media for prolonged periods (i.e., several hours) before use.

The i.v. injection of a test dose of 0.5 to 1 mL of the contrast agent before injection of the full dose has been employed in an attempt to predict severe or fatal adverse reactions. The preponderance of recent scientific literature, however, now demonstrates that this provocative test procedure is not reliably predictive of serious or fatal reactions. Severe reactions and fatalities have occurred with the test dose alone, with the full dose after a nonreactive test dose, and with or without a history of allergy. No conclusive relationship between severe or fatal reactions and antigen-antibody reactions or other manifestations of allergy has been established. A history of allergy may be more useful in predicting reactions, and warrants special attention when administering the drug. Since delayed severe reactions may occur, the patient should be kept under observation for 30 to 60 minutes following injection.

There have been reports in the literature indicating that patients on adrenergic beta-blockers may be more prone to severe adverse effects to contrast media. At the same time, treatment of allergic-anaphylactoid reactions in these patients is more difficult. Epinephrine should be administered with caution since it may not have its usual effects. On the one hand larger doses of epinephrine may be needed to overcome the bronchospasm, while on the other, these doses can be associated with excessive alpha-adrenergic stimulation with consequent hypertension, reflex bradycardia and heart-block and possible potentiation of bronchospasm. Alternatives to the use of large doses of epinephrine include vigorous supportive care such as fluids and the use of beta agonists including parenteral salbutamol or isoproterenol to overcome bronchospasm and norepinephrine to overcome hypotension.

Addition of an inotropic agent to contrast agents may produce a paradoxical depressant response which can be deleterious to the ischemic myocardium.

Under some circumstances (pH, temperature, concentrations, time), diatrizoate solutions are incompatible with promethazine hydrochloride, diphenhydramine hydrochloride, brompheniramine maleate or papaverine hydrochloride solutions.

Because of the possibility of inducing temporary oliguria with contrast media, it is wise to allow an interval of at least 48 hours before studies are repeated especially in patients with unilateral or bilateral reduction of normal renal function.

Renal toxicity has been reported in patients with liver dysfunction who have been given an oral cholecystographic agent prior to the injection of diatrizoates. In such patients the administration of Hypaque should be postponed.

Preparatory dehydration is not necessary and may be dangerous in infants, young children, the elderly, presence of multiple myeloma and azotemic patients (especially those with polyuria, oliguria, diabetes, advanced vascular disease or preexisting dehydration). The undesirable dehydration in these patients may be accentuated by the osmotic diuretic action of the medium.

When high doses are used, caution should be exercised in patients with congestive heart failure because of the transitory increase in circulatory osmotic load, and such patients should be observed for several hours to detect delayed hemodynamic disturbances.

In angiographic procedures, dehydration of the patient is unnecessary and undesirable, especially if large doses of the medium are to be used.

Special precaution is advised in patients with cerebral thrombosis or embolism, primary or metastatic cerebral lesions, subarachnoid hemorrhage, increased intracranial pressure, arterial spasm, transient ischemic attacks and in any condition when the blood-brain barrier is breached or the transit time of the contrast material through the cerebral vasculature is prolonged, since clinical deterioration, convulsions and serious temporary or permanent neurological complications (including aphasia, cortical blindness, etc.) may occur following i.v. or intraarterial injection of relatively large doses of contrast media. Such patients, and patients in clinically unstable or critical condition should undergo examinations with intravascular contrast media only if in the opinion of the physician the expected benefits outweigh the potential risks and the dose should be kept to the absolute minimum.

When a contrast medium is used with a urea washout procedure, the patient should be observed for a few hours to detect signs of undue dehydration caused by increased diuresis induced by both the medium and the urea. Ingestion of water may be required for rehydration.

The results of PBI and RAI uptake studies, which depend on iodine estimation, will not reflect thyroid function for at least 16 days following administration of iodinated urographic media. However, function tests not depending on iodine estimations, e.g., T3 resin uptake or direct thyroxine assays are not affected (for Specific Precautions, see Dosage).

Adverse Effects: Reactions accompanying the use of contrast media may vary directly with the concentration of the substance, the amount used, the technique used, and the underlying pathology.

Mild and transient adverse effects occur frequently during or shortly after injection. These include nausea, vomiting, flushing, feeling of warmth, metallic taste, tingling of lips, tongue, mouth or extremities, faintness, sweating, headache, dizziness, tremor, chills, fever.

Minor allergic reactions such as sneezing, rhinitis, nasal stuffiness, coughing, lacrimation, urticaria with or without pruritus, other skin eruptions, mucocutaneous edema and allergic glossitis have occurred.

Severe, life-threatening adverse reactions, requiring immediate emergency measures occur in approximately 1 of 2 000 examinations. These include: laryngospasm, bronchospasm, wheezing and dyspnea, status asthmaticus, angioneurotic edema, subglottic edema with signs of airway obstruction, anaphylactic shock; cardiovascular collapse with peripheral vasodilation, hypotension, tachycardia, dyspnea, cyanosis, sweating, pallor, ventricular fibrillation, cardiac arrest; CNS stimulation or depression with agitation, convulsions, coma, death.

The reported fatality rate is approximately 1 of 40 000 urographic examinations.

Rarely, immediate or delayed rigors can occur, sometimes accompanied by hyperpyrexia. Infrequently, "iodism" (salivary gland swelling) from organic iodinated compounds appears two days after exposure and subsides by the 6th day.

Occasionally, transient proteinuria, and rarely, oliguria or anuria may occur. Serious neurological complications such as hemiplegia, aphasia and cortical blindness have occurred.

S.C. extravasation, chiefly because of hypertonicity of the medium, causes transitory stinging. If the volume is small, ill effects are very unlikely. However, if s.c. extravasation is extensive, especially in poorly vascularized areas (i.e., dorsum of the foot or hand) and in the presence of vascular disease, skin slough may occur. Injection of sterile water to dilute or addition of spreading agents to speed absorption have not been successful and may aggravate the condition.

Diffuse petechiae have been described and, in several instances, were traced to contamination of syringes, gloves with talc, or fine lint.

Rarely, disseminated intravascular coagulation has occurred.

Treatment of Adverse Reactions to Contrast Media: Contrast media should be injected only by physicians thoroughly familiar with the emergency treatment of all adverse reactions to contrast media. The assistance of other trained personnel such as cardiologists, internists and anesthetists is required in the management of severe reactions.

The following are guidelines for the treatment of adverse reactions. This outline is not intended to be a complete manual on the treatment of adverse reactions to contrast media or on cardiopulmonary resuscitation. The physician should refer to the appropriate texts on the subject. Techniques may vary between institutions and individual practitioners.

Minor allergic reactions: diphenhydramine 25 to 50 mg (or other antihistamine) i.v. or i.m. This is contraindicated in epileptics. Outpatients must not drive or go home unaccompanied due to the resulting drowsiness.

Major or life-threatening reactions: A major reaction may be manifested by signs and symptoms of cardiovascular collapse, severe respiratory difficulty and nervous system dysfunction. Convulsions, coma and cardiorespiratory arrest may ensue. The following measures should be considered:

1. Start emergency therapy immediately and carefully monitor vital signs. 2. Have emergency resuscitation team summoned. Do not leave patient unattended. 3. Ensure patent airway, guard against aspiration. 4. Commence artificial respiration if patient is not breathing. 5. Administer oxygen if necessary.

6. Start external cardiac massage in the event of cardiac arrest. 7. Establish route for i.v. medication by starting infusion of appropriate solution (5% dextrose in water). 8. Judiciously administer specific drug therapy as indicated by the type and severity of the reaction. Careful monitoring is mandatory to detect adverse reactions of all drugs administered: soluble hydrocortisone 500 to 1 000 mg i.v. for all acute allergic-anaphylactic reactions; 0.2 to 0.4 mL s.c. epinephrine 1:1 000 for severe allergic reactions. In extreme emergency epinephrine 0.1 mL/minute, appropriately diluted, may be given i.v. until desired effect is obtained. Do not exceed 0.4 mL; in case of cardiac arrest epinephrine 0.1 to 0.2 mL, appropriately diluted, may be given intracardially. In the presence of anoxia, epinephrine may cause ventricular fibrillation. Caution is advised in patients on adrenergic β-blockers (see Precautions). In hypotension (carefully monitoring blood pressure): phenylephrine HCl 0.1 to 0.5 mg appropriately diluted slowly i.v. or by slow infusion or levarterenol bitartrate 4 mL of 0.2% solution in 1 000 mL of 5% dextrose by slow drip infusion. Sodium bicarbonate 5%, 50 mL i.v. every 10 minutes as needed to combat post-arrest acidosis. Atropine 0.4 to 0.6 mg i.v. to increase heart rate in sinus bradycardia. May reverse 2nd or 3rd degree block. To control convulsions: diazepam 5 to 10 mg slowly i.v., titrating the dose to the response of the patient, or phenobarbital sodium may be injected i.v. or i.m. at a rate not in excess of 30 to 60 mg/minute. Depending on the patients response, a total dose of 200 to 300 mg may be required. The dose may be repeated in 6 hours if necessary. 9. Defibrillation, administration of antiarrhythmics and additional emergency measures and drugs may be required. 10. Transfer patient to intensive care unit when feasible for further monitoring and treatment.

Dosage: Angiocardiography: Specific Precautions: Due to tonicity, viscosity and the volume administered, it has been shown in vivo and in vitro that Hypaque-M 76% may cause a number of transitory hemodynamic changes, especially in right-sided injections. When the medium is ejected from the left ventricle or introduced at the root of the ascending aorta, a brief (3 seconds) hypertensive response is usually induced, followed immediately by a decrease in aortic and peripheral blood pressures below normal levels, lasting for at least 2 minutes. This hypotensive phase may be followed by a 15 to 20 minute period of fluctuating blood pressure. With large volumes, a drop in peripheral arterial and systemic pressures and cardiac output, a rise in pulmonary arterial and right-heart pressures, bradycardia and cardiac arrhythmia result. The effects of these changes on peripheral arterial and pulmonary arterial pressures are thought to be due to mechanical blockage of the pulmonary vascular bed and clumping of red cells.

Clinical doses (up to 1 mL/kg) injected into the vena cava or right-heart outflow tract usually cause an irregular rise in right ventricular blood pressure, a slight increase in pulmonary artery blood pressure, and delayed signs of peripheral hypotension. Special care should be observed in patients with right ventricular failure, pulmonary hypertension, or obliterated pulmonary vascular beds.

Other changes reported clinically include an increase in cardiac output and atrial pressure, a decrease in myocardial contractile force, and at the peak of post injection hypotension, a marked rise in aortic and carotid blood flow, and elevation of central venous pressure. At dosage levels used in angiocardiography, the hematocrit and hemoglobin level may fall about 10 to 15% and serum osmolality may rise 10 to 12%. Blood carbon dioxide, pH and BUN levels may fall. These changes commence immediately after injection, reach a maximum in 2 to 5 minutes, and return to normal values in 10 to 15 minutes. However, after the initial rise, plasma volume may decrease and continue to fall below control levels, even beyond 30 minutes, probably due to diuresis. If repeat injections are made in rapid succession, these changes are likely to be more pronounced.

During administration of large doses of Hypaque-M 76%, continuous monitoring of vital signs is desirable. Caution is advised in the administration of large doses to patients with incipient heart failure because of the possibility of aggravation of the pre-existing condition. Hypotension should be corrected promptly since it may induce serious arrhythmias.

Precaution in Infants: Apnea, bradycardia and other arrhythmias, cerebral effects (lethargy and depression), and a tendency to acidosis are more likely to occur in cyanotic infants. It is desirable that vital signs be monitored on an intensive care basis afterwards to detect delayed adverse effects (arrhythmias, electrolyte and hemodynamic disturbances). Infants are more likely than adults to respond with convulsions, particularly after repeated injections. The amount of the total dosage in young infants is of particular importance.

Dose: Angiocardiography: The individual dose is influenced by the size of the structure to be visualized, the anticipated degree of hemodilution, and valvular competence. Weight is a minor consideration in adults. The size of each individual dose is more important than the total dosage used. When large individual doses are administered, as for contrast in the cardiac chambers and aorta, it has been suggested that 20 minutes be permitted to elapse between each injection to allow for subsidence of hemodynamic disturbances.

Catheter Angiocardiography: Adults: (Media: Hypaque-M 76%): 35 to 50 mL into the right or left chamber, or vena cava. **Children:** (Media: Hypaque-M 76%) 0.5 to 1 mL/kg for a subject with heart of normal size and intact valves and septum. For patients with stenotic lesions, 0.5 mL/kg is recommended. Doses up to 1.5 mL/kg may be required in cardiomegaly, large volume shunts or where right cardiac injection is also intended to opacify left chambers. **Young infants:** The individual dose is similar to that described under Children's dosage. It has been suggested, however, that the total dosage administered should be maintained below 2 mL/kg in infants under 2 months old in any one procedure.

I.V. Angiocardiography: Adults: 70 to 100 mL.

Aortography: Specific Precautions: During aortography by the translumbar technique, extreme care is advised to avoid inadvertent intrathecal injection since the injection of even small amounts of the contrast medium may cause convulsions, permanent sequelae, or fatality. Should the accident occur, the patient should be placed upright to confine the hyperbaric solution to a low level, anesthesia may be required to control convulsions, and if there is evidence of a large dose having been administered, a careful cerebrospinal fluid exchange washout should be considered.

The presence of a vigorous, pulsatile flow should be established before using a catheter or pressure injection technique. A small "pilot" dose (about 2 mL) should be administered to locate the exact site of needle or catheter tip to help prevent injection of the main dose into a branch of the aorta or intramurally. In the translumbar technique, severe pain during injection may indicate intramural placement and abdominal or back pain afterwards may indicate hemorrhage from the injection site. Following catheter procedures, gentle pressure hemostasis for 5 to 10 minutes is advised, followed by observation and immobilization of the limb for several hours to prevent hemorrhage from the site of arterial puncture.

Under conditions of slowed aortic circulation there is an increased likelihood of aortography causing muscle spasm. Occasional serious neurologic complications, including paraplegia, have also been reported in patients with aorto-iliac or even femoral artery bed obstruction, abdominal compression, hypotension, hypertension, spinal anesthesia, injection of vasopressors to increase contrast, and low injection sites (L 2–3). In these patients the concentration, dose, and number of repeat injections of the medium should be maintained at a minimum with appropriate intervals between injections. The position of the patient and catheter tip should be carefully evaluated.

Aortic branches: Great care is necessary to avoid entry of a large concentrated bolus into an aortic branch. Mesenteric necrosis, acute pancreatitis, renal shut down, persistent cortical blindness, aphasia, serious neurologic complications including spinal cord damage and hemiplegia or quadriplegia have been reported following inadvertent injection of a large part of the aortic dose into an aortic branch or arterial trunks providing spinal or cerebral artery branches.

A "pilot" dose should be utilized to establish correct positioning of the catheter tip. Pain or muscle spasm during the injection may require reevaluation of the procedure.

Entry of the large aortic dose into the renal artery can cause, even in the absence of symptoms, albuminuria, cylindruria, hematuria, elevated BUN, acute tubular necrosis and infarction. Also reported are coronary occlusion, hemorrhage from puncture site, retroperitoneal hemorrhage, arterial perforation by catheter or needle, thrombosis, embolism and subintimal injection with aortic dissection by the medium.

Dose: Translumbar or Retrograde (Catheter) Aortography: Adults: (Media: Hypaque-M 60% or Hypaque-M 76%): Single dose of 15 to 35 mL. Note that sufficient time should elapse between each injection to allow for subsidence of hemodynamic disturbances. **Children:** (Media: Hypaque-M 60%) The single dose is proportionately less according to age and weight, generally not exceeding 0.5 mL/kg.

Arteriography: Cerebral Arteriography: Patients should be selected with care. There is increased risk in patients who have experienced recent cerebral embolism or thrombosis. The diagnostic value of the procedure must be considered in light of the added risk to the patient.

Reactions may vary directly with the concentration of the substance, the amount used, the speed and frequency of injections, and the interval between injections. In subarachnoid hemorrhage, angiography is expected to be hazardous. In migraine, the procedure can be hazardous because of ischemic complications, particularly if performed during or soon after an attack.

Specific Adverse Reactions: With any contrast medium introduced into the cerebral vasculature, neurologic complications, including neuromuscular disorders, seizures, loss of consciousness, hemiplegia, unilateral dysesthesias, visual field defects, language disorders (aphasia), amnesia and respiratory difficulties may occur. Such untoward reactions are, for the most part, temporary, although permanent defects have been reported.

Amaurosis can occur following carotid or especially selective vertebral arteriography. It is almost always transitory (4 to 48 hours) but may be permanent.

Some investigators who are experienced in angiographic procedure emphasize the fact that reactions tend to occur after repeated injections or higher doses of the contrast medium. Other clinicians find that they occur most frequently in elderly patients. It is noteworthy that the procedure itself is attended by technical difficulties regardless of the risk the patient presents.

Dose: Adults: (Media: Hypaque-M 60%): For carotid and vertebral angiography, depending upon the method used, most clinicians employ doses of 5 to 10 mL of Hypaque-M, 60% injected at a rate not exceeding the normal flow in the carotid artery (about 5 mL/second). The dose may be repeated as indicated, however, an increased risk attends each repeat injection. In the retrograde (brachial) method, a single injection of 35 to 50 mL is generally used. Depending upon the vessel injected and the method employed, other dosages may be used as indicated. **Children:** Use a smaller dose in proportion to weight. Light anesthesia may be required in these procedures.

Selective Renal Arteriography: Be aware that a transitory increase in the resistance of the renal vascular bed may occur with disturbance of renal function and renal damage.

Dose: Adults and children over 14 years of age: (Media: Hypaque-M 60% or Hypaque-M 76%): A single dose of 5 to 8 mL is recommended. The dose may be repeated if indicated. **Children** under 14 years of age: (Media: Hypaque-M 60%) The dose is proportionate to age.

Selective Coronary Arteriography: Specific Precautions: Coronary arteriography should only be used in carefully selected patients when the value of the anticipated information outweighs the risk involved. Coronary arteriography should be deferred for 4 weeks in patients with acute myocardial infarction. Continuous ECG monitoring for early detection of arrhythmias and adequate facilities for resuscitation and cardioversion are mandatory.

The injection of large volumes of hypertonic solutions into the heart chambers can cause significant hemodynamic disturbances (see also Specific Precautions in Angiocardiography).

Specific Adverse Reactions: Most patients will have transient ECG changes during the procedure. Serious cardiac arrhythmias, including ventricular tachycardia, ventricular fibrillation and cardiac arrest have occurred. Other adverse effects include hypotension, shock, minor and life-threatening arrhythmias, anginal pain, myocardial infarction and death. These may result from the manipulation of the catheter or from administration of the medium. Dissection of coronary arteries, dislodgment of arteriosclerotic plaques, perforation, hemorrhage, and thrombosis have been reported.

Dose: Adults: (Media: Hypaque-M 76%): 4 to 10 mL injected into a coronary artery. This dose, repeated if necessary, may be administered into each coronary artery. For combined coronary arteriography with left ventriculography, the intraventricular adult dose is 35 to 50 mL injected into the left ventricle, repeated if necessary.

Peripheral Arteriography and Venography: Specific Precautions: Pulsation must be present in the artery to be injected. Extreme caution is advised in considering peripheral angiography in patients suspected of having thromboangiitis obliterans (Buerger's disease) since any procedure (even insertion of a needle or catheter) may induce a severe arterial or venous spasm. Caution is also advisable in patients with severe ischemia associated with ascending infection. Special care is required when venography is performed in patients with suspected thrombosis, phlebitis, ischemic disease, local infection or a significantly obstructed venous system. In the presence of venous stasis, vein irrigation with normal saline should be considered following the procedure.

Hypaque Parenteral (cont'd)

Specific Adverse Reactions: Adverse reactions observed during peripheral arteriography may sometimes be due to arterial trauma during the procedure (i.e., insertion of a needle or catheter, subintimal injection, perforation, etc.), as well as to the hypertonic effect of the medium. Reported adverse reactions include soreness in extremities, transient arterial spasm, extravasation, hemorrhage, hematoma formation with tamponade, injury to nerves in close proximity to artery, thrombosis, dissecting aneurysm, arteriovenous fistula (e.g., with accidental perforation of femoral artery and vein during the needling), and transient leg pain from contraction of calf muscles in femoral arteriography. Transient hypotension has been reported after intraarterial (especially brachial) injection of the medium. Also, brachial plexus injury has been reported with axillary artery injections.

Following venography especially in the presence of venous stasis, inflammatory changes, thrombosis and gangrene may occur. Thrombosis is rare if the vein is irrigated following the injection.

Dose: Peripheral Arteriography: Adults: (Media: Hypaque-M 60% or Hypaque-M 76%): For visualization of an entire extremity, diagnostic arteriograms may be obtained with 25 to 35 mL of Hypaque-M 60% introduced into the larger peripheral arteries by percutaneous needle or catheter methods. For visualization of upper or lower half of extremity only, 10 to 20 mL may be used.

Sometimes Hypaque-M 76% is preferred over less concentrated media in selected cases of femoral and brachio-axillary arteriography. The usual dose of these more concentrated media is 10 to 25 mL, which may be repeated.

Peripheral Venography: Adults: (Media: Hypaque-M 60%): For visualization of an upper extremity 10 to 20 mL is suggested. For visualization of a lower extremity 20 to 40 mL is usually sufficient.

For visualization of the great saphenous vein, the upper femoral or the iliac veins, the medium is generally injected into the great saphenous vein in the lower leg at a rate of 1 mL/second. When demonstration of the small saphenous vein, the popliteal vein, or the lower femoral vein is necessary, injection is performed in a superficial vein of the outer aspect of the foot. The axillary and subclavian veins are best delineated by introducing the medium into the median basilic vein at the rate of 1 mL/second and exposing films during the process of injection.

Intraosseous Venography: Adults: (Media: Hypaque sodium 50% is recommended for injection directly into the bone marrow in the study of venous circulation of the bone and extraosseous tissue in the immediate drainage area). After aspiration of 4 mL of marrow, 10 to 20 mL of the medium are injected.

A general anesthetic is sometimes necessary since the method is painful. Occasionally, extravasation of the contrast medium from the needle into the soft tissue may occur.

Arthrography: Specific Precautions: A strict, aseptic technique is required to avoid introducing infection. Arthrography should not be performed when there is infection in or near the joint.
Specific Adverse Reactions: Injection of Hypaque-M 60% into the joint usually causes immediate but transient discomfort. However, delayed, severe or persistent pain may occur occasionally. Severe pain often results from undue use of pressure or the injection of large volumes. Joint swelling after injection is rare. Effusion, occasionally requiring aspiration, can occur especially in patients with rheumatoid arthritis.

Dose: Adults: (Media: Hypaque-M 60%): The procedure is usually performed with analgesic premedication and under local anesthesia. The amount of medium injected depends on the capacity of the joint.
The following approximate volumes have been used in normal adult joints: knee, shoulder, hip: 5 to 15 mL; temporomandibular: 0.5 mL; other: 1 to 4 mL.

The damaged joint may require doses exceeding those for normal joints. As much fluid as possible should first be aspirated from the joint; then, the medium should be injected gently to avoid overdistention of the joint capsule. Passive manipulation is sometimes used to disperse the medium in the joint. Sometimes a 1 or 2 mL test dose is injected; immediate pain may indicate extravasation or extracapsular injection. A single injection is usually adequate for multiple exposures. Contrast is good during the first 10 minutes after injection, adequate at 10 to 15 minutes, and begins to fade at 15 to 25 minutes.

Double contrast arthrography, using a mixture of the medium and air, has been employed.

Operative, Postoperative (T tube) Cholangiography: Specific Precautions: Injection should be made slowly to prevent extravasation of the medium into the peritoneal cavity, and to minimize reflux flow into the pancreatic duct which may result in pancreatic irritation.
Specific Adverse Reactions: Adverse reactions may often be attributed to injection pressure or excessive volume of the medium, resulting in overdistention. Such pressure may produce a sensation of epigastric fullness, followed by moderate pain in the back or right upper abdominal quadrant, which will subside when injection is stopped.

Some of the medium may enter the pancreatic duct and cause pancreatic irritation with a transient serum amylase elevation 6 to 18 hours later. Occasionally, nausea, vomiting, fever, and tachycardia have been observed. Pancholangitis resulting in liver abscess or septicemia has been reported.

Dose: Adults: (Media: Hypaque sodium 50% or Hypaque-M 60%):

Operative Cholangiography: As soon as the gallbladder and ducts have been exposed surgically, if no resistance is encountered, 10 to 15 mL of a 25 to 50 or 60% solution is injected into the cystic duct or common bile duct, as indicated, or the medium may be injected directly into the gallbladder after aspiration of its contents. Before closure of the abdomen, postexploratory or completion T tube cholangiography may also be performed after exploration of the common bile duct. The usual adult dose is 10 to 15 mL.

Postoperative (T tube) Cholangiography: Delayed cholangiograms are usually made from the fifth to the tenth postoperative day prior to removal of the T tube. Ten to 15 mL of either Hypaque sodium 50% or Hypaque-M 60% is injected into the T tube, preferably under fluoroscopic control.

In the case of a dilated ductal tract, a larger volume of radiopaque medium may be required for complete filling and visualization.

Hysterosalpingography: Specific Precautions: In patients with carcinoma or in those in whom the condition is suspected, caution should be exercised to avoid possible spread of the lesion by the procedure.

The procedure should not be performed during the menstrual period or when menstrual flow is imminent, nor should it be performed when infection is present in any portion of the genital tract, including the external genitalia. The procedure must not be performed in pregnant women or in those in whom pregnancy is suspected. Its use is not advised for 6 months after termination of pregnancy or 30 days after cervical conization or endometrial curettage.
Specific Adverse Reactions: Cramping may occur during the injection and sometimes mild lower abdominal pain may be present for an hour or two afterwards. Even when the medium gains entrance into venous or lymphatic channels, systemic effects are rare. Generalized urticaria or slight transient hyperpyrexia, however, have been reported.

Dose: Adults: (Media: Hypaque sodium 50% or Hypaque-M 60%) Approximately 4 mL of either media will fill the uterine cavity and an additional 3 to 4 mL will fill the oviducts in normal subjects. A larger volume may be required in some disease states. Slow injection through a cannula is advisable, preferably under fluoroscopic control.

It is preferable to perform the procedure approximately 10 days after the patient's menstrual period. The patient should empty the bladder before the examination. An enema and vaginal douche are not essential but may be given 1 hour before the study.

Urography: Excretory Urography: (Media: Hypaque sodium 50%, Hypaque-M 60% or Hypaque-M 76%):
Specific Precautions for Excretory Urography and Nephrotomography: Some clinicians consider multiple myeloma a contraindication to the use of contrast media because of the great possibility of producing transient to fatal renal failure. Others believe that the risk of causing anuria is definite but small. If contrast media are used in the presence of multiple myeloma, dehydration should be avoided since it favors protein precipitation in renal tubules.

Due to the transitory increase in circulatory osmotic load, use with caution in patients with congestive heart failure. Such patients should be observed for several hours to detect delayed hemodynamic disturbances.

Although moderate azotemia is not considered a contraindication, care is required in patients with significant renal failure. Preparatory dehydration may be dangerous, and urinary output should be observed for 1 to 2 days in these patients.

Preparatory dehydration is not necessary and may be dangerous in infants, young children, the elderly and azotemic patients (especially those with polyuria, oliguria, diabetes, advanced vascular disease, or pre-existing dehydration). The undesirable dehydration in these patients may be accentuated by the osmotic diuretic action of the medium. Dehydration will not improve contrast quality in patients with substantial renal insufficiencies and will increase risk of contrast induced renal damage; dehydration is therefore, contraindicated.

When either of these media is used with a urea washout procedure, the patient should also be observed for a few hours to detect signs of undue dehydration caused by increased diuresis induced by both the medium and the urea. Fluid replacement may be required for rehydration.

Dose: Adults: (Media: Hypaque sodium 50% or Hypaque-M 60%): 30 to 60 mL injected i.v. in 1 to 3 minutes. **Children:** 0 to 6 months, 5 mL; 6 to 12 months, 6 to 8 mL; 1 to 2 years, 8 to 10 mL; 2 to 5 years, 10 to 12 mL; 5 to 7 years, 12 to 15 mL; 7 to 11 years, 15 to 18 mL; and 11 to 15 years, 18 to 20 mL given i.v. over 1 to 3 minutes.

Adults: (Media: Hypaque-M 76%): 25 to 50 mL injected via the antecubital vein in 1 to 3 minutes. **Children and Infants:** under 6 months, 4 mL; 6 to 12 months, 6 mL; 1 to 2 years, 8 mL; 2 to 5 years, 10 mL; 5 to 7 years, 12 mL; 8 to 10 years, 14 mL; 11 to 15 years, 16 mL.

Although diagnostic urograms are often seen in patients who have had no preliminary preparation for urography, a laxative may be taken at bedtime to eliminate gas from the intestine, unless contraindicated.

Early minute sequence films may be taken if desired as, for example, in investigating hypertension. Additionally, the urea washout technique may be employed preferably after the 30-minute film.

Nephrotomography: When the prime purpose of the examination is to intensify and prolong the nephrographic effect of the renal parenchyma, especially with tomography, the contrast medium should be injected rapidly i.v.

Drip Infusion Pyelography: (Media: Hypaque-M 18%, Hypaque-M 30%, Hypaque sodium 50% and Hypaque-M 60%):
Specific Precautions: In older patients or those with cardiac disease the rate of infusion should be slower. The drip infusion technique is useful in carefully selected patients but is not considered appropriate for routine pyelography. This technique should not be used in patients with frank or incipient congestive heart failure, or in oliguric or anuric patients.

Dose: Adults: (Media: Hypaque-M 18%): 3 to 7 mL/kg not to exceed 300 mL. (Media: Hypaque-M 30%): 2 to 4 mL/kg not to exceed 300 mL. (Media: Hypaque sodium 50%, Hypaque-M 60%): 1 to 2 mL/kg not exceeding 150 mL mixed with an equal volume of 5% dextrose in water. **Children:** reduce according to weight and age.

Administer by rapid i.v. drip through an 18 gauge needle. Infusion usually takes 6 to 10 minutes, for optimal pyelogram at 20 and 30 minutes, and for optimal cystogram at 30 to 40 minutes.

When employing drip infusion pyelography, good quality voiding cystograms and urethrograms can also be obtained. To achieve the hydration, diuresis and complete filling of the urinary tract, the reasons for the technique's advantages, large volumes of contrast medium and fluid are required. The technique is especially useful in the presence of slight to moderate azotemia where ordinary techniques often prove inadequate. Preparatory dehydration is not recommended; diuresis is better if the patient is not dehydrated.

Retrograde Cystography and Voiding Urethrocystography:
Dose: Adults: (Media: Hypaque-M 18%, Hypaque-M 30% and Hypaque-M 60%): The usual concentration used for these procedures is 30%, however, some physicians may wish to use less concentrated solutions such as Hypaque-M 18%. Should the 60% solution be used it is necessary to dilute the media with appropriate volumes of sterile water or saline before use.

After the bladder is emptied the medium is gently instilled without force, preferably under fluoroscopic control often beyond the first desire to micturate, but not beyond the point of urgency or mild discomfort. The volume required to fill the bladder to slightly less than capacity may vary from patient to patient. The volume required in adults may vary from 250 to 500 mL with an average capacity of 300 mL. Bladder capacity at birth is 20 to 50 mL. In children 3 to 5 years old, bladder capacity is 150 to 180 mL. In children older than 8 years, it is in the low adult range.

In disease, bladder capacity in adults may vary from 50 mL in a hypertonic reflex bladder to over 1 000 mL in an atonic or sensory paralytic bladder or chronic lower urinary tract obstruction.

Administration of the solution through a catheter may be by gravity flow or by syringe at the discretion of the physician. For gravity flow infusion, it should be noted that the specially designed Hypaque-M 18% and Hypaque-M 30% flask closures may be removed to allow a screw type adaptor to be used to connect the infusion set.

Retrograde Pyelography: (Media: Hypaque-M 18%, Hypaque-M 30%, Hypaque sodium 50% or Hypaque-M 60%):
Specific Precautions: Retrograde pyelography should not be performed in patients with a known active infection process or obstruction of the urinary tract.

Because of the possibility of inducing temporary suppression of urine, it is wise to avoid repetition of retrograde pyelography within 48 hours in patients with reduced renal function.

A physical incompatibility (white precipitate) following the concomitant use of a surgical lubricant containing sodium alginate, has been reported. The use of a surgical lubricant of this type, in retrograde pyelography, is therefore considered to be undesirable.

Costovertebral angle tenderness, elevated temperature and flank pain have been reported in a few patients following use of diatrizoate sodium and diatrizoate meglumine for retrograde pyelography, as have nausea, sweating and flushing. Irritation of the urinary tract mucosa attributable to the contrast agent itself may occur. The technique of retrograde pyelography may be painful, and may initiate pelvic, caliceal or ureteral spasms with consequent renal colic. A few cases of reflex anuria have been reported following retrograde pyelography.
Dose: 30% solution of Hypaque meglumine has been found to be well tolerated when used for retrograde pyelography. Alternatively Hypaque-M 18% or Hypaque-M 60% diluted to a 20 to 30% solution with sterile distilled water, or Hypaque sodium 50% likewise diluted to a 20% solution may be used. The dosage is variable according to renal pelvic capacity. In general, the following volumes may apply for unilateral study. **Adults:** 6 to 10 mL. **Children over 5 years:** 4.0 to 5.0 mL. **Children under 5 years:** 1.5 to 3.0 mL. Administration by gravity from an elevated buret is preferable. Otherwise injection should be made slowly, without force, and should be stopped at the first sign of discomfort.

I.V. Contrast Enhancement in Computerized Tomography: The entire range of Hypaque media may be useful in the image enhancement of certain intracranial lesions of various etiologies, such as some tumors, vascular lesions, and sites of active infection.

Some cerebral infarctions of recent onset may be better visualized with contrast enhancement, while others are obscured if contrast media are used (see Precautions).

The opacification of the inferior vermis following contrast medium administration has resulted in false positive diagnoses in a number of normal studies.

The use of contrast enhancement in whole body CT scanning for the demonstration of various organs has been reported. This procedure is still in its early stages of development and requires considerable, careful individualization of technique and familiarity with all factors involved.
Specific Precautions: With the higher doses used for CT in patients with brain metastases and various other cerebral or cerebrovascular lesions, the incidence of seizures and serious neurological complications can be high (1 to 10%). In these patients, the risk/benefit ratio has to be carefully evaluated and prophylactic use of a small (parenteral) dose of diazepam should be considered immediately before injection of the contrast material.

It should also be kept in mind that diabetics with existing renal impairment may develop acute renal failure when administered a large intravenous dose of radiopaque media required for contrast enhancement in computerized tomographic scanning.

Since contrast media may obscure low density lesions, producing false negative results, it is generally recommended that a non-enhanced scan be obtained prior to the contrast enhanced scan, and it should be ensured that the patient has received no injection of contrast media at least 24 hours prior to the plain CT scan.
Dose: Adults: (Media: Hypaque-M 30%, Hypaque sodium 50%, Hypaque-M 60% or Hypaque-M 76%):

For contrast scanning enhancement in computerized tomography the suggested dose of Hypaque-M 30% is 1 to 4 mL/kg but not exceeding 300 mL, by i.v. drip over a period of 10 minutes or longer. Scanning may be performed during administration and/or immediately afterwards.

The suggested i.v. dose range for either Hypaque sodium 50% or Hypaque-M 60% is 50 to 150 mL and, for Hypaque-M 76% 50 to 110 mL. Scanning may be performed immediately after completion of administration. **Children:** should be proportionately less depending on age and weight.

I.V. Digital Subtraction Arteriography: Arteriograms of diagnostic quality can be obtained following the i.v. administration of Hypaque-M, 76% employing digital subtraction and computer imaging enhancement equipment. The i.v. route of administration using these techniques has the advantage of being less invasive than the corresponding intraarterial catheter placement of the medium. The dose is administered into a peripheral vein or by using an i.v. catheter threaded proximally into larger tributaries, the femoral vein or vena cava usually by mechanical injection although sometimes by rapid manual injection. The technique has been used to visualize the aorta and most of its larger branches including carotid, cerebral, vertebral, renal, celiac, mesenterics, and the major peripheral vessels of the limbs.
Specific Precautions: The risks associated with i.v. DSA include intramural injections, rupture or dissection of venous structures with extravasation into the tissues of extremities or the mediastinum. Small test injections of contrast medium made under fluoroscopic observation to insure the catheter tip is properly positioned, and in the case of peripheral placement that the vein is of adequate size, will reduce this potential. With high pressure injection; however, the catheter tip, initially placed in a large venous structure, may still recoil into a small tributary causing rupture of a small vein with extravasation into neighboring tissues.
Dose: (Medium: Hypaque-M 76%): The usual dose of Hypaque-M 76% per injection by the i.v. digital technique is 30 to 60 mL with a range of 0.5 to 1 mL/kg administered as a bolus at a rate of 7.5 to 12.0 mL/second and up to 30 mL/second (if injection is made into a large vein e.g., vena cava) using a pressure injector. The dose and rate of injection will depend primarily on the type of equipment and technique used, with first exposures made on calculated circulation time.

Supplied: Hypaque-M 18%: Each mL of injectable solution contains: diatrizoate meglumine 18% in water for injection (85 mg/mL bound iodine). Flasks of 500 mL, boxes of 6.

Hypaque-M 30%: Each mL of injectable solution contains: diatrizoate meglumine 30% in water for injection (141 mg/mL bound iodine). Vials of 15 mL, boxes of 10; bottles of 300 mL, boxes of 6.

Hypaque Sodium 50%: Each mL of injectable solution contains: diatrizoate sodium 50% in water for injection (300 mg/mL bound iodine). Nonmedicinal ingredients: sodium carbonate, sodium hydroxide or hydrochloric acid. Vials of 50 mL, boxes of 25.

Hypaque-M 60%: Each mL of injectable solution contains: diatrizoate meglumine 60% in water for injection (283 mg/mL bound iodine. Vials of 15 mL, boxes of 10; vials of 30 and 50 mL, boxes of 25; vials of 100 mL, boxes of 10; 150 mL fill in a 300 mL flask, boxes of 6.

Hypaque-M 76%: Each mL of injectable solution contains: diatrizoate meglumine 66% and diatrizoate sodium 10% in water for injection (370 mg/mL bound iodine). Nonmedicinal ingredients: sodium carbonate, sodium hydroxide or hydrochloric acid. Vials of 100 and 200 mL, boxes of 10.

These solutions are stabilized with edetate calcium disodium. Protect from light. Unused portions must be discarded.

HYPERSTAT® I.V. INJECTION ℞

Schering

Diazoxide

Antihypertensive

Pharmacology: Diazoxide injection produces a prompt reduction in blood pressure by relaxing smooth muscle in the peripheral arterioles. Cardiac output is increased as blood pressure is reduced by diazoxide; coronary and cerebral blood flow are maintained. Renal blood flow is increased after an initial decrease. Diazoxide has no known direct action on the CNS. Patients refractory to other antihypertensive agents usually remain responsive to diazoxide.

Diazoxide is extensively bound to serum proteins (>90%). The plasma half-life is 28±8.3 hours, however, the duration of its antihypertensive effect is variable, generally lasting less than 12 hours.

Indications: The emergency reduction of blood pressure in malignant hypertension in hospitalized patients, when prompt and urgent decrease of diastolic pressure is required. Hyperstat injection is especially valuable in the emergency treatment of hypertensive crises associated with acute congestive heart failure, acute hypertensive encephalopathy, acute glomerular nephritis, cerebral hemorrhage. It is also indicated in severe pre-eclamptic toxemia or eclampsia resistant to conventional antihypertensive therapy.

Treatment with orally effective antihypertensive agents should be instituted as soon as the hypertensive emergency is controlled.

Diazoxide injection is ineffective against hypertension due to pheochromocytoma.

Contraindications: Diazoxide injection should not be used in the treatment of compensatory hypertension, such as that associated with aortic coarctation or arteriovenous shunt.

The drug should not be used in patients hypersensitive to diazoxide or other thiazides, unless the potential benefits outweigh the possible risks.

Warnings: Hypotension may occasionally result from the administration of diazoxide injection. If hypotension, severe enough to require therapy occurs, it will usually respond to the administration of sympathomimetic agents, such as norepinephrine.

Hyperglycemia occurs in the majority of patients, but usually requires treatment only in patients with diabetes mellitus; it will respond to the usual management, including insulin. Therefore, blood glucose levels should be monitored, especially in patients with diabetes or in those patients requiring multiple injections of diazoxide.

Hyperglycemia and hyperosmolar coma associated with transient cataracts developed in one infant receiving repeated daily doses of oral diazoxide. The disturbed carbohydrate metabolism was successfully treated with insulin. Cataracts have been observed in a few animals receiving repeated daily doses of i.v. or oral diazoxide.

Since diazoxide causes sodium retention, repeated injections may precipitate edema and congestive heart failure. This retention responds characteristically to diuretic agents if adequate renal function exists. It should be noted that concurrently administered thiazides may potentiate the antihypertensive, hyperglycemic, and hyperuricemia actions of diazoxide (see Drug Interactions).

Since increased volume of extracellular fluid may be a cause of treatment failure in nonresponsive patients, it may be advisable to reduce this increased volume by means of a diuretic agent (see Drug Interactions).

Although no evidence of excessive anticoagulant effects has been reported, patients, especially those who are hypoalbuminemic and receive diazoxide injection and coumarin or its derivatives, may require reduction in dosage of the anticoagulant (see Drug Interactions).

Diazoxide injection should be administered with caution to patients being treated concurrently with methyldopa or reserpine, or with drugs which act by direct peripheral vasodilatation, especially hydralazine, the nitrites and papaverine-like compounds.
Pregnancy: Like other thiazides, diazoxide crosses the placenta and published animal experiments on sheep and goats indicate it can cause hyperglycemia effects in the newborn apparently through damage to the islets of Langerhans. However, published human clinical evidence indicates the use of diazoxide in eclamptic patients is compatible with the delivery of normal infants. In any case, if diazoxide injection is administered to pregnant women, the potential benefit should be weighed against the possible hazards to the fetus. As with thiazides, diazoxide crosses the placental barrier and appears in cord blood. They may produce fetal or neonatal hyperbilirubinemia, thrombocytopenia, altered carbohydrate metabolism, and possibly other adverse reactions that have occurred in adults; similar reactions may occur with diazoxide.

Precautions: Diazoxide injection is a potent antihypertensive agent requiring close monitoring of the patient's blood pressure at frequent intervals. Its administration may occasionally cause hypotension requiring treatment with sympathomimetic drugs. Therefore, adequate facilities to treat such untoward reactions should be available when diazoxide injection is used.

Diazoxide injection should be administered only into a peripheral vein. Because the alkalinity of the solution is irritating to tissue, extravascular injection or leakage should be avoided; s.c. administration has produced inflammation and pain without subsequent necrosis. If leakage into s.c. tissue occurs, the area should be treated conservatively.

Maximal antihypertensive effects occur after rapid administration (within 30 seconds) into the vein; a slower injection may fail to reduce blood pressure or produce a very brief response.

As with any potent antihypertensive agent, diazoxide injection should be used with care in patients who have impaired cerebral or cardiac circulation, that is, patients in whom abrupt and brief reductions in blood pressure might be detrimental or those in whom concurrent tachycardia may be deleterious.

Special attention is required for patients with diabetes mellitus and those in whom retention of salt and water may present serious problems (see Warnings). Nondiabetic patients, may have a transient, reversible, and clinically insignificant increase in blood glucose following diazoxide injection.

Hyperstat I.V. Injection (cont'd)

Since peritoneal dialysis or hemodialysis can reduce levels of diazoxide in the blood, patients undergoing dialysis may require more than one injection.

Adverse Effects: Frequent and serious adverse reactions: Sodium and water retention after repeated injections, especially important in patients with impaired cardiac reserve; hyperglycemia frequently requiring treatment in diabetic patients, especially after repeated injections.
Infrequent but serious adverse reactions: Hypotension to shock levels; myocardial ischemia, usually transient but possibly leading to thrombosis and manifested by angina, atrial and ventricular arrhythmias, and marked electrocardiographic changes; cerebral ischemia, usually transient but possibly leading to thrombosis and manifested by unconsciousness, convulsions, paralysis, confusion or focal neurological deficit, such as numbness of the hands; persistent retention of nitrogenous wastes after repeated injections; hypersensitivity reactions, such as rash, leukopenia, and fever. Rarely, acute pancreatitis has been reported. Papilledema induced by plasma volume expansion secondary to the administration of diazoxide, was reported in one patient who had received 11 injections over a 22 day period.
Others: Vasodilative phenomena, such as orthostatic hypotension, sweating, flushing, and generalized or localized sensations of warmth; supraventricular tachycardia and palpitation; bradycardia; various transient neurological findings secondary to alterations in regional blood flow to the brain such as headache (sometimes throbbing), dizziness, lightheadedness, sleepiness (also reported as lethargy, somnolence or drowsiness), euphoria or "funny feeling", ringing in the ears and momentary hearing loss, and weakness of short duration; chest discomfort or non-anginal "tightness in the chest"; transient hyperglycemia in nondiabetic patients, transient retention of nitrogenous wastes, and various respiratory and gastrointestinal findings secondary to the relaxation of smooth muscle, such as dyspnea, cough and choking sensation; nausea and vomiting and/or abdominal discomfort, anorexia, alteration in taste, parotid swelling, salivation, dry mouth, lacrimation, ileus, constipation and diarrhea. Also, warmth or pain along the injected vein; cellulitis without sloughing and/or phlebitis at the site of extravasation; back pain and increased nocturia. Apprehension or anxiety, malaise and blurred vision occurred on single occasions.
Drug Interactions: Since diazoxide is highly bound to serum protein, it may displace other substances which are also bound to protein, such as bilirubin or coumarin and its derivatives, resulting in higher blood levels of these substances. A drug interaction has also been reported for oral diazoxide and phenytoin, such that their concomitant administration may result in a loss of seizure control. These potential interactions must be considered when administering diazoxide injection. The concomitant administration of diazoxide with thiazides or other commonly used potent diuretics may potentiate the hyperglycemia, hyperuricemic and antihypertensive effects of diazoxide.

Diazoxide injection should be administered with caution to patients being treated concurrently with methyldopa or reserpine, or with drugs which act by direct peripheral vasodilatation, especially hydralazine, the nitrites and papaverine-like compounds.

Overdose: Symptoms and Treatment: Overdosage of diazoxide injection may cause an undesirable hypotension. Usually, this can be controlled with sympathomimetic agents, such as norepinephrine; failure of the blood pressure to rise in response to such an agent suggests that the hypotension may have been caused by something other than diazoxide. Excessive hyperglycemia resulting from an overdosage will respond to conventional therapy.

Diazoxide may be removed from the blood by peritoneal dialysis or hemodialysis.

Dosage: Diazoxide injection is administered undiluted and rapidly by i.v. injections of 1 to 3 mg/kg, up to a maximum of 150 mg. This dose may then be repeated at intervals of 5 to 15 minutes until a satisfactory reduction in blood pressure has been achieved.

Recent studies have shown that minibolus administration of diazoxide injection (doses of 1 to 3 mg/kg repeated at intervals of 5 to 15 minutes) is as effective as the administration of 300 mg in a single dose in reducing blood pressure while offering improved safety. Minibolus administration provides a more gradual reduction in blood pressure and thus avoids the circulatory and neurological risks associated with acute hypotension.

It should only be given into a peripheral vein. Do not administer it i.m., s.c., or into body cavities. Avoid extravasation of the drug into s.c. tissues.

The response to diazoxide injection varies from patient to patient. Generally, blood pressure decreases within 5 minutes, often within 1 to 2 minutes, to the lowest level achieved. The blood pressure increases relatively rapidly in the next 10 to 30 minutes, and then more slowly over the following 2 to 12 hours, nearly reaching but rarely exceeding the pretreatment level. The response to successive injections is frequently better than that to the initial injection.

Treatment of hypertensive emergencies with diazoxide injection should be limited to a few days and a regimen of oral antihypertensive medications should be instituted as soon as possible.

With the patient recumbent, the calculated dose of diazoxide injection is administered i.v. in 30 seconds or less. Slow i.v. injection may fail to reduce the blood pressure or may produce an exceedingly short response.

Repeated administration of diazoxide injection at intervals of 4 to 24 hours usually will maintain the blood pressure below pretreatment levels until a regimen of oral antihypertensive medication becomes effective. The interval between injections may be adjusted by the duration of the response to each injection. It is usually unnecessary to continue treatment with diazoxide injection for more than 4 to 5 days.

Following the use of diazoxide injection, the blood pressure should be monitored closely until it has stabilized. Thereafter, measurements taken hourly during the balance of the effect will indicate any unusual responses. A further decrease in blood pressure at 30 minutes or more after injection should be investigated for causes other than the action of diazoxide injection. It is preferable that the patient remain recumbent for half an hour after injection. In ambulatory patients, the blood pressure should be measured with the patient standing before surveillance is ended.

Since repeated administration of diazoxide injection can lead to sodium and water retention, administration of a diuretic may be necessary both for maximal blood pressure reduction and to avoid congestive failure (see Drug Interactions).

Supplied: Each 20 mL ampul contains: diazoxide 300 mg in a clear, colorless, aqueous solution. The pH is adjusted to approximately 11.6 with sodium hydroxide. Protect from light and freezing; store between 2 and 30°C.

HYPOTEARS®
CIBA Vision

Polyvinyl Alcohol

Artificial Tears

Supplied: Each bottle contains: polyvinyl alcohol 1% (w/v). Nonmedicinal ingredients: benzalkonium chloride 0.01% (w/v) (preservative), dextrose, disodium edetate, polyethylene glycol and purified water. Plastic squeeze bottles of 15 and 30 mL with dropper tip. Store at 15 to 30°C. Keep bottle tightly closed when not in use.

HYPOTEARS® Eye Ointment
CIBA Vision

Mineral Oil—White Petrolatum

Ocular Lubricant

Supplied: Each tube contains: white petrolatum 85% (w/w) and mineral oil 15% (w/w). Preservative-free. Tubes of 3.5 g. Store at 15 to 30°C. Keep tube tightly closed when not in use.

HYSKON®
Medisan Pharmaceuticals

Dextran 70 (32% w/v) in Dextrose

Hysteroscopy Fluid

Indications: For use with the hysteroscope as an aid in distending the uterine cavity and in irrigating and visualizing its surfaces.

Contraindications: Hypersensitivity to dextran. Contraindications relative to the hysteroscopic procedure itself (e.g., *pregnancy,* endometrial carcinoma).

Precautions: When large amounts of Hyskon are employed for hysteroscopy, the possible occurrence of systemic adverse effects including plasma volume expansion, transient prolongation of bleeding time and extremely infrequent anaphylactoid reactions should be borne in mind.

Adverse Effects: To date, few adverse effects directly attributable to the use of Hyskon have been reported. For a description of adverse effects known to occur with i.v. dextran administration, refer to Macrodex monograph.

A low incidence of hypervolemia has been reported following use of large volumes of Hyskon or after infusion at increased pressures.

Dosage: Dosage is dependent on several factors, such as the type and length of the diagnostic procedure and whether or not manipulation or surgery is performed. The amount of Hyskon instilled into the uterus is usually between 50 and 100 mL.

Introduce Hyskon into the uterine cavity through the cannula of a hysteroscope under low pressure (approx. 100 mm Hg) until the uterus is sufficiently distended to permit adequate visualization. During the hysteroscopic examination, conduct the instillation at a rate that keeps the cavity suitably distended. To avoid uptake of the fluid in the tissues of the uterus and parametria and to avoid having the fluid pass into the peritoneal cavity and backwards along the side of the hysteroscope, do not use pressures greater than 150 mm Hg.

Supplied: Each 100 mL bottle contains: a clear, viscid, sterile, nonpyrogenic solution of dextran 70 (32% w/v) in dextrose (10% w/v).

Hyskon has a tendency to crystallize when subjected to temperature variations or when stored for long periods. If dextran flakes are present, heat at 100 to 110°C until complete dissolution is achieved. Keep from cold during transportation.

HYTAKEROL® Ⓟ
Sanofi

Dihydrotachysterol

Antitetany Steroid

Pharmacology: Dihydrotachysterol is hydroxylated in the liver to 25-hydroxydihydrotachysterol, which is the major circulating active form of the drug. It does not undergo further hydroxylation by the kidney and therefore is the analogue of 1,25-dihydroxyvitamin D. Dihydrotachysterol is effective in the elevation of serum calcium by stimulating intestinal calcium absorption and mobilizing bone calcium in the absence of parathyroid hormone and of functioning renal tissue. It also increases renal phosphate excretion. In contrast to parathyroid extract, dihydrotachysterol is active when taken orally, exerts a slow but persistent effect, and may be used for long periods without increasing the dosage or causing tolerance. Dihydrotachysterol is faster-acting than pharmacologic doses of vitamin D and is less persistent after cessation of treatment, thus decreasing the risk of accumulation and of hypercalcemia.

Indications: Acute, chronic and latent forms of postoperative tetany, idiopathic tetany and hypoparathyroidism.

Contraindications: In patients with hypercalcemia, hypersensitivity to the effects of dihydrotachysterol, and hypervitaminosis D.

Precautions: To prevent hypercalcemia, treatment should always be controlled by regular determinations of blood and urine calcium levels, mainly during the beginning of treatment and until the required maintenance dose has been established.

Serum calcium levels should be kept between 9 and 10 mg/mL (2.25 to 2.5 mmol/L).

The monitoring of calciuria is a convenient supplement to serum calcium determinations, but it should not be regarded as a substitute, because in hypoparathyroid patients treated with dihydrotachysterol, hypercalciuria can occur in the presence of hypocalcemia. Serum phosphate and magnesium and alkaline phosphatases may be periodically measured to monitor progress in particular situations.

In patients with renal osteodystrophy accompanied by hyperphosphatemia, maintenance of a normal serum phosphorus level by dietary phosphate restriction and/or administration of aluminum gels as intestinal phosphate binders is essential to prevent metastatic calcification.

Dihydrotachysterol should be administered with caution in patients with hypercalciuria or with a history of calcium lithiasis.

If nausea and vomiting are present, serum calcium level should be checked.

It is advisable to be very careful in using dihydrotachysterol in patients suffering from sarcoidosis, as these individuals are very sensitive to the effect of vitamin D.

Drug Interactions: Interactions with Other Medicaments and Other Forms of Interaction: Drugs with enzymatic induction effects such as phenobarbital, rifampicin and isoniazid, and anti-epileptics including phenytoin may impair the efficacy of treatment and require higher doses of dihydrotachysterol.

Concomitant therapy with thiazide diuretics and dihydrotachysterol in hypoparathyroidism may result in excessive hypercalcemia. Lowered doses of dihydrotachysterol and close monitoring of serum calcium levels are recommended.

Thyroid replacement therapy may increase clearance of dihydrotachysterol.

Cholestyramine may impair the absorption of dihydrotachysterol.

Hypercalcemia induced by excessive dosage of dihydrotachysterol may enhance the toxic effects of cardiac glycosides.

Pregnancy: As safe use in pregnancy has not been established, the use of dihydrotachysterol during pregnancy should be avoided unless, in the judgment of the physician, the potential benefits outweigh the possible hazards. Animal reproduction studies in several species have shown that hypervitaminosis D is associated with fetal abnormalities. These abnormalities were similar to the supravalvular aortic stenosis syndrome described by Black, which included infants exhibiting supravalvular aortic stenosis, elfin facies, and mental retardation.

Lactation: Dihydrotachysterol is excreted in breast milk and may cause hypercalcemia in the suckling infant. Dihydrotachysterol should not be given to women who are breastfeeding.

Adverse Effects: Adverse effects are most likely to be due to overdosage and are manifested by symptoms of hypercalcemia.

First Signs Are: loss of appetite, nausea.

More Severe Manifestations Include: vomiting, urgency of micturition, polyuria, dehydration, thirst, vertigo, stupor, headache, abdominal cramps and paralysis. The calcium and phosphorus serum concentrations are increased.

Chronic Overdosage: With chronic overdosage, calcium may be deposited in many tissues, including arteries and kidneys, leading to hypertension and renal failure.

Overdose: Symptoms: Dihydrotachysterol may be toxic in doses as low as 25 mg/day, and is manifested by symptoms of hypercalcemia. The effects of dihydrotachysterol can persist for up to 1 month after cessation of treatment.

Treatment: Chronic Overdosage: the symptoms of hypercalcemia will usually respond to withdrawal of medication, bed rest, liberal fluid intake, and use of laxatives.

Acute Overdosage: emesis or gastric lavage should be performed if ingestion of dihydrotachysterol is recent. Serum calcium estimations should be helpful in determining management.

Massive Overdosage: corticosteroids (reduced intestinal absorption of calcium) should be administered. Resistant cases may also require the administration of neutral phosphate. Several months' management may be required in such cases.

Dosage: For oral administration only. Treatment depends on the nature and the seriousness of the disorder and must be individualized. Serum calcium levels should be kept within the normal range (9 to 10 mg/mL).

The dosage can be reduced with supplementation by oral calcium lactate or gluconate (10 to 15 mg daily).

Adults and Geriatrics: Acute Cases: Initial Dose: In acute cases, 6 to 10 capsules (0.75 to 1.25 mg) may be given daily for 3 days. Serum and urinary calcium estimations should be determined 2 or 3 days following the initial treatment period.

Maintenance Dose: Usually in the range of 2 to 14 capsules (0.25 to 1.75 mg) each week, administered in divided doses. The precise dosage depends on the results of serum and urinary calcium determinations.

Chronic Cases: In chronic cases, an initial dose of 4 capsules (0.5 mg) daily or on alternate days, may be sufficient to maintain normocalcemia.

The dose usually has to be increased during menstruation and periods of unusual activity.

Children: No specific dosage recommendation.

Supplied: Each dark brown, soft capsule, imprinted with an open W contains: the equivalent of 0.125 mg of crystalline dihydrotachysterol. Nonmedicinal ingredients: caramel, cinnamyl alcohol, gelatin, glycerin, methylparaben, propylparaben, purified water, sesame oil and titanium dioxide. Energy: 1.51 kJ (0.36 kcal). Gluten-, lactose-, sucrose- and tartrazine-free. Bottles of 50.

(Shown in Product Recognition Section)

Reviewed 1999

HYTRIN® Ⓟ
Abbott

Terazosin HCl

Antihypertensive—Symptomatic Treatment of Benign Prostatic Hyperplasia (BPH)

Pharmacology: Hypertension: The antihypertensive effect of terazosin is believed to be a direct result of peripheral vasodilation. Although the exact mechanism by which the lowering of blood pressure is achieved is not known, the relaxation of the vessels appears to be produced mainly by selective blockade of alpha-1-adrenoceptors.

Benign Prostatic Hyperplasia (BPH): The reduction in the symptoms associated with BPH following administration of terazosin may be related to the changes in muscle tone produced by a blockade of alpha$_1$-adrenoceptors in the smooth muscle of the bladder neck and prostate.

Pharmacodynamics: Hypertension: Systolic and diastolic blood pressure is lowered in both the supine and standing positions. In clinical trials, blood pressure responses were measured at the end of the dosing interval (24 hours), with the usual supine response 5 to 10 mmHg systolic and 3.5 to 8 mmHg diastolic. The response in the standing position tended to be larger by 1 to 3 mmHg.

Limited measurements of peak response (2 to 3 hours after dosing) during chronic terazosin administration indicate that this response is somewhat greater than the trough (24 hour) response, suggesting some attenuation of response at 24 hours, presumably due to a fall in blood terazosin concentrations at the end of the dose interval.

The greater blood pressure effect associated with peak plasma concentrations appears to be more position dependent (greater in the standing position) than the effect of terazosin at 24 hours; in the standing position there is also a 6 to 10 beat/minute increase in heart rate in the first few hours after dosing. During the first 3 hours after dosing 12.5% of patients had a systolic pressure fall of 30 mmHg or more from supine to standing, or standing systolic pressure below 90 mmHg with a fall of at least 20 mmHg.

During controlled clinical studies, patients receiving terazosin monotherapy had a small but statistically significant decrease (a 3% fall) compared to placebo in total cholesterol and the combined low-density and very-low density lipoprotein fractions. No significant changes were observed in high-density lipoprotein fraction and triglycerides compared to placebo.

Benign Prostatic Hyperplasia (BPH): The symptoms associated with BPH are related to bladder outlet obstruction. The bladder outlet obstruction is comprised of a static obstruction due to the enlarged prostate and a dynamic obstruction which is dependent upon the sympathetically controlled tone of the smooth muscle in the prostate and the bladder neck. Stimulation of alpha$_1$-adrenoceptors in the smooth muscle of the bladder neck and the prostate causes smooth muscle contraction and an increase in muscle tone.

In three placebo-controlled studies in men with symptomatic BPH, symptom evaluation and uroflowmetric measurements were performed approximately 24 hours following dosing. Results from these studies indicated that terazosin significantly improved symptoms and peak urine flow rates over placebo.

In 30 to 70% of patients with symptomatic BPH, placebo has also shown a remarkable and sometimes dramatic effect in controlled short-term studies. The symptoms may subside or fade away without treatment in approximately 20% of patients.

Pharmacokinetics: Orally administered terazosin is essentially completely absorbed in man. Nearly all of the circulating dose is in the form of parent drug. Food has little or no effect on the bioavailability. The plasma levels of the free base peak in about 1 hour and then decline with a half-life of approximately 12 hours. Approximately 90 to 94% of the drug is bound to plasma proteins and binding is constant over the clinically observed concentration range.

Hepatic metabolism is extensive with major biliary elimination. Approximately 10% of an orally administered dose is excreted as parent drug in the urine and approximately 20% is excreted in the feces. The remainder is eliminated as metabolites. Overall approximately 40% of the administered dose is excreted in the urine and approximately 60% in the feces.

Indications: Hypertension: Terazosin is indicated in the treatment of mild to moderate hypertension. It is employed in a general treatment program in conjunction with a thiazide diuretic and/or other antihypertensive drugs as needed for proper patient response. Terazosin may be tried as a sole therapy in those patients in whom other agents caused adverse effects or are inappropriate.

Benign Prostatic Hyperplasia (BPH): Terazosin is also indicated for the treatment of symptoms of benign prostatic hyperplasia (BPH). The onset of effect is rapid, with improvement in peak flow rate and symptoms observed at 2 weeks. The effect on these variables was well maintained throughout the study duration (18 months). Terazosin does not retard or stop the progression of BPH. The long-term effects of terazosin on the incidence of surgery, acute urinary obstruction or other complications of BPH, are yet to be determined.

A number of clinical conditions can mimic symptomatic BPH (i.e., stricture of urethra, stricture of bladder neck, urinary bladder stones, neurogenic bladder dysfunction secondary to diabetes, Parkinsonism, etc.). These conditions should therefore be ruled out before terazosin therapy is initiated.

Contraindications: In individuals who have shown hypersensitivity to terazosin or its analogs.

Warnings: Syncope and "First Dose" Effect: Terazosin can cause marked hypotension, especially postural hypotension, and syncope in association with the first dose or first few doses of therapy. A similar effect can occur if therapy is re-instated following interruption for more than a few doses. Syncope has also occurred in association with rapid dosage increases or the introduction of another antihypertensive agent into the regimen of a patient taking high doses of terazosin.

Syncope is believed to be due to an excessive postural hypotensive effect, although occasionally the syncopal episode has been preceded by a bout of severe supraventricular tachycardia with heart rates of 120 to 160 beats/minute.

In studies of terazosin the incidence of syncopal episodes was approximately 1% in hypertensive patients and 0.7% in patients with BPH.

The likelihood of syncopal episodes or excessive hypotension can be minimized by limiting the initial dose of the drug to 1 mg of terazosin given at bedtime, by increasing the dosage slowly, and by introducing any additional antihypertensive drugs into the patient's regimen with caution (see Dosage).

Occupational Hazards: Patients should be advised of the possibility of syncopal and orthostatic symptoms, and to avoid driving or hazardous tasks for 12 hours after the initial dose of terazosin, after the dose is increased and after interruption of therapy when treatment is resumed. They should be cautioned to avoid situations where injury could result should syncope occur.

If syncope occurs, place the patients in the recumbent position and institute supportive measures as necessary.

Patients with a history of micturition syncope should not receive terazosin.

Concomitant administration of terazosin with verapamil to hypertensive patients may result in symptomatic hypotension and in some cases tachycardia (see Precautions).

Anaphylactoid-like Terazosin Reactions: Anaphylactoid-like reactions manifested by angioedema of the lips, tongue, pharynx, and/or laryngeal spasm have been rarely reported in patients treated with terazosin (see Adverse Effects). In such cases, terazosin should be promptly discontinued and appropriate therapy and monitoring should be provided until complete and sustained resolution of signs and symptoms has occurred.

Precautions: General: Terazosin therapy does not modify the natural history of benign prostatic hyperplasia (BPH). It does not retard or stop the progression of BPH, nor does it improve urine flow sufficiently to significantly reduce the residual urine volume. However, significant reduction of the mean residual volume have been shown in patients with baseline residual volumes of > 50 mL. The patient may continue to be at risk of developing urinary retention and other BPH complications during terazosin therapy.

Prostatic Cancer: Carcinoma of the prostate and BPH cause many of the same symptoms. These two diseases frequently coexist. Therefore, patients thought to have BPH should be examined prior to starting Hytrin therapy to rule out the presence of carcinoma of the prostate.

Orthostatic Hypotension: While syncope is the most severe orthostatic effect of terazosin (see Warnings) other symptoms of lowered blood pressure, such as dizziness, lightheadedness and palpitations are more common with one or more of these occurring in 28% of patients in clinical trials of hypertension.

In BPH clinical trials, 21% of the patients experienced one or more of the following: dizziness, hypotension, postural hypotension, syncope and vertigo.

Patients should be advised to lie down when these symptoms occur and then wait for a few minutes before standing to prevent their recurrence.

Hytrin (cont'd)

Patients with an occupation in which such events represent potential problems should be treated with particular caution.

There is evidence that the orthostatic effect of terazosin is greater, even in chronic use, shortly after dosing.

Concomitant Conditions: Terazosin should not be prescribed to patients with symptomatic BPH who have the following concomitant conditions: chronic urinary retention, high residual urine (over 200 mL), peak urine flow of 5 mL/second or less, history of prior prostatic surgery, chronic fibrous or granulomatous prostatitis, urethral stricture, history of pelvic irradiation, presence of prostatic calculi, presence of large median lobe of prostate, presence of calculi in urinary bladder, recent history of epididymitis, gross hematuria, presence of neurogenic bladder dysfunction (diabetes mellitus, Parkinsonism, uninhibited neurogenic bladder, etc.), hydronephrosis, presence of carcinoma of the prostate, patients with clinically significant renal or hepatic impairment (i.e., serum creatinine > 2 mg/dL or AST > 1.5 times the upper limit of normal (or equivalent level on the international scale).

Carcinogenesis, Mutagenesis, Impairment of Fertility: Terazosin was devoid of mutagenic potential when evaluated in vivo and in vitro.

Terazosin, administered in the feed to rats at doses of 8, 40, and 250 mg/kg/day for 2 years, was associated with a statistically significant increase in benign adrenal medullary tumors of male rats exposed to the 250 mg/kg dose. Female rats were unaffected. The drug was not oncogenic in mice when administered in feed for 2 years at a maximum tolerated dose of 32 mg/kg/day.

Effect on fertility was assessed in a standard fertility/reproductive performance study in which male and female rats were administered oral doses of 8, 30 and 120 mg/kg/day. Four of 20 male rats given 30 mg/kg and 5 of 19 male rats given 120 mg/kg failed to sire a litter. Testicular weights and morphology were unaffected by treatment. Vaginal smears at 30 and 120 mg/kg, however, appeared to contain less sperm than smears from control matings and good correlation was reported between sperm count and subsequent pregnancy.

Oral administration of terazosin for 1 or 2 years elicited a statistically significant increase in the incidence of testicular atrophy in rats exposed to 40 and 250 mg/kg/day, but not in rats exposed to 8 mg/kg/day. Testicular atrophy was also observed in dogs dosed with 300 mg/kg/day for 3 months but not after 1 year when dosed with 20 mg/kg/day.

Geriatrics: Terazosin should be used cautiously in elderly patients because of the possibility of orthostatic hypotension. There was an age-related trend towards an increased incidence of dizziness, blurred vision and syncope in elderly patients treated with this drug. Patients over 75 years of age may have limited benefit from terazosin therapy.

Children: The use of terazosin in children is not recommended since safety and efficacy have not been established.

Patients with Renal Impairment: The use of terazosin in patients with impaired renal function requires careful monitoring. Limited pharmacokinetic studies using low doses (1 mg) showed no difference in the pharmacokinetics of terazosin as compared to patients with normal renal function. Approximately 40% of oral terazosin dose is excreted by the kidney as parent drug or metabolites.

Patients with Liver Impairment: No information is available on the use of terazosin in patients with impaired liver function.

Peripheral Edema: Fluid retention resulting in weight gain may occur during terazosin therapy. In placebo-controlled monotherapy trials, male and female patients receiving terazosin gained a mean of 0.8 and 1 kg respectively, compared to losses of 0.1 and 0.5 kg respectively, in the placebo group. Both differences were significant.

Pregnancy: The safety of terazosin in pregnancy has not been established. Terazosin is not recommended during pregnancy unless potential benefits justify potential risks to mother and fetus.

In animal studies there was no teratogenic effect. In peri and postnatal development studies in rats, significantly more pups died in the group dosed with 120 mg/kg/day than in the control group during the 3 week postpartum period.

Lactation: It is not known whether terazosin is excreted in human milk. Because of possible adverse reactions in nursing infants an alternate method of infant feeding should be considered when the use of the drug is essential.

Drug Interactions: In controlled trials, terazosin has been added to diuretics and several beta-adrenergic blockers; except for the additive hypotensive effect, no unexpected interactions were observed. Terazosin has also been used in patients on a variety of concomitant therapies. While these were not formal interaction studies, no interactions were observed. Terazosin has been used concomitantly in at least 50 patients on the following drugs or drug classes: analgesic/anti-inflammatory (e.g., acetaminophen, ASA, codeine, ibuprofen, indomethacin); antibiotics (e.g. erythromycin, trimethoprim and sulfamethoxazole); anticholinergic/sympathomimetics (e.g., phenylephrine HCl, phenylpropanolamine HCl, pseudoephedrine HCl); antigout (e.g., allopurinol); antihistamines (e.g., chlorpheniramine); cardiovascular agents (e.g., atenolol, hydrochlorothiazide, methyclothiazide, propranolol); corticosteroids; gastrointestinal agents (e.g., antacid); hypoglycemics; sedatives and tranquilizers (e.g., diazepam).

Concomitant administration of terazosin with verapamil to hypertensive patients resulted in significant increases in AUC, Cmax and Cmin of terazosin. The pharmacokinetics of verapamil were not altered. Symptomatic hypotension, and in some cases tachycardia, were observed. Caution should therefore be exercised when these drugs are administered concomitantly (see Warnings).

Laboratory Tests: Long-term (6 months or longer) administration of terazosin has produced no pattern of clinically significant changes attributable to the drug in the following clinical laboratory measurements: glucose, uric acid, creatinine, BUN, liver function tests, and electrolytes. Small but statistically significant decreases in hematocrit, hemoglobin, white blood cells, total protein and albumin were observed in controlled clinical trials. These laboratory findings suggested the possibility of hemodilution. Treatment with terazosin for up to 24 months had no significant effect on prostate specific antigen (PSA) levels.

Adverse Effects: Hypertension: The incidence of adverse reactions is derived from clinical trials involving 1 986 hypertensive patients on terazosin monotherapy or combination therapy.

The most serious adverse reaction encountered with terazosin is syncope occurring in approximately 1% of patients.

The most common reactions were dizziness (18.9%), headache (14.1%), asthenia (11%), somnolence (4.8%), nasal congestion (4.6%) and palpitation (4.6%).

The most frequently reported adverse effects which resulted in termination of the drug were dizziness 3.5%, asthenia 2.1% and headache 1.8%.

The following events were reported in less than 1% of cases except as indicated in brackets. The order of presentation corresponds within each heading to the relative frequency of occurrence.

Body as a Whole: headache (14.1%), asthenia (11%), peripheral edema (3.6%), chest pain (2.2%), abdominal pain (1.5%), edema (1.3%), facial edema (1%), back pain, weight gain, allergic reactions, malaise.

Cardiovascular: palpitation (4.6%), tachycardia (2.9%), syncope (1%), postural hypotension, angina pectoris, arrhythmias, cerebrovascular accident, heart failure, hypotension (at times severe), migraine.

Digestive: nausea (3.9%), dry mouth (1.7%), diarrhea (1.3%), dyspepsia, vomiting, anorexia, gastritis, liver function abnormality, jaundice.

Nervous System: dizziness (18.9%), somnolence (4.8%), nervousness (2.2%), paresthesia (1.5%), insomnia (1.2%), incoordination, abnormal dreams, confusion, speech disorder, tremor, vertigo, seizure, depression.

Respiratory: nasal congestion (4.6%), dyspnea (2.8%), rhinitis (1.2%), sinusitis, cold symptoms, pharyngitis, asthma, increased cough, laryngeal spasm.

Skin and Appendages: sweating (1.1%), pruritus, rash, photosensitivity.

Special Senses: blurred vision (1.4%), eye disorder (1.2%), tinnitus, taste perversion.

Urogenital: impotence (1.1%), urinary frequency, dysuria.

Miscellaneous: pain in extremities (1.8%), hypokalemia, hypophosphatemia, decreased libido.

Postmarketing Experience: Body as a whole: fever, neck pain and shoulder pain anaphylaxis has rarely been reported. Cardiovascular System: vasodilation, atrial fibrillation has been reported; however, a cause and effect relationship has not been established. Digestive System: constipation and flatulence. Nervous System: anxiety. Respiratory System: bronchitis, epistaxis, and flu symptoms. Special Senses: conjunctivitis. Urogenital System: priapism, urinary tract infection, and urinary incontinence primarily reported in postmenopausal women. Musculoskeletal System: arthralgia, arthritis, joint disorder, and myalgia. Hematopoietic System: Thrombocytopenia has been reported. Metabolic/Nutritional Disorders: gout.

Benign Prostatic Hyperplasia (BPH): In clinical trials involving 1 171 patients with BPH, syncope was reported in 0.7% of patients following treatment with terazosin.

The most common reactions (≥ 1%) were dizziness (14%), asthenia (9%), headache (6.4%), somnolence (4.5%), postural hypotension (3.8%), impotence (3.5%), urinary tract infection (3.1%), pharyngitis (2.7%), dyspnea (2.5%), rhinitis (2.2%), dysuria (2%), back pain (1.8%), nausea (1.8%), flu syndrome (1.7%), rash (1.7%), sinusitis (1.7%), hypotension (1.5%), chest pain (1.5%), vertigo (1.3%), dyspepsia (1.1%), diarrhea (1%), palpitation (1%), abdominal pain (1%) and amblyopia (1%).

Postmarketing Experience: Thrombocytopenia has been reported. Atrial fibrillation has been reported; however, a cause and effect relationship has not been established. Priapism has also been reported. Anaphylaxis has rarely been reported.

Overdose: Symptoms and Treatment: Should administration of terazosin lead to hypotension, support of the cardiovascular system is of first importance. Restoration of blood pressure and normalization of heart rate may be accomplished by keeping the patient in the supine position. If this measure is inadequate, shock should first be treated with volume expanders. If necessary, vasopressors should then be used and the renal function should be monitored and supported as needed. Laboratory data indicate that terazosin is highly protein bound; therefore, dialysis may not be of benefit.

Dosage: Hypertension: The dose and the dosing intervals (12 or 24 hours) should be adjusted to the patient's individual blood pressure response.

When terazosin is being added to the existing antihypertensive therapy, the patient should be carefully monitored for the occurrence of hypotension. If a diuretic or other antihypertensive agent is being added to the terazosin regimen, dosage reduction of terazosin and retitration with careful monitoring may be necessary. The following is a guide to its administration:

Initial Dose: 1 mg of terazosin at bedtime is the starting dose for all patients and this dose should not be exceeded; compliance with this initial dosage recommendation should be strictly observed to minimize the potential for acute hypotensive episodes.

Subsequent Doses: The dose may be slowly increased to achieve the desired blood pressure response. The usual dose range is 1 to 5 mg once-a-day. Some patients may benefit from doses up to 20 mg/day which is the maximum recommended daily dose.

The blood pressure should be monitored at the end of the dosing interval to assure that control is maintained. It is also helpful to measure the blood pressure 2 to 3 hours after dosing to see if the maximum and minimum responses are similar and to evaluate symptoms.

If response to terazosin is substantially diminished at 24 hours, patients may be tried on a larger dose or twice daily dosage regimen. The latter should also be considered if adverse effects such as dizziness, palpitations or orthostatic complaints are seen 2 to 3 hours after dosing.

If terazosin administration is discontinued for several days or longer, therapy should be reinstituted using the initial dosing regimen.

Benign Prostatic Hyperplasia (BPH): The dose of terazosin should be adjusted to the patient's individual response.

Initial Dose: 1 mg of terazosin at bedtime is the starting dose for all patients, and this dose should not be exceeded for the first week. Compliance with this initial dosage should be strictly observed to minimize the potential for acute hypotensive episodes.

Subsequent Doses: The dose should be increased in a stepwise fashion at weekly intervals to 2, 5 or 10 mg once daily to achieve the desired improvement of symptoms and/or flow rates. Maintenance doses of 5 to 10 mg once daily are generally required for the clinical response. The duration and dosage of treatment should be carefully titrated. Four weeks of terazosin therapy may be required before statistically significant improvement in the objective parameters of flowmetry (peak urine flow) are obtained. Improvement in the symptoms may appear as early as 2 weeks, but may be delayed as late as 6 weeks or more. Some patients may not achieve a clinical response despite appropriate titration. Following 18 months of treatment, a complete re-evaluation of the patient's condition should be made.

Following the administration of the maximum recommended dosage, terazosin should be discontinued if improvement in uroflowmetry is not clinically significant from baseline level or improvement in the American Urology Association (AUA) scores are not translated into improvements in quality of life. Terazosin therapy should also be discontinued if terazosin side effects are more bothersome than BPH symptoms or if the patient develops a urinary complication while on terazosin therapy.

If terazosin administration is discontinued for several days or longer, therapy should be reinstituted using the initial dosing regimen.

Information for the Patient: See Blue Section—Information for the Patient "Hytrin".

Supplied: 1 mg: Each white, round tablet contains: terazosin 1 mg (as terazosin HCl dihydrate). Nonmedicinal ingredients: cornstarch, lactose, magnesium stearate, povidone and talc. Alcohol-, gluten-, paraben-, sodium-, sucrose-, sulfite- and tartrazine-free. Bottles of 100.

2 mg: Each orange round tablet contains: terazosin 2 mg (as terazosin HCl dihydrate). Nonmedicinal ingredients: cornstarch, FD&C yellow No. 6, lactose, magnesium stearate, povidone and talc. Alcohol-, gluten-, paraben-, sodium-, sucrose-, sulfite- and tartrazine-free. Bottles of 100.

5 mg: Each tan, round tablet contains: terazosin 5 mg (as terazosin HCl dihydrate). Nonmedicinal ingredients: cornstarch, iron oxide, lactose, magnesium stearate, povidone and talc. Alcohol-, gluten-, paraben-, sodium-, sucrose-, sulfite- and tartrazine-free. Bottles of 100.

10 mg: Each blue, round tablet contains: terazosin 10 mg (as terazosin HCl dihydrate). Nonmedicinal ingredients: cornstarch, FD&C Blue No. 2, lactose, magnesium stearate and talc. Alcohol-, gluten-, paraben-, sodium-, sucrose-, sulfite- and tartrazine-free. Bottles of 100.

Starter Pack: 1 strip (7) of each 1 mg and 2 mg tablets and 2 strips (2×7) of 5 mg tablets in blisters.

Store tablets at controlled room temperature (15 to 30°C).

(Shown in Product Recognition Section)

Reviewed 1998

HYZAAR® Ⓟ

MSD

Losartan Potassium—Hydrochlorothiazide

Angiotensin II Receptor Antagonist—Diuretic

Pharmacology: Hyzaar combines the actions of losartan potassium, an angiotensin II receptor antagonist, and that of a thiazide diuretic, hydrochlorothiazide.

Losartan: Losartan antagonizes angiotensin II by blocking the angiotensin type 1 (AT_1) receptor.

Angiotensin II is the primary vasoactive hormone of the renin-angiotensin system. Its effects include vasoconstriction and the stimulation of aldosterone secretion by the adrenal cortex.

Losartan, and its active metabolite, E-3174, block the vasoconstrictor and aldosterone-secreting effects of angiotensin II by selectively blocking the binding of angiotensin II to AT_1 receptors found in many tissues, including vascular smooth muscle. A second type of angiotensin II receptor has been identified as the AT_2 receptor, but it plays no known role in cardiovascular homeostasis to date. Both losartan and its active metabolite do not exhibit any agonist activity at the AT_1 receptor, and have much greater affinity, in the order of 1 000-fold, for the AT_1 receptor than for the AT_2 receptor. In vitro binding studies indicate that losartan itself is a reversible, competitive antagonist at the AT_1 receptor, while the active metabolite is 10 to 40 times more potent than losartan, and is a reversible, non-competitive antagonist of the AT_1 receptor.

Neither losartan nor its active metabolite inhibits angiotensin converting enzyme (ACE), also known as kininase II, the enzyme that converts angiotensin I to angiotensin II and degrades bradykinin, nor do they bind to or block other hormone receptors or ion channels known to be important in cardiovascular regulation.

Hydrochlorothiazide: Hydrochlorothiazide is a diuretic and antihypertensive which interferes with the renal tubular mechanism of electrolyte reabsorption. It increases excretion of sodium and chloride in approximately equivalent amounts. Natriuresis may be accompanied by some loss of potassium and bicarbonate. While this compound is predominantly a saluretic agent, in vitro studies have shown that it has a carbonic anhydrase inhibitory action which seems to be relatively specific for the renal tubular mechanism. It does not appear to be concentrated in erythrocytes or the brain in sufficient amounts to influence the activity of carbonic anhydrase in those tissues.

Hydrochlorothiazide is useful in the treatment of hypertension. It may be used alone or as an adjunct to other antihypertensive drugs. Hydrochlorothiazide does not affect normal blood pressure.

Pharmacokinetics: Losartan: Losartan is an orally active agent that undergoes substantial first-pass metabolism by cytochrome P450 enzymes. It is converted, in part, to an active carboxylic acid metabolite, E-3174, that is responsible for most of the angiotensin II receptor antagonism that follows oral losartan administration.

The terminal half-life of losartan itself is about 2 hours, and that of the active metabolite, about 6 to 9 hours. The pharmacokinetics of losartan and this metabolite are linear with oral losartan doses up to 200 mg and do not change over time. Neither losartan nor its metabolite accumulate in plasma upon repeated once-daily administration.

Following oral administration, losartan is well absorbed, with systemic bioavailability of losartan approximately 33%. About 14% of an orally-administered dose of losartan is converted to the active metabolite, although about 1% of subjects did not convert losartan efficiently to the active metabolite.

Mean peak concentrations of losartan occur at about 1 hour, and that of its active metabolite at about 3 to 4 hours. Although maximum plasma concentrations of losartan and its active metabolite are approximately equal, the AUC of the metabolite is about 4 times greater than that of losartan.

Both losartan and its active metabolite are highly bound to plasma proteins, primarily albumin, with plasma free fractions of 1.3% and 0.2% respectively. Plasma protein binding is constant over the concentration range achieved with recommended doses. Studies in rats indicate that losartan crosses the blood-brain barrier poorly, if at all.

Various losartan metabolites have been identified in human plasma and urine. In addition to the active carboxylic acid metabolite, E-3174, several inactive metabolites are formed. In vitro studies indicate that the cytochrome P450 isoenzymes 2C9 and 3A4 are involved in the biotransformation of losartan to its metabolites.

The volume of distribution of losartan is about 34 L, and that of the active metabolite is about 12 L.

Total plasma clearance of losartan is about 600 mL/min, with about 75 mL/min accounted for by renal clearance. Total plasma clearance of the active metabolite is about 50 mL/min, with about 25 mL/min accounted for by renal clearance. Both biliary and urinary excretion contribute substantially to the elimination of losartan and its metabolites.

Following oral ^{14}C-labeled losartan, about 35% of radioactivity is recovered in the urine and about 60% in the feces. Following an i.v. dose of ^{14}C-labeled losartan, about 45% of radioactivity is recovered in the urine and 50% in the feces.

Hydrochlorothiazide: Hydrochlorothiazide is not metabolized but is eliminated rapidly by the kidney. The plasma half-life is 5.6 to 14.8 hours when the plasma levels can be followed for at least 24 hours. At least 61% of the oral dose is eliminated unchanged within 24 hours. Hydrochlorothiazide crosses the placental but not the blood-brain barrier and is excreted in breast milk.

Pharmacodynamics: Losartan: Losartan inhibits the pressor effect of angiotensin II. A dose of 100 mg inhibits this effect by about 85% at peak, with 25 to 40% inhibition persisting for 24 hours. Removal of the negative feedback of angiotensin II causes a 2- to 3- fold rise in plasma renin activity, and a consequent rise in angiotensin II plasma concentration, in hypertensive patients.

Maximum blood pressure lowering, following oral administration of a single dose of losartan, as seen in hypertensive patients, occurs at about 6 hours.

In losartan-treated patients during controlled trials, there was no meaningful change in heart rate.

There is no apparent rebound effect after abrupt withdrawal of losartan therapy.

Black hypertensive patients show a smaller average blood pressure response to losartan monotherapy than other hypertensive patients.

Hydrochlorothiazide: Onset of the diuretic action following oral administration occurs in 2 hours and the peak action in about 4 hours. Diuretic activity lasts about 6 to 12 hours.

Losartan—Hydrochlorothiazide: The components of Hyzaar have been shown to have an additive effect on blood pressure reduction, reducing blood pressure to a greater degree than either component alone.

The antihypertensive effect of Hyzaar is sustained for a 24-hour period. In clinical studies of at least 1 year's duration, the antihypertensive effect was maintained with continued therapy. Despite the significant decrease in blood pressure, administration of Hyzaar had no clinically significant effect on heart rate.

Indications: For the treatment of essential hypertension in patients for whom combination therapy is appropriate.

Hyzaar is not indicated for initial therapy (see Dosage).

Losartan should normally be used in those patients in whom treatment with diuretic or beta-blocker was found ineffective or has been associated with unacceptable adverse effects.

Contraindications: In patients who are hypersensitive to any component of this product. Because of the hydrochlorothiazide component, it is also contraindicated in patients with anuria, and in patients who are hypersensitive to other sulfonamide-derived drugs.

Warnings: *Pregnancy:* Drugs that act directly on the renin-angiotensin system can cause fetal and neonatal morbidity and death when administered to pregnant women. When pregnancy is detected, Hyzaar should be discontinued as soon as possible.

The use of drugs that act directly on the renin-angiotensin system during the second and third trimesters of pregnancy has been associated with fetal and neonatal injury, including hypotension, neonatal skull hypoplasia, anuria, reversible or irreversible renal failure, and death. Oligohydramnios has also been reported, presumably resulting from decreased fetal renal function; oligohydramnios in this setting has been associated with fetal limb contractures, craniofacial deformation, and hypoplastic lung development. Prematurity, intrauterine growth retardation, and patent ductus arteriosus have also been reported, although it is not clear whether these occurrences were due to exposure to the drug. These adverse effects do not appear to have resulted from intrauterine drug exposure that has been limited to the first trimester.

Mothers whose embryos and fetuses are exposed to an angiotensin II receptor antagonist only during the first trimester should be so informed. Nonetheless, when patients become pregnant, physicians should have the patient discontinue the use of losartan potassium as soon as possible.

Rarely (probably less often than once in every thousand pregnancies), no alternative to an angiotensin II receptor antagonist will be found. In these rare cases, the mothers should be apprised of the potential hazards to their fetuses, and serial ultrasound examinations should be performed to assess the intra-amniotic environment.

If oligohydramnios is observed, losartan should be discontinued unless it is considered life-saving for the mother. Contraction stress testing (CST), a nonstress test (NST), or biophysical profiling (BPP) may be appropriate, depending upon the week of pregnancy. Patients and physicians should be aware, however, that oligohydramnios may not appear until after the fetus has sustained irreversible injury.

Infants with histories of in utero exposure to an angiotensin II receptor antagonist should be closely observed for hypotension, oliguria, and hyperkalemia. If oliguria occurs, attention should be directed toward support of blood pressure and renal perfusion. Exchange transfusion may be required as means of reversing hypotension and/or substituting for impaired renal function. Neither losartan nor the active metabolite can be removed by hemodialysis.

Thiazides cross the placental barrier and appear in cord blood. The routine use of diuretics in otherwise healthy pregnant women is not recommended and exposes mother and fetus to unnecessary hazard including fetal or neonatal jaundice, thrombocytopenia and possibly other adverse experiences which have occurred in the adult. Diuretics do not prevent development of toxemia of pregnancy and there is no satisfactory evidence that they are useful in the treatment of toxemia.

Animal Data: Losartan has been shown to produce adverse effects in rat fetuses and neonates, which include decreased

Hyzaar (cont'd)

body weight, mortality and/or renal toxicity. Significant levels of losartan and its active metabolite were shown to be present in rat milk. Based on pharmacokinetic assessments, these findings are attributed to drug exposure in late gestation and during lactation.

Hypotension: Occasionally, symptomatic hypotension has occurred after administration of losartan, in some cases after the first dose. It is more likely to occur in patients who are volume-depleted by diuretic therapy, dietary salt restriction, dialysis, diarrhea, or vomiting. In these patients, because of the potential fall in blood pressure, therapy should be started under close medical supervision. Similar considerations apply to patients with ischemic heart or cerebrovascular disease, in whom an excessive fall in blood pressure could result in myocardial infarction or cerebrovascular accident.

Azotemia: Azotemia may be precipitated or increased by hydrochlorothiazide. Cumulative effects of the drug may develop in patients with impaired renal function. If increasing azotemia and oliguria occur during treatment of severe progressive renal disease the diuretic should be discontinued.

Hypersensitivity Reactions: Sensitivity reactions to hydrochlorothiazide may occur in patients with or without a history of allergy or bronchial asthma.

The possibility of exacerbation or activation of systemic lupus erythematosus has been reported in patients treated with hydrochlorothiazide.

Precautions: Renal Impairment: As a consequence of inhibiting the renin-angiotensin-aldosterone system, changes in renal functions have been seen in susceptible individuals. In patients whose renal function may depend on the activity of the renin-angiotensin-aldosterone system, such as patients with bilateral renal artery stenosis, unilateral renal artery stenosis to a solitary kidney, or severe congestive heart failure, treatment with agents that inhibit this system has been associated with oliguria, progressive azotemia, and rarely, acute renal failure and/or death. In susceptible patients, concomitant diuretic use may further increase risk.

Use of losartan should include appropriate assessment of renal function.

Thiazides should be used with caution.

Because of the hydrochlorothiazide component, Hyzaar is not recommended in patients with severe renal impairment (creatinine clearance ≤30 mL/min).

Patients with Liver Impairment: Based on pharmacokinetic data which demonstrate significantly increased plasma concentrations of losartan and its active metabolite in cirrhotic patients after administration of Cozaar, a lower dose should be considered for patients with hepatic impairment, or a history of hepatic impairment (see Dosage).

Thiazides should be used with caution in patients with impaired hepatic function or progressive liver disease, since minor alterations of fluid and electrolyte balance may precipitate hepatic coma.

Metabolism: Hyperuricemia may occur or acute gout may be precipitated in certain patients receiving thiazide therapy.

Thiazides may decrease serum PBI levels without signs of thyroid disturbance.

Thiazides have been shown to increase excretion of magnesium; this may result in hypomagnesemia.

Thiazides may decrease urinary calcium excretion. Thiazides may cause intermittent and slight elevation of serum calcium in the absence of known disorders of calcium metabolism. Marked hypercalcemia may be evidence of hidden hyperparathyroidism. Thiazides should be discontinued before carrying out tests for parathyroid function.

Increases in cholesterol, triglyceride and glucose levels may be associated with thiazide diuretic therapy.

Valvular Stenosis: There is concern on theoretical grounds that patients with aortic stenosis might be at particular risk of decreased coronary perfusion when treated with vasodilators because they do not develop as much afterload reduction.

Lactation: It is not known whether losartan or its active metabolite are excreted in human milk, however significant levels of both of these compounds have been shown to be present in the milk of lactating rats. Thiazides appear in human milk. A decision should be made whether to discontinue nursing or discontinue the drug, taking into account the importance of the drug to the mother.

Children: Hyzaar has not been studied in children, therefore use in this age group is not recommended.

Geriatrics: No overall differences in safety were observed between elderly patients and younger patients, but appropriate caution should nevertheless be used when prescribing to the elderly, as increased vulnerability to drug effect is possible in this patient population.

Drug Interactions: Diuretics: Patients on diuretics, and especially those in whom diuretic therapy was recently instituted, may occasionally experience an excessive reduction of blood pressure after initiation of therapy with losartan. The possibility of symptomatic hypotension with losartan can be minimized by discontinuing the diuretic or increasing the salt intake prior to initiation of treatment with losartan potassium (see Warnings, Hypotension and Dosage).

Agents Increasing Serum Potassium: Since losartan decreases the production of aldosterone, potassium-sparing diuretics or potassium supplements should be given only for documented hypokalemia and with frequent monitoring of serum potassium when losartan therapy is instituted. Potassium-containing salt substitutes should also be used with caution. Concomitant thiazide diuretic use may attenuate any effect that losartan may have on serum potassium.

Lithium Salts: As with other drugs which eliminate sodium, lithium clearance may be reduced in the presence of losartan. Therefore, serum lithium levels should be monitored carefully if lithium salts are to be administered with losartan.

Lithium generally should not be given with diuretics. Diuretic agents reduce the renal clearance of lithium and add a high risk of lithium toxicity.

Digitalis: In 9 healthy volunteers, when a single oral dose of 0.5 mg digoxin was administered to patients receiving losartan for 11 days, digoxin AUC and digoxin C_{max} ratios, relative to placebo, were found to be 1.06 (90% C.I. 0.98 to 1.14) and 1.12 (90% C.I. 0.97 to 1.28), respectively. The effect of losartan on steady-state pharmacokinetics of cardiac glycosides is not known.

Thiazide-induced electrolyte disturbances may predispose to digitalis-induced arrhythmias.

Warfarin: Losartan administered for 7 days did not affect the pharmacokinetics or pharmacodynamic activity of a single dose of warfarin. The effect of losartan on steady-state pharmacokinetics of warfarin is not known.

Drugs Affecting Cytochrome P450 System: When losartan was administered to 10 healthy male volunteers as a single dose in steady-state conditions of phenobarbital, a cytochrome P450 inducer, losartan AUC, relative to baseline, was 0.80 (90% C.I. 0.72 to 0.88), while AUC of the active metabolite, E-3174, was 0.80 (90% C.I. 0.78 to 0.82).

When losartan was administered to 8 healthy male volunteers as a single dose in steady-state conditions of cimetidine, a cytochrome P450 inhibitor, losartan AUC, relative to baseline, was 1.18 (90% C.I. 1.10 to 1.27), while AUC of the active metabolite, E-3174, was 1.00 (90% C.I. 0.92 to 1.08).

d-Tubocurarine: Thiazide drugs may increase the responsiveness to tubocurarine.

Insulin: Insulin requirements in diabetic patients treated with diuretics may be increased, decreased or unchanged. Diabetes mellitus which has been latent may become manifest during thiazide administration.

Alcohol, Barbiturates or Narcotics: Diuretic potentiation of orthostatic hypotension may occur.

Corticosteroids, ACTH: Intensified electrolyte depletion, particularly hypokalemia, may occur when given concomitantly with diuretics.

Pressor Amines (e.g., norepinephrine): In the presence of diuretics possible decreased response to pressor amines may be seen but not sufficient to preclude their use.

NSAIDs: In some patients, the administration of a nonsteroidal anti-inflammatory agent can reduce the diuretic, natriuretic, and antihypertensive effects of loop, potassium-sparing and thiazide diuretics. Therefore, when Hyzaar and nonsteroidal anti-inflammatory agents are used concomitantly, the patient should be observed closely to determine if the desired effect of the diuretic is obtained.

Adverse Effects: Hyzaar has been evaluated for safety in 2 498 patients treated for essential hypertension. Of these, 1 088 were treated with Hyzaar monotherapy in controlled clinical trials. In open studies, 926 patients were treated with Hyzaar for a year or more.

The following potentially serious adverse reactions have been reported rarely with Hyzaar in controlled clinical trials: syncope, hypotension.

In controlled clinical trials, discontinuations of therapy due to clinical adverse experiences occurred in 2.4 and 2.1% of patients treated with Hyzaar and placebo, respectively.

In double-blind controlled clinical trials, the following adverse experiences were reported with losartan—hydrochlorothiazide in ≥1% of patients, regardless of drug relationship (see Table I).

Table I—Hyzaar

Adverse Experiences Reported with Losartan—Hydrochlorothiazide in ≥1% of Patients

	Losartan—Hydrochlorothiazide (n=1 088)	Losartan Alone (n=655)	Hydrochlorothiazide (n=272)	Placebo (n=187)
Body as a Whole				
Abdominal Pain	1.3	0.9	1.8	1.1
Asthenia/ Fatigue	3.1	2.9	5.1	3.7
Edema/ Swelling	1.2	0.6	2.9	1.6
Cardiovascular				
Palpitation	1.6	1.5	1.1	0
Digestive				
Diarrhea	1.6	1.8	0.4	2.1
Nausea	1.5	1.2	0	2.1
Musculoskeletal				
Back Pain	2.9	1.1	0	0.5
Nervous/Psychiatric				
Dizziness	5.8	3.7	3.7	3.2
Headache	8.0	10.5	14.0	15.0
Respiratory				
Bronchitis	1.1	1.2	0.4	1.6
Cough	2.2	2.1	1.1	2.1
Influenza	1.2	0.2	0.7	0.5
Pharyngitis	1.2	0.8	1.8	1.6
Sinusitis	1.0	0.9	2.2	0.5
Upper Respiratory Infection	5.8	4.6	5.5	4.8
Skin				
Rash	1.3	0.5	1.5	0.5

In these controlled clinical trials, dizziness was the only adverse experience, occurring in more than 1% of cases, that was reported as drug-related, and that occurred at a greater incidence in losartan—hydrochlorothiazide-treated (3.3%) than placebo-treated (2.1%) patients.

Thrombocytopenia and Adult Respiratory Distress Syndrome have been reported rarely in postmarketing experience.

In double-blind, controlled clinical trials with losartan alone, the following adverse experiences were reported at an occurrence rate of less than 1%, regardless of drug relationship: orthostatic effects, somnolence, vertigo, epistaxis, tinnitus, constipation, malaise, rash.

Other adverse experiences reported with losartan alone in open-label studies or postmarketing use, regardless of drug relationship, include diarrhea, migraine, myalgia, pruritus, taste disorder and urticaria.

Angioedema (involving swelling of the face, lips, and/or tongue), has been reported rarely in postmarketing experience with losartan.

Laboratory Test Findings: Liver Function Tests: Rarely, elevations of liver enzymes and/or serum bilirubin have occurred.

Hyperkalemia: In controlled hypertensive trials with losartan monotherapy and Hyzaar, a serum potassium >5.5 mEq/L occurred in 1.5 and 0.7% of patients, respectively. However, no patient discontinued losartan or Hyzaar therapy due to hyperkalemia.

Serum Creatinine, Blood Urea Nitrogen (BUN): Minor increases in blood urea nitrogen (1%) and serum creatinine (1%) were observed in patients with essential hypertension treated with Hyzaar. More marked increases have also been reported and were more likely to occur in patients with bilateral renal artery stenosis (see Precautions).

Minor increases in blood urea nitrogen (BUN) or serum creatinine were observed in less than 0.1% of patients with essential hypertension treated with losartan alone. In clinical studies, no patient discontinued taking losartan alone due to increased BUN or serum creatinine.

No other adverse experiences have been reported with Hyzaar which have not been reported with losartan or hydrochlorothiazide individually.

Overdose: Symptoms and Treatment: No specific information is available on the treatment of overdosage with Hyzaar. Treatment is symptomatic and supportive.
Losartan: Limited data are available in regard to overdosage in humans. The most likely manifestation of overdosage would be hypotension and tachycardia. If symptomatic hypotension should occur, supportive treatment should be instituted.

Neither losartan nor its active metabolite can be removed by hemodialysis.
Hydrochlorothiazide: The most common signs and symptoms observed are those caused by electrolyte depletion (hypokalemia, hypochloremia, hyponatremia) and dehydration resulting from excessive diuresis. If digitalis has also been administered, hypokalemia may accentuate cardiac arrhythmias.

The degree to which hydrochlorothiazide is removed by hemodialysis has not been established.

Dosage: Dosage must be individualized. The fixed combination is not for initial therapy. The dose should be determined by the titration of the individual components.

Once the patient has been stabilized on the individual components as described below, either one 50/12.5 mg tablet or 2 tablets once daily may be substituted if the doses on which the patient was stabilized are the same as those in the fixed combination (see Indications).

Hyzaar may be administered with or without food, however it should be taken consistently with respect to food intake.
Losartan Monotherapy: The usual starting dose of monotherapy is 50 mg once daily.

Dosage should be adjusted according to blood pressure response. The maximal antihypertensive effect is attained 3 to 6 weeks after initiation of therapy.

The usual dose range for losartan is 50 to 100 mg once daily. A dose of 100 mg daily should not be exceeded, as no additional antihypertensive effect is obtained with higher doses.

In most patients taking losartan 50 mg once daily, the antihypertensive effect is maintained. In some patients treated once daily, the antihypertensive effect may diminish toward the end of the dosing interval. This can be evaluated by measuring the blood pressure just prior to dosing to determine whether satisfactory control is being maintained for 24 hours. If it is not, either twice daily administration with the same total daily dosage, or an increase in the dose should be considered. If blood pressure is not adequately controlled with losartan alone, a non-potassium-sparing diuretic may be administered concomitantly.

For patients with volume-depletion, a starting dose of 25 mg once daily should be considered (see Warnings, Hypotension and Precautions, Drug Interactions).
Diuretic Treated Patients: In patients receiving diuretics, losartan therapy should be initiated with caution, since these patients may be volume-depleted and thus more likely to experience hypotension following initiation of additional antihypertensive therapy. Whenever possible, all diuretics should be discontinued 2 to 3 days prior to the administration of losartan, to reduce the likelihood of hypotension (see Warnings, Hypotension and Precautions, Drug Interactions). If this is not possible because of the patient's condition, losartan should be administered with caution and the blood pressure monitored closely. Thereafter, the dosage should be adjusted according to the individual response of the patient.
Dosage Adjustment in Renal Impairment: No initial dosage adjustment in losartan is usually necessary for patients with renal impairment, including those requiring hemodialysis. However, appropriate monitoring of these patients is recommended.

The usual regimens of therapy with Hyzaar may be followed as long as the patient's creatinine clearance is >30 mL/min. In patients with more severe renal impairment, loop diuretics are preferred to thiazides, so Hyzaar is not recommended.
Patients with Liver Impairment: Since dosage adjustment of losartan is required in patients with liver impairment, and thiazide diuretics may precipitate hepatic coma, a fixed combination product such as Hyzaar is not advisable (see Precautions, Patients with Liver Impairment).
Geriatrics: No initial dosage adjustment is necessary for most elderly patients. Appropriate caution should nevertheless be used when prescribing to the elderly, as increased vulnerability to drug effect is possible in this patient population (see Precautions, Geriatrics).

Information for the Patient: See Blue Section—Information for the Patient "Hyzaar".

Supplied: Each yellow, teardrop-shaped, film-coated tablet, marked with code MRK 717 on one side and HYZAAR on the other, contains: losartan potassium 50 mg and hydrochlorothiazide 12.5 mg. Nonmedicinal ingredients: D&C yellow No. 10 aluminum lake, hydroxypropyl cellulose, hydroxypropyl methylcellulose, lactose hydrous, magnesium stearate, microcrystalline cellulose, pregelatinized starch and titanium dioxide. Potassium: <1 mmol (4.24 mg). Push-through blister packages of 30. Store at room temperature (15 to 30°C). Keep container tightly closed.

(Shown in Product Recognition Section)

Reviewed 1998

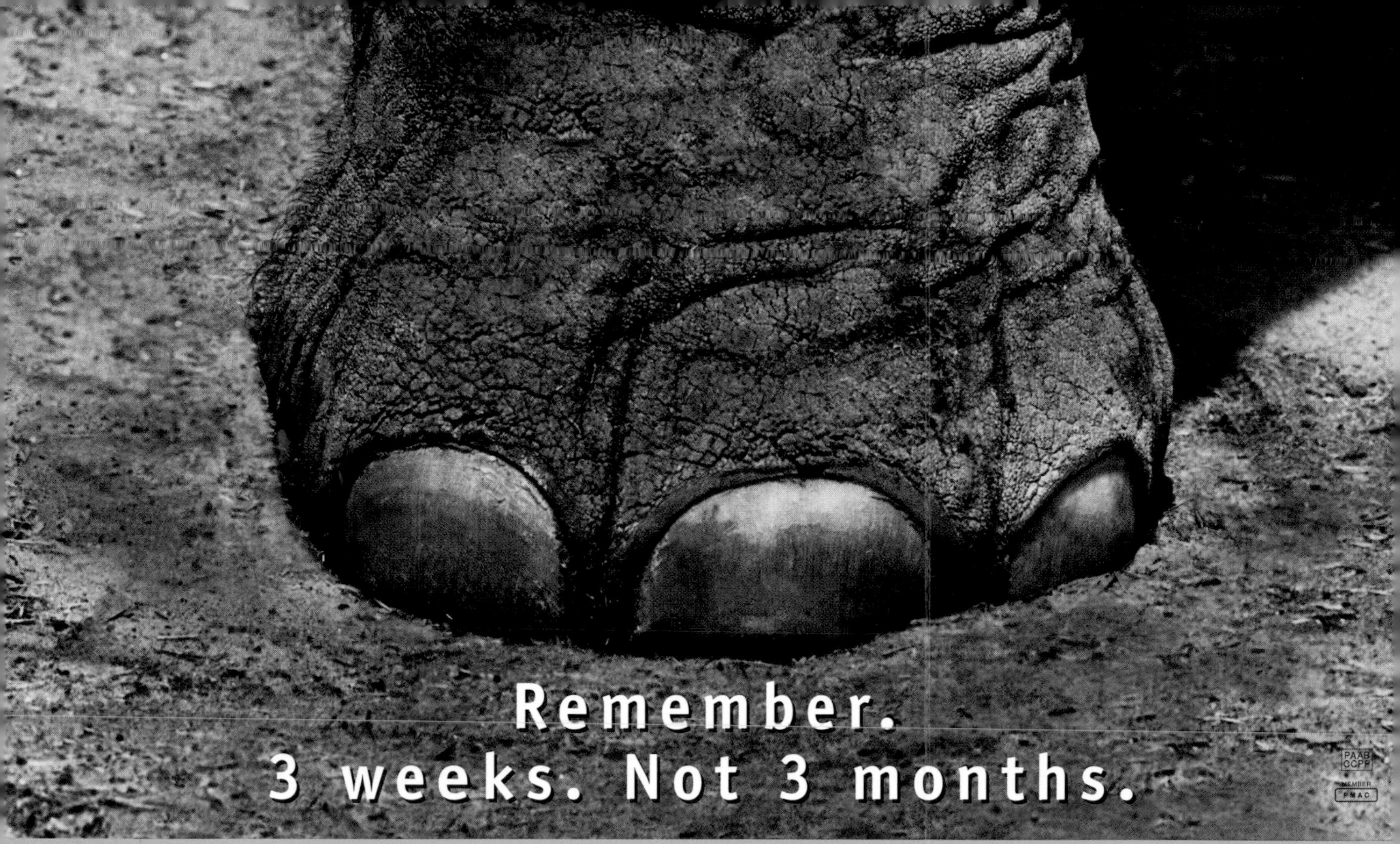

PULSE SPORANOX
200 mg B.I.D.

PULSE SPORANOX: Just 3 one-week pulses

PULSE SPORANOX* (itraconazole capsules) is the first therapy proven to treat onychomycosis of the toenail effectively with three one-week pulses.[1] That's just 21 days of pills – considerably less than any other therapeutic option.[1ab]

Stays in the nail, not the blood

With its high affinity for keratinous tissues,[2] itraconazole penetrates the nail within seven days[3c] and remains there for up to eleven months.[4de] The drug, however, rapidly clears from circulation; within a week, plasma levels are almost undetectable.[3c]

Effective and generally well tolerated

Researchers have reported clinical cure rates as high as 84% for toenail onychomycosis one year after the start of treatment.[4d] Relapse rates in toenail onychomycosis are low (<4%).[5f]
PULSE SPORANOX is generally well tolerated,[g] with a low incidence of side effects.[1,4,6,7] The most common adverse experiences during pulse therapy include abdominal pain (1.9%), nausea (1.6%), and headache (1.3%).[1]

Patients preferred the idea of pulse over continuous therapy

When given the option at the start of treatment, 100% of patients (n=28) in a recent study chose pulse dosing over a continuous three-month regimen.[8] Compliance was shown to be very good.[4h]

[a] **NOTE: Optimal clinical and mycological responses are reached 6 to 9 months after cessation of treatment.**

[b] For toenail onychomycosis, treatment begins with one week of pulse therapy (200 mg B.I.D.), followed by three weeks without pills. Three pulses are required. For fingernail onychomycosis, two pulses are required.

[c] In two healthy volunteers who received itraconazole 100 mg/d.

[d] In 25 patients treated for toenail onychomycosis with 3 one-week pulses of PULSE SPORANOX 200 mg B.I.D. Mycological cure at one year was 64%. Clinical cure defined as patients cured with or without nail malformation.

[e] In fingernails, levels begin to decline after three months due to faster growth[2]

[f] In 673 patients treated with PULSE SPORANOX 200 mg B.I.D. for 3 one-week pulses.

[g] Administration of PULSE SPORANOX with terfenadine, astemizole or cisapride is contraindicated due to the risk of cardiovascular events. Coadministration of PULSE SPORANOX with oral midazolam, triazolam, or HMG-CoA reductase inhibitors that are metabolized by the P450 3A enzyme system, such as lovastatin is also contraindicated.

[h] Confirmed by counting unused medication when patients (n=25) returned for follow-up visits.

PULSE
Pr sporanox*
(itraconazole capsules) For onychomycosis

**3 one-week pulses.
Not 3 months of pills.**

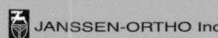

JANSSEN-ORTHO Inc.
19 Green Belt Drive, Toronto, Ontario M3C 1L9

PAAB CCPP

Due to Valtrex, this
week's episode of genital herpes
has been cancelled.

I

ICAPS®
CIBA Vision

Vitamin—Mineral Supplement

Supplied: Each white, capsule-shaped, film-coated tablet contains: beta-carotene (pro-vitamin A) 6 000 IU, vitamin C (ascorbic acid) 200 mg, vitamin E (dl-alpha tocopheryl acetate) 60 IU, riboflavin (vitamin B_2) 20 mg, zinc (zinc acetate) 30 mg, copper (HVP chelate) 1.5 mg, manganese (HVP chelate) 5 mg and selenium (HVP chelate) 30 µg. Energy: ~13.8 kJ (~3.3 kcal). Gluten-, lactose-, sucrose-, sulfite- and tartrazine-free. Bottles of 60.

ICAPS Time Release™
CIBA Vision

Vitamin—Mineral Supplement

Supplied: Each yellow, capsule-shaped, film-coated tablet contains: beta-carotene (pro-vitamin A) 7 000 IU, vitamin C (ascorbic acid) 200 mg, vitamin E (dl-alpha tocopheryl acetate) 100 IU, riboflavin (vitamin B_2) 20 mg, zinc (as acetate) 40 mg, copper (HVP chelate) 2 mg, selenium (HVP chelate) 20 µg. Nonmedicinal ingredients: carnauba wax, dicalcium phosphate, hydroxypropylmethyl cellulose, magnesium stearate, microcrystalline cellulose, natural peppermint, polyethylene glycol, polysorbate 80, silicon dioxide, titanium dioxide. Gluten-, lactose-, sucrose-, sulfite- and tartrazine-free. Bottles of 50. Keep tightly closed in a dry place at 15 to 30°C.

IDAMYCIN® Ⓟ
Pharmacia & Upjohn

Idarubicin HCl

Antineoplastic

Pharmacology: Idarubicin, either as a single agent or in combination, has been shown to be a potent antileukemic agent capable of inducing complete remission in previously untreated and in relapsed and refractory acute non-lymphocytic leukemia (ANLL) including resistant patients, and in adult and pediatric relapsed patients with acute lymphoblastic leukemia (ALL).

Idarubicin is a DNA-intercalating analog of daunorubicin which has an inhibitory effect on nucleic acid synthesis and interacts with the enzyme topoisomerase II. The modification, in position 4 of the anthracycline structure, gives the compound a high lipophilicity which results in an increased rate of cellular uptake compared with other anthracyclines.

Idarubicin has been shown to have a higher potency than daunorubicin and to be an effective agent against murine leukemias and lymphomas. In vitro studies on human and murine anthracycline-resistant cells have revealed a lower degree of cross-resistance for idarubicin in comparison with doxorubicin and daunorubicin.

Seven pharmacokinetic studies were carried out in 49 patients. The plasma concentrations of idarubicin fit a 2 or 3 compartment open model. After i.v. administration to patients with normal renal and hepatic function, idarubicin is eliminated from systemic circulation with a terminal plasma half-life ranging between 11 to 25 hours and is extensively metabolized to an active metabolite, idarubicinol, which is more slowly eliminated with a plasma half-life ranging between 41 to 69 hours. The drug is eliminated by biliary and renal excretion, mostly in the form of idarubicinol.

Studies of cellular (nucleated blood and bone marrow cells) drug concentrations in leukemic patients have shown that peak cellular idarubicin concentrations are reached a few minutes after injection. Idarubicin and idarubicinol concentrations in nucleated blood and bone marrow cells are more than a hundred times the plasma concentrations. Idarubicin disappearance rates in plasma and cells were comparable with a terminal half-life of about 15 hours. The terminal half-life of idarubicinol in cells was about 72 hours.

Protein binding was studied in vitro by equilibrium dialysis at concentrations of idarubicin and idarubicinol similar to the maximum plasma level obtained in the pharmacokinetic studies. The percent of idarubicin and idarubicinol bound to human plasma proteins at the concentration of 100 ng/mL plasma is on the average 97% and 94% respectively.

Indications: In acute nonlymphocytic leukemia (ANLL) in adults for remission induction as front-line therapy or for remission induction in relapsed or refractory patients.

Also indicated in acute lymphocytic leukemia (ALL) as second-line treatment in adults and children.

Contraindications: In patients with a history of allergic reactions to idarubicin.

Warnings: Caution: Idarubicin is a potent drug and should be used only by physicians experienced with cancer chemotherapy drugs (see Precautions). Blood counts and hepatic function tests should be performed regularly. Cardiac monitoring is advised especially in those patients who have received mediastinal radiotherapy, patients with pre-existing cardiac disease or previous therapy with anthracyclines or anthracenes at high cumulative doses.

Idarubicin is intended for use under the direction of physicians experienced in leukemia chemotherapy.

Idarubicin should not be given to patients with pre-existing bone marrow suppression induced by previous drug therapy or radiotherapy unless the benefit warrants the risk.

Pre-existing heart disease and previous therapy with anthracyclines at high cumulative doses or other potentially cardiotoxic agents are co-factors for increased risk of idarubicin-induced cardiac toxicity and the benefit to risk ratio of idarubicin therapy in such patients should be weighed before starting treatment with idarubicin.

Like most other cytotoxic agents, idarubicin has mutagenic properties and it is carcinogenic in rats.

Idarubicin is a potent bone marrow suppressant. Myelosuppression, primarily of leukocytes, will therefore occur in all patients given a therapeutic dose of this agent and careful hematologic monitoring including granulocytes, red cells and platelets is required. Facilities with laboratory and supportive resources adequate to monitor drug tolerability and protect and maintain a patient compromised by drug toxicity should be available. It must be possible to treat rapidly and completely a severe hemorrhagic condition and/or a severe infection.

Cardiac toxicity of the type described for other anthracycline compounds, manifested by clinically evident congestive heart failure or by a decrease in left ventricular ejection fraction may occur during therapy or several weeks after termination of therapy. Discontinuation of idarubicin and treatment with vasodilators, digitalis, diuretics, sodium restriction and bed-rest is indicated.

Although a cumulative dose limit cannot yet be defined, available data on patients treated with idarubicin capsules indicate that total cumulative doses up to 400 mg/m² have a low probability of cardiotoxicity.

Acute life-threatening arrhythmias have been occasionally observed during therapy.

The risk of such myocardial toxicity may be higher following concomitant or previous radiation to the mediastinal pericardial area or treatment with other potentially cardiotoxic agents or in patients with clinical situations in which the cardiac reserve is compromised (anemia, bone marrow depression, infections, leukemic pericarditis and/or myocarditis).

Available evidence appears to indicate that cardiotoxicity is cumulative across members of the anthracycline and anthracene class of drugs. Patients who have previously received daunorubicin, doxorubicin or epirubicin are at particular risk for possible cardiotoxic effects of idarubicin at a lower total dose than previously untreated patients and, therefore, should be carefully monitored.

While there is no reliable method for predicting acute congestive heart failure, cardiac function should be carefully monitored during treatment in order to minimize the risk of cardiac toxicity. Cardiomyopathy induced by anthracyclines is usually associated with persistent QRS voltage reduction, increase beyond normal limits of the systolic time interval (PEP/LVET) and decrease of the left ventricular ejection fraction (LVEF) from pretreatment baseline values. An electrocardiogram or echocardiogram and a determination of left ventricular ejection fraction by echocardiogram or by radionuclide cineangiography (MUGA scan) should be performed prior to starting therapy and during treatment with idarubicin. Early clinical diagnosis of drug-induced myocardial damage appears to influence the response to symptomatic therapy.

Idarubicin therapy should not be administered in patients with severe renal and liver impairment or in patients with uncontrolled infections unless the benefit outweighs the risk.

Since hepatic and/or renal function impairment can affect the disposition of idarubicin, liver and kidney function should be evaluated prior to, and during treatment. In a number of Phase III clinical trials, treatment was not given if bilirubin and/or creatinine serum levels exceeded 2 mg%. With other anthracyclines a 50% dose reduction is generally employed if either bilirubin levels are greater than 40 µmol/L (2.35 mg%) or creatinine levels are greater than 200 µmol/L (2.25 mg%).

Idarubicin must not be administered by i.m. or s.c. injection.

Extravasation of idarubicin during i.v. administration can cause severe local tissue necrosis. Extravasation may occur with or without an accompanying stinging or burning sensation even if blood returns well on aspiration of the infusion needle (see Dosage). If signs or symptoms of extravasation occur the injection or infusion should be terminated immediately and restarted in another vein.

Idarubicin may impart a red color to the urine for 1 to 2 days after administration and patients should be advised that this is no cause for alarm.

Pregnancy and *Lactation:* There is no conclusive information about idarubicin adversely affecting human fertility, or causing teratogenesis; however, in rats (but not rabbits) it is teratogenic and embryotoxic. Therefore, women of childbearing potential should be prescribed effective contraceptive methods and counselled on the risks of pregnancy.

If idarubicin is to be used during pregnancy, or if the patient becomes pregnant during therapy, the patient should be informed of the potential hazard to the fetus. Mothers should be advised not to breast-feed while undergoing chemotherapy with idarubicin.

Precautions: Therapy with idarubicin requires close observation of the patient and laboratory monitoring. Hyperuricemia secondary to rapid lysis of leukemic cells may be induced: blood uric acid levels should be monitored and appropriate therapy initiated if hyperuricemia develops. Appropriate measures must be taken to control any systemic infection before beginning therapy.

Extravasation of idarubicin at the site of i.v. injection can cause severe local tissue necrosis. The risk of thrombophlebitis at the injection site may be minimized by following the recommended procedure for administration.

Adverse Effects: Severe myelosuppression and cardiac toxicity are the 2 major adverse effects. Other adverse reactions include: reversible alopecia in most patients; acute nausea and vomiting; mucositis, usually involving the oral mucosa and appearing 3 to 10 days after starting treatment; esophagitis and diarrhea, fever, chills, skin rash, elevation of liver enzymes and bilirubin in about 20 to 30% of cases and 10 to 20% of cases after i.v. and oral administration, respectively. Severe and sometimes fatal infections have been associated with idarubicin alone or in combination with cytarabine. Acute toxicities such as nausea and vomiting, mucositis, diarrhea and liver dysfunction are comparable to those of daunorubicin.

Idarubicin appears to have a cardiac toxicity potential which is similar to that of daunorubicin.

The cardiotoxicity of idarubicin, taking into consideration the high risk population of leukemic patients treated, is low. Overall, the incidence of serious cardiac events has been 2.0% out of 1 204 patients receiving idarubicin via i.v. administration. If patients previously treated with anthracyclines are excluded, the overall incidence is 1.58%. When idarubicin was administered orally, the incidence of serious cardiac events (grade 3 only) was 3.2%.

Overdose: Symptoms and Treatment: Very high doses of idarubicin may be expected to cause acute myocardial toxicity within 24 hours and severe myelosuppression within 1 or 2 weeks. Treatment should aim to support the patient during this period and should utilize such measures as blood transfusions and reverse-barrier nursing. Delayed cardiac failure has been seen with the anthracyclines up to several months after the overdose. Patients should be observed carefully and if signs of cardiac failure arise, should be treated along conventional lines.

Dosage: I.V.: Acute Nonlymphocytic Leukemia (ANLL): In adults, for remission induction as front-line therapy or for remission induction in relapsed or refractory patients, the following dose schedules are recommended: (a) 12 mg/m² daily by i.v. injection for 3 days in combination with cytarabine, or (b) 8 mg/m² daily by i.v. injection as a single agent for 5 days.

Acute Lymphocytic Leukemia (ALL): As a second-line treatment, the following dose schedules are recommended: (a) in adults, 12 mg/m² daily by i.v. injection for 3 days as a single

Idamycin (cont'd)

agent, or (b) in children, 10 mg/m² daily by i.v. injection for 3 days as a single agent.

These dose schedules should, however, take into account the hematological status of the patient and the dosage of the other cytotoxic drugs when used in combination. In patients with hepatic impairment a dose reduction should be considered.

Preparation of the Solution: Caution in handling of the powder and preparation of the solution must be exercised as skin reaction associated with idarubicin may occur (refer to Guidelines for Safe Preparation and Handling).

Idarubicin 5 mg and 10 mg vials should be reconstituted with 5 mL and 10 mL respectively of either Water for Injection USP or 0.9% Sodium Chloride Injection USP to give a final concentration of 1 mg/mL of idarubicin HCl. Diluents containing bacteriostatic agents are not recommended.

The vial contents are under a negative pressure to minimize aerosol formation during reconstitution; therefore, particular care should be taken when the needle is inserted. Inhalation of any aerosol produced during reconstitution must be avoided.

Stability and Storage of Solution: The reconstituted solution is stable for 24 hours at room temperature and 48 hours under refrigeration at 2 to 8°C. The solution should be protected from exposure to direct light and any unused solution should be discarded.

Administration: Care in the administration of idarubicin will reduce the chance of perivenous infiltration. It may also decrease the chance of local reactions such as urticaria and erythematous streaking. On i.v. administration of idarubicin extravasation may occur with or without an accompanying stinging or burning sensation even if blood returns well on aspiration of the infusion needle. If any signs or symptoms of extravasation have occurred the injection or infusion should be immediately terminated and restarted in another vein. If it is known or suspected that s.c. extravasation has occurred it is recommended that intermittent ice packs (½ hour immediately, then ½ hour 4 times per day for 3 days) be placed over the area of extravasation and that the affected extremity be elevated. Because of the progressive nature of extravasation reactions, the area of injection should be frequently examined and plastic surgery consultation obtained early if there is any sign of a local reaction such as pain, erythema, edema or vesication. If ulceration begins or there is severe persistent pain at the site of extravasation, early wide excision of the involved area should be considered.

Idarubicin should be slowly administered into the tubing of a freely running i.v. infusion of Sodium Chloride Injection USP (0.9%). The tubing should be attached to a Butterfly needle or other suitable device and inserted preferably into a large vein. If possible, avoid veins over joints or in extremities with compromised venous or lymphatic drainage. The rate of administration is dependent on the size of the vein and the dosage. However, the dosage should be administered in not less than 3 to 5 minutes. Local erythematous streaking along the vein as well as facial flushing may be indicative of too rapid administration. A burning or stinging sensation may be indicative of perivenous infiltration and the infusion should be immediately terminated and restarted in another vein. Perivenous infiltration may occur painlessly.

Unless specific compatibility data are available, mixing idarubicin with other drugs is not recommended. Precipitation occurs with heparin. Prolonged contact with any solution of an alkaline pH will result in degradation of the drug.

Guidelines for Safe Preparation and Handling: Preparation and Handling: 1. Preparation of antineoplastic solutions should be done in a vertical laminar flow hood (Biological Safety Cabinet-Class II).

2. Personnel preparing idarubicin solutions should wear PVC gloves, safety glasses and protective clothing such as disposable gowns and masks. If idarubicin contacts the skin or mucosa, the area should be washed with soap and water immediately.

3. Personnel regularly involved in the preparation and handling of antineoplastics should have blood examinations on a regular basis.

Disposal: 1. Avoid contact with skin and inhalation of airborne particles by use of PVC gloves and disposable gowns and masks.

2. All needles, syringes, vials and other materials that have come in contact with idarubicin should be segregated in plastic bags, sealed and marked as hazardous waste. Incinerate at 1 000°C or higher. Sealed containers may explode if a tight seal exists.

3. If incineration is not available, idarubicin may be detoxified by adding sodium hypochlorite solution (household bleach) to the vial, in sufficient quantity to decolorize the idarubicin, taking care to vent the vial to avoid a pressure build-up of the chlorine gas that is generated. Dispose detoxified vials in a safe manner.

Needles, Syringes, Disposable and Nondisposable Equipment: Rinse equipment with an appropriate quantity of sodium hypochlorite solution. Discard the solution in the sewer system with running water and discard disposable equipment in a safe manner. Thoroughly wash nondisposable equipment in soap and water.

Spillage/Contamination: Wear gloves, mask, protective clothing. Treat spilled powder or liquid with sodium hypochlorite solution. Carefully absorb solution with gauze or towels again and place in polyethylene bag; seal, double bag and mark as hazardous waste. Dispose waste by incineration or by other methods approved for hazardous materials. Personnel involved in clean-up should wash with soap and water.

Supplied: 5 mg: Each vial contains: idarubicin HCl 5 mg. Also contains lactose NF 50 mg. Cartons of 1.

10 mg: Each vial contains: idarubicin HCl 10 mg. Also contains lactose NF 100 mg. Cartons of 1.

Store at 15 to 30°C and protect from light.

Reviewed 1999

IDARAC® Ⓟ

Sanofi

Floctafenine

Anti-inflammatory—Analgesic

Pharmacology: Floctafenine, an anthranilic acid derivative, is a nonsteroidal anti-inflammatory agent with analgesic and anti-inflammatory properties. The analgesic activity is comparable to that of other mild analgesics in the relief of acute pain. Floctafenine has been shown to inhibit in vitro biosynthesis of prostaglandins PGE_2 and $PGF_{2}\alpha$. Gastrointestinal bleeding determined by daily fecal blood loss, was shown in one clinical trial to be approximately 1.2 mL after 1 600 mg/day of floctafenine compared to 10.4 mL after 2 400 mg/day of ASA.

In normal volunteers, floctafenine was well absorbed after oral administration and peak plasma levels of floctafenine acid, the active metabolite, were attained 1 to 2 hours after administration and declined in a biphasic manner, with an initial (α phase) half-life of approximately 1 hour and a later (β phase) half-life of approximately 8 hours. Floctafenine and its metabolites do not accumulate following oral administration of multiple doses.

After oral and i.v. administration of ^{14}C labelled floctafenine, urinary excretion accounted for 40% and fecal and biliary excretion accounted for 60% of recovered radioactivity. The main urinary metabolites are floctafenic acid and its conjugate with minimal amounts of free floctafenine.

Indications: For short-term use in acute pain of mild and moderate severity.

Contraindications: As with other NSAIDs, floctafenine is contraindicated in patients with peptic ulcer or any other active inflammatory disease of the gastrointestinal tract.

Floctafenine should not be used where there is a known or suspected hypersensitivity to the drug. Because of the possibility of cross-sensitivity, floctafenine should not be used in patients in whom acetylsalicylic acid (ASA) or other nonsteroidal anti-inflammatory agents induce acute asthmatic attacks, urticaria, rhinitis or other allergic manifestations. Fatal anaphylactoid reactions may occur. On occasion, it has been observed that intermittent use may have resulted in increased sensitivity. Since severe cases of hypersensitivity reactions have been reported with floctafenine, its use in severe cardiac insufficiency and ischemic cardiomyopathy is contraindicated.

Warnings: Peptic ulceration, perforation and gastrointestinal bleeding, sometimes severe and occasionally fatal, have been reported during therapy with nonsteroidal anti-inflammatory drugs and may occur with floctafenine.

Elderly and debilitated individuals are most susceptible to adverse events from nonsteroidal anti-inflammatory drugs, the incidence of which increases with dose and duration of treatment. For such individuals, consideration should be given to a starting dose lower than usual, with individual adjustment when necessary and under close supervision (see Precautions for further information).

Floctafenine should be given under close medical supervision to patients prone to gastrointestinal tract irritation, particularly those with a history of peptic ulcer, diverticulosis or other inflammatory disease of the gastrointestinal tract. In these cases the physician must weigh the benefits of treatment against the possible hazards.

Patients taking any nonsteroidal anti-inflammatory drug including floctafenine should be instructed to contact a physician immediately if they experience symptoms of signs suggestive of peptic ulceration or gastrointestinal bleeding. These reactions can occur at any time during treatment.

Pregnancy: As floctafenic acid crosses the placental barrier, the use in women of childbearing potential requires that the likely benefit of the drug be weighed against the possible risk to the mother and fetus.

Lactation: It has been shown that floctafenic acid is slightly secreted in breast milk. Therefore, use of floctafenine in women who are nursing is not recommended.

Children: Safety and efficacy in children have not been established and therefore its use in this age group is not recommended.

The safety and efficacy of long-term use have not been clearly established.

Precautions: Renal Effects: As with other drugs that inhibit prostaglandin synthesis, floctafenine should be used with caution in patients with impaired renal function. In clinical trials dysuria, without apparent changes in renal function, was reported. The incidence of dysuria was greater in males than in females and occurred primarily in the first morning voiding. It has not been established whether dysuria is related to dose and/or duration of drug administration.

Long-term administration of nonsteroidal anti-inflammatory drugs to animals has resulted in renal papillary necrosis and other abnormal renal pathology. In humans, there have been reports of acute interstitial nephritis with hematuria, proteinuria and occasionally nephrotic syndrome.

Renal toxicity has been seen in patients treated with nonsteroidal anti-inflammatory drugs who had pre-renal conditions leading to the reduction in renal blood flow or blood volume, where the renal prostaglandins have a supportive role in the maintenance of renal perfusion. In these patients, administration of a nonsteroidal anti-inflammatory drug may cause a dose-dependent reduction in prostaglandin formation and may precipitate overt renal decompensation. Patients at greatest risk of this reaction are those with impaired renal function, heart failure, liver dysfunction, those taking diuretics, and the elderly. Discontinuation of nonsteroidal anti-inflammatory therapy is usually followed by recovery to the pretreatment state.

Floctafenine and its metabolites are eliminated from plasma by the kidneys. Therefore, in patients with impaired renal function (creatine clearance <10 mL/min), lower doses of floctafenine should be used and patients monitored.

Gastrointestinal: If peptic ulceration is suspected or confirmed, or if gastrointestinal bleeding or perforation occurs, floctafenine should be discontinued, an appropriate treatment instituted and patient closely monitored.

Hepatic Effects: As with other nonsteroidal anti-inflammatory drugs, borderline elevations of one or more liver tests may occur. These abnormalities may progress, may remain essentially unchanged, or may be transient with continued therapy. A patient with symptoms and/or signs suggesting liver dysfunction, or in whom an abnormal liver test has occurred, should be evaluated for evidence of the development of more severe hepatic reactions while on therapy with this drug. Severe hepatic reactions including jaundice and cases of fatal hepatitis have been reported with nonsteroidal anti-inflammatory drugs. Although such reactions are rare, if abnormal liver tests persist or worsen, if clinical signs and symptoms consistent with liver disease develop, or if systemic manifestations occur (e.g., eosinophilia, rash, etc.), floctafenine should be discontinued.

If floctafenine is to be used in the presence of impaired liver function, it must be done under strict observation.

Fluid and Electrolyte Balance: Fluid retention and edema have been observed in patients treated with floctafenine. Therefore, as with many other nonsteroidal anti-inflammatory drugs, the possibility of precipitating congestive heart failure in elderly patients or in those with compromised cardiac function should be borne in mind. Floctafenine should be used with caution in patients with heart failure, hypertension or other conditions predisposing to fluid retention.

Hematology: Drugs inhibiting prostaglandin biosynthesis do interfere with platelet function to some degree; therefore, patients who may be adversely affected by such an action should be carefully observed when floctafenine is administered.

Blood dyscrasias associated with the use of nonsteroidal anti-inflammatory drugs are rare, but could have severe consequences.

Infection: In common with other anti-inflammatory drugs, floctafenine may mask the usual signs of infection.

Geriatrics: As with other NSAIDs, floctafenine should be used with caution in the elderly, and the dosage adjusted individually (see Warnings).

Drug Interactions: Nonsteroidal anti-inflammatory drugs are known to be extensively bound to serum albumin. This may lead to interaction with anticoagulants, sulfonylurea, hypoglycemic agents, sulfonamides, phenytoin, lithium and certain chemotherapeutic agents such as methotrexate. Therefore, caution should be observed when these drugs are used concurrently.

Floctafenine may cause water retention and therefore could interfere with diuretics in the treatment of hypertension.

Concomitant administration of acetylsalicylic acid results in decreased peak serum concentration of nonsteroidal anti-inflammatory drugs and slight increases in both clearance and apparent half-life. The clinical significance of these changes is unknown.

In patients receiving concomitant steroid therapy, any reduction in steroid dosage should be gradual to avoid the possible complications of sudden steroid withdrawal.

No interaction with antacids has been observed.

Adverse Effects: The most commonly occurring side effects reported during therapy were:

CNS: drowsiness, dizziness, headache, insomnia, nervousness, irritability.

Gastrointestinal: nausea, diarrhea, abdominal pain or discomfort, heartburn, constipation, abnormal liver function, gastrointestinal bleeding.

Urogenital: dysuria, burning micturition, polyuria, strong smelling urine, urethritis and cystitis.

Other less frequently occurring side effects were: tinnitus, blurred vision, dry mouth, thirst, bitter taste, anorexia, stomach cramps, flatulence, hot flushes and sweating, tachycardia, weakness and tiredness.

Allergic-type Reactions: maculopapular skin rash, pruritus, urticaria, redness and itching of the face and neck. Cases of anaphylactic shock and angioedema have been reported in clinical use.

Overdose: Symptoms and Treatment: A few cases of overdose have been reported with floctafenine. No common symptoms resulting from overdosing could be distinguished among these patients. In all cases the outcome was favorable and the patients recovered well. Standard procedures to evacuate gastric contents, maintain urinary output and provide general supportive care should be employed in cases of overdose.

Dosage: Adults: 200 to 400 mg every 6 to 8 hours as required. The maximum recommended daily dose is 1 200 mg. Floctafenine is recommended for short-term management of acute pain.

The tablets should be taken with a glass of water.

Floctafenine is not recommended for use in children.

Information for the Patient: See Blue Section—Information for the Patient "Idarac".

Supplied: 200 mg: Each round, biconvex, creamy white tablet, with "W" on one side and "I" with "200" below on the other, contains: floctafenine 200 mg. Nonmedicinal ingredients: cellulose microcrystalline, cornstarch, docusate sodium, magnesium stearate and povidone. Gluten-, lactose-, sucrose-, sulfite- and tartrazine-free. Energy: 0.88 kJ (0.21 kcal). Bottles of 100 and 500.

400 mg: Each round, biconvex, creamy white tablet, with "W" on one side and "I" with "400" below on the other, contains: floctafenine 400 mg. Nonmedicinal ingredients: cellulose microcrystalline, cornstarch, docusate sodium, magnesium stearate and povidone. Gluten-, lactose-, sucrose-, sulfite- and tartrazine-free. Energy 1.72 kJ (0.41 kcal). Bottles of 100 and 500.

Store at room temperature, protect from light.

(Shown in Product Recognition Section)

IFEX® Ⓟ

Bristol

Ifosfamide

Antineoplastic Agent

> Caution: Ifosfamide is a potent drug and should be used only by physicians experienced with cancer chemotherapeutic drugs (see Warnings and Precautions). In those patients who develop bacterial, fungal or viral infections, interruption or modification of dosage should be considered. Blood counts should be taken at regular intervals. Due to the urotoxic effect of oxazaphosphorines, ifosfamide should not be administered without the use of a uroprotective agent such as mesna (see Uromitexan product monograph for Dosage).

Pharmacology: Ifosfamide is activated by metabolism in the liver by the mixed-function oxidase system of the smooth endoplasmic reticulum. The activation is induced by hydroxylation at the ring carbon atom 4. Opening of the ring results in the formation of aldo-ifosfamide, the tautomer of 4-hydroxy-ifosfamide. Two stable metabolites, 4-keto-ifosfamide and 4-carboxyifosfamide, appear in the urine. However, they have no cytotoxic activity. N,N′-bis(2-chloroethyl)-phosphoric acid diamide and acrolein are also found. The enzymatic oxidation of the chloroethyl side chains and subsequent dealkylation may produce further metabolites.

DNA is one of the main target sites of ifosfamide. In vitro, incubation of DNA with activated ifosfamide produces phosphotriesters as the predominant reaction products. The treatment of intact cell nuclei may also result in the formation of DNA-DNA crosslinks. DNA repair occurs in G-1 and G-2 stage cells. Repair capacity is more marked in less sensitive tumors. An accumulation of cells in the G-1 phase is found in tumors that respond well.

Indications: Soft Tissue Sarcoma: first-line single agent therapy; second-line single agent therapy in patients who have failed to respond or who have relapsed on other chemotherapeutic regimens.

Pancreatic Carcinoma: second-line single agent therapy in patients who have failed to respond or who have relapsed on other chemotherapeutic regimens.

Cervical Carcinoma: as a single agent or in combination with cisplatin and bleomycin in advanced or recurrent disease.

Contraindications: In individuals with a known hypersensitivity to it. It is also contraindicated in patients having severe leukopenia, thrombocytopenia, severe renal and/or hepatic impairment, cystitis, obstructions to the urine flow, or active infections. Ifosfamide should not be administered to patients with advanced cerebral arteriosclerosis.

Warnings: Urotoxic side effects, especially hemorrhagic cystitis, have been frequently associated with the use of ifosfamide. Until recently these effects resulted in cessation of therapy. The therapeutic benefit of mesna as a uroprotective agent has been demonstrated in that the incidence of urinary tract complications was reduced from 40 to 3.5%. Thus ifosfamide should always be accompanied by uroprotective treatment with mesna (see Uromitexan product monograph for Dosage).

Patients, male or female, during the reproductive period of life, should be advised of the mutagenic potential of ifosfamide. Adequate methods of contraception are recommended for such patients (see Adverse Effects).

Pregnancy and *Lactation:* Ifosfamide can be teratogenic or cause fetal resorption in experimental animals. It should not be used in pregnancy, particularly in early pregnancy, unless in the judgment of the physician the potential benefits outweigh the possible risks. As is the case with the oxazaphosphorine class of alkylating agents, ifosfamide is excreted in breast milk and breast-feeding should be terminated prior to institution of drug therapy.

Since the possibility of interference with normal wound healing has been reported with other oxazaphosphorines, therapy should not be initiated for at least 10 to 14 days after surgery.

Ifosfamide, like other alkylating agents, has been reported to have oncogenic activity in animals. Thus the possibility that it may have oncogenic potential in humans should be considered.

Precautions: Ifosfamide should be given cautiously to patients with any of the following conditions: leukopenia, thrombocytopenia, tumor-cell infiltration of the bone marrow, prior radiotherapy, prior treatment with other antineoplastic agents, brain metastases and advanced cerebral arteriosclerosis, impaired renal function, impaired hepatic function, in the presence of known infections, abnormal serum creatinine and serum albumin levels.

Because ifosfamide may exert a suppressive action in immune mechanisms, the interruption or modification of dosage should be considered for patients who develop bacterial, fungal or viral infections. This is especially true for patients receiving concomitant steroid therapy, since infections in some of these patients have been fatal.

Ifosfamide may cause significant neurologic, renal and hematologic toxicities which may prove fatal despite careful monitoring prior to and during therapy.

Prior to initiating treatment, it is necessary to exclude or correct any obstruction of the efferent urinary tract, cystitis, infections, and electrolyte imbalances.

Urinary sediment should be examined at regular intervals. Extra care is required in unilaterally nephrectomized patients, in patients with impaired renal function, and in patients pre-treated with nephrotoxic drugs (e.g., cisplatin) who obviously tolerate high-doses of ifosfamide less well. Ifosfamide should not be given until 3 months after the nephrectomy. Additional caution is also advisable in patients treated concomitantly with drugs having nephrotoxic potential (e.g., aminoglycosides and amphotericin B).

Careful monitoring is also required for patients with cerebral metastases, as ifosfamide has been associated with several CNS symptoms.

Leukocyte, erythrocyte and platelet counts should be carried out at regular intervals. There is normally a reduction in the leukocyte count beginning on approximately day 5. The nadir, depending on dosage and baseline count, tends to be reached after 8 to 10 days. Recovery occurs after 10 to 14 days and is usually complete after 2 to 3 weeks.

Neurologic manifestations consisting of somnolence, confusion, hallucinations and in some instances, coma have been reported following ifosfamide therapy. In the case of ifosfamide induced CNS symptoms, drugs acting on the CNS (e.g., antiemetics and narcotics) should be discontinued, if possible, or used with caution. The occurrence of these symptoms requires discontinuing ifosfamide therapy. These symptoms have usually been reversible and supporting therapy should be maintained until their resolution.

Drug Interactions: The concurrent use of ifosfamide may enhance the anticoagulant effect of warfarin and thus raise the risk of hemorrhages.

Adverse Effects: Urinary: Hemorrhagic cystitis, manifested by the occurrence of hematuria, dysuria, urinary frequency and occasionally urinary incontinence or retention, develops frequently in patients treated with ifosfamide. The incidence, severity and persistence of ifosfamide-induced hemorrhagic cystitis increase as the dose of the drug increases. In most instances, the hematuria resolves spontaneously upon cessation of therapy.

The urinary tract toxicity of ifosfamide can be minimized by administering a uroprotective agent such as mesna (see Uromitexan product monograph for Dosage), and ensuring adequate hydration and maintenance of fluid balance.

Granular casts in the urinary sediment have occurred mainly after high doses of ifosfamide. The cylinduria generally resolves spontaneously a few days after the last injection.

Renal parenchymal and tubular necrosis, which could lead to death, have been reported. Disorders of glomerular renal function with an increase in serum creatinine, a decrease in creatinine clearance and proteinuria occasionally occur; more frequently, disorders of tubular renal function with hyperaminoaciduria, phosphaturia, acidosis, or proteinuria occur. Severe nephropathies are rare. Predisposing factors for nephrotoxicity include the presence of renal tumors, pre-existing renal impairment, prior treatment with platinum containing drugs, and concomitant treatment with potentially nephrotoxic agents (see Precautions).

Increases and decreases in creatinine clearance are usually reversible.

Metabolic acidosis was reported in 31% of patients in one study when ifosfamide was administered at doses of 2 to 2.5 g/m²/day for 4 days.

Renal tubular acidosis, Fanconi Syndrome and renal rickets have also been reported. Close clinical monitoring of serum and urine chemistries including phosphorus, potassium, alkaline phosphatase and other appropriate laboratory studies is recommended. Appropriate replacement therapy should be administered as indicated.

Hematopoietic: Leukopenia with the risk of life-threatening infection is an expected effect and ordinarily is used as a guide to therapy. Thrombocytopenia with the risk of hemorrhage and anemia have been known to occur in a few patients.

Ifex (cont'd)

These effects are almost always reversible when therapy is interrupted. Episodes of petechial bleeding due to severe thrombocytopenia have been reported.

When ifosfamide is used in combination with other myelosuppressive agents, adjustments in dosing may be necessary.

Gastrointestinal: Nausea and vomiting are dose-related and also depend on individual sensitivity. Other gastrointestinal adverse events include anorexia, diarrhea, constipation, and stomatitis.

Effects on Gonads: Gonadal suppression, resulting in amenorrhea or azoospermia, has been reported with other oxazaphosphorines and thus may occur with ifosfamide.

Integumentary: It is ordinarily advisable to inform patients in advance of possible alopecia, a frequent complication of ifosfamide therapy. Regrowth of hair can be expected although occasionally the new hair may be of a different color or texture. Nonspecific dermatitis and inflammation of mucous membranes have been reported to occur with ifosfamide.

CNS: Cerebral side effects consist mainly of somnolence, confusion, hallucinations and depressive psychosis. Other less frequent symptoms included dizziness, disorientation, cranial nerve dysfunction, and cerebellar symptoms. Seizures of the tonic-clonic type have been reported occasionally. Isolated cases of encephalitis, generalized seizure and seizures resulting in coma have also been observed.

It is possible that the severity and incidence of cerebral effects increase with the administration of high doses, the presence of brain metastases, or advanced cerebral arteriosclerosis. The incidence and extent of cerebral effects due to ifosfamide may also be affected by the age of the patient, impaired renal clearance, pretreatment with nephrotoxic drugs, and postrenal obstructions (e.g., pelvic tumors). Other possible risk factors may include decreased levels of serum albumin or hydrogen carbonate, or concurrent high-dose treatment with antiemetic drugs.

Cardiotoxicity: Although cardiotoxicity is rarely encountered, there have been reported cases of supraventricular or ventricular arrhythmias, ST segment changes and heart failure at high doses of ifosfamide, or after pretreatment or concomitant treatment with anthracyclines. Hypertension and hypotension have been reported rarely.

Respiratory: Interstitial pulmonary fibrosis has been reported in patients treated with large doses of alkylating agents for prolonged periods. Although not reported in patients treated with ifosfamide, physicians should be aware of its possible occurrence. Pulmonary toxicities, including reports of interstitial pneumonitis and pulmonary edema, have been reported from fewer than 1% of patients.

Other: Adverse reactions in addition to those mentioned above have been noted with ifosfamide. They include infection with or without fever, hematemesis, asthenia, thrombophlebitis, increase in liver enzymes and/or bilirubin, allergic reactions, polyneuropathy, impaired or blurred vision, and increased sensitivity to irradiation. In addition, in isolated cases, syndrome of inappropriate of antidiuretic hormone (SIADH) has been reported.

Pancreatitis has been reported in isolated cases.

Overdose: Symptoms and Treatment: No specific antidote is known. Management of overdosage would include general supportive measures to sustain the patient through any period of toxicity that might occur.

Dosage: Chemotherapy with ifosfamide, as with other drugs used in cancer chemotherapy, is potentially hazardous and fatal complications can occur. It is recommended that it be administered only by physicians aware of the associated risks. Total dosage of 250 to 300 mg/kg per cycle is the usual standard. As a rule, 50 to 60 mg/kg are administered i.v., over a period of a minimum of 30 minutes, each day for 5 consecutive days. If the calculation of the dosage is based on body surface area, the recommended dosage is 2 000 to 2 400 mg/m² daily on 5 consecutive days. If a lower daily dosage or the total dosage over a longer period is indicated, ifosfamide can be given every other day (days 1, 3, 5, 7 and 9) or on 10 consecutive days in lower doses.

A treatment series should be repeated after an interval of not less than 3 to 4 weeks.

The therapeutic administration should invariably be accompanied by uroprotective treatment with mesna. Alternately, the administration of high single dose infusions is now feasible up to 5 to 8 g/m²/24 h under protection of continuous mesna infusion. The optimal use of ifosfamide in combination with other myelosuppressive agents requires dosage adjustments according to the regimen and schedule to be adopted.

Prevention of Cystitis: The concomitant administration of mesna helps to prevent the urotoxic side effects of ifosfamide which had previously limited the drug's therapeutic use. Every ifosfamide regimen should be accompanied by uroprotective treatment with mesna.

Mesna is usually given by i.v. injection concurrently with ifosfamide and 4 and 8 hours afterwards, each dose being 20% of the ifosfamide dose (see Uromitexan product monograph for Dosage).

Even with the administration of the uroprotector mesna, the daily fluid intake should be at least 2 L. If urinary excretion appears insufficient, a fast-acting diuretic such as furosemide may be administered.

Reconstitution: Preparation for I.V. Use: Reconstitute with Sterile Water for Injection as in Table I.

Table I—Ifex

Reconstitution

Vial Size	Volume to be Added	Approximate Available Volume	Approximate Average Concentration
1 g	20 mL	20 mL	50 mg/mL
3 g	60 mL	60 mL	50 mg/mL

Shake well until dissolved. The prepared solution may be further diluted to achieve concentrations of 0.6 to 20 mg/mL with any of the solutions for i.v. infusion listed below.

Solutions for I.V. Infusion: 5% Dextrose Injection USP, 0.9% Sodium Chloride USP, Lactated Ringer's Injection USP.

Stability of Solutions: Reconstituted and further diluted solutions should be used within 24 hours from the time of the initial constitution or within 72 hours when refrigerated, when stored in glass bottles, viaflex bags or PAB bags.

Note: Product should be inspected visually for particulate matter and discoloration prior to administration.

Handling and Disposal: Preparation of ifosfamide should be done in a vertical laminar flow hood (Biological Safety Cabinet—Class II). Personnel preparing ifosfamide should wear PVC gloves, safety glasses, disposable gowns and masks. All needles, syringes, vials and other materials which have come in contact with ifosfamide should be segregated and incinerated at 1 000°C or more. Sealed containers may explode. Intact vials should be returned to the manufacturer for destruction. Proper precautions should be taken in packaging these materials for transport.

Personnel regularly involved in the preparation and handling of ifosfamide should have bi-annual blood examinations.

Supplied: Each vial of sterile powder contains: ifosfamide 1 g and 3 g. Nonmedicinal ingredients: none.

Reviewed 1999

ILETIN®
ILETIN® II PORK
Lilly

Insulin

Diabetes Mellitus Therapy

Description: Insulin is a protein hormone secreted by the beta cells of the pancreatic islets of Langerhans.

The administration of suitable doses of insulin to patients with diabetes mellitus, along with controlled diet and exercise, temporarily restores their ability to metabolize carbohydrates, fats and proteins; to store glycogen in the liver; and to convert glucose to fat. When given in suitable doses at regular intervals to a patient with diabetes mellitus, the blood sugar is maintained within a reasonable range, the urine remains relatively free of sugar and ketone bodies, and diabetic acidosis and coma are prevented.

Insulin preparations differ in onset, peak and duration of action (see Table I). The addition of protamine to insulin, in the presence of zinc, produces a stable complex with less intense and more prolonged action, due to its slow solubility. The onset and duration of action is also modified by reprecipitation in the presence of sodium acetate and zinc. This modified action depends on the structure of the resulting precipitate.

Regular insulin is rapid acting while NPH and Lente are intermediate acting. Regular insulin is a clear solution, while the others are cloudy, white suspensions. Unless otherwise specified, Iletin is of mixed beef-pork origin. Iletin II Pork is of monospecies pork origin.

Regular insulin may be mixed with NPH or Lente insulin in any proportion desired.

The rapid action of the Regular Iletin is preserved when mixed with NPH Iletin preparations; independent of the time lag between mixing and administration, and independent of the proportion of Regular insulin incorporated in the mixture.

Mixtures of Lente and Regular Iletin insulins are subject to a binding phenomenon which is detectable within 15 minutes in vitro and continues for up to 24 hours. This binding increases as the ratio of Lente to Regular Iletin increases, and may be reduced by administering the dose immediately after preparation.

All mixtures are stable for at least 1 month if stored at or below room temperature and for 3 months if refrigerated. Because of this improved stability, it is feasible for the physician to prepare the mixtures during office visits for patients requiring a combination but incapable of preparing it themselves.

When the 2 types of insulin are mixed, it is important to recognize that the hypodermic syringes of different manufacturers may vary in the amount of space between the bottom line in the barrel and the needle. This is called dead space. The problem can be reduced if the patient consistently uses injection equipment of the same manufacturer and does not vary the order in which the insulins are added to the syringe.

When employing the simultaneous administration of different insulin preparations in 1 syringe, the physician's instructions concerning the order in which the materials are taken into the syringe and the degree to which the materials simultaneously measured into the syringe are mixed should be consistently followed. Under some circumstances dosage variation can result from neglect of these instructions.

The simultaneous administration of 2 insulin preparations in 1 syringe should be undertaken only if prescribed. In following the procedure all instructions for sterilizing, shaking the vial, etc. should be adhered to.

Observing aseptic technique, inject a volume of air equal to the dose into the vial of modified insulin. Withdraw the needle without withdrawing the dose. Inject air and withdraw the proper dose of regular insulin from the vial in the usual manner. Invert the vial of modified insulin several times and withdraw the dose into the syringe containing the regular insulin. Holding the syringe with the needle upright, draw an air bubble into the syringe, invert the syringe and roll the bubble through to mix. Expel the air bubble and inject in the usual manner.

Indications: Replacement therapy in the treatment of diabetes mellitus which cannot be controlled satisfactorily by dietary regulation alone. Insulin is indicated in the treatment of juvenile onset diabetes or brittle diabetes. The drug may also be indicated in maturity onset diabetes which cannot be controlled by diet alone. In addition, insulin must often be substituted for oral hypoglycemic therapy in patients with maturity onset diabetes complicated by acidosis, ketosis, diabetic coma, major surgery, fever, severe trauma, infections, serious impairment of renal or hepatic functions, thyroid or other endocrine dysfunctions, acute cardiac accidents, gangrene or Raynaud's disease, and in pregnant women. Combinations of insulin and oral hypoglycemic drugs may be used when a patient is being transferred from insulin to therapy with oral

Table I—Iletin

Characteristics of Insulin Preparations

Preparation	Buffer pH	Protein Modifier	Preservative	Approximate Peak Action (Hours)	Approximate Duration (Hours)
Regular Iletin (Neutral)	None 7.2	None	m-cresol 0.25%	2–4	5–7
NPH Iletin	Phosphate 7.2	Protamine	m-cresol 0.15% and phenol 0.06%	6–12	24–28
Lente Iletin	Acetate 7.2	None	methylparaben 0.1%	6–12	24–28

hypoglycemics. Long-term use combining insulin and oral hypoglycemic therapy is seldom warranted.

May be used to improve appetite and increase weight in selected cases of nondiabetic malnutrition e.g., anorexia nervosa.

Insulin has been used as a test for the completeness of vagotomy because of its stimulant effect on gastric secretion.

Precautions and Adverse Effects: Every diabetic patient taking insulin should carry an identification card containing pertinent medical information.

Any change of insulin should be made cautiously and only under medical supervision. Changes in strength, purity, brand, type and/or source of species may result in the need for a change in dosage. It is not possible to identify which patients will require a change in dose. Adjustment may be needed with the first dose or occur over a period of several weeks. Be aware of the possibility of symptoms of either hypoglycemia or hyperglycemia.

The number and size of daily doses and the time of administration, as well as diet and exercise, are problems that require direct and continuous medical supervision. Usually, the most satisfactory injection time is before breakfast.

Prompt recognition and appropriate management of the complications of insulin therapy are essential for safe and effective control of diabetes mellitus.

Hypoglycemia may occur in any patient receiving insulin and is most commonly manifested by hunger, nervousness, warmth and sweating, and palpitations. Patients also may experience headache, confusion, drowsiness, fatigue, anxiety, blurred vision, diplopia, or numbness of the lips, nose, or fingers. The clinical manifestations of hypoglycemia can be masked by the concomitant administration of propranolol or other beta adrenergic blockers.

Symptoms are likely to appear anytime when the blood sugar concentration falls below 40 mg/100 mL but may occur with a sudden drop in blood glucose even when the value remains above 40 mg/100 mL.

If a patient is unable to take soluble carbohydrate or fruit juice orally, hypoglycemia is treated with 10 to 20 g of dextrose in sterile solution administered i.v. If glucose is unavailable, 1 mg of glucagon may be given s.c. or i.m. every 20 minutes for 2 or 3 doses.

Local and allergic reactions are commonly seen in patients receiving insulin for the first time or when therapy is reinstated. Local inflammatory responses also result from improper cleansing of the skin, contamination of the injection site with alcohol, use of an antiseptic containing impurities or accidental intracutaneous rather than s.c. injection. Local reactions that result from skin sensitivity phenomena usually subside spontaneously. Allergic urticaria, angioedema, and anaphylactic reactions occur infrequently and may sometimes be avoided by changing the species source of insulin. Rarely, an intradermal or s.c. hyposensitization procedure may be required.

It has been observed that areas of fat atrophy (lipodystrophy) resulting from previous administration of older insulin preparations are frequently restored to normal or near normal appearance by repeated injection of current insulin preparations into, or adjacent to, the areas of fat atrophy.

Visual disturbances in uncontrolled diabetes due to refractive changes are reversed during the early phase of effective management. However, since alteration in osmotic equilibirum between the lens and ocular fluids may not stabilize for a few weeks after initiating therapy, it is wise to postpone prescribing new corrective lenses for 3 to 6 weeks.

Hormones that tend to counteract the hypoglycemic effects of insulin include growth hormone, corticotropin, glucocorticoids, thyroid hormone, and glucagon. Epinephrine not only inhibits the secretion of insulin, but also stimulates glycogen breakdown to glucose. Thus, the presence of such diseases as acromegaly, Cushing's syndrome, hyperthyroidism, and pheochromocytoma complicate the control of diabetes.

The hypoglycemic action of insulin may also be antagonized by phenytoin. Insulin's hypoglycemic action can be increased in some patients by concomitant administration of anabolic steroids, MAO inhibitors, guanethidine, alcohol, propranolol (masking effect), or other drugs affecting beta adrenergic receptors, or by daily doses of 1.5 to 6 g of salicylates.

Insulin requirements can be increased, decreased, or unchanged in patients receiving diuretics. Concomitant administration of oral contraceptives can cause a decrease in glucose tolerance in diabetic women possibly resulting in increased daily insulin requirements.

In case a meal is unavoidably omitted as a result of fever or nausea and vomiting, the next dose of insulin should not be omitted unless a urine test shows the absence of sugar or only trace amounts and the patient has not urinated for 4 hours or more. If no sugar or trace amounts are present, urine tests should be made at intervals not exceeding 4 hours.

For patients using insulin who have unavoidably omitted a meal, replace the food with similar amounts of carbohydrate in the form of orange juice or some other source of available glucose.

If the patient becomes ill from any cause, he should notify the physician immediately, have his urine tested at once, and take plenty of fluids, at least a cupful of sweetened hot tea, coffee, milk, broth, or orange juice every hour. Coma may be avoided by prompt treatment.

Avoid the use of heavily chlorinated water or chemical solutions for sterilizing the syringe prior to injection. The use of distilled or clean rainwater rather than hard water is to be preferred if the syringe is to be sterilized by boiling.

Syringes which have been used for a time may become coated with a precipitate. The opaque layer may be easily removed by a swab of cotton saturated with vinegar, and the syringe should then be thoroughly rinsed in water and sterilized. Very fine needles may become plugged with the precipitate unless cleaned with a wire after use.

Supplied: Each 10 mL multidose vial of Iletin Regular, NPH or Lente contains: 100 units/mL of the stated insulin preparation, prepared from a mixture of insulin crystals extracted from beef and pork pancreas. Each 10 mL multidose vial of Iletin II Pork Regular, NPH or Lente contains: 100 units/mL of the stated insulin preparation, prepared from insulin crystals extracted from pork pancreas.

Store in a cool place, preferably a refrigerator, and avoid freezing or high temperatures. No vial should be used in which the precipitate has become clumped or granular in appearance or has formed a deposit of solid particles on the wall of the vial. Vials in use should be kept cold and protected from strong light and their contents used as continuously as practical. A partially empty vial should be discarded if it has not been used for several weeks.

ILOSONE® Ⓟ

Lilly

Erythromycin Estolate

Antibiotic

Pharmacology: Erythromycin exerts its antibacterial action by binding the 50S ribosomal subunit of susceptible bacteria and suppressing protein synthesis. Erythromycin is usually bacteriostatic but may be bactericidal in high concentrations or against highly susceptible organisms.

Indications: For the treatment of infections caused by susceptible strains of the designated microorganisms in the diseases listed below:

Upper respiratory tract infections of mild to moderate severity caused by S. pyogenes (Group A beta-hemolytic streptococci), S. pneumoniae and H. influenzae. **Note:** not all strains of H. influenzae are susceptible to erythromycin at the concentrations of the antibiotic achieved with usual therapeutic doses.

Lower respiratory tract infections of mild to moderate severity caused by S. pyogenes (Group A beta-hemolytic streptococci), S. pneumoniae and Mycoplasma pneumoniae.

Skin and soft tissue infections of mild to moderate severity caused by S. pyogenes and S. aureus. **Note:** Resistance of staphylococci may emerge during treatment.

Primary syphilis caused by T. pallidum. Erythromycin is an alternate choice of treatment for primary syphilis in patients allergic to penicillins. Spinal fluid examinations should be performed before treatment and as part of the post-therapy follow-up.

Diphtheria caused by C. diphtheriae. As an adjunct to antitoxin, to prevent the establishment of carriers, and to eradicate the organisms in carriers.

Erythrasma caused by C. minutissimum.

Pertussis caused by B. pertussis. Erythromycin is effective in eliminating the organism from the nasopharynx of infected individuals, rendering them non-infectious. Some clinical studies suggest that erythromycin may be helpful in the prophylaxis of pertussis in exposed susceptible individuals.

Legionnaires' disease caused by L. pneumophila. Although no controlled clinical efficacy studies have been conducted, in vitro and limited clinical data suggest that erythromycin can be effective in treating Legionnaires' disease.

Chlamydial Infections: The 1988 Canadian Guidelines for the Treatment of Sexually Transmitted Diseases in Neonates, Children, Adolescents and Adults recommends erythromycin for the treatment of the following infections when caused by Chlamydia trachomatis: in newborns and infants for conjunctivitis and pneumonia. **Note:** Topical therapy alone for conjunctivitis is NOT adequate. In children under 9 years of age, in pregnant women and in nursing mothers for uncomplicated urethral, endocervical or rectal infection. In adolescents and adults, when tetracycline or doxycycline is contraindicated or not tolerated, for uncomplicated urethral, endocervical or rectal infection.

The treatment of acne vulgaris.

Specimens for bacteriologic culture should be obtained prior to therapy in order to isolate and identify the causative organisms and to determine their susceptibility to erythromycin. Therapy may be instituted before results of susceptibility studies are known; however, antibiotic treatment should be re-evaluated when the results become available or if the clinical response is not adequate.

Prophylaxis (Alpha-hemolytic Streptococci): For prophylaxis against bacterial endocarditis in patients hypersensitive to penicillin who have congenital heart disease or rheumatic or other acquired valvular heart disease when they undergo dental procedures and surgical procedures of the upper respiratory tract.

Contraindications: Erythromycin estolate is contraindicated in patients with a known history of sensitivity to this drug and in those with preexisting liver disease or dysfunction.

Concurrent therapy with astemizole or terfenadine (see Precautions, Drug Interactions).

Warnings: Erythromycin should be administered with caution to any patient who has demonstrated some form of allergy to drugs. If an allergic reaction to erythromycin occurs, administration of the drug should be discontinued. Serious hypersensitivity reactions may require epinephrine, antihistamines or corticosteroids.

There have been reports of hepatic dysfunction, with or without jaundice, occurring in patients receiving erythromycin products. If findings suggestive of significant hepatic dysfunction occur, therapy with erythromycin products should be discontinued. Erythromycin has a greater propensity to cause hepatotoxicity.

Pseudomembranous colitis has been occasionally reported to occur in association with erythromycin therapy. Therefore, it is important to consider its diagnosis in patients administered erythromycin who develop diarrhea. Mild cases of colitis may respond to drug discontinuation alone. Moderate to severe cases should be managed with fluid, electrolyte and protein supplementation as indicated. If the colitis is not relieved by discontinuation of erythromycin administration or when it is severe, consideration should be given to the administration of vancomycin or other suitable therapy. Other possible causes of the colitis should also be considered.

Precautions: Prolonged or repeated use of erythromycin may result in an overgrowth of non-susceptible bacteria or fungi and organisms initially sensitive to erythromycin. If superinfection occurs, erythromycin should be discontinued and appropriate therapy instituted.

Since erythromycin is principally excreted by the liver, caution should be exercised when erythromycin is administered to patients with impaired hepatic function.

Drug Interactions: Theophylline: Recent data from studies of erythromycin in patients reveal that its use in patients who are receiving high doses of theophylline may be associated with an increase in serum theophylline levels and potential theophylline toxicity. In case of theophylline toxicity and/or elevated serum theophylline levels, the dose of theophylline should be reduced while the patient is receiving concomitant erythromycin therapy.

Lincomycin/Clindamycin/Chloramphenicol: Erythromycin should be used with caution if administered concomitantly with these drugs. In vitro experiments have demonstrated that binding sites for erythromycin, lincomycin, clindamycin and chloramphenicol overlap and competitive inhibition may occur.

Carbamazepine/Digoxin/Phenytoin: Concomitant administration of erythromycin with carbamazepine, digoxin or phenytoin has been reported to result in elevated plasma levels of these agents, leading to toxicity in some patients.

Oral Anticoagulants: Published reports indicate that caution should be observed when erythromycin and oral anticoagulants are used concurrently since prothrombin time may be prolonged.

Triazolam: Erythromycin has been reported to decrease the clearance of triazolam and thus may increase the pharmacologic effect of triazolam.

Ilosone (cont'd)

Ergotamine: There are reports that ischemic reactions may occur when erythromycin is given concurrently with ergotamine-containing drugs.

Cyclosporine: There have been reports that there is a rise in plasma cyclosporine levels during concomitant administration of erythromycin.

Alfentanil: The concomitant use of erythromycin with alfentanil can significantly inhibit the clearance of alfentanil and may increase the risk of prolonged or delayed respiratory depression.

Terfenadine: Terfenadine undergoes metabolism in the liver by a specific cytochrome P450 isoenzyme. This metabolic pathway may be impaired in patients who are taking erythromycin, an inhibitor of this isoenzyme. Interference with this enzyme can lead to elevated terfenadine plasma levels which may be associated with QT prolongation, and increased risk of ventricular tachyarrhythmias (such as torsades de pointes, ventricular tachycardia, and ventricular fibrillation) (see Contraindications).

Astemizole: Concomitant administration of astemizole with erythromycin is contraindicated because erythromycin is known to impair the Cytochrome P450 enzyme system which also influences astemizole metabolism. There have been two reports to date of syncope with torsades de pointes requiring hospitalization in patients taking astemizole with erythromycin. In each case the QT intervals were prolonged beyond 650 milliseconds at the time of the event; one patient also received ketoconazole and the other patient also had hypokalemia (see Contraindications).

Pregnancy: The safety of erythromycin for use during pregnancy has not been established. Erythromycin crosses the placental barrier.

Lactation: The safety of erythromycin for use during breast feeding has not been established. Erythromycin is excreted in breast milk.

Children: The safety of erythromycin for use in neonates has not been established.

Adverse Effects: The most frequent adverse effects of erythromycin preparations are gastrointestinal (e.g., abdominal cramping and discomfort) and are dose related. Nausea, vomiting, and diarrhea occur infrequently with usual oral doses.

Adult erythromycin estolate administration has been associated with an infrequent occurrence of intrahepatic cholestasis.

Rarely, hepatic dysfunction, with or without jaundice, has occurred in association with erythromycin estolate administration. It may be accompanied by malaise, nausea, vomiting, abdominal colic, and fever. In some instances, severe abdominal pain may simulate the pain of biliary colic, pancreatitis, perforated ulcer, or an acute abdominal surgical problem. In other instances, clinical symptoms and liver function test results have resembled findings in extra-hepatic obstructive jaundice. If abnormalities occur, discontinue promptly. The syndrome seems to result from a form of sensitization, occurs chiefly in adults, and has been reversible when medication is discontinued.

In some cases, initial symptoms have developed after a few days of treatment, but generally they have followed 1 or 2 weeks of continuous therapy. If the above findings occur, discontinue erythromycin estolate promptly. After the drug is readministered to sensitive patients, symptoms reappear, usually within 48 hours.

Mild allergic reactions, such as urticaria and other skin rashes, have occurred. Serious allergic reactions, including anaphylaxis, have been reported rarely.

Overdose: Symptoms: Nausea, vomiting and diarrhea. Recently there has been a report of a case of erythromycin-induced pancreatitis following erythromycin overdose.

Treatment: General management may consist of supportive therapy.

Dosage: Administer orally. Infants and children 5 to 10 kg, 10 mg/kg every 6 hours, 10 to 25 kg, 125 mg every 6 hours. Adults and children over 25 kg, 250 mg every 6 hours or 500 mg every 12 hours. For severe infections, these dosages may be doubled.

If administration is desired on a twice a day schedule in either adults or children, 50% of the total daily dose may be given every 12 hours.

Streptococcal infections: In the treatment of Group A beta-hemolytic streptococcal infections, administer a therapeutic dosage of erythromycin for at least 10 days. In continuous prophylaxis of streptococcal infections in persons with a history of rheumatic heart disease, the dosage is 250 mg twice a day.

When erythromycin estolate is used prior to surgery to prevent endocarditis caused by alpha-hemolytic streptococci (viridans group), a recommended schedule for adults is 500 mg before the procedure and 250 mg every 8 hours for 4 doses afterward; for children, 30 to 50 mg/kg/day divided into 3 or 4 evenly spaced doses.

Primary syphilis: 20 to 30 g given in divided doses over a period of 10 to 15 days.

Amebic dysentery: 250 mg 4 times daily for 10 to 14 days for adults; 30 to 50 mg/kg/day in divided doses for 10 to 14 days for children.

Supplied: Liquids: 125 mg: Each 5 mL contains: erythromycin estolate equivalent to 125 mg erythromycin base in an orange flavored vehicle. Nonmedicinal ingredients: butylparaben, cellulose and sodium CMC, citric acid, edetate calcium disodium, FD&C Yellow No. 6, methylparaben, orange 0.1 valencia, propylparaben, silicone, sodium chloride, sodium citrate, sodium lauryl sulfate, sucrose and water. Energy: 37.7 kJ (9.0 kcal)/5 mL. Sodium: <1 mmol (9.75 mg)/5 mL. Tartrazine-free. Identi-Code: W 15. Bottles of 500 mL. Shake well before using. Avoid freezing. Dated item.

250 mg: Each 5 mL contains: erythromycin estolate equivalent to 250 mg erythromycin base in a cherry flavored vehicle. Nonmedicinal ingredients: amaranth, butylparaben, cellulose and sodium CMC, citric acid, edetate calcium disodium, FD&C Yellow No. 6, flavor imitation (cherry, cherry pit), imitation guarana liquid, methylparaben, propylparaben, silicone, sodium chloride, sodium citrate, sodium lauryl sulfate, sucrose and water. Energy: 29.7 kJ (7.1 kcal)/5 mL. Sodium: <1 mmol (9.75 mg)/5 mL. Tartrazine-free. Identi-Code: W 17. Bottles of 500 mL. Shake well before using. Avoid freezing. Dated item.

Pulvules: Each No. 0 capsule with ivory, opaque body, imprinted with "Ilosone 250 mg", and red, opaque cap, imprinted with "H09" contains: erythromycin estolate equivalent to erythromycin base 250 mg. Nonmedicinal ingredients: magnesium stearate, mineral oil, silica gel and talc; capsule shell and printing ink: ammonium hydroxide, benzyl alcohol, black iron oxide, butylparaben, edetate calcium disodium, ethyl alcohol, FD&C Red No. 3, FD&C Yellow No. 6, gelatin, iron oxide red, iron oxide yellow, isopropyl alcohol, methylparaben, n-butyl alcohol, propylene glycol, propylparaben, shellac, sodium lauryl sulfate, sodium propionate and titanium dioxide; may contain: dimethyl polysiloxane and potassium hydroxide. Sodium- and tartrazine-free. Bottles of 100.

IMDUR®
Astra
Isosorbide-5-Mononitrate
Antianginal

Pharmacology: As with other organic nitrates, the principal pharmacological action of isosorbide-5-mononitrate, the major active metabolite of isosorbide dinitrate (ISDN), is relaxation of vascular smooth muscle and consequent dilation of peripheral arteries and veins, especially the latter. Dilation of the veins promotes peripheral pooling of blood and decreases venous return to the heart, thereby reducing left ventricular end-diastolic pressure and pulmonary capillary wedge pressure (preload). Arteriolar relaxation reduces systemic vascular resistance, systolic arterial pressure, and mean arterial pressure (after-load). Dilation of the coronary arteries also occurs. The hemodynamic responses to isosorbide-5-mononitrate are similar to those produced by other nitrates.

Pharmacodynamics: Dosage regimens for most chronically used drugs are designed to provide plasma concentrations that are continuously greater than a minimally effective concentration. This strategy is inappropriate for organic nitrates. Prolonged administration of nitrate drugs according to traditionally recommended dosage regimens has been shown to produce tolerance. Tolerance results in a loss of efficacy. Several well-controlled clinical trials have used exercise testing to assess the antianginal efficacy of continuously delivered nitrates. In the large majority of these trials, nitrate effectiveness was indistinguishable from placebo after 24 hours (or less) of continuous therapy. Attempts to overcome tolerance by dose escalation, even to doses far in excess of those used acutely, have consistently failed. Only after nitrates have been absent from the body for several hours has their antianginal efficacy been restored. Drug-free intervals of 10 to 12 hours are known to be sufficient to restore response. The drug-free interval sufficient to avoid tolerance to isosorbide-5-mononitrate has not been completely defined. Imdur tablets during long-term use over 42 days dosed at 120 mg once daily continued to improve exercise performance at 4 hours and 12 hours after dosing but its effects (although better than placebo) are less than or at best equal to the effects of the first dose of 60 mg. Considering the pharmacokinetic profile of isosorbide-5-mononitrate and its long half-life (see Pharmacokinetics), clinical efficacy is consistent with that observed for other organic nitrates.

Pharmacokinetics: After oral administration of isosorbide-5-mononitrate as a solution or immediate-release tablets, maximum plasma concentrations of isosorbide-5-mononitrate are achieved in 30 to 60 minutes with an absolute bioavailability of approximately 100%. After i.v. administration, isosorbide-5-mononitrate is distributed into total body water in about 9 minutes with a volume of distribution of approximately 0.6 to 0.7 L/kg. Isosorbide-5-mononitrate is approximately 5% bound to human plasma proteins and is distributed into blood cells and saliva. Isosorbide-5-mononitrate is primarily metabolized by the liver, but unlike oral isosorbide dinitrate, it is not subject to first-pass metabolism. Isosorbide-5-mononitrate is cleared by denitration to isosorbide and glucuronidation as the mononitrate, with 96% of the administered dose excreted in the urine within 5 days and only about 1% eliminated in the feces. At least 6 different compounds have been detected in urine, with about 2% of the dose excreted as the unchanged drug and at least 5 metabolites. The metabolites are not pharmacologically active. Renal clearance accounts for only about 4% of total body clearance. The mean plasma elimination half-life of isosorbide-5-mononitrate is approximately 5 hours.

The disposition of isosorbide-5-mononitrate in patients with various degrees of renal insufficiency, liver cirrhosis or cardiac dysfunction was evaluated and found to be similar to that observed in healthy subjects.

The elimination half-life of isosorbide-5-mononitrate was not prolonged, and there was no drug accumulation in patients with chronic renal failure after multiple oral dosing.

Impaired liver or kidney function has no major influence on the pharmacokinetic properties.

Food intake may decrease the rate (increase in T_{max}) but not the extent (AUC) of absorption of isosorbide-5-mononitrate.

With the extended release formulation of Imdur, isosorbide-5-mononitrate is gradually released, independent of pH, over a 10-hour period, according to a first order process. This prolongation of the absorption phase results in reduced and delayed peak plasma levels compared to conventional tablets of isosorbide-5-mononitrate. After administration of 60 mg of isosorbide-5-mononitrate extended release tablets, peak plasma levels of around 3 000 nmol/L are usually obtained within approximately 4 hours. The plasma concentrations then gradually fall to around 500 nmol/L at the end of the dosage interval (24 hours after dose intake).

Indications: For the prevention of anginal attacks in patients with chronic stable angina pectoris associated with coronary artery disease.

Not intended for the immediate relief of acute attacks of angina pectoris.

Contraindications: Known hypersensitivity to isosorbide-5-mononitrate or to other nitrates or nitrites. Acute circulatory failure associated with marked hypotension (shock and states of collapse). Postural hypotension. Myocardial insufficiency due to obstruction (e.g. in the presence of aortic or mitral stenosis or of constrictive pericarditis). Increased intracranial pressure. Severe anemia.

Warnings: The benefits and safety of isosorbide-5-mononitrate in anginal patients with acute myocardial infarction or congestive heart failure have not been established. Because the effects of isosorbide-5-mononitrate are difficult to terminate rapidly, this drug is not recommended in these settings.

Abrupt withdrawal may occasionally aggravate anginal symptoms. To avoid possible withdrawal effects, the administration of isosorbide-5-mononitrate should be gradually reduced and not abruptly discontinued.

Caution should be observed in patients with severe cerebral arteriosclerosis or severe hypotension.

Precautions: Headaches or symptoms of severe hypotension, such as weakness or dizziness, particularly when arising suddenly from a recumbent position, may occur.

Caution should be exercised when using nitrates in patients prone to, or who might be affected by, hypotension. Isosorbide-5-mononitrate should therefore be used with caution in patients who may have volume depletion from diuretic therapy or in patients who have low systolic blood pressure (e.g. below 90 mmHg). Paradoxical bradycardia and increased angina pectoris may accompany nitrate-induced hypotension.

Nitrate therapy may aggravate the angina caused by hypertrophic cardiomyopathy.

In industrial workers who have had long-term exposure to unknown (presumably high) doses of organic nitrates, tolerance clearly occurs. There is, moreover, physical dependence since chest pain, acute myocardial infarction, and even sudden death have occurred during temporary withdrawal of nitrates from these workers. In clinical trials of angina patients, there are reports of anginal attacks being more easily provoked and of rebound in the hemodynamic effects soon after nitrate withdrawal. The importance of these observations to the routine, clinical use of oral isosorbide-5-mononitrate has not been fully elucidated.

Caution should be exercised in patients with arterial hypoxemia due to anemia (see Contraindications). Similarly, caution is called for in patients with hypoxemia and a ventilation/perfusion imbalance due to lung disease or ischemic heart failure. Patients with angina pectoris, myocardial infarction, or cerebral ischemia frequently suffer from abnormalities of the small airways (especially alveolar hypoxia). Under these circumstances vasoconstriction occurs within the lung to shift perfusion from areas of alveolar hypoxia to better ventilated regions of the lung. As a potent vasodilator, isosorbide-5-mononitrate could reverse this protective vasoconstriction and thus result in increased perfusion to poorly ventilated areas, worsening of the ventilation/perfusion imbalance, and a further decrease in the arterial partial pressure of oxygen.

Tolerance to isosorbide-5-mononitrate with cross tolerance to other nitrates or nitrites may occur (see Pharmacology). As tolerance to isosorbide-5-mononitrate develops, the effect of sublingual nitroglycerin on exercise tolerance, although still observable, is somewhat blunted.

Occupational Hazards: As patients may experience faintness and/or dizziness, reaction time when driving or operating machinery may be impaired, especially at the start of treatment.

Pregnancy: Teratogenic Effects: In studies designed to detect effects of isosorbide-5-mononitrate on embryo-fetal development, doses of up to 240 to 248 mg/kg/day, administered to pregnant rats and rabbits, were unassociated with evidence of such effects. No adverse effects on reproduction or fetal development were reported. These animal doses are about 100 times the maximum recommended human dose when comparison is based on body weight; when comparison is based on body surface area, the rat dose is about 17 times the human dose and the rabbit dose is about 38 times the human dose. There are no studies in pregnant women. Because animal reproduction studies are not always predictive of human response, isosorbide-5-mononitrate should be used during pregnancy only if the potential benefit justifies the potential risk to the fetus.

Non-teratogenic Effects: Neonatal survival and development and incidence of stillbirths were adversely affected when pregnant rats were administered oral doses of 750 (but not 300) mg isosorbide-5-mononitrate/kg/day during late gestation and lactation. This dose (about 312 times the human dose when comparison is based on body weight and 54 times the human dose when comparison is based on body surface area) was associated with decreases in maternal weight gain and motor activity and evidence of impaired lactation.

Lactation: It is not known whether isosorbide-5-mononitrate is excreted in human milk. Because many drugs are excreted in human milk, caution should be exercised when isosorbide-5-mononitrate is administered to a nursing mother.

Children: The safety and efficacy of isosorbide-5-mononitrate in children have not been established. Therefore, its use is not recommended.

Drug Interactions: Concomitant treatment with other vasodilators, calcium antagonists, ACE inhibitors, beta-blockers, diuretics, antihypertensives, tricyclic antidepressants, and major tranquilizers may potentiate the blood pressure lowering effect of isosorbide-5-mononitrate.

Marked symptomatic orthostatic hypotension has been reported when calcium channel blockers and organic nitrates were used in combination. Dose adjustments of either class of agents may be necessary.

Alcohol may enhance sensitivity to the hypotensive effects of nitrates.

Adverse Effects: In 17 clinical trials, both controlled and uncontrolled, 861 patients were treated with isosorbide-5-mononitrate 30 mg to 240 mg once daily, alone or in combination with β-adrenergic blocking agents. Adverse events were reported in 71% of the patients. Discontinuation of therapy due to adverse reactions was required in 8% of the patients. Most of these were discontinued because of headaches. Dizziness, myocardial infarction, nausea, and vertigo were also associated with withdrawal from these studies. The most common adverse events were headache, dizziness, fatigue, nausea and flushing.

The following adverse events were reported by >1 to 3% of patients: myocardial infarction, postural hypotension, tachycardia, angina pectoris, somnolence, coughing, paresthesia, vertigo, abdominal pain, diarrhea, flatulence, extra systoles, palpitation, aggravated angina, insomnia, dyspnea, respiratory infection, increased sweating, vasospasm, abnormal vision, back pain, musculoskeletal pain, dyspepsia, chest pain, rhinitis, constipation.

The following adverse events were reported in ≤1% of the patients: Cardiovascular: bundle branch block, cardiac failure, circulatory failure, hypotension, hypertension, syncope, arrhythmia, AV block, bradycardia, atrial fibrillation, heart murmur, abnormal heart sound, Q-wave abnormality, T-wave changes, ECG abnormal.

Dermatological: rash, pruritus, eczema, acne, rash erythematous, rash psoriaform, abnormal hair texture, skin disorder.

Gastrointestinal: duodenal ulcer, eructation, hemorrhagic gastric ulcer, gastritis, hemorrhoids, intestinal obstruction, melena, dry mouth, pharynx disorder, tooth disorder, vomiting, loose stools, glossitis.

Genitourinary: atrophic vaginitis, prostatic disorder, renal calculus, urinary bladder diverticulum, urinary tract infection, polyuria.

Miscellaneous: allergic reaction, asthenia, female breast pain, edema, feeling of warmth, fever, flu-like symptoms, malaise, rigors, earache, biliary pain, cholecystitis, hepatomegaly, diabetes mellitus, gout, weight decrease, weight increase, peripheral edema, tinnitus, epistaxis, purpura, infection, bacterial infection, cerebrovascular disorder, intermittent claudication, leg ulcer, peripheral ischemia, varicose vein, amaurosis fugax, conjunctivitis, diplopia, photophobia, moniliasis, skin nodule, tympanic membrane perforation, allergy, pain.

Musculoskeletal: arthralgia, arthritis, arthropathy, arthrosis, frozen shoulder, muscle weakness, myalgia, myositis, torticollis, tendon disorder.

Neurological: hypoesthesia, migraine, neuritis, tremor, agitation, amnesia, impaired concentration, depression, decreased libido, nervousness, paroniria, confusion, anxiety, paresis, ptosis, impotence.

Respiratory: bronchitis, bronchospasm, pharyngitis, pneumonia, rales, respiratory disorder, pulmonary infiltration, increased sputum, sinusitis, nasal congestion.

Laboratory Changes: albuminuria, hematuria, gamma GT increased, AST increased, ALT increased, hypercholesterolemia, hyperlipemia, hyperuricemia, hypocalcemia, hypokalemia, increased non-protein nitrogen, thrombocytopenia, anemia, leukopenia, leukocytosis, glycosuria.

Overdose: Symptoms and Treatment: Hemodynamic Effects: Symptoms of isosorbide-5-mononitrate overdose are generally the results of vasodilation, venous pooling, reduced cardiac output and hypotension. These hemodynamic changes may have protean manifestations, including increased intracranial pressure, with any or all of persistent throbbing headache, confusion, and moderate fever; vertigo; palpitations; visual disturbances; nausea and vomiting (possibly with colic and even bloody diarrhea); syncope (especially in the upright posture); air hunger and dyspnea, later followed by reduced ventilatory effort; diaphoresis, with the skin either flushed or cold and clammy; heart block and bradycardia; paralysis; coma; seizures and death.

No specific antagonist to the vasodilator effects of isosorbide-5-mononitrate is known, and no intervention has been subject to controlled study as a therapy of isosorbide-5-mononitrate overdose. Because the hypotension associated with isosorbide-5-mononitrate overdose is the result of venodilation and arterial hypovolemia, prudent therapy in this situation should be directed toward an increase in central fluid volume. Passive elevation of the patient's legs may be sufficient, but i.v. infusion of normal saline or similar fluid may also be necessary.

In patients with renal disease or congestive heart failure, therapy resulting in central volume expansion is not without hazard. Treatment of isosorbide-5-mononitrate overdose in these patients may be subtle and difficult, and invasive monitoring may be required.

The use of epinephrine or other vasoconstrictors is ineffective in reversing the severe hypotensive effects of overdose and is therefore contraindicated in this situation.

Dialysis is known to be ineffective in removing isosorbide-5-mononitrate from the body.

Methemoglobinemia: Methemoglobinemia has been reported in patients receiving other organic nitrates, and it may occur as a side effect of isosorbide-5-mononitrate. Nitrate ions liberated during metabolism of isosorbide-5-mononitrate can oxidize hemoglobin into methemoglobin. In patients totally without cytochrome b_5 reductase activity, about 2 mg/kg of isosorbide-5-mononitrate would be required before any of these patients manifests clinically significant (≥10%) methemoglobinemia. In patients with normal reductase function, significant production of methemoglobin would require even larger doses of isosorbide-5-mononitrate.

Methemoglobin levels are available from most clinical laboratories. The diagnosis should be suspected in patients who exhibit signs of impaired oxygen delivery despite adequate cardiac output and adequate arterial pO_2. Classically, methemoglobinemic blood is described as chocolate brown without color change on exposure to air. When methemoglobinemia is diagnosed, administration of methylene blue, 1 to 2 mg/kg i.v. may be required.

Dosage: Isosorbide-5-mononitrate, administered once daily, provides efficacy for up to 12 hours. This formulation is designed to avoid or attenuate the development of tolerance.

The recommended starting dose, for those patients who are active during the day, is 60 mg (1 tablet) once daily to be taken in the morning on arising. The dose may be increased to 120 mg (2 tablets) once daily. Rarely 240 mg may be required. To minimize the possibility of headache the dose can be titrated by initiating treatment with 30 mg (½ a tablet) for the first 2 to 4 days.

Dosage adjustments are not necessary for elderly patients or patients with altered renal or hepatic function.

The tablet may be taken whole or as divided halves.

The tablets should not be chewed or crushed, and should be swallowed together with half a glass of water.

Note: Isosorbide-5-mononitrate is not indicated for the relief of acute anginal attacks; in these situations sublingual or buccal nitroglycerin should be used.

Information for the Patient: See Blue Section—Information for the Patient "Imdur".

Supplied: Each oval, yellow, biconvex, film-coated, extended release tablet, scored on both sides and engraved A/ID on one side, contains: isosorbide-5-mononitrate 60 mg. Nonmedicinal ingredients: tablet core: aluminum silicate, colloidal silicon dioxide, hydroxypropylcellulose, magnesium stearate and paraffin; coating: hydroxypropylmethylcellulose, iron oxide yellow, paraffin, polyethylene glycol and titanium dioxide. Blister packs of 30. Bottles of 100. Store between 15 and 30°C.

(Shown in Product Recognition Section)

IMITREX® Injection/Tablets Ⓟ
IMITREX® Nasal Spray Ⓟ

Glaxo Wellcome

Sumatriptan Succinate

Sumatriptan

Migraine Therapy

Pharmacology: Sumatriptan has been shown to be effective in relieving migraine headache. It is an agonist for a vascular 5-hydroxytryptamine$_{1D}$ (5-HT$_{1D}$) receptor subtype (a member of the 5-HT$_1$ family), and has only weak affinity for 5-HT$_{1A}$ receptors and no significant activity (as measured using standard radioligand binding assays) or pharmacological activity at 5-HT$_2$, 5-HT$_3$, 5-HT$_4$, 5-HT$_{5A}$, or 5-HT$_7$ receptor subtypes, or at alpha$_1$-, alpha$_2$-, or beta-adrenergic; dopamine$_1$ or dopamine$_2$; muscarinic; or benzodiazepine receptors.

Sumatriptan activates the 5-HT$_{1D}$ receptor subtype which is present on cranial arteries, on the basilar artery and in the vasculature of dura mater. This action correlates with relief of headache. The antimigrainous effect of sumatriptan is

Imitrex (cont'd)

believed to be due to vasoconstriction of cranial arteries, which are dilated and edematous during a migraine attack.

Experimental data from animal studies shows that sumatriptan also activates 5-HT_1 receptors on peripheral terminals of the trigeminal nerve which innervates cranial blood vessels. This causes the inhibition of neuropeptide release. It is thought that such an action may contribute to the anti-migraine action of sumatriptan in humans.

Cardiovascular Effects: In vitro studies in human isolated epicardial coronary arteries suggest that the predominant contractile effect of 5-HT is mediated via 5-HT_2 receptors. However, 5-HT_1 receptors also contribute to some degree to the contractile effect seen. Transient increases in systolic and diastolic blood pressure (up to 20 mmHg) of rapid onset (within minutes), have occurred after i.v. administration of up to 64 μg/kg (3.2 mg for 50 kg subject) to healthy volunteers. These changes were not dose related and returned to normal within 10 to 15 minutes. Following oral administration of 200 mg or intranasal administration of 40 mg, however, mean peak increases in blood pressure were smaller and of slower onset than after i.v. or s.c. administration.

Pharmacokinetics: Sumatriptan is rapidly absorbed after oral, s.c. and intranasal administration. The mean bioavailability is 96% after s.c. dosing, 14% after oral dosing, and 16% after intranasal administration. The low oral and intranasal bioavailability is primarily due to metabolism (hepatic and pre-systemic) and partly due to incomplete absorption. The oral absorption of sumatriptan is not significantly affected either during migraine attacks or by food.

Following an oral dose of 100 mg, a mean C_{max} of 54 ng/mL was attained. The time to peak plasma level was variable (0.5 to 5 hours); however, 70 to 80% of C_{max} values were attained within 30 to 45 minutes of oral dosing. The mean plasma half-life was approximately 2 hours (range 1.9 to 2.2 hours).

Following a 6 mg s.c. dose (standard injection) in the deltoid region of the arm or thigh or autoinjection into the thigh, a mean C_{max} value of 60 ng/mL was attained at approximately 15 minutes. Mean plasma half-life was approximately 2 hours (range 1.7 to 2.3 hours).

Following a 5 mg, 10 mg and 20 mg intranasal dose, C_{max} values were 4.7 ng/mL, 8.5 ng/mL and 14.4 ng/mL, respectively. The time to peak plasma level was 1 to 1.5 hours. The elimination half-life is approximately 2 hours (range 1.3 to 5.4 hours). Inter-patient and intra-patient variability was noted in most pharmacokinetic parameters assessed.

Sumatriptan is extensively metabolized by the liver and cleared to a lesser extent by renal excretion. The major metabolite, the indole acetic acid analogue of sumatriptan is mainly excreted in the urine where it is present as a free acid (35%) and the glucuronide conjugate (11%). It has no known 5-HT_1 or 5-HT_2 activity. Minor metabolites have not been identified.

Plasma protein binding of sumatriptan in humans is low (14 to 21%).

No differences have been observed between the pharmacokinetic parameters in healthy elderly volunteers compared with younger volunteers (less than 65 years old).

Significant relief begins about 10 to 15 minutes following s.c. injection, 15 minutes following intranasal administration and 30 minutes following oral administration.

Indications: For the relief of migraine attacks with or without aura.

Sumatriptan is not indicated for prophylactic therapy of migraine, or for the management of hemiplegic or basilar migraine.

Contraindications: Patients with known hypersensitivity to any of the components of the formulations.

Sumatriptan is contraindicated in patients with ischemic heart disease, angina pectoris including Prinzmetal angina (coronary vasospasm), previous myocardial infarction and uncontrolled hypertension. Sumatriptan is also contraindicated in patients taking ergotamine containing preparations or ergot derivatives (such as dihydroergotamine), and in patients receiving treatment with monoamine oxidase (MAO) inhibitors or use within 2 weeks of discontinuation of MAO inhibitor therapy.

Until further data are available, the use of sumatriptan is contraindicated in patients with hemiplegic migraine, basilar migraine and in patients receiving treatment with selective 5-HT (serotonin) reuptake inhibitors and lithium.

Warnings:

There is no experience in patients with recent cerebrovascular accidents or cardiac arrhythmias (especially tachycardias). Therefore, the use of sumatriptan in these patients is not recommended.

Sumatriptan should only be used where there is a clear diagnosis of migraine headache.

As with other acute migraine therapies, before treating headaches in patients not previously diagnosed as migraineurs, and in migraineurs who present with atypical symptoms, care should be taken to exclude other potentially serious neurological conditions. There have been rare reports where patients received sumatriptan for severe headaches which subsequently were shown to have been secondary to an evolving neurological lesion (cerebrovascular accident, subarachnoid hemorrhage). In this regard, it should be noted that migraineurs may be at risk of certain cerebrovascular events (e.g., cerebrovascular accident, transient ischemic attack). However, if a patient does not respond to the first dose, the opportunity should be taken to review the diagnosis before a second dose is given.

Sumatriptan has been associated with transient chest pain and tightness which may mimic angina pectoris and may be intense. Only in rare cases have the symptoms been identified as the result of coronary vasospasm. The vasospasm may result in arrhythmia, ischemia or myocardial infarction. Serious coronary events following sumatriptan have occurred but are extremely rare. Although it is not clear how many of these can be attributed to sumatriptan, because of its potential to cause coronary vasospasm, sumatriptan should not be given to patients in whom unrecognized coronary artery disease (CAD) is likely without a prior evaluation for underlying cardiovascular disease. Such patients include postmenopausal women, males over 40, patients with risk factors for CAD (hypertension, hypercholesterolemia, obesity, diabetes, smoking, or strong family history of CAD).

Consideration should be given to administering the first dose of sumatriptan injection in the physician's office to patients in whom unrecognized coronary artery disease is comparatively likely. If the patient experiences symptoms which are severe or persistent and are consistent with angina, appropriate investigations should be carried out to check for the possibility of ischemic changes. A careful medical history should be taken before sumatriptan is prescribed to exclude pre-existing cardiovascular disease.

Sumatriptan should be used with caution in patients in whom there is a concern of ischemic heart disease, as well as in patients with arteriosclerotic diseases such as peripheral and/or cerebral vascular disease.

There have been rare reports of serious and/or life-threatening arrhythmias, including atrial fibrillation, ventricular fibrillation, ventricular tachycardia and myocardial infarction, as well as transient ischemic ST wave elevations associated with sumatriptan injection.

Sumatriptan injection should never be given i.v.

The recommended dose of sumatriptan should not be exceeded.

Precautions: Cluster Headache: There is insufficient information on the efficacy and safety of sumatriptan in the treatment of cluster headache, which is present in an older, predominantly male population. The need for prolonged use and the demand for repeated medication in this condition renders the dosing information inapplicable for cluster headache.

General: Prolonged vasospastic reactions have been reported with ergotamine. As these effects may be additive, 24 hours should elapse before sumatriptan can be taken following any ergotamine-containing preparation. Conversely, ergotamine-containing preparations should not be taken until 6 hours have elapsed following sumatriptan administration.

Sumatriptan should be used with caution in patients with a history of epilepsy or structural brain lesions which lower their convulsion threshold.

Chest, jaw or neck tightness is relatively common (3 to 5% in controlled clinical trials) after sumatriptan injection, but has only been rarely associated with ischemic ECG changes.

Sumatriptan may cause a short-lived elevation of blood pressure (see Pharmacology and Contraindications).

Occupational Hazards: Patients should be cautioned that drowsiness may occur as a result of treatment with sumatriptan. They should be advised not to perform skilled tasks e.g., driving or operating machinery if drowsiness occurs.

Concomitant Disease: Since there have been rare reports of seizures occurring, sumatriptan should be used with caution in patients with a history of epilepsy or structural brain lesions which lower their convulsive threshold.

Concomitant Medications: There have been reports of patients with known hypersensitivity to sulphonamides exhibiting an allergic reaction following administration of sumatriptan. Reactions ranged from cutaneous hypersensitivity to anaphylaxis.

Renal Impairment: The effects of renal impairment on the efficacy and safety of sumatriptan have not been evaluated. Therefore sumatriptan is not recommended in this patient population.

Hepatic Impairment: The effect of hepatic impairment on the efficacy and safety of sumatriptan has not been evaluated; however, the pharmacokinetic profile of sumatriptan in patients with moderate* hepatic impairment shows that these patients, following an oral dose of 50 mg, have much higher plasma sumatriptan concentrations than healthy subjects. Therefore, an oral dose of 50 mg may be considered in patients with hepatic impairment (see Table I).

*Assessed by aminopyrine breath test (>0.2 to 0.4 scaling units).

Table I—Imitrex Tablets

Pharmacokinetic Parameters After Oral Administration of Sumatriptan 50 mg to Healthy Volunteers and Moderately Hepatically Impaired Patients

Parameter	Mean Ratio (hepatic impaired/healthy) n=8	90% CI	p-value
AUC∞	181%	130 to 252%	0.009*
C_{max}	176%	129 to 240%	0.007*

Legend: CI=Confidence Interval.
* Statistically significant.

The pharmacokinetic parameters of 6 mg s.c. sumatriptan do not differ statistically between normal volunteers and moderately hepatically impaired subjects.

Geriatrics (>65 years): Experience of the use of sumatriptan in patients aged over 65 years is limited. Therefore the use of sumatriptan in patients over 65 years is not recommended.

Children (<18 years): The safety and efficacy of sumatriptan in children has not been established and its use in this age group is not recommended.

Pregnancy: Reproduction studies, performed in rats, have not revealed any evidence of impaired fertility, teratogenicity, or post-natal development due to sumatriptan. Reproduction studies, performed in rabbits by the oral route, have shown increased incidence of variations in cervico-thoracic blood vessel configuration in the fetuses. These effects were only seen at the highest dose tested, which affected weight gain in the dams, and at which blood levels were in excess of 50 times those seen in humans after therapeutic doses. A direct association with sumatriptan treatment is considered unlikely but cannot be excluded. Therefore, the use of sumatriptan is not recommended in pregnancy.

In a rat fertility study, oral doses of sumatriptan resulting in plasma levels approximately 150 times those seen in humans after a 6 mg s.c. dose and approximately 200 times those seen in humans after a 100 mg oral dose were associated with a reduction in the success of insemination. This effect did not occur during a s.c. study where maximum plasma levels achieved approximately 100 times those in humans by the s.c. route and approximately 150 times those in humans by the oral route.

Lactation: Sumatriptan is excreted in breast milk in animals. No data exists in humans, therefore, caution is advised when administering sumatriptan to nursing women.

Drug Interactions: Single dose pharmacokinetic drug interaction studies have not shown evidence of interactions with propranolol, flunarizine, pizotifen or alcohol. Multiple dose interaction studies have not been performed.

Adverse Effects: The most common adverse reaction associated with sumatriptan administered s.c. is transient pain (local erythema and burning sensation) at the site of injection.

Other side effects which have been reported for all routes of administration, but were more common for s.c. route, include sensations of tingling, heat, heaviness, pressure or tightness in any part of the body, chest symptoms, flushing, dizziness and feelings of weakness. Transient increases in blood pressure arising soon after treatment have been recorded. Hypotension, bradycardia, tachycardia and palpitations have been reported rarely.

Sumatriptan may cause coronary vasospasm in patients with a history of coronary artery disease, known to be susceptible to coronary artery vasospasm, and, very rarely, without prior history suggestive of coronary artery disease.

There have been rare reports of serious and/or life-threatening arrhythmias, including atrial fibrillation, ventricular fibrillation, ventricular tachycardia, myocardial infarction, and transient ischemic ST elevation associated with sumatriptan injection (see Warnings).

Fatigue and drowsiness have been reported at slightly higher rates for the oral route, as were nausea and vomiting; the relationship of the latter adverse reactions to sumatriptan is not clear. Hypersensitivity reactions to sumatriptan have been reported including anaphylactic shock, anaphylactoid reactions, rash, urticaria, pruritus and erythema.

There have been rare reports of seizures, the majority of these patients have a previous history of epilepsy or structural lesions predisposing to epilepsy (see Precautions).

Table II and Table III (on following page) list the incidence of adverse reactions reported in clinical trials undertaken with the oral formulation and the s.c. injection (see Table II), and with the intranasal formulation (see Table III on following page).

Most of the events were transient in nature and resolved within 45 minutes of s.c. administration and 2 hours of oral or intranasal administration.

Of the 3 630 patients treated with Sumatriptan nasal spray in clinical trials, there was one report of a coronary vasospasm related to Sumatriptan administration.

Minor disturbances of liver function tests have occasionally been observed with sumatriptan treatment. There is no evidence that clinically significant abnormalities occurred more frequently with sumatriptan than with placebo.

Overdose: Symptoms and Treatment: There have been no reports of overdosage with sumatriptan. Experience with doses outside of the recommended labeling are as follows: One patient received two 6 mg s.c. doses within 30 minutes and 1 patient received four 100 mg tablets within 24 hours, with no adverse events. The highest dose of sumatriptan nasal spray administered without significant adverse effects was 20 mg given 3 times daily for 4 days.

If overdosage with sumatriptan occurs, the patient should be monitored and standard supportive treatment applied as required. Toxicokinetics are not available.

The effect of hemodialysis or peritoneal dialysis on the serum concentration of sumatriptan is unknown.

Dosage: General: **Sumatriptan is indicated for the acute treatment of migraine headache with or without aura. Sumatriptan should not be used prophylactically. Sumatriptan may be given orally, s.c. or as a nasal spray.**

In selecting the appropriate formulation for individual patients, consideration should be given to the patient's preference for formulation and the patient's requirement for rapid onset of relief. Significant relief begins about 10 to 15 minutes following s.c. injection, 15 minutes following intranasal administration and 30 minutes following oral administration.

In addition to relieving the pain of migraine, sumatriptan (all formulations) has also been shown to be effective in relieving associated symptoms of migraine (nausea, vomiting, phonophobia, photophobia). Sumatriptan is equally effective when administered at any stage of a migraine attack. Long-term (12 to 24 months) clinical studies with maximum recommended doses of sumatriptan indicate that there is no evidence of the development of tachyphylaxis, or medication-induced (rebound) headache.

Twenty-four hours should elapse before sumatriptan is taken following any ergotamine-containing preparation or ergot derivative (such as dihydroergotamine). Conversely, ergotamine-containing preparations or ergot derivatives should not be taken until 6 hours have elapsed following sumatriptan administration.

Injection: Sumatriptan injection should be injected s.c. (on the outside of the thigh) using an autoinjector.

Adults: The recommended dose is a single 6 mg s.c. injection.

Clinical trials have shown that approximately 70 to 72% of patients have headache relief within 1 hour after a single s.c. injection. This number increases to 82% by 2 hours.

If adequate relief has not been attained within 2 hours, additional doses should **not** be used as they are unlikely to be of clinical benefit. Sumatriptan may be taken for subsequent attacks provided a minimum of 1 hour has elapsed since the last dose. Not more than 12 mg (two 6 mg injections) should be taken in any 24-hour period.

Table II—Imitrex Injection/Tablets

Incidence of Treatment-Emergent[a] Adverse Events Reported by at least 1% of Patients in Controlled Clinical Trials with Imitrex Tablets and Injection

Event	Tablets n=1 456	Placebo n=296	S.C. Injection n=2 665	Placebo n=868
Atypical				
Tingling	1%	<1%	9%	3%
Warm/hot sensation	1%	<1%	9%	3%
Burning sensation	<1%	0%	5%	<1%
Numbness	2%	1%	3%	2%
Feeling strange	0%	0%	1%	<1%
Cold sensation	1%	<1%	1%	<1%
Gastrointestinal				
Nausea/vomiting	14%	7%	10%	10%
Gastric symptoms, abdominal discomfort	3%	3%	1%	<1%
Dysphagia	1%	0%	<1%	<1%
Neurological				
Dizziness/vertigo	6%	2%	8%	4%
Malaise/fatigue	9%	3%	3%	1%
Drowsiness/sedation	3%	1%	3%	1%
Paresthesia	1%	0%	1%	<1%
Headache	1%	1%	2%	<1%
Syncope	1%	0%	<1%	<1%
Cardiovascular[b]				
Flushing	<1%	1%	6%	2%
Hypertension, tachycardia	<1%	0%	<2%	<1%
Bradycardia	<1%	0%	<1%	0%
Palpitations	1%	<1%	<1%	<1%
Hypotension	<1%	0%	<1%	<1%
Pallor	<1%	0%	<1%	0%
Pulsating sensation	<1%	0%	<1%	<1%
Changes in ECG	0%	0%	<1%	0%
Symptoms Potentially of Cardiac Origin[b]				
Neck pain/stiffness	3%	0%	3%	<1%
Feeling of heaviness	3%	1%	8%	1%
Feeling of tightness	<1%	0%	3%	<1%
Tight feeling in head	<1%	0%	1%	<1%
Pressure sensation	1%	<1%	6%	1%
Chest symptoms (including chest pain)	3%	<1%	5%	1%
Throat symptoms (including sore or swollen throat or throat spasms)	3%	0%	2%	<1%
Musculoskeletal				
Weakness	3%	<1%	3%	<1%
Myalgia	2%	<1%	1%	<1%
Ear, Nose and Throat				
Disturbance of nasal cavity/sinuses	<1%	1%	1%	<1%
Miscellaneous				
Injection site reactions	NA	NA	40%	17%
Sweating	2%	<1%	2%	1%
Disorder of mouth and tongue	2%	<1%	4%	2%
Disturbance of taste	11%	3%	1%	2%
Dyspnea	1%	0%	<1%	<1%

[a] Includes all events regardless of causality that occurred at a frequency of ≥1% in any Imitrex treatment group and were more frequent in this group than in the placebo group.
[b] These events are included in the table regardless of the incidence in the Imitrex group.
Legend: NA=Not Applicable.

Administration during migraine aura prior to other symptoms occurring may not prevent the development of a headache.

Patients should be advised to read the patient instruction leaflet regarding the safe disposal of syringes and needles.

Nasal Spray: The minimal effective single adult dose of sumatriptan nasal spray is 5 mg. The maximum recommended single dose is 20 mg.

If adequate relief has not been attained within 2 hours of initial treatment, additional doses should **not** be administered for the same attack as they are unlikely to be of clinical benefit. Sumatriptan may be taken for subsequent attacks provided a minimum of 2 hours has elapsed since the last dose. No more than a total of 40 mg should be taken in any 24-hour period.

Placebo-controlled clinical trials revealed the following incidence of headache relief, defined as a decrease in migraine severity from severe or moderate to mild or no pain, within 2 hours after treatment with intranasal sumatriptan at doses of 5, 10 or 20 mg (see Table IV on following page).

As shown in Table IV, optimal rates of headache relief were seen with the 20 mg dose. Single doses above 20 mg should not be used due to limited safety data and lack of increased efficacy relative to the 20 mg single dose.

Within the range of 5 to 20 mg, an increase in dose was not associated with any significant increase in the incidence or severity of adverse events other than taste disturbance (see Adverse Effects).

The nasal spray should be administered into one nostril **only.** The device is a ready to use single dose unit and **must not** be primed before administration. Patients should be advised to read the patient instruction leaflet regarding the use of the nasal spray device before administration.

Tablets: Adults: The recommended adult dose is a single 100 mg tablet.

However, based on the physician's clinical judgment, a 50 mg dose may be considered adequate. The appropriateness should be based on the patient's needs and response to treatment.

Clinical trials have shown that approximately 50 to 75% of patients have headache relief within 2 hours after oral dosing with 100 mg, and that a further 15 to 25% have headache relief by 4 hours.

If adequate relief has not been attained within 4 hours, additional doses should **not** be used as they are unlikely to be of clinical benefit. Sumatriptan may be taken to treat subsequent migraine attacks. Not more than 300 mg should be taken in any 24-hour period.

The tablet should be swallowed whole with water, not crushed, chewed or split.

Imitrex (cont'd)

Table III—Imitrex Nasal Spray

Incidence of Treatment-Emergent[a] Adverse Events Reported by at least 1% of Patients in Controlled Clinical Trials with Imitrex Nasal Spray

Event	Placebo n=741	5 mg n=496	10 mg n=1 007	20 mg n=1 249
Atypical				
Warm/hot sensation	<1%	1%	<1%	<1%
Burning sensation	<1%	<1%	<1%	1%
Gastrointestinal				
Nausea/vomiting	15%	17%	15%	16%
Neurological				
Dizziness/vertigo	<1%	1%	2%	1%
Malaise/fatigue	<1%	2%	1%	<1%
Headache	<1%	1%	<1%	<1%
Cardiovascular[b]				
Flushing	<1%	<1%	<1%	<1%
Hypertension, tachycardia	<1%	<1%	<1%	<1%
Palpitations	<1%	<1%	<1%	<1%
Pulsating sensation	0%	0%	<1%	0%
Changes in ECG	<1%	<1%	<1%	<1%
Symptoms Potentially of Cardiac Origin[b]				
Neck pain/stiffness	<1%	0%	<1%	<1%
Feeling of heaviness	<1%	<1%	<1%	<1%
Feeling of tightness	<1%	0%	<1%	<1%
Tight feeling in head	0%	0%	<1%	<1%
Pressure sensation	<1%	<1%	<1%	<1%
Chest symptoms (including chest pain)	<1%	<1%	<1%	<1%
Throat symptoms (including sore or swollen throat or throat spasms)	1%	<1%	2%	3%
Ear, Nose and Throat				
Disturbance of nasal cavity/sinuses	3%	5%	3%	4%
Throat symptoms	1%	<1%	2%	3%
Miscellaneous				
Disorder of mouth and tongue	0%	1%	<1%	<1%
Disturbance of taste	2%	15%	20%	25%

[a]Includes all events regardless of causality that occurred at a frequency of ≥1% in any Imitrex treatment group and were more frequent in this group than in the placebo group.
[b]These events are included in the table regardless of the incidence in the Imitrex group.

Table IV—Imitrex

Percentage of Patients with Headache Relief at 2 hours

Study	Placebo (n)	5 mg (n)	10 mg (n)	20 mg (n)
Study 1[a]	35% (40)	67%[b] (42)	67%[b] (39)	78%[b] (40)
Study 2[a]	42% (31)	45% (33)	66%[b] (35)	74%[b] (39)
Study 3	25% (63)	49%[b] (122)	46%[b] (115)	64%[bd] (119)
Study 4	25% (151)	not evaluated	44%[b] (288)	55%[bd] (292)
Study 5	32% (198)	44%[b] (297)	54%[bc] (293)	60%[bd] (288)
Study 6[a]	35% (100)	not evaluated	54%[b] (106)	63%[b] (202)
Study 7[a]	29% (112)	not evaluated	43% (109)	62%[b] (215)
Total	**208/695**	**232/494**	**482/985**	**722/1 195**
Weighted Average	**30%**	**47%**	**49%**	**60%**
Range	**25-42%**	**44-67%**	**43-67%**	**55-78%**

Headache relief was defined as a decrease in headache severity from severe or moderate to mild or none.
[a]comparisons between sumatriptan doses not conducted.
[b]$p \leq 0.05$ versus placebo.
[c]$p \leq 0.05$ vs 5 mg.
[d]$p \leq 0.05$ versus lower sumatriptan doses.
Legend: n=total number of patients who received treatment.

Hepatic Impairment: In patients with mild or moderate hepatic impairment, plasma sumatriptan concentrations up to two times those seen in healthy subjects have been observed. Therefore, a 50 mg dose (single tablet) may be considered in these patients (see Precautions).

Information for the Patient: See Blue Section—Information for the Patient "Imitrex Injection/Tablets/Nasal Spray".

Supplied: Injection: Each prefilled syringe contains: sumatriptan (base) 6 mg as the succinate salt, in an isotonic sodium chloride solution (total volume=0.5 mL). Also contains water for injection. Syringes are placed in a tamper-evident carrying/disposal case. Two prefilled syringes plus an autoinjector are packed in a patient starter kit. Refill pack of 2×2 prefilled syringes in a carton. Also available to physicians or hospitals in a single dose vial (total volume=0.5 mL) containing 6 mg of sumatriptan base, as the succinate salt. Store between 2 and 30°C and protect from light.

Nasal Spray: 5 mg: Each unit dose spray contains: sumatriptan (base) as the hemisulfate salt 5 mg in an aqueous buffered solution. Nonmedicinal ingredients: anhydrous dibasic sodium phosphate, monobasic potassium phosphate, purified water, sodium hydroxide and sulfuric acid. Boxes of 6 nasal spray devices (3×2 devices). Store between 2 and 30°C and protect from light.

20 mg: Each unit dose spray contains: sumatriptan (base) as the hemisulfate salt 20 mg in an aqueous buffered solution. Nonmedicinal ingredients: anhydrous dibasic sodium phosphate, monobasic potassium phosphate, purified water, sodium hydroxide and sulfuric acid. Boxes of 6 nasal spray devices (3×2 devices). Store between 2 and 30°C and protect from light.

Tablets: 50 mg: Each white, film-coated tablet contains: sumatriptan (base) 50 mg as the succinate salt. Nonmedicinal ingredients: croscarmellose sodium, lactose, magnesium stearate and microcrystalline cellulose. The tablets are coated with Opadry White containing methylhydroxypropyl cellulose, titanium dioxide and triacetin. Gluten- and tartrazine-free. Blister packs containing 6 tablets, packed in cartons of 4. Store between 2 and 30°C.

100 mg: Each pink, film-coated tablet contains: sumatriptan (base) 100 mg as the succinate salt. Nonmedicinal ingredients: croscarmellose sodium, lactose, magnesium stearate and microcrystalline cellulose. The tablets are coated with Opadry Pink containing methylhydroxypropyl cellulose, titanium dioxide triacetin and iron oxide red. Gluten- and tartrazine-free. Blister packs containing 6 tablets, packed in cartons of 4. Store between 2 and 30°C.

(Shown in Product Recognition Section)

Reviewed 1998

ImmuCyst®
Connaught

Bacillus Calmette-Guérin (BCG), substrain Connaught
Antineoplastic

Pharmacology: When administered intravesically as a cancer therapy, BCG promotes a local acute inflammatory and subacute granulomatous reaction with histiocytic and leukocytic infiltration in the urothelium and lamina propria of the urinary bladder. The local inflammatory effects are associated with an elimination or reduction of superficial cancerous lesions of the urinary bladder. The antitumor effect appears to be T-lymphocyte-dependent. The exact mechanism by which this is accomplished is unknown, but may involve expression of HLA-DR antigens on bladder urothelium and specific immunity to cells expressing both HLA-DR and BCG antigens on their cell surfaces.

General Discussion of BCG Therapy for Bladder Cancer: Carcinoma In-Situ of the Urinary Bladder: Carcinoma in-situ (CIS) may occur either alone or in association with papillary tumors, particularly those of higher grade. CIS may be multifocal, and may also be associated with multifocal pre-malignant dysplastic lesions. While trans-urethral resection (TUR) is the primary treatment for CIS, it is often not curative: some lesions may be either undetectable or unresectable or both. Furthermore, even with curative TUR, CIS is associated with a high incidence of recurrence and of recurrence of higher-stage lesions, including cancer invasive of the muscle layer of the urinary bladder (stage T2 or higher). Intravesical ImmuCyst has been studied and established as both an alternative to radical surgical treatment for CIS, and as prophylaxis for recurrence of CIS.

Papillary Tumors of the Urinary Bladder: While TUR is the primary treatment of superficial papillary tumors, these tumors have a tendency to recur and to progress. This is particularly true when there are 2 or more co-existing papillary tumors, when there has already been a recurrence of such tumors, or when there is co-existing CIS. In these circumstances, ImmuCyst has been shown to increase significantly the time to recurrence when administered intravesically for prophylactic purposes following TUR.

Efficacy of ImmuCyst: Several published studies have proven the effectiveness of ImmuCyst for patients with superficial bladder cancer at the CIS, Ta and T1 stages, including 2 multicentre controlled, randomized trials.

In the first, ImmuCyst was compared to doxorubicin HCl among patients with either CIS or recurrent papillary tumors or both. ImmuCyst was administered intravesically weekly for 6 weeks, with an additional single instillation at 3, 6, 12, 18 and 24 months following the initiation of treatment (total of 11 instillations). Doxorubicin was administered weekly for 5 weeks, with an additional 11 single monthly treatments. For patients with CIS, the complete response rate (i.e., negative biopsies and urine cytology) within 6 months of the initiation of treatment was 70% with ImmuCyst versus 34% with doxorubicin ($p<0.001$); the probability of being disease-free (i.e., having no evidence of bladder cancer) at 5 years was 45% and 18%, respectively ($p<0.001$ by proportional hazards regression model); and among complete responders, the median time to treatment failure was 39 months versus 5.1 months, respectively. Among patients with papillary tumors (Ta or T1) without CIS, the probability of being disease-free at 5 years was 37% with ImmuCyst versus 17% with doxorubicin ($p=0.015$ by proportional hazards regression model).

In the second multicenter controlled study, two treatment regimes of ImmuCyst were compared among similar patients to the first study. A 6-week induction course alone (total of 6 instillations) was compared to a more intensive regime consisting of the following: an induction course of 6 weekly treatments; after a 6-week pause, another 3 weekly treatments;

and then maintenance therapy consisting of 3 weekly instillations at 6 months after the initiation of treatment, and then every 6 months until 36 months (total of 27 instillations). Comparing the maintenance regime to the no-maintenance regime (i.e., 6-week induction course only), the following results were found: among CIS patients, the complete response rate (defined as the absence of signs of malignancy in the urinary tract at both 3 and 6 months after the first instillation) was 87% in the maintenance group versus 73% in the no-maintenance group (p=0.016). Time to recurrence was significantly increased among all patients in the maintenance group (p<0.0001); within the maintenance group, time to recurrence was significantly increased both among those with CIS (p=0.04) and among those with papillary tumors but no CIS (p<0.0001). Finally, overall survival was significantly better in the maintenance group (p=0.04).

The results are summarized in Tables I and II.

affected organs, it is often unclear to what extent such a reaction is due to an infectious process versus an inflammatory hypersensitivity reaction: hence the term "systemic reaction". Based on past clinical experience with intravesical BCG, "systemic BCG reaction" may be defined as the presence of any of the following signs, if no other etiologies for such signs are detectable: fever ≥39.5°C for ≥12 hours; fever ≥38.5°C for ≥48 hours; pneumonitis; hepatitis; other organ dysfunction outside of the genitourinary tract with granulomatous inflammation on biopsy; or the classical signs of sepsis, including circulatory collapse, acute respiratory distress, and disseminated intravascular coagulation. Although rare, a systemic BCG reaction is much more likely to occur if BCG is administered within 1 week of either trans-urethral resection or traumatic bladder catheterization that was associated with hematuria. One case of systemic BCG reaction has been

If a bacterial urinary tract infection (UTI) occurs during the course of ImmuCyst treatment, ImmuCyst instillation should be withheld until complete resolution of the bacterial UTI for 2 reasons: (1) the combination of a UTI and BCG-induced cystitis may lead to more severe adverse effects on the genitourinary tract, and (2) BCG bacilli are sensitive to a wide variety of antibiotics; antimicrobial administration may therefore diminish the efficacy of ImmuCyst. Similarly, patients undergoing antimicrobial therapy for other infections should be evaluated to assess whether the therapy might diminish the efficacy of ImmuCyst.

Intravesical treatment with ImmuCyst may induce a sensitivity to tuberculin purified protein derivative (PPD) which could complicate future interpretations of skin test reactions to tuberculin in the diagnosis of suspected mycobacterial infections. Determination of a patient's reactivity to tuberculin

Table I—ImmuCyst

Comparative Studies on Efficacy of ImmuCyst: Treatment Regimens and Complete Response Rates

	Treatment Regimen: Number of Weekly Instillations at Time (in Months) Commencing with the First Instillation i.e., Time 0 = Time of First Instillation																Total No. of Instillations	Results: CIS Patients with Complete Response within 6 Months of Initiation of Treatment		
Treatment Arm	**0**	**2**	**3**	**4**	**5**	**6**	**7**	**8**	**9**	**10**	**11**	**12**	**18**	**24**	**30**	**36**		**n**	**%**	**p**
ImmuCyst versus	6	–	1	–	–	1	–	–	–	–	–	1	1	1		–	11	64	70	p<0.001
Doxorubicin	5	1	1	1	1	1	1	1	1	1	1	1	–	–	–	–	16	67	34	
ImmuCyst Maintenance versus	6	–	3	–	–	3	–	–	–	–	–	3	3	3	3	3	27	106	87	p=0.016
ImmuCyst Induction Only	6	–	–	–	–	–	–	–	–	–	–	–	–	–	–	–	6	107	73	

Indications: For treatment of superficial transitional cell carcinoma (TCC) of the urinary bladder, regardless of antecedent intravesical treatment. Superficial TCC comprises the following: carcinoma in-situ (CIS), papillary tumors limited to the mucosa (stage Ta), papillary tumors involving the lamina propria but not the muscle layer of the bladder (stage T1), or any combination thereof.

For treatment and prophylaxis of primary or recurrent carcinoma in-situ (CIS) of the urinary bladder, and for prophylaxis following TUR of primary or recurrent stage Ta and/or T1 papillary tumors.

Contraindications: For patients: receiving immunosuppressive therapy (with drugs or radiation) or with compromised immune systems, because of the danger of a systemic BCG reaction; with active tuberculosis, because of the danger of exacerbation or of concomitant systemic BCG reaction; with current or previous evidence of a systemic BCG reaction (see Warnings and Adverse Effects, Treatment of Adverse Events); with fever, unless the cause of the fever has been determined and evaluated (see Adverse Effects, Treatment of Adverse Events); with bacterial urinary tract infection, until the infection has resolved (see Warnings); who have had a trans-urethral resection or traumatic bladder catheterization (associated with hematuria) in the previous week (see Warnings).

Warnings: Systemic BCG Reaction: A systemic BCG reaction is a systemic granulomatous illness which may occur (although rarely) subsequent to exposure to BCG. However, because it is usually difficult to isolate BCG organisms from

reported in a patient with a prosthetic aortic valve and a prior history of bacterial endocarditis; it is unknown whether these constitute risk factors for a systemic BCG reaction. Three fatalities have been reported with the use of ImmuCyst, all associated with systemic BCG reaction. One was associated with intravesical instillation in spite of traumatic catheterization in a patient with antecedent alcoholic liver disease. The second case was associated with instillation less than 1 week following transurethral resection. The third case may have been related to continued BCG treatment of a patient with an unrecognized systemic BCG reaction. The appropriate treatment of systemic BCG reaction is discussed in Adverse Effects, Treatment of Adverse Events.

Additional Warnings: Skin rash, arthralgias, and migratory arthritis are rare, and are considered to be strictly allergic reactions. The appropriate treatment is discussed in Adverse Effects, Treatment of Adverse Events.

Administration of intravesical ImmuCyst causes an inflammatory response in the bladder and has been frequently associated with transient fever, hematuria, urinary frequency and dysuria. Such reactions may to some degree be taken as evidence that BCG is evoking the desired response, but careful monitoring of urinary status is required. Infrequent associations include bacterial urinary tract infection, bladder contracture, symptomatic granulomatous prostatitis, epididymo-orchitis, ureteral obstruction, and renal abscess.

For patients with small bladder capacity, increased risk of bladder contracture should be considered in decisions to treat with ImmuCyst.

Table II—ImmuCyst

Comparative Studies on Efficacy of ImmuCyst: Number of Patients Alive and Free of Recurrence

		Results: Alive — All Patients (CIS and/or Papillary Tumors)			Free of Recurrence — CIS Patients, +/− Papillary Tumors			Free of Recurrence — Papillary Tumor Patients with No CIS		
Treatment Arm	**Median Follow-up**	**n**	**%[a]**	**p**	**n**	**%[a]**	**p**	**n**	**%[a]**	**p**
ImmuCyst versus Doxorubicin	5.4 years	127 135	65 64	NS	64 67	45 18	p<0.001	63 68	37 17	p=0.015
ImmuCyst Maintenance versus ImmuCyst Induction Only	3.2 years[c]	193[b] 199[b]	94 89	p=0.04	59[b] 63[b]	81 58	p=0.04	132 136	80 43	p=0.0001

[a] % are calculated on the basis of Kaplan-Meier estimates. p values are calculated on the basis of proportional hazards regression models.
[b] This analysis is restricted to those CIS patients who had no evidence of disease by 12 weeks from time 0.
[c] Follow-up in this study is not yet complete.

prior to administration of ImmuCyst may therefore be desirable.

Precautions: General: **Contains viable attenuated mycobacteria. Handle as infectious.**

Care must be taken during administration of intravesical ImmuCyst not to introduce contaminants into the urinary tract nor to traumatize unduly the urinary mucosa.

It is recommended that intravesical ImmuCyst not be administered any sooner than 1 week following transurethral resection.

If the physician believes that the bladder catheterization has been traumatic (e.g., associated with bleeding), then ImmuCyst should not be administered and there must be a treatment delay of at least 1 week. Subsequent treatment should be resumed as if no interruption in the schedule had occurred.

Drug Interactions: Patients must also be advised that drug combinations containing bone marrow depressants and/or immunosuppressants and/or radiation may impair the response to ImmuCyst or increase the risk of disseminated BCG reaction.

Pregnancy: Animal reproduction studies have not been conducted with ImmuCyst. It is also not known whether ImmuCyst can cause fetal harm when administered to a pregnant woman or can affect reproduction capacity. ImmuCyst should be given to a pregnant woman only if clearly needed. Women should be advised not to become pregnant while on therapy.

Lactation: A nursing woman with a systemic BCG infection could infect her infant. It is not known whether this product is excreted in human milk. Therefore, caution should be exercised when ImmuCyst is administered to a nursing woman.

Children: Safety and effectiveness in children has not been established.

Information for the Patient: Patients must be advised to check with their doctor as soon as possible if there is an increase in their existing urinary symptoms (such as frequency of voiding or painful urination), or if their symptoms persist even after receiving a number of treatments, or if any of the following symptoms develop.

More Common: Blood in urine, painful or frequent urination lasting >2 days, fever and chills lasting more than 24 hours, nausea and vomiting. Rare: cough, skin rash, high or persistent fever, joint pains, jaundice.

Urine voided for 6 hours after instillation shall be disinfected with an equal volume of 5% hypochlorite solution (undiluted household bleach) and allowed to stand for 15 minutes before flushing.

Adverse Effects: Local: The common adverse events which occurred among recipients of ImmuCyst during induction and during maintenance therapy are listed in Table III (on following page).

ImmuCyst (cont'd)

Table III—ImmuCyst

Incidence of Common Adverse Events Associated with any Instillation During Induction Versus Maintenance Therapy with ImmuCyst

	% of Patients Experiencing the Symptom or Sign Following Instillation of ImmuCyst During:		
	SWOG Study 8216: Induction Plus Maintenance (total of 11 instillations) (n=127)	**SWOG Study 8507: Induction Therapy (total of 6 instillations) (n=587)**	**SWOG Study 8507: Maintenance (total of 21 instillations) (n=247)**
Adverse Event	**%**	**%**	**%**
Dysuria	58	26	46
Urinary frequency	40	14	34
Hematuria, microscopic	39	8	9
Hematuria, gross		11	19
Urinary tract infection	18	1	1
Fever	38	17	31
Chills	34	14	32
Malaise	40	17	26

The most common local reactions are transient dysuria and urinary frequency, which occurred on at least one occasion among 26% and 14%, respectively, of patients during induction, rising to 46% and 34%, respectively, among patients during maintenance therapy. Gross hematuria has occurred among 11 to 19% of ImmuCyst recipients, while the more serious genitourinary adverse events (see Warnings) have occurred in <0.5% of recipients.

Systemic: Transient fever of <38.5°C of <48 hours duration has occurred among 17% of ImmuCyst recipients during induction and among 31% during maintenance. The serious reactions described in Warnings have occurred in <1% of ImmuCyst recipients. At the time of printing, 3 fatalities have been reported with the use of ImmuCyst.

Treatment of Adverse Events: Table IV summarizes the recommended treatment of adverse events. Irritative bladder side effects associated with ImmuCyst administration can be managed symptomatically with propantheline bromide. Acetaminophen may be administered for symptomatic relief of transient fever or irritative bladder symptoms.

BCG organisms, including the Connaught strain, are susceptible to all currently used antituberculosis drugs, with the exception of pyrazinamide. Accordingly, for more serious reactions other than the systemic BCG reaction described in Warnings—e.g., severe urinary tract adverse events or allergic reaction—isoniazid with or without rifampin should be administered for 3 to 6 months. If a systemic BCG reaction occurs, an Infectious Diseases consultation should be sought, ImmuCyst should be permanently discontinued, and triple antituberculosis therapy should be initiated promptly and continued for 6 months. Commonly, this will comprise isoniazid (300 mg daily), rifampin (600 mg daily), and ethambutol (1 000 mg daily). In the presence of signs of septic shock as a manifestation of a systemic BCG reaction, the addition of short-term corticosteroids (e.g., prednisolone, 40 mg daily) has been shown to be beneficial both in 5 patients and in an animal model, and should therefore be considered.

If a systemic BCG reaction has occurred, a report should be submitted to both the manufacturer and the appropriate health authorities. The report should include details of the treatment history with ImmuCyst, the symptoms and signs of the BCG reaction, the treatment administered for the reaction, and the response to such treatment.

Table IV—ImmuCyst

Recommended Treatment of Adverse Events Associated with ImmuCyst

Symptom, Sign or Syndrome	**Treatment**
(1) Irritative bladder symptoms <48 hours duration.	Symptomatic treatment.
(2) Irritative bladder symptoms ≥48 hours duration.	Symptomatic treatment; postpone next ImmuCyst treatment until complete resolution. If complete resolution has not occurred within 1 week, administer isoniazid (INH), 300 mg daily until complete resolution.
(3) Concomitant bacterial UTI.	Postpone next ImmuCyst treatment until completion of antimicrobial therapy and negative urine culture.
(4) Other genitourinary tract adverse events: symptomatic granulomatous prostatitis, epididymo-orchitis, ureteral obstruction, or renal abscess	Discontinue ImmuCyst. Administer INH, 300 mg daily and rifampin, 600 mg daily, for 3-6 months.
(5) Fever <38.5°C of <48 hours duration.	Symptomatic treatment with acetaminophen.
(6) Skin rash, arthralgias, or migratory arthritis.	Antihistamines or nonsteroidal anti-inflammatories. If no response, discontinue ImmuCyst and administer INH, 300 mg daily for 3 months.
(7) Systemic BCG reaction (as defined in Warnings) without signs of septic shock.	Discontinue ImmuCyst. Seek an Infectious Disease Consultation. Administer triple-drug antituberculous therapy for 6 months.
(8) Systemic BCG reaction (as defined in Warnings) with signs of septic shock.	As for (7). Consider addition of short-term high-dose systemic corticosteroids.

Legend: INH=Isoniazide.

Dosage: Treatment Schedule: Intravesical treatment of the urinary bladder should begin between 7 to 14 days after biopsy or transurethral resection. The induction treatment comprises 6 weekly intravesical treatments with ImmuCyst, each treatment dose comprising one 81 mg vial of ImmuCyst. After a 6-week pause, another dose should be given intravesically once weekly for 1 to 3 weeks. Three weekly doses should definitely be given to patients who still have evidence of bladder cancer. Clinical studies have demonstrated that the 3 doses given at 3 months significantly increased the complete response rate from 73 to 87% at 6 months (see Table I on previous page). Based on clinical studies performed with ImmuCyst, maintenance therapy following induction is recommended. This consists of 1 to 3 weekly treatments at 6 months following the initiation of treatment, and then every 6 months thereafter until 36 months.

Administration: Each dose (1 reconstituted vial) is further diluted in an additional 50 mL of sterile, preservative-free saline for a total of 53 mL (see reconstitution instructions below).

A urethral catheter is inserted into the bladder under aseptic conditions, the bladder is drained, and then 53 mL suspension of ImmuCyst is instilled slowly by gravity, following which the catheter is withdrawn.

The patient retains the suspension for as long as possible for a total of up to 2 hours. During the first 15 minutes following instillation, the patient should lie prone. Thereafter, the patient is then allowed to be up. At the end of 2 hours, all patients should void in a seated position for environmental safety reasons. Patients should be instructed to maintain adequate hydration.

Protocols for clinical trials carried out with Connaught's ImmuCyst included a percutaneous inoculation with each intravesical dose, although not all patients received it. A 0.5 mL portion of the 53 mL intravesical dose of ImmuCyst was injected percutaneously (example: on inside, upper thigh). Some studies have suggested that this may not be necessary, so the percutaneous dose may be omitted. Furthermore, if severe reactions, such as ulceration at the site or regional lymphadenitis occur, the percutaneous treatment should be discontinued.

Reconstitution of Freeze-Dried Product and Withdrawal from Rubber-Stoppered Vial: **Do not remove the rubber stoppers from the vials. Handle as infectious material.**

Reconstitute and dilute immediately prior to use, using aseptic technique in a high airflow, low traffic area (e.g., in a biocontainment cabinet). Persons handling product should wear gloves. If and when the product is handled outside of a biocontainment cabinet, persons handling the product should also wear a mask and eye protection.

ImmuCyst should not be handled by persons with a known immunologic deficiency.

ImmuCyst should be reconstituted only with the diluent provided to ensure proper dispersion of the organisms.

Apply a **sterile** piece of cotton moistened with a suitable antiseptic to the surface of the rubber stoppers of the vials of diluent and ImmuCyst.

Using a 5 mL **sterile** syringe and needle, draw into the syringe a volume of air equal to the volume of diluent in the vial. Pierce the center of the rubber stopper in the vial containing diluent with the **sterile** needle of the syringe, invert the vial, slowly inject into it the air contained in the syringe. Keeping the point of the needle immersed, withdraw into the syringe 3 mL of diluent. Then holding the syringe-plunger steady, withdraw the needle from the vial.

Using the same syringe and needle, pierce the stopper in the vial of freeze-dried material with the needle. Hold the vial of freeze-dried material upright and pull the plunger of the syringe back to the 5 mL marking on the barrel. This will create a mild vacuum in the vial. Release the plunger and allow the vacuum to pull the diluent from the syringe into the vial of freeze-dried material. After all the diluent has passed into the freeze-dried material, remove the needle and syringe. Shake the vial gently until a fine, even suspension results. Withdraw the entire contents of the reconstituted material from the vial into the same 5 mL syringe. Return the vial to an upright position before removing the syringe from the vial.

Further dilute the reconstituted material from the vial (1 dose) in an additional 50 mL of **sterile,** preservative-free saline to a final volume of 53 mL for intravesical instillation (and 0.5 mL of the 53 mL for percutaneous injection, if administered).

The product should be used immediately after reconstitution and dilution; however, it must not be used after 2 hours. Any reconstituted product which exhibits flocculation or clumping that cannot be dispersed with gentle shaking should not be used.

At no time should the reconstituted product be exposed to sunlight, direct or indirect. Exposure to artificial light should be kept to a minimum.

Special Instructions: After use, unused drug, packaging, and all equipment and materials (e.g., syringes, catheters) used for instillation of the product, should be placed immediately in a container for biohazardous materials, and discarded using suitable methods (e.g., autoclaving).

Supplied: Each vial contains: BCG 81 mg (dry weight) and monosodium glutamate 5% w/v. The reconstituted dose (1 vial) contains: $10.5 \pm 8.7 \times 10^8$ colony forming units (CFU) over the course of its shelf-life. Single dose packages of 1 vial of the freeze-dried ImmuCyst and one 3 mL vial of diluent.

Instillation medium is also available as a vial containing 50 mL of sterile, preservative-free, phosphate-buffered saline, for dilution of the reconstituted material.

ImmuCyst and the accompanying diluent should be kept in a refrigerator at a temperature between 2 and 8°C. It should not be used after the expiration date marked on the vial. At no time should the freeze-dried ImmuCyst be exposed to sunlight, direct or indirect. Exposure to artificial light should be kept to a minimum.

Reviewed 1997

IMMUNINE® VH

Baxter

Factor IX Concentrate (Human)

Blood Coagulation Factor

Pharmacology: Coagulation factor IX is one of the clotting factors found in normal human blood and is required for normal clot formation.

I.V. administration of Immunine VH, factor IX concentrate (human) vapor heated, Immuno provides an increase in plasma levels of factor IX and can temporarily correct the coagulation defect of patients with factor IX deficiency.

The in vivo recovery and half-life of Immunine VH were evaluated in 26 patients with severe hemophilia B (factor IX levels below 1%) and no bleeding at the time of testing. The patients received a single infusion of 50 to 70 units Immunine VH per kg body weight. The mean increase in the patients' factor IX plasma levels was 0.92% per administered IU factor IX per kg body weight, corresponding to a recovery of 41%. The average biological half-life was approximately 17 hours. These data are based on calculations using the new International Standard for human blood coagulation factors II, IX and X in Concentrates Code 84/681.

The effectiveness of the vapor heating process used in the manufacture of Immunine VH to inactivate virus was evaluated in in vitro spiking experiments using human immunodeficiency virus type I (HIV-1) as a target virus as well as the following model viruses: pseudorabies virus (PRV, an enveloped DNA virus as a model for hepatitis B virus), Tick-Borne encephalitis virus (TBEV, a small enveloped RNA virus as a model for HCV) and equine rhinovirus type-1 (ERV-1, a nonenveloped RNA virus as a model for hepatitis A virus). The 2-step vapor heating resulted in virus titer reductions by factors of >10.6 logs for HIV-1, >15.5 logs for TBEV, >12.0 logs for PRV, and >11.5 logs for ERV-1.

In addition to the 2-step vapor heating process, the ability of other stages in manufacture (adsorption onto DEAE-sephadex, TWEEN-80 treatment, ion exchange chromatography, hydrophobic interaction chromatography) to remove and inactivate virus was also evaluated. These steps were found to result in additional virus titer reductions by factors of >12.3 logs for HIV-1, >12.3 logs for TBEV, and 6.3 logs for PRV and 3.0 logs for ERV-1.

In prospective clinical studies as well as in postmarketing surveys, the risk of transfusion-transmitted viral infections was followed up in patients given factor concentrates of the prothrombin complex subjected to the same vapor heat treatment as Immunine VH. Using the criteria established by the ISTH, 45 patients were evaluated for non-A/non-B transmission and 27 for hepatitis B transmission. In addition, 42 patients were evaluated for HCV seroconversion, and 105 for HIV seroconversion. No cases of product related viral hepatitis or HIV transmission were observed.

Indications: Therapy and prophylaxis of bleeding episodes caused by congenital or acquired factor IX deficiency.

Contraindications: Disseminated intravascular coagulation (DIC) and/or hyperfibrinolysis. Following interruption of these processes by suitable means, Immunine VH, factor IX concentrate (human) vapor heated, Immuno should only be given for the management of life-threatening bleeding.

Warnings: This product is prepared from pooled human plasma which may contain the causative agents of hepatitis and other viral diseases. Prescribed manufacturing procedures utilized at the plasma collection centres, plasma testing laboratories, and the fractionation facilities are designed to reduce the risk of transmitting viral infection. However, the risk of the transmission of infective agents—also of hitherto unknown origin—cannot be totally excluded.

Individuals who receive infusion of blood or plasma products may develop signs and/or symptoms of some viral infections, particularly non-A/non-B hepatitis.

In patients with a risk of thrombosis (e.g., patients with a history of severe liver disease, thrombophilia, or a tentative or definite diagnosis of angina pectoris, coronary heart disease or myocardial infarction) the factor IX level should not be raised beyond 60% of normal. In addition, these patients—as well as patients receiving high doses of human blood coagulation factor IX concentrate for major surgery—should be monitored for the development of DIC and/or thrombosis.

In patients with suspected DIC, replacement therapy should be stopped immediately.

Precautions: Immunine VH, factor IX concentrate (human) vapor heated, Immuno should not be administered at a rate exceeding 2 mL/min.

If hypersensitivity reactions occur during administration of Immunine VH, the injection/infusion should be stopped. Minor reactions may be controlled by antihistamines, while the therapy of severe hypotensive reactions follows the current guidelines of shock treatment.

Immunine VH contains less than 0.1 IU heparin per mL. In case of surgical intervention in hemophilia B patients receiving replacement therapy with Immunine VH, perioperative thrombosis prophylaxis with low-dose heparin is recommended in those situations where such a prophylaxis would normally be indicated in patients having no coagulation defect.

Immunine VH contains not more than 5 μg TWEEN-80 per mL.

Appropriate vaccination should be considered in factor IX deficient patients.

Drug Interactions: No pharmacologic interactions with other drugs are currently known.

As for any blood coagulation factor concentrate, Immunine VH, factor IX concentrate (human) vapor heated, Immuno should not be mixed with other drugs. It is advisable to rinse a common venous access with isotonic saline prior to and after infusion of Immunine VH.

Pregnancy and *Lactation:* The safety of human blood coagulation factor IX concentrate for use in human pregnancy has not been established in controlled clinical trials. Therefore, human blood coagulation factor IX concentrate may be used only if clearly needed during pregnancy and lactation.

Adverse Effects: As with any infused plasma derivative, hypersensitivity reactions (e.g., fever, urticaria, nausea, vomiting, dyspnea, drop in blood pressure, shock) may occur rarely.

In rare cases, replacement therapy with human blood coagulation factor IX concentrates may lead to the formation of circulating antibodies which inhibit factor IX.

The possibility of thromboembolic complications cannot be entirely ruled out. This applies particularly to patients at risk for thrombosis and/or receiving high-dose therapy.

Overdose: Symptoms and Treatment: Based on experience with conventional prothrombin complex preparations, overdosage of factor IX concentrates may result in an increased risk of myocardial infarction, disseminated intravascular coagulation, venous thrombosis and pulmonary embolism (see Precautions).

Dosage: Hemophilia B: For the calculation of the factor IX plasma levels as specified below it is assumed that one IU of Immunine VH, factor IX concentrate (human) vapor heated, Immuno per kg body weight increases the factor IX plasma level by approximately 0.8%.

Considering the patient's preinfusion factor IX plasma level, the required dosage is administered using the following formula:

Immunine VH dose (in IU F IX)=body weight (kg)×desired increase in F IX (%)×1.2 IU/kg.

Regular determinations of the patient's factor IX plasma level are necessary for monitoring the course of therapy and calculations of appropriate maintenance doses.

Hemorrhages and Surgery: Table I indicates which factor IX plasma levels are necessary for the management of hemorrhages or for surgical prophylaxis and how long these levels need to be maintained.

In general, Immunine VH is given every 24 hours, corresponding to the biological half-life of factor IX. For surgical prophylaxis the initial dose should be administered one hour prior to surgery. In the case of major surgical interventions, 12-hour treatment intervals should be maintained during the first postoperative days.

Prophylactic Maintenance Therapy: In prophylactic maintenance therapy of severe hemophilia B, a dosage of 20 to 30 IU/kg body weight twice per week was shown to be effective. Prophylactic dosage regimens should, however, be tailored to individual needs, and the decision on the need and dosage for prophylaxis should thus be made by the treating physician.

Hemophiliacs with Inhibitor to Factor IX: Replacement therapy with human blood coagulation factor IX is usually effective only in low responder patients with an inhibitor titer of less than 10 Bethesda Units. Since the response to human blood coagulation factor IX depends on the patient's inhibitor titer, factor IX levels must be monitored frequently and the dose adjusted accordingly. In high responder inhibitor patients other therapeutic measures may be needed.

Reconstitution: Immunine VH, factor IX concentrate (human) vapor heated, Immuno is to be reconstituted only immediately before application. The solution should then be used promptly (the preparation does not contain any preservative). Any unused solution must be discarded. For reconstitution proceed as follows using aseptic technique:

1. Warm the unopened bottle containing Sterile Water for injection (diluent) to room temperature (not above 37°C).
2. Remove caps from the concentrate and diluent bottles to expose central portions of the rubber stoppers. Cleanse exposed surface of the rubber stoppers with germicidal solution and allow to dry.
3. Remove protective covering from one end of the transfer needle by twisting and pulling. Insert the exposed end through the diluent bottle stopper.
4. Remove protective covering from the other end of the transfer needle taking care not to touch the exposed end. Invert diluent bottle over the concentrate bottle and insert the free end of the transfer needle through the concentrate bottle stopper. Diluent will be drawn into the concentrate bottle by vacuum.
5. Disconnect the 2 bottles by removing the needle from the concentrate bottle stopper. Gently agitate or rotate the concentrate bottle until all material is dissolved.

Do not refrigerate after reconstitution.

Injection: 1. After reconstituting the concentrate as described under Reconstitution, attach the enclosed filter needle to a sterile disposable syringe. Insert filter needle through the concentrate bottle stopper.
2. Inject air and withdraw solution into the syringe.
3. Remove and discard the filter needle. Attach a suitable i.v. needle or winged infusion set and inject solution i.v. (maximum rate 2 mL/min).

Infusion: If administered by infusion, a disposable infusion set with adequate filter is to be used (maximum rate of infusion: 2 mL/min).

Supplied: Immunine VH, factor IX concentrate (human) vapor heated, Immuno, is a purified, sterile, freeze-dried concentrate of human blood coagulation factor IX. Immunine VH is standardized in terms of factor IX content and each vial is labeled

Table I—Immunine VH

Factor IX Plasma Levels Necessary for the Management of Hemorrhages or for Surgical Prophylaxis and Period Necessary to Maintain These Levels

Types of Hemorrhage or Surgical Intervention	Therapeutically Necessary F IX Plasma Level (% of normal)	Period During Which it is Necessary to Maintain this F IX Plasma Level
Minor, e.g., hemorrhages into joints	30%	At least 1 day, depending on the severity of the hemorrhage
Major, e.g., hemorrhages into muscles, hemorrhages into the oral cavity, mild trauma capitis, tooth extractions, surgical interventions with low risk of hemorrhage	30-50%	3-4 days, or until absorption of tissue hemorrhage or adequate wound healing
Life-threatening, e.g., gastrointestinal, intracranial, intra-abdominal, or intrathoracic hemorrhages, fractures, major surgical interventions with high risk of hemorrhage	50-75%	After 7 days factor IX levels may be lowered, but therapy should be continued for at least another 7 days or until absorption of hemorrhage or adequate wound healing

Immunine VH (cont'd)

with the factor IX content indicated in international units (IU). One IU of factor IX (based on the First International Standard for Factors II, IX and X in Coagulation Factor Concentrates Code 84/681) corresponds to the factor IX activity contained in 1 mL of fresh normal human plasma.

Immunine VH contains less than 2 IU of factors II, VII and X per mg protein; less than 0.1 IU heparin per mL and not more than 5 μg TWEEN-80 per mL.

Immunine VH is prepared from pooled human plasma.

The manufacturing process includes key stages, among them a product-specific vapor heat treatment, that have been shown to result in removal and inactivation of infectious agents.

Immunine VH is a highly purified factor IX concentrate containing only traces of other coagulation factors (less than 0.02 IU of factors II, VII and X per IU factor IX). In preclinical trials utilizing extremely high doses of Immunine VH, no thrombotic adverse reactions were observed.

Individual donations of human plasma are combined to form plasma pools. Prior to being used for manufacture of Immunine VH, each plasma pool is tested for the presence of genome sequences of the human immunodeficiency virus type 1 (HIV-1), hepatitis B virus (HBV), and hepatitis C virus (HCV) using IQ-PCR.

To prevent the transmission of infective agents by the administration of Immunine VH, prescribed procedures are used for the collection and testing of the source plasma and during the manufacture of the product. They include measures taken for donor and plasma selection, as well as virus removal and inactivation steps during manufacturing.

When stored between 2 and 8°C, Immunine VH, factor IX concentrate (human) vapor heated, Immuno is stable until the date indicated on the label. Within the indicated shelf-life, Immunine VH may temporarily be stored at room temperature (up to 25°C) for a period of 3 months. Record the period of storage at room temperature below the expiration date indicated on the package label. Discard product if stored at room temperature for greater than 3 months. Immunine VH must not be used beyond the expiration date indicated on each pack. The reconstituted solution should be used immediately after preparation (contains no preservative), it should not be refrigerated and any unused portion of it should be discarded.

Immunine VH, factor IX concentrate (human) vapor heated, Immuno, is supplied in a single dose vial accompanied by a vial of Sterile Water for Injection for diluent, USP for diluent, a sterile transfer needle and a sterile filter needle (see Table II).

Table II—Immunine VH

Single Dose Vial Accompanied by Vial of Sterile Water for Injection

Immunine VH (IU*)	Sterile Water for Injection, USP (mL)
160 to 240	5
480 to 720	5
960 to 1 440	10

*The number of IU factor IX is stated on the label of each vial.

Reviewed 1998

IMODIUM®

Janssen-Ortho/ McNeil Consumer Products

Loperamide HCl

Antidiarrheal

Pharmacology: Diarrhea may be defined as a failure or imbalance of one or a combination of activities in the gut which include secretion, absorption and motility. Loperamide has been shown to act on all of these functions via cholinergic, noncholinergic, opiate and nonopiate receptor-mediated mechanisms. In this way, loperamide effectively reduces fecal output and frequency, improves stool consistency and relieves symptoms of abdominal cramping and fecal incontinence.

Indications: As an adjunct to rehydration therapy for the symptomatic control of acute nonspecific diarrhea; for chronic diarrhea associated with inflammatory bowel disease; and for reducing the volume of discharge for ileostomies, colostomies and other intestinal resections.

Contraindications: Children under 2 years of age.

Known hypersensitivity to loperamide or any of the other components; cases in which constipation must be avoided.

Loperamide should not be used in the case of acute dysentery which is characterized by blood in stools and elevated temperature.

Loperamide must not be used in patients with acute ulcerative colitis and in pseudomembranous colitis associated with broad-spectrum antibiotics. In such patients, agents which inhibit intestinal motility or delay intestinal transit time have been reported to induce toxic megacolon. In general, loperamide should not be used when the inhibition of peristalsis is to be avoided. Discontinue loperamide therapy promptly if constipation, abdominal distention or ileus occurs or if other untoward symptoms develop.

Warnings: Children: The use of loperamide is not recommended for children under 12 years of age except on the advice of a physician (see Dosage).

Use loperamide with special caution in young children and those with compromised blood brain barrier (e.g., meningitis) because of the greater variability of response in these groups. Dehydration, particularly in young children, may further influence the variability of response to loperamide.

Since treatment of diarrhea with loperamide is only symptomatic, diarrhea should be treated causally whenever causal treatment is available. Fluid and electrolyte depletion may occur in patients who have diarrhea. The use of loperamide does not preclude the administration of appropriate fluid and electrolyte therapy.

Loperamide should be kept out of reach of children. Due to the particular ease with which the quick-dissolve tablets may be swallowed, special care should be taken when storing this product.

In case of accidental ingestion of loperamide by children, see Overdose.

Precautions: *Pregnancy:* Safe use of loperamide during pregnancy has not been established. Reproduction studies performed in the rat and the rabbit revealed no evidence of impaired fertility or harm to the fetus at dosage levels up to 30-fold the therapeutic dose for man. Therefore, loperamide should be used in pregnant women only when, in the opinion of the physician, the potential benefits outweigh the possible hazards.

Lactation: There is little information on the excretion of loperamide in human milk, but small amounts of the drug were detected in the milk of a nursing mother. Therefore, loperamide should not be administered to lactating women unless in the judgement of a physician, the potential benefits outweigh the possible risks.

Monitor patients with hepatic dysfunction for signs of CNS toxicity due to the extensive first pass metabolism of loperamide in the liver.

If improvement in symptoms of acute diarrhea is not observed within 48 hours, discontinue the use of loperamide and consult a physician.

Dependence Liability: Physical dependence to loperamide in humans has not been observed. However studies in morphine-dependent monkeys demonstrated that loperamide HCl at doses above those recommended for humans prevented signs of morphine withdrawal. However, in humans, the naloxone challenge pupil test, which when positive indicates opiate-like effects, performed after a single high dose, or after more than 2 years of therapeutic use of loperamide, was negative.

Adverse Effects: The adverse effects reported in adults during clinical trials are difficult to distinguish from symptoms associated with the diarrheal syndrome. In adults, they were generally of a minor and self-limiting nature, e.g., abdominal pain or discomfort; drowsiness or dizziness; tiredness; dry mouth; nausea and vomiting; hypersensitivity, including skin rash. Constipation and/or abdominal distention have also been reported. In some very rare cases, particularly in which the treatment information had not been respected, these effects have been associated with ileus. Opiate-like effects (CNS) have been observed in young children (under 3 years of age).

Overdose: Symptoms: In case of overdosage (including relative overdosage due to hepatic dysfunction), CNS depression (stupor, coordination abnormality, somnolence, miosis, muscular hypertonia, respiratory depression) and ileus may occur. Children may be more sensitive to CNS effects than adults.

In clinical trials, an adult who took three 20 mg doses within a 24-hour period was nauseated after the second dose and vomited after the third dose. In studies designed to examine the potential for side effects, intentional ingestion of up to 60 mg of loperamide in a single dose to healthy subjects resulted in no significant adverse effects.

Treatment: Treatment is symptomatic and supportive. Appropriate standard methods of gastrointestinal decontamination may be employed. Activated charcoal administered promptly after ingestion of loperamide can reduce the amount of drug which is absorbed into the systemic circulation by as much as 9-fold.

In the event of overdosage, patients should be monitored for signs of CNS depression for at least 48 hours. If CNS depression is observed, naloxone may be useful. Since the duration of action of loperamide is longer than that of naloxone (which is 1 to 3 hours) repeated dosing with naloxone may be required. If responsive to naloxone, vital signs must be monitored carefully for recurrence of symptoms of drug overdose for at least 48 hours after the last dose of naloxone.

Since relatively little drug is excreted in the urine, forced diuresis is not expected to be effective for loperamide overdosage.

Physicians without experience in managing loperamide overdose should seek consultation with a Regional Poison Control Centre.

Dosage: Adults: Acute Diarrhea: 4 mg initially, followed by 2 mg after each unformed stool. Clinical studies indicate that diarrheal control may be achieved after the initial dose in 50% of patients. Daily dosage should not exceed 16 mg.

The quick-dissolve tablet is fast dissolving and can be taken without fluid. The tablet disintegrates within seconds on the surface of the tongue and is swallowed with the saliva.

Chronic Diarrhea: 4 mg initially, followed by 2 mg after each unformed stool until diarrhea is controlled; thereafter the dosage should be reduced to meet individual requirements. When the optimal daily dosage has thus been established, this amount can be administered as a single daily dose or in divided doses.

The average daily maintenance dosage used in clinical trials has been 4 to 8 mg. If improvement is not observed after treatment with 16 mg/day for 10 days, symptoms are unlikely to be controlled by further administration.

Children: Acute or Chronic Diarrhea: Loperamide should be used in children only on the advice of a physician. For children up to but not including 12 years of age, the following schedule will usually fulfill initial dosage requirements. See Table I.

Table I—Imodium

Recommended First-Day Dosage Schedule

2 to 5 years:* (10-20 kg)	1 mg t.i.d. (3 mg daily dose)
5 to 8 years: (20-30 kg)	2 mg b.i.d. (4 mg daily dose)
8 to 12 years: (greater than 30 kg)	2 mg t.i.d. (6 mg daily dose)

*Imodium solid dosage forms may not be appropriate for administration to children 2 to 5 years of age.

Following the first treatment day, it is recommended that subsequent doses (1 mg/10 kg body weight) be administered only after a loose stool and not exceed the maximum daily dose.

Duration of Treatment: Loperamide may be administered for prolonged periods of time. Blood, urine, liver and kidney function, ECG and ophthalmological examinations have revealed no significant abnormalities after several years of administration. No tolerance to the antidiarrheal effect has been observed. Naloxone pupil challenge studies in patients with chronic diarrhea who have received loperamide orally for prolonged periods indicate a lack of CNS effects.

Supplied: Each light green elongated capsule shaped tablet contains: loperamide HCl 2 mg. Nonmedicinal ingredients: cellulose, colloidal silicon dioxide, D&C yellow No.10, dibasic calcium phosphate, FD&C blue No.1 and magnesium stearate. Bisulfites-, gluten-, lactose-, sodium- and tartrazine-free. Blister packs of 6, 12, 18 or 24 (supplied by McNeil Consumer Products). HDPE bottles of 100 and 500 (supplied by Janssen-Ortho). Store at room temperature, protect from light.

(Shown in Product Recognition Section)

Reviewed 1999

IMOGAM® RABIES PASTEURIZED

Connaught

Rabies Immune Globulin, Pasteurized (Human)

Immunotherapeutic Agent—Passive Immunization

Pharmacology: Infection with rabies virus characteristically produces an acute illness with rapidly progressive CNS manifestations, including anxiety, dysphagia, and convulsions, and almost invariably progresses to death. Some patients may present with paralysis.

Rabies virus is classified in the Rhabdovirus family.

Rabies virus can infect any warm blooded animal. In North America, it occurs mainly in certain wildlife species and is spread by them to domestic livestock and pets. In recent years, most reported wildlife infections in British Columbia have been in bats; in Alberta, Saskatchewan and Manitoba in skunks; in Ontario and Quebec in foxes and skunks; and in the Northwest Territories in foxes. Rabies has been reported sporadically from New Brunswick and Nova Scotia and recently outbreaks in foxes have been reported in Labrador. Although domestic dogs and cats account for less than 10% of reported animal rabies, bites of these species account for the vast majority of suspected rabies exposures in humans and thus the majority of courses of anti-rabies postexposure treatment.

Airborne transmission has been reported in the laboratory and in bat-infected caves. Transmission has also occurred by transplantation of corneas from patients dying of undiagnosed rabies. Person-to-person transmission by bite has not been documented, although the virus has been isolated from the saliva of patients.

The incubation period in humans ranges from 5 days to more than 1 year; 2 months is the average. Recently, incubation periods of many years have been confirmed by antigenic typing of strains.

Rabies virus is usually transmitted by the bite of a rabid animal but can occasionally penetrate abraded skin contaminated with the saliva of infected animals. Progress of the virus after exposure is believed to follow a neural pathway and the time between exposure and clinical rabies is a function of the proximity of the bite (or abrasion) to the CNS and the dose of virus injected. The incubation period is usually 2 to 6 weeks but can be longer. After severe bites to the face, neck or arms, it may be as short as 10 days. After initiation of the vaccine series (human diploid cell origin), it takes approximately 1 week for development of immunity to rabies; therefore, the value of immediate passive immunization with rabies antibodies in the form of Rabies Immune Globulin (Human) cannot be overemphasized.

Since reporting began in 1925, 21 persons have died of rabies in Canada. A decision on the management of a person who may have been exposed to rabies virus must be made rapidly and judiciously since delay in starting a course of vaccine reduces its effectiveness and the infection is almost always fatal. Close to 3 000 persons in Canada receive postexposure treatment each year because of exposure to rabid or suspect rabid animals.

Rabies antibody provides passive protection when given immediately to individuals exposed to rabies virus. Rabies Immune Globulin (Human) of adequate potency was used in conjunction with Rabies Vaccine of duck embryo origin. When a globulin dose of 20 IU/kg of rabies antibody was given simultaneously with the first dose of vaccine, levels of passive rabies antibody were detected 24 hours after injection in all individuals. There was minimal or no interference with the immune response to the initial and subsequent doses of vaccine, including booster doses.

Studies of Rabies Immune Globulin, Pasteurized (Human) administered with the first of 5 doses of Inactivated Human Rabies Vaccine Mérieux confirmed that passive immunization with 20 IU/kg of Rabies Immune Globulin (Human) provides maximum circulating antibody with minimum interference with the active immunization.

A recent study indicates that the neutralizing antibody levels following administration of Rabies Immune Globulin, Pasteurized (Human) with and without Rabies Vaccine (HDCV) are not significantly different from that observed following Rabies Immune Globulin (not heat treated) administered in the same manner.

A double-blind trial was conducted in 64 healthy veterinary student volunteers randomized into 4 parallel groups of 16 each, to compare the safety and antibody levels achieved following i.m. injection of Rabies Immune Globulin, Pasteurized (Human) and Rabies Immune Globulin, nonheat treated (Human). Each immune globulin was administered on day 0, either alone or in combination with the Human Diploid Cell Rabies Vaccine using the standard postexposure prophylactic schedule of day 0, 3, 7, 14 and 28.

The dosage corresponded to the postexposure recommended dose of 20 IU/kg of Rabies Immune Globulin and was administered in 3, equally divided i.m. injections of under 5 mL in either gluteus. Serum rabies antibody levels were assessed before treatment and on days 3, 7, 14, 28, 35, and 42 by the Rabies Fluorescent Focus Inhibition Test (RFFIT).

Serum antibody levels were similar in the Rabies Immune Globulin, Pasteurized (Human) and Rabies Immune Globulin, nonheat treated (Human) groups. By day 3, 60% of each group had detectable antibody titers of ≥ 0.05 IU/mL. By day 14, the geometric mean titres (with 95% confidence interval) were 19 IU/mL (11 to 38) in the Rabies Immune Globulin, Pasteurized (Human) + vaccine group and 31 IU/mL (20 to 48) in the Rabies Immune Globulin, nonheat-treated (Human) + vaccine group. These differences were not statistically different.

Both Rabies Immune Globulin, Pasteurized (Human) and Rabies Immune Globulin, nonheat-treated (Human) were safe and without serious adverse events or allergic reactions.

Indications: Rabies Immune Globulin, Pasteurized (Human) is indicated for individuals suspected of exposure to rabies, with one exception: persons who have been previously immunized with Human Diploid Cell Rabies Vaccine, (HDCV) in a pre- or postexposure treatment series receive only vaccine.

Persons previously vaccinated with a vaccine other than HDCV in whom adequate antibody levels have not been demonstrated should receive full postexposure prophylaxis with HDCV and RIG.

If indicated, Rabies Immune Globulin, Pasteurized (Human) should be administered as promptly as possible after exposure. If initiation of treatment is delayed for any reason, Rabies Immune Globulin, Pasteurized (Human) should still be given, regardless of the interval between exposure and treatment. Since vaccine-induced antibody begins to appear within 1 week, there is no value in administering rabies immune globulin more than 8 days after the first dose of a rabies vaccine course.

Recommendations for passive and/or active immunization after exposure to an animal suspected of having rabies have been outlined by the W.H.O. and by the Canadian National Advisory Committee on Immunization (NACI).

Postexposure Immunization: A decision on the management of a person who has been exposed to the risk of rabies infection must be made rapidly and judiciously since delay in starting a course of vaccine reduces its effectiveness, and the disease once established is almost always fatal.

Rabies prophylaxis must be considered in every incident where potential exposure to rabies virus has occurred. The following factors should be taken into consideration.

Species of Animal: The animals in Canada most often proven rabid are foxes, skunks, cattle, dogs, cats and bats. The distribution of animal rabies and the species involved vary considerably across Canada so it is important to consult the local medical officer of health or government veterinarian. Human exposures to livestock are usually confined to salivary contamination, with the exception of horses and swine in which biting incidents have been reported. Risk of infection following exposure to rabid cattle is low, and only about 30 cases have ever been recorded. **Squirrels, hamsters, guinea-pigs, gerbils, chipmunks, rats, mice, other rodents or rabbits and hares** are rarely found to be infected with rabies and are not known to cause human rabies in Canada and the U.S.; **their bites seldom, if ever, call for rabies prophylaxis.**

Incident: Each incident requires full investigation including an assessment of the risk of rabies in the animal species involved and the behavior of the particular animal. An **unprovoked** attack is more apt to indicate that the animal is rabid.

Nevertheless, rabid cats and dogs may become uncharacteristically quiet. Bites inflicted on a person attempting to feed or handle an apparently healthy animal should generally be regarded as **provoked.**

Type of Exposure: Exposure to rabies virus is considered to have occurred when the animal's teeth break the skin in a bite or if the animal's saliva or other potentially infectious material (such as brain tissue) comes into contact with an open wound or mucous membrane. If the virus-containing material is dry, the virus can be considered to be noninfectious. Contact with blood, urine or feces or petting a rabid animal does not constitute an exposure and is not an indication for prophylaxis. The occurrence of rabies following exposure to virus-laden aerosols in a laboratory and in a bat-infested cave has been reported. The only known cases of human-to-human transmission of rabies occurred in patients who received corneal transplants from persons who had died of unrecognized rabies. Tissues from persons who die of encephalitis of unknown etiology should not be used as donor transplants.

Because some bat bites may be less severe, and therefore more difficult to recognize, than bites inflicted by larger mammalian carnivores, rabies postexposure treatment should be considered for any physical contact with bats when bite or mucous membrane contact cannot be excluded.

Vaccination Status of Biting Animal: A small number of vaccinated animals have developed rabies. Therefore, symptoms suggesting rabies, even in a vaccinated animal, must be carefully evaluated. The vaccination history in itself should not influence the need for postexposure treatment nor the need to sacrifice the animal for assessment.

The following recommendations are intended as a guide for the management of persons following possible exposure to rabies and may need to be modified in accordance with the specific circumstances of the exposure to rabies.

Local Treatment of Wounds: **Immediate washing and flushing with soap and water, detergent, or water alone is imperative and is probably the most effective procedure in the prevention of rabies.** Suturing the wound should be avoided if possible. Tetanus prophylaxis and antibacterial drugs should be given as required.

Immunizing Agents: There are 2 types of immunizing products: **Vaccines,** which contain inactivated virus and induce an active immune response beginning in 7 to 10 days and persisting for at least a year; **Rabies Immune Globulin (RIG),** which provides rapid protection that persists for only a short period of time (half-life about 21 days).

Vaccine and immune globulin should be used concurrently for optimum postexposure prophylaxis against rabies, except in persons previously vaccinated with human diploid cell rabies vaccine (HDCV).

Postexposure Treatment Guide: The following recommendations are only a guide (see Table I). They should be applied in conjunction with knowledge of the animal species involved, circumstances of the bite or other exposure, vaccination status of the animal, and presence of rabies in the region. Local and provincial public health officials should be consulted if questions arise about the need for rabies prophylaxis.

Table I—Imogam Rabies Pasteurized Postexposure Treatment Guide

Details of Animal	Nature of Exposure	Management of Exposed Person
a) Rabid b) Suspect Rabid c) Wild animal[1] in endemic area, particularly skunk, fox, coyote, raccoon, bat	No skin or mucosal contact with animal saliva, or casual contact, e.g., petting with no possible contamination of broken skin or mucous membrane	No treatment
d) Escaped dog or cat in endemic area (unless clearly provoked)	Bite; or contamination of scratch, abrasion, open wound or mucous membrane with saliva, body fluids or tissue (except blood, urine or feces)	1. Local treatment of wound 2. RIG (local and i.m.) 3. Full course[2] of HDCV
Apparently healthy domestic dog or cat that can be held under observation for 10 days	Bite; or contamination of scratch, abrasion, open wound or mucous membrane with saliva, body fluids or tissue (except blood, urine or feces)	1. Local treatment of wound 2. At first sign of rabies in the animal during holding period give RIG (local and i.m.) and start full course of HDCV.

Legend: RIG: Rabies Immune Globulin (Human). HDCV: Human Diploid Cell Vaccine.

Notes:

1.(a)If possible, the animal should be killed and the brain tested as soon as possible; holding for observation is not recommended.

(b)Bites of squirrels, chipmunks, rats, mice, other rodents, rabbits and hares are seldom, if ever, an indication for rabies prophylaxis.

2.Vaccine may be discontinued if fluorescent antibody tests of animal killed at time of attack are negative.

Contraindications: Should not be administered in repeated doses once vaccine treatment has been initiated. Repeating the dose may interfere with maximum active immunity expected from the vaccine.

Warnings: Rabies Immune Globulin, Pasteurized (Human) is made from human plasma. Products made from human plasma may contain infectious agents, such as viruses, that can cause disease. The risk that such products will transmit an infectious agent has been reduced by screening plasma

Imogam Rabies Pasteurized (cont'd)

donors for prior exposure to certain viruses, by testing for the presence of certain current virus infections, and by inactivating and/or removing certain viruses. An alcohol fractionation procedure used to purify the immunoglobulin component removes and/or inactivates both enveloped and nonenveloped viruses. An added heat treatment process (60° C, 10 hours) further inactivates both enveloped and nonenveloped viruses (see Supplied). Despite these measures, it is still theoretically possible that known or unknown infectious agents may be present. All infections thought by a physician possibly to have been transmitted by this product should be reported by the physician or other health care provider to the Medical Director, Connaught Laboratories Limited, 1755 Steeles Avenue West, Toronto, Ontario, Canada, M2R 3T4. The physician should discuss the risks and benefits of this product with the patient. This should include information that cases of rabies have been attributed to omission of passive immunization in persons who have received rabies vaccine.

Rabies Immune Globulin, Pasteurized (Human) should be given with caution to patients with a history of prior systemic allergic reactions following the administration of human immune globulin preparations.

Persons with specific IgA deficiency have increased potential for developing antibodies to IgA and could have anaphylactic reactions to subsequent administration of blood products containing IgA.

Precautions: General: There is no contraindication to the use of rabies vaccine or rabies immune globulin if indicated following exposure to a proven rabid animal. Hypersensitive individuals should be vaccinated only under strict medical supervision.

Infiltration of wounds in some anatomical sites (finger tips) must be carried out with care in order to avoid increased pressure in the tissue compartment (compartment syndrome).

The possibility of allergic reactions in individuals sensitive to components of the product should be evaluated. Epinephrine HCl solution (1:1 000) and other appropriate agents should be available for immediate use in case an anaphylactic or acute hypersensitivity reaction occurs. Health care providers should be familiar with current recommendations for the initial management of anaphylaxis in nonhospital settings, including proper airway management.

Before administration of any product, all appropriate precautions should be taken to prevent adverse reactions. This includes a review of the patient's history with respect to possible hypersensitivity to the product or similar product, determination of previous immunization history, and the presence of any contraindications, current health status, and a current knowledge of the literature concerning the use of the product under consideration.

Special care should be taken to ensure that the product is not injected into a blood vessel.

Under no circumstances should RIG vaccine be administered in the same syringe or at the same site as Rabies Vaccine.

A separate sterile needle and syringe, or a sterile disposable unit, must be used for each individual patient to prevent the transmission of infectious agents. There have been case reports of transmission of HIV and hepatitis by failure to scrupulously observe sterile technique.

Needles should not be recapped and should be disposed of properly.

Before administration of Rabies Immune Globulin, Pasteurized (Human), health care personnel should inform the patient, parent or guardian of the benefits and risks of immunization, and also inquire about the recent health status of the patient to be injected.

Rabies Immune Globulin, Pasteurized (Human) should not be administered i.v because of the potential for serious reactions. Injection should be made i.m. and care should be taken to draw back on the plunger of the syringe before injection in order to be certain that the needle is not in a blood vessel. Although systemic reactions to immunoglobulin preparations are rare, epinephrine (1:1 000) should be available for treatment of acute anaphylactoid reactions. As with all preparations given i.m., bleeding complications may be encountered in patients with bleeding disorders.

Drug Interactions: Live virus vaccine such as measles vaccine should not be given for 4 months following Rabies Immune Globulin, Pasteurized (Human) administration because antibodies in the globulin preparation may interfere with the immune response to the vaccination. Interference may also occur if the administration of Rabies Immune Globulin, Pasteurized (Human) becomes necessary within a short time after the administration of a live viral vaccine, and if the time interval between the 2 is very short (less than 14 days), vaccination may have to be repeated.

Pregnancy: Pregnancy is not a contraindication to rabies post-exposure therapy. Based on limited data, there have been no fetal abnormalities associated with rabies vaccination. Clinical experience with other immunoglobulin preparations suggests that there are no known adverse effects on the fetus from immune globulin, but there are no reported studies indicating whether or not such adverse effects occur. Specifically animal reproduction studies have not been conducted with Rabies Immune Globulin, Pasteurized (Human). It is also not known whether Rabies Immune Globulin, Pasteurized (Human) can cause fetal harm when administered to a pregnant woman or can affect reproductive capacity. Rabies Immune Globulin, Pasteurized (Human) should be given to a pregnant woman only if clearly needed.

Adverse Effects: In a recent clinical trial involving 16 volunteers in each of 4 treatment groups, 2 subjects reported severe headaches, 1 in the Rabies Immune Globulin, Pasteurized (Human) + placebo group and one in the Rabies Immune Globulin, nonheat-treated (Human) and the Human Diploid Cell Rabies Vaccine group. One third of the volunteers reported moderately systemic reactions (headache and malaise). These were equally distributed among the 4 treatment groups with no significant differences between the groups.

Local or mild systemic adverse reactions to the globulin are infrequent and may be treated symptomatically.

Local tenderness, soreness or stiffness of the muscles may occur at the injection site and may persist for several hours after injection. Urticaria and angioedema may occur. Anaphylactic reactions although rare, have been reported following injection of human immune globulin preparations. Fever, skin reactions or chills have been reported following human rabies immunoglobulins. Rare cases of nausea, vomiting, hypotension, tachycardia and allergic-type reactions have been reported. In very rare cases, anaphylactic shock has been observed.

Physicians, nurses, and pharmacists should report any adverse occurrences temporally related to the administration of the product in accordance with local requirements and to the Medical Director, Connaught Laboratories Limited, 1755 Steeles Avenue West, Toronto, Ontario, Canada, M2R 3T4.

Dosage: Parenteral biological products should be inspected visually for extraneous particulate matter and/or discoloration before administration. If these conditions exist, the product should not be administered.

Rabies Immune Globulin, Pasteurized (Human) should be used in conjunction with rabies human diploid cell vaccine (HDCV). The recommended dose of Rabies Immune Globulin, Pasteurized (Human) is a single i.m. administration of 20 IU/kg (0.133 mL/kg) of body weight at the time of administration of the first vaccine dose. If possible up to half the dose should be used to infiltrate the wound, and the rest administered i.m., preferably in the gluteal or deltoid region. Two injections would be given in the gluteal region if the volume is greater than 5 mL.

Rabies Immune Globulin, Pasteurized (Human) should never be administered in the same syringe or into the same anatomical site as the vaccine. HDCV is never to be administered in the gluteal region. Because Rabies Immune Globulin, Pasteurized (Human) may partially suppress active production of antibody, no more than the recommended dose should be given.

The dose of 20 IU/kg body weight is the same for children and adults. The dose of Rabies Immune Globulin, Pasteurized (Human), especially following multiple wounds, may be diluted 2-to 3-fold in a solution of 0.9% sodium chloride in order to provide the full amount of human rabies immunoglobulin required for good infiltration of sites at risk of rabies.

Do not heat by placing in warm water or incubator.

When administering a dose from a rubber-stoppered vial, do not remove either the rubber stopper or the metal seal holding it in place. Aseptic technique must be used for withdrawal of each dose (see Precautions).

Before injection, the skin over the site to be injected should be cleansed with a suitable germicide.

After insertion of the needle, aspirate to ensure that the needle has not entered a blood vessel.

Do not inject i.v.

Each person who is immunized should be given a permanent personal immunization record. In addition, it is essential that the physician or nurse record the immunization history in the permanent medical record of each patient. This permanent office record should contain the name of the product, date given, dose, manufacturer and lot number.

Supplied: Imogam Rabies Pasteurized is a sterile solution of antirabies immunoglobulin (10 to 18% protein) for i.m. administration. It is prepared by cold alcohol fractionation from pooled venous plasma of individuals immunized with Rabies Vaccine prepared from human diploid cells (HDCV). The product is stabilized with 0.3 M glycine. The globulin solution has a pH of 6.8±0.4 adjusted with sodium hydroxide or hydrochloric acid. No preservatives are added.

Imogam Rabies Pasteurized is a colorless to light opalescent liquid.

A heat-treatment process step (58 to 60° C, 10 hours) to inactivate viruses has been added to further reduce risk of blood-borne viral transmission. The inactivation and removal of model and laboratory strains of enveloped and nonenveloped viruses during the manufacturing and heat treatment processes for Imogam Rabies Pasteurized has been validated by spiking experiments. Human immunodeficiency virus, type 1 (HIV-1) and type 2 (HIV-2) were selected as relevant viruses for plasma derived products. Bovine viral diarrhea virus and Sindbis virus were chosen to model hepatitis C virus. Porcine pseudorabies virus was selected to model hepatitis B virus and herpes virus. Avian reovirus was used to model nonenveloped RNA viruses and for its relative resistance to inactivation by chemical and physical methods. Finally, porcine parvovirus was selected to model human parvovirus B19 and its notable resistance to inactivation by heat treatment.

Removal and/or inactivation of the studied enveloped and nonenveloped model viruses was demonstrated at the precipitation III stage of manufacturing. In addition, inactivation was demonstrated to occur during the 10-hour (58 to 60° C) heat treatment process for the studied enveloped and nonenveloped viruses.

The product is standardized against a Standard Rabies Immune Globulin of known potency in IU for rabies antibody. Each vial is formulated to contain at least 150 IU/mL. Each mL contains: human proteins 100 to 180 mg containing (IgG-class) human rabies immunoglobulins with a minimum titre of 150 IU*/mL. Nonmedicinal ingredients: glycine, sodium chloride and water for injection. Vials of 2 mL—300 IU (150 IU/mL) which is sufficient for a child weighing 15 kg; and 10 mL—1 500 IU (150 IU/mL) which is sufficient for an adult weighing 75 kg.

* Titre determined by the Rapid Fluorescent Focus Inhibition Test (RFFIT) technique.

Store at refrigerator temperature (2 to 8° C). **Do not freeze.** Product that has been exposed to freezing should not be used. Imogam Rabies Pasteurized contains no preservatives and unused portions must be discarded immediately. Do not use after expiration date.

Reviewed 1999

IMOVANE® Ⓟ

Rhône-Poulenc Rorer

Zopiclone

Hypnotic

Pharmacology: Zopiclone, a cyclopyrrolone derivative, is a short-acting hypnotic agent. Zopiclone belongs to a novel chemical class which is structurally unrelated to existing hypnotics. However, the pharmacological profile of zopiclone is similar to that of the benzodiazepines.

In sleep laboratory studies of 1- to 21-day duration in man, zopiclone reduced sleep latency, increased the duration of sleep and decreased the number of nocturnal awakenings. Zopiclone delayed the onset of REM sleep but did not reduce consistently the total duration of REM periods. The duration of stage 1 sleep was shortened, and the time spent in stage 2 sleep increased. In most studies, stage 3 and 4 sleep tended to be increased, but no change and actual decreases have also been observed. The effect of zopiclone on stage 3 and 4 sleep differs from that of the benzodiazepines which suppress slow wave sleep. The clinical significance of this finding is not known.

With hypnotic drugs, the duration of hypnotic effect and the profile of unwanted effects may be influenced by the alpha (distribution) and beta (elimination) half-lives of the administered drug and any active metabolites formed. When half-lives are long, the drug or metabolite may accumulate during periods of nightly administration and be associated with impairments of cognitive and motor performance during waking hours. If half-lives are short, the drug and metabolites will be cleared before the next dose is ingested, and carry-over effects related to sedation or CNS depression should be minimal or absent. If the drug has a very short elimination half-life, it is possible that a relative deficiency (e.g., in relation to the receptor site) may occur at some point in the interval between each night's use. This sequence of events may account for 2 clinical findings reported to occur after several weeks of nightly use of rapidly eliminated benzodiazepines or benzodiazepine-like hypnotics: 1) increased wakefulness during the last third of the night and 2) the appearance of increased day-time anxiety (see Warnings).

During nightly use and for an extended period, pharmacodynamic tolerance or adaptation to some effects of benzodiazepines or benzodiazepine-like hypnotics may develop. However in 2 sleep laboratory studies involving 17 patients, there was an absence of tolerance with zopiclone for treatment periods of more than 4 weeks.

Rebound insomnia: A transient syndrome whereby the symptoms that led to treatment with a benzodiazepine or benzodiazepine-like agent recur in an enhanced form, may occur on withdrawal of hypnotic treatment.

Some manifestations of rebound insomnia have been reported both in sleep laboratory and clinical studies following the withdrawal of zopiclone.

Zopiclone treatment was associated with dose-related residual effects (see Precautions).

Pharmacokinetics: Absorption: Zopiclone is rapidly and well absorbed. Bioavailability is more than 75%, indicating the absence of a significant first-pass effect. After the administration of 7.5 mg doses, peak plasma concentration of 60 ng/mL were reached in less than 2 hours. Absorption was similar in males and females.

Repeated daily administration of a 7.5 mg oral dose for 14 days did not change the pharmacokinetic characteristics of zopiclone and did not lead to accumulation.

Distribution: Zopiclone is rapidly distributed from the vascular compartment (distribution half-life [$t_{1/2\alpha}$]:1.2 hours) while the elimination half-life is approximately 5 hours (range: 3.8 to 6.5 hours). Plasma protein binding is low (approximately 45% in the 25 to 100 ng/mL concentration range) and nonsaturable. The risk of drug interaction arising from displacement of bound drug is low.

Metabolism: Zopiclone is extensively metabolized by 3 major pathways; only about 4 to 5% of the drug is excreted unchanged in the urine. The principal metabolites are the N-oxide derivative (approximately 12%) which has weak pharmacological activity in animals, and the N-desmethyl metabolite (approximately 16%) which is pharmacologically inactive. Their apparent half-lives evaluated from the urinary data are approximately 4.5 and 7.4 hours, respectively. Both metabolites are excreted renally. Other metabolites resulting from oxidative decarboxylation are partly eliminated via the lung as carbon dioxide. In animals, zopiclone did not induce hepatic microsomal enzymes.

Excretion: Excretion studies, using C^{14}-zopiclone have shown that more than 90% of the administered dose was excreted over a period of 5 days, 75% being eliminated in the urine and 16% in the feces.

The low renal clearance of unchanged zopiclone (mean 8.4 mL/min) compared with that of plasma (232 mL/min) indicates that zopiclone clearance is mainly metabolic.

Special patient populations: Elderly subjects: The absolute bioavailability of zopiclone was increased (94% vs 77% in young subjects) and the elimination half-life prolonged (approximately 7 hours). Accumulation has not been observed on repeated dosing.

Patients with hepatic insufficiency: Elimination half-life was substantially prolonged (11.9 hours) and time to peak plasma levels delayed (3.5 hours). Consequently, lower doses are recommended (see Dosage).

Patients with mild to moderate renal insufficiency: The pharmacokinetics of zopiclone were not affected. Hemodialysis did not appear to increase the plasma clearance of the drug.

Lactating women: Zopiclone was present in the milk, its concentration paralleled plasma levels but was about 50% lower.

Indications: Sleep disturbance may be the presenting manifestation of a physical and/or psychiatric disorder. Consequently, a decision to initiate symptomatic treatment of insomnia should only be made after the patient has been carefully evaluated.

For the symptomatic relief of transient and short-term insomnia characterized by difficulty in falling asleep, frequent nocturnal awakenings and/or early morning awakenings.

Treatment with zopiclone should usually not exceed 7 to 10 consecutive days. Use for more than 2 to 3 consecutive weeks requires complete re-evaluation of the patient. Prescriptions for zopiclone should be written for short-term use (7 to 10 days) and it should not be prescribed in quantities exceeding a 1-month supply.

The use of hypnotics should be restricted for insomnia where disturbed sleep results in impaired daytime functioning.

Contraindications: In patients with known hypersensitivity to the drug or any component or its formulation, and in those with severe impairment of respiratory function, e.g., sleep apnea syndrome.

Warnings: Zopiclone should be used with caution in patients who in the past manifested paradoxical reactions to alcohol and/or sedative medications.

Geriatrics: The smallest possible effective dose should be prescribed for elderly patients. Inappropriate, heavy sedation in the elderly, may result in accidental events/falls.

The failure of insomnia to remit after 7 to 10 days of treatment may indicate the presence of a primary psychiatric and/ or medical illness or the presence of sleep state misperception.

Worsening of insomnia or the emergence of new abnormalities of thinking or behavior may be the consequence of an unrecognized psychiatric or physical disorder. These have also been reported to occur in association with the use of drugs that act at the benzodiazepine receptors.

Zopidone should be used with caution in patients who have myasthenia gravis or severe hepatic insufficiency.

Pregnancy: Benzodiazepines may cause fetal damage when administered during pregnancy. During the first trimester of pregnancy, several studies have suggested an increased risk of congenital malformations associated with the use of benzodiazepines.

Insufficient data are available on zopiclone to assess its safety during human pregnancy. Thus, the use of zopiclone during pregnancy is not recommended. If zopiclone is prescribed to a woman of childbearing potential, the patient should be warned of the potential risk to a fetus and advised to consult her physician regarding the discontinuation of the drug if she intends to become pregnant or suspects that she is pregnant.

During the last weeks of pregnancy, ingestion of therapeutic doses of a benzodiazepine hypnotic has resulted in neonatal CNS depression due to transplacental distribution. Similar effects can be expected to occur with zopiclone, due to its pharmacological effects.

Memory Disturbance: Anterograde amnesia of varying severity has been reported following therapeutic doses of benzodiazepines or benzodiazepine-like agents. The event is rare with zopiclone. Anterograde amnesia is a dose-related phenomenon and elderly subjects may be at particular risk.

Cases of transient global amnesia and "traveller's amnesia" have also been reported in association with benzodiazepines, the latter in individuals who have taken the drug, often in the middle of the night, to induce sleep while travelling. Transient global amnesia and traveller's amnesia are unpredictable and not necessarily dose-related phenomena. Patients should be warned not to take zopiclone under circumstances in which a full night's sleep and clearance of the drug from the body are not possible before they need again to resume full activity.

Abnormal thinking and psychotic behavioral changes: Abnormal thinking and psychotic behavioral changes have been reported to occur in association with the use of benzodiazepines and benzodiazepine-like agents including zopiclone, although rarely. Some of the changes may be characterized by decreased inhibition, e.g., aggressiveness or extroversion that seems excessive, similar to that seen with alcohol and other CNS depressants (e.g., sedative/hypnotics). Particular caution is warranted in patients with a history of violent behavior and a history of unusual reactions to sedatives including alcohol and the benzodiazepines or benzodiazepine-like agents. Psychotic behavioral changes that have been reported include bizarre behavior, hallucinations, and depersonalization. Abnormal behaviors associated with the use of benzodiazepines or benzodiazepine-like agents have been reported more with chronic use and/or high doses but they may occur during the acute, maintenance or withdrawal phases of treatment.

It can rarely be determined with certainty whether a particular instance of abnormal behaviors listed above is drug induced, spontaneous in origin, or a result of an underlying psychiatric disorder. Nevertheless, the emergence of any new behavioral sign or symptom of concern requires careful and immediate evaluation.

Confusion: The benzodiazepines and benzodiazepine-like agents affect mental efficiency, e.g., concentration, attention and vigilance. The risk of confusion is greater in the elderly and in patients with cerebral impairment.

Anxiety, restlessness: An increase in daytime anxiety and/or restlessness have been observed during treatment with zopiclone. This may be a manifestation of interdose withdrawal, due to the short elimination half-life of the drug.

Depression: Caution should be exercised if zopiclone is prescribed to patients with signs and symptoms of depression that could be intensified by hypnotic drugs. The potential for self-harm (e.g., intentional overdose) is high in patients with depression and thus, the least amount of drug that is feasible should be available to them at any one time.

Precautions: *Drug Interactions:* Zopiclone may produce additive CNS depressant effects when coadministered with alcohol, sedative antihistamines, anticonvulsants, or psychotropic medications which themselves can produce CNS depression.

Compounds which inhibit certain hepatic enzymes (particularly cytochrome P450) may enhance the activity of benzodiazepines and benzodiazepine-like agents. Examples include cimetidine or erythromycin.

Drug abuse, Dependence and Withdrawal: Withdrawal symptoms, similar in character to those noted with barbiturates and alcohol (convulsions, tremor, abdominal and muscle cramps, vomiting, sweating, dysphoria, perceptual disturbances and insomnia) have occurred following abrupt discontinuation of benzodiazepines and benzodiazepine-like agents, including zopiclone. The more severe symptoms are usually associated with higher dosages and longer usage, although patients given therapeutic dosages for as few as 1 to 2 weeks can also have withdrawal symptoms including daytime anxiety between nightly doses. Consequently, abrupt discontinuation should be avoided and a gradual dosage tapering schedule is recommended in any patient taking the drug for more than a few weeks. The recommendation for tapering is particularly important in patients with a history of seizures.

The risk of dependence is increased in patients with a history of alcoholism, drug abuse, or in patients with marked personality disorders. Interdose daytime anxiety and rebound anxiety may increase the risk of dependency in zopiclone treated patients.

As with all hypnotics, repeat prescriptions should be limited to those who are under medical supervision.

Patients With Specific Conditions: Zopiclone should be given with caution to patients with impaired hepatic or renal function, or severe pulmonary insufficiency. Respiratory depression has been reported in patients with compromised respiratory function.

Patients Requiring Mental Alertness: Because of zopiclone's CNS depressant effect, patients receiving the drug should be cautioned against engaging in hazardous occupations requiring complete mental alertness such as operating machinery or driving a motor vehicle. For the same reason, patients should be warned against the concomitant ingestion of zopiclone and alcohol or CNS depressant drugs.

Pregnancy: For teratogenic effects see Warnings. Nonteratogenic effects: A child born to a mother who is on benzodiazepines or benzodiazepine-like agents may be at risk for withdrawal symptoms from the drug during the postnatal period.

Lactation: Zopiclone is excreted in human milk, and its concentration may reach 50% of the plasma levels. Therefore, the administration of zopiclone to nursing mothers is not recommended.

Children: The safety and effectiveness of zopiclone in children and young adults below the age of 18 have not been established.

Geriatrics: Elderly patients are especially susceptible to dose-related adverse effects, such as drowsiness, dizziness, or impaired coordination. Inappropriate, heavy sedation may result in accidental events/falls. Therefore, the lowest possible dose should be used in these subjects.

Adverse Effects: The most common adverse reaction seen with zopiclone is taste alteration (bitter taste). Severe drowsiness and/or impaired coordination are signs of drug intolerance or excessive doses.

The following adverse events were observed in patients receiving zopiclone. In the absence of an established cause-effect relationship those adverse reactions that were observed more frequently with zopiclone than with a placebo are in brackets.

CNS: (somnolence), (asthenia), dizziness, (confusion), (anterograde amnesia or memory impairment), (feeling of drunkenness), (euphoria), nightmares, agitation, (anxiety or nervousness), hostility, (depression), decreased libido, (coordination abnormality), (hypotonia), tremor, muscle spasms, paresthesia, (speech disorder).

Cardiovascular: palpitations.

Digestive: dry mouth, (coated tongue), (bad breath), nausea, vomiting, dyspepsia, diarrhea, (constipation), (anorexia or increased appetite).

Respiratory: dyspnea.

Special Senses: amblyopia.

Dermatologic: rash, spots on skin, sweating. Rashes may be a sign of drug hypersensitivity; discontinue if this occurs.

Metabolic and Nutritional: weight loss.

Imovane (cont'd)

Others: (bitter taste), headache, limb heaviness, chills.

Laboratory Tests: There have been sporadic reports of abnormal laboratory test values including increase in AST, ALT or alkaline phosphatase values.

Geriatrics: Geriatric patients tended to have a higher incidence of palpitations, vomiting, anorexia, sialorrhea, confusion, agitation, anxiety, tremor and sweating than younger patients.

Overdose: Symptoms: In voluntary or accidental cases of zopiclone overdosage involving doses up to 340 mg, the principal effects reported were prolonged sleep, drowsiness, lethargy and ataxia.

Full manifestation of zopiclone overdosage can be expected to be consistent with its pharmacological activity e.g., somnolence, confusion and coma with reduced or absent reflexes.

Treatment: Treatment should be supportive and in response to clinical signs and symptoms. Respiration, pulse and blood pressure should be monitored and supported by general measures when necessary. Immediate gastric lavage should be performed. I.V. fluid should be administered and an adequate airway maintained. Hemodialysis is probably of no value. It should be borne in mind that multiple agents may have been ingested.

The benzodiazepine antagonist flumazenil, is a specific antidote in known or suspected overdose with benzodiazepines or benzodiazepine-like agents. (For conditions of use see flumazenil product monograph.)

Dosage: Treatment with zopiclone should usually not exceed 7 to 10 consecutive days. Use for more than 2 to 3 consecutive weeks requires complete re-evaluation of the patient.

The product should be taken just before retiring for the night.

Adults: The usual adult dose is 5 to 7.5 mg. The 7.5 mg dose should not be exceeded (see Precautions).

Geriatrics: In the elderly and/or debilitated patient an initial dose of 3.75 mg at bedtime is recommended. The dose may be increased to 5.0 to 7.5 mg if the starting dose does not offer adequate therapeutic effect.

Patients With Impaired Liver Function or Chronic Respiratory Insufficiency: The recommended dose is 3.75 mg depending on acceptability and efficacy. Up to 7.5 mg may be used with caution in appropriate cases.

Zopiclone is not indicated for patients under 18 years of age.

Information for the Patient: See Blue Section—Information for the Patient "Imovane".

Supplied: 5 mg: Each round, white tablet, marked IMOVANE on one side and [logo] on the other, contains: zopiclone 5 mg. Nonmedicinal ingredients: calcium phosphate dibasic, hydroxypropylmethylcellulose, lactose, magnesium stearate, maize starch, sodium starch glycolate and titanium dioxide. Blister packs in boxes of 10, 30 and 100; white high density polyethylene bottles of 100 and 500.

7.5 mg: Each oval, scored blue tablet, marked IMOVANE on one side and [logo] on the other, contains: zopiclone 7.5 mg. Nonmedicinal ingredients: acetic anhydride, calcium phosphate, carnauba wax, cellulose, croscarmellose sodium, diethyl phthalate, FD&C Blue No. 1 aluminum lake, magnesium stearate, titane oxide and zein. Amber polystyrene bottles of 100 and 500.

Store in a dry place, at room temperature (15 to 30°C). Protect from light.

(Shown in Product Recognition Section)

IMURAN® Ⓟ

Glaxo Wellcome

Azathioprine

Immunosuppressive Agent

Pharmacology: Metabolism: Azathioprine is well absorbed following oral administration. Maximum serum radioactivity occurs at 1 to 2 hours after oral ^{35}S-azathioprine and decays with a half-life of 5 hours. This is not an estimate of the half-life of azathioprine itself but is the decay rate for all ^{35}S-containing metabolites of the drug. Because of extensive metabolism, only a fraction of the radioactivity is present as azathioprine. Usual doses produce blood levels of azathioprine, and of mercaptopurine derived from it, which are low (<1 µg/mL). Blood levels are of little predictive value for therapy since the magnitude and duration of clinical effects correlate with thiopurine nucleotide levels in tissues rather than with plasma drug levels. Azathioprine and mercaptopurine are moderately bound to serum proteins (30%) and are partially dialyzable.

Azathioprine is cleaved in vivo to mercaptopurine. Both compounds are rapidly eliminated from blood and are oxidized or methylated in erythrocytes and liver; no azathioprine or mercaptopurine is detectable in urine after 8 hours. Conversion to inactive 6-thiouric acid by xanthine oxidase is an important degradative pathway, and the inhibition of this pathway in patients receiving allopurinol is the basis for the azathioprine dosage reduction required in these patients (see Precautions, Drug Interactions). Proportions of metabolites are different in individual patients, and this presumably accounts for variable magnitude and duration of drug effects. Renal clearance is probably not important in predicting biological effectiveness or toxicities, although dose reduction is practiced in patients with poor renal function.

In view of the observations by Schwartz et al. that mercaptopurine suppressed the antibody response in rabbits injected with bovine serum albumin, the effects of azathioprine on the formation of antibodies were investigated. In the suppression of the formation of antibodies in mice to sheep red cells, as determined by hemagglutinin titres, azathioprine was found to be superior to mercaptopurine. Whereas mercaptopurine was active only at its maximum tolerated dose of 75 mg/kg, azathioprine was active at 25 mg/kg and was tolerated in doses up to 60 mg/kg for the dosage schedule employed (intraperitoneal injection for 4 successive days beginning at the time of the antigenic stimulus). The anti-immune effects of azathioprine are not due entirely to the mercaptopurine derived therefrom by splitting in vivo.

Another line of evidence which suggests that part of the activity of azathioprine may be due to its reaction with sulfhydryl compounds is the potentiation of its anti-immune effect by the simultaneous administration of busulfan. (Busulfan is also known to react with sulfhydryl groups in tissues.) Thus the combination of azathioprine (10 mg/kg) and busulfan (30 mg/kg) produced a marked suppression of the antibody response whereas the minimum effective dose of azathioprine alone is 25 mg/kg; busulfan alone is inactive at its maximum tolerated dose of 40 mg/kg. The combination of mercaptopurine (25 mg/kg) and busulfan (25 mg/kg) is inactive.

Homograft Survival: Although the use of azathioprine for inhibition of renal homograft rejection is well established, the mechanism(s) for this action are somewhat obscure. The drug suppresses hypersensitivities of the cell-mediated type and causes variable alterations in antibody production. Suppression of T-cell effects, including ablation of T-cell suppression, is dependent on the temporal relationship to antigenic stimulus or engraftment. This agent has little effect on established graft rejections or secondary responses.

Alterations in specific immune responses or immunologic functions in transplant recipients are difficult to relate specifically to immunosuppression by azathioprine. These patients have subnormal responses to vaccines, low numbers of T-cells, and abnormal phagocytosis by peripheral blood cells, but their mitogenic responses, serum immunoglobulins and secondary antibody responses are usually normal.

Immunoinflammatory Response: Azathioprine suppresses disease manifestations as well as underlying pathology in animal models of autoimmune disease. For example, the severity of adjuvant arthritis is reduced by azathioprine.

The mechanisms whereby azathioprine affects autoimmune diseases are not known. Azathioprine is immunosuppressive, delayed hypersensitivity and cellular cytotoxicity tests being suppressed to a greater degree than are antibody responses. In the rat model of adjuvant arthritis, azathioprine has been shown to inhibit the lymph node hyperplasia which precedes the onset of the signs of the disease. Both the immunosuppressive and therapeutic effects in animal models are dose-related. Azathioprine is considered a slow-acting drug and effects may persist after the drug has been discontinued.

Indications: Chronic immunosuppression with this purine antimetabolite may increase risk of neoplasia. Physicians using this drug should be very familiar with this risk as well as with possible hemotologic toxicities. See below under warnings.

Renal homotransplantation: Azathioprine is indicated as an adjunct for the prevention of rejection in renal homotransplantation. Experience with over 16 000 transplants shows a 5-year patient survival of 35 to 55%, but this is dependent on donor, match for HLA antigens, anti-donor or anti B-cell alloantigen antibody and other variables. The effect of azathioprine on these variables has not been tested in controlled trials.

Rheumatoid arthritis: Azathioprine is indicated only in adult patients meeting criteria for classic or definite rheumatoid arthritis as specified by the American Rheumatism Association. Azathioprine should be restricted to patients with severe, active and erosive disease not responsive to conventional management including rest, ASA or other nonsteroidal drugs or to agents in the class of which gold is an example. Rest, physiotherapy and salicylates should be continued while azathioprine is given, but it may be possible to reduce the dose of corticosteroids in patients on azathioprine. The combined use of azathioprine with gold, antimalarials or penicillamine has not been studied for either added benefit or unexpected adverse effects. The use of azathioprine with these agents cannot be recommended.

Contraindications: Hypersensitivity to the drug.

Patients with rheumatoid arthritis previously treated with alkylating agents (cyclophosphamide, chlorambucil, melphalan or others) may have a prohibitive risk of neoplasia if treated with azathioprine.

Azathioprine should not be used in treating rheumatoid arthritis in pregnant women. Azathioprine should not be used to treat children with rheumatoid arthritis.

Warnings: Severe leukopenia and/or thrombocytopenia may occur in patients on azathioprine. Macrocytic anemia and severe bone marrow depression may also occur. Hematologic toxicities are dose related and may be more severe in renal transplant patients whose homograft is undergoing rejection. It is suggested that patients on azathioprine have complete blood counts, including platelet counts, weekly during the first month, twice monthly for the second and third months of treatment, then monthly or more frequently if dosage alterations or other therapy changes are necessary. Delayed hematologic suppression may occur. Prompt reduction in dosage or temporary withdrawal of the drug may be necessary if there is a rapid fall in, or persistently low leukocyte count or other evidence of bone marrow depression. Leukopenia does not correlate with therapeutic effect; therefore the dose should not be increased intentionally to lower the white blood cell count.

Serious infections are a constant hazard for patients receiving chronic immunosuppression, especially for homograft recipients. Fungal, viral, bacterial and protozoal infections may be fatal and should be treated vigorously. Reduction of azathioprine dosage and/or use of other drugs should be considered.

Azathioprine is mutagenic in animals and humans, carcinogenic in animals, and may increase the patient's risk of neoplasia. Renal transplant patients are known to have an increased risk of malignancy, predominantly skin cancer and reticulum cell or lymphomatous tumors. The risk of post-transplant lymphomas may be increased in patients who receive aggressive treatment with immunosuppressive drugs. The degree of immunosuppression is determined not only by the immunosuppressive regimen, but also by a number of other patient factors. The number of immunosuppressive agents may not necessarily increase the risk of post-transplant lymphomas. However, transplant patients who receive multiple immunosuppressive agents may be at risk for over-immunosuppression; therefore, immunosuppressive drug therapy should be maintained at the lowest effective levels. Information is available on the spontaneous neoplasia risk in rheumatoid arthritis, and on neoplasia following immunosuppressive therapy of other auto-immune diseases. It has not been possible to define the precise risk of neoplasia due to azathioprine. The data suggest the risk may be elevated in patients with rheumatoid arthritis, though lower than for renal transplant patients. However, acute myelogenous leukemia as well as solid tumors have been reported in patients with rheumatoid arthritis who have received azathioprine. Data on neoplasia in patients receiving azathioprine can be found under Adverse Effects.

Azathioprine has been reported to cause temporary depression in spermatogenesis and reduction in sperm viability and sperm count in mice at doses 10 times the human therapeutic dose; a reduced percentage of fertile matings occurred when animals received 5 mg/kg.

A persistent negative nitrogen balance has been observed in some patients on continuous azathioprine dosage; if this should occur, the dose should be reduced as this has been found to correct the situation.

Pregnancy: Azathioprine can cause fetal harm when administered to a pregnant woman.

Azathioprine should not be given during pregnancy or in patients of reproductive potential without careful weighing of risk versus benefit. Use of azathioprine in pregnant patients should be avoided whenever possible. If this drug is used during pregnancy or if the patient becomes pregnant while taking this drug, the patient should be apprised of the potential hazard to the fetus. Women of childbearing age should be advised to avoid becoming pregnant.

Azathioprine is teratogenic in rabbits and mice when given in doses equivalent to the human dose (5 mg/kg daily). Abnormalities included skeletal malformations and visceral anomalies.

There are no adequate and well-controlled studies in pregnant women.

Limited immunologic and other abnormalities have occurred in a few infants born of renal allograft recipients on azathioprine. In a detailed case report, documented lymphopenia, diminished IgG and IgM levels, CMV infection, and a decreased thymic shadow were noted in an infant born to a mother receiving 150 mg azathioprine and 30 mg prednisone daily throughout pregnancy. At 10 weeks most features were normalized. DeWitte et al. reported pancytopenia and severe immune deficiency in a preterm infant whose mother received 125 mg azathioprine and 12.5 mg prednisone daily. There have been 2 published reports of abnormal physical findings. Williamson and Karp described an infant born with preaxial polydactyly whose mother received azathioprine 200 mg daily and prednisone 20 mg every other day during pregnancy. Tallent et al. described an infant with a large myelomeningocele in the upper lumbar region, bilateral dislocated hips, and bilateral talipes equinovarus. The father was on long-term azathioprine therapy.

Precautions: General: The dosage which will be tolerated or will be effective will vary from patient to patient and, therefore, careful management is necessary to obtain the optimum therapeutic effect and to reduce toxicity. Caution must be exercised to observe early signs of depression of the bone marrow which may result in leukopenia and eventually thrombocytopenia and bleeding. Since this drug may have a delayed action, it is important to withdraw the medication temporarily at the first sign of an abnormally large fall in the white cell count or of abnormal depression of the bone marrow. It must be kept in mind that patients with impaired renal function may have slower elimination of the drug and a greater cumulative effect. Lower dose if there is impaired renal function. It is recommended that the drug be withheld if there is evidence of toxic hepatitis or biliary stasis.

Hematologic: There are rare individuals with an inherited deficiency of the enzyme thiopurine methyltransferase (TPMT) who may be unusually sensitive to the myelosuppressive effect of azathioprine and prone to developing rapid bone marrow suppression following the initiation of treatment with azathioprine.

Gastrointestinal: A gastrointestinal hypersensitivity reaction characterized by severe nausea and vomiting has been reported. These symptoms may also be accompanied by diarrhea, rash, fever, malaise, myalgias, elevations in liver enzymes, and occasionally, hypotension. Symptoms of gastrointestinal toxicity may often develop within the first several weeks of azathioprine therapy and are reversible upon discontinuation of the drug. The reaction can recur within hours after rechallenge with a single dose of azathioprine.

Drug Interactions: Allopurinol: The principal pathway for detoxification of azathioprine is inhibited by allopurinol. In patients receiving azathioprine, the concomitant administration of allopurinol will require a reduction in dose to approximately ⅓ to ¼ of the usual dose of azathioprine. Subsequent adjustment of doses of azathioprine should be made on the basis of therapeutic response and any toxic effects.

Other Agents Affecting Myelopoesis: Drugs which may affect leukocyte production, including co-trimoxazole, may lead to exaggerated leukopenia, especially in renal transplant recipients.

Angiotensin Converting Enzyme Inhibitors: The use of angiotensin converting enzyme inhibitors to control hypertension in patients on azathioprine has been reported to induce anemia and severe leukopenia.

Warfarin: Azathioprine may inhibit the anticoagulant effect of warfarin.

Nondepolarizing Muscle Relaxants: There is clinical evidence that azathioprine antagonizes the effect of nondepolarizing muscle relaxants such as curare, d-tubocurarine and pancuronium. Experimental data confirm that azathioprine reverses the neuromuscular blockade caused by d-tubocurarine, and show that azathioprine potentiates the neuromuscular blockade caused by succinylcholine.

Pregnancy: See Warnings.

Lactation: The use of azathioprine in nursing mothers is not recommended. Azathioprine or its metabolites are transferred at low levels, both transplacentally and in breast milk. Because of the potential for tumorigenicity shown for azathioprine, a decision should be made on whether to discontinue nursing or discontinue the drug, taking into account the importance of the drug to the mother.

Children: Safety and efficacy of azathioprine in children have not been established.

Information for the Patient: Patients being started on azathioprine should be informed of the necessity of periodic blood counts while they are receiving the drug and should be encouraged to report any unusual bleeding or bruising to their physician. They should be informed of the danger of infection while receiving azathioprine and asked to report signs and symptoms of infection to their physician. Careful dosage instructions should be given to the patient, especially when azathioprine is being administered in the presence of impaired renal function or concomitantly with allopurinol (see Drug Interactions and Dosage).

Patients should be advised of the potential risks of the use of azathioprine during pregnancy and during the nursing period. The increased risk of neoplasia following azathioprine therapy should be explained to the patient.

Adverse Effects: The principal and potentially serious toxic effects of azathioprine are hematologic and gastrointestinal. The risks of secondary infection and neoplasia are also significant (see Warnings). The frequency and severity of adverse reactions depend on the dose and duration of azathioprine as well as on the patient's underlying disease or concomitant therapies. The incidence of hematologic toxicities and neoplasia encountered in groups of renal homograft recipients is significantly higher than that in studies employing azathioprine for rheumatoid arthritis. The relative incidences in clinical studies are summarized in Table I.

Table I—Imuran

Relative Incidences of Hematologic Toxicities and Neoplasia

Toxicity	Renal Homograft	Rheumatoid Arthritis
Leukopenia		
Any Degree	>50%	28%
<2 500/mm³	16%	5.3%
Infections	20%	<1%
Neoplasia		*
Lymphoma	0.5%	
Others	2.8%	

*Data on the rate and risk of neoplasia among persons with rheumatoid arthritis treated with azathioprine are limited. The incidence of lymphoproliferative disease in patients with RA appears to be significantly higher than that in the general population. In one completed study, the rate of lymphoproliferative disease in RA patients receiving higher than recommended doses of azathioprine (5 mg/kg/day) was 1.8 cases per 1 000 patient years of follow-up, compared with 0.8 cases per 1 000 patient years of follow-up in those not receiving azathioprine. However, the proportion of the increased risk attributable to the azathioprine dosage or to other therapies (i.e., alkylating agents) received by patients treated with azathioprine cannot be determined.

Hematologic: Leukopenia and/or thrombocytopenia are dose dependent and may occur late in the course of azathioprine therapy. Dose reduction or temporary withdrawal allow reversal of these toxicities. Infection may occur as a secondary manifestation of bone marrow suppression or leukopenia, but the incidence of infection is 30 to 60 times greater in renal homotransplantation than in rheumatoid arthritis. Macrocytic anemia and/or bleeding have been reported in patients on azathioprine.

Gastrointestinal: Nausea and vomiting may occur within the first few months of azathioprine therapy, and occurred in approximately 12% of 676 rheumatoid arthritis patients. The frequency of gastric disturbance can often be reduced by administration of the drug in divided doses and/or after meals. However, in some patients, nausea and vomiting may be severe and may be accompanied by symptoms such as diarrhea, fever, malaise, and myalgias (see Precautions). Vomiting with abdominal pain may occur rarely with a hypersensitivity pancreatitis.

Hepatic: Hepatotoxicity manifest by elevation of serum alkaline phosphatase, bilirubin and/or serum transaminases is known to occur with thiopurines including azathioprine and 6-mercaptopurine. This toxic hepatitis with biliary stasis is known to occur in homograft recipients. Hepatotoxicity has been uncommon in rheumatoid arthritis patients on azathioprine (less than 1%). Hepatotoxicity following transplantation most often occurs within 6 months of transplantation and is generally reversible after interruption of azathioprine. A rare, but life-threatening hepatic veno-occlusive disease associated with chronic administration of azathioprine has been described in transplant patients and in one patient receiving azathioprine for panuveitis. Periodic measurement of serum transaminases, alkaline phosphatase and bilirubin is indicated for early detection of hepatotoxicity. If hepatic veno-occlusive disease is clinically suspected, azathioprine should be permanently withdrawn.

Others: Additional side effects of low frequency have been reported. These include skin rashes, alopecia, fever, arthralgias, diarrhea, steatorrhea, negative nitrogen balance and reversible interstitial pneumonitis.

Overdose: Symptoms: Initial symptoms are nausea and vomiting; and symptoms appearing later are leukopenia, thrombocytopenia, hepatic necrosis and anorexia.

Treatment: Administer gastric lavage and fluids; blood transfusions may be needed due to suppression of the proliferation of granulocytes.

About 30% of azathioprine is bound to serum proteins, but approximately 45% is removed during an 8-hour hemodialysis. A single case has been reported of a renal transplant patient who ingested a single dose of 7500 mg azathioprine. The immediate toxic reactions were nausea, vomiting, and diarrhea, followed by mild leukopenia and mild abnormalities in liver function. The white blood cell count, AST, and bilirubin returned to normal 6 days after the overdose.

Dosage: Renal Homotransplantation: The dose of azathioprine required to prevent rejection and minimize toxicity will vary with individual patients; this necessitates careful management. Initial dose is usually 3 to 5 mg/kg daily, beginning at the time of transplant. Azathioprine is usually given as a single daily dose on the day of, and in a minority of cases 1 to 3 days before, transplantation. Azathioprine is often initiated with the i.v. administration of the sodium salt, with subsequent use of tablets (at the same dose level) after the post-operative period. I.V. administration of the sodium salt is indicated only in patients unable to tolerate oral medications. Dose reduction to maintenance levels of 1 to 3 mg/kg daily is usually possible. The dose of azathioprine should not be increased to toxic levels because of threatened rejection. Discontinuation may be necessary for severe hematologic or other toxicity, even if rejection of the homograft may be a consequence of drug withdrawal.

Rheumatoid Arthritis: Azathioprine is usually given on a daily basis. The initial dose should be approximately 1 mg/kg (50 to 100 mg) given as a single dose or on a twice daily schedule. The dose may be increased, beginning at 6 to 8 weeks and thereafter by steps at 4-week intervals, if there are no serious toxicities and if initial response is unsatisfactory. Dose increments should be 0.5 mg/kg daily, up to a maximum dose of 2.5 mg/kg/day. Therapeutic response occurs after several weeks of treatment, usually 6 to 8; an adequate trial should be a minimum of 12 weeks. Patients not improved after 12 weeks can be considered refractory. Azathioprine may be continued long-term in patients with clinical response, but patients should be monitored carefully, and gradual dosage reduction should be attempted to reduce risk of toxicities. Maintenance therapy should be at the lowest, effective dose, and the dose given can be lowered with decremental changes of 0.5 mg/kg or approximately 25 mg daily every 4 weeks while other therapy is kept constant. The optimum duration of maintenance azathioprine has not been determined. Azathioprine can be discontinued abruptly, but delayed effects are possible.

Renal Dysfunction: Relatively oliguric patients, especially those with tubular necrosis in the immediate post-cadaveric transplant period, may have delayed clearance of azathioprine or its metabolites or be particularly sensitive to this drug and are usually given lower doses.

Parenteral Administration: **For i.v. use only.** Add 10 mL of sterile water for injection, and swirl until a clear solution results. This solution, equivalent to 100 mg azathioprine, has a pH of approximately 9.6. The solution should be prepared immediately before use and any remainder discarded. Further dilution into sterile saline or dextrose is usually made for infusion; the final volume depends on time for the infusion, usually 30 to 60 minutes but as short as 5 minutes and as long as 8 hours for the daily dose.

Reconstituted Solutions: Solution for Reconstitution: Sterile Water for Injection. See Table II.

Table II—Imuran

Reconstitution

Vial Size	Volume of Diluent To Be Added to Vial	Approximate Volume Available	Nominal Concentration per mL
100 mg	10 mL	10 mL	10 mg/mL

Imuran (cont'd)

Shake until complete dissolution.

The solution should be prepared immediately before use and any remainder discarded.

Parenteral drug products should be inspected visually for particulate matter and discoloration prior to administration, whenever solution and container permit.

I.V. Infusion: Further dilution into sterile saline or dextrose is usually made for infusion. The final volume depends on the time for the infusion, usually 30 to 60 minutes, but as short as 5 minutes and as long as 8 hours for the daily dose.

Special Instructions: Tablets and intact vials should be returned to the manufacturer for destruction. Proper precautions should be taken in packaging these materials for transport.

All materials which have come in contact with cytotoxic drugs should be segregated and incinerated at 1 000°C or more. Sealed containers may explode.

Personnel regularly involved in the preparation and handling of cytotoxic agents should have biannual blood examinations.

Supplied: Injection: Each 20 mL vial contains: the equivalent of azathioprine 100 mg as the sodium salt. Store between 15 and 25°C, protected from light.

Tablets: Each yellow to off-white, dumbbell-shaped tablet, with code number IMURAN 50 on one side and with converging scored lines on the other contains: azathioprine 50 mg. Nonmedicinal ingredients: lactose, magnesium stearate, potato starch, povidone, and stearic acid. Bottles of 100. Store in a dry place between 15 and 25°C, protected from light.

(Shown in Product Recognition Section)

Reviewed 1997

INACTIVATED POLIOMYELITIS VACCINE (DIPLOID CELL ORIGIN)—IPV

Connaught

Poliomyelitis Prophylaxis

Pharmacology: Poliomyelitis is caused by infection with 1 of the 3 antigenic types of poliovirus. Following introduction of poliovirus vaccine in Canada in 1955, the indigenous disease has been virtually eliminated.

The last significant outbreak of poliomyelitis occurred in 1978 to 1979, when there were 11 cases of paralytic disease among unimmunized contacts of imported cases. The last case of poliomyelitis attributed to imported, wild virus occurred in 1988. However, circulation of wild viruses does occur in rare circumstances, and it remains crucial that the highest possible level of vaccine-induced immunity be maintained in the population. Inactivated Poliomyelitis Vaccine (Diploid Cell Origin)—IPV, (sometimes referred to as e-IPV), is an enhanced formalin-inactivated product which has a higher potency than the original IPV. The 3 poliovirus types are propagated in human diploid cells. A primary series induces protective antibody levels in more than 99% of recipients.

The clinical data for Inactivated Poliomyelitis Vaccine (Diploid Cell Origin)—IPV were obtained from 2 centres: one in Canada (British Columbia) and the other in the U.S. (Baltimore, Maryland). Serum samples from both sites were tested for neutralizing antibody of poliovirus Types 1, 2 and 3 by the micrometabolic inhibition test at Connaught Laboratories Limited.

The clinical trial data on 3 lots of Inactivated Poliomyelitis Vaccine (Diploid Cell Origin)—IPV obtained from a study on 338 infants in British Columbia demonstrated that 2 injections of vaccine at an interval of 2 months administered to infants 2 months of age at the time of the initial injection were effective in stimulating an antibody response to each of the 3 poliovirus types.

The response to Inactivated Poliomyelitis Vaccine (Diploid Cell Origin)—IPV developed despite the presence of maternally-transmitted antibody in most of the infants at the time of the initial vaccine injection. Following the second injection of vaccine, detectable antibody (≥1:4) was present in 99.7% (of 329 children) for Types 1 and 2 and in 98.8% (of 329 children) for Type 3.

In 294 children, the third vaccine injection at 15 to 18 months of age stimulated antibody rises to each of the 3 virus types to levels much higher than those attained following the second injection. The geometric mean responses 1 month after the third dose were 1:1 922, 1:4 010 and 1:1 388 for poliovirus Types 1, 2 and 3, respectively.

The data obtained in the Baltimore trials in a group of 254 infants demonstrated that 2 injections of vaccine at an interval of 2 months administered to infants 2 months of age at the time of the initial injection were effective in stimulating an antibody response to each of the 3 poliovirus types. Following the second vaccine injection, detectable antibody (≥1:4) to Type 1 poliovirus was present in 98.8% of infants and antibody (≥1:4) to Types 2 and 3 poliovirus was present in 99.2% of infants. The response to vaccine developed despite the presence of maternally-transmitted antibody in a high percentage of the infants at the time of the initial vaccine injection.

Indications: As an active immunizing agent to be administered, as described below, for the prevention of poliomyelitis.

Contraindications: General: Immunization with Inactivated Poliomyelitis Vaccine (Diploid Cell Origin)—IPV should be deferred in the presence of any acute illness, including febrile illness. A minor afebrile illness such as mild upper respiratory infection is not usually reason to defer immunization.

Absolute Contraindications: Allergy to any component of Inactivated Poliomyelitis Vaccine (Diploid Cell Origin)—IPV (see Supplied) an anaphylactic or other allergic reaction to a previous dose of Inactivated Poliomyelitis Vaccine (Diploid Cell Origin)—IPV are contraindications to vaccination.

Elective immunization of persons over 6 months of age should be deferred during an outbreak of poliomyelitis because of the risk of provocation paralysis.

Warnings: The vaccine should be perfectly clear and colorless. Any vaccine showing particulate matter or turbidity should be discarded. If Inactivated Poliomyelitis Vaccine (Diploid Cell Origin)—IPV is used in persons with malignancies receiving immunosuppressive therapies, including irradiation, antimetabolites, alkylating agents, cytotoxic drugs, or who are otherwise immunocompromised (including HIV infected individuals), the expected immune response may not be obtained.

Corticosteroid therapy can result in immunosuppression although the exact dose and duration of therapy required to suppress the immune system is not well defined. Persons treated with high doses of systemic steroids, e.g., ≥2 mg/kg/day of prednisone orally for more than 2 weeks, should be considered to have a compromised immune system.

As with any vaccine, immunization with Inactivated Poliomyelitis Vaccine (Diploid Cell Origin)—IPV may not protect 100% of susceptible individuals.

Precautions: General: Inactivated Poliomyelitis Vaccine is the vaccine of choice for immunizing immunodeficient patients and their household contacts. Although patients with immune deficiency diseases such as combined immunodeficiency, hypogammaglobulinemia and agammaglobulinemia, those with altered immune states due to diseases such as leukemia, lymphoma or generalized malignancy, and those with immune systems compromised by therapy with corticosteroids, alkylating drugs, antimetabolites or radiation may not develop a protective immune response, Inactivated Poliomyelitis Vaccine (Diploid Cell Origin)—IPV should be administered. Because of the possibility of immunodeficiency in other members of a household in which there has been one such case, Inactivated Poliomyelitis Vaccine (Diploid Cell Origin)—IPV should be used to immunize subsequent children until the immune status of the recipient and of other children in the family is documented.

Since the vaccine contains trace amounts of bovine serum and may contain trace amounts of polymyxin B and neomycin, the possibility of allergic reactions in individuals sensitive to these substances should be borne in mind when considering the use of this vaccine.

The possibility of allergic reactions in individuals sensitive to components of the vaccine should be evaluated. Epinephrine HCl solution (1:1 000) and other appropriate agents should be available for immediate use in case an anaphylactic or acute hypersensitivity reaction occurs. Health care providers should be familiar with current recommendations for the initial management of anaphylaxis in nonhospital settings, including proper airway management.

Before administration of any vaccine, all appropriate precautions should be taken to prevent adverse reactions. This includes a review of the patient's history with respect to possible hypersensitivity to the vaccine or similar vaccine, determination of previous immunization history, and the presence of any contraindications to immunization, current health status, and a current knowledge of the literature concerning the use of the vaccine under consideration.

Special care should be taken to ensure that the product is not injected into a blood vessel.

Caution: A separate sterile needle and syringe, or a sterile disposable unit, must be used for each individual patient to prevent the transmission of infectious agents.

There have been case reports of transmission of HIV and hepatitis by failure to scrupulously observe sterile technique. In particular, the same needle and/or syringe must never be used to re-enter a multidose vial to withdraw vaccine even when it is to be used for inoculation of the same patient. This may lead to contamination of the vial contents and infection of patients who subsequently receive vaccine from the vial.

Needles should not be recapped and should be disposed of properly.

Before administration of Inactivated Poliomyelitis Vaccine (Diploid Cell Origin)—IPV health care personnel should inform the parent or guardian or the patient to be immunized of the benefits and risks of immunization, inquire about the recent health status of the patient and comply with any local requirements with respect to information to be provided to the patient before immunization.

Pregnancy: No clinical trials with inactivated poliomyelitis vaccine have been conducted on pregnant women. Although there is no convincing evidence documenting adverse effects of inactivated poliomyelitis vaccine on the pregnant women or the developing fetus, it is prudent on theoretical grounds to avoid vaccinating pregnant women.

Adverse Effects: Local reactivity at the injection site as observed during the Canadian Clinical Trials consisted of redness, hardness and pain or discomfort occurring in 14%, 4% and 12% of vaccinees, respectively, usually on the evening following injection and declining thereafter to minimal levels.

As both of the first and second Inactivated Poliomyelitis Vaccine (Diploid Cell Origin)—IPV injections were administered at the same time, but at a different site from the first and second injections of Diphtheria and Tetanus Toxoids and Pertussis Vaccine Adsorbed (DPT Adsorbed) interpretation of systemic reactivity cannot be attributed solely to either vaccine. However, the systemic reactivity associated with administration of DPT Adsorbed in previous clinical trials would tend to indicate that the DPT Adsorbed was the major contributory factor.

Physicians, nurses and pharmacists should report any adverse occurrences temporally related to the administration of the product in accordance with local requirements and to the Medical Director, Connaught Laboratories Limited, 1755 Steeles Avenue West, Toronto, Ontario, Canada M2R 3T4.

Dosage: Primary immunization of infants at or above the age of 2 months, and children up to their 7th birthday: 3 doses of **0.5 mL** each should be administered **s.c.** at intervals of 8 weeks, followed by a fourth dose of **0.5 mL** approximately 12 months after the third dose.

In infancy, the primary schedule is usually integrated with DPT Adsorbed immunization, beginning at 8 to 12 weeks of age.

Primary immunization of older children (after their 7th birthday) and adults: 2 doses of **0.5 mL** each administered **s.c.** 8 weeks apart, followed by a third dose of **0.5 mL**, approximately 12 months after the second dose.

Booster Doses: All children who have received the initial 4 doses in infancy and in early childhood should be given a booster dose of **0.5 mL** of Inactivated Poliomyelitis Vaccine (Diploid Cell Origin)—IPV before entering school.

If the fourth primary dose is administered on or after the fourth birthday, a fifth (supplementary) dose is not required at school entry.

Unless oral polio vaccine was used exclusively during the primary series and the boosting dose, the Canadian Immunization Guide recommends an additional dose at the age of 14 to 16 years. Further recall doses should be given every 10 years to persons at risk (e.g., travellers).

Adults: Routine immunization against poliomyelitis of adults living in Canada is not considered necessary.

Most adults are already immune and have a very small risk of exposure to wild polioviruses in North America. Immunization is recommended for certain adults who are at greater risk of exposure to poliovirus than the general population, including: travellers to areas or countries where poliomyelitis is epidemic or endemic; laboratory workers handling specimens which may contain polioviruses; health care workers in close contact with patients who may be excreting wild or vaccine strains of polioviruses; unvaccinated parents of infants and toddlers who are to be given OPV; unvaccinated childcare centre workers; sewage workers; residents of communities where routine immunization of infants and children has not been practised.

Adults and adolescents who are at greater risk of exposure to poliovirus than the general population (see above) may be given a single dose of IPV if more than 10 years have elapsed since the last dose of their **complete** IPV and/or OPV vaccination series.

Persons with incomplete or no immunization history under these categories should receive the remaining dose(s) of IPV regardless of the interval since the last dose (in the case of incomplete poliovirus vaccination). Non-vaccinated adults and adolescents at increased risk of exposure to poliovirus should receive the primary series of IPV. The recommended schedule is 2 doses given at a 1- to 2-month interval and a third dose given 6 to 12 months later.

The following special recommendations are made for circumstances where time will not allow at least 2 doses of IPV to be given before protection is required.

Travellers who will depart in less than 4 weeks should receive a single dose of IPV, or if not available, OPV. In both instances, the remaining doses of vaccine should be given later at the recommended intervals.

Unvaccinated parents or other household contacts of infants who are to be given OPV carry a very small risk of developing OPV-associated paralysis. It will generally not be practical for such persons to be fully protected with IPV before the infant is immunized, and the very small risk may be reduced by giving them one dose of IPV at the same time as the first dose is given to the infant. Arrangements should be made for the adults to complete their basic course of immunization.

Administration: Parenteral biological products should be inspected visually for extraneous particulate matter and/or discoloration before administration. If these conditions exist, the product should not be administered.

Shake the ampul well to distribute uniformly the solution before withdrawing each dose. Before withdrawing a dose from an ampul, tap the container first to ensure that any vaccine in the ampul neck falls to the lower portion of the ampul. Once the ampul has been opened, any of its contents not used immediately should be discarded. Aseptic technique must be used for withdrawal of each dose.

Before injection, the skin over the site to be injected should be cleansed with a suitable germicide.

After insertion of the needle, aspirate to ensure that the needle has not entered a blood vessel.

Do not inject i.v.

Each person who is immunized should be given a permanent personal immunization record. In addition, it is essential that the physician or nurse record the immunization history in the permanent medical record of each patient. This permanent office record should contain the name of the vaccine, date given, dose, manufacturer and lot number.

Supplied: Each perfectly clear and colorless, purified inactivated vaccine contains: a solution of 3 types of poliovirus, Type 1 (Mahoney), Type 2 (M.E.F.1), Type 3 (Saukett), grown in human diploid strain MRC-5 cell cultures. Formaldehyde 27 ppm and 2-phenoxyethanol 0.5% added as preservative.

By calculation, the vaccine contains 20 ppm Tween 80, 0.5% albumin (Human) and less than 1 ppm of bovine serum. Trace amounts of polymyxin B and neomycin may be present from the cell growth medium. Ampuls of 0.5 mL. Packages of 5. Store between 2 and 8°C. **Do not freeze.** Product that has been exposed to freezing should not be used. Do not use vaccine after expiration date.

Reviewed 1998

INDERAL® Ⓟ
INDERAL®-LA Ⓟ
Wyeth-Ayerst

Propranolol HCl

Beta-Adrenergic Receptor Blocking Agent

Pharmacology: Propranolol is a non-selective beta-adrenergic receptor blocking drug. It has no other autonomic nervous system activity. Propranolol is a competitive antagonist which specifically competes with beta-adrenergic receptor stimulating agents for available beta-receptor sites. When access to beta-adrenergic receptor sites is blocked by propranolol, the chronotropic, inotropic, and vasodilator responses to beta-adrenergic stimulation are decreased proportionately.

Beta-adrenergic blockade is useful in some clinical conditions in which sympathetic activity is excessive or inappropriate, and therefore, detrimental to the patient. Sympathetic stimulation is however, vital in some situations (e.g. in patients with AV block or with a severely damaged heart) and should be preserved. The basic objective of beta-adrenergic blockade is to decrease adverse sympathetic stimulation but not to the degree that impairs necessary sympathetic support. Beta-blockade may result in bronchial constriction by interfering with endogenously or exogenously induced bronchodilation (see Contraindications and Warnings).

The mechanism of the antihypertensive effects of propranolol has not been established. Among the factors that may be involved are decreased cardiac output, inhibition of renin release by the kidneys, and diminution of tonic sympathetic nerve outflow from vasomotor centers in the brain. It has been suggested, but not established, that propranolol may achieve a better antihypertensive effect in patients with normal or elevated plasma renin activity (PRA) than those with low PRA.

Propranolol may reduce the oxygen requirement of the heart at any level of effort by blocking catecholamine induced increases in the heart rate, systolic blood pressure, and the velocity and extent of myocardial contraction. On the other hand, propranolol may increase oxygen requirements by increasing left ventricular fiber length, end diastolic pressure, and systolic ejection period. When the net effect is beneficial in anginal patients, it manifests itself during exercise or stress by delaying the onset of pain and reducing the incidence and severity of anginal attacks.

Propranolol exerts antiarrhythmic effects in concentrations producing beta-adrenergic blockade, which appears to be its principal antiarrhythmic mechanism of action. Beta-adrenergic blockade is of unique importance in the management of arrhythmias caused by increased levels of circulating catecholamines or enhanced sensitivity of the heart to catecholamines (arrhythmias associated with pheochromocytoma, thyrotoxicosis, exercise).

Mechanisms of the antimigraine and antitremor effects of propranolol have not been established. The antimigraine effect may be due to inhibition of vasodilatation or arteriolar spasms over the cortex. Beta-adrenergic receptors have been demonstrated in the pial vessels of the brain. The antitremor effects may be exerted through both peripheral and central sites of action. The mechanism by which propranolol reduces the incidence of cardiovascular mortality in post-myocardial infarct patients is unknown.

Propranolol from Inderal tablets is rapidly and completely absorbed from the gastrointestinal tract and undergoes extensive presystemic (or first-pass) elimination due to its high hepatic clearance. Inter-individual variations in circulating drug concentrations due to this first-pass effect have been documented and differ according to a number of factors including genetic make-up. Peak plasma concentrations of propranolol are attained 60 to 90 minutes after administration of Inderal tablets. The plasma half-life is 2 to 3 hours whereas the duration of pharmacological effect is longer.

Inderal-LA is a special formulation of propranolol hydrochloride consisting of capsules filled with spheroids of the active drug that have a sustained-release coating.

Propranolol from Inderal-LA capsules is almost completely absorbed from the gastrointestinal tract. A large part of the absorbed drug is lost from the systemic circulation due to first-pass metabolism in the liver. The first-pass metabolism is saturable. Steady-state plasma propranolol concentrations from Inderal-LA are proportional to the dose over the range of 60 to 160 mg/day although there is considerable intersubject variation. In healthy volunteers steady state was achieved after 2 or 3 days administration of Inderal-LA.

Peak blood levels following administration of Inderal-LA capsules occur at about 6 hours and the apparent plasma half-life has been reported to be between 10 and 12 hours i.e. 2 to 3 times that of the conventional tablet formulation.

When measured at steady state over a 24-hour period the areas under the propranolol plasma concentration-time curve (AUCs) for the LA-capsules are approximately 60 to 65% of the AUCs for a comparable divided daily dose of Inderal Tablets. The lower AUCs for the Inderal-LA capsules are due to greater hepatic metabolism of propranolol because of slower absorption. Over a 24-hour period, blood levels are fairly constant for about 12 hours, then decline exponentially.

Indications: Inderal: Hypertension: It is usually used in combination with other drugs, particularly a thiazide diuretic. Propranolol can, however, in certain patients, be used alone or as an initial agent in patients in whom, in the judgment of the physician, treatment should be started with a beta-blocker rather than a diuretic. The combination of propranolol with thiazide-like diuretics and/or peripheral vasodilators has been shown to be compatible and generally more effective than propranolol alone. Experience with most commonly used antihypertensive agents has not suggested evidence of incompatibility.

Propranolol by itself is not recommended for the emergency treatment of hypertensive crisis. It is, however, sometimes used as an adjunct to counteract the unwanted effect (tachycardia) of the primary agents used in these situations.

Angina Pectoris: For the prophylaxis of angina pectoris.

Cardiac Arrhythmias: Supraventricular arrhythmias: a) paroxysmal atrial tachycardias, particularly those arrhythmias induced by catecholamines or digitalis or associated with Wolff-Parkinson-White syndrome (see Warnings); b) persistent sinus tachycardia which is noncompensatory and impairs the well-being of the patient; c) tachycardias and arrhythmias due to thyrotoxicosis when causing distress or increased hazard and when immediate effect is necessary as adjunctive, short-term (2 to 4 weeks) therapy. May be used with, but not in place of, specific therapy (see Warnings); d) persistent atrial extrasystoles which impair the well-being of the patient and do not respond to conventional measures; e) atrial flutter and fibrillation when ventricular rate cannot be controlled by digitalis alone, or when digitalis is contraindicated.

Ventricular tachycardia: Ventricular arrhythmias do not respond to propranolol as predictably as do the supraventricular arrhythmias; a) with the exception of ventricular tachycardia induced by catecholamines or digitalis, propranolol is not the drug of first choice. In critical situations when cardioversion techniques or other drugs are not indicated or are not effective, propranolol may be considered. If, after consideration of the risks involved, propranolol is used, it should be given i.v. in low dosage and very slowly (see Dosage); b) persistent premature ventricular extrasystoles which do not respond to conventional measures and impair the well being of the patient.

Tachyarrhythmias of digitalis intoxication: If digitalis induced tachyarrhythmias persist following discontinuance of digitalis and correction of electrolyte abnormalities, they are usually reversible with oral propranolol. Severe bradycardia may occur (see Symptoms and Treatment of Overdose).

I.V. propranolol is reserved for life-threatening arrhythmias. Temporary maintenance with oral therapy may be indicated (see Dosage).

Resistant tachyarrhythmias due to excessive catecholamine action during anesthesia.

Tachyarrhythmias due to excessive catecholamine action during anesthesia may sometimes arise because of release of endogenous catecholamines or administration of catecholamines. When usual measures fail in such arrhythmias, propranolol may be given i.v. to abolish them. All general inhalation anesthetics produce some degree of myocardial depression. Therefore, when propranolol is used to treat arrhythmias during anesthesia, it should be used with extreme caution and constant ECG and central venous pressure monitoring. In patients during anesthesia with agents that require catecholamine release for maintenance of adequate cardiac function, beta-blockade will impair the desired inotropic effect. Therefore, propranolol should be titrated carefully when administered for arrhythmias occurring during anesthesia.

Post-myocardial Infarction: For the reduction of cardiovascular mortality in patients who have survived the acute phase of a myocardial infarction and who are clinically stable. In the study which showed this benefit, treatment with propranolol began between 5 and 21 days after the acute phase. Data are not available as to whether benefit would ensue if the therapy were initiated later.

Migraine: The prophylaxis of migraine headache. It is not indicated for the treatment of acute migraine attacks.

Essential Tremor: The management of essential tremor.

Hypertrophic Subaortic Stenosis: The management of hypertrophic subaortic stenosis, especially for treatment of exertional or other stress induced angina, palpitations, and syncope. Propranolol also improves exercise performance. The effectiveness of propranolol in this disease appears to be due to a reduction of the elevated outflow pressure gradient which is exacerbated by beta-adrenergic receptor stimulation. Clinical improvement may be temporary.

Pheochromocytoma: After primary treatment with an alpha-adrenergic blocking agent has been instituted, propranolol may be useful as adjunctive therapy if the control of tachycardia becomes necessary before or during surgery.

It is hazardous to use propranolol unless alpha-adrenergic blocking drugs are already in use, since this would predispose to serious blood pressure rise. Blocking only the peripheral dilator (beta) action of epinephrine leaves its constrictor (alpha) action unopposed. In the event of hemorrhage or shock, producing both beta- and alpha-blockade is contraindicated since the combination prevents the increase in heart rate and peripheral vasoconstriction needed to maintain blood pressure.

In inoperable or metastatic pheochromocytoma, propranolol may be useful as an adjunct to the management of symptoms due to excessive beta-adrenergic receptor stimulation.

Inderal-LA: For maintenance therapy in the treatment of hypertension and prophylaxis of angina pectoris.

Inderal (cont'd)

As for Inderal, the combination of Inderal-LA with thiazide-like diuretics and/or peripheral vasodilators has been shown to be compatible and generally more effective than Inderal-LA alone. Experience with most commonly used antihypertensive agents has not suggested evidence of incompatibility.

Treatment must always be initiated and individual titration of dosage carried out using the conventional tablets. The long-acting formulation may be used for maintenance provided the dosage requirement is suitable.

Not indicated for the emergency treatment of hypertensive crises.

Contraindications: Bronchospasm, including bronchial asthma; allergic rhinitis during the pollen season; sinus bradycardia and greater than first degree block; cardiogenic shock; right ventricular failure secondary to pulmonary hypertension; congestive heart failure (see Warnings) unless the failure is secondary to a tachyarrhythmia treatable with propranolol.

Warnings: Cardiac Failure: Sympathetic stimulation is a vital component supporting circulatory function in congestive heart failure; therefore, inhibition by means of beta-adrenergic blockade is a potential hazard as it may further depress myocardial contractility and precipitate cardiac failure. Propranolol acts selectively without completely abolishing the inotropic action of digitalis on the heart muscle (i.e., that of supporting the strength of myocardial contractions). In patients already receiving digitalis, the positive inotropic action of digitalis may be reduced by propranolol's negative inotropic effect. The effects of propranolol and digitalis are additive in depressing AV conduction.

Patients without a History of Cardiac Failure: Continued depression of the myocardium over a period of time can, in some patients, lead to cardiac failure. In rare instances, this has been observed during propranolol therapy. Therefore, at the first sign or symptom of impending cardiac failure, patients should be fully digitalized and/or given a diuretic, and the response observed closely: a) if cardiac failure continues, despite adequate digitalization and diuretic therapy, propranolol should be withdrawn immediately; b) if tachyarrhythmia is being controlled, patients should be maintained on combined therapy and closely followed until threat of cardiac failure is over.

Abrupt Cessation of Therapy in Angina Pectoris: Severe exacerbation of angina and the occurrence of myocardial infarction have been reported in some patients with angina pectoris following abrupt discontinuation of propranolol therapy. Therefore, when discontinuation of propranolol is planned in patients with angina pectoris, the dosage should be gradually reduced over a period of about 2 weeks and the patient should be carefully observed. For patients receiving Inderal tablets, the same frequency of administration should be maintained. For patients on Inderal-LA, discontinuation can be achieved by substituting Inderal-LA 60, 80, 120 and 160 mg by the equivalent dosage of conventional Inderal tablets spread throughout the day, and then gradually reducing the dose. In situations of greater urgency, propranolol dosage should be reduced stepwise, in 4 days under close observation. If angina markedly worsens, or acute coronary insufficiency develops, it is recommended that treatment with propranolol be reinstituted promptly, at least temporarily. In addition, patients with angina pectoris should be warned against abrupt discontinuation of propranolol.

Oculomucocutaneous Syndrome: Various skin rashes and conjunctival xerosis have been reported in patients treated with beta-blockers including propranolol. A severe oculomucocutaneous syndrome, whose signs include conjunctivitis sicca and psoriasiform rashes, otitis, and sclerosing serositis has occurred with the long-term use of one beta-adrenergic blocking agent. This syndrome has not been observed with propranolol, however, physicians should be alert to the possibility of such reactions and discontinue treatment if they occur.

Patients with Thyrotoxicosis: Possible deleterious effects from long-term use of propranolol have not yet been adequately appraised. Special consideration should be given to propranolol's potential for aggravating congestive heart failure. Propranolol may mask the clinical signs of developing or continuing hyperthyroidism or its complications, and give a false impression of improvement. Therefore, abrupt withdrawal of propranolol may be followed by an exacerbation of symptoms of hyperthyroidism, including thyroid storm. This may be another instance where propranolol should be withdrawn slowly by reducing dosage. Propranolol does not distort thyroid function tests.

Patients with Wolff-Parkinson-White Syndrome: Propranolol should be used with caution since several cases have been reported in which, after propranolol treatment, the tachycardia was replaced by a severe bradycardia requiring a demand pacemaker. In one patient, this occurred after an initial dose of 5 mg of propranolol.

Patients Undergoing Elective or Emergency Surgery: The management of patients with angina, being treated with beta-blockers and undergoing elective or emergency surgery, is controversial because beta-adrenergic receptor blockade impairs the ability of the heart to respond to beta-adrenergically mediated reflex stimuli, but abrupt discontinuation of therapy with propranolol may be followed by severe complications (see Warnings). Some patients receiving beta-adrenergic blocking agents have been subject to protracted severe hypotension during anesthesia. Difficulty in restarting and maintaining the heartbeat has also been reported.

For these reasons, in patients with angina undergoing elective surgery, propranolol should be withdrawn gradually (see Warnings). According to available evidence, all clinical and physiologic effects of beta-blockade are no longer present 48 hours after cessation of medication.

In emergency surgery, since propranolol is a competitive inhibitor of beta-adrenergic receptor agonists, its effects may be reversed, if necessary, by sufficient doses of such agonists as isoproterenol or dobutamine.

Anesthesia with agents which maintain cardiac contractility by virtue of their effect on catecholamine release (e.g. ether) should be avoided in patients on propranolol therapy.

Patients prone to nonallergic Bronchospasm (e.g., chronic bronchitis, emphysema, bronchiectasis): Propranolol should be administered with caution since it may block bronchodilation produced by endogenous and exogenous catecholamine stimulation of beta-adrenergic receptors.

Patients with Diabetes and in those subject to Hypoglycemia: Because of its beta-adrenergic blocking activity, propranolol may block premonitory signs and symptoms (pulse rate and pressure changes) of acute hypoglycemia. This is especially important to keep in mind in patients with labile diabetes. Hypoglycemic attacks may be accompanied by a precipitous elevation of blood pressure.

Pregnancy: The safe use of propranolol in pregnancy has not been established. Use of any drug in pregnancy or in women of childbearing potential requires that the possible risk to mother and/or fetus be weighed against the expected therapeutic benefit. Perinatal complications, such as small placenta and intrauterine growth retardation, have been reported in a few cases where the mother took propranolol during pregnancy. Some infants born to mothers treated with propranolol were reported to have hypoglycemia and/or bradycardia.

Children: While experience with propranolol in children under 12 is limited, the indications for which this drug is recommended occur infrequently in childhood. Although reports fail to indicate that children respond in a manner different from the adult, physicians are advised to undertake treatment with caution.

Precautions: There may be increased difficulty in treating an allergic type reaction in patients on beta-blockers. In these patients, the reaction may be more severe due to pharmacological effects of beta-blockers and problems with fluid changes. Epinephrine should be administered with caution since it may not have its usual effects in the treatment of anaphylaxis. On the one hand, larger doses of epinephrine may be needed to overcome the bronchospasm, while on the other, these doses can be associated with excessive alpha adrenergic stimulation with consequent hypertension, reflex bradycardia and heart-block and possible potentiation of bronchospasm. Alternatives to the use of large doses of epinephrine include vigorous supportive care such as fluids, and the use of beta agonists including parenteral salbutamol or isoproterenol to overcome bronchospasm, and norepinephrine to overcome hypotension.

Some slowing of heart due to unopposed vagal activity is usual in patients receiving propranolol; however, occasionally severe bradycardia occurs and may lead to vertigo, syncopal attacks or orthostatic hypotension. Patients, especially those with limited cardiac reserve should be monitored for signs of excessive bradycardia. Should the patient become symptomatic the dose of propranolol should be decreased or, if necessary, the drug should be discontinued. If it is essential to correct the bradycardia i.v. atropine or isoproterenol should be considered.

It has been reported that administration of propranolol to control cardiac arrhythmias in acute myocardial infarction has caused marked reduction in cardiac output. Therefore, the doses of propranolol should be kept to the minimum in patients with severe myocardial infarction. Caution should be exercised when administering propranolol in such situations, especially when a large portion of the myocardium has been damaged due to coronary occlusion since adequate sympathetic drive should be preserved to maintain ventricular function. Prior administration of other antiarrhythmic cardiac depressant drugs, such as procainamide or quinidine may potentiate the cardiac depressant activity of propranolol. Prior digitalization may be indicated and atropine should be at hand to control bradycardia.

The combination of propranolol with a thiazide like diuretic and/or peripheral vasodilator produces a greater fall in blood pressure than either drug alone. This occurs regardless of which drug is administered first. The same degree of blood pressure control can be achieved by lower than usual dosages of each drug. Therefore, when using such combined therapy, careful monitoring of the dosages is required until the patient is stabilized.

Patients receiving catecholamine depleting drugs such as reserpine or guanethidine should be closely observed if propranolol is administered concomitantly. The added catecholamine blocking action of this drug may produce an excessive reduction of the resting sympathetic nervous activity.

In patients on long-term treatment with propranolol, laboratory determinations should be made at regular intervals. The drug should be used with caution in patients with impaired renal and hepatic functions.

Adverse Effects: The most serious adverse effects that may be encountered with propranolol are congestive heart failure and bronchospasm (see Contraindications, Warnings and Precautions).

Gastrointestinal disturbances: (anorexia, nausea, vomiting, diarrhea, abdominal pain) are the most common adverse effects reported. Other less frequently reported adverse effects are: (in descending order) cold extremities and exacerbation of Raynaud's phenomenon; congestive heart failure; sleep disturbances including vivid dreams; dizziness, fatigue and bronchospasm.

Reported adverse effects, according to organ systems are recorded below.

Cardiovascular: congestive heart failure (see Warnings); secondary effects of decreased cardiac output which could include: syncope, vertigo, lightheadedness, decreased renal perfusion and rarely, postural hypotension; intensification of AV block and hypotension; severe bradycardia; claudication and cold extremities, Raynaud's phenomenon; dyspnea; palpitations; precordial pain.

CNS: dizziness, lethargy, weakness, drowsiness, headache, insomnia, fatigue, anorexia, anxiety, mental depression, poor concentration, reversible amnesia and catatonia, vivid dreams with or without insomnia, hallucinations, paresthesia, incoordination.

Gastrointestinal: nausea, vomiting, epigastric distress, anorexia, bloating, mild diarrhea, constipation.

Respiratory: bronchospasm; laryngospasm and respiratory distress (see Contraindications and Warnings).

Dermatologic: A few cases of erythematous rashes and increase of facial acneiform lesions have been reported; urticaria; exfoliative psoriasiform eruption.

Others: reduction or loss of libido; reversible alopecia and rarely: diminution and loss of hearing; tinnitus; visual disturbances; diminished vision, conjunctivitis; thrombocytopenic purpura; pharyngitis and agranulocytosis, fever combined with aching and sore throat; flushing of the face.

Clinical Laboratory Test Findings: Elevated blood urea levels in patients with severe heart disease, elevated serum transaminase, alkaline phosphatase, and lactate dehydrogenase have been reported.

Overdose: Symptoms: Several reports in the published literature describe cases in which propranolol was used as a suicide agent. In most cases, other agents, e.g., alcohol, have also been involved. One patient who died was thought to have ingested 3 600 mg of propranolol. Survival of patients taking higher single doses has, however, also been reported. The common signs to be expected in overdosage are bradycardia, hypotension, bronchospasm, or acute cardiac failure.

Treatment: If overdosage occurs, in all cases therapy with propranolol should be discontinued and the patient observed closely. In addition the following therapeutic measures are suggested:

Bradycardia: Administer atropine incrementally in 600 μg (0.6 mg) doses. If there is no response to vagal blockade, administer isoproterenol cautiously.

Cardiac Failure: Digitalization and diuretics.

Hypotension: Vasopressors, e.g., epinephrine or levarterenol. (There is evidence that epinephrine is the drug of choice).

Bronchospasm: Administer isoproterenol and aminophylline.

Dosage: Inderal: Hypertension: Therapeutic response to a given dosage varies between patients, therefore, dosage must be individually titrated and should be carefully monitored. In the treatment of hypertension, Inderal Tablets may be started by administering the drug in 2 equal daily doses of 40 mg. This may be increased, if necessary, in one week, to 80 mg twice daily, before breakfast and at bedtime. If necessary, the drug may be increased to 160 mg twice daily. For most patients the dosage is within the range of 160 to 320 mg daily. A small number of patients may respond to 80 mg daily. Experience to date suggests that in some resistant patients increasing the dosage above 320 mg/day may have an additional effect. Doses above 320 mg/day should be given on a 3 or 4 times daily regimen.

The time course of full blood pressure response is variable. The antihypertensive effect will usually occur within 3 to 7 days after reaching the effective dose. The maximum decrease in blood pressure may occur 2 to 4 weeks after initiation of treatment.

Angina Pectoris: Dosage must be individualized. Initiate therapy with 20 to 40 mg twice daily before meals. If satisfactory response is not obtained after 1 week, dosage should be increased to 80 mg twice daily. Although individual patients may respond to any dosage level, the average optimum dosage appears to be 160 mg/day. Occasionally in resistant patients dosages as high as 320 to 400 mg/day have been administered with beneficial results. If treatment is to be discontinued, reduce dosage gradually over a period of about 2 weeks (see Warnings).

Arrhythmias: 10 to 30 mg 3 or 4 times daily, before meals and at bedtime.

Post-myocardial Infarction: Initiate therapy with a 20 mg dose. If no adverse reaction is noted, increase the dose to 40 mg three times daily. After one to two weeks increase the dose to 60 mg three time daily. If necessary, the dose may be increased to 80 mg three times daily. In a large study involving 3 837 patients, this larger dose was used in approximately 20% of patients.

Migraine: Dosage must be individualized. The initial dose is 40 mg twice daily. The dose may then be gradually increased until optimum migraine prophylaxis is achieved. The usual effective dose range is 80 to 160 mg/day.

Hypertrophic Subaortic Stenosis: 20 to 40 mg, 3 or 4 times daily, before meals and at bedtime.

Essential tremor: Dosage must be individualized. The initial dose is 80 mg daily in divided doses. The dosage may be increased to 120 to 160 mg daily for optimal effects. If a patient does not respond to the drug within this dosage range, it is unlikely that further increases in dosage will produce a therapeutic effect, although a few patients have benefited from a daily dose of 240 mg. In elderly patients, doses above 120 mg daily may increase the risk of side effects such as bradycardia, syncope and bronchospasm.

Pheochromocytoma: Preoperatively: 60 mg daily, in divided doses, for 3 days before surgery, concomitantly with an alpha-receptor blocking agent.

Malignant cases: 30 mg daily, in divided doses.

Inderal-LA: Intended for maintenance therapy in those patients requiring doses within the range of 60 to 320 mg/day. Initiation of treatment and individual titration of dosage should be carried out using the conventional tablets. Inderal-LA may be preferred for maintenance because of the convenience of once-daily dosage. Patients with angina or hypertension on a maintenance regimen within the range of 60 to 320 mg/day regular tablets taken in divided doses may be changed to the appropriate number of Inderal-LA capsules taken once daily in the morning or evening.

However, Inderal-LA should not be considered a simple mg-for-mg substitute for conventional Inderal tablets and blood levels achieved are lower than those of 2 to 4 times daily dosing with the same dose. When changing to Inderal-LA from conventional Inderal tablets, a possible need for retitration upwards should be considered, especially to maintain effectiveness at the end of the dosing interval. In most clinical settings, however, such as hypertension or angina where there is little correlation between plasma levels and clinical effect, Inderal-LA has been shown to be therapeutically equivalent to the same mg dose of conventional propranolol as assessed by 24-hour effects on blood pressure, and on 24-hour exercise responses of heart rate, systolic pressure, and rate pressure product. Inderal-LA can provide effective beta blockade for 24-hour periods.

When propranolol is combined with another antihypertensive agent which is already being administered, therapy should be initiated with conventional Inderal tablets following usual dosage recommendations. Once adequate blood pressure control has been obtained, Inderal-LA capsules may be used for maintenance provided the dosage requirement is suitable.

In the treatment of hypertension, if required, further reduction of blood pressure may be attained by the addition of diuretic and/or peripheral vasodilator. Addition of another antihypertensive agent should, however, be gradual, beginning with 50% of the usual recommended starting dose, to avoid excessive reduction of blood pressure.

Inderal Injection: I.V. administration is reserved for life-threatening arrhythmias, or those occurring under anesthesia. The usual dose is from 1 to 3 mg, administered under careful monitoring, e.g., electrocardiograph, and central venous pressure recording. The rate of administration should not exceed 1 mg/minute to avoid extreme lowering of blood pressure and cardiac arrest. Sufficient time should be allowed for the drug to reach the site of action especially when a slow circulation is present. If necessary, a second dose may be given after 2 minutes. Thereafter, additional drug should not be given in less than 4 hours. Additional propranolol should not be given once the desired alteration in rate and/or rhythm is achieved. Changeover to oral therapy should be made as soon as possible.

The i.v. product contains no preservatives. Discard the unused portion after the second dose.

Supplied: Inderal: 10 mg: Each scored, orange, round, biconvex tablet contains: propranolol HCl 10 mg. Nonmedicinal ingredients: D&C Yellow No. 10 aluminum lake, FD&C Yellow No. 6 aluminum lake, lactose, magnesium stearate, microcrystalline cellulose and stearic acid. Energy: 1.67 kJ (0.4 kcal). Alcohol-, gluten-, parabens-, sodium-, sulfites- and tartrazine-free. Bottles of 100 and 1 000.

20 mg: Each scored, light blue, hexagonal tablet contains: propranolol HCl 20 mg. Nonmedicinal ingredients: FD&C Blue No. 1 aluminum lake, lactose, magnesium stearate, microcrystalline cellulose and stearic acid. Energy: 1.67 kJ (0.4 kcal). Alcohol-, gluten-, parabens-, sodium-, sulfites- and tartrazine-free. Bottles of 100 and 1 000.

40 mg: Each scored, green, round, biconvex tablet contains: propranolol HCl 40 mg. Nonmedicinal ingredients: D&C Yellow No. 10 aluminum lake, FD&C Blue No. 1 aluminum lake, FD&C Yellow No. 6 aluminum lake, lactose, magnesium stearate, microcrystalline cellulose and stearic acid. Energy: 1.67 kJ (0.4 kcal). Alcohol-, gluten-, parabens-, sodium-, sulfites- and tartrazine-free. Bottles of 100 and 1 000.

80 mg: Each scored, yellow, round, biconvex tablet contains: propranolol HCl 80 mg. Nonmedicinal ingredients: D&C Yellow No. 10 aluminum lake, FD&C Blue No. 1 aluminum lake, FD&C Yellow No. 6 aluminum lake, lactose, magnesium stearate, microcrystalline cellulose and stearic acid. Energy: 2.51 kJ (0.6 kcal). Alcohol-, gluten-, parabens-, sodium-, sulfites- and tartrazine-free. Bottles of 100.

120 mg: Each scored, red, round, biconvex tablet contains: propranolol HCl 120 mg. Nonmedicinal ingredients: lactose, magnesium stearate, microcrystalline cellulose, red ferric oxide and stearic acid. Energy: 3.35 kJ (0.8 kcal). Alcohol-, gluten-, parabens-, sodium-, sulfites- and tartrazine-free. Bottles of 100.

Inderal-LA: 60 mg: Each white/light blue, controlled-release capsule, identified by 3 narrow bands, 1 wide band, and INDERAL-LA 60, contains: propranolol HCl 60 mg. Nonmedicinal ingredients: ethylcellulose, hydroxypropyl methylcellulose and microcrystalline cellulose; empty capsule: FD&C Blue No. 1, FD&C Red No. 3, gelatin, silicon dioxide, sodium lauryl sulfate and titanium dioxide. Energy: 0.84 kJ (0.2 kcal). Alcohol-, gluten-, lactose-, sodium-, sugar-, sulfites- and tartrazine-free. Bottles of 100.

80 mg: Each light blue, controlled-release capsule, identified by 3 narrow bands, 1 wide band, and INDERAL-LA 80, contains: propranolol HCl 80 mg. Nonmedicinal ingredients: ethylcellulose, hydroxypropyl methylcellulose and microcrystalline cellulose; empty capsule: FD&C Blue No. 1, FD&C Red No. 3, gelatin, silicon dioxide, sodium lauryl sulfate and titanium dioxide. Alcohol-, gluten-, lactose-, sodium-, sugar-, sulfites- and tartrazine-free. Energy: 0.84 kJ (0.2 kcal). Bottles 100 and 500.

120 mg: Each light blue/dark blue, controlled-release capsule, identified by 3 narrow bands, 1 wide band and INDERAL-LA 120, contains: propranolol HCl 120 mg. Nonmedicinal ingredients: ethylcellulose, hydroxypropyl methylcellulose and microcrystalline cellulose; empty capsule: FD&C Blue No. 1, FD&C Red No. 3, gelatin, silicon dioxide, sodium lauryl sulfate and titanium dioxide. Energy: 0.84 kJ (0.2 kcal). Alcohol-, gluten-, lactose-, sodium-, sugar-, sulfites- and tartrazine-free. Bottles of 100.

160 mg: Each dark blue, controlled-release capsule, identified by 3 narrow bands, 1 wide band, and INDERAL-LA 160, contains: propranolol HCl 160 mg. Nonmedicinal ingredients: ethylcellulose, hydroxypropyl methylcellulose and microcrystalline cellulose; empty capsule: FD&C Blue No. 1, gelatin and titanium dioxide. Energy: 1.26 kJ (0.3 kcal). Alcohol-, gluten-, lactose-, sodium-, sugar-, sulfites- and tartrazine-free. Bottles of 100 and 500.

Inderal Injection: Each mL contains: propranolol HCl 1 mg in aqueous solution. Nonmedicinal ingredients: citric acid and water for injection. Does not contain alcohols, gluten, parabens, sugars, sulfites or tartrazine. Vials of 1 mL, boxes of 10. Vials of 10 mL, boxes of 5.

(Shown in Product Recognition Section)

INDERIDE® Ⓟ
Wyeth-Ayerst

Propranolol HCl—Hydrochlorothiazide
Antihypertensive

Supplied: Each scored, off-white hexagonal tablet, embossed with the letter I on one side and potency on the other, contains: propranolol hydrochloride 40 mg and hydrochlorothiazide 25 mg. Nonmedicinal ingredients: ferric oxide Yellow, lactose, magnesium stearate, microcrystalline cellulose and stearic acid. Energy: 1.26 kJ (0.3 kcal). Alcohol-, gluten-, parabens-, sodium-, sulfites- and tartrazine-free. Bottles of 100.

Each scored, off-white hexagonal tablet, embossed with the letter I on one side and potency on the other, contains: propranolol hydrochloride 80 mg and hydrochlorothiazide 25 mg. Nonmedicinal ingredients: ferric oxide Yellow, lactose, magnesium stearate, microcrystalline cellulose and stearic acid. Energy: 2.1 kJ (0.5 kcal). Alcohol-, gluten-, parabens-, sodium-, sulfites- and tartrazine-free. Bottles of 100.

(Shown in Product Recognition Section)

INDOCID® Ⓟ
INDOCID® SR Ⓟ
MSD

Indomethacin
Nonsteroidal Anti-inflammatory

Pharmacology: Indomethacin is a nonsteroidal anti-inflammatory drug with marked analgesic, and antipyretic properties. It has a unique chemical structure, which differentiates it from the salicylates, corticosteroids, phenylbutazone-like compounds and colchicine. Unlike corticosteroids, it has no effect on pituitary or adrenal function.

Indomethacin is a potent inhibitor of prostaglandin synthesis in vitro. Concentrations are reached during therapy which have been demonstrated to have an effect in vivo as well.

Although indomethacin does not alter the course of the underlying disease, it has been found effective to relieve pain, reduce fever, swelling and tenderness, and increase mobility in patients with rheumatic disorders of the types listed.

Pharmacokinetics: In man, indomethacin is readily absorbed, attaining peak plasma concentrations of about 1 and 2 μg/mL at about 2 hours following single oral doses of 25 and 50 mg, respectively. Ninety percent of the orally administered indomethacin is absorbed within 4 hours. Indomethacin is eliminated via renal excretion and biliary excretion. Indomethacin undergoes appreciable enterohepatic circulation. The mean half-life of indomethacin is estimated to be about 4.5 hours. With a typical therapeutic regimen of 25 or 50 mg t.i.d., the steady state plasma concentrations of indomethacin are on average 1.4 times those following the first dose.

Indomethacin exists in the plasma as the parent drug and its desmethyl, desbenzoyl, and desmethyl-desbenzoyl metabolites, all in the unconjugated form. About 60% of an oral dosage is recovered in urine as drug and metabolites (26% as indomethacin and its glucuronide), and 33% is recovered in feces (1.5% as indomethacin).

About 90% of indomethacin is bound to protein in plasma over the expected range of therapeutic plasma concentration.

Indocid SR 75 mg capsules are designed to release 25 mg of the drug initially and the remaining 50 mg over 6 hours or longer. When measured over a 24-hour period, the cumulative amount and time-course of indomethacin absorption from a single capsule Indocid SR are similar to those of 3 doses of 25 mg capsules Indocid given at 4 to 6 hour intervals.

Indocid (cont'd)

Absorption into the systemic circulation continues over an extended period with 90% of the dose absorbed by 12 hours.

Indications: Indomethacin is not a simple analgesic and its use should be limited to the conditions listed below, particularly those cases not responding to conservative measures.
Indocid: Indocid has been effective in symptomatic treatment of selected cases of rheumatoid arthritis; ankylosing (rheumatoid) spondylitis; gout. Selected cases of severe osteoarthritis, including degenerative disease of the hip. In these conditions indomethacin may on occasion replace other commonly used agents such as corticosteroids, salicylates, phenylbutazone-like compounds, and colchicine.

The suppositories are for those patients in whom rectal administration is preferred.

Indocid SR: May be used for all the indications listed for standard Indocid suppositories except gout. Dose titration should not be attempted with Indocid SR. No long-term experience is available on Indocid SR. Limited clinical studies of 6 weeks' duration have shown that 1 capsule Indocid SR was clinically similar to one 25 mg capsule Indocid t.i.d.; and one capsule Indocid SR taken in the morning and evening was clinically similar to one 50 mg capsule Indocid t.i.d.

Rheumatoid Arthritis: Indomethacin may be used singly or in combination with other agents. However, it should not be used as a drug of first choice because of the adverse reactions that may occur with its use.

Best results (relief of pain, tenderness, swelling and stiffness) have been obtained in the acute episodes of the disease. However, in many patients with chronic rheumatoid arthritis, indomethacin produces a significant lessening of pain and stiffness within 48 hours. In other patients, treatment must be continued longer before significant subjective relief or objective evidence of decreased joint swelling and tenderness occur. In some cases of chronic rheumatoid arthritis, it may be necessary to continue treatment for at least a month before concluding that it has not produced significant benefit. Use of indomethacin may enable reduction of steroid dosage in patients receiving corticosteroids. In such instances, the steroid dosage should be reduced slowly.

Ankylosing (Rheumatoid) Spondylitis: Indomethacin frequently produces marked relief of pain and improved motion of the spine within 3 to 10 days.

Osteoarthritis: Indomethacin should be used in those cases of severe osteoarthritis which do not respond to treatment with such other drugs as the salicylates. In many cases prompt relief of pain is obtained.

Degenerative Joint Disease (Osteoarthritis) of the Hip: Indomethacin has provided relief of pain and increased range of motion in patients with degenerative joint disease of the hip.

Gout: In acute attacks of gout the response to indomethacin is usually rapid and often dramatic. Marked reduction of pain may be obtained within 2 to 4 hours. Tenderness and heat subside within 24 to 36 hours, and swelling decreases over a 3 to 5 day period.

Contraindications: As with other anti-inflammatory agents, indomethacin may mask the signs and symptoms of peptic ulcer. Indomethacin itself may cause peptic ulceration or irritation of the gastrointestinal tract. For these reasons, it should not be given to patients with active peptic ulcer, gastritis, regional enteritis, ulcerative colitis, diverticulitis or with a recurrent history of gastrointestinal lesions.

Contraindicated in patients who are hypersensitive to any component of this product, and in patients in whom acute asthmatic attacks, urticaria, or rhinitis are precipitated by ASA or other nonsteroidal anti-inflammatory agents (NSAIDs). Fatal anaphylactoid reactions have occurred in such individuals.

Indomethacin suppositories are contraindicated in subjects with a recent history of rectal bleeding or proctitis.

The drug should not be prescribed for children because safe conditions for use have not been established. In a few cases of severe juvenile rheumatoid arthritis, where indomethacin was given along with other drugs, severe reactions, including fatalities, were reported.

Warnings: Gastrointestinal: Single or multiple ulcerations, including perforation and hemorrhage of the esophagus, stomach, duodenum or small or large intestine have been reported to occur with indomethacin. Fatalities have been reported in some instances. Rarely, intestinal ulceration has been associated with stenosis and obstruction.

Gastrointestinal bleeding without obvious ulcer formation and performation of pre-existing sigmoid lesions (diverticulum, carcinoma, etc.) have occurred. Increased abdominal pain in ulcerative colitis patients or the development of ulcerative colitis and regional ileitis have been reported to occur rarely.

Indomethacin should be given under close medical supervision to patients prone to gastrointestinal tract irritation particularly those with a history of peptic ulcer, diverticulosis or other inflammatory disease of the gastrointestinal tract. In these cases the physician must weigh the benefits of treatment against the possible hazards.

Patients taking any NSAID including this drug should be instructed to contact a physician immediately if they experience symptoms or signs suggestive of peptic ulceration or gastrointestinal bleeding. These reactions can occur without warning symptoms or signs and at any time during the treatment.

Elderly, frail and debilitated patients appear to be at higher risk from a variety of adverse reactions from NSAIDs. For such patients, consideration should be given to a starting dose lower than usual, with individual adjustment when necessary and under close supervision (see Precautions).

CNS: Headache, sometimes accompanied by dizziness or lightheadedness, may occur usually early in treatment with indomethacin. Although the severity of these effects rarely requires discontinuing therapy, if headache persists despite dose reduction, indomethacin therapy should be discontinued.

Occupational Hazards: Patients should be warned that they may experience dizziness and in this event should not operate motor vehicles and should avoid potentially dangerous activities which require alertness.

Indomethacin should be used with caution in patients with psychiatric disturbances, epilepsy, or parkinsonism, since it may, in some instances, aggravate these conditions.

Pregnancy and *Lactation:* The known effects of drugs of this class on the human fetus during the third trimester of pregnancy are closure of the ductus arteriosus, platelet dysfunction with resultant bleeding, renal dysfunction or failure with oligohydramnios, gastrointestinal bleeding or perforation and myocardial degenerative changes.

Administration of indomethacin is not recommended during pregnancy or in nursing mothers.

Indomethacin is excreted in breast milk.

Precautions: Gastrointestinal: If peptic ulceration is suspected or confirmed, or if gastrointestinal bleeding or perforation occurs indomethacin should be discontinued, an appropriate treatment instituted and patient closely monitored.

There is no definitive evidence that the concomitant administration of histamine H_2-receptor antagonists and/or antacids will either prevent the occurrence of gastrointestinal side effects or allow continuation of indomethacin therapy when and if these adverse reactions appear.

Indomethacin, both capsules and suppositories, should be used with caution because of the gastrointestinal reactions which may occur. The gastrointestinal effects may be decreased by giving the oral formulations of the drug immediately after meals, with food or with antacids. The risk of continuing therapy with indomethacin in the face of such symptoms must be weighed against the possible benefits to the individual patient. Indomethacin suppositories should be given with caution to patients with any anal or rectal pathology.

Studies in normal subjects with radioactive chromate-tagged red blood cells indicate that large doses of indomethacin (50 mg 4 times a day) produce less fecal blood loss than average doses of ASA (600 mg 4 times a day). Notwithstanding, indomethacin may cause single or multiple ulceration of the stomach, duodenum, or small and large intestine. There have been reports of severe bleeding and of perforation with a few fatalities. Patients may also develop gastrointestinal bleeding with no obvious ulcer formation. If gastrointestinal bleeding occurs, discontinue using the drug. In many patients with peptic ulceration, a history of a previous ulcer was present or they were on concomitant steroids, salicylates or phenylbutazone. A possible potentiation of the ulcerogenic effect of these drugs cannot be ruled out at present. In some patients there was no history of a previous ulcer and other drugs were not being given. As a result of obvious or occult gastrointestinal bleeding some patients may manifest anemia. For this reason appropriate blood determinations are recommended periodically.

Renal Function: As with other NSAIDs, there have been reports of acute interstitial nephritis with hematuria, proteinuria, and occasionally nephrotic syndrome in patients receiving long-term administration of indomethacin.

In patients with reduced renal blood flow where renal prostaglandins play a major role in maintaining renal perfusion, administration of a nonsteroidal anti-inflammatory agent may precipitate overt renal decompensation. Patients at greatest risk of this reaction are those with renal or hepatic dysfunction, diabetes mellitus, advanced age, extracellular volume depletion, congestive heart failure, sepsis, or concomitant use of any nephrotoxic drug. A NSAID should be given with caution and renal function should be monitored in any patient who may have reduced renal reserve. Discontinuation of non-steroidal anti-inflammatory therapy is usually followed by recovery to the pretreatment state.

Increases in serum potassium concentration, including hyperkalemia, have been reported, even in some patients without renal impairment. In patients with normal renal function, these effects have been attributed to a hyporeninemic-hypoaldosteronism state (see Drug Interactions).

Since indomethacin is eliminated primarily by the kidneys, patients with significantly impaired renal function should be closely monitored; a lower daily dosage should be used to avoid excessive drug accumulation.

Hepatic Function: As with other NSAIDs, borderline elevations of one or more liver tests may occur.

Significant (3 times the upper limit of normal) elevations of ALT or AST occurred in controlled clinical trials in less than 1% of patients receiving therapy with NSAIDs. A patient with symptoms and/or signs suggesting liver dysfunction, or in whom an abnormal liver test has occurred, should be evaluated for evidence of the development of more severe hepatic reaction while on therapy with indomethacin.

If abnormal liver tests persist or worsen, if clinical signs and symptoms consistent with liver disease develop, or if systemic manifestations occur (e.g., eosinophilia, rash, etc.), therapy should be discontinued.

During long-term therapy, liver function tests should be monitored periodically. If this drug is to be used in the presence of impaired liver function, it must be done under strict observation.

Fluid and Electrolyte Balance: Fluid retention and peripheral edema have been observed in some patients taking indomethacin. Therefore, as with other NSAIDs, indomethacin should be used with caution in patients with cardiac dysfunction, hypertension, or other conditions predisposing to fluid retention.

Serum electrolytes should be monitored periodically during long-term therapy, especially in those patients at risk.

Hematology: Drugs inhibiting prostaglandin biosynthesis do interfere with platelet function to some degree; therefore patients who may be adversely affected by such an action should be carefully observed when indomethacin is administered.

Blood dycrasias associated with the use of NSAIDs are rare, but could have severe consequences.

Indomethacin, like other nonsteroidal anti-inflammatory agents, can inhibit platelet aggregation. This effect is of shorter duration than that seen with ASA and usually disappears within 24 hours after discontinuation of indomethacin. Indomethacin has been shown to prolong bleeding time (but within the normal range) in normal subjects. Because this effect may be exaggerated in patients with underlying hemostatic defects, indomethacin should be used with caution in persons with coagulation defects.

Infection: In common with other drugs which have anti-inflammatory, analgesic and antipyretic properties, indomethacin possesses the potential of masking the signs and symptoms which ordinarily accompany infectious disease. The physician must be alert to this possibility to avoid undue delay in initiating appropriate treatment of the infection. Indomethacin should be used with caution in patients with existing, but controlled, infections.

Ophthalmology: Corneal deposits and retinal disturbances, including those of the macula, have been reported in some patients with rheumatoid arthritis on prolonged therapy with indomethacin. Similar eye changes have been observed in some patients with this disease who have not received indomethacin. Nevertheless, where therapy is prolonged, it is desirable to perform ophthalmological examinations at periodic intervals.

CNS: Headache may occur, usually early in treatment with indomethacin. If headache persists despite dosage reduction therapy with indomethacin should be discontinued (see Warnings).

Hypersensitivity Reactions: Patients should be followed carefully to detect unusual manifestations of drug sensitivity, and since advancing years appear to increase the possibility of adverse reactions, indomethacin should be used with greater care in the elderly.

Drug Interactions: ASA: The use of indomethacin in conjunction with ASA or other salicylates is not recommended. Controlled clinical studies have shown that the combined use of indomethacin and ASA does not produce any greater therapeutic effect than the use of indomethacin alone. Furthermore, in one of these clinical studies, the incidence of gastrointestinal side effects was significantly increased with combined therapy.

In a study in normal volunteers, it was found that chronic concurrent administration of 3.6 g of ASA/day decreases indomethacin blood levels approximately 20%.

Antihypertensive Medications: Coadministration of indomethacin and some antihypertensive agents has resulted in an attenuation of the latter's hypotensive effect acutely, due at least in part to indomethacin's inhibition of prostaglandin synthesis. Caution should be exercised when considering the addition of indomethacin to the regimen of a patient taking one of the following antihypertensive agents: an alpha-adrenergic blocking agent (such as prazosin), an angiotensin converting enzyme inhibitor (such as captopril or lisinopril), a beta-adrenergic blocking agent, a diuretic (see Diuretics), or hydralazine.

Cyclosporine: Administration of nonsteroidal anti-inflammatory drugs concomitantly with cyclosporine has been associated with an increase in cyclosporine induced toxicity, possibly due to decreased synthesis of renal prostacyclin. NSAIDs should be used with caution in patients taking cyclosporine, and renal function should be monitored carefully.

Diflunisal: The combined use of indomethacin and diflunisal has been associated with fatal gastrointestinal hemorrhage. The coadministration of diflunisal and indomethacin results in an increase of about 30 to 35% in indomethacin plasma levels and a concomitant decrease in renal clearance of indomethacin and its conjugate. Therefore, indomethacin and diflunisal should not be used concomitantly.

Digoxin: Indomethacin given concomitantly with digoxin has been reported to increase the serum concentration and prolong the half-life of digoxin. Therefore, when indomethacin and digoxin are used concomitantly, serum digoxin levels should be closely monitored.

Phenylpropanolamine: Hypertensive crises have been reported due to oral phenylpropanolamine alone and rarely to phenylpropanolamine given with indomethacin. This additive effect is probably due at least in part to indomethacin's inhibition of prostaglandin synthesis. Caution should be exercised when indomethacin and phenylpropanolamine are administered concomitantly.

Anticoagulants: Clinical studies have shown that indomethacin did not influence the hypoprothrombinemia produced by the use of anticoagulants in patients and in normal subjects. However, when any additional drug, including indomethacin is added to the treatment of patients on anticoagulant therapy, the patient should be observed closely for alterations of the prothrombin time.

Hypoglycemic Agents: Indomethacin and hypoglycemic agents should not be used concomitantly.

Diuretics: In some patients, the administration of indomethacin can reduce the diuretic, natriuretic, and antihypertensive effects of loop, potassium-sparing, and thiazide diuretics. Therefore, when indomethacin and diuretics are used concomitantly, the patient should be observed closely to determine if the desired effect of the diuretic is obtained.

Indomethacin reduces basal plasma renin activity (PRA), as well as those elevations of PRA induced by furosemide administration, or salt or volume depletion. These facts should be considered when evaluating plasma renin activity in hypertensive patients.

It has been reported that the addition of triamterene to a maintenance schedule of indomethacin resulted in reversible acute renal failure in two of four healthy volunteers. Indomethacin and triamterene should not be administered together.

Indomethacin and potassium-sparing diuretics each may be associated with increased serum potassium levels. The potential effects of indomethacin and potassium-sparing diuretics on potassium kinetics and renal function should be considered when these agents are administered concurrently.

Most of the above effects concerning diuretics have been attributed, at least in part, to mechanisms involving inhibition of prostaglandin synthesis by indomethacin.

Beta-adrenergic Receptor Blocking Agents: A decrease in the antihypertensive effect of beta-adrenergic receptor blocking agents by NSAIDs including indomethacin has been reported. Therefore, when using a beta blocking agent to treat hypertension, patients should be observed carefully in order to confirm that the desired therapeutic effect has been obtained.

Methotrexate: Caution should be used if indomethacin is administered simultaneously with methotrexate. Indomethacin has been reported to decrease the tubular secretion of methotrexate and to potentiate toxicity.

Lithium: Indomethacin capsules 50 mg t.i.d. produced a clinically relevant elevation of plasma lithium and reduction in renal lithium clearance in psychiatric patients and normal subjects with steady state plasma lithium concentrations. This effect has been attributed to inhibition of prostaglandin synthesis. As a consequence, when indomethacin and lithium are given concomitantly, the patient should be carefully observed for signs of lithium toxicity. (Read the product monographs for the appropriate lithium preparation before use of such concomitant therapy.) In addition, the frequency of monitoring serum lithium concentration should be increased at the outset of such combination drug treatment.

Table I—Indocid SR

Adverse Reactions to Indocid SR Capsules

Incidence >1%	Incidence <1%	
Gastrointestinal		
Nausea* with or without vomiting Dyspepsia* (including indigestion, heartburn and epigastric pain) Diarrhea Abdominal distress or pain Constipation	Anorexia Bloating (includes distention) Flatulence Peptic ulcer Gastroenteritis Rectal bleeding Proctitis Single and multiple ulcerations, including perforation and hemorrhage of the esophagus, stomach, duodenum or small or large intestines Intestinal ulceration associated with stenosis and obstruction	Gastrointestinal bleeding without obvious ulcer formation and perforation of pre-existing sigmoid lesions (diverticulum, carcinoma, etc.) Development of ulcerative colitis and regional ileitis Ulcerative stomatitis Toxic hepatitis and jaundice (some fatal cases have been reported)
CNS		
Headache Dizziness* Vertigo Somnolence Depression and fatigue (including malaise and listlessness)	Anxiety (includes nervousness) Muscle weakness Involuntary muscle movements Insomnia Muzziness Psychic disturbances including psychotic episode Mental confusion Drowsiness;	Lightheadedness Syncope Paresthesia Aggravation of epilepsy and parkinsonism Depersonalization Coma Peripheral neuropathy Convulsions Dysarthria
Dermatologic		
None	Pruritus Rash Urticaria Petechiae or ecchymosis Exfoliative dermatitis Erythema nodosum	Loss of hair Stevens-Johnson syndrome Erythema multiforme Toxic epidermal necrolysis
Cardiovascular		
None	Hypertension Hypotension Tachycardia Chest pain Congestive heart failure	Arrhythmia Palpitations
Special Senses		
Tinnitus	Ocular-corneal deposits and retinal disturbances including those of the macula, have been reported in some patients on prolonged therapy with indomethacin	Blurred vision, diplopia Hearing disturbances, deafness
Hematologic		
None	Leukopenia Bone marrow depression Anemia secondary to obvious or occult gastrointestinal bleeding Aplastic anemia	Hemolytic anemia Agranulocytosis Thrombocytopenic purpura Disseminated intravascular coagulation
Genitourinary		
None	Hematuria Vaginal bleeding Proteinuria Nephrotic syndrome Interstitial nephritis	BUN elevation Renal insufficiency, including renal failure
Hypersensitivity		
None	Acute anaphylaxis Acute respiratory distress Rapid fall in blood pressure resembling a shock-like state Angioedema	Dyspnea Asthma Purpura Angiitis Pulmonary edema.
Metabolic		
None	Edema Weight gain Fluid retention Flushing or sweating	Hyperglycemia Glycosuria Hyperkalemia
Miscellaneous		
None	Epistaxis Breast changes, including enlargement and tenderness, or gynecomastia	

*Reactions occurring in 3 to 9% of patients treated with indomethacin. (Those reactions occurring in less than 3% of the patients are unmarked.)

Indocid (cont'd)

Probenecid: When indomethacin is given to patients receiving probenecid, the plasma levels of indomethacin are likely to be increased. Therefore, a lower total daily dosage of indomethacin may produce a therapeutic effect. When increases in the dose of indomethacin are made under these circumstances, they should be made cautiously and in small increments.

Clinical Lab Tests: False-negative results in the dexamethasone suppression test (DST) in patients being treated with indomethacin have been reported. Thus, results of the DST should be interpreted with caution in these patients.

Adverse Effects: The most common adverse reactions encountered with NSAIDs are gastrointestinal, of which peptic ulcer, with or without bleeding, is the most severe. Fatalities have occurred on occasion, particularly in the elderly.

The following adverse reactions for capsules have been arranged into 2 groups: (1) incidence greater than 1% and (2) incidence less than 1% (see Table I on previous page). The incidence for group (1) was obtained from 33 double-blind controlled clinical trials reported in the literature (1 092 patients). The incidence for group (2) was based on reports in clinical trials, in the literature, and on voluntary reports since marketing. The probability of a causal relationship exists between Indocid and these adverse reactions, some of which have been reported only rarely.

In controlled clinical trials, the incidence of adverse reactions to Indocid SR capsules and equal 24-hour doses of Indocid capsules were similar.

The adverse reactions reported with the capsules may occur with use of the suppositories. In addition, rectal irritation and tenesmus have been reported in patients who have received the suppositories.

The following local adverse reactions have been associated with the use of the suppositories: tenesmus, proctitis, rectal bleeding, burning, pain, discomfort and itching.

Adverse Reactions-Causal Relationship Unknown: The following additional side effects have been reported; however a causal relationship to therapy with indomethacin has not been established.

Cardiovascular: thrombophlebitis.

Hematologic: Although there have been several reports of leukemia, the supporting information is weak.

Genitourinary: urinary frequency.

Overdose: Symptoms: The following symptoms may be observed following overdosage: nausea, vomiting, intense headache, dizziness, mental confusion, disorientation, or lethargy might be observed. There have been reports of paresthesias, numbness and convulsions. Signs of gastrointestinal hemorrhage could appear but have not been reported following the acute ingestion of large amounts of indomethacin accidentally or intentionally.

Treatment: Treatment is symptomatic and supportive. The stomach should be emptied as quickly as possible if the ingestion is recent. If vomiting has not occurred spontaneously, the patient should be induced to vomit with syrup of ipecac. If the patient is unable to vomit, gastric lavage should be performed. Once the stomach has been emptied, 25 or 50 g of activated charcoal may be given. Depending on the condition of the patient, close medical observation and nursing care may be required. The patient should be followed for several days because gastrointestinal ulceration and hemorrhage have been reported as adverse reactions of indomethacin. Use of antacids may be helpful.

Dosage: In chronic disorders, treatment should be started with a dosage of 25 mg 2 or 3 times a day. By starting therapy with low dosage, increased gradually when necessary, maximum benefit will be produced with fewer adverse reactions. Always give indomethacin with food or with antacids to reduce gastric irritation.

As with all drugs, the lowest possible effective dose should be utilized for each individual patient.

The drug should not be prescribed for children because safe conditions for use have not been established.

Since advancing years appear to increase the possibility of adverse reactions, indomethacin should be used with greater care in the elderly.

Adults: Rheumatoid arthritis and ankylosing (rheumatoid) spondylitis: Initial Dosage: 25 mg 2 or 3 times a day. If the response is not adequate, increase the daily dosage by 25 mg at about weekly intervals until a satisfactory response is obtained or a dosage of 150 to 200 mg/day is reached.

If a satisfactory response is not obtained with 200 mg a day, larger doses probably will not be effective.

If adverse reactions develop as the dosage is increased, reduce the dosage to a tolerated level and maintain this for 3 to 4 weeks. If an adequate response has not been obtained, gradually increase the daily dosage by 25 mg at about weekly intervals to 150 mg to 200 mg a day.

For patients with acute rheumatoid arthritis or with acute flares of chronic rheumatoid arthritis, increase the dosage daily by 25 mg until a satisfactory response is obtained or a total daily dosage of 150 to 200 mg is reached. If adverse effects develop as the dosage is increased, the dosage should be reduced to a tolerated level for 2 or 3 days, and then gradually increased by 25 mg every few days as tolerated. After the acute phase is under control, it is often possible to reduce the daily dosage gradually to 75 to 100 mg.

Reduction of Steroid Dosage: Use of indomethacin often will permit a gradual reduction of steroid dosage by 25 to 50%. In some patients steroids can be slowly discontinued over a period of several weeks or months. The usual precautions should be observed in withdrawing steroids.

Severe Osteoarthritis and Degenerative Joint Disease of the Hip: Initial Dosage: 25 mg 2 or 3 times a day. If the response is not adequate, increase the daily dosage by 25 mg at about weekly intervals until a satisfactory response is obtained or a dosage of 150 to 200 mg a day is reached. If a satisfactory response is not obtained with 200 mg/day, larger doses will probably not be effective.

If adverse reactions develop as the dosage is increased, reduce the dosage to a tolerated level and maintain this for 3 to 4 weeks. If an adequate response has not then been obtained, gradually increase the daily dosage by 25 mg at about weekly intervals to 150 to 200 mg a day.

Gout: To Control Acute Attacks: 50 mg 3 times a day until all signs and symptoms subside. Definite relief of pain has been reported within 2 to 4 hours. Tenderness and heat usually subside in 24 to 36 hours, and swelling gradually disappears in 3 to 5 days.

Indocid SR capsules are not recommended for use in acute attacks of gout.

Use of Alternate Dosage Forms: Indocid SR: Indocid SR may be tried after the daily dose has been established using the standard capsules and found to fall within 75 to 150 mg range. Patients stabilized on 25 mg three times daily should be tried on 1 SR capsule once daily and those stabilized on 50 mg 3 times daily should be tried on one SR capsule twice daily.

Indocid Suppositories: The recommended dosage is 100 to 200 mg daily and should be individually adjusted to the patient's response and tolerance. Daily dose of 100 mg can be given as 50 mg twice daily or as 100 mg at night. Doses higher than 100 mg must be given on a twice daily schedule.

Combined Administration: One 50 mg or 100 mg suppository at bedtime, supplemented the following day by 25 mg capsules as needed up to a total of 150 to 200 mg of indomethacin. The total daily dose of Indocid (capsules and suppositories) should not exceed 200 mg.

Information for the Patient: See Blue Section—Information for the Patient "Indocid/Indocid SR".

Supplied: Indocid: 50 mg: Each white, opaque suppository contains: indomethacin 50 mg. Nonmedicinal ingredients: butylated hydroxyanisole, butylated hydroxytoluene, edetic acid, glycerin, polyethylene glycol 3350, polyethylene glycol 8000 and sodium chloride. Boxes of 30. Store below 25°C.

100 mg: Each white, opaque suppository contains: indomethacin 100 mg. Nonmedicinal ingredients: butylated hydroxyanisole, butylated hydroxytoluene, edetic acid, glycerin, polyethylene glycol 3350 and polyethylene glycol 8000. Boxes of 30. Store below 25°C.

Indocid SR: Each opaque capsule with clear body and yellow cap, printed with MSD trademark in black and "693", containing a mixture of blue and white pellets, contains: indomethacin 75 mg. Nonmedicinal ingredients: allura red, black iron oxide, confectioner's sugar, cornstarch, gelatin, hydroxypropyl methylcellulose, indigotine, magnesium stearate, microcrystalline cellulose, polyvinyl acetate-crotonic acid copolymer, quinoline yellow, sunset yellow and titanium dioxide. Blister packages of 30 and bottles of 250. Store at room temperature (15 to 30°C).

(Shown in Product Recognition Section)

Reviewed 1997

INDOCID® P.D.A. Ⓟ

MSD

Indomethacin Sodium

Nonsteroidal Anti-inflammatory Agent for Closure of Patent Ductus Arteriosus

Pharmacology: Indomethacin is a nonsteroidal, anti-inflammatory agent which inhibits prostaglandin synthesis. The disposition of indomethacin following i.v. administration (0.2 mg/kg) in preterm neonates with patent ductus arteriosus has not been extensively evaluated. Even though the plasma half-life of indomethacin was variable among premature infants, it was shown to vary inversely with postnatal age and weight. In one study of 28 evaluable infants, the plasma half-life in those infants less than 7 days old averaged 20 hours (range: 3 to 60 hours, n=18). In infants older than 7 days, the mean plasma half-life of indomethacin was 12 hours (range 4 to 38 hours, n=10). Grouping the infants by weight, mean plasma half-life in those weighing less than 1 000 g was 21 hours (range: 9 to 60 hours, n=10); in those infants weighing more than 1 000 g, the mean plasma half-life was 15 hours (range: 3 to 52 hours, n=18).

Following i.v. administration in adults, indomethacin is eliminated via renal excretion, metabolism, and biliary excretion. Indomethacin undergoes appreciable enterohepatic circulation. The mean half-life of indomethacin is estimated to be about 4 to 5 hours. Indomethacin exists in the plasma as the parent drug and its desmethyl, desbenzoyl, and desmethyl-desbenzoyl metabolites, all in the unconjugated form. About 60% of an oral dosage is recovered in urine as drug and metabolites (26% as indomethacin and its glucuronide), and 33% is recovered in feces (1.5% as indomethacin). About 99% of indomethacin is bound to protein in plasma over the expected range of therapeutic plasma concentrations.

The percent bound in neonates has not been studied. In controlled trials in premature infants, however, no evidence of bilirubin displacement has been observed as evidenced by increased incidence of bilirubin encephalopathy (kernicterus).

Indications: To close hemodynamically significant patent ductus arteriosus in premature infants weighing between 500 and 1 750 g when after 48 hours usual medical management (e.g., fluid restriction, diuretics, digitalis, respiratory support) is ineffective. Clearcut clinical evidence of a hemodynamically significant patent ductus arteriosus should be present, such as respiratory distress, a continuous murmur, a hyperactive precordium, cardiomegaly and pulmonary plethora on chest x-ray.

Indomethacin is indicated to close patent ductus arteriosus in premature infants when usual medical management is ineffective.

Contraindications: Infants with proven or suspected infection that is untreated; infants who are bleeding, especially those with active intracranial hemorrhage or gastrointestinal bleeding; infants with thrombocytopenia; infants with coagulation defects; infants with or who are suspected of having necrotizing enterocolitis; infants with significant impairment of renal function; jaundiced infants with bilirubin ≥ 10 mg/dL or those with known hepatic diseases; in infants with congenital heart disease in whom patency of the ductus arteriosus is necessary for satisfactory pulmonary or systemic blood flow (e.g., pulmonary atresia, severe tetralogy of Fallot, severe coarctation of the aorta).

Warnings: Renal: Indomethacin may cause significant reduction in urine output (50% or more) with concomitant elevations of BUN and creatinine (≥ 1.8 mg/dL), and reductions in glomerular filtration rate and creatinine clearance (see Adverse Effects). Most of the renal abnormalities reported have been reversible but some fatalities occurred. However, because adequate renal function can depend upon renal prostaglandin synthesis, indomethacin, as a prostaglandin inhibitor, may precipitate renal insufficiency, including acute renal failure, especially in infants with other conditions that may adversely affect renal function (e.g., extracellular volume depletion from any cause, congestive heart failure, sepsis, concomitant use of any nephrotoxic drug, hepatic dysfunction). When significant suppression of urine volume occurs after a dose of indomethacin, no additional dose should be given until the urine output returns to normal levels (see Contraindications).

Indomethacin in preterm infants may suppress water excretion to a greater extent than sodium excretion. This may result in hyponatremia. Renal function and serum electrolytes should be monitored (see Dosage).

CNS: Prematurity per se, is associated with an increased incidence of spontaneous intracranial hemorrhage, however, because indomethacin inhibits platelet aggregation, the potential for intracranial bleeding may be increased. A number of intracranial hemorrhages have been reported in infants who received indomethacin. However, in one multi-center study involving 405 infants, the incidence of intracranial hemorrhage in babies treated with indomethacin was not significantly higher than in the control infants.

Gastrointestinal: Clinical results indicate that major gastrointestinal bleeding was no more common in those infants receiving indomethacin than in those infants on placebo. However, gastrointestinal bleeding (e.g., chemical detection of blood in stool) was more commonly noted in those infants treated with indomethacin. Severe gastrointestinal effects have been reported in adults with various arthritic disorders treated for a prolonged period with oral indomethacin.

The following have been reported with oral use of indomethacin in adults and could occur in infants on i.v. indomethacin: irritation of the gastrointestinal tract and single or multiple gastrointestinal ulcerations. Fatalities have been reported in some instances. Rarely, intestinal ulceration has been associated with stenosis and obstruction.

Because of the occurrence, and at times severity, of gastrointestinal reactions to indomethacin the prescribing physician must be continuously alert for any sign or symptom signaling a possible gastrointestinal reaction. The risks of continuing therapy with indomethacin in the face of such symptoms must be weighed against the possible benefits to the individual patient.

Precautions: Indomethacin may mask the usual signs and symptoms of infection. Therefore, the physician must be continually on the alert for this and should use the drug with extra care in the presence of existing controlled infection.

Severe hepatic reactions have been reported in adults treated for a prolonged period with oral indomethacin for arthritic disorders. If clinical signs and symptoms consistent with liver disease develop in the neonate, or if systemic manifestations occur, indomethacin should be discontinued.

Indomethacin, like other nonsteroidal anti-inflammatory agents, can inhibit platelet aggregation. Premature infants should be observed for signs of bleeding. Indomethacin has been shown to prolong bleeding time (but within the normal range) in normal adult subjects. This effect may be exaggerated in patients with underlying hemostatic defects (see Contraindications).

The drug should be administered carefully to avoid extravascular injection or leakage as the solution may be irritating to tissue.

Drug Interactions: Digitalis: Preterm infants with patent ductus arteriosus and associated cardiac failure are frequently treated with digitalis. The half-life of digitalis in preterm infants is generally prolonged, and renal function during therapy with indomethacin is often reduced. Where both drugs are used concomitantly, the infant should be observed closely; frequent ECGs and serum digitalis levels may be required to prevent or to detect digitalis toxicity early.

Furosemide: Therapy with indomethacin may decrease the natriuretic effect of furosemide.

Aminoglycosides: In one study of premature infants treated with indomethacin and also receiving either gentamicin or amikacin, both peak and trough levels were significantly elevated for both antibiotics.

Clinical studies in adults have shown that the administration of indomethacin can reduce the natriuretic and anti-hypertensive effects of furosemide and thiazides in some patients. This response has been attributed to inhibition of renal prostaglandin synthesis by nonsteroidal anti-inflammatory drugs. Therefore, when Indocid P.D.A. is added to the treatment of an infant receiving furosemide or thiazides, or furosemide or thiazides are added to the treatment of an infant receiving Indocid P.D.A., the patient should be observed closely to determine if the desired effect of furosemide or thiazides is obtained.

Adverse Effects: In a collaborative double-blind placebo-controlled trial of 405 premature infants weighing less than or equal to 1 750 g with evidence of large ductal shunting, there was a statistically significantly greater incidence of bleeding problems in those infants treated with indomethacin than in those treated with placebo. Specifically, these bleeding disorders included gross or microscopic bleeding into the gastrointestinal tract, oozing from the skin after needle puncture, pulmonary hemorrhage, microscopic hematuria and disseminated intravascular coagulopathy. There was no statistically significant difference between treatment groups with reference to intracranial (e.g., intraventricular) hemorrhage.

The infants treated with sterile indomethacin also had a significantly higher incidence of transient oliguria and hypercreatininemia (≥1.8 mg/dL) than did the infants treated with placebo.

The incidence of retrolental fibroplasia (grades III and IV) and pneumothorax in infants treated with indomethacin were no greater than in placebo controls and were statistically significantly lower than in surgically-treated infants.

The following additional adverse reactions in infants have been reported from the collaborative study, anecdotal case reports, and from other studies using rectal, oral, or i.v. indomethacin for treatment of patent ductus arteriosus.

Cardiovascular: pulmonary hypertension, intracranial bleeding.
Gastrointestinal: gastrointestinal bleeding, abdominal distension, vomiting, melena, transient ileus and localized perforation(s) of the small and/or large intestine.
Laboratory Findings: hyponatremia, elevated serum creatinine, elevated serum potassium, elevated BUN, decreased platelet aggregation, and reduction in blood sugar including hypoglycemia.
General: increased weight gain (fluid retention); exacerbation of infection.
Renal: renal dysfunction including one or more of the following: reduced urinary output; reduced urine sodium, chloride, or potassium, urine osmolality, free water clearance, or glomerular filtration rate; uremia.

The following adverse reactions have also been reported in infants treated with indomethacin, however, a causal relationship to therapy with indomethacin has not been established. Cardiovascular: bradycardia. Respiratory: apnea, exacerbation of pre-existing pulmonary infection. Hematologic: disseminated intravascular coagulation. Metabolic: acidosis/alkalosis. Gastrointestinal: necrotizing enterocolitis. Ophthalmic: retrolental fibroplasia.

For adverse effects which have been reported in adults, please consult the monograph for Indocid.

Dosage: For i.v. administration only.

Dosage recommendations for closure of the ductus arteriosus depends on the age of the infant at the time of therapy. A course of therapy is defined as from 1 up to 3 i.v. doses of indomethacin given at 12 to 24 hours intervals, with careful attention to urinary output. If anuria or marked oliguria (urinary output 0.6 mL/kg/hr) is evident at the scheduled time of the second or third dose, no additional doses should be given until laboratory studies indicate that renal function has returned to normal.

If severe adverse reactions occur, **stop the drug.**

Dosage according to age is shown in Table I.

Table I—Indocid P.D.A.

Dosages

Age at 1st dose	Dosage (mg/kg) 1st	2nd	3rd
<48 hours	0.2	0.1	0.1
2–7 days	0.2	0.2	0.2
Over 7 days	0.2	0.25	0.25

If the ductus arteriosus closes or is significantly reduced in size after an interval of 48 hours or more from completion of the first course of indomethacin, no further doses are necessary. If during continued medical management the ductus arteriosus re-opens, a second course of 1 to 3 doses may be given, each dose separated by a 12 to 24 hours interval as described above (in the U.S. collaborative study about 10% of the infants required a second course of therapy).

If the infant remains unresponsive to therapy with indomethacin after 2 courses, surgery may be necessary for closure of the ductus arteriosus.

Directions for Use: The solution may be prepared with 2 mL of preservative-free sterile sodium chloride injection 0.9% or sterile, preservative-free water for injection. **Benzyl alcohol as a preservative has been associated with toxicity in newborns.** Therefore, all diluents should be preservative-free. With 2 mL of diluent the concentration of the solution will equal approximately 0.05 mg/0.1 mL. Any unused portion of the solution should be discarded because there is no preservative contained in the vial. A fresh solution should be prepared just prior to each administration. Once reconstituted, the indomethacin solution may be injected i.v. over 5 to 10 seconds.

Parenteral drug products should be inspected visually for particulate matter and discoloration prior to administration whenever solution and container permit.

Further dilution with i.v. infusion solutions is not recommended. Indocid P.D.A. is not buffered, and reconstitution with solutions at pH values below 6.0 may result in precipitation of the insoluble indomethacin free acid moiety.

Supplied: Each single-dose vial of sterile, lyophilized powder contains: indomethacin sodium trihydrate equivalent to 1 mg indomethacin. Boxes of 3 as a white to yellow lyophilized cake or plug. Store at room temperature (15 to 30°C). Protect from light. Store vials in carton until contents have been used.

INDOTEC® 🄿
Technilab

Indomethacin

Nonsteroidal Anti-inflammatory—Analgesic

Pharmacology: Indomethacin is a nonsteroidal anti-inflammatory drug with marked analgesic, and antipyretic properties. It has a unique chemical structure, which differentiates it from the salicylates, corticosteroids, phenylbutazone-like compounds and colchicine. Unlike corticosteroids, it has no effect on pituitary or adrenal function.

Indomethacin is a potent inhibitor of prostaglandin synthesis in vitro. Concentrations are reached during therapy which have been demonstrated to have an in vivo effect as well.

Although indomethacin does not alter the course of the underlying disease, it has been found effective to relieve pain, reduce fever, swelling and tenderness, and increase mobility in patients with rheumatic diseases, including rheumatoid arthritis, ankylosing spondylitis, osteoarthritis and gout.

Pharmacokinetics: In man, indomethacin is readily absorbed, attaining peak plasma concentrations of about 1 and 2 μg/mL at approximately 2 hours following single oral doses of 25 and 50 mg, respectively. Ninety percent of the orally administered indomethacin is absorbed within 4 hours. The suppository formulation is more rapidly and completely absorbed than the oral dose of indomethacin. Thus, C_{max} after rectal administration is lower than after oral dosing. The mean half-life of indomethacin is estimated to be about 4.5 hours. With a typical therapeutic regimen of 25 or 50 mg t.i.d., the steady-state plasma concentrations of indomethacin are on average 1.4 times those following the first dose.

Indomethacin exists in the plasma as the parent drug and its desmethyl, desbenzoyl, and desmethyl-desbenzoyl metabolites, all in the unconjugated form. About 60% of an oral dosage is recovered in urine as drug and metabolites (26% as indomethacin and its glucuronide), and 33% is recovered in feces (1.5% as indomethacin).

About 90% of indomethacin is bound to protein in plasma over the expected range of therapeutic plasma concentration.

Indications: Indomethacin is not a simple analgesic, and its use should be limited to the conditions listed below, particularly those cases not responding to conservative measures.

Indomethacin has been found effective in the symptomatic treatment of: selected cases of rheumatoid arthritis; ankylosing (rheumatoid) spondylitis; gout; selected cases of severe osteoarthritis, including degenerative disease of the hip.

In these conditions indomethacin may on occasion replace other commonly used agents such as corticosteroids, salicylates, phenylbutazone-like compounds and colchicine.

Indomethacin suppositories are for those patients in whom rectal administration is preferred.

Rheumatoid Arthritis: Indomethacin may be used singly or in combination with other agents. However, it should not be used as a drug of first choice because of the adverse reactions that may occur with its use.

Best results (relief of pain, tenderness, swelling and stiffness) have been obtained in the acute episodes of the disease. However, in many patients with chronic rheumatoid arthritis, indomethacin will produce a significant lessening of pain and stiffness within 48 hours. In other patients, treatment must be continued longer before significant subjective relief or objective evidence of decreased joint swelling and tenderness occur. In some cases of chronic rheumatoid arthritis, it may be necessary to continue treatment for at least a month before concluding that it has not produced significant benefit. Use of indomethacin may enable reduction of steroid dosage in patients receiving corticosteroids. In such instances, the steroid dosage should be reduced slowly.

Ankylosing (Rheumatoid) Spondylitis: Indomethacin frequently produces marked relief of pain and improved motion of the spine within 3 to 10 days.

Osteoarthritis: Indomethacin should be used in those cases of severe osteoarthritis which do not respond to treatment with other drugs such as the salicylates. In many cases prompt relief of pain is obtained.

Degenerative Joint Disease (Osteoarthritis) of the Hip: Indomethacin may be used to provide relief of pain and increased range of motion in patients with degenerative joint disease of the hip.

Indotec (cont'd)

Gout: In acute attacks of gout the response to indomethacin is usually rapid and often dramatic. Marked reduction of pain may be obtained within 2 to 4 hours. Tenderness and heat subside within 24 to 36 hours, and swelling decreases over a 3- to 5-day period.

Contraindications: Active peptic ulcer, a history of recurrent ulceration or active inflammatory disease of the gastrointestinal system.

Known or suspected hypersensitivity to the drug or other NSAIDs. The potential for cross-reactivity between different NSAIDs must be kept in mind.

Indomethacin should not be used in patients with the complete or partial syndrome of nasal polyps, or in whom asthma, anaphylaxis, urticaria, rhinitis or other allergic manifestations are precipitated by ASA or other NSAIDs. Fatal anaphylactoid reactions have occurred in such individuals. As well, individuals with the above medical problems are at risk of a severe reaction even if they have taken NSAIDs in the past without any adverse effects.

Significant hepatic impairment or active liver disease.

Severely impaired or deteriorating renal function (creatinine clearance <30 mL/minute). Individuals with lesser degrees of renal impairment are at risk of deterioration of their renal function when prescribed NSAIDs and must be monitored.

Indomethacin is not recommended for use with other NSAIDs because of the absence of any evidence demonstrating synergistic benefits and the potential for additive side effects.

Indomethacin suppositories are contraindicated in subjects with a recent history of rectal bleeding or proctitis.

Warnings: Gastrointestinal System: Serious gastrointestinal toxicity, such as peptic ulceration, perforation and gastrointestinal bleeding, **sometimes severe and occasionally fatal** can occur at any time, with or without symptoms in patients treated with NSAIDs including indomethacin.

Minor upper gastrointestinal problems, such as dyspepsia, are common, usually developing early in therapy. Physicians should remain alert for ulceration and bleeding in patients treated with NSAIDs, even in the absence of previous gastrointestinal tract symptoms.

In patients observed in clinical trials of such agents, symptomatic upper gastrointestinal ulcers, gross bleeding, or perforation appear to occur in approximately 1% of patients treated for 3 to 6 months and in about 2 to 4% of patients treated for 1 year. The risk continues beyond 1 year and possibly increases.

The incidence of these complications increases with increasing dose.

Indomethacin should be given under close medical supervision to patients prone to gastrointestinal tract irritation, particularly those with a history of peptic ulcer, diverticulosis or other inflammatory disease of the gastrointestinal tract such as ulcerative colitis and Crohn's disease. In these cases, the physician must weigh the benefits of treatment against the possible hazards.

Physicians should inform patients about the signs and/or symptoms of serious gastrointestinal toxicity and instruct them to contact a physician immediately if they experience persistent dyspepsia or other symptoms or signs suggestive of gastrointestinal ulceration or bleeding.

Because serious gastrointestinal tract ulceration and bleeding can occur without warning symptoms, physicians should follow chronically treated patients by checking their hemoglobin periodically and by being vigilant for the signs and symptoms of ulceration and bleeding and should inform the patients of the importance of this follow-up.

If ulceration is suspected or confirmed, or if gastrointestinal bleeding occurs, indomethacin should be discontinued immediately, appropriate treatment instituted and the patient monitored closely.

No studies, to date, have identified any group of patients **not** at risk of developing ulceration and bleeding. A prior history of serious gastrointestinal events and other factors such as excess alcohol intake, smoking, age, female gender and concomitant oral steroid and anticoagulant use have been associated with increased risk.

Studies to date show that all NSAIDs can cause gastrointestinal tract adverse events. Although existing data does not clearly identify differences in risk between various NSAIDs, this may be shown in the future.

Geriatrics: Patients older than 65 years and frail or debilitated patients are most susceptible to a variety of adverse reactions from NSAIDs; the incidence of these adverse reactions increases with dose and duration of treatment. In addition, these patients are less tolerant to ulceration and bleeding. Most reports of fatal gastrointestinal events are in this population. Older patients are also at risk of lower esophageal ulceration and bleeding.

For such patients, consideration should be given to a starting dose lower than the one usually recommended, with individual adjustment when necessary and under close supervision (see Precautions).

Cross-sensitivity: Patients sensitive to any one of the NSAIDs may also be sensitive to any of the other NSAIDs.

Aseptic Meningitis: In occasional cases, with some NSAIDs, the symptoms of aseptic meningitis (stiff neck, severe headaches, nausea and vomiting, fever or clouding of consciousness) have been observed. Patients with autoimmune disorders (systemic lupus erythematosus, mixed connective tissue diseases, etc.) seem to be predisposed. Therefore, in such patients, the physician must be vigilant to the development of this complication.

Pregnancy, Labor and *Lactation:* The known effects of drugs of this class on the human fetus during the third trimester of pregnancy are closure of the ductus arteriosis, platelet dysfunction with resultant bleeding, renal dysfunction or failure with oligohydramnios, gastrointestinal bleeding or perforation and myocardial degenerative changes.

Administration of indomethacin is therefore not recommended during pregnancy or in nursing mothers.

Children: **The drug should not be prescribed for children as safe conditions for use have not been established. In a few cases of severe juvenile rheumatoid arthritis, where indomethacin was given along with other drugs, severe reactions, including fatalities, were reported.**

Other: Occupational Hazards: Patients should be warned that they may experience dizziness and in this event should not operate motor vehicles and should avoid potentially dangerous activities which require alertness.

Indomethacin should be used with caution in patients with psychiatric disturbances, epilepsy, or parkinsonism, since it may, in some instances, aggravate these conditions.

Precautions: Gastrointestinal: There is no definitive evidence that the concomitant administration of histamine H_2-receptor antagonists and/or antacids will either prevent the occurrence of gastrointestinal side effects or allow the continuation of indomethacin therapy when and if these adverse reactions appear.

Indomethacin, both capsules and suppositories, should be used with caution because of the gastrointestinal reactions which may occur. The gastrointestinal effects may be decreased by giving the oral formulations of the drug immediately after meals, with food or with antacids. The risk of continuing therapy with indomethacin in the face of such symptoms must be weighed against the possible benefits to the individual patient. Indomethacin suppositories should be given with caution to patients with any anal or rectal pathology.

Studies in normal subjects with radioactive chromate-tagged red blood cells indicate that large doses of indomethacin (50 mg 4 times a day) produce less fecal blood loss than average doses of ASA (600 mg 4 times a day). Indomethacin however may cause single or multiple ulceration of the stomach, duodenum, or small and large intestine. There have been reports of severe bleeding and of perforation with a few fatalities. Patients may also develop gastrointestinal bleeding with no obvious ulcer formation. If gastrointestinal bleeding occurs, the drug should be discontinued. In many patients with peptic ulceration, a history of a previous ulcer was present or they were on concomitant steroids, salicylates or phenylbutazone. A possible potentiation of the ulcerogenic effect of these drugs cannot be ruled out at present. In some patients there was no history of a previous ulcer and other drugs were not being given. As a result of obvious or occult gastrointestinal bleeding some patients may manifest anemia. For this reason appropriate blood determinations are recommended periodically.

Renal Function: Long-term administration of NSAIDs to animals has resulted in renal papillary necrosis and other abnormal renal pathology. In humans, there have been reports of acute interstitial nephritis with hematuria, proteinuria, and occasionally nephrotic syndrome.

A second form of renal toxicity has been seen in patients with prerenal conditions leading to the reduction in renal blood flow or blood volume, where the renal prostaglandins have a supportive role in the maintenance of renal perfusion. In these patients, administration of a NSAID may cause a dose-dependent reduction in prostaglandin formation and may precipitate overt renal decompensation. Patients at greatest risk of this reaction are those with impaired renal function, heart failure, liver dysfunction, those taking diuretics, and the elderly. Discontinuation of nonsteroidal anti-inflammatory therapy is usually followed by recovery to the pretreatment state.

Indomethacin and its metabolites are eliminated primarily by the kidneys; therefore, the drug should be used with great caution in patients with impaired renal function. In these cases, utilization of lower doses of indomethacin should be considered and patients carefully monitored.

During long-term therapy kidney function should be monitored periodically.

Increases in serum potassium concentration, including hyperkalemia, have been reported, even in some patients without renal impairment. In patients with normal renal function, these effects have been attributed to a hyporeninemic-hypoaldosteronism state (see Drug Interactions).

Since indomethacin is eliminated primarily by the kidneys, patients with significantly impaired renal function should be closely monitored; a lower daily dosage should be used to avoid excessive drug accumulation.

Genitourinary Tract: Some NSAIDs are known to cause persistent urinary symptoms (bladder pain, dysuria, urinary frequency), hematuria or cystitis. The onset of these symptoms may occur at any time after the initiation of therapy with an NSAID. Some cases have become severe on continued treatment. Should urinary symptoms occur, treatment with indomethacin **must be stopped immediately** to obtain recovery. This should be done before any urological investigations or treatments are carried out.

Hepatic Function: As with other NSAIDs, borderline elevations of one or more liver function tests may occur in up to 15% of patients. These abnormalities may progress, may remain essentially unchanged, or may be transient with continued therapy. Significant (3 times the upper limit of normal) elevations of ALT or AST occurred in controlled clinical trials in less than 1% of patients receiving therapy with NSAIDs. A patient with symptoms and/or signs suggesting liver dysfunction, or in whom an abnormal liver test has occurred, should be evaluated for evidence of the development of more severe hepatic reaction while on therapy with this drug. Severe hepatic reactions including jaundice and cases of fatal hepatitis have been reported with NSAIDs.

Although such reactions are rare, if abnormal liver tests persist or worsen, if clinical signs and symptoms consistent with liver disease develop, or if systemic manifestations occur (e.g., eosinophilia, rash, etc.), this drug should be discontinued.

During long-term therapy, liver function tests should be monitored periodically. If there is a need to prescribe this drug in the presence of impaired liver function, it must be done under strict observation.

Fluid and Electrolyte Balance: Fluid retention and edema have been observed in patients treated with indomethacin. Therefore, as with many other NSAIDs, the possibility of precipitating congestive heart failure in elderly patients or those with compromised cardiac function should be borne in mind. Indomethacin should be used with caution in patients with heart failure, hypertension or other conditions predisposing to fluid retention.

With nonsteroidal anti-inflammatory treatment there is a potential risk of hyperkalemia, particularly in patients with conditions such as diabetes mellitus or renal failure; elderly patients; or in patients receiving concomitant therapy with β-adrenergic blockers, angiotensin converting enzyme inhibitors or some diuretics. Serum electrolytes should be monitored periodically during long-term therapy, especially in those patients who are at risk.

Hematology: Drugs inhibiting prostaglandin biosynthesis do interfere with platelet function to varying degrees; therefore, patients who may be adversely affected by such an action should be carefully observed when indomethacin is administered.

Blood dyscrasias (such as neutropenia, leukopenia, thrombocytopenia, aplastic anemia and agranulocytosis) associated with the use of NSAIDs are rare, but could occur with severe consequences.

Indomethacin, like other NSAIDs, can inhibit platelet aggregation. This effect is of shorter duration than that seen with ASA and usually disappears within 24 hours after discontinuation of indomethacin. Indomethacin has been shown to prolong bleeding time (but within the normal range) in normal subjects. Because this effect may be exaggerated in patients with underlying hemostatic defects, indomethacin should be used with caution in persons with coagulation defects.

Infection: In common with other anti-inflammatory drugs, indomethacin may mask the usual signs of infection.

Ophthalmology: Blurred and/or diminished vision has been reported with the use of indomethacin and other NSAIDs. If such symptoms develop, this drug should be discontinued and an ophthalmologic examination performed; ophthalmic examination should be carried out at periodic intervals in any patient receiving this drug for an extended period of time.

CNS: Some patients may experience drowsiness, dizziness, vertigo, insomnia or depression with the use of indomethacin. If patients experience these side effects, they should exercise caution in carrying out activities that require alertness.

Headaches may occur, usually early in treatment with indomethacin. If headaches persist despite dosage reduction, therapy with indomethacin should be discontinued (see Warnings).

Hypersensitivity Reactions: Patients should be followed carefully to detect unusual manifestations of drug sensitivity, and since advancing years appear to increase the possibility of adverse reactions, indomethacin should be used with greater care in the elderly.

Drug Interactions: ASA or other NSAIDs: The use of indomethacin in addition to any other NSAID, including those over the counter ones (such as ASA and ibuprofen) is not recommended due to the possibility of additive side effects.

Controlled clinical studies have shown that the combined used of indomethacin and ASA does not produce any greater therapeutic effect than the use of indomethacin alone. Furthermore, in one of these clinical studies, the incidence of gastrointestinal side effects was significantly increased with combined therapy.

In a study in normal volunteers, it was found that chronic concurrent administration of 3.6 g of ASA/day decreases indomethacin blood levels approximately 20%.

Digoxin: Indomethacin given concomitantly with digoxin has been reported to increase the serum concentration and prolong the half-life of digoxin. Therefore, when indomethacin and digoxin are used concomitantly, serum digoxin levels should be closely monitored.

Anticoagulants: Numerous studies have shown that the concomitant use of NSAIDs and anticoagulants increases the risk of gastrointestinal adverse events such as ulceration and bleeding.

Because prostaglandins play an important role in hemostasis, and NSAIDs affect platelet function, concurrent therapy of indomethacin with warfarin requires close monitoring to be certain that no change in anticoagulant dosage is necessary.

Clinical studies have shown that indomethacin did not influence the hypoprothrombinemia produced by the use of anticoagulants in patients and in normal subjects. However, when any additional drug, including indomethacin is added to the treatment of patients on anticoagulant therapy, the patient should be observed closely for alterations of the prothrombin time.

Oral Hypoglycemics: Indomethacin and hypoglycemic agents should not be used concomitantly.

Diuretics: In some patients, the administration of indomethacin can reduce the diuretic, natriuretic, and antihypertensive effects of loop, potassium-sparing, and thiazide diuretics. Therefore, when indomethacin and diuretics are used concomitantly, the patient should be observed closely to determine if the desired effect of the diuretic is obtained.

Indomethacin reduces basal plasma renin activity (PRA), as well as those elevations of PRA induced by furosemide administration, or salt or volume depletion. These facts should be considered when evaluating plasma renin activity in hypertensive agents.

It has been reported that the addition of triamterene to a maintenance schedule of indomethacin resulted in reversible acute renal failure in 2 of 4 healthy volunteers. Indomethacin and triamterene should not be administered together.

Indomethacin and potassium-sparing diuretics each may be associated with increased serum potassium levels. The potential effects of indomethacin and potassium-sparing diuretics on potassium kinetics and renal function should be considered when these agents are administered concurrently.

Most of the above effects concerning diuretics have been attributed, at least in part, to mechanisms involving inhibition of prostaglandin synthesis by indomethacin.

Antihypertensives: Coadministration of indomethacin and some antihypertensive agents has resulted in an attenuation of the latter's hypotensive effect acutely, due at least in part to indomethacin's inhibition of prostaglandin synthesis. Caution should be exercised when considering the addition of indomethacin to the regimen of a patient taking one of the following antihypertensive agents; an alpha-adrenergic blocking agent (such as prazosin), an angiotensin converting enzyme inhibitor (such as captopril or lisinopril), a beta adrenergic blocking agent, a diuretic (see Diuretics), or hydralazine.

A decrease in the antihypertensive effect of beta-adrenergic receptor blocking agents by NSAIDs including indomethacin has been reported. Therefore, when using a beta-blocking agent to treat hypertension, patients should be observed carefully in order to confirm that the desired therapeutic effect has been obtained.

Glucocorticoids: Numerous studies have shown that the concomitant use of NSAIDs and oral glucocorticoids increases the risk of gastrointestinal side effects such as ulceration and bleeding. This is especially the case in older (>65 years of age) individuals.

Methotrexate: Caution should be used if indomethacin is administered simultaneously with methotrexate. Indomethacin has been reported to decrease the tubular secretion of methotrexate and to potentiate toxicity.

Lithium: Indomethacin 50 mg t.i.d. produced a clinically relevant elevation of plasma lithium and reduction in renal lithium clearance in psychiatric patients and normal subjects with steady-state plasma lithium concentrations. This effect has been attributed to inhibition of prostaglandin synthesis resulting in renal vasoconstriction and decreased lithium excretion. As a consequence, when indomethacin and lithium are given concomitantly, the patient should be carefully observed for signs of lithium toxicity. (Read the product monographs for the appropriate lithium preparation before use of such concomitant therapy). In addition, the frequency of monitoring serum lithium concentration should be increased at the outset of such combination drug treatment.

Other Drug Interactions: Cyclosporine: Administration of NSAIDs concomitantly with cyclosporine has been associated with an increase in cyclosporine-induced toxicity, possibly due to decreased synthesis of renal prostacyclin. NSAIDs should be used with caution in patients taking cyclosporine, and renal function should be monitored carefully.

Diflunisal: The combined used of indomethacin and diflunisal has been associated with fatal gastrointestinal hemorrhage. The coadministration of diflunisal and indomethacin results in an increase of about 30 to 35% in indomethacin plasma levels and a concomitant decrease in renal clearance of indomethacin and its conjugate. Therefore, indomethacin and diflunisal should not be used concomitantly.

Probenecid: When indomethacin is given to patients receiving probenecid, the plasma levels of indomethacin are likely to be increased. Therefore, a lower total daily dosage of indomethacin may produce a therapeutic effect. When increases in the dose of indomethacin are made under these circumstances, they should be made cautiously and in small increments.

Phenylpropanolamine: Hypertensive crises have been reported due to oral phenylpropanolamine alone and rarely to phenylpropanolamine given with indomethacin. This additive effect is probably due at least in part to indomethacin's inhibition of prostaglandin synthesis. Caution should be exercised when indomethacin and phenylpropanolamine are administered concomitantly.

Clinical Laboratory Tests: False-negative results in the dexamethasone suppression test (DST) in patients being treated with indomethacin have been reported. Thus, results of the DST should be interpreted with caution in these patients.

Adverse Effects: The most common adverse reactions encountered with NSAIDs are gastrointestinal, of which peptic ulcer, with or without bleeding, is the most severe. Fatalities have occurred, particularly in the elderly.

The following adverse reactions for capsules have been arranged into 2 groups: (1) incidence greater than 1%; and (2) incidence less than 1%. The incidence for group (1) was obtained from 33 double-blind controlled clinical trials reported in the literature (1 092 patients). The incidence for group (2) was based on reports in clinical trials, in the literature, and on voluntary reports since marketing. The probability of a causal relationship exists between indomethacin and these adverse reactions, some of which have been reported only rarely (see Table I on following page).

In controlled clinical trials, the incidence of adverse reactions to indomethacin SR capsule and equal 24-hour doses of indomethacin capsules were similar.

The adverse reactions reported with indomethacin capsules may occur with use of the suppositories. In addition, rectal irritation and tenesmus have been reported in patients who have received the suppositories.

Gastrointestinal: Incidence >1%: nausea* with or without vomiting; dyspepsia* (including indigestion, heartburn and epigastric pain); diarrhea; abdominal distress or pain; constipation.

Incidence < 1%: anorexia; bloating (includes distention); flatulence; peptic ulcer; gastroenteritis; rectal bleeding; proctitis; single and multiple ulcerations, including perforation and hemorrhage of the esophagus, stomach, duodenum or small or large intestines; intestinal ulceration associated with stenosis and obstruction; gastrointestinal bleeding without obvious ulcer formation and perforation of pre-existing sigmoid lesions (diverticulum, carcinoma, etc.); development of ulcerative colitis and regional ileitis; ulcerative stomatitis; toxic hepatitis and jaundice (some fatal cases have been reported).

CNS: Incidence >1%: headache; dizziness*; vertigo; somnolence; depression and fatigue (including malaise and listlessness).

Incidence < 1%: anxiety (includes nervousness); muscle weakness; involuntary muscle movements; insomnia; muzziness; psychic disturbances including psychotic episode; mental confusion; drowsiness, lightheadedness; syncope; paresthesia; aggravation of epilepsy and parkinsonism; depersonalization; coma; peripheral neuropathy; convulsions; dysarthria.

Dermatologic: Incidence >1%: none.

Incidence <1%: pruritus; rash; urticaria; petechiae or ecchymosis; exfoliative dermatitis; erythema nodosum; loss of hair; Stevens-Johnson syndrome; erythema multiforme; toxic epidermal necrolysis.

Cardiovascular: Incidence >1%: none.

Incidence <1%: hypertension; hypotension; tachycardia; chest pain; congestive heart failure; arrhythmia; palpitations.

Special Senses: Incidence >1%: tinnitus.

Incidence <1%: Ocular-corneal deposits and retinal disturbances including those of the macula, have been reported in some patients on prolonged therapy with indomethacin; blurred vision, diplopia; hearing disturbances, deafness.

Hematologic: Incidence >1%: none.

Incidence <1%: leukopenia; bone marrow depression; anemia secondary to obvious or occult gastrointestinal bleeding; aplastic anemia; hemolytic anemia; agranulocytosis; thrombocytopenic purpura; disseminated intravascular coagulation.

Genitourinary: Incidence >1%: none.

Incidence <1%: hematuria; vaginal bleeding; proteinuria; nephrotic syndrome; interstitial nephritis; BUN elevation; renal insufficiency, including renal failure.

Hypersensitivity: Incidence >1%: none.

Incidence <1%: acute anaphylaxis; acute respiratory distress; rapid fall in blood pressure resembling a shock-like state; angioedema; dyspnea; asthma; purpura; angiitis; pulmonary edema.

Metabolic: Incidence >1%: none.

Incidence <1%: edema; weight gain; fluid retention; flushing or sweating; hyperglycemia; glycosuria; hyperkalemia.

Miscellaneous: Incidence >1%: none.

Incidence <1%: epistaxis; breast changes, including enlargment and tenderness, or gynecomastia.

*Reactions occurring in 3 to 9% of patients treated with indomethacin. (Those reactions occurring in less than 3% of the patients are unmarked.)

The following local adverse reactions have been associated with the use of indomethacin suppositories: tenesmus, proctitis, rectal bleeding, burning, pain, discomfort and itching.

The following additional side effects have been reported; however a causal relationship to therapy with indomethacin has not been established.

Cardiovascular: thrombophlebitis.

Hematologic: Although there have been several reports of leukemia, the supporting information is weak.

Genitourinary: urinary frequency.

Overdose: Symptoms: Relatively little experience is available recording overdosage with indomethacin. Nausea, vomiting, intense headache, dizziness, mental confusion, disorientation, or lethargy may be observed. There have been reports of paresthesia, numbness, and convulsions. Signs of gastrointestinal hemorrhage could appear but have not been reported following the acute ingestion of large amounts of indomethacin accidentally or intentionally.

Treatment: Symptomatic and supportive treatment include emptying the stomach as quickly as possible by emesis or lavage if the ingestion is recent. If vomiting has not occurred spontaneously, the patient should be induced to vomit with syrup of ipecac. If the patient is unable to vomit, gastric lavage should be performed. Once the stomach has been emptied, 25 or 50 g of activated charcoal may be given. Depending on the condition of the patient, close medical observation and nursing care may be required. The patient should be followed for several days because gastrointestinal ulceration and hemorrhage have been reported as adverse reactions of indomethacin. Use of antacids may be helpful.

Dosage: In chronic disorders, treatment should be started with a dosage of 25 mg 2 or 3 times a day. By starting therapy with low dosage, increased gradually when necessary, maximum benefit will be produced with fewer adverse reactions.

Always give indomethacin with food, immediately after meals, or with antacids to reduce gastric irritation.

Indotec (cont'd)

Table I—Indotec

Tabulation of Frequency of Adverse Reactions

Body System	Frequency of Adverse Reactions	
	Frequent (Incidence >1%)	**Rare (Incidence <1%)**
Gastrointestinal	Nausea* with or without vomiting; dyspepsia* (including indigestion, heartburn and epigastric pain), diarrhea, abdominal distress or pain, constipation.	Anorexia; bloating (including distention); flatulence; peptic ulcer; gastroenteritis; rectal bleeding; proctitis; single and multiple ulcerations, including perforation and hemorrhage of the esophagus, stomach, duodenum or small or large intestines; intestinal ulceration associated with stenosis and obstruction; gastrointestinal bleeding without obvious ulcer formation and perforation of pre-existing sigmoid lesions (diverticulum, carcinoma, etc.); development of ulcerative colitis and regional ileitis; ulcerative stomatitis; toxic hepatitis and jaundice (some fatal cases have been reported).
CNS	Headache; dizziness*; vertigo; somnolence; depression and fatigue (including malaise and listlessness).	Anxiety (includes nervousness); muscle weakness; involuntary muscle movements; insomnia; muzziness; psychic disturbances including psychotic episode; mental confusion; drowsiness; lightheadedness; syncope; paresthesia; aggravation of epilepsy and parkinsonism; depersonalization; coma; peripheral neuropathy; convulsions; dysarthria.
Dermatologic	None.	Pruritus; rash; urticaria; petechiae or ecchymosis; exfoliative dermatitis; erythema nodosum; loss of hair; Stevens-Johnson syndrome; erythema multiforme; toxic epidermal necrolysis.
Cardiovascular	None.	Hypertension; hypotension; tachycardia; chest pain; congestive heart failure; arrhythmia; palpitations.
Special Senses	Tinnitus.	Ocular-corneal deposits and retinal disturbances including those of the macula, have been reported in some patients on prolonged therapy with indomethacin; blurred vision; diplopia; hearing disturbances; deafness.
Hematologic	None.	Leukopenia; bone marrow depression; anemia secondary to obvious or occult gastrointestinal bleeding; aplastic anemia; hemolytic anemia; agranulocytosis; thrombocytopenic purpura; disseminated intravascular coagulation.
Genitourinary	None.	Hematuria; vaginal bleeding; proteinuria; nephrotic syndrome; interstitial nephritis; BUN elevation; renal insufficiency, including renal failure.
Hypersensitivity	None.	Acute anaphylaxis; acute respiratory distress; rapid fall in blood pressure resembling a shock-like state; angioedema; dyspnea; asthma; purpura; angiitis; pulmonary edema.
Metabolic	None.	Edema; weight gain; fluid retention; flushing or sweating; hyperglycemia; glycosuria; hyperkalemia.
Miscellaneous	None.	Epistaxis; breast changes, including enlargement and tenderness or gynecomastia.

*Reactions occurring in 3 to 9% of patients treated with indomethacin. (Those reactions occurring in less than 3% of the patients are unmarked.)

As with all drugs, the lowest possible effective dose should be utilized for each individual patient.

Children: The drug should not be prescribed for children because safe conditions for use have not been established.

Geriatrics: Since advancing years appear to increase the possibility of adverse reactions, indomethacin should be used with greater care in the elderly.

Adult Dosage Recommendations: Rheumatoid Arthritis and Ankylosing (Rheumatoid) Spondylitis: Initial Dosage: 25 mg 2 or 3 times a day. If the response is not adequate, increase the daily dosage by 25 mg at about weekly intervals until a satisfactory response is obtained or a dosage of 150 to 200 mg/day is reached. If a satisfactory response is not obtained with 200 mg a day, larger doses probably will not be effective.

If adverse reactions develop as the dosage is increased, reduce the dosage to a tolerated level and maintain this for 3 to 4 weeks. If an adequate response has not been obtained, gradually increase the daily dosage by 25 mg at about weekly intervals to 150 to 200 mg daily.

For patients with acute rheumatoid arthritis or with acute flares of chronic rheumatoid arthritis, increase the dosage daily by 25 mg until a satisfactory response is obtained or a total daily dosage of 150 to 200 mg is reached. If adverse effects develop as the dosage is increased, the dosage should be reduced to a tolerated level for 2 or 3 days, and then, gradually increased by 25 mg every few days as tolerated. After the acute phase is under control, it is often possible to reduce the daily dosage gradually to 75 to 100 mg.

Reduction of Steroid Dosage: Use of indomethacin often will permit a gradual reduction of steroid dosage by 25 to 50%. In some patients, steroids can be slowly discontinued over a period of several weeks or months. The usual precautions should be observed in withdrawing steroids.

Severe Osteoarthritis and Degenerative Joint Disease of the Hip: Initial dosage: 25 mg 2 or 3 times a day. If the response is not adequate, increase the daily dosage by 25 mg at about weekly intervals until a satisfactory response is obtained or a dosage of 150 to 200 mg a day is reached. If a satisfactory response is not obtained with 200 mg a day, larger doses will probably not be effective.

If adverse reactions develop as the dosage is increased, reduce the dosage to a tolerated level and maintain this for 3 to 4 weeks. If an adequate response has not then been obtained, gradually increase the daily dosage by 25 mg at about weekly intervals to 150 to 200 mg daily.

Gout: To control acute attacks: 50 mg 3 times a day until all signs and symptoms subside. Definite relief of pain has been reported within 2 to 4 hours. Tenderness and heat usually subside in 24 to 36 hours, and swelling gradually disappears in 3 to 5 days.

Use of Alternate Dosage Forms: Suppositories: The recommended dosage is 100 to 200 mg daily and should be individually adjusted to the patient's response and tolerance. Daily dose of 100 mg can be given as 50 mg twice daily or as 100 mg at night. Doses higher than 100 mg must be given on a twice daily schedule.

Combined administration: One 50 mg or 100 mg suppository at bedtime, supplemented the following day by 25 mg capsules as needed up to a total of 150 mg to 200 mg of indomethacin. The total daily dose of indomethacin (capsules and suppositories) should not exceed 200 mg.

Children: Indomethacin should not be prescribed for children because safe conditions for use have not been established (see Warnings).

Information for the Patient: See Blue Section—Information for the Patient "Indotec".

Supplied: Capsules: 25 mg: Each opaque blue and white capsule imprinted with INDOTEC 25 and "TEC" contains: indomethacin 25 mg. Nonmedicinal ingredients: black iron oxide, colloidal silicon dioxide, D&C yellow #10 aluminum lake, FD&C blue #1 aluminum lake, FD&C blue #2 aluminum lake, FD&C red #3, FD&C red #40 aluminum lake, gelatin, lactose, magnesium stearate, microcrystalline cellulose, pregelatinized cornstarch, shellac, silicon dioxide, sodium lauryl sulfate and titanium dioxide. Gluten- and tartrazine-free. Bottles of 100, 500 and 1 000. Store between 15 and 30°C. Protect from light and moisture. Store in a tight container.

50 mg: Each opaque blue and white capsule, imprinted with INDOTEC 50 and "TEC" contains: indomethacin 50 mg. Nonmedicinal ingredients: black iron oxide, colloidal silicon dioxide, D&C yellow #10 aluminum lake, FD&C blue #1 aluminum lake, FD&C blue #2 aluminum lake, FD&C red #3, FD&C red #40 aluminum lake, gelatin, lactose, magnesium stearate, microcrystalline cellulose, pregelatinized cornstarch, shellac, silicon dioxide, sodium lauryl sulfate and titanium dioxide. Gluten- and tartrazine-free. Bottles of 100 and 500. Store between 15 and 30°C. Protect from light and moisture. Store in a tight container.

Suppositories: 50 mg: Each torpedo-shaped, smooth surface, yellowish-white suppository contains: indomethacin 50 mg. Nonmedicinal ingredients: butylated hydroxyanisole, butylated hydroxytoluene, EDTA, glycerin, polyethylene glycol and sodium chloride. Boxes of 30. Store below 30°C. Protect from light and elevated humidity. Keep away from excessive heat. Preserve in well-closed containers, at controlled room temperature.

100 mg: Each torpedo-shaped, smooth surface, yellowish-white suppository contains: indomethacin 100 mg. Nonmedicinal ingredients: butylated hydroxyanisole, butylated hydroxytoluene, EDTA, glycerin, polyethylene glycol and sodium chloride. Boxes of 30. Store below 30°C. Protect from light and elevated humidity. Keep away from excessive heat. Preserve in well-closed containers, at controlled room temperature.

Reviewed 1999

INFANTOL®

Carter Horner

Multivitamins

Dietary Supplement

Supplied: Drops: Each 0.5 mL of flavored, light golden brown, clear, fat free, water soluble liquid contains: vitamin A 1 600 IU (as palmitate), vitamin D 400 IU, vitamin B_1 1.25 mg, riboflavin 2 mg (as riboflavin 5′-phosphate sodium), ascorbic acid 50 mg, niacinamide 12.5 mg and vitamin B_6 1.2 mg. Nonmedicinal ingredients: corn oil, flavor, glycerin, paraben, polysorbate, propylene glycol, sodium benzoate, sodium cyclamate, sorbitol and tocopherol. pH: 3.4 to 3.6. Energy: 5.9 kJ (1.4 kcal)/0.5 mL. Sodium: <1 mmol (1.5 mg). Alcohol-, gluten- and tartrazine-free. Dropper bottles of 30 mL.

Liquid: Each 5 mL of yellow, opaque, viscous, citrus flavored, water miscible liquid contains: vitamin A 1 600 IU (as palmitate), vitamin B_1 1.25 mg, riboflavin 2 mg (as riboflavin 5′-phosphate sodium), ascorbic acid 80 mg, vitamin D 400 IU, niacinamide 10 mg and vitamin B_6 1.2 mg. Nonmedicinal ingredients: alcohol, corn oil, flavors, parabens, polysorbate, sodium cyclamate, sorbitol, simethicone, tocopherol and xanthan gum. Hydrochloric acid and sodium hydroxide to adjust the pH. pH: 3.9 to 4.1. Energy: 24.3 kJ (5.8 kcal)/5 mL. Sodium: <1 mmol (7 mg). Gluten- and tartrazine-free. Bottles of 350 mL.

INFLAMASE® FORTE Ⓟ
INFLAMASE® MILD Ⓟ

CIBA Vision

Prednisolone Sodium Phosphate

Ophthalmic Anti-inflammatory

Supplied: Inflamase Forte (1%): Each bottle contains: prednisolone sodium phosphate 10 mg/mL (equivalent to 9.1 mg of prednisolone phosphate or 8 mg prednisolone) in a sterile aqueous solution. Nonmedicinal ingredients: benzalkonium chloride 0.01% w/v (preservative), dibasic sodium phosphate, disodium edetate, monobasic sodium phosphate, purified water and sodium chloride. Plastic squeeze bottles of 5 and 10 mL with dropper tip.

Inflamase Mild (1/8%): Each bottle contains: prednisolone sodium phosphate 1.25 mg/mL (equivalent to 1.14 mg of prednisolone phosphate or 1 mg prednisolone) in a sterile aqueous solution. Nonmedicinal ingredients: benzalkonium chloride 0.01% w/v (preservative), dibasic sodium phosphate, disodium edetate, monobasic sodium phosphate, purified water and sodium chloride. Plastic squeeze bottles of 5 mL with dropper tip.

Store at 15 to 30°C. Protect from light. Keep bottle tightly closed when not in use.

INFUFER® ℞

Sabex

Iron Dextran

Hematinic—Iron Supplement

Pharmacology: After i.m. injection, iron dextran is absorbed from the injection site into the capillaries and the lymphatic system. Circulating iron dextran is dissociated by the reticuloendothelial system. The ferric iron is transported by transferrin and incorporated into hemoglobin and storage sites. Only traces of unmetabolized iron dextran are excreted in urine, bile or feces. The drug is negligibly removed by hemodialysis. Most of the i.m. injection of iron dextran is absorbed within 72 hours, with the remainder absorbed over 3 to 4 weeks.

The half-life of i.v. administered [^{59}Fe] iron dextran to iron deficient subjects has ranged from 5 hours to more than 20 hours; however, these values do not represent loss of iron from the body, and accumulation of iron to potentially toxic levels should be avoided.

Iron status following iron dextran administration by i.v. infusion was assessed in 8 chronic hemodialysis patients (3 female, 5 male; mean age 54±9.9 years) not receiving parenteral iron or r-HuEPO (recombinant human erythropoietin) therapy within the previous 8 weeks. Iron dextran was administered in doses of 100 mg diluted in 100 mL of NaCl 0.9%, during the last hour of successive dialysis sessions (usually 2 to 3 sessions per week) until the total dose was attained (mean total dose of 950±220 mg). An initial test dose of 25 mg was administered over 5 minutes, the patient observed for 15 minutes for anaphylaxis, and the remaining 75 mg dose administered over 1 hour. Iron dextran increased the iron status in these chronic hemodialysis patients. Plasma ferritin and transferrin saturation values increased significantly at the first time point assessed. Plasma ferritin values remained elevated for at least 4 weeks post-completion of dosing, while transferrin saturation values remained elevated only during the iron dextran administration period. Hemoglobin (Hb) and hematocrit tended to increase, with levels 4 weeks post-completion of dosing significantly higher than the time at which half the iron dextran dose had been administered. The greater increase in Hb was observed in patients with a baseline ferritin of <100 µg/L compared to ferritin values of >100 µg/L. Therefore, the presence of both a transferrin saturation <20% and plasma ferritin <100 µg/L may improve the identification of hemodialysis patients who will often respond to parenteral iron with an increase in Hb.

Iron status following iron dextran administration by i.v. infusion was assessed in 14 r-HuEPO (recombinant human erythropoietin)-treated hemodialysis patients who completed the study (3 female, 11 male; mean age 59±5.2 years; mean r-HuEPO dose per week 11 429±2 142 units) not receiving parenteral iron therapy within the previous 12 months. Iron dextran was administered in doses of 100 mg diluted in 100 mL NaCl 0.9%, during the last half-hour of hemodialysis. Doses were given once a week for 10 consecutive weeks, for a total dose of 1 000 mg. An initial test dose of 25 mg was administered and the patient observed for 1 hour for anaphylaxis. Iron dextran had a significant impact on the ferritin levels, which is reflective of the patient's iron stores. Significant increases in serum iron and transferrin saturation were observed, with a peak at 8 weeks following initiation of iron dextran therapy. These changes did not translate into an increase in hemoglobin levels. For patients concurrently taking r-HuEPO, 20% of those enrolled (5/25) experienced an adverse reaction to iron dextran. Hypertension was observed in 2 patients (one 3 hours following the test dose, the other during the second dose at week 2). In addition, 1 patient had an anaphylactic response to the test dose. Finally, in the 5 patients who experienced adverse reactions, the following were observed: dizziness, headache, faintness, unconsciousness, distress, palpitations, increased heart rate and blood flow, hypotension, chest pain, flushing, cyanosis, diarrhea, limb cramps, shortness of breath, urticaria and itching.

Indications: For treatment of patients with documented iron deficiency in whom oral administration is unsatisfactory or impossible. It may be administered by i.m. injection or by i.v. infusion. **I.V. infusion must be confined to the hospital treatment of patients for whom the i.m. route or other forms of therapy are inappropriate or are not available.**

Contraindications: Hypersensitivity to the product. All anemias not associated with iron deficiency.

Iron dextran is not to be used during the acute phase of infectious kidney disease, not to be given i.v. to patients with a history of asthma and not to be administered concomitantly with oral iron preparations.

Warnings: The parenteral use of complexes of iron and carbohydrates has resulted in anaphylactic-type reactions. Deaths associated with such administration have been reported. Therefore, iron dextran should be used only in those patients in whom the indications have been clearly established and laboratory investigations confirm an iron deficient state not amenable to oral iron therapy.

Large i.v. doses, such as those used with total dose infusions (TDIs) have been associated with an increased incidence of adverse effects. The adverse effects frequently are delayed (1 to 2 days) and include one or more of the following symptoms: arthralgia, backache, chills, dizziness, moderate to high fever, headache, malaise, myalgia, nausea and vomiting. The onset is usually 24 to 48 hours after administration and symptoms generally subside within 3 to 4 days. Similar symptoms reported following i.m. injection usually subside within 3 to 7 days. The estimate of risk/benefit should take into consideration the potential for a delayed reaction.

Iron dextran injection should be used with extreme care in patients with serious impairment of liver function.

Iron dextran injection should not be used during the acute phase of infectious kidney disease.

Adverse reactions experienced following administration of iron dextran injection may exacerbate cardiovascular complications in patients with pre-existing cardiovascular disease.

Animal studies have shown a risk of carcinogenesis associated with the i.m. injection of iron-carbohydrate complexes. Sarcomas were produced when large doses were given to rodents or when small doses were injected repeatedly into the same site in rodents and rabbits.

The long latent period between the injection of a potential carcinogen and the appearance of a tumor makes it impossible to measure accurately the risk in man. There have, however, been several reports in the literature describing tumors at the injection site in humans who had previously received i.m. injections of iron dextran.

Precautions: Unwarranted therapy with parenteral iron will cause excess storage of iron with the consequent possibility of exogenous hemosiderosis. Such iron overload is particularly apt to occur in patients with hemoglobinopathies and other refractory anemias that might be erroneously diagnosed as iron deficiency anemias.

Iron dextran injection should be used with caution in individuals with histories of significant allergies and/or asthma.

Anaphylaxis and other hypersensitivity reactions have been reported after uneventful test doses as well as therapeutic doses of iron dextran injection. Therefore, administration of subsequent test doses during therapy should be considered (see Dosage).

Epinephrine should be immediately available in the event of acute hypersensitivity reactions. The usual dose of epinephrine is 0.5 mL of a 1:1 000 solution, by s.c. or i.m. injection. Note: Patients using beta-blocking agents may not respond adequately to epinephrine, and they may require isoproterenol or similar beta-agonist agents.

Patients with rheumatoid arthritis may have an acute exacerbation of joint pain and swelling following the administration of iron dextran injection.

There have been published reports, from New Zealand, associating the use of i.m. iron dextran in neonates with an increased incidence of gram-negative sepsis, primarily due to E. coli.

Information for the Patient: Patients should be advised of the potential adverse reactions associated with the use of iron dextran injection (see Adverse Effects).

Drug/Laboratory Test Interactions: Large doses of iron dextran (5 mL or more) have been reported to give a brown color to serum from a blood sample drawn 4 hours after administration. Iron dextran injection may cause falsely elevated values of serum bilirubin and falsely decreased values of serum calcium.

Serum iron determinations by colorimetric assays may not be meaningful for 3 weeks following the administration of iron dextran.

Serum ferritin peaks approximately 7 to 9 days after an i.v. dose and slowly returns to baseline after about 3 weeks.

Examination of the bone marrow for iron stores may not be meaningful for prolonged periods following therapy with iron dextran injection because residual iron dextran may remain in the reticuloendothelial cells.

Bone scans involving 99m Tc-diphosphonate have been reported to show a dense, crescentic area of activity in the buttocks, following the contour of the iliac crest, 1 to 6 days after i.m. injections of iron dextran.

Bone scans with 99m Tc-labeled bone seeking agents, in the presence of high serum ferritin levels or following iron dextran infusions, have been reported to show reduction of bony uptake, marked renal activity and increased blood pool and soft tissue accumulation.

Pregnancy: Iron dextran has been shown to be teratogenic and embryocidal in nonanemic mice, rats, rabbits, dogs and monkeys when given in doses of about 3 times the maximum human dose. No consistent adverse fetal effects were observed in mice, rats, rabbits, dogs and monkeys at doses of 50 mg iron/kg or less. Fetal and maternal toxicity have been reported in monkeys at a total i.v. dose of 90 mg iron/kg over a 14-day period. Similar effects were observed in mice and rats after administration of a single dose of 125 mg iron/kg. Fetal abnormalities in rats and dogs were observed at doses of 250 mg iron/kg and higher. The animals used in these tests were not iron deficient. There are no adequate and well-controlled studies in pregnant women. **Iron dextran injection should be used in pregnant women only if the potential benefit justifies the potential risk to the fetus.**

Placental Transfer: Various animal studies have demonstrated placental transfer of iron dextran complex, and studies in pregnant humans have demonstrated inconclusive results.

It appears that some iron does reach the fetus, but the form in which it crosses the placenta is not clear.

Lactation: Caution should be exercised when iron dextran is administered to a nursing woman. Traces of unmetabolized iron dextran are excreted in human milk.

Children: **Not recommended for use in infants under 4 months of age (see Dosage).**

Adverse Effects: Severe/Fatal: Anaphylactic reactions to iron dextran injection, including fatal anaphylaxis, have been reported. Such reactions which occur most often within the first several minutes of administration are generally characterized by the sudden onset of respiratory difficulty and/or cardiovascular collapse.

The incidence of these acute hypersensitivity reactions has been estimated between 0.1 to 0.6% (see Warnings). (See Precautions pertaining to immediate availability of epinephrine.) Administration must be stopped **immediately** when signs of an anaphylactoid reaction are seen.

Mild/moderate: Delayed reactions may occur (see Warnings). In a surveillance program of 1 260 patients treated with total dose infusion of iron dextran injection, the overall reaction rate was 29.8%, with 14.3% immediate reactions occurring on the day of infusion and 17.7% delayed reactions occurring on later days; 2.1% of patients experienced both immediate and delayed reactions. (Severe reactions were recorded in 5.3% of patients.)

Cardiovascular: chest pain, chest tightness, shock, hypotension, hypertension, tachycardia, flushing, arrhythmias. (Flushing and hypotension may occur from too rapid i.v. administration.)

Dermatologic: urticaria, pruritus, purpura, rash.

Gastrointestinal: abdominal pain, nausea, vomiting, diarrhea.

Hematologic/Lymphatic: leukocytosis, lymphadenopathy.

Musculoskeletal/Soft Tissue: arthralgia, arthritis (may represent reactivation in patients with quiescent rheumatoid arthritis, see Precautions), myalgia; backache; sterile abscess, atrophy/fibrosis (i.m. injection site); brown skin and/or underlying tissue discoloration (staining), soreness or pain at or near i.m. injection sites; cellulitis; swelling; inflammation; local phlebitis at or near i.v. injection site.

Neurologic: convulsions, seizures, syncope, headache, weakness, unresponsiveness, paresthesia, febrile episodes, chills, dizziness, disorientation, numbness.

Respiratory: respiratory arrest, dyspnea, bronchospasm.

Urologic: hematuria.

Delayed Reactions: arthralgia, backache, chills, dizziness, fever, headache, malaise, myalgia, nausea, vomiting (see Warnings).

Miscellaneous: febrile episodes, sweating, shivering, chills, malaise, altered taste.

Overdose: Symptoms and Treatment: Overdosage with iron dextran injection is unlikely to produce acute adverse reactions. Excessive doses beyond the requirements for restoration of hemoglobin and replenishment of iron stores may lead to hemosiderosis. Periodic monitoring of serum ferritin levels may be helpful in recognizing adverse accumulation of iron in concurrent medical conditions such as chronic renal failure, Hodgkin's disease and rheumatoid arthritis.

Dosage: Oral iron should be discontinued prior to administration of iron dextran.

Infufer (cont'd)

Dosage is calculated specifically for each patient dependent upon body weight, age, sex and degree of anemia, using a dosage table or some suitable formula. It is preferred that iron dextran be given by the i.m. route, unless there are valid reasons for i.v. administration. The i.v. infusion of iron dextran should be restricted to hospital usage only.

Dosage Determinations in Patients with Iron Deficiency Anemia: Periodic hematologic determination of hemoglobin and hematocrit should be used as a guide for monitoring hematological response. As iron storage may lag behind the appearance of normal blood morphology, other tests, such as serum iron, total iron binding capacity, serum ferritin and percent saturation of transferrin, may be needed for detecting and monitoring the iron deficient state of the patient.

Reticulocyte count should increase within a few days of iron dextran administration.

Serum ferritin levels may not correlate with body iron stores in patients on chronic renal dialysis who are also receiving iron dextran complex.

Although there are significant variations in body build and weight distribution among males and females, Table I and the accompanying formula represent a convenient means for estimating the total iron required. This total iron requirement reflects the amount of iron needed to restore hemoglobin concentration to normal or near normal levels plus an additional allowance to provide adequate replenishment of iron stores in most individuals with moderately or severely reduced levels of hemoglobin. It should be remembered that iron deficiency anemia will not appear until essentially all iron stores have been depleted. Thus, therapy should aim at not only the restoration of hemoglobin but also the replenishment of iron stores.

Factors contributing to the formula include:

$$\frac{\text{mg blood iron}}{\text{lb body weight}} = \frac{\text{mL blood}}{\text{lb body weight}} \times \frac{\text{g hemoglobin}}{\text{mL blood}} \times \frac{\text{mg iron}}{\text{g hemoglobin}}$$

a) Blood volume 65 mL/kg of body weight. b) Normal hemoglobin (males and females), over 15 kg (33 lbs) 14.8 g/100 mL, 15 kg (33 lbs) or less 12 g/100 mL. c) Iron content of hemoglobin 0.34%. d) Hemoglobin deficit. e) Weight.

Based on the above factors, individuals with normal hemoglobin levels will have approximately 33 mg of blood iron/kg (15 mg/lb).

Note: The formula and accompanying table are applicable for dosage determinations only in patients with iron deficiency anemia; they are not to be used for dosage determinations in patients requiring iron replacement for blood loss.

The total amount of iron dextran in mL required to treat the anemia and replenish iron stores may be approximated as follows: For Adults and Children over 15 kg (33 lbs): See Table I.

Alternatively, the total dose may be calculated as follows:

Dose (mL)=0.0442 (Desired Hb−Observed Hb)×LBW+(0.26×LBW).

Based on: Desired Hb=the target Hb in g/dL. Observed Hb=the patient's current hemoglobin in g/dL. LBW=Lean body weight in kg. A patient's lean body weight (or actual body weight if less than lean body weight) should be utilized when determining dosage. To convert the patient's weight from pounds to kg: patient's weight in pounds/2.2=weight in kg. For males: LBW=50 kg+2.3 kg for each inch of patient's height over 5 feet. For females: LBW=45.5 kg+2.3 kg for each inch of patient's height over 5 feet.

Children 5 to 15 kg (11 to 33 lbs): See Table I. Iron dextran should not normally be given in the first 4 months of life (see Precautions, Children).

Alternatively, the total dose may be calculated as follows:

Dose (mL)=0.0442 (Desired Hb−Observed Hb)×W+(0.26×W).

Based on: Desired Hb=the target Hb in g/dL. (Normal Hb for children 15 kg or less is 12 g/dL.) Observed Hb=the patient's current Hb in g/dL. W=Weight in kg. To convert the patient's weight from pounds to kg: Patient's weight in pounds/2.2=weight in kg.

Iron Replacement for Blood Loss: Some individuals sustain blood losses on an intermittent or repetitive basis. Such blood losses may occur periodically in patients with hemorrhagic diatheses (familial telangiectasia, hemophilia, gastrointestinal bleeding) and on a repetitive basis from procedures such as renal hemodialysis.

Iron therapy in these patients should be directed toward replacement of the equivalent amount of iron represented in the lost blood. **The table and formulae presented under iron deficiency anemia are not applicable for simple iron replacement values.**

Quantitative estimates of the individual's periodic blood loss and hematocrit during the bleeding episode provide a convenient method for the calculation of the required iron dose.

The formula shown below is based on the approximation that 1 mL of normocytic, normochromic red cells contains 1 mg of elemental iron:

Replacement iron (in mg)=Blood loss (in mL)×hematocrit.

Example: Blood loss of 500 mL with 20% hematocrit.

Replacement iron=500×0.20=100 mg.

$$\text{Infufer dose} = \frac{100 \text{ mg}}{50 \text{ mg/mL}} = 2 \text{ mL.}$$

Administration: The total amount of iron dextran required for the treatment of iron deficiency anemia or iron replacement for blood loss is determined from the table or appropriate formula (see Dosage).

I.M. Injection: **Prior to receiving their first therapeutic dose, all patients should be given an i.m. test dose of 0.5 mL gradually.** The test dose should be administered in the same recommended test site and by the same technique as described in the last paragraph of this section. Although anaphylactic reactions known to occur following iron dextran administration are usually evident within a few minutes or sooner, it is recommended that at least an hour or longer elapse before the remainder of the initial therapeutic dose is given.

If no adverse reactions are observed, iron dextran can be given according to the following schedule until the calculated total amount required has been reached. Each day's dose should ordinarily not exceed 0.5 mL (25 mg of iron) for infants under 5 kg (11 lbs); 1 mL (50 mg of iron) for children under 10 kg (22 lbs); and 2 mL (100 mg of iron) for other patients. It is recommended that these be **given as a graded series of injections starting with a test dose of 0.5 mL (25 mg elemental iron),** 1 mL, then 2 mL, while the patient is observed carefully for adverse reactions. The injections should be administered gradually. If the patient is moderately active, injections may be given daily into alternate buttocks. In inactive or bedridden patients, the frequency of injections should be reduced to once or twice weekly.

Deep i.m. injection in the upper outer quadrant of the buttock, using a Z-track technique (with displacement of the skin laterally prior to injection) insures absorption and will help to avoid staining of the skin. A 5 cm needle is recommended for the adult of average size.

The i.m. route of administration is to be used unless there are valid reasons for i.v. administration.

I.V. Infusion: Prior to receiving their first therapeutic dose, all patients should be given a test dose of 0.5 mL (equivalent to 25 mg elemental iron) by i.v. infusion administered slowly over at least 5 minutes at a rate of not more than 5 drops/minute. If the test dose is well tolerated, the rate of infusion may be increased progressively to 45 to 60 drops/minute (3 to 4 mL/minute).

Anaphylactoid reactions are usually evident within a few minutes. **If at any time during the i.v. administration, any signs of a hypersensitivity reaction or intolerance are detected, administration must be stopped immediately.** Resuscitative equipment should be available, and the reactions treated with 0.5 mL of aqueous epinephrine 1:1 000 given s.c. with general supportive measures, followed by either oral or parenteral antihistamines and/or corticosteroids (see Precautions).

Iron dextran may be administered in large volumes via the Total Dose Infusion technique for the hospital treatment of patients for whom the i.m. route or other forms of therapy are inappropriate or are not available.

The i.v. route should not be used for patients with a history of asthma. If the i.v. route is judged necessary for patients with a history of allergy, effective antihistamine cover should be given before administration of the iron dextran.

Total Dose Infusion (TDI) Technique: The total amount of calculated iron dextran required is added aseptically immediately before use to the required volume, usually 500 mL of sterile NaCl 0.9% or Dextrose 5% solution. The use of Dextrose 5% solution has been associated with a higher incidence of local pain and phlebitis.

A test dose of 25 mg of elemental iron should be administered slowly over 5 minutes at an infusion rate not exceeding 5 drops/minute. If no hypersensitivity reaction occurs following an observation period of at least 1 hour, the remainder of the dose may be infused over 1 to 3 hours, or as much as 6 to 8 hours at an infusion rate of 3 to 4 mL/minute. The vein should then be flushed with about 10 mL of saline. Patients should be observed closely during the infusion and for at least 1 hour after it is completed.

The i.m. route of administration is to be used unless there are valid reasons for i.v. administration.

Preparation of Infusion Solutions: For i.v. infusion with dilution, iron dextran may be diluted in NaCl 0.9% or Dextrose 5%. The diluted preparations are chemically stable for 24 hours at room temperature. Discard unused portion.

Solutions of iron dextran in Dextrose 5% solution must not be autoclaved, because precipitation may occur. Other agents should not be added to iron dextran infusions, nor should iron dextran be added to blood for transfusion.

Iron dextran has been reported to be incompatible with oxytetracycline and with sulfadiazine sodium in i.v. infusion.

Table I—Infufer

Total Infufer Requirement For Hemoglobin Restoration and Iron Stores Replacement

Patient Lean Body Weight		mL Requirement of Infufer Based on Observed Hemoglobin of							
kg	**lb**	**3 g/dL**	**4 g/dL**	**5 g/dL**	**6 g/dL**	**7 g/dL**	**8 g/dL**	**9 g/dL**	**10 g/dL**
5	11	3	3	3	3	2	2	2	2
10	22	7	6	6	5	5	4	4	3
15	33	10	9	9	8	7	7	6	5
20	44	16	15	14	13	12	11	10	9
25	55	20	18	17	16	15	14	13	12
30	66	23	22	21	19	18	17	15	14
35	77	27	26	24	23	21	20	18	17
40	88	31	29	28	26	24	22	21	19
45	99	35	33	31	29	27	25	23	21
50	110	39	37	35	32	30	28	26	24
55	121	43	41	38	36	33	31	28	26
60	132	47	44	42	39	36	34	31	28
65	143	51	48	45	42	39	36	34	31
70	154	55	52	49	45	42	39	36	33
75	165	59	55	52	49	45	42	39	35
80	176	63	59	55	52	48	45	41	38
85	187	66	63	59	55	51	48	44	40
90	198	70	66	62	58	54	50	46	42
95	209	74	70	66	62	57	53	49	45
100	220	78	74	69	65	60	56	52	47
105	231	82	77	73	68	63	59	54	50
110	242	86	81	76	71	67	62	57	52
115	253	90	85	80	75	70	64	59	54
120	264	94	88	83	78	73	67	62	57

Table values were calculated based on a normal adult hemoglobin of 14.8 g/dL for body weights greater than 15 kg (33 lbs) and a hemoglobin of 12 g/dL for body weights less than or equal to 15 kg (33 lbs).

Preparation of Infusion Solutions: See Table II.

Table II—Infufer

Preparation of Infusion Solutions

	Amount of Infufer	Amount of Diluent*
Total Dose Infusion	Total Calculated Dose	500 mL
Infusion Following Hemodialysis	2 mL (100 mg iron)	100 mL

*Diluent may be sterile 0.9% NaCl or Dextrose 5% solution. Note that Dextrose 5% solution has been associated with a higher incidence of local pain and phlebitis.

Note: Do not mix iron dextran with other medications or add to parenteral nutrition solutions for i.v. infusion.

Parenteral drug products should be inspected visually for particulate matter and discoloration prior to administration whenever the solution and container permit.

Infusion Following Hemodialysis Procedure: Chronic hemodialysis patients who develop anemia may be administered iron dextran in 100 mg doses diluted in 100 mL of NaCl 0.9% during the last hour of successive dialysis sessions until the total dose is attained. A test dose of 25 mg of elemental iron should be administered slowly over 5 minutes, and the patient monitored for adverse reactions over a 1-hour period before continuing with the initial infusion, as described previously.

Supplied: Each mL of injection contains: elemental iron 50 mg as an iron dextran complex and sodium chloride 0.9% in water for injection. Sodium hydroxide or hydrochloric acid may be used to adjust pH. Preservative-free. Single use, clear glass vials of 2 mL, boxes of 10. Single use, clear glass vials of 5 mL, boxes of 5. Store between 15 and 25°C. Do not freeze.

Reviewed 1998

INHIBACE® Ⓟ

Roche

Cilazapril

Angiotensin Converting Enzyme Inhibitor

Pharmacology: Cilazapril is an angiotensin converting enzyme (ACE) inhibitor, which is used in the treatment of hypertension and congestive heart failure.

Cilazapril suppresses the renin-angiotensin-aldosterone system and thereby reduces both supine and standing systolic and diastolic blood pressures. Renin is an enzyme that is released by the kidneys into the circulation to stimulate the production of angiotensin I, an inactive decapeptide. Angiotensin I is converted by ACE to angiotensin II, a potent vasoconstrictor. Angiotensin II also stimulates aldosterone secretion, leading to sodium and fluid retention. After absorption, cilazapril, a pro-drug, is hydrolyzed to cilazaprilat, the active metabolite, which prevents the conversion of angiotensin I to angiotensin II by inhibition of ACE. Following the administration of cilazapril, plasma ACE activity is inhibited more than 90% within 2 hours at therapeutic doses. Plasma renin activity (PRA) and angiotensin I concentrations are increased and angiotensin II concentrations and aldosterone secretion are decreased. The increase in PRA comes as a result of the loss of negative feedback on renin release caused by the reduction in angiotensin II. The decreased aldosterone secretion may lead to small increases in serum potassium along with sodium and fluid loss. In patients with normal renal function, serum potassium usually remains within the normal range during cilazapril treatment. Mean serum potassium values increased by 0.02 mEq/L in patients with a normal baseline serum creatinine and by 0.11 mEq/L in patients with a raised serum creatinine. In patients concomitantly taking potassium-sparing diuretics, potassium levels may rise.

ACE is identical to kininase II. Therefore, cilazapril may interfere with the degradation of the vasodepressor peptide bradykinin. The role that this plays in the therapeutic effects of cilazapril is unknown.

The antihypertensive effect of cilazapril is usually apparent within the first hour after administration, with maximum effect observed between 3 and 7 hours after dosing. Supine and standing heart rates remain unchanged. Reflex tachycardia has not been observed. Small, clinically insignificant alterations of heart rate may occur.

At recommended doses, the effect of cilazapril in hypertensive patients and in patients with congestive heart failure is maintained for up to 24 hours. In some patients, blood pressure reduction may diminish toward the end of the dosage interval. Blood pressure should be assessed after 2 to 4 weeks of therapy, and dosage adjusted if required. The antihypertensive effect of cilazapril is maintained during long-term therapy. No rapid increase in blood pressure has been observed after abrupt withdrawal of cilazapril.

The antihypertensive effect of angiotensin converting enzyme inhibitors is generally lower in black patients than in non-blacks.

In hypertensive patients with moderate to severe renal impairment, the glomerular filtration rate and renal blood flow remained in general unchanged with cilazapril.

In patients with congestive heart failure the renin-angiotensin-aldosterone and the sympathetic nervous systems are generally activated leading to enhanced systemic vasoconstriction and to the promotion of sodium and water retention. By suppressing the renin-angiotensin-aldosterone system, cilazapril improves loading conditions in the failing heart by reducing systemic vascular resistance (afterload) and pulmonary capillary wedge pressure (preload) in patients on diuretics and/or digitalis. The onset of action of cilazapril occurs within 1 to 2 hours, reaching its maximum effect within 2 to 4 hours after the first dose. The exercise tolerance of these patients was increased and was associated with an improvement of clinical symptomatology. Patients studied belonged primarily to New York Heart Association Class II and III. The effect of cilazapril on survival in patients with heart failure has not been evaluated.

Pharmacokinetics: Cilazapril is well absorbed and rapidly converted to the active form, cilazaprilat. Peak plasma concentrations, and times to peak plasma concentrations for cilazapril and cilazaprilat following the oral administration of 0.5 to 5 mg cilazapril are given in Table I.

Table I—Inhibace

Pharmacokinetics

Oral Dose (mg)	Cilazapril C_{max} (ng/mL)	Cilazapril t_{max} (h)	Cilazaprilat C_{max} (ng/mL)	Cilazaprilat t_{max} (h)
0.5	17.0	1.1	5.4	1.8
1.0	33.9	1.1	12.4	1.8
2.5	82.7	1.1	37.7	1.9
5.0	182.0	1.0	94.2	1.6

Maximum plasma concentrations of cilazaprilat are reached within 2 hours after administration of cilazapril.

Maximum ACE inhibition is greater than 90% after 1 to 5 mg cilazapril. Maximum ACE inhibition is 70 to 80% after 0.5 mg cilazapril. Dose proportionality is observed following the administration of 1 to 5 mg cilazapril. Apparent non-proportionality is observed at 0.5 mg reflective of the binding to ACE. The higher doses of cilazapril are associated with longer duration of maximum ACE inhibition.

The absolute bioavailability of cilazaprilat after oral administration of cilazapril is 57% based on urinary recovery data. (The absolute bioavailability of cilazaprilat after oral administration of cilazaprilat is 19%.) Ingestion of food immediately before the administration of cilazapril reduces the average peak plasma concentration of cilazaprilat by 29%, delays the peak by 1 hour and reduces the bioavailability of cilazaprilat by 14%. These pharmacokinetic changes have little influence on plasma ACE inhibition.

Cilazaprilat is eliminated unchanged by the kidneys. The total urinary recovery of cilazaprilat after i.v. administration of 2.5 mg is 91%. Total clearance is 12.3 L/hour and renal clearance is 10.8 L/hour. The total urinary recovery of cilazaprilat following the oral administration of 2.5 mg cilazapril is 52.6%.

Half-lives for the periods 1 to 4 hours and 1 to 7 days after the i.v. administration of 2.5 mg cilazaprilat are 0.90 and 46.2 hours respectively. These data suggest the saturable binding of cilazaprilat to ACE. The early elimination phase corresponds to the clearance of free drug. During the terminal elimination phase, almost all of the drug is bound to enzyme. Following the oral administration of 0.5, 1, 2.5 and 5 mg cilazapril, terminal elimination phase half-lives for cilazaprilat are 48.9, 39.8, 38.5 and 35.8 hours respectively.

After multiple dose, daily administration of 2.5 mg cilazapril for 8 days, pharmacokinetic parameter values for intact cilazapril after the last dose are similar to the first dose. For cilazaprilat, peak plasma concentrations are achieved at the same time but are 30% higher after the last dose. Trough plasma concentrations and areas under the curve are 20% higher. The terminal elimination phase half-life after the last dose is 53.8 hours. The effective half-life of accumulation for cilazaprilat is 8.9 hours.

Following the administration of 1 mg cilazapril to healthy elderly and young volunteers, the elderly group experienced greater peak plasma concentrations of cilazaprilat and areas under the curve (39% and 25%, respectively) and lower total clearance and renal clearance (20% and 28%, respectively) than the younger volunteers.

In patients with renal impairment, peak plasma concentrations of cilazaprilat, times to peak plasma concentrations, early elimination phase half-lives, areas under the curve and 24 hour plasma concentrations all increase as creatinine clearance decreases. The changes in these parameters are small for patients with creatinine clearances of 40 mL/min or more. Cilazaprilat clearance (total and renal) decreases in parallel with creatinine clearance. Cilazaprilat is not eliminated in patients with complete renal failure. Hemodialysis reduces concentrations of both cilazapril and cilazaprilat to a limited extent.

Following the administration of 1 mg cilazapril in patients with moderate to severe compensated liver cirrhosis, peak plasma concentrations of cilazapril and cilazaprilat are increased (57% and 28% respectively), attained 30 minutes and 45 minutes earlier, and total clearances are decreased (51% and 31% respectively), in comparison to healthy subjects. The renal clearance and early and terminal elimination phase half-lives of cilazaprilat are decreased 52%, 42% and 62% respectively.

In patients with congestive heart failure the clearance of cilazaprilat is correlated with the creatinine clearance. Thus, dosage adjustments beyond those recommended for patients with impaired renal functions (see Dosage, Congestive Heart Failure) should not be necessary.

Indications: The treatment of mild to moderate essential hypertension. Cilazapril may be used alone or in combination with thiazide-type diuretics. Cilazapril is also indicated in the treatment of congestive heart failure as an adjunctive therapy with digitalis and/or diuretics.

In using cilazapril consideration should be given to the risk of angioedema (see Warnings).

Hypertension: Cilazapril should normally be used in those patients in whom treatment with a diuretic or a beta-blocker was found ineffective or has been associated with unacceptable adverse effects.

Cilazapril can also be tried as an initial agent in those patients in whom use of diuretics and/or beta-blockers is contraindicated or in patients with medical conditions in which these drugs frequently cause serious adverse effects.

The safety and efficacy of cilazapril in renovascular hypertension has not been established and therefore, its use in this condition is not recommended.

The safety and efficacy of concomitant use of cilazapril with antihypertensive agents other than thiazide diuretics have not been established.

Congestive Heart Failure: Cilazapril is indicated in the treatment of congestive heart failure as adjunctive therapy in patients who have not responded adequately to digitalis and/or diuretics. There is limited data on New York Heart Association Class IV patients (see Pharmacology). Treatment with cilazapril should be initiated in patients with congestive heart failure under close medical supervision.

When used in pregnancy during the second and third trimesters, ACE inhibitors can cause injury or even death of the developing fetus. When pregnancy is detected, cilazapril should be discontinued as soon as possible (see Warnings, Pregnancy and Precautions, Information for the Patient).

Contraindications: In patients who are hypersensitive to cilazapril, in patients with a history of angioedema related to previous treatment with an ACE inhibitor and in patients with ascites.

Warnings: Angioedema: Angioedema has been reported in patients treated with cilazapril. Angioedema associated with laryngeal edema and/or shock may be fatal. If angioedema occurs, cilazapril should be promptly discontinued and appropriate therapy instituted without delay. The patient should be followed carefully until the swelling has resolved. Swelling confined to the face, lips and mouth usually resolves without treatment, although antihistamines may provide symptomatic relief. Swelling of the tongue, glottis or larynx, may cause airway obstruction; therefore, s.c. epinephrine (0.5 mL 1:1 000) should be administered promptly when indicated.

The incidence of angioedema during ACE inhibitor therapy has been reported to be higher in black than in non-black patients.

Patients with a history of angioedema unrelated to ACE inhibitor therapy may be at an increased risk of angioedema while receiving an ACE inhibitor (see Contraindications).

Hypotension: Occasionally, symptomatic hypotension has occurred after administration of cilazapril usually after the first dose or when the dose had been increased. It is more likely

Inhibace (cont'd)

to occur in patients with sodium or volume depletion in connection with diuretic therapy, dietary salt restriction, dialysis, diarrhea or vomiting. Patients with congestive heart failure, especially those vigorously treated with loop diuretics, may experience excessive hypotension in response to ACE inhibitors. Because of the potential fall in blood pressure in these patients, therapy should be started under very close medical supervision. Such patients should be followed closely for the first 2 weeks of treatment and whenever the dose of cilazapril and/or diuretic is increased. Similar considerations may apply to patients with ischemic heart or cerebrovascular disease in whom an excessive fall in blood pressure could result in a myocardial infarction or cerebrovascular accident (see Adverse Effects).

In patients with severe heart failure, whose renal function may depend on the activity of the renin-angiotensin-aldosterone system, treatment with ACE inhibitors, including cilazapril, may be associated with oliguria and/or progressive azotemia and rarely acute renal failure and/or death.

If hypotension occurs, the patient should be placed in supine position and, if necessary, receive an i.v. infusion of normal saline. A transient hypotensive response does not necessitate discontinuation of cilazapril. Once the blood pressure has increased after volume expansion, cilazapril therapy may be continued. If symptoms persist, the dosage should be reduced or the drug discontinued.

Two elderly male patients, with a history of previous myocardial infarctions, on high diuretic dosage (240 mg and 120 mg of furosemide daily, respectively) for congestive heart failure NYHA Class III died within 8 hours after the addition of a single dose of 2.5 mg of cilazapril.

Neutropenia/Agranulocytosis: Agranulocytosis and bone marrow depression have been caused by ACE inhibitors. Cases of leukopenia and neutropenia have rarely been reported in patients treated with cilazapril. However, in no patient could a causal relationship to cilazapril be established. Periodic monitoring of white blood cell counts should be considered, especially in patients with collagen vascular disease and renal disease.

Pregnancy: ACE inhibitors can cause fetal and neonatal morbidity and mortality when administered to pregnant women. Several dozen cases have been reported in the world literature. When pregnancy is detected, cilazapril should be discontinued as soon as possible.

In rare cases (probably less than 0.01% of pregnancies) in which no alternative to ACE inhibitors therapy will be found, the mother should be apprised of the potential hazards to the fetus. Serial ultrasound examinations should be performed to assess fetal development and well-being and the volume of amniotic fluid.

If oligohydramnios is observed, cilazapril should be discontinued unless it is considered life-saving for the mother. A non-stress test (NST), and/or a biophysical profiling (BPP) may be appropriate, depending upon the week of pregnancy. If concerns regarding fetal well-being still persist, a contraction stress testing (CST) should be considered. Patients and physicians should be aware, however, that oligohydramnios may not appear until after the fetus has sustained irreversible injury.

Infants with a history of in utero exposure to ACE inhibitors should be closely observed for hypotension, oliguria, and hyperkalemia. If oliguria occurs, attention should be directed toward support of blood pressure and renal perfusion. Exchange transfusion or dialysis may be required as a means of reversing hypotension and/or substituting for impaired renal function, however, limited experience with those procedures has not been associated with significant clinical benefit. Dialysis clearance was estimated to be 2.4 L/hour for cilazapril and 2.2 to 2.8 L/hour for cilazaprilat.

Human Data: It is not known whether exposure limited to the first trimester of pregnancy can adversely affect fetal outcome. The use of ACE inhibitors during the second and third trimesters of pregnancy has been associated with fetal and neonatal injury including hypotension, neonatal skull hypoplasia, anuria, reversible or irreversible renal failure and death. Oligohydramnios has also been reported, presumably resulting from decreased fetal renal function; oligohydramnios in this setting has been associated with fetal limb contractures, craniofacial deformation, and hypoplastic lung development. Prematurity and patent ductus arteriosus have also been reported, although it is not clear whether these occurrences were due to the ACE inhibitor exposure.

Animal Data: In fertility and general reproduction performance testing in rats, dosing with 50 mg/kg/day of cilazapril resulted in greater implantation losses, less viable fetuses, smaller pups, and dilatation of the renal pelvis in the pups. No teratogenic effects and no adverse effects on postnatal pup development were observed in rats and cynomolgus monkeys during embryotoxicity testing. In the rats, however, at a dose of 400 mg/kg/day, renal cavitation was observed in the pups. In peri- and post-natal toxicity testing in rats, dosing with 50 mg/kg/day resulted in greater pup mortality, smaller pups, and delayed unfolding of the pinna. On administration ^{14}C-cilazapril to pregnant mice, rats and monkeys, radioactivity was measured in the fetuses.

Precautions: Impaired Renal Function: As a consequence of inhibiting the renin-angiotensin-aldosterone system, changes in renal function have been seen in susceptible individuals. In patients whose renal function may depend on the activity of the renin-angiotensin-aldosterone system, such as patients with bilateral renal artery stenosis, unilateral renal artery stenosis to a solitary kidney, or severe congestive heart failure, treatment with agents that inhibit this system has been associated with oliguria, progressive azotemia, and rarely, acute renal failure and/or death. In susceptible patients, concomitant diuretic use may further increase risk.

Use of cilazapril should include appropriate assessment of renal function.

Anaphylactoid Reactions during Membrane Exposure: Anaphylactoid reactions have been reported in patients dialyzed with high-flux membranes (e.g., polyacrylonitrile [PAN]) and treated concomitantly with an ACE inhibitor. Dialysis should be stopped immediately if symptoms such as nausea, abdominal cramps, burning, angioedema, shortness of breath and severe hypotension occur. Symptoms are not relieved by antihistamines. In these patients, consideration should be given to using a different type of dialysis membrane or a different class of antihypertensive agent.

Anaphylactoid Reactions during LDL Apheresis: Rarely, patients receiving ACE inhibitors during low density lipoprotein (LDL) apheresis with dextran sulfate have experienced life-threatening anaphylactoid reactions. These reactions were avoided by temporarily withholding ACE inhibitor therapy prior to each apheresis.

Anaphylactoid Reactions during Desensitization: There have been isolated reports of patients experiencing sustained life threatening anaphylactoid reactions while receiving ACE inhibitors during desensitizing treatment with hymenoptera (bees, wasps) venom. In the same patients, these reactions have been avoided when ACE inhibitors were temporarily withheld for at least 24 hours, but they have reappeared upon inadvertent rechallenge. Cilazapril use must therefore be interrupted before the start of desensitization therapy. In this situation, cilazapril must not be replaced by a beta-blocker.

Hyperkalemia: In clinical trials, elevated serum potassium (greater than 5.5 mEq/L) was observed in approximately 0.7% of hypertensive patients and 0.8% of congestive heart failure patients receiving cilazapril. In most cases these were isolated values which resolved despite continued therapy; however, in one case the patient discontinued treatment. Risk factors for the development of hyperkalemia may include renal insufficiency, diabetes mellitus, and the concomitant use of agents to treat hypokalemia (see Drug Interactions and Adverse Effects).

Valvular Stenosis: There is concern on theoretical grounds that patients with aortic stenosis might be at particular risk of decreased coronary perfusion when treated with vasodilators because they do not develop as much afterload reduction.

Surgery/Anesthesia: In patients undergoing major surgery or during anesthesia with agents that produce hypotension, cilazapril blocks angiotensin II formation, secondary to compensatory renin release. This may result in arterial hypotension which can be corrected by volume expansion.

Patients With Impaired Liver Function: Hepatitis (hepatocellular and/or cholestatic), jaundice, elevations of liver enzymes and/or serum bilirubin have occurred during therapy with other ACE inhibitors in patients with or without pre-existing liver abnormalities. In most cases the changes were reversed on discontinuation of the drug.

Elevations of liver enzymes and/or serum bilirubin have been reported for cilazapril (see Adverse Effects). Jaundice was also spontaneously reported in 1 patient worldwide. Should the patient receiving cilazapril experience any unexplained symptoms particularly during the first weeks or months of treatment, it is recommended that a full set of liver function tests and any other necessary investigation be carried out. Discontinuation of cilazapril should be considered when appropriate.

There are no adequate studies in patients with cirrhosis and/or liver dysfunction. Cilazapril should be used with particular caution in patients with pre-existing liver abnormalities. In such patients baseline liver function tests should be obtained before administration of the drug and close monitoring of response and metabolic effects should apply.

Cough: A dry, persistent cough, which usually disappears only after withdrawal or lowering of the dose of cilazapril, has been reported.

Such possibility should be considered as part of the differential diagnosis of the cough.

Lactation: In rats, it has been shown that after the oral administration of cilazapril, cilazaprilat is excreted in milk.

It is not known whether cilazapril and/or cilazaprilat are excreted in human breast milk. Caution should be exercised when cilazapril is administered to nursing mothers.

Children: The safety and effectiveness of the use of cilazapril in children have not been established. Therefore, use in this age group is not recommended.

Geriatrics: Although clinical experience has not identified differences in response between the elderly and younger patients, greater sensitivity of some older individuals cannot be ruled out. In elderly patients with congestive heart failure on high diuretic dosage, the recommended starting dose of cilazapril 0.5 mg must be strictly followed (see Warnings, Hypotension and Dosage).

Drug Interactions: Diuretic Therapy: Patients concomitantly taking ACE inhibitors and diuretics, and especially those in whom diuretic therapy was recently instituted, may occasionally experience an excessive reduction of blood pressure after initiation of therapy. The possibility of hypotensive effects after the first dose of cilazapril can be minimized by either discontinuing the diuretic, or increasing the salt intake prior to initiation of treatment with cilazapril. If it is not possible to discontinue the diuretic, the starting dose of cilazapril should be reduced and the patient should be closely observed for several hours following initial dose and until blood pressure has stabilized (see Warnings and Dosage).

Agents Increasing Serum Potassium: Since cilazapril decreases aldosterone production, elevation of serum potassium may occur. Potassium sparing diuretics such as spironolactone, triamterene or amiloride, or potassium supplements should be given only for documented hypokalemia and with caution since they may lead to a significant increase in serum potassium particularly in patients with renal impairment. Therefore, if concomitant use for such agents is indicated, their dosage should be reduced when cilazapril is initiated and serum potassium and renal function should be monitored carefully. Salt substitutes containing potassium should also be used with caution.

Agents Causing Renin Release: The antihypertensive effect of cilazapril is augmented by antihypertensive agents that cause renin release (e.g., diuretics).

Agents Affecting Sympathetic Activity: Agents affecting sympathetic activity (e.g., ganglionic blocking agents or adrenergic neuron blocking agents) should be used with caution. Beta-adrenergic blocking drugs may add some further antihypertensive effect to cilazapril.

Inhibitors of Endogenous Prostaglandin Synthesis: Concomitant administration of a nonsteroidal anti-inflammatory drug (NSAID) may reduce the antihypertensive effect of cilazapril. The introduction of therapy with cilazapril (2.5 mg once daily) in hypertensive patients receiving indomethacin (50 mg twice daily) did not result in a reduction in blood pressure. However, the introduction of therapy with indomethacin (50 mg twice daily) in hypertensive patients receiving cilazapril (2.5 mg once daily) did not attenuate the blood pressure lowering effects of cilazapril. The interaction does not appear to occur in patients treated with cilazapril prior to the administration of a NSAID. There was no evidence of a pharmacokinetic interaction between cilazapril and indomethacin.

Digoxin: No pharmacodynamic or pharmacokinetic interactions (and no increase in plasma digoxin concentrations) were observed when cilazapril therapy (5 mg once daily) was administered to healthy volunteers receiving digoxin (0.25 mg twice daily).

Lithium Salts: As with other drugs which eliminate sodium, lithium elimination may be reduced. Therefore, the serum lithium levels should be monitored carefully if lithium salts are to be administered.

Information for the Patient: Angioedema: Angioedema, including laryngeal edema, may occur especially following the first dose of cilazapril. Patients should be so advised and told to report immediately any signs or symptoms suggesting angioedema (swelling of face, extremities, eyes, lips, tongue, difficulty in breathing) and to take no more drug until they have consulted with the prescribing physician. Should the tongue and/or larynx be involved, the physician should be consulted immediately.

Hypotension: Patients should be cautioned to report light-headedness, especially during the first few days of cilazapril therapy. If actual syncope occurs, the patients should be told to discontinue the drug until they have consulted with the prescribing physician.

All patients should be cautioned that excessive perspiration and dehydration may lead to an excessive fall in blood pressure because of reduction in fluid volume. Other causes of volume depletion such as vomiting or diarrhea may also lead to a fall in blood pressure; patients should be advised to consult with their physician.

Neutropenia: Patients should be advised to report promptly any indication of infection (e.g., sore throat, fever) since this may be an early sign of neutropenia.

Impaired Liver Function: Patients should be advised to return to the physician if he/she experiences any symptoms possibly related to liver dysfunction. This would include "viral-like symptoms" in the first weeks to months of therapy (such as fever, malaise, muscle pain, rash or adenopathy which are possible indicators of hypersensitivity reactions), or if abdominal pain, nausea or vomiting, loss of appetite, jaundice, itching or any other unexplained symptoms occur during therapy.

Hyperkalemia: Patients should be advised not to use potassium supplements or salt substitutes containing potassium without consulting their physician.

Surgery: Patients planning to undergo surgery and/or anesthesia should be told to inform their physician that they are taking an ACE inhibitor.

Pregnancy: Since the use of cilazapril during pregnancy can cause injury and even death of the developing fetus, patients should be advised to report promptly to their physician if they become pregnant.

Adverse Effects: Cilazapril has been evaluated for safety in 5 450 patients treated for essential hypertension and in 1 106 patients treated for congestive heart failure.

Of these, 2 586 hypertensive and 900 congestive heart failure patients were treated with cilazapril in controlled clinical trials. Cilazapril was evaluated for long-term safety in 798 hypertensive and 264 congestive heart failure patients treated for 1 year or longer.

The most severe adverse reactions reported in the 5 450 patients treated with cilazapril for hypertension included: angioedema/face edema (0.1%), postural hypotension (0.3%), orthostatic hypotension (2.1%), myocardial infarction (0.1%), cerebrovascular disorder (0.04%), renal failure (0.09%), and thrombocytopenic purpura (0.02%). In the 1 106 patients treated with cilazapril for congestive heart failure, the most serious adverse reactions were: postural hypotension (1.6%), symptomatic hypotension (1.2%), myocardial infarction (0.3%), renal failure (0.1%), and cardiogenic shock (1 patient) (see Warnings, Hypotension).

Hypotension and syncope, each reported in 0.1% of the hypertensive patients treated with cilazapril, were reported in 2.1% and 0.8% of the congestive heart failure patients treated with cilazapril.

Discontinuation of therapy was required in 63 (2.4%) of the hypertensive patients and 143 (12.9%) of the congestive heart failure patients.

The most frequent adverse reactions reported in controlled clinical trials (≥1% and more frequent than in placebo treated patients) were: See Table II.

Table II—Inhibace

Adverse Reactions

	Hypertension n=2 586	Congestive Heart Failure n=900
Headache	5.1%	3.2%
Dizziness	3.0%	8.2%
Fatigue	2.1%	2.6%
Cough	1.8%	7.5%
Nausea	1.3%	2.9%
Asthenia	0.3%	1.6%
Palpitation	0.2%	1.2%

Other adverse reactions occurring in less than 1% of the 5 450 hypertension patients and the 1 106 congestive heart failure patients treated with cilazapril were:

Cardiovascular: chest pain, angina pectoris, tachycardia, atrial fibrillation, arrhythmia, flushing.

In the patient population treated with cilazapril for congestive heart failure, there were reports of bradycardia, AV block, extra systoles, cardiac failure and cardiac decompensation.

Renal: micturition frequency, polyuria, dysuria, uremia, renal pain.

Hematologic: epistaxis, anemia, purpura.

Gastrointestinal: dyspepsia, abdominal pain, diarrhea, constipation, vomiting, flatulence, GI bleeding, rectum bleeding, anorexia.

Dermatologic/Allergic: rash (includes maculo-papular rash and erythematous rash), dermatitis, pruritus, urticaria, angioedema (including face edema).

Nervous System: increased sweating, paresthesia, hypoesthesia, impotence, decreased libido, depression, anxiety, dry mouth, vertigo, migraine, tremor, dysphonia, ataxia, confusion, somnolence, insomnia, nervousness.

Musculoskeletal: myalgia, leg cramps, arthralgia.

Special Senses: tinnitus, abnormal vision, photophobia, conjunctivitis, taste perversion.

Respiratory: rhinitis, sinusitis, pharyngitis, bronchitis, respiratory tract infection, dyspnea, bronchospasm.

In the congestive heart failure patient database the overall incidence of dyspnea was 3.1%. Dyspnea however was less frequent after cilazapril than after placebo.

Metabolic: gout.

Body as a Whole: malaise, hot flushes, pain, edema, rigors.

Postmarketing Experience: Treatment with ACE inhibitors has been associated with, rarely, the following: hemolytic anemia, pemphigus and Stevens-Johnson syndrome.

Abnormal Laboratory Findings: Hematology: Patients had clinically relevant changes in platelet (0.4% and 0.7%), neutrophil (1.9% and 1.4%) or white blood cell counts (1.3% and 0.7%) while treated for hypertension and congestive heart failure respectively.

Leukopenia and neutropenia: Leukopenia was observed in 0.2% (10/3 580) and 0% (0/1 163) and neutropenia in 0.4% (22/5 720) and 0.6% (7/1 163) of the hypertensive and congestive heart failure patients respectively. Most of these were single transient occurrences; 1 case with 2 successive abnormalities showed no associated clinical symptoms.

Liver Function Tests: Clinically relevant changes in the values associated with liver function (AST, ALT, GGTP, LDH, total bilirubin and alkaline phosphatase) occurred in 0.1% (bilirubin) to 1.1% (ALT, GGTP) of the hypertensive patients and in 0.8% (LDH) to 2.9% (ALT) of the congestive heart failure patients. Most of these abnormalities were transient.

Renal: Clinically relevant changes in renal function test results (BUN or serum creatinine concentrations) occurred in 0.6% or less of the hypertensive patients and in 2.6% and 0.9% respectively of the congestive heart failure patients.

Hyperkalemia: (see Precautions).

Creatinine: Serum creatinine values >2 mg/dL were reported in 1.3% (44/3 468) of the hypertensive patients. Two thirds of these patients had renal impairment at baseline. Serum creatinine values >2.8 mg/dL were reported in 0.4% (5/1 163) of the congestive heart failure patients. Of these, 4 of the 5 had abnormal serum creatinine values at baseline.

Proteinuria (≥2+ dipstick reaction or excretion of ≥1 g/24h): Proteinuria considered remotely, possibly or probably related to therapy was reported in 0.5% (17/3 421) of the hypertensive patients. Five patients had prior renal impairment. In congestive heart failure patients, 1.4% (16/1 106) experienced potentially clinically relevant proteinuria.

Other: In congestive heart failure patients, hyperglycemia considered remotely, possibly or probably related to therapy was reported in 0.2% (2/1 106) patients.

Overdose: Symptoms and Treatment: Limited data are available with regard to overdosage in humans. The most likely clinical manifestation would be symptoms attributable to severe hypotension, which should be normally treated by i.v. volume expansion with normal saline.

Hemodialysis removes cilazapril and cilazaprilat from the general circulation to a limited extent.

Dosage: Dosage must be individualized.

Initiation of therapy requires consideration of recent antihypertensive drug treatment, the extent of blood pressure elevation, salt restriction, and other pertinent clinical factors. The dosage of other antihypertensive agents being used with cilazapril may need to be adjusted.

The dose should always be taken at about the same time each day.

Hypertension: Monotherapy: The recommended initial dose is 2.5 mg once daily. Dosage should be adjusted according to blood pressure response, generally, at intervals of at least 2 weeks. The usual dose range is 2.5 to 5 mg once daily. Minimal additional blood pressure lowering effects were achieved with a dose of 10 mg once daily. A dose of 10 mg should not be exceeded.

In most patients, the antihypertensive effect of cilazapril is maintained with a once a day dosing regimen. In some patients treated once daily, the antihypertensive effect may diminish toward the end of the dosing interval. This can be evaluated by measuring blood pressure just prior to dosing to determine whether satisfactory control is being maintained for 24 hours. If it is not, either twice daily administration with the same total daily dose, or an increase in dose should be considered. If blood pressure is not adequately controlled with cilazapril alone, a non-potassium-sparing diuretic may be administered concomitantly. After the addition of a diuretic, it may be possible to reduce the dose of cilazapril.

Concomitant Diuretic Therapy: In patients receiving diuretics, cilazapril therapy should be initiated with caution, since they are usually volume depleted and more likely to experience hypotension following ACE inhibition. Whenever possible, all diuretics should be discontinued 2 to 3 days prior to the administration of cilazapril to reduce the likelihood of hypotension (see Warnings). If this is not possible because of the patient's condition, cilazapril should be started at 0.5 mg once daily and the blood pressure closely monitored after the first dose until stabilized. Thereafter, the dose should be adjusted according to individual response.

Dosage in Geriatrics (over 65 Years): Cilazapril treatment should be initiated with 1.25 mg (half of a 2.5 mg tablet) once daily or less, depending on the patient's volume status and general condition. Thereafter, the dose of cilazapril must be adjusted according to individual tolerability, response, and clinical status.

Dosage Adjustment in Renal Impairment: see Precautions, Anaphylactoid Reactions during Membrane Exposure. The following dose schedules are recommended in patients with hypertension: see Table III.

Table III—Inhibace

Dosage Adjustment in Renal Impairment

Creatinine Clearance	Initial Dose of Inhibace	Maximal Dose of Inhibace
>40 mL/min	1 mg once daily	5 mg once daily
10–40 mL/min	0.5 mg once daily	2.5 mg once daily
<10 mL/min	0.25–0.5 mg once or twice a week according to blood pressure response	

Hemodialysis Patients: Cilazapril should be administered on days when dialysis is not performed and the dosage should be adjusted according to blood pressure response.

Dosage Adjustment in Hepatic Impairment: Should patients with liver cirrhosis require treatment with cilazapril, treatment should be initiated with caution at a dose of 0.5 mg once daily or less as significant hypotension may occur (see Precautions).

Congestive Heart Failure: Cilazapril can be used as adjunctive therapy with digitalis and/or diuretics in patients with congestive heart failure. Therapy should be initiated under close medical supervision. Blood pressure and renal function should be monitored both before and during treatment with cilazapril because severe hypotension and more rarely, renal failure have been reported (see Warnings and Precautions).

Initiation of therapy requires consideration of recent diuretic therapy and the possibility of severe salt/volume depletion. If possible, the dose of diuretic should be reduced before beginning treatment, to reduce the likelihood of hypotension. Serum potassium should also be monitored (see Warnings and Precautions, Drug Interactions).

Therapy with cilazapril should be initiated with a recommended starting dose of 0.5 mg once daily under close medical surpervision. **In elderly patients with congestive heart failure on high diuretic dosage the recommended starting dose of cilazapril 0.5 mg must be strictly followed (see Warnings).**

The dose should be increased to the lowest maintenance dose of 1 mg daily, usually within a 5 day period, according to tolerability and clinical status. Further titration within the usual maintenance dose of 1 mg to 2.5 mg daily should be carried out based on patient response, clinical status and tolerability.

The usual maximum dose is 2.5 mg once daily. A few patients have been titrated to 5 mg once daily with some additional benefits being achieved. However only limited data is available in congestive heart failure patients treated with 5 mg once daily.

Dosage Adjustment in Patients with Congestive Heart Failure and Renal Impairment or Hyponatremia: Reduced dosage may be required for patients with congestive heart failure and renal

Inhibace (cont'd)

impairment or hyponatremia depending on the creatinine clearance. The following dosing is recommended: see Table IV.

Table IV—Inhibace

Dosage Adjustment in Patients with Congestive Heart Failure and Renal Impairment or Hyponatremia

Creatinine Clearance	Initial Dose of Inhibace	Maximal Dose of Inhibace
>40 mL/min	0.5 mg once daily	2.5 mg once daily
10-40 mL/min	0.25-0.5 mg once daily	2.5 mg once daily
<10 mL/min	0.25-0.5 mg once or twice a week according to blood pressure response	

Supplied: 1 mg: Each yellow, oval-shaped, single-scored, biconvex, film-coated tablet, imprinted CIL 1, contains: cilazapril 1 mg as cilazapril monohydrate. Nonmedicinal ingredients: cornstarch, hydroxypropyl methylcellulose, iron oxide, lactose, sodium stearyl fumarate, talc and titanium dioxide. Bottles of 100.

2.5 mg: Each pinkish-brown, oval-shaped, single-scored, biconvex, film-coated tablet, imprinted CIL 2.5, contains: cilazapril 2.5 mg as cilazapril monohydrate. Nonmedicinal ingredients: cornstarch, hydroxypropyl methylcellulose, iron oxide, lactose, sodium stearyl fumarate, talc and titanium dioxide. Bottles of 100.

5 mg: Each reddish-brown, oval-shaped, single-scored, biconvex tablet, imprinted CIL 5, contains: cilazapril 5 mg as cilazapril monohydrate. Nonmedicinal ingredients: cornstarch, hydroxypropyl methylcellulose, iron oxide, lactose, sodium stearyl fumarate, talc and titanium dioxide. Bottles of 100.

Store 15 to 30°C. Keep container tightly closed.

(Shown in Product Recognition Section)

Reviewed 1998

INNOHEP® Ⓟ

Leo

Tinzaparin Sodium

Anticoagulant—Antithrombotic

Pharmacology: Tinzaparin is a low molecular weight (LMW) heparin, produced by enzymatic depolymerization of conventional heparin from porcine mucosa. It possesses antithrombotic activity mediated through antithrombin III.

Pharmacokinetics: The pharmacokinetics of tinzaparin after a single s.c. injection have been studied in clinical trials by the measurement of plasma levels of anti-Xa activity, anti-IIa activity and APTT activity (see Table I).

Table I—Innohep

Pharmacokinetics

	anti-Xa activity	anti-IIa activity	APTT activity
Absorption T½ after s.c.	199.5 min	256.7 min	
Bioavailability	90.1%	66.8%	
Elimination T½	81.9 min	71.3 min	35.3 min
Apparent volume of distribution	4.0 L	10.9 L	4.0 L
Time for peak activity	4-6 hours	4-6 hours	

Results from clinical trials, however, have not demonstrated that plasma levels of any of these activities correlate to either the antithrombotic effect or the bleeding risk. The plasma level of anti-Xa activity may only be used as a measure of the amount of tinzaparin anti-Xa active molecules in plasma. It is not recommended as a tool for monitoring treatment efficacy with tinzaparin.

In orthopedic hip or knee replacement surgery, patients may have a very high risk of developing postoperative deep venous thrombosis and also may have a high risk of bleeding. Therefore, careful precise dosing of conventional unfractionated heparin is required. Results from clinical trials with tinzaparin indicate that there is a close relationship between plasma levels of anti-Xa activity and body weight. This indicates that dosing according to body weight is the best way to obtain precise dosing.

Tinzaparin, 75 anti-Xa IU/kg s.c. once daily following hip or knee replacement surgery, has been shown to be safe and effective for the prevention of deep-vein thrombosis in a randomized double-blind trial versus adjusted dose warfarin. Tinzaparin was equally effective as warfarin treatment in hip surgery and superior to warfarin in preventing thromboembolic events in knee replacement.

Indications: For the treatment of deep vein thrombosis.

In the management of the prevention of postoperative venous thromboembolism in patients undergoing orthopedic surgery.

Tinzaparin may be used in the management of the prevention of postoperative venous thromboembolism in patients undergoing general surgery who are at high risk of developing postoperative venous thromboembolism (see Precautions, Selection of General Surgery Patients).

Postoperative administration of tinzaparin does not preclude other prophylactic modalities including physical and mechanical methods of adjunct therapy.

Contraindications: Tinzaparin must **not** be administered by i.m. injection due to the risk of hematoma. Where possible, i.m. injections should be avoided in patients during anticoagulant treatment. Allergy and hypersensitivity to tinzaparin. Acute or subacute septic endocarditis. History of thrombocytopenia or in patients in whom an in vitro platelet-aggregation test in the presence of tinzaparin is positive. Uncontrolled severe hypertension. Generalized hemorrhage tendency and other conditions/diseases involving an increased risk of hemorrhage. Hemophilia or major blood clotting disorders. Severe liver damage. Uremia. Acute cerebral insults. Active bleeding from a local lesion such as an acute ulcer or ulcerating carcinoma.

Warnings: Tinzaparin should be used with care in patients with severe liver or kidney insufficiency, uncontrolled arterial hypertension or a history of gastrointestinal ulceration.

Children and *Pregnancy:* There is currently no clinical experience with tinzaparin in pregnant women and children. In two clinical studies performed in pregnant women during second trimester using tinzaparin in a dose of 35 to 40 anti-Xa IU/kg, no transplacental passage of anti-Xa and anti-IIa activities was demonstrated. In rabbits no placental passage of anti-Xa and anti-IIa activity could be demonstrated after s.c. doses of 1 750 anti-Xa IU/kg body weight of tinzaparin. Toxicological studies have shown that no embryotoxic or teratogenic effects were found. Tinzaparin should not be used in pregnant women and in children unless the therapeutic benefits to the patients outweigh the possible risks to the fetus and the patients.

Lactation: It is not known whether tinzaparin is excreted in breast milk of nursing mothers. Mothers receiving tinzaparin should avoid breast-feeding.

Innohep contains sodium bisulfite, which may cause allergic reactions including anaphylactic symptoms and life-threatening or less severe asthmatic episodes in certain susceptible people.

The overall prevalence of sulfite sensitivity in the general population is unknown. Sulfite sensitivity is seen more frequently in asthmatics than in nonasthmatic people.

There have been cases of intraspinal hematomas with the concurrent use of LMW heparin and spinal/epidural anesthesia resulting in long-term or permanent paralysis. The risk of these events may be higher with the use of postoperative indwelling epidural catheters. Tinzaparin should be used concurrently with spinal/epidural anesthesia only when therapeutic benefits to the patient outweigh the possible risks. Appropriate guidelines, precautions, monitoring and followup procedures should be followed (see Adverse Effects, Spinal/Epidural Anesthesia).

Precautions: Tinzaparin should not be administered by i.m. injection due to the risk of hematoma. Where possible i.m. injections should be avoided in patients during anticoagulant treatment.

Tinzaparin should be used with caution in conjunction with drugs which affect either platelet function or the coagulation system (i.e., salicylates, vitamin K antagonists and dextran).

Laboratory Tests: Administration of 75 anti Xa IU/kg in hip and knee surgery patients may be associated with bleeding. In the event of excessive blood loss from the surgical wound, the first injection of tinzaparin should be deferred, until the bleeding has stopped. Clinical studies found no correlation between anti-Xa, anti-IIa, or APTT ratios and bleeding complications. Therefore, there is no need for extensive monitoring of these activities. A fall in thrombocyte counts has been observed yet no direct association to tinzaparin has been identified.

As a precautionary measure, platelet counts should be determined prior to the start of treatment with tinzaparin and, subsequently, twice weekly for the duration of treatment. An in vitro platelet-aggregation test in the presence of tinzaparin should be performed in patients with a history of heparin-induced thrombocytopenia. In case of negative results, treatment with tinzaparin may be instituted but the patient must be closely monitored and platelet counts determined at least once daily. A positive result contraindicates tinzaparin.

In the case of minor bleeding, the drug should be postponed or withdrawn. When serious bleeding requires reversal of tinzaparin, protamine sulfate (1% solution) by slow infusion will neutralize tinzaparin. The effect of protamine sulfate should be monitored by the APTT. (For more information, please see Overdose: Symptoms and Treatment.)

Selection of General Surgery Patients: Tinzaparin may be used as an adjunct in the prevention of postoperative venous thromboembolism in patients undergoing general surgery who are at high risk of developing postoperative venous thromboembolism.

General surgery patients, who have one or more of the following risk factors, are at high risk of developing postoperative venous thromboembolism: previous venous thromboembolism, varicose veins, obesity, heart failure, malignancy, previous long bone fracture of lower limb, bed rest more than 5 days prior to surgery, predicted duration of surgery more than 30 minutes, and age 60 years or above.

<u>*Drug Interactions:*</u> There has been no clinical experience with the possible interaction between tinzaparin and other drugs other than ASA. No evidence of an interaction between tinzaparin and ASA on the **anti-Xa or anti-IIa activities** was found. The **bleeding time** increased on the combined treatment in 7/8 subjects as expected with regard to the ASA intake, though no significant influence on the platelet aggregation was found. The bleeding time was prolonged by an average of 3 to 4 minutes (within a variance of 4 to 7.25 minutes) on the final day of 3 consecutive days of ASA intake (300 mg daily). Bleeding time did not exceed 10 to 12 minutes (upper normal limit), nor did any patient experience clinically evident bleeding. Tinzaparin alone or in combination with ASA was well tolerated in clinical studies with only occasional bruising at the injection site seen.

ASA inhibits platelet aggregation and is often recommended in the prevention of arterial thrombi formation. Heparin and LMW heparin primarily inhibit fibrin formation on the surface of platelet aggregates. Theoretically, maximal antithrombotic effect of the two compounds may be achieved when combined. The combined use of several substances influencing hemostasis will increase the risk of bleeding complications, and caution must be exercised particularly in patients at risk of developing bleeding complications. Many patients presenting for thromboprophylaxis may be ASA consumers since ASA is recommended as prophylaxis against myocardial infarction in many countries. Therefore, tinzaparin should be used with caution in conjunction with drugs which affect the platelet function or the coagulation system (i.e., oral anticoagulants, inhibitors of platelet aggregation, nonsteroidal anti-inflammatory agents, preparations containing ASA, vitamin K antagonists and dextran).

Adverse Effects: Hemorrhage is the main complication that can result from tinzaparin treatment. However, the clinical trials with tinzaparin in the dosages recommended have not been associated with hemorrhage to any clinically significant degree.

Frequent reactions (>1/100): General: hematoma at injection site—uncomplicated. Liver: transient increase in aminotransferase levels—not clinically relevant.

Less frequent reactions: Skin: rash—uncomplicated.

Rare (<1/1 000): General: allergic reactions (has not been reported). Blood: bleeding—clinical relevance depend on the site and severity of bleeding; thrombocytopenia—clinical relevance unknown.

Liver: As with conventional heparin, a significant but transient increase of the liver transaminases has been noted following administration of tinzaparin in doses of 50 anti-Xa IU/kg body weight once daily, as well as in higher doses. The increased levels of liver transaminases observed in the tinzaparin studies were most probably induced by the treatment. The conclusion agrees with observations made in association with treatment using heparins. The exact mechanism associated with the increased levels of liver transaminases has not been fully elucidated. However, no consistent irreversible liver damage has ever been demonstrated due to this known heparin effect.

Clinical studies have suggested that the transaminase increase seems to be dose dependent and requires more than 3 days of treatment to appear. Following the administration of tinzaparin in a dose of 150 anti-Xa IU/kg twice daily; however, all subjects showed increased plasma levels of AST and ALT from a mean of 17.8 to 128.5 U/mL and 19.3 to 257 U/mL respectively. These elevations correspond to a 7- to 12-fold increase as compared to the post-study evaluation performed within 7 days of study completion. Transaminase levels normalized within 2 weeks of the last dose of tinzaparin.

In summary, tinzaparin administered in doses of 50 anti-Xa IU/kg body weight once daily, 75 anti-Xa IU/kg once daily, and 150 anti-Xa IU/kg twice daily, for 5 consecutive days results in markedly increased but reversible liver transaminases levels (especially ALT). Normalization of these levels occurred within 2 to 4 weeks. Clinical studies involving administration of standard heparin in doses up to 10 000 IU given i.v. every 6 hours or s.c. in doses of 5 000 IU every 8 hours or twice daily, have yielded the same effect.

Spinal/Epidural Anesthesia: There have been cases of intraspinal hematomas with the concurrent use of LMW heparin and spinal/epidural anesthesia resulting in long-term or permanent paralysis (incidence: 1:45 000). Tinzaparin should only be used concurrently with spinal/epidural anesthesia when the therapeutic benefits to the patient outweigh the possible risks. If LMW heparin is used concurrently with spinal/epidural anesthesia, experts have suggested that no spinal invasion should be attempted for 12 hours following the dose of LMW heparin and that the next dose should be held until at least 2 hours after the spinal/epidural anesthesia procedure. The same rules are applied to the withdrawal or manipulation of the catheter. Careful vigilance for neurological signs is recommended, with rapid diagnosis and treatment, if such signs occur.

Overdose: Symptoms and Treatment: Bleeding is a symptom of tinzaparin overdose. In recommended doses, there should be no need for an antidote but in the event of accidental administration of an overdose, protamine sulfate should be given. There is no clinical experience with overdose, but studies in animals indicate that the dose of protamine sulfate required to neutralize the hemorrhagic effects is greater for tinzaparin than for unfractionated heparin. The effect of protamine sulfate should be monitored by the APTT. Excess bleeding is not seen in animal experiments when the APTT is brought within the normal range. If transfusions are required, fresh frozen plasma is preferred.

In the case of minor bleeding, the drug should be postponed or withdrawn. When serious bleeding requires reversal of tinzaparin, protamine sulfate (1% solution) by slow infusion will neutralize tinzaparin. No more than 50 mg should be administered, using a very slow i.v., during a 10-minute period. Each mg of protamine sulfate neutralizes approximately 100 anti-Xa IU tinzaparin.

Dosage: Prevention of postoperative venous thromboembolism in **general surgery** patients: tinzaparin 3 500 anti-Xa IU (available in a prefilled syringe) given by s.c. injection 2 hours before surgery followed by 3 500 anti-Xa IU once daily for 7 to 10 days.

Prevention of postoperative venous thromboembolism in **orthopedic surgery** patients: **Hip Surgery:** Tinzaparin 50 anti-Xa IU/kg body weight given by s.c. injection 2 hours before surgery followed by 50 anti-Xa IU/kg body weight once daily for 7 to 10 days; **or** tinzaparin 75 anti-Xa IU/kg body weight given postoperatively by s.c. injection once daily for 7 to 10 days.

Knee Surgery: Tinzaparin 75 anti-Xa IU/kg body weight given postoperatively by s.c. injection once daily for 7 to 10 days.

For convenience, the following prefilled syringes are available for dosing by body weight (see Table II).

Table II—Innohep

Availability of Prefilled Syringes for Dosing by Body Weight

	Preoperative 50 anti-Xa IU/kg	Postoperative 75 anti-Xa IU/kg
Doses per syringe	**Body weight**	**Body weight**
3 500 anti-Xa IU	60-80 kg	35-55 kg
4 500 anti-Xa IU	80-100 kg	50-70 kg

Patients outside of these weight ranges should be dosed on an individual basis.

Treatment of deep vein thrombosis: tinzaparin 175 anti-Xa IU/kg of body weight, once daily.

No dose modifications are necessary for the use of tinzaparin in elderly patients. There is no experience of use in children.

Information for the Patient: See Blue Section—Information for the Patient "Innohep".

Supplied: Syringes: 10 000 anti-Xa IU/mL: Each mL of sterile solution contains: tinzaparin sodium 10 000 anti-Xa IU. Nonmedicinal ingredients: sodium acetate•3H_2O, sodium hydroxide* and water for injection (*quantity sufficient for pH adjustment). pH range of the final solution is 5.0 to 7.5. Preservative-free. Unit dose syringes of 0.35 mL and 0.45 mL.

20 000 anti-Xa IU/mL: Each mL of sterile solution contains: tinzaparin sodium 20 000 anti-Xa IU. Nonmedicinal ingredients: sodium metabisulfite, sodium hydroxide* and water for injection (*quantity sufficient for pH adjustment). pH range of the final solution is 5.0 to 7.5. Preservative-free. Unit dose graduated syringes of 0.5 mL, 0.7 mL and 0.9 mL.

Vials: 10 000 anti-Xa IU/mL: Each mL of sterile solution contains: tinzaparin sodium 10 000 anti-Xa IU. Nonmedicinal ingredients: benzyl alcohol, sodium hydroxide*, sodium metabisulfite and water for injection (*quantity sufficient for pH adjustment). pH range of the final solution is 5.0 to 7.5. Multidose vials of 2 mL.

20 000 anti-Xa IU/mL: Each mL of sterile solution contains: tinzaparin sodium 20 000 anti-Xa IU. Nonmedicinal ingredients: benzyl alcohol, sodium hydroxide*, sodium metabisulfite and water for injection (*quantity sufficient for pH adjustment). pH range of the final solution is 5.0 to 7.5. Multidose vials of 2 mL.

Store at 15 to 25°C. Protect from light.

Reviewed 1998

INOCOR® Ⓟ

Sanofi

Amrinone Lactate

Inotrope—Vasodilator

Pharmacology: Amrinone is a positive inotropic agent with vasodilatory activity, different in structure and mode of action from either digitalis glycosides or catecholamines. Its mechanism of action has not been fully elucidated. Experimental evidence indicates that it is not a beta-adrenergic agonist. It inhibits myocardial cyclic adenosine monophosphate phosphodiesterase (c-AMPase) activity and increases cellular levels of c-AMP. Unlike digoxin, it does not inhibit sodium-potassium adenosine tri-phosphatase activity.

Vasodilatory effect of amrinone is the result of direct relaxant effect on vascular smooth muscle. The drug reduces both the afterload and preload.

Following an i.v. loading dose (1 to 2 minutes) of 0.68 to 1.2 mg/kg to normal volunteers, amrinone had a volume of distribution of 1.2 L/kg. Following a distributive phase half-life of about 4.6 minutes in plasma, amrinone had a mean apparent first-order terminal elimination half-life of about 3.6 hours.

In patients with congestive heart failure receiving infusions of amrinone the mean apparent first-order terminal elimination half-life was 5.8 hours. Following loading doses of 1.5 to 3.5 mg/kg, steady-state plasma levels of about 2.4 μg/mL were maintained during infusion of 5 to 10 μg/kg/min. Amrinone has been shown in one study to be 10 to 22% bound to human plasma protein by ultrafiltration in vitro, and in another study 36 to 49% bound by either ultrafiltration or equilibrium dialysis.

The drug is excreted in man as both unchanged amrinone and several metabolites (N-glycolyl, N-acetate, 0-glucuronide and N-glucuronide), primarily via the urine. Oral amrinone is 92% bioavailable relative to i.v. amrinone. Approximately 63% of an oral dose was excreted in the urine over a 72-hour period. In the first 8 hours, 51% appeared as amrinone in the urine, with 5% as the N-acetate, 8% as the N-glycolate, and less than 5% for each glucuronide. Approximately 18% of the dose was excreted in the feces in 72 to 96 hours.

In a 24-hour nonradioactive i.v. study, 10 to 40% of the dose was excreted in the urine as unchanged amrinone. The N-acetyl metabolite represented less than 2% of the dose.

In patients with depressed myocardial function, amrinone produces a prompt increase in cardiac output due to its inotropic and vasodilator actions.

Following a single i.v. bolus dose of amrinone of 0.75 to 3 mg/kg in patients with congestive heart failure, dose related increases in cardiac output occur (a maximum of about 28% increase at 0.75 mg/kg to about 61% increase at 3 mg/kg). The peak effect occurs within 10 minutes at all doses. The duration of effect depends upon dose, lasting about ½ hour at 0.75 mg/kg and approximately 2 hours at 3 mg/kg.

Over the same range of doses, pulmonary capillary wedge pressure and total peripheral resistance show dose related decreases (mean maximum decreases of 29% in pulmonary capillary wedge pressure and 29% in systemic vascular resistance). At doses up to 3.0 mg/kg, dose related decreases in diastolic pressure (up to 13%) have been observed. Mean arterial pressure decreases (9.7%) at the dose of 3.0 mg/kg.

The changes in hemodynamic parameters are maintained during continuous i.v. infusion and for several hours following the infusion with no evidence of tachyphylaxis.

Amrinone is effective even in fully digitalized patients. Its inotropic effects are independent of those of digitalis. In heart failure patients, it produces positive inotropic effects without increasing myocardial oxygen demand or causing clinically significant increases in heart rate.

Most patients have been studied hemodynamically for periods up to 24 hours. Some patients have been maintained on infusions of amrinone for longer periods and demonstrated consistent hemodynamic and clinical effects. The duration of therapy should depend on patient responsiveness.

Indications: For the short-term management of severe congestive heart failure. Because of limited experience and potential for serious adverse effects (see Adverse Effects), amrinone should only be used in patients who can be closely monitored and have not responded adequately to digitalis, diuretics, and/or vasodilators. It has been used concomitantly with other agents including digitalis, diuretics, and vasodilators.

Contraindications: In patients with hypersensitivity to amrinone or sensitivity to bisulfites.

Warnings: Allergic Reactions: Amrinone contains sodium metabisulfite, which may cause allergic-type reactions including anaphylactic symptoms and life-threatening or less severe asthmatic episodes in certain susceptible people. The overall prevalence of sulfite sensitivity in the general population is unknown and probably low. Sulfite sensitivity is seen more frequently in asthmatic than in nonasthmatic people.

Reduction of Blood Platelet Counts: Administration of amrinone resulted in platelet count reductions to below 100 000/mm³ in 2.4% of patients. Blood platelet counts should be determined before and during amrinone therapy. Clinically significant lowering of platelet counts warrants consideration of reduction or discontinuation of amrinone therapy. Amrinone therapy should be discontinued if platelet count is ≤50 000/mm³.

Platelet reduction appears to be dose-related. This reduction may be due to a decrease in platelet survival time which is postulated to be due to direct amrinone binding. Bone marrow examinations were normal in several patients who developed thrombocytopenia while receiving amrinone. There is no evidence relating platelet reduction to immune response or to a platelet activating factor. Asymptomatic platelet count reduction (to <150 000/mm³) may be reversed within 1 week of a decrease in drug dosage.

Acute M.I.: Amrinone injection is not recommended in the acute phase of myocardial infarction as insufficient data are available to support its use for this indication.

Hepatic: Hepatotoxicity has been observed in man in 0.2% of patients following i.v. administration. There have been rare reports of increases in hepatic enzymes, bilirubin elevation and jaundice.

It is advisable to perform liver function tests before and during therapy. If alterations in liver enzymes occur together with clinical symptoms suggesting an idiosyncratic hypersensitivity reaction, therapy should be promptly discontinued.

Exceptionally, excessive hypotension has been reported when amrinone was used concurrently with disopyramide.

Concurrent administration with disopyramide should be undertaken with caution until additional clinical experience is available.

Precautions: Amrinone **should not be used in severe obstructive aortic or pulmonic valvular disease** in lieu of surgical relief of the obstruction. Like other inotropic agents, it may aggravate outflow tract obstruction in conditions like hypertrophic subaortic stenosis.

During i.v. therapy, blood pressure and heart rate should be monitored and the **rate of infusion** decreased in patients showing hypotension. At the same time, dosage of concomitant medications (e.g., vasodilators) should be readjusted as required. In addition, pulmonary capillary wedge pressure and cardiac index should be obtained to demonstrate patient responsiveness whenever possible.

Fluid and electrolyte changes and serum creatinine should be carefully monitored during amrinone therapy.

Patients who have been extensively dehydrated by vigorous diuretic therapy may have insufficient cardiac filling pressure to respond adequately to amrinone, in which case correction or adjustment of fluids/electrolytes and diuretic dosage is essential to obtain satisfactory response with amrinone. Potassium loss due to excessive diuresis may predispose digitalized patients to arrhythmia. Therefore hypokalemia should be corrected by potassium supplementation in advance of or during use. Improvement in cardiac output with resultant diuresis may necessitate a reduction in the dose of diuretic.

Inocor (cont'd)

In patients with **atrial fibrillation or flutter,** digitalis should be administered concomitantly to control the possible enhanced atrioventricular conduction induced by amrinone. In such cases, and in those with **multifocal or runs of premature ventricular contractions,** careful dose titration and close electrocardiographic monitoring is advisable, during i.v. therapy. As supraventricular and ventricular arrhythmias have been observed in the high-risk population treated, and as the potential for arrhythmia, present in heart failure itself, may be increased by many drugs or combination of drugs, patients receiving amrinone should be closely monitored during infusion.

Plasma levels of amrinone may rise higher than expected during the infusion period in some congestive heart failure patients in whom associated compromised renal and hepatic perfusion is present. In these cases especially careful monitoring of hemodynamic response and/or plasma levels is necessary.

Pregnancy: There are no adequate studies in pregnant women. Amrinone should not be used during pregnancy unless the potential benefit to the patient justifies the potential risk to the fetus.

Lactation: Caution should be exercised when amrinone is administered to a nursing woman, since it is not known whether it is excreted in human milk.

Children: Safety and effectiveness in children have not been established. Amrinone should only be used when the potential benefits outweigh the potential risks.

Drug Interactions: No specific drug interaction study has been done in humans with injectable amrinone.

Amrinone has been used concurrently with the following drugs: digitalis glycosides, quinidine, propranolol, metoprolol, prazosin, hydralazine, captopril, isosorbide dinitrate, nitroglycerin, lidocaine, furosemide, ethacrynic acid, hydrochlorothiazide, chorthalidone, spironolactone, potassium supplements, insulin, heparin, warfarin sodium and diazepam. No serious adverse effects due to the interaction between these drugs and amrinone were reported. However, careful dosage readjustments of concurrent medication may be required.

Disopyramide (see Warnings).

Chemical Interactions: A chemical interaction occurs slowly over a 24 hour period when the i.v. solution of amrinone is mixed **directly** with dextrose (glucose)-containing solutions. **Therefore, amrinone injection should not be diluted with solutions that contain dextrose (glucose) prior to injection.**

A chemical interaction occurs immediately, which is evidenced by the formation of a precipitate when furosemide is injected into an i.v. line of an infusion of amrinone. Therefore, furosemide should not be administered in i.v. lines containing amrinone.

Adverse Effects: Thrombocytopenia: Administration of amrinone resulted in platelet count reductions to below 100 000/mm³ in 2.4% of the patients (see Warnings).

Gastrointestinal Effects: nausea (1.7%), vomiting (0.9%), abdominal pain (0.4%), anorexia (0.4%) and diarrhea.

Cardiovascular Effects: Ventricular arrhythmias including ventricular tachycardia, ventricular fibrillation, or ventricular ectopy have been reported in patients receiving amrinone. Supraventricular arrhythmia including tachycardia, flutter and bradycardia have also been described, as well as hypotension.

Hepatotoxicity: liver enzymes elevation (0.2%) (see Warnings).

Other: Additional adverse reactions observed in i.v. amrinone clinical studies include fever (0.9%), chest pain (0.2%), and burning at site of injection (0.2%). Rarely headache, chills, hematuria, pneumothorax, yellowing of the nails, burning and cutaneous necrosis at the injection site, anemia and leukocytosis have also been reported.

Hypersensitivity: There have been reports of several apparent hypersensitivity reactions in patients treated with oral amrinone for about two weeks. The oral formulation is not marketed. Signs and symptoms were variable but included pericarditis, pleuritis, interstitial pneumonitis and ascites (1 case), myositis with interstitial shadowing on chest x-ray and elevated sedimentation rate (1 case) and vasculitis with nodular pulmonary densities, hypoxemia, and jaundice (1 case). The first patient died, not necessarily of the possible reaction, while the last two resolved with discontinuation of therapy. None of the cases were rechallenged so that attribution to amrinone is not certain, but possible hypersensitivity reactions should be considered in any patient maintained for a prolonged period on amrinone.

Renal Function Tests: Abnormalities of renal function tests and isolated cases of renal failure have been reported. The contribution of the underlying heart failure to these abnormalities is not clear.

Overdose: Symptoms and Treatment: Because of its vasodilatory and inotropic effect, amrinone injection in excessive doses may produce hypotension and/or arrhythmia. If hypotension or arrhythmia does occur, amrinone administration should be reduced or stopped. No antidote is known, but general measures for circulatory support should be taken.

It is suggested dialysis be considered when clinically necessary.

A death has been reported with a massive accidental overdose of amrinone (840 mg over 3 hours by initial bolus and infusion), although causal relation is uncertain. Diligence should be exercised during product preparation and administration.

Dosage: Adequate facilities and personnel must be available for monitoring the cardiac and circulatory response.

Monitoring central venous pressure (CVP) may be valuable in the assessment of hypotension and fluid balance management. Prior correction or adjustment of fluid/electrolytes may be necessary to obtain satisfactory response.

Inspect ampuls visually and do not use if evidence of particulate matter or discoloration.

Protect amrinone ampuls from prolonged exposure to light. Ampul packaging is light resistant for protection during storage in original containers. Store at room temperature.

Administer i.v. as supplied or dilute in normal (0.9%), or half normal saline solution to a concentration of 1 to 3 mg/mL. Use diluted solutions within 24 hours.

A chemical interaction occurs slowly when the i.v. solution of amrinone is mixed directly with glucose (dextrose) solutions. Solutions of amrinone must not be diluted with glucose solutions prior to injection. However, amrinone may be injected into running glucose infusions through a Y-connector or directly into the tubing.

A chemical interaction occurs immediately, which is evidenced by the formation of a precipitate when furosemide is injected into an i.v. line of an amrinone infusion. Therefore, furosemide should not be administered in i.v. lines containing amrinone.

Initiate therapy with a 0.75 mg/kg loading dose given slowly over 2 to 3 minutes. Continue therapy with maintenance infusion of 5 to 10 μg/kg/minute. Based on clinical response, an additional loading dose of 0.75 mg/kg may be given 30 minutes after the initiation of therapy. Maintain infusion at approximately 5 to 10 μg/kg/minute such that the total daily dose (including loading doses) does not exceed 10 mg/kg. In a limited number of patients a dosage regimen up to 18 mg/kg/day was used. However be cautioned about the possibility of increased incidence of adverse reactions with a dosage higher than 10 mg/kg/day. The rate of administration should be adjusted according to the patient's response. Reduce or titrate the infusion downward based on clinical responsiveness or occurrence of untoward effects. In most patients amrinone was administered up to 24 hours. Its administration is not recommended for a period over 24 hours unless the potential benefit clearly exceeds the risk of longer therapy.

Table I is provided as an example of applicable dosages and flow-rates when using a specific dilution (2.5 mg amrinone/mL) of the original (5 mg/mL) ampuls.

Supplied: Each mL of clear, yellow solution contains: amrinone 5 mg as amrinone lactate. Nonmedicinal ingredients: sodium metabisulfite and water for injection. pH adjusted to 3.2 to 4.0 with lactic acid or sodium hydroxide. The total concentration of lactic acid can vary between 5.0 mg/mL and 7.5 mg/mL. Gluten-, lactose- and tartrazine-free. Ampuls of 20 mL, boxes of 5.

Protect from prolonged exposure to light. Ampul packaging is light resistant for protection during storage in original containers. Store at room temperature.

Reviewed 1999

Table I—Inocor

Amrinone I.V. Dosage Guide (refers to 1:1 dilution of 5 mg/mL ampul in normal or half-normal saline to a final concentration of 2.5 mg/mL)

Patient's Weight (kg)	5 μg/kg/min	6 μg/kg/min	7 μg/kg/min	8 μg/kg/min	9 μg/kg/min	10 μg/kg/min
	Flow Rate in mL/hour					
30	3.6	4.3	5.0	5.8	6.5	7.2
35	4.2	5.0	5.9	6.7	7.6	8.4
40	4.8	5.8	6.7	7.7	8.6	9.6
45	5.4	6.5	7.6	8.6	9.7	10.8
50	6.0	7.2	8.4	9.6	10.8	12.0
55	6.6	7.9	9.2	10.6	11.9	13.2
60	7.2	8.6	10.1	11.5	13.0	14.4
65	7.8	9.4	10.9	12.5	14.0	15.6
70	8.4	10.1	11.8	13.4	15.1	16.8
75	9.0	10.8	12.6	14.4	16.2	18.0
80	9.6	11.5	13.4	15.3	17.3	19.2
85	10.2	12.2	14.3	16.3	18.3	20.4
90	10.8	13.0	15.1	17.3	19.4	21.6
95	11.4	13.7	15.9	18.2	20.5	22.8
100	12.0	14.4	16.8	19.2	21.6	24.0

INSULIN HUMAN (Biosynthetic) Preparations
NOVOLIN®ge Preparations
Novo Nordisk

Insulin Human (Biosynthetic)
Antidiabetic Agent

Pharmacology: Novolin®**ge** Biosynthetic Human Insulin is a polypeptide structurally identical to natural human insulin.

Novolin®**ge** is produced by recombinant DNA technology, using Saccharomyces cerevisiae (baker's yeast). The content of immunoreactive peptides derived from the used microorganism (yeast) is undetectable (less than 1 ppm by weight of the dry insulin) as determined by enzyme linked immunoabsorbent assay.

When administered in appropriate regular doses to patients with diabetes mellitus and who follow a controlled diet and exercise program, Novolin®**ge** temporarily restores their ability to metabolize carbohydrates, protein and fats.

The Novolin®**ge** insulin formulations differ with respect to onset, peak and duration of action. These times reflect averages and can vary depending upon the individual patient. The standard time action characteristics can be located in Table I (on following page).

Novolin®ge Toronto, (Insulin Injection, Human Biosynthetic) is a clear, colorless neutral solution of human insulin with a short duration of action. The effect of Novolin®**ge** Toronto after s.c. administration begins after approximately 0.5 hours, is maximal between 2.5 and 5 hours and terminates after approximately 8 hours.

Novolin®ge NPH (Insulin Isophane, Human Biosynthetic) is a cloudy neutral suspension of human isophane insulin with an intermediate duration of action. The effect of Novolin®**ge** NPH begins after approximately 1.5 hours, is maximal between 4 and 12 hours and terminates after approximately 24 hours.

Novolin®ge Lente (Insulin Zinc Suspension-Medium, Human Biosynthetic) is a cloudy neutral suspension of human insulin with an intermediate duration of action. Thirty percent (30%) of the insulin is present in amorphous form and 70% in crystalline form. The effect of Novolin®**ge** Lente begins after approximately 2.5 hours, is maximal between 7 and 15 hours and terminates after approximately 22 hours.

Novolin®ge Ultralente (Insulin Zinc Suspension—Prolonged, Human Biosynthetic) is a cloudy neutral suspension of human insulin with a prolonged duration of action. The insulin is present in crystalline form. The effect of Novolin®**ge** Ultralente begins after approximately 4 hours, is maximal between 8 and 24 hours and terminates after approximately 28 hours.

Table I—Insulin Human (Biosynthetic) Preparations/Novolin®ge Preparations

Standard Time Action Characteristics of the Novolin®ge Preparations

Biosynthetic Human Insulin Preparations	Description	Buffer pH	Zinc Content mg/1 000 Units	Protein Modifier	Preservative	Onset (Hours)	Approx. Peak (Hours)	Duration (Hours)
Short Acting								
Novolin®ge Toronto Insulin Injection, (Regular)	clear, colorless solution of zinc insulin crystals plus glycerin	none 7–7.8	0.1–0.4	none	m-cresol 0.3%	0.5	2.5–5	8
Intermediate Acting								
Novolin®ge NPH Insulin Isophane	cloudy, white suspension of a crystalline complex of zinc insulin crystals and protamine plus glycerin and NaCl	phosphate 7–7.8	0.1–0.4	protamine	m-cresol 0.15% phenol 0.065%	1.5	4–12	24
Novolin®ge Lente Insulin Zinc Suspension—Medium	cloudy, white suspension of zinc insulin complex in crystalline (approx. 70%) and amorphous form plus NaCl	acetate 7–7.8	1.2–2.5	none	methylparaben 0.1%	2.5	7–15	22
Long Acting								
Novolin®ge Ultralente Insulin Zinc Suspension—Prolonged	cloudy, white suspension of insulin complex in crystal form plus NaCl	acetate 7–7.8	1.2–2.5	none	methylparaben 0.1%	4	8–24	28
Premixed								
Novolin®ge 10/90 Insulin Injection (10%) and Insulin Isophane (90%)	cloudy, white suspension containing a mixture of Novolin®ge Toronto 10% and Novolin®ge NPH 90% plus glycerin	phosphate 7–7.8	0.1–0.4	protamine	m-cresol 0.15% phenol 0.065%	0.5	2–12	24
Novolin®ge 20/80 Insulin Injection (20%) and Insulin Isophane (80%)	cloudy, white suspension containing a mixture of Novolin®ge Toronto 20% and Novolin®ge NPH 80% plus glycerin	phosphate 7–7.8	0.1–0.4	protamine	m-cresol 0.15% phenol 0.065%	0.5	2–12	24
Novolin®ge 30/70 Insulin Injection (30%) and Insulin Isophane (70%)	cloudy, white suspension containing a mixture of Novolin®ge Toronto 30% and Novolin®ge NPH 70% plus glycerin	phosphate 7–7.8	0.1–0.4	protamine	m-cresol 0.15% phenol 0.065%	0.5	2–12	24
Novolin®ge 40/60 Insulin Injection (40%) and Insulin Isophane (60%)	cloudy, white suspension containing a mixture of Novolin®ge Toronto 40% and Novolin®ge NPH 60% plus glycerin	phosphate 7–7.8	0.1–0.4	protamine	m-cresol 0.15% phenol 0.065%	0.5	2–12	24
Novolin®ge 50/50 Insulin Injection (50%) and Insulin Isophane (50%)	cloudy, white suspension containing a mixture of Novolin®ge Toronto 50% and Novolin®ge NPH 50% plus glycerin	phosphate 7–7.8	0.1–0.4	protamine	m-cresol 0.15% phenol 0.065%	0.5	2–12	24

Novolin®ge Premixed Insulin Preparations: Novolin®ge 10/90, Novolin®ge 20/80, Novolin®ge 30/70, Novolin®ge 40/60, Novolin®ge 50/50: These are a series of premixed insulins containing various proportions of Novolin®ge Toronto and Novolin®ge NPH, respectively, in the proportions indicated by the ratio in the product name. The mixtures are cloudy, neutral suspensions with an intermediate duration of action. The strength of the initial effect is dependent on the amount of Novolin®ge Toronto in the mixture. The effect of Novolin®ge mixtures begins after approximately 0.5 hours, is maximal between 2 and about 12 hours and terminates after approximately 24 hours.

Novolin®ge Lente, Novolin®ge NPH or Novolin®ge Ultralente may be mixed with Novolin®ge Toronto in order to meet the requirements of individual patients with diabetes as determined by the physician.

Indications: For the treatment of insulin-requiring patients with diabetes.

Only Novolin®ge Toronto, using i.v. administration, should be used for the treatment of emergencies, such as diabetic coma and pre-coma, and in patients with diabetes undergoing surgery. See also Contraindications.

Contraindications: Insulin is contraindicated in hypoglycemia (see Hypoglycemia and Overdose: Treatment).

Novolin®ge Lente, Novolin®ge Ultralente, Novolin®ge NPH and Novolin®ge premixed insulin preparations should not be administered i.v. or i.m., nor are they suitable for the treatment of diabetic coma.

Warnings: Novolin®ge Toronto should not be used if it is not water-clear and colorless. Due to the risk of precipitation in some pump catheters, Novolin®ge Toronto is not recommended for use in insulin pumps.

Novolin®ge Lente, Novolin®ge Ultralente, Novolin®ge NPH and Novolin®ge premixed insulin suspensions should not be used if the precipitate has become lumpy or granular in appearance or has formed a deposit of solid particles on the wall of the vial or cartridge. These insulin suspensions should also not be used if the contents remain clear after the vial or cartridge has been shaken carefully.

To avoid possible transmission of disease, a Penfill® cartridge must not be used by more than 1 person.

A few patients have reported that after being transferred to human insulin, the early warning symptoms for hypoglycemia were less pronounced than they were with animal-source insulin. Such patients should frequently measure their blood glucose and consult their doctor for dose adjustments, if necessary.

Insulin should not be used after the expiration date printed on the package.

Novolin®ge in vials: A U-100 syringe should always be used. Failure to use the correct syringe can lead to dosage errors.

Insulin should only be mixed as directed by the physician. Novolin®ge Toronto should only be mixed in the syringe with insulins of equal purity (eg., Novolin®ge Lente, Novolin®ge NPH or Novolin®ge Ultralente). The order of mixing and brand or model of syringe should be specified by the physician. In general when longer-acting insulins are mixed with short-acting soluble insulins, the short-acting insulin should be drawn into the syringe first. When mixing regular insulin with insulin zinc suspensions, the insulin mixture should be injected immediately.

Novolin®ge Penfill® cartridges are designed only for use in Novolin-Pen® systems. If treatment involves 2 insulins in Penfill® cartridges, a separate Novolin-Pen® system should be used for each type of insulin.

Novolin®ge Penfill® must not be refilled.

Use only Novolin®ge Penfill® cartridges and NovoFine® needles with Novolin-Pen® systems. NovoFine® needles should be removed after each injection. If the needle is not removed, changes in ambient temperature can result in some liquid being expelled from the cartridge. In the case of insulin suspensions, removal of supernatant liquid can cause an increase in insulin concentration (i.e. strength) within the cartridge.

Precautions: Stress or illness may increase insulin requirements. In these instances, patients should contact their physician and carefully control and monitor their blood glucose. The concomitant use of corticosteroids, oral contraceptives, diuretics, tricyclic antidepressants and the initiation of thyroid hormone replacement therapy may lead to an increase in insulin requirements. If a beta-adrenergic blocking agent or a MAO inhibitor is added to the patient's treatment, adjustment of the insulin dosage may be necessary.

An insulin reaction (hypoglycemia) may occur if the patient takes too much insulin, misses meals or exercises more than usual (see Hypoglycemia and Overdose: Treatment).

Insulin Human (Biosynthetic) Preparations/ Novolin®ge Preparations (cont'd)

Patients with diabetes should be instructed to carry a few lumps of sugar, candies or biscuits to prevent the progression of a hypoglycemic reaction, should one occur. The patient with diabetes should make relatives and close work-mates aware that he/she is diabetic and instruct them regarding signs and symptoms of hypoglycemia and assistance in the event of a hypoglycemic reaction. An unconscious person should not be given anything to eat or drink as choking is possible.

Diabetic ketosis, ketoacidosis or coma may develop if patient takes less insulin than needed. This could be due to increased insulin demand during illness or infection, neglect of diet, omission or maladministration of prescribed insulin doses. A developing ketoacidosis will be revealed by urine tests which show large amounts of sugar and acetone. The symptoms of thirst, large urine volumes, loss of appetite, fatigue, dry skin and deep and rapid breathing come on gradually, usually over a period of some hours or days. If hyperglycemia is not treated, it can cause diabetic coma or death.

Pregnancy and *Lactation:* During pregnancy and lactation, diabetes may become more difficult to manage. On the other hand, optimal metabolic control not only during pregnancy, but also prior to conception has proven to be beneficial in reducing the risk of miscarriage and malformation of the fetus. Patients with diabetes who have become pregnant or desire to become pregnant should consult their doctor for advice. Insulin ingested with the mother's milk has not been associated with any risk for the baby.

Adverse Effects: At initiation of insulin therapy, edema and refraction anomalies may occur. These conditions are usually of a transitory nature.

Occasionally, transitory redness, swelling, and itching at the injection site can either be caused by the insulin as such or the preservative used in the preparation. These reactions will often be of a non-specific and transitory nature. In very rare cases lipoatrophy or lipohypertrophy can develop at the injection site. Patients should change the injection site to avoid this side effect.

If, in exceptional cases, redness at the injection site quickly spreads as rash and blisters over the whole body, immediate medical attention is required. This is extremely rare with the use of Novolin®**ge** (Insulin, Human Biosynthetic).

Hypoglycemia and Overdose: Treatment: Hypoglycemia may occur if the patient with diabetes administers too much insulin, misses meals or exercises more than usual. The first symptoms can come on suddenly and may include hunger, cold sweat, rapid heartbeat, nervousness or shakiness. If untreated, the situation may progress to unconsciousness.

In rare cases, the nature and intensity of hypoglycemia warning symptoms may change. This has been observed in patients with long duration of diabetes (with diabetic neuropathy), after changes of regimen and in patients on strict metabolic control. However, if severe hypoglycemia is not treated it may cause temporary or permanent brain damage or death.

A few patients have reported that after being transferred to human insulin, the early warning symptoms for hypoglycemia were less pronounced than they were with animal-source insulin. Such patients should frequently measure their blood glucose and consult their doctor for dose adjustment, if necessary.

In the event of an overdose, if the patient is conscious, glucose should be given orally. Where the patient is unconscious, an i.m, s.c. or i.v. injection of glucagon should be given and oral carbohydrate administered when the patient responds. Alternatively i.v. glucose may be administered; it **must** be given if there is no response to glucagon.

Dosage: Novolin®**ge** is made in one strength, 100 units/mL. The dosage is determined by the physician in accordance with the needs of the patient.

Novolin®**ge** Toronto when used alone is usually given 3 or more times daily. Novolin®**ge** Toronto may also be used in combination with longer-acting insulins of equal purity to suit the needs of the individual patients. It may be given s.c., i.m. or i.v. The s.c. injection of Novolin®**ge** Toronto should be followed by a meal within approximately 30 minutes of administration.

Novolin®**ge** Lente may be given once daily or more usually twice daily. It is administered by s.c. injection.

Novolin®**ge** Ultralente is usually given once daily, often in the evening. It is administered by s.c. injection.

Novolin®**ge** NPH is usually given once or twice daily. It is administered by s.c. injection.

Novolin®**ge** Premixed Insulin Preparations: Novolin®**ge** 10/90, Novolin®**ge** 20/80, Novolin®**ge** 30/70, Novolin®**ge** 40/60, Novolin®**ge** 50/50 are usually given once or twice daily, especially when a strong initial effect is desired. They are administered by s.c. injection. The injection of Novolin®**ge** premixed insulins should be followed by a meal within approximately 30 minutes of administration.

Insulin suspensions should be carefully shaken to ensure that the contents are uniformly mixed before injection of each dose.

Mixing Insulin: In vitro studies demonstrate an interaction occurs when zinc from Lente preparations (i.e., Novolin®**ge** Lente and Novolin®**ge** Ultralente) is mixed with insulin injection such as Novolin®**ge** Toronto. This binding may result in a blunting of the timing of onset of the Novolin®**ge** Toronto. The degree of interaction has been shown to be dependent on the ratio of regular to longer acting insulin and on the time between mixing and injection. However, when mixing Novolin®**ge** Toronto and Novolin®**ge** NPH the blunting effect is not observed and the rapid onset of Novolin®**ge** Toronto is preserved.

Novolin-Pen® systems are insulin delivery devices for use with Novolin®**ge** Penfill® insulin cartridges and NovoFine® needles. Novolin-Pen® 3 has a dial-a-dose selector which allows delivery of 2 to 70 units of insulin in increments of 1 unit from a 3 mL Penfill® cartridge. Novolin-Pen® 1.5 has a dial-a-dose selector which allows 2 to 40 units of insulin to be delivered in increments of 1 unit from a 1.5 mL Penfill® cartridge.

The following are general prescribing guidelines: **New Patients:** Although each patient must be assessed individually, initial stabilization on multiple injections of Novolin®**ge** Toronto is recommended. Following this, most patients will respond well to a regimen of Novolin®**ge** Lente twice daily; Novolin®**ge** NPH once or twice daily; or Novolin®**ge** Ultralente once daily. Usually small amounts of Novolin®**ge** Toronto are added to cover the morning and evening meals. Alternatively, Novolin®**ge** premixed insulin preparations may be given once or twice daily.

Transfer of Patients: When patients are transferred from other insulins to Novolin®**ge**, the change should be made as directed by the physician according to the following general guidelines:

When a switch is made from mixed species (porcine/bovine) or bovine insulin to human insulin a dosage adjustment may be required dependent upon dosage, purity, species and formulation of the insulin(s) currently administered. Variations in glycemic control may occur and adjustments in therapy should be made under the guidance of a physician. For patients currently controlled on porcine monocomponent or other highly purified human or porcine insulins, no dosage change is anticipated other than the routine adjustments made in order to maintain stable diabetic control.

Patients currently on self-prepared mixtures may be transferred to the closest available Novolin®**ge** fixed mixture preparation.

Any patient on a total daily dose of greater than 100 units of insulin may need to be closely monitored by the physician when transferring to a different insulin preparation, preferably in hospital.

Supplied: Vials of 10 mL. Insulin cartridges of 1.5 and 3 mL. All in a strength of 100 units/mL. Novolin®**ge** preparations are available in the following presentations (see Table II).

Storage: Insulin preparations including Penfill® cartridges should be stored between 2 and 10°C. They should not be exposed to heat or sunlight, and should never be frozen.

A vial in use can be kept at room temperature (max. 25°C) for 1 month. Novolin®**ge** Penfill® when used in Novolin-Pen® systems can be in-use or carried as a spare for up to 1 month at ambient temperature (max. 37°C). When in use, Novo Nordisk injection devices and their cartridges should not be refrigerated.

Insulin should not be used after the expiry date printed on the package.

Novo Nordisk cannot be held responsible for malfunctions occurring as a consequence of using Novo Nordisk insulin or insulin delivery systems in combination with products that do not meet Novo Nordisk specifications or quality standards.

(Shown in Product Recognition Section)

Reviewed 1997

Table II—Insulin Human (Biosynthetic) Preparations/Novolin®ge Preparations

Availability of Novolin®ge Preparations

10 mL vials	1.5 mL Penfill® cartridges	3 mL Penfill® cartridges
Novolin®**ge** Toronto	Novolin®**ge** Toronto Penfill®	Novolin®**ge** Toronto Penfill®
Novolin®**ge** NPH	Novolin®**ge** NPH Penfill®	Novolin®**ge** NPH Penfill®
Novolin®**ge** Lente	Novolin®**ge** 30/70 Penfill®	Novolin®**ge** 10/90 Penfill®
Novolin®**ge** Ultralente		Novolin®**ge** 20/80 Penfill®
Novolin®**ge** 30/70		Novolin®**ge** 30/70 Penfill®
		Novolin®**ge** 40/60 Penfill®
		Novolin®**ge** 50/50 Penfill®

Note: Delivery devices for the 3 mL Penfill® cartridges (Novolin-Pen® 3) and the 1.5 mL Penfill® cartridges (Novolin-Pen® 1.5) as well as the NovoFine® needles are described under separate sections.

INTAL® INHALER
INTAL® SYNCRONER®

Rhône-Poulenc Rorer

Sodium Cromoglycate

Asthma Prophylaxis

Pharmacology: In vitro and in vivo animal studies have shown that sodium cromoglycate inhibits sensitized mast cell degranulation which occurs after exposure to specific antigens. Sodium cromoglycate acts by inhibiting the release of mediators from mast cells. Studies show that sodium cromoglycate indirectly blocks calcium ions from entering the mast cell, thereby preventing mediator release.

Sodium cromoglycate inhibits both the immediate and non-immediate bronchoconstrictive reactions to inhaled allergens. Sodium cromoglycate also attenuates bronchospasm caused by exercise, toluene diisocyanate, ASA, cold air, sulfur dioxide and environmental pollutants in some patients.

Sodium cromoglycate has no intrinsic bronchodilator antihistaminic or anti-inflammatory activity.

Indications: As an adjunct in the management of intrinsic and extrinsic asthma. It is used on a continuous basis to prevent the symptoms associated with asthma.

Also indicated for use in the prevention of bronchospasm induced by known precipitating factors such as exercise, cold air, allergens and environmental pollutants.

Contraindications: Hypersensitivity to any of its components.

Warnings: Sodium cromoglycate has no role in the treatment of an acute attack of asthma, especially status asthmaticus.

Severe anaphylactic reactions can occur after sodium cromoglycate administration. The recommended dosage should be decreased in patients with decreased renal or hepatic function. Sodium cromoglycate should be discontinued if the patient develops eosinophilic pneumonia (or pulmonary infiltrates with eosinophilia).

The number of inhalations per day should be specified to the patient. **Regular dosage is important and treatment must not be discontinued abruptly,** especially when benefit has been obtained. **If troublesome symptoms occur,** particularly breathlessness at rest, no benefit is likely to be obtained by increasing the dosage above 16 mg/day, and the **patient should be advised to consult his physician immediately,** so that additional measures can be instituted if necessary.

Precautions: Mild throat irritation, coughing and transient bronchospasm may occur. Very rarely, severe bronchospasm associated with a marked fall in pulmonary function has been reported. In such cases treatment shoud be stopped and should not be reintroduced.

Possible immunologic changes resulting in reactions, such as, polymyositis, pneumonitis and heart failure, urticaria and anaphylaxis have been reported.

Fluorocarbon propellants may be hazardous if they are deliberately abused. Inhalation of high concentrations of aerosol sprays has brought about cardiovascular toxic effects and even death, especially under conditions of hypoxia. However, evidence attests to the relative safety of aerosols when used properly and with adequate ventilation.

Pregnancy: There are no adequate and well controlled studies in pregnant women. However, during clinical use there have been, to date, no reports of adverse effects on the fetus that could be ascribed to the use of sodium cromoglycate. Nevertheless, as with all medications, caution must be exercised during pregnancy.

Lactation: It is not known whether this drug is excreted in human milk; therefore, caution should be exercised when sodium cromoglycate is administered to a nursing woman, and the attending physician must make a benefit/risk assessment in regard to its use in this situation.

Adverse Effects: In controlled studies the most frequently reported adverse reactions attributed to sodium cromoglycate treatment were: throat irritation or dryness, bad taste, cough, wheeze and nausea.

Bronchospasm [sometimes severe, associated with precipitous fall in pulmonary function (FEV_1)], laryngeal edema (rare), nasal congestion (sometimes severe) and pharyngeal irritation have been reported.

Adverse reactions which occur infrequently and are associated with administration of the drug are: anaphylaxis, angioedema, dizziness, dysuria and urinary frequency, joint swelling and pain, lacrimation, headache, rash, swollen parotid gland, urticaria, pulmonary infiltrates with eosinophilia, substernal burning and myopathy.

The following adverse reactions have been reported as rare events and it is unclear whether they are attributable to the drug: anemia, exfoliative dermatitis, hemoptysis, hoarseness, myalgia, nephrosis, periarteritic vasculitis, pericarditis, peripheral neuritis, photodermatitis, sneezing, drowsiness, nasal itching, nasal bleeding, nasal burning, serum sickness, stomach ache, polymyositis, vertigo and liver disease.

Overdose: Symptoms and Treatment: There have been no reported cases in humans of overdosage of the drug. Symptomatic treatment is suggested should overdosage occur.

Dosage: Adults and Children over 6 Years of Age: Sodium chromoglycate is used on a continuous basis to prevent the symptoms of asthma and has no role in the treatment of acute attacks.

Initial Treatment: Two puffs four times daily at 4 to 6 hourly intervals. In more severe cases or during periods of high antigen challenge, the interval between doses may be 3 hours (i.e., up to 16 puffs daily may be taken).

For protection against bronchospasm induced by exercise, sodium cromoglycate should be used 15 to 30 minutes beforehand.

Maintenance Therapy: When adequate response has been obtained, frequency of inhalations may be reduced to 2 puffs every 8 to 12 hours (i.e., 4 to 6 puffs/day). If chest symptoms are troublesome at night, it is important that the final dose be taken, if awakened, during the night.

Patients should be warned against suddenly discontinuing therapy when symptoms have been partially or completely controlled by sodium cromoglycate.

Concomitant Therapy: Other asthma therapy should be continued until clinical improvement permits a progressive reduction in dosage. However, sodium cromoglycate alone may prevent symptoms of mild to moderate asthma, especially in children and young adults.

In severe asthma, particularly in older patients, sodium cromoglycate therapy alone is insufficient to prevent symptoms. In a proportion of such cases, significant improvement can be obtained by combining sodium cromoglycate with corticosteroid therapy, even when inadequate relief is obtained from either drug alone.

In steroid-dependent patients the addition of sodium cromoglycate to the regimen may permit a slow, progressive and significant reduction in maintenance dose of steroids.

Reduction or Withdrawal of Corticosteroids: The dangers of sudden withdrawal of corticosteroids are well recognized, particularly in steroid-treated patients who have received long-term administration of oral steroids, or injections of adrenocorticotrophic hormone (ACTH).

When the physician attempts to reduce the corticosteroid dosage, it is important that the reduction be gradual and that close surveillance and frequent examination of the patient is maintained. It should be remembered that adrenal cortex is suppressed by the administration of oral steroids, and that in both oral steroid and ACTH therapy, the ability of the patient to react to stress is usually impaired. In such patients, acute renal insufficiency and severe asthma can be precipitated by an increase in stress and/or reduction or withdrawal of either steroid or ACTH therapy. In order to identify such a risk in patients who have received long-term steroid therapy, and where substantial reduction or complete withdrawal of corticosteroid is contemplated, it is advisable to assess adrenal and pituitary function.

Method of Reducing Steroid Dosage: The reduction in the daily maintenance dose of steroids should be stepwise at a suggested rate equivalent to about 1%/day (e.g., a maintenance dose of 10 mg prednisolone/day is reduced to 9 mg/day after 1 week). The gradual reduction should be continued until either the patient cannot tolerate a further reduction, or it is found possible to withdraw corticosteroids completely.

Note: If troublesome symptoms recur during the period of reduction, the daily dose should be raised immediately. A larger increase in the steriod dose may be essential at times, as a temporary measure, to control a severe relapse induced by antigen challenge, infections or stress. The **increased physical or mental activity resulting from subjective improvement can also constitute a stress.** When symptoms are brought under control, a progressive reduction may be attempted as before.

Method of Withdrawing ACTH: The same principles apply as discussed above. In practice, either the number of units of ACTH per injection can be reduced, or the interval between injections can be extended (e.g., from 1/day, to 1 on alternate days, to 1 biweekly).

Withdrawal of Sodium Cromoglycate Therapy: As the action of sodium cromoglycate is essentially preventive, continuity of therapy is important in patients who have gained benefit. If, for any reason, sodium cromoglycate is withdrawn, a suggested regimen for withdrawal is to reduce the sodium cromoglycate dosage gradually over a period of 1 week. It should be borne in mind that symptoms of asthma may recur when the drug is discontinued.

Caution: In cases where sodium cromoglycate has permitted a reduction in the maintenance dose of steroids, it is recommended that the steroid dose first be restored to at least pre-sodium cromoglycate level at the commencement of withdrawal of sodium cromoglycate, followed by slow reduction of the steroid dose to tolerance. This is to avoid risk of acute relapse. It is also recommended that adrenal function be assessed before restoring the pre-sodium cromoglycate steroid dose.

Information for the Patient: See Blue Section—Information for the Patient "Intal Inhaler/Intal Syncroner".

Supplied: Inhaler: Each actuation contains sodium cromoglycate (micronized) 1 mg. Nonmedicinal ingredients: dichlorodifluoromethane, dichlorotetrafluoroethane and sorbitan trioleate. Pressurized aerosol containers of 10 mL delivering either 112 or 200 metered inhalations.

Syncroner: Each actuation contains: sodium cromoglycate (micronized) 1 mg. Nonmedicinal ingredients: dichlorodifluoromethane, dichlorotetrafluoroethane and sorbitan trioleate. Pressurized aerosol containers of 10 mL delivering 200 metered inhalations.

Intal Syncroner differs from Intal Inhaler in the design of the mouthpiece only. The Syncroner is an elongated mouthpiece of approximately 8 cm in length, with a portion of its upper surface cut away.

Store at room temperature. Contents under pressure. Do not place in hot water or near radiators, stoves or other sources of heat. Do not puncture or incinerate container or store at temperatures over 30°C.

INTAL® SPINCAPS® Ⓟ
INTAL® NEBULIZER SOLUTION Ⓟ

Rhône-Poulenc Rorer

Sodium Cromoglycate

Bronchial Asthma Prophylaxis

Pharmacology: In vitro and in vivo animal studies have shown that sodium cromoglycate inhibits sensitized mast cell degranulation which occurs after exposure to specific antigens. Sodium cromoglycate acts by inhibiting the release of mediators from mast cells. Studies show that sodium cromoglycate indirectly blocks calcium ions from entering the mast cell, thereby preventing mediator release.

Sodium cromoglycate inhibits both the immediate and non-immediate bronchoconstrictive reactions to inhaled allergens. Sodium cromoglycate also attenuates bronchospasm caused by exercise, toluene diisocyanate, ASA, cold air, sulfur dioxide and environmental pollutants in some patients.

Sodium cromoglycate has no intrinsic bronchodilator antihistaminic or anti-inflammatory activity.

Indications: As an adjunct in the management of intrinsic and extrinsic asthma. It is used on a continuous basis to prevent the symptoms associated with asthma.

Also indicated for use in the prevention of bronchospasm induced by known precipitating factors such as exercise, cold air, allergens, and environmental pollutants.

Contraindications: Hypersensitivity to any of its components.

Warnings: Sodium cromoglycate has no role in the treatment of an acute attack of asthma, especially status asthmaticus.

Severe anaphylactic reactions can occur after sodium cromoglycate administration. The recommended dosage should be decreased in patients with decreased renal or hepatic function. Sodium cromoglycate should be discontinued if the patient develops eosinophilic pneumonia (or pulmonary infiltrates with eosinophilia).

The number of inhalations per day should be specified to the patient. **Regular dosage is important and treatment must not be discontinued abruptly,** especially when benefit has been obtained. **If troublesome symptoms occur,** particularly breathlessness at rest, no benefit is likely to be obtained by increasing the dosage above 8 cartridges or ampuls per day, and the **patient should be advised to consult his physician immediately,** so that additional measures can be instituted if necessary.

Precautions: Mild throat irritation, coughing and transient bronchospasm may occur. Very rarely, severe bronchospasm associated with a marked fall in pulmonary function has been reported. In such cases treatment should be stopped and should not be reintroduced.

Possible immunologic changes resulting in reactions, such as, polymyositis, pneumonitis and heart failure, urticaria and anaphylaxis have been reported.

Pregnancy: There are no adequate and well-controlled studies in pregnant women. However, during clinical use there have been, to date, no reports of adverse effects on the fetus that could be ascribed to the use of sodium cromoglycate. Nevertheless, as with all medications, caution must be exercised during pregnancy.

Lactation: It is not known whether this drug is excreted in human milk; therefore, caution should be exercised when sodium cromoglycate is administered to a nursing woman, and the attending physician must make a benefit/risk assessment in regard to its use in this situation.

Adverse Effects: In controlled clinical studies the most frequently reported adverse reactions attributed to sodium cromoglycate treatment were: throat irritation or dryness, bad taste, cough, wheeze and nausea.

Bronchospasm [sometimes severe, associated with precipitous fall in pulmonary function (FEV_1)], laryngeal edema (rare), nasal congestion (sometimes severe) and pharyngeal irritation have been reported.

Adverse reactions which occur infrequently and are associated with administration of the drug are: anaphylaxis, angioedema, dizziness, dysuria and urinary frequency, joint swelling and pain, lacrimation, headache, rash, swollen parotid gland, urticaria, pulmonary infiltrates with eosinophilia, substernal burning and myopathy.

The following adverse reactions have been reported as rare events and it is unclear whether they are attributable to the drug: anemia, exfoliative dermatitis, hemoptysis, hoarseness, myalgia, nephrosis, periarteritic vasculitis, pericarditis, peripheral neuritis, photodermatitis, sneezing, drowsiness, nasal itching, nasal bleeding, nasal burning, serum sickness, stomach ache, polymyositis, vertigo and liver disease.

Overdose: Symptoms and Treatment: There have been no reported cases in humans of overdosage of the drug. Symptomatic treatment is suggested should overdosage occur.

Dosage: Adults and Children: Sodium cromoglycate is used on a continuous basis to prevent the symptoms of asthma and has no role in the treatment of acute attacks.

Intal Spincaps are administered by specially developed inhalers which enable efficient and controlled dosage—1) the Spinhaler turbo-inhaler and 2) and the Intal Halermatic automatic piercing inhaler.

Intal Nebulizer Solution is recommended for use in a Wright nebulizer or a suitable equivalent operated at an air flow rate of 6 to 8 L/minute and equipped with a suitable face mask.

Initial Treatment: One Spincap or one ampul of Nebulizer Solution 4 times daily at 4 to 6 hourly intervals. In more severe cases, or during periods of high antigen challenge, the interval between doses may be reduced to 3 hours (i.e., up to 8 Spincaps or ampuls daily may be taken).

For protection against bronchospasm induced by exercise, sodium cromoglycate should be used 15 to 30 minutes beforehand.

Maintenance Therapy: When adequate response has been obtained, the frequency of inhalations may be reduced to 1 Spincap or 1 ampul of Nebulizer Solution every 8 to 12 hours

Intal Spincaps/Intal Nebulizer Solution (cont'd)

(i.e., 2 or 3 Spincaps or ampuls/day). If chest symptoms are troublesome at night, it is important that the final dose be taken, if awakened, during the night.

Patients should be warned against suddenly discontinuing therapy when symptoms have been partially or completely controlled by sodium cromoglycate.

Concomitant Therapy: Other asthma therapy should be continued until clinical improvement permits a progressive reduction in dosage. However, sodium cromoglycate alone may prevent symptoms of mild to moderate asthma, especially in children and young adults.

In severe asthma, particularly in older patients, sodium cromoglycate therapy alone is insufficient to prevent symptoms. In a proportion of such cases, significant improvement can be obtained by combining sodium cromoglycate with corticosteroid therapy, even when inadequate relief is obtained from either drug alone.

In steroid-dependent patients, the addition of sodium cromoglycate to the regimen may permit a slow, progressive and significant reduction in maintenance dose of steroids.

Reduction or Withdrawal of Corticosteroids: The dangers of sudden withdrawal of corticosteroids are well recognized, particularly in steroid-treated patients who have received long-term administration of oral steroids, or ACTH injections.

When the physician attempts to reduce the corticosteroid dosage, it is important that the reduction should be gradual and that close surveillance and frequent examination of the patient is maintained. It should be remembered that the adrenal cortex is suppressed by the administration of oral steroids, and that in both oral steroid and ACTH therapy, the ability of the patient to react to stress is usually impaired. In such patients, acute renal insufficiency and severe asthma can be precipitated by an increase in stress and/or reduction or withdrawal of either steroid or ACTH therapy. In order to identify such a risk in patients who have received long-term steroid therapy and where substantial reduction or complete withdrawal of corticosteroid is contemplated, it is advisable to assess adrenal and pituitary function.

Method of Reducing Steroid Dosage: The reduction in the daily maintenance dose of steroids should be stepwise at a suggested rate equivalent to about 1%/day (e.g., a maintenance dose of 10 mg prednisolone/day is reduced to 9 mg/day after 1 week). The gradual reduction should be continued until either the patient cannot tolerate a further reduction, or it is found possible to withdraw corticosteroids completely.

Note: If troublesome symptoms recur during the period of reduction, the daily dose should be raised immediately. A larger increase in the steroid dose may be essential at times, as a temporary measure, to control a severe relapse induced by antigen challenge, infections or stress. The **increased physical or mental activity resulting from subjective improvement can also constitute a stress.** When symptoms are brought under control, a progressive reduction may be attempted as before.

Method of Withdrawing ACTH: The same principles apply as discussed above. In practice, either the number of units of ACTH per injection can be reduced, or the interval between injections can be extended (e.g., from 1/day, to 1 on alternate days, to 1 biweekly).

Withdrawal of Sodium Cromoglycate Therapy: As the action of sodium cromoglycate is essentially preventive, continuity of therapy is important in patients who have gained benefit. If, for any reason, sodium cromoglycate is withdrawn, a suggested regimen for withdrawal is to reduce the sodium cromoglycate dosage gradually over a period of 1 week. It should be borne in mind that symptoms of asthma may recur when the drug is discontinued.

Caution: In cases where sodium cromoglycate has permitted a reduction in the maintenance dose of steroids, it is recommended that the steroid dose first be restored to at least the pre-sodium cromoglycate level at the commencement of withdrawal of sodium cromoglycate, followed by slow reduction of the steroid dose to tolerance. This is to avoid risk of acute relapse. It is also recommended that adrenal function be assessed before restoring the pre-sodium cromoglycate steroid dose.

Administration of **Spincaps:** Administration by inhalation of the contents of a Spincaps cartridge is only possible by the correct use of the Spinhaler or the Intal Halermatic. It is desirable to demonstrate the use of the Spinhaler or the Intal Halermatic to each patient for whom sodium cromoglycate therapy is prescribed. In practice, they are very simple to operate, provided they are used strictly according to the following instructions:

Spinhaler: The Spinhaler turbo-inhaler is essentially a tube-like inhaler in which the movement of the inspired air causes a small propeller to rotate and vibrate at high speed. When a Spincap cartridge is fitted in this device, its gelatin envelope is perforated by moving the grey sleeve of the Spinhaler. During deep and rapid inspiration through the device the contents of the cartridge are dispersed into the inspired air by the action of the propeller. In this way, the drug particles are carried deep into the lungs to the site where their action is required.

The Spinhaler consists of: A **tubular body** threaded at one end to receive the mouthpiece, and with an air inlet at the other end. The body is fitted with a grey sleeve which can slide from its normal position against the air inlet, to the mouthpiece and back again. The body unscrews from the mouthpiece; **The propeller,** inside the tubular body which rotates on a stainless steel spindle. It has a slotted cup into which a Spincap can be fitted; **The mouthpiece,** fitted with a stainless steel spindle.

Loading and Inhaling the Dose: 1. To prepare the Spinhaler for use—hold the appliance vertically **with the white mouthpiece downwards** and unscrew the body from the mouthpiece.

2. Insert the **colored** end of the Spincap firmly into the cup on the propeller. Check that the propeller rotates freely.

3. Screw the mouthpiece back into position.

4a. **Still holding the Spinhaler vertically** (mouthpiece downwards), force the grey sleeve downwards as far as it will go and then back to its original position. (This step may be repeated a second time for optimal piercing.)

4b. The Spincap has now been pierced and the appliance is ready for use.

5. **Inhaling Procedure:** Hold the Spinhaler well away from your mouth. Breathe out as fully as possible.

6. Now put the mouthpiece of the Spinhaler between your lips with air inlet held slightly upwards. Close your lips, but keep your teeth apart, and draw in a deep breath through the Spinhaler as rapidly as possible. You should hear and feel the high speed vibration made by the rotating propeller.

7. Hold your breath for a few seconds and remove the Spinhaler from your mouth.

8. Breathe out completely, holding the Spinhaler well away from your face. Repeat inhaling procedure several times until the Spincap is empty.

9. Discard Spincap and return Spinhaler to its container.

Note: Patients who experience mild hoarseness following inhalation may benefit by taking a drink of water immediately after using the Spinhaler.

Care of Spinhaler: 1. Brush propeller blades weekly to remove powder and dust.

2. Alternatively, it may be necessary to dismantle the Spinhaler and wash the parts in warm water, **including the inside of the shaft** (by moving the propeller on and off the spindle underwater).

3. Shake out the excess water, **especially from inside the propeller shaft.** Allow to dry in a warm place before reassembly. The Spinhaler will not function properly unless the propeller shaft is clean and dry.

Always handle the Spincap cartridges with clean dry hands and keep the Spinhaler in a dry place at room temperature.

It is advisable to carry the Spinhaler in the container provided. Failure to do so could result in dust and debris entering the apparatus and such foreign matter might then be inhaled when the spinhaler is in use.

Halermatic: The Halermatic, automatic piercing inhaler is an insufflator device used to facilitate the administration of Spincaps.

When a Spincap is fitted in this device its gelatin envelope is perforated automatically when the device is reassembled. During deep and rapid inspiration through the device the contents of the cartridge are dispersed into the inspired air. In this way, the drug particles are carried deep into the lungs to the site where their action is required.

The Halermatic consists of: **The body,** which contains the Spincap slot, a rotation chamber, and the piercing needles; **The mouthpiece,** which has air inlets that line up with air inlet channels in the body through which air moves to allow the Spincap to spin within the rotation chamber dispensing the contents of the cartridge into the inspired air. The mouthpiece also has a grid through which the powder must pass on its way into the lungs; **The cover,** which fits over the mouthpiece protecting the grid and air inlets from dust and debris. The cover has a storage compartment for spincaps. The cover storage compartment is threaded to receive **the cap.**

How to Load the Halermatic: Cartridges should only be inserted immediately prior to use.

1. Remove the mouthpiece cover and then pull off the mouthpiece.

2. Push a Spincap cartridge firmly down to the bottom of the slot.

3. Slide the mouthpiece back onto the body pushing down **slowly** as far as it will go. This action pierces the cartridge and lifts it into the rotation chamber—the inhaler is now ready to use.

Note: Step 3 must not be repeated as the cartridge must be pierced once only.

How to use The Halermatic: 1. Breathe out as far as possible holding the device away from the mouth.

2. Tilt the head back and breathe in **quickly** and **steadily** through the mouthpiece, keeping the lips closed around it. Be sure not to obstruct the flow of Intal into the lungs with teeth or tongue.

3. Hold your breath to keep the Intal in the lungs as long as possible, remove the device from your mouth and then breathe out.

4. Repeat steps 1 to 3 until all the powder has been inhaled.

5. If the throat becomes dry or irritated, drink a little water before and after inhalation.

6. If there is any difficulty, be sure: the device is clean; the air inlets are not obstructed when breathing in, (e.g., by your fingers); the cartridge is free to rotate. Do not place the cartridge back in the slot if it is already pierced; the cartridge has been pierced. If not, begin again by pushing the cartridge back into the slot.

Cleaning the Halermatic: 1. Brush away powder deposits daily with a brush.

2. When powder deposits build up, wipe away with a lightly dampened cloth.

3. The mouthpiece may be washed separately if necessary. **Do not wet the blue-based body of the Halermatic and be sure the mouthpiece grid is dry before reassembling the device.**

Spincap cartridges may be carried in the special compartment on the top of the Halermatic, for 1 day only. Ensure that the storage compartment is kept tightly closed to exclude humidity.

Replace the Halermatic every 6 months.

Always handle the Spincap cartridges with clean, dry hands and keep the Halermatic in a dry place at room temperature.

Information for the Patient: See Blue Section—Information for the Patient "Intal Spincaps/Intal Nebulizer Solution".

Supplied: Cartridges: Each single dose, yellow/clear, hard gelatin cartridge imprinted Fisons and Intal-p, contains: sodium cromoglycate (micronized) 20 mg. Nonmedicinal ingredients: erythrosine CL 45430, gelatin, iron oxide and quinoline Yellow CL 47005. Sodium: <1 mmol (1.8 mg)/ cartridge. Lactose- and tartrazine-free. Boxes of 100 in moisture-proof aluminum blister packs of 10 cartridges. Store in a dry place, at room temperature. Do not refrigerate.

Solution: Each mL of sterile solution contains: sodium cromoglycate (micronized) 1% w/v (10 mg/mL). Nonmedicinal ingredients: purified water. Sodium: <1 mmol (1.8 mg)/ ampul. Ampuls of 2 mL, cartons of 48. Store at room temperature. Do not refrigerate. Protect from direct sunlight.

(Shown in Product Recognition Section)

INTRALIPID® 10%
INTRALIPID® 20%
INTRALIPID® 30%

Pharmacia & Upjohn

Fat Emulsions

I.V. Nutrition

Pharmacology: Intralipid acts as an energy source in patients for whom the usual i.v. therapy would not be adequate and as a source of essential fatty acids to prevent essential fatty acid deficiency.

Providing sufficient amounts of calories to satisfy basal metabolic requirements plus the additional needs imposed by disease and/or surgical stress can be difficult and sometimes even impossible. If the i.v. route has to be used and only carbohydrates are given as an energy source large amounts of fluid or very hypertonic solutions must be employed. Fat has an energy value a little more than twice that of carbohydrates, and is therefore an excellent source of energy for use in parenteral nutrition. By including fat emulsion in the nutritional program a balanced i.v. nutrition can be achieved.

Moreover, Intralipid is practically isotonic with blood which makes it possible to infuse large amounts of energy providing substrate in a small volume of fluid via peripheral veins. This property makes possible peripheral vein infusion of solutions that otherwise have to be administered by central veins, (see Dosage, Administration).

Fat emulsions may be used to supply up to 40% of the nonprotein energy requirements of the patient. Each mL of Intralipid 10% contains 4.6 kJ (1.1 kcal), each mL of Intralipid 20% contains 8.4 kJ (2.0 kcal) and each mL of Intralipid 30% contains 12.6 kJ (3.0 kcal). Half a litre (1 bottle) of Intralipid 10%, Intralipid 20% and Intralipid 30% thus contains 2.3 MJ (550 kcal), 4.2 MJ (1 000 kcal) and 6.3 MJ (1 500 kcal), respectively. Particle size and biological properties are similar to those of natural chylomicrons.

The i.v. administered fat is utilized as an energy source by the organism in the same manner as orally ingested fat, as demonstrated in a number of investigations and by different methods e.g., growth experiments. Parenterally administered fat is utilized rapidly by the body for energy purposes.

The elimination of fat from the blood stream after i.v. administration has been studied in the dog, rabbit and in man by determination of the plasma triglyceride content.

Studies in the dog and man have demonstrated that after infusion of Intralipid, fat particles are cleared from the blood stream in a manner similar to that of chylomicrons. The rate of elimination of fat emulsion is dependent both on the capacity of the chylomicron receptor sites in the capillary walls of different organs and the rate of blood flow in these vessels.

Significant amounts of Intralipid are removed by skeletal muscle (47%), splanchnic viscera (25%), myocardium (14%) and s.c. tissue (13%), with no removal observed in the liver.

Even after the i.v. administration of large doses of fat no losses occur via the urine or feces.

Indications: Should be used as an energy source in patients for whom the usual i.v. fluid therapy would not be adequate and as a source of essential fatty acids to prevent essential fatty acid deficiency.

Pre- and postoperative nutritional disorders, in which an increased administration of energy is necessary.

Nutritive disorders resulting from decreased or inhibited intestinal absorption. Such disorders may be due to tumors of the digestive tract, or to acute or chronic intestinal diseases, such as ulcerative colitis or terminal ileitis.

In burn cases where the energy requirements can be excessive. In these cases every energy supplement is of the utmost importance. Even if the patients are able to take nourishment by mouth, difficulties are often encountered in supplying sufficient amounts of energy in the diet. The administration of i.v. fat is, therefore, indicated in such cases.

Prolonged states of unconsciousness e.g., following trauma, or intoxication, if tube feeding is inadvisable or impossible.

Cachexia due to serious diseases in organs other than the alimentary tract, e.g., metastasized tumors, systemic diseases.

Impaired renal function in which adequate energy supply is essential to reduce protein breakdown.

Essential fatty acid deficiency. To prevent clinical manifestations during parenteral nutrition.

Contraindications: Only in conditions characterized by severely disordered fat metabolism such as in severe liver damage, acute myocardial infarction and shock, is Intralipid contraindicated.

Warnings: Fat metabolism may be disturbed in patients with special diseases and conditions. In these cases, fat elimination must be checked daily. For instructions see Precautions.

Pregnancy: The safety of Intralipid for use in pregnancy has not yet been established; therefore, it should not be used in pregnant women, unless, in the judgment of the physician, its use is deemed absolutely necessary to the welfare of the patient.

Rare cases of hypersensitivity have been observed in patients allergic to soybean protein, egg yolk and egg whites.

Precautions: Patients with Special Diseases and Conditions: Fat metabolism may be disturbed in conditions such as renal insufficiency, uncompensated diabetes, certain forms of liver insufficiency, metabolic disorders and sepsis. When i.v. fat is considered to be indicated in patients with the above mentioned disorders, fat elimination should be checked daily (see Fat Elimination Test) and the dosage adjusted to the patient's capacity for fat elimination. In cases of verified or suspected liver insufficiency, liver function must be closely followed.

If increased levels of transaminases, alkaline phosphatases or bilirubin appear, further infusion of Intralipid should be postponed, or the dosage decreased, until normalization is achieved.

Children: Very low birth weight preterm infants and small for gestational age infants clear i.v. fat emulsion more slowly than term infants and are at a greater risk of developing hyperlipidemia. This has the potential risk for lowering oxygen tension. The rate of infusion of Intralipid should be as slow as possible, the daily dose preferably administered continuously over 24 hours by infusion pump. The infant's ability to eliminate infused fat from the circulation must be carefully monitored. The lipemia must clear prior to proceeding to the next daily infusion.

Due to the lack of experience, Intralipid 30% is not recommended for use in infants and children.

Fat Elimination Test: Before the beginning of infusion in the morning a citrated blood sample is drawn, preferably when the patient is still in a fasting state. The blood sample is centrifuged at 20 to 25 Hz (or 1 200 to 1 500 rpm). If the plasma is then strongly opalescent or milky, the planned infusion is postponed. In the great majority of cases, plasma is completely clear 12 hours after the infusion of the daily dose. In patients with no suspected metabolic disturbances this test should be carried out once a week.

Laboratory Tests: Interference: Lipemic serum interferes with colorimetric laboratory analyses. To avoid this, blood samples should be drawn in the morning prior to infusion of Intralipid.

Adverse Effects: Adverse reactions reported to occur during and/or following infusion of Intralipid include: fever, chills, nausea, vomiting, headache, back or chest pain with dyspnea and cyanosis.

Overdose: Symptoms and Treatment: When fat emulsion is given in amounts exceeding the capacity of fat elimination the following symptoms may occur: hyperlipemia, hepatosplenomegaly, jaundice, hemolytic anemia, prolonged clotting time and thrombocytopenia. All symptoms clear in days to weeks after cessation of fat infusion.

Dosage: Adults: Dosage should normally not exceed 2 g of fat/kg body weight/day (20 mL, 10 mL and 6.7 mL/kg of Intralipid 10%, 20% and 30%, respectively). In raised energy requirements, the supply of Intralipid can be increased but should not, without special precautions, exceed a quantity corresponding to 3 g fat (30 mL, 15 mL and 10 mL of Intralipid 10%, 20% and 30%, respectively)/kg body weight/day.

Prevention of Essential Fatty Acid Deficiency: The recommended minimum requirement is approximately 4% of the caloric intake. In most patients, this can be supplied as 500 mL of Intralipid 10% administered i.v. twice weekly.

The drip rate is adjusted to about 2 to 3 mL/minute for Intralipid 10% and about 1 to 2 mL/minute of Intralipid 20% at which rates 500 mL can be infused in 3 to 5 hours and 5 to 9 hours, respectively. The infusion time for 500 mL must not be shorter than 3 and 5 hours, respectively. The infusion should be started at half the infusion rate during the first 30 minutes, under supervision.

A daily supplement of 333 mL of Intralipid 30% (100 g fat) is regarded as sufficient to meet the basal metabolic requirements of a 70 kg patient on total parenteral nutrition. The drip rate is adjusted to 0.6 to 1 mL/minute at which rate 333 mL can be infused over a period of 5 to 10 hours. The rate of infusion should not exceed 333 mL of Intralipid 30% over a 5-hour period. The infusion should be started at half the infusion rate during the first 30 minutes, under supervision.

Children: The infant's ability to eliminate fat should govern the dosage (see Contraindications and Precautions). Recommended dosage per 24 hours is 0.5 to 4 g fat/kg body weight equivalent to 2.5 to 20 mL Intralipid 20% and 5 to 40 mL Intralipid 10%/kg body weight, respectively. Recommended initial dose in very low birth weight infants and small for gestational age infants is 0.5 g fat/kg body weight per 24 hours. The dose should be increased in relation to the infant's ability to eliminate fat, which should be checked daily (see Fat Elimination Test). The daily dose should preferably be administered continuously over 24 hours by infusion pump. Due to the lack of experience, Intralipid 30% is not recommended for use in infants.

Administration: Intralipid must not be mixed with electrolyte or nutrient solutions, nor must drugs or vitamins be added to the emulsion in the infusion bottle other than drugs or vitamins especially formulated for addition to fat emulsions. The simultaneous administration of Intralipid and amino acid solutions or carbohydrate can be achieved, using separate infusion sets where the two liquids are allowed to mix in a Y-tube just before the i.v. needle. Filters should not be used with i.v. fat emulsion. The remaining contents of a partly used bottle must be discarded and should not be stored for later use.

Supplied: Intralipid 10%: 1 000 mL contain: purified soybean oil 100 g, purified egg phospholipids 12 g, glycerol anhydrous 22 g, water for injection q.s. ad 1 000 mL. pH is adjusted with sodium hydroxide to pH approximately 8. Energy content/L: 4.6 MJ (1 100 kcal). Osmolality (approx.): 300 mOsm/kg water. Bottles of 500 mL.

Intralipid 20%: 1 000 mL contain: purified soybean oil 200 g, purified egg phospholipids 12 g, glycerol anhydrous 22 g, water for injection q.s. ad 1 000 mL. pH is adjusted with sodium hydroxide to pH approximately 8. Energy content/L: 8.4 MJ (2 000 kcal). Osmolality (approx.): 350 mOsm/kg water. Bottles of 100, 250 and 500 mL.

Intralipid 30%: 1 000 mL contain: purified soybean oil 300 g, purified egg phospholipids 12 g, glycerol anhydrous 16.7 g, water for injection q.s. ad 1 000 mL. pH is adjusted with sodium hyroxide to pH approximately 7.5. Energy content/L: 12.6 MJ (3 000 kcal). Osmolality (approx.): 310 mOsm/kg water. Bottles of 333 mL.

Store at controlled room temperature below 25°C. Do not freeze.

Reviewed 1998

INTRON A®

Schering

Interferon alfa-2b

Biological Response Modifier

Pharmacology: Interferon alfa-2b has exhibited antiproliferative effects in preclinical studies employing both cell culture systems and human tumor xenografts in animals, and has demonstrated significant immunomodulatory activity in vitro. Interferon alfa-2b also inhibits viral replication in vitro and in vivo.

Interferons exert their cellular activities by binding to specific membrane receptors on the cell surface. The results of several studies suggest that, once bound to the cell membrane, interferon initiates a complex sequence of intracellular events that include the induction of certain enzymes. It is thought that this process, at least in part, is responsible for the various cellular responses to interferon, including inhibition of virus replication in virus-infected cells, suppression of cell proliferation and such immunomodulation activities as enhancement of the phagocytic activity of macrophages and augmentation of the specific cytotoxicity of lymphocytes for target cells. All of these activities possibly contribute to interferon's therapeutic effects.

Pharmacokinetics: The pharmacokinetics of interferon alfa-2b injection were studied in 12 healthy male volunteers following single doses of 5 million IU/m² administered i.m., s.c. and as a 30-minute i.v. infusion in a cross-over design. Interferon concentrations were determined using a radioimmunoassay (RIA) with a detection limit equal to 10 IU/mL. The mean serum interferon concentrations following i.m. and s.c. injections were comparable.

The maximum serum concentrations obtained via these routes were approximately 18 to 116 IU/mL and occurred 3 to 12 hours after administration. The elimination half-lives of interferon following both i.m. and s.c. injections were approximately 2 to 3 hours. Serum levels were below the detection limit 16 hours post-injection. After i.v. administration, serum interferon levels peaked (135 to 273 IU/mL) by the end of the infusion, then declined at a slightly more rapid rate than after s.c. or i.m. drug administration, becoming undetectable 4 hours after the infusion. The elimination half-life was approximately 2 hours. Urine levels of interferon following a single dose (5 million IU/m²) were below the detection limit following each of the 3 routes of administration.

In another study, the pharmacokinetics of interferon alfa-2b were studied in 12 healthy male volunteers following single 10 million IU doses administered s.c., i.m. and as a 30-minute i.v. infusion. The mean serum level profiles of interferon following s.c. and i.m. injections were comparable. The maximum serum levels obtained at 6 to 8 hours after injection were approximately 150 to 180 IU/mL. The elimination half-lives of interferon following both s.c. and i.m. injections were approximately 6 to 7 hours. Serum levels were below the detection limit of 25 IU/mL, 24 hours after the injections. Serum levels of interferon after i.v. administration peaked (546 IU/mL) by the end of the infusion, then declined rapidly with time, becoming undetectable 4 hours after the infusion. Urine levels of interferon were below the detection limit following each of the 3 routes of administration.

There are no pharmacokinetic data available for the intralesional route of administration.

Indications: Chronic Hepatitis Non-A, Non-B/C: For the treatment of chronic hepatitis Non-A, Non-B/C (NANB/C) in patients 18 years or older with compensated liver disease who have a history of blood or blood product exposure and/or are HCV

Intron A (cont'd)

antibody positive. Studies in these patients demonstrated that interferon alfa-2b can produce normalization of ALT, clearance of serum HCV RNA and improvement in liver histology.

Chronic Active Hepatitis B: For the treatment of chronic active hepatitis B in patients 18 years of age or older with compensated liver disease and who have evidence of viral replication. Patients must be serum HBsAg positive for at least 6 months and have HBV replication, as demonstrated by positive serum HBeAg, with elevated serum ALT.

Studies in these patients demonstrated that interferon alfa-2b therapy can produce virologic remission of this disease (loss of serum HBeAg and HBV-DNA) and normalization of serum aminotransferases. Interferon alfa-2b therapy resulted in the loss of serum HBsAg in some responding patients.

Interferon alfa-2b is not indicated for the treatment of patients who are chronic carriers of hepatitis B surface antigen (HBsAg) but lack evidence of viral replication (serum HBeAg negative).

Chronic Myelogenous Leukemia: For the treatment of patients with chronic myelogenous leukemia (CML). Studies have demonstrated a greater likelihood of response to interferon alfa-2b therapy in patients who are in the chronic phase of the disease.

Thrombocytosis Associated with CML: Thrombocytosis is frequently associated with CML. During the clinical experience accumulated to date, approximately one-quarter (26%) of the patients diagnosed with CML had concomitant thrombocytosis, with a baseline platelet count of greater than 500×10^9/L. Platelet control was achieved in all patients within 2 months of treatment. At no time were monthly platelet counts $< 80 \times 10^9$/L.

Multiple Myeloma: Interferon alfa-2b maintenance is a therapeutic option for multiple myeloma patients who achieved objective remission on induction therapy (i.e., melphalan and prednisone). In the relatively older patient poplulation, the potential interferon-mediated benefit of prolonged remission duration must be weighed against the toxicity associated with interferon therapy. The approach to these patients should be individualized.

Non-Hodgkin's Lymphoma: As adjuvant treatment of high tumor burden follicular lymphoma (Stage 3 or 4) in combination with appropriate chemotherapy, such as a CHOP-like regimen.

Malignant Melanoma: As adjuvant to surgical treatment in patients 18 years of age or older with malignant melanoma who are free of disease but at high risk for systemic recurrence, within 56 days of surgery.

AIDS-Related Kaposi's Sarcoma: For the treatment of select patients, above 18 years of age with AIDS-Related Kaposi's Sarcoma. Studies have demonstrated a greater likelihood of response in patients who are without systemic symptoms, who have limited lymphadenopathy and who have a relatively intact immune system.

Hairy Cell Leukemia: For the treatment of patients with hairy cell leukemia either following or replacing splenectomy.

Basal Cell Carcinoma: Interferon alfa-2b, administered intralesionally, should be considered as an alternative treatment for patients with primary superficial and noduloulcerative basal cell carcinoma, where surgery or radiation are considered inappropriate. The basal cell lesion should be subtyped prior to initiation of treatment since no data exist for the use of interferon alfa-2b in the following conditions: 1) recurrent basal cell carcinoma; 2) genetic or nevoid basal cell carcinoma; 3) basal cell carcinoma with evidence of deep tissue involvement; 4) morphealike basal cell carcinoma.

Condylomata Acuminata: For intralesional treatment of selected patients with condylomata acuminata involving external surfaces of the genital and perianal areas.

In selecting patients for interferon alfa-2b treatment, the physician should consider the nature of the patient's lesion and the patient's past treatment history, in addition to the patient's ability to comply with the treatment regimen. Interferon alfa-2b therapy offers an additional approach to treatment in condylomata and is particularly useful for those patients who do not respond satisfactorily to other treatment modalities (e.g., podophyllin resin, surgery, cryotherapy, chemotherapy, and laser therapy), or whose lesions are more readily treatable by interferon alfa-2b than by other treatments.

Contraindications: Hypersensitivity to interferon alfa-2b or any of its components.

Warnings: Variations in dosage, routes of administration, and adverse reactions exist among different brands of interferon. Therefore, do not use different brands of interferon in any single treatment regimen.

General: Pulmonary infiltrates, pneumonitis and pneumonia, including fatality, have been observed rarely in interferon-alfa treated patients. The etiology has not been defined. Any patient developing fever, cough, dyspnea or other respiratory symptoms should have a chest x-ray taken. If the chest x-ray shows pulmonary infiltrates or there is evidence of pulmonary function impairment, the patient should be monitored closely, and, if appropriate, interferon-alfa treatment should be discontinued. While this has been reported more often in patients with chronic hepatitis non-A, non-B/C treated with interferon-alfa, it has also been reported in patients with oncologic diseases treated with interferon-alfa. These symptoms have been reported more frequently when shosaikoto, a Chinese herbal medication, has been administered concomitantly with interferon-alfa.

Patients with a pre-existing psychiatric condition or a history of severe psychiatric disorder should not be treated with interferon alfa-2b. Therapy should be discontinued for any patient developing severe depression during treatment.

AIDS-Related Kaposi's Sarcoma: Interferon alfa-2b should not be used for patients with rapidly progressive visceral disease. Patients receiving concomitant zidovudine (AZT) have had a higher incidence of neutropenia than that expected with zidovudine alone. Careful monitoring of the WBC counts is indicated in all patients who are myelosuppressed and in all patients receiving other myelosuppressive medications. The effects of interferon alfa-2b when administered in association with drugs used in the treatment of AIDS-related disease are unknown.

Chronic Hepatitis Non-A, Non-B/C and Chronic Active Hepatitis B: Patients with decompensated liver disease, autoimmune hepatitis, a history of autoimmune disease or immune suppressed transplant recipients should not be treated with interferon alfa-2b. There are reports of worsening liver disease, including jaundice, hepatic encephalopathy, hepatic failure and death following interferon alfa-2b therapy in patients with decompensated liver disease.

Patients with chronic hepatitis B with evidence of decreasing hepatic synthetic function, such as decreasing albumin levels or prolongation of prothrombin time, may be at increased risk of clinical decompensation if a flare of aminotransferases occurs. In considering these patients for interferon alfa-2b therapy, the potential risks must be evaluated against the potential benefits of treatment.

Pregnancy: Interferon alfa-2b has been shown to have abortifacient effects in Macaca mulatta (rhesus monkeys) at 90 and 180 times the i.m. or s.c. dose of 2 million IU/m². Although abortion was observed in all dose groups (7.5 million, 15 million, and 30 million IU/kg), it was only statistically significant versus control at the mid- and high-dose groups (corresponding to 90 and 180 times the i.m. or s.c. dose of 2 million IU/m²). There are no adequate and well-controlled studies in pregnant women. Interferon alfa-2b should be used during pregnancy only if the potential benefit justifies the potential risk to the fetus.

Lactation: It is not known whether the components of this drug are excreted in human milk. Because many drugs are excreted in human milk and because of the potential for serious adverse reactions from interferon alfa-2b in nursing infants, a decision to use or discontinue the drug should be based on a benefit to risk assessment.

Effect on Fertility: Interferon may impair fertility. In studies of interferon use in nonhuman primates, menstrual cycle abnormalities have been observed. Decreased serum estradiol and progesterone concentrations have been reported in women treated with human leukocyte interferon. Therefore, fertile women should not receive interferon alfa-2b injection unless they are using effective contraception during the treatment period. When interferon alfa-2b is used by fertile men, a possible effect on fertility should be considered.

Precautions: Patients should be cautioned not to change brands of interferon without medical consultation as a change in dosage may result.

Acute serious hypersensitivity reactions (e.g., urticaria, angioedema, bronchoconstriction, anaphylaxis) have been observed rarely during interferon alfa-2b therapy. If such a reaction develops, the drug should be discontinued and appropriate medical therapy instituted immediately. Transient rashes do not necessitate interruption of treatment.

There have been reports of interferon exacerbating preexisting conditions of psoriasis. Therefore, interferon alfa-2b should be used in these patients only if the potential benefit justifies the potential risk.

Hepatotoxicity, including fatality, has been observed rarely in interferon alfa-2b treated patients. Any patient developing liver function abnormalities during treatment should be monitored closely and if appropriate, treatment should be discontinued.

Because of the fever and other flu-like symptoms associated with interferon alfa-2b administration, it should be used cautiously in patients with debilitating medical conditions, such as those with a history of cardiovascular disease (e.g., unstable angina, uncontrolled congestive heart failure), pulmonary disease (e.g., chronic obstructive pulmonary disease) or diabetes mellitus prone to ketoacidosis.

While fever may be associated with interferon therapy, other causes of persistent fever should be ruled out. Caution should also be observed in patients with coagulation disorders (e.g., thrombophlebitis, pulmonary embolism) or severe myelosuppression.

Patients with a history of myocardial infarction and/or previous or current arrhythmic disorders, who require interferon alfa-2b therapy, should be closely monitored (see Laboratory Tests). Those patients who have pre-existing cardiac abnormalities and/or are in advanced stages of cancer, should have ECGs taken prior to and during the course of treatment. Cardiac arrhythmias (primarily supraventricular) usually respond to conventional therapy but may require dose modification or discontinuation of interferon alfa-2b therapy.

Transient reversible cardiomyopathy was reported in approximately 2% of the AIDS-Related Kaposi's Sarcoma patients treated with interferon alfa-2b. Cardiomyopathy has also been reported in AIDS patients not receiving interferon alfa-2b therapy. Baseline chest x-rays are suggested and should be repeated if clinically indicated.

Adequate hydration should be maintained in patients undergoing inferferon alfa-2b therapy since hypotension related to fluid depletion has been seen in some patients during therapy and up to 2 days post-therapy. Fluid replacement may be necessary.

Retinal hemorrhages, cotton-wool spots, and retinal artery or vein obstruction have been observed rarely in patients treated with interferon alfa, including interferon alfa-2b. The etiologic explanation for these findings has not yet been established. These events appear to occur after use of the drug for several months, but also have been reported after shorter treatment periods. Diabetes mellitus or hypertension have been present in some patients. Any patient complaining of changes in visual acuity or visual fields, or reporting other ophthalmologic symptoms during treatment with interferon alfa-2b, should have an eye examination. Because the retinal events may have to be differentiated from those seen with diabetic or hypertensive retinopathy, a baseline ocular examination is recommended prior to treatment with interferon in patients with diabetes mellitus or hypertension.

CNS effects manifested by depression, confusion and other alterations of mental status have been observed in some interferon alfa-2b-treated patients, and suicidal ideation and attempted suicide have been observed rarely. These adverse effects have occurred in patients treated with recommended doses as well as in patients treated with higher interferon alfa-2b doses. More significant obtundation and coma have been observed in some patients, usually elderly, treated at higher doses. While these effects are generally reversible upon discontinuation of therapy, in a few patients full resolution took up to 3 weeks. Very rarely, seizures have occurred with high doses of interferon alfa-2b. Narcotics, hypnotics or sedatives should be administered with caution concomitantly with interferon alfa-2b.

Administration of interferon alfa-2b in combination with other chemotherapeutic agents may lead to increased risk of toxicity (severity and duration), which may be life-threatening or fatal as a result of the concomitantly administered drug. The most commonly reported potentially life-threatening or fatal adverse events include mucositis, diarrhea, neutropenia, renal impairment, and electrolyte disturbance. Because of the risk of increased toxicity, careful adjustments of doses are required for interferon alfa-2b and for the concomitant chemotherapeutic agents.

In the presence of thyroid dysfunction, interferon alfa-2b treatment may be initiated or continued only if TSH levels can be maintained in the normal range by medication. Discontinuation of interferon alfa-2b therapy has not reversed thyroid dysfunction occurring during treatment.

Children: Safety and effectiveness have not been established in patients below the age of 18 years.

Laboratory Tests: In addition to those tests normally required for monitoring patients, the following laboratory tests are recommended for all patients on interferon alfa-2b therapy prior to beginning treatment and then periodically thereafter: standard hematologic tests–including hemoglobin, complete and differential white blood cell counts and platelet count; blood chemistries–including electrolytes, calcium, liver enzyme tests and serum creatinine and TSH.

The hematologic parameters of the patients should be followed closely as part of the treatment, and also because a certain degree of myelodepression has been detected in some patients under treatment with interferon alfa-2b.

Mild to moderate leukopenia and elevated serum liver enzyme (AST) levels have been reported with intralesional administration of interferon alfa-2b; therefore, the monitoring of these laboratory parameters should be considered.

For specific laboratory testing recommendations on chronic hepatitis Non-A, Non-B/C and chronic active hepatitis B, see Dosage.

Adverse Effects: Systemic Administration: The most commonly reported adverse effects were fever, fatigue, headache and myalgia (flu-like symptoms). Fever and fatigue were reversible within 72 hours of interruption or cessation of treatment and were dose related.

Common adverse effects include rigors, anorexia and nausea.

Less common adverse effects include vomiting, diarrhea, arthralgia, asthenia, somnolence, dizziness, dry mouth, alopecia, flu-like symptoms (unspecified), back pain, depression, malaise, pain, increased sweating, taste alteration, irritability, insomnia, confusion, impaired concentration and hypotension.

Rarely reported adverse reactions include abdominal pain, rash, nervousness, injection site disorders, paresthesia, herpes simplex, pruritus, eye pain, anxiety, epistaxis, coughing, pharyngitis, pulmonary infiltrates, pneumonitis and pneumonia, impaired consciousness, weight decrease, facial edema, dyspnea, dyspepsia, tachycardia, hypertension, increased appetite, decreased libido, hypoesthesia, taste alteration, loose stool, gingival bleeding, leg cramps, neuropathy, polyneuropathy, rhabdomyolysis (sometimes serious), hearing disorder, renal failure, renal insufficiency, nephrotic syndrome, and diabetes mellitus/hyperglycemia. Hyperthyroidism or hypothyroidism have also been observed rarely. Hepatotoxicity, including fatality, has been observed rarely (see Precautions).

Cardiovascular adverse reactions, particularly arrhythmia, appeared to be correlated mostly with pre-existing cardiovascular disease and prior cardiotoxic therapy. Transient reversible cardiomyopathy has been reported rarely in patients without prior evidence of cardiac disease. Very rarely reported adverse reactions include pancreatitis, cardiac ischemia and myocardial infarction.

Clinically significant laboratory abnormalities, most frequently occurring at doses greater than 10 million IU daily, include reduction in granulocyte and white blood cell counts; decreases in hemoglobin level and platelet count; increases in alkaline phosphatase, lactate dehydrogenase (LDH), serum creatinine, serum urea nitrogen, and TSH levels. Increase in serum ALT/AST levels have been noted as an abnormality in some non-hepatitis subjects and also in some patients with chronic hepatitis B coincident with clearance of viral DNAp.

There were no new or unusual toxicities associated with the use of interferon alfa-2b for the treatment of malignant melanoma. The most commonly reported adverse reactions were gastrointestinal events, hematologic events, hepatic toxicity, neurologic toxicity, vomiting, chills, fatigue, fever and myalgia. In the surgical adjuvant trial involving 280 patients, 100% of patients treated with interferon alfa-2b experienced at least 1 adverse event compared to 43% for the observation patients. Severe adverse events occurred in 78% of interferon alfa-2b treated patients versus 6% of observation patients. Sixty-five percent of patients had at least 1 dose modification due to toxicity. Twenty-four percent of patients discontinued interferon alfa-2b treatment due to adverse events.

The following adverse reactions were reported to be possibly or probably treatment-related in the trial involving 143 interferon alfa-2b treated patients. The most commonly reported adverse reactions were fatigue, fever, myalgia, anorexia, nausea, headache and chills. Less common adverse reactions were depression, diarrhea, alopecia, taste alteration, dizziness, rash, pain (unspecified), dyspnea, paresthesia, influenza-like symptoms, confusion, bleeding, coughing, increased sweating, arthralgia, malaise and insomnia.

Intralesional Administration: Most reported adverse reactions were mild to moderate, transient and rapidly reversible. The incidence of reported adverse reactions in the patients treated for condylomata acuminata appears to increase in proportion to the number of lesions treated and consequently, is dose related.

The most common adverse reactions are flu-like symptoms, (rigors/chills, fever, headache, myalgia and malaise). Other commonly reported side effects include nausea, fatigue, dizziness, arthralgia, back pain and injection site reactions (burning, itching, pain and injection site bleeding). In patients treated for condylomata acuminata injection site reactions appear to be due to manipulation of the lesion rather than the interferon alfa-2b therapy.

Rarely reported side effects include diarrhea, somnolence, depression, pain, dyspepsia, increased sweating, unspecified flu-like symptoms, confusion, weakness, vomiting, flushing, leg cramps, asthenia, taste perversion, dermatitis and pruritus.

Low white blood cell counts, elevated serum liver enzyme (AST) levels and low platelet counts have been reported in some patients with intralesional administration of interferon alfa-2b. Most of these laboratory findings were transient, rapidly reversible and mild to moderate in severity.

Reported adverse reactions and abnormal laboratory test values observed in patients who were re-treated for condylomata acuminata with interferon alfa-2b were qualitatively and quantitatively similar to those reported above.

The following adverse events have been reported very rarely after administration of interferon alfa-2b: Blood Disorders: hemolytic anemia, granulocytopenia, leukopenia, increased gamma globulins, coagulation disorder.

Body as a Whole: dehydration, hypercalcemia, cachexia, peripheral edema, lymphadenopathy, periorbital edema, malignant hyperpyrexia, transplant rejection, acidosis, ascites.

Cardiovascular: palpitations, postural hypotension, chest pain, chest pain substernal, bradycardia, cardiac failure, cardiomyopathy, atrial fibrillation, arrhythmia, extrasystole, angina pectoris, thrombophlebitis, peripheral ischemia.

Central and Peripheral Nervous System: amnesia, stupor, convulsions, hypertonia, hyperesthesia, hot flashes, migraine, encephalopathy, tremor, coma, extrapyramidal disorder, paresis, speech disorder, dysphonia, syncope, tinnitus, vertigo, abnormal coordination, ataxia, aphasia, CNS dysfunction, abnormal gait, hyperkinesia, dystonia, paralysis, hyperparesthesia.

Endocrine: gynecomastia, virilism, aggravation of diabetes mellitus, hyperglycemia, adrenal hypercorticism.

Gastrointestinal: eructation, stomatitis, stomatitis ulcerative, constipation, tenesmus, ileus, thirst, melena, increased saliva, esophagitis, rectal bleeding after stool, dysphagia, gastrointestinal hemorrhage, gastric ulcer, gingivitis, gum hyperplasia, rectal hemorrhage, oral leukoplakia, gastrointestinal mucosal discoloration, abdominal distention, flatulence, tongue discoloration, glossitis, taste loss, discolored feces.

Liver and Biliary: abnormal hepatic function tests, bilirubinemia, jaundice, right upper quadrant pain, hepatosplenomegaly, splenomegaly, hepatic encephalopathy.

Musculoskeletal: bone pain, muscle weakness, arthritis, arthrosis, myopathy.

Psychiatric Disorders: agitation, emotional lability, personality disorder, abnormal thinking, abnormal dreaming, sleep disorder, dysphonia, flushing, hypokinesia, suicide attempt, paroniria, apathy, aggravated depression, neurosis, aggressive reaction, feeling of ebriety, hallucination, dementia, paranoid reactions.

Reproduction: impotence, leukorrhea, menorrhagia, uterine bleeding, vaginal hemorrhage, amenorrhea.

Resistance Mechanism Disorders (i.e., altered resistance to infection): stye, conjunctivitis, viral and fungal infections, moniliasis, sepsis.

Respiratory: hypoxia, stridor, nasal congestion, pneumonia, sinusitis, rhinitis, rhinorrhea, bronchospasm, cyanosis, wheezing, pleural pain, sneezing, nonproductive coughing, pulmonary embolism, pulmonary edema, laryngitis, cold.

Skin and Appendages: urticaria, acne, nail disorders, hypertrichosis, purpura, peripheral ischemia, furunculosis, nonherpetic cold sores, epidermal necrolysis, lacrimal gland disorder, cyanosis of the hand, photosensitivity, skin discoloration, chloasma, abnormal hair texture, increased hair growth, skin depigmentation, dermatitis lichenoides, melanosis, vitiligo, dry skin, dermatitis, erythema, maculopapular rash, pustular rash, clammy skin, injection site reaction.

Urinary: micturition disorder, nocturia, polyuria, hematuria, micturition frequency, cystitis, oliguria, nephrosis, urinary incontinence, hyperuricemia.

Visual and Auditory Disorders: photophobia, blurred vision, abnormal vision, diplopia, dry eyes, oculomotor nerve paralysis, retinal disorder, retinal hemorrhage, night blindness, twitching, earache, deafness, hyperacusis.

Overdose: Symptoms and Treatment: Distinction between the therapeutic dose of interferon alfa-2b and overdose has not been clearly defined. Symptoms of overdose may include amplification of the adverse effects, notably flu-like symptoms, leukopenia or thrombocytopenia and increased serum liver enzyme levels. The severity of the adverse reactions can be ameliorated by adjusting the dose level and schedule, or in some cases termination of interferon alfa-2b therapy. Cardiovascular side effects such as hypotension and arrhythmia may require supportive therapy.

Dosage: Interferon alfa-2b injection may be administered using either sterilized glass or plastic disposable syringes.

In general, the dosage may be adjusted according to the patient's tolerance to the medication. If severe adverse reactions develop, the dosage should be modified (50% reduction) or therapy should be temporarily discontinued until the adverse reactions abate. If persistent or recurrent intolerance develops following adequate dosage adjustment, or if the disease progresses rapidly, treatment with interferon alfa-2b should be discontinued.

For maintenance dosage regimens administered s.c. or i.m., the patient may self-administer the dose at the discretion of the physician.

Laboratory Tests: Standard hematologic tests and blood chemistries (complete blood count and differential, platelet count, electrolytes, liver enzymes, including serum ALT, serum bilirubin, and albumin, serum protein, and serum creatinine) should be conducted in all patients prior to and periodically during treatment with interferon alfa-2b. Thyroid stimulating hormone (TSH) levels must be within normal limits prior to initiation of interferon alfa-2b therapy. Any patient developing symptoms consistent with possible thyroid dysfunction during interferon alfa-2b therapy should have an evaluation of thyroid function.

In patients treated for hepatitis, the recommended testing schedule is at weeks 1, 2, 4, 8, 12, 16, and every other month, thereafter, throughout treatment. If ALT flares (≥ 2 times baseline) during interferon alfa-2b therapy, interferon alfa-2b may be continued unless signs or symptoms of liver failure are observed. During ALT flare, liver function tests for prothrombin time, ALT, alkaline phosphatase, albumin and bilirubin levels should be performed at 2 week intervals.

Chronic Hepatitis Non-A, Non-B/C: The recommended dosage of interferon alfa-2b is 3 million IU administered s.c. or i.m. 3 times/week for up to 18 months. Most patients who respond demonstrate improvement in ALT levels within 12 weeks. Some patients who fail to respond to 3 million IU may benefit from higher doses of up to 10 million IU 3 times/week.

Current clinical experience in patients who remain on interferon alfa-2b for 12 to 18 months indicates that a higher proportion of patients demonstrated a sustained response after longer durations of therapy than those who discontinued therapy after 6 months.

Patients who relapse following therapy may be retreated with the same dosage regimen to which they had previously responded.

A liver biopsy should be performed to establish the diagnosis of chronic hepatitis. Patients should be tested for the presence of antibody to HCV and other causes of chronic hepatitis, including autoimmune hepatitis should be excluded. Prior to initiation of interferon alfa-2b therapy, the physician should establish that the patient has compensated liver disease with no evidence of hepatic failure. Serum bilirubin, serum albumin, and serum creatinine should be within normal limits.

Prior to initiation of interferon alfa-2b therapy, CBC and platelet counts should be evaluated in order to establish baselines for monitoring potential toxicity. During treatment with interferon alfa-2b, these tests should be evaluated at weeks 1 and 2, and monthly thereafter. ALT levels should be evaluated after 2, 12 and 24 weeks of therapy to assess response to treatment.

Thyroid stimulating hormone (TSH) must be within normal limits upon initiation of interferon alfa-2b treatment. Patients with pre-existing thyroid abnormalities may be treated if TSH levels can be maintained in the normal range by medication.

Chronic Active Hepatitis B: The recommended dosage of interferon alfa-2b is 30 to 35 million IU/week, administered s.c. or i.m. either as 5 million IU daily or 10 million IU 3 times/week, for 16 weeks.

Prior to initiation of therapy, a liver biopsy may be useful in establishing a diagnosis of chronic hepatitis. The physician should establish that the patient has compensated liver disease. The following patient entrance criteria for compensated liver disease were used in the clinical studies:

No history of hepatic encephalopathy, variceal bleeding, ascites, or other clinical signs of decompensation; bilirubin: normal; albumin: stable and within normal limits; prothrombin time: <3 seconds prolonged; WBC: ≥4 000/mm³; platelets: ≥100 000/mm³.

Patients with other causes of chronic hepatitis should be excluded. CBC and platelet counts should be evaluated prior to initiation of interferon alfa-2b therapy in order to establish baselines for monitoring potential toxicity. These tests should

Intron A (cont'd)

be repeated at treatment weeks 1, 2, 4 and monthly thereafter. Liver function tests, including serum ALT, albumin and bilirubin, should be evaluated after 1, 2, 4, 8, 12 and 16 weeks of therapy. HBeAg, HBsAg, and ALT should be evaluated at the end of therapy, as well as at 3 and 6 months post-therapy, since patients may become virologic responders during the 6-month period following the end of treatment.

For patients with decreases in granulocyte or platelet counts, the following guidelines for dose modifications were used in the clinical trials: See Table I.

Table I—Intron A

Laboratory Values for Dose Modification

Dose	Granulocytes	Platelets
Reduce 50%	<750/mm³	<50 000/mm³
Interrupt	<500/mm³	<30 000/mm³

Interferon alfa-2b therapy was resumed at 50% or increased to 100% of the initial dose when granulocytes and/or platelets increased above the appropriate values.

A transient increase in ALT ≥2 times baseline value (flare) can occur during interferon alfa-2b therapy for chronic active hepatitis B. In clinical trials, this flare generally occurred 8 to 12 weeks after initiation of therapy and was more frequent in responders (63%, 24/38) than in nonresponders (27%, 13/48). However, coincident elevation in bilirubin ≥3 mg/dL occurred infrequently (2%, 2/85). When ALT flare occurs, in general interferon alfa-2b therapy should be continued unless signs and symptoms of liver failure are observed. During ALT flare, clinical symptomatology and liver function tests including ALT, albumin and bilirubin, should be monitored at approximately 2-week intervals.

Chronic Myelogenous Leukemia: The recommended dosage of interferon alfa-2b is 4 to 5 million IU/m² administered daily s.c. Dosages as little as 0.5 million IU/m² or as high as 10 million IU/m² may be necessary to achieve or maintain control of the white blood cell count. When the white blood cell count is controlled, the dosage may be administered 3 times/week (every other day). The dosage may be adjusted according to the patient's tolerance to the medication.

Treatment should be initiated as early as possible after diagnosis, and continued until complete hematological response is achieved or for a maximum of 18 months. Responding patients generally show a hematologic response within 2 to 3 months of treatment. These patients should continue to be treated until a complete hematologic response is obtained, as defined by a white blood cell (WBC) count of 3 to 4 x 10⁹/L. All patients with a complete hematological response should further continue treatment in order to achieve a cytogenetic response which in some patients may not occur until 2 years after treatment initiation.

In patients, who at the time of initiation of therapy with interferon alfa-2b, present with extremely high white blood cell counts leading to possible life-threatening complications, consideration should be given to concomitant interventions such as leukapheresis in order to quickly lower the white blood cell count. Once the immediate risk to the patient has been reduced, interferon alfa-2b therapy should be initiated.

Thrombocytosis Associated with CML: The recommended dosage for the control of thrombocytosis in CML is the same as that recommended above for the treatment of CML. Dose adjustments made for the control of the white blood cell counts should also be appropriate to control platelet counts.

Multiple Myeloma: In patients who are in the plateau phase following inductive chemotherapy, interferon alfa-2b may be administered as monotherapy, s.c., at a dose of 3 million IU/m², 3 times a week (every other day).

Treatment should continue unless clear disease progresses or severe intolerance occurs.

Non-Hodgkin's Lymphoma: When used adjunctively with chemotherapy, the recommended dosage of interferon alfa-2b is 5 million IU 3 times/week on alternate days administered s.c. for a duration of 18 months.

The standard chemotherapeutic treatment for patients with high tumor burden follicular lymphomas is the administration of a combination chemotherapy regimen. Most of these regimens are related to the well-known CHOP [cyclophosphamide, doxorubicin, vincristine, and prednisone] regimen such as the CHVP regimen of doxorubicin, cyclophosphamide, teniposide and prednisolone.

At diagnosis, most follicular lymphoma patients have a disseminated disease, stage III or stage IV. Despite this advanced disease, many patients have an indolent course and survive several years after diagnosis. A wait and watch approach may be appropriate for these patients, especially if their tumor burden is low. Treatment is frequently initiated without delay for patients with high-tumor burden such as bulky lymphadenopathy, major organ obstruction or compression syndromes, malignant effusions, bone marrow failure, or rapidly enlarging tumors.

Malignant Melanoma: The recommended interferon alfa-2b treatment regimen includes an induction treatment of 5 consecutive days/week for 4 weeks as an i.v. infusion at a dose of 20 million IU/m², followed by a maintenance treatment of 3 times/week for 48 weeks as a s.c. injection, at a dose of 10 million IU/m². Therapy should be administered for a total of 1 year unless the disease progresses.

Induction therapy is administered as a 20-minute i.v. infusion of interferon alfa-2b in 100 mL of normal saline.

If severe adverse reactions develop during interferon alfa-2b treatment, particularly if granulocytes decrease to <500/mL or ALT/AST rises to >5×upper limit of normal, treatment should be temporarily discontinued until the adverse reaction abates. Interferon alfa-2b treatment should be restarted at 50% of the previous dose. If intolerance persists after dose adjustment or if granulocytes decrease to <250/mL or ALT/AST rises to >10×upper limit of normal, interferon alfa-2b therapy should be discontinued. In the clinical trial, patients were able to maintain clinical benefit in conjunction with appropriate dose modifications.

For patients treated for malignant melanoma, liver function and white blood cell and differential counts should be monitored weekly during the induction phase of therapy and monthly during the maintenance phase of therapy.

AIDS-Related Kaposi's Sarcoma: The recommended dosage of interferon alfa-2b is 30 million IU/m² 3 times/week administered s.c. or i.m.

When patients initiate therapy at 30 million IU/m² 3 times/week, the average dose tolerated at the end of 12 weeks of therapy is approximately 75% of the weekly dose and 50% of the weekly dose at the end of 24 weeks of therapy.

Lesion measurements and blood counts should be performed prior to initiation of therapy and should be monitored periodically during treatment to determine whether response to treatment or disease stabilization has occurred.

When disease stabilization or a response to treatment occurs, treatment should continue until there is no further evidence of tumor or until discontinuation is required by evidence of a severe opportunistic infection or adverse effect.

Hairy Cell Leukemia: The recommended dosage of interferon alfa-2b is 2 million IU/m² administered s.c. 3 times/week (every other day).

Prior to initiation of therapy, tests should be performed to quantitate peripheral blood hemoglobin, platelets, granulocytes and hairy cells and bone marrow hairy cells. These parameters should be monitored periodically during treatment to determine whether response to treatment has occurred. The normalization of one or more hematologic variables usually begins within 2 months of initiation of therapy. Improvement in all 3 hematologic variables (granulocyte count, platelet count and hemoglobin level) may require 6 months or more of therapy.

If a patient does not respond within 6 months, treatment should be discontinued. If a response to treatment does occur, treatment usually should be continued until no further improvement is observed and the laboratory parameters have been stable for about 3 months. It is not known whether continued treatment after that point is beneficial.

Basal Cell Carcinoma: The lesion to be injected should be cleaned first with a sterile alcohol pad. The intralesional injection should be made into the base and substance of the lesion using a fine needle (30 gauge) and a 1 mL syringe. Care should be taken not to go too deeply beneath the lesion. S.C. injection should be avoided. For lesions with an initial area below 2 cm², inject 0.15 mL of reconstituted solution containing 1.5 million IU interferon alfa-2b (see Reconstitution) into the lesion 3 times/week on alternate days, for 3 weeks. The cumulative dose administered per lesion should be 13.5 million IU. As many as 3 lesions can be treated at one time.

Large superficial and noduloulcerative basal cell lesions (lesions with an area between 2 and 10 cm²) should be treated 3 times/week for 3 weeks with 0.5 million IU/cm² of the lesion's initial size (the minimum dose being 1.5 million IU and the maximum dose being 5.0 million IU). Only one large lesion should be treated at a time.

The improvement in clinical status (appearance, size, erythema, etc.) of the treated lesion is a reliable predictor of biopsy-proven cures. Therefore, the clinical status should be monitored periodically after treatment end. Improvement in disease signs usually begins at approximately 8 weeks after treatment initiation. If no clinical improvement on the lesion is observed after 8 to 12 weeks, excision should be reconsidered.

Condylomata Acuminata: Inject 1 million IU of interferon alfa-2b (0.1 mL of reconstituted interferon alfa-2b solution) into each lesion 3 times/week on alternate days, for 3 weeks. Only the 10 million IU vial of interferon alfa-2b when reconstituted with 1 mL of designated diluent results in an isotonic solution at the desired concentration of 1 million IU/0.1 mL. The injection should be administered intralesionally using a Tuberculin or similar syringe and a 25 to 30 gauge needle. The needle should be directed at the center of the base of the wart and at an angle almost parallel to the plane of the skin (approximating that in the commonly used PPD test). This will deliver the interferon to the dermal core of the lesion, infiltrating the lesion and causing a small wheal. Care should be taken not to go beneath the lesion too deeply; s.c. injection should be avoided, since this area is below the base of the lesion. Do not inject too superficially since this will result in possible leakage, infiltrating only the keratinized layer, and not the dermal core. As many as 5 lesions can be treated at one time. To reduce side effects, interferon alfa-2b injections may be administered in the evening, when possible. Additionally, acetaminophen may be administered at the time of injection to alleviate some of the potential side effects.

The maximum response usually occurs 4 to 8 weeks after initiation of the first treatment course. If results at 12 to 16 weeks after the initial treatment course has concluded are not satisfactory, a second course of treatment using the above dosage schedule may be instituted providing that clinical symptoms and signs, or changes in laboratory parameters (liver function tests, WBC and platelets) do not preclude such a course of action.

Patients with 6 to 10 condylomata may receive a second (sequential) course of treatment at the above dosage schedule, to treat up to 5 additional condylomata per course of treatment. Patients with greater than 10 condylomata may receive additional sequences depending on how large a number of condylomata are present.

Concomitant Therapy: Acetaminophen has been used successfully to alleviate the symptoms of fever and headache which can occur with interferon alfa-2b therapy. The recommended acetaminophen dosage is 500 mg to 1 g given 30 minutes before administration of interferon alfa-2b. The maximum dosage of acetaminophen to be given is 1 g 4 times daily. In order to properly assess the source of fever, adjunctive acetaminophen should be limited to a maximum of 5 consecutive days unless otherwise specified by the prescribing physician.

A synergistic adverse effect on the white blood cell count may occur when interferon alfa-2b is administered concomitantly with zidovudine. Patients receiving the two agents concomitantly have had a dose-dependent higher incidence of neutropenia than expected when zidovudine is administered alone.

Interactions between interferon alfa-2b and other drugs have not been fully evaluated. Caution should be exercised when administering interferon alfa-2b in combination with other potentially myelosuppressive agents.

Reconstitution: Interferon alfa-2b lyophilized powder should be reconstituted with accompanying Bacteriostatic Water for Injection USP (preserved with benzyl alcohol, 0.9%), as diluent. If the patient is allergic to benzyl alcohol or if it is preferred by the physician, Sterile Water for Injection may be used.

S.C. or I.M. Administration: Using a sterile syringe and needle, inject 1 mL of Bacteriostatic Water for Injection USP (preserved with benzyl alcohol, 0.9%), supplied, or Sterile Water for Injection into the vial. Agitate gently to hasten complete dissolution of the powder. The appropriate dose should then be withdrawn with a sterile syringe and injected slowly s.c. or i.m.

Intralesional Administration: An isotonic solution of interferon alfa-2b is recommended for the treatment of basal cell carcinoma. Only the 10 million IU vial of Intron A when reconstituted with 1 mL of designated diluent results in an isotonic solution at the desired concentration of 1 million IU/0.1 mL. Reconstitution of other vial sizes to prepare the dilution required for intralesional use will result in a hypertonic solution.

I.V. Administration: The lyophilized powder form of interferon alfa-2b should be reconstituted by adding 1 mL of the provided diluent to the vial. The calculated amount of interferon for the appropriate dose then should be withdrawn from the vial(s), added to 100 mL of Sterile Normal Saline solution, and administered over 20 minutes. **No other drug can be infused concomitantly with Intron A.**

Intron A ready-to-use solution is not recommended for i.v. administration unless it is pre-filtered prior to use. A 0.2-micron filter can be used.
Compatibility with Other I.V. Fluids: In addition to i.v. normal saline solution, Intron A, at final concentrations of 50 000 to 1 million IU/mL is stable and compatible in the following mixtures for up to 24 hours at refrigerated or at room temperature in glass bottles: Ringers Injection, Amino Acid Injections, Lactate Ringers Injection, 5% Sodium Bicarbonate Injection.

The admixtures remained stable for the 6-hour infusion period through an administration set.
Stability and Storage: Store lyophilized powder and ready-to-use solution between 2 and 8°C.
Reconstituted Lyophilized Intron A: Diluted with Bacteriostatic Water for Injection USP (preserved with benzyl alcohol, 0.9%)—supplied with Intron A: If stored between 2 and 8°C, use within 30 days. If stored between 15 and 30°C, use within 14 days. Diluted with Sterile Water for Injection: Store at 2 to 30°C; use within 24 hours.

The reconstituted solution is clear and colorless to light yellow in color. The reconstituted material, as for all parenteral drug products, should be inspected visually for particulate matter and discoloration prior to administration.

Information for the Patient: See Blue Section–Information for the Patient "Intron A".

Supplied: Lyophilized Powder with Diluent: Each vial contains: 3, 5, 10 or 18 $\times 10^6$ IU of interferon alfa-2b, aminoacetic acid, sodium phosphate dibasic anhydrous, sodium phosphate monobasic monohydrate and human albumin and 1 vial of 1 mL Bacteriostatic Water for Injection USP (preserved with benzyl alcohol, 0.9%). Store between 2 and 8°C.

Ready-to-Use Solution: Each mL contains: 5×10^6 IU of interferon alfa-2b, sodium phosphate dibasic anhydrous, sodium phosphate monobasic monohydrate, glycine, human albumin, methylparaben, propylparaben, q.s. water for injection to make 1 mL. Vials of 2 and 5 mL. Store between 2 and 8°C.

Reviewed 1999

INTROPIN® Ⓟ

DuPont Pharma

Dopamine HCl

Sympathomimetic

Pharmacology: Dopamine exerts an inotropic effect on the myocardium resulting in an increased cardiac output. Dopamine produces less increase in myocardial oxygen consumption than isoproterenol and its use is usually not associated with a tachyarrhythmia. Clinical studies indicate that dopamine at low and intermediate therapeutic doses usually increases systolic and pulse pressure with either no effect or a slight increase in diastolic pressure, and total peripheral resistance is usually unchanged.

Blood flow to peripheral vascular beds may decrease while mesenteric flow increases. Dopamine has also been reported to dilate the renal vasculature presumptively by activation of a "dopaminergic" receptor. This action is accompanied by increases in glomerular filtration rate, renal blood flow, and sodium excretion. An increase in urinary output produced by dopamine is usually not associated with a decrease in osmolality of the urine.
Note: Dopamine is a rapidly acting compound. Cardiovascular effects are usually evident within 10 minutes and renal response usually occurs within 30 minutes. The half-life of dopamine is approximately 1.75 minutes.

Indications: For the correction of hemodynamic imbalances present in the shock syndrome due to myocardial infarction, trauma, endotoxic septicemia, open heart surgery, renal failure and chronic cardiac decompensation as in congestive failure.

Where appropriate, restoration of blood volume with a suitable plasma expander or whole blood should be instituted or completed prior to dopamine administration.

Patients most likely to respond adequately to dopamine are those in whom physiological parameters, such as urine flow, myocardial function, and, blood pressure, have not undergone profound deterioration. The shorter the time interval between onset of signs and symptoms and initiation of therapy with volume correction and dopamine, the better the prognosis.
Poor Perfusion of Vital Organs: Urine flow appears to be one of the better diagnostic signs by which adequacy of vital organ perfusion can be monitored. Nevertheless, the physician should also observe the patient for signs of reversal of confusion or comatose condition. Loss of pallor, increase in toe temperature and/or adequacy of nail bed capillary filling may also be used as indices of adequate dosage. Clinical studies have shown that when dopamine is administered before urine flow has diminished to levels approximating 0.5 mL/minute, prognosis is more favorable. Nevertheless, in a number of oliguric or anuric patients, dopamine administration has resulted in an increase in urine flow which in some cases reached normal levels. Dopamine may also increase urine flow in patients whose output is within normal limits and thus may be of value in reducing the degree of pre-existing fluid accumulation. It should be noted that at doses above those optimal for the individual patient, urine flow may decrease, necessitating reduction of dosage. Concurrent administration of dopamine and diuretic agents may produce an additive or potentiating effect.
Low Cardiac Output: Increased cardiac output is related to dopamine's direct inotropic effect on the myocardium. Increased cardiac output at low or moderate doses appears to be related to a favorable prognosis. Increase in cardiac output has been associated with either a static or decreased systemic vascular resistance (SVR). Static or decreased SVR associated with low or moderate increments in cardiac output is believed to be a reflection of differential effects on specific vascular beds with increased resistance in peripheral beds (i.e., femoral) and concomitant decrease in mesenteric and renal vascular beds. Redistribution of blood flow parallels these changes so that an increase in cardiac output is accompanied by an increase in mesenteric and renal blood flow. In many instances, the renal fraction of the total cardiac output has been found to increase. Increase in cardiac output produced by dopamine usually is not associated with substantial decreases in systemic vascular resistance.
Hypotension: Hypotension due to inadequate cardiac output can be managed by administration of low to moderate doses of dopamine, which have little effect on SVR. At high therapeutic doses, dopamine's alpha-adrenergic activity becomes more prominent and thus may correct hypotension due to diminished SVR. As in the case of other circulatory decompensation states, prognosis is better in patients whose blood pressure and urine flow have not undergone profound deterioration. Therefore, it is suggested that the physician administer dopamine as soon as a definite trend towards decreased systolic and diastolic pressure becomes evident.

Contraindications: Pheochromocytoma.

Warnings: Sensitivity to sulfites: Intropin contains sodium metabisulfite, a sulfite that may cause allergic-type reactions including anaphylactic symptoms and life-threatening or less severe asthmatic episodes in certain susceptible people. The overall prevalence of sulfite sensitivity in the general population is unknown, and probably low. Sulfite sensitivity is seen more frequently in asthmatic than in nonasthmatic people.
Note: Dopamine should not be administered in the presence of uncorrected tachyarrhythmias or ventricular fibrillation.

Do **not** add Intropin to any alkaline diluent solution, since the drug is inactivated in alkaline solution.

Patients who have been treated with MAO inhibitors prior to the administration of dopamine will require substantially reduced dosage. Dopamine is metabolized by MAO, and inhibition of this enzyme prolongs and potentiates the effect of dopamine. Reduce starting dose in such patients to at least 10% of the usual dose.

Cyclopropane or halogenated hydrocarbon anesthetics increase cardiac autonomic irritability and therefore seem to sensitize the myocardium to the action of certain intravenously administered catecholamines. Use dopamine with **extreme caution** in patients inhaling cyclopropane or halogenated hydrocarbon anesthetics.
Pregnancy: Animal studies have revealed no evidence of teratogenic effects from dopamine. The drug may be used in pregnant women when, in the judgement of the physician the expected benefits outweigh the potential for risk to the fetus.
Children: The safety and efficacy of this drug in children has not been established. Dopamine has been used in a limited number of pediatric patients, but such use has been inadequate to fully define proper dosage and limitations for use.

Precautions: Prior to dopamine treatment hypovolemia should be fully corrected, if possible, with either whole blood or plasma as indicated.

If a disproportionate rise in the diastolic pressure (i.e. a marked decrease in the pulse pressure) or a decrease in urine flow is observed in patients receiving dopamine, the infusion rate should be decreased and the patient observed carefully for further evidence of predominant vasoconstrictor activity, unless such an effect is desired.
Extravasation: Check the infusion site frequently for free flow since several cases of necrosis and sloughing of surrounding tissue due to extravasation have been reported. Infuse dopamine into a large vein whenever possible to prevent the possibility of extravasation into tissue adjacent to the infusion site. Large veins of the antecubital fossa are preferred to veins in the dorsum of the hand or ankle. Less suitable infusion sites should be used only if the patient's condition requires immediate attention. The physician should switch to more suitable sites as rapidly as possible.
Important: Peripheral Ischemia: No clinical experience exists in which phentolamine has been administered as an antidote for peripheral ischemia due to dopamine. However, the following is suggested, based on experience with other catecholamines: to prevent sloughing and necrosis in ischemic areas, infiltrate the area as soon as possible with 10 to 15 mL of saline solution containing from 5 to 10 mg of phentolamine, an α-adrenergic blocking agent. A syringe with a fine hypodermic needle should be used, and the solution liberally infiltrated throughout the ischemic area. Sympathetic blockage with phentolamine causes immediate and conspicuous local hyperemic changes if the area is infiltrated within 12 hours. **Phentolamine should be given as soon as possible after the extravasation is noted.**
Peripheral Vasoconstriction: Several cases of severe vasoconstriction leading to vascular stasis and gangrene of the extremities have been reported after dopamine administration. Patients with preexisting vascular disease such as cold injury, atherosclerosis, Raynaud's disease and diabetic endarteritis seem to be particularly prone to severe peripheral vasoconstriction. Monitor patients closely for any changes in color or temperature of the skin in the extremities. If a change in skin color or temperature occurs which is thought to be the result of compromised circulation to the extremities, weigh the benefits of continued dopamine infusion against the risk of possible necrosis. As noted above, phentolamine should be available on a standby basis as an antidote for peripheral vasoconstriction.

Close monitoring of urine flow, cardiac output and blood pressure during dopamine infusion is necessary as in the case of any adrenergic agent.

Dopamine, particularly when infused in high doses, may facilitate disturbances in impulse formation such as ectopic beats, tachycardia, sinus bradycardia, sinus arrhythmia. With the occurrence of these symptoms, use dopamine with extreme caution, and if necessary reduce the dosage or if warranted, stop the dopamine infusion.

Dopamine administration in patients with primary pulmonary hypertension can cause pulmonary vasoconstriction which may be detrimental to the condition of these patients.

When dopamine is administered concurrently with diuretics, extra caution should be taken because it may produce an additive or potentiating effect.

Adverse Effects: The most frequent adverse reactions observed in clinical evaluation of dopamine included ectopic beats, nausea, vomiting, tachycardia, anginal pain, palpitation, dyspnea, headache, hypotension and vasoconstriction.
Extravasation: Sloughing and necrosis of surrounding tissue due to extravasation when dopamine was infused into small veins has been reported.
Peripheral Vasoconstriction: Peripheral ischemic changes leading to vascular stasis and gangrene have been reported. Patients with preexisting vascular disease may be particularly sensitive to dopamine's vasoconstrictive effects (see Precautions).

Other adverse reactions which have been reported infrequently were aberrant conduction, bradycardia, piloerection, widened QRS complex, azotemia and elevated blood pressure.

Overdose: Symptoms and Treatment: In case of accidental overdosage, as evidenced by excessive blood pressure elevation, reduce rate of administration or temporarily discontinue dopamine until patient's condition stabilizes. Since dopamine's duration of action is quite short, no additional remedial measures are usually necessary. If these measures fail to stabilize the patient's condition, consider the use of the short-acting alpha adrenergic blocking agent, phentolamine.

Dosage: Intropin must be diluted before administration to patients.
Dilution: Transfer contents of 1 ampul or vial (yielding 5 mL of solution containing 200 mg dopamine) by aseptic technique to either a 250 or 500 mL bottle of 1 of the following sterile i.v. solutions: Sodium Chloride Injection USP; Dextrose (5%) Injection USP; Dextrose (5%) and Sodium Chloride (0.9%) Injection USP; 5% Dextrose in 0.45% Sodium Chloride Solution; Dextrose (5%) in Lactated Ringer's Solution; Sodium Lactate (1/6 Molar) Injection USP; Lactated Ringer's Injection USP.

These dilutions will yield a final concentration for administration as follows: 250 mL dilution: 800 μg/mL of dopamine; 500 mL dilution: 400 μg/mL of dopamine.

Intropin (cont'd)

Intropin has been found to be stable for a minimum of 24 hours after dilution in the sterile i.v. solutions listed above. However, as with all i.v. admixtures, dilution should be made just prior to administration. Furthermore, all unused solution from the ampul or vial should be discarded.

Do **not** add Intropin Injection to 5% Sodium Bicarbonate or other alkaline i.v. solutions, since the drug is inactivated in alkaline solution.

See also Indications for additional information on patient's management.

Administration Rate: After dilution, Intropin is administered i.v. through a suitable i.v. catheter or needle.

An i.v. drip chamber or other suitable metering device is essential for controlling the rate of flow in drops/minute. Each patient must be individually titrated to the desired hemodynamic and/or renal response with dopamine. In titrating to the desired increase in systolic blood pressure, the optimum dosage rate for renal response may be exceeded, thus necessitating a reduction in rate after the hemodynamic condition is stabilized.

Administration at rates greater than 50 μg/kg/min has been used in advanced circulatory decompensation states.

If unnecessary fluid expansion is of concern, adjustment of drug concentration may be preferred over increasing the flow rate of a less concentrated dilution.

Regimen: 1. When appropriate, increase blood volume with whole blood or plasma until central venous pressure is 10 to 15 cm H_2O or pulmonary venous pressure is 14 to 18 mm Hg.
2. Begin administration of diluted solution at doses of 2 to 5 μg/kg/min dopamine in patients who are likely to respond to modest increments of heart force and renal perfusion.

In more seriously ill patients, begin administration of diluted solution at doses of 5 μg/kg/min dopamine and increase gradually using 5 to 10 μg/kg/min increments up to 20 to 50 μg/kg/min as needed. Check the urine output frequently, especially if doses of dopamine in excess of 50 μg/kg/min are required. Should urine flow begin to decrease in the absence of hypotension, consider a dopamine dosage reduction. Multiclinic trials have shown that more than 50% of the patients were satisfactorily maintained on doses of dopamine less than 20 μg/kg/min. In patients who do not respond to these doses with adequate arterial pressure or urine flow, additional increments of dopamine may be employed in an effort to produce an appropriate arterial pressure and central perfusion.
3. Treatment of all patients requires constant evaluation of therapy in terms of the blood volume, augmentation of myocardial contractility and distribution of peripheral perfusion. Adjust dopamine dosage according to the patient's response.
4. As with all potent i.v. administered drugs, care should be taken to control the rate of administration so as to avoid inadvertent administration of a bolus of drug.

Supplied: Each 5 mL ampul or single-dose vial contains: dopamine HCl 40 mg/mL (equivalent to 32.3 mg base). Nonmedicinal ingredients: sodium metabisulfite and water for injection USP. Tartrazine-free. Boxes of 10. Intropin is stable for a period of 5 years in ampul and 3 years in vial at room temperature (15 to 30°C).

INVIRASE™ ℞

Roche

Saquinavir Mesylate

HIV Protease Inhibitor—Antiretroviral Agent

Pharmacology: Saquinavir is a selective inhibitor of the viral pol-encoded aspartic protease which cleaves precursor molecules into the structural proteins of the mature virion core and activates reverse transcriptase during the HIV growth cycle. Because of these functions, this protease is essential for the release of infectious virus (as proved by active site mutagenesis).

Saquinavir is a potent (Ki ≤ 0.12 nM) inhibitor of HIV proteases. No inhibition of human aspartyl or other proteases has been seen even at a concentration of 10 μM, indicating high selectivity (at least 50 000-fold). Experiments in cell culture indicate that saquinavir produces an additive to synergistic effect against HIV in double and triple combination with various reverse transcriptase inhibitors (including zidovudine, didanosine and zalcitabine), without enhanced cytotoxicity.

Two mutations have been identified in the protease gene which contribute to genotypic saquinavir resistance (G48V and L90M). After 1 year of therapy, at least 1 of these mutations has occurred in 31% of patients taking saquinavir in combination with zidovudine [ZDV] or zalcitabine [ddC]), and in 45% of patients taking saquinavir monotherapy (600 mg t.i.d.). Genotypic evidence suggests that patients with these mutations will not develop broad cross-resistance to other protease inhibitors. Evidence also suggests that combination therapy with ZDV or ddC decreases the emergence of reduced sensitivity to saquinavir in culture (=phenotypic resistance): after 1 year of therapy, reduced sensitivity to saquinavir has been seen in 38% of patients treated with saquinavir plus ZDV or ddC, vs 45% of patients treated with saquinavir monotherapy (600 mg t.i.d.). Additionally, dual therapy with saquinavir and ZDV appears to restrict the emergence of ZDV resistance.

Saquinavir must be taken anytime within 2 hours following a meal. The extent of absorption (as reflected by AUC) after a 600 mg oral dose in fasting healthy volunteers was substantially increased when given following food, from 24 to 161 ng·h/mL. The presence of food also increased the time taken to achieve maximum concentration from 2.4 to 3.8 hours, and substantially increased the mean maximum plasma concentrations (C_{max}) from 3.0 to 35.5 ng/mL. The effect of food has been shown to be present for up to 2 hours after food intake. Additionally, exposure to saquinavir was doubled ($AUC_{(0-12)}$ increased from 183.2 ng·h/mL to 374.4 ng·h/mL) when saquinavir was coadministered with "double-strength" grapefruit juice; and increased by 40% ($AUC_{(0-12)}$ from 183.2 ng·h/mL to 238.1 ng·h/mL) when taken with normal strength grapefruit juice in a single dose study.

Following administration of a 600 mg oral dose to healthy volunteers in the presence of food, the mean absolute bioavailability is 4%. This low bioavailability is thought to be due to a combination of incomplete absorption (approximately 30%) and extensive first pass metabolism.

The mean steady-state volume of distribution following i.v. administration of a 12 mg dose of saquinavir is 700 L, indicating extensive partitioning into tissues. Saquinavir shows a high degree of protein binding (approximately 98%), which is independent of concentration over the range 15 to 700 ng/mL. Greater than 96% of a radiolabelled i.v. dose appears in the feces within 48 hours, indicating extensive hepatic clearance. Hepatic metabolism is P450-mediated, of which >90% is the work of one isozyme (CYP3A4). Renal excretion is a very minor route of elimination for saquinavir (<4%). Systemic clearance is rapid, 80 L/h, which is close to hepatic plasma flow. Systemic clearance was constant after i.v. doses of 6, 36 and 72 mg infused over 3 hours. The mean residence time of the drug was found to be 7 hours.

After single and multiple oral doses as capsules (25 to 600 mg) in the presence of food, the increase in exposure (50-fold) was greater than directly proportional to the increase in dose (24-fold). Accumulation following multiple dosing (25 to 600 mg t.i.d.) in HIV-infected patients is modest: AUC was increased 150% at steady state compared to single doses.

Indications: In combination with reverse transcriptase inhibitor (RTI) nucleoside analogues for the treatment of advanced HIV infection. This indication is based on changes in surrogate markers in patients who initiated saquinavir concomitantly with zalcitabine or zalcitabine and zidovudine. Results available from limited uncontrolled open-label studies suggest that saquinavir in combination with other RTI nucleoside analogues also produces improvement in surrogate markers.

Patients in these studies had prolonged prior antiretroviral therapy and CD4 cell counts less than 300/mm³. RTI nucleoside analogues used in open-label clinical trials include lamivudine, stavudine, didanosine, zalcitabine and zidovudine. There are no results available from clinical trials confirming the clinical benefit of combination therapy with saquinavir on HIV disease progression or survival.

Contraindications: Patients with clinically significant hypersensitivity to saquinavir or to any components contained in the capsule.

Warnings: The indication for saquinavir for the treatment of HIV infection is based on changes in surrogate markers. At present there are no results from controlled clinical trials evaluating the effect of regimens containing saquinavir on survival or the clinical progression of HIV infection, such as the occurrence of opportunistic infections or malignancies.

New onset diabetes mellitus, exacerbation of pre-existing diabetes mellitus and hyperglycemia have been reported during postmarketing surveillance in HIV-infected patients receiving protease inhibitor therapy. Some patients required either initiation or dose-adjustment of insulin or oral hypoglycemic agents for the treatment of these events. In some cases diabetic ketoacidosis has occurred. In those patients who discontinued protease inhibitor therapy, hyperglycemia persisted in some cases. Because these events have been reported voluntarily during clinical practice, estimates of frequency cannot be made and a causal relationship between protease inhibitor therapy and these events has not been established.

Precautions: General: When saquinavir is prescribed in combination with other antiretroviral therapies, physicians should refer to the appropriate Product Monographs for safety and prescribing information.

Hemophiliac Patients: There have been reports of increased bleeding including spontaneous skin hematomas and hemarthrosis in patients with Hemophilia Type A and Type B treated with protease inhibitors. In some patients, additional Factor VIII was given. In more than half of the reported cases, treatment with protease inhibitors was continued or re-introduced. There is no proven relationship between protease inhibitors and such bleeding, however, the frequency of bleeding episodes should be closely monitored in patients on saquinavir.

Children and Geriatrics: The safety and efficacy of saquinavir in HIV-infected children (younger than 13 years) has not been established. Only limited experience is available in elderly patients (older than 60 years).

Patients with Hepatic Impairment: Therapeutic studies with saquinavir included patients with a range of hepatic impairment from mild to moderate. In these patients, exposure to saquinavir was not correlated with laboratory markers of hepatic impairment. Increases in saquinavir plasma concentrations might be expected in patients with severe hepatic impairment; however, such patients have not been investigated and should therefore be treated with caution.

Patients with Renal Impairment: Therapeutic studies with saquinavir included patients with a range of renal impairment from mild to moderate. In these patients, exposure to saquinavir was not correlated with laboratory markers of renal impairment. Although renal clearance is only a minor elimination pathway for saquinavir, no data are available in patients with more severe renal impairment. Clinical judgment should be exercised when administering saquinavir to patients with renal insufficiency.

Drug Interactions: Combination therapy of saquinavir with zalcitabine (ddC) and/or zidovudine has been studied in adults with advanced HIV-disease, and been shown **not** to alter the rate or severity of known major toxicities previously associated with the use of zalcitabine and zidovudine. Data from pharmacokinetic studies also suggest that the absorption, metabolism and elimination of each drug is unchanged when they are administered together as triple combination therapy.

Concomitant use of ketoconazole (200 mg daily) and saquinavir (600 mg t.i.d.) caused a 1.5-fold increase in plasma concentrations of saquinavir, with no increase in the elimination half-life or any change in the absorption rate. This was due to inhibition of the P450 isozyme (CYP3A4) responsible for the metabolism of saquinavir. Ketoconazole pharmacokinetics were not affected by this coadministration. Dose adjustment should not be required for tolerability reasons when these compounds are coadministered. A similar interaction could occur with other compounds in this class, such as fluconazole, itraconazole and miconazole, or with other inhibitors of the CYP3A4 isozyme of P450.

Rifampicin (600 mg daily) was shown to decrease plasma concentrations of saquinavir by 80%, due to its induction of the CYP3A4 isozyme of cytochrome P450. The use of rifampicin in combination with saquinavir could therefore result in subtherapeutic concentrations of saquinavir. Rifabutin (300 mg daily) has also been shown to reduce saquinavir plasma concentration by 40% when these 2 compounds are coadministered. Considering the extensive hepatic metabolism of saquinavir, coadministration with other compounds known for their potential to induce hepatic enzymes (i.e., phenytoin, carbamazepine, alcohol or barbiturates) may result in decreased plasma concentrations of saquinavir. The potential reduction in effectiveness of saquinavir therapy should be considered when using such drugs concomitantly.

During the absorption phase of saquinavir, the high presystemic concentrations of saquinavir may decrease the activity of the CYP3A4 isozyme. Other compounds which are substrates of CYP3A4 (i.e., nifedipine and other calcium channel blockers, clindamycin, terfenadine) may compete with saquinavir for their metabolism, possibly resulting in increased plasma concentrations of the concomitant medications. Patients receiving saquinavir in combination with such drugs should be monitored for any toxicities associated with these medications.

Ritonavir is a potent inhibitor of the CYP3A4 isozyme of cytochrome P450, which is responsible for the metabolism of saquinavir. Because of this activity, combining these 2 protease inhibitors will likely result in substantially increased plasma levels of saquinavir. No data regarding potential interactions between saquinavir and other protease inhibitors are currently available.

Pregnancy and *Lactation:* Reproduction studies with saquinavir in rats have shown no embryotoxicity or teratogenicity at plasma exposures (AUC values) up to 5 times those achieved with human use (1 800 mg/day), or in rabbits at dose levels up to 24 times the recommended human dose. There are however, no adequate or well controlled studies of saquinavir in pregnant women. Because animal reproduction studies are not always predictive of human response, saquinavir should be used during pregnancy only if the potential benefits to the mother are considered to outweigh the potential risks to the fetus.

It is not known whether saquinavir is excreted in human milk. Because many drugs are excreted in human milk, it is advisable to caution mothers against breast-feeding while taking saquinavir. Animal studies indicate that administration of saquinavir to rats through the lactation period at plasma concentrations (AUC values) up to 5 times those achieved with the human dose (1 800 mg/day) had no effect on the survival, growth or development of offspring to weaning.

Adverse Effects: The majority of adverse reactions observed in clinical trials were of mild intensity. The most frequently reported reactions concerned the gastrointestinal tract, with diarrhea, abdominal discomfort and nausea being the most common.

Saquinavir has been shown not to alter the rate or severity of known major toxicities previously associated with the use of zalcitabine (ddC) and/or zidovudine (ZDV), or to produce unexpected toxicities when used in combination with ddC and/or ZDV. For comprehensive dose adjustment recommendations and drug-associated adverse reactions for either ddC or ZDV, physicians should refer to the Product Monograph for each of these drugs.

Data from 2 double-blind North American trials are displayed in Table I. Patients in these trials were randomized to receive treatment with either saquinavir+ZDV, saquinavir+ZDV+ddC, or ZDV+ddC (Protocol NV14255); or, saquinavir monotherapy, ddC monotherapy, or saquinavir+ddC (Protocol NV14256). In NV14255, 197 patients were treated with saquinavir 600 mg t.i.d.; a total of 170 completed at least 24 weeks of treatment. In NV14256, 306 subjects from the surrogate analysis were treated with saquinavir 600 mg t.i.d.; a total of 259 completed more than 16 weeks of treatment. Table I summarizes the clinical adverse events (considered at least possibly related or of unknown relationship to study drug, and of moderate or greater intensity) which occurred in ≥2% of patients. The comprehensive safety database of 688 patients receiving saquinavir in all clinical trials also includes data from 185 patients in 3 double-blind, randomized European studies who completed at least 16 weeks of saquinavir treatment. Pooled data from these studies are consistent with the findings in Table I.

Table I—Invirase

Percent of Patients with Adverse Events (at Least Possibly Related or of Unknown Relationship to Study Drug, and of Moderate or Greater Intensity) which Occurred with a Frequency of ≥2% in NV14255 or NV14256

	NV14255 (ACTG229)			NV14256		
Body System/Adverse Event	**SAQ+ZDV (n=99)**	**SAQ+ddC+ZDV (n=98)**	**ddC+ZDV (n=100)**	**ddC (n=145)**	**SAQ (n=159)**	**SAQ+ddC (n=147)**
Gastrointestinal						
Diarrhea	3.0	1.0	—	1.4	3.8	3.4
Abdominal Discomfort	2.0	3.1	4.0	1.4	1.3	0.7
Nausea	—	3.1	3.0	0.7	1.9	0.7
Dyspepsia	2.0	1.0	2.0	2.1	—	0.7
Abdominal Pain	—	1.0	2.0	0.7	1.9	0.7
Mucosa Damage	—	—	4.0	1.4	—	0.7
Buccal Mucosa Ulceration	2.0	2.0	2.0	9.0	2.5	4.1
Nervous System						
Headache	2.0	2.0	2.0	4.1	0.6	0.7
Paresthesia	2.0	3.1	4.0	0.7	1.0	1.0
Extremity Numbness	2.0	1.0	4.0	—	—	0.7
Dizziness	—	2.0	1.0	—	—	—
Peripheral Neuropathy	—	1.0	2.0	5.5	—	4.8
Body as a Whole						
Asthenia	6.1	9.2	10.0	0.7	1.3	0.7
Appetite Disturbances	—	1.0	2.0	—	—	—
Skin and Appendages						
Rash	—	—	3.0	0.7	1.3	1.4
Pruritus	—	—	2.0	—	—	—
Musculoskeletal Disorders						
Musculoskeletal Pain	2.0	2.0	4.0	—	0.6	0.7
Myalgia	1.0	—	3.0	1.4	—	—

Legend: SAQ: Invirase (saquinavir mesylate).
ZDV: zidovudine.
ddC: zalcitabine.

Table II—Invirase

Percentage of Patients (by Treatment Group) with Marked* Laboratory Abnormalities in Protocols NV14255 and NV14256

	NV14255 (ACTG229)			NV14256		
Parameter	**SAQ+ZDV (n=99)**	**SAQ+ZDV+ddC (n=98)**	**ZDV+ddC (n=100)**	**ddC (n=145)**	**SAQ (n=159)**	**SAQ+ddC (n=147)**
Biochemistry						
Calcium (high)	1	—	—	<1	—	—
Creatinine Phosphokinase	10	12	7	4	3	6
Glucose (low)	—	—	—	3	4	1
Glucose (high)	—	—	—	—	<1	<1
Phosphorus	2	1	—	—	—	—
Potassium	—	—	—	1	<1	<1
Serum Amylase	2	1	1	<1	<1	1
AST	2	2	—	3	<1	<1
ALT	—	3	1	3	<1	<1
Total Bilirubin	1	—	—	—	<1	—
Uric Acid	—	—	1	NA	NA	NA
Hematology						
Neutrophils (low)	2	2	8	—	—	—
Hemoglobin (low)	—	—	1	—	—	—
Platelets (low)	—	—	2	—	—	<1

*Marked Laboratory Abnormality: change from Grade 0 to 3 or 4; or from Grade 1 to 4.

Although most adverse events reported during the above studies were mild or moderate in severity, the following serious adverse events have been reported during clinical trials and/or postmarketing experience with saquinavir and were considered possibly related to use of this drug: confusion, ataxia and weakness; acute myeloblastic leukemia; hemolytic anemia; attempted suicide; Stevens-Johnson syndrome; seizures; severe cutaneous reaction associated with increased liver function tests; isolated elevation of transaminases, thrombophlebitis; headache; exacerbation of chronic liver disease with Grade 4 elevated LFTs, jaundice, ascites and right/left upper quadrant abdominal pain; pancreatitis leading to death; nephrolithiasis; hepatitis; diabetes mellitus, bullous skin eruption and polyarthritis; portal hypertension.The clinical trial database for saquinavir consists of >6 000 patients, with over 100 patients followed for >2 years.

The following clinical adverse events (possibly or probably related to study drug, all severities) occurred with a frequency of <2% in the saquinavir arms of 2 North American studies (NV14255 and NV14256).

Body as a Whole: fever, wasting syndome, allergic reaction, chest pain, weight decrease, shivering.

Cardiovascular: hypertension.

Endocrine/Metabolic: hyperglycemia.

Gastrointestinal: vomiting, constipation, eructation, stomatitis, discolored feces, glossitis, frequent bowel movements, gastralgia, gastritis, gastrointestinal inflammation, pancreatitis, tooth disorder.

Hematologic: neutropenia, thrombocytopenia.

Musculoskeletal: stiffness, arthralgia.

Neurological: ataxia, confusion, dry mouth, convulsions, dysesthesia, tremor.

Psychological: insomnia, euphoria, anxiety, reduced intellectual ability, irritability, agitation, hallucination, somnolence, depression.

Resistance Mechanisms: staphylococcal infection.

Respiratory: pharyngitis, dyspnea, laryngitis, rhinitis.

Skin: sweating increased, hot flushes, skin pigment changes, acne, dermatitis, folliculitis.

Special Senses: visual disturbances, taste alteration, xerophthalmia.

Urinary: micturition disorder.

Laboratory Values: No consistent alterations in standard laboratory tests have been associated with the use of saquinavir. Table II shows the laboratory shift data in studies NV14255 and NV14256 for those tests where any patient had a change from grade 0 to abnormality grade 3 or higher, or from grade 1 to grade 4.

Overdose: Symptoms and Treatment: One patient exceeded the recommended daily dose of 1 800 mg by ingesting 8 g in a single dose. The patient was treated with induction of emesis within 2 to 4 hours of ingestion. No toxicities or sequelae were noted. In exploratory clinical studies, oral doses of saquinavir up to 7 200 mg/day have been relatively well tolerated. In cases of saquinavir overdose, vital signs should be monitored, and symptoms treated as they arise. Patients may also benefit from treatment with activated charcoal.

Dosage: The recommended dosage is 600 mg (3×200 mg capsules) taken every 8 hours (q8h), anytime within 2 hours after a meal or substantial snack. Total daily dose is 1 800 mg. Saquinavir should be administered in combination with reverse transcriptase inhibitor nucleoside analogues.

Monitoring of Patients: Clinical chemistry tests should be performed prior to initiating therapy with saquinavir and reverse transcriptase inhibitor nucleoside analogues, and at appropriate intervals thereafter.

Dose Adjustments: For recipients of combination therapy with saquinavir and reverse transcriptase inhibitor nucleoside analogues, dose adjustments of any single drug should be based on the known toxicity profile of that individual drug.

Information for the Patient: See Blue Section—Information for the Patient ''Invirase''.

Supplied: Each hard gelatin, light brown and green capsule, imprinted with Roche and 0245 on opaque shells, contains: saquinavir 200 mg, present as saquinavir mesylate. Nonmedicinal ingredients: lactose, magnesium stearate, microcrystalline cellulose, povidone, sodium starch glycolate and talc. Capsule shell: gelatin, indigotine, iron oxide and titanium dioxide. Glass or plastic (HDPE) bottles of 270. Keep in tightly closed container at room temperature (15 to 30°C).

(Shown in Product Recognition Section)

Reviewed 1999

IONAMIN® ◊

Rhône-Poulenc Rorer

Phentermine (Resin Complex)

Anorexiant

Pharmacology: Phentermine is a sympathomimetic amine with pharmacologic activity similar to the prototype drug of this class used in obesity, amphetamine (d- and dl-amphetamine). Actions include CNS stimulation and elevation of blood pressure. Tachyphylaxis and tolerance have been demonstrated with all drugs of this class in which these phenomena have been looked for.

Drugs of this class used in obesity are commonly known as anorectics or anorexigenics. It has not been established, however, that the action of such drugs in treating obesity is primarily one of appetite suppression. Other CNS actions or metabolic effects may be involved.

Adult obese subjects instructed in dietary management and treated with anorectic drugs, lose more weight on the average than those treated with placebo and diet, as determined in relatively short-term clinical trials.

The magnitude of increased weight loss of drug-treated patients over placebo-treated patients is only a fraction of a pound a week (less than 500 g). The rate of weight loss is greatest in the first weeks of therapy for both drug and placebo subjects and tends to decrease in succeeding weeks. The possible origins of the increased weight loss due to the various drug effects are not established. The amount of weight loss associated with the use of an anorectic drug varies from trial to trial, and the increased weight loss appears to be related in part to variables other than the drugs prescribed, such as the physician-investigator, the population treated and the diet prescribed. Studies do not permit conclusions as to the relative importance of the drug and nondrug factors on weight loss. The natural history of obesity is measured in years; whereas, the studies cited are restricted to a few weeks or months duration. Thus, the total impact of drug-induced weight loss over that of diet alone must be considered clinically limited. The bioavailability of phentermine has been studied in humans in which blood levels of phentermine were measured by a gas-chromatography method. Blood levels obtained with the 15 and 30 mg resin-complex formulations indicated slower absorption with a reduced but prolonged peak concentration and without a significant difference in prolongation of blood levels when compared with the same doses of phentermine hydrochloride. The clinical significance of these differences is not known. In clinical trials establishing the efficacy of phentermine, a single daily dose produced an effect comparable to that produced by other regimens of anorectic drug therapy.

Indications: As a short-term (i.e., a few weeks) adjunct to continued dietary treatment in the medical management of obesity in patients who have not responded to an appropriate weight reducing diet alone. Phentermine is recommended only for obese patients with an initial body mass index ≥ 30 kg/m^2, or ≥ 27 kg/m^2 in the presence of other risk factors (e.g., hypertension, diabetes, hyperlipidemia).

The limited usefulness of agents of this class (see Pharmacology) should be measured against possible risk factors inherent in their use such as those described below. See Table I.

Table I—Ionamin

Body Mass Index (BMI), kg/m²

Weight (pounds)	**Height (feet, inches)** 5′0″	5′3″	5′6″	5′9″	6′0″	6′3″
140	**27**	25	23	21	19	18
150	**29**	**27**	24	22	20	19
160	31	**28**	26	24	22	20
170	33	30	**28**	25	23	21
180	35	32	**29**	**27**	25	23
190	37	34	31	**28**	26	24
200	39	36	32	30	**27**	25
210	41	37	34	31	**29**	26
220	43	39	36	33	30	**28**
230	45	41	37	34	31	**29**
240	47	43	39	36	33	30
250	49	44	40	37	34	31

Patients with BMI values of 27 to 29 may be candidates for Ionamin therapy if they also have a concomitant risk factor (e.g., hypertension, diabetes, hyperlipidemia).

Patients with BMI values ≥ 30 may be candidates for Ionamin therapy.

Contraindications: Advanced arteriosclerosis, symptomatic cardiovascular disease, moderate to severe hypertension, hyperthyroidism, known hypersensitivity, or idiosyncrasy to the sympathomimetic amines, glaucoma.

Agitated states.

Patients with a history of drug abuse.

During or within 14 days following the administration of MAO inhibitors (hypertensive crises may result).

Tricyclic Antidepressant (hypertensive crises may result or cardiac arrhythmia).

Warnings: Primary Pulmonary Hypertension: **Anorexigens increase the risk of developing primary pulmonary hypertension, an often fatal disorder.**

Although phentermine was not identified, an epidemiological study has indicated that use of other anorexigens for longer than 3 months was associated with a 23-fold increase in the risk of developing Primary Pulmonary Hypertension (PPH). There was no significant increase in risk for persons who had used these agents for 3 months or less. Obesity itself (body mass index ≥ 30 kg/m^2) was also independently associated with an increase of about two-fold in the risk of developing PPH. In the general population, the yearly occurrence of PPH is estimated to be about 1 to 2 cases per 1 000 000 persons. Therefore, the estimated risk associated with the long-term use of anorexigen drugs is about 23 to 46 cases per million persons exposed per year. The study further suggested that the risk of PPH rises with increasing duration of use of these drugs. The effect of intermittent compared to continuous use of anorexigens on the risk of PPH has not been determined.

The onset of aggravation of exertional dyspnea, or unexplained symptoms of angina pectoris, syncope, or lower extremity edema suggest the possibility of occurrence of pulmonary hypertension. Under these circumstances, treatment should be immediately discontinued, and the patient should be evaluated for the possible presence of PPH.

If tolerance to the anorectic effect develops, the recommended dose should not be exceeded in an attempt to increase the effect: rather, the drug should be discontinued.

Occupational Hazards: Phentermine may impair the ability of the patient to engage in potentially hazardous activities such as operating machinery or driving a motor vehicle; the patient should, therefore, be cautioned accordingly.

When using CNS active agents, consideration must always be given to the possibility of adverse interactions with alcohol.

Drug Dependence: Phentermine is related chemically and pharmacologically to amphetamine (d- and dl-amphetamine) and other stimulant drugs that have been extensively abused. The possibility of abuse of phentermine should be kept in mind when evaluating the desirability of including a drug as part of a weight reduction program. Abuse of amphetamine (d- and dl-amphetamine) and related drugs may be associated with intense psychological dependence and severe social dysfunction. There are reports of patients who have increased the dosage of some of these drugs to many times that recommended. Abrupt cessation following prolonged high dosage administration results in extreme fatigue and mental depression; changes are also noted on the sleep EEG. Manifestations of chronic intoxication with anorectic drugs include severe dermatoses, marked insomnia, irritability, hyperactivity and personality changes. The most severe manifestation of chronic intoxication is psychosis, often clinically indistinguishable from schizophrenia.

Pregnancy: Safe use in pregnancy has not been established. Use of phentermine by women who are or may become pregnant requires that the potential benefit be weighed against the possible hazard to mother and infant.

Children: Phentermine is not recommended for use in children under 12 years of age.

Precautions: Caution is to be exercised in prescribing phentermine for patients with even mild hypertension. Insulin requirements in diabetes mellitus may be altered in association with the use of phentermine and the concomitant dietary regimen.

Phentermine may decrease the hypotensive effect of adrenergic neuron blocking drugs. The least amount feasible should be prescribed or dispensed at one time in order to minimize the possibility of overdosage.

Adverse Effects: Cardiovascular: palpitation, tachycardia, elevation of blood pressure, primary pulmonary hypertension (see Warnings).

CNS: overstimulation, restlessness, dizziness, insomnia, euphoria, dysphoria, tremor, headache; rarely psychotic episodes at recommended doses with some drugs in this class.

Gastrointestinal: dryness of the mouth, unpleasant taste, diarrhea, constipation, other gastrointestinal disturbances.

Allergic: urticaria.

Endocrine: impotence, changes in libido.

Overdose: Symptoms and Treatment: Manifestations of acute overdosage may include restlessness, tremor, hyperreflexia, rapid respiration, confusion, assaultiveness, hallucinations, panic states. Fatigue and depression usually follow the central stimulation. Cardiovascular effects include arrhythmias, hypertension, or hypotension and circulatory collapse. Gastrointestinal symptoms include nausea, vomiting, diarrhea and abdominal cramps. Overdosage of pharmacologically similar compounds has resulted in fatal poisoning, usually terminating in convulsions and coma.

Management of acute phentermine intoxication is largely symptomatic and includes lavage and sedation with a barbiturate. Experience with hemodialysis or peritoneal dialysis is inadequate to permit recommendation in this regard. I.V. phentolamine has been suggested on pharmacologic grounds for possible acute, severe hypertension, if this complicates overdosage.

Dosage: 1 capsule daily, before breakfast or 10 to 14 hours before retiring. For individuals exhibiting greater drug responsiveness, Ionamin 15 will usually suffice. Ionamin 30 is recommended for less responsive patients. Not recommended for use in children under 12 years of age.

Phentermine should be used for a duration of no more than a few weeks (see Warnings).

Supplied: 15 mg: Each yellow and gray capsule, printed with "IONAMIN", "15", and "E" in black, contains: phentermine 15 mg as the cationic exchange resin complex. Nonmedicinal ingredients: calcium phosphate, D&C Yellow No. 10, FD&C Yellow No. 6, gelatin, iron oxide, lactose, magnesium stearate and titanium dioxide. Energy: 1.5 kJ (0.22 kcal). Bottles of 100.

30 mg: Each yellow capsule, printed with "IONAMIN", "30", and "E" in black, contains: phentermine 30 mg as the cationic exchange resin complex. Nonmedicinal ingredients: calcium phosphate, D&C Yellow No. 10, FD&C Yellow No. 6, gelatin, lactose, magnesium stearate, polacrilin potassium and titanium dioxide. Energy: 0.9 kJ (0.013 kcal). Bottles of 100 and 400.

(Shown in Product Recognition Section)

Reviewed 1998

IONIL®

Galderma

Salicylic Acid—Benzalkonium Chloride

Antiseborrheic

Supplied: Each bottle of shampoo contains: salicylic acid 2% and benzalkonium chloride 0.2%. Nonmedicinal ingredients: alcohol SD-40, laureth-4, laureth-23, purified water and tetrasodium EDTA. Plastic bottles of 235 and 470 mL.

IONIL-T®

Galderma

Benzalkonium Chloride—Tar

Antiseborrheic

Supplied: Each bottle of shampoo contains: benzalkonium chloride 0.2% and coal tar solution USP 4.25%. Nonmedicinal ingredients: alcohol SD-40, isopropyl alcohol, laureth-4, laureth-23, purified water and tetrasodium EDTA. May also contain citric acid to adjust pH. Plastic bottles of 235 and 470 mL.

IONIL-T® PLUS

Galderma

Coal Tar

Antiseborrheic

Supplied: Each bottle of shampoo contains: coal tar 2%. Nonmedicinal ingredients: citric acid, D&C yellow #10, DMDM hydantoin, edetate disodium, fragrance, FD&C blue #1, glycol distearate, lauramide DEA, laureth-4, laureth-23, potassium cocoyl hydrolyzed collagen, purified water, quaternium-22, sodium laureth sulfate, talloweth-60 myristyl glycol and TEA lauryl sulfate. Plastic bottles of 235 mL.

IOPIDINE® 1% ℞
IOPIDINE® 0.5% ℞

Alcon

Apraclonidine HCl

Controls Postsurgical Intraocular Pressure Glaucoma Therapy

Pharmacology: Apraclonidine is a relatively selective alpha adrenergic agonist and does not have significant membrane stabilizing (local anesthetic) activity. When instilled into the eye, apraclonidine has the action of reducing intraocular pressure. The precise mechanism of the ocular hypotensive action of apraclonidine is not completely established at this time. Aqueous fluorophotometry studies in man suggest that apraclonidine's predominant action may be related to a reduction of aqueous formation.

Apraclonidine is a partial agonist for alpha 1 and alpha 2 adrenergic receptors. The affinity of apraclonidine for alpha 2 receptors, as measured by competitive radioligand binding studies, is higher than its affinity towards alpha 1 receptors.

The onset of action with apraclonidine can usually be noted within 1 hour and the maximum intraocular pressure reduction usually occurs 3 to 5 hours after application of a single dose.

Indications: 1%: To control or prevent postsurgical elevations in intraocular pressure that occur in patients after anterior segment laser ophthalmic surgery including argon laser trabeculoplasty, argon laser iridotomy and neodymium:yttrium aluminum garnet (Nd:YAG) laser posterior capsulotomy.

0.5%: For adjunctive use in lowering intraocular pressure and may be used as a short-term therapy in glaucoma patients on maximally tolerated medical therapy who require an additional IOP reduction.

The largest body of clinical data regarding the efficacy of apraclonidine as an adjunctive drug has been obtained in patients using timolol as the primary therapy. However, apraclonidine has also been found effective in combination with topical betaxolol, carbachol, dipivefrin, echothiophate, epinephrine, levobunolol and pilocarpine and systemic acetazolamide and methazolamide.

The addition of apraclonidine 0.5% to patients already using 2 aqueous suppressing drugs (i.e., beta-blocker plus carbonic anhydrase inhibitor) as part of their maximally tolerated medical therapy may not provide much additional benefit. Since apraclonidine 0.5% is an aqueous suppressing drug, the addition of a third aqueous suppressant may not significantly reduce IOP.

Contraindications: Hypersensitivity to any component of this medication or to clonidine. Also contraindicated in patients receiving MAO inhibitors.

Warnings: Since apraclonidine is a potent depressor of intraocular pressure, patients who develop exaggerated reductions in intraocular pressure should be closely monitored.

Although the acute administration of 2 drops of apraclonidine 1% has minimal effect on heart rate or blood pressure in clinical studies evaluating patients undergoing anterior segment laser surgery, the preclinical pharmacologic profile of this drug suggests that caution should be observed in treating patients with severe cardiovascular disease including hypertension.

The possibility of a vasovagal attack occurring during laser surgery should be considered and caution used in patients with history of such episodes.

Use of apraclonidine 0.5% can lead to an allergic-like reaction characterized wholly or in part by the symptoms of hyperemia, pruritus, discomfort, tearing, foreign body sensation and edema of the lids and conjunctiva. If ocular allergic-like symptoms occur, apraclonidine 0.5% therapy should be discontinued. The allergic-like reaction associated with apraclonidine use may be masked by seasonal allergic conjunctivitis.

Not for injection. Topical ophthalmic use only.

Precautions: General: (Glaucoma Therapy): Although the topical use of apraclonidine 0.5% has not been studied in renal failure patients, structurally related clonidine undergoes a significant increase in half-life in patients with severe renal impairment. Close monitoring of patients with impaired renal function is advised if they are candidates for topical apraclonidine 0.5% solution therapy. Close monitoring of patients with impaired liver function is also advised as the systemic dosage form of clonidine is partly metabolized in the liver.

Apraclonidine 0.5% should be used with caution in patients with coronary insufficiency, recent myocardial infarction, cerebrovascular disease, chronic renal failure, Raynaud's disease, or thromboangiitis obliterans. Caution and monitoring of depressed patients are advised since apraclonidine has been rarely associated with depression.

Occupational Hazards: Apraclonidine 0.5% can cause dizziness and somnolence. Patients who engage in hazardous activities requiring mental alertness should be warned of the potential for a decrease in mental alertness while using apraclonidine 0.5% solution.

Drug Interactions: No specific drug interactions with topical glaucoma drugs (betaxolol, carbachol, dipivefrin, echothiophate, epinephrine, levobunolol, pilocarpine, timolol) or systemic medications (acetazolamide, methazolamide) were identified in clinical studies of apraclonidine 0.5%. The possibility of an additive or potentiating effect with CNS depressants (alcohol, barbiturates, opiates, sedatives, anesthetics) should be borne in mind. Tricyclic antidepressants have been reported to blunt the hypotensive effect of systemic clonidine. It is not known whether the concurrent use of these agents with apraclonidine can lead to a reduction in IOP lowering effect. No data on the level of circulating catecholamines after apraclonidine withdrawal are available. Caution, however, is advised in patients taking tricyclic antidepressants which can affect the metabolism and uptake of circulating amines.

Since apraclonidine may reduce pulse and blood pressure, caution in using drugs such as beta-blockers (ophthalmic and systemic), antihypertensives, and cardiac glycosides is advised. Patients using cardiovascular drugs concurrently with Apraclonidine should have their pulse and blood pressure frequently monitored. Caution should be exercised with simultaneous use of clonidine and other similar pharmacologic agents.

Carcinogenesis, Mutagenesis, Impairment of Fertility: In a series of 5 in vitro cell assays and 1 in vivo, apraclonidine was nonmutagenic. There was no significant increase in tumor incidence or type following 2 years of oral administration of apraclonidine to rats at dose levels 20 times the maximum recommended human dose or in mice at dose levels 12 times the maximum recommended human dose. Reproduction and fertility studies in rats showed no adverse effect on male or female fertility at doses 5 to 10 times the maximum recommended human dose.

Pregnancy: There are no adequate and well-controlled studies in pregnant women. Apraclonidine should be used during pregnancy only if the potential benefit justifies the potential risk to the fetus.

Teratogenicity studies with apraclonidine in rabbits and rats at doses up to 3 mg/kg/day in rabbits (60 times the maximum recommended human dose) and 0.3 mg/kg/day in rats (6 times the maximum recommended human dose) showed no evidence of fetal malformations, although embryotoxicity was evident at the high dose level in the rabbit study. Dose-related maternal toxicity was evident in both the rat and rabbit studies.

Lactation: It is not known if topically applied apraclonidine is excreted in human milk. However, systemic clonidine can be found in mother's milk, and a decision should be made whether to discontinue apraclonidine 0.5% use in nursing women or continue therapy, taking into account the importance of the drug to the mother. For surgical use, a decision should be considered to discontinue nursing temporarily for the 1 day apraclonidine 1% solution is used.

Children: Safety and effectiveness in children have not been established.

Adverse Effects: Surgical Use: The following adverse events were reported in association with the use of apraclonidine 1% in laser surgery: upper lid elevation (1.3%), conjunctival blanching (0.4%), and mydriasis (0.4%).

Glaucoma Therapy: Use of apraclonidine 0.5% can lead to an allergic-like reaction characterized wholly or in part by the symptoms of hyperemia, pruritus, discomfort, tearing, foreign body sensation, and edema of the lids and conjunctiva. If ocular allergic-like symptoms occur, therapy should be discontinued.

The overall discontinuation rate in clinical studies with apraclonidine 0.5% was 16%. The most commonly reported events leading to discontinuation included (in decreasing order of frequency) hyperemia, pruritus, discomfort, tearing, dry mouth, lid edema, and foreign body sensation.

The following adverse reactions (incidence) were reported in clinical studies of apraclonidine 0.5% as being related to therapy:

Ocular: hyperemia (11.9%), pruritus (11.3%), discomfort (7.2%), tearing (4.8%), foreign body sensation (2.7%), lid edema (2.4%), dry eye (2.1%), blurred vision (1.8%), blanching (1.5%), conjunctivitis (1.5%), lid margin crusting (1.2%), conjunctival edema (0.9%), discharge (0.9%), abnormal vision (0.9%), pain (0.6%), lid disorder (0.6%), edema (0.6%), lid erythema (0.6%), irritation (0.3%), keratitis (0.3%), blepharitis (0.3%), blepharoconjunctivitis (0.3%), photophobia (0.3%), conjunctival follicles (0.3%), scleritis (0.3%), keratopathy (0.3%), lid scales (0.3%), corneal infiltrate (0.3%), corneal staining (0.3%).

Body as a Whole: headache (2.7%), asthenia (2.1%), chest pain (0.6%), abnormal coordination (0.3%), malaise (0.3%).

Cardiovascular: peripheral edema (0.3%), arrhythmia (0.3%). Although no reports of bradycardia related to apraclonidine 0.5% were available from clinical studies, the possibility of its occurrence based on apraclonidine's alpha 2 agonist effect should be considered.

CNS: somnolence (1.2%), dizziness (1.2%), depression (0.6%), nervousness (0.6%), insomnia (0.3%), paresthesia (0.3%).

Digestive System: dry mouth (12.8%), constipation (1.5%), nausea (0.6%).

Musculoskeletal: myalgia (0.3%).

Respiratory System: dry nose (3.3%), rhinitis (1.2%), dyspnea (0.3%), pharyngitis (0.3%).

Skin: contact dermatitis (0.3%), dermatitis (0.3%).

Special Senses: taste perversion (3.6%), parosmia (0.3%).

This listing is presented in Table I and lists treatment-related adverse reactions which occurred at an incidence rate of 2% or more during placebo-controlled clinical studies of apraclonidine 0.5%.

Table I—Iopidine 0.5%

Adverse Effects

Coded Adverse Event	Single Therapy n=183		Adjunctive+ Maximal Therapy n=152		Placebo n=160	
Ocular	n	%	n	%	n	%
Pruritus	24	13.1	14	9.2	1	0.6
Discomfort	19	10.4	5	3.3	7	4.4
Hyperemia	15	8.2	25	16.4	5	3.1
Tearing	11	6.0	5	3.3	1	0.6
Dry Eye	6	3.3	1	0.7	1	0.6
Foreign Body Sensation	5	2.7	4	2.6	1	0.6
Lid Edema	5	2.7	3	2.0	0	
Blanching	5	2.7	0		1	0.6
Blurred Vision	2	1.1	4	2.6	1	0.6
Conjunctivitis	2	1.1	3	2.0	0	
Nonocular						
Body as a Whole						
Headache	8	4.4	1	0.7	0	
Asthenia	7	3.8	0		3	1.9
CNS						
Somnolence	4	2.2	0		1	0.6
Dizziness	1	0.5	3	2.0	0	
Digestive						
Dry Mouth	39	21.3	4	2.6	16	10.0
Constipation	5	2.7	0		0	
Respiratory						
Dry Nose	11	6.0	0		1	0.6
Rhinitis	4	2.2	0		0	
Special Senses						
Taste Perversion	10	5.5	2	1.3	2	1.3

Overdose: Symptoms and Treatment: Overdose is unlikely with topical ocular instillation, as the volume of exposure is limited by the capacity of the cul-de-sac. The small volume packaging and unique design of the Drop-Tainer limit the potential for accidental overdosage by ingestion. Signs of toxicity of apraclonidine in animals include lethargy, decreased activity, loss of appetite, hypothermia, decreased GI motility and constipation. Following oral administration of apraclonidine to monkeys, plasma levels 100 times greater than those seen in human plasma level studies were associated with moderate signs of toxicity, including lethargy, hypoactivity, and loss of appetite; no significant target organ toxicities were found. Acute oral toxicity studies in rats and mice resulted in LD_{50} values of 64 and 5 mg/kg, respectively. While higher doses usually caused deaths within 24 hours, lower doses often resulted in delayed deaths.

While no instances of human ingestion of apraclonidine are known, overdose with the oral form of clonidine has been reported to cause hypotension, transient hypertension, asthenia, vomiting, irritability, diminished or absent reflexes, lethargy, somnolence, sedation or coma, pallor, hypothermia, bradycardia, conduction defects, arrhythmias, dryness of the

Iopidine (cont'd)

mouth, miosis, apnea, respiratory depression, hypoventilation, and seizure.

Treatment of an oral overdose includes supportive and symptomatic therapy; a patent airway should be maintained. Gastric lavage i.v. fluids, atropine, dopamine, tolazoline, furosemide and diazoxide have been reported to be useful in treating the systemic symptoms associated with oral clonidine overdose. Hemodialysis is of limited value, since a maximum of 5% of circulating drug is removed.

Dosage: 1%: 1 drop of apraclonidine 1% should be instilled in the scheduled operative eye 1 hour before initiating anterior segment laser surgery and a second drop should be instilled in the same eye immediately upon completion of the laser surgical procedure. Use a separate container for each single-drop dose and discard each container after use.

0.5%: 1 to 2 drops of apraclonidine 0.5% should be instilled in the affected eye(s) 2 or 3 times daily. Since apraclonidine 0.5% will be used with other ocular glaucoma therapies, an approximate 5-minute interval between instillation of each medication should be practiced to prevent washout of the previous dose. **Not for injection into the eye. Not for oral ingestion.**

Supplied: 1%: Each mL of sterile, isotonic, aqueous solution contains: apraclonidine HCl USP 1.15% equivalent to apraclonidine base 1% with benzalkonium chloride 0.01% as preservative. Nonmedicinal ingredients: hydrochloric acid, purified water, sodium acetate, sodium chloride and sodium hydroxide. Plastic ophthalmic dispensers of 0.1 mL. Pouches of 2. These dispensers are enclosed in a foil overwrap as an added barrier to evaporation.

0.5%: Each mL of sterile, isotonic, aqueous solution contains: apraclonidine HCl USP 0.575% equivalent to apraclonidine base 0.5% with benzalkonium chloride 0.01% as preservative. Nonmedicinal ingredients: hydrochloric acid, purified water, sodium acetate, sodium chloride and sodium hydroxide. Plastic Drop-Tainer dispensers of 5 and 10 mL.

Store between 2 and 30°C. Do not freeze. Protect from light.

IPECAC SYRUP

General Monograph, CPhA

Emetic

This monograph has been compiled by CPhA. It may contain information different from that approved by Therapeutic Products Programme, Health Canada, and the pharmaceutical manufacturers' approval has not been requested.

Pharmacology: Ipecac induces vomiting by both gastric irritation and central stimulation of the chemoreceptor trigger zone.

Approximately 95% of patients vomit within 15 to 30 minutes of administration of a therapeutic dose and vomiting usually persists for 30 minutes to 2 hours. Approximately 28 to 60% of an ingested toxin will be removed by emesis if ipecac is given within 5 minutes following ingestion of the toxin. If given 1 hour after, a maximum of 30% of the toxin will be removed.

Indications: To induce vomiting in the early management of certain oral poisonings. Ideally, ipecac should be given on the advice of a Poison Control Centre or physician, especially in the case of infants and children.

Contraindications: Situations where emesis is contraindicated, include: poisoning involving strong acids or alkalies, unconscious, semicomatose or severely inebriated patients, patients experiencing convulsions and patients who have lost the gag reflex.

Warnings: The use of ipecac syrup in patients who have ingested petroleum distillates is controversial. Use may be considered in: poisonings involving petroleum distillates when product contains a more toxic ingredient such as heavy metals or pesticides; mixed poisonings where the quantity ingested is certain to be toxic.

Administration of ipecac syrup and the resulting vomiting may induce convulsions in patients who have ingested CNS stimulants. Care must be taken when administering ipecac syrup in these situations.

Ipecac syrup should be used with caution in cases of poisonings involving CNS depressants since loss of consciousness may occur before emesis has resulted.

Precautions: Do not use ipecac fluid extract in place of ipecac syrup since it is 14 times more concentrated. Activated charcoal should not be administered until after ipecac syrup has induced emesis and vomiting is complete.

If vomiting does not occur after 2 doses of ipecac syrup, gastric lavage should be performed.

Care should be taken to avoid aspiration of vomitus in young children and infants because of their poorly developed gag reflex.

Administration of ipecac syrup should not preclude the use of other emergency measures. Its use may be advised after consultation with a Poison Control Centre or physician as a preliminary measure prior to transporting the patient to hospital.

Pregnancy: Safety has not been established. Ipecac syrup should be used during pregnancy only when potential benefit outweighs risk.

Lactation: Data are not available.

Adverse Effects: When used in the treatment of drug overdose or poisoning, ipecac syrup does not usually cause systemic toxicity. Protracted or prolonged vomiting, diarrhea and lethargy may occasionally occur.

Toxicity may occur in patients with eating disorders who chronically consume large amounts of ipecac syrup. Myopathy, with manifestations of muscle weakness and pain, hyporeflexia, tenderness and stiffness, has been the major presenting adverse effect. Cardiotoxicity including hypotension, cardiac failure and more severely arrhythmias, may be serious and potentially fatal.

Protracted vomiting produced by the chronic ingestion of ipecac syrup may cause some metabolic abnormalities, dental abnormalities, eosophagitis, gastric reflux, Mallory-Weiss syndrome, parotid gland enlargement and aspiration pneumonitis.

Dosage: Do not use ipecac fluid extract in place of ipecac syrup. Ipecac should be given as soon as possible after ingestion of a toxin, ideally within 1 hour. Dose should be followed by 1 to 2 glasses of water since ipecac is ineffective when the stomach is empty. Administration with milk can prolong the time to vomiting because it decreases the irritant action of ipecac on the stomach.

Adults: 15 to 30 mL.

Children 1 to <12 years: 15 mL.

Children 6 months to <1 year: 5 to 10 mL.

If vomiting has not occurred within 15 to 20 minutes, the dose may be repeated once in adults and children over 12 years.

Reviewed 1997

IRON SALTS

General Monograph, CPhA

Anemia Therapy

This monograph has been compiled by CPhA. It may contain information different from that approved by Therapeutic Products Programme, Health Canada, and the pharmaceutical manufacturers' approval has not been requested.

Pharmacology: Iron is an important component of a number of enzymes necessary for energy transfer. It is also present in hemoglobin and myoglobin and is important in the metabolism of catecholamines and the functioning of neutrophils.

Administration of iron preparations corrects erythropoietic abnormalities which are due to deficiency of iron. Iron does not stimulate erythropoiesis nor does it correct hemoglobin disturbances not caused by iron deficiency. In fact, it may cause iron storage disease or iron toxicity when used in these conditions.

Administration of iron also relieves other symptoms of iron deficiency such as soreness of the tongue, dysphagia, dystrophy of the nails and skin, and fissuring of the angles of the lips.

Pharmacokinetics: Absorption of iron is influenced by many factors including the form in which it is administered, the dose, the status of the patient's iron stores, the degree of erythropoiesis, and the patient's diet. Absorption will be increased in iron deficient individuals. Ferrous iron passes through gastrointestinal mucosal cells directly into the blood and is immediately bound to transferrin which transports iron to the bone marrow where it is incorporated into hemoglobin. Maximal absorption takes place in the duodenum and proximal jejunum; therefore, iron may not be as well absorbed from slow-release and delayed-release preparations which may bypass the site of optimal absorption.

The body has no physiological route for the excretion of excess iron. Most of the iron liberated by destruction of hemoglobin is conserved and reused. Normal daily excretion of iron from cell desquamation varies from 0.5 to 2 mg. The average monthly loss of iron in normal menstruation is 12 to 30 mg.

Frequent blood donors, pregnant women, burn victims, individuals on hemodialysis, or with intestinal diseases (celiac, Crohn's, sprue, inflammatory bowel disease) and premature infants may require prophylactic therapy.

In its 1991 policy statement, the The Canadian Paediatric Society states that term infants who are not breast-fed should receive iron-fortified formula from birth, and that term breast-fed infants do not require supplemental iron until after 6 months of age.

Indications: Prevention and treatment of iron deficiency anemias.

Contraindications: Hemosiderosis, hemochromatosis. Iron compounds are also contraindicated in the treatment of anemia other than iron deficiency. Administration of iron to premature infants with vitamin E deficiency may precipitate red cell hemolysis. Therefore, vitamin E deficiency should also be corrected if possible.

Because of the risk of iron overload, oral and parenteral iron therapy should not be used concomitantly.

Precautions: Prolonged administration of iron should be avoided except in patients with continued bleeding, malabsorption syndromes that benefit from additional iron therapy or repeated pregnancies.

Orally administered iron salts may not be well absorbed in patients with steatorrhea and those who have had a partial gastrectomy.

Liquid iron preparations may stain the teeth on continued use. Stains may be prevented to a large extent by taking the dose through a straw, first mixing it with water or fruit juice, and by following the dose with a drink of plain water or juice. Brushing the teeth with sodium bicarbonate or hydrogen peroxide 3% will usually remove existing stains.

Drug Interactions: Iron may decrease the absorption of the following drugs: etidronate, tetracycline, penicillamine, quinolone antibiotics, levodopa, methyldopa and levothyroxine. It is recommended that administration of these drugs with iron be separated by at least 2 hours. Patients should be monitored for inadequate clinical response and switched to alternative therapy if necessary.

Administration of iron and either vitamin E or chloramphenicol may impair the hematological response to iron.

Concomitant administration of antacids (containing aluminum and magnesium salts or sodium bicarbonate or calcium carbonate) or cholestyramine may impair the absorption of iron.

Drug-Laboratory Test Interactions: Because iron preparations can color the feces black, large amounts may interfere with the guaiac test for occult blood in stool.

Pregnancy: No adverse effects have been reported with intake of normal daily requirements.

Lactation: At therapeutic doses, amount excreted in breast milk is not significant to affect infant.

Children: Deaths have occurred in children from as little as 400 mg of elemental iron. Severe reactions, including fatalities, have resulted. Patients should be warned about the extreme danger to children of accidental iron poisoning.

In infants, large chronic doses of iron may interfere with the assimilation of phosphorus and cause severe rickets.

Adverse Effects: Oral ingestion of iron preparations may be associated with gastrointestinal discomfort (such as nausea) or epigastric pain, dose related bowel effects (such as constipation or diarrhea) and dark stools. Untoward effects usually subside with continuation of therapy. Other measures may be helpful such as taking doses with or after meals, or initiating therapy at lower doses and gradually increasing to the therapeutic dose.

Liquid iron preparations may stain teeth (see Precautions).

Overdose: Iron poisoning is rare in adults, but serious acute toxicity may occur in children. The estimated lethal dose of iron is 200 to 300 mg/kg. Toxicity following ingestion of greater than 60 mg/kg is likely. However, toxicity following doses of 20 to 60 mg/kg has been observed.

Symptoms: Acute poisoning with iron has 4 distinct phases. Signs and symptoms may occur within about 30 minutes or may be delayed for several hours. The first phase, which may last up to 6 hours, includes symptoms such as epigastric pain, nausea, vomiting, diarrhea, melena and hematemesis that may be associated with drowsiness, pallor, cyanosis, lassitude, shock, coagulopathy, acidosis and coma. Following this first phase, there may be a transient period of apparent recovery which may last up to 24 hours. The third phase, occurring from 4 to 48 hours post ingestion, may be manifested by metabolic acidosis, hypotension, convulsions, fever, hepatic dysfunction or necrosis, renal failure, and later progress to circulatory collapse, coma and death. Possible intestinal scarring and obstruction may occur 2 to 4 weeks post-ingestion as part of the fourth phase.

Treatment: Obtain CBC, blood glucose, electrolytes and serum iron level. In severe overdose also obtain PT, PTT and liver function tests. Remove as much iron as possible from the gastrointestinal tract, using ipecac syrup or gastric lavage. Use tepid water. Administration of magnesium citrate cathartic or surgical removal of iron tablets may be required if other methods are unsuccessful. Maintain fluid and electrolyte balance.

Parenteral deferoxamine may be used when serum iron level is >63 μmol/L. Peak level generally occurs 3 to 6 hours after ingestion; however, it may be longer after ingestion of enteric coated or sustained release preparations. Patients who develop a WBC > 15×10^9/L or blood glucose >8.3 mmol/L are more likely to have toxic iron levels and should be admitted to hospital and administered deferoxamine if they develop symptoms. Hemodialysis is of little value in cases of iron poisoning.

Dosage: In preventing iron deficiency, adequate dietary intake is preferred over supplementation whenever possible. For a listing of food sources of iron, see Mineral Food Sources in the Clin-Info section.

The recommended daily intake of iron to prevent deficiency is 0.3 mg in infants less than 4 months and 6 to 8 mg in older infants and children. Adolescents and adults should receive 8 to 13 mg daily. An additional 5 mg/day is recommended in the second trimester of pregnancy with an additional 10 mg/day in the third trimester. Additional iron is not usually required during the first trimester or lactation. For a complete listing of the daily requirements of iron and other vitamins and minerals, see Recommended Nutrient Intake in the Clin-Info section.

Calculation of dosage for iron preparations should always be in terms of the elemental iron to be administered rather than in terms of the iron salt. Commonly used oral iron salts and their approximate elemental iron equivalents are listed in Table I.

Table I—Iron Salts

Comparison of Elemental Iron Content

Iron Salt	Strength	Approximate Elemental Iron Content (mg)	% of Elemental Iron
Ferrous Ascorbate	275 mg	33	12
Ferrous Fumarate	200 mg	65	33
Ferrous Gluconate	300 mg	35	11.6
Ferrous Sulfate	300 mg	60	20

For iron deficient adults, 50 to 100 mg of elemental iron given orally 3 times daily is usually adequate. Absorption is optimal in the fasting state. To lessen gastrointestinal intolerance, lower doses may be administered initially, and the medication may be given with or after meals. After 4 or 5 days the dose may be gradually increased. After the hemoglobin returns to normal, oral therapy should be continued for 3 to 6 months to replenish stores.

Iron deficient children may receive 4 to 6 mg/kg elemental iron daily in 3 divided doses.

Reviewed 1998

ISMO®

Wyeth-Ayerst

Isosorbide-5-Mononitrate

Antianginal

Pharmacology: As with other organic nitrates, the principal pharmacological action of isosorbide-5-mononitrate, the major active metabolite of isosorbide dinitrate, is relaxation of vascular smooth muscle and consequent dilation of peripheral arteries and veins, especially the latter. Dilation of the veins promotes peripheral pooling of blood and decreases venous return to the heart, thereby reducing left ventricular end-diastolic pressure and pulmonary capillary wedge pressure (preload). Arteriolar relaxation reduces systemic vascular resistance, systolic arterial pressure, and mean arterial pressure (after-load). Dilation of the coronary arteries also occurs. The hemodynamic responses to isosorbide-5-mononitrate are similar to those produced by other nitrates.

Pharmacodynamics: Dosing regimens for most chronically used drugs are designed to provide plasma concentrations that are continuously greater than a minimally effective concentration. This strategy is inappropriate for organic nitrates. Prolonged administration of nitrate drugs according to traditionally recommended dosage regimens has been shown to produce tolerance. Tolerance results in a loss of efficacy. Several well-controlled clinical trials have used exercise testing to assess the antianginal efficacy of continuously-delivered nitrates. In the large majority of these trials, nitrate effectiveness was indistinguishable from placebo after 24 hours (or less) of continuous therapy. Attempts to overcome tolerance by dose escalation, even to doses far in excess of those used acutely, have consistently failed. Only after nitrates have been absent from the body for several hours has their antianginal efficacy been restored. Drug-free intervals of 10 to 12 hours are known to be sufficient to restore response. The drug-free interval sufficient to avoid tolerance to isosorbide-5-mononitrate has not been completely defined. In the only regimen of twice-daily isosorbide-5-mononitrate the 2 doses are given 7 hours apart. This asymmetric twice-daily regimen provides antianginal efficacy for up to 12 hours (i.e. 7 hours between doses and 5 hours after second dose). Considering the pharmacokinetic profile of isosorbide-5-mononitrate and its long half-life (see Pharmacokinetics), clinical efficacy is consistent with that observed for other organic nitrates.

Pharmacokinetics: In humans, isosorbide-5-mononitrate is not subject to significant first pass metabolic changes in liver. The absolute bioavailability of isosorbide-5-mononitrate from tablets is nearly 100%. The absorption is rapid, and maximum serum concentrations are achieved 30 to 60 minutes after dosing. The volume of distribution of isosorbide-5-mononitrate is approximately 0.6 L/kg, and less than 4% is bound to plasma proteins. It is cleared from the serum by denitration to isosorbide; glucuronidation to the mononitrate glucuronide; and denitration/hydration to sorbitol. None of these metabolites is vasoactive. Less than 1% of administered isosorbide-5-mononitrate is eliminated in the urine.

The overall elimination half-life of isosorbide-5-mononitrate is about 5 hours; the rate of clearance is the same in healthy young adults, in patients with various degrees of renal, hepatic, or cardiac dysfunction, and in the elderly.

Indications: For the prevention of anginal attacks in patients with chronic stable angina pectoris associated with coronary artery disease.

Not intended for the immediate relief of acute attacks of angina pectoris.

Contraindications: Known hypersensitivity to isosorbide mononitrate or to other nitrates or nitrites. Acute circulatory failure associated with marked hypotension (shock and states of collapse). Postural hypotension. Myocardial insufficiency due to obstruction (e.g. in presence of aortic or mitral stenosis or of constrictive pericarditis). Increased intracranial pressure. Increased intraocular pressure. Severe anemia.

Warnings: The benefits and safety of isosorbide-5-mononitrate in anginal patients with acute myocardial infarction or congestive heart failure have not been established. Because the effects of isosorbide mononitrate are difficult to terminate rapidly, this drug is not recommended in these settings.

Precautions: Headaches or symptoms of severe hypotension, such as weakness or dizziness, particularly when arising suddenly from a recumbent position, may occur.

Caution should be exercised when using nitrates in patients prone to, or who might be affected by hypotension. Isosorbide-5-mononitrate should therefore be used with caution in patients who may have volume depletion from diuretic therapy or in patients who have low systolic blood pressure (e.g., below 90 mmHg). Paradoxical bradycardia and increased angina pectoris may accompany nitrate-induced hypotension.

Nitrate therapy may aggravate the angina caused by hypertrophic cardiomyopathy.

In industrial workers who have had long-term exposure to unknown (presumably high) doses of organic nitrates, tolerance clearly occurs. There is moreover, physical dependence since chest pain, acute myocardial infarction, and even sudden death have occurred during temporary withdrawal of nitrates from these workers. In clinical trials of angina patients, there are reports of anginal attacks being more easily provoked and of rebound in the hemodynamic effects soon after nitrate withdrawal. The importance of these observations to the routine, clinical use of oral isosorbide mononitrate has not been fully elucidated.

Caution should be exercised in patients with arterial hypoxemia due to anemia (see Contraindications). Similarly, caution is called for in patients with hypoxemia and a ventilation/perfusion imbalance due to lung disease or ischemic heart failure. Patients with angina pectoris, myocardial infarction, or cerebral ischemia frequently suffer from abnormalities of the small airways (especially alveolar hypoxia). Under these circumstances vasoconstriction occurs within the lung to shift perfusion from areas of alveolar hypoxia to better ventilated regions of the lung. As a potent vasodilator, isosorbide-5-mononitrate could reverse this protective vasoconstriction and thus result in increased perfusion to poorly ventilated areas, worsening of the ventilation/perfusion imbalance, and a further decrease in the arterial partial pressure of oxygen.

Tolerance to isosorbide-5-mononitrate with cross tolerance to other nitrates or nitrites may occur (see Pharmacology). As tolerance to isosorbide-5-mononitrate develops, the effect of sublingual nitroglycerin on exercise tolerance, although still observable, is somewhat blunted.

Occupational Hazards: As patients may experience faintness and/or dizziness, reaction time when driving or operating machinery may be impaired, especially at the start of treatment.

Pregnancy: In rats receiving isosorbide-5-mononitrate 500 mg/kg/day (125 times the human exposure comparing body surface area) there were small but statistically significant increases in the rates of prolonged gestation, prolonged parturition, stillbirth, and neonatal death; and there were small but statistically significant decreases in birth weight, live litter size, and pup survival. At 250 mg/kg/day, no adverse effects on reproduction and development were reported.

In rats and rabbits receiving isosorbide-5-mononitrate at up to 250 mg/kg/day, no developmental abnormalities, fetal abnormalities, or other effects on reproductive performance were detected; these doses are larger than the maximum recommended human dose by factors between 70 (body-surface-area basis in rabbits) and 310 (body-weight basis, in either species).

There are no studies in pregnant women. Isosorbide-5-mononitrate should be used during pregnancy only if the potential benefit justifies the potential risk to the fetus.

Lactation: It is not known whether isosorbide-5-mononitrate is excreted in human milk. Because many drugs are excreted in human milk, caution should be exercised when isosorbide-5-mononitrate is used to treat a nursing woman.

Children: The safety and effectiveness of isosorbide-5-mononitrate in children have not been established. Therefore, its use is not recommended.

Drug Interactions: Concomitant treatment with other vasodilators, calcium antagonists, ACE inhibitors, beta-blockers, diuretics, antihypertensives, tricyclic antidepressants and major tranquilizers may potentiate the blood pressure lowering effect of isosorbide-5-mononitrate.

Alcohol may enhance sensitivity to the hypotensive effects of nitrates.

Information for the Patient: Patients should be told that in order to maintain the antianginal efficacy of isosorbide-5-mononitrate tablets they must carefully follow the prescribed schedule of dosing (2 doses taken 7 hours apart) in a 24-hour period. For most patients, this can be accomplished by taking the first dose on awakening and the second dose 7 hours later.

As with other nitrates, headache may occur during therapy with isosorbide-5-mononitrate. Patients who get these headaches, should not alter the schedule of their treatment with isosorbide-5-mononitrate, since loss of headache may be associated with simultaneous loss of antianginal efficacy. Headaches may be relieved by the use of standard analgesics, such as ASA or acetaminophen.

Treatment with isosorbide-5-mononitrate may be associated with light-headedness on standing, especially just after rising from a recumbent or seated position. This effect may be more frequent in patients who have also consumed alcohol.

Adverse Effects: In controlled clinical trials 20 mg twice daily of isosorbide-5-mononitrate was administered to 219 patients alone or in combination with beta-adrenergic blocking agents. Adverse reactions were reported in 47% of patients. Discontinuation of therapy due to adverse reactions was required in 11% of patients. Most of these discontinued because of headache. Dizziness, nausea and chest pain were also frequently associated with withdrawal from these studies. The most common adverse reactions (incidence of at least 1%) were: headache, nausea, dizziness, flu-like symptoms, chest pain and rash.

In addition, the following adverse reactions were reported with an incidence lower than 1% in controlled as well as other studies in which 3 344 patients received 5 to 240 mg/day in a variety of regimens: Cardiovascular: angina pectoris,

Ismo (cont'd)

arrhythmias, atrial fibrillation, hypotension, palpitations, postural hypotension, premature ventricular contractions, supraventricular tachycardia, syncope.
Dermatological: pruritus, rash.
Gastrointestinal: abdominal pain, diarrhea, dyspepsia, tenesmus, vomiting.
Genitourinary: dysuria, impotence, urinary frequency.
Miscellaneous: asthenia, blurred vision, cold sweat, diplopia, edema, malaise, neck stiffness, rigors.
Musculoskeletal: arthralgia.
Neurological: agitation, anxiety, confusion, dyscoordination, hypoesthesia, hypokinesia, increased appetite, insomnia, nervousness, nightmares.
Respiratory: bronchitis, pneumonia, upper respiratory tract infection.

Extremely rarely, ordinary doses of organic nitrates have caused methemoglobinemia; for further discussion of its diagnosis and treatment see Overdose: Symptoms and Treatment.

Overdose: Symptoms and Treatment: Hemodynamic Effects: Symptoms of isosorbide-5-mononitrate overdose are generally the results of vasodilation, venous pooling, reduced cardiac output and hypotension. These hemodynamic changes may have protean manifestations, including increased intracranial pressure, with any or all of persistent throbbing headache, confusion, and moderate fever; vertigo; palpitations; visual disturbances; nausea and vomiting (possibly with colic and even bloody diarrhea); syncope (especially in the upright posture); air hunger and dyspnea, later followed by reduced ventilatory effort; diaphoresis, with the skin either flushed or cold and clammy; heart block and bradycardia; paralysis; coma; seizures and death.

No specific antagonist to the vasodilator effects of isosorbide-5-mononitrate is known, and no intervention has been subject to controlled study as a therapy of isosorbide-5-mononitrate overdose. Because the hypotension associated with isosorbide-5-mononitrate overdose is the result of venodilation and arterial hypovolemia, prudent therapy in this situation should be directed toward an increase in central fluid volume. Passive elevation of the patient's legs may be sufficient, but i.v. infusion of normal saline or similar fluid may also be necessary.

In patients with renal disease or congestive heart failure, therapy resulting in central volume expansion is not without hazard. Treatment of isosorbide-5-mononitrate overdose in these patients may be subtle and difficult, and invasive monitoring may be required.

The use of epinephrine or other arterial vasoconstrictors are ineffective in reversing the severe hypotensive effects of overdose and are therefore contraindicated in this situation.

Dialysis is known to be ineffective in removing isosorbide-5-mononitrate from the body.

Methemoglobinemia: Methemoglobinemia has been reported in patients receiving other organic nitrates, and it may occur as a side effect of isosorbide-5-mononitrate. Nitrate ions liberated during metabolism of isosorbide-5-mononitrate can oxidize hemoglobin into methemoglobin. In patients totally without cytochrome b_5 reductase activity, about 2 mg/kg of isosorbide-5-mononitrate would be required before any of these patients manifests clinically significant ($\geq$ 10%) methemoglobinemia. In patients with normal reductase function, significant production of methemoglobin would require even larger doses of isosorbide-5-mononitrate.

Methemoglobin levels are available from most clinical laboratories. The diagnosis should be suspected in patients who exhibit signs of impaired oxygen delivery despite adequate cardiac output and adequate arterial pO_2. Classically, methemoglobinemic blood is described as chocolate brown without color change on exposure to air. When methemoglobinemia is diagnosed, administration of methylene blue, 1 to 2 mg/kg i.v., may be required.

Dosage: The daily dosage schedule is designed to avoid or attenuate the development of tolerance of isosorbide-5-mononitrate. Patients should be watched carefully for an increase in angina pectoris during the drug-free period. Adjustment of background medication may be required.

The recommended dose of isosorbide-5-mononitrate is 20 mg twice daily given 7 hours apart. For those patients who are active during the day, this can be accomplished by taking the first dose upon awakening and the second dose 7 hours later. Dosage adjustments are not necessary for elderly patients or patients with altered renal or hepatic function.

The 20 mg twice daily dose should not be exceeded and doses lower than that are not recommended. Limited clinical experience has shown that the 10 mg twice daily dose was not unequivocally better than placebo, while the effect of the 40 mg twice daily dose was similar to that of the 20 mg dose. The 60 mg twice daily dose appeared to be less effective and was associated with an increased incidence of adverse reactions and a rebound phenomenon.

Supplied: Each orange, biconvex, round, film-coated tablet, engraved with "ISMO 20" on one side and "W" on the other side, contains: isosorbide-5-mononitrate 20 mg. Nonmedicinal ingredients: alcohol, FD&C Yellow No. 6 aluminum lake, D&C Yellow No. 10 aluminum lake, hydroxypropyl cellulose, hydroxypropyl methylcellulose, lactose, magnesium stearate, microcrystalline cellulose, polyethylene glycol, polysorbate, povidone USP, silicon dioxide colloidal, sodium starch glycolate and titanium dioxide. Bottles of 100. Store at controlled room temperature, between 15 and 30°C. Dispense in tight containers.

(Shown in Product Recognition Section)

ISOCAL®
Mead Johnson

Therapeutic Nutrient

Indications: Nutritionally complete and well-balanced to provide the total dietary needs of most tube-fed patients.

Precautions: Give additional water as needed to meet the patient's requirements. Particular attention should be given to water supply for comatose and unconscious patients and others who cannot express the usual sensations of thirst. Additional water is important also when renal concentrating ability is impaired, when there is extensive breakdown of tissue protein, or when water requirements are high, as in fever.

Dosage: Not for parenteral use. Isocal should be administered by slow, continuous drip. It is ready-to-feed, and may be fed initially at full strength. The rate (mL/hour) may be adjusted for acutely ill patients to enhance tolerance. Tube feedings should be at room temperature. Bedside reservoir hang time for Isocal should not exceed 6 to 8 hours. Additional water should be supplied to maintain adequate urinary output. Shake well before using. Unused Isocal should be covered, kept refrigerated, and used within 48 hours of opening.

All current commercially available standard tube feedings are formulated to be low in sodium. This allows for flexibility while still meeting the requirements for a standard patient. A protocol to add sodium should be established and followed for patients on long-term tube feeds or for patients with unresolving diarrhea.

Supplied: Isocal is an isotonic, nutritionally balanced tube feeding. It provides 100% Canadian adult RNI for all vitamins and minerals in 1 250 mL and is formulated specifically for tube fed patients to assure acceptance and tolerance. Each ready to use 250 mL with easy open top, or 945 mL can contains: water, maltodextrin, caseinates (from casein and sodium and calcium hydroxides), canola oil, MCT oil (medium chain triglycerides 40% of total fat), sugar, soya protein isolate, potassium citrate, calcium phosphate dibasic, sodium citrate, magnesium chloride, calcium citrate, potassium chloride, magnesium phosphate dibasic, artificial vanilla flavor, sodium ascorbate, calcium chloride, lecithin, mono & diglycerides, choline chloride, carrageenan and essential vitamins and minerals (selenium, chromium, molybdenum). Glucose-, gluten-, lactose- and tartrazine-free. Each can supplies 419 kJ (100 kcal)/100 mL. Osmolality: 300 mOsm/kg water. Cases of 24 (250 mL), cases of 12 (945 mL).

ISOCAL® HN
Mead Johnson

Therapeutic Nutrient

Indications: A complete liquid diet formulated to provide well balanced nutrition when used as the sole source of nourishment, particularly in tube fed patients who have normal digestive function.

The non-protein-calorie-to-nitrogen ratio of Isocal HN is indicated for patients with burns, sepsis, major injury and surgery. When protein needs are increased with increasing levels of stress; e.g., protein requirement for basic maintenance is 1 g/kg IBW. For trauma patients with surgery, surgery patients with sepsis or tumor with multiple therapy, protein requirement is 1.75 g/kg IBW.

Precautions: Give additional water as needed to meet the patient's requirements. Particular attention should be given to water supply for comatose and unconscious patients and others who cannot express the usual sensations of thirst. Additional water is important also when renal concentrating ability is impaired, when there is extensive breakdown of tissue protein, or when water requirements are high, as in fever.

Dosage: Isocal HN can be initiated at full strength. The rate (mL/hour) may be adjusted for acutely ill patients to enhance tolerance. Tube feedings should be at room temperature and may be given by slow continuous drip or at intervals. Bedside reservoir hang time for Isocal HN should not exceed 6 to 8 hours.

Unopened Isocal HN should be stored at room temperature. After opening, unused Isocal HN should be covered and refrigerated and used within 48 hours.

Supplied: Isocal HN is a high-nitrogen, isotonic, nutritionally balanced tube feeding. It provides 100% Canadian adult RNIs for all vitamins, minerals and protein in 1 250 mL. The formulation is designed specifically to meet the increased requirements of stressed patients.

Each ready to use 250 mL with easy open top can contains: water, maltodextrin, caseinates (from casein and sodium and calcium hydroxides), canola oil, MCT oil (medium chain triglycerides 40% of total fat), soy protein isolate, magnesium chloride, potassium citrate, polyglycerol esters of fatty acids, potassium phosphate dibasic, calcium phosphate monobasic, sodium citrate, sodium ascorbate, choline chloride, potassium chloride, carrageenan and essential vitamins and minerals (selenium, chromium, molybdenum). Glucose-, gluten-, lactose-, sucrose- and tartrazine-free. Energy: 419 kJ (100 kcal)/100 mL. Osmolality: 270 mOsm/kg water. Cases of 24.

ISOCAL® with Fibre
Mead Johnson

Therapeutic Nutrient

Indications: A complete liquid diet formulated to provide the nutrient density of Isocal with the associated advantages of fibre.

Precautions: Give additional water as needed to meet the patient's requirements. Particular attention should be given to water supply for comatose and unconscious patients and others who cannot express the usual sensations of thirst. Additional water is important also when renal concentrating ability is impaired, when there is extensive breakdown of tissue protein, or when water requirements are high, as in fever.

Dosage: Not for parenteral use. Isocal with Fibre should be administered by slow, continuous drip. It is ready-to-feed, and may be fed initially at full strength. The rate (mL/hour) may be adjusted for acutely ill patients to enhance tolerance.

Tube feedings should be at room temperature. Bedside reservoir hang time for Isocal with Fibre should not exceed 6 to 8 hours.

Additional water should be supplied to maintain adequate urinary output. Shake well before using. Unused Isocal should be covered, kept refrigerated, and used within 48 hours of opening.

All current commercially available standard tube feedings are formulated to be low in sodium. This allows for flexibility while still meeting the requirements for a standard patient. A protocol to add sodium should be established and followed for patients on long-term tube feeds or for patients with unresolving diarrhea.

Supplied: Isocal with Fibre is isotonic, has a bland, unsweetened taste. MCT Oil, as a component of the fat source, is easily digested and well absorbed. Isocal with Fibre provides 100% Canadian adult RNI for all vitamins and minerals in 1 250 mL or kcal. Each ready to use 250 mL with easy open top contains: water, maltodextrin, caseinates (from casein and sodium and calcium hydroxides), canola oil, soy polysaccharides, MCT oil (medium chain triglycerides 40% of total fat), sugar, potassium citrate, calcium phosphate dibasic, sodium citrate, magnesium chloride, calcium citrate, potassium chloride, magnesium phosphate dibasic, artificial vanilla flavor, sodium ascorbate, calcium chloride, lecithin, mono & diglycerides, choline chloride, carrageenan and essential vitamins and minerals (selenium, chromium, molybdenum). Glucose-, gluten-, lactose- and tartrazine-free. Each can supplies 419 kJ (100 kcal)/100 mL. Osmolality: 300 mOsm/kg water. Cases of 24.

ISOFLURANE ℞
Technilab

Inhalation Anesthetic

Supplied: Contains isoflurane USP 100%. Amber-colored bottles of 100 mL. Store between 15 and 30°C.

New Product 1998

ISOFLURANE, USP ℞
Abbott

Inhalation Anesthetic

Supplied: Amber-colored bottles of 100 and 250 mL. Store at controlled room temperature (15 to 25°C). Isoflurane contains no additives.

ISOFLURANE, USP ℞
Schein Pharmaceutical

Inhalation Anesthetic

Supplied: Amber-colored bottles of 100 and 250 mL.

New Product 1998

ISOMIL® Preparations
Abbott

Milk-Free Formula

Nutritional Formula

Indications: For infants and children with an allergy or sensitivity to cow's milk. A feeding following diarrhea. A feeding for patients with disorders for which lactose should be avoided: lactase deficiency, lactose intolerance and galactosemia.

Precautions: Shake can well before opening. Shake bottle well before feeding.

Dosage: The number of mL to be offered to the baby in 24 hours is determined by the physician for each infant. A suggested feeding schedule is available on request from the manufacturer.

Supplied: Liquid, Concentrated (undiluted): Contains: water, liquid corn syrup, sucrose, soy protein isolate, high oleic sunflower oil or high oleic safflower oil, coconut oil, soy oil, modified cornstarch, minerals (calcium phosphate, potassium citrate, potassium chloride, magnesium chloride, sodium chloride, ferrous sulfate, zinc sulfate, cupric sulfate, manganese sulfate, potassium iodide), mono- and diglycerides, soy lecithin, vitamins (ascorbic acid, alpha-tocopheryl acetate, niacinamide, calcium pantothenate, vitamin A palmitate, thiamine hydrochloride, riboflavin, pyridoxine hydrochloride, vitamin K_1 [phylloquinone], folic acid, biotin, vitamin D_3, cyanocobalamin), calcium carrageenan, L-methionine, choline chloride, taurine and L-carnitine.

Liquid Ready To Feed: Contains: water, liquid corn syrup, sucrose, soy protein isolate, high oleic sunflower oil or high oleic safflower oil, coconut oil, soy oil, minerals (calcium citrate, calcium phosphate, potassium phosphate, potassium chloride, potassium citrate, magnesium chloride, ferrous sulfate, sodium chloride, copper sulfate, zinc sulfate, manganese sulfate, potassium iodide), mono- and diglycerides, soy lecithin, vitamins (ascorbic acid, alpha-tocopheryl acetate, niacinamide, calcium pantothenate, vitamin A palmitate, thiamine hydrochloride, riboflavin, pyridoxine hydrochloride, vitamin K_1[phylloquinone], folic acid, biotin, vitamin D_3, cyanocobalamin), calcium carrageenan, choline chloride, L-methionine, taurine and L-carnitine.

Powder: Contains: corn syrup solids, sucrose, soy protein isolate, high oleic sunflower oil or high oleic safflower oil, coconut oil, soy oil, minerals (calcium phosphate, potassium citrate, potassium chloride, magnesium chloride, calcium carbonate, ferrous sulfate, sodium chloride, zinc sulfate, cupric sulfate, potassium iodide), vitamins (ascorbic acid, alpha-tocopheryl acetate, niacinamide calcium pantothenate, vitamin A palmitate, thiamine hydrochloride, riboflavin, pyridoxine hydrochloride, vitamin K_1[phylloquinone], folic acid, biotin, vitamin D_3, cyanocobalamin), L-methionine, choline chloride, taurine and L-carnitine. See Table I.

Note: Ingredients may differ slightly between ready-to-feed, concentrate and powder presentations of Isomil. The user should consult the can label for exact composition.

Table I—Isomil Preparations

Analysis	100 mL	
Energy	285 (68)	kJ (kcal)
Carbohydrate	6.8	g
Fat	3.7	g
Protein	1.7	g
Ash	0.4	g
Vitamin A	200	IU
Vitamin D_3	40	IU
Vitamin E	2	IU
Vitamin C	5.5	mg
Niacin	0.9	mg
Pantothenic Acid	0.5	mg
Riboflavin	0.06	mg
Thiamine	0.04	mg
Vitamin B_6	0.04	mg
Vitamin K_1	0.01	mg
Folic Acid	0.01	mg
Biotin	0.003	mg
Vitamin B_{12}	0.0003	mg
Sodium	30	mg
Potassium	73	mg
Chloride	42	mg
Calcium	70	mg
Phosphorus	50	mg
Magnesium	5	mg
Iron	1.2	mg
Zinc	0.5	mg
Copper	0.05	mg
Manganese	0.02	mg
Iodine	0.01	mg
Choline	8.2	mg
Taurine	4.5	mg
Carnitine	1.13	mg

Preparation and Dilution: Instructions for each form are available on the can label.

Liquid Concentrated: Cans of 385 mL, cases of 12.

Liquid Ready-to-Feed (prediluted): Cans of 235 mL, cases of 12. Cans of 945 mL, cases of 6.

Powder: Tins of 400 g, cases of 12. For hospital use: Bottles of 120 mL, cases of 48.

Store unopened liquid and powder at room temperature. Prepared bottles and opened can (covered) should be refrigerated and used within 48 hours. Opened powder should be stored in a cool, dry place (but not in refrigerator) and used within 1 month. Formula remaining in bottle after feeding should be discarded.

ISONIAZID ℞
General Monograph, CPhA

INH

Isonicotinic Acid Hydrazide

Isonicotinylhydrazide

Antimycobacterial

> This monograph has been compiled by CPhA. It may contain information different from that approved by Therapeutic Products Programme, Health Canada, and the pharmaceutical manufacturers' approval has not been requested.

Pharmacology: Isoniazid is a bactericidal agent active against organisms of the genus Mycobacterium, specifically M. tuberculosis, M. bovis and M. kansasii. It is a highly specific agent, ineffective against other microorganisms. The mode of action is unknown but the drug is firmly bound to actively growing, sensitive, tubercle bacilli and does not affect these organisms when they are in the metabolic resting state.

When used alone in the treatment of tuberculosis, resistant strains emerge very rapidly; when combined with other antituberculosis agents the emergence of resistant strains may be delayed or prevented. When isoniazid is used alone in the prophylaxis of tuberculosis, the development of resistance does not appear to be a major problem.

Pharmacokinetics: Isoniazid is rapidly and almost completely absorbed, and peak blood levels are reached in about 1 to 2 hours. Bioavailability is reduced when isoniazid is administered with food. It diffuses readily into all body fluids (including cerebrospinal, pleural, and ascitic), tissues, organs, and excreta (saliva, sputum and feces). The drug also passes through the placental barrier and into milk in concentrations comparable to those in the plasma. Isoniazid is < 10% bound to plasma proteins.

Isoniazid is metabolized by the liver mainly by acetylation and dehydrazination. The N-acetylhydrazine metabolite is believed to be responsible for the hepatotoxic effects seen in patients treated with isoniazid. The rate of acetylation is genetically determined. Approximately 50% of blacks and Caucasians are slow inactivators; the majority of Inuit and Orientals are rapid inactivators. The half-life in fast acetylators is 1 to 2 hours while in slow acetylators it is 2 to 5 hours. Elimination is largely independent of renal function, however the half-life may be prolonged in liver disease. The rate of acetylation has not been shown to significantly alter the effectiveness of isoniazid. However, slow acetylation may lead to higher blood concentrations with chronic administration of the drug, with an increased risk of toxicity. Isoniazid and its metabolites are excreted in the urine with 75 to 95% of the dose excreted in 24 hours. Small amounts are also excreted in saliva, sputum and feces. Isoniazid is removed by hemodialysis and peritoneal dialysis.

Indications: Used in conjunction with other antituberculosis agents in the treatment of pulmonary and extrapulmonary tuberculosis and alone in the prophylaxis of tuberculosis.

Contraindications: Patients who develop severe hypersensitivity reactions to isoniazid, including drug-induced hepatitis; acute liver disease of any etiology.

Warnings: Severe and sometimes fatal hepatitis associated with isoniazid therapy may occur and may develop even after months of treatment. Serum AST levels become elevated in about 10 to 20% of patients, usually during the first few months of therapy, but it can occur at any time. Usually enzyme levels return to normal despite continuance of the drug, but in some cases progressive liver dysfunction occurs. The risk of developing hepatitis is increased with pre-existing liver disease, increasing age, concurrent use of other hepatotoxic medications and excessive or chronic use of alcohol. Patients given isoniazid should be carefully monitored and interviewed regularly. Patients should be instructed to report immediately any of the prodromal symptoms of hepatitis, such as fatigue, weakness, malaise, anorexia, nausea or vomiting. If symptoms and signs suggestive of hepatic damage are detected, an alternative agent should be used since continued use of isoniazid in these patients may cause a more severe form of liver damage. If isoniazid must be reinstituted, this should be done only after symptoms and laboratory abnormalities have cleared. Therapy should be reinitiated in very small and gradually increasing doses, and withdrawn immediately if there is any indication of recurrent liver involvement.

Precautions: Isoniazid may cause mild or severe hepatic dysfunction (see Warnings).

Hypersensitivity reactions, including rash, fever, lymphadenopathy or vasculitis have occurred rarely and usually develop within 3 to 7 weeks of starting therapy. If these signs or symptoms occur, isoniazid should be discontinued and reinstituted very gradually, if necessary, after the reaction resolves.

Optic neuritis has been reported as a rare complication. Periodic ophthalmoscopic examinations during isoniazid therapy are recommended when visual symptoms occur.

It is believed that isoniazid competes with pyridoxyl phosphate for the enzyme apotryptophanase which may lead to symptoms of pyridoxine (vitamin B_6) deficiency. Pyridoxine administration can prevent and reverse peripheral neuropathy complicating isoniazid use. Prophylactic pyridoxine administration (e.g., 10 to 50 mg/day) should probably be given routinely in individuals predisposed to develop peripheral neuropathies secondary to isoniazid therapy (e.g., patients who are malnourished, pregnant, alcoholic, diabetic, HIV-infected, or patients receiving higher doses of isoniazid).

Drug Interactions: Because the chemotherapy of tuberculosis involves the use of at least 2 drugs, the possible adverse reactions of each drug should be borne in mind as well as the potential for drug interactions.

Aluminum Hydroxide Gel: Decreases gastrointestinal absorption of isoniazid; isoniazid should be administered at least 1 hour before the antacid.

Anticonvulsants: Isoniazid inhibits hepatic metabolism of carbamazepine and phenytoin, resulting in increased anticonvulsant concentrations and toxicity in some patients. If isoniazid and carbamazepine or phenytoin are administered concurrently, serum concentrations of the anticonvulsant should be monitored, the patient observed for evidence of toxicity and the dosage of the anticonvulsant should be reduced accordingly.

Isoniazid (cont'd)

Cycloserine: In combination with isoniazid may result in increased cycloserine CNS side effects such as dizziness or drowsiness.
Disulfiram: Coordination difficulties and psychotic episodes have occurred in patients receiving isoniazid and disulfiram; concurrent administration of the drugs should be avoided.
Ketoconazole: Concentrations may be decreased by isoniazid, possibly decreasing the antifungal effect.
Rifampin: Hepatotoxicity has been reported to occur more frequently when rifampin and isoniazid are given concurrently. The incidence may be higher in slow isoniazid acetylators, those receiving high doses of isoniazid or those with preexisting liver disease.
Others: In addition, isoniazid may cause inhibition of metabolism of the following: acetaminophen, corticosteroids, diazepam, oral anticoagulants, primidone and theophyllines. The patient should be observed for increased effect or toxicity of these agents.
Pregnancy: Although safe use of isoniazid during pregnancy has not been definitely established, isoniazid has been used to treat clinical tuberculosis in pregnant women. If a risk vs. benefit analysis results in a decision to use isoniazid during pregnancy, prophylactic pyridoxine supplementation is recommended.

Prophylactic isoniazid therapy is best postponed until after delivery, unless the woman is likely to have been recently infected or has other high risk medical conditions such as HIV infection.
Lactation: No adverse effects have been reported, but there is a potential risk of peripheral neuritis or hepatic damage. Breast-fed infants should be carefully observed for evidence of adverse effects.

Adverse Effects: Toxic effects are usually encountered only with higher doses of isoniazid, and their incidence is reportedly higher in slow inactivators. The incidence of adverse effects at a dose of 10 mg/kg has been reported to be approximately 15%.
CNS: Peripheral neuropathy (occurs most often in the malnourished and is usually preceded by paresthesias of the feet and hands) is the most common (see Precautions). Convulsions, toxic encephalopathy, optic neuritis and atrophy, and toxic psychosis may occur rarely.
Gastrointestinal: nausea, vomiting, epigastric distress.
Hepatic: elevated serum aminotransferases (ALT, AST) and bilirubin concentrations (10 to 20%), hepatitis with or without jaundice. Isoniazid-associated, occasionally severe and sometimes fatal hepatitis is generally considered an unpredictable hypersensitivity reaction (see Warnings).
Hematologic: agranulocytosis, hemolytic, sideroblastic or aplastic anemia; thrombocytopenia; eosinophilia.
Hypersensitivity: fever, skin eruptions (morbilliform, maculopapular, purpuric, or exfoliative), lymphadenopathy, vasculitis. Hypersensitivity reactions usually occur in the first 3 to 7 weeks of therapy (see Precautions).
Metabolic and Endocrine: pyridoxine deficiency, pellagra, hyperglycemia, metabolic acidosis, gynecomastia.
Miscellaneous: rheumatic syndrome and systemic lupus erythematosus like syndrome.

Overdose: Symptoms: Manifestations of isoniazid overdosage usually become apparent within 30 minutes to 3 hours following ingestion. Nausea, vomiting, dizziness, slurring of speech, blurring of vision and visual hallucinations (including bright colors and strange designs), are among the early manifestations. With marked overdosage, respiratory distress and CNS depression, progressing rapidly from stupor to profound coma, are to be expected, along with severe, intractable seizures. Severe metabolic acidosis, acetonuria and hyperglycemia are typical laboratory findings.

Treatment: Treatment of overdosage consists of establishment of an airway, controlling of seizures with diazepam or barbiturates, i.v. injection of large doses of pyridoxine (e.g., a gram-for-gram dose equivalent to the amount of isoniazid ingested). See Vitamin B_6 General Monograph. If seizures are under control and ingestion occurred within the past 2 to 3 hours, gastric lavage should be performed. I.V. sodium bicarbonate may be used to correct metabolic acidosis if necessary. Forced osmotic diuresis should be used to increase renal clearance over several hours, with monitoring of fluid intake and output. Hemodialysis or peritoneal dialysis may be helpful in severe cases.

Dosage: Isoniazid is given orally, as a single daily dose. Absorption is optimal if taken on an empty stomach but it may be taken with food if gastrointestinal irritation occurs.

Treatment of Tuberculosis: In conjunction with other agents, the adult dose is 5 to 10 mg/kg/day, to a maximum of 300 mg, for a minimum of 6 months. When intermittent therapy regimens are used, the adult dose of isoniazid is 15 mg/kg 2 or 3 times weekly, to a maximum of 900 mg per dose.
Children: 10 to 20 mg/kg once daily to a maximum of 300 mg. Intermittent therapy in children: 20 to 40 mg/kg 2 or 3 times weekly, to a maximum of 900 mg per dose.

Prophylaxis of Tuberculosis: Isoniazid is generally used alone for preventive therapy, for a period of 6 to 12 months. Adults: 300 mg once daily. Children: 10 to 15 mg/kg once daily, to a maximum of 300 mg.

For high-risk individuals who are likely to be noncompliant and whose prophylactic therapy needs to be directly observed, a dose of 15 mg/kg twice weekly, to a maximum of 900 mg per dose, may be considered as an alternative to daily therapy.

Reviewed 1999

ISOPRINOSINE® ℞
Rivex Pharma

Inosiplex

Subacute Sclerosing Panencephalitis Therapy

Pharmacology: Mechanism(s) that might explain the results of the clinical studies employing inosiplex have not been completely elucidated. However, possible antiviral and immunomodulating properties of this drug may be involved.

Serum uric acid concentration rose with increasing inosiplex doses. Hyperuricemic levels (greater than 7.5 mg%) were seen at doses equal to or exceeding 3 g/day. At doses of 4 g/day, about 60% of the subjects had serum uric acid levels in excess of 7 mg%; 30% of the subjects exceeded 7.5 mg%. Urinary uric acid excretion was also elevated after inosiplex administration. The time for urine normalization was usually longer than that required for normalization of serum uric acid level. In 1 case, uricosuria was found to last more than 9 days, and another case was reported in which 3 weeks were required to restore uric acid excretion to normal level.

Inosiplex is composed of inosine and the p-acetamidobenzoic acid salt of N, N-dimethylamido-2-propanol. The principal metabolite (about 80%) of p-acetamidobenzoic acid is O-acylglucuronide and the principal metabolite of N, N-dimethylamine-2-propanol is N, N-dimethylamino- 2-propanol-N-oxide. Virtually 100% of the metabolites was recovered in urine within 8 through 24 hours postadministration period. Each of the compoments of inosiplex is rapidly metabolized, the inosine and p-acetamidobenzoic acid more extensively than N, N-dimethylamino-2-propanol.

Indications: May be beneficial in retarding neurological deterioration and prolonging life in patients with slowly progressive subacute sclerosing panencephalitis (SSPE). Inosiplex is not indicated for any condition other than SSPE.

Contraindications: None for SSPE patients.

Warnings: Because the purine (inosine) moiety of inosiplex is rapidly catabolized to uric acid, resulting in elevations of serum and uric acid, it should be used with care in patients with a history of gout, urolithiasis, nephrolithiasis, or renal dysfunction. Uricosuric agents may be administered to patients with severely elevated serum uric acid levels.

Precautions: *Pregnancy:* Specific studies on the effects of inosiplex on animal reproduction have been performed and were negative. However, well-controlled trials concerning fetal risk and impairment of fertility in humans are not available. Therefore, care should be taken in the use of inosiplex by pregnant women and women of childbearing age, and the risks involved should be assessed.

Adverse Effects: Other than potential problems arising from uric acid metabolism, no adverse physiological reactions have been unequivocally associated with inosiplex therapy.

Overdose: Symptoms and Treatment: Toxic effects from an overdose of inosiplex have not been observed. Since the drug is rapidly metabolized, reduction in dosage or withdrawal from treatment with symptomatic general management of signs and symptoms would generally suffice should any unfoward reaction occur. Similar management would apply to an accidental overdose.

Dosage: Adults and Children: The recommended dosage is 50 mg/kg/day, up to a maxium of 3 g/day, administered orally in 3 to 4 equally divided doses during waking hours.

Supplied: Each white, round, scored tablet contains: inosiplex 500 mg. Nonmedicinal ingredients: magnesium stearate, microcrystalline cellulose, povidone, pregelatinized cornstarch and stearic acid. Tartrazine-free. Amber glass bottles of 100. Store at room temperature.

Reviewed 1998

ISOPTIN® ℞
Knoll

Verapamil HCl

Antianginal—Antiarrhythmic—Antihypertensive Agent

Pharmacology: Angina and Arrhythmia: Verapamil is a calcium ion influx inhibitor (calcium entry blocker or calcium ion antagonist). The mechanism of the antianginal and antiarrhythmic effects of verapamil is believed to be related to its specific cellular action of selectively inhibiting transmembrane influx of calcium in cardiac muscle, coronary and systemic arteries and in cells of the intracardiac conduction system. Verapamil blocks the transmembrane influx of calcium through the slow channel (calcium ion antagonism) without affecting to any significant degree the transmembrane influx of sodium through the fast channel. This results in a reduction of free calcium ions available within cells of the above tissues.

Verapamil's antiarrhythmic effects are believed to be brought about largely by its action on the sinoatrial (SA) and atrioventricular (AV) nodes. Verapamil depresses AV nodal conduction and prolongs functional refractory periods. Verapamil does not alter the normal atrial action potential or intraventricular conduction time, but depresses amplitude, velocity of depolarization and conduction in depressed atrial fibres. Through this action, it interrupts re-entrant pathways and slows the ventricular rate.

Verapamil may shorten the antegrade effective refractory period of the accessory bypass tract. Acceleration of ventricular rate and/or ventricular fibrillation has been reported in patients with atrial flutter or atrial fibrillation and a coexisting accessory AV pathway following administration of verapamil (see Warnings, Conduction Disturbance). Verapamil has a local anesthetic action that is 1.6 times that of procaine on an equimolar basis.

Verapamil is a potent smooth muscle relaxant with vasodilatory properties, as well as a depressant of myocardial contractility, and these effects are largely independent of autonomic influences. Its antianginal action in exertional angina seems to result from a decrease in resistance in the systemic vasculature, as well as from a direct effect on myocardial contraction. The net pharmacologic effect is a decrease in myocardial oxygen consumption. Verapamil's effectiveness in vasospastic angina is due to a decrease in coronary vascular tone.
Essential Hypertension: Verapamil exerts antihypertensive effects by inducing peripheral vasodilation and reducing peripheral vascular resistance usually without reflex tachycardia. Verapamil does not blunt hemodynamic response to isometric or dynamic exercise.

Verapamil depresses AV nodal conduction and prolongs functional refractory periods. Verapamil does not alter the normal atrial action potential or intraventricular conduction time, but depresses amplitude, velocity of depolarization and conduction in depressed atrial fibres.

Verapamil may shorten the antegrade effective refractory period of the accessory bypass tract. Acceleration of ventricular rate and/or ventricular fibrillation has been reported in patients with atrial flutter or atrial fibrillation and a coexisting accessory AV pathway following administration of verapamil (see Warnings, Conduction Disturbance). Verapamil has a local anesthetic action that is 1.6 times that of procaine on an equimolar basis.

Verapamil is a potent smooth muscle relaxant with vasodilatory properties, as well as a depressant of myocardial contractility, and these effects are largely independent of autonomic influences.

Compared to baseline, verapamil does not affect electrolytes, glucose and creatinine. The hypotensive effect of verapamil is not blunted by an increase in sodium intake.

In hypertensive normolipidemic patients, verapamil had no effects on plasma lipoprotein fractions.
Pharmacodynamics: In a study in 5 healthy males, the S enantiomer was found to be 8 to 20 times more active than the R enantiomer in slowing AV conduction. In another study using septal strips isolated from the left ventricle of 5 patients with mitral disease, the S enantiomer was 8 times more potent than the R enantiomer in reducing myocardial contractility.
Pharmacokinetics: Verapamil is a racemic mixture consisting of equal portions of the R enantiomer and the S enantiomer.

More than 90% of the orally administered dose of verapamil is absorbed. Upon oral administration, there is rapid stereoselective biotransformation during the first pass of verapamil through the portal circulation. The systemic concentrations of R and S enantiomers are dependent upon the route and the rate of administration and the rate and extent of release from the dosage forms.

The following bioavailability information was obtained from healthy volunteers and not from the populations most likely to be treated with verapamil.

In a study in 5 healthy volunteers with oral immediate-release verapamil, the systemic bioavailability varied from 33 to 65% for the R enantiomer and from 13 to 34% for the S enantiomer. The S enantiomer is pharmacologically more active than the R enantiomer (see Pharmacodynamics).

There is a nonlinear correlation between the verapamil dose administered and verapamil plasma levels. In early dose titration with verapamil, a relationship exists between total verapamil (R and S combined) plasma concentration and prolongation of the PR interval. The mean elimination half-life in single-dose studies of immediate release verapamil ranged from 2.8 to 7.4 hours. In these same studies, after steady-state was reached, the half-life increased to a range from 4.5 to 12.0 hours (after less than 10 consecutive doses given 6 hours apart). Half-life of verapamil may increase during titration. Aging decreases the clearance and elimination of verapamil.

In healthy men, orally administered verapamil undergoes extensive metabolism by the cytochrome P450 system in the liver. The particular isoenzymes involved are CYP3A4, CYP1A2, and CYP2C family. Thirteen metabolites have been identified in urine. Norverapamil can reach steady-state plasma concentrations approximately equal to those of verapamil itself. The cardiovascular activity of norverapamil appears to be approximately 20% that of verapamil. Approximately 70% of an administered dose is excreted as metabolites in the urine and 16% or more in the feces within 5 days. About 3 to 4% is excreted in the urine as unchanged drug. R-verapamil is 94% bound to plasma albumin, while S-verapamil is 88% bound. In addition, R-verapamil is 92% and S-verapamil 86% bound to alpha-1 acid glycoprotein. The degree of biotransformation during the first pass of verapamil may vary according to the status of the liver in different patient populations. In patients with hepatic insufficiency, metabolism is delayed and elimination half-life prolonged up to 14 to 16 hours (see Warnings, Hepatic Insufficiency and Dosage).

Verapamil crosses the placental barrier and can be detected in umbilical vein blood at delivery. Verapamil is excreted in human milk.

A study was conducted in which 240 mg single oral doses of Isoptin standard release (fasting) and Isoptin sustained release (fed) tablets were given to 12 young, healthy males (19 to 37 years old) in a randomized, crossover (7-day washout) study. Serial blood samples for drug determination were taken over a 48 hour period. The pharmacokinetic data from this study is summarized in Table I.

Table I—Isoptin

Pharmacokinetic Data

	Isoptin Standard Release Tablet (240 mg)		**Isoptin Sustained Release Tablet (240 mg)**	
Parameter	R-verapamil	S-verapamil	R-verapamil	S-verapamil
C_{max}, ng/mL	258	59.0	60.1	11.3
T_{max}, h	1.46	1.58	10.8	11.8
AUC_{0-48}, ng/mL/h	1 250	261	918	150

Influence of Food: Administration of Isoptin tablets with food results in marked prolongation of T_{max} (45 to 75%) and slight decreases in C_{max} (about 15%) and AUC (1 to 8%). Food thus produces a slight decrease in bioavailability (AUC), but a narrower peak-to-trough ratio.

Indications: Chronic stable angina of effort. Angina resulting from coronary artery spasm. Obstructive hypertrophic cardiomyopathy, where surgery is not otherwise indicated. Atrial fibrillation or flutter with rapid ventricular response not otherwise controllable with digitalis preparations. Follow-up treatment to the use of injectable verapamil in paroxysmal supraventricular tachycardia.

Verapamil is indicated in the treatment of mild to moderate essential hypertension. Verapamil should normally be used in those patients in whom treatment with diuretics or beta-blockers has been associated with unacceptable adverse effects.

Verapamil can be tried as an initial agent in those patients in whom the use of diuretics and/or beta-blockers is contraindicated or in patients with medical conditions in which these drugs frequently cause serious adverse effects.

Combination of verapamil with a diuretic has been found to be compatible and showed additive antihypertensive effect. Concomitant use of Isoptin SR with an angiotensin converting enzyme inhibitor has been shown to be compatible and to have additive blood pressure lowering effects.

Verapamil should not be used concurrently with beta adrenoreceptor blockers in the treatment of hypertension (see Precautions, Drug Interactions).

Safety of concurrent use of verapamil with other antihypertensive agents has not been established and such use cannot be recommended at this time.

Contraindications: Complicated myocardial infarction (patients who have ventricular failure manifested by pulmonary congestion). Severe congestive heart failure and/or severe left ventricular dysfunction (i.e., ejection fraction <40%), unless secondary to a supraventricular tachycardia amenable to oral verapamil therapy. Cardiogenic shock. Severe hypotension. Second- or third-degree AV block. Sick Sinus Syndrome (see Warnings). Marked bradycardia. Hypersensitivity to the drug. Patients with atrial flutter or atrial fibrillation and an accessory bypass tract (e.g., Wolff-Parkinson-White, Lown-Ganong-Levine syndromes) (see Warnings).

Warnings: General: In patients with angina or arrhythmias using antihypertensive drugs, the additional hypotensive effect of verapamil should be taken into consideration.

Heart Failure: Because of the drug's negative inotropic effect, verapamil should not be used in patients with poorly compensated congestive heart failure, unless the failure is complicated by or caused by a dysrhythmia. If verapamil is used in such patients, they must be digitalized prior to treatment. It has been reported that digoxin plasma levels may increase with chronic verapamil administration (see Precautions, Drug Interactions, Digoxin). The use of verapamil in the treatment of hypertension is not recommended in patients with heart failure caused by systolic dysfunction.

Hypotension: Hypotensive symptoms of lethargy and weakness with faintness have been reported following single oral doses and even after some months of treatment. In some patients it may be necessary to reduce the dose.

Conduction Disturbance: Verapamil slows conduction across the AV node and rarely may produce second- or third-degree AV block, bradycardia and in extreme cases, asystole.

Verapamil causes dose-related suppression of the SA node. In some patients, sinus bradycardia may occur, especially in patients with a sick sinus syndrome (SA nodal disease), which is more common in older patients (see Contraindications).

Bradycardia: The total incidence of bradycardia (ventricular rate less than 50 beats/min) was 1.4% in controlled studies. Asystole in patients other than those with sick sinus syndrome is usually of short duration (few seconds or less), with spontaneous return to AV nodal or normal sinus rhythm. If this does not occur promptly, appropriate treatment should be initiated immediately (see Overdose: Symptoms and Treatment).

Accessory Bypass Tract (Wolff-Parkinson-White or Lown-Ganong-Levine): Verapamil may result in significant acceleration of ventricular response during atrial fibrillation or atrial flutter in the Wolff-Parkinson-White (WPW) or Lown-Ganong-Levine syndromes after receiving i.v. verapamil. Although a risk of this occurring with oral verapamil has not been established, such patients receiving oral verapamil may be at risk and its use in these patients is contraindicated (see Contraindications).

Concomitant Use with Beta-blockers: Generally, oral verapamil should not be given to patients receiving beta-blockers since the depressant effects on myocardial contractility, heart rate and AV conduction may be additive. However, in exceptional cases when, in the opinion of the physician, concomitant use in angina and arrhythmias is considered essential, such use should be instituted gradually under careful supervision. If combined therapy is used, close surveillance of vital signs and clinical status should be carried out and the need for continued concomitant treatment periodically assessed.

Verapamil gives no protection against the dangers of abrupt beta-blocker withdrawal and such withdrawal should be done by the gradual reduction of the dose of beta-blocker. Then verapamil may be started with the usual dose.

Patients with Hypertrophic Cardiomyopathy: In 120 patients with hypertrophic cardiomyopathy who received therapy with verapamil at doses up to 720 mg/day, a variety of serious adverse effects was seen. Three patients died in pulmonary edema; all had severe left ventricular outflow obstruction and a past history of left ventricular dysfunction. Eight other patients had pulmonary edema and/or severe hypotension, abnormally high (greater than 20 mm Hg) pulmonary wedge pressure and a marked left ventricular outflow obstruction were present in most of these patients. Concomitant administration of quinidine (see Precautions, Drug Interactions) preceded the severe hypotension in 3 of the 8 patients (2 of whom developed pulmonary edema). Sinus bradycardia occurred in 11% of the patients, second-degree AV block in 4%, and sinus arrest in 2%. It must be appreciated that this group of patients had a serious disease with a high mortality rate. Most adverse effects responded well to dose reduction, but in some cases, verapamil use had to be discontinued.

Elevated Liver Enzymes: Elevation of transaminase with and without concomitant elevations in alkaline phosphatase and bilirubin have been reported. Several published cases of hepatocellular injury produced by verapamil have been proven by rechallenge. Clinical symptoms of malaise, fever, and/or right upper quadrant pain, in addition to elevation of AST, ALT and alkaline phosphatase have been reported. Periodic monitoring of liver function in patients receiving verapamil is therefore prudent.

Hepatic Insufficiency: Because verapamil is extensively metabolized by the liver, it should be administered cautiously to patients with impaired hepatic function, since the elimination half-life of verapamil in these patients is prolonged 4-fold (from 3.7 to 14.2 hours). A decreased dosage should be used in patients with hepatic insufficiency and careful monitoring for abnormal prolongation of the PR interval or other signs of excessive pharmacologic effect should be carried out (see Pharmacology, Pharmacokinetics and Dosage).

Renal Insufficiency: About 70% of an administered dose of verapamil is excreted as metabolites in the urine. In one study in healthy volunteers, the total body clearance after i.v. administration of verapamil was 12.08 mL/min/kg, while in patients with advanced renal disease it was reduced to 5.33 mL/min/kg. This pharmacokinetic finding suggests that renal clearance of verapamil in patients with renal disease is decreased. In 2 studies with oral verapamil no difference in pharmacokinetics could be demonstrated.

Therefore, until further data are available, verapamil should be used with caution in patients with impaired renal function. These patients should be carefully monitored for abnormal prolongation of the PR interval or other signs of excessive pharmacologic effect (see Dosage).

Precautions: Atypical lens changes and cataracts were observed in beagle dog studies at high doses. This has been concluded to be species-specific for the beagle dog. (These ophthalmological changes were not seen in a second study.) No similar changes have been observed in long-term prospective human ophthalmological trials.

Verapamil does not alter total serum calcium levels. However, one report suggested that calcium levels above the normal range may decrease the therapeutic effect of verapamil.

Patients with Attenuated (Decreased) Neuromuscular Transmission: It has been reported that verapamil decreases neuromuscular transmission in patients with Duchenne's muscular dystrophy, and that verapamil prolongs recovery from the neuromuscular blocking agent vercuronium. It may be necessary to decrease the dosage of verapamil when it is administered to patients with attenuated neuromuscular transmission.

Geriatrics: Caution should be exercised when verapamil is administered to elderly patients (≥65 years) especially those prone to developing hypotension or those with a history of cerebrovascular insufficiency (see Dosage and Pharmacology, Pharmacokinetics). The incidence of adverse reactions is approximately 4% higher in the elderly. The adverse reactions occurring more frequently include dizziness and constipation. Serious adverse events associated with heart block have occurred in the elderly.

Pregnancy: Teratology and reproduction studies have been performed in rabbits and rats at oral doses up to 1.5 (15 mg/kg/day) and 6 (60 mg/kg/day) times the human oral daily dose, respectively, and have revealed no evidence of teratogenicity or impaired fertility. In rats, however, this multiple of the human dose was embryocidal and retarded fetal growth and development, probably because of adverse maternal effects reflected in reduced weight gains of the dams. This oral dose has also been shown to cause hypotension in rats.

There are no studies in pregnant women. However, verapamil crosses the placental barrier and can be detected in umbilical vein blood at delivery. Verapamil is not recommended for use in pregnant women unless the potential benefits outweigh potential risks to mother and fetus.

Labor and Delivery: It is not known whether the use of verapamil during labor or delivery has immediate or delayed

Isoptin (cont'd)

adverse effects on the fetus, or whether it prolongs the duration of labor or increases the need for forceps delivery or other obstetric intervention.

Lactation: Verapamil is excreted in human milk. Because of the potential for adverse reactions in nursing infants from verapamil, nursing should be discontinued while verapamil is administered.

Children: The safety and dosage regimen of verapamil in children has not yet been established.

Drug Interactions: As with all drugs, care should be exercised when treating patients with multiple medications. Calcium channel blockers undergo biotransformation by the cytochrome P450 system. Coadministration of verapamil with other drugs which follow the same route of biotransformation may result in altered bioavailability of verapamil or these drugs. Dosages of similarly metabolized drugs, particularly those of low therapeutic ratio, and especially in patients with renal and/or hepatic impairment, may require adjustment when starting or stopping concomitantly administered verapamil to maintain optimum therapeutic blood levels.

Drugs known to be inhibitors of the cytochrome P450 system include: azole antifungals, cimetidine, cyclosporine, erythromycin, quinidine, terfenadine, warfarin.

Drugs known to be inducers of the cytochrome P450 system include: phenobarbital, phenytoin, rifampin.

Drugs know to be biotransformed via P450 include: benzodiazepines, flecainide, imipramine, propafenone, theophylline.

Alcohol: Verapamil may increase blood alcohol concentrations and prolong its effects.

Antineoplastic Agents: Verapamil inhibits P-glycoprotein mediated transport of antineoplastic agents out of tumor cells, resulting in their decreased metabolic clearance. Dosage adjustments of antineoplastic agents should be considered when verapamil is administered concomitantly.

Antihypertensive Agents: Verapamil administered concomitantly with other antihypertensive agents such as vasodilators, ACE inhibitors, and diuretics may have an additive effect on lowering blood pressure. In patients with angina or arrhythmias using antihypertensive drugs, this additional hypotensive effect should be taken into consideration. Verapamil should not be combined with beta-blockers for the treatment of hypertension. Concomitant use of verapamil and alpha-adrenoreceptor blockers may result in excessive fall in blood pressure in some patients as observed in one study following the concomitant administration of verapamil and prazosin.

ASA: Potential adverse reactions in terms of bleeding due to synergistic antiplatelet effects of the two agents should be taken into consideration in patients taking ASA and verapamil concomitantly.

Beta-Adrenergic Blockers: The concomitant administration of verapamil with beta-blockers can result in severe adverse effects (see Warnings).

Carbamazepine: The concomitant oral administration of verapamil and carbamazepine may potentiate the effects of carbamazepine neurotoxicity. Symptoms include nausea, diplopia, headache, ataxia or dizziness.

Cimetidine: Two clinical trials have shown a lack of significant verapamil interaction with cimetidine. A third study showed cimetidine reduced verapamil clearance and increased elimination half-life.

Cyclosporine: Verapamil therapy may increase serum levels of cyclosporine.

Digoxin: Verapamil treatment increases serum digoxin levels by 50 to 75% during the first week of therapy, and this can result in digitalis toxicity. In patients with hepatic cirrhosis the influence of verapamil on digoxin kinetics is magnified. Verapamil may reduce total body clearance and extrarenal clearance of digitoxin by 27 and 29% respectively. Maintenance and digitalization doses should be reduced when verapamil is administered and the patient should be reassessed to avoid over- or underdigitalization. Whenever overdigitalization is suspected, the daily dose of digitalis should be reduced or temporarily discontinued. On discontinuation of verapamil use, the patient should be reassessed to avoid underdigitalization.

Disopyramide: Until data on possible interactions between verapamil and disopyramide are obtained, disopyramide should not be administered within 48 hours before or 24 hours after verapamil administration.

Flecainide: A study in healthy volunteers showed that the concomitant administration of flecainide and verapamil may have additive effects on myocardial contractility, AV conduction, and repolarization. Concomitant therapy with flecainide and verapamil may result in additive negative inotropic effect and prolongation of atrioventricular conduction.

Inhalation Anesthetics: When used concomitantly, inhalation anesthetics and calcium antagonists, such as verapamil, should be titrated carefully because additive hemodynamic depressive effects have been observed.

Lithium: Increased sensitivity to the effects of lithium (neurotoxicity) has been reported during concomitant verapamil-lithium therapy with either no change or an increase in serum lithium levels. However, the addition of verapamil has also resulted in the lowering of serum lithium levels in patients receiving chronic stable oral lithium. Patients receiving both drugs must be monitored carefully.

Neuromuscular Blocking Agents: Clinical data and animal studies suggest that verapamil may potentiate the activity of neuromuscular blocking agents (curare-like and depolarizing). It may be necessary to decrease the dose of verapamil and/or the dose of the neuromuscular blocking agent when the drugs are used concomitantly.

Nitrates, Diuretics: No cardiovascular adverse effects have been attributed to any interaction between these agents and verapamil.

Phenobarbital: Phenobarbital therapy may increase verapamil clearance.

Quinidine: In a small number of patients with hypertrophic cardiomyopathy, concomitant use of verapamil and quinidine resulted in significant hypotension. Until further data are obtained combined therapy of verapamil and quinidine in patients with hypertrophic cardiomyopathy should probably be avoided. The electrophysiologic effects of quinidine and verapamil on AV conduction were studied in 8 patients. Verapamil significantly counteracted the effects of quinidine on AV conduction. There has been a report of increased quinidine levels during verapamil therapy.

Rifampin: Therapy with rifampin may markedly reduce oral verapamil bioavailability.

Sulfinpyrazone: Increased clearance and decreased bioavailability of verapamil may occur.

Theophylline: Verapamil may inhibit the clearance and increase the plasma levels of theophylline.

Adverse Effects: In 4 826 patients treated with Isoptin immediate release tablets for arrhythmias, angina or hypertension, the overall adverse reaction rate in these patients was 37.1% and the dropout rate was 10.2%. The majority of these patients were seriously ill and treated under emergency drug regulations.

The most common adverse reactions were: constipation (7.3%), dizziness (3.2%) and nausea (2.7%). In hypertension studies, constipation occurred in 18.5% of patients on Isoptin and 4.7% of patients on Isoptin SR.

The most serious adverse reactions reported with verapamil are heart failure (1.8%), hypotension (2.5%), AV block (1.2%) and rapid ventricular response (see Warnings).

The following adverse reactions divided by body system have been reported in clinical trials or marketing experience. When incidences are shown, they are calculated based on the 4 954 (4 826+128) patient base.

Cardiovascular: hypotension 2.5%; edema 2.1%; CHF/pulmonary edema 1.9%; bradycardia 1.4%; AV block, total (1°, 2°, 3°) 1.2%, 2° and 3° 0.8%.

CNS: dizziness 3.2%, headache 2.2%, fatigue 1.7%.

Gastrointestinal: constipation 7.3%, nausea 2.7%.

The following reactions were reported in 1% or less of patients: Cardiovascular: flushing, angina pectoris, atrioventricular dissociation, chest pain, claudication, myocardial infarction, palpitations, purpura, syncope, severe tachycardia, developing or worsening of heart failure, development of rhythm disturbances, ventricular dysrhythmias, painful coldness and numbness of extremities.

CNS: cerebrovascular accident, confusion, equilibrium disorders, insomnia, muscle cramps, paresthesia, psychotic symptoms, shakiness, somnolence, excitation, depression, rotary nystagmus, vertigo, tremor, extrapyramidal disorders, muscle fatigue, hyperkinesis.

Gastrointestinal: diarrhea, dry mouth, gastrointestinal distress, gingival hyperplasia, vomiting.

Respiratory: dyspnea, bronchospasm.

Urogenital: gynecomastia, increased frequency of urination, spotty menstruation, oligomenorrhea, impotence.

Hematologic and Lymphatic: ecchymosis or bruising.

Skin: arthralgia and rash, exanthema, hair loss, hyperkeratosis, macules, sweating, urticaria, Stevens-Johnson syndrome, erythema multiforme, pruritus.

Special Senses: blurred vision, diplopia.

Hepatotoxicity with elevated enzymes (AST, ALT, alkaline phosphatase) and bilirubin levels, jaundice and associated symptoms of hepatitis with cholestasis have been reported (see Warnings).

Isolated cases of angioedema have been reported. Angioedema may be accompanied by breathing difficulty.

In clinical trials related to the control of ventricular response in digitalized patients who had atrial fibrillation or flutter, ventricular rates below 50 at rest occurred in 15% of patients and asymptomatic hypotension occurred in 5% of patients.

Overdose: Symptoms: Based on reports of intentional overdosage of verapamil, the following symptoms have been observed. Hypotension occurs, varying from transient to severe. Conduction disturbances seen included: prolongation of AV conduction time, AV dissociation, nodal rhythm, ventricular fibrillation and ventricular asystole.

Treatment: Treatment of overdosage should be supportive. Gastric lavage should be undertaken even later than 12 hours after ingestion, if no gastrointestinal motility is present. Beta-adrenergic stimulation or parenteral administration of calcium solutions may increase calcium ion influx across the slow channel. These pharmacologic interventions have been effectively used in treatment of overdosage with verapamil. Clinically significant hypotensive reactions should be treated with vasopressor agents. AV block is treated with atropine and cardiac pacing. Asystole should be handled by the usual Advanced Cardiac Life Support measures including the use of vasopressor agents, e.g., isoproterenol HCl. Verapamil is not removed by hemodialysis.

Suggested Treatment of Acute Cardiovascular Adverse Reactions: See Table II. Actual treatment and dosage should depend on the severity of the clinical situation and the judgment of the treating physician. Patients with hypertrophic cardiomyopathy treated with verapamil should not be administered positive inotropic agents (marked by asterisks in Table II).

Dosage: Isoptin should be taken with food (see Pharmacology, Pharmacokinetics, Influence of Food).

Angina Pectoris: Usual starting dose in adults is 80 mg 3 to 4 times daily. This may be increased to 120 mg 3 to 4 times daily until optimum response is obtained. The dose should not be increased beyond 480 mg/day. In some cases the dose may be decreased following clinical improvement.

Obstructive Hypertrophic Cardiomyopathy: Usual starting dose is 80 to 120 mg 3 to 4 times daily, and occasionally patients may require doses up to 600 to 720 mg/day.

Paroxysmal Supraventricular Tachycardia: Oral treatment should replace i.v. therapy as soon as possible. It can be administered in adults in the same dosage schedule as for angina pectoris. Duration of treatment will depend on the underlying cause and history of recurrence. At this time there is insufficient data to establish a safe and effective oral dose for children.

Table II—Isoptin

Suggested Treatment of Acute Cardiovascular Adverse Effects

Adverse Reaction	Proven Effective Treatment	Treatment with Good Theoretical Rationale	Supportive Treatment
Shock, cardiac failure, severe hypotension	Calcium salt, e.g., calcium gluconate i.v. Metaraminol bitartrate i.v.*	Dopamine HCl i.v.* Dobutamine HCl i.v.*	I.V. fluids Trendelenburg position
Bradycardia, AV block, asystole	Isoproterenol HCl i.v.* Atropine sulfate i.v. Cardiac pacing	—	I.V. fluids (slow drip)
Rapid ventricular rate (due to antegrade conduction in flutter/fibrillation with WPW or LGL syndrome)	DC cardioversion (high energy may be required) Procainamide i.v. Lidocaine HCl i.v.	—	I.V. fluids (slow drip)

*positive inotropic agent.

Atrial Fibrillation and Flutter with Rapid Ventricular Response: Verapamil tablets may be administered to adults not completely controlled with digitalis preparations. The same dosage as for angina pectoris can be used but the physician should be aware that digoxin plasma levels may increase with verapamil administration and downward adjustment of the digoxin dose may be necessary (see Precautions, Drug Interactions).

Mild to Moderate Essential Hypertension: (see Indications).

The dosage should be individualized by titration depending on patient tolerance and responsiveness to verapamil.

The usual initial adult dose is 80 mg 3 times a day. If required, the dose may be increased up to 160 mg 3 times a day. A maximum daily dose of 480 mg should not be exceeded.

The antihypertensive effects of verapamil tablets are evident within the first week of therapy. Optimal doses are usually lower in patients also receiving diuretics since additive antihypertensive effects can be expected.

Geriatrics: Lower dosage may be warranted in elderly patients (≥65 years) (see Precautions, Geriatrics). The dosage should be carefully and gradually adjusted depending on patient tolerability and response. Consideration can be given to beginning titration using one Isoptin SR 120 mg tablet once a day since no suitable strength of standard tablet is available.

Patients with Impaired Hepatic and Renal Function: Verapamil tablets should be administered cautiously to patients with liver or renal function impairment. The dosage should be carefully and gradually adjusted depending on patient tolerance and response. These patients should be monitored carefully for abnormal prolongation of the PR interval or other signs of overdosage. At this time, verapamil tablets should not be used in patients with severe hepatic dysfunction (see Warnings, Hepatic Insufficiency).

Supplied: 80 mg: Each round, yellow, sugar-coated tablet contains: verapamil HCl 80 mg. Nonmedicinal ingredients: acacia, calcium carbonate, carnauba wax, cellulose, cornstarch, gelatin, lactose, magnesium stearate, povidone, quinoline yellow lake, silicon dioxide, sodium carboxymethylcellulose, sucrose, talc and titanium dioxide. Bottles of 250.

120 mg: Each round, white, sugar-coated tablet contains: verapamil HCl 120 mg. Nonmedicinal ingredients: acacia, calcium carbonate, carnauba wax, cellulose, cornstarch, gelatin, lactose, magnesium stearate, povidone, silicon dioxide, sodium carboxymethylcellulose, sucrose, talc and titanium dioxide. Bottles of 250.

(Shown in Product Recognition Section)

Reviewed 1999

ISOPTIN® I.V. Ⓟ

Knoll

Verapamil HCl

Antiarrhythmic

Pharmacology: Mode of Action: The mechanism of action of verapamil is believed to be related to its specific cellular action of selectively inhibiting transmembrane influx of calcium in cardiac muscle, coronary and systemic arteries and in cells of the intracardiac conduction system.

Verapamil blocks the transmembrane influx of calcium ion through the slow channel (calcium ion antagonism) without affecting to any significant degree the transmembrane influx of sodium through the fast channel. This results in a reduction of free calcium ions available within the cells of the above tissues.

Verapamil's antiarrhythmic effects are believed to be brought about largely by its action on the sinus and atrioventricular nodes. Electrical activity in the SA and AV nodes depends, to a large extent, upon calcium influx through the slow channel. By inhibiting this influx, verapamil slows AV conduction and prolongs the effective refractory period within the AV node in a rate-related manner. This effect results in a reduction of the ventricular rate in patients with atrial flutter and/or atrial fibrillation and a rapid ventricular response.

Verapamil does not alter the normal atrial action potential or intraventricular conduction time, but depresses amplitude, velocity of depolarization and conduction in depressed atrial fibers.

By interrupting re-entry at the AV node, verapamil can restore normal sinus rhythm in patients with paroxysmal supraventricular tachycardias (PSVT), including PSVT associated with Wolff-Parkinson-White syndrome.

It has no effect on conduction across accessory bypass tracts.

The vasodilatory effect of verapamil appears to be due to its effect on blockade of calcium channels as well as α-receptors. Verapamil does not induce peripheral arterial spasm.

Verapamil has a local anesthetic action that is 1.6 times that of procaine on an equimolar basis. It is not known whether this action is important at the doses used in man.

Verapamil does not alter total serum calcium levels.

Pharmacokinetics: The onset of action of a single i.v. injection is usually 1 to 2 minutes, with peak effect occurring between 3 to 5 minutes and virtual dissipation of the hemodynamic effects between 10 to 20 minutes.

Verapamil is absorbed rapidly. From a comparison of the areas under the time concentration curves of total plasma radioactivity, following oral and i.v. administration, as well as based on cumulative urinary excretion, absorption has been calculated at 90 to 92%. The absolute bioavailability of unchanged verapamil is about 10 to 20% because of an intense first-pass metabolism.

The elimination of unchanged substance from the plasma after i.v. administration occurs with a half-life between 3.5 and 7.4 hours. Total radioactivity, however, is eliminated with a half-life of about 24 hours.

Elimination half-life may be prolonged in the elderly.

The binding of verapamil to plasma protein is about 90%. Sixty-three to 70% of a radioactive dose was eliminated in the urine after oral as well as i.v. administration and up to 16% was excreted in the feces.

In healthy men, orally administered verapamil undergoes extensive metabolism in the liver, 12 metabolites having been identified, most in only trace amounts. The chief metabolites are the primary and secondary amines and norverapamil.

Verapamil is metabolized through the cytochrome P450 system. The particular isoenzymes involved are CYP 3A4, CYP 1A2, and the CYP 2C family.

Hemodynamics: Verapamil reduces afterload and myocardial contractility. The commonly used i.v. dose of 5 to 10 mg produces transient, usually asymptomatic, reduction in normal systemic arterial pressure, systemic vascular resistance and contractility; left ventricular filling pressure is slightly increased. In most patients, including those with organic cardiac disease, the negative inotropic action of verapamil is countered by reduction of afterload, and cardiac index is usually not reduced. However, in patients with moderately severe to severe cardiac dysfunction (pulmonary wedge pressure above 20 mm Hg, ejection fraction less than 30%), acute worsening of heart failure may be seen. Peak therapeutic effects occur within 3 to 5 minutes after a bolus injection.

Indications: Rapid conversion to sinus rhythm of paroxysmal supraventricular tachycardias, including those associated with accessory bypass tracts (Wolff-Parkinson-White [W-P-W] and Lown-Ganong-Levine [L-G-L] syndromes). When clinically advisable, appropriate vagal maneuvers (e.g., Valsalva maneuver) should be attempted prior to verapamil administration.

Temporary control of rapid ventricular rate in atrial flutter or atrial fibrillation **except** when the atrial flutter and/or atrial fibrillation are associated with accessory bypass tracts (Wolff-Parkinson-White [W-P-W] and Lown-Ganong-Levine [L-G-L] syndromes).

Because a small fraction (<1%) of patients treated with verapamil respond with life-threatening adverse responses (rapid ventricular rate in atrial flutter/fibrillation and an accessory bypass tract, marked hypotension, or extreme bradycardia/asystole (see Contraindications and Warnings), the use of i.v. verapamil should, if possible, be in a treatment setting with monitoring and resuscitation facilities, including DC-cardioversion capability (see Overdose: Symptoms and Treatment). Cardioversion has been used safely and effectively after i.v. verapamil.

Contraindications: Acute myocardial infarction.

Severe congestive heart failure (unless secondary to a supraventricular tachycardia amenable to verapamil therapy).

Cardiogenic shock or severe hypotension.

Second- or third-degree AV block (except in patients with a functioning artificial ventricular pacemaker.

Sick sinus syndrome (except in patients with a functioning artificial ventricular pacemaker).

Concomitant use of injectable verapamil with beta-blockers and cardiac depressant drugs.

The use of i.v. verapamil with these drugs can produce a reduction in myocardial contractility. This myocardial depressant effect (independent of changes in heart rate) can be significant in patients with impaired left ventricular performance. On rare occasions, the concomitant administration of i.v. beta-blockers and i.v. verapamil has resulted in serious adverse reactions, especially in patients with severe cardiomyopathy, congestive heart failure or recent myocardial infarction. Accordingly, i.v. verapamil and i.v. beta adrenergic blocking drugs should not be administered in close proximity to each other (i.e., within a few hours).

Patients with atrial flutter or atrial fibrillation and an accessory bypass tract (e.g., Wolff-Parkinson-White, Lown-Ganong-Levine syndromes) are at risk to develop ventricular tachyarrhythmia including ventricular fibrillation if verapamil is administered. Therefore, the use of verapamil in these patients is contraindicated.

Ventricular Tachycardia: Administration of i.v. verapamil to patients with wide-complex ventricular tachycardia (QRS ≥0.12 sec) can result in marked hemodynamic deterioration and ventricular fibrillation. Proper pretherapy diagnosis and differentiation from wide complex supraventricular tachycardia (based on a 12 lead ECG) is imperative in the emergency room setting.

Hypersensitivity to the drug.

Warnings: Verapamil should be given as a slow i.v. injection over at least a 2 minute period of time (see Dosage).

Heart Failure: Because of the drug's negative inotropic effect, verapamil should not be used in patients with poorly compensated congestive heart failure, unless the failure is complicated by or caused by an arrhythmia. If verapamil is used in such patients, they must be digitalized prior to treatment. Continuous monitoring is mandatory when i.v. verapamil is used in digitalized patients. It has been reported that digoxin plasma levels may increase with chronic oral administration (see Warnings, Concomitant Antiarrhythmic Therapy).

Hypotension: Severe hypotension has occasionally occurred following i.v. administration of the drug. On rare occasions, this has been followed by loss of consciousness. If severe hypotension develops, verapamil should be promptly discontinued and vasoconstrictor substances used as described in Overdose: Symptoms and Treatment.

I.V. verapamil often produces a decrease in blood pressure below baseline levels that is usually transient and asymptomatic, but may result in dizziness. Administration of i.v. calcium chloride or calcium gluconate prior to i.v. administration of verapamil may prevent this hemodynamic response.

In patients using antihypertensive drugs, the additional hypotensive effect should be taken into consideration.

Ventricular Fibrillation: I.V. administration may precipitate ventricular fibrillation. Patients with atrial flutter/fibrillation and an accessory AV pathway (e.g. Wolff-Parkinson-White or Lown-Ganong-Levine syndromes) may develop increased antegrade conduction across the aberrant pathway bypassing the AV node, producing a very rapid ventricular response after receiving verapamil (or digitalis). This has been reported in 1% of the patients treated in controlled double blind trials. Treatment is usually DC cardioversion. Cardioversion has been used safely and effectively after i.v. verapamil (see Overdose: Symptoms and Treatment).

Bradycardia/Asystole: Verapamil slows conduction across the AV node and rarely may produce second or third degree AV block, bradycardia and in extreme cases, asystole. This is more likely to occur in patients with a sick sinus syndrome (SA nodal disease), which is more common in older patients (see Contraindications).

A total incidence of bradycardia (ventricular rate less than 60 beats/min) was 1.2% in controlled i.v. and oral studies. Asystole in patients other than those with sick sinus syndrome is usually of short duration (few seconds or less) with spontaneous return to AV nodal or normal sinus rhythm. If this does not occur promptly, appropriate treatment should be initiated immediately (see Overdose: Symptoms and Treatment).

Impaired Hepatic or Renal Function: Because verapamil is extensively metabolized in the liver, decreased dosage should be used in patients with hepatic insufficiency.

About 70% of an administered dose of verapamil is excreted as metabolites in the urine. Therefore, verapamil should be used cautiously in patients with impaired renal function.

Patients with impaired hepatic and/or renal function should be monitored carefully for abnormal prolongation of the PR interval or other signs of excessive pharmacologic effects.

Verapamil cannot be removed by hemodialysis.

Duchenne's Muscular Dystrophy: I.V. verapamil can precipitate respiratory muscle failure in these patients and should, therefore, be used with caution.

Increased Intracranial Pressure: I.V. verapamil has been seen to increase intracranial pressure in patients with supratentorial tumors at the time of anesthesia induction. Caution should be taken and appropriate monitoring performed.

Concomitant Antiarrhythmic Therapy: Digitalis Glycosides: I.V. verapamil has been used concomitantly with digitalis preparations without the occurrence of serious adverse effects. However, since both drugs slow AV conduction, patients should be monitored for AV block or excessive bradycardia.

Isoptin I.V. (cont'd)

Verapamil produces a significant increase in serum digoxin concentration. This effect is dose dependent and occurs with continued administration of verapamil. This phenomenon has been at least partially explained by reduced renal excretion of digoxin. As digoxin toxicity may therefore occur, the dose of digoxin may need downward adjustment in patients who are receiving verapamil concomitantly.

Lidocaine: Two deaths have been reported in patients receiving both verapamil and lidocaine i.v.

Beta-adrenergic Blockers: On rare occasions, the concomitant administration of verapamil with beta-blockers has resulted in severe adverse effects, especially in patients with severe cardiomyopathy, congestive heart failure or recent myocardial infarction (see Contraindications).

Verapamil gives no protection against the dangers of abrupt beta-blocker withdrawal; any such withdrawal should be by gradual reduction of the dose of beta-blocker.

Disopyramide: Until data on possible interactions between disopyramide and verapamil are available, disopyramide should not be administered within 48 hours before or 24 hours after verapamil.

Procainamide: I.V. verapamil has been administered to a small number of patients receiving oral procainamide without the occurrence of serious adverse effects.

Quinidine: I.V. verapamil has been administered to a small number of patients receiving oral quinidine without the occurrence of serious adverse effects. However, several patients have been described in whom the combination resulted in an exaggerated hypotensive response presumably from the combined ability of both drugs to antagonize the effects of catecholamines on α-adrenergic receptors. Caution should therefore be used when employing this combination of drugs.

Flecainide: A study in healthy volunteers showed that the concomitant administration of flecainide and verapamil have additive effects on myocardial contractility, AV conduction, and repolarization. Concomitant therapy with flecainide and verapamil may result in an additive negative inotropic effect and prolongation of atrioventricular conduction.

Precautions: Sick Sinus Syndrome: Precaution should be taken when treating any supraventricular arrhythmia on an emergency basis as it may be caused by an undiagnosed sick sinus syndrome (see Contraindications and Warnings).

Heart Block: Development of second or third degree AV block or unifascicular, bifascicular or trifascicular bundle branch block requires reduction in subsequent doses or discontinuation of verapamil and institution of appropriate therapy, if needed (see Overdose: Symptoms and Treatment).

Premature Ventricular Contractions: During conversion to normal sinus rhythm, or marked reduction in ventricular rate, a few benign complexes of unusual appearance (sometimes resembling premature ventricular contractions) may be seen after treatment with verapamil. Similar complexes are seen during spontaneous conversion of supraventricular tachycardias, after DC cardioversion and other pharmacologic therapy. These complexes appear to have no clinical significance.

Pregnancy: Teratology and reproduction studies in animals have not revealed any evidence of impaired fertility or teratogenic potential. There are no studies in pregnant women. In all patients of childbearing potential, anticipated benefits must be weighed against possible hazards.

Preliminary studies have shown that unchanged drug crosses the placental barrier.

Labor and Delivery: There have been few controlled studies to determine whether the use of verapamil during labor or delivery has immediate or delayed adverse effects on the fetus, or whether it prolongs the duration of labor or increases the need for forceps delivery or other obstetric intervention. Such adverse experiences have not been reported in the literature, despite a long history of use of i.v. verapamil in Europe in the treatment of cardiac side effects of beta-adrenergic agonist agents used to treat premature labor.

Lactation: Verapamil crosses the placental barrier and can be detected in umbilical vein blood at delivery. Also, verapamil is excreted in human milk. Because of the potential for adverse reactions in nursing infants from verapamil, nursing should be discontinued while verapamil is administered.

Children: Controlled studies with verapamil have not been conducted in pediatric patients, but uncontrolled experience with i.v. administration in more than 250 patients, about half under 12 months of age and about 25% newborn, indicates that results of treatment are similar to those in adults. In rare instances, however, severe hemodynamic side effects — some of them fatal — have occurred following the i.v. administration of verapamil in neonates and infants. Caution should therefore be used when administering verapamil to this group of pediatric patients.

Drug Interactions: As with all drugs, care should be exercised when treating patients with multiple medications. Calcium channel blockers undergo biotransformation by the cytochrome P450 system. Coadministration of verapamil with other drugs which follow the same route of biotransformation may result in altered bioavailability of verapamil or these drugs. Dosages of similarly metabolized drugs, particularly those of low therapeutic ratio, and especially in patients with renal and/or hepatic impairment, may require adjustment when starting or stopping concomitantly administered verapamil to maintain optimum therapeutic blood levels.

Drugs known to be inhibitors of the cytochrome P450 system include: azole antifungals, cimetidine, cyclosporine, erythromycin, quinidine, terfenadine, warfarin.

Drugs known to be inducers of the cytochrome P450 system include: phenobarbital, phenytoin, rifampin.

Drugs known to be biotransformed via P450 include: benzodiazepines, flecainide, imipramine, propafenone, theophylline.

Alpha-adrenergic Blockers: Concomitant use of verapamil with α-adrenergic blockers may result in an exaggerated hypotensive response.

Antineoplastic Agents: Verapamil inhibits P-glycoprotein mediated transport of antineoplastic agents out of tumor cells, resulting in their decreased metabolic clearance. Dosage adjustments of antineoplastic agents should be considered when verapamil is administered concomitantly.

ASA: Potential adverse reactions in terms of bleeding due to synergistic antiplatelet effects of the two agents should be taken into consideration in patients taking verapamil and ASA concomitantly.

Carbamazepine: Verapamil therapy may increase carbamazepine concentrations during combined therapy. This may produce carbamazepine side effects such as diplopia, headache, ataxia or dizziness.

Cimetidine: The interaction between cimetidine and chronically administered verapamil has not been studied. In acute studies of healthy volunteers, clearance of verapamil was either reduced or unchanged.

Concomitant Antiarrhythmic Therapy: See Warnings.

Cyclosporine: Verapamil therapy may increase serum levels of cyclosporine.

Dantrolene: Two animal studies suggest concomitant i.v. use of verapamil and dantrolene sodium may result in cardiovascular collapse. There has also been one report of hyperkalemia and myocardial depression following the coadministration of oral verapamil and i.v. dantrolene.

Inhalation Anesthetics: Animal experiments have shown that inhalation anesthetics depress cardiovascular activity by decreasing the inward movement of calcium ions. When used concomitantly, inhalation anesthetics and calcium antagonists (such as verapamil) should be titrated carefully to avoid excessive cardiovascular depression.

Lithium: Increased sensitivity to the effects of lithium (neurotoxicity) has been reported during concomitant verapamil-lithium therapy with either no change or an increase in serum lithium levels. The addition of verapamil, however, has also resulted in the lowering of serum lithium levels in patients receiving chronic stable oral lithium. Patients receiving both drugs must be monitored carefully.

Neuromuscular Blocking Agents: Clinical data and animal studies suggest that verapamil may potentiate the activity of depolarizing and nondepolarizing neuromuscular blocking agents. It may be necessary to decrease the dose of verapamil and/or the dose of the neuromuscular blocking agent when the drugs are used concomitantly.

Phenobarbital: Phenobarbital therapy may increase verapamil clearance.

Plasma Bound Drugs: As verapamil is highly bound to plasma proteins, it should be administered with caution to patients receiving other highly protein bound drugs.

Rifampin: Therapy with rifampin may markedly reduce oral verapamil bioavailability.

Adverse Effects: The incidence of all adverse reactions, including those seen with both the oral and i.v. use of verapamil is about 10.6% with 6.7% associated with oral administration. Approximately 1.4% of these patients required discontinuation of the drug because of side effects. The most common adverse effect seen with oral verapamil is constipation, while hypotension and bradycardia are most common with its i.v. use.

In rare cases of hypersensitive patients, broncholaryngeal spasm accompanied by itch and urticaria have been reported.

Isolated cases of angioedema have been reported. Angioedema may be accompanied by breathing difficulty. One case of anaphylactic shock following i.v. verapamil has also been reported.

The following adverse reactions were reported with i.v. verapamil use in controlled clinical trials involving 324 patients:

Cardiovascular: symptomatic hypotension (1.5%); bradycardia (1.2%); severe tachycardia (1%). The worldwide experience in open clinical trials in more than 7 900 patients was similar.

CNS: dizziness (1.2%); headache (1.2%). Occasional cases of seizures during verapamil injection have been reported.

Gastrointestinal: nausea (0.9%); abdominal discomfort (0.6%).

Respiratory: In rare cases of hypersensitive patients, bronchо-laryngeal spasm accompanied by itch and urticaria have been reported.

Miscellaneous: The following reactions were reported at low frequency: Skin reactions, exanthema, urticaria, pruritus, muscular cramps, arthralgia, emotional depression, confusion, rotary nystagmus, diplopia, impaired vision, sleepiness, insomnia, muscle fatigue, diaphoresis, painful coldness and numbness in the extremities, paresthesia, hyperkinesia, impotence.

Overdose: Symptoms and Treatment: Hypotension occurs, varying from transient to severe. Conduction disturbances seen included: prolongation of AV conduction time, AV dissociation, nodal rhythm, ventricular fibrillation and ventricular asystole.

Treatment of overdosage should be supportive and individualized (see Table I). Beta-adrenergic stimulation and/or parenteral administration of calcium solutions (calcium chloride or calcium gluconate) may increase calcium ion flux across the slow channel. These pharmacologic interventions have been effectively used in treatment of deliberate overdosage with oral verapamil.

Clinically significant hypotensive reactions should be treated with vasopressor agents.

AV block should be treated with atropine and cardiac pacing. Asystole should be handled by the usual measures including isoproterenol hydrochloride, other vasopressor agents, or cardiopulmonary resuscitation.

Verapamil cannot be removed by hemodialysis.

Actual treatment and dosage should depend on the severity of the clinical situation and the judgment and experience of the treating physician.

Dosage: Verapamil should be given as a slow i.v. injection over at least a 2 minute period of time, in hospital, where

Table I—Isoptin I.V.

Suggested Treatment of Acute Cardiovascular Adverse Reactions

Adverse Reaction	Proven Effective Treatment	Supportive Treatment
Hypotension requiring treatment	Calcium chloride (i.v.) Norepinephrine bitartrate (i.v.) Metaraminol bitartrate (i.v.) Isoproterenol HCl (i.v.) Dopamine (i.v.)	I.V. fluids Trendelenburg position
Bradycardia, AV block, Asystole	Isoproterenol HCl (i.v.) Calcium chloride (i.v.) Cardiac pacing Norepinephrine bitartrate (i.v.) Atropine (i.v.)	I.V. fluids (slow drip)
Rapid ventricular rate (due to antegrade conduction in flutter/fibrillation with W-P-W or L-G-L syndromes)	DC cardioversion (high energy may be required) Procainamide (i.v.) Lidocaine HCl (i.v.)	I.V. fluids (slow drip)

coronary care facilities are available and continuous ECG and blood pressure monitoring are performed.

Verapamil injection should be inspected visually for particulate matter and discoloration prior to administration.

Admixing verapamil with albumin, amphotericin B, hydralazine HCl and trimethoprim with sulfamethoxazole should be avoided. Verapamil will precipitate in any solution with a pH above 6.

The dosage regimen for verapamil should be individualized for each patient based on response and tolerance. Injections should be continued only to the point where therapeutic effect has been achieved, at which point the i.v. infusion may be terminated, i.e., before the total recommended dose has been administered. Its i.v. use may be accompanied by a hypotensive response which can be precipitous, by a rapid ventricular rate, extreme bradycardia, or asystole.

An i.v. preparation of calcium chloride or calcium gluconate should be available in the event of any adverse hemodynamic phenomenon. Concomitant use of beta-blockers is contraindicated.

The recommended i.v. doses are as follows: Adults: Initial dose: 5 to 10 mg (0.075 to 0.15 mg/kg body weight) given as an i.v. bolus over at least 2 minutes.

Repeat Dose: 10 mg (0.15 mg/kg body weight) 30 minutes after the first dose if the initial response is not adequate. An optimal interval for subsequent i.v. doses has not been determined, and should be individualized for each patient.

Older Patients: The dose should be administered over at least 3 minutes to minimize the risk of untoward drug effects.

Children: Initial Dose: 0 to 1 year: 0.1 to 0.2 mg/kg body weight (usual single dose range 0.75 to 2 mg) should be administered as an i.v. bolus over at least 2 minutes under continuous ECG monitoring.

1 to 15 years: 0.1 to 0.3 mg/kg body weight (usual single dose range 2 to 5 mg) should be administered as an i.v. bolus over at least 2 minutes. Do not exceed 5 mg.

Repeat Dose: 0 to 1 year: 0.1 to 0.2 mg/kg body weight (usual single dose range 0.75 to 2 mg) 30 minutes after the first dose if the initial response is not adequate (under continuous ECG monitoring). An optimal interval for subsequent doses has not been determined and should be individualized for each patient.

1 to 15 years: 0.1 to 0.3 mg/kg body weight (usual single dose range 2 to 5 mg) 30 minutes after the first dose if the initial response is not adequate. An optimal interval for subsequent doses has not been determined and should be individualized for each patient.

Do not exceed 10 mg as a single dose.

Oral treatment should replace i.v. therapy as soon as possible, when the physician wishes to continue treatment with verapamil. Duration of treatment will depend on the underlying cause and history of recurrence.

Stability: Isoptin injection is physically compatible and chemically stable for at least 24 hours at 25°C protected from light in the following large volume parenteral solutions in glass, polyvinyl chloride and polyolefin containers at a nominal concentration of 40 mg/L: 5% Dextrose, 0.9% Sodium Chloride, Ringer's, Ringer's Lactate and combinations thereof.

Supplied: Each mL of sterile, clear, colorless aqueous solution, contains: verapamil HCl 2.5 mg and sodium chloride 8.5 mg. pH adjusted with hydrochloric acid and/or sodium hydroxide. Preservative-free. Clear glass ampuls of 2 mL. Clear glass, single use vials of 2 and 4 mL. Packages of 10. Store between 15 and 30°C. Do not freeze. Protect from light. Do not use beyond the expiry date indicated on the label.

Reviewed 1999

ISOPTIN® SR Ⓟ

Knoll

Verapamil HCl

Antihypertensive Agent

Pharmacology: Verapamil is a calcium ion influx inhibitor (calcium entry blocker or calcium ion antagonist) that exerts its pharmacological effects by modulating the influx of ionic calcium across the cell membrane of the arterial smooth muscle as well as in conducting and contractile myocardial cells.

Verapamil exerts antihypertensive effects by inducing vasodilation and reducing peripheral vascular resistance usually without reflex tachycardia. Verapamil does not blunt hemodynamic response to isometric or dynamic exercise.

Verapamil depresses AV nodal conduction and prolongs functional refractory periods. Verapamil does not alter the normal atrial action potential or intraventricular conduction time, but depresses amplitude, velocity of depolarization and conduction in depressed atrial fibres.

Verapamil may shorten the antegrade effective refractory period of the accessory bypass tract. Acceleration of ventricular rate and/or ventricular fibrillation has been reported in patients with atrial flutter or atrial fibrillation and a coexisting accessory AV pathway following administration of verapamil (see Warnings, Conduction Disturbance). Verapamil has a local anesthetic action that is 1.6 times that of procaine on an equimolar basis.

Verapamil is a potent smooth muscle relaxant with vasodilatory properties, as well as a depressant of myocardial contractility, and these effects are largely independent of autonomic influences.

Compared to baseline, verapamil does not affect electrolytes, glucose, and creatinine. The hypotensive effect of verapamil is not blunted by an increase in sodium intake.

In hypertensive normolipidemic patients, verapamil had no effects on plasma lipoprotein fractions.

Pharmacodynamics: In a study in 5 healthy males, the S enantiomer was found to be 8 to 20 times more active than the R enantiomer in slowing AV conduction. In another study using septal strips isolated from the left ventricle of 5 patients with mitral disease, the S enantiomer was 8 times more potent than the R enantiomer in reducing myocardial contractility.

Pharmacokinetics: Isoptin SR is a racemic mixture consisting of equal portions of the R enantiomer and the S enantiomer. More than 90% of the orally administered dose of Isoptin SR is absorbed. Upon oral administration, there is rapid stereoselective biotransformation during the first pass of verapamil through the portal circulation. The systemic concentrations of R and S enantiomers are dependent upon the route and the rate of administration and the rate and extent of release from the dosage forms.

The following bioavailability information was obtained from healthy volunteers and not from the populations most likely to be treated with verapamil.

In a study in 5 healthy volunteers with oral immediate-release verapamil, the systemic bioavailability varied from 33 to 65% for the R enantiomer and from 13 to 34% for the S enantiomer. The S enantiomer is pharmacologically more active than the R enantiomer (see Pharmacodynamics).

There is a nonlinear correlation between the verapamil dose administered and verapamil plasma levels. In early dose titration with verapamil, a relationship exists between total verapamil (R and S combined) plasma concentration and prolongation of the PR interval. The mean elimination half-life in single-dose studies of immediate release verapamil ranged from 2.8 to 7.4 hours. In these same studies, after steady-state was reached, the half-life increased to a range from 4.5 to 12 hours (after less than 10 consecutive doses given 6 hours apart). Half-life of verapamil may increase during titration. Aging decreases the clearance and elimination of verapamil.

In a randomized, multiple-dose study in 44 healthy young subjects, administration of Isoptin SR 240 mg with food produced peak plasma concentrations at approximately 8 hours postdose of 188 and 76 ng/mL and AUC's (0 to 24 hours) of 2 553 and 1 046 ng•h/mL for the R and S enantiomers, respectively. Similar results were demonstrated for plasma norverapamil.

In healthy men, orally administered verapamil undergoes extensive metabolism by the cytochrome P450 system in the liver. The particular isoenzymes involved are CYP3A4, CYP1A2, and CYP2C family. Thirteen metabolites have been identified in urine. Norverapamil can reach steady-state plasma concentrations approximately equal to those of verapamil itself. The cardiovascular activity of norverapamil appears to be approximately 20% that of verapamil. Approximately 70% of an administered dose is excreted as metabolites in the urine and 16% or more in the feces within 5 days. About 3 to 4% is excreted in the urine as unchanged drug. R-verapamil is 94% bound to plasma albumin, while S-verapamil is 88% bound. In addition, R-verapamil is 92% and S-verapamil 86% bound to alpha-1 acid glycoprotein. The degree of biotransformation during the first pass of verapamil may vary according to the status of the liver in different patient populations. In patients with hepatic insufficiency, metabolism is delayed and elimination half-life prolonged up to 14 to 16 hours (see Warnings, Hepatic Insufficiency and Dosage).

Verapamil crosses the placental barrier and can be detected in umbilical vein blood at delivery. Verapamil is excreted in human milk.

A study was conducted in which 240 mg single oral doses of Isoptin Standard Release (fasting) and Isoptin Sustained Release (fed) tablets were given to 12 young, healthy males (19 to 37 years old) in a randomized, crossover (7-day washout) study. Serial blood samples for drug determination were taken over a 48 hour period. The pharmacokinetic data from this study is summarized in Table I.

Table I—Isoptin SR

Pharmacokinetic Data

Parameters	Isoptin Standard Release Tablet (240 mg)		Isoptin Sustained Release Tablet (240 mg)	
	R-verapamil	S-verapamil	R-verapamil	S-verapamil
C_{max}, ng/mL	258	59.0	60.1	11.3
T_{max}, h	1.46	1.58	10.8	11.8
AUC_{0-48}, ng/mL/h	1 250	261	918	150

The steady-state pharmacokinetic data from a study in which 11 volunteers were treated with the sustained release formulation twice daily at 12 hourly intervals and with the standard release formulation 3 times daily at 8 hourly intervals for 5 days is summarized in the Table II.

Table II—Isoptin SR

Pharmacokinetic Data

Parameters	Standard Release 120 mg Tablet[b] (360 mg daily)	Sustained Release 240 mg Tablet[b] (360 mg daily)	Sustained Release 240 mg Tablet[a] (480 mg daily)
C_{max} (ng/mL)	289.4	250.5	298.4
C_{min} (ng/mL)	80.1	110.7	152.0
T_{max} (h)	1.4	4.5	4.4
$T_{1/2}$ (h)	6.1	8.2	8.7
$AUC_{0-\infty}$ (ng/mL/h)	1 850	3 466	4 484
AUC_{0-36} (ng/mL/h)	1 809	3 154	4 116

[a] last dose=240 mg.
[b] last dose=120 mg.

The data have been calculated from samples taken at frequent intervals for 36 hours after the last dose.

Influence of Food: Administration of Isoptin SR with food results in marked prolongation of T_{max} (45 to 75%) and slight decreases in C_{max} (about 15%) and AUC (1 to 8%). Food thus produces a slight decrease in bioavailability (AUC), but a narrower peak-to-trough ratio.

Indications: In the treatment of mild to moderate essential hypertension. Verapamil should normally be used in those patients in whom treatment with diuretics or beta-blockers has been associated with unacceptable adverse effects.

Verapamil can be tried as an initial agent in those patients in whom the use of diuretics and/or beta-blockers is contraindicated or in patients with medical conditions in which these drugs frequently cause serious adverse effects.

Concomitant use of verapamil with a diuretic or an angiotensin converting enzyme inhibitor has been shown to be compatible and to have additive blood pressure lowering effects.

Verapamil should not be used concurrently with beta adrenoreceptor blockers in the treatment of hypertension (see Precautions, Drug Interactions).

Safety of concurrent use of verapamil with other antihypertensive agents has not been established and such use cannot be recommended at this time.

Contraindications: Complicated myocardial infarction (patients who have ventricular failure manifested by pulmonary congestion). Severe congestive heart failure and/or severe left ventricular dysfunction (i.e. ejection fraction <40%), unless secondary to a supraventricular tachycardia amenable to oral verapamil therapy. Cardiogenic shock. Severe hypotension. Second- or third-degree AV block. Sick Sinus syndrome (see Warnings). Marked bradycardia. Hypersensitivity to the drug. Patients with atrial flutter or atrial fibrillation and an accessory bypass tract (e.g., Wolff-Parkinson-White, Lown-Ganong-Levine syndromes) (see Warnings).

Warnings: General: In patients with angina or arrhythmias using antihypertensive drugs, the additional hypotensive effect of verapamil should be taken into consideration.

Heart Failure: Because of the drug's negative inotropic effect, verapamil should not be used in patients with poorly compensated congestive heart failure, unless the failure is complicated by or caused by a dysrhythmia. If verapamil is used in such patients, they must be digitalized prior to treatment.

It has been reported that digoxin plasma levels may increase with chronic verapamil administration (see Precautions, Drug

Isoptin SR (cont'd)

Interactions, Digoxin). The use of verapamil in the treatment of hypertension is not recommended in patients with heart failure caused by systolic dysfunction.

Hypotension: Hypotensive symptoms of lethargy and weakness with faintness have been reported following single oral doses and even after some months of treatment. In some patients it may be necessary to reduce the dose.

Conduction Disturbance: Verapamil slows conduction across the AV node and rarely may produce second or third degree AV block, bradycardia and in extreme cases, asystole.

Verapamil causes dose-related suppression of the SA node. In some patients, sinus bradycardia may occur, especially in patients with a sick sinus syndrome (SA nodal disease), which is more common in older patients (see Contraindications).

Bradycardia: The total incidence of bradycardia (ventricular rate less than 50 beats/min) was 1.4% in controlled studies. Asystole in patients other than those with sick sinus syndrome is usually of short duration (few seconds or less), with spontaneous return to AV nodal or normal sinus rhythm. If this does not occur promptly, appropriate treatment should be initiated immediately (see Overdose: Symptoms and Treatment).

Accessory Bypass Tract (Wolff-Parkinson-White or Lown-Ganong-Levine): Verapamil may result in significant acceleration of ventricular response during atrial fibrillation or atrial flutter in the Wolff-Parkinson-White (WPW) or Lown-Ganong-Levine syndromes after receiving i.v. verapamil. Although a risk of this occurring with oral verapamil has not been established, such patients receiving oral verapamil may be at risk and its use in these patients is contraindicated (see Contraindications).

Concomitant Use with Beta-blockers: Generally, oral verapamil should not be given to patients receiving beta-blockers since the depressant effects on myocardial contractility, heart rate and AV conduction may be additive. However, in exceptional cases when in the opinion of the physician concomitant use in angina and arrhythmias is considered essential, such use should be instituted gradually under careful supervision. If combined therapy is used, close surveillance of vital signs and clinical status should be carried out and the need for continued concomitant treatment periodically assessed.

Verapamil gives no protection against the dangers of abrupt beta-blocker withdrawal and such withdrawal should be done by the gradual reduction of the dose of beta-blocker. Then verapamil may be started with the usual dose.

Patients with Hypertrophic Cardiomyopathy: In 120 patients with hypertrophic cardiomyopathy who received therapy with verapamil at doses up to 720 mg/day, a variety of serious adverse effects was seen. Three patients died in pulmonary edema; all had severe left ventricular outflow obstruction and a past history of left ventricular dysfunction. Eight other patients had pulmonary edema and/or severe hypotension, abnormally high (greater than 20 mm Hg) pulmonary wedge pressure and a marked left ventricular outflow obstruction were present in most of these patients. Concomitant administration of quinidine (see Precautions, Drug Interactions) preceded the severe hypotension in 3 of the 8 patients (2 of whom developed pulmonary edema). Sinus bradycardia occurred in 11% of the patients, second degree AV block in 4%, and sinus arrest in 2%. It must be appreciated that this group of patients had a serious disease with a high mortality rate. Most adverse effects responded well to dose reduction, but in some cases, verapamil use had to be discontinued.

Elevated Liver Enzymes: Elevation of transaminase with and without concomitant elevations in alkaline phosphatase and bilirubin have been reported. Several published cases of hepatocellular injury produced by verapamil have been proven by rechallenge. Clinical symptoms of malaise, fever, and/or right upper quadrant pain, in addition to elevation of AST, ALT and alkaline phosphatase have been reported. Periodic monitoring of liver function in patients receiving verapamil is therefore prudent.

Hepatic Insufficiency: Because verapamil is extensively metabolized by the liver, it should be administered cautiously to patients with impaired hepatic function, since the elimination half-life of verapamil in these patients is prolonged 4-fold (from 3.7 to 14.2 hours). A decreased dosage should be used in patients with hepatic insufficiency and careful monitoring for abnormal prolongation of the PR interval or other signs of excessive pharmacologic effect should be carried out (see Pharmacology, Pharmacokinetics and Dosage).

Renal Insufficiency: About 70% of an administered dose of verapamil is excreted as metabolites in the urine. In one study in healthy volunteers, the total body clearance after i.v. administration of verapamil was 12.08 mL/min/kg, while in patients with advanced renal disease it was reduced to 5.33 mL/min/kg. This pharmacokinetic finding suggests that renal clearance of verapamil in patients with renal disease is decreased. In 2 studies with oral verapamil no difference in pharmacokinetics could be demonstrated. Therefore, until further data are available, verapamil should be used with caution in patients with impaired renal function. These patients should be carefully monitored for abnormal prolongation of the PR interval or other signs of excessive pharmacologic effect (see Dosage).

Precautions: Atypical lens changes and cataracts were observed in beagle dog studies at high doses. This has been concluded to be species-specific for the beagle dog. (These ophthalmological changes were not seen in a second study). No similar changes have been observed in long-term prospective human ophthalmological trials.

Verapamil does not alter total serum calcium levels. However, one report suggested that calcium levels above the normal range may decrease the therapeutic effect of verapamil.

Patients with Attenuated (Decreased) Neuromuscular Transmission: It has been reported that verapamil decreases neuromuscular transmission in patients with Duchenne's muscular dystrophy, and that verapamil prolongs recovery from the neuromuscular blocking agent vecuronium. It may be necessary to decrease the dosage of verapamil when it is administered to patients with attenuated neuromuscular transmission.

Geriatrics: Caution should be exercised when verapamil is administered to elderly patients (≥65 years) especially those prone to developing hypotension or those with a history of cerebrovascular insufficiency (see Dosage and Pharmacology, Pharmacokinetics). The incidence of adverse reactions is approximately 4% higher in the elderly. The adverse reactions occurring more frequently include dizziness and constipation. Serious adverse events associated with heart block have occurred in the elderly.

Pregnancy: Teratology and reproduction studies have been performed in rabbits and rats at oral doses up to 1.5 (15 mg/kg/day) and 6 (60 mg/kg/day) times the human oral daily dose, respectively, and have revealed no evidence of teratogenicity or impaired fertility. In rat, however, this multiple of the human dose was embryocidal and retarded fetal growth and development, probably because of adverse maternal effects reflected in reduced weight gains of the dams. This oral dose has also been shown to cause hypotension in rats.

There are no studies in pregnant women. However, verapamil crosses the placental barrier and can be detected in umbilical vein blood at delivery. Verapamil is not recommended for use in pregnant women unless the potential benefits outweigh potential risks to mother and fetus.

Labor and Delivery: It is not known whether the use of verapamil during labor or delivery has immediate or delayed adverse effects on the fetus, or whether it prolongs the duration of labor or inceases the need for forceps delivery or other obstetric intervention.

Lactation: Verapamil is excreted in human milk. Because of the potential for adverse reactions in nursing infants from verapamil, nursing should be discontinued while verapamil is administered.

Children: The safety and dosage regimen of verapamil in children has not yet been established.

Drug Interactions: As with all drugs, care should be exercised when treating patients with multiple medications. Calcium channel blockers undergo biotransformation by the cytochrome P450 system. Coadministration of verapamil with other drugs which follow the same route of biotransformation may result in altered bioavailability of verapamil or these drugs. Dosages of similarly metabolized drugs, particularly those of low therapeutic ratio, and especially in patients with renal and/or hepatic impairment, may require adjustment when starting or stopping concomitantly administered verapamil to maintain optimum therapeutic blood levels.

Drugs known to be inhibitors of the cytochrome P450 system include: azole antifungals, cimetidine, cyclosporine, erythromycin, quinidine, terfenadine, warfarin.

Drugs known to be inducers of the cytochrome P450 system include: phenobarbital, phenytoin, rifampin.

Drugs known to be biotransformed via P450 include: benzodiazepines, flecainide, imipramine, propafenone, theophylline.

Alcohol: Verapamil may increase blood alcohol concentrations and prolong its effects.

Antineoplastic Agents: Verapamil inhibits P-glycoprotein mediated transport of antineoplastic agents out of tumor cells, resulting in their decreased metabolic clearance. Dosage adjustments of antineoplastic agents should be considered when verapamil is administered concomitantly.

Antihypertensive Agents: Verapamil administered concomitantly with antihypertensive agents such as vasodilators, ACE inhibitors, and diuretics may have an additive effect on lowering blood pressure. In patients with angina or arrhythmias using antihypertensive drugs, this additional hypotensive effect should be taken into consideration. Verapamil should not be combined with beta-blockers for the treatment of hypertension. Concomitant use of verapamil and alpha-adrenoceptor blockers may result in excessive fall in blood pressure in some patients as observed in one study following the concomitant administration of verapamil and prazosin.

ASA: Potential adverse reactions in terms of bleeding due to synergistic antiplatelet effects of the two agents should be taken into consideration in patients taking ASA and verapamil concomitantly.

Beta-Adrenergic Blockers: The concomitant administration of verapamil with beta-blockers can result in severe adverse effects (see Warnings).

Carbamazepine: The concomitant oral administration of verapamil and carbamazepine may potentiate the effects of carbamazepine neurotoxicity. Symptoms include nausea, diplopia, headache, ataxia or dizziness.

Cimetidine: Two clinical trials have shown a lack of significant verapamil interaction with cimetidine. A third study showed cimetidine reduced verapamil clearance and increased elimination half-life.

Cyclosporine: Verapamil therapy may increase serum levels of cyclosporine.

Digoxin: Verapamil treatment increases serum digoxin levels by 50 to 75% during the first week of therapy, and this can result in digitalis toxicity. In patients with hepatic cirrhosis the influence of verapamil on digoxin kinetics is magnified. Verapamil may reduce total body clearance and extrarenal clearance of digitoxin by 27 and 29% respectively. Maintenance and digitalization doses should be reduced when verapamil is administered and the patient should be reassessed to avoid over- or underdigitalization. Whenever overdigitalization is suspected, the daily dose of digitalis should be reduced or temporarily discontinued. On discontinuation of verapamil use, the patient should be reassessed to avoid underdigitalization.

Disopyramide: Until data on possible interactions between verapamil and disopyramide are obtained, disopyramide should not be administered within 48 hours before or 24 hours after verapamil administration.

Flecainide: A study in healthy volunteers showed that the concomitant administration of flecainide and verapamil may have additive effects on myocardial contractility, AV conduction, and repolarization. Concomitant therapy with flecainide and verapamil may result in additive negative inotropic effect and prolongation of atrioventricular conduction.

Inhalation Anesthetics: When used concomitantly, inhalation anesthetics and calcium antagonists, such as verapamil, should be titrated carefully because additive hemodynamic depressive effects have been observed.

Lithium: Increased sensitivity to the effects of lithium (neurotoxicity) has been reported during concomitant verapamil-lithium therapy with either no change or an increase in serum lithium levels. However, the addition of verapamil has also resulted in the lowering of serum lithium levels in patients receiving chronic stable oral lithium. Patients receiving both drugs must be monitored carefully.

Neuromuscular Blocking Agents: Clinical data and animal studies suggest that verapamil may potentiate the activity of neuromuscular blocking agents (curare-like and depolarizing). It may be necessary to decrease the dose of verapamil and/or the dose of the neuromuscular blocking agent when the drugs are used concomitantly.

Nitrates, Diuretics: No cardiovascular adverse effects have been attributed to any interaction between these agents and verapamil.

Phenobarbital: Phenobarbital therapy may increase verapamil clearance.

Quinidine: In a small number of patients with hypertrophic cardiomyopathy, concomitant use of verapamil and quinidine resulted in significant hypotension. Until further data are obtained combined therapy of verapamil and quinidine in patients with hypertrophic cardiomyopathy should probably be avoided. The electrophysiologic effects of quinidine and verapamil on AV conduction were studied in 8 patients. Verapamil significantly counteracted the effects of quinidine on AV conduction. There has been a report of increased quinidine levels during verapamil therapy.

Rifampin: Therapy with rifampin may markedly reduce oral verapamil bioavailability.

Sulfinpyrazone: Increased clearance and decreased bioavailability of verapamil may occur.

Theophylline: Verapamil may inhibit the clearance and increase the plasma levels of theophylline.

Adverse Effects: In 4 826 patients treated with Isoptin immediate release tablets for arrhythmias, angina or hypertension, the overall adverse reaction rate in these patients was 37.1% and the dropout rate was 10.2%. The majority of these patients were seriously ill and treated under emergency drug regulations.

In controlled pivotal studies with 128 patients treated with Isoptin SR tablets for hypertension the overall adverse reaction rate was 21.7% and the dropout rate was 3.9%.

The most common adverse reactions were: constipation (7.3%), dizziness (3.2%), and nausea (2.7%). In hypertension studies, constipation occurred in 18.5% of patients on Isoptin and 4.7% of patients on Isoptin SR.

The most serious adverse reactions reported with verapamil are heart failure (1.8%), hypotension (2.5%), AV block (1.2%) and rapid ventricular response (see Warnings).

The following adverse reactions divided by body system have been reported in clinical trials or marketing experience. When incidences are shown, they are calculated based on the 4 954 (4 826+128) patient base.

Cardiovascular: hypotension 2.5%; edema 2.1%; CHF/pulmonary edema 1.9%; bradycardia 1.4%; AV block, total (1°, 2°, 3°) 1.2%, 2° and 3° 0.8%.

CNS: dizziness 3.2%, headache 2.2%, fatigue 1.7%.

Gastrointestinal: constipation 7.3%, nausea 2.7%.

The following reactions were reported in 1% or less of patients: Cardiovascular: flushing, angina pectoris, atrioventricular dissociation, chest pain, claudication, myocardial infarction, palpitations, purpura, syncope, severe tachycardia, developing or worsening of heart failure, development of rhythm disturbances, ventricular dysrhythmias, painful coldness and numbness of extremities.

CNS: cerebrovascular accident, confusion, equilibrium disorders, insomnia, muscle cramps, paresthesia, psychotic symptoms, shakiness, somnolence, excitation, depression, rotary nystagmus, vertigo, tremor, extrapyramidal disorders, muscle fatigue, hyperkinesis.

Gastrointestinal: diarrhea, dry mouth, gastrointestinal distress, gingival hyperplasia, vomiting.

Respiratory: dyspnea, bronchospasm.

Urogenital: gynecomastia, increased frequency of urination, spotty menstruation, oligomenorrhea, impotence.

Hematologic and Lymphatic: ecchymosis or bruising.

Skin: arthralgia and rash, exanthema, hair loss, hyperkeratosis, macules, sweating, urticaria, Stevens-Johnson syndrome, erythema multiforme, pruritus.

Special Senses: blurred vision, diplopia.

Hepatotoxicity with elevated enzymes (AST, ALT, alkaline phosphatase) and bilirubin levels, jaundice and associated symptoms of hepatitis with cholestasis have been reported (see Warnings).

Isolated cases of angioedema have been reported. Angioedema may be accompanied by breathing difficulty.

In clinical trials related to the control of ventricular response in digitalized patients who had atrial fibrillation or flutter, ventricular rates below 50 at rest occurred in 15% of patients and asymptomatic hypotension occurred in 5% of patients.

Overdose: Symptoms: Based on reports of intentional overdosage of verapamil, the following symptoms have been observed. Hypotension occurs, varying from transient to severe. Conduction disturbances seen included: prolongation of AV conduction time, AV dissociation, nodal rhythm, ventricular fibrillation and ventricular asystole.

Treatment: Treatment of overdosage should be supportive. Gastric lavage should be undertaken, even later than 12 hours after ingestion, if no gastrointestinal motility is present. Beta-adrenergic stimulation or parenteral administration of calcium solutions may increase calcium ion influx across the slow channel.

These pharmacologic interventions have been effectively used in treatment of overdosage with verapamil. Clinically significant hypotensive reactions should be treated with vasopressor agents. AV block is treated with atropine and cardiac pacing. Asystole should be handled by the usual Advanced Cardiac Life Support measures including the use of vasopressor agents, e.g. isoproterenol HCl. Verapamil is not removed by hemodialysis.

In case of overdosage with large amounts of Isoptin SR, it should be noted that the release of the active drug and the absorption in the intestine may take more than 48 hours. Depending on the time of ingestion, incompletely dissolved tablets may be present along the entire length of the gastrointestinal tract which function as active drug depots. Extensive elimination measures are indicated, such as induced vomiting, removal of the contents of the stomach and the small intestine under endoscopy, intestinal lavage and high enemas.

Table III—Isoptin SR

Suggested Treatment of Acute Cardiovascular Adverse Effects

Adverse Reaction	Proven Effective Treatment	Treatment with Good Theoretical Rationale	Supportive Treatment
Shock, cardiac failure, severe hypotension	Calcium salt, e.g., calcium gluconate i.v. Metaraminol bitartrate i.v.*	Dopamine HCl i.v.* Dobutamine HCl i.v.*	I.V. fluids Trendelenburg position
Bradycardia, AV block, asystole	Isoproterenol HCl i.v.* Atropine sulfate i.v. Cardiac pacing	—	I.V. fluids (slow drip)
Rapid ventricular rate (due to antegrade conduction in flutter/fibrillation with WPW or LGL syndrome)	DC cardioversion (high energy may be required) Procainamide i.v. Lidocaine HCl i.v.	—	I.V. fluids (slow drip)

*positive inotropic agent.

Suggested Treatment of Acute Cardiovascular Adverse Reactions: See Table III. Actual treatment and dosage should depend on the severity of the clinical situation and the judgement of the treating physician. Patients with hypertrophic cardiomyopathy treated with verapamil should not be administered positive inotropic agents (marked by asterisks in Table III).

Dosage: Crushing or chewing Isoptin SR tablets is not recommended since the sustained-release effect will be altered by damage to the tablet structure. The Isoptin SR 240 mg tablet may be split in half.

Mild to Moderate Essential Hypertension: Isoptin SR tablets should be taken with food (see Pharmacology, Pharmacokinetics, Influence of Food). The dosage should be individualized by titration depending on patient tolerance and responsiveness to verapamil. Titration should be based on therapeutic efficacy and safety, evaluated weekly and approximately 24 hours after the previous dose.

The usual initial adult dose is 180 to 240 mg/day. If required, the dose may be increased up to 240 mg twice a day. A maximum daily dose of 480 mg should not be exceeded.

Recommended dosing intervals for specific daily dosages are given in Table IV.

Table IV—Isoptin SR

Recommended Dosing Intervals

Total Daily Isoptin SR Dose	Recommended Dosing Intervals
180 mg	Once each morning with food
240 mg	Once each morning with food
360 mg	180 mg each morning plus 180 mg each evening, with food or 240 mg each morning plus 120 mg each evening, with food
480 mg	240 mg each morning plus 240 mg each evening with food

The antihypertensive effects of Isoptin SR are evident within the first week of therapy. Optimal doses are usually lower in patients also receiving diuretics since additive antihypertensive effects can be expected.

Geriatrics: Lower dosages of Isoptin SR i.e. 120 mg a day, may be warranted in elderly patients (i.e., 65 years and older) (see Precautions, Geriatrics). The dosage should be carefully and gradually adjusted depending on patient tolerability and response.

Impaired Liver and Renal Function: Isoptin SR should be administered cautiously to patients with liver or renal function impairment. The dosage should be carefully and gradually adjusted depending on patient tolerance and response. These patients should be monitored carefully for abnormal prolongation of the PR interval or other signs of overdosage. Isoptin SR should not be used in severe hepatic dysfunction (see Warnings, Hepatic Insufficiency).

Switching from Isoptin to Isoptin SR: When switching from Isoptin to Isoptin SR the total daily dose in mg may remain the same.

Special Note to Pharmacists: The Isoptin SR 240 mg tablet may be split in half. Crushing Isoptin SR tablets is not recommended since the sustained-release effect will be altered by damage to the tablet structure. Use of Isoptin SR 120 mg is recommended.

Supplied: 120 mg: Each off-white, biconvex, round, film-coated tablet, with SR 120 embossed on one side, KNOLL on the other side, contains: verapamil HCl 120 mg. Nonmedicinal ingredients: cellulose, hydroxypropyl methylcellulose, magnesium stearate, polyethylene glycol, povidone, sodium alginate, talc, titanium dioxide and wax. Bottles of 100.

180 mg: Each light-pink, football-shaped, film coated tablet with KNOLL on one side and SR, scored, 180 on the other, contains: verapamil HCl 180 mg. Nonmedicinal ingredients: cellulose, hydroxypropyl methylcellulose, magnesium stearate, polyethylene glycol, povidone, red iron oxide, sodium alginate, talc, titanium dioxide and wax. Bottles of 100.

240 mg: Each light-green, scored, capsule-shaped, film-coated tablet, with 2 triangles embossed on one side, contains: verapamil HCl 240 mg. Nonmedicinal ingredients: cellulose, hydroxypropyl methylcellulose, indigotine lake, magnesium stearate, polyethylene glycol, povidone, quinoline yellow lake, sodium alginate, talc, titanium dioxide and wax. Bottles of 100 and 500.

(Shown in Product Recognition Section)

ISOPTO® ATROPINE 🄿

Alcon

Atropine Sulfate

Mydriatic—Cycloplegic—Anticholinergic

Supplied: Each Drop-Tainer dispenser contains: a sterile, buffered ophthalmic solution with 1% atropine sulfate. Preserved with benzalkonium chloride. Nonmedicinal ingredients: boric acid, hydrochloric acid, 0.5% hydroxylpropyl methylcellulose, purified water and sodium hydroxide. Drop-Tainer dispensers of 5 mL.

ISOPTO® CARBACHOL 🄿

Alcon

Carbachol

Miotic—Cholinergic

Supplied: Each Drop-Tainer dispenser contains: a sterile, buffered, isotonic solution with carbachol 1.5% or 3%. Preserved with benzalkonium chloride. Nonmedicinal ingredients: boric acid, hydrochloric acid, 1% hydroxypropyl methylcellulose, purified water, sodium borate, sodium chloride and sodium hydroxide. Drop-Tainer dispensers of 15 mL.

ISOPTO® CARPINE 🄿

Alcon

Pilocarpine HCl

Miotic—Cholinergic

Supplied: Each Drop-Tainer dispenser contains: a sterile, buffered solution of pilocarpine HCl 0.5%, 1%, 2%, 4%, or 6%. Preserved with benzalkonium chloride. Nonmedicinal ingredients: boric acid, citric acid, hydrochloric acid, 0.5% hydroxypropyl methylcellulose, purified water, sodium chloride, sodium citrate and sodium hydroxide. Drop-Tainer dispensers of 15 mL.

ISOPTO® HOMATROPINE
Alcon

Homatropine HBr
Mydriatic—Cycloplegic—Anticholinergic

Supplied: Each Drop-Tainer dispenser contains: a sterile, buffered solution of homatropine HBr 2% or 5%. Preservative: benzalkonium chloride (in 2%); benzethonium chloride (in 5%). Nonmedicinal ingredients: 0.5% hydroxypropyl methylcellulose, hydrochloric acid and/or sodium hydroxide, polysorbate 80, purified water and sodium chloride. Drop-Tainer dispensers of 15 mL.

ISOPTO® TEARS
Alcon

Hydroxypropyl Methylcellulose
Artificial Tears

Supplied: Each Drop-Tainer dispenser contains: a sterile, buffered, isotonic solution of hydroxypropyl methylcellulose 0.5% or 1%. Nonmedicinal ingredients: benzalkonium chloride, dibasic sodium phosphate, monobasic sodium phosphate, purified water, sodium chloride and sodium citrate. Drop-Tainer dispensers of 15 mL.

ISORDIL®
Wyeth-Ayerst

Isosorbide Dinitrate
Coronary Vasodilator

Pharmacology: The basic action of isosorbide dinitrate is the relaxation of smooth muscle. Relaxation of peripheral vascular smooth muscle and pooling results in the reduction of preload and afterload on the left ventricle. The effect of the long acting nitrate appears to be mainly peripheral. Although isosorbide dinitrate dilates the coronary arteries there is no incontrovertible evidence that it relieves ischemic heart pain by increasing coronory blood flow.

When administered sublingually, isosorbide dinitrate has an onset of action of 2 to 5 minutes and lasts 1 to 2 hours. After oral administration, relief of angina pectoris begins in 30 minutes and lasts 4 to 6 hours.

Isosorbide dinitrate is metabolized to 2-isosorbide mononitrate and 5-isosorbide mononitrate. After a single oral dose, 80 to 100% of the amount absorbed is excreted in the urine within 24 hours, chiefly as metabolites.

Indications: The prophylaxis of ischemic heart pain associated with coronary insufficiency. Isosorbide dinitrate may reduce the number, duration and severity of anginal attacks, exercise tolerance may be increased and nitroglycerin requirements curtailed.

Contraindications: Although isosorbide dinitrate may be used for the control of angina pectoris occurring after myocardial infarction, it is suggested that treatment be withheld in the presence of cardiogenic shock, or if there is a risk of shock developing. Hypersensitivity to isosorbide dinitrate.

Warnings: Data supporting the use of nitrites during the early days of the acute phase of myocardial infarction (the period during which clinical and laboratory findings are unstable) are insufficient to establish safety.

Precautions: Use isosorbide dinitrate with caution in patients with glaucoma. Isosorbide dinitrate is a potent vasodilator and causes a slight decrease in mean blood pressure (approx. 10 to 15 mm Hg) in some patients when used in therapeutic doses. Caution should be exercised in using the drug in patients who are prone to, or might be affected by, hypotension. In patients with renal insufficiency, isosorbide dinitrate should be used with caution since the hypotensive effect may cause a dangerous reduction in renal blood flow.

Tolerance to this drug and cross tolerance to other nitrites and nitrates may occur.

Adverse Effects: As with nitroglycerin and other nitrates, vascular headache occurs and it may be severe and persistent. This adverse effect occurs most frequently at the beginning of therapy. Headache usually can be controlled by temporary dosage reduction, concomitant administration of suitable analgesics or by administering the drug during meals. These headaches usually disappear within 1 week of continuous, uninterrupted therapy. It is usually best to advise the patient of their possible occurrence and of their importance in regard to the prevention of angina. Drug and/or exfoliative dermatitis occasionally occur. Signs of cerebral ischemia associated with postural hypotension such as weakness, transient episodes of dizziness may occasionally develop. Cutaneous vasodilatation with flushing may occur. Rarely, a marked sensitivity to the hypotensive effects of the drug and severe response (nausea, vomiting, restlessness, perspiration and collapse) can occur and alcohol may enhance this effect. Isosorbide dinitrate can antagonize the effects of histamine or epinephrine, acetylcholine and similar agents.

Overdose: Symptoms: Related to vasodilatation; cutaneous flushing, headache, nausea, dizziness and hypotension.

Treatment: Gastric lavage. Symptomatic and supportive therapy should include ventilation with oxygen and vasopressor amines if indicated (norepinephrine is suitable).

Dosage: Sublingual Tablets (tablets dissolve in 20 seconds in the mouth): 5 to 10 mg sublingually, every 2 to 4 hours for the prophylaxis of acute angina; may be supplemented by a dose of 5 to 10 mg sublingually prior to stressful situations likely to provoke an attack of angina.

Oral Titradose Tablets: 5 to 30 mg orally 4 times daily, according to therapeutic and patient response.

Supplied: 5 mg: Each pink, sublingual tablet with a depressed dot, contains: isosorbide dinitrate 5 mg. Nonmedicinal ingredients: cornstarch, FD&C Red Aluminum Lake, lactose, magnesium stearate and microcrystalline cellulose. Energy: 0.50 kJ (0.12 kcal)/tablet. Gluten- and tartrazine-free. Bottles of 100.

10 mg: Each white, scored, titradose tablet, imprinted ISORDIL 10, contains: isosorbide dinitrate 10 mg. Nonmedicinal ingredients: lactose, magnesium stearate, microcrystalline cellulose and polacrilin potassium. Energy: 2.72 kJ (0.65 kcal). Gluten- and tartrazine-free. Bottles of 100, 500 and 2 500.

30 mg: Each white, scored titradose tablet, imprinted ISORDIL 30, contains: isosorbide dinitrate 30 mg. Energy: 3.85 kJ (0.92 kcal). Nonmedicinal ingredients: magnesium stearate, microcrystalline cellulose and polacrilin potassium. Gluten- and tartrazine-free. Bottles of 100, 500 and 2 500.

(Shown in Product Recognition Section)

ISOSOURCE®
Novartis Nutrition

Therapeutic Nutrient

Indications: A standard tube feeding (nasogastric, nasoduodenal or jejunal) for patients with normal gastrointestinal function, when low-residue feeding is required.

Because it is slightly flavored, Isosource may be appropriate for oral administration in patients experiencing altered or heightened taste perceptions (e.g., individuals undergoing radiation and chemotherapy treatment).

Precautions: Not for parenteral administration.

Dosage: 1 500 mL or 7 520 kJ (6 cans) (1 800 kcal) provides at least 100% of the Canadian RNI (adult males, 25 to 49) for protein and essential vitamins and minerals. Isosource is ready to use and does not require dilution with water. It may be fed at room temperature or chilled.

Follow a physician's or dietitian's instructions for tube feedings. When initiating feeding, the flow rate, volume and dilution are dependent on patient condition and tolerance. Care should be taken to avoid contamination of this product during preparation and administration. Additional fluid requirements should be met by giving water orally with or after feedings, or when flushing the feeding tube.

Oral: For oral feeding, it may be used as a sole source of nutrition or as a supplement with and between meals for added nutritional support.

Supplied: Each 250 mL ready-to-use can or 1 000 mL closed system bottle contains: ⓤ-D water, maltodextrin, sodium and calcium caseinates, corn syrup solids, modified coconut oil (medium chain triglycerides), canola oil, soy protein isolate, potassium citrate, calcium phosphate tribasic, sodium citrate, soy lecithin, magnesium chloride, sodium ascorbate, choline chloride, potassium chloride, molybdenum yeast, selenium yeast, carrageenan, *artificial flavor, chromium yeast, niacinamide, zinc sulfate, alpha tocopheryl acetate, ferrous sulfate, D-calcium pantothenate, copper gluconate, manganese sulfate, thiamine hydrochloride, pyridoxine hydrochloride, riboflavin, vitamin A palmitate, biotin, folic acid, potassium iodide, vitamin K_1, *maltol, cyanocobalamin and vitamin D_3. See Table I.

*These ingredients do not appear in bottled products.

Energy Distribution: protein 14%, fat 30%, carbohydrate 56%; 500 kJ (120 kcal)/100 mL.

Table I—Isosource

Analysis	100 mL	
Energy	500 (120)	kJ (kcal)
Protein	4.3	g
Carbohydrate	16.7	g
Fat	4.2	g
Linoleic Acid	0.4	g
Sodium	120	mg
Potassium	167	mg
Vitamin A	333	IU
Vitamin C	20	mg
Thiamine	0.2	mg
Riboflavin	0.23	mg
Niacin	2.67	mg
Calcium	66.8	mg
Iron	1.2	mg
Vitamin D	26.7	IU
Vitamin E	3.0	IU
Vitamin B_6	0.27	mg
Folic Acid	0.027	mg
Vitamin B_{12}	0.0008	mg
Phosphorus	66.8	mg
Iodine	0.013	mg
Magnesium	26.7	mg
Zinc	1.67	mg
Copper	0.13	mg
Biotin	0.04	mg
Pantothenic Acid	1.33	mg
Vitamin K	0.006	mg
Choline	33.3	mg
Chloride	113	mg
Manganese	0.33	mg
Selenium	0.01	mg
Chromium	0.01	mg
Molybdenum	0.02	mg
Osmolality	360	mOsm/kg water

Isosource is a high nutrient density, low-residue, essentially isotonic (360 mOsm/kg water) feeding. It provides a calorie-to-nitrogen ratio of 173:1, which is suggested as reasonable for effective protein utilization; it contains essential fatty acids as well as medium-chain triglycerides to facilitate rapid, effective fat absorption; it will not contribute to lactose-associated diarrhea as it is lactose-free.

Cans of 250 mL, cases of 24. Closed system bottles of 1 000 mL, cases of 6. Store unopened at room temperature. Once opened, store covered in refrigerator and use within 24 hours.

Reviewed 1997

ISOSOURCE® HN
Novartis Nutrition

Therapeutic Nutrient

Indications: A high nitrogen, complete liquid tube feeding (nasogastric, nasoduodenal or jejunal) for patients with normal gastrointestinal function, when low-residue feeding is required.

Because it is slightly flavored, Isosource HN may be appropriate for oral administration in patients experiencing altered or heightened taste perceptions (e.g., individuals undergoing radiation and chemotherapy treatment).

Precautions: Not for parenteral administration.

Dosage: 1 500 mL or 7 520 kJ (6 cans) (1 800 kcal) provides at least 100% of the Canadian RNI (adult males, 25 to 49) for protein and essential vitamins and minerals. Isosource HN is ready to use and does not require dilution with water. It may be fed at room temperature or chilled.

Follow a physician's or dietitian's instructions for tube feedings. When initiating feeding, the flow rate, volume and dilution are dependent on patient condition and tolerance. Care should be taken to avoid contamination of this product during preparation and administration. Additional fluid requirements should be met by giving water orally with or after feedings, or when flushing the feeding tube.

Oral: For oral feeding, it may be used as a sole source of nutrition or as a supplement with and between meals for added nutritional support.

Supplied: Each 250 mL ready-to-use can or 1 000 mL closed system bottle contains: ⓤ-D water, maltodextrin, sodium and calcium caseinates, corn syrup solids, modified coconut oil (medium chain triglycerides), canola oil, soy protein isolate, potassium citrate, calcium phosphate tribasic, soy lecithin, magnesium chloride, sodium ascorbate, sodium citrate, choline chloride, potassium chloride, molybdenum yeast, selenium yeast, carrageenan, *artificial flavor, chromium yeast, niacinamide, zinc sulfate, alpha tocopheryl acetate, ferrous sulfate, D-calcium pantothenate, copper gluconate, manganese sulfate, thiamine hydrochloride, pyridoxine hydrochloride, riboflavin, vitamin A palmitate, biotin, folic acid, potassium iodide, vitamin K_1, *maltol, cyanocobalamin and vitamin D_3. See Table I.

*These ingredients do not appear in bottled product.

Energy Distribution: protein 18%, fat 30%, carbohydrate 52%; 500 kJ (120 kcal)/100 mL.

Table I—Isosource HN

Analysis	100 mL	
Energy	500 (120)	kJ (kcal)
Protein	5.3	g
Carbohydrate	15.7	g
Fat	4.2	g
Linoleic Acid	0.4	g
Sodium	107	mg
Potassium	167	mg
Vitamin A	333	IU
Vitamin C	20	mg
Thiamine	0.2	mg
Riboflavin	0.23	mg
Niacin	2.67	mg
Calcium	66.8	mg
Iron	1.2	mg
Vitamin D	26.7	IU
Vitamin E	3.0	IU
Vitamin B_6	0.27	mg
Folic Acid	0.027	mg
Vitamin B_{12}	0.0008	mg
Phosphorus	66.8	mg
Iodine	0.013	mg
Magnesium	26.7	mg
Zinc	1.67	mg
Copper	0.13	mg
Biotin	0.04	mg
Pantothenic Acid	1.33	mg
Vitamin K	0.006	mg
Choline	33.3	mg
Chloride	113	mg
Manganese	0.33	mg
Selenium	0.01	mg
Chromium	0.01	mg
Molybdenum	0.02	mg
Osmolality	330	mOsm/kg water

Isosource HN is a high nutrient density, low-residue, essentially isotonic (330 mOsm/kg water) feeding. It provides a calorie-to-nitrogen ratio of 141:1, which is suggested as reasonable for effective protein utilization; it contains essential fatty acids and medium-chain triglycerides to facilitate rapid, effective fat absorption; it will not contribute to lactose-associated diarrhea as it is lactose-free.

Cans of 250 mL, cases of 24. Closed system bottles of 1 000 mL, cases of 6. Store unopened at room temperature. Once opened, store covered in refrigerator and use within 24 hours.

Reviewed 1997

ISOSOURCE® VHN

Novartis Nutrition

Therapeutic Nutrient

Indications: A high nitrogen, fibre containing, complete liquid tube feeding (nasogastric, nasoduodenal or jejunal) for patients with normal gastrointestinal function. Recommended for both short-term and long-term feeding. Not recommended when a low residue tube feeding is required.

Precautions: Not for parenteral administration.

Dosage: 1 250 mL or 5 220 kJ (5 cans or 1 250 kcal) provides at least 100% of the Canadian RNI (adult males, 25 to 49) for protein and essential vitamins and minerals.

Ready-to-use: Feed at room temperature. Follow a physician's or dietitian's directions. When initiating feedings, the flow rate, volume and dilution are dependent on the patient's condition and tolerance. Care should be taken to avoid contamination of the product during preparation and administration. Additional fluid requirements should be met by giving water orally with or after feedings or when flushing the feeding tube.

Feeding should be initiated at a slow rate. Rate and volume of feeding can be increased gradually over 48 hours if well tolerated. If intolerance develops, return to previously tolerated rate or dilute formula to half strength until desired rate is achieved, then switch to full strength. Do not alter strength and volume at the same time. Rinse the tube with 20 to 30 mL water after each intermittent feeding or every 3 to 4 hours during continuous feeding to avoid clogging and provide additional water.

Supplied: Each 250 mL ready-to-use can contains: Ⓤ-D water, maltodextrin, sodium and calcium caseinates, modified coconut oil (medium chain triglycerides), soy cotyledon, canola oil, soybean oil, potassium citrate, calcium phosphate tribasic, sodium citrate, artificial flavor, soy lecithin, sodium ascorbate, potassium chloride, magnesium chloride, choline choride, magnesium oxide, L-carnitine, taurine, molybdenum yeast, selenium yeast, chromium yeast, zinc sulfate, alpha tocopheryl acetate, ferrous sulfate, niacinamide, D-calcium pantothenate, copper gluconate, manganese sulfate, thiamine HCl, pyridoxine HCl, riboflavin, beta carotene, vitamin A palmitate, folic acid, biotin, potassium iodide, vitamin K_1, maltol, cyanocobalamin, vitamin D_3. See Table I.

Energy Distribution: protein 25%, fat 25%, carbohydrate 50%; 418 kJ (100 kcal)/100 mL. Contains 2.5 g/250 mL of dietary fibre (from soy cotyledon).

Table I—Isosource VHN

Analysis	100 mL	
Energy	418 (100)	kJ (kcal)
Protein	6.2	g
Carbohydrate	12.8	g
Fat	2.9	g
Linoleic Acid	0.4	g
Dietary Fibre	1.0	g
Sodium	128	mg
Potassium	160	mg
Vitamin A*	288	IU
Vitamin C	24	mg
Thiamine	0.24	mg
Riboflavin	0.27	mg
Niacin	3.2	mg
Calcium	80	mg
Iron	1.44	mg
Vitamin D	27.2	IU
Vitamin E	4.8	IU
Vitamin B_6	0.32	mg
Folic Acid	0.048	mg
Vitamin B_{12}	0.00096	mg
Phosphorus	80	mg
Iodine	0.013	mg
Magnesium	32	mg
Zinc	2.4	mg
Copper	0.16	mg
Biotin	0.036	mg
Pantothenic Acid	1.6	mg
Vitamin K	0.008	mg
Choline	40	mg
Chloride	136	mg
Manganese	0.4	mg
Selenium	0.008	mg
Chromium	0.012	mg
Molybdenum	0.02	mg
L-carnitine	12.8	mg
Taurine	12.8	mg
Osmolality	300	mOsm/kg water

*Includes vitamin A activity from beta carotene.

IsoSource VHN is a complete, high protein, isotonic liquid formula with fibre. It is designed to meet the needs of patients with increased protein requirements. IsoSource VHN contains medium-chain triglycerides for enhanced fat absorption and the trace elements selenium, chromium and molybdenum as well as L-carnitine, taurine and beta carotene.

Cans of 250 mL (vanilla), cases of 24. Store unopened at room temperature. Once opened, store covered in refrigerator and use within 24 hours.

Reviewed 1998

ISOTAMINE® Ⓟ

ICN

Isoniazid

Tuberculostatic Agent

Supplied: Syrup: Each mL of strawberry flavored syrup contains: isoniazid, USP 10 mg. Nonmedicinal ingredients: citric acid, glycerin, methylparaben, propylparaben, sodium citrate and flavor. Bottles of 500 mL.

Tablets: Each white, scored, compressed tablet, imprinted ICN I22, contains: isoniazid, USP 300 mg. Nonmedicinal ingredients: colloidal silicon dioxide, magnesium stearate and microcrystalline cellulose. Bottles of 100 and 1 000.

ISOTREX® Ⓟ

Stiefel

Isotretinoin

Acne Therapy

Pharmacology: Isotretinoin is a drug known to improve cystic acne when taken orally. It has also shown similar activity when used for treating less severe forms of acne. While its mechanism of action is not known, studies have shown that oral isotretinoin can decrease sebum secretion and sebaceous gland size. It also affects the keratinization of the stratum corneum. These processes are important to the pathogenesis of acne vulgaris. Topical isotretinoin appears to have similar properties. It is also known that a structurally related drug, tretinoin, is effective in the treatment of acne vulgaris when used topically. Since the oral use of drugs often exposes the patient to much larger quantities of drug, systemic side effects can occur as is the case with oral isotretinoin. The topical use of drugs in dermatology can often treat the disease locally without the systemic side effects.

Indications: For the topical treatment of acne vulgaris.

Contraindications: In persons who demonstrate hypersensitivity to any of the listed ingredients.

Warnings: Isotrex is intended for external use only and should be kept away from eyes, nose, mouth, and other mucous membranes because of its irritant effect.

Do not apply to eyelids or to the skin at the corners of the eyes and mouth. Avoid the angles of the nose and nasolabial fold (if treatment in these areas is necessary, apply very sparingly). Topical use may induce severe local erythema and peeling at the site of application. If the degree of local irritation warrants, patients should be directed to use the medication less frequently, discontinue use temporarily or discontinue use altogether.

Pregnancy: **Topical isotretinoin should be used by women of childbearing years only after contraceptive counselling. It is recommended that topical isotretinoin should not be used by pregnant women.**

There have been rare reports of birth defects among babies born to women exposed to topical tretinoin during pregnancy. However, there are no well-controlled prospective studies of the use of topical tretinoin in pregnant women. A retrospective study of mothers exposed to topical tretinoin during the first trimester of pregnancy found no increase in the incidence of birth defects. **Oral** isotretinoin has been associated with teratogenicity in humans. As with all retinoids, isotretinoin administered **orally** at high doses is teratogenic in animals. **Topical** reproduction studies have been performed in rabbits at maximally tolerable dermal doses up to 60 times human dose (assuming the human dose to be 800 mg of gel/day) and have revealed no evidence of harm to the fetus due to isotretinoin when applied as Isotrex gel. **Topical** retinoid teratology studies in rats and rabbits have been inconclusive.

Lactation: **It is not known whether isotretinoin is excreted in human milk. Nevertheless, a decision should be made whether to discontinue the drug taking into account the importance of the drug to the mother.**

Precautions: Concomitant topical acne therapy should be used with caution because a cumulative irritant effect may occur, especially with the use of peeling, desquamating, or abrasive agents.

Adverse Effects: During clinical trials, 4 of 171 patients treated with isotretinoin 0.05% gel discontinued use because of irritation. Most patients experienced some erythema (109 of 171) or peeling (104 of 171). Some patients experienced severe erythema (7 of 171) or peeling (4 of 171). Transient burning, stinging, itching, or scaling were also reported.

Overdose: Symptoms and Treatment: Acute overdosage of isotretinoin gel in humans has not been reported to date.

Dosage: The gel should be applied twice daily, in the morning and before retiring, using enough medication to cover the entire affected area.

Information for the Patient: See Blue Section—Information for the Patient "Isotrex".

Isotrex (cont'd)

Supplied: Each g of gel contains: isotretinoin 0.05% in an alcohol-base gel. Nonmedicinal ingredients: alcohol anhydrous, butylated hydroxytoluene and hydroxypropyl cellulose. Metal tubes of 30 g. Store at 15 to 30°C.

ISUPREL®

Sanofi

Isoproterenol HCl

Sympathomimetic

Indications: Inhalation solution: Symptomatic relief of bronchial asthma and in cases of emphysema, bronchitis and other chronic bronchopulmonary disorders in which bronchospasm is a complicating factor.

Injectable form is particularly suitable for the treatment and prevention of (1) Adams-Stokes syndrome and other episodes of heart block, except when caused by ventricular tachycardia or fibrillation (2) cardiac arrest (3) mild or transient episodes of heart block not requiring electric shock or pacemaker therapy (4) laryngobronchospasm during anesthesia (5) as adjunctive therapy in shock.

Contraindications: Patients with known hypersensitivity to isoproterenol or any other component of this drug. Patients with tachycardia or heart block caused by digitalis intoxication; ventricular arrhythmias which require inotropic therapy and coronary insufficiency (angina pectoris).

Precautions: Use with caution in patients sensitive to sympathomimetic amines and in the presence of hypertension, cardiovascular disorders (including coronary artery disease and coronary insufficiency), diabetes, hyperthyroidism, in patients with a potential for cardiac arrhythmias and in those patients receiving MAO inhibitors. Potent inhalational anesthetics such as halothane may sensitize the myocardium to effects of sympathomimetic amines.

Occasionally, patients have been reported to develop severe paradoxical airway resistance with repeated, excessive use of aerosol preparations containing sympathomimetic amines. The cause of this refractory state is unknown. It is advisable that in such instances the use of the aerosol be discontinued immediately and alternative therapy instituted, since in the reported cases the patients did not respond to other forms of therapy until the aerosol was withdrawn. Deaths have been reported following excessive use of aerosol preparations containing sympathomimetic amines, the exact cause of which is unknown. Cardiac arrest was noted in several instances.

Isoproterenol injection, by increasing myocardial oxygen requirements while decreasing effective coronary perfusion, may have a deleterious effect on the injured or failing heart. Most experts discourage its use as the initial agent in treating cardiogenic shock following myocardial infarction. However, when a low arterial pressure has been elevated by other means, isoproterenol injection may produce beneficial hemodynamic and metabolic effects.

In a few patients, presumably with organic disease of the AV node and its branches, isoproterenol injection has paradoxically been reported to worsen heart block or to precipitate Adams-Stokes attacks during normal sinus rhythm or transient heart block.

Solution and injection may contain sodium metabisulfite, a sulfite that may cause allergic-type reactions including anaphylactic symptoms and life-threatening or less severe asthmatic episodes in susceptible people. The overall prevalence of sulfite sensitivity in the general population is unknown and probably low. Sulfite sensitivity is seen more frequently in asthmatic than in nonasthmatic people.

Isoproterenol injection should generally be started at the lowest recommended dose. This may be gradually increased, if necessary, while carefully monitoring the patient. Doses sufficient to increase the heart rate to more than 130 beats/minute may increase the likelihood of inducing ventricular arrhythmias. Such increases in heart rate will also tend to increase cardiac work and oxygen requirements which may adversely affect the failing heart or the heart with a significant degree of arteriosclerosis.

Particular caution is necessary in administering isoproterenol injection to patients with coronary artery disease, coronary insufficiency, diabetes, hyperthyroidism and sensitivity to sympathomimetic amines.

Adequate filling of the intravascular compartment by suitable volume expanders is of primary importance in most cases of shock, and should precede the administration of vasoactive drugs. In patients with normal cardiac function, determination of central venous pressure is a reliable guide during volume replacement. If evidence of hypoperfusion persists after adequate volume replacement, isoproterenol injection may be given.

In addition to the routine monitoring of systemic blood pressure, heart rate, urine flow, and the ECG, the response to therapy should also be monitored by frequent determination of the central venous pressure and blood gases. Patients in shock should be closely observed during isoproterenol injection administration. If the heart rate exceeds 110 beats/minute, it may be advisable to decrease the infusion rate or temporarily discontinue the infusion. Determinations of cardiac output and circulation time may also be helpful. Appropriate measures should be taken to ensure adequate ventilation. Careful attention should be paid to acid-base balance and to the correction of electrolyte disturbances. In cases of shock associated with bacteremia, suitable antimicrobial therapy is, of course, imperative.

Drug Interactions: Isoproterenol injection and epinephrine should not be administered simultaneously because both drugs are direct cardiac stimulants and their combined effects may induce serious arrhythmias. The drugs may, however, be administered alternatively provided a proper interval has elapsed between doses.

Isoproterenol should be used with caution, if at all, when potent inhalational anesthetics such as halothane are employed because of potential to sensitize the mycocardium to effects of sympathomimetic amines.

Isoproterenol should not be used with tricyclic antidepressants or MAO inhibitors since the effects of isoproterenol may be magnified.

Pregnancy and *Lactation:* It is not known whether isoproterenol can cause fetal harm when administered to a pregnant woman or can affect reproduction capacity.

Isoproterenol should be given to a pregnant woman only if clearly needed. It is also not known whether this drug is excreted in human milk. Because many drugs are excreted in human milk, caution should be exercised when isoproterenol is administered to a nursing woman.

Adverse Effects: The following reactions to isoproterenol injection have been reported: CNS: nervousness, headache, dizziness.

Cardiovascular: tachycardia, palpitations, angina, Adams-Stokes attacks, pulmonary edema, hypertension, hypotension, ventricular arrhythmias, tachyarrhythmias.

In a few patients, presumably with organic disease of the AV node and its branches, isoproterenol injection has been reported to precipitate Adams-Stokes seizures during normal sinus rhythm or transient heart block.

Other: flushing of the skin, sweating, mild tremors, weakness, nausea and vomiting.

Overdose: Symptoms and Treatment: In case of accidental overdosage as evidenced mainly by tachycardia or other arrhythmias, palpitations, angina, hypotension, or hypertension, reduce rate of administration or discontinue isoproterenol injection until patient's condition stabilizes. Blood pressure, pulse, respiration, and ECG should be monitored.

It is not known whether isoproterenol is dialyzable.

Dosage: Parenteral: Isoproterenol injection 1:5 000 should generally be started at the lowest recommended dose and the rate of administration gradually increased if necessary while carefully monitoring the patient. The usual route of administration is by i.v. infusion or bolus injection. In dire emergencies, the drug may be administered by intracardiac injection. If time is not of the utmost importance, initial therapy by i.m. or s.c. injection is preferred.

There are no well-controlled studies in children to establish appropriate dosing; however, the American Heart Association recommends an initial infusion rate of 0.1 μg/kg/minute, with the usual range being 0.1 μg/kg/minute to 1.0 μg/kg/minute.

Cardiac disorders: s.c. or i.m. injection of 200 μg (1 mL of 1:5 000 solution), i.v. injection of 20 to 60 μg (1 to 3 mL of 1:50 000 solution). I.V. infusion of solution containing 1 mg in 250 mL of 5% glucose at a rate of 1.25 mL (5 μg) per minute. Intracardiac injection of 200 μg (1 mL of 1:5 000 solution). Laryngobronchospasm: i.v. injection of from 10 to 20 μg (0.5 to 1 mL of 1:50 000 solution). To prepare 1:50 000 solution dilute 1 mL of 1:5 000 solution to 10 mL with 5% dextrose in water or sodium chloride injection, USP. Adjunctive therapy in shock: i.v. infusion of 1 mg in 500 mL of 5% dextrose in water administered at a rate of 0.5 μg to 5 μg/minute. Infusion rate (up to 30 μg/minute in advanced shock) should be adjusted on the basis of heart rate, central venous pressure, systemic blood pressure and urine flow. If the heart rate exceeds 110 beats/minute, it may be advisable to decrease the infusion rate or temporarily discontinue the infusion.

Solution: Do not use if a precipitate or pinkish to brownish discoloration is observed. Nebulizer solutions should be freshly prepared daily. Isuprel 1:200 solution may be administered by hand nebulizer, compressed air or oxygen operated nebulizer, or by intermittent positive pressure breathing (IPPB) devices.

Acute bronchial asthma: Hand Nebulizer: Depending on the frequency of treatment and the type of nebulizer used, place a volume of Isuprel solution, sufficient for not more than 1 day's treatment, in the nebulizer using the dropper provided. In time, the patient can learn to adjust the volume required. For adults and children, administer the 1:200 solution by hand bulb nebulization in a dosage of 5 to 15 deep inhalations (using an all glass or plastic nebulizer). If after 5 to 10 minutes inadequate relief is observed, these doses may be repeated once more. If the acute attack recurs, treatments may be repeated up to 5 times daily if necessary. Close patient monitoring is necessary (see Precautions).

Bronchospasm in chronic obstructive lung disease: hand bulb nebulizer: Isuprel 1:200 aerosol solution may be administered daily at not less than 3- to 4-hour intervals for subacute bronchospastic attacks as part of a programmed treatment regimen in patients with chronic obstructive lung disease with a reversible bronchospastic component. An adequate dose is usually 5 to 15 deep inhalations.

Nebulization of compressed air or oxygen: A method often used in patients with severe chronic obstructive lung disease is to deliver the Isuprel mist in more dilute form over a longer period of time. The purpose is, not so much to increase the dose supplied, as to achieve progressively deeper bronchodilatation and thus insure that the mist achieves maximum penetration of the finer bronchioles. Dilute 0.5 mL of Isuprel 1:200 solution to 2 to 2.5 mL with water or isotonic saline to achieve a use concentration of 1:800 to 1:1 000 for this method. The diluted solution is then placed in a nebulizer connected to either a source of compressed air or oxygen. Regulate the flow rate to suit the particular nebulizer so that the diluted isoproterenol solution will be delivered over approximately 10 to 20 minutes. A treatment may be repeated up to 5 times daily if necessary. Although the total delivered dose of Isuprel is somewhat higher than with treatment regimens employing the hand bulb nebulizer, patients usually tolerate it well because of the greater dilution and longer application time factors.

Intermittent Positive Pressure Breathing (IPPB): Diluted solutions of isoproterenol 1:200 are used in a programmed regimen for the treatment of reversible bronchospasm in patients with chronic obstructive lung disease who require IPPB therapy. These devices generally have a small nebulizer, usually of 3 to 5 mL capacity, on a patient operated side arm. The effectiveness of IPPB therapy is greatly enhanced by the simultaneous use of aerosolized bronchodilators. As with compressed air or oxygen operated nebulizers, the usual regimen is to place 0.5 mL of Isuprel 1:200 solution diluted to 2 to 2.5 mL with water or isotonic saline in the nebulizer cup and follow the IPPB manufacturer's operating instructions. IPPB bronchodilator treatments are usually administered over 15 to 20 minutes, up to 5 times daily if necessary.

Children's dosage: In general, the technique of Isuprel aerosol solution administration to children is similar to that of adults, since children's smaller ventilatory exchange capacity automatically provides proportionally smaller aerosol intake. Generally, the 1:200 solution should be used for an acute attack of bronchospasm, and no more than 0.25 mL of the 1:200 solution should be used for each 10 to 15 minute programmed treatment in chronic bronchospastic disease.

Supplied: Ampuls: Each mL of injectable solution contains: isoproterenol HCl 1:5 000. Nonmedicinal ingredients: lactic acid, sodium chloride, sodium lactate and sodium metabisulfite in water for injection. Ampuls of 1 mL, boxes of 5. Ampuls of 5 mL, boxes of 10.

Solution: Each mL of inhalation solution contains: isoproterenol HCl 1:200. (Each 6 drops is equivalent to 0.25 mL.) Nonmedicinal ingredients: citric acid, chlorobutanol, glycerin, sodium chloride and sodium metabisulfite in purified water. Bottles of 10 mL.

Reviewed 1999

Look for CPhA general monographs to provide additional drug information. These are shaded gray and listed in the WHITE SECTION of the *CPS*.

IVEEGAM IMMUNO®

Baxter

Immune Globulin (Human), I.V.

Passive Immunizing Agent

Pharmacology: Immune globulin for i.m. use is known to cause anaphylactoid reactions when given i.v. Osterreichisches Institut für Haemoderivate has developed animal models which permit the testing of a preparation's potential for causing anaphylactoid reactions.

The tests have shown that hypotensive, leukopenic, and bronchospastic substances are present in Cohn Fraction II, which is used for the preparation of Iveegam Immuno. Osterreichisches Institut für Haemoderivate has developed manufacturing processes which reduce these substances by 2 or 3 log steps. Assays are performed on each lot of the final product to guarantee that only traces of contaminants, if any, are present. Clinical experience has shown that lots meeting these criteria will minimize or exclude the occurrence of side effects in recipients.

The safety of Iveegam Immuno has been demonstrated in several preclinical and clinical studies.

The effectiveness of the manufacturing process of Iveegam Immuno to remove and/or inactivate virus was validated in in vitro spiking experiments using Human Immunodeficiency virus type I (HIV-1) as a target virus as well as the following model viruses: Pseudorabies virus (PRV, an enveloped DNA virus as a model for hepatitis B virus), Tick-Borne Encephalitis virus (TBEV, a small enveloped RNA virus as a model for HCV) and Equine Rhinovirus type-1 (ERV-1, a nonenveloped RNA virus as a model for hepatitis A virus). It was demonstrated that Immuno's modified Cohn-fractionation process combined with hydrolase treatment and polyethylene glycol precipitation used in the manufacture of Iveegam Immuno is capable of providing an overall reduction factor of >19.7 for HIV-1, >20.7 for TBEV, >19.0 for PRV and >24.6 for ERV-1. (According to the Commission of European Communities, Note for Guidance: "Validation of Virus Removal and Inactivation Procedures" III/8115/89-EN.)

Sixteen lots of Iveegam Immuno were used in the treatment of 14 patients with idiopathic thrombocytopenia in both the U.S. and Italy. The patients were followed for HIV-1 antibody between 2 to 27 months after initial product administration. None of the patients tested positive for anti-HIV-1.

To evaluate the risk of hepatitis non-A/non-B virus transmission by Iveegam Immuno, 2 chimpanzees were treated with a total of 218 and 254 g respectively, of product from 2 lots of Iveegam Immuno on a chronic basis over 8 months. None of the 2 animals had signs indicative of non-A/non-B hepatitis virus infection.

These findings were corroborated in a clinical study conducted in Poland. In this study 21 lots were given to 6 patients who were tested for ALT levels at biweekly intervals and followed up for a total of 106 4-month periods. None of the patients had an increase in ALT levels exceeding 2.5 times the upper normal limit.

The safety and efficacy of Iveegam Immuno has been demonstrated in clinical studies both in the U.S. and Europe. In a study conducted by Rosen et al. at the Children's Hospital Medical Center in Boston, Mass., from 1981 to 1983, 300 infusions were given to 16 patients with primary immunodeficiencies for an average time period of 14 months. Only 2 mild adverse reactions (0.7%) were observed. Patients accepted and tolerated the infusions well. The average dose applied per patient per month was 220 mg/kg. Using this dosage regime, a continuous increase of preinfusion serum IgG levels could be observed in 14 of the 16 patients. This increase continued after 6 months of therapy and levelled off after 1 year of treatment. The efficacy measured by increase of preinfusion serum immune globulin levels, and estimated on clinical grounds, was satisfactory and highly superior to the i.m. globulin regime. The ability to deliver larger doses with greater frequency has clearly been life-saving in 2 of the 16 patients.

Other studies conducted in Europe from the end of 1979 to mid 1983 in which a total of 1 956.37 g Iveegam Immuno were administered in 1 028 doses showed a rate of adverse reactions of less than 1%.

Indications: For replacement therapy in patients with primary and secondary antibody deficiency syndromes. The extent of impairment of antibody production may vary substantially and can involve all immune globulin classes, or only one immune globulin class, as well as IgG subclasses. Antibody deficiency syndromes with normal or elevated serum immune globulin levels have also been described. Patients with different forms of primary antibody deficiency are unduly susceptible to infections mainly with pyogenic microorganisms and may develop life-threatening bacterial infections or chronic lung diseases. Replacement therapy with Iveegam Immuno has been shown to be beneficial, and treatment should be started in patients with severe antibody deficiency syndromes even if no clinical symptoms or infections are apparent. Agammaglobulinemic patients might develop meningoencephalitis due to ECHO virus infection. This potentially fatal disease has been successfully treated with high dose immune globulin. I.V. immune globulin is preferable to the i.m. regime, because it allows for the delivery of high doses, the increase of serum IgG levels is fast, and infusions are not painful.

Replacement therapy is indicated in patients with hypo-and agammaglobulinemia, transient antibody deficiency syndrome in infancy, antibody deficiency with elevated IgM, antibody deficiency with normal IgM in combined IgG-IgA deficiency (see Precautions); isolated IgA deficiency with severe recurrent viral or bacterial infections (these patients often have additional IgG_2 and IgG_4 subclass deficiency) (see Precautions); IgG subclass deficiency, and patients with normal or elevated serum immune globulin levels who have been shown to be unable to produce antibodies.

Patients with combined immunodeficiency and severe combined immunodeficiency have in addition to a T-cell defect an impairment of antibody production as well, and may benefit from replacement therapy with Iveegam Immuno, even though this therapy will not correct the cellular immune defect.

Secondary antibody deficiencies may develop as consequence of protein loss, increased catabolism or decreased antibody production or a combination of these in the course of different underlying conditions and diseases. Patients with antibody deficiency syndromes, if unduly susceptible to infections, may benefit from treatment with Iveegam Immuno. These antibody deficiency syndromes may occur: in severe protein enteropathy; after major surgical intervention, e.g., gastrointestinal malignancies; in burn patients; in patients with malignancies; in patients with diseases of the hematopoietic and lymphoreticular system; after irradiation and/or cytostatic therapy.

Contraindications: Individuals who are known to have had an anaphylactic or severe systemic response to immune serum globulin (human). For individuals with selective IgA deficiencies, see Precautions.

Warnings: Iveegam Immuno should only be administered i.v. as the i.m. route has not yet been evaluated. This product is manufactured using components of human blood which may contain the causative agent of hepatitis and other viral diseases. Prescribed manufacturing procedures utilized in blood collection centres and the plasma testing laboratories are designed to reduce the risk of transmitting viral infection. However, the risk of the transmission of infective agents—also of hitherto unknown origin—cannot be totally excluded. Iveegam Immuno can, on occasion, cause a precipitous fall in blood pressure and the clinical picture of anaphylaxis even when the patient is not known to be sensitive to immune globulin preparations. These reactions are sometimes related to the rate of infusion. Accordingly, the infusion rate given under "Dosage" should be closely followed, at least until the physician has had sufficient experience with a given patient. The patient's vital signs should be monitored continuously and careful observation made for any symptoms throughout the entire infusion. Epinephrine should be available for treatment of any acute anaphylactoid reaction.

Although moderate and severe anaphylactoid reactions have not been observed in any of the clinical studies with this product, their occurrence cannot be ruled out. Investigators using other immune globulin products for i.v. use have described true anaphylactic reactions following administration. These reactions have been attributed to the presence of immune globulin A in certain preparations, while high level circulating IgA antibodies have been demonstrated or assumed to be present in the patients.

Anaphylactic reactions have also been explained in certain instances by antigen-antibody interactions if patients had antigenemia and the respective antibodies were in the product.

If anaphylactic or anaphylactoid reactions occur, the injection or infusion is to be discontinued immediately. Antihistamines (H1-receptor and H2-receptor blockers) and/or steroids and/or sympathicomimetics, given i.v., have proven effective antidotes. It is advisable that these medications be available for the treatment of such reactions, should they occur.

The administration of high doses of Iveegam Immuno may cause temporary increase in serum glucose in diabetics.

Precautions: General: Patients with severe antibody deficiency syndromes may react more readily to the infusion of homologous immune globulin. Such patients can be treated with Iveegam Immuno according to Table I.

Table I—Iveegam Immuno

Treatment Schedule for Patients with Severe Antibody Deficiency Syndromes

Infusion Number	Total Single Doses	Further Dilutions of the 5% Preparation	Infusion Rate
1st	5 mg/kg	1:10	1.0 mL/min
2nd	10 mg/kg	1:10	1.5 mL/min
3rd	20 mg/kg	1:10	2.0 mL/min
4th	30 mg/kg	1:5	1.5 mL/min
5th	50 mg/kg	1:5	2.0 mL/min
6th and further	100 mg/kg or higher (see Dosage)	—	2.0 mL/min

2 infusions/day at 6 hourly intervals, on consecutive days

Patients with IgA deficiency with severe recurrent viral or bacterial respiratory infections or with isolated IgA deficiency (and additional IgG_2 and IgG_4 deficiency), who may develop severe anaphylactic reactions after infusion of i.v. immune globulin, should receive the first infusion in the hospital under medical supervision.

Drug Interactions: Because antibodies in immune globulins may interfere with the immunogenic response to live virus vaccines, e.g., measles, mumps or rubella, vaccination should be postponed to 3 months after the last administration of immune globulin.

Pregnancy: Animal reproduction studies have not been carried out with this product. It is also not known whether Iveegam Immuno can cause fetal harm when administered to a pregnant woman or can affect reproduction capacity. The product should be given to a pregnant woman only if clearly needed.

Adverse Effects: Iveegam Immuno is a specially purified preparation for i.v. administration. Although years of experience have shown the preparation to be particularly well tolerated, adverse reactions cannot be ruled out completely.

As with any i.v. immunoglobulin, untoward reactions (e.g., flushing of the face, rashes, itching, headache, chest tightness, anxiety, malaise, rise in temperature, chills, slight elevation of blood pressure, tachycardia, difficulty of breathing, backache) may occur. Severe reactions with sudden onset of dyspnea, nausea, vomiting, circulatory collapse, loss of consciousness and fever are more common in patients with antibody deficiencies.

In clinical studies with Iveegam Immuno the rate of adverse reactions was less than 1%. Only minor reactions occurred.

In many cases adverse reactions as listed above can be avoided by slowing of the infusion rate. If hypersensitivity reactions (e.g., flushing of the face, chest tightness, drop in blood pressure) occur, the infusion must be discontinued immediately. In the case of anaphylactic reactions or shock, therapy should follow the current guidelines of shock treatment.

I.V. dosages of antihistamines, steroids and/or sympathomimetics are effective treatment and should always be available.

After minor reactions have subsided, further treatment may be attempted using diluted solutions, lower doses, and/or shorter intervals (e.g., administer a lower dose in 2 infusions a day).

Dosage: Parenteral drug products should be inspected visually for particle matter and discoloration prior to administration whenever solution and container permit. Reconstituted vials found to contain product with either should not be used. In most cases a dosage of 200 mg/kg/month is sufficient for treatment. If required, the dosage may be increased up to 4-fold and/or intervals shortened.

In cases of hypo- or agammaglobulinemia the serum IgG levels should be monitored by measurements prior to each infusion until a preinfusion level of a minimum of 400 mg/100 mL is reached. With adequate doses given at regular intervals it can be expected that a steady increase of the preinfusion values will occur over a period of 6 to 12 months until a plateau of the preinfusion level is reached. If clinical results are not fully satisfactory with this preinfusion level of 400 mg/100 mL, attempts should be made to reach a preinfusion level of 600 mg/100 mL and more. Experience has shown that this may be achieved by increasing the dose to 500 to 600 mg/kg/month.

Reconstitution: Reconstitution with the Sterile Water for Injection provided in each pack results in a 5% solution. 1. Remove

Iveegam Immuno (cont'd)

protective caps from the concentrate and solvent bottles and disinfect rubber stoppers of both bottles. 2. Remove protective covering from one end of the accompanying double-ended needle and insert the exposed needle through the diluent bottle stopper. 3. Remove protective cap from the other end of the double-ended needle. Do not touch exposed needle end! 4. Turn diluent bottle upside down and insert free end of the needle into the concentrate bottle stopper to half its length. Diluent will be drawn into the concentrate bottle by vacuum. 5. Disconnect the 2 bottles leaving the needle on the solvent bottle. Accelerate reconstitution by gently agitating or rotating the concentrate bottle. 6. Administer the solution directly using the accompanying infusion set with filter.

Reconstitution of the freeze-dried powder of Iveegam Immuno with the accompanying Sterile Water for Injection, yields a solution of the following composition: functionally intact monomeric IgG 50 mg/mL±5 mg/mL; total protein content 55 mg/mL±5 mg/mL; sodium chloride 3 mg/mL±1 mg/mL; stabilizer: glucose 50 mg/mL ±5 mg/mL.

Iveegam Immuno must be administered i.v. immediately after reconstitution. The rate of administration should be generally 1 mL up to a maximum of 2mL/minute for the 5% solution.

If lower immune globulin concentrations are desired, the 5% solution of Iveegam Immuno can be diluted with isotonic saline or isotonic sugar solutions (glucose, levulose).

Supplied: Iveegam Immuno is a sterile, freeze-dried concentrate of immune globulines G prepared from pooled human plasma. Plasma units are obtained from blood banks and from licensed plasmapheresis centers in the U.S. and Europe. The source material is subjected to a modified cold ethanol fractionation process according to COHN. From the immunoglobulin fraction thus obtained, Iveegam Immuno is manufactured in a multistep procedure.

The major manufacturing steps include: elimination of IgA by adsorption onto ion exchangers; inactivation and removal of viruses and substances causing adverse reactions by treatment with immobilized hydrolases; isolation of aggregate-free immunoglobulin G by fractionated precipitation with polyethylene glycol (PEG).

The individual steps of this manufacturing process also lead to the reduction and inactivation of potentially present viral contaminants. The treatment with immobilized hydrolases is an additional virus inactivation measure incorporated into the manufacture of Iveegam Immuno.

In the manufacture of Iveegam Immuno, the immune globulins remain unaltered in their native form, the biological half-life unimpaired and the Fc-function of the antibody molecule intact.

Single dose infusion vials of 5 000 mg of freeze-dried immune globulin (for i.v. use) accompanied by 100 mL vial of Sterile Water for Injection, 1 sterile double-ended needle and 1 infusion set with filter. Store at 2 to 8°C. Any vial that has been entered should be used promptly. Partially used vials should be discarded. Do not use after expiration date. Do not use if turbid. Avoid freezing, which may damage the diluent bottle.

Reviewed 1998

J

JECTOFER® Pr

Astra

Iron-Sorbitol-Citric Acid Complex, Dextrin-Stabilized

Intramuscular Hematinic

Pharmacology: Many of the properties of iron sorbitol result from its relatively low molecular weight. It is rapidly absorbed from the injection site and is stable in tissue fluids. Two-thirds of the injected dose is absorbed from an i.m. site within 3 hours, most of it directly into the blood circulation and, to a lesser extent, via lymphatics. Within approximately 10 days, little or no residue of iron remains at the injection site.

Absorption is followed by a rapid increase in serum iron concentration. In man, maximum plasma levels are attained in about 2 hours and return to normal values within 24 hours. This pattern of absorption is repeated in day-by-day injections and appears to be constant from patient to patient.

Clearance from the circulation is rapid. A proportion of the absorbed complex immediately gives up its iron directly to transferrin in the plasma and thus is available for marrow utilization and hemoglobin synthesis without intermediate metabolism. During this period, serum transferrin is fully saturated. The amount of iron sorbitol taken up by the liver and bone marrow is determined by iron status. A larger proportion is taken up by the liver in nonanemic patients than in the iron deficient. The main route of plasma clearance is via reticuloendothelial uptake in the liver from which iron is released to plasma transferrin for utilization. A fraction of the iron is taken up by renal convoluted tubules, appearing there as ferritin which is mobilized and cleared from the tubules in the course of some weeks.

Iron sorbitol has no effect on blood clotting at the concentrations achieved clinically.

Indications: Treatment of iron deficiency anemia. Replenishment of storage iron.

Absolute Indications: In cases where intestinal malabsorption may occur; when oral iron produces gastrointestinal intolerance.

Practical Indications: In cases where oral iron is contraindicated because of diseases or disorders of the gastrointestinal tract e.g., peptic ulceration; failure of patient to cooperate in oral iron therapy; in late pregnancy when an assured response to iron is needed; in cases of chronic blood loss when it is desired to avoid the use of blood transfusion.

Note: Iron sorbitol can only replace iron loss. In acute hemorrhage when the amount of blood loss may be considerable, attention must be given to the replacement of blood volume in the form of blood transfusion or blood substitutes or other volume expanders, according to the clinical situation, as well as to the replacement of iron loss.

Contraindications: Anemias not due to iron deficiency: e.g., hemolytic anemia, aplastic or hypoplastic anemia, acute leukemia, thalassemia, untreated megaloblastic anemias; acute pyelonephritis; acute liver disease; early pregnancy (see Precautions); known sensitivity to iron sorbitol.

Warnings: Iron sorbitol is for i.m. use only.

Iron sorbitol, a low molecular weight complex, contains 6% dialyzable iron. If given i.v., this fraction will rapidly saturate the transferrin and the excess can cause a toxic reaction, i.e., hypotension, flushing, dizziness and vomiting. When iron sorbitol is given i.m. the iron release proceeds at a controlled rate, greatly reducing the potential for a toxic reaction.

Iron sorbitol may form a grey precipitate when refrigerated. Do not use if precipitate forms and/or solution is unclear (see Supplied).

Precautions: Iron sorbitol should be administered only by i.m. injection in the treatment of accurately diagnosed iron deficiency anemia (see Warnings). If expected results are not obtained during or following the course of treatment, a complicating illness or an inaccurate diagnosis should be suspected. Do not continue without establishing the reason for failure to respond as it may be possible that iron sorbitol is not indicated.

The importance of using the correct recommended dose in relation to body weight is emphasized (1.5 mg iron/kg), especially in patients who are already markedly underweight (see Adverse Effects).

Iron sorbitol should not be administered concurrently with oral iron medication. Such concurrent administration has been reported to produce an increase in the incidence of side effects.

As with other iron therapy, iron sorbitol is not effective in anemia of rheumatoid arthritis and in anemias of infection unless iron deficiency is present.

Pregnancy: It is highly unlikely that iron sorbitol will cause fetal abnormalities when administered to women in late pregnancy.

There have been a few reports of abortion and congenital malformation after iron sorbitol in early pregnancy. In view of the severe conditions in the patients treated with iron sorbitol, and the use of concomitant medication, a relation between the events and the drug does not seem to be proven. However, the use of iron sorbitol in the first 3 or 4 months of pregnancy is not recommended.

Drug Interactions: The concomitant administration of chloramphenicol may delay the response to iron therapy in patients with iron deficiency anemia. Most likely this effect is due to the bone marrow depressing properties of chloramphenicol.

Adverse Effects: Initial local discomfort, sometimes described as painful, may be experienced at the site of injection. Temporary skin discoloration at the injection site may occur. In a very small percentage of cases the injection may be followed by a localized or generalized urticaria.

A transient metallic taste is common, which may be accompanied by a temporary loss of taste. Nausea, vomiting, diarrhea, headache, dizziness, sweating and flushing of the face may occur. Hematuria has been reported.

Severe systemic reactions with cardiac involvement are seen mostly in connection with overdose. Those reported include sensations of pressure in the chest, circulatory failure, hypertension, syncope, hypotension, arrhythmia, palpitation, AV block, bradycardia, atrial fibrillation and tachycardia.

In general, the systemic side effects mentioned above have been observed more commonly when doses higher than those recommended were given. This generally occurs in patients who are underweight or in those with anemias that are not, or only in part due to iron deficiency (see Contraindications). In such cases the transferrin saturation is often high. For this reason, iron sorbitol should not be administered concurrently with oral iron medication. Similar systemic reactions may rarely occur in severely debilitated or sensitive patients given recommended doses. In such cases the amount of the single daily dose should be reduced.

Isolated cases of anaphylactoid reactions have been reported.

Overdose: There have been 10 cases of overdoses reported to date: One case involved a 4-month-old infant who received 44 mg Fe/kg. Two children <3 years received 50 mg Fe. One of these children was on concomitant ampicillin. All 3 patients died.

Four reports describe patients with malabsorption diseases and who were underweight (43 to 49 kg). All 4 patients were given 1 to 6 injections of 100 mg Fe/injection. Two of the patients died and 2 recovered with sequelae. Another 2 patients had diarrhea of long duration, one received 5 injections of 100 mg Fe/injection, the other, 1 injection of 100 mg Fe. Both patients recovered. In 1 case the patient was inadvertently given an i.v. injection of 200 mg Fe. The patient recovered.

Symptoms: The systemic reactions reported in overdosage are generally dose related. The reported symptoms are dizziness, nausea, vomiting, diarrhea, sweating, palpitations, pressure sensations in the chest and hypotension. The more severe reactions reported are circulatory collapse and cardiac arrhythmias (in 1 case ventricular tachycardia).

Treatment: Close clinical observation and laboratory monitoring are essential. Treatment should be adapted to the severity of overdose with reference to serum iron and total iron-binding capacity.

When the patient exhibits symptoms of systemic iron poisoning, chelation therapy with parenterally administered deferoxamine is indicated. The recommended dosing regimen for deferoxamine is 15 mg/kg/h by continuous i.v. infusion. The infusion is continued until the patient is symptom-free and the corrected serum iron concentration is normal or low. For severely ill patients, higher infusion rates might be needed.

Rehydration, acidosis- and electrolyte correction should be initiated as soon as possible. If a vasopressor is needed, dopamine has been suggested. Liver and kidney function should be monitored.

Dosage: For i.m. injection only (see Warnings).

Adults: The recommended single daily dose for injection is calculated on the basis of 1.5 mg iron/kg body weight. The calculated dose may be administered daily or every other day until hemoglobin values reach the normal range. The single daily injection of more than 2 mL of iron sorbitol is not recommended. Two mL iron sorbitol contains the recommended single daily dose (100 mg) for an adult of 70 kg body weight.

The total course of single daily doses should be adjusted according to the severity of the anemia. To increase the Hb value by 10 g/L it is necessary to administer, by the parenteral route, approximately 200 mg of elemental iron for women and 250 mg for men. Corresponding amounts to achieve an increase of 1% Hb are approximately 35 mg of iron for women and 45 mg for men. In addition, about 250 to 1 000 mg elemental iron are required for the replenishment of iron stores.

Dosage Guide: Adults: Table I may be used as a practical guide to dosage.

Table I—Jectofer

Dosage Guide for Adults

Patient's Weight (kg)	Single Daily Dose in mL Calculated	Total Number of Single Daily Doses for a Course of Treatment Calculated from a Hemoglobin Value of:								
		35	40	45	50	55	60	65	70	%Hb
		53	60	68	75	83	90	98	105	g Hb/L
35	1.0									
40	1.2									
50	1.5	24	22	20	18	16	14	12	10	
60	1.8									
70	2.0									

Note: In addition to the number suggested above, another 5 to 10 additional doses should be given to adults to replenish stores.

Children: The recommended single daily dose for injection is similarly calculated on the basis of 1.5 mg iron/kg body weight. The calculated daily dose should be administered daily or every other day until hemoglobin values reach the normal range.

Dosage Guide: Children: Table II may be used as a practical guide to dosage.

Table II—Jectofer

Dosage Guide for Children

Patient's Weight (kg)	Single Daily Dose in mL Calculated	Total Number of Single Daily Doses for a Course of Treatment Calculated from a Hemoglobin Value of:							
		40	45	50	55	60	65	70	% Hb
		60	68	75	83	90	98	105	g Hb/L
7	0.20								
10	0.30								
12	0.35	22	20	18	16	14	12	10	
16	0.50								
27	0.80								

I.M. Injection Technique: 1. After loading the syringe with the appropriate dose of iron sorbitol, change to a new, dry needle.

2. Use a fine needle to ensure a deep i.m. injection even in an obese patient. A needle 50 mm in length with an outside diameter of 0.7 mm (22 gauge) is suitable in most cases. As a rule, the needle should not be shorter than 40 mm and not longer than 80 mm.

3. The injection is given into the upper outer quadrant of the buttock to avoid accidental injection into a large nerve or blood vessel. Alternate sides should be used for subsequent injections.

4. A Z-track technique should be used to prevent leakage along the needle track. The skin over the injection site is moved firmly to one side and held in this position until the needle has been inserted.

5. Insert the needle for deep i.m. injection.

6. Check that the needle point is not in a blood vessel. Exert a gentle pull on the plunger as if to withdraw it. There should be firm resistance to movement of the plunger. If the needle is in a blood vessel, the plunger will yield to the pull and blood will enter the syringe, although this may escape observation because of the dark colored solution.

7. Inject slowly without any force. Withdraw the needle quickly after about 10 seconds. As the skin and s.c. tissue resumes

Jectofer (cont'd)

a normal position, this completes the Z-track procedure. Do not massage the site of injection. The patient should rest lying down for 5 minutes after the injection.

Note: When using iron sorbitol only freshly opened ampuls should be used. On no account should an opened ampul be retained for later use.

Supplied: Each mL of clear, dark brown, sterile colloidal solution contains: iron 50 mg (as a complex of ferric iron, sorbitol and citric acid, stabilized with dextrin). Sorbitol for injection is added to strengthen the complex. Sodium hydroxide and/or hydrochloric acid to adjust pH to 7.2 to 7.9. Single-use ampuls of 2 mL, boxes of 10. Store at room temperature (15 to 30°C). **Do not refrigerate.** Lower temperatures may disturb the colloid resulting in the formation of a grey precipitate. If a precipitate forms and/or solution is unclear, discard and do not use.

Reviewed 1998

JE-VAX®

Connaught

Japanese Encephalitis Virus Vaccine Inactivated

Active Immunizing Agent

Pharmacology: Japanese encephalitis (JE), a mosquito-borne arboviral Flavivirus infection is the leading cause of viral encephalitis in Asia.

Infection leads to overt encephalitis in only 1 of 20 to 1 000 cases. Encephalitis usually is severe, resulting in a fatal outcome in 25% of cases and residual neuropsychiatric sequelae in 50% of cases. JE acquired during the first or second trimesters of pregnancy may cause intrauterine infection and miscarriage. Infections that occur during the third trimester of pregnancy have not been associated with adverse outcomes in newborns.

The virus is transmitted in an enzootic cycle among mosquitoes and vertebrate amplifying hosts, chiefly domestic pigs and, in some areas, wild Ardeid (wading) birds. Viral infection rates in mosquitoes range from <1 to 3%. These species are prolific in rural areas where their larvae breed in ground pools and flooded rice fields. Thus all elements of the transmission cycle are prevalent in rural areas of Asia and human infections occur principally in this setting. Because vertebrate amplifying hosts and agricultural activities may be situated within and at the periphery of cities, human cases occasionally are reported from urban locations.

JE virus is transmitted seasonally in most areas of Asia. The seasonal patterns of viral transmission are correlated with the abundance of vector mosquitoes and of vertebrate amplifying hosts. Although the abundance of vector mosquitoes fluctuates with rainfall and with the impact of the rainy season in some tropical locations, irrigation associated with agricultural practices is a more important factor affecting vector abundance, and transmission may occur year round. Thus the periods of greatest risk for JE viral transmission vary regionally and within countries, and from year to year.

In areas where JE is endemic, annual incidence ranges from 1 to 10 per 10 000 people. Cases occur primarily in children under 10 years of age. Seroprevalence studies in these endemic areas indicate nearly universal exposure by adulthood (calculating from a ratio of asymptomatic to symptomatic infection of 200 to 1, approximately 10% of the susceptible population is infected per year). In addition to children <10 years, an increase in JE incidence has been observed in the elderly.

Challenge experiments in passively protected mice have defined the levels of neutralizing antibody that may be considered protective for humans. Mice passively immunized to achieve a neutralizing antibody titre of $\geq 1{:}10$ were protected from a JE virus challenge of $10^5 LD_{50}$, a viral dose thought to be transmitted by an infected mosquito.

The efficacy of the BIKEN Nakayama-NIH strain Japanese Encephalitis Virus Vaccine Inactivated was demonstrated in a placebo-controlled, randomized clinical trial in Thai children, sponsored by the U.S. Army. In this trial, children between 1 and 14 years of age received BIKEN monovalent Nakayama-NIH strain (n=21 628) or a bivalent vaccine containing the Nakayama-NIH and Beijing JE virus strains (n=22 080) or tetanus toxoid as a placebo (n=21 516). Immunization consisted of 2 s.c. 1 mL doses of vaccine, except in children under 3 years of age who receive two 0.5 mL doses. One case (5 cases/100 000) of JE occurred in the monovalent vaccine group, 11 cases (51 cases/100 000) in the placebo group. The observed efficacy of both monovalent and bivalent vaccines was 91% (95% confidence interval, 54 to 98%). Side effects of vaccination, including headache, sore arm, rash and swelling were reported at rates similar to those in the placebo group, usually less than 1%. Symptoms did not increase after the second dose. It should be noted that a schedule of 2 doses, separated by 7 days, as employed in this trial, may be appropriate for use in residents of endemic or epidemic areas, where pre-existing exposure to Flaviviruses may contribute to the immune response.

Experience from the Centers for Disease Control and Prevention, and a controlled immunogenicity trial performed in U.S. military personnel demonstrated the need for a 3-dose vaccination schedule for persons not native to JE virus endemic areas. The CDC experience demonstrated that neutralizing antibody was produced in fewer than 80% of vaccinees following 2 doses of vaccine in U.S. travelers and antibody levels declined substantially in most vaccinees within 6 months. The U.S. Army studied the immunogenicity of Je-Vax in 538 volunteers. Two 3-dose regimens were evaluated (Day 0, 7 and 14 or Day 0, 7 and 30). All vaccine recipients demonstrated neutralizing antibodies at 2 months and 6 months after initiation of vaccination. The schedule of Day 0, 7 and 30 produced higher antibody responses than the Day 0, 7 and 14 schedule. Two hundred and seventy-three of the original study participants were tested at 12 months post-vaccination and there was no longer a statistical difference in antibody titres between the 2 vaccination regimens.

The full duration of protection is unknown. Of U.S. Army volunteers completing a 3-dose regimen, 252 agreed to receive a booster dose of vaccine 1 year after the primary series. All boosted participants still had antibody 12 months after the booster. Protective levels of neutralizing antibody persisted for 24 months (2 years) in all 21 persons who had not received a booster. Definitive recommendations cannot be given on the timing of booster doses at this time.

Indications: Provides active immunization against JE for persons 1 year of age and older. For the recommended primary immunization series see Dosage.

Je-Vax should be considered for use in persons who plan to reside in or travel to areas where JE is endemic or epidemic during a transmission season. The incidence of JE in the location of intended stay, the conditions of housing, nature of activities, duration of stay, and the possibility of unexpected travel to high-risk areas are factors that should be considered in the decision to administer vaccine. Vaccination should generally be considered for travelers of any age who will spend 3 weeks or more in rural areas during the seasons of transmission of endemic or epidemic JE; proximity to areas of rice culture or of pig farming increases the risk of acquiring JE. Depending on the epidemic circumstances, vaccine should be considered for persons spending less than 3 weeks whose activities, such as extensive outdoor activities in rural areas, place them at particularly high risk for exposure.

In all instances, travelers are advised to take personal precautions to reduce exposure to mosquito bites.

The decision to use Je-Vax should balance the risks for exposure to the virus and for developing illness; the availability and acceptability of repellents and other alternative measures; and the side effects of vaccination. Assessments should be interpreted cautiously because risk can vary within areas and from year to year and available data are incomplete. Although Je-Vax is reactogenic, rates of serious allergic reactions (generalized urticaria and/or angioedema) are low (approximately 1 to 104 per 10 000).

Advanced age may be a risk factor for developing symptomatic illness after infection. JE acquired during pregnancy carries the potential for intrauterine infection and fetal death. These factors should be considered when advising the elderly or pregnant women who plan to visit JE endemic areas.

There are no data on the safety and efficacy of Je-Vax in infants under 1 year of age. Whenever possible, immunization of infants should be deferred until they are 1 year of age or older.

Research Laboratory Workers: Laboratory acquired JE has been reported in 22 cases. JE virus may be transmitted in a laboratory setting through needle sticks and other accidental exposures. Vaccine-derived immunity presumably protects against exposure through these percutaneous routes. Exposure to aerosolized JE virus, and particularly to high concentrations of virus, such as may occur during viral purification, potentially could lead to infection through mucous membranes and possibly directly into the CNS through the olfactory epithelium. It is unknown whether vaccine derived immunity protects against such exposures, but immunization is recommended for all laboratory workers with a potential for exposure to infectious JE virus.

As with any vaccine, vaccination with Je-Vax may not result in protection in all individuals. Long-term protection, as demonstrated by persistence of neutralizing antibody for more than 2 years, has not yet been shown.

Contraindications: Adverse reactions to a prior dose of JE vaccine manifesting as generalized urticaria and angioedema are considered to be contraindications to further vaccination.

JE vaccine is produced in mouse brains and should not be administered to persons with a proven or suspected hypersensitivity to proteins of rodent or neural origin. **Hypersensitivity to thimerosal is a contraindication to vaccination.**

Warnings: Adverse reactions to JE vaccine manifesting generalized urticaria or angioedema may occur within minutes following vaccination. A possibly related reaction has occurred as late as 17 days after vaccination. Most reactions occur within 10 days with the majority occurring within 48 hours (see Adverse Effects).

Vaccinees should be observed for 30 minutes after vaccination and warned about the possibility of delayed generalized urticaria, often in a generalized distribution or angioedema of the extremities, face and oropharynx, especially of the lips.

Vaccinees should be advised to remain in areas where they have ready access to medical care for 10 days after receiving a dose of JE vaccine.

Persons should not embark on international travel within 10 days of Je-Vax Japanese Encephalitis Virus Vaccine Inactivated immunization because of the possibility of delayed allergic reactions. However, if departure is imminent and will occur in less than 10 days, an assessment to use Je-Vax must balance i) the risk of exposure the traveller will have to JE virus infection (if unvaccinated, or if an incomplete vaccine series given), and ii) the risk of having a delayed allergic reaction in the absence of accessible medical care.

Vaccinees should be instructed to seek medical attention immediately upon symptoms of any serious or unusual reaction, particularly, angioedema of the extremities, face and oropharynx, especially of the lips.

Persons with a past history of urticaria after hymenoptera envenomation, drugs, physical or other provocations, or of idiopathic cause appear to have a greater risk of developing reactions to JE vaccine (relative risk 9.1, 95% confidence interval 1.8 to 50.9). This history should be considered when weighing risks and benefits of the vaccine for an individual patient. When patients with such a history are offered JE vaccine, they should be alerted to their increased risk for reaction and monitored appropriately. There are no data supporting the efficacy of prophylactic antihistamines or steroids in preventing JE vaccine-related allergic reactions.

Precautions: General: Epinephrine Injection (1:1 000) must be immediately available should an acute anaphylactic reaction occur due to any component of the vaccine.

Prior to injection of any vaccine, all known precautions should be taken to prevent adverse reactions. This includes a review of the patient's history with respect to possible sensitivity to this vaccine, a similar vaccine or allergic disorder in general (see Contraindications).

A separate, sterile syringe and needle or a disposable unit should be used for each patient to prevent transmission of infectious agents from person to person. Needles should not be recapped and should be disposed of properly.

Although substantial neutralizing antibody titres are elicited by Japanese Encephalitis Virus Vaccine Inactivated in more than 90% of U.S. travelers without history of prior JE immunization or of prior exposure to JE, the precise relationship between antibody level and efficacy has not been established even though these titres persisted for at least 2 years after immunization.

The decision to administer Je-Vax should balance the risks for exposure to the virus and for developing illness, the availability and acceptability of repellents and other alternative protective measures, and the side effects of vaccination.

Drug Interactions: There are no data on the effect of concurrent administration of other vaccines, drugs (e.g., chloroquine, mefloquine) or biologicals on the safety and immunogenicity of Je-Vax.

Carcinogenesis, Mutagenesis, Impairment of Fertility: No studies have been performed to evaluate carcinogenicity, mutagenic potential, or impact on fertility.

Pregnancy: Animal reproduction studies have not been conducted with Japanese Encephalitis Virus Vaccine. It is not known whether Japanese Encephalitis Virus Vaccine can cause fetal harm when administered to a pregnant woman or can affect reproductive capacity. Pregnant women who must travel to an area where risk of JE is high should be immunized when the theoretical risks of immunization are outweighed by the risk of infection to the mother and developing fetus. Japanese Encephalitis Virus Vaccine should be given to a pregnant woman only if clearly needed.

Lactation: It is not known whether Je-Vax is excreted in human milk. Because many drugs are excreted in human milk, caution should be exercised when Je-Vax is administered to a nursing woman.

Children: Safety and efficacy of JE vaccine in infants under 1 year of age have not been established.

Adverse Effects: JE vaccine is associated with a moderate frequency of local and mild systemic adverse effects. Tenderness, redness, swelling and other local effects have been reported in about 20% of vaccinees (<1 to 31%). Systemic side effects, principally fever, headache, malaise, rash, and other reactions, such as chills, dizziness, myalgia, nausea, vomiting and abdominal pain have been reported in approximately 10% of vaccinees.

In a study conducted by the CDC less than 5% of the 1 756 U.S. travelers immunized with a 3-dose regimen of the vaccine reported headache, flu-like symptoms, fever, and other systemic complaints. Hives and facial swelling were reported in 0.2 and 0.1% of vaccinees, respectively. Local soreness occurred in 5.9% and local redness in 2.9%. There was no increase in the number or severity of reactions with increasing numbers of doses.

The U.S. Army studied 4 034 personnel from 1987 to 1989. Using a 2- or 3-dose regimen of JE vaccine, arm soreness was described in 22.7%, local redness in 4.8%, headache in 15.2%, and a febrile episode in 5.5%. In another trial evaluating the safety and immunogenicity of a 3-dose immunizing series (Day 0, 7 and 30 or Day 0, 7 and 14), performed in 538 adult volunteers in 1990, the Army determined that local soreness and redness occurred in 21% of vaccinees after the first dose, then decreased with subsequent injections ($p<0.0001$, Chi-square for downward trend). Systemic symptoms including feverishness, headache and rash occurred in 5% of vaccinees after the first dose, then decreased with subsequent injections ($p<0.001$, Chi-square for downward trend). Participants who received the third dose on Day 14 reported more side effects than those who received the injection on Day 30. Among these volunteers, 252 received a booster injection of vaccine 1 year after receiving the dose of the primary series. Side effects reported after the booster injection included local symptoms of soreness (24.5%) and redness (6.1%) at the injection site and systemic complaints of headache (4.9%), fever (1.6%), and rash (0.8%). Less than 1% of all reported symptoms was graded as severe. No generalized urticaria or anaphylaxis was reported.

Since 1989, an apparently new pattern of adverse reactions has been reported among vaccinees in Europe, North America and Australia. The reactions have been characterized by urticaria, often in a generalized distribution, or angioedema of the extremities, face, especially of the lips and oropharynx. Three vaccine recipients developed respiratory distress. Distress or collapse due to hypotension or other causes led to hospitalization in several cases. Most reactions were treated successfully with antihistamines or oral steroids; however, some patients were hospitalized for parenteral steroid therapy. Three patients developed an erythema multiforme or erythema nodosum and some patients had joint swelling. Some vaccinees complained of generalized itching without objective evidence of a rash.

An important feature of the reactions has been the interval between vaccination and onset of symptoms. Reactions after a first vaccine dose occurred after a median of 12 hours after immunization (88% of reactions occurred within 3 days). The interval between administration of a second dose and onset of symptoms generally was longer, (median 3 days and possibly as long as 2 weeks). Reactions have occurred after a second or third dose, when preceding doses were received uneventfully.

Between November 1991 and May 1992, the U.S. Navy immunized 35 253 U.S. personnel (marines, other military and dependents) with Japanese Encephalitis Virus Vaccine Inactivated on Okinawa. The overall reaction rate, 62.4 per 10 000 vaccinees (95% confidence interval 54.2 to 70.6) includes persons reporting urticaria, angioedema, generalized itching and wheezing. The reaction rate per 10 000 vaccinees was 26.7 (95% confidence interval 21.3 to 32.1), 30.8 (95% confidence interval 24.6 to 37.0) or 12.2 (95% confidence interval 7.9 to 16.5) after the first, second or third dose, respectively. These reactions were generally mild to moderate in severity. Nine out of 35 253 persons immunized were hospitalized (2.6 per 10 000 vaccinees) primarily to allow administration of i.v. steroids for refractory urticaria. None of these reactions were considered life-threatening.

A case-control study conducted as part of the JE immunization campaign in Okinawa found that persons developing these reactions after JE vaccination were more likely to have had a past history of urticaria after hymenoptera envenomation, drugs, physical or other provocations of idiopathic origins (relative risk 9.1, 95% confidence interval 1.8 to 50.9). The vaccine constituents responsible for these adverse reactions have not been identified.

Other serious adverse events reported following vaccination include (1) one case of Guillain-Barré syndrome after JE vaccination has been reported in the United States since 1984, however, this patient was diagnosed as having mononucleosis 3 weeks before the onset of weakness; (2) one case of urticaria, hepatitis and respiratory failure 1 week after dose 2 (this person showed effusion and infiltrate on chest x-ray and eosinophilia), and (3) one case of respiratory and renal failure 1 week after a dose (this 26-month-old male had infiltrate on chest x-ray and acid fast bacilli in sputum); and (4) one case of newly diagnosed hypertension in a young adult male presenting with a headache several hours after receiving dose one. The etiology of these adverse events is unknown.

Sudden death occurred approximately 60 hours after receiving the first dose of JE vaccine in a 21-year-old U.S. military person with a history of recurrent hypersensitivity and an episode of possible anaphylaxis. This person also received the third dose of plague vaccine approximately 12 to 15 hours prior to the death. There was no evidence of urticaria or angioedema. Cause of death was not established at autopsy.

Surveillance of JE vaccine-related complication in Japan from 1965 to 1973 disclosed neurologic events (primarily encephalitis, encephalopathy, seizures, and peripheral neuropathy) in 1 to 2.3 per million vaccinees. Very rarely, deaths occurred with vaccine-associated encephalitis. Between 1987 and 1989, 2 cases of neurologic dysfunction were reported from Japan; one of these was a transverse myelitis, while the second included seizures, cranial nerve paresis, cerebellar ataxia, and behavior disorder. In 1992, 2 cases of acute disseminated encephalomyelitis were reported from Japan; one occurred 14 days after the second dose and the second occurred 17 days after a booster dose of JE vaccine. Both cases recovered. One case of Bell's Palsy was reported from Thailand.

Reporting of Adverse Events: Reporting by parents and patients of all adverse events occurring after antigen administration should be encouraged. Health care providers should report any occurrences temporally related to the administration of the product in accordance with provincial and federal statutory requirements.

Health care providers also should report these events to the Department of Medical Affairs, Connaught Laboratories Limited.

Dosage: Parenteral drug products should be inspected visually for extraneous particulate matter and/or discoloration prior to administration whenever solution and container permit. If either of these conditions exist, the vaccine should not be administered.

For persons 3 years of age and older, a single dose is 1 mL of vaccine. **For children 1 year to 3 years of age, a single dose is 0.5 mL of vaccine.** (see Primary Immunization Schedule).

Single-Dose Vial of Lyophilized Vaccine: Remove plastic tab of flip-off cap. **Do not remove rubber stopper.** Cleanse stopper with a suitable disinfectant. Reconstitute only with the supplied 1.3 mL of Sterile Diluent (water for injection). Shake vial thoroughly.

Primary Immunization Schedule: The recommended primary immunization series is 3 doses of 1 mL each for individuals>3 years of age given s.c. on days 0, 7 and 30. **For children 1 to 3 years of age a series of 3 doses of 0.5 mL each should be given s.c. on days 0, 7 and 30.** An abbreviated schedule of days 0, 7 and 14 can be used when the longer schedule is impractical because of time constraints. (When it is impossible to follow one of the above recommended schedules, 2 doses given a week apart will induce antibodies in approximately 80% of vaccinees; however, this 2-dose regimen should not be used except under unusual circumstances.) The last dose should be given at least 10 days before the commencement of international travel to ensure an adequate immune response and access to medical care in the event of delayed adverse reactions.

A booster dose of 1 mL **(0.5 mL for children from 1 to 3 years of age)** may be given after 2 years. In the absence of firm data on the persistence of antibody after primary immunization, a definite recommendation cannot be made on the spacing of boosters beyond 2 years.

There are no data on the safety and efficacy of JE vaccine in infants under 1 year of age. Whenever possible, immunization of infants should be deferred until they are 1 year of age or older.

The skin at the site of injection first should be cleansed and disinfected. **Shake the vial well** to uniformly distribute the suspension before withdrawing the dose.

When Japanese Encephalitis Virus Vaccine Inactivated and any other vaccines are given concurrently, separate syringes and separate sites should be used.

Each person who is immunized should be given a permanent personal immunization record. In addition, it is essential that the health care provider also maintain a permanent record of the immunization history of each individual. This office record should contain the name of the vaccine, date given, manufacturer and lot number.

Supplied: Japanese Encephalitis Virus Vaccine Inactivated is a sterile, lyophilized vaccine for s.c. use, prepared by inoculating mice intracerebrally with Japanese encephalitis (JE) virus, "Nakayama-NIH" strain, manufactured by The Research Foundation for Microbial Diseases of Osaka University ("BIKEN"). Infected brains are harvested and homogenized in phosphate buffered saline, pH 8.0. The homogenate is centrifuged and the supernatant inactivated with formaldehyde, then processed to yield a partially purified, inactivated virus suspension. This is further purified by ultra-centrifugation through 40% w/v sucrose. Thimerosal (mercury derivative) is added as a preservative to a final concentration of 0.007%. The suspension is then lyophilized in final containers and sealed under dry nitrogen atmosphere. The Sterile Diluent (water for injection), contains no preservative. Each 1 mL dose contains approximately gelatin 500 μg, less than 100 μg of formaldehyde, and less than 50 ng of mouse serum protein. No myelin basic protein can be detected at the detection threshold of the assay (<2 ng/mL). Prior to reconstitution, the vaccine is a white caked powder, and after reconstitution the vaccine is a colorless transparent liquid. The potency of JE vaccine is determined by immunizing mice with either the test vaccine or the JE reference vaccine. Neutralizing antibodies are measured in a plaque neutralization assay performed on sera from the immunized mice. The potency of the test vaccine must be no less than that of the reference vaccine.

Boxes of 5 single dose vials with 5×1.3 mL vials of Sterile Diluent (water for injection). Boxes of 3 single dose vials with 3×1.3 mL vials of Sterile Diluent (water for injection). Store between 2 and 8°C. **Do not freeze.** After reconstitution the vaccine should be stored between 2 and 8°C and used within 8 hours. **Do not freeze reconstituted vaccine.**

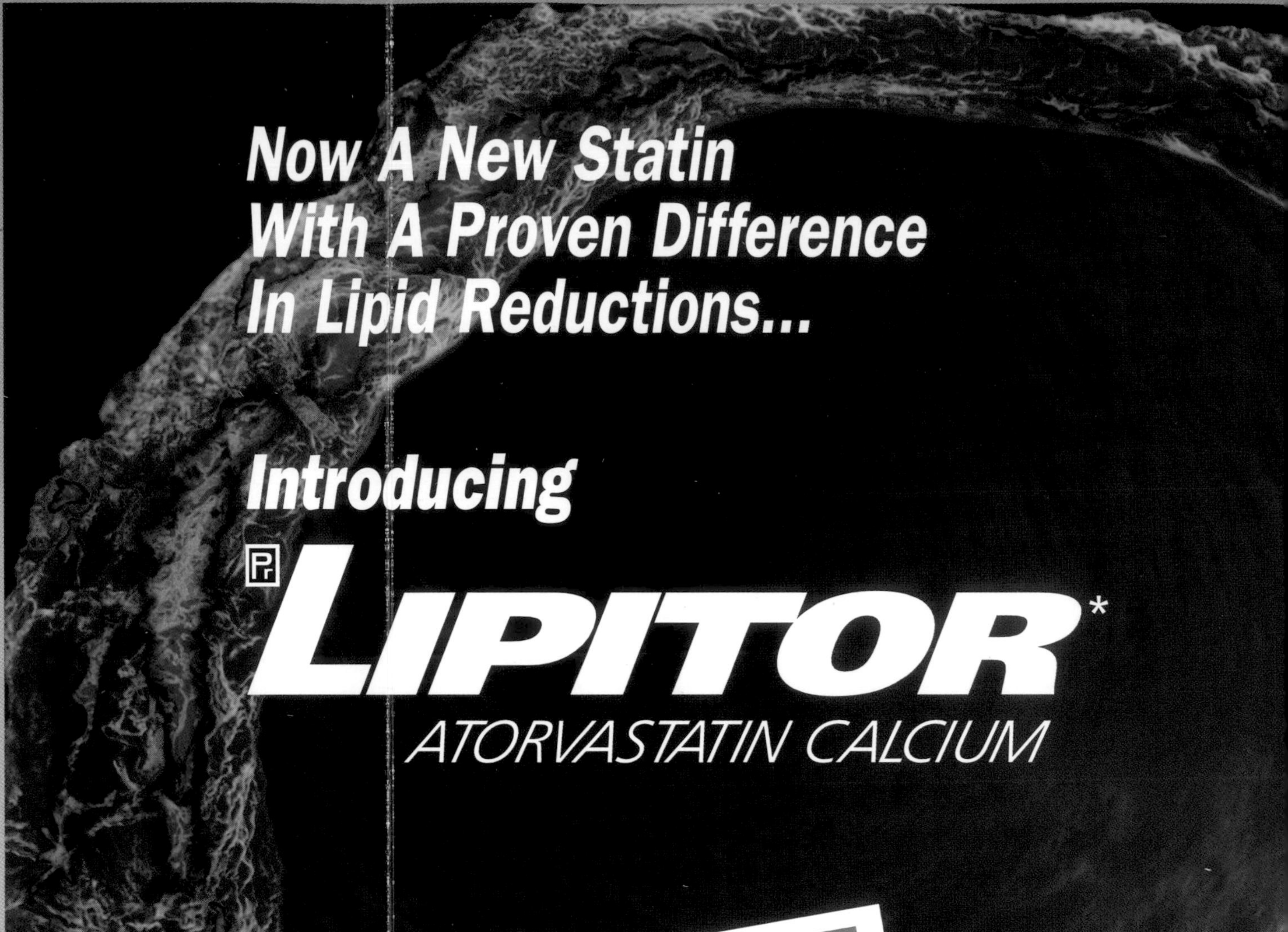
Now A New Statin
With A Proven Difference
In Lipid Reductions...
Introducing
Pr LIPITOR*
ATORVASTATIN CALCIUM
NOW AVAILABLE ON ALL
PROVINCIAL FORMULARIES!††
††Pending in Prince Edward Island

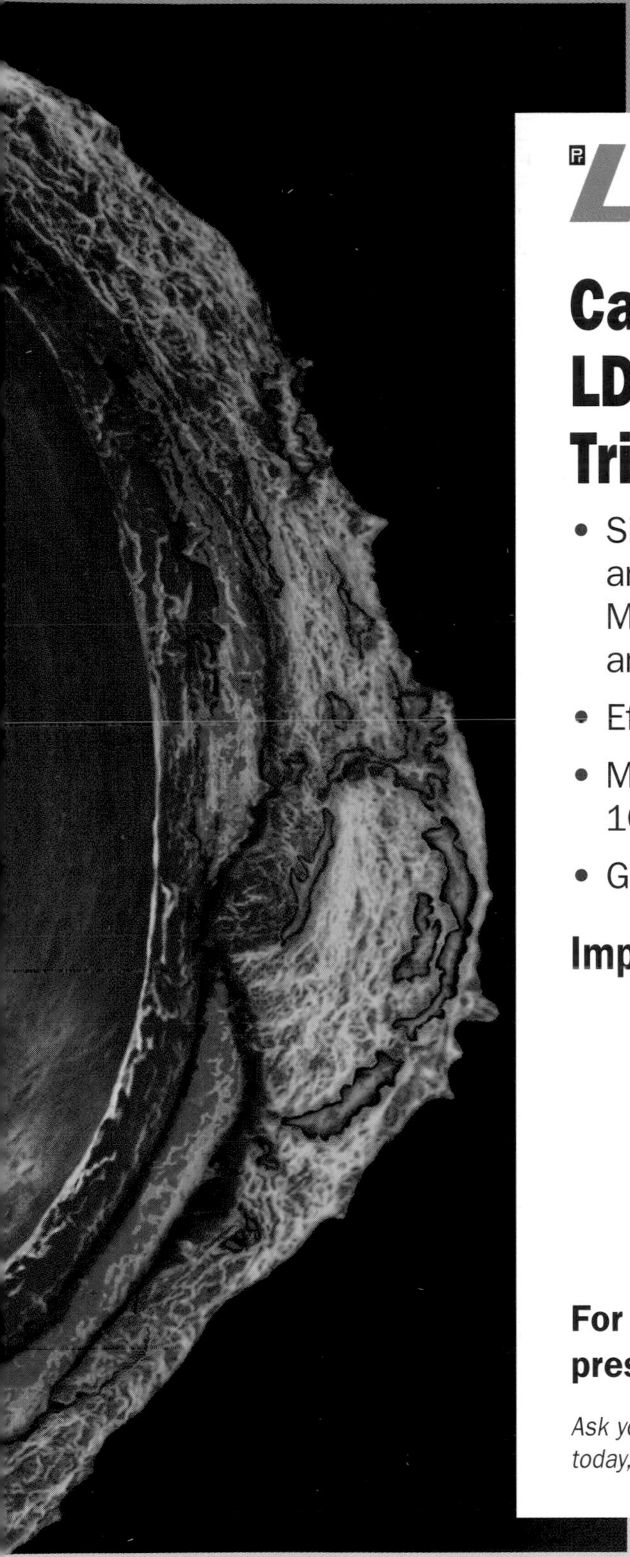

LIPITOR*

ATORVASTATIN CALCIUM

Can dramatically lower LDL-C by 39-60% and Triglycerides by 19-37%*[1]

- Significantly greater reductions in both LDL-C and Triglycerides than Zocor®, Pravachol® and Mevacor® at starting doses (results at 16 weeks and 1 year)[‡2,3,4]
- Effective in a wide range of patients[1]
- Most patients will be managed on the recommended 10 mg once-a-day dose[5]
- Generally well-tolerated[1]

Impressive lipid effects...*[1]

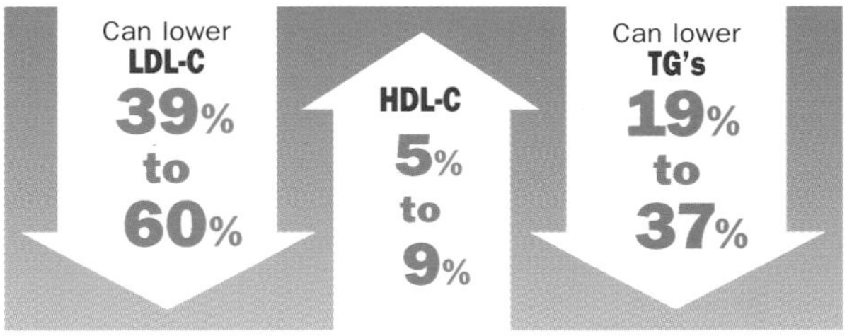

For your next patient requiring a statin, prescribe LIPITOR 10 mg.

Ask your Parke-Davis or Pfizer Canada Inc. representative about New LIPITOR today, or call the LIPITOR toll-free Medical Information line at: 1-888-776-7747.

PARKE-DAVIS

*TM Warner-Lambert Export Limited
Parke-Davis Div.
Warner-Lambert Canada Inc., lic. use
Scarborough, ONT M1L 2N3

98-37/E/J/DPS

Co-promoted with

Pfizer

We're part of the cure†

Pfizer Canada Inc.
Kirkland, Quebec H9J 2M5

† TM Pfizer Inc. used under license

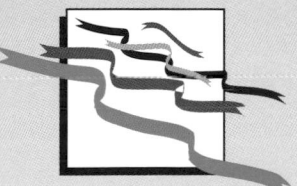

LIPITOR*

ATORVASTATIN CALCIUM

ACHIEVING NEW LEVELS OF LIPID CONTROL

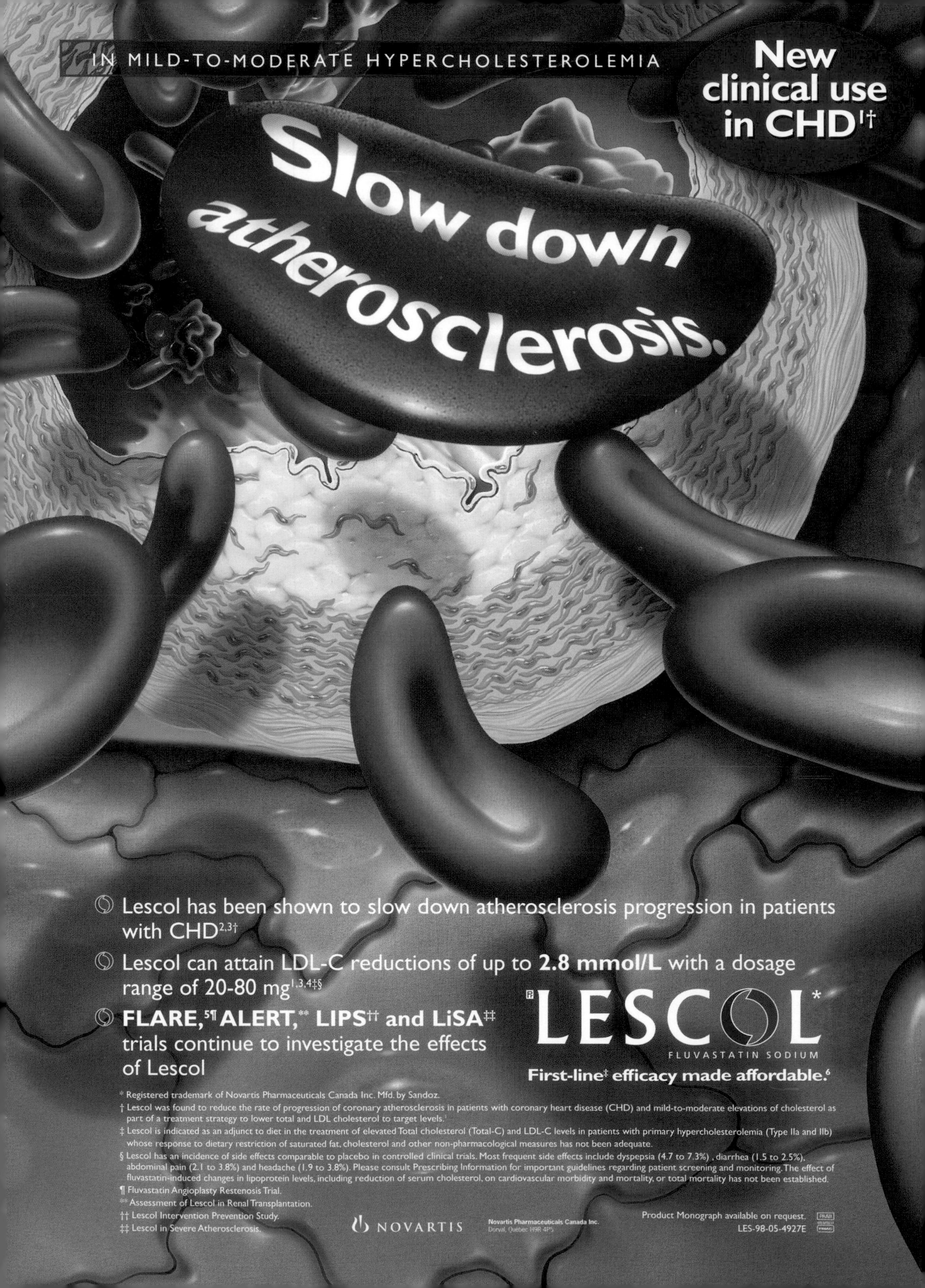

IN MILD-TO-MODERATE HYPERCHOLESTEROLEMIA
New clinical use in CHD[1†]
Slow down atherosclerosis.
Lescol has been shown to slow down atherosclerosis progression in patients with CHD[2,3†]
Lescol can attain LDL-C reductions of up to **2.8 mmol/L** with a dosage range of 20-80 mg[1,3,4‡§]
FLARE,[5¶] ALERT,[**] LIPS[††] and LiSA[‡‡] trials continue to investigate the effects of Lescol
LESCOL*
FLUVASTATIN SODIUM
First-line[‡] efficacy made affordable.[6]
* Registered trademark of Novartis Pharmaceuticals Canada Inc. Mfd. by Sandoz.
† Lescol was found to reduce the rate of progression of coronary atherosclerosis in patients with coronary heart disease (CHD) and mild-to-moderate elevations of cholesterol as part of a treatment strategy to lower total and LDL cholesterol to target levels.[1]
‡ Lescol is indicated as an adjunct to diet in the treatment of elevated Total cholesterol (Total-C) and LDL-C levels in patients with primary hypercholesterolemia (Type IIa and IIb) whose response to dietary restriction of saturated fat, cholesterol and other non-pharmacological measures has not been adequate.
§ Lescol has an incidence of side effects comparable to placebo in controlled clinical trials. Most frequent side effects include dyspepsia (4.7 to 7.3%) , diarrhea (1.5 to 2.5%), abdominal pain (2.1 to 3.8%) and headache (1.9 to 3.8%). Please consult Prescribing Information for important guidelines regarding patient screening and monitoring. The effect of fluvastatin-induced changes in lipoprotein levels, including reduction of serum cholesterol, on cardiovascular morbidity and mortality, or total mortality has not been established.
¶ Fluvastatin Angioplasty Restenosis Trial.
** Assessment of Lescol in Renal Transplantation.
†† Lescol Intervention Prevention Study.
‡‡ Lescol in Severe Atherosclerosis.
NOVARTIS
Novartis Pharmaceuticals Canada Inc.
Dorval, Québec H9R 4P5
Product Monograph available on request.
LES-98-05-4927E

K

KABIKINASE® Ⓟ

Pharmacia & Upjohn

Streptokinase

Thrombolytic Agent

Pharmacology: Streptokinase is a purified preparation of a bacterial protein elaborated by group C beta-hemolytic streptococci. It acts with plasminogen to form an activator complex which converts plasminogen to plasmin in both the blood and blood-clots. Plasmin is a proteolytic enzyme with a special affinity for fibrin. It degrades fibrin clots as well as fibrinogen and other plasma proteins. The plasma half-life of the activator complex is about 20 minutes.

As streptokinase possesses weak streptococcal antigenicity it is initially neutralized by circulating antibodies found in human blood. Only after administration of excess streptokinase exceeding the level of antibodies is the fibrinolytic state achieved. Thrombolysis may start as soon as the complex of streptokinase and plasminogen is present within the thrombus.

I.V. infusion of streptokinase is followed by increased fibrinolytic activity. This hyperfibrinolytic effect disappears within a few hours after discontinuation, but a prolonged thrombin time, due to a decrease in plasma levels of fibrinogen and an increase in the amount of circulating fibrin degradation products may persist for 12 to 24 hours.

Indications: Acute Myocardial Infarction: For use in the management of acute myocardial infarction, for the lysis of intracoronary thrombi, the improvement of ventricular function, reduction of mortality associated with acute myocardial infarct, when administered by either the i.v. or intracoronary route, as well as for the reduction of infarct size and congestive heart failure associated with acute myocardial infarct when administered by the i.v. route. Earlier administration of streptokinase is correlated with greater clinical benefit.

Pulmonary Embolism: For the lysis of objectively diagnosed (angiography or lung scan) pulmonary emboli, involving obstruction of blood flow to a lobe or multiple segments, with or without unstable hemodynamics.

Deep Vein Thrombosis: For the lysis of objectively diagnosed (preferably ascending venography), acute, extensive thrombi of the deep veins such as those involving the popliteal and more proximal vessels.

Arterial Thrombosis and Embolism: For the lysis of acute arterial thrombi and emboli. Streptokinase is not indicated for arterial emboli originating from the left side of the heart due to the risk of new embolic phenomena such as cerebral embolism.

Arteriovenous Cannulae Occlusion: For clearing of totally or partially occluded arteriovenous cannulae as an alternative to surgical intervention when acceptable flow cannot otherwise be achieved.

Contraindications: Because thrombolytic therapy increases the risk of bleeding, streptokinase is contraindicated in the following situations: severe allergy to streptokinase; active internal bleeding; recent (within 2 months) cerebrovascular accident, intracranial or intraspinal surgery (see Warnings); intracranial neoplasm.

Warnings: Bleeding: The aim of streptokinase therapy is the production of sufficient amounts of plasmin for the lysis of intravascular deposits of fibrin. However, fibrin deposits, which provide hemostasis such as those occurring at sites of needle punctures, are also lysed and bleeding may occur from these sites.

Severe bleeding complications requiring transfusion are extremely rare (0.3 to 0.5%) following i.v. high-dose brief duration streptokinase therapy in acute myocardial infarction. Combined therapy with low-dose ASA does not appear to increase the risk of major bleeding. However, the addition of ASA to streptokinase may cause a slight increase in the risk of minor bleeding (3.1% without ASA vs 3.9% with ASA).

In order to minimize the risk of bleeding during treatment with streptokinase, venipunctures and physical handling of the patient should be performed carefully and as infrequently as possible. I.M. injections should not be given. Should an arterial puncture be necessary during i.v. therapy, it is preferable to use an upper extremity vessel. Pressure should be exerted for at least 30 minutes, a pressure dressing applied, and the puncture site checked frequently for evidence of bleeding.

In the following conditions the risks of therapy may be increased and should be weighed against the potential benefits: prior severe allergic reaction to streptokinase (see Contraindications); recent (within 10 days) serious gastrointestinal bleeding, major surgery, obstetrical delivery, organ biopsy, puncture of a noncompressible vessel, trauma including external cardiac compression; severe, uncontrolled hypertension; potential for cardiac emboli, e.g., mitral valve disease with atrial fibrillation; bacterial endocarditis; hemostatic defects including those secondary to severe renal and hepatic disease; pregnancy; cerebrovascular disease; diabetic hemorrhagic retinopathy; ulcerative lesions within the last 6 months e.g., peptic ulcer, ulcerative colitis or diverticulitis; active tuberculosis; tumors; septic thrombophlebitis or occluded cannula at severely infected site; any condition in which bleeding constitutes a significant hazard or would be particularly difficult to manage.

Should serious spontaneous bleeding (uncontrolled by local pressure) occur, the infusion of streptokinase should be terminated immediately and treatment instituted as described under Adverse Effects.

Arrhythmias: Rapid lysis of coronary thrombi has been shown to cause reperfusion atrial or ventricular dysrhythmias requiring immediate treatment. Careful monitoring for arrhythmia is recommended during and immediately following administration of streptokinase for acute myocardial infarction.

Occurrence of Hypotension: Occasionally, severe hypotension, not secondary to bleeding or anaphylaxis, has been observed during i.v. streptokinase infusion (1 to 10% of patients). Patients should be monitored closely and should symptomatic or alarming hypotension occur, appropriate treatment should be administered. This treatment may include a decrease in the streptokinase infusion rate.

Precautions: General: Treatment with streptokinase should be instituted as soon as possible preferably within 7 days after the onset of thrombotic event. Any delay in therapy to evaluate the effect of heparin therapy decreases the potential for optimal efficacy.

Internal bleeding, when it does occur, may be more difficult to manage than that which occurs with conventional anticoagulant therapy. **Streptokinase should only be used in hospitals where any necessary emergency care and the recommended diagnostic and monitoring techniques are available.**

Streptokinase may not be effective if administered between 5 days and 6 months of a prior streptokinase administration or streptococcal infections, because of the increased likelihood of resistance due to a high titre of neutralizing antibodies.

Noncardiogenic pulmonary edema has been reported rarely in patients treated with streptokinase. The risk appears to be greatest in patients who have large myocardial infarctions and are undergoing thrombolytic therapy by the intracoronary route.

Rarely, polyneuropathy has been temporally related to the use of streptokinase.

Should pulmonary embolism or recurrent pulmonary embolism occur during streptokinase therapy, the originally planned course of therapy should be completed in an attempt to lyse these emboli. While pulmonary embolism may occasionally occur during streptokinase treatment the incidence is no greater than when patients are treated with heparin alone.

Patient Monitoring with Coagulation Tests: I.V. administration of streptokinase will cause marked decreases in plasminogen and fibrinogen levels and increases in thrombin time (TT), activated partial thromboplastin time (APTT), and prothrombin time (PT), which usually normalize within 12 to 24 hours. These changes may also occur in some patients with intracoronary administration of the drug.

Before commencing and during thrombolytic therapy, it is desirable to obtain the TT, APTT, PT, hematocrit and platelet counts in order to assess the hemostatic status of the patient.

Children: Safety and effectiveness in children has not been established.

Geriatrics: Caution must be exercised in patients >75 years of age.

Pregnancy: Safe use of streptokinase during pregnancy has not been established and treatment should be undertaken only if clearly needed. Thrombolytic therapy should be avoided within the first 18 weeks of pregnancy because of the risk of placental separation.

Lactation: There is no information regarding the use of streptokinase in lactating women. It is not known whether streptokinase is excreted in breast milk nor whether it has harmful effects on the newborn. It is recommended that breast-feeding be discontinued in a woman who is to receive streptokinase.

Drug Interactions: There is an increased risk of hemorrhage in patients who are receiving or who have recently received heparin, coumarin derivatives, or drugs that affect platelet formation (e.g., ASA, phenylbutazone, dipyridamole and nonsteroidal anti-inflammatory drugs [NSAIDs]).

Streptokinase alone or in combination with antiplatelet agents and anticoagulants may cause bleeding complications. Careful monitoring is essential.

In the treatment of acute myocardial infarction, low dose ASA when not otherwise contraindicated can be administered with streptokinase.

Anticoagulation Treatment Following Streptokinase: Optimal treatment in acute myocardial infarction with anticoagulants after thrombolysis is not yet established.

However, anticoagulant therapy for other indications should follow treatment with streptokinase to prevent rethrombosis. Heparin therapy should not be started earlier than 4 hours after administration of streptokinase.

Until information regarding the interaction between streptokinase and tissue plasminogen activator (tPA) is available, special care should be taken if such a combination is considered.

Adverse Effects: Bleeding: The reported incidence of bleeding (major or minor) has not been correlated with the indication, dose, route and duration of administration.

Minor bleeding from punctures and surgical sites can occur with a reported incidence of approximately 3 to 4%. If such bleeding occurs, local measures should be taken to control the bleeding. Minor bleeding can usually be managed without interrupting the treatment. However, when thrombolytic therapy is continued, do not reduce the dose as this will increase the conversion of plasminogen to plasmin which may increase bleeding.

Ongoing menstrual bleeding may be aggravated.

Severe internal bleeding involving gastrointestinal, genitourinary, intracerebral and retroperitoneal site may occur. Several fatalities due to cerebral and other serious internal hemorrhage have occurred during thrombolytic therapy.

Major hemorrhagic episodes, requiring transfusion, have occurred with an incidence of approximately 0.3%. There is increased risk of bleeding where anticoagulants are to be used. In one study (Thrombolysis in Myocardial Infarction [TIMI] trial), which required both invasive techniques and administration of anticoagulants, a frequency of 15.6% of major bleeding was reported.

Should uncontrollable bleeding occur, streptokinase infusion should be terminated immediately rather than slowing the rate of administration or reducing the dose of streptokinase. In cases of severe uncontrolled bleeding tranexamic acid by slow i.v. injection will reverse the fibrinolytic action of streptokinase. Plasma volume expanders may be used to correct the hemostatic deficiency. Other alternatives are human red blood cells or fresh whole blood.

Fever: Although streptokinase is nonpyrogenic in standard animal tests, approximately one third of patients treated with it have shown slight elevations in body temperature. This slight increase of temperature occurs 5 to 8 hours after starting the administration of streptokinase and generally returns to normal spontaneously after 24 hours. An antipyretic dose of ASA should not be used with streptokinase due to increased risk of bleeding.

Allergic Reactions: Allergic reactions have been reported in less than 5% of the patients. Reactions attributed to possible anaphylaxis have been rarely observed (about 0.1%). These ranged in severity from minor breathing difficulty to bronchospasm, periorbital swelling or angioneurotic edema. Other milder allergic effects such as urticaria, itching, flushing, nausea, headache and musculoskeletal pain have also been observed.

Mild or moderate reactions may be managed with concomitant antihistamine and/or corticosteroid therapy. Severe allergic reactions require immediate discontinuation of streptokinase. Adrenergics, antihistamines or corticosteroids should be administered as required.

Kabikinase (cont'd)

Hypotension: Hypotension, sometimes severe, not secondary to bleeding or anaphylaxis has been observed during i.v. streptokinase infusion in 1 to 10% of patients. Patients should be monitored and, if symptomatic or alarming hypotension occurs, appropriate treatment administered, which may include a decrease in the i.v. streptokinase infusion rate. Smaller hypotensive effects are common and have not required treatment.

Overdose: Symptoms and Treatment: In general, overdosage of streptokinase does not cause any increased bleeding reactions. If a very high dose of streptokinase is given most of the plasminogen molecules will form a complex with streptokinase and there will be less free plasminogen available to be converted to plasmin.

Should serious uncontrolled bleeding occur as a result of overdosage, the infusion of streptokinase and any other concomitant anticoagulant should be discontinued immediately. Bleeding can be reversed and blood loss effectively managed with appropriate replacement therapy (see Adverse Effects).

Dosage: Streptokinase should be administered by volumetric infusion pump. Do not use drop counting infusion method since streptokinase may alter droplet size.

Acute Myocardial Infarction: I.V. infusion of 1 500 000 IU of streptokinase administered at a constant rate over 30 or 60 minutes.

Intracoronary administration of 250 000 IU at a constant rate over 30 or 60 minutes.

Streptokinase treatment for coronary thrombosis should be undertaken only in medical centres where coronary arteriography is an established routine and appropriate after treatment is available.

Streptokinase should be administered as soon as possible after the onset of symptoms of myocardial infarction. The greatest benefit in reduction of mortality occurred when streptokinase was administered within 4 hours but a demonstrable benefit has been reported up to 24 hours.

Deep Venous Thrombosis, Pulmonary Embolism and Arterial Thrombosis and Embolism: Streptokinase treatment by i.v. infusion into a peripheral vein should be initiated as soon as possible after onset of thrombotic event, preferably no later than 7 days after onset. Any delay in instituting lytic therapy to evaluate the effect of heparin therapy decreases the potential for optimal efficacy.

Since human exposure to streptococci is common, antibodies to streptokinase (streptokinase resistance) are found normally. Thus a loading dose of streptokinase, sufficient to neutralize the resistance is required. A dose of 250 000 IU streptokinase infused into a peripheral vein over 30 minutes has been found appropriate in over 90% of patients, followed by a maintenance dose of 100 000 IU/h (see Table I for details).

Table I—Kabikinase

Dosage Schedule

Indication	Loading Dose	Maintenance Dose
Pulmonary Embolism	250 000 IU over 30 minutes	100 000 IU/h for 24 hours (72 hours if concurrent DVT is suspected)
Deep Vein Thrombosis (DVT)	250 000 IU over 30 minutes	100 000 IU/h for 72 hours
Arterial Thrombosis or Embolism	250 000 IU over 30 minutes	100 000 IU/h for 24 to 72 hours

It is important that the infusion is given at a constant rate. If possible, this should be followed by a phlebographic check. If no clinical effect is noted after 3 days, treatment should be discontinued. Streptokinase therapy may be continued for an additional 1 to 3 days if considered necessary.

Treatment with streptokinase should always be followed by anticoagulant therapy. If heparin therapy is given it should be started not earlier than 4 hours after the termination of streptokinase infusion for safety reasons.

Arteriovenous Cannulae Occlusion: Before using streptokinase, an attempt should be made to clear the cannulae by careful syringe technique, using heparinized saline solution. If adequate flow is not re-established, streptokinase may be employed. Allow the effect of any pretreatment anticoagulants to diminish.

Table II—Kabikinase

Dilutions and Infusion Rates

IU	Vials Required	Set Pump Infusion Rate* (mL/h) Volume of Dilution 50 mL	150 mL	250 mL	500 mL
Acute Myocardial Infarction					
Intracoronary Artery Administration					
250 000 in 30 minutes	1×750 000	33	100	167	—
250 000 in 60 minutes	1×750 000	17	50	84	—
I.V. Infusion					
1 500 000 in 30 minutes	2×750 000 or 1×1 500 000	100	300	500	—
1 500 000 in 60 minutes	2×750 000 or 1×1 500 000	50	150	250	—
Deep Vein Thrombosis, Pulmonary Embolism or Arterial Thrombosis and Embolism					
Loading Dose					
250 000 in 30 minutes	1×750 000	33	100	167	—
Maintenance Dose					
100 000/h (see Table I for infusion duration)	1×750 000 2×750 000 or 1×1 500 000	7 3	20 10	33 17	67 33

* Depending upon the type of infusion pump available, the dosage rate may have to be adjusted with corresponding adjustment of total volume of the solution. Values are expressed to nearest whole integers.

Instill 250 000 IU streptokinase (in 5 mL reconstituted solution) into each occluded limb of the cannulae slowly. Clamp off cannulae limb(s) for 2 hours. Observe the patient closely for possible adverse effects.

Aspirate contents of infused cannulae limb(s), flush with saline, and reconnect cannulae.

Reconstituted Solutions: Reconstitute the contents of each 250 000 IU and 750 000 IU vial of streptokinase with 5 mL Sodium Chloride Injection USP and each 1 500 000 IU vial with 10 mL Sodium Chloride Injection USP. Sterile water for injection can also be used to reconstitute the lyophilized streptokinase. Add the diluent slowly to the vial directing it at the side of the container rather than into the lyophilized powder. For dissolution, gently swirl the vial. Avoid shaking to prevent foaming.

Because Kabikinase contains no preservatives, the solution should be reconstituted immediately before use. The reconstituted solution is stable for up to 24 hours at 2 to 8°C. Discard unused reconstituted drug.

Further Dilution: The reconstituted solution is transferred to infusion solution bottles containing either sodium chloride injection USP or 5% Dextrose solution. The diluted solution is intended for i.v. or intracoronary administration. Table II presents some suggested dilutions and corresponding infusion rates for Kabikinase.

Arteriovenous Cannulae: Use the reconstituted solution (5 mL) without further dilution. Instill into the occluded part of the cannulae slowly.

The vials of streptokinase after reconstitution and dilution should be inspected visually for particulate matter and discoloration prior to administration whenever solution and container permit. The albumin (human) may impart a slightly yellow color to the drug after reconstitution. Particulate or discolored solution should be discarded.

The diluted infusion solution should be used immediately. However, it is stable within 12 hours when stored at room temperature below 25°C.

Do not add other medications to the container of streptokinase.

Supplied: 750 000 IU: Each 8 mL clear glass vial of sterile, lyophilized powder contains: purified streptokinase 750 000 IU. Single vials.

1 500 000 IU: Each 10 mL clear glass vial of sterile, lyophilized powder contains: purified streptokinase 1 500 000 IU. Single vials.

Nonmedicinal ingredients: albumin (human), disodium phosphate anhydrous (added as dodecahydrate), sodium dihydrogen phosphate anhydrous (added as dihydrate) and sodium-L-glutamate anhydrous. The vials are fitted with bromobutyl freeze-drying stoppers and secured with aluminum overseals and flip off caps. Store the unopened vials at room temperature below 25°C. The product is stable up to the expiration date indicated on the package.

KADIAN® Ⓝ

Knoll

Morphine Sulfate

Opioid Analgesic

Pharmacology: Morphine is an opioid analgesic which exerts an agonist effect at specific, saturable opioid receptors in the CNS and other tissues. Morphine produces diverse pharmacological effects in man including analgesia, suppression of the cough reflex, respiratory depression due to a reduction in the responsiveness of the respiratory centre to carbon dioxide, nausea and emesis through direct stimulation of the chemoreceptor trigger-zone (CTZ), mood changes including euphoria and dysphoria, sedation, mental clouding, alterations in both the endocrine and autonomic nervous systems, and a decrease in gastrointestinal motility leading to constipation.

Pharmacokinetics: Morphine is rapidly absorbed from the gastrointestinal tract, nasal mucosa, lung and after s.c. and i.m. injection. When administered orally it is subject to extensive but variable first pass metabolism, and only about 40% of the administered dose reaches the central compartment.

Once absorbed, morphine is distributed to skeletal muscle, kidneys, liver, intestinal tract, lungs, spleen and brain. It crosses the placental membranes and has been found in breast milk. About 30 to 35% of morphine is reversibly protein bound.

Although a small fraction of morphine (less than 5%) is demethylated, for all practical purposes, virtually all morphine is converted to glucuronide metabolites including morphine-3-glucuronide and morphine-6-glucuronide. The glucuronide system has very high capacity and is not easily saturated even in disease. Studies in healthy subjects and cancer patients have shown that the glucuronide metabolite to morphine mean molar ratios (based on AUC) are similar following single doses of Kadian and morphine sulfate solution. The morphine to morphine-3-glucuronide to morphine-6-glucuronide mean molar ratios (based on AUC) are approximately 1:26:4, similar to those occurring with morphine sulfate solution.

There has been no evaluation of Kadian in patients with impaired hepatic and renal function. Pharmacokinetic parameters of morphine show considerable inter-subject variation. The average volume of distribution (Vd) is approximately 4 L/kg, and the terminal half-life is 2 to 4 hours.

Following oral administration, the dose normalized extent of absorption (AUC) of morphine from Kadian is similar to that obtained from morphine solutions. However, the rate of absorption of morphine from Kadian is significantly slower.

A single 50 mg oral dose of Kadian in 30 healthy male subjects resulted in a mean peak plasma morphine concentration of 8.1 ng/mL (C_{max}) at 8.5 hours (T_{max}). The extent of absorption was unaffected by food, but the T_{max} was slightly delayed to 10 hours. However, this is not clinically significant. Kadian can be administered with or without food.

When Kadian is given on a fixed dosing regimen, steady state is achieved within about 2 days.

The pharmacokinetic characteristics of Kadian administered once daily for a 7 day period have been investigated in 24 patients with moderate-severe chronic cancer pain requiring opioid analgesia. The mean pharmacokinetic values were calculated from steady-state plasma morphine data and adjusted to a dose of 100 mg (see Table I).

Table I—Kadian

Mean Pharmacokinetic Values

Parameter	Mean±S.D.
C_{max} (ng/mL)	37.3±14.0
T_{max} (h)	10.3±3.3
AUC (ng·h/mL)	501±193
C_{min} (ng/mL)	9.9±5.2
T≥0.75 C_{max} (h)	6.0±3.0

C_{max}=maximum observed plasma morphine concentration.
T_{max}=time to reach C_{max}.
AUC=area under the plasma concentration time curve.
C_{min}=minimum plasma morphine concentration.
T≥0.75 C_{max}=time for which the plasma morphine concentration is greater than or equal to 75% of the C_{max}.

Morphine is excreted primarily in the urine as morphine-3-glucuronide and morphine-6-glucuronide. A small amount of the glucuronide metabolites is excreted in the bile, and there is some minor enterohepatic cycling. Seven to 10% of administered morphine is excreted in the feces. Morphine-6-glucuronide has been shown to be pharmacologically active. Because accumulation of this metabolite has been observed in patients with renal disease, caution should be exercised in patients with clinically significant impairment of renal function.

Indications: For the relief of severe chronic pain requiring the prolonged use of an oral opioid preparation.

Contraindications: Patients with known hypersensitivity to morphine, morphine salts or any of the capsule components, acute or severe bronchial asthma or other obstructive airway disease, respiratory depression, cor pulmonale, biliary colic, gastrointestinal obstruction, particularly paralytic ileus, cardiac arrhythmias, acute alcoholism, delirium tremens, severe CNS depression, convulsive disorder, increased cerebrospinal or intracranial pressure, head injury, brain tumor, suspected surgical abdomen, or concurrent MAO inhibitors or within 14 days of such therapy (see Precautions, Drug Interactions).

Warnings: Impaired Respiration: Respiratory depression is the chief hazard of all morphine preparations. Respiratory depression occurs more frequently in elderly and debilitated patients, and in those suffering from conditions accompanied by hypoxia or hypercapnia when even moderate therapeutic doses may significantly decrease pulmonary ventilation.

Morphine should be used with extreme caution in patients with chronic obstructive pulmonary disease or cor pulmonale and in patients having a substantially decreased respiratory reserve, hypoxia, hypercapnia or preexisting respiratory depression. In such patients, even usual therapeutic doses of morphine may increase airway resistance and decrease respiratory drive to the point of apnea. Severe pain antagonizes the respiratory depressant effects of morphine.

Head Injury and Increased Intracranial Pressure: The respiratory depressant effects of morphine with carbon dioxide retention and secondary elevation of cerebrospinal fluid pressure may be markedly exaggerated in the presence of head injury, other intracranial lesions, or a preexisting increase in intracranial pressure. Morphine produces effects which may obscure neurological signs of further increases in pressure in patients with head injuries. Morphine should only be administered under such circumstances when considered essential, and then, with extreme caution.

Hypotensive Effect: Morphine, like all opioid analgesics, may cause severe hypotension in an individual whose ability to maintain blood pressure has already been compromised by a reduced blood volume, or a concurrent administration of drugs such as phenothiazines or general anesthetics (see Precautions, Drug Interactions). Morphine may produce orthostatic hypotension in ambulatory patients.

Morphine, like all opioid analgesics, should be administered with caution to patients in circulatory shock, as vasodilation produced by the drug may further reduce cardiac output and blood pressure.

Gastrointestinal Motility: Morphine should not be given to patients with gastrointestinal obstruction, particularly paralytic ileus, as there is a risk of the product remaining in the stomach for an extended period and the subsequent release of a bolus of morphine when normal gut motility is restored.

As with any other solid dose morphine formulation, diarrhea may reduce morphine absorption.

Drug Abuse and Dependence: Morphine has a potential for physical and psychological dependence. However, this is not a prime concern in the management of terminally ill patients or patients in severe pain. Abrupt cessation or a sudden reduction in dose after prolonged use may result in withdrawal symptoms. The opioid agonist abstinence syndrome is characterized by some or all of the following symptoms: restlessness, lacrimation, rhinorrhea, yawning, perspiration, gooseflesh, restless sleep or "yen" and mydriasis during the first 24 hours. These symptoms often increase in severity and over the next 72 hours may be accompanied by increasing irritability, anxiety, weakness, twitching and spasms of muscles, kicking movements, severe backache, abdominal and leg pains, abdominal and muscle cramps, hot and cold flashes, insomnia, nausea, anorexia, vomiting, intestinal spasm, diarrhea, coryza and repetitive sneezing, increase in body temperature, blood pressure, respiratory rate and heart rate. Because of excessive loss of fluids through sweating, vomiting and diarrhea, there is usually marked weight loss, dehydration, ketosis, and disturbances in acid base balance. Cardiovascular collapse can occur. Most observable symptoms disappear in 5 to 14 days without treatment; however, there appears to be a phase of secondary or chronic abstinence which may last for 2 to 6 months characterized by insomnia, irritability and muscle aches.

If treatment of physical dependence of patients on morphine is necessary, detoxification may be achieved by a gradual dosage reduction. Gastrointestinal disturbance or dehydration should be treated appropriately.

Infants born to mothers who are physically dependent on opioid analgesics may also be physically dependent and may exhibit withdrawal symptoms. These infants may have respiratory depression at birth (see Precautions).

Tolerance: Tolerance, in which increasingly large doses are required in order to produce the same degree of analgesia, may develop upon repeated administration of morphine. The dose of morphine may need to be increased to maintain adequate pain relief (see Dosage).

Pregnancy: Animal reproduction studies have not been performed using morphine. It is not known whether morphine can cause fetal damage when administered throughout pregnancy or if it can affect reproductive capacity in humans. Pregnant patients should be given morphine only when the benefits clearly outweigh potential risks to the fetus.

Precautions: General: Kadian is intended for use in patients who require more than several days of continuous treatment with a potent opioid analgesic.

As with any potent opioid, it is critical to adjust the dosing regimen of morphine for each patient individually, taking into account the patient's prior analgesic treatment experience. Although it is clearly impossible to enumerate every consideration that is important to the selection of the initial dose of morphine, attention should be given to the points listed under Dosage.

Cordotomy: Patients who are scheduled for cordotomy or other interruption of pain transmission pathways should not receive morphine within 24 hours of the procedure.

Special Risk Groups: Morphine should be administered with caution, and in reduced dosages in elderly or debilitated patients; patients with severe renal or hepatic insufficiency or impaired pulmonary function; patients with Addison's disease; myxedema; hypothyroidism; prostatic hypertrophy or urethral stricture.

Caution should also be exercised in the administration of morphine to patients with CNS depression; toxic psychosis; acute alcoholism or delirium tremens; severe kyphoscoliosis; convulsive disorders; about to undergo biliary surgery and patients with acute pancreatitis secondary to biliary tract disease.

Occupational Hazards: Driving and Operating Dangerous Machinery: Morphine may impair the mental and/or physical abilities needed to perform potentially hazardous activities such as driving a car or operating machinery. Patients must be cautioned accordingly. Patients should also be warned about the potential combined effects of morphine with other CNS depressants, including other opioids, phenothiazines, sedatives, sedative/hypnotics and alcohol (see Drug Interactions).

Labor/Delivery: Morphine is not recommended for use in women during and immediately before labor. The effects of opioid analgesics are unpredictable. They may prolong labor by temporarily reducing the strength, duration and frequency of uterine contractions, or conversely they may tend to shorten labor by increasing the rate of cervical dilatation. Infants born to mothers receiving opioid analgesics during labor should be observed closely for signs of respiratory depression. Naloxone HCl should be available for reversal of narcotic-induced respiratory depression.

Lactation: As morphine is excreted in human milk, breast-feeding is not recommended while a patient is receiving morphine. Withdrawal symptoms have been observed in breast-fed infants when maternal administration of morphine is stopped.

Drug Interactions: CNS Depressants: Morphine should be used with great caution and in reduced dosage in patients concurrently receiving other CNS depressants including sedatives, hypnotics, general anesthetics, phenothiazines, other tranquilizers and alcohol because of the risk of respiratory depression, hypotension and profound sedation or coma. When such combined therapy is contemplated, the dose of one or both agents should be reduced.

Muscle Relaxants: Morphine may enhance the neuromuscular blocking action of skeletal relaxants and produce an increased degree of respiratory depression.

Mixed Agonist/Antagonist Opioid Analgesics: From a theoretical perspective, mixed agonist/antagonist opioid analgesics (e.g., pentazocine and buprenorphine) should **not** be administered to a patient who has received or is receiving a course of therapy with a pure opioid agonist analgesic. In these patients, mixed agonist/antagonist analgesics may reduce the analgesic effect or may precipitate withdrawal symptoms.

MAO Inhibitors: The concurrent use of MAO inhibitors and opioid drugs such as morphine can cause anxiety, confusion and significant depression of respiration, sometimes leading to coma. Morphine should not be given to patients taking MAO inhibitors or within 14 days of stopping such treatment.

Cimetidine: There is a report of confusion and severe respiratory depression when a hemodialysis patient was administered morphine and cimetidine.

Diuretics: Morphine reduces the efficacy of diuretics by inducing the release of antidiuretic hormone. Morphine may also lead to acute retention of urine by causing spasm of the sphincter of the bladder, particularly in men with prostatism.

Adverse Effects: The adverse reactions caused by morphine are essentially the same as those observed with other oral and parenteral opioid analgesics. They include the following major hazards: respiratory depression, apnea and to a lesser degree, circulatory depression, respiratory arrest, shock and cardiac arrest.

Most Common Adverse Effects: constipation, dizziness, dysphoria, euphoria, lightheadedness, nausea, sedation, vomiting, sweating.

Sedation: Most patients receiving morphine will experience initial drowsiness. This usually disappears in 3 to 5 days and is not a cause for concern unless it is excessive, or accompanied with unsteadiness or confusion. Excessive or persistent sedation should be investigated. Factors to be considered should include concurrent sedative medications, the presence of hepatic or renal insufficiency, exacerbated respiratory failure, tolerance to the dose used especially in older patients, disease severity and the patient's general condition. If the dose of morphine has been reduced and pain is not adequately controlled, the dose may be carefully increased again after a few days.

Dizziness and Unsteadiness: May be associated with morphine-induced postural hypotension, particularly in elderly or debilitated patients. The dosage should be adjusted according to individual needs but, because of reduced clearance, dosage may be lower in patients over 50 years of age.

Nausea and Vomiting: Nausea and vomiting are common after single doses of morphine or as an early undesirable effect of regular opioid therapy. The prescription of a suitable antiemetic should be considered. The frequency of nausea and vomiting usually decreases within a week or so but may persist due to opioid-induced gastric stasis.

Constipation: Most patients suffer from constipation while taking opioids on a chronic basis. Some patients, particularly those who are elderly, debilitated or bedridden may become impacted. Patients must be cautioned accordingly and laxatives, softeners and other appropriate treatments should be initiated at the beginning of opioid therapy.

Other adverse reactions include: Cardiovascular: flushing of the face, chills, tachycardia, bradycardia, palpitations, faintness, syncope, hypotension and hypertension.

CNS: euphoria, dysphoria, weakness, insomnia, dizziness, confusional symptoms and occasionally hallucinations, disorientation, headache, tremor, muscle rigidity, agitation, uncoordinated muscle movements, seizures, increased intracranial pressure, hypothermia, paresthesia, dyspnea, alterations in mood (nervousness, apprehension, depression, floating feelings).

Gastrointestinal: dry mouth, anorexia, constipation, laryngospasm, colic, taste alterations and biliary colic.

Kadian (cont'd)

Genitourinary: urine retention or hesitancy, reduced libido or potency.
Endocrine: A syndrome of inappropriate antidiuretic hormone secretion characterized by hyponatremia secondary to decreased free-water excretion may occur (monitoring of electrolytes may be necessary).
Visual Disturbances: blurred vision, nystagmus, diplopia and miosis.
Dermatologic: pruritus, urticaria, other skin rashes and edema, diaphoresis.
Withdrawal (Abstinence) Syndrome: Chronic use of opioid analgesics may be associated with the development of physical dependence. An abstinence syndrome may be precipitated when opioid administration is suddenly discontinued or opioid antagonists administered.

Withdrawal symptoms that may be observed after discontinuation of opioid use include body aches, diarrhea, piloerection, anorexia, nervousness or restlessness, rhinorrhea, sneezing, tremors or shivering, abdominal colic, nausea, sleep disturbance, unusual increase in sweating and yawning, weakness, tachycardia and unexplained fever. With appropriate dose adjustments and gradual withdrawal these symptoms are usually mild.

Overdose: Symptoms: Acute overdosage with morphine is manifested by respiratory depression, somnolence progressing to stupor or coma, skeletal muscle flaccidity, cold and clammy skin, constricted pupils, and sometimes bradycardia and hypotension.

Treatment: Primary attention should be given to the establishment of a patent airway and institution of assisted or controlled ventilation. The pure opioid antagonist, naloxone HCl, is a specific antidote against respiratory depression which results from opioid overdose. Naloxone (usually 0.4 to 2 mg) should be administered i.v. However, because its duration of action is relatively short, the patient must be carefully monitored until spontaneous respiration is reliably re-established. Morphine will continue to release and add to the morphine load for periods longer than the action of a single dose of antagonist, and the management of morphine overdosage should be modified accordingly. If the response to naloxone is suboptimal or not sustained, additional naloxone may be administered as needed, or given by continuous i.v. infusion to maintain alertness and respiratory function. There is no information available about the cumulative dose of naloxone that may be safely administered.

Naloxone should not be administered in the absence of clinically significant respiratory or circulatory depression secondary to morphine overdosage. Naloxone should be administered cautiously to persons who are known or suspected to be physically dependent on morphine. In such cases, an abrupt or complete reversal of opioid effects may precipitate an acute withdrawal syndrome. The severity of the withdrawal syndrome produced will depend on the degree of physical dependence and the dose of the antagonist administered. If it is necessary to treat serious respiratory depression in the physically dependent patient, the antagonist should be administered with extreme care and by titration with smaller than usual doses of the antagonist.

Supportive measures (including oxygen, vasopressors) should be employed in the management of circulatory shock and pulmonary edema accompanying overdose as indicated. Cardiac arrest or arrhythmias may require cardiac massage or defibrillation.

Gastric contents may need to be emptied as this can be useful in removing unabsorbed drug, particularly when a sustained-release formulation has been taken.

Morphine toxicity may be a result of overdosage but because of the large inter-individual variation in sensitivity to opioids it is difficult to assess the exact dose of any opioid that is toxic or lethal. The toxic effects of morphine tend to be overshadowed by the presence of pain or tolerance. Patients having chronic morphine therapy have been known to take in excess of 3 000 mg/day with no apparent toxic effects being present.

Dosage: See Warnings and Precautions. **Kadian capsules contain sustained-release pellets which should not be chewed or crushed. Taking chewed or crushed Kadian pellets could lead to the rapid release and absorption of a potentially toxic dose of morphine.**

The capsules are to be administered once daily (every 24 hours).

Selection of the initial dose of morphine should take into account the following: the total daily dose, potency and characteristics of previous opioid analgesics (e.g., pure agonists or mixed agonist/antagonist); the reliability of the relative potency estimate used to calculate the dose of morphine required (potency estimates vary with the route of administration); the degree of opioid tolerance; the patient's general condition and medical status; and type and severity of pain.

Individual dosing requirements vary considerably based on each patient's size, weight, severity of pain, and medical and analgesic history.

Patients over the age of 50 tend to require much lower doses of morphine than do younger patients. In elderly and debilitated patients and those with impaired respiratory function or significantly decreased renal function, the initial dose should be one half of the usual recommended dose.

For patients who have difficulty swallowing, Kadian capsules may be opened and the sustained-release pellets may be administered in the following way: the pellets may be sprinkled onto a small amount of soft foods (such as yogurt, apple sauce or jam). This should be taken within 30 minutes of sprinkling. The pellets must not be chewed or crushed, and the mouth should be rinsed to ensure that all pellets have been swallowed.

The use of opioid analgesics for the relief of chronic pain, including cancer pain, should be only part of a complete approach to pain control which should include other types of treatment or drug therapy, nondrug measures and psychosocial support.

If signs of excessive opioid effects are observed early in the dosing interval, the next dose should be reduced. If this adjustment leads to inadequate analgesia, that is, breakthrough pain occurs, a supplemental dose of a short acting analgesic may be given. If breakthrough pain repeatedly occurs at the end of a dose interval, it is generally an indication for dosage increase, not more frequent administration. However, where judged necessary, Kadian may be administered more frequently than every 24 hours. The dosing interval should not be reduced below every 12 hours. As experience is gained, adjustments can be made to obtain an appropriate balance between pain relief and opioid side effects.

For essential information on the important details of the management of cancer pain, the reader may wish to consult the following resources: Cancer Pain: A Monograph on the Management of Cancer Pain. Health and Welfare, Canada. Twycross, R.G. and Lack, S.A. Symptom control in far advanced cancer: Pain relief.

Because of the sustained release properties of Kadian, dosage increases should generally be separated by 48 hours.

When properly ingested, no evidence of dose dumping was observed in any of the patients receiving their full daily dose of morphine in the every 24 hours arms of the various steady-state studies.

Use of Kadian as the First Opioid Analgesic: There has been no systematic evaluation of Kadian as an initial opioid analgesic in the management of pain. Because it may be more difficult to titrate a patient using a controlled release morphine, it is ordinarily advisable to begin treatment using an immediate release formulation.

For patients currently receiving opioids, the following dosing recommendations should be considered.

Conversion from Immediate Release Oral Morphine Formulations to Kadian: Patients on Immediate Release oral morphine formulations may be converted to Kadian by administering the patient's total daily morphine dose as Kadian capsules on an every 24 hours dosing regimen. Dose is then adjusted as needed.

The first dose of Kadian should be taken with the last dose of any immediate-release opioid medication due to the prolonged T_{max} after administration of Kadian.

Conversion from Sustained-Release Oral Morphine Formulations to Kadian: Patients on sustained-release oral morphine formulations may be converted to Kadian by administering the patient's total daily morphine dose as Kadian capsules on an every 24 hours dosing regimen at the time of the next scheduled dose of morphine.

Conversion from Parenteral Morphine or Other Parenteral or Oral Opioids to Kadian: If Kadian is administered as the initial oral morphine drug product, particular care must be exercised in the conversion process. Because of uncertainty about an inter-subject variation in relative estimates of opioid potency and cross tolerance, initial dosing regimens should be conservative; that is, an underestimation of the 24 hours oral morphine requirements is preferred to an overestimate. To this end, initial individual doses of Kadian should be estimated conservatively.

Estimates of the relative potency of opioids are only approximate and are influenced by route of administration, individual patient differences, and possibly, by an individual's medical condition.

Consequently, it is difficult to recommend any fixed rule for converting a patient to Kadian directly. The following general points should be considered: Parenteral to Oral Morphine Ratio: Estimates of the oral to parenteral potency of morphine vary. Some authorities suggest that a dose of oral morphine only 2 to 3 times the daily parenteral morphine requirement may be sufficient in chronic use settings.

Other Parenteral or Oral Opioids to Oral Morphine: Because there are no data on these types of analgesic substitutions, specific recommendations are not possible. Physicians are advised to refer to published relative potency data, keeping in mind that such ratios are only approximate (see Table II). In general, it is safer to underestimate the daily dose of Kadian required and rely upon ad hoc supplementation to deal with inadequate analgesia.

Table II—Kadian

Opioid Analgesics: Approximate Analgesic Equivalences[a]

Drug	Equivalent Dose (mg)[b] (compared to morphine 10 mg i.m.)		Duration of Action (hours)
	Parenteral	Oral	
Strong Opioid Agonists			
Morphine (single dose)	10	60[c]	3-4
(chronic dose)	10	20-30[c]	3-4
Hydromorphone	1.5-2	6-7.5	2-4
Anileridine	25	75	2-3
Levorphanol	2	4	4-8
Meperidine[d]	75	300	1-3
Oxymorphone	1.5	5 (rectal)	3-4
Methadone[e]	—	—	—
Heroin	5-8	10-15	3-4
Weak Opioid Agonists			
Codeine	120	200	3-4
Oxycodone	5-10	10-15[f]	2-4
Propoxyphene	50	100	2-4
Mixed Agonist-Antagonists[g]			
Pentazocine[d]	60	180	3-4
Nalbuphine	10	—	3-6
Butorphanol	2	—	3-4

[a] References:
Cancer Pain: A Monograph on the Management of Cancer Pain, Health and Welfare Canada 1984. Foley K.M., New Engl J. Med 313:84-95,1985. Aronoff, G.M. and Evans, W.O., In: Evaluation and Treatment of Chronic Pain, 2nd Ed., G.M. Aronoff (Ed.), Williams and Wilkins, Baltimore, pp.359-368,1992. Cherny, N.I. and Portenoy, R.K., In: Textbook of Pain, 3rd Ed., P.D. Wall and R. Melzack (Eds.), Churchill Livingstone, London, pp.1437-1467,1994.
[b] Most of this data was derived from single-dose, acute pain studies and should be considered an approximation for selection of doses when treating chronic pain.
[c] For acute pain, the oral or rectal dose of morphine is 6 times the injectable dose. However, for chronic dosing, clinical experience indicates that this ratio is 2-3:1 (i.e., 20-30 mg of oral or rectal morphine is equivalent to 10 mg of parenteral morphine).
[d] These drugs are not recommended for the management of chronic pain.
[e] Extremely variable equianalgesic dose. Patients should undergo individualized titration starting at an equivalent to 1/10 of the morphine dose.
[f] In combination with acetaminophen or ASA. For acute pain, single entity oral oxycodone is twice as potent as oral morphine.
[g] Mixed agonist-antagonists can precipitate withdrawal in patients on pure opioid agonists.

Conversion from Kadian to Other Controlled-Release Oral Morphine Formulations: Kadian is not bioequivalent to other controlled-release morphine preparations. Conversion from Kadian to the same daily dose of other controlled-release morphine preparations may lead to an initial change in the clinical status of the patient and close observation is recommended.

Conversion from Kadian to Parenteral Opioids: When converting a patient from Kadian to parenteral opioids, it is best to assume that the parenteral to oral potency is high. **Note that this is the converse of the strategy used when the direction of conversion is from the parenteral to oral formulations. In both cases however, the aim is to estimate the new dose conservatively.** For example, to estimate the required 24-hour dose of morphine for i.m. use, one could employ a conversion of 1 mg of morphine i.m. for every 6 mg of morphine as Kadian. Therefore, the i.m. 24-hour dose would have to be divided by 6 and administered every 4 hours.

This approach is recommended because it is least likely to cause overdose. However, for chronic dosing, clinical experience indicates that this ratio is 2-3:1 and individual titration is recommended (i.e., 20 to 30 mg of oral or rectal morphine is equivalent to 10 mg of parenteral morphine).

Opioid analgesic agents do not effectively relieve dysesthetic pain, post-herpetic neuralgia, stabbing pains, activity-related pain, and some forms of headache. This does not mean that patients with advanced cancer suffering these types of pain should not be given an adequate trial of opioid analgesics. However, such patients may need to be referred early on for other types of pain therapy. Pain without nociception is usually not opioid-responsive.

Dose Titration: Dose titration is the key to success with morphine therapy. Proper optimization of doses scaled to the relief of the individual's pain should aim at the regular administration of the lowest dose of morphine which will maintain the patient free of pain at all times. Dose adjustments should be based on the patient's clinical response. Higher doses may be justified in some patients to cover periods of physical activity.

Because of the sustained release properties of Kadian, dosage adjustments should generally be separated by 48 hours. If dose increments turn out to be required, they should be proportionately greater at lower dose levels (in terms of percentage of the previous dose), than when adjusting a higher dose.

Adjustment or Reduction of Dosage: During the first 2 or 3 days of effective pain relief, the patient may exhibit drowsiness or sleep for prolonged periods. This can be misinterpreted as the effect of excessive analgesic dosing rather than the first sign of relief in a pain-exhausted patient. The dose, therefore, should be maintained for at least 3 days before reduction, provided that the sedation is not excessive or associated with unsteadiness and symptoms of confusion, and that respiratory activity and other vital signs are adequate. If excessive sedation persists, the reason(s) for such an effect must be sought. Some of these are concomitant sedative medications, hepatic or renal failure, exacerbated respiratory failure, higher doses than tolerated by an older patient, or an illness which is more severe than previously recognized. If it is necessary to reduce the dose, it can be carefully increased again after 2 or 4 days if it is obvious that the pain is not being well-controlled.

Following successful relief of severe pain, periodic attempts to reduce the opioid dose should be made. Smaller doses or complete discontinuation of the opioid analgesic may become feasible due to a change in the patient's condition or improved mental state.

Children: The use of morphine in children has not been evaluated.

Geriatrics: Morphine should be administered with caution and in reduced dosages in elderly patients.

Information for the Patient: See Blue Section—Information for the Patient "Kadian".

Supplied: 20 mg: Each size 4 capsule, clear cap imprinted with K20 and clear body imprinted with 2 black bands, contains: morphine sulfate 20 mg as creamy-white to light tan polymer-coated sustained-release pellets. Nonmedicinal ingredients: diethyl phthalate, ethylcellulose, gelatin, hypromellose, maize starch, methacrylic acid copolymer, polyethylene glycol, sucrose, talc and a black ink containing ammonium hydroxide, potassium hydroxide, propylene glycol and shellac and the coloring agent E172. Gluten-free. Bottles of 100.

50 mg: Each size 2 capsule, clear cap imprinted with K50 and clear body imprinted with 3 black bands, contains: morphine sulfate 50 mg as creamy-white to light tan polymer-coated sustained-release pellets. Nonmedicinal ingredients: diethyl phthalate, ethylcellulose, gelatin, hypromellose, maize starch, methacrylic acid copolymer, polyethylene glycol, sucrose, talc and a black ink containing ammonium hydroxide, potassium hydroxido, propylono glycol and chellac and the coloring agent E172. Gluten-free. Bottles of 100.

100 mg: Each size 0 capsule, clear cap imprinted with K100 and clear body imprinted with 4 black bands, contains: morphine sulfate 100 mg as creamy-white to light tan polymer-coated sustained-release pellets. Nonmedicinal ingredients: diethyl phthalate, ethylcellulose, gelatin, hypromellose, maize starch, methacrylic acid copolymer, polyethylene glycol, sucrose, talc and a black ink containing ammonium hydroxide, potassium hydroxide, propylene glycol and shellac and the coloring agent E172. Gluten-free. Bottles of 50.

Store below 25°C. Protect from light and moisture.

(Shown in Product Recognition Section)

Reviewed 1997

KAOCHLOR®-10
KAOCHLOR®-20
Pharmacia & Upjohn

Potassium Chloride

Potassium Replacement Therapy

Indications: The treatment of potassium deficiency.

Warnings: If administered full strength, Kaochlor-20 will cause gastrointestinal irritation.

Precautions: Potassium therapy should not be started unless urinary output is adequate. Use only under supervision of a physician.

Dosage: Kaochlor-10: The usual adult dosage is 20 mEq in 100 mL of water once or twice daily after meals. Citrus fruit juices or citrated soft drinks may be used in place of water to dilute Kaochlor-10.

Kaochlor-20: The usual adult dosage is 40 mEq in 175 mL of water once or twice daily after meals. Citrus fruit juices such as orange juice or citrated soft drinks may be used in place of water to dilute Kaochlor-20.

Supplied: Kaochlor-10: Each 15 mL supplies: 20 mEq of elemental potassium and chloride (as potassium chloride 1.5 g), dicalite, ethyl alcohol, methylparaben, artificial orange juice flavor, sodium cyclamate, sorbitol, sucrose, tartrazine and water. Bottles of 500 mL.

Kaochlor-20: Each 15 mL supplies: 40 mEq of elemental potassium and chloride (as potassium chloride 3 g), citric acid, D&C Red #33, dicalite, ethyl alcohol, imitation cherry oil, methylparaben, sodium cyclamate and water. Bottles of 500 mL.

Protect from excessive heat or cold.

Reviewed 1997

KAON®
Pharmacia & Upjohn

Potassium Gluconate

Potassium Replacement Therapy

Indications: Treatment of potassium deficiency.

Precautions: Potassium therapy should not be started unless urinary output is adequate. Use only under supervision of a physician.

Dosage: 15 mL twice daily supplies 40 mEq of elemental potassium. Larger doses should be given with water or after meals to avoid a saline laxative effect.

Supplied: Each 15 mL supplies: 20 mEq of elemental potassium (as potassium gluconate 4.68 g). Nonmedicinal ingredients: artificial grape flavor, benzyl acetate, citric acid, D&C Red #33, ethyl alcohol, FD&C Blue #1, glucono delta lactone, methylparaben, potassium hydroxide, sodium cyclamate, sorbitol and water. Bottles of 500 mL. Protect from excessive heat or cold.

KAOPECTATE®
Johnson & Johnson • Merck

Attapulgite

Antidiarrheal

Indications: Fast relief of diarrhea and cramps.

Warnings: Do not use for more than 2 days or in the presence of high fever unless directed by a physician. Do not use if stools are bloody; consult a physician. If diarrhea persists, consult a physician. Keep this and all medications out of the reach of children.

Oral Suspensions: Children's: Infants and children less than 3 years old, only as directed by a physician.

Extra and Regular Strength: Infants and children, only as directed by a physician.

Tablets: Chewable: Do not use in infants or children under 3 years of age, unless directed by a physician.

Extra Strength: Do not use in infants and children under 6 years of age, unless directed by a physician.

Regular Strength: Do not use in infants and children under 6 years of age, unless directed by a physician.

Dosage: Oral Suspensions: Extra Strength: Not to exceed 6 doses in 24 hours. Adults and children over 12 years: 30 mL of suspension. Children 6 to 12 years: 15 mL of suspension. Children under 6 years: as directed by a physician.

Regular Strength and Children's: Not to exceed 7 doses in 24 hours. Adults and children over 12 years: 30 mL of suspension. Children 6 to 12 years: 15 mL of suspension. Children 3 to 6 years: 7.5 mL of suspension. Infants and children: as directed by a physician.

Tablets: Chewable: Adults: 4 tablets initially then 4 tablets after each subsequent bowel movement. Not to exceed 28 tablets in 24 hours. Children 6 to 12 years: 2 tablets initially then 2 tablets after each subsequent bowel movement. Not to exceed 14 tablets in 24 hours. Children 3 to 6 years: 1 tablet initially then 1 tablet after each subsequent bowel movement. Not to exceed 7 tablets in 24 hours. **Chew tablets thoroughly and swallow.**

Extra Strength: Adults: 2 tablets initially then 2 tablets after each subsequent bowel movement. Not to exceed 12 tablets in 24 hours. Children 6 to 12 years: 1 tablet initially then 1 tablet after each subsequent bowel movement. **Swallow tablets with water. Do not chew.**

Regular Strength: Adults: 2 tablets initially, then 2 tablets after each subsequent bowel movement. Not to exceed 14 tablets in 24 hours. Children 6 to 12 years: 1 tablet initially, then 1 tablet after each subsequent bowel movement. Not to exceed 7 tablets in 24 hours. **Swallow whole tablets with water. Do not chew.**

Supplied: Oral Suspensions: Children's: Each 15 mL of cherry-flavored suspension contains: activated attapulgite 600 mg. Nonmedicinal ingredients: FD&C red No. 40, flavor, glucono-delta-lactone, magnesium aluminum silicate, methylparaben, purified water, sorbic acid, sucrose, titanium dioxide and xanthan gum. Energy: 28.7 kJ (7.1 kcal)/15 mL. Sodium: <1 mmol (4.88 mg)/15 mL. Gluten-, lactose- and tartrazine-free. Bottles of 180 mL. Protect from freezing.

Extra Strength: Each 15 mL of peppermint-flavored suspension contains: activated attapulgite 750 mg. Nonmedicinal ingredients: flavor, glucono-delta-lactone, magnesium aluminum silicate, methylparaben, purified water, sorbic acid, sucrose, titanium dioxide and xanthan gum. Energy: 29.7 kJ (7.1 kcal)/15 mL. Sodium: <1 mmol (4.88 mg)/15 mL. Gluten-, lactose- and tartrazine-free. Bottles of 250 and 350 mL. Protect from freezing.

Regular Strength: Each 15 mL of vanilla-flavored suspension contains: activated attapulgite 600 mg. Nonmedicinal ingredients: flavor, glucono-delta-lactone, magnesium aluminum silicate, methylparaben, purified water, sorbic acid, sucrose, titanium dioxide and xanthan gum. Energy: 29.7 kJ (7.1 kcal)/15 mL. Sodium: <1 mmol (2.2 mg)/15 mL. Gluten-, lactose- and tartrazine-free. Bottles of 250 and 350 mL. Protect from freezing.

Tablets: Chewable: Each pink with white specks tablet contains: activated attapulgite 300 mg. Nonmedicinal ingredients: cornstarch, D&C red No. 27, D&C red No. 30, dextrose, flavor, magnesium stearate, sucrose and titanium dioxide. Energy: 23.9 kJ (5.7 kcal). Sodium: <1 mmol (1 mg). Gluten-, lactose- and tartrazine-free. Blister packs of 16. Store at room temperature.

Extra Strength: Each white, capsule-shaped tablet contains: activated attapulgite 750 mg. Nonmedicinal ingredients: carnauba wax, croscarmellose sodium, hydroxypropyl cellulose, hydroxypropyl methylcellulose, parabens, pectin, propylene glycol, sucrose, synthetic black iron oxide, titanium dioxide and zinc stearate. Energy: <4.2 kJ (1 kcal). Sodium: <1 mmol (1 mg). Gluten-, lactose- and tartrazine-free. Blister packs of 15. Store at room temperature.

Regular Strength: Each white, ellipsoidal tablet contains: activated attapulgite 600 mg. Nonmedicinal ingredients: carnauba wax, croscarmellose sodium, hydroxypropyl cellulose, hydroxypropyl methylcellulose, parabens, pectin, propylene glycol, sucrose, synthetic black iron oxide, titanium dioxide and zinc stearate. Energy: <4.2 kJ (1 kcal). Sodium: <1 mmol (1 mg). Gluten-, lactose- and tartrazine-free. Blister packs of 15. Store at room temperature.

KAYEXALATE® ℞
Sanofi

Sodium Polystyrene Sulfonate

Cation Exchange Resin

Pharmacology: Sodium polystyrene sulfonate is not absorbed from the gastrointestinal tract. As the resin passes along the intestine or is retained in the colon after administration by

Kayexalate (cont'd)

enema, the sodium ions are partially released and are replaced by potassium ions. For the most part, this action occurs in the large intestine, which excretes potassium ions to a greater degree than does the small intestine. The efficiency of this process is limited and unpredictably variable. It commonly approximates the order of 33% but the range is so large that definite indices of electrolyte balance must be clearly monitored. Metabolic data are unavailable.

Indications: Treatment of hyperkalemia.

Contraindications: Sodium polystyrene sulfonate should not be administered to patients with the following conditions: serum potassium <5 mmol/L; history of hypersensitivity to polystyrene sulfonate resins; obstructive bowel disease.

Sodium polystyrene sulfonate should not be administered **orally** to neonates or in neonates with reduced gut motility (postoperatively or drug induced).

Warnings: Alternative Therapy in Severe Hyperkalemia: Since effective lowering of serum potassium with sodium polystyrene sulfonate may take hours to days, treatment with this drug alone may be insufficient to rapidly correct severe hyperkalemia associated with states of rapid tissue breakdown (e.g., burns and renal failure). In such instances, some form of dialysis (peritoneal or hemo-) may be imperative.

If hyperkalemia is so marked as to constitute a medical emergency (e.g., serum potassium above 7.5 mmol/L), immediate treatment with i.v. glucose and insulin, or i.v. sodium bicarbonate may be necessary as a temporary measure to lower serum potassium while other long-term potassium lowering therapy is being prepared.

Hypokalemia: Sodium polystyrene sulfonate therapy can precipitate serious potassium deficiency. It is imperative, therefore, to determine serum potassium concentrations at least daily and more frequently when indicated. Therapy should be discontinued as soon as serum potassium falls below 5 mmol/L. Since intracellular potassium deficiency is not always reflected by serum potassium concentrations, the concentration at which treatment with this resin should be discontinued must be determined individually for each patient. Important aids in making this determination are the patient's clinical condition and ECG.

Early clinical signs of severe hypokalemia include a pattern of irritable confusion and delayed thought processes. Severe hypokalemia is often associated with a lengthened QT interval, widening, flattening or inversion of the T wave, and the appearance of U waves on the ECG. Also, cardiac arrhythmias may occur, such as premature atrial, nodal and ventricular contractions and supraventricular and ventricular tachycardias. Marked hypokalemia can also be manifested by severe muscle weakness, at times extending into frank paralysis. The toxic effects of digitalis on the heart, especially various ventricular arrhythmia and AV nodal dissociation, are likely to be exaggerated by hypokalemia, even in the face of serum digoxin concentrations in the normal range.

During the resin's action in the intestinal tract, sodium is released mole for mole with potassium uptake. (A single dose of sodium polystyrene sulfonate (15 g) contains approximately 60 mmol of sodium.) Therefore, exercise caution when it is administered to patients who cannot tolerate even a small increase in sodium loads (i.e., severe congestive heart failure, severe hypertension or marked edema or renal damage). In such instances compensatory restriction of sodium intake from other sources may be indicated.

Like all cation exchange resins, sodium polystyrene sulfonate is not totally selective (for potassium) in its actions, and small amounts of other cations such as magnesium and calcium can also be lost during treatment. Patients receiving sodium polystyrene sulfonate should be monitored for all applicable electrolyte disturbances.

The patient should be positioned carefully when ingesting the resin, in order to avoid aspiration, which could lead to bronchopulmonary complications.

In the event of clinically significant constipation, treatment with the resin should be discontinued until normal bowel motion is resumed. To reduce any tendency to fecal impaction, constipation should be treated with sorbitol (from 10 to 20 mL of 70% syrup every 2 hours as needed). Sorbitol added to enemas of sodium polystyrene sulfonate has been implicated in cases of colonic necrosis. Although inadequate post-treatment colon irrigation cannot be ruled out as a factor, it is prudent to exclude sorbitol from resin enemas. Magnesium-containing laxatives should not be used.

Children and Neonates: In neonates, sodium polystyrene sulfonate should not be given by the **oral** route. In both children and neonates, particular care should be observed with rectal administration. Excessive dosage or inadequate dilution could result in impaction of the resin.

Drug Interactions: Cation Donating Agents: May reduce the effectiveness of the resin in binding potassium.

Aluminum Hydroxide: Intestinal obstruction due to concretions of aluminum hydroxide has been reported when aluminum hydroxide was combined with the resin.

Digitalis Drugs: The toxic effects of digitalis on the heart, especially various ventricular arrhythmias and AV nodal dissociation, are likely to be exaggerated if hypokalemia is allowed to develop.

Systemic alkalosis has been reported after cation-exchange resins were administered orally in combination with nonabsorbable cation-donating antacids and laxatives. Magnesium hydroxide should not be administered with sodium polystyrene sulfonate, since this may reduce the resin's potassium exchange capability.

Sorbitol in Enemas: (See Adverse Effects.)

Pregnancy and *Lactation:* Sodium polystyrene sulfonate is not absorbed from the gastrointestinal tract. No data are available concerning the use of polystyrene sulfonate resins in humans during either pregnancy or lactation.

Adverse Effects: Sodium polystyrene sulfonate may cause some degree of gastric irritation. Anorexia, nausea, vomiting and constipation may occur especially if high doses are given. Hypokalemia, hypocalcemia, and significant sodium retention may also occur. Occasionally diarrhea develops. Large doses in elderly individuals may cause fecal impaction. These effects may be obviated through usage of the resin in enemas as described under Dosage. Rare instances of colonic necrosis have been reported, apparently due to either inadequate or no lavage after use of sorbitol. Intestinal obstruction due to concretions of aluminum hydroxide when used in combination with sodium polystyrene sulfonate has been reported.

Fecal impaction following rectal administration in children and gastrointestinal concretions following oral administration to neonates have been reported.

Some cases of acute bronchitis and/or bronchopneumonia associated with inhalation of particles of sodium polystyrene sulfonate have been described.

Overdose: Symptoms and Treatment: Biochemical disturbances resulting from overdosage may give rise to clinical signs and symptoms of hypokalemia, including irritability, confusion, delayed thought processes, muscle weakness, hyporeflexia, and eventually frank paralysis. Apnea may be a serious consequence of the progression. Electrocardiographic changes may be consistent with hypokalemia; cardiac arrhythmia may occur. Hypocalcemic tetany may occur. Appropriate measures should be taken to correct serum electrolytes. The resin should be removed from the alimentary tract by appropriate use of laxatives or enemas.

Dosage: Suspensions of this drug should be freshly prepared and not stored beyond 24 hours. Sodium polystyrene sulfonate powder should not be heated as heating may alter the exchange properties of the resin.

Adults, Including the Elderly: Oral: The average daily adult dose of the resin is 15 to 60 g. This is provided by administering 15 g (approximately 4 level teaspoonfuls) of Kayexalate 1 to 4 times daily. 1 g of resin contains 4.1 mmol of sodium; 1 level teaspoonful contains approximately 3.5 g of resin and 15 mmol of sodium. (A heaping teaspoonful may contain as much as 10 to 12 g of resin.) Since the in vivo efficiency of sodium-potassium exchange resins is approximately 33%, about one third of the resin's actual sodium content is being delivered to the body.

Give each dose as a suspension in a small quantity of water or, for greater palatability, in syrup but not in orange juice or other fruit juices that are known to contain potassium. The amount of fluid usually ranges from 20 to 100 mL, depending on the dose, or may be simply determined by allowing 3 to 4 mL/g of resin.

The resin may be introduced into the stomach through a plastic tube and, if desired, mixed with a diet appropriate for a patient in renal failure.

Rectal: The resin may also be given, although with less effective results, in a daily enema. Thirty to 50 g of resin is given once or twice daily at 6-hour intervals. Each dose is administered as a warm emulsion (at body temperature) in 150 to 200 mL of aqueous vehicle (such as plain water, 10% dextrose in water, or equal parts of water and 2% methylcellulose suspension). Sorbitol is not contraindicated, however, see Adverse Effects regarding inadequate or no lavage following its use. The emulsion should be agitated gently during administration. The enema should be retained for as long as possible and followed by a cleansing enema.

After the initial cleansing enema, a soft, large size (French 28) rubber tube is inserted into the rectum for a distance of about 20 cm, with the tip well into the sigmoid colon, and taped in place. The resin is then suspended in the appropriate amount of water or 10% dextrose (in water) at body temperature and introduced by gravity, while the particles are kept in suspension by stirring. The suspension is flushed with 50 or 100 mL of saline solution, following which the tube is clamped and left in place. If back leakage occurs, the hips are elevated on pillows or a knee-chest position is taken temporarily. A somewhat thicker suspension may be used, but care should be taken that no paste is formed, because the latter has a greatly reduced exchange surface and will be particularly ineffective, if deposited in the rectal ampulla. The suspension is kept in the sigmoid colon for several hours, if possible. The colon is irrigated with a nonsodium containing solution at body temperature in order to remove the resin. Two quarts of flushing solution may be necessary. The returns are drained constantly through a Y tube connection. Particular attention should be paid to this cleansing enema when sorbitol has been used.

It should be noted that the rectal route of administration should be reserved for patients who are vomiting or who have uper gastrointestinal tract problems, including paralytic ileus. The rectal route may also be used simultaneously with oral administration in cases where more rapid initial results are desirable.

The intensity and duration of therapy depends upon the severity and resistance of hyperkalemia.

Children: Oral: In smaller children and infants, lower doses should be employed. Calculation of the dose may be based upon the exchange rate of 1 mmol of potassium/g of resin. An appropriate initial dose is 1 g/kg body weight daily in divided doses in acute hyperkalemia. For maintenance therapy, dosage may be reduced to 0.5 g/kg body weight daily.

Rectal: When refused by mouth, the resin may be given rectally using a dose at least as great as that which would have been given orally. The resin should be suspended in a proportional amount of 10% dextrose in water. Following retention of the enema, the colon should be irrigated to ensure adequate removal of the resin.

Neonates: Since it is advised that the oral route should not be employed, only rectal administration should be considered. With rectal administration, the minimum effective dosage within the range of 0.5 to 1 g/kg of resin should be employed. The resultant suspension should be diluted as for adults. Following administration of resin, the colon should be adequately irrigated to ensure recovery of the resin.

Supplied: Light brown, to brown, finely powdered sodium polystyrene sulfonate, a cation-exchange resin prepared in the sodium phase with an in vivo exchange capacity of approximately 1 mmol (in vitro approximately 3.1 mmol) of potassium/g. Sodium: 4.1 mmol (100 mg)/g. Gluten, lactose-, starch-, sucrose- and tartrazine-free. Jars of 454 g.

Reviewed 1999

K-DUR®
Key

Potassium Chloride

Potassium Supplement

Pharmacology: Potassium ion is the principal intracellular cation of most body tissues. Potassium ions participate in a number of essential physiological processes including the maintenance of intracellular tonicity, the transmission of nerve impulses, the contraction of cardiac, skeletal and smooth muscle and the maintenance of normal renal function. Potassium depletion may occur whenever the rate of potassium loss exceeds the rate of potassium intake. Such depletion usually develops slowly as a consequence of prolonged therapy with oral diuretics, primary or secondary hyperaldosternism, diabetic ketoacidosis, severe diarrhea, or inadequate replacement of potassium in patients on prolonged parenteral nutrition. Potassium depletion due to these causes is usually accompanied by a concomitant deficiency of chloride and is manifested by hypokalemia and metabolic alkalosis.

K-Dur tablets contain microcrystalloids which disperse upon disintegration of the tablet. The microcrystalloids are formulated to provide a controlled release of potassium chloride. The dispersibility of the microcrystalloids and the controlled release of ions from them are intended to minimize the possibility of high local concentrations of potassium within the gastrointestinal tract.

Indications: For the treatment of patients with hypokalemia with or without metabolic alkalosis in the treatment of digitalis intoxication, and for the treatment of patients with hypokalemic familial periodic paralysis.

For the prevention of potassium depletion when the dietary intake is inadequate in the following conditions: patients receiving digitalis and diuretics for congestive heart failure, selected patients with hypertension on long-term diuretic therapy, hepatic cirrhosis with ascites, states of aldosterone excess with normal renal function, potassium-losing nephropathy, and with certain diarrheal states.

Contraindications: In patients with hyperkalemia since a further increase in potassium concentration in such patients can produce cardiac arrest. Hyperkalemia may complicate any of the following conditions: acute and chronic renal failure, systemic acidosis such as diabetic acidosis, acute dehydration, extensive tissue breakdown as in severe burns, adrenal insufficiency, or the administration of a potassium-sparing diuretic (e.g. spironolactone, triamterene), or other drugs causing hyperkalemia such as captopril and enalapril.

Slow release potassium chloride preparations have produced esophageal ulceration in certain cardiac patients with esophageal compression due to enlarged left atrium. The administration of these preparations is contraindicated in such patients as well as in patients with dysphagia.

All solid dosage forms of potassium supplements are contraindicated in any patients in whom there is cause for arrest or delay in tablet passage through the gastrointestinal tract. In these instances, potassium supplementation should be with a liquid preparation.

Warnings: Hyperkalemia: In patients with impaired mechanisms for excreting potassium, the administration of potassium salts can produce hyperkalemia and cardiac arrest. This occurs most commonly in patients given potassium by the i.v. route but may also occur in patients given potassium orally. Potentially fatal hyperkalemia can develop rapidly and be asymptomatic. The use of potassium salts in patients with chronic renal disease, or any other condition which impairs potassium excretion, requires particularly careful monitoring of the serum potassium concentration and appropriate dosage adjustment. Hyperkalemia has the potential to promote quinidine toxicity.

Hypokalemia: Hypokalemia should not be treated by the concomitant administration of potassium salts and a potassium-sparing diuretic (e.g. spironolactone, triamterene) or other drugs causing hyperkalemia such as captopril or enalapril since the simultaneous administration of these agents can produce severe hyperkalemia. Hypokalemia in patients with metabolic acidosis should be treated with an alkalinizing potassium salt such as potassium acetate, potassium bicarbonate or potassium citrate.

Gastrointestinal Lesions: Potassium chloride tablets have produced stenotic and/or ulcerative lesions of the small bowel and deaths, in addition to upper gastrointestinal bleeding. These lesions are caused by a high localized concentration of potassium ions in the region of a rapidly dissolving tablet, which injures the bowel wall and thereby produces obstruction, hemorrhage or perforation.

The frequency of gastrointestinal lesions with potassium chloride is, at present, unknown. The drug should be discontinued immediately and the possibility of bowel obstruction or perforation considered if severe vomiting, abdominal pain, distention, or gastrointestinal bleeding occurs. All oral potassium preparations should be prescribed with particular caution in patients with a history of peptic ulcer.

Precautions: The treatment of potassium depletion, particularly in the presence of cardiac disease, renal disease, or acidosis, requires careful attention to acid-base balance and appropriate monitoring of the serum electrolytes, the ECG and the clinical status of the patient.

Potassium supplements should be used with caution in diseases associated with heart block since increased serum potassium may increase the degree of block.

Since anticholinergic agents have the potential to slow gastrointestinal motility, caution should be exercised when prescribing solid oral potassium preparations to patients concurrently receiving anticholinergic agents.

Pregnancy and *Lactation:* Because of gastrointestinal hypomotility associated with pregnancy, solid oral potassium supplements should be given to pregnant women only if clearly needed.

Adverse Effects: The most common adverse reactions to oral potassium salts are nausea, vomiting, abdominal discomfort and diarrhea. These symptoms are due to irritation of the gastrointestinal tract and are best avoided by increasing fluid intake when possible, taking the dose with meals or reducing the dose. Intestinal bleeding, ulceration, perforation and obstruction have been reported in patients treated with solid dosage forms of potassium salts and may occur with K-Dur (see Contraindications and Warnings).

One of the most severe adverse effects is hyperkalemia (see Contraindications, Warnings and Overdose). Skin rash has been reported rarely with potassium preparations.

Overdose: Overdosage from therapeutic doses of solid oral potassium salts in persons with normal excretory mechanism rarely occurs; however, if excretory mechanisms are impaired, potentially fatal hyperkalemia may occur. Acute (accidental or intentional) overdosages of solid oral potassium salts have resulted in severe and/or fatal hyperkalemia.

Symptoms: Overdosage with potassium is characterized chiefly by cardiovascular, neuromuscular and gastrointestinal disturbances.

Cardiovascular: ECG changes, hypotension and shock, bundle-branch block, ventricular arrhythmias, ventricular fibrillation leading possibly to cardiac arrest.

Neuromuscular: paresthesia, areflexia, convulsions, flaccid paralysis of striated muscle leading possibly to respiratory paralysis.

Gastrointestinal: nausea, vomiting, diarrhea and abdominal cramps.

Hyperkalemia: It is important to recognize that hyperkalemia is usually asymptomatic and may be manifested only by an increased serum potassium concentration and characteristic ECG changes which include increased amplitude and peaking of the T-wave, and flattening or absence of the P-wave. As hyperkalemia worsens prolongation of the PR interval, widening of the QRS complex with ST segment depression and arrhythmias may develop.

Widening of the QRS complex is one of the most ominous signs and indicates the need for aggressive treatment.

Treatment: The plasma concentration and ECG must be monitored in every case of potassium overdosage, as well as serum electrolytes, BUN, glucose and arterial blood gases.

ECG signs of hyperkalemia (tall peaked T-waves, PR prolongation, disappearance of P-waves, QRS widening, heart block) are indications for immediate treatment.

In severe hyperkalemia (plasma potassium exceeded 8 mmol/L or ECG abnormalities include absence of P-wave, presence of widened QRS complex or ventricular arrhythmia): administer i.v. 300 to 500 mL/hour of 10% dextrose solution containing 10 to 20 units of insulin/1 000 mL. Correct acidosis, if present, with i.v. sodium bicarbonate (44 to 132 mmol/L of glucose solution). Administer 10 to 30 mL of 10% calcium gluconate i.v. over 1 to 5 minutes under continuous ECG monitoring.

Administer cation exchange resin by high retention enema. 30 to 50 g sodium polystyrene sulfonate suspended in 100 mL warm aqueous sorbital solution should be kept in the sigmoid colon for several hours, if possible. The colon is then irrigated with non-sodium containing solution to remove the resin. Repeated enemas can be administered, or the resin given repeatedly by mouth to maintain a physiologic potassium concentration.

Hemodialysis or peritoneal dialysis may be of use, particularly in patients with renal failure.

In moderately severe hyperkalemia (plasma potassium between 6.5 and 8 mmol/L or ECG peaking of T-wave): administer i.v. 300 to 500 mL/hour of 10% dextrose solution containing 10 to 20 units of insulin/1 000 mL. Correct acidosis, if present, with i.v. sodium bicarbonate (44 to 132 mmol/L of glucose solution). Correct hyponatremia and hypovolemia, if present.

Once the patient's cardiac state has been stabilized, in the case of a recent acute ingestion of K-Dur, consideration should be given to the evacuation of the stomach. When overdosage is the result of chronic therapeutic ingestion, the drug should be discontinued immediately as well as potassium containing foods and medications and also potassium sparing diuretics.

Dosage: The usual dietary intake of potassium by the average adult is 40 to 80 mmol (3 000 to 6 000 mg)/day.

Potassium depletion sufficient to cause hypokalemia usually requires the loss of 200 or more mmol (15 000 mg) of potassium from the total body store.

Dosage must be adjusted to the individual needs of each patient but is typically in the range of 20 mmol (1 500 mg)/day for the prevention of hypokalemia to 40 to 100 mmol (3 000 to 7 500 mg)/day or more for the treatment of potassium depletion (see Table I).

Table I—K-Dur

Dosage		
K-Dur Tablets	**For Prevention**	**For Treatment**
20 mmol (1 500 mg)	1 tablet/day 20 mmol (1 500 mg)	2 to 5 tablets/day 40 to 100 mmol (3 000 to 7 500 mg)

If more than one 20 mmol tablet is prescribed/day, the total daily dosage should be divided into 2 or more separate doses.

Tablets should be taken with a glass of water or other liquid.

Patients having difficulty swallowing whole tablets may try one of the following alternate methods of administration. Break the tablet in half, and take each half separately with a glass of water; or prepare an aqueous suspension as follows: Place the whole tablet in approximately one-half glass of water (115 mL). Allow 2 to 3 minutes for the tablet to disintegrate. Stir for about half a minute after the tablet has disintegrated. Drink the entire contents of the glass immediately. Add another small quantity of water, stir and drink immediately. Aqueous suspensions of K-Dur tablets that are not taken immediately should be discarded. The use of other liquids for suspending the tablets is not recommended.

Supplied: Each capsule-shaped, white to off-white, mottled sustained release tablet, imprinted "K-DUR 20" on one side and scored on the other, contains: potassium chloride 20 mmol (1 500 mg). Nonmedicinal ingredients: crospovidone, ethylcellulose, hydroxypropylcellulose, magnesium stearate and microcrystalline cellulose. Bottles of 100. Unit dose boxes of 50 strip of 10 tablets (hospital use only). Keep tightly closed. Store at controlled room temperature 14 to 30°C.

(Shown in Product Recognition Section)

KEFLEX® Ⓟ

Lilly

Cephalexin

Antibiotic

Pharmacology: Cephalexin is bactericidal against many gram-positive and gram-negative organisms. In vitro tests demonstrate that the cephalosporins are bactericidal through their inhibition of cell wall synthesis. Cephalexin is active against the following organisms in vitro:

Beta-hemolytic and other streptococci (many strains of enterococci; e.g. S. faecalis, are resistant).

Staphylococci, including coagulase-positive, coagulase-negative, and beta-lactamase (penicillinase) producing strains (a few strains of staphylococci are resistant to cephalexin).

S. pneumoniae; E. coli; P. mirabilis; K. pneumoniae; H. influenzae; B. catarrhalis.

Cephalexin is not active against most strains of Enterobacter sp., P. morganii or P. vulgaris. It has no activity against Pseudomonas or Herellea sp. When tested by in vitro methods, staphylococci exhibit cross resistance between cephalexin and methicillin type antibiotics.

Cephalexin is well absorbed orally to produce effective blood levels within 1 hour. Less than 10% of absorbed drug is bound to serum protein in concentrations above 1 µg/mL. More than 80% is excreted as cephalexin in the urine. Cephalexin is acid stable. Food in the stomach causes a delay in onset, a lower peak and a prolongation of blood concentrations. Approximately 10% less drug is excreted in the urine of patients taking food than in that of fasting subjects.

Indications: The treatment of bacterial infections of the respiratory tract including otitis media, genitourinary tract, bones and joints, skin, and soft tissues when the infection is caused by susceptible organisms. Culture and susceptibility studies should be performed.

Contraindications: Patients with known allergy to the cephalosporin group of antibiotics.

Warnings: Before therapy with cephalexin is instituted, careful inquiry should be made concerning previous hypersensitivity reactions to cephalosporins, penicillins or other drugs. Cephalexin should be given only with caution to penicillin-sensitive patients. There is some evidence of cross-allergenicity between the penicillins and the cephalosporins. Patients have been reported to have had severe reactions (including anaphylaxis) to both.

Antibiotics including cephalexin should be administered with caution, and then only when absolutely necessary, to any

Keflex (cont'd)

patient who has demonstrated some form of allergy, particularly to drugs. Of 12 917 clinical trial patients, 462 had histories of penicillin allergy. Twenty-one of them (about 4.6%) were among those in whom possible allergic reactions to cephalexin were observed.

Pseudomembranous colitis has been reported with virtually all broad-spectrum antibiotics including cephalexin; therefore, it is important to consider its diagnosis in patients administered cephalexin who develop diarrhea in association with the use of antibiotics. Such colitis may range in severity from mild to life-threatening.

Treatment with broad-spectrum antibiotics including cephalexin may alter the normal flora of the colon and may permit overgrowth of clostridia. Studies indicate that a toxin produced by Clostridium difficile is one primary cause of antibiotic-associated colitis.

Mild cases of pseudomembranous colitis usually respond to drug discontinuance alone. In moderate to severe cases, management should include sigmoidoscopy, appropriate bacteriologic studies, and fluid, electrolyte, and protein supplementation. When the colitis does not improve after the administration of cephalexin has been discontinued, or when it is severe, consideration should be given to the administration of oral vancomycin. Other causes of colitis should be ruled out.

Precautions: As is the case with all drugs, patients should be followed carefully so that any adverse effects or unusual manifestations of drug idiosyncrasy may be detected. If an allergic reaction to cephalexin occurs, the drug should be discontinued and the patient treated with the usual agents (e.g. epinephrine, antihistamines, pressor amines, or corticosteroids).

Prolonged use of cephalexin will result in the overgrowth of nonsusceptible organisms. Careful observation of the patient is essential. If superinfection occurs during therapy, appropriate measures should be taken.

Administer cephalexin with caution in the presence of impaired renal function. Under such conditions, careful clinical observation and laboratory studies should be made because safe dosage may be lower than that usually recommended.

If cephalexin is to be used for long-term therapy, periodic monitoring of hematologic, renal and hepatic functions should be done.

Indicated surgical procedures should be performed in conjunction with antibiotic therapy; e.g. the incision and drainage of abscesses.

Pregnancy: Safety of this product for use during pregnancy has not been established.

Positive direct Coombs' tests have been reported during treatment with the cephalosporin antibiotics. In hematologic studies or in transfusion cross matching procedures when antiglobulin tests are performed on the minor side or in Coombs' testing of newborns whose mothers have received cephalosporin antibiotics before parturition, it should be recognized that a positive Coombs' test may be due to the drug.

Cephalexin may produce a false positive reaction for glucose in the urine with Benedict's or Fehling's solution or with Clinitest tablets, but not with Tes-Tape (Glucose Enzymatic Test Strip, USP).

Adverse Effects: Of 12 917 patients treated with Keflex in formal clinical trials, 771 (6%) reported adverse events, of which 385 (3%) were judged to be drug-related. 462 of these patients had known sensitivity to penicillin, 4.6% reacted. The incidence of reported side effects was as follows:
Gastrointestinal: diarrhea 1.3%, nausea 1.0%, vomiting 0.6%, dyspepsia/gastrointestinal upset 0.2%, abdominal cramp/pain 0.1%, anorexia 0.1%.
Hypersensitivity: skin rash 0.7%, urticaria 0.3%.
CNS: headache 0.1%.
Genitourinary: genital moniliasis 0.8%, vaginitis 0.4%, pruritus vulvae 0.2%.

Other adverse reactions experienced less frequently include: glossitis/stomatitis, oral moniliasis, pruritus ani, gastroenteritis, fever, pruritus, a positive direct Coombs', allergy/anaphylaxis, intertrigo, angioedema, dizziness, paresthesia, somnolence, visual hallucination/diplopia, insomnia, tremor, leukorrhea, dysuria, malaise/fatigue, superinfection, myalgia/back pain, nuchal swelling, dyspnea, cardiac arrhythmia and vasodilatation.

Laboratory Tests: 170 patients (1.3%) had abnormal laboratory values. There was no consistent pattern of abnormality and only 2 patients were withdrawn from studies as a result of these findings.
Hematological: eosinophilia 0.4%.
Biochemical: elevated alkaline phosphatase 0.2%, elevated AST 0.3%, elevated ALT 0.2%.
Renal: elevated BUN 0.1%.

Other abnormal values reported less frequently included: elevated creatinine, bilirubin and cholesterol: decreased platelets, hemoglobin and/or hematocrit.

The following adverse reactions have been reported during postmarketing experience:
Gastrointestinal: Symptoms of pseudomembranous colitis may appear either during or after antibiotic treatment. Nausea and vomiting have been reported. The most frequent side effect has been diarrhea. It was very rarely severe enough to warrant cessation of therapy. Dyspepsia and abdominal pain have also occurred. As with some penicillins and some other cephalosporins, transient hepatitis and cholestatic jaundice have been reported.
Hypersensitivity: Allergic reactions in the form of rash, urticaria, angioedema, erythema multiforme, Stevens-Johnson syndrome, or toxic epidermal necrolysis have been observed. These reactions usually subsided upon discontinuation of the drug. In some of these reactions, supportive therapy may be necessary. Anaphylaxis has also been reported.
Other reactions have included genital and anal pruritus, genital moniliasis, vaginitis and vaginal discharge, dizziness, fatigue, headache, agitation, confusion, hallucinations, arthralgia, arthritis, and joint disorder. Reversible interstitial nephritis, eosinophilia, neutropenia, leukopenia, thrombocytopenia and slight elevations in AST and ALT have been reported.

Vertigo, tinnitus, hearing loss, and behavioral changes in young children have been reported with cephalexin use.

Overdose: Symptoms: Symptoms of oral overdose may include nausea, vomiting, epigastric distress, diarrhea, and hematuria. If other symptoms are present, it is probably secondary to an underlying disease state, an allergic reaction, or toxicity due to ingestion of a second medication.

Treatment: Unless 5 to 10 times the normal dose of cephalexin has been ingested, gastrointestinal decontamination should not be necessary.

Protect the patient's airway and support ventilation and perfusion. Meticulously monitor and maintain, within acceptable limits, the patient's vital signs, blood gases, serum electrolytes, etc. Absorption of drugs from the gastrointestinal tract may be decreased by giving activated charcoal, which, in many cases, is more effective than emesis or lavage; consider charcoal instead of or in addition to gastric emptying. Repeated doses of charcoal over time may hasten elimination of some drugs that have been absorbed. Safeguard the patient's airway when employing gastric emptying or charcoal.

Forced diuresis, peritoneal dialysis, hemodialysis, or charcoal hemoperfusion have not been established as beneficial for an overdose of cephalexin; however, it would be extremely unlikely that one of these procedures would be indicated.

Dosage: Cephalexin is administered orally. Adults: The dosage ranges from 1 to 4 g daily in divided doses. The usual adult dose is 1 g/day in divided doses every 6 hours. For more severe infections or those caused by less susceptible organisms, larger doses may be needed. If daily doses of cephalexin greater than 4 g are required, parenteral cephalosporins, in appropriate doses should be considered.
Children: The recommended daily dosage is 25 to 50 mg/kg administered in divided doses every 6 hours. See Table I.

Table I—Keflex

Dosage in Children—Suspension

Child's Weight	125 mg/5 mL	250 mg/5 mL
10 kg	½ to 1 tsp. q.i.d.	
20 kg	1 to 2 tsp. q.i.d.	½ to 1 tsp. q.i.d.
40 kg	2 to 4 tsp. q.i.d.	1 to 2 tsp. q.i.d.
	OR	
10 kg	1 to 2 tsp. b.i.d.	—
20 kg	2 to 4 tsp. b.i.d.	1 to 2 tsp. b.i.d.
40 kg	4 to 8 tsp. b.i.d.	2 to 4 tsp. b.i.d.

In severe infections, the dosage may be doubled.

For the treatment of bacterial pharyngitis caused by S. pyogenes group A, and, acute cystitis, the daily dosage may be divided into 2 and given every 12 hours.

In the treatment of beta-hemolytic infections, administer antibiotic therapy for at least 10 days.

To obtain maximum peak levels, administer cephalexin on an empty stomach.

Supplied: Suspension: 125 mg/5 mL: Each 5 mL of flavored suspension, Identi-Code W 21, contains: the equivalent of cephalexin 125 mg (mauve granules). Nonmedicinal ingredients: FD&C Red No. 40, imitation guarana flavor, methylcellulose, silicone, sodium lauryl sulfate and sucrose. Energy: 52.0 kJ (12.4 kcal)/5 mL. Sodium: <1 mmol (0.032 mg)/5 mL. Tartrazine-free. Bottles of 100 and 200 mL.

250 mg/5 mL: Each 5 mL of flavored suspension, Identi-Code W 68, contains: the equivalent of cephalexin 250 mg (peach granules). Nonmedicinal ingredients: FD&C Yellow No. 40, imitation guarana flavor, methylcellulose, silicone, sodium lauryl sulfate and sucrose. Energy: 50.5 kJ (12.1 kcal)/5 mL. Sodium: <1 mmol (0.032 mg)/5 mL. Tartrazine-free. Bottles of 100 and 200 mL.

Tablets: 250 mg: Each peach tablet, Identi-Code U 57, contains: cephalexin 250 mg. Nonmedicinal ingredients: glycerin, hydroxypropyl methylcellulose, magnesium stearate, starch, stearic acid powder and sodium starch glycolate; coating: iron oxide red, iron oxide yellow, methylcellulose, titanium dioxide and talc. Sodium- and tartrazine-free. Bottles of 100.

500 mg: Each peach tablet, Identi-Code U 49, contains: cephalexin 500 mg. Nonmedicinal ingredients: glycerin, hydroxypropyl methylcellulose, magnesium stearate, povidone and sodium starch glycolate; coating: iron oxide red, iron oxide yellow, methylcellulose, titanium dioxide and talc. Sodium- and tartrazine-free. Bottles of 100.

KEFLIN® Ⓟ

Lilly

Cephalothin Sodium

Antibiotic

Pharmacology: In vitro tests demonstrate that the cephalosporins are bactericidal by the inhibition of cell wall synthesis. Cephalothin is a broad spectrum antibiotic for parenteral administration. After administration of a 500 mg dose i.m. to normal volunteers, the average peak serum antibiotic level at ½ hour was 10 µg/mL; with a 1 g dose, the average was about 20 µg/mL. Following a single 1 g i.v. dose of cephalothin, blood levels have been about 30 µg/mL at 15 minutes, have ranged from 3 to 12 µg/mL at 1 hour, and have declined to about 1 µg/mL at 4 hours. With continuous infusion at the rate of 500 mg/hour, levels have been from 14 to 20 µg/mL of serum. Dosages of 2 g given i.v. over a 30-minute period have produced serum concentrations of 80 to 100 µg/mL ½ hour after the infusion; levels ranged from 10 to 40 µg/mL at 1 hour and from 3 to 6 µg/mL at 2 hours and were not assayable after 5 hours.

Assayable levels are not achieved after oral administration of cephalothin. Effectiveness of orally administered cephalothin has not been demonstrated in the treatment of enteric infections or in preoperative bowel preparation.

Sixty to 70% of an i.m. dose is excreted by the kidneys in the first 6 hours; this results in high urine concentrations e.g., 800 µg/mL of urine after a 500 mg dose and 2 500 µg/mL following 1 g. Probenecid slows tubular excretion and almost doubles peak blood levels.

Spinal-fluid levels have ranged from 0.4 to 1.4 µg/mL in a child and from 0.15 to 5 µg/mL in adults with meningeal inflammatory states. The antibiotic passes readily into other body fluids, e.g., pleural, joint, and ascitic fluids. Studies of amniotic fluid and cord blood show prompt transfer of the drug across the placenta.

Following single 1 g i.m. doses of cephalothin, peak maternal levels were reached between 31 and 45 minutes after injection; the peak levels in the infants occurred about 15 minutes later. All plasma levels in the infants were far below those of the mother.

Secondary aqueous-humor levels have averaged 0.5 µg/mL 30 minutes after a single 1 g i.v. dose. The antibiotic has been detected in bile.

Sensitivity Plate Tests: If the Bauer-Kirby-Sherris-Turck method of disc sensitivity testing is used, a disc containing 30 µg cephalothin should give a zone of over 17 mm when tested against a cephalothin-sensitive bacterial strain, and a zone of over 14 mm with an organism of intermediate sensitivity.

Indications: May be indicated for the treatment of serious infections caused by susceptible strains of the designated microorganisms in the diseases listed below. Culture and susceptibility studies should be performed. Clinical judgment and anticipated bacteriological findings may permit the start of therapy before results of susceptibility studies are obtained.

Respiratory tract infections caused by S. pneumoniae, staphylococci [beta-lactamase and nonbeta-lactamase (penicillinase) producing], S. pyogenes, Klebsiella spp., and H. influenzae spp.
Skin and soft-tissue infections, including peritonitis caused by staphylococci (beta-lactamase and nonbeta-lactamase producing), S. pyogenes, E. coli, P. mirabilis, and Klebsiella spp.
Genitourinary tract infections caused by E. coli, P. mirabilis, and Klebsiella sp.
Septicemia, including endocarditis, caused by S. pneumoniae, staphylococci (beta-lactamase and nonbeta-lactamase producing), S. pyogenes, S. viridans, E. coli, P. mirabilis, and Klebsiella sp.
Meningitis caused by S. pneumoniae, S. pyogenes, and staphylococci (beta-lactamase and nonbeta-lactamase producing).
Note: Inasmuch as only low levels of cephalothin are found in the cerebrospinal fluid, the drug is not reliable in the treatment of meningitis and cannot be recommended for that purpose. Cephalothin has, however, proved to be effective in a number of cases of meningitis and may be considered for unusual circumstances in which other, more reliably effective antibiotics cannot be used.
Bone and joint infections caused by staphylococci (beta-lactamase and nonbeta-lactamase-producing).

Evidence indicates that perioperative administration of cephalothin may help to reduce the incidence of postoperative infections in patients undergoing surgical procedures involving contaminated or potentially contaminated sites. It may also be effective in patients at risk of serious infection when undergoing "clean" bone and open heart surgery, gynecological, obstetric, urologic, head and neck and other types of surgery. Cephalothin is not at present recommended in surgery related to the lower gastrointestinal tract or certain other sites where anaerobic organisms such as bacteroides tend to prevail.

Past experience has generally involved 1 or 2-day postoperative administration of cephalothin followed by oral antibiotics. Longer courses of therapy may be desirable when prosthetic devices are surgically implanted (see Dosage).
Note: If the susceptibility tests show that the infecting organism is resistant to cephalothin, other appropriate antibiotic therapy should be initiated.

Contraindications: Hypersensitivity to cephalosporin antibiotics.

Warnings: Before cephalothin therapy is instituted, careful inquiry should be made concerning previous hypersensitivity reactions to cephalosporins and penicillin. Cephalosporin C derivatives should only be given cautiously in penicillin sensitive patients.

Serious acute hypersensitivity reactions may require epinephrine and other emergency measures.

There is some evidence of partial crossallergenicity of the penicillins and the cephalosporins. Patients have been reported to have had severe reactions (including fatal anaphylaxis) to both drugs.

Antibiotics, including cephalothin, should be administered cautiously, and then only when absolutely necessary, to any patient who has demonstrated some form of allergy, particularly to drugs.

Pseudomembranous colitis has been reported with virtually all broad-spectrum antibiotics including cephalothin; therefore, it is important to consider its diagnosis in patients administered cephalothin who develop diarrhea in association with the use of antibiotics. Such colitis may range in severity from mild to life-threatening.

Treatment with broad-spectrum antibiotics including cephalothin may alter the normal flora of the colon and may permit overgrowth of clostridia. Studies indicate that a toxin produced by C. difficile is one primary cause of antibiotic-associated colitis.

Mild cases of pseudomembranous colitis usually respond to drug discontinuance alone. In moderate to severe cases, management should include sigmoidoscopy, appropriate bacteriologic studies, and fluid, electrolyte, and protein supplementation. When the colitis does not improve after the administration of cephalothin has been discontinued, or when it is severe, consideration should be given to the administration of oral vancomycin. Other causes of colitis should be ruled out.

Precautions: Patients should be followed carefully so that any side effects or unusual manifestations of drug idiosyncrasy may be detected. If an allergic reaction to cephalothin occurs, the drug should be discontinued and the patient treated with the usual agents (epinephrine, antihistamines, pressor amines, or corticosteroids).

Although cephalothin rarely produces alteration in kidney function, evaluation of renal status is recommended, especially in seriously ill patients receiving maximum doses. Patients with impaired renal function should be placed on the special dosage schedule recommended under Dosage. Usual doses in such individuals may result in excessive serum concentrations.

The administration of inappropriately large doses of parenteral cephalosporins may cause seizures, particularly in patients with renal impairment.

Where potentially nephrotoxic agents such as potent diuretics or aminoglycoside antibiotics are administered prior to or in conjunction with cephalosporins, the risk of nephrotoxicity may be increased and renal function should be monitored.

When i.v. doses of cephalothin larger than 6 g daily are given by infusion for periods longer than 3 days, they may be associated with thrombophlebitis, and the veins may have to be alternated. The use of small i.v. needles in the larger available veins may be preferred.

Prolonged use of cephalothin may result in the overgrowth of non-susceptible organisms. Constant observation of the patient is essential. If superinfection occurs during therapy, appropriate measures should be taken.

Pregnancy: Safety of this product for use during pregnancy has not been established.

A false-positive reaction for glucose in the urine may occur with Benedict's or Fehling's solution or with Clinitest tablets, but not with Tes-Tape (Glucose Enzymatic Test Strip, USP).

Adverse Effects: Maculopapular rash, urticaria, reactions resembling serum sickness, and anaphylaxis have been reported. Eosinophilia and drug fever have been observed to be associated with other allergic reactions. These reactions are most likely to occur in patients with a history of allergy, particularly to penicillin.

Neutropenia, thrombocytopenia, and hemolytic anemia have been reported. Some individuals, particularly those with azotemia, have developed positive direct Coombs tests during cephalothin therapy.

Transient rise in AST and alkaline phosphatase has been noted.

Rise in BUN and decreased creatinine clearance have been reported, particularly in patients with prior renal impairment. The role of cephalothin in renal changes is difficult to assess, because other factors predisposing to prerenal azotemia or to acute renal failure usually have been present. With larger than recommended doses renal impairment has been reported.

Pain, induration, tenderness, and elevation of temperature have been reported following repeated i.m. injections. Thrombophlebitis has occurred and is usually associated with daily doses over 6 g given by infusion for more than 3 days.

Symptoms of pseudomembranous colitis may appear either during or after antibiotic treatment. Diarrhea, nausea and vomiting have been reported rarely.

Overdose: Symptoms and Treatment: Daily doses up to 12 g have been used successfully without evidence of untoward systemic effects.

The administration of inappropriately large doses of parenteral cephalosporins may cause seizures, particularly in patients with renal impairment. Dosage reduction is necessary when renal function is impaired (see Dosage). If seizures occur, the drug should be promptly discontinued; anticonvulsant therapy may be administered if clinically indicated. Hemodialysis may be considered in cases of overwhelming overdosage.

As is the case with all new drugs, patients should be followed carefully so that any side effects or unusual manifestations of drug idiosyncrasy may be detected. If an allergic reaction to cephalothin occurs, the drug should be discontinued and the patient treated with the usual agents (e.g., epinephrine, antihistamines, pressor amines, or corticosteroids).

Dosage: Keflin has been shown to be physically compatible with most commonly used i.v. fluids and electrolyte solutions. In general, it is not compatible with compounds of high molecular weight or with alkaline earth metals. Its addition to solutions having a pH below 4 or above 8.5 is not advised.

The usual adult dosage range is 500 mg to 2 g of cephalothin every 4 to 6 hours. A dosage of 500 mg every 6 hours is adequate in uncomplicated pneumonia, furunculosis with cellulitis, and most urinary tract infections. In severe infections, this may be increased by giving the injections every 4 hours or, when the desired response is not obtained, by raising the dose to 1 g. In life-threatening infections, doses up to 2 g every 4 hours may be required.

To reduce the incidence of postoperative infection in contaminated or potentially contaminated surgery, 2 g administered i.v. just prior to surgery, 2 g during surgery (if the procedure is prolonged), and 2 g every 6 hours for 1 or 2 days postoperatively is recommended. Continuation with oral antibiotics may be considered. Longer periods of cephalothin administration may also be desirable in selected surgical procedures.

When renal function is reduced, an i.v. loading dose of 1 to 2 g may be given. Continued dosage schedule should be determined by degree of renal impairment, severity of infection, and sensitivity of the causative organism. The maximum doses administered should be based on the following recommendations (see Table I).

Table I—Keflin

Maximum Doses

Renal Function Status	Maximum Adult Dosage (Maintenance)
Mild Impairment (C_{cr}=80–50 mL/min)	2 g q6h
Moderate Impairment (C_{cr}=50–25 mL/min)	1.5 g q6h
Severe Impairment (C_{cr}=25–10 mL/min)	1 g q6h
Marked Impairment (C_{cr}=10–2 mL/min)	0.5 g q6h
Essentially No Function (C_{cr}= <2 mL/min)	0.5 g q8h

In infants and children, the dosage should be proportionately less in accordance with age, weight, and severity of infection. Daily administration of 100 mg/kg (80 to 160 mg/kg) in divided doses has been found effective for most infections susceptible to cephalothin.

Antibiotic therapy in β-hemolytic streptococcal infections should continue for at least 10 days. In staphylococcal infections, surgical procedures, such as incision and drainage, should be carried out in all cases when indicated.
Administration: I.M.: Cephalothin should be given by deep i.m. injection into a large muscle mass, such as the gluteus or lateral aspect of the thigh, to minimize pain and induration and the possible formation of s.c. sterile abscess.
I.V.: The i.v. route may be preferable for patients with bacteremia, septicemia, or other severe or life-threatening infections who may be poor risks because of lowered resistance resulting from such debilitating conditions as malnutrition, trauma, surgery, diabetes, heart failure, or malignancy, particularly if shock is present or impending. For these infections in patients with normal renal function, the i.v. dosage is 4 to 12 g of cephalothin daily. In conditions such as septicemia, 6 to 8 g/day may be given i.v. for several days at the beginning of therapy; then, depending on the clinical response and laboratory findings, the dosage may gradually be reduced.
Intermittent I.V.: Administration: For intermittent i.v. administration, a solution containing 1 g cephalothin in 10 mL of diluent may be slowly injected directly into the vein over a period of 3 to 5 minutes or may be given through the tubing when the patient is receiving parenteral solutions.

Intermittent i.v. infusion with a Y-type administration set can also be accomplished while bulk i.v. solutions are being infused. However, during infusion of the solution containing cephalothin, it is desirable to discontinue the other solution. When this technique is employed, careful attention should be paid to the volume of the solution containing cephalothin so that the calculated dose will be infused. See Reconstitution for specific package information.
Continuous I.V. Infusion: For continuous i.v. infusion, 2 g of cephalothin, diluted and well mixed with Sterile Water for Injection, may be added to an i.v. bottle containing 5% dextrose, normal saline solution, Lactated Ringer's Injection, USP, Dextrose 5% in Lactated Ringer's Injection or 5% dextrose with 0.02% sodium bicarbonate. The choice of solution and the volume to be employed are dictated by fluid and electrolyte management.
Intraperitoneal: In peritoneal dialysis procedures, cephalothin has been added to dialysis fluid in concentrations up to 6 mg/100 mL and instilled into the peritoneal space throughout an entire dialysis (16 to 30 hours). Careful assay procedures have shown that 44% of the administered drug was absorbed into the bloodstream. Serum levels of 10 μg/mL were reported, with no evidence of accumulation and no untoward local or systemic reactions.

The intraperitoneal administration of solutions containing 0.1 to 4% cephalothin in saline has been used in treating patients with peritonitis or contaminated peritoneal cavities.

Keflin (cont'd)

(The total daily dosage of cephalothin should take into account the amount given by the intraperitoneal route.)
Reconstitution: I.M.: Reconstitute with Sterile Water for Injection. See Table II.

Table II—Keflin

Reconstitution I.M.

Vial Size	Volume to be Added	Approximate Available Volume	Approximate Average Concentration
1 g	4.5 mL	5 mL	200 mg/mL

Shake well until dissolved.
I.V.: Solutions for Reconstitution: Sterile Water for Injection, 5% Dextrose Injection, 0.9% Sodium Chloride Injection. See Table III.

Table III—Keflin

Reconstitution I.V.

Vial Size	Volume to be Added	Approximate Available Volume	Approximate Average Concentration
1 g	10 mL	10.5 mL	95 mg/mL

Shake well until dissolved. The prepared solution may be further diluted to the desired volume with any of the solutions for i.v. infusion listed below.
Solutions for I.V. Infusion: 0.9% Sodium Chloride Injection, 5% Dextrose Injection, 5% Dextrose and 0.9% Sodium Chloride Injection, 5% Dextrose and 0.45% Sodium Chloride Injection, 5% Dextrose and 0.2% Sodium Chloride Injection, 5% Dextrose and 0.15% Potassium Chloride Injection, 5% Osmitrol in Water for Injection, Sodium Lactate Injection (M/6), Normosol-M in D5-W, Ionosol-B in 5% Dextrose Injection, Ringer's Injection, Acetated Ringers Injection, Lactated Ringers in 5% Dextrose Injection.
Stability: Reconstituted Keflin should be used within 8 hours when stored at room temperature or within 72 hours when refrigerated.

Keflin solutions reconstituted with bacteriostatic diluent and used for i.m. administration as multiple-dose containers should be used within 7 days when stored under refrigeration.

A concentrated solution of Keflin may take on a pale straw color when freshly mixed. This will darken upon standing at room temperature. Dark brown solutions should not be used.

I.V. infusion should be completed within 24 hours after preparing the solution. For prolonged infusions, replace with a freshly prepared solution at least every 24 hours.

Supplied: Each vial of sterile powder contains: cephalothin 1 g as cephalothin sodium and sodium bicarbonate 30 mg as buffer.

KEFUROX® Ⓟ

Lilly

Cefuroxime Sodium

Antibiotic

Pharmacology: In vitro tests demonstrate that the bactericidal action of cefuroxime results from the inhibition of the transpeptidase and carboxypeptidase enzymes, thus inhibiting cell wall synthesis.

Indications: For the treatment of patients with infections caused by susceptible strains of the designated organisms in the following diseases:
Lower Respiratory Tract Infections: Pneumonia caused by S. pneumoniae. H. influenzae including ampicillin-resistant strains, Klebsiella species, S. aureus including ampicillin-resistant (but not methicillin-resistant) strains. S. pyogenes and E. coli.
Urinary Tract Infections: Caused by E. coli and Klebsiella species.
Soft Tissue Infections: Caused by S. aureus including ampicillin-resistant (but not methicillin-resistant) strains. S. pyogenes and E. coli, Klebsiella species.
Gonorrhea: Caused by N. gonorrhea including ampicillin resistant strains.
Meningitis: Caused by S. aureus including ampicillin-resistant (but not methicillin-resistant) strains, S. pneumoniae, H. influenzae, and N. meningitis.
Bone and Joint infections: Caused by S. aureus (penicillinase and non-penicillinase producing strains).

Specimens for bacteriologic culture should be obtained prior to therapy in order to identify the causative organisms and to determine their susceptibility to cefuroxime. Therapy may be instituted before results of susceptibility testing are known. However, modification of the treatment may be required once these results become available.
Prevention: The pre-operative prophylactic administration of cefuroxime may prevent the growth of susceptible disease causing bacteria and thereby may reduce the incidence of certain post-operative infections: in patients undergoing surgical procedures (e.g. vaginal hysterectomy) that are classified as clean contaminated or potentially contaminated: in patients undergoing open heart surgery in whom infections at the operative site would present a serious risk.

If signs of infection occur postoperatively, specimens for culture should be obtained for identification of causative organism and appropriate antimicrobial therapy should be instituted.

Contraindications: Persons who have shown Type 1 hypersensitivity to cephalosporin antibiotics.

Warnings: Before therapy with cefuroxime is instituted, careful inquiry should be made to determine whether the patient has had previous hypersensitivity reactions to cefuroxime, cephalosporins, penicillins or other drugs. Cefuroxime should be administered with caution to any patient who has demonstrated some form of allergy, particularly to drugs. There is clinical and laboratory evidence of partial cross allergenicity of the cephalosporins and penicillins. If an allergic reaction to cefuroxime occurs, discontinue treatment with the drug. Serious acute hypersensitivity reactions may require epinephrine and other emergency measures.

Pseudomembranous colitis has been reported to be associated with treatment of cefuroxime (and other broad-spectrum antibiotics). Therefore, it is important to consider its diagnosis in patients administered cefuroxime who develop diarrhea. Treatment with broad-spectrum antibiotics including cefuroxime, alters the normal flora of the colon and may permit overgrowth of Clostridia. Studies indicate that a toxin produced by C. difficile is one primary cause of antibiotic associated colitis.

Mild cases of colitis may respond to drug discontinuance alone. Moderate to severe cases, should be managed with fluid, electrolyte and protein supplementation as indicated. When the colitis does not improve after administration of cefuroxime has been discontinued, or when it is severe, consideration should be given to the administration of oral vancomycin or other suitable therapy. Other possible causes of colitis should also be considered.

Precautions: Cefuroxime should be administered with caution to individuals with a history of gastrointestinal disease, particularly colitis.

Although cefuroxime rarely produces alterations in kidney function, evaluation of renal status during therapy is recommended, especially in seriously ill patients receiving the maximum doses. Cephalosporins should be given with caution to patients receiving concurrent treatment with potent diuretics and aminoglycosides as these regimens are suspected of adversely affecting renal function.

The total daily dose of cefuroxime should be reduced in patients with transient or persistent renal insufficiency (see Dosage), because high and prolonged serum antibiotic concentrations can occur in such individuals from usual doses.

Patients with altered renal or hepatic function should be carefully monitored during therapy with cefuroxime.

Prolonged use of cefuroxime may result in the overgrowth of non-susceptible organisms. Careful observation of the patient is essential. If superinfection occurs during therapy, appropriate measures should be taken.
Pregnancy: The safety of cefuroxime in the treatment of infections during pregnancy has not been established. If the administration of cefuroxime to pregnant patients is considered necessary, its use requires that the potential benefits be weighed against the possible hazards to the fetus.
Lactation: Cefuroxime is excreted in human milk in low concentrations (0.5 mg/L). The clinical significance of this is unknown, therefore, caution should be exercised when cefuroxime is administered to a nursing mother.
Geriatrics: The elimination of cefuroxime may be reduced due to impairment of renal function.
Laboratory Test Changes: A false-positive reaction for glucose in the urine may occur with Benedict's or Fehling's solution or with Clinitest tablets, but not with Test-Tape (Glucose Enzymatic Test Strip, USP). A false negative reaction may occur in the ferricyanide test for blood glucose, and a high reading is possible in the alkaline picrate test for creatinine.

Adverse Effects: The most common adverse effects observed during treatment have been local reactions following i.v. administration.
Local Reactions: Thrombophlebitis, pain on i.m. injection when using sterile water as the diluent, stiffness and inflammatory reaction within the injection site have all been reported.

Other adverse reactions observed include: Hypersensitivity: rash and eosinophilia, urticaria, pruritus and anaphylaxis. Drug fever has also been observed with cephalosporins.
Gastrointestinal Tract: diarrhea and nausea.
Blood: Decreased hemoglobin and hematocrit have been observed as well as transient eosinophilia and positive Coombs' test. Neutropenia and leukopenia were less common.
Hepatic: transient rise in AST and ALT, alkaline phosphatase, LDH and serum bilirubin.
Renal: increases in serum creatinine and/or BUN and a decreased creatinine clearance.
Other: drowsiness, loose stools, faint feeling, sweating, palpitation and Candida intertrigo.

Overdose: Symptoms and Treatment: Other than general supportive treatment, no specific antidote is known.

The administration of inappropriately large doses of parenteral cephalosporins may cause seizures, particularly in patients with renal impairment. Dosage reduction is necessary when renal function is impaired (see Dosage). If seizures occur, the drug should be promptly discontinued; anticonvulsant therapy may be administered if clinically indicated. Dialysis may be considered in cases of overwhelming overdosage.

Dosage: Cefuroxime may be administered i.v. after reconstitution. Dosage and route of administration should be determined by the severity of infection, susceptibility of the causative organisms and condition of the patient. The i.v. route is preferable for patients with severe or life-threatening infections.

The usual duration of treatment is 5 to 14 days. For β-hemolytic Streptococcal infections, therapy should be continued for at least 10 days.
Patients with Normal Renal Function: Adults: The usual adult dosage range is 750 mg every 8 hours.

In uncomplicated urinary tract infections and soft tissue infections a 750 mg dose every 8 hours is recommended. In life-threatening or complicated infections or gram negative infections of the lower respiratory tract, 1.5 g 3 times daily may be required.

For bone and joint disease, a dosage of 1.5 g i.v. every 8 hours (4.5 g/day) is recommended. Surgical intervention should be performed when indicated as an adjunct to cefuroxime therapy. Oral antibiotics should be administered when appropriate following the completion of parenteral administration of cefuroxime.

In bacterial meningitis the dose should not exceed 3 g every 8 hours.
Infants, Children: In bacterial meningitis, the usual dosage is 200 to 240 mg/kg/day i.v. in divided doses every 6 to 8 hours. Dosages may be reduced to 100 mg/kg/day after 3 days of clinical improvement (not to exceed the maximum adult dose)*.

The usual pediatric dosage for most other infections due to susceptible organisms is 30 to 100 mg/kg/day in 2 to 3 divided doses. For children >3 months, the dosage is usually 60 mg/kg/day.

For bone and joint infections, a dosage between 70 to 150 mg/kg/day administered i.v. every 8 hours is recommended, to be followed by a course of oral antibiotics.

Doses in excess of the maximum adult dose should not be used in infants and children.
Neonates (up to 1 Month): In the first few weeks of life, the serum half-life of cefuroxime can be 3 to 5 times that in adults. Infections in neonates should be treated with dosages in the range 30 to 100 mg/kg/day in 2 or 3 equally divided doses.

For bacterial meningitis, a dosage of 100 mg/kg/day i.v. in 2 or 3 equally divided doses should be employed*.
*Bacterial Meningitis in Children: Delayed sterilization of cerebrospinal fluid has been reported occasionally in children treated with cefuroxime for bacterial meningitis. Moderate to severe hearing impairment has occasionally occurred as a complication of meningitis in children treated with cefuroxime.
Note: As a general principle, antibiotic therapy should be continued for a minimum of 48 to 72 hours after the patient becomes asymptomatic or after evidence of bacterial eradication has been obtained; a minimum of 10 days of treatment

is recommended in infections caused by group A β-hemolytic streptococci in order to guard against the risk of rheumatic fever or glomerulonephritis; frequent bacteriologic and clinical appraisal is necessary during therapy of chronic urinary tract infections and may be required for several months after therapy has been completed; persistent infections may require longer treatment; doses smaller than those indicated above should not be used.

Prevention: Clean contaminated or potentially contaminated surgical procedures: The recommended dose is 1.5 g of cefuroxime administered i.v. just prior to surgery.

This may be supplemented with 750 mg at 8 and 16 hours when surgery is prolonged.

In general, prophylactic administration is usually not required after the end of surgical procedures, however, intraoperative administrations should be considered if the surgical procedure is lengthy.

In many surgical procedures, continuing prophylactic administration of any antibiotic does not appear to be associated with a reduced incidence of subsequent infection, but will increase the possibility of adverse reactions and the development of bacterial resistance.

Open Heart Surgery: The recommended dosage is 1.5 g of cefuroxime administered i.v. at the induction of anesthesia and every 12 hours thereafter for 48 hours.

Patients with Impaired Renal Function: When renal function is impaired, a reduced dosage must be employed. The dosage should be determined by the degree of renal impairment and the susceptibility of the causative organism (see Table I).

Table I—Kefurox

Dosage in Adults with Reduced Renal Function

Creatinine Clearance mL/min/1.73m²	Creatinine Clearance mL/s/1.73m²	Dose	Frequency
>20	>0.33	750 mg–1.5 g	Every 8 hours
10–20	0.17–0.33	750 mg	Every 12 hours
<10	<0.17	750 mg	Every 24 hours

For adults with severe infections who require doses higher than recommended in Table I, serum levels of cefuroxime should be monitored and dosage adjusted accordingly.

Insufficient information is available to recommend specific dosages for children with renal impairment. Consideration should be given to adjusting the frequency of administration consistent with the recommendations for renally impaired adults in Table I.

Since cefuroxime is dialyzable, patients on hemodialysis should be given a further dose at the end of the dialysis.

When only serum creatinine is available, the following formula (based on sex, weight and age of the patient) may be used to convert this value into creatinine clearance. The serum creatinine should represent a steady state of renal function.

Males:

$$\text{Creatinine Clearance (mL/min)} = \frac{\text{Weight (kg)} \times (140-\text{age})}{72 \times \text{serum creatinine (mg/dL)}}$$

Females: 0.85×above value.

Administration: Cefuroxime should be given i.v., especially for patients with bacterial septicemia or other severe or life-threatening infections or for patients who may be poor risks because of lowered resistance, particulary if shock is present or impending.

Direct I.V. (Bolus) Injection: Slowly inject the solution into a vein over a period of 3 to 5 minutes or give it through the tubing system by which the patient is also receiving other i.v. solutions.

I.V. Infusion: I.V. infusion should be given over a period of 30 minutes.

For Intermittent I.V. Infusion with a Y-Type Administration Set: Dosing can be accomplished through the tubing system by which the patient may be receiving other i.v. solutions. However, during infusion of the solution containing cefuroxime it is advisable to temporarily discontinue administration of any other solutions at the same site.

For Continuous I.V. Infusion: Cefuroxime may also be administered over a longer period of time.

Note: If therapy with cefuroxime is carried out in combination with an aminoglycoside antibiotic, either, each of these antibiotics should be administered at different sites, or cefuroxime and aminoglycosides may be administered sequentially by intermittent i.v. infusion. After the administration of 1 of the 2 drugs, the tubing is carefully and thoroughly flushed with an approved solution for reconstitution and then the other drug solution is administered. An aminoglycoside should not be mixed with cefuroxime in the same container.

Reconstitution: I.V.: Solutions for Reconstitution: Sterile Water for Injection: Reconstitute as shown in Table II.

Table II—Kefurox

Method of Reconstitution for I.V. Use

Vial Size	Diluent to be Added to Vial	Volume to be Withdrawn	Approximate Average Concentration
750 mg (vial 7271)	7.5 mL	Total (8 mL)	100 mg/mL
1.5 g (vial 7272)	14 mL	Total (15 mL)	100 mg/mL

The prepared solution may be further diluted to the desired volume with any of the solutions for i.v. infusion listed below. Vials intended for further dilution should be reconstituted immediately prior to dilution.

Pharmacy Bulk Vial: The availability of the Bulk Pharmacy Vial is restricted to hospitals with a recognized i.v. admixture program.

Cefuroxime does not contain any preservatives. The Pharmacy Bulk Vial is intended for multiple dispensing for i.v. use only, employing a single puncture.

Reconstitution: Pharmacy Bulk Vial: Solutions for Reconstitution: Sterile Water for Injection. Reconstitute as shown in Table III.

Table III—Kefurox

Method of Reconstitution for the Pharmacy Bulk Vial

Vial Size	Diluent to be Added to Vial	Volume to be Withdrawn	Approximate Average Concentration
7.5 g (Vial 7275)	77 mL	Total (81 mL)*	99 mg/mL

*8 mL of solution contains 750 mg of cefuroxime; 15 mL of solution contains 1.5 g of cefuroxime.

Use reconstituted stock solution within 8 hours, and further diluted solutions within 8 hours if kept at room temperature and 48 hours if refrigerated from time of initial puncture.

Solutions for I.V. Infusion: 0.9% Sodium Chloride Injection, 5% Dextrose Injection, 5% Dextrose and 0.9% NaCl Injection, 5% Dextrose and 0.45% NaCl Injection, 5% Dextrose and 0.225% NaCl Injection, Ringer's Injection USP, Lactated Ringer's Injection USP, 10% Dextrose Injection, M/6 Sodium Lactate Injection.

Stability and Storage: Dry Powder: The vials should be protected from light and stored at 15 to 25°C.

Solutions and Suspensions: When the 750 mg and 1.5 g vials are reconstituted as directed with Sterile Water for Injection, the solutions for i.v. administration maintain satisfactory potency for 8 hours at room temperature (25°C) or for 48 hours under refrigeration.

Diluted solutions at concentrations of between 1 mg/mL and 30 mg/mL may be stored for up to 12 hours at room temperature (25°C) or 48 hours under refrigeration.

Note: Parenteral drug products should be inspected visually for particulate matter and discoloration prior to administration whenever solution and container permit.

As with other cephalosporins, cefuroxime powder, solutions and suspensions tend to darken, without adversely affecting potency.

Supplied: Pharmacy Bulk Vials: Each vial contains: sterile cefuroxime sodium, USP, 7.5 g/100 mL (vial 7275).

Vials: Each vial contains: sterile cefuroxime sodium, USP 750 mg/10 mL (vial 7271) or 1.5 g/20 mL (vial 7272).

Reviewed 1998

KEFZOL® Ⓟ

Lilly

Cefazolin Sodium

Antibiotic

Pharmacology: In vitro tests demonstrate that the bactericidal action of the cephalosporins results from inhibition of cell wall synthesis. Cefazolin is active against the following organisms in vitro: S. aureus (penicillin-sensitive and penicillin-resistant). S. pyogenes and other strains of streptococci including S. pneumoniae (many strains of enterococci are resistant). E. coli; P. mirabilis; E. aerogenes; H. influenzae; Klebsiella sp.

Most strains of E. cloacae and indole positive Proteus (P. vulgaris, M. morganii, P. rettgeri) are resistant. Methicillin-resistant staphylococci, Serratia, Pseudomonas, Mima, and Herellea sp. are almost uniformly resistant to cefazolin.

Clinical pharmacology studies in patients hospitalized with infections indicate that cefazolin produces mean peak serum levels approximately equivalent to those seen in normal volunteers.

In a study (using normal volunteers) of constant i.v. infusion with dosages of 3.5 mg/kg for 1 hour (approximately 250 mg) and 1.5 mg/kg the next 2 hours (approximately 100 mg) cefazolin produced a steady serum level at the third hour of approximately 28 µg/mL. The average half-life after i.v. injection of a single 1 g dose was 1.4 hours.

In controlled studies on adult normal volunteers receiving 1 g four times a day for 10 days, CBC, AST, ALT, bilirubin, alkaline phosphatase, BUN, creatinine, and urinalysis showed no clinically significant changes attributable to cefazolin.

Cefazolin is excreted unchanged in the urine in the biologically active form. Sixty to 89% of a 500 mg i.m. dose is excreted in the first 6 hours. In several studies, as much as 86% of cefazolin was recovered in the urine within 24 hours. Following the i.m. administration of 1 g doses of cefazolin, peak urine concentrations of 4 040 to 4 560 µg/mL were attained.

Studies of cord blood show prompt transfer of cefazolin across the placenta. Cefazolin is present in very low concentrations in the milk of nursing mothers.

Cefazolin is removed from serum primarily by glomerular filtration at the rate of 64 mL/min/1.73 m².

Cefazolin is present in the bile in varying concentrations.

Indications: Cefazolin may be indicated in the treatment of the following infections caused by susceptible strains of the designated microorganisms.

Respiratory tract infections due to S. pneumoniae, Klebsiella species, H. influenzae, S. aureus (penicillinase-producing and non-producing), and S. pyogenes.

Cefazolin is effective in the eradication of streptococci from the nasopharynx; however, data establishing the efficacy of cefazolin in the subsequent prevention of rheumatic fever are not available at present.

Genitourinary tract infections due to E. coli, P. mirabilis and Klebsiella species.

Skin and soft-tissue infections due to S. aureus (penicillinase-producing and non-producing) and S. pyogenes and other strains of streptococci.

Bone and joint infections due to S. aureus.

Septicemia due to S. pneumoniae, S. aureus (pencillinase-producing and non-producing), P. mirabilis, E. coli, and Klebsiella species.

Endocarditis due to S. aureus (pencillinase-producing and non-producing) and S. pyogenes.

Contraindications: In persons who have shown hypersensitivity to cephalosporin antibiotics.

Warnings: Before cefazolin therapy is instituted, careful inquiry should be made concerning previous hypersensitivity reactions to cephalosporins and penicillin. Cephalosporin C derivatives should only be given cautiously in penicillin-sensitive patients. Serious acute hypersensitivity reactions may require pressor amines, antihistamines or corticosteroids and other emergency measures.

There is some evidence of partial cross-allergenicity of the penicillins and the cephalosporins. Patients have been reported to have had severe reactions (including fatal anaphylaxis) to both drugs.

Antibiotics, including cefazolin, should be administered cautiously and then only when absolutely necessary, to any patient who has demonstrated some form of allergy, particularly to drugs.

Pseudomembranous colitis has been reported with virtually all broad-spectrum antibiotics including cefazolin. Therefore, it is important to consider its diagnosis in patients who administered cefazolin who develop diarrhea. Such colitis may range in severity from mild to life-threatening.

Treatment with broad-spectrum antibiotics including cefazolin, may alter the normal flora of the colon and may permit overgrowth of Clostridia. Studies indicate that a toxin produced by C. difficile is one primary cause of antibiotic-associated colitis.

Mild cases of pseudomembranous colitis usually respond to drug discontinuance alone. In moderate to severe cases, management should include sigmoidoscopy, appropriate bacteriologic studies, and fluid, electrolyte, and protein supplementation. When the colitis does not improve after the

Kefzol (cont'd)

administration of cefazolin has been discontinued, or when it is severe, consideration should be given to the administration of oral vancomycin. Other causes of colitis should be ruled out.

Precautions: Prolonged use of cefazolin may result in the overgrowth of nonsusceptible organisms. Careful clinical observation of the patient is essential. If superinfection occurs during therapy, appropriate measures should be taken.

To avoid unnecessarily high serum concentrations of cefazolin in patients with impaired renal function, as evidenced by elevated BUN or creatinine or decreased creatinine clearance or urine/plasma creatinine ratio, these patients should be treated according to the dosage schedule given below (see Dosage).

The intrathecal administration of cefazolin is not an approved route of administration for this antibiotic; in fact, there have been reports of severe CNS toxicity including seizures when cefazolin was administered in this manner.

Pregnancy: Safety of this product for use during pregnancy has not been established.

Lactation: The concentrations of cefazolin in mother's milk was very low. Levels less than 0.9 µg/mL were found only in isolated milk samples after i.m. administration of 500 mg 3 times daily for 2 days. Caution should be exercised when cefazolin is administered to a nursing woman.

Children: Since safety for use in premature infants and in infants under 1 month of age has not been established, the use of cefazolin in these patients is not recommended.

A false-positive reaction for glucose in the urine may occur with Benedict's or Fehling's solution or with Clinitest tablets, but not with Tes-Tape (Glucose Enzymatic Test Strip, USP).

Positive direct and indirect antiglobulin (Coombs') tests have occurred; these may also occur in neonates whose mothers received cephalosporins before delivery.

Adverse Effects: The following reactions have been reported:

Hypersensitivity: drug fever, skin rash, vulvar pruritus, eosinophilia and anaphylaxis have occurred.

Blood: neutropenia, leukopenia, thrombocytopenia, and positive direct and indirect Coombs' tests have occurred.

Renal: Transient rise in BUN levels has been observed without clinical evidence of renal impairment. Interstitial nephritis and other renal disorders have been reported rarely. Most patients experiencing these reactions have been seriously ill and were receiving multiple drug therapies. The role of cefazolin in the development of nephropathies has not been determined.

Hepatic: Transient rise in AST, ALT and alkaline phosphatase levels has been observed rarely. As with some penicillins and some other cephalosporins, transient hepatitis and cholestatic jaundice have been reported rarely.

Gastrointestinal: Symptoms of pseudomembranous colitis may appear either during or after antibiotic therapy. Nausea, anorexia, vomiting, diarrhea, oral candidiasis (oral thrush) and cheilitis have been reported.

Other: Pain at injection site after i.m. administration has occurred, some with induration. Phlebitis at site of injection has been noted. Other reactions have included genital and anal pruritus, genital moniliasis and vaginitis.

Drug Interactions: Probenecid may decrease renal tubular secretion of cephalosporins when used concurrently, which results in increased and more prolonged cephalosporin blood levels.

Overdose: Symptoms: Toxic signs and symptoms following an overdose of cefazolin may include pain, inflammation, and phlebitis at the injection site. The administration of inappropriately large doses of parenteral cephalosporins may cause dizziness, paresthesias, and headaches. Seizures may occur following overdosage with some cephalosporins, particularly in patients with renal impairment in whom accumulation is likely to occur. Laboratory abnormalities that may occur after an overdose include elevations in creatinine, BUN, liver enzymes and bilirubin, a positive Coombs' test, thrombocytosis, thrombocytopenia, eosinophilia, leukopenia, and prolongation of the prothrombin time.

Treatment: In managing overdosage, consider the possibility of multiple drug overdoses, interaction among drugs, and unusual drug kinetics in your patient.

If seizures occur, the drug should be discontinued promptly; anticonvulsant therapy may be administered if clinically indicated. Protect the patient's airway and support ventilation and perfusion. Meticulously monitor and maintain, within acceptable limits, the patient's vital signs, blood gases, serum electrolytes, etc.

In cases of severe overdosage, especially in a patient with renal failure, combined hemodialysis and hemoperfusion may be considered if response to more conservative therapy fails. However, no data supporting such therapy are available.

Dosage: May be administered i.m. or i.v. after reconstitution.

The intrathecal administration of cefazolin is not an approved route of administration for this antibiotic; in fact, there have been reports of severe CNS toxicity including seizures when cefazolin was administered in this manner.

The usual dosages for adults are given in Table I.

Table I—Kefzol

Usual Adult Dosage

Type of infection	Dose	Frequency
Pneumococcal pneumonia	500 mg	q12h
Mild infections caused by susceptible gram-positive cocci	250 to 500 mg	q8h
Acute uncomplicated urinary tract infections	1 g	q12h
Moderate to severe infections	500 mg to 1 g	q6 to 8h

Cefazolin has been administered in dosages of 6 g/day in serious infections such as endocarditis.

In patients with renal impairment, cefazolin is not readily excreted; therefore, blood levels should be monitored. After a loading dose of 500 mg, the following recommendations (see Table II) for maintenance dosage may be used as an approximate guide.

Blood levels of cefazolin remain fairly high in spite of dialysis, hence, blood levels should be monitored routinely in these patients.

Children: In children, a total daily dosage of 25 to 50 mg/kg of body weight divided into 2 to 4 equal doses is effective for most mild to moderate severe infections. Total daily dosage may be increased to 100 mg/kg of body weight for severe infections. See Table III.

In children with mild to moderate impairment (creatinine clearance of 70 to 40 mL/min), 60% of the normal daily dose given in divided doses q12h should be sufficient. In patients with moderate impairment (creatinine clearance of 40 to 20 mL/min), 25% of the normal daily dose given in divided doses q12h should be sufficient. In children with severe impairment (creatinine clearance of 20 to 5 mL/min), 10% of the normal daily dose given q24h should be adequate. All dosage recommendations apply after an initial loading dose.

Duration of therapy in most infections should be 5 to 10 days. In the treatment of beta-hemolytic streptococcal infections, a minimum of 10 days therapy should be considered.

Administration: I.M.: Cefazolin should be injected well within the body of a large muscle mass such as the upper outer quadrant of the gluteus maximus or lateral part of the thigh.

I.V.: The i.v. route is preferable for patients with septicemia, peritonitis, or other severe or life-threatening infections.

Direct I.V. (bolus) Injection: The reconstituted solution should be injected slowly over a period of 3 to 5 minutes. Do not inject in less than 3 minutes.

Intermittent I.V. Infusion: The reconstituted solution may be administered through the tubing of an administration set while any of the i.v. solutions (see Solutions for I.V. Infusion) are being infused. During infusion of the solution containing cefazolin, it is desirable to discontinue administration of the other solution. Careful account should be made of the volume of the cefazolin solution being administered so that the calculated dose will be infused.

Continuous I.V. Infusion: The further diluted solutions of cefazolin should be administered over a longer period of time.

Reconstitution: **Shake well** and inspect visually for particulate matter prior to administration. If particulate matter is evident in reconstituted fluids, the drug solutions should be discarded.

I.M.: Solutions for Reconstitution: Sterile Water for Injection or Bacteriostatic Water for Injection. See Table IV.

Table IV—Kefzol

Reconstitution for I.M. Use

Vial Size	Volume to be Added	Approximate Available Volume	Approximate Average Concentration
500 mg	2.0 mL	2.2 mL	225 mg/mL
	3.8 mL	4.0 mL	125 mg/mL
1 g	2.5 mL	3.0 mL	334 mg/mL

Table II—Kefzol

Maintenance Dosage of Kefzol in Adults with Reduced Renal Function

Renal Function	BUN* (mg%)	Creatinine Clearance (mL/min)	Dosage: Mild to Moderate Infection	Dosage: Moderate to Severe Infection	Serum Half-Life (hours)
Mild Impairment	20–34	70–40	250 to 500 mg q12h	500 mg to 1.25 g q12h	3–5
Moderate Impairment	35–49	40–20	125 to 250 mg q12h	250 to 600 mg q12h	6–12
Severe Impairment	50–75	20–5	75 to 150 mg q24h	150 to 400 mg q24h	15–30
Essentially No function	≥75	≤5	37.5 to 75 mg q24h	75 to 200 mg q24h	30–40

* If used to estimate degree of renal impairment, BUN concentrations should reflect a steady state of renal azotemia.

Table III—Kefzol

Guide for Pediatric Dosage

25 mg/kg/day Dilution: 125 mg/mL

Weight	Single dose q.i.d. (q 6 hours)		Single dose t.i.d. (q 8 hours)		Single dose b.i.d. (q 12 hours)	
kg	mg	Volume (mL)	mg	Volume (mL)	mg	Volume (mL)
5	31	0.3	42	0.3	62	0.5
10	62	0.5	85	0.7	125	1.0
15	94	0.8	125	1.0	188	1.5
20	125	1.0	167	1.3	250	2.0
25	156	1.3	208	1.7	312	2.5

50 mg/kg/day Dilution: 225 mg/mL

Weight	Single dose q.i.d. (q 6 hours)		Single dose t.i.d. (q 8 hours)		Single dose b.i.d. (q 12 hours)	
kg	mg	Volume (mL)	mg	Volume (mL)	mg	Volume (mL)
5	62	0.3	85	0.4	125	0.6
10	125	0.5	167	0.7	250	1.1
15	185	0.8	250	1.0	375	1.7
20	250	1.0	333	1.5	500	2.2
25	310	1.4	416	1.9	625	2.8

Shake well until dissolved.
I.V.: Solutions for Reconstitution: Sterile Water for Injection, Sodium Chloride Injection or 5% Dextrose Injection. See Table V and Table VI.

Table V—Kefzol

Reconstitution for I.V. Use

Vial Size	Volume to be Added	Approximate Available Volume	Approximate Average Concentration
500 mg	10.0 mL	10.2 mL	49 mg/mL
1 g	10.0 mL	10.5 mL	95 mg/mL

Shake well until dissolved. The prepared solution may be further diluted to the desired volume with any of the solutions for i.v. infusion listed below.

Table VI—Kefzol

Reconstitution for Pharmacy Bulk Vial

Vial Size	Volume to be Added	Approximate Available Volume	Approximate Average Concentration
10 g	45.0 mL	50 mL	200 mg/mL
10 g	96.0 mL	100 mL	100 mg/mL

Solutions for I.V. Infusion: Sodium Chloride Injection, 5% or 10% Dextrose Injection, 5% Dextrose in Lactated Ringer's Injection, 5% Dextrose and 0.9% Sodium Chloride Injection (also may be used with 5% Dextrose and 0.45% or 0.2% Sodium Chloride Injection), Lactated Ringer's Injection, Invert Sugar 5% or 10% in Sterile Water for Injection, Ringer's Injection, 5% Sodium Bicarbonate in Sterile Water for Injection.
Extended Use of I.V. Admixtures: Although i.v. admixtures may often be physically and chemically stable for longer periods, **due to microbiological considerations, they are usually recommended for use within the maximum of 24 hours at 25°C or 72 hours at 2 to 8°C.**

Hospital and institutions that have recognized admixture programs and use validated aseptic techniques for preparation of i.v. solutions, may extend the storage times for Kefzol in admixtures with 5% Dextrose Injection or 0.9% Sodium Chloride Injection in Viaflex bags, in concentrations of 5 to 80 mg/mL, to 21 days when stored at 2 to 8°C.
Warning: As with all parenteral products, i.v. admixtures should be inspected visually for clarity, particulate matter, precipitate, discoloration and leakage prior to administration, whenever solution and container permit. Solutions showing haziness, particulate matter, precipitate, discoloration or leakage should not be used.
Stability and Storage: Vials: Vials should be stored at 25°C.
Solutions: Reconstituted Kefzol solutions should be used within 24 hours when stored at 25°C or within 96 hours when stored at 2 to 8°C. Reconstituted solutions may range in color from pale yellow to yellow without a change in potency.

Kefzol solutions reconstituted with bacteriostatic diluent and used for i.m. administration as multiple-dose containers should be used within 7 days when stored at 2 to 8°C.

The Pharmacy Bulk Vial is intended for multiple dispensing for i.v. use only, employing a single puncture. Following reconstitution, the solution should be dispensed and diluted for use within 8 hours. Any unused reconstituted solution should be discarded after 8 hours.

Supplied: Vials: 500 mg: Each vial contains: cefazolin sodium 500 mg (equivalent to cefazolin). Preservative-free. Vials of 10 mL.

1 g: Each vial contains: cefazolin sodium 1 g (equivalent to cefazolin). Preservative-free. Vials of 10 mL.

Pharmacy Bulk Vials: Each Pharmacy Bulk vial contains: cefazolin sodium 10 g (equivalent to cefazolin). Preservative-free. Pharmacy Bulk Vials of 100 mL. **The availability of the Pharmacy Bulk Vials is restricted to hospitals with a recognized I.V. Admixture Program.**

ADD-Vantage Vial: Each ADD-vantage vial contains: cefazolin sodium 1 g (equivalent to cefazolin). The ADD-Vantage vials are to be used with Abbott Laboratories' ADD-Vantage Antibiotic Diluent Container containing: 0.9% Sodium Chloride Injection, USP, 50 mL or 100 mL; or 5% Dextrose Injection, USP, 50 mL or 100 mL. The resulting solution should be used within 8 hours.

Readers are encouraged to photocopy the cardiac arrest algorithms found in the CLIN-INFO SECTION.

KEMADRIN® Ⓡ
Glaxo Wellcome

Procyclidine HCl
Antispasmodic Agent

Pharmacology: Procyclidine is a synthetic antispasmodic compound of relatively low toxicity. It has been shown to be useful for the symptomatic treatment of parkinsonism (paralysis agitans) and extrapyramidal dysfunction caused by antipsychotic agents.

Pharmacologic tests have shown that procyclidine has an atropine-like action and exerts an antispasmodic effect on smooth muscle. It is a potent mydriatic and inhibits salivation. It has no sympathetic ganglion-blocking activity in doses as high as 4 mg/kg, as measured by the lack of inhibition of the response of the nictitating membrane to preganglionic electrical stimulation.

Indications: The treatment of parkinsonism (paralysis agitans), including the postencephalitic, arteriosclerotic and idiopathic types. Partial control of the parkinsonism symptoms is the usual therapeutic accomplishment. Procyclidine is usually more efficacious in the relief of rigidity than tremor; but tremor, fatigue, weakness and sluggishness are frequently beneficially influenced. It can be used as a single agent in mild and moderate cases. For the control of more severe cases, other drugs may be added to procyclidine therapy as indications warrant.

Clinical results in the treatment of parkinsonism indicate that most patients experience subjective improvement characterized by a feeling of well-being and increased alertness, together with diminished salivation and a marked improvement in muscular coordination as demonstrated by objective tests of manual dexterity, and by increased ability to carry out ordinary self-care activities. While the drug exerts a mild atropine-like action and therefore causes mydriasis, this may be kept minimal by careful adjustment of the daily dosage.

Procyclidine also relieves symptoms of extrapyramidal dysfunction (dystonia, dyskinesia, akathisia and parkinsonism) induced by drug therapy of psychosis, such as may accompany the use of phenothiazine or Rauwolfia compounds. In addition to minimizing the extrapyramidal symptoms induced by antipsychotic drugs, the drug effectively controls sialorrhea resulting from neuroleptic medication. At the same time, freedom from the side effects induced by antipsychotic drugs, as provided by the administration of procyclidine, permits a more sustained treatment of the patient's mental disorder.

Contraindications: In patients with myasthenia gravis and should not be used in angle-closure glaucoma (although simple type glaucomas do not appear to be adversely affected.)

Warnings: Children: Safety and efficacy have not been established in the pediatric age group; therefore, the use of procyclidine in this age group requires that the potential benefits be weighed against the possible hazards to the child.
Pregnancy and *Lactation:* The safe use of this drug in pregnancy has not been established; therefore, the use of procyclidine in pregnancy, lactation, or in women of childbearing age requires that the potential benefits be weighed against the possible hazards to the mother and child.

Precautions: Conditions in which inhibition of the parasympathetic nervous system is undesirable, such as tachycardia and urinary retention (such as may occur with marked prostatic hypertrophy), require special care in the administration of the drug. Hypotensive patients who receive the drug should be observed closely.

Untoward CNS effects such as inability to concentrate, memory difficulties, restlessness, confusion and disorientation may occur, particularly in the elderly. If these symptoms are not recognized as being related to procyclidine administration, and dosage is not reduced or the drug discontinued, the patient may become agitated and confused, and develop hallucinations, psychotic symptoms or acute delirium. Toxic psychotic reactions may occasionally be produced by procyclidine when used to control drug-induced extrapyramidal symptoms. This may lead to confusion in diagnosis between the exacerbation of symptoms of the psychotic disease being treated and those of procyclidine toxicity.

Adverse Effects: Anticholinergic effects are most common, but can usually be minimized or eliminated by careful adjustment of dosage to a level just sufficient for adequate control of symptoms and by giving the drug during or after meals. These effects include dry mouth, blurred vision, slurred speech, mydriasis, gastrointestinal disturbances (such as nausea, vomiting, epigastric distress and constipation), dysuria, giddiness, lightheadedness, tachycardia, and muscle weakness. Acute suppurative parotitis as a complication of dry mouth has been reported.

CNS effects include impaired memory, inability to concentrate, confusion, restlessness, disorientation, agitation, hallucinations, and acute toxic psychosis (see Precautions). Occasional allergic reactions, such as skin rash, have been reported.

Overdose: Symptoms: drowsiness, giddiness, dry mouth, nausea, vomiting, mental confusion, excitement, convulsions.

Treatment: Gastric lavage and, if needed, symptomatic relief with paraldehyde and/or neostigmine.

Dosage: Parkinsonism: The dosage of the drug for the treatment of parkinsonism depends upon the age of the patient, the etiology of the disease, and individual responsiveness. Therefore, the dosage must remain flexible to permit adjustment to the individual tolerance and requirements of each patient. In general, younger and postencephalitic patients require and tolerate a somewhat higher dosage than older patients and those with arteriosclerosis.
Patients Who Have Received No Other Therapy: The usual dose of procyclidine for initial treatment is 2.5 mg administered 3 times daily after meals. If well tolerated, this dose may be gradually increased to 5 mg 3 times a day and occasionally 5 mg given at bedtime. In some cases, smaller doses may be employed with good therapeutic results.

Occasionally, a patient is encountered who cannot tolerate a bedtime dose of procyclidine. In such cases it may be desirable to adjust dosage so that the bedtime dose is omitted and the total daily requirement is administered in 3 equal daytime doses.

Procyclidine is best administered during or after meals to minimize the development of side reactions.
To Transfer Patients to Procyclidine from Other Therapy: To change to Kemadrin brand from other antiparkinsonian therapy, gradually substitute 2.5 mg 3 times daily for all or part of other drug; increase procyclidine dosage and decrease original drug until level of maximum benefit is reached with procyclidine alone.
Drug-Induced Extrapyramidal Symptoms: For treatment of symptoms of extrapyramidal dysfunction induced by antipsychotic drugs during the therapy of mental disorders, the dosage of procyclidine will depend on the severity of side effects associated with antipsychotic administration. In general, the larger the dosage of the antipsychotic agent the more severe the associated symptoms, including rigidity and tremors, will be. Accordingly, the procyclidine dosage should be adjusted to suit the needs of the individual patient and to provide maximum relief of the symptoms induced. A convenient method to establish the daily dosage of procyclidine is to begin with the administration of 2.5 mg 3 times daily after meals. This dosage may be increased by 2.5 mg daily until the patient obtains relief of symptoms. In most cases excellent results will be obtained with 10 to 20 mg daily.

Supplied: Tablets: Each white, round, biconvex, scored tablet, imprinted with KEMADRIN and S3A contains: procyclidine HCl 5 mg. Nonmedicinal ingredients: cornstarch, lactose and magnesium stearate. Bottles of 1 000. Store between 15 and 30°C. Keep in a dry place.

Elixir: Each 5 mL of clear, vanilla peppermint-flavored elixir contains: procyclidine HCl 2.5 mg. Nonmedicinal ingredients: alcohol, citric acid, glycerin, methylparaben, oil of orange, oil of peppermint, purified water, sodium benzoate, sorbitol solution 70% and vanillin. Bottles of 500 mL. Store between 15 and 30°C.

(Shown in Product Recognition Section)

Reviewed 1997

KEMSOL® Ⓡ
Carter Horner

Dimethylsulfoxide
Scleroderma Therapy

Pharmacology: The mode of action of dimethylsulfoxide (DMSO) as a treatment for scleroderma is unknown.

DMSO's dermal absorption in humans revealed DMSO serum concentrations after 5 minutes. The peak serum concentrations were reached from 4 to 6 hours.

DMSO is metabolized to dimethylsulfone in the liver. Levels of the metabolite were detected in serum and urine 2 hours following application, with maximal concentrations between 36 and 72 hours.

Kemsol (cont'd)

Indications: Topical treatment of the dermatological manifestations of scleroderma (general progressive sclerosis) and of localized scleroderma (morphea).

Contraindications: Patients with known eye disease, renal or liver dysfunction, history of allergy or skin sensitivity to DMSO.

Use of DMSO in children and infants is contraindicated unless the potential benefit outweighs the risks involved.

Pregnancy and *Lactation:* DMSO's safety in pregnant or lactating women has not been established and therefore is not recommended in their treatment.

Application of DMSO to mucous membranes is not advisable.

Precautions: Heavy DMSO dosage in the dog, rabbit, pig and monkey, particularly by the oral route, has resulted in abnormal eye changes, changes in lens refractive index and/or the appearance of concentric rings in the lens and lens opacities (rabbit only). No change in the human eye has been positively associated with the use of DMSO but regular periodic and full eye examinations including slit lamp examination must be given before and during treatment. DMSO should not be used under occlusive dressings, or as a vehicle for other drugs. DMSO applied to already infected skin may induce invasion by certain microorganisms. Repeated application of the drug may lessen its effectiveness in some individuals.

Occupational Hazards: As DMSO may cause mild sedation or drowsiness, warn the patient not to drive or operate machinery until these effects have disappeared.

At a minimum of 3 month intervals during DMSO treatment, in addition to the eye examinations, patients must be investigated with respect to biochemical parameters, particularly renal and liver functions.

Avoid contact of synthetic fabrics with skin wetted with DMSO.

Adverse Effects: Most patients experience a garlic like odor in the breath and a particular taste in the mouth 15 to 20 minutes after dermal application.

A mild erythematous localized dermatitis occurs in many patients; occasionally, a generalized dermatitis may occur. Sensations of warmth, burning, irritation and itching at the application site have been experienced. Headache, nausea, dizziness and sedation also have been reported.

No significant abnormalities have been determined in AST, ALT, total protein, albumin/globulin ratios, BUN, bilirubin, alkaline phosphatase and prothrombin time in patients treated with DMSO externally.

(i) Proteinuria was observed in a number of patients treated topically with DMSO and 1 of these subsequently died from renal failure,

(ii) noted during the same clinical studies were ketonuria, bilirubinemia and increased alkaline phosphatase, and

(iii) although the incidence of these developments was relatively low, their occurrence (especially proteinuria) to any significant degree, in any patients being treated with DMSO, should be cause for considering discontinuation of therapy.

Overdose: Symptoms: Excessive or allergic skin manifestations.

Treatment: Symptomatic.

Dosage: Adults, 2 mL (usually sufficient to treat 20 sq. cm. of skin) applied to lesions 3 times daily. Doses exceeding 30 mL/day are not recommended. Apply drug by means of a swab held by forceps to clean, dry skin, free of any other drug or chemical.

Supplied: Each bottle of clear, colorless solution contains: dimethylsulfoxide 70%. Nonmedicinal ingredients: purified water. Alcohol-, gluten- and tartrazine-free. Amber bottles of 250 mL.

KENACOMB® Preparations

Westwood-Squibb

Triamcinolone Acetonide—Neomycin—Nystatin—Gramicidin Compound

Dermatoses Therapy

Indications: Corticosteroid-responsive inflammatory or pruritic dermatoses caused, threatened or complicated by infection due to bacteria and/or candida. Pruritus ani and pruritus vulvae (cream only). The 0.025% formulations are for use on extensive lesions, or dermatoses which are chronic, mild, or highly susceptible to topical corticosteroid therapy, or for maintenance therapy of dermatoses previously controlled by a 0.1% formulation.

Contraindications: Tuberculous and most viral lesions of the skin, including herpes simplex, vaccinia and varicella. Fungal lesions of the skin, except candidiasis. Patients with a history of hypersensitivity to any of the components. Not for ophthalmic use; not to be applied to the external auditory canal of patients with perforated eardrums or patients with otitis media. Occlusive therapy contraindicated in patients with atopic dermatitis.

Precautions: Because of the potential hazard of nephrotoxicity and ototoxicity, avoid prolonged use or use of large amounts in the treatment of skin infections following burns, trophic ulceration and other conditions where absorption of neomycin is possible.

As with any antibiotic preparation, prolonged use may result in overgrowth of nonsusceptible organisms, including fungi other than Candida. Constant observation of the patient is essential. Should superinfection due to nonsusceptible organisms occur, Kenacomb should be discontinued and appropriate therapy instituted.

Although adrenal suppression and other systemic adverse effects are rare with topical corticosteroid preparations, their possible occurrence must be kept in mind, particularly when these preparations are used over large areas or for an extended period of time. Occasionally, a patient who has been on prolonged therapy may develop symptoms of steroid withdrawal when the medication is stopped.

The use of occlusive dressings is not recommended with products containing anti-infective agents.

If local irritation or sensitization develops, the preparation should be discontinued and appropriate therapy instituted.

Patients should be advised to inform subsequent physicians of the prior use of corticosteroids.

When applied to moist intertriginous areas, oleaginous ointments in general may be irritating and are not recommended.

Pregnancy and *Lactation:* The safety of topical steroid preparations during pregnancy and lactaction has not been absolutely established; therefore, the potential benefit of use should be weighed against possible hazard to the fetus or the nursing infant.

Articles in current medical literature indicate an increase in the incidence of patients allergic to neomycin. Neomycin itself may cause an allergic otitis externa. Systemic neomycin toxicity has occurred rarely following topical administration; tinnitis and deafness have been reported. The possibility of such a reaction should be borne in mind.

Topical steroids should be used with caution on lesions close to the eye.

Prolonged use of topical corticosteroid products may produce atrophy of the skin and subcutaneous tissues, particularly on flexor surfaces and on the face. If this is noted, discontinue use of the corticosteroid.

Topical corticosteroids should be used with caution in patients with stasis dermatitis and other skin diseases associated with impaired circulation.

If a symptomatic response is not noted within a week, discontinue the local application of corticosteroids and re-evaluate the patient.

Gramicidin absorption following topical administration is unlikely; however, hemolysis may occur should the drug enter the blood. If gramicidin is allowed to come in close proximity to the sub-arachnoid space, a chemical arachnoiditis may occur.

The possibility of hypersensitivity to ethylenediamine, a constituent of Kenacomb cream, should be borne in mind.

Adverse Effects: Hypersensitivity to nystatin is extremely uncommon. Sensitivity reactions following the topical use of gramicidin or triamcinolone acetonide are rarely encountered. Neomycin: see Precautions. Burning, itching, irritation, dryness, erythema, folliculitis, hypertrichosis, acneiform eruptions, tinnitus, deafness and hypopigmentation have been reported with topical corticosteroids.

When steroid preparations are used for long periods in intertriginous areas or under occlusive dressings, striae may occur. Damage to collagen, which constitutes a middle layer of the tympanic membrane, may occur. Delayed healing and systemic effects, including adrenal suppression and subcapsular cataracts, may occur if absorbed in appreciable amounts.

Dosage: Cream: Rub into affected areas 2 to 3 times daily.
Ointment: Apply a thin film to the affected areas 2 to 3 times daily.
Mild Cream and Ointment: 3 or 4 times daily.

Supplied: Cream: Each g contains: triamcinolone acetonide 1 mg, neomycin base (as sulfate) 2.5 mg, gramicidin 250 µg, nystatin 100 000 units. The cream is formulated in a perfumed aqueous vanishing cream base which permits its use even in moist intertriginous areas. Nonmedicinal ingredients: alcohol, aluminum hydroxide, ceteareth-20, cetearyl alcohol, ethylenediamine, fragrance, hydrochloric acid, methylparaben, petrolatum, polysorbate, propylene glycol, propylparaben, simethicone, sorbitol, titanium dioxide and water. Tubes of 15, 30 and 60 g.

Ointment: Each g contains: triamcinolone acetonide 1 mg, neomycin base (as sulfate) 2.5 mg, gramicidin 250 µg, nystatin 100 000 units. The ointment is formulated in protective Plastibase (Squibb plasticized hydrocarbon gel), a polyethylene and mineral oil gel base. Nonmedicinal ingredients: mineral oil and polyethylene. Tubes of 15, 30 and 60 g.

Mild Cream: Each g contains: triamcinolone acetonide 0.025%, neomycin base (as sulfate) 2.5 mg, gramicidin 250 µg, nystatin 100 000 units. The cream is formulated in a perfumed aqueous vanishing cream base which permits its use even in moist intertriginous areas. Nonmedicinal ingredients: alcohol, aluminum hydroxide, ceteareth-20, cetearyl alcohol, ethylenediamine, fragrance, hydrochloric acid, methylparaben, petrolatum, polysorbate, propylene glycol, propylparaben, simethicone, sorbitol, titanium dioxide and water. Tubes of 30 g.

Mild Ointment: Each g contains: triamcinolone acetonide 0.025%, neomycin base (as sulfate) 2.5 mg, gramicidin 250 µg, nystatin 100 000 units. The ointment is formulated in protective Plastibase (Squibb plasticized hydrocarbon gel), a polyethylene and mineral oil gel base. Nonmedicinal ingredients: mineral oil and polyethylene. Tubes of 30 g.

KENALOG®

Westwood-Squibb

Triamcinolone Acetonide

Topical Corticosteroid

Indications: The relief of inflammatory manifestations of corticosteroid responsive dermatoses, including atopic dermatitis, contact dermatitis, eczematous dermatitis, neurodermatitis, seborrheic dermatitis, insect bites, lichen simplex chronicus, exfoliative dermatitis, stasis dermatitis, nummular eczema, psoriasis and pruritus ani and vulvae (creams only).

Contraindications: Tuberculous, fungal and most viral diseases of the skin such as herpes simplex, vaccinia and varicella; hypersensitivity to any of the components of the preparations. Corticosteroid preparations are not intended for ophthalmic use, nor should they be applied in the external auditory canal of patients with perforated eardrums.

Precautions: *Pregnancy* and *Lactation:* Although topical steroids have not been reported to have an adverse effect on the fetus, the safety of topical steroid preparations during pregnancy and lactation has not been absolutely established. Weigh the potential benefits against possible hazard to the fetus or nursing infant.

If irritation develops, discontinue the product and institute appropriate therapy.

If a symptomatic response is not noted within a week, discontinue the local application of corticosteroids and re-evaluate the patient.

In the presence of an infection, use appropriate antifungal or antibacterial agents. If a favorable response does not occur promptly, discontinue the corticosteroid until the infection has been adequately controlled.

Use cautiously in patients with stasis dermatitis and other skin diseases associated with impaired circulation, and on lesions close to the eye.

When applied to moist intertriginous areas, oleaginous ointments in general may be irritating and are not recommended.

If extensive areas are treated or if the occlusive technique is used, the possibility exists of increased systemic absorption of the corticosteroid and suitable precautions should be taken. Occasionally, a patient who has been on prolonged therapy, especially occlusive therapy, may develop symptoms of steroid withdrawal when the medication is stopped. For patients with extensive lesions, it may be preferable to use a sequential approach, treating one portion of the body at a time.

Thermal homeostasis may be impaired if large areas of the body are covered; discontinue use of the occlusive dressing if elevation of the body temperature occurs.

If the occlusive dressing technique is employed, exercise caution with regard to the use of plastic films which are often flammable and also, may pose a suffocation hazard for children.

If superinfection develops during the use of occlusive dressings, discontinue the technique and institute appropriate antimicrobial therapy.

Prolonged use of topical corticosteroid products may produce atrophy of the skin and of subcutaneous tissues, particularly on flexor surfaces and on the face. If this is noted, discontinue the use of topical corticosteroids.

Patients should be advised to inform subsequent physicians of the prior use of corticosteroids.

Adverse Effects: The following local adverse reactions have been reported with topical corticosteroids, either with or without occlusive dressings: burning sensation, itching, irritation, dryness, folliculitis, secondary infection, skin atrophy, miliaria, hypertrichosis, acneiform eruptions, laceration of the skin and hypopigmentation, pustules, pyoderma, atrophy of subcutaneous tissue, telangiectasia, adrenal suppression and erythema. Contact sensitivity to a particular dressing material or adhesive may occur occasionally. When steroid preparations are used for long periods in intertriginous areas or under occlusive dressings, striae may occur.

Posterior subcapsular cataracts have been reported following systemic use of corticosteroids.

Overdose: Symptoms: Mild, reversible suppression of adrenal function, ecchymoses of the skin, peptic ulceration, hypertension, aggravation of infection, hirsutism, acne, edema and muscle weakness.

Treatment: Discontinue corticosteroid and treat symptomatically.

Dosage: Kenalog Cream: Rub into affected area 2 or 3 times daily.

Kenalog Ointment: Apply lightly to the affected area 2 or 3 times daily.

The ointments are preferable for dry, scaly lesions; the creams for moist, weeping lesions.

Occlusive Dressing Technique: Gently rub a small amount of Kenalog cream or ointment on the lesion until the cream or ointment disappears. Then reapply, leaving a thin coating and cover with a pliable non porous film. For convenience apply the cream or ointment intermittently (12 hour occlusion during the night) followed by reapplication without occlusion, during the day.

Frequency of changing dressings is best determined on an individual basis. Reapplication of the preparation is essential at each dressing change.

Supplied: Cream: Each g contains: triamcinolone acetonide USP 0.1% in an aqueous vanishing cream base. Nonmedicinal ingredients: ceteareth-20, cetearyl alcohol, petrolatum, propylene glycol, simethicone, sorbitol and water. Tubes of 30 g. Store at room temperature.

Ointment: Each g contains: 0.1% triamcinolone acetonide USP in Plastibase (Squibb plasticized hydrocarbon gel containing a polyethylene and mineral oil gel base). Nonmedicinal ingredients: mineral oil and polyethylene. Tubes of 30 g. Store at room temperature.

KENALOG® in ORABASE Ⓟ

Westwood-Squibb

Triamcinolone Dental Paste

Dental Corticosteroid

Pharmacology: Triamcinolone is a synthetic corticosteroid which possesses anti-inflammatory, antipruritic, and antiallergic action. The emollient dental paste acts as an adhesive vehicle for applying the active medication to the oral tissues. The vehicle provides a protective covering which may serve to temporarily reduce the pain associated with oral irritation.

Indications: Adjunctive treatment and temporary relief of symptoms associated with oral inflammatory lesions and ulcerative lesions resulting from trauma.

Contraindications: Fungal, viral or bacterial infections of the mouth or throat. Hypersensitivity to any of the components.

Precautions: *Pregnancy:* Safe use of this preparation during pregnancy has not been established with respect to possible adverse reactions upon fetal development; therefore, it should not be used in women of childbearing potential and particularly during early pregnancy unless the potential benefits outweigh the possible hazards.

Patients with tuberculosis, peptic ulcer or diabetes mellitus should not be treated with any corticosteroid preparation without the advice of the patient's physician. It should be borne in mind that the normal defensive reponses of the oral tissues are depressed in patients receiving topical corticosteroid therapy. Virulent strains of oral microorganisms may multiply without producing the usual symptoms of oral infections.

The small amount of steroid released when the preparation is used as recommended makes systemic effects very unlikely; however, they are a possibility when topical corticosteroid preparations are used over a long period of time.

If local irritation or sensitization should develop, discontinue the preparation and institute appropriate therapy.

Adverse Effects: Prolonged administration may elicit the adverse reactions known to occur with systemic steroid preparations; e.g., adrenal suppression, alteration of glucose metabolism, protein catabolism, peptic ulcer activation and others. These are usually reversible and disappear when the hormone is discontinued.

Dosage: Press a small dab (about 6 mm) to the lesion until a thin film develops. A larger quantity may be required for coverage of some lesions. For optimal results use only enough to coat the lesion with a thin film. Do not rub in. Attempting to spread this preparation may result in a granular, gritty sensation and cause it to crumble. After application, however, a smooth, slippery film develops.

Apply at bedtime to permit steroid contact with the lesion throughout the night. Depending on the severity of symptoms, it may be necessary to apply the preparation 2 or 3 times a day, preferably after meals. If significant regeneration or repair of oral tissues has not occurred in 7 days, additional investigation into the etiology of the oral lesion is advised.

Supplied: Each g contains: triamcinolone acetonide 1 mg (0.1%) in Orabase, protective emollient vehicle containing gelatin, pectin and sodium carboxymethylcellulose in Plastibase (plasticized hydrocarbon gel). Nonmedicinal ingredients: gelatin, mineral oil, pectin, polyethylene and sodium carboxymethylcellulose. Tubes of 7.5 g. Keep tightly closed.

KENALOG®-10 Injection Ⓟ

Westwood-Squibb

Triamcinolone Acetonide

Corticosteroid

Pharmacology: Naturally occurring glucocorticoids (e.g., hydrocortisone), which also have salt-retaining properties, are used as replacement therapy in adrenocortical deficiency states. Synthetic analogs such as triamcinolone are primarily used for their potent anti-inflammatory effects in disorders of many organ systems.

Glucocorticoids cause profound and varied metabolic effects. In addition, they modify the body's immune responses to diverse stimuli.

Indications: Intra-Articular: For intra-articular or intrabursal administration, and for injections into tendon sheaths, as adjunctive therapy for short-term administration in the following conditions: synovitis of osteoarthritis, rheumatoid arthritis, acute and subacute bursitis, acute gouty arthritis, epicondylitis, acute nonspecific tenosynovitis, and post-traumatic osteoarthritis.

Intradermal: Intralesional administration is indicated for the treatment of keloids, discoid lupus erythematosus, necrobiosis lipoidica diabeticorum, alopecia areata, and localized hypertrophic, infiltrated, inflammatory lesions of: lichen planus, psoriatic plaques, granuloma annulare, and lichen simplex chronicus (neurodermatitis).

Contraindications: Corticosteroids are generally contraindicated in patients with systemic infections. Kenalog-10 is also contraindicated in patients with a sensitivity to the medicinal or nonmedicinal ingredients.

The preparation should not be injected into infected areas.

Warnings: Because Kenalog-10 is a suspension, it should **not** be administered i.v..

Kenalog-10 is a long-acting preparation, and is **not** suitable for use in acute situations.

Prolonged use of corticosteroids may produce posterior subcapsular cataracts or glaucoma with possible damage to the optic nerve. Prolonged use may also enhance the likelihood of secondary ocular infections.

Average and large doses of hydrocortisone or cortisone can cause elevation of blood pressure, salt and water retention, and increased excretion of potassium. These effects are less likely to occur with the synthetic derivatives except when they are used in large doses; dietary salt restriction and potassium supplementation may be necessary (see Precautions). All corticosteroids increase calcium excretion, which may be associated with osteoporosis or aggravate preexisting osteoporosis.

Corticosteroids may mask some signs of infection, and new infections may appear during their use. There may be decreased resistance and inability to localize infection when corticosteroids are used. In addition, patients who are on immunosuppressant drugs including corticosteroids are more susceptible to infections than those not taking these drugs. Moreover, chickenpox and measles can have a more serious or even fatal course in patients on corticosteroids. In such children, or adults receiving corticosteroids who have not had these diseases, particular care should be taken to avoid exposure. If exposed, therapy with varicella zoster immune globulin (VZIG) or pooled i.v. immunoglobulin (IVIG), as appropriate, may be indicated. If chickenpox or herpes zoster develops, treatment with antiviral agents may be considered. Similarly, corticosteroids should be used with great caution in patients with Strongyloides (threadworm) infestation because corticosteroid-induced immunosuppression may lead to Strongyloides hyperinfection and dissemination with widespread larval migration, often accompanied by severe enterocolitis and potentially fatal Gram-negative septicemia.

Patients should not be vaccinated or immunized while on corticosteroid therapy, especially on high doses, because of a lack of antibody response predisposing to medical complications, particularly neurological ones.

The use of triamcinolone in patients with active tuberculosis should be restricted to those cases of fulminating or disseminated tuberculosis in which the corticosteroid is used for the management of the disease in conjunction with an appropriate antituberculous regimen. Chemoprophylaxis should be used in patients with latent tuberculosis or tuberculin reactivity who are taking corticosteroids.

Rare instances of anaphylactoid reactions have occurred in patients receiving parenteral corticosteroid therapy. Appropriate precautionary measures should be taken prior to administration, especially when the patient has a history of allergy to any drug.

Adequate studies to demonstrate the safety of Kenalog-10 use by intraturbinal, subconjunctival, sub-tenons, and retrobulbar injection have not been performed. Therefore, it is not recommended to administer Kenalog-10 by these routes.

Pregnancy and *Lactation:* Many corticosteroids have been shown to be teratogenic in laboratory animals at low doses. Since adequate human reproduction studies have not been performed with corticosteroids, the use of these drugs in pregnancy, nursing mothers, or women of childbearing potential requires that the possible benefits of the drug be weighed against the potential hazards to the mother and the embryo, fetus, or breast-fed infant. Other systemic corticosteroids have been shown to appear in breast milk and to slightly elevate (by 1%) the risk of cleft palate in human fetuses. Infants born to mothers who have received substantial doses of corticosteroids during pregnancy should be carefully observed for signs of adrenal suppression.

Children: Because corticosteroids can suppress growth, the development of infants and children on prolonged corticosteroid therapy should be carefully observed. Caution should be used in the event of exposure to chickenpox, measles or other communicable diseases. Children should not be vaccinated or immunized while on corticosteroid therapy (see Warnings). Corticosteroids may also affect endogenous steroid production.

Precautions: Drug induced adrenocortical insufficiency may occur with corticosteroids and persist for months after discontinuation of therapy; therefore, in any situation of stress such as trauma, surgery or severe illness occurring during that period, hormone therapy should be reinstituted. Since mineralocorticoid secretion may be impaired, salt and/or a mineralocorticoid should be administered concurrently.

There is an enhanced corticosteroid effect in patients with hypothyroidism and in those with cirrhosis.

Corticosteroids should be used cautiously in patients with ocular herpes simplex because of possible corneal perforation.

Psychiatric disturbances may appear when corticosteroids are used. These can include insomnia, depression (sometimes severe), euphoria, mood swings, psychotic symptoms and personality changes. Pre-existing emotional instability or psychosis may also be aggravated by corticosteroids. The use of antidepressant drugs does not relieve and may exacerbate adrenocorticoid-induced mental disturbances.

Corticosteroids should be used with caution in the following conditions: Nonspecific ulcerative colitis (if there is a probability of perforation, abscess, or other pyogenic infection); diverticulitis; recent intestinal anastomoses; active or latent peptic ulcer; renal insufficiency; acute glomerulonephritis; chronic nephritis; hypertension; congestive heart failure;

Kenalog-10 Injection (cont'd)

thrombophlebitis; thromboembolism; osteoporosis; exanthema; Cushing's syndrome; diabetes mellitus; convulsive disorders; metastatic carcinoma; myasthenia gravis.

Although therapy with Kenalog-10 may ameliorate symptoms of inflammation, it does not obviate the need to treat the cause.

Intra-articular injection of a corticosteroid may produce systemic as well as local effects. The inadvertent injection of the suspension into the soft tissues surrounding a joint may lead to the occurrence of systemic effects and is the most common cause of failure to achieve the desired local results.

Following intra-articular steroid therapy, patients should be specifically warned to avoid overuse of joints in which symptomatic benefit has been obtained. Otherwise an increase in joint deterioration can occur.

Overdistention of the joint capsule and deposition of steroid along the needle track should be avoided in intra-articular injection, since this may lead to s.c. atrophy.

Corticosteroids should not be injected into unstable joints. Repeated intra-articular injection may in some cases itself result in instability of the joint. In selected cases, particularly where repeated injections are given, x-ray follow-up is suggested.

An increase in joint discomfort has seldom occurred. A marked increase in pain accompanied by local swelling, further restriction of joint motion, fever, and malaise are suggestive of a septic arthritis. If these complications should appear, and the diagnosis of septic arthritis is confirmed, administration of triamcinolone should be stopped, and antimicrobial therapy should be instituted immediately and continued for 7 to 10 days after all evidence of infection has disappeared. Appropriate examination of any joint fluid present is necessary to exclude a septic process. Injection of a steroid into a previously infected joint should therefore be avoided. Repeated injection into inflamed tendons has been followed by tendon rupture. Therefore, it should also be avoided.

Like other potent corticosteroids, triamcinolone should be used under close clinical supervision. Triamcinolone can cause elevation of blood pressure, salt and water retention, and increased potassium and calcium excretion necessitating dietary salt restriction and potassium supplementation. Edema may occur in the presence of renal disease with a fixed or decreased glomerular filtration rate.

During prolonged therapy, **an adequate protein intake is essential** to counteract the tendency to gradual weight loss sometimes associated with negative nitrogen balance, wasting and weakness of skeletal muscles.

Menstrual irregularities may also occur with corticosteroid treatment.

In peptic ulcer, recurrence may be asymptomatic until perforation or hemorrhage occurs. Long-term adrenocortical therapy may itself produce hyperacidity or peptic ulcer. Therefore, antiulcer therapy is recommended.

Continued supervision of the patient after termination of triamcinolone therapy is essential, since there may be a sudden reappearance of severe manifestations of the disease for which the patient was treated.

Patients should be advised to inform subsequent physicians of the prior use of corticosteroids.

Geriatrics: The common adverse effects of systemic corticosteroids such as osteoporosis or hypertension may be associated with more serious consequences in old age. Close clinical supervision is recommended.

Occupational Hazards: The effects of corticosteroid therapy on the ability to drive or operate machinery have not been studied.

<u>*Drug Interactions*</u>: Amphotericin B injection and Potassium-Depleting Agents: Patients should be observed for hypokalemia.

Anticholinesterases: Effects of the anticholinesterase agent may be antagonized.

Anticoagulants, Oral: Corticosteroids may potentiate or decrease anticoagulant action. Patients receiving oral anticoagulants and corticosteroids should therefore be closely monitored.

Antidiabetics: Corticosteroids may increase blood glucose; diabetic control should be monitored, especially when corticosteroids are initiated, discontinued, or changed in dosage.

Antitubercular Drugs: Isoniazid serum concentrations may be decreased.

Cyclosporine: Monitor for evidence of increased toxicity of cyclosporine when the two are used concurrently.

Digitalis Glycosides: Coadministration may enhance the possibility of digitalis toxicity.

Estrogens, Including Oral Contraceptives: Corticosteroid half-life and concentration may be increased and clearance decreased.

Hepatic Enzyme Inducers (e.g., barbiturates, phenytoin, carbamazepine, rifampin): There may be increased metabolic clearance of Kenalog-10 injection. Patients should be carefully observed for possible diminished effect of steroid, and the dosage of Kenalog-10 injection should be adjusted accordingly.

Human Growth Hormone (e.g., somatrem): The growth-promotion effect of somatrem may be inhibited.

Ketoconazole: Corticosteroid clearance may be decreased, resulting in increased effects.

Nondepolarizing Muscle Relaxants: Corticosteroids may decrease or enhance the neuromuscular blocking action.

Nonsteroidal Anti-inflammatory Agents (NSAIDS): Corticosteroids may increase the incidence and/or severity of gastrointestinal bleeding and ulceration associated with NSAIDS. Also, corticosteroids can reduce serum salicylate levels and therefore decrease their effectiveness. Conversely, discontinuing corticosteroids during high-dose salicylate therapy may result in salicylate toxicity. ASA should be used cautiously in conjunction with corticosteroids in patients with hypoprothrombinemia.

Thyroid Drugs: Metabolic clearance of adrenocorticoids is decreased in hypothyroid patients and increased in hyperthyroid patients. Changes in thyroid status of the patient may necessitate adjustment in adrenocorticoid dosage.

Vaccines: Neurological complications and lack of antibody response may occur when patients taking corticosteroids are vaccinated (see Warnings).

Laboratory Test Interactions: Corticosteroids may affect the nitroblue tetrazolium test for bacterial infection, producing false-negative results.

Adverse Effects: Undesirable reactions following intra-articular administration of the preparation have included postinjection flare, transient pain, irritation at the injection site, sterile abscesses, hyper- or hypopigmentation, Charcot-like arthropathy, and occasional increase in joint discomfort; following intradermal administration, rare instances of blindness associated with intralesional therapy around the face and head, transient local discomfort, sterile abscesses, hyper- or hypopigmentation, cutaneous and s.c. atrophy (which usually disappears, unless the basic disease process is itself atrophic) have occurred.

Since systemic absorption may occasionally occur with intra-articular or other local administration, patients should be watched closely for the following adverse reactions which may be associated with any corticosteroid therapy:

General: anaphylactoid reactions; aggravation or masking of infections.

Cardiovascular: hypertension, syncope, congestive heart failure, arrhythmias, necrotizing angiitis, thromboembolism, thrombophlebitis.

Fluid and Electrolyte Disturbances: sodium retention, fluid retention associated with hypertension or congestive heart failure, potassium loss which may lead to cardiac arrhythmias or ECG changes, and hypokalemic alkalosis.

Musculoskeletal: muscle weakness, fatigue, steroid myopathy, loss of muscle mass, osteoporosis, vertebral compression fractures, delayed healing of fractures, aseptic necrosis of femoral and humeral heads, pathologic fractures of long bones, and spontaneous fractures.

Gastrointestinal: peptic ulcer with possible subsequent perforation and hemorrhage, pancreatitis, abdominal distention, ulcerative esophagitis.

Dermatologic: impaired wound healing, thin fragile skin, petechiae and ecchymoses, facial erythema, increased sweating, purpura, striae, hirsutism, acneiform eruptions, lupus erythematosus-like lesions, hives, rash, suppressed reactions to skin tests.

Neuropsychiatric: convulsions, increased intracranial pressure with papilledema (pseudotumor cerebri) usually after treatment, vertigo, headache, insomnia, neuritis, parasthesias, and aggravation of pre-existing psychiatric conditions, depression (sometimes severe), euphoria, mood swings, psychotic symptoms and personality changes.

Endocrine: menstrual irregularities; development of the cushingoid state; suppression of growth in children; secondary adrenocortical and pituitary unresponsiveness, particularly in times of stress (e.g., trauma, surgery, or illness); decreased carbohydrate tolerance; manifestations of latent diabetes mellitus; and increased requirements for insulin or oral hypoglycemic agents in diabetics.

Ophthalmic: posterior subcapsular cataracts, increased intraocular pressure, glaucoma, and exophthalmos, corneal perforation.

Metabolic: hyperglycemia, glycosuria, and negative nitrogen balance due to protein catabolism.

Overdose: Symptoms and Treatment: Chronic: The symptoms of glucocorticoid overdose may include confusion, anxiety, depression, gastrointestinal cramping or bleeding, ecchymosis, moon face and hypertension. After long-term use, rapid withdrawal can result in acute adrenal insufficiency (which also may occur in times of stress); Cushingoid changes can result from continued use of large doses.

Acute: There is no specific treatment for overdose, but supportive therapy should be instituted and, if gastrointestinal bleeding occurs, it should be treated as peptic ulcer.

Dosage: Intra-articular or intrabursal and tendon sheaths: The initial dose of Kenalog-10 for intra-articular or intrabursal administration and for injection into tendon sheaths may vary from 2.5 to 5 mg (0.25 to 0.5 mL) for smaller joints and from 5 to 15 mg (0.5 to 1.5 mL) for larger joints, depending on the specific disease entity being treated. Single injections into several joints, up to a total of 20 mg (2 mL) or more, have been given without incident.

Intradermal: The initial dose of triamcinolone will vary depending upon the specific disease entity being treated but should be limited to 1 mg (0.1 mL) per injection site, since larger volumes are more likely to produce cutaneous atrophy.

Multiple sites separated by 1 cm or more may be injected, keeping in mind that the greater the **total** volume employed the more corticosteroid becomes available for systemic absorption and systemic effects. Such injections may be repeated, if necessary, at weekly or less frequent intervals.

Localization of Dose: The lower dosages in the initial dosage range of triamcinolone may produce the desired effect when the corticosteroid is administered to provide a localized concentration. The site and volume of the injection should be carefully considered when triamcinolone is administered for this purpose.

General: The initial dosage should be maintained or adjusted until a satisfactory response is noted. If after a reasonable period of time there is a lack of satisfactory clinical response, Kenalog-10 should be gradually discontinued and the patient transferred to other appropriate therapy.

Dosage requirements are variable and must be individualized on the basis of the disease under treatment and the response of the patient. Dosage adjustments may be necessary in accordance with changes in clinical status.

Administration: **Strict aseptic technique is mandatory.** The vial should be shaken before use to ensure a uniform suspension. Prior to withdrawal, the suspension should be inspected for clumping or granular appearance (agglomeration). An agglomerated product results from exposure to freezing temperatures and should not be used. After withdrawal, inject without delay to prevent settling in the syringe. Careful technique should be employed to avoid the possibility of entering a blood vessel or introducing infection.

Injection Technique: For treatment of joints, the usual intra-articular injection techniques should be followed. If an excessive amount of synovial fluid is present in the joint, some, but not all, should be aspirated to aid in the relief of pain and to prevent undue dilution of the steroid.

With intra-articular or intrabursal administration, and with injection of Kenalog-10 into tendon sheaths or ganglia, prior use of a local anesthetic may often be desirable. Care should be taken with this kind of injection, particularly in the deltoid region, to avoid injecting the suspension into the tissues surrounding the site, since this may lead to tissue atrophy.

For treatment of ganglia, Kenalog-10 injection is injected directly into the cyst cavity.

In treating acute tenosynovitis, care should be taken to ensure that the injection of Kenalog-10 is made into the tendon sheath rather than the tendon substance. Epicondylitis may be treated by infiltrating the preparation into the area of greatest tenderness.

Intralesional: For treatment of dermal lesions, Kenalog-10 should be injected directly into the lesion, i.e., intradermally or s.c. For accuracy of dosage measurement and ease of administration, it is preferable to employ a tuberculin syringe and a small bore needle (23 to 25 gauge). Ethyl chloride spray may be used to alleviate the discomfort of the injection.

Safety in Handling: Due to the high potency of this drug and its potential for absorption through the skin, persons who handle Kenalog-10 should avoid skin and eye contact, as well as inhalation of airborne drug.

Supplied: Each mL of sterile, aqueous suspension contains: triamcinolone acetonide 10 mg. Nonmedicinal ingredients: benzyl alcohol, carboxymethylcellulose sodium, hydrochloric acid, polysorbate, sodium chloride, sodium hydroxide and water. pH between 5.0 and 7.5. At the time of manufacture, the air in the container is replaced by nitrogen. Vials of 5 mL.

Store at controlled room temperature (15 to 30°C), avoid freezing and protect from light.

Reviewed 1998

KENALOG®-40 Injection Ⓟ
Westwood-Squibb

Triamcinolone Acetonide
Corticosteroid

Pharmacology: Naturally occurring glucocorticoids (e.g., hydrocortisone), which also have salt-retaining properties, are used as replacement therapy in adrenocortical deficiency states. Synthetic analogs such as triamcinolone are primarily used for their potent anti-inflammatory effects in disorders of many organ systems.

Glucocorticoids cause profound and varied metabolic effects. In addition, they modify the body's immune responses to diverse stimuli.

Kenalog-40 has an extended duration of effect which may be permanent, or sustained over a period of several weeks. Studies indicate that following a single i.m. dose of 60 to 100 mg of triamcinolone acetonide, adrenal suppression occurs within 24 to 48 hours and then gradually returns to normal, usually in 30 to 40 days. This finding correlates closely with the extended duration of therapeutic action achieved with the drug.

Indications: I.M.: The i.m. administration is indicated for systemic corticosteroid therapy in such conditions as dermatoses, or generalized rheumatoid arthritis and other connective tissue disorders. It is also indicated for allergic diseases; however, for acute allergic reactions, epinephrine is the drug of choice, steroid therapy being adjunctive.

I.M. administration is particularly valuable in such conditions when oral corticosteroid therapy is not feasible. Triamcinolone is not an agent of choice in the treatment of adrenocortical insufficiency or the salt-losing form of the adrenogenital syndrome.

Intra-Articular: For intra-articular or intrabursal administration, and for injections into tendon sheaths, as adjunctive therapy for short-term administration in the following conditions: synovitis of osteoarthritis; rheumatoid arthritis; acute and subacute bursitis; acute gouty arthritis; epicondylitis; acute nonspecific tenosynovitis; and post-traumatic osteoarthritis.

Contraindications: Corticosteroids are contraindicated in patients with systemic infections. I.M. corticosteroid preparations are contraindicated for idiopathic thrombocytopenic purpura. Kenalog-40 is also contraindicated in patients with a sensitivity to the medicinal or non-medicinal ingredients.

Warnings: Because Kenalog-40 is a suspension, it should **not** be administered i.v.. The s.c. route of administration must not be used, due to the possibility of local atrophy.

Adequate studies to demonstrate the safety of Kenalog-40 use by intraturbinal, subconjunctival, sub-tenons, and retrobulbar injection have not been performed. Therefore, it is not recommended to administer Kenalog-40 by these routes. Several instances of blindness have been reported following injection of corticosteroid suspensions into the nasal turbinates and intralesional injection about the head. Therefore, these routes are not recommended.

Kenalog-40 is a long-acting preparation and is not suitable for use in acute situations. To avoid drug-induced adrenal insufficiency, supportive dosage may be required in times of stress (such as trauma, surgery or severe illness) both during treatment with Kenalog-40 and for a year afterwards.

Prolonged use of corticosteroids may produce posterior subcapsular cataracts or glaucoma, with possible damage to the optic nerve. Prolonged use may also enhance the likelihood of secondary ocular infections.

Average and large doses of hydrocortisone or cortisone can cause elevation of blood pressure, salt and water retention, and increased excretion of potassium. These effects are less likely to occur with the synthetic derivatives except when they are used in large doses; dietary salt restriction and potassium supplementation may be necessary (see Precautions). All corticosteroids increase calcium excretion, which may be associated with or aggravate preexisting osteoporosis.

Corticosteroids may mask some signs of infection, and new infections may appear during their use. There may be decreased resistance and inability to localize infection when corticosteroids are used. In addition, patients who are on immunosuppressant drugs including corticosteroids are more susceptible to infections than those not taking these drugs. Moreover, chickenpox and measles can have a more serious or even fatal course in patients on corticosteroids. In such children, or adults receiving corticosteroids who have not had these diseases, particular care should be taken to avoid exposure. If exposed, therapy with varicella zoster immune globulin (VZIG) or pooled i.v. immunoglobulin (IVIG), as appropriate, may be indicated. If chickenpox or herpes zoster develops, treatment with antiviral agents may be considered. Similarly, corticosteroids should be used with great caution in patients with Strongyloides (threadworm) infestation because corticosteroid-induced immunosuppression may lead to Strongyloides hyperinfection and dissemination with widespread larval migration, often accompanied by severe enterocolitis and potentially fatal Gram-negative septicemia.

Patients should not be vaccinated or immunized while on corticosteroid therapy, especially on high doses, because of a lack of antibody response predisposing to medical complications, particularly neurological ones.

The use of triamcinolone in patients with active tuberculosis should be restricted to those cases of fulminating or disseminated tuberculosis in which the corticosteroid is used for the management of the disease in conjunction with an appropriate antituberculous regimen. Chemoprophylaxis should be used in patients with latent tuberculosis or tuberculin reactivity who are taking corticosteroids.

Rare instances of anaphylactoid reactions have occurred in patients receiving parenteral corticosteroid therapy. Appropriate precautionary measures should be taken prior to administration, especially when the patient has a history of allergy to any drug.

Unless a **deep** i.m. injection is given, local atrophy is likely to occur. (For recommendations on injection techniques, see Dosage.) Due to the significantly higher incidence of local atrophy when the material is injected into the deltoid area, this injection site should be avoided in favor of the gluteal area.

Pregnancy and *Lactation:* Many corticosteroids have been shown to be teratogenic in laboratory animals at low doses. Since adequate human reproduction studies have not been performed with corticosteroids, the use of these drugs in pregnancy, nursing mothers, or women of child-bearing potential requires that the possible benefits of the drug be weighed against the potential hazards to the mother and the embryo, fetus, or breast-fed infant. Other systemic corticosteroids have been shown to appear in breast milk and to slightly elevate (by 1%) the risk of cleft palate in human fetuses. Infants born to mothers who have received substantial doses of corticosteroids during pregnancy should be carefully observed for signs of adrenal suppression.

Children: This preparation is not recommended for children under 6 years of age. Because corticosteroids can suppress growth, the development of children on prolonged corticosteroid therapy should be carefully observed. Caution should be used in the event of exposure to chickenpox, measles or other communicable diseases. Children should not be vaccinated or immunized while on corticosteroid therapy (see Warnings). Corticosteroids may also affect endogenous steroid production.

Precautions: Drug induced adrenocortical insufficiency may occur with corticosteroids and persist for months after discontinuation of therapy; therefore, in any situation of stress (such as trauma, surgery or severe illness) occurring during that period, hormone therapy should be reinstituted. Since mineralocorticoid secretion may be impaired, salt and/or a mineralocorticoid should be administered concurrently.

There is an enhanced corticosteroid effect in patients with hypothyroidism and in those with cirrhosis.

Corticosteroids should be used cautiously in patients with ocular herpes simplex because of possible corneal perforation.

Psychiatric disturbances may appear when corticosteroids are used. These can include insomnia, depression (sometimes severe), euphoria, mood swings, psychotic symptoms and personality changes. Pre-existing emotional instability or psychosis may also be aggravated by corticosteroids. The use of antidepressant drugs does not relieve and may exacerbate adrenocorticoid-induced mental disturbances.

Corticosteroids should be used with caution in the following conditions: nonspecific ulcerative colitis (if there is a probability of perforation, abscess, or other pyogenic infection); diverticulitis; recent intestinal anastomoses; active or latent peptic ulcer; renal insufficiency; acute glomerulonephritis; chronic nephritis; hypertension; congestive heart failure; thrombophlebitis; thromboembolism; osteoporosis; exanthema; Cushing's syndrome; diabetes mellitus; convulsive disorders; metastatic carcinoma; myasthenia gravis.

Although therapy with Kenalog-40 may ameliorate symptoms of inflammation, it does not obviate the need to treat the cause.

Intra-articular injection of a corticosteroid may produce systemic as well as local effects. The inadvertent injection of the suspension into the soft tissues surrounding a joint may also lead to the occurrence of systemic effects, and is the most common cause of failure to achieve the desired local results.

Following intra-articular steroid therapy, patients should be specifically warned to avoid overuse of joints in which symptomatic benefit has been obtained. Otherwise an increase in joint deterioration can occur.

Overdistention of the joint capsule and deposition of steroid along the needle track should be avoided in intra-articular injection, since this may lead to s.c. atrophy.

Corticosteroids should not be injected into unstable joints. Repeated intra-articular injection may in some cases itself result in instability of the joint. In selected cases, particularly where repeated injections are given, x-ray follow-up is suggested.

An increase in joint discomfort has seldom occurred. A marked increase is pain accompanied by local swelling, further restriction of joint motion, fever, and malaise are suggestive of a septic arthritis. If these complications should appear, and the diagnosis of septic arthritis is confirmed, administration of triamcinolone should be stopped, and antimicrobial therapy should be instituted immediately and continued for 7 to 10 days after all evidence of infection has disappeared. Appropriate examination of any joint fluid present is necessary to exclude a septic process. Injection of a steroid into a previously infected joint should therefore be avoided. Repeated injection into inflamed tendons has been followed by tendon rupture. Therefore, it should also be avoided.

Like other potent corticosteroids, triamcinolone should be used under close clinical supervision. Triamcinolone can cause elevation of blood pressure, salt and water retention, and increased potassium and calcium excretion necessitating dietary salt restriction and potassium supplementation. Edema may occur in the presence of renal disease with a fixed or decreased glomerular filtration rate.

During prolonged therapy, **an adequate protein intake is essential** to counteract the tendency to gradual weight loss sometimes associated with negative nitrogen balance, wasting and weakness of skeletal muscles.

Menstrual irregularities may also occur with corticosteroid treatment.

In peptic ulcer, recurrence may be asymptomatic until perforation or hemorrhage occurs. Long-term adrenocortical therapy may itself produce hyperacidity or peptic ulcer. Therefore, antiulcer therapy is recommended.

Continued supervision of the patient after termination of triamcinolone therapy is essential, since there may be a sudden reappearance of severe manifestations of the disease for which the patient was treated.

Patients should be advised to inform subsequent physicians of the prior use of corticosteroids.

Geriatrics: The common adverse effects of systemic corticosteroids such as osteoporosis or hypertension may be associated with more serious consequences in old age. Close clinical supervision is recommended.

Occupational Hazards: The effects of corticosteroid therapy on the ability to drive or operate machinery have not been studied.

<u>*Drug Interactions*</u>: Amphotericin B Injection and Potassium-Depleting Agents: Patients should be observed for hypokalemia.

Anticholinesterases: Effects of the anticholinesterase agent may be antagonized.

Anticoagulants, Oral: Corticosteroids may potentiate or decrease anticoagulant action. Patients receiving oral anticoagulants and corticosteroids should therefore be closely monitored.

Antidiabetics: Corticosteroids may increase blood glucose; diabetic control should be monitored, especially when corticosteroids are initiated, discontinued, or changed in dosage.

Antitubercular Drugs: Isoniazid serum concentrations may be decreased.

Cyclosporine: Increased activity of both cyclosporine and corticosteroids may occur when the two are used concurrently.

Digitalis Glycosides: Coadministration may enhance the possibility of digitalis toxicity.

Estrogens, Including Oral Contraceptives: Corticosteroid half-life and concentration may be increased and clearance decreased.

Hepatic Enzyme Inducers (e.g., barbiturates, phenytoin, carbamazepine, rifampin): There may be increased metabolic clearance of Kenalog-40 injection. Patients should be carefully observed for possible diminished effect of steroid, and the dosage of Kenalog-40 injection should be adjusted accordingly.

Human Growth Hormone (e.g., somatrem): The growth-promoting effect of somatrem may be inhibited.

Kenalog-40 Injection (cont'd)

Ketoconazole: Corticosteroid clearance may be decreased, resulting in increased effects.
Nondepolarizing Muscle Relaxants: Corticosteroids may decrease or enhance the neuromuscular blocking action.
Nonsteroidal Anti-inflammatory Agents (NSAIDS): Corticosteroids may increase the incidence and/or severity of gastrointestinal bleeding and ulceration associated with NSAIDS. Also, corticosteroids can reduce serum salicylate levels and therefore decrease their effectiveness. Conversely, discontinuing corticosteroids during high-dose salicylate therapy may result in salicylate toxicity. ASA should be used cautiously in conjunction with corticosteroids in patients with hypoprothrombinemia.
Thyroid Drugs: Metabolic clearance of adrenocorticoids is decreased in hypothyroid patients and increased in hyperthyroid patients. Changes in thyroid status of the patient may necessitate adjustment in adrenocorticoid dosage.
Vaccines: Neurological complications and lack of antibody response may occur when patients taking corticosteroids are vaccinated (see Warnings).
Laboratory Test Interactions: Corticosteroids may affect the nitroblue tetrazolium test for bacterial infection, producing false-negative results.

Adverse Effects: Following administration by any route: General: anaphylactoid reactions; aggravation or masking of infections.
Cardiovascular: hypertension, syncope, congestive heart failure, arrhythmias, necrotizing angiitis, thromboembolism, thrombophlebitis.
Fluid and Electrolyte Disturbances: sodium retention, fluid retention associated with hypertension or congestive heart failure, potassium loss which may lead to cardiac arrhythmias or ECG changes, hypokalemic alkalosis.
Musculoskeletal: muscle weakness, fatigue, myopathy, loss of muscle mass, osteoporosis, vertebral compression fractures, delayed healing of fractures, aseptic necrosis of femoral and humeral heads, pathologic fractures of long bones, spontaneous fractures.
Gastrointestinal: peptic ulcer with possible subsequent perforation and hemorrhage, pancreatitis, abdominal distention, ulcerative esophagitis.
Dermatologic: impaired wound healing, thin fragile skin, petechiae and ecchymoses, facial erythema, increased sweating, purpura, striae, hirsutism, acneiform eruptions, lupus erythematosus-like lesions, hives, rash, suppressed reactions to skin tests.
Neuropsychiatric: convulsions, increased intracranial pressure with papilledema (pseudotumor cerebri) usually after treatment, vertigo, headache, insomnia, neuritis, parasthesias, aggravation of pre-existing psychiatric conditions, depression (sometimes severe), euphoria, mood swings, psychotic symptoms and personality changes.
Endocrine: menstrual irregularities; development of the cushingoid state; suppression of growth in children; secondary adrenocortical and pituitary unresponsiveness, particularly in times of stress (e.g., trauma, surgery, or illness); decreased carbohydrate tolerance; manifestations of latent diabetes mellitus; and increased requirements for insulin or oral hypoglycemic agents in diabetics.
Ophthalmic: posterior subcapsular cataracts, increased intraocular pressure, glaucoma, and exophthalmos, corneal perforation.
Metabolic: hyperglycemia, glycosuria, and negative nitrogen balance due to protein catabolism.
Following I.M. Administration: Severe pain has been reported following i.m. administration. Sterile abscesses, cutaneous and s.c. atrophy, hyperpigmentation, hypopigmentaion and Charcot-like arthropathy have also occurred.
Intra-Articular Administration: Undesirable reactions have included postinjection flare, transient irritation at the injection site, sterile abscesses, hyper-or hypopigmentation, Charcot-like arthropathy and occasional increase in joint discomfort (see Precautions).

Overdose: Symptoms and Treatment: Chronic: The symptoms of glucocorticoid overdose may include confusion, anxiety, depression, gastrointestinal cramping or bleeding, ecchymosis, moon face and hypertension. After long-term use, rapid withdrawal can result in acute adrenal insufficiency (which also may occur in times of stress); Cushingoid changes can result from continued use of large doses.
Acute: There is no specific treatment for acute overdose, but supportive therapy should be instituted and, if gastrointestinal bleeding occurs, it should be managed.

Dosage: General: The initial dose of Kenalog-40 may vary from 2.5 to 60 mg/day depending on the specific disease entity being treated (see below). In less severe conditions, lower doses generally suffice, while in other patients, higher initial doses may be required. Usually the parenteral dosage range is one-third to one-half the oral dose, given every 12 hours. In life-threatening situations, administration of higher dosages may be justified.

The initial dosage should be maintained or adjusted until a satisfactory response is noted. If after a reasonable period of time there is a lack of satisfactory clinical response, Kenalog-40 should be gradually discontinued and the patient transferred to other appropriate therapy.

Dosage requirements are variable and must be individualized on the basis of the disease under treatment and the response of the patient. The lowest possible dose of corticosteroid should be used to control the condition being treated. After a favorable response is noted, the proper maintenance dosage should be determined by decreasing the initial drug dosage in small decrements at appropriate time intervals down to the lowest dosage which will maintain the desired clinical response. Constant monitoring of drug dosage is necessary. Dose adjustments may be necessary in accordance with changes in clinical status. Patient exposure to stressful situations not directly related to the disease may necessitate increasing the dosage. After long-term therapy, it is recommended that Kenalog-40 be withdrawn gradually.
Systemic: Adults and children over 12 years of age: The suggested initial dose is 60 mg (1.5 mL), **injected deeply into the gluteal muscle.** Atrophy of s.c. fat may occur if the injection is not properly given. Dosage is usually adjusted within the range of 40 to 80 mg, depending upon patient response and duration of relief. However, some patients may be well controlled on doses as low as 20 mg or less.
Hay Fever or Pollen Asthma: Patients with hay fever or pollen asthma who are not responding to pollen administration and other conventional therapy may obtain a remission of symptoms lasting throughout the pollen season after a single injection of 40 to 100 mg (1 to 2.5 mL).
Children 6 to 12 years: The suggested initial dose is 40 mg (1 mL), although dosage depends more on the severity of symptoms than on age or weight. There is insufficient clinical experience with Kenalog-40 to recommend its use in children under 6 years of age.
Local: Intra-articular or intrabursal administration and for injection into tendon sheaths: A single local injection of triamcinolone is frequently sufficient, but several injections may be needed for adequate relief of symptoms.
Initial Dose: 2.5 to 5 mg (0.063 to 0.125 mL) for smaller joints and from 5 to 15 mg (0.125 to 0.375 mL) for larger joints, depending on the specific disease entity being treated. For adults, doses up to 10 mg (0.25 mL) for smaller areas and up to 40 mg (1 mL) for larger areas have usually been sufficient. Single injections into several joints, up to a total of 80 mg (2 mL), have been given without undue reactions.
Administration: General: **Strict aseptic technique is mandatory.** The vial should be shaken before use to ensure a uniform suspension. Prior to withdrawal, the suspension should be inspected for clumping or granular appearance (agglomeration). An agglomerated product results from exposure to freezing temperatures and should not be used. After withdrawal, Kenalog-40 should be injected without delay to prevent settling in the syringe. Careful technique should be employed to avoid the possibility of entering a blood vessel or introducing infection.
Systemic: For systemic therapy, injection should be made **deeply into the gluteal muscle** (see Warnings). For adults, a minimum needle length of 4 cm is recommended. In obese patients, a longer needle may be required. Use alternative sites for subsequent injections.
Local: For treatment of joints, usual intra-articular injection techniques should be followed. If an excessive amount of synovial fluid is present in the joint, some, but not all, should be aspirated to aid in the relief of pain and to prevent undue dilution of the steroid.

With intra-articular or intrabursal administration, and with injection into tendon sheaths, prior use of a local anesthetic may often be desirable. Care should be taken with this kind of injection, particularly in the deltoid region, and with injection into tendon sheaths to avoid injecting the suspension into the tissues surrounding the site, since this may lead to tissue atrophy.

In treating acute nonspecific tenosynovitis, care should be taken to ensure that the injection of the corticosteroid is made into the tendon sheath rather than the tendon substance. Epicondylitis may be treated by infiltrating the preparation into the area of greatest tenderness.

Safety in Handling: Due to the high potency of this drug and its potential for absorption through the skin, persons who handle Kenalog-40 should avoid skin and eye contact, as well as inhalation of airborne drug.

Supplied: Each mL of sterile, aqueous suspension contains: triamcinolone acetonide 40 mg. Nonmedicinal ingredients: benzyl alcohol, carboxymethylcellulose sodium, hydrochloric acid, polysorbate, sodium chloride, sodium hydroxide and water. pH is between 5.0 and 7.5. At the time of manufacture, the air in the container is replaced by nitrogen. Vials of 1 and 5 mL. Store at controlled room temperature (15 to 30°C), avoid freezing and protect from light.

Reviewed 1998

KERALYT®
Westwood-Squibb

Salicylic Acid Gel

Keratolytic

Supplied: Each 55 g tube contains: salicylic acid 6% in a propylene glycol-ethanol gel with 20% alcohol. Nonmedicinal ingredients: hydroxypropylcellulose, propylene glycol, SD alcohol G 1-B and water.

KETALAR® Ⓟ
Parke-Davis

Ketamine HCl

Parenteral General Anesthetic

Pharmacology: Ketamine is a cataleptic, analgesic and anesthetic agent devoid of sedative or hypnotic properties, distinguishing it from the commonly used barbiturates.

It produces an anesthetic state characterized by profound analgesia, normal pharyngeal-laryngeal reflexes and normal or slightly enhanced skeletal muscle tone. Mild cardiac stimulation and occasionally respiratory depression occur.

The anesthetic state produced by ketamine has been termed dissociative anesthesia' in that it appears to selectively interrupt association pathways of the brain before producing somesthetic sensory blockade. It may selectively depress the thalamoneocortical system before significantly obtunding the more ancient cerebral centres and pathways (reticular activating and limbic systems).

Ketamine is rapidly absorbed following parenteral administration. Animal experiments indicated that ketamine was rapidly distributed into body tissues, with relatively high concentrations appearing in body fat, liver, lung and brain; lower concentrations were found in the heart, skeletal muscle and blood plasma. Placental transfer of the drug was found to occur in pregnant dogs and monkeys. No significant degree of binding to serum albumin was found with ketamine.

Studies in human subjects resulted in the mean recovery of 91% of the dose in the urine and 3% in the feces. Peak plasma levels averaged about 0.75 μg/mL and CSF levels were about 0.2 μg/mL, 1 hour after dosing.

Ketamine undergoes N-demethylation and hydroxylation of the cyclohexanone ring, with the formation of water-soluble conjugates which are excreted in the urine. Further oxidation also occurs with the formation of a cyclohexanone derivative. The unconjugated N-demethylated metabolite was found to be less than one sixth as potent as ketamine. The unconjugated demethyl cyclohexanone derivative was found to be less than one tenth as potent as ketamine. Repeated doses of ketamine administered to animals did not produce any detectable increase in microsomal enzyme activity.

Indications: As the sole anesthetic agent for recommended diagnostic and surgical procedures. Although best suited to short procedures, ketamine can be used, with additional doses, for longer procedures.
Note: If skeletal muscle relaxation is desired, a muscle relaxant should be used. In surgical procedures involving visceral pain pathways, ketamine should be supplemented with an agent which obtunds visceral pain.

For the induction of anesthesia prior to the administration of other general anesthetic agents.

To supplement low potency agents such as nitrous oxide.

Contraindications: History of cerebrovascular accident; cases where a significant elevation of blood pressure would constitute a serious hazard, such as in patients with severe hypertension; severe cardiac decompensation; in surgery of the pharynx, larynx, or bronchial tree unless adequate muscle relaxants are used; hypersensitivity to the drug.

Precautions: Ketamine is for use only by or under the direction of physicians and oral surgeons experienced in administering general anesthetics and in maintenance of an airway and in the control of respiration.

Cardiac function should be continually monitored during the procedure in patients found to have hypertension or cardiac decompensation.

Barbiturates and ketamine, being chemically incompatible because of precipitate formation, should not be injected from the same syringe.

Barbiturates and narcotics, being CNS depressants, may prolong recovery time if used concurrently with ketamine.

Respiratory depression may occur with overdosage or too rapid administration of ketamine, in which case supportive ventilation should be employed. Mechanical support of respiration is preferred to administration of analeptics.

An increase in cerebrospinal fluid pressure has been reported following the administration of ketamine. Therefore, special caution should be exercised when using ketamine in cases with preexisting elevated intracranial pressure, and in those cases with normal intracranial pressure in which, in the opinion of the physician, a rise in such pressure would entail special risks.

Pregnancy: Although animal studies of teratogenicity, fertility, and reproduction indicated the safety of ketamine, its safe use in human pregnancy has not been established.

Because pharyngeal reflexes are maintained, mechanical stimulation of the pharynx should be avoided unless adequate muscle relaxants are used. Precautions should be taken in patients with upper respiratory infection because of the increased danger of respiratory difficulties, such as laryngospasm, in these cases.

Resuscitative equipment should be available and ready for use.

The initial i.v. dose should be administered over a period of 60 seconds. More rapid administration may result in respiratory depression and enhanced pressor response.

During recovery from anesthesia the patient may go through a phase of emergence reaction characterized by vivid dreams, confusion (with or without psychomotor activity), excitement, irrational behavior and occasionally hallucinations. In 12 283 procedures, postanesthetic emergence responses were broken down into parameters and the incidence of reaction is shown in Table I.

Table I—Ketalar

Postanesthetic Emergence Responses

Reaction	Number	%	% in 15 to 35 yr. age group
Dreams, pleasant or not specified	679	5.44	9.6
Dreams, unpleasant	199	1.62	3.1
Hallucinations	152	1.23	1.6
Confusion, with and without vocalization	327	2.66	4.7
Excitement or irrational behavior	111	0.89	1.8
Psychic abnormalities	62	0.51	0.8
Overall rate*		11.00	19.4

* Some procedures have multiple emergence reactions, therefore the overall rate is less than the sum of the reactions.

Table I indicates that emergence reactions are more common in the 15 to 35 year group.

The reactions tabled above occurred in the majority of instances in patients in whom droperidol or diazepam had not been used as premedications.

Long-term follow up observations of 221 patients (140 with ketamine, 81 with other anesthetic agents) have not revealed any residual psychological effects.

The incidence of emergence reactions may be reduced if verbal, tactile and visual stimulation of the patient is avoided during the recovery period, certainly until the patient is fully conscious and able to be returned to the ward. These precautions do not preclude the monitoring of vital signs.

Hypnotic doses of ultrashort acting thiobarbiturates (50 to 100 mg i.v.) can be used to terminate severe emergence reactions. Diazepam, 5 mg i.v., has also been used to terminate emergence reactions.

During anesthesia the eyelids may remain retracted. During recovery they close. Premature stimulation during recovery in the presence of nystagmus and diplopia may precipitate retching, nausea, or frank vomiting.

Purposeless movements of extremities may occur during the course of anesthesia. These movements do not imply a light plane and are not indicative of the need for additional doses of the anesthetic.

Adverse Effects: Cardiovascular: Ketamine may cause a temporary augmentation of the pulse rate and blood pressure. Elevation of blood pressure begins shortly after injection, reaches a maximum within a few minutes and usually returns to preanesthetic values within 15 minutes after injection. The median peak rise has ranged from 20 to 25% of preanesthetic values. Depending on the condition of the patient, this elevation of blood pressure may be considered a beneficial effect, or in others, an adverse reaction. If elevation of blood pressure would be considered adverse to the patient, the benefit to risk ratio should be carefully determined. Maintaining or moderately increasing blood pressure may be beneficial to some patients, as those in shock or those in whom reduction in blood pressure is contraindicated (see Precautions).

Hypotension, arrhythmia, and bradycardia have rarely been observed.

Respiratory: Respiration is not greatly affected. Mild stimulation sometimes occurs, but respiratory depression, moderate and transient (less than 30 seconds), also occurs in a small percentage of patients. Laryngospasm and other forms of airway obstruction have occurred during ketamine anesthesia.

Psyche: During emergence from anesthesia the patient may go through a phase of vivid dreaming, with or without psychomotor activity, manifested by confusion and irrational behavior (see Precautions). These reactions are transient and have been observed less often in children than in adults. They appear to be similar to those observed following the use of other general anesthetic agents.

Tonic and clonic movements sometimes resembling convulsive seizures have occurred in a few patients receiving ketamine. These movements do not imply a light plane and are not indicative of the need for additional doses of the anesthetic.

EEG recordings were made in 14 patients receiving ketamine. Although 1 of these patients exhibited slight twitching of the arms and legs, none showed EEG changes to suggest seizure reactions.

Epileptiform attacks have been observed in a few patients following ketamine administration. However, ketamine has been used successfully in patients known to be suffering from epilepsy.

Gastrointestinal: Anorexia, nausea, or vomiting are minimal, allowing the great majority of patients to take liquids by mouth shortly after regaining consciousness.

Increased salivation may occur unless an antisialagogue is used.

Ophthalmic: Blurred vision and nystagmus are not uncommon findings during the recovery period.

Ketamine causes a small transient increase in intraocular pressure. However, it has been used in patients with glaucoma without causing any deterioration in this condition.

General: Except for rare reports of local pain and exanthema at the injection site, ketamine is well tolerated by the patient when administered either by the i.v. or i.m. route. Transient erythema and morbilliform rash have been reported.

Overdose: Symptoms and Treatment: Respiratory depression can result from an overdosage of ketamine. Supportive ventilation should be employed. Mechanical support of respiration that will maintain adequate blood oxygen saturation and carbon dioxide elimination is preferred to administration of analeptics.

Ketamine has a wide margin of safety; several instances of unintentional administration of overdoses of ketamine (up to 10 times of the usually required dose) have been followed by prolonged but complete recovery.

Dosage: Ketamine has been safely used alone when the stomach was not empty. However, since the need to use supplementary anesthetic or muscle relaxant agents cannot always be predicated, it is preferable not to give anything by mouth for at least 6 hours before elective surgery. Ketamine is recommended for use in patients whose stomach is not empty when in the judgment of the physician the benefits of the drug outweigh the possible hazards.

Atropine, scopolamine, or other antisecretory agents should be given at an appropriate interval prior to induction.

Certain drugs such as droperidol or diazepam have been used i.m. in an attempt to reduce the incidence of emergence reactions: sufficient data have not yet been accumulated to constitute thorough documentation. The incidence of emergence reactions is reduced as experience with the drug is gained.

As with other general anesthetic agents, the individual response to ketamine is somewhat varied depending on the dose, route of administration, and age of patient, so that dosage recommendation cannot be absolutely fixed. The drug should be titrated to the patient's requirements.

Because of rapid induction following the initial i.v. injection, the patient should be in a supported position during administration.

The onset of action of ketamine is rapid; an i.v. dose of 2 mg/kg (1 mg/lb) usually produces surgical anesthesia within 30 seconds after injections, with the anesthetic effect usually lasting 5 to 10 minutes. If a longer effect is desired, additional increments can be administered i.v. or i.m. to maintain anesthesia without producing significant cumulative effects.

I.M. doses, from experience primarily in children, in a range of 9 to 13 mg/kg (4 to 6 mg/lb) usually produce surgical anesthesia within 3 to 4 minutes following injection, with the anesthetic effect usually lasting 12 to 25 minutes.

Ketamine as sole anesthetic agent:

Induction: I.V.: The initial dose of ketamine administered i.v. may range from 1.0 to 4.5 mg/kg (0.5 to 2 mg/lb). The average amount required to produce 5 to 10 minutes of surgical anesthesia has been 2.0 mg/kg (1 mg/lb). Ketamine should be administered slowly (over a period of 60 seconds). More rapid administration may result in respiratory depression and enhanced pressor response.

I.M.: The initial dose of ketamine administered i.m. may range from 6.5 to 13.0 mg/kg (3 to 6 mg/lb). A dose of 10 mg/kg (5 mg/lb) will usually produce 12 to 25 minutes of surgical anesthesia.)

Maintenance: Increments of 50% to the full induction dose, either i.v. or i.m. may be repeated as needed for maintenance of anesthesia. Nystagmus, movements in response to stimulation, and vocalization may indicate lightening of anesthesia.

Ketamine used prior to administration of other general anesthetics: Ketamine is clinically compatible with the commonly used general and local anesthetic agents when an adequate respiratory exchange is maintained.

When ketamine is used as an induction agent, prior to the administration of other general anesthetic agents:

1. The full induction dose of ketamine should be given i.v. over 60 seconds.
2. At the completion of the induction dose of ketamine, the anesthetist should proceed immediately with the chosen general anesthetic procedure. A second dose of ketamine (half the original induction dose) may be required at 5 to 8 minutes following the initial induction dose when using an agent such as methoxyflurane where some considerable time is required for full surgical anesthesia to be established with the gaseous anesthetic. Otherwise lightening in the depth of anesthesia may occur and the patient may enter the stage of excitement, associated with vocalization and purposeful movements.

Recovery: Following the procedure the patient should be observed but left undisturbed. This does not preclude the monitoring of vital signs.

Supplied: 10 mg: Each mL contains: ketamine HCl equivalent to 10 mg ketamine base. Steri-Vials of 20 mL.

50 mg: Each mL contains: ketamine HCl equivalent to 50 mg ketamine base. Steri-Vials of 10 mL.

The solution for i.v. or i.m. use contains 1:10 000 benzethonium chloride as a preservative (pH 3.5 to 5.5). The 10 mg/mL solution has been made isotonic with sodium chloride (2.6 mg/5 mL).

KIDROLASE® Ⓟ

Rhône-Poulenc Rorer

L-asparaginase

Antileukemic Agent

Pharmacology: Asparaginase, which does not have any apparent effect on the principal body functions, exerts an antitumor activity which is directly related to its catalytic action upon the hydrolysis of the extracellular asparagine into aspartic acid and ammonia. This action is exerted on certain neoplastic cells which are unable to synthesize the asparagine needed for their own growth and which must rely upon the extracellular asparagine supply to assure their development.

At high dosages, asparaginase also shows a marked immunosuppressive effect which has been measured in various in vivo and in vitro tests. Both cell mediated and humoral immunities are affected by this inhibitory effect.

Asparaginase has been shown to exert an antiviral effect on 3 DNA viruses: vaccina virus, myxoma virus and herpes simplex. This effect seems to be associated with an action of the enzyme on a cellular reaction requiring asparagine and essential to the replication of the DNA molecule.

Kidrolase (cont'd)

Indications: Mainly indicated to induce remissions in acute lymphoblastic leukemia. Remissions have also been obtained in cases of acute myeloblastic and acute myelomonocytic leukemia although these conditions are less sensitive to the action of asparaginase. Favorable results have sometimes been obtained with the enzyme in certain cases of lymphosarcoma, reticulosarcoma, Hodgkin's disease, chronic lymphocytic leukemia and melanosarcoma.

Precautions: Asparaginase may be used for maintenance or reinduction treatment; however, if a relapse occurs during maintenance treatment, attempt reinduction with another agent.

Pregnancy: Animal studies have shown that asparaginase possesses embryotoxic and teratogenic activity; therefore, it should not be used in pregnant patients unless the benefits to the patient outweigh the possible risks to the fetus.

Asparaginase may induce allergic reactions. Since the intradermal test has proven unreliable in detecting patient sensitivity (i.e. reactions have been observed after a negative intradermal test and vice versa) and these reactions regress rapidly with i.v. corticosteroid therapy, corticosteroids should be administered for a day or two before initiating reinduction treatment. Furthermore, at the time of injection, the appropriate facilities, personnel and drugs required to treat anaphylactic shock should be readily available.

At the beginning of treatment, watch closely for uricemia and, if necessary, administer allopurinol for as long as required.

Hyperglycemia has been observed in a number of patients; therefore, during treatment, watch for glycemia especially in patients with uncontrolled diabetes.

Adverse Effects: Gastrointestinal: Nausea and vomiting which generally appear at the beginning of treatment may be directly attributable to the drug or may be secondary to BUN elevation and hyperuricemia. These adverse effects are rather frequent but rarely severe enough to necessitate withdrawal of treatment. Diarrhea and abdominal pain have been observed infrequently; the precise cause is unknown.

Rarely, intestinal perforation has occurred; a causal relationship with L-asparaginase therapy has not been established.

Allergic: Within ½ to 1 hour following injection, hypersensitivity reactions consisting of cutaneous manifestations, edema or, rarely, anaphylactic reactions have been observed. The latter have occurred after initial injection but are mainly observed between the fifth and the ninth administrations.

Although allergic reactions rarely occur when the enzyme is administered i.v. on a daily basis, the incidence is slightly more frequent following i.m. intermittent administration and the incidence becomes even greater with intermittent i.v. injection.

Hepatic: Hepatic function disturbances occur frequently and may, in some cases, warrant interruption of treatment. Hypocholesterolemia, hypoalbuminemia, increased alkaline phosphatase and AST levels are frequently observed. A mild ALT elevation and an increase in beta- and gammaglobulins as shown by protein electrophoresis have also been noted. While asparaginase induced hepatotoxicity is mainly mild and regressive, severe and fatal jaundice can occur in severely debilitated patients. Perform hepatic function tests at least once a week during therapy and stop therapy if significant changes in test values are noted. If reinduction is contemplated, ensure that hepatic function is normal.

Hematologic: A moderate hypofibrinemia which is sometimes associated with variable decreases of some factors of the prothrombin complex has been noted. Interruption of therapy rapidly corrects this effect. Check hemostatic function periodically during therapy. Bone marrow aplasia is exceptional and the hematological toxicity of the drug is not increased by concomitant usage with other antileukemic drugs; nevertheless, the usual blood and bone marrow determinations should be done.

CNS: Rarely, in adults, mild depression associated with personality disorders, disorientation, delusion, convulsions and pseudo-parkinsonism has been noted.

Miscellaneous: renal failure; septicemia during a period of bone marrow aplasia; fever due, either to the disease itself, or to the treatment; less frequently, weight loss, hyperglycemia, acute pancreatitis and respiratory distress with retrosternal pressure.

Dosage: Kidrolase is provided in sealed dry powder vials which are stable for up to 24 months at 5°C. Each vial of the powdered enzyme is reconstituted with 4 mL of sterile water for injection. Rotate gently, do not shake. The reconstituted solution can be kept in the refrigerator for 14 days.

Administer either i.m. or i.v. by infusion in an isotonic glucose solution or normal saline which does not contain a preservative.

Daily administration (usual method and less likely to cause adverse effects): Dosage varies from 200 to 1 000 IU/kg/day for 28 consecutive days. Thereafter, if complete remission is obtained, institute maintenance therapy; otherwise continue induction treatment for an additional 14 days.

Intermittent administration: Asparaginase may also be administered intermittently with 3 injections per week for 4 weeks by administration of 400 IU/kg on Monday and Wednesday and 600 IU/kg on Friday. After this period, institute maintenance therapy if complete remission is obtained; otherwise, continue the treatment for another 14 days.

Intermittent i.v. administration produces anaphylactic reactions 3 times more frequently than does i.m. injections. Consequently, the i.m. route is preferred for intermittent administration.

When asparaginase is used concomitantly with other antileukemic drugs, administer full doses as outlined above.

The choice of dose and method of administration should be made following an evaluation of the particular circumstances relevant to each case.

Supplied: Each lyophilized vial contains: 10 000 IU of L-asparaginase. Nonmedicinal ingredients: glycine and sodium hydroxide. Boxes of 1.

KLEAN-PREP®

Rivex Pharma

Polyethylene Glycol 3350—Electrolytes

Laxative

Pharmacology: Klean-Prep is a balanced electrolyte solution containing polyethylene glycol 3350, sodium sulfate, potassium chloride, sodium chloride and sodium bicarbonate. The solution prepared as recommended is iso-osmotic. It has been found that very little net absorption or secretion of electrolytes from the bowel occurs with this mixture. The sodium sulfate inhibits net sodium absorption, and the other electrolytes prevent net absorption or secretion of other ions, so that the patient can ingest large volumes of the solution to effect bowel cleansing without significant changes in water and electrolyte balance.

It is known that sodium is actively absorbed (against an electrochemical gradient) by the intestinal mucosa when the accompanying anion is chloride. However, sodium absorption is markedly reduced when sulfate is substituted for chloride. Total gut perfusion with this product is, thus, not associated with significant sodium and water absorption. The solution is useful in cleansing the colon of patients who are about to undergo gastrointestinal examinations (barium x-rays, colonoscopy, etc.) or surgical procedures requiring a clean colon. Fordtran and his colleagues have recommended that oral ingestion of 1.2 to 1.8 L/hour until 4 L have been consumed, would result in satisfactory cleansing of the colon. Orally administered Klean-Prep induces diarrhea which rapidly cleanses the bowel, usually within 3 to 4 hours.

Polyethylene glycol 3350 acts as an osmotic agent and the electrolyte concentration results in virtually no net absorption or secretion of ions. Large volumes may be administered without significant changes in water or electrolyte balance.

Indications: For cleansing of the bowel prior to colonoscopy, barium enema x-ray examination or surgical procedures requiring a clean colon.

Contraindications: In patients with gastrointestinal obstruction, gastric retention, bowel perforation, severe colitis or toxic megacolon.

Warnings: No additional ingredients, flavorings, etc. should be added to the solution before administration.

Precautions: Patients with impaired gag reflex or a stuporous or unconscious state or who are otherwise prone to regurgitation or aspiration, should be observed during the administration of Klean-Prep, especially if it is given via nasogastric tube. If gastrointestinal obstruction or perforation is suspected, appropriate studies should be performed to rule out these contraindications before administering Klean-Prep.

Pregnancy: Animal reproduction studies have not been conducted with Klean-Prep. It is also not known whether Klean-Prep can cause fetal harm when it is administered to a pregnant woman or whether it can affect reproductive capacity. Klean-Prep should be given to a pregnant woman only if clearly needed.

Children: Safety and effectiveness in children have not been established.

Long-term studies have not been done on animals to determine carcinogenic potential or effects on reproduction.

Adverse Effects: Klean-Prep administration is associated with a low incidence of side effects, primarily nausea, abdominal fullness and bloating and occasional cramps and vomiting. These side effects are transient and usually subside rapidly.

Dosage: The recommended dose for adults is 4 L of solution prior to gastrointestinal examination or procedures. The usual procedure is to have the patient drink 250 mL every 10 minutes until the 4 L is consumed or the rectal effluent is clear. Rapid drinking of each portion is preferred rather than drinking small amounts continuously. The first bowel movement should occur approximately 1 hour after the start of administration. Patient acceptance may be improved by chilling the solution before administration (but not serving with ice). If the patient is unable or unwilling to drink the solution, it may be administered via nasogastric tube.

Various regimens have been used. Ideally, the patient should fast approximately 3 to 4 hours prior to Klean-Prep ingestion, but in no case should solid foods be given for at least 2 hours before the solution is administered. One method is to schedule patients for examination at mid-morning, allowing the patient 3 hours for drinking and 1 hour waiting period to completed bowel evacuation. Another method is to administer Klean-Prep on the evening before the examination, particularly if the patient is to have a barium enema. No food except clear liquids are permitted after Klean-Prep administration and prior to examination.

Supplied: Each sachet of powder for oral administration as a solution following reconstitution contains: polyethylene glycol 3350, 59 g; sodium sulfate 5.68 g; sodium bicarbonate 1.68 g; sodium chloride 1.46 g and potassium chloride 0.74 g.

When made up to a 1 L volume with water, the solution contains: polyethylene glycol 3350, 17.6 mmol/L; sodium 125 mmol/L; sulfate 40 mmol/L; chloride 35 mmol/L; bicarbonate 20 mmol/L and potassium 10 mmol/L.

Four sachets of 1 L in a clear, graduated 1 L container for reconstitution. Makes 4 L of solution. Store in a dry place at room temperature. When reconstituted, keep solution refrigerated. Use reconstituted solution within 72 hours. Discard unused portion.

K-LOR®

Abbott

Potassium Chloride

Potassium Supplement

Supplied: Each packet of natural fruit flavored powder of potassium chloride for oral solution USP contains: potassium 20 mEq and chloride 20 mEq provided by potassium chloride 1.5 g. Nonmedicinal ingredients: calcium cyclamate, colloidal silicon dioxide, FD&C yellow #6, flavor (grapefruit and pineapple), malic acid, maltodextrin, potassium citrate and water for injection. Energy: <8.4 kJ (2 kcal)/packet. Alcohol-, gluten-, lactose-, paraben-, sodium-, sucrose-, sulfite- and tartrazine-free. Packets of 3 g, cartons of 30.

K-LYTE®
K-LYTE®/Cl

Roberts

Potassium Citrate
Potassium Chloride

Potassium Supplement

Indications: Oral potassium supplement for the therapy or prophylaxis of potassium deficiency. Especially useful for routine use with thiazide diuretics or corticosteroid hormones to replace excessive potassium losses.

Contraindications: In ventricular fibrillation, hyperkalemia of any etiology, in association with Addison's disease, salt losing adrenal hyperplasia, in extensive tissue breakdown as in severe burns, acute dehydration and heat cramps. Renal impairment with oliguria or azotemia. Increased sensitivity to potassium administration, e.g., in congenital paramyotonia or adynamia episodica hereditaria.

Warnings: In patients with impaired mechanisms for excreting potassium, e.g. chronic renal disease, administration of potassium salts can produce hyperkalemia and cardiac arrest. This occurs most commonly in patients given i.v. potassium but may also occur in patients given oral potassium. Potentially fatal hyperkalemia can develop rapidly and be asymptomatic. Careful monitoring of the serum potassium concentration and appropriate dosage adjustment is recommended.

Caution is advised with concomitant administration of potassium and potassium sparing diuretics e.g., spironolactone or triamterene, since hyperkalemia may develop. Hypokalemia in patients with metabolic acidosis should be treated with an alkalinizing potassium salt such as the acetate, bicarbonate, gluconate or citrate.

In patients on a low salt diet particularly, hypokalemic hypochloremic alkalosis is a possibility that may require chloride as well as potassium supplementation.

Precautions: The treatment of potassium depletion, particularly in the presence of cardiac disease, renal disease or acidosis, requires careful attention to acid base balance and appropriate monitoring of serum electrolytes, the ECG and the patient's clinical status.

Use potassium with caution in diseases associated with heart block since increased serum potassium may increase the degree of block.

Adverse Effects: Nausea, vomiting and diarrhea have been reported. These symptoms are due to irritation of the gastrointestinal tract and are best avoided by dissolving each dose completely in the stated amount of water, increasing fluid intake when possible, taking the dose with meals or reducing dose.

Overdose: Symptoms: In patients under normal conditions of exertion, concentrations of potassium in the blood of greater than 4 mmol (mEq)/L, and in the urine of greater than 2.0 g/24 hours, may indicate hyperkalemia.

Paresthesia of the extremities, listlessness, mental confusion, weakness, paralysis, hypotension, cardiac arrhythmias, heart block and cardiac arrest may occur. ECG changes include increased amplitude and peaking of the T waves, depression of the ST segment, reduction in the amplitude of the R wave, widening of the QRS complex, prolongation of the PR interval and a decrease in the amplitude and ultimately disappearance of the P wave. Widening of the QRS complex is one of the most ominous signs and indicates the need for aggressive treatment.

Frequently hyperkalemia is asymptomatic and may be manifested only by increased serum potassium concentration and characteristic electrocardiographic changes as above.

Treatment: 1. Eliminate foods and medications containing potassium, and discontinue potassium sparing diuretics. 2. I.V. administration of 300 to 500 mL/hour of 10% dextrose solution containing 10 to 20 units of crystalline insulin/1 000 mL. 3. Correct acidosis, if present, with i.v. sodium bicarbonate. 4. Use exchange resins, hemodialysis or peritoneal dialysis. 5. In the presence of life threatening cardiac arrhythmias, to antagonize the cardiac toxicity, administer i.v. 10 to 50 mL calcium gluconate 10% over 1 to 5 mins. Continuous ECG monitoring is mandatory.

In treating hyperkalemia in digitalized patients, too rapid a lowering of the serum potassium concentration can produce digitalis toxicity.

Dosage: In general a daily dose exceeding 60 mmol (mEq) should not be required.

Adults: Completely dissolve 1 K-Lyte tablet in 85 to 115 mL of cold or ice water, or 1 dose (7.8 g pouch) of K-Lyte/Cl powder in 180 mL of cold or ice water and administer 2 to 4 times daily, depending upon the patient's requirements.

Note: K-Lyte or K-Lyte/Cl should be taken with meals and sipped slowly over a 5 to 10 minute period.

The usual dietary intake of potassium is 40 to 80 mmol (mEq)/day. Potassium depletion sufficient to cause hypokalemia usually requires the loss of 200 or more mmol (mEq) of potassium from the total body store.

If given concomitantly in chronic diuretic therapy, administer on alternating days.

Prevention of hypokalemia: supplementally, approximately 20 to 40 mmol (mEq)/day.

Treatment of depletion: 40 to a maximum of 100 mmol (mEq) daily.

Supplied: K-Lyte: Each effervescent, orange or lime flavored and colored tablet, when dissolved in water, contains: potassium citrate 2.5 g or elemental potassium 25 mmol (mEq). Boxes of 30 individually foil wrapped tablets.

K-Lyte/Cl: Each dose of 7.8 g powder contains: potassium chloride 1.86 g [25 mmol (mEq) of potassium and 25 mmol (mEq) of chloride]. Fruit flavored powder available in boxes of 30 "unit dose" pouches (7.8 g each). Energy: 88.7 kJ (21.2 kcal)/7.8 g dose.

KOĀTE®-HP
Bayer
Antihemophilic Factor (Human)
Hemophilia A Therapy

Supplied: Each bottle of sterile, nonpyrogenic, stable, purified, dried concentrate contains: human antihemophilic factor (AHF, Factor VIII, AHG) which has been treated with tri-n-butylphosphate (TNBP) and polysorbate 80. Single use bottles of 250 IU (5 mL); 500 IU (5 mL); 1 000 IU (10 mL); 1 500 IU (10 mL). A sterile, double-ended transfer needle, sterile filter needle and sterile administration set are also provided.

Each bottle contains the labelled amount of antihemophilic factor activity, expressed in International Units (IU). One IU, as defined by the World Health Organization Standard for Blood Coagulation Factor VIII, human, is approximately equal to the level of AHF found in 1 mL of fresh pooled human plasma. The final product when reconstituted as directed contains not more than (NMT) 5 units heparin/mL, NMT 1 500 ppm polyethylene glycol (PEG), NMT 0.05 M glycine, NMT 25 ppm polysorbate 80, NMT 5 ppm tri-n-butyl phosphate (TNBP), NMT 3 mmol calcium chloride, NMT 1 ppm aluminum, NMT 0.06 M histidine, and NMT 10 mg/mL albumin (human).

Store under refrigeration 2 to 8°C. Storage of lyophilized powder at room temperature (up to 25°C) for 6 months, such as in home treatment situations, may be done without loss of factor VIII activity. Freezing should be avoided as breakage of the diluent bottle might occur.

KOFFEX® DM
Rougier
Dextromethorphan HBr
Antitussive

Supplied: Solution (sucrose-free): Each 5 mL of orange, melon-flavored solution contains: dextromethorphan HBr 15 mg. Energy: 29.8 kJ (7 kcal). Alcohol-, gluten-, parabens-, sucrose-, sulfite- and tartrazine-free. Bottles of 100, 250 and 2 000 mL.

Syrup: Each 5 mL of syrup contains: dextromethorphan HBr 15 mg. Energy: 51 kJ (12 kcal). Alcohol-, gluten-, parabens-, sulfite- and tartrazine-free. Bottles of 100, 250 and 2 000 mL.

KOGENATE®
Bayer
Antihemophilic Factor (Recombinant)
Antihemophilic—Coagulation Factor

Pharmacology: The clinical trial of antihemophilic factor (recombinant) has included 168 patients, enrolled over a 55 month period. A total of 16 186 infusions have been utilized in this trial. The study was conducted in several stages.

Pharmacokinetics: Initial pharmacokinetic studies were conducted in 17 asymptomatic hemophilic patients, comparing pharmacokinetics of plasma-derived antihemophilic factor (human) (pdAHF) and Kogenate. The mean biologic half-life of rAHF was 15.8 hours. The mean biologic half-life of pdAHF in the same individuals was 13.9 hours. A similar degree of shortening of the activated partial thromboplastin time was seen with both rAHF and pdAHF. The mean in vivo recovery of rAHF was similar to pdAHF, with a linear dose-response relationship. The recovery and half-life of rAHF was consistent with initial results following 13 weeks of exclusive treatment with Kogenate. Subsequently, 826 recovery studies were conducted in 58 hemophilic patients participating in later clinical studies. Mean recovery from this group was 2.48% per IU/kg infused.

Fourteen subjects from initial pharmacokinetic studies commenced home treatment with rAHF. Forty-four additional subjects were then enrolled who treated themselves at home exclusively with rAHF. A total of 12 730 infusions have been administered under this portion of the study, of which 1 021 were given in clinic for recovery studies, 7 339 were given for treatment of bleeds, 4 361 were given as prophylaxis, 5 for minor surgery not requiring hospitalization and 4 for unspecified reason.

Forty-eight patients have received rAHF on 63 occasions for surgical procedures or in-hospital treatment of serious hemorrhage. Eleven received rAHF for the first time in this study, while 37 were already on study or study participants under an investigation of previously untreated patients. Hemostasis has been satisfactory in all cases, with no adverse reactions.

In a study of previously untreated patients, a total of 3 254 infusions have been administered to 96 patients over a 48 month enrollment period. Hemostasis was successfully achieved in all cases.

During the analytical characterization of Kogenate, analyses for carbohydrate structure revealed the presence of terminal galactose $\alpha 1 \rightarrow 3$ galactose residues. Since naturally occurring antibody to this structure has been reported in humans, a trial in 18 patients was performed in which the half-life and recovery of rAHF with high levels of this carbohydrate residue was compared to that with Kogenate, which contains low levels of this structure. As in the normal population, all patients had pre-existing endogenous antibody to galactose $\alpha 1 \rightarrow 3$ galactose in titers ranging from 1:320 to 1:5 120 and no significant change in antibody level was noted during the study. While the mean recovery for Kogenate in the study, 2.76%/IU/kg (N=43), was significantly different from that of rAHF with high levels of residues, 2.43%/IU/kg (N=155; p=0.0001), the recovery for rAHF with high levels of galactose $\alpha 1 \rightarrow 3$ galactose is not significantly different from the 2.48%/IU/kg recovery obtained in the larger study from the 58 patients treated with Kogenate mentioned above. Based on these results, the galactose $\alpha 1 \rightarrow 3$ galactose residue appears to have no clinical significance.

Indications: For the treatment of classical hemophilia (hemophilia A) in which there is a demonstrated deficiency of activity of the plasma clotting factor, factor VIII. Antihemophilic factor (recombinant) provides a means of temporarily replacing the missing clotting factor in order to correct or prevent bleeding episodes, or in order to perform emergency and elective surgery in hemophiliacs.

Antihemophilic factor (recombinant) can also be used for treatment of hemophilia A in certain patients with inhibitors to factor VIII. In clinical studies of antihemophilic factor (recombinant), patients who developed inhibitors on study continued to manifest a clinical response when inhibitor titers were less than 10 Bethesda Units (B.U.) per mL. When an inhibitor is present, the dosage requirement for factor VIII is variable. The dosage can be determined only by clinical response, and by monitoring of circulating factor VIII levels after treatment (see Dosage).

Antihemophilic factor (recombinant) does not contain von Willebrand's factor and therefore is not indicated for the treatment of von Willebrand's diseases.

Contraindications: Due to the fact that antihemophilic factor (recombinant) contains trace amounts of mouse protein (maximum 0.03 ng/IU rAHF) and hamster protein (maximum 0.04 ng/IU rAHF), it should be administered with caution to individuals with previous hypersensitivity to pdAHF or known hypersensitivity to biologic preparations with trace amounts of murine or hamster proteins.

Assays to detect seroconversion to mouse and hamster protein were conducted on all patients on study. No patient has developed specific antibody titers against these proteins after commencing study, and no allergic reactions have been associated with rAHF infusions. Although no reactions were observed, patients should be warned of the theoretical possibility of a hypersensitivity reaction, and alerted to the early signs of such a reaction (e.g., hives, generalized urticaria, wheezing and hypotension). Patients should be advised to discontinue use of the product and contact their physician if such symptoms occur.

Warnings: None.

Precautions: General: Antihemophilic factor (recombinant) is intended for the treatment of bleeding disorders arising from a deficiency in factor VIII. This deficiency should be proven prior to administering antihemophilic factor (recombinant).

The development of circulating neutralizing antibodies to factor VIII may occur during the treatment of patients with hemophilia A. In a study of previously untreated patients, inhibitor antibodies have developed in 17 of 92 patients (18.5%) who have had at least one follow-up titer. The incidence of antibodies is 15/56 (26.7%) in patients with severe disease (<2% factor VIII), 2/18 (11%) in patients with moderate disease (2 to 5% factor VIII) and 0/18 in patients with mild disease (>5% factor VIII). Ten of the antibodies were high titer (>10 Bethesda Units), 3 were low titer, and 4 were low titer and transient. Studies most closely resembling the design of the study of inhibitor development with antihemophilic factor (recombinant) have reported incidences of inhibitor formation ranging between 18.4 and 52% for patients treated with pdAHF. The incidence of inhibitor formation in previously untreated patients treated with antihemophilic factor (recombinant) appears to be consistent with that

Kogenate (cont'd)

reported in the literature; however, the true immunogenicity of antihemophilic factor (recombinant) is not known at present. Patients treated with rAHF should be carefully monitored for the development of antibodies to rAHF by appropriate clinical observation and laboratory tests.

Product administration and handling of the infusion set and needles must be done with caution. Percutaneous puncture with a needle contaminated with blood can transmit infectious viruses including HIV (AIDS) and hepatitis. Obtain immediate medical attention if injury occurs.

Place needles in sharps container after single use. Discard all equipment including any reconstituted Kogenate product in accordance with biohazard procedures.

Carcinogenesis, Mutagenesis, Impairment of Fertility: In vitro evaluation of the mutagenic potential of antihemophilic factor (recombinant) failed to demonstrate reverse mutation of chromosomal aberrations at doses substantially greater than the maximum expected clinical dose. In vivo evaluation of rAHF using doses ranging between 10 and 40 times the expected clinical maximum also indicated that antihemophilic factor (recombinant) does not possess a mutagenic potential. Long-term investigations of carcinogenic potential in animals have not been performed.

Children: Antihemophilic factor (recombinant) has been proven to be safe and efficacious in newborns and children while under investigation as previously treated (n=21) and previously untreated patients (n=96) (see Pharmacology).

Pregnancy: Category C: Animal reproduction studies have not been conducted with antihemophilic factor (recombinant). It is also not known whether antihemophilic factor (recombinant) can cause fetal harm when administered to a pregnant woman or can affect reproduction capacity. It should be given to a pregnant woman only if clearly needed.

Adverse Effects: During the clinical studies conducted in previously treated patients, 47 out of 12 932 infusions (0.36%) were associated with 58 reported minor adverse reactions. Of these, 19 reactions were local to the injection site (e.g., burning, pruritus, erythema); and 39 were systemic complaints (dizziness, nausea, chest discomfort, sore throat, cold feet, unusual taste in mouth, and slight decrease in blood pressure). In the study with previously untreated patients, 3 254 infusions have been associated with 11 minor adverse reactions (0.34%); 2 reports of erythema at the injection site; 1 of facial flushing related to the infusion; 1 report of diarrhea; 2 reports of nonspecific rash; 2 reports of fever; and 3 reports of emesis. No serious reactions have been reported, and all reactions have been self-limited.

Dosage: Each bottle of antihemophilic factor (recombinant) has the rAHF content in international units per bottle stated on the label of the bottle. The reconstituted product must be administered i.v. by either direct syringe injection or drip infusion. The product must be administered within 3 hours after reconstitution.

General Approach to Treatment and Assessment of Treatment Efficacy: The dosages described below are presented as general guidance. It should be emphasized that the dosage required for hemostasis must be individualized according to the needs of the patient, the severity of the deficiency, the severity of the hemorrhage, the presence of inhibitors, and the factor VIII level desired. It is often critical to follow the course of therapy with factor VIII level assays.

The clinical effect of antihemophilic factor (recombinant) is the most important element in evaluating the effectiveness of treatment. It may be necessary to administer more antihemophilic factor (recombinant) than would be estimated in order to attain satisfactory clinical results. If the calculated dose fails to attain the expected factor VIII levels, or if bleeding is not controlled after administration of the calculated dosage, the presence of a circulating inhibitor in the patient should be suspected. Its presence should be sustantiated and the inhibitor level quantitated by appropriate laboratory tests. When an inhibitor is present, the dosage requirement for rAHF is extremely variable and the dosage can be determined only by the clinical response.

Some patients with low titer inhibitors (<10 B.U.) can be successfully treated with factor VIII without a resultant anamnestic rise in inhibitor titer. Factor VIII levels and clinical response to treatment must be assessed to insure adequate response. Use of alternative treatment products, such as Factor IX Complex concentrates, Antihemophilic Factor (Porcine) or Anti-inhibitor Coagulant Complex, may be necessary for patients with anamnestic responses to factor VIII treatment and/or high titer inhibitors.

Calculation of Dosage: The in vivo percent elevation in factor VIII level can be estimated by multiplying the dose of rAHF per kilogram of body weight (IU/kg) by 2%. This method of calculation is based on clinical findings by Abildgaard et al., and is illustrated in the following examples:

$$\text{Expected \% factor VIII increase} = \frac{\text{units administered} \times 2\%/\text{IU/kg}}{\text{body weight (kg)}}$$

$$\text{Example for a 70 kg adult: } \frac{1\,400\ \text{IU} \times 2\%/\text{IU/kg}}{70\text{kg}} = 40\%$$

or

$$\text{Dosage required (IU)} = \frac{\text{body weight (kg)} \times \text{desired \% factor VIII increase}}{2\%/\text{IU/kg}}$$

$$\text{Example for a 15 kg child: } \frac{15\ \text{kg} \times 100\%}{2\%/\text{IU/kg}} = 750\ \text{IU required}$$

The dosage necessary to achieve hemostasis depends upon the type and severity of the bleeding episode, according to the following general guidelines: Mild Hemorrhage: Mild superficial or early hemorrhages may respond to a single dose of 10 IU per kg, leading to an in vivo rise of approximately 20% in the factor VIII level. Therapy need not be repeated unless there is evidence of further bleeding.

Moderate Hemorrhage: For more serious bleeding episodes (e.g., definite hemarthroses, known trauma), the factor VIII level should be raised to 30 to 50% by administering approximately 15 to 25 IU/kg. If further therapy is required, a repeat infusion can be given at 12 to 24 hours.

Severe Hemorrhage: In patients with life-threatening bleeding or possible hemorrhage involving vital structures (e.g., CNS, retropharyngeal and retroperitoneal spaces, iliopsoas sheath), the factor VIII level should be raised to 80 to 100% of normal in order to achieve hemostasis. This may be achieved with an initial rAHF antihemophilic factor (recombinant) dose of 40 to 50 IU/kg and a maintenance dose of 20 to 25 IU/kg every 8 to 12 hours.

Surgery: For major surgical procedures, the factor VIII level should be raised to approximately 100% by giving a preoperative dose of 50 IU/kg. The factor VIII level should be checked to assure that the expected level is achieved before the patient goes to surgery. In order to maintain hemostatic levels, repeat infusions may be necessary every 6 to 12 hours initially, and for a total of 10 to 14 days until healing is complete. The intensity of factor VIII replacement therapy required depends on the type of surgery and postoperative regimen employed. For minor surgical procedures, less intensive treatment schedules may provide adequate hemostasis.

Prophylaxis: Factor VIII concentrates may also be administered on a regular schedule for prophylaxis of bleeding, as reported by Nilsson, et al.

Reconstitution (see package insert for illustrations): Vacuum Transfer: 1. Warm the unopened diluent and the concentrate to room temperature (NMT 37°C). 2. After removing the plastic flip-top caps, aseptically cleanse the rubber stoppers of both bottles. 3. Remove the protective cover from the plastic transfer-needle cartridge with tamper-proof seal and penetrate the stopper of the diluent bottle. 4. Remove the remaining portion of the plastic cartridge, invert the diluent bottle and penetrate the rubber seal on the concentrate bottle with the needle at an angle. Alternate method of transferring sterile water: with a sterile needle and syringe, withdraw the appropriate volume of diluent and transfer to the bottle of lyophilized concentrate. 5. The vacuum will draw the diluent into the concentrate bottle. Hold the diluent bottle at an angle to the concentrate bottle in order to direct the jet of diluent against the wall of the concentrate bottle. Avoid excessive foaming. 6. After removing the diluent bottle and transfer needle, swirl continuously until completely dissolved. 7. After the concentrate powder is completely dissolved, withdraw solution into the syringe through the filter needle which is supplied in the package. Replace the filter needle with the administration set provided and inject i.v. Note: Firmly grasp one or both wings to perform venipuncture: do not use the postuse needle shield for this purpose. 8. After infusion, lock postuse needle shield in place using one of the following methods: a: One-hand technique: Hold tubing in hand and advance needle shield with thumb and index finger until locked over needle tip. b: Two-hand technique: Hold wing stationary and slide needle shield forward with other hand until locked over needle tip. 9. If the same patient is to receive more than 1 bottle, the contents of 2 bottles may be drawn into the same syringe through a separate unused filter needle before attaching the vein needle.

Rate of Administration: The rate of administration should be adapted to the response of the individual patient, but administration of the entire dose in 5 to 10 minutes or less is well-tolerated.

Parenteral drug products should be inspected visually for particulate matter and discoloration prior to administration, whenever solution and container permit.

Supplied: Each bottle of sterile, nonpyrogenic stable, purified, dried concentrate which has been manufactured by recombinant DNA technology, contains: antihemophilic factor (recombinant) 250, 500 or 1 000 IU.

Antihemophilic factor (recombinant) is produced by Baby Hamster Kidney (BHK) cells into which the human factor VIII (FVIII) gene has been introduced. It is a highly purified glycoprotein consisting of multiple peptides including an 80 kD and various extensions of the 90 kD subunit. It has the same biological activity as FVIII derived from human plasma. In addition to the use of the classical purification methods of ion exchange chromatography and size exclusion chromatography, monoclonal antibody immunoaffinity chromatography is utilized along with other steps designed to purify recombinant factor VIII (rAHF) and remove contaminating substances. The final preparation is stabilized with Albumin (Human) and lyophilized. The concentration of antihemophilic factor (recombinant) is approximately 100 IU/mL. Preservative-free.

Each vial contains the labelled amount of rAHF in international units (IU). One IU, as defined by the World Health Organization standard for blood coagulation factor VIII, human, is approximately equal to the level of factor VIII activity found in 1.0 mL of fresh pooled human plasma.

The final product when reconstituted as directed contains the following excipients: 10 to 30 mg glycine/mL; not more than (NMT) 500 µg imidazole/1 000 IU; NMT 600 µg polysorbate 80/1 000 IU; 2 to 5 mmol calcium chloride; 100 to 130 mEq/L sodium; 100 to 130 mEq/L chloride and 4 to 10 mg albumin (human)/mL. The product must be administered by the i.v. route.

Store under refrigeration (2 to 8°C). Storage of lyophilized powder at room temperature (up to 25°C) for 3 months, such as in home treatment situations, may be done without loss of factor VIII activity. Freezing should be avoided, as breakage of the diluent bottle might occur. Do not use beyond expiration date indicated on the bottle.

K-10®

SmithKline Beecham

Potassium Chloride

Potassium Replacement Therapy

Supplied: Each 15 mL contains: potassium chloride 1.5 g (supplying 20 mEq of elemental potassium). Nonmedicinal ingredients: calcium cyclamate, citric acid, glycerin, lemon flavor, orange flavor and sodium benzoate. Bottles of 500 mL.

KWELLADA-P™

R & C

Permethrin

Topical Scabicide

Pharmacology: Permethrin, a synthetic pyrethroid, has a broad spectrum of insecticidal activity combined with high potency when applied topically to insects.

Like other pyrethroids, permethrin is a sodium channel toxin. In susceptible nerve cells small amounts of permethrin cause a change in the kinetics of the sodium channel. Although the activation of the sodium current in unaffected, the rate of inactivation of the current is greatly slowed. This tail current, even at low doses, is adequate to cause repetitive activity. One normal action potential, in the presence of permethrin, leads to a series of abnormal action potentials. Consequently, there is a repetitive firing of the neuron.

Clinical studies have demonstrated that permethrin is active against S. scabiei, scabies. In clinical trials 5% permethrin was found to be an effective treatment for scabies. After one application of 5% permethrin lotion 93% of patients were cured at 28 days. At the interim assessment at 14 days 37% were already cured and 61% were improving.

Only a very minimal amount of permethrin is absorbed when applied topically. In a bioavailability study it was determined that <0.032% of a topically applied dose of 5% permethrin lotion was absorbed.

Indications: For the treatment of scabies S. scabiei. One application is usually adequate to eradicate the infestation of scabies. If new lesions appear or live scabies mites are seen, a second treatment can occur 7 to 10 days after the initial treatment.

Contraindications: Patients with a known sensitivity or reaction to permethrin, any synthetic pyrethroid or pyrethrin or to chrysanthemums.

Warnings: Permethrin should be discontinued if hypersensitivity occurs.

Precautions: General: If permethrin lotion comes in contact with the eyes it can cause irritation. If this occurs, the eyes should be rinsed. During a scabies infestation the skin is often irritated resulting in erythema, edema and pruritus. These symptoms can be temporarily exacerbated after treatment, with pruritus often persisting for several weeks after treatment. This is not an adverse reaction to the permethrin lotion, nor is it a treatment failure.

Children: Permethrin lotion is safe and efficacious in children over 2 months of age. The safety and efficacy of permethrin has not been established in children under the age of 2 months.

Pregnancy: Safety has not been established during controlled clinical trials for use in pregnant women. Permethrin should be used when the expected benefits outweigh the potential risks.

Lactation: Because it is not known whether permethrin is excreted during lactation, consideration should be given to discontinuing nursing during treatment with permethrin lotion or withholding treatment if it is not possible to discontinue nursing.

Adverse Effects: Clinical trials have indicated that adverse reactions are reported infrequently. Adverse reactions which do occur are usually mild and resolve rapidly. They are local in nature.

In clinical trials burning, stinging and tingling were the most frequently reported adverse events with fewer than 1% of patients reporting them. The next most frequently reported event was pruritus followed by erythema which was reported by less than 0.02% of patients. Pruritus is not considered to be an adverse reaction to permethrin because pruritus characteristically remains for several weeks after successful treatment. The itching gradually subsides with the natural loss of the upper layer of skin.

Overdose: Symptoms and Treatment: There has been no incidence of ingestion of permethrin lotion.

If permethrin lotion is accidently ingested, vomiting can be induced.

Dosage: Prior to application the skin should be clean, dry and cool. A hot bath should not be taken prior to treatment. The lotion should be thoroughly massaged into the skin from the neck to the soles of the feet, paying particular attention to the areas between fingers and toes, under the fingernails and toenails, wrists, armpits, genital area and buttocks. Permethrin lotion disappears when rubbed gently into the skin; therefore, it is not necessary for the patient to apply the medication until it remains detectable on the skin. If the hands are washed with soap and water during the treatment period, permethrin lotion should be reapplied.

The patient should put on clean clothes and leave the lotion in place for 12 to 14 hours. The lotion should then be thoroughly washed off during a shower or bath. Patients should again change into clean clothes.

One treatment is usually adequate to eliminate the scabies. However, if live scabies mites are present or new skin lesions appear a second application can be given 7 to 10 days later.

Permethrin should be shaken before use.

Information for the Patient: See Blue Section—Information for the Patient "Kwellada-P".

Supplied: Each mL of lotion contains: permethrin 5% (w/w) cis-trans ratio of 25:75. Nonmedicinal ingredients: carbomer, edetate sodium, imidurea, methylparaben, polysorbate, propylene glycol, propylparaben, purified water, sorbitan monolaurate and sodium hydroxide. Plastic bottles of 50 and 200 mL. Store between 15 and 30°C.

New Product 1998

KYTRIL™ Ⓟ

SmithKline Beecham

Granisetron HCl

Antiemetic

Pharmacology: Granisetron is a selective antagonist of 5-hydroxytryptamine (5-HT_3) receptors. Following exposure to emetogenic cancer chemotherapy, mucosal enterochromaffin cells release serotonin which stimulates 5-HT_3 receptors located peripherally on vagal nerve terminals and centrally in the nucleus tractus solitarus. The antiemetic effect of granisetron appears to involve antagonism of the serotonin-induced stimulation of vagal afferent activity.

Radioligand binding studies have demonstrated that granisetron has negligible affinity for other 5-HT receptors or for dopamine D_2 receptor binding sites.

In healthy subjects, granisetron produced no consistent or clinically significant changes in pulse rate, blood pressure or ECG. There was no evidence of an effect on psychomotor performance at i.v. doses of up to 200 μg/kg i.v. Granisetron did not affect the plasma levels of prolactin or aldosterone at single i.v. doses of up to 300 μg/kg or after repeat i.v. doses of 40 μg/kg for 5.5 days.

Following single and multiple oral doses, granisetron slowed colonic transit in normal volunteers.

Pharmacokinetics: Injection: In adult cancer patients undergoing chemotherapy and in healthy volunteers, infusion of a single 40 μg/kg dose of granisetron produced the following mean pharmacokinetic data (see Table I).

Oral: In healthy volunteers and adult cancer patients undergoing chemotherapy, administration of oral granisetron produced the following mean pharmacokinetic data (see Table II).

Metabolism: The clearance of granisetron occurs predominantly through hepatic metabolism. Biotransformation pathways involve N-demethylation and aromatic ring oxidation followed by conjugation.

Excretion: In normal volunteers, the urinary excretion of unchanged granisetron averages 12% of the administered dose over a period of 48 hours, while the remainder of the dose is excreted as metabolites, 47% in the urine and 34% in the feces. The metabolism of granisetron involves N-demethylation and aromatic ring oxidation followed by conjugation.

Plasma Protein Binding and Distribution: Granisetron is extensively distributed between plasma and red blood cells with a mean volume of distribution of approximately 3 L/kg. Plasma protein binding is approximately 65%.

Cancer Patients: Following i.v. administration, mean terminal elimination half-life values are approximately twice as long in cancer patients as they are in healthy adult volunteers, while clearance values are decreased by approximately 50% (see Table I). Available data do not allow a formal comparison of elimination half-life or clearance between volunteers and cancer patients receiving oral granisetron.

Elderly: In elderly (mean age 71 years) subjects after single i.v. doses of 40 μg/kg, pharmacokinetic parameters were within the range found for non-elderly subjects (mean age 29 years). Although the elimination half-life was prolonged and the total plasma clearance reduced in the elderly relative to the young subject group, no significant differences were determined between the two groups with regard to maximum plasma concentration or area under the plasma concentration time curve values (see Table I).

Renally Impaired Patients: Although renal clearance was decreased in subjects with severe renal impairment (N=11) relative to normal volunteers (N=12), total plasma clearance was numerically higher in this renally impaired group (43 L/h) than in the normal volunteers (32 L/h). Mean area under the plasma concentration time curve values were similar for the 2 subject groups.

Hepatically Impaired Patients: A pharmacokinetic study in patients with hepatic impairment due to neoplastic liver involvement showed that total clearance was approximately halved and mean area under the plasma concentration time curve (AUC) values were approximately doubled compared to patients without hepatic impairment.

Clinical Trials: Injection: Granisetron has been shown to prevent nausea and vomiting associated with single-day and repeat-cycle cancer chemotherapy.

In a double-blind, placebo-controlled study in 28 cancer patients, granisetron, administered as a single i.v. infusion of 40 μg/kg, was significantly more effective than placebo in preventing nausea and vomiting induced by cisplatin chemotherapy (see Table III on following page).

Single-day Chemotherapy: Granisetron was evaluated in a double-blind, randomized dose response study of 353 patients stratified for high (>80 to 120 mg/m²) or low (50 to 79 mg/m²) cisplatin dose. Response rates of patients for both cisplatin strata are given in Table IV (on following page).

The 10, 20 and 40 μg/kg doses were more effective than the 5 μg/kg dose in preventing nausea and vomiting within 24 hours of chemotherapy administration. The 10 μg/kg dose was at least as effective as the higher doses.

Table I—Kytril

Pharmacokinetic Parameters in Adult Cancer Patients Undergoing Chemotherapy and in Volunteers, Following a Single i.v. 40 μg/kg Dose of Kytril Injection

	Peak Plasma Concentration (ng/mL)	Terminal Phase Plasma Half-Life (h)	AUC (ng.h/mL)	Total Clearance (L/h)
Cancer Patients				
(n=14)				
Mean	63.8[a]	8.95[a]	167[a]	25.8[a]
Range	18.0 to 176	0.90 to 31.1	26.0 to 294	8.92 to 95.2
Young Adult Volunteers				
21 to 42 years				
(n=20)				
Mean	64.3[b]	4.91[b]	89.7[b]	51.8[b]
Range	11.2 to 182	0.88 to 15.2	15.6 to 201	11.3 to 176
Elderly Volunteers				
65 to 81 years				
(n=20)				
Mean	57.0[b]	7.69[b]	115[b]	27.1[b]
Range	14.6 to 153	2.65 to 17.7	37.7 to 240	10.9 to 58.4

[a]5 minute infusion.
[b]3 minute infusion.

Table II—Kytril

Pharmacokinetic Parameters [Mean (range)] In Adult Cancer Patients Undergoing Chemotherapy and in Volunteers Following Oral Kytril

	Peak Plasma Concentration (ng/mL)	Terminal Plasma Half-Life (h)	Area Under Curve (ng.h/mL)	Total Clearance (L/h)
Cancer Patients				
1.0 mg b.i.d., 7 days (n=24)	8.19 (1.97 to 18.4)	N.D.[a]	54.2 (10.2 to 126)	34.1 (7.94—98.0)
Volunteers				
single dose (n=25)				
1.0 mg	4.10 (0.58 to 7.37)	8.74 (2.40 to 19.9)	43.7 (2.85 to 142)	53.3 (7.04 to 351)
2.5 mg	9.44 (1.68 to 19.5)	7.24 (2.54 to 17.0)	105 (7.75 to 319)	67.2 (7.84 to 323)

[a]Not determined after oral administration.

Kytril (cont'd)

Table III—Kytril

Prevention of Chemotherapy - Induced Nausea and Vomiting - Single-Day Cisplatin Therapy[a]

	Granisetron	Placebo	P value
Number of Patients	14	14	
Response Over 24 h			
Complete Response[b]	93%	7%	<0.001
No Vomiting	93%	14%	<0.001
No More Than Mild Nausea	93%	7 %	<0.001

[a]Cisplatin administration began within 10 minutes of Kytril infusion and continued for 1.5 to 3.0 hours. Mean cisplatin doses were 86 mg/m² in the Kytril group and 80 mg/m² in the placebo group.
[b]No vomiting and no moderate or severe nausea.

Table IV—Kytril

Prevention of Chemotherapy - Induced Nausea and Vomiting - Single-Day High-Dose and Low-Dose Cisplatin Therapy[a]

Granisetron Dose (μg/kg)	5	10	20	40
Number of Patients	82	90	88	93
Complete Response[b] (%)	23	48[c]	48[c]	44[c]
No Vomiting (%)	32	54[c]	53[c]	48[c]
No Nausea (%)	22	46[c]	38[c]	38[c]

[a]Cisplatin administration began within 10 minutes of granisetron infusion and continued 2 hours (mean). Mean cisplatin dose was 82 mg/m².
[b]No vomiting and no rescue medication.
[c]$p<0.05$ vs 5 μg/kg.

Repeat Cycle Chemotherapy: Two single blind, active-controlled studies have been performed in which granisetron was administered to a total of 246 chemotherapy-naive patients with malignant disease receiving cytostatic therapy (≥15 mg/m²/day cisplatin, ≥1.2 g/m²/day ifosfamide, and ≥120 mg/m²/day etoposide) for 5 days. Granisetron was administered as a daily 40 μg/kg i.v. dose 5 minutes before the infusion of the cytostatic with up to two additional 40 μg/kg i.v. doses permitted over each 24 hour period. In both studies, response rates (percentage of patients with no vomiting and no more than mild nausea in the 24 hour period following granisetron administration) were observed to decline with repeated treatment, decreasing from 87 to 90% at day 1 to 70 to 71% at day 3, and 67 to 73% at day 5.

Co-Administration with Dexamethasone: A randomized, double-blind, placebo-controlled trial compared the safety and efficacy of i.v. granisetron (3 mg) plus 8 mg dexamethasone phosphate with that of i.v. granisetron alone (3 mg) in the prevention of emesis induced by cytotoxic chemotherapy. A total of 278 patients received one of the following agents as their main cytotoxic therapy, either as a single agent or in combination with other cytotoxic agents: carboplatin >300 mg/m², cisplatin >20 mg/m² to <50 mg/m², dacarbazine >350 mg/m² to <500 mg/m², cyclophosphamide >500 mg/m² in combination, doxorubicin >40 mg/m² as single agent, doxorubicin >25 mg/m² in combination, epirubicin >75 mg/m² as single agent, epirubicin >50 mg/m² in combination. Patients received chemotherapy on Day 0 and were followed up to a further 6 days.

For the efficacy parameter of total control, there was a significantly better response in the granisetron/dexamethasone group than the granisetron/placebo group on Day 0 ($p=0.020$) [95% CI (2.2%, 24.2%)] (see Table V).

Table V—Kytril

Summary of Total Control* on Day 0 [Number (%) of Patients]

	Treatment Group		
	Kytril/ Dexamethasone (n=141)	Kytril/Placebo (n=137)	P-value
Day 0	103 (73.0%)	82 (59.9%)	0.020

*Patients with no vomiting, no nausea, no rescue therapy and not withdrawn.

In addition, a statistically significant difference between the treatment groups was observed over the 7 day period for the parameters of time to first rescue medication, time to first vomiting episode and time to first moderate/severe nausea.

Oral: Oral granisetron prevents nausea and vomiting associated with emetogenic cancer therapy as shown by 24-hour efficacy data from three double-blind studies. The first trial compared oral granisetron doses of 0.25 mg to 2.0 mg b.i.d. in 930 cancer patients receiving, principally, cyclophosphamide, carboplatin, or cisplatin (20 mg/m² to 50 mg/m²) as chemotherapeutic agents. Table VI summarizes the results of this study. The 1 mg b.i.d. dose of oral granisetron was demonstrated to produce the highest therapeutic benefit.

Table VI—Kytril

Prevention of Nausea and Vomiting 24 Hours Post-Chemotherapy[a] (Percentage of Patients)

	Oral Kytril Dose			
	0.25 mg b.i.d. (n=229)	0.5 mg b.i.d. (n=235)	1.0 mg b.i.d. (n=233)	2.0 mg b.i.d. (n=233)
Efficacy Measures	%	%	%	%
Complete Response[b]	61	70[c]	81[c,d]	72[c]
No Vomiting	66	77[c]	88[c]	79[c]
No Nausea	48	57	63[c]	54

[a]Chemotherapy included oral and injectable cyclophosphamide, carboplatin, cisplatin (20 to 50 mg/m²), dacarbazine, doxorubicin, epirubicin.
[b]No vomiting, no moderate or severe nausea, no rescue medication, and not withdrawn/discontinued during treatment period.
[c]Statistically significant ($p<0.01$) vs 0.25 mg b.i.d.
[d]Statistically significant ($p<0.01$) vs 0.5 mg b.i.d.

A second double-blind randomised trial compared oral granisetron 1 mg, b.i.d., oral granisetron-plus-dexamethasone and metoclopramide-plus-dexamethasone in 357 patients receiving cisplatin (mean dose >80 mg/m²). The complete response rate for the granisetron-plus-dexamethasone regimen was significantly better than for granisetron alone, or the metoclopramide-plus-dexamethasone regimen. Table VII summarizes the results of this study.

The third study compared once daily versus twice daily dosing regimes with 2 mg/day of oral granisetron in 700 patients. Approximately 50% of patients who received granisetron 2 mg daily administered either as a single dose (n=344) or in divided doses (n=356), were free of emetic episodes and nausea and did not require antiemetic rescue treatment during the 24-hour post-chemotherapy period.

The continued efficacy of granisetron tablets 2 mg daily or 1 mg b.i.d., administered on the day of chemotherapy only, has not been investigated beyond the 24 hour post-chemotherapy period. It is not known whether additional doses confer efficacy beyond 24 hours.

No controlled study has been performed to compare the antiemetic efficacy of granisetron tablets and granisetron injection at the recommended therapeutic doses.

Table VII—Kytril

Prevention of Nausea and Vomiting 24 Hours Post-High Dose Cisplatin Therapy (Percentage of Patients)

	Antiemetic Regimen		
Efficacy Measures	Oral Kytril 1.0 mg b.i.d. (n=119) %	Oral Kytril 1.0 mg b.i.d. plus Dexamethasone 12 mg i.v. (n=117) %	Metoclopramide 7 mg/kg i.v. plus Dexamethasone 12 mg i.v. (n=121) %
Complete Response[a]	52	65[b]	52
No Vomiting	56	66	52
No Nausea	45	57	39

[a]No emetic episodes, no moderate or severe nausea, no rescue medication, and not withdrawn/discontinued during treatment period.
[b]Statistically significant ($p<0.05$) vs oral Kytril alone and vs metoclopramide-plus dexamethasone.

Indications: For the prevention of nausea and vomiting associated with emetogenic cancer chemotherapy, including high dose cisplatin.

Contraindications: In patients with a known hypersensitivity to the drug or to any component of its formulations.

Precautions: Carcinogenesis: Granisetron has been associated with an increased occurrence of hepatocellular tumors in carcinogenicity studies performed in rodents at doses in excess of the recommended human dose. Although the clinical significance of these findings has not been determined, the use of this drug should be restricted to the treatment of nausea and vomiting in patients undergoing emetogenic cancer chemotherapy. The recommended dosage of granisetron should not be exceeded.

Granisetron was administered to rats in the diet in a 24 month carcinogenicity study. The incidence of hepatocellular carcinomas and adenomas was significantly increased in male rats treated at doses of 5 mg/kg/day and in rats of both sexes treated with 25 mg/kg/day. No increase in the rate of occurrence of liver tumors was observed in the 1 mg/kg/day treatment group (100 times the recommended human dose given i.v.).

In another 24 month carcinogenicity study, mice were administered granisetron in the diet at doses of 1, 5, and 50 mg/kg/day. There was a statistically significant increase in the incidence of hepatocellular carcinomas in males and hepatocellular adenomas in females dosed with 50 mg/kg/day. No statistically significant increase in liver tumors was observed in mice at a dose of 5 mg/kg/day (500 times the recommended human dose given i.v.).

Gastrointestinal: Granisetron may reduce lower bowel motility, patients with signs of sub-acute intestinal obstruction should be monitored following administration of granisetron.

Pregnancy: The use of granisetron in pregnant women has not been studied and is not recommended.

Reproduction studies performed in pregnant rats given granisetron at i.v. dosages up to 9 mg/kg/day and pregnant rabbits at i.v. dosage up to 3 mg/kg/day revealed no evidence of impaired fertility or harm to the fetus due to granisetron.

Lactation: It is not known whether granisetron is excreted in human milk. Nursing is not recommended during treatment with granisetron.

Children: The safety and efficacy of granisetron has not been adequately studied in children or adolescents under 18 years of age.

Geriatrics: During clinical trials, 713 patients 65 years of age or older received i.v. granisetron and of 325 patients 65 years of age or older who received oral granisetron, 298 were 65 to 74 years of age and 27 were 75 years of age or older. The efficacy and safety of granisetron did not appear to be age dependent.

Drug Interactions: No pharmacodynamic interaction was found between single 160 μg/kg i.v. doses of granisetron and single oral doses of 2.5 mg lorazepam or 3 mg haloperidol. Pharmacokinetic interactions with these drugs were not investigated.

The pharmacokinetic characteristics of a single 40 μg/kg i.v. dose of granisetron were not significantly different whether it was administered alone or following 8 days of treatment with the hepatic enzyme inhibitor, cimetidine (200 mg q.i.d.).

Granisetron does not induce or inhibit the cytochrome P_{450} drug metabolizing enzyme system.

Occupational Hazards: In healthy subjects, no clinically relevant effects on resting EEG or on the performance of psychometric tests were observed after i.v. granisetron at any dose tested (up to 200 μg/kg). There are no data on the effect of granisetron on the ability to drive. As there have been occasional reports of somnolence in clinical studies, patients should be advised to avoid driving a car or operating hazardous machinery until they are reasonably certain that the drug treatment does not affect them adversely.

Adverse Effects: Most Common Adverse Events: Table VIII gives the frequencies of the 6 adverse events most commonly reported by patients receiving i.v. or oral granisetron in single-day chemotherapy trials. Table VIII does not include those events that are commonly associated with chemotherapy or the underlying malignant disease. I.V. granisetron was given as a single dose. Oral granisetron was given either as a single dose or divided dose for 1, 7, or 14 days. Patients received cancer chemotherapy which consisted primarily of cisplatin or cyclophosphamide regimens. During the 24-hour period following i.v. granisetron administration, i.v. fluids were also given. Adverse events were recorded over 7 days when granisetron was given on a single day and up to 28 days when granisetron was administered for 7 or 14 days. In the absence of a placebo group, the relationship of observed adverse events to granisetron treatment is difficult to judge. The only two common adverse experiences recognised to be causally related to granisetron are constipation and headache. As with other drugs of this class, rare cases of hypersensitivity reactions, sometimes severe (e.g., anaphylaxis, shortness of breath, hypotension, urticaria) have been reported.

Table VIII—Kytril

Principal Adverse Events in Clinical Trials of Single-Day Chemotherapy

	Percentage of Patients with Event I.V. Kytril (10-40 μg/kg) (n=1 519)	Percentage of Patients with Event Oral Kytril (1 mg b.i.d. or 2 mg daily) (n=1 322)
Headache	14%	22%
Asthenia	5%	15%
Somnolence	4%	2%
Diarrhea	5%	8%
Constipation	4%	17%
Abdominal Pain	3%	6%

Adverse Experience Reports: The safety profile of granisetron has been evaluated in 3 269 patients receiving i.v. granisetron (2 to 160 μg/kg) and 2 600 patients receiving oral granisetron (0.25 to 20 mg) in single-day and multiple-day clinical trials with emetogenic cancer therapies. In the listings which follow, a COSTART-based dictionary terminology has been used to classify reported adverse experiences. The frequencies presented, therefore, represent the proportion of the patients who experienced an event of the type cited on at least one occasion while receiving granisetron Experiences are further classified within body system categories and enumerated in order of decreasing frequency using the following definitions: frequent experiences are defined as those occurring on one or more occasion in at least 1/100 patients; infrequent adverse experiences as those occurring in less than 1/100 but at least 1/1 000 patients; rare experiences as those occurring in less than 1/1 000 patients.

Many adverse experiences are observed in cancer chemotherapy patients. All adverse experiences are included except those for which the drug cause was remote, those reported in terms so general as to be uninformative and those already listed in Table VIII.

Body as a Whole: Frequent: abdominal pain. Infrequent: abdomen enlarged, chills, fever, malaise. Rare: allergic reaction, chest pain.

Cardiovascular: Infrequent: hypertension, hypotension, migraine, syncope, vasodilatation. Rare: arrhythmia, bradycardia, palpitation, postural hypotension, tachycardia, ventricular arrhythmia.

Digestive System: Frequent: decreased appetite. Infrequent: dry mouth, dyspepsia, flatulence, jaundice, liver function tests abnormal, nausea. Rare: gastrointestinal hemorrhage, hepatic coma, ileus, liver damage, melena, vomiting.

Hemic and Lymphatic: Rare: anemia, coagulation time increased, eosinophilia, leukopenia, thrombocytopenia.

Metabolic and Nutritional: Infrequent: hypokalemia. Rare: bilirubinemia, edema, hyperphosphatemia, hyponatremia.

Nervous System: Infrequent: agitation, anxiety, dizziness, drugged feeling, insomnia, nervousness, paresthesia, tremor. Rare: coma, depersonalisation, grand mal convulsion, vertigo.

Respiratory: Infrequent: dyspnea, hiccup. Rare: epistaxis, rhinitis, sinusitis.

Skin and Appendages: Infrequent: pruritus, rash, sweating. Rare: photosensitivity.

Special Searches: Rare: puncture site pain.

Special Senses: Infrequent: taste perversion. Rare: abnormal vision.

Urogenital: Infrequent: dysuria. Rare: urinary incontinence.

Overdose: Symptoms and Treatment: There is no specific antidote for granisetron overdosage. In the case of overdosage, symptomatic treatment should be given. Overdose with both the i.v. and oral formulations has been reported. Overdosage of up to 38.5 mg of granisetron injection has been reported without symptoms or with the occurrence of a slight headache.

Dosage: Injection: The recommended dosage of granisetron is 10 μg/kg infused i.v. over 5 minutes, beginning within 30 minutes before initiation of chemotherapy only on the day(s) when chemotherapy is given.

Oral: The recommended dosage of oral granisetron is 2 mg on the day of chemotherapy. This may be administered either as a single dose (2×1 mg) 1 hour before chemotherapy or as a divided dose of 1 mg 1 hour before chemotherapy followed by a second 1 mg dose 12 hours post-chemotherapy. The need for additional doses beyond 24 hours post-chemotherapy has not been investigated.

Geriatrics, Renally Impaired: Available clinical data suggest that dosage reductions may not be necessary in these patient populations.

Hepatically Impaired: The clearance of granisetron is reduced by half in patients with hepatic impairment. The dose response of granisetron in patients with hepatic impairment has not been determined.

Diluted Solutions: Infusion Preparation: To prepare the recommended dose of 10 μg/kg, take the contents of the 1 mL single use vial and dilute with infusion fluid to a total volume of 50 mL in any of the following solutions: 0.9% sodium chloride, 0.18% sodium chloride and 4% dextrose, 5% dextrose, Hartmann's solution, sodium lactate, mannitol.

Required Volume of Diluted Infusion by Body Weight: see Table IX.

Table IX—Kytril

Required Volume of Diluted Infusion by Body Weight

Patient Weight (kg)	40	50	60	70	80	90	100
Required Volume of Diluted Solution (mL)	20	25	30	35	40	45	50

Granisetron has been shown to be stable for at least 24 hours in these solutions, when stored at ambient temperature in normal indoor illumination (natural daylight supplemented by fluorescent light). As with all parenteral drug products, i.v. admixtures should be inspected visually for clarity, particulate matter, precipitate, discoloration and leakage prior to administration, whenever solution and container permit. Appropriate precautions should be taken to maintain the sterility of the infusion solution once prepared.

Pharmaceutical Precautions: As a general precaution, Kytril should not be mixed in solution with other drugs. Prophylactic administration of Kytril should be completed prior to the start of cytostatic therapy.

Information for the Patient: See Blue Section—Information for the Patient "Kytril".

Supplied: Injection: Each mL single use vial contains: granisetron HCl 1 mg, sodium chloride 0.9%, water for injection and hydrochloric acid and/or sodium hydroxide for pH adjustment. Clear glass single use vials, boxes of 1. Store between 5 and 30°C. Protect from light.

Tablets: Each white, triangular, biconvex, film-coated tablet, contains: granisetron HCl equivalent to granisetron 1 mg. Nonmedicinal ingredients: hydroxypropyl methylcellulose, lactose, magnesium stearate, microcrystalline cellulose, sodium starch glycolate and Opadry YS-1-7003 (hydroxypropyl methylcellulose, titanium dioxide, polyethylene glycol and polysorbate 80). Blister cards of 2 and 10. Store at controlled room temperature (15 to 30°C).

(Shown in Product Recognition Section)

Reviewed 1997

L

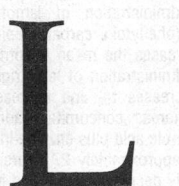

LAC-HYDRIN®
Westwood-Squibb

Ammonium Lactate

Moisturizer

Indications: For the treatment of moderate to severe dry skin and scaling (xerosis), and hyperkeratotic conditions such as ichthyosis, and for the temporary relief of itching associated with these conditions.

Contraindications: Abraded or inflamed skin. Known sensitivity to any of the ingredients.

Precautions: If irritation develops, use should be discontinued. For external use only.

Dosage: Apply to the affected areas twice daily or as often as physician directs. In cases of severe dry skin, improvement may be evident within 1 week. If symptoms persist, discontinue use and consult physician.

Supplied: Each plastic bottle contains: ammonium lactate 12% in a humectant lotion base. pH: 4.5 to 5.5. Nonmedicinal ingredients: ammonium hydroxide, cetyl alcohol, fragrance, glycerin, glyceryl stearate/PEG-100 stearate, laureth-4, magnesium aluminum silicate, methylcellulose, methylparaben, mineral oil, PEG-40 stearate, propylene glycol, propylparaben and water. Plastic bottles of 225 mL.

LACRI-LUBE® S.O.P.®
Allergan

Petrolatum—Mineral Oil Compound

Ocular Lubricant

Supplied: Each g of sterile, bland, nonmedicated, preservative-free ophthalmic ointment contains: white petrolatum USP, mineral oil USP and lanolin alcohols NF. Tubes of 3.5 and 7 g.

LACRISERT®
MSD

Hydroxypropyl Cellulose

Ophthalmic Insert

Indications: In patients with moderate to severe dry eye syndromes, including keratoconjunctivitis sicca, especially in patients who remain symptomatic after an adequate trial of therapy with artificial tear solutions. Exposure keratitis. Decreased corneal sensitivity.

Contraindications: Hypersensitivity to hydroxypropyl cellulose.

Precautions: Instructions for inserting and removing Lacrisert should be carefully followed.
Occupational Hazards: Because this product may produce transient blurring of vision, patients should be instructed to exercise caution when operating hazardous machinery or driving a motor vehicle.

Adverse Effects: The following adverse reactions have been reported in patients treated with Lacrisert, but were in most instances mild and transient: transient blurring of vision (see Precautions), ocular discomfort or irritation, matting or stickiness of eyelashes, photophobia, hypersensitivity, edema of the eyelids, hyperemia, tearing.

Dosage: One Lacrisert ophthalmic insert in each eye once daily is usually sufficient to relieve the symptoms associated with moderate to severe dry eye syndromes. Individual patients may require more flexibility in the use of Lacrisert, some patients may require twice daily use for optimal results.

In some patients, the concomitant administration of a replacement tear solution at the time of insertion may be of benefit. Clinical experience with Lacrisert indicates that in some patients several weeks may be required before satisfactory improvement of symptoms is achieved.

Lacrisert is inserted into the inferior cul-de-sac of the eye beneath the base of the tarsus.
Note: Occasionally Lacrisert is inadvertently expelled from the eye, especially in patients with shallow conjunctival fornices or when the eye is rubbed. The patient should be cautioned against rubbing the eye(s) containing Lacrisert, especially upon awakening, so as to not dislodge or expel the insert. If required, another Lacrisert ophthalmic insert may be inserted. If experience indicates that transient blurred vision develops in an individual patient, the patient may want to remove Lacrisert a few hours after insertion to avoid this. Another Lacrisert ophthalmic insert may be inserted if needed.

If Lacrisert causes worsening of symptoms, the patient should be instructed to inspect the conjunctival sac to make certain Lacrisert is in the proper location, deep in the inferior cul-de-sac of the eye, beneath the base of the tarsus. If these symptoms persist, Lacrisert should be removed and the patient should contact the practitioner.

Supplied: A rod-shaped, water-soluble, ophthalmic preparation made of hydroxypropyl cellulose, 5 mg. It contains no preservatives or other ingredients. Packages of 60 units, together with illustrated instructions and a special applicator for removing Lacrisert from the unit dose blister and inserting it into the eye. A spare applicator is included in each package.

Illustrated instructions are included in each package, but initially patients must be instructed in the correct method of insertion. While in the ophthalmologist's office, the patient should read the instructions, then practise insertions and removal of Lacrisert until proficiency is achieved.

(Shown in Product Recognition Section)

LACTAID®
McNeil Consumer Products

Lactase Enzyme

Lactose Digestant

Pharmacology: Converts the disaccharide lactose via hydrolysis into its monosaccharide components, glucose and galactose.
Tablets: In vivo activity has been demonstrated with drug administration at time of milk consumption and at time of consumption of other lactose containing solid and liquid foods.
Drops: Fifteen drops will hydrolyze nearly all of the lactose in 1 L of milk at refrigerator temperature (6°C) in 24 hours. 1 L of any type of milk will contain approximately 50 g lactose prior to lactose hydrolysis.

Indications: Lactase insufficiency either suspected because of gastrointestinal disturbances (bloating, flatulence, diarrhea) after consumption of milk or milk products or identified by a lactose tolerance test, or a breath hydrogen test after lactose challenge.

Precautions: Lactase deficient diabetics should be made aware that milk sugar (lactose) which was previously indigestible by them will now be metabolized and provide calories which must be accounted for in their diet (e.g., 50 g of lactose will yield 25 g of glucose and 25 g of galactose sugar each of which may be converted to energy by metabolism).

Galactosemics may not have milk in any form, lactase enzyme modified or not.
Drug Interactions: No drug interactions reported.

Adverse Effects: The most frequently reported adverse effects to the tablets are gastrointestinal in nature, sometimes mimicking the symptoms of lactose intolerance. No reactions of any kind were observed from the liquid drops. Total reactions were estimated at under 0.1% of users.

Overdose: Symptoms and Treatment: Overdose has not been reported with this drug.

Dosage: Drops: Add up 15 drops to each L of milk to convert nearly all of the lactose.
Tablets: Extra Strength: 2 tablets to be taken **just before** eating a meal or food which contains lactose. The tablet can either be swallowed or chewed.

Regular Strength: 3 tablets to be taken **just before** eating a meal or food which contains lactose. The tablet can either be swallowed or chewed. Dosage requirements may vary substantially between individuals and between situations.
Ultra Caplets: 1 caplet to be taken just before eating a meal or food which contains lactose. The caplet must be swallowed whole.

Supplied: Drops: Each mL of solution contains: lactase (β-D-galactosidase derived from Kluyveromyces lactis yeast). Nonmedicinal ingredients: glycerin and water. Dropper bottles of 6.5 and 15.5 mL. Sufficient to treat 30 and 75 L respectively, with doses of 5 drops/L. Treats 10 and 25 L respectively, with doses of 15 drops/L.

Tablets: Extra Strength: Each tablet contains: at least 4 500 FCC lactase units of β-D-galactosidase from Aspergillus oryzae. Nonmedicinal ingredients: cellulose, dextrose, magnesium stearate, mannitol and sodium citrate. Packages of 12, 40 and 80.

Regular Strength: Each tablet contains: at least 3 000 FCC lactase units of β-D-galactosidase from Aspergillus oryzae. Nonmedicinal ingredients: cellulose, dextrose, magnesium stearate, mannitol and sodium citrate. Packages of 15†, 50† and 100.

Ultra Caplets: Each caplet contains: at least 9 000 FCC lactase units of β-D-galactosidase from Aspergillus oryzae. Nonmedicinal ingredients: cellulose, colloidal silicon dioxide, dextrose, magnesium stearate and sodium citrate. Packages of 2, 20 and 40.

†Container provided with a child-resistant closure.

(Shown in Product Recognition Section)

LACTICARE® AHA
Stiefel

Lactic Acid—Sodium Pyrrolidone Carboxylate

Emollient

Supplied: Each mL of lotion contains: lactic acid 5% (an alpha-hydroxy acid) and sodium pyrrolidone carboxylate 2.5% in a viscous oil in water lotion base. Nonmedicinal ingredients: carbomer 940 NF, cetyl alcohol, dehydroacetic acid, DMDM hydantoin, fragrance, glyceryl stearate blend, isopropyl palmitate, mineral oil, myristyl lactate, polyethylene glycol ether complex, purified water USP and sodium hydroxide. Polyethylene bottles of 225 mL with dispenser cap.

LACTRASE®
Rivex Pharma

Lactase

Lactose Digestant

Pharmacology: Lactose is a nonabsorbable disaccharide found as a common constituent in most dairy products. Under normal conditions, dietary lactose is hydrolyzed in the jejunum and proximal ileum by beta-D-galactosidase or lactase. Lactase is produced in the brush border of the columnar epithelial cells of the intestinal villi. Lactase hydrolyzes lactose into 2 monosaccharides, glucose and galactose, that are readily absorbed by the intestine.

Though lactase is normally present in adequate quantities in infants, in many populations its concentration naturally declines starting at about 4 to 5 years of age and is low in a substantial number of individuals by their teens or early 20's. Within certain geographic and ethnic groups, especially in adult Blacks, Orientals, Indians, and Eastern European Jews, the lactase activity may be low even earlier. Although many of them can easily digest smaller quantities of lactose in milk, after consumption of an excessive volume of milk or dairy products, they may exhibit symptoms of lactose intolerance.

When available lactase is insufficient to split the lactose, the unabsorbable sugar remains in the small intestine for an extended period, presenting an osmotic load that increases and retains intraluminal fluid and intensifies intestinal motility; thus the individual reports a bloated feeling and cramps. The undigested lactose is decomposed by the intestinal flora in the lower intestine and excessive carbon dioxide and hydrogen is produced. These gases contribute to flatulence and increased abdominal discomfort. The lactic acid and other short chain acids raise the osmolality, hinder fluid reabsorption and decrease transit time of the contents of the colon, leading to diarrhea. Often hydrogen is noticed in the expired breath of a lactase deficient patient.

Indications: For individuals exhibiting symptoms of lactose intolerance or lactase insufficiency as identified by a lactose tolerance test or by symptoms of gastrointestinal disturbances after consumption of milk or dairy products.

Precautions: It should be noted that in diabetic persons who use Lactrase, the milk sugar will be metabolically available and may result in increased blood glucose levels. Individuals

Lactrase (cont'd)

with galactosemia may not have milk in any form, lactase enzyme modified or not.

Adverse Effects: Virtually unknown.

Dosage: Generally, 1 or 2 capsules taken orally with milk or dairy products is all that is necessary to digest the milk sugar contained in a normal serving. If the patient is more intolerant to lactose, the patient may need more than 2 capsules; increase the dose until the correct dose is found. Lactrase capsules are safe to take and higher doses will be well tolerated.

If the patient prefers, milk can also be pretreated; simply add the contents from 1 to 2 capsules to each L of milk, shake gently, and store the milk in the refrigerator for 24 hours. Lactrase will break down milk sugars to digestible simple sugars. Lactrase powder will not alter the appearance of milk; however, the taste may be slightly sweeter than untreated milk.

If the patient cannot swallow capsules, the contents of the capsules can be sprinkled onto their favorite dairy product before consuming. Lactrase will not alter the taste of the dairy product when used in this manner.

Supplied: Each opaque orange and opaque white capsule imprinted with "SCHWARZ" and "505" contains: standardized lactase 250 mg. Nonmedicinal ingredients: magnesium stearate and maltodextrin. Gluten-, lactose- and tartrazine-free. Bottles of 100.

LAMICTAL® ℞

Glaxo Wellcome

Lamotrigine

Antiepileptic

Pharmacology: Lamotrigine is a drug of the phenyltriazine class chemically unrelated to existing antiepileptic drugs (AEDs).

Lamotrigine is thought to act at voltage-sensitive sodium channels to stabilize neuronal membranes and inhibit the release of excitatory amino acid neurotransmitters (e.g. glutamate, aspartate) that are thought to play a role in the generation and spread of epileptic seizures.

Clinical Trials: In placebo-controlled clinical studies, lamotrigine has been shown to be effective in reducing seizure frequency and the number of days with seizures when added to existing antiepileptic drug therapy in adult patients with partial seizures, with or without generalized tonic-clonic seizures, that are not satisfactorily controlled.

Studies have also been conducted using lamotrigine monotherapy in patients (n=443) newly diagnosed with epilepsy (partial seizures, with or without secondary generalization or primary generalized tonic clonic). Results have shown comparable efficacy (time to first seizure, seizure frequency, percentage of patients seizure-free) with fewer side effects than currently approved therapies.

Clinical trials have also demonstrated that patients (any seizure type) can be converted to lamotrigine monotherapy from polytherapy with significant numbers of patients maintaining or improving seizure control. Efficacy was maintained during longterm treatment (up to 152 weeks).

Pharmacokinetics: Adults: Lamotrigine is rapidly and completely absorbed following oral administration, reaching peak plasma concentrations 1.4 to 4.8 hours (T_{max}) post-dosing. When administered with food, the rate of absorption is slightly reduced, but the extent remains unchanged. Following single lamotrigine doses of 50 to 400 mg, peak plasma concentration (C_{max}=0.6–4.6 μg/mL) and the area under the plasma concentration-versus-time curve (AUC=29.9–211 h•μg/mL) increase linearly with dose. The time-to-peak concentration, elimination half-life ($t_{1/2}$) and volume of distribution (Vd/F) are independent of dose. The $t_{1/2}$ averages 33 hours after single doses and Vd/F ranges from 0.9 to 1.4 L/kg. Following repeated dosing in healthy volunteers for 14 days, the $t_{1/2}$ decreased by an average of 26% (mean steady state $t_{1/2}$ of 26.4 hours) and plasma clearance increased by an average of 33%. In a single-dose study where healthy volunteers were administered both oral and i.v. doses of lamotrigine, the absolute bioavailability of oral lamotrigine was 98%.

Lamotrigine is approximately 55% bound to human plasma proteins. This binding is unaffected by therapeutic concentrations of phenytoin, phenobarbital or valproic acid. Lamotrigine does not displace other antiepileptic drugs (carbamazepine, phenytoin, phenobarbital) from protein binding sites.

Lamotrigine is metabolized predominantly in the liver by glucuronic acid conjugation. The major metabolite is an inactive 2-N-glucuronide conjugate that can be hydrolyzed by β-glucuronidase. Approximately 70% of an oral lamotrigine dose is recovered in urine as this metabolite.

Geriatrics: The pharmacokinetics of lamotrigine in 12 healthy elderly volunteers (≥65 years) who each received a single oral dose of lamotrigine (150 mg) were not different from those in healthy young volunteers. (However, see Precautions, Geriatrics and Dosage.)

Renal Impairment: The pharmacokinetics of a single oral dose of lamotrigine (100 mg) were evaluated in 12 individuals with chronic renal failure (with mean creatinine clearance of 13 mL/min) who were not receiving other antiepileptic drugs. In this study, the elimination half-life of unchanged lamotrigine was prolonged (by an average of 63%) relative to individuals with normal renal function (see Precautions, Renal Failure and Dosage).

Hemodialysis: In 6 hemodialysis patients, the elimination half-life of unchanged lamotrigine was doubled off dialysis, and reduced by 50% on dialysis, relative to individuals with normal renal function.

Hepatic Impairment: The pharmacokinetics of lamotrigine in patients with impaired liver function has not been evaluated.

Gilbert's Syndrome: Gilbert's syndrome (idiopathic unconjugated hyperbilirubinemia) does not appear to affect the pharmacokinetic profile of lamotrigine.

Concomitant Antiepileptic Drugs: In patients with epilepsy, concomitant administration of lamotrigine with enzyme-inducing AEDs (phenytoin, carbamazepine, primidone or phenobarbital) decreases the mean lamotrigine $t_{1/2}$ to 13 hours. Concomitant administration of lamotrigine with valproic acid significantly increases $t_{1/2}$ and decreases the clearance of lamotrigine, whereas concomitant administration of lamotrigine with valproic acid plus enzyme-inducing AEDs can prolong $t_{1/2}$ up to approximately 27 hours. Acetaminophen was shown to slightly decrease the $t_{1/2}$ and increase the clearance of lamotrigine. The key lamotrigine parameters for adult patients and healthy volunteers are summarized in Table I.

Indications: As adjunctive therapy for the management of patients with epilepsy who are not satisfactorily controlled by conventional therapy. Also indicated for use as monotherapy following withdrawal of concomitant antiepileptic drugs.

Contraindications: Patients with known hypersensitivity to lamotrigine or to any components of the formulation.

Warnings: Severe, potentially life-threatening rashes have been reported in association with the use of lamotrigine. These reports, occurring in approximately one in every thousand adults, have included Stevens-Johnson syndrome and, rarely, toxic epidermal necrolysis. Rare deaths have been reported.

The incidence of severe, potentially life-threatening rash in pediatric patients appears higher than that reported in adults using lamotrigine; specifically, reports from clinical

Table I—Lamictal

Mean Pharmacokinetic Parameters in Adult Patients with Epilepsy or Healthy Volunteers

		Healthy Young Volunteers		**Patients with Epilepsy**		
	Lamictal Administered	**Lamictal**	**Lamictal + Valproic Acid**[b]	**Lamictal + Enzyme-Inducing AEDs**	**Lamictal + Valproic Acid**	**Lamictal + Valproic Acid + Enzyme-Inducing AEDs**
T_{max} (h)	Single Dose	2.2 (0.25–12.0)[a]	1.8 (1.0–4.0)	2.3 (0.5–5.0)	4.8 (1.8–8.4)	3.8 (1.0–10.0)
	Multiple Dose	1.7 (0.5–4.0)	1.9 (0.5–3.5)	2.0 (0.75–5.93)	ND	ND
$t_{1/2}$	Single Dose	32.8 (14.0–103.0)	48.3 (31.5–88.6)	14.4 (6.4–30.4)	58.8 (30.5–88.8)	27.2 (11.2–51.6)
	Multiple Dose	25.4 (11.6–61.6)	70.3 (41.9–113.5)	12.6 (7.5–23.1)	ND	ND
Plasma Clearance (mL/min/kg)	Single Dose	0.44 (0.12–1.10)	0.30 (0.14–0.42)	1.10 (0.51–2.22)	0.28 (0.16–0.40)	0.53 (0.27–1.04)
	Multiple Dose	0.58 (0.24–1.15)	0.18 (0.12–0.33)	1.21 (0.66–1.82)	ND	ND

Legend: ND=Not done.

[a]Range of individual values across studies.

[b]Valproic acid administered chronically (Multiple Dose Study) or for 2 days (Single Dose Study).

Table II—Lamictal

Effect of Concomitant AEDs on Rash Associated with Lamictal in All Controlled and Uncontrolled Clinical Trials Regardless of Dosing Escalation Scheme

AED Group	**Total Patient Number**	**All Rashes**	**Withdrawal Due to Rash**	**Hospitalization in Association with Rash**
Enzyme-Inducing AEDs[a]	1 788	9.2%	1.8%	0.1%
Enzyme-Inducing AEDs[a] + VPA	318	8.8%	3.5%	0.9%
VPA ± Non-Enzyme-Inducing AEDs[b]	159	20.8%	11.9%	2.5%
Non-Enzyme-Inducing AEDs[b]	27	18.5%	0.0%	0.0%

[a]Enzyme-inducing AEDs include carbamazepine, phenobarbital, phenytoin and primidone.

[b]Non-enzyme-inducing AEDs include clonazepam, clobazam, ethosuximide, methsuximide, vigabatrin and gabapentin.

Table III—Lamictal

Effect of the Initial Daily Dose[a] of Lamictal in the Presence of Concomitant AEDs, on the Incidence of Rash Leading to Withdrawal of Treatment in Add-On Clinical Trials

AED Group	**Enzyme-Inducing AEDs**[b]		**Enzyme-Inducing AEDs**[b] **+ VPA**		**VPA ± Non-Enzyme-Inducing AEDs**[c]	
Lamictal Average Daily Dose (mg)	**Total Patient Number**	**Percentage of Patients Withdrawn**	**Total Patient Number**	**Percentage of Patients Withdrawn**	**Total Patient Number**	**Percentage of Patients Withdrawn**
12.5	9	0.0	10	0.0	51	7.8
25	3	0.0	7	0.0	58	12.1
50	182	1.1	111	0.9	35	5.7
100	993	1.4	179	4.5	15	40.0
≥125	601	2.8	11	18.2	0	0.0

[a]Average daily dose in week 1.

[b]Enzyme-inducing AEDs include carbamazepine, phenobarbital, phenytoin and primidone.

[c]Non-enzyme-inducing AEDs include clonazepam, clobazam, ethosuximide, methsuximide, vigabatrin and gabapentin.

trials suggest that as many as 1 in 50 to 1 in 100 pediatric patients may develop a potentially life-threatening rash. it bears emphasis, that lamotrigine is not currently approved for use in patients below the age of 18 (see Precautions).

A higher incidence of serious dermatologic events (see Precautions, Skin-related Events, Tables II and III (on previous page); see also Dosage) has been associated with more rapid initial titration dosing (exceeding the recommended initial dose or exceeding the recommended dose escalation), and use of concomitant valproic acid.

Nearly all cases of serious rashes associated with lamotrigine have occurred within 2 to 8 weeks of treatment initiation. However, isolated cases have been reported after prolonged treatment (e.g., 6 months). Accordingly, duration of therapy cannot be relied upon as a means to predict the potential risk signalled by the first appearance of a rash.

Although benign rashes also occur with lamotrigine, it is not possible to predict reliably which rashes will prove to be life-threatening. Accordingly, all patients who develop rash should be promptly evaluated and lamotrigine withdrawn immediately, unless the rash is clearly not drug related.

Hypersensitivity Reactions: Rash has also been reported as part of a hypersenstitivity syndrome associated with a variable pattern of systemic symptoms including fever, lymphadenopathy, facial edema and abnormalities of the blood and liver. The syndrome shows a wide spectrum of clinical severity and may rarely lead to disseminated intravascular coagulation (DIC) and multiorgan failure. It is important to note that early manifestations of hypersensitivity (e.g., fever, lymphadenopathy) may be present even though rash is not evident. If such signs and symptoms are present, the patient should be evaluated immediately and lamotrigine discontinued if an alternative etiology cannot be established.

Prior to initiation of treatment with lamotrigine, the patient should be instructed that a rash or other signs or symptoms of hypersensitivity (e.g., fever, lymphadenopathy) may herald a serious medical event and that the patient should report any such occurrence to a physician immediately.

Precautions: Drug Discontinuation: Abrupt discontinuation of any antiepileptic drug (AED) in a responsive patient with epilepsy may provoke rebound seizures. In general, withdrawal of an AED should be gradual to minimize this risk. Unless safety concerns require a more rapid withdrawal, the dose of lamotrigine should be tapered over a period of at least 2 weeks (see Dosage).

Occupational Hazards: Patients with uncontrolled epilepsy should not drive or handle potentially dangerous machinery. During clinical trials common adverse effects included dizziness, ataxia, drowsiness, diplopia and blurred vision. Patients should be advised to refrain from activities requiring mental alertness or physical coordination until they are sure that lamotrigine does not affect them adversely.

Skin-Related Events: In controlled studies of adjunctive lamotrigine therapy, the incidence of rash (usually maculopapular and/or erythematous) in patients receiving lamotrigine was 10% compared with 5% in placebo patients. The rash usually occurred within the first 6 weeks of therapy and resolved during continued administration of lamotrigine. Lamotrigine was discontinued because of rash in 1.1% of patients in controlled studies and 3.8% of all patients in all studies. The rate of rash-related withdrawal in clinical studies was higher with more rapid initial titration dosing, and in patients receiving concomitant valproic acid (VPA), particularly in the absence of enzyme-inducing AEDs (see Table II and III (on previous page); see also Warnings and Dosage).

Increased incidence of rash-related withdrawal was seen when initial doses were higher and titration more rapid than recommended under Dosage.

Drug Interactions: Antiepileptic Drugs (AEDs): Lamotrigine does not affect the plasma concentrations of concomitantly administered enzyme-inducing AEDs. Antiepileptic drugs that induce hepatic drug-metabolizing enzymes (phenytoin, carbamazepine, phenobarbital, primidone) increase the plasma clearance and reduce the elimination half-life of lamotrigine (see Pharmacology).

Valproic acid reduces the plasma clearance and prolongs the elimination half-life of lamotrigine (see Pharmacology). When lamotrigine was administered to 18 healthy volunteers already receiving valproic acid, a modest decrease (25% on average) in the trough steady-state valproic acid plasma concentrations was observed over a 3-week period, followed by stabilization. However, the addition of lamotrigine did not affect the plasma concentration of valproic acid in patients receiving enzyme-inducing AEDs in combination with valproic acid (see Precautions, Skin-Related Events).

Table IV—Lamictal

Treatment-Emergent Adverse Experience Incidence in Placebo-Controlled Clinical Studies[a]

Body System/Adverse Experience[b]	Percent of Patients Receiving Lamictal (and other AEDs) (n=711)	Percent of Patients Receiving Placebo (and other AEDs) (n=419)	Percent of Patients Receiving Lamictal (and other AEDs) Who Were Discontinued (n=711)
Body as a Whole			
Headache	29.1	19.1	1.3
Accidental Injury	9.1	8.6	0.1
Asthenia	8.6	8.8	0.3
Flu Syndrome	7.0	5.5	0.0
Pain	6.2	2.9	0.1
Back Pain	5.8	6.2	0.0
Fever	5.5	3.6	0.1
Abdominal Pain	5.2	3.6	0.1
Infection	4.4	4.1	0.0
Neck Pain	2.4	1.2	0.0
Malaise	2.3	1.9	0.3
Seizure Exacerbation	2.3	0.5	0.3
Digestive			
Nausea	18.6	9.5	1.3
Vomiting	9.4	4.3	0.3
Diarrhea	6.3	4.1	0.3
Dyspepsia	5.3	2.1	0.1
Constipation	4.1	3.1	0.0
Tooth Disorder	3.2	1.7	0.0
Musculoskeletal			
Myalgia	2.8	3.1	0.0
Arthralgia	2.0	0.2	0.0
Nervous			
Dizziness	38.4	13.4	2.4
Ataxia	21.7	5.5	0.6
Somnolence	14.2	6.9	0.0
Incoordination	6.0	2.1	0.3
Insomnia	5.6	1.9	0.4
Tremor	4.4	1.4	0.0
Depression	4.2	2.6	0.0
Anxiety	3.8	2.6	0.0
Convulsion	3.2	1.2	0.3
Irritability	3.0	1.9	0.1
Speech Disorder	2.5	0.2	0.1
Memory Decreased	2.4	1.9	0.0
Respiratory			
Rhinitis	13.6	9.3	0.0
Pharyngitis	9.8	8.8	0.0
Cough Increased	7.5	5.7	0.0
Respiratory Disorder	5.3	5.5	0.1
Skin and Appendages			
Rash	10.0	5.0	1.1
Pruritus	3.1	1.7	0.3
Special Senses			
Diplopia	27.6	6.7	0.7
Blurred Vision	15.5	4.5	1.1
Vision Abnormality	3.4	1.0	0.0
Urogenital			
Female Patients	**(n=365)**	**(n=207)**	
Dysmenorrhea	6.6	6.3	0.0
Menstrual Disorder	5.2	5.8	0.0
Vaginitis	4.1	0.5	0.0

[a] Patients in these studies were receiving 1 to 3 concomitant enzyme-inducing antiepileptic drugs in addition to Lamictal or placebo. Patients may have reported multiple adverse experiences during the study or at discontinuation. Thus, patients may be included in more than one category.

[b] Adverse Experiences reported by at least 2% of patients treated with Lamictal are included.

Oral Contraceptives: In a study of 12 female volunteers, lamotrigine did not affect plasma concentrations of ethinyl estradiol and levonorgestrel following administration of the oral contraceptive pill. However, as with the introduction of other chronic therapy in patients taking oral contraceptives, the patient should be asked to report any change in the menstrual bleeding pattern.

Drugs Depressing Cardiac Conduction: See Patients with Special Diseases and Conditions.

Drug/Laboratory Test Interactions: Lamotrigine has not been associated with any assay interferences in clinical laboratory tests.

Geriatrics: The safety and efficacy of lamotrigine in elderly patients with epilepsy have not been systematically evaluated in clinical trials. Caution should thus be exercised in dose selection for an elderly patient, recognizing the more frequent hepatic, renal and cardiac dysfunctions and limited experience with lamotrigine in this population.

Children: The safety and efficacy of lamotrigine in children under 18 years of age have not yet been established (see Warnings).

Obstetrics: *Pregnancy:* Studies in mice, rats and rabbits given lamotrigine orally or i.v. revealed no evidence of teratogenicity; however, maternal and secondary fetal toxicity were observed. Studies in rats and rabbits indicate that lamotrigine crosses the placenta; placental and fetal levels of lamotrigine were low and comparable to levels in maternal plasma. Because animal reproduction studies are not always predictive of human response, lamotrigine should only be used during pregnancy if the benefits of therapy outweigh the risks associated with it.

Clinical trials data indicate that lamotrigine has no effect on blood folate concentrations in adults; however, its effects during human fetal development are unknown.

Labor and Delivery: The effect of lamotrigine on labor and delivery in humans is unknown.

Lamictal (cont'd)

Lactation: Lamotrigine is excreted in human milk. Because of the potential for adverse reactions from lamotrigine in nursing infants, breast-feeding while taking this medication is not recommended.

Patients with Special Diseases and Conditions: Clinical experience with lamotrigine in patients with concomitant illness is limited. Caution is advised when using lamotrigine in patients with diseases or conditions that could affect the metabolism or elimination of the drug.

Renal Failure: A study in individuals with chronic renal failure (not receiving other AEDs) indicated that the elimination half-life of unchanged lamotrigine is prolonged relative to individuals with normal renal function (see Pharmacology). Use of lamotrigine in patients with severe renal impairment should proceed with caution.

Impaired Liver Function: There is no experience with the use of lamotrigine in patients with impaired liver function. Caution should be exercised in dose selection for patients with this condition.

Cardiac Conduction Abnormalities: One placebo-controlled trial that compared electrocardiograms at baseline and during treatment, demonstrated a mild prolongation of the PR interval associated with lamotrigine administration. The prolongation was statistically significant but clinically insignificant. Patients with significant cardiovascular disease or electrocardiographic abnormalities were, however, systematically excluded from clinical trials. Thus, lamotrigine should be used with caution in patients with cardiac conduction abnormalities, and in patients taking concomitant medications which depress AV conduction.

Dependence Liability: No evidence of abuse potential has been associated with lamotrigine, nor is there evidence of psychological or physical dependence in humans.

Laboratory Tests: The use of lamotrigine does not require routine monitoring of any clinical laboratory parameters or plasma levels of concomitant AEDs.

Adverse Effects: Rarely, serious skin rashes, including Stevens-Johnson syndrome and toxic epidermal necrolysis (Lyell's syndrome) have been reported. The latter condition carries a high mortality (see Warnings).

Adverse experiences in patients receiving lamotrigine were generally mild, occurred within the first 2 weeks of therapy, and resolved without discontinuation of the drug.

Commonly Observed: The most commonly observed adverse experiences associated with the use of adjunctive therapy with lamotrigine (incidence of at least 10%) were dizziness, headache, diplopia, somnolence, ataxia, nausea and asthenia.

Dizziness, diplopia, ataxia and blurred vision were dose-related and occurred more commonly in patients receiving carbamazepine in combination with lamotrigine than in patients receiving other enzyme-inducing AEDs with lamotrigine. Reduction of the daily dose and/or alteration of the timing of doses of concomitant antiepileptic drugs and/or lamotrigine may reduce or eliminate these symptoms. Clinical data suggest a higher incidence of rash in patients who are receiving concomitant valproic acid, or non-inducing AEDs (see Warnings and Precautions, Skin-Related Events, Table II).

Adverse Events Associated with Discontinuation of Treatment: Across all studies, the most common adverse experiences associated with discontinuation of lamotrigine were rash, dizziness, headache, ataxia, nausea, diplopia, somnolence, seizure exacerbation, asthenia and blurred vision. In controlled clinical trials, 6.9% of the 711 patients receiving lamotrigine discontinued therapy due to an adverse experience, versus 2.9% of the 419 patients receiving placebo. Of 3 501 patients and volunteers who received lamotrigine in premarketing clinical studies, 358 (10.2%) discontinued therapy due to an adverse experience.

Serious Adverse Events Associated with Discontinuation of Treatment: Discontinuation due to an adverse experience classified as serious occurred in 2.3% of patients and volunteers who received lamotrigine in the premarketing studies. Rash accounted for almost half of the discontinuations due to serious adverse experiences. More rapid initial titration dosing of lamotrigine, and concomitant use of valproic acid were associated with higher incidences of rash-related withdrawal in clinical studies (see Warnings and Precautions, Skin-Related Events, Table III on previous pages).

Controlled Add-on Clinical Studies: Table IV (on previous page) enumerates adverse experiences that occurred with an incidence of 2% or greater among refractory patients with epilepsy treated with lamotrigine.

Other Events Observed During Clinical Studies: During clinical testing, multiple doses of lamotrigine were administered to 3 501 patients and volunteers. The conditions and duration of exposure to lamotrigine during these clinical studies varied greatly. Studies included monotherapy and pediatric trials. A substantial proportion of the exposure was gained in open, uncontrolled clinical studies. Adverse experiences associated with exposure to lamotrigine were recorded by clinical investigators using terminology of their own choosing. Consequently, it is not possible to provide a meaningful estimate of the proportion of individuals experiencing adverse events without first grouping similar types of adverse experiences into a smaller number of standardized event categories.

Since the adverse experiences reported occurred during treatment with lamotrigine in combination with other antiepileptic drugs, they were not necessarily caused by lamotrigine.

The following adverse events have been reported on one or more occasions by at least 1% of patients and volunteers exposed to lamotrigine: anorexia, weight gain, amnesia, concentration disturbance, confusion, emotional lability, nervousness, nystagmus, paresthesia, thinking abnormality and vertigo. (All types of events are included except those already listed in Table IV on previous page.)

Monotherapy Clinical Studies: Withdrawals due to adverse events were reported in 42 (9.5%) of newly diagnosed patients treated with lamotrigine monotherapy. The most common adverse experiences associated with discontinuation of lamotrigine were rash (6.1%), asthenia (1.1%), headache (1.1%), nausea (0.7%) and vomiting (0.7%).

Other Events Observed During Clinical Practice and from "Compassionate Plea" Patients: In addition to the adverse experiences reported during clinical testing of lamotrigine, the following adverse experiences have been reported in patients receiving lamotrigine marketed in other countries and from worldwide "compassionate plea" patients. These adverse experiences have not been listed above and data are insufficient to support an estimate of their incidence or to establish causation. The listing is alphabetized: apnea, erythema multiforme, esophagitis, hematemesis, hemolytic anemia, pancreatitis, pancytopenia and progressive immunosuppression.

Overdose: Symptoms and Treatment: During the clinical development program, the highest known overdose of lamotrigine occurred in a 33-year old female who ingested between 4 000 and 5 000 mg lamotrigine that corresponded to a plasma level of 52 μg/mL 4 hours after the ingestion. The patient presented to the emergency room comatose and remained comatose for 8 to 12 hours, returned to almost normal over the next 24 hours, and completely recovered by the third day.

There are no specific antidotes for lamotrigine. Following a suspected overdose, hospitalization of the patient is advised. General supportive care is indicated, including frequent monitoring of vital signs and close observation of the patient. If indicated, emesis should be induced or gastric lavage should be performed. It is uncertain whether hemodialysis is an effective means of removing lamotrigine from the blood. In 6 renal failure patients, about 20% of the amount of lamotrigine in the body was removed during 4 hours of hemodialysis.

Dosage: Adults: Lamotrigine is intended for oral administration and may be taken with or without food. Lamotrigine should be added to the patient's current antiepileptic therapy.

Valproic acid more than doubles the elimination half-life of lamotrigine and reduces the plasma clearance by 50%; conversely, hepatic enzyme-inducing drugs such as carbamazepine, phenytoin, phenobarbital, and primidone reduce the elimination half-life of lamotrigine by 50% and double the plasma clearance (see Pharmacology). These clinically important interactions require dosage schedules of lamotrigine as summarized in Table V.

Lamotrigine does not alter plasma concentrations of concomitantly administered enzyme-inducing AEDs, and therefore, they do not usually require dose adjustment to maintain therapeutic plasma concentrations. For patients receiving lamotrigine in combination with other AEDs, an evaluation of all AEDs in the regimen should be considered if a change in seizure control or an appearance or worsening of adverse experiences is observed. If there is a need to discontinue therapy with lamotrigine, a step-wise reduction of dose over at least 2 weeks (approximately 50% per week) is recommended unless safety concerns require a more rapid withdrawal (see Precautions).

The relationship of plasma concentration to clinical response has not been established for lamotrigine. Dosing of lamotrigine should be based on therapeutic response. In controlled clinical studies, doses of lamotrigine that were efficacious generally produced steady-state trough plasma lamotrigine concentrations of 1 to 4 μg/mL in patients receiving one or more concomitant AEDs. Doses of lamotrigine producing this plasma concentration range were well tolerated. As with any antiepileptic drug, the oral dose of lamotrigine should be adjusted to the needs of the individual patient, taking into consideration the concomitant AED therapy the patient is receiving.

Because of an increased risk of rash, the recommended initial dose and subsequent dose escalations of lamotrigine should not be exceeded (see Warnings).

There have been no controlled studies to establish the effectiveness or optimal dosing regimen of add-on lamotrigine therapy in patients receiving only non-enzyme-inducing AEDs or valproic acid. However, available data from open clinical trials indicate that the addition of lamotrigine under these conditions is associated with a higher incidence of serious rash or rash-related withdrawal, even at an initial titration dose of 12.5 mg daily (see Precautions, Skin Related Events, Table III; see also Warnings). The potential medical benefits of addition of lamotrigine under these conditions must be weighed against the increased risk of serious rash. If use of lamotrigine under these conditions is considered clinically indicated, titration dosing should proceed with extreme caution, especially during the first 6 weeks of treatment.

Withdrawal of Concomitant AEDs: Concomitant AEDs may be decreased over a 5-week period, by approximately 20% of the original dose every week. However, a slower taper may be used if clinically indicated. During this period, the dose of lamotrigine administered will be dependent upon the effect of the drug being withdrawn on the pharmacokinetics of lamotrigine, together with the overall clinical response of the patient. The withdrawal of enzyme inducing AEDs (i.e., phenytoin, phenobarbital, primidone, and carbamazepine) will result in an approximate doubling of the $t_{1/2}$ of lamotrigine. Under these conditions, it may be necessary to reduce the dose of lamotrigine. In contrast, the withdrawal of enzyme inhibiting AEDs (i.e., valproic acid) will result in a decrease in the $t_{1/2}$ of lamotrigine and may require an increase in the dose of lamotrigine.

Geriatrics: There is little experience with the use of lamotrigine in elderly patients. Caution should thus be exercised in dose selection for an elderly patient, recognizing the more frequent hepatic, renal and cardiac dysfunctions.

Patients with Impaired Renal Function: The elimination half-life of lamotrigine is prolonged in patients with impaired renal

Table V—Lamictal

Recommended Dosage Schedule for Adults			For Information[b]
	Patients Taking		
Treatment Week	Enzyme-Inducing AEDs[a] With Valproic Acid	Enzyme-Inducing AEDs[a] Without Valproic Acid	Patients Taking Valproic Acid Only
Weeks 1 + 2	25 mg once a day	50 mg once a day	25 mg every other day
Weeks 3 + 4	25 mg twice a day	50 mg twice a day	25 mg once a day
Usual Maintenance	50–100 mg twice a day To achieve maintenance doses may be increased by 25–50 mg every 1 to 2 weeks.	150–250 mg twice a day To achieve maintenance, doses may be increased by 100 mg every 1 to 2 weeks.	50–100 mg twice a day To achieve maintenance, doses may be increased by 25–50 mg every 1 to 2 weeks.

[a]Enzyme-inducing AEDs include carbamazepine, phenobarbital, phenytoin, and primidone.
[b]Column reflects dosage recommendations in the United Kingdom and is provided for information.

function (see Pharmacology). Caution should be exercised in dose selection for patients with impaired renal function.

Patients with Impaired Hepatic Function: There is no experience with the use of lamotrigine in patients with impaired liver function. Because lamotrigine is metabolized by the liver, caution should be exercised in dose selection for patients with this condition.

Children: Dosage recommendations for children under 18 years of age are not yet established.

Information for the Patient: See Blue Section—Information for the Patient "Lamictal".

Supplied: 25 mg: Each white, scored, shield-shaped tablet, engraved with "LAMICTAL" and "25", contains: lamotrigine 25 mg. Nonmedicinal ingredients: cellulose, lactose, magnesium stearate, povidone and sodium starch glycolate. Bottles of 100.

100 mg: Each peach, scored, shield-shaped tablet, engraved with "LAMICTAL" and "100", contains: lamotrigine 100 mg. Nonmedicinal ingredients: cellulose, lactose, magnesium stearate, povidone, sunset yellow FCF lake and sodium starch glycolate. Bottles of 100.

150 mg: Each cream, scored, shield-shaped tablet, engraved with "LAMICTAL" and "150", contains: lamotrigine 150 mg. Nonmedicinal ingredients: cellulose, ferric oxide (yellow), lactose, magnesium stearate, povidone and sodium starch glycolate. Bottles of 60.

Store at controlled room temperature (15 to 30°C) in a dry place and protect from light.

(Shown in Product Recognition Section)

Reviewed 1998

LAMISIL® Ⓟ

Novartis Pharmaceuticals

Terbinafine HCl

Antifungal

Pharmacology: Terbinafine is an allylamine which has a broad spectrum of antifungal activity. At low concentrations terbinafine is fungicidal against dermatophytes, molds and certain dimorphic fungi. The activity against yeasts is fungicidal or fungistatic, depending on the species.

Terbinafine interferes specifically with fungal sterol biosynthesis by inhibition of squalene epoxidase in the fungal cell membrane. This leads to a deficiency in ergosterol and to an intracellular accumulation of squalene, resulting in fungal cell death. The enzyme squalene epoxidase is not linked to the cytochrome P450 system, hence terbinafine does not influence the metabolism of hormones or other drugs. When given orally, the drug concentrates rapidly in skin, hair and nails at levels associated with fungicidal activity.

The cream has a rapid onset of action and can be effective with a short duration of treatment.

Pharmacokinetics: Oral: A single oral dose of 250 mg terbinafine results in peak plasma concentrations of 0.97 μg/mL within 2 hours after administration. The absorption half-life is 0.8 hour and the distribution half-life is 4.6 hours. The bioavailability of terbinafine is moderately increased by a fat-rich meal, but not sufficiently to require dosing adjustments.

Terbinafine binds strongly to plasma proteins (99%). It rapidly diffuses through the dermis and concentrates in the lipophilic stratum corneum. Terbinafine is also secreted in sebum, thus achieving high concentrations in hair follicles, hair and in sebum-rich skin. There is also evidence that terbinafine is distributed into the nail plate within the first few weeks of commencing therapy, resulting in a rapid onset of action.

Biotransformation results in metabolites with no antifungal activity, which are excreted predominantly in the urine. The terminal elimination half-life is 17 hours. There is no evidence of accumulation. No age-dependent changes in pharmacokinetics have been observed but the elimination rate may be reduced in patients with renal or hepatic impairment, resulting in higher blood levels of terbinafine (see Warnings).

Topical: Less than 5% of the dose is absorbed after topical application to humans; systemic exposure is thus very slight.

Indications: The treatment of fungal infections of the skin and nails caused by dermatophytes such as Trichophyton (e.g., T. rubrum, T. mentagrophytes, T. verrucosum, T. violaceum), M. canis and E. floccosum.

Oral: Oral terbinafine is indicated in the treatment of onychomycosis (fungal infection of the nail) caused by dermatophyte fungi. Where oral therapy is considered appropriate owing to the site, severity or extent of the infection, terbinafine tablets may also be indicated in the treatment of tineal skin infections (tinea corporis, tinea cruris and tinea pedis).

Note: Oral terbinafine is not effective in pityriasis versicolor.

Topical: Cream: Topical terbinafine is indicated in the treatment of fungal infections of the skin caused by dermatophytes such as Trichophyton, as well as yeast infections of the skin, principally those caused by the genus Candida (e.g., Candida albicans). The cream is also indicated in the treatment of pityriasis (tinea) versicolor due to P. orbiculare (also known as M. furfur).

Spray: The spray is indicated in the treatment of fungal infections of the skin caused by dermatophytes such as trichophyton. The spray is also indicated in the treatment of pityriasis (tinea) versicolor due to P. orbiculare (also known as M. furfur).

Note: Topical terbinafine is not effective in onychomycosis.

Contraindications: In patients with a hypersensitivity to terbinafine or any of the excipients (see Supplied).

Warnings: Clinical studies in patients with liver dysfunction and impaired renal function suggest that the elimination rate of orally administered terbinafine may be reduced in these patients. Consequently, patients with pre-existing stable chronic liver dysfunction or impaired renal function (creatinine clearance less than 50 mL/minute or serum creatinine of more than 300 μmol/L) should receive half the regular dose of oral terbinafine and be carefully monitored (see Precautions and Dosage).

Cases of significant hepatobiliary dysfunction as well as isolated cases of blood dyscrasias have been reported in patients treated with oral terbinafine (see Precautions and Adverse Effects).

Precautions: General: Terbinafine should be kept out of the reach of children.

Terbinafine cream and spray are for external use only. Contact with the eyes should be avoided. The spray should not be used on the face. In case of accidental contact with the eyes, rinse eyes thoroughly with running water and consult a physician if any symptoms persist. In case of accidental inhalation, patients should be advised to consult a physician if any symptoms develop and persist.

The spray should be used with caution in patients with lesions where alcohol could be irritating.

Patients should report any signs and symptoms which may suggest hepatobiliary dysfunction or a blood dyscrasia so that terbinafine treatment can be discontinued and/or appropriate laboratory testing can be done. Such signs and symptoms would include unusual fatigue, anorexia, jaundice, dark urine, pale stools and pruritus, or sore throat and fever.

In those patients at a higher risk for developing hepatic dysfunction (e.g., those receiving terbinafine concomitantly with potentially hepatotoxic drugs; those with a history of significant alcohol intake or suspicion of liver disorder) performing liver function tests at baseline and periodically during terbinafine treatment may be of value.

Pregnancy and *Lactation:* Fetal toxicity and fertility studies in animals suggest no adverse effects.

There is very limited clinical experience with terbinafine in pregnant women; therefore, unless the potential benefits outweigh any potential risks, terbinafine tablets should not be used during pregnancy.

Terbinafine is excreted in breast milk; therefore, mothers receiving oral treatment with terbinafine should not breastfeed. However, with the cream and spray treatment, the small amounts absorbed through the skin are unlikely to affect the infant.

Geriatrics: There is no evidence to suggest that healthy elderly patients require different dosages or experience adverse effects different from those of younger patients. The possibility of pre-existing impairment of liver or kidney function should be considered in this age group (see Warnings).

Children: There is limited experience with terbinafine in children.

Drug Interactions: Tablets: According to the results from studies undertaken in vitro and in healthy volunteers, terbinafine shows negligible potential to inhibit or induce the clearance of drugs that are metabolized via the cytochrome P450 system (e.g., cyclosporine, tolbutamide or oral contraceptives). Some cases of menstrual irregularities have been reported in patients taking terbinafine concomitantly with oral contraceptives, although the incidence of these disorders remains within the background incidence of patients taking oral contraceptives alone. On the other hand, the plasma clearance of terbinafine may be accelerated by drugs which induce metabolism (such as rifampicin) and may be reduced by drugs which inhibit cytochrome P450 (such as cimetidine). Where coadministration of such agents is necessary the dosage of terbinafine may need to be adjusted accordingly.

Cream and Spray: No drug interactions are known to date.

Carcinogenesis: An increase in liver tumors was observed in male rats at the highest dose level (69 mg/kg) during the lifetime (123 weeks) carcinogenicity study. The changes included increased enzyme activity, peroxisome proliferation and altered triglyceride metabolism. The changes have been shown to be species specific since they were not seen in mice or monkeys.

Adverse Effects: Tablets: In general terbinafine is well tolerated. Side effects are mild to moderate in severity, and transient. The most common are gastrointestinal symptoms (fullness, loss of appetite, dyspepsia, nausea, mild abdominal pain, diarrhea) or nonserious forms of skin reactions (rash, urticaria).

There have been isolated reports of serious skin reactions (e.g., Stevens-Johnson Syndrome, Toxic Epidermal Necrolysis). If progressive skin rash occurs, treatment with terbinafine should be discontinued.

A few cases of hair loss have been reported, although a clear causal relationship remains to be established.

Rarely, terbinafine may cause taste disturbances, including taste loss, which usually recover within several weeks after discontinuation of the drug.

Oral terbinafine has been rarely associated with systemic allergic reactions, including urticaria, angioedema, arthralgia, arthritis, serum-sickness like reactions and anaphylactoid reactions.

Hepatobiliary dysfunction has been rarely reported in association with terbinafine treatment. Liver function tests should be performed if a patient develops unexplained nausea, anorexia or tiredness. If liver function tests are found to be abnormal in a patient, or if a patient presents with overt symptoms of liver dysfunction, terbinafine should be discontinued.

The estimated reporting incidence of the development of clinically significant signs and symptoms of hepatobiliary dysfunction for which no other cause was apparent, and in which terbinafine was considered the possible causative agent is approximately 1:45 000. Extremely rare cases (less than 1:1 000 000 exposed patients) of liver failure with fatal outcome have been reported following treatment with oral terbinafine. A causal relationship has not been established.

Worldwide, of the estimated 4.7 million patients treated with terbinafine as of August 1996, there have been 8 cases of agranulocytosis, 1 case of pancytopenia and 10 cases of thrombocytopenia, which are possibly related to terbinafine. One case of thrombotic thrombocytopenic purpura (TTP) has been reported. The mechanism of TTP and its induction are not completely known. The role of terbinafine in the development of TTP in the reported case cannot be established.

In clinical trials adverse events occurred in 10.4% of patients receiving the recommended dose. Of these, 5% were mild to moderate gastrointestinal events, 3% were skin reactions (rash or urticaria) and the remainder were miscellaneous nonspecific events such as malaise or tiredness.

Table I (on following page) lists adverse events observed in clinical trials with oral terbinafine, by organ system.

Cream and Spray: Redness, itching or stinging occasionally occur at the site of application; however, treatment rarely has to be discontinued for this reason. These symptoms should be distinguished from allergic reactions which are rare but require discontinuation of the drug. In clinical trials, adverse reactions were recorded in 33 of the 1 757 (1.8%) patients who received terbinafine cream and in 39 of the 898 (4.3%) patients who received the terbinafine spray.

Overdose: Symptoms and Treatment: A few cases of accidental overdosage of up to 5 g have been reported. After intake, the patients presented with headache, nausea, epigastric pain and dizziness. The recommended treatment of overdosage consists of eliminating the drug primarily by the administration of activated charcoal and, if needed, of symptomatic supportive therapy.

No case of overdoage has been reported with terbinafine cream or spray. Should, however, terbinafine cream or spray be inadvertently ingested, adverse effects similar to those observed with an overdosage of terbinafine tablets are to be expected. The alcohol content (23.5%) of the spray has to be taken into account.

Dosage: Tablets: The bioavailability of terbinafine is moderately increased by a fat-rich meal, but not sufficiently to require dosing adjustments.

Adults: 250 mg daily.

Note: In tineal skin infections, terbinafine tablets should be used when oral therapy is considered appropriate owing to the site, severity or extent of the infection.

Lamisil (cont'd)

Table I—Lamisil Tablets

Adverse Effects

Organ System Adverse Event	**Lamisil 250 mg (n=998)**	(%)
Skin (overall)	27	2.7
Erythema or rash	9	0.9
Urticaria	5	0.5
Eczema	1	0.1
Pruritus	4	0.4
Other	8	0.8
Gastrointestinal (overall)	52	5.2
Diarrhea and/or cramps	10	1.0
Nausea and/or vomiting	11	1.1
Fullness	5	0.5
Sickness	1	0.1
Gastrointestinal irritation, dyspepsia, gastritis	22	2.2
Other	3	0.3
CNS (overall)	12	1.2
Headache	9	0.9
Concentration	2	0.2
Other	1	0.1
Other (overall)	11	1.1
Tiredness, fatigue	3	0.3
Pain (back, knee, legs, feet, kidney)	1	0.1
Change of taste or dry mouth	1	0.1
Other	6	0.6
Laboratory Adverse Changes (overall)	2	0.2
Hypoglycemia	1	0.1
Elevated liver enzymes	1	0.1
Total	104	10.4

Patients with Renal or Hepatic Impairment: The elimination rate may be reduced in patients with renal or hepatic impairment. The dose should be reduced by half in these patients (see Warnings and Precautions).

Duration of Treatment: The duration of treatment varies according to the indication and the severity of infection (see Table II).

Table II—Lamisil Tablets

Duration of Treatment

Indication	**Duration of Treatment**
Onychomycosis (of fingers and toes)[a]	6 weeks-3 months
Skin Infections[b]	
Tinea pedis (interdigital and plantar/moccasin type)	2-6 weeks
Tinea corporis, cruris	2-4 weeks

[a] In patients with fingernail infections or toenail infections other than the big toe, or in younger patients, treatment periods of less than 3 months may be adequate. In patients with infections of the big toenail, treatment for 3 months is usually sufficient, although some patients may require treatment for 6 months or longer. Poor nail outgrowth during the first weeks of treatment may enable identification of those patients in whom longer therapy is required.

In onychomycosis the optimal clinical effect is seen some months after mycological cure and cessation of treatment. This is related to the period required for outgrowth of healthy nail tissue.

[b] Complete resolution of the signs and symptoms may not occur until several weeks after mycological cure.

Cream: The cream can be applied once or twice daily. The affected areas should be cleansed and dried thoroughly before application of terbinafine cream. The cream should be applied to the affected skin and surrounding area in a thin layer and rubbed in lightly. In the case of intertriginous infections (submammary, interdigital, intergluteal, inguinal) the application may be covered with a gauze strip, especially at night.

The duration of treatment varies with the indication and is dependent on the severity of the infection (see Table III).

Table III—Lamisil Cream

Duration of Treatment

Indication	**Duration of Treatment**
Tinea corporis/cruris	1 week
Tinea pedis	1 week
Cutaneous Candidiasis	1-2 weeks*
Pityriasis versicolor	2 weeks

*Two weeks of treatment with terbinafine cream produced slightly improved efficacy over treatment for 1 week. The difference in outcome may not be clinically significant.

Many patients treated with shorter durations of therapy (1 to 2 weeks) continue to improve during the 2 to 4 weeks after therapy has been completed. As a consequence, patients should not be considered therapeutic failures until they have been observed for a period of 2 to 4 weeks after cessation of treatment.

Relief of clinical symptoms usually occurs within a few days. Irregular use or premature discontinuation of treatment increases the risk of recurrence. If there are no signs of improvement after 2 weeks, the diagnosis should be verified.

Spray: The spray is applied once or twice daily, depending on the indication. The affected areas should be cleansed and dried thoroughly before application of the spray. A sufficient amount of solution should be applied to wet the treatment area(s) thoroughly, and to cover the affected skin and surrounding area.

The duration of treatment varies with the indication and is dependent on the severity of the infection (see Table IV).

Table IV—Lamisil Spray

Duration of Treatment

Indications	**Duration of Treatment**
Tinea pedis	1 week once a day
Tinea corporis/cruris	1 week once a day
Pityriasis versicolor	1 week twice a day

Relief of clinical symptoms usually occurs within a few days. Irregular use or premature discontinuation of treatment increases the risk of recurrence. If there are no signs of improvement after 2 weeks the diagnosis should be verified.

Information for the Patient: See Blue Section—Information for the Patient "Lamisil Tablets".

Supplied: Cream: Each g of white, smooth, glossy cream contains: terbinafine HCl 10 mg. Nonmedicinal ingredients: benzyl alcohol, cetyl alcohol, cetyl palmitate, isopropyl myristate, polysorbate 60, purified water, sodium hydroxide, sorbitan monostearate and stearyl alcohol. Tubes of 30 g. Store at temperatures between 15 and 30°C.

Spray: Each g of clear solution contains: terbinafine HCl 10 mg. Nonmedicinal ingredients: cetomacrogol 1 000, ethanol, propylene glycol and water. Alcohol: 23.5% w/w. Bottles of 30 mL. Store at temperatures between 15 and 30°C.

Tablets: Each round, whitish/yellow uncoated tablet, scored on one side and embossed "Lamisil 250", contains: terbinafine 250 mg, present as the hydrochloride salt. Nonmedicinal ingredients: cellulose microcrystalline, magnesium stearate, methylhydroxypropylcellulose, silica, colloidal anhydrous and sodium carboxymethyl starch. Blister strips of 14, cartons of 14 and 28. Store at temperatures between 15 and 30°C. Protect from light.

(Shown in Product Recognition Section)

Reviewed 1999

LANOHEX® SKIN CLEANSER
Rougier

Phenoxetol
Antibacterial Skin Cleanser

Indications: An all-purpose skin cleanser for personal hygiene, diaper rash and acne treatment as well as folliculitis and impetigo.

Precautions: If a mild irritation appears discontinue use for a few days. Apply an emollient lotion, and resume using this product. Avoid scrubbing. During extremely cold or extremely dry weather, the auxiliary use of an emollient cream or lotion is recommended. If foam gets into the eyes, rinse thoroughly with lukewarm water only.

Dosage: Wet area requiring cleansing. Pour a few drops of Lanohex on the hands or on a soft facecloth. Massage gently for 1 minute to cause abundant foaming. Rinse thoroughly. Repeat the operation for 1 minute. Rinse thoroughly. Dry gently with a towel. Never use a brush to cause foaming. Always rinse skin thoroughly before drying.

Supplied: Each bottle contains: phenoxetol (beta-phenoxyethanol) 1.7% in a hypoallergenic detergent base with an acid pH. Nonmedicinal ingredients: ammonium chloride, EDTA, F-106-D (detergent), glycerin, parabens (methyl, propyl, butyl), Solulan (water soluble lanolin derivative) and tartrazine. Plastic bottles of 115, 450 and 5 000 mL.

LANOXIN® Ⓟ
Glaxo Wellcome

Digoxin
Cardiotonic Glycoside

Pharmacology: The influence of digitalis glycosides on the myocardium is dose related, and involves both direct action on cardiac muscle and the specialized conduction system, and indirect actions on cardiovascular system mediated by the autonomic nervous system. The indirect actions mediated by the autonomic nervous system involve a vagomimetic action, which is responsible for the effects of digitalis on the sinoatrial (SA) and atrioventricular (AV) nodes; and also a baroreceptor sensitization which results in increased carotid sinus nerve activity and enhanced sympathetic withdrawal for any given increment in mean arterial pressure. The pharmacologic consequences of these direct and indirect effects are: an increase in the force and velocity of myocardial systolic contraction (positive inotropic action); a slowing of heart rate (negative chronotropic effect); and decreased conduction velocity through the AV node. In higher doses, digitalis increases sympathetic outflow from the CNS to both cardiac and peripheral sympathetic nerves. This increase in sympathetic activity may be an important factor in digitalis cardiac toxicity. Most of the extracardiac manifestations of digitalis toxicity are also mediated by the CNS.

Pharmacokinetics: Gastrointestinal absorption of digoxin is a passive process. Absorption of Lanoxin digoxin from tablets is 60 to 80%. When digoxin tablets are taken after meals, the rate of absorption is slowed, but the total amount of digoxin absorbed is usually unchanged. When taken with meals high in bran fibre; however, the amount absorbed from an oral dose may be reduced.

In some patients, orally administered digoxin is converted to cardioinactive reduction products (e.g., dihydrodigoxin) by colonic bacteria in the gut. Data suggest that 1 in 10 patients treated with digoxin tablets will degrade 40% or more of the ingested dose.

Following drug administration, a 6- to 8-hour distribution phase is observed. This is followed by a much more gradual serum concentration decline, which is dependent on digoxin elimination from the body. The peak height and slope of the early portion (absorption/distribution phases) of the serum concentration-time curve are dependent upon the route of administration and the absorption characteristics of the formulation. Clinical evidence indicates that the early high serum concentrations do not reflect the concentration of digoxin at its site of action, but that with chronic use, the steady-state postdistribution serum levels are in equilibrium with tissue levels and correlate with pharmacologic effects. In individual patients, these postdistribution serum concentrations are linearly related to maintenance dosage and may be useful in evaluating therapeutic and toxic effects (see Dosage, Serum digoxin concentrations).

Digoxin is concentrated in tissues and therefore has a large apparent volume of distribution. Digoxin crosses both the blood-brain barrier and the placenta. At delivery, serum digoxin concentration in the newborn is similar to the serum level in the mother. Approximately 20 to 25% of plasma digoxin is bound to protein. Serum digoxin concentrations are not significantly altered by large changes in fat tissue weight, so that its distribution space correlates best with lean (ideal) body weight, not total body weight.

Pharmacologic Response: The approximate times to onset of effect and to peak effect of all the Lanoxin preparations are given in Table I (on following page).

Table I—Lanoxin

Pharmacologic Response

Product	Time to Onset of Effect[a]	Time to Peak Effect[a]
Lanoxin Tablet	0.5–2 hours	2–6 hours
Lanoxin Elixir	0.5–2 hours	2–6 hours
Lanoxin Injection/I.M.	0.5–2 hours	2–6 hours
Lanoxin Injection/I.V.	5–30 minutes[b]	1–4 hours

[a]Documented for ventricular response rate in atrial fibrillation, inotropic effect and electrocardiograph changes.
[b]Depending upon rate of infusion.

Elimination of digoxin follows first-order kinetics (that is, the quantity of digoxin eliminated at any time is proportional to the total body content). Following i.v. administration to normal subjects, 50 to 70% of a digoxin dose is excreted unchanged in the urine. Renal excretion of digoxin is proportional to glomerular filtration rate and is largely independent of urine flow. In subjects with normal renal function, digoxin has a half-life of 1.5 to 2 days. The half-life in anuric patients is prolonged to 4 to 6 days. Digoxin is not effectively removed from the body by dialysis, exchange transfusion or during cardiopulmonary bypass because most of the drug is in the tissue rather than circulating in the blood.

Indications: Congestive Heart Failure: The increased cardiac output resulting from the inotropic action of digoxin ameliorates the disturbances characteristic of heart failure (venous congestion, edema, dyspnea, orthopnea and cardiac asthma).

Digoxin is more effective in low output (pump) failure than in "high output" heart failure secondary to arteriovenous fistula, anemia, infection hyperthyroidism, or bronchopulmonary insufficiency.

Digoxin is usually continued after failure is controlled unless some known precipitating factor is corrected. Studies have shown, however, that even though hemodynamic effects can be demonstrated in almost all patients, corresponding improvement in the signs and symptoms of heart failure is not necessarily apparent. Therefore, in patients in whom digoxin may be difficult to regulate, or in whom the risk of toxicity may be great (e.g., patients with unstable renal function or whose potassium levels tend to fluctuate) a cautious withdrawal of digoxin may be considered. If digoxin is discontinued, the patient should be regularly monitored for clinical evidence of recurrent heart failure.

Atrial Fibrillation: Digoxin reduces ventricular rate through increased AV nodal block and thereby improves hemodynamics. Palpitation, precordial distress or weakness are relieved and concomitant congestive heart failure ameliorated. Digoxin should be continued in doses necessary to maintain the desired ventricular rate.

Atrial Flutter: Digoxin slows the heart and regular sinus rhythm may appear. Frequently the flutter is converted to atrial fibrillation with a controlled ventricular response. Stopping digitalis at this point may be followed by restoration of sinus rhythm, especially if the flutter is of the paroxysmal type. It is preferable, however to continue digitalis if failure ensues or if atrial flutter is a frequent occurrence. (Electrical cardioversion is often the treatment of choice for atrial flutter. See discussion of cardioversion in Precautions).

Paroxysmal Atrial Tachycardia (PAT): Digoxin may convert PAT to sinus rhythm by slowing conduction through the AV node. If heart failure has ensued or paroxysms occur frequently, digoxin should be continued. In infants, digoxin is usually continued for 3 to 6 months after a single episode of PAT to prevent recurrence.

Contraindications: Digitalis glycosides are contraindicated in ventricular fibrillation.

In a given patient, an untoward effect requiring permanent discontinuation of other digitalis preparations usually constitutes a contraindication to digoxin. Hypersensitivity to digoxin itself is a contraindication to its use. Allergy to digoxin, though rare, does occur. It may not extend to all such preparations, and another digitalis glycoside may be tried with caution.

Warnings: Digitalis alone or with other drugs has been used in the treatment of obesity. This use of digoxin or other digitalis glycosides is unwarranted. Moreover, since they may cause potentially fatal arrhythmias or other adverse effects, the use of these drugs solely for the treatment of obesity is dangerous.

Anorexia, nausea, vomiting and arrhythmias may accompany heart failure or may be indications of digitalis intoxication. Clinical evaluation of the cause of the symptoms should be attempted before further digitalis administration. In such circumstances determination of the serum digoxin concentration may be an aid in deciding whether or not digitalis toxicity is likely to be present. If the possibility of digitalis intoxication cannot be excluded, cardiac glycosides should be temporarily withheld, if permitted by the clinical situation.

Patients with renal insufficiency require smaller than usual maintenance doses of digoxin (see Dosage).

Heart failure accompanying acute glomerulonephritis requires extreme care in digitalization. Relatively low loading and maintenance doses and concomitant use of antihypertensive drugs may be necessary and careful monitoring is essential. Digoxin should be discontinued as soon as possible, especially if a therapeutic trial does not result in improvement. Patients with severe carditis, such as carditis associated with rheumatic fever or viral myocarditis, are especially sensitive to digoxin-induced disturbances of rhythm.

Newborn infants display considerable variability in their tolerance to digoxin. Premature and immature infants are particularly sensitive and dosage must not only be reduced but must be individualized according to their degree of maturity. Impaired renal function must also be carefully taken into consideration.

Note: Digitalis glycosides are an important cause of accidental poisoning in children.

Precautions: General: If the patient has been given digoxin during the previous week or any other less rapidly excreted drug of the digitalis group during the previous 2 weeks, the dose of digoxin must be reduced accordingly. Digoxin toxicity develops more frequently and lasts longer in patients with renal impairment because of the decreased excretion of digoxin. Therefore, it should be anticipated that dosage requirements will be decreased in patients with moderate to severe renal disease (see Dosage). Because of impaired renal function and excretion in elderly patients, they frequently require lower than recommended doses. Because of the prolonged half-life, a longer period of time is required to achieve an initial or new steady-state concentration in patients with renal impairment than in patients with normal renal function.

In patients with hypokalemia, toxicity may occur despite serum digoxin concentrations within the normal range, because potassium depletion sensitizes the myocardium to digoxin. Therefore, it is desirable to maintain normal serum potassium levels in patients being treated with digoxin. Hypokalemia may result from diuretic, amphotericin B or corticosteroid therapy, and from peritoneal or hemodialysis or mechanical suction of gastrointestinal secretions. It may also accompany malnutrition, diarrhea, prolonged vomiting, old age, long-standing heart failure, long-standing wasting diseases and treatment with ion-exchange resins or carbenoxolone. In general, rapid changes in serum potassium or other electrolytes should be avoided, and i.v. treatment with potassium should be reserved for special circumstances as described below (see Overdose: Symptoms and Treatment).

Calcium, particularly when administered rapidly by the i.v. route, may produce serious arrhythmias in digitalized patients. Hypercalcemia from any cause predisposes the patient to digitalis toxicity. On the other hand, hypocalcemia can nullify the effects of digoxin in man; thus digoxin may be ineffective until serum calcium is restored to normal. These interactions are related to the fact that calcium affects contractility and excitability of the heart in a manner similar to digoxin.

Hypomagnesemia may predispose to digitalis toxicity. If low magnesium levels are detected in a patient on digoxin, replacement therapy should be instituted.

Quinidine and verapamil cause a rise in serum digoxin concentration, with the implication that digitalis intoxication may result. This rise appears to be proportional to the dose. The effect is mediated by a reduction in digoxin clearance and, in the case of quinidine, decreased volume of distribution as well. Due to the considerable variability of these interactions, digoxin dosage should be carefully individualized when patients receive coadministered medications.

Certain antibiotics may increase digoxin absorption in patients who convert digoxin to inactive metabolites in the gut (see Pharmacology, Pharmacokinetics). Recent studies have shown that specific colonic bacteria in the lower gastrointestinal tract convert digoxin to cardioinactive reduction products, thereby reducing its bioavailability. Although inactivation of these bacteria by antibiotics is rapid, the serum digoxin concentration will rise at a rate consistent with the elimination half-life of digoxin. The magnitude of rise in serum digoxin concentrations relates to the extent of bacterial inactivation, and may be as much as 2-fold in some cases.

Patients with acute myocardial infarction or severe pulmonary disease may be unusually sensitive to digoxin-induced disturbances of rhythm. Atrial arrhythmias associated with hypermetabolic states (e.g., hyperthyroidism) are particularly resistant to digoxin treatment. Large doses of digoxin are not recommended as the only treatment of these arrhythmias and care must be taken to avoid toxicity if large doses of digoxin are required. In hypothyroidism the digoxin requirements are reduced. Digoxin responses in patients with compensated thyroid disease are normal.

Reduction of digoxin dosage may be desirable prior to electrical cardioversion to avoid induction of ventricular arrhythmias, but the physician must consider the consequences of rapid increase in ventricular response to atrial fibrillation if digoxin is withheld 1 to 2 days prior to cardioversion. If there is a suspicion that digitalis toxicity exists, elective cardioversion should be delayed. If it is not prudent to delay cardioversion, the energy level selected should be minimal at first and carefully increased in an attempt to avoid precipitating ventricular arrhythmias.

Incomplete AV block, especially in patients with Stokes-Adams attacks, may progress to advanced or complete heart block if digoxin is given. Heart failure in these patients can usually be controlled by other measures and by increasing the heart rate. If digitalization is essential, electrical pacing of the ventricles may be indicated. In some patients with sinus node disease (i.e., Sick Sinus Syndrome), digoxin may worsen sinus bradycardia or sinoatrial block.

In patients with Wolff-Parkinson-White Syndrome and atrial fibrillation, digoxin can enhance transmission of impulses through the accessory pathway. This effect may result in extremely rapid ventricular rates and even ventricular fibrillation.

Digoxin may worsen the outflow obstruction in patients with idiopathic hypertrophic subaortic stenosis (IHSS). Unless cardiac failure is severe, it is doubtful whether digoxin should be employed.

Patients with chronic constrictive pericarditis may fail to respond to digoxin. In addition, slowing of the heart rate by digoxin in some patients may further decrease cardiac output.

Patients with heart failure from amyloid heart disease or constrictive cardiomyopathies respond poorly to treatment with digoxin.

Digoxin is not indicated for the treatment of sinus tachycardia unless it is associated with heart failure.

Digoxin may produce false positive ST-T changes in the electrocardiogram during exercise testing.

Dosage of digoxin must be carefully titrated and differences in the bioavailability of parenteral preparations, elixirs and tablets taken into account when changing patients from one preparation to another. I.M. injection of digoxin is extremely painful and offers no advantages unless other routes of administration are contraindicated.

Laboratory Tests: Patients receiving digoxin should have their serum electrolytes and renal function (BUN and/or serum creatinine) assessed periodically; the frequency of assessments will depend on the clinical setting. For discussion of serum digoxin concentrations, see Dosage.

Drug Interactions: Potassium-depleting corticosteroids and diuretics may be major contributing factors to digitalis toxicity. Calcium, particularly if administered rapidly by the i.v. route, may produce serious arrhythmias in digitalized patients. Quinidine and verapamil cause a rise in serum digoxin concentration, with the implication that digitalis intoxication may result. Certain antibiotics increase digoxin absorption in patients who inactivate digoxin by bacterial metabolism in the lower intestine, so that digitalis intoxication may result. Propantheline and diphenoxylate, by decreasing gut motility, may increase digoxin absorption. Antacids, kaolin-pectin, sulfasalazine, neomycin, cholestryramine, phenytoin and certain anticancer drugs may interfere with intestinal digoxin absorption, resulting in unexpectedly low serum concentrations. Thyroid administration to a digitalized hypothyroid patient may increase the dose requirement of digoxin. Concomitant use of digoxin and sympathomimetics increases the risk of cardiac arrhythmias because both enhance ectopic pacemaker activity. Succinylcholine may cause a sudden extrusion of potassium from muscle cells and may thereby cause arrhythmias in digitalized patients. Although β-adrenergic blockers or calcium channel blockers and digoxin may be useful in combination to control atrial fibrillation, their additive effects on AV node conduction can result in complete heart block.

Carcinogenesis, Mutagenesis, Impairment of Fertility: There have been no long-term studies performed in animals to evaluate carcinogenic potential.

Pregnancy: Teratogenic Effects: Animal reproduction studies have not been conducted with digoxin. It is also not known whether digoxin can cause fetal harm when administered to a pregnant woman or can affect reproduction capacity, although there have been no reports of teratogenic effects following the use of digoxin in pregnancy since its availability in 1929. Digoxin should be given to pregnant women only if clearly needed.

Lanoxin (cont'd)

Lactation: Studies have shown that digoxin concentrations in the mother's serum and milk are similar. However, the estimated daily dose to a nursing infant will be far below the usual infant maintenance dose. Therefore, this amount should have no pharmacologic effect upon the infant. Nevertheless, caution should be exercised when digoxin is administered to a nursing woman.

Adverse Effects: The frequency and severity of adverse reactions to digoxin depend on the dose and route of administration, as well as on the patient's underlying disease or concomitant therapies (see Precautions). The overall incidence of adverse reactions have been reported as 5 to 20% with 15 to 20% of them being considered serious (1 to 4% of patients receiving digoxin). Evidence suggests that the incidence of toxicity has decreased since the introduction of the serum digoxin assay and improved standardization of digoxin tablets. Cardiac toxicity accounts for about one-half, gastrointestinal disturbances for about one-fourth, and CNS and other toxicity for about one-fourth of these adverse reactions.

Adults: Cardiac: Unifocal or multiform ventricular premature contractions, especially in bigeminal or trigeminal patterns, are the most common arrhythmias associated with digoxin toxicity in adults with heart disease. Persistent bigeminy at rest but not on exercise when the sinus rate increases has traditionally been acceptable in the management of some arrhythmias. This suggests approaching toxicity and a lower dose of digoxin plus a small dose of a beta-blocker may give better control.

Ventricular tachycardia may result from digitalis toxicity. Atrioventricular (AV) dissociation, accelerated junctional (nodal) rhythm and atrial tachycardia with block are also common arrhythmias caused by digoxin overdosage.

Excessive slowing of the pulse is a clinical sign of digoxin overdosage. AV block (Wenckebach) of increasing degree may proceed to complete heart block.

Note: The electrocardiogram is fundamental in determining the presence and nature of these cardiac disturbances. Digoxin may also induce other changes in the ECG (e.g., PR prolongation, ST depression), which represent digoxin effect and may or may not be associated with digitalis toxicity.

Gastrointestinal: Anorexia, nausea, vomiting, and less commonly, diarrhea are common early symptoms of overdosage. However, uncontrolled heart failure may also produce such symptoms.

It is inadvisable to rely on nausea as an early warning of excessive digoxin as arrhythmias may occur first.

CNS: Visual disturbances (blurred or yellow vision), headache, weakness, apathy and psychosis can occur.

Other: Gynecomastia is occasionally observed.

Infants and Children: Toxicity differs from the adult in a number of respects. Anorexia, nausea, vomiting, diarrhea and CNS disturbances may be present but are rare as initial symptoms in infants. Cardiac arrhythmias are more reliable signs of toxicity. Digoxin in children may produce any arrhythmia. The most commonly encountered are conduction disturbances or supraventricular tachyarrhythmias, such as atrial tachycardia with or without block and junctional (nodal) tachycardia. Ventricular arrhythmias are less common. Sinus bradycardia may also be a sign of impending digoxin intoxication, especially in infants, even in the absence of first-degree heart block. Any arrhythmia or alteration in cardiac conduction that develops in a child taking digoxin should initially be assumed to be a consequence of digoxin intoxication.

Overdose: Symptoms and Treatment: Arrhythmias: Adults: Digoxin should be discontinued until all signs of toxicity are gone. Discontinuation may be all that is necessary if toxic manifestations are not severe and appear only near the expected time for maximum effect of the drug.

Correction of factors that may contribute to toxicity such as electrolyte disturbances, hypoxia, acid-base disturbances and removal of aggravating agents such as catecholamines, should also be considered. Potassium salts may be indicated particularly if hypokalemia is present. Potassium administration may be dangerous in the setting of massive digitalis overdosage (see Massive Overdose subsection below). Potassium chloride in divided oral doses totaling 3 to 6 g of the salt (40 to 80 mEq K^+) for adults may be given provided renal function is adequate (see Infants and Children subsection below for potassium recommendation).

When correction of the arrhythmia is urgent and the serum potassium concentration is low or normal, potassium should be administered i.v. in 5% dextrose injection. For adults, a total of 40 to 80 mEq (diluted to a concentration of 40 mEq/500 mL) may be given at a rate not exceeding 20 mEq/hour, or slower if limited by pain due to local irritation. Additional amounts may be given if the arrhythmia is uncontrolled and potassium well-tolerated. ECG monitoring should be performed to watch for any evidence of potassium toxicity (e.g., peaking of T waves) and to observe the effect on the arrhythmia. The infusion may be stopped when the desired effect is achieved.

Note: Potassium should not be used and may be dangerous in heart block due to digoxin, unless primarily related to supraventricular tachycardia.

Other agents that have been used for the treatment of digoxin intoxication include lidocaine, procainamide, propranolol and phenytoin, although use of the latter must be considered experimental. Quinidine, procainamide, and beta-adrenergic blocking agents should be used with caution when AV block is a component of digitalis intoxication as they may exaggerate this arrhythmic property.

In advanced heart block, atropine and/or temporary ventricular pacing may be beneficial. Digibind (digoxin immune Fab [ovine]) can be used to reverse potentially life-threatening digoxin (or digitoxin) intoxication. Improvement in signs and symptoms of digitalis toxicity usually begins within 0.5 hour of Digibind administration. Each 38 mg vial of Digibind will neutralize 0.5 mg digoxin (which is a usual body store of an adequately digitalized 70 kg patient). For further information consult the Digibind package insert or product monograph.

Infants and Children: See Adults section for general recommendations for the treatment of arrhythmias produced by overdosage and for cautions regarding the use of potassium.

If a potassium preparation is used to treat toxicity, it may be given orally in divided doses totaling 1 to 1.5 mEq K^+/kg body weight (1 g of potassium chloride contains 13.4 mEq K^+). When correction of the arrhythmia with potassium is urgent, approximately 0.5 mEq/kg of potassium/hour may be given i.v., with careful ECG monitoring. The i.v. solution of potassium should be dilute enough to avoid local irritation; however, especially in infants, care must be taken to avoid i.v. fluid overload.

Massive Digitalis Overdose: Manifestations of life-threatening toxicity include severe ventricular arrhythmias such as ventricular tachycardia or ventricular fibrillation, or progressive bradyarrhythmias such as severe sinus bradycardia or second- or third-degree heart block not responsive to atropine. An overdosage of more than 10 mg of digoxin in previously healthy adults or 4 mg in previously healthy children or overdosage resulting in steady-state serum concentrations greater than 10 ng/mL, often results in cardiac arrest.

Severe digitalis intoxication can cause life-threatening elevation in serum potassium concentration by shifting potassium from inside to outside the cell resulting in hyperkalemia. Administration of potassium supplements in the setting of massive intoxication may be hazardous.

Digibind, (digoxin immune Fab [Ovine]), may be used at a dose equimolar to digoxin in the body to reverse the effects of ingestion of a massive overdose. The decision to administer Digibind before the onset of toxic manifestations will depend on the likelihood that life-threatening toxicity will occur (see above). For further information consult the Digibind package insert or product monograph.

Patients with massive digitalis ingestion should receive large doses of activated charcoal to prevent absorption and bind digoxin in the gut during enteroenteric recirculation. Emesis or gastric lavage may be indicated especially if ingestion has occurred within 30 minutes of the patient's presentation at the hospital. Emesis should not be induced in patients who are obtunded. If a patient presents more than 2 hours after ingestion or already has toxic manifestations, it may be unsafe to induce vomiting or attempt passage of a gastric tube, because such maneuvres may induce an acute vagal episode that can worsen digitalis-toxic arrhythmias.

Dosage: Recommended dosages are average values that may require considerable modification because of individual sensitivity or associated conditions. Diminished renal function is the most important factor requiring modification of recommended doses.

In deciding the dose of digoxin, several factors must be considered:

1. The disease being treated. Atrial arrhythmias may require larger doses than heart failure.
2. The body weight of the patient. Doses should be calculated based upon lean or ideal body weight.
3. The patient's renal function, preferably evaluated on the basis of creatinine clearance.
4. Age is an important factor in infants and children.
5. Concomitant disease states, drugs or other factors likely to alter the expected clinical response to digoxin (see Precautions and Drug Interactions).

Digitalization may be accomplished by either of 2 general approaches that vary in dosage and frequency of administration, but reach the same endpoint in terms of total amount of digoxin accumulated in the body.

1. Rapid digitalization may be achieved by administering a loading dose based upon projected peak body digoxin stores, then calculating the maintenance dose as a percentage of the loading dose.
2. More gradual digitalization may be obtained by beginning an appropriate maintenance dose, thus allowing digoxin body stores to accumulate slowly. Steady-state serum digoxin concentrations will be achieved in approximately 5 half-lives of the drug for the individual patient. Depending upon the patient's renal function, this will take between 1 and 3 weeks.

Adults: Rapid Digitalization with a Loading Dose: Peak body digoxin stores of 8 to 12 µg/kg should provide therapeutic effect with minimum risk of toxicity in most patients with heart failure and normal sinus rhythm. Larger stores (10 to 15 µg/kg) are often required for adequate control of ventricular rate in patients with atrial flutter or fibrillation. Because of altered digoxin distribution and elimination, projected peak body stores for patients with renal insufficiency should be conservative [(i.e., 6 to 10 µg/kg) (see Precautions)].

The loading dose should be based on the projected peak body stores and administered in several portions, with roughly half the total given as the first dose. Additional fractions of this planned total dose may be given at 6- to 8-hour intervals, **with careful assessment of clinical response before each additional dose.**

If the patient's clinical response necessitates a change from the calculated dose of digoxin, then calculation of the maintenance dose should be based upon the amount actually given.

In previously undigitalized patients, a single initial Lanoxin Tablet dose of 0.5 to 0.75 mg (500 to 750 µg) usually produces a detectable effect in 0.5 to 2 hours that becomes maximal in 2 to 6 hours. Additional doses of 0.125 to 0.375 mg (125 to 375 µg) may be given cautiously at 6- to 8-hour intervals until clinical evidence of an adequate effect is noted. The usual amount of Lanoxin Tablets that a 70 kg patient requires to achieve 8 to 15 µg/kg peak body stores is 0.75 to 1.25 mg (750 to 1 250 µg).

Although peak body stores are mathematically related to loading doses and are utilized to calculate maintenance doses, they do not correlate with measured serum concentrations. This discrepancy is caused by digoxin distribution within the body during the first 6 to 8 hours following a dose. Serum concentrations drawn during this time are usually not interpretable.

The maintenance dose should be based upon the percentage of the peak body stores lost each day through elimination. The following formula has had wide clinical use:

$$\text{Maintenance dose} = \frac{\text{Peak body stores}}{\text{(i.e., Loading Dose)}} \times \frac{\text{\% Daily Loss}}{100}$$

Where % Daily Loss = 14+Ccr/5

Ccr is creatinine clearance, corrected to 70 kg body weight or 1.73 m^2 body surface area. For adults, if only serum creatinine concentrations (Scr) are available, a Ccr (corrected to 70 kg body weight) may be estimated in men as (140-Age)/Scr. For women, this result should be multiplied by 0.85.

Note: This equation cannot be used for estimating creatinine clearance in infants or children.

A common practice involves the use of Lanoxin Injection to achieve rapid digitalization, with conversion to Lanoxin Tablets for maintenance therapy. If patients are switched from i.v. to oral digoxin formulations, allowances must be made for the differences in bioavailability when calculating maintenance dosages.

Gradual Digitalization with a Maintenance Dose: Table II (on following page) provides average Lanoxin Tablet daily maintenance dose requirements for patients with heart failure based upon lean body weight and renal function.

Example: Based on Table II (on following page), a patient in heart failure with an estimated lean body weight of 70 kg and a Ccr of 60 mL/min, should be given a 0.25 mg (250 µg) Lanoxin Tablet each day, usually taken after the morning meal. Steady-state serum concentration should not be anticipated before 11 days.

Table II—Lanoxin

Usual Lanoxin Maintenance Dose Requirements (μg) for Estimated Peak Body Stores of 10 μg/kg

		Lean Body Weight (kg)							
		50	60	70	80	90	100		
	0	63[a,b]	125	125	125	188[c]	188	22	
	10	125	125	125	188	188	188	19	
	20	125	125	188	188	188	250	16	Number
Corrected	30	125	188	188	188	250	250	14	days
Ccr	40	125	188	188	250	250	250	13	before
(mL/min/	50	188	188	250	250	250	250	12	steady-
70 kg)	60	188	188	250	250	250	375	11	state
	70	188	250	250	250	250	375	10	achieved
	80	188	250	250	250	375	375	9	
	90	188	250	250	250	375	500	8	
	100	250	250	250	375	375	500	7	

[a]63 μg=0.063 mg.
[b]½ of 125 μg tablet or 125 μg every other day.
[c]1½ of 125 μg tablet.

Infants and Children: Digitalization must be individualized. Divided daily dosing is recommended for infants and young children. Children over 10 years of age require adult dosages in proportion to their body weight.

In the newborn period, renal clearance of digoxin is diminished and suitable dosage adjustments must be observed. This is especially pronounced in the premature infant. Beyond the immediate newborn period, children generally require proportionally larger doses than adults on the basis of body weight or body surface area.

Lanoxin Injection Pediatric can be used to achieve rapid digitalization, with conversion to an oral Lanoxin formulation for maintenance therapy. If patients are switched from i.v. to oral digoxin tablets or elixir, allowances must be made for differences in bioavailability when calculating maintenance dosages.

I.M. injection of digoxin is extremely painful and offers no advantages unless other routes of administration are contraindicated.

Digitalizing and daily maintenance doses for each age group are given in Table III and should provide therapeutic effect with minimum risk of toxicity in most patients with heart failure and normal sinus rhythm. Larger doses are often required for adequate control of ventricular rate in patients with atrial flutter or fibrillation.

The loading dose should be administered in several portions, with roughly half the total given as the first dose. Additional fractions of this planned total dose may be given at 6- to 8-hour intervals, **with careful assessment of clinical response before each additional dose.** If the patient's clinical response necessitates a change from the calculated dose of digoxin, then calculation of the maintenance dose should be based upon the amount actually given.

Table III—Lanoxin

Usual Digitalizing and Maintenance Dosages for Lanoxin Tablets in Children with Normal Renal Function Based on Lean Body Weight

Age	Digitalizing[a] Dose (μg/kg)	Daily[b] Maintenance Dose (μg/kg)
2 to 5 years	30 to 40	25 to 35% of oral loading dose[c]
5 to 10 years	20 to 35	
Over 10 years	10 to 15	

[a]I.V. digitalizing doses are 80% of oral digitalizing doses.
[b]Divided daily dosing is recommended in children under 10 years of age.
[c]Projected or actual digitalizing dose providing clinical response.

More gradual digitalization can also be accomplished by beginning an appropriate maintenance dose. The range of percentages provided in Table III can be used in calculating this dose for patients with normal renal function. In children with renal disease, digoxin dosing must be carefully titrated based upon clinical response.

Long-term use of digoxin is indicated in many children who have been digitalized for acute heart failure, unless the cause is transient. Children with severe congenital heart disease, even after surgery, may require digoxin for prolonged periods.

It cannot be overemphasized that both the adult and pediatric dosage guidelines provided are based upon average patient response and substantial individual variation can be expected. Accordingly, ultimate dosage selection must be based upon clinical assessment of the patient.

Serum Digoxin Concentrations: Measurement of serum digoxin concentrations can be helpful to the clinician in determining the state of digitalization and in assigning certain probabilities to the likelihood of digoxin intoxication. Studies in adults considered adequately digitalized (without evidence of toxicity) show that about two-thirds of such patients have serum digoxin levels ranging from 0.8 to 2.0 ng/mL. Patients with atrial fibrillation or atrial flutter require and appear to tolerate higher levels than do patients with other indications. On the other hand, in adult patients with clinical evidence of digoxin toxicity, about two-thirds will have serum digoxin levels greater than 2.0 ng/mL. Thus, whereas levels less than 0.8 ng/mL are infrequently associated with toxicity, levels greater than 2.0 ng/mL are often associated with toxicity. Values in between are not very helpful in deciding whether a certain sign or symptom is more likely to be caused by digoxin toxicity or by something else. There are rare patients who are unable to tolerate digoxin even at serum concentrations below 0.8 ng/mL. Some researchers suggest that infants and young children tolerate slightly higher serum concentrations than do adults.

To allow adequate time for equilibration of digoxin between serum and tissue, **sampling of serum concentrations for clinical use should be at least 6 to 8 hours after the last dose,** regardless of the route of administration or formulation used. On a twice daily dosing schedule, there will be only minor differences in the serum digoxin concentrations whether sampling is done at 8 or 12 hours after a dose. After a single daily dose, the concentration will be 10 to 25% lower when sampled at 24 hours versus 8 hours, depending upon the patient's renal function. Ideally, sampling for assessment of steady state concentration should be done just before the next dose.

If a discrepancy exists between the reported serum concentration and the observed clinical response, the clinician should consider the following possibilities: 1. Analytical problems in the assay procedure. 2. Inappropriate serum sampling time. 3. Administration of a digitalis glycoside other than digoxin. 4. Conditions (described in Warnings and Precautions) causing an alteration in the sensitivity of the patient to digoxin. 5. The patient falls outside the norm in his response to or handling of digoxin. This decision should be reached only after exclusion of the other possibilities and generally should be confirmed by additional correlations of clinical observations with serum digoxin concentrations.

The serum concentration data should always be interpreted in the overall clinical context and an isolated serum concentration value should not be used alone as a basis for increasing or decreasing digoxin dosage.

Adjustment of Maintenance Dose in Previously Digitalized Patients: Digoxin maintenance doses in individual patients on steady-state digoxin can be adjusted upward or downward in proportion to the ratio of the desired versus the measured serum concentration. For example, a patient at steady-state on 0.125 mg (125 μg) of digoxin/day with the measured serum concentration of 0.7 ng/mL, should have the dose increased to 0.25 mg/day (250 μg) to achieve a steady-state serum concentration of 1.4 ng/mL, **assuming the serum digoxin concentration measurement is correct, renal function remains stable during this time and the needed adjustment is not the result of a problem with compliance.**

Dosage Adjustment When Changing Preparations: The difference in bioavailability between injectable Lanoxin and Lanoxin Elixir Pediatric or Lanoxin Tablets must be considered when changing patients from one dosage form to another.

I.M. injection of digoxin is extremely painful and offers no advantages unless other routes of administration are contraindicated.

Supplied: Injections: Each mL contains: digoxin CSD 0.05 mg (50 μg) (pediatric) or 0.25 mg (250 μg). Nonmedicinal ingredients: alcohol, anhydrous citric acid, propylene glycol and sodium phosphate. Lanoxin pediatric injection: ampuls of 1 mL. Lanoxin injection: ampuls of 2 mL. Store between 15 to 30°C and protect from light.

Pediatric Elixir: Each mL of clear, light-green colored liquid with a lime odor and taste, contains: digoxin 0.05 mg (50 μg). Nonmedicinal ingredients: alcohol 11.5 mL/100 mL of elixir, citric acid, D&C Green No. 5, D&C Yellow No. 10, lime oil concentrate, methylparaben, propylene glycol, sodium phosphate, sucrose and water. Tartrazine-free. Bottles of 115 mL with calibrated dropper. Store between 15 to 30°C.

Tablets: 0.0625 mg: Each round, peach, flat-faced, bevelled-edge tablet with code LANOXIN U3A, contains: digoxin 0.0625 mg (62.5 μg). Nonmedicinal ingredients, FD&C Yellow No. 6, lactose, magnesium stearate, pregelatinized starch and starch (corn and potato). Tartrazine-free. Bottles of 100.

0.125 mg: Each round, yellow, flat-faced tablet, with code LANOXIN Y3B on the same side as score mark, contains: digoxin 0.125 mg (125 μg). Nonmedicinal ingredients: FD&C Yellow No. 6, D&C Yellow No. 10, lactose, magnesium stearate, pregelatinized starch and starch (corn and potato). Tartrazine-free. Bottles of 100 and 1 000.

0.25 mg: Each round, white, biconvex tablet, with code LANOXIN X3A on same side as score mark, contains: digoxin 0.25 mg (250 μg). Nonmedicinal ingredients: lactose, magnesium stearate, pregelatinized starch and starch (corn and potato). Dye- and tartrazine-free. Bottles of 100 and 1 000.

Store between 15 to 30°C in a dry place and protect from light.

(Shown in Product Recognition Section)

Reviewed 1998

LANSOŸL®
LANSOŸL® SUGAR-FREE

Axcan Pharma

Mineral Oil

Laxative

Indications: Intestinal lubricant indicated in the treatment of occasional transient constipation as well as to lessen the strain of evacuation after surgery, during and after pregnancy, and in cases of aneurysm, myocardial infarction, hypertension, cardiovascular disease and hernia.

Contraindications: Presence of abdominal pain, fever, nausea and vomiting. Concomitant administration of a surface-active laxative, such as docusate calcium or sodium sulfosuccinate, which emulsifies the oil in droplets and increases its absorption.

Warnings: Not to be used for periods exceeding 1 week unless under physician's advice. Prolonged excessive use of mineral oil reduces absorption of fat-soluble vitamins (A, D, E and K); a vitamin K deficiency could increase the effect of anticoagulants. Oral administration must be avoided after anorectal surgery since mineral oil may cause pruritus ani and thus interfere with tissular healing.

Prolonged use of laxatives may cause chronic constipation.

Dosage: Lansoÿl: Children (6 to 12 years): 5 to 20 mL/day. Children over 12 and adults: 15 to 60 mL/day. The administration of a single dose at bedtime is recommended.

Lansoÿl Sugar-Free: Children under 6 years: consult a physician. Children (6 to 12 years): 5 to 15 mL daily. Children (12 years and older) and adults: 15 to 45 mL daily. The administration of a single dose at night upon retiring is usually recommended.

Supplied: Lansoÿl: Each 225 g bottle contains: a red raspberry-flavored jelly containing 78% of mineral oil. Nonmedicinal ingredients: citric acid, gelatin, mixture of natural and artificial aromas, red cochenille, sugar syrup and water. Sodium: <1 mmol (0.22 mg)/15 g. Energy: 38 kJ (9 kcal)/15 g. Unit dose of 15 g, boxes of 10.

Lansoÿl Sugar-Free: Each 215 g bottle contains: a red raspberry-flavored jelly containing 78% of mineral oil. Nonmedicinal ingredients: aromatic flavors, citric acid, gelatin, lactulose syrup, red cochenille A, sodium saccharine and sorbitol (4 kcal/unidose). Unit dose of 15 g, boxes of 10.

(Shown in Product Recognition Section)

Reviewed 1997

LANVIS® Pr

Glaxo Wellcome

Thioguanine

Antileukemic Agent

Pharmacology: Thioguanine is a close relative of mercaptopurine and like the latter is an antimetabolite which blocks purine metabolism. It causes depletion of human bone marrow producing neutropenia, reticulopenia, anemia, thrombocytopenia, and prolongation of clotting time. The protracted but reversible aplasia of bone marrow closely resembles the effects of ionizing radiations. In man, thioguanine is extensively converted to 2-amino-6-methyl-mercaptopurine which is much less toxic and less effective than the parent compound. Unlike mercaptopurine and azathioprine, its metabolism is not inhibited by the xanthine oxidase inhibitor, allopurinol.

Lanvis (cont'd)

Thioguanine has multiple metabolic effects and at present it is not possible to designate one major site of action. Its tumor inhibitory properties may be due to one or more of its effects on (a) feedback inhibition of de novo purine synthesis; (b) inhibition of purine nucleotide interconversions; or (c) incorporation into the DNA and the RNA. The net consequence of its actions is a sequential blockade of the synthesis and utilization of the purine nucleotides.

Clinical studies have shown that the absorption of an oral dose of thioguanine in man is incomplete and variable, averaging approximately 30% of the administered dose (range: 14 to 46%). Following oral administration of ^{35}S-6-thioguanine, total plasma radioactivity reached a maximum at 8 hours and declined slowly thereafter. The parent drug represented only a very small fraction of the total plasma radioactivity at any time, being virtually undetectable throughout the period of measurements.

Thioguanine is extensively metabolized in vivo. There are 2 principal catabolic routes: methylation to 2-amino-6-methylthiopurine and deamination to 2-hydroxy-6-mercaptopurine, followed by oxidation to 6-thiouric acid. Deamination and subsequent oxidation to thiouric acid occurs only to a small extent. The product of deamination by guanase, 6-thioxanthine is inactive, having negligible antitumor activity. This pathway of thioguanine inactivation is not dependent on the action of xanthine oxidase, and an inhibitor of that enzyme (such as allopurinol) will not block the detoxification of thioguanine even though the inactive 6-thioxanthine is normally further oxidized by xanthine oxidase to thiouric acid before it is eliminated. The product of methylation, 2-amino-6-methylthiopurine, is also substantially less active and less toxic than thioguanine, and its formation is likewise unaffected by the presence of allopurinol. Appreciable amounts of inorganic sulfate are also found in urine, presumably arising from further metabolism of the methylated derivatives.

The oral administration of radiolabeled thioguanine revealed only trace quantities of parent drug in the urine. However, the methylated metabolite, 2-amino-6-methylthiopurine (MTG), appeared very early, rose to a maximum 6 to 8 hours after drug administration, and was still being excreted after 12 to 22 hours. Radiolabeled sulfate appeared somewhat later than MTG but was the principal metabolite after 8 hours. Thiouric acid and some unidentified products were found in the urine in small amounts.

Plasma levels decay biexponentially with initial and terminal half-lives of 3 and 5 to 9 hours respectively.

Thioguanine is incorporated into the DNA and the RNA of human bone marrow cells. Studies with i.v. ^{35}S-6-thioguanine have shown that the amount of thioguanine incorporated into nucleic acids is more than 100 times higher after 5 daily doses than after a single dose. With the 5-dose schedule, from one-half to virtually all of the guanine in the residual DNA was replaced by thioguanine. Tissue distribution studies of ^{35}S-6-thioguanine in mice showed only traces of radioactivity in the brain after oral administration. Thioguanine concentrations in human cerebrospinal fluid (CSF) have not been measured, but observations on tissue distribution in animals, together with the lack of CNS penetration by the closely related compound, mercaptopurine, suggest that thioguanine does not reach therapeutic concentrations in the CSF.

Monitoring of plasma levels of thioguanine during therapy is of questionable value. There is technical difficulty in determining plasma concentrations, which are seldom greater than 1 to 2 μg/mL after a therapeutic oral dose. More significantly, thioguanine enters rapidly into the anabolic and catabolic pathways for purines, and the active intracellular metabolites have appreciably longer half-lives than the parent drug. The biochemical effects of a single dose of thioguanine are evident long after the parent drug has disappeared from the plasma. Because of this rapid metabolism of thioguanine to active intracellular derivatives, hemodialysis would not be expected to appreciably reduce toxicity of the drug.

In some animal tumors, resistance to the effect of thioguanine correlates with the loss of HGPRTase activity and the resulting inability to convert thioguanine to thioguanylic acid. However, other resistance mechanisms, such as increased catabolism of TGMP by a nonspecific phosphatase, may be operative. Although not invariable, it is usual to find cross-resistance between thioguanine and its close analogue, mercaptopurine.

Indications: For the treatment of acute leukemia. It has also been used for the treatment of chronic granulocytic (myelocytic, myeloid, myelogenous) leukemia. Although superior results are generally obtained with busulfan in the treatment of chronic granulocytic leukemia, thioguanine may be useful during periods of thrombocytopenia induced by busulfan or other therapy. Cross-resistance exists between thioguanine and mercaptopurine and generally it is not to be expected that patients who no longer respond to mercaptopurine will respond to thioguanine, or vice versa. Thioguanine is not effective for the treatment of chronic lymphocytic leukemia or solid tumors.

Contraindications: Should not be used in patients whose disease has demonstrated prior resistance to this drug. In animals and man, there is usually complete cross-resistance between mercaptopurine and thioguanine.

Should not be given to patients with previous hypersensitivity reaction to the drug or any of its components.

Warnings: Thioguanine is a potent drug and should be used only by physicians experienced with cancer chemotherapeutic drugs. Blood counts should be taken weekly. Discontinue or reduce the dosage immediately at the first sign of abnormal depression of the bone marrow.

The most consistent, dose-related toxicity is bone marrow suppression. This may be manifested by anemia, leukopenia, thrombocytopenia, or any combination of these. Any one of these findings may also reflect progression of the underlying disease. Since thioguanine may have a delayed effect, it is important to withdraw the medication temporarily at the first sign of an abnormally large decrease in any of the formed elements of the blood. Blood counts should be made at least once weekly. Life-threatening infections and bleeding have been observed as consequences of thioguanine-induced granulocytopenia and thrombocytopenia.

It is recommended that evaluation of the hemoglobin concentration or hematocrit, total white blood cell count and differential count, and quantitative platelet count be obtained frequently while the patient is on thioguanine therapy. In cases where the cause of fluctuations in the formed elements in the peripheral blood is obscure, bone marrow examination may be useful for the evaluation of marrow status. The decision to increase, decrease, continue, or discontinue a given dosage of thioguanine must be based not only on the absolute hematologic values, but also upon the rapidity with which changes are occurring. In many instances, particularly during the induction phase of acute leukemia, complete blood counts will need to be done more frequently in order to evaluate the effect of the therapy. The dosage of thioguanine may need to be reduced when this agent is combined with other drugs whose primary toxicity is myelosuppression.

The effect of thioguanine on the immunocompetence of patients is unknown.

Pregnancy: Drugs of this type have potential teratogenic activity and the benefits and risks must be weighed before use during pregnancy. Whenever possible, use of the drug should be deferred until after the first trimester of pregnancy.

Precautions: General: A few cases of jaundice have been reported in patients with leukemia who received thioguanine. Among these were 2 adult male patients and 4 children with acute myelogenous leukemia, and an adult male with acute lymphocytic leukemia who developed veno-occlusive hepatic disease while receiving chemotherapy for their leukemia. Six patients had received cytarabine prior to treatment with thioguanine, and some were receiving other chemotherapy in addition to thioguanine when they became symptomatic. While veno-occlusive hepatic disease has not been reported in patients treated with thioguanine alone, it is recommended that thioguanine be withheld if there is evidence of toxic hepatitis or biliary stasis, and that appropriate clinical and laboratory investigations be initiated to establish the etiology of the hepatic dysfunction. Deterioration in liver function studies during thioguanine therapy should prompt discontinuation of treatment and a search for an explanation of the hepatotoxicity.

During remission induction particularly, when rapid cell lysis is occurring, adequate precautions should be taken to avoid hyperuricemia and/or hyperuricosuria and the risk of uric acid nephropathy.

There are rare individuals with an inherited deficiency of the enzyme thiopurine methyltransferase (TPMT) who may be unusually sensitive to the myelosuppressive effect of thioguanine and prone to developing rapid bone marrow depression following the initiation of treatment with thioguanine.

Since the enzyme hypoxanthine guanine phosphoribosyltransferase is responsible for the conversion of thioguanine to its active metabolite, it is possible that patients deficient in this enzyme, such as those suffering from Lesch-Nyhan syndrome, may be resistant to thioguanine.

Pregnancy: As with all cytotoxic chemotherapy, adequate contraceptive precautions should be advised when either partner is receiving thioguanine (see Warnings).

Lactation: It is not known whether thioguanine is excreted in human milk. Because of the potential for tumorigenicity shown for thioguanine, a decision should be made whether to discontinue nursing or to discontinue the drug, taking into account the importance of the drug to the mother.

Carcinogenesis, Mutagenesis, Impairment of Fertility: In view of its action on cellular DNA, thioguanine is potentially mutagenic and carcinogenic, and consideration should be given to the theoretical risk of carcinogenesis when thioguanine is administered.

Patients with Special Diseases and Conditions: Consideration should be given to reducing the dosage in patients with impaired hepatic or renal function.

Drug Interactions: Mercaptopurine: There is usually complete cross-resistance between mercaptopurine and thioguanine.

Busulfan: In one study, 12 of approximately 330 patients receiving continuous busulfan and thioguanine therapy for treatment of chronic myelogenous leukemia were found to have esophageal varices associated with abnormal liver function tests. Subsequent liver biopsies were performed in 4 of these patients, all of which showed evidence of nodular regenerative hyperplasia. Duration of combination therapy prior to the appearance of esophageal varices ranged from 6 to 45 months. With the present analysis of the data, no cases of hepatotoxicity have appeared in the busulfan alone arm of the study. Long-term continuous therapy with thioguanine and busulfan should be used with caution.

Laboratory Tests: It is advisable to monitor liver function tests (serum transaminases, alkaline phosphatase, bilirubin) at weekly intervals when first beginning therapy and at monthly intervals thereafter. It may be advisable to perform liver function tests more frequently in patients with known pre-existing liver disease or in patients who are receiving thioguanine with other hepatotoxic drugs. Patients should be instructed to discontinue thioguanine immediately if clinical jaundice is detected (see Precautions, General).

Adverse Effects: The most frequent adverse reaction to thioguanine is myelosuppression. The induction of complete remission of acute myelogenous leukemia usually requires combination chemotherapy in dosages which produce marrow hypoplasia. Since consolidation and maintenance of remission are also affected by multiple drug regimens whose component agents cause myelosuppression, pancytopenia is observed in nearly all patients. Dosages and schedules must be adjusted to prevent life-threatening cytopenias whenever these adverse reactions are observed.

Hyperuricemia frequently occurs in patients receiving thioguanine as a consequence of rapid cell lysis accompanying the antineoplastic effect. Adverse effects can be minimized by increased hydration, urine alkalinization, and the prophylactic administration of a xanthine oxidase inhibitor such as allopurinol. Unlike mercaptopurine and azathioprine, thioguanine may be continued in the usual dosage when allopurinol is used conjointly to inhibit uric acid formation.

Gastrointestinal: Less frequent adverse reactions include nausea, vomiting, anorexia, and stomatitis. Intestinal necrosis and perforation have been reported in patients who received multiple drug chemotherapy including thioguanine. Esophageal varices have been reported in patients receiving continuous busulfan and thioguanine therapy for treatment of chronic myelogenous leukemia (see Precautions, Drug Interactions).

While on the whole no significant clinical difference between thioguanine and mercaptopurine has been noted with respect to action or side effects, it has been observed that occasionally patients may experience better gastrointestinal tolerance to one or another drug of this type.

Hepatic Effects: Liver enzyme and other liver function studies are occasionally abnormal. If jaundice, hepatomegaly, or anorexia with tenderness in the right hypochondrium occurs, thioguanine should be withheld until the exact etiology can be determined. There have been reports of veno-occlusive liver disease occurring in patients who received combination chemotherapy including thioguanine (see Precautions, General).

One case of centrilobular hepatic necrosis was reported in a patient who had been treated for acute myelogenous leukemia with high cumulative doses of thioguanine and cytosine arabinoside. This patient was also taking oral contraceptives.

Overdose: Symptoms and Treatment: Signs and symptoms of overdosage may be immediate, such as nausea, vomiting, malaise, hypertension, and diaphoresis; or delayed, such as myelosuppression and azotemia. It is not known whether thioguanine is dialyzable. Hemodialysis is thought to be of marginal use due to the rapid incorporation of thioguanine into active metabolites with long persistence.

There is no known pharmacologic antagonist of thioguanine. The drug should be discontinued immediately if unintended toxicity occurs during treatment. Severe hematologic toxicity may require supportive therapy with platelet transfusions for bleeding, and granulocyte transfusions and antibiotics if sepsis is documented. If a patient is seen immediately following an accidental overdosage of the drug, it may be useful to induce emesis.

Dosage: The dosage must be carefully adjusted for each patient to obtain optimum benefit without toxic effects. The usual initial dose is approximately 2 mg/kg body weight/day, orally. If after 4 weeks on this dosage there is no clinical improvement and no leukocyte depression, the dosage may be cautiously increased to 3 mg/kg/day.

The total daily dose may be given at one time. It is usually calculated to the closest multiple of 20 mg. Although the effect usually occurs slowly over a period of 2 to 4 weeks, occasionally there may be a rapid fall in leukocyte count within 1 or 2 weeks. This may occur in some adults with acute leukemia and high total leukocyte counts as well as in certain adults with chronic granulocytic leukemia. For this reason it is important to observe such patients closely.

It is advisable to provide maintenance therapy, usually 2 mg/kg/day to provide a sustained remission and avoid early relapse. Unlike mercaptopurine and azathioprine, thioguanine may be continued in the usual dosage when allopurinol is used conjointly to inhibit uric acid formation.

Special Instructions: All materials which have come in contact with cytotoxic drugs should be segregated and incinerated at 1 000°C or more.

Tablets should be returned to the manufacturer for destruction. Proper precautions should be taken in packaging these materials for transport.

Personnel regularly involved in the preparation and handling of cytotoxic agents should have biannual blood examinations.

Care should be taken when handling or halving the tablets so as not to contaminate hands or to inhale the drug.

Supplied: Each pale, greenish-yellow, biconvex tablet, plain on one side and scored on the other side, with Wellcome on the upper half and U3B on the lower half, contains: thioguanine 40 mg. Nonmedicinal ingredients: gum acacia, lactose, magnesium stearate, potato starch and stearic acid. Bottles of 25. Store between 15 and 25°C, in a dry place.

(Shown in Product Recognition Section)

Reviewed 1998

LARGACTIL® Ⓟ

Rhône-Poulenc Rorer

Chlorpromazine

Antipsychotic—Antiemetic

Supplied: Injectable: Each mL contains: chlorpromazine base 25 mg (as the hydrochloride). Nonmedicinal ingredients: ascorbic acid, potassium metabisulfite, sodium chloride, sodium sulfite and water for injection. Ampuls of 2 mL. Boxes of 10. Protect from light or discoloration may occur. Discard if markedly discolored.

Liquid: 25 mg/5 mL: Each 5 mL of colorless liquid contains: chlorpromazine base 25 mg (as the hydrochloride). Nonmedicinal ingredients: alcohol, ascorbic acid, citric acid, ethyl vanillin, glycerin, peach flavor, purified water, sodium benzoate and sucrose. Alcohol: 0.5% v/v. Energy: 62.9 kJ (15.0 kcal)/ 5 mL. Sucrose: 3.9 g/5 mL. Tartrazine-free. Bottles of 500 mL. Protect from light or discoloration may occur. Discard if markedly discolored.

100 mg/5 mL: Each 5 mL of yellow liquid contains: chlorpromazine base 100 mg (as the hydrochloride). Nonmedicinal ingredients: alcohol, artificial fruit flavor, citric acid, D&C Yellow No. 10, ethyl vanillin, glycerin, purified water, sodium benzoate and sucrose. Alcohol: 0.5% v/v. Energy: 80.0 kJ (14.1 kcal)/5 mL. Sucrose: 3.6 g/5 mL. Tartrazine-free. Bottles of 500 mL and 2 000 mL. Protect from light or discoloration may occur. Discard if markedly discolored.

Oral Drops: Each mL of brown solution contains: chlorpromazine base 40 mg (4%) (as the hydrochloride). Nonmedicinal ingredients: alcohol, artificial and natural custard flavor, caramel, citric acid, glycerin, purified water, sucrose and terpeneless orange oil. Alcohol: 17.5% v/v. Energy: 7.2 kJ (1.7 kcal)/mL. Sucrose: 200 mg. Bottles of 100 mL with calibrated dropper. Protect from light or discoloration may occur. Discard if markedly discolored.

Suppositories: Each rectal suppository contains: chlorpromazine base 100 mg (as the hydrochloride). Nonmedicinal ingredients: hydrogenated vegetable glycerides. Tartrazine-free. Boxes of 10. Store in a cool place.

(Shown in Product Recognition Section)

LARIAM® Ⓟ

Roche

Mefloquine HCl

Antimalarial Agent

Pharmacology: Mefloquine acts on the asexual intraerythrocytic forms of the human malaria parasites: P. falciparum, P. vivax, P. malariae and P. ovale.

Mefloquine is also effective against malaria parasites resistant to other antimalarials such as chloroquine, proguanil, pyrimethamine and pyrimethamine-sulfonamide combinations.

Resistance to P. falciparum to mefloquine has been reported, mainly in parts of South-East Asia. Cross-resistance between mefloquine and halofantrine has been observed.

Pharmacokinetics: Absorption: The absolute oral bioavailabilty of mefloquine has not been determined since an i.v. formulation is not available. The bioavailability of the tablet formulation compared with an oral solution was over 85%. The presence of food significantly enhances the rate and extent of absorption, leading to about a 40% increase in bioavailability. Plasma concentrations peak 6 to 24 hours (median, about 17 hours) after a single dose of mefloquine. Maximum plasma concentrations in µg/L are roughly equivalent to the dose in mg (for example, a single 1 000 mg dose produces a maximum concentration of about 1 000 µg/L). At a dose of 250 mg once weekly, maximum steady-state plasma concentrations of 1 000 to 2 000 µg/L are reached after 7 to 10 weeks.

Distribution: In healthy adults, the apparent volume of distribution is approximately 20 L/kg, indicating extensive tissue distribution. Mefloquine may accumulate in parasitized erythrocytes at an erythrocyte-to-plasma concentration ratio of about 2. Protein binding is about 98%. clinical experience suggests a minimal suppressive plasma concentration of mefloquine in the order of 600 µg/L.

Mefloquine crosses the placenta (see Warnings, Pregnancy). Excretion into breast milk appears to be minimal (see Precautions, Lactation).

Metabolism: Two metabolites have been identified in humans. The main metabolite, 2-8-bis-trifluoromethyl-4-quinoline carboxylic acid, is inactive against P. falciparum. In a study in healthy volunteers, the carboxylic acid metabolite appeared in plasma 2 to 4 hours after a single oral dose of mefloquine. Maximum plasma concentrations of the metabolite, which were about 50% higher than those of mefloquine, were reached after 2 weeks. Thereafter, plasma levels of the main metabolite and mefloquine declined at a similar rate. The area under the plasma concentration-time curve (AUC) of the main metabolite was 3 to 5 times larger than that of the parent drug.

The other metabolite, an alcohol, was present in only minute amounts.

Elimination: In 15 studies in healthy adults, the mean elimination half-life of mefloquine varied between 2 and 4 weeks, with an average of about 3 weeks. Total clearance, which is essentially hepatic, is in the order of 30 mL/min. There is evidence that mefloquine is excreted mainly in the bile and feces. In volunteers, urinary excretion of unchanged mefloquine and its main metabolite accounted for about 9% and 4% of the dose, respectively. Concentrations of their metabolites could not be measured in the urine.

During long-term prophylaxis, the elimination half-life of mefloquine remains unchanged.

Indications: Prophylaxis: For the prophylaxis of P. falciparum and P. vivax malaria infections, including prophylaxis of chloroquine-resistant strains of P. falciparum.

Treatment of Acute Malaria Infections: For the treatment of mild to moderate acute malaria caused by mefloquine-susceptible strains of P. falciparum (both chloroquine-susceptible and resistant strains) or by P. vivax.

Note: In case of life-threatening, serious or overwhelming malaria infections due to P. falciparum, patients should be treated with an i.v. antimalarial drug. Following completion of i.v. treatment, mefloquine may be given orally to complete the course of therapy.

Patients with acute P. vivax malaria, treated with mefloquine, are at high risk of relapse because mefloquine does not eliminate exoerythrocytic (hepatic phase) parasites. To avoid relapse, after initial treatment of the acute infection with mefloquine, patients should subsequently be treated with an 8-aminoquinoline (e.g., primaquine).

There are insufficient clinical data to document the effect of mefloquine in malaria caused by P. ovale or P. malariae.

Contraindications: In patients with a known hypersensitivity to mefloquine or related compounds, e.g., quinine, quinidine, chloroquine.

Patients with a history of psychiatric disturbances (including depression) or convulsions should not be prescribed mefloquine prophylactically since mefloquine may precipitate these conditions.

Warnings: Concomitant administration of mefloquine and quinine, quinidine, chloroquine, or drugs producing beta-adrenergic blockade may produce electrocardiographic abnormalities or cardiac arrest. Because of the danger of a potentially fatal prolongation of the QTc interval, halofantrine must not be given simultaneously with or subsequent to mefloquine. Concomitant administration of mefloquine, quinine, quinidine or chloroquine may increase the risk of convulsions (see Precautions, Drug Interactions).

In patients with epilepsy, mefloquine, especially when used in high doses, may increase the risk of convulsions. Therefore, in such patients, mefloquine should be used only for curative treatment and only if there are compelling medical reasons.

In patients with impaired liver function the elimination of mefloquine may be prolonged, leading to higher plasma levels.

Pregnancy: Mefloquine crosses the placenta. Administered at 5 to 20 times the therapeutic dose in man, mefloquine was teratogenic in mice and rats and embryotoxic in rabbits. The safety of mefloquine use during the first trimester has not been established. Available data indicate that mefloquine is safe and effective in pregnancy beyond 16 weeks. Women of childbearing potential should be advised to practise contraception during malaria prophylaxis with mefloquine and for 3 months after the last dose.

Pregnancy has no clinically relevant effect on the pharmacokinetics of mefloquine.

Precautions: General: Occupational Hazards: Caution should be exercised with regard to driving, piloting airplanes, operating machines, or any other activity requiring alertness and fine motor coordination, as dizziness, a disturbed sense of balance and other disorders of the central and peripheral nervous system have been reported during and up to 3 weeks after the use of mefloquine (see Adverse Effects). During prophylactic use, if signs of unexplained anxiety, depression, restlessness or confusion are noticed, these may be considered prodromal to a more serious event. In these cases, the drug must be discontinued.

Mefloquine should be taken with caution in patients suffering from cardiac conduction disorders. Parenteral studies in animals show that mefloquine, a myocardial depressant, possesses 20% of the antifibrillatory action of quinidine and produces 50% of the increase in the PR interval reported with quinine. The effect of mefloquine on the compromised cardiovascular system has not been evaluated. In patients with cardiac disease, the benefits of mefloquine therapy should be weighed against the possibility of adverse effects.

During clinical trials, this drug was not administered for longer than 1 year. If the drug is to be administered for a prolonged period, periodic evaluations including liver function tests should be performed, if feasible. Although retinal abnormalities seen in humans with long-term chloroquine use have not been observed with mefloquine use, long-term feeding of mefloquine to rats resulted in dose-related ocular lesions (retinal degeneration, retinal edema and lenticular opacity at 12.5 mg/kg/day and higher). Therefore, periodic ophthalmic examinations are recommended.

<u>*Drug Interactions:*</u> Drug-drug interactions with mefloquine have not been explored in detail.

Concomitant administration of mefloquine and quinine, quinidine, or chloroquine may produce electrocardiographic abnormalities. If quinine or quinidine are to be used in the initial treatment of severe malaria, mefloquine administration should be delayed for at least 12 hours after the final dose of either of these drugs. Caution should also be exercised with other drugs that alter cardiac conduction (e.g., antiarrhythmics, β-adrenergic blocking agents, calcium channel blockers, antihistamines or H_1-blocking agents (astemizole, terfenadine), tricyclic antidepressants and phenothiazines) since they may contribute to a prolongation of the QTc interval.

There is evidence that the use of halofantrine after mefloquine causes a significant lengthening of the QTc interval. Clinically significant QTc interval prolongation has not been found with mefloquine alone.

A patient with previous myocardial infarction suffered a cardiopulmonary arrest 5 hours after taking mefloquine. Propranolol and chloroquine were also taken. That patient recovered fully.

Concomitant administration of mefloquine with quinine, quinidine or chloroquine may increase the risk of convulsions.

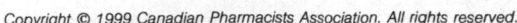

Patients taking mefloquine while taking valproic acid had loss of seizure control and lower than expected valproic acid

Lariam (cont'd)

blood levels. Therefore, patients concurrently taking antiseizure medication, including valproic acid, carbamazepine, phenobarbital, and phenytoin, and mefloquine should have the blood level of their antiseizure medication monitored and the dosage adjusted appropriately.

In clinical trials, the concomitant administration of sulfadoxine and pyrimethamine did not alter the adverse reaction profile.

When mefloquine is taken concurrently with oral live typhoid vaccines, attenuation of immunization cannot be excluded. Vaccinations with attenuated live bacteria should therefore be completed at least 3 days before the first dose of mefloquine.

A controlled clinical study was carried out in 20 subjects to investigate a potential interaction between mefloquine and alcohol. The blood alcohol concentrations attained in the patients taking mefloquine (0.3 to 0.5 mg/mL), did not impair coordinated psychomotor activities. A single case in the literature reports a transient severe psychiatric disturbance, suggesting an adverse reaction to mefloquine associated with a heavy ingestion of alcohol (600 mL of whisky).

Mefloquine is highly bound (98%) to plasma proteins.

Impairment of Fertility: Fertility studies with mefloquine in rats have demonstrated adverse effects on fertility in males at the high dose (50 mg/kg/day) and in females at the mid and high dose (20 and 50 mg/kg/day). Administration of 250 mg/week of mefloquine (base) to adult males for 22 weeks failed to reveal any deleterious effects on human spermatozoa.

Lactation: Based on a study in a few subjects, low concentrations (3 to 4%) of mefloquine were excreted in human milk following a dose equivalent to 250 mg of the free base. The amount of mefloquine excreted in the milk is of no prophylactic value to the infant. Caution should be exercised when mefloquine is administered to a nursing woman.

Children: Two studies were conducted to look at the effects of mefloquine on children living in endemic areas for P. falciparum. All children in these studies had at least a low level of parasitemia and 18 to 40% had significant parasitemia with or without mild malaria symptoms. When given 20 to 30 mg/kg of mefloquine as a single dose, nausea and vomiting occurred in approximately 10 to 20%, and dizziness was seen in approximately 40% of children. The incidence of adverse reactions was higher than that observed in adults.

Experience with mefloquine in infants less than 3 months old or weighing less than 5 kg is limited. No relevant age-related changes have been observed in the pharmacokinetics of mefloquine.

Geriatrics: No relevant age-related changes have been observed in the pharmacokinetics of mefloquine.

Renal Insufficiency: No pharmacokinetic studies have been performed in patients with renal insufficiency since only a small proportion of the drug is eliminated renally.

Other: Pharmacokinetic differences have been observed between various ethnic populations. In practice, however, these are of minor importance compared with host immune status and sensitivity of the parasite.

In vitro and in vivo studies showed no hemolysis associated with G-6-PD deficiency.

Adverse Effects: Overall the most frequently reported adverse events are nausea, vomiting, dizziness or vertigo, loss of balance, headache, somnolence, sleep disorders (insomnia, abnormal dreams), loose stools or diarrhea, and abdominal pain.

At the doses used for treatment of acute malaria infections, the symptoms possibly attributable to drug administration cannot be distinguished from those symptoms usually attributable to the disease itself.

Among subjects who received mefloquine for prophylaxis of malaria, the most frequently observed adverse experiences are nausea, vomiting, headache and dizziness. These adverse events are generally mild and may decrease with prolonged use.

Less frequently reported adverse events include: Central and Peripheral Nervous System: sensory and motor neuropathies (including paresthesia), convulsions or seizures, visual disturbances, tinnitus and vestibular disorders, tremor, abnormal coordination, ataxia, emotional problems (anxiety, panic attacks, restlessness, depressive moods, aggression, agitation, psychotic or paranoid reactions), forgetfulness, confusion, hallucinations.

Note: In the literature, the incidence of serious neuropsychiatric adverse drug reactions (e.g., seizures, psychotic reactions) with mefloquine has been reported at 1/215 following treatment and 1/13 000 following prophylactic use.

Cardiovascular: circulatory disturbances (hypotension, hypertension, flushing, syncope), tachycardia or palpitations, bradycardia, irregular pulse, extrasystoles and other transient cardiac conduction alterations. Isolated cases of AV-block have been reported. Cardiopulmonary arrest was reported in one patient shortly after ingesting a single prophylactic dose of mefloquine while concomitantly using propranolol (see Warnings and Precautions).

Skin: rash, exanthema, erythema, urticaria, pruritus, hair loss. Isolated cases of erythema multiforme and Stevens-Johnson syndrome have been reported.

Musculoskeletal: muscle weakness, muscle cramps, myalgia, arthralgia.

General Symptoms: asthenia, malaise, fatigue, fever, chills, loss of appetite. Isolated cases of encephalopathy have been reported.

Adverse reactions to mefloquine may occur or persist up to several weeks after the last dose.

Laboratory Abnormalities: Decreased hematocrit, transient elevation of transaminases, leukopenia or leukocytosis, and thrombocytopenia.

Overdose: Symptoms and Treatment: The following procedure is recommended in case of overdosage: Induce vomiting or perform gastric lavage, as appropriate. Monitor cardiac function (if possible by ECG) and neuropsychiatric status for at least 24 hours. Provide symptomatic and intensive supportive treatment as required, particularly for cardiovascular disturbances.

Dosage: Mefloquine should be taken with food, and with at least 240 mL of liquid. All dosage instructions relate to the mefloquine base. The tablets may be crushed and suspended in a small amount of water, milk or other beverage for administration to small children and other persons unable to swallow them whole.

Prophylaxis: The recommended prophylactic dose of mefloquine is approximately 5 mg/kg once weekly. The first dose should be taken at least 1 week before arrival in an endemic area. Weekly doses should always be taken on the same day of the week. To reduce the risk of malaria after leaving an endemic area, prophylaxis must be continued for 4 additional weeks.

If it is not possible to initiate therapy 1 week before arrival in an endemic area, data from the literature indicate that a loading dose of mefloquine can be given in order to rapidly achieve effective blood levels of the drug; in adults weighing over 45 kg this is 1 tablet (250 mg mefloquine) daily for 3 days, followed by 1 tablet weekly during exposure and for 4 weeks after leaving an endemic area.

The use of a loading dose may also permit an assessment of drug tolerance before travel and allows a change to a suitable alternative if required. Consideration may also be given to initiating mefloquine prophylaxis 2 to 3 weeks prior to departure in order to determine tolerance to mefloquine and allow time to substitute other antimalarials if required.

Adults and children weighing over 45 kg: In persons over 45 kg, the prophylactic dose is 250 mg of mefloquine (1 tablet) once weekly.

Children and adults weighing less than 45 kg: The weekly dose decreases in proportion to body weight: >30 to 45 kg: ¾ tablet; >20 to 30 kg: ½ tablet; 5 to 20 kg: ¼ tablet.

Experience with mefloquine in infants less than 3 months old or weighing less than 5 kg is limited. Children weighing between 5 and 10 kg will receive a higher prophylactic dose of mefloquine than the recommended 5 mg/kg; however the tablet cannot be accurately subdivided into less than ¼ tablet.

When prophylaxis with mefloquine fails, physicians should carefully evaluate which antimalarial to use for therapy. Regarding the use of halofantrine, see Warnings and Precautions.

Treatment: **The recommended total therapeutic dose of mefloquine for nonimmune patients is 20 to 25 mg/kg.** A lower total dose of 15 mg/kg may suffice for partially immune individuals. Thus, **nonimmunes** weighing over 45 kg should receive a total of 1 250 to 1 500 mg mefloquine (5 to 6 tablets) while **partially immune patients** of the same weight should receive 750 to 1 000 mg (3 to 4 tablets) (see Table I).

A second full dose should be given to patiens who vomit less than 30 minutes after receiving the drug. If vomiting occurs 30 to 60 minutes after a dose, an additional half-dose should be given.

Patients with acute P. vivax malaria treated with mefloquine are at high risk of relapse because mefloquine does not eliminate exoerythrocytic (hepatic phase) parasites. To avoid relapse after initial treatment of the acute infection with mefloquine, patients should subsequently be treated with an 8-aminoquinoline (e.g., primaquine) in order to eliminate liver forms.

If a full treatment course with mefloquine does not lead to improvement within 48 to 72 hours, alternative treatments should be considered. When breakthrough malaria occurs during mefloquine prophylaxis, physicians should carefully evaluate which antimalarial to use for therapy. Regarding the use of halofantrine, see Warnings and Precautions.

Mefloquine can be given for servere acute malaria after an initial course of i.v. quinine lasting at least 2 to 3 days. Interactions leading to adverse events can largely be prevented by allowing an interval of at least 12 hours after the last dose of quinine.

Information for the Patient: See Blue Section—Information for the Patient "Lariam".

Supplied: Each cross-scored (both sides), white, cylindrical, biplane tablet with bevelled edges imprinted ROCHE with hexagon on one side, contains: mefloquine base 250 mg as mefloquine HCl. Nonmedicinal ingredients: ammonium-calcium alginate, cornstarch, crospovidone, lactose, magnesium stearate, microcrystalline cellulose, poloxamer and talc. Blister packs of 8. Store at 15 to 30°C. The tablets are sensitive to moisture and should remain in their blister until consumed.

(Shown in Product Recognition Section)

Reviewed 1999

Table I—Lariam

Recommended Total Therapeutic Dosages of Lariam Tablets Relative to Body Weight and Immune Status[a]

	Nonimmune patients	Partially immune patients
<20 kg[b]	¼ tablet per 2.5-3 kg of weight 1 tablet per 10-12 kg of weight	¼ tablet per 4 kg of weight 1 tablet per 16 kg of weight
20-30 kg	2-3 tablets	1½-2 tablets
30-45 kg	3-4 tablets	2-3 tablets
45-60 kg	5 tablets	3 tablets
>60 kg[c]	6 tablets	4 tablets

[a] Splitting the total curative dosages into 2 to 3 doses (e.g., 3+1, 3+2, 3+2+1 tablets) taken 6 to 8 hours apart may reduce the occurrence or severity of adverse effects (see Adverse Effects).

[b] Experience with Lariam in infants less than 3 months old or weighing less than 5 kg is limited.

[c] There is no specific experience with total dosages of more than 6 tablets in very heavy patients.

LASIX® Ⓟ

Hoechst Marion Roussel

Furosemide

Diuretic

Pharmacology: Animal experiments using stop-flow and micropuncture techniques have demonstrated that furosemide inhibits sodium reabsorption in the ascending limb of Henle's loop as well as in both proximal and distal tubules. The action of furosemide on the distal tubule is independent of any inhibitory effect on carbonic anhydrase or aldosterone.

Furosemide may promote diuresis in cases which have previously proved resistant to other diuretics.

Furosemide has no significant pharmacological effects other than on renal function.

Absorption, Metabolism and Excretion: In man, furosemide is rapidly absorbed from the gastrointestinal tract. The diuretic effect of furosemide is apparent within 1 hour following oral administration and the peak effect occurs in the first or second hour. The duration of action is 4 to 6 hours but may continue up to 8 hours. Following i.v. administration of the drug, the diuresis occurs within 30 minutes and the duration of action is about 2 hours.

Urinary excretion is accomplished both by glomerular filtration and proximal tubular secretion, together this accounts for roughly only 2/3 of the ingested dose, the remainder being excreted in the feces. A small fraction is metabolized by cleavage of the side chain.

Table I—Lasix

Elimination Kinetics

Subjects	Route of Administration	Dose (mg)	Rate of Administration	Biliary Excretion	Max. Serum Concentration	t½ Hr
Normal	Oral	40	—	10 to 15%	<1 µg/mL	4.0
Normal	I.V.	40	Bolus	10 to 15%	2.5 µg/mL	4.5

Table I summarizes the elimination kinetics of furosemide.

Indications: The treatment of edema associated with congestive heart failure, cirrhosis of the liver and renal disease, including nephrotic syndrome as well as other edematous states amenable to diuretic therapy.

Furosemide can also be used alone in the control of mild to moderate hypertension or in combination with other antihypertensive agents in the treatment of more severe cases. Hypertensive patients who cannot be adequately controlled with thiazides will probably also not be adequately controllable with furosemide alone.

Parenteral furosemide is indicated when a rapid onset and an intense diuresis is desired e.g., acute pulmonary edema, cerebral edema. Parenteral furosemide is also indicated when oral therapy is precluded because of interference with intestinal absorption or for other reasons. Parenteral furosemide, by virtue of its therapeutic indications, will be generally administered to patients in hospital or outpatient clinics. However, in case of emergency where parenteral furosemide is administered outside this setting, the recommended dosage should be closely adhered to and the patient kept under close observation.

Contraindications: Complete renal shutdown. If increasing azotemia and oliguria occur during treatment of severe progressive renal disease, the drug should be discontinued. Therapy with furosemide should not be initiated in patients with hepatic coma and precoma or in states of electrolyte depletion until the basic condition is improved or corrected.

Severe hyponatremia, hypokalemia, hypovolemia or hypotension must be regarded as contraindications until serum electrolytes and fluid balance and blood pressure have been restored to normal levels.

Furosemide is also contraindicated in patients with a known history of hypersensitivity to this compound.

As furosemide may be capable of displacing bilirubin from albumin at least in vitro, it should not be administered to jaundiced newborn infants or to infants suffering from diseases (e.g., Rh incompatibility, familial non-hemolytic jaundice, etc.) with the potential of causing hyperbilirubinemia and possibly kernicterus.

Warnings: Furosemide is a potent diuretic which if given in excessive amounts can lead to a profound diuresis with water and electrolyte depletion. Therefore, careful medical supervision is required, and dose and dose schedule have to be adjusted to the individual patient's needs (see Dosage).

Cases of tinnitus and reversible deafness have been reported. There have also been some reports of cases, the majority in children undergoing renal transplantation, in which permanent deafness has occurred. In these latter cases, the onset of deafness was usually insidious and gradually progressive up to 6 months after furosemide therapy. Hearing impairment is more likely to occur in patients with severely reduced renal function who are given large doses of furosemide parenterally, at a rate exceeding 4 mg/min or in patients who are also receiving drugs known to be ototoxic.

Sulfonamide diuretics have been reported to decrease arterial responsiveness to pressor amines and to enhance the effect of tubocurarine. Great caution should be exercised in administering curare or its derivatives to patients undergoing therapy with furosemide and it is advisable to discontinue furosemide for 1 week prior to any elective surgery.

Pregnancy: The teratogenic and embryotoxic potential of furosemide in humans is unknown. The drug should not be used in pregnant women or in women of childbearing potential unless in the opinion of the attending physician the benefits to the patient outweigh the possible risk to the fetus.

Lactation: It should be noted that diuretics may partially inhibit lactation and that furosemide passes into the breast milk.

Precautions: General: During long-term therapy a high-potassium diet is recommended. Potassium supplements may be required especially when high doses are used for prolonged periods. Particular caution with potassium levels is necessary when the patient is on digitalis glycosides, potassium-depleting steroids, or in the case of infants and children. Potassium supplementation, diminution in dose, or discontinuation of furosemide therapy may be required.

Since rigid sodium restriction is conducive to both hyponatremia and hypokalemia, strict restriction in sodium intake is not advisable in patients receiving furosemide therapy.

Furosemide parenteral administered in doses up to 100 mg should be injected slowly (1 to 2 minutes) when the i.v. route is used.

Furosemide may lower the state of patient alertness and/or reactivity particularly at the start of treatment, as a result of a reduction in blood pressure and of other adverse reactions. (see Adverse Effects).

Geriatrics: Excessive diuresis induced by furosemide may result in dehydration and reduction of blood volume, with circulatory collapse and with the possibility of vascular thrombosis and embolism particularly in elderly patients. Furosemide may cause electrolyte depletion.

Children: In children, urge to defecate, complaints of abdominal pain and cramping have been reported after i.v. furosemide. An association of these symptoms with a low serum calcium and/or a low calcium:protein ratio is possible. Calcium levels should be monitored when children are to receive i.v. furosemide for durations longer than a few days. Furosemide may lower serum calcium levels, and rare cases of tetany have been reported. Accordingly, periodic serum calcium concentrations should be obtained.

Special Diseases and Conditions: Increases in blood glucose and alterations in glucose tolerance tests with abnormalities of the fasting and 2-hour postprandial blood sugar levels have been observed. Rare cases of precipitation of diabetes mellitus have been reported.

Asymptomatic hyperuricemia can occur and gout may rarely be precipitated.

It may be advisable to hospitalize patients with hepatic cirrhosis and ascites prior to initiating therapy. Sudden alterations of fluid and electrolyte balance in patients with cirrhosis may precipitate hepatic coma; therefore, strict observation is necessary during the period of diuresis. Supplemental potassium chloride and, if required, an aldosterone antagonist, are helpful in preventing hypokalemia and metabolic alkalosis.

Laboratory Tests: Frequent serum electrolyte and CO_2 content determinations should be performed during the first few months of therapy and periodically thereafter. It is essential to replace electrolyte losses and to maintain fluid balance so as to avoid any risk of electrolyte depletion (hyponatremia, hypochloremia, hypokalemia, hypomagnesemia or hypocalcemia), hypovolemia, or hypotension.

Checks on urine and blood glucose should be made at regular intervals especially in diabetics and in those suspected of latent diabetes when receiving furosemide. Increases in blood glucose and alterations in glucose tolerance tests with abnormalities of the fasting and 2-hour postprandial blood sugar levels have been observed.

Frequent BUN determinations during the first few months of therapy and periodically thereafter, as well as regular observations for possible occurrences of blood dyscrasias, liver damage or idiosyncratic reactions are advisable.

Drug Interactions: Sulfonamide diuretics have been reported to decrease arterial responsiveness to pressor amines and to enhance the effect of tubocurarine or curare-type muscle relaxants.

In edematous hypertensive patients being treated with antihypertensive agents, care should be taken to reduce the dose of these drugs when furosemide is administered, since furosemide potentiates their hypotensive effect. Especially in combination with ACE inhibitors, a marked hypotension may be seen sometimes progressing to shock. The concomitant administration of furosemide with ACE inhibitors may lead to deterioration in renal function and, in isolated cases, to acute renal failure.

Since furosemide is a sulfonamide derivative, it should be used with caution in patients with known sulfonamide sensitivity.

In case of concomitant abuse of laxatives, the risk of an increased potassium loss should be considered.

Glucocorticoids, carbenoxolone and licorice may also increase potassium loss.

It has been reported in the literature that diuretics such as furosemide may enhance the nephrotoxicity of cephaloridine. Therefore the simultaneous administration of both drugs is not advisable.

Administration of furosemide to diabetic patients may result in possible decrease of diabetic control. Dosage adjustments of the anti-diabetic agent may be needed.

Renal clearance of lithium is decreased in patients receiving furosemide, and lithium toxicity may result.

Concurrent administration of furosemide and sucralfate should be avoided, as sucralfate reduces the absorption of furosemide and hence weakens its effect.

Patients receiving high doses of salicylates in conjunction with furosemide may experience salicylate toxicity at lower doses because of competition for renal excretory sites.

Nonsteroidal anti-inflammatory drugs (e.g., indomethacin, acetylsalicylic acid) may attenuate the effect of furosemide and may cause renal failure in case of pre-existing hypovolemia. Probenecid and anticonvulsant drugs (phenytoin, carbamazepine, phenobarbital) may also attenuate the effect of furosemide.

Clinical studies have shown that the administration of indomethacin can reduce the natriuretic and antihypertensive effect of furosemide in some patients. This response has been attributed to inhibition of prostaglandin synthesis by indomethacin. Therefore, when indomethacin is added to the treatment of a patient receiving furosemide or furosemide is added to the treatment of a patient receiving indomethacin, the patient should be closely observed to determine if the desired effect of furosemide is obtained. Indomethacin blocks the furosemide-induced increase in plasma-renin activity. This fact should be kept in mind when evaluating plasma-renin activity in hypertensive patients.

Hearing impairment is more likely to occur in patients who are also receiving drugs known to be ototoxic (e.g., aminoglycosides antibiotics, ethacrynic acid and cisplatin) (see Warnings).

Administration of furosemide i.v. within 24 hours after the ingestion of chloral hydrate has caused the sensation of heat, sweating, restlessness, nausea, rise in blood pressure and tachycardia in isolated cases.

Pediatrics: Renal calcifications (nephrolithiasis and nephrocalcinosis), from barely visible on x-ray to staghorn, have occurred in some severely premature infants treated with furosemide i.v. for edema due to patent ductus arteriosus and hyaline membrane disease. The concurrent use of chlorothiazide has been reported to decrease hypercalciuria and to dissolve some calculi.

When administered to premature infants with respiratory distress syndrome in the first few weeks of life, diuretic treatment with furosemide may accentuate the risk of a patent ductus arteriosus.

Adverse Effects: Adverse reactions are categorized by body system: Metabolic: Electrolyte depletion has occurred during therapy with furosemide, especially in patients receiving higher doses with a restricted salt intake. Electrolyte depletion manifests itself by adverse reactions attributed to various body systems: weakness, dizziness, drowsiness, polyuria, polydipsia, orthostatic hypotension, lethargy, leg cramps, sweating, bladder spasms, anorexia, vomiting, mental confusion and meteorism (see Precautions).

Transient elevations of BUN have been observed, especially in patients with renal insufficiency.

As with other diuretics, there may be a transient rise in serum creatinine, uric acid (this may lead to gout attack in predisposed patients), cholesterol and triglyceride levels during furosemide treatment.

Treatment with furosemide has occasionally caused some deterioration in cases of manifest diabetes, or has made latent diabetes manifest.

Pre-existing metabolic alkalosis (e.g., in decompensated cirrhosis of the liver) may be aggravated.

Cardiovascular: Too vigorous diuresis may induce orthostatic hypotension or acute hypotensive episodes.

In extreme cases, hypovolemia may lead to dehydration, circulatory collapse and thrombophilia. Thrombophlebitis and emboli have been reported.

CNS and Special Senses: At the commencement of treatment, excessive diuresis may give rise, especially in elderly patients, to a feeling of pressure in the head, dizziness, dryness of the mouth or blurring of vision.

Paresthesia, vertigo, and xanthopsia have been reported.

Cases of tinnitus and reversible deafness have been reported. There have also been some reports of cases, the majority in children undergoing renal transplantation, in which permanent deafness has occurred. In these latter cases, the onset of deafness is usually insidious and gradually progressive up to 6 months after furosemide therapy. Hearing impairment is more likely to occur in patients with severely reduced

Lasix (cont'd)

renal function who are given large doses of furosemide parenterally, at a rate exceeding 4 mg/min or in patients who are also receiving drugs known to be ototoxic (see Warnings).

Dermatologic and Hypersensitivity: Various forms of dermatitis, including urticaria, erythema multiforme, exfoliative dermatitis, pruritus and epidermolysis bullosa have occurred.

Dermatologic and hypersensitivity reactions to furosemide also include purpura, photosensitivity, rash. Systemic hypersensitivity reactions include vasculitis, interstitial nephritis and necrotizing angiitis. Anaphylactic shock is rare and can occur with the i.v. administration of furosemide.

Hematologic: Anemia, eosinophilia, leukopenia and thrombocytopenia (with purpura) have occurred, as well as agranulocytosis, aplastic anemia and hemolytic anemia.

Urogenital: Symptoms of obstructed micturition (e.g., in hydronephrosis, prostatic hypertrophy, ureterostenosis) may become manifest or may be aggravated during medication with diuretics.

Gastrointestinal: In children, urge to defecate, complaints of abdominal pain and cramping have been reported after furosemide i.v. (see Precautions). Pancreatitis, anorexia, jaundice (intrahepatic cholestatic jaundice) oral and gastric burning, diarrhea, nausea, vomiting and constipation have been reported. Rare occurrences of sweet taste have been reported.

Other: In addition, the following adverse reactions have been reported: transient pain at injection site following i.m. injection and paradoxical swelling.

Overdose: Symptoms: Dehydration, electrolyte depletion and hypotension may be caused by overdosage or accidental ingestion. In cirrhotic patients, overdosage may precipitate hepatic coma.

Treatment: The drug should be discontinued and appropriate corrective treatment applied: replacement of excessive fluid and electrolyte losses; serum electrolytes, carbon dioxide level and blood pressure should be determined frequently. Adequate drainage must be assured in patients with urinary bladder outlet obstruction (such as prostatic hypertrophy).

Dosage: Adults: Oral: Edema: The usual initial dose is 40 to 80 mg. Ordinarily a prompt diuresis ensues and the starting dose can then be maintained or even reduced. If a satisfactory diuresis has not occurred within 6 hours, succeeding doses should be increased by increments of 20 to 40 mg, if necessary. Maximum daily dose: 200 mg. Once the effective single dose has been determined, it may be repeated 1 to 3 times a day.

The mobilization of edema may be most efficiently and safely accomplished by utilizing an intermittent dosage schedule in which furosemide is given for 2 to 4 consecutive days each week. With doses exceeding 120 mg/day, careful clinical and laboratory observations are particularly advisable.

Hypertension: A dosage schedule of 20 to 40 mg twice daily is recommended. Individualized therapy is of great importance. Careful observations for changes in blood pressure must be made when furosemide is used with other antihypertensive drugs, especially during initial therapy. The dosage of other agents must be reduced by at least 50% as soon as furosemide is added to the regimen to prevent an excessive drop in blood pressure. As the blood pressure falls under the potentiating effect of furosemide, a further reduction in dosage, or even discontinuation of other antihypertensive drugs may be necessary. It is further recommended, if 40 mg twice daily does not lead to a clinically satisfactory response, to add other antihypertensive agents, rather than an increase in the dose of furosemide.

Parenteral: Parenteral furosemide should not be added into the tubing of a running infusion solution.

Edema: Usual initial dose is 20 to 40 mg injected as a single dose i.m. or i.v. I.V. injections should be given slowly over a period of 1 to 2 minutes. Ordinarily, a prompt diuresis ensues.

If the diuretic response with a single dose of 20 to 40 mg is not satisfactory it may be increased by increments of 20 mg not sooner than 2 hours after the previous dose until the desired diuretic effect has been obtained. Maximum daily dose: 100 mg. Once the effective single dose has been determined, it should then be given once or twice daily.

Parenteral therapy should be replaced by treatment with furosemide tablets as soon as this is practical.

Acute Pulmonary Edema: The following schedule is recommended: 40 mg are to be slowly injected i.v. followed by another 40 mg i.v. 1 to 1.5 hours later if indicated by the patient's condition.

Children: Oral and Parenteral: Therapy should be instituted in the hospital, in carefully selected patients, under close observation with frequent monitoring of serum electrolytes.

Parenteral furosemide should not be added into the tubing of a running infusion solution.

Orally or parenterally, the initial dose should be in the range of 0.5 to 1.0 mg/kg body weight.

The total daily dose (given in divided doses of 6 to 12 hours apart) should not exceed 2 mg/kg orally or 1 mg/kg parenterally. In the newborn and in premature babies, the daily dose should not exceed 1 mg/kg.

An intermittent dosage schedule should be adopted as soon as possible using the minimum effective dose at the longest possible intervals. Particular caution with regard to potassium levels is always desirable when furosemide is used in infants and children.

Supplied: Oral Solution: Each mL of clear, yellowish-orange solution contains: furosemide 10 mg. Bottles of 25 mL (with calibrated dropper) and 120 mL (with calibrated spoon). Protect from light.

Parenteral: Each mL of injectable sterile solution contains: 10 mg of furosemide pH: 9.1. Ampuls of 2 mL, boxes of 5 and 50; ampuls of 4 mL, boxes of 5 and 50. Multidose vials of 30 mL (nonmedicinal ingredients: benzyl alcohol 9.0 mg/mL, edetate disodium, sodium chloride for isotonicity and sodium hydroxide for pH adjustment), cartons of 10.

Tablets: 20 mg: Each white, round tablet (Code DLF) contains: furosemide 20 mg. Amber bottles of 300, boxes of 30.

40 mg: Each yellow, round, scored tablet (Code Lasix 40) contains: furosemide 40 mg. Amber bottles of 500, boxes of 30.

80 mg: Each yellow, flat, oblong tablet, scored both sides (Code DKF) contains: furosemide 80 mg. Amber bottles of 30 and 300.

(Shown in Product Recognition Section)

LASIX® SPECIAL Pr

Hoechst Marion Roussel

Furosemide

Diuretic

Pharmacology: Animal experiments using stop-flow and micropuncture techniques have demonstrated that furosemide inhibits sodium reabsorption in the ascending limb of Henle's loop as well as in both proximal and distal tubules. The action of furosemide on the distal tubule is independent of any inhibitory effect on carbonic anhydrase or aldosterone.

The diuretic effect of furosemide is exerted even when glomerular filtration is markedly impaired. Furosemide may promote diuresis in cases which have previously proved resistant to other diuretics.

Furosemide has no significant pharmacological effects other than on renal function.

Absorption, Metabolism and Excretion: In man, furosemide is rapidly absorbed from the gastrointestinal tract. The diuretic effect of furosemide is apparent within 1 hour following oral administration and the peak effect occurs in the first or second hour. The duration of action is 4 to 6 hours but may continue up to 8 hours. Following i.v. administration of the drug, the diuresis occurs within 30 minutes and the duration of action is about 2 hours.

Urinary excretion is accomplished both by glomerular filtration and proximal tubular secretion, together this accounts for roughly only 2/3 of the ingested dose, the remainder being excreted in the feces. A small fraction is metabolized by cleavage of the side chain.

Table I summarizes the elimination kinetics of furosemide in both normal subjects and patients with renal insufficiency.

Indications: Lasix Special 500 mg tablets and 250 mg ampuls are high-dosage formulations of furosemide and are intended exclusively for patients with severely impaired renal function. They are to be used under strict medical supervision only within a hospital setting (see Dosage).

High doses of furosemide may be used as an adjuvant treatment of oliguria and in the promotion of diuresis in the treatment of edema; in selected patients with acute renal failure, e.g., in the postoperative phase and in association with septic infections; in selected patients with chronic renal failure with fluid retention, both in the predialysis phase and when dialysis has become unavoidable, especially in the presence of acute pulmonary edema; in selected patients with the nephrotic syndrome with severe impairment of renal function, e.g., in chronic glomerular nephritis, lupus erythematosus and Kimmelstiel-Wilson syndrome.

Contraindications: In patients with complete renal shutdown and glomerular filtration rate below 5 mL/minute. **In patients whose glomerular filtration rate is above 20 mL/minute. In such cases, it might cause extremely severe water and electrolyte losses.**

Patients with hepatic cirrhosis, with renal failure due to poisoning with nephrotoxic or hepatotoxic substances and in patients with renal failure accompanied by hepatic coma and precoma.

Severe hyponatremia, hypokalemia, hypovolemia or hypotension must be regarded as contraindications until serum electrolytes and fluid balance and blood pressure have been restored to normal levels.

Known history of hypersensitivity to furosemide.

Children: As furosemide may be capable of displacing bilirubin from albumin at least in vitro, it should not be administered to jaundiced newborn infants or to infants suffering from diseases (e.g., Rh incompatibility, familial non-hemolytic jaundice, etc.) with the potential of causing hyperbilirubinemia and possibly kernicterus.

Warnings: Furosemide is a potent diuretic which if given in excessive amounts can lead to a profound diuresis with water and electrolyte depletion. Therefore, careful medical supervision is required, and dose and dose schedule have to be adjusted to the individual patient's needs (see Dosage).

Cases of tinnitus and reversible deafness have been reported. There have also been some reports of cases, the majority in children undergoing renal transplantation, in which permanent deafness has occurred. In these latter cases, the onset of deafness was usually insidious and gradually progressive up to 6 months after furosemide therapy. Hearing impairment is more likely to occur in patients with severely reduced renal function who are given large doses of furosemide parenterally, at a rate exceeding 4 mg/minute or in patients who are also receiving drugs known to be ototoxic.

Sulfonamide diuretics have been reported to decrease arterial responsiveness to pressor amines and to enhance the effect of tubocurarine. Great caution should be exercised in administering curare or its derivatives to patients undergoing therapy with furosemide and it is advisable to discontinue furosemide for 1 week prior to any elective surgery.

Pregnancy: The teratogenic and embryotoxic potential of furosemide in humans is unknown. The drug should not be used in pregnant women or in women of childbearing potential unless in the opinion of the attending physician the benefits to the patient outweigh the possible risk to the fetus.

Lactation: It should be noted that diuretics may partially inhibit lactation and that furosemide passes into the breast milk.

Precautions: General: During long-term therapy a high-potassium diet is recommended. Potassium supplements may be required especially when high doses are used for prolonged periods. Particular caution with potassium levels is necessary when the patient is on digitalis glycosides, potassium-depleting steroids, or in the case of infants and children. Potassium supplementation, diminution in dose, or discontinuation of furosemide therapy may be required.

Since rigid sodium restriction is conducive to both hyponatremia and hypokalemia, strict restriction in sodium intake is not advisable in patients receiving furosemide therapy.

Furosemide may lower the state of patient alertness and/or reactivity particularly at the start of treatment as a result of a reduction in blood pressure and other adverse reactions (see Adverse Effects).

Table I—Lasix Special

Elimination Kinetics in Normal Subjects and Patients with Renal Insufficiency

Subjects	Route of Administration	Dose (mg)	Rate of Administration	Biliary Excretion	Max. Serum Concentration	t½ Hr
Normal	Oral	40	—	10 to 15%	<1 μg/mL	4.0
Normal	I.V.	40	Bolus	10 to 15%	2.5 μg/mL	4.5
Renal insufficiency	I.V.	1 000	25 mg/min	60%	53 μg/mL	13.5
Renal insufficiency	I.V.	1 000	4 mg/min	—	29 μg/mL	—

During treatment with furosemide in high-dosage formulations (250 mg ampuls or 500 mg tablets), extreme care must always be taken to adjust dosage to individual requirements. Rate of infusion must not exceed 4 mg/minute.

Geriatrics: Excessive diuresis induced by furosemide may result in dehydration and reduction of blood volume, with circulatory collapse and with the possibility of vascular thrombosis and embolism particularly in elderly patients. Furosemide may cause electrolyte depletion.

Children: In children, urge to defecate, complaints of abdominal pain and cramping have been reported after i.v. furosemide. An association of these symptoms with a low serum calcium and/or a low calcium: protein ratio is possible. Calcium levels should be monitored when children are to receive i.v. furosemide for durations longer than a few days. Furosemide may lower serum calcium levels, and rare cases of tetany have been reported. Accordingly, periodic serum calcium levels should be obtained.

Patients with Special Diseases and Conditions: Increases in blood glucose and alterations in glucose tolerance tests with abnormalities of the fasting and 2-hour postprandial blood sugar levels have been observed. Rare cases of precipitation of diabetes mellitus have been reported. Asymptomatic hyperuricemia can occur and gout may rarely be precipitated.

Laboratory Test: Frequent serum electrolyte and CO_2 content determinations should be performed during the first few months of therapy and periodically thereafter. It is essential to replace electrolyte losses and to maintain fluid balance so as to avoid any risk of electrolyte depletion (hyponatremia, hypochloremia, hypokalemia, hypomagnesemia or hypocalcemia), hypovolemia, or hypotension.

Checks on urine and blood glucose should be made at regular intervals especially in diabetics and in those suspected of latent diabetes when receiving furosemide. Increases in blood glucose and alterations in glucose tolerance tests with abnormalities of the fasting and 2-hour postprandial blood sugar levels have been observed.

Frequent BUN determinations during the first few months of therapy and periodically therafter, as well as regular observations for possible occurrence of blood dyscrasias, liver damage or idiosyncratic reactions are advisable.

Drug Interactions: Sulfonamide diuretics have been reported to decrease arterial responsiveness to pressor amines and to enhance the effect of tubocurarine or curare-type muscle relaxants.

In edematous hypertensive patients being treated with antihypertensive agents, care should be taken to reduce the dose of these drugs when furosemide is administered, since this drug potentiates their hypotensive effect.

Especially in combination with ACE inhibitors, a marked hypotension may be seen sometimes progressing to shock. The concomitant administration of furosemide with ACE-inhibition may lead to deterioration in renal function and, in isolated cases, to acute renal failure.

Since furosemide is a sulfonamide derivative, it should be used with caution in patients with known sulfonamide sensitivity.

In case of concomitant abuse of laxatives, the risk of an increased potassium loss should be considered.

Glucocorticoids, carbenoxolone and licorice may also increase potassium loss.

It has been reported in the literature that diuretics such as furosemide may enhance the nephrotoxicity of cephaloridine. Therefore the simultaneous administration of both drugs is not advisable.

Administration of furosemide to diabetic patients may result in possible decrease of diabetic control. Dosage adjustments of the antidiabetic agent may be needed.

Renal clearance of lithium is decreased in patients receiving furosemide, and lithium toxicity may result.

Concurrent administration of furosemide and sucralfate should be avoided, as sucralfate reduces the absorption of furosemide and hence weakens its effect.

Patients receiving high doses of salicylates in conjunction with furosemide may experience salicylate toxicity at lower doses because of competition for renal excretory sites.

Nonsteroidal anti-inflammatory drugs (e.g., indomethacin, ASA) may attenuate the effect of furosemide and may cause renal failure in case of pre-existing hypovolemia. Probenecid and anticonvulsants drugs (phenytoin, carbamazepine, phenobarbital) may also attenuate the effect of furosemide.

Clinical studies have shown that the administration of indomethacin can reduce the natriuretic and antihypertensive effect of furosemide in some patients. This response has been attributed to inhibition of prostaglandin synthesis by indomethacin. Therefore, when indomethacin is added to the treatment of a patient receiving furosemide, or furosemide is added to the treatment of a patient receiving indomethacin, the patient should be closely observed to determine if the desired effect of furosemide is obtained. Indomethacin blocks the furosemide-induced increase in plasma-renin activity. This fact should be kept in mind when evaluating plasma-renin activity in hypertensive patients.

Hearing impairment is more likely to occur in patients who are also receiving drugs known to be ototoxic (e.g., aminoglycosides antibiotics, ethacrynic acid and cisplatin) (see Warnings).

Administration of i.v. furosemide within 24 hours after the ingestion of chloral hydrate has caused the sensation of heat, sweating, restlessness, nausea, rise in blood pressure and tachycardia in isolated cases.

Pediatrics: Renal calcifications (nephrolithiasis and nephrocalcinosis), from barely visible on x-ray to staghorn, have occurred in some severely premature infants treated with i.v. furosemide for edema due to patent ductus arteriosus and hyaline membrane disease. The concurrent use of chlorothiazide has been reported to decrease hypercalciuria and to dissolve some calculi.

When administered to premature infants with respiratory distress syndrome in the first few weeks of life, diuretic treatment with furosemide may accentuate the risk of a patent ductus arteriosus.

Adverse Effects: Adverse reactions are categorized below by body system.

Metabolic: Electrolyte depletion has occurred during therapy with furosemide, especially in patients receiving higher doses with a restricted salt intake. Electrolyte depletion manifests itself by adverse reactions attributed to various body systems: weakness, dizziness, drowsiness, polyuria, polydipsia, orthostatic hypotension, lethargy, leg cramps, sweating, bladder spasms, anorexia, vomiting, mental confusion and meteorism (see Precautions).

Transient elevations of BUN have been observed, especially in patients with renal insufficiency.

As with other diuretics, there may be a transient rise in serum creatinine, uric acid (this may lead to gout attack in predisposed patients), cholesterol and trigylceride levels during furosemide treatment.

Treatment with furosemide has occasionally caused some deterioration in cases of manifest diabetes, or has made latent diabetes manifest.

Pre-existing metabolic alkalosis (e.g., decompensated cirrhosis of the liver) may be aggravated.

Cardiovascular: Too vigorous diuresis may induce orthostatic hypotension or acute hypotensive episodes.

In extreme cases, hypovolemia may lead to dehydration, circulatory collapse and thrombophilia. Thrombophlebitis and emboli have been reported.

CNS and Special Senses: At the commencement of treatment, excessive diuresis may give rise, especially in elderly patients, to a feeling of pressure in the head, dizziness, dryness of the mouth or blurring of vision.

Paresthesia, vertigo and xanthopsia have been reported.

Cases of tinnitus and reversible deafness have been reported. There have also been some reports of cases, the majority in children undergoing renal transplantation, in which permanent deafness has occurred. In these latter cases, the onset of deafness is usually insidious and gradually progressive up to 6 months after furosemide therapy. Hearing impairment is more likely to occur in patients with severely reduced renal function who are given large doses of furosemide parenterally, at a rate exceeding 4 mg/minute or in patients who are also receiving drugs known to be ototoxic (see Warnings).

Dermatologic and Hypersensitivity: Various forms of dermatitis, including urticaria, erythema multiforme, exfoliative dermatitis, pruritus and epidermolysis bullosa have occurred. Dermatologic and hypersensitivity reactions to furosemide also include purpura, photosensitivity, rash. Systemic hypersensitivity reactions include vasculitis, interstitial nephritis and necrotizing angiitis. Anaphylactic shock is rare and can occur with the i.v. administration of furosemide.

Hematologic: Anemia, eosinophilia, leukopenia and thrombocytopenia (with purpura) have occurred, as well as agranulocytosis, aplastic anemia and hemolytic anemia.

Urogenital: Symptoms of obstructed micturition (e.g., in hydronephrosis, prostatic hypertrophy, ureterostenosis) may become manifest or may be aggravated during medication with diuretics.

Gastrointestinal: In children, urge to defecate, complaints of abdominal pain and cramping have been reported after i.v. furosemide (see Precautions). Pancreatitis, anorexia, jaundice (intrahepatic cholestatic jaundice) oral and gastric burning, diarrhea, nausea, vomiting and constipation have been reported. Rare occurrence of sweet taste have been reported.

Other reactions: In addition, the following adverse reactions have been reported: transient pain at injection site following i.m. injection and paradoxical swelling.

Overdose: Symptoms: Dehydration, electrolyte depletion and hypotension may be caused by overdosage or accidental ingestion.

Treatment: The drug should be discontinued and appropriate corrective treatment applied: replacement of excessive fluid and electrolyte losses; serum electrolytes, carbon dioxide level and blood pressure should be determined frequently. Adequate drainage must be assured in patients with urinary bladder outlet obstruction (such as prostatic hypertrophy).

Dosage: The high-dosage formulations, furosemide 250 mg (solution for i.v. infusion) and furosemide 500 mg (tablets), are intended exclusively for selected patients with severely impaired glomerular filtration (GFR of less than 20 mL/min but greater than 5 mL/min), who have not responded to conventional doses of furosemide (see Indications).

When furosemide is used in high doses careful attention must be paid to the following points: If the patient is in shock, hypovolemia and hypotension must be corrected by appropriate measures before starting therapy. Any serious abnormalities of serum electrolytes or acid-base balance must be corrected beforehand. When treating patients with conditions likely to interfere with micturition, such as prostatic hypertrophy or disturbed consciousness, it is absolutely essential to ensure free urinary drainage. Because of the wide and unpredictable individual variations in responsiveness it is important to adjust dosage and route of administration to individual needs. Once the desired rise in urinary output has begun, exact balance of water intake and water output must be maintained throughout the course of treatment, so as to avoid hypovolemia or hypotension. Careful electrolyte replacement is also necessary.

The dosage of high strength furosemide given below is for adults only. The dosage regimen for children has not yet been determined. The administration of large doses of furosemide in children has been associated with permanent deafness (see Warnings).

Parenteral: If conventional doses (40 to 80 mg i.v.) fail to produce an adequate diuresis within 30 minutes, infusion treatment with Lasix Special 250 mg may be started:

Infusion fluid: Lasix Special for i.v. use is a mildly buffered alkaline solution. Lasix Special can be added to 5% Dextrose in Water, Isotonic Saline or Lactated Ringer's Injection when mixed as directed and prepared immediately before use. Furosemide may precipitate in and therefore is incompatible with solutions in which the pH of the resulting mixture is less than 5.5.

Furosemide should not be added into the tubing of a running infusion solution. It should also not be mixed with any other drugs in the infusion bottle.

Initial dose: 250 mg (25 mL ampul) are mixed with 250 mL of a suitable solution (see above) and given by i.v. drip **at a rate not exceeding 4 mg/minute (infusion time for 275 mL is approximately 1 hour).**

Additional dose: Should the initial dose fail to produce an adequate increase (at least 40 to 50 mL/hour) in urinary output, a second infusion of 500 mg (appropriately diluted) should be started 1 hour after the conclusion of the first. The duration of this infusion is determined by the maximum rate of furosemide 4 mg/minute. A maximum daily dose of 1 000 mg should not be exceeded.

For hypervolemic patients, it is advisable to give the high-dosage formulation of furosemide undiluted, or in a suitable volume (e.g., 250 mg in 50 mL) of infusion fluid so as to avoid the risk of overhydration. **I.V. Infusions of the undiluted solution must be given with the aid of a motor-driven precision syringe so as to make sure that the upper limit of furosemide 4 mg (0.4 mL)/minute is not exceeded.**

If a satisfactory diuretic response is achieved (40 to 50 mL/hour), the effective dose can be repeated every 24 hours.

Parenteral therapy should be replaced by treatment with furosemide 500 mg tablets as soon as this is practical.

Oral: Initial dose: The dose which has been found to produce an effective diuresis when given i.v. is used as the initial dose orally.

Additional dose: Should the initial dose fail to produce an adequate increase (at least 40 to 50 mL) in urinary output within 4 to 6 hours, the dose may be raised by 250 to 500 mg at a time.

For selected patients with advanced chronic renal failure, diuretic therapy may be started with furosemide orally. If conventional doses (80 to 160 mg orally) fail to produce an

Lasix Special (cont'd)

adequate diuresis, a single dose of 250 mg is given as a starting dose. If a satisfactory diuresis does not ensue within 4 to 6 hours, the initial dose may be doubled to 500 mg.

The criterion of optimal dosage is a urinary output of at least 2.5 L/day. A maximum daily dose of 1 000 mg should not be exceeded.

Supplied: Ampuls: Each 25 mL amber ampul contains: furosemide 250 mg (10 mg/mL) in a sterile solution at a pH of 9.1. Boxes of 10.

Tablets: Each yellow, round, quarter-scored tablet (Code DLX) contains: furosemide 500 mg. Amber bottles of 20.

(Shown in Product Recognition Section)

LAXILOSE®
Technilab

Lactulose
Laxative

Supplied: Each mL of solution contains: lactulose 667 mg. Nonmedicinal ingredients: FD&C Yellow #6 and purified water. Bottles of 500 mL and 1 L.

LECTOPAM® Ⓟ
Roche

Bromazepam
Anxiolytic—Sedative

Pharmacology: Bromazepam is a benzodiazepine with anxiolytic and sedative properties which are of value in the symptomatic relief of pathological anxiety in psychoneurotic patients.

The absolute bioavailability of unchanged, orally administered bromazepam is 60%, and peak blood levels are achieved within 2 hours after administration. On average, 70% of bromazepam is bound to plasma proteins. Bromazepam is metabolized in the liver, and has a elimination half-life of 20 hours (the half-life may be longer in elderly patients). Over a 72-hour interval, 69% of a 12 mg oral dose was recovered in the urine, in the form of conjugated 3-hydroxybromazepam and conjugated 2-(2-amino-5-bromo-3-hydroxybenzoyl)-pyridine.

Indications: For the short-term, symptomatic relief of manifestations of excessive anxiety in patients with anxiety neurosis.

Benzodiazepines are only indicated when the disorder is severe, disabling or subjecting the individual to extreme distress.

Contraindications: In patients with known hypersensitivity to benzodiazepines, myasthenia gravis, severe hepatic insufficiency, severe respiratory insufficiency, or sleep apnea syndrome.

Warnings: Bromazepam is not recommended for use in patients with depressive disorders or psychosis. Patients should be advised against the concurrent use of alcohol and other CNS depressant drugs. Patients with known or presumed dependence from alcohol or drugs should not take benzodiazepines, except in rare situations under medical supervision.

Children: Because of the lack of sufficient clinical experience, bromazepam is not recommended for use in patients less than 18 years of age.

Occupational Hazards: Since bromazepam has a CNS depressant effect, patients should be warned against driving, operating dangerous machinery, or engaging in other hazardous activities requiring mental alertness and physical coordination, and should be cautioned that the effects of alcohol on such activities may be increased.

Pregnancy: The safety of use of bromazepam in pregnancy has not been established. Therefore, bromazepam should not be used during pregnancy. Several studies have suggested an increased risk of congenital malformations associated with the use of the benzodiazepines, such as chlordiazepoxide and diazepam, and meprobamate, during the first trimester of pregnancy. Since bromazepam is also a benzodiazepine derivative, its administration is rarely justified in women of childbearing potential. Administration of bromazepam during the last 3 months of pregnancy or during labor is allowed only in the event of a strict medical indication as, due to the pharmacological action of the product, effects on the neonate can be expected, such as hypothermia, hypotonia and moderate respiratory depression. Moreover, infants born to mothers who took benzodiazepines chronically during the later stages of pregnancy may have developed physical dependence and may be at some risk for developing withdrawal symptoms in the postnatal period. If the drug is prescribed to a woman of childbearing potential, she should be warned to consult her physician regarding discontinuation of the drug if she plans to become or suspects that she is pregnant. If the drug is prescribed to a woman of childbearing potential, she should be warned to consult her physician regarding discontinuation of the drug if she plans to become or suspects that she is pregnant.

Lactation: Bromazepam and its metabolites are probably excreted in human milk. Therefore, this drug should not be given to nursing mothers.

Precautions: Geriatrics: Elderly and debilitated patients, or those with organic brain syndrome, have been found to be prone to CNS depression after even low doses of benzodiazepines. Therefore, medication should be initiated in these patients with very low initial doses, and increments should be made gradually, depending on the response of the patient, in order to avoid oversedation or neurological impairment. The initial dose for the elderly or debilitated patients should not exceed 3 mg.

Dependence Liability: Bromazepam should not be administered to individuals prone to drug abuse. The risk of dependence increases with dose and duration of treatment; it is also greater in predisposed patients with a history of alcohol or drug abuse. Caution should be observed in all patients who are considered to have potential for psychological dependence.

Withdrawal symptoms similar to those occurring with other drugs of this class including alcohol, have been observed after abrupt discontinuation of the drug. These include irritability, nervousness, insomnia, agitation, tremors, convulsions, diarrhea, abdominal cramps, vomiting, memory impairment, headache, muscle pain, extreme anxiety, tension, restlessness, and confusion. In severe cases the following symptoms may occur: derealization, depersonalization, hyperacusis, numbness and tingling of the extremities, hypersensitivity to light, noise and physical contact, hallucinations, or epileptic seizures. Since these symptoms are similar to those for which the patient is being treated, it may appear that he/she has suffered a relapse upon discontinuation of the drug. It is suggested that the drug should be withdrawn gradually, if the individual is suspected of being dependent, or the drug perhaps has been used in prolonged high doses.

Mental and Emotional Disorders: It should be recognized that suicidal tendencies may be present in patients with emotional disorders and that protective measures and appropriate treatment may be necessary and should be instituted without delay.

Since excitement and other paradoxical reactions can result from the use of anxiolytic sedatives in psychotic patients, bromazepam should not be used in ambulatory patients suspected of having psychotic tendencies.

As with other benzodiazepines, bromazepam should not be used in individuals with physiological anxiety or normal stresses of daily living, but only in the presence of disabling manifestations of an appropriate pathological anxiety disorder. These drugs are not effective in patients with characterological and personality disorders or those with obsessive-compulsive disorders. Bromazepam is also not recommended for management of depressive or psychotic disorders.

Impaired Hepatic or Renal Function: In patients with impaired hepatic or renal function, it is recommended to initiate therapy, if necessary, at a very low dose and to increase the dosage only to the extent that such an increase is compatible with the degree of residual function of these organs. Such patients should be followed closely and have periodic laboratory assessments.

Laboratory Tests: If bromazepam should be administered for repeated cycles of therapy, periodic blood counts and liver function tests are advisable.

Drug Interactions: Bromazepam may potentiate or interact with the effects of other CNS acting drugs such as alcohol, narcotics, hypnotics, sedative antihistamines, antipsychotics, anxiolytics/sedatives, anesthetics, antidepressants and anticonvulsants. Therefore, if bromazepam is to be combined with other drugs acting on the CNS, careful consideration should be given to the pharmacology of the agent involved because of possible additive or potentiation of drug effects. In the case of narcotic analgesics enhancement of euphoria may also occur, leading to an increase in psychological dependence. Patients should also be advised against the simultaneous use of other CNS depressant drugs and should be cautioned not to take alcohol during the administration of bromazepam because of the potentiation of effects that might occur.

Although not known for bromazepam, there is a possibility that compounds which inhibit certain hepatic enzymes (particularly cytochrome P450) may enhance the activity of benzodiazepines that are metabolized by these enzymes.

Cisapride may lead to a temporary increase of the effects of bromazepam due to an increased rate of absorption.

Adverse Effects: The most frequently reported adverse reactions have been drowsiness, ataxia and dizziness. Release of hostility and other paradoxical effects such as irritability, excitability, restlessness, agitation, delusion, rages, nightmares, hallucinations, psychosis, inappropriate behavior and other adverse behavioral effects are known to occur with the use of benzodiazepines. If these occur, use of the drug should be discontinued.

Anterograde amnesia may also occur using therapeutic doses of benzodiazepines, the risk increasing with higher doses.

Other side effects less frequently reported, listed by body systems, include the following:

Neurologic: blurred or double vision, headache, seizures, slurred speech, difficulty in depth perception.

Psychiatric: mental confusion, depression, nervousness, sleep disorders, euphoria, lethargy, stupor, numbed emotions, reduced alertness.

Gastrointestinal: dry mouth, nausea, nonspecific gastrointestinal disturbances, vomiting.

Musculoskeletal: muscle spasm, muscle weakness.

Cardiovascular: hypotension, palpitations, tachycardia.

Dermatologic: pruritus, rash.

Genitourinary: incontinence, change in libido.

Hematologic: decreased hemoglobin and hematocrit, increased and decreased WBC.

Hepatic: elevations of alkaline phosphatase, bilirubin, AST, ALT.

Miscellaneous Blood Chemistry: increased and decreased blood sugar levels.

Overdose: Symptoms: Overdosage manifestations include drowsiness, somnolence, ataxia, impaired vision, depressed reflexes and finally coma. Hypotension, hypotonia and respiratory depression and very rarely death may occur with large overdoses.

Treatment: Vital signs should be monitored and general supportive measures should be employed as indicated. Special attention should be paid to respiratory and cardiac function in intensive care. Flumazenil may be useful as an antagonist.

Gastric lavage (with the airway protected) should be instituted as soon as possible. Vomiting may be included within 1 hour if the patient is fully awake. If there is no advantage in emptying the stomach, activated charcoal should be given to reduce absorption. The value of dialysis has not been determined.

As is frequently the case in intentional overdose, the probability of multiple agents having been ingested should be considered.

Dosage: The dosage of bromazepam must be individualized and carefully titrated in order to avoid excessive sedation or mental and motor impairment. Short courses of treatment should usually be the rule for the symptomatic relief of excessive anxiety and the initial course of treatment should not last longer than 1 week without reassessment of the need for a limited extension. If necessary, drug dosage can be adjusted after 1 week of treatment. Initially, not more than 1 week's supply of the drug should be provided and automatic prescription renewals should not be allowed. Subsequent prescriptions, when required, should be limited to a short course of therapy.

It may be useful to inform the patient when treatment is started that it will be of limited duration and to explain precisely how the dosage will be progressively decreased. It is important that the patient should be aware of the possibility of rebound phenomena that may occur while the drug is being discontinued.

Adults: Initially; 6 to 18 mg/day in equally divided doses, depending on the severity of symptoms and response of the patient. Treatment should be initiated by lower doses and adjusted as necessary. The optimal dosage may range from 6 to 30 mg daily in individual patients, in divided doses. There is limited experience with higher doses up to 60 mg daily.

Elderly and Debilitated Patients: The initial daily dose in these patients should not exceed 3 mg in divided doses. This dosage can be carefully adjusted, depending on tolerance and reponse of the patient.

Supplied: 1.5 mg: Each white cylindrical biplane tablet with beveled edges and scored on one side, engraved ROCHE 1.5 on the other side contains: bromazepam 1.5 mg. Nonmedicinal ingredients: microcrystalline cellulose, lactose 96 mg, talc and magnesium stearate. Energy: 1.5 kJ (0.4 kcal). Gluten-, paraben-, sodium-, sulfite- and tartrazine-free. Bottles of 100 and 500.

3 mg: Each pink cylindrical biplane tablet with beveled edges and scored on one side, engraved ROCHE 3 on the other side contains: bromazepam 3 mg. Nonmedicinal ingredients: microcrystalline cellulose, lactose 94 mg, talc, magnesium stearate and erythrosine aluminum lake. Energy: 1.5 kJ (0.4 kcal). Gluten-, paraben-, sodium-, sulfite- and tartrazine-free. Bottles of 100 and 500.

6 mg: Each yellow-green cylindrical biplane tablet with beveled edges and scored on one side, engraved ROCHE 6 on the other side contains: bromazepam 6 mg. Nonmedicinal ingredients: microcrystalline cellulose, lactose 91 mg, talc, magnesium stearate, iron oxide and indigotine aluminum lake. Energy: 1.5 kJ (0.4 kcal). Gluten-, paraben-, sodium-, sulfite- and tartrazine-free. Bottles of 100 and 500.

Store at 15 to 30°C.

(Shown in Product Recognition Section)

Reviewed 1999

LEDERCILLIN® VK ℞

Wyeth-Ayerst

Potassium Phenoxymethyl Penicillin

Antibiotic

Supplied: 400 000 units: Each round, white, scored tablet, engraved "LL" on one side and "L10" on the other, contains: potassium phenoxymethyl penicillin 400 000 units. Nonmedicinal ingredients: calcium phosphate dibasic granulation, magnesium stearate, microcrystalline cellulose and sodium citrate anhydrous. Sodium: <1 mmol (2.14 mg). Tartrazine-free. Bottles of 100.

800 000 units: Each round, white, scored tablet, engraved "LL" on one side and "L9" on the other side, contains: potassium phenoxymethyl penicillin 800 000 units. Nonmedicinal ingredients: calcium phosphate dibasic granulation, magnesium stearate, microcrystalline cellulose and sodium citrate anhydrous. Sodium: <1 mmol (4.28 mg). Tartrazine-free. Bottles of 100.

LEDERLE LEUCOVORIN® CALCIUM ℞

Wyeth-Ayerst

Citrovorum Factor

Folic Acid Derivative

Pharmacology: Lederle Leucovorin Calcium (calcium folinate), the calcium salt of folinic acid (citrovorum factor), is a mixture of the diastereoisomers of the 5-formyl derivative of tetrahydrofolic acid. The biologically active compound of the mixture is the (-)-L-isomer. It is a metabolite of folic acid and an essential coenzyme for nucleic acid synthesis.

Leucovorin is a reduced form of folic acid, which is readily converted to other reduced folic acid derivatives (e.g., tetrahydrofolate).

Because it does not require reduction by dihydrofolate reductase as does folic acid, leucovorin is not affected by blockage of this enzyme by folic acid antagonists (dihydrofolate reductase inhibitors). This allows purine and thymidine synthesis, and thus DNA, RNA and protein synthesis, to occur. Leucovorin may limit methotrexate action on normal cells by competing with methotrexate for the same transport processes into the cell. Leucovorin rescues bone marrow and gastrointestinal cells from methotrexate but has no apparent effect on pre-existing methotrexate nephrotoxicity.

Leucovorin is extensively converted to 5-methyltetrahydrofolate in the intestine prior to absorption. In this form, it is a major component of the total active human serum folate. Oral absorption is saturable at doses above 25 mg.

Leucovorin enhances the cytotoxicity of fluoropyrimidines such as 5-fluorouracil (5-FU) by their metabolites, methylene tetrahydrofolate and fluorodeoxyuridine monophosphate, forming a stable ternary complex with thymidylate synthase, and thereby, decreasing intracellular levels of that enzyme and the product thymidylate. The cell then dies as a result of thymine starvation.

Caution: Do not administer leucovorin intrathecally.

Indications: To diminish the toxicity and counteract the effect of impaired methotrexate elimination. To treat the megaloblastic anemias due to folate deficiency, as in sprue, nutritional deficiency, megaloblastic anemias of pregnancy and infancy. For pre-treatment followed by 5-fluorouracil to prolong survival in the palliative treatment of patients with advanced colorectal cancer. For modulation of 5-FU as adjuvant therapy for patients with Dukes' B and C colon cancer.

Contraindications: Not to be administered for the treatment of pernicious anemia or other megaloblastic anemias where vitamin B_{12} is deficient. A hematologic remission may occur while neurologic manifestations continue to progress.

Warnings: Since leucovorin may enhance the toxicity of fluorouracil, leucovorin/fluorouracil combination therapy for advanced colorectal cancer should be administered under the supervision of a physician experienced in the use of antimetabolite cancer chemotherapy. Particular care should be taken in the treatment of elderly or debilitated colorectal cancer patients, as these patients may be at increased risk of severe toxicity. Deaths from severe enterocolitis, diarrhea and dehydration have been reported in elderly patients receiving leucovorin and fluorouracil. Concomitant granulocytopenia and fever were present in some but not all of the patients.

In the treatment of accidental overdosages of folic acid antagonists, leucovorin should be administered as promptly as possible. As the time interval between the administration of antifolate and leucovorin increases, the effectiveness of leucovorin in counteracting toxicity decreases. Monitoring of the serum MTX concentration is essential in determining the optimal dose and duration of therapy. Delayed MTX excretion may be caused by a third space fluid accumulation (i.e., ascites, pleural effusion), renal insufficiency, low pH of urine, or inadequate hydration. Under such circumstances, higher doses of leucovorin or prolonged administration may be indicated. Do not administer leucovorin intrathecally.

Cryodesiccated powder reconstituted with Bacteriostatic Water for Injection containing benzyl alcohol should only be used at doses below 10 mg/m^2 (see Precautions).

Treatment-related deaths have been sporadically reported in patients treated with leucovorin plus fluorouracil combination therapy regimens. In general, diarrhea or stomatitis/mucositis are the first indications that severe and potentially life-threatening toxicity could develop. Patients who experience these symptoms while receiving any combination therapy regimen incorporating leucovorin plus fluorouracil should be carefully followed and further therapy should be withheld until these symptoms resolve.

Leucovorin enhances the toxicity of fluorouracil. When these drugs are administered concurrently in the palliative therapy of advanced colorectal cancer, the dosage of fluorouracil must be reduced. Although the toxicities observed in patients treated with the combination of leucovorin plus fluorouracil are qualitatively similar to those observed in patients treated with fluorouracil alone, gastrointestinal toxicities (particularly stomatitis and diarrhea) are observed more commonly and may be more severe in patients receiving the combination (see Precautions).

Therapy with leucovorin/fluorouracil must not be initiated or continued in patients who have symptoms of gastrointestinal toxicity of any severity, until those symptoms have resolved. Patients with diarrhea must be monitored with particular care until the diarrhea has resolved, as rapid clinical deterioration leading to death can occur. Elderly or debilitated patients are at greater risk for severe toxicity receiving this therapy.

Seizures and/or syncope have been reported rarely in cancer patients receiving leucovorin, usually in association with fluoropyrimidine administration, and most commonly in those with CNS metastases or other predisposing factors; however, a causal relationship has not been established.

Precautions: Because of the Ca^{++} content of leucovorin solutions, no more than 160 mg of leucovorin should be injected i.v./minute.

If the cryodesiccated powder is reconstituted with Bacteriostatic Water for Injection containing 0.9% benzyl alcohol doses greater than 10 mg/m^2 are not recommended due to the benzyl alcohol content. If greater doses are required (see Dosage), leucovorin calcium for injection (cryodesiccated powder) should be reconstituted with Sterile Water for Injection USP and used immediately, or the preservative-free liquid form, leucovorin calcium injection should be used.

Leucovorin should not be mixed in the same infusion as 5-fluorouracil as a precipitate may form.

<u>*Drug Interactions:*</u> Folic acid in large amounts may counteract the antiepileptic effect of phenobarbital, phenytoin and primidone, and increase the frequency of seizures in susceptible children.

Preliminary animal and human studies have shown that small quantities of systemically administered leucovorin enter the CSF primarily as 5-methyltetrahydrofolate and, in humans, remain 1 to 3 orders of magnitude lower than the usual methotrexate concentrations following intrathecal administration. However, high doses of leucovorin may reduce the efficacy of intrathecally administered methotrexate.

Leucovorin may enhance the toxicity of fluorouracil (see Warnings).

Pregnancy: Teratogenic Effects: Reproduction studies have been performed in rats and rabbits at doses at least 50 times the human dose and have revealed no evidence of harm to the fetus due to leucovorin.

There are, however, no adequate and well-controlled studies in pregnant women. Because animal reproduction studies are not always predictive of human response, this drug should be used during pregnancy only if clearly needed.

Lactation: It is not known whether this drug is excreted in human milk. Because many drugs are excreted in human milk, caution should be exercised when leucovorin is administered to a nursing mother.

Children: See Drug Interactions.

Adverse Effects: Allergic sensitization, including anaphylactoid reactions and urticaria, has been reported following both oral and parenteral administration of folinic acid. In combination regimens, the toxicity profile of 5-FU is enhanced by leucovorin. The most common manifestations are mucositis, stomatitis, leukopenia, and/or diarrhea which may be dose-limiting. In clinical trials with this drug combination, these toxicities were found to be reversible with appropriate modification of 5-FU administration.

Overdose: Symptoms and Treatment: Folic acid is a water soluble vitamin converted in the body by the action of folate reductase to folinic acid (Leucovorin) which is rapidly eliminated in the urine.

Folic acid has low acute and chronic toxicities in man. No adverse effects have been noted in adults after the ingestion of 400 mg/day for 5 months or 10 mg/day for 5 years.

Excessive amounts of leucovorin may nullify the chemotherapeutic affect of folic acid antagonists.

Dosage: Impaired Methotrexate Elimination or Accidental Overdosage: Leucovorin rescue should begin as soon as possible after an inadvertent overdosage and within 24 hours of methotrexate administration when there is delayed excretion (see Warnings). Leucovorin 10 mg/m^2 should be administered i.v., i.m. or orally every 6 hours until the serum methotrexate level is less than 10^{-8}M. In the presence of gastrointestinal toxicity, nausea or vomiting, leucovorin should be administered parenterally. Because absorption is saturable, doses greater than 25 mg should be given i.v.

Serum creatinine and methotrexate levels should be determined at 24-hour intervals. If the 24-hour serum creatinine has increased 50% over baseline or if the 24-hour methotrexate level is greater than 5×10^{-6}M or the 48-hour level is greater than 9×10^{-7}M, the dose of leucovorin should be increased to 100 mg/m^2 i.v. every 3 hours until the methotrexate level is less than 10^{-8}M.

Hydration (3 L/day) and urinary alkalinization with $NaHCO_3$ should be employed concomitantly. The bicarbonate dose should be adjusted to maintain the urine pH at 7.0 or greater.

Megaloblastic Anemia Due to Folic Acid Deficiency: Up to 1 mg daily. There is no evidence that doses greater than 1 mg daily have greater efficacy than doses of 1 mg. The loss of folate in the urine becomes roughly logarithmic as the amount administered exceeds 1 mg.

Advanced Colorectal Cancer: Leucovorin is administered at 200 mg/m^2 by slow i.v. injection immediately prior to dosing with 370 mg/m^2 5-FU (fluorouracil) by slow i.v. injection, for 5 consecutive days.

This 5-day treatment course may be repeated at 4-week (28-day) intervals, provided that the patient has completely recovered from the toxic effects of the prior treatment course.

In subsequent treatment courses, the dosage of fluorouracil should be adjusted based on patient tolerance of the prior treatment course. The daily dosage of fluorouracil should be reduced by 20% for patients who experienced moderate hematologic or gastrointestinal toxicity in the prior treatment course, and by 30% for patients who experienced severe toxicity. For patients who experienced no toxicity in the prior treatment course, fluorouracil dosage may be increased by 10%. Leucovorin dosages are not adjusted for toxicity.

Adjuvant Therapy for Patients with Dukes B and C Colon Cancer: Leucovorin is administered i.v. as a 2-hour infusion

Lederle Leucovorin Calcium (cont'd)

at a dosage of 500 mg/m² weekly for 6 consecutive weeks followed by a 2-week rest. This regimen is repeated for a total of 6 cycles.

Treatment is repeated 21 days after the sixth dose of the previous course. Fluorouracil (5/FU) is administered at a dose of 500 mg/m², on the same schedule as leucovorin, i.v. via bolus 1 hour after the i.v. has been started.

Do not administer leucovorin intrathecally.

Supplied: Powder: 50 mg: Each vial of lyophilized powder contains: leucovorin (as calcium) 50 mg. Also contains sodium chloride 40 mg and sodium hydroxide and/or hydrochloric acid to adjust pH. Preservative-free. Boxes of 10. Store at 15 to 30°C.

350 mg: Each vial of lyophilized powder contains: leucovorin (as calcium) 350 mg. Also contains sodium chloride 140 mg and sodium hydroxide and/or hydrochloric acid to adjust pH. Preservative-free. Single vials, boxes of 10. Store at 15 to 30°C.

Tablets: Each round, light yellow, scored tablet, engraved "LL5" and "U2", contains: leucovorin (as calcium) 5 mg. Nonmedicinal ingredients: lactose, magnesium stearate, microcrystalline cellulose, sodium starch glycolate and starch pregelatinized. Tartrazine-free. Bottles of 24 and 100. Store at 15 to 30°C.

Vials: Each mL of solution contains: leucovorin (as calcium) 10 mg. Also contains sodium chloride 7.7 mg and sodium hydroxide and/or hydrochloric acid to adjust pH. Preservative-free. Vials of 35 mL, boxes of 10. Store between 2 to 8°C. Avoid freezing.

Reviewed 1997

LENOLTEC No. 1, 2 & 3 Ⓝ
LENOLTEC No. 4 Ⓝ

Technilab

Acetaminophen—Caffeine—Codeine
Acetaminophen—Codeine

Analgesic—Antipyretic

Supplied: Lenoltec No. 1: Caplets: Each white, uncoated caplet, imprinted TEC and 1 on one side, reverse side plain, contains: acetaminophen 300 mg, caffeine 15 mg and codeine phosphate 8 mg. Nonmedicinal ingredients: colloidal silicon dioxide, crospovidone, magnesium stearate, microcrystalline cellulose, povidone, pregelatinized starch, sodium croscarmellose and stearic acid. Energy: 0.51 kJ (0.123 kcal). Bottles of 30, 100 and 200.

Tablets: Each round, white, uncoated tablet, imprinted TEC and 1 on one side, reverse side plain, contains: acetaminophen 300 mg, caffeine 15 mg and codeine phosphate 8 mg. Nonmedicinal ingredients: colloidal silicon dioxide, crospovidone, magnesium stearate, microcrystalline cellulose, povidone, pregelatinized starch, sodium croscarmellose and stearic acid. Energy: 0.51 kJ (0.123 kcal). Bottles of 100.

Lenoltec No. 2: Each round, white, uncoated tablet, with slightly beveled edges, imprinted TEC and 2 on one side, reverse side plain, contains: acetaminophen 300 mg, caffeine 15 mg and codeine phosphate 15 mg. Nonmedicinal ingredients: colloidal silicon dioxide, crospovidone, magnesium stearate, microcrystalline cellulose, povidone, pregelatinized starch, sodium croscarmellose and stearic acid. Energy: 0.52 kJ (0.125 kcal). Bottles of 500.

Lenoltec No. 3: Each round, white, uncoated tablet, with slightly beveled edges, imprinted TEC and 3 on one side, reverse side plain, contains: acetaminophen 300 mg, caffeine 15 mg and codeine phosphate 30 mg. Nonmedicinal ingredients: colloidal silicon dioxide, crospovidone, magnesium stearate, microcrystalline cellulose, povidone, pregelatinized starch, sodium croscarmellose and stearic acid. Energy 0.64 kJ (0.152 kcal). Bottles of 500.

Lenoltec No. 4: Each round, white, uncoated tablet, with slightly beveled edges, imprinted TEC and 4 on one side, reverse side plain, contains: acetaminophen 300 mg and codeine phosphate 60 mg. Nonmedicinal ingredients: colloidal silicon dioxide, crospovidone, magnesium stearate, microcrystalline cellulose, povidone, pregelatinized starch, sodium croscarmellose and stearic acid. Energy: 0.5 kJ (0.118 kcal). Bottles of 100 and 500.

Alcohol-, gluten-, paraben-, sucrose-, sulfite- and tartrazine-free. Keep bottle tightly closed. Store at room temperature. Do not use if neckband is damaged.

LERITINE® Injection Ⓝ
LERITINE® Tablets Ⓝ

Frosst

Anileridine Phosphate
Anileridine HCl

Opioid Analgesic

Pharmacology: Anileridine, a synthetic opioid, is a strong analgesic. The chief pharmacologic action is exerted on the CNS. The analgesic effects usually are prompt in onset either orally or parenterally (approximately within 15 minutes). Duration of action is about 2 or 3 hours.

Respiratory depression, when it occurs, is of shorter duration than that seen with morphine or meperidine when equipotent analgesic doses are used.

Anileridine is absorbed by all routes of administration and is metabolized chiefly in the liver. Very little is excreted in the urine.

Indications: For the relief of moderate to severe pain (e.g., angina pectoris, renal colic, biliary colic, and pain associated with extensive burns, fractures, and carcinoma). In acute congestive heart failure for rest and relief of apprehension. In oral surgery for relief of pain including that of exodontia.

Anileridine also is useful in support of anesthesia and postoperatively. Satisfactory preoperative use has been reported.

Anileridine provides good obstetric analgesia alone and with both scopolamine and barbiturates. With the use of this analgesic, patients frequently relax and sleep between labor pains. Thus some degree of amnesia may be obtained.

Contraindications: The presence of respiratory depression; should be used with great caution, if at all, when respiratory failure is a possibility, as in head injury or brain tumor. Known hypersensitivity to the drug or any of the nonmedicinal ingredients of the preparations. Anileridine should not be used in patients 12 years of age and under because clinical experience in this age group is limited.

Warnings: As with morphine and meperidine, the possibility of addiction to anileridine should be kept in mind. The addiction potential of anileridine is regarded as being equal to that of morphine, inasmuch as anileridine will suppress completely the withdrawal symptoms of morphine addiction. Anileridine should not be given unnecessarily nor should its use be prolonged unduly.

As with other opioid analgesics, anileridine should be used with extreme caution in cases of severe hepatic insufficiency, severe CNS depression or coma, or in patients with head injuries and conditions in which intracranial pressure is increased, myxedema, Addison's Disease, acute alcoholism, delirium tremens, convulsive disorders, and in patients taking MAO inhibitors.

Pregnancy: Safe use in pregnancy has not been established with regard to the possibility of adverse effects upon fetal development. Therefore, anileridine should be used in patients who are pregnant or in women of child bearing age only when the potential benefits outweigh the possible hazards.

The sudden i.v. injection of a dose greater than 10 mg may result in severe respiratory depression and/or apnea, hypotension and cardiac arrest. Therefore, anileridine should not be given by direct i.v. injection, except in extreme emergencies when time or lack of facilities will not permit the use of a diluted preparation (5 to 10 mg/10 mL saline 0.9%).

Precautions: Respiratory depression and, to a lesser degree, circulatory depression are the chief hazards attending the use of this analgesic. Respiratory depression occurs most frequently in the elderly, and debilitated patients and in those suffering from conditions accompanied by hypoxia or hypercapnia when even moderate therapeutic doses may dangerously decrease pulmonary ventilation. Anileridine should be given very cautiously to patients in shock, since the depressant effect upon respiration may act indirectly to further reduce the circulating blood volume, cardiac output, and blood pressure.

If deep respiratory depression and circulatory collapse appear to be imminent in those patients after the administration of anileridine, the administration of naloxone may assist in counteracting these effects.

Drug Interactions: Special caution should be observed when anileridine is used with other opioids, sedatives, some phenothiazines or anesthetics, since these agents may enhance respiratory and circulatory depression.

Adverse Effects: Nausea and vomiting occur occasionally, and slight transient hypotension and bradycardia may be noted. Dizziness, perspiration, a feeling of warmth, dry mouth, visual difficulty, itching, euphoria, restlessness, nervousness and excitement have been reported.

Overdose: Symptoms and Treatment: Primary attention should be given to the reestablishment of adequate respiratory exchange through provision of a patent airway and institution of assisted or controlled ventilation. Parenteral fluids and other supportive measures should be employed as indicated.

The opioid antagonist, naloxone HCl, is a specific antidote against respiratory depression.

An appropriate dose of naloxone HCl should be administered parenterally, preferably by the i.v. route and simultaneously with efforts at resuscitation. With anileridine overdosage the following treatment is recommended.

Naloxone HCl: Adults: 0.4 mg i.v., i.m. or s.c. If an immediate response is not observed the dose may be repeated at 2 to 3 minute intervals.

Children and Newborn: 0.01 mg/kg i.v., i.m. or s.c. may be repeated at 2 to 3 minute intervals.

Note: In a patient addicted to opioids, the use of an opioid antagonist may precipitate an acute withdrawal syndrome. The severity of this syndrome will depend on the amount of opioid which has been used and the amount of antagonist given.

Dosage: Oral: Adults: 25 to 50 mg, repeated every 6 hours if necessary. A dose of 50 mg, or more frequent repeat doses, may be desirable for extremely severe pain, but neither is advised for ambulatory patients outside of home or hospital.

Parenteral: S.C. and I.M.: Adults: 25 to 50 mg repeated every 4 to 6 hours. For more severe pain 75 to 100 mg may be given, and smaller, more frequent dosages may be necessary. The total 24 hour dosage of this drug should be no more than 200 mg.

When used preoperatively in adults, doses of 50 to 75 mg, especially when given with scopolamine, have made the patient drowsy and cooperative at induction of anesthesia.

I.V. use in support of anesthesia: Since the i.v. route is employed, anileridine should be used only in the hands of a competent anesthesiologist. **During and directly following such use of the drug, provisions for oxygen administration and controlled respiration should be immediately available.**

The drug frequently has been given i.v. without ill effect, but certain hazards nevertheless exist. The threshold of safety for a single i.v. dose of anileridine is relatively low and depends largely on the rate of administration. Severe respiratory depression has resulted from the i.v. injection of this analgesic during surgical anesthesia. As with similar agents, it may cause prolonged apnea when given rapidly i.v. in one dose. This effect is rare with a dose of 10 mg or less. Furthermore, it should be remembered that sedatives, other opioid analgesics, some phenothiazines and anesthetics may increase the likelihood of respiratory depression. If respiratory depression due to anileridine occurs, it may be reversed by naloxone.

Anileridine injection should be well diluted and introduced into the vein **slowly.** For adults, from 50 to 100 mg should be added to 500 mL of 5% dextrose solution, and 5 to 10 mg injected slowly followed by the amount desired at a relatively slow drip (approximately 0.6 mg/minute depending on individual need and response). **The sudden injection of more than 10 mg may produce apnea, hypotension, and cardiac arrest.** It has been reported that an adequate amount of drug, infused intermittently instead of continuously, has been effective for about 25 to 40 minutes.

Note: Direct i.v. injection of undiluted solution should not be employed except in grave emergency when time or facilities preclude dilution of the drug.

Parenteral Use in Obstetrics: For analgesia during labor, 50 mg of anileridine may be injected i.m. or s.c. If necessary this dose may be repeated, usually in 3 to 4 hours, for a total dosage of 100 to 200 mg. For rapid action 10 mg **in dilution** may be given i.v. **slowly** at the same time that 40 mg is injected i.m. or s.c.

Care should be taken at all times, and especially with i.v. use, to avoid opioid-induced respiratory depression of either the mother or the infant. Labor may be slowed in some instances and infant respiratory depression has been reported. Rarely is the depression marked. The closer to delivery the drug is given, the greater the likelihood of respiratory depression of the newborn.

Approximate Opioid Analgesic Equivalences: The potency of anileridine lies between that of meperidine and morphine, please refer to Table I for approximate analgesic equivalences of anileridine with respect to other opioid analgesics.

Table I—Leritine

Opioid Analgesics: Approximate Analgesic Equivalences[a]

Drug	Equivalent Dose (mg)[b] (compared to morphine 10 mg i.m.) Parenteral	Oral	Duration of Action (hours)
Strong Opioid Agonists			
Morphine (single dose)	10	60	3-4
(chronic dose)	10	20-30[c]	3-4
Hydromorphone	1.5-2	6-7.5	2-4
Anileridine	25	75	2-3
Levorphanol	2	4	4-8
Meperidine[d]	75	300	1-3
Oxymorphone	1.5	5 (rectal)	3-4
Methadone[e]			
Heroin	5-8	10-15	3-4
Weak Opioid Agonists			
Codeine	120	200	3-4
Oxycodone	5-10	10-15	2-4
Propoxyphene	50	100	2-4
Mixed Agonist-Antagonists[f]			
Pentazocine[d]	60	180	3-4
Nalbuphine	10		3-6
Butorphanol	2		3-4

[a]Cancer Pain: A Monograph on the Management of Cancer Pain, Health and Welfare Canada, 1984.
Foley KM. New Engl J Med 1985; 313: 84-95.
Aronoff GM, Evans WO: Evaluation and Treatment of Chronic Pain. 2nd Ed. In Aronoff GM, ed. Williams and Wilkins, Baltimore, 1992, 359-68.
Cherny NI, Portenoy RK: Textbook of Pain. 3rd Ed. In: Wall PD, Melzack R, eds. Churchill Linvingstone, London, 1994: 1437-67.

[b]Most of these data were derived from single-dose, acute pain studies and should be considered an approximation for selection of doses when treating chronic pain.

[c]For acute pain, the oral dose of morphine is 6 times the injectable dose. However, for chronic dosing, this ratio becomes 2 and 3:1, possibly due to the accumulation of active metabolites.

[d]These drugs are not recommended for the management of chronic pain.

[e]Extremely variable equianalgesic dose. Patients should undergo personalized titration starting at an equivalent to 1/10 of the morphine dose.

[f]Mixed agonist-antagonists can precipitate withdrawal in patients on pure opioid agonists.

Supplied: Injection: Each mL of clear, colorless liquid contains: anileridine phosphate 25 mg. Nonmedicinal ingredients: phosphoric acid, sodium bisulfite and water for injection. Ampuls of 1 mL, boxes of 25. Store at room temperature (15 to 30°C) and protect from excessive heat and light.

Tablets: Each white, biconvex-shaped, compressed tablet, 0.79 cm in diameter, with a special symbol on one side, contains: anileridine HCl equivalent to anileridine base 25 mg. Nonmedicinal ingredients: calcium phosphate dibasic, hydroxypropyl methylcellulose, magnesium stearate and sodium bisulfite. Gluten-, lactose- and tartrazine-free. Bottles of 100. Store at room temperature (15 to 30°C) and protect from light.

(Shown in Product Recognition Section)

Reviewed 1997

LESCOL®

Novartis Pharmaceuticals

Fluvastatin Sodium

Lipid Metabolism Regulator

Pharmacology: Fluvastatin is a fully synthetic HMG-CoA reductase inhibitor and is hydrophilic. Fluvastatin is a racemate of two erythro enantiomers of which one exerts the pharmacological activity.

Fluvastatin is a competitive inhibitor of HMG-CoA reductase, which is responsible for the conversion of 3-hydroxy-3-methylglutaryl-coenzyme A (HMG-CoA) to mevalonate, a precursor of sterols, including cholesterol. The inhibition of cholesterol biosynthesis reduces the cholesterol in hepatic cells, which stimulates the synthesis of LDL receptors and thereby increases the uptake of LDL particles. The ultimate result of these mechanisms is a reduction of the plasma total cholesterol (total-C) and low density lipoprotein cholesterol (LDL-C) concentrations.

Epidemiologic and clinical studies have associated the risk of coronary artery disease (CAD) with elevated levels of Total-C, LDL-C and decreased levels of HDL-C. These abnormalities of lipoprotein metabolism are considered as major contributors to the development of the disease. Other factors, e.g., interactions between lipids/lipoproteins and endothelium, platelets and macrophages, have also been incriminated in the development of human atherosclerosis and of its complications.

Fluvastatin is rapidly and completely (98%) absorbed following oral administration to fasted volunteers. The drug is also completely absorbed, even when administered up to 4 hours postprandial, but at a reduced rate.

Fluvastatin is targeted to, and sequestered by the liver. Therefore, absolute bioavailability based on systemic blood concentrations is about 25%. At doses above 20 mg, given in the fasted state, absolute bioavailability can be dose dependent. Fluvastatin has a volume of distribution of approximately 30 L. More than 98% of the circulating drug is bound to plasma albumin.

Following administration of ^{3}H-fluvastatin to healthy volunteers, excretion of radioactivity was about 5% in the urine and 90% in the feces. Fluvastatin accounted for less than 2% of the total radioactivity excreted. The beta elimination half-life for fluvastatin is 1.2 hours.

Fluvastatin is predominantly metabolized by the hepatic microsomal CYP2C9 subclass of the P450 cytochromes. It is not metabolized to a significant extent by other cytochrome subclasses, including CYP3A4.

Pharmacokinetics: Fluvastatin is not a pro-drug. It is absorbed rapidly and completely (98%) following oral administration to fasted volunteers. The drug is also completely absorbed, even when administered up to 4 hours postprandial, but at a reduced rate (C_{max} is reduced by 40 to 70%). Fluvastatin is targeted to, and sequestered by the liver; therefore, absolute bioavailability based on systemic blood concentrations is about 25%. At doses above 20 mg given in the fasted state, absolute bioavailability can be dose dependent. Dose-normalized values at 40 mg were 20 to 40% higher than at 20 mg in the fasted state. The volume of distribution (VD_{ss}) for the drug is calculated to be approximately 30 L. More than 98% of the circulating drug is bound to plasma albumin, and this binding is unaffected by drug concentration.

Fluvastatin is predominantly metabolized by the hepatic microsomal CYP2C9 subclass of the P450 cytochromes. It is not metabolized to a significant extent by other cytochrome subclasses, including CYP3A4. Interactions between fluvastatin and drugs metabolized by the CYP2C9 or CYP3A4 subclasses of the P450 cytochromes may occur in some patients.

Following administration of ^{3}H-fluvastatin to healthy volunteers, excretion of radioactivity was about 5% in the urine and 90% in the feces, and fluvastatin accounted for less than 2% of the total radioactivity excreted. The plasma clearance for fluvastatin in man is calculated to be approximately 40 L/hour. Steady-state plasma concentrations show no evidence of fluvastatin accumulation following administration of up to 80 mg daily for 25 days. However, under conditions of maximum rate of absorption (i.e., fasting), systemic exposure to fluvastatin is increased 33 to 53% compared to a single 20 or 40 mg dose. This increase in systemic exposure may result from saturation of uptake and sequestration of fluvastatin by the liver when fluvastatin is administered under fasting conditions. After single (or multiple) 20 and 40 mg (40 and 80 mg/day) oral doses of fluvastatin, no differences in the fluvastatin elimination half-life are observed. The beta elimination half-life for fluvastatin is 1.2 hours (range of 0.53 to 3.1 hours).

The extent of absorption of fluvastatin 20 mg capsules is equivalent to that of a solution of fluvastatin except that the time to peak under fasted conditions is about 0.7 hours following administration of the capsule compared to about 0.4 hours for the solution. Following ingestion of a single 20 mg fluvastatin capsule under fasted conditions, measurable plasma concentrations of fluvastatin appear systemically within 10 minutes after dosing and reach a peak of 147 ± 86 ng/mL at 0.66 ± 0.3 hours. Fluvastatin, like the other HMG-CoA reductase inhibitors, has variable bioavailability. The coefficient of variation (based on the inter-subject variability) was 47 to 57% for AUC, and 58 to 69% for C_{max}.

Results from an overnight pharmacokinetic evaluation following steady-state (15 weeks) administration of fluvastatin with the evening meal or 4 hours after the evening meal, showed no significant difference in AUC and no apparent difference in the lipid-lowering effects between the two treatment groups. The administration of fluvastatin with the evening meal resulted in a 2-fold decrease in C_{max} and more than a 2-fold increase in t_{max} as compared to patients receiving the drug 4 hours after the evening meal.

The effects of gender and age on the pharmacokinetics of fluvastatin were evaluated in 4 patient subgroups; young and elderly, males and females. All patients were administered 20 mg fluvastatin daily, at least 2 hours after the evening meal, for 21 days. Overnight pharmacokinetic evaluations indicate that for the general patient population, plasma concentrations of fluvastatin do not significantly vary either as a function of age or gender.

In a single-dose study the kinetics of fluvastatin in subjects with cirrhosis (n=11) and in healthy age- and sex-matched subjects (n=11) were compared. The mean AUC and C_{max} parameters were about 2.5 times higher in the subjects with hepatic insufficiency. There was a 28% decrease in plasma clearance and a 31% smaller volume of distribution. No apparent difference was observed in the plasma elimination half-lives for the two groups.

In a study conducted in 14 healthy volunteers, coadministration of diclofenac 25 mg/day and fluvastatin 40 mg/day for 8 days resulted in a significant increase in the fluvastatin $AUC_{(0-9)}$ and C_{max} on day 8 when compared to baseline (54 and 77%, respectively). Diclofenac C_{max} and AUC were increased (60 and 25%, respectively) and oral clearance decreased by 16% on day 8 when compared to baseline.

In a study conducted in 19 stable renal transplant patients with hypercholesterolemia receiving cyclosporine A concomitantly with fluvastatin 20 mg/day, the AUC for fluvastatin was increased by 1.9 times (94%) compared to that of control subjects from another study who had received the same dose of fluvastatin. The C_{max} was increased by 30% but the T_{max} remained unchanged. Published data show that plasma trough concentrations of cyclosporine A are not significantly changed during coadministration with fluvastatin 20 mg/day. In patients receiving cyclosporine A in combination with fluvastatin, liver enzymes and CK levels should be carefully monitored and the dose of fluvastatin adjusted, if necessary. At present, no data are with doses above 40 mg/day.

Biotransformation pathways for fluvastatin include. a) hydroxylation of the indole ring at the 5- and 6-positions; b) N-dealkylation; and c) beta-oxidation. The major circulating blood components are fluvastatin and the pharmacologically inactive N-desisopropyl-propionic acid metabolite. The hydroxylated metabolites have pharmacological activity but do not circulate systemically. Both enantiomers of fluvastatin are metabolized in a similar manner resulting in only minor differences in systemic exposure.

Indications: Therapy with lipid-altering agents should be considered a component of multiple risk factor intervention in those individuals at increased risk for atherosclerosis vascular disease due to hypercholesterolemia. Fluvastatin should be used in addition to a diet restricted in saturated fat and cholesterol when the response to diet and other nonpharmacological measures alone has been inadequate.

Hypercholesterolemia: The therapeutic indication for fluvastatin is as an adjunct to diet (at least equivalent to the American Heart Association (AHA) Step 1 Diet) in the treatment of elevated total cholesterol (total-C) and LDL-C levels in patients with primary hypercholesterolemia (Type IIa and IIb) whose response to dietary restriction of saturated fat and cholesterol and other nonpharmacological measures has not been adequate.

Therapy with lipid-altering agents should be considered only after secondary causes for hyperlipidemia such as poorly controlled diabetes mellitus, hypothyroidism, nephrotic syndrome, dysproteinemias, obstructive liver disease, other medication, or alcoholism, have been excluded. Prior to initiation of fluvastatin, a lipid profile should be performed to measure total C, HDL-C and TG. For patients with TG <4.52 mmol/L (<400 mg/dL), LDL-C can be estimated using the following equation:

$$\text{LDL-C (mmol/L)} = \text{total-C} - \text{HDL-C} - 0.37 \text{ TG.}$$

For TG levels >4.52 mmol/L (>400 mg/dL), this equation is less accurate and LDL-C concentrations should be determined by ultracentrifugation. In many hypertriglyceridemic patients, LDL-C may be low or normal despite elevated total-C. In such cases, as with other HMG-CoA reductase inhibitors, fluvastatin is not indicated.

Since the goal of treatment is to lower LDL-C, LDL-C levels should be used to initiate and assess treatment response. Only if LDL-C levels are not available, should the total-C be used to monitor therapy.

Lescol (cont'd)

Fluvastatin has not been studied in conditions where the major abnormality is elevation of chylomicrons, VLDL, or IDL (i.e., hyperlipoproteinemia Types I, III, IV or V).

Coronary Heart Disease: Fluvastatin was also found to reduce the rate of progression of atherosclerosis in patients with coronary artery disease and mild to moderate elevations of cholesterol as part of a treatment strategy to lower total and LDL cholesterol to target levels. In a placebo controlled trial including such patients*, fluvastatin monotherapy reduced the rate of progression of atherosclerosis as evaluated by quantitative coronary angiography (QCA). This effect however was not accompanied by a statistically significant improvement in the clinical endpoints (new occurrence or worsening of angina, coronary revascularization procedures [PTCA] or CABG surgery, myocardial infarction [MI] and total mortality) within the 2.5 years of treatment. This trial, however, was not designed to demonstrate a reduction in the risk of coronary morbidity and mortality.

*Lipoprotein and Coronary Atherosclerosis Study (LCAS).

Contraindications: Hypersensitivity to any component of this medication. Fluvastatin is contraindicated in patients with active liver disease or unexplained, persistent clinically relevant elevations in serum transaminases (see Warnings).

Pregnancy and *Lactation:* As with other drugs of this class, fluvastatin is contraindicated during pregnancy and in nursing mothers (see Precautions).

Warnings: Pharmacokinetic Interactions: The use of HMG-CoA reductase inhibitors has been associated with rhabdomyolysis, which may be more frequent when they are coadministered with drugs that inhibit the same cytochrome P450 isoenzyme system (CYP 3A4, CYP 2C9 or CYP 2D6). The various HMG-CoA reductase inhibitors differ with respect to the P450 isoenzyme involved in their metabolism. Fluvastatin is predominantly metabolized by the CYP2C9 subclass of the P450 cytochromes. It is not metabolized to a significant extent by other cytochrome subclasses, including CYP3A4 (see Warnings, Muscle Effects and Precautions, Drug Interactions).

Hepatic Effects: Biochemical abnormalities of liver function have been associated with HMG-CoA reductase inhibitors and other lipid-lowering agents.

Overall, 25 of 2 373 patients (1.1 %) treated with fluvastatin in worldwide controlled clinical trials developed marked persistent elevations (to more than 3 times the upper limit of normal) in transaminase levels requiring discontinuation of treatment in 14 (0.6%) patients. The incidence of such elevations varied from 0.9% at 20 mg/day to 1.9% at 80 mg/day.

In all clinical trials (controlled and uncontrolled), ranging from 28 to 71.2 weeks of exposure, 33 of 2 969 (1.1%) patients had persistent transaminase elevations requiring discontinuation of treatment in 19 (0.6%) patients. In the majority of patients, these abnormal biochemical findings were asymptomatic.

It is recommended that liver function tests be performed at baseline and 12 weeks after initiation of treatment as well as after an increase in the dose, and periodically thereafter (i.e. semi-annually). Particular attention should be paid to patients who develop elevated serum transaminase levels, and in these patients, measurements should be repeated promptly and then performed more frequently.

If the transaminase levels show evidence of progression, particularly if they rise to 3 times the upper limit of normal and are persistent, the drug should be discontinued.

Fluvastatin should be used with caution in patients who consume substantial quantities of alcohol (>14 drinks/week) and/or have a past history of liver disease. Active liver disease or unexplained transaminase elevations are contraindications to the use of fluvastatin; if such condition develops during therapy, the drug should be discontinued.

Muscle Effects: CPK: Transient elevations of creatine phosphokinase (CPK) levels have been seen in fluvastatin-treated patients but have usually been of no clinical significance.

Myalgia and muscle cramps have also been associated with fluvastatin therapy.

Myopathy has been reported in isolated cases with fluvastatin. Two cases were in patients receiving placebo. The incidence of myopathy in fluvastatin-treated patients compares favorably with that in placebo. Rhabdomyolysis with renal dysfunction secondary to myoglobinuria has been reported with other drugs of this class. Rhabdomyolysis has been reported in isolated cases with fluvastatin (see Precautions, Drug Interactions and Cytochrome P450).

Myopathy should be considered in patients with diffuse myalgias, muscle tenderness or weakness and/or marked elevations of creatinine phosphokinase (10 times the upper limit of normal).

An increased risk of myopathy has been reported with HMG-CoA reductase inhibitors when administered concomitantly with immunosuppressive drugs, including cyclosporine, gemfibrozil, erythromycin, or niacin at lipid lowering doses.

Therefore, the benefits and risks of using HMG-CoA reductase inhibitors concomitantly with immunosuppressive drugs, erythromycin, or other drugs metabolized by the P450 enzyme system, fibrates or lipid-lowering doses of niacin should be carefully considered (see Pharmacokinetic Interactions and Precautions, Drug Interactions and Cytochrome P450).

There is limited experience to date with the use of fluvastatin together with cyclosporine. In a study conducted in 19 stable renal transplant patients receiving cyclosporine A concomitantly with fluvastatin 20 mg/day, the AUC for fluvastatin was increased by 1.9 times (94%). Published data indicate that the trough concentration of cyclosporine A was not changed (see Pharmacology, Pharmacokinetics). At present, since no data with doses above 40 mg/day are available, this dosage should not be exceeded in patients receiving cyclosporine A.

Myopathy has not been observed in clinical trials involving small numbers of patients who were treated with fluvastatin together with niacin at lipid lowering doses.

The use of fibrates alone or in combination with HMG-CoA reductase inhibitors has been occasionally associated with myopathy. In short-term studies involving a small number of patients, myopathy was not reported during administration of benzafibrate and fluvastatin at doses of 40 and 60 mg/day. To date, the 80 mg/day dose has not been evaluated with bezafibrate.

Interruption of therapy with fluvastatin should be considered in any patient with an acute serious condition suggestive of myopathy or having a risk factor predisposing to the development of renal failure or rhabdomyolysis, such as severe acute infection, hypotension, major surgery, trauma, severe metabolic, endocrine or electrolyte disorders and uncontrolled seizures.

Patients should be advised to report promptly unexplained muscle pain, tenderness or weakness, particularly if accompanied by malaise or fever.

Precautions: The effect of fluvastatin-induced changes in lipoprotein levels, including reduction of serum cholesterol, on cardiovascular morbidity and mortality, or total mortality has not been established.

General: Before instituting therapy with fluvastatin, an attempt should be made to control hypercholesterolemia with appropriate diet, exercise, weight reduction in overweight and obese patients, and to treat other underlying medical problems (see Indications). The patient should be advised to inform subsequent physicians of the prior use of fluvastatin or any other lipid metabolism regulator.

Homozygous Familial Hypercholesterolemia: Fluvastatin has not been evaluated in patients with rare homozygous familial hypercholesterolemia. HMG-CoA reductase inhibitors are less or not effective in this subgroup of hypercholesterolemic patients.

Effect on Lipoprotein(A) [Lp(a)]: In some patients the beneficial effect of lowered total cholesterol and LDL cholesterol levels may be partly blunted by a concomitant increase in the Lp(a) levels. Until further experience is obtained from controlled clinical trials, it is suggested, where feasible, that Lp(a) measurements be carried out in patients placed on therapy with fluvastatin.

Effect on CoQ_{10} Levels (Ubiquinone): A significant decrease in plasma CoQ_{10} levels in patients treated with fluvastatin and other statins has been observed in short-term clinical trials. The clinical significance of a potential long-term statin-induced deficiency of CoQ_{10} has not yet been established. It has been reported that a decrease in myocardial ubiquinone levels could lead to impaired cardiac function in patients with borderline congestive heart failure.

Renal Impairment: Because fluvastatin does not undergo significant renal excretion, modification of dosage should not be necessary in patients with mild to moderate renal impairment (creatinine clearance >30 mL/min).

As there is no experience with fluvastatin in patients with severe renal insufficiency (creatinine > 260 μmol/L, i.e., creatinine clearance < 30 mL/min), its use cannot be recommended in this patient population.

Endocrine Function: HMG-CoA reductase inhibitors interfere with cholesterol synthesis and as such could theoretically blunt adrenal and/or gonadal steroid production.

Fluvastatin exhibited no effect upon non-stimulated cortisol levels, FSH (males only) or thyroid metabolism as assessed by TSH. Small declines in total testosterone have been noted in treated groups, but no commensurate elevation in LH occurred. However, the effects of HMG-CoA reductase inhibitors on male fertility have not been studied in an adequate number of patients. The effects, if any, on the pituitary-gonadal axis in premenopausal women are unknown.

Patients treated with fluvastatin who develop clinical evidence of endocrine dysfunction should be evaluated appropriately. Caution should be exercised if an HMG-CoA reductase inhibitor or other agent used to lower cholesterol levels is administered to patients receiving other drugs (e.g., ketoconazole, spironolactone or cimetidine) that may decrease the levels of endogenous steroid hormones.

Effect on Lens: Current data from long-term clinical trials do not indicate an adverse effect of fluvastatin on the human lens.

Pregnancy: **Fluvastatin is contraindicated during pregnancy** (see Contraindications).

Data on the use of fluvastatin in pregnant women is limited. A few reports have been received of congenital anomalies in infants whose mothers were treated during a critical period of pregnancy with other HMG-CoA reductase inhibitors. During the clinical progam, a total of 5 women who were receiving fluvastatin became pregnant and were discontinued from the studies. Of these 5 women, 3 gave birth to healthy babies, one experienced an ectopic pregnancy which was attributed to a severely scarred fallopian tube; and one spontaneously aborted.

Atherosclerosis is a chronic process and discontinuation of lipid metabolism regulators during pregnancy should have little impact on the outcome of long-term therapy of primary hypercholesterolemia. Cholesterol and other products of cholesterol biosynthesis are essential components for fetal development (including synthesis of steroids and cell membranes). Since HMG-CoA reductase inhibitors decrease cholesterol synthesis and possibly the synthesis of other biologically active substances derived from cholesterol, they may cause fetal harm when administered to pregnant women.

Fluvastatin should be administered to women of childbearing age only when such patients are highly unlikely to conceive and have been informed of the potential hazards. If the patient becomes pregnant while taking this class of drug, therapy should be discontinued and the patient apprised of the potential hazard to the fetus (see Contraindications).

Lactation: It is not known whether fluvastatin is excreted in human milk. Because many drugs are excreted in human milk and because of the potential for serious adverse reactions in nursing infants from fluvastatin, women receiving fluvastatin should not breast-feed (see Contraindications).

Children: Limited experience with the use of other HMG-CoA reductase inhibitors is available in children. Safety and effectiveness of fluvastatin in children have not been established.

Geriatrics: The effect of age on the pharmacokinetics of fluvastatin was evaluated. Results indicate that for the general patient population plasma concentrations of fluvastatin do not vary either as a function of age or gender (see Pharmacology, Pharmacokinetics).

Drug Interactions: **Concomitant Therapy With Other Lipid Metabolism Regulators: Combined drug therapy should be approached with caution as information from controlled studies is limited.**

A drug interactive effect (pharmacokinetic and/or clinical) has been shown for the following drugs in combination with fluvastatin.

Cholestyramine: The cholesterol-lowering effects of fluvastatin and the bile acid sequestrant, cholestyramine, are additive.

Administration of fluvastatin concomitantly 2 to 4 hours after cholestyramine, results in fluvastatin decreases of more than 50% for the fluvastatin AUC and 50 to 80% for the fluvastatin C_{max}. However, administration of fluvastatin 4 hours after cholestyramine resulted in a clinically significant additive effect in reducing total-C and LDL-C compared with that achieved with either component drug (see Dosage).

Gemfibrozil/Fenofibrate/Niacin: Myopathy, including rhabdomyolysis, has occurred in patients who were receiving coadministration of HMG-CoA reductase inhibitors with fibric acid derivatives and niacin (in lipid lowering doses), particularly in subjects with pre-existing renal insufficiency (see Warnings, Muscle Effects). Fluvastatin has been safely administered concomitantly with nicotinic acid, gemfibrozil and bezafibrate in clinical studies. In short-term studies involving a small number of patients, myopathy was not reported during administration of bezafibrate and fluvastatin at doses of 40 and 60 mg/day. To date, the 80 mg/day dose has not been evaluated with bezafibrate.

Other Concomitant Therapy: Cimetidine/Ranitidine/Omeprazole: Concomitant administration of fluvastatin with cimetidine, ranitidine and omeprazole results in a significant increase in the fluvastatin C_{max} (43, 70 and 50%, respectively) and AUC (24 to 33%), with an 18 to 23% decrease in apparent oral plasma clearance (Cl/F).

Digoxin: In a crossover study involving 18 patients chronically receiving digoxin, concomitant administration of a single 40 mg dose of fluvastatin had no effect on digoxin AUC and small but clinically insignificant increases in the digoxin C_{max} and urinary clearance were noted.

Rifampin: Administration of fluvastatin to subjects pretreated with rifampin results in significant reduction in C_{max} (59%) and AUC (51%) of fluvastatin, with a large increase (95%) in plasma clearance.

Antipyrine: Administration of fluvastatin does not influence the metabolism and excretion of antipyrine, either by induction or inhibition.

Beta-adrenergic Blocking Drugs: Concomitant administration of propranolol has no effect on the bioavailability of fluvastatin sodium.

Warfarin: In vitro protein binding studies demonstrated no interaction at therapeutic concentrations. In a drug interaction study, the concomitant use of fluvastatin and warfarin did not alter the plasma levels and prothrombin times compared to warfarin alone. However, since other drugs of this class have been shown to enhance the anticoagulant effect of warfarin, caution is advised when administering warfarin concomitantly with fluvastatin.

Cytochrome P450: Fluvastatin is predominantly metabolized by the hepatic microsomal CYP2C9 subclass of the P450 cytochromes. It is not metabolized to a significant extent by other cytochrome subclasses, including CYP3A4. The clearance of drugs which are also CYP2C9 substrates may decrease when coadministered with fluvastatin. However, for those CYP2C9-metabolized drugs which have been studied directly, including diclofenac, tolbutamide, and warfarin, the effect on clearance is small and no clinically significant drug interactions of fluvastatin with other CYP2C9 substrates have been demonstrated. Caution should nevertheless be exercised with concomitant use of drugs metabolized by the CYP2C9 subclass of the P450 cytochromes such as phenytoin, oral anticoagulants (e.g., warfarin), oral hypoglycemic agents (e.g., tolbutamide, chlorpropamide) and NSAIDs (e.g., diclofenac) (see Warnings, Muscle Effects).

In addition, since fluvastatin demonstrates a moderate affinity for the CYP 3A4 isoenzyme, drugs or common agents such as grapefruit juice that inhibit this enzyme (immunosuppressants, azole-type antifungal agents, macrolide antibiotics or antidepressants) may represent a potential, at least in some patients, for drug interactions when combined with fluvastatin (see Warnings, Pharmacokinetics Interactions and Muscle Effects).

Patients with Severe Hypercholesterolemia: Higher dosages (80 mg/day) required for some patients with severe hypercholesterolemia are associated with increased plasma levels of fluvastatin. Caution should be exercised in such patients who are also significantly renally impaired, elderly, or are also concomitantly being administered digoxin, or CYP 450 inhibitors (See Warnings, Pharmacokinetic Interactions and Muscle Effects and Precautions, Drug Interactions).

Although specific interaction studies were not performed with all drugs listed below, in clinical studies, fluvastatin was used concomitantly with angiotensin-converting enzyme (ACE) inhibitors, beta-blockers, calcium-channel blockers, oral sulphonylureas, antacids, diuretics and NSAIDs without evidence to date of clinically significant interactions.

Immunosuppressive Drugs, Erythromycin: See Warnings, Muscle Effects.

Laboratory Interactions: The HMG-CoA reductase inhibitors may cause elevation of creatinine phosphokinase and transaminase levels (see Warnings). In the differential diagnosis of chest pain in a patient on fluvastatin, cardiac and noncardiac fractions of these enzymes should be determined.

Adverse Effects: In all clinical studies (controlled and uncontrolled), 1% (32/2 969) of fluvastatin patients were discontinued due to adverse experiences attributed to study drug (mean exposure of approximately 16 months ranging in duration from 1 to more than 36 months). This results, in controlled studies, in an exposure adjusted incidence of 0.8 % per patient year in fluvastatin patients compared to an incidence of 1.1 % in placebo patients. Adverse events were usually mild and transient. Clinical adverse reactions of positive or uncertain relationship to study medication occuring at a frequency

Table I—Lescol

Adverse Reactions

Adverse Event	Lescol 20 mg/day (N=1 425) (%)	40 mg/day (N=1 136) (%)	80 mg/day (N=369) (%)	Placebo (N=960) (%)
Gastrointestinal				
Dyspepsia	4.7	4.8	7.3	2.3
Constipation	2.8	1.8	2.4	2.5
Abdominal Pain	2.7	2.1	3.8	2.0
Flatulence	2.5	1.9	1.6	2.2
Diarrhea	2.5	1.5	1.6	2.1
Nausea	2.0	1.6	0.8	1.4
Eructation	1.4	0.6	0.5	1.1
Musculoskeletal				
Myalgia	1.7	1.8	2.7	2.3
Arthralgia	1.4	1.4	1.4	1.5
Back Pain	1.0	0.8	1.1	1.6
CNS				
Dizziness	0.9	1.1	0.5	1.8
Abnormal Vision	1.0	0.9	1.1	1.4
Psychiatric				
Insomnia	1.9	1.3	0.3	0.9
Respiratory				
Upper Respiratory Infection	1.1	0.9	2.4	1.9
Integumentary				
Rash	1.5	0.8	1.9	1.6
Miscellaneous				
Headache	3.8	2.7	1.9	3.0
Fatigue	1.8	1.5	0.5	1.8
Chest Pain	0.3	0.9	1.4	0.5

$\geq$ 1 % in controlled clinical trials with fluvastatin are shown in Table I.

Other clinical adverse reactions of positive or uncertain relationship to study medication occuring in 0.5 to 1.0% of patients receiving 20 to 80 mg fluvastatin monotherapy in controlled clinical trials (N=2 326) are listed below:

Gastrointestinal: vomiting, gastritis.

Musculoskeletal: arthritis.

CNS: conjunctivitis, paresthesia.

Respiratory: rhinitis.

Integumentary: pruritus.

Miscellaneous: leg pain, influenza-like symptoms, allergy.

The following effects have been reported with drugs of this class: Skeletal: myopathy, rhabdomyolysis (see Warnings), muscle cramping/pain.

Neurological: paresthesia, peripheral neuropathy, psychiatric disturbances/anxiety.

Hypersensitivity Reactions: An apparent hypersensitivity syndrome has been reported rarely with other HMG-CoA reductase inhibitors and has included one or more of the following features: anaphylaxis, angioedema, lupus erythematous-like syndrome, polymyalgia rheumatica, vasculitis, purpura, thrombocytopenia, leukopenia, hemolytic anemia, positive antinuclear antibody (ANA), erythrocytes sedimentation rate (ESR) increase, arthritis, arthralgia, urticaria, asthenia, photosensitivity, fever, chills, flushing, malaise, dyspnea, toxic epidermal necrolysis, erythema multiform, including Stevens-Johnson syndrome.

Gastrointestinal: hepatitis, cholestatic jaundice, anorexia, vomiting.

Skin: alopecia.

Miscellaneous: asthenia, sweating, hot flushes.

Overdose: Symptoms: The maximum single oral dose of fluvastatin received by healthy volunteers was 60 mg. No clinically significant adverse experiences were seen at this dose. There has been a single report of two children, one 2 year old and the other 3 years of age, either of whom may have possibly ingested fluvastatin. The maximum amount of fluvastatin ingested was 80 mg (4×20 mg capsules). Vomiting was induced by ipecac in both children and no capsules were noted in their emesis. Neither child experienced any adverse symptoms and both recovered from the incident without problems.

Treatment: Should an accidental overdose occur, administration of activated charcoal is recommended. In the case of very recent oral intake, gastric lavage may be considered.

Treatment should be symptomatic. The dialyzability of fluvastatin and its metabolites in man is not known at present.

Dosage: Prior to initiating fluvastatin, the patient should be placed on a standard cholesterol-lowering diet (at least equivalent to the American Heart Association (AHA) Step 1 Diet), which should be continued during treatment. If appropriate, a program of weight control and physical exercise should be implemented.

The recommended starting dose is 20 mg once daily to be taken in the evening or at bedtime. The recommended dosing range is 20 to 80 mg/day. The daily dose regimen of 80 mg should be administered in divided doses, i.e., 40 mg b.i.d. Fluvastatin should be taken with or after meals. Since the maximal reductions in LDL-C are seen within 4 weeks of administration of a given dose, periodic lipid determinations should be performed with dosage adjusted to a maximum of 40 mg twice a day, according to the patient's response.

The therapeutic effect of fluvastatin is maintained with prolonged administration.

Cholesterol levels should be monitored periodically and consideration should be given to reducing the dosage of fluvastatin if cholesterol levels fall below the targeted range, such as that recommended by the Second Report of the U.S. National Cholesterol Education Program (NCEP).

Severe Hypercholesterolemia: In patients with severe hypercholesterolemia, higher dosages (80 mg/day) may be required (see Warnings, Pharmacokinetic Interactions and Muscle Effects and Precautions, Drug Interactions).

Concomitant Therapy: (see Precautions).

Patients with Renal Insufficiency: (see Precautions).

Information for the Patient: See Blue Section—Information for the Patient "Lescol".

Supplied: 20 mg: Each brown opaque cap and light brown opaque body gelatin capsule contains: fluvastatin 20 mg (from fluvastatin sodium 21.06 mg). Sandoz Triangle ⚠ printed twice and "20" in white ink on the cap; "Lescol" and product logo in red ink on the body. Nonmedicinal ingredients: calcium carbonate, magnesium stearate, microcrystalline cellulose, pregelatinized starch, sodium bicarbonate and talc. Capsule shell and printing ink: ammonium hydroxide, benzyl alcohol, n-butyl alcohol, butylparaben, carboxymethylcellulose sodium, edetate calcium disodium, ethyl alcohol, gelatin, iron oxide black, iron oxide red, iron oxide yellow, isopropyl alcohol, methylparaben, polyvinylpyrrolidone, propylene glycol, propylparaben, shellac, silicon dioxide, sodium hydroxide, sodium laurel sulfate, sodium propionate and titanium dioxide. Bottles of 100.

40 mg: Each brown opaque cap and gold opaque body gelatin capsule contains: fluvastatin 40 mg (from fluvastatin sodium 42.12 mg). Sandoz Triangle ⚠ printed twice and "40" in white ink on the cap; "Lescol" and product logo in red ink on the body. Nonmedicinal ingredients: calcium carbonate, magnesium stearate, microcrystalline cellulose, pregelatinized starch, sodium bicarbonate and talc. Capsule shell and printing ink: ammonium hydroxide, benzyl alcohol, n-butyl alcohol,

Lescol (cont'd)

butylparaben, carboxymethylcellulose sodium, edetate calcium disodium, ethyl alcohol, gelatin, iron oxide black, iron oxide red, iron oxide yellow, isopropyl alcohol, methylparaben, polyvinylpyrrolidone, propylene glycol, propylparaben, shellac, silicon dioxide, sodium hydroxide, sodium laurel sulfate, sodium propionate and titanium dioxide. Bottles of 100.

Store between 15 and 30°C in a tight container. Protect from light and humidity.

(Shown in Product Recognition Section)

Reviewed 1999

LEUCOVORIN CALCIUM INJECTION ℞

Faulding

Citrovorum Factor

Folic Acid Derivative

Pharmacology: Leucovorin is a reduced form of folic acid, which is readily converted to other reduced folic acid derivatives (e.g., tetra-hydrofolate). Because it does not require reduction by dihydrofolate reductase as does folic acid, leucovorin is not affected by blockages of this enzyme by folic acid antagonists (dihydrofolate reductase inhibitors). This allows purine and thymidine synthesis, and thus DNA, RNA and protein synthesis, to occur. Leucovorin may limit methotrexate action on normal cells by competing with methotrexate for the same transport processes into the cell.

Leucovorin enhances the cytotoxicity of fluoropyrimidines such as fluorouracil by their metabolites, methylene tetrahydrofolate and fluorodeoxyuridine monophosphate, forming a stable ternary complex with thymidylate synthase, and thereby, decreasing intracellular levels of that enzyme and the product thymidylate. The cell then dies as a result of thymine starvation.

Indications: To diminish the toxicity and counteract the effects of overdosage of folic acid antagonists.

To diminish the systemic toxicity of methotrexate after administration of methotrexate as a chemotherapeutic agent, as part of chemotherapeutic treatment programs in the management of several forms of cancer.

To treat megaloblastic anemias **due to folate deficiency,** as in sprue and other nutritional deficiencies; and megaloblastic anemias of pregnancy and infancy (see Contraindications).

For pre-treatment followed by fluorouracil to prolong survival in the palliative treatment of patients with advanced colorectal cancer.

Contraindications: Leucovorin is improper therapy for pernicious anemia or other megaloblastic anemias secondary to a deficiency of vitamin B_{12}. Its use can lead to an apparent response of the hematopoietic system, but neurological damage may occur or progress if already present.

Caution: Leucovorin Injection should not be administered intrathecally.

Warnings: In cases of overdosage of folic acid antagonists, prompt administration of leucovorin calcium is essential; if a period of more than 4 hours intervenes, the treatment may be ineffective due to the time delay. Monitoring of the serum MTX concentration is essential in determining the optimal dose of leucovorin to give and duration of therapy. Delayed MTX excretion may be an indication of a third space fluid accumulation (i.e. ascites, pleural effusion), renal insufficiency, low pH of urine or inadequate hydration. Higher doses of leucovorin or prolonged administration may be indicated in such cases. Leucovorin has no apparent effect on pre-existing methotrexate nephrotoxicity.

In general diarrhea and/or stomatitis/mucositis are the first indications that severe and potentially life-threatening toxicity could develop. Patients who experience these symptoms while receiving any combination therapy regimen involving leucovorin and fluorouracil should be carefully monitored, generally these symptoms are easily controllable by reducing the dose of fluorouracil. Treatment-related deaths have been sporadically reported in patients receiving leucovorin/fluorouracil combination therapy.

Leucovorin enhances the toxicity of fluorouracil. When these drugs are administered concurrently in the palliative therapy of advanced colorectal cancer, the dosage of fluorouracil must be reduced. Although the toxicities observed in patients treated with the combination of leucovorin and fluorouracil are qualitatively similar to those observed in patients treated with fluorouracil alone, gastrointestinal toxicities (particularly stomatitis and diarrhea) are observed more commonly and may be more severe in patients receiving the combination therapy. Generally these symptoms are easily controllable by reducing the dose of fluorouracil.

Therapy with leucovorin/fluorouracil must not be initiated or continued in patients who have symptoms of gastrointestinal toxicity of any severity, until those symptoms have resolved. Patients with diarrhea must be closely monitored until the diarrhea has resolved, as rapid clinical deterioration leading to death can occur.

Geriatrics: Elderly or debilitated patients are at greater risk for severe toxicity receiving this therapy.

Precautions: General: Leucovorin should be used with caution after chemotherapeutically administered methotrexate when the following medical problems exist: aciduria (urine pH less than 7); ascites; dehydration (**Note:** inadequate hydration including that secondary to vomiting may also result in increased methotrexate toxicity); gastrointestinal obstruction; pleural or peritoneal effusions; renal function impairment (**Note:** risk of methotrexate toxicity is increased because elimination of methotrexate may be impaired and accumulation may occur; even small doses of methotrexate may lead to severe myelosuppression and mucositis; larger doses and/or increased duration of leucovorin treatment may be necessary).

Patient monitoring is recommended when leucovorin is administered as part of methotrexate chemotherapy programs. Monitoring may include creatinine clearance determinations prior to therapy; plasma or serum methotrexate determinations to detect developing renal function impairment (an increase of greater than 50% within 24 hours is associated with severe renal toxicity); urine pH determination (recommended every 6 hours to ensure that the pH remains greater than 7 to minimize the risk of methotrexate nephropathy). Leucovorin has no apparent effect on pre-existing methotrexate nephrotoxicity.

Pregnancy, Reproduction and *Lactation:* Problems have not been documented. It is not known whether leucovorin is excreted in breast milk.

Geriatrics: No information is available regarding the use of leucovorin in geriatrics.

Elderly patients are at greater risk of developing severe toxicity when treated with the combination of leucovorin plus fluorouracil for the palliative treatment of colorectal cancer.

Children: Leucovorin may increase the frequency of seizures in susceptible children.

Drug Interactions: The following drugs or combinations containing these drugs may interact with leucovorin with clinical significance: anticonvulsants, barbiturate or anticonvulsants, hydantoin; primidone (large doses of leucovorin may counteract the anticonvulsant effects of these medications); diaminopyrimidines (there is some evidence that concomitant administration of leucovorin and trimethoprim (or co-trimoxazole) may inhibit the antibiotic effect of trimethoprim).

Leucovorin, administered concomitantly with methotrexate, may nullify the antitumor chemotherapeutic effect of the latter drug (see Dosage).

Leucovorin has been administered simultaneously with pyrimethamine without interfering with its antimalarial therapy.

Leucovorin enhances the cytotoxicity and toxicity of fluorouracil.

Adverse Effects: Allergic reactions, wheezing, skin rash, hives or itching, occur rarely. In combination regimens, the toxicity of fluorouracil is enhanced by leucovorin. The most common manifestations are mucositis, stomatitis, leukopenia, and/or diarrhea which may be dose limiting. In clinical trials with this drug combination, these toxicities were found to be easily controllable by appropriately reducing the dose of fluorouracil.

Overdose: Symptoms and Treatment: Leucovorin has very low acute and subchronic toxicity in animals. There has been no experience with overdosage of parenteral leucovorin in humans.

Dosage: Leucovorin calcium injection may be administered as received by i.m. injection or i.v. injection, or it may be diluted for i.v. infusion (see Dilution for I.V. Infusion).

Due to calcium content of leucovorin solution, no more than 160 mg/minute of leucovorin should be injected i.v.

Treatment of Overdosage of Folic Acid Antagonists: In cases of overdosage of folic acid antagonists, prompt administration of leucovorin calcium is essential; if a period of more than 4 hours intervenes, the treatment may be ineffective.

The dose of leucovorin calcium should be equal to or greater than the suspected dose of folic acid antagonist.

Where large doses of methotrexate have been given, leucovorin may be administered by i.v. infusion in doses up to 75 mg within 12 hours, followed by 12 mg i.m. every 6 hours for 4 doses. In less severe overdosage, 6 to 12 mg of leucovorin may be given i.m. every 6 hours for 4 doses, until the serum methotrexate level is less than 10^{-8}M.

Use after Chemotherapy with Methotrexate: The dosage and scheduling of doses of leucovorin varies, but it is normally given about 6 to 24 hours following methotrexate administration, in amounts equal to the weight of methotrexate given.

Serum creatinine and methotrexate levels should be determined at 24-hour intervals. If the 24-hour serum creatinine has increased 50% over baseline or if the 24-hour methotrexate level is greater than 5×10^{-6}M or the 48-hour level is greater than 9×10^{-7}M, the dose of leucovorin should be increased to 100 mg/m^2 i.v. every 3 hours until the methotrexate level is less than 10^{-8}M.

Hydration (3 L/day) and urinary alkalinization with $NaHCO_3$ should be employed concomitantly. The bicarbonate dose should be adjusted to maintain the urine pH at 7 or greater.

In most cases, leucovorin should not be administered simultaneously with systemic methotrexate, since the therapeutic effect of the antimetabolite may be nullified. However, when methotrexate is administered by intra-arterial (regional perfusion) or intrathecal injection, leucovorin may be given (i.m., i.v. or orally) concomitantly, to offset systemic methotrexate toxicity without abolishing the local activity of the cytotoxic drug.

Treatment of Megaloblastic Anemia: For treatment of megaloblastic anemia due to folate deficiency, the dose should not exceed 1 mg daily. The duration of therapy depends on the hematologic response to the drug. Oral leucovorin is preferred to parenteral therapy, except where cases of severe vomiting impair drug absorption when administered orally.

Treatment of Advanced Colorectal Cancer: Leucovorin is administered at 200 mg/m^2 by slow i.v. injection prior to dosing with 370 mg/m^2 fluorouracil by slow i.v. injection, for 5 consecutive days.

This 5-day treatment course may be repeated at 4-week (28-day) intervals, provided that the patient has completely recovered from the toxic effects of the prior treatment course.

In subsequent treatment courses, the dosage of fluorouracil should be adjusted based on patient tolerance of the prior treatment course. The daily dosage of fluorouracil should be reduced by 20% for patients who experienced moderate hematologic or gastrointestinal toxicity in the prior treatment course, and by 30% for patients who experienced severe toxicity. For patients who did not experience toxicity in the prior treatment course, fluorouracil dosage may be increased by 10%. Leucovorin dosages are not adjusted for toxicity.

Note: Since leucovorin may enhance the toxicity of fluorouracil, combination therapy consisting of Leucovorin and Fluorouracil for advanced colorectal cancer should be administered under the supervision of a physician experienced in the use of antimetabolite cancer chemotherapy. Particular care should be taken in the treatment of elderly or debilitated colorectal cancer patients, as these patients may be at increased risk of severe toxicity. Death from severe enterocolitis, diarrhea and dehydration have been reported in elderly patients receiving leucovorin and fluorouracil. Concomitant granulocytopenia and fever were present in some but not all of the patients.

Stability and Storage: Store refrigerated (2 to 8°C) and protect from light.

Dilution for I.V. Infusion: When required for i.v. infusion, the injection may be diluted with 5% Dextrose Injection, 0.9% Sodium Chloride Injection, Lactated Ringer's Injection or Ringer's Injection to give a final concentration of 0.05 mg/mL leucovorin. These dilutions may be stored for 24 hours at room temperature. Due to the possibility of antimicrobial contamination, unused solution should be discarded after that time.

Dilutions with the hypertonic infusion solutions, 10% Dextrose Injection and 5% Dextrose in 0.9% Sodium Chloride Injection, may also be prepared to a final concentration of 0.05 mg/mL of leucovorin. However these dilutions should be stored for no longer than 8 hours at room temperatures. Unused solution should be discarded after that time.

Dispensing of Pharmacy Bulk Vials: Leucovorin calcium injection, 10 mg/mL, is supplied as 500 mg in 50 mL of sterile, unpreserved, isotonic solution as a pharmacy bulk vial.

The use of pharmacy bulk vials is restricted to hospitals with a recognized i.v. admixture program. The pharmacy bulk vial is intended for single puncture, multiple dispensing, and for i.v. use only.

Contents of the pharmacy bulk vials should be dispensed within 8 hours of the initial entry because of the potential for microbial contamination. Discard any unused portion. The diluted solutions, prepared from the pharmacy bulk vial, should be used within 24 hours if kept at room temperature from the time of the initial entry into the pharmacy bulk vial. However, the product diluted with hypertonic infusion solutions are restricted to 8 hours if kept at room temperature from the time of the initial entry into the pharmacy bulk vial.

Pharmacy bulk vials contain no preservatives. Care must be taken to minimize the potential for inadvertant introduction of microorganisms during manipulation in the hospital environment.

Warning: As with all parenteral drug products, i.v. admixtures should be inspected visually for clarity, particulate matter, precipitate, discoloration and leakage prior to administration, whenever solution and container permit. Solutions showing haziness, particulate matter, precipitate, discoloration or leakage should not be used.

Supplied: Each mL of sterile, isotonic solution contains: leucovorin 10 mg (as the calcium salt) in water for injection with sodium chloride 8.5 mg. Preservative-free. Sodium hydroxide or hydrochloric acid may be used for pH adjustment. Single dose vials of 5 mL (50 mg/5 mL). Pharmacy bulk vials of 50 mL (500 mg/50 mL) for i.v. administration only. The pharmacy bulk vial is supplied to hospitals with a recognized i.v. admixture program only.

LEUCOVORIN CALCIUM INJECTION USP Ⓟ

Novopharm

Citrovorum Factor

Folic Acid Derivative

Supplied: Each mL of solution contains: leucovorin 10 mg (as the calcium salt). Nonmedicinal ingredients: sodium chloride, sodium hydroxide and water for injection. Vials of 5 mL, boxes of 10. Vials of 50 mL.

LEUKERAN® Ⓟ

Glaxo Wellcome

Chlorambucil

Antineoplastic Agent

Pharmacology: Chlorambucil is an aromatic nitrogen mustard derivative which acts as a bifunctional alkylating agent. Alkylation takes place through the formation of a highly reactive ethylenimonium radical. A probable mode of action involves cross-linkage of the ethylenimonium derivative between two strands of helical DNA and subsequent interference with replication.

After oral administration of carbon-14 labelled chlorambucil, maximum plasma radioactivity occurs between 40 and 70 minutes later. Studies have shown that chlorambucil disappears from the plasma with a mean terminal phase half-life of 1.5 hours and that its urinary excretion is low. A high level of urinary radioactivity after oral or i.v. administration of carbon-14 labelled chlorambucil indicates that the drug is well absorbed after oral dosage.

Chlorambucil and its metabolites are extensively bound to plasma and tissue proteins. In vitro, chlorambucil is 99% bound to plasma proteins, specifically albumin. Cerebrospinal fluid levels of chlorambucil have not been determined. Evidence of human teratogenicity suggests that the drug crosses the placenta.

Chlorambucil is extensively metabolized in the liver primarily to phenylacetic acid mustard which has antineoplastic activity. The peak plasma levels of chlorambucil and phenylacetic acid mustard are similar, approximating 1 μg/mL; however, the metabolite's half-life is 1.6 times greater than that of the parent drug. Chlorambucil and its major metabolite spontaneously degrade in vivo forming monohydroxy and dihydroxy derivatives. After a single dose of radiolabelled chlorambucil (carbon-14), approximately 15 to 60% of the radioactivity appears in the urine after 24 hours. Less than 1% of the urinary radioactivity is in the form of chlorambucil or phenylacetic acid mustard. In summary, the pharmacokinetic data suggest that oral chlorambucil undergoes rapid gastrointestinal absorption and plasma clearance and that it is almost completely metabolized, having extremely low urinary excretion.

Indications: Treatment of chronic lymphocytic leukemia, malignant lymphomas including lymphosarcoma, giant follicular lymphoma and Hodgkin's disease. It is not curative but produces remissions, some of which may be striking in a substantial portion of patients.

Contraindications: Should not be administered to patients who are resistant to the drug or who have developed hypersensitivity to it. There may be cross-hypersensitivity (skin rash) between chlorambucil and other alkylating agents.

Chlorambucil should not be used within 4 weeks of a full course of radiation or chemotherapy.

Warnings: Caution: Chlorambucil is a potent drug product and should be used only by physicians experienced with cancer chemotherapeutic drugs. Blood counts should be taken once or twice weekly. Discontinue or reduce the dosage upon evidence of abnormal depression of the bone marrow (see Contraindications and Precautions).

Chlorambucil, a derivative of nitrogen mustard, is a potent drug. It is for use only under the direction of physicians experienced in the administration of cancer chemotherapeutic drugs.

Rare instances of skin rash progressing to erythema multiforme, toxic epidermal necrolysis, or Stevens-Johnson's syndrome have been reported. Chlorambucil should be discontinued promptly in patients who develop skin reactions.

Pregnancy: When cytotoxic drugs are used in pregnancy, the possible teratogenic effect on the fetus should be kept in mind. It is therefore advisable to delay treatment with these drugs as long as possible and certainly until after the first three months of pregnancy.

Lactation: Mothers receiving chlorambucil should not breastfeed.

Precautions: Since chlorambucil is capable of producing irreversible bone marrow depression, blood counts should be monitored once or twice weekly in patients under treatment.

At therapeutic dosage, chlorambucil depresses lymphocytes and has less effect on neutrophil and platelet counts and on hemoglobin levels. Discontinuation of chlorambucil is not necessary at the first sign of a fall in neutrophils but it must be remembered that the fall may continue for 10 days or more after the last dose.

When lymphocytic infiltration of the bone marrow is present, or the bone marrow is hypoplastic, the daily dose should not exceed 0.1 mg/kg body weight.

Patients with evidence of impaired renal function should be carefully monitored as they are prone to additional myelosuppression associated with azotemia.

Development of acute leukemia after chlorambucil therapy for chronic lymphocytic leukemia has been reported. However it was not clear whether the acute leukemia was part of the natural history of the disease or if the chemotherapy was the cause.

A comparison of patients with ovarian cancer who received alkylating agents with those who did not, showed that the use of alkylating agents including chlorambucil, significantly increased the incidence of acute leukemia.

Acute myelogenous leukemia has been reported in a small proportion of patients receiving chlorambucil as long-term adjuvant therapy for breast cancer.

The leukemogenic risk must be balanced against the potential therapeutic benefit when considering the use of chlorambucil.

Children with nephrotic syndrome may have an increased risk of seizures if administered concurrent chlorambucil. As with any potentially epileptogenic drug, caution should be exercised when administering chlorambucil to patients with a history of seizure disorder, head trauma, or receiving other potentially epileptogenic drugs.

Drug Interactions: Animal studies indicate that patients who receive phenylbutazone may require a reduction of the standard chlorambucil doses because of the possibility of enhanced chlorambucil toxicity.

Patients with Impaired Hepatic Function: Consideration should be given to dose reduction in patients with gross hepatic dysfunction.

Impairment of Fertility, Teratogenic Effects, Mutagenesis: Chlorambucil may cause suppression of ovarian function. Amenorrhea has been reported following chlorambucil therapy.

Azoospermia has been observed as a result of therapy with chlorambucil although it is estimated that a total dose of at least 400 mg is necessary.

Varying degrees of recovery of spermatogenesis have been reported in patients with lymphoma following treatment with chlorambucil in total doses of 410 to 2 600 mg.

As with other cytotoxic agents chlorambucil is potentially teratogenic.

As with all cytotoxic chemotherapy, adequate contraceptive precautions should be advised when either partner is receiving chlorambucil.

Chlorambucil has been shown to cause chromatid or chromosome damage in man.

Children: The safety and effectiveness in children have not been established.

Adverse Effects: The most common side effect is bone marrow suppression. Although bone marrow suppression frequently occurs, it is usually reversible if the chlorambucil is withdrawn early enough. However, irreversible bone marrow failure has been reported.

Gastrointestinal disturbances such as nausea and vomiting, diarrhea and oral ulceration occur infrequently. Other side effects may be encountered but usually only when the therapeutic dosage has been exceeded.

Severe interstitial pulmonary fibrosis has occasionally been reported in patients with chronic lymphocytic leukemia on long-term chlorambucil therapy. Pulmonary fibrosis may be reversible on withdrawal of chlorambucil.

Skin hypersensitivity (including rare reports of skin rash progressing to erythema multiforme, toxic epidermal necrolysis, and Stevens-Johnson syndrome) has been reported (see Warnings).

Other reported adverse reactions include hepatotoxicity and jaundice, drug fever, peripheral neuropathy, interstitial pneumonia, sterile cystitis, infertility, leukemia, and secondary malignancies (see Precautions).

Seizures have occurred in children with nephrotic syndrome treated with chlorambucil and dose related focal fits in adults have been reported (see Precautions).

Overdose: Symptoms and Treatment: Reversible pancytopenia was the main finding of inadvertent overdose of chlorambucil. Neurological toxicity ranging from agitated behavior and ataxia to multiple grand mal seizures has also occurred. As there is no known antidote, the blood picture should be closely monitored and general supportive measures should be instituted together with appropriate blood transfusion if necessary. Chlorambucil is not diazylable.

Dosage: Chronic Lymphocytic Leukemia: Treatment with chlorambucil is usually started after the patient has developed symptoms or when there is evidence of impaired bone marrow function (but not marrow failure) as indicated by the peripheral blood count.

Initially, chlorambucil is given at the dose of 0.15 mg/kg/day until the total leukocyte count is formed to 10 000/μL. Treatment may be resumed 4 weeks after the end of the first course and continued at a dosage of 0.1 mg/kg/day.

In a proportion of patients, usually after about 2 years of treatment, the blood leukocyte count is reduced to the normal range, enlarged spleen and lymph nodes become impalpable and the proportion of lymphocytes in the bone marrow is reduced to less than 20%.

Patients with evidence of bone marrow failure should first be treated with prednisolone and evidence of marrow regeneration should be obtained before commencing treatment with chlorambucil.

Non-Hodgkin's Lymphoma: Used as a single agent, the usual dosage is 0.1 to 0.2 mg/kg/day for 4 to 8 weeks initially. Maintenance therapy is then given either by a reduced daily dosage or intermittent courses of treatment.

Chlorambucil is useful in the management of patients with advanced lymphocytic lymphoma and those who have relapsed after radiotherapy.

There is no significant difference in the overall response rate obtained with chlorambucil as a single agent and combination chemotherapy in patients with advanced non-Hodgkin's lymphocytic lymphoma.

Hodgkin's Disease: Used as a single agent, a typical dosage is 0.2 mg/kg/day for 4 to 8 weeks. Chlorambucil is usually included in combination therapy and a number of regimes have been used. Chlorambucil may also be used as an alternative to nitrogen mustard with a reduction in toxicity but similar therapy results.

Special Instructions: Tablets should be returned to the manufacturer for destruction. Proper precautions should be taken in packaging those materials for transport.

All materials which have come in contact with cytotoxic drugs should be segregated and incinerated at 1 000°C or more. Sealed containers may explode.

Personnel regularly involved in the preparation and handling of cytotoxic agents should have bi-annual blood examinations.

Provided the outer coating is intact, there is no risk to handling. Chlorambucil tablets should not be divided.

Supplied: Each white ellipsoid, sugar-coated tablet, imprinted (with edible black ink) with "635" on one side, contains: chlorambucil 2 mg. Nonmedicinal ingredients: confectioner's sugar, lactose, magnesium stearate and pregelatinized cornstarch; tablet coating: carnauba wax (No. 1 Yellow), liquid sucrose, pharmaceutical glaze, polysorbate 60, powdered

Leukeran (cont'd)

acacia and wheat starch. Bottles of 25. Store at a temperature between 15 and 25°C in a dry place.

(Shown in Product Recognition Section)

Reviewed 1998

LEUSTATIN® ℞

Janssen-Ortho

Cladribine

Antineoplastic—Chemotherapeutic Agent

Warning: Cladribine should be administered under the supervision of a qualified physician experienced in the use of antineoplastic therapy.

Suppression of bone marrow function should be anticipated. This is usually reversible and appears to be dose-dependent. Significant and prolonged lymphopenia has been noted.

Serious neurological toxicity (including irreversible paraparesis and quadriparesis) has been reported in patients who received cladribine injection by continuous infusion at high doses (4 to 9 times the recommended dose for hairy cell leukemia). Neurologic toxicity appears to demonstrate a dose relationship, however, severe neurological toxicity has been reported rarely following treatment with standard cladribine dose regimens.

Acute nephrotoxicity has been observed with high doses of cladribine (4 to 9 times the recommended dose for hairy cell leukemia), especially when given concomitantly with other nephrotoxic agents/therapies.

Pharmacology: Cladribine (also commonly known as 2-chloro-2′-deoxy-ß-D-adenosine) is a synthetic antineoplastic agent. The selective toxicity of cladribine towards certain normal and malignant lymphocyte and monocyte populations is based on the relative activities of deoxycytidine kinase, and deoxynucleotidase. Like some other deoxypurine nucleosides, cladribine crosses the cell membrane by facilitated diffusion. In cells with a high ratio of deoxycytidine kinase to deoxynucleotidase, it is phosphorylated by deoxycytidine kinase to 2-chloro-2′-deoxy-ß-D-adenosine monophosphate (2-CdAMP). Since cladribine is resistant to deamination by adenosine deaminase and there is little deoxynucleotidase in lymphocytes and monocytes, 2-CdAMP accumulates intracellularly and is subsequently converted into the active triphosphate deoxynucleotide, 2-chloro-2′-deoxy-ß-D-adenosine triphosphate (2-CdATP). It is postulated that cells with high deoxycytidine kinase and low deoxynucleotidase activities will be selectively killed by cladribine as toxic deoxynucleotides accumulate intracellularly.

Cells containing high concentrations of deoxynucleotides are unable to properly repair single-strand DNA breaks. The broken ends of DNA activate the enzyme poly (ADP-ribose) polymerase resulting in NAD and ATP depletion and disruption of cellular metabolism. There is evidence, also, that 2-CdATP is incorporated into the DNA of dividing cells, resulting in impairment of DNA synthesis. Thus cladribine can be distinguished from other chemotherapeutic agents affecting purine metabolism in that it is cytotoxic to both actively dividing and quiescent lymphocytes and monocytes, inhibiting both DNA synthesis and repair.

Pharmacokinetics: In one study following 7 days of continuous infusion of i.v. cladribine (0.09 mg/kg/day), the mean steady-state serum concentration was estimated to be 5.7 ng/mL with an estimated systemic clearance of 663.5 mL/hr/kg. Accumulation of cladribine over the 7 day treatment period was not noted.

In a second study, following a 2 hour infusion of cladribine (0.12 mg/kg), the mean end-of-infusion plasma cladribine concentration was 48±19 ng/mL. The mean harmonic terminal half-life was 5.4 hours. Mean values for clearance and steady-state volume of distribution were 978±422 mL/hr/kg and 4.52±2.82 L/kg, respectively.

In patients with Hairy Cell Leukemia (HCL) there does not appear to be a relationship between serum concentrations and ultimate clinical outcome.

Cladribine is bound approximately 20% to plasma proteins.

Except for limited understanding of the mechanism of cellular toxicity and route of excretion, no other information is available on the metabolism of cladribine in humans. An average of 18% of the administered dose has been reported to be excreted in urine of patients with solid tumors during a 5-day continuous i.v. infusion of 3.5 to 8.1 mg/m²/day of cladribine. Other investigators reported an approximately 30% of urinary recovery of cladribine during the first 24 hour post-infusion period during 5-day 2-hour i.v. infusion of 3.5 to 10.5 mg/m²/day of cladribine in patients with solid tumors and during 5-day 2-hour i.v. infusion of 6 to 12 mg/m²/day of cladribine in 10 patients with leukemia or lymphoma. The effect of renal and hepatic impairment on the elimination of cladribine has not been investigated in humans.

Indications: For the treatment of patients with Hairy Cell Leukemia.

Contraindications: In those patients who are hypersensitive to this drug or any of its components.

Warnings: General: Cladribine should be administered under the supervision of a qualified physician experienced in the use of antineoplastic therapy.

Suppression of bone marrow function should be anticipated. This is usually reversible and appears to be dose-dependent. Significant and prolonged lymphopenia has been noted.

High doses (4 to 9 times the recommended dose for Hairy Cell Leukemia), in conjunction with cyclophosphamide and total body irradiation as preparation for bone marrow transplantation, have been associated with severe, irreversible, neurologic toxicity (paraparesis/quadriparesis) and/or acute renal insufficiency in 45% of patients treated for 7 to 14 days. In patients with Hairy Cell Leukemia treated with the recommended dose (0.09 mg/kg/day for 7 days), no nephrotoxicity has been reported.

Bone Marrow Suppression: Severe bone marrow suppression, including neutropenia, anemia and thrombocytopenia, have been commonly observed in patients treated with cladribine, especially at high doses. The myelosuppressive effects of cladribine were most notable during the first month following treatment. Forty-four per cent of patients received transfusions with RBCs and 14% received platelets during Month 1. Most patients in the clinical studies had hematologic impairment as a manifestation of active Hairy Cell Leukemia. Consequently care should be taken to distinguish disease-related bone marrow suppression from that which may result following treatment with cladribine. (During the first 2 weeks after treatment initiation, Mean Platelet Count, Absolute Neutrophil Count (ANC) and Hemoglobin concentration declined and subsequently increased with normalization of mean counts by Day 12, Week 5 and Week 8, respectively). Proceed carefully in patients with severe bone marrow impairment of any etiology since further suppression of bone marrow function should be anticipated.

Fever: Fever (T≥37.8°C) was associated with the use of cladribine in approximately two-thirds of patients (131/196) in the first month of therapy. Virtually all of these patients were treated empirically with parenteral antibiotics. Overall, 47% (93/196) of all patients had fever in the setting of neutropenia (ANC≤1 000×10⁶/L), including 62 patients (32%) with severe neutropenia (ANC≤500×10⁶/L) (see Adverse Effects).

Effects of High Doses: Nephrotoxicity and neurotoxicity were observed in patients undergoing bone marrow transplantation for acute leukemia, who were treated with high doses of cladribine (4 to 9 times the recommended dose). In patients with Hairy Cell Leukemia treated with the recommended treatment regimen (0.09 mg/kg/day for 7 consecutive days), there have been no reports of nephrotoxicities. Deviations from the dosing regimen recommended for Hairy Cell Leukemia are not advised.

Pregnancy: Fetotoxicity: Cladribine is teratogenic in mice and rabbits and consequently has the potential to cause fetal harm when administered to a pregnant woman. A significant increase in variations of fetal growth/development (i.e., increases in cervical ribs, irregularly-shaped exoccipital bones, and variations in sternal ossification) was observed in mice receiving 1.5 mg/kg/day (4.5 mg/m²) and increased resorptions, reduced litter size and increased fetal malformations were observed when mice received 3 mg/kg/day (9 mg/m²). Fetal death and malformations were observed in rabbits that received 3 mg/kg/day (33 mg/m²). No fetal effects were seen in mice at 0.5 mg/kg/day (1.5 mg/m²) or in rabbits at 1 mg/kg/day (11 mg/m²).

Although there is no evidence of teratogenicity due to cladribine in humans, other drugs which inhibit DNA synthesis (e.g., methotrexate and aminopterin) have been reported to be teratogenic in humans. Cladribine has been shown to be embryotoxic in mice when given at doses equivalent to the recommended dose. Cladribine should not be given during pregnancy. There are no adequate and well-controlled studies in pregnant women. If cladribine is used during pregnancy or if the patient becomes pregnant while taking this drug, the patient should be apprised of the potential hazard to the fetus. Women of childbearing age should be advised to avoid becoming pregnant.

Precautions: General: Cladribine is a potent antineoplastic agent with potentially significant toxic side effects. It should be administered only under the supervision of a physician experienced with the use of cancer chemotherapeutic agents. Patients undergoing therapy should be closely observed for signs of hematologic and non-hematologic toxicity. Careful hematologic monitoring (assessment of peripheral blood counts), particularly during the first 4 to 8 weeks post-treatment, is recommended to detect the development of anemia, neutropenia and thrombocytopenia. Since fever is a frequently observed side effect during the first month on therapy, patients should be kept well hydrated. As with other potent chemotherapeutic agents, monitoring of renal and hepatic function is also recommended, especially in patients with underlying kidney or liver dysfunction (see Warnings, Adverse Effects and Dosage).

Rare cases of tumor lysis syndrome have been reported in patients treated with cladribine with other hematologic malignancies having a high tumor burden.

Cladribine must be diluted in designated i.v. solutions prior to administration (see Dosage).

Children: Safety and effectiveness in children have not been established. In a Phase I study involving patients 1 to 21 years old with relapsed acute leukemia, cladribine was given by continuous i.v. infusion in doses ranging from 3 to 10.7 mg/m²/day for 5 days (one-half to twice the dose recommended in Hairy Cell Leukemia). In this study, the dose-limiting toxicity was severe myelosuppression with profound neutropenia and thrombocytopenia. At the highest dose (10.7 mg/m²/day), 3 of 7 patients developed irreversible myelosuppression and fatal systemic bacterial or fungal infections. No unique toxicities were noted in this study (see Warnings and Adverse Effects).

Benzyl Alcohol as a Diluent: Benzyl alcohol is a constituent of the recommended diluent for the 7-day infusion solution. Benzyl alcohol has been reported to be associated with a fatal "Gasping Syndrome" in premature infants (see Dosage).

Impairment of Fertility: When administered i.v. to Cynomolgus monkeys, cladribine has been shown to cause suppression of rapidly generating cells, including testicular cells. The effect on human fertility is unknown.

Pregnancy: See Warnings.

Lactation: It is not known whether this drug is excreted in human milk. Cladribine should not be given to a nursing mother.

Effects on Renal and Hepatic Function: Acute renal insufficiency has developed in some patients receiving high doses of cladribine. In one study following a 1 hour infusion, the recovery of cladribine in the urine over a 24 hour period was between 10 to 30% of the administered dose. There are inadequate data on dosing of patients with renal or hepatic insufficiency. Therefore, caution is advised when administering cladribine to patients with known or suspected renal or hepatic insufficiency (see Warnings).

Drug Interactions: There are no known drug interactions with cladribine. Caution should be exercised if cladribine is administered before, after or in conjunction with other drugs known to cause immunosuppression or myelosuppression (see Warnings).

Laboratory Tests: During and following treatment, the patient's hematologic profile should be monitored regularly to determine the degree of hematopoietic suppression. In the clinical studies, following reversible declines in all cell counts, the mean Platelet Count reached 100×10⁹/L by Day 12, the mean Absolute Neutrophil Count reached 1 500×10⁶/L by Week 5 and the mean Hemoglobin reached 12 g/dL by Week 8. After peripheral counts have normalized, bone marrow aspiration and biopsy should be performed to confirm response to treatment with cladribine. Febrile events should be investigated with appropriate laboratory and radiologic studies. Periodic assessment of renal function and hepatic function should be performed as clinically indicated.

Mutagenesis: As expected for compounds in this class, the actions of cladribine yield DNA damage. In mammalian cells in culture, cladribine caused the accumulation of DNA strand breaks. Cladribine was also incorporated into DNA of human lymphoblastic leukemia cells. Cladribine was not mutagenic in vitro and did not induce unscheduled DNA synthesis in primary rat hepatocyte cultures. However, cladribine was clastogenic both in vitro (chromosome abberrations in Chinese hamster ovary cells) and in vivo (mouse bone marrow micronucleus test).

Adverse Effects: Safety data are based on 196 patients with Hairy Cell Leukemia: the original cohort of 124 patients plus an additional 72 patients enrolled at the same 2 centres after the original enrollment cutoff.

In Month 1 of the clinical trials for Hairy Cell Leukemia, severe neutropenia was noted in 70% of patients, fever in

69%, and infection was documented in 28%. Other adverse experiences reported frequently during the first 14 days after initiating treatment included: fatigue (45%), nausea (28%), rash (27%), headache (22%) and injection site reactions (19%). Most of the non-hematologic adverse experiences were mild to moderate in severity.

Myelosuppression: Myelosuppression was frequently observed during the first month after starting treatment. Neutropenia (ANC $<500\times10^6$/L) was noted in 70% of patients, compared with 26% in whom it was present initially. Severe anemia (hemoglobin <8.5 g/dL) developed in 37% of patients, compared with 10% initially and thrombocytopenia (platelets $<20\times10^9$/L) developed in 12% of patients, compared with 4% in whom it was noted initially. During the first month, 54 of 196 patients (28%) exhibited documented evidence of infection: serious infections (e.g., septicemia, pneumonia) were reported in 6% of all patients; the remainder were mild or moderate. Several deaths were attributable to infection and/or complications related to the underlying disease. During the second month, the overall rate of documented infection was 6%; these infections were mild to moderate and no severe systemic infections were seen. After the third month, the monthly incidence of infection was either less than or equal to that of the months immediately preceding cladribine therapy.

Fever and Infection: Fever was a frequently observed side effect during the first month on study. During the first month, 11% of patients experienced severe fever (i.e., ≥40°C). Since fever may be accompanied by increased fluid loss, patients should be kept well hydrated during treatment. Since the majority of fevers occurred in neutropenic patients, patients should be closely monitored during the first month of treatment and empiric antibiotics should be initiated as clinically indicated. Although 69% of patients developed fevers, less than one-third of febrile events were associated with documented infection. Given the known myelosuppressive effects of cladribine, practitioners should carefully evaluate the risks and benefits of administering this drug to patients with active infections (see Warnings).

Documented infections were noted in fewer than one-third of febrile episodes. Of the 196 patients studied, 19 were noted to have a documented infection in the month prior to treatment. In the month following treatment, there were 54 episodes of documented infection: 23 (42%) were bacterial, 11 (20%) were viral and 11 (20%) were fungal. Seven of eight documented episodes of herpes zoster occurred during the month following treatment. Fourteen of sixteen episodes of documented fungal infections occurred in the first 2 months following treatment. Virtually all of these patients were treated empirically with antibiotics.

Effects on Lymphocytes: Analysis of lymphocyte subsets indicates that treatment with cladribine is associated with prolonged depression of the CD4 counts and transient suppression of CD8 counts. Prior to treatment, the mean CD4 count was 766/μL. The mean CD4 count nadir, which occurred 4 to 6 months following treatment was 272/μL. Fifteen months after treatment, mean CD4 counts remained below 500/μL. CD8 counts behaved similarly, though increasing counts were observed after 9 months. There were no associated opportunistic infections reported during this time.

Bone Marrow Hypocellularity: Another event of unknown clinical significance includes the observation of prolonged bone marrow hypocellularity. Bone marrow hypocellularity of <35% was noted after 4 months in 42 of 124 patients (34%) treated in the 2 pivotal trials. This hypocellularity was noted as late as Day 1 010. It is not known whether the hypocellularity is the result of disease related marrow fibrosis or if it is the result of cladribine toxicity. There was no apparent clinical effect on the peripheral blood counts.

Rash: The vast majority of rashes were mild and occurred in patients who were receiving or had recently been treated with other medications (e.g., allopurinol or antibiotics) known to cause rash.

Nausea: Most episodes of nausea were mild, not accompanied by vomiting, and did not require treatment with antiemetics. In patients requiring antiemetics, nausea was easily controlled, most frequently with chlorpromazine.

Adverse reactions reported during the first 2 weeks following treatment initiation (regardless of relationship to drug) by ≥5% of patients are listed in Table I.

Adverse experiences related to i.v. administration included: Injection site reactions (9%): (i.e., redness, swelling, pain), thrombosis (2%), phlebitis (2%) and a broken catheter (1%). These appear to be related to the infusion procedure and/or indwelling catheter, rather than the medication or the vehicle. From Day 15 to the last follow-up visit, the only events reported by ≥5% of patients were: fatigue (11%), rash (10%), headache (7%), cough (7%) and malaise (5%).

Table I—Leustatin

Adverse Reactions Reported by ≥5% of Patients During the First 2 Weeks Following Treatment Initiation (regardless of relationship to drug)

Body System	Adverse Event
Body as a Whole	fever, chills, fatigue, asthenia, malaise, trunk pain, diaphoresis
Gastrointestinal System	nausea, decreased appetite, constipation, vomiting, diarrhea, abdominal pain
Hemic/Lymphatic System	purpura, petechiae, epistaxis
Nervous System	headache, dizziness, insomnia
Cardiovascular System	edema, tachycardia
Respiratory System	abnormal breath sounds, abnormal chest sounds, cough, shortness of breath
Skin/Subcutaneous Tissue	rash, injection site reactions, pruritus, pain, erythema
Musculoskeletal System	myalgia, arthralgia

Deaths: Of the 196 patients with Hairy Cell Leukemia entered in the 2 trials, there were 8 deaths following treatment. Of these, 6 were of infectious etiology, including 3 pneumonias, and 2 occurred in the first month following cladribine therapy. Of the 8 deaths, 6 occurred in previously treated patients who were refractory to α-interferon.

The following additional adverse events have been reported since the drug became commercially available. These adverse events have been reported primarily in patients who received multiple courses of cladribine.

Hematologic: bone marrow suppression with prolonged pancytopenia, including some reports of aplastic anemia; hemolytic anemia which was reported in patients with lymphoid malignancies, occuring within the first few weeks following treatment; hypereosinophilia.

Hepatic: reversible, generally mild increases in bilirubin and transaminases.

Nervous System: neurological toxicity, however, severe neurotoxicity has been reported rarely following treatment with standard cladribine dosing regimens.

Respiratory: pulmonary interstitial infiltrates; in most cases, an infectious etiology was identified.

Skin/S.C.: urticaria, hypereosinophilia. In isolated cases Stevens-Johnson and toxic epidermal necrolysis have been reported in patients who were receiving or had recently been treated with other medications (e.g., allopurinol or antibiotics) known to cause these syndromes. Opportunistic infections have occurred in the acute phase of treatment due to the immunosuppression mediated by cladribine.

Effects of High Doses: In a Phase I investigational study using cladribine in high doses (4 to 9 times the recommended dose for Hairy Cell Leukemia) as part of a bone marrow transplant conditioning regimen, which also included high dose cyclophosphamide and total body irradiation, acute nephrotoxicity and delayed onset neurotoxicity were observed. Thirty-one poor-risk patients with drug-resistant acute leukemia in relapse (29 cases) or non-Hodgkins lymphoma (2 cases) received doses of cladribine for 7 to 14 days prior to bone marrow transplantation. During cladribine infusion, 8 patients experienced gastrointestinal symptoms. While the bone marrow was initially cleared of all hematopoietic elements, including tumor cells, leukemia eventually recurred in all treated patients. Within 7 to 13 days after starting treatment with cladribine, 6 patients (19%) developed manifestations of renal dysfunction (i.e., acidosis, anuria, elevated serum creatinine, etc.) and 5 required dialysis. Several of these patients were also being treated with other medications having known nephrotoxic potential. Renal dysfunction was reversible in 2 of these patients. In the 4 patients whose renal function had not recovered at the time of death, autopsies were performed; in 2 of these, evidence of tubular damage was noted. Eleven patients (35%) experienced delayed onset neurologic toxicity. In the majority, this was characterized by progressive irreversible motor weakness (paraparesis/quadriparesis) of the upper and/or lower extremities, first noted 35 to 84 days after starting high dose therapy with cladribine. Non-invasive testing (electromyography and nerve conduction studies) was consistent with demyelinating disease.

Axonal peripheral polyneuropathy was observed in a dose escalation study at the highest dose levels (approximately 4 times the recommended dose for Hairy Cell Leukemia) in patients not receiving cyclophosphamide or total body irradiation. Severe neurological toxicity has been reported rarely following treatment with standard cladribine dosing regimens.

Effect on Renal and Hepatic Function: Acute renal insufficiency has developed in some patients receiving high doses of cladribine. In one study following a 1 hour infusion, the recovery of cladribine in the urine over a 24 hour period was between 10 to 30% of the administered dose. In addition, there are inadequate data on dosing of patients with renal or hepatic insufficiency. Therefore, caution is advised when administering cladribine to patients with known or suspected renal or hepatic insufficiency (see Warnings).

Overdose: Symptoms and Treatment: High doses of cladribine have been associated with: irreversible neurologic toxicity (paraparesis/quadriparesis), acute nephrotoxicity, and severe bone marrow suppression resulting in neutropenia, anemia and thrombocytopenia (see Warnings and Adverse Effects). There is no known specific antidote to overdosage. Treatment of overdosage consists of discontinuation of cladribine, careful observation and appropriate supportive measures. It is not known whether cladribine can be removed from the circulation by any form of dialysis or hemofiltration.

Dosage: The recommended dose and schedule for Hairy Cell Leukemia is a single course given by continuous infusion for 7 consecutive days at a dose of 0.09 mg/kg/day. Deviations from this dosage regimen are not advised. If the patient does not respond to the initial course of cladribine treatment for hairy-cell leukemia, it is unlikely that he/she will benefit from additinal courses. Physicians should consider delaying or discontinuing the drug if neurotoxicity or renal toxicity occurs (see Warnings).

Specific risk factors predisposing to increased toxicity from cladribine have not been defined. In view of the known toxicities of agents of this class, it would be prudent to proceed carefully in patients with known or suspected renal insufficiency or severe bone marrow impairment of any etiology. Patients should be monitored closely for hematologic or non-hematologic toxicity (see Warnings and Precautions).

Effect on Renal and Hepatic Function: Acute renal insufficiency has developed in some patients receiving high doses of cladribine. In one study following a 1 hour infusion, the recovery of cladribine in the urine over a 24 hour period was between 10 to 30% of the administered dose. In addition, there are inadequate data on dosing of patients with renal or hepatic insufficiency. Therefore, caution is advised when administering cladribine to patients with known or suspected renal or hepatic insufficiency (see Warnings and Adverse Effects).

The potential hazards associated with cytotoxic agents are well established and proper precautions should be taken when handling, preparing, and administering cladribine. The use of disposable gloves and protective garments is recommended. If cladribine comes in contact with the skin or mucous membranes, wash the involved surface immediately with copious amounts of water. Several guidelines on this subject have been published.

Reconstituted Solutions: Cladribine must be diluted with the designated diluent prior to administration. **Since the drug product does not contain any antimicrobial preservative or bacteriostatic agent, aseptic technique and proper environmental precautions must be observed in preparation of cladribine solutions.**

Preparation of a Single Daily Dose (see Table II): Add the calculated dose (0.09 mg/kg or 0.09 mL/kg) of cladribine to an infusion bag containing 500 mL of 0.9% Sodium Chloride Injection, USP. Infuse continuously over 24 hours. Repeat daily for a total of 7 consecutive days. **The use of 5% dextrose as a diluent is not recommended because of increased degradation of cladribine.** Admixtures of cladribine are chemically and physically stable for at least 24 hours at room temperature under normal room fluorescent light in Baxter Viaflex PVC infusion containers.

Table II—Leustatin

Preparation of a Single Daily Dose

	Dose of Leustatin Injection	Recommended Diluent	Quantity of Diluent
24-hour infusion method	0.09 mg/kg 1(day)×0.09 mg/kg	0.9% Sodium Chloride Injection	500 mL

Preparation of a 7-Day Infusion (see Table III on following page): The 7-day infusion solution should only be prepared with Bacteriostatic 0.9% Sodium Chloride Injection, USP (0.9% benzyl alcohol preserved). In order to minimize the risk of microbial contamination, both cladribine and the diluent should be passed through a sterile 0.22 μ disposable hydrophilic syringe filter as each solution is being introduced into the infusion reservoir. First add the calculated dose of cladribine (7 days×0.09 mg/kg) to the infusion reservoir through the

Leustatin (cont'd)

sterile filter. Then add a calculated amount of Bacteriostatic 0.9% Sodium Chloride Injection, USP (0.9% benzyl alcohol preserved) also through the filter to bring the total volume of the solution to 100 mL. After completing solution preparation, clamp off the line, disconnect and discard the filter. Aseptically aspirate air bubbles from the reservoir as necessary using the syringe and a dry second sterile filter or a sterile vent filter assembly. Reclamp the line and discard the syringe and filter assembly. Infuse continuously over 7 days. Solutions prepared with Bacteriostatic Sodium Chloride Injection for individuals weighing more than 85 kg may have reduced preservative effectiveness due to greater dilution of the benzyl alcohol preservative. Admixtures for the 7-day infusion have demonstrated acceptable chemical and physical stability for at least 7 days in SIMS Deltec Inc. Medication Cassettes.

Table III—Leustatin

Preparation of a 7-Day Infusion

	Dose of Leustatin Injection	Recommended Diluent	Quantity of Diluent
7-day infusion method (use sterile 0.22 μ filter when preparing infusion solution)	7(days)×0.09 mg/kg	Bacteriostatic 0.9% Sodium Chloride Injection, USP (0.9% benzyl alcohol)	q.s. to 100 mL

Since limited compatibility data are available, adherence to the recommended diluents and infusion systems is advised. Solutions containing cladribine should not be mixed with other i.v. drugs or additives or infused simultaneously via a common i.v. line, since compatibility testing has not been performed. Preparations containing benzyl alcohol should not be used in neonates (see Warnings).

If the same i.v. line is used for sequential infusion of several different drugs, the line should be flushed with a compatible diluent before and after infusion of cladribine.

Care must be taken to assure the sterility of prepared solutions. Once diluted, solutions of cladribine should be administered promptly or stored in the refrigerator (2 to 8°C) for no more than 8 hours prior to start of administration. Vials of cladribine are for single-use only. Any unused portion should be discarded in an appropriate manner.

Parenteral drug products should be inspected visually for particulate matter and discoloration prior to administration, whenever solution and container permit. A precipitate may occur during the exposure of cladribine to low temperatures; it may be resolubilized by allowing the solution to warm naturally to room temperature and by shaking vigorously. **Do not heat or microwave.**

Handling and Diposal: The potential hazards associated with cytotoxic agents are well established and proper precautions should be taken when handling, preparing and administering cladribine. The use of disposable gloves and protective garments is recommended. If cladribine comes in contact with the skin or mucous membranes, wash the involved surface immediately with copious amounts of water. Several guidelines on this subject have been published. Refer to your institution's guidelines for disposal of cytotoxic waste.

Stability and Storage: When vials and infusion solutions are stored between 2 to 8°C protected from light, unopened vials are stable until the expiration date indicated on the package. Freezing does not adversely affect the solution. If freezing occurs, thaw naturally to room temperature. **Do not** heat or microwave. Once thawed, the vial is stable until expiry if refrigerated. **Do not** refreeze. Once diluted, solutions containing cladribine should be administered promptly or stored in the refrigerator (2 to 8°C) for no more than 8 hours prior to administration. Store refrigerated 2 to 8°C. Protect from light during storage.

Supplied: Each mL of sterile, preservative-free, isotonic solution contains: cladribine 1 mg and sodium chloride 9 mg as an inactive ingredient. Phosphoric acid and/or dibasic sodium phosphate may have been added to adjust the pH. pH: 5.5 to 8.0. Single use clear flint glass 20 mL vials of 10 mL (1 mg/mL).

Reviewed 1999

LEVAQUIN® Ⓟ
Janssen-Ortho

Levofloxacin

Antibacterial

Pharmacology: Levofloxacin is a synthetic broad spectrum antibacterial agent for oral and i.v. administration.

Levofloxacin is the l-isomer of the racemate, ofloxacin, a quinolone antibacterial agent. The antibacterial activity of ofloxacin resides primarily in the l-isomer. The mechanism of action of levofloxacin and other quinolone antibacterials involves inhibition of DNA gyrase (bacterial topoisomerase II), an enzyme required for DNA replication, transcription, repair and recombination.

Pharmacokinetics: Absorption: Oral: Levofloxacin is rapidly and essentially completely absorbed after oral administration. Peak plasma concentrations are usually attained 1 to 2 hours after oral dosing. The absolute bioavailability of a 500 mg oral dose of levofloxacin is approximately 99%. Levofloxacin pharmacokinetics are linear and predictable after single and multiple oral dosing regimens. Steady state is reached within 48 hours following a 500 mg once daily regimen. The peak and trough plasma concentrations attained following multiple once daily oral 500 mg regimens were approximately 5.7 μg/mL and 0.5 μg/mL respectively. There was no clinically significant effect of food on the extent of absorption of levofloxacin. Oral administration with food slightly prolongs the time to peak concentration by approximately 1 hour and slightly decreases the peak concentration by approximately 14%. Therefore, levofloxacin can be administered without regard to food.

I.V.: Following a single 60 minute i.v. infusion of 500 mg of levofloxacin to healthy volunteers, the mean peak plasma concentration attained was 6.2 μg/mL. Levofloxacin pharmacokinetics are linear and predictable after single and multiple i.v. dosing regimens. Steady-state is reached within 48 hours following a 500 mg once daily regimen. The peak and trough plasma concentrations attained following multiple once daily i.v. 500 mg regimens were approximately 6.4 μg/mL and 0.8 μg/mL respectively.

The plasma concentration profile of levofloxacin after i.v. administration is similar and comparable in extent of exposure (AUC) to that observed for levofloxacin tablets when equal doses (mg/mg) are administered. Therefore, the oral and i.v. routes of administration can be considered interchangeable.

Distribution: The mean volume of distribution of levofloxacin generally ranges from 89 to 112 L after single and multiple 500 mg doses, indicating widespread distribution into body tissues. Levofloxacin penetrates into blister fluid. The blister fluid to plasma AUC ratio is approximately 1. Levofloxacin also penetrates into lung tissues. Lung tissue concentrations were generally 2- to 5-fold higher than plasma concentrations and ranged from approximately 2.4 to 11.3 μg/g over a 24-hour period after a single 500 mg oral dose.

Levofloxacin is 24 to 38% bound to serum proteins across all species studied. Levofloxacin binding to serum proteins is independent of the drug concentration.

Metabolism: Levofloxacin is stereochemically stable in plasma and urine and does not invert metabolically to its enantiomer, D-ofloxacin. Levofloxacin undergoes limited metabolism in humans and is primarily excreted as unchanged drug (87%) in the urine within 48 hours.

Excretion: The major route of elimination of levofloxacin in humans is as unchanged drug in urine. The mean terminal plasma elimination half-life of levofloxacin ranges from approximately 6 to 8 hours following single or multiple doses of levofloxacin given orally or i.v.

Summary of Pharmacokinetics: The mean (±SD) pharmacokinetic parameters of levofloxacin determined under single and steady state conditions following oral or i.v. doses of levofloxacin are summarized in Table I.

Factors Influencing the Pharmacokinetics: Special Populations: Geriatrics: There are no significant differences in levofloxacin pharmacokinetics between young and elderly subjects when the subjects' differences in creatinine clearance are taken into consideration. Drug absorption appears to be unaffected by age. Levofloxacin dose adjustment based on age alone is not necessary.

Children: The pharmacokinetics of levofloxacin in pediatric patients have not been studied.

Gender: There are no significant differences in levofloxacin pharmacokinetics between male and female subjects when

Table I—Levaquin

Summary of Pharmacokinetics Parameters (mean ± S.D.)

Regimen	N	C_{max} (μg/mL)	T_{max} (h)	AUC[a] (μg·h/mL)	CL/F (mL/min)	Vd/F (L)	$t_{1/2}$ (h)	CL_R (mL/min)
Single dose								
250 mg p.o.[b]	15	2.8±0.4	1.6±1.0	27.2±3.9	156±20	ND	7.3±0.9	142±21
500 mg p.o.[b,c]	23	5.1±0.8	1.3±0.6	47.9±6.8	178±28	ND	6.3±0.6	103±30
500 mg i.v.[b]	23	6.2±1.0	1.0±0.1	48.3±5.4	175±20	90±11	6.4±0.7	112±25
Multiple dose								
500 mg q24h p.o.[b]	10	5.7±1.4	1.1±0.4	47.5±6.7[d]	175±25	102±22	7.6±1.6	116±31
500 mg q24h i.v.[b]	10	6.4±0.8	ND	54.6±11.1[d]	158±29	91±12	7.0±0.8	99±28
500 mg q12h p.o.[b]	20	7.8±1.1	1.3±0.6	59.0±11.8[e]	144±30	102±16	8.0±1.1	104±26
500 mg q12h i.v.[b]	10	7.9±1.1	ND	49.6±7.3[e]	172±23	112±17	7.7±0.9	115±28
500 mg or 250 mg q24h i.v. patients with bacterial infections[f]	272	8.7±4.0[g]	ND	72.5±51.2[d,g]	154±72	111±58	ND	ND
500 mg p.o. single dose, effects of gender and age								
male[h]	12	5.5±1.1	1.2±0.4	54.4±18.9	166±44	89±13	7.5±2.1	126±38
female[i]	12	7.0±1.6	1.7±0.5	67.7±24.2	136±44	62±16	6.1±0.8	106±40
young[j]	12	5.5±1.0	1.5±0.6	47.5±9.8	182±35	83±18	6.0±0.9	140±33
elderly[k]	12	7.0±1.6	1.4±0.5	74.7±23.3	121±33	67±19	7.6±2.0	91±29
500 mg p.o. single dose, patients with renal insufficiency								
CL_{CR} 50-80 mL/min	3	7.5±1.8	1.5±0.5	95.6±11.8	88±10	ND	9.1±0.9	57±8
CL_{CR} 20-49 mL/min	8	7.1±3.1	2.1±1.3	182.1±62.6	51±19	ND	27±10	26±13
CL_{CR} <20 mL/min	6	8.2±2.6	1.1±1.0	263.5±72.5	33±8	ND	35±5	13±3
hemodialysis	4	5.7±1.0	2.8±2.2	ND	ND	ND	76±42	ND
CAPD	4	6.9±2.3	1.4±1.1	ND	ND	ND	51±24	ND

[a] AUC for 0-∞ reported, unless otherwise specified.
[b] healthy males 18-53 years of age.
[c] Absolute bioavailability.
[d] $AUC_{0-24\,h}$.
[e] $AUC_{0-12\,h}$.
[f] including 500 mg q48h for 8 patients with moderate renal impairment (CL_{CR} 20-50 mL/min) and infections of the respiratory tract or skin.
[g] dose-normalized values (to 500 mg dose), estimated by population pharmacokinetic modeling.
[h] healthy males 22-75 years of age.
[i] healthy females 18-80 years of age.
[j] young healthy male and female subjects 18-36 years of age.
[k] healthy elderly male and female subjects 66-80 years of age.
ND=Not Determined.
F=0.99±0.08.

subjects' differences in creatinine clearance are taken into consideration. Dose adjustment based on gender alone is not necessary.
Renal Insufficiency: Clearance of levofloxacin is reduced and plasma elimination half-life is prolonged in patients with impaired renal function (creatinine clearance ≤80 mL/min), and may require dosage adjustment in such patients to avoid accumulation. Neither hemodialysis nor continuous ambulatory peritoneal dialysis (CAPD) is effective in removal of levofloxacin from the body, indicating supplemental doses of levofloxacin are not required following hemodialysis or CAPD (see Precautions, Renal and Dosage).
Hepatic Insufficiency: Pharmacokinetics studies in hepatically impaired patients have not been conducted. Due to the limited extent of levofloxacin metabolism, the pharmacokinetics of levofloxacin are not expected to be affected by hepatic impairment.
Bacterial Infection: The pharmacokinetics of levofloxacin in patients with community-acquired bacterial infections are comparable to those observed in healthy subjects.

Indications: For the treatment of adults with bacterial infections caused by susceptible strains of the designated microorganisms in the infections listed.
Note: Since i.v. and oral formulations are interchangeable, i.v. administration is recommended only when it offers a route of administration advantageous to the patient (e.g., patient cannot tolerate oral dosage form).
Upper Respiratory Tract: Acute sinusitis (mild to moderate) due to S. pneumoniae, H. influenzae and M. catarrhalis.
Lower Respiratory Tract: Acute exacerbations of chronic bronchitis (mild to moderate) due to S. aureus, S. pneumoniae, H. influenzae, H. parainfluenzae and M. catarrhalis.

Community-acquired pneumonia (mild, moderate and severe* infections) due to S. aureus, S. pneumoniae, H. influenzae, H. parainfluenzae, K. pneumoniae, M. catarrhalis, C. pneumoniae, L. pneumophila and M. pneumoniae.
*Note: In 3 North American clinical studies, of 655 patients treated with levofloxacin for community-acquired pneumonia, 45 clinically and microbiologically evaluable patients were defined as severely ill by study criteria and met American Thoracic Society criteria for severe (American Thoracic Society, 1993). Clinical success (cure and improvement) was achieved in 98% of these 45 patients. Data on the treatment of patients with severe Legionella pneumonia is limited to one patient.
Skin and Skin Structure: Uncomplicated skin and skin structure infections (mild to moderate) due to S. aureus and S. pyogenes.

Complicated skin and skin structure infections (mild to moderate) due to E. faecalis, S. aureus, S. pyogenes, E. cloacae, E. coli, K. pneumoniae, P. mirabilis and P. aeruginosa.
Urinary Tract: Complicated urinary tract infections (mild to moderate) due to E. faecalis, E. cloacae, E. coli, K. pneumoniae, P. mirabilis and P. aeruginosa.

Acute pyelonephritis (mild to moderate) caused by E. coli.

Appropriate culture and susceptibility tests should be performed before treatment in order to isolate and identify organisms causing the infection and to determine their susceptibility to levofloxacin. Therapy with levofloxacin may be initiated before results of these tests are known; once results become available, appropriate therapy should be continued.

As with other drugs in this class, some strains of P. aeruginosa may develop resistance fairly rapidly during treatment with levofloxacin. Culture and susceptibility testing performed periodically during therapy will provide not only the therapeutic effect of the antimicrobial agent but also the possible emergence of bacterial resistance.

Contraindications: Persons with a history of hypersensitivity to levofloxacin, quinolone antimicrobial agents, or any other components of this product. Levofloxacin is also contraindicated in persons with a history of tendinitis or tendon rupture associated with the use of any member of the quinolone group of antimicrobial agents.

Warnings: The safety and efficacy of levofloxacin in children, adolescents (under the age of 18 years), pregnant women, and nursing mothers have not been established (see Precautions: Children, Pregnancy and Lactation).

The oral and i.v. administration of levofloxacin increased the incidence and severity of osteochondrosis in immature rats and dogs. Other quinolones also produce similar erosions in the weight bearing joints and other signs of arthropathy in immature animals of various species. Consequently, levofloxacin should not be used in pre-pubertal patients.
Sexually Transmitted Diseases: Levofloxacin is not indicated for the treatment of syphilis or gonorrhea. Levofloxacin is not effective in the treatment of syphilis. Antimicrobial agents used in high doses for short periods of time to treat gonorrhea may mask or delay the symptoms of incubating syphilis. All patients with gonorrhea should have a serologic test for syphilis at the time of diagnosis. Patients treated with antimicrobial agents with limited or no activity against T. pallidum should have a follow-up serologic test for syphilis after 3 months.
Hypersensitivity Reactions: Serious and occasionally fatal hypersensitivity and/or anaphylactic reactions have been reported in patients receiving therapy with quinolones including levofloxacin. These reactions often occur following the first dose. Some reactions have been accompanied by cardiovascular collapse, hypotension/shock, seizure, loss of consciousness, tingling, angioedema (including tongue, laryngeal, throat or facial edema/swelling), airway obstruction (including bronchospasm, shortness of breath and acute respiratory distress), dyspnea, urticaria, itching and other serious skin reactions. Levofloxacin should be discontinued immediately at the first appearance of a skin rash or any other sign of hypersensitivity. Serious acute hypersensitivity reactions may require treatment with epinephrine and other resuscitative measures, including oxygen, i.v. fluids, antihistamines, corticosteroids, pressor amines and airway management, as clinically indicated (see Adverse Effects.)

Serious and sometimes fatal events, some due to hypersensitivity, and some due to uncertain etiology, have been reported rarely in patients receiving therapy with quinolones including levofloxacin. These events may be severe and generally occur following the administration of multiple doses. Clinical manifestations may include one or more of the following: fever, rash or severe dermatologic reactions (e.g., toxic epidermal necrolysis, Stevens-Johnson syndrome); vasculitis; arthralgia; myalgia; serum sickness; allergic pneumonitis; interstitial nephritis; acute renal insufficiency or failure; hepatitis; jaundice; acute hepatic necrosis or failure; anemia, including hemolytic and aplastic; thrombocytopenia, including thrombotic thrombocytopenic purpura; leukopenia; agranulocytosis; pancytopenia; and/or other hematologic abnormalities. The administration of levofloxacin should be discontinued immediately at the first appearance of a skin rash or any other sign of hypersensitivity and supportive measures instituted (see Adverse Effects.)
CNS and Psychiatric Effects: Convulsions and toxic psychoses have been reported in patients receiving quinolones, including levofloxacin. Quinolones may also cause increased intracranial pressure and CNS stimulation which may lead to tremors, restlessness, anxiety, lightheadedness, dizziness, confusion and hallucinations, paranoia, depression, nightmares, insomnia and, rarely, suicidal thoughts or acts. These reactions may occur following the first dose. If these reactions occur in patients receiving levofloxacin, the drug should be discontinued and appropriate measures instituted. As with all quinolones, levofloxacin should be used with caution in patients with a known or suspected CNS disorder that may predispose to seizures or lower the seizure threshold (e.g., severe cerebral arteriosclerosis, epilepsy) or in the presence of other risk factors that may predispose to seizures or lower the seizure threshold (e.g., alcohol abuse, certain drug therapy such as NSAIDs and theophylline, renal dysfunction.) Levofloxacin should be used with caution in patients with unstable psychiatric illness (see Precautions, Drug Interactions and Adverse Effects).
Gastrointestinal Effects: Pseudomembranous colitis has been reported with nearly all antibacterial agents, including levofloxacin, and may range in severity from mild to life-threatening. Therefore, it is important to consider this diagnosis in patients who present with diarrhea subsequent to the administration of any antibacterial agent.

Treatment with antibacterial agents alters the normal flora of the colon and may permit overgrowth of clostridia. Studies indicate a toxin produced by C. difficile is one primary cause of "antibiotic-associated colitis".

After the diagnosis of pseudomembranous colitis has been established, therapeutic measures should be initiated. Mild cases of pseudomembranous colitis usually respond to drug discontinuation alone. In moderate to severe cases, consideration should be given to management with fluids and electrolytes, protein supplementation, and treatment with an antibacterial drug clinically effective against C. difficile colitis (see Adverse Effects).
Musculoskeletal Effects: Ruptures of the shoulder, hand and Achilles tendons that required surgical repair or resulted in prolonged disability have been reported in patients receiving quinolones. Levofloxacin should be discontinued if the patient experiences pain, inflammation, or rupture of a tendon. Patients should rest and refrain from exercise until the diagnosis of tendinitis or tendon rupture has been confidently excluded. Tendon rupture can occur during or after therapy with quinolones, including levofloxacin (see Contraindications).

Precautions: Although levofloxacin is soluble, adequate hydration of patients receiving levofloxacin should be maintained to prevent the formation of a highly concentrated urine. Crystalluria has been observed rarely in patients receiving other quinolones when associated with high doses and an alkaline urine. Although crystalluria was not observed in clinical trials with levofloxacin, patients are encouraged to remain adequately hydrated.

As with any antimicrobial drug, periodic assessment of organ system functions, including renal, hepatic, and hematopoietic, is advisable during prolonged therapy (see Warnings and Adverse Effects).
I.V. Administration: Because rapid or bolus i.v. injection may result in hypotension, **levofloxacin injection should only be administered by slow i.v. infusion over a period of 60 minutes** (see Dosage).
Renal: In patients with impaired renal function (creatinine clearance ≤80 mL/min), adjustment of the dosage regimen may be necessary to avoid the accumulation of levofloxacin due to decreased clearance. Administer levofloxacin with caution in the presence of renal insufficiency. Careful clinical observation and appropriate laboratory studies should be performed prior to and during therapy since elimination of levofloxacin may be reduced (see Dosage and Pharmacology).
Phototoxicity: Moderate to severe phototoxicity reactions have been observed in patients exposed to direct sunlight while receiving drugs in this class. Excessive exposure to sunlight should be avoided. However, in clinical trials with levofloxacin, phototoxicity has been observed in less than 0.1% of patients. Therapy should be discontinued if phototoxicity (e.g., skin eruption) occurs.
Pregnancy: There are no adequate and well-controlled studies in pregnant women. Levofloxacin should be used during pregnancy only if the potential benefit justifies the potential risk to the fetus (see Warnings).
Lactation: Levofloxacin has not been measured in human milk. Based upon data from ofloxacin, it can be presumed that levofloxacin can be excreted in human milk. Because of the potential for serious adverse reactions from levofloxacin in nursing infants, a decision should be made whether to discontinue nursing or to discontinue the drug, taking into account the importance of the drug to the mother (see Warnings).
Children: Safety and effectiveness in children and adolescents below the age of 18 years have not been established. Levofloxacin like other quinolones, causes arthropathy and osteochondrosis in juvenile animals of several species (see Warnings).
Disturbances of Blood Glucose: As with other quinolones, disturbances of blood glucose, including symptomatic hyper-and hypoglycemia, have been reported, usually in diabetic patients receiving concomitant treatment with an oral hypoglycemic agent (e.g., glyburide/glibenclamide) or with insulin. In these patients, careful monitoring of blood glucose is recommended. If a hypoglycemic reaction occurs in a patient being treated with levofloxacin, discontinue levofloxacin immediately and appropriate therapy should be initiated (see Drug Interactions and Adverse Effects).
Drug Interactions: Antacids, Sucralfate, Metal Cations, Multivitamins: Levaquin Tablets: Due to the chelation of levofloxacin by multivalent cations, concurrent administration of Levaquin tablets with antacids containing calcium, magnesium, or aluminum, as well as sucralfate, metal cations such as iron, and multivitamin preparations with zinc may interfere with the gastrointestinal absorption of levofloxacin resulting in systemic levels considerably lower than desired. These agents should be taken at least 2 hours before or 2 hours after levofloxacin tablet administration.
Levaquin Injection: There are no data concerning an interaction of i.v. quinolones with oral antacids, sucralfate, multivitamins, or metal cations. Levofloxacin should not be coadministered with any solution containing multivalent cations, e.g., magnesium, through the same i.v. line (see Dosage, Preparation of Parenteral Products for Administration).
Theophylline: No significant effect of levofloxacin on the plasma concentrations, AUC and other disposition parameters for theophylline was detected in a clinical study involving 14 healthy volunteers. Similarly, no apparent effect of theophylline on levofloxacin absorption and disposition was observed. However, concomitant administration of other quinolones with theophylline has resulted in prolonged elimination, elevated serum theophylline levels, and a subsequent increase in the risk of theophylline-related adverse reactions in the patient population. Therefore, theophylline levels should be closely monitored and theophylline dosage adjustments made, if appropriate, when levofloxacin is coadministered. Adverse

Levaquin (cont'd)

reactions, including seizures, may occur with or without an elevation in serum theophylline level (see Warnings).

Warfarin: No significant effect of levofloxacin on the peak plasma concentrations, AUC, and other disposition parameters for R-and S-warfarin was detected in a clinical study involving healthy volunteers. No significant change in prothrombin time was noted in the presence of levofloxacin. Similarly, no apparent effect of warfarin on levofloxacin absorption and disposition was observed. However, since some quinolones have been reported to enhance the effects of oral anticoagulant warfarin or its derivatives in the patient population, the prothrombin time or other suitable coagulation test should be closely monitored if a quinolone antimicrobial is administered concomitantly with warfarin or its derivatives.

Cyclosporine: No significant effect of levofloxacin on the peak plasma concentrations, AUC, and other disposition parameters for cyclosporine was detected in a clinical study involving healthy volunteers. However, elevated serum levels of cyclosporine have been reported in the patient population when co-administered with some other quinolones. Levofloxacin C_{max} and k_e were slightly lower while T_{max} and $t_{1/2}$ were slightly longer in the presence of cyclosporine than those observed in other studies without concomitant medication. The differences, however, are not considered to be clinically significant. Therefore, no dosage adjustment is required for levofloxacin or cyclosporine when administered concomitantly.

Digoxin: No significant effect of levofloxacin on the peak plasma concentrations, AUC, and other disposition parameters for digoxin was detected in a clinical study involving healthy volunteers. Levofloxacin absorption and disposition kinetics were similar in the presence or absence of digoxin. Therefore, no dosage adjustment for levofloxacin or digoxin is required when administered concomitantly.

Probenecid and Cimetidine: No significant effect of probenecid or cimetidine on the rate and extent of levofloxacin absorption was observed in a clinical study involving healthy volunteers. The AUC and $t_{1/2}$ of levofloxacin were 27 to 38% and 30% higher, respectively, while CL/F and CL_R were 21 to 35% lower during concomitant treatment with probenecid or cimetidine compared to levofloxacin alone. Although the differences were statistically significant, the changes were not high enough to warrant dosage adjustment for levofloxacin when probenecid or cimetidine is co-administered.

NSAIDs: The concomitant administration of a NSAID with a quinolone, including levofloxacin, may increase the risk of CNS stimulation and convulsive seizures (see Warnings: CNS and Psychiatric Effects).

Antidiabetic agents: Disturbances of blood glucose, including hyperglycemia and hypoglycemia, have been reported in patients treated concomitantly with quinolones and an antidiabetic agent. Therefore, careful monitoring of blood glucose is recommended when these agents including levofloxacin are co-administered.

Zidovudine: Levofloxacin absorption and disposition in HIV-infected subjects with or without concomitant zidovudine treatment were similar. Therefore, no dosage adjustment for levofloxacin appears to be required when co-administered with zidovudine. The effect of levofloxacin on zidovudine pharmacokinetics has not been studied.

Adverse Effects: In North American Phase 2 and 3 Clinical Trials involving 3 158 subjects the incidence of treatment emergent adverse events in patients treated with levofloxacin was 41.2% which was comparable to controls. The majority of adverse events were considered to be mild to moderate with 4.7% of patients considered to have severe adverse events. Among patients receiving multiple dose therapy, 3.7% discontinued therapy with levofloxacin due to adverse experiences. The incidence of adverse reactions which were considered to be probably or definitely related to treatment with levofloxacin was 6.2%.

In clinical trials, the adverse events in Table II were characterized as probably or definitely related to drug therapy for patients receiving multiple doses of levofloxacin.

In clinical trials, the most frequently reported adverse events occurring in >2% of the study population regardless of drug relationship, were: nausea 6.6%, injection site reaction 5.6%, diarrhea 5.4%, headache 5.4%, constipation 3.1%, i.v. injection site pain 2.7%, dizziness 2.5%, insomnia 2.9% and vomiting 2.1%.

Additional events occurring in clinical trials at rates indicated regardless of relationship to drug or route of administration are shown in Table III.

Table II—Levaquin

Adverse Events Considered likely to be Drug-related (n=3 158)

Body System	Event	Percentage of patients with ADR
Body as a Whole	fatigue	0.1
	malaise	0.1
	edema	0.1
Special Senses	taste perversion	0.2
Nervous System	dizziness	0.3
	insomnia	0.3
	somnolence	0.2
	anorexia	0.1
	anxiety	0.1
	headache	0.1
	sleep disorders	0.1
	nervousness	0.1
	tremor	0.1
Gastrointestinal	diarrhea	1.2
	nausea	1.2
	flatulence	0.5
	abdominal pain	0.3
	dyspepsia	0.3
	vomiting	0.2
	constipation	0.1
	stomatitis	0.3
Genital/Reproductive	vaginitis	0.8
	genital moniliasis	0.3
	leukorrhea	0.1
Skin/Hypersensitivity	rash	0.3
	increased sweating	0.1
	urticaria	0.1
I.V. Injection Site	inflammation	0.8
Disorders	pain	1.5
	reaction	1.3

Events occurring at a frequency lower than 0.3% regardless of drug relationship but considered medically important include: Cardiovascular: angina pectoris, arrhythmia, atrial and ventricular fibrillation, bradycardia, cardiac arrest, cardiomyopathy, circulatory failure, coronary thrombosis, embolism-blood clot, heart block, hypotension, palpitations, phlebitis, postural hypotension, syncope, supraventricular tachycardia, thrombosis (arterial).

CNS/Psychiatric: abnormal co-ordination, abnormal dreaming, aggressive reaction, cerebrovascular disorder, coma, confusion, convulsions (seizures), delirium, depression, emotional lability, hallucination, impaired concentration, manic reaction, mental deficiency, paralysis, paranoia, sleep disorders, speech disorder, stupor, vertigo.

Gastrointestinal: esophagitis, gastrointestinal hemorrhage, pseudomembranous colitis, stomatitis.

Hematopoietic: abnormal platelets, anemia, granulocytopenia, leukocytosis, leukopenia, lymphadenopathy, thrombocytopenia, WBC abnormal (not otherwise specified).

Liver/Biliary/Pancreas: abnormal hepatic function, hepatic coma, increased LDH, jaundice, pancreatitis.

Metabolic: dehydration, aggravated diabetes mellitus, hypoglycemia, hyperkalemia, weight decrease.

Musculoskeletal: arthritis, muscle weakness, rhabdomyolysis, tendinitis.

Renal/Urinary: abnormal renal function, acute renal failure.

Respiratory: ARDS, asthma.

Special Senses: abnormal vision, diplopia.

Skin/Hypersensitivity: anaphylactoid reaction, erythema nodosum, photosensitivity.

In clinical trials using multiple-dose therapy, ophthalmologic abnormalities, including cataracts and multiple punctate lenticular opacities, have been noted in patients undergoing treatment with other quinolones. The relationship of the drugs to these events is not presently established.

Crystalluria and cylindruria have been reported with other quinolones.

Laboratory abnormalities seen in ≥2% of the patients receiving multiple doses of levofloxacin: decreased glucose 2.4% and decreased lymphocytes 2.2%. It is not known whether these abnormalities were caused by the drug or the underlying condition being treated.

Postmarketing Adverse Reactions: Additional serious adverse events reported with levofloxacin regardless of drug relationship include: agranulocytosis, allergic pneumonitis, amnesia, anaphylactic shock, anaphylactoid reaction, angioedema, aplastic anemia, apnea, DIC, dysphonia, EEG abnormal, encephalopathy, eosinophilia, erythema multiforme, glomerulonephritis, hemolytic anemia, hepatitis, interstitial pneumonia, interstitial nephritis, laryngeal edema, liver failure, multi-system organ failure, myositis, nephrosis, pancytopenia, Stevens-Johnson syndrome, thrombocytopenic purpura, tendon rupture, toxic epidermal necrolysis and vasodilation.

Overdose: Symptoms and Treatment: In the event of an acute overdosage, the stomach should be emptied. The patient should be observed and appropriate hydration maintained. Levofloxacin is not efficiently removed by hemodialysis or peritoneal dialysis.

Dosage: The dosage of levofloxacin tablets and i.v. for **Patients with Normal Renal Function** (i.e., CL_{CR} > 80 mL/min) is described in the Table IV (on following page). For patients with altered renal function (i.e., CL_{CR} ≤ 80 mL/min), see the **Patients with Impaired Renal Function** subsection. The dose of levofloxacin i.v. should be administered by slow infusion over 60 minutes.

Patients with Impaired Renal Function: On the basis of the altered levofloxacin disposition pharmacokinetics in subjects with impaired renal function, dose adjustment is recommended for patients with impaired renal function as shown in Table V (on following page) (see Pharmacology, Renal Insufficiency).

Table III—Levaquin

Adverse Event Without Regard to Relationship to Drug or Route of Administration (n=3 158)

Body System	0.3 to <0.5%	0.5 to <1.0%	1 to 2%
Body as a Whole	asthenia malaise	fatigue dry mouth fever edema	pain chest pain back pain
Special Senses	conjunctivitis tinnitus	taste perversion	
Nervous System/Psychiatric Disorders	tremor paresthesia	anxiety agitation anorexia nervousness somnolence	
Cardiovascular	cardiac failure myocardial infarction hypertension		
Respiratory	coughing	dyspnea pharyngitis rhinitis	
Gastrointestinal			abdominal pain dyspepsia flatulence
Genital/Reproductive	genital moniliasis	genital pruritus	vaginitis
Skin/Hypersensitivity	urticaria purpura	increased sweating skin disorder	rash pruritus injection site inflamed
Musculoskeletal	myalgia	arthralgia	

Table IV—Levaquin

Dosing Chart for Patients with Normal Renal Function

Infection[a]	Unit Dose	Freq.	Duration[b]	Daily Dose
Exacerbation of Chronic Bronchitis	500 mg	q24h	7 days	500 mg
Comm. Acquired Pneumonia	500 mg	q24h	7-14 days (10-14 days for severe infections)	500 mg
Sinusitis	500 mg	q24h	10-14 days	500 mg
Uncomplicated SSSI	500 mg	q24h	7-10 days	500 mg
Complicated SSSI	500 mg	q12h	7-14 days	1 000 mg
Complicated UTI	250 mg	q24h	10 days	250 mg
Acute pyelonephritis	250 mg	q24h	10 days	250 mg

[a]Due to the designated pathogens (see Indications).
[b]Total therapy duration. When appropriate, patients may be converted from the injection to an equivalent dose of the tablets.

Table V—Levaquin

Dosing Chart for Patients with Impaired Renal Function

Renal Status	Initial Dose	Subsequent Dose
Acute Respiratory Infections/Uncomplicated SSSI		
CL_{CR} from 50 to 80 mL/min	No dosage adjustment required	
CL_{CR} from 20 to 49 mL/min	500 mg	250 mg q24h
CL_{CR} from 10 to 19 mL/min	500 mg	250 mg q48h
Hemodialysis	500 mg	250 mg q48h
CAPD	500 mg	250 mg q48h
Complicated UTI/Acute Pyelonephritis		
CL_{CR} ≥20 mL/min	No dosage adjustment required	
CL_{CR} from 10 to 19 mL/min	250 mg	250 mg q48h
Complicated SSSI		
CL_{CR} from 50 to 80 mL/min	500 mg	500 mg q24h
CL_{CR} from 20 to 49 mL/min	500 mg	250 mg q24h
CL_{CR} from 10 to 19 mL/min	500 mg	250 mg q48h
Hemodialysis	500 mg	250 mg q48h
CAPD	500 mg	250 mg q48h

Legend: CL_{CR}=creatinine clearances.
CAPD=Chronic ambulatory peritoneal dialysis.

When only the serum creatinine is known, the following formula may be used to estimate creatinine clearance.

Men: Creatinine Clearance (mL/min)

$$= \frac{\text{Weight (kg)} \times (140-\text{age})}{72 \times \text{serum creatinine (mg/dL)}}$$

Women: 0.85×the value calculated for men.

The serum creatinine should represent a steady state of renal function.

Tablets: Levofloxacin can be administered without regard to food. Doses should be administered at least 2 hours before or 2 hours after antacids containing magnesium or aluminum, sucralfate, metal cations such as iron, and multivitamin preparations with zinc.

I.V.: **Caution: Rapid or bolus i.v. infusion must be avoided.** Levofloxacin injection should be infused i.v. slowly over a period of not less than 60 minutes. The injection should only be administered by i.v. infusion. It is not for i.m., intrathecal, intraperitoneal, or s.c. administration (see Precautions).

Single-use vials require dilution prior to administration. The concentration of the resulting diluted solution should be 5 mg/mL prior to administration (see Preparation of Patenteral Products for Administration).

This parenteral drug product should be inspected visually for particulate matter prior to administration. Samples containing visible particles should be discarded.

Since no preservative or bacteriostatic agent is present in this product, aseptic technique must be used in preparation of the final parenteral solution. **Since the vials are for single-use only, any unused portion remaining in the vial should be discarded. When used for split dosing, the full content of the vial should be withdrawn at once using a single-entry procedure and a second dose should be prepared and stored for subsequent use** (see Stability and Storage).

Since only limited data are available on the compatibility of levofloxacin i.v. injection with other i.v. substances, **additives or other medications should not be added to the injection in single-use vials or infused simultaneously through the same i.v. line.** If the same i.v. line is used for sequential infusion of several different drugs, the line should be flushed before and after infusion of levofloxacin injection with an infusion solution compatible with levofloxacin injection and with any other drug(s) administered via this common line.

Preparation of Parenteral Products for Administration: Single-use Vials: The injection is supplied in single-use vials containing a concentrated levofloxacin solution with the equivalent of 500 mg of levofloxacin in water for injection. The 20 mL vials contain 25 mg of levofloxacin/mL. **These single-use vials must be further diluted with an appropriate solution prior to i.v. administration** (see Compatible Intravenous Solutions). The concentration of the resulting diluted solution should be 5 mg/mL prior to administration.

As with all parenteral products, i.v. admixture should be inspected visually for clarity, discoloration, particulate matter, precipitate, and leakage prior to administration whenever solution and container permit. Samples containing visible particles should be discarded.

Since no preservative or bacteriostatic agent is present in this product, aseptic technique must be used in preparation of the final parenteral solution. **Since the vials are for single-use only, any unused portion remaining in the vial should be discarded. When used for split dosing, the full content of the vial should be withdrawn at once using a single-entry procedure and a second dose should be prepared and stored for subsequent use** (see Stability and Storage).

Since only limited data are available on the compatibility of levofloxacin i.v. injection with other i.v. substances, **additives or other medications should not be added to the injection in single-use vials or infused simultaneously through the same i.v. line.** If the same i.v. line is used for sequential infusion of several different drugs, the line should be flushed before and after infusion of levofloxacin injection with an infusion solution compatible with levofloxacin injection and with any other drug(s) administered via this common line.

Prepare the desired dosage of levofloxacin according to Table VI.

Table VI—Levaquin

Preparation of Parenteral Products

Desired Dosage Strength	From 20 mL Vial Withdraw Volume	Volume of Diluent	Infusion Time
250 mg	10 mL	40 mL	60 min
500 mg	20 mL	80 mL	60 min

For example, to prepare a 500-mg dose using the 20 mL vial (25 mg/mL), withdraw 20 mL and dilute with a compatible i.v. solution to a total volume of 100 mL.

Compatible I.V. Solutions: Any of the i.v. solutions in Table VII may be used to prepare a 5 mg/mL levofloxacin solution with the approximate pH values.

Table VII—Levaquin

Compatible I.V. Solutions

I.V. Fluids	Levofloxacin Injection Solution
0.9% Sodium Chloride Injection, USP	4.71
5% Dextrose Injection, USP	4.58
5% Dextrose/0.9% NaCl Injection	4.62
5% Dextrose in Lactated Ringers	4.92
Plasma-Lyte 56/5% Dextrose Injection	5.03
5% Dextrose, 0.45% Sodium Chloride, and 0.15% Potassium Chloride Injection	4.61
Sodium Lactate Injection (M/6)	5.54

Premix in Single-use Flexible Containers: The injection is also supplied in 100 mL flexible containers containing a premixed, ready-to-use levofloxacin solution in D_5W for single-use. The fill volume is either 50 or 100 mL. **No further dilution of this preparation is necessary. Each 100 mL Premix flexible container already contains a dilute solution with the equivalent of 500 mg of levofloxacin (5 mg/mL) in 5% Dextrose (D_5W).**

This parenteral drug product should be inspected visually for clarity, discoloration, particulate matter, precipitate and leakage prior to administration. Samples containing visible particles should be discarded.

Since the Premix flexible containers are for single-use only, any unused portion should be discarded.

Since only limited data are available on the compatibility of levofloxacin i.v. injection with other i.v. substances, **additives or other medications should not be added to levofloxacin injection in flexible containers or infused simultaneously through the same i.v. line.** If the same i.v. line is used for sequential infusion of several different drugs, the line should be flushed before and after infusion of levofloxacin Injection with an infusion solution compatible with levofloxacin injection and with any other drug(s) administered via this common line.

Instructions for the Use of Levaquin Injection Premix in Flexible containers: To open: 1. Tear outer wrap at the notch and remove solution container. 2. Check the container for minute leaks by squeezing the inner bag firmly. If leaks are found, or if the seal is not intact, discard the solution, as the sterility may be compromised. 3. Do not use if the solution is cloudy or a precipitate is present. 4. Use sterile equipment. 5. **Warning: Do not use flexible containers in series connections.** Such use could result in air embolism due to residual air being drawn from the primary container before administration of the fluid from the secondary container is complete.

Preparation for Administration: 1. Close flow control clamp of administration set. 2. Remove cover from port at bottom of container. 3. Insert piercing pin of administration set into port with a twisting motion until the pin is firmly seated. **Note: See full directions on administration set carton.** 4. Suspend container from hanger. 5. Squeeze and release drip chamber to establish proper fluid level in chamber during infusion of the injection in Premix Flexible Containers. 6. Open flow control clamp to expel air from set. Close clamp. 7. Regulate rate of administration with flow control clamp.

Stability and Storage: Tablets: Store at controlled room temperature (15 to 30°C) in well-closed containers.

Injection: When stored under recommended conditions, the injection, as supplied in 20 mL vials and 100 mL flexible containers, is stable through the expiration date printed on the label.

Single-use vials should be stored at 2 to 30°C and protected from light.

Premix in flexible containers should be stored at 2 to 25°C; however, brief exposure up to 40°C does not adversely affect the product. Avoid excessive heat and protect from freezing and light.

Stability of Injection Following Dilution: The injection, when diluted in a compatible i.v. fluid to a concentration of 5 mg/mL, is stable for 24 hours when stored at or below 25°C and for 72 hours when stored under refrigeration at 5°C in plastic i.v. containers. Solutions that are diluted in a compatible i.v. solution and frozen in glass bottles or plastic i.v. containers are stable for 6 months when stored at −20°C. **Thaw frozen solutions at room temperature (25°C) or in a refrigerator (8°C). Do not force thaw by microwave irradiation or water bath immersion. Do not refreeze after initial thawing.**

Supplied: Injection: 5 mg/mL: Each mL of sterile, non-pyrogenic premixed, ready-to-use solution contains: levofloxacin 5 mg in 5% Dextrose (D_5W). pH: 3.8 to 5.8. Solutions of hydrochloric acid and/or sodium hydroxide may have been added to adjust the pH. Preservative-free. Single-use flexible containers of 100 mL with a fill volume of 50 or 100 mL, cases of 12.

No further dilution of this preparation is necessary. Consequently, each 100 mL premix flexible container with a fill volume of either 50 or 100 mL already contains a dilute solution with the equivalent of either 250 or 500 mg of levofloxacin (5 mg/mL) in 5% Dextrose (D_5W).

25 mg/mL: Each mL of sterile, clear yellow to greenish-yellow solution contains: levofloxacin 25 mg in water for injection. pH: 3.8 to 5.8. Solution may contain hydrochloric acid and/or sodium hydroxide for pH adjustment. Preservative-free. Single-use vials of 20 mL, cartons of 1. **Single-use vials require dilution prior to administration.** See Dosage, Preparation for Administration.

Tablets: 250 mg: Each modified rectangular, film-coated, terra cotta pink tablet contains: levofloxacin 250 mg. Nonmedicinal ingredients: crospovidone, hydroxypropyl methylcellulose, magnesium stearate, microcrystalline cellulose, polyethylene glycol, polysorbate 80, synthetic red iron oxide and titanium dioxide. Bottles of 50.

Levaquin (cont'd)

500 mg: Each modified rectangular, film-coated, peach tablet contains: levofloxacin 500 mg. Nonmedicinal ingredients: crospovidone, hydroxypropyl methylcellulose, magnesium stearate, microcrystalline cellulose, polyethylene glycol, polysorbate 80, synthetic red and yellow oxides and titanium dioxide. Bottles of 50.

(Shown in Product Recognition Section)

New Product 1998

LEVOBUNOLOL HYDROCHLORIDE ℞

Rivex Ophthalmics

Glaucoma Therapy

Supplied: 0.25%: Each mL of sterile ophthalmic solution contains: levobunolol HCl 0.25%. Nonmedicinal ingredients: benzalkonium chloride 0.004% (as preservative), edetate disodium, polyvinyl alcohol 1.4%, potassium phosphate, purified water, sodium chloride, sodium metabisulfite and sodium phosphate. Hydrochloric acid and/or sodium hydroxide may be added to adjust pH. Plastic bottles with controlled-drop tips of 10 mL.

0.5%: Each mL of sterile ophthalmic solution contains: levobunolol HCl 0.5%. Nonmedicinal ingredients: benzalkonium chloride (as preservative), edetate disodium, polyvinyl alcohol, potassium phosphate, purified water, sodium chloride, sodium metabisulfite and sodium phosphate. Hydrochloric acid and/or sodium hydroxide may be added to adjust pH. Plastic bottles with controlled-drop tips of 5, 10 and 15 mL.

LEVOPHED®

Sanofi

Norepinephrine Bitartrate

Sympathomimetic

Pharmacology: Norepinephrine functions as a powerful peripheral vasoconstrictor (alpha-adrenergic action) and as a potent inotropic stimulator of the heart and dilator of coronary arteries (beta-adrenergic action). Both of these actions result in an increase in systemic blood pressure and coronary artery blood flow. Cardiac output will vary reflexly in response to systemic hypertension but is usually increased in hypotensive man when the blood pressure is raised to an optimal level. In myocardial infarction accompanied by hypotension. norepinephrine usually increases aortic blood pressure, coronary artery blood flow, and myocardial oxygenation, thereby helping to limit the area of myocardial ischemia and infarction. Venous return is increased and the heart tends to resume a more normal rate and rhythm than in the hypotensive state.

In hypotension that persists after correction of blood volume deficits, norepinephrine helps raise the blood pressure to an optimal level and establish a more adequate circulation.

In myocardial infarction norepinephrine has been shown to increase greatly the patient survival rate. Norepinephrine not only corrects systemic shock (through cardiotonic and peripheral vasoconstrictor action), but also markedly dilates the coronary arteries, thereby increasing coronary blood flow, reducing the area of ischemia and promoting myocardial oxygenation. There is increased venous return and the heart tends to resume a more normal rate and rhythm.

On the coronary arteries norepinephrine causes about two and one half times the degree of vasodilatation that epinephrine produces and therefore has a greater effect in increasing coronary flow. It has only a slight effect on sugar metabolism, its hyperglycemic action being far less pronounced than epinephrine, and is not contraindicated in diabetic patients.

Note: With norepinephrine administration, bradycardia sometimes occurs, probably as a direct result of the rise in blood pressure to normal levels.

Indications: The restoration and maintenance of blood pressure in acute hypotensive or shock states, such as surgery, trauma, myocardial infarction, pheochromocytomectomy, sympathectomy, spinal anesthesia, septicemia, drug reactions, poliomyelitis, blood transfusion reactions, and hemorrhage. Because of the selective peripheral vasoconstrictive action of norepinephrine, pooled or stagnant blood in the dilated capillaries is driven into the central circulation, thus maintaining vital functions (e.g. brain, heart, kidneys, etc.) Also a useful adjunct in treating cardiac arrest and profound hypotension.

Contraindications: Use in patients who are hypotensive from blood volume deficits is contraindicated except as an emergency measure to maintain coronary and cerebral artery perfusion until blood volume replacement therapy can be completed. If norepinephrine is continuously administered to maintain blood pressure in the absence of blood volume replacement, the following may occur: severe peripheral and visceral vasoconstriction, decreased renal perfusion and urine output, poor systemic blood flow despite "normal" blood pressure, tissue hypoxia, and lactate acidosis.

Norepinephrine should also not be given to patients with mesenteric or peripheral vascular thrombosis (because of the risk of increasing ischemia and extending the area of infarction) unless, in the opinion of the attending physician, the administration of norepinephrine is necessary as a life-saving procedure.

Cyclopropane and halothane anesthetics increase cardiac autonomic irritability and therefore seem to sensitize the myocardium to the action of i.v. administered epinephrine or levarterenol. Hence, the use of norepinephrine during cyclopropane and halothane anesthesia is generally considered contraindicated because of the risk of producing ventricular trachycardia or fibrillation. The same type of cardiac arrhythmias may result from the use of norepinephrine in patients with profound hypoxia or hypercarbia.

Warnings: Norepinephrine should be used with extreme caution in patients receiving MAO inhibitors or antidepressants of the triptyline or imipramine types, because severe, prolonged hypertension may result.

Norepinephrine contains sodium metabisulfite, a sulfite that may cause allergic-type reactions including anaphylactic symptoms and life-threatening or less severe asthmatic episodes in certain susceptible people. The overall prevalence of sulfite sensitivity in the general population is unknown. Sulfite sensitivity is seen more frequently in asthmatic than in non-asthmatic people.

Precautions: Avoid Hypertension: Because of the potency of norepinephrine and because of varying response to pressor substances, the possibility always exists that dangerously high blood pressure may be produced with overdoses of this pressor agent. It is desirable, therefore, to record the blood pressure every 2 minutes from the time administration is started until the desired blood pressure is obtained, then every 5 minutes if administation is to be continued. The rate of flow must be watched constantly, and the patient should never be left unattended while receiving norepinephrine. Headache may be a symptom of hypertension due to overdosage.

Site of infusion: Whenever possible, norepinephrine should be given into a large vein, particularly an antecubital vein because, when administered into this vein, the risk of necrosis of the overlying skin from prolonged vasoconstriction is apparently very slight. Some authors have indicated that the femoral vein is also an acceptable route of administration. A catheter tie-in technique should be avoided, if possible, since the obstruction to blood flow around the tubing may cause stasis and increased local concentration of the drug. Occlusive vascular diseases (for example, atherosclerosis, arteriosclerosis, diabetic endarteritis, Buerger's disease) are more likely to occur in the lower than in the upper extremity. Therefore, one should avoid the veins of the leg or dorsum of the hand in elderly patients, or in those suffering from such disorders. Gangrene has been reported in a lower extremity when norepinephrine was given in an ankle vein.

Extravasation: **The infusion site should be checked frequently for free flow.** Care should be taken to avoid extravasation of norepinephrine into the tissues, as local necrosis might ensure due to the vasoconstrictive action of the drug. **Blanching along the course of the infused vein,** sometimes without obvious extravasation, has been attributed to vasa vasorum constriction with increased permeability of the vein wall, permitting some leakage. This also may progress on rare occasions to superficial slough, particularly during infusion into leg veins, in elderly patients or in those suffering from obliterative vascular disease. Hence, if blanching occurs, consideration should be given to the advisability of changing the infusion site at intervals to allow the effects of local vasoconstriction to subside.

Important: Antidote for Extravasation Ischemia: To prevent sloughing and necrosis in areas in which extravasation has taken place, the area should be infiltrated as soon as possible with 10 to 15 mL of saline solution containing from 5 to 10 mg of phentolamine, an adrenergic blocking agent. A syringe with a fine hypodermic needle is used, and the solution is infiltrated liberally throughout the area, which is easily identified by its cold, hard, and pallid appearance. Sympathetic blockage with phentolamine causes immediate and conspicuous local hyperemic changes if the area is infiltrated within 12 hours. Therefore, phentolamine should be given as soon as possible after the extravasation is noted.

Some investigators add phentolamine (5 to 10 mg) directly to the infusion flask because it is believed that the drug used in this manner is an effective antidote against sloughing should extravasation occur, whereas the systemic vasopressor activity of the norepinephrine is not impaired.

Two investigators stated that, in the treatment of patients with severe hypotension following **myocardial infarction,** thrombosis in the infused vein and perivenous reactions and necrosis may usually be prevented if 10 mg of heparin are added to each 500 mL of infusion fluid (5% dextrose) containing norepinephrine.

Sympathetic nerve block has also been suggested.

Pregnancy and *Lactation:* It is not known whether norepinephrine can cause fetal harm when administered to a pregnant woman or can affect reproduction capacity. It should be given to a pregnant woman only if clearly needed. It is not known whether this drug is excreted in human milk. Because many drugs are excreted in human milk, caution should be exercised when norepinephrine is administered to a nursing woman.

Adverse Effects: Body as a Whole: Ischemic injury due to potent vasoconstrictor action and tissue hypoxia.

Cardiovascular: bradycardia, probably as a reflex result of a rise in blood pressure, arrhythmias.

Nervous System: anxiety, transient headache.

Respiratory: respiratory difficulty.

Skin and Appendages: Extravasation necrosis at injection site.

Prolonged administration of any potent vasopressor may result in plasma volume depletion which should be continuously corrected by appropriate fluid and electrolyte replacement therapy. If plasma volumes are not corrected, hypotension may recur when norepinephrine is discontinued, or blood pressure may be maintained at the risk of severe peripheral and visceral vasoconstriction (e.g., decreased renal perfusion) with diminution in blood flow and tissue perfusion with subsequent tissue hypoxia and lactic acidosis and possible ischemic injury. Gangrene of extremities has been rarely reported.

Overdoses or conventional doses in hypersensitive persons (e.g., hyperthyroid patients) cause severe hypertension with violent headache, photophobia, stabbing retrosternal pain, pallor, intense sweating, and vomiting.

Overdose: Symptoms and Treatment: Overdosage with norepinephrine may result in headache, severe hypertension, reflex bradycardia, marked increase in peripheral resistance and decreased cardiac output. In case of accidental overdosage, as evidenced by excessive blood pressure elevation, discontinue the drug until the condition of the patient stabilizes.

Dosage: Restoration of Blood Pressure in Acute Hypotensive States: Add 4 mL of the solution to 1 000 mL of dextrose solution 5% or dextrose in saline (1 mL of dilution contains 4 μg of norepinephrine base): Fluids containing dextrose are protection against significant loss of potency due to oxidation. Administration in saline solution alone is not recommended. Inject i.v. (preferably through polyethylene tubing) through a drip bulb. After observing the response to an initial dose of 2 to 3 mL (from 8 to 12 μg of base) per minute, adjust the flow to establish and maintain the desired blood pressure, which usually is from 80 to 100 mm Hg systolic in previously normotensive patients (and even lower in patients in hemorrhagic or hypovolemic shock, pending replacement of circulating blood volume). In previously hypertensive patients, it is recommended that the blood pressure should be raised no higher than 40 mm Hg below the preexisting systolic pressure. The average maintenance dose ranges from 0.5 to 1 mL (2 to 4 μg base) per minute. Great individual variation occurs in the dose required to attain and maintain an adequate blood pressure. In all cases, dosage of norepinephrine should be titrated according to the response of the patient. Occasionally much larger or even enormous daily doses (as high as 68 mg base or 17 ampuls) may be necessary if the patient remains hypotensive, but occult blood volume depletion should always be suspected and corrected when present. Central venous pressure monitoring is usually helpful in detecting and treating this situation. If large volumes of fluid are needed, administer a more dilute solution than 4 μg/mL. Conversely, when the fluid volume should be restricted (e.g., in congestive heart failure), higher concentrations than 4 μg/mL may be used. Continue therapy until the patient can maintain normotension (from hours up to 6 days). Gradually reduce infusion rate: avoid abrupt withdrawal. Whole blood or plasma, if indicated, should be administered separately (e.g., by Y tube from separate bottles). Before administering drug, refer to detailed information in package circular.

Adjunctive Treatment in Cardiac Arrest: Norepinephrine is usually administered i.v. during cardiac resuscitation to restore and maintain an adequate blood pressure after an effective heartbeat and ventilation have been established by other means. (Norepinephrine's powerful beta-adrenergic stimulating action is also thought to increase the strength and effectiveness of systolic contractions once they occur.)
Average Dosage: To maintain systemic blood pressure during the management of cardiac arrest, norepinephrine is used in the same manner as described under Restoration of Blood Pressure in Acute Hypotensive States.

Supplied: Each mL of solution contains: norepinephrine bitartrate equivalent to 1 mg (base). Also contains sodium metabisulfite and sodium chloride to make isotonic in water for injection. Ampuls of 4 mL, boxes of 10.

LEVOTEC ℞

Technilab

Levothyroxine Sodium

Hypothyroidism Therapy

Pharmacology: Levothyroxine sodium is the monosodium salt of the levorotatory isomer of thyroxin (tetraiodothyronine), the principal hormone secreted by the normal thyroid gland.

Following oral administration, the absorption of levothyroxine is incomplete and variable (50 to 75%), especially when taken with food. Once absorbed, synthetic levothyroxine is indistinguishable from the endogenous hormone.

Levothyroxine is nearly totally bound to serum proteins and has an elimination half-life of 6 to 7 days in the euthyroid subject. Half-life is shortened in hyperthyroidism and prolonged in hypothyroidism and in pregnancy. Deiodination of levothyroxine (T4) to 1-triiodothyronine (T3) occurs in various tissues, particularly liver and kidney. T3 is approximately 4 times as potent as T4 on a weight basis.

The mechanism of action of thyroid hormones is not completely understood. The principal effect is to increase the metabolic rate of body tissues. Thyroid hormones have both catabolic and anabolic effects, and are therefore involved in normal metabolism, growth and development, especially the development of the CNS in infancy.

Indications: Specific hormonal replacement or supplemental therapy in the presence of hypothyroidism of any etiology, with the exception of transient hypothyroidism during the recovery phase of subacute thyroiditis.

As a pituitary TSH suppressant, in the treatment or prevention of various types of euthyroid goiters, including thyroid nodules, subacute or chronic lymphocytic thyroiditis (Hashimoto's disease), multinodular goiter and in the management of thyroid cancer.

As a diagnostic agent in suppression tests to aid in the diagnosis of suspected mild hyperthyroidism or thyroid gland autonomy.

Contraindications: Patients with hypersensitivity to any of the active or extraneous constituents of the tablets, and in patients with thyrotoxicosis, acute myocardial infarction or uncorrected adrenal insufficiency.

Warnings: *Lactation:* In euthyroid lactating mothers, levothyroxine (endogenous or exogenous) may be secreted into breast milk in amounts sufficient to mask signs of hypothyroidism in the suckling infant.

The use of levothyroxine, along or combined with other drugs, in the treatment of obesity or infertility in patients who are not hypothyroid has been shown to be ineffective and potentially harmful. In the treatment of obesity with hypothyroidism, large doses may produce serious or even life-threatening manifestations of toxicity, particularly when given in association with sympathomimetic amines such as those used for their anorectic effects.

Precautions: *Pregnancy:* Levothyroxine does not readily cross the placenta, and when successfully employed to render or maintain the patient in an euthyroid state, therapy is considered to be warranted in pregnant patients.
Lactation: Minimal amounts of thyroid hormones are secreted in human milk. Although thyroid hormones are not associated with serious adverse reactions and does not have known tumorigenic potential, caution should be exercised when therapy is administered to nursing patients. Generally however, adequate replacement doses of levothyroxine are needed to maintain normal lactation.
Children: Treatment should be initiated immediately upon diagnosis and maintained for life, unless transient hypothyroidism is suspected. In which case, therapy may be interrupted for 2 to 8 weeks after the age of 3 years in order to reassess their condition. Cessation of therapy is justified in patients who have maintained a normal TSH during those 2 to 8 weeks.

Due to the profound effects of thyroid hormones on energy-requiring metabolic processes, the administration of levothyroxine to a hypothyroid patient may unmask occult cardiovascular, endocrine or metabolic disease.

Hypothyroidism of long standing is associated with atherogenesis, which may or may not fully manifest itself in the hypometabolic state. In such cases levothyroxine should be administered with extreme caution employing low initial dosage increased slowly by small increments, as even a gradual restoration of normal metabolic rate may result in development or exacerbation of myocardial ischemia and angina. In some patients, cardiovascular status may be so compromised that the metabolic demands of the euthyroid state cannot be met, despite the employment of appropriate antianginal therapy. Clinical judgment may then dictate a less-than-complete restoration of thyroid status.

Hypothyroidism decreases the sensitivity to oral anticoagulants. Prothrombin time should be closely monitored in thyroid treated patients on oral anticoagulants and dosage of the latter agents adjusted on the basis of frequent prothrombin time determinations. In infants, excessive doses of thyroid hormone preparations may produce craniosynostosis.

Endocrine disorders such as diabetes mellitus, diabetes insipidus, Addison's disease (adrenal insufficiency) and hypopituitarism are characterized by signs and symptoms which may be diminished in severity or obscured by hypothyroidism.

Treatment with levothyroxine may require that appropriate adjustments in therapy for these concomitant disorders be made. In particular, when hypothyroidism is accompanied by adrenal insufficiency (such as in panhypopituitarism), appropriate adrenocortical replacement therapy should be instituted prior to commencement of treatment with levothyroxine in order to prevent the possible precipitation of Addisonian crisis.

Slightly excessive dosage of thyroid agents were previously recommended for replacement therapy in congenital hypothyroidism (cretinism), since it was thought that slight underdosage was harmful while slightly excessive dosage was not. However, it is currently recommended that excessive dosage be avoided since minimal brain damage has occurred in children with thyrotoxicosis during infancy and excessive dosage may accelerate bone age and cause premature craniosynostosis (see Dosage).

The intestinal absorption of levothyroxine may be impaired in patients with certain malabsorption states, particularly celiac sprue (gluten enteropathy). Higher dosages of levothyroxine may be required in such patients, especially during exacerbations of the enteropathy.
Geriatrics: Levothyroxine should be used with caution in elderly patients who may be more sensitive to the effects of thyroid hormones (see Dosage).
Drug Interactions: Thyroid hormones potentiate the hypoprothrombinemic effects of oral anticoagulant agents such as warfarin. When treatment with levothyroxine is initiated in patients receiving oral anticoagulants, the prothrombin time should be determined frequently and the anticoagulant dosage reduced appropriately.

Administration of levothyroxine to a diabetic patient may result in an increase in the patient's requirements for insulin and/or hypoglycemic medication (see above).

Cholestyramine resin binds levothyroxine in the intestinal tract and substantially impairs its absorption. When the two agents must be used concurrently the levothyroxine dose should be taken at least 1 hour before or 4 hours after the dose of cholestyramine, with regular monitoring of thyroid function.

Phenytoin competes with thyroid hormones for serum protein binding sites, resulting in an increase in the unbound fractions of T3 and T4 and an enhanced thyroid effect. Dosage reduction may be necessary in sensitive patients.

Administration of phenytoin to patients stabilized on levothyroxine may necessitate a reduction in the dosage of the latter.

Phenobarbital induces hepatic enzymes and increases the rate of degradation of thyroid hormones. The dosage of levothyroxine may need to be increased when concurrent therapy with phenobarbital is employed.

Beta-adrenergic blocking agents may decrease peripheral conversion of T4 to T3, thereby reducing the efficacy of exogenous levothyroxine.

Estrogens increase serum thyroxin-binding globulin levels, thereby decreasing the unbound fractions of T3 and T4. Administration of estrogen-containing preparations (such as oral contraceptives) to hypothyroid patients may cause an increase in their levothyroxine requirements.

Patients receiving thyroid replacement therapy who undergo anesthesia with ketamine should be closely monitored for possible hypertension and tachycardia.

Concurrent use of sympathomimetic agents or tricyclic antidepressants with thyroid hormones may result in enhanced effects of either medication. In patients with coronary artery disease receiving thyroid replacement therapy, administration of sympathomimetic agents increases the risk of coronary insufficiency.

If coadministered with cardiac glycosides, adjustment of dosage of cardiac glycoside may be necessary.
Laboratory Test Interactions: Various physiologic and pathologic conditions or certain drugs can interfere with thyroid function tests and their interpretation. Serum thyroxin-binding globulin (TBG) is increased in pregnancy, on estrogen therapy, or in patients using estrogen-containing oral contraceptives. Infectious hepatitis may also increase serum TBG concentration. Decreased TBG is found in patients on androgen or corticosteroid therapy and also in cases of nephrosis and acromegaly. Some drugs such as phenylbutazone and salicylates bind competitively to TBG or thyroxin-binding prealbumin. Familial hyper- or hypo-thyroxin-binding globulinemias have been reported.

Adverse Effects: Adverse reactions to levothyroxine are confined to hypersensitivity to or intolerance of an ingredient of the tablets, and toxicity due to overdosage of levothyroxine (see Overdose: Symptoms and Treatment).

Overdose: Symptoms and Treatment: Overdosage with levothyroxine can be expected to produce the typical signs and symptoms of thyrotoxicosis. These may include weight loss, increased appetite, palpitations, nervousness, diarrhea, abdominal cramps, sweating, tachycardia, increased pulse and blood pressures, angina pectoris, cardiac dysrhythmias, tremors, headache, insomnia, heat intolerance, fever and dysmenorrhea.

Severe overdosage is equivalent to thyroid storm and may be manifested by coma, cardiac decompensation, and possibly death secondary to cardiac dysrhythmia or failure. The effects of acute overdosage of levothyroxine may take several days to appear.

The manifestations of levothyroxine overdosage should be managed by discontinuation of levothyroxine for 2 to 7 days followed by resumption of treatment with lower doses.

The management of acute severe overdosage should consist principally of reducing absorption of the drug and counteracting central and peripheral effects, mainly those of increased sympathetic nervous activity. Initially, the stomach should be emptied immediately by inducing emesis or by gastric lavage. If the patient is comatose, having seizures, or lacks the gag reflex, gastric lavage may be performed if an endotracheal tube with cuff inflated is in place to prevent aspiration of vomitus. Oxygen may be administered and ventilation maintained. If congestive heart failure develops, cardiac glycosides may be administered. Measures to control fever, hypoglycemia, or fluid loss should be initiated as necessary. A β-adrenergic blocking agent may be useful to counteract many of the effects of increased sympathetic activity. Provided no contraindications for its use exist, propranolol may be administered i.v. in a dosage of 1 to 3 mg every 10 minutes, or orally in a dosage of 80 to 100 mg/day. However, propylthiouracil and other antithyroid agents are **not** effective in the treatment of thyrotoxicosis due to overdosage of exogenous levothyroxine.

Dosage: Dosage of levothyroxine must be carefully adjusted according to individual requirements and response. The age and general physical condition of the patients and the severity and duration of hypothyroid symptoms determine the initial dosage and rate at which dosage may be increased to the eventual maintenance dosage (see Precautions). Adjustment of levothyroxine dosage should be based mainly on the patient's clinical response and confirmed by appropriate laboratory tests. Laboratory tests alone should not be relied upon to guide therapy.

For purposes of conversion, levothyroxine sodium (T4) 100 μg is usually considered equivalent to desiccated thyroid 60 mg, thyroglobulin 60 mg, or liothyronine sodium (T3) 25 μg. However, these are rough guidelines only and do not obviate the careful re-evaluation of a patient when switching thyroid hormone preparations.
Adults: For the management of mild hypothyroidism, the usual initial dose is 50 μg once daily. Dosage may be increased in increments of 25 to 50 μg/day at intervals of 2 to 4 weeks until the desired response is obtained.

For the management of severe hypothyroidism the usual initial dosage is 12.5 to 25 μg once daily. Dosage may be increased by increments of 25 to 50 μg/day at intervals of 2 to 4 weeks until the desired response is obtained. The usual maintenance dosage for full replacement therapy is 100 to 200 μg/day, although certain patients may require higher dosages. Failure to respond adequately to dosages exceeding

Levotec (cont'd)

300 to 400 μg/day is rare and should prompt re-evaluation of the diagnosis, or suggest the presence of malabsorption or patient noncompliance.

Geriatrics: Patients with Hypothyroidism: The usual initial dosage is 12.5 to 50 μg once daily. Dosage may be increased at intervals of 3 to 8 weeks until the desired response is obtained. Thyroid hormone replacement requirements are about 25% lower in patients over the age of 60 years than in younger adults.

Infants and Children: In infants and children, it is essential to achieve rapid and complete thyroid replacement because of the critical importance of thyroid hormones in sustaining growth and maturation, including the normal development of the CNS. In general, the dosage requirements of children, on a per body weight basis, are higher than those of adults. Levothyroxine tablets may be given to infants and children unable to swallow intact tablets by crushing the appropriate dose and suspending it in a small amount of water or formula, in cooked cereal or apple sauce. Do not store the suspension for any period of time.

The recommended replacement dosages of levothyroxine, to be administered in a single daily dose, are as follows (see Table I).

Table I—Levotec

Recommended Pediatric Dosage for Congenital Hypothyroidism

Age	Dose/Day (μg)	Daily Dose/kg of Body Weight (μg)
0-6 months	25-50	8-10
6-12 months	50-75	6-8
1-5 years	75-100	5-6
6-12 years	100-150	4-5

Prematures: Neonates weighing less than 2 kg and neonates at risk of cardiac failure may receive an initial dosage of 25 μg once daily; dosage may be increased to 50 μg once daily in 4 to 6 weeks.

Supplied: 25 μg: Each round, orange, scored tablet, engraved with 25 and "M" on one side, and blank on the other side, contains: levothyroxine sodium USP 25 μg. Nonmedicinal ingredients: dibasic calcium phosphate, D&C Yellow #10, FD&C Red #40, starch, stearic acid, and talc. Bottles of 100 and 1 000.

50 μg: Each round, white, scored tablet engraved with 50 and "M" on one side, and blank on the other side, contains: levothyroxine sodium USP 50 μg. Nonmedicinal ingredients: dibasic calcium phosphate, starch, stearic acid, and talc. Coloring agents-free. Bottles of 100 and 1 000.

75 μg: Each round, violet, scored tablet, engraved with 75 and "M" on one side, and blank on the other side, contains: levothyroxine sodium USP 75 μg. Nonmedicinal ingredients: dibasic calcium phosphate, FD&C Blue #1, FD&C Red #40, starch, stearic acid, and talc. Bottles of 100 and 1 000.

100 μg: Each round, yellow, scored tablet, engraved with 100 and "M" on one side, and blank on the other side, contains: levothyroxine sodium USP 100 μg. Nonmedicinal ingredients: dibasic calcium phosphate, FD&C Yellow #5, FD&C Yellow #6, starch, stearic acid, and talc. Bottles of 100 and 1 000.

112 μg: Each round, rose, scored tablet, engraved with 112 and "M" on one side, and blank on the other side, contains: levothyroxine sodium USP 112 μg. Nonmedicinal ingredients: dibasic calcium phosphate, FD&C Red #40, starch, stearic acid, talc and titanium dioxide. Bottles of 100 and 1 000.

125 μg: Each round, brown, scored tablet, engraved with 125 and "M" on one side, and blank on the other side, contains: levothyroxine sodium USP 125 μg. Nonmedicinal ingredients: dibasic calcium phosphate, FD&C Blue #1, FD&C Red #40, starch, stearic acid, and talc. Bottles of 100 and 1 000.

150 μg: Each round, blue, scored tablet, engraved with 150 and "M" on one side, and blank on the other side, contains: levothyroxine sodium USP 150 μg. Nonmedicinal ingredients: dibasic calcium phosphate, FD&C Blue #1, starch, stearic acid, and talc. Bottles of 100 and 1 000.

175 μg: Each round, lilac, scored tablet, engraved with 175 and "M" on one side, and blank on the other side, contains: levothyroxine sodium USP 175 μg. Nonmedicinal ingredients: dibasic calcium phosphate, FD&C Blue #1, FD&C Red #40, starch, stearic acid, and talc. Bottles of 100 and 1 000.

200 μg: Each round, pink, scored tablet, engraved with 200 and "M" on one side, and blank on the other side, contains: levothyroxine sodium USP 200 μg. Nonmedicinal ingredients: dibasic calcium phosphate, FD&C Red #3, starch, stearic acid, and talc. Bottles of 100 and 1 000.

300 μg: Each round, green, scored tablet, engraved with 300 and "M" on one side, and blank on the other side, contains: levothyroxine sodium USP 300 μg. Nonmedicinal ingredients: D&C Yellow #10, dibasic calcium phosphate, FD&C Blue #1, FD&C Yellow #6, starch, stearic acid, and talc. Bottles of 100 and 1 000.

Store between 15 and 30°C. Protect from light.

New Product 1998

LEVOVIST®
Berlex Canada

Galactose—Palmitic Acid
Ultrasound Contrast Agent

Pharmacology: Levovist is an ultrasound contrast agent consisting of granules which are composed of 99.9% galactose and 0.1% palmitic acid. Prior to use, Levovist must be reconstituted with sterilized water for injections and shaken vigorously by hand for 5 to 10 seconds. After injection of the suspension into a peripheral vein, Levovist leads to temporarily enhanced ultrasound echoes from the heart chambers and blood vessels. The distinct amplification of the ultrasound echo is caused primarily by micron-sized air bubbles, which are formed after suspension of the granules in water. Mediated by the palmitic acid additive, they remain stable for several minutes while in transit through the lungs and heart, and subsequent vascular bed before dissolving in the blood stream.

The pharmacokinetic investigation of Levovist was performed with the concentration of 400 mg/mL and injection volumes of 35 and 70 mL.

Galactose and palmitic acid are physiological substances with rapid metabolism.

After i.v. administration of Levovist, the galactose microparticles quickly dissolve in the blood stream. Galactose is rapidly distributed to the extracellular space and extracted by the liver. In the liver cells, galactose is converted to galactose-1-phosphate, then to glucose-1-phosphate, and glucose-6-phosphate which can enter the various pathways of glucose metabolism. Galactose is excreted via the kidneys if the plasma galactose level exceeds 50 mg/100 mL.

Palmitic acid is one of the most common fatty acids present in the human body. This 16-carbon atom and fully saturated fatty acid is one of the major constituents of the fats in the blood. Being highly miscible with the membranes of the cells, it immediately diffuses into the fat cells where it follows the usual metabolic process.

The plasma half-lives of galactose and palmitic acid, in adults, are in the range of 10 to 15 minutes and 1 to 4 minutes, respectively.

Depending on hepatic function, a prolonged elimination half-life can be expected. The elimination rate may therefore be reduced in cases of liver dysfunction and in neonates. As ethanol decreases the rate of galactose conversion in the liver, it may also prolong the half-life.

Results from clinical trials with Levovist show that within the range of recommended dosages (from 10 mL of 200 mg/mL, up to 8 mL of 400 mg/mL), Levovist produces no clinically relevant effects on physiological functions. Transient hemodynamic effects were observed at doses of 70 mL of the 400 mg/mL concentration injected as a bolus, which is more than 8-fold greater than the maximum recommended diagnostic dose.

Indications: One- and two-dimensional Doppler sonographic blood flow imaging in patients with insufficient Doppler signal intensity. B-mode contrast echocardiography.

Contraindications: Levovist should not be administered to patients with galactosemia.

Warnings: In patients with severe cardiovascular insufficiency close to cardiac decompensation (i.e., NYHA stage IV), the total osmotic load caused by the Levovist injections must be considered carefully.

Levovist must be prepared according to instructions (see Dosage) in order to ensure safe administration of the product.

Precautions: *Pregnancy:* The safe use of Levovist during pregnancy has not been established. Therefore, it should not be used unless the benefits outweigh the risks.

Children: The safety and effectiveness of Levovist in children have not been established.

Drug Interactions: The interaction of Levovist with other compounds has not been investigated.

Adverse Effects: The safety of Levovist was evaluated in 1 819 patients during clinical trials for Doppler sonography and B-mode echocardiography. No serious adverse events were reported during the clinical trials. Most adverse events experienced by patients were transient, and graded as mild or moderate in severity. The most frequently reported adverse events were: vasodilatation [sensation of warmth] (6.2%), injection site pain (3.9%), paresthesia (3.9%) and pain (1.4%).

Spontaneous adverse events having an incidence of <1%:
Cardiovascular: hypertension, hypotension, tachycardia, bradycardia, chest pain, and thrombophlebitis.
Injection Site: injection site reaction and inflammation. Slight local intolerance reactions after an accidental paravenous administration of Levovist might occur. In this case, symptomatic treatment is recommended (e.g., immobilisation, cold compresses and observation).
CNS: dizziness, headache, asthenia, chills and convulsion.
Body as a Whole: body odor.
Special Senses: taste perversion and abnormal vision.
Respiratory: dyspnea, increased cough, lung edema and hyperventilation.
Digestive: nausea, vomiting and dry mouth.
Skin and Appendages: pruritus and rash.
Musculoskeletal: myalgia and dystonia.
Urogenital: urinary urgency.

Overdose: Symptoms and Treatment: The risk of accidental poisoning with Levovist is extremely low.

An overdose of Levovist should be treated by prompt initiation of symptomatic therapy. For symptoms of osmotic diuresis: monitor the serum electrolytes and intravascular volume, and correct when necessary. For symptoms of hypervolemia: i.v. administration of diuretics (e.g., furosemide).

Dosage: Amplification of the ultrasound echo is dependent on the concentration of the microparticle suspension and the volume injected. After having prepared the suspension by adding the appropriate amount of sterilized water for injections and shaking it vigorously by hand for 5 to 10 seconds, let the suspension stand for 2 minutes before withdrawing into a syringe. The use of excessive negative pressure when the suspension is drawn into the syringe is to be avoided. Care must be taken to remove any visible air bubbles before injection. Levovist should be injected into a large vein (e.g., antecubital vein). The following dosages are recommended (see Table I).

Table I—Levovist

One-and Two-Dimensional Doppler Sonography	Volume (mL)	Concentration (mg/mL)
Vascular Doppler Sonography		
For adults with:		
Moderately-well detectable but diagnostically unsatisfactory Doppler signals	10-16	200
Weak Doppler signals, (e.g., in the presence of small vessels, lesion vascularity, low blood flow or unfavorable scanning conditions)	10	300
Very weak or absent Doppler signals	8	400
Doppler Echocardiography of the Right and Left Heart Chambers		
Adults:		
Usual dose	10-16	200
For the examination of the right heart chambers only	5-10	200
Transesophageal echocardiography	10	200
In cases of very weak or nondetectable Doppler signals and for the clarification of mitral insufficiency	10	300

Table II—Levovist

B-Mode Contrast Echocardiography

	Volume (mL)	Concentration (mg/mL)
Adults:		
Usual dose	10	300
For examination of the right heart chambers only	5-10	300
In cases of unfavorable sound conduction conditions	5-8	400
Transesophageal echocardiography	5	300
Stress echocardiography	8	400

The i.v. injection should be done continuously (approximately 1 to 2 mL/s) in order to have homogeneous enhancement effects in the Doppler recording. To ensure that the total dose of Levovist is systemically delivered, the injection should be followed by a 5 to 10 mL normal saline flush.

A repeat injection of Levovist may be necessary in special cases, e.g., in order to examine several sectional planes. To achieve a stronger effect or longer duration of enhancement, the dose may be increased, particularly by choosing a higher concentration. The duration of the increased signal strength is usually 1 to 2 minutes for Doppler echocardiographic examinations, and 2 to 4 minutes for Doppler vascular examinations.

Additional injections can be repeated at 5-minute intervals. The maximum recommended dose is 6 injections of the highest single dose.

B-Mode Contrast Echocardiography: See Table II.

The i.v. injection should be given as bolus. To ensure that the total dose of Levovist is systemically delivered, the injection should be followed by a 5 to 10 mL normal saline flush. This can improve the reproducibility of the quantitatively measurable contrast effects. To facilitate the injection of the saline solution without delay, the use of a 3-way connector is recommended.

Additional injections can be repeated at 5-minute intervals. The maximum recommended dose is 6 injections of the highest single dose.

Reconstituted Suspensions: Prior to use, Levovist is reconstituted with sterilized water for injection. The concentration of the microparticle suspension and thereby the degree of the contrast effect produced by the microbubbles can be adjusted to the respective clinical demand by adding different specific amounts of sterilized water for injections (see Table III).

Table III—Levovist

Reconstitution

Vial Size	Volume of Water to be Added to the Vial (mL)	Approximate Available Volume (mL)*	Levovist Concentration (mg microparticles/mL)
4 g	17	19.5	approximately 200
	11	13.5	approximately 300
	8	10.5	approximately 400

*Withdrawable volume is approximately 1 to 2 mL less.

Special Instructions: Preparation of the Levovist Suspension: Withdraw the appropriate amount of sterilized water for injection using the syringe. Remove the plastic cap from the vial containing the granules without disturbing the flanged metal cap. Pierce the rubber stopper with the minispike. Attach the syringe to the minispike, and transfer the water into the vial of Levovist granules. Prepare the suspension by immediately shaking vigorously by hand for 5 to 10 seconds. Do not use shaking devices or an ultrasound bath. Let the suspension stand for 2 minutes before use. Withdraw the ready-for-use, homogeneous, milky Levovist suspension through the minispike into the syringe and administer within 10 minutes of preparation.

The granules and sterilized water for injections should be at room temperature before making the suspension. After reconstitution, drawing the suspension up too quickly and warming the vial by holding it in the hand for a prolonged period should be avoided. This is necessary to prevent a decrease of the microbubble concentration and the formation of larger air bubbles due to the degassing processes. It is recommended to perform the injection via a flexible indwelling cannula with an adequate gauge size (e.g., 19 to 20 G). As usual, care must be taken to remove any macroscopically visible air bubbles from the suspension before injection. Should a slight sedimentation of the microparticles occur during standing time, resuspend the preparation by gently rotating it immediately before injection. Any suspension not used at one examination session must be discarded.

Supplied: Each g of granules contains: galactose 999 mg and palmitic acid 1 mg. Maximum osmolality at 37°C (solution): 200 mg/mL, ~1 175 mOsm/kg; 300 mg/mL, ~1 965 mOsm/kg; 400 mg/mL, ~2 894 mOsm/kg. Effective osmolality at 25°C (filtrate): 200 mg/mL, ~910 mOsm/kg; 300 mg/mL, ~980 mOsm/kg; 400 mg/mL, ~950 mOsm/kg. Viscosity at 25°C (ready-for-use suspension): 200 mg/mL, ~1.4 mPa·s; 300 mg/mL, ~3.6 mPa·s; 400 mg/mL, ~8.0 mPa·s. Viscosity at 25°C (filtrate): 200 mg/mL, 1.4 mPa·s; 300 mg/mL, 1.4 mPa·s; 400 mg/mL, 1.4 mPa·s.

The reconstituted suspensions have a stability of approximately 15 minutes in the vial without any loss of echogenicity. Vials of 4 g, cartons of 1 vial of granules, one 19 mL ampul of sterilized water for injection, one 20 mL disposable syringe and 1 minispike. Store at room temperature (15 to 30°C). Protect from light.

New Product 1998

LEVSIN®

Rivex Pharma

Hyoscyamine Sulfate

Antispasmodic

Pharmacology: Hyoscyamine inhibits specifically the actions of acetylcholine on structures innervated by postganglionic cholinergic nerves and on smooth muscles that respond to acetylcholine but lack cholinergic innervation. These peripheral cholinergic receptors are present in the autonomic effector cells of the smooth muscle, cardiac muscle, the sinoatrial node, the atrioventricular node, and the exocrine glands. It is completely devoid of any action in the autonomic ganglia. Hyoscyamine inhibits gastrointestinal propulsive motility and decreases gastric acid secretion. Hyoscyamine also controls excessive pharyngeal, tracheal, and bronchial secretions.

Hyoscyamine is absorbed totally and completely by sublingual administration as well as oral administration. Once absorbed, hyoscyamine disappears rapidly from the blood and is distributed throughout the entire body. The half-life of hyoscyamine is 3.5 hours and the majority of drug is excreted in the urine unchanged within the first 12 hours. Only traces of this drug are found in breast milk. Hyoscyamine passes the blood brain barrier and placenta barrier.

Indications: Adjunct therapy in the treatment of peptic ulcer. To control gastric secretion, visceral spasm and hypermotility in spastic colitis, spastic bladder, cystitis, pylorospasm, and associated abdominal cramps. Used in functional intestinal disorders to reduce symptoms such as those seen in mild dysenteries, diverticulitis and acute enterocolitis. Adjunctive therapy in irritable bowel syndrome (irritable colon, spastic colon, mucous colitis) and functional gastrointestinal disorders. Adjunctive therapy in the treatment of neurogenic bladder and neurogenic bowel disturbances (including the splenic flexure syndrome and neurogenic colon). Also for infant colic (drops). In combination with morphine or other narcotics in symptomatic relief of biliary and renal colic; as a drying agent in the relief of symptoms of acute rhinitis; parkinsonism to reduce rigidity and hyperhidrosis; and in therapy of poisoning by anticholinesterase agents.

Hyoscyamine may be used to reduce pain and hypersecretion in pancreatitis. Hyoscyamine may be used in certain cases of partial heart block associated with vagal activity.

Contraindications: Glaucoma, obstructive uropathy (for example, bladder neck obstruction due to prostatic hypertrophy); obstructive disease of the gastrointestinal tract (as in achalasia, pyloroduodenal stenosis); paralytic ileus; intestinal atony of the elderly or debilitated patients; unstable cardiovascular status in acute hemorrhage; severe ulcerative colitis; toxic megacolon complicating ulcerative colitis; myasthenia gravis.

Warnings: In the presence of high environmental temperature, heat prostration can occur (fever and heat stroke due to decreased sweating). Diarrhea may be an early symptom of incomplete intestinal obstruction, especially in patients with ileostomy or colostomy; treatment with this drug would be inappropriate and possibly harmful.

Occupational Hazards: Drowsiness or blurred vision may occur. In this event, the patient should be warned not to engage in activities requiring mental alertness such as operating a motor vehicle or other machinery or to perform hazardous work while taking this drug.

Psychosis has been reported in sensitive individuals given anticholinergic drugs. CNS signs and symptoms include confusion, disorientation, short-term memory loss, hallucinations, dysarthria, ataxia, coma, euphoria, decreased anxiety, fatigue, insomnia, agitation and mannerisms, and inappropriate affect. These CNS signs and symptoms usually resolve within 12 to 48 hours after discontinuation of the drug.

Precautions: Use with caution in patients with autonomic neuropathy, hyperthyroidism, coronary heart disease, congestive heart failure, cardiac arrhythmias, hypertension and renal failure. Investigate any tachycardia before giving any anticholinergic drug since they may increase the heart rate. Use with caution in patients with hiatal hernia associated with reflux esophagitis.

Occupational Hazards: Hyoscyamine may cause drowsiness, dizziness or blurred vision; observe caution before driving, using machinery or performing other tasks requiring mental alertness.

Use of hyoscyamine may decrease sweating resulting in heat prostration, fever or heat stroke; febrile patients or those who may be exposed to elevated environmental temperatures should use caution.

Drug Interactions: Additive adverse effects resulting from cholinergic blockade may occur when hyoscyamine is administered concomitantly with other antimuscarinics, amantadine, haloperidol, phenothiazines, MAO inhibitors, tricyclic antidepressants or some antihistamines.

Antacids may interfere with the absorption of hyoscyamine. Administer before meals; antacids after meals.

Carcinogenesis, Mutagenesis, Impairment of Fertility: No long-term studies in animals have been performed to determine the carcinogenic, mutagenic, or impairment of fertility potential of hyoscyamine; however, over 30 years of marketing experience shows no demonstrable evidence of a problem.

Pregnancy: Animal reproduction studies have not been conducted with hyoscyamine. It is also not known whether it can cause fetal harm when administered to a pregnant woman or can affect reproduction capacity. It should be given to a pregnant woman only if clearly needed.

Lactation: Hyoscyamine is excreted in human milk. Caution should be exercised when it is administered to a nursing woman.

Adverse Effects: Not all of the following adverse reactions have been reported with hyoscyamine. The following adverse reactions have been reported for pharmacologically similar drugs with anticholinergic/antispasmodic action. Adverse reactions may include dryness of the mouth, urinary hesitancy and retention, blurred vision, tachycardia, palpitations, mydriasis, cycloplegia, increased ocular tension, loss of taste, headache, nervousness, drowsiness, weakness, dizziness, insomnia, nausea, vomiting, impotence, suppression of lactation, constipation, bloated feeling, allergic reactions or drug idiosyncrasies, urticaria and other dermal manifestations, ataxia, speech disturbance, some degree of mental confusion and/or excitement (especially in elderly persons), and decreased sweating.

Overdose: Symptoms: Headache, nausea, vomiting, blurred vision, dilated pupils, hot dry skin, dizziness, dryness of the mouth, difficulty in swallowing, and CNS stimulation.

Treatment: Immediate lavage of the stomach and injection of physostigmine 0.5 to 2 mg i.v. and repeat as

Levsin (cont'd)

necessary up to a total of 5 mg. Fever may be treated symptomatically (tepid water sponge baths, hypothermic blanket). Excitement to a degree which demands attention may be managed with sodium thiopental 2% solution given slowly i.v. or chloral hydrate (100-200 mL of a 2% solution) by rectal infusion. In the event of progression of the curare-like effect to paralysis of the respiratory muscles, artificial respiration should be instituted and maintained until effective respiratory action returns.

Dosage: Dosage may be adjusted according to the conditions and severity of symptoms. The tablets may be taken sublingually or orally.

Adults: 1 or 2 tablets every 4 hours or as needed.

Supplied: Each pale blue-green, octagonal, scored tablet, engraved with SCHWARZ logo and 532, contains: hyoscyamine sulfate 0.125 mg. Nonmedicinal ingredients: colloidal silicon dioxide, dextrates, FD&C Green #3, mannitol, natural peppermint flavor, purified water and stearic acid. Gluten- and tartrazine-free. Bottles of 100.

LIBRAX® Ⓟ
Roche

Chlordiazepoxide HCl—Clidinium Bromide

Anxiolytic—Anticholinergic

Supplied: Each No. 4 hard gelatin capsule with green, opaque cap and body, imprinted ROCHE C and LIBRAX (black ink) alternating between cap and body, contains: chlordiazepoxide HCl 5 mg and clidinium bromide 2.5 mg. Nonmedicinal ingredients: cornstarch, fast green FCF, gelatin, lactose (104 mg), quinolone yellow WS, talc and titanium dioxide. Energy: 2.1 kJ (0.5 kcal). Gluten-, paraben-, sodium-, sulfite- and tartrazine-free. Bottles of 100 and 500. Protect from light. Store at 15 to 30°C.

(Shown in Product Recognition Section)

LIDEMOL® Ⓟ
Medicis

Fluocinonide

Topical Corticosteroid

Indications: For topical therapy of corticosteroid-responsive acute and chronic skin eruptions where an anti-inflammatory, anti-allergenic and antipruritic activity in the topical management is required.

Contraindications: Untreated bacterial, tubercular, fungal and most viral lesions of the skin (including herpes simplex, vaccinia and varicella) and untreated purulent bacterial infections. Hypersensitivity to any of the components.

Warnings: *Pregnancy* and *Lactation:* The safety of topical corticosteroids during pregnancy or lactation has not been established. The potential benefit of topical corticosteroids, if used during pregnancy or lactation, should be weighed against possible hazard to the fetus or the nursing infant.

Not for ophthalmic use.

Precautions: Not recommended for use under occlusive dressings.

Apply cautiously on lesions close to the eye. Severe irritation is possible if these formulations contact the eye. Should this occur, immediate flushing of the eye with a large volume of water is recommended.

Prolonged use of topical corticosteroid products may produce atrophy of the skin and of s.c. tissues, particularly on flexor surfaces and on the face. If this is noted, discontinue its use.

Use with caution in patients with stasis dermatitis and other skin diseases associated with impaired circulation.

If a symptomatic response is not noted within a few days to a week, the local applications of corticosteroids should be discontinued and the patient re-evaluated.

During the use of topical corticosteroids, secondary infections may occur.

Although hypersensitivity reactions have been rare with topically applied steroid products, the drug should be discontinued and appropriate therapy instituted if there are signs of reaction.

In cases of bacterial infections of the skin, appropriate antibacterial agents should be used as primary therapy. If it is considered necessary, the topical corticosteroid product may be used as an adjunct to control inflammation, erythema and itching.

Patients should be advised to inform subsequent physicians of the prior use of corticosteroids.

Significant systemic absorption may result when steroids are applied over large areas of the body. To minimize the possibility, when long-term therapy is anticipated, interrupt treatment periodically or treat one area of the body at a time. Laboratory Tests: Urinary free cortisol test and ACTH stimulation test may be helpful in evaluating HPA axis suppression.

Adverse Effects: The following adverse skin reactions have been reported with the use of topical steroids: dryness, burning, itching, local irritation, striae, skin atrophy, atrophy of s.c. tissues, telangiectasia, hypertrichosis, change in pigmentation and secondary infection. Adrenal suppression has also been reported following topical corticosteroid therapy. Posterior subcapsular cataracts have been reported following systemic use of corticosteroids.

Overdose: Symptoms and Treatment: There is no specific antidote. Perform gastric lavage.

In the case of hypercorticism and/or adrenal suppression, discontinue therapy.

Dosage: This product is suitable when an emollient effect is desired. Apply gently a small amount onto the affected area 2 to 4 times daily as needed. This product is not to be used under occlusive conditions.

Supplied: Each tube contains: fluocinonide 0.05% in a water washable, aqueous emollient base. Nonmedicinal ingredients: cetyl alcohol, citric acid, mineral oil, polysorbate 60, propylene glycol, sorbitan monostearate and stearyl alcohol. Ethylene glycol-, lanolin-, parabens- and phenolic compounds-free. Tubes of 15 and 60 g. Store at controlled room temperature, 15 to 30°C.

LIDEX® Ⓟ
Medicis

Fluocinonide

Topical Corticosteroid

Indications: For topical therapy of corticosteroid-responsive acute and chronic skin eruptions where an anti-inflammatory, anti-allergenic and antipruritic activity in the topical management is required.

Contraindications: Untreated bacterial, tubercular, fungal and most viral lesions of the skin (including herpes simplex, vaccinia and varicella). Contraindicated in individuals with a history of hypersensitivity to any of the components.

Warnings: *Pregnancy* and *Lactation:* The safety of topical corticosteroids during pregnancy or lactation has not been established. The potential benefit of topical corticosteroids, if used during pregnancy or lactation, should be weighed against possible hazard to the fetus or the nursing infant.

Not for ophthalmic use.

Precautions: Not recommended for use under occlusive dressings.

Apply cautiously on lesions close to the eye. Severe irritation is possible if these formulations contact the eye. Should this occur, immediate flushing of the eye with a large volume of water is recommended.

Prolonged use of topical corticosteroid products may produce atrophy of the skin and of s.c. tissues, particularly on flexor surfaces and on the face. If this is noted, discontinue its use.

Use with caution in patients with stasis dermatitis and other skin diseases associated with impaired circulation.

If a symptomatic response is not noted within a few days to a week, the local applications of corticosteroids should be discontinued and the patient re-evaluated.

During the use of topical corticosteroids, secondary infections may occur.

Although hypersensitivity reactions have been rare with topically applied steroid products, the drug should be discontinued and appropriate therapy instituted if there are signs of reaction.

In cases of bacterial infections of the skin, appropriate antibacterial agents should be used as primary therapy. If it is considered necessary, the topical corticosteroid product may be used as an adjunct to control inflammation, erythema and itching.

Patients should be advised to inform subsequent physicians of the prior use of corticosteroids.

Significant systemic absorption may result when steroids are applied over large areas of the body. To minimize the possibility, when long-term therapy is anticipated, interrupt treatment periodically or treat one area of the body at a time. Laboratory Tests: Urinary free cortisol test and ACTH stimulation test may be helpful in evaluating HPA axis suppression.

Adverse Effects: The following adverse skin reactions have been reported with the use of topical steroids: dryness, burning, itching, local irritation, striae, skin atrophy, atrophy of s.c. tissues, telangiectasia, hypertrichosis, change in pigmentation and secondary infection. Adrenal suppression has also been reported following topical corticosteroid therapy. Posterior subcapsular cataracts have been reported following systemic use of corticosteroids.

Overdose: Symptoms and Treatment: There is no specific antidote, but gastric lavage should be performed.

In the case of hypercorticism and/or adrenal suppression, discontinue therapy.

Dosage: The cream is recommended for moist, weeping lesions. The ointment is suitable when an emollient effect is desired.

A small amount of cream or ointment should be applied gently on the affected skin area, 2 to 4 times daily, depending on the severity of the condition.

It is recommended that the cream or ointment not be used under occlusive conditions.

Supplied: Cream: Each tube contains: fluocinonide 0.05% in a greaseless, nonstaining, water washable, hydrophilic cream base designed for optimal release of the active ingredients. Nonmedicinal ingredients: citric acid, 1,2, 6-hexanetriol, polyethylene glycol 6 000, propylene glycol and stearyl alcohol. Ethylene glycol-, lanolin-, parabens- and phenolic compounds-free. Tubes of 60 g.

Ointment: Each tube contains: fluocinonide 0.05% in an ointment base providing optimal release of fluocinonide while retaining the occlusive and emollient effects desirable in an ointment. Nonmedicinal ingredients: Amerchol CAB, propylene carbonate, propylene glycol and white petrolatum. Ethylene glycol-, lanolin-, parabens- and phenolic compounds-free. Tubes of 60 g.

Store at room temperature. Avoid excessive heat above 40°C.

LIDOCAINE HCl 0.4% and 0.8% in 5% DEXTROSE for I.V. INFUSION

Baxter

Antiarrhythmic Agent

Supplied: Each mL of i.v. infusion contains: lidocaine HCl 0.4%, 0.8% in 5% dextrose. Viaflex Plus plastic (polyvinyl chloride) containers in the following sizes and concentrations: see Table I.

Table I—Lidocaine HCl 0.4% and 0.8% in 5% Dextrose for I.V. Infusion

Supplied		
Total Volume (mL)	Total Lidocaine HCl Content (mg)	Lidocaine HCl Concentration (mg/mL)
250	1 000	4
250	2 000	8
500	2 000	4

Do not store above 30°C. Protect from freezing.

LIDOCAINE PARENTERAL

Abbott

Lidocaine HCl

Antiarrhythmic Agent

Supplied: Single i.v. Injection: Each 5 mL ABBOJECT Disposable Syringe and 25-G, 5/8″ or 21-G, 1½″ needle contains: lidocaine HCl 2%. Also contains: hydrochloric acid, sodium chloride, sodium hydroxide and water for injection. Boxes of 10.

Medication, fluid path and needle are sterile and non-pyrogenic if caps and needle-guard are in place and the package has not been damaged or opened.

Single-dose: Each 2 mL ampul contains: lidocaine HCl 1%. Also contains: hydrochloric acid, sodium chloride, sodium hydroxide and water for injection. Boxes of 50.

Multiple-dose: Each 20 or 50 mL fliptop vial contains: lidocaine HCl 1%. Boxes of 50. Also contains methylparaben added as preservative. Also contains: hydrochloric acid, sodium chloride, sodium hydroxide and water for injection.

Each 20 mL fliptop vial contains: lidocaine HCl 2%. Also contains: hydrochloric acid, methylparaben, sodium chloride, sodium hydroxide and water for injection. Boxes of 50.

Lidocaine and Epinephrine: Each 20 mL fliptop vial contains: lidocaine HCl 1 or 2% and epinephrine (1:100 000). Also contains: citric acid, hydrochloric acid, methylparaben, sodium chloride, sodium hydroxide, sodium metabisulfite and water for injection.Boxes of 25.

Continuous i.v. infusion: Each mL contains: lidocaine HCl 0.4% in Dextrose 5% for i.v. infusion (Lidocaine 0.4% D5-W). Also contains: hydrochloric acid, sodium chloride, sodium hydroxide and water for injection. Plastic bags of 250 and 500 mL.

LIDOCAINE PARENTERAL

Bioniche

Lidocaine HCl

Lidocaine HCl—Epinephrine

Local Anesthetic

Supplied: See Table I. Lidocaine parenteral solutions are available in plastic ampuls, single use glass vials and multi-dose glass vials. Plastic ampuls and single use glass vials are preservative-free. Multidose glass vials also contain methylparaben. Vials containing epinephrine also contain metabisulfite. All solutions should be stored at room temperature (15 to 30°C).

Table I—Lidocaine Parenteral

Availability	Plastic Ampuls[a,b] (mL)		Single Use[b] Vials (mL)				Multidose Vials (mL)	
Concentration	2	5	10	20	30	50	20	50
1% Lidocaine HCl	◇	◇	◇				◇	◇
2% Lidocaine HCl	◇	◇	◇	◇			◇	◇
2%/1:100 000[c] Lidocaine HCl with epinephrine							◇	◇

[a]B.P. Std.
[b]Without preservative.
[c]Contains sodium metabisulfite as an antioxidant.

LIDODAN™ Endotracheal
LIDODAN™ Ointment
LIDODAN™ Viscous

Odan

Lidocaine HCl

Lidocaine

Lidocaine HCl

Topical Anesthetic

Supplied: Endotracheal: Each metered dose contains; lidocaine HCl 12 mg (equivalent to 10 mg lidocaine base). Nonmedicinal ingredients: sodium hydroxide and/or hydrochloric acid to adjust pH 5.0 to 7.0 and water for injection. Nonaerosol spray bottles of 30 mL with a metered dose valve. Single pak: 1 bottle with 1 × 20 cm stainless steel nozzle. Three pak: 3 × 30 mL nonaerosol spray bottles. Nozzle pak: 2 × 20 cm stainless steel nozzles. Clean stainless steel nozzles may be steam sterilized at 121°C for 15 minutes. Store at room temperature 15 to 30°C. Protect from freezing.

Ointment: Each g contains: lidocaine USP 50 mg (5%) in a water miscible ointment base. Nonmedicinal ingredients: polyethylene glycols and propylene glycol. Tubes of 15 and 30 g.

Viscous: Each mL contains: lidocaine HCl USP 20 mg (2%). Nonmedicinal ingredients: amaranth, cellulose gum, methylparaben, perfume, propylparaben, purified water and sodium cyclamate. Gluten- and tartrazine-free. Unbreakable natural polyethylene bottles of 50 and 100 mL with child-resistant closures. Store at room temperature: 15 to 30°C.

LIDOSPORIN® Cream
LIDOSPORIN® Ear Drops

Warner-Lambert Consumer Healthcare

Polymyxin B Sulfate—Gramicidin—Lidocaine HCl

Polymyxin B Sulfate—Lidocaine HCl

Antibiotic—Anesthetic—Antipruritic

Indications: Cream: Topical relief of pain and itching; also for the treatment and prevention of infections in minor cuts, wounds, and burns.

Ear Drops: The prevention of exacerbations and treatment of infection due to susceptible organisms, relief of pain and itching associated with otitis externa, including "swimmer's ear", otitis media (if tympanic membrane is perforated), postoperative aural cavities, furunculosis.

Contraindications: Hypersensitivity to any of the components.

Precautions: As with other antibiotic preparations, prolonged use may result in overgrowth of nonsusceptible organisms. Appropriate measures should be taken if this occurs.

If burning or itching increases or persists, discontinue use and consult a physician.

Although the otic solution does not require refrigeration, some patients may prefer to warm the medication before using and they should be cautioned to avoid heating the solution above body temperature so as to prevent loss of antibiotic potency.

Overdose: Symptoms and Treatment: Treatment is symptomatic.

Dosage: Cream: A small quantity of the cream may be applied 2 to 5 times daily, as required. If the skin condition permits, the cream should be gently rubbed into the affected areas.

Ear Drops: After cleansing and thorough but gentle drying, instill 3 or 4 drops into the infected ear, 3 or 4 times daily. For infants and children, 2 or 3 drops are suggested. Solution may be applied by saturating a gauze or cotton wick which may be left in the canal for 24 to 48 hours, keeping the wick moist by adding a few drops of solution as required.

Supplied: Cream: Each g contains: polymyxin B sulfate 10 000 units, gramicidin 250 μg (0.25 mg), lidocaine HCl 50 mg, in a smooth, white, water washable vanishing cream base with a pH of approximately 5.0. Nonmedicinal ingredients: mineral oil, paraben, petrolatum, polysorbate, propylene glycol, sodium hydroxide, water and wax. Tubes of 15 and 30 g.

Ear Drops: Each mL contains: polymyxin B sulfate 10 000 units, lidocaine HCl 50 mg (5%). Nonmedicinal ingredients: cupric sulfate, hydrochloric acid, propylene glycol and water. Plastic dropper bottles of 10 mL.

Store between 15 to 25°C.

LINCOCIN® Ⓟ

Pharmacia & Upjohn

Lincomycin HCl Monohydrate

Antibiotic

Pharmacology: The mode of action of lincomycin is the inhibition of protein synthesis by the inhibition of the binding of aminoacyl sRNA to the messenger ribosome complex at the 50S ribosomal unit.

Lincomycin is absorbed rapidly after oral administration, reaching peak levels in 2 to 4 hours. Levels above the minimum inhibitory concentration for most gram-positive organisms are maintained for 6 to 8 hours. I.M. administration of lincomycin produces peak serum levels in 30 minutes with detectable levels persisting for 24 hours after a 600 mg dose.

I.V. infusions of lincomycin over a 2 hour interval yield therapeutic levels for 14 hours.

Indications: The treatment of serious infections due to sensitive gram positive organisms (staphylococci, including penicillinase-producing staphylococci, streptococci and pneumococci) when the patient is intolerant of, or the organism resistant to other appropriate antibiotics.

Also indicated in the treatment of osteomyelitis, when the causative organism has been found to be sensitive to lincomycin.

Contraindications: In patients previously found to be hypersensitive to the drug or patients who have previously been found hypersensitive to clindamycin.

Until further clinical experience is obtained, lincomycin is not indicated in the newborn.

Warnings: Use of lincomycin has been associated with severe colitis which may be fatal. The major cause of this condition is a toxin produced by C. difficile. The condition manifests as a spectrum of symptoms from watery to severe diarrhea, fever, abdominal cramps and leukocytosis. This may be accompanied by the passage of blood and mucous which may result in peritonitis, shock and toxic megacolon if the drug is not discontinued and/or the condition treated.

Positive diagnosis can be made by performing an endoscopy, culture of the stool for C. difficile and performing a selective assay for the toxin(s) produced by C. difficile.

Antibiotic associated colitis may occur 2 to 3 weeks after lincomycin administration and is more likely to be severe in elderly or debilitated patients.

Mild cases showing minimal mucosal changes may respond to drug discontinuance. More severe cases, including those

Lincocin (cont'd)

showing ulceration or pseudomembrane formation, are treated with fluid, electrolyte and protein supplementation. The primary treatment for antibiotic associated colitis is vancomycin, 125 to 500 mg every 6 hours for 7 to 14 days. Where vancomycin is contraindicated, oral bacitracin 25 000 IU 4 times daily for 7 to 10 days may be used as an alternative. In critically ill patients, oral vancomycin 500 mg every 6 hours should be used.

Anticholinergics and antiperistaltic agents may worsen the condition. Other causes of colitis should be considered.

It should be noted that serious relapses have occurred up to 1 month after apparently successful treatment. A relatively prolonged period of continuing observation is therefore recommended.

Lincomycin should not be administered undiluted i.v. All i.v. doses should be given by infusion over a period of 30 to 120 minutes. Cases of cardiopulmonary arrest have been reported during the treatment of severe endocarditis when large i.v. doses (over 4 g) were given rapidly without dilution. These reactions do not occur when the drug is diluted as noted under Dosage.

This product contains benzyl alcohol. Benzyl alcohol has been reported to be associated with a fatal "Gasping Syndrome" in premature infants.

Precautions: General: Should be used with caution in those patients with a history of gastrointestinal disease, specifically colitis.

Lincomycin is not indicated for use in the treatment of meningitis as the levels within the cerebral spinal fluid do not reach an adequate concentration to combat this infection.

No serious renal or neurologic abnormalities have been reported to date. No ototoxicity has been demonstrated in any of a large number of patients treated with lincomycin.

Pregnancy: Limited experience with 322 women receiving lincomycin orally at a dosage of 500 mg 4 times/day for 7 days during pregnancy revealed no ill effect in the mother or the fetus. One hundred and ten of these patients were treated in the first trimester of pregnancy, 105 in the second trimester and 107 in the third trimester. All were suffering from cervicitis and/or vaginitis of bacterial origin in conjunction with their pregnancy. One hundred and twelve of the children, ages 6½ to 7½ years, from these patients have been examined and compared with a control group of 65 children born at the same time in the same hospital. Lincomycin treatment did not result in any drug related abnormalities (physical, dental or developmental) when compared with the control group.

Since safe conditions for the parenteral use of lincomycin in pregnancy have not been established, its use in such patients should involve careful consideration of expected benefits and possible risks.

Lactation: Lincomycin has been reported in breast milk at concentrations of 0.5 to 2.4 μg/mL.

Patients with Special Diseases and Conditions: The serum half-life of lincomycin is increased in those patients with impaired renal or hepatic function. Therefore, consideration should be given to reducing the frequency of administration in these patients.

Since adequate data are not yet available in patients with pre-existing endocrine or metabolic diseases, its use in such patients is not recommended at this time unless special clinical circumstances so indicate. Efficacy of lincomycin in the prophylactic treatment of rheumatic fever has not been established.

Drug Interactions: In vitro studies have shown antagonistic activity between lincomycin and erythromycin; therefore, these agents should not be used concurrently.

Because lincomycin has been shown to have neuromuscular blocking properties which may enhance the action of other neuromuscular blocking agents, it should be used with caution in patients receiving such agents.

Laboratory Tests: The use of antibiotics occasionally results in overgrowth of non-susceptible organisms—particularly yeasts. Should superinfections occur, appropriate measures should be taken. No direct relationship of the drug to liver disease has been established. However, it is recommended that all patients receiving treatment for longer than 1 or 2 weeks have liver function tests performed. If abnormal tests appear, the drug should be discontinued unless, in the opinion of the physician, the drug should be continued for the treatment of a serious infection.

Table I—Lincocin

Dosages

	Oral[a] (Capsules)	I.M. (Sterile Solution)	I.V. (Sterile Solution)
Adults	500 mg q8h	600 mg (2 mL) every 24 hrs	600 mg (2 mL) every 8 to 12[c] hours. Administer as infusion in 250 mL or more of 5% glucose in water or normal saline over a period of 30 to 120 minutes.
Severe	500 mg q6h	600 mg (2 mL) every 12 hrs	
Children[b]	20 mg/kg/day in 3 or 4 equal doses	10 mg/kg every 24 hrs	10 to 20 mg/kg/day in 2 or 3 doses at 8 to 12 hour intervals. Administer as infusion diluted as for adults.
Severe	60 mg/kg/day in 3 or 4 equal doses	10 mg/kg every 12 hrs	

[a]For optimal absorption, it is recommended that nothing be given by mouth except water for a period of 1 hour before and 2 hours after lincomycin administration.

[b]Over 1 month of age.

[c]All doses may be increased in more severe infections. Doses as high as 8.4 g/day, for 7 days, in 4 divided doses of 2 100 mg in an infusion of 250 mL, of normal saline, over a period of 120 minutes, were well tolerated in normal volunteers.

During clinical studies of lincomycin in the therapy of infectious disease, a few cases of neutropenia and/or leukopenia were reported. No cases of irreversible toxicity to the hematopoietic system have been reported; however, it is recommended that blood counts be obtained early and repeated periodically during the course of lincomycin therapy.

Adverse Effects: The following adverse reactions have been reported with the use of lincomycin:

Gastrointestinal: nausea, vomiting, abdominal distress and persistent diarrhea (see Warnings) and, with oral preparations, esophagitis.

Hematopoietic: neutropenia, leukopenia, agranulocytosis, and thrombocytopenic purpura have been reported. There have been rare reports of aplastic anemia and pancytopenia in which lincomycin could not be ruled out as the causative agent.

Hypersensitivity Reactions: Hypersensitivity reactions such as angioneurotic edema, serum sickness and anaphylaxis have been reported, some of these in patients sensitive to penicillin. Rare instances of erythema multiforme, some resembling Stevens-Johnson syndrome, have been associated with lincomycin administration.

Skin and Mucous Membranes: Pruritus, skin rashes, urticaria, vaginitis, and rare instances of exfoliative and vesiculobullous dermatitis have been reported.

Liver: Jaundice and abnormal liver function tests (particularly elevation of serum transaminase) have been observed during lincomycin therapy.

Cardiovascular: Instances of hypotension following parenteral administration have been reported, particularly after too rapid administration. Rare instances of cardiopulmonary arrest have been reported after too rapid i.v. administration (see Dosage).

Local Reactions: Local irritation, pain, induration, and sterile abscess formation have been seen with i.m. injection. Thrombophlebitis has been reported with i.v. injection. These reactions can be minimized by deep i.m. injection and avoidance of indwelling i.v. catheters.

Overdose: Symptoms and Treatment: No cases of large overdosage have been reported. It would be expected however that should overdosage occur, gastrointestinal side effects, including abdominal pain, nausea, vomiting and diarrhea, might be seen.

Overdosage should be treated with simple gastric lavage. No specific antidote is known.

Dosage: See Table I.

In ß-hemolytic streptococcal infections, continue treatment for at least 10 days to diminish the likelihood of subsequent rheumatic fever or glomerulonephritis.

Reconstituted Solutions: Lincocin (600 mg/2 mL and 1 800 mg/6 mL) was found to be compatible with 500 mL of the following solutions for a period of 24 hours at room temperature: 5% Dextrose in Water, 5% Dextrose in Saline, 10% Dextrose in Water, 10% Dextrose in Saline, Invert sugar 10%, Polysal M with 5% dextrose, Ringer's Solution, Sodium lactate 1/6 molar.

Compatibility was determined by a study which indicated no appreciable change in the pH of the resultant mixture and no loss of potency of the lincomycin when diluted as indicated above.

Supplied: Capsules: Each No. 0, hard gelatin capsule with light blue, opaque body and dark blue, opaque cap branded with Lincocin 500 on both parts contains: lincomycin HCl monohydrate equivalent to lincomycin base 500 mg. Sodium: <1 mmol (0.2 mg). Nonmedicinal ingredients: lactose, magnesium stearate and talc. Bottles of 100.

Sterile Solution: Each mL of sterile solution contains: lincomycin HCl monohydrate equivalent to lincomycin base 300 mg. Also contains benzyl alcohol. Vials of 2 and 10 mL.

(Shown in Product Recognition Section)

LIORESAL® Ⓟ

Novartis Pharmaceuticals

Baclofen

Muscle Relaxant—Antispastic

Pharmacology: Baclofen's precise mechanisms of action are not fully known. It inhibits both monosynaptic and polysynaptic reflexes at the spinal level, probably by hyperpolarization of afferent terminals, although actions at supraspinal sites may also occur and contribute to its clinical effect. Although baclofen is an analog of the putative inhibitory neurotransmitter gamma-aminobutyric acid (GABA), there is no conclusive evidence that actions on GABA systems are involved in the production of its clinical effects.

Peak plasma concentrations of baclofen are achieved within 2 hours and the plasma half-life is 2 to 4 hours.

In man, a single 10 mg oral dose of baclofen is rapidly and almost completely absorbed whereas absorption of 20 mg and 40 mg doses is less complete. Animal studies indicate rapid distribution throughout the body except to the CNS where concentrations are lower than average. The decay in CNS concentration is, however, slower than the decay from other tissues.

About 85% of a single oral dose is excreted unchanged in the urine. The remaining 15% is mainly deaminated to β-(p-chlorophenyl)-γ-hydroxybutyric acid within 24 hours. Baclofen is about 30% bound to serum proteins.

Indications: The alleviation of signs and symptoms of spasticity resulting from multiple sclerosis. May also be of some value in patients with spinal cord injuries and other spinal cord diseases.

Contraindications: Baclofen hypersensitivity.

Warnings: Abrupt Drug Withdrawal: Following abrupt withdrawal of baclofen, visual and auditory hallucinations, convulsions (status epilepticus), dyskinesia, confusion, psychotic, manic or paranoid states, anxiety with tachycardia and sweating, insomnia and worsening of spasticity have occurred. Therefore, except for serious adverse reactions, reduce the dose slowly when the drug is discontinued (over a period of approximately 1 to 2 weeks).

Impaired Renal Function: Because baclofen is primarily excreted unchanged through the kidneys, it should be given with caution and it may be necessary to reduce the dosage.

Stroke: Baclofen has not significantly benefited patients with stroke. These patients have also shown poor tolerability to the drug.

Pregnancy and *Lactation:* Safe use of baclofen during pregnancy or lactation has not been established. Baclofen crosses the placental barrier. High doses are associated with an increased incidence of abdominal hernias in the fetuses of rats and of ossification defects in those of rats and rabbits. Therefore, the drug should be administered to pregnant patients or women of childbearing potential only when the potential benefits outweigh the possible hazards.

Precautions: Children: Safe use of baclofen in children under age 12 has not been established and it is, therefore, not recommended for use in children.

Occupational Hazards: Because of the possibility of sedation, patients should be cautioned regarding the operation of automobiles or dangerous machinery and activities made hazardous by decreased alertness.

Patients should also be cautioned that baclofen's CNS effects may be additive to those of alcohol and other CNS depressants.

Use baclofen with caution where spasticity is utilized to sustain upright posture and balance in locomotion, or whenever spasticity is utilized to obtain increased function.

Exercise extreme caution in patients with epilepsy or a history of convulsive disorders. In such patients, monitor the clinical state and EEG at regular intervals during therapy, as deterioration in seizure control and EEG has been reported occasionally in patients taking baclofen.

Use caution in treating patients with, or with a history of, peptic ulceration, elderly patients with cerebrovascular disorders and in patients with respiratory, hepatic, or renal failure.

Baclofen should be used with caution in patients with underlying bladder sphincter hypertonia, since acute retention of urine may occur.

Patients with psychiatric disorders such as psychosis, schizophrenia, or confusional states should be treated cautiously with baclofen and kept under close surveillance, since exacerbation of these conditions may occur with baclofen treatment.

The following laboratory tests have been found to be abnormal in a few patients receiving baclofen: AST, alkaline phosphatase and blood sugar (all elevated). Therefore, in patients with liver diseases or diabetes mellitus, appropriate laboratory tests should be performed periodically in order to ensure that no drug-induced changes in these underlying diseases have occurred.

Drug Interactions: The concomitant administration of baclofen and tricyclic antidepressants may potentiate the pharmacological effects of baclofen, resulting in pronounced muscular hypotonia.

The concurrent use of MAO inhibitors and baclofen may result in increased CNS depressant effects; therefore, caution is advised and the dosage of one or both agents should be adjusted accordingly.

Since combined treatment with baclofen and antihypertensives is likely to increase the fall in blood pressure, the dosage of antihypertensive medication should be adjusted accordingly.

In patients with Parkinson's disease receiving treatment with baclofen and levodopa plus carbidopa, there have been several reports of mental confusion, hallucinations and agitation.

Isolated cases of increased blood glucose concentrations have reported with baclofen; dosage adjustments of antidiabetic agents (oral and insulin) may therefore be necessary with combined baclofen treatment.

Caution should be exercised when administering baclofen and magnesium sulfate (or other neuromuscular blocking agents), since a synergistic effect may theoretically occur.

Lactation: Baclofen is excreted in human milk. As a general rule, nursing should not be undertaken while a patient is on a drug.

Adverse Effects: Adverse effects most frequently occur at the start of treatment, particularly if the dosage is increased too rapidly, if large doses are administered, and in the elderly patient. However, these effects are often transient and can be alleviated or eliminated by decreasing the dosage; they are seldom severe enough to warrant withdrawal of the medication. In elderly patients or those patients with cerebrovascular disorder or a history of psychiatric illness, more serious adverse reactions may occur, such as hallucinations and confusion.

The most common adverse reactions associated with baclofen are transient drowsiness, daytime sedation, dizziness, weakness and fatigue. Others reported:

Neuropsychiatric: headache (<10%), insomnia (<10%), and rarely, euphoria, excitement, depression, confusion, hallucinations, paresthesia, nightmares, muscle pain, tinnitus, slurred speech, coordination disorder, tremor, rigidity, dystonia, ataxia, blurred vision, nystagmus, strabismus, miosis, mydriasis, diplopia, dysarthria, epileptic seizures, lowered convulsion threshold, and respiratory depression.

Cardiovascular: hypotension (<10%), rare instances of dyspnea, palpitation, chest pain, syncope.

Gastrointestinal: nausea (approx. 10%), constipation (<10%), and rarely, dry mouth, anorexia, taste disorder, abdominal pain, vomiting, diarrhea, positive test for occult blood in stool.

Genitourinary: urinary frequency (<10%), and rarely, enuresis, urinary retention, dysuria, impotence, inability to ejaculate, nocturia, hematuria.

Other: instances of rash, pruritus, ankle edema, excessive perspiration, weight gain, nasal congestion, visual disturbances, hepatic function disorders and paradoxical increase in spasticity.

Muscular hypotonia of a degree sufficient to make walking or movement difficult may occur, but is usually relieved by readjusting the dosage. For this purpose, the daytime dose may be reduced and the evening dose increased.

Some of the CNS and genitourinary symptoms reported may be related to the underlying disease rather than to drug therapy.

Overdose: Symptoms: Symptoms of overdosage are predominantly those of CNS depression and include drowsiness, impairment of consciousness, respiratory depression, coma, seizures, confusion, hallucinations, agitation, accommodation disorders, absent pupillary reflexes, muscular hypotonia, myoclonia, hyporeflexia or areflexia, hypotension, bradycardia, hypothermia, peripheral vasodilatation, nausea, vomiting, diarrhea, increased salivation, and elevated LDH, AST, AP and blood glucose values.

The signs and symptoms may be further aggravated by coadministration of a variety of other agents including alcohol, diazepam and tricyclic antidepressants.

Treatment: There is no specific antidote. The treatment is symptomatic. In the alert patient, empty the stomach promptly by induced emesis followed by lavage. Administer activated charcoal and if necessary, saline laxatives. In the obtunded patient, secure the airway with a cuffed endotracheal tube before beginning lavage (do not induce emesis).

Maintain adequate respiratory exchange; do not use respiratory stimulants. Muscular hypotonia may involve the respiratory muscles and require assisted respiration. Institute measures to support cardiovascular function. Maintain a high urinary output since baclofen is excreted mainly by the kidneys. For this purpose, generous quantities of fluid should be administered, possibly together with a diuretic. Dialysis is indicated in severe poisoning associated with renal failure. In the event of convulsions, administer diazepam i.v. with caution.

Dosage: The determination of baclofen's optimal dosage requires individual titration. Start therapy at a low dosage and increase gradually until optimum effect is achieved (usually between 40 to 80 mg daily).

The following dosage titration schedule is suggested: 5 mg 3 times daily for 3 days; 10 mg 3 times daily for 3 days; 15 mg 3 times daily for 3 days; 20 mg 3 times daily for 3 days.

Thereafter, additional increases may be necessary but the total daily dose should not exceed a maximum of 80 mg daily (20 mg 4 times daily).

Utilize the lowest dose compatible with an optimal response. If benefits are not evident after a reasonable trial period, withdraw patients slowly from the drug (see Warnings).

Supplied: 10 mg: Each white to off-white, oval, flat-faced, bevel-edged tablet, engraved GEIGY on one side and engraved KJ on the other (fully bisected between the K and J), contains: baclofen 10 mg. Nonmedicinal ingredients: cellulose compounds, cornstarch, magnesium stearate and polyvinylpyrrolidone. Energy: 8.6 kJ (2.05 kcal). Alcohol-, bisulfite-, gluten-, lactose-, parabens-, sodium- and tartrazine-free. Bottles of 100 and 500.

D.S. 20 mg: Each white to off-white, capsule-shaped tablet, engraved GEIGY on one side and engraved GW on the other, (fully bisected between the G and W), contains: baclofen 20 mg. Nonmedicinal ingredients: cellulose compounds, cornstarch, magnesium stearate and polyvinylpyrrolidone. Energy: 1.7 kJ (0.41 kcal). Alcohol-, bisulfite-, gluten-, lactose-, parabens-, sodium- and tartrazine-free. Bottles of 100.

(Shown in Product Recognition Section)

LIORESAL® Intrathecal Ⓟ

Novartis Pharmaceuticals

Baclofen

Muscle Relaxant—Antispastic

Pharmacology: The precise mechanisms of action of baclofen as a muscle relaxant and antispastic agent are not fully understood. Baclofen inhibits both monosynaptic and polysynaptic reflex transmission at the spinal level, possibly by decreasing excitatory neurotransmitter release from primary afferent terminals. Actions at supraspinal sites may also contribute to its clinical effect. Baclofen is an analogue of the inhibitory neurotransmitter gamma-aminobutyric acid (GABA), and may exert its effects by stimulation of the $GABA_B$ receptor subtype.

Baclofen has been shown to have general CNS depressant properties as indicated by the production of sedation with tolerance, somnolence, ataxia and respiratory and cardiovascular depression.

Neuromuscular transmission is not affected by baclofen. Baclofen exerts an antinociceptive effect. In neurological diseases associated with spasm of the skeletal muscles, the clinical effects of baclofen take the form of a beneficial action on reflex muscle contractions and of marked relief from painful spasm, automatism, and clonus.

Intrathecal baclofen, when introduced directly into the spinal subarachnoid space, permits the attainment of effective CSF concentrations with resultant plasma concentrations 100 times lower than those occurring following oral administration.

Clinical use in special patient populations: Intrathecal baclofen has also been used for the treatment of 21 patients with spinal cord disease and 18 patients with cerebral palsy.

A small number of patients with tetanus (7 patients) have been treated with intrathecal baclofen to reduce hyperreflexia, clonus, and trismus.

The safety and efficacy of intrathecal baclofen in these patient populations has not been systematically evaluated.

Pharmacodynamics: Intrathecal Bolus: The onset of action is generally 0.5 to 1 hour after administration of an intrathecal bolus dose. Peak spasmolytic effect is seen at approximately 4 hours after dosing and effects may last 4 to 8 hours. Onset, peak response, and duration of action may vary with individual patients depending on the dose and severity of symptoms.

Continuous Infusion: The antispastic action is first seen at 6 to 8 hours after initiation of continuous infusion. Maximum efficacy is observed in 24 to 48 hours.

Pharmacokinetics: The pharmacokinetics of cerebrospinal fluid (CSF) clearance of intrathecal baclofen, calculated from intrathecal bolus or continuous infusion studies, approximate CSF turnover, suggesting elimination is by bulk-flow removal of CSF. Direct infusion into the spinal subarachnoid space bypasses absorption processes and allows exposure to the receptor sites in the dorsal horn of the spinal cord.

Intrathecal bolus: After a bolus lumbar injection of 50 or 100 µg intrathecal baclofen in 7 patients, the average CSF elimination half-life was 1.51 hours over the first 4 hours and the average CSF clearance was approximately 30 mL/h.

Continuous infusion: A study, conducted in 10 patients, suggests that the mean CSF clearance for continuous intrathecal infusion of baclofen is approximately 30 mL/h.

After single intrathecal bolus injection/short-term infusion the volume of distribution, calculated from CSF levels, ranges from 22 to 157 mL.

Continuous intrathecal infusion daily doses of 50 to 1 200 µg result in lumbar CSF concentrations of baclofen as high as 130 to 1 240 ng/mL at steady state. According to the half-life measured in the CSF, CSF steady-state concentrations will be reached within 1 to 2 days. Concurrent plasma concentrations of baclofen during intrathecal administration are expected to be low (0 to 5 ng/mL).

Limited pharmacokinetic data suggest that a lumbar-cisternal baclofen concentration gradient of about 4:1 is established during continuous baclofen infusion. This is based upon simultaneous CSF sampling via cisternal and lumbar tap during continuous baclofen infusion at the lumbar level in doses associated with therapeutic efficacy; the interpatient variability was great. This is of clinical importance insofar as spasticity in the lower extremities can be effectively treated with little effect on the upper limbs and with fewer CNS adverse reactions due to effects on the brain centres.

Indications: For the management of patients with severe spasticity due to spinal cord injury or multiple sclerosis who are unresponsive to oral baclofen or who experience unacceptable side effects at effective oral doses.

Intrathecal baclofen therapy may be considered as an alternative to destructive neurosurgical procedures.

Prior to implantation of a device for chronic intrathecal infusion, patients must demonstrate a positive clinical response to an intrathecal baclofen screening trial (See Dosage).

Intrathecal baclofen has been used in patients with spasticity of cerebral origin, e.g., spasticity following hypoxic encephalopathy, head injury, or stroke; however, clinical experience is limited.

Contraindications: Known or suspected hypersensitivity to baclofen.

The drug should not be administered by the i.v., i.m., s.c. or epidural routes.

Lioresal Intrathecal (cont'd)

Warnings: Because of the possibility of potential life-threatening CNS depression, cardiovascular collapse and/or respiratory failure, physicians must be adequately trained in chronic intrathecal infusion therapy.

Specific instructions for programming and/or refilling the implantable pump are given by the pump manufacturers, and must be strictly adhered to. Consult pump manufacturer's literature for information on the appropriate use and care of these devices.

Because of the risks associated with the screening procedure and the adjustment of dosage following pump implantation, these phases must be conducted in a medically supervised and adequately equipped environment (see Dosage).

Resuscitative equipment should be available.

The pump system should not be implanted until the patient's response to bolus intrathecal injection of intrathecal baclofen has been properly evaluated and found to be clinically safe and effective.

Following surgical implantation of the pump, particularly during the initial phase of pump use the patient should be monitored closely until it is certain that the patient's response to the infusion is acceptable and reasonably stable.

On each occasion that the dosing rate of the pump and/or the concentration of intrathecal baclofen in the reservoir is adjusted, close medical monitoring is required until it is certain that the patient's response to the infusion is acceptable and reasonably stable.

It is mandatory that the patient and all those involved in the care of the patient receive adequate information regarding the risks of this mode of treatment. All medical personnel and care givers should be instructed in 1) the signs and symptoms of overdose, 2) procedures to be followed in the event of overdose and 3) proper home care of the pump or insertion site.

Overdose: Signs of overdose may appear suddenly or insidiously (see Overdose: Symptoms and Treatment).

Abrupt Drug Withdrawal: Sudden cessation of intrathecal baclofen, especially after doses exceeding the normal dose range, results in a hyperactive state with rapid and uncontrolled spasms and increased rigidity to intolerable levels, lasting for several days. Following abrupt withdrawal of oral baclofen, visual and auditory hallucinations, convulsions (status epilepticus), dyskinesia, confusion, psychotic, manic, or paranoid states, anxiety with tachycardia and sweating, insomnia and—as a rebound phenomenon—temporary aggravation of spasticity have occurred. Therefore, except for serious adverse reactions and overdose related emergencies, the dose should always be reduced slowly when the drug is discontinued (over a period of approximately 1 to 2 weeks).

Precautions: Screening: Patients should be infection-free prior to the screening trial with intrathecal baclofen because the presence of a systemic infection may interfere with an assessment of the patient's response to bolus intrathecal baclofen.

Careful monitoring of respiratory and cardiovascular functions is essential during initial test dose administrations (screening phase), especially in patients with cardiopulmonary disease and respiratory muscle weakness as well as those being treated concomitantly with benzodiazepine-type preparations or opiates, who are at higher risk of respiratory depression.

Pump implantation: Patients should be infection-free prior to pump implantation because the presence of infection may increase the risk of surgical complications. Moreover, a systemic infection may complicate attempts to adjust the dose.

Patient monitoring: Following surgical implantation of the pump, particularly during the initial phases of pump use, and on each occasion that the dosing rate of the pump and/or the concentration of baclofen in the reservoir is adjusted, the patient should be monitored closely until it is certain that the patient's response to the infusion is acceptable and stable.

Pump adjustment and titration: In most patients, it will be necessary to increase the dose gradually over time to maintain effectiveness; a sudden requirement for substantial dose escalation typically indicates a catheter complication (i.e., catheter kink or dislodgement).

Reservoir Filling: Reservoir refilling must be performed by fully trained and qualified personnel following the directions provided by the pump manufacturer. Refill intervals should be carefully calculated to prevent depletion of the reservoir, as this would result in the return of severe spasticity. Depending on individual daily dose requirements and the flow rate of the pump, refill intervals generally vary between 1 and 3 months.

Strict aseptic filling is required to avoid microbial contamination and serious infection. A period of observation appropriate to the clinical situation should follow each refill or manipulation of the drug reservoir.

Extreme caution must be used when filling an implantable pump equipped with an injection port that allows direct access to the intrathecal catheter. Direct injection into the catheter through the access port may cause a life-threatening overdose.

In order to prevent excessive weakness and falling, intrathecal baclofen should be used with caution when spasticity is needed to sustain upright posture and balance in locomotion or whenever spasticity is used to maintain function.

It may be important to maintain some degree of muscle tone and allow occasional spasms to help support circulatory function and possibly prevent the formation of deep vein thrombosis.

An attempt should be made to discontinue concomitant oral antispastic medication to avoid possible overdose or adverse drug interactions, preferably before initiating baclofen infusion, with careful monitoring by the physician. However, abrupt reduction or discontinuation of concomitant antispastics during chronic intrathecal therapy with baclofen should be avoided.

Occupational Hazards: Drowsiness has been reported in some patients on intrathecal baclofen. Patients should be cautioned regarding the operation of automobiles or dangerous machinery, and activities made hazardous by decreased alertness.

Geriatrics: Several patients over the age of 65 years have been treated with intrathecal baclofen during the clinical trials without specific problems. Elderly patients may be more susceptible to the side effects of oral baclofen in the titration stage and this may also apply to intrathecal baclofen. However, as doses are individually titrated there is not likely to be a particular problem in treating elderly patients.

Children: Clinical experience with intrathecal baclofen in patients under 18 years of age is limited and safe use in this age group has not been established.

Pregnancy: Safe use of intrathecal baclofen during pregnancy has not been established. Baclofen crosses the placental barrier. High doses of oral baclofen are associated with an increased incidence of omphaloceles (abdominal hernias) in the fetuses of rats and of ossification defects in those of rats and rabbits. Therefore, the drug should be administered to pregnant patients or women of childbearing potential only when, in the judgment of the physician, the potential benefits outweigh the possible hazards.

Lactation: In mothers taking oral baclofen in therapeutic doses, the active substance passes into the breast milk. It is not known whether detectable levels of drug are present in breast milk of nursing mothers receiving intrathecal baclofen. As a general rule, nursing should be undertaken while a patient is receiving intrathecal baclofen only if the potential benefits outweigh the possible risks to the infant.

Patients with Special Diseases and Conditions: In patients with abnormal CSF flow, the spread of the drug and therefore, the distribution of antispastic activity may be inadequate.

Patients suffering from psychotic disorders, schizophrenia, confusional states, or Parkinson's disease should be treated cautiously with intrathecal baclofen and kept under careful surveillance, because exacerbations of these conditions have been observed with oral baclofen administration.

Special attention should be given to patients known to suffer from epilepsy since seizures have occasionally been reported during overdose with, and withdrawal from, intrathecal baclofen as well as in patients maintained on therapeutic doses of intrathecal baclofen.

Intrathecal baclofen should be used with caution in patients with a history of autonomic dysreflexia. The presence of nociceptive stimuli or abrupt withdrawal of intrathecal baclofen may cause an autonomic dysreflexic episode.

Baclofen should be used with caution in patients with cerebrovascular or respiratory insufficiency, as these conditions may be exacerbated by baclofen.

Interaction of intrathecal baclofen with underlying, non CNS related diseases is unlikely because the systemic availability of the drug after intrathecal administration is substantially lower than after oral administration. Nevertheless, observations after oral baclofen therapy suggest that caution should be exercised in the following situations: history of peptic ulcers, pre-existing sphincter hypertonia, impaired hepatic or renal function.

In rare instances elevated AST, alkaline phosphatase and glucose levels in the serum have been recorded when using oral baclofen.

Drug Interactions: There is inadequate systemic experience with the use of baclofen intrathecal in combination with other medications to predict specific drug-drug interactions. The combined use of morphine and intrathecal baclofen was responsible for hypotension in 1 patient. The potential for this combination to cause dyspnea or other CNS symptoms cannot be excluded.

The coadministration of other intrathecal agents with intrathecal baclofen has not been tested and the safety of these combinations is unknown.

The CNS depressant effects of alcohol and other compounds affecting the CNS may be additive to the effects of intrathecal baclofen.

When using oral baclofen, concurrent treatment with tricyclic antidepressants may potentiate the effect of baclofen, resulting in pronounced muscular hypotonia. Therefore, caution is advised when using intrathecal baclofen in this combination.

Since concomitant treatment with oral baclofen and antihypertensives is likely to increase antihypertensive effects, it is recommended that blood pressure is checked and if necessary, the dosage of antihypertensive medication adjusted accordingly.

Information to be Provided to the Patient: See Information for the Patient.

Adverse Effects: Baclofen has been shown to have general CNS depressant properties, causing sedation, somnolence, and respiratory and cardiovascular depression.

The most commonly reported adverse events with intrathecal baclofen in clinical trials were drowsiness, weakness in the lower extremities, dizziness/lightheadedness and seizures. Adverse events reported during controlled and uncontrolled studies in the United States of America are shown in Table I.

A causal link between events observed and the administration of baclofen cannot be reliably assessed in many cases, since many of the adverse events reported are known to occur in association with the underlying conditions being treated.

Adverse events associated with the delivery system (e.g., catheter dislocation, pocket infection, meningitis, overdose due to wrong manipulation of the device) are in addition to those listed below.

In a fatal case of a child (causality with baclofen uncertain), inflammatory signs in the posterior horns and signs of arachnoiditis in proximity of the catheter tip were observed. This corresponds to observations in dogs, where chronic inflammatory reactions to the foreign body of the catheter were observed, independently of baclofen concentration.

Table I—Lioresal Intrathecal

Incidence of Most Frequent Adverse Events in U.S. Clinical Trials

	Number of Patients Reporting Events (%)		
Adverse Event	**Screening (N=244)**	**Titration (N=214)**	**Maintenance (N=214)**
Drowsiness	13 (5.3%)	11 (5.1%)	18 (8.4%)
Weakness, Lower Extremities	1 (0.4%)	11 (5.1%)	15 (7.0%)
Dizziness/Lightheadedness	6 (2.4%)	5 (2.3%)	12 (5.6%)
Seizures	1 (0.4%)	4 (1.9%)	11 (5.1%)
Headache	0 (0%)	3 (1.4%)	9 (4.2%)
Nausea/Vomiting	3 (1.2%)	5 (2.3%)	3 (1.4%)
Numbness/Itching/Tingling	2 (0.8%)	1 (0.5%)	8 (3.7%)
Hypotension	3 (1.2%)	0 (0%)	5 (2.3%)
Blurred Vision	0 (0%)	2 (0.9%)	5 (2.3%)
Constipation	0 (0%)	2 (0.9%)	5 (2.3%)
Hypotonia	2 (0.8%)	3 (1.4%)	2 (0.9%)
Slurred Speech	0 (0%)	1 (0.5%)	6 (2.8%)
Coma (Overdose)	0 (0%)	4 (1.9%)	3 (1.4%)
Lethargy	1 (0.4%)	0 (0%)	4 (1.9%)
Weakness, Upper Extremities	1 (0.4%)	0 (0%)	4 (1.9%)
Hypertension	1 (0.4%)	2 (0.9%)	2 (0.9%)
Dyspnea	1 (0.4%)	2 (0.9%)	1 (0.5%)

In addition to the more common adverse events reported above, the following adverse events were observed during clinical trials elsewhere or reported by clinicians using intrathecal baclofen on a humanitarian basis.

CNS: Occasional: sedation, accommodation disorders/double vison. Rare: respiratory depression, hypothermia, nystagmus, dysphagia, insomnia, somnolence, fatigue, decreased coordination, memory loss, confusion/disorientation, anxiety,

depression, suicide ideation and attempt, euphoria, dysphoria, hallucinations, paranoia.
Cardiovascular: Occasional: bradycardia. Rare: deep vein thrombosis, skin flushing, paleness, pulmonary embolism.
Gastrointestinal tract: Rare: dry mouth, diarrhea, decreased appetite, dehydration, ileus, decreased taste.
Respiratory: Occasional: bradypnea.
Genitourinary: Rare: urinary incontinence, sluggish bladder, bladder spasm, sexual dysfunction.
Skin and appendages: Rare: urticaria, alopecia, facial edema, diaphoresis.

Overdose: Special attention must be given to recognizing the signs and symptoms of overdosage at all times, especially during the initial "screening" and "dose titration" phase of treatment and also during reintroduction of intrathecal baclofen after a period of interruption of therapy.

Symptoms: Signs of overdose may appear suddenly or insidiously.

Less sudden and/or less severe forms of overdose may present with signs of drowsiness, lightheadedness, dizziness, somnolence, seizures, loss of consciousness, excessive salivation, nausea and/or vomiting and cephalad progression of hypotonia. Respiratory depression, apnea, and coma result from serious overdosage.

Serious overdose may occur, for example, by inadvertent delivery of catheter contents during catheter patency/position analysis. Errors in programming, excessively rapid dose increases, and concomitant treatment with oral baclofen are other possible causes of overdosage. Possible pump malfunction should also be investigated.

Symptoms of severe intrathecal baclofen overdose (coma) were reported in a sensitive adult patient after receiving a 25 µg intrathecal bolus dose.

Treatment: There is no specific antidote for treating overdoses of intrathecal baclofen, however, the following steps should generally be undertaken. 1. Residual baclofen solution should be removed from the pump as soon as possible. 2. Patients with respiratory depression should be intubated if necessary, until the drug is eliminated.

If lumbar puncture is not contraindicated, consideration should be given in the early stage of the intoxication to withdrawing 30 to 40 mL of CSF to reduce CSF baclofen concentration.

Institute measures to support cardiovascular function.

In the event of convulsions, administer diazepam i.v. with caution.

Anecdotal reports suggest that i.v. physostigmine may reverse central side effects, notably drowsiness and respiratory depression.

Caution in administering physostigmine i.v. is advised, however, because its use has been associated with the induction of seizures, bradycardia, and cardiac conduction disturbances.

A test dose of 0.5 mg i.v. is given initially. Give 1 to 2 mg slowly i.v. (over 2 minutes). Patients should be monitored closely during this time. If no clinical changes or cholinergic signs occur within 15 to 30 minutes, an additional 1 to 2 mg may be cautiously administered. Repeat doses of 1 to 2 mg i.v. every 30 minutes up to 2 hours. Physostigmine may not be effective in reversing large overdoses and patients may need to be maintained with respiratory support.

As the CNS effects of physostigmine may wear off rapidly, it is important to monitor the patient continuously.

Physostigmine is the only drug of this class that may be used. Neostigmine should not be used as it does not have any CNS effects.

If symptoms of cholinergic toxicity develop, physostigmine should be discontinued.

Dosage: Establishment of the optimum dose schedule requires that each patient undergoes an initial screening phase with intrathecal bolus, followed by a very careful individual dose titration prior to maintenance therapy. This is due to the great variability in the effective individual therapeutic dose.
General: **The first dose should be performed with resuscitative equipment on stand-by.**

Patients must be monitored closely in a fully equipped and staffed environment during the screening phase and dose titration period immediately following implant. Resuscitative equipment should be available for immediate use in case of life-threatening or intolerable adverse reactions. Implantation of pumps should only be performed in experienced centres in order to minimize the risks in the perioperative phase.
Screening phase: Prior to initiation of chronic infusion of intrathecal baclofen, patients must demonstrate a response to intrathecal baclofen bolus in a screening trial. A test bolus dose of baclofen is usually administered via a lumbar puncture or an intrathecal catheter to elicit a response. For this purpose low concentration ampuls of 0.05 mg/mL are available.

The usual initial test dose is 25 µg or 50 µg and is stepped up by 25 µg increments at 24 hours apart, until an approximately 4- to 8-hour response is observed; the dose should be given by barbotage over at least 1 minute. If an adverse reaction occurs at a dose of 25 µg, a lower dose, such as 10 µg may be tested.

Patients should demonstrate a positive clinical response in order to be considered responders to treatment. A positive clinical response is characterized by a significant decrease in muscle tone and/or frequency and/or severity of spasms. There is great variability in sensitivity to intrathecal baclofen.

Patients who do not respond to a 100 µg test dose should not be given further increases of dose or be considered for continuous intrathecal infusion. However, in rare instances some patients, particularly those with spasticity of cerebral origin, have received higher test bolus doses.
Dose titration phase: After confirmation that the patient is responsive to intrathecal baclofen by means of test bolus doses, intrathecal infusion is established using a suitable delivery system (see Drug delivery devices).

To determine the initial total daily dose of intrathecal baclofen following implant, the screening dose which gave a positive effect should be doubled and administered over a 24-hour period, unless the efficacy of the bolus dose was maintained for more than 12 hours. In this case the starting daily dose should be the screening dose delivered over a 24-hour period. No dose increases should be administered in the first 24 hours.

After the first 24 hours, the dosage should be adjusted slowly on a daily basis to achieve the desired effect, with dosage increments limited to 10 to 30% to avoid possible overdosing. With programmable pumps, the dose should be increased only once every 24 hours. For nonprogrammable pumps with a 76 cm catheter delivering 1 mL/day, intervals of 48 hours are suggested for evaluation of response. If the daily dose has been significantly increased and no clinical effect is achieved, check for proper pump function and catheter patency.

The clinical goal is to maintain muscle tone as close to normal as possible, and to minimize the frequency and severity of spasms without inducing intolerable side effects.

There is limited experience with doses greater than 1 000 µg/day.
Maintenance therapy: The lowest dose giving an adequate response should be used. Most patients require gradual increases in dose over time to maintain optimum response during chronic therapy due to decreased responsiveness to therapy or to progress of the disease.

The daily dose may be gradually increased by 10 to 30% to maintain adequate symptom control by adjusting the dosing rate of the pump and/or the concentration of intrathecal baclofen in the reservoir. The daily dose may also be reduced by 10 to 20% if patients experience side effects. A sudden requirement for substantial dose escalation suggests a catheter complication (i.e., catheter kink or dislodgement) or pump malfunction.

Maintenance dosage for long-term continuous infusion of intrathecal baclofen ranges from 10 to 1 200 µg/day, most patients being adequately maintained on 300 to 800 µg/day. The specific concentration that should be used depends upon the total daily dose required as well as the delivery rate of the pump. Please consult pump manufacturer's manual for specific recommendations.

During long-term treatment approximately 10% of patients become refractory to increasing doses. There is not sufficient experience to make firm recommendations for tolerance management; however, in 17 patients, the use of a "drug holiday" by switching for 10 to 14 days to intrathecal preservative-free morphine sulfate has been reported as an effective approach to the management of tolerance. After a few days the sensitivity to baclofen may be restored; treatment should be resumed at the initial continuous infusion dose and followed by a titration phase to avoid overdose accidents. This must be performed in a hospital unit.

Regular clinical review remains a necessity throughout to assess dosage requirements, functioning of the delivery system, and monitoring for possible adverse drug reactions or evidence of infection.
Delivery regimen: Intrathecal baclofen is most often administered in a continuous infusion mode immediately following implant. After the patient has stabilized with regard to daily dose and functional status, and provided the pump allows it, a more complex mode of delivery may be started to optimize control of spasticity at different times of the day. For example, patients who have increased spasm at night may require a 20% increase in their hourly infusion rate. Changes in flow rate should be programmed to start 2 hours before the time of desired clinical effect.
Drug delivery devices: Intrathecal administration of baclofen through an implanted delivery system should only be undertaken by physicians with the necessary knowledge and experience. Specific instructions for programming and/or refilling the implantable pump are given by the pump manufacturers, and must be strictly adhered to. Consult pump manufacturer's literature for information on the appropriate use and care of these devices.

Evidence demonstrating the efficacy of intrathecal baclofen was obtained using the Medtronic SynchroMed Infusion System and the Infusaid Infusion System. Other pumps proven to be suitable for intrathecal baclofen administration may be used.

The Medtronic SynchroMed Infusion System and the Infusaid Infusion System are implantable drug delivery systems with refillable reservoirs which, after general or local anesthesia, are implanted in a s.c. pocket usually on the abdominal wall. Both devices are connected to an intrathecal catheter that passes subcutaneously to the subarachnoid space.

The Medtronic SynchroMed Infusion System has an 18 mL drug reservoir and may be programmed to different flow rates such as single bolus, periodic boluses, continuous and complex continuous. However, the lithium battery of the pump has a life span of 3 to 4 years and therefore requires replacement.

The Infusaid Infusion System has a 50 mL drug reservoir. This pump does not contain a battery and therefore does not require replacement. Since this device is not programmable, the dose titration phase must occur prior to implantation. As a result, single bolus doses are used in the titration phase. Complex delivery modes over 24 hours cannot be achieved with this system.

Intrathecal baclofen proved to be stable in the implanted SynchroMed Infusion System for 11 weeks and in the Infusaid pumps for 28 days.

Details regarding the availability and use of these drug delivery devices can be obtained from the manufacturers: Medtronic of Canada Ltd., 6733 Kitimat Road, Mississauga, Ontario, L5N 1W3. 1 (800) 268 5346; Fax: 1 (905) 826 6620. Minogue Medical (Canadian Distributors of Infusaid pumps), Suite 902, 1140 de Maisonneuve West, Montreal, Quebec, H3A 1M8. 1 (514) 287 1644; Fax: 1 (514) 287 0853.

General guidelines regarding the use of all implantable systems are located under Precautions.

Before using other systems, it must be confirmed that the technical specifications, including chemical stability of baclofen in the reservoir fulfil the requirements for safe and effective use of intrathecal baclofen. Please consult pump manufacturer's manual for this information.
Parenteral Products: Instructions for use/handling: Intrathecal baclofen is intended for intrathecal injection and continuous intrathecal infusion as indicated by the delivery specifications of the infusion system.

Each ampul is intended for single use only. Discard any unused portion.

Parenteral drug products should be inspected for particulate matter and discoloration prior to administration whenever solution and container permit.

The concentration to be used depends upon the total daily dose required as well as the delivery rate of the pump. Please consult manufacturer's manual for specific recommendations.

For patients who require concentrations other than 0.05 mg/mL, 0.5 mg/mL or 2 mg/mL, intrathecal baclofen must be diluted, under aseptic conditions, with sterile preservative-free sodium chloride injection and used immediately.

As a rule baclofen ampuls for intrathecal administration should not be mixed with other infusion or injection solutions. Dextrose proved to be incompatible due to a chemical reaction with baclofen.

Information for the Patient: See Blue Section—Information for the Patient "Lioresal Intrathecal".

Supplied: 0.05 mg/mL: Each mL of clear, colorless solution contains: baclofen 0.05 mg for intrathecal administration. Nonmedicinal ingredients: sodium chloride and water for injection. Ampuls of 1 mL. Cartons of 5.

0.5 mg/mL: Each mL of clear, colorless solution contains: baclofen 0.5 mg for intrathecal administration. Nonmedicinal

Lioresal Intrathecal (cont'd)

ingredients: sodium chloride and water for injection. Ampuls of 20 mL. Cartons of 5.

2 mg/mL: Each mL of clear, colorless solution contains: baclofen 2 mg for intrathecal administration. Nonmedicinal ingredients: sodium chloride and water for injection. Ampuls of 5 mL. Cartons of 5.

Protect from heat (store at 15 to 30°C). Do not freeze. Do not heat sterilize.

(Shown in Product Recognition Section)

LIOTEC

Technilab

Baclofen

Muscle Relaxant—Antispastic

Supplied: 10 mg: Each white, oval, flat, beveled-edged bisected tablet, reverse side inscribed TEC 102A, contains: baclofen USP 10 mg. Nonmedicinal ingredients: colloidal silicon dioxide, dibasic calcium phosphate, lactose, magnesium stearate, microcrystalline cellulose and sodium starch glycolate. Bottles of 100 and 500.

20 mg: Each white, capsule-shaped tablet, reverse side inscribed TEC 102B, contains: baclofen USP 20 mg. Nonmedicinal ingredients: colloidal silicon dioxide, dibasic calcium phosphate, lactose, magnesium stearate, microcrystalline cellulose and sodium starch glycolate. Bottles of 100.

Store between 15 and 30°C. Protect from heat and humidity.

New Product 1998

LIPACTIN®

Novartis Consumer Health

Heparin Sodium—Zinc Sulfate

Symptomatic Treatment of Herpes Simplex I

Pharmacology: Lipactin is composed of heparin and zinc for topical application. Topical application of heparin produces accumulation of the heparin molecules in the corium of the skin while insignificant amounts are absorbed through the skin. Oral administration of heparin is associated with negligible anticoagulant effect as heparin is immediately metabolized in the gastrointestinal tract and not absorbed from aqueous solution.

Absorption of zinc through broken skin when applied in the concentrations used in Lipactin does not produce significant increases in serum and tissue concentrations of zinc.

Clinical studies have indicated Lipactin significantly reduces the duration of pain associated with HSV I infections when compared with placebo. There is also a statistically significant increase in the rate of healing of perioral and lip lesions when compared to placebo preparations.

One study compared Lipactin to placebo in 54 patients with Herpes labialis. In the Lipactin treated group (n=23), 96% had resolution of at least 2 of their initial symptoms within 3 days. This compared to the placebo group (n=31) in which only 45% of patients had resolution of 2 or more symptoms within the first 3 days. The same study demonstrated that 83% of the patients in the Lipactin group were completely healed within 7 days, compared to 26% in the placebo group.

Indications: For the relief and management of symptoms due to lip and perioral infections of Herpes Simplex Virus type I. This includes Herpes labialis, Herpes febrilis, fever blisters and cold sores.

Early initiation of therapy, within 3 days of the onset of signs and symptoms of infection or re-infection, has been found to produce faster healing than treatment commenced after 3 days of symptoms.

Treatment should be continued until healing is complete or to a maximum of 14 days, whichever comes first.

Contraindications: In individuals who are hypersensitive to heparin sodium, zinc sulfate or parabens.

Warnings: For external use only. The gel is **not** for ophthalmic use.

Children and *Pregnancy:* Safe use of the gel in children or in pregnant women has not been established. Use only as directed by a physician in children and pregnant women.

Precautions: If the symptoms of the infection persist or become more severe or wide-spread with treatment, use of the medication should be discontinued and a physician consulted.

Adverse Effects: In a few cases, a mild transient burning sensation has been experienced at the site of application.

Isolated cases of local hypersensitivity reactions have been reported; in such cases, use of the product should be discontinued.

Dosage: Apply Lipactin to the affected area(s) 3 to 6 times a day. A sufficient quantity of the gel should be applied to adequately cover all lesions and a margin of healthy skin surrounding them.

Therapy should be initiated as early as possible following the onset of signs and/or symptoms, i.e. tingling, burning, vesiculation etc. Treatment should be continued until healing is complete or to a maximum of 14 days, whichever comes first.

Supplied: Each g of clear, colorless, odorless gel contains: heparin sodium 160 USP units and zinc sulfate 5 mg. Nonmedicinal ingredients: glycerin, methyl parahydroxybenzoate, polysorbate, propyl parahydroxybenzoate, sodium carboxymethylcellulose and water. Alcohol- and bisulfite-free. Tubes of 3 g.

LIPIDIL MICRO®

Fournier

Fenofibrate (Micronized)

Lipid Metabolism Regulator

Pharmacology: Fenofibrate lowers elevated serum lipids by decreasing the low density lipoprotein (LDL) fraction rich in cholesterol and the very low density lipoprotein (VLDL) fraction rich in triglycerides. In addition, fenofibrate increases the high density lipoprotein (HDL) cholesterol fraction.

Fenofibrate appears to have a greater depressant effect on the very low density lipoproteins (VLDL) than on the low density lipoproteins (LDL). Therapeutic doses of fenofibrate produce variable elevations of HDL cholesterol, a reduction in the content of the total low density lipoproteins cholesterol, and a substantial reduction in the triglyceride content of very low density lipoproteins.

The mechanism of action of fenofibrate has not been definitely established. Work carried out to date suggests that fenofibrate enhances the liver elimination of cholesterol as bile salts, inhibits the biosynthesis of triglycerides and enhances the catabolism of VLDL by increasing the activity of lipoprotein lipase, has an inhibitory effect on the biosynthesis of cholesterol by modulating the activity of HMG-CoA reductase.

Pharmacokinetics: After oral administration with food, fenofibrate is rapidly hydrolyzed into fenofibric acid, the active metabolite.

Fenofibrate's absorption is low and variable when the product is administered under fasting conditions. Fenofibrate's absorption is increased when the compound is given with food. In man it is mainly excreted through the kidney. Half-life is about 20 hours. In patients with severe renal failure, significant accumulation was observed with a large increase in the half-life. Therefore, the dose of fenofibrate may need to be reduced, depending on the rate of creatinine clearance.

The long half-life led Laboratoires Fournier to develop a once daily formulation. The micronized formulation of fenofibrate (Lipidil Micro) offers in the order of 33% greater bioavailability than the nonmicronized fenofibrate formulation. Thus, a single 200 mg capsule daily of Lipidil Micro is bioequivalent to three 100 mg capsules of nonmicronized fenofibrate. In comparison with nonmicronized fenofibrate formulation, the absorption of micronized fenofibrate is less influenced by fat content of the diet.

Indications: As an adjunct to diet and other therapeutic measures for: 1. Treatment of patients with hypercholesterolemia, Fredrickson classification Type IIa and IIb mixed hyperlipidemias, to regulate lipid levels (reduce serum triglycerides and LDL cholesterol levels and increase HDL cholesterol). 2. Treatment of adult patients with very high serum triglyceride levels, Fredrickson classification Type IV and Type V hyperlipidemias, who are at a high risk of sequelae and complications (i.e., pancreatitis) from their hyperlipidemia.

Micronized fenofibrate alone may not be an adequate therapy in some patients with familial combined hyperlipidemia with Type IIb and Type IV hyperlipoproteinemia.

Initial therapy for hyperlipidemia should include a specific diet (at least an equivalent of the American Heart Association (AHA) Step 1 diet), weight reduction and an exercise program; and for patients with diabetes mellitus, good diabetic control.

Contraindications: Hepatic or severe renal dysfunction (creatinine clearance <20 mL/min), including primary biliary cirrhosis. Pre-existing gallbladder disease (see Warnings). Hypersensitivity to fenofibrate, or other drugs of the fibrate class.

Pregnancy and *Lactation:* The drug should not be used in pregnant or lactating patients.

Fenofibrate is not indicated for the treatment of Type I hyperlipoproteinemia.

Warnings: *Drug Interactions:* Concomitant Oral Anticoagulants: Caution should be exercised when anticoagulants are given in conjunction with fenofibrate. The dosage of anticoagulants should be reduced to maintain the prothrombin time at the desired level to prevent bleeding complications. Careful monitoring of prothrombin time is therefore recommended until it has been definitely determined that the prothrombin level has been stabilized.

Statins and Cyclosporine: Severe myositis and rhabdomyolysis have occurred when a statin or cyclosporine was administered in combined therapy with a fibrate. Therefore, the benefits and risks of using fenofibrate concomitantly with these drugs should be carefully considered.

MAO Inhibitors: MAO inhibitors with hepatotoxic potential must not be administered together with fibrates such as fenofibrate as they may increase the risk of hepatotoxicity.

Sulfonylureas and Insulin: It has been previously reported that the fibrates may potentiate the effects of these classes of drug. This effect has not yet been documented in the case of fenofibrate. No case of hypoglycemia or hypoglycemic reaction has been reported to date.

Children: Limited experience is available in children and adolescents, at the dose of 5 mg/kg/day nonmicronized formulation. However, safety and effectiveness has not been established in this sub-population.

Pregnancy: Strict birth control procedures must be exercised by women of childbearing potential. If pregnancy occurs despite birth control procedures, fenofibrate should be discontinued. Women who are planning pregnancy should discontinue fenofibrate several months prior to conception.

Lactation: In the absence of information concerning the presence of fenofibrate in human breast milk, fenofibrate should not be used by nursing mothers.

Cholelithiasis: Fenofibrate may increase cholesterol excretion into the bile and may lead to cholelithiasis. If cholelithiasis is suspected, gallbladder studies are indicated. Fenofibrate therapy should be discontinued if gallstones are found.

Fenofibrate clinically and pharmacologically shows similarities with clofibrate. Physicians prescribing fenofibrate should also be familiar with the risks and benefits of clofibrate.

In long-term animal toxicity and carcinogenicity studies, fenofibrate has been shown to be tumorigenic for the liver in male rats at 12 times the human dose. At this dose level in male rats, there was also an increase in benign Leydig cell tumors. Pancreatic acinar cell tumors were increased in male rats at 9 and 40 times the human dose. However, mice and female rats were unaffected at similar doses. Florid hepatocellular peroxisome proliferation has been observed following fenofibrate administration to rats. Such changes have not been found in the human liver after up to 3.5 years of fenofibrate administration.

Since a relationship between reduction of mortality from coronary artery disease and total mortality has not been established, fenofibrate should be administered only to those patients described in Indications. If a significant serum lipid response is not obtained in 3 months, fenofibrate should be discontinued. If fenofibrate is chosen for treatment, the prescribing physician should discuss the proposed therapy and inform the patient of the expected benefits and potential risks which may be associated with long-term administration (see Precautions).

Precautions: Initial Therapy: Before instituting fenofibrate therapy, attempts should be made to control serum lipids with appropriate diet, exercise and weight loss in obese patients. Other medical problems, such as diabetes mellitus and hypothyroidism, should also be controlled. In patients at high risk, consideration should be given to the control of other risk factors such as smoking, excessive alcohol intake, hormonal contraceptive use, and inadequately controlled hypertension.

Long-term Therapy: Because long-term administration of fenofibrate is recommended, the potential risks and benefits should be carefully weighed. Adequate pretreatment laboratory studies should be performed to ensure that patients have elevated serum cholesterol and/or triglycerides or low HDL-cholesterol levels. Periodic determination of serum lipids, fasting glucose, creatinine and ALT should be considered during fenofibrate treatment, particularly during the first months of therapy.

Reproduction Studies: Standard tests for teratology, fertility and peri- and post-natal effects in animals have shown a relative absence of risk; however, embryotoxicity has occurred in animals at maternally toxic doses.

Hematologic Changes: Mild hemoglobin, hematocrit and white blood cell decreases have been observed occasionally in patients following initiation of fenofibrate therapy. However, these levels stabilize during long-term administration. Periodic blood counts are recommended during the first 12 months of fenofibrate administration.

Liver Function: Abnormal liver function tests have been observed occasionally during fenofibrate administration, including elevations of transaminases, and decreases or, rarely, increases in alkaline phosphatase. However, these abnormalities disappear when therapy with fenofibrate is discontinued. Therefore, periodic liver function tests (AST, ALT and GGT [if originally elevated]) in addition to other baseline tests are recommended after 3 to 6 months and at least yearly thereafter. Fenofibrate therapy should be terminated if abnormalities persist. Fenofibrate may increase cholesterol excretion into the bile and may lead to cholelithiasis.

Hepatobiliary Disease: In patients with a past history of jaundice or hepatic disorder, fenofibrate should be used with caution.

Skeletal Muscle: Treatment with drugs of the fibrate class has been associated on rare occasions with rhabdomyolysis, or myositis, usually in patients with impaired renal function. Myopathy should be considered in any patient with diffuse myalgias, muscle tenderness or weakness and/or marked elevation of creatinine phosphokinase levels.

Patients should be advised to report promptly unexplained muscle pain, tenderness or weakness, particularly if accompanied by malaise or fever. CPK levels should be assessed in patients reporting these symptoms, and fenofibrate therapy should be discontinued if markedly elevated CPK levels (10 times the upper limit of normal) occur or myopathy is diagnosed.

Drug Interactions (see also Warnings): Resins: When a fibrate is used concurrently with cholestyramine or any other resin, an interval of at least 2 hours should be maintained between the administration of the two drugs, since the absorption of fibrates are impaired by cholestyramine.

Estrogens: Since estrogens may lead to a rise in lipid levels, the prescribing of fibrates in patients taking estrogens or estrogen-containing contraceptives must be critically considered on an individual basis.

Renal Function: In patients with hypoalbuminemia, e.g., nephrotic syndrome, and in patients with renal insufficiency, the dosage of fibrates must be reduced and renal function should be monitored regularly (see Precautions, Skeletal muscle and Dosage). Fenofibrate is not removed by hemodialysis and should not be used in dialysis patients.

Adverse Effects: Clinical adverse effects of fenofibrate therapy have been reported at an incidence between 2 and 15% with a mean of 6.3% in European trials of less than 12 months duration. In longer term studies, the incidence was between 7 and 14% with a mean of 11.3%. The most frequently reported adverse effects include: Gastrointestinal: epigastric distress, flatulence, abdominal pain, nausea, diarrhea, constipation.

Dermatologic: erythema, pruritus, urticaria.

Musculoskeletal: muscle pain and weakness, arthralgia.

CNS: headache, dizziness, insomnia.

Miscellaneous: decreased libido, hair loss, weight loss.

In 2 separate controlled clinical studies conducted in the U.S., a total of 191 patients on fenofibrate (116 Type II and 75 Type IV/V patients) were evaluated for adverse effects versus 183 patients on placebo (111 Type II and 72 Type IV/V patients). Listed in Table I are the adverse reactions considered by the investigators to be possibly or probably related to treatment, and reported by more than 1% of the patients receiving fenofibrate in these trials.

Table I—Lipidil Micro

Number (%) of Patients Reporting Adverse Reactions

U.S. Multicenter Studies
Type II study (6-month treatment)
Type IV/V Study (2-month treatment)

Adverse Reactions	Nonmicronized Fenofibrate (n=191)	Placebo (n=183)
Gastrointestinal		
Dyspepsia	6(3.1)	8(4.4)
Flatulence	6(3.1)	5(2.7)
Nausea	4(2.1)	3(1.6)
Abdominal pain	4(2.1)*	2(1.1)
Constipation	3(1.6)	1(0.5)
Skin and Appendages		
Pruritus	6(3.1)*	1(0.5)
Rash	6(3.1)	1(0.5)
Hives	3(1.6)	—
Body as a Whole		
Fatigue	4(2.1)	2(1.1)
Musculoskeletal		
Arthralgia	3(1.6)*	—

*One patient reported multiple adverse effects.

In these studies, the difference between the numbers of nonmicronized fenofibrate and placebo patients reporting these adverse reactions was not statistically significant ($p > 0.05$). While the nature of the adverse reactions reported was similar in both studies, these reactions were observed in most cases at a higher frequency in the longer term, 6-month trial in Type II patients.

Adverse reactions for micronized fenofibrate at recommended therapeutic doses in clinical trials have shown a comparable profile with those described for the nonmicronized fenofibrate formulation.

Surveillance in countries in which fenofibrate has been marketed for up to 20 years, such as France, Germany and the United Kingdom, indicates that clinical adverse effects reported include gastrointestinal complaints, painful muscles, skin disorders typically classified as pruritus, urticaria or erythema, loss of weight, impotence, diverse nervous complaints, hair loss, gallstones, pancreatitis and hepatitis.

Laboratory Parameters: In most trials, sporadic and transient increases in aminotransferase levels have been associated with the use of fenofibrate. The reported frequency of AST and ALT elevations was variable; in the U.S. clinical trials, elevations above twice the upper limit of normal were observed in 6.8% of the patients treated with fenofibrate, versus 1.6% of the patients on placebo. Values usually return to normal without interruption of treatment. On some occasions, more severe elevations of transaminases (above twice the upper limit of normal values) were noted; such rises subside when fenofibrate therapy is discontinued (see Precautions). Reductions in alkaline phosphatase levels have also been observed.

Mild decreases in hemoglobin, hematocrit and white blood cell counts have been observed occasionally in patients following initiation of fenofibrate therapy. However, these levels stabilize during long-term administration. In addition, a decrease in haptoglobin concentration has been observed in some patients with Type IV hyperlipidemia during long-term use of fenofibrate. However, this decrease in haptoglobin was not associated with any other sign of blood dyscrasia and/or hemolysis.

The mean plasma levels of urea and creatinine showed increases, particularly during long-term fenofibrate treatment, most of them remaining within the limits of normal values.

Fenofibrate also has the potential to provoke CPK elevations and changes in hematologic parameters which generally subside when the drug is discontinued (see Precautions).

Overdose: Symptoms and Treatment: While there has been no reported case of overdosage, symptomatic and supportive measures should be taken. Because fenofibric acid (the main metabolite of fenofibrate) is highly bound to plasma proteins, hemodialysis should not be considered.

Dosage: The recommended dose for micronized fenofibrate is one 200 mg capsule daily taken with the main meal.

Information for the Patient: See Blue Section—Information for the Patient "Lipidil Micro".

Supplied: Each orange, hard gelatin capsule contains: micronized fenofibrate 200 mg. Nonmedicinal ingredients: lactose, magnesium stearate, pregelatinized starch, reticulated polyvinyl pyrrolidone and sodium laurylsulfate. Boxes of 30. Keep at room temperature. Avoid excessive humidity.

(Shown in Product Recognition Section)

Reviewed 1997

LIPISORB®

Mead Johnson

Therapeutic Nutrient

Indications: A nutritionally complete liquid diet specifically designed for patients with fat malabsorption (e.g., inflammatory bowel disease, cystic fibrosis, short bowel syndrome and HIV infection). It provides complete vitamins and minerals with a readily absorbed fat blend. This vanilla flavored beverage can be fed orally or as a tube feeding.

Dosage: As prescribed by a physician. Tube feeding may be initiated at full strength (30 or 40 kcal/30 mL) or diluted 1:1 with water, based on patient's condition. If diluted, concentration should be increased as tolerated to full strength to achieve prescribed nutrient intake. The patient's fluid needs should be monitored and additional water given as needed. Administration via infusion pump is suggested. Bedside reservoir hang time for Lipisorb should not exceed 6 to 8 hours.

Reconstituted powder should be covered, refrigerated and used within 24 hours. Opened cans of Lipisorb powder should be kept covered and stored in a cool, dry place up to 30 days.

Supplied: A readily absorbable fat blend made up of 86% medium chain triglycerides makes Lipisorb appropriate for the total nutritional support of patients with fat malabsorption. It provides 100% Canadian adult RNI for all vitamins and minerals and protein in 2 100 mL. Glucose-, gluten-, lactose- and tartrazine-free. Each can of powder contains: corn syrup solids, MCT oil, sugar, corn oil, artificial vanilla flavor, soy lecithin, salt and essential vitamins and minerals. Provides 2 067 kJ (490 kcal)/100 g. Osmolality: 320 mOsm/kg water. Cases of 6 (340 g).

LIPITOR™ ℞

Parke-Davis

Atorvastatin Calcium

Lipid Metabolism Regulator

Pharmacology: Atorvastatin is a synthetic lipid-lowering agent. It is a selective, competitive inhibitor of 3-hydroxy-3-methylglutaryl-coenzyme A (HMG-CoA) reductase. This enzyme catalyzes the conversion of HMG-CoA to mevalonate, which is an early and rate-limiting step in the biosynthesis of cholesterol.

Atorvastatin lowers plasma cholesterol and lipoprotein levels by inhibiting HMG-CoA reductase and cholesterol synthesis in the liver and by increasing the number of hepatic low density lipoprotein (LDL) receptors on the cell-surface for enhanced uptake and catabolism of low density lipoprotein (LDL).

Atorvastatin reduces LDL-cholesterol (LDL-C) and the number of LDL particles, and lowers very low density lipoprotein-cholesterol (VLDL-C) and serum triglycerides (TG), as well as the number of apolipoprotein B (apo B) containing particles.

Pharmacokinetics: Atorvastatin is rapidly absorbed after oral administration; maximum plasma concentrations occur within 1 to 2 hours. Atorvastatin tablets are 95 to 99% bioavailable compared to solutions.

Mean distribution of atorvastatin is approximately 565 L. Atorvastatin is ≥98% bound to plasma proteins. Atorvastatin is extensively metabolized by cytochrome P450 3A4 to ortho- and para-hydroxylated derivatives and various beta-oxidation products. Approximately 70% of circulating inhibitory activity for HMG Co-A reductase is attributed to active metabolites.

Atorvastatin and its metabolites are eliminated by biliary excretion. Less than 2% of a dose of atorvastatin is recovered in urine following oral administration. Mean plasma elimination half-life of atorvastatin in humans is approximately 14 hours, but the half-life of inhibitory activity for HMG-CoA reductase is 20 to 30 hours due to the contribution of longer-lived active metabolites.

Indications: As an adjunct to diet, at least equivalent to the American Heart Association (AHA) Step 1 diet, for the reduction of elevated total cholesterol, LDL-C, triglycerides (TG) and apolipoprotein B (apo B) in hyperlipidemic and dyslipidemic

Lipitor (cont'd)

conditions, when response to diet and other nonpharmacological measures alone has been inadequate, including: primary hypercholesterolemia (Type IIa); combined (mixed) hyperlipidemia (Type IIb), including familial combined hyperlipidemia, regardless of whether cholesterol or triglycerides are the lipid abnormality of concern; heterozygous familial hypercholesterolemia.

In clinical trials, atorvastatin (10 to 80 mg/day) significantly improved lipid profiles in patients with a wide variety of hyperlipidemic and dyslipidemic conditions. In 2 dose-response studies in mildly to moderately hyperlipidemic patients (Fredrickson Types IIa and IIb), atorvastatin reduced the levels of total cholesterol (29 to 45%), LDL-C (39 to 60%), apo B (32 to 50%), TG (19 to 37%), and increased HDL-C levels (5 to 9%). Comparable responses were achieved in patients with heterozygous familial hypercholesterolemia, non-familial forms of hypercholesterolemia, combined hyperlipidemia, including familial combined hyperlipidemia and patients with non-insulin dependent diabetes mellitus. In patients with hypertriglyceridemia TG >3.95 mmol/L (>350 mg/dL), atorvastatin lowered TG levels by 27 to 42%.

Limited data are available in homozygous familial hypercholesterolemia (FH). An open-label study with atorvastatin 80 mg/day in homozygote FH patients showed a LDL-C lowering of 30% for patients not on plasmapheresis and of 31% for patients who continued plasmapheresis. A LDL-C lowering of 35% was observed in receptor defective patients and of 19% in receptor negative patients.

Prior to initiating therapy with atorvastatin, secondary causes should be excluded for elevations in plasma lipid levels (e.g., poorly controlled diabetes mellitus, hypothyroidism, nephrotic syndrome, dysproteinemias, obstructive liver disease, and alcoholism), and a lipid profile performed to measure total cholesterol, LDL-C, HDL-C, and TG. For patients with TG <4.52 mmol/L (<400 mg/dL), LDL-C can be estimated using the following equation:

LDL-C (mmol/L)=total cholesterol −[(0.37×(TG)+HDL-C)]
LDL-C (mg/dL)=total cholesterol −[(0.2×(TG)+HDL-C)]

For patients with TG levels >4.52 mmol/L (>400 mg/dL), this equation is less accurate and LDL-C concentrations should be determined by ultracentrifugation.

Contraindications: Hypersensitivity to any component of this medication. Active liver disease or unexplained persistent elevations of serum transaminases exceeding 3 times the upper limit of normal (see Warnings).
Pregnancy and *Lactation* (see Precautions).

Warnings: Pharmacokinetic Interactions: The use of HMG-CoA reductase inhibitors has been associated with severe myopathy, including rhabdomyolysis, which may be more frequent when they are coadministered with drugs that inhibit the cytochrome P450 enzyme system. Atorvastatin is metabolized by cytochrome P450 isoform 3A4 and as such may interact with agents that inhibit this enzyme (see Warnings, Muscle Effects and Precautions, Drug Interactions and Cytochrome P450-mediated Interactions).
Hepatic Effects: In clinical trials, persistent increases in serum transaminases greater than 3 times the upper limit of normal occurred in <1% of patients who received atorvastatin. When the dosage of atorvastatin was reduced, or when drug treatment was interrupted or discontinued, serum transaminase levels returned to pretreatment levels. The increases were generally not associated with jaundice or other clinical signs or symptoms. Most patients continued treatment with a reduced dose of atorvastatin without clinical sequelae.

Liver function tests should be performed before the initiation of treatment, and periodically thereafter. Special attention should be paid to patients who develop elevated serum transaminase levels, and in these patients measurements should be repeated promptly and then performed more frequently.

If increases in alanine aminotransferase (ALT) or aspartate aminotransferase (AST) show evidence of progression, particularly if they rise to greater than 3 times the upper limit of normal and are persistent, the dosage should be reduced or the drug discontinued.

Atorvastatin should be used with caution in patients who consume substantial quantities of alcohol and/or have a past history of liver disease. Active liver disease or unexplained transaminase elevations are contraindications to the use of atorvastatin; if such a condition should develop during therapy, the drug should be discontinued.
Muscle Effects: Myopathy, defined as muscle aching or muscle weakness in conjunction with increases in creatinine phosphokinase (CPK) values to greater than 10 times the upper limit of normal, should be considered in any patient with diffuse myalgia, muscle tenderness or weakness, and/or marked elevation of CPK. Patients should be advised to report promptly unexplained muscle pain, tenderness or weakness, particularly if accompanied by malaise or fever. Atorvastatin therapy should be discontinued if markedly elevated CPK levels occur or myopathy is diagnosed or suspected.

The risk of myopathy during treatment with HMG-CoA reductase inhibitors is increased with concurrent administration of cyclosporine, fibric acid derivatives, erythromycin, niacin (nicotinic acid), azole antifungals or nefazodone. As there is no experience to date with the use of atorvastatin given concurrently with these drugs, with the exception of a pharmacokinetic study with erythromycin, the benefits and risks of such combined therapy should be carefully considered (see Precautions, Drug Interactions).

Rhabdomyolysis has been reported in very rare cases with atorvastatin (see Precautions, Drug Interactions).

Rhabdomyolysis with renal dysfunction secondary to myoglobinuria has also been reported with HMG-CoA reductase inhibitors. Atorvastatin therapy should be temporarily withheld or discontinued in any patient with an acute serious condition suggestive of a myopathy or having a risk factor predisposing to the development of renal failure secondary to rhabdomyolysis (such as severe acute infection, hypotension, major surgery, trauma, severe metabolic, endocrine and electrolyte disorders, and uncontrolled seizures).

Precautions: General: **The effects of atorvastatin-induced changes in lipoprotein levels, including reduction of serum cholesterol on cardiovascular morbidity or mortality or total mortality have not been established.**

Before instituting therapy with atorvastatin, an attempt should be made to control elevated serum lipoprotein levels with appropriate diet, exercise, and weight reduction in overweight patients, and to treat other underlying medical problems (see Indications). Patients should be advised to inform subsequent physicians of the prior use of atorvastatin or any other lipid-lowering agents.
Effect on the Lens: Current long-term data from clinical trials do not indicate an adverse effect of atorvastatin on the human lens.
Effect on Ubiquinone (CoQ_{10}) Levels: Significant decreases in circulating ubiquinone levels in patients treated with atorvastatin and other statins have been observed. The clinical significance of a potential long-term statin-induced deficiency of ubiquinone has not been established. It has been reported that a decrease in myocardial ubiquinone levels could lead to impaired cardiac function in patients with borderline congestive heart failure.
Effect on Lipoprotein (a): In some patients, the beneficial effect of lowered total cholesterol and LDL-C levels may be partly blunted by a concomitant increase in Lp(a) levels. Until further experience is obtained, it is suggested, where feasible, that measurements of serum Lp(a) be followed up in patients placed on atorvastatin therapy.
Hypersensitivity: An apparent hypersensitivity syndrome has been reported with other HMG-CoA reductase inhibitors which has included 1 or more of the following features: anaphylaxis, angioedema, lupus erythematous-like syndrome, polymyalgia rheumatica, vasculitis, purpura, thrombocytopenia, leukopenia, hemolytic anemia, positive ANA, ESR increase, eosinophilia, arthritis, arthralgia, urticaria, asthenia, photosensitivity, fever, chills, flushing, malaise, dyspnea, toxic epidermal necrolysis, erythema multiforme, including Stevens-Johnson syndrome. Although to date hypersensitivity syndrome has not been described as such, atorvastatin should be discontinued if hypersensitivity is suspected.
Pregnancy: **Atorvastatin is contraindicated during pregnancy (see Contraindications).**

Atherosclerosis is a chronic process and discontinuation of lipid-lowering drugs during pregnancy should have little impact on the outcome of long-term therapy of primary hypercholesterolemia. Cholesterol and other products of cholesterol biosynthesis are essential components for fetal development (including synthesis of steroids and cell membranes). Since HMG-CoA reductase inhibitors decrease cholesterol synthesis and possibly the synthesis of other biologically active substances derived from cholesterol, they may cause harm to the fetus when administered to pregnant women. There are no data on the use of atorvastatin during pregnancy. Atorvastatin should be administered to women of childbearing age only when such patients are highly unlikely to conceive and have been informed of the potential hazards. If the patient becomes pregnant while taking atorvastatin, the drug should be discontinued and the patient apprised of the potential risk to the fetus.

Lactation: In rats, milk concentrations of atorvastatin are similar to those in plasma. It is not known whether this drug is excreted in human milk. Because of the potential for adverse reactions in nursing infants, women taking atorvastatin should not breast-feed (see Contraindications).
Children: Treatment experience in a pediatric population is limited to doses of atorvastatin up to 80 mg/day for 1 year in 8 patients with homozygous familial hypercholesterolemia. No clinical or biochemical abnormalities were reported in these patients.
Geriatrics: Treatment experience in adults 70 years or older (N=221) with doses of atorvastatin up to 80 mg/day has demonstrated that the safety and effectiveness of atorvastatin in this population was similar to that of patients <70 years of age. Pharmacokinetic evaluation of atorvastatin in subjects over the age of 65 years indicates an increased AUC. As a precautionary measure, the lowest dose should be administered initially.
Renal Insufficiency: Plasma concentrations and LDL-C lowering efficacy of atorvastatin are similar in patients with moderate renal insufficiency compared with patients with normal renal function. However, since several cases of rhabdomyolysis have been reported in patients with a history of renal insufficiency of unknown severity, as a precautionary measure and pending further experience in renal disease, the lowest dose (10 mg/day) of atorvastatin should be used in these patients. Similar precautions apply in patients with severe renal insufficiency (creatinine clearance <30 mL/min); the lowest dosage should be used and implemented cautiously (see Warnings, Muscle Effects; Precautions, Drug Interactions).

Refer also to Dosage.
Endocrine Function: HMG-CoA reductase inhibitors interfere with cholesterol synthesis and as such might theoretically blunt adrenal and/or gonadal steroid production. Clinical studies with atorvastatin and other HMG-CoA reductase inhibitors have suggested that these agents do not reduce plasma cortisol concentration or impair adrenal reserve and do not reduce basal plasma testosterone concentration. However, the effects of HMG-CoA reductase inhibitors on male fertility have not been studied in adequate numbers of patients. The effects, if any, on the pituitary-gonadal axis in premenopausal women are unknown. Patients treated with atorvastatin who develop clinical evidence of endocrine dysfunction should be evaluated appropriately. Caution should be exercised if an HMG-CoA reductase inhibitor or other agent used to lower cholesterol levels is administered to patients receiving other drugs (e.g., ketoconazole, spironolactone or cimetidine) that may decrease the levels of endogenous steroid hormones.
Drug Interactions: Concomitant Therapy with Other Lipid Metabolism Regulators: Combined drug therapy should be approached with caution as information from controlled studies is limited.
Bile Acid Sequestrants: Patients With Mild to Moderate Hypercholesterolemia: LDL-C reduction was greater when atorvastatin 10 mg and colestipol 20 g were coadministered (−45%) than when either drug was administered alone (−35% for atorvastatin and −22% for colestipol).

Patients With Severe Hypercholesterolemia: LDL-C reduction was similar (−53%) when atorvastatin 40 mg and colestipol 20 g were coadministered when compared with that of atorvastatin 80 mg alone. Plasma concentration of atorvastatin was lower (approximately 26%) when atorvastatin 40 mg plus colestipol 20 g were coadministered compared with atorvastatin 40 mg alone.

However, the combination drug therapy was less effective in lowering the triglycerides than atorvastatin monotherapy in both types of hypercholesterolemic patients. When atorvastatin is used concurrently with colestipol or any other resin, an interval of at least 2 hours should be maintained between the two drugs, since the absorption of atorvastatin may be impaired by the resin.
Fibric Acid Derivatives (Gemfibrozil, Fenofibrate, Bezafibrate) and Niacin (Nicotinic Acid): Although there is no experience with the use of atorvastatin given concurrently with fibric acid derivatives and niacin, the benefits and risks of such combined therapy should be carefully considered. The risk of myopathy during treatment with other drugs in this class is increased with concurrent administration (see Warnings, Muscle Effects).
Coumarin Anticoagulants: Atorvastatin had no clinically significant effect on prothrombin time when administered to patients receiving chronic warfarin therapy.

Digoxin: Coadministration of multiple doses of atorvastatin and digoxin increased steady-state plasma digoxin concentrations by approximately 20%. Patients taking digoxin should be monitored closely and appropriately.

Oral Contraceptives: Coadministration of atorvastatin with an oral contraceptive, containing 1 mg norethindrone and 35 μg ethinyl estradiol, increased plasma concentrations (AUC levels) of norethindrone and ethinyl estradiol by approximately 30% and 20%, respectively. These increases should be considered when selecting an oral contraceptive.

Antacids: Administration of aluminum and magnesium based antacids, such as Maalox TC suspension, with atorvastatin decreased plasma concentrations of atorvastatin by approximately 35%. LDL-C reduction was not altered but the triglyceride-lowering effect of atorvastatin may be affected.

Cimetidine: Administration of cimetidine with atorvastatin did not alter plasma concentrations or LDL-C lowering efficacy of atorvastatin, however, the triglyceride-lowering effect of atorvastatin was reduced from 34 to 26%.

Cytochrome P450-mediated Interactions: Atorvastatin is metabolized by the cytochrome P450 isoenzyme, CYP 3A4. Erythromycin, a CYP 3A4 inhibitor, increased atorvastatin plasma levels by 40%. Coadministration of CYP 3A4 inhibitors, such as grapefruit juice, macrolide antibiotics (including erythromycin), immunosuppressants (cyclosporine), azole antifungal agents (i.e., itraconazole, ketoconazole), or some antidepressants (e.g., nefazodone), may have the potential to increase plasma concentrations of HMG CoA reductase inhibitors, including atorvastatin. Caution should thus be exercised with concomitant use of these agents (see Warnings, Pharmacokinetic Interactions, Muscle Effects; Dosage).

In a study with healthy subjects, coadministration of maximum doses of both atorvastatin (80 mg) and terfenadine (120 mg), a CYP 3A4 substrate, was shown to produce modest increases in AUC values. The QTc interval remained unchanged. However, since an interaction between these two drugs cannot be excluded in patients with predisposing factors for arrhythmia, (e.g., pre-existing prolonged QT interval, severe coronary artery disease, hypokalemia), caution should be exercised when these agents are coadministered (see Warnings, Pharmacokinetic Interactions and Dosage).

Antipyrine: Antipyrine was used as a nonspecific model for drugs metabolized by the microsomal hepatic enzyme system (cytochrome P450 system). Atorvastatin had no effect on the pharmacokinetics of antipyrine, thus interactions with other drugs metabolized via the same cytochrome isozymes are not expected.

Erythromycin: In healthy individuals, plasma concentrations of atorvastatin increased approximately 40% with coadministration of atorvastatin and erythromycin, a known inhibitor of cytochrome P450 3A4 (see Warnings, Muscle Effects).

Other Concomitant Therapy: Caution should be exercised with concomitant use of immunosuppressive agents and azole antifungals (see Warnings, Muscle Effects).

In clinical studies, atorvastatin was used concomitantly with antihypertensive agents and estrogen replacement therapy without evidence of clinically significant adverse interactions. Interaction studies with specific agents have not been conducted.

Patients with Severe Hypercholesterolemia: Higher drug dosages (80 mg/day) required for some patients with heterozygous familial hypercholesterolemia or severe hypercholesterolemia are associated with increased plasma levels of atorvastatin. **Caution should be exercised in such patients who are also severely renally impaired, elderly, or are concomitantly being administered digoxin or CYP 3A4 inhibitors (see Warnings, Pharmacokinetic Interactions, Muscle Effects; Precautions, Drug Interactions and Dosage).**

Drug/Laboratory Test Interactions: Atorvastatin may elevate serum transaminase and creatinine phosphokinase levels (from skeletal muscle). In the differential diagnosis of chest pain in a patient on therapy with atorvastatin, cardiac and noncardiac fractions of these enzymes should be determined.

Adverse Effects: Atorvastatin is generally well-tolerated. Adverse reactions have usually been mild and transient. In controlled clinical studies (placebo-controlled and active-controlled comparative studies with other lipid lowering agents) involving 2 502 patients, <2% of patients were discontinued due to adverse experiences attributable to atorvastatin. Of these 2 502 patients, 1 721 were treated for at least 6 months and 1 253 for 1 year or more.

Adverse experiences occurring at an incidence ≥1% in patients participating in placebo-controlled clinical studies of atorvastatin and reported to be possibly, probably or definitely drug related are shown in Table I.

Table I—Lipitor

Associated Adverse Events Reported in ≥1% of Patients in Placebo Controlled Clinical Trials

	Placebo % (n=270)	Lipitor % (n=1 122)
Gastrointestinal		
Constipation	1	1
Diarrhea	1	1
Dyspepsia	2	1
Flatulence	2	1
Nausea	0	1
Nervous System		
Headache	2	1
Miscellaneous		
Pain	<1	1
Myalgia	1	1
Asthenia	<1	1

The following additional adverse events were reported in clinical trials; not all events listed below have been associated with a causal relationship to atorvastatin therapy: muscle cramps, myositis, myopathy, paresthesia, peripheral neuropathy, pancreatitis, hepatitis, cholestatic jaundice, anorexia, vomiting, alopecia, pruritus, rash, impotence, hyperglycemia and hypoglycemia.

Postmarketing Experience: Very rare reports of severe myopathy with or without rhabdomyolysis have been reported (see Warnings, Muscle Effects; Precautions, Renal Insufficiency and Drug Interactions).

Ophthalmologic Observations: see Precautions.

Laboratory Tests: Increases in serum transaminase levels have been noted in clinical trials (see Warnings).

Overdose: Symptoms and Treatment: There is no specific treatment for atorvastatin overdosage. Should an overdose occur, the patient should be treated symptomatically and supportive measures instituted as required. Due to extensive drug binding to plasma proteins, hemodialysis is not expected to significantly enhance atorvastatin clearance.

Dosage: Patients should be placed on a standard cholesterol-lowering diet [at least equivalent to the American Heart Association (AHA) Step 1 diet] before receiving atorvastatin, and should continue on this diet during treatment. If appropriate, a program of weight control and physical exercise should be implemented.

Primary Hypercholesterolemia and Combined (Mixed): Hyperlipidemia, Including Familial Combined Hyperlipidemia: The recommended dose of atorvastatin is 10 mg once a day. The majority of patients achieve and maintain target cholesterol levels with atorvastatin 10 mg/day. A significant therapeutic response is evident within 2 weeks, and the maximum response is usually achieved within 2 to 4 weeks. The response is maintained during chronic therapy.

Doses can be given at any time of the day, with or without food, and should preferably be given in the evening. Doses should be individualized according to baseline LDL-C levels, the desired LDL-C target (such as that recommended by the U.S. National Cholesterol Education Program [NCEP] and/or the Canadian Consensus Conference Guidelines), the goal of therapy and the patient's response. Adjustments of dosage, if necessary, should be made at intervals of 4 weeks or more. The recommended dose range for most patients is 10 to 40 mg/day. The maximum dose is 80 mg/day, which may be required in a minority of patients (see severe hypercholesterolemia). **Cholesterol levels should be monitored periodically and consideration should be given to reducing the dosage of atorvastatin if cholesterol falls below the targeted range such as that recommended by guidelines.**

Table II—Lipitor

Dose-Response in Patients with Mild to Moderate Hypercholesterolemia (Mean % Change from Baseline)[a]

Lipid Parameter	Lipitor Dose (mg/day) 10 (N=22)	20 (N=20)	40 (N=21)	80 (N=23)
Total-C: 7.1 mmol/L[b] (273 mg/dL)[b]	−29	−33	−37	−45
LDL-C: 4.9 mmol/L[b] (190 mg/dL)[b]	−39	−43	−50	−60

[a]Results are pooled from 2 dose-response studies.
[b]Mean baseline values.

The following reductions in total cholesterol and LDL-C levels have been observed in 2 dose-response studies, and may serve as a guide to treatment of patients with mild to moderate hypercholesterolemia (see Table II).

Severe Hypercholesterolemia: In patients with severe hypercholesterolemia, including heterozygous familial hypercholesterolemia, higher dosages (up to 80 mg/day) may be required (see Warnings, Muscle Effects and Precautions, Drug Interactions).

Concomitant Therapy: See Precautions, Drug Interactions.

Renal Insufficiency: See Precautions.

Information for the Patient: See Blue Section—Information for the Patient "Lipitor".

Supplied: 10 mg: Each white, elliptical, film-coated tablet, coded "10" on one side and "PD 155" on the other, contains: atorvastatin calcium 10 mg. Nonmedicinal ingredients: calcium carbonate, candelilla wax, croscarmellose sodium, hydroxypropyl cellulose, lactose monohydrate, magnesium stearate, microcrystalline cellulose, hydroxypropyl methylcellulose, polyethylene glycol, talc, titanium dioxide, polysorbate 80 and simethicone emulsion. Bottles of 90.

20 mg: Each white, elliptical, film-coated tablet, coded "20" on one side and "PD 156" on the other, contains: atorvastatin calcium 20 mg. Nonmedicinal ingredients: calcium carbonate, candelilla wax, croscarmellose sodium, hydroxypropyl cellulose, lactose monohydrate, magnesium stearate, microcrystalline cellulose, hydroxypropyl methylcellulose, polyethylene glycol, talc, titanium dioxide, polysorbate 80 and simethicone emulsion. Bottles of 90.

40 mg: Each white, elliptical, film-coated tablet, coded "40" on one side and "PD 157" on the other, contains: atorvastatin calcium 40 mg. Nonmedicinal ingredients: calcium carbonate, candelilla wax, croscarmellose sodium, hydroxypropyl cellulose, lactose monohydrate, magnesium stearate, microcrystalline cellulose, hydroxypropyl methylcellulose, polyethylene glycol, talc, titanium dioxide, polysorbate 80 and simethicone emulsion. Bottles of 90.

Store at controlled room temperature 15 to 25°C.

(Shown in Product Recognition Section)

Reviewed 1999

LIQUIFILM® FORTE

Allergan

Polyvinyl Alcohol

Ocular Lubricant

Supplied: Each mL contains: polyvinyl alcohol 3%. Nonmedicinal ingredients: benzalkonium chloride 0.005% (as preservative), edetate disodium, sodium chloride, sodium phosphate dibasic and sodium phosphate monobasic. Plastic dropper bottles of 15 mL.

LIQUIFILM® TEARS

Allergan

Polyvinyl Alcohol

Ocular Lubricant

Supplied: Each mL contains: polyvinyl alcohol 1.4%. Nonmedicinal ingredients: benzalkonium chloride 0.005% (as preservative), edetate disodium, sodium chloride, sodium phosphate dibasic and sodium phosphate monobasic. Plastic dropper bottles of 15 and 30 mL.

LIQUOR CARBONIS DETERGENS

Odan

Coal Tar Solution

Antipsoriatic

Supplied: Each plastic, amber bottle contains: coal tar solution USP 20%. Bottles of 500 mL.

LISINOPRIL Ⓟ

General Monograph, CPhA

see ACE INHIBITORS

LITHANE™ Ⓟ

Pfizer

Lithium Carbonate

Antimanic Agent

Pharmacology: Although lithium is useful for its antimanic effect and in preventing relapses in patients with a clearcut diagnosis of bipolar affective disorder, it has very little, if any, direct effect on moods, normal or abnormal.

Lithium alters sodium transport in nerve and muscle cells, effects a shift toward intraneuronal metabolism of catecholamines and has an inhibitory action on the intracellular formation of cyclic AMP. However, the specific biochemical mechanism of action of lithium in mania is still largely unkown.

Lithium is inactive in most screening psychopharmacological tests but it produces marked potentiation of amphetamine hyperactivity in animals. It does not appear to protect against the action of stimulant and convulsive drugs and produces only slight potentiation of CNS depressants.

ECG changes with lithium have been reported in both animals and man.

Pharmacokinetics: Lithium ions are rapidly absorbed from the gastrointestinal tract following oral administration of lithium. Peak plasma lithium concentrations are reached 2 to 4 hours after lithium administration. The distribution of lithium in the body approximates that of total body water, but its passage across the blood-brain barrier is slow and at equilibration the CSF lithium level reaches only approximately half the plasma concentration.

Lithium is excreted primarily in urine with less than 1% being eliminated with the feces. Lithium is filtered by the glomeruli and 80% of the filtered lithium is reabsorbed in the tubules, probably by the same mechanism responsible for sodium reabsorption. The renal clearance of lithium is proportional to its plasma concentration. The half-life of elimination of lithium is approximately 24 hours. A low salt intake resulting in low tubular concentration of sodium will increase lithium reabsorption and might result in retention or intoxication.

Renal lithium clearance is, under ordinary circumstances, remarkably constant in the same individual but decreases with age and falls when sodium intake is lowered. The dose necessary to maintain a given concentration of serum lithium depends on the ability of the kidney to excrete lithium. However, renal lithium excretion may vary greatly between individuals and lithium dosage must, therefore, be adjusted individually. In clinical reports, it has been noted that serum lithium may rise an average of 0.2 to 0.4 mmol/L after intake of 300 mg and 0.3 to 0.6 mmol/L after intake of 600 mg of lithium carbonate. It has been suggested that manic patients retain larger amounts of lithium during the active manic phase, but studies have been unable to confirm a clear difference in excretion patterns. However, patients in a manic state seem to have an increased tolerance to lithium.

Balance studies indicate that lithium may produce a transitory diuresis with increase in sodium and potassium excretion. A period of equilibrium or slight retention may follow, but persistent polyuria may occur in some patients. There is evidence that therapeutic doses of lithium decrease the 24-hour exchangeable sodium. Longitudinal metabolic studies have demonstrated cumulative lithium retention in some patients without undue rise in plasma lithium values, indicating a possible intracellular retention of lithium. There is some evidence that lithium may affect the metabolism of potassium, magnesium and calcium.

Indications: In the treatment of acute manic episodes in patients with manic-depressive disorders. Maintenance therapy has been found useful in preventing or diminishing the frequency of subsequent relapses in bipolar manic-depressive patients (with a strong history of mania).

Contraindications: Patients with significant cardiovascular or renal disease. It is also contraindicated in patients with evidence of severe debilitation or dehydration, sodium depletion, brain damage and in conditions requiring low sodium intake.

Warnings: Lithium therapy requires reaching plasma levels of lithium which are relatively close to the toxic level. Since lithium is excreted primarily by the kidney, adequate renal function and adequate salt and fluid intake (2 500 to 3 000 mL) are essential in order to avoid lithium accumulation and intoxication. Thus, a decision to initiate lithium therapy should be preceded by a thorough clinical examination and evaluation of each patient, including laboratory determinations, ECG, and a very careful assessment of renal function.

Means of obtaining accurate determination of serum lithium levels should be available, since frequent serum determinations are required specially during the initial period of treatment. Lithium toxicity is closely related to serum lithium levels and during treatment they should usually not exceed 1.5 mmol/L, if serious adverse reactions and lithium intoxication are to be avoided. This lithium level refers to a blood sample drawn before the patient has had his/her first lithium dose of the day, therefore, 9 to 12 hours after his/her last dose of drug. Serum lithium levels should usually be monitored 3 times weekly during the initial period of administration and periodically as required thereafter. If lithium levels exceed 1.5 to 2 mmol/L, the drug should be discontinued and, if appropriate, administration resumed at a lower level after 24 hours. Prodromal toxic signs such as fatigue, muscular weakness, incoordination, drowsiness, coarse tremors, diarrhea and vomiting, provide a sensitive warning of lithium intoxication.

In view of the limited dosage range of lithium compared to other psychotropic agents, particular care is required for the patient to receive exactly the prescribed number of lithium capsules.

Good kidney function and adequate salt and fluid intake are essential to maintain lithium excretion. When sodium intake is lowered, lithium excretion is reduced. Diminished intake or excessive loss of salt and fluids, as a result of vomiting, diarrhea, perspiration or use of diuretics will also increase lithium retention. Thus, lithium should not be given to patients on a salt-free diet and sodium depletion must be carefully avoided. Therefore, it is essential for the patient to maintain a normal diet including adequate salt and fluid intake during lithium therapy. Salt supplements and additional fluids may be required if excessive losses occur. Lithium should generally not be given to patients receiving diuretics, since the risk of lithium toxicity is very high in such patients. If diuretics are used during lithium therapy the serum lithium concentration must be closely monitored.

Chronic lithium therapy may be associated with diminution of renal concentrating ability, occasionally presenting as nephrogenic diabetes insipidus, with polyuria and polydipsia. Such patients should be carefully managed to avoid dehydration with resulting lithium retention and toxicity. This condition is usually reversible when lithium is discontinued. Morphologic changes with glomerular and interstitial fibrosis and nephron atrophy have been reported in patients on chronic lithium therapy. Morphological changes have also been seen in manic depressive patients never exposed to lithium. The relationship between renal functional and morphologic changes and their association with lithium therapy have not been established.

When kidney function is assessed for baseline data prior to starting lithium therapy or thereafter, routine urinalysis and other tests may be used to evaluate tubular function (e.g., urine specific gravity or osmolality following a period of water deprivation, or 24-hour urine volume) and glomerular function (e.g., serum creatinine or creatinine clearance). During lithium therapy, progressive or sudden changes in renal function, even within the normal range, indicate the need for re-evaluation of treatment.

An encephalopathic syndrome (characterized by weakness, lethargy, fever, tremulousness and confusion, extrapyramidal symptoms, leukocytosis, elevated serum enzymes, BUN and FBS) followed by irreversible brain damage has occurred in a few patients treated with lithium plus haloperidol. A causal relationship between these events and the concomitant administration of lithium and haloperidol has not been established; however, patients receiving such combined therapy should be monitored closely for early evidence of neurologic toxicity and treatment discontinued promptly if such signs appear (see Precautions, Drug Interactions). The possibility of similar adverse interactions with other antipsychotic medication exists (see Precautions, Drug Interactions).

Outpatients and their families should be warned that patients must discontinue lithium therapy and contact their physician immediately if such clinical signs of lithium toxicity as diarrhea, vomiting, tremor, mild ataxia, drowsiness, fatigue or muscular weakness occur.

There is evidence of decreased tolerance to lithium once the acute manic episode breaks. Therefore, when the acute attack subsides, the dosage should be reduced rapidly in order to produce serum lithium levels no higher than between 0.6 and 1.2 mmol/L.

Precautions: General: Periodic review and monitoring of kidney and cardiovascular function is advisable during therapy with lithium carbonate. Other laboratory tests should be performed as indicated by the patient's clinical condition. The appearance of signs of toxicity or a rise in the blood level of lithium after the dosage is stabilized should alert the physician to determine the reasons for lithium accumulation.

Patients with Special Diseases and Conditions: Cardiovascular Disease: Patients with underlying cardiovascular disease should be observed carefully for signs of arrhythmias.

Thyroid Disorder: Since the formation of nontoxic goiters has been reported during lithium therapy, the thyroid gland should be examined before treatment and appropriate thyroid function tests performed. Nontoxic goiters reported during prolonged lithium therapy have disappeared following discontinuation of the medication. Treatment with small doses of thyroxin or desiccated thyroid in patients who develop a diffuse nontoxic goiter may stop further growth or lead to shrinkage of the gland.

Concomitant Infection: In addition to sweating and diarrhea, concomitant infection with elevated temperatures may also necessitate a temporary reduction or cessation of medication.

Pregnancy or Women of Childbearing Potential: Lithium should not be used during pregnancy or in women of childbearing potential unless it cannot be substituted by other appropriate therapy and in the opinion of the physician the expected benefits outweigh the possible hazards to the fetus.

In various animal species lithium affects reproduction and has been noted to have teratogenic effects. A group of spontaneous reports concerning 37 mothers who received lithium during pregnancy included 2 who gave birth to infants with congenital malformations. Data from lithium birth registries suggest that the drug may increase the incidence of cardiac and other anomalies, especially Ebstein's anomaly.

When possible, lithium should be withdrawn for at least the first trimester unless it is determined that this would seriously endanger the mother.

If this drug is used during pregnancy, or if the patient becomes pregnant while taking the drug, the patient should be apprised for the potential hazards to the fetus.

When lithium is used during pregnancy, serum lithium concentrations should be carefully monitored and dosage adjusted if necessary since renal clearance of the drug and distribution of the drug into erythrocytes may be increased during pregnancy. Pregnant women receiving lithium may have subtherapeutic serum lithium concentrations if dosage of the drug is not increased during pregnancy. Immediately postpartum, renal clearance of lithium may decrease to pre-pregnancy levels; therefore, to decrease the risk of postpartum lithium intoxication, dosage of the drug should be reduced from 1 week before parturition.

Lactation: Lithium is excreted in human milk (concentrations of 33 to 50% of those in the mother's serum). Nursing should not be undertaken during lithium therapy except in rare and unusual circumstances where, in the opinion of the physician, the potential benefits to the mother outweigh possible hazards to the child.

Geriatrics: Geriatric patients appear to be more susceptible to adverse effects even when lithium levels are therapeutic.

Children: Since information regarding the safety and effectiveness of lithium in children under 12 years of age is not available, its use in such patients is not recommended. There has been a report of a transient syndrome of acute dystonia and hyperreflexia occurring in a 15 kg child who ingested 300 mg of lithium.

Discontinuation of Therapy: The majority of patients do not experience withdrawal symptoms or rebound phenomenon upon cessation of long-term lithium therapy. In view of the occasional reports of sudden relapses occurring with abrupt discontinuation, gradual discontinuation is recommended unless abrupt withdrawal is necessary because of toxicity.

Drug Interactions: Diuretics or Angiotensin Converting Enzyme (ACE) Inhibitors: Caution should be exercised when lithium and diuretics or ACE inhibitors are used concomitantly because sodium loss may reduce the renal clearance of lithium and increase serum lithium levels with risk of lithium toxicity. When such combinations are used, the lithium dosage may need to be decreased and more frequent monitoring of lithium plasma levels is recommended (see Warnings).

Haloperidol: It has been proposed that haloperidol and lithium could have a combined inhibitory effect on striatal adenylate cyclase. If haloperidol and lithium are used concomitantly, careful attention should be given to the dose of both agents as well as to early detection of neurotoxicity, particularly in the presence of one or more predisposing factors which include large doses of one or both drugs, the presence of acute mania, failure to discontinue drugs when adverse effects occur, pre-existing brain damage, a history of extrapyramidal symptoms with neuroleptic therapy alone, the concurrent use of anticholinergic antiparkinsonian drugs, and the presence of other physiologic disturbances such as infection, fever, or dehydration (see Warnings).

Phenothiazines: Both pharmacokinetic interactions and clinical toxicity with the combined use of phenothiazines and lithium have been described. Lithium-induced reductions in plasma chlorpromazine levels, phenothiazine-induced increases in red cell uptake of lithium and chlorpromazine-induced increases in renal lithium excretion have been reported. Clinically, occasional cases of neurotoxicity have been reported and may be more likely to occur with thioridazine than other phenothiazines, when combined with lithium. Therefore, the clinician should be alert for altered response to either drug when used in combination and when either drug is withdrawn.

Non-steroidal Anti-inflammatory Drugs (NSAIDs): NSAIDs have been reported to increase significantly, steady state plasma lithium levels. In some cases lithium toxicity has resulted from such interactions. In a patient stabilized on lithium and NSAIDs, discontinuation of the NSAIDs may result in inadequate serum lithium concentrations. When such combinations are used, increased plasma lithium level monitoring is recommended.

Selective Serotonin Reuptake Inhibitors (SSRI) Drugs: Lithium may enhance the serotonergic effects of SSRI drugs. Coadministration of lithium with SSRI drugs may lead to a higher incidence of serotonin associated side effects and lithium toxicity.

Fluvoxamine: Several cases of adverse reactions including convulsions have been reported in patients receiving concomitant lithium and fluvoxamine.

Fluoxetine: There have been reports of both increased and decreased lithium levels when lithium was used concomitantly with fluoxetine. Cases of lithium toxicity have been reported.

Sertraline: In placebo-controlled study in normal volunteers sertraline did not alter steady-state concentrations or renal clearance of lithium. However, there was a high incidence of apparently treatment-related side effects with the combination in this study, tremors being the most frequently observed. There is no clinical experience with lithium in sertraline treated patients.

Therefore, combined use of lithium and SSRI drugs should be carried out with caution. Lithium levels should be monitored when these drugs are administered concomitantly, so that appropriate adjustments to the lithium dose may be made if necessary.

Carbamazepine: Several cases of neurotoxicity (in the absence of toxic serum lithium concentrations) have been reported in patients receiving lithium and carbamazepine, but the combination has also been used to advantage in some manic patients. Patients should be monitored for evidence of lithium toxicity when carbamazepine is given concomitantly. It is not yet established whether plasma lithium concentrations are useful in monitoring this interaction since the carbamazepine might increase the effect of lithium without increasing plasma lithium concentrations.

Neuromuscular Blocking Agents: In patients receiving chronic lithium therapy, the action of neuromuscular blocking agents (e.g., succinylcholine, pancuronium) may be prolonged.

Theophylline: Theophylline enhances the renal clearance of lithium in most patients, thus tending to reduce serum lithium concentrations. When initiating lithium therapy in a patient on chronic theophylline, lithium dosage requirements may be higher than anticipated. When initiating theophylline therapy in a patient on chronic lithium, there may be reduced lithium response. Monitoring of serum lithium concentration is recommended.

Calcium Channel Blockers (CCBs): The addition of verapamil or diltiazem to patients stabilized on lithium therapy may result in neurotoxicity. The CCB effects may be additive to that of lithium on transmitter secretion in the nervous system. The use of CCBs in the treatment of patients with bipolar disorders receiving lithium should be commenced carefully with observation for neurotoxic effects. The therapeutic range of lithium may need to be toward the lower end when a CCB is coadministered.

Propranolol: Limited clinical data suggest that propranolol may increase lithium serum concentrations, and its co-administration with lithium may produce bradycardia. Pending further data, patients maintained on lithium should be monitored for changed lithium serum concentrations or exaggerated beta-blocker effects.

Tricyclic Antidepressants: Both lithium and tricyclic antidepressants lower the seizure threshold. An additive effect is possible.

Potassium Iodide: The hypothyroidic and goitrogenic effects of lithium carbonate and potassium iodide (and possibly other iodides) may be additive if the 2 drugs are used concurrently.

Diazepam: An isolated case has been reported of serious hypothermia during concurrent treatment with lithium and diazepam. Since hypothermia is potentially fatal if it occurs and its general incidence is not known, it would be prudent to watch for this interaction during concurrent treatment.

Sodium Bicarbonate: Patients on combined sodium bicarbonate and lithium therapy should be monitored for decreased lithium effects. Lithium blood levels may be helpful in assessing this interaction.

Sodium Chloride: Patients on salt-restricted diets who receive lithium are prone to developing symptoms of lithium toxicity. In contrast, increased sodium intake has been associated with reduced therapeutic response to lithium. Extremely large or small intakes of sodium chloride should be avoided in patients receiving lithium (see Warnings).

Urea: Limited clinical experience indicates that urea may enhance the renal excretion of lithium resulting in reduced lithium serum concentrations.

Other: Isolated cases of lithium toxicity have been reported to be induced by concomitant administration of mazindol, methyldopa and phenytoin.

Adverse Effects: Mild side effects may be encountered with lithium even when serum lithium values remain below 1 mmol/L. The most frequent side effects are the initial postabsorptive symptoms, believed to be associated with a rapid rise in serum lithium levels. They include, gastrointestinal discomfort, nausea, vertigo, muscle weakness and a dazed feeling and frequently disappear after stabilization of therapy. The more common and persistent adverse reactions are: fine tremor of the hands, and, at times, fatigue, thirst, and polyuria. These do not necessarily require reduction of dosage.

Mild to moderate toxic reactions may occur at lithium levels from 1.5 to 2 mmol/L, and moderate to severe reactions at levels above 2 mmol/L.

A number of patients may experience lithium accumulation during initial therapy, increasing to toxic levels and requiring immediate discontinuation of the drug. Some elderly patients with lower renal clearances for lithium may also experience different degrees of lithium toxicity, requiring reduction or temporary withdrawal of medication. However, in patients with normal renal clearance the toxic manifestations appear to occur in a fairly regular sequence related to serum lithium levels. The usually transient gastrointestinal symptoms are the earliest side effects to occur. A mild degree of fine tremor of the hands may persist throughout therapy. Thirst and polyuria may be followed by increased drowsiness, ataxia, tinnitus and blurred vision, indicating early intoxication. As intoxication progresses the following manifestations may be encountered: confusion, increasing disorientation, muscle twitchings, hyperreflexia, nystagmus, seizures, diarrhea, vomiting, and eventually coma and death.

The following adverse effects have been reported and are usually related to serum lithium levels: Gastrointestinal: anorexia, nausea, vomiting, diarrhea, abdominal pain and weight loss.

Neuromuscular: general muscle weakness, ataxia, tremor, muscle hyperirritability, (fasciculation, twitchings, especially of facial muscles and clonic movements of the limbs), choreoathetotic movement and hyperactive deep tendon reflexes.

Neurological: Cases of pseudotumor cerebri (increased intracranial pressure and papilledema) have been reported with lithium use. If undetected, this condition may result in enlargement of the blind spot, constriction of visual fields and eventual blindness due to optic atrophy. Lithium should be discontinued, if clinically possible, if this syndrome occurs.

Central and Peripheral Nervous System: urinary and fecal incontinence, slurred speech, blackout spells, seizures, cranial nerve involvement, psychomotor retardation, somnolence, toxic confusional states, restlessness, stupor and coma.

Cardiovascular: arrhythmia, hypotension, peripheral circulatory failure, cardiac collapse and peripheral edema.

ECG Changes: reversible flattening, isoelectricity or inversion of T-waves.

EEG Changes: diffuse slowing, widening of frequency spectrum, potentiation and disorganization of background rhythm. Sensitivity to hyperventilation and paroxysmal bilateral synchronous delta activity have also been described.

Autonomic Nervous System: blurred vision, dry mouth.

Thyroid Abnormalities: Euthyroid goiter and/or hypothyroidism (including myxedema) accompanied by lower T_3 and T_4. Iodine uptake may be elevated (see Precautions). Paradoxically, rare cases of hyperthyroidism have been reported.

Genitourinary: albuminuria, oliguria, polyuria and glycosuria.

Dermatologic: drying and thinning of hair, anesthesia of skin, chronic folliculitis, xerosis cutis, alopecia, exacerbation of psoriasis, rash, and pruritus.

Allergic: allergic vasculitis.

Metabolic and Nutritional Disorders: thirst, hyperglycemia, and dehydration.

Hematopoietic and Lymphatic: anemia, leukopenia, leukocytosis.

General: general fatigue, leg ulcers, metallic taste, and slight elevation of plasma magnesium.

Miscellaneous Reactions Unrelated to Dosage Are: transient electroencephalographic and electrographic changes, hyperthyroidism, worsening of organic brain syndromes, excessive weight gain, edematous swelling of ankles or wrists. A single report has been received of the development of painful discoloration of fingers and toes and coldness of the extremities within one day of the starting of treatment of lithium. The mechanism through which these symptoms (resembling Raynaud's Syndrome) developed is not known. Recovery followed discontinuance.

Serious reactions to long-term therapy: In addition to other possible adverse reactions, the main concern during chronic lithium therapy centres on kidney function, the thyroid, parathyroid, the bones and skin.

Overdose: Symptoms: Lithium toxicity is closely related to the concentration of lithium in the blood and is usually associated with serum levels in excess of 2 mmol/L. Early signs of toxicity which may occur at lower serum levels were described under Adverse Effects and usually respond to reduction of dosage. Lithium intoxication has been preceded by the appearance or aggravation of the following symptoms: sluggishness, drowsiness, lethargy, coarse tremors or muscle twitchings, loss of appetite, vomiting, and diarrhea. Occurrence of these symptoms requires immediate cessation of medication and careful clinical reassessment and management. Signs and symptoms of lithium intoxication have already been described under Adverse Effects.

In 8 cases of lithium poisoning described by Schou, the patients frequently developed muscle rigidity with hyperactive deep reflexes, generalized muscle tremors or fasciculations, attacks of hyperextension of the limbs with gasping and wide opening of the eyes, and sometimes epileptic seizures and various neurological dysfunction. There was progressive impairment of consciousness and in some patients coma. EEG changes in some patients consisted of decrease of alpha activity and increase of theta and delta activity, the latter at times paroxysmal with maximum activity frontally. Periods of beta activity with sharp waves were also observed. The kidney function was probably impaired in several patients. Three of these patients died, all of pulmonary complications.

Treatment: No specific antidote for lithium poisoning is known. The treatment of lithium poisoning is symptomatic. Early symptoms of lithium toxicity can usually be treated by reduction or cessation of dosage of the drug and resumption of treatment at a lower dose after 24 to 48 hours. In severe cases of lithium poisoning, the first and foremost goal of treatment consists of elimination of this ion from the organism. Treatment of lithium poisoning is 1) lavage 2) correction of fluid and electrolyte imbalance, and 3) regulation of kidney function. Sodium depletion in particular must be corrected. However, administration of large amounts of sodium in the absence of depletion of this electrolyte has not been very successful in many as a means of speeding lithium excretion. Lithium excretion may be facilitated by the judicious use of the intravenous urea, sodium bicarbonate, acetazolamide or aminophylline. Hemodialysis is an effective and rapid means of removing the ion from the severely toxic patient or in the presence of impaired renal function. Infection prophylaxis, regular chest x-rays and preservation of adequate respiration are essential.

Dosage: Since lithium acts without the production of "sedation", some prefer it to neuroleptics or use these to supplement lithium therapy and obtain rapid control of overt manic behavior. Lithium also has a useful indication in those cases that fail to respond to neuroleptics.

Selection of patients and approach to lithium therapy: The results of lithium therapy depend largely on the nature and course of the illness itself, rather than on the symptoms. The selection of patients for long-term treatment requires a

Lithane (cont'd)

clearcut diagnosis of primary affective disorder, the condition for which the stabilizing effects of lithium have been found useful. The variables that have been more consistently associated with response to lithium therapy in patients with a primary affective disorder are: the good quality of remissions with good function and no significant symptomatology during the free intervals between previous episodes of illness; low frequency of episodes, typically 1 or 2 (and not more than 3 or 4) per year, and symptomatology during the acute episodes that meet strict criteria for a primary affective disorder (DSM-III: Research Diagnostic Criteria).

Screening for lithium candidates should include at least a medical history and physical examination with emphasis on the CNS, urinary, cardiovascular, gastrointestinal and endocrine systems and the skin. It should also include: routine 24-hour urine volume, serum creatinine, record of weight, an ECG, possibly electrolytes and TSH, and for long-term treatment, creatinine clearance and a urine concentration test. Other examinations and tests should be used when indicated. Monitoring lithium treatment should include, for each visit, mental status, physical examination, weight, 12-hour serum lithium and a check for lithium side effects and compliance. It should also include serum creatinine every 2 months, plasma thyroid hormone and TSH every 6 to 12 months, particularly in female patients, and attention to renal and thyroid function should be maintained throughout, with tests used for baseline screening repeated as required.

The first objective of treatment is to establish an effective and safe daily dosage of lithium with the aid of standardized 12-hour serum lithium levels maintained within the therapeutic range, as high as necessary for efficacy, and with the patient as much as possible free of significant side effects. Three daily doses should be used initially, at least until the daily dosage is established. The next aim is to move to an optimal dose, which should be as low as possible, consistent with protection against relapse. During follow-up, an adjustment to lower dosages may be required to minimize adverse effects, and a change in the lithium preparation used and/or the frequency of dosing, either towards multiple doses or towards a single dose, may be necessary to handle absorption-related adverse effects or concern over possible renal toxicity. Intermittent lithium treatment in carefully selected patients has been recommended by some lithium experts, but should not be undertaken without careful planning and great caution. The cooperation of patients and relatives is required throughout.

Before deciding on the institution of long-term treatment, it is essential to establish that the patient has clearly responded to a course of stabilizing lithium therapy and that the risk of such therapy is acceptable. Maintaining a patient with a lithium non-responsive condition on long-term therapy poses an unacceptable risk. A decision with regards to long-term therapy can be made during a time-limited trial of lithium therapy with frequent reassessment of outcome. The following are among the factors to be reassessed before a decision is made: careful reconfirmation of the diagnosis of primary affective disorder, the health status of the patient, the side effects of lithium therapy experienced by the patient, and the response to treatment. Assessment of response to treatment is based strictly on firm evidence of relapse prevention during a reasonable trial period, but can be assisted by consideration of the predictors of response outlined above. Great pains should be taken to exclude false responders and false non-responders. It should also be borne in mind that non-responders are more susceptible to the adverse effects of lithium.

Acute mania: The therapeutic dose of lithium for the treatment of acute mania should be based primarily on the patient's clinical condition. It must be individualized for each patient according to blood levels and clinical response. Manic patients usually require serum lithium levels in excess of 1 mmol/L, and the dosage should be adjusted to obtain serum levels between 1 and 1.5 mmol/L (in blood samples drawn before the patient has had his/her first lithium dose of the day).

In properly screened adult patients, the suggested initial daily dosage for acute mania is 1 800 mg (approximately 50 mmol), divided into 3 doses. In view of the large variability of renal lithium excretion between individuals, it is suggested that lithium treatment be started at a dose between 600 and 900 mg/day, reaching a level of 1 200 to 1 800 mg in divided doses on the second day. Depending on the patient's clinical condition, the initial dosage should be adjusted to produce the desired serum lithium level. The weight of the patient should also influence the choice of the initial dose.

Lithium should be used cautiously and in reduced doses in the elderly patient, usually in the range of 600 to 1 200 mg/day. Serum lithium levels should be monitored frequently and kept below 1.5 mmol/L.

Long-term Control: After the acute manic episode subsides, usually within a week, the dosage of lithium should be rapidly reduced to achieve serum levels between 0.6 and 1.2 mmol/L (with the level kept below 1.5 mmol/L), since there is evidence at this time of a decreased tolerance to lithium. The average suggested dosage at this stage is 900 mg/day (approximately 25 mmol), divided into 3 doses, with a range usually between 600 and 1 200 mg/day. If a satisfactory response is not obtained in 14 days, lithium therapy should be discontinued. When the manic attack is controlled, lithium administration should be maintained during the expected duration of the manic phase, since early withdrawal might lead to relapse. It is essential to maintain clinical supervision of the patient and monitor lithium levels as required during treatment (see Warnings and Precautions).

Lithium may be used concomitantly with neuroleptic drugs, (see Warnings and Precautions, Drug Interactions).

Serum lithium levels in uncomplicated cases receiving maintenance therapy during remission should be monitored at least every 2 months.

Patients abnormally sensitive to lithium may exhibit toxic signs at serum levels of 1 to 1.4 mmol/L. Elderly patients often respond to reduced dosage and may exhibit signs of toxicity at serum levels ordinarily tolerated by other patients. Note: Blood samples for serum lithium determinations should be drawn immediately prior to the next dose when lithium concentrations are relatively stable (i.e., 8 to 12 hours after the previous dose). Total reliance must be placed on serum levels alone. Accurate patient evaluation requires both clinical and laboratory analysis.

Supplied: 150 mg: Each ivory #3, hard gelatin capsule contains: lithium carbonate 150 mg; capsule shell: also contains gelatin, silicon dioxide, sodium lauryl sulfate, titanium dioxide and dyes FD&C Yellow #6 and D&C Yellow #10. Tartrazine-free. Opaque plastic bottles of 100 and 1 000.

300 mg: Each green and ivory #1, hard gelatin capsule contains: lithium carbonate 300 mg; capsule shell: also contains gelatin, silicon dioxide, sodium lauryl sulfate, titanium dioxide and dyes FD&C Yellow #6, D&C Yellow #10 and FD&C Green #3. Tartrazine-free. Opaque plastic bottles of 1 000.

Store at 15 to 30°C.

(Shown in Product Recognition Section)

LITHIUM ℞

General Monograph, CPhA

Antimanic Agent

This monograph has been compiled by CPhA. It may contain information different from that approved by Therapeutic Products Programme, Health Canada, and the pharmaceutical manufacturers' approval has not been requested.

Pharmacology: Lithium is a monovalent cation which competes at cellular sites with other cations in the body. Cations are involved in the synthesis, storage, release and reuptake of neurotransmitters. The pathogenesis of mania appears to be affected by neurotransmitters such as dopamine and norepinephrine. Lithium alters sodium transport in nerve and muscle cells and may reduce concentrations of catecholamine neurotransmitters and inhibit the intracellular formation of cyclic AMP. However, the specific biochemical mechanism of lithium action in the control of mania is unknown.

Unlike other antimanic agents, lithium does not possess general sedative properties.

Lithium may alter renal function and cause a mild nephrogenic diabetes insipidus which presents as polyuria. Sodium and potassium excretion are increased and renal concentrating ability and water reabsorption are decreased. Polyuria may persist in some patients even when the drug is discontinued (see Warnings).

ECG changes with lithium have been reported.

Lithium is available as lithium carbonate in several regular and extended release oral dosage forms and as lithium citrate in oral syrup form.

Pharmacokinetics: Lithium is well absorbed from the gastrointestinal tract with peak plasma concentrations occurring between 1 and 3 hours after administration. Peak plasma concentrations following administration of extended release preparations are not reached for 4 to 12 hours. Lithium does not undergo biotransformation in the liver. Steady-state concentrations are reached in 4 days with the onset of antimanic effect usually occurring within 5 to 7 days. Full therapeutic effects may not be achieved for 10 to 21 days following initiation of therapy.

Lithium is widely distributed into most body tissues. It crosses the blood-brain barrier. CSF lithium concentrations are approximately half of plasma concentrations. Lithium does not bind to plasma proteins. Elimination half-life is 24 hours and is increased to 36 hours in geriatric patients and to between 40 and 50 hours in patients with impaired renal function.

Lithium is excreted primarily in the urine with less than 1% of the drug being eliminated in the feces. Small amounts are also excreted in sweat. Lithium is filtered by the glomeruli with 80% being reabsorbed in the tubules. In patients with normal renal function, 50 to 80% of a single dose is excreted in the urine within 24 hours. Renal lithium excretion does vary between individuals and dosage must be individually adjusted. Renal clearance is decreased in geriatric patients and increased in younger patients and during pregnancy. Sodium loading or depletion does affect renal clearance of the drug. A low salt intake resulting in low tubular concentration of sodium increases lithium reabsorption and may result in retention or intoxication. Polyuria does not increase renal clearance of the drug. Lithium is removed by hemodialysis.

Routine serum drug concentration monitoring is necessary (see Warnings, Precautions and Dosage). It has been suggested that manic patients retain larger amounts of lithium during the active manic phase, but recent studies have been unable to confirm a clear difference in excretion patterns. However, patients in a manic state may have an increased tolerance to lithium.

Indications: In the treatment of acute manic and hypomanic episodes in patients with bipolar disorder. Maintenance therapy has been found useful in preventing or diminishing the frequency of subsequent manic episodes in patients with bipolar disorder (with a strong history of mania).

Contraindications: Patients with significant renal or cardiovascular disease, severe debilitation or dehydration or sodium depletion and patients receiving diuretics. The risk of lithium toxicity is increased in such patients. If the psychiatric indication is life-threatening and if such a patient fails to respond to other measures, lithium treatment may be undertaken at low doses with extreme caution, including dosage adjustments based on daily serum lithium determinations. In such instances, hospitalization is necessary.

Warnings: Lithium toxicity is closely related to serum lithium levels and can occur at levels close to the therapeutic range. Facilities for prompt and accurate serum lithium determinations should be available before initiating therapy.

The ability to tolerate lithium is greater during the acute manic phase and decreases when manic symptoms subside (see Dosage).

Impaired Renal Function: Chronic lithium therapy is frequently associated with a decrease in renal concentrating capacity with development of thirst, polyuria, mycturia, weight gain and altered kidney function tests and occasionally presents as nephrogenic diabetes insipidus. Such patients should be carefully managed to avoid dehydration with resulting lithium retention and toxicity. Impaired renal function during chronic therapy may be only partially reversible when lithium is discontinued.

Prevention of renal toxicity and other toxic effects of long-term therapy requires a firm diagnosis of bipolar manic depressive illness, careful screening for pre-existing renal and other diseases, establishment of standardized 12 hour serum lithium levels which are as low as possible yet clinically effective, maintaining control of treatment by monitoring serum lithium levels and exercising clinical and laboratory surveillance over possible side effects or signs of lithium intoxication, exercising maximum control of at-risk patients, insuring that long-term lithium therapy is maintained only when clinical response has been clearly established, and adjusting the dosage schedule and formulation used in order to temporarily obtain periods of low lithium concentrations in the kidney.

Glomerular sclerosis and interstitial fibrosis as well as tubular lesions have been reported in patients on chronic lithium therapy.

During lithium therapy, progressive or sudden changes in renal function, even within the normal range, indicate the need for re-evaluation of treatment including dosage and frequency of lithium administration and a reassessment of the risk-benefit ratio of long-term lithium therapy.

Pregnancy: Administration of lithium during pregnancy may result in an increased incidence of cardiac and other anomalies, especially Ebstein's anomaly. Nephrogenic diabetes insipidus, euthyroid goiter and hypoglycemia have also occurred in women treated with lithium during pregnancy. Lithium should not be used during pregnancy or in women of childbearing potential unless it cannot be substituted by other appropriate therapy and if the expected benefits outweigh the possible hazards to the child.

If lithium is used during pregnancy, serum lithium concentrations should be carefully monitored and the dosage adjusted if necessary since renal clearance and distribution of the drug into erythrocytes may be increased during pregnancy. Pregnant women receiving lithium may have subtherapeutic serum lithium concentrations if the dosage is not increased during pregnancy. Immediately postpartum, renal clearance of lithium may decrease to pre-pregnancy levels. To decrease the risk of postpartum lithium intoxication, dosage of the drug should be reduced 1 week prior to parturition or when labor begins.

Lactation: Lithium is excreted into breast milk. Mothers receiving lithium should not breast-feed their infants.

Children: Information regarding the safety and efficacy of lithium in children under 12 years of age is not available. The use of lithium in children is not recommended.

Precautions: Maintain patients on lithium therapy under careful clinical and laboratory control throughout treatment. If serious adverse reactions and lithium intoxication are to be avoided, serum lithium concentrations during treatment should not exceed 1.5 mmol/L (see Geriatrics). This lithium concentration refers to a blood sample drawn before the patient has taken the first lithium dose of the day, therefore, 9 to 12 hours after the last dose administered. Serum lithium concentrations should usually be monitored 3 times weekly and blood studies and urinalysis weekly during the initial period of administration and as required thereafter. If lithium levels exceed 1.5 to 2 mmol/L, discontinue the drug and, if appropriate, resume administration at a lower dose after 24 hours.

Changes in sodium intake may significantly alter the renal elimination of lithium. Decreasing sodium intake may lead to decreased clearance of lithium and vice versa. Patients should be advised to maintain adequate sodium and fluid intake and to avoid substantial changes in either. They should also be cautioned to avoid dehydration and to report prolonged vomiting, diarrhea or fever to their physician.

Prodromal toxic signs such as fatigue, muscular weakness, incoordination, drowsiness, coarse tremors, diarrhea and vomiting provide a sensitive warning of lithium intoxication. The patient and his family should be warned to notify the physician immediately if any such adverse reactions should occur. The appearance of signs of toxicity or a rise in the blood concentration of lithium after the dosage is stabilized should alert the physician to determine the reasons for lithium accumulation.

There is evidence of decreased tolerance to lithium once the acute manic episode breaks. Therefore, when the acute attack subsides, the dosage should be reduced rapidly in order to produce serum lithium concentrations no higher than between 0.6 and 1.0 mmol/L.

In view of the limited dosage range of lithium compared to other psychotropic agents, particular care is required for the patient to receive exactly the prescribed number of lithium tablets or capsules.

Extended-release lithium carbonate tablets should be swallowed whole or broken in half. They should not be chewed or crushed. See product monograph.

There have been reports of withdrawal symptoms following lithium discontinuation. Thus, gradual discontinuation is recommended unless abrupt withdrawal is necessary because of toxicity.

Periodic review and monitoring of kidney and cardiovascular function is advisable during therapy with lithium. Patients with underlying cardiovascular disease should be observed carefully for signs of arrhythmias. Perform other laboratory tests as indicated by the patient's clinical condition.

Since the formation of nontoxic goiters has been reported during lithium therapy, examine the thyroid gland before treatment and perform appropriate thyroid function tests. Nontoxic goiters reported during prolonged lithium therapy have disappeared following discontinuation of the medication. Treatment with small doses of thyroxine in patients who develop a diffuse nontoxic goiter may stop further growth or lead to shrinkage of the gland.

Geriatrics: Elderly patients appear to be more susceptible to adverse effects and may experience a higher incidence of neurotoxicity at lithium concentrations considered therapeutic for younger adults. Certain groups of elderly patients are particularly vulnerable, including those with neurological disease, cardiovascular disorders, renal impairment and those over 80 years of age. Reports suggest that lithium serum concentrations should be in the therapeutic range of 0.4 to 0.8 mmol/L or lower and not in excess of 1 mmol/L.

Occupational Hazards: Lithium may cause dizziness or decreased mental alertness. Patients should be appropriately cautioned regarding the operation of motor vehicles or hazardous machinery.

Drug Interactions: ACE Inhibitors: Concomitant administration of lithium and ACE inhibitors may increase the risk of lithium toxicity. Frequently monitor lithium levels during concurrent therapy.

Anticonvulsants: Concurrent use of lithium and carbamazepine or phenytoin might result in an increased risk of CNS toxicity.

Calcium Channel Blockers: Concomitant administration of lithium and calcium channel blockers may increase the risk of neurotoxicity.

Diuretics: Patients stabilized on lithium therapy who receive a thiazide diuretic may require a reduction of lithium dosage to avoid accumulation and toxicity, since there is often a 20 to 40% reduction of renal lithium clearance. Furosemide appears to be less likely to affect lithium clearance.

Fluoxetine: Concomitant administration of lithium and fluoxetine may increase the risk of lithium toxicity or serotonin syndrome.

Haloperidol: An encephalopathy resembling the malignant neuroleptic syndrome (characterized by weakness, lethargy, fever, tremulousness and confusion, extrapyramidal symptoms, leukocytosis, elevated serum enzymes, BUN and fasting blood sugar) followed by irreversible brain damage has occurred in a few patients treated with both lithium and haloperidol. A causal relationship between these events and concomitant administration of lithium and haloperidol has not been clearly established; however, patients receiving such combined therapy should be monitored closely for early evidence of neurological toxicity such as rigidity and/or hyperpyrexia and treatment discontinued promptly if such signs appear.

Iodides: Concomitant administration of lithium and iodides may increase the hypothyroid effects of either of these medications.

Methyldopa: Concomitant administration of lithium and methyldopa may increase the risk of lithium toxicity.

Metronidazole: Concomitant administration of lithium and metronidazole may cause renal retention of lithium, leading to lithium toxicity. If possible, lithium should be discontinued during therapy with metronidazole.

Neuromuscular Blockers: The action of neuromuscular blockers may be prolonged in patients receiving lithium. A temporary omission of a few doses of lithium can reduce the risks of this interaction.

NSAIDs: Indomethacin, mefanemic acid, phenylbutazone, piroxicam and ibuprofen have been reported to increase steady-state plasma lithium levels by 30 to 60%. There is evidence that other NSAIDs may have a similar effect. When such combinations are used, increased frequency of monitoring plasma lithium levels is recommended.

Phenothiazines: Both pharmacokinetic interactions and clinical toxicity with the combined use of these agents have been described. Lithium-induced reductions in plasma chlorpromazine levels, phenothiazine-induced increases in red blood cell uptake of lithium and chlorpromazine-induced increases in renal lithium excretion have been reported. Clinically, occasional cases of neurotoxicity have been reported and may be more likely to occur with thioridazine than other phenothiazines, when combined with lithium. The clinician should be alert for altered response to either drug when used in combination and when either drug is withdrawn.

Sodium Bicarbonate: Concomitant administration of lithium and sodium bicarbonate may enhance lithium excretion. A higher dose of lithium may be required in these patients.

Tetracycline: Concomitant administration of lithium and tetracycline may increase the risk of lithium toxicity.

Theophylline: The administration of aminophylline or theophylline to patients on lithium may require increased lithium doses to maintain the psychotropic effects of the drug.

Adverse Effects: Mild adverse effects may be encountered even when serum lithium values remain below 1 mmol/L. The most frequent adverse effects are the initial postabsorptive symptoms, believed to be associated with a rapid rise in serum lithium concentrations. They include, gastrointestinal discomfort, nausea, vertigo, muscle weakness and a dazed feeling and frequently disappear after stabilization of therapy. The more common and persistent adverse reactions are: fine tremor of the hands, and, at times, fatigue, thirst, polyuria and nephrogenic diabetes insipidus. These do not necessarily require reduction of dosage.

Mild to moderate toxic reactions may occur at lithium concentrations from 1.5 to 2 mmol/L, and moderate to severe reactions at concentrations above 2 mmol/L (see Precautions, Geriatrics).

A number of patients may experience lithium accumulation during initial therapy, increasing to toxic concentrations and requiring immediate discontinuation of the drug. Some elderly patients with lower renal clearances for lithium may also experience different degrees of lithium toxicity, requiring reduction or temporary withdrawal of medication. However, in patients with normal renal clearance the toxic manifestations appear to occur in a fairly predictable sequence related to serum lithium concentrations. The usually transient gastrointestinal symptoms are the earliest side effects to occur. A mild degree of fine tremor of the hands may persist throughout therapy. Thirst and polyuria may be followed by increased drowsiness, ataxia, tinnitus and blurred vision, indicating early intoxication. As intoxication progresses the following manifestations may be encountered: confusion, increasing disorientation, muscle twitchings, hyperreflexia, nystagmus, seizures, diarrhea, vomiting, and eventually coma and death.

The following adverse effects have been reported and appear to be related to serum lithium concentrations:

Autonomic Nervous System: blurred vision, dry mouth.

Cardiovascular: arrhythmia, hypotension, ECG changes consisting of flattening or inversion of T waves, peripheral circulatory failure, cardiac collapse.

CNS: anesthesia of the skin, slurred speech, blurring of vision, blackout spells, headache, seizures, cranial nerve involvement, psychomotor retardation, somnolence, toxic confusional states, restlessness, stupor, coma, acute dystonia. EEG changes recorded consisted of diffuse slowing, widening of the frequency spectrum, potentiation and disorganization of background rhythm. Sensitivity to hyperventilation and paroxysmal bilateral synchronous delta activity have also been described.

Dermatologic: dryness and thinning of the hair, leg ulcers, skin rash, pruritus and exacerbation of psoriasis.

Gastrointestinal: anorexia, nausea, vomiting, diarrhea.

Genitourinary: diabetes insipidus (see Warnings), albuminuria, oliguria, polyuria, glycosuria.

Hematologic: anemia, leukopenia, leukocytosis.

Hypersensitivity: allergic vasculitis.

Metabolic: transient hyperglycemia, slight elevation of plasma magnesium, goiter.

Neurologic: general muscle weakness, ataxia, tremor, muscle hyperirritability, (fasciculation, twitchings, especially of facial muscles and clonic movements of the limbs), choreoathetotic movement, hyperactive deep tendon reflexes.

Thyroid Abnormalities: euthyroid goiter and/or hypothyroidism (including myxedema) accompanied by lower T_3 and T_4 levels and elevated TSH. Iodine^{131} uptake may be elevated. On average, 5 to 15% of patients on long-term lithium therapy manifest clinical signs or have altered serum hormone levels (see Precautions). Paradoxically, rare cases of hyperthyroidism have been reported.

Miscellaneous: general fatigue, dehydration, weight loss, tendency to sleep, lethargy, transient scotomata, metallic taste, peripheral edema.

Hypercalcemia, associated with lithium-induced hyperparathyroidism, has also been reported.

Overdose: Symptoms: Lithium toxicity is closely related to the concentration of lithium in the blood and is usually associated with serum concentrations in excess of 2 mmol/L. Early signs of toxicity which may occur at lower serum concentrations (see Adverse Effects) usually respond to a reduction in dosage. Lithium intoxication has been preceded by the appearance or aggravation of the following symptoms: sluggishness, drowsiness, lethargy, coarse hand tremor or muscle twitchings, loss of appetite, vomiting, and diarrhea. Occurrence of these symptoms requires immediate cessation of medication and careful clinical reassessment and management.

Treatment: Early symptoms of lithium toxicity can usually be treated by reduction or cessation of dosage of the drug and resumption of treatment at a lower dose after 24 to 48 hours. In severe lithium poisoning, induce emesis with ipecac syrup. In patients who are comatose or experiencing seizures initiate gastric lavage. Emesis is most effective if started within 30 minutes of ingestion. Activated charcoal does not absorb lithium but may be of value if multiple drug ingestion is suspected. Measure serum lithium levels every 3 hours until the serum lithium level is below 1 mmol/L. Toxicity is related to drug serum concentration and duration of exposure. Maintain fluid and electrolyte balance. Maintain urine output

Lithium (cont'd)

and sodium excretion by administering i.v. sodium chloride. Administration of large amounts of sodium in the absence of sodium depletion has not been shown to be successful in speeding lithium excretion. Lithium excretion may be increased by the use of i.v. sodium bicarbonate, mannitol or acetazolamide. Treat arrhythmias with standard drugs for type of arrhythmia observed. Treat hypotension with i.v. fluids and by placing the patient in the Trendelenburg position. If unresponsive, dopamine or norepinephrine may be required. Hypertension does not usually require pharmacologic intervention. Infection prophylaxis, regular chest x-ray and preservation of adequate respiration are also necessary.

Hemodialysis is the treatment of choice when the above measures fail to improve the patients clinical condition, reduce the serum lithium level or the serum lithium level is >3.5 mmol/L. Hemodialysis is more effective than peritoneal dialysis, but peritoneal dialysis is somewhat effective and can be used if hemodialysis is not available.

Dosage: The results of lithium therapy depend largely on the nature and course of the illness itself, rather than on the symptoms. The selection of patients for long-term treatment requires a clearcut diagnosis of primary affective disorder.

Patients likely to have a good response to lithium therapy typically have had fewer than 2 episodes per year. During acute epidoses, these patients experience symptoms which meet the DSM-IV criteria for primary affective disorder; they also experience remissions which are free of significant symptomatology.

Screening of patients should include a medical history and physical examination with emphasis on the CNS, urinary, cardiovascular, gastrointestinal and endocrine systems as well as the skin. It should also include: routine 24-hour urine volume, serum creatinine, record of weight and ECG. Electrolytes and TSH should also be measured and for long-term treatment, a creatinine clearance and a urine concentration test should also be performed.

Once therapy is initiated monitoring of the patient should include: mental status, physical examination, weight, 12-hour serum lithium and a check for lithium side effects and compliance. It should also include serum creatinine every 2 months, plasma thyroid hormone and TSH every 6 to 12 months, particularly in female patients.

Serum lithium levels should be maintained within the therapeutic range, as high as necessary for efficacy and with the patient free of significant adverse effects. Three daily doses should be used initially, at least until the daily dosage is established. Adjustments in dosage may be required to minimize adverse effects and a change in the lithium preparation used and/or the frequency of dosing, either towards multiple doses or towards a single dose, may be necessary to handle absorption-related adverse effects or concern over possible renal toxicity.

Before starting long-term therapy, it is essential to establish that the patient has clearly responded to a course of stabilizing therapy and that the risk of such therapy is acceptable. Reassess the following: the diagnosis of primary affective disorder; the health status of the patient; the side effects of lithium therapy experienced by the patient and the response to treatment.

Maintaining a patient with a lithium nonresponsive condition on long-term therapy poses an unacceptable risk. These patients are more susceptible to the adverse effects of lithium.

The therapeutic dose for the treatment of acute mania should be based primarily on the patient's clinical condition. It must be individualized for each patient according to blood concentrations and clinical response. For manic patients, the dosage should be adjusted to obtain serum concentrations between 0.8 and 1.2 mmol/L (in blood samples drawn before the patient has taken the first lithium dose of the day).

In properly screened adult patients, the suggested initial daily dosage for acute mania is 900 to 1 800 mg (15 to 20 mg/kg), divided into 3 doses. In view of the large variability of renal lithium excretion between individuals, it is suggested that lithium treatment be started at a dose between 600 and 900 mg/day, reaching a level of 1 200 to 1 800 mg in divided doses on the second day. Depending on the patient's clinical condition, the initial dosage should be adjusted to produce the desired serum lithium concentration. The weight of the patient should also influence the choice of the initial dose.

After the acute manic episode subsides, usually within a week, the dosage should be rapidly reduced to achieve serum concentrations between 0.6 and 1.0 mmol/L (with the concentration kept below 1.5 mmol/L), since there is evidence at this time of a decreased tolerance to lithium. The average suggested dosage at this stage is 900 mg/day, divided into 3 doses, with a range usually between 450 and 1 200 mg/day. If a satisfactory response is not obtained in 14 days, discontinue lithium therapy. When the manic attack is controlled, maintain lithium administration during the expected duration of the manic phase, since early withdrawal might lead to relapse.

Once patients are stabilized on a maintenance dose with a multiple dosing schedule and once stable therapeutic blood levels are reached, the dosage schedule may be changed to a once daily regimen. The total daily dose, when administered as a single dose, may be approximately 5 to 30% lower than when given in divided doses over the day. It is essential to maintain clinical supervision of the patient and to monitor serum lithium levels both when using the divided daily dosage regimen and when transferring to the once daily administration dosage regimen (see Precautions).

In uncomplicated cases receiving maintenance therapy during remission, serum lithium levels should be monitored at least every 2 months. Blood samples for serum lithium determination should be drawn immediately prior to the next dose. Total reliance must not be placed on serum levels. Adequate patient evaluation requires both clinical assessment and laboratory analysis.

Elderly and debilitated patients, and those with significant renal impairment should be prescribed lithium with particular caution (see Precautions, Geriatrics). Starting dose should not exceed 300 mg/day accompanied by frequent serum level monitoring. Serum concentrations of 0.4 to 0.6 mmol/L are usually effective in elderly patients and should not exceed 1 mmol/L.

Children: Lithium is not recommended for routine use in children under 12 years of age.

Reviewed 1999

LIVOSTIN™ EYE DROPS ℞

CIBA Vision

Levocabastine HCl

Histamine H_1-antagonist

Pharmacology: Levocabastine is a potent, fast-acting and highly selective histamine H_1-antagonist with a sustained duration of action.

Within 10 to 15 minutes of topical application to the eyes, levocabastine inhibits: itching, redness and chemosis induced by conjunctival provocation with histamine; itching, redness, chemosis, eyelid swelling, and tearing induced by conjunctival provocation with allergens; and itching and redness induced by conjunctival provocation with compound 48/80.

Orally-administered levocabastine provides a dose dependent inhibition of skin reactions to intradermal histamine. After topical application to the eyes levocabastine did not produce clinically significant systemic antihistamine effects in patients.

Levocabastine eye drops (2 drops/eye 3 times daily), under acute and steady state conditions, are devoid of CNS effects, as evaluated by objective and subjective psychoperformance tests and measures of general CNS activity.

Following topical application to the eyes, the absorption of levocabastine was incomplete and the absolute bioavailability of levocabastine instilled in the eyes could be estimated at approximately 30% in patients with allergic conjunctivitis and up to 60% in healthy volunteers.

Indications: The symptomatic management of seasonal allergic conjunctivitis.

Contraindications: In patients with hypersensitivity to any of the ingredients.

Warnings: Children: Levocabastine is not recommended for use in children under the age of 12 years except on the advice of a physician. Clinical experience in children under 5 years of age is limited with ocular levocabastine.

Precautions: As with all ophthalmic preparations containing benzalkonium chloride, patients are advised not to wear soft (hydrophilic) contact lenses while under treatment with levocabastine eye drops.

Pregnancy and *Lactation:* There are no clinical trials on the use of levocabastine eye drops in pregnant or nursing women; therefore, levocabastine eye drops should not be used during pregnancy, except if the potential benefit justifies the potential risk to the fetus.

Geriatrics: The safety and efficacy of topical levocabastine have not been established in patients greater than 65 years of age.

Adverse Effects: The most frequent side effect encountered with levocabastine eye drops is eye irritation. Most side effects are transient and rarely necessitate discontinuation of therapy. See Table I.

Table I—Livostin Eye Drops

Incidence of the most frequent* adverse experiences in patients treated with Livostin eye drops or placebo eye drops

Organ System	Incidence (%) Livostin Eye Drops (n=599)	Placebo Eye Drops (n=215)
Ocular	**19.9**	**18.6**
Eye irritation	16.4	15.8
Dry conjunctiva	<1.0	0.0
The others (blurred vision, eye discharge, eyelid edema, eye pain and abnormal lacrimation) were <1.0% for both the Livostin and placebo group.		
CNS	**6.0**	**9.3**
Headache	3.5	4.2
Somnolence	2.0	5.1
Insomnia	<1.0	0.0
Respiratory System	**4.2**	**5.1**
Coughing	1.0	1.4
Epistaxis	1.0	<1.0
Nasal congestion	<1.0	0.0
Rhinorrhea	<1.0	1.4
The others (nasal irritation, itchy throat, pharyngitis and dyspnea) were <1.0% for both the Livostin and placebo groups.		
Other		
Tiredness	2.0	1.4
Dry mouth	1.0	4.2
Fever	<1.0	0.0
Rash	<1.0	0.0
Generalized pruritus	<1.0	<1.0
Pruritus	<1.0	0.0
Nausea	<1.0	0.0

*Reported more than once in the Livostin group.

Overdose: Symptoms and Treatment: There has been no experience with overdosage of levocabastine eye drops. Treatment should include general supportive measures.

Dosage: Adults and children (12 to 65 years old): 1 drop (15 μg/drop) instilled in each eye, 2 times daily. The dose may be increased to 1 drop 3 to 4 times daily.

It is not useful to continue the treatment for more than 3 days if no improvement is seen. There are no clinical studies to support continuous treatment durations of greater than 16 weeks.

As levocabastine eye drops are available as a microsuspension, the bottle should be shaken before each application. Levocabastine eye drops should be used within 1 month of the first opening of the bottle. Patients should be instructed to take appropriate measures to avoid contamination.

Supplied: Each mL of white sterile ophthalmic microsuspension contains: levocabastine HCl equivalent to levocabastine 0.5 mg. Nonmedicinal ingredients: benzalkonium chloride 0.15 mg as preservative, disodium edetate, disodium phosphate, hypromellose, monosodium phosphate, polysorbate 80, propylene glycol and water. pH 6 to 8. Plastic bottles of 10 mL containing 5 mL of microsuspension. Store between 15 and 30°C.

LIVOSTIN® NASAL SPRAY ℞

Janssen-Ortho

Levocabastine HCl

Histamine H_1-antagonist

Pharmacology: Levocabastine is a potent, fast-acting and highly selective histamine H_1-antagonist with a sustained duration of action.

Within 10 minutes of topical application to the nose, levocabastine inhibits sneezing, itchy nose and rhinorrhea induced by nasal provocation with allergens.

Orally-administered levocabastine provides a dose dependent inhibition of skin reactions to intradermal histamine. After repeated topical application to the nose, topical and systemic antihistamine effects contribute to overall clinical outcome. Although systemic effects may contribute to the therapeutic effects of levocabastine nasal spray, this is not accompanied by any sedative effects.

Levocabastine nasal spray (2 sprays/nostril 3 times daily), under acute and steady state conditions, is devoid of CNS effects, as evaluated by objective and subjective psychoperformance tests and measures of general CNS activity.

Following topical application to the nose, the absorption of levocabastine was incomplete and the absolute bioavailability of levocabastine administered in the nose could be estimated at 60 to 80% in healthy volunteers and in patients with allergic rhinitis.

Indications: The symptomatic treatment of allergic rhinitis (sneezing, itchy nose, runny nose).

Contraindications: In patients with hypersensitivity to any of the ingredients.

Warnings: *Pregnancy* and *Lactation:* There are no clinical trials on the use of levocabastine nasal spray in pregnant or nursing women, therefore, levocabastine nasal spray should not be used during pregnancy, except if the potential benefit justifies the potential risk to the fetus.

Children: Levocabastine nasal spray is not recommended for use in children under the age of 12 years except on the advice of a physician. Clinical experience with nasal levocabastine is absent in children under 5 years of age.

Occupational Hazards: Effects on Driving Ability and Use of Machinery: Levocabastine will generally not cause clinically relevant sedation nor does it impair psychomotor performance as compared with placebo. Levocabastine nasal spray, therefore, would not be expected to interfere with the ability to drive a car or operate machinery. Should drowsiness occur, caution is advised.

Precautions: Since levocabastine is excreted renally, caution should be exercised when administering levocabastine nasal spray to patients with renal impairment.

Geriatrics: The safety and efficacy of topical levocabastine has not been established in patients greater than 65 years of age.

Drug Interactions: Interaction with alcohol or any other drug was never reported in clinical trials. In specially designed studies, there was no evidence of potentiation of alcohol or diazepam by levocabastine nasal spray used in normal dosages.

Adverse Effects: The most frequent side effect encountered with levocabastine nasal spray is nasal irritation. In post-marketing experience, allergic reactions have rarely been reported. Most side effects are transient and rarely necessitate discontinuation of therapy. See Table I.

Table I—Livostin Nasal Spray

Incidence of the Most Frequent[a] Adverse Experiences in Patients Treated With Livostin or Placebo Nasal Spray

Organ System	Incidence (%) Livostin Nasal Spray (n=702)	Placebo Nasal Spray (n=427)
Respiratory System	**10.4**	**9.6**
nasal irritation	5.4	5.6
epistaxis	1.0	<1.0
Coughing, throat irritation, respiratory disorder, aggravated nasal obstruction and nasal pruritus were <1.0% in the Livostin group and not reported in the placebo group. The others (dry nose, rhinorrhea, dyspnea, itchy throat) were <1.0% for both the Livostin and placebo groups.		
CNS	**7.7**	**7.0**
somnolence	3.8	3.5
headache	3.1	3.0
dizziness	<1.0	<1.0
Ocular	**3.0**	**2.1**
eye irritation[b]	2.6	1.9
Other		
dry mouth	3.3	2.6
tiredness	1.4	<1.0
Facial edema, rash, decreased hearing, pruritus of external ear and taste perversion were <1.0% in the Livostin group and not reported in the placebo group. The others (abdominal pain, increased appetite, nausea and increased weight) were <1.0% for both the Livostin and placebo groups.		

[a]Reported more than once in the Livostin group.
[b]The eye irritation observed in the Livostin nasal spray group was mostly reported by the patients receiving both the Livostin nasal spray and eye drops.

Overdose: Symptoms and Treatment: There have not been any reports of overdosage of levocabastine nasal spray. Some sedation after accidental intake of the contents of the bottle cannot be excluded.

In the case of accidental ingestion, the patient should be advised to drink plenty of fluids in order to accelerate the renal elimination of levocabastine. Treatment should include general supportive measures.

Dosage: Adults and children (12 to 65 years old): 2 sprays (50 µg/spray)/nostril, 2 times daily. The dose may be increased to 2 sprays 3 to 4 times daily.

It is not useful to continue the treatment for more than 3 days if no improvement is seen. There are no clinical studies to support continuous treatment durations of greater than 10 weeks.

As levocabastine nasal spray is available as a microsuspension, the bottle should be shaken before each application. Patients should be instructed to clear the nasal passages prior to administering the spray and to inhale through the nose during spraying. Before using the pump delivery system for the first time, the pump reservoir should be filled up by priming until a fine spray is delivered.

Supplied: Each mL of white microsuspension contains: levocabastine HCl equivalent to levocabastine 0.5 mg. Nonmedicinal ingredients: benzalkonium chloride, disodium edetate, disodium phosphate, hypromellose, monosodium phosphate, polysorbate 80, propylene glycol and water. pH 6 to 8. Plastic bottles of 15 mL containing 15 mL of microsuspension. Store at room temperature (15 to 30°C).

(Shown in Product Recognition Section)

Reviewed 1999

LOCACORTEN® VIOFORM® Ⓟ

Novartis Pharmaceuticals

Flumethasone Pivalate—Clioquinol

Topical Corticosteroid—Antibacterial—Antifungal

Pharmacology: Flumethasone pivalate is a moderately potent difluorinated corticosteroid ester with anti-inflammatory, antipruritic and vasoconstrictive properties. As it is a privalate, its anti-inflammatory action is concentrated at the site of application. This local effect on diseased areas results in a prompt decrease in inflammation, exudation and itching.

Clioquinol, the antimicrobial component of Locacorten Vioform, is active against a broad spectrum of pathogenic microorganisms, including fungi (e.g. Candida, Microsporum, Trichophyton) and gram-positive bacteria (e.g. Staphylococci). Clioquinol has only a slight inhibitory effect on gram-negative bacteria. Clioquinol exerts a bacteriostatic, rather than a bactericidal action.

Locacorten Vioform combines the antifungal and antibacterial effects of clioquinol with the anti-inflammatory and antipruritic effects of flumethasone.

Indications: Initial treatment of corticosteroid-responsive inflammatory skin disorders complicated by bacterial and/or fungal infections, with appropriate systemic antibiotics if necessary, such as: seborrheic dermatitis, atopic dermatitis, localized neurodermatitis, contact dermatitis, intertrigo, superficial forms of pyoderma (e.g., impetigo) and of dermatomycosis in which acute inflammation is a prominent feature.

The cream has a slightly drying effect primarily useful for moist, weeping lesions and in intertriginous areas.

Contraindications: Viral infections of the skin (e.g., chickenpox, skin eruptions following vaccination, herpes simplex, herpes zoster), tuberculosis of the skin, syphilis, rosacea, acne vulgaris, and perioral dermatitis.

Known hypersensitivity to flumethasone pivalate or to corticosteroids in general, hydroxyquinolines, clioquinol, or other quinoline derivatives, iodine, as well as to any other components of Locacorten Vioform.

Application to ulcerated areas.

Application to the eye.

Children: Children under 2 years of age.

Warnings: *Pregnancy* and *Lactation:* The safety of Locacorten Vioform during pregnancy or lactation has not been established. Animal studies have shown that corticosteroids may induce fetal abnormalities in pregnant animals. The relevance of this finding to human use has not been elucidated. It is not known whether the active substance passes into the breast milk when applied topically. Therefore, the potential benefit of topical corticosteroids during pregnancy (particularly in the first 3 months), or lactation, should be weighed against possible hazard to the fetus or the nursing infant.

Precautions: Application to relatively large and/or eroded areas, treatment for longer than 1 week, as well as use under occlusive dressings may lead to a marked increase in protein-bound iodine (PBI) and should therefore be avoided.

Provided the preparation is used as recommended, unwanted systemic effects are unlikely to occur. On basic medical grounds, the possibility of a clinically important effect on adrenocortical function should nevertheless be borne in mind, particularly if the preparation is used under occlusion, over large areas of the body, in pediatrics and in patients undergoing prolonged therapy.

If no improvement occurs within 1 week, therapy should be discontinued; it is then advisable to identify and treat the causative pathogens.

Locacorten Vioform should not be used to treat bacterial or mycotic skin diseases in which acute inflammation is not present.

If in exceptional cases Locacorten Vioform is applied in large amounts, the patient should be kept under regular medical supervision.

Patients should, as a general rule, be advised to inform subsequent physicians of the prior use of corticosteroids.

Locacorten Vioform should not be allowed to come into contact with the conjunctiva.

Locacorten Vioform should not be used in the external auditory canal if the ear drum is perforated.

In patients suffering from hepatic and/or renal failure, caution is indicated.

Locacorten Vioform may turn yellow when exposed to air and may cause staining of the skin, nails, hair or fabrics.

Interactions: Topical use of clioquinol, as well as other iodine-containing compounds, may increase the amount of protein-bound iodine (PBI) in patients with normal thyroid function and therefore may interfere with some thyroid function tests (such as PBI, radioactive iodine and butanol-extractable iodine). These tests should not be performed within a period shorter than 1 month following the use of Locacorten Vioform. Other thyroid function tests, such as the T_3 resin sponge test or the T_4 determination, are unaffected by clioquinol.

The ferric chloride test for phenylketonuria may yield a false-positive result when clioquinol is present in the urine.

Adverse Effects: Occasionally: signs of irritation such as burning sensation, itching or skin rash at the site of application; hypersensitivity reactions.

Isolated cases: mild skin atrophy due to flumethasone.

If an exacerbation or an allergic type reaction occurs, treatment with Locacorten Vioform should be discontinued.

Local adverse reactions reported during topical treatment with glucocorticoids include contact allergy, changes in skin pigmentation, and secondary infections. Topically applied glucocorticoids may give rise to striae rubrae distensae, telangiectasia, purpura, skin atrophy or steroid acne, especially if applied for prolonged periods of time, under occlusive dressings, to large areas or to permeable areas (e.g., face, axillae).

Overdose: Symptoms and Treatment: Application to extensive or eroded areas of skin may lead to increased PBI values within 1 week. Elevated PBI values may also occur where relatively small areas of skin are treated for more than 1 week. If signs and symptoms resembling those of thyrotoxicosis occur, the preparation should be withdrawn at once.

Dosage: Should be applied to the affected areas in a thin layer 2 to 3 times daily.

Use of Locacorten Vioform under occlusive dressings is not recommended as the resulting humid conditions may promote secondary infection with nonsensitive organisms and also may increase the possibility of elevated PBI.

Information for the Patient: See Blue Section—Information for the Patient "Locacorten Vioform".

Supplied: Each tube of off-white water soluble cream contains: flumethasone pivalate 0.02% and clioquinol 3%. Nonmedicinal ingredients: cetyl alcohol, cetyl palmitate, glycerin, petrolatum, phenoxyethanol, sodium lauryl sulfate, stearyl alcohol and water. Tubes of 15 and 50 g. Protect from heat (store between 15 and 30°C) and freezing.

Reviewed 1999

LOCACORTEN® VIOFORM® Eardrops Ⓟ

Novartis Pharmaceuticals

Flumethasone Pivalate—Clioquinol

Topical Aural Corticosteroid—Antibacterial—Antifungal

Pharmacology: Flumethasone pivalate is a moderately potent difluorinated glucocorticoid with anti-inflammatory, antipruritic, and vasoconstrictive properties. As it is a pivalate, its action is concentrated at the site of application. This local

Locacorten Vioform Eardrops (cont'd)

effect on diseased areas results in a prompt decrease in inflammation, exudation and itching.

Clioquinol, the antimicrobial component of Locacorten Vioform Eardrops, is active against a broad spectrum of pathogenic micro-organisms, including fungi (e.g., Candida, Microsporum, Trichophyton) and gram-positive bacteria (e.g., Staphylococci). Clioquinol has only a slight inhibitory effect on gram-negative bacteria. Clioquinol exerts a bacteriostatic rather than a bactericidal action.

The polyethylene glycol vehicle is inert, non-irritant and viscous. This vehicle softens the cerumen and ensures prolonged contact of the active ingredients with the surface of the ear canal.

Indications: Otitis externa; otomycosis including that due to aspergillus niger.

Contraindications: Perforation of the eardrum (suspected or verified).

Viral (e.g., chicken pox) or syphilitic skin infections; tuberculosis of the skin; skin eruptions following vaccination.

Known hypersensitivity to flumethasone pivalate or to corticosteroids in general, to hydroxyquinolines, clioquinol, or other quinoline derivatives, iodine, as well as to any other components of Locacorten Vioform eardrops (see Supplied).

Application to the eye.

Children: Use is contraindicated in children under 2 years of age.

Warnings: *Pregnancy* and *Lactation:* Safety during pregnancy or lactation has not been established. Studies have shown that corticosteroids may induce fetal abnormalities in pregnant animals. The relevance of this finding to human use has not been elucidated. It is not known whether the active substances pass into breast milk when applied topically. Therefore, the potential benefit of this product during pregnancy (particularly during the first 3 months) or lactation, should be weighed against possible hazard to the fetus or the nursing infant.

Precautions: Prior to beginning therapy, the eardrum should be checked by the physician. Locacorten Vioform should not be used if there is a risk that perforation of the eardrum may occur or has occurred.

Topical use of clioquinol-containing preparations may lead to a marked increase in protein-bound iodine (PBI) (see Overdose: Symptoms and Treatment).

Provided the preparation is used as recommended unwanted systemic effects are unlikely to occur. On basic medical grounds, the possibility of a clinically important effect on adrenocortical function should nevertheless be borne in mind, particularly in pediatric use and in patients undergoing prolonged therapy.

If no improvement occurs within 1 week, therapy should be discontinued; the pathogens should then be identified and treated.

Patients should, as a general rule, be advised to inform subsequent physicians of the prior use of corticosteroids.

Locacorten Vioform eardrops should not be allowed to come into contact with the conjunctiva (see Contraindications).

Locacorten Vioform may turn yellow when exposed to air and may cause staining of the skin, nails, hair or fabrics.

Drug Interactions: Topical use of clioquinol, as well as other iodine-containing compounds, may increase the amount of protein-bound iodine (PBI) in patients with normal thyroid function and therefore may interfere with some thyroid function tests (such as PBI, radioactive iodine and butanol-extractable iodine). These tests should not be performed within 1 month of Locacorten Vioform eardrops use. Other thyroid function tests, such as the T_3 resin sponge test or the T_4 determination, are unaffected by clioquinol.

The ferric chloride test for phenylketonuria may yield a false-positive result when clioquinol is present in the urine.

Adverse Effects: Occasionally: signs of irritation such as burning sensation, itching or skin rash at the site of application; hypersensitivity reactions.

If an exacerbation or allergic type reaction occurs, treatment with Locacorten Vioform eardrops should be discontinued.

Overdose: Symptoms and Treatment: Poisoning due to accidental ingestion is not expected since a bottle of Locacorten Vioform eardrops contains far less active ingredients than the upper safe limit of a single oral dose for either component.

Application of clioquinol-containing preparations to extensive or eroded areas of skin may lead to increased PBI values within 1 week. Elevated PBI values may also occur where relatively small areas of skin are treated for more than 1 week. If signs and symptoms resembling those of thyrotoxicosis occur, the preparation should be withdrawn at once.

Dosage: Thorough cleansing of the external ear is essential for successful treatment. If a copious and offensive discharge is present, the meatus may initially require gentle syringing. Thereafter the passage may be kept clean by wiping as necessary.

Two to 3 drops should be instilled twice daily.

The solution may be warmed to body temperature prior to application by holding the bottle in the hands. Heating above body temperature should be avoided.

To ensure correct administration of the drug, the patient or another person should be instructed both on how to clean the outer ear and apply the ear drops. The patient should be either sitting or lying down with the treated ear turned upwards during application. This position should be maintained for 1 to 2 minutes following the application.

Free drainage of the ear encourages healing; however, in severe cases it may be desirable to pack the ear lightly with a gauze strip moistened with the solution, replacing this dressing as necessary, at least once every 24 hours.

To avoid contamination of the ear drops, contact of the dropper with any surface (including the ear) should be avoided.

Treatment should normally not exceed 10 days.

Information for the Patient: See Blue Section—Information for the Patient "Locacorten Vioform".

Supplied: Each dispenser of clear solution contains: flumethasone pivalate 0.02% and clioquinol 1%. Nonmedicinal ingredients: polyethylene glycol. Parabens- and tartrazine-free. Plastic controlled-drop dispenser of 10 mL, cartons of 1. Protect from heat (store between 15 and 30°C) and light. The eardrops may turn yellow when exposed to air and may cause staining of the skin, nails, hair or fabrics.

Reviewed 1998

LOCASALEN® Ⓟ

Novartis Pharmaceuticals

Flumethasone Pivalate—Salicylic Acid

Topical Corticosteroid—Squamolytic

Pharmacology: Locasalen exhibits pronounced anti-inflammatory, anti-allergic antiproliferative and antipruritic effects. Flumethasone pivalate, a topical corticoid of proven efficacy, is in solution in the ointment base rather than as suspended microcrystals and attains a higher degree of penetration into the skin where it remains active in the epidermis for a long period of time.

The salicylic acid component facilitates transepidermal penetration and also contributes therapeutic properties which are beneficial in respect of the indications of Locasalen. In a lipophilic base of this type salicylic acid 3% is squamolytic and mildly keratolytic, softening the horny layer of normal and hyperkeratotic skin and enhancing penetration. It also displays a significant antiseptic effect against bacteria and fungi. Even though no pH can be determined in this type of vehicle an acidogenic effect is exerted on contact with aqueous media (surface of the skin), to reinforce or restore the physiological acidity of the epidermal hydrolipidic mantle. The epidermoplastic effect promotes normalization of pathological cornification processes.

Lipophilic in character, the fatty ointment base spreads easily and readily penetrates (facilitating release of flumethasone pivalate), leaving a thin oily film on the skin, rendering it hydrophobic. The ointment can passively absorb a certain volume of water at and below body temperature while the outer layer of ointment remains hydrophobic. Evaporation does not take place and by virtue of this occlusive effect Locasalen will block insensible perspiration, slight sensible perspiration and the loss of heat to the atmosphere, thereby exerting a lubricating and emollient action, and also rehydration of the skin. The ointment adheres well to dry skin but for cosmetic reasons, can be rubbed into the skin with remaining traces removable by dabbing the area with a dry tissue. Locasalen is easily removed with soap and water or a skin cleansing agent. The ointment does not stain clothes or bed linen.

Indications: The treatment of subacute to hyperchronic, inflammatory and/or dysplastic skin diseases, as well as hyperkeratotic conditions in particular. Its indications thus include: chronic constitutional eczema or neurodermatitis; and chronic exogenous eczema irrespective of origin (e.g. skin disorders due to attrition), occupational eczema, chronic eczema of microbial or mycotic origin, tylotic eczema, hyperkeratosis as encountered in ichthyosis or chronic dyshidrosis, pustulosis of the palms and soles, lichen planus and chronic cutaneous lupus erythematosus and psoriasis.

Contraindications: Tuberculosis of the skin, syphilitic skin infections, viral and acute fungal infections of the skin, rosacea, perioral dermatitis, acne vulgaris. Systemic fungal infections. This preparation is not for ophthalmic use. Locasalen is contraindicated in individuals with a history of hypersensitivity to its components, to corticosteroids in general or to other salicylates.

Corticosteroids are also contraindicated in untreated bacterial infection.

Warnings: Locasalen is not indicated in acute weeping or subacute exudative stages.

In children and patients with marked renal insufficiency, repeated applications to extensive areas of skin should be avoided because transcutaneous absorption of the salicylic acid component might possibly give rise to systemic effects.

Likewise corticosteroids are known to be absorbed percutaneously. Since a moderate decrease in adrenocortical function has been reported, the risk of systemic side effects should be borne in mind. In patients requiring applications of Locasalen to extensive areas and/or under occlusive dressings, adrenal function should be carefully monitored.

All contact of the drug with the eyes, mouth and mucous membranes should be avoided.

Pregnancy: Animal experiments relevant to the safety assessment of corticosteroids, although not specifically conducted with Locasalen, have shown either teratogenic potential or other adverse effects on the embryo and/or fetus. However, no reports on adverse effects with Locasalen in human pregnancy have been received to date.

When using Locasalen in pregnancy, the risk-benefit relationship must be carefully considered and the therapy should be clearly indicated. However, the use of Locasalen in large amounts, on large areas of skin (especially under occlusive dressings), or for prolonged periods of time should be avoided during pregnancy.

Lactation: It is not known whether the active substances of Locasalen and/or their metabolite(s) pass into the breast milk when the preparation is applied topically. For safety reasons, nursing mothers should not use the product.

Precautions: If sensitivity or idiosyncratic reactions occur Locasalen should be discontinued and appropriate measures taken.

Patients should be advised to inform subsequent physicians of the prior use of corticosteroids.

In the presence of an infection, the use of an appropriate antifungal or antibacterial agent should be instituted. If a favorable response does not occur promptly, Locasalen should be discontinued until the infection has been adequately controlled. During the use of topical corticosteroids secondary infections may occur.

Application under occlusive dressings should be of limited duration and confined to small areas of diseased skin. Occlusive dressing should not be applied if there is an elevation of temperature.

In infants and small children, whose skin is more sensitive, Locasalen should be used with caution.

Prolonged use of topical corticosteroid products may produce atrophy of the skin and of subcutaneous tissues, particularly on flexor surfaces and on the face. Therefore, long-term treatment, especially of the facial skin, should always be avoided. The use of Locasalen should be discontinued if the above reactions are noted.

In exceptional cases where Locasalen is applied in large amounts, to large areas of skin, or under occlusive dressings, this should only be done if the patient is kept under close medical supervision.

The product should be used with caution in patients with stasis dermatitis and other skin diseases associated with impaired circulation.

Locasalen should not be allowed to come into contact with the conjunctiva.

Adverse Effects: The local tolerability of Locasalen proved to be very good. Cases in which local irritation made it advisable to discontinue the medication accounted for less than 2% of the total number of patients treated. Adverse reactions consist mainly of local reddening of the skin, desquamation, pruritus and smarting.

In isolated cases, mild skin atrophy due to flumethasone pivalate has also been observed.

Locasalen contains no preservatives, odor correcting agents, emulsifiers, stabilizers or antibiotic supplement which have been recognized as potential sensitizers. Hypersensitivity to salicylic acid can occur; however, the incidence in the population as a whole is approximately 0.2%.

Treatment should be discontinued if severe irritation or sensitization develops.

Systemic side effects attributable to the transcutaneous absorption of salicylic acid have not been reported. Absorption of salicylic acid does occur; however, investigations have shown that irrespective of the amount of Locasalen employed, and even applied under occlusive dressings, plasma concentrations of salicylic acid did not exceed ordinary therapeutic levels as a result of transcutaneous absorption. The risk of systemic side effects however should be borne in mind, particularly when using the preparation in pediatrics. Investigations have shown that under extreme conditions—where 40 to 60 g of ointment were applied daily to 89 to 90% of the body surface under occlusive dressings—plasma cortisol and urinary steroids have been observed to decrease below normal levels. This decrease proved transitory and was not accompanied by any clinical symptoms. Isolated cases of Cushing's syndrome have been reported.

When occlusive dressings are used, pustules, miliaria, folliculitis and pyoderma may occur. The following local adverse skin reactions have been reported with the use of topical steroids: dryness, itching, burning, local irritation, acneiform eruptions, skin atrophy, atrophy of s.c. tissues, hypertrichosis, folliculitis, change in pigmentation, secondary infection and contact allergy. Adrenal suppression has also been reported following topical corticosteroid therapy. Posterior subcapsular cataracts have been reported following systemic use of corticosteroids.

Topical corticosteroids may also give rise to striae rubrae distensae, telangiectasia, purpura or steroid acne, particularly if applied for prolonged periods of time, to large areas, under occlusive dressings, or to areas of increased skin permeability, such as the face of axillae.

Overdose: Symptoms and Treatment: Poisoning due to accidental ingestion is not anticipated. No specific antidote exists hence treatment of overdosage is symptomatic.

Dosage: As a rule Locasalen should be applied once or twice daily when dressings are not used and once daily when employed under occlusive dressing. It is not usually necessary to cover the treated area. The thickness of the layer should vary depending on the nature and severity of the skin disorder, since in this way it is possible to regulate moisture retention. In cases in which transitory exudation must be anticipated, Locasalen should be applied in a very thin layer, thereby allowing larger quantities of moisture to be released through the film of ointment. Locasalen can also exert an occlusive effect but only if applied in a thick layer. It penetrates well into the skin and, when rubbed in thoroughly, leaves on the skin a transparent oily film, that can be removed with soap and water or a skin cleanser. Excess film can be removed relatively well with paper tissues, leaving scarcely any perceptible sheen.

Supplied: Each g of ointment, colorless, soft to moderately firm in consistency with a smooth, homogeneous surface appearance contains: flumethasone pivalate 0.02% and salicylic acid 3%. Nonmedicinal ingredients: lanolin, propylene glycol and white petrolatum. Tartrazine-free. Tubes of 15 and 50 g.

LOESTRIN™ 1.5/30 ℞

Parke-Davis

Norethindrone Acetate—Ethinyl Estradiol

Oral Contraceptive

Pharmacology: Loestrin 1.5/30 achieves its contraceptive effect primarily by inhibition of ovulation through gonadotrophin suppression.

It is well-established that oral contraceptives containing estrogen and progestogen affect hypothalamic, pituitary and ovarian functions. They may alter many other physiological systems. Although the exact mechanisms of action are incompletely understood, there is universal agreement that the inhibition of the ovulatory peak of luteinizing hormone (LH) is a constant and contributing factor. Oral contraceptives may exert their contraceptive action in at least 4 ways: alteration of the physical and chemical properties of the cervical mucus, thereby inhibiting sperm penetration; endometrial changes hindering implantation; inhibition of ovulation; subtle changes in the hypothalamic-pituitary-ovarian axis with possible altered corpus luteum function. The steroid profiles quite often indicate either an absence of or insufficient luteal activity, or a significant and gradual decrease in several of the indices of luteal function.

Probably none of these factors alone accounts for the high degree of anti-fertility effect of any oral contraceptive. They may all play a part in the production of effective contraception.

Indications: Conception control.

Contraindications: Thrombophlebitis, thromboembolic disorders or a history of these conditions; history of/or actual cerebrovascular disorders; history of/or actual myocardial infarction or coronary arterial disease; active liver disease; history of/or actual benign or malignant liver tumors; known or suspected carcinoma of the breast; known or suspected estrogen-dependent neoplasia; undiagnosed abnormal vaginal bleeding; any ocular lesion arising from ophthalmic vascular disease, such as partial or complete loss of vision or defect in visual fields; when pregnancy is suspected or diagnosed.

Warnings: Predisposing Factors for Coronary Artery Disease: Cigarette smoking increases the risk of serious cardiovascular side effects and mortality. Birth control pills increase this risk, especially with increasing age. Convincing data are available to support an upper age limit of 35 years for oral contraceptive use in women who smoke.

Other women who are independently at high risk for cardiovascular disease include those with diabetes, hypertension, abnormal lipid profile, or a family history of these. Whether oral contraceptives accentuate this risk is unclear.

In low risk, non-smoking women of any age, the benefits of oral contraceptive use outweigh the possible cardiovascular risks associated with low dose formulations. Consequently, oral contraceptives may be prescribed for these women up to the age of menopause.

> Cigarette smoking increases the risk of serious adverse effects on the heart and blood vessels. This risk increases with age and becomes significant in oral contraceptive users over 35 years of age. Women should be counselled not to smoke.

Discontinue medication at the earliest manifestation of:

A. Thromboembolic and cardiovascular disorders such as: thrombophlebitis, pulmonary embolism, cerebrovascular disorders, myocardial ischemia, mesenteric thrombosis and retinal thrombosis.

B. Conditions which predispose to venous stasis and to vascular thrombosis, e.g. immobilization after accidents or confinement to bed during long-term illness. Other non-hormonal methods of contraception should be used until regular activities are resumed. For use of oral contraceptives when surgery is contemplated, see Precautions.

C. Visual defects, partial or complete.

D. Papilledema, or ophthalmic vascular lesions.

E. Severe headache of unknown etiology or worsening of pre-existing migraine headache.

Precautions: Physical Examination and Follow-up: Before oral contraceptives are used, a thorough history and physical examination should be performed, including a blood pressure determination. Breasts, liver, extremities and pelvic organs should be examined. A Papanicolaou smear should be taken if the patient has been sexually active.

The first follow-up visit should be done 3 months after oral contraceptives are prescribed. Thereafter, examinations should be performed at least once a year or more frequently if indicated. At each annual visit, examination should include those procedures that were done at the initial visit as outlined above or per recommendations of the Canadian Workshop on Screening for Cancer of the Cervix. For women who had 2 consecutive negative Pap smears, screening could be continued every 3 years up to the age of 69.

Pregnancy: Oral contraceptives should not be taken by pregnant women. However, if conception accidently occurs while taking the pill, there is no conclusive evidence that the estrogen and progestin contained in the oral contraceptive will damage the developing child.

Lactation: In breastfeeding women, the use of oral contraceptives results in the hormonal components being excreted in breast milk and may reduce its quantity and quality. If the use of oral contraceptives is initiated after the establishment of lactation, there does not appear to be any effect on the quantity and quality of the milk. There is no evidence that low dose oral contraceptives are harmful to the nursing infant.

Hepatic Function: Patients who have had jaundice including a history of cholestatic jaundice during pregnancy should be given oral contraceptives with great care and under close observation.

The development of severe generalized pruritus or icterus requires that the medication be withdrawn until the problem is resolved.

If a patient develops jaundice which proves to be cholestatic in type, the use of oral contraceptives should not be resumed. In patients taking oral contraceptives, changes in the composition of the bile may occur and an increased incidence of gallstones has been reported.

Hepatic nodules (adenoma and focal nodular hyperplasia) have been reported, particularly in long-term users of oral contraceptives. Although these lesions are extremely rare, they have caused fatal intra-abdominal hemorrhage and should be considered in women presenting with an abdominal mass, acute abdominal pain, or evidence of intra-abdominal bleeding.

Hypertension: Patients with essential hypertension whose blood pressure is well-controlled may be given oral contraceptives but only under close supervision. If a significant elevation of blood pressure in previously normotensive or hypertensive subjects occurs at any time during the administration of the drug, cessation of medication is necessary.

Migraine and Headache: The onset or exacerbation of migraine or the development of headache of a new pattern which is recurrent, persistent or severe, requires discontinuation of oral contraceptives and evaluation of the cause.

Diabetes: Current low dose oral contraceptives exert minimal impact on glucose metabolism. Diabetic patients, or those with a family history of diabetes, should be observed closely to detect any worsening of carbohydrate metabolism. Patients predisposed to diabetes who can be kept under close supervision may be given oral contraceptives. Young diabetic patients whose disease is of recent origin, well-controlled, and not associated with hypertension or other signs of vascular disease such as ocular fundal changes, should be monitored more frequently while using oral contraceptives.

Ocular Disease: Patients who are pregnant or are taking oral contraceptives, may experience corneal edema that may cause visual disturbances and changes in tolerance to contact lenses, especially of the rigid type. Soft contact lenses usually do not cause disturbances. If visual changes or alterations in tolerance to contact lenses occur, temporary or permanent cessation of wear may be advised.

Breasts: Increasing age and a strong family history are the most significant risk factors for the development of breast cancer. Other established risk factors include obesity, nulliparity and late age at first full-term pregnancy. The identified groups of women that may be at increased risk of developing breast cancer before menopause are long-term users of oral contraceptives (more than 8 years) and starters at early age. In a few women, the use of oral contraceptives may accelerate the growth of an existing but undiagnosed breast cancer. Since any potential increased risk related to oral contraceptive use is small, there is no reason to change prescribing habits at present.

Women receiving oral contraceptives should be instructed in self-examination of their breasts. Their physicians should be notified whenever any masses are detected. A yearly clinical breast examination is also recommended because, if a breast cancer should develop, estrogen-containing drugs may cause a rapid progression.

Vaginal Bleeding: Persistent irregular vaginal bleeding requires assessment to exclude underlying pathology.

Fibroids: Patients with fibroids (leiomyomata) should be carefully observed. Sudden enlargement, pain, or tenderness requires discontinuance of the use of oral contraceptives.

Emotional Disorders: Patients with a history of emotional disturbances, especially the depressive type, may be more prone to have a recurrence of depression while taking oral contraceptives. In cases of a serious recurrence, a trial of an alternate method of contraception should be made which may help to

Loestrin 1.5/30 (cont'd)

clarify the possible relationship. Women with premenstrual syndrome (PMS) may have a varied response to oral contraceptives, ranging from symptomatic improvement to worsening of the condition.

Laboratory Tests: Results of laboratory tests should be interpreted in the light that the patient is on oral contraceptives. The following laboratory tests are modified.

A. Liver function tests: Aspartate serum transaminase (AST): variously reported elevations. Alkaline phosphatase and gamma glutamine transaminase (GGT): slightly elevated.

B. Coagulation tests: Minimal elevation of test values reported for such parameters as Factors VII, VIII, IX and X.

C. Thyroid function tests: Protein binding of thyroxine is increased as indicated by increased total serum thyroxine concentrations and decreased T_3 resin uptake.

D. Lipoproteins: Small changes of unproven clinical significance may occur in lipoprotein cholesterol fractions.

E. Gonadotropins: LH and FSH levels are suppressed by the use of oral contraceptives. Wait 2 weeks after discontinuing the use of oral contraceptives before measurements are made.

Tissue Specimens: Pathologists should be advised of oral contraceptive therapy when specimens obtained from surgical procedures and Pap smears are submitted for examination.

Return to Fertility: After discontinuing oral contraceptive therapy, the patient should delay pregnancy until at least 1 normal spontaneous cycle has occurred in order to date the pregnancy. An alternative contraceptive method should be used during this time.

Amenorrhea: Women having a history of oligomenorrhea, secondary amenorrhea, or irregular cycles may remain anovulatory or become amenorrheic following discontinuation of estrogen-progestin combination therapy.

Amenorrhea, especially if associated with breast secretion, that continues for 6 months or more after withdrawal, warrants a careful assessment of hypothalamic-pituitary function.

Thromboembolic Complications—Post-surgery: There is an increased risk of post-surgery thromboembolic complications in oral contraceptive users, after major surgery. If feasible, oral contraceptives should be discontinued and an alternative method substituted at least 1 month prior to **major** elective surgery. Oral contraceptives should not be resumed until the first menstrual period after hospital discharge following surgery.

<u>*Drug Interactions:*</u> The concurrent administration of oral contraceptives with other drugs may result in an altered response to either agent. Reduced effectiveness of the oral contraceptive, should it occur, is more likely with the low dose formulations. It is important to ascertain all drugs that a patient is taking, both prescription and nonprescription, before oral contraceptives are prescribed.

Refer to the revised 1994 Report on Oral Contraceptives, Health and Welfare Canada, for possible drug interactions with oral contraceptives.

Non-contraceptive Benefits of Oral Contraceptives: Several health advantages other than contraception have been reported.

1. Combination oral contraceptives reduce the incidence of cancer of the endometrium and ovaries.
2. Oral contraceptives reduce the likelihood of developing benign breast disease.
3. Oral contraceptives reduce the likelihood of development of functional ovarian cysts.
4. Pill-users have less menstrual blood loss and have more regular cycles, thereby reducing the chance of developing iron-deficiency anemia.
5. The use of oral contraceptives may decrease the severity of dysmenorrhea and premenstrual syndrome, and may improve acne vulgaris, hirsutism, and other androgen-mediated disorders.
6. Other non-contraceptive benefits are outlined in the revised 1994 Report on Oral Contraceptives, Health and Welfare Canada.

> Oral contraceptives **do not protect** against sexually transmitted diseases (STDs) including HIV/AIDS. For protection against STDs, it is advisable to use latex condoms **in combination with** oral contraceptives.

Adverse Effects: An increased risk of the following serious adverse reactions has been associated with the use of oral contraceptives: thrombophlebitis; pulmonary embolism; mesenteric thrombosis; neuro-ocular lesions, e.g., retinal thrombosis; myocardial infarction; cerebral thrombosis; cerebral hemorrhage; hypertension; benign hepatic tumors; gallbladder disease.

The following adverse reactions also have been reported in patients receiving oral contraceptives: nausea and vomiting, usually the most common adverse reaction, occurs in approximately 10% or less of patients during the first cycle. Other reactions, as a general rule, are seen less frequently or only occasionally.

Other reactions, as a general rule, are seen less frequently or only occasionally: gastrointestinal symptoms (such as abdominal cramps and bloating); breakthrough bleeding; spotting; change in menstrual flow; dysmenorrhea; amenorrhea during and after treatment; temporary infertility after discontinuance of treatment; edema; chloasma or melasma which may persist; breast changes: tenderness, enlargement, and secretion; change in weight (increase or decrease); endocervical hyperplasias; possible diminution in lactation when given immediately postpartum; cholestatic jaundice; migraine; increase in size of uterine leiomyomata; rash (allergic); mental depression; reduced tolerance to carbohydrates; vaginal candidiasis; premenstrual-like syndrome; intolerance to contact lenses; change in corneal curvature (steepening); cataracts; optic neuritis; retinal thrombosis; changes in libido; chorea; changes in appetite; cystitis-like syndrome; rhinitis; headache; nervousness; dizziness; hirsutism; loss of scalp hair; erythema multiforme; erythema nodosum; hemorrhagic eruption; vaginitis; porphyria; impaired renal function; Raynaud's phenomenon; auditory disturbances; hemolytic uremic syndrome; pancreatitis.

Overdose: Symptoms and Treatment: In case of overdosage or accidental ingestion by children, the physician should observe the patient closely although no medication is required. Gastric lavage should be given if considered necessary.

Dosage: Information for the Patient on How to Take the Birth Control Pill:

1. **Read these directions:**
   - before you start taking your pills, and
   - any time you are not sure what to do.
2. **Look at your pill pack** to see if it has 21 or 28 pills:
   - 21-Pill Pack: 21 active pills (with hormones) taken daily for 3 weeks, and then take no pills for 1 week
   or
   - 28-Pill Pack: 21 active pills (with hormones) taken daily for 3 weeks, and then 7 "reminder" pills (no hormones) taken daily for 1 week.

Also check (1) where to start and (2) direction to take pills in.

3. You may wish to use a second method of birth control (e.g., latex condoms and spermicidal foam or gel) for the first 7 days of the first cycle of pill use. This will provide a back-up in case pills are forgotten while you are getting used to taking them.
4. When receiving any medical treatment, be sure to tell your doctor that you are using birth control pills.
5. **Many women have spotting or light bleeding, or may feel sick to their stomach during the first 3 months on the pill.** If you do feel sick, do not stop taking the pill. The problem will usually go away. If it does not go away, check with your doctor or clinic.
6. **Missing pills also can cause some spotting or light bleeding,** even if you make up the missed pills. You also could feel a little sick to your stomach on the days you take 2 pills to make up for missed pills.
7. **If you miss pills at any time, you could get pregnant. The greatest risks for pregnancy are:**
   - when you start a pack late, and
   - when you miss pills at the beginning or at the very end of the pack.
8. **Always be sure you have ready:**
   - **another kind of birth control** (such as latex condoms and spermicidal foam or gel) to use as a back-up in case you miss pills, and
   - **an extra, full pack of pills.**
9. **If you have vomiting or diarrhea, or if you take some medicines,** such as antibiotics, your pills may not work as well. Use a back-up method, such as latex condoms and spermicidal foam or gel, until you can check with your doctor or clinic.
10. **If you forget more than 1 pill 2 months in a row,** talk to your doctor or clinic about how to make pill-taking easier or about using another method of birth control.
11. **If your questions are not answered here, call your doctor or clinic.**

When to start the first pack of pills: Be sure to read these instructions:

- before you start taking your pills, and
- any time you are not sure what to do.

Decide with your doctor or clinic what is the best day for you to start taking your first pack of pills. Your pills may be either a 21-day or a 28-day type.

A. 21-Day Combination: With this type of birth control pill, you are 21 days on pills with 7 days off pills. You must not be off the pills for more than 7 days in a row.

1. **The first day of your menstrual period (bleeding) is Day 1 of your cycle.** Your doctor may advise you to start taking the pills on Day 1, on Day 5, or on the first Sunday after your period begins. If your period starts on Sunday, start that same day.

   Loestrin 1.5/30 (21's) is recommended for a Day 1 start.
   - Label the pack by selecting the appropriate day label strip that starts with Day 1 of your menstrual period (counting the first day of menstrual flow as Day 1). Place the strip in the space where you see the words "Place Day Label Here." Having the compact dispenser labelled with the correct day of the week will help remind you to take your tablet every day.
   - On Day 1 of your menstrual cycle, take your first tablet, beginning with the first tablet in the top row (where you see the word "start"). This tablet should correspond to the day of the week that you are taking your first tablet. To remove the tablet, push it through the back of the compact dispenser.
   - On the following day, take the next tablet in the row, always proceeding from left to right. Each new row will always begin on the same day of the week.
2. Take 1 pill at approximately the same time every day for 21 days; **then take no pills for 7 days.** Start a new pack on the 8th day. You will probably have a period during the 7 days off the pill. (This bleeding may be lighter and shorter than your usual period.) Always have a new compact ready to start each cycle (refills may be obtained by giving pharmacist the number on the prescription label).

B. 28-Day Combination: With this type of birth control pill, you take 21 pills which contain hormones and 7 pills which contain no hormones.

1. **The first day of your menstrual period (bleeding) is Day 1 of your cycle.** Your doctor may advise you to start taking the pills on Day 1, on Day 5, or on the first Sunday after your period begins. If your period starts on Sunday, start that same day.

   Loestrin 1.5/30 (28's) is recommended for a Day 1 start.
   - Label the pack by selecting the appropriate day label strip that starts with Day 1 of your menstrual period (counting the first day of menstrual flow as Day 1). Place the strip in the space where you see the words "Place Day Label Here." Having the compact dispenser labelled with the correct day of the week will help remind you to take your tablet every day.
   - On Day 1 of your menstrual cycle, take your first tablet, begining with the first tablet in the top row (where you see the word "start"). This tablet should correspond to the day of the week that you are taking your first tablet. To remove the tablet, push it through the back of the compact dispenser.
   - On the following day, take the next tablet in the row, always proceeding from left to right. Each new row will always begin on the same day of the week.
2. Take 1 pill at approximately the same time every day for 28 days. Begin a new pack the next day, **not missing any days on the pills.** Your period should occur during the last 7 days of using that pill pack. Always have a new compact ready to start each new cycle (refills may be obtained by giving pharmacist the number on the prescription label).

What to do during the month:

1. **Take a pill at approximately the same time every day until the pack is empty.**
   - Try to associate taking your pill with some regular activity like eating a meal or going to bed.
   - Do not skip pills even if you have bleeding between monthly periods or feel sick to your stomach (nausea).
   - Do not skip pills even if you do not have sex very often.
2. **When you finish a pack:**
   - **21 pills: Wait 7 days** to start the next pack. You will have your period during that week.
   - **28 pills:** Start the next pack **on the next day.** Take 1 pill every day. Do not wait any days between packs.

What to do if you miss pills: Table I outlines the actions you should take if you miss 1 or more of your birth control pills.

Table I—Loestrin 1.5/30

What To Do If You Miss Pills

Day 1 Start

Miss 1 Pill

Take it as soon as you remember, and take the next pill at the usual time. This means that you might take 2 pills in 1 day.

Miss 2 Pills In A Row

First 2 Weeks:
1. Take 2 pills the day you remember and 2 pills the next day.
2. Then take 1 pill a day until you finish the pack.
3. Use a back-up method of birth control if you have sex in the 7 days after you miss the pills.

Third Week:
1. Safely dispose of the rest of the pill pack and start a new pack that same day.
2. Use a back-up method of birth control if you have sex in 7 days after you miss the pills.
3. You may not have a period this month.

If you miss 2 periods in a row, call your doctor or clinic.

Miss 3 Or More Pills In A Row

Anytime in the cycle:
1. Safely dispose of the rest of the pill pack and start a new pack that same day.
2. Use a back-up method of birth control if you have sex in the 7 days after you miss the pills.
3. You may not have a period this month.

If you miss 2 periods in a row, call your doctor or clinic.

Note: 28-Day Pack: If you forget any of the 7 "reminder" pills (without hormones) in Week 4, just safely dispose of the pills you missed. Then keep taking 1 pill each day until the pack is empty. You do not need to use a back-up method.

Always be sure you have on hand:
- a back-up method of birth control (such as latex condoms and spermicidal foam or gel) in case you miss pills, and
- an extra, full pack of pills.

If you forget more than 1 pill 2 months in a row, talk to your doctor or clinic. Talk about ways to make pill-taking easier or about using another method of birth control.

Information for the Patient: See Blue Section—Information for the Patient "Oral Contraceptives".

Supplied: Each green tablet contains: norethindrone acetate 1.5 mg and ethinyl estradiol 30 μg. Nonmedicinal ingredients: acacia, D&C Yellow No. 10, FD&C Blue No. 1, FD&C Yellow No. 6, lactose, magnesium stearate, starch, sugar and talc. Each pale orange tablet contains the following inactive ingredients: acacia, D&C Yellow No. 10, FD&C Red No. 3, lactose, magnesium stearate, starch, sugar and talc. Energy: 0.8 kJ (0.2 kcal). Gluten-, paraben-, sodium-, sulfite- and tartrazine-free. Credit-card dispensers of 21 tablets (green) and 28 tablets (21 green tablets and 7 pale orange inert tablets). Packages of 5.

(Shown in Product Recognition Section)

LOFENALAC®
Mead Johnson
Phenylketonuria Therapy

Indications: For use as basic food in low phenylalanine dietary management of infants and children with phenylketonuria.

Contraindications: Should not be used except for children with phenylketonuria.

Precautions: Phenylalanine intake must be carefully controlled to prevent excessive blood levels and urinary excretion, and still provide enough for growth. Phenylalanine blood levels should be determined regularly. Physical and mental development should be carefully followed. Symptoms of phenylalanine deprivation may include lethargy, nausea, vomiting and fever.

Dosage: Mix with water to desired concentration and caloric value. Normal dilution—1 packed level measuring scoop of powder (9.3 g)/57 mL of water—or 139 g made up with water to 946 mL of formula. This dilution supplies approximately 84 kJ (20 kcal)/30 mL.

Supplied: Powder: A balanced low phenylalanine food made from a casein hydrolysate low in phenylalanine. Carbohydrate from glucose polymers and tapioca starch. Vitamins and minerals are included. Cans of 454 g with measure enclosed.

LOMINE
Riva
Dicyclomine HCl
Antispasmodic

Supplied: Each blue capsule contains: dicyclomine HCl 10 mg, USP. Nonmedicinal ingredients: colloidal silicon dioxide, lactose and magnesium stearate. Bottles of 500 and 1 000.

LOMOTIL® Ⓝ
Searle
Diphenoxylate HCl—Atropine Sulfate
Antidiarrheal

Pharmacology: The mode of action of diphenoxylate in the bowel is similar to that of morphine and related drugs. Gastrointestinal propulsion is inhibited through a direct action on the smooth muscle, resulting in a decrease in peristaltic action and a consequent increase in transit time.

Indications: As an adjunct in the management of diarrhea. Bacterially-induced diarrhea should be treated with appropriate antimicrobial therapy.

Contraindications: Known hypersensitivity to diphenoxylate or atropine; patients who are jaundiced; the treatment of diarrhea associated with pseudomembranous enterocolitis; diarrhea caused by enterotoxin producing bacteria.

Warnings: This medication should be kept out of the reach of children since accidental overdose may cause severe or even fatal respiratory depression. Lomotil is not recommended for use in children under 2 years of age. Dosage recommendations should be strictly adhered to, especially in children.

Pregnancy and *Lactation:* The use of Lomotil during pregnancy, lactation or in women of childbearing potential requires that the expected benefits of the drug be weighed against any possible hazard to the mother and child. Effects of diphenoxylate or atropine may be evident in the infants of nursing mothers taking Lomotil (since these compounds are excreted in breast milk).

Precautions: General: Occupational Hazards: Lomotil may produce drowsiness or dizziness. The patient should be cautioned regarding activities that require mental alertness, such as driving or operating dangerous machinery.

Slowing of intestinal motility by an agent such as Lomotil does not preclude the need for appropriate fluid and electrolyte replacement. Dehydration may further influence the variability of response to Lomotil and may predispose to delayed diphenoxylate intoxication. Drug-induced inhibition of peristalsis may result in fluid retention in the colon which may further aggravate dehydration and electrolyte imbalance. If severe dehydration or electrolyte imbalance is present, withhold Lomotil until appropriate corrective therapy has been initiated.

Children: Lomotil should be used with special caution, since signs of atropinism may occur even with recommended doses, particularly in patients with Down's Syndrome. Lomotil should be used with special caution in young children because of their variable response.

Patients with Special Diseases and Conditions: Lomotil should be used with extreme caution in patients with cirrhosis and other hepatic disease and in all patients with abnormal liver function tests, since hepatic coma may be precipitated.

In some patients with acute ulcerative colitis, agents which inhibit intestinal motility or delay intestinal transit time have been reported to induce toxic megacolon. Consequently, patients with acute ulcerative colitis should be carefully observed and Lomotil therapy should be discontinued promptly if abdominal distension occurs or if other untoward symptoms develop.

Dependence Liability: Addiction to (dependency on) Lomotil is theoretically possible at high dosage. Therefore, the recommended dosage should not be exceeded. Because of the structural and pharmacological similarity of diphenoxylate to meperidine and similar drugs with a definite addiction potential, Lomotil should be administered with considerable caution to patients who are receiving addicting drugs, to individuals known to be addiction-prone, or to those whose histories suggest that they may increase the dosage on their own initiative. Because a subtherapeutic dose of atropine has been added to the diphenoxylate, to discourage deliberate overdosage, there should be strict observance of the contraindications and precautions relative to the use of atropine.

Drug Interactions: Lomotil may potentiate the action of barbiturates, tranquilizers and alcohol. Therefore, the patient should be closely observed when these medications are used concomitantly.

Since the chemical structure of diphenoxylate is similar to that of meperidine, the concurrent use of Lomotil with MAO inhibitors may in theory precipitate a hypertensive crisis.

Adverse Effects: The most frequently reported adverse effect is nausea. Other symptoms which have been reported at therapeutic doses are: Nervous System: drowsiness, coma, lethargy, sedation/drowsiness, restlessness, dizziness, insomnia, headache, blurring of vision, depression, euphoria, confusion, paresthesia, malaise.

Respiratory: respiratory depression.

Gastrointestinal: vomiting, anorexia, nausea, abdominal bloating, cramps, paralytic ileus, toxic megacolon, pancreatitis.

Allergy: anaphylaxis, pruritus, skin eruption, giant urticaria, angioneurotic edema.

Atropine effects such as dryness of the skin and mucous membranes, hyperthermia, tachycardia, urinary retention and flushing may also occur, especially in children.

Overdose: Symptoms: Initial signs may include dryness of the skin and mucous membranes, mydriasis, restlessness, flushing, hyperthermia and tachycardia followed by lethargy or coma, hypotonic reflexes, nystagmus, pinpoint pupils and respiratory depression. Cardiac arrest has occurred in children.

Treatment: Treat all possible Lomotil overdoses as serious and maintain medical observation for at least 48 hours.

Gastric lavage, establishment of a patent airway and possibly mechanically assisted respiration are advised. Undertake gastric lavage with due caution in an unconscious patient, preferably following insertion of a cuffed endotracheal tube. If the patient is not comatose, administration of a slurry of activated charcoal may be indicated.

Narcotic antagonists such as naloxone HCl may be used for the treatment of respiratory depression caused by narcotic drugs or pharmacologically-related compounds, such as Lomotil.

Naloxone HCl Dosage in Adults: Naloxone HCl may be administered to adults at a dose of 0.4 mg i.v. Additional doses of 0.4 mg may be given at 2- or 3-minute intervals until adequate improvement in pulmonary ventilation is demonstrated. Subsequent injections of this drug must be governed by the degree of respiratory depression present and should be titrated accordingly. Since the duration of action of naloxone HCl is short in comparison to that of diphenoxylate, improvement of respiration after its administration may be followed by subsequent respiratory depression. It should be noted that although signs of overdosage and respiratory depression may not be evident with Lomotil after ingestion, respiratory depression may occur 12 to 30 hours later. Consequently, continuous observation is necessary until the effect of diphenoxylate on respiration, which may persist for many hours, has passed. The period of observation should extend over at least 48 hours, preferably under continuous hospital care.

Naloxone HCl Dosage in Children: For known or suspected narcotic overdosage, the initial dosage of naloxone HCl in children is 0.005 to 0.01 mg/kg body weight when given i.v., i.m. or s.c. This dose may be repeated as for adults above. If necessary, naloxone HCl can be diluted with sterile water for injection.

Dosage: Adults: The usual initial dose is 5 mg (2 tablets) 3 or 4 times daily (20 mg/24 hours in divided doses is the maximum recommended dosage). An individual maintenance dose can be subsequently determined. Downward adjustment should be made as soon as initial control of symptoms is accomplished. The maintenance dose may be as low as ¼ of the dose required for initial control.

Children: **Not for use in children under 2 years of age (see Warnings and Precautions).**

Lomotil (cont'd)

The recommended initial dosage determined by the child's weight, is 0.3 to 0.4 mg/kg **daily** in divided doses. For convenience, **approximate** dosage (in children of average weight) may be determined by Table I.

Table I—Lomotil

Approximate Dosage in Children of Average Weight

Age	Approximate Body Weight	Total Daily Dose
2 to 5 years	15-20 kg	2.5 mg b.i.d.
6 to 8 years	20-27 kg	2.5 mg t.i.d.
9 to 12 years	27-36 kg	2.5 mg q.i.d.
13 years and above	—	5 mg q.i.d.

As with adult therapy, adjustment of dosage downward should be made as soon as initial control of symptoms is accomplished.

These pediatric schedules are the best approximation of an average dose recommendation which should be adjusted according to the overall nutritional status and degree of dehydration encountered in the child. The recommended doses must not be exceeded.

Supplied: Each round, white tablet, with "SEARLE" debossed on one side and "61" on the other side, contains: diphenoxylate HCl 2.5 mg and atropine sulfate 0.025 mg. Nonmedicinal ingredients: acacia, cornstarch, magnesium stearate, mineral oil, sorbitol, sucrose and talc. Bottles of 250. Store at temperatures below 30°C and protect from light.

(Shown in Product Recognition Section)

Reviewed 1997

LONITEN® ℞

Pharmacia & Upjohn

Minoxidil

Antihypertensive

Pharmacology: Minoxidil is an orally effective direct acting peripheral vasodilator that reduces elevated systolic and diastolic blood pressure by decreasing peripheral vascular resistance.

Minoxidil does not directly stimulate the heart or electrolyte reabsorption by the kidney. However, because of peripheral dilatation, minoxidil elicits a reflex mediated increase in cardiac output, salt and water retention, and a rise in plasma renin activity. These adverse effects are diminished by the simultaneous administration of a diuretic and a beta-adrenergic blocking agent or other sympathetic nervous system suppressant.

Minoxidil is at least 95% absorbed from the gastrointestinal tract. Plasma levels of the drug reach maximum within the first hour and decline rapidly thereafter. The average plasma half-life in man is 4.2 hours. Approximately 90% of the administered drug is metabolized, predominantly by conjugation with glucuronic acid at the N-oxide position in the pyrimidine ring but also by conversion to more polar products.

Known metabolites exert much less pharmacologic effect than minoxidil itself, and all are excreted principally in the urine. Minoxidil does not bind to plasma proteins, and its renal clearance corresponds to the glomerular filtration rate. In the absence of functional renal tissue, minoxidil and its metabolites can be removed by hemodialysis, although this does not rapidly reverse its pharmacological effect.

The extent and time-course of blood pressure reduction by minoxidil do not correspond closely to its concentration in plasma. After a single oral dose, blood pressure usually starts to decline within one half hour, and reaches a minimum between 2 and 3 hours and recovers at an arithmetically linear rate of about 30%/day. The total duration of effect is approximately 72 hours. When minoxidil is administered chronically, the time required to achieve maximum effect on blood pressure is inversely related to the size of the dose.

Indications: Because of the potential for serious adverse effects, minoxidil is indicated only in the treatment of severe hypertension that is symptomatic or associated with target organ damage and is not manageable with maximum therapeutic doses of a diuretic plus two other antihypertensive drugs. At the present time, use in milder degrees of hypertension is not recommended because the benefit—risk relationship in such patients has not been defined.

Contraindications: Pheochromocytoma because minoxidil may reflexly stimulate secretion of catecholamines from the tumor; pulmonary hypertension associated with mitral stenosis; hypersensitivity to minoxidil or any components of the preparation.

Warnings: Salt and water retention; congestive heart failure—concomitant use of an adequate diuretic is required: Minoxidil must usually be administered concomitantly with a diuretic adequate to prevent fluid retention and possible congestive heart failure; a high-ceiling (loop) diuretic is almost always required. Body weight should be monitored closely. If minoxidil is used without a diuretic, retention of several hundred milli-equivalents of salt and corresponding volumes of water can occur within a few days, leading to increased plasma and interstitial fluid volume and local and generalized edema. Diuretic treatment, alone or in combination with restricted salt intake, will usually minimize fluid retention, although reversible edema did develop in approximately 10% of nondialysis patients so treated. Diuretic effectiveness was limited mostly by disease related impaired renal function. The condition of patients with pre-existing congestive heart failure occasionally deteriorated in association with fluid retention although because of the fall in blood pressure (reduction of afterload), more than twice as many improved than worsened. Rarely, refractory fluid retention may require discontinuation of minoxidil. Provided that the patient is under close medical supervision, it may be possible to resolve refractory salt retention by discontinuing minoxidil for 1 or 2 days and then resuming treatment in conjunction with vigorous diuretic therapy.

Concomitant treatment to prevent tachycardia is usually required: Minoxidil increases the heart rate. This increase can be partly or entirely prevented by the concomitant administration of a beta-adrenergic blocking drug or other sympathetic nervous system suppressant. Round-the-clock effectiveness of the sympathetic suppressant should be assured. In addition, angina may worsen or appear for the first time during minoxidil treatment, probably because of the increased oxygen demands associated with increased heart rate and cardiac output. This can usually be prevented by sympathetic blockade.

Pericarditis, Pericardial effusion and Tamponade: Although there is no evidence of a causal relationship, there have been multiple reports of pericarditis occurring in association with minoxidil. Pericardial effusion, occasionally with tamponade, has been observed in about 3% of treated patients not on dialysis, especially those with inadequate or compromised renal function. Although in many cases the pericardial effusion was associated with a connective tissue disease, the uremic syndrome, congestive heart failure or marked fluid retention, there have been instances in which these potential causes of effusion were not present. Patients should be observed closely for any suggestion of a pericardial disorder, and echocardiographic studies should be carried out if suspicion arises. More vigorous diuretic therapy, dialysis, pericardiocentesis or surgery may be required. If the effusion persists, withdrawal of therapy should be considered in light of other means of controlling the hypertension and the patient's clinical status.

Interaction with Guanethidine: Although minoxidil does not itself cause orthostatic hypotension, its administration to patients already receiving guanethidine can result in profound orthostatic effects. If at all possible guanethidine should be discontinued well before minoxidil is begun. Where this is not possible, minoxidil therapy should be started in the hospital and the patient should remain institutionalized until severe orthostatic effects are no longer present or the patient has learned to avoid activities that provoke them.

Hazard of Rapid Control of Blood Pressure: In patients with very severe blood pressure elevation, too rapid control of blood pressure, especially with i.v. agents, can precipitate cerebrovascular accidents and myocardial infarction. Although such events have not been unequivocally associated with minoxidil use, total experience is limited at present.

Any patient with malignant hypertension should have initial treatment with minoxidil carried out in a hospital setting, both to assure that blood pressure is falling and to assure that it is not falling more rapidly than intended.

Cardiac Lesions in Animals: In non-primate animal studies, minoxidil produced several types of myocardial lesions as well as other adverse cardiac effects. These included necrotic and hemorrhagic lesions of the myocardium and papillary muscles and cardiac hypertrophy and dilatation. As greater experience with minoxidil has accumulated, it has become apparent that these cardiac lesions so described in the dog, minipig and other non-primates do not occur in humans.

Human autopsy experience has revealed the following: Among 242 autopsies performed on patients who received minoxidil tablets, cardiac pathology was detected in only 8 instances. In every instance, the conclusion has been reached that the human heart lesions were decidedly different in individual elements and constellation of changes from both the atrial and ventricular lesions seen in animals. Among 224 autopsies performed on patients never exposed to minoxidil tablets, the cardiac pathology observed, especially in the right atrium, entirely encompassed the pathologic findings seen in the minoxidil cases. The inference of these observations is that the pathologic findings in hearts of minoxidil treated hypertensive patients were not attributable to minoxidil administration, but rather to disease processes which were common to patients in these 2 studies.

Precautions: Monitor fluid and electrolyte balance and body weight (see Warnings).

Observe patients for signs and symptoms of pericarditis, pericardial effusions and tamponade (see Warnings).

Abnormal hair growth is a common occurrence (see Adverse Effects). This is especially disturbing to women and children and patients should be thoroughly informed about this effect.

When using a concomitant sympatholytic to prevent tachycardia, careful attention to adjusting the dosages of the beta-blocker or other sympathetic nervous system suppressant is required for maximum safety and efficacy (see Dosage, Concomitant Therapy).

When using a concomitant diuretic to prevent or treat fluid retention, careful attention to adjusting the dosage of the diuretic is required for maximum safety and efficacy (see Dosage, Concomitant Therapy).

Minoxidil has not been used in patients who have had a myocardial infarction within the preceding month. It is possible that a reduction of arterial pressure with minoxidil might further limit blood flow to the myocardium, although this might be compensated by decreased oxygen demand because of lower blood pressure.

Possible hypersensitivity to minoxidil, manifested as a skin rash, including rare reports of bullous eruptions and Stevens-Johnson syndrome, has been seen.

Renal failure or dialysis patients may require smaller doses of minoxidil and should have close medical supervision to prevent exacerbation of renal failure or precipitation of cardiac failure.

If minoxidil therapy must be discontinued in a patient who has been treated effectively, the drug should be phased out gradually or replaced with another antihypertensive agent. Careful monitoring of the patient's blood pressure during the treatment adjustment is necessary.

Pregnancy: The safety for use of minoxidil in pregnancy has not been established. Minoxidil has been shown to reduce the conception rate in rats and to show evidence of increased fetal absorption in rabbits when administered at 5 times the human dose. There was no evidence of teratogenic effects in rats and rabbits. Minoxidil should be used during pregnancy only if the potential benefit justifies the potential risk to the fetus.

Lactation: This drug has been reported to be excreted in human milk. As a general rule, nursing should not be undertaken while a patient is on minoxidil.

Children: Use in children has been limited to date particularly in infants. The recommendations under Dosage can be considered only a rough guide and careful titration is essential.

Patient Information: The patient should be made fully aware of the importance of continuing all prescribed antihypertensive medications and of the nature of symptoms that would suggest fluid overload (see Blue Section—Information for the Patient "Loniten").

Adverse Effects: Salt and water retention (see Warnings): Temporary edema, developed in 7% of patients who were not edematous at the start of therapy.

Pericarditis, pericardial effusion and tamponade (see Warnings).

Hypertrichosis: Elongation, thickening, and enhanced pigmentation of fine body hair are seen in about 80% of patients. This develops within 3 to 6 weeks after starting therapy. It is usually first noticed on the temples, between the eyebrows, between the hairline and the eyebrows, or in the sideburn area of the upper lateral cheek, later extending to the back, arms, legs, and scalp. Upon discontinuation of minoxidil, new hair growth stops, but 1 to 6 months may be required for restoration to pretreatment appearance. No endocrine abnormalities have been found to explain the abnormal hair growth; thus, it is hypertrichosis without virilism.

ECG Changes: Changes in direction and magnitude of the ECG T waves occur in approximately 60% of patients treated with minoxidil. In rare instances a large negative amplitude of the T wave may encroach upon the ST segment, but the ST segment is not independently altered. These changes usually disappear with continuance of treatment and revert to the

pretreatment state if minoxidil is discontinued. No symptoms have been associated with these changes.
Miscellaneous: Breast tenderness, rash (see Precautions) and gastrointestinal intolerance developed in less than 1% of patients.
Altered Laboratory Findings: Effects of hemodilution-hematocrit, hemoglobin, and erythrocyte count usually fall about 7% initially and then recover to pretreatment levels; thrombocytopenia and leukopenia have been rarely reported; alkaline phosphatase increased varyingly without other evidence of liver or bone abnormality; serum creatinine increased an average of 6% and BUN slightly more, but later declined to pretreatment levels.

Overdose: Symptoms: There have been only a few instances of deliberate or accidental overdosage with minoxidil. When exaggerated hypotension is encountered, it is most likely to occur in association with residual sympathetic nervous system blockade from previous therapy (guanethidine-like effects of alpha-adrenergic blockade).

Treatment: The recommended treatment is i.v. administration of normal saline. Sympathomimetic drugs, such as norepinephrine or epinephrine, should be avoided because of their excessive cardiac stimulating action. Phenylephrine, angiotensin II, vasopressin and dopamine, which reverse the effects of minoxidil, should only be used if inadequate perfusion of a vital organ is evident.

Dosage: Adults and children over 12 years of age: The recommended initial daily dosage of minoxidil is 5 mg given in 2 divided doses. Daily dosage can be increased to 10, 20 and 40 mg in divided doses, at 3-day intervals or longer, if required for optimum blood pressure control. The effective dosage range is usually 10 to 40 mg/day. In certain patients, doses up to a maximum of 100 mg/day may be attempted, recognizing the probability of an increase in the incidence and severity of adverse reactions.
Children under 12 years of age: The initial recommended daily dosage is 0.2 mg/kg minoxidil in 2 divided doses. The dosage may be increased by 0.1 to 0.2 mg/kg/day increments, at 3-day intervals or longer, until optimum blood pressure control is achieved. The effective dosage range is usually 0.25 to 1 mg/kg/day. The maximum recommended dose is 50 mg/day.
Frequency of Dosage Adjustment: Dosage must be titrated carefully according to individual response. Intervals between dosage adjustments normally should be at least 3 days since the full response to a given dose is not obtained for at least that amount of time. Where a more rapid management of hypertension is required, a 5 mg dose can be given every 6 hours if the patient is hospitalized and carefully monitored (see Warnings).
Dose Frequency: The magnitude of within-day fluctuation of arterial pressure during therapy with minoxidil is directly proportional to the extent of pressure reduction. When the targeted blood pressure has been reached, a change from twice daily to once daily dosing with minoxidil may be tried in those patients in whom the diastolic pressure has been reduced less than 30 mmHg. If supine diastolic pressure has been reduced more than 30 mmHg, the twice daily dosage schedule should be maintained.
Concomitant Therapy: Diuretics: To prevent fluid retention and possible congestive heart failure, minoxidil must be used in conjunction with a high ceiling (loop) diuretic in patients relying on renal function for maintaining salt and water balance. Diuretics have been used at the following dosages when starting therapy with minoxidil: hydrochlorothiazide (50 mg twice daily) or other thiazides at equi-effective dosage; chlorthalidone (50 to 100 mg once daily); furosemide (40 mg twice daily).

If excessive salt and water retention results in a weight gain of more than 2 kg, diuretic therapy should be changed to furosemide; if the patient is already taking furosemide, dosage should be increased in accordance with the patient's requirements. Rarely, refractory fluid retention may require discontinuation of minoxidil. Provided that the patient is under close medical supervision, it may be possible to resolve refractory fluid retention by discontinuing minoxidil for 1 or 2 days and then resuming treatment in conjunction with vigorous diuretic therapy.

In dialysis patients also receiving diuretic therapy, use of minoxidil may create the need to raise diuretic dosage or to increase the frequency or duration of dialysis in order to maintain salt and water balance.
Sympathetic Nervous System Suppressants: The preferred agent to achieve sympathetic nervous system suppression is a beta-blocker equivalent to a propranolol dosage of 80 to 160 mg/day. Higher doses may be required when patients, pretreated with a beta-blocker, have an increase in heart rate exceeding 20 beats/minute or when simultaneous introduction of minoxidil and a beta-blocker causes an increase in heart rate exceeding 10 beats/minute.

If beta-blockers are contraindicated, methyldopa (250 to 750 mg twice daily) may be used instead. Methyldopa must be given for at least 24 hours before starting therapy with minoxidil because of the delay in the onset of methyldopa's action. Limited clinical experience indicates that clonidine may also be used to prevent tachycardia induced by minoxidil; the usual dosage is 0.1 to 0.2 mg twice daily.

Sympathetic nervous system suppressants may not completely prevent an increase in heart rate due to minoxidil but usually do prevent tachycardia. Typically, patients receiving a beta-blocker prior to initiation of therapy with minoxidil have a bradycardia and can be expected to have an increase in heart rate toward normal when minoxidil is added. When treatment with minoxidil and a beta-blocker or other sympathetic nervous system suppressant are begun simultaneously, their opposing cardiac effects usually nullify each other, leading to little change in heart rate.

Information for the Patient: See Blue Section—Information for the Patient "Loniten".

Supplied: 2.5 mg: Each round, white tablet scored and embossed with a "U" and 121 on one side and 2½ on the other contains: minoxidil 2.5 mg. Nonmedicinal ingredients: cornstarch, lactose, magnesium stearate, microcrystalline cellulose and silicon dioxide. Gluten-free. Bottles of 100.

10 mg: Each round, white tablet scored and embossed with a "U" and 137 on one side and 10 on the other contains: minoxidil 10 mg. Nonmedicinal ingredients: cornstarch, lactose, magnesium stearate, microcrystalline cellulose and silicon dioxide. Gluten-free. Bottles of 100.

(Shown in Product Recognition Section)

LOPERACAP Ⓟ
ICN

Loperamide HCl
Antidiarrheal

Supplied: Each light green, capsule-shaped tablet contains: loperamide HCl USP 2 mg. Nonmedicinal ingredients: D&C yellow #10, FD&C blue #1, lactose, magnesium stearate, microcrystalline cellulose, pregelatinized starch and sodium starch glycolate. Bottles of 100 and 500.

LOPID® Ⓟ
Parke-Davis

Gemfibrozil
Antihyperlipidemic Agent

Pharmacology: Gemfibrozil is a lipid regulating agent which decreases serum triglycerides and total cholesterol, and increases high density lipoprotein cholesterol. The lipid-lowering changes occur primarily in the very low density lipoprotein (VLDL) fraction (S_f 20 to 400) rich in triglycerides and to a lesser extent in the low density lipoprotein (LDL) fraction (S_f0 to 20) rich in cholesterol. Gemfibrozil treatment of patients with elevated triglycerides due to Type IV hyperlipoproteinemia may cause a rise in LDL-cholesterol. In addition, gemfibrozil increases the high density lipoprotein (HDL) cholesterol subfractions, HDL_2 and HDL_3, as well as apolipoproteins AI and AII.

Epidemiological studies have shown that both low HDL-cholesterol and high LDL-cholesterol are independent risk factors for coronary heart disease. Depending on the type of hyperlipidemia, pharmacological intervention with gemfibrozil raises HDL-cholesterol and may lower LDL-cholesterol, and may be associated with reduced morbidity due to coronary heart disease as reported in the Helsinki Heart Study, a 5 year primary prevention Phase IV clinical trial.

The mechanism of action has not been definitely established. In man, gemfibrozil has been shown to inhibit peripheral lipolysis and to decrease the hepatic extraction of free fatty acids, thus reducing hepatic triglyceride production. Gemfibrozil also inhibits the synthesis and increases clearance of VLDL carrier apolipoprotein B, leading to a decrease in VLDL.

Animal studies suggest that gemfibrozil may, in addition to elevating HDL cholesterol (HDL-C), reduce incorporation of long-chain fatty acids into newly formed triglycerides, accelerate turnover and removal of cholesterol from the liver, and increase excretion of cholesterol in the feces.

Indications: An adjunct to diet and other therapeutic measures for treatment of adult patients with very high serum triglyceride levels, Fredrickson classification Type IV and V hyperlipidemias, who are at high risk of sequelae and complications (i.e. pancreatitic) from their hyperlipidemia.

Treatment of patients with hypercholesterolemia, Type IIa and IIb mixed dyslipidemias, to regulate lipid levels (reduce serum triglycerides and LDL cholesterol levels and increase HDL cholesterol).

Gemfibrozil alone may not be adequate therapy in some patients with familial combined hyperlipidemia with Type IIb and IV hyperlipoproteinemia.

Initial therapy for hyperlipidemia should include a specific diet, weight reduction, and an exercise program and for patients with diabetes mellitus, a good diabetic control.

Contraindications: Hepatic and renal dysfunction, including primary biliary cirrhosis; pre-existing gallbladder disease (see Precautions); hypersensitivity to gemfibrozil; the drug should not be used in pregnant or lactating patients; treatment of Type I hyperlipoproteinemia.

Warnings: Drug Interactions: When gemfibrozil and lovastatin were used concomitantly, there have been reports of severe myositis with markedly elevated creatine kinase (CK) and myoglobinuria (rhabdomyolysis). When myoglobinuria is severe, acute renal failure may ensue. Therefore, lovastatin should not be used concomitantly with gemfibrozil.

Caution should be exercised when anticoagulants are given in conjunction with gemfibrozil. The dosage of the anticoagulant should be reduced to maintain the prothrombin time at the desired level to prevent bleeding complications. Frequent prothrombin determinations are advisable until it has been definitely determined that the prothrombin level has stabilized.

Reduced bioavailability of gemfibrozil may result when given simultaneously with resin-granule drugs such as colestipol. Administration of the drugs 2 hours or more apart is recommended.

Gemfibrozil clinically, pharmacologically and chemically shows similarities with clofibrate. Physicians prescribing gemfibrozil should also be familiar with the risks and benefits of clofibrate.

Long-term studies with gemfibrozil have been conducted in rats and mice at 1 and 10 times the human dose. The incidence of benign liver nodules and liver carcinomas was significantly increased in high dose male rats. The incidence of liver carcinomas was increased also in low dose males, but the increase was not statistically significant ($p>0.05$). In high dose female rats, there was a significant increase in the combined incidence of benign and malignant liver neoplasms. There were no statistically significant differences from controls in the incidence of liver tumors in male and female mice, but the doses tested were lower than those shown to be carcinogenic with other fibrates. Liver and testicular cell tumors were increased in male rats.

Electron microscopy studies have demonstrated a florid hepatic peroxisome proliferation following gemfibrozil administration to male rats. Such changes have not been found in the liver of patients treated with this drug.

Toxicology studies in male rats revealed a dose-related increase of benign Leydig cell tumors. Subcapsular bilateral cataracts occurred in 10% and unilateral in 6.3% of the high dose males.
Cholelithiasis: Gemfibrozil may increase cholesterol excretion into the bile leading to cholelithiasis. If cholelithiasis is suspected, gallbladder studies are indicated. Drug therapy should be discontinued if gallstones are found.

Since a reduction of total mortality has not been demonstrated, gemfibrozil should be administered only in those patients described in the Indications section. If a significant serum lipid response is not obtained in 3 months, gemfibrozil should be discontinued.

If gemfibrozil is chosen for treatment, the prescribing physicians should discuss the proposed therapy and inform the patient of the expected benefits and potential risks which may be associated with long-term administration (see Precautions).
Children: Safety and efficacy in children have not been established.
Pregnancy: Strict birth control procedures must be exercised by women of childbearing potential. If pregnancy occurs despite birth control procedures, gemfibrozil should be discontinued.

Women who are planning pregnancy should discontinue gemfibrozil several months prior to conception.
Lactation: Because of the potential for tumorigenicity shown for gemfibrozil in rats, a decision should be made whether to

Lopid (cont'd)

discontinue nursing or discontinue the drug, taking into account the importance of the drug to the mother.

Precautions: Initial Therapy: Before instituting gemfibrozil therapy, attempts should be made to control serum lipids and lipoproteins with appropriate diet, exercise, weight loss in obese patients, and control of diabetes mellitus.

Long-term Therapy: Because long-term administration of gemfibrozil is recommended, pretreatment clinical chemistry studies should be performed to ensure that the patient has elevated serum lipid or low HDL cholesterol levels. Periodic determinations of serum lipids should be done during gemfibrozil administration, including measurement of LDL-cholesterol/HDL-cholesterol ratio, particularly in Type IV hyperlipoproteinemic patients.

Impairment of Fertility: Administration of approximately 3 and 10 times the human dose to male rats for 10 weeks resulted in a dose-related decrease of fertility. Subsequent studies demonstrated that this effect was reversed after a drug-free period of about 8 weeks, and it was not transmitted to their offspring.

Hematologic Changes: Mild hemoglobin, hematocrit and white cell decreases have been observed in occasional patients following initiation of gemfibrozil therapy. The levels then stabilize during long-term administration. Rarely, severe anemia, leukopenia, thrombocytopenia, eosinophilia and bone marrow hypoplasia have been reported. Therefore, periodic blood count determinations are recommended during the first 12 months of gemfibrozil administration.

Liver Function: Abnormal liver function tests have been observed occasionally during gemfibrozil administration, including elevations of AST, ALT, LDH, creatine kinase, bilirubin and alkaline phosphatase. These are usually reversible when the drug is discontinued. Therefore periodic liver function studies are recommended and gemfibrozil therapy should be terminated if abnormalities persist.

Hepatobiliary Disease: In patients with past history of jaundice or hepatic disorder, gemfibrozil should be used with caution.

Cardiac Arrhythmias: Although no clinically significant abnormalities occurred that could be attributed to gemfibrozil, the possibility exists that such abnormalities may occur.

Adverse Effects: Premarketing Studies: Gemfibrozil has been carefully evaluated in over 3 000 patients having received the drug in monitored clinical studies prior to marketing. Symptoms reporting during the controlled phase in studies of 805 subjects were considered for safety. The symptoms listed in Table I are those which occurred in at least 5 patients and all skin reactions whatever their incidence. The principal symptoms for which incidence was greater with gemfibrozil than with placebo involved the gastrointestinal system. Nausea and vomiting, and abdominal and epigastric pain occurred more often in the gemfibrozil group than in the placebo group. However, the incidence was low: nausea, 4.3% with gemfibrozil vs 3.8% with placebo; vomiting, 2.3% vs 0.8%; abdominal pain, 6.4% vs 4.2%; and epigastric pain, 3.4% vs 1.7%.

Additional adverse reactions that have been reported, where a causal relationship to treatment with gemfibrozil is probable, are:

Gastrointestinal: cholestatic jaundice, pancreatitis. CNS: somnolence, peripheral neuritis, depression, decreased libido. Genitourinary: impotence. Musculoskeletal: arthralgia, synovitis, myalgia, myopathy, myasthenia, rhabdomyolysis (see Warnings, Drug Interactions). Integumentary: exfoliative dermatitis, photosensitivity. Immune: angioedema, laryngeal edema.

Postmarketing Study (Helsinki Heart Study): The long-term safety of gemfibrozil was established in the Helsinki Heart Study, a 5-year primary prevention Phase IV clinical trial. In the double-blind phase of the Helsinki Heart Study, 2 046 patients received gemfibrozil for up to 5 years. Table II lists the most frequently reported adverse events and includes those occurring in at least 1% of all subjects treated with gemfibrozil. Dyspepsia, abdominal pain, acute appendicitis and atrial fibrillation occurred more often in the gemfibrozil group than the placebo group, while all other adverse events were similar in frequency between the two groups.

Overdose: Symptoms and Treatment: Overdosage has been reported with gemfibrozil. In 1 case of accidental overdosage, where a child ingested 9 g of gemfibrozil, nonspecific symptoms of nausea and vomitting were reported. The patient fully recovered.

Symptomatic supportive measures should be taken should overdosage occur.

Table I—Lopid

Incidence of Symptoms Reported in Controlled Premarketing Studies

Symptom	Gemfibrozil (n=529)	Placebo (n=236)
Body as a Whole		
Dizziness	2.8%	4.2%
Chest pain	2.1%	1.7%
Fatigue	0.9%	0.4%
Integumentary		
Rash	2.5%	1.3%
Pruritus	0.8%	1.3%
Dermatitis	0.6%	0.4%
Urticaria	0.2%	0.0%
Musculoskeletal		
Pain in extremities	1.5%	1.7%
Gastrointestinal		
Abdominal pain	6.4%	4.2%
Diarrhea	4.9%	5.1%
Nausea	4.3%	3.8%
Epigastric pain	3.4%	1.7%
Vomiting	2.3%	0.8%
Flatulence	1.5%	2.1%
Endocrine		
Gout	0.9%	0.8%
CNS		
Headache	2.3%	4.2%
Paresthesia	0.9%	0.4%
Special Senses		
Blurred vision	1.1%	0.8%
Number of Patients Withdrawn for Clinical Symptoms	**1.3%**	**1.3%**

Table II—Lopid

Incidence of Adverse Events in Controlled Phase of Helsinki Heart Study

Adverse Event	Gemfibrozil (n=2 046)	Placebo (n=2 035)
Body as a Whole		
Fatigue	3.8%	3.5%
Headache	1.2%	1.1%
Digestive System		
Dyspepsia	19.6%	11.9%
Abdominal pain	9.8%	5.6%
Diarrhea	7.2%	6.5%
Flatulence	5.3%	5.2%
Nausea and/or vomiting	2.5%	2.1%
Constipation	1.4%	1.3%
Acute appendicitis	1.2%	0.6%
Nervous System		
Vertigo	1.5%	1.3%
Skin and Appendages		
Eczema	1.9%	1.2%
Rash	1.7%	1.3%
Number of Patients Withdrawn Due to Adverse Events	**10.4%**	**7.3%**

Dosage: Adults: The recommended dose is 1 200 mg administered in 2 divided doses (two 300 mg capsules or one 600 mg tablet twice a day) 30 minutes before the morning and evening meal. The maximum recommended daily dose is 1 500 mg.

Supplied: 300 mg: Each maroon and white capsule contains: gemfibrozil 300 mg. Nonmedicinal ingredients: Capsule: cornstarch, polysorbate 80 and silica gel. Capsule shell: contains: colloidal silicon dioxide, FD&C Blue No. 1, FD&C Red No. 3, gelatin, sodium lauryl sulfate and titanium dioxide. Energy: 3.4 kJ (0.8 kcal). Gluten-, lactose-, paraben-, sodium-, sulfite- and tartrazine-free. Bottles of 100 and 250.

600 mg: Each white, ellipsoidal, film-coated tablet, imprinted "Lopid 600 mg" on one side and "Parke-Davis" on the other, contains: gemfibrozil 600 mg. Nonmedicinal ingredients: calcium stearate, candelilla wax, colloidal silicon dioxide, hydroxypropylmethylcellulose, hydroxypropylcellulose, methylparaben, microcrystalline cellulose, Opacode Black, polyethylene glycol, polysorbate 80, pregelatinized starch, propylparaben and titanium dioxide. Energy: 2.0 kJ (0.47 kcal). Gluten-, lactose-, paraben-, sodium-, sulfite- and tartrazine-free. Bottles of 100 and 250.

Store below 30°C.

(Shown in Product Recognition Section)

LOPRESOR® ℞

Novartis Pharmaceuticals

Metoprolol Tartrate

Beta-adrenergic Receptor Blocking Agent

Pharmacology: Metoprolol is a β-adrenergic receptor-blocking agent. In vitro and in vivo animal studies have shown that it has a preferential effect on the β_1-adrenoreceptors, chiefly located in cardiac muscle. This preferential effect is not absolute, however, and at higher doses, metoprolol also inhibits β_2-adrenoreceptors, chiefly located in the bronchial and vascular musculature. Metoprolol has no membrane-stabilizing or partial agonism (intrinsic sympathomimetic activities). It is used in the treatment of hypertension, angina pectoris and to reduce mortality in patients with myocardial infarction.

The mechanism of the antihypertensive effect has not been established. Among the factors that may be involved are: a) competitive ability to antagonize catecholamine-induced tachycardia at the β-receptor sites in the heart, thus decreasing heart rate, cardiac contractility and cardiac output; b) inhibition of renin release by the kidneys; c) inhibition of the vasomotor centres.

By blocking catecholamine-induced increases in heart rate, in velocity and extent of myocardial contraction, and in blood pressure, metoprolol reduces the oxygen requirements of the heart at any given level of effort, thus making it useful in the long-term management of angina pectoris. However, in patients with heart failure, β-adrenergic receptor blockade may increase oxygen requirements by increasing left ventricular fiber length and end-diastolic pressure (preload).

The mechanisms involved in reducing mortality in patients with acute myocardial infarction are not fully understood.

Pharmacokinetics: In humans, absorption of metoprolol is rapid and complete. Plasma levels following oral administration, however, approximate 50% of levels following i.v. administration, indicating about 50% first-pass metabolism.

Intersubject plasma levels achieved are highly variable after oral administration, although they show good reproducibility within each individual. Peak plasma concentrations are attained after approximately 1.5 to 2 hours with conventional metoprolol formulations, and after approximately 4 to 5 hours with slow-release formulations. Upon repeated oral administration, the percentage of the dose systemically available is higher than after a single dose and also increases dose dependently. Ingestion with food may raise the systemic availability of an oral dose by approximately 20 to 40%. Only a small fraction of the drug (about 12%) is bound to human serum albumin. Elimination is mainly by biotransformation in the liver, and the plasma half-life averages 3.5 hours (range: 1 to 9 hours). The total clearance rate of an i.v. dose is approximately 1 L/min and the protein binding rate is approximately 10%. Less than 5% of an oral dose of metoprolol is recovered unchanged in the urine; the rest is excreted by the kidneys as metabolites that appear to have no clinical significance.

The systemic availability and half-life of metoprolol in patients with renal failure do not differ to a clinically significant degree from those in normal subjects; however metabolite excretion is impaired. Since the resulting metabolite accumulation has no effect on the β-blocking effects, no reduction in dosage is usually needed in patients with chronic renal failure.

Liver impairment may increase metoprolol bioavailability and reduce total clearance.

Pharmacodynamics: Significant beta-blocking effect (as measured by reduction of exercise heart rate) occurs within 1 hour after oral administration, and its duration is dose-related. For example, a 50% reduction of the maximum effect after single oral doses of 20, 50, and 100 mg occurred at 3.3, 5.0 and 6.4 hours, respectively, in normal subjects. After repeated oral dosages of 100 mg twice daily, a significant reduction in exercise systolic blood pressure was evident at 12 hours.

Pharmacokinetic and Pharmacodynamic Relationship: Following i.v. administration of metoprolol, the half-life of the distribution phase is approximately 12 minutes; the urinary recovery of unchanged drug is approximately 10%. When the drug was infused over a 10-minute period, in normal volunteers, maximum β-blockade was achieved at approximately 20 minutes. Doses of 5 mg and 15 mg yielded a maximal reduction in exercise-induced heart rate of approximately 10% and 15%, respectively. The effect on exercise heart rate decreased linearly with time at the same rate for both doses, and disappeared at approximately 5 hours and 8 hours for the 5 mg and 15 mg doses, respectively.

Equivalent maximal β-blocking effect is achieved with oral and i.v. doses in the ratio of approximately 2.5:1.

There is a linear relationship between the log of plasma levels and reduction of exercise heart rate. However, antihypertensive activity does not appear to be related to plasma levels. Because of variable plasma levels attained with a given dose and lack of a consistent relationship of antihypertensive activity to dose, selection of proper dosage requires individual titration.

In several studies of patients with acute myocardial infarction, i.v. followed by oral administration of metoprolol caused a reduction in heart rate, systolic blood pressure, and cardiac output. Stroke volume, diastolic blood pressure, and pulmonary artery end diastolic pressure remained unchanged.

The SR formulation produced lower peak metoprolol plasma concentrations than the regular tablets in studies with volunteers. Between 4 to 6 hours both concentration curves were similar. During the 8- to 24-hour period concentrations were higher after the SR tablets.

Indications: Hypertension: Metoprolol is indicated for mild or moderate hypertension. Usually combined with other antihypertensive agents (thiazide diuretics), it may be tried alone when the physician judges that a beta-blocker rather than a diuretic, should be the initial treatment.

Combining metoprolol with a diuretic or peripheral vasodilator has been found to be compatible and generally more effective than metoprolol alone. Limited experience with other antihypertensive agents has not shown evidence of incompatibility with metoprolol.

Metoprolol is not recommended for the emergency treatment of hypertensive crises.

Angina Pectoris: Metoprolol is indicated for the long-term treatment of angina pectoris due to ischemic heart disease.

Myocardial Infarction: Metoprolol is indicated in the treatment of hemodynamically stable patients with definite or suspected acute myocardial infarction to reduce cardiovascular mortality.

Treatment with i.v. metoprolol can be initiated as soon as the patient's clinical condition allows (see Dosage, Contraindications and Warnings).

Alternatively, in patients with proven myocardial infarction, oral treatment can begin within 3 to 10 days of the acute event (see Dosage). Data are not available as to whether benefit would ensue if the treatment is initiated later.

Clinical trials have shown that patients with unconfirmed myocardial infarction received no benefit from early drug therapy.

Contraindications: Metoprolol should not be used in the presence of: known hypersensitivity to metoprolol and derivatives, Lopresor components; sinus bradycardia; sick sinus syndrome; second and third degree A-V block; right ventricular failure secondary to pulmonary hypertension; overt heart failure; cardiogenic shock; severe peripheral arterial circulatory disorders; anesthesia with agents that produce myocardial depression (e.g., ether); the i.v. form is also contraindicated in the presence of asthma and other obstructive respiratory diseases (for oral treatment, see Precautions, Bronchospastic Diseases).

Myocardial Infarction Patients – Additional Contraindications: In patients with a heart rate <45 beats/min; significant heart block greater than first degree (PR interval ≥ 0.24 s); systolic blood pressure <100 mmHg; or moderate to severe cardiac failure (see Warnings).

Warnings: Cardiac Failure: Special caution should be exercised when administering metoprolol to patients with a history of heart failure. Sympathetic stimulation is a vital component supporting circulatory function in congestive heart failure, and inhibition with β-blockade always carries the potential hazard of further depressing myocardial contractility and precipitating cardiac failure. The positive inotropic action of digitalis may be reduced by the negative inotropic effect of metoprolol when the two drugs are used concomitantly. The effects of β-blockers and digitalis are additive in depressing A-V conduction. This also applies to combinations with calcium-antagonists of the verapamil type or some antiarrhythmics (see Drug Interactions).

In patients without a history of cardiac failure, continued depression of the myocardium over a period of time can, in some cases, lead to cardiac failure and/or hypotension (systolic blood pressure ≤ 90 mmHg). Therefore, at the first sign or symptom of impending cardiac failure, patients should be fully digitalized and/or given a diuretic and the response observed closely. If cardiac failure continues, despite adequate digitalization and diuretic therapy, metoprolol therapy should be reduced or withdrawn.

Abrupt Cessation of Therapy: Patients with angina should be warned against abrupt discontinuation of metoprolol. There have been no reports of severe exacerbation of angina and of myocardial infarction or ventricular arrhythmias in patients with angina pectoris, following abrupt discontinuation of beta-blocker therapy. The last 2 complications may occur with or without preceding exacerbation of angina pectoris. Therefore, when discontinuation of metoprolol is planned in patients with angina pectoris or previous myocardial infarction, the dosage should be reduced gradually over a period of about 2 weeks. The patient should be carefully observed. The same frequency of administration should be maintained. In situations of greater urgency, metoprolol therapy should be discontinued stepwise and with closer observation. If angina markedly worsens or acute coronary insufficiency develops, it is recommended that treatment with metoprolol be reinstituted promptly, at least temporarily.

Patients should be warned against interruption or discontinuation of therapy without the physician's advice. Because coronary artery disease is common and may be unrecognized, it is prudent not to discontinue metoprolol therapy abruptly even in patients treated only for hypertension.

Oculomucocutaneous Syndrome: Various skin rashes and conjunctival xerosis have been reported with β-blockers, including metoprolol. Oculomucocutaneous syndrome, a severe syndrome whose signs include conjunctivitis sicca and psoriasiform rashes, otitis, and sclerosing serositis, has occurred with the chronic use of one β-adrenergic receptor-blocking agent (practolol). This syndrome has not been observed with metoprolol or any other such agent. However, physicians should be alert to the possibility of such reactions and should discontinue treatment in the event they occur.

Severe Sinus Bradycardia: Severe sinus bradycardia may occur after β_1-adrenergic receptor blockade with metoprolol because of unopposed vagal activity. Very rarely a pre-existing AV conduction disorder of moderate degree may become aggravated, possibly leading to AV block. In such cases, dosage should be reduced or gradually withdrawn. Atropine, isoproterenol or dobutamine should be considered in patients with acute myocardial infarction.

Thyrotoxicosis: Although metoprolol has been used successfuly for the symptomatic (adjuvant) therapy of thyrotoxicosis, possible deleterious effects from long-term use of metoprolol have not been adequately appraised. Beta-blockade may mask the clinical signs of continuing hyperthyroidism or its complications, and give a false impression of improvement. Therefore, abrupt withdrawal of metoprolol may be followed by an exacerbation of the symptoms of hyperthyroidism, including thyroid storm.

Myocardial Infarction Patients – Additional Warnings: Acute Intervention: During acute intervention in myocardial infarction, i.v. metoprolol should only be used by experienced staff under circumstances where resuscitation and monitoring equipment is available.

Cardiac Failure: Depression of the myocardium with metoprolol may lead to cardiac failure (see general Warnings). Special caution should be exercised when administering metoprolol to patients with a history of cardiac failure or those with minimal cardiac reserve. Should failure occur, treatment should be as described in Warnings.

Severe Sinus Bradycardia: Severe sinus bradycardia may occur with the use of metoprolol (see general Warnings). Acute myocardial infarction (particularly inferior infarcts) may significantly decrease sinus rate. If the rate falls below 40 beats/min, especially with signs of decreased cardiac output, administer atropine (0.25 to 0.5 mg) i.v. If atropine treatment is unsuccessful, discontinue metoprolol and consider cautious administration of isoproterenol or installation of a cardiac pacemaker.

AV Conduction: Metoprolol slows AV conduction and may produce significant first- (PR interval ≥ 0.24 s), second-, or third-degree heart block. Acute myocardial infarction may also produce heart block. If heart block occurs, discontinue metoprolol and administer atropine (0.25 to 0.5 mg) i.v. If atropine treatment is unsuccessful, consider cautious administration of isoproterenol or installation of a cardiac pacemaker.

Hypotension: If hypotension (systolic blood pressure ≤ 90 mmHg) occurs, metoprolol should be discontinued, and the hemodynamic status of the patient and the extent of myocardial damage carefully assessed. Invasive monitoring of central venous, pulmonary capillary wedge, and arterial pressures may be required. Appropriate therapy with fluids, positive inotropic agents, balloon counterpulsation, or other treatment modalities should be instituted. If hypotension is associated with sinus bradycardia or AV block, treatment should be directed at reversing these (see above).

Precautions: Bronchospastic Diseases: Patients with bronchospastic diseases should, in general, not receive β-blockers. Because of its relative β_1-selectivity, however, metoprolol may be used with caution in patients with bronchospastic disease who do not respond to, or cannot tolerate, other antihypertensive treatment. Since β_1-selectivity is not absolute, a β_2-stimulating agent should be administered concomitantly, and the lowest possible dose of metoprolol should be used. In these circumstances it would be prudent initially to administer metoprolol in smaller doses 3 times daily, instead of larger doses 2 times daily, to avoid the higher plasma levels associated with the longer dosing interval (see Dosage).

Because it is unknown to what extent β_2-stimulating agents may exacerbate myocardial ischemia and the extent of infarction, these agents should not be used prophylactically in patients with proven or suspected acute myocardial infarction. If bronchospasm not related to congestive heart failure occurs, metoprolol should be discontinued. A theophylline derivative or a β_2-agonist may be administered cautiously, depending on the clinical condition of the patient. Both theophylline derivatives and β_2-agonists may produce serious cardiac arrhythmias.

Diabetes and Hypoglycemia: Metoprolol should be administered cautiously to spontaneously hypoglycemic or diabetic patients (especially those with labile diabetes) who are receiving insulin or oral hypoglycemic agents. β-adrenergic receptor blockers may mask the premonitory signs and symptoms of acute hypoglycemia.

Liver Function: Metoprolol should be used with caution in patients with impaired liver function. Liver function tests should be performed at regular intervals during long-term treatment (see Pharmacology, Pharmacokinetics).

Allergen Immunotherapy: There may be increased difficulty in treating an allergic type reaction in patients on β-blockers. In these patients, the reaction may be more severe due to pharmacologic effects of the β-blockers and problems with fluid changes. Epinephrine should be administered with caution since it may not have its usual effects in the treatment of anaphylaxis. On the one hand, larger doses of epinephrine may be needed to overcome the bronchospasm, while on the other, these doses can be associated with excessive alpha-adrenergic stimulation with consequent hypertension, reflex bradycardia and heart block and possible potentiation of bronchospasm. Alternatives to the use of large doses of epinephrine include vigorous supportive care such as fluids and the use of β-agonists including parenteral salbutamol or isoproterenol, to overcome bronchospasm and norepinephrine to overcome hypotension.

Patients Undergoing Surgery: Angina patients should be gradually withdrawn from metoprolol prior to elective surgery. Beta-blockade impairs cardiac response to β-andrenergically-mediated reflex stimuli. Protracted severe hypotension during anesthesia, and difficulty in restarting and maintaining the heartbeat in patients receiving β-blocking drugs, have been reported.

Follow the recommendations under Warnings, Abrupt Cessation of Therapy to avoid severe complications associated with abrupt withdrawal. All clinical and pharmacological effects should disappear within 48 hours of the last dose.

Since metoprolol is a competitive β-adrenergic receptor agonist inhibitor, its effects may be reversed, if necessary, by sufficient doses of agonists such as isoproterenol or dobutamine.

Peripheral Artery Disorders: Metoprolol may aggravate the symptoms of peripheral arterial circulatory disorders, mainly due to its blood pressure lowering effect.

Pheochromocytoma: Where a β-blocker is prescribed for a patient known to be suffering from a pheochromocytoma, an alpha-blocker should be given concomitantly.

Occupational Hazards, Reaction Time: β-blockers may adversely affect the patient's reaction time. Patients should be advised to avoid operating automobiles and machinery or engaging in other tasks requiring alertness until the patient's response to metoprolol therapy has been determined.

Pregnancy: Metoprolol crosses the placental barrier. Since metoprolol has not been studied in human pregnancy, the drug should not be given to pregnant women. The use of any drug in patients of child-bearing potential requires that the anticipated benefit be weighed against the possible hazards.

Lactation: Metoprolol is excreted in breast milk. If drug use is essential, patients should stop nursing.

Children: The safety and efficacy of metoprolol in children has not been established.

Geriatrics: Caution is indicated when using metoprolol in elderly patients. An excessively pronounced decrease in blood pressure or pulse rate may cause the blood supply to vital organs to fall to inadequate levels.

Drug Interactions: Antihypertensives: Metoprolol dosage should be adjusted to the individual requirements of the patient especially when used concomitantly with other antihypertensive agents (see Dosage).

Lopresor (cont'd)

MAO Inhibitors and Adrenergic Neuron-blockers: Closely monitor patients receiving MAO inhibitors or catecholamine-depleting drugs (such as reserpine or guanethidine). The added β-adrenergic-blockade of metoprolol may excessively reduce sympathetic activity. Metoprolol should not be combined with other β-blockers.
Calcium Channel Blockers: As with other β-blockers, metoprolol should not be given together with verapamil type calcium-antagonists. However, in exceptional cases, when the physician considers concomitant use essential, such use should be instituted gradually in a hospital setting under careful supervision. Negative inotropic, dromotropic and chronotropic effects may occur when metoprolol is given together with calcium antagonists. Verapamil and diltiazem reduce metoprolol clearance.
Antiarrhythmic Agents: β-blockers may enhance the negative inotropic and negative dromotropic effect of antiarrhythmic agents such as quinidine and amiodarone.
Clonidine Withdrawal Syndrome: The hypertensive crisis which may follow clonidine withdrawal may be accentuated in the presence of β-blockade. Withdrawing the β-blocker several days before the clonidine may reduce the danger of rebound effects.
Oral Antidiabetics: The dosage of oral antidiabetics may have to be readjusted in patients receiving β-blockers (see Precautions).
NSAIDs: Concurrent treatment with indomethacin may decrease the antihypertensive effect of β-blockers.
Hepatic Enzyme-Inducers and Enzyme-Inhibitors: Hepatic enzyme-inducing and enzyme-inhibiting substances may exert an influence on the plasma level of metoprolol. The plasma concentration of metoprolol is lowered by rifampicin, and may be raised by cimetidine, ranitidine and propafenone.
Lidocaine: Metoprolol may reduce the clearance of lidocaine.
α-Adrenergic Stimulants (Cold Remedies, Nasal Drops): Exaggerated hypertensive responses can be produced when β-blockers are combined with α-adrenergic agonists.
Inhalation Anesthetics: β-blockers enhance the cardiodepression produced by certain anesthetics (see Precautions, Patients Undergoing Surgery).
Alcohol: Metoprolol may modify the pharmacokinetics (decrease the elimination rate) of alcohol.

Adverse Effects: The most common adverse events reported are exertional tiredness, gastrointestinal disorders, and disturbances of sleep patterns. The most serious adverse events reported are congestive heart failure, bronchospasm and hypotension.

Reported adverse effects according to organ systems are:
Cardiovascular: secondary effects of decreased cardiac output which include: syncope, vertigo, light-headedness and postural hypotension; second and third degree AV block (see Contraindications); congestive heart failure (see Warnings); severe bradycardia; lengthening of PR interval; sinus arrest; cardiac arrhythmias; palpitations; chest pains; hot flushes; edema; cold extremities; Raynaud's phenomenon; claudication; gangrene in patients with pre-existing severe peripheral circulatory disorders.

In a placebo-controlled study in patients with acute myocardial infarction the incidence of the following cardiovascular reactions were as shown in Table I.

Table I—Lopresor

Incidence of Cardiovascular Reactions

	Metoprolol	Placebo
Hypotension (systolic BP <90 mmHg)	27.4%	23.2%
Bradycardia (heart rate <40 beats/min)	15.9%	6.7%
Second- or third-degree heart block	4.7%	4.7%
First-degree heart block (PR≥0.24 s)	5.3%	1.9%
Heart failure	27.5%	29.6%

CNS: headache, dizziness, mental depression, light-headedness, vivid dreams/nightmares, vertigo, anxiety, decreased mental alertness, weakness, fatigue, sedation, somnolence or insomnia, hallucination, paresthesia, personality disorder.
Gastrointestinal: diarrhea, constipation, flatulence, nausea and vomiting, abdominal pain, heartburn, dryness of mouth, hepatitis.
Respiratory: shortness of breath, bronchospasm, status asthmaticus, wheezing, rhinitis.
Allergic/Dermatological (see Warnings): skin rash (exanthema, urticaria, psoriasiform and dystrophic skin lesions), sweating, pruritus, photosensitivity.
Ear, Eye, Nose and Throat (EENT): tinnitus, hearing difficulties when doses exceed those recommended, dry and/or itchy eyes, conjunctivitis, blurred vision and nonspecific visual disturbances.
Miscellaneous: muscle cramps, exertional tiredness, weight gain, loss of hair, decreased libido, Peyronie's disease, arthritis.
Clinical Laboratory: The following laboratory parameters have been elevated on rare occasions: transaminases, BUN, alkaline phosphatase and bilirubin.
Hematology: Isolated cases of thrombocytopenia and leukopenia.

Overdose: Symptoms: The most common signs to be expected with overdosage of a β-adrenoreceptor agent are hypotension, bradycardia, congestive heart failure, bronchospasm and hypoglycemia. Atrioventricular block, cardiogenic shock and cardiac arrest may develop. In addition, impairment of consciousness (or even coma), nausea, vomiting and cyanosis may occur.

Concomitant ingestion of alcohol, antihypertensives, quinidine, or barbiturates aggravate the signs and symptoms.

The first manifestations of overdosage set in 20 minutes to 2 hours after drug administration.

Treatment: If overdosage occurs, in all cases therapy with metoprolol should be discontinued, the patient hospitalized and observed closely. Remove any drug remaining in the stomach by induction of emesis or gastric lavage. In addition, if required, the following therapeutic measures are suggested. 1. Bradycardia and Hypotension: Atropine 1 to 2 mg initially should be given i.v. If a satisfactory effect is not achieved, norepinephrine or dopamine may be administered after preceding treatment with atropine. (See Precautions concerning the use of epinephrine in patients.) In cases of hypoglycemia β-blocked glucagon (1 to 10 mg) can be administered. 2. Heart block (second or third degree): Isoproterenol or transvenous cardiac pacemaker. 3. Congestive heart failure: Conventional therapy. 4. Bronchospasm: I.V. aminophylline or a β_2-agonist. 5. Hypoglycemia: I.V. glucose.

It should be remembered that metoprolol is a competitive antagonist of isoproterenol and hence large doses of isoproterenol can be expected to reverse many of the effects of excessive doses of metoprolol. However, the complications of excess isoproterenol, e.g. hypotension and tachycardia, should not be overlooked.

Dosage: Hypertension: Metoprolol is usually used in conjunction with other antihypertensive agents, particularly a thiazide diuretic, but may be used alone (see Indications).

The dose must always be adjusted to the individual requirements of the patient, in accordance with the following guidelines.

Metoprolol treatment should be initiated with doses of 50 mg b.i.d. If an adequate response is not seen after 1 week, dosage should be increased to 100 mg b.i.d. In some cases the daily dosage may need to be increased by further 100 mg increments at intervals of not less than 2 weeks up to a maximum of 200 mg b.i.d., which should not be exceeded. The usual maintenance dose is within the range of 100 to 200 mg daily.

When metoprolol is combined with another antihypertensive agent which is already being administered, metoprolol should be added initially at a dose of 50 mg b.i.d. After 1 or 2 weeks the daily dosage may be increased if required, in increments of 100 mg, at intervals of not less than 2 weeks, until adequate blood pressure control is obtained.
Angina Pectoris: The recommended dosage range is 100 to 400 mg/day in divided doses. Initiate treatment with 50 mg b.i.d. for the first week. If response is not adequate, the daily dosage should be increased by 100 mg for the next week. The usual maintenance dose is 200 mg/day. The need for further increases should be closely monitored at weekly intervals and the dosage increased in 100 mg increments to a maximum of 400 mg/day in 2 or 3 divided doses. A metoprolol dose of 400 mg/day should not be exceeded.
Slow-release Tablets: Treatment must always be initiated and individual titration of dosage carried out using the regular tablets. The SR formulation may be preferred for maintenance because of the convenience of once-daily administration. Lopresor SR tablets should be taken in the morning and swallowed whole.

Lopresor SR 100 mg is intended for maintenance dosing in those patients requiring 100 mg metoprolol/day.

Lopresor SR 200 mg is intended for maintenance dosing in those patients requiring doses of 200 mg/day.
Tablet Residue in Feces: After the active substance has diffused out of the insoluble core of the Lopresor SR Tablet, the tablet residue is excreted in a softened form and may be found in the feces.
Myocardial Infarction: In addition to the usual contraindications: **Only patients with suspected acute myocardial infarction who meet the following criteria are suitable for therapy as described below:** systolic blood pressure≥100 mmHg; heart rate* ≥45 beats/minute; PR interval <0.24 seconds; rales*: <10 cm; adequate peripheral circulation.
*Extreme caution should be exercised when giving i.v. metoprolol to patients with heart rate between 45 and 60 and/or pulmonary rales less than 10 cm.

Therapy should be discontinued in patients if the heart rate drops below 45 or the systolic blood pressure drops below 100 mmHg.
Early Treatment: During the early phase of definite or suspected acute myocardial infarction, treatment with metoprolol can be initiated as soon as possible after the patient's arrival in the hospital. Such treatment should be initiated in a coronary care or similar unit immediately after the patient's hemodynamic condition has stabilized.

Treatment in this early phase should begin with the i.v. administration of 3 bolus injections of 5 mg each. The injections should be given at approximately 2-minute intervals. During the i.v. administration, blood pressure, heart rate, and ECG should be carefully monitored. If any of the injections are associated with adverse cardiovascular effects, i.v. administration should be stopped immediately and the patient should be observed carefully and appropriate therapy instituted.

In patients who tolerate the full i.v. dose (15 mg), metoprolol tablets, 50 mg every 6 hours, should be initiated 15 minutes after the last i.v. dose and continued for 48 hours. Thereafter, patients should receive a maintenance dosage of 100 mg twice daily (see Late Treatment).

Patients who appear not to tolerate the full i.v. dose should be started on either 25 or 50 mg every 6 hours (depending on the degree of intolerance) 15 minutes after the last i.v. dose or as soon as their clinical condition allows. In patients with severe intolerance, treatment with metoprolol should be discontinued (see Warnings).
Late Treatment (for proven myocardial infarction patients only): Patients with contraindications to treatment during the early phase of myocardial infarction, patients who appear not to tolerate the full early treatment, and patients in whom the physician wishes to delay therapy for any other reason should be started on metoprolol tablets, 100 mg twice daily, as soon as their clinical condition allows. Treatment can begin within 3 to 10 days of the acute event. Therapy should be continued for at least 3 months. Although the efficacy of treatment beyond 6 months has not been conclusively established data from studies with other β-blockers suggest that the treatment should be continued for 1 to 3 years.
Note: Ampuls: Metoprolol ampuls are single dose ampuls intended for i.v. injection. All parenteral drug products should be inspected for particulate matter and discoloration prior to administration whenever solution and container permit. Discard any unused portion or solution with particulate matter or discoloration.

Supplied: Ampuls: Each mL of aqueous, clear, injectable solution contains: metoprolol tartrate 1 mg. Also contains sodium chloride 9 mg. Alcohol-, bisulfite-, gluten-, lactose-, parabens- and tartrazine-free. Ampuls of 5 mL. Cartons of 5.

Protect ampuls from heat (store between 2 to 30°C) and light.

Tablets: 50 mg: Each light red, film-coated, capsule-shaped tablet embossed 51/51 and scored on one side and embossed Geigy on the other, contains: metoprolol tartrate 50 mg. Nonmedicinal ingredients: carnauba wax, cellulose compounds, lactose, magnesium stearate, peridone, polyethylene glycol, silicon dioxide, sodium carboxymethyl starch and talc. Energy: 1.05 kJ (0.25 kcal). Sodium: <1 mmol (0.06 mg). Alcohol-, bisulfite-, gluten-, parabens- and tartrazine-free. Bottles of 100 and 500.

100 mg: Each light blue, film-coated, capsule-shaped tablet embossed 71/71 and scored on one side and embossed Geigy on the other, contains: metoprolol tartrate 100 mg. Nonmedicinal ingredients: carnauba wax, cellulose compounds, lactose, magnesium stearate, peridone, polyethylene glycol, silicon dioxide, sodium carboxymethyl starch and talc. Energy: 1.05 kJ (0.25 kcal). Sodium: <1 mmol (0.12 mg). Alcohol-, bisulfite-, gluten-, parabens- and tartrazine-free. Bottles of 100 and 500.

Slow-Release Tablets: 100 mg: Each round, film-coated, orange-brown tablet, embossed GEIGY on one side and KR/100 engraved on the other, contains: metoprolol tartrate 100 mg in a slow-release formulation. Nonmedicinal ingredients: carnauba wax, castor oil compounds, cellulose compounds, iron oxides, magnesium stearate, phosphates polysorbate, talc and titanium dioxide. Energy: 1.05 kJ (0.26 kcal). Alcohol-, bisulfite-, gluten-, lactose-, parabens-, sodium- and tartrazine-free. Bottles of 100 and 250.

200 mg: Each round, film-coated, light yellow tablet, embossed GEIGY on one side and CDC on the other, contains: metoprolol tartrate 200 mg in a slow-release formulation. Nonmedicinal ingredients: carnauba wax, castor oil compounds, cellulose compounds, iron oxides, magnesium stearate, phosphates polysorbate, talc and titanium dioxide. Energy: 1.05 kJ (0.26 kcal). Alcohol-, bisulfite-, gluten-, lactose-, parabens-, sodium- and tartrazine-free. Bottles of 100 and 250.

Protect tablets from heat (store between 2 and 30°C), light and humidity.

(Shown in Product Recognition Section)

Reviewed 1997

LOPROX®

Hoechst Marion Roussel

Ciclopirox Olamine

Topical Antifungal

Pharmacology: Ciclopirox is a synthetic broad spectrum antifungal agent that inhibits the growth of pathogenic dermatophytes, yeasts, and M. furfur. It exhibits fungicidal activity in vitro against isolates of T. rubrum, T. mentagrophytes, E. floccosum, M. canis and C. albicans.

The mode of action of ciclopirox olamine was studied mainly in C. albicans. It is presumed that ciclopirox mediated growth inhibition or death of fungal cells is primarily caused by in vitro cellular depletion of some essential substrates and/or ions and that such effects are brought about through blockage of their uptake from the medium.

No data on mechanism of action are available for dermatophytes.

Penetration studies in human cadaverous skin with tagged ciclopirox cream 1% showed the presence of 0.8 and 1.6% of the dose in stratum corneum 1.5 to 6 hours after application. The levels in the dermis were still 10 to 15 times above the minimum inhibitory concentrations.

Autoradiographic studies with human cadaverous skin showed that ciclopirox penetrates through the epidermis, hair follicles, into the dermis, hair and the sebaceous gland with a depot or reservoir in the stratum corneum.

Pharmacokinetic studies in males with tagged ciclopirox cream 1% showed an average of 1.3% absorption of the dose. The cream was applied topically under occlusion to the back, with a total penetration time of 6 hours. Excretion occurred via the kidney, with biological half-life of 1.7 hours. Two days after application only 0.01% of the dose applied could be found in the urine.

Draize Human Sensitization Assay, 21-Day Cumulative Irritancy study, Phototoxicity study and Photo-Draize study conducted in a total of 142 healthy male subjects showed no contact sensitization of the delayed hypersensitivity type, no irritation, no phototoxicity and no photo-contact sensitization due to ciclopirox olamine cream 1%. The ingredients of ciclopirox lotion 1% are qualitatively the same as those of ciclopirox cream 1%.

Microbiology: Ciclopirox can be best described as a broad spectrum antimycotic agent with significant antibacterial activity. It is also effective against several protozoa.

Indications: For the topical treatment of the following dermal infections; tinea pedis, tinea cruris and tinea corporis due to T. rubrum, T. mentagrophytes, E. floccosum, M. canis; cutaneous candidiasis (moniliasis) due to C. albicans; and tinea (pityriasis) versicolor due to M. furfur.

It is not proposed for vaginal application.

Contraindications: In individuals who have shown hypersensitivity to any of the product components.

Warnings: Not for ophthalmic use.

Precautions: If a reaction suggesting sensitivity or chemical irritation should occur with the use of ciclopirox, treatment should be discontinued and appropriate therapy instituted.

Pregnancy: Reproduction studies have been performed in the mouse, rat, rabbit and monkey (via various routes of administration) at doses 10 times or greater than the topical human dose. No significant evidence of impaired fertility or harm to the fetus due to the use of ciclopirox has been revealed. However, a higher incidence of systemic absorption of ciclopirox in the rat was noted in the group given 30 mg/kg orally as compared to controls. There are, however, no adequate or well-controlled studies in pregnant women. Because animal reproduction studies are not always predictive of human response, this drug should be used during pregnancy only if clearly needed.

Lactation: It is not known whether this drug is excreted in human milk. Because many drugs are excreted in human milk, caution should be exercised when ciclopirox is administered to nursing women.

Children: Safety and effectiveness in children below the age of 10 years have not been established.

Adverse Effects: Ciclopirox is well tolerated with a low incidence of adverse reactions reported in clinical trials. Ciclopirox cream had a 0.4% incidence of adverse reactions in controlled clinical trials. These included pruritus at the site of application, worsening of clinical signs and symptoms and mild to severe burning reported in a few cases.

In a controlled clinical trial with 89 patients using ciclopirox lotion and 89 patients using the vehicle, the incidence of adverse reactions was low. The side effects included pruritus occurring in 3 patients and burning, which occurred in 1 patient.

Overdose: Symptoms and Treatment: There have been no clinical reports of acute overdosage with ciclopirox cream or lotion by any route of administration.

From acute toxicity studies of ciclopirox cream 1% in adult rats, oral doses of 36 g/kg produced no evidence of toxic signs.

Dosage: Gently massage into the affected and surrounding skin areas twice daily, in the morning and evening, for a minimum of 4 weeks. Clinical improvement with relief of pruritus and other symptoms usually occurs within the first week of treatment. If a patient shows no clinical improvement after 2 weeks of treatment with ciclopirox the diagnosis should be redetermined. Patients with tinea versicolor usually exhibit clinical and mycological clearing after 2 weeks of treatment.

Supplied: Cream: Each tube contains: ciclopirox olamine USP 1%. Nonmedicinal ingredients: benzyl alcohol, cetyl alcohol, cocamide DEA, lactic acid, mineral oil, myristyl alcohol, octyldodecanol, polysorbate 60, sorbitan monostearate, stearyl alcohol, and purified water. Tubes of 15 and 30 g.

Lotion: Each bottle contains: ciclopirox olamine USP 1%. Nonmedicinal ingredients: benzyl alcohol, cetyl alcohol, cocamide DEA, lactic acid, mineral oil, myristyl alcohol, octyldodecanol, polysorbate 60, sorbitan monostearate, stearyl alcohol, and purified water. Bottles of 30 mL.

Store at room temperature below 25°C.

LORAZEPAM

General Monograph, CPhA

see BENZODIAZEPINES

LOSEC®

Astra

Omeprazole Magnesium

H^+, K^+-ATPase Inhibitor

Note: When used in combination with amoxicillin, clarithromycin or metronidazole, the product monographs for those agents must be consulted and followed.

Pharmacology: Omeprazole inhibits the gastric enzyme H^+, K^+-ATPase (the proton pump) which catalyzes the exchange of H^+ and K^+. It is effective in the inhibition of both basal acid secretion and stimulated acid secretion. The inhibition is dose dependent. Daily oral doses of 20 mg and higher, showed a consistent and effective acid control. Information from clinical trials in patients with duodenal ulcers in remission indicate that omeprazole 20 mg tablets demonstrate the same inhibition of stimulated acid secretion and similar effect on 24 hour intragastric pH as omeprazole 20 mg capsules. The mean decrease in peak acid output after pentagastrin stimulation was approximately 70%, after 5 days of dosing with omeprazole 20 mg tablet once daily.

The equivalence of two 10 mg omeprazole tablets to one 20 mg omeprazole tablet has been demonstrated by a bioequivalence study in healthy volunteers.

Treatment with omeprazole alone has been shown to suppress, but not eradicate H. pylori, a bacterium that is strongly associated with acid peptic disease. Approximately 90 to 100% of patients with duodenal ulcers, and 80% of patients with gastric ulcer, are infected with H. pylori. Clinical evidence indicates a synergistic effect between omeprazole and certain antibiotics in achieving eradication of H. pylori. Eradication of H. pylori is associated with symptom relief, healing of mucosal lesions, decreased rate of duodenal ulcer recurrence and long-term remission of peptic ulcer disease, and reducing the need for prolonged antisecretory therapy.

There is no statistically significant change in the bioavailability (AUC, C_{max}) of amoxicillin during concomitant treatment with omeprazole, in healthy volunteers.

There is an increase in the bioavailability (AUC) and half-life of omeprazole, and bioavailability (AUC) and C_{max} of clarithromycin, during concomitant administration, in healthy volunteers.

There is no statistically significant change in the bioavailability (AUC, C_{max}) of metronidazole during concomitant treatment with omeprazole, in healthy volunteers.

Omeprazole tablets are absorbed rapidly. Food has no effect on the bioavailability of the tablet. Peak plasma levels occur on average within 2 hours. The 20 mg tablet and the 20 mg capsule are not bioequivalent in terms of plasma omeprazole AUC, C_{max} and T_{max}. Omeprazole 20 mg tablets demonstrate, after repeated dosing, increased plasma omeprazole AUC (18%) and maximum concentration (41%) in comparison to omeprazole 20 mg given as capsules.

The omeprazole capsule (as a multiple unit formulation) is usually emptied gradually from the stomach into the intestine. In contrast to the capsule, the tablet (as a single unit formulation) will enter the intestine and dissolve as one unit. Consequently, the absorption and first pass metabolism of the tablet take place only during a very limited period. This may be one of the reasons for the difference observed in the pharmacokinetic variables of the two formulations.

The antisecretory effect of omeprazole is directly proportional to the AUC; it is not dependent on the plasma concentration at any given time. Omeprazole is 95% bound to plasma proteins.

Omeprazole undergoes first-pass metabolism by the cytochrome P-450 2C19 system, mainly in the liver. Following i.v. administration and oral administration (capsules) of omeprazole, 80% of the dose is recovered as urinary metabolites. The remaining 20% is excreted in the feces.

Omeprazole 20 mg tablets and 20 mg capsules have an equivalent pharmacodynamic effect assessed by the inhibition of stimulated acid secretion and effect on 24-hour intragastric pH.

Indications: In the treatment of conditions where a reduction of gastric acid secretion is required, such as: duodenal ulcer; gastric ulcer; NSAID-associated gastric and duodenal ulcers; reflux esophagitis; symptomatic gastroesophageal reflux disease (GERD), i.e., heartburn and regurgitation; Zollinger-Ellison syndrome (pathological hypersecretory condition); eradication of H. pylori.

Omeprazole, in combination with clarithromycin and either amoxicillin or metronidazole, is indicated for the treatment of patients with peptic ulcer disease associated with H. pylori infection. The optimal timing for eradication therapy in patients whose ulcer is not clinically active (i.e., asymptomatic) remains to be determined. See Table I and Table II (on following page).

Patients who fail to have their infection eradicated may be considered to have H. pylori resistant to the antimicrobials used in the eradication regimen. Therefore, therapy involving alternative effective antimicrobial agents should be considered (if re-treating).

It has been demonstrated that resistance to metronidazole is a negative predictive factor, decreasing the eradication rate of H. pylori obtained with triple therapy (omeprazole, metronidazole and clarithromycin) by 10 to 20%. The addition of omeprazole to metronidazole and clarithromycin appears to reduce the effect of primary resistance and the development of secondary resistance compared to antimicrobials alone.

Contraindications: Hypersensitivity to omeprazole or any of the components of this medication (see Supplied).

Warnings: When gastric ulcer is suspected, the possibility of malignancy should be excluded before therapy with omeprazole is instituted, as treatment with this drug may alleviate symptoms and delay diagnosis.

Pregnancy: The safety in pregnancy has not been established. Omeprazole should not be administered to pregnant women unless the expected benefits outweigh the potential risks.

Lactation: It is not known if omeprazole is secreted in human milk. It should not be given to nursing mothers unless its use is considered essential.

Children: The safety and effectiveness of omeprazole in children have not yet been established.

Precautions: Geriatrics: Elderly subjects showed increased bioavailability (36%), reduced total plasma clearance (to

Losec (cont'd)

Table I—Losec

Results of studies in patients with a history of duodenal ulcer who were H. pylori positive

	Treatment	Eradication Rate APT or ITT Analysis	Eradication Rate PP Analysis
Study 1	omeprazole 20 mg + amoxicillin 1 000 mg + clarithromycin 500 mg, all twice daily for 1 week	96%	98%
	omeprazole 20 mg + metronidazole 400 mg* + clarithromycin 250 mg, all twice daily for 1 week	95%	94%
Study 2	omeprazole 20 mg + amoxicillin 1 000 mg + clarithromycin 500 mg, all twice daily for 1 week	94%	95%
	omeprazole 20 mg + metronidazole 400 mg* + clarithromycin 250 mg, all twice daily for 1 week	87%	91%

*500 mg metronidazole appears to be equivalent to 400 mg with regards to efficacy and safety.

Study 1: Patients included in the APT and PP analyses were assessed for H. pylori status by UBT pre- and post-treatment, n=684 (APT analysis).

Study 2: Patients included in the ITT and PP analyses were assessed for H. pylori status by UBT and culture pre- and post-treatment, n=514 (ITT analysis).

Table II—Losec

Results of studies in patients with active peptic ulcer who were H. pylori positive (ITT analysis)

	Treatment	Eradication Rate (PP analysis)	Ulcer Healing Rate (post-treatment)	Rate of Patients in Remission (6 months after cessation of therapy)
Study 3	omeprazole 20 mg + amoxicillin 1 000 mg + clarithromycin 500 mg, all twice daily for 1 week	78% (87%)	92%	88%
	omeprazole 20 mg + metronidazole 400 mg* + clarithromycin 250 mg, all twice daily for 1 week	85% (92%)	94%	92%
Study 4	omeprazole 20 mg + amoxicillin 1 000 mg + clarithromycin 500 mg, all twice daily for 1 week	79% (83%)	94%	83%
	omeprazole 20 mg + metronidazole 400 mg* + clarithromycin 250 mg, all twice daily for 1 week	86% (93%)	96%	92%

*500 mg metronidazole appears to be equivalent to 400 mg with regards to efficacy and safety.

Study 3: Patients with duodenal ulcer, included in the ITT analysis, were assessed for H. pylori status by UBT and histology pre- and post-treatment, n=146 (ITT analysis).

Study 4: Patients with gastric ulcer, included in the ITT analysis, were assessed for H. pylori status by UBT and histology pre- and post-treatment, n=145 (ITT analysis).

250 mL/min) and prolonged (50%) elimination half-life (to 1 hour) (data obtained from studies with i.v. administration of omeprazole and oral administration of omeprazole capsules). The daily dose in elderly patients should, as a rule, not exceed 20 mg (see Dosage).

Patients With Hepatic Insufficiency: Patients with impaired liver function showed a 75% increase in bioavailability, reduced total plasma clearance (to 67 mL/min), and a 4-fold prolongation of the elimination half-life (to 2.8 hours) (data obtained from studies with i.v. administration of omeprazole and oral administration of omeprazole capsules). A dose of 20 mg omeprazole capsules given once daily to these patients for 4 weeks was well tolerated, with no accumulation of omeprazole or its metabolites. The daily dose in patients with severe liver disease should, as a rule, not exceed 20 mg (see Dosage).

Patients With Renal Insufficiency: The disposition of intact omeprazole is unchanged in patients with impaired renal function and no dose adjustment is needed in these patients (data obtained from studies with i.v. administration of omeprazole and oral administration of omeprazole capsules) (see Dosage).

Information on the bioavailability of omeprazole 20 mg tablet in elderly patients, in patients with hepatic insufficiency, and in patients with renal insufficiency, as well as information on drug interactions are not currently available.

Carcinogenicity: The rat carcinogenicity study (24 months) revealed a gradual development from gastric ECL-cell hyperplasia to carcinoids at the end of their normal life span during administration with 14 to 140 mg/kg/day of omeprazole. No metastasis developed. No carcinoids developed during 18 months' high-dose treatment of mice (14 to 140 mg/kg/day). Similarly, administration of omeprazole up to 28 mg/kg/day in dogs for 7 years did not cause any carcinoids.

The gastric carcinoids in rats were related to sustained hypergastrinemia secondary to acid inhibition and not to omeprazole per se. Similar observations have been made after administration of histamine H_2-receptor blockers and also in partially fundectomised rats.

Short-term treatment and long-term treatment with omeprazole capsules in a limited number of patients for up to 6 years have not resulted in any significant pathological changes in gastric oxyntic endocrine cells.

Drug Interactions: The absorption of some drugs might be altered due to the decreased intragastric acidity. Thus, it can be predicted that the absorption of ketoconazole will decrease during omeprazole treatment, as it does during treatment with other acid secretion inhibitors or antacids.

Omeprazole is metabolized by the cytochrome P-450 system (CYP), mainly in the liver. The pharmacokinetics of the following drugs, which are also metabolized through the cytochrome P-450 system, have been evaluated during concomitant use of omeprazole capsules in humans: aminopyrine, antipyrine, diazepam, phenytoin, warfarin, theophylline, propranolol, metoprolol, lidocaine, quinidine, ethanol, piroxicam, diclofenac and naproxen.

Aminopyrine and Antipyrine: After 14 days' administration of 60 mg omeprazole once daily, the clearance of aminopyrine was reduced by 19%; the clearance of antipyrine was reduced by 14%. After 14 days' administration of 30 mg once daily, no significant changes in clearance were noted.

Diazepam, Warfarin and Phenytoin: As omeprazole is metabolized through cytochrome P-450 2C19, it can alter the metabolism and prolong elimination of diazepam, warfarin (R-warfarin) and phenytoin.

Diazepam: Following repeated dosing with omeprazole 40 mg once daily, the clearance of diazepam was decreased by 54%. The corresponding decrease after omeprazole 20 mg was 26%.

Warfarin: Concomitant administration of omeprazole 20 mg in healthy subjects had no effect on plasma concentrations of the (S)-enantiomer of warfarin, but caused a slight, though statistically significant increase (12%) in the less potent (R)-enantiomer concentrations. A small but statistically significant increase (11%) in the anticoagulant effect of warfarin was also seen. Concomitant treatment with omeprazole 20 mg daily did not change coagulation time in patients on continuous treatment with warfarin.

Phenytoin: Following 3 weeks' treatment with omeprazole 20 mg once daily, the steady-state plasma levels of phenytoin in epileptic patients already receiving concomitant phenytoin treatment were not significantly affected. Urinary excretion of phenytoin and its main metabolite were also unchanged.

After single i.v. and oral doses of omeprazole capsules 40 mg in young, healthy volunteers, the clearance of phenytoin was decreased by 15 to 20%, and half-life was prolonged by 20 to 30%. Following repeated dosing with omeprazole 40 mg once daily, the elimination half-life of phenytoin was increased by 27%. Thus, there appears to be a dose dependent inhibition of elimination of phenytoin by omeprazole.

Patients receiving phenytoin and warfarin should be monitored to determine if it is necessary to adjust the dosage of these drugs when taken concomitantly with omeprazole.

Results from a range of interaction studies with omeprazole versus other drugs indicate that omeprazole, 20 to 40 mg given repeatedly, has no influence on other clinically relevant isoforms of CYP, as shown by the lack of metabolic interaction with substrates for CYP 1A2 (caffeine, phenacetin, theophylline), CYP 2C9 (S-warfarin), CYP 2D6 (metoprolol, propranolol), CYP 2E1 (ethanol), and CYP 3A (cyclosporine, lidocaine, quinidine, estradiol).

Theophylline: No effects on oral or i.v. theophylline kinetics have been observed after repeated once daily doses of 40 mg omeprazole.

Propranolol and Metoprolol: No effects on propranolol kinetics were observed in a steady-state trial with 20 mg of omeprazole daily. Similarly, no effects on steady-state plasma levels of metoprolol were observed after concomitant treatment with 40 mg omeprazole daily.

Lidocaine: No interaction with a single i.v. dose of lidocaine or its active metabolite, MEGX, was found after 1 week's pretreatment with omeprazole 40 mg once daily. There were no interactions between omeprazole and lidocaine or MEGX concerning pharmacokinetic variables.

Quinidine: After 1 week of omeprazole 40 mg once daily, no effect was observed on the kinetics or pharmacodynamics of quinidine.

Ethanol: There was no significant effect on the pharmacokinetics of ethanol after omeprazole 20 mg.

Piroxicam, Diclofenac and Naproxen: There was no significant effect on the steady-state pharmacokinetics of piroxicam, diclofenac, and naproxen following repeated dosing with omeprazole 20 mg, in healthy volunteers.

No interaction with food after repeated dosing of omeprazole tablets has been found. No interaction with antacids administered concomitantly with omeprazole (given as capsules) has been found.

Adverse Effects: Omeprazole is well tolerated. Most adverse reactions have been mild and transient, and have shown no consistent relationship with treatment. Adverse events have been recorded during controlled clinical investigations in 2 764 patients exposed to omeprazole (data taken from controlled clinical studies with omeprazole capsules) or reported from routine use. In a controlled clinical trial comparing omeprazole to placebo, the prevalence of adverse events with omeprazole 40 mg once daily was similar to that with placebo. In short-term comparative double-blind studies with histamine H_2-receptor antagonists, there was no significant difference in the prevalence of adverse events between omeprazole capsules and the H_2-receptor antagonists. An extensive evaluation of laboratory variables has not revealed any significant changes during omeprazole treatment which are considered to be clinically important.

The following adverse events (at a rate of more than 1%) have been reported in individuals receiving omeprazole capsules in controlled clinical situations: diarrhea (2.8%); headache (2.6%); flatulence (2.3%); abdominal pain (1.7%); constipation (1.3%); and dizziness/vertigo (1.1%).

In addition, the following adverse events were reported in clinical trials or were reported from routine use:

Skin: Rarely, rash and/or pruritus. In isolated cases photosensitivity, erythema multiforme and alopecia.

Musculoskeletal: In isolated cases arthralgia, muscular weakness and myalgia.

Central and Peripheral Nervous System: Rarely dizziness, paresthesia, somnolence, insomnia and vertigo. In isolated cases reversible mental confusion, agitation, depression and hallucination occurring predominantly in severely ill patients.

Gastrointestinal: nausea and vomiting. In isolated cases dry mouth, stomatitis and gastrointestinal candidiasis.

Hepatic: In rare cases, increased liver enzyme levels. In isolated cases encephalopathy in patients with pre-existing severe liver disease, hepatitis with or without jaundice and hepatic failure.

Endocrine: In isolated cases gynecomastia.

Hematologic: In isolated cases, patients have developed leukopenia and thrombocytopenia, agranulocytosis and pancytopenia.
Other: Rarely, malaise. Hypersensitive reactions including urticaria (rarely) and, in isolated cases, angioedema, fever, bronchospasm and interstitial nephritis and anaphylactic shock. In isolated cases increased sweating, peripheral edema, blurred vision and taste disturbances.
H. pylori Eradication Combination Therapy: The following adverse events (at a rate of more than 1%), were recorded during controlled clinical trials in 493 patients receiving omeprazole, amoxicillin and clarithromycin: diarrhea (28%), taste disturbances (15%), headache (5%), flatulence (4%), nausea (3%), abdominal pain (2%), ALT increased (1%), epigastric pain (1%), pharyngitis (1%) and glossitis (1%).

The following adverse events (at a rate of more than 1%) were recorded during controlled clinical trials in 494 patients receiving omeprazole, metronidazole and clarithromycin: taste disturbances (14%), diarrhea (13%), headache (6%), ALT increased (6%), flatulence (5%), nausea (5%), AST increased (5%), dyspepsia (3%), dry mouth (2%), dizziness/vertigo (2%), epigastric pain (1%), pharyngitis (1%), eructation (1%) and fatigue (1%).

Clinical experience with the use of omeprazole 20 mg tablet is limited. In 2 short-term studies (20 mg tablet once daily for a maximum duration of 7 days) in a limited number of patients with duodenal ulcer in remission, the adverse event profile seen with the omeprazole 20 mg tablet is similar to that seen with the omeprazole 20 mg capsule.

Overdose: Symptoms and Treatment: No information is available on the effects of higher doses in man, and specific recommendations for treatment cannot be given. Single oral doses of up to 400 mg of omeprazole capsules have not resulted in any severe symptoms, and no specific treatment has been needed. As in all cases where overdosing is suspected, treatment should be supportive and symptomatic. Any unabsorbed material should be removed from the gastrointestinal tract, and the patient should be carefully monitored.

The oral LD_{50} of omeprazole in male and female rats and mice was greater than 4 000 mg/kg. In dogs, the only sign of acute toxicity was vomiting which occurred at doses of approximately 600 mg/kg.

When used in combination with antibiotics, the prescribing information/product monograph for those antibiotics should be consulted.

Dosage: Omeprazole 20 mg tablets and omeprazole 20 mg capsules have an equivalent effect on the inhibition of stimulated acid secretion and on 24-hour intragastric pH. These data support the conclusion that omeprazole 20 mg tablet and capsule can be used with equivalent efficacy in the treatment of conditions where a reduction of gastric acid secretion is required.
Duodenal Ulcer: Acute Therapy: The recommended adult oral dose is 20 mg given once daily. Healing usually occurs within 2 weeks. For patients not healed after this initial course of therapy, an additional 2 weeks of treatment is recommended.
Refractory Patients: In patients with duodenal ulcer refractory to other treatment regimens, the recommended adult dose is 20 to 40 mg given once daily. Healing is usually achieved within 4 weeks in such patients.
Maintenance Therapy for Duodenal Ulcer: Over 95% of duodenal ulcer patients are H. pylori-positive, and should be treated with eradication therapy, as described below. A small percentage of patients who are H. pylori-negative will experience a disease recurrence and will require maintenance treatment with an antisecretory agent. The recommended omeprazole dose is 10 mg once daily, increased to 20 to 40 mg once daily as necessary.
Gastric Ulcer: Acute Therapy: The recommended adult dose is 20 mg given once daily. Healing usually occurs within 4 weeks. For patients not healed after this initial course of therapy, an additional 4 weeks of treatment is recommended.
Refractory Patients: In patients with gastric ulcer refractory to other treatment regimens, the recommended adult dose is 40 mg given once daily. Healing is usually achieved within 8 weeks.
Maintenance Therapy for Gastric Ulcer: About 80% of gastric ulcer patients are H. pylori-positive, and should be treated with eradication therapy, as described below. A small percentage of patients who are H. pylori-negative will experience a disease recurrence and will require maintenance treatment with an antisecretory agent. The recommended omeprazole dose is 20 mg once daily, increased to 40 mg once daily as necessary.
NSAID-Associated Gastric or Duodenal Ulcers: The issue of whether or not eradication of H. pylori in patients with NSAID-associated ulcers might have beneficial preventive effects has not yet been settled.
Acute Therapy: In patients with NSAID-associated gastric or duodenal ulcers, the recommended adult dose is 20 mg given once daily. Symptom resolution is rapid and healing usually occurs within 4 weeks. For those patients not healed after this initial course of therapy, an additional 4 weeks of treatment is recommended.
Maintenance Therapy: For the prevention of relapse in patients with NSAID-associated gastric or duodenal ulcers, the recommended adult dose is 20 mg given once daily, for up to 6 months.
H. pylori Associated Peptic Ulcer Disease: Omeprazole, Amoxicillin and Clarithromycin Triple Therapy: The recommended dose for eradication of H. pylori is omeprazole 20 mg, amoxicillin 1 000 mg and clarithromycin 500 mg, all twice daily for 7 days.
Omeprazole, Metronidazole and Clarithromycin Triple Therapy: The recommended dose for eradication of H. pylori is omeprazole 20 mg, metronidazole 500 mg and clarithromycin 250 mg, all twice daily for 7 days.

To ensure healing and/or symptom control, further treatment with 20 mg omeprazole once daily for up to 3 weeks is recommended for patients with active duodenal ulcer, and with 20 to 40 mg omeprazole once daily for up to 12 weeks for patients with active gastric ulcer.

Patient compliance with treatment regimens for the eradication of H. pylori has been demonstrated to have a positive effect on eradication outcome. In clinical trials, patients treated with triple therapy regimens have shown high compliance rates.

Susceptibility testing (MIC values derived from the Agar dilution method) of H. pylori to metronidazole and clarithromycin is available for 486 primary isolates from patients with a history of duodenal ulcer in one European study. Resistance to metronidazole (MIC >8 mg/L) was detected in 131 strains (27%), while 9 strains (2%) were resistant to clarithromycin (MIC >1 mg/L). Secondary resistance to metronidazole developed in strains from 4 patients treated with omeprazole/metronidazole/clarithromyin. Similarly, in those patients treated with omeprazole/metronidazole/clarithromycin or omeprazole/amoxicillin/clarithromycin combinations, secondary resistance to clarithromycin developed in strains from 4 patients. For amoxicillin, the MIC values at pretherapy or post-therapy did not indicate any primary, or the development of secondary, resistance to H. pylori.
Reflux Esophagitis: Acute Therapy: The recommended adult dose is 20 mg given once daily. In most patients, healing occurs within 4 weeks. For patients not healed after this initial course of therapy, an additional 4 weeks of treatment is recommended.
Refractory Patients: For patients with reflux esophagitis refractory to other treatment regimens, the recommended adult dose is 40 mg given once daily. Healing is usually achieved within 8 weeks.
Maintenance Therapy for Reflux Esophagitis: For the long-term management of patients with healed reflux esophagitis, 10 mg omeprazole (given as capsules) once daily has been found to be effective in controlled clinical trials of 12 months' duration, and in continuous maintenance treatment, in a limited number of patients, for a period of up to 6 years. Therefore, the recommended adult dose of omeprazole tablets for maintenance treatment of patients with healed reflux esophagitis is 10 mg given once daily. In the case of recurrence, the dose can be increased to 20 to 40 mg once daily.
Symptomatic Gastroesophageal Reflux Disease: (i.e., Heartburn and Regurgitation): The recommended adult dose is 20 mg given once daily. Symptom relief should be rapid. If symptom control is not achieved after 4 weeks, further investigation is recommended. Since some patients respond adequately to 10 mg given once daily, individual dose adjustment should be considered. For the maintenance of symptom relief in patients with gastroesophageal reflux disease (i.e., heartburn and regurgitation) the recommended adult dose is 10 mg given once daily.
Zollinger-Ellison Syndrome: The dose used in the treatment of Zollinger-Ellison syndrome will vary with the individual patient.

The recommended initial dose is 60 mg, given once daily. More than 90% of the patients with the severe form of the disease and inadequate response to other therapies have been adequately controlled with doses of 20 to 120 mg omeprazole capsules daily. With doses greater than 80 mg, the dose should be divided and given twice daily. Doses should be adjusted to the individual patient's need and should continue as long as clinically indicated. Doses up to 120 mg omeprazole capsules 3 times daily have been administered.
Patients With Renal Insufficiency: No dose adjustment is required (see Precautions).
Patients with Hepatic Insufficiency: No dose adjustment is required. The daily dose should not exceed 20 mg (see Precautions).
Geriatrics: No dose adjustment is required. The daily dose should not exceed 20 mg (see Precautions).

The tablets should be swallowed whole with sufficient water.
Storage: Omeprazole tablets are moisture sensitive and are therefore provided in blister compliance packages suitable for direct distribution to the patient. Store in a dry place at controlled room temperature (15 to 30°C).

Information for the Patient: See Blue Section—Information for the Patient "Losec".

Supplied: 10 mg: Each pink, circular and biconvex delayed release tablet, printed $^{LOSEC}_{10}$ on both sides, contains: omeprazole magnesium anhydrous 10.3 mg (equivalent to omeprazole 10 mg). Nonmedicinal ingredients: hydroxypropyl methylcellulose, iron oxide, mannitol, methacrylic acid copolymer, microcrystalline cellulose, paraffin, polyethylene glycol, sodium starch glycolate, sodium stearyl fumarate, talc and titanium dioxide. Press-through blister compliance strips in cartons of 28. Dispense in original container.

20 mg: Each red-brown, circular, biconvex delayed release tablet, printed $^{LOSEC}_{20}$ on both sides, contains: omeprazole magnesium anhydrous 20.6 mg (equivalent to omeprazole 20 mg). Nonmedicinal ingredients: hydroxypropyl methylcellulose, iron oxide, mannitol, methacrylic acid copolymer, microcrystalline cellulose, paraffin, polyethylene glycol, sodium starch glycolate, sodium stearyl fumarate, talc and titanium dioxide. Press-through blister compliance packs in cartons of 14 and 28 and in 10×10 unit dose blister packages. Dispense in the original container.

(Shown in Product Recognition Section)

Reviewed 1999

LOSEC® 1-2-3 A™
Astra
Omeprazole Magnesium—Amoxicillin—Clarithromycin
H. pylori Associated Peptic Ulcer Disease

Note: Regimen consists of omeprazole magnesium 20 mg, amoxicillin 1 000 mg and clarithromycin 500 mg. All twice daily for 7 days. For further details on this triple therapy for treatment of H. pylori eradication, consult the Losec product monograph. For additional safety information on amoxicillin and clarithromycin, consult the product monographs.

LOSEC® 1-2-3 M™
Astra
Omeprazole Magnesium—Metronidazole—Clarithromycin
H. pylori Associated Peptic Ulcer Disease

Note: Regimen consists of omeprazole magnesium 20 mg, metronidazole 500 mg and clarithromycin 250 mg. All twice daily for 7 days. For further details on this triple therapy for treatment of H. pylori eradication, consult the Losec product monograph. For additional safety information on metronidazole and clarithromycin, consult the product monographs.

LOTENSIN® ℞
Novartis Pharmaceuticals
Benazepril HCl
Angiotensin Converting Enzyme Inhibitor

Pharmacology: Benazepril is an angiotensin converting enzyme (ACE) inhibitor which is used in the treatment of hypertension.

Benazepril, after hydrolytic bioactivation to benazeprilat, inhibits angiotensin converting enzyme (ACE), a peptidyl dipeptidase catalyzing the conversion of angiotensin I to the vasoconstrictor angiotensin II. Angiotensin II also stimulates aldosterone secretion by the adrenal cortex, leading to sodium resorption and potassium secretion by the distal renal tubules.

Inhibition of ACE results in a decrease in plasma angiotensin II, leading to decreased vasoconstriction and a small decrease in aldosterone secretion and plasma aldosterone concentrations. Although the decrease in aldosterone is small,

Lotensin (cont'd)

it can result in small increases in serum potassium. Slight increases in serum potassium have been observed in some hypertensive patients treated with benazepril alone. Essentially no change in mean serum potassium was seen in patients treated with benazepril and a thiazide diuretic (see Precautions).

Removal of inhibition of renin secretion by angiotensin II leads to increased plasma renin activity (due to removal of negative feedback of renin release).

ACE is identical to kininase II. Thus, benazepril may interfere with degradation of the potent peptide vasodilator, bradykinin. Whether increased levels of bradykinin play a role in the therapeutic effects of benazepril is unknown.

While the mechanism through which benazepril lowers blood pressure is believed to be primarily suppression of the renin-angiotensin-aldosterone system, benazepril has an antihypertensive effect even in patients with low renin hypertension. In particular, benazepril was antihypertensive in all races studied, although it was somewhat less effective in blacks than in non-blacks.

Pharmacokinetics: Following oral administration of benazepril, peak plasma concentrations of benazepril are reached within 0.5 to 1 hour. The extent of absorption is at least 37% as determined by urinary recovery of unchanged drug and its metabolites. Following absorption, benazepril is rapidly hydrolyzed to its active metabolite, benazeprilat. Peak plasma concentrations of benazeprilat are reached 1 to 2 hours after drug intake in the fasting state and 2 to 4 hours after drug intake in the nonfasting state. While the rate of absorption may be slowed by the presence of food in the gastrointestinal tract, the systemic availability of benazeprilat is not affected. Benazeprilat is eliminated predominantly by renal excretion and has an effective accumulation half-life of 10 to 11 hours. The serum protein binding of benazepril is about 97%, and that of benazeprilat about 95%.

Benazepril is almost completely metabolized to benazeprilat, and to the glucuronide conjugates of benazepril and benazeprilat. Only trace amounts of an administered dose of Lotensin can be recovered in the urine as unchanged benazepril, while about 20% of the dose is excreted as benazeprilat, 4% as benazepril glucuronide, and 8% as benazeprilat glucuronide. The kinetics of benazepril are approximately dose-proportional within the dosage range (10 to 40 mg).

The disposition of benazepril and benazeprilat in patients with mild to moderate renal insufficiency (creatinine clearance >30 mL/min [0.5 mL/s]) is similar to that in patients with normal renal function. In patients with creatinine clearance <30 mL/min [0.5 mL/s], peak benazeprilat levels and the initial (alpha phase) half-life increase, and time to steady state may be delayed (see Dosage).

In patients with hepatic dysfunction due to cirrhosis, levels of benazeprilat are essentially unaltered. The pharmacokinetics of benazepril and benazeprilat do not appear to be influenced by age.

Pharmacodynamics: Administration of benazepril to patients with mild to moderate essential hypertension results in a reduction of both supine and standing blood pressure usually with little or no orthostatic change. Symptomatic postural hypotension is infrequent, although it may occur in patients who are salt- and/or volume-depleted (see Warnings).

After administration of a single oral dose, the onset of antihypertensive activity occurs at approximately 1 hour, with maximum reduction of blood pressure achieved by 2 to 4 hours, in most patients. At recommended doses given once daily, antihypertensive effects have persisted for at least 24 hours. In dose-response studies using once daily dosing in mild to moderate essential hypertensive patients, the minimally effective daily dose of benazepril was 10 mg. In studies comparing the same daily dose of benazepril given as a single morning dose or as a twice daily dose, blood pressure reductions at the time of morning trough blood levels were greater with the divided regimen.

During chronic therapy, the maximum reduction in blood pressure with any dose is generally achieved after 1 to 2 weeks. Abrupt withdrawal of benazepril has not been associated with a rapid increase in blood pressure.

When benazepril is given together with thiazide-type diuretics, its blood pressure lowering effect is approximately additive.

Efficacy and safety appear to be the same for elderly (>65 years of age) and younger adult patients given the same daily dosages.

Indications: In the treatment of mild to moderate essential hypertension. It may be used alone or in association with thiazide diuretics.

In using benazepril, consideration should be given to the risk of angioedema (see Warnings).

Benazepril should normally be used in those patients in whom treatment with a diuretic or a beta-blocker was found ineffective or has been associated with unacceptable adverse effects.

Benazepril can also be tried as an initial agent in those patients in whom use of diuretics and/or beta-blockers is contraindicated or in patients with medical conditions in which these drugs frequently cause serious adverse effects.

The safety and efficacy of benazepril in congestive heart failure and renovascular hypertension have not been established and therefore, its use in these conditions is not recommended.

The safety and efficacy of concurrent use of benazepril with antihypertensive agents other than thiazide diuretics have not been established.

Pregnancy: **When used in pregnancy during the second and third trimesters, ACE inhibitors can cause injury or even death of the developing fetus. When pregnancy is detected, ACE inhibitors should be discontinued as soon as possible (see Warnings, Pregnancy and Information for the Patient).**

Contraindications: In patients with known hypersensitivity to this product or any of its components and in patients with a history of angioedema related to previous treatment with an ACE inhibitor.

Warnings: Angioedema: Angioedema has been reported in patients with ACE inhibitors, including benazepril. Angioedema associated with laryngeal involvement may be fatal. If laryngeal stridor or angioedema of the face, tongue, or glottis occurs, benazepril should be discontinued immediately, the patient treated appropriately in accordance with accepted medical care, and carefully observed until the swelling disappears. In instances where swelling is confined to the face and lips, the condition generally resolves without treatment, although antihistamines may be useful in relieving symptoms. Where there is involvement of tongue, glottis or larynx, likely to cause airway obstruction, appropriate therapy (including, but not limited to 0.3 to 0.5 mL of s.c. epinephrine solution 1:1 000) should be administered promptly (see Adverse Effects).

Patients with a history of angioedema unrelated to ACE inhibitor therapy may be at increased risk of angioedema while receiving an ACE inhibitor (see Contraindications).

Hypotension: Occasionally, symptomatic hypotension has occurred after administration of benazepril usually after the first or second dose or when the dose was increased. It is more likely to occur in patients who are volume depleted by diuretic therapy, dietary salt restriction, dialysis, diarrhea, or vomiting. In patients with ischemic heart disease or cerebrovascular disease, an excessive fall in blood pressure could result in a myocardial infarction or cerebrovascular accident (see Adverse Effects). Because of the potential fall in blood pressure in these patients, therapy with benazepril should be started under close medical supervision. Such patients should be followed closely for the first weeks of treatment and whenever the dose of benazepril is increased. In patients with severe congestive heart failure, with or without associated renal insufficiency, ACE inhibitor therapy may cause excessive hypotension and has been associated with oliguria, and/or progressive azotemia, and rarely, with acute renal failure and/or death.

If hypotension occurs, the patient should be placed in a supine position and, if necessary, receive an i.v. infusion of normal saline. A transient hypotensive response is not a contraindication to further treatment, which usually can be continued without difficulty once the blood pressure has increased after volume expansion. However, lower doses of benazepril and/or reduced concomitant diuretic therapy should be considered.

Neutropenia/Agranulocytosis: Agranulocytosis and bone marrow depression have been caused by ACE inhibitors. Current experience with benazepril shows the incidence to be rare and a causal relationship to the administration of benazepril has not been established. Periodic monitoring of white blood cell counts should be considered, especially in patients with collagen vascular disease and/or renal disease.

Pregnancy: ACE inhibitors can cause fetal and neonatal morbidity and mortality when administered to pregnant women. Several dozen cases have been reported in the world literature. When pregnancy is detected, benazepril should be discontinued as soon as possible.

In rare cases (probably less than 1 in every 1 000 pregnancies) in which there is no alternative to ACE inhibitor therapy, patients should be apprised of the potential hazards to their fetuses. Serial ultrasound examinations should be performed to assess fetal development and well-being in addition to the volume of amniotic fluid.

If oligohydramnios is observed, benazepril should be discontinued unless it is considered life-saving for the mother. A non-stress test (NST), and/or biophysical profiling (BPP) may be appropriate, depending upon the week of pregnancy. If concerns regarding fetal well-being still persist, a contraction stress testing (CST) should be considered. Patients and physicians should be aware, however, that oligohydramnios may not appear until after the fetus has sustained irreversible injury.

Infants with a history of exposure to ACE inhibitors in utero should be closely observed for hypotension, oliguria, and hyperkalemia. If oliguria occurs, attention should be directed toward support of blood pressure and renal perfusion. Exchange transfusion or dialysis may be required as a means of reversing hypotension and/or substituting for impaired renal function, however, experience with these procedures is limited and they have not been associated with significant clinical benefit. Hemodialysis has little effect on the clearance of benazepril and benazeprilat.

Human Data: It is not known whether exposure limited to the first trimester of pregnancy can adversely affect fetal outcome. Use of ACE inhibitors during the second and third trimesters of pregnancy has been associated with fetal and neonatal injury including hypotension, neonatal skull hypoplasia, anuria, reversible or irreversible renal failure and death. Oligohydramnios has also been reported, presumably resulting from decreased fetal renal function; oligohydramnios in this setting has been associated with fetal limb contracture, craniofacial deformation and hypoplastic lung development. Prematurity and patent ductus arteriosus have also been reported, although it is not clear whether these occurrences were due to the ACE inhibitor exposure.

Animal Data: Dose related maternal toxicity was observed in studies of pregnant rats, mice and rabbits at doses of 250 mg/kg, 150 mg/kg and 1 mg/kg respectively. No embryotoxic or teratogenic effects of benazepril were seen at doses up to 250 mg/kg in rats (300 times the maximum recommended dose in humans), 150 mg/kg in mice (90 times the maximum recommended dose in humans) and 5 mg/kg in rabbits (more than 3 times the maximum recommended dose in humans).

Precautions: Renal Impairment: As a consequence of inhibiting the renin-angiotensin-aldosterone system, changes in renal function have been seen in susceptible individuals. In patients whose renal function may depend on the activity of the renin-angiotensin-aldosterone system, such as patients with bilateral renal artery stenosis, unilateral renal artery stenosis to a solitary kidney, or severe congestive heart failure, treatment with agents that inhibit this system has been associated with oliguria, progressive azotemia, and rarely, acute renal failure and/or death. In susceptible patients, concomitant diuretic use may further increase risk.

Use of benazepril should include appropriate assessment of renal function.

In patients with severe heart failure, whose renal function may depend on the activity of the renin-angiotensin-aldosterone system, treatment with ACE inhibitors, including benazepril, may be associated with oliguria and/or progressive azotemia and rarely acute renal failure and/or death.

Anaphylactoid Reactions During Membrane Exposure: Anaphylactoid reactions have been reported in patients dialyzed with high-flux membranes (e.g., polyacrylonitrile [PAN]) and treated concomitantly with an ACE inhibitor. Dialysis should be stopped immediately if symptoms such as nausea, abdominal cramps, burning, angioedema, shortness of breath and severe hypotension occur. Symptoms are not relieved by antihistamines. In these patients consideration should be given to using a different type of dialysis membrane or a different class of antihypertensive agents.

Anaphylactoid Reactions During Desensitization: There have been isolated reports of patients experiencing sustained life threatening anaphylactoid reactions while receiving ACE inhibitors during desensitizing treatment with hymenoptera (bees, wasps) venom. In the same patients, these reactions have been avoided when ACE inhibitors were temporarily withheld for at least 24 hours, but they have reappeared upon inadvertent rechallenge.

Hyperkalemia and Potassium-Sparing Diuretics: Elevated serum potassium (>5.5 mEq/L) was observed in 1.1% of hypertensive patients in clinical trials treated with benazepril alone and in 0.4% treated with benazepril and hydrochlorothiazide. In most cases these were isolated values which resolved despite continued therapy. Hyperkalemia was a cause of discontinuation of therapy in less than 0.1% of hypertensive patients.

Risk factors for the development of hyperkalemia may include renal insufficiency, diabetes mellitus, and the concomitant use of agents to treat hypokalemia (see Drug Interactions).

Valvular Stenosis: There is concern on theoretical grounds that patients with aortic stenosis might be at particular risk of decreased coronary perfusion when treated with vasodilators because they do not develop as much afterload reduction.

Surgery/Anesthesia: ACE inhibitors may augment the hypotensive effects of anesthetics and analgesics. In patients undergoing surgery or during anesthesia with agents that produce hypotension, benazepril will block the angiotensin II formation that could otherwise occur secondary to compensatory renin release. Hypotension that occurs as a result of this mechanism can be corrected by volume expansion.

Patients with Impaired Liver Function: Hepatitis (hepatocellular and/or cholestatic), elevations of liver enzymes and/or serum bilirubin have occurred during therapy with ACE inhibitors in patients with or without pre-existing liver abnormalities. In most cases the changes were reversed on discontinuation of the drug.

Elevations of liver enzymes and/or serum bilirubin have been reported with benazepril (see Adverse Effects). Should the patient receiving benazepril experience any unexplained symptoms particularly during the first weeks or months of treatment, it is recommended that a full set of liver function tests and any other necessary investigations be carried out. Discontinuation of benazepril should be considered when appropriate.

There are no adequate studies in patients with cirrhosis and/or liver dysfunction. Benazepril should be used with particular caution in patients with pre-existing liver abnormalities. In such patients baseline liver function tests should be obtained before administration of the drug and close monitoring of response and metabolic effects should apply.

Cough: A dry, persistent cough, which usually disappears only after withdrawal or lowering of the dose of benazepril has been reported. Such possibility should be considered as part of the differential diagnosis of the cough.

Lactation: Ingestion of 20 mg daily for 3 days resulted in detectable levels of benazeprilat in breast milk (0.3% of those found in plasma). In general, benazepril should not be administered to nursing mothers.

Children: Safety and effectiveness of benazepril in children have not been established; therefore, its use in this age group is not recommended.

Geriatrics: Although clinical experience has not identified differences in response between the elderly (>65 years) and younger patients, greater sensitivity of some older individuals cannot be ruled out.

Drug Interactions: Concomitant Diuretic Therapy: Patients concomitantly taking ACE inhibitors and diuretics, and especially those in whom diuretic therapy was recently instituted, may occasionally experience an excessive reduction of blood pressure after initiation of therapy. The possibility of hypotensive effects after the first dose of benazepril can be minimized by either discontinuing the diuretic or increasing the salt intake prior to initiation of treatment with benazepril. If it is not possible to discontinue the diuretic, the starting dose of benazepril should be reduced and the patient should be closely observed for several hours following initial dose and until blood pressure has stabilized (see Warnings and Dosage).

Agents Causing Renin Release: The antihypertensive effect of benazepril is augmented by antihypertensive agents that cause renin release (e.g., diuretics).

Agents Increasing Serum Potassium: Since benazepril decreases aldosterone production, increases of serum potassium may occur. Potassium sparing diuretics (e.g., spironolactone, triamterene, amiloride, etc.) or potassium supplements should be given only for documented hypokalemia and with caution and frequent monitoring of serum potassium, since they may lead to a significant increase in serum potassium. Salt substitutes which contain potassium should also be used with caution.

Agents Affecting Sympathetic Activity: Agents affecting sympathetic activity (e.g., ganglionic blocking agents or adrenergic neuron blocking agents) may be used with caution. ß-adrenergic blocking agents add some further antihypertensive effect to benazepril.

Indomethacin: Indomethacin may diminish the antihypertensive efficacy of concomitantly administered benzepril.

Oral Anticoagulants: Multiple dose interaction studies failed to identify any clinically important effects on the serum concentrations, the degree of protein binding or the anticoagulant effect (measured by prothrombin time) of warfarin and nicoumalone. The bioavailability of benazeprilat was not assessed during the coadministration of benazepril with warfarin or nicoumalone.

Lithium: Increased lithium levels and symptoms of lithium toxicity have been reported in patients receiving ACE inhibitors during therapy with lithium. These drugs should be coadministered with caution and frequent monitoring of serum lithium levels is recommended. If a diuretic is also used, the risk of lithium toxicity may be increased.

Hydrochlorothiazide, Chlorthalidone and Furosemide: The bioavailability of benazepril was not altered when single doses were administered concomitantly with the diuretics hydrochlorothiazide, chlorthalidone or furosemide.

ASA: No important changes in pharmacokinetic parameters occurred when single doses of benazepril were administered concomitantly with ASA.

Digoxin: In a single dose interaction study of benazepril with multiple doses of digoxin, no important changes in pharmacokinetic parameters were observed.

Amlodipine/Nifedipine: Benazepril has been used concomitantly with the calcium channel blockers amlodipine and nifedipine, without evidence of clinically important adverse interactions.

Other: In separate single or multiple dose pharmacokinetic interaction studies, the bioavailability of benazepril was not altered by coadministration with propranolol, naproxen, atenolol, nifedipine, amlodipine or cimetidine.

Information for the Patient: Note: As with many other drugs, certain advice to patients being treated with benazepril is warranted. This information is intended to aid in the safe and effective use of this medication. It is not a disclosure of all possible adverse experiences or intended effects.

Angioedema: Angioedema, including laryngeal edema, may occur especially following the first dose of benazepril. Patients should be so advised and told to report immediately any signs or symptoms suggesting angioedema, such as swelling of face, extremities, eyes, lips, tongue, difficulty in swallowing or breathing. They should immediately stop taking benazepril and consult with their physician.

Hypotension: Patients should be cautioned to report lightheadedness, especially during the first few days of benazepril therapy. If actual syncope occurs, the patient should be told to discontinue the drug and consult with their physician.

All patients should be cautioned that excessive perspiration and dehydration may lead to an excessive fall in blood pressure because of reduction in fluid volume. Other causes of volume depletion such as vomiting or diarrhea may also lead to a fall in blood pressure, patients should be advised to consult with their physician.

Agranulocytosis/Neutropenia: Patients should be told to report promptly to their physician any indication of infection (e.g., sore throat, fever), as this may be a sign of neutropenia.

Impaired Liver Function: Patients should be advised to return to their physician if he/she experiences any symptoms possibly related to liver dysfunction. This would include "viral-like symptoms" in the first weeks to months of therapy (such as fever, malaise, muscle pain, rash or adenopathy which are possible indicators of hypersensitivity reactions), or if abdominal pain, nausea or vomiting, loss of appetite, jaundice, itching or any other unexplained symptoms occur during therapy.

Hyperkalemia: Patients should be told not to use salt substitutes containing potassium without consulting their physician.

Pregnancy: Since the use of benazepril during pregnancy can cause injury and even death of the developing fetus, patients should be advised to report promptly to their physician if they become pregnant.

Adverse Effects: Benazepril has been evaluated for safety in over 6 000 hypertensive patients. Over 400 elderly patients have participated in controlled hypertension trials. Long-term safety has been assessed in more than 700 patients treated for 1 year or more. There was no increase in the incidence of adverse reactions in elderly patients given the same daily dose. The overall frequency of adverse reactions was not related to duration of therapy or total daily dose.

The most severe adverse reactions occurring in clinical trials with benazepril were: angioedema (full clinical syndrome, 1 case; edema of lips or face without the other manifestations of angioedema, 0.5%), hypotension (0.3%), postural hypotension (0.4%) and syncope (0.1%). Hypotension or postural dizziness was a cause for discontinuation of therapy in <0.2% of patients treated with benazepril alone. Myocardial infarction and cerebral vascular accident occurred, possibly secondary to excessive hypotension in high risk patients (see Warnings).

The most frequent clinical adverse reactions in placebo-controlled clinical trials with benazepril monotherapy (N=964) were headache (6.2%), dizziness (3.6%), fatigue (2.4%), somnolence (1.6%), postural dizziness (1.5%), nausea (1.3%) and cough (1.2%). Discontinuation of therapy due to adverse experiences was required in 4% of patients treated with benazepril.

Adverse reactions occurring in 1% or more of the 2 004 patients in controlled hypertension trials who were treated with benazepril monotherapy, are listed in Table I.

Table I—Lotensin

Adverse Reactions in Controlled Hypertension Trials

Body System	Patients (N=2 004)
Nervous System	
Headache	10.2%
Dizziness	4.2%
Somnolence	1.1%
Vertigo	1.1%
Respiratory	
Upper respiratory symptoms	5.4%
Increased cough	3.4%
Flu symptoms	1.2%
Gastrointestinal	
Nausea	2.5%
Abdominal pain	2.4%
Diarrhea	2.0%
Dyspepsia	1.2%
Musculoskeletal	
Musculoskeletal pain	2.6%
Other	
Fatigue	3.6%
Rhinitis	2.4%
Pharyngitis	1.7%
Back pain	1.7%
Chest pain	1.2%

Clinical adverse reactions occurring in less than 1% of patients treated with benazepril in controlled and uncontrolled clinical trials, and postmarketing experience, are listed below by body system: Incidence less than 1%:

Body as Whole: asthenia.

Cardiovascular: excessive hypotension, angina pectoris, palpitations, myocardial infarction, cerebrovascular accident, arrhythmia.

Digestive: constipation, gastritis, vomiting, flatulence, melena, abdominal pain, pancreatitis.

Musculoskeletal: arthritis, arthralgia, myalgia.

Nervous: anxiety, depression, hypertonia, insomnia, nervousness, paresthesia, incoordination, decreased libido.

Respiratory: dyspnea, asthma, bronchitis.

Dermatologic: apparent hypersensitivity reactions (manifested by dermatitis, pruritus, or rash), photosensitivity, pemphigus, Stevens-Johnson syndrome and flushing.

Special Senses: tinnitus and taste disorders.

Urogenital: impaired renal function, impotence, urinary frequency.

Hematologic: leukopenia, eosinophilia, hemolytic anemia and thrombocytopenia.

Allergic and Immune Reactions: angioedema, lip and/or facial edema.

Abnormal Laboratory Findings: hyperkalemia (see Precautions).

Creatinine, Blood Urea Nitrogen: Increases in serum creatinine (>150% of baseline) were observed in 2% of patients treated with benazepril alone. Less than 0.1% of these patients developed simultaneous increases in blood urea nitrogen and serum creatinine. Increases are more likely to occur in patients receiving concomitant diuretic therapy than in those on benazepril alone. These increases often reversed on continued therapy.

Neutropenia: Neutrophil counts of less than 1 500/mm^3 occurred in 2% of patients treated with benazepril alone. No patient was discontinued from a study because of a low neutrophil or white blood cell (WBC) count. No patient developed a persistent neutrophil count <1 000/mm^3 and no patient developed a serious infection in association with a reduced neutrophil or WBC count. No patient treated with benazepril developed agranulocytosis (see Warnings).

Hemoglobin: Decreases in hemoglobin (a low value and a decrease of 5 g/dL) occurred in only 1 of 2 014 patients receiving benazepril alone and in 1 of 1 357 patients receiving benazepril plus a diuretic.

Hepatic: Elevations of liver enzymes and/or serum bilirubin have occurred (see Precautions).

Lotensin (cont'd)

Other: Elevations of uric acid and blood glucose have been reported, as have scattered incidents of hyponatremia and proteinuria.

Overdose: Symptoms and Treatment: No data are available on overdosage in humans.

The most likely clinical manifestation of overdosage would be symptoms attributable to severe hypotension, for which the usual treatment is i.v. infusion of normal saline solution.

If ingestion is recent, then emesis should be induced. Although the active metabolite, benazeprilat, is only slightly dialyzable, renal dialysis may be useful in overdosed patients with severely impaired renal function.

Dosage: Dosage must be individualized. Initiation of therapy requires consideration of recent antihypertensive drug treatment, the extent of blood pressure elevation and salt restriction. The dosage of other antihypertensive agents being used with benazepril may need to be adjusted.

Monotherapy: The recommended initial dose of benazepril is 10 mg once daily. Dosage should be adjusted according to blood pressure response, generally, at intervals of at least 2 weeks. The usual maintenance dose is 20 mg daily. The maximum daily dose of benazepril is 40 mg.

In some patients treated once daily, the antihypertensive effect may diminish towards the end of the dosing interval. This can be evaluated by measuring blood pressure just prior to dosing to determine whether satisfactory control is being maintained for 24 hours. If it is not, either twice daily administration with the same total daily dose, or an increase in dose should be considered.

If blood pressure is not controlled with benazepril alone, a diuretic may be added. After the addition of a diuretic, it may be possible to reduce the dose of benazepril.

Concomitant Diuretic Therapy: Symptomatic hypotension occasionally may occur following the initial dose of benazepril and is more likely in patients who are currently being treated with a diuretic. The diuretic should, if possible, be discontinued for 2 to 3 days before beginning therapy with benazepril to reduce the likelihood of hypotension (see Warnings). If the diuretic cannot be discontinued, an initial dose of 5 mg benazepril should be used with careful medical supervision for several hours and until blood pressure has stabilized. The dosage of benazepril should subsequently be titrated (as described above) to the optimal response.

Dosage Adjustment in Renal Impairment: The usual dose of benazepril is recommended for patients with a creatinine clearance >30 mL/min [0.5 mL/s]. For patients with severe renal impairment (creatinine clearance of <30 mL/min [0.5 mL/s]), the initial daily dose is 5 mg. Titration must be individualized. The dosage may be titrated upwards to 10 mg/day. For further reductions in blood pressure the addition of a diuretic or another antihypertensive should be considered or alternatively, the dose of benazepril can be increased.

Information for the Patient: See Blue Section—Information for the Patient "Lotensin".

Supplied: 5 mg: Each light yellow, capsule-shaped, biconvex, film-coated tablet, engraved CG on one side and LV on the other side, fully bisected on both sides between the C and G, and the L and V, contains: benazepril HCl 5 mg. Nonmedicinal ingredients: cellulose compounds, colloidal silicon dioxide, cornstarch, hydrogenated castor oil, iron oxide, lactose, polyethylene glycol, povidone, talc and titanium dioxide. Bottles of 100.

10 mg: Each dark yellow, capsule-shaped, biconvex, film-coated tablet, engraved CG on one side and HO on the other side, fully bisected on both sides between the C and G, and the H and O, contains: benazepril HCl 10 mg. Nonmedicinal ingredients: cellulose compounds, colloidal silicon dioxide, cornstarch, hydrogenated castor oil, iron oxide, lactose, polyethylene glycol, povidone, talc and titanium dioxide. Bottles of 100.

20 mg: Each reddish-orange, capsule-shaped, biconvex, film-coated tablet, engraved CG on one side and HP on the other side, fully bisected on both sides between the C and G, and the H and P, contains: benazepril HCl 20 mg. Nonmedicinal ingredients: cellulose compounds, colloidal silicon dioxide, cornstarch, hydrogenated castor oil, iron oxide, lactose, polyethylene glycol, povidone, talc and titanium dioxide. Bottles of 100.

Protect from heat (i.e., store at 15 to 30°C) and humidity.

(Shown in Product Recognition Section)

LOTRIDERM® Ⓟ

Schering

Clotrimazole—Betamethasone Dipropionate

Topical Antifungal—Corticosteroid

Pharmacology: Betamethasone dipropionate with clotrimazole combines the anti-inflammatory, antipruritic and vasoconstrictive activity of betamethasone dipropionate with the antifungal activity of clotrimazole. The primary action of clotrimazole is against dividing and growing organisms, possibly through reaction with the cell membrane.

Indications: For the topical treatment of the following fungal dermal infections complicated by inflammatory pruritus: tinea pedis, tinea cruris and tinea corporis due to T. rubrum, T. mentagrophytes, E. floccosum, and M. canis.

Contraindications: Patients who are sensitive to betamethasone dipropionate, clotrimazole, other corticosteroids or imidazoles, or to any one of the components in this preparation.

Topical steroids are contraindicated in untreated bacterial and tubercular infections involving the skin and in certain viral diseases such as herpes simplex, chickenpox and vaccinia.

Warnings: Lotriderm should not be used in or near the eyes since this preparation is not formulated for ophthalmic use.

Pregnancy: There are no adequate and well-controlled studies in pregnant women on teratogenic effects of a topically applied combination of clotrimazole and betamethasone dipropionate. Therefore, this cream should be used during pregnancy only if the potential benefit justifies the potential risk to the fetus.

Drugs containing corticosteroids should not be used extensively on pregnant patients in large amounts or for prolonged periods of time.

Lactation: Since it is not known whether the components of Lotriderm Cream are excreted in human milk, caution should be exercised when this product is administered to a nursing woman.

Children: Any of the side effects that have been reported following systemic use of corticosteroids, including adrenal suppression, may also occur with topical corticosteroids, especially in infants and children.

Systemic absorption of topical corticosteroids will be increased if extensive body surface areas are treated or if the occlusive technique is used. Suitable precautions should be taken under these conditions or when long-term use is anticipated, particularly in infants and children. Pediatric patients may demonstrate greater susceptibility to topical corticosteroid-induced HPA axis suppression and Cushing's syndrome than mature patients because of a larger skin surface area to body weight ratio. Use of topical corticosteroids in children should be limited to the least amount compatible with an effective therapeutic regimen. Chronic corticosteroid therapy may interfere with growth and development of children.

Precautions: Systemic absorption of topical corticosteroids has produced reversible hypothalamic-pituitary-adrenal (HPA) axis suppression, manifestations of Cushing's syndrome, hyperglycemia and glucosuria in some patients.

Significant systemic absorption may occur when steroids are applied over large areas of the body. To minimize this possibility when long-term therapy is anticipated, interrupt treatment periodically or treat one area of the body at a time (see Dosage). Therefore, patients receiving a large dose of a potent topical steroid applied to a large surface area should be evaluated periodically for evidence of HPA axis suppression by using the urinary free cortisol and ACTH stimulation tests. If HPA axis suppression is noted, an attempt should be made to withdraw the drug, to reduce the frequency of application, or to substitute a less potent steroid. Recovery of HPA axis function is generally prompt and complete upon discontinuation of the drug. Infrequently, signs and symptoms of steroid withdrawal may occur, requiring supplemental systemic corticosteroids.

If irritation or hypersensitivity develops with the use of the cream, treatment should be discontinued and appropriate therapy instituted.

Suitable precautions should be taken in using topical corticosteroids in patients with stasis dermatitis and other skin diseases with impaired circulation.

Prolonged use of corticosteroid preparations may produce striae or atrophy of the skin or s.c. tissue. If this occurs, treatment should be discontinued.

Patients should be advised to inform subsequent physicians of the prior use of corticosteroids.

Children: Safety and effectiveness in children below the age of 12 have not been established with Lotriderm Cream.

Pediatric patients may demonstrate greater susceptibility to topical corticosteroid-induced HPA axis suppression and Cushing's syndrome than mature patients because of a larger skin surface area to body weight ratio.

Hypothalamic-pituitary-adrenal (HPA) axis suppression, Cushing's syndrome and intracranial hypertension have been reported in children receiving topical corticosteroids. Manifestations of adrenal suppression in children include linear growth retardation, delayed weight gain, low plasma cortisol levels and absence of response to ACTH stimulation. Manifestations of intracranial hypertension include bulging fontanelles, headaches and bilateral papilledema.

Administration of topical dermatologics containing a corticosteroid to children should be limited to the least amount compatible with an effective therapeutic regimen. Chronic corticosteroid therapy may interfere with the growth and development of children.

Laboratory tests: If there is a lack of response to the cream, appropriate microbiological studies should be repeated to confirm the diagnosis and rule out other pathogens before instituting another course of antimycotic therapy.

The following tests may be helpful in evaluating HPA axis suppression due to the corticosteroid component: urinary free cortisol test and ACTH stimulation test.

Adverse Effects: The following adverse reactions have been reported in connection with the use of Lotriderm cream: paresthesia in 5 of 270 patients (1.85%), maculopapular rash, edema, and secondary infection, each in 1 of 270 (0.37%) patients.

Adverse reactions reported with the use of clotrimazole are as follows: erythema, stinging, blistering, peeling, edema, pruritus, urticaria and general irritation of the skin.

The following local adverse reactions are reported infrequently when topical corticosteroids are used as recommended. These reactions are listed in an approximate decreasing order of occurrence: burning, itching, irritation, dryness, folliculitis, hypertrichosis, acneiform eruptions, hypopigmentation, perioral dermatitis, allergic contact dermatitis, maceration of the skin, secondary infection, skin atrophy, striae and miliaria.

Overdose: Symptoms and Treatment: No specific antidote is available and treatment should be symptomatic.

Betamethasone Dipropionate: Excessive or prolonged use of topical corticosteroids can suppress pituitary-adrenal function, resulting in secondary adrenal insufficiency, and produce manifestations of hypercorticism, including Cushing's disease.

Clotrimazole: Overdosage by topical clotrimazole administration is highly improbable, since application of C^{14} labeled clotrimazole to intact or diseased skin under occlusive dressing for 6 hours did not yield measurable quantities (lower detection limit 0.001 μg/mL) of radioactive material in the sera of human subjects.

Treatment: Appropriate symptomatic treatment of corticosteroid overdosage is indicated. Acute hypercorticoid symptoms are usually reversible. Treat electrolyte imbalance, if necessary. In cases of chronic toxicity, slow withdrawal of corticosteroids is advised.

Dosage: A thin film of cream should be applied to cover completely the affected and surrounding skin areas twice daily, in the morning and at night, for 2 weeks in tinea cruris and tinea corporis and for 4 weeks in tinea pedis. The use of the cream for longer than 4 weeks is not recommended.

Clinical improvement, with relief of erythema and pruritus, usually occurs within 3 to 5 days of treatment. If a patient with tinea cruris and tinea corporis shows no clinical improvement after 1 week of treatment, the diagnosis should be reviewed. In tinea pedis, the treatment should be applied for 2 weeks prior to making that decision. Treatment with Lotriderm should be discontinued if the condition persists after 2 weeks in tinea cruris and tinea corporis and after 4 weeks in tinea pedis. Alternate therapy may then be instituted, if indicated, with an appropriate antifungal preparation.

Lotriderm cream should **not** be used with occlusive dressings.

Supplied: Each g of white to off-white cream contains: clotrimazole USP 10 mg and betamethasone (as dipropionate USP) 0.5 mg in a hydrophilic emollient cream. Nonmedicinal ingredients: benzyl alcohol, ceteareth-30, cetostearyl alcohol, mineral oil, phosphoric acid, propylene glycol, purified water, sodium phosphate and white petrolatum. Sodium hydroxide to adjust pH. Tubes of 15 and 50 g. Store between 2 and 30°C.

For comparative information on Calcium Salts: Oral or Parenteral, see the CPhA General Monograph in the WHITE SECTION.

LOVENOX® Ⓟ

Rhône-Poulenc Rorer

Enoxaparin Sodium

Anticoagulant—Antithrombotic

Pharmacology: Enoxaparin is a low molecular weight heparin fragment, which is obtained by controlled depolymerization of natural heparin from porcine intestinal mucosa. It possesses antithrombotic action. Enoxaparin is composed of molecules with and without a specially characterized pentasaccharide, the antithrombin binding site, that is essential for high affinity binding to the plasma protein antithrombin (formerly referred to as antithrombin III). With a molecular weight range of 3 500-5 000 Daltons (versus 15 000 Daltons for heparin), the enoxaparin molecule is too small to bind simultaneously to thrombin and antithrombin, the primary anticoagulant factor in blood.

The mechanism of action of enoxaparin is antithrombin-dependent. It acts mainly by accelerating the rate of the neutralization of certain activated coagulation factors by antithrombin, but other mechanisms may also be involved. Enoxaparin potentiates preferentially the inhibition of coagulation factors Xa and IIa and only slightly affects other hemostatic mechanisms such as clotting time. The antithrombotic effect of enoxaparin is well correlated to the inhibition of factor Xa.

The ratio of anti-Xa/anti-IIa activity is greater than 4 with enoxaparin (whereas this ratio is equal to 1 with heparin). This dissociation between anti-Xa and anti-IIa activities has been shown in experimental models with an antithrombotic activity comparable to that of heparin while the bleeding effect is reduced. In man, clinical trials have not shown a causal relationship between the ratio of anti-Xa/anti-IIa activity and clinical/pharmacological effect.

Enoxaparin cannot be measured directly in the blood stream. Rather the effect on clotting mechanisms is measured. Heparin dosage is monitored by both prolongation of APTT, and by anti-Xa activity. For enoxaparin, the APTT may not be significantly prolonged relative to unfractionated heparin at prophylactic doses, and at therapeutic doses APTT prolongation is not used to measure the therapeutic effect of enoxaparin. Enoxaparin potency is described in international anti-Xa units (e.g., 30 mg=3 000 IU).

Pharmacokinetics: The pharmacokinetics of enoxaparin have been studied on the basis of plasma levels of anti-Xa activity.

Following a single s.c. injection, enoxaparin is rapidly and almost completely absorbed, with peak plasma activity appearing after 3 hours. Maximum anti-Xa levels and AUCs are positively correlated to the dose levels; between the doses of 20 and 80 mg s.c., maximum anti-Xa levels range from 1.58 (±0.35) to 7.44 (±1.47) μg/mL and the AUCs range from 11.79 (±3.30) to 70.76 (±15.49) h·μg·mL^{-1}.

The t½ of plasma anti-Xa activity is between 4.18 (±2.21) and 3.46 (±0.86) hours and the mean residence time (MRT) of anti-Xa activity is about 6 hours, independent of the dose (between 20 and 80 mg s.c.), although anti-Xa activity can still be measured after 12 hours.

Information from a clinical trial with a very small number of volunteers indicates that enoxaparin, as detected by anti-factor Xa activity, does not appear to cross the placental barrier, at least during the second trimester of pregnancy.

Following repeated s.c. doses of enoxaparin the T_{max} for anti-Xa activity remained at 3 hours and there was no evidence of accumulation or alterations in distribution and clearance.

Enoxaparin is weakly metabolized in the liver by desulfation and depolymerization. Small amounts of the drug are eliminated by the kidneys in the intact or slightly degraded form.

In the elderly, peak concentration (T_{max}) was delayed by approximately 1 hour and there was some lengthening of both the apparent half-life (t½) and the mean residence time (MRT). There were no significant changes in the pharmacokinetic profiles of enoxaparin in elderly patients or in hemodialyzed patients with renal failure when compared to those of healthy subjects.

The dose and frequency of dosing do not have to be modified in elderly patients or dialyzed patients with renal insufficiency.

In nondialyzed patients with severe renal impairment (mean renal creatinine clearance: 11.4 mL/min), total clearance of enoxaparin was 1.9 times slower and the apparent half-lives of absorption and elimination 1.7 times more prolonged than in healthy subjects. These effects suggest that dose modifications may have to be considered in patients with severe renal impairment who are not hemodialyzed, when repeated high doses are required.

Indications: For the prophylaxis of thromboembolic disorders (deep vein thrombosis) in patients undergoing: orthopedic surgery of the hip or knee; high-risk abdominal, gynecological, or urological surgeries; colorectal surgery.

For the treatment of deep vein thrombosis and pulmonary embolism.

For the treatment of unstable angina and non-Q-wave myocardial infarction, concurrently with ASA.

Contraindications: Enoxaparin must **not** be administered by the i.m. route. Allergy to enoxaparin or any of its constituents. Acute or subacute bacterial endocarditis. Major blood clotting disorders. History of thrombocytopenia with enoxaparin or in patients in whom an in vitro platelet-aggregation test in the presence of enoxaparin is positive. Active gastric or duodenal ulcer. Hemorrhagic cerebrovascular accident (except if there are systemic emboli). Severe untreated hypertension. Diabetic or hemorrhagic retinopathy. Other conditions or diseases involving an increased risk of hemorrhage. Injuries to and operations on the brain, spinal cord, eyes and ears.

Warnings: Enoxaparin should be used with care in patients with hepatic insufficiency, renal insufficiency or a history of gastrointestinal ulceration.

Determination of anti-factor Xa levels in plasma is the only method available for monitoring enoxaparin activity. The effect of enoxaparin on global clotting tests such as APTT, PT and TT is dose-dependent. At lower doses, used in prophylaxis, enoxaparin does not prolong these tests. At higher doses, APTT prolongation is observed but treatment cannot be monitored with these tests.

There have been cases of intra-spinal hematomas with the concurrent use of enoxaparin and spinal/epidural anesthesia resulting in long-term or permanent paralysis. The risk of these events may be higher with the use of post-operative indwelling epidural catheters or by the concomitant use of drugs affecting hemostasis: nonsteroidal anti-inflammatory drugs (NSAIDs), platelet inhibitors, or other drugs affecting coagulation. The risk also appears to be increased by traumatic or repeated epidural or spinal procedure. **Enoxaparin should only be used concurrently with spinal/epidural anaesthesia when the therapeutic benefits to the patients outweigh the possible risks.** When used concurrently, no spinal invasion should be performed for at least 12 hours following the last dose of enoxaparin and the next dose should be held until at least 2 hours after the anaesthetic procedure. The same rules apply to the withdrawal or manipulation of the catheter. Careful vigilance for neurological signs is recommended with rapid diagnosis and treatment if signs occur (see also Adverse Effects).

Enoxaparin should be used with caution in the presence of known hypersensitivity to heparin and/or low molecular weight heparins (see Precautions).

Enoxaparin dosage should be carefully monitored in patients with severely impaired renal function. The main route of elimination is via the kidney. The half-life for anti-Xa activity in patients with impaired renal function is much longer than for people with normal renal function (t½=5.12 h in patients with chronic renal failure vs 2.94 h in young healthy volunteers).

Except under special circumstances enoxaparin should not be used when abortion is imminent or threatened. It may be used in such cases only when, in the opinion of the physician, the increased risk of bleeding is outweighed by the risk of thrombosis and thromboembolism.

Pregnancy, Lactation and Children: The safety of enoxaparin in pregnant women and in children has not been established, although it is known that the drug does not appear to cross the placental barrier, at least during the second trimester, and that it exhibited no embryotoxic or teratogenic effects in experimental animals. Enoxaparin should not be used in pregnant women and in children unless the therapeutic benefits to the patients outweigh the possible risks.

There has been no experience with enoxaparin during human lactation. Mothers receiving enoxaparin should avoid breast-feeding.

Use in Unstable Coronary Artery Disease: When thrombolytic treatment is considered appropriate, the concomitant use of an anticoagulant such as enoxaparin is not recommended since there is no data available on this combination therapy.

Precautions: Enoxaparin cannot be used interchangeably (unit for unit) with unfractionated heparin (UFH) or other low molecular weight heparins (LMWHs) as they differ in their manufacturing process, molecular weight distribution, anti-Xa and anti-IIa activities, units and dosages. Special attention and compliance with instructions for use of each specific product is required during any change in treatment.

Biochemical Monitoring: Enoxaparin has only a moderate prolonging effect on clotting time assays such as APTT or thrombin time. For lab monitoring of effect, anti-Xa methods are recommended. Prolongation of APTT during therapy with enoxaparin to the same extent as with unfractionated heparin should only be used as a criteria of overdose. Dose increases aimed at prolonging APTT to the same extent as with unfractionated heparin could cause overdose and bleeding.

Enoxaparin is administered s.c. and, therefore, the individual patient's antifactor Xa activity level will not remain within the range that would be expected with unfractionated heparin by continuous i.v. infusion throughout the entire dosing interval. The peak plasma antifactor Xa level occurs 3 to 4 hours after s.c. administration. The mean maximum plasma antifactor Xa activity achieved is approximately 1.0 and 1.5 antifactor Xa IU/mL following s.c. administration of 1 mg/kg and 1.5 mg/kg doses in healthy volunteers, respectively. In patients treated with enoxaparin 1.0 mg/kg twice daily for proximal deep vein thrombosis, mean peak plasma anti-Xa levels were 0.91 IU/mL. In patients given enoxaparin 1.0 mg/kg twice daily for acute treatment of unstable angina, peak anti-Xa activity levels were 1.0 -1.1 IU/mL. At steady-state in patients given a 1.5 mg/kg qd regimen for treatment of DVT, mean peak activity was 1.7 IU anti-Xa/mL. The steady-state is practically achieved at the second or the third dose depending on the dosage regimen, once or twice daily, respectively. Enoxaparin should be administered as directed in the Dosage section.

Patient Monitoring: As with all anti-thrombotic agents, there is a risk of systemic bleeding with enoxaparin administration. Consequently, therapy should not be started before primary hemostasis has been established and preferably no sooner than 12 hours after surgery (see Dosage). Care should be taken with enoxaparin use in high dose treatment of newly operated patients.

After treatment is initiated patients should be carefully monitored for bleeding complications. This may be done by regular physical examination of the patients, close observation of the surgical drain and periodic measurements of hemoglobin and anti-factor Xa determinations. Bleeding complications may be considered major if hemoglobin is decreased by 2 g/dL or if a transfusion of 2 or more units has been required. With normal prophylactic doses, enoxaparin does not modify global clotting tests of activated partial thromboplastin time (APTT), prothrombin time (PT) and thrombing clotting time (TT). Therefore, treatment cannot be monitored with these tests.

Enoxaparin is administered s.c. and, therefore, the individual patient's antifactor Xa activity level will not remain within the range that would be expected with unfractionated heparin by continuous i.v. infusion throughout the entire dosing interval. The peak plasma antifactor Xa level occurs 3 to 4 hours after s.c. administration. The mean maximum plasma antifactor Xa activity achieved is approximately 1.0 and 1.5 antifactor Xa IU/mL following s.c. administration of 1 mg/kg and 1.5 mg/kg doses in healthy volunteers, respectively. In patients treated with enoxaparin 1.0 mg/kg twice daily for proximal deep vein thrombosis, mean peak plasma anti-Xa levels were 0.91 IU/mL. In patients given enoxaparin 1.0 mg/kg twice daily for acute treatment of unstable angina, peak anti-Xa activity levels were 1.0 to 1.1 IU/mL. At steady state in patients given a 1.5 mg/kg qd regimen for treatment of DVT, mean peak activity was 1.7 IU anti-Xa/mL. The steady-state is practically achieved at the second or the third dose depending on the dosage regimen, once or twice daily, respectively. Enoxaparin should be administered as directed in the Dosage section.

Platelets: Platelet counts should be determined prior to the commencement of treatment with enoxaparin and, subsequently, twice weekly for the duration of therapy.

Caution is recommended when administering enoxaparin to patients with congenital or drug-induced thrombocytopenia, or platelet defects.

In patients who have a history of heparin-induced thrombocytopenia (HIT), the risk of this occurrence for the individual patient in response to the low molecular weight heparins cannot be estimated, but would be expected to be increased relative to the general population. The frequency of this potentially life-threatening event that has been observed during clinical development of enoxaparin was observed in patients who had received one course of therapy only. Since the frequency of HIT in patients who had received more than one course of therapy of enoxaparin is not known, the physician should weigh all the therapeutic options before deciding on the antithrombotic therapy in patients with a history of HIT. If enoxaparin is prescribed, an in vitro platelet aggregation test should be performed prior to instituting enoxaparin. A positive result contraindicates enoxaparin. With a negative result, treatment with enoxaparin may be instituted, but patients must be monitored with particular care to include platelet counts at least once daily.

Cardiovascular: See Contraindications and Warnings.

Lovenox (cont'd)

Lipid Metabolism: Enoxaparin increases lipolytic activity, although to a lesser degree than heparin.
Selection of General Surgery Patients: Risk factors associated with postoperative venous thromboembolism following general surgery include history of venous thromboembolism, varicose veins, obesity, heart failure, malignancy, previous long bone fracture of a lower limb, bed rest for more than 5 days prior to surgery, predicted duration of surgery of more than 30 minutes, age 60 years or above.
Geriatrics: Age is highly correlated to risk of thrombosis. No increased bleeding tendency has been observed in the clinical studies with enoxaparin in elderly patients with normal kidney and liver function. No dose reduction should be necessary unless kidney or liver function is impaired.
Drug Interactions: There have been no pharmacologic/toxicologic studies into the possible interaction between enoxaparin and other drugs. Because of the possibility of an interaction with blood clotting mechanisms, caution should be exercised if enoxaparin is combined with any of the following drugs: oral anticoagulants, inhibitors of platelet aggregation, nonsteroidal anti-inflammatory agents, preparations containing ASA or dextran. For information concerning the antidote in cases of excess, see Overdose: Symptoms and Treatment.

Adverse Effects: Bleeding: As with any antithrombotic treatment, hemorrhagic manifestations can occur. Injection site hematomas are a common side effect with enoxaparin occurring at a frequency of 5% or less with lower (prophylaxis) doses to 10% or more with higher (treatment) doses.

The incidence of major hemorrhagic complications during enoxaparin treatment has been low and generally did not differ from that observed with unfractionated heparin. Patients taking enoxaparin are at risk for major bleeding complications when the plasma anti-factor Xa levels approach 2.0 IU/mL. Other risk factors associated with bleeding on therapy with heparins include a serious concurrent illness, chronic heavy alcohol consumption, use of platelet inhibiting drugs, renal failure, age and possibly, the female gender. Petechiae or easy bruising may precede frank hemorrhage. Bleeding may range from minor local hematoma to major hemorrhage. The early signs of bleeding may include epistaxis, hematuria, or melena. Bleeding may occur at any site and may be difficult to detect; such as retroperitoneal bleeding. Bleeding may also occur from surgical sites.

There have been cases of intra-spinal hematomas with the concurrent use of low molecular weight heparins and spinal/epidural anesthesia resulting in long-term or permanent paralysis (incidence of 1:45 000). See also Warnings.
Liver: Transient, asymptomatic elevations of liver transaminases (AST and ALT) to greater than three times the upper limit of normal has been observed in up to 6% of patients taking enoxaparin. This is a consistent finding with all members of the LMWH class, as well as with unfractionated heparin. The mechanism associated with the increased levels of liver transaminases has not been elucidated. No consistent irreversible liver damage has been observed. Transaminase levels returned to normal within 3 to 7 days after discontinuation of enoxaparin.
Hypersensitivity: Thrombocytopenia, skin rash, and allergic reactions are rare, but occur with all low molecular weight heparins. Enoxaparin should be discontinued in patients showing local or systemic allergic responses. Anaphylactoid reactions to unfractionated heparin and the low molecular weight heparins have been observed rarely.
Skeletal: Osteopenic effects of enoxaparin have not been reported, possibly because enoxaparin has not been given to many patients for the long-term. Since this symptom has been reported as an adverse effect after long-term treatment with unfractionated heparin at high doses, the risk of osteoporosis cannot be ruled out.
Lipid Metabolism: Enoxaparin increases lipolytic activity, although to a lesser degree than heparin.

Overdose: Symptoms and Treatment: Hemorrhage is the major clinical sign of overdosage. In case of accidental overdosage, the platelet count and other coagulation parameters should be measured. Minor bleeding rarely requires specific therapy and reducing or delaying subsequent doses of enoxaparin is usually sufficient. Enoxaparin should be discontinued in cases of major bleeding. Protamine (either the sulphate or hydrochloride salt) should be administered in more serious cases.

The anticoagulant effect of the drug is inhibited by protamine. A slow i.v. injection of protamine will almost completely neutralize the anticoagulant activity of enoxaparin (i.e., the anti-IIa activity); however, the anti-Xa activity is only partially neutralized (maximum about 60%). The dose of protamine should be identical to the dose of enoxaparin injected, that is, 1 mg or 100 units of protamine to neutralize the anti-IIa activity generated by 1 mg enoxaparin. Particular care should be taken to avoid overdosage with protamine. The half-life of enoxaparin should be taken into account when calculating the neutralizing dose of protamine to avoid overdosage. The rate of administration of protamine should not exceed 50 mg in any 10-minute period since administration that is too rapid can cause severe hypotensive and anaphylactoid-like reactions.

Dosage: Enoxaparin is administered by s.c. injection only and is not to be injected by any other route or added to i.v. solutions. The s.c. injection of enoxaparin should be carried out with the patient in the decubitus position. Inject in the s.c. cellular tissue of the anterolateral and posterolateral abdominal girdle, alternatively on the left and right sides. With the thickness of skin held between the operator's thumb and finger, introduce the entire length of the needle vertically into the skin.
Prophylaxis in Conjunction with Orthopedic Surgery: Enoxaparin should be administered between 12 and 24 hours after orthopedic surgery, after primary hemostasis has been established. When using enoxaparin supplied in prefilled syringes of 0.3 mL, administer 30 mg (3 000 IU) enoxaparin, the contents of 1 syringe, every 12 hours, by the s.c. route in the abdomen. When using the multiple-dose vial, which also contains 10 mg/0.1 mL enoxaparin sterile solution, a tuberculin syringe or the equivalent is recommended to assure accurate withdrawal of the appropriate volume of drug. The usual duration of treatment is from 7 to 14 days.
Prophylaxis in Conjunction with Abdominal or Colorectal Surgery: Enoxaparin should be administered between 2 hours prior to surgery. When using enoxaparin supplied in prefilled syringes of 0.4 mL, administer 40 mg (4 000 IU) enoxaparin, the contents of 1 syringe, every 24 hours, by the s.c. route in the abdomen. When using the multiple-dose vial, which also contains 10 mg/0.1 mL enoxaparin sterile solution, a tuberculin syringe or the equivalent is recommended to assure accurate withdrawal of the appropriate volume of drug. The usual duration of treatment is from 7 to 10 days for a maximum of 12 days.
Treatment of Deep Vein Thrombosis with or without Pulmonary Embolism: Enoxaparin can be administered s.c. either as a single injection of 1.5 mg/kg or as twice daily injections of 1 mg/kg.

The 1.5 mg/kg body weight daily dose is the equivalent of 150 IU/kg and should be given once daily at the same time every day. The single daily dose should not exceed 18 000 IU. The expected plasma anti-Xa levels during s.c. treatment, when enoxaparin is used as the reference standard, would be <0.3 IU anti-Xa/mL before injection and <1.7 IU anti-Xa/mL 3 to 4 hours postinjection. The measurement of plasma anti-Xa circulating activities depends on the experimental conditions of the assay, particularly on the reference standard used.

In patients with complicated thromboembolic disorders, a dose of 1 mg/kg administered twice daily is recommended. This is the equivalent of 100 IU/kg. The expected plasma anti-Xa levels during s.c. treatment, when enoxaparin is used as the reference standard, would be <0.3 IU anti-Xa/mL before injection and <1.15 IU anti-Xa/mL 3 to 4 hours postinjection.

Oral anticoagulant therapy should be initiated as soon as possible and enoxaparin should be continued until a therapeutic anticoagulant effect has been achieved (INR: 2 to 3), in general for approximately 7 days.

An investigator-driven study in patients with chronic renal insufficiency at 0.5 mk/kg s.c. showed that the elimination of enoxaparin is delayed in patients with renal failure compared to young healthy volunteers ($t_{1/2}$=5.12 vs 2.94 h). Based on these results and in the absence of multiple dose kinetic data at higher doses, enoxaparin dosage should be carefully monitored when treating patients with severely impaired renal function particularly when using high doses.
Treatment of Unstable Angina and non-Q-wave Myocardial Infarction: The recommended dose of enoxaparin is 1 mg/kg every 12 hours by s.c. injection. This is the equivalent of 100 IU/kg. The maximum dose should not exceed 10 000 IU/12 hours. The expected plasma anti-Xa levels during s.c. treatment would be <0.3 IU anti-Xa/mL before injection and <1.15 IU anti-Xa/mL 3 to 4 hours after injection. Treatment should continue for a minimum of 2 days until clinical stabilization has been achieved, in general for up to 8 days. Concomitant therapy with ASA (100 to 325 mg once daily) is recommended.
Important: The prefilled syringes are ready for use and no attempt should be made to expel air prior to giving the injection.

Under normal conditions of use, enoxaparin does not modify global clotting tests of activated partial thromboplastin time (APTT), prothrombin time (PT) and thrombin clotting time (TT). Therefore treatment cannot be monitored with these tests. The plasma levels of the drug can be verified by measuring anti-Xa and anti-IIa activities.

Information for the Patient: See Blue Section—Information for the Patient "Lovenox".

Supplied: Multiple-dose Vials: Each multiple-dose vial contains: enoxaparin sodium 300 mg in 3 mL water for injection (concentration 10 mg/0.1 mL) and 1.5% (m/v) benzyl alcohol as a preservative.

Prefilled Syringes: 30 mg/0.3 mL: Each syringe contains: enoxaparin sodium 30 mg in 0.3 mL water for injection. The solution is preservative-free and intended for use as a single-dose injection. Prefilled syringes of 0.3 mL, cartons of 10, each in individual blister pack.

40 mg/0.4 mL: Each syringe contains: enoxaparin sodium 40 mg in 0.4 mL water for injection. The solution is preservative-free and intended for use as a single-dose injection. Prefilled syringes of 0.4 mL, cartons of 10, each in individual blister pack.

60 mg/0.6 mL: Each syringe contains: enoxaparin sodium 60 mg in 0.6 mL water for injection. The solution is preservative-free and intended for use as a single-dose injection. Prefilled syringes of 0.6 mL, cartons of 10, each in individual blister pack.

80 mg/0.8 mL: Each syringe contains: enoxaparin sodium 80 mg in 0.8 mL water for injection. The solution is preservative-free and intended for use as a single-dose injection. Prefilled syringes of 0.8 mL, cartons of 10, each in individual blister pack.

100 mg/1.0 mL: Each syringe contains: enoxaparin sodium 100 mg in 1.0 mL water for injection. The solution is preservative-free and intended for use as a single-dose injection. Prefilled syringes of 1.0 mL, cartons of 10, each in individual blister pack.

The pH of the syringe and multiple-dose solution is 5.5 to 7.5 with an approximate anti-factor Xa activity of 100 IU/1 mg of drug (with reference to the WHO First International Low Molecular Weight Heparin Reference Standard). Nitrogen is used in the headspace to inhibit oxidation. Store at room temperature (15 to 25°C). Protect from heat.

Reviewed 1999

LOXAPAC® ℞
Wyeth-Ayerst

Loxapine

Antipsychotic Agent

Pharmacology: Loxapine, a tricyclic dibenzoxazepine antipsychotic agent, which is chemically distinct from the phenothiazines, thioxanthenes and butyrophenones, produces pharmacological responses in various animal species which are characteristic of those seen with the majority of antipsychotic drugs.

Loxapine is an antipsychotic drug which exhibits many of the actions common to this broad class of drugs. Loxapine has proven to be of value in the management of both acute and chronic schizophrenia. As in the case of other antipsychotics, the mode of action has not been clearly established, but is postulated to involve changes in synaptic transmission at the subcortical level of the brain, resulting in strong inhibition of spontaneous motor activity.

Absorption of orally administered loxapine tablets, oral concentrate, and i.m. injection in man is rapid and virtually complete following a single 25 mg dose. After administration of the oral concentrate somewhat higher and earlier peak serum levels may be expected initially than after tablet administration. When the i.m. administration was compared to the oral administration, the mean serum concentrations of unmetabolized loxapine were approximately twice as high after i.m. injection of 25 mg as they were after equivalent oral dosage during the period of 1 to 4 hours. Signs of sedation in normal volunteers appear generally within 30 minutes for oral and parenteral administration. Duration of sedation is essentially the same with either the tablets or the oral concentrate and may last through a 12-hour period. The duration and intensity of sedation produced by the i.m. formulation in normal volunteers have been less than those observed following oral administration. (Average: 1 hour with the i.m. solution and close to 3 hours with the oral administration.) When multiple doses were given by the oral or i.m. route, the onset and duration of sedative effects were generally comparable. Initially, sedation occurred within 1.5 hours of the dose and lasted 8 hours: thereafter the duration was shortened to 1 to 2.5 hours. Loxapine is metabolized extensively, essentially no unchanged parent drug being excreted in urine or feces. The serum half-life of loxapine is approximately 3 hours. The serum concentration time curve of total drug related materials (loxapine plus metabolites), as shown by studies with radio-labelled drug, is biphasic in nature and shows larger half-lives, i.e., 5 hours for the alpha-phase and 19 hours for the beta-phase.

Five metabolites have been identified in the urine—loxapine N-oxide, 8-hydroxyloxapine, 7-hydroxyloxapine, 8-hydroxyamoxapine and 7-hydroxyamoxapine. The phenolic metabolites are excreted in the urine largely in the form of conjugates and in the feces primarily in the free form. In man, the greater proportion of the dose (56 to 70%) is excreted in the urine.

Indications: The management of the manifestations of schizophrenia.

Contraindications: Comatose or severe drug induced depressed states (alcohol, barbiturates, narcotics, etc.), individuals with known hypersensitivity to the drug, patients with circulatory collapse.

Warnings: Tardive Dyskinesia: A syndrome consisting of potentially irreversible, involuntary, dyskinetic movements may develop in patients treated with conventional antipsychotic drugs. Although the prevalence of tardive dyskinesia with conventional antipsychotics appears to be highest among the elderly, especially elderly women, it is impossible to rely upon prevalence estimates to predict, at the beginning of treatment, which patients are likely to develop the syndrome.

Both the risk of developing tardive dyskinesia and the likelihood that it will become irreversible are believed to increase as the duration of treatment and the total cumulative dose of antipsychotic drugs administered to the patient increase. However, the syndrome can develop, although much less commonly, after relatively brief treatment periods at low doses. There is no known treatment for established cases of tardive dyskinesia, although the syndrome may remit, partially or completely, if antipsychotic drug treatment is withdrawn. Antipsychotic drug treatment itself, however, may suppress (or partially suppress) the signs and symptoms of tardive dyskinesia and thereby may possibly mask the underlying process. The effect that symptom suppression has upon the long-term course of the syndrome is unknown.

Given this consideration, loxapine should be prescribed in a manner that is most likely to minimize the risk of the occurrence of tardive dyskinesia. As with any antipsychotic drug, chronic loxapine use should be reserved for patients who appear to be obtaining substantial benefit from the drug. In such patients, the smallest dose and the shortest duration of treatment should be sought. The need for continued treatment should be reassessed periodically.

If signs and symptoms of tardive dyskinesia appear in a patient on loxapine, drug discontinuation should be considered. However, some patients may require treatment with loxapine despite the presence of the syndrome.

Neuroleptic Malignant Syndrome: A potentially fatal symptom complex sometimes referred to as Neuroleptic Malignant Syndrome (NMS) has been reported in association with antipsychotic drugs. Clinical manifestations of NMS are hyperpyrexia, muscle rigidity, altered mental status and evidence of autonomic instability (irregular pulse or blood pressure, tachycardia, diaphoresis and cardiac dysrhythmias).

The diagnostic evaluation of patients with this syndrome is complicated in arriving at a diagnosis. It is important to identify cases where the clinical presentation includes both serious medical illness (e.g., pneumonia, systemic infection, etc.) and untreated or inadequately treated extrapyramidal signs and symptoms (EPS). Other important considerations in the differential diagnosis include central anticholinergic toxicity, heat stroke, drug fever and primary CNS pathology.

The management of NMS should include (1) immediate discontinuation of antipsychotic drugs and other drugs not essential to concurrent therapy, (2) intensive symptomatic treatment and medical monitoring and (3) treatment of any concomitant serious medical problems for which specific treatment is available. There is no general agreement about specific pharmacological treatment regimens for uncomplicated NMS.

If a patient requires antipsychotic drug treatment after recovery from NMS, the potential reintroduction of drug therapy should be carefully considered. The patient should be carefully monitored, since recurrences of NMS have been reported.

Pregnancy and *Lactation:* Safe use of loxapine during pregnancy or lactation has not been established; therefore, its use in pregnancy, in nursing mothers or in women of childbearing potential requires that the benefits of treatment be weighed against the possible risks to mother and child.

Children: Studies have not been performed in children; therefore, this drug is not recommended for use in children below the age of 16.

Occupational Hazards: Loxapine, like other antipsychotics, may impair mental and/or physical abilities, especially during the first few days of therapy. Therefore, ambulatory patients should be warned about activities requiring alertness (e.g., operating vehicles or machinery) and about concomitant use of alcohol and other CNS depressants.

This drug is not recommended for use in cases suffering from blood dyscrasias or liver disease of significant severity.

Loxapine has not been evaluated for the management of behavioral complications in patients with mental retardation and therefore cannot be recommended in these patients.

Precautions: Loxapine should be used with extreme caution in patients with a history of convulsive disorders, since it lowers the convulsive threshold. Seizures have been reported in epileptic patients receiving loxapine at antipsychotic dose levels and may occur even with maintenance of routine anticonvulsant drug therapy.

Loxapine has an antiemetic effect in animals. Since this effect may also occur in man, loxapine may mask signs of overdosage of toxic drugs and may obscure conditions such as intestinal obstruction and brain tumor.

Use loxapine with caution in patients with cardiovascular disease. Increased pulse rate and transient hypotension have both been reported in patients receiving antipsychotic doses. In the presence of severe hypotension requiring vasopressor therapy, the preferred drugs would be levarterenol or phenylephrine. The use of epinephrine in these cases should be avoided.

Although clinical experience has not demonstrated ocular toxicity, careful observation should be made for pigmentary retinopathy and lenticular pigmentation, since these have been observed in some patients receiving certain other antipsychotic drugs for prolonged periods.

Because of possible anticholinergic action, the drug should be used with caution in patients with glaucoma or a tendency to urinary retention, particularly with concomitant administration of anticholinergic type of antiparkinson medication.

Neuroleptic drugs elevate prolactin levels; the elevation persists during chronic administration. Tissue culture experiments indicate that approximately one-third of human breast cancers are prolactin-dependent in vitro, a factor of potential importance if the prescription of these drugs is contemplated in a patient with a previously detected breast cancer. Although disturbances such as galactorrhea, amenorrhea, gynecomastia and impotence have been reported, the clinical significance of elevated serum prolactin levels is unknown for most patients. An increase in mammary neoplasms has been found in rodents after chronic administration of neuroleptic drugs. Neither clinical studies, nor epidemiologic studies conducted to date, however, have shown an association between chronic administration of these drugs and mammary tumorigenesis; the available evidence is considered too limited to be conclusive at this time.

There have been reports of excessive stupor, significant reduction in respiratory rate, and, in one patient, hypotension when loxapine and lorazepam were given concomitantly.

Withdrawal Emergent Neurological Signs: Abrupt withdrawal after short-term administration of antipsychotic drugs does not generally pose problems. However, transient dyskinetic signs are experienced by some patients on maintenance therapy after abrupt withdrawal. The signs are very similar to those described under Tardive Dyskinesia, except for duration. Although it is not known whether gradual withdrawal of antipsychotic drugs will decrease the incidence of withdrawal emergent neurological signs, gradual withdrawal would appear to be advisable.

Adverse Effects: CNS: The incidence of sedation following loxapine administration has been less than that of certain aliphatic phenothiazines and slightly more than the piperazine phenothiazines. Drowsiness, usually mild, may occur at the beginning of therapy or when dosage is increased. It usually subsides with continued loxapine therapy. Dizziness, faintness, headache, staggering gait, shuffling gait, muscle twitching, weakness, insomnia, agitation, tension, seizures, akinesia, slurred speech, numbness, paresthesia and confusional states have been reported. Neuroleptic malignant syndrome has been reported (see Warnings).

Extrapyramidal Reactions: Neuromuscular (extrapyramidal) reactions during loxapine administration have been reported frequently, often during the first few days of treatment. In most patients, these reactions involved Parkinson-like symptoms such as tremor, rigidity, excessive salivation and masked facies. Akathisia (motor restlessness) also has been reported relatively frequently. These symptoms are not usually severe and can be controlled by reduction of loxapine dosage or by administration of antiparkinson drugs in usual dosage.

Dystonic and dyskinetic reactions have occurred less frequently, but may be more severe and may occur during the first few days of treatment. Dystonias include spasms of muscles of the neck and face, tongue protrusion and oculogyric movement. Dyskinetic reaction has been described in the form of choreoathetoid movements. These reactions sometimes require reduction or temporary withdrawal of loxapine dosage in addition to appropriate counteractive drugs.

Tardive Dyskinesia: As with all antipsychotic agents, tardive dyskinesia may appear in some patients on long-term therapy or may appear after drug therapy has been discontinued. The risk appears to be greater in elderly patients on high dose therapy, especially females. The symptoms are persistent and in some patients appear to be irreversible. The syndrome is characterized by rhythmical involuntary movement of the tongue, face, mouth or jaw (e.g., protrusion of tongue, puffing of cheeks, puckering of mouth, chewing movements). Sometimes these may be accompanied by involuntary movements of the extremities.

There is no known effective treatment for tardive dyskinesia; antiparkinson agents usually do not alleviate the symptoms of this syndrome. It is suggested that all antipsychotic agents be discontinued if these symptoms appear. Should it be necessary to reinstitute treatment, or increase the dosage of the agent, or switch to a different antipsychotic agent, the syndrome may be masked. The physician may be able to reduce the risk of this syndrome by minimizing the unnecessary use of neuroleptic drugs and reducing the dose or discontinuing the drug, if possible, when manifestations of this syndrome are recognized, particularly in patients over the age of 50. It has been reported that fine vermicular movements of the tongue may be an early sign of the syndrome and if the medication is stopped at that time the syndrome may not develop.

Autonomic: Dry mouth, nasal congestion, constipation, blurred vision, urinary retention and paralytic ileus have occurred.

Cardiovascular: Tachycardia, hypotension, hypertension, lightheadedness and syncope have been reported. A few cases of ECG changes similar to those seen with phenothiazines have been reported. It is not known whether these were related to loxapine administration.

Hematologic: Rarely, agranulocytosis, thrombocytopenia and leukopenia.

Gastrointestinal: Nausea and vomiting have been reported in some patients. Hepatocellular injury (i.e., AST/ALT elevation) has been reported in association with loxapine administration and rarely, jaundice and/or hepatitis questionably related to loxapine treatment.

Dermatological: Dermatitis, edema (puffiness of face), pruritus and seborrhea have been reported with loxapine. The possibility of photosensitivity and/or phototoxicity occurring has not been excluded; skin rashes of uncertain etiology have been observed in a few patients during hot summer months.

Endocrine: Rarely, galactorrhea, amenorrhea, gynecomastia and menstrual irregularity of uncertain etiology have been reported.

Other Adverse Reactions: Weight gain, weight loss, dyspnea, ptosis, hyperpyrexia, flushed facies, and polydipsia have been reported in some patients.

Overdose: Symptoms: Would be expected to range from mild depression of the CNS and cardiovascular systems to profound hypotension, respiratory depression and unconsciousness. The possibility of occurrence of extrapyramidal symptoms and/or convulsive seizures should be kept in mind.

Treatment: No specific antidote is known. The treatment of overdosage would be essentially symptomatic and supportive. Early gastric lavage might be expected to be beneficial as might be extended dialysis. Additional supportive measures include the administration of oxygen and i.v. fluids. Centrally acting emetics may have little effect because of loxapine's antiemetic action. In addition, emesis should be avoided because of the possibility of aspiration of vomitus. Avoid analeptics, which may cause convulsions.

Severe hypotension might be expected to respond to the administration of levarterenol or phenylephrine. **Epinephrine should not be used since its use in a patient with partial adrenergic blockade may further lower the blood pressure.** Severe extrapyramidal reactions should be treated with anticholinergic antiparkinson agents or diphenhydramine HCl, and anticonvulsant therapy should be initiated as indicated.

Renal failure following loxapine overdosage has also been reported.

Loxapac (cont'd)

Dosage: Loxapine is administered orally, usually in divided doses 2 to 4 times a day. Daily dosage should be adjusted to the individual patient's needs, as assessed by the severity of symptoms and previous history of response to antipsychotic drugs. Initial dosage of 10 mg twice daily is recommended, although in severely disturbed patients, initial dosage up to a total of 50 mg daily may be desirable. Based on initial response to the drug, dosage may then be increased fairly rapidly over the first 7 to 10 days until there is effective control of psychotic symptoms. The usual therapeutic range is 60 to 100 mg daily. However, as with other antipsychotic drugs, some patients respond to lower dosage and others require higher dosage for optimal benefit. Daily dosage higher than 250 mg is not recommended. For maintenance therapy, dosage should be reduced to the lowest level compatible with symptom control; many patients have been maintained satisfactorily at dosages in the range of 20 to 60 mg daily.

I.M. Administration: Loxapine i.m. is utilized in patients whose symptoms render oral medication temporarily impractical. During clinical trials, there were no reports of significant local tissue reaction.

Loxapine is administered by i.m. (not i.v.) injection in doses of 12.5 mg (1/4 mL) to 50 mg (1 mL) at intervals of 4 to 6 hours or longer, both dose and interval depending on patient response. Many patients have responded satisfactorily to twice-daily dosage. As described above for oral administration, attention is directed to the necessity for dosage adjustment on an individual basis over the early days of loxapine administration.

Once the desired symptomatic control is achieved and the patient is able to take medication orally, loxapine should be administered in tablet or oral concentrate form.

Supplied: Injectable: For i.m. use only. Not for i.v. use. Each 1 mL ampul contains: loxapine HCl equivalent to loxapine 50 mg for i.m. injection. Nonmedicinal ingredients: polysorbate 80, polypropylene glycol and Water for Injection with hydrochloric acid or sodium hydroxide to adjust the pH to approximately 6.0. Tartrazine-free. Boxes of 10.

Oral Concentrate: Each mL of clear, colorless solution (pH: 5.0 to 6.5) contains: loxapine 25 mg as loxapine HCl. Nonmedicinal ingredients: hydrochloric acid, propylene glycol and purified water. Should be mixed with orange or grapefruit juice shortly before administration. Bottles with a dropper calibrated to deliver 10, 15, 20 and 25 mg and a syringe calibrated to deliver 2.5, 5.0, 7.5, 10.0, 12.5 or 15.0 mg. Expiration date: 2 years following date of manufacture. Bottles of 100 mL.

Tablets: 5 mg: Each yellow, scored, round, convex, film-coated tablet, engraved "LL" in script over "5" on one side and "x" above and "1" below the score on the other contains: loxapine 5 mg as the succinate salt. Nonmedicinal ingredients: alginic acid, calcium phosphate dibasic dihydrate, D&C Yellow No. 10 Aluminum Lake, FD&C Yellow No. 6 Aluminum Lake, hydroxypropyl methylcellulose, magnesium stearate, mineral oil, mineral oil light, sodium lauryl sulfate, starch, starch pregelatinized, stearic acid and titanium dioxide. Tartrazine-free. Bottles of 100 and 500.

10 mg: Each light green, scored, round, convex, film-coated tablet, engraved "LL" in script over "10" on one side and "x" to the left and "2" to the right of the score on the other contains: loxapine 10 mg as the succinate salt. Nonmedicinal ingredients: calcium phosphate dibasic dihydrate, D&C Yellow No. 10 Aluminum Lake, FD&C Blue No. 1 Aluminum Lake, FD&C Yellow No. 6 Aluminum Lake, hydroxypropyl methylcellulose, magnesium stearate, methylcellulose, mineral oil, mineral oil light, sodium lauryl sulfate, starch, starch pregelatinized, stearic acid and titanium dioxide. Tartrazine-free. Bottles of 100 and 500.

25 mg: Each pink, scored, round, convex, film-coated tablet, engraved "LL" in script over "25" on one side and "x" to the left and "3" to the right of the score on the other contains: loxapine 25 mg as the succinate salt. Nonmedicinal ingredients: calcium phosphate dibasic dihydrate, D&C Red No. 30 Aluminum Lake, hydroxypropyl methylcellulose, magnesium stearate, methylcellulose, mineral oil, mineral oil light, sodium lauryl sulfate, starch, starch pregelatinized, stearic acid and titanium dioxide. Tartrazine-free. Bottles of 100 and 500.

50 mg: Each white, scored, round, convex, film-coated tablet, engraved "LL" in script over "50" and "x" to the left and "4" to the right of the score on the other contains: loxapine 50 mg as the succinate salt. Nonmedicinal ingredients: calcium phosphate dibasic dihydrate, hydroxypropyl methylcellulose, magnesium stearate, methylcellulose, mineral oil light, sodium lauryl sulfate, starch, starch pregelatinized, stearic acid and titanium dioxide. Tartrazine-free. Bottles of 100 and 500.

Store all preparations at room temperature (15 to 30°C).

Reviewed 1997

LOZIDE® Ⓟ

Servier

Indapamide Hemihydrate

Diuretic—Antihypertensive Agent

Pharmacology: Indapamide is a diuretic antihypertensive agent. The mechanism whereby indapamide exerts its action in the control of hypertension is not completely elucidated: both renal and extrarenal actions may be involved. The renal site of action is the proximal part of the distal tubule and the ascending part of Henle's loop. Sodium and chloride ions are excreted in approximately equivalent amounts. The increased delivery of sodium to the distal tubular exchange site results in increased potassium excretion and hypokalemia.

Pharmacokinetics: Indapamide is rapidly and completely absorbed after oral administration. Peak blood levels are obtained after 1 to 2 hours. Indapamide is concentrated in the erythrocytes and is 79% bound to plasma proteins and to erythrocytes.

It is taken up by the vascular wall in smooth vascular muscle according to its high lipid solubility. Seventy per cent of a single oral dose is eliminated by the kidneys and 23% by the gastrointestinal tract. Indapamide is metabolized to a marked degree, the unchanged product representing approximately 5% of the total dose found in the urine during the 48 hours following administration. Elimination of indapamide from the plasma is biphasic with half-lives of 14 and 25 hours respectively.

Indications: The management of essential hypertension. It may be tried as a sole therapeutic agent in the treatment of mild to moderate hypertension. Normally indapamide, as other diuretics, is used as the initial agent in multiple drug regimens.

Contraindications: Anuria, progressive and severe oliguria, hepatic coma. Known hypersensitivity to indapamide or to other sulfonamide derivatives.

Warnings: Electrolyte changes observed with indapamide become severe at doses above 2.5 mg/day. Therefore the maximum daily dose should not exceed this dose.

Hypokalemia may occur at all doses with consequent weakness, cramps, and cardiac dysrhythmias. Hypokalemia is a particular hazard in digitalized patients; dangerous or fatal arrhythmias may be precipitated.

Hypokalemia occurs commonly with diuretics; electrolyte monitoring is essential particularly in patients who would be at increased risk from hypokalemia, such as patients with cardiac arrhythmias or those who are receiving concomitant cardiac glycosides.

Patients with renal insufficiency receiving indapamide should be carefully monitored. If increasing azotemia and oliguria occur during treatment, the diuretic should be discontinued.

Hyperuricemia may occur during administration of indapamide. Rarely gout has been reported. Blood uric acid levels should be monitored, particularly in patients with a history of gout who should continue to receive appropriate treatment.

Precautions: Patients receiving indapamide should be carefully observed and serum electrolytes monitored for signs and symptoms of fluid or electrolyte imbalance; namely hyponatremia, hypochloremia and hypokalemia. BUN, uric acid, and glucose levels should also be assessed during therapy. Hypokalemia, an ever present hazard with most diuretics, will be more common in association with concomitant steroid or ACTH therapy and with inadequate electrolyte intake. The serum potassium should be determined at regular intervals and potassium supplementation instituted when indicated (see Warnings).

The signs of electrolyte imbalance are: dryness of the mouth, thirst, weakness, lethargy, drowsiness, restlessness, muscle pains or cramps, muscle fatigue, hypotension, oliguria, gastrointestinal disturbances such as nausea and vomiting, tachycardia and ECG changes.

Special caution should be used in treating patients with severe hepatic disease since diuretics may induce metabolic alkalosis in cases of potassium depletion which may precipitate episodes of hepatic encephalopathy.

Orthostatic hypotension may occur and may be potentiated by alcohol, barbiturates, narcotics or concurrent therapy with other antihypertensives.

When indapamide is given with other nondiuretic antihypertensive agents, the effects on blood pressure are additive.

Sulfonamide derivatives have been reported to exacerbate or activate systemic lupus erythematosus. These possibilities should be kept in mind with the use of indapamide although no case has been reported to date.

Severe dermatological adverse reactions, some accompanied by systemic manifestations, have been rarely reported with the use of indapamide. In the majority of cases, the condition subsided within 14 days following discontinuation of indapamide therapy (see Adverse Effects).

Caution should be observed when administering the drug to patients with severely impaired renal function, since the drug is excreted primarily by the renal route.

Although indapamide exerts minimal effect on glucose metabolism, insulin requirements may be affected in diabetics and hyperglycemia and glycosuria may occur in patients with latent diabetes.

Calcium excretion is decreased by diuretics pharmacologically related to indapamide. After 6 to 8 weeks of indapamide 1.25 mg treatment and in long-term studies of hypertensive patients with higher doses of indapamide, however, serum concentrations of calcium increased only slightly with indapamide. Prolonged treatment with drugs pharmacologically related to indapamide may in rare instances be associated with hypercalcemia and hypophosphatemia secondary to physiologic changes in the parathyroid gland; however, the common complications of hyperparathyroidism, such as renal lithiasis, bone resorption, and peptic ulcer, have not been seen. Treatment should be discontinued before tests for parathyroid function are performed. Like the thiazides, indapamide may decrease serum PBI levels without signs of thyroid disturbance.

The antihypertensive effect of the drug may be enhanced in the patient postsympathectomy.

Pregnancy: Since indapamide has not been studied in human pregnancy, the drug should not be given to pregnant women. The use in patients of childbearing potential requires that the anticipated benefit be weighed against possible hazards.

Lactation: It is unknown whether or not indapamide appears in breast milk. Indapamide should not be administered to nursing mothers. If use of the drug is deemed essential, the patient should stop nursing.

Children: The safety and effectiveness have not been established.

Adverse Effects: The safety data presented under this section involves 2 different databases and was obtained at 2 different time periods. For the earliest database (indapamide 2.5 mg), consisting mainly of European studies performed before 1980, adverse events were collected with respect to a possible causal relationship to treatment, whereas for the most recent database (indapamide 1.25 mg), consisting exclusively of North American studies, adverse events were collected irrespective of such a causal relationship. This explains why the overall incidence of adverse events at the 2.5 mg dose appears to be lower than at the 1.25 mg dose (see below).

Most adverse events for both dosages, 1.25 mg and 2.5 mg, have been mild or moderate.

The adverse reactions represent data from clinical studies involving a total of 992 patients given indapamide 2.5 mg: 349 patients from 4 placebo controlled studies treated for 8 to 12 weeks; 356 patients from 6 active controlled studies treated for 6 up to more than 52 weeks; 287 patients from 4 uncontrolled studies treated for 6 up to 40 weeks.

The overall rate of adverse events, with respect to a possible causal relationship to the drug, was 29% and discontinuation of therapy due to adverse events was required in 5.6% of patients.

The most severe and common adverse event is the electrolyte imbalance. Electrolyte changes reported include hypokalemia (14.2%; requiring potassium supplementation 6%; with clinical symptoms 1.2%), hypochloremia (9.4%) and hyponatremia (3.1%).

The other changes observed in laboratory parameters are minor and infrequent: elevation in blood uric acid (8.6%), blood glucose (6.0%), BUN (5.7%) and blood creatinine (3.6%).

The most frequent adverse events (incidence ≥1%) reported for patients treated with indapamide 2.5 mg were: headache (3.4%), vertigo (2.2%), dizziness (1.9%), asthenia (1.7%) and muscle cramps (1.2%).

All other adverse events occured at an incidence of less than 1% and included by body system:

Central Nervous: drowsiness, sleepiness, insomnia, weakness, lethargy and visual disturbance.
Gastrointestinal: nausea, anorexia, dryness of mouth, gastralgia, vomiting, diarrhea and constipation.
Musculoskeletal: joint pain, back pain and weakness of legs.
Cardiovascular: orthostatic hypotension, tachycardia and ECG changes (nonspecific ST-T change, U waves, left ventricular strain).
Urogenital: impotence, modification of libido and polyuria.
Dermatological: rash and pruritus.
Endocrine: gout.
Other: tinnitus, malaise, fainting and sweat.

In placebo-controlled studies involving 306 patients given indapamide 1.25 mg and 319 given placebo for up to 8 weeks, the overall incidence of adverse events, irrespective of causal relationship, was about 50% in both indapamide and placebo groups. In the indapamide 1.25 mg group, 4.2% of patients discontinued treatment because of adverse events.

In these studies, 20% of patients treated with indapamide 1.25 mg had at least 1 potassium value below 3.4 mEq/L.

The most frequently reported adverse events (incidence ≥1%) in the indapamide 1.25 mg group were: headache (17%), infection (12%), pain (8%), dizziness (7%), back pain (5%), rhinitis (5%), asthenia (4%), dyspepsia (4%), flu syndrome (3%), hypertonia (3%), sinusitis (3%), chest pain (2%), constipation (2%), cough (2%), diarrhea (2%), edema (2%), nausea (2%), pharyngitis (2%), conjunctivitis (1%), nervousness (1%) and ECG abnormalities (nonspecific ST-T changes (7%), sinus bradycardia (3%), arrhythmia (2%) or tachycardia (2%)).

All other clinical adverse events occured at an incidence of less than 1%. These are the following:
Central Nervous: agitation, amnesia, anxiety, ataxia, coordination abnormality, depression, dream abnormality, hyperesthesia, insomnia, migraine, paresthesia, somnolence, twitching and vertigo.
Gastrointestinal: increased appetite, dry mouth, GI carcinoma, GI disorders, duodenitis, dysphagia, esophagitis, flatulence, gastritis, gastroenteritis, oral moniliasis, proctitis, rectal disorders, rectal hemorroids, stomatitis, tooth disorders and vomiting.
Musculoskeletal: arthralgia, arthritis, bone disorders, joint disorders, bone fracture, bone pain, chondrodystrophy, myalgia, myasthenia and myopathy.
Cardiovascular: angina pectoris, bundle branch block, ventricular extrasystoles, atrial fibrillation, atrial flutter, hypertension, postural hypotension, palpitations, syncope, supraventricular tachycardia and vasodilation.
Urogenital: dysmenorrhea, dysuria, impotence, urinary tract infection, nocturia, oliguria, urinary frequency or urgency, renal pain or calculus, prostate disorders and vaginitis.
Respiratory: bronchitis, dyspnea, laryngitis, lung disorder and sputum increase.
Dermatological: acne, application site reaction, exfoliative dermatitis, nail disorder, skin nodule, rash, bullous eruption and sweat.
Metabolic and nutritional: diabetes mellitus and gout.
Special senses: amblyopia, ear disorders, ear pain, otitis, photophobia, taste perversion, tinnitus and vision abnormality.
Other: thyroid disorder, ecchymosis, allergic reaction, edema face, fever, hernia, malaise and monilia.
Postmarketing experience: Among the less common suspected adverse reactions reported, the following, which are not included elsewhere in the product monograph, have been published in the medical literature and/or are classified as serious or potentially serious: Stevens-Johnson syndrome, bullous eruption, photosensitivity with bullae, erythroderma, purpura, epidermal necrolysis, erythema multiforme, angioedema, cataract, acute myopia, optic neuritis, ventricular arrhythmia, torsades de pointe, stroke, acute hypersensitivity reaction leading to interstitial nephritis and renal failure, anemia, agranulocytosis, metabolic alcalosis, hyperosmolar coma, dehydration, hepatitis, pancreatitis, lithium toxicity, rhabdomyolysis, vasculitis, fever.

One case of synergetic effect of clofibrate with indapamide leading to hyponatremia, hypokalemia, hypoosmolarity, nausea and progressive loss of consciousness.

Relationship with the administration of indapamide has not been proved in all cases.

Overdose: Symptoms: There have been no reports of overdosage. Based on the pharmacological activities of indapamide, overdosage may lead to excessive diuresis with electrolyte depletion. In cirrhotic patients, overdosage might precipitate hepatic coma.

Treatment: There is no specific antidote. Treatment is symptomatic and supportive. Discontinue drug. Induce emesis or perform gastric lavage. Correct dehydration, electrolyte imbalance, hepatic coma and hypotension by established procedures.

Dosage: One 1.25 mg tablet/day taken in the morning as a single dose. If the response is not satisfactory after 4 to 8 weeks, the dose may be increased to a maximum of 2.5 mg as a single dose taken in the morning. If the antihypertensive response to indapamide is insufficient, an increase in dosage is not recommended (see Warnings).

Instead a nondiuretic antihypertensive agent should be added to the drug regimen. Alternatively if in the opinion of the physician, an important diuretic effect is desirable for the patient's control, a different diuretic which allows for dose titration could be tried instead of indapamide.

Supplied: 1.25 mg: Each round, orange, film-coated tablet, with S embossed on one side, contains: indapamide hemihydrate 1.25 mg. Blister-packs of 30 and 100.

2.5 mg: Each pink sugar-coated tablet contains: indapamide hemihydrate 2.5 mg. Tartrazine-free. Blister-packs of 30 and 100.

(Shown in Product Recognition Section)

Reviewed 1997

LUDIOMIL® Ⓟ
Novartis Pharmaceuticals

Maprotiline HCl
Antidepressant

Pharmacology: Maprotiline has been shown to exhibit an antidepressant action.

Maprotiline strongly inhibits the uptake of norepinephrine in the brain and peripheral tissues, but has a notable lack of serotonergic uptake inhibition. It has markedly less pronounced alpha-adrenergic blocking activity than amitriptyline. Maprotiline has a strong antihistaminic activity and a weaker anticholinergic activity. Maprotiline also exerts a sedative effect on the anxiety component of depressive illness.

It is postulated that maprotiline exerts its antidepressant action by inhibition of presynaptic uptake of catecholamines, thereby increasing their concentration at the synaptic clefts in the brain. In single doses, the effect of maprotiline on the EEG included an increase in the alpha-wave density, a decrease of the alpha-wave frequency and an increase in the alpha-wave amplitude. However, as with other tricyclic antidepressants, maprotiline lowers the convulsive threshold.

In one as yet uncorroborated "sleep study", it appears that maprotiline increased the REM phase of sleep in depressed patients, from its initially reduced base line, whereas imipramine reduced the REM phase of sleep.

Pharmacokinetics: Maprotiline is slowly, but completely, absorbed after oral administration. Serum protein binding is 88 to 90%. The half-life of unchanged maprotiline is relatively long, ranging from 27.4 to 57.6 hours. The mean systemic clearance is 514 mL/min.

After repeated doses of 150 mg maprotiline daily, steady state plasma concentrations between 100 and 400 ng/mL were reached in the second week. The same plasma levels are attained whether the daily dosage is given as a single dose of 150 mg, in 2 fractions of 75 mg or 3 fractions of 50 mg.

Maprotiline is metabolized by N-demethylation, deamination, aliphatic and aromatic hydroxylations and by formation of aromatic methoxy derivatives. Maprotiline is excreted primarily in the urine. Within 21 days after a single dose, 57% of the total dose is excreted in the urine, with about 30% in the bile. Only 2 to 4% of the dose is excreted unchanged in the urine. Ninety percent of the amount excreted in the urine consists of metabolites, 75% in the form of glucuronides.

Steady state plasma concentrations for a given dose are higher in elderly patients (aged >60 years) than in younger patients. The half-life and renal excretion of maprotiline are not significantly affected by impaired renal function (creatinine clearance: 24 to 37 mL/min), provided that hepatic function is still normal. Urinary excretion of metabolites is reduced, although this reduction is offset by increased fecal elimination of metabolites through biliary excretion.

Indications: The treatment of endogenous depressive illness, including the depressed phase of bipolar (manic-depressive) disorders, unipolar (psychotic) depression, and involutional melancholia. Maprotiline may also be useful in selected patients suffering severe depressive neurosis.

Contraindications: In patients who have known or suspected hypersensitivity to the drug or its excipients, or have known or suspected hypersensitivity to tricyclic antidepressants belonging to the dibenzazepine group.

Maprotiline should not be given in conjunction with, or within 14 days before or after treatment with a MAO inhibitor (see Precautions, Drug Interactions). The concomitant treatment with selective, reversible MAO-A inhibitors, such as moclobemide, is also contraindicated. Hypertensive crises, hyperactivity, hyperpyrexia, spasticity, severe convulsions or coma, and death have been reported in patients receiving such combinations.

Maprotiline is contraindicated during the acute recovery phase following a myocardial infarction and in the presence of acute congestive heart failure.

Maprotiline is contraindicated in patients with existing liver or kidney damage and should not be administered to patients with a history of blood dyscrasias.

Maprotiline is contraindicated in patients with glaucoma, as the condition may be aggravated due to the atropine-like effects of the drug.

Maprotiline should not be used in patients with known or suspected convulsive disorders since it is known to lower the seizure threshold (see Warnings).

Warnings: Seizures: Tricyclic agents are known to lower the convulsive threshold and maprotiline should, therefore, be used with extreme caution in patients with a history of convulsive disorders and other predisposing factors, e.g., brain damage of varying etiology, concomitant use of neuroleptics, alcoholism and withdrawal from alcohol, and concomitant use with other drugs that lower the seizure threshold. It appears that the occurrence of seizures is dose dependent. Therefore, the recommended total daily doses should not be exceeded (see Dosage).

Seizures have been reported in patients without a history of seizures who were treated with maprotiline at therapeutic dose levels. However, in some of these patients other confounding factors such as concomitant medications known to lower seizure threshold were also present. The risk of seizures may be increased when maprotiline is taken concomitantly with phenothiazines, when the dosage of benzodiazepines is rapidly tapered in patients receiving maprotiline, or when the recommended dosage of maprotiline is rapidly exceeded. While a cause-and-effect relationship has not been established, the risk of seizures may be reduced by: initiating therapy at a low dose; maintaining the initial dosage for 2 weeks before raising it gradually in small increments (see Dosage) due to the long half-life of maprotiline (average 51 hours); keeping the maintenance dosage at a minimally effective level (dosages below 200 mg/day); cautious alteration in, or avoidance of, concomitant prescribing of drugs that lower the seizure threshold (i.e., phenothiazines) or rapid tapering of benzodiazepines.

Concurrent administration of electroconvulsive therapy and maprotiline may be hazardous and such treatment should be limited to patients for whom it is essential. Physicians should discuss with patients the risk of taking maprotiline while engaging in activities in which a sudden loss of consciousness could result in serious injury to the patient or others, e.g., the operation of complex machinery, driving, swimming, or climbing.

Cardiovascular: Tricyclic antidepressants, particularly in high doses, have been reported to produce sinus tachycardia, changes in conduction time and arrhythmias. A few instances of unexpected death have been reported in patients with cardiovascular disorders. Myocardial infarction and stroke have also been reported with drugs of this class. Therefore, maprotiline should be administered with extreme caution to patients with a history of cardiovascular disorders, especially those with cardiovascular insufficiency, conduction disorders (e.g., atrioventricular block grades I to III) or other arrhythmias, those with circulatory lability and elderly patients. Maprotiline also has a hypotensive action which may be detrimental in these circumstances. In such cases, treatment should be initiated at low doses with progressive increases only if required and tolerated, and the patients should be under close surveillance at all dosage levels. Monitoring of cardiac function and the ECG is indicated in such patients as well as in the elderly.

Use in Concomitant Illness: Caution should be observed when prescribing maprotiline for hyperthyroid patients or for patients receiving thyroid medication. Transient cardiac arrhythmias have occurred in rare instances in patients who have been receiving other tricyclic compounds concomitantly with thyroid medication.

Because of its anticholinergic properties, maprotiline should be used with caution in patients with increased intraocular pressure, narrow angle glaucoma or urinary retention, particularly in the presence of prostatic hypertrophy.

Tricyclic antidepressants may give rise to paralytic ileus, particularly in the elderly and in hospitalized patients. Therefore, appropriate measures should be taken if constipation occurs.

Ludiomil (cont'd)

Caution is called for when employing maprotiline in patients with tumors of the adrenal medulla (e.g., pheochromocytoma, neuroblastoma), in whom the drug may provoke a hypertensive crisis.

Children: Maprotiline is **not** recommended for use in children since safety and efficacy in the pediatric age group have not been established (cases of sudden death in children treated with maprotiline have been reported).

Maprotiline should be kept in a safe place, well out of reach of children.

Pregnancy: The safety of use in pregnant women has not been established. Therefore, maprotiline should not be administered to women of childbearing potential, or during pregnancy, unless, in the opinion of the physician, the expected benefit to the patient outweighs the potential risk to the fetus. Withdrawal symptoms including tremors, dyspnea, lethargy, colic, irritability, hypotonia/hypertonia, convulsions and respiratory depression have been reported in neonates whose mothers received tricyclic antidepressants during the third trimester of pregnancy. To avoid such symptoms, maprotiline should, if possible, be gradually withdrawn at least 7 weeks before the calculated date of confinement.

Lactation: Maprotiline passes into breast milk. After repeated administration of 150 mg/day for 5 days, concentrations of maprotiline in breast milk exceeded that in blood by a factor of 1.3 to 1.5. Therefore, maprotiline should be gradually withdrawn or the infant weaned if the patient is breast-feeding.

Precautions: Suicide: The possibility of a suicide attempt is inherent in depression. These patients should be carefully supervised during treatment with maprotiline and hospitalization or concomitant electroconvulsive therapy may be required. One study in which maprotiline was given as prophylactic treatment for unipolar depression suggested an increase in suicidal behavior in the treated group. To minimize the risk of an intentional overdose by a depressed patient, prescriptions for maprotiline should be written for the smallest possible quantity of the drug consistent with good patient management.

Psychosis, Mania-Hypomania and Other Neuropsychiatric Phenomena: In patients treated with tricyclic antidepressants, activation of latent schizophrenia or aggravation of existing psychotic manifestations in schizophrenic patients may occur. Patients with manic-depressive tendencies may experience hypomanic or manic shifts. Hyperactive or agitated patients may become over-stimulated. A reduction in dose or discontinuation of maprotiline should be considered under these circumstances.

In predisposed and elderly patients, tricyclic antidepressants may, particularly at night, provoke pharmacogenic (delirious) psychoses that disappear within a few days of withdrawing the drug.

Occupational Hazards: Since maprotiline may produce sedation, particularly during the initial phase of therapy, patients should be cautioned about the danger of engaging in activities requiring mental alertness, judgment and physical coordination.

Cardiovascular: Before initiating treatment, it is advisable to check the patient's blood pressure, because individuals with hypotension or a labile circulation may react to the drug with a fall in blood pressure. Regular measurements of blood pressure should be performed in suceptible patients. Postural hypotension may be controlled by reducing the dosage or administering circulatory stimulants.

ECG abnormalities have been observed in patients treated with maprotiline. The most common ECG changes were premature ventricular contractions (PVCs), ST-T wave changes, and abnormalities in intraventricular conduction. These changes were rarely associated with significant clinical symptoms. Nevertheless, caution is necessary when treating patients with heart disease, as well as elderly subjects. In these patients cardiac function should be monitored and ECG examinations performed during long-term therapy. Gradual dose titration is also recommended.

Hepatic Changes: Isolated cases of obstructive jaundice have been reported. Caution is indicated in treating patients with known liver disease and periodic monitoring of hepatic function is recommended in such patients.

Hematological Changes: Isolated cases of bone marrow depression with agranulocytosis have been reported. Leukocyte and differential blood cell counts are recommended in patients receiving treatment with maprotiline over prolonged periods, and should be performed for patients who develop fever, an influenzal infection or sore throat. In the event of an allergic skin reaction, maprotiline should be withdrawn.

Withdrawal Symptoms: A variety of withdrawal symptoms have been reported in association with abrupt discontinuation of maprotiline, including dizziness, nausea, vomiting, headache, malaise, sleep disturbance, hyperthermia and irritability. In addition, such patients may experience a worsening of psychiatric status. While the withdrawal effects of maprotiline have not been systematically evaluated in controlled trials, they are well known with closely related tricyclic antidepressants. It is recommended that the dosage be tapered gradually and the patient monitored carefully during discontination. Sudden withdrawal of maprotiline may result in serious hypotension.

Metabolic Effects: Tricyclic antidepressants have been associated with porphyrinogenicity in susceptible patients.

Renal Function: It is advisable to monitor renal function during long-term therapy with tricyclic antidepressants.

Dental Effects: Lengthy treatment with tricyclic antidepressants can lead to an increased incidence of dental caries.

Lacrimation: Decreased lacrimation and accumulation of mucoid secretions, due to the anticholinergic properties of tricyclic antidepressants, may cause damage to the corneal epithelium in patients with contact lenses.

Drug Interactions: Patients should be warned that, while taking maprotiline, their responses to alcoholic beverages, other CNS depressants (e.g., barbiturates, benzodiazepines or general anesthetics) or anticholinergic agents (e.g., atropine, antihistamines, biperiden, levodopa) may be exaggerated.

When tricyclic antidepressants are given in combination with anticholinergics or neuroleptics with an anticholinergic action, hyperexcitation states or delirium may occur, as well as attacks of glaucoma.

Tricyclic antidepressants should not be employed in combination with antiarrhythmic agents of the quinidine type (see Warnings, Cardiovascular).

Since maprotiline may diminish or abolish the antihypertensive effects of guanethidine, bethanidine, clonidine, reserpine or alpha-methyldopa, patients requiring concomitant treatment for hypertension should be given antihypertensives of a different type (e.g., diuretics, vasodilators, beta-blockers).

Maprotiline may potentiate the cardiovascular effects of norepinephrine or epinephrine, amphetamine, as well as nasal drops and local anesthetics containing sympathomimetics (e.g., isoprenaline, ephedrine, phenylephrine).

Fluoxetine, fluvoxamine and other selective serotonin reuptake inhibitors (SSRIs) may increase the activity and plasma concentrations of tricyclic antidepressants with corresponding adverse effects.

Caution should be exercised if maprotiline is administered together with cimetidine or methylphenidate since these drugs have been shown to inhibit the metabolism of several tricyclic antidepressants. Clinically significant increases in plasma levels of maprotiline may occur, necessitating a dosage reduction.

Substances which activate the hepatic mono-oxygenase enzyme system (e.g., barbiturates, carbamazepine, phenytoin, nicotine and oral contraceptives) may lower plasma concentrations of tricyclic antidepressants and so reduce their antidepressive effects. In addition, maprotiline may increase plasma levels of phenytoin and carbamazepine, therefore, it may be necessary to adjust the dosage of these drugs.

Maprotiline should not be administered for a period of at least 14 days after the discontinuation of treatment with MAO inhibitors due to the potential for severe interactions (see Contraindications). The same caution should also be observed when administering a MAO inhibitor after previous treatment with maprotiline.

Maprotiline should be discontinued prior to elective surgery for as long as clinically feasible, since little is known about the interaction with general anesthetics.

Concomitant treatment with neuroleptic agents (e.g., phenothiazines and butyrophenones) may result in increased plasma concentrations of maprotiline, a lowered convulsion threshold and seizures. Combination with thioridazine may produce severe cardiac arrhythmias. No such effects are known to occur in combination with diazepam, but it might be necessary to lower the dosage of maprotiline if administered concomitantly with alprazolam or disulfiram.

Tricyclic antidepressants may potentiate the anticoagulant effect of coumarin drugs by inhibiting hepatic metabolism of these drugs. Careful monitoring of plasma prothrombin is therefore advised.

Comedication with oral sulfonylureas or insulin may potentiate their hypoglycemic effect. Diabetic patients should monitor their blood glucose levels when treatment with maprotiline has been initiated or discontinued.

If administered concomitantly with estrogens, the dose of maprotiline should be reduced since steroid hormones inhibit the metabolism of maprotiline.

Adverse Effects: Adverse reactions with maprotiline have been mild and transient, usually disappearing with continued treatment or following a reduction in the dosage. Adverse reactions do not always correlate with plasma levels or dose. It is often difficult to differentiate certain adverse reactions from symptoms of depression such as fatigue, sleep disturbances, agitation, anxiety, constipation and dry mouth.

The most common adverse reactions reported with maprotiline are due to its anticholinergic, largely autonomic, effects which include: dry mouth, day sedation, vertigo, blurred vision, constipation, headache and nervousness.

If severe neurological or psychiatric reactions occur, maprotiline should be withdrawn.

Elderly patients are particularly susceptible to anticholinergic, psychiatric, neurological and cardiovascular effects.

The following adverse reactions have been reported either with maprotiline or other similar tricyclic antidepressant drugs: (Frequency estimates: Frequent $>10\%$; Occasional >1 to 10%; Rare >0.01 to 1%; Isolated cases $<0.01\%$).

Neurological: Frequent: tremors. Occasional: dizziness, headache, paresthesia (numbness, tingling sensation, symptoms suggestive of peripheral neuropathy), delirium. Rare: epileptic seizures. Isolated cases: tinnitus, incoordination, ataxia, alterations in EEG patterns, extrapyramidal symptoms, myoclonus, speech disorders, weakness.

Behavioral: Occasional: drowsiness, fatigue, insomnia, confusional states with hallucinations (particularly in geriatric patients and patients suffering from Parkinson's disease), anxiety, agitation, restlessness, nightmares, hypomania, mania, decrease in memory, feeling of unreality. Rare: activation of latent psychosis. Isolated cases: aggressiveness.

Anticholinergic: Frequent: dry mouth and rarely associated sublingual adenitis, blurred vision, disturbances of visual accommodation, constipation, perspiration, hot flushes. Occasional: delayed micturition, dilation of the urinary tract. Isolated cases: mydriasis, glaucoma, paralytic ileus.

Cardiovascular: Frequent: hypotension, particularly orthostatic hypotension with associated vertigo, sinus tachycardia, ECG changes (including flattening or inversion of T wave, depressed S-T segments) in patients of normal cardiac status. Occasional: arrhythmia, disturbances in cardiac conduction (e.g., widening of QRS complex, PQ changes, bundle-branch block), palpitation, syncope. Isolated cases: hypertension, congestive heart failure, myocardial infarction, heart block, asystole, stroke, peripheral vasospastic reactions.

Hematologic: Isolated cases: agranulocytosis, eosinophilia, leukopenia, purpura and thrombocytopenia may occur as an idiosyncratic response.

Gastrointestinal: Occasional: nausea, vomiting, anorexia, abdominal cramps. Rare: diarrhea, elevated transaminases. Isolated cases: bitter taste, stomatitis, epigastric distress, black tongue, dysphagia, increased salivation, hepatitis with or without jaundice.

Respiratory: Isolated cases: bronchospasm.

Endocrine: Frequent: weight gain. Occasional: increased or decreased libido, impotence. Isolated cases: gynecomastia in the male, breast enlargement and galactorrhea in the female, testicular swelling, elevation or depression of blood sugar levels, weight loss, inappropriate antidiuretic hormone (SIADH) secretion syndrome.

Allergic or Toxic: Occasional: skin rash, urticaria. Isolated cases: petechiae, itching, photosensitization (avoid excessive exposure to sunlight), edema (general or of face and tongue), drug fever, obstructive jaundice, nasal congestion, alopecia, allergic alveolitis (pneumonia) with or without eosinophilia, systemic anaphylactic/anaphylactoid reactions including hypotension.

Withdrawal Symptoms: Abrupt cessation of treatment with tricyclic antidepressants after prolonged administration may occasionally produce nausea, vomiting, abdominal pain, diarrhea, insomnia, nervousness, anxiety, headache and malaise. These symptoms are not indicative of addiction.

Overdose: Since children may be more sensitive than adults to acute overdosage with tricyclic antidepressants, and since fatalities in children have been reported, effort should be made to avoid potential overdose, particularly in this age group.

Symptoms: These may vary in severity depending upon factors such as the amount of drug absorbed, the interval between drug ingestion and the start of treatment and the age of the patient. Accidental ingestion in children should be regarded as serious and potentially fatal.

Symptoms generally appear within 4 hours of ingestion and reach maximum severity after 24 hours. Owing to delayed absorption (increased anticholinergic effect due to overdose), long half-life and enterohepatic recycling of the drug, the patient may be at risk for up to 4 to 6 days.

Symptoms may include drowsiness, stupor, ataxia, vomiting, cyanosis, restlessness, agitation, delirium, severe perspiration, hyperactive reflexes, muscle rigidity, athetoid and choreiform movements and/or convulsions. Hyperpyrexia, mydriasis, bowel and bladder paralysis, oliguria or anuria and respiratory depression may occur.

Hypotension and initial hypertension may occur. However, the usual finding is increasing hypotension which may eventually lead to shock. Serious cardiovascular disturbances are frequently present, including tachycardia, cardiac arrhythmias (flutter, atriofibrillation, premature ventricular beats and ventricular tachycardia) as well as impaired myocardial conduction, atrioventricular and intraventricular block, ECG abnormalities (such as widened QRS complexes and marked S-T shifts), signs of congestive heart failure and cardiac arrest. Coma may ensue.

One case of acute intoxication with 5 g of maprotiline in a 58 year old woman has been reported, in which full recovery occurred. Other cases of recorded clinical recovery have been reported in the dose range of 1.6 to 2 g of maprotiline. A 22 year old woman, however, died from cardiac arrest 5 days after ingestion of 3 g of the drug. Fatal outcomes have also been reported in combined intoxication with tricyclic antidepressants, sedatives or hypnotics in the maprotiline dose range of 2 to 10 g.

Treatment: Patients in whom overdosage is suspected should be admitted to hospital without delay. No specific antidote is available and treatment is essentially symptomatic and supportive.

Gastric lavage or aspiration should be performed promptly and is recommended up to 12 hours or even more after the overdose, since the anticholinergic effect of the drug may delay gastric emptying. Administration of activated charcoal may help reduce absorption of the drug. As maprotiline is largely protein bound, forced diuresis, peritoneal dialysis and hemodialysis are unlikely to be of value.

Treatment should be designed to insure maintenance of the vital functions. An open airway should be maintained in comatose patients and assisted ventilation instituted, if necessary, but respiratory stimulants should not be used. Hyperpyrexia should be controlled by external measures, such as ice packs and cooling sponge baths. Acidosis may be treated by cautious administration of sodium bicarbonate. Adequate renal function should be maintained.

ECG monitoring in an intensive care unit is recommended in all patients, particularly in the presence of ECG abnormalities, and should be maintained for several days after the cardiac rhythm has returned to normal. Unexpected deaths attributed to cardiac arrhythmias have been reported several days following an apparent recovery from tricyclic antidepressant overdose. Correction of hypoxia and acidosis, if present, may be beneficial. Correction of metabolic acidosis and low potassium concentrations by means of bicarbonate i.v. and potassium substitution may also be effective for treatment of arrhythmias. If bradyarrhythmia or AV block occur, consider temporary insertion of a cardiac pacemaker. Because of its effect on cardiac conduction, digitalis should be used only with caution. If rapid digitalization is required for the treatment of congestive heart failure, special care should be exercised in using the drug.

External stimulation should be minimized to reduce the tendency to convulsions. If convulsions occur, anticonvulsants (preferably i.v. diazepam) should be administered. Barbiturates may intensify respiratory depression, particularly in children, and aggravate hypotension and coma. Paraldehyde may be used in some children to counteract muscular hypertonus and convulsions with less likelihood of causing respiratory depression. If the patient fails to respond rapidly to anticonvulsants, artificial ventilation should be instituted. Prompt control of convulsions is essential since they aggravate hypoxia and acidosis and may thereby precipitate cardiac arrhythmias and arrest.

Shock should be treated with supportive measures such as i.v. fluids, plasma expanders, and oxygen. The use of corticosteroids in shock is controversial and may be contraindicated in tricyclic antidepressant overdose. Hypotension usually responds to elevation of the foot of the bed. Pressor agents, (but **not** epinephrine) should be given cautiously, if indicated. In the event of reduced myocardial function, consider recourse to treatment with dopamine or dobutamine by i.v. drip.

Since it has been reported that physostigmine may cause severe bradycardia, asystole and seizures, its use is not recommended in cases of overdosage with maprotiline.

Deaths by deliberate or accidental overdosage have occurred with this class of drugs. Since the propensity for suicide is high in depressed patients, a suicide attempt by other means may occur during the recovery phase. The possibility of simultaneous ingestion of other drugs should also be considered.

Dosage: Patients should be kept under medical surveillance during treatment with maprotiline.

The dosage of maprotiline should be individualized according to the requirements of each patient. Treatment should be initiated at the lowest recommended dose and increased gradually, noting carefully the clinical response and any evidence of intolerance. It should be kept in mind that a lag in therapeutic response usually occurs at the onset of therapy, lasting from several days to a few weeks. Increasing the dosage does not normally shorten this latent period and may increase the incidence of side effects.

Initial Dosage: Adults: The recommended initial dosage is 75 mg daily 2 or 3 divided doses. Because of the long half-life of maprotiline, this dosage should usually be maintained for 2 weeks. It may then be increased gradually in increments of 25 mg as necessary and tolerated, preferably by adding to the late afternoon or bedtime dose. The maximum recommended dose in outpatients is 150 mg daily, although doses up to 200 mg may be required in some patients. In the treatment of severely depressed hospitalized patients, a higher initial dose of 100 mg daily in 2 or 3 divided doses may be indicated. The usual optimal dose in these patients is 150 mg daily, but some patients may require up to 225 mg in divided doses. When these higher doses are used, it is essential to exclude a history of convulsive disorders.

Elderly and Debilitated Patients: In general, lower dosages are recommended for these patients, and doses should only be increased in gradual increments. This approach is particularly important in elderly patients, since these individuals generally show a more marked response to maprotiline than patients in younger age groups. The initial recommended dose is 10 mg 3 times daily, with very gradual increments, depending on tolerance and response, up to 75 mg daily in divided doses. A maintenance dose of 50 to 75 mg daily is usually satisfactory. Blood pressure and cardiac rhythm should be checked frequently, particularly in patients who have unstable cardiovascular function.

Maintenance Dosage: Dosage during maintenance therapy should be kept at the lowest effective level. Medication should be continued for the expected duration of the depressive episode in order to minimize the possibility of relapse following clinical improvement.

When a maintenance dosage has been established as described above, maprotiline may be administered in a single daily dose at bedtime, provided such a dosage regimen is well tolerated. However, if the total daily dose exceeds 150 mg, it should be administered in divided doses.

Supplied: 10 mg: Each cream-colored, round, film-coated, biconvex tablet, engraved CIBA on one side and CO on the other, contains: maprotiline HCl 10 mg. Nonmedicinal ingredients: cellulose compounds, colloidal silicon dioxide, cornstarch, iron oxides, lactose, magnesium stearate, polysorbates, stearic acid, talc, titanium dioxide and tribasic calcium phosphate. Energy: 1.1 kJ (0.26 kcal). Bottles of 100.

25 mg: Each orange-brown, round, beveled-edged, film-coated, biconvex tablet, engraved CIBA on one side and DP on the other, contains: maprotiline HCl 25 mg. Nonmedicinal ingredients: cellulose compounds, colloidal silicon dioxide, cornstarch, iron oxides, lactose, magnesium stearate, polysorbates, stearic acid, talc, titanium dioxide and tribasic calcium phosphate. Energy: 0.91 kJ (0.21 kcal). Bottles of 100.

50 mg: Each brownish-yellow, round, beveled-edged, film-coated, biconvex tablet, engraved CIBA on one side and ER on the other, contains: maprotiline HCl 50 mg. Nonmedicinal ingredients: cellulose compounds, colloidal silicon dioxide, cornstarch, iron oxides, lactose, magnesium stearate, polysorbates, stearic acid, talc, titanium dioxide and tribasic calcium phosphate. Energy: 0.92 kJ (0.22 kcal). Bottles of 100.

75 mg: Each reddish-brown, round, film-coated, biconvex tablet, engraved CIBA on one side and FS with bisect on the other, contains: maprotiline HCl 75 mg. Nonmedicinal ingredients: cellulose compounds, colloidal silicon dioxide, cornstarch, iron oxides, lactose, magnesium stearate, polysorbates, stearic acid, talc, titanium dioxide and tribasic calcium phosphate. Energy: 1.3 kJ (0.32 kcal). Bottles of 100.

Alcohol-, bisulfite-, gluten-, parabens-, sodium- and tartrazine-free. Protect from heat (store between 2 and 30°C). Keep out of reach of children.

(Shown in Product Recognition Section)

Reviewed 1997

LUPRON® Ⓟ
LUPRON DEPOT®
3.75 mg/7.5 mg Ⓟ

Abbott/TAP Pharmaceuticals

Leuprolide Acetate
Leuprolide Acetate for Depot Suspension

Gonadotropin–releasing Hormone Analog for Management of Central Precocious Puberty in Children

Pharmacology: Leuprolide is a synthetic nonapeptide analog of naturally occurring gonadotropin releasing hormone (GnRH or LHRH). The analog possesses greater potency than the natural hormone. When administered as indicated, leuprolide acts as a potent inhibitor of gonadotropin production. It is chemically unrelated to steroids.

Unlike steroid hormones leuprolide exerts specific action on the pituitary gonadotrophs and the human reproductive tract.

This specificity reduces the likelihood of secondary adverse effects such as gynecomastia, thromboembolism, edema, liver and gallbladder involvement.

Human studies indicated that following an initial stimulation of gonadotropins, chronic stimulation with leuprolide results in suppression or "downregulation" of these hormones and consequent suppression of ovarian and testicular steroidogenesis. These effects are reversible on discontinuation of drug therapy.

Leuprolide is not active when given orally. In adults, bioavailability by s.c. administration is comparable to that by i.v. administration. Leuprolide has a plasma half-life of 2.9 hours.

Two chronic studies involving the treatment of children with central precocious puberty (CPP), demonstrated that following the administration of leuprolide injection and/or leuprolide for depot suspension, stimulated and basal gonadotropins are reduced to prepubertal levels. Testosterone and estradiol are reduced to prepubertal levels in males and females, respectively, and a reduction of gonadotropins will allow for normal physical and psychological growth and development. Natural maturation occurs when gonadotropins return to pubertal levels following discontinuation of leuprolide.

The following physiological effects have been noted with the chronic administration of leuprolide in (CPP) patients: Skeletal Growth: A measurable increase in body length can be noted since the epiphyseal plates will not close prematurely. Organ Growth: Reproductive organs will return to a prepubertal state. Menses: Menses, if present, will cease.

I.M. injection of leuprolide for depot suspension provides plasma concentrations of leuprolide over a period of 1 month.

In a study of 22 children with central precocious puberty, doses of leuprolide for depot suspension were given every 4 weeks and plasma levels were determined according to weight categories as summarized in Table I.

Table I—Lupron/Lupron Depot

Determination of Leuprolide Plasma Levels According to Weight Categories in Children with Central Precocious Puberty

Patient Weight Range (kg)	Group Weight Average (kg)	Dose (mg)	Trough Plasma Leuprolide Level Mean ± SD (ng/mL)*
20.2–27.0	22.7	7.5	0.77±0.033
28.4–36.8	32.5	11.25	1.25±1.06
39.3–57.5	44.2	15.0	1.59±0.65

*Group average values determined at Week 4 immediately prior to leuprolide injection. Drug levels at 12 and 24 weeks were similar to respective 4 week levels.

Pharmacokinetics: Absorption: A single dose of leuprolide for depot suspension 3.75 mg was administered by i.m. injection to healthy adult female volunteers. The absorption of leuprolide was characterized by an initial increase in plasma concentration, with peak concentration ranging from 4.6 to 10.2 ng/mL at 4 hours post-dosing. However, intact leuprolide and an inactive metabolite could not be distinguished by the assay used in the study. Following the initial rise, leuprolide concentrations started to plateau within 2 days after dosing and remained relatively stable for about 4 to 5 weeks with plasma concentrations of about 0.30 ng/mL.

Following a single leuprolide for depot suspension 7.5 mg i.m. injection to adult patients, the mean peak leuprolide plasma concentration was almost 20 ng/mL at 4 hours and

Lupron/Lupron Depot 3.75 mg/7.5 mg (cont'd)

then declined to 0.36 ng/mL at 4 weeks. However, intact leuprolide and an inactive major metabolite could not be distinguished by the assay used in the study. Undetectable leuprolide plasma concentrations have been observed during chronic leuprolide for depot suspension 7.5 mg administration, but testosterone levels appear to be maintained at castrate levels.

Distribution: The mean steady-state volume of distribution of leuprolide following i.v. bolus administration to healthy male volunteers was 27 L. In vitro binding to human plasma proteins ranged from 43 to 49%.

Metabolism: In healthy male volunteers, a 1 mg bolus of leuprolide administered i.v. revealed that the mean systemic clearance was 7.6 L/h, with a terminal elimination half-life of approximately 3 hours based on a 2 compartment model.

In rats and dogs, administration of ^{14}C-labelled leuprolide was shown to be metabolized to smaller inactive peptides, pentapeptide (Metabolite I), tripeptide (Metabolite II and II) and dipeptide (Metabolite IV). These fragments may be further catabolized.

The major metabolite (M-I) plasma concentrations measured in 5 prostate cancer patients reached mean maximum concentration 2 to 6 hours after dosing and were approximately 6% of the peak parent drug concentration. One week after dosing, mean plasma M-I concentrations were approximately 20% of leuprolide concentrations.

Excretion: Following administration of leuprolide for depot suspension 3.75 mg to 3 patients, less than 5% of the dose was recovered as parent and M-I metabolite in the urine.

Special Populations: The pharmacokinetics of the drug in hepatic and renal impaired patients have not been determined.

A pharmacokinetic study of leuprolide acetate in children has not been performed.

Indications: In the treatment of children with central precocious puberty. Children should be selected using the following criteria: 1. Clinical diagnosis of CPP (idiopathic or neurogenic) with onset of secondary sexual characteristics earlier than 8 years in females and 9 years in males. 2. Clinical diagnosis should be confirmed prior to initiation of therapy as follows: (a) Confirmation of diagnosis by a pubertal response to a GnRH stimulation test. The sensitivity and methodology of this assay must be undertstood. (b) Bone age advanced 1 year beyond the chronological age. 3. Baseline evaluation should also include: (a) height and weight measurements; (b) sex steroid levels; (c) adrenal steroid level to exclude congenital adrenal hyperplasia; (d) beta human chorionic gonadotropin level to rule out a chorionic gonadotropin secreting tumor; (e) pelvic/adrenal/testicular ultrasound to rule out a steroid secreting tumor; (f) computerized tomography of the head to rule out intracranial tumor.

Contraindications: In patients with hypersensitivity to the drug or its components or similar nonapeptides. Isolated cases of anaphylaxis have been reported.

Pregnancy: Leuprolide for depot suspension is contraindicated in women who are or may become pregnant while receiving the drug. When administered on day 6 of pregnancy at test dosages of 0.00024, 0.0024 and 0.024 mg/kg (1/1 200 to 1/12 the human pediatric dose) to rabbits, it produced a dose-related increase in major fetal abnormalities. Similar studies in rats failed to demonstrate an increase in fetal malformations. There was increased fetal mortality and decreased fetal weights with the 2 higher doses of leuprolide for depot suspension in rabbits and with the highest dose (0.024 mg/kg) in rats. The effects on fetal mortality are logical consequences of the alterations in hormonal levels brought about by this drug. Therefore, the possibility exists that spontaneous abortion may occur if the drug is administered during pregnancy.

Lactation: It is not known whether leuprolide for depot suspension is excreted in human milk; therefore, it should not be administered to a nursing mother.

Warnings: During the early phase of therapy, gonadotropins and sex steroids rise above baseline because of the natural stimulatory effect of the drug. An increase in clinical signs and symptoms may therefore be observed (see Pharmacology).

Noncompliance with the drug regimen or inadequate dosing may result in inadequate control of the pubertal process. The consequences of poor control include the return of pubertal signs such as menses, breast development, and testicular growth. The long-term consequences of inadequate control of gonadal steroid secretion are unknown, but may include a further compromise of adult stature.

Precautions: General: Patients with known allergies to benzyl alcohol, vehicle ingredient of leuprolide injection, may present symptoms of hypersensitivity, usually local, in the form of erythema and induration at the injection site.

Response to leuprolide should be monitored 1 to 2 months after the start of therapy with a GnRH stimulation test and sex steroid levels. Measurement of bone age for advancement should be done every 6 to 12 months.

Sex steroids may increase or rise above prepubertal levels if the dose is inadequate (see Warnings). Once a therapeutic dose has been established, gonadotropin and sex steroid levels will decline to prepubertal levels.

Dependence Liability: No drug-dependence has been reported with the use of leuprolide.

Drug Interactions: No pharmacokinetic based drug-drug interaction studies have been conducted.

Leuprolide being 46% bound to plasma proteins, and a peptide that is primarily degraded by peptidase and not by cytochrome P450 enzymes as noted in specific studies, drug interactions would not be expected to occur.

Drug/Laboratory Test Interactions: Administration of leuprolide for depot suspension 3.75 mg in women results in suppression of the pituitary-gonadal system. Normal function is usually restored within 4 to 12 weeks after treatment is discontinued. Diagnostic tests of pituitary-gonadal function conducted during treatment and within 4 to 8 weeks after discontinuation of leuprolide for depot suspension therapy may therefore be misleading.

Effect on Clinical Laboratory Tests: As expected (see Pharmacology), leuprolide administration will initially affect selected serum and urine parameters in the first week of treatment: elevation of BUN, creatinine, acid phosphatase, testosterone and dihydrotestosterone can be expected. With chronic administration, these high values will usually return to normal, or drop below baselines in the case of testosterone, dihydrotestosterone and acid phosphatase.

Adverse Effects: Potential exacerbation of signs and symptoms during the first few weeks of the treatment (see Precautions) is a concern in patients with rapidly advancing central precocious puberty.

In 2 studies of children with central precocious puberty, in 2% or more of the patients receiving the drug, the following adverse reactions were reported to have a possible or probable relationship to drug as ascribed by the treating physician. Reactions considered not drug related are excluded. See Table II.

Table II—Lupron/Lupron Depot

Adverse Reactions

	Number of Patients N=397	(%)
Body as a Whole		
General pain	6	(2)
Integumentary		
Acne/seborrhea	8	(2)
Injection site reactions including abscess	21	(5)
Rash including erythema multiforme	8	(2)
Urogenital		
Vaginitis/bleeding/discharge	8	(2)

In these same studies, the following adverse reactions were reported in less than 2% of the patients.

Body as a Whole: body odor, fever, headache, infection, hypertrophy.

Cardiovascular: syncope, vasodilation.

Digestive: dysphagia, gingivitis, nausea/vomiting.

Endocrine: accelerated sexual maturity.

Metabolic and Nutritional Disorders: peripheral edema, weight gain.

Nervous System: nervousness, personality disorder, somnolence, emotional liability.

Respiratory: epistaxis.

Integumentary: alopecia, skin striae, urticaria.

Urogenital: cervix disorder, gynecomastia/breast disorders, urinary incontinence.

Postmarketing Surveillance: During postmarketing surveillance which include other dosage forms, the following adverse events were reported: Cardiovascular: hypotension.

Hemic and Lymphatic: decreased WBC.

Central/Peripheral Nervous System: peripheral neuropathy, spinal fracture/paralysis.

Integumentary: rash, urticaria, photosensitivity reactions.

Musculoskeletal: tenosynovitis-like symptoms.

Urogenital: prostate pain.

Miscellaneous: injection site reactions including pain, inflammation, sterile abscess, induration and hematoma.

Isolated cases of anaphylaxis have been reported. Symptoms consistent with an anaphylactoid or asthmatic process have been rarely reported.

Overdose: Symptoms and Treatment: In rats, s.c. administration of 250 to 500 times the recommended human pediatric dose, expressed on a per body weight basis resulted in dyspnea, decreased activity, and local irritation at the injection site.

There is no clinical experience with the effects of an acute overdose. Because the acute animal toxicity of the drug is low, adverse effects are not expected. No difference in adverse reactions was observed in patients who received either 1 or 10 mg/day leuprolide for up to 3 years or 20 mg/day for up to 2 years.

Dosage: The dose must be individualized for each child. The dose is based on a mg/kg ratio of drug to body weight. Younger children require higher doses on a mg/kg ratio.

For each dosage form, after 1 to 2 months of initiating therapy or changing doses, the child must be monitored with a GnRH stimulation test, sex steroids, and Tanner staging to confirm downregulation. Measurements of bone age for advancement should be monitored every 6 to 12 months. The dose should be titrated upward until no progression of the condition is noted either clinically and/or by laboratory parameters.

The first dose found to result in adequate downregulation can probably be maintained for the duration of therapy in most children. However, there are insufficient data to guide dosage adjustments as patients move into higher weight categories after beginning therapy at very young ages and low dosages. It is recommended that adequate downregulation be verified in such patients whose weight has increased significantly while on therapy.

As with other drugs administered chronically by injection, the injection site should be varied periodically.

Discontinuation of leuprolide should be considered before age 11 for females and age 12 for males.

Lupron: The recommended starting dose is 50 μg/kg/day administered as a **single s.c. injection.** If total downregulation is not achieved, the dose should be titrated upward by 10 μg/kg/day to a maximum of 100 μg/kg/day. This dose will be considered the maintenance dose.

Note: As with other parenteral products, inspect container's solution for discoloration and particulate matter before each use.

Lupron Depot: The recommended starting dose is 0.3 mg/kg/4 weeks (minimum 7.5 mg) administered as a **single i.m. injection.** The starting dose will be dictated by the child's weight: ≤25 kg: 7.5 mg; >25-37.5 kg: 11.25 mg; >37.5 kg: 15 mg.

If total downregulation is not achieved, the dose should be titrated upward in increments of 3.75 mg every 4 weeks to a maximum of 15 mg/month. This dose will be considered the maintenance dose.

The lyophilized microspheres are to be reconstituted and administered **monthly** as a **single i.m. injection.**

Special Instructions for Use: **Leuprolide for depot suspension must be administered under the supervision of a physician.**

The lyophilized microspheres are to be reconstituted and administered **monthly** as a single i.m. injection, in accord with the following directions: Vial and Ampul: 1. Using a syringe with a 22 gauge needle, withdraw **1 mL of diluent** from the ampul, and inject it into the vial. (Extra diluent is provided; any remaining diluent should be discarded.) 2. Shake well to thoroughly disperse particles to obtain a uniform, homogeneous suspension. (The suspension will appear milky.) 3. Withdraw the entire contents of the vial into the syringe and inject it as directed (**once a month**) at the time of reconstitution. Any reconstituted suspension not used immediately should be discarded.

Prefilled Dual-chamber Syringe: 1. Screw the white plunger into the end stopper until the stopper begins to turn. 2. Remove and discard the tamper evident tab around the base of the needle. 3. Holding the syringe upright, release the diluent by **slowly pushing** the plunger until the first stopper is at the blue line in the middle of the barrel. 4. Gently shake the syringe to thoroughly mix the particles to form a uniform suspension. The suspension will appear milky. 5. If the microspheres (particles) adhere to the stopper, tap the syringe against your finger. 6. Then remove the needle guard and advance the plunger to expel the air from the syringe. 7. At the time of reconstitution, inject the entire contents of the syringe i.m. as you would for a normal injection.

As with other drugs administered by injection, the injection site should be varied periodically.

Although the suspension has been shown to be stable for 24 hours following reconstitution, since the product does not contain a preservative, the suspension should be discarded if not used immediately.

Information for the Patient: See Blue Section—Information for the Patient "Lupron/Lupron Depot 3.75 mg/7.5 mg".

Supplied: Lupron: Each mL contains: leuprolide acetate 5 mg. Nonmedicinal ingredients: benzyl alcohol, sodium chloride and sterile water for injection. The pH may have been adjusted with sodium hydroxide and/or acetic acid. Multiple dose vials of 2.8 mL for s.c. use. Also supplied as 14-day kits. Each 14-day Patient Administration Kit contains: 1 vial of Lupron, 28 swabs and 14 syringes, Patient Information Leaflet, Instruction for Use Leaflet and Package Insert. Keep refrigerated between 2 and 8°C.

Lupron Depot Kits (Vial and Ampul): 3.75 mg (1-month slow release): Each single-dose vial contains: leuprolide acetate 3.75 mg. Sterile lyophilized microspheres composed of leuprolide acetate incorporated in a biodegradable copolymer of lactic and glycolic acids. Nonmedicinal ingredients: DL-lactic and glycolic acids copolymer, D-mannitol and purified gelatin.

7.5 mg (1-month slow release): Each single-dose vial contains: leuprolide acetate 7.5 mg. Sterile lyophilized microspheres composed of leuprolide acetate incorporated in a biodegradable copolymer of lactic and glycolic acids. Nonmedicinal ingredients: DL-lactic and glycolic acids copolymer, D-mannitol and purified gelatin.

Each mL of the accompanying ampul of sterile diluent contains: carboxymethylcellulose sodium, D-mannitol, polysorbate 80, water for injection and acetic acid to control pH. Supplied as kits. Each kit contains 1 vial of Lupron Depot (1-month SR), 1 ampul of sterile diluent, 1 syringe with 22 G needle, 1 additional 22 G needle, 2 alcohol swabs, Special Instructions for Use, Patient Information Leaflet and Package Insert. Store vials, kits and sterile diluent at controlled room temperature between 15 and 30°C. Protect from freezing.

Prefilled Syringes: 3.75 mg (1-month slow release): Each prefilled dual-chamber syringe contains: leuprolide acetate for depot suspension 3.75 mg (1-month slow release). Sterile lyophilized microspheres composed of leuprolide incorporated in a biodegradable copolymer of lactic acid and glycolic acids. Nonmedicinal ingredients: DL-lactic and glycolic acids copolymer, D-mannitol and purified gelatin. The rear chamber of diluent contains: carboxymethylcellulose sodium, D-mannitol, glacial acetic acid USP to control pH, polysorbate 80 and water for injection.

7.5 mg (1-month slow release): Each prefilled dual-chamber syringe contains: leuprolide acetate for depot suspension 7.5 mg (1-month slow release). Sterile lyophilized microspheres composed of leuprolide incorporated in a biodegradable copolymer of lactic acid and glycolic acids. Nonmedicinal ingredients: DL-lactic and glycolic acids copolymer, D-mannitol and purified gelatin. The rear chamber of diluent contains: carboxymethylcellulose sodium, D-mannitol, glacial acetic acid USP to control pH, polysorbate 80 and water for injection.

Store prefilled syringes at controlled room temperature between 15 and 30°C. Protect from freezing. Supplied as single-dose kits. Each kit contains 1 prefilled dual-chamber syringe with 23 G needle, 2 alcohol swabs, Special Instruction for Use, Patient Information Leaflet and Package Insert.

During the manufacturing process, acetic acid is lost, leaving the peptide.

Reviewed 1999

LUPRON® ℞
LUPRON DEPOT® 7.5 mg/ 22.5 mg ℞

Abbott

Leuprolide Acetate
Leuprolide Acetate for Depot Suspension

Gonadotropin-releasing Hormone Analog

Pharmacology: Leuprolide is a synthetic nonapeptide analog of naturally occurring gonadotropin-releasing hormone (GnRH or LHRH). The analog possesses greater potency than the natural hormone. When administered as indicated, leuprolide acts as a potent inhibitor of gonadotropin production. It is chemically unrelated to steroids.

Unlike steroid hormones, leuprolide exerts specific action on the pituitary gonadotrophs and the human reproductive tract. This specificity reduces the likelihood of secondary adverse effects such as gynecomastia, thromboembolism, edema, liver and gallbladder involvement.

Bioavailability by s.c. administration is comparable to i.v. administration. Leuprolide has a plasma half-life of 2.9 hours.

I.M. injections of leuprolide for depot suspension 7.5 mg (1-month SR) and 22.5 mg (3-month SR) provide plasma concentrations of leuprolide acetate over a period of 1 and 3 months, respectively.

General: Animal and human studies indicate that, following an initial stimulation, chronic administration of leuprolide results in the inhibition of gonadotropin production. Consequently, ovarian or testicular steroidogenesis is suppressed. The therapeutic effect of leuprolide in the treatment of hormone-dependent tumors, such as in prostatic cancer, results from the reduction in serum gonadotropins and gonadal steroids.

Chronic administration of leuprolide has resulted in inhibition of tumor growth (prostatic tumors in Noble and Dunning male rats, 7–12-dimethylbenz[α]-anthracene (DMBA)-induced mammary tumors in female rats) as well as atrophy of the reproductive organs. An additional mechanism of action, a direct effect on the gonads by down-regulation of the gonadotropin receptors, is suggested in some animal studies.

In humans, s.c. administration of single daily doses of leuprolide results in an initial increase in circulating levels of luteinizing hormone (LH) and follicle-stimulating hormone (FSH), leading to a transient increase in the levels of the gonadal steroids (testosterone and dihydrotestosterone in males and estrone and estradiol in premenopausal females). However, continuous administration results in decreased levels of LH and FSH in all patients. In males, testosterone is reduced to castrate levels. In premenopausal females, estrogens are reduced to postmenopausal levels. These decreases occur within 2 to 4 weeks after initiation of treatment, and are maintained as long as treatment continues. Castrate levels of testosterone in prostatic cancer patients have been demonstrated for periods of up to 5 years.

Pharmacokinetics: Absorption: Following a single leuprolide for depot suspension 7.5 mg (1-month SR) injection to adult patients, the mean peak leuprolide plasma concentration was almost 20 ng/mL at 4 hours and then declined to 0.36 ng/mL at 4 weeks. However, intact leuprolide and an inactive major metabolite could not be distinguished by the assay used in the study. Undetectable leuprolide plasma concentrations have been observed during chronic leuprolide for depot suspension 7.5 mg (1-month SR) administration, but testosterone levels appear to be maintained at castrate levels.

The pharmacokinetic profile of leuprolide for depot suspension 22.5 mg (3-month SR) was characterized in 23 orchiectomized prostate cancer patients. Following a single injection of the 3-month formulation of leuprolide for depot suspension 22.5 mg (3-month SR), a mean peak plasma leuprolide concentration of 48.9 ng/mL was observed at 4 hours and then declined to 0.67 ng/mL at 12 weeks. Leuoprolide appeared to be released at a constant rate following the onset of steady-state level during the third week after dosing, providing steady plasma concentrations through the 12-week dosing interval. Detectable levels of leuprolide were present at all measurement points in all patients during this 12-week period. The initial burst, followed by the rapid decline to a steady-state level, was similar to the release pattern seen with the monthly formulation.

Distribution: The mean steady-state volume of distribution of leuprolide following i.v. bolus administration to healthy male volunteers was 27 L. In vitro binding to human plasma proteins ranged form 43 to 49%.

Metabolism: In healthy male volunteers, a 1 mg bolus of leuprolide administered i.v. revealed that the mean systemic clearance was 7.6 L/h, with a terminal elimination half-life of approximately 3 hours based on a 2-compartment model.

In rats and dogs, administration of ^{14}C-labelled leuprolide was shown to be metabolized to smaller inactive peptides, pentapeptide (Metabolite I), tripeptide (Metabolite II and III) and dipeptide (Metabolite IV). These fragments may be further catabolized.

The major metabolite (M-I) plasma concentrations measured in 5 prostate cancer patients reached mean maximum concentration 2 to 6 hours after dosing and were approximately 6% of the peak parent drug concentration. One week after dosing, mean plasma M-I concentrations were approximately 20% of leuprolide concentrations.

Excretion: Following administration of leuprolide for depot suspension 3.75 mg (1-month SR) to 3 patients, less than 5% of the dose was recovered as parent and M-I metabolite in the urine.

Special Populations: The pharmacokinetics of the drug in hepatic- and renal-impaired patients have not been determined.

Indications: In the palliative treatment of sex hormone responsive advanced (stage D_2) carcinoma of the prostate.

Contraindications: General: Patients with hypersensitivity to the drug or its components or similar nonapeptides. Isolated cases of anaphylaxis have been reported.

Warnings: Prostatic Cancer: Isolated cases of short-term worsening of signs and symptoms have been reported during initiation of leuprolide therapy: they are sometimes, but not necessarily, associated with a stimulation of the pituitary gland and an initial increase in the levels of circulating gonadal hormones.

Worsening of symptoms may contribute to paralysis with or without fatal complications. For patients at risk, the physician may consider initiating therapy with daily leuprolide injection for the first 2 weeks. Worsening of clinical conditions may occasionally require discontinuation of therapy and/or surgical intervention.

Urinary signs and symptoms may worsen in patients with a previous history of obstructive uropathy. Therefore, these patients should be closely monitored during the first week of therapy (see Precautions).

Patients with metastatic vertebral lesions should begin leuprolide therapy under close supervision (see Precautions).

Long-term administration of leuprolide will cause suppression of pituitary gonadotropins and gonadal hormone production with clinical symptoms of hypogonadism. The reversibility of this effect has not yet been established.

Leuprolide for depot suspension 22.5 mg (3-month SR) is also contraindicated in females and children.

Precautions: General: Patients with known allergies to benzyl alcohol, vehicle ingredient of leuprolide injection, may present symptoms of hypersensitivity, usually local, in the form of erythema and induration at the injection site.

Prostatic Cancer: Leuprolide is occasionally associated with an acute worsening of bone pain and urinary signs and symptoms during the first week of therapy (see Warnings). These effects sometimes occurred in association with a transient rise in testosterone and dihydrotestosterone with peak levels 50 to 100% over basal at 72 hours.

Bone pain was reported in approximately 10% of patients. Pain varied in intensity (mild to serious) and in frequency, usually requiring the symptomatic and supportive use of mild oral analgesics together with rest. Some patients required parenteral narcotics.

Urinary obstruction may occur in patients with a previous history of obstructive uropathy. In these cases, catheterization may be necessary.

Patients on leuprolide therapy should be followed on a regular basis with physical examinations and laboratory tests (including testosterone, dihydrotestosterone, prostate-specific antigen (PSA), and prostatic acid phosphatase or acid phosphatase).

The effects of leuprolide on bone lesions may be monitored by bone scans, while its effects on prostatic lesions may be monitored by ultrasonography, and/or CT scan in addition to digital rectal examination.

I.V. pyelogram, ultrasonography, or CT scan may be also utilized to diagnose or assess the status of obstructive uropathy.

Changes in Bone Density: Bone loss can be expected as part of natural aging and can also be anticipated during medically induced hypoandrogenic status caused by long-term use of leuprolide. In patients with significant risk factors for decreased bone mineral content and/or bone mass such as family history of osteoporosis, chronic use of corticosteroids or anticonvulsants or chronic abuse of alcohol or tobacco, leuprolide may pose additional risk. In these patients, risk versus benefit must be weighed carefully before initiation of leuprolide therapy.

Dependence Liability: No drug-dependence has been reported with the use of leuprolide.

Drug Interactions: No pharmacokinetic based drug-drug interaction studies have been conducted.

Leuprolide being 46% bound to plasma proteins, and a peptide that is primarily degraded by peptidase and not by cytochrome P450 enzymes as noted in specific studies, drug interactions would not be expected to occur.

Drug/Laboratory Test Interactions: Administration of leuprolide in therapeutic doses results in suppression of the pituitary-gonadal system. Normal function is usually restored within 4 to 12 weeks after treatment is discontinued. Diagnostic tests of pituitary-gonadal function conducted during treatment and within 4 to 8 weeks after discontinuation of

Lupron/Lupron Depot 7.5 mg/22.5 mg (cont'd)

leuprolide for depot suspension therapy may therefore be misleading.

Effect on Clinical Laboratory Tests: As expected, leuprolide administration will initially affect selected serum and urine parameters in the first week of treatment: elevation of BUN, creatinine, acid phosphatase, testosterone and dihydrotestosterone can be expected. With chronic administration, these high values will usually return to normal, or drop below baseline in the case of testosterone, dihydrotestosterone and acid phosphatase.

Response to leuprolide and leuprolide for depot suspension should be monitored by measuring serum levels of testosterone, as well as prostate-specific antigen and prostatic acid phosphatase.

Adverse Effects: Prostatic Cancer: Some side effects seen with leuprolide are due to specific pharmacologic action, namely increases and decreases in sex hormone levels.

In clinical studies, an initial rise in serum testosterone levels usually occurred in nonorchiectomized patients during the first week of treatment.

This occasionally was associated with a worsening of signs and symptoms, usually an increase in bone pain (see Warnings and Precautions). In some cases, temporary renal impairment was accompanied by mental confusion, joint pain, nausea and vomiting. In each case, leuprolide administration was continued and the symptoms subsided in 1 to 2 weeks.

The relationship of these observations to leuprolide administration is unknown.

The potential for exacerbation of signs and symptoms during the first few weeks of treatment is a concern in patients with vertebral metastases and/or in patients with severe obstructive uropathy which, if aggravated, may lead to neurological problems such as temporary weakness and/or paresthesia of the lower limbs or worsening of urinary symptoms, such as hematuria and urinary tract obstruction.

Lupron: The following adverse reactions documented in 2 clinical studies are considered to be leuprolide treatment related: hot flashes (49 to 55%), impotence/decrease in libido (3 to 10%), local reactions at injection site/ecchymosis/erythema (4 to 15%), decrease in testicular size/atrophic genitalia (7 to 13%), and itching rash (3%).

The following additional adverse reactions have been reported with leuprolide injection. Reactions considered not drug-related are excluded.

Cardiovascular: congestive heart failure, ECG changes/ischemia, high blood pressure, hypotension, myocardial infarction, murmur, phlebitis/thrombosis, pulmonary emboli, transient ischemic attack/stroke, cardiac arrhythmias.

Gastrointestinal: constipation, dysphagia, gastrointestinal bleeding, gastrointestinal disturbance, hepatic dysfunction, peptic ulcer, rectal polyps, anorexia.

Endocrine: breast tenderness or pain, libido increase, thyroid enlargement, gynecomastia.

Hemic and Lymphatic: anemia, decreased WBC.

Musculoskeletal: ankylosing spondylosis, joint pain, pelvic fibrosis, myalgia, spasms.

Central/Peripheral Nervous System: anxiety, blurred vision, dizziness/lightheadedness, headache, hearing disorder, sleep disorders, lethargy, memory disorder, mood swings, nervousness, numbness, paresthesia, peripheral neuropathy, spinal fracture/paralysis, syncope/blackouts, taste disorders.

Respiratory: cough, pleural rub, pneumonia, pulmonary fibrosis, pulmonary infiltrate, respiratory disorders, sinus congestion.

Integumentary: carcinoma of skin/ear, dry skin, ecchymosis, hair loss, itching, pigmentation, skin lesions.

Urogenital: bladder spasms, incontinence, penile swelling, prostate pain, urinary obstruction, urinary tract infection, hematuria.

Miscellaneous: depression, hypoglycemia, hypoproteinemia, increased BUN, increased creatinine, infection/inflammation, ophthalmologic disorders, swelling (temporal bone), asthenia, fatigue, fever.

Leuprolide Acetate for Depot Suspension: In a clinical trial of leuprolide for depot suspension 7.5 mg (1-month SR), the following adverse reactions were reported to have a possible or probable relationship to drug as ascribed by the treating physician in 5% or more of the patients receiving the drug. Reactions considered not drug-related are excluded. See Table I.

In this same study, the following adverse reactions were reported in less than 5% of the patients on leuprolide for depot suspension 7.5 mg (1-month SR):

Cardiovascular: angina, cardiac arrhythmia.

Table I—Lupron Depot 7.5 mg

Adverse Reactions	Lupron Depot 7.5 mg N=56	(%)
Cardiovascular		
Edema	7	(12.5)
Gastrointestinal		
Nausea/vomiting	3	(5.4)
Endocrine		
*Decreased testicular size	3	(5.4)
*Hot flashes	33	(58.9)
*Impotence	3	(5.4)
Central/Peripheral Nervous System		
General pain	4	(7.1)
Respiratory		
Dyspnea	3	(5.4)
Miscellaneous		
Asthenia	3	(5.4)
Laboratory: Elevations of certain parameters were observed, but it is difficult to assess these abnormalities in this population.		
LDH (greater than 2 times normal values)	3	(5.4)
Alkaline Phosphatase (greater than 1.5 times normal values)	5	(8.9)

*Physiologic effect of decreased testosterone.

Endocrine: gynecomastia, libido decrease.

Gastrointestinal: anorexia, diarrhea.

Integumentary: dermatitis, local skin reactions, hair growth.

Miscellaneous: asthenia, diabetes, fever/chills, hard nodule in throat, increased calcium, weight gain, increased uric acid, AST (greater than 2 times normal values).

Musculoskeletal: bone pain, myalgia.

Central/Peripheral Nervous System: paresthesia, insomnia.

Respiratory: dyspnea, hemoptysis.

Urogenital: dysuria, frequency/urgency, hematuria, testicular pain.

In 2 clinical trials of leuprolide for depot suspension 22.5 mg (3-month SR), the following adverse reactions were reported to have a possible or probable relationship to drug as ascribed by the treating physician in 5% or more of the patients receiving the drug. **Often, causality is difficult to assess in patients with metastatic prostate cancer.** Reactions considered not drug-related are excluded. See Table II.

Table II—Lupron Depot 22.5 mg

Adverse Reactions	Lupron Depot 22.5 mg N=94 (%)
Body as a Whole	
Asthenia	7 (7.4)
General pain	25 (26.6)
Headache	6 (6.4)
Injection site reaction	13 (13.8)
Cardiovascular	
Hot flashes/sweats*	55 (58.5)
Digestive	
Gastrointestinal disorders	15 (16.0)
Musculoskeletal	
Joint disorders	11 (11.7)
Central/Peripheral Nervous System	
Dizziness/Vertigo	6 (6.4)
Insomnia/Sleep disorders	8 (8.5)
Neuromuscular disorders	9 (9.6)
Respiratory	
Respiratory disorders	6 (6.4)
Skin and Appendages	
Skin reaction	8 (8.5)
Urogenital	
Testicular atrophy*	19 (20.2)
Urinary disorders	14 (14.9)

*Physiologic effect of decreased testosterone.

In these same studies, the following adverse reactions were reported in less than 5% of the patients on leuprolide for depot suspension 22.5 mg (3-month SR).

Body as a Whole: enlarged abdomen, fever.

Cardiovascular: arrhythmia, bradycardia, heart failure, hypertension, hypotension, varicose vein.

Digestive: anorexia, duodenal ulcer, increased appetite, thirst/dry mouth.

Hemic and Lymphatic Systems: anemia, lymphedema.

Metabolic and Nutritional Disorders: dehydration, edema.

Central/Peripheral Nervous System: anxiety, delusions, depression, hypesthesia, libido decreased*, nervousness, paresthesia.

Respiratory: epistaxis, pharyngitis, pleural effusion, pneumonia.

Special Senses: abnormal vision, amblyopia, dry eyes, tinnitus.

Urogenital: gynecomastia, impotence*, penis disorders, testis disorders.

Laboratory: Abnormalities of certain parameters were observed, but are difficult to assess in this population. The following were recorded in ≥ 5% of patients: increased BUN, hyperglycemia, hyperlipidemia (total cholesterol, LDL-cholesterol, triglycerides), hyperphosphatemia, abnormal liver function tests, increased PT, increased PTT. Additional laboratory abnormalities reported were: decreased platelets, decreased potassium and increased WBC.

*Physiologic effect of decreased testosterone.

Postmarketing Surveillance: The following adverse events have been reported during postmarketing surveillance: Cardiovascular: hypotension.

Hemic and Lymphatic: decreased WBC.

Central/Peripheral Nervous System: peripheral neuropathy, spinal fracture/ paralysis.

Integumentary: rash, urticaria, photosensitivity reactions.

Musculoskeletal: tenosynovitis-like symptoms.

Urogenital: prostate pain.

Miscellaneous: injection site reactions including pain, inflammation, sterile abscess, induration, and hematoma.

Isolated cases of anaphylaxis have been reported.

Symptoms consistent with an anaphylactoid or asthmatic process have been rarely reported.

Overdose: Symptoms and Treatment: In rats, s.c. administration of 250 to 500 times the recommended human dose/kg results in dyspnea, decreased activity, and local irritation at the injection site.

There is no clinical experience with the effects of an acute overdose. Because the acute animal toxicity of the drug is low, adverse effects are not expected. No difference in adverse reactions was observed in patients who received either 1 or 10 mg/day leuprolide for up to 3 years or 20 mg/day for up to 2 years.

Dosage: Prostatic Cancer: **Lupron:** The recommended dose is 1 mg (0.2 mL), as a **single daily s.c. injection.**

Note: As with all parenteral products, inspect container's solution for discoloration and particulate matter before each use.

Lupron Depot 7.5 mg (1-month SR): The recommended dose is 7.5 mg administered **monthly** as a **single i.m. injection,** after reconstitution with the special diluent (see Special Instructions for Use and Information for the Patient).

As with other drugs administered chronically by injection, the injection site should be varied periodically.

Lupron Depot 22.5 mg (3-month SR): The recommended dose is 22.5 mg administered as a **single i.m. injection once every 3 months**, after reconstitution with the special diluent (see Special Instructions for Use and Information for the Patient). Due to different release characteristics, a fractional dose of this 3-month depot formulation is not equivalent to the same dose of the monthly formulation and should therefore not be given.

Special Instructions for Use: **Lupron Depot must be administered under the supervision of a physician.**

The lyophilized microspheres contained in the vial are to be reconstituted prior to i.m. administration, in accord with the following directions:

Lupron Depot 7.5 mg (1-month SR): Vial and Ampul: 1. Using a syringe with a 22 gauge needle, withdraw **1 mL of diluent** from the ampul, and inject it into the vial. (Extra diluent is provided; any remaining unused portion should be discarded). 2. Shake well to thoroughly disperse particles to obtain a uniform, homogeneous suspension. (The suspension will appear milky.) 3. Withdraw the entire contents of the vial into the syringe and inject it as directed **(once a month)**, at the time of reconstitution. Any reconstituted suspension not used immediately, should be discarded.

Prefilled Dual-chamber Syringe: 1. Screw the white plunger into the end stopper until the stopper begins to turn. 2. Remove and discard the tamper-evident tab around the base of the needle. 3. Holding the syringe upright, release the diluent by **slowly pushing** the plunger until the first stopper is at the blue line in the middle of the barrel. 4. Gently shake the syringe to thoroughly mix the particles to form a uniform suspension. The suspension will appear milky. 5. If the microspheres (particles) adhere to the stopper, tap the syringe against your finger. 6. Then remove the needle guard and advance the plunger to expel the air from the syringe. 7. At the time of reconstitution, inject the entire contents of the syringe i.m. as you would for a normal injection.

Although the suspension has been shown to be stable for 24 hours following reconstitution, since the product does not contain a preservative, the suspension should be discarded if not used immediately.

Lupron Depot 22.5 mg (3-month SR): Vial and Ampul: 1. Using a syringe with a 22 gauge needle, withdraw **1.5 mL of diluent** from the ampul, and inject it into the vial. (Extra diluent is provided; any remaining unused portion should be discarded.) 2. Shake well to thoroughly disperse particles to obtain a uniform, homogeneous suspension. (The suspension will appear milky.) 3. Withdraw the entire contents of the vial into the syringe and inject it as directed **(once every 3 months)**, at the time of reconstitution. The suspension settles very quickly following reconstitution; therefore, it is preferable that Lupron Depot 22.5 mg (3-month SR) be mixed and used immediately. Reshake suspension if settling occurs. Any reconstituted suspension not used immediately, should be discarded.

Prefilled Dual-chamber Syringe: 1. Screw the white plunger into the end stopper until the stopper begins to turn. 2. Remove and discard the tamper-evident tab around the base of the needle. 3. Holding the syringe upright, release the diluent by **slowly pushing** the plunger until the first stopper is at the blue line in the middle of the barrel. 4. Gently shake the syringe to thoroughly mix the particles to form a uniform suspension. The suspension will appear milky. 5. If the microspheres (particles) adhere to the stopper, tap the syringe against your finger. 6. Then remove the needle guard and advance the plunger to expel the air from the syringe. 7. Inject the entire contents of the syringe i.m. as you would for a normal injection. The suspension settles very quickly following reconstitution: therefore, it is strongly recommended that Lupron Depot 22.5 mg (3-month SR) be mixed and used immediately. Reshake suspension if settling occurs.

As with other drugs administered by injection, the injection site should be varied periodically.

Information for the Patient: See Blue Section—Information for the Patient "Lupron/Lupron Depot 7.5 mg/22.5 mg".

Supplied: Lupron: Each mL contains: leuprolide acetate 5 mg. Nonmedicinal ingredients: benzyl alcohol sodium chloride and sterile water for injection. The pH may have been adjusted with sodium hydroxide and/or acetic acid. Sterile multiple dose vials of 2.8 mL for s.c. use. Supplied as vials and 14-day or 28-day kits. Each patient administration kit contains: 14-day: 1 vial of Lupron, 28 swabs, 14 syringes, Patient Information Leaflet, Instructions for Use Leaflet, and Package Insert; 28-day: 2 vials of Lupron, 56 swabs and 28 syringes, Patient Information Leaflet, Instructions for Use leaflet, and Package Insert. Keep refrigerated between 2 and 8°C.

Lupron Depot: 7.5 mg (1-month slow release): Each single-dose vial contains: leuprolide acetate for depot suspension 7.5 mg.

Sterile lyophilized microspheres containing leuprolide acetate incorporated in a biodegradable copolymer of lactic and glycolic acids. Nonmedicinal ingredients: DL-lactic and glycolic acids copolymer and D-mannitol and purified gelatin.

Each mL of the accompanying ampul of sterile diluent contains: carboxymethylcellulose sodium, D-mannitol, polysorbate, water for injection and glacial acetic acid USP to control pH. Store diluent at controlled room temperature between 15 and 30°C. Protect from freezing. Supplied as kits. Each kit contains 1 vial of Lupron Depot, 1 ampul of sterile diluent, 1 syringe with 22 gauge needle, 1 additional 22 gauge needle, 2 alcohol swabs and Patient Information Leaflet, Special Instructions for Use and Package Insert.

22.5 mg (3-month slow release): Each single-dose vial contains: leuprolide acetate for depot suspension 22.5 mg.

Sterile lyophilized microspheres containing leuprolide acetate incorporated in a biodegradable copolymer of lactic and glycolic acids. Nonmedicinal ingredients: D-mannitol and polylactic acid.

Each mL of the accompanying ampul of sterile diluent contains: carboxymethylcellulose sodium, D-mannitol, polysorbate, water for injection and glacial acetic acid USP to control pH. Store diluent at controlled room temperature between 15 and 30°C. Protect from freezing. Supplied as kits. Each kit contains 1 vial of Lupron Depot, 1 ampul of sterile diluent, 1 syringe with 22 gauge needle, 1 additional 22 gauge needle, 2 alcohol swabs and Patient Information Leaflet, Special Instructions for Use and Package Insert.

Prefilled syringes: 7.5 mg (1-month slow release): Each prefilled dual-chamber syringe contains: leuprolide acetate for depot suspension 7.5 mg. Sterile lyophilized microspheres containing leuprolide acetate incorporated in a biodegradable copolymer of lactic and glycolic acids. Nonmedicinal ingredients: DL-lactic and glycolic acids copolymers, D-mannitol and purified gelatin. The rear chamber of diluent contains: carboxymethylcellulose sodium, D-mannitol, glacial acetic acid USP to control pH, polysorbate and water for injection. Store at controlled room temperature between 15 and 30°C. Protect from freezing. Supplied in single dose kits containing 1 prefilled dual-chamber syringe with 23 gauge needle, 2 alcohol swabs, Patient Information Leaflet, Special Instructions for Use, and Package Insert.

22.5 mg (3-month slow release): Each prefilled dual-chamber syringe contains: leuprolide acetate for depot suspension 22.5 mg. Sterile lyophilized microspheres containing leuprolide acetate incorporated in a biodegradable copolymer of polylactic acid. Nonmedicinal ingredients: D-mannitol and polylactic acid. The rear chamber of diluent contains: carboxymethylcellulose sodium, D-mannitol, glacial acetic acid USP to control pH, polysorbate and water for injection. Store at controlled room temperature between 15 and 30°C. Protect from freezing. Supplied in single dose kits containing 1 prefilled dual-chamber syringe with 23 gauge needle, 2 alcohol swabs, Patient Information Leaflet, Special Instructions for Use, and Package Insert.

Reviewed 1999

LUPRON® DEPOT® 3.75 mg Ⓟ

Abbott

Leuprolide Acetate for Depot Suspension

Gonadotropin-releasing Hormone Analog

Pharmacology: Leuprolide is a synthetic nonapeptide analog of naturally occurring gonadotropin-releasing hormone (GnRH or LHRH). The analog possesses greater potency than the natural hormone. When administered as indicated, leuprolide acts as a potent inhibitor of gonadotropin production. It is chemically unrelated to steroids.

Unlike steroid hormones, leuprolide exerts specific action on the pituitary gonadotrophs and the human reproductive tract.

This specificity reduces the likelihood of secondary adverse effects such as gynecomastia, thromboembolism, edema, liver and gallbladder involvement.

Bioavailability by s.c. administration is comparable to i.v. administration. Leuprolide has a plasma half-life of 2.9 hours.

I.M. injection of leuprolide for depot suspension 3.75 mg (1-month SR) provides effective plasma concentrations of leuprolide acetate over a period of 1 month.

General: Animal and human studies indicate that, following an initial stimulation, chronic administration of leuprolide results in the inhibition of gonadotropin production. Consequently, ovarian or testicular steroidogenesis is suppressed. The therapeutic effect of leuprolide in the treatment of hormone-dependent tumors, such as in prostatic cancer, results from the reduction in serum gonadotropins and gonadal steroids.

Chronic administration of leuprolide has resulted in inhibition of tumor growth (prostatic tumors in Noble and Dunning male rats, 7-12-dimethylbenz[α]-anthracene(DMBA)-induced mammary tumors in female rats) as well as atrophy of the reproductive organs. An additional mechanism of action, a direct effect on the gonads by down-regulation of the gonadotropin receptors, is suggested in some animal studies.

In humans, s.c. administration of single daily doses of leuprolide results in an initial increase in circulating levels of luteinizing hormone (LH) and follicle-stimulating hormone (FSH), leading to a transient increase in the levels of the gonadal steroids (testosterone and dihydrotestosterone in males and estrone and estradiol in premenopausal females). However, continuous administration results in decreased levels of LH and FSH in all patients. In males, testosterone is reduced to castrate levels. In premenopausal females, estrogens are reduced to postmenopausal levels. These decreases occur within 2 to 4 weeks after initiation of treatment and are maintained as long as treatment continues.

Endometriosis: Endometriosis is a gynecologic disorder wherein endometrial tissue is found to be established in sites outside the endometrial cavity. As definitive diagnosis can only be made during surgery, the true incidence of the disease is unknown.

The etiology of the disease is unclear. An accepted theory of the etiology of endometriosis is the retrograde flow of menstrual fluid with subsequent implantation of viable fragments of endometrium within the pelvic cavity (Sampson's theory). However, this theory does not explain the extra-pelvic sites of endometriosis such as the limbs, thoracic cavity and elsewhere. It has also been suggested that chronic irritation of the peritoneum by menstrual blood may be causative. Another theory is that endometrial tissues are displaced into an implant in new sites during surgery. Genetic and immunologic factors may account for spontaneous endometriosis in a small segment of the population. It is also believed that endometriosis may be caused by lymphatic and hematogenous spread of normal endometrium to distant sites.

Endometriosis may be treated both surgically and medically. Since endometriosis resolves after oophorectomy and menopause, surgical castration may be used to treat the disease. A menopausal state may also be achieved medically. The resultant hypoestrogenic environment results in atrophic changes in both the uterine and ectopic endometrial tissue.

Leuprolide achieves a menopausal state by suppression of the pituitary-ovarian axis by inhibiting the output of gonadotropins (FSH and LH) from the pituitary gland.

In female volunteers receiving a single dose of leuprolide for depot suspension 3.75 mg (1-month SR) i.m., an initial burst of leuprolide in plasma was observed. Mean plasma leuprolide levels of approximately 0.23 to 0.34 ng/mL were maintained over a period of 4 to 5 weeks, and then slowly tapered off, becoming undetectable 8 weeks after injection.

Pharmacokinetics: Absorption: A single dose of leuprolide for depot suspension 3.75 mg (1-month SR) was administered by i.m. injection to healthy female volunteers. The absorption of leuprolide was characterized by an initial increase in plasma concentration, with peak concentration ranging from 4.6 to 10.2 ng/mL at 4 hours postdosing. However, intact leuprolide and an inactive metabolite could not be distinguished by the assay used in the study. Following the initial rise, leuprolide concentrations started to plateau within 2 days after dosing and remained relatively stable for about 4 to 5 weeks with plasma concentrations of about 0.3 ng/mL.

Distribution: The mean steady-state volume of distribution of leuprolide following i.v. bolus administration to healthy male volunteers was 27 L. In vitro binding to human plasma proteins ranged from 43 to 49%.

Metabolism: In healthy male volunteers, a 1 mg bolus of leuprolide administered i.v. revealed that the mean systemic clearance was 7.6 L/h, with a terminal elimination half-life of approximately 3 hours based on a 2-compartment model.

In rats and dogs, administration of ^{14}C-labelled leuprolide was shown to be metabolized to smaller inactive peptides, pentapeptide (Metabolite I), tripeptide (Metabolite II and III) and dipeptide (Metabolite IV). These fragments may be further catabolized.

The major metabolite (M-I) plasma concentrations measured in 5 prostate cancer patients reached mean maximum concentration 2 to 6 hours after dosing and were approximately 6% of the peak parent drug concentration. One week after dosing, mean plasma M-I concentrations were approximately 20% of leuprolide concentrations.

Excretion: Following administration of leuprolide for depot suspension 3.75 mg (1-month SR) to 3 patients, less than 5% of the dose was recovered as parent and M-I metabolite in the urine.

Special Populations: The pharmacokinetics of the drug in hepatic-and renal-impaired patients have not been determined.

Indications: In the treatment of endometriosis, for a period of 6 months.

Leuprolide for depot suspension can be used as sole therapy where it may provide symptomatic relief for women close to menopause who do not desire surgery, or as an adjunct to surgery.

Experience with leuprolide for depot suspension for the management of endometriosis has been limited to women 18 years of age and older.

Contraindications: General: In patients with hypersensitivity to the drug or its components, or similar nonapeptides.

Isolated cases of anaphylaxis have been reported.

Pregnancy: Leuprolide for depot suspension is contraindicated in women who are or may become pregnant while receiving the drug. When administered on day 6 of pregnancy at test dosages of 0.00024, 0.0024, and 0.024 mg/kg (1/300 to 1/3 the 3.75 mg leuprolide for depot suspension human dose) to rabbits, leuprolide produced a dose-related increase in major fetal abnormalities. Similar studies in rats failed to demonstrate an increase in fetal malformations. There was increased fetal mortality and decreased fetal weights with the 2 higher doses of leuprolide for depot suspension in rabbits and with the highest dose (0.024 mg/kg) in rats. The effects on fetal mortality are logical consequences of the alterations in hormonal levels brought about by this drug. Therefore, the possibility exists that spontaneous abortion may occur if the drug is administered during pregnancy.

Lupron Depot 3.75 mg (cont'd)

Patients treated with leuprolide for depot suspension should use nonhormonal methods of contraception.

Leuprolide for depot suspension is also contraindicated in patients with undiagnosed abnormal vaginal bleeding as well as in patients who are breast-feeding.

Warnings: General: Isolated cases of short-term worsening of signs and symptoms have been reported during initiation of leuprolide therapy: they are sometimes, but not necessarily, associated with a stimulation of the pituitary gland.

During the early phase of therapy, sex steroids temporarily rise above baseline because of the physiologic effect of the drug. Therefore, an increase in clinical signs and symptoms may be observed during the initial days of therapy, but these will dissipate with continued therapy at adequate doses.

Worsening of the clinical condition may occasionally require discontinuation of therapy and/or surgical intervention.

Pregnancy: Before initiating treatment with leuprolide for depot suspension, pregnancy must be ruled out (see Precautions).

Precautions: General: Patients on leuprolide therapy should be assessed on a regular basis by their attending physician.

Endometriosis: Changes in Bone Density: Since bone loss can be anticipated as part of natural menopause, it may also be expected to occur during a medically induced hypoestrogenic state caused by the long-term use of leuprolide for depot suspension. For a period of up to 6 months, this bone loss should not be important.

In patients with significant risk factors for decreased bone mineral content and/or bone mass such as chronic alcohol and/or tobacco use, presumed or strong family history of osteoporosis or chronic use of drugs that can reduce bone mass such as anticonvulsants or corticosteroids, leuprolide for depot suspension may pose an additional risk. In these patients, risk versus benefit must be weighed carefully before therapy with leuprolide for depot suspension is instituted.

Retreatment cannot be recommended since safety data for retreatment are not available. If the symptoms of endometriosis recur after a course of therapy, and further treatment with leuprolide for depot suspension 3.75 mg (1-month SR) is contemplated, it is recommended that bone density be assessed before retreatment begins to ensure that values are within normal limits.

A controlled study in endometriosis patients showed that vertebral bone density, as measured by dual energy x-ray absorptiometry (DEXA), decreased by an average of 4.1% at 6 months compared with the pretreatment value.

For those patients who were tested at 6 or 12 months after discontinuation of therapy, the mean bone density returned to 2.6% of pretreatment.

Earlier studies in endometriosis patients, utilizing quantitative computed tomography (QCT), demonstrated that in the few patients who were retested at 6 and 12 months, partial to complete recovery of bone density was recorded in the post-treatment period. Use of leuprolide for depot suspension for longer than 6 months or in the presence of other known risk factors for decreased bone mineral content may cause additional bone loss.

Changes in Laboratory Values During Treatment: Plasma Enzymes: During clinical trials with leuprolide for depot suspension, regular laboratory monitoring revealed that AST levels were more than twice the upper limit of normal in only one patient. There was no other clinical or laboratory evidence of abnormal liver function.

Lipids: At enrolment, 4% of leuprolide for depot suspension 3.75 mg (1-month SR) patients and 1% of the danazol patients had total cholesterol values above the normal range. These patients also had cholesterol values above the normal range at the end of treatment. Of those patients whose pretreatment cholesterol values were in the normal range, 7% of leuprolide for depot suspension patients and 9% of the danazol patients had post-treatment values above the normal range.

The mean (±SEM) pretreatment values for total cholesterol from all patients were 4.63 (0.08) mmol/L in the leuprolide for depot suspension 3.75 mg (1-month SR) group and 4.54 (0.08) mmol/L in the danazol group. At the end of treatment, the mean values for total cholesterol from all patients were 5.01 mmol/L in the leuprolide for depot suspension group and 5.03 mmol/L in the danazol group. These increases from the pretreatment values were statistically significant ($p < 0.03$) in both groups.

Triglycerides were increased above the upper limit of normal in 12% of the patients who received leuprolide for depot suspension 3.75 mg (1-month SR) and in 6% of the patients who received danazol.

At the end of treatment, HDL cholesterol fractions decreased below the lower limit of the normal range in 2% of leuprolide for depot suspension 3.75 mg (1-month SR) patients compared with 54% of those receiving danazol. LDL cholesterol fractions increased above the upper limit of the normal range in 6% of the patients receiving leuprolide for depot suspension 3.75 mg (1-month SR) compared with 23% of those receiving danazol. There was no increase in the LDL/HDL ratio in patients receiving leuprolide for depot suspension 3.75 mg (1-month SR), but there was approximately a 2-fold increase in the LDL/HDL ratio in patients receiving danazol. The clinical implication of these changes in this patient population for a restricted therapeutic period is unclear.

Isolated elevations of AST were observed in leuprolide- and danazol-treated patients.

Other Changes: In comparative studies, the following changes were seen in approximately 5 to 8% of patients. Leuprolide for depot suspension was associated with elevations of LDH and phosphorus, and decreases in WBC counts, and danazol therapy was associated with increases in hematocrit, platelet count and LDH.

The safety of retreatment as well as treatment beyond 6 months with leuprolide for depot suspension has not been established.

Pregnancy: Safe use of the drug in pregnancy has not been established; therefore a nonhormonal method of contraception should be used during treatment. Patients should be advised that if they miss or postpone a dose of leuprolide for depot suspension, ovulation may occur with the potential for conception. If a patient becomes pregnant during treatment, she should discontinue treatment and consult her physician.

Since menstruation should stop with effective doses of leuprolide for depot suspension, the patient should notify her physician if regular menstruation persists. Patients missing successive doses of leuprolide for depot suspension may experience breakthrough bleeding.

Before initiating treatment with leuprolide for depot suspension, pregnancy must be ruled out.

Lactation: It is not known whether leuprolide is excreted in human milk; therefore, leuprolide for depot suspension should not be administered to a nursing mother.

Dependence Liability: No drug-dependence has been reported with the use of leuprolide.

Drug Interactions: No pharmacokinetic based drug-drug interaction studies have been conducted.

Leuprolide being 46% bound to plasma proteins, and a peptide that is primarily degraded by peptidase and not by cytochrome P450 enzymes as noted in specific studies, drug interactions would not be expected to occur.

Drug/Laboratory Test Interactions: Administration of leuprolide for depot suspension in therapeutic doses results in suppression of the pituitary-gonadal system. Normal function is usually restored within 4 to 12 weeks after the treatment is discontinued. Diagnostic tests of pituitary-gonadal function conducted during the treatment and within 4 to 8 weeks after discontinuation of leuprolide for depot suspension therapy may therefore be misleading.

Adverse Effects: Estradiol levels may increase during the first weeks following the initial injection, but then decline to basal levels. This transient increase in estradiol can be associated with temporary worsening of signs and symptoms (see Warnings).

Endometriosis: In 2 controlled clinical trials treating endometriosis, one comparing leuprolide for depot suspension 3.75 mg (1-month SR) with danazol (800 mg/day) and the other with placebo, the following adverse reactions (see Table I) were reported to have a possible or probable relationship to study drugs as ascribed by the treating physician in 5% or more of the patients receiving the drug.

In these same studies, the following were reported in less than 5% of patients receiving leuprolide for depot suspension.

Cardiovascular: palpitations, syncope, tachycardia.

Gastrointestinal: dry mouth, thirst, appetite changes.

Table I—Lupron Depot 3.75 mg

Adverse Effects	Lupron Depot N=166 (%)	Danazol N=136(%)	Placebo N=31(%)
	Number of Reports (%)		
Cardiovascular			
edema	12 (7)	17 (13)	1 (3)
Gastrointestinal			
nausea/vomiting	21 (13)	17 (13)	1 (3)
gastrointestinal disturbances[a]	11 (7)	8 (6)	1 (3)
Endocrine			
hot flashes/sweats[a]	139 (84)	77 (57)	9 (29)
breast changes, tenderness/pain[a]	10 (6)	12 (9)	0 (0)
decreased libido[a]	19 (11)	6 (4)	0 (0)
androgen-like effects	22 (13)	44 (32)[b]	1 (3)
virilism	0 (0)	1 (1)	0 (0)
acne	17 (10)	27 (20)	0 (0)
seborrhea	2 (1)	5 (4)	0 (0)
hirsutism	2 (1)	9 (7)	1 (3)
voice alteration	1 (1)	2 (1)	0 (0)
Musculoskeletal			
myalgia[a]	1 (1)	7 (5)	0 (0)
joint disorder[a]	14 (8)	11 (8)	0 (0)
Central/Peripheral Nervous System			
depression/emotional lability[a]	36 (22)	27 (20)	1 (3)
headaches[a]	53 (32)	30 (22)	2 (6)
dizziness	19 (11)	4 (3)	0 (0)
insomnia/sleep disorders[a]	2 (1)	4 (3)	0 (0)
general pain	31 (19)	22 (16)	1 (3)
neuromuscular disorders[a]	11 (7)	17 (13)	0 (0)
nervousness[a]	8 (5)	11 (8)	0 (0)
paresthesias	12 (7)	11 (8)	0 (0)
Integumentary			
skin reactions	17 (10)	20 (15)	1 (3)
Urogenital			
vaginitis[a]	46 (28)	23 (17)	0 (0)
Miscellaneous			
asthenia	5 (3)	9 (7)	0 (0)
weight gain/loss	22 (13)	36 (26)	0 (0)

[a]Physiologic effect of decreased estrogen.
[b]Individual percentages equal 33% due to rounding.
Reactions considered not drug related are excluded.

Central/Peripheral Nervous System: anxiety*, personality disorder, memory disorder, delusions.
Integumentary: ecchymosis, alopecia, hair disorder.
Urogenital: dysuria*, lactation.
Miscellaneous: ophthalmologic disorders*, lymphadenopathy.
* Physiologic effect of decreased estrogen.
Postmarketing Surveillance: The following events have been reported during postmarketing surveillance: Cardiovascular: hypotension.
Gastrointestinal: hepatic dysfunction.
Hemic and Lymphatic: decreased WBC.
Central/Peripheral Nervous System: peripheral neuropathy, spinal fracture/paralysis.
Respiratory: dyspnea.
Integumentary: rash, urticaria, photosensitivity reactions.
Musculoskeletal: tenosynovitis-like symptoms.
Urogenital: menstrual disorders.
Miscellaneous: injection site reactions including pain, inflammation, sterile abscess, induration and hematoma.

Isolated cases of anaphylaxis have been reported. Symptoms consistent with an anaphylactoid or asthmatic process have been rarely reported.

Like other drugs in this class, mood swings, including depression, have been reported as a physiologic effect of decreased sex steroids. There have been very rare reports of suicidal ideation and attempt. Many, but not all, of these patients had a history of depression or other psychiatric illness. Patients should be counselled on the possibility of worsening of depression.

Overdose: Symptoms and Treatment: In rats, s.c. administration of 250 to 500 times the recommended human dose, expressed on a per body weight basis, results in dyspnea, decreased activity and local irritation at the injection site. There is no evidence at present that there is a clinical counterpart of this phenomenon.

In early clinical trials using daily s.c. leuprolide in patients with prostate cancer, doses as high as 20 mg/day for up to 2 years caused no adverse effects differing from those observed with the 1 mg/day dose.

Dosage: Endometriosis: The recommended dose is 3.75 mg administered **monthly** as a **single i.m. injection,** after reconstitution with the special diluent (see Special Instructions for Use and Patient Information). The treatment course is for 6 months.

Retreatment cannot be recommended since safety data for retreatment are not available. If the symptoms of endometriosis recur after a course of therapy, and further treatment with leuprolide for depot suspension 3.75 mg (1-month SR) is contemplated, it is recommended that bone density be assessed before retreatment begins to ensure that values are within normal limits.

As with other drugs administered by injection, the injection site should be varied periodically.
Special Instructions for Use: **Leuprolide for depot suspension must be administered under the supervision of a physician.**

The lyophilized microspheres are to be reconstituted and administered **monthly** as a single i.m. injection, in accord with the following directions:
Vial and Ampul: 1. Using a syringe with a 22 gauge needle, withdraw **1 mL of diluent** from the ampul, and inject it into the vial. (Extra diluent is provided; any remaining diluent should be discarded.) 2. Shake well to thoroughly disperse particles to obtain a uniform, homogeneous suspension (the suspension will appear milky). 3. Withdraw the entire contents of the vial into the syringe and inject it as directed (**once a month**) at the time of reconstitution. Any reconstituted suspension not used immediately should be discarded.
Prefilled Dual-chamber Syringe: 1. Screw the white plunger into the end stopper until the stopper begins to turn. 2. Remove and discard the tamper evident tab around the base of the needle. 3. Holding the syringe upright, release the diluent by **slowly pushing** the plunger until the first stopper is at the blue line in the middle of the barrel. 4. Gently shake the syringe to thoroughly mix the particles to form a uniform suspension. The suspension will appear milky. 5. If the microspheres (particles) adhere to the stopper, tap the syringe against your finger. 6. Then remove the needle guard and advance the plunger to expel the air from the syringe. 7. At the time of reconstitution, inject the entire contents of the syringe i.m. as you would for a normal injection.

As with other drugs administered by injection, the injection site should be varied periodically.

Although the suspension has been shown to be stable for 24 hours following reconstitution, since the product does not contain a preservative, the suspension should be discarded if not used immediately.

Information for the Patient: See Blue Section—Information for the Patient "Lupron Depot 3.75 mg".

Supplied: Kits (Vial and Ampul): Each single-dose vial contains: leuprolide acetate for depot suspension 3.75 mg (1-month slow release). Sterile lyophilized microspheres which is leuprolide acetate incorporated in a biodegradable copolymer of lactic and glycolic acids. Nonmedicinal ingredients: DL-lactic and glycolic acids copolymer, D-mannitol and purified gelatin. Each mL of the accompanying ampul of sterile diluent contains: carboxymethylcellulose sodium, D-mannitol, polysorbate 80, water for injection and glacial acetic acid, USP to control pH. During the manufacturing process, acetic acid is lost, leaving the peptide. Store vials and kits at controlled room temperature between 15 and 30°C. Protect from freezing. Supplied as kits. Each kit contains: 1 vial of Lupron Depot, 1 ampul (2 mL) of sterile diluent, 1 syringe with 22G needle, 1 additional 22G needle, 2 alcohol swabs, Special Instructions for Use, Patient Information Leaflet and Package Insert.

Prefilled Syringes: Each prefilled dual-chamber syringe contains: leuprolide acetate for depot suspension 3.75 mg (1-month slow release). Sterile lyophilized microspheres which is leuprolide acetate incorporated in a biodegradable copolymer of lactic and glycolic acids. Nonmedicinal ingredients: DL-lactic and glycolic acids copolymer, D-mannitol and purified gelatin. The rear chamber of diluent contains: carboxymethylcellulose sodium, D-mannitol, glacial acetic acid, USP to control pH, polysorbate 80 and water for injection USP. During the manufacturing process, acetic acid is lost, leaving the peptide. Store at controlled room temperature between 15 and 30°C. Protect from freezing. Supplied as single-dose kits. Each kit contains: 1 prefilled dual-chamber syringe with 23G needle, 2 alcohol swabs, Special Instructions for Use, Patient Information Leaflet and Package Insert.

Reviewed 1999

LUTREPULSE™ ℞

Ferring

Gonadorelin Acetate

Ovulatory Agent

Pharmacology: Gonadorelin is a synthetic decapeptide that has the same amino acid sequence as endogenous gonadotropin-releasing hormone (GnRH) synthesized in the human hypothalamus and in various neurons terminating in the hypothalamus. Its pharmacological and toxicological profile is therefore identical to that of endogenous GnRH.

Under physiologic conditions, GnRH is released by the hypothalamus in a pulsatile fashion. The primary effect of GnRH is the synthesis and release of luteinizing hormone (LH) in the anterior pituitary gland. GnRH also stimulates the synthesis and release of follicle stimulating hormone (FSH), but this effect is less pronounced. LH and FSH subsequently stimulate the gonads to produce steroids which are instrumental in regulating reproductive hormonal status. Unlike human menopausal gonadotropin (hMG) which supplies pituitary hormones, pulsatile administration of gonadorelin replaces defective hypothalamic secretion of GnRH. Gonadorelin for pulsatile injection approximates the natural hormonal secretory pattern, causing pulsatile release of pituitary gonadotropins. Accordingly, gonadorelin for pulsatile injection is useful in treating conditions of infertility caused by defective GnRH stimulation from the hypothalamus.

The following information summarizes clinical efficacy of gonadorelin administered by pulsatile i.v. or s.c. injection to patients with primary hypothalamic amenorrhea.

In 48 patients with primary hypothalamic amenorrhea (HA) 94% (45/48) patients ovulated and 58% (25/43) patients became pregnant (5 patients did not desire pregnancy).

Treatment was successful even in those patients who failed past attempts at ovulation induction by other methods.

Following i.v. or s.c. injection of GnRH into normal subjects and/or hypogonadotropic patients, plasma GnRH concentrations rapidly declined with initial and terminal half-lives of 2 to 10 min and 10 to 40 min, respectively. In these studies, high clearance values (500 to 1 500 L/day) and low volumes of distribution (9 to 15 L) were calculated. The pharmacokinetics of GnRH in normal subjects and in hypogonadotropic patients were similar. GnRH was rapidly metabolized to various biologically inactive peptide fragments which are readily excreted in urine. Renal failure, but not hepatic disease, prolonged the half-life and reduced the clearance of GnRH.

A comparison of gonadorelin to hCG or hCG + gonadorelin for corpus luteum maintenance revealed the information in Table I.

Table I—Lutrepulse

Comparison of Lutrepulse to hCG or hCG+Lutrepulse for Corpus Luteum Maintenance

	hCG	Lutrepulse	hCG+Lutrepulse
Delivered	43/63 (68%)	19/26 (73%)	19/25 (76%)
Aborted	20/63 (32%)	7/26 (27%)	6/25 (24%)

Gonadorelin alone is therefore able to maintain the corpus luteum during pregnancy.

Indications: For the induction of ovulation in women with primary hypothalamic amenorrhea.
Differential Diagnosis: Proper diagnosis is critical for successful treatment with gonadorelin. It must be established that hypothalamic amenorrhea or hypogonadism is, in fact, due to a deficiency in quantity or pulsing of endogenous GnRH. The diagnosis of hypothalamic amenorrhea or hypogonadism is based on the exclusion of other causes of the dysfunction, since there is currently no practical technique to directly assess hypothalamic function. Prior to initiation of therapy with gonadorelin the physician should rule out disorders (other than abnormalities of GnRH secretion), that can cause amenorrhea and involve most often general health, reproductive organs, CNS, anterior pituitary, thyroid, adrenals or other endocrine or metabolic disorders.

Contraindications: Women with any condition that could be exacerbated by pregnancy. For example, pituitary prolactinoma should be considered one such condition. Additionally, any history of sensitivity to gonadorelin or any component of this product is a contraindication.

Patients who have ovarian cysts should not receive gonadorelin.

Gonadorelin is intended to initiate events including the production of reproductive hormones (e.g., estrogens and progesterone). Therefore, any condition that may be worsened by reproductive hormones, such as a hormonally-dependent tumor, is a contraindication to the use of gonadorelin.

Warnings: Therapy with gonadorelin should be conducted by physicians familiar with pulsatile GnRH delivery and the clinical ramifications of ovulation induction. While there have been few cases of hyperstimulation (<1%), this possibility must be considered. If hyperstimulation should occur, therapy should be discontinued and spontaneous resolution can be expected. The preservation of the endogenous feedback mechanisms makes severe hyperstimulation (with ascites and pleural effusion) rare. However, the physician should be aware of the possibility and be alert for any evidence of ascites, pleural effusion, hemoconcentration, rupture of a cyst, fluid or electrolyte imbalance, or sepsis.

Multiple pregnancy is a possibility that can be minimized by careful attention to the recommended doses and ultrasonographic monitoring of the ovarian response to therapy. Following a baseline pelvic ultrasound, follow-up studies should be conducted at a minimum on day 7 and day 14 of therapy.

As with any parenteral medication, scrupulous attention to asepsis is important. The infusion area must be monitored as with all indwelling parenteral approaches.

Precautions: General: Ovarian hyperstimulation has been reported. This may be related to pulse dosage or concomitant use of other ovulation stimulators. Hyperstimulation may be a greater risk in patients where spontaneous variations in endogenous GnRH secretion occur. Multiple follicle development, multiple pregnancy and spontaneous termination of pregnancy have been reported. Multiple pregnancy can be minimized by appropriate monitoring of follicle formation; nonetheless, the patient and her partner should be advised of the frequency (12%) and potential risks of multiple pregnancy before starting treatment.

Ovarian hyperstimulation, a syndrome of sudden ovarian enlargement, ascites with or without pain, and/or pleural effusion, is rare with pulsatile GnRH therapy. Among 268 patients participating in clinical trials, one case of moderate hyperstimulation has been reported, but this cycle included concomitant use of clomiphene citrate. In contrast, menotropins (hMG) with hCG, have been variously reported to cause some degree of hyperstimulation in up to 50% of conception cycles, and severe hyperstimulation may occur in up to 1.3% of all cycles.

Several cases of allergic reactions to synthetic LHRH have been reported in the published scientific literature. Most of

Lutrepulse (cont'd)

the reports described urticaria following administration of synthetic LHRH although one case described a serious anaphylactic reaction. In cases where it has been investigated, the allergic reactions were associated with anti-LHRH antibodies in the patient's serum. The s.c. route of administration of synthetic LHRH would bear a greater risk of antibody induction compared to i.v. administration. In one study, the incidence of circulating antibodies in patients treated with pulsatile s.c. LHRH was found to be 3%. Some patients who develop antibodies to LHRH may become refractory to treatment.

Gonadorelin should be administered with a suitable pulsatile pump and suitable infusion catheters. The patient should be provided with detailed oral and written instructions regarding infusion pump usage and potential sepsis in order to minimize the frequency of infusion pump malfunction and inflammation, infection, mild phlebitis or hematoma at the catheter site.

Laboratory Tests: Following a diagnosis of primary hypothalamic amenorrhea, initiation of gonadorelin therapy may be monitored by the following: 1. Ovarian ultrasound—baseline, and at least weekly while the patient is on therapy or until ovulation has been documented. 2. Estradiol serum level to assess ovarian response. 3. Mid-luteal phase serum progesterone to confirm ovulation. 4. Recording of basal body temperature. 5. Clinical observation of infusion site at each visit and as needed. 6. Physical examination including pelvic at regularly scheduled visits.

Drug Interactions: None are known. Gonadorelin should not be used concomitantly with other ovulation stimulators.

Drug/Laboratory Test Interactions: None are known.

Carcinogenesis, Mutagenesis, Impairment of Fertility: Since GnRH is a natural substance normally present in humans, long-term studies in animals have not been performed to evaluate carcinogenic potential. Mutagenicity testing was not done.

Pregnancy: Reproductive studies (teratology and embryotoxicity) performed in rats and rabbits have not revealed any evidence of harm to the fetus due to gonadorelin acetate. There was no evidence of teratogenicity when gonadorelin was administered i.v. up to 120 μg/kg/day (>70 times the recommended human dose of 5 μg per pulse) in rats and rabbits.

Studies in pregnant women have shown that gonadorelin does not increase the risk of abnormalities when administered during the first trimester of pregnancy. It appears that the possibility of fetal harm is remote, if the drug is used during pregnancy. In clinical studies, 47 pregnant patients have used gonadorelin during the first trimester of pregnancy (51 pregnancies) and the drug had no apparent adverse effect on the course of pregnancy. Available follow-up reports on infants born to these women revealed no adverse effects or complications that were attributable to gonadorelin. Nevertheless, because the studies in humans cannot rule out the possibility of harm, gonadorelin should be used during pregnancy only for maintenance of the corpus luteum in ovulation induction cycles.

Lactation: It is not known whether this drug is excreted in human milk. There is no indication for use of gonadorelin in a nursing woman.

Children: Not applicable.

Adverse Effects: The majority of adverse effects are associated with the parenteral route of administration of the drug and are generally confined to superficial thrombophlebitis and injection site irritation.

Adverse reactions have been reported in approximately 10% of treatment regimens in pivotal clinical trials. Ten of 268 patients interrupted therapy because of an adverse reaction but subsequently resumed treatment. One other subject did not resume treatment.

In clinical studies involving 268 women, one case of moderate ovarian hyperstimulation has been reported. This cycle included concomitant use of clomiphene. This low incidence of hyperstimulation appears to be due to the preservation of normal feedback mechanisms of the pituitary-ovarian axis. Despite the preservation of feedback mechanisms, some incidents of multiple follicle development, multiple pregnancy and spontaneous termination of pregnancy have been reported. In clinical studies involving 142 pregnancies, delivery information was available on 89 pregnancies. Eleven of these gonadorelin-induced pregnancies (12%) were multiple (10 sets of twins, 1 set of triplets).

The following adverse reactions are related to use of an infusion pump: inflammation, infection, mild phlebitis, or hematoma at the catheter site. Additionally, infusion set malfunction and interruption of infusion may occur; this has no known adverse effect other than interruption of therapy.

Anaphylaxis (bronchospasm, tachycardia, flushing, urticaria, induration at injection site) has been reported with the related polypeptide hormone gonadorelin hydrochloride (Factrel). Antibody formation has occurred in approximately 3% of patients treated with Factrel via the s.c. route. In some cases, these appear to be related to a decreased effectiveness of the drug.

Ovarian Cancer: Ovarian cancer has been reported in a very small number of infertile women who have been treated with fertility drugs. A causal relationship between treatment with fertility drugs and ovarian cancer has not been established.

Overdose: Symptoms and Treatment: Continuous, non-pulsatile exposure to gonadorelin could temporarily reduce pituitary responsiveness. If the pump should malfunction and deliver the entire contents of the 3.2 mg system, no harmful effects would be expected. Bolus doses as high as 3 000 μg of gonadorelin hydrochloride have not been harmful. Pituitary hyperstimulation and multiple follicle development can be minimized by adhering to recommended doses, and appropriate monitoring of follicle formation (see Precautions).

The LD_{50} values (mg/kg) in the mouse are >400, >3 000, and >4 000 when GnRH is administered i.v., s.c. and orally, respectively. The LD_{50} values (mg/kg) in the rat are >200, >2 000, and >3 000 when GnRH is administered i.v., s.c. and orally, respectively.

Administration of 640 μg/kg in monkeys as a single i.v. bolus resulted in no compound-related effects in clinical observations or gross morphologic evaluations.

Dosage: Dosages between 1 and 20 μg have been successfully used in clinical studies. The recommended dose in primary hypothalamic amenorrhea is 5 μg every 90 minutes, administered either s.c. or i.v. This is delivered using the 0.8 mg solution at 50 μL per pulse. Sixty-eight percent of the 5 μg every 90 minutes regimens induced ovulation in patients with primary hypothalamic amenorrhea, when administered i.v.

Some women may require a reduction in the recommended dose of 5 μg should laboratory testing and patient monitoring indicate an inappropriate response. While most primary hypothalamic amenorrhea patients will ovulate during the first cycle of 5 μg therapy, some may be refractory to this dose. The recommended treatment interval before dose adjustment is 21 days. It may be necessary to raise the dose cautiously, and in stepwise fashion if there is no response after 3 treatment intervals. All dose changes should be carefully monitored for inappropriate response.

Table II can be used to calculate the dose per pulse when individualizing treatment.

Table II—Lutrepulse

Calculation of the Dose per Pulse

Vial Size	Volume of Diluent	Volume/pulse	Dose/pulse
0.8 mg	8 mL	25 μL	2.5 μg
0.8 mg	8 mL	50 μL	5 μg
3.2 mg	8 mL	25 μL	10 μg
3.2 mg	8 mL	50 μL	20 μg

The response to gonadorelin usually occurs within 2 to 3 weeks after therapy initiation. When ovulation occurs, therapy should be continued for another 2 weeks to maintain the corpus luteum. Lutrepulse dose and dosing frequency should remain the same.

Administration: Gonadorelin is to be reconstituted aseptically with 8 mL of the diluent provided (isotonic sterile sodium chloride for injection). The drug product should be reconstituted immediately prior to use and transferred to a plastic reservoir. First withdraw 8 mL of the saline diluent and then inject it onto the lyophile (drug product) cake. The product is shaken for a few seconds to produce a solution which should be clear, colorless, and free of particulate matter. Parenteral drug products should be inspected visually for particulate matter and discoloration prior to administration, whenever solution and container permit. If particulate matter or discoloration are present, the solution should not be used.

The reconstituted solution is administered either i.v. or s.c. using a suitable pulsatile pump. The pump could be set to deliver either 25 or 50 μL of solution, based upon the dose selected, over a pulse period of 1 minute, and at a pulse frequency of 90 minutes. If 50 μL per pulse is used with a pulse frequency of 90 minutes, the 8 mL of solution should last 7 days. If 25 μL per pulse is used with a pulse frequency of 90 minutes, the 8 mL of solution should last 14 days.

Supplied: Each 10 mL vial of lyophilized, sterile powder contains: gonadorelin acetate 0.8 or 3.2 mg (gonadorelin base 0.73 mg and 2.91 mg respectively) and mannitol 10 mg as a carrier. Packages of 1 vial and a 10 mL vial of sterile, isotonic sodium chloride diluent. The product is stable when stored at room temperature (15 to 30°C) in the unopened package. The reconstituted solution is stable for up to 45 days at 24 to 37°C when stored in vials and reservoir bags, and remains stable and uncontaminated for up to 16 hours in catheter tubing.

LUVOX® Ⓟ

Solvay Pharma

Fluvoxamine Maleate

Antidepressant—Antiobsessional Agent

Pharmacology: The antidepressant and antiobsessional actions of fluvoxamine are believed to be related to its selective inhibition of presynaptic serotonin re-uptake in brain neurones.

There is minimum interference with noradrenergic processes, and, in common with several other specific inhibitors of serotonin uptake, fluvoxamine has very little in vitro affinity for α_1, α_2, β_1, $dopamine_2$, $histamine_1$, $serotonin_1$, $serotonin_2$ or muscarinic receptors.

Pharmacokinetics: In healthy volunteers, fluvoxamine is well absorbed after oral administration. Following a single 100 mg oral dose, peak plasma levels of 31 to 87 ng/mL were attained 1.5 to 8 hours-postdose. Peak plasma levels and AUCs (0 to 72 hours) are directly proportionate to dose after single oral doses of 25, 50 and 100 mg.

Following single doses, the mean plasma half-life is 15 hours, and slightly longer (17 to 22 hours), during repeated dosing. Steady-state plasma levels are usually achieved within 10 to 14 days. The pharmacokinetic profile in the elderly is similar to that in younger patients.

In a dose proportionality study involving fluvoxamine at 100, 200 and 300 mg/day for 10 consecutive days in 30 normal volunteers, steady-state was achieved after about a week of dosing. Maximum plasma concentrations at steady-state occurred within 3 to 8 hours of dosing and reached concentrations averaging 88, 283 and 546 ng/mL, respectively. Thus, fluvoxamine had nonlinear pharmacokinetics over this dose range, i.e., higher doses of fluvoxamine produced disproportionately higher concentrations than predicted from the lower dose.

Metabolism and Elimination: Fluvoxamine undergoes extensive hepatic transformation, mainly via oxidative demethylation, to at least 9 metabolites, which are excreted by the kidney. Ninety-four percent of an oral radioactive dose is recovered in the urine within 48 hours. The 2 major metabolites showed negligible pharmacological activity. In vitro binding of fluvoxamine to human plasma proteins is about 77% at drug concentrations up to 4 000 ng/mL.

Indications: Depression: For the symptomatic relief of depressive illness.

The effectiveness of fluvoxamine in long-term use (i.e., for more than 5 to 6 weeks) has not been systematically evaluated in controlled trials. Therefore, the physician who elects to use fluvoxamine for extended periods should periodically re-evaluate the long-term usefulness of the drug for the individual patient.

Obsessive-Compulsive Disorder: Fluvoxamine has been shown to significantly reduce the symptoms of obsessive-compulsive disorder. The obsessions or compulsions must be experienced as intrusive, markedly distressing, time consuming, or interfering significantly with the person's social or occupational functioning.

The efficacy of fluvoxamine has been studied in double-blind, placebo-controlled clinical trials conducted in obsessive-compulsive outpatients. The usefulness of fluvoxamine for long-term use (i.e., for more than 10 weeks) has not been systematically evaluated in controlled trials. Therefore, the physician who elects to use fluvoxamine for extended periods should periodically re-evaluate the long-term usefulness of the drug for the individual patient.

Contraindications: In patients with known hypersensitivity to the drug.

Fluvoxamine should not be administered together with MAO inhibitors. At least 2 weeks should elapse after discontinuation of MAO inhibitor therapy before fluvoxamine treatment is initiated. MAO inhibitors should not be introduced within 2 weeks of cessation of therapy with fluvoxamine.

Precautions: Seizures: Convulsions have been reported rarely during fluvoxamine administration. Caution is recommended when the drug is administered to patients with a history of seizures. If seizures occur during fluvoxamine administration, the drug should be discontinued.

ECT: Concurrent administration with electroshock therapy should be avoided because of the absence of experience in this area.

Hepatic Enzymes: Treatment with fluvoxamine has been rarely associated with increases in hepatic enzymes, usually accompanied by symptoms. Fluvoxamine administration should be discontinued in such cases.

Combination with Alcohol: Fluvoxamine may potentiate the effects of alcohol and increase the level of psychomotor impairment.

Occupational Hazards: Cognitive and Motor Disturbances: Sedation may occur in some patients. Therefore, patients should be cautioned about participating in activities requiring complete mental alertness, judgment and physical coordination—such as driving an automobile or performing hazardous tasks—until they are reasonably certain that treatment with fluvoxamine does not affect them adversely.

Suicide: The possibility of a suicide attempt is inherent in depression and may persist until significant remission occurs. Therefore, high-risk patients should be closely supervised throughout therapy and consideration should be given to the possible need for hospitalization. In order to minimize the opportunity for overdosage, prescriptions for fluvoxamine should be written for the smallest quantity of drug consistent with good patient management.

Concomitant Illness: Fluvoxamine has not been evaluated or used to any appreciable extent in patients with a recent history of myocardial infarction or unstable heart disease. Patients with these diagnoses were systematically excluded from premarketing clinical studies.

Pregnancy and *Lactation:* Safe use of fluvoxamine during pregnancy and lactation has not been established. Like other antidepressants, fluvoxamine is excreted via human milk in small quantities. Therefore, it should not be administered to women of childbearing potential or nursing mothers unless, in the opinion of the treating physician, the expected benefits to the patient outweigh the possible hazards to the child or fetus.

Children: Safety and efficacy in children under 18 years of age have not been established.

Drug Interactions: Combined use of fluvoxamine and MAO inhibitors is contraindicated (see Contraindications).

An increase in tricyclic antidepressant blood levels has also been reported in patients taking fluvoxamine concomitantly.

Lithium, and possibly tryptophan, may enhance the serotonergic effects of fluvoxamine; these combinations should therefore be used with caution. The serotonergic effects may also be enhanced when fluvoxamine and other agents, including sumatriptan and SSRI's, are used in combination. This may, on rare occasions, result in a serotonergic syndrome.

Fluvoxamine may prolong the elimination of drugs which are metabolized by oxidation in the liver, and a clinically significant interaction is more likely when the second agent has a narrow therapeutic index, as is the case with warfarin, phenytoin, theophylline, clozapine and carbamazepine. Such combinations should therefore be administered with caution, and consideration be given to lowering the dose of the second agent. In interaction studies, a 5-fold increase in plasma levels of propranolol and a 65% increase in warfarin plasma levels were seen during concurrent administration of fluvoxamine. An absence of pharmacokinetic interaction has been seen with digoxin and atenolol, which are not significantly metabolized in the liver.

Cytochrome P450 Isozyme (IID6): Like other selective serotonin reuptake Inhibitors, fluvoxamine inhibits the specific hepatic cytochrome P450 isozyme (IID6) which is responsible for the metabolism of debrisoquine and sparteine. Although the clinical significance of this effect has not been established, inhibition of IID6 may lead to elevated plasma levels of coadministered drugs which are metabolized by this isozyme. Drugs metabolized by cytochrome P450IID6 include the tricyclic antidepressants (e.g., nortriptyline, amitriptyline, imipramine, and desipramine), phenothiazine neuroleptics (e.g., perphenazine and thioridazine), and Type 1C antiarrhythmics (e.g., propafenone and flecainide).

Adverse Effects: Commonly Observed: In clinical trials, the most commonly observed adverse events associated with fluvoxamine administration, and not seen at an equivalent incidence among placebo-treated patients, were gastrointestinal complaints, including nausea (sometimes accompanied by vomiting), constipation, anorexia, diarrhea and dyspepsia; CNS complaints, including somnolence, dry mouth, nervousness, insomnia, dizziness, tremor and agitation; and asthenia. Abnormal (mostly delayed) ejaculation was frequently reported by patients with obsessive-compulsive disorder, primarily at doses over 150 mg/day.

Adverse Events Leading to Discontinuation of Treatment: Approximately 14% (14.4%) of 34 587 patients who received fluvoxamine in clinical trials discontinued treatment due to an adverse event. The more common events causing discontinuation from depression trials included nausea and vomiting, insomnia, agitation, headache, abdominal pain, somnolence, dizziness, asthenia and anorexia. The most common events causing discontinuation in patients suffering from obsessive-compulsive disorder included insomnia, asthenia and somnolence.

Incidence of Adverse Experiences: Adverse events with an incidence of ≥ 5% reported in double-blind, placebo-controlled clinical trials in depression and in obsessive-compulsive disorder are presented in Table I for each indication.

During premarketing and postmarketing studies, multiple doses of fluvoxamine were administered to approximately 34 587 patients. All events with an incidence of > 0.01% are listed, regardless of relation to drug, except those in terms so general as to be uninformative. Events are further classified within body system categories and enumerated in order of decreasing frequency using the following definitions: frequent (occurring on 1 or more occasions in at least 1% of patients), infrequent (occurring in less than 1%, but at least 0.1% of patients), or rare (occurring in less than 0.1% but at least in 0.01% of patients). Multiple events may have been reported by a single patient. It is important to emphasize that although the events reported did occur during treatment with fluvoxamine, they were not necessarily caused by it.

Nervous: Frequent: agitation, anxiety, dizziness, insomnia, nervousness, somnolence, thinking abnormal, tremor, vertigo.

Infrequent: abnormal dreams, abnormal gait, akathisia, amnesia, apathy, ataxia, confusion, depersonalization, depression, drug dependence, emotional lability, euphoria, hallucinations, hostility, hyperkinesia, hypertonia, hypoesthesia, hypokinesia, incoordination, increased salivation, libido decreased, libido increased, manic reaction, neurosis, paresthesia, psychotic depression, stupor, twitching, vasodilatation.

Rare: akinesia, CNS neoplasia, CNS stimulation, coma, convulsion, delirium, delusions, dysarthria, dyskinesia, dystonia, extrapyramidal syndrome, hemiplegia, hyperesthesia, hypotonia, hysteria, myoclonus, neuralgia, neuropathy, paralysis, paranoid reaction, psychosis, reflexes decreased, schizophrenic reaction, screaming syndrome, torticollis, trismus.

Digestive: Frequent: anorexia, constipation, diarrhea, dry mouth, dyspepsia, nausea, vomiting.

Infrequent: colitis, dysphagia, eructation, flatulence, gastritis, gastroenteritis, increased appetite, thirst.

Rare: biliary pain, esophagitis, fecal incontinence, gastrointestinal carcinoma, gastrointestinal hemorrhage, gingivitis, glossitis, hematemesis, hepatitis, jaundice, liver function tests abnormal, melena, mouth ulceration, rectal hemorrhage, stomatitis, tenesmus, tongue discoloration, tongue edema, tooth disorder.

Cardiovascular: Frequent: palpitation.

Infrequent: angina pectoris, hypertension, hypotension, migraine, postural hypotension, syncope, tachycardia.

Rare: arrhythmia, bradycardia, cerebrovascular accident, extrasystoles, hemorrhage, myocardial infarct, pallor, peripheral vascular disorder, shock.

Body as a Whole: Frequent: abdominal pain, asthenia, headache, malaise.

Table I—Luvox

Treatment—Emergent Adverse Experience Incidence (≥ 5%) in Placebo-Controlled Clinical Trials for Depression and Obsessive-Compulsive Disorder[a]

	Percentage of Patients Reporting Event			
	Depression		OCD	
Body System/Adverse Event	**Fluvoxamine (N=222)**	**Placebo (N=192)**	**Fluvoxamine (N=160)**	**Placebo (N=160)**
Nervous				
Somnolence	26.2	9.0	26.9	9.4
Agitation	15.7	8.9	3.8	0
Insomnia	14.4	10.4	31.3	15.0
Dizziness	14.8	13.5	9.4	4.4
Tremor	10.8	4.7	8.1	0.6
Hypokinesia	8.1	3.6	—	—
Hyperkinesia	6.7	8.9	—	—
Depression	4.0	4.2	6.3	4.4
Nervousness	2.2	1.6	15.6	5.0
Anxiety	2.3	2.1	9.4	6.9
Libido decreased	—	—	7.5	1.9
Thinking abnormal	—	—	6.9	3.8
Digestive				
Nausea	36.5	10.9	28.8	6.9
Dry mouth	25.7	23.9	11.9	3.1
Constipation	18.0	6.8	14.4	8.8
Anorexia	14.9	6.3	5.0	3.1
Diarrhea	5.9	6.3	11.9	8.8
Dyspepsia	3.2	0	13.8	9.4
Body as a Whole				
Headache	21.6	18.7	20.0	23.8
Pain	5.9	3.7	4.4	1.3
Asthenia	4.9	3.2	28.8	9.4
Infection	—	—	11.3	9.4
Abdominal pain	3.6	3.6	5.6	8.1
Flu syndrome	—	—	5.0	3.8
Skin				
Sweating increased	11.2	12.5	6.9	1.9
Respiratory				
Pharyngitis	—	—	6.3	5.0
Rhinitis	1.3	2.6	5.6	1.9
Special Senses				
Accommodation abnormal	6.3	6.3	—	—
Taste perversion	3.2	3.1	5.0	0
Urogenital				
Urinary frequency	2.2	1.6	5.0	1.3
Abnormal ejaculation	1.4	0	17.9[b]	0

[a] Dosage titration at study initiation varied between the depression and OCD trials. In depression, fluvoxamine was administered: Day 1, 50 mg hs; Day 2, 100 mg; Day 3, 150 mg then titrated to response. In OCD, fluvoxamine was administered: Days 1 to 4, 50 mg; Days 5 to 8, 100 mg, Days 9 to 14, 150 mg then titrated to response.

[b] Corrected for gender (males: n=78).

Luvox (cont'd)

Infrequent: accidental injury, allergic reaction, back pain, chest pain, chills, fever, flu syndrome, infection, neck pain, pain, suicide attempt.
Rare: abdomen enlarged, chills and fever, face edema, halitosis, hangover effect, hernia, neck rigidity, overdose, pelvic pain.
Skin: Frequent: sweating increased.
Infrequent: pruritus, rash.
Rare: acne, alopecia, dry skin, eczema, furunculosis, herpes simplex, herpes zoster, maculopapular rash, psoriasis, urticaria.
Respiratory: Infrequent: dyspnea, pharyngitis, rhinitis.
Rare: asthma, bronchitis, cough increased, epistaxis, hiccup, hyperventilation, laryngismus, laryngitis, pneumonia, sinusitis, voice alternation, yawn.
Special Senses: Infrequent: abnormal vision, amblyopia, hyperacusis, taste perversion, tinnitus.
Rare: abnormality of accommodation, blepharitis, conjunctivitis, deafness, diplopia, dry eyes, ear pain, eye pain, lacrimation disorder, mydriasis, parosmia, photophobia, taste loss.
Musculoskeletal: Infrequent: arthralgia, arthrosis, myalgia, myasthenia, tetany.
Rare: arthritis, bone pain, leg cramps, pathological fracture, rheumatoid arthritis.
Urogenital: Infrequent: abnormal ejaculation, dysuria, impotence, metrorrhagia, urinary frequency, urinary incontinence.
Rare: amenorrhea, anorgasmia, breast pain, cystitis, dysmenorrhea, female lactation, hematuria, kidney pain, leukorrhea, menorrhagia, nocturia, polyuria, prostatic disorder, urinary retention, urinary tract infection, urinary urgency, vaginitis.
Metabolic and Nutritional: Frequent: weight gain.
Infrequent: peripheral edema, weight loss.
Rare: alcohol intolerance, dehydration, edema, obesity.
Hematic and Lymph Systems: Rare: anemia, cyanosis, ecchymosis, lymphadenopathy, thrombocytopenia.
Hyponatremia: Hyponatremia has been reported in association with other antidepressants, though rarely with fluvoxamine.

Adverse effects following discontinuation of treatment: Symptoms, including headache, nausea, dizziness and anxiety, have been reported after discontinuation of other antidepressants, though rarely after abrupt discontinuation of fluvoxamine.

Anecdotal spontaneous reports, from the marketplace, but not from clinical trials, have been collected for the following adverse experiences: angioedema, galactorrhea, and photosensitivity.

Overdose: Symptoms: More than 300 cases of overdosage with fluvoxamine, alone or in combination with other compounds, have been reported. The most common symptoms of overdosage include gastrointestinal complaints (nausea, vomiting and diarrhea), somnolence and dizziness. Cardiac events (tachycardia, bradycardia, hypotension), liver function disturbances, convulsions and coma have also been reported. Among more than 300 patients reported to have taken deliberate overdoses of fluvoxamine, there have been 30 deaths, all but 1 of which occurred in patients who were confirmed to have taken multiple medications. The highest documented dose of fluvoxamine ingested by a patient is 12 g; this patient recovered completely with symptomatic treatment only.

Treatment: There is no specific antidote to fluvoxamine. In situations of overdosage, the stomach should be emptied as soon as possible after tablet ingestion and symptomatic treatment initiated. The repeated use of medicinal charcoal is also recommended. Due to the large distribution volume of fluvoxamine, forced diuresis or dialysis is unlikely to be of benefit.

Dosage: Depression: Adults: Treatment should be initiated at the lowest possible dose (50 mg) given once daily at bedtime, and then increased to 100 mg daily at bedtime after a few days, as tolerated. The effective daily dose usually lies between 100 and 200 mg, and should be adjusted gradually according to the individual response of the patient, up to a maximum of 300 mg. Dosage increases should be made in 50 mg increments. Doses above 150 mg should be divided so that a maximum of 150 mg is given in the bedtime dose. Tablets should be swallowed with water and without chewing.
Obsessive-Compulsive Disorder: Treatment should be initiated at the lowest possible dose (50 mg) given once daily at bedtime, and then increased to 100 mg daily at bedtime after a few days, as tolerated. The effective daily dose usually lies between 100 and 300 mg, and should be adjusted gradually according to the individual response of the patient, up to a maximum of 300 mg. If no improvement is observed within 10 weeks, treatment with fluvoxamine should be reconsidered. Dosage increases should be made in 50 mg increments. Doses above 150 mg should be divided so that a maximum of 150 mg is given in the bedtime dose. Fluvoxamine should be swallowed with water and without chewing.
Hepatic or Renal Insufficiency: Patients with hepatic or renal insufficiency should begin treatment with a low dose and be carefully monitored.
Children: The safety and effectiveness of fluvoxamine in children under 18 years of age have not been established.
Geriatrics: Since there is limited clinical experience in the geriatric age group, caution is recommended when administering fluvoxamine to elderly patients.

Information for the Patient: See Blue Section—Information for the Patient "Luvox"

Supplied: 50 mg: Each film-coated, biconvex, round, scored, white tablet, stamped "291" twice on one side and a stylized "S" on the other, contains: fluvoxamine maleate 50 mg. Nonmedicinal ingredients: colloidal anhydrous silica, hydroxypropyl methylcellulose, maize starch, mannitol, polyethylene glycol, pregelatinized starch, sodium stearyl fumarate, talc and titanium dioxide. Gluten-, lactose-, sodium metabisulfite- and tartrazine-free. Bottles of 100.

100 mg: Each film-coated, biconvex, oval, scored, white tablet, stamped "313" twice on one side and a stylized "S" on the other contains: fluvoxamine maleate 100 mg. Nonmedicinal ingredients: colloidal anhydrous silica, hydroxypropyl methylcellulose, maize starch, mannitol, polyethylene glycol, pregelatinized starch, sodium stearyl fumarate, talc and titanium dioxide. Gluten-, lactose-, sodium metabisulfite- and tartrazine-free. Bottles of 100.

Preserve in well-closed containers. Store in a dry place at temperatures not below 0°C and not above 30°C.

(Shown in Product Recognition Section)

LYDERM Ⓟ
Taro
Fluocinonide
Topical Corticosteroid

Supplied: Each g of cream contains: fluocinonide 0.05% in a base consisting of stearyl alcohol, polyethylene glycols, propylene glycol, 1, 2, 6-hexanetriol, glycerin and citric acid. Tubes of 15 and 60 g. Jars of 400 g.

LYDONIDE Ⓟ
Technilab
Fluocinonide
Topical Corticosteroid

Supplied: Cream: Each g contains: fluocinonide 0.05% in a water miscible cream base. Nonmedicinal ingredients: caprylic/capric triglycerides, cetearyl alcohol, ceteareth-12, ceteareth-20, chlorocresol, citric acid, propylene glycol and purified water. Tubes of 60 g.

Emollient Cream: Each g contains: fluocinonide 0.05% in a water miscible cream base. Nonmedicinal ingredients: ceteareth-20, cetyl alcohol, chlorocresol, citric acid, glyceryl stearate, light mineral oil, petrolatum, polysorbate 60, propylene glycol and purified water. Tubes of 60 g.

Ointment: Each g contains: fluocinonide 0.05% in an ointment base. Nonmedicinal ingredients: petrolatum, propylene carbonate and propylene glycol. Tubes of 60 g.

Store at room temperature, between 15 and 30°C.

LYSODREN Ⓟ
Bristol
Mitotane
Antineoplastic

Pharmacology: Mitotane is an adrenal cytotoxic agent, and can cause adrenal inhibition, apparently without cellular destruction. Its biochemical mechanism of action is unknown. Available data suggest that the drug modifies the peripheral metabolism of steroids as well as directly suppressing the adrenal cortex. In man, mitotane administration alters cortisol's extra-adrenal metabolism, leading to a reduction in measurable 17-hydroxy corticosteroids, even though plasma corticosteroid concentrations do not fall. The drug apparently causes increased formation of 6-beta-hydroxy cortisol.

Approximately 40% of oral mitotane is absorbed, and approximately 10% is recovered in the urine as a water soluble metabolite. A small amount is excreted in the bile and the balance is stored in the tissues. When administered parenterally, approximately 25% of the dose is found in the urine as a water soluble metabolite.

Both unchanged drug and a metabolite were measured during and after dosing. The concentrations in patients receiving doses from 5 to 15 g/day varied from 7 to 90 μg/mL of unchanged mitotane and 29 to 54 μg/mL of the metabolite. These studies indicated no relationship between blood concentrations and therapeutic and/or toxic effects.

Following discontinuation of the drug, blood concentrations fell, but persisted for several weeks. In most patients, blood concentrations became undetectable after 6 to 9 weeks. In 1 patient who had received a total of 1 900 g of mitotane, high blood concentrations were found 10 weeks after stopping the drug. Autopsy data have provided evidence that mitotane is found in most body tissues. Fat tissues were the primary storage site. In 1 patient a very large number of tissues were examined and the drug was found in essentially every tissue.

Mitotane appears to be partly converted to a water soluble metabolite. This material has not been characterized, but is only found in the urine and blood of patients receiving mitotane. Examination of bile was made and found to contain no unchanged mitotane. There was metabolite in the bile, and this would indicate that biliary excretion is a significant route of removal of this metabolite from the body.

There is no evidence of a cure as a consequence of mitotane administration. A number of patients have been treated intermittently, treatment being restarted when severe symptoms reappear. Patients often do not respond after the third or fourth such course. Experience accumulated to date suggest that continuous treatment with the maximum possible mitotane dosage would be the best approach.

There was significant reduction in tumor mass following mitotane administration in about 50%, and a significant reduction in elevated steroid excretion in about 80% of the evaluable patients studied to date. Clinical effectiveness can be shown by reduction in tumor mass, reduction in pain, weakness or anorexia, and reduction of steroid symptoms.

Indications: Mitotane is indicated only in the treatment of inoperable adrenal cortical carcinoma of both functional and nonfunctional type.

Contraindications: Known hypersensitivity to mitotane.

Precautions: Mitotane should be temporarily discontinued immediately following shock or severe trauma since adrenal suppression is its prime action. Exogenous steroids should also be administered in such circumstances, since the depressed adrenal may not immediately start to secrete steroids.

Administer mitotane with caution to patients with liver disease in addition to metastatic lesion of the adrenal cortex, since mitotane's metabolism may be interfered with and the drug may accumulate.

All possible tumor tissue should be surgically removed from large metastatic masses before mitotane administration is instituted. This is necessary to minimize the possibility of infarction and hemorrhage in the tumor due to a rapid, positive effect of the drug.

Long-term continuous administration of high doses of mitotane may lead to brain damage and impairment of function. Conduct behavioral and neurological assessments at regular intervals when continuous mitotane treatment exceeds 2 years.
Pregnancy and *Lactation:* Mitotane's safety in pregnancy or lactation has not been established. Treatment of women who are, or who may become pregnant, should be undertaken only after consideration of the benefits versus the possibility of harm to mother and child.

Adrenal insufficiency may develop in patients treated with mitotane; consider adrenal steroid replacement for these patients.
Occupational Hazards: Since sedation, lethargy, vertigo, and other CNS adverse effects can occur, caution ambulatory patients about driving, operating machinery, and other hazardous pursuits requiring mental and physical alertness.

Mitotane appears to induce drug metabolizing enzymes in both experimental animals and man. Consequently, the dosage of other drugs given concurrently with mitotane may require adjustment in order to achieve the desired therapeutic effect.

Adverse Effects: A very high percentage of patients treated with mitotane have shown at least one type of adverse effect.

The main types of adverse reactions consist of the following: 1. Gastrointestinal disturbances, which consisted of anorexia, nausea or vomiting, and in some cases diarrhea, occurred in about 80% of the patients. 2. CNS effects occurred in 40% of the patients and consisted primarily of depression as manifested by lethargy and somnolence (25%), and dizziness or vertigo (15%). 3. Skin toxicity was observed in about 15% of the cases. In some instances, however, this adverse effect subsided while the patients were maintained on the drug.

Infrequently occurring adverse effects involve the eye (visual blurring, diplopia, lens opacity, toxic retinopathy); the genitourinary system (hematuria, hemorrhagic cystitis, albuminuria); cardiovascular system (hypertension, orthostatic hypotension, flushing); and some miscellaneous complaints including generalized aching, hyperpyrexia, and lowered PBI.

Overdose: Symptoms and Treatment: Mitotane would have an emetic effect if an overdose occurred.

Dosage: Start the patient at 9 to 10 g of mitotane/day in divided doses, either 3 or 4 times daily since most patients will have adverse effects initially irrespective of starting dosage. If severe adverse effects appear, reduce the dose until the maximum tolerated dose is achieved. If the patient can tolerate higher doses and improved clinical response appears possible, increase the dose until adverse reactions interfere.

Experience has shown that the maximum tolerated dose (MTD) will vary from 2 to 16 g/day, but has usually been 8 to 10 g/day. The highest doses used in the studies to date were 18 to 19 g/day.

Treatment should be instituted in the hospital until a stable dosage regimen is achieved.

Continue treatment as long as clinical benefits are observed. Maintenance of clinical status or slowing of growth of metastatic lesions can be considered clinical benefits if they can clearly be shown to have occurred.

If no clinical benefits are observed after 3 months at the maximum tolerated dose, the case may be considered a clinical failure. However, 10% of the patients who showed a measurable response required more than 3 months at the MTD.

Early diagnosis and prompt institution of treatment improve the probability of a positive clinical response.

Supplied: Each scored, biconvex tablet contains: mitotane 500 mg. Nonmedicinal ingredients: microcrystalline cellulose, polyethylene glycol, silicon dioxide and starch. Bottles of 100.

LYTEPREP™

Therapex

Electrolytes

Gastrointestinal Lavage

Supplied: Each unidose jug contains: sodium sulfate 22.74 g, sodium bicarbonate 6.74 g, sodium chloride 5.86 g, potassium chloride 2.97 g and 236 g polyethylene glycol 3350 in powdered form. When reconstituted to 4 L, the solution contains: sodium 125 mmol/L, potassium 10 mmol/L, sulfate 40 mmol/L, bicarbonate 20 mmol/L, chloride 35 mmol/L and polyethylene glycol 17.6 mmol/L. Keep solution refrigerated and use within 48 hours. Discard unused portion.

983

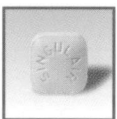

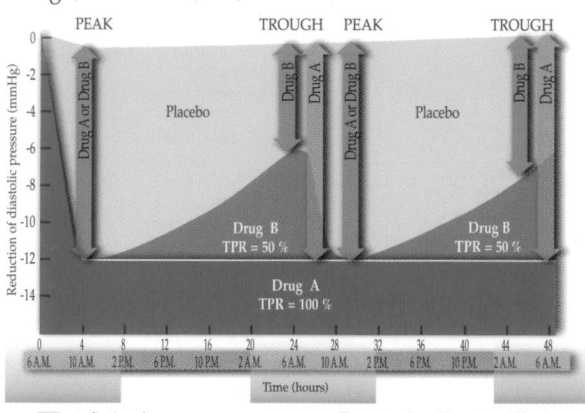

M

MAALOX®

Novartis Consumer Health

Magnesium Hydroxide—Aluminum Hydroxide

Antacid

Indications: For the treatment and relief of the symptoms of peptic ulcer, gastritis and hyperacidity.

Contraindications: Not to be given to patients who are severely debilitated or suffering from kidney failure, alkalosis or hypermagnesemia.

Precautions: Magnesium salts, in the presence of renal insufficiency, may cause CNS depression. Aluminum hydroxide, in the presence of low phosphorus diets, may cause phosphorus deficiency. Aluminum salts tend to cause constipation.

Antacids can interfere with the absorption of iron preparations and/or tetracyclines.

Overdose: Symptoms: Diarrhea is the only symptom of overdosage to be expected in the normal patient. In the presence of marked renal insufficiency, the possibility of magnesium intoxication exists; which will be manifested by dryness of mouth, drowsiness, stupor and respiratory depression.

Treatment: Massive overdosage should be treated by gastric lavage and by catharsis with castor oil or other laxatives not containing magnesium. Should symptoms of magnesium intoxication be present, calcium gluconate should be administered i.v.

Dosage: Suspension: Adults, 10 to 20 mL taken 20 minutes to 1 hour after meals and upon retiring. May be mixed with water or milk. In gastritis, however, undiluted administration is recommended.

Tablets: Adults, 1 or 2 tablets, well chewed, 20 minutes to 1 hour after meals and at bedtime. May be followed with milk or water.

Supplied: Suspension: Each 5 mL of mint-flavored, or cherry-flavored, creamy, colloidal suspension contains: magnesium hydroxide 200 mg, aluminum hydroxide dried gel USP 225 mg (equivalent to 172 mg aluminum hydroxide). Nonmedicinal ingredients: calcium saccharin flavors, guar gum, methylparaben, propylparaben, sorbitol and water. Energy: 3.86 kJ (0.22 kcal)/5 mL. Sodium: <1 mmol (0.92 mg)/5 mL. Tartrazine-free. Bottles of 350 mL (mint- and cherry-flavored) and 770 mL (mint-flavored). Protect from freezing.

Tablets: Each round, flat-faced, beveled, white (mint-flavored) or pink (cherry-flavored), chewable tablet, engraved "Maalox" on one side and on the other side, contains: magnesium hydroxide 200 mg and aluminum hydroxide dried gel USP 200 mg (equivalent to 153 mg aluminum hydroxide). Nonmedicinal ingredients: flavors, glycerin, magnesium stearate, mannitol, sodium saccharin, sorbitol and talc. Energy: 4.9 kJ (1.18 kcal). Sodium: <1 mmol (0.93 mg). Tartrazine-free. Bottles of 50 (mint- or cherry-flavored) and 100 (mint-flavored).

MAALOX® HRF

Novartis Consumer Health

Magnesium Alginate—Aluminum Hydroxide-Magnesium Carbonate—Magnesium Carbonate

Gastroesophageal Reflux Therapy

Pharmacology: The liquid or tablets when chewed, produce a viscous demulcent antacid foam barrier which floats on the stomach contents serving as a protective barrier for the esophagus against reflux of gastric contents. The alkaline foam readily flows into the esophagus during reflux aiding in the neutralization of refluxed gastric acids. Maalox HRF also reduces the frequency of reflux episodes.

Indications: For symptomatic relief of heartburn, acid indigestion and stomach acid reflux.

Precautions: The divalent cations of magnesium and aluminum interfere with the absorption of tetracycline, iron and phosphate. Patients suffering from renal failure or those taking any form of tetracycline should not use Maalox HRF. Maalox HRF may decrease the absorption of certain drugs such as digoxin, indomethacin, isoniazid, etc.

Adverse Effects: Nausea, vomiting, eructation and flatulence.

Overdose: Symptoms and Treatment: Should overdose occur, gastric distention may result and is best treated conservatively.

Dosage: Adults: 10 to 20 mL or 2 to 4 tablets after meals and at bedtime, or as directed by a physician.

Supplied: Suspension: Each 10 mL of pale green, mint-flavored suspension contains: magnesium alginate 500 mg, aluminum hydroxide-magnesium carbonate codried gel 280 mg and magnesium carbonate 350 mg. Nonmedicinal ingredients: calcium carbonate, calcium cyclamate, D&C Yellow #10, FD&C Blue #1, FD&C Yellow #6, flavors, methylparaben, potassium bicarbonate, propylparaben, sorbitol, water and xanthan gum. Sodium: <1 mmol (<1 mg)/mL. Sucrose- and tartrazine-free. Bottles of 350 mL. Protect from freezing.

Tablets: Each round, flat-faced, beveled, pale green, mint-flavored, chewable tablet engraved "Maalox HRF" on one side and on the other side, contains: magnesium alginate 250 mg, aluminum hydroxide-magnesium carbonate codried gel 180 mg and magnesium carbonate 160 mg. Nonmedicinal ingredients: cornstarch, D&C Yellow #10, FD&C Blue #2, flavors, magnesium stearate, potassium bicarbonate and sugar. Sodium: <1 mmol (<3 mg)/tablet. Tartrazine-free. Bottles of 30.

MAALOX H2 ACID CONTROLLER™

Novartis Consumer Health

Famotidine

Histamine H_2 Receptor Antagonist

Pharmacology: Famotidine is a competitive inhibitor of histamine H_2-receptors. The primary clinically important pharmacologic activity of famotidine is inhibition of gastric juice secretion. Famotidine reduces the acid and pepsin content, as well as the volume, of basal, nocturnal, and stimulated gastric secretion.

Indications: In the treatment of the following conditions where a controlled reduction of gastric secretion is required, such as acid indigestion, heartburn, sour or upset stomach. It is also indicated for the prevention of these symptoms when associated with the consumption of food and/or beverage.

Contraindications: Hypersensitivity to any component of this medication.

Precautions: General: In clinical trials, patients with other underlying acid gastrointestinal diseases (e.g., duodenal ulcer, gastric ulcer) did not experience complications; in general, they did not exhibit a clinically significant deterioration in their condition. However, if patients have difficulty swallowing or if abdominal discomfort persists, the underlying cause should be determined. Symptomatic response to therapy with famotidine does not preclude the presence of gastric malignancy.

Patients with severe kidney disease, previous history of ulcer disease complications, severe coexisting illness, those who are experiencing unintended weight loss in association with dyspeptic symptoms, and those who are middle-aged or older with new or recently changed dyspeptic symptoms should consult a physician before commencing therapy with famotidine.

Patients consuming nonsteroidal anti-inflammatory drugs may have dyspepsia as a side effect of these medicines and should consult a physician or a pharmacist before taking famotidine.

Therapy should not exceed 2 weeks of continuous treatment without medical consultation.

Drug Interactions: Studies with famotidine in man, in animal models, and in vitro have shown no significant interference with the disposition of compounds metabolized by the hepatic microsomal enzymes, e.g., cytochrome P450 system. Compounds tested in man have included warfarin, theophylline, phenytoin, diazepam, aminopyrine and antipyrine. Indocyanine green as an index of hepatic blood flow and/or hepatic drug extraction has been tested and no significant effects have been found.

Concomitant use of aluminum hydroxide/magnesium hydroxide at commonly used doses, does not influence the pharmacodynamics or bioavailability of famotidine. Famotidine does not affect gastric alcohol dehydrogenase and, consequently, blood ethanol levels.

Pregnancy: Reproductive studies have been performed in rats and rabbits at oral doses of up to 2 000 and 500 mg/kg/day, respectively (approximately 2 500 and 625 times the maximum recommended prescription human dose [80 mg], respectively), and have revealed no evidence of impaired fertility or harm to the fetus due to famotidine. There are, however, no adequate or well-controlled studies in pregnant women.

Since the safe use of famotidine in pregnant women has not been established, pregnant women should not use famotidine unless directed otherwise by a physician.

Lactation: Famotidine is detectable in human milk. Nursing mothers should either stop this drug or should stop nursing.

Children: Safety and effectiveness in children have not been established. Famotidine should not be administered to children under 12 years of age.

Geriatrics: No dosage adjustment is required based on age.

Adverse Effects: Famotidine has been demonstrated to be generally well tolerated. Adverse reactions reported in ≥1% of patients were headache and dizziness. These occurred with comparable frequency in patients treated with placebo.

Laboratory parameters may be affected during treatment with famotidine, but the changes are usually not considered serious. Among the laboratory changes that were reported during clinical trials were increases in AST, ALT, and WBC count, and decreases in hemoglobin and hematocrit. These changes were rarely of clinical significance.

No famotidine-treated patients/subjects had to be discontinued from therapy because of laboratory adverse experiences.

During marketed use of prescription doses, which are higher than those recommended for nonprescription use, the following adverse reactions have been reported; urticaria, liver enzymes abnormalities, cholestatic jaundice, anaphylaxis and angioedema. Toxic epidermal necrolysis has been reported very rarely with H_2-receptor antagonists.

The following adverse reactions have been reported; however, a causal relationship to therapy with famotidine has not been established: agitation, confusion, hallucinations, grand mal seizures, rare cases of impotence, thrombocytopenia, pancytopenia, leukopenia and agranulocytosis.

Gynecomastia has been reported rarely. In most cases that were followed up, it was reversible after discontinuing treatment.

Overdose: Symptoms and Treatment: There is no experience to date with deliberate overdosage. Doses of up to 800 mg/day have been employed in patients with pathological hypersecretory conditions with no serious adverse effects. In the event of overdosage, treatment should be symptomatic and supportive. Unabsorbed material should be removed from the gastrointestinal tract, the patient should be monitored, and supportive therapy should be employed.

The oral LD_{50} of famotidine in male and female rats and mice was >5 000 mg/kg.

Dosage: Adults and children 12 years of age or older: 10 mg, as required to relieve symptoms. For prevention of acid-related symptoms associated with the consumption of food and/or beverage: 10 mg 1 hour before eating. Repeat if symptoms return, up to a maximum of 20 mg in a 24-hour period.

Therapy should not exceed 2 weeks of continuous treatment without medical consultation.

Concomitant Use with Antacids: Antacids may be given concomitantly if needed.

Supplied: Each light yellow, round, biconvex, film-coated tablet engraved "10" on one side, contains: famotidine 10 mg. Nonmedicinal ingredients: carnauba wax, colloidal silicon dioxide, croscarmellose sodium, dextrates, hydroxypropyl methylcellulose, magnesium stearate, polyethylene glycol, titanium dioxide and yellow ferric oxide. Unit dose packages of 2, 6, 12 and 30. Store at room temperature (15 to 30°C). Protect from light and moisture.

New Product 1998

Patients should be informed of potential "occupational hazards" which may be induced by medications. Look for this heading under precautions in product monographs.

MAALOX® PLUS

Novartis Consumer Health

Magnesium Hydroxide—Aluminum Hydroxide— Simethicone

Antacid—Antiflatulent

Indications: For symptomatic relief of hyperacidity, acid indigestion, heartburn and gas.

Contraindications: Alkalosis; hypermagnesemia; where distention may be due to partial or complete intestinal obstruction. Not recommended for severely debilitated patients or those with impaired renal function.

Precautions: See Maalox monograph.

Overdose: Symptoms and Treatment: See Maalox monograph.

Dosage: Suspension: Adults, 10 to 20 mL taken 20 minutes to 1 hour after meals and upon retiring. May be mixed with milk or water, except in gastritis, when undiluted administration is recommended.

Tablets: Each tablet is approximately equivalent to 5 mL of the suspension. Adults, 2 to 4 tablets well chewed, 20 minutes to 1 hour after meals and at bedtime. May be followed with water or milk.

Supplied: Suspension: Each 5 mL of mint- or lemon-flavored, creamy, colloidal suspension contains: magnesium hydroxide 200 mg, aluminum hydroxide dried gel USP 225 mg (equivalent to 172 mg aluminum hydroxide) and simethicone 25 mg. Nonmedicinal ingredients: calcium saccharin, flavors, guar gum, hydroxypropyl cellulose, methylparaben, microcrystalline cellulose, propylparaben, sodium carboxymethylcellulose, sorbitol and water. Energy: 3.78 kJ (0.9 kcal)/5 mL. Sodium: <1 mmol (0.92 mg)/5 mL mint; <1 mmol (0.95 mg)/5 mL (lemon). Sucrose- and tartrazine-free. Bottles of 350 mL (lemon). Bottles of 350 and 770 mL (mint). Protect from freezing.

Tablets: Each round, flat-faced, beveled, green (mint-flavored), yellow (lemon-flavored) or pink (cherry-flavored), chewable tablet, engraved "Maalox Plus" on one side and LOGO on the other side, contains: magnesium hydroxide 200 mg, aluminum hydroxide dried gel USP 200 mg (equivalent to 153 mg aluminum hydroxide) and simethicone 25 mg. Nonmedicinal ingredients: citric acid, cornstarch, D&C Red #30, D&C Yellow #10, dextrose, FD&C Blue #1, flavors, magnesium stearate, mannitol, sodium saccharin, sorbitol, sucrose and talc. Energy: 11.7 kJ (2.8 kcal). Sodium: <1 mmol (0.94 mg) (mint); <1 mmol (1.0 mg) (lemon). Tartrazine-free. Bottles of 50 tablets and roll packs of 12 tablets.

MAALOX® PLUS EXTRA STRENGTH

Novartis Consumer Health

Magnesium Hydroxide—Aluminum Hydroxide—Simethicone

Antacid—Antiflatulent

Indications: For symptomatic relief of hyperacidity, acid indigestion, heartburn and gas.

Contraindications: Alkalosis; hypermagnesemia; where distention may be due to partial or complete intestinal obstruction. Not recommended for severely debilitated patients or those with impaired renal function.

Precautions: Magnesium salts, in the presence of renal insufficiency, may cause CNS depression. Aluminum hydroxide, in the presence of low phosphorus diets, may cause phosphorus deficiency. Aluminum salts tend to cause constipation.

Antacids can interfere with the absorption of iron preparations and/or tetracyclines.

Overdose: Symptoms: Diarrhea is the only symptom of overdosage to be expected in the normal patient. In the presence of marked renal insufficiency, the possibility of magnesium intoxication exists, which will be manifested by dryness of the mouth, drowsiness, stupor and respiratory depression.

Treatment: Massive overdosage should be treated by gastric lavage and by catharsis with castor oil or other laxatives not containing magnesium. Should symptoms of magnesium intoxication be present, calcium gluconate should be administered i.v.

Dosage: Adults: 10 to 20 mL or 1 to 3 tablets taken 20 minutes to 1 hour after meals and at bedtime, or as directed by a physician.

Supplied: Suspension: Each 5 mL of mint-flavored or cherry-flavored, creamy, colloidal suspension contains: magnesium hydroxide 450 mg, aluminum hydroxide dried gel USP 500 mg (equivalent to 383 mg aluminum hydroxide) and simethicone 40 mg. Nonmedicinal ingredients: calcium saccharin, FD&C Red #10, flavors, guar gum, methylparaben, propylparaben, sorbitol and water. Sodium: <1 mmol (1.2 mg)/5 mL. Lactose-, sucrose- and tartrazine-free. Bottles of 350 mL. Protect from freezing.

Tablets: Each round, flat-faced, beveled, pink, cherry-flavored, chewable tablet, engraved "ES Maalox Plus" on one side and on the other side, contains: magnesium hydroxide 350 mg, aluminum hydroxide dried gel USP 350 mg (equivalent to 268 mg aluminum hydroxide) and simethicone 30 mg. Nonmedicinal ingredients: citric acid, dextrose, D&C Red #30, flavors, glycerin, magnesium stearate, mannitol, saccharin, sorbitol, starch, sucrose and talc. Tartrazine-free. Bottles of 40.

MAALOX® TC

Novartis Consumer Health

Magnesium Hydroxide—Aluminum Hydroxide

Antacid

Indications: A high potency antacid for the treatment and relief of the symptoms of peptic ulcer and severe hyperacidity related disorders.

Contraindications: Alkalosis, hypermagnesemia; where distention may be due to partial or complete intestinal obstruction. Not recommended for severely debilitated patients or those with impaired renal function.

Precautions: Magnesium salts in the presence of renal insufficiency may cause CNS depression. Aluminum hydroxide, in the presence of low phosphorus diets may cause phosphorus deficiency. Aluminum salts tend to cause constipation. Magnesium salts tend to cause loose stools.

Do not administer concomitantly with tetracycline antibiotics or iron preparations.

Dosage: 5 to 10 mL 4 times a day, taken 20 minutes to 1 hour after meals and at bedtime. Higher dose regimens may be employed under the direct supervision of a physician in the treatment of active peptic ulcer disease.

Supplied: Suspension: Each 5 mL of sucrose-free, mint-flavored, suspension contains: aluminum hydroxide dried gel USP 600 mg (equivalent to 459 mg aluminum hydroxide) and magnesium hydroxide 300 mg. Nonmedicinal ingredients: flavor, guar gum, methylparaben, propylparaben, sorbitol and water. Energy: 12.5 kJ (3.0 kcal)/5 mL. Sodium: <1 mmol (0.95 mg)/5 mL. Tartrazine-free. Bottles of 350 mL. Protect from freezing.

Tablets: Each round, flat-faced, beveled, white, mint-flavored, chewable tablet, engraved "Maalox TC" on one side and on the other side, contains: magnesium hydroxide 300 mg and aluminum hydroxide dried gel USP 600 mg (equivalent to 459 mg aluminum hydroxide). Nonmedicinal ingredients: flavors, glycerin, light mineral oil, magnesium stearate, mannitol, sorbitol, sucrose and water. Energy: 12.5 kJ (3.0 kcal). Sodium: <1 mmol (0.98 mg). Tartrazine-free. Bottles of 40.

MACROBID® P

Procter & Gamble Pharmaceuticals

Nitrofurantoin Monohydrate—Nitrofurantoin Macrocrystals

Urinary Tract Antibacterial

Pharmacology: Nitrofurantoin is reduced by bacterial flavoproteins to reactive intermediates which inactivate or alter bacterial ribosomal proteins and other macromolecules. As a result of such inactivations, the vital biochemical processes of protein synthesis, aerobic energy metabolism, DNA synthesis, RNA synthesis and cell wall synthesis are inhibited. The broad-based nature of this mode of action may explain the lack of acquired bacterial resistance to nitrofurantoin, as the necessary multiple and simultaneous mutations of the target macromolecules would likely be lethal to the bacteria.

Each MacroBID capsule contains 2 forms of nitrofurantoin. Twenty-five percent is macrocrystalline nitrofurantoin, which has slower dissolution and absorption than nitrofurantoin monohydrate. The remaining 75% is nitrofurantoin monohydrate contained in a powder blend which, upon exposure to gastric and intestinal fluids, forms a gel matrix that releases nitrofurantoin over time.

Following a single 100 mg dose, the extent and rate of nitrofurantoin excretion in the urine are similar for 100 mg capsules of MacroBID and 50 or 100 mg capsules of Macrodantin. Nitrofurantoin bioavailability can be increased by as much as 40% when MacroBID is administered with food. Approximately 20 to 25% of a single dose of MacroBID is recovered in the urine unchanged over 24 hours and drug concentrations inhibitory of bacterial growth are reached or exceeded in the urine. Plasma levels attained with MacroBID usually do not exceed 1 μg/mL and are not considered systemically therapeutic.

Indications: The treatment of acute uncomplicated urinary tract infections, e.g., cystitis, when due to susceptible strains of E. coli and S. saprophyticus.

MacroBID is not indicated for treatment of associated renal cortical or perinephric abscesses.

MacroBID is not indicated for therapy of any systemic infections or for use in prostatitis.

Contraindications: Anuria, oliguria or significant impairment of renal function (creatinine clearance under 60 mL/min or clinically significant elevated serum creatinine) are contraindications to therapy with this drug. Treatment of this type of patient carries an increased risk of toxicity because of impaired excretion of the drug. For the same reason, the drug is much less effective under these circumstances.

The drug is contraindicated in pregnant patients during labor and delivery, or when the onset of labor is imminent, and in infants under 1 month of age, because of the possibility of hemolytic anemia in the fetus or the newborn infant due to their immature erythrocyte enzyme systems (glutathione instability).

MacroBID capsule therapy is also contraindicated in those patients with known hypersensitivity to nitrofurantoin.

Warnings: Acute, subacute and chronic pulmonary reactions have been observed in patients treated with nitrofurantoin products (see Adverse Effects). If these reactions occur, the drug should be withdrawn and appropriate measures taken. Reports have cited pulmonary reactions as a contributing cause of death.

Chronic pulmonary reactions (diffuse interstitial pneumonitis or pulmonary fibrosis, or both) can develop insidiously. These reactions occur rarely and generally in patients receiving therapy for 6 months or longer. Close monitoring of the pulmonary condition of patients receiving long-term therapy is warranted and requires that the benefits of therapy be weighed against potential risks (see Adverse Effects).

Hepatic reactions, including hepatitis, hepatic necrosis, cholestatic jaundice and chronic active hepatitis, occur rarely. Fatalities have been reported. The onset of chronic active hepatitis may be insidious, and patients should be monitored periodically for changes in liver function. If hepatitis occurs the drug should be withdrawn immediately and appropriate measures taken.

Peripheral neuropathy (including optic neuritis) may occur with nitrofurantoin therapy; this may become severe or irreversible. Fatalities have been reported. Predisposing conditions such as renal impairment (creatinine clearance under 60 mL/min or clinically significant elevated serum creatinine), anemia, diabetes mellitus, electrolyte imbalance, vitamin B deficiency and debilitating disease may enhance such occurrence. Patients receiving long-term therapy should be monitored periodically for changes in renal function. If numbness or tingling occurs, discontinue use.

Cases of hemolytic anemia of the primaquine sensitivity type have been induced by nitrofurantoin. The hemolysis appears to be linked to a glucose-6-phosphate dehydrogenase deficiency in the red blood cells of the affected patients. This deficiency is found in 10% of blacks and a small percentage of ethnic groups of Mediterranean and Near-Eastern origin. Any sign of hemolysis is an indication to discontinue the drug. Hemolysis ceases when the drug is withdrawn.

Pseudomonas is the organism most commonly implicated in superinfections in patients with nitrofurantoin preparations. Carcinogenesis, Mutagenesis and Impairment of Fertility: Nitrofurantoin presented evidence of carcinogenic activity in female $B_6C_3F_1$ mice as shown by increased incidences of tubular adenomas, benign mixed tumor and granulosa cell tumors of the ovary. In male F344/N rats, there were increased incidences of uncommon kidney tubular cell neoplasms, osteosarcomas of the bone, and neoplasms of the s.c. tissue. In one study involving 3 s.c. injections of 75 mg/kg nitrofurantoin to pregnant female mice, lung papillary adenomas were observed in the F1 generation.

Nitrofurantoin was not carcinogenic when fed to female Holtzman rats for 44.5 weeks or to female Sprague-Dawley rats for 75 weeks. Two chronic rodent bioassays utilizing male and female Sprague-Dawley rats and 2 chronic bioassays in Swiss mice and BDF_1 mice revealed no evidence of carcinogenicity.

Nitrofurantoin has demonstrated mutagenic potential in a variety of laboratory assays conducted in vitro with mammalian and nonmammalian cells exposed to therapeutically attainable and higher concentrations. Point and possibly other types of mutations were observed in bacteria, yeast and fungi. Damage to DNA or inhibition of DNA synthesis was produced in human fibroblasts and lymphocytes, and Chinese hamster ovaries and lung fibroblasts.

In vivo tests on rodents utilizing a wide range of doses demonstrated similar potential. DNA damage to liver, lung, spleen and kidney were observed in rat (alkaline elution test), immature red blood cells (rat micronucleus test) and sperm (H-test in mouse). Some test results were negative such as the sex-linked recessive lethal assay in Drosophila where nitrofurantoin was administered by feeding or injection.

The significance of the carcinogenicity and mutagenicity findings relative to the therapeutic use of nitrofurantoin in humans is unknown. Because of the potential toxicity of nitrofurantoin when used for long-term therapy, the benefits of long-term therapy should be weighed against potential risks (see Dosage).

The administration of high doses of nitrofurantoin to rats causes temporary spermatogenic arrest, which is reversible on discontinuing the drug. Doses of 10 mg/kg/day or greater in healthy human males may, in certain unpredictable instances, produce slight to moderate spermatogenic arrest with a decrease in sperm count.

Precautions: *Drug Interactions:* Antacids containing magnesium trisilicate, when administered concomitantly with nitrofurantoin, reduce both the rate and extent of absorption. The mechanism for this interaction probably is adsorption of drug onto the surface of magnesium trisilicate. Nitrofurantoin should not be given along with drugs which may produce impaired renal function. Uricosuric drugs, such as probenecid and sulfinpyrazone, may inhibit renal tubular secretion of nitrofurantoin. The resulting increase in serum levels may increase toxicity and the decreased urinary levels could lessen its efficacy as a urinary tract antibacterial.

Drug/Laboratory Test Interactions: As a result of administration of nitrofurantoin, a false-positive reaction for glucose in the urine may occur. This has been observed with Benedict's and Fehling's solution but not with the glucose enzymatic test.

Antimicrobial Antagonism: Antagonism has been demonstrated in vitro between nitrofurantoin and quinolone antimicrobials. Although the clinical significance of this finding is unknown, concomitant MacroBID and quinolone therapy should be approached with caution.

Pregnancy: Several reproduction studies performed in rabbits and rats with low multiples of human doses and plasma levels revealed no evidence of general reproductive effects, impaired fertility or harm to the fetus. However, in one published study in which pregnant mice were administered 250 mg/kg s.c. on 3 days, growth retardation and a low incidence of malformations were observed. These effects were not observed at 100 mg/kg. In another controlled study in which cultured rat embryos were exposed for 26 hours to concentrations of 48 μg/mL all were malformed. None of those exposed to 60 μg/mL of nitrofurantoin survived.

The relevance of these findings to humans is uncertain. There are, however, no adequate well-controlled studies in pregnant women. Though animal reproduction studies are not always predictive of human response, this drug should not be used during pregnancy unless clearly needed.

Labor and Delivery: Nitrofurantoin should not be given to women during labor and delivery, or when the onset of labor is imminent (see Contraindications).

Lactation: Nitrofurantoin has been detected in trace amounts in breast milk. Caution should be exercised when the nitrofurantoin is administered to a nursing woman, especially if the infant is known or suspected to have a glucose-6-phosphate dehydrogenase deficiency (see Contraindications).

Children: Nitrofurantoin is contraindicated in infants under 1 month of age (see Contraindications and Dosage).

Adverse Effects: In limited clinical trials, MacroBID 100 mg capsule b.i.d demonstrated an equivalent side effect profile to Macrodantin 50 mg q.i.d.

In clinical trials of MacroBID the most frequent clinical adverse events that were reported as possibly or probably drug-related were nausea (8%), headache (6%), and flatulence (1.5%).

The following additional clinical adverse events have been reported with the use of nitrofurantoin: Respiratory: Chronic, subacute or acute pulmonary hypersensitivity reactions may occur with the use of nitrofurantoin (see Warnings). Chronic pulmonary reactions generally occur in patients who have received continuous treatment for 6 months or longer. Malaise, dyspnea on exertion, cough and altered pulmonary function are common manifestations which can occur insidiously. Radiologic and histologic findings of diffuse interstitial pneumonitis or fibrosis, or both, are also common manifestations of the chronic pulmonary reaction. Fever is rarely prominent. The severity of chronic pulmonary reactions and the degree of their resolution appear to be related to the duration of therapy after the first clinical signs appear. Pulmonary function may be impaired permanently even after cessation of nitrofurantoin therapy. The risk is greater when pulmonary reactions are not recognized early.

In subacute pulmonary reactions, fever and eosinophilia occur less often than in the acute form. Upon cessation of therapy, recovery may require several months. If the symptoms are not recognized as being drug related and nitrofurantoin is not stopped, the symptoms may become more severe.

Acute reactions are commonly manifested by fever, chills, cough, chest pain, dyspnea, pulmonary infiltration with consolidation or pleural effusion on x-ray, and eosinophilia. Acute reactions usually occur within the first week of treatment and are reversible with cessation of therapy. Resolution often is dramatic.

Changes in ECG may occur associated with pulmonary reactions.

Collapse and cyanosis have seldom been reported.

Gastrointestinal: diarrhea, dyspepsia, abdominal pain, constipation, emesis, sialadenitis, pancreatitis.

Pseudomembranous colitis, including that due to an overgrowth by C. difficile, has been reported rarely with the use of nitrofurantoin.

Hepatic: hepatic reactions, including hepatitis, cholestatic jaundice, chronic active hepatitis and hepatic necrosis occur rarely (see Warnings).

Neurologic: peripheral neuropathy, including optic neuritis (see Warnings).

Dizziness, drowsiness, amblyopia, asthenia, vertigo and nystagmus also have been reported with the use of nitrofurantoin.

Benign intracranial hypertension has seldom been reported.

Confusion, depression, euphoria and psychotic reactions have been reported rarely.

Dermatologic: Alopecia. Exfoliative dermatitis and erythema multiforme (including Stevens-Johnson syndrome) have been reported rarely.

Allergic Reactions: Lupus-like syndrome associated with pulmonary reaction to nitrofurantoin has been reported. Also, angioedema; maculopapular, erythematous or eczematous eruptions; pruritus; urticaria; anaphylaxis; arthralgia; myalgia; drug fever; chills; and malaise have been reported.

Hematologic: Glucose-6-phosphate dehydrogenase deficiency anemia (see Warnings), agranulocytosis, leukopenia, granulocytopenia, hemolytic anemia, thrombocytopenia, megaloblastic anemia and eosinophilia have occurred. In most cases, these hematologic abnormalities resolved following cessation of therapy. Aplastic anemia has been reported rarely.

Miscellaneous: As with other antimicrobial agents, superinfections with resistant organisms, e.g., Pseudomonas species or Candida species, may occur with the use of nitrofurantoin. Superinfections have been limited to the genitourinary tract.

Increased AST, increased ALT, decreased hemoglobin and increased serum phosphorus.

Nitrofurantoin may cause a rust yellow to brown discoloration of the urine. The clinical significance is unknown.

Overdose: Symptoms: Occasional incidents of acute overdosage of nitrofurantoin have not resulted in any specific symptomatology other than vomiting.

Treatment: In case vomiting does not occur soon after an excessive dose, induction of emesis is recommended. There is no specific antidote for nitrofurantoin but a high fluid intake should be maintained to promote urinary excretion of the drug. It is dialyzable.

Dosage: Adults and Children over 12 years: 100 mg twice a day for 7 days (maximum 200 mg/day).

MacroBID should be taken every 12 hours with food or milk to minimize gastric upset.

Therapy for acute urinary tract infections should be continued for 7 days or for at least 3 days after sterility of the urine is obtained. Continued infection indicates the need for re-evaluation.

Information of the Patient: See Blue Section—Information for the Patient "MacroBID".

Supplied: Each opaque, black and yellow, hard shell gelatin capsule, imprinted "MacroBID" on the black portion and "Norwich Eaton" on the yellow portion contains: the equivalent of 100 mg of nitrofurantoin in the form of nitrofurantoin macrocrystals and nitrofurantoin monohydrate. Nonmedicinal ingredients: carbomer 934P, compressible sugar, corn starch, D&C Yellow No. 10, edible gray ink, FD&C Blue No. 1, FD&C Red No. 40, gelatin, lactose, magnesium stearate, povidone, talc, and titanium dioxide. Bottles of 100. Store at controlled room temperature (15 to 30°C).

Reviewed 1999

MACRODANTIN® Ⓟ

Procter & Gamble Pharmaceuticals

Nitrofurantoin Macrocrystals

Urinary Tract Antibacterial

Pharmacology: Nitrofurantoin is reduced by bacterial flavoproteins to reactive intermediates which inactivate or alter bacterial ribosomal proteins and other macromolecules. As a result of such inactivations, the vital biochemical processes of protein synthesis, aerobic energy metabolism, DNA synthesis, RNA synthesis and cell wall synthesis are inhibited. The broad-based nature of this mode of action may explain the lack of acquired bacterial resistance to nitrofurantoin, as the necessary multiple and simultaneous mutations of the target macromolecules would likely be lethal to the bacteria.

Macrodantin is a larger crystal form of nitrofurantoin. The absorption of Macrodantin is slower and its urinary excretion somewhat less when compared to nitrofurantoin tablets. At therapeutic doses, low drug concentrations are observed in blood, with therapeutic concentrations achieved only in the urine. A number of patients who cannot tolerate nitrofurantoin tablets can take Macrodantin without nausea.

Nitrofurantoin taken orally is rapidly absorbed from the gastrointestinal tract and appears to be widely distributed. Based upon urine recovery levels its bioavailability may be increased by as much as 40% when administered with food. In one study in which healthy male adults were provided a single 100 mg capsule of Macrodantin with food the C_{max}, t_{max}, and elimination $t_{1/2}$ were respectively 100 μg/mL, 3.6 hrs, and 1.13 hours in urine. Plasma levels do not normally exceed 1 μg/mL following therapeutic administration of Macrodantin to subjects with normal kidney function. Levels far exceeding those in plasma have been reported for human bile, seminal fluid and kidney. About 20 to 25% of a single dose of Macrodantin is recovered in the urine and about 1.5% of urine contents are metabolized. Little is known about nitrofurantoin metabolism and the rate or extent of its excretion by other routes in humans.

Indications: The treatment of urinary tract infections, e.g., cystitis, when due to susceptible strains of E. coli, enterococci, S. aureus and certain susceptible strains of Klebsiella species, Enterobacter species and Proteus species.

It is not indicated for treatment of associated renal cortical or perinephric abscesses.

Nitrofurantoin is not indicated for therapy of any systemic infections or for use in prostatitis.

Contraindications: Anuria, oliguria or significant impairment of renal function (creatinine clearance under 60 mL/min or clinically significant elevated serum creatinine) are contraindications to therapy with this drug. Treatment of this type of patient carries an increased risk of toxicity because of impaired excretion of the drug. For the same reason, the drug is much less effective under these circumstances.

Nitrofurantoin is contraindicated in pregnant patients during labor and delivery, or when the onset of labor is imminent, and in infants under 1 month of age, because of the possibility of hemolytic anemia in the fetus or the newborn infant due to their immature erythrocyte enzyme systems (glutathione instability).

Macrodantin capsule therapy is also contraindicated in those patients with known hypersensitivity to nitrofurantoin.

Warnings: Acute, subacute and chronic pulmonary reactions have been observed in patients treated with nitrofurantoin products (see Adverse Effects). If these reactions occur, the drug should be withdrawn and appropriate measures taken. Reports have cited pulmonary reactions as a contributing cause of death.

Chronic pulmonary reactions (diffuse interstitial pneumonitis or pulmonary fibrosis, or both) can develop insidiously. These reactions occur rarely and generally in patients

Macrodantin (cont'd)

receiving therapy for 6 months or longer. Close monitoring of the pulmonary condition of patients receiving long-term therapy is warranted and requires that the benefits of therapy be weighed against potential risks (see Adverse Effects).

Hepatic reactions, including hepatitis, hepatic necrosis, cholestatic jaundice and chronic active hepatitis, occur rarely. Fatalities have been reported. The onset of chronic active hepatitis may be insidious, and patients should be monitored periodically for changes in liver function. If hepatitis occurs the drug should be withdrawn immediately and appropriate measures taken.

Peripheral neuropathy (including optic neuritis) may occur with nitrofurantoin therapy; this may become severe or irreversible. Fatalities have been reported. Predisposing conditions such as renal impairment (creatinine clearance under 60 mL/min or clinically significant elevated serum creatinine), anemia, diabetes mellitus, electrolyte imbalance, vitamin B deficiency and debilitating disease may enhance such occurrence. Patients receiving long-term therapy should be monitored periodically for changes in renal function. If numbness or tingling occurs, discontinue use.

Cases of hemolytic anemia of the primaquine sensitivity type have been induced by nitrofurantoin. The hemolysis appears to be linked to a glucose-6-phosphate dehydrogenase deficiency in the red blood cells of the affected patients. This deficiency is found in 10% of blacks and a small percentage of ethnic groups of Mediterranean and Near-Eastern origin. Any sign of hemolysis is an indication to discontinue the drug. Hemolysis ceases when the drug is withdrawn.

Pseudomonas is the organism most commonly implicated in superinfections in patients with nitrofurantoin preparations.

Carcinogenesis, Mutagenesis and Impairment of Fertility: Nitrofurantoin presented evidence of carcinogenic activity in female $B_6C_3F_1$ mice as shown by increased incidences of tubular adenomas, benign mixed tumor and granulosa cell tumor of the ovary. In male F344/N rats, there were increased incidences of uncommon kidney tubular cell neoplasms, osteosarcomas of the bone and neoplasms of the s.c. tissue. In one study involving three s.c. injections of 75 mg/kg nitrofurantoin to pregnant female mice, lung papillary adenomas were observed in the F1 generation.

Nitrofurantoin was not carcinogenic when fed to female Holtzman rats for 44.5 weeks or to female Sprague-Dawley rats for 75 weeks. Two chronic rodent bioassays utilizing male and female Sprague-Dawley rats and 2 chronic bioassays in Swiss mice and BDF_1 mice revealed no evidence of carcinogenicity.

Nitrofurantoin has demonstrated mutagenic potential in a variety of laboratory assays conducted in vitro with mammalian and nonmammalian cells exposed to therapeutically attainable and higher concentrations. Point and possibly other types of mutations were observed in bacteria, yeast and fungi. Damage to DNA or inhibition of DNA synthesis was produced in human fibroblasts and lymphocytes, and Chinese hamster ovaries and lung fibroblasts.

In vivo tests on rodents utilizing a wide range of doses demonstrated similar potential. DNA damage to liver, lung, spleen and kidney were observed in rat (alkaline elution test), immature red blood cells (rat micronucleus test) and sperm (H-test in mouse). Some test results were negative such as the sex-linked recessive lethal assay in Drosophila where nitrofurantoin was administered by feeding or injection.

The significance of the carcinogenicity and mutagenicity findings relative to the therapeutic use of nitrofurantoin in humans is unknown. Because of the potential toxicity of nitrofurantoin when used for long-term therapy, the benefits of long-term therapy should be weighed against potential risks (see Dosage).

The administration of high doses of nitrofurantoin to rats causes temporary spermatogenic arrest, which is reversible on discontinuing the drug. Doses of 10 mg/kg/day or greater in healthy human males may, in certain unpredictable instances, produce slight to moderate spermatogenic arrest with a decrease in sperm count.

Precautions: *Drug Interactions:* Antacids containing magnesium trisilicate, when administered concomitantly with nitrofurantoin, reduce both the rate and extent of absorption. The mechanism for this interaction probably is adsorption of drug onto the surface of magnesium trisilicate. Nitrofurantoin should not be given along with drugs which may produce impaired renal function. Uricosuric drugs, such as probenecid and sulfinpyrazone, may inhibit renal tubular secretion of nitrofurantoin. The resulting increase in serum levels may increase toxicity and the decreased urinary levels could lessen its efficacy as a urinary tract antibacterial.

Drug/Laboratory Test Interactions: As a result of administration of nitrofurantoin, a false-positive reaction for glucose in the urine may occur. This has been observed with Benedict's and Fehling's solution but not with the glucose enzymatic test.

Pregnancy: Several reproduction studies performed in rabbits and rats with low multiples of human doses and plasma levels revealed no evidence of general reproductive effects, impaired fertility or harm to the fetus. However, in one published study in which pregnant mice were administered 250 mg/kg s.c. on 3 days, growth retardation and a low incidence of malformations were observed. These effects were not observed at 100 mg/kg. In another controlled study in which cultured rat embryos were exposed for 26 hours to concentrations of 48 µg/mL all were malformed. None of those exposed to 60 µg/mL of nitrofurantoin survived.

The relevance of these findings to humans is uncertain. There are, however, no adequate well-controlled studies in pregnant women. Though animal reproduction studies are not always predictive of human response, this drug should not be used during pregnancy unless clearly needed.

Labor and Delivery: Nitrofurantoin should not be given to women during labor and delivery, or when the onset of labor is imminent (see Contraindications).

Lactation: Nitrofurantoin has been detected in trace amounts in breast milk. Caution should be exercised when the nitrofurantoin is administered to a nursing woman, especially if the infant is known or suspected to have a glucose-6-phosphate dehydrogenase deficiency.

Children: Nitrofurantoin is contraindicated in infants under 1 month of age (see Contraindications and Dosage).

Adverse Effects: The following clinical adverse events have been reported with the use of nitrofurantoin: Respiratory: Chronic, subacute or acute pulmonary hypersensitivity reactions may occur with the use of nitrofurantoin (see Warnings). Chronic pulmonary reactions generally occur in patients who have received continuous treatment for 6 months or longer. Malaise, dyspnea on exertion, cough and altered pulmonary function are common manifestations which can occur insidiously. Radiologic and histologic findings of diffuse interstitial pneumonitis or fibrosis, or both, are also common manifestations of the chronic pulmonary reaction. Fever is rarely prominent. The severity of chronic pulmonary reactions and the degree of their resolution appear to be related to the duration of therapy after the first clinical signs appear. Pulmonary function may be impaired permanently even after cessation of nitrofurantoin therapy. The risk is greater when pulmonary reactions are not recognized early.

In subacute pulmonary reactions, fever and eosinophilia occur less than in the acute form. Upon cessation of therapy, recovery may require several months. If the symptoms are not recognized as being drug related and nitrofurantoin is not stopped, the symptoms may become more severe.

Acute reactions are commonly manifested by fever, chills, cough, chest pain, dyspnea, pulmonary infiltration with consolidation or pleural effusion on x-ray, and eosinophilia. Acute reactions usually occur within the first week of treatment and are reversible with cessation of therapy. Resolution often is dramatic.

Changes in ECG may occur associated with pulmonary reactions.

Collapse and cyanosis have seldom been reported.

Gastrointestinal: Diarrhea, dyspepsia, abdominal pain, constipation, emesis, sialadenitis, pancreatitis.

Hepatic: Hepatic reactions, including hepatitis, cholestatic jaundice, chronic active hepatitis and hepatic necrosis occur rarely (see Warnings).

Neurologic: Peripheral neuropathy, including optic neuritis (see Warnings).

Dizziness, drowsiness, amblyopia, asthenia, vertigo and nystagmus also have been reported with the use of nitrofurantoin.

Benign intracranial hypertension has seldom been reported.

Confusion, depression, euphoria and psychotic reactions have been reported rarely.

Dermatologic: Alopecia. Exfoliative dermatitis and erythema multiforme (including Stevens-Johnson syndrome) have been reported rarely.

Allergic Reactions: Lupus-like syndrome associated with pulmonary reaction to nitrofurantoin has been reported. Also, angioedema; maculopapular, erythematous or eczematous eruptions; pruritus; urticaria; anaphylaxis; arthralgia; myalgia; drug fever; chills; and malaise have been reported.

Hematologic: Glucose-6-phosphate dehydrogenase deficiency anemia (see Warnings), agranulocytosis, leukopenia, granulocytopenia, hemolytic anemia, thrombocytopenia, megaloblastic anemia and eosinophilia have occurred. In most cases, these hematologic abnormalities resolved following cessation of therapy. Aplastic anemia has been reported rarely.

Miscellaneous: As with other antimicrobial agents, superinfections with resistant organisms, e.g., Pseudomonas species or Candida species, may occur with the use of nitrofurantoin. Superinfections have been limited to the genitourinary tract.

Increased AST, increased ALT, decreased hemoglobin and increased serum phosphorus.

Nitrofurantoin may cause a rust-yellow to brown discoloration of the urine.

Overdose: Symptoms: Occasional incidents of acute overdosage of nitrofurantoin have not resulted in any specific symptomatology other than vomiting.

Treatment: In case vomiting does not occur soon after an excessive dose, induction of emesis is recommended. There is no specific antidote for nitrofurantoin but a high fluid intake should be maintained to promote urinary excretion of the drug. It is dialyzable.

Dosage: Adults: 50 to 100 mg 4 times a day. Children: Dosage should be calculated on the basis of 5 to 7 mg/kg of body weight/24 hours given in divided doses 4 times a day (contraindicated in infants under 1 month).

Macrodantin may be given with food or milk to further minimize gastric upset.

Therapy should be continued for at least 1 week or for at least 3 days after sterility of the urine is obtained. Continued infection indicates the need for re-evaluation.

For long-term suppressive therapy in adults, a reduction of dosage to 50 to 100 mg once daily at bedtime may be adequate. See Warnings section regarding risks associated with long-term therapy. For long-term suppressive therapy in children, doses as low as 1 mg/kg/24 hours, given in a single or in 2 divided doses, may be adequate.

Supplied: 50 mg: Each opaque, yellow and white capsule, coded with 2 black bars and Macrodantin, 50 mg, 0149, 0008, contains: nitrofurantoin macrocrystals 50 mg. Nonmedicinal ingredients: edible black ink, carnauba wax, gelatin, lactose, starch, talc and titanium dioxide, and may contain FD&C Yellow #6 and D&C Yellow #10. Bisulfite-, gluten-, paraben-, sodium- and tartrazine-free. Bottles of 100 and 500.

100 mg: Each opaque, yellow capsule, coded with 3 black bars and Macrodantin, 100 mg, 0149, 0009, contains: nitrofurantoin macrocrystals 100 mg. Nonmedicinal ingredients: edible black ink, carnauba wax, gelatin, lactose, starch, talc and titanium dioxide, and may contain FD&C Yellow #6 and D&C Yellow #10. Bisulfite-, gluten-, paraben-, sodium- and tartrazine-free. Bottles of 100 and 500.

Avoid excessive heat (over 40°C).

Reviewed 1999

MAGLUCATE™
Pharmascience

Magnesium Gluconate

Magnesium Supplement

Supplied: Each white compressed tablet, identified PMS contains: magnesium gluconate USP 500 mg (29.31 mg of magnesium) equivalent to 2.41 mEq magnesium. Bottles of 100.

MAGNESIUM-ROUGIER
Rougier

Magnesium Glucoheptonate

Magnesium Supplement

Indications: In hypomagnesemic states: malnutrition, excessive gastrointestinal losses due to severe diarrhea or prolonged vomiting, malabsorption syndrome, liver cirrhosis, diabetic acidosis, chronic alcoholism, electrolyte abnormalities following the use of potent diuretics.

Contraindications: Renal insufficiency.

Precautions: Magnesium forms insoluble chelates with tetracyclines, thus inhibiting antibiotic absorption. Therefore, concomitant administration of magnesium and tetracyclines should be avoided.

Administer magnesium cautiously in conjunction with drugs which affect electrolyte balance: diuretics, corticosteroids, cardiovascular agents.

When barbiturates, narcotics or other CNS depressants are administered concomitantly with magnesium, their dosage should be adjusted carefully because of the additive central depressive effects of magnesium.

Prolonged administration should be conducted under close medical supervision.

Overdose: Symptoms: The absence or depression of deep tendon reflexes; drowsiness, heart block and respiratory paralysis may also occur.

Treatment: I.V. administration of 5 to 10 mEq. of calcium as gluconate (10 to 20 mL of 10% calcium gluconate) is usually adequate for reversal of heart block or respiratory depression. In extreme cases, peritoneal dialysis using a dialysate free of magnesium or hemodialysis may be necessary.

Dosage: Adults: 15 to 30 mL 1 to 3 times per day, with meals. Average dose: 15 mL 4 times per day.

Supplied: Each mL of amber-yellow, transparent, raspberry-flavored solution contains: magnesium glucoheptonate 100 mg (5 mg elemental magnesium). Energy: 23.12 kJ (5.44 kcal)/5 mL. Bottles of 500 and 2 000 mL.

MAGNESIUM SULFATE

Abbott

Anticonvulsant—Electrolyte Replenisher

Pharmacology: Magnesium (Mg++) is an important cofactor for enzymatic reactions and plays an important role in neurochemical transmission and muscular excitability.

As a nutritional adjunct in hyperalimentation, the precise mechanism of action for magnesium is uncertain. Early symptoms of hypomagnesemia (less than 1.5 mEq/L) may develop as early as 3 to 4 days or within weeks. Predominant deficiency effects are neurological, e.g., muscle irritability, clonic twitching and tremors. Hypocalcemia and hypokalemia often follow low serum levels of magnesium. While there are large stores of magnesium present intracellularly and in the bones of adults, these stores often are not mobilized sufficiently to maintain plasma levels. Parenteral magnesium therapy repairs the plasma deficit and causes deficiency symptoms and signs to cease.

Magnesium prevents or controls convulsions by blocking neuromuscular transmission and decreasing the amount of acetylcholine liberated at the end plate by the motor nerve impulse. Magnesium is said to have a depressant effect on the CNS, but it does not adversely affect the mother, fetus or neonate when used as directed in eclampsia or pre-eclampsia. Normal plasma magnesium levels range from 1.5 to 2.5 or 3.0 mEq/L.

As plasma magnesium rises above 4 mEq/L, the deep tendon reflexes are first decreased and then disappear as the plasma level approaches 10 mEq/L. At this level, respiratory paralysis may occur. Heart block also may occur at this or lower plasma levels of magnesium.

Magnesium acts peripherally to produce vasodilation. With low doses only flushing and sweating occur, but larger doses cause lowering of blood pressure. The central and peripheral effects of magnesium poisoning are antagonized to some extent by i.v. administration of calcium.

With i.v. administration, the onset of anticonvulsant action is immediate and lasts about 30 minutes. Following i.m. administration, the onset of action occurs in about 1 hour and persists for 3 to 4 hours. Effective anticonvulsant serum levels range from 2.5 or 3.0 to 7.5 mEq/L. Magnesium is excreted solely by the kidney at a rate proportional to the plasma concentration and glomerular filtration.

Indications: For replacement therapy in magnesium deficiency, especially in acute hypomagnesemia accompanied by signs of tetany similar to those observed in hypocalcemia. In such cases, the serum magnesium (Mg++) level is usually below the lower limit of normal (1.5 to 2.5 or 3.0 mEq/L) and the serum calcium (Ca++) level is normal (4.3 to 5.3 mEq/L) or elevated.

In total parenteral nutrition, magnesium sulfate may be added to the nutrient admixture to correct or prevent hypomagnesemia which can arise during the course of therapy.

Magnesium sulfate injection is also indicated as a parenteral anticonvulsant for the prevention and control of seizures (convulsions) in severe toxemia of pregnancy. When used judiciously, it effectively prevents and controls the convulsions of eclampsia without producing deleterious depression of the CNS of the mother or infant. However, other effective drugs are available for this purpose.

Magnesium sulfate injection may be used to control hypertension, encephalopathy and convulsions associated with acute nephritis in children. However, other drugs such as barbiturates, reserpine or hydralazine should be tried first.

Contraindications: I.V. magnesium should not be given to mothers with toxemia of pregnancy during the 2 hours preceding delivery.

Warnings: I.V. use in eclampsia should be reserved for immediate control of life-threatening convulsions.

Parenteral use in the presence of renal insufficiency may lead to magnesium intoxication.

Precautions: Because magnesium is removed from the body solely by the kidneys, the drug should be used with caution in patients with renal impairment. Urine output should be maintained at a level of 100 mL every 4 hours. Monitoring serum magnesium levels and the patient's clinical status is essential to avoid the consequences of overdosage in toxemia. Clinical indications of a safe dosage regimen include the presence of the patellar reflex (knee jerk) and absence of respiratory depression (approximately 16 breaths or more/minute). Serum magnesium levels usually sufficient to control convulsions range from 3 to 6 mg/100 mL (2.5 to 5.0 mEq/L). The strength of the deep tendon reflexes begins to diminish when magnesium levels exceed 4 mEq/L. Reflexes may be absent at 10 mEq magnesium/L, where respiratory paralysis is a potential hazard. An injectable calcium salt should be immediately available to counteract the potential hazards of magnesium intoxication in eclampsia.

Fifty percent magnesium sulfate injection must be diluted to a concentration of 20% or less prior to i.v. infusion. Rate of administration should be slow and cautious, to avoid producing hypermagnesemia. The 50% solution also should be diluted to 20% or less for i.m. injection in infants and children.

Pregnancy: Studies in pregnant women have not shown that magnesium sulfate injection increases the risk of fetal abnormalities if administered during all trimesters of pregnancy. If this drug is used during pregnancy, the possibility of fetal harm appears remote. However, because studies cannot rule out the possibility of harm, magnesium sulfate injection should be used during pregnancy only if clearly needed.

When administered by continuous i.v. infusion (especially for infusion lasting more than 24 hours preceding delivery) to control convulsions in toxemic mothers, the newborn may show signs of magnesium toxicity, including neuromuscular or respiratory depression (see Overdose: Symptoms and Treatment).

Drug Interactions: CNS Depressants: When barbiturates, opiates, general anesthetics, or other CNS depressants are administered concomitantly with magnesium sulfate, dosage of these agents must be carefully adjusted because of the additive central depressant effects.

Neuromuscular Blocking Agents: Excessive neuromuscular blockade has occurred in patients receiving parenteral magnesium sulfate and a neuromuscular blocking agent; these drugs should be administered concomitantly only with caution.

Cardiac Glycosides: Magnesium salts should be administered with extreme caution in digitalized patients, because serious changes in cardiac conduction, which can result in heart block, may occur if administration of calcium is required to treat magnesium toxicity.

Adverse Effects: The adverse effects of parenterally administered magnesium usually are the result of magnesium intoxication. These include flushing, sweating, hypotension, depressed reflexes, flaccid paralysis, hypothermia, circulatory collapse, cardiac and CNS depression proceeding to respiratory paralysis. Hypocalcemia, with signs of tetany secondary to magnesium sulfate therapy for eclampsia, has been reported.

Overdose: Symptoms and Treatment: Magnesium intoxication is manifested by a sharp drop in blood pressure and respiratory paralysis. Disappearance of the patellar reflex is a useful clinical sign to detect the onset of magnesium intoxication. In the event of overdosage, artificial ventilation must be provided until a calcium salt can be injected i.v. to antagonize the effects of magnesium.

In adults, i.v. administration of 5 to 10 mEq of 10% calcium gluconate will usually reverse respiratory depression or heart block due to magnesium intoxication. In extreme cases, peritoneal dialysis or hemodialysis may be required.

Hypermagnesemia in the newborn may require resuscitation and assisted ventilation via endotracheal intubation or intermittent positive pressure ventilation, as well as i.v. calcium.

Dosage: Both i.v. and i.m. administration are appropriate. I.M. administration of the undiluted 50% solution results in therapeutic plasma levels in 60 minutes, whereas i.v. doses will provide a therapeutic level almost immediately. The rate of i.v. injection should generally not exceed 1.5 mL of a 10% concentration (or its equivalent)/minute, except in severe eclampsia with seizures.

Solutions for i.v. infusion must be diluted to a concentration of 20% or less prior to administration. The diluents commonly used are 5% Dextrose Injection USP and 0.9% Sodium Chloride Injection USP. Deep i.m. injection of the undiluted (50%) solution is appropriate for adults, but the solution should be diluted to a 20% concentration prior to such injection in children.

Magnesium Deficiency: In the treatment of mild magnesium deficiency, the usual adult dose is 1 g, equivalent to 8.12 mEq of magnesium (2 mL of the 50% solution) injected i.m. every 6 hours for 4 doses (equivalent to a total of 32.5 mEq of magnesium/24 hours). For severe hypomagnesemia, as much as 2 mEq (0.5 mL of the 50% solution)/kg of body weight may be given i.m. within a period of 4 hours if necessary. Alternatively, 5 g (approximately 40 mEq) can be added to 1 L of 5% Dextrose Injection USP or 0.9% Sodium Chloride Injection USP for slow i.v. infusion over a 3-hour period.

Total Parenteral Nutrition: In total parenteral nutrition, maintenance requirements for magnesium are not precisely known. The maintenance dose recommended for adults is 5 to 8 mEq magnesium/L of TPN solution; typical daily adult intake ranges from 10 to 24 mEq. For infants, the recommended intake ranges from 0.25 to 0.6 mEq/kg/day.

Eclampsia: In severe pre-eclampsia or eclampsia, the total initial dose is 10 to 14 g of magnesium sulfate. I.V., a dose of 4 to 5 g in 250 mL of 5% Dextrose Injection USP or 0.9% Sodium Chloride Injection USP may be infused. Simultaneously, i.m. doses of up to 10 g (10 mL of the undiluted 50% solution in each buttock) are given. Alternatively, the initial i.v. dose of 4 g may be given by diluting the 50% solution to a 10 or 20% concentration; the diluted fluid (40 mL of a 10% solution or 20 mL of a 20% solution) may then be injected i.v. over a period of 3 to 4 minutes. Subsequently, 4 to 5 g (8 to 10 mL of the 50% solution) are injected i.m. into alternate buttocks every 4 hours, depending on the continuing presence of the patellar reflex and adequate respiratory function. Therapy should continue until paroxysms cease. A serum magnesium level of 6 mg/100 mL is considered optimal for control of seizures. A total daily (24 hour) dose of 30 to 40 g should not be exceeded and less should be used if the patient is anuric.

Nephritic Seizures: In children with nephritic seizures, the 50% concentration should be diluted to a 20% solution for i.m. injection. The dose for children is 20 to 40 mg (0.1 to 0.2 mL of a 20% solution)/kg of body weight, administered i.m. as needed, to control seizures.

Stability and Storage: Store at controlled room temperature (15 to 30°C).

Parenteral drug products should be inspected visually for particulate matter and discoloration prior to administration, whenever solution and container permit.

Do not administer unless solution is clear and container is undamaged. Discard unused portion.

Supplied: Each mL contains: magnesium sulfate 500 mg. May contain sulfuric acid and/or sodium hydroxide for pH adjustment. The pH is 6.0 (5.5 to 7.0). The 50% concentration has an osmolarity of 4.06 mOsm/mL (calc.). The solution contains no bacteriostat, antimicrobial agent or added buffer (except for pH adjustment). Any unused portion remaining in container should be discarded within 24 hours of initial use. Ampuls of 10 mL, boxes of 25. Also supplied, syringes of 5 and 10 mL, boxes of 10.

MAGNEVIST®

Berlex Canada

Gadopentetate Dimeglumine

Contrast Enhancement Agent for Magnetic Resonance Imaging (MRI)

Pharmacology: Gadopentetate dimeglumine was developed as a contrast agent for diagnostic use in magnetic resonance imaging (MRI). Gadolinium is a rare earth element. Its ion (Gd^{+++}) has 7 unpaired electrons and, therefore, shows paramagnetic properties. Gd^{+++} has a strong effect on the hydrogen-proton spin-lattice relaxation time (T_1), which causes the observed contrast enhancement in MRI scans. By chelation of Gd^{+++} with diethylenetriamine pentaacetic acid (DTPA), a strongly paramagnetic, well-tolerated, stable complex (gadopentetate dimeglumine salt) is obtained.

Magnevist (cont'd)

The free gadolinium ion is unsuitable for clinical use due to high toxicity, however, the metal chelate is metabolically inert. The organic component of the chelate is not measurably metabolized and the metal does not dissociate. After i.v. injection of gadopentetate dimeglumine, the meglumine ion completely dissociates from the gadopentetate. The hydrophylic chelate is distributed only in the extracellular water and does not cross the intact blood-brain barrier. Gadopentetate is excreted unchanged in the urine. It is rapidly eliminated by the kidneys with a clearance identical to that of inulin (no tubular reabsorption).

Pharmacokinetics: The pharmacokinetic profile of i.v. administered gadopentetate dimeglumine in normal subjects conforms to a 2 compartment open model with a mean distribution half-life of about 0.2 hours and a mean elimination half-life of about 1.6 hours. Approximately 80% of the dose was excreted in the urine within 6 hours and 93% within 24 hours post injection of a 0.1 mmol/kg dose. Excretion in the feces amounted to <0.1% over 5 days. There was no detectable biotransformation, dissociation or decomposition of gadopentetate.

Gadopentetate dimeglumine has no pharmacodynamic effect when administered as indicated with the exception of slightly increased plasma osmolality.

Indications: By i.v. injection, for contrast enhancement during cranial and spinal MRI investigations in adults and children, to detect lesions associated with abnormal vascularity, or those thought to alter the blood-brain barrier.

Contraindications: Should not be administered to patients who are known or suspected of being hypersensitive to it.

Warnings: The decision to use gadopentetate dimeglumine must be made after careful evaluation of the risk-benefit in patients with a history of allergic disposition or bronchial asthma, since experience shows that these patients suffer more frequently than others from hypersensitivity reactions.

In very rare cases anaphylactoid reactions, including anaphylactic shock, may occur after i.v. injection of gadopentetate dimeglumine. It is important for prompt action in the event of such incidents to be familiar with the practice of emergency measures. To permit immediate countermeasures to be taken in emergencies, appropriate drugs and instruments (e.g., endotracheal tube and ventilator) should be readily available.

Deoxygenated sickle cell erythrocytes have been shown in in vitro studies to align perpendicular to a magnetic field which may result in vaso-occlusive complications in vivo. The enhancement of magnetic moment by gadopentetate dimeglumine may possibly potentiate sickle erythrocyte alignment. Gadopentetate dimeglumine in patients with sickle cell anemia and other hemoglobinopathies has not been studied.

No studies have been conducted in children with severe renal or hepatic dysfunction, clinically unstable or uncontrolled hypertension, or in premature infants.

MRI procedures which involve the use of gadopentetate dimeglumine by injection should be carried out by physicians who have the prerequisite training and a thorough knowledge of the particular procedure to be performed.

Precautions: General: Gadopentetate dimeglumine is to be administered strictly by i.v. injection. It will cause tissue irritation and pain if administered extravascularly or if it leaks interstitially.

A sweet taste may be experienced briefly by patients receiving a bolus injection of gadopentetate dimeglumine i.v.

Hemolytic States: Gadopentetate dimeglumine alters red blood cell morphology resulting in transient, slight, extravascular (splenic) hemolysis with increased serum iron and total bilirubin levels. Although this effect was of no clinical significance during clinical trials, caution is advised in patients with hepatic disease and/or hemolytic states.

Convulsive States: While there is no evidence suggesting that gadopentetate dimeglumine directly precipitates convulsion, the possibility that it may decrease the convulsive threshold in susceptible patients cannot be ruled out. Precautionary measures should be taken with patients predisposed to seizure, e.g., close monitoring and availability of injectable anticonvulsants (see Dosage).

Pregnancy: There are no studies on the use of gadopentetate dimeglumine in pregnant women. Gadopentetate dimeglumine should not be used during human pregnancy unless the potential benefit justifies the potential risk to the fetus.

Lactation: Transfer of gadopentetate dimeglumine into the milk of lactating mothers can occur. Thus breast-feeding should be interrupted for 24 hours postadministration of gadopentetate dimeglumine and the milk discarded during this period.

Geriatrics: No special precautions are required for elderly patients.

Adverse Effects: General: Most adverse reactions develop soon after injection, however the possibility of delayed reactions cannot be ruled out. The most frequently reported adverse reactions following administration of gadopentetate dimeglumine are shown in Table I.

Table I—Magnevist

Adverse Reactions	
Headache	8.7%*
in some cases severe	1.3%
Injection Site Discomfort	6.7%
Nausea	3.2%
Localized Pain in Other Parts of the Body (back, ear, eye, teeth)	2.8%
Hypersensitivity-type Skin and Mucosal Reactions	2.1%
Dizziness	1.5%
Vomiting	1.2%
Paresthesia	1.2%

*42.3% of all cases of headache were considered unrelated to gadopentetate dimeglumine administration.

Adverse reactions occurred in 11 of 319 (3.4%) pediatric patients receiving gadopentetate dimeglumine in clinical trials (headache, vasodilatation, dizziness, diarrhea, ear pain, tachycardia, fever, edema, seizure, vomiting, nausea and urticaria). This adverse reaction profile is consistent with the adverse reaction profile observed in adults.

Gadopentetate dimeglumine will cause tissue irritation and pain if administered extravascularly.

Transient increases or decreases in blood pressure may occur after the administration of gadopentetate dimeglumine. These changes are generally of little consequence although 3 clinically significant cases of hypotension have occurred 2 to 6 hours after gadopentetate dimeglumine injection. A relationship to the contrast medium could not be determined, however caution should be exercised by the patient when driving or operating machinery.

Serious or severe adverse effects associated with gadopentetate dimeglumine have been rare in clinical experience. Postmarketing anaphylactic reactions have been reported, but are very rare. Convulsions were reported in 3 patients with a history of seizures.

Laboratory Changes: Reversible mild elevations over baseline in serum iron and total bilirubin occur in most patients after receiving gadopentetate dimeglumine. These changes do not appear to be clinically relevant. Other disturbances in laboratory values (transient increases in liver function tests) have not been associated with the use of gadopentetate dimeglumine.

Adverse Drug Reaction Profile: The following adverse reactions, listed according to body system, have been reported after administration of gadopentetate dimeglumine.

Cardiovascular: hypotension, vasodilatation, pallor, phlebitis, nonspecific ECG changes, substernal pain, angina.

CNS: headache, dizziness, agitation, paresthesia, tinnitus, visual field defect, convulsions, hyperesthesia.

Gastrointestinal: nausea, vomiting, gastrointestinal distress, stomach pain, thirst, increased salivation, taste abnormality.

Respiratory: dry mouth, throat irritation, rhinorrhea, wheezing, sneezing, laryngismus, cough, dyspnea/apnea.

Cutaneous/Mucous Membranes: rash, sweating, urticaria, pruritus.

Miscellaneous: injection site discomfort (coldness, burning, warmth, pain), teeth pain, generalized weakness, fever, localized edema, tiredness, anaphylactoid reactions (characterized by cardiovascular, respiratory and cutaneous symptoms), conjunctivitis.

Laboratory Tests: transient elevation of serum iron and bilirubin levels.

The following other adverse events were reported. A causal relationship has neither been established nor refuted.

Cardiovascular: hypertension, tachycardia, syncope, death related to myocardial infarction or other undetermined causes.

CNS: diplopia, migraine, anxiety, drowsiness, nystagmus, stupor.

Gastrointestinal: constipation, diarrhea, anorexia.

Cutaneous/Mucous Membranes: facial edema, erythema, epidermal necrolysis.

Miscellaneous: localized pain (back, ear, eye).

Overdose: Symptoms and Treatment: In the event of inadvertent overdosage or in the case of severely impaired renal function, gadopentetate dimeglumine can be removed from the body by extracorporeal hemodialysis.

Dosage: Special preparation of the patient for examination with gadopentetate meglumine is not required; however, precautionary measures should be taken with patients predisposed to seizure, e.g., close monitoring and availability of injectable anticonvulsants (see Precautions). The usual safety rules for MRI (e.g., exclusion of ferromagnetic vascular clips) must be observed.

Young children, infants and neonates may require sedation prior to undergoing an MRI examination, in order to eliminate movement artifacts.

The following dosage guidelines apply to adults and children (including neonates and infants):

Recommended Dose: 0.2 mL/kg (0.1 mmol/kg).

Route of Administration: i.v. (into a large vein, if possible).

Rate of Administration: 10 mL/min or as a bolus injection at 10 mL/15 sec.

Maximum Total Dose: 20 mL.

To ensure complete injection of the contrast medium, the injection should be followed by a 5 mL normal saline flush.

If strong clinical suspicion of an intracranial or intraspinal lesion persists, despite a normal MRI scan, the diagnostic yield of the examination may be increased by giving another injection of gadopentetate dimeglumine equivalent to the original total dose within 30 minutes and performing MRI again.

Gadopentetate dimeglumine should not be drawn into the syringe until immediately before use. Any unused portion must be discarded upon completion of the procedure.

T_1-weighted scanning sequences are particularly suitable for contrast-enhanced examinations.

Gadopentetate dimeglumine has been shown to be effective in a wide range of field strengths (0.14 to 1.5 Tesla).

Important Note: The imaging procedure should be completed within **1 hour** since optimal contrast is generally observed in cranial investigations within 27 minutes following injection of gadopentetate dimeglumine and in spinal investigations during the early postadministration phase (10 to 30 minutes).

In neonates and infants, optimal CNS contrast has been observed to persist for several hours after gadopentetate dimeglumine administration.

Supplied: Each mL of sterile, clear colorless to slightly yellow aqueous i.v. injection solution, contains: gadopentetic acid dimeglumine salt 469.01 mg (equivalent to 0.5 mmol/mL). Nonmedicinal ingredients: diethylenetriamine pentaacetic acid and meglumine. Osmolality: 1 960 mOsm/kg H_2O at 37°C. Single dose vials of 10, 15 and 20 mL packaged in individual cartons. Store at 15 to 30°C and protect from light.

Reviewed 1998

MAJEPTIL® Ⓟ

Rhône-Poulenc Rorer

Thioproperazine Mesylate

Neuroleptic

Pharmacology: Thioproperazine is a potent neuroleptic with antipsychotic properties.

Thioproperazine has a marked cataleptic and antiapomorphine activity associated with relatively slight sedative, hypothermic and spasmolytic effects. It is virtually without antiserotonin and hypotensive action and has no antihistaminic property.

Indications: All types of acute and chronic schizophrenia, including those which did not respond to the usual neuroleptics; manic syndromes.

Contraindications: Comatose or depressive states including those induced by CNS depressants; Parkinson's disease; blood dyscrasias; in patients with spastic diseases and in senile patients with pre-existing Parkinson-like symptoms; in children under 3 years of age and in patients generally sensitive to phenothiazines.

Precautions: Before starting treatment with thioproperazine, it is recommended to ascertain that the cardiovascular system and the liver and kidney functions are unimpaired.

Treatment should be initiated preferably by the oral route with a low initial dosage, increased progressively.

Since thioproperazine may potentiate the action of general anesthetics, morphine-like analgesics, barbiturates, alcohol, and other CNS depressants, care should be exercised when these agents are given with it.

The antiemetic effect of thioproperazine may obscure symptoms such as vomiting and nausea, normally associated with some types of organic disease (intestinal obstruction and brain tumor).

Thiproperazine should be used cautiously in patients with a history of seizures.

Pregnancy: The safety of thioproperazine in pregnant women has not been clearly established, therefore it should not be used during the first trimester of pregnancy.

Warnings: Treatment should be discontinued if a severe neurologic syndrome is observed, especially when hypertonia is accompanied by dysphagia and/or marked autonomic disturbances.

Adverse Effects: Neuromuscular (extrapyramidal) reactions are the most frequently observed. They are usually dose-related and generally subside when the dose is reduced or when the drug is temporarily discontinued. Administration of an antiparkinsonian agent is usually, but not always, effective in reversing the neuromuscular reactions associated with this and other phenothiazines.

Anxiety or apathy, elation or depression, drowsiness and/or insomnia are not infrequently observed.

Occasional disturbances of accommodation, rare cases of headache and exceptionally, cases of nausea and vomiting, constipation or diarrhea have been reported. Lacrimation, sialorrhea and profuse sweating are more frequent. Oliguria may occur.

Overdose: Symptoms: Overdosage may result in severe extrapyramidal symptoms with dysphagia, marked sialorrhea, persistent and rapidly increasing hyperthermia, pulmonary syndrome, state of shock with pallor and profuse sweating, which may be followed by collapse and coma.

Treatment: There is no specific antidote. When mild symptoms are present (e.g., in regular therapy) corrective measures are usually sufficient:

Administration of thioproperazine should be discontinued.

Against Dyskinetic Manifestations: An antiparkinsonian or chloral hydrate, but the latter should be used with caution, as it may further depress the respiration.

In the presence of severe symptoms (e.g., in cases of overdosage) in addition to the above corrective measures, the following supportive treatment should be carried out:

Gastric Lavage: Because of the antiemetic effect of thioproperazine, centrally acting emetics will remain ineffective.

In cases of severe hypotension or collapse: norepinephrine and adrenocortical hormones to restore blood pressure. Since phenothiazines are known to reverse the pressor action of epinephrine, the latter should **not** be used as it may further lower blood pressure.

Against Respiratory Depression: oxygen inhalation and, if necessary, tracheal intubation.

Against Dehydration: i.v. infusion of dextrose in normal saline.

Against Respiratory Infection: broad spectrum antibiotics.

Dosage: Initial Treatment: Adults: Oral route (usual route of administration): It is recommended to start treatment at a low dosage of about 5 mg per day in a single dose or in divided doses. This initial dosage is gradually increased by the same amount every 2 to 3 days until the usual effective dosage of 30 to 40 mg per day is reached. In some cases higher dosages of 90 mg or more per day, are necessary to control the psychotic manifestations.

Children: Oral Route: In children over 10 years: Start treatment with a daily dosage of 1 to 3 mg following the method of treatment described for adults.

Maintenance Therapy: Adults and Children: Dosage should be reduced gradually to the lowest effective level, which may be as low as a few mg per day and maintained as long as necessary.

Other Method of Treatment: Occasionally, thioproperazine is prescribed in the form of discontinuous treatment at 5 or 10 mg, 3 times a day, until the onset of severe extrapyramidal symptoms. Then, treatment is discontinued until spontaneous full recovery from these symptoms. The same course of therapy is repeated for at least 3 consecutive treatments. Discontinuous treatment should be reserved for resistant cases, and performed in hospitalized patients, under close medical supervision.

Supplied: Each scored orange tablet contains: thioproperazine base (as the mesylate) 10 mg. Nonmedicinal ingredients: acetic anhydride, calcium phosphate, carnauba wax, cellulose, colloidal silicon dioxide, diethyl phthalate, FD&C Yellow No 6 aluminum lake, magnesium stearate, polacrilin potassium, sodium oleate, titane oxide and zein. Tartrazine-free. Bottles of 100 and 500.

(Shown in Product Recognition Section)

MALARONE™ Ⓟ

Glaxo Wellcome

Atovaquone—Proguanil HCl

Antimalarial

Pharmacology: The constituents of Malarone, interfere with 2 different pathways involved in the biosynthesis of pyrimidines required for nucleic acid replication. Atovaquone is a selective inhibitor of parasite mitochondrial electron transport. Proguanil exerts its effect primarily by means of the metabolite cycloguanil, a dihydrofolate reductase inhibitor. Inhibition of dihydrofolate reductase in the malaria parasite disrupts deoxythymidylate synthesis. These two mechanisms are believed to be the prime explanation of the synergy observed when used in combination.

Pharmacokinetics: There are no pharmacokinetic interactions between atovaquone and proguanil at the recommended dose. Tables I, II and III summarize a number of the pharmacokinetic parameters for atovaquone and proguanil.

of atovaquone in children compared to adults. This is also shown by the 2-fold lower elimination half-life of atovaquone in children compared to adults. Atovaquone clearance is also higher in oriental adults compared to European adults.

Absorption: Atovaquone is a highly lipophilic compound with low aqueous solubility. Dietary fat taken with atovaquone increases the rate and extent of absorption. When taken with a standard breakfast containing 23 g of fat, AUC was increased 2 to 3 times and C_{max} 5 times compared to the fasting state. Patients should take Malarone tablets with food (see Dosage).

Proguanil is rapidly and extensively absorbed regardless of food intake.

Distribution: Atovaquone is highly protein bound (>99%) but does not displace other highly protein bound drugs in vitro, indicating that significant drug interactions arising from displacement are unlikely. Proguanil is 75% protein bound. In human plasma the binding of atovaquone and proguanil were unaffected by the presence of the other.

Metabolism: There is no evidence that atovaquone is metabolized and there is negligible excretion of atovaquone in urine

Table I—Malarone

Atovaquone, Proguanil and Cycloguanil Geometric Means and Point Estimates for Combined Versus Separate Malarone Tablets in Adults

Parameter	Geometric Means Combined	Geometric Means Separate	Combined/Separate ratio×100 (%)	90% Confidence Interval (%)
Atovaquone				
AUC_{0-24} (h·µg/mL)[a]	193	180	108	(100, 116)
$AUC_{0-\infty}$ (h·µg/mL)[b]	510	549	93	(79, 110)
C_{max} (µg/mL)	11.5	10.5	110	(102, 118)
$t_{1/2}$ (h)	60.5	59.7	103	(96, 111)
Proguanil (PG)				
AUC_{0-24} (h·ng/mL)[a]	5819	6296	92	(86, 99)
$AUC_{0-\infty}$ (h·ng/mL)[b]	5998	6437	93	(84, 103)
C_{max} (ng/mL)	509	548	93	(87, 99)
$t_{1/2}$ (h)	14.5	13.7	106	(100, 113)
Cycloguanil (CG)				
AUC_{0-24} (h·ng/mL)[a]	1187	1297	92	(86, 98)
$AUC_{0-\infty}$ (h·ng/mL)[b]	1213	1313	92	(83, 103)
C_{max} (ng/mL)	94	97	97	(92, 102)
$t_{1/2}$ (h)	11.8	11.1	106	(93, 120)
AUC_{CG}/AUC_{PG}	0.21	0.22	94	(86, 103)

[a] AUC_{0-24}: Trapezoidal area under plasma curve from last dose until 24h postdose.
[b] $AUC_{0-\infty}$: Trapezoidal area under plasma curve from last dose until final measured concentration, extrapolated from last concentration to infinity, corrected for concentration predose. At true steady-state, this is equivalent to $AUC_{0-\infty}$ for a single dose.

The pharmacokinetics of atovaquone, proguanil and cycloguanil were characterized following daily oral administration of separate tablets of atovaquone and proguanil HCl in 9 children (mean±SD of 9±2 years of age) for 3 consecutive days. Administration of tablets was based on mg/kg body weight basis (see Table II).

Table II—Malarone

Administration of Tablets Based on mg/kg Body Weight Basis

Body Weight (kg)	Atovaquone Dose (mg)	Proguanil Base Dose (mg)	Proguanil HCl Dose (mg)
11 to 20	250	85.6	100
21 to 30	500	171.2	200
31 to 40	750	256.8	300

The lower atovaquone AUC and C_{max} values in Thai children compared to European adults is related to a higher clearance

with the parent drug being predominantly (>90%) eliminated unchanged in feces.

Proguanil is partially metabolized with less than 40% being excreted unchanged in the urine. Its metabolites cycloguanil and 4-chlorophenylbiguanide are also excreted in the urine.

Elimination: The elimination half-life of atovaquone is about 2 to 3 days in adults and 1 to 2 days in children 6 to 12 years of age.

The elimination half-lives of proguanil and cycloguanil are about 12 to 15 hours in both adults and children 6 to 12 years of age.

Indications: For the treatment of acute, uncomplicated P. falciparum malaria when oral treatment is appropriate.

Malarone has been shown to be effective in areas where P. falciparum may be resistant to some other antimalarials.

The indication is based on 5 controlled clinical studies conducted in 466 patients (adults and children) receiving concurrent atovaquone and proguanil at the recommended dose (see Dosage). Most of the patients were residents of malaria

Table III—Malarone

Atovaquone, Proguanil and Cycloguanil Pharmacokinetic Parameters (Mean, Range) in Thai Children (9 children in ages ranging from 6 to 12 years)

Parameter	Atovaquone	Proguanil	Cycloguanil
$AUC_{0-\infty}$[a,b]	162 (56-413)	4 646 (2436-6132)	787 (138-1442)
C_{max}[c]	5.1 (2.1-7.8)	306 (152-462)	44 (15-101)
$t_{1/2}$ (h)	32 (23-50)	14.9 (9.8-19.4)	14.6 (11.8-18.2)
Clearance/F (mL/h/kg)	162 (41-296)	1 600 (1112-3421)	
t_{max} (h)	11 (6-24.1)	8 (6-12.1)	7.5 (6-12.1)

[a] $AUC_{0-\infty}$ units h·µg/mL for atovaquone, h·ng/mL for proguanil and cycloguanil.
[b] $AUC_{0-\infty}$: Trapezoidal area under the plasma curve from last dose until final measured concentration, extrapolated from last concentration to infinity, corrected for concentration predose. At true steady-state, this is equivalent to $AUC_{0-\infty}$ for a single dose.
[c] C_{max} units: µg/mL for atovaquone, ng/mL for proguanil and cycloguanil.

Malarone (cont'd)

endemic areas and may have had previous malaria infections that could have conferred a degree of immunity.

Contraindications: Individuals with known hypersensitivity to atovaquone or proguanil or any component of the formulation (see Supplied).

Warnings: Malarone has not been evaluated for the treatment of cerebral malaria or other severe manifestations of complicated malaria including hyperparasitemia, pulmonary edema or renal failure.

In the event of recrudescent infections due to P. falciparum, patients should be treated with a different antimalarial.

Because absorption of atovaquone may be reduced in patients with severe diarrhea, or gastrointestinal disorders, alternative therapy should be considered in such patients. However, if Malarone were to be used in these patients parasitemia should be closely monitored.

Parasitemia should be closely monitored in patients receiving concurrent rifampin or metoclopramide (see Precautions, Drug Interactions).

Precautions: General: Patients who have a history of epilepsy or psychiatric illness should take Malarone with caution (see Adverse Effects).

Absorption of orally administered atovaquone is significantly reduced when fasting. Therefore alternative therapy with other agents should be considered for patients who are not able to consume food.

Geriatrics: Since no studies have been carried out in the elderly, no special precautions or dosage adjustments can be recommended in this age group.

Pregnancy: There are no studies in pregnant women. Malarone should be considered for use in pregnancy only if the expected benefit to the mother justifies the potential risk to the fetus and mother.

There is no evidence of teratogenicity in animal reproductive studies with atovaquone alone. Studies in rats on proguanil alone or in combination with atovaquone show no evidence of teratogenic effects. However, animal studies are not always predictive of human response.

Lactation: It is not recommended that mothers receiving Malarone breast-feed their babies. It is not known whether atovaquone is excreted in human milk. Proguanil is excreted in human milk in small quantities. In a rat study, the atovaquone concentrations in milk were 30% of the concurrent atovaquone concentrations in maternal plasma.

The amount of atovaquone or proguanil found in human breast milk would not provide adequate treatment for the infant against malaria.

Children: Malarone is not recommended for treatment of children under 3 years of age. Table IV shows the number of children in various age groups who were treated with Malarone in clinical studies.

Table IV—Malarone

Number of Children in Various Age Groups who Were Treated with Malarone

Age (Years)	Number
<3.0	None
3.0 to <7	58
7.0 to <10	27
10.0 to <13	25
13.0 to <17	12
Total	**122**

Renal Impairment: Malarone has not been specifically studied in patients with renal impairment.

The lack of renal elimination of atovaquone implies that renal failure would have little effect on atovaquone elimination. Despite the known renal elimination of proguanil and cycloguanil, clinically significant accumulation is unlikely given the short duration of treatment. To date, no special precautions or dosage adjustment for patients with renal impairment have been identified.

Hepatic Impairment: Malarone has not been specifically studied in patients with hepatic impairment.

The metabolic route of elimination of proguanil is via the liver. Atovaquone elimination is substantially liver dependent. Clinically significant accumulation of proguanil and atovaquone is unlikely given the short duration of treatment. To date, no special precautions or dosage adjustment for patients with hepatic impairment have been identified.

Drug Interactions: Parasitemia should be closely monitored in patients receiving tetracycline, rifampin or metoclopramide concurrently with Malarone. Concomitant treatment with metoclopramide and rifampin have been associated with significant decreases in plasma concentrations of atovaquone. Increased clearance of atovaquone when coadministered with tetracycline, leading to 40% lower atovaquone concentrations has been observed.

Malarone should not be administered in combination with other antimalarial drugs. Interactions between Malarone and other antimalarial drugs have not been studied.

Atovaquone is highly protein bound (>99%) but does not displace other highly protein bound drugs in vitro, indicating that significant drug interactions arising from displacement are unlikely.

Adverse Effects: As Malarone contains atovaquone and proguanil, the type and severity of adverse reactions associated with each of the compounds may be expected. The most common adverse experiences reported while receiving treatment with atovaquone are: rash, nausea, diarrhea, headache, vomiting, fever and insomnia. The most common adverse experiences reported while receiving treatment with proguanil are: anorexia, nausea, vomiting, abdominal pain, diarrhea, mouth ulcers, stomatitis and headache. At the doses employed for the treatment of malaria, adverse reactions have generally been mild and of limited duration. There has been no evidence of increased toxicity following concurrent administration of the two compounds.

Of the 7 severe or treatment limiting adverse experiences reported in clinical trials with atovaquone and proguanil, 3 were considered to be treatment related; two were reports of nausea and/or vomiting and 1, a report of an anaphylactic reaction. Two subjects receiving atovaquone/proguanil had seizures; in 1 of these cases the patient successfully continued treatment. Both subjects had a prior history of seizures and the investigators did not consider the events to be exacerbated by Malarone treatment. During clinical trials, 2 subjects receiving atovaquone monotherapy experienced psychiatric symptoms. One subject had a history of psychiatric illness and the other a history of drug and alcohol abuse. Studies of this size and design would only be able to detect adverse events at a rate of 1:150 (95% CI).

Table V provides a summary of the adverse events reported in clinical trials with Malarone tablets. Abdominal pain, headache, anorexia, nausea, vomiting, diarrhea and coughing were the most commonly reported adverse experiences.

A similar profile of clinical adverse events was reported in children with malaria treated with atovaquone and proguanil in phase III trials as occurred in the adult studies.

Abnormalities in liver function tests (elevated bilirubin and transaminases) were reversible and not associated with untoward clinical events.

Overdose: Symptoms and Treatment: There have been no reports of overdosage with Malarone. In cases of suspected overdosage, symptomatic and supportive therapy should be given as appropriate.

Dosage: The daily dose should be taken with food or a milky drink at the same time each day (see Precautions). In the event of vomiting within 1 hour of dosing, a repeat dose should be taken. Should vomiting continue, alternative therapy should be considered or the patient's parasitemia should be monitored.

Adults: 4 tablets as a single dose for 3 consecutive days.

Children (see Precautions, Children): See Table VI.

Clearance of atovaquone and proguanil following oral administration of Malarone is dependent on body weight. Although the C_{max} and AUC for atovaquone and proguanil were lower in children than in adults, the clinical cure rates in children were comparable to those seen in adults.

Table VI—Malarone

Dosage—Children

Body Weight	Dosage
11-20 kg	1 tablet daily for 3 consecutive days.
21-30 kg	2 tablets as a single dose for 3 consecutive days.
31-40 kg	3 tablets as a single dose for 3 consecutive days.
>40 kg	Dose as for adults.

Supplied: Each pink, round biconvex film-coated tablet, branded GX CM3, contains: atovaquone 250 mg and proguanil base 85.6 mg (equivalent to proguanil HCl 100 mg). Nonmedicinal ingredients: low-substituted hydroxypropyl cellulose, macrogol 400, magnesium stearate, microcrystalline cellulose, poloxamer 188, polyethylene glycol, povidone K30, sodium starch glycollate; film-coating suspension (pink color

Table V—Malarone

Adverse Events Considered by Investigators to be Attributable to Study Medication, Occurring in ≥1% of Adults with Malaria in Completed Phase III Studies

Adverse Event	Malarone (n=304)	PYR+S (n=81)	MFQ (n=91)	ADQ (n=71)	C±PYR+S* (n=55)
Gastrointestinal					
Abdominal Pain	15% (45)	21% (17)	0%	8% (6)	0%
Vomiting	12% (35)	15% (12)	0%	25% (18)	2% (1)
Nausea	11% (32)	14% (11)	2% (2)	21% (15)	2% (1)
Diarrhea	8% (25)	11% (9)	0%	7% (5)	2% (1)
Anorexia	5% (15)	5% (4)	1% (1)	13% (9)	2% (1)
Hepatomegaly	2% (6)	6% (5)	0%	0%	0%
Constipation	1% (2)	0%	0%	0%	0%
Dyspepsia	1% (2)	0%	0%	0%	0%
Nervous/Psychiatric					
Headache	8% (25)	31% (25)	1% (1)	7% (5)	0%
Dizziness	3% (8)	11% (9)	0%	11% (8)	2% (1)
Insomnia	1% (3)	4% (3)	0%	25% (18)	0%
Body as a Whole					
Asthenia	7% (20)	16% (13)	0%	3% (2)	0%
Back Pain	1% (2)	4% (3)	0%	0%	0%
Abnormal Liver Function Tests					
ALT	6% (18)	6% (5)	7% (6)	0%	0%
AST	5% (16)	5% (4)	7% (6)	0%	0%
Bilirubin	2% (7)	0%	1% (1)	0%	0%
Cardiovascular					
Hypotension, postural	2% (6)	17% (14)	0%	0%	0%
Palpitations	2% (5)	0%	0%	6% (4)	0%
Cutaneous					
Pruritus	2% (6)	2% (2)	0%	46% (33)	0%
Rash	1% (2)	0%	0%	0%	0%
Musculoskeletal					
Myalgia	3% (8)	6% (5)	0%	4% (3)	0%
Erythropoietic					
Splenomegaly	1% (4)	2% (2)	0%	0%	0%
Respiratory					
Coughing	1% (3)	0%	0%	2% (2)	0%

Legend: PYR=pyrimethamine, S=sulfadoxine, MFQ=mefloquine, ADQ=amodiaquine, C=chloroquine.
*Data for both comparator groups of chloroquine alone plus pyrimethamine and sulfadoxine.

concentrate OY-S-24972): macrogol 400, methylhydroxypropylcellulose, red iron oxide and titanium dioxide. Blister packs of 12. Store between 15 and 30°C.

(Shown in Product Recognition Section)

New Product 1998

MALTLEVOL®
MALTLEVOL®-12
Carter Horner

Multivitamins

Dietary Supplement

Indications: As a multivitamin dietary supplement and for iron deficiency anemia.

Contraindications: Hemosiderosis, hemochromatosis, hemolytic anemia.

Precautions: Oral iron preparations may aggravate existing peptic ulcer, regional enteritis and ulcerative colitis. Iron compounds taken orally can impair the absorption of tetracycline antibiotics. Antacids given concomitantly with iron compounds decrease iron absorption.

Adverse Effects: Rarely, in iron-sensitive patients, mild gastrointestinal upsets may occur.

Overdose: Symptoms and Treatment: Symptomatic.

Dosage: 15 mL 3 times daily before meals.

Supplied: Maltlevol: Each 45 mL (maximum daily dose) contains: vitamin A 5 000 IU, vitamin D 400 IU, vitamin E 25 IU, vitamin B_1 2 mg, riboflavin 2 mg, vitamin B_6 1.5 mg, niacinamide 10 mg, iron 108 mg as ferric ammonium citrate in a dark brown, opaque, viscous sherry wine base with malt taste. Nonmedicinal ingredients: alcohol, caramel color, citric acid, flavors, paraben, polysorbate, pure malt extract, simethicone emulsion, sodium alginate, sodium benzoate, sucrose and tocopherols. Sodium hydroxide to adjust pH. pH: 5.4 to 5.6. Alcohol: 15%. Energy: 41 kJ (9.8 kcal)/5 mL. Sodium: <1 mmol (5 mg)/15 mL. Gluten- and tartrazine-free. Bottles of 350 mL.

Maltlevol-12: Each 45 mL (maximum daily dose) contains: vitamin B_{12} 14 μg, vitamin A 6 000 IU, vitamin B_1, 4.5 mg, riboflavin 3 mg, vitamin B_6 3 mg, niacinamide 30 mg, vitamin D 400 IU, vitamin E 25 IU, iron 108 mg as ferric ammonium citrate in a caramel brown, translucent, sweet base of sherry wine. Nonmedicinal ingredients: alcohol, caramel color, citric acid, flavors, parabens, polysorbate, simethicone emulsion, sodium cyclamate, sodium hydrogen phosphate, sorbitol, sucrose and tocopherol. Sodium hydroxide and hydrochloric acid to adjust pH. pH: 4.4 to 4.6. Alcohol: 16%. Energy: 32.76 kJ (7.8 kcal)/5 mL. Sodium: <1 mmol (12 mg)/15 mL. Gluten- and tartrazine-free. Bottles of 350 mL.

MALTLEVOL®-M
Carter Horner

Multivitamins—Minerals

Nutritional Supplement

Indications: For nutritional reinforcement; pre- and postoperatively and during pregnancy and lactation.

Contraindications, Precautions and Adverse Effects: See Maltlevol/Maltlevol 12.

Overdose: Symptoms and Treatment: Treatment is symptomatic.

Dosage: 1 tablet daily or as prescribed.

Supplied: Each lemon yellow, film coated, oblong, biconvex tablet with rounded ends and intagliated Maltlevol-M on one side, contains: vitamin A 5 000 IU, vitamin D 400 IU, vitamin E 25 IU, ascorbic acid 150 mg, vitamin B_1, 3 mg, riboflavin 1 mg, vitamin B_6 1 mg, vitamin B_{12} 3 μg, niacinamide 10 mg, iron (as ferrous sulfate) 4 mg, calcium (as dibasic calcium phosphate) 161 mg, phosphorus (as dibasic calcium phosphate) 125 mg and copper (as cupric sulfate) 1 mg. Nonmedicinal ingredients: alumina, cellulose, D&C Yellow No. 10, FD&C Blue No. 2, FD&C Yellow No. 6, glycerin, magnesium stearate, povidone, propylene glycol, starch (corn) and titanium dioxide. May contain traces of peanut oil. Energy: 0.4 kJ (0.1 kcal). Tartrazine-free. Bottles of 60.

(Shown in Product Recognition Section)

MANDELAMINE®
Parke-Davis

Methenamine Mandelate

Urinary Anti-infective

Supplied: Each brown, film-coated tablet contains: methenamine mandelate 500 mg. Nonmedicinal ingredients: calcium stearate, isopropyl alcohol, povidone, silica and stearic acid; coating: candelilla wax, hydroxypropylmethylcellulose, opaspray brown and propylene glycol. Energy: 0 kcal. Gluten-, lactose-, paraben-, sodium-, sulfite- and tartrazine-free. Bottles of 100.

(Shown in Product Recognition Section)

MANDOL® Ⓟ
Lilly

Cefamandole Nafate

Antibiotic

Pharmacology: Cefamandole, a semisynthetic cephalosporin antibiotic, possesses properties similar to other members of this group, but has a broader spectrum of activity particularly with respect to the treatment of Gram-negative bacillary infections.

Cefamandole has been shown to be active against the following organisms in vitro:

Gram-positive: β-hemolytic and other strains of streptococci including S. pneumoniae (many strains of S. faecalis are resistant), Staphylococci, both penicillin-resistant and sensitive including S. epidermidis and many methicillin-resistant strains.

Gram-negative: H. influenzae including ampicillin-resistant strains. E. coli. Enterobacter sp. (many strains of E. cloacae are resistant). K. pneumoniae. P. mirabilis. Indole-positive Proteus sp., including P. morganii, P. rettgeri and some strains of P. vulgaris. Salmonella sp. including S. typhosa. Serratia sp. (many strains of S. marcescens and other Serratia sp. are resistant).

Anaerobic Organisms: Bacteroides, Clostridia, Peptococci, Peptostreptococci.

High concentrations of cefamandole may be required for clinical efficacy against some strains of Proteus, Enterobacter, Serratia, and Bacteroides.

Pseudomonas organisms are resistant to cefamandole.

β-Lactamase Stability: Cefamandole is resistant to hydrolysis by β-lactamase from S. aureus (penicillinase), and by β-lactamases (sometimes referred to as cephalosporinases) from certain members of the Enterobacteriacae family.

Susceptibility testing continues to be the most effective method to determine the usefulness of a specific antibiotic in treating an infection.

The O-formyl group of cefamandole nafate is rapidly hydrolyzed to cefamandole sodium when a solution is prepared using an appropriate diluent. The sodium carbonate in Mandol enhances the hydrolysis rate and does not affect cefamandole serum concentrations after i.v. or i.m. administration. In vivo studies have demonstrated that cefamandole sodium is the major circulating antibiotic (85 to 89% of total plasma concentration). No apparent differences in cefamandole serum concentration and total urinary excretion were observed when cefamandole nafate was compared with cefamandole sodium.

Cefamandole nafate i.m. administration to normal subjects resulted in detectable cefamandole concentrations within 15 minutes. Mean peak concentrations of approximately 13 and 25 μg/mL were attained after 0.5 and 1.0 g i.m. doses, respectively. The time to achieve peak concentrations ranged from 30 to 120 minutes. Cefamandole was excreted in urine, with approximately 43 to 77% of the dose being recovered in 0 to 8 hours. Results for cefamandole disposition were comparable between adult patients and infants or children whose ages ranged from 3 months to 13 years, respectively.

I.V. administration of a single 1 g cefamandole nafate dose resulted in a mean cefamandole serum concentration of 139 μg/mL at 10 minutes. This concentration declined to 0.8 μg/mL at 4 hours. Following single doses of 2, 3 and 4 g, serum concentrations were 240, 533 and 666 μg/mL respectively at 10 minutes and these declined to 2.2, 2.9 and 3.9 μg/mL respectively at 4 hours. Assayable concentrations were present for 8 hours after 2 and 4 g doses. Multiple dose studies performed on normal subjects receiving 4 g of cefamandole nafate on various regimens for 4 or 5 days or even longer periods produced no evidence of accumulation.

Cefamandole's half-life is dependent on the administration route, e.g., 34 minutes and 59 minutes after i.v. and i.m. administration, respectively.

Cefamandole is excreted by glomerular filtration as well as by active tubular secretion. Since 65 to 80% of an i.m. or i.v. dose is excreted over an 8 hour period, high urinary concentrations result, i.e., an average of 359 μg/mL following a 500 mg i.m. dose and 816 μg/mL after a 1 g i.v. dose. Probenecid slows tubular excretion and doubles the peak serum concentration and the duration of measurable serum concentrations.

In the presence of renal impairment, urinary excretion of cefamandole is slower. A study comparing 14 patients with normal kidney function to 9 patients with impaired renal function showed that, after a 500 mg i.m. dose, total urinary excretion values over 7.5 hours were significantly lower in the patients with renal impairment. Following a 1 g dose, a difference was still apparent but considered to be not significant. In one study, serum half-life of cefamandole in patients with normal renal function averaged 1.7 hours, whereas the average half-life in patients with varying degrees of kidney impairment (serum creatinine >1.6 mg/100 mL) was 3 hours. On the basis of these data, and because cefamandole is excreted almost exclusively by the kidneys, the dosage should be adjusted according to the degree of renal impairment.

The antibiotic reaches therapeutic concentrations in pleural and joint fluids and in bile and bone.

Indications: Cefamandole may be indicated in the treatment of the following infections caused by susceptible organisms: lower respiratory tract infections such as pneumonia and pulmonary complications resulting from cystic fibrosis; urinary tract infections; septicemia; soft tissue and postsurgical infections such as peritonitis, cellulitis, abscesses, wound infections; bone and joint infections.

Perform appropriate culture and susceptibility studies. On the basis of clinical judgment and anticipated bacteriological findings, therapy may be instituted before results of susceptibility studies are obtained. Antibiotic treatment may be modified once these results become available.

Contraindications: Hypersensitivity to cephalosporin antibiotics.

Warnings: Before therapy with cefamandole is instituted, careful inquiry should be made concerning previous hypersensitivity reactions to cephalosporins, penicillins or other drugs. Cephalosporin C derivatives should be given with caution to penicillin-sensitive patients.

Antibiotics including cefamandole should be administered with caution, and then only when absolutely necessary, to any patient who has demonstrated some form of allergy, particularly to drugs.

As is the case with all new drugs, patients should be followed carefully so that adverse reactions or unusual manifestations of drug idiosyncrasy may be detected. If an allergic reaction to cefamandole occurs, the drug should be discontinued and the patient treated with the usual agents (e.g., epinephrine, antihistamines, pressor amines or corticosteroids).

In newborn infants, accumulation of cephalosporin-class antibiotics (with a resulting prolongation of drug half-life) has been reported.

Pseudomembranous colitis has been reported with virtually all broad-spectrum antibiotics, including cefamandole. Therefore, it is important to consider its diagnosis in patients administered cefamandole who develop diarrhea. Such colitis may range in severity from mild to life-threatening.

Treatment with broad-spectrum antibiotics including cefamandole may alter the normal flora of the colon and may permit overgrowth of clostridia. Studies indicate that a toxin produced by C. difficile is one primary cause of antibiotic-associated colitis.

Mild cases of pseudomembranous colitis usually respond to drug discontinuance alone. In moderate to severe cases, management should include sigmoidoscopy, appropriate bacteriologic studies, and fluid, electrolyte, and protein supplementation. When the colitis does not improve after the administration of cefamandole has been discontinued, or when it is severe, consideration should be given to the administration of oral vancomycin.

Precautions: *Pregnancy:* Cefamandole's safety in the treatment of infections during pregnancy has not been established. Therefore, if the drug's administration to pregnant patients is considered necessary, weigh the potential benefits against the possible hazards to the fetus.

Although cefamandole rarely produces alterations in kidney function, evaluation of renal status is recommended, especially in seriously ill patients receiving high doses. Place

Mandol (cont'd)

patients with impaired renal function on the special dosage schedule (see Dosage), because doses in these individuals are likely to produce excessive serum concentrations.

Studies suggest that the concurrent use of potent diuretics such as furosemide and ethacrynic acid may increase the risk of renal toxicity with cephalosporins. Nephrotoxicity has been reported following concomitant administration of aminoglycoside antibiotics and cephalosporins.

In a few patients receiving cefamandole, nausea, vomiting and vasomotor instability with hypotension and peripheral vasodilation occurred following ingestion of ethanol. These effects are probably due to the inhibition of acetaldehyde dehydrogenase which causes accumulation of acetaldehyde when ethanol is administered concomitantly.

Hypoprothrombinemia, with or without bleeding, has been reported rarely, but it has been promptly reversed by administration of vitamin K. Such episodes usually have occurred in elderly, debilitated, or otherwise compromised patients with deficient stores of vitamin K. Treatment of such individuals with antibiotics possessing Gram-negative and/or anaerobic activity is thought to alter the number and/or type of intestinal bacterial flora, with consequent reduction in synthesis of vitamin K. Prophylactic administration of vitamin K may be indicated in such patients, especially when procedures such as intestinal sterilization are performed.

Erythropenia and decreases in hematocrit values and hemoglobin concentrations have been observed.

Prolonged use of cefamandole may result in the overgrowth of nonsusceptible organisms. Constant patient observation is essential. If superinfection occurs during therapy, take appropriate measures.

Some individuals have developed positive direct Coombs' test during treatment with cephalosporin antibiotics.

In patients treated with cefamandole, a false positive reaction for glucose in the urine may occur with Benedict's or Fehling's solution or with Clinitest tablets but not with Tes-Tape (Glucose Enzymatic Test Strip USP). A false positive test for protein in the urine can occur with acid or denaturization precipitation tests.

Adverse Effects: Hypersensitivity: Maculopapular rash, urticaria, eosinophilia, anaphylaxis and drug fever have been reported. These reactions are most likely to occur in patients with a history of allergy, particularly to penicillin.

Blood: Thrombocytopenia has been reported rarely. Neutropenia has been reported, especially in long courses of treatment. Some individuals have developed positive direct Coomb's test during cephalosporin treatment. Erythropenia and decreases in hematocrit values and hemoglobin concentrations have been observed.

Hepatic: Transient increases in AST, ALT, alkaline phosphatase and bilirubin concentrations have been noted. Transient hepatitis or cholestatic jaundice occurred in a few patients.

Renal: BUN increases and decreased creatinine clearance have been reported, particularly in patients with prior renal impairment.

Local: Pain on i.m. injection, phlebitis and thrombophlebitis have occurred infrequently.

Gastrointestinal: Symptoms of pseudomembranous colitis may appear either during or after antibiotic treatment. Nausea and vomiting have been reported rarely. As with some penicillins and some other cephalosporins, transient hepatitis and colistatic jaundice have been reported rarely.

Overdose: Symptoms and Treatment: The administration of inappropriately large doses of parenteral cephalosporins may cause seizures, particularly in patients with renal impairment. Dosage reduction is necessary when renal function is impaired (see Dosage). If seizures occur, the drug should be promptly discontinued; anticonvulsant therapy may be administered if clinically indicated. Hemodialysis may be considered in cases of overwhelming overdosage.

Other than general supportive treatment, no specific antidote is known. Although cefamandole is poorly dialyzed, the rate of removal by hemodialysis is slightly better than that by peritoneal dialysis.

Dosage: After reconstitution, cefamandole may be administered i.v. or i.m. Dosage and route of administration should be determined by the severity of infection, susceptibility of the causative organisms, and condition of the patient.

Adults: The usual daily i.v. or i.m. dosage is 500 mg to 1 g every 4 to 8 hours (i.e., 1.5 to 6 g/day). Higher doses may be required for some bone and joint infections and those infections due to anaerobic organisms. In severe infections, the usual dosage is 1 g every 4 to 6 hours.

In life-threatening infections, doses up to 2 g every 4 hours may be needed (i.e., 12 g/day). The duration of treatment should normally not exceed 2 weeks. Antibiotic therapy for β-hemolytic streptococcal infections should continue for at least 10 days (see Infants and Children).

A dosage of 500 mg every 6 hours is adequate for uncomplicated pneumonia and soft tissue infections.

A dosage of 500 mg every 8 hours is sufficient for mild urinary tract infections. One g may be administered every 8 hours in moderate infections and every 4 to 6 hours in severe infections.

The i.v. route may be preferable for patients with septicemia, localized parenchymal abscesses such as intra-abdominal abscess and peritonitis or other severe or life threatening infections in patients who may be poor risks because of lowered resistance.

For infections in patients with normal renal function, the i.v. dosage is 3 to 12 g/day. In conditions such as septicemia, initiate treatment with 6 to 12 g/day; then, depending on the clinical response and laboratory findings, gradually reduce the dosage.

Infants and Children: Administration of 50 to 100 mg/kg/day in equally divided doses every 4 to 8 hours has been effective in children for most infections susceptible to cefamandole. This may be increased to a total daily dose of 150 mg/kg (not to exceed the maximum adult dose) for serious infections.

Note: As a general principle, antibiotic therapy should be continued for a minimum of 48 to 72 hours after the patient becomes asymptomatic or after evidence of bacterial eradication has been obtained; a minimum of 10 days of treatment is recommended in infections caused by group A beta-hemolytic streptococci in order to guard against the risk of rheumatic fever or glomerulonephritis; frequent bacteriologic and clinical appraisal is necessary during therapy of chronic urinary tract infections and may be required for several months after therapy has been completed; persistent infections may require longer treatment; doses smaller than those indicated above should not be used.

Impaired Renal Function: For adults, when renal function is impaired, employ a reduced dosage and monitor the serum concentration closely. After an initial loading dose of 1 to 2 g (depending on the severity of infection), calculate the maintenance dosage (see Table I) relative to the degree or renal impairment, severity of infection and susceptibility of the causative organism.

Table I—Mandol

Maintenance Dosage in Patients with Impaired Function

Creatinine Clearance (mL/min/1.73 m²)*: 0 | 10 | 20 | 30 | 40 | 50 | 60 | 70 | 80 | 90 | 100

Renal Function	**0**	**Marked Impairment**	**Severe Impairment**	**Moderate Impairment**	**Mild Impairment**	**Normal**	
Dosage Schedule	0.5 g q 8 h or 0.75 g q 12 h	0.67 g q 8 h or 1.0 g q 12 h	1.0 g q 6 h or 1.25 g q 8 h	1.5 g q 6 h or 2.0 g q 8 h	1.5 g q 4 h or 2.0 g q 6 h	2 g q 4 h	Life-threatening infections-maximum dosage
	0.25 –0.5 g q 12 h	0.5–0.75 g q 12 h	0.5–1.0 g q 8 h	0.75–1.5 g q 8 h	0.75–1.5 g q 6 h	1 –2 g q 6 h	Less severe infections

* See Clin-Info Section for SI conversion to mL/s.

When only serum creatinine concentrations are known, the following formula (based on the patient's sex, weight and age) may be used to approximate the creatinine clearance (mL/min). The serum creatinine should represent a steady state of renal function.

$$\text{Males: } \frac{\text{Weight (kg)} \times (140 - \text{age})}{72 \times \text{serum creatinine (mg/dL)}}$$

Females: $0.85 \times$ above value.

Note: Although cefamandole is poorly dialyzed, the rate of removal by hemodialysis is slightly better than that by peritoneal dialysis.

Note: Consider concomitant administration of aminoglycoside antibiotics such as tobramycin in certain cases of sepsis and serious infections, particularly in immunosuppressed patients, as initial therapy while awaiting culture and susceptibility results. Antibiotic treatment may be modified once these results have become available. Monitor renal function carefully especially if high doses are to be given.

Mandol and aminoglycosides should **not** be mixed in the same vial, infusion container or volume control chamber.

Note: I.M. administration is not recommended for anaerobic infections which require the i.v. administration of about 2 g every 4 to 6 hours to attain adequate concentrations.

Reconstitution: For i.m. use, reconstitute Mandol with sterile water for injection, bacteriostatic water for injection, 0.9% sodium chloride injection or bacteriostatic sodium chloride injection. Use 3 mL for the 1 g vial. Mandol is sometimes difficult to dissolve and requires vigorous shaking. Dissolution is facilitated by keeping the powder at the stopper end of the vial while adding the diluent to the other end of the vial.

Carbon dioxide for sodium carbonate develops inside the reconstituted vial during storage. This pressure may be dissipated prior to withdrawing the vial contents, or the pressure may be used to aid withdrawal by inverting the vial over the syringe needle and allowing the contents to flow into the syringe. Employ proper aseptic techniques at all times. When used as multiple dose containers, reconstitute with bacteriostatic water for injection or bacteriostatic sodium chloride injection.

I.M.: For i.m. administration, inject Mandol into a large muscle mass (such as the gluteus or lateral part of the thigh) to minimize pain.

Direct I.V. (Bolus) Injection: The reconstituted solution should be injected slowly over a period of 3 to 5 minutes.

Intermittent I.V. Infusion: For Mandol administration during the infusion of other i.v. fluids, a Y type administration set or volume control set may be used. During infusion of the solution containing Mandol, discontinue administration of the other solution. Careful attention should be paid to the infused volume of the Mandol solution to ensure administration of the correct dose.

Note: If therapy with cefamandole is carried out in combination with an aminoglycoside antibiotic, either, each of these antibiotics should be administered at different sites, or cefamandole and the aminoglycoside should be administered sequentially by intermittent i.v. infusion. After the administration of 1 of the 2 drugs, the tubing should be flushed very carefully and thoroughly with an approved solution for reconstitution and then administer the other drug solution. An aminoglycoside should not be mixed with cefamandole in the same container.

For i.v. administration, Mandol may be administered by i.v. injection or by either continuous or intermittent infusion. Reconstitute with sterile water for injection or, if required, bacteriostatic water for injection. Shake well until dissolved. The reconstituted Mandol must be further diluted to desired volume with any of the solutions for i.v. infusion.

For direct i.v. injection or intermittent i.v. infusion, reconstitute each g of Mandol with 10 to 20 mL of diluent and administer slowly over a 3- to 5-minute period.

For continuous i.v. infusion, reconstitute each g of Mandol with 10 mL of sterile water for injection. This solution may be added to an i.v. bottle/bag containing any of the solutions for i.v. infusion listed below. The following i.v. infusion fluids are compatible with Mandol and may be used as diluents: 0.9% sodium chloride injection; 5% and 10% dextrose injection; 5% dextrose and 0.9%, 0.45%, or 0.2% sodium chloride injection; lactated Ringer's and 5% dextrose.

Storage: Reconstituted Mandol Solutions stored at room temperature must be discarded after 24 hours or after 72 hours if stored under refrigeration.

Further diluted infusion mixtures should be prepared immediately before use and any unused portion must be discarded.

Incompatibility: Mandol should not be added to blood products, protein hydrolysates or amino acids. It should not be mixed with an aminoglycoside.

Supplied: Each 10 mL dry powder, rubber stoppered vial contains: 1 g (equivalent to cefamandole 1 g and sodium carbonate 63 mg; sodium content: 3.3 mmol (77 mg)/vial). Each 25 mL rubber stoppered vial contains: cefamandole nafate 2 g (equivalent to cefamandole 2 g and sodium carbonate 126 mg; sodium: 6.6 mmol (154 mg)/vial).

MANERIX® ℞
Roche

Moclobemide

Antidepressant

Pharmacology: Moclobemide is a short-acting, reversible inhibitor of monoamine oxidase (MAO). It is a benzamide derivative which inhibits the deamination of serotonin, norepinephrine and dopamine. This action leads to increased concentrations of these neurotransmitters, which may account for the antidepressant activity of moclobemide.

MAOs are currently subclassified into 2 types, A and B, which differ in their substrate specificity. Moclobemide preferentially inhibits MAO-A; at a 300 mg dose, the inhibition of MAO-A is approximately 80%, while that of MAO-B is approximately 20 to 30%. The estimated MAO-A inhibition is short-lasting (maximum 24 hours) and reversible.

Pharmacokinetics: Volunteers: General: Following oral administration, moclobemide was 98% absorbed from the gastrointestinal tract. Due to hepatic first pass effect, absolute bioavailability was approximately 55% after single doses, but 90% after multiple doses. The apparent volume of distribution was approximately 1.2 L/kg, indicating extensive tissue distribution.

Moclobemide was extensively metabolized, largely via oxidative reactions on the morpholine moiety of the molecule. While 95% of the administered dose is excreted in the urine, less than 1% of this is in the unchanged form. Active metabolites recovered in vitro or in animal experiments are present only at very low concentrations in the systemic circulation in man. Moclobemide was 50% bound to plasma proteins, mainly to albumin. The presence of food reduced the rate, but not the extent of moclobemide absorption.

Single Dose: Following the administration of a 100 mg single oral dose of moclobemide to healthy subjects, peak plasma concentrations ranged from 488 ng/mL to 1 450 ng/mL (mean C_{max}: 849 ng/mL) and were reached in 0.5 to 3.5 hours (mean t_{max}: 49 min). The elimination half-life was 1.5 hours. Up to 200 mg, the pharmacokinetics of moclobemide were linear. At higher doses, nonlinear pharmacokinetics were observed. In a dose range of 400 mg to 1 200 mg, maximum plasma concentrations increased and clearance decreased in a non-dose-proportional manner. With increasing doses, the elimination half-life also became prolonged.

Multiple Dose: During the second week of a 100 mg t.i.d. dosing regimen in healthy subjects, the steady-state trough concentrations of moclobemide ranged between 114 ng/mL and 517 ng/mL. An increase in the dose to 150 mg t.i.d. resulted in a greater than proportional increase in moclobemide steady-state trough concentrations, namely to concentrations ranging between 346 ng/mL and 1 828 ng/mL.

Patients: Hepatic Impairment, Single Dose: In patients with liver cirrhosis, the administration of a single 100 mg dose of moclobemide resulted in approximately a threefold increase in peak plasma concentrations (C_{max}: 1 607 ng/mL), and elimination half-life ($t_{1/2\beta}$=4 h), while clearance decreased about fourfold (Cl 337 mL/min).

Renal Impairment, Single Dose: In patients with renal insufficiency, the administration of a single 100 mg dose of moclobemide did not appreciably alter the pharmacokinetics of the drug, except for an increase in absorption time.

Elderly Patients, Single and Multiple Dose: Following a 100 mg t.i.d. dosing regimen in elderly subjects (65 to 77 years old), C_{max} and AUC values were somewhat higher than in young subjects (21 to 34 years old), namely 1 498 versus 950 ng/mL and 5 571 versus 3 102 ng·h/mL, respectively. Clearance in the elderly was reduced (19.7 versus 32.3 L/h).

Slow Metabolizers: Because moclobemide is partly metabolized by polymorphic isozymes (CYP2C19 and CYP2D6), blood levels of the drug can be affected in patients with genetically or drug-induced poor metabolism. Approximately 2% of the Caucasian population and 15% of the Asian population can be genetically phenotyped as slow metabolizers with respect to oxidative hepatic metabolism. It was found that the area under the curve (AUC) measurement in slow metabolizer subjects was approximately 1.5 times greater than in extensive metabolizer subjects for the same dose of moclobemide. This increase is within the normal range of variation (up to twofold) typically seen in patients.

Indications: For the symptomatic relief of depressive illness.

Contraindications: In patients with a known hypersensitivity to the drug. As with any other exogenous compound the possibility of hypersensitivity reaction should be considered in susceptible patients. Symptoms of hypersensitivity may include rash and edema. Moclobemide is also contraindicated in patients in an acute confusional state.

In a clinical study designed to test the interaction between moclobemide and a tricyclic antidepressant (clomipramine), severe adverse reactions emerged and the study was terminated. Data involving other tricyclic antidepressants is limited. Consequently, the concomitant use of moclobemide and tricyclic antidepressants is contraindicated.

Clinical data are not available on the concomitant use of moclobemide and selective serotonin reuptake inhibitors or other available MAO inhibitors. Therefore, until such data becomes available, moclobemide should not be administered in combination with these agents.

Although there is limited experience with the concomitant use of moclobemide and narcotics, death has occurred in patients receiving a conventional MAO inhibitor and meperidine (pethidine) given concomitantly. Therefore, moclobemide should not be used in combination with meperidine.

Children: As the safety and effectiveness of moclobemide in children below the age of 18 have not been established, pediatric use is not recommended.

Precautions: General: The possibility of suicide in depressed patients is inherent in their illness and may persist until remission occurs. Therefore, patients must be carefully supervised during all phases of treatment with moclobemide. Prescriptions in potentially suicidal patients should be written for a limited supply only.

In patients with thyrotoxicosis or pheochromocytoma, conventional MAO inhibitors may precipitate a hypertensive reaction. Because there are no data available on the use of moclobemide in such patients, caution is advised when prescribing moclobemide to these subjects.

Occupational Hazards: Patients should be cautioned against driving an automobile or performing hazardous tasks until they are certain of the effect that moclobemide has on them.

Pregnancy: Safety of use in pregnancy has not been established. Therefore, moclobemide is not recommended in women who may be pregnant, unless, in the opinion of the physician, the expected benefits to the patient markedly outweigh the possible risk to the fetus.

Lactation: Clinical data suggests that small quantities of moclobemide are excreted in human milk. Therefore, moclobemide is not recommended in nursing mothers unless the anticipated benefits outweigh the potential harm to the infant.

Hepatic Dysfunction: In patients with severe liver dysfunction, the daily dose of moclobemide should be substantially reduced to one-third or one-half of the standard dose (see Pharmacology, Pharmacokinetics).

Renal Dysfunction: Single-dose pharmacokinetic data suggest that no dosage adjustment may be required in patients with impaired renal function (see Pharmacology, Pharmacokinetics). However, multiple dose studies with moclobemide have not been performed in patients with renal dysfunction, therefore, moclobemide should be used with caution in this patient population. In normal volunteers, the absolute bioavailability almost doubles following multiple dosing as compared to a single dose.

Drug Interactions: Cimetidine: Cimetidine doubles the AUC (area under the plasma concentration-time curve) of moclobemide and is expected to approximately double moclobemide steady-state concentrations.

In patients receiving moclobemide concomitantly with cimetidine, a 50% reduction in the dosage of moclobemide may be necessary.

Tyramine: During studies conducted at the maximum recommended moclobemide dose of 600 mg/day, the mean dose of tyramine required to produce a 30 mm Hg increase in systolic blood pressure was 148±50 mg (76 to 200 mg) when moclobemide was administered immediately after tyramine. The threshold dose of tyramine was reduced to 84±23 mg (54 to 112 mg) when the sequence of administration was reversed so that moclobemide was administered 1 hour before tyramine. These findings indicate that the potentiation of tyramine may be minimized by administering moclobemide after, instead of prior to, a tyramine-enriched meal. There is limited experience in patients who took moclobemide before meals. Most clinical trial protocols specified that the drug be taken immediately after meals.

Treatment with moclobemide does not necessitate special dietary restrictions. In clinical studies it was demonstrated that up to 100 mg tyramine can be safely ingested during treatment with moclobemide 600 mg/day when moclobemide was given after meals. This amount of tyramine, 100 mg, corresponds to 1 000 g to 2 000 g mild or 200 g strong cheese, or to 70 g Marmite yeast extract.

As a safety measure, patients should be urged to report immediately the abrupt occurrence of any of the following symptoms; occipital headache, palpitations, neck stiffness, tachycardia or bradycardia or other atypical or unusual symptoms not previously experienced.

Other Antidepressants: Concomitant Use: Clinical interaction studies between moclobemide and a tricyclic antidepressant (clomipramine) resulted in severe adverse reactions (see Contraindications). Data involving other tricyclic antidepressants is limited. Therefore, the concomitant use of moclobemide and tricyclic antidepressants is contraindicated.

Clinical data are not available on the concomitant use of moclobemide and selective serotonin re-uptake inhibitors, or conventional MAO inhibitors. Therefore, until clinical data become available, moclobemide should not be administered in combination with these agents.

Sequential Use: Treatment with a tricyclic antidepressant may be initiated following the discontinuation of moclobemide with a short washout period of no less than 2 days.

When switching patients from serotonergic antidepressants to a conventional MAO inhibitor, it is standard practice to allow for a washout period equivalent to at least 4 to 5 half-lives of the previously administered drug or any active metabolites. This recommendation also applies to moclobemide.

Fluoxetine: An exception is fluoxetine; at least 5 weeks should elapse between its discontinuation and initiation of treatment with moclobemide.

Buspirone: To date, there is no experience regarding the co-administration of moclobemide and buspirone. Therefore, patients should be carefully monitored should concomitant administration be implemented.

Antipsychotics: In depressed patients with schizophrenic or schizoaffective disorder, psychotic symptoms may be exacerbated during treatment with moclobemide. There is little experience regarding the concomitant use of moclobemide and antipsychotic drugs. Therefore, patients should be carefully monitored should concomitant treatment be undertaken.

Alcohol: Excessive alcohol consumption should be avoided. Alcohol interaction studies were performed at blood alcohol concentrations of 0.05%. However, no studies were conducted at blood alcohol concentrations recognized as legally intoxicating.

Anesthetic Agents: While specific data on the use of moclobemide in patients undergoing anesthesia are not available, based on the reversible action and short elimination half-life (see Pharmacology), moclobemide should be discontinued no less than 2 days before the administration of anesthetic agents, especially spinal or local anesthetic agents that contain epinephrine.

In animals, moclobemide has been shown to potentiate the effects of opiates. The combination of moclobemide and meperidine (pethidine) is not recommended (see Contraindications). Other opioid analgesics should be used with extreme caution, if at all, and a dosage adjustment may be necessary for these drugs.

Sympathomimetics: Following multiple oral doses of moclobemide (total dose: 600 mg/day), a phenylephrine-induced increase in systolic blood pressure was potentiated (1.6 times) after i.v. administration. Patients should be advised to avoid the concomitant use of all sympathomimetic amines (e.g., amphetamine and ephedrine like compounds contained in many proprietary cold, hay fever or weight-reducing preparations), until further studies have been conducted.

Dextromethorphan: In isolated cases, the coadministration of moclobemide and dextromethorphan resulted in adverse events, including vertigo, tremor, nausea and vomiting. Since cough and cold medicines may contain dextromethorphan, they should not be taken without prior consultation with the physician, such that nondextromethorphan containing alternatives may be given.

Antihypertensives: Clinical trials with moclobemide have shown inconsistent effects on the blood pressure of hypertensive patients. Therefore, careful monitoring is recommended during initial treatment.

Manerix (cont'd)

Adverse Effects: Table I lists the adverse events reported during clinical trials in which 1 922 patients were treated with 50 to 600 mg/day moclobemide for depressive illness. Limited experience in 60 patients treated with 601 to 750 mg/day of moclobemide suggests that the incidence of adverse reactions may increase at higher doses.

Table I—Manerix

Clinical Adverse Events > 1%

Organ System	**Adverse Event**	**%** **Moclobemide (n=1 922)**	**Placebo (n=271)**
CNS	headache, pressure in head	8.0	11.1
	insomnia, sleep disturbances	7.3	4.8
	dizziness	5.1	8.1
	tremor	5.0	3.0
	increased agitation	4.5	2.6
	restlessness, nervousness	4.1	2.6
	sleepiness, somnolence	3.7	5.5
	tiredness, sedation	3.0	4.1
	increased anxiety, acute anxiety state	2.8	2.2
	weakness or faintness	1.2	1.8
Gastrointestinal	nausea	5.2	4.8
	constipation	3.9	3.3
	gastrointestinal pain epigastric discomfort	2.3	2.6
	sickness	1.9	1.1
	diarrhea	1.8	1.1
	abdominal fullness abdominal pain	1.6	1.5
	vomiting	1.6	0.4
Cardiovascular	tachycardia, palpitations	3.8	3.3
	hypotension	3.0	0.4
	orthostatic, reactive hypotension	2.3	3.3
Anticholinergic	dry mouth	9.2	10.7
Miscellaneous	sweating	2.4	2.2
	blurred vision	1.8	1.1
	increase/loss of appetite	1.3	1.8

Other clinical adverse events with an incidence of <1% in clinical trials, or reported in postmarketing surveillance, are as follows: Psychiatric: difficulties falling asleep, nightmares/dreams, hallucinations, memory disturbances, confusion, disorientation, delusions, increased depression, excitation/irritability, hypomanic symptoms, aggressive behavior, apathy, tension.

Central and Peripheral Nervous System: migraine, extrapyramidal effects, tinnitus, paresthesia, dysarthria.

Gastrointestinal: heartburn, gastritis, meteorism, indigestion.

Cardiovascular: hypertension, bradycardia, extrasystoles, angina/chest pain, phlebitic symptoms, flushing.

Dermatological/Mucocutaneous: exanthema/rash, allergic skin reaction, itching, gingivitis, stomatitis, dry skin, conjunctivitis, pruritus, urticaria.

Genitourinary: disturbances of micturition (dysuria, polyuria, tenesmus) metrorrhagia, prolonged menstruation.

Miscellaneous: general malaise, skeletal/muscular pain, altered taste sensations, hot flushes/cold sensation, photopsia, dyspnea, visual disturbances.

Laboratory Abnormalities: Laboratory examinations were performed in a total of 1 401 patients during clinical trials with moclobemide. Reductions were observed in leukocyte, AST and ALT values, however, these reductions were attributed to raised baseline values returning to normal, and were not considered clinically relevant. No other laboratory abnormalities were noted during clinical trials.

In postmarket surveillance, there appeared to be a low incidence of raised liver enzymes, without associated clinical sequelae.

Overdose: Symptoms: Signs and symptoms of overdosage with moclobemide include nausea, vomiting, drowsiness, disorientation, slurred speech, amnesia, reduced reflexes, agitation, hypertension and convulsions. One patient remained stuporous for 36 hours following an overdose with 1 550 mg moclobemide. All abnormal laboratory values and vital signs returned to within normal range 1 to 5 days after overdosage. No organ toxicity was reported.

Treatment: The treatment of overdosage should consist of general supportive measures. Gastric lavage or induction of emesis, activated charcoal and fluid control may be of benefit.

As with other antidepressants, mixed overdoses of moclobemide with other drugs (e.g., agents active on the CNS), could be life-threatening. Serotonergic syndrome and death have been reported after combined overdose of moclobemide and other antidepressants. Therefore, such patients should be closely monitored so that appropriate care and treatment may be given.

Dosage: Note: Moclobemide should always be taken after meals (see Precautions, Drug Interactions).

Usual Adult Dosage: The administration of moclobemide should be initiated at 300 mg daily dose (in 2 divided doses), and increased gradually to a maximum of 600 mg/day if needed, noting carefully the clinical response and any evidence of intolerance. Individual patient response may allow for a reduction of the daily dose. As with other antidepressants, it should be kept in mind that there may be a lag time in therapeutic response. There is no evidence that increasing the dosage rapidly shortens this latent period and may, in fact, increase the incidence of side effects. Furthermore, because bioavailability of moclobemide has been shown to increase over the first week of dosing (see Pharmacology, Pharmacokinetics), the initial daily dose of 300 mg should not be increased until after this first week of therapy.

Liver Dysfunction: When hepatic metabolism is severely impaired by hepatic disease or inhibited by a drug that affects microsomal mixed function oxidase activity (e.g., cimetidine), the daily dose of moclobemide should be reduced to one-third or one-half of the standard dose.

Renal Dysfunction: Single-dose pharmacokinetic data suggest that no dosage adjustment may be required in patients with impaired renal function. However, multiple-dose studies with moclobemide have not been performed in patients with renal dysfunction, therefore, moclobemide should be used with caution in this patient population. In normal volunteers, the absolute bioavailability almost doubles following multiple dosing as compared to a single dose.

Geriatrics: No dosage adjustments are necessary in elderly patients.

Cimetidine: Cimetidine doubles the AUC (area under the plasma concentration-time curve) of moclobemide and is expected to approximately double moclobemide steady-state concentrations (see Precautions, Drug Interactions).

In patients receiving moclobemide concomitantly with cimetidine, a 50% reduction in the dosage of moclobemide may be necessary.

Information for the Patient: See Blue Section—Information for the Patient "Manerix".

Supplied: 150 mg: Each pale yellow, single-scored, biconvex, film-coated tablet imprinted ROCHE 150 on one side, single scored on the other, contains: moclobemide 150 mg. Nonmedicinal ingredients: cornstarch, ethylcellulose, iron oxide, lactose, magnesium stearate, methylhydroxypropyl cellulose, polyethylene glycol, povidone, sodium starch glycolate, talc and titanium dioxide. Gluten-, parabens-, sucrose-, sulfites- and tartrazine-free. Bottles of 100.

300 mg: Each white, single scored, biconvex, film-coated tablet imprinted ROCHE 300 on one side and single scored on the other, contains: moclobemide 300 mg. Nonmedicinal ingredients: cornstarch, ethylcellulose, lactose, magnesium stearate, methylhydroxypropyl cellulose, polyethylene glycol, povidone, sodium starch glycolate, talc and titanium dioxide. Bottles of 100.

Store at 15 to 30°C.

(Shown in Product Recognition Section)

Reviewed 1999

MANNITOL

Abbott

Osmotic Diuretic

Supplied: Each mL contains: mannitol 250 mg. Nonmedicinal ingredients: hydrochloric acid, sodium bicarbonate and water for injection. Vials of 50 mL, boxes of 25.

MARCAINE®

Sanofi

Bupivacaine HCl

Local Anesthetic

Pharmacology: Bupivacaine stabilizes the neuronal membrane and prevents both the generation and the conduction of nerve impulses, thereby exerting local anesthetic action.

The onset of action is rapid, and anesthesia is long lasting. The advantage of bupivacaine over other local anesthetics is in the prolonged duration of effective anesthesia. It is to be noted however, that the duration of action of a local anesthetic is dependent on a number of factors including site of injection, route of administration, concentration and volume. It has also been noted that there is a period of analgesia that persists after the return of sensation, during which time the need for strong analgesics is reduced.

When administered in recommended doses and concentrations, bupivacaine does not ordinarily produce irritation or tissue damage, and does not cause methemoglobinemia.

Following injection of bupivacaine for caudal, epidural, or peripheral nerve block in man, peak levels of bupivacaine in the blood are reached in 30 to 45 minutes, followed by a gradual decline to insignificant levels during the next 3 to 6 hours.

The plasma elimination half-life of bupivacaine in adults is 2.7 hours (range 1.2 to 4.6 hours). In infants the half-life ranges from 6 to 22 hours, thus it is significantly longer than in adults. Half-life is also prolonged in the elderly.

Local anesthetics are bound to plasma proteins in varying degrees. The highly lipophilic agents, such as bupivacaine, are far more highly protein-bound than the more hydrophilic compounds. Bupivacaine is approximately 95% protein-bound in normal adults. If plasma protein concentrations are decreased, more of the free drug will be available to exert activity.

Because of its amide structure, bupivacaine is metabolized primarily in the liver. The major metabolite of bupivacaine is pipecoloxylidine, a dealkylated derivative. Patients with hepatic disease may be more susceptible to the potential toxicities of the amide-type local anesthetics. The kidney is the main excretory organ for most local anesthetics and their metabolites. Urinary excretion is affected by renal perfusion and factors affecting urinary pH.

Local anesthetics appear to cross the placenta by passive diffusion. The rate and degree of diffusion is governed by the degree of plasma protein binding, the degree of ionization, and the degree of lipid solubility.

Fetal/maternal ratios of local anesthetics appear to be inversely related to the degree of plasma protein binding because only the free, unbound drug is available for placental transfer. Bupivacaine with a high protein binding capacity (95%) has a low fetal/maternal ratio (0.2 to 0.4).

Indications: For the production of local or regional anesthesia and analgesia in infiltration procedures, peripheral nerve blocks, retrobulbar block, and caudal, epidural and subarachnoid (spinal) blocks.

Contraindications: Known hypersensitivity to local anesthetics of the amide type or to other components of bupivacaine solutions (see Supplied); the presence of inflammation and/or sepsis near the proposed injection site; severe shock; heart block.

Bupivacaine is contraindicated for i.v. regional anesthesia (Bier Block).

Spinal Use: With the exception of certain serious diseases of the central nervous system or of the lumbar vertebral column, most anesthesiologists consider the following conditions to be only **relative contraindications** to spinal anesthesia. The decision as to whether or not spinal anesthesia should be used for an individual case depends on the individual physician's appraisal of the advantages as opposed to the risks and on his ability to cope with the complications that may arise. Disease of the cerebrospinal system, such as meningitis, spinal fluid block, cranial or spinal hemorrhage, increased intracranial pressure, tumors and syphilis. Shock. This should be treated before any anesthetic is administered. However, in emergency operations, spinal anesthesia may at times be considered the method of choice. Profound anemia, cachexia and when death is imminent. Sepsis with positive blood cultures. High Blood Pressure. Spinal anesthesia should be well tolerated if particular care is taken to prevent a sudden or appreciable fall in blood pressure. Low Blood Pressure. The use of suitable pressor agents and methods of controlling the diffusion of the anesthetic should remove the principal objection to spinal anesthesia in patients with low blood pressure. Highly nervous and sensitive persons. Preoperative medication should overcome this difficulty. Visceral perforation, bowel strangulation, acute peritonitis. Some surgeons object to contraction of the gastrointestinal musculature; others, however, consider, the associated arrest of peristalsis an advantage. With gastrointestinal hemorrhage, spinal anesthesia should be used with caution or may even be contraindicated. Cardiac decompensation, massive pleural effusion, and increased intra-abdominal pressure (e.g., fullterm pregnancy, massive ascites, large tumor). High spinal anesthesia should not be used in patients with these conditions unless the Trendelenburg position can be omitted or the intra-abdominal pressure released slowly.

Warnings: Resuscitative equipment and drugs should be readily available when any local anesthetic is used. The highest (0.75%) isotonic concentration is not recommended for obstetrical anesthesia. There have been reports of cardiac arrest with difficult resuscitation or death following its use for epidural anesthesia in obstetrical patients. Resuscitation has been difficult or impossible despite apparently adequate preparation and appropriate management. Cardiac arrest has occurred after convulsions resulting from systemic toxicity, probably following unintentional intravascular injection.

Bupivacaine should not be used in obstetrical paracervical block anesthesia. Its use in this technique has resulted in fetal bradycardia and death.

Bupivacaine with epinephrine 1:200 000 or other vasopressors should not be used concomitantly with ergot-type oxytocic drugs because severe persistent hypertension may occur.

Bupivacaine with epinephrine 1:200 000 or other vasopressors should be used with extreme caution in patients receiving MAO inhibitors or antidepressants of the imipramine type because severe hypertension may occur.

Epinephrine-containing solutions should not be injected into tissues supplied by end arteries, for example, fingers and toes, ears, the nose and the penis.

It is essential that aspiration for blood or cerebrospinal fluid be done prior to injecting any local anesthetic, both the original dose and all subsequent doses, to avoid intravascular or subarachnoid injection. During the performance of spinal anesthesia, a free flow of cerebrospinal fluid is indicative of entry into the subarachnoid space. However, aspiration should be performed before the anesthetic solution is injected to confirm entry into the subarachnoid space and to avoid intravascular injection.

Mixing or the prior or intercurrent use of any other local anesthetic with bupivacaine is not recommended because of insufficient data regarding the interaction and safety of such mixtures.

Bupivacaine with epinephrine 1:200 000 contains sodium metabisulfite, a sulfite that may cause allergic-type reactions including anaphylactic symptoms and life-threatening or less severe asthmatic episodes in certain susceptible people. The overall prevalence of sulfite sensitivity in the general population is unknown and probably low. Sulfite sensitivity is seen more frequently in asthmatic than in nonasthmatic people.

Precautions: The safety and effectiveness of local anesthetics depend upon proper dosage, correct technique, adequate precautions, and readiness for emergencies. Resuscitative equipment, oxygen and resuscitative drugs should be available for immediate use. During major nerve blocks, the patient should have a functioning i.v. line in place, providing ready access to the circulation, for the administration of emergency drugs should an adverse reaction occur. The lowest dosage that gives effective anesthesia should be used, to avoid high plasma levels and serious systemic side effects. The rapid injection of a large volume of local anesthetic solution should be avoided and fractional (incremental) doses should be used when feasible.

The following precautions apply to all local anesthetics: Select needles of proper length and bevel for the technique employed. Inject slowly with frequent aspirations and if blood is aspirated, relocate the needle. Inadvertent intravascular injection may cause serious complications. Absorption is more rapid when injections are made into highly vascular tissues. In caudal or epidural anesthesia, abandon the method if the subarachnoid space has been entered, as shown by aspiration of spinal fluid. However, a negative aspiration is not 100% reliable.

Injection of repeated doses of bupivacaine may cause a significant increase in blood concentrations due to accumulation of the drug or its metabolites or slow metabolic degradation. Tolerance to elevated blood levels varies with the status of the patient. Debilitated, elderly and acutely ill patients may require reduced doses commensurate with age and physical condition.

The decision to use a local anesthetic containing a vasoconstrictor in patients with peripheral vascular disease, will depend on the physician's appraisal of the relative advantages and risks.

Dose related cardiac arrhythmias may occur if preparations containing epinephrine are employed in patients during or immediately following the administration of halothane, cyclopropane, trichloroethylene or other related agents. In deciding whether to use these products concurrently in the same patient, the combined action of both agents upon the myocardium, the concentration and volume of vasoconstrictor used, and the time since injection, when applicable, should be taken into account.

Because amide-type local anesthetics, such as bupivacaine, are metabolized in the liver, these drugs should be used cautiously in patients with hepatic disease. Local anesthetics should also be used with caution in patients with impaired cardiovascular function because they may be less able to compensate for functional changes associated with the prolongation of AV conduction produced by these drugs.

Local anesthetics which contain preservatives, i.e., those supplied in multiple dose vials, should not be used for caudal or epidural anesthesia.

Spinal Use: In addition to the above noted precautions, when administering bupivacaine, hyperbaric solution for spinal anesthesia, the patient's blood pressure should be carefully monitored. Spinal anesthesia is usually associated with a fall in arterial blood pressure due to sympathetic blockade.

Epidural Use: It is recommended that a test dose be administered initially and the effects monitored before a full dose is given. However, the optimal formulation and usefulness of the test dose in obstetrics are being debated. Generally 2 to 3 mL of 0.5% bupivacaine containing 1:200 000 epinephrine be administered to check that the spinal canal or a blood vessel has not been entered while locating the epidural needle or catheter. In the event of spinal injection clinical signs of spinal block would become evident in a few minutes. In the event of intravascular injection a transient increase in pulse rate and/or systolic blood pressure is usually detectable with a monitor. The other symptoms and signs of "epinephrine response" are less dependable. Concomitantly administered medications may modify these responses. When reinforcing doses are required the test dose should be used again to check the catheter location. However, an intravascular or subarachnoid injection is still possible even if results of the test dose are negative.

Head and Neck Area: Relatively small doses of local anesthetics injected into the head and neck area, including retrobulbar, and stellate ganglion blocks, may produce adverse reactions similar to systemic toxicity seen with unintentional intravascular injections of larger doses. The injection procedures require the utmost care. Confusion, convulsions, respiratory depression and/or respiratory arrest, and cardiovascular stimulation or depression have been reported. These reactions may be due to intra-arterial injection of the local anesthetic with retrograde flow to the cerebral circulation. They may also be due to puncture of the dural sheath of the optic nerve during retrobulbar block with diffusion of any local anesthetic along the subdural space to the midbrain. Patients receiving these blocks should have their circulation and respiration monitored and be constantly observed. Resuscitative equipment and personnel for treating adverse reactions should be immediately available.

Ophthalmic Surgery: Clinicians who perform retrobulbar blocks should be aware that there have been reports of respiratory arrest following local anesthetic injection. Prior to retrobulbar block, as with all other regional procedures, the immediate availability of equipment, drugs and personnel to manage respiratory arrest or depression, convulsions, and cardiac stimulation or depression should be assured. As with other anesthetic procedures, patients should be constantly monitored following ophthalmic blocks for signs of these adverse reactions, which may occur following relatively low total doses. A concentration of 0.75% bupivacaine is indicated for retrobulbar block; however, this concentration is not indicated for any other peripheral nerve block, including the facial nerve, and not indicated for local infiltration, including the conjunctiva.

When bupivacaine 0.75% is used for retrobulbar block, complete corneal anesthesia usually precedes onset of clinically acceptable external ocular muscle akinesia. Therefore, presence of akinesia rather than anesthesia alone should determine readiness of the patient for surgery.

Pregnancy: Decreased pup survival in rats and an embryocidal effect in rabbits have been observed when bupivacaine was administered to these species in doses comparable, respectively, to 9 and 5 times the maximal recommended daily human dose (400 mg).

There are no adequate and well controlled studies in pregnant women of the effect of bupivacaine on the developing fetus. Bupivacaine should be used during pregnancy only if the potential benefit justifies the potential risk to the fetus.

Obstetrics: The highest (0.75%) isotonic concentration is not recommended for obstetrical anesthesia (see Warnings). This, however does not exclude the use of isotonic bupivacaine 0.25% or 0.50% or the spinal use of the hyperbaric bupivacaine 0.75% in dextrose at term for obstetrical anesthesia or analgesia.

Bupivacaine is contraindicated for obstetrical paracervical block anesthesia (see Warnings). Local anesthetics rapidly cross the placenta and when used for epidural, caudal or pudendal block anesthesia, can cause varying degrees of maternal, fetal and neonatal toxicity. However, the fetal/maternal ratio for bupivacaine is relatively low.

Lactation: It is not known whether local anesthetics are excreted in human milk. However, because many drugs are excreted in human milk, caution should be exercised when bupivacaine is administered to a nursing woman.

Bupivacaine has been reported to be excreted in human milk suggesting that the nursing infant could be theoretically exposed to a dose of the drug. Because of the potential for serious adverse reactions in nursing infants from bupivacaine, a decision should be made whether to discontinue nursing or not administer bupivacaine, taking into account the importance of the drug to the mother.

Children: The 0.25 and 0.5% solutions of bupivacaine, with or without epinephrine, are recommended in children **older** than 2 years. For the appropriate concentration and dosage see Dosage section.

Until further experience is gained, the following restrictions apply to the use of bupivacaine: isotonic bupivacaine solutions with or without epinephrine are not recommended for spinal use; the 0.75% isotonic solution of bupivacaine with or without epinephrine is not recommended in patients younger than 12 years.

Bupivacaine spinal (0.75% hyperbaric solution in dextrose) is not recommended for spinal use in patients younger than 18 years.

Drug Interactions: The administration of local anesthetic solutions containing epinephrine or norepinephrine to patients receiving MAO inhibitors or tricyclic antidepressants may produce severe, prolonged hypertension. Concurrent use of these agents should generally be avoided. In situations when concurrent therapy is necessary, careful patient monitoring is essential. Concurrent administration of vasopressor drugs and of ergot-type oxytocic drugs may cause severe, persistent hypertension or cerebrovascular accidents. Phenothiazines and butyrophenones may reduce or reverse the pressor effect of epinephrine. Administration of H_2 blockers prior to epidural anesthesia is inadvisable since toxic levels of local anesthetic may result.

Adverse Effects: Reactions to bupivacaine are characteristic of those associated with amide type local anesthetics. A major cause of adverse reactions to this group of drugs is excessive

Marcaine (cont'd)

plasma levels, which may be due to overdosage, inadvertent intravascular injection, or slow metabolic degradation.

The most commonly encountered adverse reactions which demand immediate countermeasures involve the CNS and the cardiovascular system. The adverse reactions are usually dose-related and due to high plasma levels which may result from overdosage, rapid absorption from the injection site, diminished tolerance or from unintentional intravascular injection. Factors influencing plasma protein binding, e.g., diseases which alter protein synthesis or competition of other drugs for protein binding, may diminish individual tolerance.

The CNS effects are characterized by excitation or depression. The first manifestation may be anxiety, nervousness, dizziness, blurred vision, or tremors, followed by drowsiness, convulsions, unconsciousness, and possibly respiratory arrest. Since excitement may be transient or absent, the first manifestation may be drowsiness, sometimes merging into unconsciousness and respiratory arrest. Other CNS effects may be nausea, vomiting, chills, constriction of the pupils or tinnitus. The cardiovascular manifestations of excessive plasma levels may include depression of the myocardium, blood pressure changes (usually hypotension), decreased cardiac output, heart block, bradycardia, ventricular arrhythmias including ventricular tachycardia and ventricular fibrillation, and cardiac arrest.

Allergic reactions are characterized by cutaneous lesions (e.g., urticaria, edema), and other manifestations of allergy.

Neurologic reactions following epidural or caudal anesthesia may include: high or total spinal block, urinary retention; fecal and urinary incontinence, loss of perineal sensation and sexual function; persistent anesthesia, paresthesia, and paralysis of the lower extremities; headache and backache; and slowing of labor and increased incidence of forceps delivery.

Reactions due to systemic absorption may be slow or rapid in onset. Those of rapid onset include respiratory depression, cardiovascular collapse and cardiac arrest. This type of reaction necessitates a high degree of preparedness since it can occur with little warning.

In some subjects, bupivacaine may produce marked peripheral vasoconstriction in unanesthetized areas which may last for several hours.

Spinal use: The most commonly encountered adverse reactions which demand immediate countermeasures are hypotension due to loss of sympathetic tone and respiratory paralysis or underventilation due to cephalid extension of the motor level of anesthesia. These may lead to cardiac arrest if untreated. In addition, one or several of the following complications or side effects may be observed during or after spinal anesthesia. 1. Meningitis. With the employment of an aseptic technique, septic meningitis should be practically nonexistent. Some instances of aseptic meningitis, with fever, neck rigidity, and cloudy spinal fluid, have been reported with the use of other spinal anesthetics. The course is usually brief and benign, terminating in complete recovery. In a few, permanent paralysis (sometimes terminating fatally) and sensory disturbances have been observed. This type of meningitis has also been observed in rare instances following ordinary diagnostic lumbar puncture. 2. Palsies. These are rare and affect either the extraocular muscles or the legs and the anal and vesical sphincters (cauda equina syndrome). Paralysis of extraocular muscles usually clears up spontaneously by the third or fourth week. Cauda equina and lumbosacral cord complications (usually consisting of arachnoiditis and demyelinization) result in loss or impairment of motor and sensory function of the saddle area (bladder, rectum) and one or both legs. The complications have occurred after the use of most, if not all, spinal anesthetics. The loss or impairment of motor function may be permanent or partial recovery may slowly occur. Various explanations for such complications have been advanced, such as hypersensitivity or intolerance to the anesthetic agent with a resultant myelolytic or neurotoxic effect; pooling of relatively high concentrations of anesthetic solution around the cauda equina and spinal cord before diffusion; and accidental injection of irritating antiseptics or detergents (as when syringes are incompletely cleansed or when ampul storage solution enters a cracked ampul). Hence, most anesthesiologists prefer to autoclave ampuls in order to destroy bacteria on the exterior before opening. 3. Headache. This may largely be prevented by using a small gauge needle to prevent spinal fluid leakage and by placing the patient in the supine position after operation and providing adequate hydration. 4. Nausea and vomiting. These may be due to a drop in blood pressure, undue intra-abdominal manipulation or to preoperative medication.

Overdose: Symptoms and Treatment: Acute emergencies from local anesthetics are generally related to high plasma levels encountered during therapeutic use of local anesthetics or to unintended subarachnoid injection of local anesthetic solution. The first consideration in the management of the emergencies is prevention, best accomplished by careful and constant monitoring of cardiovascular and respiratory vital signs and the patient's state of consciousness after each local anesthetic injection.

The first step in the management of systemic toxic reactions, as well as underventilation or apnea, consists of the immediate establishment and maintenance of a patent airway and assisted or controlled ventilation with 100% oxygen. Supportive treatment of the cardiovascular system includes i.v. fluids and, when appropriate, vasopressors (such as epinephrine or ephedrine which enhance myocardial contractility).

If necessary, use drugs to control convulsions. A bolus i.v. injection of succinylcholine will paralyze the patient without depressing the CNS or cardiovascular system and facilitate ventilation. A bolus i.v. dose of diazepam or thiopental will permit ventilation and counteract central nervous system stimulation, but these drugs also depress CNS, respiratory, and cardiac function, add to possible depression, and may result in apnea. I.V. barbiturates, anticonvulsant agents, or muscle relaxants should only be administered by those familiar with their use. For specific techniques and procedures, refer to standard textbooks.

Recent clinical data from patients experiencing local anesthetic-induced convulsions demonstrated rapid development of hypoxia, hypercarbia and acidosis with bupivacaine within a minute of the onset of convulsions. These observations suggest that oxygen consumption and carbon dioxide production are greatly increased during local anesthetic convulsions and emphasize the importance of immediate and effective ventilation with oxygen which may avoid cardiac arrest. If cardiac arrest should occur, successful outcome may require prolonged resuscitative efforts.

Dosage: As with all local anesthesias, the dosage varies and depends upon the area to be anesthetized, the vascularity of the tissues, the number of neuronal segments to be blocked, the depth of anesthesia and degree of muscle relaxation required, individual tolerance, the technique of anesthesia, and the physical condition of the patient. The lowest dosage needed to provide effective anesthesia should be administered.

In recommended doses, bupivacaine produces complete sensory block, but the effect on motor function differs between the 3 concentrations.

0.25% when used for caudal, epidural or peripheral nerve block, produces incomplete motor block. Should be used for operations in which muscle relaxation is not important, or when another means of providing muscle relaxation is used concurrently. Onset of action may be slower than with the 0.5 or 0.75% solutions.

0.50% provides motor blockade for caudal, epidural, or nerve block, but muscle relaxation may be inadequate for operations in which complete muscle relaxation is essential.

0.75% provides complete motor block. This concentration is recommended only for epidural block (single dose) in abdominal operations requiring complete muscle relaxation without the aid of other medication, and for retrobulbar anesthesia. It is not recommended for epidural block in obstetrical patients.

The duration of anesthesia with bupivacaine is such that, for most procedures, a single dose is sufficient. Maximum dosage limit must be individualized in each case after evaluating the patient's size and physical status and the usual rate of systemic absorption from a particular injection site. Most experience to date is with single doses of bupivacaine, up to 225 mg with epinephrine 1:200 000 and 175 mg without epinephrine; more or less drug may be used depending on individualization of each case. The maximum doses of bupivacaine are considered to apply to a healthy, 70 kg young male, however, it is not recommended that they be exceeded in heavier persons.

At present there is insufficient clinical evidence with multiple dosage or intermittent dose techniques to permit precise recommendations for such procedures to be given. However, limited clinical experience in this area of use indicates that bupivacaine may be repeated in 3 to 6 hours up to a maximum dose of 400 mg in 24 hours. The duration of anesthetic effect may be prolonged by the addition of epinephrine.

The 0.75% concentration of isotonic bupivacaine is not recommended for obstetrical anesthesia or analgesia (see Warnings). The 0.5% and 0.25% concentrations of isotonic bupivacaine and the 0.75% hyperbaric solution of bupivacaine in dextrose are recommended at term for obstetrical anesthesia and analgesia.

Table I is presented as a guide to the use of bupivacaine in adults. The doses shown have generally proved satisfactory for the average patient. They may require adjustment in relation to age and the physical condition of the patient.

Children: Until further experience is gained, the following restrictions apply to the use of bupivacaine; isotonic bupivacaine solutions with or without epinephrine are not recommended for spinal use; the 0.75% isotonic solution of bupivacaine with or without epinephrine is not recommended in patients younger than 12 years; spinal bupivacaine HCl 0.75% hyperbaric solution in dextrose is not recommended for spinal use in patients younger than 18 years.

The 0.25 and 0.5% solutions of bupivacaine, with or without epinephrine, are recommended in children **older** than 2 years. For the appropriate suggested concentrations and dosage see Table II (on following page).

Spinal Use: Bupivacaine for spinal anesthesia is available as a 0.75% hyperbaric solution. The smallest dose required to produce the desired result should be administered and the dosage should be reduced for elderly and debilitated patients and patients with cardiac and/or liver disease. The use of the hyperbaric solution should permit improved control of the extent of anesthesia since the solution will have a higher specific gravity than spinal fluid (see Table III on following page).

Bupivacaine in dextrose (0.75% hyperbaric solution) is not recommended in pediatric patients younger than 18 years of age.

Table I—Marcaine

Recommended Concentrations and Dosage for Adults

Type of Block	Concentration	Each Dose mL	Each Dose mg	Motor Block[a]
Local Infiltration	0.25%	up to max.	up to max.	
Epidural[c]	0.75%[b]	10–20	75–150	Complete
	0.50%	10–20	50–100	Moderate to Complete
	0.25%	10–20	25–50	Partial to Moderate
Epidural[c] Test dose	0.50% with epinephrine	2–3	10–15 (10–15 μg epinephrine)	—
Caudal	0.50%	15–30	75–150	Moderate to Complete
	0.25%	15–30	37.5–75	Moderate
Peripheral Nerves	0.50%	5–30	25–150	Moderate to Complete
	0.25%	5–60	12.5–150	Moderate to Complete
Retrobulbar	0.75%	2– 4	15–30	Complete
Sympathetic	0.25%	20–50	50–125	—

[a]With continuous (intermittent) techniques in caudal and epidural block, using 0.25 and 0.5% solutions, repeat doses increase the degree of motor block. For intermittent epidural anesthesia, use maximum increments of 3 to 5 mL of 0.5% bupivacaine with sufficient time between doses to detect any toxic effects. The first dose of 0.5% may produce complete motor block. In most intercostal nerve blocks for intra-abdominal surgery, the 0.25% concentration has produced satisfactory motor blockade.

[b]For single dose use: not for intermittent technique. Not for obstetrical anesthesia.

[c]Use of an appropriate test dose is recommended prior to injecting the full epidural dose (see Precautions).

Table II—Marcaine

Recommended Concentration and Dosage for Children

Type of Block	Concentration	mL/kg	mg/kg
Caudal	0.25%	0.4–0.8	1–2
	0.5%	0.2–0.4	1–2
Lumbar/Epidural	0.25%	0.6–1.0	1.5–2.5
	0.5%	0.3–0.5	1.5–2.5
Penile	0.25% (without epinephrine)	0.1–0.2	0.3–0.5
	0.5% (without epinephrine)	0.06–0.1	0.3–0.5
Intercostal	0.25% (with epinephrine)	0.8–1.2	2–3
	0.5% (with epinephrine)	0.4–0.6	2–3
Local infiltration for hernia repair	0.25%	0.2–0.8	0.5–2
	0.5%	0.1–0.4	0.5–2

Note: These bupivacaine concentrations and doses are recommended for anesthesia and/or analgesia, with the understanding that such use may be supplementary to light general anesthesia.

Table III—Marcaine

Suggested Adult Dosage Limits for Spinal Anesthesia

Extent of Anesthesia	Bupivacaine 0.75% Hyperbaric Solution Dosage (mL)	(mg)	Injection Site (lumbar interspace)
Low Spinal and Saddle block for perineal operations	0.8–1.06	6–8	4th
Median Spinal for operations on lower abdomen	1.06–1.6	8–12	3rd or 4th
High Spinal for operations on upper abdomen	1.6–2	12–15	2nd, 3rd or 4th

The extent and degree of spinal anesthesia depend on: (1) the dose of anesthetic (see Table III), (2) the specific gravity of the anesthetic solution, (3) the volume of solution administered, (4) the force of injection, (5) the level of puncture and (6) the position of the patient during and immediately after injection. The lateral recumbent position is the customary one for injection; however, when both perineal and abdominal anesthesia are required, the sitting position may be preferred. After preliminary antiseptic preparation of the back, the spinal interspace to be punctured is marked and anesthetized with 1 to 2 mL of 0.25% bupivacaine HCl solution.

Ephedrine (25 mg) may be administered if needed to maintain blood pressure.

After the spinal anesthetic has been administered the specific gravity of the solution injected determines which position the patient should be placed in, at least for the first 15 to 20 minutes. Continuous sensory tests should be made by gentle strokes with a sharp instrument or by pinching the skin, comparing the sensitivity to that of the inside of the forearm. Since hypalgesia always precedes anesthesia, it is necessary to determine the line of demarcation between hypalgesia and normal sensation, to avoid extension of anesthesia above the desired segment.

After injection of a 0.75% hyperbaric solution for spinal anesthesia, the patient is immediately placed on his back and the table tilted to a 10 to 20 degree Trendelenburg position in order to allow the solution to flow cephalad. Under no circumstances should a patient be left in a head down position longer than 1 minute from the start of injection without testing the height of anesthesia. The neck is sharply flexed by supporting the head on a double pillow. When hypalgesia is extended to the desired height, the table is promptly brought to the horizontal position and time (about 10 to 20 minutes) allowed for the anesthetic agent to become fixed.

Supplied: Isotonic Solutions: These solutions are not for spinal anesthesia. Solutions of bupivacaine HCl that do not contain epinephrine may be autoclaved. Autoclave at 15 pound pressure, 121°C for 15 minutes. Do not use if solution is discolored or contains a precipitate.

0.25%: Each mL contains: bupivacaine HCl 2.5 mg. Single dose vials of 10 mL (without preservative); boxes of 5. Single dose vials of 20 mL (without preservative); boxes of 5. Multiple dose vials of 50 mL (with methylparaben as preservative); boxes of 1.

0.5%: Each mL contains: bupivacaine HCl 5 mg. Single dose vials of 10 mL (without preservative); boxes of 5. Single dose vials of 20 mL (without preservative); boxes of 5. Multiple dose vials of 50 mL (with methylparaben as preservative); boxes of 1.

0.75%: Each mL contains: bupivacaine HCl 7.5 mg. Single dose vials of 20 mL (without preservative); boxes of 5.

Bupivacaine HCl with epinephrine 1:200 000 (as bitartrate): These solutions should not be autoclaved and should be protected from light. Do not use if solution is pinkish or darker than slightly yellow or contains a precipitate.

0.25% with epinephrine 1:200 000: Each mL contains: bupivacaine HCl 2.5 mg. Single dose vials of 20 mL (without preservative); boxes of 5.

0.5% with epinephrine 1:200 000: Each mL contains: bupivacaine HCl 5 mg. Single dose ampuls of 3 mL (without preservative); boxes of 10. Single dose vials of 20 mL (without preservative); boxes of 5.

These solutions are made isotonic with NaCl and the pH is adjusted with NaOH or HCl. The pH range for solutions without epinephrine is 4 to 6.5 and for solutions with epinephrine is 3.3 to 5.5. Each mL of solution with epinephrine contains epinephrine bitartrate 0.0091 mg and, as nonmedicinal ingredients, sodium metabisulfite, monothioglycerol and ascorbic acid as antioxidants, sodium lactate buffer and edetate calcium disodium as stabilizer.

0.75% Hyperbaric Solution for Spinal Use Only: Each mL of solution contains: bupivacaine HCl 7.5 mg and dextrose 82.5 mg in Water for Injection. The pH is adjusted between 4 and 6.5 with NaOH or HCl. The solution may be autoclaved once at 15 pound pressure, 121°C for 15 minutes. Do not administer any solution which is discolored or contains particulate matter. Single dose ampuls of 2 mL; boxes of 10.

MARINOL® Ⓝ

Sanofi

Dronabinol

Antiemetic

Pharmacology: Dronabinol, also known as delta-9-tetrahydrocannabinol has been shown to have psychotropic and antiemetic activity. Dronabinol can produce changes in mood, decrease in cognitive performance and memory, decrease in ability to control drives and impulses, and altered perception of reality, particularly altered time sense.

Pharmacokinetics: Dronabinol is readily absorbed from the gastrointestinal tract. The systemic availability, following oral administration, is 10 to 20% relative to an i.v. dose indicating extensive first pass metabolism. Maximum plasma concentrations appear approximately 2 to 3 hours after oral dosing. Dronabinol has a long half-life (approximately 60 hours) due to sequestration in body tissues and to enterohepatic recirculation.

Dronabinol is metabolized chiefly in the liver where it is converted to 11-hydroxy-Δ^9-tetrahydrocannabinol and more than 20 other metabolites. The 11-hydroxy-metabolite is psychoactive and appears in the plasma in roughly the same quantities as the parent drug. It has a terminal half-life of approximately 15 to 18 hours.

Biliary excretion is the major route of elimination. Within 72 hours following oral administration, approximately 50% of the dose is recovered in the feces; another 10 to 15% appears in the urine either unchanged or as a metabolite.

Indications: In the treatment of severe nausea and vomiting associated with cancer chemotherapy.

Dronabinol is a psychotropic agent which may produce physical and psychological dependence and has the potential to be abused. Dronabinol is scheduled as a narcotic and as such cannot be used or prescribed except for its recognized indication; namely severe nausea and vomiting associated with cancer chemotherapy.

Prescription of dronabinol should be limited to the amount necessary for a single course of antinauseant therapy (i.e. a few days).

Contraindications: Dronabinol should not be given to patients sensitive to marijuana, other cannabinoids or sesame oil. Dronabinol should not be given to patients with a history of psychotic disorders or those judged to be intolerant of the drug.

Warnings: Dronabinol can produce physical and psychological dependence and has the potential for being abused. Dronabinol has complex effects on the CNS. These can result in changes of mood, decrease in cognitive performance and memory, decrease in ability to control drives and impulses, and alteration of the perception of reality. Because of its potential to alter the mental state, dronabinol should be used only as indicated and under circumstances that permit close medical supervision of the patient.

Drug administration should be discontinued in patients experiencing a psychotic reaction and the patient should be closely observed in an appropriate setting until his/her mental state returns to normal.

Occupational Hazards: Patients should be warned not to drive or engage in activities requiring unimpaired judgment and coordination.

Pregnancy and *Lactation:* The safe use of dronabinol during pregnancy has not been established.

There is evidence that dronabinol is excreted in human breast milk and may be absorbed by the nursing baby. Because the effects on the infant of chronic exposure to dronabinol and its metabolites are unknown, nursing mothers should not use it.

Precautions: Dronabinol may cause an increase in sympathomimetic activity. It should be administered with caution to patients with cardiovascular problems, such as tachyarrhythmias, angina pectoris or hypertension.

Dronabinol should not be used in manic depressive or schizophrenic patients as symptoms may be unmasked by cannabinoids. Use dronabinol with caution, if at all, in patients receiving other psychoactive drugs.

Information for the Patient: Patients should be alerted to the additive effects of dronabinol and barbiturates. They should be warned not to drive or engage in activities requiring unimpaired judgment and coordination until the effects of dronabinol have completely subsided.

Adverse Effects: During controlled clinical trials, the most commonly encountered events were drowsiness, dizziness and transient impairment of sensory and perceptual functions. Psychotropic effects can be observed in most patients. Easy laughing, elation and heightened awareness, often termed a "high", was described in 24% of dronabinol patients in the reported clinical trials.

Table I lists in order of decreasing frequency the adverse reactions experienced by dronabinol treated patients participating in controlled clinical trials.

Table I—Marinol

Frequency of Adverse Effects from Controlled Studies

Body System/ Adverse Reactions	Marinol (n=317) %	Control (n=263) %	Placebo (n=68) %
CNS			
Drowsiness	48	33	49
Dizziness	21	5	1
Anxiety	16	3	24
Muddled thinking	12	1	1
Perceptual difficulties	11	1	0
Coordination impairment	9	2	10
Irritability/Weird feeling	7	3	0
Depression	7	3	15
Weak, Sluggish	6	3	
Headache	6	4	4
Hallucinations	5	0	0
Memory lapse	5	1	0
Unsteadiness, ataxia	4	1	0
Paranoia	2	0	0
Depersonalization	2	0	0
Disorientation, confusion	1	0	2
Autonomic Nervous System			
Dry mouth	3	1	1
Paresthesia	3	0	1
Visual distortions	3	0	0
Cardiovascular			
Tachycardia	1	1	0
Postural hypotension	1	0	0

In addition to the events enumerated above, the following have been reported at a frequency below 1%: CNS: tinnitus, nightmares.

Autonomic Nervous System: speech difficulty, facial flushing, perspiring.

Cardiovascular: syncope.

Gastrointestinal: diarrhea, fecal incontinence.

Musculoskeletal: muscular pains.

Marinol (cont'd)

Overdose: Symptoms and Treatment: Signs and symptoms of overdosage are an extension of the psychotomimetic and physiologic effects of dronabinol.

Overdosage may be considered to have occurred at prescribed dosage if disturbing psychiatric symptoms have occurred. In such case, the patient should be closely observed in a quiet environment and supportive measures, including reassurance, should be used.

Dosage: The bioavailability of dronabinol by the oral route is variable.

Initial Dose: 5 mg/m² given 1 to 3 hours prior to administration of chemotherapy.

Repeat Dose: 5 mg/m² every 2 to 4 hours following chemotherapy, when necessary, for a total of not more than 4 to 6 doses/day usually for 1 or 2 days.

Should 5 mg/m² prove ineffective and in the absence of significant side effects, the dose may be increased by 2.5 mg/m² increments to a maximum of 10 mg/m² per dose. Caution should be exercised since the incidence and severity of disturbing psychiatric adverse reactions increase significantly at these doses.

Supplied: 2.5 mg: Each white, soft gelatin capsule, identified RL, contains: dronabinol 2.5 mg. Nonmedicinal ingredients: gelatin, glycerin, methylparaben, propylparaben, sesame oil, titanium dioxide and purified water. Bottles of 25.

5 mg: Each brown, soft gelatin capsule, identified RL, contains: dronabinol 5 mg. Nonmedicinal ingredients: gelatin, glycerin, methylparaben, propylparaben, sesame oil, titanium dioxide and purified water. Bottles of 25.

10 mg: Each orange, soft gelatin capsule, identified RL, contains: dronabinol 10 mg. Nonmedicinal ingredients: gelatin, glycerin, methylparaben, propylparaben, sesame oil, titanium dioxide and purified water. Bottles of 25.

Store in a cool place, in well sealed amber containers.

MARVELON® Ⓟ

Organon

Desogestrel—Ethinyl Estradiol

Oral Contraceptive

Pharmacology: Combination oral contraceptives act by suppression of gonadotropins. Although the primary mechanism of this action is inhibition of ovulation, other alterations include changes in the cervical mucus (which increase the difficulty of sperm entry into the uterus) and the endometrium (which reduce the likelihood of implantation).

Desogestrel, the progestogen component of Marvelon, displays low androgenic activity in relation to its progestogenic effects and may increase the HDL/LDL ratio and apoprotein A-1/B ratio without affecting HDL_2. Like other oral contraceptives, these changes in lipid profile can be associated with an increase in triglycerides.

Indications: Conception control.

Contraindications: History of/or actual thrombophlebitis or thromboembolic disorders. History of/or actual cerebrovascular disorders. History of/or actual myocardial infarction or coronary arterial disease. Active liver disease or history of/or actual benign or malignant liver tumors. Known or suspected carcinoma of the breast. Known or suspected estrogen-dependent neoplasia. Undiagnosed abnormal vaginal bleeding. Any ocular lesion arising from ophthalmic vascular disease, such as partial or complete loss of vision or defect in visual fields. When pregnancy is suspected or diagnosed.

Warnings: Predisposing Factors for Coronary Artery Disease: Cigarette smoking increases the risk of serious cardiovascular side effects and mortality. Birth control pills increase this risk, especially with increasing age. Convincing data are available to support an upper age limit of 35 years for oral contraceptive use in women who smoke.

Other women who are independently at high risk for cardiovascular disease include those with diabetes, hypertension, abnormal lipid profile, or a family history of these. Whether oral contraceptives accentuate this risk is unclear.

In low-risk, nonsmoking women of any age, the benefits of oral contraceptive use outweigh the possible cardiovascular risks associated with low dose formulations. Consequently, oral contraceptives may be prescribed for these women up to the age of menopause.

> Cigarette smoking increases the risk of serious adverse effects on the heart and blood vessels. This risk increases with age and becomes significant in oral contraceptive users over 35 years of age. Women should be counselled not to smoke.

Discontinue medication at the earliest manifestation of:

A. Thromboembolic and cardiovascular disorders such as: thrombophlebitis, pulmonary embolism, cerebrovascular disorders, myocardial ischemia, mesenteric thrombosis and retinal thrombosis.

B. Conditions which predispose to venous stasis and to vascular thrombosis, e.g., immobilization after accidents or confinement to bed during long-term illness. Other nonhormonal methods of contraception should be used until regular activities are resumed. For use of oral contraceptives when surgery is contemplated, see Precautions.

C. Visual defects, partial or complete.

D. Papilledema, or ophthalmic vascular lesions.

E. Severe headache of unknown etiology or worsening of pre-existing migraine headache.

Precautions: Physical Examination and Follow-up: Before oral contraceptives are used, a thorough history and physical examination should be performed, including a blood pressure determination. Breasts, liver, extremities and pelvic organs should be examined. A Papanicolaou smear should be taken if the patient has been sexually active.

The first follow-up visit should be done 3 months after oral contraceptives are prescribed. Thereafter, examinations should be performed at least once a year, or more frequently if indicated. At each annual visit, examination should include those procedures that were done at the initial visit as outlined above or per recommendations of the Canadian Task Force on the Periodic Health Examination.

Pregnancy: Oral contraceptives should not be taken by pregnant women. However, if conception accidentally occurs while taking the pill, there is no conclusive evidence that the estrogen and progestin contained in the oral contraceptive will damage the developing child.

Lactation: In breast-feeding women, the use of oral contraceptives results in the hormonal components being excreted in breast milk and may reduce its quantity and quality. If the use of oral contraceptives is initiated after the establishment of lactation, there does not appear to be any effect on the quantity and quality of the milk. There is no evidence that low dose oral contraceptives are harmful to the nursing infant.

Hepatic Function: Patients who have had jaundice including a history of cholestatic jaundice during pregnancy should be given oral contraceptives with great care and under close observation.

The development of severe generalized pruritus or icterus requires that the medication be withdrawn until the problem is resolved.

If the jaundice should prove to be cholestatic in type, the use of oral contraceptives should not be resumed. In patients taking oral contraceptives, changes in the composition of the bile may occur and an increased incidence of gallstones has been reported. Hepatic nodules (adenoma and focal nodular hyperplasia) have been reported, particularly in long-term users of oral contraceptives. Although these lesions are extremely rare they have caused fatal intra-abdominal hemorrhage and should be considered in women presenting with an abdominal mass, acute abdominal pain or evidence of intra-abdominal bleeding.

Hypertension: Patients with essential hypertension whose blood pressure is well controlled may be given oral contraceptives but only under close supervision. If a significant elevation of blood pressure in previously normotensive or hypertensive subjects occurs at any time during the administration of the drug, cessation of medication is necessary.

Migraine and Headache: The onset or exacerbation of migraine or the development of headache of a new pattern which is recurrent, persistent or severe requires discontinuation of oral contraceptives and evaluation of the cause.

Diabetes: Current low dose oral contraceptives exert minimal impact on glucose metabolism. Diabetic patients, or those with a family history of diabetes, should be observed closely to detect worsening of carbohydrate metabolism. Patients predisposed to diabetes who can be kept under close supervision may be given oral contraceptives. Young diabetic patients

Table I—Marvelon

Drugs Which May Decrease the Efficacy of Oral Contraceptives

Class of Compound	Drug	Proposed Mechanism	Suggested Management
Anticonvulsants	Carbamazepine Ethosuximide Phenobarbital Phenytoin Primidone	Induction of hepatic microsomal enzymes: Rapid metabolism of estrogen and increased binding of progestin and ethinyl estradiol to SHBG.	Use higher dose OCs (50 µg ethinyl estradiol), another drug or another method.
Antibiotics	Ampicillin Cotrimoxazole Penicillin	Enterohepatic circulation disturbance, intestinal hurry.	For short course, use additional method or use another drug. For long course, use another method.
	Rifampin	Increased metabolism of progestins. Suspected acceleration of estrogen metabolism.	Use another method.
	Chloramphenicol Metronidazole Neomycin Nitrofurantoin Sulfonamides Tetracyclines	Induction of hepatic microsomal enzymes. Also disturbance of enterohepatic circulation.	For short course, use additional method or use another drug. For long course, use another method.
	Troleandomycin	May retard metabolism of OCs, increasing the risk of cholestatic jaundice.	
Antifungal	Griseofulvin	Stimulation of hepatic metabolism of contraceptive steroids may occur.	Use another method.
Sedatives and Hypnotics	Benzodiazepines Barbiturates Chloral hydrate Glutethimide Meprobamate	Induction of hepatic microsomal enzymes.	For short course, use additional method or another drug. For long course, use another method or higher dose OCs.
Antacids		Decreased intestinal absorption of progestins.	
Other Drugs	Phenylbutazone Antihistamines Analgesics Antimigraine preparations Vitamin E	Reduced OC efficacy has been reported. Remains to be confirmed.	

whose disease is of recent origin, well-controlled and not associated with hypertension or other signs of vascular disease such as ocular fundal changes should be monitored more frequently while using oral contraceptives.

Ocular Disease: Patients who are pregnant or are taking oral contraceptives may experience corneal edema that may cause visual disturbances and changes in tolerance to contact lenses, especially of the rigid type. Soft contact lenses usually do not cause disturbances. If visual changes or alterations in tolerance to contact lenses occur, temporary or permanent cessation of wear may be advised.

Breasts: Increasing age and a strong family history are the most significant risk factors for the development of breast cancer. Other established risk factors include obesity, nulliparity and late age at first full-term pregnancy. The identified groups of women that may be at increased risk of developing breast cancer before menopause are long-term users of oral contraceptives (more than 8 years) and starters at early age. In a few women, the use of oral contraceptives may accelerate the growth of an existing but undiagnosed breast cancer. Since any potential increased risk related to oral contraceptive use is small, there is no reason to change prescribing habits at present.

Women receiving oral contraceptives should be instructed in self-examination of their breasts. Their physicians should be notified whenever any masses are detected. A yearly clinical breast examination is also recommended because, if a breast cancer should develop, estrogen-containing drugs may cause a rapid progression.

Vaginal Bleeding: Persistent irregular vaginal bleeding requires assessment to exclude underlying pathology.

Fibroids: Patients with fibroids (leiomyomata) should be carefully observed. Sudden enlargement, pain or tenderness requires discontinuation of the use of oral contraceptives.

Emotional Disorders: Patients with a history of emotional disturbances, especially the depressive type, may be more prone to have a recurrence of depression while taking oral contraceptives. In cases of a serious recurrence, a trial of an alternate method of contraception should be made which may help to clarify the possible relationship. Women with premenstrual syndrome (PMS) may have a varied response to oral contraceptives, ranging from symptomatic improvement to worsening of the condition.

Laboratory Tests: Results of laboratory tests should be interpreted in the light that the patient is on oral contraceptives. The following laboratory tests are modified.

A. Liver function tests: Aspartate serum transaminase (AST): variously reported elevations. Alkaline phosphatase and gamma glutamine transaminase (GGT): slightly elevated.

B. Coagulation tests: Minimal elevation of test values reported for such parameters as prothrombin and Factors VII, VIII, IX and X.

C. Thyroid function tests: Protein binding of thyroxine is increased as indicated by increased total serum thyroxine concentrations and decreased T_3 resin uptake.

D. Lipoproteins: Small changes of unproven clinical significance may occur in lipoprotein cholesterol fractions.

E. Gonadotropins: LH and FSH levels are suppressed by the use of oral contraceptives. Wait 2 weeks after discontinuing the use of oral contraceptives before measurements are made.

Tissue Specimens: Pathologists should be advised of oral contraceptive therapy when specimens obtained from surgical procedures and Pap smears are submitted for examination.

Return to Fertility: After discontinuing oral contraceptive therapy, the patient should delay pregnancy until at least 1 normal spontaneous menstrual cycle has occurred in order to date the pregnancy. An alternative contraceptive method should be used during this time.

Amenorrhea: Women having a history of oligomenorrhea, secondary amenorrhea or irregular cycles may remain anovulatory or become amenorrheic following discontinuation of estrogen-progestin combination therapy. Amenorrhea, especially if associated with breast secretion, that continues for 6 months or more after withdrawal warrants a careful assessment of hypothalamic-pituitary function.

Thromboembolic Complications—Post-surgery: There is an increased risk of post-surgery thromboembolic complications in oral contraceptive users, after major surgery. If feasible, oral contraceptives should be discontinued and an alternative method substituted at least 1 month prior to **major** elective surgery. Oral contraceptives should not be resumed until the first menstrual period after hospital discharge following surgery.

Drug Interactions: The concurrent administration of oral contraceptives with other drugs may result in an altered response to either agent [see Table I (on previous page) and Table II]. Reduced effectiveness of the oral contraceptive, should it

Table II—Marvelon

Modification of Other Drug Action by Oral Contraceptives

Class of Compound	Drug	Modification of Other Drug Action	Suggested Management
Alcohol		Possible increased levels of ethanol or acetaldehyde.	Use with caution.
Alpha-II Adrenoreceptor Agents	Clonidine	Sedation effect increased.	Use with caution.
Anticoagulants	All	OCs increase clotting factors, decrease efficacy. However, OCs may potentiate action in some patients.	Use another method.
Anticonvulsants	All	Fluid retention may increase risk of seizures.	Use another method.
Antidiabetic Drugs	Oral hypoglycemics and insulin	OCs may impair glucose tolerance and increase blood glucose.	Use low dose estrogen and progestin OC or another method. Monitor blood glucose.
Antihypertensive Agents	Guanethidine and methyldopa	Estrogen component causes sodium retention, progestin has no effect.	Use low estrogen OC or use another method.
	Beta-blockers	Increased drug effect (decreased metabolism).	Adjust dose of drug if necessary. Monitor cardiovascular status.
Antipyretics	Acetaminophen	Increased renal clearance.	Dose of drug may have to be increased.
	Antipyridine	Impaired metabolism.	Decrease dose of drug.
	ASA	Effects of ASA may be decreased by the short-term use of OCs.	Patients on chronic ASA therapy may require an increase in ASA dosage.
Aminocaproic Acid		Theoretically, a hypercoagulable state may occur because OCs augment clotting factors.	Avoid concomitant use.
Betamimetic Agents	Isoproterenol	Estrogen causes decreased response to these drugs.	Adjust dose of drug as necessary. Discontinuing OCs can result in excessive drug activity.
Caffeine		The actions of caffeine may be enhanced as OCs may impair the hepatic metabolism of caffeine.	Use with caution.
Cholesterol Lowering Agents	Clofibrate	OCs may increase the clearance of clofibrate leading to decreased levels of clofibrate.	Use with caution.
Corticosteroids	Prednisone	Markedly increased serum levels.	Possible need for decrease in dose.
Cyclosporine		May lead to an increase in cyclosporine levels and hepatotoxicity.	Monitor hepatic function. The cyclosporine dose may have to be decreased.
Folic Acid		OCs have been reported to impair folate metabolism.	
Meperedine		Possible increased analgesia and CNS depression due to decreased metabolism of meperidine.	Use combination with caution.
Phenothiazine Tranquilizers	All phenothiazines, reserpine and similar drugs	Estrogen potentiates the hyperprolactinemia effect of these drugs.	Use other drugs or lower dose OCs. If galactorrhea or hyperprolactinemia occurs, use other method.
Sedatives and Hypnotics	Chlordiazepoxide Lorazepam Oxazepam Diazepam	Increased effect (increased metabolism).	Use with caution.
Theophylline	All	Decreased oxidation, leading to possible toxicity.	Use with caution. Monitor theophylline levels.
Tricyclic Antidepressants	Clomipramine (possibly others)	Increased side effects; i.e., depression.	Use with caution.
Vitamin B_{12}		OCs have been reported to reduce serum levels of Vitamin B_{12}.	

occur, is more likely with the low-dose formulations. It is important to ascertain all drugs that a patient is taking, both prescription and nonprescription, before oral contraceptives are prescribed.

Non-contraceptive Benefits of Oral Contraceptives: Several health advantages other than contraception have been reported.

1. Combination oral contraceptives reduce the incidence of cancer of the endometrium and ovaries.
2. Oral contraceptives reduce the likelihood of developing benign breast disease and, as a result, decrease the incidence of breast biopsies.
3. Oral contraceptives reduce the likelihood of development of functional ovarian cysts.
4. Pill-users have less menstrual blood loss and have more regular cycles, thereby reducing the chance of developing iron-deficiency anemia.
5. The use of oral contraceptives may decrease the severity of dysmenorrhea and premenstrual syndrome, and may improve acne vulgaris, hirsutism and other androgen-mediated disorders.
6. Oral contraceptives decrease the incidence of acute pelvic inflammatory disease and, thereby, reduce as well the incidence of ectopic pregnancy.
7. Oral contraceptives have potential beneficial effects on endometriosis.

Oral contraceptives **do not protect** against sexually transmitted diseases (STDs) including HIV/AIDS. For protection against STDs, it is advisable to use latex condoms **in combination with** oral contraceptives.

Adverse Effects: An increased risk of the following serious

Marvelon (cont'd)

adverse reactions has been associated with the use of oral contraceptives: thrombophlebitis, pulmonary embolism, mesenteric thrombosis, neuro-ocular lesions, e.g., retinal thrombosis, myocardial infarction, cerebral thrombosis, cerebral hemorrhage, hypertension, benign hepatic tumors, gallbladder disease, congenital anomalies.

The following adverse reactions also have been reported in patients receiving oral contraceptives: Nausea and vomiting, usually the most common adverse reaction, occurs in approximately 10% or less of patients during the first cycle. Other reactions, as a general rule, are seen less frequently or only occasionally, as follows: gastrointestinal symptoms (such as abdominal cramps and bloating), breakthrough bleeding, spotting, change in menstrual flow, dysmenorrhea, amenorrhea during and after treatment, temporary infertility after discontinuance of treatment, edema, chloasma or melasma which may persist, breast changes (tenderness, enlargement and secretion), change in weight (increase or decrease), endocervical hyperplasias, possible diminution in lactation when given immediately postpartum, cholestatic jaundice, migraine, increase in size of uterine leiomyomata, rash (allergic), mental depression, reduced tolerance to carbohydrates, vaginal candidiasis, premenstrual-like syndrome, intolerance to contact lenses, change in corneal curvature (steepening), cataracts, optic neuritis, retinal thrombosis, changes in libido, chorea, changes in appetite, cystitis-like syndrome, rhinitis, headache, nervousness, dizziness, hirsutism, loss of scalp hair, erythema multiforme, erythema nodosum, hemorrhagic eruption, vaginitis, porphyria, impaired renal function, Raynaud's phenomenon, auditory disturbances, hemolytic uremic syndrome, pancreatitis.

Overdose: Symptoms and Treatment: Serious ill effects have not been reported following acute ingestion of large doses of oral contraceptives by young children. Overdosage may cause nausea, and withdrawal bleeding may occur in females.

Dosage: Information for the Patient on How to Take the Birth Control Pill:

1. **Read these directions:**
   - before you start taking your pills, and
   - any time you are not sure what to do.
2. **Look at your pill pack** to see if it has 21 or 28 pills:
   - 21-Pill Pack: 21 active pills (with hormones) taken daily for 3 weeks, and then take no pills for 1 week

   or
   - 28-Pill Pack: 21 active pills (with hormones) taken daily for 3 weeks, and then 7 "reminder" pills (no hormones) taken daily for 1 week.

Also check the pill pack for instructions on (1) where to start and (2) directions to take pills (see package insert for illustrations).

3. You may wish to use a second method of birth control (e.g., latex condoms and spermicidal foam or gel) for the first 7 days of the first cycle of pill use. This will provide a back-up in case pills are forgotten while you are getting used to taking them.
4. When receiving any medical treatment, be sure to tell your doctor that you are using birth control pills.
5. **Many women have spotting or light bleeding or may feel sick to their stomach during the first 3 months on the pill.** If you do feel sick, do not stop taking the pill. The problem will usually go away. If it does not go away, check with your doctor or clinic.
6. **Missing pills also can cause some spotting or light bleeding,** even if you make up the missed pills. You also could feel a little sick to your stomach on the days you take 2 pills to make up for missed pills.
7. **If you miss pills at any time, you could get pregnant. The greatest risks for pregnancy are:**
   - when you start a pack late, and
   - when you miss pills at the beginning or at the very end of the pack.
8. **Always be sure you have ready:**
   - **another kind of birth control** (such as latex condoms and spermicidal foam or gel) to use as a back-up in case you miss pills, and
   - **an extra, full pack of pills.**
9. **If you have vomiting or diarrhea, or if you take some medicines,** such as antibiotics, your pills may not work as well. Use a back-up method, such as latex condoms and spermicidal foam or gel, until you can check with your doctor or clinic.
10. **If you forget more than 1 pill 2 months in a row,** talk to your doctor or clinic about how to make pill-taking easier or about using another method of birth control.

Table III—Marvelon

What To Do If You Miss Pills

Sunday Start	Day 1 Start
Miss 1 pill	**Miss 1 pill**
Take it as soon as you remember, and take the next pill at the usual time. This means that you might take 2 pills in one day.	Take it as soon as you remember, and take the next pill at the usual time. This means that you might take 2 pills in one day.
Miss 2 pills in a row	**Miss 2 pills in a row**
First 2 Weeks: 1. Take 2 pills the day you remember and 2 pills the next day. 2. Then take 1 pill a day until you finish the pack. 3. Use a back-up method of birth control if you have sex in the 7 days after you miss the pills.	**First 2 Weeks:** 1. Take 2 pills the day you remember and 2 pills the next day. 2. Then take 1 pill a day until you finish the pack. 3. Use a back-up method of birth control if you have sex in the 7 days after you miss the pills.
Third Week: 1. Keep taking 1 pill a day until Sunday. 2. On Sunday, safely discard the rest of the pack and start a new pack that day. 3. Use a back-up method of birth control if you have sex in the 7 days after you miss the pills. 4. You may not have a period this month. **If you miss 2 periods in a row, call your doctor or clinic.**	**Third Week:** 1. Safely dispose of the rest of the pill pack and start a new pack that same day. 2. Use a back-up method of birth control if you have sex in the 7 days after you miss the pills. 3. You may not have a period this month. **If you miss 2 periods in a row, call your doctor or clinic.**
Miss 3 or more pills in a row	**Miss 3 or more pills in a row**
Anytime in the Cycle: 1. Keep taking 1 pill a day until Sunday. 2. On Sunday, safely discard the rest of the pack and start a new pack that day. 3. Use a back-up method of birth control if you have sex in the 7 days after you miss the pills. 4. You may not have a period this month. **If you miss 2 periods in a row, call your doctor or clinic.**	**Anytime in the Cycle:** 1. Safely dispose of the rest of the pill pack and start a new pack that same day. 2. Use a back-up method of birth control if you have sex in the 7 days after you miss the pills. 3. You may not have a period this month. **If you miss 2 periods in a row, call your doctor or clinic.**

11. **If your questions are not answered here, call your doctor or clinic.**

When to start the first pack of pills: Be sure to read these instructions:
- before you start taking your pills, and
- any time you are not sure what to do.

Decide with your doctor or clinic what is the best day for you to start taking your first pack of pills. Your pills may be either a 21-day or a 28-day type.

A. 21-Day Combination: With this type of birth control pill, you are 21 days on pills with 7 days off pills. You must not be off the pills for more than 7 days in a row.

1. **The first day of your menstrual period (bleeding) is Day 1 of your cycle.** Your doctor may advise you to start taking the pills on Day 1 or on the first Sunday after your period begins. If your period starts on Sunday, start that same day.
2. Take 1 pill at approximately the same time every day for 21 days; **then take no pills for 7 days.** Start a new pack on the eighth day. You will probably have a period during the 7 days off the pill. (This bleeding may be lighter and shorter than your usual period.)

B. 28-Day Combination: With this type of birth control pill, you take 21 pills which contain hormones and 7 pills which contain no hormones.

1. **The first day of your menstrual period (bleeding) is Day 1 of your cycle.** Your doctor may advise you to start taking the pills on Day 1 or on the first Sunday after your period begins. If your period starts on Sunday, start that same day.

   For Day 1 start: Label the dispenser by selecting the appropriate day label strip that starts with Day 1 of your menstrual period (first day of menstruation is Day 1).

   or

   For Sunday start: Label the dispenser by selecting the day label strip that starts with Sunday.

   Place the day label strip in the space where you see the words "Place Day Label Here". Having the dispenser labelled with the days of the week will help remind you to take your pill every day.
2. Take 1 pill at approximately the same time every day for 28 days. Begin a new pack the next day, **not missing any days on the pills.** Your period should occur during the last 7 days of using that pill pack.

What to do during the month:

1. **Take a pill at approximately the same time every day until the pack is empty.**
   - Try to associate taking your pill with some regular activity like eating a meal or going to bed.
   - Do not skip pills even if you have bleeding between monthly periods or feel sick to your stomach (nausea).
   - Do not skip pills even if you do not have sex very often.
2. **When you finish a pack:**
   - **21 pills: Wait 7 days** to start the next pack. You will have your period during that week.
   - **28 pills:** Start the next pack **on the next day.** Take 1 pill every day. Do not wait any days between packs.

What to do if you miss pills: Table III outlines the actions you should take if you miss 1 or more of your birth control pills. Match the number of pills missed with the appropriate starting time for your type of pill pack.

Note: 28-Day Pack: If you forget any of the 7 "reminder" pills (without hormones) in Week 4, just safely dispose of the pills you missed. Then keep taking 1 pill each day until the pack is empty. You do not need to use a back-up method.

Always be sure you have on hand:
- a back-up method of birth control (such as latex condoms and spermicidal foam or gel) in case you miss pills, and
- an extra, full pack of pills.

If you forget more than 1 pill 2 months in a row, talk to your doctor or clinic. Talk about ways to make pill-taking easier or about using another method of birth control.

Information for the Patient: See Blue Section—Information for the Patient "Oral Contraceptives".

Supplied: Marvelon 21: Each white, round tablet contains: desogestrel 0.15 mg and ethinyl estradiol 0.03 mg. Nonmedicinal ingredients: colloidal silicon dioxide, hydroxypropyl methylcellulose, lactose, polyethylene glycol, povidone, starch, stearic acid, talc, titanium dioxide and vitamin E. Blister dispensers of 21.

Marvelon 28: Each white, round tablet contains: desogestrel 0.15 mg and ethinyl estradiol 0.03 mg. Nonmedicinal ingredients: colloidal silicon dioxide, hydroxypropyl methylcellulose, lactose, polyethylene glycol, povidone, starch, stearic acid, talc, titanium dioxide and vitamin E. Each green, round tablet contains the following inactive ingredients: hydroxypropyl methylcellulose, indigotine blue, iron oxide, lactose, magnesium stearate, polyethylene glycol, starch, titanium dioxide and talc. Blister dispensers of 21 white tablets and 7 green tablets.

Store between 15 and 30°C.

(Shown in Product Recognition Section)

MATERNA®

Wyeth-Ayerst

Multivitamins—Minerals

Prenatal/Postpartum Supplement

Indications: A multivitamin-mineral product for use as a dietary supplement during pregnancy, lactation and postpartum.

Contraindications: Iron therapy is contraindicated in the presence of hemochromatosis, hemosiderosis, hemolytic anemia.

Precautions: Folic acid may obscure pernicious anemia in that the peripheral blood picture may revert to normal while neurological manifestations remain progressive.

Oral iron preparations may aggravate existing peptic ulcer, regional enteritis and ulcerative colitis.

Iron compounds taken orally can impair the absorption of tetracycline antibiotics. Antacids given concomitantly with iron compounds decrease iron absorption.

Adverse Effects: Rarely, in iron-sensitive patients, mild gastrointestinal upsets may occur.

Dosage: One tablet daily or as prescribed.

Supplied: Each light pink, oval, scored, film-coated tablet, engraved "MATERNA" and "U24", contains: beta-carotene (a source of vitamin A) 1 500 IU, vitamin A (as vitamin A acetate) 1 500 IU, vitamin D (cholecalciferol) 250 IU, vitamin E (as dl-alpha tocopheryl acetate) 30 IU, vitamin C (ascorbic acid) 100 mg, folic acid 1 mg, vitamin B_1 (thiamine mononitrate) 3 mg, vitamin B_2 (riboflavin) 3.4 mg, vitamin B_6 (pyridoxine hydrochloride) 10 mg, niacinamide 20 mg, vitamin B_{12} (cyanocobalamin) 12 μg, biotin 30 μg, pantothenic acid (calcium pantothenate) 10 mg, calcium (as calcium carbonate) 250 mg, magnesium (as magnesium oxide) 50 mg, iodine (as potassium iodide) 0.15 mg, iron (as ferrous fumarate) 60 mg, copper (as cupric oxide) 2 mg, zinc (as zinc oxide) 25 mg, chromium (as chromium chloride) 25 μg, molybdenum (as sodium molybdate) 25 μg, manganese (as manganese sulfate) 5 mg, selenium (as sodium selenate) 25 μg. Nonmedicinal ingredients: crospovidone, FD&C Red No. 40 aluminum lake, hydroxypropyl methylcellulose, lactose, magnesium stearate, mineral oil light, polysorbate 80, sodium lauryl sulfate, stearic acid, syloid, titanium dioxide and triethyl citrate. Lactose: 1 mg. Tartrazine-free. Bottles of 100.

MAVIK™ Ⓟ

Knoll

Trandolapril

Angiotensin Converting Enzyme Inhibitor

Pharmacology: Trandolapril is a nonsulfydryl angiotensin converting enzyme (ACE) inhibitor, which is used in the treatment of mild to moderate essential hypertension and following acute myocardial infarction in stabilized patients with left ventricular dysfunction.

Angiotensin converting enzyme (ACE) is a peptidyl dipeptidase that catalyzes the conversion of angiotensin I to the pharmacologically active substance, angiotensin II, which is a vasopressor agent. In addition, angiotensin II stimulates aldosterone secretion by the adrenal cortex. Inhibition of angiotensin converting enzyme results in a decreased plasma angiotensin II level. The resulting lack of negative feedback on renal renin secretion leads to an increased plasma renin activity.

Angiotensin converting enzyme is identical to kininase II. Thus, trandolapril administration may interfere with the degradation of the potent peptide vasodilator bradykinin, which may contribute to the therapeutic activity of trandolapril. Trandolapril is a prodrug, which is hydrolyzed to its diacid form, trandolaprilat, a potent ACE inhibitor.

The antihypertensive effect of trandolapril is due to a reduction in peripheral vascular resistance with little or no change in cardiac output and heart rate. The decrease in blood pressure is not accompanied by water or sodium retention. No modification was found in the urinary excretion of chloride and potassium. Administration of trandolapril to patients with essential hypertension results in reduction of both supine and standing blood pressure.

Pharmacokinetics: Following a single oral administration of trandolapril to healthy volunteers, trandolapril was detectable in the plasma 30 minutes later with peak concentrations reached within 1 hour. Trandolaprilat, the active metabolite, reached peak plasma concentrations after approximately 6 hours. Plasma concentrations of both trandolapril and trandolaprilat were dose dependent. While food can delay the rate of absorption of trandolapril, there is no clinically significant effect on other pharmacokinetic and pharmacodynamic parameters of trandolaprilat.

Approximately 40 to 60% of an administered oral dose of trandolapril is absorbed. Trandolapril undergoes extensive first-pass metabolism in the liver, and this is the reason that its bioavailability is low: 7.5% (ranging from 4 to 14%). In the liver it is transformed into its biologically active diacid form, trandolaprilat. Trandolaprilat itself is poorly absorbed after oral administration. Minor metabolic pathways lead to the formation of diketopiperazine derivatives of trandolapril and trandolaprilat. These molecules have no ACE inhibitory activity. Glucuronide conjugated derivatives of trandolapril and trandolaprilat are also produced.

With once-daily dosing, a steady-state of trandolaprilat plasma concentrations is reached within 4 days in healthy male and female subjects as well as in patients with chronic renal failure. Similar results were found in young (<65 years) as well as old (≥65 years) male and female patients suffering from mild to moderate essential hypertension. As is the case with several other ACE inhibitors, trandolaprilat has a polyphasic elimination profile with a slow terminal phase, probably the result of binding to ACE and a subsequently slow dissociation from the enzyme. The effective half-life for accumulation of trandolaprilat has been estimated to be in the range of 16 to 24 hours. The accumulation ratio as measured in hypertensive patients was about 1.5. Trandolapril's elimination half-life is on average 0.7 hours. Eighty percent of the circulating trandolapril and up to 94% of the circulating trandolaprilat are bound to plasma proteins. The protein binding is not saturable for trandolapril but is saturable for trandolaprilat.

In healthy male volunteers the excretion, in urine and feces, of trandolapril following an 8 mg single oral dose of ^{14}C-labelled drug is virtually complete after 7 days (99±3%): 82% of the dose was eliminated in 48 hours and 93% of the dose in 72 hours. In this dual route of excretion, urinary and fecal recoveries accounted for 33 and 66% of the total excretion, respectively. Trandolaprilat represents 46% of the urinary and 57% of the fecal excretion. The glucuronide derivatives of trandolapril and trandolaprilat excreted represent each about 13% of total urinary excretion and, 2 and 4% of total fecal excretion. The diketopiperazine of trandolaprilat was 7% of the total urinary excretion. The amounts of trandolapril excreted unchanged and the corresponding diketopiperazine are negligible (<0.5% of the dose).

Over the first 16 to 20 hours following oral administration of trandolapril, there is a rapid elimination phase of trandolaprilat. Beyond this time, there is a prolonged terminal elimination phase. No adjustment in dosage is necessary when elderly patients are treated with trandolapril.

In patients with creatinine clearance ≤30 mL/min/1.73 m², the C_{max} and AUC of trandolaprilat were approximately doubled after repeated oral administration, as compared to those of normal subjects.

In patients with moderate to severe impairment of liver function, plasma trandolapril levels were approximately 10 times higher than in healthy subjects. The plasma concentrations of trandolaprilat and the quantities excreted in the urine were also increased, although to a lesser degree. The dose should therefore be reduced in these patients.

In one study, cirrhotic patients who received a single dose of trandolapril 2 mg exhibited a 9-fold increase in trandolapril C_{max} and AUC values. The C_{max} and AUC values of trandolaprilat were about doubled.

Pharmacodynamics: Administration of trandolapril to patients with mild to moderate essential hypertension results in a reduction of both supine and standing blood pressure usually with little or no orthostatic change or change in heart rate. Symptomatic postural hypotension is infrequent, although this may occur in patients who are salt- and/or volume-depleted (see Warnings).

In mild to moderate hypertensive patients, significant reductions in blood pressure were seen at 2 hours and peak antihypertensive effects were seen after approximately 8 hours. At the recommended doses, antihypertensive effects are maintained throughout the 24-hour dosing interval in most patients who responded to trandolapril. Abrupt withdrawal of trandolapril has not resulted in rapid increase in blood pressure.

Following single oral therapeutic doses in healthy male volunteers, a rapid onset of ACE inhibition was observed. The peak inhibition was reached between 2 and 4 hours after the initial dose.

The effectiveness of trandolapril appears to be similar in the elderly (over 65 years of age) and younger adult patients given the same daily doses.

The antihypertensive effect of ACE inhibitors is generally lower in black patients than in nonblacks.

The antihypertensive effect of trandolapril and thiazide diuretics used concurrently is greater than that seen with either drug used alone.

Indications: Essential Hypertension: In the treatment of patients with mild to moderate essential hypertension. It may be used alone or in association with thiazide diuretics.

Trandolapril should normally be used in patients in whom treatment with a diuretic or a beta-blocker was found ineffective or has been associated with unacceptable adverse effects.

Trandolapril can also be tried as an initial agent in those patients in whom use of diuretics and/or beta-blockers are contraindicated or in patients with medical conditions in which these drugs frequently cause serious adverse effects.

The safety and efficacy of trandolapril in patients with renovascular hypertension have not been established and therefore, its use in these conditions is not recommended.

Treatment Following Acute Myocardial Infarction: Following acute myocardial infarction in clinically stable patients with left ventricular dysfunction, with or without symptoms of heart failure, to improve survival and reduce hospitalizations for heart failure.

Sufficient experience in the treatment of patients with severe heart failure (NYHA class IV) immediately after myocardial infarction is not yet available.

General: In using trandolapril, consideration should be given to the risk of angioedema (see Warnings).

Pregnancy: **When used in pregnancy during the second and third trimesters, ACE inhibitors can cause injury or even death of the developing fetus. When pregnancy is detected trandolapril should be discontinued as soon as possible (see Warnings, Pregnancy and Information for the Patient).**

Contraindications: In patients who are hypersensitive to this drug, or to any ingredient in the formulation, or in those patients who have a history of angioedema.

Warnings: Angioedema: Angioedema has been reported in patients taking ACE inhibitors, including trandolapril. Angioedema associated with laryngeal involvement may be fatal. If laryngeal stridor or angioedema of the face, tongue, or glottis occurs, trandolapril should be discontinued immediately, the patient treated appropriately in accordance with accepted medical care, and carefully observed until the swelling disappears. In instances where swelling is confined to the face and lips, the condition generally resolves without treatment. Where there is involvement of tongue, glottis, or larynx, likely to cause airway obstruction, appropriate therapy (including, but not limited to 0.3 to 0.5 mL of s.c. epinephrine solution 1:1 000) should be administered promptly (see Adverse Effects).

Patients with a history of angioedema unrelated to ACE inhibitor therapy may be at increased risk of angioedema while receiving an ACE inhibitor (see Contraindications).

The incidence of angioedema during ACE inhibition therapy has been reported to be higher in black than in nonblack patients.

Hypotension: Symptomatic hypotension has occurred after administration of trandolapril, usually after the first or second dose or when the dose was increased. It is more likely to occur in patients who are volume depleted as a result of diuretic therapy, dietary salt restriction, dialysis, diarrhea, or vomiting. In patients with ischemic heart disease or cerebrovascular disease, an excessive fall in blood pressure could result in a myocardial infarction or cerebrovascular accident (see Adverse Effects). Because of the potential fall in blood pressure in these patients, therapy with trandolapril should be started under close medical supervision. Such patients should be followed closely for the first weeks of treatment and whenever the dose of trandolapril is increased. In patients with severe congestive heart failure, with or without associated renal insufficiency, ACE inhibitor therapy may cause excessive hypotension and has been associated with oliguria, and/or progressive azotemia, and rarely, with acute renal failure and/or death.

If hypotension occurs, the patient should be placed in a supine position and, if necessary, receive an i.v. infusion of 0.9% sodium chloride. A transient hypotensive response is not a contraindication to further doses which can be given usually without difficulty once the blood pressure has increased after volume expansion. However, lower doses of trandolapril and/or reduced concomitant diuretic therapy should be considered.

If hypotension develops in patients receiving treatment following acute myocardial infarction, consideration should be given to discontinuation of trandolapril (see Adverse Effects, Treatment Following Myocardial Infarction, and Dosage, Treatment Following Myocardial Infarction).

Neutropenia/Agranulocytosis: Agranulocytosis and bone marrow depression have been caused by ACE inhibitors. Current experience with trandolapril shows the incidence to be rare. Periodic monitoring of white blood cell counts should be considered, especially in patients with collagen vascular disease and/or renal disease.

Pregnancy: ACE inhibitors can cause fetal and neonatal morbidity and mortality when administered to pregnant women. Several dozen cases have been reported in the world literature. When pregnancy is detected, trandolapril should be discontinued as soon as possible.

Mavik (cont'd)

In rare cases (probably less than 1 in every 1 000 pregnancies) in which no alternative to ACE inhibitor therapy will be found, the mother(s) should be apprised of the potential hazard(s) to her (their) fetus(es). Serial ultrasound examinations should be performed to assess fetal development and well-being and the volume of amniotic fluid.

If oligohydramnios is observed, trandolapril should be discontinued unless it is considered life-saving for the mother. A nonstress test (NST), and/or a biophysical profiling (BPP) may be appropriate, depending upon the week of pregnancy. If concerns regarding fetal well-being still persist, a contraction stress testing (CST) should be considered.

Patients and physicians should be aware, however, that oligohydramnios may not appear until the fetus has sustained irreversible injury.

Infants with a history of in utero exposure to ACE inhibitors should be closely observed for hypotension, oliguria, and hyperkalemia. If oliguria occurs, attention should be directed toward support of blood pressure and renal perfusion. Exchange transfusion or dialysis may be required as a means of reversing hypotension and/or substituting for impaired renal function; however, limited experience with those procedures has not been associated with significant clinical benefit. It is not known if trandolapril or trandolaprilat can be removed from the body by hemodialysis.

Human Data: It is not known whether exposure limited to the first trimester of pregnancy can adversely affect fetal outcome. The use of ACE inhibitors during the second and third trimesters of pregnancy has been associated with fetal and neonatal injury including hypotension, neonatal skull hypoplasia, anuria, reversible or irreversible renal failure, and death. Oligohydramnios has also been reported, presumably resulting from decreased fetal renal function; oligohydramnios in this setting has been associated with fetal limb contractures, craniofacial deformation, and hypoplastic lung development. Prematurity and patent ductus arteriosus have also been reported, although it is not clear whether these occurrences were due to the ACE inhibitor exposure.

Animal Data: Teratology studies in the rat were carried out at doses of 0, 100, 300 or 1 000 mg/kg/day. An increased incidence of minor defects (dilation of renal pelvis and ureters) over control values was found at the 1 000 mg/kg/day dose series. In fertility studies, where doses of 0, 1, 10 or 100 mg/kg/day were used, the incidence of pelvic cavitation and dilated ureters was increased with the 10 and 100 mg/kg/day dose.

Teratology studies were carried out in the rabbit both without and with electrolyte supplementation. In 2 studies without supplementation covering the dose range 0.1 to 0.8 mg/kg, maternal deaths were seen at all doses with a dose-related incidence. These were associated with fetal toxicity and increased fetal loss. No teratological effect was seen. Supplementation with electrolytes allowed doses of 2 to 8 mg/kg to be given: maternal toxicity was again seen, particularly at 8 mg/kg with weight loss and abortion. No teratological effect was seen.

Two teratology studies were carried out in the cynomolgus monkey (doses of 0, 10, 50 or 250 mg/kg/day and also 5, 25 or 125 mg/kg/day): dosing was on days 20 to 50 of gestation with examination of the fetuses following cesarean section on day 100. Abortions were 3/10, 6/10, 5/11 and 7/10 at respectively 0, 10, 50 or 250 mg/kg/day and 1/10, 4/10, 4/10 and 7/10 at 0, 5, 25 or 125 mg/kg/day. Apart from 1 animal with a kinked tail in the group receiving 250 mg/kg/day, no other evidence of teratological effects attributable to treatment were observed.

Precautions: Renal Impairment: As a consequence of inhibiting the renin-angiotensin-aldosterone system, changes in renal function have been seen in susceptible individuals. In patients whose renal function may depend on the activity of the renin-angiotensin-aldosterone system, such as patients with bilateral renal artery stenosis, unilateral renal artery stenosis to a solitary kidney, or severe congestive heart failure, treatment with agents that inhibit this system has been associated with oliguria, progressive azotemia, and rarely, acute renal failure and/or death. In susceptible patients, concomitant diuretic use may further increase risk.

Use of trandolapril should include appropriate assessment of renal function.

Anaphylactoid Reactions During Membrane Exposure: Anaphylactoid reactions have been reported in patients dialyzed with high-flux membranes (e.g., polyacrylonitrile [PAN]) and treated concomitantly with an ACE inhibitor. Dialysis should be stopped immediately if symptoms such as nausea, abdominal cramps, burning, angioedema, shortness of breath and severe hypotension occur. Symptoms are not relieved by antihistamines. In these patients consideration should be given to using a different type of dialysis membrane or a different class of antihypertensive agents.

Anaphylactoid Reactions during LDL Apheresis: Rarely, patients receiving ACE inhibitors during low density lipoprotein apheresis with dextran sulfate have experienced life-threatening anaphylactoid reactions. These reactions were avoided by temporarily withholding ACE inhibitor therapy prior to each apheresis.

Anaphylactoid Reactions During Desensitization: There have been isolated reports of patients experiencing sustained life-threatening anaphylactoid reactions while receiving ACE inhibitors during desensitization treatment with hymenoptera (bees, wasps) venom. In the same patients, these reactions have been avoided when ACE inhibitors were temporarily withheld for at least 24 hours, but they have reappeared upon inadvertent rechallenge.

Hyperkalemia and Potassium-sparing Diuretics: Increases in serum potassium (upper limit of normal range 5 mmol/L) were observed in approximately 2.2% of patients in clinical trials treated with trandolapril. In most cases these resolved despite continued therapy. Hyperkalemia was not a cause of discontinuation of therapy in any hypertensive patient. Risk factors for the development of hyperkalemia may include renal insufficiency, diabetes mellitus, and the concomitant use of agents to treat hypokalemia or other drugs associated with increases in serum potassium (see Precautions, Drug Interactions).

Surgery/Anesthesia: In patients undergoing surgery or anesthesia with agents producing hypotension, trandolapril will block angiotensin II formation secondary to compensatory renin release. If hypotension occurs and is considered to be due to this mechanism, it may be corrected by volume repletion.

Aortic Stenosis: There is concern, on theoretical grounds, that patients with aortic stenosis might be at particular risk of decreased coronary perfusion when treated with vasodilators.

Patients with Impaired Liver Function: Trandolapril should be used with caution in patients with pre-existing liver abnormalities. In such patients baseline liver function tests should be obtained before administration of the drug and close monitoring of response and metabolic effects should apply.

Hepatitis (hepatocellular and/or cholestatic), elevations of liver enzymes and/or serum bilirubin have occurred during therapy with ACE inhibitors in patients with or without pre-existing liver abnormalities. In most cases the changes were reversed on discontinuation of the drug.

Elevations of liver enzymes and/or serum bilirubin have been reported with trandolapril (see Adverse Effects). Should the patient receiving trandolapril experience any unexplained symptoms particularly during the first weeks or months of treatment, it is recommended that a full set of liver function tests and any other necessary investigations be carried out. Discontinuation of trandolapril should be considered when appropriate (see Pharmacology, Pharmacokinetics).

Lactation: Trandolapril is not recommended in nursing mothers as there are no studies available. Following administration of radiolabelled trandolapril to lactating rats, radioactivity was measured in the milk.

Children: The safety and effectiveness of trandolapril in children have not been established; therefore use in this group is not recommended.

Geriatrics: Although clinical experience has not identified differences in response between the elderly (≥65 years) and younger patients (<65 years), greater sensitivity of some older individuals cannot be ruled out (see Pharmacology, Pharmacodynamics).

Cough: As with other ACE inhibitors, dry, persistent cough, which usually disappears only after withdrawal or lowering of the dose of trandolapril, has been reported. Such possibility should be considered as part of the differential diagnosis of cough.

Drug Interactions: Alcohol: Alcohol enhances the bioavailability of ACE inhibitors.

Concomitant Diuretic Therapy: Patients concomitantly taking ACE inhibitors and diuretics, and especially those in whom diuretic therapy was recently instituted, may occasionally experience an excessive reduction of blood pressure after initiation of therapy. The possibility of adverse hypotensive effects after the first dose of trandolapril can be minimized by either discontinuing the diuretic or increasing the salt intake prior to initiation of treatment with trandolapril. If it is not possible to discontinue the diuretic, the starting dose of trandolapril should be reduced and the patient should be closely observed for several hours following the initial dose until blood pressure has stabilized (see Warnings and Dosage).

Agents Increasing Serum Potassium: Since trandolapril decreases aldosterone production, elevation of serum potassium may occur. Potassium sparing diuretics such as spironolactone, triamterene or amiloride, or potassium supplements should be given only for documented hypokalemia and with caution and frequent monitoring of serum potassium, since a significant increase in serum potassium could occur.

Salt substitutes which contain potassium should be used with caution.

Agents Causing Renin Release: The antihypertensive effect of trandolapril is augmented by antihypertensive agents that cause renin release (e.g., diuretics).

Lithium: Increased serum lithium levels and symptoms of lithium toxicity have been reported in patients receiving concurrently ACE inhibitors and lithium. Lithium based drugs should be administered with caution, and frequent monitoring of serum lithium levels is recommended. If a diuretic is also used, the risk of lithium toxicity may be further increased.

Antacids: They decrease the bioavailability of ACE inhibitors (it is recommended to ingest these products separately).

Digoxin: In one open-label study conducted in 8 healthy male volunteers, in which multiple therapeutic doses of both trandolapril and digoxin were administered, no changes were found in serum levels of trandolapril, trandolaprilat and digoxin. Pharmacodynamically the combination had a synergistic effect on left ventricular functions, as evidenced by the improvement in systolic time-intervals.

Warfarin: In a multidose, double-blind, placebo-controlled, pharmacodynamic interaction study with 20 healthy volunteers administered trandolapril (2 mg) and therapeutic doses of warfarin, no clinically significant effects on the anticoagulant properties of warfarin were found.

Nifedipine SR: A study evaluating the potential pharmacokinetic and pharmacodynamic interaction between nifedipine (20 mg) (sustained release) and trandolapril (4 mg) was conducted in 12 healthy male volunteers. After a single dose, no pharmacokinetic or pharmacodynamic interaction was found between the two products.

Nonsteroidal Anti-inflammatory Agents: The antihypertensive effects of ACE inhibitors may be reduced with concomitant administration of nonsteroidal anti-inflammatory agents. As with other ACE inhibitors, the combination of trandolapril with nonsteroidal anti-inflammatory agents predisposes to a risk of hyperkalemia particularly in cases of renal failure.

Allopurinol, Cytostatic, Immunosuppressive Agents, Systemic Corticosteroids or Procainamide: Concomitant administration with ACE inhibitors may lead to an increased risk of leukopenia.

Information for the Patient: Angioedema: Angioedema, including laryngeal edema, may occur especially following the first dose of trandolapril. Patients should be so advised and told to report immediately any signs or symptoms suggesting angioedema, such as swelling of face, extremities, eyes, lips, tongue, difficulty in swallowing or breathing. They should immediately stop taking trandolapril and consult with their physician (see Warnings).

Hypotension: Patients should be cautioned to report lightheadedness, especially during the first few days of trandolapril therapy. If actual syncope occurs, the patients should be told to discontinue the drug and consult with their physician.

All patients should be cautioned that excessive perspiration and dehydration may lead to an excessive fall in blood pressure because of reduction in fluid volume. Other causes of volume depletion such as vomiting or diarrhea may also lead to a fall in blood pressure, patients should be advised to consult with their physician.

Agranulocytosis/Neutropenia: Patients should be told to report promptly to their physician any indication of infection (e.g., sore throat, fever) as this may be a sign of neutropenia (see Warnings and Adverse Effects).

Impaired Liver Function: Patients should be advised to return to their physician if they experience any symptoms possibly related to liver dysfunction. This would include "viral-like symptoms" in the first weeks to months of therapy (such as fever, malaise, muscle pain, rash or adenopathy which are possible indicators of hypersensitivity reactions), or if abdominal pain, nausea or vomiting, loss of appetite, jaundice, itching or any other unexplained symptoms occur during therapy.

Hyperkalemia: Patients should be told not to use salt substitutes or foods containing potassium without consulting their physician (see Precautions).

Pregnancy: Since the use of trandolapril during pregnancy can cause injury and even death of the developing fetus, patients should be advised to report promptly to their physician if they become pregnant.

Adverse Effects: Essential Hypertension: The safety experience in controlled and open-label studies includes 1 988 patients with mild to moderate essential hypertension who received trandolapril therapy. Of these, 265 patients were 65 years of age or older. In placebo and active drug-controlled trials, 1 409 patients received trandolapril. In open-label trials, 1 098 received trandolapril therapy, of which 212 continued treatment for 24 months, 689 for at least 12 months, and 911 for at least 6 months.

Severe adverse events occurring in controlled clinical trials (n=1 049) with doses of trandolapril ranging from 0.5 mg to 8 mg included headache (1.8%), pharyngitis (1%), nausea (0.3%), dizziness (0.3%), hot flushes (0.3%), bronchitis (0.3%), arthralgia (0.3%), pancreatitis (0.3%), tachycardia (0.2%), stomatitis (0.2%), urinary tract infection (0.2%).

One serious adverse event was judged to be possibly related to trandolapril therapy. This involved a rapid supraventricular arrhythmia with atrial flutter which occurred in a 68-year-old male patient with a known history of heart disease.

The adverse events ≥1%, and premature discontinuations due to these events, in controlled trials (N=1 409), regardless of relationship to treatment are shown in Table I.

Table I—Mavik

Adverse Events

Body System	Controlled Clinical Trials N=1 409 Adverse Event Incidence %	Discontinuations %
Body as a Whole		
Infection	1.0	0.1
Malaise	2.5	0.2
Asthenia	3.4	0.1
Flu Syndrome	2.0	—
Gastrointestinal		
Nausea	2.6	0.7
Gastrointestinal Pain	1.9	0.1
Diarrhea	0.9	
Nervous System		
Dizziness	4.9	0.1
Headache	7.8	0.9
Vertigo	1.2	1.1
Respiratory		
Cough Increased	2.3	3.0*
Upper Respiratory Infection	4.9	—
Bronchitis	2.7	—
Pharyngitis	1.4	—
Rhinitis	1.0	—
Dermatologic		
Urticaria	0.9	—

*Includes all patients exposed to trandolapril in controlled and open-label trials.

Treatment Following Acute Myocardial Infarction: In a survival study in patients with left ventricular dysfunction following myocardial infarction, 876 patients randomized to trandolapril, and 873 to placebo, were treated for an average of 2 years.

The most serious adverse events occurring more frequently than with placebo included dizziness (2.6 %) and hypotension (1.5 %). The most frequent clinical adverse events occurring more frequently with placebo were cough, dizziness and hypotension.

The adverse events with an incidence ≥ 3%, occurring in a higher percentage of trandolapril treated patients than in placebo treated patients, regardless of relationship to treatment are presented in Table II. The incidence of premature discontinuations, due to these adverse events, are also presented.

Rash (2.7%), cerebral ischemia (2.6%), thrombocytopenia (2.4%), uremia (2.3%), stomach ulcer (2.2%), diarrhea (2.1%), atrial flutter (1.8%), sepsis (1.0%) and taste perversion (1.0%) were noted to occur in a frequency greater than placebo.

General: Adverse events <1% irrespective of relationship to treatment in clinical trials and postmarketing experience include:

Body as a Whole: abnormal feeling, abdominal pain, pain in extremities and myalgia.

Cardiovascular: palpitation, hypotension, chest pain, syncope, hypertension, migraine, tachycardia, edema, angina pectoris myocardial infarction, postural hypotension.

Dermatologic: urticaria, pruritus, rash, pemphigus, Stevens-Johnson syndrome.

Table II—Mavik

Adverse Events

Body System	Adverse Events: Trandolapril (n=876) %	Adverse Events: Placebo (n=873) %	Discontinuations: Trandolapril (n=876) %	Discontinuations: Placebo (n=873) %
Body as a Whole				
Asthenia	3.0	2.4	0.7	0.3
Cardiovascular				
Coronary Artery Disorder	7.3	6.1	0.9	1.0
Hypotension	10.3	4.9	2.1	0.8
Peripheral Vascular Disorder	3.8	1.8	0.2	0.2
Syncope	5.4	3.1	0.2	0.1
Ventricular Tachycardia	4.3	3.9	0.2	0.6
Gastrointestinal				
Dyspepsia	5.4	4.5	0.3	0.2
Gastritis	3.3	3.0	0.1	0.0
Metabolic and Nutritional Disorders				
BUN Increased	8.7	7.2	0.7	0.1
Creatinine Increased	4.5	2.4	1.0	0.5
Hyperkalemia	4.9	2.6	0.1	0.0
Hyperuricemia	14.2	13.2	0.1	0.1
Hypocalcemia	4.5	3.7	0.0	0.1
Hypoproteinemia	4.5	4.2	—	—
Musculoskeletal				
Myalgia	4.1	2.9	0.0	0.1
Nervous System				
Dizziness	22.6	16.8	4.0	1.8
Respiratory				
Cough Increased	33.9	21.0	4.5	1.5

Gastrointestinal: vomiting, constipation, dyspepsia, anorexia, hepatitis, pancreatitis, esophagitis.

Nervous: anxiety, depression, paresthesia, sleep disorder, decreased libido, hot flushes, somnolence, insomnia, sweating, tremor, cerebrovascular accident.

Respiratory: dyspnea, epistaxis.

Hematologic: leukopenia, thrombocytopenia, hemolytic anemia.

Metabolic and Nutritional Disorder: edema, peripheral edema.

Urogenital System: kidney failure, urinary tract infection, polyurea.

Other Adverse Events: gout, impotence, tinnitus, abnormal vision, arthralgia, dry mouth, taste disorders, increased sweating, myoclonus, anaphylactoid reactions, glaucoma, leukocytoclastic vasculitis.

Rare cases of angioedema affecting the face, extremities, lips, tongue, glottis and/or larynx have been reported in patients treated with ACE inhibitor, including trandolapril.

A symptom complex has been reported which may include fever, vasculitis, myalgia, arthralgia/arthritis, a positive ANA, elevated ESR, eosinophilia and leukocytosis. Rash, photosensitivity or other dermatologic manifestations may also occur.

Clinical Laboratory Test Findings: increased creatinine, increased lactic dehydrogenase, increased alkaline phosphatase, increased blood urea nitrogen, occasional elevation of transaminases, increased bilirubin, hyperglycemia.

Overdose: Symptoms and Treatment: No data are available regarding overdosage of trandolapril in humans. The most likely clinical manifestation would be symptoms attributable to severe hypotension, which should normally be treated by i.v. volume expansion with normal saline. It is not known if trandolapril or trandolaprilat can be removed from the body by hemodialysis.

Dosage: Essential Hypertension: Dosage must be individualized. Initiation of therapy requires consideration of recent antihypertensive drug treatment, the extent of blood pressure elevation and salt restriction. The dosage of other antihypertensive agents being used with trandolapril may need to be adjusted.

The drug may be taken before, during or after meals.

Monotherapy: The recommended initial dosage is 1 mg once daily. Dosage should be adjusted according to blood pressure response at intervals of 2 to 4 weeks up to a maximum of 4 mg once daily. The usual maintenance dose is 1 to 2 mg once daily.

In some patients treated once daily, the antihypertensive effect may diminish towards the end of the dosing interval. This can be evaluated by measuring blood pressure just prior to dosing to determine whether satisfactory control is being maintained for 24 hours. If it is not, an increase in dose should be considered. If blood pressure is not controlled with trandolapril alone, a diuretic may be added.

Diuretic-treated Patients: Symptomatic hypotension occasionally may occur following the initial dose and is more likely in patients who are currently being treated with a diuretic. The diuretic should, if possible, be discontinued for 2 to 3 days before beginning therapy with trandolapril to reduce the likelihood of hypotension (see Warnings). If the diuretic cannot be discontinued, an initial dose of 0.5 mg trandolapril should be used with careful medical supervision for several hours and until blood pressure has stabilized. The dosage of trandolapril should subsequently be titrated to the optimal response.

Renal Impairment: For patients with a creatinine clearance below 30 mL/min/1.73 m², the recommended initial dose is 0.5 mg once daily. Dosage may be titrated upward until blood pressure is controlled or to a maximum total daily dose of 1 mg.

In patients with severe renal impairment (creatinine clearance below 10 mL/min/1.73 m²) a daily dosage of 0.5 mg in a single dose should not be exceeded.

Liver Impairment: The recommended initial dose is 0.5 mg once daily.

A single oral dose of 2 mg of trandolapril was administered to patients with hepatic cirrhosis. Compared to healthy subjects receiving the same dose, C_{max} and AUC values of trandolapril increased by approximately 9 times; C_{max} and AUC of trandolaprilat were nearly doubled (see Pharmacology, Pharmacokinetics and Precautions, Patients with Impaired Liver Function).

Geriatrics: In elderly patients with normal renal and hepatic function, no dosage adjustment is necessary (see Precautions, Geriatrics).

However, as some elderly patients may be particularly susceptible to ACE inhibitors, administration of low initial doses and evaluation of the blood pressure response and of the renal function at the beginning of the treatment is recommended.

Treatment Following Acute Myocardial Infarction: Dosage should be individualized. Initiation of therapy requires consideration of concomitant medication and baseline blood pressure in hemodynamically stable patients.

A starting dose of 1 mg trandolapril once daily should be initiated no earlier than the third day following acute myocardial infarction in patients with left ventricular dysfunction.

After 2 days at 1 mg once daily, the dose should be increased to 2 mg once daily. For patients who cannot tolerate this dose, the 1 mg once daily dose can be maintained.

After 1 month, patients tolerating the 2 mg once daily dose should have their dosage increased to 4 mg once daily. Again, for patients who cannot tolerate the 4 mg once daily dose, the 2 mg once daily dose can be maintained.

The dose must be reduced when it is clinically necessary (see Warnings, Hypotension). If hypotension preventing the patient from standing or walking is observed and is not explained by other factors, the dose must be reduced.

Mavik (cont'd)

For patients with renal or liver impairment, a starting dose no higher than 0.5 mg once daily should be instituted.

Information for the Patient: See Blue Section—Information for the Patient "Mavik".

Supplied: 0.5 mg: Each red opaque body and yellow opaque cap, no. 4 gelatin capsule, contains: trandolapril 0.5 mg. Nonmedicinal ingredients: maize starch, lactose, povidone and sodium stearyl fumarate; capsule cap: titanium dioxide and yellow iron oxide; capsule body: erythrosine, titanium dioxide and yellow iron oxide. HDPE plastic bottles of 100.

1 mg: Each red opaque body and orange opaque cap, no. 4 gelatin capsule, contains: trandolapril 1 mg. Nonmedicinal ingredients: maize starch, lactose, povidone and sodium stearyl fumarate; capsule cap: titanium dioxide and yellow iron oxide; capsule body: erythrosine, titanium dioxide and yellow iron oxide. HDPE plastic bottles of 100.

2 mg: Each red opaque body and red opaque cap, no. 4 gelatin capsule, contains: trandolapril 2 mg. Nonmedicinal ingredients: maize starch, lactose, povidone and sodium stearyl fumarate; capsule cap: erythrosine, titanium dioxide and yellow iron oxide; capsule body: erythrosine, titanium dioxide and yellow iron oxide. HDPE plastic bottles of 100.

Store in original container at room temperature, below 25°C and not beyond the date indicated on the container.

Reviewed 1999

MAXERAN® Ⓟ

Hoechst Marion Roussel

Metoclopramide HCl

Modifier of Upper Gastrointestinal Tract Motility—Antiemetic

Pharmacology: Metoclopramide is a benzamide derivative, structurally related to procainamide and sulpiride. As with sulpiride, it has dopamine-antagonist activity with selective affinity for D-2 (non-adenylate cyclase-linked) receptors. The behavioral, motor, and neuroendocrine effects of metoclopramide have been linked to its antidopaminergic activity.

Metoclopramide has antiemetic properties, which are believed to result from its action on the chemoreceptor trigger zone. A peripheral mechanism of action also may be involved.

Metoclopramide increases resting pressure in the lower esophageal sphincter and the gastric fundus, and gives rise to an increase in the amplitude of peristaltic movements in the esophagus, gastric antrum and small intestine. These actions result in hastened esophageal clearance, accelerated gastric emptying and shortened transit time through the small bowel. These effects are blocked by atropine and opioids but not by vagotomy. Metoclopramide elevates serum prolactin and also causes transient increases in circulating aldosterone levels. These effects are thought to be due to blockade of dopamine receptors at the pituitary and adrenocortical cellular level.

Following i.v. administration, peak plasma levels occur within minutes, and between 45 to 90 minutes after oral administration. The elimination half-life is approximately 3 to 5 hours. In patients with impaired renal function, the half-life is prolonged and may reach 14 hours or more. About 20% of the drug is eliminated unchanged in the urine, and 30 to 40% is eliminated as the sulfate conjugate. There is a first-pass effect after oral administration, and bioavailability varies between 30 to 70%. Metoclopramide is 15 to 20% bound to plasma proteins.

In some patients, metoclopramide may produce sedation, drowsiness, galactorrhea, menstrual disorders and extrapyramidal reactions. Extrapyramidal symptoms are more frequent at higher than recommended doses, but occur with therapeutic doses, particularly in children and in patients with impaired renal or hepatic function. Tardive dyskinesia has been reported following discontinuation of long-term treatment with metoclopramide.

Indications: An adjunct in the management of delayed gastric emptying associated with subacute and chronic gastritis or following vagotomy and pyloroplasty and other surgical procedures.

Metoclopramide has also been found useful as an adjunct to facilitate small bowel intubation.

Metoclopramide has been found useful as an adjunct to facilitate gastroduodenal evacuation of barium meals and improve radiological visualization of the gastroduodenal region in patients with gastric atonia, pylorospasm, spasm of the duodenal bulb, or with mechanical gastric outlet obstruction. Metoclopramide has also been shown to accelerate small bowel transit of the barium meal and to facilitate fluoroscopy of the terminal ileum.

Metoclopramide, when used preoperatively by the oral route, may be useful to reduce postoperative vomiting induced by narcotics.

Contraindications: Should not be used whenever stimulation of gastrointestinal motility might be dangerous; i.e., in the presence of gastrointestinal hemorrhage, mechanical obstruction or perforation. Metoclopramide is contraindicated in patients with known sensitivity or intolerance to the drug.

Warnings: Metoclopramide elevates prolactin levels and the elevation persists during chronic administration. Tissue culture experiments indicate that approximately ⅓ of human breast cancers are prolactin-dependent **in vitro,** a factor of potential importance if the prescription of metoclopramide is contemplated in a patient with previously detected breast cancer. Although disturbances such as galactorrhea, amenorrhea, gynecomastia and impotence have been reported with prolactin-elevating drugs, the clinical significance of elevated serum prolactin levels is unknown for most patients. An increase in mammary neoplasms has been found in rodents after chronic administration of prolactin-stimulating neuroleptic drugs. Neither clinical studies nor epidemiologic studies conducted to date, however, have shown an association between chronic administration of these drugs and mammary tumorigenesis; the available evidence is too limited to be conclusive at this time.

Metoclopramide should not be used in patients with epilepsy or extrapyramidal symptoms unless the expected benefits outweigh the risk of increased frequency and severity of seizures or extrapyramidal reactions.

Pregnancy: The safe use of metoclopramide in pregnancy has not been established. Therefore, it should not be used in pregnant women, unless, in the opinion of the physician, the expected benefits to the patient outweigh potential risks to the fetus.

Children: Daily dose should not exceed 0.5 mg/kg, since with higher doses extrapyramidal symptoms frequently occur.

Precautions: The recommended dosage of metoclopramide should usually not be exceeded since a further increase in dosage will not produce a corresponding increase in clinical response.

Drug Interactions: Anticholinergic drugs antagonize the effects of metoclopramide on gastrointestinal motility. Metoclopramide should not be used in conjunction with ganglioplegic or neuroleptic drugs since potentiation of effects might occur. The sedative effects of metoclopramide may be potentiated by sedatives, hypnotics, narcotics and anxiolytics.

Metoclopramide may decrease the absorption of drugs from the stomach (e.g. digoxin) whereas absorption from the small bowel may be accelerated (e.g., acetaminophen, tetracyclines, levodopa, ethanol).

Care should be exercised when metoclopramide is administered in combination with a MAO inhibitor. In an animal study, pre-treatment with a MAO inhibitor increased the toxicity of i.v. metoclopramide.

In patients with pheochromocytoma, i.v. administered metoclopramide may cause an hypertensive crisis. These crisis may be controlled by i.v. phentolamine.

Adverse Effects: Drowsiness, fatigue and lassitude occur in approximately 10% of patients at the usual recommended dosage. Less frequent adverse reactions, occurring in approximately 5% of patients are insomnia, headache, dizziness and bowel disturbances. Galactorrhea and menstrual disorders have also been reported.

The more serious adverse reactions associated with the use of metoclopramide are parkinsonism and/or other extrapyramidal reactions. These consist often of a feeling of restlessness, facial spasms, involuntary movements and in some cases, torticollis, muscular twitching, trismus, oculogyric crisis, and opisthotonos. Dystonic reactions resembling tetanus have been reported. Extrapyramidal side effects appear to occur more frequently at dosages higher than the usual recommended dosage. Tardive dyskinesia, which in some cases appears to be irreversible, has been reported after discontinuation of long-term metoclopramide therapy. Therefore, prolonged treatment with metoclopramide should be avoided.

Overdose: Symptoms: Symptoms of overdosage may include drowsiness, disorientation and extrapyramidal reactions. Anticholinergic, antiparkinson drugs or antihistamines with anticholinergic properties such as diphenhydramine have effectively controlled extrapyramidal reactions. Symptoms are self-limiting and usually disappear within 24 hours.

Treatment: Management of overdosage consists of gastric emptying, close observation and supportive therapy.

Hemodialysis removes relatively little metoclopramide probably because of the small amount of the drug in blood relative to tissues. Similarly, continuous ambulatory peritoneal dialysis does not remove significant amounts of drug. It is unlikely that dosage would need to be adjusted to compensate for losses through dialysis. Dialysis is not likely to be an effective method of drug removal in overdose situations. Methemoglobinemia has occurred in premature and fullterm neonates who were given overdoses of metoclopramide (1 to 4 mg/kg/day orally, i.m. or i.v. for 1 to 3 or more days). Methemoglobinemia has not been reported in neonates treated with 0.5 mg/kg/day in divided doses. Methemoglobinemia can be reversed by i.v. administration of methylene blue.

Dosage: Note: **The total adult and pediatric daily dosage must not exceed 0.5 mg/kg/body weight.**

Delayed Gastric Emptying: Adults: 5 to 10 mL (5 to 10 mg) 3 or 4 times a day before meals, depending upon response and body weight.

Children (5 to 14 years): 2.5 to 5 mL (2.5 to 5 mg) 3 times a day before meals, depending on response and body weight.

Diagnostic Radiology: Adults: 20 mL (20 mg) 5 to 10 minutes before barium swallow.

Renal or Hepatic Impairment: Since metoclopramide is excreted principally through the kidneys, in those patients whose creatinine clearance is below 40 mL/min, therapy should be initiated at approximately one-half the recommended dosage. Depending upon clinical efficacy and safety considerations, the dosage may be increased or decreased as appropriate.

See Overdose section for information regarding dialysis. Metoclopramide undergoes minimal hepatic metabolism, except for simple conjugation. Its safe use has been described in patients with advanced liver disease whose renal function was normal.

Supplied: Each mL contains: metoclopramide HCl 1 mg. Nonmedicinal ingredients: artificial and natural orange flavors, citric acid, FD&C Yellow No. 6, methylparaben, natural apricot flavor, propylparaben, purified water and sorbitol. Bottles of 500 mL.

(Shown in Product Recognition Section)

MAXIDEX® Ⓟ

Alcon

Dexamethasone

Ophthalmic Anti-inflammatory

Supplied: Ophthalmic Ointment: Each tube of sterile ointment contains: dexamethasone 0.1% in a white petrolatum base. Nonmedicinal ingredients: liquid lanolin, methylparaben and propylparaben. Tubes of 3.5 g.

Ophthalmic Suspension: Each sterile Drop-Tainer dispenser contains: 0.1% dexamethasone. Preserved with benzalkonium chloride. Nonmedicinal ingredients: citric acid, edetate disodium, 0.5% hydroxypropyl methylcellulose, polysorbate 80, purified water, sodium chloride and sodium phosphate. Drop-Tainer dispensers of 5 mL.

MAXIPIME™ Ⓟ

Bristol-Myers Squibb

Cefepime HCl

Antibiotic

Pharmacology: Cefepime is a semi-synthetic broad spectrum cephalosporin antibiotic intended for i.m. or i.v. administration. Cefepime is a bactericidal agent that acts by inhibition of bacterial cell wall synthesis. It has a broad spectrum of activity against a wide range of gram-positive and gram-negative bacteria.

Pharmacokinetics: The average plasma concentrations of cefepime in normal adult males at various times following single

30-minute infusions and single i.m. injections of 500 mg, 1 g and 2 g are summarized in Table I.

Table I—Maxipime

Mean Plasma Concentrations of Cefepime (μg/mL)

Cefepime Dose	0.5 h	1 h	2 h	4 h	8 h	12 h
			I.V.			
500 mg	38.2	21.6	11.6	5.0	1.4	0.2
1 g	78.7	44.5	24.3	10.5	2.4	0.6
2 g	163.1	85.8	44.8	19.2	3.9	1.1
			I.M.			
500 mg	8.2	12.5	12.0	6.9	1.9	0.7
1 g	14.8	25.9	26.3	16.0	4.5	1.4
2 g	36.1	49.9	51.3	31.5	8.7	2.3

The average elimination half-life of cefepime is approximately 2 hours, and does not vary with respect to dose over the range of 250 mg to 2 g. There was no accumulation in healthy subjects receiving doses up to 2 g i.v. every 8 hours for a period of 9 days. Total body clearance averages 120 mL/minute. The average renal clearance of cefepime is 110 mL/minute, suggesting that the compound is eliminated almost exclusively by renal mechanisms, primarily glomerular filtration. Urinary recovery of unchanged cefepime represents approximately 85% of dose, resulting in high concentrations of cefepime in the urine. The serum protein binding of cefepime averages 16.4% and is independent of its concentration in the serum. The average steady-state volume of distribution is 18 L.

Following i.m. administration, cefepime is completely absorbed. The pharmacokinetics of cefepime administered i.m. are linear over the range of 500 mg to 2 g and do not vary with respect to treatment duration.

Children: Cefepime pharmacokinetics have been evaluated in pediatric patients following single and multiple 50 mg/kg doses on q8h (n=29) and q12h (n=13) schedules. The mean (±SD) age of the patients was 3.6 (±3.3) years, and ranged from 2.1 months to 11.2 years. Following a single i.v. dose, total body clearance and the steady-state volume of distribution averaged 3.3 (±1.0) mL/min/kg and 0.3 (±0.1) L/kg, respectively. The overall mean elimination half-life was 1.7 (±0.4) hours. The urinary recovery of unchanged cefepime was 60.4 (±30.4)% of the administered dose, and renal clearance was the primary pathway of elimination, averaging 2.0 (±1.1) mL/min/kg. There were no significant differences in the pharmacokinetics of cefepime among pediatric patients of various ages or between male (n=25) and female patients (n=17). There was no evidence of accumulation of cefepime in patients treated for up to 14 days with either regimen. The absolute bioavailability of cefepime after an i.m. dose of 50 mg/kg was 82.3 (±15.6)% in 8 patients. The exposure to cefepime, including minimum plasma concentrations at steady state, following a 50 mg/kg i.v dose in a pediatric patient is comparable to that in adults treated with a 2 g i.v. dose.

Indications: In the treatment of the following infections when caused by susceptible strains of the designated microorganisms: Adults: Lower respiratory tract infections: nosocomial and community acquired pneumonia caused by P. aeruginosa, S. aureus (methicillin-susceptible strains), S. pneumoniae, E. coli and H. influenzae.

Acute exacerbations of chronic bronchitis caused by S. pneumoniae and H. influenzae.

Uncomplicated and complicated urinary tract infections, including pyelonephritis caused by P. aeruginosa, E. coli, K. pneumoniae and P. mirabilis.

Due to the nature of the underlying conditions which usually predispose patients to Pseudomonas infections of the lower respiratory and urinary tracts, a good clinical response accompanied by bacterial eradication may not be achieved despite evidence of in vitro sensitivity.

Skin and skin structure infections caused by S. aureus (methicillin-susceptible strains), S. pyogenes (Group A streptococci) and P. aeruginosa.

Peritonitis due to gangrenous and perforated appendicitis caused by E. coli.

Bacterial septicemia caused by E. coli, S. pneumoniae and K. pneumoniae.

Empiric Therapy in Febrile Neutropenic Patients: Cefepime as monotherapy is indicated for empiric treatment of febrile neutropenic patients. In patients at high risk for severe infection (including patients with a history of recent bone marrow transplantation, with hypotension at presentation, with an underlying hematologic malignancy, or with severe or prolonged neutropenia), antimicrobial monotherapy may not be appropriate. Insufficient data exist to support the efficacy of cefepime monotherapy in such patients.

Specimens for bacteriologic culture should be obtained prior to therapy in order to identify the causative organisms and to determine their susceptibilities to cefepime.

Treatment with cefepime may be instituted empirically before results of susceptibility studies are known; however, modification of the antibiotic treatment may be required once these results become available.

In patients who are at risk of infection due to an anaerobic organism, concurrent initial therapy with an antianaerobic agent such as metronidazole or clindamycin is recommended before the causative organism(s) is (are) known. When such concomitant treatment is appropriate, the recommended doses of both antibiotics should be given according to the severity of the infection and the patient's condition.

Children: In pediatric patients for the treatment of infections listed below when caused by susceptible bacteria:

Lower respiratory tract infections: nosocomial and community acquired pneumonia caused by P. aeruginosa, S. aureus (methicillin-susceptible strains), S. pneumoniae, E. coli, and H. influenzae.

Uncomplicated and complicated urinary tract infections, including pyelonephritis caused by P. aeruginosa, E. coli, K. pneumoniae, and P. mirabilis.

Skin and skin structure infections caused by S. aureus (methicillin-susceptible strains), S. pyogenes (Group A streptococci), and P. aeruginosa.

Empiric Therapy in Febrile Neutropenic Patients: Cefepime as monotherapy is indicated for empiric treatment of febrile neutropenic patients. In patients at high risk for severe infection (including patients with a history of recent bone marrow transplantation, with hypotension at presentation, with an underlying hematologic malignancy, or with severe or prolonged neutropenia), antimicrobial monotherapy may not be appropriate. Insufficient data exist to support the efficacy of cefepime monotherapy in such patients.

Specimens for bacteriologic culture should be obtained prior to therapy in order to identify the causative organisms and to determine their susceptibilities to cefepime.

Treatment with cefepime may be instituted empirically before results of susceptibility studies are known; however, modification of the antibiotic treatment may be required once these results become available.

Contraindications: In patients who have had previous hypersensitivity reactions to cefepime or the cephalosporin class of antibiotics, penicillins or other beta-lactam antibiotics.

Warnings: Before therapy with cefepime is instituted, careful inquiry should be made to determine whether the patient has had previous immediate hypersensitivity reactions to cefepime, cephalosporins, penicillins or other beta-lactam antibiotics. Antibiotics should be administered with caution to any patient who has demonstrated some form of allergy, particularly to drugs. If an allergic reaction to cefepime occurs, discontinue the drug and institute supportive treatment as appropriate (e.g., maintenance of ventilation, pressor amines, antihistamines, corticosteroids). Serious immediate hypersensitivity reactions may require epinephrine and other supportive therapy.

Pseudomembranous colitis has been reported with virtually all broad-spectrum antibiotics including cefepime; therefore, it is important to consider this diagnosis in patients who develop diarrhea in association with the use of antibiotics.

Treatment with broad-spectrum antibiotics alters the normal flora of the colon and may permit overgrowth of clostridia. Studies indicate that a toxin produced by C. difficile is a primary cause of antibiotic-associated colitis.

After the diagnosis of pseudomembranous colitis has been established, therapeutic measures should be initiated. Mild cases of pseudomembranous colitis may respond to drug discontinuation alone. In moderate to severe cases, management should include fluids and electrolytes and protein supplementation. When colitis does not improve after drug discontinuation or when it is severe, it should be treated with an antibiotic clinically effective against C. difficile. Other causes of colitis should also be considered.

Precautions: General: As with other antibiotics, prolonged use of cefepime may result in overgrowth of nonsusceptible organisms. Should superinfection occur during therapy, appropriate measures should be taken.

Cefepime should be used with caution in individuals with a history of gastrointestinal disease, particularly colitis.

Drug Interactions: The combination of cefepime with an aminoglycoside has been shown to be synergistic in vitro. Although there is no evidence that cefepime adversely affects renal function at normal therapeutic doses, the usual precautions with respect to combining a cephalosporin with an aminoglycoside should be applied.

Pregnancy: There are no adequate and well-controlled studies in pregnant women.

Reproduction studies performed in mice and rats showed no evidence of fetal damage at dose levels equivalent to (mouse) or slightly greater (rat) than the maximum human daily dose when the daily doses are compared to those in man on a mg/m² basis. Because animal reproduction studies are not always predictive of human response, this drug should be used during pregnancy only if the potential benefit justifies the potential risk.

Lactation: Cefepime is excreted in human breast milk in very low concentrations. Although less than 0.01% of a 1 g i.v. dose is excreted in milk, caution should be used when cefepime is administered to a nursing woman.

Children: The safety and effectiveness of cefepime in the treatment of uncomplicated and complicated urinary tract infections (including pyelonephritis), uncomplicated skin and skin structure infections, pneumonia (nosocomial and community acquired), and as empiric therapy in febrile neutropenic patients, have been established in the age groups 2 months up to 12 years. Use of cefepime in these age groups is supported by evidence from adequate and well-controlled studies of cefepime in adults with additional pharmacokinetic and safety data from pediatric trials (see Pharmacology and Adverse Effects).

Safety and effectiveness in pediatric patients below the age of 2 months have not been established. However, accumulation of other cephalosporin antibiotics in newborn infants (resulting from prolonged drug half-life in this age group) has been reported.

Geriatrics: Healthy elderly male and female volunteers (≥65 years old) who received a single 1 g i.v. dose of cefepime had higher area under the curve (AUC) and lower renal clearance values when compared to younger subjects. However, this appeared to be a function of the decrease in creatinine clearance with increasing age. In patients with age-normalized renal function, a dosage adjustment of cefepime is not necessary.

In clinical studies, the safety and efficacy of cefepime were comparable in elderly patients and nonelderly adult patients receiving the usual recommended adult dose.

Hepatic Impairment: The pharmacokinetics of cefepime were unaltered in patients with impaired hepatic function who received a single 1 g dose. Therefore, dosage adjustments are not required in patients with hepatic impairment.

Renal Impairment: Elimination half-life is prolonged in patients with various degrees of renal insufficiency, with a linear relationship between total body clearance and creatinine clearance. This serves as the basis for dosage adjustment recommendations in this group of patients (see Dosage). The average half-life is 13 hours in patients with severe renal impairment requiring hemodialysis and 19 hours in those requiring continuous ambulatory peritoneal dialysis.

Cystic Fibrosis: The pharmacokinetics of cefepime do not change to a clinically significant degree in patients with cystic fibrosis. It is not necessary to alter the dosage of cefepime in this patient population.

Adverse Effects: Cefepime is generally well tolerated. In clinical trials (N=5 598) the most common adverse events were gastrointestinal symptoms and hypersensitivity reactions. Adverse events considered to be of probable relationship to cefepime are listed below.

Events that occurred at an incidence of >0.1 to 1% (except where noted) were:

Hypersensitivity: rash (1.8%), pruritus, urticaria.

Gastrointestinal: nausea, vomiting, oral moniliasis, diarrhea (1.2%), colitis (including pseudomembranous colitis).

CNS: headache.

Other: fever, erythema.

Events that occurred between 0.05 to 0.1% were: abdominal pain, constipation, vasodilation, dyspnea, dizziness, paresthesia, genital pruritus, taste perversion, chills, unspecified moniliasis, vaginal moniliasis, urogenital infection and vaginitis.

Events of clinical significance that occurred at an incidence of < 0.05% included anaphylaxis and seizures.

Local reactions at the site of i.v. infusion occurred in 5.2% of patients; these included phlebitis (2.9%) and inflammation (0.1%). I.M. administration of cefepime was very well tolerated with 2.6% of patients experiencing pain or inflammation at the injection site.

At the higher dose of 2 g q8h in febrile neutropenia, the incidence of probably related adverse events was higher among 1 048 patients who received this dose of cefepime in

Maxipime (cont'd)

clinical trials. They consisted of rash (4%), diarrhea (3%), nausea (2%), vomiting (1%), pruritus (1%), fever (1%) and headache (1%).

Laboratory test abnormalities that developed during clinical trials in patients with normal baseline values were transient. Those that occurred at a frequency between 1 and 2% (unless noted) were: elevations in ALT (3.6%), AST (2.5%), alkaline phosphatase, total bilirubin, prothrombin time, and partial thromboplastin time (2.8%); anemia, eosinophilia and positive Coombs' test without hemolysis (18.7%) also occurred. Additionally, increased phosphorous, decreased phosphorous (2.8%), increased calcium, decreased calcium (which was more common in elderly patients) and increased potassium were observed.

As with some other cephalosporins, transient elevations of blood urea nitrogen and/or serum creatinine and transient thrombocytopenia were observed in 0.5 to 1% of patients. Transient leukopenia and neutropenia were also seen (<0.5%). During postmarketing experience, agranulocytosis has been reported rarely.

Renal insufficiency and hepatic failure have been reported in conjunction with cefepime treatment. However, a causative relationship to cefepime therapy has not been determined. During postmarketing experience, encephalopathy has been reported in patients with renal impairment who received unadjusted doses of cefepime.

The following adverse events and altered laboratory tests have been reported for cephalosporin-class antibiotics: Stevens-Johnson syndrome, erythema multiforme, toxic epidermal necrolysis, toxic nephropathy, aplastic anemia, hemolytic anemia, hemorrhage, hepatic dysfunction including cholestasis, false positive test for urinary glucose and pancytopenia.

A similar safety profile has been experienced in infants and children relative to the adult population. No specific concerns have been identified.

Overdose: Symptoms and Treatment: Cefepime is eliminated primarily by the kidneys. In case of severe overdosage, especially in patients with compromised renal function, hemodialysis will aid in the removal of cefepime from the body. Peritoneal dialysis is of no value.

Dosage: Can be administered either i.v. or i.m. The dosage and route of administration should be determined according to the susceptibility of the causative organisms, the severity of the infection, and the condition and renal function of the patient. Guidelines for dosage of cefepime in adults with normal renal function are provided in Table II.

Pediatrics (aged 2 months up to 12 years with normal renal function): Usual Recommended Dosages: Empiric treatment of febrile neutropenia: Patients >2 months of age with body weight ≤40 kg: 50 mg/kg i.v q8h for 7 to 10 days.

Pneumonia, urinary tract infections, skin and skin structure infections: Patients >2 months of age with body weight ≤40 kg: 50 mg/kg i.v q12h for 10 days.

Experience with the use of cefipime in pediatric patients <2 months of age is limited.

For pediatric patients with body weights >40 kg, adult dosing recommendations apply (see Table II). For patients older than 12 years who are ≤40 kg, the dosage recommendations for younger patients ≤40 kg should be used. Dosage in pediatric patients should not exceed the maximum recommended dosage in adults (2 g q8h). Experience with i.m. administration in pediatric patients is limited.

Infection: The usual duration of therapy is 7 to 10 days; however, more severe infections may require longer treatment.

Table III—Maxipime

Maintenance Dosing Schedule in Adult Patients With Renal Impairment

Creatinine Clearance (mL/min/1.73 m²)	Creatinine Clearance (mL/s/1.73 m²)	Normal Recommended Maintenance Schedule: 1 g q12h	2 g q12h	2 g q8h
>50	>0.8	Usual maintenance dose, no adjustment necessary		
30-50	0.5-0.8	1 g q24h	2 g q24h	1 g q8h
11-29	0.18-0.48	500 mg q24h	1 g q24h	2 g q24h
≤10	≤0.17	250 mg q24h	500 mg q24h	1 g q24h

Impaired Hepatic Function: No adjustment is necessary for patients with impaired hepatic function.

Impaired Renal Function: There is no need to adjust dosage in the elderly unless renal impairment is present.

Cefepime is excreted by the kidneys almost exclusively by glomerular filtration. Therefore, in patients with impaired renal function (creatinine clearance ≤50 mL/min), the dose of cefepime should be adjusted to compensate for the slower rate of renal elimination. The initial dose of cefepime is the same as in patients with normal renal function. An estimate of creatinine clearance should be made to determine the appropriate maintenance dose. The recommended maintenance doses of cefepime in patients with renal insufficiency are presented in Table III.

When only serum creatinine is available, the following formulas may be used to estimate creatinine clearance. The serum creatinine should represent a steady state of renal function:

Males:

$$\text{Creatinine clearance (mL/min/1.73m}^2\text{)} = \frac{\text{Weight (kg)} \times (140-\text{age})}{72 \times \text{serum creatinine (mg/dL)}}$$

or

$$\text{Creatinine clearance (mL/s/1.73m}^2\text{)} = \frac{\text{Weight (kg)} \times (140-\text{age})}{49 \times \text{serum creatinine } (\mu\text{mol/L})}$$

Females: 0.85×value calculated using formula for males.

Children With Impaired Renal Function: Since urinary excretion is the primary route of elimination of cefepime in pediatric patients (see Pharmacology), an adjustment of the dosage of cefepime should also be considered in patients <12 years of age with renal impairment.

A dose of 50 mg/kg in patients aged 2 months up to 12 years is comparable to a dose of 2 g in an adult. As recommended in Table III, the same increase in interval between doses and/or reduction in dose should be used. When only serum creatinine is available, creatinine clearance may be estimated using either of the following methods (proposed by Schwartz or Dechaux, et al):

$$\text{Creatinine clearance (mL/min/1.73 m}^2\text{)} = \frac{0.55 \times \text{height (cm)}}{\text{serum creatinine (mg/dL)}}$$

or

$$\text{Creatinine clearance (mL/s/1.73 m}^2\text{)} = \frac{0.52 \times \text{height (cm)}}{\text{serum creatinine (mg/dL)}} - 3.6$$

Dialysis Patients: In patients undergoing hemodialysis, approximately 68% of the total amount of cefepime present in the body at the start of dialysis will be removed during a 3-hour dialysis period. A repeat dose, equivalent to the initial dose, should be given at the completion of each dialysis session.

In patients undergoing continuous ambulatory peritoneal dialysis, cefepime may be administered at the same doses recommended for patients with normal renal function, i.e., 500 mg, 1 g or 2 g (depending on the severity of the infection) at a dosage interval of every 48 hours.

Route of Administration: I.V.: The i.v. route of administration is preferable for patients with severe or life-threatening infections, particularly if the possibility of shock is present.

For direct i.v. injection, the solution reconstituted as recommended (see Reconstitution and Compatibility) should be slowly injected directly into the vein over a period of 3 to 5 minutes. Alternatively, the injection can be made into the tubing of an administration set while the patient is receiving a compatible i.v. fluid.

For continuous i.v. infusion, reconstitute the 1 or 2 g vial as recommended (see Reconstitution and Compatibility) and add an appropriate quantity of the resulting solution to one of the compatible i.v. fluids in an i.v. administration set. The resulting solution should be administered over a period of approximately 30 minutes.

For intermittent i.v. infusion, a Y-tube administration set can be used with compatible solutions. However, during infusion of a solution containing cefepime, it is desirable to discontinue the other solution.

I.M.: Reconstituted as recommended (see Reconstitution and Compatibility) to a final concentration of 280 mg/mL and given by deep i.m. injection into a large muscle mass (such as the upper outer quadrant of the gluteus maximus).

Although cefepime can be constituted with 0.5 or 1% lidocaine HCl, it is usually not required since cefepime causes little or no pain upon i.m. administration.

Reconstitution: I.M. Injection: The following diluents may be used for constituting cefepime for i.m. injection: sterile water for injection, 0.9% sodium chloride injection, 5% dextrose injection, bacteriostatic water for injection with paraben(s), bacteriostatic water for injection with benzyl alcohol, 0.5 or 1% lidocaine HCl. See Table IV.

Table IV—Maxipime

Reconstitution Table—I.M. Injection

Vial Size (g)	Volume of Diluent to be Added (mL)	Approximate Available Volume (mL)	Approximate Cefepime Concentration* (mg/mL)
1.0	2.4	3.6	280

* Approximate cefepime concentration includes overages used during manufacturing.

Direct I.V. Injection: Constitute cefepime with 10 mL of sterile water for injection, 5% dextrose injection or 0.9% sodium chloride injection, as directed in Table V.

Table V—Maxipime

Reconstitution Table—Direct I.V. Injection

Vial Size (g)	Volume of Diluent to be Added (mL)	Approximate Available Volume (mL)	Approximate Cefepime Concentration* (mg/mL)
1.0	10	11.3	100
2.0	10	12.5	160

* Approximate cefepime concentration includes overages used during manufacturing.

I.V. Infusion: Constitute the 1 g or 2 g vial as recommended and add an appropriate quantity of the resulting solution to one of the compatible i.v. fluids in an i.v. administration set.

At concentrations between 1 and 40 mg/mL, cefepime is compatible with the following i.v. infusion fluids: 0.9% sodium chloride injection, 5% or 10% dextrose injection, M/6 sodium lactate injection, 5% dextrose and 0.9% sodium chloride injection, Lactated Ringers and 5% dextrose injection and Normosol-R and Normosol-M in 5% dextrose injection.

Compatibility: Cefepime, prepared in 0.9% sodium chloride or 5% dextrose injection at a concentration of 4 mg of cefepime/mL, is stable for 72 hours under refrigeration (2 to 8°C) when admixed with: heparin (10 or 50 U/mL), potassium chloride (10 or 40 mEq/mL), theophylline (0.8 mg/mL in 5% dextrose injection).

Cefepime at a concentration of 40 mg/mL in 0.9% sodium chloride solution or 5% dextrose injection was found to be compatible with amikacin (6 mg/mL).

Solutions of cefepime, like solutions of most beta-lactam antibiotics, should not be added to solutions of ampicillin,

Table II—Maxipime

Recommended Dosage Schedule for Adults (12 years and older) With Normal Renal Function

Site and Type of Infection	Dose (g)	Route	Frequency	Duration (days)
Mild to moderate urinary tract infection (uncomplicated and complicated), including pyelonephritis	0.5-1	i.v. or i.m.	q12h	7-10
Mild to moderate infections including pneumonia, bronchitis and skin and skin-structure infections	1	i.v. or i.m.	q12h	10
Severe infections including pneumonia, septicemia and complicated intra-abdominal infections	2	i.v.	q12h	10
Empiric therapy in febrile neutropenic patients[a]	2	i.v.	q8h	7[b]

[a]Cefepime has also been used in combination with an aminoglycoside or a glycopeptide in patient populations which excluded high risk patients (see Indications).

[b]Or until resolution of neutropenia.

metronidazole, vancomycin, gentamicin, tobramycin sulfate or netilmicin sulfate because of physical or chemical incompatibility. However, if concurrent therapy with cefepime is indicated, each of these antibiotics can be administered separately to the same patient.

As with all parenteral products, i.v. admixtures should be inspected visually for clarity, particulate matter, precipitation, discoloration and leakage prior to administration whenever solution and container permit.

Stability and Storage: Store dry powder at room temperature (15 to 30°C) and protect from light. The dry powder may also be stored in the refrigerator (2 to 8°C), protected from light.

Solutions for i.m. or i.v. use reconstituted as well as diluted as recommended with sterile water for injection, 0.9% sodium chloride injection or 5% dextrose injection are stable for 72 hours when stored under refrigeration (2 to 8°C) and protected from light. Solutions reconstituted as well as diluted with diluents other than those listed above should be used immediately after reconstitution.

Note: Parenteral drugs should be inspected visually for particulate matter before administration, and not used if particulate matter is present.

As with other cephalosporins, the color of reconstituted solutions of cefepime may darken (colorless to amber) on storage, nevertheless, the product potency is not adversely affected.

Supplied: Each single use vial of dry powder contains: cefepime HCl equivalent to 1 g and 2 g of cefepime activity. Nonmedicinal ingredients: L-arginine 725 mg per g of cefepime.

Reviewed 1999

MAXITROL® Ⓟ

Alcon

Dexamethasone—Neomycin—Polymyxin B

Anti-inflammatory—Antibiotic

Supplied: Ophthalmic Ointment: Each g of sterile ointment contains: polymyxin B sulfate 6 000 units, neomycin (as sulfate) 3.5 mg and dexamethasone 1 mg (0.1%) in a white petrolatum base. Nonmedicinal ingredients: anhydrous lanolin, methylparaben and propylparaben. Tubes of 3.5 g.

Ophthalmic Suspension: Each mL contains: dexamethasone 1 mg (0.1%), neomycin (as sulfate) 3.5 mg and polymyxin B sulfate 6 000 units. Preserved with benzalkonium chloride. Nonmedicinal ingredients: hydrochloric acid and/or sodium hydroxide (to adjust pH), 0.5% hydroxypropyl methylcellulose, polysorbate 20, purified water and sodium chloride. Drop-Tainer dispensers of 5 mL.

M.C.T.® OIL

Mead Johnson

Medium Chain Triglycerides Oil

Fat Modified Diets

Indications: A dietary supplement for use in the nutritional management of children and adults who cannot efficiently digest and absorb conventional long chain food fats.

Precautions: In persons with advanced cirrhosis of the liver, large amounts of medium chain triglycerides in the diet may result in elevated blood and spinal fluid levels of medium chain fatty acids (MCFA), due to impaired hepatic clearance of these fatty acids, which are rapidly absorbed via the portal vein. These elevated levels have been reported to be associated with reversible coma and pre coma in certain subjects with advanced cirrhosis, particularly with portacaval shunts. Therefore, diets containing high levels of medium chain triglyceride fat should be used with caution in persons with hepatic cirrhosis and complications thereof, such as portacaval shunts or tendency to encephalopathy.

Dosage: 15 mL 3 to 4 times per day. M.C.T. Oil should be mixed with fruit juices, used on salads and vegetables, incorporated into sauces for use on fish, chicken, or lean meat, or used in cooking or baking.

Supplied: Each 15 mL of bland tasting, light yellow colored oil weighs 14 g and contains 115 calories. M.C.T. Oil provides 8.3 calories/g. It is a lipid fraction of coconut oil and consists primarily of the triglycerides of C_8 and C_{10} saturated fatty acids. Approximate fatty acid percentages are: shorter than C_6 maximum 6%, C_8 (Caprylic) 60 to 80%, C_{10} (capric) 18 to 32%, C_{12} and higher maximum 4%. Amber bottles of 500 mL, cases of 6.

MD-76®

Mallinckrodt

Diatrizoate Meglumine—Diatrizoate Sodium

Radiopaque Medium

Pharmacology: Following intravascular injection, MD-76 is rapidly transported through the bloodstream to the kidneys and is excreted unchanged in the urine by glomerular filtration. When urinary tract obstruction is severe enough to block glomerular filtration, the agent appears to be excreted by the tubular epithelium.

Renal accumulation is sufficiently rapid that the period of maximal opacification of the renal passages may begin as early as 5 minutes after injection. In infants and small children excretion takes place somewhat more promptly than in adults, so that maximal opacification occurs more rapidly and is less sustained. The normal kidney eliminates the contrast medium almost immediately. In nephropathic conditions, particularly when excretory capacity has been altered, the rate of excretion varies unpredictably, and opacification may be delayed for 30 minutes or more after injection; with severe impairment opacification may not occur. Generally, however, the medium is concentrated in sufficient amounts and promptly enough to permit a thorough evaluation of the anatomy and physiology of the urinary tract.

Intravascular injection also opacifies those vessels in the path of flow of the medium, permitting visualization until the circulating blood dilutes the concentration of the medium. Thus selective angiography may be performed following injection directly into veins or arteries.

Injectable iodinated contrast agents are excreted either through the kidneys or through the liver. These 2 excretory pathways are not mutually exclusive, but the main route of excretion seems to be related to the affinity of the contrast medium for serum albumin. Diatrizoate salts are poorly bound to serum albumin, and are excreted mainly through the kidneys.

The liver and small intestine provide the major alternate route of excretion. In patients with severe renal impairment, the excretion of this contrast medium through the gallbladder and into the small intestine sharply increases.

Diatrizoate salts cross the placental barrier in humans and are excreted unchanged in human milk.

Computerized Tomography of the Head: When used for contrast enhancement in computed tomographic brain scanning, the degree of enhancement is directly related to the amount of iodine administered. Rapid injection of the entire dose yields peak blood iodine concentrations immediately following the injection, which fall rapidly over the next 5 to 10 minutes. This can be accounted for by the dilution in the vascular and extracellular fluid compartments which causes an initial sharp fall in plasma concentration. Equilibration with the extracellular compartments is reached by about 10 minutes; thereafter the fall becomes exponential. Maximum contrast enhancement frequently occurs after peak blood iodine levels are reached. The delay in maximum contrast enhancement can range from 5 to 40 minutes, depending on the peak iodine levels achieved and the cell type of the lesion. This lag suggests that the contrast enhancement of the image is at least in part dependent on the accumulation of iodine within the lesion and outside the blood pool, although the mechanism by which this occurs is not clear.

In brain scanning, the contrast medium (MD-76) does not accumulate in normal brain tissue due to the presence of the blood brain barrier. The increase in x-ray absorption in the normal brain is due to the presence of the contrast agent within the blood pool. A break in the blood brain barrier, such as occurs in malignant tumors of the brain, allows accumulation of the contrast medium within the interstitial tumor tissue; adjacent normal brain tissue does not contain the contrast medium.

The image enhancement of non-tumoral lesions, such as arteriovenous malformations and aneurysms, is probably dependent on the iodine content of the circulation blood pool.

Computerized Tomography of the Body: In non-neural tissues (during CT of the body), MD-76 diffuses rapidly from the vascular to the extravascular space. Increase in x-ray absorption is related to blood flow, concentration of the contrast medium and extraction of the contrast medium by interstitial tissue since no barrier exists; contrast enhancement is thus due to the relative differences in extravascular diffusion between normal and abnormal tissue, quite different than that in the brain.

Enhancement of CT with MD-76 may be of benefit in establishing diagnoses of certain lesions in some sites with greater assurance than is possible with unenhanced CT and in supplying additional features of the lesions. In other cases, the contrast medium may allow visualization of lesions not seen with CT alone or may help to define suspicious lesions seen with unenhanced CT.

The pharmacokinetics of MD-76 in normal and abnormal tissue has been shown to be variable. Contrast enhancement appears to be greatest within 30 to 90 seconds after bolus administration, thus greatest enhancement can be detected by a series of consecutive 2 to 3 second scans (Dynamic CT Scanning) during this time period. Dynamic scanning may improve enhancement and diagnostic assessment of tumors and other lesions such as an abscess, occasionally revealing more extensive disease. A cyst, or similar non-vascularized lesion may be distinguished from vascularized solid lesions by comparing enhanced and unenhanced scans; the non-vascularized lesions show no change in CT number, the vascularized lesions would show an increase. The latter might be benign, malignant or normal, but it is unlikely that it would be a cyst, hematoma or other non-vascularized lesion.

Indications: In excretory urography, aortography, pediatric angiocardiography, peripheral arteriography, selective renal arteriography, selective visceral arteriography, selective coronary arteriography with or without left ventriculography, I.V. contrast enhancement of computed tomography and for i.v. digital subtraction angiography.

Contraindications: Known hypersensitivity to diatrizoic acid; anuria or severe oliguria.

Warnings: Serious or fatal reactions have been associated with the administration of iodine containing radiopaque media. It is of utmost importance to be completely prepared to treat any contrast medium reaction.

Serious neurologic sequelae, including permanent paralysis, have been reported following injections of concentrated contrast media into arteries supplying the spinal cord. The injection of a contrast medium should never be made following the administration of vasopressors since they strongly potentiate neurologic effects (see Precautions pertaining to Aortography).

A previous reaction to a contrast medium or a history of iodine sensitivity is not an absolute contraindication to the use of MD-76. However, extreme caution should be exercised in injecting these patients and prophylactic therapy should be considered (see Precautions, General).

In patients with subarachnoid hemorrhage, a rare association between contrast administration and clinical deterioration, including convulsions and death, has been reported. Therefore, administration of intravascular iodinated ionic contrast media in these patients should be undertaken with extreme caution and only if in the opinion of the physician the expected benefits outweigh the potential risks.

A definite risk exists in the use of intravascular contrast agents in patients who are known to have multiple myeloma. In such instances there has been anuria resulting in progressive uremia, renal failure and eventually death. Although neither the contrast agent nor dehydration has separately proved to be the cause of anuria in myeloma, it has been speculated that the combination of both may be the causative factor. The risk in myelomatous patients is not a contraindication to the procedures; however, partial dehydration in the preparation of these patients for the examination is not recommended since this may predispose to the precipitation of myeloma protein in the renal tubules. No form of therapy, including dialysis, has been successful in reversing this effect. Myeloma, which occurs most commonly in persons over age 40, should be considered before intravascular administration of a contrast agent.

Administration of radiopaque materials to patients known or suspected to have pheochromocytoma should be performed with extreme caution. If, in the opinion of the physician, the possible benefits of such procedures outweigh the considered risks, the amount of radiopaque medium injected should be kept to an absolute minimum. The blood pressure should be assessed throughout the procedure and measures for treatment of a hypertensive crisis should be available.

Contrast media have been shown to promote the phenomenon of sickling in individuals who are homozygous for sickle cell disease when the material is injected i.v. or intra-arterially.

MD-76 (cont'd)

Avoid accidental introduction of this preparation into the subarachnoid space since even small amounts may produce convulsions and possible fatal reactions.

Convulsions have occurred in patients with primary or metastatic cerebral lesions following the administration of contrast media for contrast enhancement of CT brain images.

In computed tomography, it has been reported that in low density lesions, false negative results may be produced following contrast media administration, i.e., contrast media may obscure low-density lesions. Steps should be taken to insure that patients undergoing computed tomography have received no injections of water-soluble contrast media at least 24 hours prior to examination. The necessity to obtain a non-enhanced CT scan prior to the administration of MD-76 has to be assessed by the physician.

Precautions: General: Diagnostic procedures which involve the use of radiopaque contrast agents should be carried out under the direction of personnel with the prerequisite training and with a thorough knowledge of the particular procedure to be performed (see Adverse Effects).

Preparatory dehydration is dangerous and may contribute to acute renal failure in infants, young children, the elderly, patients with pre-existing renal insufficiency, patients with advanced vascular disease, diabetic patients and those with multiple myeloma.

Severe, life-threatening reactions suggest hypersensitivity to the radiopaque agent, which has prompted the use of several pre-testing methods, none of which can be relied upon to predict severe reactions. Many authorities question the value of any pre-test. A history of bronchial asthma or allergy, a family history of allergy, or a previous reaction to a contrast agent warrant special attention. Such a history, by suggesting histamine sensitivity and a consequent proneness to reactions, may be more accurate than pre-testing in predicting the likelihood of a reaction, although not necessarily the severity or type of reaction in the individual case.

Prophylactic therapy including corticosteroids and antihistamines should be considered for patients who present a strong allergic history, a previous reaction to a contrast medium, or a positive pre-test, since in these patients the incidence of reaction is 2 to 3 times that of the general population. Adequate doses of corticosteroids should be started early enough prior to contrast medium injection to be effective and should continue through the time of injection and for 24 hours after injection.

Antihistamines may be administered if considered necessary by the physician. When used, antihistamines should be administered within 30 minutes of the contrast media injection.

The sensitivity test most often performed is the slow injection of 0.5 to 1.0 mL of the radiopaque medium, administered i.v., prior to injection of the full dose. It should be noted that the absence of a reaction to the test dose does not preclude the possibility of a reaction to the full dose. If the test dose (or subsequent diagnostic injection) causes an untoward response, the examination should be terminated and appropriate measures taken to combat the adverse reaction. In rare instances, reactions to the test dose itself may be extremely severe; therefore, close observation of the patient, and facilities for emergency treatment, are indicated.

Renal toxicity has been reported in a few patients with liver dysfunction who were given oral cholecystographic agents followed by intravascular iodinated radiopaque agents, and also in patients with occult renal disease, notably diabetics and hypertensives. Administration of MD-76 should be postponed in patients with hepatic or biliary disorder who have recently taken a cholecystographic agent. In infants, young children, in diabetics, in patients with multiple myeloma and in cases of impaired renal function, there should be no fluid restriction and every attempt made to maintain normal hydration, prior to contrast medium administration, since dehydration is the single most important factor influencing further renal impairment. The possibility of thrombosis should be borne in mind when percutaneous techniques are employed.

Injection of MD-76 should be undertaken with extreme caution in patients with severe concomitant hepatic and renal disease. Consideration must be given to the functional ability of the kidneys before injecting this preparation.

Caution should be exercised in performing contrast medium studies in patients with endotoxemia and/or those with elevated body temperatures.

General anesthesia may be indicated in the performance of some procedures in young and uncooperative children and in selected adult patients; however, a higher incidence of adverse reactions has been reported in these patients, and may be attributable to the inability of the patient to identify untoward symptoms or to the hypotensive effect of anesthesia which can prolong the circulation time and increase the duration of contact of the contrast agent.

Recent reports of thyroid storm occurring following the intravascular use of iodinated radiopaque agents in patients with hyperthyroidism or with an autonomously functioning thyroid nodule, suggest that this additional risk be evaluated in such patients before use of this drug. Iodine containing contrast agents may alter the results of thyroid function tests which depend on iodine estimation, e.g., PBI and radioactive iodine uptake studies. Such tests, if indicated, should be performed prior to the administration of this preparation.

Contrast agents may interfere with some chemical determinations made on urine specimens; therefore, urine should be collected before administration of the contrast medium or 2 or more days afterwards.

Pregnancy: Category B: Diatrizoate sodium and diatrizoate meglumine administered i.v. cross the placenta and are evenly distributed in fetal tissues. No teratogenic effects attributable to diatrizoate sodium or diatrizoate meglumine have been observed in teratology studies performed in animals. There are, however, no adequate and well-controlled studies in pregnant women. Because animal teratology studies are not always predictive of human response, this agent should be used during pregnancy only if clearly needed.

Lactation: Diatrizoate salts are excreted unchanged in human milk. Because of the potential for adverse effects in nursing infants, bottle feedings should be substituted for breast feedings for at least 24 hours following the administration of this drug. Therefore, a decision should be made whether to discontinue nursing or not to administer the drug, taking into account the importance of the drug to the mother.

(Precautions for specific procedures receive comment under that procedure.)

Adverse Effects: General: Adverse reactions accompanying the use of iodine-containing intravascular contrast agents are usually mild and transient, although severe and life-threatening reactions, including fatalities, have occurred. Because of the possibility of severe reactions to the procedure and/or the radiopaque medium, appropriate emergency facilities and well-trained personnel should be available to treat both conditions. Emergency facilities and personnel should remain available for 30 to 60 minutes following the procedure since severe delayed reactions have been known to occur.

Nausea, vomiting, flushing, or a generalized feeling of warmth are the reactions seen most frequently with intravascular injection. Symptoms which may occur include chills, fever, sweating, headache, dizziness, pallor, weakness, severe retching and choking, wheezing, a rise or fall in blood pressure, facial or conjunctival petechiae, urticaria, pruritus, rash and other eruptions, edema, cramps, tremors, itching, sneezing and lacrimation. Antihistaminic agents may be of benefit; rarely such reactions may be severe enough to require discontinuation of dosage.

Although local tissue tolerance is usually good, there have been a few reports of a burning or stinging sensation or numbness and of venospasm or venous pain, and partial collapse of the injected vein. Neutropenia or thrombophlebitis may occur. Tissue necrosis has occurred with extravasation. Severe reactions which may require emergency measures may take the form of a cardiovascular reaction characterized by peripheral vasodilatation with resultant hypotension and reflex trachycardia, dyspnea, agitation, confusion, convulsions, and cyanosis progressing to unconsciousness. Or, the histamine-liberating effect of these compounds may induce an allergic-like reaction which may range in severity from rhinitis or angioneurotic edema to laryngeal or bronchial spasm or anaphylactoid shock.

Extremely rare cases of disseminated intravascular coagulation resulting in death have been reported. Renal shutdown or other nephropathy may occur.

In addition to the adverse reactions described above, adverse reactions may sometimes occur as a consequence of the procedure for which the contrast agent is used. Adverse reactions in excretion urography have included cardiac arrest, ventricular fibrillation, anaphylaxis with severe asthmatic reaction, and flushing due to generalized vasodilation. In aortography, the risks of procedures include injury to the aorta and neighboring organs, pleural puncture, renal damage including infarction and acute tubular necrosis with oliguria and anuria, accidental selective filling of the right renal artery during the translumbar approach, spinal cord injury and pathology associated with the syndrome of transverse myelitis, generalized petechiae, and death following hypotension, arrhythmia, and anaphylactoid reactions. Adverse reactions in pediatric angiocardiography have included arrhythmia and death. During peripheral arteriography, complications have occurred including hemorrhage from the puncture site, thrombosis of the vessel, and brachial plexus palsy following axillary artery injections. During selective coronary arteriography with or without left ventriculography most patients will have transient ECG changes. Ventricular tachycardia, ventricular fibrillation, other arrhythmias and cardiac arrest may result from manipulation of the catheter during the procedure or administration of the medium. Other reactions may include hypotension, chest pain, and myocardial infarction. Transient elevation of creatinine phosphokinase has occurred in approximately 30% of patients tested. Fatalities have been reported. Complications due to the procedure include hemorrhage, thrombosis, pseudoaneurysms at the puncture site, and dislodgement of arteriosclerotic placques. Dissection of the coronary vessels and transient sinus arrest have occurred rarely.

Adverse reactions in selective renal arteriography include nausea, vomiting, hypotension and hypertension.

Post-arteriographic changes in laboratory studies include transient elevations in BUN, serum creatinine, glucose and serum enzymes.

Overdose: Symptoms and Treatment: Overdosage may occur. The adverse effects of overdosage are life-threatening and affect mainly the pulmonary and cardiovascular system. The symptoms may include cyanosis, bradycardia, acidosis, pulmonary hemorrhage, convulsions, coma and cardiac arrest. Treatment of an overdose is directed toward the support of all vital functions and prompt institution of specific therapy.

Diatrizoate salts are dialyzable.

Treatment of Adverse Effects: Contrast media should be administered only by physicians thoroughly familiar with the emergency treatment of all adverse reactions to contrast media. The assistance of other trained personnel such as cardiologists, internists and anesthetists is required in the management of severe reactions.

A guideline for the treatment of adverse reactions is presented below. This outline is not intended to be a complete manual on the treatment of adverse reactions to contrast media or on cardio-pulmonary resuscitation. The physician should refer to the appropriate texts on the subject.

It is also realized that institutions or individual practitioners will already have appropriate systems in effect and that circumstances may dictate the use of additional or different measures.

Minor Allergic Reactions (if considered necessary): The i.v. or i.m. administration of an antihistamine such as diphenhydramine; 25 to 50 mg is generally sufficient (contraindicated in epileptics). The resulting drowsiness makes it imperative to ensure that out-patients do not drive or go home unaccompanied.

Major or Life-threatening Reactions: A major reaction may be manifested by signs and symptoms of cardiovascular collapse, severe respiratory difficulty and nervous system dysfunction. Convulsions, coma and cardio-respiratory arrest may ensue. The following measures should be considered: Start emergency therapy immediately, carefully monitoring vital signs. Have emergency resuscitation team summoned: do not leave patient unattended. Ensure patent airway: guard against aspiration. Commence artificial respiration if patient is not breathing. Administer oxygen, if necessary. Start external cardiac massage in the event of cardiac arrest. Establish route for i.v. medication by starting infusion of appropriate solution (5% dextrose in water). Judiciously administer specific drug therapy as indicated by the type and severity of the reaction. Careful monitoring is mandatory to detect adverse reactions of all drugs administered: a) soluble hydrocortisone 500 to 1 000 mg i.v. for all acute allergic-anaphylactic reactions. b) epinephrine 1:1 000 solution (in the presence of anoxia it may cause ventricular fibrillation). i) 0.2 to 0.4 mL s.c. for severe allergic reactions. ii) in extreme emergency 0.1 mL/minute, appropriately diluted, may be given i.v. until desired effect is obtained. Do not exceed 0.4 mL. iii) in case of cardiac arrest 0.1 to 0.2 mL, appropriately diluted, may be given intracardially. c) In hypotension (carefully monitoring blood pressure): i) phenylephrine HCl 0.1 to 0.5 mg appropriately diluted slowly i.v. or by slow infusion or ii) levarterenol bitartrate 4 mL of 0.2% solution in 1 000 mL of 5% dextrose by slow drip infusion. d) Sodium bicarbonate 5%; 50 mL i.v. every 10 minutes as needed to combat post-arrest acidosis. e) Atropine 0.4 to 0.6 mg i.v. to increase heart rate in sinus bradycardia. May reverse 2nd or 3rd degree block. f) To control convulsions: i) pentobarbital sodium 50 mg in fractional doses slowly i.v. (contraindicated if cyanosis is present) or ii) diazepam 5 to 10 mg slowly i.v. titrating the dose to the response of the patient. Defibrillation, administration of antiarrhythmics and additional emergency measures and drugs may be required. Transfer patient to intensive care unit when feasible for further monitoring and treatment.

Dosage: MD-76 should be at body temperature when injected, and may need to be warmed before use. If kept in a syringe before injection, it should be protected from exposure to strong light. Discard unused portion.

Under no circumstances should either corticosteroids or antihistamines be mixed in the same syringe with the contrast medium because of a potential for chemical incompatibility.

Parenteral drug products should be inspected visually for particulate matter and discoloration prior to administration.

Excretory Urography: Patient Preparation: Appropriate preparation of the patient is desirable for optimal results. In adults and older children, a low residue diet is recommended for the day preceding the examination and a laxative is given the evening before the examination, unless contraindicated.

Precautions: In addition to the general precautions previously described, infants and young children should not have fluid restrictions prior to excretory urography. Injection of MD-76 represents an osmotic load which, if superimposed on increased serum osmolality due to partial dehydration, may magnify hypertonic dehydration (see Warnings and Precautions, General concerning preparatory dehydration).

Maintenance of adequate fluid intake is particularly desirable in uremic patients and patients with impaired renal function, multiple myeloma or diabetes. Adequate visualization may be difficult or impossible to attain in uremic patients or others with severely impaired renal function (see Precautions, General).

Usual Dosage: The dose range for adults is 20 to 40 mL; the usual dose is 20 mL; children require proportionately less. Suggested dosages are as follows: under 6 months of age: 4 mL; 6 to 12 months: 6 mL; 1 to 2 years: 8 mL; 2 to 5 years: 10 mL; 5 to 7 years: 12 mL; 8 to 10 years: 14 mL; 11 to 15 years: 16 mL. In adults, when the smaller dose has provided inadequate visualization, or when poor visualization is anticipated, the 40 mL dose may be given.

The preparation is given by i.v. injection. If flushing or nausea occur during administration, injection should be slowed or briefly interrupted until the side effects have disappeared.

In patients with renal dysfunction, optimal visualization may be delayed until 30 minutes or more after injection.

Aortography: MD-76 may be administered by accepted techniques to visualize the aorta and its major branches. Normal hydration should be maintained.

Warnings: In addition to the warnings previously described, during aortography by the translumbar technique, extreme care is advised to avoid inadvertent intrathecal injection since the injection of even small amounts of the contrast medium may cause convulsions, permanent sequelae, or fatality. Should the accident occur, the patient should be placed upright to confine the hyperbaric solution to a low level, anesthesia may be required to control convulsions, and if there is evidence of a large dose having been administered, a careful cerebrospinal fluid exchange-washout should be considered.

Precautions: In addition to the general precautions previously described, the hazards of aortography include those associated with the particular technique employed, the contrast medium and the underlying pathology which warrants the procedure.

In order to prevent the inadvertent injection of a large dose into a branch of the aorta or intramurally, the position of the catheter tip or needle should be carefully evaluated. A small dose of 1 to 2 mL should be administered to locate the exact site of the needle or catheter tip. Inadvertent direct injection of contrast medium into brachiocephalic vessels may result in significant slowing of heart rate, peripheral hypotension and severe CNS reactions, including convulsions. Toxic effects may also be produced if large quantities of contrast medium are injected directly into aortic branches such as the renal artery, and repetitive injection of the recommended clinical dosage may be hazardous.

Occasional serious neurologic complications, including paraplegia and quadriplegia have been reported and may be attributable to an excessive dose being injected into arterial trunks supplying the spinal arteries or to prolonged contact time of the concentrated contrast medium on the CNS tissue. Conditions which can contribute to prolonged contact time include decreased circulation, aortic occlusions distal to the site of injection, abdominal compression, hypotension, general anesthesia or the administration of vasopressors. When these conditions exist or occur, the necessity of performing or continuing the procedure should be carefully evaluated and the dose and number of repeat injections should be maintained at a minimum with appropriate intervals between injections.

Severe pain, paresthesia, or peripheral muscle spasm during injection may require discontinuance of the procedure and a reevaluation of the placement of the catheter tip or needle.

Following catheter procedures, gentle pressure hemostatis is advised, followed by observation and immobilization of the limb for several hours to prevent hemorrhage from the site of arterial puncture.

Usual Dosage: For adults and children over 16 years of age, the usual dose is 15 to 40 mL as a single injection, repeated if indicated. Children require less in proportion to weight.

Since the medium is given by rapid injection in this procedure, patients should be watched for untoward reactions during the injection. Unless general anesthesia is employed, patients should be warned that they may feel some transient pain or burning during the injection followed by a feeling of warmth immediately afterwards.

Pediatric Angiocardiography: Angiocardiography with MD-76 may be performed by injection into the large peripheral vein or by direct catheterization of the heart.

Patient Preparation: Normal patient hydration should be maintained. Appropriate preanesthetic medication should be given.

Warnings: In addition to the general warnings previously described, the inherent risks of angiocardiography in cyanotic infants and patients with chronic pulmonary emphysema must be weighed against the necessity for performing this procedure. In pediatric angiocardiography, a dose of 10 to 20 mL may be particularly hazardous in infants weighing less than 7 kg. This risk is probably significantly increased if these infants have pre-existing right heart strain, right heart failure, and effectively decreased or obliterated pulmonary vascular beds.

Adverse Effects: In addition to the adverse reactions previously described, clinical studies in man, and related animal experiments, have suggested that the hypertonicity of diatrizoate contrast agents produces significant hemodynamic effects, especially in right-sided injections. Large volumes of such agents cause a drop in peripheral arterial and systemic pressures and cardiac output, a rise in pulmonary arterial and right-heart pressures, bradycardia, and regular ectopic beats. Resulting effects on peripheral arterial and pulmonary arterial pressures are postulated to be due to mechanical blockage of the pulmonary vascular bed and clumping of red cells.

Hypertonic solutions cause a decrease in hematocrit in vitro and in vivo, and shrinkage of red blood cells.

It is suggested that hemodynamic changes be monitored and that pressures considered abnormal under roentgenographic conditions be allowed to return to a pre-angiographic level before continuation of radiopaque injection; this usually takes 15 minutes.

Usual Dosage: The suggested single dose for children under 5 years of age is 10 to 20 mL, depending on the size of the child. For children 5 to 10 years of age, single doses of 20 to 30 mL are recommended. The dose may be repeated if required.

Peripheral Arteriography: MD-76 may be injected into the peripheral arterial circulation. Injection is made into the femoral or subclavian artery by the percutaneous or operative method.

Patient Preparation: The procedure is normally performed with local or general anesthesia (see Precautions, General). Premedication may be employed as indicated.

Precautions: In addition to the general precautions previously described, hypotension or moderate decreases in blood pressure seem to occur frequently with intra-arterial (brachial) injections; therefore, the blood pressure should be monitored during the immediate 10 minutes after injection; this blood pressure change is transient and usually requires no treatment. Extreme caution during injection of the contrast agent is necessary to avoid extravasation and fluoroscopy is recommended. This is particularly important in patients with severe arterial disease.

Adverse Effects: In addition to the adverse reactions previously described, since the contrast agent is given by rapid injection, pain and flushing of the skin may occur. Patients not under general anesthesia may experience nausea and vomiting or a transient feeling of warmth. Vascular spasm occurs rarely as does thrombosis of the vessel and brachial plexus palsy following axillary artery injection.

Usual Adult Dosage: For visualization of an entire extremity, a single dose of 20 to 40 mL is suggested; for the upper or lower half of the extremity only, 10 to 20 mL is usually sufficient. The dose for children is reduced in proportion to body weight.

Selective Renal Arteriography: Usual Adult Dosage: The usual dose is 5 to 10 mL injected into either or both renal arteries via femoral artery catheterization. This dose may be repeated as necessary; cumulative total doses up to 60 mL have been given.

Selective Visceral Arteriography: Usual Adult Dosage: The usual dose for injections into the superior mesenteric artery is 40 mL with a range of 30 to 50 mL; inferior mesenteric artery, usual dose of 15 mL with a range of 10 to 25 mL; celiac artery, usual dose of 40 mL with a range of 30 to 50 mL; hepatic artery, usual dose of 25 mL with a range of 15 to 35 mL; splenic artery, usual dose of 35 mL with a range of 30 to 40 mL. These doses may be repeated as necessary.

Selective Coronary Arteriography with or without Left Ventriculography: Precautions: In addition to the general precautions previously described, it is recommended that this procedure should not be performed for approximately 4 weeks following the diagnosis of myocardial infarction. Mandatory prerequisites to the procedure are experienced personnel, ECG monitoring apparatus, and adequate facilities for resuscitation and cardioversion.

Patients should be monitored continuously by ECG throughout the procedure.

Usual Adult Dosage: 4 to 10 mL injected into either coronary artery and repeated as necessary. For left ventriculography the usual dose is 35 to 50 mL injected into the left ventricles and repeated as necessary. The total dose for combined selective coronary arteriography and left ventriculography should not exceed 200 mL.

I.V. Contrast Enhancement in Computed Tomography (CT): Computed Tomography of the Brain: Tumors: MD-76 may be useful to enhance the demonstration of the presence and extent of certain malignancies such as: gliomas including malignant gliomas, glioblastomas, astrocytomas, oligodendrogliomas and gangliomas; ependymomas, medulloblastomas, meningiomas, neuromas; pinealomas; pituitary adenomas; craniopharyngiomas; germinomas; and metastatic lesions.

The usefulness of contrast enhancement for the investigation of the retrobulbar space and in cases of low grade or infiltrative glioma has not been demonstrated.

In cases where lesions have calcified, there is less likelihood of enhancement. Following therapy, tumors may show decreased or no enhancement.

Non-Neoplastic Conditions: The use of MD-76 may be beneficial in the image enhancement of non-neoplastic lesions. Cerebral infarctions of recent onset may be better visualized with the contrast enhancement, while some infarctions are obscured if contrast media are used. The use of iodinated contrast media results in contrast enhancement in about 60% of cerebral infarctions studied from 1 week to 4 weeks from the onset of symptoms.

Sites of active infection may also be enhanced following contrast medium administration.

Arteriovenous malformations and aneurysms will show contrast enhancement. In the case of these vascular lesions, the enhancement is probably dependent on the iodine content of the circulating blood pool.

Hematomas and intraparenchymal bleeders seldom demonstrate any contrast enhancement. However, in cases of intraparenchymal clot, for which there is no obvious clinical explanation, contrast medium administration may be helpful in ruling out the possibility of associated arteriovenous malformation.

The opacification of the inferior vermis following contrast medium administration has resulted in false positive diagnoses in a number of normal studies.

Body Computed Tomography: MD-76 may be administered when necessary to visualize vessels and organs in patients undergoing CT of the chest, abdomen and pelvis.

Because unenhanced scanning may provide adequate information in the individual patient, the decision to employ contrast enhancement, which may be associated with additional risk and increased radiation exposure, should be based upon a careful evaluation of clinical, other radiological and unenhanced CT findings.

Continuous or multiple scans separated by intervals of 1 to 3 seconds during the first 30 to 90 seconds post-injection of the contrast medium (dynamic CT scanning) provide enhancement of diagnostic significance. Subsets of patients in whom delayed body CT scans might be helpful have not been identified.

Inconsistent results have been reported and abnormal and normal tissues are usually isodense during the time frame used for delayed CT scanning. The risks of such indiscriminate use of contrast media are well known and such use is not recommended. At present, consistent results have been documented using dynamic CT techniques only.

Warnings: Patients with diabetes mellitus and impaired renal function are considered to be at greater risk to develop acute

MD-76 (cont'd)

renal failure following the injection of large doses of contrast media required for contrast enhancement in CT scanning.

Convulsions have occurred in patients with primary or metastatic cerebral lesions following the administration of iodine-containing radiopaque media for enhancement of CT brain images.

Patient Preparation: No special patient preparation is required for contrast enhancement in computerized tomography. However, it is advisable to insure that patients are well hydrated prior to examination. In patients undergoing abdominal or pelvic examination, opacification of the bowel may be valuable in scan interpretation.

Precautions: In addition to the general precautions previously described, it is advisable to insure that patients are adequately hydrated prior to examination. Patient motion, including respiration, can markedly effect image quality, therefore, patient cooperation is essential. The use of an intravascular contrast medium can obscure tumors in patients undergoing CT evaluation of the liver resulting in a false negative diagnosis.

Usual Dosage: Computerized Tomography of the Brain: 1.3 mL/kg not to exceed 120 mL in adults and a proportionally smaller amount in children depending on age and weight. In most cases, scanning may be performed immediately after completion of administration. However, when fast scanning equipment (less than 1 minute) is used, consideration should be given to waiting approximately 5 minutes to allow for maximum contrast enhancement.

Usual Adult Dosage: Body Computed Tomography: MD-76 may be administered by i.v. bolus injection, by rapid infusion, or by a combination of both.

For vascular opacification, a bolus injection of 25 to 50 mL may be used, repeated as necessary. When prolonged arterial or venous phase enhancement is required and for the enhancement of specific lesions, a rapid infusion of 100 mL may be used.

I.V. Digital Subtraction Angiography (I.V. DSA): I.V. DSA is a radiographic modality which allows dynamic imaging of the arterial system following i.v. injection of iodinated x-ray contrast media through the use of image intensification, enhancement of the iodine signal and digital processing of the image data. Temporal subtraction of the images obtained during the first arterial pass of the injected contrast medium from images obtained before and after contrast medium injection yield images which are devoid of bone and soft tissue.

Areas that have been examined by i.v. DSA are the heart, including coronary by-pass grafts; the pulmonary arteries; the arteries of the brachiocephalic circulation; the aortic arch; the abdominal aorta and its major branches including the celiac, mesenterics and renal arteries; the iliac arteries; and the arteries of the extremities.

Patient Preparation: No special patient preparation is required for DSA. However, it is advisable to insure that patients are well hydrated prior to examination.

Precautions: In addition to the general precautions previously described, the risks associated with DSA are those usually attendant with catheter procedures and include intramural injections, vessel dissection or rupture and tissue extravasation. Small test injections of contrast medium made under fluoroscopic observation to insure the catheter tip is properly positioned, and in the case of peripheral placement that the vein is of adequate size, will reduce the potential for intramural injections, vessel dissection or tissue extravasation occurring.

Patient motion, including respiration and swallowing, can result in marked image degradation yielding non-diagnostic studies. Therefore, patient cooperation is essential.

Adverse Effects: See Adverse Effects, General.

Usual Adult Dosage: MD-76 may be injected either centrally, into the superior or inferior vena cava, or peripherally into an appropriate arm vein. For central injections, catheters may be introduced at the antecubital fossa into either the basilic or cephalic vein or at the leg into the femoral vein and advanced to the distal segment of the corresponding vena cava. For peripheral injections, the catheter is introduced at the antecubital fossa into an appropriate size arm vein. In order to reduce the potential for extravasation during peripheral injection, a catheter of approximately 20 cm in length should be employed.

Depending on the area to be imaged, the usual dose range is 20 to 60 mL. Injections may be repeated as necessary.

Central catheter injections are usually made with a power injection with an injection rate of between 10 and 30 mL/second. When making peripheral injections, rates of 12 to 20 mL/second should be used, depending on the size of the vein. Also, since contrast medium may remain in the arm vein for an extended period following injection, it may be advisable to flush the vein, immediately following injection with an appropriate volume (20 to 25 mL) of 5% dextrose in water or normal saline.

Supplied: Each mL of sterile aqueous solution contains: diatrizoate meglumine 660 mg (iodine 37%), diatrizoate sodium 100 mg, edetate calcium disodium 0.110 mg as a sequestering agent and monobasic sodium phosphate 0.125 mg as a buffer. Sodium: <1 mmol (3.66 mg)/mL. Vials of 50 mL, boxes of 12; bottles of 100 mL fill/150 mL, boxes of 12; bottles of 150 mL, boxes of 12; bottles of 200 mL fill/250 mL, boxes of 12. Pharmacy Bulk Vial: Multiple dispensing bottles of 500 mL, boxes of 12.

Store between 15 to 30°C. Protect from light. Protect from freezing. Discard unused portion.

MEASLES VIRUS VACCINE, LIVE ATTENUATED (DRIED)

Connaught

Vaccine

Pharmacology: Measles Virus Vaccine, Live, Attenuated (Dried) is prepared in avian leucosis-free chick embryo fibroblast cultures from the Edmondston Strain of attenuated measles virus, obtained from Dr. J.F. Enders and given an additional 69 passages in chick embryo cell cultures. The diluent for reconstitution for the 1 dose vial is Water for Injection (WFI). The diluent for reconstitution for the 10 dose vial is Phosphate Buffered Saline with 40 to 70 ppm Tween 80.

The clinical trial of Measles Virus Vaccine, Live, Attenuated (Dried) involved 5 lots of vaccine and was administered to 378 individuals between 11 to 17 months of age. Serologic response 4 weeks following vaccination equal to or greater than 1:8 by hemagglutination-inhibition test (method I) was demonstrated in 99% of the 374 vaccinees for whom serum samples were available and in 97% by virus neutralization test (method II).

The serum sero-conversion rate for individual vaccine lots ranged from 98 to 100% by test method I and from 92 to 100% by test method II. The overall geometric mean-titre was 36.0 by test method I, with the titre ranging from 31.2 to 39.8 for the individual lots. The overall geometric mean-titre was 21.8 by test method II, with the titre ranging from 16.9 to 27.0 for individual vaccine lots.

Similar results were obtained in a previous clinical trial of 1 142 vaccinees of whom 98% demonstrated post-vaccine serologic response equal to or greater than 1:8 by hemagglutination-inhibition test.

Indications: For the active immunization of children against measles (rubeola). It does not protect against German measles (rubella).

This vaccine is recommended routinely for all children at, or as soon as practicable after, their first birthday. If a goal of measles elimination is adopted, a second dose of measles vaccine is required. It is given at 4 to 6 years of age. The minimum interval between the 2 doses should be at least 1 month.

Measles vaccine is also recommended for children and adolescents who have never had documented measles or who have received live attenuated vaccine before the age of 12 months and for persons of any age known to be seronegative. Routine primary immunization of adults born prior to 1957 is not usually necessary because they are very likely to have acquired immunity by natural infection.

Children, who, in accordance with previous recommendations, received vaccine prior to 1 year of age, or who were given a dose of further attenuated vaccine accompanied by immune globulin, human, may not be fully protected. It is recommended that such children be revaccinated with live measles vaccine.

Despite the risk of local reaction (see Adverse Effects), persons who have previously been given inactivated vaccine alone or followed by live vaccine within 3 months should be revaccinated with live vaccine to avoid the severe atypical form of natural measles that may occur.

Contraindications: Immunization with Measles Virus Vaccine, Live, Attenuated (Dried) should be deferred in the presence of any acute illness, including febrile illness. Minor illness, such as the common cold, are very prevalent in children and are not contraindications to immunization; however, febrile illness is a reason to defer immunization.

Allergic reaction to any component of Measles Virus Vaccine, Live, Attenuated (Dried) is a contraindication to vaccination.

Elective immunization should be deferred during an outbreak of poliomyelitis.

Measles Virus Vaccine, Live, Attenuated (Dried) should **not** be administered to any individual whose immune mechanism is impaired as the result of disease, injury, or therapy including the following: (a) individuals with blood dyscrasias, lymphomas, or other generalized malignancies, (b) individuals undergoing treatment with immunosuppressive agents of any kind or with primary immunodeficiency, e.g. agammaglobulinemia, dysgammaglobulinemia, hypogammaglobulinemia.

Pregnancy: Measles Virus Vaccine, Live, Attenuated (Dried) should **not** be administered to pregnant women, since the possible effect of attenuated measles virus on the fetus is not known.

If a measles-susceptible woman is exposed to measles during pregnancy, one should consider the possibility of providing temporary passive immunity through the administration of immune globulin, human.

Human Immunodeficiency Virus (HIV) Infected Persons: Measles Virus Vaccine, Live, Attenuated, (Dried) is recommended for asymptomatic and symptomatic HIV-infected children since no increased incidence or severity of adverse events has been observed following vaccination of such children, and severe disease and fatalities have been associated with natural infection. Because the immune response may be impaired, such children should receive IG following recognized exposures to measles, HIV-infected infants who are receiving IGIV prophylaxis are unlikely to respond to Measles Virus Vaccine and, therefore, vaccine need not be administered.

Warnings: If Measles Virus Vaccine, Live, Attenuated (Dried) is used in persons with malignancies, receiving immunosuppressive therapy, or who are otherwise immunocompromised, the expected immune response may not be obtained.

As with any vaccine, vaccination with Measles Virus Vaccine, Live Attenuated (Dried) may not protect 100% of susceptible individuals.

Precautions: Live measles vaccine is grown in chick fibroblast cultures and not in eggs. Egg albumin and yolk components are absent from these cultures. Hypersensitivity reactions very rarely follow the administration of live measles vaccine. Most of these reactions are considered minor and consist of wheal and flare or urticaria at the injection site. With over 190 million doses of measles vaccine distributed in the USA, there have been less than 10 reported cases of immediate severe allergic reactions in children who had histories of anaphylactoid reactions to egg ingestion. Extreme caution should be exercised if the vaccine is administered to persons with a history of anaphylactoid reactions subsequent to egg ingestion. Egg allergies which are not anaphylactoid in nature and allergies to chicken and feathers do not appear to constitute an increased risk of reaction to the vaccine. The attending physician must weigh the benefits of immunization against the potential risks of hypersensitivity reactions.

General: The possibility of allergic reactions in individuals sensitive to components of the vaccine should be evaluated. Epinephrine HCl solution (1:1 000) should be available for immediate use in case an anaphylactic or acute hypersensitivity reaction occurs.

Prior to an injection of any vaccine, all known precautions should be taken to prevent adverse reactions. This includes a review of the patient's history with respect to possible hypersensitivity to the vaccine or similar vaccine.

Special care should be taken to ensure that the injection does not enter a blood vessel.

A separate, sterile syringe and needle or a sterile disposable unit should be used for each individual patient to prevent transmission of hepatitis or other infectious agents from one person to another. Do not recap needles after vaccine administration.

Administer the vaccine s.c., do **not** administer i.v.

Children: The vaccine should be given with caution to children with a history of febrile convulsions.

Drug Interactions: Administration of the vaccine should be deferred at least 3 months after administration of human immune globulin, plasma or whole blood. If repeated or large amounts of these substances have been given, a longer interval should be allowed.

Administration of attenuated live-virus measles vaccine may temporarily depress tuberculin skin sensitivity. Therefore, if a tuberculin test is to be done, it should be scheduled before administering measles vaccine or on the day of vaccination with reading 48 to 72 hours later. Otherwise, it should be postponed for 4 to 6 weeks. This avoids the possibility of a false-negative response. Although tuberculosis may be exacerbated by natural measles infection, there is no evidence that measles vaccine has such effect.

One live vaccine may interfere with the effectiveness of another, and to minimize this possibility, 2 or more live vaccines should preferably be administered at different sites with separate syringes either on the same day or be separated by an interval of at least 1 month. Simultaneous administration of Measles Virus Vaccine, Live, Attenuated (Dried) and inactivated vaccines may be performed provided the vaccines are administered separately and at different sites with separate syringes with observance of the precautions that apply to the individual vaccines.

Adverse Effects: Local erythema and/or swelling around the site of injection are not uncommon and regional lymphadenopathy may occur rarely.

Fever or mild rash, or both, may occur 5 to 12 days after administration of Measles Virus Vaccine, Live, Attenuated (Dried). Based on clinical trials, the febrile response would be expected to be mild, $\leq$37.7°C in 48–57%, moderate 37.8–39.4°C in 39–47% and high $>$39.4°C in 4–5% of recipients. With high temperatures the possibility of development of convulsions is present.

Rash may occur in 12 to 16% of vaccinees and is usually minimal.

Reactions which may be temporally associated with administration of measles vaccine such as encephalitis and encephalopathy have been reported to occur approximately once per million doses. Following natural measles infections, the incidence of such neurological disorders is approximately one per thousand reported cases.

There have been reports of subacute sclerosing panencephalitis (SSPE) in individuals who have no history of measles but who have received measles vaccine. However, studies have shown that the incidence of SSPE in measles vaccine recipients (about one case per million doses of vaccine distributed) is significantly less than the 5 to 10 SSPE cases per million cases of natural measles. It would appear that measles vaccine significantly reduces the chance of developing SSPE by protecting against measles.

Local reactions characterized by marked swelling, redness and vesiculation at the injection site of attenuated live virus measles vaccines have occurred in children who have previously received killed measles vaccine.

On rare occasions, more severe reactions have been reported. These included prolonged high fevers and extensive local reactions which required hospitalization.

Health care providers should report any adverse occurrences temporally related to the administration of the product in accordance with local requirements and report to the Medical Director at Connaught Laboratories Limited, 1755 Steeles Avenue West, Toronto, Ontario, Canada, M2R 3T4.

Dosage: One dose of 0.5 mL of Measles Virus Vaccine, Live, Attenuated (Dried) s.c., at 12 months of age, or as soon as possible thereafter. If a goal of measles elimination is adopted, a second dose of 0.5 mL Measles Virus Vaccine is required. It is given at 4 to 6 years of age. The minimum interval between the 2 doses should be at least 1 month.

Parenteral biological products should be inspected visually prior to and following vaccine reconstitution for extraneous particulate matter and/or discoloration prior to administration. If these conditions exist, vaccine should not be administered.

The vaccine should be administered by **s.c.** injection which may conveniently be made near the insertion of the deltoid muscle. The vaccine **must not** be injected i.v. The site of the injection should be prepared with a suitable antiseptic.

Caution: A new sterile plastic disposable syringe should be used for each injection of the vaccine because certain preservatives, antiseptics and detergents will inactivate the live measles virus in the vaccine (see Precautions).

Withdrawing the Sterile Diluent from a Sealed Glass Ampul: Tap the ampul to ensure that the diluent is in the lower portion rather than the neck of the ampul. Wipe the neck of the ampul with a suitable antiseptic. Using a **sterile** piece of cotton or a **sterile** towel, break off the top of the ampul at the scored line (no file is required). Then with a **sterile** syringe and needle withdraw the required volume (see Reconstitution) of sterile diluent from the ampul, holding the syringe in such a way that the point is kept immersed throughout the withdrawal.

Withdrawing the Sterile Diluent from a Rubber-Stoppered Vial: Do not remove the rubber stopper from the vial.

Apply a **sterile** piece of cotton moistened with a suitable antiseptic to the surface of the rubber stopper of the vial of sterile diluent and allow to dry. Then with a **sterile** syringe pierce the centre of the rubber stopper, invert the vial, slowly inject into it the air contained in the syringe, and, keeping the point of the needle immersed, withdraw into the syringe 0.6 mL of sterile diluent. Then holding the syringe-plunger steady, withdraw the needle from the vial.

Reconstitution of Freeze-Dried Vaccine: Do not remove the rubber stopper from the vial.

Apply a **sterile** piece of cotton with a suitable antiseptic to the surface of the rubber stopper of the vial of vaccine. Holding the plunger of the syringe containing the diluent, pierce the centre of the rubber stopper in the vial and inject the required volume of sterile diluent into the freeze-dried vaccine. Do not try to force all of the diluent into the vial at once as this will create pressure. It is necessary to gradually allow air to escape into the syringe by intermittently aspirating air from the vial while injecting the diluent into the vial. Do not remove the needle from the stopper until the required volume of diluent has been injected. The **required volume** for reconstitution is 0.6 mL for the single dose vial and 6 mL for the 10 dose vial. Shake the vial gently until a fine, even suspension results. **Avoid foaming** since this will prevent withdrawal of the proper dose. Withdraw the required dose (0.5 mL) of the reconstituted vaccine into the syringe.

Carefully insert the needle into the subcutaneous tissue. **In order to avoid i.v. injection,** pull back on the plunger of the syringe to make certain that no blood is withdrawn before injecting the vaccine.

The vaccine should be used immediately after reconstitution and any reconstituted vaccine not used within 8 hours **must** be discarded.

Supplied: 1 single dose vial of vaccine with 1 vial or ampul of 0.6 mL sterile diluent for the reconstitution of a single dose and in a 10 dose vial of vaccine with 1 ampul of 6 mL sterile diluent for the reconstitution of 10 doses.

The vaccine is freeze-dried in single and multidose vials. Each dose contains not less than 1 000 $TCID_{50}$ of measles virus.

The freeze-dried vaccine and sterile diluent should be stored and transported between 2 and 8°C. **Do not freeze.** Reconstituted vaccine **must** be protected from light and maintained at 2 to 8°C.

Reviewed 1997

MEDROL® Ⓟ

Pharmacia & Upjohn

Methylprednisolone

Glucocorticoid

Indications: Endocrine Disorders: Primary or secondary adrenocortical insufficiency (hydrocortisone or cortisone is the first choice; synthetic analogs may be used in conjunction with mineralocorticoids where applicable; in infancy mineralocorticoid supplementation is of particular importance). Congenital adrenal hyperplasia. Nonsuppurative thyroiditis. Hypercalcemia associated with cancer.

Nonendocrine Disorders: Rheumatic Disorders: As adjunctive therapy for short-term administration (to tide the patient over an acute episode or exacerbation) in: psoriatic arthritis; rheumatoid arthritis, including juvenile rheumatoid arthritis (selected cases may require low-dose maintenance therapy); ankylosing spondylitis; acute and subacute bursitis; acute nonspecific tenosynovitis; acute gouty arthritis; post-traumatic osteoarthritis; synovitis of osteoarthritis; epicondylitis.

Collagen Diseases: During an exacerbation or as maintenance therapy in selected cases of: systemic lupus erythematosus; systemic dermatomyositis (polymyositis); acute rheumatic carditis; polymyalgia rheumatica; giant cell arteritis.

Dermatologic Diseases: pemphigus; bullous dermatitis herpetiformis; severe erythema multiforme (Stevens-Johnson syndrome); exfoliative dermatitis; mycosis fungoides; severe psoriasis; severe seborrheic dermatitis.

Allergic States: Control of severe or incapacitating allergic conditions intractable to adequate trials of conventional treatment: seasonal or perennial allergic rhinitis; serum sickness; bronchial asthma; drug hypersensitivity reactions; contact dermatitis; atopic dermatitis.

Ophthalmic Diseases: Severe acute and chronic allergic and inflammatory processes involving the eye and its adenexa such as: allergic corneal marginal ulcers; herpes zoster ophthalmicus; anterior segment inflammation; diffuse posterior uveitis and choroiditis; sympathetic ophthalmia; allergic conjunctivitis; keratitis; chorioretinitis; optic neuritis; iritis and iridocyclitis.

Respiratory Diseases: symptomatic sarcoidosis; Löeffler's syndrome not manageable by other means; berylliosis; fulminating or disseminated pulmonary tuberculosis when used concurrently with appropriate antituberculous chemotherapy; aspiration pneumonitis.

Hematologic Disorders: idiopathic thrombocytopenic purpura in adults; secondary thrombocytopenia in adults; acquired (autoimmune) hemolytic anemia; erythroblastopenia (RBC anemia); congenital (erythroid) hypoplastic anemia.

Neoplastic Diseases: For palliative management of: leukemias and lymphomas in adults; acute leukemia of childhood.

Edematous States: To induce a diuresis or remission of proteinuria in the nephrotic syndrome, without uremia, of the idiopathic type or that due to lupus erythematosus.

Gastrointestinal Diseases: To tide the patient over a critical period of the disease in: ulcerative colitis; regional enteritis.

Nervous System: acute exacerbations of multiple sclerosis; management of edema associated with brain tumor.

Miscellaneous: Tuberculous meningitis with subarachnoid block or impending block when used concurrently with appropriate antituberculous chemotherapy. Trichinosis with neurologic or myocardial involvement.

Organ Transplantation.

Contraindications: Systemic fungal infections; known hypersensitivity to methylprenisolone or the inactive ingredients in Medrol tablets.

Warnings: In patients on corticosteroid therapy subjected to unusual stress, increased dosage of rapidly acting corticosteroids before, during, and after the stressful situation is indicated.

Corticosteroids may mask some signs of infection, and new infections may appear during their use. There may be decreased resistance and inability to localize infection when corticosteroids are used. Infections with any pathogen including viral, bacterial, fungal, protozoan or helminthic infections, in any location in the body, may be associated with the use of corticosteroids alone or in combination with other immunosuppressive agents that affect cellular immunity, or neutrophil function. These infections may be mild, but can be severe and at times fatal. With increasing doses of corticosteroids, the rate of occurrence of infectious complication increases.

Prolonged use of corticosteroids may produce posterior subcapsular cataracts, glaucoma with possible damage to the optic nerves, and may enhance the establishment of secondary ocular infections due to fungi or viruses. Allergic reactions (e.g., angioedema) may occur.

Average and large doses of hydrocortisone or cortisone can cause elevation of blood pressure, salt and water retention, and increased excretion of potassium. These effects are less likely to occur with the synthetic derivatives except when used in large doses. Dietary salt restriction and potassium supplementation may be necessary. All corticosteroids increase calcium excretion.

Administration of live or live, attenuated vaccines is contraindicated in patients receiving immunosuppressive doses of corticosteroids. Killed or inactivated vaccines may be administered to patients receiving immunosuppressive doses of corticosteroids; however, the response to such vaccines may be diminished. Indicated immunization procedures may be undertaken in patients receiving nonimmunosuppressive doses of corticosteroids.

The use of methylprednisolone in active tuberculosis should be restricted to those cases of fulminating or disseminated tuberculosis in which the corticosteroid is used for the management of the disease in conjunction with an appropriate antituberculous regimen.

If corticosteroids are indicated in patients with latent tuberculosis or tuberculin reactivity, close observation is necessary as reactivation of the disease may occur. During prolonged corticosteroid therapy, these patients should receive chemoprophylaxis.

There is no universal agreement on whether corticosteroids per se are responsible for peptic ulcers encountered during therapy; however, glucocorticoid therapy may mask the symptoms of peptic ulcer so that perforation or hemorrhage may occur without significant pain.

Osteoporosis is a common but infrequently recognized adverse effect associated with a long-term use of large doses of glucocorticoid.

Growth may be suppressed in children receiving long-term daily, divided dose glucocorticoid therapy and use of such regimen should be restricted to the most urgent indication. Alternate day glucocorticoid therapy usually avoids or minimizes this side effect.

Host defenses are impaired in patients receiving large doses of glucocorticoids and this effect increases susceptibility to fungus infections as well as bacterial and viral infections.

Pregnancy: Some animal studies have shown that corticosteroids, when administered to the mother at high doses, may cause fetal malformations. Adequate human reproductive studies have not been done with corticosteroids. Therefore,

Medrol (cont'd)

the use of this drug in pregnancy, nursing mothers, or women of childbearing potential requires that the benefits of the drug be carefully weighed against the potential risk to the mother and embryo or fetus. Since there is inadequate evidence of safety in human pregnancy, this drug should be used in pregnancy only if clearly needed.

Corticosteroids readily cross the placenta. Infants born of mothers who have received substantial doses of corticosteroids during pregnancy must be carefully observed and evaluated for signs of adrenal insufficiency. There are no known effects of corticosteroids on labor and delivery.

Lactation: Corticosteroids are excreted in breast milk.

Precautions: Drug-induced adrenocortical insufficiency may be minimized by gradual reduction of dosage. This type of relative insufficiency may persist for months after discontinuation of therapy; therefore, in any situation of stress occurring during that period, hormone therapy should be reinstituted. Since mineralocorticoid secretion may be impaired, salt and/or mineralocorticoid should be administered concurrently.

There is an enhanced effect of corticosteroids on patients with hypothyroidism and in those with cirrhosis.

Corticosteroids should be used cautiously in patients with ocular herpes simplex because of possible corneal perforation.

The lowest possible dose of corticosteroid should be used to control the condition under treatment, and when reduction in dosage is possible, the reduction should be gradual.

Psychic derangements may appear when corticosteroids are used ranging from euphoria, insomnia, mood swings, personality changes, and severe depression to frank psychotic manifestations. Also, existing emotional instability or psychotic tendencies may be aggravated by corticosteroids.

Corticosteroids should be used with caution in nonspecific ulcerative colitis if there is a probability of impending perforation, abscess or other pyogenic infection; diverticulitis; fresh intestinal anastomoses; active or latent peptic ulcer, renal insufficiency; hypertension; osteoporosis; or myasthenia gravis.

Because complications of treatment with glucocorticoids are dependent on the size of the dose and the duration of treatment, a risk/benefit decision must be made in each individual case as to dose and duration of treatment and as to whether daily or intermittent therapy should be used.

Kaposi's sarcoma has been reported to occur in patients receiving corticosteroid therapy. Discontinuation of corticosteroids may result in clinical remission.

Carcinogenesis, mutagenesis, impairment of fertility: There is no evidence that corticosteroids are carcinogenic, mutagenic, or impair fertility.

Lactation: Corticoids are excreted in breast milk.

Drug Interactions: The pharmacokinetic interactions listed below are potentially clinically important. Mutual inhibition of metabolism occurs with concurrent use of cyclosporin and methylprednisolone, therefore it is possible that adverse events associated with the individual use of either drug may be more apt to occur. Convulsions have been reported with concurrent use of methylprednisolone and cyclosporin. Drugs that induce hepatic enzymes such as phenobarbital, phenytoin and rifampin may increase the clearance of methylprednisolone and may require increase in methylprednisolone dose to achieve desired response. Drugs such as troleandomycin and ketoconazole may inhibit the metabolism of methylprednisolone and thus decrease its clearance. Therefore the dose of methylprednisolone should be titrated to avoid steroid toxicity. Methylprednisolone may increase the clearance of chronic high dose ASA. This could lead to a decrease in salicylate serum levels or increase the risk of salicylate toxicity when methylprednisolone is withdrawn. ASA should be used cautiously in conjunction with corticosteroids in patients suffering from hypoprothrombinemia. The effect of methylprednisolone on oral anticoagulants is variable. There are reports of enhanced as well as diminished effects of anticoagulant when given concurrently with corticosteroids. Therefore coagulation indices should be monitored to maintain the desired anticoagulant effect.

Adverse Effects: Note: The following are typical for all systemic corticosteroids. Their inclusion in this list does not necessarily indicate that the specific event has been observed with this particular formulation.

Fluid and electrolyte disturbances: sodium retention; fluid retention; congestive heart failure in susceptible patients; potassium loss, hypokalemic alkalosis; hypertension.

Musculoskeletal: muscle weakness; steroid myopathy; osteoporosis; vertebral compression fractures; aseptic necrosis; pathologic fractures; loss of muscle mass; tendon rupture—particularly of the Achilles tendon.

Gastrointestinal: peptic ulceration with possible perforation and hemorrhage; gastric hemorrhage; pancreatitis; esophagitis; perforation of the bowel.

Dermatologic: impaired wound healing; thin fragile skin; petechiae and ecchymoses; facial erythema; increased sweating.

Metabolic: negative nitrogen balance due to protein catabolism.

Neurological: increased intracranial pressure; pseudotumor cerebri; psychic derangements; seizures.

Endocrine: menstrual irregularities; development of Cushingoid state; suppression of pituitary/adrenal axis; decreased carbohydrate tolerance; manifestations of latent diabetes mellitus; increased requirements for insulin or oral hypoglycemic agents in diabetes; suppression of growth in children.

Ophthalmic: posterior subcapsular cataracts; increased intraocular pressure; exophthalmos; glaucoma.

Immune System: masking of infections; latent infections becoming active; opportunistic infections; hypersensitivity reactions including anaphylaxis; may suppress reactions to skin tests.

Increases in ALT, AST and alkaline phosphatase have been observed following corticosteroid treatment. These changes are usually small, not associated with any clinical syndrome and are reversible upon discontinuation.

Dosage: The initial dosage of methylprednisolone may vary from 4 to 48 mg as methylprednisolone/day depending on the specific disease entity being treated. In situations of less severity, lower doses will generally suffice while in selected patients higher initial doses may be required. Clinical situations in which high dose therapy may be indicated include multiple sclerosis (200 mg/day), cerebral edema (200 to 1 000 mg/day), and organ transplantation (up to 7 mg/kg/day). If after a reasonable period of time there is a lack of satisfactory clinical response, methylprednisolone should be discontinued and the patient transferred to other appropriate therapy. If after long-term therapy the drug is to be stopped, it is recommended that it be withdrawn gradually rather than abruptly.

After a favorable response is noted, the proper maintenance dosage should be determined by decreasing the initial drug dosage in small decrements at appropriate time intervals until the lowest dosage which will maintain an adequate clinical response is reached. It should be kept in mind that constant monitoring is needed in regard to drug dosage. Included in the situations which may make dosage adjustments necessary are changes in clinical status secondary to remissions or exacerbations in the disease process, the patient's individual drug responsiveness, and the effect of patient exposure to stressful situations not directly related to the disease entity under treatment; in this latter situation it may be necessary to increase the dosage of methylprednisolone for a period of time consistent with the patient's condition.

It should be emphasized that dosage requirements are variable and must be individualized on the basis of the disease under treatment and the response of the patient.

ADT Alternate Day Therapy: Alternate day therapy is a corticosteroid dosing regimen in which twice the usual daily dose of corticosteroid is administered every other morning. The purpose of this mode of therapy is to provide a patient requiring long-term, pharmacologic dose treatment with the beneficial effects of corticoids while minimizing certain undesirable effects, including pituitary-adrenal suppression, the Cushingoid state, corticoid withdrawal symptoms, and growth suppression in children.

Directions for Medrol Dosepak: 1st day: 2 tablets before breakfast, 1 tablet after lunch and after supper, and 2 tablets at bedtime.

2nd day: 1 tablet before breakfast. 1 tablet after lunch and after supper, and 2 tablets at bedtime.

3rd day: 1 tablet before breakfast, after lunch, after supper and at bedtime.

4th day: 1 tablet before breakfast, after lunch and at bedtime.

5th day: 1 tablet before breakfast and at bedtime.

6th day: 1 tablet before breakfast.

Supplied: 4 mg: Each white, elliptical, cross-scored tablet, engraved "Upjohn 56", contains: methylprednisolone 4 mg. Nonmedicinal ingredients: calcium stearate, cornstarch, lactose, mineral oil and sucrose. Gluten-free. Bottles of 100. Dosepack units of 21.

16 mg: Each white, elliptical, cross-scored tablet, engraved "Medrol 16", contains: methylprednisolone 16 mg. Nonmedicinal ingredients: calcium stearate, cornstarch, lactose, mineral oil and sucrose. Gluten-free. Bottles of 100.

(Shown in Product Recognition Section)

Reviewed 1997

MEDROL® Acne Lotion Ⓟ

Pharmacia & Upjohn

Methylprednisolone—Aluminum Chlorhydroxide—Sulfur

Acne Therapy

Pharmacology: Medrol Acne Lotion has an anti-inflammatory action by virtue of its content of methylprednisolone, as astringent and antiperspirant action by virtue of its content of aluminum chlorhydroxide and a keratolytic effect by virtue of its sulfur content. Sulfur has also demonstrated some antibacterial activity at the concentration used.

Indications: For the control of acne vulgaris in the adolescent and young adult. Also useful in some cases of acne rosacea and seborrheic dermatitis.

Contraindications: In tuberculosis of the skin and in the presence of skin viral diseases such as herpes simplex, vaccinia and varicella. Also contraindicated in patients known to be sensitive to any ingredients in this lotion.

Warnings: *Pregnancy:* Corticosteroids are generally teratogenic in laboratory animals when administered systemically at relatively low dosage levels. The more potent corticosteroids have been shown to be teratogenic after dermal application in laboratory animals. There are no adequate and well-controlled studies in pregnant women on teratogenic effects from topically applied corticosteroids. Therefore, topical corticosteroids should be used during pregnancy only if the potential benefit justifies the potential risk to the fetus. Drugs of this class should not be used extensively on pregnant patients, in large amounts, or for prolonged periods of time.

Precautions: General: If irritation develops, topical corticosteroids should be discontinued and appropriate therapy instituted.

In the presence of dermatological infections, the use of an appropriate antifungal or antibacterial agent should be instituted. If a favorable response does not occur promptly, the corticosteroid should be discontinued until the infection has been adequately controlled.

Avoid contact with the eyes. If there are signs of irritation or sensitivity, application should be discontinued. The patient should be advised to inform subsequent physicians of the prior use of corticosteroids.

Systemic absorption of topical corticosteroids has produced reversible hypothalamic-pituitary-adrenal (HPA) axis suppression, manifestations of Cushing's syndrome, hyperglycemia, and glucosuria in some patients. Conditions which augment systemic absorption include the application of the more potent steroids, use over large surface areas, prolonged use, and the addition of occlusive dressings. Therefore, patients receiving a large dose of a potent topical steroid applied to a large surface area or under an occlusive dressing should be evaluated periodically for evidence of HPA axis suppression by using the urinary free cortisol and ACTH stimulation tests. If HPA axis suppression is noted, an attempt should be made to withdraw the drug, to reduce the frequency of application, or to substitute a less potent steroid. Recovery of HPA axis function is generally prompt and complete upon discontinuation of the drug. Infrequently, signs and symptoms of steroid withdrawal may occur, requiring supplemental systemic corticosteroids.

Children: Children may absorb proportionally larger amounts of topical corticosteroids than mature patients because children have a larger skin surface area to body weight ratio. This could lead to greater susceptibility to topical corticosteroid-induced HPA axis suppression and Cushing's syndrome.

HPA axis suppression, Cushing's syndrome, and intracranial hypertension have been reported in children receiving topical corticosteroids. Manifestations of adrenal suppression in children include linear growth retardation, delayed weight gain, low plasma cortisol levels, and absence of response to ACTH stimulation. Manifestations of intracranial hypertension include bulging fontanelles, headaches and bilateral papilledema.

Administration of topical corticosteroids to children should be limited to the least amount compatible with an effective therapeutic regimen. Chronic corticosteroid therapy may interfere with the growth and development of children.

Lactation: It is not known whether topical administration of corticosteroids could result in sufficient systemic absorption to produce detectable quantities in breast milk. Systemically administered corticosteroids are secreted into breast milk in quantities not likely to have a deleterious effect on the infant. Nevertheless, caution should be exercised when topical corticosteroids are administered to a nursing woman.

Laboratory Tests: The following tests may be helpful in evaluating the HPA axis suppression: urinary free cortisol test; ACTH stimulation test.
Information for the Patient: Patients using topical corticosteroids should receive the following information and instructions:
1. This medication is to be used as directed by the physician. It is for external use only. Avoid contact with the eyes.
2. Patients should be advised not to use this medication for any disorder other than for which it was prescribed.
3. The treated skin area should not be bandaged or otherwise covered or wrapped as to be occlusive unless directed by the physician.
4. Patients should report any signs of local adverse reactions especially under occlusive dressing.
5. Parents of pediatric patients should be advised not to use tight-fitting diapers or plastic pants on a child being treated in the diaper area, as these garments may constitute occlusive dressings.

Adverse Effects: The following local adverse reactions have been reported with topical corticosteroids, but may occur more frequently with the use of occlusive dressings. These reactions are listed in a an approximate decreasing order of occurrence: burning, itching, irritation, dryness, folliculitis, hypertrichosis, acneiform eruptions, hypopigmentation, perioral dermatitis, allergic contact dermatitis, maceration of the skin, secondary infection, skin atrophy, striae, and miliaria.

If excessive dryness of the skin occurs, reduce amount and frequency of application of Medrol Acne Lotion. This effect is more commonly seen in patients with fair complexions or sensitive skin. Localized atrophy or striae have been reported with the use of topical corticosteroids particularly when used in the intertriginous areas. The remote possibility of systemic corticosteroid absorption does exist, particularly if extensive areas are treated or treatment is maintained for prolonged periods. It is estimated that 0.18 mg of methylprednisolone acetate would be absorbed daily if the contents of a 30 mL bottle were used over a period of 7 days.

Overdose: Symptoms and Treatment: No cases have been reported. Excessive applications should be immediately removed with mild soap and water.

Accidental ingestion has not been reported. Should this occur, vomiting should be induced and appropriate measures taken to treat any irritation of the oral mucosa which might occur. The absorption of a single high dose of methylprednisolone should cause no concern.

Dosage: The lotion should be applied to all lesions once or twice a day taking care to avoid contact with the eyes. The skin should be washed with a bland soap prior to each application. The frequency of application will vary from person to person depending on his susceptibility to the drying effect of the lotion. To obtain satisfactory results, dryness of the skin should be produced, but not to the point of flaking or peeling.

In patients with very sensitive skin, application every other day may control acne lesions.

Supplied: Each mL contains: methylprednisolone acetate 2.5 mg, aluminum chlorhydroxide complex 100 mg, sulfur 50 mg. Nonmedicinal ingredients: butylparaben, cetyl palmitate, lexemul AR, methylcellulose, methylparaben, perfume oil, polysorbate 80, polysorbate 85, propylene glycol, polyethylene glycol, and purified water. Gluten-free. Plastic squeeze bottles of 75 mL.

MEDROL® VERIDERM® Cream

Pharmacia & Upjohn

Methylprednisolone

Topical Glucocorticoid

Indications: Noninfected dermatoses, including allergic dermatoses, pruritus ani and vulvae, atopic and seborrheic dermatitis and contact dermatitis, induced by poison ivy, cosmetics, chemicals or drugs.

Contraindications: Tuberculosis of the skin, herpes simplex, vaccinia, varicella and other cutaneous infections for which an effective agent is not available for simultaneous application. Do not use in the eye or in patients sensitive to any of the components.

Precautions: Although untoward effects associated with the use of topical corticosteroids are uncommon and not to be expected from ordinary use, sensitization, irritation and failure of therapeutic response have been noted in rare instances. Application to extensive areas, too frequent application, or application under occlusive dressings may result in systemic absorption with symptoms of adrenal suppression, localized atrophy and striae. If secondary bacterial infection exists or supervenes, concomitant antimicrobial therapy is indicated.

Convulsions have been reported with concurrent use of methylprednisolone and cyclosporine. Since concurrent use of these agents results in a mutal inhibition of metabolism, it is possible that convulsions and other adverse events associated with the individual use of either drug may be more apt to occur.

Pregnancy: The safety of the use of topical steroid preparations during pregnancy has not been fully established. Therefore, steroids should not be used unnecessarily during pregnancy or for prolonged periods of time.

Adverse Effects: The following adverse skin reactions have been reported rarely with the use of topical steroids: dryness, itching, burning, local irritation, striae, hypopigmentation, atrophy and secondary infection. When occlusive dressings are used, pustules, folliculitis and pyoderma may occur.

Dosage: Careful cleansing of the affected skin should precede the application of a small amount of ointment. Initially, application may be made 1 to 3 times a day. Frequency of application may be reduced after control has been achieved.

Supplied: Each g contains: methylprednisolone acetate 2.5 mg (0.25%) in Veriderm, a skin lipid base. Nonmedicinal ingredients: butyl hydrolytol, butyl hydroxyan, butylparaben, cetyl palmitate, cetyl alcohol, cholesterol, corn oil, glycerin, lexemul ar, methylparaben, mineral oil, oleic acid, oleyl alcohol, perfume oil, polyoxyl 40 stearate, sorbitan monooleate, squalene, stearic acid, stearyl alcohol, tocopherol and water. Tubes of 25 and 50 g.

MEFOXIN®

MSD

Cefoxitin Sodium

Antibiotic

Pharmacology: In vitro studies demonstrate that the bactericidal action of cefoxitin, a cephamycin derived from cephamycin C, results from the inhibition of bacterial cell wall synthesis. Evidence suggests that the methoxy group in the 7α position is responsible for the resistance of cefoxitin to degradation by bacterial beta-lactamases.

Cefoxitin is poorly absorbed orally in humans.

Cefoxitin, administered parenterally, produces high serum and urine concentrations. It is excreted virtually unchanged (up to 6% is excreted as the deacylated metabolite) as active cefoxitin by the kidneys, and has a mean terminal serum half-life of approximately 1 hour in adults. The mean terminal serum half-life in neonates 0 to 7 days of age is 5.6$\pm$0.5 hours, in neonates 7 days to 1 month of age 2.5$\pm$0.5 hours and in infants 1 to 3 months of age 1.7$\pm$0.4 hours. Cefoxitin passes rapidly into the bile. Probenecid slows tubular excretion and increases and prolongs blood levels. Lidocaine had no effect on cefoxitin's absorption or elimination.

Indications: Treatment: The treatment of the following infections when due to susceptible organisms: intra-abdominal infections such as peritonitis and intra-abdominal abscess, gynecological infections such as endometritis and pelvic cellulitis, septicemia, urinary tract infections (including those caused by S. marcescens and Serratia spp.), lower respiratory tract infections, bone and joint infections caused by S. aureus, soft tissue infections such as cellulitis, abscesses and wound infections.

Appropriate culture and susceptibility studies should be performed to determine the susceptibility of the causative organism(s) to cefoxitin. Therapy may be started while awaiting the results of these tests; however, treatment modification may be required once these results become available.

Organisms particularly appropriate for therapy with cefoxitin are: Gram-Positive: staphylococci, penicillinase producing and nonproducing; streptococci excluding enterococci.
Gram-negative (beta-lactamase producing and nonproducing strains): E. coli; Klebsiella species (including K. pneumoniae); Proteus, indole positive and negative; H. influenzae; Providencia species.
Anaerobes: B. fragilis.

Cefoxitin may also be appropriate for the treatment of infections involving susceptible strains of both aerobic and anaerobic bacteria.

Clinical experience has demonstrated that cefoxitin can be administered to patients who are also receiving carbenicillin, gentamicin, tobramycin, or amikacin (see Precautions).

Prophylactic Use: Cefoxitin may be administered perioperatively (preoperatively, intraoperatively and postoperatively) to patients undergoing vaginal or abdominal hysterectomy and abdominal surgery when there is a significant risk of postoperative infection or where the occurrence of postoperative infection is considered to be especially serious.

In patients undergoing cesarean section, intraoperative (after clamping the umbilical cord) and postoperative use of cefoxitin may reduce the incidence of surgery related postoperative infections.

Effective prophylactic use depends on the time of administration. Cefoxitin usually should be given ½ to 1 hour before the operation. Prophylactic administration should usually be stopped within 12 hours. It has been generally reported that continuing administration of any antibiotic beyond 24 hours following surgery increases the possibility of adverse reactions but, in the majority of surgical procedures, does not reduce the incidence of subsequent infection.

If signs of postsurgical infection should appear, specimens for culture should be obtained for identification of the causative organism(s) so that appropriate treatment may be instituted.

Contraindications: Hypersensitivity to cefoxitin or to the cephalosporin group of antibiotics.

Warnings: Before cefoxitin therapy is instituted, careful inquiry should be made to determine whether the patient has had previous hypersensitivity reactions to cefoxitin, cephalosporins, penicillins or other drugs. Cefoxitin should be given with caution to penicillin-sensitive patients.

There is some clinical and laboratory evidence of partial cross-allergenicity between cephamycins and the other beta-lactam antibiotics, penicillins and cephalosporins. Severe reactions (including anaphylaxis) have been reported with most beta-lactam antibiotics.

Pseudomembranous colitis has been reported with virtually all antibiotics including cefoxitin. This colitis can range from mild to life-threatening in severity. Antibiotics should therefore be prescribed with caution in individuals with a history of gastrointestinal disease, particularly colitis. It is important to consider a diagnosis of pseudomembranous colitis in patients who develop diarrhea in association with antibiotic use. While studies indicate that a toxin produced by C. difficile is one primary cause of antibiotic-associated colitis, other causes should also be considered.

Any patient who has demonstrated some form of allergy, particularly to drugs, should receive antibiotics including cefoxitin with caution.

If an allergic reaction to cefoxitin occurs, administration of the drug should be discontinued. Serious hypersensitivity reactions may require treatment with epinephrine and other emergency measures.

Precautions: General: Prolonged use of cefoxitin may result in the overgrowth of nonsusceptible organisms. Repeated evaluation of the patient's condition is essential and if superinfection occurs during therapy, appropriate measures should be taken. Should an organism become resistant during antibiotic therapy, another antibiotic should be substituted.
Children: In children 3 months of age or older, higher doses of cefoxitin (100 mg/kg/day and above) have been associated with an increased incidence of eosinophilia and elevated AST.
Pregnancy: The safety of cefoxitin in the treatment of infections during pregnancy has not been established. If the administration of cefoxitin during pregnancy is considered necessary, its use requires that the anticipated benefits be weighed against possible hazards to the fetus. Reproductive and teratogenic studies performed in mice and rats have revealed no evidence of impaired fertility or harm to the fetus due to cefoxitin.

There are no controlled studies in pregnant women.
Lactation: Cefoxitin is excreted in human milk. Caution should be exercised if use is indicated.
Patients with Special Diseases and Conditions: Renal Insufficiency: The total daily dosage should be reduced when cefoxitin is administered to patients with transient or persistent reduction of urinary output due to renal insufficiency (see Dosage) because high and prolonged serum antibiotic concentrations can occur from usual doses.
Drug Interactions: Increased nephrotoxicity has been reported following concomitant administration of cephalosporins and aminoglycoside antibiotics.
Laboratory Tests: In patients treated with cefoxitin a false-positive reaction to glucose in the urine may occur with Benedict's or Fehling's solutions but not with the use of specific glucose oxidase methods.

Using the Jaffe Method falsely high creatinine values in serum may occur if serum concentrations of cefoxitin exceed

Mefoxin (cont'd)

100 μg/mL. Serum samples from patients treated with cefoxitin should not be analyzed for creatinine if withdrawn within 2 hours of drug administration.

High concentrations of cefoxitin in the urine may interfere with measurement of urinary 17-hydroxy-corticosteroids by the Porter-Silber reaction and produce false increases of modest degree in the levels reported.

Adverse Effects: Cefoxitin is generally well tolerated. Adverse reactions rarely required cessation of treatment and usually have been mild and transient.

Local: Thrombophlebitis has occurred with i.v. administration. Some degree of pain and tenderness is usually experienced after i.m. injections using water. Induration has occasionally been reported.

Allergic: Rash (including exfoliative dermatitis, and toxic epidermal necrolysis), urticaria, pruritus, eosinophilia, fever and other allergic reactions including anaphylaxis, interstitial nephritis and angioedema have been reported.

Gastrointestinal: Diarrhea, including pseudomembranous colitis can appear during or after antibiotic treatment. Nausea and vomiting have been reported rarely.

Hematologic: Eosinophilia, leukopenia, neutropenia, hemolytic anemia, thrombocytopenia and bone marrow depression have been reported. Some individuals, particularly those with azotemia may develop positive direct Coombs' tests during therapy with cefoxitin.

Liver Function: Transient elevations in AST, ALT, serum LDH, serum alkaline phosphatase and jaundice have been reported.

Cardiovascular Function: hypotension.

Renal Function: Elevations in serum creatinine and/or BUN have been observed. As with the cephalosporins, acute renal failure has been reported rarely. Cefoxitin's role in changes in renal function tests is difficult to assess, since factors predisposing to prerenal azotemia or to impaired renal function have often been present.

Musculoskeletal: worsening myasthenia gravis (single case).

Overdose: Symptoms and Treatment: Other than general supportive treatment, no specific antidote is known. Cefoxitin can be eliminated by dialysis in patients with renal insufficiency.

Dosage: Cefoxitin may be administered i.v. or i.m. as required (see below Reconstitution for each route).

The i.v. route is preferable for patients with bacteremia, bacterial septicemia, or other severe or life-threatening infections, or for patients who may be poor risks because of lowered resistance resulting from such debilitating conditions as malnutrition, trauma, surgery, diabetes, heart failure, or malignancy, particularly if shock is present or impending.

Therapeutic Use: Adults: The usual adult dosage is 1 or 2 g every 6 to 8 hours. Dosage and route of administration should be determined by severity of infection, susceptibility of the causative organisms, and condition of the patient. The usual adult dosages are shown in Table I.

Table I—Mefoxin

Usual Adult Dosage

Type of Infection	Daily Dosage	Frequency and Route
Uncomplicated forms* of infections such as pneumonia, urinary tract infection, soft tissue infection	3-4 g	1 g every 6 to 8 hours i.v. or i.m.
Moderately severe or severe infections	6-8 g	1 g every 4 hours or 2 g every 6 to 8 hours i.v.
Infections commonly needing antibiotics in higher dosage (i.e., gas gangrene)	12 g	2 g every 4 hours or 3 g every 6 hours i.v.

*Including patients in whom bacteremia is absent or unlikely.

Therapy may be started while awaiting the results of susceptibility testing.

Antibiotic therapy for group A beta-hemolytic streptococcal infections should be maintained for at least 10 days to guard against the risk of rheumatic fever or glomerulonephritis. In staphylococcal and other infections involving a collection of pus, surgical drainage should be carried out where indicated.

Adults with Impaired Renal Function: Cefoxitin may be used in patients with reduced renal function but a reduced dosage should be employed and it is advisable to monitor serum levels in patients with severe impairment.

In adults with renal insufficiency, an initial loading dose of 1 to 2 g should be given. After a loading dose, the following recommendations for **maintenance dosage** may be used as a guide. See Table II.

Table II—Mefoxin

Maintenance Dosage in Adults with Reduced Renal Function

Renal Function	Creatinine Clearance mL/min	Dose	Frequency
Mild impairment	50-30	1–2 g	every 8–12 hours
Moderate impairment	29-10	1–2 g	every 12–24 hours
Severe impairment	9–5	0.5–1 g	every 12–24 hours
Essentially no function	<5	0.5–1 g	every 24–48 hours

In patients undergoing hemodialysis, the loading dose of 1 to 2 g should be given after each hemodialysis and the maintenance dose should be given as indicated in Table II.

Neonates (including premature infants), infants and children (see Warnings for Neonates under Administration): See Table III.

Table III—Mefoxin

Dosage in Neonates, Infants and Children

Premature Infants* with Body Weights Above 1 500 g	20–40 mg/kg every 12 h i.v.
Neonates*	
0–1 week of age	20–40 mg/kg every 12 h i.v.
1–4 weeks of age	20–40 mg/kg every 8 h i.v.
Infants* 1 month to 2 years of age	20–40 mg/kg every 6 h or every 8 h i.m. or i.v.
Children	20–40 mg/kg every 6 h or every 8 h i.m. or i.v.

*Clinical data are insufficient to recommend use of the i.m. formulation in infants less than 3 months of age.

In severe infections, the total daily dosage in infants and children may be increased to 200 mg/kg, but not to exceed 12 g/day.

Cefoxitin is not recommended for the therapy of meningitis. If meningitis is suspected, an appropriate antibiotic should be used.

At present there are insufficient data to recommend a specific dosage for children with impaired renal function. However, if the administration of cefoxitin is deemed to be essential the dosage should be modified consistent with the recommendations for adults (see Table II).

Prophylactic Use: Vaginal or Abdominal Hysterectomy, Abdominal Surgery and Cesarean Section: For prophylactic use, a 3-dose regimen of cefoxitin is recommended as follows: Vaginal or Abdominal Hysterectomy and Abdominal Surgery: 2 g i.m. or i.v. just prior to surgery (approximately ½ to 1 hour before initial incision). The second and third 2 g doses should be administered at 2- to 6-hour intervals after the initial dose.

Cesarean Section: The first dose of 2 g should be administered i.v. as soon as the umbilical cord has been clamped. The second and third 2 g doses should be given i.v. or i.m. 4 and 8 hours after the first dose.

Administration: Warning for Neonates: Solutions containing preservatives should not be used for injection or for flushing catheters in treating neonates.

Benzyl alcohol as a preservative in bacteriostatic water for injection and bacteriostatic sodium chloride injection has been associated with toxicity in neonates. Data are unavailable on the toxicity of other preservatives in this age group. Therefore, any diluent used with cefoxitin in the treatment of neonates should be free of any preservative.

I.M.: Cefoxitin should be injected into a large muscle mass such as the upper outer quadrant of the buttock (i.e., gluteus maximus); aspiration is necessary to avoid inadvertent injection into a blood vessel.

I.V.: The i.v. route is preferable for patients with severe or life-threatening infections.

Cefoxitin may be administered by i.v. injection either by continuous or intermittent infusion. The reconstituted cefoxitin must be further diluted to desired volume with any of the diluents recommended.

Intermittent I.V. Administration: A solution of cefoxitin in sterile water for injection may be administered slowly over a period of 3 to 5 minutes. Using an infusion system cefoxitin may be given through the tubing by which the patient is receiving other parenteral solutions. However, during infusion of the solution containing cefoxitin, it is advisable to temporarily discontinue administration of any other infusion solution at the same site (by using an appropriate i.v. infusion set). Any unused portion must be discarded.

Continuous I.V. Infusions: A solution of cefoxitin may be added to an i.v. bottle containing an appropriate i.v. infusion fluid in the amount calculated to give the desired antibiotic dose. Butterfly or scalp vein-type needles are preferred for this type of infusion.

Reconstitution: I.M.: Solutions for reconstitution: sterile water for injection or bacteriostatic water for injection (see Warnings for Neonates under Administration) or 0.5% lidocaine HCl injection (without epinephrine). Reconstitute as directed in Table IV.

Table IV—Mefoxin

Reconstitution Table—I.M.

Strength	Amount of Diluent to be Added (mL)*	Approximate Withdrawable Volume (mL)	Approximate Average Concentration (mg/mL)
1 g vial	2	2.5	400
2 g vial	4	5.0	400

*Shake to dissolve and let stand until clear.

I.V. Solutions for reconstitution: sterile water for injection or 0.9% Sodium Chloride Injection or 5% and 10% Dextrose Injection. Vials (1 and 2 g): Reconstitute as directed in Table V.

Table V—Mefoxin

Reconstitution Table—I.V.

Strength	Amount of Diluent to be Added (mL)*	Approximate Withdrawable Volume (mL)	Approximate Average Concentration (mg/mL)
1 g vial	10	10.5	95
2 g vial	10 or 20	11.1 or 21.0	180 or 95

* Shake to dissolve and let stand until clear.

Pharmacy Bulk Vial: The 10 g Pharmacy Bulk Vial contains many single doses for multiple dispensing. The closure shall be penetrated only one time after reconstitution (single puncture). Any unused stock solution remaining after a period of 8 hours should be promptly discarded. Reconstitute as directed in Table VI.

Table VI—Mefoxin

Reconstitution Table—Pharmacy Bulk Vial

Strength	Amount of Diluent to be Added (mL)*	Approximate Withdrawable Volume (mL)	Approximate Average Concentration (mg/mL)
10 g vial	43 or 93	49 or 98.5	200 or 100

*Shake to dissolve and let stand until clear.

The Pharmacy Bulk Vial is intended for use in hospitals with a recognized I.V. admixture program, and is restricted to **the preparation of admixtures for infusion. It is not for direct infusion.**

Direct I.V. Injection: Reconstitute as directed in Table V.

Intermittent I.V. infusion: Reconstitute as directed in Table V.

Continuous I.V. Infusion: Reconstitute with sterile water for injection. The primary solution may be further diluted to the desired volume with any of the solutions of i.v. infusion listed below:

Solutions for I.V. Infusion: 0.9% Sodium Chloride Injection, 5% or 10% Dextrose Injection, 5% Dextrose and 0.9% Sodium Chloride Injection, 5% Dextrose Injection with 0.2% or 0.45% saline solution, Ringer's Injection, 5% Dextrose Injection with 0.02% Sodium Bicarbonate Solution, Lactated Ringer's Injection, 5% Dextrose in Lactated Ringer's Injection, 5% or 10% Invert Sugar in water, 10% Invert Sugar in saline solution, 5% Sodium Bicarbonate Injection, M/6 Sodium Lactate solution, Normosol-M in D5-W, Ionosol B w/Dextrose 5%, Mannitol 5% and 2.5%, Mannitol 10%.

Mefoxin has also been found compatible when admixed in i.v. infusions with the following: Heparin 0.1 unit/mL (at room temperature 8 hours), Heparin 100 units/mL, Insulin in normal saline, Insulin in 10% invert sugar.

ADD-Vantage Vials: When administering cefoxitin using the ADD-Vantage drug delivery system, cefoxitin sterile powder is added directly to a single-dose flexible plastic ADD-Vantage diluent container.

Solutions for Reconstitution: Use Abbott Laboratories' ADD-Vantage diluent containers containing 50 or 100 mL of either: 5% Dextrose Injection or 0.9% Sodium Chloride Injection. Reconstitute as directed in Table VII.

Table VII—Mefoxin

Reconstitution Table (Add-Vantage Vials)

ADD-Vantage Vial Size	Amount of Diluent to be Added (mL)*	Approximate Withdrawable Volume (mL)	Approximate Average Concentration (mg/mL)
1 g vial	50 or 100	50 or 100	20 or 10
2 g vial	50 or 100	50 or 100	40 or 20

* Shake to dissolve and let stand until clear.

Instructions for Use (ADD-Vantage): To Open Diluent Container: Peel overwrap from the corner and remove container. Some opacity of the plastic due to moisture absorption during the sterilization process may be observed. This is normal and does not affect the solution quality or safety. The opacity will diminish gradually.

To Assemble Vial and Flexible Diluent Container (use aseptic technique): see package insert for figures:

1) Remove the protective covers from the top of the vial and the vial port on the diluent container as follows: a) To remove the breakaway vial cap, swing the pull ring over the top of the vial and pull down far enough to start the opening. Pull the ring approximately half way around the cap and then pull straight up to remove the cap. b) To remove the vial port cover, grasp the tab on the pull ring, pull up to break the 3 tie strings, then pull back to remove the cover.

2) Screw the vial into the vial port until it will go no further. **The vial must be screwed in tightly to assure a seal.** This occurs approximately ½ turn (180°) after the first audible click. The clicking sound does not assure a seal; the vial must be turned as far as it will go. **Note:** Once vial is seated, do not attempt to remove.

3) Recheck the vial to assure that it is tight by trying to turn it further in the direction of assembly.

4) Label appropriately.

To Prepare Admixture:

1) Squeeze the bottom of the diluent container gently to inflate the portion of the container surrounding the end of the drug vial.

2) With the other hand, push the drug vial down into the container telescoping the walls of the container. Grasp the inner cap of the vial through the walls of the container.

3) Pull the inner cap from the drug vial. Verify that the rubber stopper has been pulled out, allowing the drug and diluent to mix.

4) Mix container contents thoroughly and use within the specified time.

Preparation for Administration (use aseptic technique):

1) Confirm the activation and admixture of vial contents.

2) Check for leaks by squeezing container firmly. If leaks are found, discard unit as sterility may be impaired.

3) Close flow control clamp of administration set.

4) Remove cover from outlet port at bottom of container.

5) Insert piercing pin of administration set into port with a twisting motion until the pin is firmly seated. **Note:** See full directions on administration set carton.

6) Lift the free end of the hanger loop on the bottom of the vial, breaking the 2 tie strings. Bend the loop outward to lock it in the upright position, then suspend container from hanger.

7) Squeeze and release drip chamber to establish proper fluid level in chamber.

8) Open flow control clamp and clear air from set. Close clamp.

9) Attach set to venipuncture device. If device is not indwelling, prime and make venipuncture.

10) Regulate rate of administration with flow control clamp.

Warning: Do not use flexible containers in series connections.

Stability of Solutions: Store powder below 30°C. The powder and solutions tend to darken, depending on storage conditions; however, product potency is not adversely affected.

Storage: Vials: Reconstituted solution for i.m. injection and i.v. injection should be used within 24 hours if kept at room temperature (15 to 30°C) or 72 hours if stored under refrigeration (2 to 8°C).

The further diluted solutions for i.v. infusion should be used within 12 hours if kept at room temperature (15 to 30°C) or 24 hours if stored under refrigeration (2 to 8°C).

ADD-Vantage Vials: Prepared as directed, ADD-Vantage vials should be used within **12 hours** if kept at room temperature or **36 hours** if stored under refrigeration (2 to 8°C).

Dark brown solution should not be used.

Parenteral drug products should be inspected visually for particulate matter and discoloration prior to administration whenever solution and container permit.

Incompatibility: Solutions of Mefoxin, like those of most beta-lactam antibiotics, should not be added to aminoglycoside solutions (e.g., gentamicin sulfate, tobramycin sulfate, amikacin sulfate) because of potential interaction.

Supplied: ADD-Vantage Vials: Each ADD-Vantage vial of sterile powder contains: cefoxitin 1 or 2 g as sodium salt for i.v. use. Boxes of 10.

Pharmacy Bulk Vials: Each bottle of Pharmacy Bulk solution contains: cefoxitin 10 g as sodium salt for i.v. use. Boxes of 6.

Vials: Each vial of dry white to off-white sterile powder contains: cefoxitin 1 or 2 g as sodium salt for i.m. and i.v. use. Boxes of 10.

Solutions of cefoxitin sodium range from clear to light amber in color. The pH of freshly constituted solutions ranges from 4.2 to 7.0. Each g of cefoxitin sodium contains approximately 2.3 mmol sodium.

Reviewed 1999

MEGACE® Ⓟ
MEGACE® OS Ⓟ
Bristol

Megestrol Acetate

Antineoplastic—Progestogen—Antianorexic—Anticachectic
Antianorexic—Anticachectic

Pharmacology: The precise mechanism of action by which megestrol produces its antineoplastic effects is unknown at present. Pharmacologic doses of megestrol exerted a direct cytotoxic effect on human breast cancer cells in vitro and proved capable of modifying and abolishing the stimulatory effects of estrogen on breast cancer cell lines.

Megestrol interacts with progesterone receptors to stimulate cell maturation through a progestin-inducing mechanism. It has also been shown to have certain androgenic properties and may also modify glucocorticoid action by binding to the glucocorticoid receptor.

In previously untreated breast cancer patients with ER+PR+ receptor status, endocrine therapy has been shown to produce responses in up to 81% of patients.

Inhibition of persistent endometrial hyperplasia and of persistent endometrial adenocarcinoma was observed upon administration of megestrol in doses of 160 mg/day. Megestrol partially inhibited expression of estrogen dependent secretory proteins and certain constituent proteins in the rat uterine epithelium.

Metastatic carcinoma of the prostate responds to a variety of hormone manipulations that decrease the level of androgens in androgen-sensitive tissue. The primary mechanism of action of megestrol and DES is the suppression of luteinizing hormone from the pituitary gland, which leads to suppression of serum androgens arising from the testicle.

Megestrol may have other mechanisms of action as well, including an antiandrogen activity, suppression of adrenal androgens, and possibly the inhibition of enzymes, e.g., 5 α-reductase, critical to androgen metabolism within the prostate. The precise mechanism of action by which megestrol produces its antianorexic and anticachectic effects is also unknown at present. The gain in weight associated with megestrol is associated with increased appetite, an increase in fat and body cell mass.

Pharmacokinetics: In 24* healthy male volunteers (age 19 to 44 years) who received 160 mg of megestrol given as a 40 mg q.i.d. regimen, the oral absorption of Megace appeared to be variable. Peak drug levels for the first 40 mg dose ranged from 10 to 56 ng/mL (mean 27.6 ng/mL) and the times to peak concentrations ranged from 1 to 3 hours (mean 2.2 hours). Plasma elimination half-life ranged from 9.9 to 104.9 hours (mean 34.2 hours). The steady state plasma concentrations for a 40 mg q.i.d. regimen have not been established.

*Pharmacokinetic data from 1 patient excluded due to unusually high drug levels.

Plasma steady-state pharmacokinetics of Megace OS were evaluated in 10 adult cachectic male patients (age 26 to 49 years) with acquired immunodeficiency syndrome (AIDS) and an involuntary weight loss greater than 10% of baseline. Patients received a single oral dose of 800 mg/day of megestrol for 21 days. Plasma concentration data obtained on day 21 were evaluated for up to 48 hours past the last dose. A high degree of interpatient variability in rate and extent of absorption was observed. Median peak plasma concentration (C_{max}) of megestrol was 602 ng/mL (range 77 to 1 670 ng/mL). Median area under the concentration versus time-curve (AUC) was 7 547 ng.h/mL (range 1 550 to 27 090 ng.h/mL) and median T_{max} value was 5 h (range 1 to 8 hours).

Steady-state plasma pharmacokinetics of Megace OS were evaluated in 24 asymptomatic HIV seropositive male patients (age 21 to 40 years). Patients received single oral dose of 750 mg of megestrol for 14 days. The mean plasma concentration (C_{max}) of megestrol was 490 ng/mL (range 156 to 1 169 ng/mL). The mean area under the concentration vs time curve (AUC) was 6 779 h.ng/mL (range 1 826 to 14 094 h.ng/mL) and median T_{max} was 3 hours (range 0 to 8 hours).

Estimates of plasma levels of megestrol are dependent on the measurement method used. Plasma levels depend on intestinal and hepatic inactivation of the drug, which may be affected by intestinal tract motility, intestinal bacteria, concomitant antibiotic administration, body weight, diet and hepatic function.

Pharmacodynamics: A single oral dose of radioactive megestrol given to 1 male produced a maximum blood level in 1 to 3 hours and gradually fell over a 24-hour period. Megestrol when given orally to women exhibited an average excretion of 86.2% (range 83.1 to 94.7%), fecal excretion accounted for 19.8% (range 7.7 to 30.3%) and urinary excretion for 66.4% (range 56.5 to 78.4%). The biological half-life for doses of 60 to 90 mg was 3.5 days. The half-life of a 160 mg dose was 37.6 hours. The excretion occurred as 3 glucuronide conjugates with hydroxylation occurring at either the 2-α, or the 6-methyl position or at both positions. Other metabolites occur but only account for 5 to 8% of the dose.

Respiratory excretion and fat storage may account for the fraction of an administered dose not found in urine or feces.

Indications: Tablets: For adjunctive or palliative treatment of recurrent, inoperable or metastatic carcinoma of the breast and endometrium and for palliative treatment of hormone responsive advanced (Stage D_2) carcinoma of the prostate. Megestrol should not be used in lieu of currently accepted procedures such as surgery and radiation. Objective or subjective responses or arrest of tumor growth may occur for one to several months while on therapy.

Megestrol is also indicated in male or female patients for the treatment of anorexia, cachexia or weight loss secondary to metastatic cancer.

Oral Suspension: For the treatment of anorexia, cachexia, or an unexplained significant weight loss in patients with a diagnosis of acquired immunodeficiency syndrome (AIDS).

Contraindications: In those people who are sensitive to megestrol or any ingredients in the dosage forms. Megestrol preparations should not be used as a diagnostic test for pregnancy.

Warnings: *Pregnancy:* **The use of progestational agents during the first 4 months of pregnancy is not recommended.**

Progestational agents have been used beginning within the first trimester of pregnancy in an attempt to prevent habitual abortion or treat threatened abortion. There is no adequate evidence that such use is effective and there is evidence of potential harm to the fetus when such drugs are given during the first 4 months of pregnancy. Furthermore, in the vast majority of women, the cause of abortion is a defective ovum, which progestational agents could not be expected to influence. In addition, the use of progestational agents, with their uterine-relaxant properties, in patients with fertilized defective ova may cause a delay in spontaneous abortion.

Several reports suggest an association between intrauterine exposure to progestational drugs in the first trimester of pregnancy and genital abnormalities in male and female fetuses. The risk of hypospadias, 5 to 8 per 1 000 male births in the general population, may be approximately doubled with exposure to these drugs. There are insufficient data to quantify the risk to exposed female fetuses, but insofar as some of these drugs induce mild virilization of the external genitalia of the female fetus, and because of the increased association of hypospadias in the male fetus, it is prudent to avoid the use of these drugs during the first trimester of pregnancy.

If the patient is exposed to megestrol during the first 4 months of pregnancy or if she becomes pregnant while taking this drug, she should be apprised of the potential risks to the fetus. Women of childbearing potential should be advised to avoid becoming pregnant.

Megestrol oral suspension is not intended for prophylactic use to avoid weight loss.

Precautions: General: Therapy with megestrol oral suspension for weight loss should only be instituted after treatable causes of weight loss are sought and addressed. These treatable

Megace (cont'd)

causes include malignancies, systemic infections, gastrointestinal disorders affecting absorption, endocrine disease and renal or psychiatric disease.

Although the glucocorticoid effects of megestrol oral suspension in HIV-infected individuals have not been evaluated, laboratory evidence of adrenal suppression has been observed rarely in patients shortly after discontinuation of megestrol oral suspension therapy. The significance of these findings has not been fully established.

Effects of megestrol oral suspension on HIV viral replication have not been determined.

Use megestrol tablets and oral suspension with caution in patients with a history of thrombophlebitis. Close, customary surveillance is indicated as in any patient being treated for recurrent or metastatic cancer. Patients receiving large doses of progestational agents such as megestrol continuously for prolonged periods should be observed closely for possible adrenal cortical suppression.

Children: Safety and effectiveness in children have not been established.

Lactation: Because many drugs are excreted in human breast milk and because of the potential for adverse reactions in nursing infants, nursing should be discontinued when receiving megestrol therapy.

HIV Infected Women: Although megestrol has been used extensively in women for the treatment of endometrial and breast cancers, its use in HIV infected women has been limited. All 10 women in clinical trials reported breakthrough bleeding.

Drug Interactions: Possible interactions of megestrol with concomitant medications have not been investigated.

Information for the Patient: Patients should be advised to use megestrol as directed and report any adverse reaction experiences to their physician. Women of childbearing potential should be advised to avoid becoming pregnant and should exercise adequate contraceptive control. If patients become pregnant while taking megestrol, they should promptly notify their physician.

Adverse Effects: Weight gain is a frequent side effect of megestrol when it is used in patients with cancer of the breast or endometrium. This gain has been associated with increased appetite. It is this effect which forms the basis for use of megestrol in patients with anorexia, cachexia or weight loss. Weight gain is associated with an increase in fat and body cell mass.

Untoward reactions that have been reported to occur in patients receiving megestrol include nausea, vomiting, edema, and breakthrough uterine bleeding and occur in approximately 1 to 2% of patients. Gynecomastia and loss of hearing have also been reported. Dyspnea, heart failure, hypertension, hot flashes, mood changes, cushingoid facies, tumor flare (with or without hypercalcemia), hyperglycemia, alopecia, carpal tunnel syndrome and rash have also occurred.

Thromboembolic phenomenon including thrombophlebitis and pulmonary embolism (in some cases fatal) have also been reported.

Laboratory evidence of pituitary-adrenal axis abnormalities has been observed in patients treated with megestrol. Although the significance of these laboratory findings has not been fully established, clinically apparent adrenal insufficiency has been reported to occur rarely in patients shortly after megestrol was discontinued. Patients should be observed for clinical evidence of adrenocortical insufficiency when megestrol is abruptly withdrawn.

In patients with advanced, non-endocrine-sensitive cancer who received doses of megestrol up to 480 mg/day in a clinical trial for anorexia and weight loss, dyspnea, nausea, edema, pain, lethargy and urinary diarrhea were observed commonly. Constipation and urinary frequency also have been reported in patients who received high doses of megestrol in other clinical trials.

In clinical trials involving patients with acquired immune deficiency syndrome receiving megestrol oral suspension, only impotence was reported in at least 5% of patients treated with megestrol.

Overdose: Symptoms and Treatment: Usual safety measures as with the overdose of any medication should be instituted. However, no serious unexpected side effects have resulted from studies involving megestrol administered in dosages as high as 1 600 mg/day for 6 months or more. Megestrol has not been tested for dialyzability; however, due to its low solubility, it is postulated that dialysis would not be an effective means of treating overdose.

Dosage: For the following indications, at least 2 months of continuous treatment is considered an adequate period for determining the efficacy of megestrol tablets and oral suspension.

Tablets: Palliative or Adjunctive Treatment of Breast Carcinoma: 160 mg or 125 mg/m² daily (40 mg 4 times a day or 160 mg daily).

Endometrial Carcinoma: 80 to 320 mg or 62.5 to 250 mg/m² daily in divided doses (40 to 80 mg 1 to 4 times daily or one to two 160 mg tablets daily).

Palliative Treatment of Hormone Responsive Advanced (Stage D_2) Carcinoma of the Prostate: 120 mg (93.8 mg/m²) as a single daily dose in combination with diethylstilbestrol tablet, 0.1 mg.

Anorexia, Cachexia, or Significant Weight Loss in Patients with Cancer: Usual adult dose: 400 to 800 mg as a single daily dose.

Oral Suspension: Anorexia, Cachexia, or Significant Weight Loss in Patients with a Diagnosis of Acquired Immunodeficiency Syndrome (AIDS): Usual adult dose: 400 to 800 mg as a single daily dose (10 to 20 mL/day). Ten mL of oral suspension contain 400 mg of megestrol.

Shake container well before use.

Supplied: Tablets: 40 mg: Each light blue, scored tablet contains: megestrol acetate 40 mg. Nonmedicinal ingredients: acacia, cornstarch, dibasic calcium phosphate, FD&C blue No. 1, lactose, magnesium stearate and colloidal silicon dioxide. Tartrazine-free. Bottles of 100.

160 mg: Each white oval, scored, tablet contains: megestrol acetate 160 mg. Nonmedicinal ingredients: lactose, magnesium stearate, microcrystalline cellulose, povidone, colloidal silicon dioxide and sodium starch glycolate. Tartrazine-free. Bottles of 30.

Oral Suspension: Each mL of lemon-lime flavored oral suspension contains: megestrol acetate 40 mg. Nonmedicinal ingredients: anhydrous citric acid, natural and artificial lemon-lime flavor, polyethylene glycol 1 450, polysorbate 80, purified water, sodium benzoate, sodium citrate dihydrate, sucrose and xanthan gum. Bottles of 120, 240 and 480 mL.

Store at room temperature (15 to 30°C). Protect from temperatures above 30°C.

(Shown in Product Recognition Section)

Reviewed 1998

MEGRAL® Ⓟ

Glaxo Wellcome

Ergotamine Tartrate—Cyclizine HCl—Caffeine Hydrate

Migraine Therapy

Indications: The treatment of vascular headache, migraine and related conditions where distention of cranial vessels appears to be the cause.

Contraindications: Sepsis, occlusive vascular disease (thromboangiitis obliterans, luetic arteritis, severe arteriosclerosis, coronary artery disease, thrombophlebitis, Raynaud's disease), thyrotoxicosis, anemia, renal or hepatic disease, hypertension, angina pectoris, peptic ulcer, infectious states, malnutrition, severe pruritus, pregnancy, lactation. Hypersensitivity to any of the components. Ergotamine should not be used prophylactically.

Precautions: Avoid prolonged administration or dosage in excess of that recommended, because of the danger of ergotism and gangrene. Use the minimum effective dosage of ergotamine necessary since individual sensitivity to the arterial effects of ergotamine varies considerably. Doses of ergotamine as small as 2 mg have caused signs of arterial insufficiency, but this is a very rare occurrence. Discontinue use if symptoms of arterial insufficiency develop.

Megral should be used with caution in patients with infective hepatitis because of an increased risk of precipitating peripheral ischemia.

Repeated doses of ergotamine have occasionally been associated with renal artery spasm and loss of renal function.

Occupational Hazards: Caution patients not to operate vehicles or hazardous machinery until their response to the drug has been determined.

Since the depressant effects of antihistamines are additive to those of other drugs affecting the CNS, caution patients against drinking alcoholic beverages or taking hypnotics, sedatives, psychotherapeutic agents or other drugs with CNS depressant effects during antihistaminic therapy.

In rare instances, patients, particularly those who have used the medication indiscriminately over long periods of time, may display withdrawal symptoms consisting primarily of headache upon discontinuation of the product.

Drug Interactions: The concomitant use of ergot alkaloids and beta-blocking agents increases the risks of peripheral vasoconstriction.

Vomiting and peripheral ischemia have been reported after concomitant use of ergot alkaloids and the antibiotics erythromycin and oleandomycin.

Adverse Effects: Unpleasant adverse effects which may occur include nausea and vomiting, weakness in the legs, muscle pains in the extremities, numbness and tingling of fingers and toes, precordial distress and pain, and transient tachycardia or bradycardia. Localized edema and itching may occur in the rare sensitive patient.

Many of these effects are the result of reduced arteriolar blood flow and are usually relieved by withdrawing therapy. Failure to recognize the early symptoms of arterial insufficiency has on rare occasions led to irreversible vascular change after therapeutic use of ergotamine.

Overdose: Symptoms: Nausea, tachycardia, hypotonia, peripheral ischemia, vomiting, salivation, weakness, tremor, fall of blood pressure, convulsions, peripheral vascular spasms, abdominal colic, respiratory depression, stupor and coma.

Treatment: Gastric lavage, fluids, diuretics, cathartics (sodium sulfates), amyl nitrite inhalation. Some success has been reported with sodium nitroprusside, starting at a rate of 25 μg/minute and increasing at 15 minute intervals to 100 μg/minute. Peritoneal dialysis and forced diuresis may help to eliminate ergotamine from the body.

Dosage: Initially, ¼ to 1 tablet with a little water at the first warning of an attack, then ½ to 1 tablet every half-hour; not more than 3 tablets should be taken for any single attack. No more than 6 tablets should be taken per week. Children, ¼ to ½ tablet.

Supplied: Each white, biconvex, press-coated tablet with code number WELLCOME A4A on same side as score mark, contains: ergotamine tartrate 2 mg, cyclizine HCl 50 mg, caffeine hydrate 100 mg. Nonmedicinal ingredients: amaranth, cornstarch, dextrose, docusate sodium, gelatin, lactose, liquid glucose, magnesium stearate and sodium metabisulfite. When cut in half, the tablet reveals a pink core. Bottles of 50. Store at 15 to 25°C and keep dry.

(Shown in Product Recognition Section)

MELLARIL® Ⓟ

Novartis Pharmaceuticals

Thioridazine HCl

Tranquilizer—Antipsychotic

Pharmacology: The basic pharmacological profile of thioridazine is similar to that of other phenothiazines, but there are significant differences in the clinical spectrum when compared with other agents of this class. The distinctive features of thioridazine are its low propensity to cause extrapyramidal side effects and its low antiemetic activity.

Thioridazine has a wide therapeutic margin. At low and medium doses it relieves tension and anxiety, and acts against multiple symptoms (e.g., agitation, depression, sleep disturbances) of nonpsychotic mental disorders. At higher doses, thioridazine is effective in controlling the symptoms of psychotic disorders.

Pharmacokinetics: Thioridazine is rapidly and completely absorbed from the gastrointestinal tract. Maximum plasma concentrations are reached 2 to 4 hours after ingestion. The average systemic bioavailability is approximately 60%. The relative distribution volume is about 10 L/kg and protein binding is high (more than 95%). Thioridazine is metabolized in the liver with some of the resulting metabolites (e.g., mesoridazine, sulforidazine) possessing pharmacodynamic properties similar to those of the parent compound. Excretion is mainly via the feces (50%), but also via the kidney (less than 4% as unchanged drug, about 30% as metabolites). Plasma elimination half-life is approximately 10 hours. Thioridazine crosses the placenta, and passes into breast milk.

Indications: General Medicine: anxiety, tension, mixed states of anxiety and depression, agitation, emotional disturbances accompanied by anxiety and tension, psychosomatic disorders, sleep disturbances.

Geriatrics: senile agitation and confusional states, anxiety and mixed states of anxiety and depression, insomnia.

Pediatrics: anxiety, tension, difficulties with concentration, sleep disturbances, behavioral disorders such as agitation, hyperactivity or aggressiveness.
Psychiatry: multiple symptoms of psychotic and nonpsychotic mental disorders, the latter including anxiety, tension, agitation, depressed mood, sleep disturbances; intractable pain.

Thioridazine is particularly useful: in chronic hospitalized psychotic patients; in psychotic outpatients; in geriatric patients suffering from severe agitation, anxiety or mixed states of anxiety and depression, often associated with various degrees of an organic brain syndrome; during alcohol withdrawal for the relief of symptoms such as anxiety, agitation, hostility, or hallucinations; as an adjuvant treatment in agitated depression; in children with severe behavioral disorders such as emotional instability, hyperexcitability, excessive motor activity, and aggressiveness.

Contraindications: In patients with a history of hypersensitivity to other phenothiazines. Also in patients with severe CNS depression or comatose states from any cause, severe cardiovascular disease, bone marrow depression, or a history of blood dyscrasia.

Thioridazine should not be given to children under 1 year of age.

Precautions: Caution is required in patients with narrow-angle glaucoma, prostatic hypertrophy, or cardiovascular disease (severe cardiovascular disease is a contraindication).

Hypotension (which is usually orthostatic) may occur, especially in females, the elderly, and in alcoholic patients. The administration of epinephrine should be avoided in the treatment of drug-induced hypotension in view of the fact that phenothiazines may induce a reverse-epinephrine effect.

As with other phenothiazines, benign repolarization changes such as prolongation of the Q-T interval, flattening of the T wave and the appearance of a U wave have been reported. These changes are usually confined to high doses and are more likely to occur when potassium blood levels are low. Like all phenothiazines, thioridazine may induce arrhythmias.

Sudden and unexplained death, apparently due to arrhythmias or cardiac arrest, has been reported. Previous brain damage or seizures may also be predisposing factors. High doses should be avoided in patients with a history of seizures.

Convulsive seizures have been reported but are infrequent. However, thioridazine has been shown to be helpful in the treatment of behavioral disorders in epileptic patients. In such cases, anticonvulsant medication should be continued and dosage adjustment considered (see Drug Interactions).

Leukopenia and agranulocytosis have been reported but are infrequent. A complete blood count is recommended before the initiation of therapy, especially if long-term treatment is anticipated. Blood counts should be carried out regularly during the first few months of therapy and should be done immediately whenever clinical signs suggestive of blood dyscrasia occur.

Pigmentary retinopathy has been observed after long-term treatment, mostly in patients receiving doses exceeding the recommended maximum of 800 mg/day. Patients receiving higher doses of phenothiazines for prolonged periods should have complete eye examinations at regular intervals.

In patients with liver disease, regular monitoring of liver function is necessary.

Occupational Hazards: Where patients are participating in activities requiring complete mental alertness (e.g., driving vehicles, operating machinery), administer the phenothiazine cautiously since impairment of reactions may occur with large doses and during early treatment.

Pregnancy and *Lactation:* Safe use of thioridazine in human pregnancy has not been established. Therefore, thioridazine should not be administered to pregnant women (particularly during the first trimester of pregnancy) unless the expected benefit to the patient clearly outweighs the potential risk to the fetus. Thioridazine may appear in human breast milk and therefore mothers receiving thioridazine should not breastfeed.

Children: Thioridazine should be kept out of the reach of children.

Drug Interactions: Phenothiazines may enhance the CNS-depressant effects of alcohol, antihistamines and other CNS depressants as well as atropine and phosphorus insecticides; the antimuscarinic effects of anticholinergic agents; and the inhibitory cardiac effects of quinidine.

Use of epinephrine in the treatment of phenothiazine-induced hypotension may induce a reverse-epinephrine effect.

Phenothiazines may reduce the antiparkinsonian effects of levodopa.

Phenothiazines may lower the seizure threshold in epileptic patients. Dosage adjustment of anticonvulsant medication may be necessary.

Owing to their adrenolytic action, phenothiazines may reduce the pressor effect of adrenergic vasoconstrictors.

Concurrent use with MAO inhibitors may prolong and intensify the sedative and antimuscarinic effects of phenothiazines.

Concomitant use of lithium may aggravate extrapyramidal symptoms and neurotoxicity caused by neuroleptic agents. Early signs of lithium toxicity may be masked by the antiemetic effect of phenothiazines.

Concurrent use with β-adrenergic blocking agents may result in an increased plasma concentration of phenothiazines.

Antacids and antidiarrheal drugs may inhibit the absorption of phenothiazines.

Adverse Effects: Not all of the following adverse reactions have been observed with every phenothiazine derivative, but they have been reported with one or more and should be considered when drugs of this class are administered.
CNS: drowsiness, sedation, nocturnal confusion, hyperactivity, lethargy, psychotic reactions, restlessness, disturbances of accommodation, vertigo and headache.

Extrapyramidal reactions (including Parkinsonism with motor retardation, rigidity, mask-like facies, tremor, salivation), dystonic reactions (including facial grimacing, tics, trismus, torticollis, opisthotonos, oculogyric crises), tremor, muscular rigidity, akinesia, akathisia.

As with all antipsychotic agents, tardive dyskinesia may appear in some patients on long-term therapy or may occur after drug therapy has been discontinued. This risk seems to be greater in elderly patients on high-dose therapy, especially females. The symptoms are persistent and in some patients appear to be irreversible.

All antipsychotic agents should be discontinued if tardive dyskinesia develops. Should it be necessary to reinstitute treatment, increase the dosage of the agent, or switch to a different antipsychotic agent, the syndrome may be masked. It has been reported that fine vermicular movements of the tongue may be an early sign of the syndrome and if the medication is stopped at that time, the syndrome may not develop.

Slowing of the EEG has been reported.

Behavioral Reactions: oversedation, impaired psychomotor function, paradoxical effects (such as agitation, excitement, insomnia, bizarre dreams, aggravation of psychotic symptoms), toxic confusional states.
Cardiovascular Effects: orthostatic hypotension, tachycardia, ECG changes (see Precautions).
Autonomic Nervous System: dry mouth, fainting, nasal stuffiness, photophobia, miosis, blurred vision.
Blood Dyscrasias: agranulocytosis, leukopenia, granulocytopenia, eosinophilia, thrombocytopenia, anemia, aplastic anemia, pancytopenia.
Gastrointestinal: anorexia, gastric irritation, nausea, vomiting, constipation, diarrhea, obstipation, paralytic ileus, pallor.
Hepatotoxicity: jaundice, biliary stasis.
Endocrine System: menstrual irregularities, altered libido, gynecomastia, galactorrhea, breast engorgement, weight change, edema, false positive pregnancy tests, disturbances of erection and of ejaculation (failure or priapism).
Urinary Disturbances: retention, incontinence.
Skin Reactions: itching, rash, hypertrophic papillae of the tongue, erythema, exfoliative dermatitis, contact dermatitis, photosensitivity.
Allergic Reactions: fever, laryngeal edema, angioneurotic edema, asthma.
Retinal Pigmentation: retinal pigmentation has been observed in psychiatric patients taking doses in excess of the maximum recommended daily dose of 800 mg over long periods of time (see Precautions).
Others: hyperpyrexia. Rare cases described as parotid swelling have been reported.
Neuroleptic Malignant Syndrome: As with other neuroleptic drugs, a symptom complex sometimes referred to as neuroleptic malignant syndrome (NMS) has been reported. Cardinal features of NMS are hyperpyrexia, muscle rigidity, altered mental status (including catatonic signs), and evidence of autonomic instability (irregular pulse or blood pressure). Additional signs may include elevated CPK, myoglobinuria (rhabdomyolysis), and acute renal failure. NMS is potentially fatal and requires symptomatic treatment and immediate discontinuation of neuroleptic treatment.

Overdose: Symptoms: 1) Drowsiness, confusion, disorientation, followed in more severe cases by coma and areflexia. 2) Dry mouth, nasal congestion, blurred vision. 3) Postural hypotension which may be early in onset, severe, and persistent. 4) Respiratory depression may be a late manifestation of severe phenothiazine intoxication. 5) Motor restlessness, hyperreflexia, and convulsions. 6) Hypothermia. 7) Cardiac abnormalities, including arrhythmia, tachycardia.

Note: Acute extrapyramidal symptoms, such as dystonia and oculogyric crisis, have not been reported with acute thioridazine overdosage, but are possible.

Treatment: There is no specific antidote for acute phenothiazine poisoning. Therefore, treatment is directed at minimizing the amount of drug absorbed, eliminating the absorbed drug from the body, and combating the toxic effects of the overdose. Elimination of the offending drug: 1) Emesis: If the patient is conscious, induce vomiting with syrup of ipecac (15 to 30 mL). Unlike other phenothiazines, thioridazine's antiemetic effect is very low. 2) Perform gastric lavage followed by the administration of activated charcoal if the pharyngeal and laryngeal reflexes are present, and if less than 4 hours have elapsed since ingestion. Do not attempt gastric lavage on an unconscious patient unless cuffed endotracheal intubation has been performed to prevent aspiration and pulmonary complications. 3) Catharsis: Following gastric lavage, a saline cathartic (sodium or magnesium sulfate 30 g in 250 mL of water) may be introduced and left in the stomach. 4) Encourage diuresis with the administration of i.v. fluids assisted, if necessary, by 100 to 150 mL 25% mannitol solution given slowly i.v. Mannitol should not be mixed with blood in a transfusion set, as red cell crenation and agglutination may occur. 5) Exchange transfusion: In children, exchange transfusion may be indicated to remove most of the circulating drug which is strongly bound to plasma proteins.

Note: Peritoneal dialysis and hemodialysis have been found ineffective in the treatment of acute phenothiazine poisoning.

Maintenance of Adequate Pulmonary Ventilation: Perform pharyngeal and tracheal suction diligently to remove excess mucous secretions. Judicious administration of oxygen is also indicated. However, oxygen without assisted respiration must be used with caution, as its use in hypoventilation hypoxia may result in further respiratory depression and hypercapnia. In more critical cases, endotracheal intubation or tracheotomy, with or without assisted respiration, may be necessary.
Correction of Hypotension: 1) Mild cases: The usual head down position and other supportive measures may be adequate. 2) Severe cases: Vasopressors (dopamine, norepinephrine) may be given i.v. with the usual precautions and serial blood pressure monitoring.
Caution: Epinephrine should not be administered in phenothiazine overdosage. Phenothiazine derivatives may reverse the usual blood pressure elevating action and cause a further lowering of pressure.
General Supportive Measures: 1) Good nursing care is of prime importance, particularly in the comatose patient, and should include regular observation and accurate recording of the vital signs and depth of coma, maintenance of a free airway, frequent turning and other routine measures usually adopted with unconscious patients. 2) Careful supervision and recording of fluid intake and output is essential. 3) Because hypothermia may occur in phenothiazine intoxication, maintain normal body temperature and avoid overheating.

Dosage: All dosages must be adjusted to meet the individual requirements of the patients.

It is recommended that the initial dose be at the lower end of the ranges mentioned below and be gradually increased until the fully effective level is reached. In underweight patients, in patients with liver or kidney disease, and in the elderly a particularly low initial dose followed by small increments are recommended. The daily amounts of thioridazine are usually given in 2 to 4 divided doses.

The maximum daily dose is 800 mg.

Psychiatry: Mild mental and emotional disturbances: 30 to 75 mg daily; moderate disturbances: 50 to 200 mg daily; severe disturbances (e.g., schizophrenic, manic or toxic psychoses and agitated depressions), ambulatory outpatients: 150 to 400 mg daily; severe disturbances, hospitalized patients: 200 to 800 mg daily.
General Medicine: Mild conditions: 10 mg 3 times daily; moderate disturbances: 50 to 200 mg daily.
Geriatrics: Most geriatric patients will require 25 mg 3 times daily.
Children: Thioridazine is not intended for children under 2 years of age and is contraindicated in children under 1 year of age. For children aged 2 to 12, the dosage of thioridazine ranges from 0.5 mg/kg to a maximum of 3.0 mg/kg per day. For children with moderate disorders, 10 mg 2 or 3 times a day is the usual starting dose. For hospitalized, severely disturbed, or psychotic children, 25 mg 2 or 3 times daily is the usual starting dose. Dosage may be increased gradually until optimum therapeutic effect is obtained or the maximum has been reached.

Supplied: Solution: Each mL of solution contains: thioridazine HCl USP 30 mg. Nonmedicinal ingredients: ethanol, flavor

Mellaril (cont'd)

cherry (artificial), methylparaben, propylparaben, purified water and sorbitol. Alcohol: 24.5 mg. Bottles of 115 mL with calibrated droppers.

Suspension: Each 5 mL of fruit-flavored suspension contains: thioridazine (base) 10 mg. Nonmedicinal ingredients: carboxymethylcellulose, castor oil, flavor apricot (artificial), microcrystalline cellulose, microcrystalline sodium, purified water and sorbitol. Bottles of 230 mL.

Protect from light.

(Shown in Product Recognition Section)

MENINGOCOCCAL POLYSACCHARIDE VACCINE, GROUPS A, C, Y AND W-135 COMBINED, MENOMUNE®

Connaught

Vaccine

Pharmacology: Meningitis can be caused by a variety of microorganisms including several sero-groups of meningococci. This vaccine will not stimulate protection against infections caused by organisms other than Groups A, C, Y and W-135 meningococci. It has been demonstrated that the presence of human serum bactericidal antibodies to meningococcal antigens is strongly correlated with immunity to meningococcal disease. Studies have shown that meningococcal polysaccharides induce the formation of such antibodies in man. Subsequently large scale field studies in South Africa showed group A polysaccharide vaccine to be 100% effective in preventing systemic disease caused by group A organisms occurring 2 weeks or longer after immunization. In addition large scale field studies in the U.S. Army showed group C polysaccharide vaccine to be at least 87% effective in preventing systemic disease caused by group C organisms. A study performed using 5 lots of Meningococcal Polysaccharide Vaccine, Groups A and C Combined in 4 343 adults showed at least a 4 fold increase of bactericidal antibodies to both group A and C in 95% of subjects. A study performed using 4 lots of Meningococcal Polysaccharide Vaccine, Groups A, C, Y and W-135 Combined in 150 adults showed at least a 4 fold increase in bactericidal antibodies to all groups in greater than 90% of the subjects.

A study was conducted in 73 children 2 to 12 years of age. Post-immunization sera were not obtained on 4 children. Therefore, the seroconversion rates were based on 69 paired samples. Seroconversion rates as measured by bactericidal antibody were: Group A–72%, Group C–58%, Group Y–90% and Group W-135–82%. Seroconversion rates as measured by a 2-fold rise in antibody titres based on Solid Phase Radioimmunoassay were: Group A–99%, Group C–99%, Group Y–97% and Group W-135–89%.

In recent years, the reported incidence of meningococcal disease in Canada has ranged between 200 and 300 cases (20% infants). Mortality has varied from 5 to 15% and about one quarter of the deaths are infants.

As with any vaccine, vaccination with Meningococcal Polysaccharide Vaccine, Groups A, C, Y and W-135 Combined may not protect 100% of susceptible individuals. Protective antibody levels may be achieved within 10 to 14 days after vaccination.

Indications: Primarily in persons 2 years of age and older at risk in epidemic or highly endemic areas. Vaccination should also be considered for household or institutional contacts of meningococcal disease as an adjunct to appropriate antibiotic chemoprophylaxis. Medical and laboratory personnel at risk of exposure to meningococcal disease should also be considered for vaccination. Vaccine may be of benefit for some travelers planning to visit countries recognized as having epidemic meningococcal disease. The quadrivalent vaccine also should be used to prevent meningococcal disease in populations clearly demonstrated to be at increased risk, such as military recruits.

Vaccine should be administered to adults and children 2 years of age or older with functional or anatomic asplenia. Whenever possible, vaccine should be given at least 10 to 14 days before splenectomy.

Contraindications: Immunization should be deferred during the course of any acute illness.

It is a contraindication to administer the vaccine to individuals known to be sensitive to thimerosal or any other component of the vaccine.

Warnings: If the vaccine is used in persons receiving immunosuppressive therapy, the expected immune response may not be obtained.

Precautions: As with any injection of biological materials, epinephrine HCl (1:1 000) should be immediately available as a precautionary measure should an acute anaphylactoid reaction occur.

Prior to an injection of any vaccine, all known precautions should be taken to prevent side reactions. This includes a review of the patient's history with respect to possible sensitivity to the vaccine or similar vaccines.

Special care should be taken to avoid injecting the vaccine intradermally or i.v. since clinical studies have not been done to establish safety and efficacy of the vaccine using these routes of administration.

A separate sterile syringe and needle should be used for each individual patient to prevent transmission of hepatitis B virus or other infectious agents from person to person.

Pregnancy: Safety in pregnant women has not been established. It is prudent not to use them unless there is a substantial risk of infection.

Animal reproduction studies have not been conducted with Meningococcal Polysaccharide Vaccine Groups A, C, Y and W-135. It is also not known whether this product can cause fetal harm when administered to a pregnant woman or can affect reproduction capacity. This product should not be given to a pregnant woman unless in the opinion of the attending physician vaccination is clearly required.

Children: There are no data on safety and efficacy of this vaccine when administered to children under 2 years of age.

Adverse Effects: The incidence and kinds of reactions reported in adults and children in clinical studies are presented in Table I. As with the administration of any biological, one should expect possible hypersensitivity reactions.

Table I—Meningococcal Polysaccharide Vaccine Groups A, C, Y and W-135 Combined, Menomune

Systemic or Local Reactions Encountered with Vaccine			
	Systemic Reactions (%)		
	None	**Mild**	**Moderate**
Headache	94.7	4.1	1.2
Malaise	97.4	2.6	0
Chills	98.3	1.7	0
Oral Temperature°C	36.7–37.2° (96.5%)	37.8–38.3° (3.1%)	38.3° (0.4%)
	Local Reactions (%)		
	None	**Mild**	**Moderate**
Pain	57.4	17.5	25.1
Tenderness	46.7	24.2	29.1
Diameter of Local Reaction	0	<2 cm	≥2 cm
Erythema	67.5	31.7	0.8
Induration	86.9	8.3	4.8

Epinephrine HCl Solution (1:1 000) always must be immediately available to combat unexpected anaphylactic or other allergic reactions.

Health-care providers should report any occurrences temporally related to the administration of the product in accordance with provincial and federal statutory requirements.

Dosage: Inspect visually for extraneous particulate matter and/or discoloration prior to administration. Reconstitute the vaccine using only the diluent supplied for this purpose. Draw the volume of diluent shown on the diluent label into a suitable size syringe and inject into the vial containing the vaccine. Shake vial until the vaccine is dissolved. Administer the vaccine s.c.

The immunizing dose is a single injection of 0.5 mL s.c.

The vaccine can be given at the same time as other immunizations if needed.

There are no data on the incidence and degree of reactions following booster doses of quadrivalent meningococcal vaccine.

Each person who is immunized should be given a permanent personal immunization record. In addition, it is essential that the health care provider also maintain a permanent record of the immunization history of each individual. This office record should contain the name of the vaccine, date given, dose, manufacturer and lot number.

Jet Injector Use: Inspect visually for extraneous particulate matter and/or discoloration prior to administration.

Using a syringe and needle of suitable size and aseptic precautions, transfer the volume of diluent shown on the diluent label into the vial containing the vaccine. Shake vial until the vaccine is dissolved.

Administer **only** with automatic hypodermic jet apparatus. **50 dose vial not to be utilized in needle and syringe method of immunization.** If absolutely necessary, syringes and needles may be used with such containers with caution; however, the full 50 doses may not be obtained. Discard partially used vial of vaccine.

Immunization consists of a single injection of 0.5 mL given s.c. Special care should be taken by using the deltoid area to avoid injecting the vaccine intradermally or i.v. since clinical studies have not been done to establish safety and efficacy of the vaccine using these routes of administration.

Any unused reconstituted vaccine remaining in a vial which has been administered with a Jet Injector Apparatus should be discarded and **not** retained for later use.

Note: During use it is possible that the nozzle of the Jet Injector Apparatus may become contaminated with blood or serum. If this occurs, the nozzle should be cleansed and sterilized before continued use to prevent the possibility of transmission of hepatitis B virus and other infectious agents.

Supplied: The vaccine is a freeze-dried preparation of the group-specific polysaccharide antigens from Neisseria meningitidis, Group A, Group C, Group Y and Group W-135 for s.c. injection. The diluent is sterile pyrogen-free distilled water to which thimerosal (mercury derivative) 1:10 000 is added as a preservative. After reconstitution with diluent as indicated on the label, each 0.5 mL dose contains 50 µg of "isolated product "from each Group A, C, Y and W-135 in isotonic sodium chloride solution preserved with thimerosal (mercury derivative). Each dose of vaccine also contains 2.5 mg to 5 mg of lactose added as a stabilizer. The vaccine when reconstituted is a clear colorless liquid.

1 Dose Vial of vaccine, with vial of 0.6 mL diluent.

10 Dose Vial of vaccine, with vial of 6 mL diluent, for administration with needle and syringe (may be used with jet injector although the desired number of doses may not be obtained).

50 Dose Vial of vaccine, with vial of 27.5 mL diluent, for jet injector use only.

Store freeze-dried vaccine and reconstituted vaccine, when not in use, between 2 to 8°C. Discard remainder of 10 dose vials of vaccine within 5 days after reconstitution. The single dose vial should be used within 24 hours of reconstitution. Any unused reconstituted vaccine remaining in a 50 dose vial should be discarded and **not** retained for later use.

Reviewed 1997

MEPERIDINE Ⓝ

General Monograph, CPhA

see OPIOID ANALGESICS

MEPERIDINE Ⓝ

Abbott

Meperidine Hydrochloride

Opioid Analgesic

Supplied: Ampuls: Each mL contains: meperidine HCl 10 mg, 25 mg, 50 mg, 75 mg or 100 mg. Nonmedicinal ingredients: hydrochloric acid and water for injection. Bisulfites-free. Ampuls of 1 mL. Boxes of 100.

Cartridge: Each mL contains: meperidine HCl 10 mg. Nonmedicinal ingredients: acid acetic glacial, sodium acetate anhydrous and water for injection. Bisulfites-free. Cartridge (single dose vial) of 30 mL for Patient-Controlled-Analgesia infusor (PCA).

MEPRON® Ⓟ

Glaxo Wellcome

Atovaquone

Antiprotozoal Agent

Pharmacology: Atovaquone is a hydroxy-1,4-naphthoquinone, an analog of ubiquinone, with antipneumocystis activity. The mechanism of action against P. carinii has not been fully elucidated.

Pharmacokinetics: The pharmacokinetics of atovaquone has been studied in healthy volunteers, HIV-infected adults with varying stages and manifestations of HIV infection and in immunocompromised children. The half-life of atovaquone is long (2 to 3 days) due to presumed enterohepatic cycling and eventual fecal elimination. There is no evidence that the drug is metabolized in man.

Atovaquone is extensively bound to plasma proteins (>99.9%).

The bioavailability of atovaquone is highly dependent on formulation and diet. The atovaquone oral suspension formulation, which has now replaced the atovaquone tablets, has atovaquone particles significantly smaller than those in the tablet formulation, provides an approximately two-fold increase in atovaquone bioavailability in the fasting or fed state compared to the tablet formulation studied under the same conditions. The bioavailability of the oral suspension can be increased approximately two- to three-fold when administered with meals. Fat has been shown to enhance absorption significantly.

During a multiple-dose study of 4 HIV-seropositive asymptomatic volunteers, the relative oral bioavailability of the tablet formulation decreased at doses above 750 mg once daily with food.

In another multiple-dose escalation study conducted in AIDS patients, lack of dose proportionality was also demonstrated with the tablet formulation; however there was a modest increase in concentrations.

Indications: For the acute oral treatment of mild to moderate P. carinii pneumonia (PCP) in patients who are intolerant to trimethoprim-sulfamethoxazole (TMP-SMX).

The efficacy of atovaquone in patients who are failing therapy with TMP-SMX, has not been systematically studied (see Warnings).

The indication is based on the results of a comparative pharmacokinetic studies of the oral suspension and tablet formulations and clinical efficacy studies of the tablet formulation which established a relationship between atovaquone plasma concentration and successful treatment. The results of a randomized double-blind trial comparing atovaquone tablets to TMP-SMX in AIDS patients with mild to moderate PCP (defined as an alveolar-arterial oxygen diffusion gradient [(A-a)DO_2] ≤45 mmHg and PaO_2 ≥60 mmHg on room air); and a randomized trial comparing atovaquone tablets and i.v. pentamidine isethionate in patients with mild to moderate PCP intolerant to trimethoprim or sulfa-antimicrobials. These studies are summarized below:

TMP-SMX Comparative Study: This double-blind trial initiated in 1990 was designed to compare the safety and efficacy of atovaquone tablets to that of TMP-SMX for the treatment of AIDS patients with histologically confirmed PCP. Only patients with mild to moderate PCP were eligible for enrollment.

A total of 408 patients were enrolled into the trial at 37 study centres. Eighty-six patients without histologic confirmation of PCP were excluded from the efficacy analyses. Of the 322 patients with histologically confirmed PCP, 160 were randomized to receive atovaquone tablets and 162 to TMP-SMX.

Study participants randomized to atovaquone treatment were to receive 750 mg atovaquone (three 250 mg tablets) 3 times daily for 21 days and those randomized to trimethoprim-sulfamethoxazole were to receive 320 mg TMP plus 1 600 mg SMX 3 times daily for 21 days.

All patients were evaluated for their response to treatment. Each patient was classified as a therapy success or failure. Therapy success was defined as improvement in clinical and respiratory measures persisting at least 4 weeks after cessation of therapy. Therapy failures included lack of response, treatment discontinuation due to an adverse experience, and unevaluable.

There was a significant difference (p=0.03) in mortality rates between the treatment groups. Among the 322 patients with confirmed PCP, 13 of 160 patients treated with atovaquone tablets and 4 of 162 patients receiving TMP-SMX died during the 21-day treatment course or an 8-week follow-up period. In the intent-to-treat analysis for all 408 randomized patients there were 16 deaths in the atovaquone tablets arm and 7 in the TMP-SMX arm (p=0.051).

This difference in mortality between the 2 treatment groups appeared to be partially due to a disproportionate number of fatal bacterial infections in the atovaquone tablets group. Four of the 13 atovaquone tablets-treated patients died of PCP, tablets while 5 of the 13 died of a combination of bacterial infections and PCP. A correlation between plasma concentrations and death was demonstrated; in general, patients with lower atovaquone plasma concentrations were more likely to die than patients with higher atovaquone plasma concentrations.

Sixty-two percent (62%) of patients on atovaquone tablets and 64% of patients on TMP-SMX were classified as protocol-defined therapy successes. The therapeutic outcomes are presented in Table I.

Table I—Mepron

Outcome of Treatment for PCP-Positive Patients Enrolled in the TMP-SMX Comparative Study

Outcome of Therapy*	Number of Patients (% of Total): Mepron Tablets (n=160)	Number of Patients (% of Total): TMP-SMX (n=162)	P Value
Therapy Success	99 (62%)	103 (64%)	0.75
Therapy Failure			
Lack of Response	28 (17%)	10 (6%)	<0.01
Adverse Experience	11 (7%)	33 (20%)	<0.01
Unevaluable	22 (14%)	16 (10%)	0.28
Required Alternative PCP Therapy During Study	55 (34%)	55 (34%)	0.95

*As defined by the protocol and described in study description above.

The failure rate due to lack of response was significantly larger for patients receiving atovaquone tablets, while the failure rate due to adverse experiences was larger for patients receiving TMP-SMX.

There were no significant differences in the effect of either treatment on additional indicators of response (i.e., arterial blood gas measurements, vital signs, serum LDH levels, clinical symptoms, and chest radiographs).

Pentamidine Comparative Study: This open, randomized trial initiated in 1991, was designed to compare the safety and efficacy of atovaquone tablets to that of pentamidine for the treatment of histologically confirmed mild or moderate PCP among AIDS patients. Approximately 80% of the patients had a history of, or were currently experiencing, intolerance to trimethoprim or sulfa-antimicrobials.

Patients randomized to atovaquone were to receive 750 mg atovaquone (three 250 mg tablets) 3 times daily for 21 days, and those randomized to pentamidine isethionate were to receive a 3 to 4 mg/kg single i.v. infusion daily for 21 days.

It was anticipated that patients intolerant of TMP-SMX would present in either of 2 ways. They would either have a known intolerance and would represent a primary therapy group, or their intolerance would first become evident during treatment for the current episode of PCP and would represent a study group for salvage therapy.

A total of 135 PCP-positive patients were enrolled: 110 were in the primary therapy group and 25 were in the salvage therapy group.

There was no difference in mortality rates between the treatment groups. Among the 135 patients with confirmed PCP, 10 of 70 patients treated with atovaquone tablets and 9 of 65 patients treated with pentamidine died during the 21-day treatment course or an 8-week follow-up period. Three of the 10 patients treated with atovaquone tablets died of PCP while another 3 patients died with a combination of bacterial infections and PCP. The contribution of PCP in these latter deaths is unclear. One patient died of sepsis, 1 died of lymphoma, 1 died of complications of AIDS and 1 died of refractory pneumothorax. Two of 9 patients treated with pentamidine died of PCP while another 3 patients died with a combination of bacterial infections and PCP. The contribution of PCP in these latter deaths is unclear. One each died of a cerebral mycotic aneurysm and disseminated C. immitis and 2 patients died of complications of AIDS. In the intent-to-treat analysis for all randomized patients, there were 11 deaths in the atovaquone tablets arm and 12 deaths in the pentamidine arm. For those patients for whom day 4 atovaquone plasma concentration are available, 3 of 5 (60%) patients with concentrations <5 µg/mL died during participation in the study. However, only 2 of 21 (9%) patients with day 4 plasma concentrations >5 µg/mL died. The therapeutic outcomes are presented in Table II.

Data on Chronic Use: Atovaquone oral suspension has not been systematically evaluated as a chronic suppressive agent to prevent the development of PCP in patients at high risk for P. carinii disease. In a pilot-dosing study of chronic dosing of atovaquone tablets in AIDS patients, 5 of 31 patients had PCP breakthroughs: one patient at a dose of 750 mg once daily (after 20 days), three patients at 750 mg twice daily (after 14, 70, and 97 days), and one patient at 1500 mg twice daily (after 74 days). The dose used in the acute treatment studies (750 mg 3 times daily) was not studied and, therefore, there are no data on the rate of breakthrough at this dose. Based on these limited observations, no recommendation can be made as to the use of atovaquone oral suspension for prophylaxis.

Contraindications: Patients who develop, or have history of, potentially life-threatening allergic reactions to any of the components of the formulation.

Warnings: Clinical experience with atovaquone has been limited to patients with mild to moderate PCP [(A-a)DO_2 ≤45 mmHg]. Treatment of more severe episodes of PCP has not been systematically studied with this agent. Also, the efficacy of atovaquone tablets in patients who are failing therapy with TMP-SMX has not been systematically studied and, therefore, cannot be recommended. Atovaquone has not been evaluated as an agent for PCP prophylaxis.

Precautions: General: Absorption of orally administered atovaquone is limited but can be significantly increased when the drug is taken with food. Atovaquone plasma concentrations have been shown to correlate with the likelihood of successful treatment and survival. Therefore, parenteral therapy with other agents should be considered for patients who have difficulty taking atovaquone with food (see Pharmacology). Gastrointestinal disorders may limit absorption of orally administered drugs. Patients with these disorders also may not achieve plasma concentrations of atovaquone associated with response to therapy in controlled trials.

Based upon the spectrum of in vitro antimicrobial activity, atovaquone is not effective therapy for concurrent pulmonary conditions such as bacterial, viral or fungal pneumonia or mycobacterial diseases. Clinical deterioration in patients may be due to other pathogens, as well as progressive PCP. All patients with acute PCP should be carefully evaluated for all other possible causes of pulmonary disease and treated with additional agents as appropriate.

Geriatrics: Atovaquone has not been systematically evaluated in patients greater than 65 years of age. Caution should be exercised when treating elderly patients reflecting the greater frequency of decreased hepatic, renal and cardiac function in this population.

Infants and Young Children: There are no efficacy studies in children. Clinical experience with atovaquone in the pediatric population is limited to a pharmacokinetic and safety study. No children under 4 months of age participated in the Phase I trial.

Pregnancy: There are no adequate and well-controlled studies in pregnant women. Atovaquone should be used during pregnancy only if the potential benefit justifies the potential risk to the fetus.

Lactation: It is not known whether atovaquone is excreted in human milk. Because many drugs are excreted in human milk, caution should be exercised when administering atovaquone to a nursing mother. In a rat study, atovaquone concentrations in the milk were 30% of the concurrent atovaquone concentrations in the maternal plasma.

Table II—Mepron

Outcome of Treatment for PCP-Positive Patients Enrolled in the Pentamidine Comparative Study

Outcome of Therapy	Primary Treatment: Mepron Tablets (n=56)	Primary Treatment: Pentamidine (n=53)	P Value	Salvage Treatment: Mepron (n=14)	Salvage Treatment: Pentamidine (n=11)	P Value
Therapy Success	32 (57%)	21 (40%)	0.09	13 (93%)	7 (64%)	0.14
Therapy Failure						
Lack of Response	16 (29%)	9 (17%)	0.18	0	0	
Adverse Experience	2 (3.6%)	19 (36%)	<0.01	0	3 (27%)	0.07
Unevaluable	6 (11%)	4 (8%)	0.75	1 (7%)	1 (9%)	1.00
Required Alternative PCP Therapy During Study	19 (34%)	29 (55%)	0.04	0	4 (36%)	0.03

Mepron (cont'd)

Drug Interactions: Atovaquone is highly bound to plasma protein (>99.9%). Therefore, caution should be used when administering atovaquone concurrently with other highly plasma protein bound drugs with narrow therapeutic indices, as competition for binding sites may occur. The extent of plasma protein binding of atovaquone in human plasma is not affected by the presence of therapeutic concentrations of phenytoin (15 μg/mL), nor is the binding of this drug affected by the presence of atovaquone.

Laboratory Tests: It is not known if atovaquone interferes with clinical laboratory test or assay results.

Information for the Patient: The importance of taking the prescribed dose of atovaquone oral suspension should be stressed. Patients should be instructed to take their daily doses with meals as the presence of food will significantly improve the absorption of the drug.

The oral suspension should be shaken gently before use.

Adverse Effects: Because many patients who participated in clinical trials with atovaquone tablets had complications of advanced HIV disease, it was often difficult to distinguish adverse events caused by the drug from those caused by underlying medical conditions. There were no life-threatening or fatal adverse experiences caused by atovaquone tablets.

Table III summarizes all the clinical adverse experiences reported by ≥5% of the study population during the TMP-SMX comparative study of atovaquone tablets (n=408), regardless of attribution.

Table III—Mepron

Treatment-Emergent Adverse Experiences in the TMP-SMX Comparative PCP Treatment Study

Treatment-Emergent Adverse Experience	Number of Patients with Treatment-Emergent Adverse Experience (% of Total) Mepron Tablets (n=203)		TMP-SMX (n=205)	
Body as a whole				
Asthenia	17	(8%)	16	(8%)
Fever	28	(14%)	52	(25%)*
Headache	33	(16%)	44	(22%)
Gastrointestinal				
Diarrhea	39	(19%)*	15	(7%)
Constipation	7	(3%)	35	(17%)*
Abdominal Pain	9	(4%)	15	(7%)
Vomiting	29	(14%)	72	(35%)*
Nausea	43	(21%)	90	(44%)*
Monilia, Oral	11	(5%)	21	(10%)
Nervous				
Dizziness	7	(3%)	17	(8%)*
Insomnia	20	(10%)	18	(9%)
Skin				
Rash (including maculopapular)	47	(23%)	69	(34%)*
Pruritus	11	(5%)	18	(9%)
No. Patients Discontinuing Therapy due to an Adverse Experience	19	(9%)	50	(24%)*
No. Patients Reporting at least one Adverse Experience	127	(63%)	134	(65%)

*p=<0.05.

Although an equal percentage of patients receiving atovaquone tablets and TMP-SMX reported at least 1 adverse experience, more patients receiving TMP-SMX required discontinuation of therapy due to an adverse event. Nine percent of patients receiving atovaquone tablets were prematurely discontinued from therapy due to an adverse event versus 24% of patients receiving TMP-SMX. Eight patients receiving atovaquone tablets had therapy discontinued due to development of rash. The majority of cases of rash among patients receiving atovaquone tablets were mild and did not require the discontinuation of dosing. The only other clinical adverse experience which led to premature discontinuation of atovaquone tablets dosing by more than 1 patient was the development of vomiting (n=2). The most common adverse experience requiring discontinuation of dosing in the TMP-SMX group was rash (n=16).

Laboratory test abnormalities reported for ≥5% of the study population during the treatment period are summarized in Table IV. Five patients treated with atovaquone tablets and 15 patients treated with TMP-SMX had therapy prematurely discontinued due to elevations in ALT/AST. In general, patients treated with atovaquone tablets developed fewer abnormalities in measures of hepatocellular function (ALT, AST, alkaline phosphatase) or amylase values than patients treated with TMP/SMX.

Table IV—Mepron

Treatment-Emergent Laboratory Abnormalities

Laboratory Test Abnormality	Number of Patients Developing a Laboratory Test Abnormality % of Total Patients Mepron Tablets	TMP-SMX
Anemia (Hgb <8.0 g/dL)	6%	7%
Neutropenia (ANC <750 c/mm³)	3%	9%
Elevated ALT (>5×ULN)	6%	16%
Elevated AST (>5×ULN)	4%	14%
Elevated Alkaline Phosphate (>2.5×ULN)	8%	6%
Elevated Amylase (>1.5×ULN)	7%	12%
Hyponatremia (<0.96×LLN)	7%	26%

Legend: ULN=upper limit of normal range.
LLN=lower limit of normal range.
ANC=absolute neutrophil count.

Table V summarizes the clinical adverse experiences reported by ≥5% of the study population during the comparative trial of atovaquone tablets and i.v. pentamidine (n=144), regardless of attribution. A slightly lower percentage of patients who received atovaquone tablets reported occurrence of adverse events than did those who received pentamidine (63% vs 72%).

Table V—Mepron

Treatment-Emergent Adverse Experiences in the Pentamidine Comparative PCP Treatment Study

Treatment-Emergent Adverse Experience	Number of Patients with Treatment-Emergent Adverse Experience (% of Total) Mepron Tablets (n=73)		Pentamidine (n=71)	
Body as a whole				
Asthenia	6	(8%)	10	(14%)
Fever	29	(40%)	18	(25%)
Headache	13	(18%)	20	(28%)
Pain	7	(10%)	7	(10%)
Cardiovascular				
Hypotension	1	(1%)	7	(10%)[a]
Gastrointestinal				
Diarrhea	15	(21%)	22	(31%)
Dyspepsia	4	(5%)	7	(10%)
Abdominal Pain	7	(10%)	8	(11%)
Vomiting	10	(14%)	12	(17%)
Nausea	16	(22%)	26	(37%)
Monilia, Oral	7	(10%)	2	(3%)
Anorexia	5	(7%)	7	(10%)
Metabolic				
Hypoglycemia	1	(1%)	11	(15%)[a]
Nervous				
Anxiety	5	(7%)	7	(10%)
Dizziness	6	(8%)	10	(14%)
Insomnia	14	(19%)	10	(14%)
Respiratory				
Sinusitis	5	(7%)	4	(6%)
Rhinitis	4	(5%)	5	(7%)
Cough	10	(14%)[a]	1	(1%)
Skin				
Rash	16	(22%)	9	(13%)
Sweat	7	(10%)	2	(3%)
Special Senses				
Taste Perversion	2	(3%)	9	(13%)[a]
No. Patients Discontinuing Therapy due to an Adverse Experience	5	(7%)	29	(41%)[b]
No. Patients Reporting at least one Adverse Experience	46	(63%)	51	(72%)

[a]p=<0.05.
[b]p=<0.001.

However, only 7% of patients discontinued treatment with atovaquone tablets due to adverse events, while 41% of patients who received pentamidine discontinued treatment for this reason (p=<0.001). Of the 5 patients who discontinued therapy with atovaquone, 3 reported rash (4%). Rash was not severe in any patient. No other reason for discontinuation of atovaquone tablets was cited more than once. The most frequently cited reasons for discontinuation of pentamidine therapy were hypoglycemia [8 patients (11%)] and vomiting [6 patients (9%)].

Laboratory test abnormalities reported in ≥5% of patients in the pentamidine comparative study are presented in Table VI. Laboratory abnormality was reported as the reason for discontinuation of treatment in 2 of 73 patients who received atovaquone tablets. One patient (1%) had elevated creatinine and BUN levels and one patient (1%) had elevated amylase levels. Laboratory abnormalities were the sole or contributing factor in 14 patients who prematurely discontinued pentamidine therapy. In the 71 patients who received pentamidine, laboratory parameters most frequently reported as reasons for discontinuation were hypoglycemia (11%), elevated creatinine levels (6%), and leukopenia (4%).

Table VI—Mepron

Treatment-Emergent Laboratory Test Abnormalities in the Pentamidine Comparative PCP Treatment Study

Laboratory Test Abnormalities	Patients Developing a Laboratory Test Abnormality (% of Total) Mepron Tablets	Pentamidine
Anemia (Hgb <8.0 g/dL)	4%	9%
Neutropenia (ANC <750 c/mm³)	5%	9%
Hyponatremia (<0.96×LLN)	10%	10%
Hyperkalemia (>1.18×ULN)	0%	5%
Alkaline Phosphatase (>2.5×ULN)	5%	2%
Hyperglycemia (>1.8×ULN)	9%	13%
Elevated AST (>5×ULN)	0%	5%
Elevated Amylase (>1.5×ULN)	8%	4%
Elevated Creatinine (>1.5×ULN)	0%	7%

Legend: ULN=upper limit of normal range.
LLN=lower limit of normal range.
ANC: absolute neutrophil count.

Overdose: Symptoms and Treatment: There have been no reports of overdosage from the tablet or oral suspension administration of atovaquone.

Dosage: Adults: The recommended oral dose is 750 mg (5 mL) administered with food twice a day (total daily dose 1 500 mg) for 21 days.

Failure to administer with food may result in lower plasma concentrations and may limit response to therapy.

Supplied: Each 5 mL of bright yellow suspension, with a sweet, fruity flavor, contains: atovaquone 750 mg. Nonmedicinal ingredients: benzyl alcohol, flavor (tutti frutti), poloxamer 188, purified water, saccharin sodium and xanthan gum. Bottles of 210 mL with child resistant cap. Store at 15 to 25°C. Keep in tight, light resistant containers. **Do not freeze.**

(Shown in Product Recognition Section)

Reviewed 1997

MERCODOL® with DECAPRYN® Ⓝ

Hoechst Marion Roussel

Hydrocodone Bitartrate—Etafedrine HCl Sodium Citrate—Doxylamine Succinate

Antihistaminic—Antitussive—Decongestant

Indications: The treatment of cough associated with inflamed mucosa, which does not respond to products of lesser potency.

Contraindications: Patients receiving MAO inhibitors, sensitivity to any of the components.

Precautions: Before prescribing medication to suppress or modify cough, it is important to ascertain that the underlying cause of the cough is identified, that modification of the cough does not increase the risk of clinical or physiologic complications, and that appropriate therapy for the primary disease is provided.

Use with caution in patients with hypertension, diabetes mellitus, hyperthyroidism, cardiac disorders, glaucoma, or peripheral vascular disorders.

In young children the respiratory centre is especially susceptible to the depressant action of narcotic cough suppressants. Benefit to risk ratio should be carefully considered, especially in children with respiratory embarrassment, e.g., croup. Estimation of dosage relative to the child's age and weight is of great importance.

Pregnancy: Since hydrocodone crosses the placental barrier, its use in pregnancy is not recommended.

As hydrocodone may inhibit peristalsis, patients with chronic constipation should be given this product only after weighing the potential therapeutic benefit against the hazards involved.

Mercodol with Decapryn contains hydrocodone—may be habit-forming.

Occupational Hazards: Patients should be cautioned not to operate vehicles or hazardous machinery until their response to the drug has been determined.

Since the depressant effects of antihistamines are additive to those of other drugs affecting the CNS, patients should be cautioned against drinking alcoholic beverages or taking hypnotics, sedatives, psychotherapeutic agents or other drugs with CNS depressant effects during antihistaminic therapy.

Adverse Effects: Drowsiness, dizziness, nausea, nervousness, palpitation, or increased blood pressure seldom occur.

Overdose: Symptoms: Slow pulse, flushed face, feeling of lightness in head, temporary anuria, nausea and vomiting, gastric pain, convulsive motions, tremor, respiratory paralysis, extreme general vasodilation.

Treatment: Naloxone HCl.

Dosage: Adults: 5 mL every 3 to 5 hours but not more than 30 mL in any 24-hour period. Children 6 to 12 years of age, 2.5 to 5 mL—with a maximum of 15 mL in any 24-hour period. Children 1 to 6 years: 1.25 to 2.5 mL with a maximum of 3 doses in any 24-hour period.

Supplied: Each mL contains: hydrocodone bitartrate 0.33 mg, etafedrine HCl 3.33 mg, sodium citrate 40 mg, doxylamine succinate 1.2 mg. Nonmedicinal ingredients: alcohol, artificial blackcurrant flavor, benzoic acid, butylparaben, FD&C Blue No. 1, FD&C Red No. 2, FD&C Yellow No. 6, glycerin, menthol, natural tolu flavor, purified water, sucrose and thyme oil. Energy: 63.6 kJ (15.2 kcal)/5 mL. Bottles of 100 mL and 2 L.

MERITENE®
Novartis Nutrition
Therapeutic Nutrient

Indications: As a supplement or as a tube feeding, recommended whenever protein needs are increased and energy requirements are moderate. Meritene Powder provides 18 g protein and 275 kcal (1 150 kJ)/serving.

Precautions: Not for parenteral use.

Dosage: Oral: As a supplement with or between meals: 1 to 3 servings daily, 1 150 to 3 450 kJ (275 to 825 kcal), 18 g protein to 54 g protein. When used as the sole daily feeding: should be administered to meet individual nutrition requirements; 1 040 mL or 4 600 kJ (4 servings of 32.4 g Meritene powder in 240 mL whole milk or 1 100 kcal) provides at least 100% of the Canadian RNI (adult males, 25 to 49) for protein and essential vitamins and minerals.

Tube Feeding: Follow a physician's or dietitian's directions. When initiating feeding, the flow rate, volume and dilution are dependent on patient tolerance. Care should be taken to avoid contamination of this product during preparation and administration. Additional fluid requirements should be met by giving water orally with or after feedings, or when flushing the feeding tube.

Supplied: Each 32.4 g contains: skim milk powder, corn syrup solids, partially hydrogenated soybean oil, magnesium sulfate, ascorbic acid, natural and artificial vanilla flavor, soy lecithin, ferrous sulfate, zinc sulfate, alpha tocopheryl acetate, niacinamide, copper gluconate, manganese sulfate, D-calcium pantothenate, vitamin A palmitate, pyridoxine hydrochloride, thiamine hydrochloride, folic acid, BHA (to preserve freshness), biotin, vitamin K_1, choline bitartrate, tricalcium phosphate, potassium iodide, riboflavin, cyanocobalamin. See Table I.

Energy Distribution: protein 26%, fat 29%, carbohydrate 45%; 440 kJ (110 kcal)/100 mL.

Table I—Meritene

Analysis	100 mL (mixed with whole milk)	
Energy	440 (110)	kJ (kcal)
Protein	6.9	g
Carbohydrate	11	g
Fat	3.6	g
Linoleic Acid	0.1	g
Sodium	96	mg
Potassium	300	mg
Vitamin A	440	IU
Vitamin C	8.3	mg
Thiamine	0.21	mg
Riboflavin	0.34	mg
Niacin	1.9	mg
Calcium	230	mg
Iron	1.7	mg
Vitamin D	33	IU
Vitamin E	1.9	IU
Vitamin B_6	0.22	mg
Folic Acid	0.038	mg
Vitamin B_{12}	0.0009	mg
Phosphorus	190	mg
Iodine	0.016	mg
Magnesium	38	mg
Zinc	1.7	mg
Copper	0.19	mg
Biotin	0.032	mg
Pantothenic Acid	0.96	mg
Choline	21	mg
Chloride	210	mg
Manganese	0.38	mg
Osmolality	690	mOsm/kg water

Meritene has a calorie-to-nitrogen ratio of 96:1. Gluten-free.

Cans of 908 g (chocolate, strawberry, vanilla, eggnog), cases of 6 (168 servings/case).

MERREM® Ⓟ
Zeneca
Meropenem
Antibiotic

Pharmacology: Meropenem is a broad spectrum, β-lactamase-resistant, carbapenem antibiotic for parenteral administration.

The bactericidal activity of meropenem results from the inhibition of bacterial cell wall synthesis. Meropenem readily penetrates through the cell wall of most gram-positive and gram-negative bacteria to reach penicillin binding protein (PBP) targets. Its greatest affinity is for PBP 2 of E. coli, PBP 2 and 3 of P. aeruginosa and 1, 2 and 4 of S. aureus.

Meropenem is stable in the presence of all serine β-lactamases (both penicillinases and cephalosporinases) produced by gram-positive and gram-negative bacteria.

Pharmacokinetics: At the end of a 30-minute i.v. infusion of a single dose of meropenem in healthy, male volunteers, mean peak plasma concentrations are approximately 23 μg/mL for the 500 mg dose, 49 μg/mL for the 1 g dose and 115 μg/mL for the 2 g dose.

I.V. bolus injections of a 1 g dose of meropenem over 2 minutes, 3 minutes and 5 minutes were compared in a 3-way crossover trial in healthy male volunteers. This resulted in peak plasma levels of 110, 91 and 94 μg/mL, respectively.

A 5-minute i.v. bolus injection of meropenem in healthy, male volunteers results in mean peak plasma levels of approximately 52 μg/mL for the 500 mg dose and 112 μg/mL for the 1 g dose.

At doses of 500 mg, mean plasma levels of meropenem decline to 1 μg/mL or less, 6 hours after administration.

In subjects with normal renal function, the elimination half-life of meropenem is approximately 1 hour. Approximately 70% of the administered dose is recovered unchanged in the urine over 12 hours, after which little further urinary excretion is detectable. Urinary concentrations of meropenem in excess of 10 μg/mL are maintained for at least 5 hours at the 500 mg dose. No clinically important accumulation of meropenem in plasma or urine was observed with regimens using 500 mg administered every 8 hours or 1 g administered every 6 hours in volunteers with normal renal function. Plasma protein binding of meropenem is approximately 2%.

There is one metabolite which is microbiologically inactive. In healthy subjects, the AUC for this metabolite was approximately 10% of the AUC for meropenem.

Meropenem penetrates well into most body fluids and tissues. However, it does not penetrate readily into cerebrospinal fluid or aqueous humor in the absence of inflammation at the sites. In children and adults with bacterial meningitis, meropenem concentrations in the cerebrospinal fluid, after i.v. administration of recommended doses, are in excess of those required to inhibit susceptible bacteria.

The pharmacokinetics of meropenem in children over age 2 are essentially similar to those in adults. The elimination half-life for meropenem was approximately 1.5 hours in children of age 3 months to 2 years. The pharmacokinetics for children are linear for doses of 10, 20 and 40 mg/kg and the peak plasma concentrations and AUC values are similar to those seen in healthy adult volunteers after 500 mg, 1 g and 2 g doses, respectively.

Pharmacokinetic studies of meropenem in patients with renal insufficiency have shown that the plasma clearance of meropenem correlates with creatinine clearance. Dosage adjustments are necessary in subjects with renal impairment (see Dosage). A pharmacokinetic study with meropenem in elderly patients with renal insufficiency has shown that a reduction in plasma clearance of meropenem correlates with age-associated reduction in creatinine clearance.

A pharmacokinetic study of meropenem in patients with hepatic impairment has shown no effects of liver disease on the pharmacokinetics of meropenem.

Indications: For treatment of the following infections when caused by susceptible strains of the designated microorganisms: Lower Respiratory Tract: Community-acquired pneumonia caused by S. aureus (β-lactamase-producing and non-β-lactamase-producing), S. pneumoniae, E. coli and H. influenzae (β-lactamase-producing and non-β-lactamase-producing).

Nosocomial pneumonia caused by S. aureus (non-β-lactamase-producing), E. coli, H. influenzae (non-β-lactamase-producing), K. pneumoniae and P. aeruginosa.

Urinary Tract: Complicated urinary tract infections caused by E. cloacae, E. coli, K. pneumoniae, P. aeruginosa and S. marcescens.

Intra-abdominal: Complicated intra-abdominal infections caused by S. milleri, S. mitior, S. sanguis, C. freundii, E. cloacae, E. coli, K. oxytoca, K. pneumoniae, M. morganii, P. aeruginosa, B. distasonis, B. fragilis, B. ovatus, B. thetaiotaomicron, B. uniformis, B. vulgatus, C. perfringens, Clostridium species, E. lentum, Fusobacterium species and Peptostreptococcus species.

Clinical trials of meropenem in patients with complicated intra-abdominal infections have demonstrated that the efficacy against E. faecalis is 71%.

Gynecologic: Gynecologic infections caused by E. faecalis, S. aureus (β-lactamase-producing and non-β-lactamase producing), S. epidermidis (non-β-lactamase-producing), E. coli, Fusobacterium species, P. bivia, P. disiens, P. intermedia and Peptostreptococcus species.

Pelvic inflammatory disease caused by S. epidermidis (non-β-lactamase-producing), S. agalactiae, E. coli, N. gonorrhoeae (non-β-lactamase-producing) and P. bivia.

Note: Meropenem has no activity against C. trachomatis. Additional antimicrobial coverage is required if this pathogen is expected.

Skin and Skin Structure: Uncomplicated skin and skin structure infections caused by S. aureus (β-lactamase-producing and non-β-lactamase-producing), S. agalactiae, S. pyogenes and E. coli.

Bacterial Meningitis: Bacterial meningitis caused by S. pneumoniae, H. influenzae (β-lactamase-producing and non-β-lactamase-producing) and N. meningitidis.

Note: There is limited adult efficacy data for meropenem in the treatment of bacterial meningitis. Support for the adult meningitis indication is largely provided by pediatric data.

Bacterial Septicemia: Bacterial septicemia caused by E. coli.

Therapy with meropenem may be initiated on the basis of clinical judgment before results of sensitivity testing are available. Continuation of therapy should be re-evaluated on the basis of bacteriological findings and on the patient's clinical condition. Regular sensitivity testing is recommended when treating P. aeruginosa infections.

Contraindications: Patients with known hypersensitivity to any component of this product or in patients who have demonstrated anaphylactic reactions to β-lactam antibiotics.

Warnings: Serious and occasionally fatal hypersensitivity (anaphylactic) reactions have been reported in patients receiving therapy with β-lactam antibiotics. These reactions

Merrem (cont'd)

are more likely to occur in individuals with a history of sensitivity to multiple allergens.

There have been reports of individuals with a history of penicillin hypersensitivity who have experienced severe reactions when treated with another β-lactam antibiotic. Before initiating therapy with meropenem, careful inquiry should be made concerning previous hypersensitivity reactions to penicillins, cephalosporins, other β-lactam antibiotics, and other allergens. If an allergic reaction to meropenem occurs, discontinue the drug immediately. Anaphylactic reactions require immediate treatment with epinephrine. Oxygen, i.v. steroids, antihistamines and airway management, including intubation, may be required.

Pseudomembranous colitis has been reported with many antibiotics, including meropenem; therefore, it is important to consider this diagnosis in patients who develop diarrhea in association with antibiotic use. This colitis may range in severity from mild to life threatening.

Treatment with antibacterial agents alters the normal flora of the colon and may permit overgrowth of Clostridia. Studies indicated that a toxin produced by C. difficile is one primary cause of antibiotic-associated colitis.

After the diagnosis of pseudomembranous colitis has been established, therapeutic measures should be initiated. Mild cases of pseudomembranous colitis usually respond to drug discontinuation alone. In moderate to severe cases, consideration should be given to management with fluids and electrolytes, protein supplementation, and treatment with an antibacterial drug effective against C. difficile.

Meropenem should not be used to treat infections caused by methicillin resistant staphylococci.

Precautions: General: As with other broad-spectrum antibiotics, prolonged use of meropenem may result in overgrowth of nonsusceptible organisms. Repeated evaluation of the patient is essential. If superinfection does occur during therapy, appropriate measures should be taken.

Meropenem, like all β-lactam antibiotics, has the potential to cause seizures. Diminished renal function and CNS lesions may increase the risk of seizures. When meropenem is indicated in patients with these risk factors, caution is advised.

Children: The safety and effectiveness of meropenem have been established only for those infants and children 3 months of age and older.

The use of meropenem in pediatric patients with bacterial meningitis is supported by evidence from adequate and well controlled studies in the pediatric population. Use of meropenem in pediatric patients for all other indications, as listed in the Indications section, is supported by evidence from adequate and well controlled studies in adults with additional data from pediatric pharmacokinetic studies and controlled clinical trials in pediatric patients (see Dosage, Children).

Note: Inadequate data are available to support the pediatric indications for nosocomial pneumonia and for septicemia.

Pregnancy: There are no adequate and well-controlled studies in pregnant women. Because animal reproduction studies are not always predictive of human response, this drug should be used during pregnancy only if clearly needed. Reproduction studies have been performed in rats and Cynomolgus monkeys at doses up to 1 000 mg/kg/day (approximately 16 times the usual human dose of 1 g every 8 hours). These studies revealed no evidence of impaired fertility or harm to the fetus due to meropenem although there were slight changes in fetal body weight at doses of 240 mg/kg/day and above in rats.

Lactation: It is not known whether meropenem is excreted in human milk. Therefore, caution should be exercised when considering the administration of meropenem to a nursing woman.

Liver Disease: Patients with pre-existing liver disorders should have their liver function monitored during treatment with meropenem.

Drug Interactions: Probenecid competes with meropenem for active tubular secretion and thus inhibits the renal excretion of meropenem with the effect of increasing the elimination half-life and plasma concentration of meropenem. The coadministration of probenecid with meropenem is neither required nor recommended.

Other than probenecid, no specific drug interaction studies were conducted.

Adverse Effects: Local Adverse Reactions: Meropenem is generally well tolerated. The following adverse reaction frequencies were derived from all clinical trials in 2 676 patients treated with meropenem administered i.v. and in 481 patients treated with an i.m. injection formulation of meropenem. Local adverse clinical reactions that were reported as possibly, probably or definitely related to therapy with meropenem were: inflammation at the injection site 2.4%, phlebitis/thrombophlebitis 0.8%, injection site reaction 0.7%, pain at the injection site 0.2% and edema at the injection site 0.1%.

Systemic Adverse Reactions: Systemic adverse clinical reactions that were reported as possibly, probably or definitely related to meropenem and occurring in greater than 0.2% of the patients were: diarrhea (2.6%), nausea/vomiting (1.2%), rash (1.2%), pruritus (0.6%), headache (0.4%), urticaria (0.3%), vaginal moniliasis (0.4%), oral moniliasis (0.2%) and fever (0.2%).

Additional adverse systemic clinical reactions reported as possibly, probably or definitely related to meropenem and occurring in less than 0.2% of the patients are listed below within each body system in order of decreasing frequency.

Body as a Whole: abdominal pain, moniliasis, chills, infection, pain.

Nervous System: agitation, convulsions, dizziness, hallucinations, paresthesias, neuropathy.

Skin and Appendages: sweating.

Urogenital System: vaginitis.

Special Senses: taste perversion.

Digestive System: constipation.

Metabolic/Nutritional: peripheral edema.

Adverse Laboratory Changes: Adverse laboratory changes that were reported as possibly, probably or definitely related to meropenem occurring in greater than 0.2% of the patients were as follows: Hepatic: increased ALT, AST, alkaline phosphatase, LDH and bilirubin.

Hematologic: increased platelets, increased eosinophils, abnormal prothrombin time, abnormal partial thromboplastin time, decreased platelets, positive direct or indirect Coombs' test and decreased WBC.

Renal: increased creatinine and increased BUN.

Children: Drug-related diarrhea (5%) and increases in platelets (7%) appear to occur more frequently in pediatric patients than in adults treated with meropenem.

Overdose: Symptoms: Intentional overdosing of meropenem is unlikely, although accidental overdosing might occur if large doses are given to patients with reduced renal function. The largest dose of meropenem administered in clinical trials has been 2 g given i.v. every 8 hours to adult patients with normal renal function and 40 mg/kg every 8 hours to children with normal renal function. At these dosages, no adverse pharmacological effects were observed.

Treatment: No specific information is available for the treatment of meropenem overdosage. In the event of an overdose, meropenem should be discontinued and general supportive treatment given until renal elimination takes place. Meropenem and its metabolite are readily dialyzable and effectively removed by hemodialysis; however, no information is available on the use of hemodialysis to treat overdosage.

The i.v. LD_{50} of meropenem in mice and rats is more than 2 500 mg/kg and is approximately 2 000 mg/kg in dogs.

Dosage: Adults: The usual dose is 500 mg to 1 g by i.v. infusion every 8 hours, depending on type and severity of infection, the known or suspected susceptibility of the pathogens and the condition of the patient (see Table I). Doses up to 2 g every 8 hours have been used. Meropenem should be given by i.v. infusion over approximately 15 to 30 minutes or as an i.v. bolus injection (5 to 20 mL) over approximately 5 minutes.

The recommended dose to be given for adults is shown in Table I.

Table I—Merrem

Recommended Dose—Adults

Type of Infection	Dose	Dosage Interval
Complicated urinary tract	500 mg	every 8 hours
Uncomplicated skin and skin structure	500 mg	every 8 hours
Gynecologic and pelvic inflammatory disease	500 mg	every 8 hours
Lower respiratory		
Community-acquired pneumonia	500 mg	every 8 hours
Nosocomial pneumonia	1 g	every 8 hours
Complicated intra-abdominal	1 g	every 8 hours
Meningitis	2 g	every 8 hours
Septicemia	1 g	every 8 hours

Impaired Renal Function: Dosage should be reduced in patients with creatinine clearance less than 51 mL/min (see Table II).

Table II—Merrem

Dosage in Impaired Renal Function

Creatinine Clearance (mL/min)	Dose (dependent on type of infection)	Dosing Interval
26-50	recommended dose (500 mg to 2 000 mg)	every 12 hours
10-25	one-half recommended dose	every 12 hours
<10	one-half recommended dose	every 24 hours

Meropenem is removed by hemodialysis; if continued treatment with meropenem is necessary, the dose, based on the infection type and severity, should be administered at the completion of the hemodialysis procedure to reinstitute effective treatment.

There are no data on appropriate doses in patients requiring dialysis.

Adults with Hepatic Insufficiency: No dosage adjustment is necessary in patients with hepatic dysfunction as long as renal function is normal.

Geriatrics: Dosage adjustment is recommended for the elderly with an estimated or measured creatinine clearance value below 50 mL/min (see Impaired Renal Function).

Children: For infants and children over 3 months of age and weighing up to 50 kg, the recommended dose of meropenem is 10 to 40 mg/kg every 8 hours, depending on type and severity of infection, the known or suspected susceptibility of the pathogens and the condition of the patient (see Table III). Children weighing over 50 kg require the adult dosage. Meropenem should be given as an i.v. infusion over approximately 15 to 30 minutes or as an i.v. bolus injection (5 to 20 mL) over approximately 5 minutes.

Table III—Merrem

Recommended Dose—Children

Type of Infection	Dose (mg/kg)	Dosing Interval
Complicated urinary tract	10	every 8 hours
Uncomplicated skin and skin structure	10–20	every 8 hours
Community acquired pneumonia	10–20	every 8 hours
Complicated intra-abdominal	20	every 8 hours
Meningitis	40	every 8 hours

There are no data on appropriate doses for children with renal impairment.

Parenteral Products: Compatibility of meropenem with other drugs has not been established. Meropenem should not be mixed with or physically added to solutions containing other drugs.

Freshly prepared solutions of meropenem should be used whenever possible. Solutions of meropenem should not be frozen.

Parenteral drug products should be inspected visually for particulate matter and discoloration prior to administration, whenever solution and container permit.

I.V. Bolus Administration: Reconstitute injection vials (500 mg/20 mL and 1 g/30 mL) with Sterile Water for Injection (see Table IV). Shake to dissolve and let stand until clear.

Table IV—Merrem

Reconstitution for I.V. Bolus

Vial Size	Amount of Diluent Added (mL)	Approximate Withdrawable Volume (mL)	Approximate Average Concentration (mg/mL)
500 mg/20 mL	10	10	50
1 g/30 mL	20	20	50

Meropenem injection vials reconstituted with Sterile Water for Injection for bolus administration (up to 50 mg/mL) may be stored for up to 2 hours at controlled room temperature 15 to 25°C or for up to 12 hours at 4°C.

Infusion: Injection vials may be reconstituted, then the resulting solution added to an i.v. container and further diluted with an appropriate infusion fluid (see Table V on following page).

Stability in Plastic I.V. Bags: Solutions prepared for infusion (meropenem concentrations ranging from 1 to 20 mg/mL) may be stored in plastic i.v. bags with diluents as shown in Table V (on following page). Diluted i.v. infusion solutions

Table V—Merrem

Diluents

Diluent	Number of Hours Stable at Controlled Room Temperature 15 to 25°C	Number of Hours Stable at 4°C
Sodium Chloride 0.9% Injection	4	24
Dextrose 5% Injection	1	4
Dextrose 10% Injection	1	2
Dextrose 5% and Sodium Chloride 0.9% Injection	1	2
Dextrose 5% and Sodium Chloride 0.2% Injection	1	4
Potassium Chloride 0.15% in Dextrose 5% Injection	1	6
Sodium Bicarbonate 0.02% in Dextrose 5% Injection	1	6
Dextrose 5% Injection in Normosol-M	1	8
Dextrose 5% Injection in Ringers Lactate Injection	1	4
Dextrose 2.5% and Sodium Chloride 0.45% Injection	3	12
Mannitol Injection 2.5%	2	16
Ringers Injection	4	24
Ringers Lactate Injection	4	12
Sodium Lactate Injection 1/6 N	2	24
Sodium Bicarbonate 5% Injection	1	4

should be inspected visually for discoloration, haziness, particulate matter and leakage prior to administration, whenever solution and container permit. Discard unused portion.

Stability in Plastic Syringes, Tubing and I.V. Infusion Sets: Solutions of meropenem (concentrations ranging from 1 to 20 mg/mL) in Water for Injection or Sodium Chloride 0.9% Injection (for up to 4 hours) or in Dextrose 5% Injection (for up to 2 hours) at controlled room temperatures 15 to 25°C are stable in plastic syringes, plastic tubing, drip chambers, and volume control devices of common i.v. infusion sets.

Supplied: Vials: 500 mg: Each vial of dry powder contains: meropenem trihydrate equivalent to meropenem anhydrous 500 mg and sodium carbonate equivalent to sodium 45.1 mg. Vials of 20 mL.

1 g: Each vial of dry powder contains: meropenem trihydrate equivalent to meropenem anhydrous 1 g and sodium carbonate equivalent to sodium 90.2 mg. Vials of 30 mL.

Store between 15 and 30°C.

Reviewed 1998

MERSYNDOL® with CODEINE Ⓝ

Hoechst Marion Roussel

Acetaminophen—Codeine Phosphate—Doxylamine Succinate

Analgesic

Pharmacology: Acetaminophen is the major metabolite of phenacetin and acetanilid. Acetaminophen is an effective and fast-acting analgesic which acts centrally to relieve mild to moderate pain. Animal and clinical studies have shown acetaminophen to have antipyretic and analgesic activity equal to that of ASA.

Unlike the salicylates, acetaminophen does not interfere with tubular secretion of uric acid, nor does it affect acid-base balance at normal therapeutic doses. Acetaminophen does not interfere with hemostasis and does not inhibit platelet aggregation.

Acetaminophen is rapidly and completely absorbed from the gastrointestinal tract. Approximately 85% of a 1 g dose is recovered from the urine in 24 hours. About 3% is excreted unchanged, the balance being conjugated principally to the glucuronide or sulfate. Peak plasma concentrations of the free and conjugated drug are achieved ½ to 1 hour after oral administration. The plasma half-life of the unchanged drug is about 2 hours. Like the salicylates, acetaminophen reduces fever by a direct effect on the heat-regulating centres to increase dissipation of body heat.

Allergic reactions are rare with acetaminophen but have occurred. This drug may be useful in asthmatic patients sensitive to salicylates; however, patients with salicylate induced urticaria or angioedema can suffer cross-reactivity with acetaminophen.

Small amounts of acetaminophen are normally converted to a highly reactive metabolite by hepatic microsomal enzymes. At therapeutic doses, the small amounts of the active metabolite so formed are rapidly inactivated by hepatic glutathione and removed by renal excretion. However, where hepatic glutathione has been rapidly depleted by a large dose of acetaminophen, covalent binding of the metabolite to liver-cell macromolecules occurs and is presumed to be responsible for the hepatic cell necrosis. Prompt administration of acetylcysteine is indicated to prevent acetaminophen-induced hepatic necrosis (see Overdose).

Codeine phosphate and the other opiates cause a selective relief of pain by raising the threshold for pain. Codeine also exerts antitussive action by directly depressing the cough centre. Codeine phosphate is an effective oral analgesic which provides relief from mild to moderate pain. The abuse potential of codeine is lower than that of other opiates.

Doxylamine succinate belongs to the ethanolamine class of antihistamines which are associated with a tendency to induce sedation. Its sedative effect is useful in reducing the restlessness and allaying the anxiety which can perpetuate or increase pain. It has antinauseant and antiemetic activity. Its anticholinergic effects tend to lessen rhinorrhea.

Indications: For relief of headaches, cold symptoms, muscular aches and pains, and neuralgia.

Contraindications: Hypersensitivity to acetaminophen, codeine, or doxylamine. Pre-existing respiratory depression or embarrassment.

Precautions: Occupational Hazards: Patients should be cautioned not to operate vehicles or hazardous machinery until their response to the drug has been determined. Since the depressant effects of antihistamines are additive to those of other drugs affecting the CNS, patients should be cautioned against drinking alcoholic beverages or taking tranquilizers, hypnotics, sedatives, psychotherapeutic agents or other drugs with CNS depressant effects during antihistaminic therapy.

Products containing codeine should not be given for prolonged periods. Codeine phosphate may occasionally cause constipation. Codeine may be habit-forming.

In patients with asthma or pulmonary emphysema, indiscriminate use may precipitate respiratory insufficiency resulting from increased viscosity of bronchial secretions and suppression of the cough reflex.

Use with caution in sedated or debilitated patients, in patients who have undergone thoracotomies or laparotomies, since suppression of the cough reflex may lead to retention of secretions postoperatively in these patients.

Hepatic failure is known to occur occasionally with the long-term use of acetaminophen. Agranulocytosis, renal papillary necrosis and with higher doses, fatal liver damage and very rare complications of treatment with acetaminophen may occur.

Pregnancy and *Lactation:* Safe use in pregnancy has not been established in human studies, therefore, this medication should not be used during pregnancy unless, in the opinion of the prescribing doctor, the potential benefits outweigh the potential risks. There is epidemiological evidence of safety in pregnancy for acetaminophen and doxylamine succinate. There is inadequate evidence of safety of codeine in pregnancy but it has been in wide use for many years without apparent ill consequence. Since codeine phosphate crosses the placental barrier, its use in pregnancy is not recommended. No data are available on the use of Mersyndol during pregnancy and lactation.

Adverse Effects: Acetaminophen: The incidence of gastrointestinal upset is less than after salicylate administration.

Hepatic toxicity has been associated with acetaminophen overdose. Phenobarbital increases the activity of microsomal enzymes which produce a toxic metabolite and therefore acetaminophen's hepatotoxicity may be enhanced. Thus, concomitant ingestion of phenobarbital may increase the likelihood of liver necrosis in acetaminophen overdose.

Nonfatal nepatic damage is usually reversible. There have been reports of kidney damage, disturbances in clotting mechanisms, metabolic acidosis, hypoglycemia, neutropenia, agranulocytosis, thrombocytopenia, methemoglobinemia and myocardial necrosis.

The chronic ingestion of alcohol may be implicated in the increasing potential for hepatic toxicity. Abnormal liver function has been associated with therapeutic doses ranging from 3 to 8 g/day. In patients with compromised liver function, acetaminophen could exacerbate liver insufficiency.

Renal papillary necrosis has been reported following prolonged acetaminophen administration of up to 19 g per day. There have been no authenticated reports of renal papillary necrosis with therapeutic doses of acetaminophen alone. Renal insufficiency may occur as an effect secondary to liver failure.

Anemia has been reported in patients with gastrointestinal bleeding who were often analgesic abusers, had chronic gastric ulcers or where gastrointestinal bleeding was already present.

Rarely, asthmatic attacks have been precipitated by acetaminophen.

Skin rashes and fixed dermatitis with pruritus have been rarely reported.

Codeine phosphate: Adverse reactions due to codeine phosphate may include drowsiness, nausea, vomiting and constipation. Infrequent adverse effects include palpitation, pruritus and, rarely, hyperhidrosis and agitation have been reported. Respiratory depression is seen with higher dosages. Habituation or true addiction should be guarded against.

Doxylamine succinate: Drowsiness, vertigo, nervousness, epigastric pain, headache, palpitation, diarrhea, disorientation, irritability, convulsions, urinary retention, or insomnia have been reported.

Other: Other infrequently observed side effects are anorexia, depression, dizziness and dry mouth.

Overdose: Symptoms and Treatment: Acetaminophen: In adults, hepatotoxicity may occur after ingestion of a single dose of 10 to 15 g (200 to 250 mg/kg) of acetaminophen; a dose of 25 g or more is potentially fatal.

Reports have indicated hepatic necrosis with a single dose of 6 g and death occurring with a single dose of 13 g. Nonfatal overdoses of 12.5 to 31.5 g have also been reported. However, it is generally agreed that consumption of more than 50% of the toxic dose, e.g., 7.5 g in adults and 140 to 150 mg/kg in children could initiate liver damage.

The earliest symptoms of overdose with acetaminophen are nausea, vomiting, sweating and pallor. This initial period is frequently followed by an asymptomatic phase of 24 to 48 hours after which hepatic damage may become evident. Elevation in hepatic enzymes, AST, ALT are noted. BUN remains low. Hepatic function is altered as measured by bilirubin and prothrombin time. The liver enlarges with marked right upper quadrant pain and tenderness.

After 3 to 5 days, jaundice, hypoglycemia, encephalopathy, cardiomyopathy, renal failure, hepatic coma and death may occur.

Factors contributing to an accurate evaluation of toxicity include: the amount of drug ingested and more significantly, the serum acetaminophen concentration measured optimally, after 4 hours of ingestion.

When serum determinations of acetaminophen are above 150 μg/mL at 4 hours, or above 40 μg/mL at 12 hours following the estimated time of ingestion, the patient is at risk of liver damage and antidotal therapy should be instituted immediately.

An additional reliable indicator of possible hepatic injury is the serum half-life. The normal half-life of acetaminophen in a healthy adult is 2 hours. If the serum half-life exceeds 4 hours, it can be assumed that hepatic necrosis will occur; if the half-life exceeds 12 hours hepatic coma is a likely possibility.

Treatment of acetaminophen overdosage includes ipecac induced emesis or gastric lavage which should, when possible, commence within 4 hours of drug ingestion. Activated charcoal is effective only when given within 1 to 2 hours of the alleged overdose. Prior to antidotal treatment with acetylcysteine, residual activated charcoal must be removed by gastric lavage with water.

Acetylcysteine is effective orally. A loading dose of 140 mg/kg is given as a single dose. A maintenance dose of 70 mg/kg is then given every 4 hours for 17 doses. If nausea

Mersyndol with Codeine (cont'd)

and vomiting occurs within 1 hour of the loading or maintenance dose, the entire dose should be repeated. Acetylcysteine 20% solution may be diluted to a 5% concentration with a soft drink or fruit juice to make it more palatable. This mixture should be consumed within 1 hour of preparation.

The use of i.v. acetylcysteine is recommended when oral therapy is not feasible or practical. A loading dose, 150 mg/kg of sterile acetylcysteine 20% is infused in 200 mL D5W over 15 minutes, followed by an infusion of 50 mg/kg in 500 mL D5W over 4 hours, and finally 100 mg/kg in 1 000 mL D5W during the next 16 hours. The total dose is 300 mg/kg administered over 20 hours.

Codeine phosphate: May result in euphoria, dysphoria, visual disturbances, hypotension and coma or death from respiratory depression.

In an evaluation of codeine intoxication in children, symptoms ranked by decreasing order of frequency included: sedation, rash, miosis, vomiting, itching, ataxia and swelling of the skin. Respiratory failure may occur. Blood concentrations of codeine ranged from 1.4 to 5.6 μg/mL in 8 adults whose deaths were attributed primarily to codeine overdosage.

Intubation measures aimed at supporting respiration, and the administration of a narcotic antagonist, e.g., naloxone, should be considered to counteract the effects of an overdose of codeine phosphate.

Doxylamine succinate: Dryness of mouth, dilated pupils, sleepiness, vertigo, mental confusion, restlessness or tachycardia. Reactions associated with doxylamine succinate overdosage may vary from CNS depression to stimulation. Stimulation is particularly likely in children. Atropine-like signs and symptoms (dry mouth, fixed, dilated pupils, flushing) and gastrointestinal symptoms may also occur.

Dosage: Adults and children over 12 years: 1 to 2 tablets every 4 hours as required. Do not exceed 12 tablets in a 24-hour period.

Supplied: Each round, flat, white tablet with a stylized S contains: acetaminophen 325 mg, codeine phosphate 8 mg and doxylamine succinate 5 mg. Nonmedicinal ingredients: cellulose, cornstarch, magnesium stearate, povidone, silicon dioxide and sodium carboxymethylcellulose. Bisulfites-, gluten-, lactose-, parabens- and tartrazine-free. Bottles of 100. Blister packages of 24.

(Shown in Product Recognition Section)

Reviewed 1999

MESASAL™ Ⓟ

SmithKline Beecham

5-Aminosalicylic Acid Enteric Coated

Lower Gastrointestinal Anti-inflammatory

Pharmacology: 5-Aminosalicylic acid (5-ASA) is considered to be the active component of sulfasalazine. Although its mode of action has not been definitely elucidated, 5-ASA is thought to have a topical anti-inflammatory effect which is produced by inhibition of prostaglandin and/or leukotriene synthesis.

The tablets have an acrylic based resin coating which is specifically designed to release 5-ASA in the terminal ileum and colon. Urinary recovery studies have shown that 35% of the 5-ASA is absorbed. The absorbed 5-ASA is rapidly acetylated and excreted mainly by the kidney.

Detectable plasma levels of 5-ASA were seen 4 hours after a single oral dose of tablets (2×250 mg). Peak plasma levels of 5-ASA and N-acetyl-5-ASA were 1.2 and 1.9 μg/mL, respectively, and occurred 6.5 to 7 hours post-dosing. Mean steady-state plasma levels of 5-ASA and N-acetyl-5-ASA using a 500 mg 3 times a day dosage schedule are 0.7 and 1.2 μg/mL, respectively.

Except for a delay of 1.5 to 3 hours in time to peak of 5-ASA and N-acetyl-5-ASA plasma levels, the pharmacokinetics are essentially the same in fasted and fed subjects.

Indications: The management of acute ulcerative colitis and the prevention of relapse of active ulcerative colitis.

Contraindications: Hypersensitivity to salicylates; in cases of hemorrhagic diathesis; in patients with existing gastric and duodenal ulcers; in patients with urinary tract obstruction; in children under 2 years of age.

Warnings: In cases of severe liver and kidney disorders, caution should be exercised.

Pregnancy and *Lactation:* 5-ASA should not be prescribed during the last weeks of pregnancy or during lactation. In the first 3 months of pregnancy, treatment is recommended only if potential benefits outweigh the possible risks.

Children: There is limited experience with respect to the use of this drug in children; potential benefits should be weighed against possible risks.

Precautions: *Drug Interactions:* Caution should be exercised when 5-ASA and sulfonylureas are prescribed concomitantly since the blood-sugar reducing effect of sulfonylureas may be enhanced. Interactions with coumarins, methotrexate, probenecid, sulfinpyrazone, spironolactone, furosemide and rifampicin cannot be excluded.

In long-term therapy, periodic urinalysis should be conducted. Caution should be exercised when therapy is first initiated in patients known to be allergic to sulfasalazine.

Adverse Effects: In controlled clinical trials in 395 patients who received 5-ASA, the following adverse reactions were reported: headache (3.0%), nausea (2.0%), abdominal pain (1 to 5%) and diarrhea (1.5%). Rash (including pruritus and urticaria) has also been reported. Other adverse effects common to salicylates, such as occasional transitory abnormal liver function tests or hypersensitivity reactions, may be expected to occur rarely. There have been a few spontaneous reports of pancreatitis, acute and chronic interstitial nephritis and pericarditis, associated with 5-ASA therapy.

Overdose: Symptoms and Treatment: There is no specific antidote. Gastric lavage should be employed, followed by promotion of diuresis by the i.v. infusion of an electrolyte solution.

Dosage: During the acute inflammatory stage and in long-term maintenance therapy, 5-ASA must be taken reliably and consistently by the patient in order to ensure therapeutic success.

Although symptomatic relief may be seen as early as 3 to 21 days, therapy should be continued depending on clinical findings.

The following dosage regimens are recommended: Adults: The tablets should be swallowed whole before meals with plenty of fluid.

For the management of acute ulcerative colitis, 1.5 g to 3 g daily in divided doses.

For prevention of relapses of acute ulcerative colitis, 1.5 g daily in divided doses.

Supplied: Each oval, red-orange enteric coated tablet contains: 5-aminosalicylic acid 500 mg. Nonmedicinal ingredients: calcium stearate, glycine, iron oxide (red), iron oxide (yellow), methacrylic acid copolymer, microcrystalline cellulose, polyethylene glycol 6 000, povidone, silicon dioxide, sodium carbonate, sodium croscarmellose, talc and titanium dioxide. Mesasal tablets are acrylic coated to prevent release of 5-ASA until the tablets reach the terminal ileum and proximal colon. Polyethylene bottles of 100.

(Shown in Product Recognition Section)

Reviewed 1997

M-ESLON® Ⓝ

Rhône-Poulenc Rorer

Morphine Sulfate

Opioid Analgesic

Pharmacology: Morphine is an opioid analgesic which exerts an agonist effect at specific, saturable opioid receptors in the CNS and other tissues. In man, morphine produces a variety of effects including analgesia, constipation from decreased gastrointestinal motility, suppression of the cough reflex, respiratory depression from reduced responsiveness of the respiratory centre to CO_2, nausea and vomiting via stimulation of the CTZ, changes in mood including euphoria and dysphoria, sedation, mental clouding, and alterations of the endocrine and autonomic nervous systems.

The psychological effects are of longer duration than that of analgesia. Morphine-induced analgesia is relatively selective in that other sensory modalities (touch, vision, hearing) are not affected. Moderate doses of morphine are effective in relieving clinical (pathological) pain and increasing pain threshold to tolerate pain. The capacity to perceive the sensation of pain may be relatively unaltered. The analgesic effects of morphine are due to its CNS action, i.e., limbic system, hypothalamus, and centrally induced endocrinological effect. At present, the exact mechanism by which opiates exert their effects remains unknown.

Pharmacokinetics: Morphine is readily absorbed from the gastrointestinal tract and after s.c. or i.m. injection. Due to first-pass metabolism in the liver, the effect of an oral dose is less than after parenteral administration. With repeated regular dosing, orally administered morphine is about one-third as potent as when given by i.m. injection. Morphine is primarily excreted in the urine as morphine-3-glucuronide. About 7 to 10% of a dose of morphine is excreted in the feces via the bile.

The morphine sulfate extended release capsules produce peak morphine levels at steady state in approximately 3 to 4 hours following administration. In human pharmacokinetic studies, they have been shown to have an extended release action, when compared to oral morphine sulfate syrup, as characterized by a flatter peak serum concentration curve which took longer to attain; the elimination half-life was significantly lengthened. Therapeutic levels are maintained over a period of 12 hours.

This product has not been compared to any slow-release morphine preparation on the Canadian market, and therefore is not interchangeable.

Indications: The symptomatic relief of severe pain.

Contraindications: Should not be given to patients with: hypersensitivity to opiate opioids; acute asthma or other obstructive airway disease and acute respiratory depression; cor pulmonale; cardiac arrhythmias; acute alcoholism; severe cirrhosis; delirium tremens; severe CNS depression, convulsive disorders; increased cerebrospinal or intracranial pressure; head injury or brain tumor (may cause marked exaggeration of cerebrospinal fluid pressure and mask the clinical course); suspected surgical abdomen; surgical anastomosis (opioids may cause increase in intraluminal pressure); after surgery of the biliary tract; surgical anastomosis; hypotension; concomitant MAO inhibitors (or within 14 days of such therapy).

Warnings: This product has not been compared to slow-release morphine preparation on the Canadian market, and therefore is not interchangeable.

Drug Dependence: As with other opioids, tolerance and physical dependence tend to develop upon repeated administration of morphine and there is potential for abuse of the drug and for development of strong psychological dependence. The morphine sulfate extended release capsules should therefore be prescribed and handled with the high degree of caution appropriate to the use of a drug with strong abuse potential. Drug abuse is not, however, a problem in patients with severe pain in which morphine is appropriately indicated. On the other hand, in the absence of a clear indication for a strong opioid analgesic, drug-seeking behavior must be suspected and resisted, particularly in patients with a history of, or propensity for drug abuse. Withdrawal symptoms may occur following abrupt discontinuation of morphine therapy or upon administration of an opioid antagonist. Therefore, patients on prolonged therapy should be withdrawn gradually from the drug if it is no longer required for pain control.

Severe pain antagonizes the subjective and respiratory depressant actions of morphine. Should pain suddenly subside, these effects may rapidly become manifest. Patients who are scheduled for cordotomy or other interruption of pain transmission pathways should not receive the morphine sulfate extended release capsules within 24 hours of the procedure.

Pregnancy: Animal studies indicate that morphine may be teratogenic at high doses in mice and may cause an increased incidence of abortions and reduced birth weight in rabbits. In humans, it is not known whether morphine can cause fetal harm when administered during pregnancy or can affect reproductive capacity. The morphine sulfate extended release capsules should be given to pregnant patients only if clearly needed and when the anticipated benefits outweigh the risks to the fetus and the mother. Infants born to mothers who are physically dependent on opioids exhibit withdrawal symptoms, such as generalized tremors, hypertonicity, hyperalertness, sleeplessness, excessive crying, vomiting, diarrhea, yawning, and occasional fever.

Precautions: General: The respiratory depressant effects of morphine, and the capacity to elevate cerebrospinal fluid pressure, may be greatly increased in the presence of an already elevated intracranial pressure produced by trauma. Also, morphine may produce confusion, miosis, vomiting and other side effects which obscure the clinical course of patients with head injury. In such patients, morphine must be used with extreme caution and only if it is judged to be essential.

Morphine should be used with extreme caution in patients with chronic pulmonary disease; substantially decreased respiratory reserve, preexisting respiratory depression, hypoxia or hypercapnia. Such patients are often less sensitive to the stimulatory effects of carbon dioxide on the respiratory centre and the respiratory depressant effects of morphine may reduce respiratory drive to the point of apnea.

Morphine administration may result in severe hypotension in patients whose ability to maintain adequate blood pressure is compromised by reduced blood volume, or concurrent administration of such drugs as phenothiazines or certain anesthetics.

Morphine may obscure the diagnosis or clinical course of patients with acute abdominal conditions.

Morphine may cause a decrease in systemic vascular resistance in patients with myocardial infarction. A transient fall in systemic arterial pressure may result, leading to severe hypotension. Administered in large doses, morphine may cause severe hypotension even in the supine patient.

Special Risk Groups: Morphine should be administered with caution, and in reduced dosages, to elderly or debilitated patients, to patients with severely reduced hepatic or renal function, and in patients with Addison's disease, hypothyroidism, prostatic hypertrophy or urethral stricture, hypopituitarism, anemia, severe malnutrition, fulminant ulcerative colitis, untreated myxedema.

Labor/Delivery and *Lactation:* Morphine crosses the placental barrier and its administration during labor can produce respiratory depression in the neonate. Morphine has been detected in human breast milk. Caution should be exercised if morphine is administered to a nursing mother.

Occupational Hazards: Morphine may impair the mental and/or physical abilities needed for certain potentially hazardous activities such as driving a car or operating machinery. Patients should be cautioned accordingly.

Patients should also be cautioned about the combined effects of morphine with other CNS depressants, including other opioids, phenothiazines, sedative/hypnotics and alcohol.

Drug Interactions: Generally, the effects of morphine may be antagonized by acidifying agents and potentiated by alkalinizing agents.

Anticholinergics: The concomitant use of anticholinergics with opioids, including morphine, may result in an increased risk of severe constipation and urinary retention.

Opioid Antagonists: Concomitant use of opioid antagonists may result in reversal of analgesia, and may precipitate withdrawal symptoms in patients who are physically dependent on narcotics.

CNS Depressants: CNS depressants, such as other opioids, alcohol, anesthetics, antihistamines, barbiturates, beta-blockers, chloral hydrate, glutethimide, hypnotics, MAO inhibitors, phenothiazines, pyrazolidone, sedatives, skeletal muscle relaxants and tricyclic antidepressants may enhance the depressant effects of morphine. Concurrent use may result in potentiation of CNS depression and death may occur. If used concurrently with CNS depressants, dosage adjustment may be required.

Amphetamines: Amphetamines potentiate the analgesic effect of morphine.

Oral Anticoagulants: Morphine may increase the anticoagulant activity of coumarin and other anticoagulants.

Adverse Effects: The major hazards associated with morphine, as with other opioid analgesics, are respiratory depression and, to a lesser degree, circulatory depression. Respiratory arrest, shock and cardiac arrest have occurred following oral or parenteral use of morphine.

Most Common Adverse Effects Requiring Medical Attention: The most frequently observed side effects of opioid analgesics such as morphine are sedation, nausea and vomiting, constipation and sweating.

Sedation: Most patients experience initial drowsiness partly for pharmacokinetic reasons and partly because patients often recuperate from prolonged fatigue after the relief of persistent pain. Drowsiness usually clears in 3 to 5 days and is usually not a reason for concern providing that it is not excessive, or associated with unsteadiness or confusional symptoms. If excessive sedation persists the reason for it must be sought. Some of these are: concomitant sedative medications, hepatic or renal failure, exacerbated respiratory failure, higher doses than tolerated in an older patient, or the patient is actually more severely ill than realized. If it is necessary to reduce the dose, it can be carefully increased again after 3 or 4 days if it is obvious that the pain is not being well controlled. Dizziness and unsteadiness may be caused by postural hypotension particularly in elderly or debilitated patients. It can be alleviated if the patient lies down. Because of the slower clearance in patients over 50 years of age, an appropriate dose in this age group may be as low as half or less the usual in the younger age group.

Nausea and Vomiting: Nausea and vomiting occur frequently after single doses of opioids or as an early unwanted effect of regular opioid therapy. When instituting prolonged therapy for chronic pain the routine prescription of antiemetic should be considered. Patients taking the equivalent of a single dose of 20 mg or more of morphine every 4 hours (60 mg of morphine sulfate extended release capsules every 12 hours) usually require an antiemetic during early therapy. Small doses of prochlorperazine or haloperidol are the most frequently prescribed antiemetics. Nausea and vomiting tend to lessen in a week or so but may persist due to opioid-induced gastric stasis. In such patients, metoclopramide is often useful.

Constipation: Practically all patients become constipated while taking opioids on a persistent basis. In some instances, particularly the elderly or bedridden, patients may become impacted. It is essential to caution the patients in this regard and to institute an appropriate regimen of bowel management at the start of prolonged opioid therapy. Softeners, laxatives and other appropriate measures should be used as required.

CNS: euphoria, dysphoria, weakness, insomnia, dizziness, headache, agitation, tremor, uncoordinated muscle movements, visual disturbances, confusional symptoms and occasionally hallucinations.

Gastrointestinal: dry mouth, anorexia, constipation, cramps, taste alterations and biliary tract spasm.

Genitourinary: urinary retention or hesitance, reduced libido or potency.

Cardiovascular: supraventricular tachycardia, postural hypotension, palpitations, faintness and syncope.

Endocrine: A syndrome of inappropriate antidiuretic hormone secretion characterized by hyponatremia secondary to decreased free-water excretion may be prominent (monitoring of electrolytes may be necessary).

Allergic: pruritus, urticaria, other skin rashes and edema.

Withdrawal (Abstinence) Syndrome: Physical dependence with or without psychological dependence tend to occur on chronic administration. An abstinence syndrome may be precipitated when opioid administration is discontinued or opioid antagonists administered. The following withdrawal symptoms may be observed after opioids are discontinued: body aches, diarrhea, gooseflesh, loss of appetite, nervousness or restlessness, runny nose, sneezing, tremors or shivering, stomach cramps, nausea, trouble with sleeping, unusual increase in sweating and yawning, weakness, tachycardia and unexplained fever. With appropriate medical use of opioids and gradual withdrawal from the drug, these symptoms are usually mild.

Overdose: Symptoms: Serious morphine overdosage is characterized by respiratory depression (reduced respiratory rate and/or tidal volume; Cheyne-Stokes respiration; cyanosis), extreme somnolence progressing to stupor or coma, flaccidity of skeletal muscle, cold or clammy skin, and sometimes hypotension and bradycardia. Severe overdosage may result in apnea, circulatory collapse, cardiac arrest and death. Convulsions may occur in young children.

Treatment: Primary attention should be given to the establishment of adequate respiratory exchange through provision of a patent airway and controlled or assisted ventilation. The opioid antagonist naloxone is a specific antidote against respiratory depression due to overdosage or as a result of unusual sensitivity to morphine. An appropriate dose of this antagonist should therefore be administered, preferably by the i.v. route. The usual initial i.v. adult dose of naloxone is 0.4 mg or higher. Concomitant efforts at respiratory resuscitation should be carried out. Since the duration of action of morphine, particularly extended release formulations, may exceed that of the antagonist, the patient should be under continued surveillance and doses of the antagonist should be repeated as needed to maintain adequate respiration.

An antagonist should not be administered in the absence of clinically significant respiratory or cardiovascular depression. Oxygen, i.v. fluids, vasopressors and other supportive measures should be used as indicated.

Note: In an individual physically dependent on opioids, the administration of the usual dose of opioid antagonist will precipitate an acute withdrawal syndrome. The severity of this syndrome will depend on the degree of physical dependence and the dose of antagonist administered. The use of opioid antagonists in such individuals should be avoided if possible. If an opioid antagonist must be used to treat serious respiratory depression in the physically dependent patient, the antagonist should be administered with extreme care by using dosage titration, commencing with 10 to 20% of the usual recommended initial dose.

Evacuation of gastric contents may be useful in removing unabsorbed drug, particularly when an extended release formulation has been taken.

Dosage: This product has not been compared to any slow-release morphine preparation on the Canadian market, and therefore is not interchangeable.

Administration and dosing of morphine should be individualized bearing in mind the properties of the drug. In addition, the nature and severity of the pain or pains experienced, and the total condition of the patient must be taken into account. Of special importance is other medication given previously or concurrently.

As with other strong opioid analgesics, use of morphine for the management of persistent pain should be preceded by a thorough assessment of the patient and diagnosis of the specific pain or pains and their causes. Use of opioids for the relief of chronic pain, including cancer pain, all important as it may be, should be only one part of a comprehensive approach to pain control including other treatment modalities or drug therapy, non-drug measures and psychosocial support.

For essential information on the important details of the management of cancer pain, the reader may wish to consult the following resource: Cancer Pain: A Monograph on the Management of Cancer Pain. Health and Welfare Canada.

Initial Adult Dose: Individual dosing requirements vary considerably based on each patient's age, weight, severity of pain, and medical and analgesic history.

The most frequent initial dose is 30 mg every 12 hours.

The capsules may be opened, and the microgranules given mixed with soft food, liquids or by gastric tube or gastrotomy to dysphagic (e.g. E.N.T. cancer) patients who can benefit from the analgesia obtained from an extended release preparation.

Patients over the age of 50 tend to require much lower doses of morphine than the younger age group. In elderly and debilitated patients and those with impaired respiratory function or significantly decreased renal function, the initial dose should be one-half the usual recommended dose.

Patients currently receiving other oral morphine immediate release formulations may be transferred to M-Eslon capsules at the same total daily morphine dosage, equally divided into two 12-hourly M-Eslon doses.

For patients who are receiving an alternate opioid, the "oral morphine equivalent" of the analgesic presently being used should be determined. Having determined the total daily dosage of the present analgesic, Table I can be used to calculate the approximate daily oral morphine dosage that should provide equivalent analgesia. This total daily oral morphine dosage should then be equally divided in two 12 hourly M-Eslon doses.

Table I—M-Eslon

Opioids: Approximate Analgesic Equivalences[a]

Drug	**Equivalent Dose (mg)[b] i.m.**	**oral**
Agonists		
Morphine sulfate	10	20–30[c]
Codeine phosphate	120	200
Hydromorphone (Dilaudid)	2	4
Levorphanol (Levo-Dromoran)	2	4
Oxycodone (Percodan, Percocet)		10–15
Anileridine (Leritine)	25	75
Meperidine (pethidine, Demerol)	75	300
Oxymorphone (Numorphan)	1.5	(Supp 5 mg)
Methadone	10	20
Heroin	5–8	10–15
Agonist-Antagonists		
Pentazocine (Talwin)	60	180
Nalbuphine (Nubain)	10	
Butorphanol	2	

[a] Adapted from Cancer Pain: A Monograph on the Management of Cancer Pain, Minister of Supply and Services Canada, 1984.

[b] Most of this data was derived from single-dose, acute pain studies and should be considered a rough approximation for initial selection of doses when treating chronic cancer pain.

[c] The oral/i.m. potency ratio of 1/3 to 1/2 for morphine is based on clinical experience in chronic pain.

Dose titration is the key to success with morphine therapy. **Proper optimization of doses scaled to the relief of the individual's pain should aim at the regular administration of the lowest dose of morphine which will maintain the patient free of pain at all times.** Dose adjustments should be based on the patient's clinical response. Higher doses may be justified in some patients to cover periods of physical activity.

Because of the extended release properties of M-Eslon capsules, dosage adjustments should generally be separated by 48 hours. If dose increments turn out to be required, they should be proportionately greater at the lower dose level (in terms of percentage of previous dose), than when adjusting a higher dose. The usual recommended dose (every 12 hours)

M-Eslon (cont'd)

increments are 30, 60, 90, 120, 150, 180, 200 mg. Above the 200 mg/dose (400 mg/day) increments should be by 30 to 60 mg/dose.

Morphine sulfate extended release capsules are designed to allow 12-hourly dosing. If "breakthrough" pain repeatedly occurs at the end of a dose interval, it is generally an indication for a dosage increase, not more frequent administration. However, where judged necessary for optimization of drug effects, the product may be administered every 8 hours. More frequent (than every 8 hours) administration is not recommended.

Adjustment or Reduction of Dosage: During the first 2 or 3 days of effective pain relief, the patient may exhibit drowsiness or sleep for prolonged periods. This can be misinterpreted as the effect of excessive analgesic dosing rather than the first sign of relief in a patient exhausted by pain. The dose, therefore, should be maintained for at least 3 days before reduction, provided the sedation is not excessive or associated with unsteadiness and confusional symptoms, and respiratory activity and other vital signs are adequate. If excessive sedation persists, the reason(s) for such an effect must be sought. Some of these are: concomitant sedative medications, hepatic or renal failure, exacerbated respiratory failure, higher doses than tolerated by an older patient, or the patient is actually more severely ill than realized. If it is necessary to reduce the dose, it can be carefully increased again after 3 or 4 days if it is obvious that the pain is not being well controlled.

Following successful relief of severe pain, periodic attempts to reduce the opioid dose should be made. Smaller doses or complete discontinuation of the opioid analgesic may become feasible due to a change in the patient's condition or improved mental state.

Opioid agents do not relieve effectively dysesthetic pain, post-herpetic neuralgia, stabbing pains, activity-related pain, and some forms of headache. This is not to say that patients with advanced cancer suffering from some of these forms of pain should not be given an adequate trial of opiate analgesics, but it may be necessary to refer such patients at an early time for other forms of pain therapy. Pain without nociception does not respond to opioids.

Information for the Patient: See Blue Section—Information for the Patient "M-Eslon".

Supplied: 10 mg: Each #4 hard gelatin capsule, printed with the logo, "M-ESLON" and "10" in black, opaque white cap and body, contains: morphine sulfate 10 mg in the form of extended release microgranules. Nonmedicinal ingredients: dibutyl sebacate, ethylcellulose, gelatin, polyethylene glycol, starch, sucrose, talc and titanium dioxide. Tartrazine-free.

15 mg: Each #4 hard gelatin capsule, printed with the logo, "M-ESLON" and "15" in black, opaque yellow cap and transparent natural body, contains: morphine sulfate 15 mg in the form of extended release microgranules. Nonmedicinal ingredients: dibutyl sebacate, ethylcellulose, FD&C No. 10, gelatin, polyethylene glycol, starch, sucrose, talc and titanium dioxide. Tartrazine-free.

30 mg: Each #4 hard gelatin capsule, printed with the logo, "M-ESLON" and "30" in black, opaque pink cap and transparent natural body contains: morphine sulfate 30 mg in the form of extended release microgranules. Nonmedicinal ingredients: dibutyl sebacate, ethylcellulose, FD&C Red No. 3, gelatin, polyethylene glycol, starch, sucrose, talc and titanium dioxide. Tartrazine-free.

60 mg: Each #3 hard gelatin capsule, printed with the logo, "M-ESLON" and "60" in black, opaque orange cap and transparent natural body, contains: morphine sulfate 60 mg in the form of extended release microgranules. Nonmedicinal ingredients: dibutyl sebacate, ethylcellulose, FD&C Yellow No. 6, gelatin, polyethylene glycol, starch, sucrose, talc and titanium dioxide. Tartrazine-free.

100 mg: Each #2 hard gelatin capsule, printed with the logo, "M-ESLON" and "100" in black, opaque white cap and transparent natural body, contains: morphine sulfate 100 mg in the form of extended release microgranules. Nonmedicinal ingredients: dibutyl sebacate, ethylcellulose, gelatin, polyethylene glycol, starch, sucrose, talc and titanium dioxide. Tartrazine-free.

200 mg: Each #0 hard gelatin capsule, printed with the logo, "M-ESLON" and "200" in black, transparent natural cap and body, contains: morphine sulfate 200 mg in the form of extended release microgranules. Nonmedicinal ingredients: dibutyl sebacate, ethylcellulose, gelatin, polyethylene glycol, starch, sucrose and talc. Tartrazine-free.

Cartons containing blister packs of 20. White, opaque polypropylene bottles of 50 with tamper-evident polyethylene caps. Store at room temperature and protect from excessive heat.

(Shown in Product Recognition Section)

MESTINON® Ⓟ
MESTINON®-SR Ⓟ

ICN

Pyridostigmine Bromide

Antimyasthenic—Cholinergic

Pharmacology: Pyridostigmine is a cholinergic agent which acts primarily by the inhibition of cholinesterase. It enhances cholinergic action by facilitating the transmission of impulses across neuromuscular junctions. It also has a direct cholinomimetic effect on skeletal muscle and possibly on autonomic ganglion cells and neurons of the CNS. Because of its quaternary ammonium structure, moderate doses of pyridostigmine do not cross the blood-brain barrier to produce CNS effects. Extremely high doses, however, produce CNS stimulation followed by CNS depression, in addition to a depolarizing neuromuscular blockade.

Pyridostigmine is an analog of neostigmine. However, it differs from neostigmine in certain clinically significant respects; for example, pyridostigmine is more effectively absorbed from the alimentary tract than is neostigmine; with equipotent doses, pyridostigmine has a slower onset and longer duration of action, and produces fewer gastrointestinal side effects than neostigmine. After oral administration, Mestinon generally has an onset of action of 20 minutes and a duration of action of approximately 6 hours; as for Mestinon-SR, it has an onset of action of 30 to 60 minutes and a duration of action of 6 to 12 hours.

Indications: For the symptomatic treatment of myasthenia gravis. In acute myasthenic crises where difficulty in breathing and swallowing is present, the parenteral form should be used. The patient can be transferred to the oral form as soon as it can be tolerated.

Contraindications: In patients with known hypersensitivy to anticholinesterase agents. Because of the presence of the bromide ion, this product should not be used in patients with a prior history of reaction to bromides. It is also contraindicated in patients with peritonitis or mechanical obstruction of the intestinal or urinary tract.

Warnings: Pyridostigmine should be used with caution in patients with epilepsy, bronchial asthma, bradycardia, recent coronary occlusion, vagotonia, hyperthyroidism, cardiac arrhythmias or peptic ulcer. Large oral doses of the drug should be avoided in patients with megacolon or decreased gastrointestinal motility. In these patients, the drug may accumulate and result in toxicity when gastrointestinal motility is restored.

Precautions: General: Although failure of patients to show clinical improvement may reflect underdosage, it can also be indicative of overdosage. It is important to differentiate between myasthenic crisis and cholinergic crisis caused by overdosage of pyridostigmine. Both conditions result in extreme muscle weakness but require radically different treatment (see Overdose: Symptoms and Treatment).

Information for the Patient: Complete restoration of muscle strength is rare in myasthenia gravis, and patients should be cautioned not to increase their dose, in an attempt to relieve their symptoms, without consulting their physician. The patient should be encouraged to keep a daily record of his or her condition to assist the physician in determining an optimal therapeutic regimen.

Drug Interactions: Atropine antagonizes the muscarinic effects of pyridostigmine and this interaction may be utilized to counteract the effects of pyridostigmine (see Overdose: Symptoms and Treatment).

Pyridostigmine does not antagonize, and in fact may prolong the phase I block of **depolarizing** muscle relaxants such as succinylcholine or decamethonium.

Certain antibiotics, especially neomycin, streptomycin and kanamycin, have a mild but definite nondepolarizing blocking action which may accentuate neuromuscular block. These antibiotics should be used in the myasthenic patient only where definitely indicated, and then careful adjustment should be made of adjunctive anticholinesterase dosage.

Local and some general anesthetics, antiarrhythmic agents and other drugs that interfere with neuromuscular transmission should be used cautiously, if at all, in patients with myasthenia gravis; the dose of pyridostigmine may have to be increased accordingly.

In severe myasthenia gravis, neostigmine has been used in combination with pyridostigmine to provide the benefits of short and long-term activity; because of the possibility of reduced intestinal motility and increased toxicity, this combination should be used only under strict medical supervision.

Carcinogenesis, Mutagenesis and Impairment of Fertility: Carcinogenicity and mutagenicity studies have not been performed with pyridostigmine.

A fertility and general reproductive performance study was performed in rats at dosages of 15 and 40 mg/kg/day. There were no adverse effects on pregnancy rate, average number of implantation sites, average number of embryos per dam, percent resorptions, duration of gestation, litter size, pup viability or pup growth.

Pregnancy: Teratogenic effects: Pregnancy category B: Reproductive studies have been performed in rats at dosages up to 40 mg/kg/day (2 times the maximum recommended human dose; 4.6 times the average recommended dose). These studies have revealed no evidence of impaired fertility or harm to the fetus due to pyridostigmine. There are, however, no adequate and well controlled studies in pregnant women. However, pyridostigmine, like other cholinesterase inhibitors, contains a quaternary ammonium and, therefore, would be expected to cross the placenta only to a limited extent. Because animal reproductive studies are not always predictive of human response, this drug should be used during pregnancy only if clearly needed.

Nonteratogenic effects: Of newborn infants whose mothers have received anticholinesterase drugs for treatment of myasthenia gravis, 10 to 20% were observed to have transient muscular weakness.

Lactation: It is not known whether pyridostigmine is excreted in human milk. Because many drugs are excreted in human milk, and because of the potential for serious adverse reactions from pyridostigmine in nursing infants, a decision should be made whether to discontinue nursing or to discontinue the drug, taking into account the importance of the drug to the mother.

Children: See Dosage.

Adverse Effects: Side effects are generally due to an exaggeration of pharmacological effects of which increased salivation and fasciculation are the most common. Abdominal cramps and diarrhea may also occur.

The following additional adverse reactions have been reported following the use of pyridostigmine: Respiratory: increased bronchial secretions.

Gastrointestinal: nausea, vomiting, increased peristalsis.

Musculoskeletal: muscle cramps.

Dermatologic: urticaria, rash.

Miscellaneous: miosis, diaphoresis, weakness, allergic reactions.

Overdose: Symptoms and Treatment: As is true of all anticholinesterase agents, overdosage of pyridostigmine can cause cholinergic crisis, which is characterized by increasing muscle weakness and which, through involvement of the muscles of respiration, may result in death. Myasthenic crisis, due to an increase in the severity of the disease, is also accompanied by extreme muscle weakness, and thus may be difficult to distinguish from cholinergic crisis on a symptomatic basis. However, such differentiation is extremely important, because increases in the dose of pyridostigmine or other drugs in this class in the presence of cholinergic crisis or of a refractory or "insensitive" state could have grave consequences. The two types of crises may be differentiated by the use of edrophonium chloride as well as by clinical judgment.

Treatment of the two conditions differs radically. Whereas the presence of **myasthenic crisis** requires more intensive anticholinesterase therapy, **cholinergic crisis** calls for the prompt **withdrawal** of all drugs of this type. The immediate use of atropine in cholinergic crisis is also recommended. A syringe containing 1 mg of atropine sulfate should be immediately available to be given in aliquots i.v. to counteract severe cholinergic reactions.

Atropine also may be used to abolish or minimize gastrointestinal side effects or other muscarinic reactions; but such use, by masking signs of overdosage, can lead to inadvertent induction of cholinergic crisis.

Dosage: The dosage, route and frequency of administration depend on the requirements and clinical response of the patients. The dosage schedule should be adjusted for each patient and changed as the need arises. Dosage requirements in patients with myasthenia gravis may vary from day to day, according to remissions and exacerbations of the disease and the physical and emotional stress suffered by the patient. Larger portions of the label daily dose may be given at times when the patient is more prone to fatigue (afternoon, mealtimes, etc.).

In the initial treatment of myasthenia gravis, oral pyridostigmine should be started at a dosage smaller than that required to produce maximum strength, and daily dosage gradually increased at intervals of 48 hours or more. Changes in oral dosage may take several days to show results. When a further increase in dosage produces no corresponding increase in muscle strength, dosage should be reduced to the previous level so that the patient receives the smallest dose necessary to produce maximum strength.

Note: For information on a diagnostic test for myasthenia gravis, and for the evaluation and stabilization of anticholinesterase therapy, see product monograph on Tensilon.

The immediate effect of a Mestinon-SR 180 mg tablet is about equal to that of a 60 mg conventional tablet; however, the duration of drug action, although varying in individual patients, averages 2½ times that of a 60 mg dose. One to three 180 mg tablets, once or twice daily (180 mg to 1.08 g a day), will usually be sufficient to control symptoms; however, the needs of individual patients may vary markedly from this average. For optimal control, it may be necessary to use conventional tablets or syrup in conjunction with Mestinon-SR therapy. Mestinon-SR tablets are particularly useful for bedtime administration in patients who are very weak upon awakening.

Mestinon and Mestinon-SR tablets should be swallowed whole. Do not crush. However, in certain cases, Mestinon and Mestinon-SR tablets, can be cut in half; but Mestinon-SR tablets should not be crushed or quartered since this would destroy too much of the sustained release matrix.

Due to the slow-release mechanism of the tablet, the matrix may pass through the intestinal system intact. However, it should be noted that the medicinal ingredient has been released through the gastrointestinal tract over an 8 to 12 hour passing time and only the matrix is rejected.

Supplied: Mestinon: Each white, flat compressed tablet, cross-scored on one side and embossed MESTINON 60-ICN on the other, contains: pyridostigmine bromide 60 mg. Nonmedicinal ingredients: lactose, silicone dioxide and stearic acid. Energy: 4.6 kJ (1.1 kcal). Gluten-, paraben-, sodium-, sulfite- and tartrazine-free. Bottles of 100.

Mestinon-SR: Each capsule-shaped, flattened on 2 sides with a single score on 1 face, light straw colored tablet, embossed ICN M180, contains: pyridostigmine bromide 180 mg. Nonmedicinal ingredients: calcium phosphate, carnauba wax, isopropyl alcohol and magnesium stearate. Energy: 2.3 kJ (0.5 kcal). Gluten-, lactose-, paraben-, sodium-, sulfite- and tartrazine-free. Bottles of 30.

Store in a dry place between 15 and 30°C, in a well-closed container with the desiccant enclosed.

Note: Because of the hygroscopic nature of the Mestinon and Mestinon-SR tablets, mottling may occur. This does not affect their efficacy.

Reviewed 1997

METAMUCIL® Preparations

Procter & Gamble

Psyllium Hydrophilic Mucilloid

Laxative—Fibre Supplement

Indications: The relief of chronic, atonic, spastic and rectal constipation and for the constipation accompanying pregnancy, convalescence and advanced age. As adjunctive therapy in the constipation of mucous and ulcerative colitis and diverticulitis. To provide supplementary dietary fibre in special dietary programs. Also useful in the management of hemorrhoids and following anorectal surgery.

Contraindications: Presence of nausea, vomiting, fever, abdominal pain or symptoms of an acute abdomen, intestinal obstruction, fecal impaction, undiagnosed rectal bleeding or dysphagia. The Instant Mix preparation is contraindicated in patients who must severely restrict their dietary sodium intake, including patients with congestive heart failure.

Precautions: Sensitization to psyllium has occurred in some individuals. Therefore, Metamucil may cause an allergic reaction in people sensitive to inhaled or ingested psyllium powder.

Do not take a laxative within 2 hours of taking any other medicine.

Taking this product without adequate fluid may cause it to swell and block the throat or esophagus and cause choking. Do not take Metamucil if you have difficulty swallowing. If you have chest pain, vomiting or difficulty in swallowing or breathing after taking the product, seek immediate medical attention.

Notice to Health Care Professionals: To minimize the potential for allergic reaction, health care professionals who frequently dispense powdered psyllium products should avoid inhaling airborne dust while dispensing these products.

Handling and Dispensing: To minimize generating airborne dust, spoon the product from the canister into a glass according to label directions

Powder: Original Texture, Unflavored: Each dose of 7 g contains hydrous dextrose 51% (3.6 g total) which provides approximately 25 calories. Smooth Texture Orange: Each dose of 12.24 g contains: sucrose 68% (8.3 g) which provides approximately 50 calories. Contains no added sodium (<5 mg/dose).

Powder: Sugar-Free: Unflavored Smooth Texture: Each dose of 5.8 g contains: sodium <5 g and provides 20 calories. Also contains magnesium sulfate. Sugar-free. Smooth Texture Orange: Each dose of 5.8 g contains: no sugar or added sodium (<5 mg/dose), and provides 20 calories. Contains phenylalanine, 25 mg/dose.

Keep this medication out of reach of children.

Dosage: Because of its gradual mode of action, therapy should be taken for 2 to 3 days to become fully effective. Do not interrupt dosage during this time.

Metamucil may cause temporary gastrointestinal distress (cramping, flatulence, bloating). To minimize the potential for this effect, the dosage level may be gradually increased up to the daily recommended dose during the first 1 to 2 weeks.

Adults: 1 rounded teaspoonful of Sugar-Free Smooth Texture Orange Powder or Sugar-Free Smooth Texture Unflavored Powder or Original Texture Unflavored Powder; 1 rounded tablespoon for Smooth Texture Orange Powder (sugared) in 240 mL of cool liquid. An additional glass of liquid by itself is recommended. The Powder or Sugar-Free Powder can also be mixed with other suitable liquids, e.g., fruit juice. Drink without delay when mixed.

This dose may be taken 1 to 3 times daily depending on the condition being treated, its severity and individual response. Children: 6 years of age and over: one half the adult dose 1 to 3 times/day, the dose being adjusted for patient size and need. Each dose is taken in 240 mL or more of water or other suitable liquids.

Supplied: Powder, Smooth Texture and Sugar-Free Powder and Original Texture, Unflavored, contains: dietary fibre (natural and gluten-free) derived from the refined husk of the psyllium seed (Plantago ovata).

Powder: Original Texture, Unflavored: Each rounded teaspoonful of buff colored, unflavored powder (approximately 7 g) contains: psyllium hydrophilic mucilloid 3.4 g. Nonmedicinal ingredients: sucrose (3.56 g). Sodium: <1 mmol (5 mg)/dose. Bottles of 300, 530 and 800 g.

Smooth Texture Orange: Each rounded tablespoon (12.24 g) of fine orange powder contains: psyllium hydrophilic mucilloid 3.4 g. Nonmedicinal ingredients: citric acid, D&C Yellow #10, FD&C Yellow #6, orange flavor and sucrose. Sucrose: 8.3 g. Bottles of 65 doses (800 g).

Powder: Sugar-Free: Smooth Texture Unflavored: Each rounded teaspoonful (5.4 g) of smooth, beige powder contains: psyllium hydrophilic mucilloid 3.4 g. Nonmedicinal ingredients: citric acid and maltodextrin. Sodium: <1 mmol (5 mg)/dose. Bottles of 45 doses (275 g).

Smooth Texture Orange: Each rounded teaspoonful (5.8 g) of fine orange powder contains: psyllium hydrophilic mucilloid 3.4 g. Nonmedicinal ingredients: aspartame, citric acid, FD&C Yellow #6, orange flavor and maltodextrin. Bottles of 114 doses (660 g), 65 doses (410 g) and 45 doses (275 g) and boxes of 30 single dose packets.

Reviewed 1998

METANDREN® ♦

Novartis Pharmaceuticals

Methyltestosterone

Oral Androgen

Indications: In the male: replacement therapy in hypogonadism, eunuchoidism, the climacteric, and other conditions due to loss, atrophy or hypofunction of the testes. In the female: palliation of androgen-responsive, advancing, inoperable breast cancer in women who are more than 1 year, but less than 5 years, postmenopausal or who have been proven to have a hormone dependent tumor, as shown by previous beneficial response to castration.

Contraindications: Severe liver damage, cardiac or renal decompensation, hypercalcemia, prepuberal males, pregnancy, and in male patients with suspected or proven carcinoma of the prostate or breast. Do not give to elderly, asthenic males who may react adversely to overstimulation by androgens.

Precautions: Alterations in liver function tests, such as increases in bromsulphalein retention and AST levels, and rarely jaundice, have been reported with methyltestosterone. These changes appear to be directly related to the dose of the drug. Therefore, in the presence of any changes in liver function tests, reduce dosage or discontinue the drug. Use cautiously in young boys to avoid possible premature epiphyseal closure or precocious sexual development. Since androgens can produce virilization in females, watch for hoarseness or deepening of the voice, acne, hirsutism, enlarged clitoris, stimulation of libido, and menstrual irregularities. Androgens may cause retention of sodium and water, occasionally producing edema. Therefore, use cautiously in patients with cardiac or renal disease. Hypercalcemia may occur, particularly in immobilized patients; withdraw the drug if this occurs.

Adverse Effects: In addition to reactions listed under Precautions, hypersensitivity and gynecomastia may occur rarely. Prolonged administration or excessive dosage may cause inhibition of testicular function in the male, resulting in oligospermia and decrease in ejaculatory volume. If priapism occurs, withdraw therapy temporarily.

There have been rare reports of hepatocellular carcinoma, particularly in association with long-term therapy, in patients receiving methyltestosterone or other androgenic anabolic steroids.

Dosage: Since patients vary widely in requirements, dosage must be strictly individualized. Daily requirements are best administered in divided doses. Table I is suggested as a guide.

Table I—Metandren

Dosage	Tablets
In the male:	
Hypogonadism Maintenance	10 to 40 mg daily
Eunuchoidism Maintenance	10 to 40 mg daily
In the female:	
Carcinoma of the breast	100 mg twice daily for 2 to 4 weeks then halved if response is evident

Supplied: 10 mg: Each white, round, biconvex, scored tablet, fully bisected between J and L, imprinted CIBA on one side and JL on the other, contains: methyltestosterone 10 mg. Nonmedicinal ingredients: cornstarch, gelatin, lactose, magnesium stearate and talc. Energy: 3.7 kJ (0.89 kcal). Alcohol-, bisulfite-, gluten-, parabens-, sodium- and tartrazine-free. Bottles of 100.

25 mg: Each white, round, biconvex, scored tablet, fully bisected between K and M, imprinted CIBA on one side and KM on the other, contains: methyltestosterone 25 mg. Nonmedicinal ingredients: cornstarch, gelatin, lactose, magnesium stearate and talc. Energy: 3.5 kJ (0.83 kcal). Alcohol-, bisulfite-, gluten-, parabens-, sodium- and tartrazine-free. Bottles of 100.

METED® Shampoo

Medicis

Salicylic Acid—Sulfur

Antipsoriatic—Antiseborrheic

Supplied: Each bottle contains: salicylic acid 3% and sulfur 5%. Plastic bottles of 120 mL.

METFORMIN Ⓟ

BDH

Metformin HCl

Oral Antihyperglycemic Agent

Supplied: Each white, convex tablet, marked "MF" on one side and "G" on the other, contains: metformin HCl 500 mg. Nonmedicinal ingredients: magnesium stearate and povidone. Bottles of 100 and 500. Store between 15 and 30°C.

METHOTREXATE Ⓟ

Wyeth-Ayerst

Methotrexate Sodium

Antimetabolite

> Caution: Methotrexate should be used only by physicians whose knowledge and experience includes the use of antimetabolite therapy.

Pharmacology: Methotrexate is a folate antagonist.

Methotrexate inhibits dihydrofolate reductase (DHFR), the enzyme that reduces folic acid to tetrahydrofolic acid. Tetrahydrofolate must be regenerated via the DHFR-catalyzed reaction in order to maintain the intracellular pool of tetrahydrofolate one-carbon derivatives for both thymidylate and purine nucleotide biosynthesis. The inhibition of DHFR by folate antagonists (methotrexate) results in a deficiency in the cellular pools of thymidylate and purines and thus in a decrease in nucleic acid synthesis. Therefore, methotrexate interferes with DNA synthesis, repair, and cellular replication.

Methotrexate is most active against rapidly multiplying cells, because its cytotoxic effects occur primarily during the S phase of the cell cycle. Since cellular proliferation in malignant tissues is greater than in most normal tissues, methotrexate may impair malignant growth without irreversible damage to normal tissues. As a result, actively proliferating tissues such as malignant cells, bone marrow, fetal cells, buccal and intestinal mucosa, and cells of the urinary bladder are in general more sensitive to DHFR inhibition effects of methotrexate.

The cytotoxicity of methotrexate results from 3 important actions: inhibition of DHFR, inhibition of thymidylate synthase, and alteration of the transport of reduced folates. The affinity of DHFR to methotrexate is far greater than its affinity for folic acid or dihydrofolic acid, therefore, large doses of folic acid given simultaneously will not reverse the effects of methotrexate. However, leucovorin calcium, a derivative of tetrahydrofolic acid may block the effects of methotrexate if given shortly after the antineoplastic agent. Methotrexate in high doses, followed by leucovorin rescue, is used as a part of the treatment of patients with nonmetastatic osteosarcoma.

The original rationale for high dose methotrexate therapy was based on the concept of selective rescue of normal tissues by leucovorin. More recent evidence suggests that high dose methotrexate may also overcome methotrexate resistance caused by impaired active transport, decreased affinity of dihydrofolic acid reductase for methotrexate, increased levels of dihydrofolic acid reductase resulting from gene amplification, or decreased polyglutamation of methotrexate. The actual mechanism of action is unknown.

Methotrexate has immunosuppressive activity, this may be a result of inhibition of lymphocyte multiplication. The mechanisms of action in the management of rheumatoid arthritis of the drug is not known, although suggested mechanisms have included immunosuppressive and/or anti-inflammatory effects.

In psoriasis, the rate of production of epithelial cells in the skin is greatly increased over normal skin. This differential in proliferation rates is the basis for the use of methotrexate to control the psoriatic process.

Orally administered methotrexate is absorbed rapidly in most, but not all patients and reaches peak serum levels in 1 to 4 hours. Methotrexate is generally completely absorbed following parenteral administration, and after i.m. injection peak serum concentrations occur in 30 to 60 minutes.

The terminal half-life reported for methotrexate is approximately 3 to 10 hours for patients receiving treatment for psoriasis, or rheumatoid arthritis or low dose antineoplastic therapy (less than 30 mg/m²). For patients receiving high doses of methotrexate, the terminal half-life is 8 to 15 hours.

Excretion of single daily doses occurs through the kidneys in amounts form 80 to 90% within 24 hours. Repeated doses daily result in more sustained serum levels and some retention of methotrexate over each 24-hour period, which may result in accumulation of the drug within the tissues. The liver cells appear to retain certain amounts of the drug for prolonged periods even after a single therapeutic dose. Methotrexate is retained in the presence of impaired renal function and may increase rapidly in the serum and in the tissue cells under such conditions. Methotrexate does not penetrate the blood cerebrospinal fluid barrier in therapeutic amounts when given orally or parenterally. High concentrations of the drug, when needed, may be attained by direct intrathecal administration.

Methotrexate has been detected in human breast milk. The highest breast milk to plasma concentration ratio reached was 0.08:1.

Indications: Two major fields of indication exists for methotrexate: neoplastic diseases and Disease Modifying Antirheumatic Drug (DMARD).

Neoplastic Diseases: choriocarcinoma: methotrexate—as single chemotherapy or in combination with other drugs; intermediate-, or high-grade non-Hodgkin's Lymphoma (NHL) as part of ProMACE-CytaBOM, ProMACE-MOPP, Magrath protocols; breast Ca-: as part of CMF; acute lymphoblastic leukemia (ALL)- as maintenance therapy; head and neck Ca- in combination with other chemotherapies(CT); Gastric Ca- palliative combination chemotherapy; metastasis of unknown primary—as palliative combination chemotherapy; osteogenic sarcoma (adjuvant)—high-dose methotrexate with Leucovorin Rescue (HDMTX-LV); bladder Ca (advanced)—as part of M-VAC; leptomeningeal spread of malignancies (carcinomatosis/leukemia/lymphoma) as a single chemotherapy or alternating with Ara-C; Burkitt's lymphoma; advanced stages of childhood lymphoma (III and IV, St. Jude's Children's Research Hospital Staging System) and advanced cases of mycosis fungoides.

Disease Modifying Antirheumatic Drug (DMARD): The use of MTX as DMARD in the following diseases where standard therapeutic interventions fail: severe disabling psoriasis/psoriatic arthritis; severe disabling rheumatoid arthritis (RA) and severe, disabling seronegative arthritides.

In the treatment of psoriasis, methotrexate should be restricted to severe recalcitrant, disabling psoriasis, which is not adequately responsive to other forms of therapy, but only when the diagnosis has been established after dermatologic consultation.

Contraindications: *Pregnancy:* Methotrexate can cause fetal death or teratogenic effects when administered to a pregnant woman. Methotrexate is contraindicated in pregnant patients with psoriasis or rheumatoid arthritis and should be used in the treatment of neoplastic diseases only when the potential benefit outweighs the risk to the fetus. Women of childbearing potential should not be started on methotrexate until pregnancy is excluded and should be fully counselled on the serious risk to the fetus (see Precautions) should they become pregnant while undergoing treatment. Pregnancy should be avoided if either partner is receiving methotrexate; during and for a minimum of 3 months after therapy for male patients, and during and for at least 1 ovulatory cycle after therapy for female patients (see Warnings).

Lactation: Because of the potential for serious adverse reactions from methotrexate in breast-fed infants, it is contraindicated in nursing mothers.

Patients with psoriasis or rheumatoid arthritis with alcoholism, alcoholic liver disease or other chronic liver disease should not receive methotrexate.

Patients with psoriasis or rheumatoid arthritis who have overt or laboratory evidence of immunodeficiency syndromes should not receive methotrexate.

Patients with psoriasis or rheumatoid arthritis who have preexisting blood dyscrasias, such as bone marrow hypoplasia, leukopenia, thrombocytopenia or significant anemia, should not receive methotrexate.

Patients with a known hypersensitivity to methotrexate should not receive the drug.

Warnings:

> **Deaths have been reported with the use of methotrexate in the treatment of malignancy, psoriasis, and rheumatoid arthritis. The use of methotrexate high-dose regimens recommended for osteosarcoma requires meticulous care (see Dosage). High-dosage regimens for other neoplastic diseases are investigational and a therapeutic advantage has not been established.**
>
> **Because of the possibility of serious toxic reactions the patient should be informed by the physician of the risks involved and should be under a physician's constant supervision.**
>
> *Pregnancy:* **Methotrexate has been reported to cause fetal death and/or congenital anomalies. Therefore, it is not recommended for women of childbearing potential unless there is clear medical evidence that the benefits can be expected to outweigh the considered risks. Pregnant patients with psoriasis or rheumatoid arthritis should not receive methotrexate (see Contraindications).**
>
> **Methotrexate formulations and diluents containing preservatives must not be used for intrathecal or high dose methotrexate therapy.**

Malignant lymphomas, which may regress following withdrawal of methotrexate, may occur in patients receiving low-dose methotrexate and, thus, may not require cytotoxic treatment. Discontinue methotrexate first and, if the lymphoma does not regress, appropriate treatment should be instituted.

Like other cytotoxic drugs, methotrexate may induce "tumor lysis syndrome" in patients with rapidly growing tumors. Appropriate supportive and pharmacologic measures may prevent or alleviate this complication.

Periodic monitoring for toxicity, including CBC with differential and platelet counts, and liver and renal function tests is a mandatory part of methotrexate therapy. Liver biopsies prior to MTX therapy are not indicated routinely. Liver function tests (LFTs) should be determined prior to the initiation of therapy with MTX and they should be monitored regularly throughout therapy. Patients at increased risk for impaired methotrexate elimination (e.g., renal dysfunction, pleural effusions, or ascites) should be monitored more frequently (see Precautions).

Methotrexate therapy in patients with impaired renal function should be undertaken with extreme caution, and at reduced dosages, because renal dysfunction will prolong methotrexate elimination.

Methotrexate exits slowly from third-space compartments (e.g., pleural effusions or ascites). This results in a prolonged terminal plasma half-life and unexpected toxicity. In patients with significant third-space accumulations, it is advisable to evacuate the fluid before treatment and to monitor plasma methotrexate levels.

Methotrexate causes hepatotoxicity, fibrosis and cirrhosis, but generally only after prolonged use. Acutely, liver enzyme elevations are frequently seen, these are usually transient and asymptomatic, and also do not appear predictive of subsequent hepatic disease. Liver biopsy after sustained use often shows histologic changes, and fibrosis and cirrhosis have been reported; these latter lesions often are not preceded by symptoms or abnormal liver function tests (see Precautions).

Methotrexate-induced lung disease is a potentially dangerous lesion, which may occur acutely at any time during therapy and which has been reported at doses as low as 7.5 mg/week. It is not always fully reversible. Pulmonary symptoms (especially a dry, nonproductive cough) may require interruption of treatment and careful investigation.

Methotrexate should be used with caution in patients with impaired bone marrow function and previous or concomitant wide field radiotherapy. Methotrexate may produce marked bone marrow depression, with resultant anemia, leukopenia, and/or thrombocytopenia.

Diarrhea and ulcerative stomatitis require interruption of therapy; otherwise, hemorrhagic enteritis and death from intestinal perforation may occur.

Unexpectedly severe (sometimes fatal) marrow suppression and gastrointestinal toxicity have been reported with concomitant administration of methotrexate (usually in high dosage) along with some nonsteroidal anti-inflammatory drugs (NSAIDs) (see Precautions, Drug Interactions).

Bone marrow and mucosal toxicity of methotrexate depend on: i) dose and ii) duration of exposure of high levels ($>2\times10^{-8}$ mmol/L) (0.02 micromolar) of MTX. Since the critical time factor has been defined for these organs as being 42 hours in humans, this has the following implications: when high doses of methotrexate are employed (>1 g/m^2) drug levels in serum should be monitored; when drug levels exceeding (2×10^{-8} mmol/L) (0.02 micromolar) the above for >42 hours may forecast significant toxicity; when toxicity can be minimized by appropriate administration of Leucovorin calcium; when high-dose MTX (HDMTX) is employed it is imperative to alkalinize the urine in order to pevent crystallization of methotrexate and its 7-hydroxy metabolite in the urine, which may lead to acute renal failure.

Severe, occasionally fatal, skin reactions have been reported following single or multiple doses of methotrexate. Reactions have occurred within days of oral i.m., i.v., or intrathecal methotrexate administration. Recovery has been reported with discontinuation of therapy (see Precautions, Organ System Toxicity, Skin).

Potentially fatal opportunistic infections, especially P. carinii pneumonia, may occur with methotrexate therapy.

Precautions: General: Methotrexate has the potential for serious toxicity (see boxed Warnings). Toxic effects may be related in frequency and severity to dose or frequency of administration but have been seen at all doses. Because they can occur at any time during therapy, it is necessary to follow patients on methotrexate closely. Most adverse reactions are reversible if detected early. When such reactions do occur, the drug should be reduced in dosage or discontinued and appropriate corrective measures should be taken. If necessary, this could include the use of leucovorin calcium (see Overdose: Symptoms and Treatment). If methotrexate therapy is reinstituted, it should be carried out with caution, with adequate consideration of further need for the drug and with increased alertness as to possible recurrence of toxicity.

Geriatrics: The clinical pharmacology of methotrexate has not been well studied in older individuals. Due to diminished hepatic and renal function as well as decreased folate stores in this population, relatively low doses should be considered, and these patients should be closely monitored for early signs of toxicity.

Children: Safety and effectiveness in children have not been established, other than in cancer chemotherapy.

Pregnancy: See Contraindications.

Carcinogenesis, Mutagenesis and Impairment of Fertility: No controlled human data exist regarding the risk of neoplasia with methotrexate. Methotrexate has been evaluated in a number of animal studies for carcinogenic potential with inconclusive results. Although there is evidence that methotrexate causes chromosomal damage to animal somatic cells and human bone marrow cells, the clinical significance remains uncertain. Assessment of the carcinogenic potential of methotrexate is complicated by conflicting evidence of an increased risk of certain tumors in rheumatoid arthritis. Benefit should be weighed against this potential risk before using methotrexate alone or in combination with other drugs, especially in children or young adults. Methotrexate causes embryotoxicity, abortion, and fetal defects in humans. It has also been reported to cause impairment of fertility, oligospermia and menstrual dysfunction in humans, during and for a short period after cessation of therapy.

Lactation: See Contraindications.

Patients with Special Diseases and Conditions (Organ System Toxicity): Gastrointestinal: If vomiting, diarrhea, or stomatitis occur, which may result in dehydration, methotrexate should be discontinued until recovery occurs. Methotrexate should be used with extreme caution in the presence of peptic ulcer disease or ulcerative colitis.

Hematologic: Methotrexate can suppress hematopoiesis and cause anemia, leukopenia, and/or thrombocytopenia. In patients with malignancy and pre-existing hematopoietic impairment, the drug should be used with caution, if at all. In controlled clinical trials in rheumatoid arthritis (n=128), leukopenia (WBC $<3\,000$/mm^3) was seen in 2 patients, thrombocytopenia (platelets $<1\,000\,000$/mm^3) in 6 patients, and pancytopenia in 2 patients.

In psoriasis and rheumatoid arthritis, methotrexate should be stopped immediately if there is a significant drop in blood counts. In the treatment of neoplastic diseases, methotrexate should be continued only if the potential benefit warrants the risk of severe myelosuppression. Patients with profound granulocytopenia and fever should be evaluated immediately and usually require parenteral broad-specturm antibiotic therapy.

Hepatic: Methotrexate has the potential for acute (elevated transaminases) and chronic (fibrosis and cirrhosis) hepatotoxicity. Chronic toxicity is potentially fatal; it generally has occurred after prolonged use (generally 2 years or more) and after a total dose of at least 1.5 g. In studies in psoriatic patients, hepatotoxicity appeared to be a function of total cumulative dose and appeared to be enhanced by alcoholism, obesity, diabetes and advanced age. An accurate incidence rate has not been determined; the rate of progression and reversibility of lesions is not known. Special caution is indicated in the presence of pre-existing liver damage or impaired hepatic function.

Liver function tests, including serum albumin, should be performed periodically prior to dosing but are often normal in the face of developing fibrosis or cirrhosis. These lesions may be detectable only by biopsy.

In psoriasis, the usual recommendation is to obtain a liver biopsy at a total cumulative dose of 1.5 g. Moderate fibrosis or any cirrhosis normally leads to discontinuation of the drug; mild fibrosis normally suggests a repeat biopsy in 6 months. Milder histologic findings such as fatty change and low grade portal inflammation are relatively common pretherapy. Although these mild changes are usually not a reason to avoid or discontinue methotrexate therapy, the drug should be used with caution.

Clinical experience with liver disease in rheumatoid arthritis is limited, but the same risk factors would be anticipated. Liver function tests are also usually not reliable predictors of histological changes in this population.

When to perform a liver biopsy in rheumatoid arthritis patients has not been established, either in terms of cumulative methotrexate dose or duration of therapy. There is a combined reported experience in 217 rheumatoid arthritis patients with liver biopsies both before and during treatment (after a cumulative dose of at least 1 500 mg) and in 714 patients with a biopsy only during treatment. There are 64 (7%) cases of fibrosis and 1 (0.1%) case of cirrhosis. Of the 64 cases of fibrosis, 60 were deemed mild. The reticulin stain is more sensitive for early fibrosis and its use may increase these figures. It is unknown whether even longer use will increase these risks.

Infection or Immunologic States: Methotrexate should be used with extreme caution in the presence of active infection, and is usually contraindicated in patients with overt or laboratory evidence of immunodeficiency syndromes. Immunization may be ineffective when given during methotrexate therapy. Immunization with live virus vaccines is generally not recommended. There have been reports of disseminated vaccinia infections after smallpox immunization in patients receiving methotrexate therapy. Hypogammaglobulinemia has been reported rarely.

Potentially fatal opportunistic infections, especially Pneumocystis carinii pneumonia, may occur with methotrexate therapy. When a patient presents with pulmonary symptoms, the possibility of Pneumocystis carinii should be considered.

Neurologic: There have been reports of leukoencephalopathy following i.v. administration of methotrexate to patients who have had craniospinal irradiation. Serious neurotoxicity, frequently manifested as generalized or focal seizures, has been reported with unexpectedly increased frequency among pediatric patients with acute lymphoblastic leukemia who were treated with intermediate-dose i.v. methotrexate (1 g/m^2). Symptomatic patients were commonly noted to have leukoencephalopathy and/or microangiopathic calcifications on diagnostic imaging studies. Chronic leukoencephalopathy has also been reported in patients with osteosarcoma who received repeated doses of high-dose methotrexate with leucovorin rescue even without cranial irradiation. Discontinuation of methotrexate does not always result in complete recovery.

A transient acute neurologic syndrome has been observed in patients treated with high-dosage regimens. Manifestations of this neurologic disorder may include behavioral abnormalities, focal sensorimotor signs and abnormal reflexes. The exact cause is unknown.

After the intrathecal use of methotrexate, the CNS toxicity which may occur can be classified as follows: chemical arachnoiditis manifested by such symptoms as headache, back pain, nuchal rigidity, and fever; paresis, usually transient, manifested by paraplegia associated with involvement with one or more spinal nerve roots; leukoencephalopathy manifested by confusion, irritability, somnolence, ataxia, dementia, and occasionally major convulsions.

Pulmonary: Pulmonary symptoms (especially a dry nonproductive cough) or a nonspecific pneumonitis occurring during methotrexate therapy may be indicative of a potentially dangerous lesion and require interruption of treatment and careful investigation. Although clinically variable, the typical patient with methotrexate induced lung disease presents with fever, cough, dyspnea, hypoxemia, and an infiltrate on chest x-ray; infection needs to be excluded. This lesion can occur at all dosages.

Renal: High doses of methotrexate used in the treatment of osteosarcoma may cause renal damage leading to acute renal failure. Nephrotoxicity is due primarily to the precipitation of methotrexate and 7-hydroxymethotrexate in the renal tubules. Close attention to renal function including adequate hydration, urine alkalinization and measurement of serum methotrexate and creatinine levels are essential for safe administration.

Skin: Severe, occasionally fatal, dermatologic reactions, including toxic epidermal necrolysis, Stevens-Johnson syndrome, exfoliative dermatitis, skin necrosis, and erythema multiforme, have been reported in children and adults, within days of oral, i.m., i.v., or intrathecal methotrexate administration. Reactions were noted after single or multiple, low, intermediate or high doses of methotrexate in patients with neoplastic and non-neoplastic diseases.

Other Precautions: Methotrexate should be used with extreme caution in the presence of debility.

Lesions of psoriasis may be aggravated by concomitant exposure to ultraviolet radiation. Radiation dermatitis and sunburn may be "recalled" by the use of methotrexate.

<u>*Drug Interactions:*</u> NSAIDs should not be administered prior to or concomitantly with the high doses of methotrexate used in the treatment of osteosarcoma. Concomitant administration of some NSAIDs with high-dose methotrexate therapy has been reported to elevate and prolong serum methotrexate levels, resulting in deaths from severe hematologic and gastrointestinal toxicity.

Caution should be used when NSAIDs and salicylates are administered concomitantly with lower doses of methotrexate. These drugs have been reported to reduce the tubular secretion of methotrexate thereby enhancing its toxicity.

Despite the potential interactions, studies of methotrexate in patients with rheumatoid arthritis have usually included concurrent use of constant dosage regimens of NSAIDs, without apparent problems. It should be appreciated however, that the doses used in rheumatoid arthritis (7.5 to 15 mg/week) are somewhat lower than those used in psoriasis and that larger doses could lead to unexpected toxicity.

Methotrexate is partially bound to serum albumin, and toxicity may be increased because of displacement by certain drugs, such as salicylates, phenylbutazone, phenytoin, and sulfonamides. Renal tubular transport is also diminished by probenecid; use of methotrexate with this drug should be carefully monitored.

In the treatment of patients with osteosarcoma, caution must be exercised if high-dose methotrexate is administered in combination with a potentially nephrotoxic chemotherapeutic agent (e.g., cisplatin). Methotrexate clearance is decreased by cisplatinum.

Although not documented, other nephrotoxic drugs such as aminoglycosides, amphotericin B, cyclosporin could theoretically increase methotrexate toxicity by decreasing its elimination.

Oral antibiotics such as tetracycline, chloramphenicol, and nonabsorbable broad-spectrum antibiotics, may decrease intestinal absorption of methotrexate or interfere with the enterohepatic circulation by inhibiting bowel flora and suppressing metabolism of the drug by bacteria. For example: neomycin, polymyxin B, nystatin, vancomycin **decrease** methotrexate absorption, whereas kanamycin **increases** methotrexate absorption.

Trimethoprim/sulfamethoxazole has been reported rarely to increase bone marrow suppression in patients receiving methotrexate, probably by an additive antifolate effect.

Vitamin preparations containing folic acid or its derivatives may decrease responses to systemically administered methotrexate. Preliminary animal and human studies have shown that small quantities of i.v. administered leucovorin enter the CSF primarily as 5-methyltetrahydrofolate and, in humans, remain 1 to 3 orders of magnitude lower than the usual methotrexate concentrations following intrathecal administration. However, high doses of leucovorin may reduce the efficacy of intrathecally administered methotrexate. Folate deficiency states may increase methotrexate toxicity.

Laboratory Tests: Patients undergoing methotrexate therapy should be closely monitored so that toxic effects are detected promptly. Baseline assessment should include a complete blood count with differential and platelet counts, hepatic enzymes, renal function tests, and a chest x-ray. During therapy of rheumatoid arthritis and psoriasis, monitoring of these parameters is recommended: hematology at least monthly, and liver and renal function every 1 to 3 months. More frequent monitoring is usually indicated during antineoplastic therapy. During initial or changing doses, or during periods of increased risk or elevated methotrexate blood levels (e.g., dehydration), more frequent monitoring may also be indicated.

Methotrexate (cont'd)

A relationship between abnormal liver function tests and fibrosis or cirrhosis of the liver has not been established. Transient liver function test abnormalities are observed frequently after methotrexate administration and are usually not cause for modification of methotrexate therapy. Transient liver function test abnormalities are observed frequently after methotrexate administration and are usally not cause for modification of methotrexate therapy. Persistent liver function test abnormalities just prior to dosing and/or depression of serum albumin may be indicators of serious liver toxicity and require evaluation.

Pulmonary function tests may be useful if methotrexate-induced lung disease is suspected, especially if baseline measurements are available.

Information for Patients: Patients should be informed of the early signs and symptoms of toxicity, of the need to see their physician promptly if they occur, and the need for close follow-up, including periodic laboratory tests to monitor toxicity.

Both the physician and pharmacist should emphasize to the patient that the recommended dose is taken weekly in rheumatoid arthritis and psoriasis, and that mistaken daily use of the recommended dose has led to fatal toxicity.

Patients should be informed of the potential benefit and risk in the use of methotrexate. The risk of effects on reproduction should be discussed with both male and female patients taking methotrexate.

Adverse Effects: In general, the incidence and severity of acute side effects are related to dose, frequency of administration, and the duration of the exposure to significant blood levels of methotrexate to the target organs. The most serious reactions are discussed above under patients with special diseases and conditions (organ system toxicity) in the precaution section. That section should also be consulted when looking for information about adverse reactions with methotrexate.

The most frequently reported adverse reactions include ulcerative stomatitis, leukopenia, nausea, and abdominal distress. Other frequently reported adverse effects are malaise, undue fatigue, chills and fever, dizziness and decreased resistance to infection.

Other adverse reactions that have been reported with methotrexate are listed below by organ system. In the oncology setting, concomitant treatment and the underlying disease make specific attribution of a reaction to methotrexate difficult.

Hematopoietic: Methotrexate can suppress hematopoiesis and cause anemia, leukopenia, and/or thrombocytopenia (see Precautions, Organ Toxicity).

Alimentary System: gingivitis, pharyngitis, stomatitis, anorexia, nausea, vomiting, diarrhea, hematemesis, melena, gastrointestinal ulceration and bleeding, enteritis, pancreatitis.

Cardiovascular: pericarditis, pericardial effusion, hypotension, and thromboembolic events (including arterial thrombosis, cerebral thrombosis, deep vein thrombosis, retinal vein thrombosis, thrombophlebitis, and pulmonary embolus.

CNS: headaches, drowsiness, blurred vision. Aphasia, hemiparesis, paresis and convulsions have also occurred following administration of methotrexate. Following low doses, there have been occasional reports of transient subtle cognitive dysfunction, mood alteration, or unusual cranial sensations, leukoencephalopathy, or encephalopathy.

Infection: There have been case reports of sometimes fatal opportunistic infections in patients receiving methotrexate therapy for neoplastic and non-neoplastic diseases. P. carinii pneumonia was the most common infection. Other reported infections included nocardiosis, histoplasmosis, cryptococcosis, Herpes zoster, H. simplex hepatitis, and disseminated H. simplex.

Pulmonary System: Interstitial pneumonitis deaths have been reported, and chronic interstitial obstructive pulmonary disease has occasionally occurred.

Skin: erythematous rashes, pruritus, urticaria, photosensitivity, pigmentary changes, alopecia, ecchymosis, telangiectasia, acne, furunculosis, erythema multiforme, toxic epidermal necrolysis, Stevens-Johnson syndrome skin necrosis, and exfoliative dermatitis.

Urogenital System: severe nephropathy or renal failure, azotemia, cystitis, hematuria; defective oogenesis or spermatogenesis, transient oligospermia, menstrual dysfunction, vaginal discharge and gynecomastia; infertility, abortion, fetal defects.

Rarer Reactions: related to or attributed to the use of methotrexate such as nodulosis, vasculitis, herpes zoster, sepsis, arthralgia/myalgia, loss of libido/impotence, diabetes, osteoporosis, sudden death, lymphomas and tumor lysis syndrome. A few cases of anaphylactoid reactions have been reported.

Adverse Reactions Reported in Rheumatoid Arthritis: Incidence greater than 10%: elevated liver enzymes 15%, nausea/vomiting 10%. Incidence 3 to 10%: stomatitis, thrombocytopenia. Incidence 1 to 3%: rash/pruritus/dermatitis, alopecia, diarrhea, dizziness, leukopenia and pancytopenia.

For complete information, refer to the Adverse Effects Section of the Product Monograph for Rheumatrex.

Adverse Reactions in Psoriasis: The adverse reaction rates reported are very similar to those in the rheumatoid arthritis studies (see the Adverse Effects Section of the Product Monograph for Rheumatrex).

Overdose: Symptoms and Treatment: see Precautions, Organ System Toxicity.

Discontinue or reduce dosage at the first sign of ulceration or bleeding, diarrhea, or marked depression of the hematopoietic system.

Leucovorin is indicated to diminish the toxicity and counteract the effect of inadvertently administered overdosages of methotrexate. Leucovorin administration should begin as promptly as possible. As the time interval between methotrexate administration and leucovorin initiation increases, the effectiveness of leucovorin in counteracting toxicity decreases. Monitoring of the serum methotrexate concentration is essential in determining the optimal dose and duration of treatment with leucovorin (see Dosage).

In cases of massive overdosage, hydration and urinary alkalinization may be necessary to prevent the precipitation of methotrexate and/or its metabolites in the renal tubules. Neither hemodialysis nor peritoneal dialysis has been shown to improve methotrexate elimination.

Dosage: Neoplastic Diseases: Oral administration in tablet form is often preferred when low doses are being administered since absorption is rapid and effective serum levels are obtained. Methotrexate injection and for injection may be given by the i.m., i.v., intra-arterial, intrathecal or intraventricular (via Ommaya reservoir into the CNS) routes. The preserved formulation contains benzyl alcohol and must not be used for intrathecal, intraventricular, or high-dose therapy.

Parenteral drug products should be inspected visually for particulate matter and discoloration prior to administration, whenever solution and container permit.

Methotrexate may only be administered by physicians experienced in the treatment of neoplasia. The oncologist should consult the current literature for the treatment regimen to be used. Typical dosages reported in the literature for the following malignancies are:

Breast Cancer: The initial doses of CMF will be cyclophosphamide 100 mg/m² p.o. days 1 through 14, methotrexate 40 mg/m² i.v. day 1, 8, and 5—Fluorouracil 600 mg/m² i.v. day 1, 8. Cycle length will be 28 days ("2 weeks-on, 2 weeks-off"). In patients over 60 years of age, the dosage of methotrexate will be 30 mg/m² i.v. day 1, 8.

If total bilirubin exceeds 1.5 mg/dL, decrease the dose of methotrexate only by 50%.

Bladder Cancer: Typical dosage regimens for bladder cancer are the CMV Regimen and the M-VAC Regimen which are represented in Tables I and II.

Table I—Methotrexate

CMV Regimen[a] for Bladder Cancer

Drugs[b]	Days		
	1	2	8[c]
Cisplatin[d]		100	
Vinblastine	4		40
Methotrexate[e]	30		4

[a] All doses in mg/m² with cycles repeated on day 22.
[b] Patients >70 years old receive 80% of all doses; if vomiting persists to day 8, no drug is given.
[c] Major dose modifications for both drugs depending on myelosuppression.
[d] For each cycle adjust cisplatin to 100% for Ccr >60 mL/min; 50% of dose for Ccr 50-60 mL/min; none for Ccr <50 mL/min.
[e] No drug for a decrease on day 8 of >30 mL/min compared to day 1 or Ccr <50 mL/min or Cr >1.8 mg/dL.

Table II—Methotrexate

M-VAC Regimen[a] for Bladder Cancer

Drugs	Days			
	1	2	15	22[c]
Methotrexate	30		30	30
Vinblastine		3	3	3
Doxorubicin		30[b]		
Cisplatin		70		

[a] All doses in mg/m² with cycles repeated every 28 to 32 days.
[b] Patients having prior pelvic irradiation equivalent to >2 500 rad in 5 days, reduce the dose of doxorubicin 15 mg/m².
[c] No doses given when the WBC <2 500 cells/mm³, platelets >100 000 cells/mm³ or mucositis present.

Head and Neck Cancer: Methotrexate remains the standard of therapy for patients with recurrent or metastatic disease. It has been given in a wide variety of doses and schedules (a few of which are represented in Table III).

Table III—Methotrexate

Methotrexate Schedules* for Head and Neck Cancer

0.8 mg/kg every 4 days i.v.
25–50 mg every 4 to 7 days
60 mg/m² weekly iv. or 40 mg/m² biweekly i.v.
40–60 mg/m² weekly i.v.
80 mg/m² for 30 h every 2 weeks with escalation to toxicity
40 mg/m² weekly i.v.
40–200 mg/m² i.v. on days 1, 4 weekly; leucovorin on days 2,5
60 mg/m² i.v. weekly

* excerpt from Devita, et al: CANCER 3rd Ed, p. 496.

For palliation of patients with advanced, incurable disease and acceptable renal function, it is appropriate to begin oral or i.v. methotrexate with weekly doses of 40 to 50 mg/m² or biweekly doses of 15 to 20 mg/m² and escalate the dose in weekly increments until either mild toxicity or therapeutic response is achieved.

Gastric Cancer: A regimen used in a clinical trial in Belgium in patients with resectable gastric cancer follows: methotrexate (1.5 g/m² i.v. day 1), +5-fluorouracil (1.5 g/m² i.v.) +leucovorin (15 mg/m² orally or i.v. every 6 hours for 72 hours)+ adriamycin (30 mg/m² i.v. day 15). The schedule is repeated on day 29 for 6 cycles.

Choriocarcinoma and Similar Trophoblastic Diseases: Methotrexate is administered orally or i.m. in doses of 15 to 30 mg daily for a 5-day course. Such courses are usually repeated for 3 to 5 times as required, with rest periods of 1 or more weeks interposed between courses, until any manifesting toxic symptoms subside. The effectiveness of therapy is ordinarily evaluated by 24-hour quantitative analysis of urinary chorionic gonadotropin hormone (beta-HCG), which should return to normal or less than 50 IU/24 hrs usually after the third or fourth course and usually be followed by a complete resolution of measurable lesions in 4 to 6 weeks. One to two courses of methotrexate after normalization of beta-HCG is usually recommended. Before each course of the drug careful clinical assessment is essential. Cyclic combination therapy of methotrexate with other antitumor drugs has been reported as being useful.

Since hydatidiform mole may precede choriocarcinoma, prophylactic chemotherapy with methotrexate has been recommended.

Chorioadenoma destruens is considered to be an invasive form of hydatidiform mole. Methotrexate is administered in these disease states in doses similar to those recommended for choriocarcinoma.

Lymphomas: In Burkitt's tumor, Stages I and II, methotrexate has produced prolonged remissions in some cases. Recommended dosage is 10 to 25 mg/day orally for 4 to 8 days. In Stage III, methotrexate is commonly given concomitantly with other antitumor agents. Treatment in all stages usually consists of several courses of the drug interposed with 7 to 10 day rest periods. Lymphosarcomas in Stage III may respond to combined drug therapy with methotrexate given in doses of 0.625 to 2.5 mg/kg daily.

The treatment of choice for localized histologically aggressive lymphoma is primary combination chemotherapy with or without involved filed radiation therapy. Frequently used regimens for intermediate-, or high-grade NHL that include methotrexate include groups: the ProMACE/MOPP, ProMACE-CytaBOM, Magrath Protocols. Represented in Table IV (on following page) for example, is the ProMACE CytaBOM Regimen.

Table IV—Methotrexate

ProMACE-CytaBOM Regimen

ProMACE-CytaBOM	Day 1	Day 8	Day 14	Day 15–21
Cyclophosphamide 650 mg/m² i.v.	x			No therapy
Doxorubicin 25 mg/m² i.v.	x			
Etoposide 120 mg/m² i.v.	x			
Cytarabine 300 mg/m² i.v.		x		
Bleomycin 5 mg/m² i.v.		x		
Vincristine 1.4 mg/m² i.v.		x		
Methotrexate 120 mg/m² i.v.		x with leucovorin rescue		
Prednisone 60 mg/m² po	x ————	————	———— x	
Cotrimoxazole 2 po b.i.d. throughout 6 cycles of therapy				

In early stage childhood non-Hodgkin's lymphoma methotrexate is used effectively in combination chemotherapy regimens.

Mycosis Fungoides: Therapy with methotrexate appears to produce a clinical response 70% of the time, but chemotherapy is not curative. Dosage is usually 2.5 to 10 mg daily by mouth for several weeks or months. Dose levels of drug and adjustment of dose regimen by reduction or cessation of drug are guided by patient response and hematologic monitoring. Methotrexate has also been given i.m. in doses of 50 mg once weekly or 25 mg 2 times weekly.

Leukemia: Acute lymphoblastic leukemia (ALL) in children and young adolescents is the most responsive to present day chemotherapy. In young adults and older patients, clinical remission is more difficult to obtain and early relapse is more common.

Methotrexate alone or in combination with steroids was used initially for induction of remission in acute lymphoblastic leukemias (ALL). More recently corticosteroid therapy, in combination with other antileukemic drugs or in cyclic combinations with methotrexate included, has appeared to produce rapid and effective remissions. When used for induction, methotrexate in doses of 3.3 mg/m² in combination with 60 mg/m² of prednisone, given daily, produced remissions in 50% of patients treated, usually within a period of 4 to 6 weeks. Methotrexate in combination with other agents appears to be the drug of choice for securing maintenance of drug-induced remissions. When remission is achieved and supportive care has produced general clinical improvement, maintenance therapy is initiated, as follows: methotrexate is administered 2 times weekly either by mouth or i.m. in total weekly doses of 30 mg/m². It has also been given in doses of 2.5 mg/kg i.v. every 14 days. If and when relapse does occur, reinduction of remission can again usually be obtained by repeating the initial induction regimen.

A variety of combination chemotherapy regimens have been used for both induction and maintenance therapy in acute lymphoblastic leukemia (ALL). The physician should be familiar with recent advances in antileukemic therapy.

Meningeal Leukemia: In the treatment of prophylaxis of meningeal leukemia, methotrexate must be administered intrathecally.

For intrathecal administration, preservative-free methotrexate is diluted to a concentration of 1 mg/mL in an appropriate sterile, preservative-free medium such as 0.9% Sodium Chloride Injection, USP.

The cerebrospinal fluid volume is dependent on age and not on body surface area. The CSF is at 40% of the adult volume at birth and reaches the adult volume in several years.

Intrathecal methotrexate administration at a dose of 12 mg/m² (maximum 15 mg) has been reported to result in low CSF methotrexate concentrations and reduced efficacy in children and high concentrations and neurotoxicity in adults. The following dosage regimen is based on age instead of body surface area (see Table V).

Table V—Methotrexate

Meningeal Leukemia: Dosage

Age (years)	Dose (mg)
<1	6
1	8
2	10
3 or older	12

In one study in patients under the age of 40, this dosage regimen appeared to result in more consistent CSF methotrexate concentrations and less neurotoxicity. Another study in children with acute lymphocytic leukemia compared this regimen to a dose of 12 mg/m² (maximum 15 mg), a significant reduction in the rate of CNS relapse was observed in the group whose dose was based on age.

Because the CSF volume and turnover may decrease with age, a dose reduction may be indicated in elderly patients.

For the treatment of meningeal leukemia, intrathecal methotrexate may be given at intervals of 2 to 5 days. However, administration at intervals of less than 1 week may result in increased subacute toxicity. Methotrexate is administered until the cell count of the cerebrospinal fluid returns to normal. At this point one additional dose is advisable. For prophylaxis against meningeal leukemia, the dosage is the same as for treatment except for the intervals of administration. On this subject, it is advisable for the physician to consult the medical literature.

Untoward side effects may occur with any given intrathecal injection and are commonly neurological in character. Large doses may cause convulsions. Methotrexate given by the intrathecal route appears significantly in the systemic circulation and may cause systemic methotrexate toxicity. Therefore, systemic antileukemic therapy with the drug should be appropriately adjusted, reduced, or discontinued. Focal leukemic involvement of the CNS may not respond to intrathecal chemotherapy and is best treated with radiotherapy.

Leptomeningeal Carcinomatosis: Intrathecal administration of methotrexate as a single-drug or in combination regimens, is the most common therapy for carcinomatous leptomeningitis.

Treatment is optimally administered through an Ommaya reservoir and is usually started with methotrexate (10 mg/m²) given twice weekly until the cerebrospinal fluid cytology becomes negative. The treatment regimen is gradually decreased, first to a weekly course, and eventually to a single administration every 2 months.

Osteosarcoma: An effective adjuvant chemotherapy regimen requires the administration of several cytotoxic chemotherapeutic agents. In addition to high-dose methotrexate with leucovorin rescue, these agents may include doxorubicin, cisplatin, and the combination of bleomycin, cyclophosphamide and dactinomycin (BCD) in the doses and schedule shown in Table VI. The starting dose for high-dose methotrexate treatment is 12 g/m². If this dose is not sufficient to produce a peak serum methotrexate concentration of 1 000 micromolar (10^{-3} mol/L) at the end of the methotrexate infusion, the dose may be escalated to 15 g/m² in subsequent treatments. If the patient is vomiting or is unable to tolerate oral medication, leucovorin is given i.v. or i.m. at the same dose and schedule.

When these higher doses of methotrexate are to be administered, the following safety guidelines should be closely observed.

Guidelines for Methotrexate Therapy with Leucovorin Rescue: Administration of methotrexate should be delayed until recovery if: the WBC count is less than 1 500/µL; the neutrophil count is less than 200/µL; the platelet count is less than 75 000/µL; the serum bilirubin level is greater than 1.2 mg/dL; the ALT level is greater than 450 U; mucositis is present, until there is evidence of healing and persistent pleural effusion is present; this should be drained dry prior to infusion.

Adequate renal function must be documented. Serum creatinine must be normal, and creatinine clearance must be greater than 60 mL/min, before initiation of therapy. Serum creatinine must be measured prior to each subsequent course of therapy. If serum creatinine has increased by 50% or more compared to a prior value, the creatinine clearance must be measured and documented to be greater than 60 mL/min (even if the serum creatinine is still within the normal range).

Table VI—Methotrexate

Osteosarcoma: Dosage and Schedule

Drug[a]	Dose[a]	Treatment Week After Surgery
Methotrexate	12 g/m² i.v. as 4 hour infusion (starting dose)	4,5,6,7,11, 12,15,16,29, 30,44,45
Leucovorin	15 mg orally every 6 hours for 10 doses starting at 24 hours after start of methotrexate infusion	
Doxorubicin[b] as a single drug	30 mg/m²/day i.v.×3 days	8,17
Doxorubicin[b]	50 mg/m² i.v.	20,23,33,36
Cisplatin[b]	100 mg/m² i.v.	20,23,33,36
Bleomycin[b]	15 units/m² i.v.×2 days	2,13,26,39,42
Cyclophosphamide[b]	600 mg/m² i.v.×2 days	2,13,26,39,42
Dactinomycin[b]	0.6 mg/m² i.v.×2 days	2,13,26,39,42

[a] Link MP, Goorin AM, Miser AW, et al: The effect of adjuvant chemotherapy on relapse-free survival in patients with osteosarcoma of the extremity. N Engl J of Med 1986; 314(No.25):1600–1606.

[b] See each respective package insert for full prescribing information. Dosage modifications may be necessary because of drug-induced toxicity.

Patients must be well hydrated, and must be treated with sodium bicarbonate for urinary alkalinization. Administer 1 000 mL/m² of i.v. fluid over 6 hours prior to initiation of the methotrexate infusion. Continue hydration at 125 mL/m²/h (3 L/m²/day) during the methotrexate infusion, and for 2 days after the infusion has been completed. Alkalinize urine to maintain pH above 7 during methotrexate infusion and leucovorin calcium therapy. This can be accomplished by the administration of sodium bicarbonate orally or by incorporation into a separate i.v. solution.

Repeat serum creatinine and serum methotrexate 24 hours after starting methotrexate and at least once daily until the methotrexate level is below 5×10^{-8} mol/L (0.05 micromolar).

Table VII (on following page) provides guidelines for leucovorin calcium dosage based upon serum methotrexate levels.

Patients who experience delayed early methotrexate elimination are likely to develop nonreversible oliguric renal failure. In addition to appropriate leucovorin therapy, these patients require continuing hydration and urinary alkalinization, and close monitoring of fluid and electrolyte status, until the serum methotrexate level has fallen to below 0.05 micromolar and the renal failure has resolved.

Some patients will have abnormalities in methotrexate elimination, or abnormalities in renal function following methotrexate administration, which are significant but less severe than the abnormalities described in Table VII (on following page). These abnormalities may or may not be associated with significant clinical toxicity. If significant clinical toxicity is observed, leucovorin rescue should be extended for an additional 24 hours (total 14 doses over 84 hours) in subsequent courses of therapy. The possibility that the patient is taking other medications which interact with methotrexate (e.g., medications which may interfere with methotrexate binding to serum albumin, or elimination) should always be reconsidered when laboratory abnormalities or clinical toxicities are observed.

Psoriasis and Rheumatoid Arthritis: The patient should be fully informed of the risks involved and should be under constant supervision of the physician (see Precautions, Information for Patients). For complete information refer to the Product Monograph for Rheumatrex (see Dosage).

All dosage schedules should be continually tailored to the individual patient. An initial test dose may be given prior to the regular dosing schedule to detect any extreme sensitivity to adverse effects (see Adverse Effects). Maximal myelosuppression usually occurs in 7 to 10 days.

Methotrexate (cont'd)

Table VII—Methotrexate

Leucovorin Rescue Schedules Following Treatment with Higher Doses of Methotrexate

Clinical Situation	Laboratory Findings	Leucovorin Dosage and Duration
Normal Methotrexate Elimination	Serum methotrexate level approximately 10 micromolar at 24 hours after administration, 1 micromolar at 48 hours, and less than 0.2 micromolar at 72 hours.	15 mg po, i.m. or i.v. q. 6 hours for 60 hours (10 doses starting at 24 hours after start of methotrexate infusion).
Delayed Late Methotrexate Elimination	Serum methotrexate level remaining above 0.2 micromolar at 72 hours, and more than 0.05 micromolar at 96 hours after administration.	Continue 15 mg po, i.m. or i.v. q. 6 hours, until methotrexate level is less than 0.05 micromolar.
Delayed Early Methotrexate Elimination and/or Evidence of Acute Renal Injury	Serum methotrexate level of 50 micromolar or more at 24 hours, or 5 micromolar or more at 48 hours after administration, **or;** a 100% or greater increase in serum creatinine level at 24 hours after methotrexate administration (e.g., an increase from 0.5 mg/dL to a level of 1 mg/dL or more).	150 mg i.v. q. 3 hours, until methotrexate level is less than 1 micromolar; then 15 mg i.v. q. 3 hours, until methotrexate level is less than 0.05 micromolar.

Psoriasis: Recommended Starting Dose Schedules: 1. Weekly single oral, i.m. or i.v. dose schedule: 10 to 25 mg/week until adequate response is achieved. 2. Divided oral dose schedule: 2.5 mg at 12 hour intervals for 3 doses.

Dosages in each schedule may be gradually adjusted to achieve optimal clinical response; 30 mg/week should not ordinarily be exceeded.

Once optimal clinical response has been achieved, each dosage schedule should be reduced to the lowest possible amount of drug and to the longest possible rest period. The use of methotrexate may permit the return to conventional topical therapy, which should be encouraged.

Rheumatoid Arthritis: Recommended Starting Dosage Schedules: 1. Single oral doses of 7.5 mg once weekly. 2. Divided oral dosages of 2.5 mg at 12-hour intervals for 3 doses given as a course once weekly.

Dosages in each schedule may be adjusted gradually to achieve an optimal response, but not ordinarily to exceed a total weekly dose of 20 mg.

Therapeutic response usually begins within 3 to 6 weeks and the patient may continue to improve for another 12 weeks or more.

For complete information refer to the Product Monograph for Rheumatrex (see Dosage).

Reconstitution: See Table VIII. Methotrexate sodium for injection (lyophilized powder, 20 mg/vial) contains no preservative. Reconstitute immediately before use with an appropriate sterile, preservative-free medium, such as Sterile Water for Injection, USP. It is recommended that each vial of lyophilized powder should be reconstituted with 2 to 10 mL of such media, depending on the final concentration desired.

For intrathecal use, the solution is made in a strength of 1 mg/mL using an appropriate, sterile, preservative-free medium such as Sodium Chloride Injection, USP.

Table VIII—Methotrexate

Reconstitution

Vial Size	Volume of Diluent to Be Added	Approximate Available Volume	Nominal Concentration (mg/mL)
20 mg	2 mL	2 mL	10
	4 mL	4 mL	5
	10 mL	10 mL	2
	20 mL	20 mL	1

Unused reconstituted material should be discarded due to the possibility of microbial growth.

Infusion of Liquid or Reconstituted Powder Products: For further dilution (as in i.v. infusion) methotrexate is stable for up to 24 hours in glass at room temperature in the commonly used infusion solutions such as water for injection, USP, dextrose 5% and 10% in water, dextrose 10% in normal saline, Ringer's injection USP, lactated Ringer's injection USP, normal saline, and 5% sodium bicarbonate.

Since methotrexate is poorly soluble in acid media, use of potassium chloride solution is not advisable.

If a preservative-free diluent is used, the solution should be used immediately because of the possibility of microbial growth. It is advisable to protect diluted solutions from light.

Due to the number of brands available, stability data of methotrexate in plastic syringes and bags are not available.

Unused preservative-free products should be discarded due to the possibility of microbial growth.

Incompatibilities: Other drugs should not be mixed with methotrexate in the same infusion bottle.

Contact with acidic solutions should be avoided since methotrexate is sparingly soluble in acid media and precipitation may occur.

See Precautions for clinical incompatibilities.

Special Instructions: Safe Handling and Disposal: Methotrexate is a potent antineoplastic drug. Good medical practice will minimize exposure of persons involved with frequent handling of this drug as outlined below:

Handling: Methotrexate or solutions of methotrexate have no vesicant properties and do not show acute toxicity on topical contact with the skin or mucous membranes. However, persons involved with handling cytotoxic drugs should avoid contact with skin and inhalation of airborne particles. Preparation of antineoplastic solutions should be done in a vertical laminar flow hood (Biological Safety Cabinet—Class II). Personnel preparing methotrexate solutions should wear PVC gloves, safety glasses and protective clothing such as disposable gowns and masks. Personnel regularly involved in the preparation and handling of antineoplastics should have bi-annual blood examinations.

Disposal: Avoid contact with skin and inhalation of airborne particles by use of PVC gloves and disposable gowns and masks. All needles, syringes, vials, and other materials for disposal which have come in contact with methotrexate should be segregated in plastic bags, sealed and marked as hazardous waste. Incinerate at 1 000°C or higher. Sealed containers may explode if a tight seal exists. Tablets: Place container and tablets in a plastic bag, seal, and mark as hazardous waste. Incinerate at 1 000°C or higher. If incineration is not available, rinse all needles, syringes, tubing and other materials for disposal which have come in contact with methotrexate solutions with water and discard in the sewer system with running water. Rinse vials with the appropriate quantity of water with the aid of a hypodermic syringe. Withdraw the solution and discard in the sewer system with running water. Dispose of rinsed equipment and vials in a safe manner.

Tablets: Dissolve tablets in a suitable quantity of normal sodium hydroxide (40 g/L of water*) and discard in the sewer system with running water.

* Use appropriate safety equipment such as goggles and gloves while working with sodium hydroxide since it can cause severe burns.

Cleaning: Non-disposable equipment that has come in contact with methotrexate solutions may be rinsed with water and washed thoroughly with soap and water.

Spillage/Contamination: Wear gloves, mask, protective clothing. Place spilled material in an appropriate container (i.e., cardboard for broken glass) and then in a polyethylene bag; absorb remains with gauze pads or towels; wash area with water and absorb with gauze or towels again and place in bag; seal, double bag and mark as a hazardous waste. Dispose of waste by incineration or by other methods approved for hazardous materials. Personnel involved in cleanup should wash with soap and water.

Supplied: Parenteral: Solutions: Each vial contains: methotrexate sodium in solution equivalent to methotrexate 50 mg (25 mg/mL). Nonmedicinal ingredients: benzyl alcohol, sodium chloride, sodium hydroxide and water for injection. Tartrazine-free. Vials of 2 mL, boxes of 10.

Each vial contains: methotrexate sodium 55 mg in solution equivalent to methotrexate 50 mg (25 mg/mL). Nonmedicinal ingredients: sodium hydroxide and water for injection. Preservative- and tartrazine-free. Vials of 2 mL, boxes of 10.

Lyophilized Powder: Each vial contains: methotrexate sodium powder 22 mg equivalent to methotrexate 20 mg. Nonmedicinal ingredients: sodium hydroxide. Preservative- and tartrazine- free. Boxes of 10.

Store all parenteral products between 15 to 25°C. Use preservative-free products immediately after preparation and discard unused portion of these opened vials. Avoid freezing. Protect from light.

Tablets: Each round, yellow, scored tablet, engraved "2.5" and "M1", contains: methotrexate sodium equivalent to methotrexate 2.5 mg. Nonmedicinal ingredients: cornstarch, lactose and magnesium stearate. Dye- and tartrazine-free. Bottles of 100. Store at 15 to 30°C. Protect from light.

Reviewed 1999

METHOTREXATE SODIUM INJECTION USP Ⓟ

Faulding

Antimetabolite

Pharmacology: Methotrexate is an antimetabolite which competitively inhibits the enzyme folic acid reductase. During DNA synthesis and cellular reproduction, folic acid is reduced to tetrahydrofolic acid by the enzyme folic acid reductase. By interfering with the reduction of folic acid, methotrexate interferes with tissue cell reproduction. Generally, the most sensitive cells to the antimetabolite effect of methotrexate are those cells which are most actively proliferating such as malignant cells, dermal epithelium, buccal and intestinal mucosa, bone marrow, fetal cells and cells of the urinary bladder. Because the proliferation of cells in malignant tissues is greater than in most normal tissues, methotrexate may impair the growth of the malignant tissues without causing irreversible damage to normal tissues.

The basis for the use of methotrexate in psoriasis lies in the fact that the rate of production of the epithelial cells in this skin condition are greatly increased over normal and thus methotrexate affects the psoriatic tissues which are reproducing at a greater rate than the normal skin cells.

Indications: Antineoplastic Chemotherapy: For the treatment of gestational choriocarcinoma, and in patients with chorioadenoma destruens and hydatidiform mole.

For the palliation of acute and subacute lymphocytic and meningeal leukemia. The greatest effect of methotrexate is in the palliation of acute lymphoblastic (stem-cell) leukemia.

Methotrexate is also effective in the treatment of the advanced stages (III and IV, Peters' Staging System) of lymphosarcoma, especially in children, and in advanced stages of mycosis fungoides.

Psoriasis Chemotherapy: Because of the high risk attending its use, methotrexate is only indicated in the symptomatic control of severe, recalcitrant, disabling psoriasis, which is not adequately responsive to other forms of therapy, but only when the diagnosis has been established and the need for therapy has been confirmed by dermatologic consultation.

Contraindications: *Pregnancy:* Methotrexate has caused fetal deaths and congenital abnormalities.

Methotrexate is contraindicated in the presence of preexisting blood dyscrasias, such as bone marrow hypoplasia, leukopenia, thrombocytopenia and anemia. Kidney disease. Liver disease including fibrosis, cirrhosis, recent or active hepatitis. Active infectious disease. Active peptic ulcer. Ulcerative colitis.

Warnings: Methotrexate is a potent and potentially fatal drug and should be used only by physicians experienced with cancer chemotherapeutic drugs (see Precautions). Renal and hepatic function must be assessed prior to therapy and frequently during therapy. Blood counts should be taken once or twice weekly.

Methotrexate should be used only by physicians who are experienced in providing antimetabolite chemotherapy.

Methotrexate, preservative-free is recommended for intrathecal administration to eliminate the possibility of preservative toxicity.

Patients should be fully informed by the physician of the risk of fatal or severe toxic reactions involved with the administration of methotrexate and they should be under the physician's constant supervision.

It is recommended that a liver biopsy be taken prior to methotrexate therapy and periodically thereafter during methotrexate therapy.

Methotrexate therapy is not recommended in patients who are known to ingest excessive quantities of alcohol. The concomitant use of hepatotoxic drugs and alcohol should be avoided.

During the treatment of psoriasis with methotrexate, deaths have been reported. Although the reasons for the sudden deaths have not been completely explained, it appears that they may be due to hypersensitivity reactions.

Methotrexate should be restricted to severe recalcitrant, disabling psoriasis, which is not adequately responsive to other forms of therapy and only when the diagnosis of psoriasis has been established following dermatologic consultation.

Methotrexate is toxic to the hematopoietic system and may produce depression of the bone marrow, anemia, leukopenia, thrombocytopenia and bleeding.

At high or prolonged doses, methotrexate may be hepatotoxic. Liver atrophy, necrosis, cirrhosis, fatty changes and periportal fibrosis have been reported. Hepatic function should be determined prior to initiation of methotrexate treatment, as changes may occur without previous signs of gastrointestinal or hematologic toxicity. Furthermore, hepatic function should be monitored regularly throughout each course of therapy.

The concomitant use of steroidal anti-inflammatory drugs may potentiate methotrexate toxicity.

In men and women of fertile age, steps should be taken to avoid conception during methotrexate therapy. The risk of genetic abnormalities may persist after discontinuing methotrexate therapy. Thus, it is advised that both men and women avoid intercourse leading to conception for an indefinite period (at least 8 weeks) after taking methotrexate to ensure the re-establishment of normal germinal cells.

Interruption of methotrexate therapy as a result of toxicity is indicated in the following situations: ulcerative stomatitis, severe diarrhea, hemorrhagic enteritis, hepatic fibrosis or cirrhosis, impaired liver function, impaired renal function, suppression of the hematopoietic system.

Precautions: Methotrexate has a high potential for toxicity which is usually dose-related.

Before using methotrexate the physician should be familiar with the various characteristics and established clinical usage of methotrexate.

Methotrexate patients should be kept under appropriate supervision so that signs and symptoms of toxicity or adverse effects may be detected and evaluated as early as possible.

The use of methotrexate in chemotherapy requires pretreatment and periodic hematologic evaluations as a result of its hematopoietic suppressive effects.

Methotrexate administration should be discontinued if an unexpected large drop in white blood cell count occurs and appropriate therapy instituted.

The drug should be used with caution, if at all, in patients with malignant disease in which there is pre-existing bone marrow aplasia, leukopenia, thrombocytopenia or anemia.

Because methotrexate is excreted primarily by the kidneys, impaired renal function can lead to drug accumulation with resultant toxicity or even additional renal damage. Therefore, pre-existing kidney disease is considered a contraindication to methotrexate therapy. It is recommended that the renal status of the patients proposed for methotrexate therapy be determined prior to beginning therapy and at appropriate intervals during therapy. Caution should be taken if significant renal damage is present, and drug dosage should be reduced or discontinued until renal function is improved or restored.

The following laboratory tests should be carried out as part of the clinical evaluation and monitoring of patients on methotrexate therapy: complete hemogram, hematocrit, urinalysis and renal function tests. A liver biopsy is mandatory. A chest x-ray is recommended.

The reason for the above tests is to determine any pre-existing organ function or system impairment. Tests should be performed prior to, during and after termination of therapy. If high-dose long-term therapy is used, it is imperative that liver biopsy and bone marrow aspiration studies be completed.

Drug Interactions: Methotrexate is bound in part to serum albumin after absorption, and toxicity may be increased because of displacement by certain drugs, such as salicylates, sulfonamides, diphenylhydantoin and some antibacterials such as tetracycline, chloramphenicol and para-aminobenzoic acid. These drugs, especially salicylates and sulfonamides, whether antibacterial, hypoglycemic or diuretic, should not be given concurrently until the significance of these findings is established.

Because of the potential for drug interaction, corticosteroids should not be given concurrently with methotrexate.

Vitamin preparations containing folic acid or its derivatives may alter responses to methotrexate.

Use methotrexate with extreme caution when infection is present and in patients with peptic ulcer, ulcerative colitis or general debilitation. Also exercise caution with the use of methotrexate in young children and in the elderly.

Bacterial infection may be a threat or may occur if profound leukemia occurs during therapy. In this instance the drug should be discontinued and appropriate antibiotic therapy instituted. If severe bone marrow depression occurs, blood or platelet transfusions may be required.

The possible immunosuppressant action of methotrexate should be taken into consideration when considering the use of the drug in patients where immune responses are important or essential.

When considering the use of methotrexate for chemotherapy, clinicians must evaluate the need and potential value of the drug against the risks, adverse reactions or toxic effects.

Most adverse effects are reversible if detected early. When adverse reactions occur, the dosage should be reduced or the drug discontinued and appropriate corrective action taken according to the clinical judgment of the physician. Caution should be taken when reinstituting methotrexate therapy and adequate consideration given to the need for further drug administration as well as being alert to the possible recurrence of toxicity.

Adverse Effects: The most common adverse reactions include ulcerative stomatitis, leukopenia, nausea and abdominal distress. Others reported are malaise, undue fatigue, chills and fever, dizziness and decreased resistance to infection. In general, the incidence and severity of side effects are considered to be dose-related. Adverse reactions as reported for the various systems are as follows:

Skin: erythematous rashes, pruritus, urticaria, photosensitivity, depigmentation, alopecia, ecchymosis, telangiectasia, acne, furunculosis. Lesions of psoriasis may be aggravated by concomitant exposure to ultraviolet radiation.

Blood: bone marrow depression, leukopenia, thrombocytopenia, anemia, hypogammaglobulinemia, hemorrhage from various sites, septicemia.

Alimentary: gingivitis, pharyngitis, stomatitis, anorexia, vomiting, diarrhea, hematemesis, melena, gastrointestinal ulceration and bleeding, enteritis, hepatic toxicity resulting in acute liver atrophy, necrosis, fatty metamorphosis, periportal fibrosis or hepatic cirrhosis.

Urogenital: renal failure, azotemia, cystitis, hematuria, defective oogenesis or spermatogenesis, transient oligospermia, menstrual dysfunction, infertility, abortion, fetal defects, severe nephropathy.

CNS: headaches, drowsiness, blurred vision. Aphasia, hemiparesis, paresis and convulsions have occurred, possibly related to hemorrhage or to complications from intra-arterial catheterization. Convulsion, paresis and Guillain-Barré syndrome, increased cerebrospinal fluid pressure have followed intrathecal administration.

Other reactions related to or attributed to the use of methotrexate, such as pneumonitis, metabolic changes, precipitating diabetes, osteoporotic effects, abnormal tissue cell changes and even sudden death have been reported. Although not completely explained as yet, the sudden death would appear to point to the possibility of hypersensitivity reactions.

Overdose: Symptoms and Treatment: Discontinue or reduce dosage at the first sign of ulceration or bleeding, diarrhea or marked depression of hematopoietic system.

Leucovorin (citrovorum factor) is a potent agent for neutralizing the immediate toxic effects of methotrexate on the hematopoietic system. When large doses or overdoses are given, calcium leucovorin may be administered by i.v. infusion in doses up to 75 mg within 12 hours, followed by 12 mg i.m. every 6 hours for 4 doses. Where average doses of methotrexate appear to have an adverse effect, 6 to 12 mg of leucovorin calcium may be given i.m. every 6 hours for 4 doses. In general, where overdosage is suspected, the dose of leucovorin should be equal to or higher than the dose of methotrexate and is best administered within the first hour. Use of leucovorin calcium after an hour's delay is much less effective.

Dosage: Antineoplastic Chemotherapy: Sodium methotrexate for injection may be given by i.m., i.v. or intra-arterial routes. The preparation without preservatives could also be used for intrathecal administration. It is recommended that initial treatment takes place with the patient under hospital supervision.

Administration of methotrexate tablets is often preferred over the parenteral route. Absorption is rapid and effective serum levels are obtained in 1 to 2 hours. Methotrexate sodium parenteral may be given by i.m., i.v., intra-arterial or intrathecal route. Initial treatment is usually undertaken with the patient under hospital care.

A guideline of a ratio of 1:30 is given for the conversion of mg/kg body weight to mg/m^2 of body surface area. The conversion factor usually varies between 1:20 and 1:40, depending on age and body build.

Choriocarcinoma and similar trophoblastic diseases: Methotrexate is administered in doses of 15 to 30 mg daily for a 5 day course. Such courses are usually repeated 3 to 5 times, as required, with rest periods of 1 or more weeks interposed between courses until any manifesting toxic symptoms subside. The effectiveness of therapy is ordinarily evaluated by 24-hour quantitative analysis of urinary chorionic gonadotropin hormone (CGH), which should return to normal or less than 50 IU/24 hours, usually after the third or fourth course, with a complete resolution of measurable lesions in 4 to 6 weeks. One to two courses of methotrexate after normalization of CGH are usually recommended. Before each course of the drug, careful clinical assessment is essential. Cyclic combination therapy of methotrexate with other antitumor drugs has been reported as being useful.

Since hydatidiform mole may precede or be followed by choriocarcinoma, prophylactic chemotherapy with methotrexate has been recommended. Chorioadenoma destruens is considered to be an invasive form of hydatidiform mole. Methotrexate is administered in these disease states in doses similar to those recommended for choriocarcinoma.

Leukemia: Acute lymphatic (lymphoblastic) leukemia in children and young adolescents is the most responsive to present day chemotherapy. In young adults and older patients, clinical remission is more difficult to obtain and early relapse is more common. In chronic lymphatic leukemia, the prognosis for adequate response is less encouraging.

Methotrexate alone or in combination with steroids was used initially for induction of remission of lymphoblastic leukemias. More recently, corticosteroid therapy in combination with other antileukemic drugs or in cyclic combinations with methotrexate appears to produce rapid and effective remissions. When used for induction, methotrexate in doses of 3.3 mg/m^2 in combination with prednisone 60 mg/m^2, given daily, produced remission in 50% of patients treated, usually within a period of 4 to 6 weeks. Methotrexate alone or in combination with other agents appears to be the drug of choice for securing maintenance of drug-induced remissions. When remission is achieved and supportive care has produced general clinical improvement, maintenance therapy is initiated as follows: methotrexate is administered 2 times weekly in doses of 30 mg/m^2. It has also been given in doses of 2.5 mg/kg i.v. every 14 days. If and when relapse occurs, reinduction of remission can usually be obtained by repeating the initial induction regime. A variety of dosage schedules for both induction and maintenance of remission with various combinations of alkylating and anti-folic agents have been proposed. Multiple drug therapy with several agents, including methotrexate, given concomitantly is gaining increasing support in both the acute and chronic forms of leukemia. The physician should become familiar with the new advances in antileukemia therapy.

Acute granulocytic leukemia is rare in children but common in adults. This form of leukemia responds poorly to chemotherapy and remissions are short with relapses common, and resistance to therapy develops rapidly.

Meningeal leukemia: Some patients with leukemia are subject to leukemic invasion of the CNS. This may result in characteristic signs or symptoms or may remain silent and be diagnosed only by examination of the CSF, which contains leukemic cells. The CSF should be examined in all leukemic patients. Since the penetration of methotrexate into the CSF is minimal, adequate therapy requires intrathecal administration. Some clinicians have given such chemotherapy in a prophylactic regime, but such a procedure is of doubtful value, and the more common approach is to treat such patients who manifest leukemic involvement by direct intrathecal instillation of methotrexate.

Methotrexate is administered by intrathecal injection of the sodium salt in solution in doses of 0.2 to 0.5 mg/kg body weight. Administration is at intervals of 2 to 5 days and is usually repeated until the cell count of the CSF returns to normal. At this point, 1 additional dose is advised. A second common course of administration is methotrexate 12 mg/m^2 once weekly for 2 weeks then once monthly. Large doses may cause convulsions. Untoward side effects may occur with any given intrathecal injection and are commonly neurological in

Methotrexate Sodium Injection USP (cont'd)

character. Methotrexate given by intrathecal route appears significantly in the systemic circulation and may cause systemic toxicity. Therefore, systemic antileukemic therapy with the drug should be appropriately adjusted, reduced or discontinued. Focal leukemic involvement of the CNS may not respond to intrathecal chemotherapy and is best treated with radiotherapy.

Lymphomas: In Burkitt's tumor, stages I-II, methotrexate has produced prolonged remissions in some cases. Recommended dosage is 10 to 25 mg/day orally for 4 to 8 days. In stage III, methotrexate is commonly given concomitantly with other antitumor agents. Treatment in all stages usually consists of several courses of the drug interposed with 7 to 10 day rest periods. Lymphosarcomas in stage III may respond to combined drug therapy with methotrexate given in doses of 0.625 mg to 2.5 mg/kg daily. Hodgkin's disease responds poorly to methotrexate and to most types of chemotherapy.

Mycosis fungoides: Therapy with methotrexate appears to produce clinical remission in one-half of the cases treated. Dosage is usually 2.5 to 10 mg daily by mouth for weeks or months. Dose levels of drug and adjustment to dose regimen with reduction or cessation of drug are guided by patient response and hematologic monitoring.

Psoriasis Chemotherapy: **The patient should be fully informed of the risks involved and should be under constant supervision of the physician.**

Methotrexate therapy should be restricted to patients whose psoriasis is so extensive or severe that it seriously interferes with physical, emotional or economic well-being and is not adequately controlled by standard, topically applied anti-psoriatic therapy. Methotrexate therapy has been widely used for patients and has provided effective therapy. Most studies indicate that about three-quarters of patients benefit from the treatment.

Either oral or parenteral methotrexate may be used for the treatment of psoriasis. With the use of methotrexate for injection, the following dosage schedule is recommended: weekly intermittent i.v. large doses; divided oral doses, intermittent over 36 hours.

These schedules should be continually tailored to the individual patient. Dose schedules cited below pertain to an average 70 kg adult. An initial test dose 1 week prior to initiation of therapy is recommended to detect any idiosyncrasy. A suggested dose range is 5 to 10 mg parenterally.

Recommended Starting Dose Schedules: Weekly single oral, i.m. or i.v. dose schedule: 10 to 25 mg per week until adequate response is achieved. With this dosage schedule, 50 mg per week should ordinarily not be exceeded.

Divided oral dose schedule: 2.5 mg at 12-hour intervals for 3 doses or at 8-hour intervals for 4 doses each week. With this dosage schedule, 30 mg per week should not be exceeded.

Dosage may be gradually adjusted to achieve optimal clinical response, but not to exceed the maximum stated for each schedule.

Once optimal clinical response has been achieved, the dosage should be reduced to the lowest amount of the drug and to the longest possible rest period. The use of methotrexate may permit the return to conventional topical therapy, which should be encouraged.

Assessment of renal function, liver function and blood elements should be made by history, physical examination and laboratory tests (such as CBC, urinalysis, serum creatinine, liver function studies and liver biopsy) before beginning methotrexate therapy and before re-instituting methotrexate therapy after a rest period. Appropriate steps should be taken to avoid conception during and for at least 8 weeks following methotrexate therapy.

Dilution: Methotrexate Sodium Injection USP may be diluted with any of the solutions for i.v. infusion listed below in a concentration range of 0.4 mg/mL to 2 mg/mL. Dilutions should be used within 24 hours if kept at room temperature. Unused solution should be discarded after this time in order to avoid risk of microbial contamination.

Solutions: 0.9% Sodium Chloride Injection, 5% Dextrose Injection, 4% Dextrose and 0.18% Sodium Chloride Injection and Ringer's Injection.

Pharmacy Bulk Vials: The availability of Pharmacy Bulk Vials is restricted to hospitals with a recognized i.v. admixture program only.

Pharmacy Bulk Vials are intended for multiple dispensing **for i.v. use only** employing a single puncture (see Special Instructions, Handling and Disposal of Cytotoxic Drugs).

The Pharmacy Bulk Vial content should be dispensed within 8 hours. Any unused solution should be discarded within 8 hours. The diluted solutions prepared from the Pharmacy Bulk Vial should be used within 24 hours, when kept at room temperature, from the time of initial puncture of the Pharmacy Bulk Vial.

Pharmacy Bulk Vials contain no preservatives. Care must be taken to minimize the potential for inadvertent introduction of micro-organism during manipulation in the hospital environment.

Special Instructions—Handling and Disposal of Cytotoxic Drugs: Preparation of all antineoplastic agents should be done in a vertical laminar flow hood. Personnel preparing parenteral antineoplastic agents should wear PVC gloves, safety glasses, disposable gowns and masks. All needles, syringes, vials, ampuls and other materials which have come in contact with cytotoxic drugs should be segregated and incinerated at 1 000°C or more. Sealed containers may explode. Intact and unopened vials should be returned to the manufacturer for destruction. Proper precautions should be taken in packaging these materials for transport. If incineration is not available, the material should be neutralized usually with 5% sodium hypochlorite and/or 5% sodium thiosulfate, placed in sealed containers and deposited in land fill sites, according to local regulations. Personnel regularly involved in the preparation and handling of cytotoxic agents should have bi-annual blood examinations.

Supplied: Pharmacy Bulk Vials: 25 mg/mL: Each mL of sterile, **unpreserved,** isotonic solution contains: methotrexate (as methotrexate sodium USP) 25 mg. Vials of 20, 40 and 200 mL.

Vials: 10 mg/mL: Each mL of sterile, **unpreserved,** isotonic solution contains: methotrexate (as methotrexate sodium USP) 10 mg. Vials of 2 mL.

25 mg/mL: Each mL of sterile, **unpreserved,** isotonic solution contains: methotrexate (as methotrexate sodium USP) 25 mg. Vials of 2 mL.

Each mL of sterile, **preserved,** isotonic solution contains: methotrexate (as methotrexate sodium USP) 25 mg. Vials of 2 and 20 mL.

Store below 25°C. Protect from light.

METHOTREXATE SODIUM INJECTION USP ℞

Novopharm

Antimetabolite

Supplied: Each mL of sterile solution contains: methotrexate sodium 25 mg. Nonmedicinal ingredients: sodium chloride and water for injection. Sodium hydroxide and/or hydrochloric acid may be used for pH adjustment. Preservative-free. May be administered by i.m., i.v., intra-arterial, intraventricular or intrathecal (via Ommaya reservoir) routes. Clear glass vials of 2 and 20 mL.

METHOTREXATE TABLETS USP ℞

Faulding

Antimetabolite

Pharmacology: Methotrexate is an antimetabolite which competitively inhibits the enzyme folic acid reductase. During DNA synthesis and cellular reproduction, folic acid is reduced to tetrahydrofolic acid by the enzyme folic acid reductase. By interfering with the reduction of folic acid, methotrexate interferes with tissue cell reproduction. Generally, the most sensitive cells to the antimetabolite effect of methotrexate are those cells which are most actively proliferating such as malignant cells, dermal epithelium, buccal and intestinal mucosa, bone marrow, fetal cells and cells of the urinary bladder. Because the proliferation of cells in malignant tissues is greater than in most normal tissues, methotrexate may impair the growth of the malignant tissues without causing irreversible damage to normal tissues.

The basis for the use of methotrexate in psoriasis lies in the fact that the rate of production of the epithelial cells in this skin condition are greatly increased over normal and thus methotrexate affects the psoriatic tissues which are reproducing at a greater rate than the normal skin cells.

The mechanism of action of methotrexate in rheumatoid arthritis has not been elucidated; it may affect immune function. In vitro studies suggest methotrexate may inhibit DNA precursor uptake by stimulated mononuclear cells. One report in an animal polyarthritis model has shown partial correction of spleen cell hyporesponsiveness and suppression of interleukin 2 production, as responses to methotrexate.

Although methotrexate clearly ameliorates symptoms of inflammation (pain, swelling, stiffness), there is no evidence that it induces remission of rheumatoid arthritis, nor has a beneficial effect been demonstrated on bone erosions and other radiologic changes which result in impaired joint use, functional disability and deformity.

Pharmacokinetics: The absorption of methotrexate orally administered in small doses (approximately 30 mg/m²) is rapid and complete, whereas with oral doses in excess of 80 mg/m² absorption is less than complete. About a third of an oral dose of methotrexate is metabolized by intestinal bacteria during absorption. Pretreatment with oral neomycin decreases and with kanamycin increases the gastrointestinal absorption of oral methotrexate.

The plasma disposition of methotrexate is multiexponential. Due to differences in sampling schedule and assay methods, widely varying estimates of elimination half-life ($t_{1/2}\beta$) of 6 to 69 hours of methotrexate have been reported. The long half-life may either be due to enterohepatic circulation of methotrexate and/or its metabolites or a slow elimination of dihydrofolate reductase (DHFR) bound methotrexate. The plasma clearance of methotrexate following small clinical doses is about 80 mL/min but may become saturated at high doses (20 g). During high dose infusions, the peak plasma level is proportional to dose up to 200 mg/kg. The pharmacokinetics of low doses of methotrexate in patients with rheumatoid arthritis closely resembles the pattern in patients receiving intermediate and high doses for the treatment of neoplasia.

Methotrexate is transported across cellular membranes via a carrier-mediated active process. At high concentrations, when the carrier route is saturated, passive diffusion assumes greater importance.

Methotrexate is not highly bound to plasma proteins (approximately 50%). However, being highly ionized at physiological pH, the drug does not accumulate in the cerebrospinal fluid to any appreciable extent, necessitating intrathecal administration in the treatment of cerebral and meningeal metastases.

Renal excretion is the major route of elimination of methotrexate (approximately 80%), the drug being actively secreted in the renal tubule by the general organic acid transport system. Hence, the renal clearance of methotrexate is decreased by the concomitant administration of organic acids, such as salicylate. The renal clearance of methotrexate is correlated with endogenous creatinine clearance.

Biliary excretion of methotrexate constitutes less than 10% of the administered dose. Other extrarenal routes of excretion such as secretion into human breast milk and saliva are negligible.

Methotrexate is extensively metabolized intracellularly to polyglutamate derivates. The major metabolite is 4-amino-4-deoxy-N^{10}-methylpteroic acid. Small amounts (approximately 11%) of 7-hydroxymethotrexate have also been found in urine of patients receiving high dose methotrexate therapy. Except for the poly-y-glutamates, all of the reported metabolites are less effective than methotrexate as an inhibitor of dihydrofolate reductase. As determined by inhibition of DNA synthesis, normal tissues are sensitive to low levels of methotrexate (10^{-8}M). Furthermore, toxicity with methotrexate is related to duration of exposure as well as to the dose or plasma concentration.

Resistance in tumor cells is related to one or more of the following biochemical phenomena: decreased membrane transport of methotrexate, altered dihydrofolate reductase, which has reduced affinity for methotrexate, increased levels of dihydrofolate reductase due to amplification of the gene controlling dihydrofolate reductase synthesis, decreased formation of methotrexate polyglutamates and decreased activity of thymidylate synthetase.

Indications: Neoplastic Diseases: For the treatment of gestational choriocarcinoma, and in patients with chorioadenoma destruens and hydatidiform mole.

For the palliation of acute and subacute lymphocytic leukemia. The greatest effect of methotrexate is in the palliation of acute lymphoblastic (stem-cell) leukemia.

Methotrexate is also effective in the treatment of the advanced stages (III and IV, Peters Staging System) of lymphosarcoma, especially in children, and in advanced stages of mycosis fungoides.

Psoriasis: For the symptomatic control of severe, recalcitrant, disabling disease which has not responded adequately to other therapies, following established diagnosis and after dermatologic consultation. It is important to determine that a psoriasis "flare" is not due to undiagnosed disease affecting immune response.

Rheumatoid Arthritis: In the management of selected adults with severe, active, classical or definite rheumatoid arthritis (American Rheumatism Association criteria), who have shown insufficient response to an adequate trial of first-line therapy with a nonsteroidal anti-inflammatory drug (NSAID), and usually a trial of at least one disease modifying antirheumatic drug (DMARD).

ASA, NSAIDs and/or low dose steroids may be continued, although increased toxicity with concomitant NSAIDs including salicylates may be expected (see Pharmacology, Pharmacokinetics and Precautions, Drug Interactions). Steroids must be reduced gradually in patients who respond to methotrexate. Combined use of methotrexate with gold, penicillamine, hydroxychloroquine, sulfasalazine, immunosuppressive therapy or cytotoxic agents has not been studied and may increase the risk of toxicity. Physiotherapy, where indicated, should be continued.

Contraindications: Methotrexate is contraindicated in the following conditions:

Pregnancy and *Lactation:* Methotrexate has caused fetal deaths and congenital abnormalities.

The presence of pre-existing blood dyscrasias, such as bone marrow hypoplasia, leukopenia, thrombocytopenia, anemia. Kidney disease. Liver disease including fibrosis, cirrhosis, recent or active hepatitis, or known alcoholism in patients with rheumatoid arthritis or psoriasis. Active infectious disease and during immunization procedures. Active peptic ulcer. Ulcerative colitis. Overt or laboratory evidence of immunodeficiency syndromes in patients with psoriasis or rheumatoid arthritis. Known hypersensitivity to methotrexate.

Warnings: Caution: Methotrexate is a potent and potentially fatal drug and should be used only by physicians experienced with cancer chemotherapeutic drugs (see Precautions). Renal and hepatic function must be assessed prior to therapy and frequently during therapy. Blood counts should be taken once or twice weekly. Patients should be informed by the physician of the risks involved and should be under a physician's constant supervision. Deaths have been reported with the use of methotrexate in the treatment of rheumatoid arthritis.

Because of the possibility of serious toxicity, the use of methotrexate in psoriasis and rheumatoid arthritis is indicated only in the symptomatic control of severe, recalcitrant, disabling disease, which is not adequately responsive to other forms of therapy, and only after the diagnosis has been established and the need for therapy has been confirmed by appropriate consultation.

In the treatment of rheumatoid arthritis, methotrexate use should be restricted to patients with severe, recalcitrant, disabling disease, which is not adequately responsive to other forms of therapy, and only when the diagnosis has been established and after appropriate consultation.

Methotrexate therapy is not recommended in patients who are known to ingest excessive quantities of alcohol. The concomitant use of hepatotoxic drugs and alcohol should be avoided.

During the treatment of psoriasis with methotrexate, deaths have been reported. Although the reasons for the sudden deaths have not been completely explained, it appears that they may be due to hypersensitivity reactions.

Methotrexate-induced lung disease is a potentially dangerous lesion, which may occur acutely at any time during therapy and which has been reported at doses as low as 7.5 mg/week. It is not always fully reversible. Pulmonary symptoms (especially a dry, nonproductive cough) may require interruption of treatment and careful investigation.

Methotrexate is toxic to the hematopoietic system and may produce depression of the bone marrow, anemia, leukopenia, thrombocytopenia and bleeding.

Unexpectedly severe (sometimes fatal) marrow suppression and gastrointestinal toxicity have been reported with concomitant administration of methotrexate (usually in high dosage) along with some nonsteroidal anti-inflammatory drugs.

Methotrexate causes hepatotoxicity, fibrosis and cirrhosis, but generally only after prolonged use. Acutely, liver enzyme elevations are frequently seen, these are usually transient and asymptomatic, and also do not appear predictive of subsequent hepatic disease. Liver biopsy after sustained use often shows histologic changes, and fibrosis and cirrhosis have been reported; these latter lesions often are not preceded by symptoms or abnormal liver function tests.

The concomitant use of nonsteroidal anti-inflammatory drugs may potentiate methotrexate toxicity.

In men and women of fertile age, steps should be taken to avoid conception during methotrexate therapy. The risk of genetic abnormalities may persist after discontinuing methotrexate therapy. Thus, it is advised that both men and women avoid intercourse leading to conception for an indefinite period (at least 8 weeks) after taking methotrexate to ensure the reestablishment of normal germinal cells.

Periodic monitoring for toxicity, including CBC with differential and platelet counts, and liver and renal function tests is a mandatory part of methotrexate therapy. Periodic liver biopsies may be indicated in some situations. Patients at increased risk for impaired methotrexate elimination (e.g. renal dysfunction, pleural effusions or ascites) should be monitored more frequently (see Precautions).

Diarrhea and ulcerative stomatitis require interruption of therapy; otherwise, hemorrhagic enteritis and death from intestinal perforation may occur.

Methotrexate therapy in patients with impaired renal function should be undertaken with extreme caution, and at reduced dosages, because renal dysfunction will prolong methotrexate elimination.

Interruption of methotrexate therapy as a result of toxicity is indicated in the following situations: ulcerative stomatitis, severe diarrhea, hemorrhagic enteritis, hepatic fibrosis or cirrhosis, impaired liver function, impaired renal function, suppression of the hematopoietic system, pulmonary symptoms (especially a dry non-productive cough) or a non-specific pneumonitis, pregnancy.

Precautions: General: Methotrexate has a high potential for toxicity which is usually dose related. Most adverse reactions are reversible if detected early. When such effects or reactions do occur, the drug should be reduced in dosage or discontinued and appropriate corrective measures should be taken, according to the clinical judgment of the physician. Reinstitution of methotrexate therapy should be carried out with caution, with adequate consideration of further need for the drug and alertness as to possible recurrence of toxicity.

Methotrexate patients should be kept under appropriate supervision so that signs and symptoms of toxicity or adverse effects may be detected and evaluated as early as possible.

The use of methotrexate requires pretreatment and periodic hematologic evaluations as a result of its hematopoietic suppressive effects. Hematopoietic suppression may occur abruptly and while on an apparently safe dosage. In severe bone marow depression, blood or platelet transfusions may be necessary.

In rheumatoid arthritis and psoriasis, methotrexate should be stopped immediately if there is a significant drop in blood counts. In the treatment of neoplastic diseases, methotrexate should be continued only if the potential benefit warrants the risks of severe myelosuppression. Patients with profound granulocytopenia and fever should be evaluated immediately and usually require parenteral broad-spectrum antibiotic therapy.

The drug should be used with caution, if at all, in patients with malignant disease in which there is pre-existing bone marrow aplasia, leukopenia, thrombocytopenia or anemia.

The clinical pharmacology of methotrexate has not been well studied in older individuals. Due to diminished hepatic and renal function as well as decreased folate stores in this population, these patients should be closely monitored for early signs of toxicity and relatively low doses should be considered.

Because methotrexate is excreted primarily by the kidneys, impaired renal function can lead to drug accumulation with resultant toxicity or even additional renal damage. Therefore, pre-existing kidney disease is considered a contraindication to methotrexate therapy. It is recommended that the renal status of the patients proposed for methotrexate therapy be determined prior to beginning therapy and at appropriate intervals during therapy. Caution should be taken if significant renal damage is present, and drug dosage should be reduced or discontinued until renal function is improved or restored. If stomatitis, vomiting, diarrhea or decreased fluid intake occur which may result in dehydration, methotrexate should be discontinued until recovery ensues.

Use methotrexate with extreme caution when infection is present and in patients with peptic ulcer, ulcerative colitis or general debilitation. Also exercise caution with the use of methotrexate in young children, the elderly and in the presence of a significant third space (e.g. pleural effusion).

Bacterial infection may be a threat or may occur if profound leukopenia occurs during therapy. In this instance the drug should be discontinued and appropriate antibiotic therapy instituted. If severe bone marrow depression occurs, blood or platelet transfusions may be required.

The possible immunosuppressant action of methotrexate should be taken into consideration when considering the use of the drug in patients where immune responses are important or essential. Therefore, immunization may be ineffective and immunization with live virus is contraindicated.

When considering the use of methotrexate for chemotherapy, clinicians must evaluate the need and potential value of the drug against risks, adverse reactions or toxic effects.

The physician and pharmacist should emphasize to the patient with rheumatoid arthritis, that the recommended dose is taken weekly, and that mistaken daily use of the recommended dose has led to fatal toxicity (see Information for the Patient). When methotrexate is discontinued, a "flare" of arthritis usually occurs within 3 to 6 weeks.

Laboratory Tests: The following laboratory tests should be carried out as part of the clinical evaluation and monitoring of patients on methotrexate therapy: complete hemogram, hematocrit, urinalysis, renal function tests and liver function tests. Periodic liver biopsy may be indicated in some situations. A chest x-ray is recommended.

Tests should be performed prior to, during and after termination of therapy. If high-dose, long-term therapy is used, it is imperative that liver biopsy and bone marrow aspiration studies be completed.

During therapy of rheumatoid arthritis, monitoring of these parameters is recommended: hematology at least monthly, and liver and renal function every 1 to 3 months. More frequent monitoring is usually indicated during antineoplastic therapy. During initial or changing doses, or during periods of increased risk of elevated methotrexate blood levels (e.g. dehydration), more frequent monitoring may also be indicated.

A relationship between abnormal liver function tests and fibrosis or cirrhosis of the liver has not been established. Transient liver function test abnormalities are observed frequently after methotrexate administration and are usually not causes for modification of methotrexate therapy. Persistent liver function test abnormalities just prior to dosing and/or depression of serum albumin may be indicators of serious liver toxicity and require evaluation.

Liver function tests, including serum albumin, should be performed periodically prior to dosing but are often normal in the face of developing fibrosis or cirrhosis. These lesions may be detectable only by biopsy.

Pulmonary function tests may be useful if methotrexate-induced lung disease is suspected, especially if baseline measurements are available.

Drug Interactions: Methotrexate is bound in part to serum albumin after absorption, and toxicity may be increased because of displacement by certain drugs, such as salicylates, phenylbutazone, sulfonamides and phenytoin. These drugs, especially salicylates and sulfonamides, whether hypoglycemic or diuretic, should not be given concurrently until the significance of these findings is established.

Nonsteroidal anti-inflammatory drugs should not be administered prior to or concomitantly with the high doses of methotrexate used in the treatment of osteosarcoma. Concomitant administration of some NSAIDs with high dose methotrexate therapy has been reported to elevate and prolong serum methotrexate levels, thereby enhancing gastrointestinal toxicity.

Caution should be used when NSAIDs and salicylates are administered concomitantly with lower doses of methotrexate. These drugs have been reported to reduce the tubular secretion of methotrexate in an animal model and may enhance its toxicity.

Despite the potential interactions, studies of methotrexate in patients with rheumatoid arthritis have usually included concurrent use of dosage regimens of NSAIDs, without apparent problems. It should be appreciated however, that the doses used in rheumatoid arthritis (7.5 to 15 mg/week) are somewhat lower than those used in psoriasis and that larger doses could lead to unexpected toxicity.

Vitamin preparations containing folic acid or its derivatives may alter responses to methotrexate.

Oral antibiotics such as tetracycline, chloramphenicol and non-absorbable broad-spectrum antibiotics may decrease intestinal absorption of methotrexate or interfere with the enterohepatic circulation by inhibiting bowel flora and suppressing metabolism of the drug by bacteria.

Trimethoprim/sulfamethoxazole has been reported rarely to increase bone marrow suppression in patients receiving methotrexate, probably by an additive antifolate effect.

Adverse Effects: The most common adverse reactions include ulcerative stomatitis, leukopenia, nausea and abdominal distress. Others reported are malaise, undue fatigue, chills and fever, dizziness and decreased resistance to infection. In general, the incidence and severity of side effects are considered to be dose-related. Adverse reactions as reported for the various systems are as follows: Skin: erythematous rashes, pruritus, urticaria, photosensitivity, depigmentation, alopecia, ecchymosis, telangiectasia, acne, furunculosis. Lesions of psoriasis may be aggravated by concomitant exposure to

Methotrexate Tablets USP (cont'd)

ultraviolet radiation. Radiation dermatitis and sunburn may be reactivated by methotrexate.
Blood: bone marrow depression, leukopenia, thrombocytopenia, anemia, hypogammaglobulinemia, hemorrhage from various sites, septicemia.
Alimentary: gingivitis, pharyngitis, stomatitis, anorexia, nausea, vomiting, diarrhea, hematemesis, melena, gastrointestinal ulceration and bleeding, enteritis, significant elevation of liver enzymes, hepatic toxicity resulting in acute liver atrophy, necrosis, fatty metamorphosis, periportal fibrosis or hepatic cirrhosis.
Urogenital: renal failure, azotemia, cystitis, hematuria, defective oogenesis or spermatogenesis, transient oligospermia, menstrual dysfunction, infertility, abortion, fetal defects, severe nephropathy.
Pulmonary: pulmonary symptoms (especially a dry, nonproductive cough) or a nonspecific pneumonitis occurring during methotrexate therapy may be indicative of a potentially dangerous lesion and require interruption of treatment and careful investigation. Although clinically variable, the typical patient with methotrexate-induced lung disease presents with fever, cough, dyspnea, hypoxemia, and an infiltrate on chest x-ray; infection needs to be excluded. This lesion can occur at all dosages.
CNS: headaches, drowsiness, blurred vision, dizziness, tinnitus. Aphasia, hemiparesis, paresis and convulsions have occurred, possibly related to hemorrhage or to complications from intra-arterial catheterization. Convulsion, paresis and Guillain-Barré syndrome, and increased cerebrospinal fluid pressure have followed intrathecal administration. Following low doses, occasional patients have reported transient subtle cognitive dysfunction, mood alteration or unusual cranial sensations.

Other reactions related to or attributed to the use of methotrexate, such as pneumonitis, metabolic changes, precipitating diabetes, osteoporotic effects, loss of libido/impotence, abnormal tissue cell changes and even sudden death have been reported. Although not completely explained as yet, the sudden death would appear to point to the possibility of hypersensitivity reactions. A few cases of anaphylactoid reactions have been reported.

Overdose: Symptoms and Treatment: Discontinue or reduce dosage at the first sign of ulceration or bleeding, diarrhea or marked depression of hematopoietic system. In cases of massive overdosage, hydration and urinary alkalinization may be necessary to prevent the precipitation of methotrexate and/or its metabolites in the renal tubules. The bicarbonate dose should be adjusted to maintain a urinary pH at 7 or greater.

Leucovorin (citrovorum factor) is a potent agent for neutralizing the immediate toxic effects of methotrexate on the hematopoietic system. When large doses or overdoses are given, calcium leucovorin may be administered by i.v. infusion in doses up to 75 mg within 12 hours, followed by 12 mg i.m. every 6 hours for 4 doses. Where average doses of methotrexate appear to have an adverse effect, 6 to 12 mg of leucovorin calcium may be given i.m. every 6 hours for 4 doses. In general, where overdosage is suspected, the dose of leucovorin should be equal to or higher than the dose of methotrexate and is best administered within the first hours. Use of leucovorin calcium after an hour's delay is much less effective.

Serum samples should be assayed for creatinine levels and methotrexate levels at 24 hour intervals. If the 24 hour serum creatinine level has increased 50% over baseline or if the 24 hour methotrexate level is $>5 \times 10^{-6}$M or the 48 hour methotrexate level is 9×10^{-7}M or higher, the doses of leucovorin should be increased to 100 mg/m² i.v. every 3 hours until the methotrexate level is $<10^{-8}$M. The infusion rate for leucovorin should not exceed 16 mL (160 mg leucovorin)/minute.

Dosage: Neoplastic Disease: Absorption of methotrexate tablets is rapid, and effective serum levels are obtained in 1 to 2 hours. Alternatively, methotrexate sodium parenteral may be given by i.m., i.v. intra-arterial or intrathecal route (see package insert or product monograph for Methotrexate Sodium Injection Faulding).

A guideline ratio of 1:30 is given for the conversion of mg/kg body weight to mg/m² of body surface area. The conversion factor actually varies between 1:20 and 1:40, depending on age and body build.
Choriocarcinoma and Similar Trophoblastic Diseases: Methotrexate is administered in doses of 15 to 30 mg daily for a 5-day course. Such courses are usually repeated for 3 to 5 times, as required, with rest periods of 1 or more weeks interposed between courses until any manifesting toxic symptoms subside. The effectiveness of therapy is ordinarily evaluated by 24 hour quantitative analysis of urinary chorionic gonadotrophin (CGH), which should return to normal or less than 50 IU/24 hours, usually after the third or fourth course, with a complete resolution of measurable lesions in 4 to 6 weeks. One to 2 courses of methotrexate after normalization of CGH are usually recommended. Before each course of the drug, careful clinical assessment is essential. Cyclic combination therapy of methotrexate with other anti-tumor drugs has been reported as being useful.

Since hydatidiform mole may precede or be followed by choriocarcinoma, prophylactic chemotherapy with methotrexate has been recommended. Chorioadenoma destruens is considered to be an invasive form of hydatidiform mole. Methotrexate is administered in these disease states in doses similar to those recommended for choriocarcinoma.
Leukemia: Acute lymphatic (lymphoblastic) leukemia in children and young adolescents is the most responsive. In young adults and older patients, clinical remission is more difficult to obtain and early relapse is more common. In chronic lymphatic leukemia, the prognosis for adequate response is less encouraging.

Methotrexate alone or in combination with steroids was used initially for induction of remission of lymphoblastic leukemia. More recently, corticosteroid therapy in combination with other antileukemic drugs or in cyclic combinations with methotrexate appears to produce rapid and effective remissions. When used for induction, methotrexate in doses of 3.3 mg/m² in combination with prednisone 60 mg/m², given daily, produced remission in 50% of patients treated, usually within a period of 4 to 6 weeks. Methotrexate alone or in combination with other agents appears to be the drug of choice for securing maintenance of drug-induced remissions. When remission is achieved and supportive care has produced general clinical improvement, maintenance therapy is initiated as follows: Methotrexate is administered 2 times weekly in doses of 30 mg/m². If and when relapse occurs, reinduction of remission can usually be obtained by repeating the initial induction regime. A variety of dosage schedules for both induction and maintenance of remission with various combinations of alkylating and antifolic agents, have been proposed. Multiple drug therapy with several agents, including methotrexate, given concomitantly is gaining increasing support in both the acute and chronic forms of leukemia. The physician should familiarize himself with new advances in antileukemia therapy.

Acute granulocytic leukemia is rare in children but common in adults. This form of leukemia responds poorly to chemotherapy and remissions are short with relapses common, and resistance to therapy develops rapidly.
Lymphomas: In Burkitt's tumor, stages I to II, methotrexate has produced prolonged remissions in some cases. Recommended dosage is 10 to 25 mg/day orally for 4 to 8 days. In stage III, methotrexate is commonly given concomitantly with other antitumor agents. Treatment in all stages usually consists of several courses of the drug interposed with 7 to 10 day rest periods. Lymphosarcomas in stage III may respond to combined drug therapy with methotrexate given in doses of 0.625 mg to 2.5 mg/kg daily. Hodgkin's disease responds poorly to methotrexate and to most types of chemotherapy.
Mycosis Fungoides: Therapy with methotrexate appears to produce clinical remission in one-half of the cases treated. Dosage is usually 2.5 to 10 mg daily by mouth for weeks or months. Dose levels of drug and adjustment of dose regimen with reduction or cessation of drug are guided by patient response and hematologic monitoring.
Psoriasis Chemotherapy: **The patient should be fully informed of the risks involved and should be under constant supervision of the physician.**

Methotrexate therapy should be restricted to patients whose psoriasis is so extensive or severe that it seriously interferes with physical, emotional or economic well being and is not adequately controlled by standard, topically applied antipsoriatic therapy. Methotrexate therapy has been widely used for patients and has provided effective therapy. Most studies indicate that about three quarters of patients benefit from the treatment. Methotrexate tablets may be used for the treatment of psoriasis. Either of the following are dosage schedules recommended: 1. Weekly intermittent large doses. 2. Divided doses, intermittent over 36 hours. These schedules should be continually tailored to the individual patient. Example dose schedules cited below pertain to an average 70 kg adult. An initial test dose 1 week prior to initiation of therapy is recommended to detect any idiosyncrasy.
Recommended Starting Dose Schedules: Weekly Single Oral Dose Schedule: 10 to 25 mg/week until adequate response is achieved. With this dosage schedule, 50 mg/week should ordinarily not be exceeded.
Divided Oral Dose Schedule: 2.5 mg at 12-hour intervals for 3 doses or at 8-hour intervals for 4 doses each week. With this dosage schedule, 30 mg/week should not be exceeded.

Dosage may be gradually adjusted to achieve optimal clinical response, but not to exceed the maximum stated for each schedule. Once optimal clinical response has been achieved, the dosage should be reduced to the lowest amount of drug and to the longest possible rest period. The use of methotrexate may permit the return to conventional topical therapy, which should be encouraged.

Assessment of renal function, liver function and blood elements should be made by history, physical examination and laboratory tests (such as CBC, urinalysis, serum creatinine, liver function studies and liver biopsy) before beginning methotrexate therapy and before re-instituting methotrexate therapy after a rest period. Appropriate steps should be taken to avoid conception during and for at least 8 weeks following methotrexate therapy.
Rheumatoid Arthritis: The patient should be fully informed of the risks involved and should be under constant supervision by the physician. Assessment of hematologic, hepatic, renal and pulmonary function should be made by history, physical examination, and laboratory tests before beginning, periodically during, and berfore reinstituting methotrexate therapy (see Precautions). Appropriate measures should be taken to avoid conception during methotrexate therapy (see Contraindications and Precautions).

Both the physician and the pharmacist should emphasize to the patient the importance of the weekly dosage regimens; mistaken daily use may cause serious and sometimes life-threatening or fatal toxicity.

All schedules should be continually tailored to the individual patient. An initial test dose may be given prior to the regular dosing schedule to detect any extreme sensitivity to adverse effects. Complete blood count with platelets should be evaluated 7 to 10 days later.

Recommended starting dosage schedules are: 1. Single doses of 7.5 mg (3 × 2.5 mg tablets) once weekly or 2. Divided dosages of 2.5 mg at 12-hour intervals for 3 doses given as a course once weekly.

Dosages in each schedule may be increased to 15 mg/week after 6 weeks in non-responsive patients. If necessary dosage may be gradually increased further to achieve optimal response, but not ordinarily to exceed a total weekly dose of 20 mg. Limited experience shows a significant increase in the incidence and severity of serious toxic reactions, especially bone marrow suppression, at doses greater than 20 mg.

Once response has been achieved, each schedule should be reduced, if possible, to the lowest possible effective dose. Although rare, some patients may be maintained on a dose of 2.5 mg/week. Therapeutic response usually begins within 3 to 6 weeks and the patient may continue to improve for another 12 weeks or more.

The optimal duration of therapy is unknown. Limited data available from long-term studies indicate that the initial clinical improvement is maintained for at least 2 years with continued therapy. When methotrexate is discontinued, the arthritis usually worsens within 3 to 6 weeks.
Safe Handling and Disposal: Methotrexate is a potent antineoplastic drug. Good medical practice will minimize exposure of persons involved with frequent handling of this drug outlined below.
Handling: 1. Methotrexate does not show acute toxicity on topical contact with the skin and mucous membrane. However, persons involved with handling cytotoxic drugs should avoid contact with skin and inhalation of airborne particles.
2. Personnel regularly involved in preparation and handling of antineoplastics should have bi-annual blood examinations.
Disposal: 1. Avoid contact with skin and inhalation of airborne particles by use of PVC gloves and disposable gowns and masks.
2. Tablets: Place container and tablets in a plastic bag, seal, and mark as hazardous waste. Incinerate at 1 000°C or higher.
3. If incineration is not available, dissolve tablets in a suitable quantity of 1N sodium hydroxide solution, and autoclave the mixture for 1 hour. Discard in the sewer system with copious amounts of running water.
Cleaning: Non-disposable equipment that has come in contact with methotrexate may be rinsed with water and washed thoroughly with soap and water.

Information for the Patient: See Blue Section—Information for the Patient "Methotrexate Tablets".

Supplied: Each small, round, yellow, uncoated tablet, engraved with M2.5/F, contains: methotrexate USP 2.5 mg.

No preservatives or coloring agents. Bottles of 100. Store at room temperature 15 to 25°C).

Patients with rheumatoid arthritis should receive the 2.5 mg dosage form and should be informed of the Information for the Patient.

METHOXACET METHOXACET-C Ⓝ

Technilab

Methocarbamol—Acetaminophen Methocarbamol—Acetaminophen—Codeine Phosphate

Muscle Relaxant—Analgesic

Supplied: Methoxacet: Each green and white laminated caplet, green layer scored and white layer engraved "TEC", contains: methocarbamol 400 mg and acetaminophen 325 mg. Nonmedicinal ingredients: crospovidone, FD&C blue #1 aluminum lake, FD&C yellow #10 aluminum lake, magnesium stearate, microcrystalline cellulose, povidone, pregelatinized starch, sodium croscarmellose and stearic acid. Blisters of 18. Bottles of 100 and 500.

Methoxacet-C⅛: Each uncoated, blue and white laminated caplet, blue layer scored, white layer engraved "TEC", contains: methocarbamol 400 mg, acetaminophen 325 mg and codeine phosphate 8 mg. Nonmedicinal ingredients: crospovidone, FD&C blue #1 aluminum lake, magnesium stearate, microcrystalline cellulose, povidone, pregelatinized starch, sodium croscarmellose and stearic acid. Blisters of 18. Bottles of 100.

Store between 15 to 30°C.

New Product 1998

METHOXISAL METHOXISAL-C Ⓝ

Technilab

Methocarbamol—ASA Methocarbamol—ASA—Codeine Phosphate

Muscle Relaxant—Analgesic

Supplied: Methoxisal: Each pink and white laminated caplet contains: methocarbamol 400 mg and ASA 325 mg. Nonmedicinal ingredients: D&C red #30 aluminum lake, microcrystalline cellulose, povidone, simethicone, sodium croscarmellose and stearic acid. Blisters of 18. Bottles of 100 and 500.

Methoxisal-C1/8: Each yellow and white laminated caplet, yellow layer scored, white layer engraved "TEC", contains: methocarbamol 400 mg, ASA 325 mg and codeine phosphate 8 mg. Nonmedicinal ingredients: FD&C yellow #6 aluminum lake, FD&C yellow #10 aluminum lake, microcrystalline cellulose, povidone, simethicone, sodium croscarmellose and stearic acid. Blisters of 18. Bottles of 100.

Methoxisal-C1/4: Each orange and white laminated caplet, orange layer scored, white layer engraved "TEC", contains: methocarbamol 400 mg, ASA 325 mg and codeine phosphate 16.2 mg. Nonmedicinal ingredients: D&C red #30 aluminum lake, FD&C yellow #10 aluminum lake, microcrystalline cellulose, povidone, simethicone, sodium croscarmellose and stearic acid. Bottles of 100 and 500.

Methoxisal-C1/2: Each coral and white laminated caplet, coral layer scored, white layer engraved "TEC", contains: methocarbamol 400 mg, ASA 325 mg and codeine phosphate 32.4 mg. Nonmedicinal ingredients: FD&C yellow #6 aluminum lake, microcrystalline cellulose, povidone, simethicone, sodium croscarmellose and stearic acid. Bottles of 100 and 500.

Store between 15 and 30°C.

New Product 1998

METHYLENE BLUE

Bioniche

Tetramethylthionine Chloride Trihydrate

Methemoglobinemia—Diagnostic Aid

Pharmacology: Methylene Blue activates a normally dormant reductase enzyme system which reduces the methylene blue to leucomethylene blue, which in turn is able to reduce methemoglobin to hemoglobin. Methylene Blue is absorbed from the gastrointestinal tract. It is believed to be reduced in the tissues to the leuco form which is slowly excreted, mainly in the urine together with some unchanged drug. Methylene Blue imparts a blue color to urine and faeces. In large doses Methylene Blue can produce methemoglobinemia.

Indications: Used in the treatment of methemoglobinemia. Also used as a bacteriological stain, as a dye in diagnostic procedures such as fistula detection, and for the delineation of certain body tissues during surgery.

Contraindications: In patients with severe renal impairment or a known hypersensitivity to the drug.

Precautions: Methemoglobin concentration should be closely monitored during treatment as Methylene Blue can produce methemoglobinemia in large doses.

Methylene Blue should be used with caution in the treatment of toxic methemoglobinemia; high doses can cause hemolytic anemias and patients with glucose-6-phosphate dehydrogenase (G6PD) deficiencies are particularly susceptible.

A rapid disappearance of cyanosis in response to Methylene Blue would be expected within one hour but might not occur if the patient has erythrocyte G6PD or NADPH-diaphorase deficiency or if methemoglobinemia is due to the ingestion of compounds such as aniline or dapsone. A second dose has been recommended if cyanosis does not disappear within 1 hour of Methylene Blue administration but results of a study in animals and of a patient with aniline poisoning indicated that an increased dosage of Methylene Blue might be of no additional benefit and could be potentially dangerous in that it could enhance Heinz body formation.

Methylene Blue should not be injected s.c. as it may cause necrotic abscesses. It should not be given by intrathecal injection as neural damage has occurred. Methylene Blue should be used with caution in patients with glucose-6-phosphate dehydrogenase deficiency.

Pregnancy and *Lactation:* Although intra-amniotic injection of Methylene Blue has been used to diagnose premature rupture of fetal membranes or to identify separate amniotic sacs in twin pregnancies, there have been several reports of hemolytic anemia (Heinz-body anemia) and hyperbilirubinemia in neonates exposed to Methylene Blue in the amniotic cavity. In most cases, exchange transfusions and/or phototherapy are required to control the jaundice.

Adverse Effects: After i.v. administration Methylene Blue may cause nausea, vomiting, abdominal and chest pain, headache, dizziness, mental confusion, profuse sweating, and hypertension; with very high doses methemoglobinemia and hemolysis may occur.

Dosage: For the treatment of drug-induced methemoglobinemia as in nitrite poisoning, Methylene Blue is administered i.v. as a 1% solution in doses of 1 to 2 mg/kg body weight injected over a period of several minutes. A repeat dose may be given after 1 hour if required.

Supplied: Each mL of sterile solution contains: tetramethylthionine chloride trihydrate 10 mg in water for injection. Nonmedicinal ingredients: sodium hydroxide and hydrochloric acid to adjust pH. Ampuls of 1 and 5 mL, boxes of 10. Store at room temperature (15 to 30°C).

METHYLENE BLUE INJECTION USP

Faulding

Indicator Dye

Supplied: Each mL of sterile solution for parenteral use contains: methylene blue USP 10 mg in water for injection. Ampuls of 5 mL, boxes of 5. Store at room temperature. Protect from light.

METHYLPREDNISOLONE Ⓟ

General Monograph, CPhA

see CORTICOSTEROIDS: SYSTEMIC
see CORTICOSTEROIDS: TOPICAL

...Drug identification problem? Consult the PRODUCT RECOGNITION SECTION.

METHYLPREDNISOLONE SODIUM SUCCINATE FOR INJECTION USP Ⓟ

Faulding

Glucocorticoid—Anti-inflammatory

Pharmacology: Methylprednisolone is a synthetic adrenocortical steroid derivative with predominantly glucocorticoid properties possessing anti-inflammatory and immunosuppressive action.

Methylprednisolone belongs to the pharmacologic class of glucocorticoid/anti-inflammatory drugs which, following systemic absorption, diffuse across cell membranes and complex with specific cytoplasmic receptors. These complexes may enter the cell nucleus, bind to DNA and stimulate transcription of mRNA. Subsequent cellular responses result in a variety of local and systemic effects. Anti-inflammatory processes such as edema, fibrin deposition, decreased prostaglandin/thromboxane synthesis, capillary dilation, migration of leukocytes, phagocytosis stage of wound healing and cicatrization are inhibited. Immune reactions are suppressed. Metabolically, protein catabolism and increased gluconeogenesis along with decreased peripheral utilization of glucose leads to glycogen storage in the liver, increased blood glucose concentration and insulin resistance (diabetogenic effect). During therapy lipolysis is inhanced and abnormal distribution of fat may result (Cushingoid effect). Skeletal calcium is mobilized and lost via renal excretion. Glucocorticoids in general augment renal glomerular filtration and promote urate excretion.

In respect of electrolyte and water balance, sodium tends to be reabsorbed and potassium and hydrogen excreted resulting in water retention and risk of hypokalemic alkalosis.

Methylprednisolone has a greater anti-inflammatory potency than prednisolone and has less tendency than prednisolone to induce sodium and water retention.

Methylprednisolone has the same metabolic and anti-inflammatory actions as hydrocortisone. When given parenterally and in equimolar quantities, the 2 compounds are equivalent in biologic activity. The relative potency of methylprednisolone and hydrocortisone, following i.v. administration, is at least 4 to 1. This is in good agreement with the relative oral potency of methylprednisolone and hydrocortisone.

A water-soluble corticosteroid salt should be administered i.v. to achieve a rapid onset of action.

Cortisone and prednisone are reduced to their pharmacologically active forms, hydrocortisone and prednisolone respectively. Pharmacologically active compounds are then metabolized primarily in the liver to biologically inactive compounds. Inactive metabolites, primarily glucuronides and sulfates are excreted by the kidneys. Small amounts of unmetabolized drug are excreted in urine and bile.

Indications: Management of conditions known to be responsive to prednisone or prednisolone where anti-inflammatory action or immunosuppression or adrenocortical supplementation and replacement is required.

For most indications, glucocorticoid administration provides symptomatic relief, but has no effect on the underlying disease process. Use of these medications does not eliminate the need for other therapies that may be required.

Situations in which a rapid and intense hormonal effect is required. These include the following:

Hypersensitivity and Dermatologic Conditions: Status asthmaticus, anaphylactic reactions, drug reactions, contact dermatitis, urticaria, generalized neurodermatitis, reactions to insect bites, pemphigus foliaceous and vulgaris, exfoliative dermatitis, erythema multiforme.

Ulcerative Colitis: In addition to the above conditions, colonic installations of methylprednisolone for injection in retention enemas or by continuous drip have been shown to be a useful adjunct in the treatment of patients with ulcerative colitis.

Anaphylactic Reactions: Epinephrine or norepinephrine should be administered first for an immediate hemodynamic effect followed by i.v. injection of methylprednisolone and other accepted procedures. There is evidence that the corticoids through their prolonged hemodynamic effect are of value in preventing recurrent attacks of acute anaphylactic reactions.

Sensitivity Reactions: Such as in serum sickness, allergic dermatosis (urticaria) and reactions to insect bites, methylprednisolone is capable of providing relief within 0.5 to 2 hours. In some asthmatic patients it may be advantageous to administer methylprednisolone by slow i.v. drip over a period of hours.

As Adjunctive Therapy in Fulminating Acute Systemic Lupus Erythematosus and Acute Rheumatic Fever, and to Relieve Pain During the Acute Manifestations of Gout: May be given by slow i.v. administration over a period of several minutes.

Methylprednisolone Sodium Succinate for Injection USP (cont'd)

Thereafter, the patient should be placed on i.m. or oral therapy as required for continued relief of symptoms. In these conditions, other accepted measures of therapy should also be instituted.

Shock: In severe hemorrhagic or traumatic shock, adjunctive use of i.v. methylprednisolone may aid in achieving hemodynamic restoration. [Although there are no well-controlled (double-blind placebo) clinical trials, data from experimental animal models indicate that methylprednisolone may be useful in hemorrhagic and traumatic shock. See also Warnings regarding septic shock.] Corticoid therapy should not replace standard methods of combatting shock, but present evidence indicates that concurrent use of large doses of corticoids with other measures may improve survival rates.

Organ Transplants: Corticosteroids both parenterally and orally in high doses have been used following organ transplantation as part of multifaceted attempts to reduce the rejection phenomenon. Methylprednisolone is suitable for such indications.

Cerebral Edema: Corticosteroid therapy as an adjunct to the usual forms of therapy for cerebral edema has been used for many years. Cerebral edema associated with acute craniocerebral injuries and intracranial hematomas of traumatic origin has been treated with methylprednisolone with some improvement in overall survival rate and reduction of permanent disability following such conditions. Administration immediately prior to intracranial surgery and in the immediate postoperative period has reduced the duration of postoperative complications related to cerebral edema.

Acute Spinal Cord Injury: The use of methylprednisolone in high dose has resulted in improvement in motor and sensory recovery. Treatment should begin within 8 hours of injury.

Contraindications: Untreated systemic fungal infections.

Hypersensitivity to methylprednisolone, or other corticosteroids, or to any of its ingredients.

Except when used for short-term or emergency therapy as in acute sensitivity reactions, methylprednisolone is contraindicated in patients with arrested tuberculosis, herpes simplex keratitis, acute psychoses, Cushing's syndrome, peptic ulcer, markedly elevated serum creatinine, vaccinia and varicella.

Warnings: Glucocorticoid-induced suppression of HPA (Hypothalamic-Pituitary-Adrenal) function is dependent on dose and duration of treatment. Recovery occurs gradually as the steroid dose is reduced and withdrawn. Suppression persists for a period of time after withdrawal depending on dose and length of treatment time.

In patients on corticosteroid therapy subjected to unusual stress, increased dosage of rapidly acting corticosteroids before, during and after the stressful situation is indicated. Corticosteroids may mask some signs of infection, and new infections may appear during their use. There may be decreased resistance and inability to localize infection when corticosteroids are used.

If corticosteroids have to be used in the presence of fungal or bacterial infections, institute appropriate anti-infective therapy.

Prolonged use of corticosteroids may produce posterior subcapsular cataracts or glaucoma with possible damage to the optic nerves, and may enhance the establishment of secondary ocular infections due to fungi or viruses.

Average and large doses of corticosteroids can cause elevation of blood pressure, salt and water retention, and increased excretion of potassium. These effects are less likely to occur with the synthetic derivatives except when used in large doses. Dietary salt restriction and potassium supplementation may be necessary. All corticosteroids increase calcium excretion. While on corticosteroid therapy, patients should not be vaccinated against measles. **Other immunization procedures should not be undertaken in patients who are on corticosteroids, especially on high doses, because of possible hazards of neurological complications and lack of antibody response.**

The use of corticosteroids in active tuberculosis should be restricted to those cases of fulminating or disseminated tuberculosis in which the corticosteroid is used for the management of the disease in conjunction with an appropriate antituberculous regimen. If corticosteroids are indicated in patients with latent tuberculosis or tuberculin reactivity, close observation is necessary as reactivation of the disease may occur. During prolonged corticosteroid therapy, these patients should receive chemoprophylaxis.

Patients who are on drugs which suppress the immune system are more susceptible to infections than healthy individuals. Chicken pox and measles can have a more serious or even fatal course in non-immune children or adults who are on corticosteroids. In such children or adults who have not had these diseases, particular care should be taken to avoid exposure. The contribution of the underlying disease and/or prior corticosteroid treatment to the risk is not known. If exposed to chicken pox, prophylaxis with varicella zoster immune globulin (VZIG) may be indicated. If exposed to measles, prophylaxis with pooled i.m. immunoglobulin (IG) may be indicated. If chicken pox develops, treatment with antiviral agents may be considered.

Recent studies do not establish the efficacy of methylprednisolone in septic shock and suggest that increased mortality may occur in some subgroups at higher risk (i.e., elevated serum creatinine greater than 2.0 mg% or secondary infections).

Because rare instances of anaphylactoid (e.g., bronchospasm) reactions have occurred in patients receiving parenteral corticosteroid therapy, appropriate precautionary measures should be taken prior to administration, especially when the patient has a history of allergy to any drug.

Should bacteriostatic water for injection be used for reconstitution, note that benzyl alcohol has been reported to be associated with a fatal ''Gasping syndrome'' in premature infants.

Precautions: During prolonged corticosteroid therapy, routine laboratory studies such as urinalysis, 2-hour postprandial blood sugar determinations, blood pressure monitoring, body weight and chest X-ray should be performed at regular intervals. If doses of methylprednisolone are high, serum potassium should be monitored regularly. Serious consideration of upper gastrointestinal studies should be contemplated when patients complain of gastric symptoms while on this medication. Prolonged therapy above 8 mg/day is associated with doses exceeding 40 mg/day.

Drug-induced secondary adrenocortical insufficiency may be minimized by gradual reduction of dosage. This type of relative insufficiency may persist for months after discontinuation of therapy; therefore, in any situation of stress occurring during that period, hormone therapy should be reinstituted. Since mineralocorticoid secretion may be impaired, salt and/or mineralocorticoids should be administered concurrently.

Children: Growth and development of infants and children on prolonged corticosteroid therapy should be carefully observed. Administration of corticosteroids to children should be limited to the least amount compatible with an effective therapeutic regimen.

Pediatric patients demonstrate greater susceptibility to corticosteroid-induced HPA axis suppression and Cushing's syndrome than mature patients. HPA axis suppression, Cushing's syndrome and intracranial hypertension have been reported in children taking oral corticosteroids. Manifestations of adrenal suppression in children include linear growth retardation, delayed weight gain, low plasma cortisol levels and absence of response to ACTH stimulation. Manifestations of intracranial hypertension include bulging fontanelles, headaches and bilateral papilloedema.

General Use: There is an enhanced effect of corticosteroids in patients with hypothyroidism and in those with cirrhosis of the liver.

Corticosteroids should be used cautiously in patients with ocular herpes simplex because of possible corneal perforation.

The lowest possible dose of corticosteroid should be used to control the condition under treatment and, when reduction in dosage is possible, the reduction should be gradual.

Psychic derangements may appear when corticosteroids are used, ranging from euphoria, insomnia, mood swings, personality changes and severe depression to frank psychotic manifestations. Also, existing emotional instability or psychotic tendencies may be aggravated by corticosteroids.

Following prolonged therapy, psychological and/or physiological dependence may develop. Withdrawal of glucocorticoids may result in symptoms of the glucocorticoid withdrawal syndrome including: fever, myalgia, arthralgia and malaise. This may occur in patients even without evidence of adrenal insufficiency.

ASA and other NSAIDs should be used cautiously in conjunction with corticosteroids in hypoprothrombinemia.

Corticosteroids Should be Used With Caution in the Following Clinical Conditions: Nonspecific ulcerative colitis (if there is a probability of impending perforation), abscess or other pyogenic infection, diverticulitis, fresh intestinal anastomoses, active or latent peptic ulcer, renal insufficiency, hypertension, osteoporosis, cardiac disease, thromboembolic disorders and diabetes mellitus.

In myasthenia gravis, hospitalization with careful observation is recommended because transient worsening of symptoms, possibly leading to respiratory distress, may precede clinical improvement.

There are reports of cardiac arrhythmias and/or circulatory collapse and/or cardiac arrest following the rapid administration or large i.v. doses of methylprednisolone (greater than 0.5 g administered over a period of less than 10 minutes). Bradycardia has been reported during or after the administration of large doses of methylprednisolone and may be unrelated to the speed or duration of infusion.

Since complications of treatment with glucocorticoids are dependent on the size of the dose and the duration of treatment, a risk/benefit decision must be made in each individual case as to dose and duration of treatment and as to whether daily or intermittent therapy should be used.

Patients should be warned not to discontinue the use of methylprednisolone abruptly or without medical supervision, to advise any medical attendants that they are taking methylprednisolone and to seek medical advice at once should they develop fever or other signs of infection.

Corticosteroids may mask some signs of infection and new infections may appear during their use. There may be decreased resistance and inability to localize infection when corticosteroids are used.

Adequate adrenocortical supportive therapy including ACTH must be employed promptly if the patient is subjected to any unusual stress such as surgery, trauma or severe infection.

Persons who are on immunosuppressant doses of corticosteroids should be warned to avoid exposure to chicken pox or measles. Patients should also be advised that if they are exposed, medical advice should be sought without delay (See Warnings).

Steroids may increase or decrease motility and number of spermatozoa in some male patients. However, it is not known whether reproductive capacity in humans is adversely affected.

Carcinogenicity and Mutagenicity: There is no evidence that corticosteroids are carcinogenic.

Drug Interactions: Although no unusual drug interactions have been detected during clinical trials, the same precautions should be exercised as for other glucocorticoids. It is recommended to increase the maintenance dose of glucocorticoids if the following drugs are administered at the same time: anticonvulsants (phenobarbital, phenytoin), certain antibiotics (rifampin), anticoagulants (coumarin) and bronchodilators (ephedrine). If the patient receiving glucocorticoids is treated at the same time with some other antibiotics (erythromycin), ketoconazole, estrogens or preparations containing estrogens, a reduction in the dose of methylprednisolone is recommended. Since methylprednisolone is metabolized in the liver, the possibility remains that concomitant administration of other hepatically metabolized drugs may lead to interactions (e.g., barbiturates).

Anticholinesterase effects may be antagonized in myasthenia gravis. Toxicity may be enhanced when cyclosporin and glucocorticoids are combined in organ transplant patients. Coadministration with digitalis glycosides may enhance the possibility of digitalis toxicity associated with hypocalcemia. Isoniazid and salicylate serum concentrations may be decreased upon coadministration with glucocorticoids.

Potassium-depleting agents (e.g., thiazide diuretics) may enhance hypocalcemia and hypokalemia secondary to glucocorticoid use. Coadministration with nonsteroidal anti-inflammatories may increase the risk of gastrointestinal ulceration. Immunologic response to vaccines and toxoids is reduced by glucocorticoids which may also potentiate the replication of organisms in attenuated vaccines (e.g., measles). Glucocorticoids may alter laboratory or radiological tests for serum T_3 or serum protein-bound iodine, may decrease T_4 minimally or decrease the uptake of ^{131}iodine.

Immunization procedures may be undertaken in patients who are receiving corticosteroids as **replacement** therapy (e.g., Addison's disease).

Convulsions have been reported with concurrent use of methylprednisolone and cyclosporine. Since concurrent administration of these agents results in a mutual inhibition of metabolism, it is possible that convulsions and other adverse events associated with the individual use of either drug may be more apt to occur.

Pregnancy: Methylprednisolone (corticosteroid) has been shown to be teratogenic in various animal species when given in doses equivalent to the human dose. There are no adequate and well-controlled studies in pregnant women. Methylprednisolone should be used during pregnancy only if the potential benefit justifies the potential risk to the fetus. Animal studies in which methylprednisolone has been given to pregnant rodents and rabbits have yielded an increased incidence of cleft palate in the offspring.

Infants born to mothers who have received substantial doses of corticosteroids during pregnancy should be carefully observed for signs of hypoadrenalism.

Lactation: Methylprednisolone is excreted in breast milk. Caution should be exercised when methylprednisolone is administered to a nursing woman.

Adverse Effects: Corticosteroids have a potential for multiple adverse effects. There are essentially 2 types of toxicity observed when administered in therapeutic dosages: withdrawal effects, which could produce life-threatening adrenal insufficiency; and high dosage over long periods, which could produce fluid/electrolyte disturbances, hyperglycemia, increased susceptibility to infections, peptic ulceration, osteoporosis, myopathy, behavioral disturbances, cataracts, or Cushing's habitus. Single doses, or short courses of therapy (over several days) usually have less harmful effects. The approach to therapy should follow logical and rational sequence of: (i) attempting to control the condition with more conventional mode(s) of management; (ii) weighing the benefits of steroid therapy against the risks; (iii) commencing therapy with a high loading dose, reducing to the minimum effective dosage as soon as possible.

General Adverse Events for Prednisone or Prednisolone: Fluid and Electrolyte Disturbances: sodium retention, fluid retention, congestive heart failure in susceptible patients, potassium loss, hypokalemic alkalosis, hypertension.

Musculoskeletal: muscle weakness, steroid myopathy, loss of muscle mass, osteoporosis, vertebral compression fractures, aseptic necrosis of femoral and humeral heads, pathologic fracture of long bones.

Gastrointestinal: peptic ulcer with possible perforation and hemorrhage, pancreatitis, abdominal distention, ulcerative esophagitis.

Dermatologic: impaired wound healing, thin fragile skin, petechiae and ecchymoses, facial erythema, increased sweating, may suppress reactions to skin test.

Metabolic: negative nitrogen balance due to protein catabolism.

Neurological: convulsions, increased intracranial pressure with papilloedema (pseudotumor cerebri) usually after treatment, vertigo, headache.

Endocrine: menstrual irregularities; development of cushingoid state; secondary adrenocortical and pituitary unresponsiveness, particularly in times of stress, as in trauma, surgery or illness; suppression of growth in children; decreased carbohydrate tolerance, manifestations of latent diabetes mellitus, increased requirements for insulin or oral hypoglycemic agents in diabetics.

Ophthalmic: posterior subcapsular cataracts, increased intraocular pressure, glaucoma, exophthalmos.

The following additional reactions are related to parenteral corticosteroid therapy: anaphylactic reaction with or without circulatory collapse, cardiac arrest, bronchospasm, cardiac arrhythmias, hypotension or hypertension.

Overdose: Symptoms and Treatment: There is no clinical symptom of acute overdosage with this drug. Methylprednisolone is dialysable. The metabolism and excretion of methylprednisolone is similar to that of other corticosteroids. Continuous overdosage would require careful gradual reduction of dosage in order to prevent the occurrence of acute adrenal insufficiency.

For corticosteroids in general, anaphylactic and hypersensitivity reactions depending on their severity may be treated with antihistamines with or without epinephrine.

In the absence of specific rescue therapy, treatment is to be symptomatic and supportive.

Since injections of slightly soluble corticosteroids may produce atrophy at the site of injection, i.m. injections of these products should be made deeply into gluteal muscle; repeated i.m. injections at the same site should be avoided and these products should not be administered s.c.

Dosage: The minimum effective dosage should be sought once clinical control of the disease is obtained. Withdrawal should be slow and gradual in order to avoid glucocorticoid withdrawal syndrome.

Dosage ranges for corticosteroids are extremely wide and patient responses are quite variable. Dosage should be individualized according to the diagnosis, severity, prognosis, probable duration of disease, patient response and tolerance. For infants and children, the recommended dosage should be governed by the same considerations rather than by strict adherence to the ratio indicated by age or body weight.

As Adjunctive Therapy in Life-threatening Conditions (e.g., shock states): The recommended dose of methylprednisolone is 30 mg/kg, given i.v. over a period of at least 30 minutes. The large doses may be repeated every 4 to 6 hours for up to 48 hours.

Acute Spinal Cord Injury: For treatment of acute spinal cord injury, administer i.v. 30 mg methylprednisolone/kg of body weight in a bolus dose over a 15-minute period, followed by a 45-minute pause, and then a continuous infusion of 5.4 mg/kg/h for 23 hours. There should be a separate i.v. site for the infusion pump. The treatment should begin within 8 hours of injury.

Ulcerative Colitis: Methylprednisolone in doses of 40 to 120 mg administered as retention enemas or by continuous drip 3 to 7 times weekly for periods of 2 or more weeks has been shown to be a useful adjunct in the treatment of some patients with ulcerative colitis. Many patients can be controlled with 40 mg administered in 1 to 10 fluid ounces of water depending on the degree of involvement of the inflamed colonic mucosa. Other accepted therapeutic measures should, of course, be instituted.

In Other Indications: Initial dosage will vary from 10 to 500 mg depending on the clinical problem being treated. Larger doses may be required for short-term management of severe, acute conditions. Therapy may be initiated by administering methylprednisolone i.v. over a period of at least 5 minutes (e.g., doses up to 250 mg) to at least 30 minutes (e.g., doses greater than 250 mg). Subsequent doses may be given i.v. or i.m. at intervals dictated by the patient's response and clinical condition. Corticosteroid therapy is an adjunct to, and not replacement for, conventional therapy.

Methylprednisolone may be administered by i.v. or i.m. injection or by i.v. infusion, the preferred method for initial emergency use being i.v. injection. To administer i.v. (or i.m.) injection, prepare solution as directed (see Directions for Reconstitution).

The lowest possible dose of corticosteroid should be used to control the condition under treatment and, when reduction in dosage is possible, the reduction should be gradual.

Since complications of treatment with glucocorticoids are dependent on the size of the dose and the duration of treatment, a risk/benefit decision must be made in each individual case as to dose and duration of treatment and as to whether daily or intermittent therapy should be used.

Alternate day therapy (ADT) in which a single dose is administered every other morning is the dosage regimen of choice for long-term corticosteroid treatment.

Morning administration of the drug simulates the natural circadian rhythm of corticosteroid secretion which is high in the morning and low in the evening. This regimen provides relief of symptoms while minimizing adrenal suppression, cushingoid state, withdrawal symptoms and growth suppression in children. Intermediate acting agents should be used for alternate day therapy (see Table I).

Table I provides a comparison of glucocorticoid equivalence.

Table I—Methylprednisolone Sodium Succinate for Injection USP

Corticosteroid Comparison Chart

Drug	Biologic Half-life (hours)	Equivalent Anti-inflammatory Dose (mg)*	Relative Mineralo-corticoid Potency
Glucocorticoids:			
Short-acting	8-12		
Cortisone		25	2
Hydrocortisone		20	2
Intermediate acting	18-36		
Methylprednisolone		4	0
Prednisolone		5	1
Prednisone		5	1
Triamiconolone		4	0
Long-acting	36-54		
Betamethasone		0.6	0
Dexamethasone		0.75	0
Mineralocorticoid:			
Fludrocortisone	12-24	10	125

*Equivalent doses are general approximations and may not apply to all diseases or routes of administration. Duration of HPA axis suppression and degree of mineralocorticoid activities must be considered separately.

Stability and Storage: Store intact vials at 15 to 25°C. Protect from light.

Reconstituted Solution: When reconstituted with Bacteriostatic Water for Injection, the resulting solution may be stored for up to 48 hours at 15 to 25°C. When reconstituted with Sterile Water for Injection, the resulting solution may be stored for up to 24 hours at 15 to 25°C due to risk of microbial contamination. The solution with a slight haze should be discarded. Discard unused portion.

Directions for Reconstitution: 1. Remove the protective plastic flip-top seal. 2. Swab the rubber stopper with an antiseptic solution and introduce the required quantity of the diluent by means of a syringe into the vial. 3. Shake the vial thoroughly to dissolve the powder content. 4. Withdraw the dose in the usual manner with the help of a syringe; unused portion should be discarded.

Reconstitute with Sterile Water for Injection, or, if required, Bacteriostatic Water for Injection as follows (see Table II).

Table II—Methylprednisolone Sodium Succinate for Injection USP

Reconstitution Table

Size (mg/vial)	Quantity of Diluent (mL)	Approximative Withdrawable Volume (mL)	Nominal Concentration (mg/mL)
500	7.8	8	62.5
1 000	15.6	16	62.5

Parenteral drug products should be inspected visually for particulate matter and discoloration prior to administration. Do not use if solution is cloudy or contains a precipitate.

Preparation of Solutions for I.V. Infusion: First prepare the solution for injection as directed. Further dilution should be done immediately after reconstitution.

If desired, the medication may be administered in diluted solutions by admixing the reconstituted product with 0.9% Sodium Chloride Injection or with Dextrose 5% Injection. Concentrations of 1 mg/mL are physically and chemically stable for 24 hours at 15 to 25°C.

Parenteral drug products should be inspected visually for particulate matter and discoloration prior to administration, whenever solution and container permit.

Compatibility: The compatibility and stability of methylprednisolone in solutions and with other drugs in i.v. admixtures is dependent on admixture pH, concentration, time, temperature, and ability of methylprednisolone to solubilize itself. Thus, to avoid compatibility and stability problems, whenever possible it is recommended that methylprednisolone for injection be administered separate from other drugs and as either i.v. push, through an i.v. medication chamber, or as an i.v. "piggy-back" solution.

Supplied: 500 mg: Each vial of sterile, lyophilized powder contains: methylprednisolone 500 mg as the sodium succinate. Nonmedicinal ingredients: disodium hydrogen phosphate and sodium dihydrogen phosphate. Clear glass vials, boxes of 1 [including a vial of Bacteriostatic Water for Injection (benzyl alcohol 0.9% v/v)] of 10 mL.

1 g: Each vial of sterile, lyophilized powder contains: methylprednisolone 1 g as the sodium succinate. Nonmedicinal ingredients: disodium hydrogen phosphate and sodium dihydrogen phosphate. Clear glass vials, boxes of 1 [including a vial of Bacteriostatic Water for Injection (benzyl alcohol 0.9% v/v)] of 20 mL.

New Product 1998

METIMYD® Ⓟ

Schering

Prednisolone—Sulfacetamide Compound

Ophthalmic Corticosteroid—Antibacterial

Indications: Inflammatory and allergic disease of the eye especially when antibacterial effect is desired.

Contraindications: Tuberculosis, fungal and most viral lesions of the eye (herpes simplex/dendritic keratitis): vaccinia; varicella; acute purulent conjunctivitis and acute purulent blepharitis and in those persons who have shown hypersensitivity to any of its components.

Precautions: Extended use of topical steroid therapy may cause increased intraocular pressure in certain individuals. It is advisable that intraocular pressure be checked frequently. In those diseases causing thinning of the cornea, perforation has been known to occur with the use of topical steroids. Prolonged use may result in overgrowth of nonsusceptible organisms, including fungi. Appropriate measures should be taken if superinfection occurs. A few individuals may be sensitive to one or more components of this product. If any reactions indicating sensitivity are observed, discontinue use.

Metimyd (cont'd)

The protracted use of topical corticosteroids in the eye has been rarely associated with the development of posterior subcapsular cataracts.

Pregnancy: The safety of intensive or protracted use of topical corticosteroids during pregnancy has not been substantiated.

Dosage: Administration should be adjusted to the specific needs of the individual; 2 or 3 drops should be instilled into the conjunctival sac every hour or two during the day and less often at night until response is favorable. The dosage should be reduced thereafter.

Supplied: Each mL of sterile suspension contains: microcrystalline prednisolone acetate USP 5 mg (0.5%) suspended in an isotonic buffered and preserved solution of sulfacetamide sodium USP 100 mg (10%). Nonmedicinal ingredients: benzalkonium chloride, edetate disodium, phenylethyl alcohol, sodium phosphate dibasic, sodium phosphate monobasic, sodium thiosulfate, tyloxapol and water. Dropper bottles of 5 mL. Store in a cool place.

METRETON® Ⓟ

Schering

Prednisone Acetate—Chlorpheniramine Maleate—Ascorbic Acid

Glucocorticoid—Antihistamine

Pharmacology: Metreton combines the anti-inflammatory and antiallergic effects of the corticosteroid prednisone with the antihistaminic activity of chlorpheniramine. In addition, Metreton tablets contain ascorbic acid.

By using prednisone and chlorpheniramine in combination, comparable results usually are obtained with smaller amounts of corticosteroid than when the corticosteroid is given alone.

Indications: For the relief of hay fever, allergic rhinitis, intractable asthma and other allergic states.

Contraindications: Systemic fungal infections; hypersensitivity to prednisone, to other corticosteroids or to any component of Metreton.

Precautions: Prednisone: Dosage adjustments may be required with remission or exacerbation of the disease process, the patient's individual response to therapy and exposure of the patient to emotional or physical stress such as serious infection, surgery or injury. Monitoring may be necessary for up to 1 year following cessation of long-term or high-dose corticosteroid therapy. Drug induced secondary adrenocortical insufficiency may be minimized by gradual dosage reduction. This type of relative insufficiency may persist for months after discontinuation of therapy, therefore, in any stress situation occurring during that period, reinstitute hormone therapy. If the patient is receiving steroids already, the dosage may have to be increased.

The lowest possible dose of corticosteroid should be used to control the condition under treatment. A gradual dosage reduction is recommended.

Corticosteroid effect is enhanced in patients with hypothyroidism or in those with cirrhosis.

Cautious use of corticosteroids is advised in patients with ocular herpes simplex because of possible corneal perforation.

Psychic derangements may appear with corticosteroid therapy. Existing emotional instability or psychotic tendencies may be aggravated by corticosteroids.

Corticosteroids should be used with caution in: nonspecific ulcerative colitis, if there is a probability of impending perforation, abscess, or other pyogenic infection; diverticulitis; fresh intestinal anastomoses; active or latent peptic ulcer; renal insufficiency; hypertension; osteoporosis; and myasthenia gravis.

Since complications of glucocorticoid treatment are dependent on dosage and duration of treatment, a risk/benefit decision must be made with each patient.

Corticosteroids may mask some signs of infection, and new infections may appear during use. When corticosteroids are used, decreased resistance and inability to localize infection may occur.

Prolonged corticosteroid use may produce posterior subcapsular cataracts (especially in children), glaucoma with possible damage to the optic nerves, and may enhance secondary ocular infections due to fungi or viruses.

Corticosteroid therapy may cause hyperacidity or peptic ulcer. Since the appearance of a peptic ulcer may be asymptomatic until perforation or hemorrhage occurs, take x-rays when treatment is prolonged or when there is gastric distress. An ulcer regimen, including an antacid, should be considered as a prophylactic measure during prolonged therapy.

Average and large doses of corticosteroids can cause elevation of blood pressure, salt and water retention, and increased excretion of potassium. These effects are less likely to occur with the synthetic derivatives except when used in large doses. Dietary salt restriction and potassium supplementation may be considered. All corticosteroids increase calcium excretion. Since mineralocorticoid secretion may be impaired, salt and/or a mineralocorticoid should be administered concurrently.

While on corticosteroid therapy patients should not be vaccinated against smallpox. Conversely, patients with vacinia should not receive corticosteroid therapy. Other immunization procedures should not be undertaken in patients receiving corticosteroids, especially high doses, because of possible hazards of neurological complications and lack of antibody response.

Patients who are on immunosuppressant doses of corticosteroids should be warned to avoid exposure to chickenpox or measles, and if exposed, to obtain medical advice. This is of particular importance in children.

Corticosteroid therapy in active tuberculosis should be restricted to those cases of fulminating or disseminated tuberculosis in which the corticosteroid is used in conjunction with an appropriate antituberculous regimen.

If corticosteroids are indicated in patients with latent tuberculosis, close observation is necessary since reactivation of the disease may occur. During prolonged corticosteroid therapy, patients should receive chemoprophylaxis.

Growth and development of children on prolonged corticosteroid therapy should be followed carefully, since corticosteroid administration can disturb growth rates and inhibit endogenous corticosteroid production in these patients.

Corticosteroid therapy may alter the motility and number of spermatozoa in some patients.

Pregnancy and *Lactation:* Since adequate human reproduction studies have not been done with corticosteroids, the use of these drugs in pregnancy, nursing mothers or women of child bearing potential requires that the possible benefits of the drug be weighed against the potential hazards to the mother and fetus or infant. Infants born of mothers who have received substantial doses of corticosteroids during pregnancy should be carefully observed for signs of hypoadrenalism.

Advise patients to inform subsequent physicians of the prior use of corticosteroids.

Chlorpheniramine Maleate: Metreton should be used with caution in patients with narrow angle glaucoma, stenosing peptic ulcer, pyloroduodenal obstruction, prostatic hypertrophy or bladder neck obstruction, cardiovascular disease including hypertension, in those with increased intraocular pressure or hyperthyroidism.

Occupational Hazards: Patients should be warned about engaging in activities requiring mental alertness, such as driving a car or operating appliances, machinery, etc.

Conventional antihistamines may cause dizziness, sedation, and hypotension in patients over 60 years of age.

Children: Safety and effectiveness have not been established in children under 2 years of age.

Drug Interactions: Concurrent use of phenobarbital, phenytoin, rifampin or ephedrine may enhance the rate of metabolism and clearance of corticosteroids, thereby reducing their therapeutic effects. May inhibit the response to somatotropin.

Patients receiving both a corticosteroid and an estrogen should be observed for excessive corticosteroid effects.

Concurrent use of corticosteroids with potassium-depleting diuretics may enhance hypokalemia. Concurrent use of corticosteroids with cardiac glycosides may enhance the possibility of arrhythmias or digitalis toxicity associated with hypokalemia. Corticosteroids may enhance the potassium depletion caused by amphotericin B. In all patients taking any of these drug therapy combinations, serum electrolyte determinations, particularly potassium levels, should be monitored closely.

Concurrent use of corticosteroids with coumarin-type anticoagulants may increase or decrease the anticoagulant effect, possibly requiring adjustment in dosage.

Combined effects of noncorticosteroid drugs or alcohol with glucocorticoids may result in an increased occurrence or increased severity of gastrointestinal ulceration.

Corticosteroids may decrease blood salicylate concentrations. ASA should be used cautiously in conjunction with corticosteroids in hypoprothrombinemia.

Corticosteroids may affect the nitroblue tetrazolium test for bacterial infection and produce false negative results.

Dose adjustments of an antidiabetic drug may be necessary when corticosteroids are given to diabetics.

MAO inhibitors prolong and intensify the effects of antihistamines; severe hypotension may occur. Concomitant use of antihistamines with alcohol, tricyclic antidepressants, barbiturates or other CNS depressants may potentiate the sedative effect of chlorpheniramine maleate. Antihistamines may inhibit the action of oral anticoagulants.

Adverse Effects: The physician should be alerted to the possibility of any adverse effects associated with the use of corticosteroids and antihistamines, especially of the sedating type.

Prednisone: Adverse reactions to this component are the same as those reported with other corticosteroids and they are related to dose and duration of therapy.

Adverse reactions reported for corticosteroids include: Fluid and Electrolyte Disturbances: sodium retention, potassium loss, hypokalemic alkalosis; fluid retention, congestive heart failure in susceptible patients; hypertension.

Musculoskeletal: muscle weakness, corticosteroid myopathy, loss of muscle mass; aggravation of myasthenic symptoms in myasthenia gravis; osteoporosis; vertebral compression fractures; aseptic necrosis of femoral and humeral heads; pathologic fracture of long bones; tendon rupture.

Gastrointestinal: peptic ulcer with possible subsequent perforation and hemorrhage; pancreatitis, abdominal distention; ulcerative esophagitis.

Dermatologic: impaired wound healing, skin atrophy, thin fragile skin; petechiae and ecchymoses; facial erythema; increased sweating; suppressed reactions to skin tests; reactions such as allergic dermatitis, urticaria, angioneurotic edema.

Neurologic: convulsions; increased intracranial pressure with papilledema (pseudotumor cerebri) usually after treatment; vertigo; headache.

Endocrine: menstrual irregularities; development of cushingoid state; suppression of fetal intrauterine or childhood growth; secondary adrenocortical and pituitary unresponsiveness, particularly in times of stress, as in trauma, surgery or illness; decreased carbohydrate tolerance, manifestations of latent diabetes mellitus, increased requirements of insulin or oral hypoglycemic agents in diabetics.

Ophthalmic: posterior subcapsular cataracts; increased intraocular pressure, glaucoma; exophthalmos.

Metabolic: negative nitrogen balance due to protein catabolism.

Psychiatric: euphoria, mood swings; severe depression to frank psychotic manifestations; personality changes; hyperirritability; insomnia.

Other: anaphylactoid or hypersensitivity and hypotensive or shock-like reactions.

Chlorpheniramine Maleate: Adverse reactions to this component have been the same as those reported with other conventional (sedating) antihistamines, and rarely cause toxicity. Slight to moderate drowsiness is the most frequent side effect of chlorpheniramine maleate. Adverse effects of sedating antihistamines vary in incidence and severity. Among these are cardiovascular, hematologic (pancytopenia, thrombocytopenia, hemolytic anemia), neurologic (confusion, hallucinations, tremor), gastrointestinal (urinary retention), respiratory adverse reactions and mood changes. The most common effects include sedation, sleepiness, dizziness, disturbed coordination, epigastric distress, rash, dry mouth and thickening of bronchial secretions.

Overdose: Symptoms: Metreton is a combination product and, therefore, the potential toxicity of each of its components must be considered. Toxicity from a single excessive dose of Metreton results primarily from the chlorpheniramine maleate component.

A single excessive dose of a corticosteroid should not be expected to produce acute symptoms. Except at the most extreme dosages, a few days of excessive glucocorticosteroid dosing is unlikely to produce harmful results in the absence of specific contraindications, such as in patients at particular risk due to underlying conditions or on concomitant medications likely to interact adversely with the prednisone component.

Overdosage reactions with conventional (sedating) antihistamines may vary from CNS depression (sedation, apnea, diminished mental alertness, cardiovascular collapse) to stimulation (insomnia, hallucinations, tremor, convulsions) to death. Other signs and symptoms may include dizziness, tinnitus, ataxia, blurred vision and hypotension. In children, stimulation is dominant, as are atropine-like signs and symptoms (dry mouth, fixed, dilated pupils, flushing, fever, and gastrointestinal symptoms). Hallucinations, incoordination, and convulsions of the tonic-clonic type may occur. In adults, a cycle consisting of depression with drowsiness and coma, and an excitement phase leading to convulsions followed by depression may occur.

Treatment: Acute overdosage should be treated immediately by inducing emesis or by the administration of gastric lavage. Dialysis has not been found helpful. Treatment of the signs and symptoms is symptomatic and supportive. Stimulants should **not** be used. Vasopressors may be used to treat hypotension. Convulsions are best treated with short-acting depressants, such as thiopental. Maintain adequate fluid intake and monitor electrolytes in serum and urine, with particular attention to sodium and potassium balance. Treat electrolyte imbalance if necessary.

Dosage: Average initial dosage will be 1 or 2 tablets after meals and at bedtime and is not to exceed 8 tablets daily. After 2 weeks of therapy, patients should be re-evaluated to determine whether Metreton dosage can be reduced. As improvement occurs, the dosage should be reduced gradually to the minimum maintenance level and discontinued where possible.

When symptoms of respiratory allergies are adequately controlled, slow withdrawal of the combination product and treatment with an antihistamine alone should be considered.

Supplied: Each white tablet contains: prednisone acetate USP 2.5 mg, chlorpheniramine maleate USP 2 mg and ascorbic acid USP 75 mg. Nonmedicinal ingredients: cornstarch, lactose, magnesium stearate, povidone. Tartrazine-free. Bottles of 100.

(Shown in Product Recognition Section)

Reviewed 1997

METROCREAM™ Ⓟ
METROGEL® Ⓟ

Galderma

Metronidazole

Antirosacea Agent

Pharmacology: Metronidazole topical preparations are particularly effective against the inflammatory, papulopustular component of rosacea. The mechanisms by which topical metronidazole acts in reducing inflammatory lesions of rosacea are unknown, but may include an anti-bacterial and/or an anti-inflammatory effect.

Serum metronidazole levels have been shown to be below detection limits (<25 ng/mL) at the majority of time points after administration of topical metronidazole. At the time points that it could be detected, topical metronidazole produced blood levels (C_{max} 40.6 ng/mL) that were approximately 80% less than a similar dose administered orally (C_{max} 212 ng/mL). Therefore, with normal usage, topical metronidazole results in minimal blood levels of metronidazole.

Pharmacokinetics: Metronidazole is rapidly and nearly totally absorbed after oral administration. The drug is not significantly bound to serum proteins and distributes well to all body compartments with the lowest concentration found in fat. Metronidazole is excreted primarily in the urine as parent drug, oxidative metabolites, and conjugates.

Studies on the topical administration of 1 g of topical gel to the face (7.5 mg of metronidazole) of 10 rosacea patients showed a maximum serum concentration of 66 ng/mL in 1 patient. This concentration is approximately 100 times less than concentrations afforded by a single 250 mg oral tablet. The serum metronidazole concentrations were below the detectable limits (25 ng/mL) of the assay at the majority of time points in all patients. Three of the patients had no detectable serum concentrations of metronidazole at any time point. The mean dose of gel applied during clinical studies was 600 mg, which represents 4.5 mg of metronidazole per application. Therefore, under normal usage levels, the formulation affords minimal serum concentrations of metronidazole.

An *in vitro* study with 0.75% metronidazole topical cream and gel demonstrates that the penetration of metronidazole into the layers of the skin is comparable.

Indications: For topical application in the treatment of inflammatory papules, pustules, and erythema of rosacea. Patients with dry or sensitive skin may prefer using the cream formulation.

Contraindications: In individuals with a history of hypersensitivity to metronidazole, or other ingredients of the formulations.

Warnings: Avoid contact with the eyes. Topical metronidazole has been reported to cause tearing of the eyes. It should not be used in or close to the eye. If contact does occur, flush with water.

Children: Safety and effectiveness in children have not been established.

Pregnancy: There has been no experience to date with the use of metronidazole in pregnant patients. Metronidazole crosses the placental barrier and enters the fetal circulation rapidly. No fetotoxicity was observed after oral metronidazole in rats or mice. However, because animal reproduction studies are not always predictive of human response, this drug should be used during pregnancy only after careful assessment of the risk/benefit ratio.

Lactation: Even though metronidazole blood levels are significantly lower after topical than after oral administration a decision should be made whether to discontinue nursing or to discontinue the drug, taking into account the importance of the drug to the mother. After oral administration, metronidazole is secreted in breast milk in concentrations similar to those found in the plasma.

Mutagenicity and Carcinogenicity: Information from preclinical studies indicates that metronidazole and its principal metabolite are mutagenic in bacteria and that tumors were observed in animal studies after oral administration of metronidazole. The relevance of these findings to the topical use of metronidazole in humans is unknown. The anaerobic or hypoxic conditions that might lead to the production of genotoxic compounds are unlikely to occur in topical use. There is no conclusive evidence after 30 years of clinical use of systemic metronidazole for either a genotoxic or carcinogenic potential.

Exposure to Sun: Exposure to excessive sunlight, including sunlamps and tanning beds, should be avoided when using the topical gel or cream (based on studies in hairless mice treated with intraperitoneal metronidazole).

Precautions: Because of the minimal absorption of metronidazole, and consequently its insignificant plasma concentration after topical administration, the systemic adverse experiences reported with the oral form of the drug should not be expected with the metronidazole topical gel or cream.

General: Avoid contact with the eyes. Topical metronidazole has been reported to cause tearing of the eyes. If contact with the eyes does occur, flush with water. If a reaction suggesting local irritation occurs, patients should be directed to use the medication less frequently, discontinue use temporarily, or discontinue use until further instructions. Metronidazole is a nitroimidazole and should be used with care in patients with evidence of, or a history of, blood dyscrasia. Although rosacea is a chronic disease, data on the long-term use of the topical gel or cream in rosacea is not available. In controlled clinical trials, patients were treated for 12 weeks (see Dosage).

Drug Interactions: Drug interactions are less likely with topical administration but should be kept in mind when metronidazole is prescribed for patients who are receiving anticoagulant treatment. Oral metronidazole has been reported to potentiate the anticoagulant effect of coumarin and warfarin resulting in a prolongation of prothrombin time. Oral metronidazole also interacts with alcohol, producing a disulfiram-like reaction. Although this adverse reaction has not been reported with topical application of metronidazole, a drug interaction of metronidazole-alcohol is a possibility.

Dermatological Sensitivity: There were no reports of contact dermatitis attributed to the topical gel or cream during clinical trials. However, there have been reports of contact dermatitis/allergic reaction reported as post marketing adverse experiences (see Adverse Effects). Physicians should be aware of the possibility of skin sensitivity reactions and of cross-sensitization with other imidazole preparations, such as clotrimazole and tioconazole.

Adverse Effects: The patient safety database included 114 evaluable patients that participated in controlled and uncontrolled metronidazole topical gel trials. Adverse experiences attributed to the use of MetroGel are summarized in Table I.

In controlled clinical trials with MetroCream, the patient safety database included 71 evaluable patients. Adverse experiences attributed to the use of MetroCream are summarized in Table II.

Since commercialization of MetroGel, the following post marketing adverse experiences have been reported: contact dermatitis/allergic reaction; local irritation, redness, itching and burning; treatment failure (worsening of rosacea); watery eyes (tearing); metallic taste; tingling or numbness of the extremities; nausea; other (zoster lesion, pustules on nose and vesicular bullous eruptions). A causal relationship with topical metronidazole has not been unequivocally established for these adverse experiences.

Overdose: Symptoms and Treatment: There is no human experience with overdosage of metronidazole.

Massive ingestion may produce vomiting and slight disorientation. There is no specific antidote. Ipecac syrup or gastric lavage; then activated charcoal followed by a saline cathartic is suggested. Treatment should include symptomatic and supportive therapy.

Dosage: Apply and rub in a thin film of the topical gel or cream twice daily, morning and evening, to entire affected areas after washing. Significant therapeutic results should be noticed within 3 weeks. Clinical studies have demonstrated continuing improvement through 9 weeks of therapy. The dosage required for long-term administration is uncertain (see Precautions).

Areas to be treated should be cleansed before application of metronidazole. Patients may use cosmetics after application of metronidazole.

Supplied: MetroCream: The white, smooth, emollient cream, contains: metronidazole 0.75%. Nonmedicinal ingredients: emulsifying wax, glycerin, isopropyl palmitate, purified water, sorbitol, lactic acid and/or sodium hydroxide with benzyl alcohol as preservative. Tubes of 45 g.

MetroGel: The clear, colorless gel, contains: metronidazole 0.75%. Nonmedicinal ingredients: carbopol 940, edetate disodium, propylene glycol, purified water and sodium hydroxide with methylparaben and propylparaben as preservatives. Tubes of 30 g.

Store at room temperature (15 to 30°C).

Reviewed 1997

Table I—MetroCream/MetroGel

Adverse Experiences Attributed to the Use of MetroGel

Body System/ Adverse Experience	Incidence (no. of patients)	Severity	Follow-up Treatment
Skin			
irritation	1.8% (2)	mild	none required
dryness	1.8% (2)	mild	none required
transient redness	1.8% (2)	mild	none required
burning	0.9% (1)	mild	none required
Ocular			
watery (tearing) eyes	0.9% (1)	mild	none required

Table II—MetroCream/MetroGel

Adverse Experiences Attributed to the Use of MetroCream

Body System/ Adverse Experience	Incidence (no. of patients)	Severity	Follow-up Treatment
Skin			
discomfort	2.8% (2)	moderate	none required
(burning & stinging)		moderate	drug discontinued
rosacea worsening	1.4% (1)	mild	drug discontinued
facial erythema	1.4% (1)	moderate	drug discontinued
irritation	1.4% (1)	moderate	drug discontinued
pruritus	1.4% (1)	moderate	none required

METRONIDAZOLE

General Monograph, CPhA

Antibacterial—Antiprotozoal

This monograph has been compiled by CPhA. It may contain information different from that approved by Therapeutic Products Programme, Health Canada, and the pharmaceutical manufacturers' approval has not been requested.

Pharmacology: Metronidazole is amebicidal, trichomonacidal and bactericidal. A chemically reactive, reduced form of metronidazole is thought to be responsible for the drug's activity. The reduced substrate affects anoxic or hypoxic cells causing loss of the helical structure of DNA, strand breakage and impairment of cellular function.

The spectrum of activity of metronidazole includes the following: Anaerobic gram-negative bacilli, including most Bacteroides species, Fusobacterium and Veillonella; anaerobic gram-positive cocci including Clostridium, Eubacterium, Peptococcus and Peptostreptococcus. Metronidazole is also active against H. pylori, G. vaginalis and the protozoa E. histolytica, T. vaginalis and G. lamblia. Metronidazole acts primarily against the trophozoite forms of E. histolytica and has limited activity against the encysted forms.

Metronidazole is not active against fungi, viruses and most other aerobic or facultative anaerobic bacteria, i.e., Actinomyces, Lactobacillus and P. acnes.

The mechanisms by which topical metronidazole reduces inflammatory lesions of rosacea are unknown.

Pharmacokinetics: Following oral administration, metronidazole is well absorbed from the gastrointestinal tract. Peak serum levels following an oral dose occur in 1 to 2 hours.

With normal usage, only trace amounts of metronidazole are found in the serum following topical application of a 0.75% gel to the skin. Following vaginal administration of a 5 g dose of a 0.75% gel, systemic absorption is minimal (equivalent to 2% of the mean serum concentration achieved following a single 500 mg oral dose). Metronidazole is less than 20% bound to serum proteins and is widely distributed in the body. It reaches all tissues and fluids, with CSF concentrations reaching approximately 43% of serum concentrations. The drug crosses the placenta and is distributed into breast milk. Metronidazole is metabolized in the liver. It is excreted primarily in the urine as metabolites, with 20% of a dose excreted as unchanged drug. The half-life of metronidazole in adults ranges between 6 and 12 hours. Accumulation may occur in patients with severely impaired hepatic function; dosage reduction may be indicated. Dosage adjustment is generally unnecessary in patients with decreased renal function.

Metronidazole is removed by hemodialysis but is not significantly removed by peritoneal dialysis.

Indications: Bacterial Infections: The treatment of serious infections caused by susceptible anaerobic bacteria, such as B. fragilis (and other species of Bacteroides), Clostridium, Fusobacterium, Peptococcus, and Peptostreptococcus species.

Metronidazole has been used orally in the treatment of antibiotic-induced diarrhea and colitis, including mild to moderate cases of pseudomembranous colitis caused by C. difficile.

In mixed aerobic and anaerobic infections, consideration should be given to the concomitant administration of an antibiotic appropriate for the treatment of the aerobic component of the infection (see Warnings).

Metronidazole is used in multiple-drug regimens for the treatment of H. pylori-associated peptic ulcer disease.

Bacterial Vaginosis: The 1995 Canadian STD Guidelines recommended metronidazole for the treatment of this condition.

Periodontal Infections: Metronidazole is used in the treatment of periodontal infections. It is also used as an adjunct in the treatment of acute necrotizing ulcerative gingivitis (ANUG) caused by spirochetes, fusobacteria, and Bacteroides species.

Protozoal Infections: Trichomonal infections in men and women. Hepatic and intestinal amebiasis. Giardiasis.

Rosacea: For topical application in the treatment of inflammatory papules, pustules and erythema of rosacea.

Contraindications: Hypersensitivity to metronidazole or other nitroimidazole derivatives.

Metronidazole should not be administered to patients with active neurological disorders or a history of blood dyscrasia.

Warnings: Metronidazole has no direct activity against aerobic or facultative anaerobic bacteria. In patients with mixed aerobic-anaerobic infections, appropriate concomitant antibiotics active against the aerobic component should be considered.

Convulsive seizures and peripheral neuropathy, characterized by numbness, tingling, pain, or weakness in the hands or feet, have been reported in patients treated with metronidazole (administered orally or i.v.). If abnormal neurologic symptoms occur, treatment must be discontinued immediately.

Precautions: When metronidazole is used in the treatment of trichomoniasis, sexual contacts should be treated concurrently regardless of symptomatology. To minimize the risk of reinfection and transmission, patients should be advised to abstain from intercourse or to use a condom during intercourse for the duration of treatment.

When metronidazole is used in the treatment of acute intestinal amebiasis and amebic liver abscess caused by E. histolytica, sequential treatment with an intraluminal amebicide (such as iodoquinol or paromomycin) is recommended. Metronidazole is not indicated in cases of asymptomatic amebiasis, as it has limited activity against encysted E. histolytica.

Transient eosinophilia and leukopenia have been observed during treatment with metronidazole.

Studies using chronic, oral administration of metronidazole in rats and mice have shown it to be carcinogenic and tumorigenic. Metronidazole has not been shown to be carcinogenic or tumorigenic in humans.

Treatment with metronidazole should be discontinued if ataxia or any other symptom of CNS involvement occurs.

Patients with severe hepatic disease metabolize metronidazole slowly with resultant accumulation of metronidazole and its metabolites in the plasma. Accordingly, for such patients, doses of metronidazole below those usually recommended should be administered and with caution.

Drug Interactions: Alcohol: Patients taking metronidazole should be warned against consuming alcohol (during therapy and for 24 hours post-treatment) because of a possible disulfiram-like reaction.

Anticoagulants: Metronidazole has been reported to potentiate the anticoagulant effect of warfarin resulting in a prolongation of prothrombin time. This possible drug interaction should be considered when metronidazole is prescribed for patients on this type of anticoagulant therapy.

Barbiturates: metronidazole metabolism may be enhanced causing reduced serum concentrations.

Disulfiram: Administering disulfiram and metronidazole together may result in confusion and psychotic reactions because of combined toxicity.

Lithium: Initiation of metronidazole therapy has been associated with increased serum lithium levels and, in a few cases, signs of lithium toxicity.

Pregnancy: Metronidazole crosses the placental barrier. Metronidazole should be withheld during the first trimester. In addition, it is advisable that administration be avoided during the second and third trimesters; however, if metronidazole treatment is considered necessary, its use requires that the potential benefits be weighed against the possible risks.

Lactation: Metronidazole is distributed into milk. Any unnecessary exposure to metronidazole should be avoided. If a nursing mother is treated with metronidazole, the breast milk should be expressed and discarded during treatment. Breast-feeding can be resumed 24 to 48 hours after treatment.

Children: Controlled studies in children are limited.

Adverse Effects: Cardiovascular: palpitation and chest pain.

CNS: peripheral neuropathy, convulsive seizures, transient ataxia, dizziness, drowsiness, confusion, insomnia and headache.

Peripheral neuropathies have been reported in a few patients receiving prolonged treatment with large doses of metronidazole. It would appear that the occurrence is not directly related to the daily dosage and that an important predisposing factor is the continuation of oral and/or i.v. medication for several weeks or months.

Profound neurological deterioration, within 2 hours after metronidazole administration, has been reported. The occurrence is not directly related to the dose.

Dermatologic: rash and pruritus. With topical use: dry skin, skin irritation, stinging or burning of the skin.

Gastrointestinal: diarrhea, nausea, vomiting, unpleasant metallic taste, anorexia, epigastric distress, dyspepsia, constipation, antibiotic-associated pseudomembranous colitis, dry mouth, glossitis, stomatitis, candidiasis (oral).

Genitourinary: dysuria, proliferation of C. albicans in the vagina, vaginal dryness and burning. Darkening of urine has been reported; this is probably due to a metabolite of metronidazole and has no clinical significance. With vaginal administration: burning or increased frequency of urination, vulvitis, burning or irritation of penis of sexual partner.

Hematologic: transient eosinophilia or leukopenia.

Hypersensitivity: Erythematous rash, urticaria, serum sickness-like reactions have been reported rarely.

Local Reactions: Thrombophlebitis has occurred with i.v. administration.

Metabolic: Gynecomastia has been reported rarely.

Overdose: Symptoms: Severe toxicity following overdosage with metronidazole is uncommon. Massive ingestion may cause vomiting, nausea, anorexia and headache. Insomnia, drowsiness, depression and darkening of urine may also occur.

Treatment: There is no specific antidote. Symptomatic and supportive therapy is usually sufficient.

Dosage: Metronidazole is available as: an injection; oral capsules and tablets; vaginal gel, cream and inserts; topical cream or gel.

Anaerobic Infections: Duration of therapy depends upon clinical and bacteriological assessment. Treatment for 7 days should be satisfactory for most infections. However, in cases where infection sites cannot be drained or which are liable to endogenous recontamination by anaerobic pathogens, longer treatment may be required.

Adults: Oral: 500 mg every 8 hours (7.5 mg/kg every 6 to 8 hours), to a maximum of 4 g/24 hours.

I.V.: 500 mg by i.v. infusion every 8 hours (7.5 mg/kg every 6 to 8 hours), to a maximum of 4 g/24 hours. The injection should be infused i.v. at the rate of 5 mL/minute.

Children: 30 mg/kg/day i.v. in 3 divided doses or 15 to 30 mg/kg/day orally in 3 to 4 divided doses.

Antibiotic-associated Pseudomembranous Colitis: Adults: Doses of 750 mg to 2 g daily given in 3 or 4 divided doses for 7 to 14 days have been used.

H. pylori-associated Peptic Ulcer Disease: Adults: metronidazole 500 mg orally twice daily for 7 days together with a proton pump inhibitor and clarithromycin. Alternate regimens include metronidazole 250 mg orally 4 times daily for 7 days together with a proton pump inhibitor, bismuth subsalicylate and tetracycline.

Bacterial Vaginosis: The Canadian STD Guidelines 1995 recommend in adults a dose of 500 mg orally twice daily for 7 days. Alternatively, metronidazole gel 0.75%, one applicatorful invtravaginally twice daily for 5 days or metronidazole 2 g orally in a single dose can be used. Routine treatment of male sexual partners is not necessary.

Trichomoniasis: The Canadian STD Guidelines 1995 recommend all cases and their sexual contacts should be treated regardless of symptoms. In adults, metronidazole 2 g orally as a single dose is recommended.

Alternate regimens include 250 mg orally 3 times daily for 7 days or 500 mg twice daily for 5 days.

Children: 15 to 20 mg/kg/day orally in 3 divided doses (maximum 250 mg 3 times daily) for 7 days or 40 mg/kg (maximum 2 g) in a single dose.

Amebiasis: Adults: Acute intestinal amebiasis or amebic hepatic abscess: 750 mg 3 times daily for 10 days. Treatment should be followed with a course of a luminal amebicide (see Precautions).

Children: 35 to 50 mg/kg/day in 3 divided doses for 10 days.

Giardiasis: Adults: 2 g daily for 3 days (preferably given at bedtime with food). Alternatively, 250 mg 3 times daily for 5 to 7 days.

Children: 15 mg/kg/day in 3 divided doses for 5 to 7 days. Alternatively, single daily dose treatment has been used, as follows: <25 kg: 35 mg/kg once daily for 3 days; 25 to 40 kg: 50 mg/kg once daily for 3 days (preferably given at bedtime with food); >40 kg: adult dose is given.

Periodontal Infections: The usual oral dose is 250 mg 3 times daily for 3 to 5 days. For severe infections, the oral dose is 500 mg twice daily for 3 to 5 days. As an adjunct in ANUG the usual oral dose is 250 mg 3 times daily for 3 to 5 days or for 7 to 10 days in more severe disease.

Rosacea: Topical metronidazole is applied to the affected areas twice daily, morning and evening, for 9 weeks.

Reviewed 1999

METRONIDAZOLE INJECTION

Abbott

Antibacterial Agent

Supplied: Each mL of sterile, nonpyrogenic, isotonic solution, in a single-dose flexible container (PVC) contains: metronidazole 5 mg, sodium chloride for tonicity adjustment with dibasic sodium phosphate anhydrous and citric acid anhydrous as buffers. Each 100 mL contains: 14 mmol sodium. Osmolarity: 290 mOsm/L (approx.). pH 5.7 (approx.). Containers of 100 mL. Store at room temperature (15° to 30°C). Protect from light.

Incompatibility: Do not mix with sodium lactate 5% w/v injection and dextrose 10% w/v injection.
Reconstitution: The injection is a ready to use solution: no dilution or buffering is required.

MEVACOR® Ⓟ
MSD

Lovastatin
Lipid Metabolism Regulator

Pharmacology: Lovastatin is a cholesterol-lowering agent isolated from a strain of A. terreus. After oral ingestion, lovastatin, which is an inactive lactone, is hydrolyzed to the corresponding β-hydroxyacid form. This principal metabolite is a specific inhibitor of 3-hydroxy-3-methylglutaryl-coenzyme A (HMG-CoA) reductase.

This enzyme catalyzes the conversion of HMG-CoA to mevalonate, which is an early and rate-limiting step in the biosynthesis of cholesterol.

Lovastatin reduces cholesterol production by the liver and induces some changes in cholesterol transport and disposition in the blood and tissues. The mechanism(s) of this effect is believed to involve both reduction of the synthesis of low density lipoprotein (LDL), and an increase in LDL catabolism as a result of induction of the hepatic LDL receptors.

Lovastatin has complex pharmacokinetic characteristics.
Pharmacokinetics: Lovastatin is a lactone which is readily hydrolyzed in vivo to the corresponding β-hydroxyacid, a potent inhibitor of HMG-CoA reductase. Inhibition of HMG-CoA reductase is the basis for an assay in pharmacokinetic studies of the β-hydroxyacid metabolites (active inhibitors) and, following base hydrolysis, active plus latent inhibitors (total inhibitors) in plasma following administration of lovastatin.

Following an oral dose of ^{14}C-labeled lovastatin to man, 10% of the dose was excreted in urine and 83% in feces. The latter represents absorbed drug equivalents excreted in bile, as well as any unabsorbed drug. As a consequence of extensive hepatic extraction of lovastatin, the availability of drug to the general circulation is low and variable. In a single dose study in 4 hypercholesterolemic patients, it was estimated that less than 5% of an oral dose of lovastatin reaches the general circulation as active inhibitors. Following administration of lovastatin tablets the coefficient of variation, based on between-subject variability, was approximately 40% for the area under the curve of total inhibitory activity in the general circulation.

Both lovastatin and its β-hydroxyacid metabolite are highly bound (>95%) to human plasma proteins. Animal studies demonstrated that lovastatin crosses the blood-brain and placental barriers.

The major active metabolites present in human plasma are the β-hydroxyacid of lovastatin, its 6'-hydroxy, 6'-hydroxymethyl, and 6'-exomethylene derivatives. Peak plasma concentrations of both active and total inhibitors were attained within 2 to 4 hours of dose administration. While the recommended therapeutic dose range is 20 to 80 mg/day, linearity of inhibitory activity in the general circulation was established by a single dose study employing lovastatin tablet dosages from 60 to as high as 120 mg. With a once-a-day dosing regimen, plasma concentrations of total inhibitors over a dosing interval achieved a steady-state between the second and third days of therapy and were about 1.5 times those following a single dose. When lovastatin was given under fasting conditions, plasma concentrations of both active and total inhibitors were on average about two-thirds those found when lovastatin was administered immediately after a standard test meal.

In a study of patients with severe renal insufficiency (creatinine clearance 0.167 to 0.5 mL/s [10 to 30 mL/min]), the plasma concentrations of total inhibitors after a single dose of lovastatin were approximately 2-fold higher than those in healthy volunteers.

Indications: As an adjunct to diet, at least equivalent to the American Heart Association (AHA) Step 1 diet, for the reduction of elevated total and Low Density Lipoprotein Cholesterol (LDL-C) levels in patients with primary hypercholesterolemia (Types IIa and IIb),* when the response to diet and other nonpharmacological measures alone has been inadequate.

*A disorder of lipid metabolism characterized by elevated serum cholesterol levels in association with normal triglyceride levels (Type IIa) or with increased triglyceride levels (Type IIb).

After establishing that the elevation in plasma lipids represents a primary disorder not due to secondary conditions such as poorly-controlled diabetes mellitus, hypothyroidism, the nephrotic syndrome, liver disease, or dysproteinemias, it should be determined that patients for whom treatment with lovastatin is being considered have an elevated LDL-C level as the cause for an elevated total serum cholesterol. This may be particularly relevant for patients with total triglycerides over 4.52 mmol/L (400 mg/dL) or with markedly elevated High Density Lipoprotein Cholesterol (HDL-C) values, where non-LDL lipoprotein fractions may contribute significantly to total cholesterol levels without apparent increase in cardiovascular risk. In general, LDL-C may be estimated according to the following equation:

LDL-C(mmol/L) = Total cholesterol − [(0.37×triglycerides) + HDL-C]
LDL-C(mg/dL) = Total cholesterol − [(0.16×triglycerides) + HDL-C]

When total triglycerides are greater than 4.52 mmol/L (400 mg/dL) this equation is not applicable. In such patients, LDL-C may be obtained by ultra-centrifugation.

Lovastatin was also found to slow the progression of coronary atherosclerosis in patients with coronary heart disease as part of a treatment strategy to lower total and LDL-cholesterol to target levels. In 2 trials including this type of patients, i.e., in a secondary prevention intervention, lovastatin monotherapy was shown to slow the progression of coronary atherosclerosis as evaluated by computerized quantitative coronary angiography (QCA). This effect, however, was not accompanied by an improvement in the clinical endpoints (death, fatal/nonfatal myocardial infarction, hospitalization for unstable angina, and coronary revascularization procedure [PTCA and CABG]) within the 2 to 2½ years' period of treatment. These trials, however, were not designed to demonstrate a reduction in the risk of coronary morbidity and mortality.

The effect of lovastatin on the progression of atherosclerosis in the coronary arteries has been corroborated by similar findings in another vasculature. In a trial including hyperlipidemic patients with early, asymptomatic carotid lesions and without known coronary artery disease, the effect of therapy with lovastatin on carotid atherosclerosis was assessed by B-mode ultrasonography. There was a significant regression of carotid lesions in patients receiving lovastatin alone compared to those receiving placebo alone. The predictive value of changes in the carotid vasculature for stroke has not yet been established. In the lovastatin group there was a significant reduction in the number of patients with major cardiovascular events relative to the placebo group (5 vs 14) and a significant reduction in all-cause mortality (1 vs 8). This trial should be viewed as supportive and complementary to the others mentioned above. However, it was not powered to demonstrate a reduction in the risk of coronary morbidity and mortality. A larger trial of longer duration is needed to clarify the effect of lovastatin in monotherapy on clinical events (see Warnings).

Contraindications: Hypersensitivity to any component of this medication. Active liver disease or unexplained persistent elevations of serum transaminases. Pregnancy and Lactation (see also Precautions).

Warnings: The effect of lovastatin-induced changes in lipoprotein levels, including reduction of serum cholesterol, on cardiovascular morbidity or mortality or total mortality has not been established.

Hepatic Effects: In the initial controlled clinical trials performed in 695 patients, marked persistent increases (to more than 3 times the upper limit of normal) in serum transaminases occurred in 1.6% of adult patients who received lovastatin for at least 1 year (see Adverse Effects and Laboratory Tests). When the drug was interrupted or discontinued in these patients, the transaminase levels fell slowly to pretreatment levels. The increases usually appeared 3 to 12 months after the start of therapy with lovastatin. In most cases they were not associated with jaundice or other clinical signs or symptoms (see Precautions, Drug Interactions and Adverse Effects, Postmarketing Experience).

In a 48-week Expanded Clinical Evaluation of Lovastatin (EXCEL study) performed in 8 245 patients suffering from moderate hypercholesterolemia, the incidence of marked (more than 3 times the upper limit of normal) increases in serum transaminases on successive testing was 0.1% in patients receiving a placebo and 0.1% at 20 mg/day, 0.9% at 40 mg/day and 1.5% at 80 mg/day in patients administered lovastatin. A significant lovastatin dose-related trend was noted for confirmed serum transaminase elevation >3 times the ULN.

It is recommended that liver function tests be performed at baseline and periodically thereafter in all patients. Particular attention should be paid to patients who develop elevated serum transaminase levels, and in these patients, measurements should be repeated promptly and then performed more frequently.

If the transaminase levels show evidence of progression, particularly if they rise to 3 times the upper limit of normal and are persistent, the drug should be discontinued.

The drug should be used with caution in patients who consume substantial quantities of alcohol and/or have a past history of liver disease. Active liver disease or unexplained serum transaminase elevations are contraindications to the use of lovastatin; if such condition develops during therapy, the drug should be discontinued.

Moderate elevations of serum transaminases (less than 3 times the upper limit of normal) have been reported following therapy with lovastatin (see Adverse Effects). These changes were not specific to lovastatin and were also observed with comparative lipid metabolism regulators. They generally appeared within the first 3 months after initiation of therapy, were often transient and were not accompanied by any other symptoms. They did not necessitate interruption of treatment.
Muscle Effects: **CPK:** Transient elevations of creatine phosphokinase (CPK) levels are commonly seen in lovastatin-treated patients but have usually been of no clinical significance.

Myalgia and muscle cramps have also been associated with lovastatin therapy.

Myopathy has occurred rarely and should be considered in any patient with diffuse myalgias, muscle tenderness and/or weakness and/or marked elevation of creatine phosphokinase (10 times the upper limit of normal). There have been reports of severe rhabdomyolysis that precipitated acute renal failure. Therapy with lovastatin should be discontinued if marked elevation of CPK levels occurs, or if myopathy is diagnosed or suspected.

In the EXCEL study comparing lovastatin to placebo in 8 245 patients, myopathy (defined as a CPK elevation >10 times the ULN with associated muscle symptoms) occurred in 1 patient in the lovastatin 40 mg/day group (0.1%) and in 4 patients in the 80 mg/day group (0.2%).

The EXCEL study, however, excluded patients with factors known to be associated with an increased risk of myopathy, including rhabdomyolysis.

These factors include pre-existing renal insufficiency (usually as a consequence of long-standing diabetes), concomitant therapy with cyclosporine, gemfibrozil, or lipid-lowering doses of niacin, and erythromycin (see Precautions, Drug Interactions).

Rhabdomyolysis with or without renal impairment has been reported in seriously ill patients receiving erythromycin concomitantly with lovastatin.

In the initial clinical trials, about 30% of patients on immunosuppressive therapy, including cyclosporine, developed myopathy within a year after starting therapy with lovastatin. The corresponding incidence figures for concomitant therapy with gemfibrozil and niacin were approximately 5% and 2% respectively. Most of these patients were taking lovastatin 40 to 80 mg/day. In 7 subsequent reports, 148 cyclosporine-treated transplant patients (105 cardiac and 43 renal) received concurrent lovastatin 10 to 60 mg/day (the vast majority receiving 20 mg/day) for periods of 3 to 41 months with 1 reported case of rhabdomyolysis (0.6%) and 1 case of significant CPK elevations.

Therefore, the benefits and risks of using lovastatin concomitantly with immunosuppressive drugs, erythromycin, fibrates or lipid-lowering doses of niacin should be carefully considered. In patients receiving lovastatin without these concomitant therapies, the incidence of myopathy was approximately 0.1%.

In 6 patients with cardiac transplants taking immunosuppressive therapy including cyclosporine, concomitantly with lovastatin 20 mg/day, the average plasma level of active metabolites derived from lovastatin was elevated to approximately 4 times the expected levels. In this group the therapeutic response also appeared to be proportionately higher, relative to the dosage used.

Because of an apparent relationship between increased plasma levels of active metabolites derived from lovastatin and myopathy, the daily dosage in patients taking immunosuppressants should not exceed 20 mg/day (see Dosage). Even at this dosage, the benefits and risks of using lovastatin in patients taking immunosuppressants should be carefully considered.

Rhabdomyolysis with renal failure has been reported in a renal transpant patient receiving cyclosporine and itraconazole shortly after a dose increase in the systemic antifungal agent itraconazole. Another transplant patient on cyclosporine and a different HMG-CoA reductase inhibitor experienced muscle weakness accompanied by marked elevation of CPK following the initiation of systemic itraconazole therapy. The HMG-CoA reductase inhibitors and the azole derivative antifungal agents

Mevacor (cont'd)

inhibit cholesterol biosynthesis at different points in the biosynthetic pathway. In patients receiving cyclosporine, lovastatin should be temporarily discontinued if systemic azole derivative antifungal therapy is required; patients not taking cyclosporine should be carefully monitored if systemic azole derivative antifungal therapy is required.

Interruption of therapy with lovastatin should be considered in any patient with an acute, serious condition, suggestive of a myopathy or having a risk factor predisposing to the development of renal failure or rhabdomyolysis, such as severe acute infection, hypotension, major surgery, trauma, severe metabolic, endocrine or electrolyte disorders and uncontrolled seizures.

Patients should be advised to report promptly unexplained muscle pain, tenderness or weakness, particularly if accompanied by malaise or fever.

Precautions: General: Before instituting therapy with lovastatin, an attempt should be made to control hypercholesterolemia with appropriate diet, exercise, weight reduction in overweight and obese patients, and to treat other underlying medical problems (see Indications). The patient should be advised to inform subsequent physicians of the prior use of lovastatin or any other lipid metabolism regulator.

Homozygous Familial Hypercholesterolemia (FH): Lovastatin is not effective or is less effective in patients with rare homozygous familial hypercholesterolemia because these patients have no or very low levels of LDL receptor activity. Lovastatin appears to be more likely to raise serum transaminases (see Adverse Effects) in these homozygous patients.

Effect on the Lens: Current long-term data from clinical trials do not indicate an adverse effect of lovastatin on the human lens.

Effect on Lipoprotein(a) [Lp(a)]: In some patients the beneficial effect of lowered total cholesterol and LDL cholesterol levels may be partly blunted by a concomitant increase in the Lp(a) levels. Until further experience is obtained from controlled clinical trials, it is suggested, where feasible, that Lp(a) measurements be carried out in patients placed on therapy with lovastatin.

Effect on CoQ_{10} Levels (Ubiquinone): A significant decrease in plasma CoQ_{10} levels in patients treated with lovastatin and other statins has been observed in short-term clinical trials. The clinical significance of a potential long-term statin-induced deficiency of CoQ_{10} has not yet been established.

Hypersensitivity: Although to date hypersensitivity syndrome has not been described as such, in few instances eosinophilia and skin eruptions appear to be associated with lovastatin treatment. If hypersensitivity is suspected, lovastatin should be discontinued.

Pregnancy: **Lovastatin is contraindicated during pregnancy.**

Atherosclerosis is a chronic process and the discontinuation of lipid metabolism regulators during pregnancy should have little impact on the outcome of long-term therapy of primary hypercholesterolemia. Moreover, cholesterol and other products of the cholesterol biosynthesis pathway are essential components for fetal development, including synthesis of steroids and cell membranes. Because of the ability of inhibitors of HMG-CoA reductase such as lovastatin to decrease the synthesis of cholesterol and possibly other products of the cholesterol biosynthesis pathway, lovastatin may cause fetal harm when administered to a pregnant woman.

A few reports have been received of congenital anomalies in infants whose mothers were treated during a critical period of pregnancy with HMG-CoA reductase inhibitors including lovastatin.

Lovastatin should be administered to women of childbearing age only when such patients are highly unlikely to conceive. If the patient becomes pregnant while taking this drug, it should be discontinued and the patient apprised of the potential hazard to the fetus.

Lactation: It is not known whether lovastatin is excreted in human milk. Because many drugs are excreted in human milk and because of the potential for serious adverse reactions in nursing infants from lovastatin, women taking the drug should not nurse their infants (see Contraindications).

Children: Limited experience is available in children. However, safety and effectiveness in children have not been established.

Geriatrics: In patients over 60 years, efficacy appeared similar to that seen in the population as a whole, with no apparent increase in the frequency of clinical or laboratory adverse findings.

Impaired Renal Function: Because lovastatin does not undergo significant renal excretion, modification of dosage should not be necessary in patients with moderate renal insufficiency.

In patients with severe renal insufficiency (creatinine clearance <0.5 mL/s [30 mL/min]), dosages above 20 mg/day should be carefully considered and, if deemed necessary, implemented cautiously (see Warnings, Muscle Effects).

Endocrine Function: HMG-CoA reductase inhibitors interfere with cholesterol synthesis and as such might theoretically blunt adrenal and/or gonadal steroid production. Clinical studies with lovastatin have shown that this agent does not reduce plasma cortisol concentration or impair adrenal reserve, and does not reduce basal plasma testosterone concentration. However, the effects of HMG-CoA reductase inhibitors on male fertility have not been studied in adequate number of patients. The effects, if any, on the pituitary-gonadal axis in premenopausal women are unknown.

Patients treated with lovastatin who develop clinical evidence of endocrine dysfunction should be evaluated appropriately. Caution should be exercised if an HMG-CoA reductase inhibitor or other agent used to lower cholesterol levels is administered to patients receiving other drugs (e.g., ketoconazole, spironolactone, or cimetidine) that may decrease the levels of endogenous steroid hormones.

Drug Interactions: Concomitant Therapy with other Lipid Metabolism Regulators: **Combined drug therapy should be approached with caution as information from controlled studies is limited.**

Bile Acid Sequestrants: Preliminary evidence suggests that the cholesterol-lowering effects of lovastatin and the bile acid sequestrant, cholestyramine, are additive.

When lovastatin is used concurrently with cholestyramine or any other resin, an interval of at least 2 hours should be maintained between the two drugs, since the absorption of lovastatin may be impaired by the resin.

Gemfibrozil, Fenofibrate and Niacin: Myopathy, including rhabdomyolysis, has occurred in patients who were receiving coadministration of lovastatin with fibric acid derivatives and niacin, particularly in subjects with pre-existing renal insufficiency (see Warnings).

Erythromycin: See Warnings, Muscle Effects.

Angiotensin-Converting Enzyme Inhibitors: Hyperkalemia associated with myositis (myalgia and elevated CPK) has been reported in the case of a single patient with insulin-dependent diabetes mellitus and mild renal insufficiency who received lovastatin concomitantly with an angiotensin-converting enzyme inhibitor (lisinopril).

Coumarin Anticoagulants: Clinically evident bleeding and/or increased prothrombin time have been reported occasionally in patients taking coumarin anticoagulants concomitantly with lovastatin. Careful monitoring of prothrombin time is therefore recommended in such cases.

Digoxin: In patients with hypercholesterolemia, concomitant administration of lovastatin and digoxin resulted in no effect on digoxin plasma concentrations.

Beta-Adrenergic Blocking Drugs: In healthy volunteers, the coadministration of propranolol and lovastatin resulted in a slight decrease of the AUC of lovastatin and its metabolites as well as in a significant decrease of the C_{max} for the lovastatin metabolites.

The clinical interpretation of this phenomenon is difficult as it may indicate a greater uptake of lovastatin by the liver.

There was no clinically relevant interaction reported in patients who have been receiving lovastatin concomitantly with beta-adrenergic blocking agents.

Antipyrine: Antipyrine was used as a model for drugs metabolized by the microsomal hepatic enzyme system (cytochrome P450 system). Lovastatin had no effect on the pharmacokinetics of antipyrine.

Other Concomitant Therapy: Caution should be exercised with concomitant use of immunosuppressants and itraconazole (see Warnings).

Although specific interaction studies were not performed, in clinical studies, lovastatin was used concomitantly with calcium-channel blockers (such as verapamil HCl, nifedipine and diltiazem HCl) and a number of diuretics and nonsteroidal anti-inflammatory drugs (NSAIDs), hypoglycemic drugs (chlorpropamide, glipizide, glyburide, insulin), without evidence of clinically significant adverse interactions.

Drug/Laboratory Test Interactions: Lovastatin may elevate creatine phosphokinase and transaminase levels (see Adverse Effects, Laboratory Tests). In the differential diagnosis of chest pain in a patient on therapy with lovastatin, cardiac and noncardiac fractions of these enzymes should be determined.

Adverse Effects: Lovastatin was compared to placebo in 8 245 patients with hypercholesterolemia (total cholesterol 6.2 to 7.8 mmol/L) in a randomized, double-blind, parallel, 48-week Expanded Clinical Evaluation of Lovastatin (EXCEL study). Clinical adverse reactions reported as possible, probably or definitely drug-related in any treatment group are shown in Table I.

Other clinical adverse reactions reported as possibly, probably or definitely drug-related in 0.5 to 1% of patients in any drug-treated group are listed below. In all these cases the incidence on drug and placebo was not statistically different.

Body as a whole: chest pain.

Gastrointestinal: acid regurgitation, dry mouth, vomiting.

Musculoskeletal: leg pain, shoulder pain, arthralgia.

Nervous System/Psychiatric: insomnia, paresthesia.

Skin: alopecia, pruritus.

Special Senses: eye irritation.

No significant difference was found among the different treatment group including placebo in the incidence of serious clinical adverse experiences including death due to CHD, nonfatal myocardial infarction, cancer, and deaths due to all causes. This study was not designed or powered to evaluate the incidence of these serious clinical adverse experiences. The EXCEL study included a minority of patients at risk of or with coronary artery disease; however, its findings cannot be extrapolated in this respect to other segments of the high-risk population.

Laboratory Tests: Marked persistent increases of serum transaminases have been noted (see Warnings).

Other liver function test abnormalities including elevated alkaline phosphatase and bilirubin have been reported. In the EXCEL study, 7.3% of the patients on lovastatin had elevations of CPK levels of at least twice the normal value on one or more occasions compared to 6.2% on placebo.

Table I—Mevacor

Adverse Reactions	**Placebo (n=1 663) %**	**Mevacor 20 mg q p.m. (n=1 642) %**	**Mevacor 40 mg q p.m. (n=1 645) %**	**Mevacor 20 mg b.i.d. (n=1 646) %**	**Mevacor 40 mg b.i.d. (n=1 649) %**
Body as a Whole					
Asthenia	1.4	1.7	1.4	1.5	1.2
Gastrointestinal					
Abdominal pain	1.6	2.0	2.0	2.2	2.5
Constipation	1.9	2.0	3.2	3.2	3.5
Diarrhea	2.3	2.6	2.4	2.2	2.6
Dyspepsia	1.9	1.3	1.3	1.0	1.6
Flatulence	4.2	3.7	4.3	3.9	4.5
Nausea	2.5	1.9	2.5	2.2	2.2
Musculoskeletal					
Muscle cramps	0.5	0.6	0.8	1.1	1.0
Myalgia	1.7	2.6	1.8	2.2	3.0
CNS					
Dizziness	0.7	0.7	1.2	0.5	0.5
Headache	2.7	2.6	2.8	2.1	3.2
Skin					
Rash	0.7	0.8	1.0	1.2	1.3
Special Senses					
Blurred vision	0.8	1.1	0.9	0.9	1.2

The EXCEL study, however, excluded patients with factors known to be associated with an increased risk of myopathy (see Warnings, Muscle Effects and Precautions, Drug/Laboratory Test Interactions).
Nervous System: Visual evoked response, nerve conduction measurements and electromyography in over 30 patients showed no evidence of neurotoxic effects of lovastatin.
Effect on the Lens: (See Precautions).
Postmarketing Experience: The following additional side effects have been reported since the drug was marketed: hepatitis, cholestatic jaundice, vomiting, anorexia, paresthesia peripheral neuropathy and psychic disturbances including anxiety, alopecia, erythema multiforme, including Stevens-Johnson's syndrome; toxic epidermal necrolysis.

An apparent hypersensitivity syndrome has been reported rarely which has included one or more of the following features: anaphylaxis, angioedema, lupus-like syndrome, polymyalgia rheumatica, vasculitis, thrombocytopenia, leukopenia, eosinophilia, hemolytic anemia, positive ANA, ESR increase, arthritis, arthralgia, urticaria, asthenia, photosensitivity, fever, flushing, chills, dyspnea and malaise.

Overdose: Symptoms and Treatment: Five healthy human volunteers have received up to 200 mg of lovastatin as a single dose without clinically significant adverse experiences. A few cases of accidental overdosage have been reported; no patients had any specific symptoms and all patients recovered without sequelae. The maximum dosage taken was 5 to 6 g.

In the event of overdosage, treatment should be symptomatic and supportive, liver function should be monitored, and appropriate therapy instituted. Until further experience is obtained, no specific therapy of overdosage can be recommended.

The dialyzability of lovastatin and its metabolites in man is not known.

Dosage: The patient should be placed on at least an equivalent of the American Heart Association (AHA) Step 1 diet before receiving lovastatin and should continue on this diet during treatment with lovastatin. If appropriate, a program of weight control and physical exercise should be implemented.
Patients with Hypercholesterolemia: The usual starting dose is 20 mg/day given as a single dose with the evening meal. Single daily doses given with the evening meal have been shown to be more effective than the same dose given with the morning meal, perhaps because cholesterol is synthesized mainly at night. Adjustments of dosage, if required, should be made at intervals of not less than 4 weeks, to a maximum of 80 mg daily given in single doses or divided doses with the morning and evening meals. Divided doses (i.e., twice daily) tend to be slightly more effective than single daily doses.

Cholesterol levels should be monitored periodically and consideration should be given to reducing the dosage of lovastatin if cholesterol levels fall below the targeted range, such as that recommended by the Second Report of the U.S. National Cholesterol Education Program (NCEP).
Patients with Established Coronary Heart Disease: In the trials involving patients with coronary heart disease and administered lovastatin with (colestipol) or without concomitant therapy, the dosages used were 20 to 80 mg daily, given in single or divided doses. In the 2 trials which utilized lovastatin alone, the dose was reduced if total plasma cholesterol decreased to below 2.85 mmol/L or if LDL-cholesterol decreased to below 2.1 mmol/L, respectively.
Concomitant Therapy: See Precautions, Drug Interactions: Concomitant Therapy with Other Lipid Metabolism Regulators.

In patients taking immunosuppressive drugs concomitantly with lovastatin, the maximum recommended dosage of lovastatin is 20 mg/day (see Warnings, Muscle Effects).

Information for the Patient: See Blue Section—Information for the Patient "Mevacor".

Supplied: 20 mg: Each light blue-colored, octagon-shaped, flat, beveled-edge, scored tablet, engraved with 731/731 on one side and MEVACOR on the other side, contains: lovastatin 20 mg. Nonmedicinal ingredients: butylated hydroxyanisole, indigotine on alumina, lactose, magnesium stearate, microcrystalline cellulose and pregelatinized starch. Blister packages of 30, bottles of 500.

40 mg: Each green-colored, octagon-shaped, flat, beveled-edge tablet, engraved with 732 on one side and MEVACOR on the other side, contains: lovastatin 40 mg. Nonmedicinal ingredients: butylated hydroxyanisole, indigotine and quinoline yellow, both on alumina substratum, lactose, magnesium stearate, microcrystalline cellulose and pregelatinized starch. Blister packages of 30, bottles of 250.

Keep container tightly closed and store at 15 to 30°C. Protect from light.

(Shown in Product Recognition Section)

Reviewed 1997

MEXITIL® Ⓟ

Boehringer Ingelheim

Mexiletine HCl

Antiarrhythmic

Pharmacology: Mexiletine is a class 1B antiarrhythmic agent based on the classification system of Vaughan-Williams with local anesthetic properties, similar in structure and activity to lidocaine.

Mexiletine blocks the fast sodium channel in cardiac tissues, especially the Purkinje network, without involvement of the autonomic system. Mexiletine reduces the rate of rise and amplitude of the action potential and decreases automaticity (increases the threshold of excitability) in the Purkinje fibers. It shortens the action potential duration and, to a lesser extent, decreases the effective refractory period in the Purkinje fibers. It does not usually alter conduction velocity, although it may slow conduction in patients with pre-existing conduction abnormalities. In those with pre-existing sick sinus syndrome, mexiletine produces a more pronounced depression of the sinus rate and/or prolongation of sinus node recovery time. It does not significantly affect resting membrane potential or sinus node automaticity, left ventricular function, systolic arterial blood pressure, atrioventricular (AV) conduction velocity, or QRS or QT intervals.

Hemodynamic studies with oral mexiletine in patients with normal or abnormal myocardial function have shown that the drug has usually only minor effects on cardiac output, pulmonary capillary wedge pressure, left ventricular end-diastolic pressure, pulmonary diastolic pressure, blood pressure or heart rate. Small increases in vascular resistance without significant negative inotropic effects have also been observed.

Some studies with i.v. mexiletine showed evidence of impaired myocardial contractility after drug treatment. In patients with a history of cardiac decompensation, depression of heart function has been observed.

Mexiletine is well absorbed from gastrointestinal tract and peak plasma levels occur within 2 to 4 hours following an oral dose. Systemic bioavailability of mexiletine is about 90%. The apparent volume of distribution is large (5 to 10 L/kg) reflecting the extensive uptake of the drug by tissues. Protein binding of mexiletine has been estimated to be 55 to 70%.

The optimal plasma range is approximately 0.5 to 2 µg/mL. The therapeutic efficacy as well as the frequency of side effects proportionately increases as the blood level rises. Little therapeutic response is seen with levels under 0.5 µg/mL and a significant increase in side effects, particularly those in CNS, have been observed when plasma levels exceed 2 µg/mL.

Mexiletine is primarily eliminated by hepatic metabolism with about 10% being excreted unchanged in urine. In man, the main metabolites are 4-hydroxy-mexiletine, hydroxymethyl mexiletine and their corresponding alcohols which are devoid of antiarrhythmic activity. The most active metabolite is N-methylmexiletine which is 20% as potent as mexiletine. The urinary excretion of this metabolite in man is less than 0.5%.

Mexiletine shows insignificant first pass elimination. In patients with ventricular arrhythmias, the elimination half-life ($t_{1/2}$) is about 12.1 ± 4.0 hours (mean±SD) as compared to 9.7 ± 1.9 hours in normal volunteers. The renal clearance of drug is increased by urinary acidosis.

Delayed and incomplete absorption as well as prolonged elimination ($t_{1/2}$ approximately 24 hours) has been associated with an acute myocardial infarction.

Prolongation of the $t_{1/2}$ was also observed in patients with hepatic impairment ($t_{1/2}$ approximately 25 hours), reduced renal function (creatinine clearance 10 mL/min: $t_{1/2}$=15.7 hours, creatinine clearance 11 to 40 mL/min: $t_{1/2}$=13.4 hours) and in patients free of hepatic or renal involvement but with severe left ventricular failure ($t_{1/2}$=about 15.4 hours±5.8 hours) (see Precautions, Drug Interactions).

Indications:

No antiarrhythmic drug has been shown to reduce the incidence of sudden death in patients with asymptomatic ventricular arrhythmias. Most antiarrhythmic drugs have the potential to cause dangerous arrhythmias; some have been shown to be associated with an increased incidence of sudden death. In light of the above, physicians should carefully consider the risk and benefits of antiarrhythmic therapy for all patients with ventricular arrhythmias.

Mexiletine is indicated for the treatment of documented life-threatening ventricular arrhythmias, such as sustained ventricular tachycardia. Mexiletine may also be used for the treatment of patients with documented symptomatic ventricular arrhythmias when the symptoms are of sufficient severity to require treatment. Because of the proarrhythmic effects of mexiletine its use should be reserved for patients in whom, in the opinion of the physician, the benefit of treatment clearly outweighs the risks.

For patients with sustained ventricular tachycardia, mexiletine therapy should be initiated in the hospital. Hospitalization may also be required for certain other patients depending on their cardiac status and underlying cardiac disease.

The effects of mexiletine in patients with recent myocardial infarction have not been adequately studied and, therefore, its use in this condition cannot be recommended.

Contraindications: In the presence of: known hypersensitivity to the drug or local anesthetics of amide type (e.g. pramoxine); second or third degree AV block in the absence of a pacemaker; cardiogenic shock.

Warnings: Mortality: The results of the Cardiac Arrhythmia Suppression Trial (CAST) in post-myocardial infarction patients with asymptomatic ventricular arrhythmias showed a significant increase in mortality and in non-fatal cardiac arrest rate in patients treated with encainide or flecainide compared with a matched placebo-treated group. CAST was continued using a revised protocol with the moricizine and placebo arms only. The trial was prematurely terminated because of a trend towards an increase in mortality in the moricizine treated group.

The applicability of these results to other populations or other antiarrhythmic agents is uncertain, but at present it is prudent to consider these results when using any antiarrhythmic agent.
Proarrhythmic Effects: Mexiletine has been reported to aggravate or induce arrhythmias in some patients. In the 398 patients studied in North American controlled clinical trials in whom evaluation was possible, mexiletine induced or aggravated pre-existing arrhythmias in 3.8%. The incidence as reported in the literature has ranged from 8 to 29%.

In the subgroup of patients with life-threatening arrhythmias subjected to programmed electrical stimulation or to exercise, 10 to 15% of the patients had exacerbation of their arrhythmias.

Precautions: Congestive Heart Failure or Hypotension: Mexiletine should be used with caution in such patients because of its potential for depressing myocardial contractility.
AV Block: If a ventricular pacemaker is operative, patients with second or third degree AV block may be treated with mexiletine if continuously monitored.
Conduction Abnormalities: Caution should be exercised when mexiletine is used in patients with first degree AV block, pre-existing sinus node dysfunction (e.g., sick sinus syndrome) or intraventricular conduction abnormalities.
Blood Dyscrasias: Blood dyscrasias were not seen in the controlled trials, but in the compassionate use program, leukopenia, neutropenia, agranulocytosis and thrombocytopenia have been reported in a small number of patients. Although causal relationship has not been clearly established, such a relationship cannot be excluded. Therefore, it is recommended that careful hematologic monitoring should be carried out in patients on mexiletine. Hemogram including WBC differential and platelet count should be performed prior to initiation of therapy. If significant hematologic changes are observed, the patients should be carefully evaluated, and, if warranted, mexiletine should be discontinued. Blood counts usually returned to normal within one month of discontinuation (see Adverse Effects).
Patients with Liver Disease: Since mexiletine is metabolized in the liver, and hepatic impairment has been reported to prolong the elimination half-life of mexiletine, patients with liver disease should be followed carefully while receiving mexiletine. The same caution should be observed in patients with hepatic dysfunction secondary to congestive heart failure.
Liver Injury: Abnormalities of the liver function and rare instances of severe liver injury, including hepatic necrosis, have been reported in association with mexiletine treatment. It is recommended that patients in whom an abnormal liver test has occurred, or who have signs or symptoms suggesting liver dysfunction, be carefully evaluated. If persistent or worsening elevation of hepatic enzymes is detected, consideration should be given to discontinuing therapy.
Urinary pH: Since renal excretion of mexiletine is highly increased with acidification of urine, concurrent drug therapy or dietary regimens which may markedly alter urinary pH should be avoided during therapy.

Mexitil (cont'd)

Seizures: Mexiletine should be used with caution in patients with known seizure disorders. In the compassionate use programme, seizures were reported in approximately 0.2% of the patients with or without a prior history of seizures. Therapy was discontinued in 28% of those patients.

Occupational Hazards: Because mexiletine can cause CNS effects such as lightheadedness/dizziness, tremor and coordination difficulty, patients should be cautioned about engaging in activities requiring mental alertness, judgement and physical coordination (such as driving an automobile or operating machinery) when these effects occur.

Hypokalemia: Antiarrhythmic drugs may be ineffective in patients with hypokalemia. Therefore, any potassium deficit should be corrected as part of the management of ventricular arrhythmia.

Pregnancy: The safety of mexiletine in pregnancy has not been established. The expected benefits of using mexiletine when pregnancy is present or suspected must be weighed against possible hazards to the fetus. Studies in animals showed no embryotoxic nor teratogenic effects.

Lactation: It has been reported that mexiletine appears in human milk in concentrations similar to those observed in plasma. Therefore, if the use of mexiletine is deemed essential, an alternative method of infant feeding should be considered.

Children: The efficacy and safety of mexiletine in children has not been established and, therefore, its use in this age group is not recommended.

Drug Interactions: Tocainide/Lidocaine: Concomitant use of mexiletine and lidocaine or tocainide may lead to potentiation of adverse effects involving the CNS.

Other Cardiovascular Agents: Mexiletine has been used clinically with cardiac glycosides, other antiarrhythmic agents (quinidine, procainamide, disopyramide), diuretics and anticoagulants without evidence of serious untoward effects. In some cases addition of another antiarrhythmic achieved improved control of ventricular ectopy. It is however possible that concurrent use may produce additive effects and dosage adjustments may be necessary.

Mexiletine has no effect on digoxin serum levels.

Hepatic Enzyme Inducers: Drugs which induce hepatic enzymes such as phenytoin, rifampicin and phenobarbital increase non-renal clearance of mexiletine and therefore an increase in dosage may be required when these agents are started during mexiletine administration. Similarly, stopping therapy may call for a decrease in mexiletine dosage.

Cimetidine: Cimetidine has been reported to have a variety of effects on mexiletine absorption and plasma levels. During concurrent therapy, the patient should be carefully monitored for the emergence of adverse effects.

Theophylline: There have been rare reports of increased serum levels of theophylline following the concomitant administration of theophylline and mexiletine. Adverse effects typical of elevated serum levels of theophylline (i.e., nausea, vomiting, tremor) have occurred. Patients should be observed during concomitant therapy with the 2 drugs, and serum theophylline levels should be monitored. A reduction in the theophylline dose may be required.

Metoclopramide: Metoclopramide through its action on gastric motility, produces faster absorption and higher peak blood levels of mexiletine. No change in the maintenance dosage is required as bioavailability is not altered.

Agents which Alter Gastrointestinal Activity: Narcotic analgesics, anticholinergics and magnesium—aluminum hydroxide delay the absorption of mexiletine. The bioavailability and clearance of mexiletine are not altered and therefore no change in the maintenance dosage of mexiletine is recommended in patients receiving these drugs.

Adverse Effects: The most common adverse reactions to mexiletine were upper gastrointestinal distress (22%), lightheadedness (8.6%) and tremor (8%). These were generally mild and were reversible with a reduction in dose or discontinuation of therapy. The adverse effect judged to be most severe was the induction or aggravation of pre-existing arrhythmia (see Warnings). Approximately 16% of patients had mexiletine discontinued because of side effects. Upper gastrointestinal distress was the adverse effect most commonly responsible for discontinuation of mexiletine.

Adverse experiences (incidence ≥1%) (see Table I) were observed among 10 321 patients treated with mexiletine in controlled and open clinical trials. The majority of patients were seriously ill and undergoing multiple drug therapy.

Adverse effects occurring in less than 1% of patients are indicated below in decreasing order of incidence.

Table I—Mexitil

Adverse Events (Incidence ≥1%)

	Incidence %	Adverse Event
Cardiovascular (see Warnings)	1.0	Arrhythmia
	1.0	Palpitations
	1.0	Congestive Heart Failure
CNS	8.6	Lightheadedness
	8.0	Tremor
	3.1	Coordination difficulties
	2.5	Changes in sleep habits
	2.3	Weakness
	2.2	Fatigue
	1.8	Nervousness
	1.7	Clouded sensorium
	1.5	Paresthesias
	1.2	Depression
Gastrointestinal	22.0	Upper gastrointestinal distress
	2.3	Changes in appetite
	2.0	Constipation
	1.7	Abdominal pain/cramps/discomfort
	1.2	Diarrhea
	1.0	Dry mouth
Respiratory	1.0	Dyspnea
Other	2.1	Vision problems
	1.7	Rash
	1.4	Headache

Cardiovascular: (0.1% to 1%) chest pain, hypotension, syncope, angina/angina-like pain, bradycardia, edema, hot flashes, atrioventricular block/conduction disturbances, hypertension. (<0.1%) cardiogenic shock.

CNS: (0.1% to 1%) short-term memory loss, speech difficulties, tinnitus, convulsions, hallucinations, psychosis, malaise. (<0.1%) loss of consciousness.

Dermatological: (0.1% to 1%) diaphoresis, loss of hair, dry skin. Rare cases of exfoliative dermatitis and Stevens-Johnson Syndrome have been reported in association with mexiletine treatment.

Digestive: (0.1% to 1%) abdominal gas/bloating, dysphagia, hiccups, altered taste, salivary changes. (<0.1%) upper gastrointestinal inflammation, upper gastrointestinal bleeding, peptic ulcer, esophageal ulceration. There have been rare reports of severe hepatitis/acute hepatic necrosis.

Genitourinary: (0.1% to 1%) impotence/decreased libido, urinary hesitancy/retention. (<0.1%) renal failure.

Hematological: thrombocytopenia (0.16 %), neutropenia (0.16%), agranulocytosis (0.16%), leukopenia (0.11%). Agranulocytosis was reported in 8 patients (including 2 patients with myelofibrosis) in the emergency use program. It occurred mostly after 1 to 6 weeks of therapy. All patients were also receiving procainamide and/or other drugs known to be associated with hematological disorders. Four patients died. Systemic Lupus Erythematosus was also reported in the emergency use program at a ratio of 4/10 000.

Other: (0.1% to 1%) arthralgia, difficulty swallowing, fever. (<0.1%) arthritis.

Laboratory: (0.1% to 1%) abnormal liver function tests, positive ANA.

Approximately 2% of the patients in the mexiletine compassionate use programme had elevations of AST greater than or equal to 3 times the upper limit of normal. These elevations frequently occurred in association with identifiable clinical events (e.g., CHF, myocardial infarction) and therapeutic measures (e.g., blood transfusion, other medications). These elevations were often asymptomatic and transient, usually not associated with elevated bilirubin levels and usually did not require discontinuation of mexiletine therapy. Marked elevations of AST (>1 000 U/L) were seen before death in 4 patients with end-stage cardiac disease (severe CHF, cardiogenic shock).

In foreign marketing experience, rare instances of severe liver injury, including hepatic necrosis, have been reported in association with mexiletine treatment (see Precautions).

In postmarketing experience, there have been isolated, spontaneous reports of pulmonary changes including pulmonary fibrosis during mexiletine therapy with or without other drugs or diseases that are known to produce pulmonary toxicity. A causal relationship to mexiletine therapy has not been established.

Overdose: Symptoms: Overdosage of mexiletine has resulted in nausea, hypotension, bradycardia, paresthesia, left bundle branch block, asystole, convulsions and death.

Treatment: Should be supportive and may include gastric lavage and atropine for cardiovascular complications. Animal studies have shown that benzodiazepines protect against mexiletine induced convulsions. Acidification of the urine enhances mexiletine elimination.

Eleven cases of overdose have been reported; 3 were fatal. One fatality involved a healthy 22 year old male who ingested approximately 4.4 g of mexiletine. His symptoms were paresthesias, nausea and generalized convulsions.

On admission to the hospital, his pulse rate was 15 beats/minute, his blood pressure was unrecordable and an ECG showed complete heart block with a slow escape rhythm followed by ventricular asystole. He was unresponsive to all therapy. The blood level of mexiletine was 34 to 37 μg/mL at the time of death.

Another fatality involved a male who started convulsing at home after taking an unknown quantity of mexiletine. The convulsions were uncontrolled by diazepam, phenytoin and phenobarbital and the patient died following aspiration and ventricular fibrillation. A post mortem at 26 hours found cardiac blood levels of 25 μg/mL.

Details on the third fatality are not available.

Dosage: The optimal dosage should be individually determined based upon patient's response and tolerance.

The recommended starting dose is 200 mg 3 times daily. This may be increased to a maximum of 1 200 mg daily, given in 3 or 4 divided doses. Dosage adjustment should take place in steps of 100 mg 3 times daily. A minimum of 3 days between each dosage change is required. The dosage usually associated with therapeutic response is between 600 and 900 mg daily. A small proportion of patients and those with severe liver disease may require smaller doses such as 100 mg 3 to 4 times daily, as such doses have been shown to provide effective plasma levels in some patients.

In patients in whom rapid control of ventricular arrhythmia is required, a loading dose of 400 mg may be administered. This should be followed by 200 mg given 3 times daily commencing 8 hours after the loading dose has been given.

Mexiletine should be administered with ample liquid, food and/or an antacid.

Information on the appropriate regimen for the transfer from i.v. lidocaine to mexiletine is lacking.

When transferring from lidocaine to mexiletine, the lidocaine infusion should be stopped when the first oral dose of mexiletine is administered. The infusion line should be kept in place in case the arrhythmia reappears and requires additional lidocaine to suppress it. Consideration should be given to the similarity of the adverse effects of lidocaine and mexiletine and the possibility that they may be additive.

Supplied: 100 mg: Each orange/scarlet, hard, gelatin capsule contains: mexiletine HCl 100 mg. Nonmedicinal ingredients: colloidal silica, magnesium stearate and maize starch. Boxes of 100 (blister packed).

200 mg: Each scarlet, hard, gelatin capsule contains: mexiletine HCl 200 mg. Nonmedicinal ingredients: colloidal silica, magnesium stearate and maize starch. Boxes of 100 (blister packed).

Store between 15 and 30°C in an air-tight container.

MICANOL®

Canderm Pharma

Anthralin

Psoriasis Treatment

Pharmacology: Micanol cream provides the action of anthralin in a pharmaceutically elegant base formulated to minimize staining and irritation. With successful treatment, scales will be removed and the lesions will flatten. The lesions will take time to blanch after flattening has occurred.

Indications: For the treatment of psoriasis.

Contraindications: Do not use on areas of skin where inflammation is present. Use only on quiescent or chronic patches and not in acute eruptions.

Warnings: For external use only. Avoid contact with eyes, mucous membranes or genitals. In case of contact, rinse with water. Discontinue use if condition worsens. Do not ingest this product since it is a cathartic. Do not use on the face or areas of blistered, raw or oozing skin and avoid contact with unaffected areas of skin. If irritation, dryness or redness is noted on adjacent normal skin, reduce frequency of application. If any reaction indicating sensitivity is observed, discontinue use.

When washing, avoid using hot water and soaps as this may cause increased staining. Temporary discoloration of hair may occur in persons with white or grey hair.

May stain skin, hair, fingernails, clothing, bed linen, basin or bathtub. If staining occurs, it will wear off in several weeks.

Wash hands thoroughly after using.

Precautions: To be used only on the advice of a physician. Test area the size of a quarter 24 hours before use. If no irritation occurs, continue use. For adult use only.
Children: Not for use in children except on the advice of a physician.

Dosage: Apply to affected area once daily. Leave on affected area between 10 and 30 minutes, as directed by a physician, and wash off with cool water (no soap).
Scalp Use: Wash hair with shampoo, rinse with water and apply cream while hair is still damp. Rub the cream well into psoriatic lesions. Leave on for 10 to 30 minutes, as directed by a physician, then rinse hair and scalp thoroughly with cool water to remove any surplus cream. Finally, shampoo the hair.

Supplied: Each g of aqueous base cream contains: anthralin USP 1% or 3% w/w. Nonmedicinal ingredients: citric acid, glyceryl monolaurate, glyceryl monomyristate, purified water and sodium hydroxide. Tubes of 50 g. Store at 15 to 25°C. Keep out of reach of children. External use only.

New Product 1998

MICATIN®
McNeil Consumer Products

Miconazole Nitrate
Topical Antifungal

Pharmacology: Miconazole exhibits broad spectrum in vitro fungistatic activity; e.g., against species of the genus Candida. Studies with C. albicans indicate that at low concentrations, miconazole acts primarily on the yeast cell membrane resulting in selective inhibition of the uptake of precursors of RNA and DNA (purines) and mucopolysaccharide (glutamine).

In addition, in vitro antibacterial activity has been reported with Gram-positive bacilli and cocci.

Indications: Topical treatment of dermatophytes and Candida infections and lesions caused by mixed infections involving susceptible organisms e.g., tinea pedis (athlete's foot), tinea cruris, tinea corporis and tinea versicolor caused by dermatophytes.

Miconazole is also effective in cutaneous candidiasis, excluding moderate to severe candidal paronychia. Among the organisms against which miconazole has been found to be effective are T. rubrum, T. mentagrophytes, T. interdigitale, E. floccosum, M. canis, M. gypseum, and species of Candida (including C. albicans) and M. furfur.

Contraindications: Sensitivity to any of the components.

Precautions: If irritation occurs, or there is no improvement following the full treatment period (see Dosage), discontinue use and see a doctor. Avoid contact with the eyes; if this happens, rinse thoroughly with water. For external use only. Do not use in children under 2 years of age unless directed by a doctor. Do not use for infections of the nails.

Adverse Effects: Rarely, mild pruritus, irritation and burning at the site of application have been reported.

Dosage: Cleanse skin with soap and water and dry thoroughly. Apply (or spray) a thin layer over the affected area morning and night for the full treatment period. If there is no improvement within 2 weeks, consult a doctor. Otherwise, continue treatment for 1 to 2 weeks after symptoms have disappeared, up to a maximum of 4 weeks. Jock itch and ringworm usually require 2 weeks to resolve, while athlete's foot may require 4 weeks.

When treating athlete's foot, pay special attention to the spaces between toes; wear well-fitting, ventilated shoes and cotton socks.

The cream should be applied sparingly and smoothed in well to avoid maceration effects. Massage treated area gently until Micatin disappears.

Early clinical improvement (1 to 2 weeks) has been seen in the treatment of infections caused by dermatophytes and Candida species and in mixed infections, but resistant lesions may take longer to clear. If a patient shows no clinical improvement after 30 days of treatment, reconsider the diagnosis.

Supplied: Cream: Each tube of cream contains: miconazole nitrate 2% in a water miscible, white to off-white cream base. Nonmedicinal ingredients: benzoic acid, butylated hydroxyanisole, mineral oil, peglicol 5 oleate, pegoxol 7 stearate and purified water. Tubes of 15 and 30 g.

Spray: Each 90 or 120 g can contains: miconazole nitrate 2% (as a percent of nonvolatile ingredients). Nonmedicinal ingredients: alcohol, hydrocarbon propellant, stearalkonium hectorite, sorbitan sesquioleate and talc.

(Shown in Product Recognition Section)

Reviewed 1999

MICOZOLE
Taro

Miconazole Nitrate
Antifungal

Indications: For the local treatment of vulvovaginal candidiasis (moniliasis) and has been shown to be effective in both pregnant and nonpregnant women and in women taking oral contraceptives.

Miconazole, a synthetic imidazole derivative, exhibits a broad spectrum of antimicrobial activity for the use in the systemic treatment and local treatment of vaginal and topical fungal infections. It is particularly active against Candida species, Trichophyton species, Epidermophyton species and Microsporum species as well as possessing some activity against gram-positive bacteria.

The exact mechanism of miconazole's antifungal activity has not been fully established. The primary site of action appears to be the cell membrane. Studies with C. albicans indicate that at low concentrations, miconazole acts primarily on the yeast cell membrane resulting in selective inhibition of the uptake of precursors of RNA and DNA (purines) and mucopolysaccharides (glutamine). Depending on dose and duration of exposure, yeast cells show progressive degradation of cytoplasmic organelles and the cell wall. Growth, cell permeability and respiration of C. albicans are inhibited at low miconazole concentrations. These observations indicate that miconazole may have multiple actions and/or pathways to inhibit and/or kill microbial cells.

Contraindications: Patients known to be hypersensitive to miconazole or to any of its components.

Warnings: The vaginal cream is used to treat the symptoms of a vaginal yeast infection, which include itching and burning of the vagina and, sometimes, a white discharge.

A physician should be consulted if there is no improvement in 3 days, if the symptoms have not disappeared within 7 days, or if abdominal pain, fever or foul-smelling vaginal discharge occur before or during treatment with this medication.

Pregnancy, Lactation and Children: This product should not be used except on the advice of a physician in pregnant or nursing women or in children under 12 years of age.

A physician should be consulted if symptoms recur within 2 months.

This product should be discontinued if a skin rash or new irritation occurs.

If you are at increased risk for sexually transmitted diseases, have multiple partners or change partners often, consult a doctor before starting each treatment.

Precautions: If sensitization or a new irritation occurs from intravaginal use, discontinue use. Avoid contact of miconazole vaginal cream with the eyes; if this happens, rinse thoroughly with water.

As unrecognized diabetes has intractable candidiasis as a presenting symptom the appropriate urine/blood studies may be indicated in patients unresponsive to treatment. It may be necessary to repeat microbiological studies to confirm the diagnosis of vulvovaginal candidiasis and to rule out the presence of other pathogens and concomitant disease, in any case not responsive to therapy.

During vaginal therapy, it is advisable to postpone sexual relations until treatment is finished.

Pregnancy: Miconazole cream, like other imidazoles, has low toxicity and is safe for use during pregnancy when administered intravaginally; however it should only be used in pregnant or nursing women on the advice of a physician.

Pregnant patients should be advised to exercise caution is the use of the vaginal applicator.

Follow-up reports on infants born to 167 of 263 pregnant patients (some follow-up reports are not yet available) who participated in North American clinical evaluations of miconazole cream 2% described no complications or adverse effects attributed to the therapeutic agent. Nevertheless, since miconazole is absorbed in small quantities from the human vagina, miconazole vaginal cream should be used in the first trimester only when the physician considers it essential to the welfare of the patient.

Children: No information is available on the relationship of age to the effects of vaginal miconazole application. However, it is advisable not to use the vaginal preparation on children under 12 years of age except on the advice of a physician. Do not use on children under 2 years of age.

Lactation: It is not known whether miconazole is excreted in breast milk. Although no appreciable systemic absorption has been noted, do not use either preparation while nursing except on the advice of a physician.

Adverse Effects: Miconazole preparations are generally well tolerated. On rare occasions, it has been reported that patients treated with miconazole cream have experienced vulvovaginal burning, mild pruritus, irritation (<0.5%) and edema and hives at the site of application (<0.1%).

Few side effects are associated with miconazole. The most frequently reported side effects during treatment with systemic miconazole are listed in decreasing order of frequency. Phlebitis, pruritus, nausea, fever, chills, rash, vomiting, anemia, drowsiness, diarrhea, hyperlipidemia, anorexia, rushes, thrombocytosis, leukopenia, hyponatremia, hypotension and pain on injection.

Miconazole topical preparations are generally well-tolerated. The most common adverse effects encountered with vaginal miconazole therapy include vulvovaginal burning, itching, irritation, edema and hives.

The safety of miconazole cream has been characterized by its minimal systemic absorption and the fact that no teratogenic effects have been reported.

Overdose: Symptoms and Treatment: Overdose of miconazole in humans has not been reported to date. In mice, rats, guinea pigs and dogs, the LD_{50} values were found to be 578.1, >640, 275.9 and >160 mg/kg, respectively.

Dosage: Administer one 5 g applicator of cream intravaginally once daily at bedtime for 7 consecutive days. The course of therapy may be repeated if the patient remains symptomatic and other possible pathogens have been ruled out.

Tampons should not be used during treatment since they may absorb some of the medication. Patients should be advised to dry the vaginal area well after bathing and avoid damp clothing (e.g., bathing suits), avoid feminine hygiene sprays and cleanse the vaginal area from front to back after using the toilet.

Supplied: Each g of vaginal cream contains: miconazole nitrate 2%. Nonmedicinal ingredients: apricot kernel oil/PEG-6, benzoic acid, butylated hydroxytoluene, mineral oil, PEG-6-32 stearate/glycol stearate and purified water. Tubes of 45 g sufficient for one 7-day course of therapy. Packages include a consumer information leaflet and 1 reusable applicator. Each tube of vaginal cream has sufficient cream for the treatment period and sufficient cream for extravaginal use, if necessary. Each full applicator supplies miconazole nitrate 100 mg in 5 g cream. Store at 15 to 30°C. Protect from freezing.

Reviewed 1998

MICRO-K EXTENCAPS®
MICRO-K-10 EXTENCAPS®
Wyeth-Ayerst

Microencapsulated Potassium Chloride
Potassium Supplement

Pharmacology: Potassium ions participate in a number of physiological processes including the maintenance of intracellular tonicity; the transmission of nerve impulses; the contraction of cardiac, skeletal and smooth muscle; and the maintenance of normal renal function. Depletion may occur whenever the rate of potassium loss through renal excretion and/or loss from the gastrointestinal tract exceeds the rate of potassium intake.

Micro-K Extencaps (600 mg) (8 mEq K+) and Micro-K-10 Extencaps (750 mg) (10 mEq K+) are hard gelatin capsules, containing small, microencapsulated, crystalline, dispersible particles of potassium chloride. Each particle is microencapsulated with a polymeric coating which allows for controlled release of potassium and chloride ions. The dispersibility of the microcapsules and the controlled release of ions are

Micro-K Extencaps (cont'd)

intended to minimize the likelihood of high localized concentrations of potassium chloride and resultant mucosal ulceration within the gastrointestinal tract.

The polymeric coating forming the microcapsules functions as a water-permeable membrane. Fluids pass through the membrane and gradually dissolve the potassium chloride. In this manner, slow and sustained release of potassium chloride from the coated particles into the gastrointestinal tract occurs over a period of 4 to 8 hours.

Indications: For the prevention of potassium depletion when the dietary intake of potassium is inadequate for this purpose. Also indicated for the treatment of potassium depletion in patients with hypokalemia and metabolic alkalosis, and in the treatment of chronic digitalis intoxication.

The prophylactic administration of potassium may be indicated in patients receiving digitalis and diuretics for the treatment of congestive heart failure, and hepatic cirrhosis with ascites. May be indicated in selected patients with hypertension on long-term diuretic therapy, hyperaldosteronism states with normal renal function, the nephrotic syndrome and certain diarrheal states.

Contraindications: Patients with hyperkalemia, since a further increase in serum potassium concentration in such patients can produce cardiac arrest. Hyperkalemia may complicate any of the following conditions: acute and chronic renal failure, systemic acidosis such as diabetic acidosis, acute dehydration, extensive tissue breakdown as in severe burns, adrenal insufficiency or the administration of a potassium-sparing diuretic (e.g. spironolactone, triamterene), or other drugs causing hyperkalemia such as captopril and enalapril.

Patients with renal impairment with oliguria or azotemia.

Patients who may have an increased sensitivity to potassium administration, e.g., in congenital paramyotonia, or adynamia episodica hereditaria.

All solid dosage forms of potassium supplements are contraindicated in any patient in whom there is cause for arrest or delay in tablet passage through the gastrointestinal tract. In these instances, potassium supplementation should be with a liquid preparation. Long-acting potassium chloride preparations have produced esophageal ulceration in certain cardiac patients with esophageal compression due to an enlarged left atrium. Micro-K Extencaps are therefore contraindicated in such patients as well as in patients with dysphagia.

Warnings: In patients with impaired mechanisms for excreting potassium, the administration of potassium salts can produce hyperkalemia and cardiac arrest. This occurs most commonly in patients given potassium by the i.v. route but may also occur in patients given potassium orally. Potentially fatal hyperkalemia can develop rapidly and be asymptomatic. The use of potassium salts in patients with chronic renal disease, or any other condition which impairs potassium excretion, requires particularly careful monitoring of the serum potassium concentration and appropriate dosage adjustment. Hypokalemia has the potential to promote quinidine toxicity (see Contraindications).

Hypokalemia should not be treated by the concomitant administration of potassium salts and a potassium-sparing diuretic (e.g. spironolactone, triamterene) or other drugs causing hyperkalemia such as captopril or enalapril, since the simultaneous administration of these agents can produce severe hyperkalemia. Hypokalemia in patients with metabolic acidosis should be treated with an alkalinizing potassium salt such as potassium acetate, potassium bicarbonate or potassium citrate (see Contraindications).

Potassium chloride tablets have produced stenotic and/or ulcerative lesions of the small bowel, and deaths. These lesions are caused by a high localized concentration of potassium ions in the region of a rapidly dissolving tablet, which injures the bowel wall and thereby produces obstruction, hemorrhage or perforation. Micro-K is formulated from microencapsulated crystalline particles of potassium chloride. The sustained release of potassium chloride from the microcaps is intended to minimize the possibility of a high local concentration of potassium ion near the bowel wall. Micro-K should be discontinued immediately and the possibility of bowel obstruction or perforation considered if severe vomiting, abdominal pain, distention or gastrointestinal bleeding occurs (see Contraindications).

All oral potassium preparations should be prescribed with particular caution in patients with a history of peptic ulcer.

Precautions: The treatment of potassium depletion, particularly in the presence of cardiac disease, renal disease or acidosis, requires careful attention to acid-base balance and appropriate monitoring of serum electrolytes, the electrocardiogram and the clinical status of the patient.

Potassium supplements should be used with caution in diseases associated with heart block since increased serum potassium may increase the degree of block.

Since anticholinergic agents have the potential to slow gastrointestinal motility, caution should be exercised when prescribing solid oral potassium preparations to patients concurrently receiving anticholinergic agents (see Contraindications, Warnings).

Pregnancy: Because of gastrointestinal hypomotility associated with pregnancy, solid oral potassium supplements should be given to pregnant women only if clearly needed.

Children: Safety and effectiveness in children have not been established. Keep out of reach of children.

Adverse Effects: The most common adverse reactions are nausea, vomiting, diarrhea and abdominal discomfort. These symptoms are due to irritation of the gastrointestinal tract and can be reduced by increasing fluid intake when possible, by taking the dose with meals or by reducing the dose. One of the most severe adverse effects of potassium supplementation is hyperkalemia. Skin rash has been reported rarely. Intestinal bleeding, ulceration, perforation and stenosis have been reported in patients treated with solid dosage forms of potassium salts, but there appears to be less likelihood of this occurring with Micro-K.

Overdose: Overdosage from therapeutic doses of solid oral potassium salts in persons with normal excretory mechanism rarely occurs; however, if excretory mechanisms are impaired, potentially fatal hyperkalemia may occur. Acute (accidental or intentional) overdosages of solid oral potassium salts have resulted in severe and/or fatal hyperkalemia.

Symptoms: Overdosage with potassium is characterized chiefly by cardiovascular, neuromuscular and gastrointestinal disturbances.

Cardiovascular: ECG changes, hypotension and shock, bundle-branch block, ventricular arrhythmias, ventricular fibrillation leading possibly to cardiac arrest.

Neuromuscular: paresthesia, areflexia, convulsions, flaccid paralysis of striated muscle leading possibly to respiratory paralysis.

Gastrointestinal: nausea, vomiting, diarrhea and abdominal cramp.

It is important to recognize that hyperkalemia is usually asymptomatic and may be manifested only by an increased serum potassium concentration and characteristic electrocardiographic changes, which include increased amplitude and peaking of the T wave, and flattening or absence of P wave. As hyperkalemia worsens, prolongation of the P-R interval, widening of the QRS complex with S-T segment depression and arrhythmias may develop.

Widening of the QRS complex is one of the most ominous signs and indicates the need for aggressive treatment.

Treatment: The plasma concentration and electrocardiogram must be monitored in every case of potassium overdosage, as well as serum electrolytes, BUN, glucose and arterial blood gases.

Electrocardiographic signs of hyperkalemia (tall peaked T waves, P-R prolongation, disappearance of P waves, QRS widening, heart block) are indications for immediate treatment.

In severe hyperkalemia (plasma potassium exceeds 8 mEq/L or ECG abnormalities include absence of P wave, presence of widened QRS complex or ventricular arrhythmia): Administer i.v. 300 to 500 mL/h of 10% dextrose solution containing 10 to 20 units of insulin/1 000 mL.

Correct acidosis, if present, with intravenous sodium bicarbonate (44 to 132 mEq/L of glucose solution).

Administer 10 to 30 mL of 10% calcium gluconate i.v. over 1 to 5 minutes under continuous ECG monitoring.

Administer cation exchange resin by high retention enema. 100 mL of warm aqueous solution of sorbitol containing 30 to 50 g of sodium polystyrene sulfonate should be kept in the sigmoid colon for several hours, if possible. The colon is then irrigated with a non-sodium containing solution to remove the resin. Repeated enemas can be administered, or the resin given repeatedly by mouth, to maintain a physiologic potassium concentration.

Hemodialysis or peritoneal dialysis may be of use, particularly in patients with renal failure.

In moderately severe hyperkalemia (plasma potassium between 6.5 and 8 mEq/L or ECG peaking of T wave): Administer i.v. 300 to 500 mL/h of 10% dextrose solution containing 10 to 20 units insulin/1 000 mL.

Correct acidosis, if present, with intravenous sodium bicarbonate (44 to 132 mEq/L of glucose solution).

Correct hyponatremia and hypovolemia, if present.

Once the patient's cardiac state has been stabilized, in the case of a recent **acute** ingestion of Micro-K, consideration should be given to the evacuation of the stomach. When overdosage is the result of **chronic** therapeutic ingestion, Micro-K should be discontinued immediately as well as potassium containing foods and medications and also potassium-sparing diuretics.

Dosage: The usual dietary intake of potassium by the average adult is 40 to 80 mEq/day. Potassium depletion sufficient to cause hypokalemia usually requires the loss of 200 or more mEq of potassium from the total body store.

Dosage must be adjusted to the individual needs of each patient but typically is approximately 20 mEq/day for the prevention of hypokalemia and 40 to 100 mEq/day for the treatment of potassium depletion (see Table I).

Table I—Micro-K Extencaps

Dosage

	For Prevention	For Treatment
Micro-K Extencaps (8 mEq K+)	2 or 3 Extencaps/day (16–24 mEq K+)	5 to 12 Extencaps/day (40–96 mEq K+)
Micro-K–10 Extencaps (10 mEq K+)	2 Extencaps/day (20 mEq K+)	4 to 10 Extencaps/day (40–100 mEq K+)

If more than 2 Extencaps are prescribed per day, the total daily dosage should be divided into two or more separate doses. These capsules should not be crushed or chewed, but administered whole and taken with water. Those patients having difficulty swallowing the capsules may be advised to sprinkle the contents onto a spoonful of soft food to facilitate ingestion.

Supplied: Micro-K Extencaps: Each hard gelatin capsule, opaque pale orange body and cap, monogrammed respectively "AYERST" and "Micro-K" in black contains: potassium chloride 600 mg (8 mEq K+). Nonmedicinal ingredients: magnesium stearate and sodium lauryl sulfate. Empty capsule: FD&C Yellow No. 6, gelatin, silicon dioxide, sodium lauryl sulfate and titanium dioxide. Energy: <1 kJ (<1 kcal). Sodium: <1 mmol (0.048 mg). Alcohol-, gluten-, lactose-, parabens-, sugars-, sulfites- and tartrazine-free. Bottles of 100 and 500.

Micro-K-10 Extencaps: Each hard gelatin capsule, opaque white body and opaque pale orange cap, monogrammed respectively "AYERST" and "Micro-K-10" in black contains: potassium chloride 750 mg (10 mEq K+). Nonmedicinal ingredients: magnesium stearate and sodium lauryl sulfate. Empty capsule: FD&C Yellow No. 6, gelatin, silicon dioxide, sodium lauryl sulfate and titanium dioxide. Energy: <1 kJ (<1 kcal). Sodium: <1 mmol (0.060 mg). Alcohol-, gluten-, lactose-, parabens-, sugars-, sulfites- and tartrazine-free. Bottles of 100 and 500.

(Shown in Product Recognition Section)

MICROLAX®

Pharmacia & Upjohn

Micro-Enema

Indications: Rectal constipation; or, as directed by a physician, to facilitate rectoscopic or sigmoidoscopic examination.

Adverse Effects: No severe reactions have been reported. Very occasionally slight cramps or tenesmus may occur.

Dosage: Adults and children: the contents of 1 tube (5 mL) administered rectally but a second tube may be needed in severe cases; children under 3 years, insert only half the length of the nozzle into the rectum. Defecation can normally be expected within 5 to 20 minutes. No lubrication of the tip of the nozzle is necessary, 1 drop pressed out of the tip before application will facilitate insertion into the rectum.

Supplied: Each mL contains: sodium citrate dihydrate, sodium lauryl sulfoacetate, glycerin, sorbitol, sorbic acid, and distilled water q.s. in a disposable plastic tube fitted with a flexible enema tip about 5 cm long. Tubes of 5 mL. Boxes of 4, 12 and 50.

...Seeking additional information? Consult the health organization directory in the CLIN-INFO SECTION.

MICRONOR® Ⓟ

Janssen-Ortho

Norethindrone

Oral Contraceptive

Pharmacology: The mechanism of contraception action of Micronor tablets is multicausal, primarily at the local pelvic level and secondarily at the systemic level. The hormonal effect is mainly progestational.

Pelvic effects include changes in the cervical mucus and endometrium. Systemic effects involve mainly the inhibition of secretion of pituitary gonadotropins which in turn prevents follicular maturation and ovulation.

Studies by Moghissi, Beck, Fortier and Lefebvre, and others suggest the following priority of causes: 1. Inhibitory cervical mucus changes including increased viscosity and cell content, with inhibition of sperm transport or migration. Changes in cervical mucus reach their peak 3 to 4 hours after Micronor pill intake and the possibility of sperm penetration remains low for 16 to 19 hours. 2. Suppression of FSH levels and the LH surge. 3. Abnormal ovulation and deficient corpus luteum function. (Serum progesterone levels may be suppressed in the second half of the menstrual cycle when they are usually low, i.e., dysphasic.) Serum estrogens may be increased above normal early in the cycle. 4. Endometrial changes (progestational) unfavorable to implantation.

Indications: Conception control.

Micronor tablets contain a low dosage of norethindrone without the addition of an estrogen agent. Progestin-only pills are often called "Progestin-only pills" or the "Minipill".

Contraindications: Progestin-only pills should not be used by women who currently have the following conditions: when pregnancy is suspected or diagnosed; active liver disease or history of/or actual benign or malignant liver tumors; known or suspected carcinoma of the breast; undiagnosed abnormal vaginal bleeding; hypersensitivity to any component of this product.

Warnings: Progestin-only pills have less progestin than the combined birth control pill (or the "Pill") which contains both an estrogen and a progestin. Therefore, this product monograph does not discuss the serious health risks that have been associated with the estrogen component of combined oral contraceptives (COCs).

> Cigarette smoking increases the risk of serious adverse effects on the heart and blood vessels. This risk increases with age and becomes significant in oral contraceptive users over 35 years of age. Women should be counselled not to smoke.

Ectopic Pregnancy: The incidence of ectopic pregnancies for progestin-only oral contraceptive users is 5 per 1 000 woman-years. Up to 10% of pregnancies reported in clinical studies of progestin-only oral contraceptive users are extrauterine. Although symptoms of ectopic pregnancy should be watched for, a history of ectopic pregnancy need not be considered a contraindication to use of this contraceptive method. Health providers should be alert to the possibility of an ectopic pregnancy in women who become pregnant or complain of lower abdominal pain while on progestin-only oral contraceptives.

Delayed Follicular Atresia/Ovarian Cysts: If follicular development occurs, atresia of the follicle is sometimes delayed and the follicle may continue to grow beyond the size it would attain in a normal cycle. Generally these enlarged follicles disappear spontaneously. Often they are asymptomatic; in some cases they are associated with mild abdominal pain. Rarely they may twist or rupture, requiring surgical intervention.

Carcinoma of the Breast and Reproductive Organs: Some epidemiological studies of oral contraceptive users have reported an increased relative risk of developing breast cancer, particularly at a younger age and apparently related to duration of use. These studies have predominately involved combined oral contraceptives and there is insufficient data to determine whether the use of progestin-only pills similarly increases the risk. Women with breast cancer should not use oral contraceptives because the role of female hormones in breast cancer has not been fully determined.

Some studies suggest that oral contraceptive use has been associated with an increase in the risk of cervical intraepithelial neoplasia in some populations of women. However, there continues to be controversy about the extent to which such findings may be due to differences in sexual behavior and other factors. There is insufficient data to determine whether the use of progestin-only pills increases the risk of developing cervical intraepithelial neoplasia.

Headache: Discontinue medication at the earliest manifestation of severe headache of unknown etiology or worsening of pre-existing migraine headache.

Vaginal Bleeding: Irregular menstrual patterns are common among women using progestin-only oral contraceptives. If genital bleeding is suggestive of infection, malignancy or other abnormal conditions, such nonpharmocologic causes should be ruled out. If prolonged amenorrhea occurs, the possibility of pregnancy should be evaluated.

Precautions:

> **Sexually Transmitted Diseases**
>
> Birth control pills **do not protect** against sexually transmitted diseases (STDs), including HIV/AIDS. For protection against STDs, it is advisable to use latex condoms **in combination with** birth control pills.

Physical Examination and Follow-up: Before oral contraceptives are used, a thorough history and physical examination should be performed, including a blood pressure determination. Breasts, liver, extremities and pelvic organs should be examined. A Papanicolaou smear should be taken if the patient has been sexually active.

The first follow-up visit should be done 3 months after oral contraceptives are prescribed. Thereafter, examinations should be performed at least once a year or more frequently if indicated. At each annual visit, examination should include those procedures that were done at the initial visit as outlined above or per recommendations of the Canadian Workshop on Screening for Cancer of the Cervix. Their suggestion was that, for women who had 2 consecutive negative Pap smears, screening could be continued every 3 years up to the age of 69.

Pregnancy: Oral contraceptives should not be taken by pregnant women. However, if conception accidentally occurs while taking the pill, there is no conclusive evidence that the progestin contained in the oral contraceptive will damage the developing child.

Lactation: If the use of oral contraceptives is initiated after the establishment of lactation, there does not appear to be any effect on the quantity and quality of the milk. There is no evidence that low dose oral contraceptives are harmful to the nursing infant.

No adverse effects have been found on breast-feeding performance or on the health, growth or development of the infant. Small amounts of progestin pass into the breastmilk, resulting in steroid levels in infant plasma of 1 to 6% of the levels of maternal plasma.

Migraine and Headache: The onset or exacerbation of migraine or the development of headache of a new pattern which is recurrent, persistent or severe, requires discontinuation of oral contraceptives and evaluation of the cause.

Carbohydrate and Lipid Metabolism: Some users may experience slight deterioration in glucose tolerance, with increases in plasma insulin, but women with diabetes mellitus who use progestin-only oral contraceptives do not generally experience changes in their insulin requirements. Nonetheless, prediabetic and diabetic women in particular should be carefully monitored while taking progestin-only pills.

Lipid metabolism is occassionally affected in that HDL, HDL_2 and apolipoprotein A-I and A-II may be decreased; hepatic lipase may be increased. There is usually no effect on total cholesterol, HDL_3, LDL or VLDL.

Emotional Disorders: Patients with a history of emotional disturbances, especially the depressive type, may be more prone to have a recurrence of depression while taking oral contraceptives. In cases of a serious recurrence, a trial of an alternate method of contraception should be made which may help to clarify the possible relationship. Women with premenstrual syndrome (PMS) may have a varied response to oral contraceptives, ranging from symptomatic improvement to worsening of the condition.

Laboratory Tests: The following endocrine tests may be affected by progestin-only oral contraceptive use: sex hormone-binding globulin (SHBG) concentrations may be decreased; thyroxine concentrations may be decreased, due to a decrease in thyroid-binding globulin (TBG).

Results of laboratory tests should be interpreted in the light that the patient is on oral contraceptives. LH and FSH levels are suppressed by the use of oral contraceptives. Wait 2 weeks after discontinuing the use of oral contraceptives before measurements are made.

Tissue Specimens: Pathologists should be advised of oral contraceptive therapy when specimens obtained from surgical procedures and pap smears are submitted for examination.

Return to Fertility: The limited available data indicate a rapid return of normal ovulation and no delay to fertility following discontinuation of progestin-only oral contraceptives.

Amenorrhea: Women having a history of oligomenorrhea, secondary amenorrhea, or irregular cycles may remain anovulatory or become amenorrheic following discontinuation of progestin therapy. Amenorrhea, especially if associated with breast secretion, that continues for 6 months or more after withdrawal, warrants a careful assessment of hypothalamic-pituitary function.

Drug Interactions: The effectiveness of progestin-only pills is reduced by hepatic-inducing drugs such as the anticonvulsants phenytoin, carbamazepine, and barbiturates and the antituberculosis drug rifampin. No significant interaction has been found with broad-spectrum antibiotics (see Table I). It is important to ascertain all drugs that a patient is taking, both prescription and nonprescription, before oral contraceptives are prescribed.

Refer to Oral Contraceptives 1994 (Chapter 8), Health Canada, for possible drug interactions with OC's.

Adverse Effects: Adverse reactions reported with the use of progestin-only pills include: Menstrual irregularity is the most frequently reported side effect; frequent and irregular bleeding are common, while long duration of bleeding episodes and amenorrhea are less likely; headache, breast tenderness, nausea, and dizziness are increased among progestin-only oral contraceptive users in some studies; androgenic side effects such as acne, hirsutism, and weight gain occur rarely.

Overdose: Symptoms and Treatment: In case of overdose or accidental ingestion by children, the physician should observe the patient closely although generally no treatment is required. Gastric lavage may be utilized if considered necessary. There have been no reports of serious ill effects from overdosage.

Dosage: Information for the Patient on How to Take Micronor Tablets (Progestin-only Pills):

1. **Read these directions:**
   - before you start taking your pills, and
   - any time you are not sure what to do.
2. **Look at your pill pack:**
   - 28-Pill Pack: 28 active pills (with hormones) taken daily for 28 days.

Also check the pill pack for instructions on (1) where to start and (2) directions to take pills (see package insert for illustrations).

3. You may wish to use a second method of birth control (e.g., latex condoms and spermicidal foam or gel) for the first 48 hours of the first cycle of pill use. This will provide

Table I—Micronor

Drugs Which May Decrease the Efficacy of Oral Contraceptives

Class of Compound	Drug	Proposed Mechanism	Suggested Management
Anticonvulsants	Carbamazepine Ethosuximide Phenobarbital Phenytoin Primidone	Induction of hepatic microsomal enzymes: Increased binding of progestin to SHBG.	Use higher dose OCs (50 µg ethinyl estradiol), another drug or another method.
Antituberculosis	Rifampin	Increased metabolism of progestins.	Use another method.
Sedatives and Hypnotics	Benzodiazepines Barbiturates Chloral hydrate Glutethimide Meprobamate	Induction of hepatic microsomal enzymes.	For short course, use additional method or another drug. For long course, use another method or higher dose OCs.

Micronor (cont'd)

a back-up in case pills are forgotten while you are getting used to taking them.

4. When receiving any medical treatment, be sure to tell your doctor that you are using birth control pills.
5. **Many women have spotting or light bleeding or may feel sick to their stomach during the first 3 months on the pill.** If you do feel sick, do not stop taking the pill. The problem will usually go away. If it does not go away, check with your doctor or clinic. The most common side effect of progestin-only pills is a change in menstrual bleeding. Your period may be either late or early and you may have some spotting.
6. **Missing pills also can cause some spotting or light bleeding,** even if you make up the missed pills. You also could feel a little sick to your stomach on the days you take 2 pills to make up for missed pills.
7. **If you miss pills at any time, you could get pregnant. The greatest risks for pregnancy are:**
   - when you start a pack late, and
   - if you are more than 3 hours late in taking your pill or you miss 1 or more pills.
8. **Always be sure you have ready:**
   - **another kind of birth control** (such as latex condoms and spermicidal foam or gel) to use as a back-up method in case you miss a pill, or take it more than 3 hours late, and
   - **an extra, full pack of pills.**
9. **If you experience vomiting or diarrhea, or if you take some medicines,** such as antibiotics, your pills may not work as well. Use a back-up method, such as latex condoms and spermicidal foam or gel, until you can check with your doctor or clinic.
10. **If you forget more than 1 pill 2 months in a row,** talk to your doctor or clinic about how to make pill-taking easier or about using another method of birth control.
11. **If your questions are not answered here, call your doctor or clinic.**

When to start the first pack of Progestin-only pills: Be sure to read these instructions:

- before you start taking your pills, and
- any time you are not sure what to do.

Your Micronor tablets are in a 28 day pill package. With this type of birth control pill, you take 28 pills which contain only one hormone, a progestin.

Starting Progestin-only Pills:

1. **The first day of your menstrual period (bleeding) is Day 1 of your cycle.** With Micronor, it is best to start your first package of progestin-only pills on the first day of your menstrual period (Day 1)*. Then you simply continue taking one tablet every single day until your VARIDATE DIALPAK Tablet Dispenser is empty. Without missing a day, start taking Micronor from your new VARIDATE DIALPAK Tablet Dispenser.

*If you decide to take your first progestin-only pill on another day, use an additional method of birth control (such as latex condoms and spermicidal foam or gel) everytime you have sex during the next 48 hours.

2. If you have had a miscarriage or an abortion, you can start progestin-only pills the next day.
3. Take 1 pill at the same time every day for 28 days. Begin a new pack the next day, **not missing any days on the pills.** Your period should occur during the last 7 days of using that pill pack. Micronor Tablets are taken every day — even when you are having some menstrual bleeding.

Follow these steps carefully (see package insert for illustrations): To set the package to the first day of your period insert a coin into the middle slot and turn the inner wheel counterclockwise until that day appears in the window. The example shown is for a **Sunday** start. Your first green tablet is below the "V" notch as shown. Ensure that the tab marked "Lift Out" is set over this tablet. Break off the tab and begin tablet taking. To take your second and all subsequent tablets, turn the clear outer cover clockwise to the next available tablet. Take 1 tablet every day for 28 days, completing all green tablets. When you take your last tablet, be sure to set your next package for the following day, i.e., last tablet taken **Tuesday,** set next package for **Wednesday. Important:** Remember to take a tablet each day without interruption.

If you are breast-feeding:

1. **If you are fully breast-feeding** (not giving your baby any food or formula), you may start taking your pills 6 weeks after delivery.
2. **If you are partially breast-feeding** (giving your baby some food or formula), you should start taking your pills 3 weeks after delivery.

If you are switching pills:

1. If you are switching from the combined pills to progestin-only pills, and you were on a 21-day regimen, take the first progestin-only pill the day after you finish the last **active** combined pill. If you have been on a 28-day regimen, do not take any of the 7 **inactive** pills from the combined pill pack. You should know that many women have irregular periods after switching to progestin-only pills, but this is normal and to be expected.
2. If you are switching from progestin-only pills to the combined pills, take the first **active** combined pill on the first day of your period, even if your progestin-only pill pack is not finished.
3. If you are breast-feeding, you can switch to another method of birth control at anytime, except do not switch to the combined pills until you stop breast-feeding or at least until 6 months after delivery.

What to Do During the Month:

1. **Take a pill at the same time every day until the pack is empty.** Progestin-only pills must be taken at the same time every day since its action is time dependent. Every time you take a pill more than 3 hours late, and especially if you miss a pill, you are more likely to get pregnant.
   - Try to associate taking your pill with some regular activity like eating a meal or going to bed.
   - Do not skip pills even if you have bleeding between monthly periods or feel sick to your stomach (nausea).
   - Do not skip pills even if you do not have sex very often.
2. **When you finish a pack:**
   - **28 pills:** Start the next pack **on the next day.** Take 1 pill every day. Do not wait any days between packs.

What to Do if You Miss Pills: If you are more than 3 hours late or miss taking your progestin-only pills:

1. Take a missed pill as soon as you remember you missed it.
2. Then go back to taking progestin-only pills at your regular time.
3. But be sure to use a back-up method (such as a condom and/or a spermicide) everytime you have sex for the next 48 hours.

If you are not sure what to do about the pills you have missed, keep taking progestin-only pills and use a back-up method until you can talk to your doctor or clinic.

Always be sure you have on hand:

- a back-up method of birth control (such as latex condoms and spermicidal foam or gel) in case you miss pills, and
- an extra, full pack of pills.

If you forget more than 1 pill 2 months in a row, talk to your doctor or clinic. Talk about ways to make pill-taking easier or about using another method of birth control.

Information for the Physician: Counselling Issues: The following points should be discussed with prospective users before prescribing progestin-only oral contraceptives:

- the necessity of taking pills at the same time every day, including throughout all bleeding episodes.
- the need to use a back-up method such as condoms and spermicides for the next 48 hours whenever a progestin-only oral contraceptive is taken 3 or more hours late.
- the potential side effects of progestin-only oral contraceptives, particularly menstrual irregularities.
- the need to inform the clinician of prolonged episodes of bleeding, amenorrhea or severe abdominal pain.
- the importance of using an effective barrier method in addition to progestin-only oral contraceptives if a woman is at risk of contracting or transmitting STDs/HIV.

Information for the Patient: See Blue Section—Information for the Patient "Oral Contraceptives".

Supplied: Each green, unscored tablet, with ORTHO 0.35 engraved on each side, contains: norethindrone 0.35 mg. Nonmedicinal ingredients: D&C Yellow No. 10, FD&C Green No. 5 Aluminum Lake, lactose, magnesium stearate, polyvinylpyrrolidone and starch. Tartrazine-free. A 28-day VARIDATE DIALPAK Tablet Dispenser contains a 4-week supply of tablets. Store between 15 and 30°C.

(Shown in Product Recognition Section)

Reviewed 1999

MIDAMOR® Ⓟ

MSD

Amiloride HCl

Antikaliuretic—Diuretic

Pharmacology: Amiloride is an antikaliuretic drug with mild natriuretic diuretic and antihypertensive activity. The activities may be additive to the effects of thiazides or other saluretic-diuretic agents. The principal use is to conserve potassium in selected patients receiving kaliuretic-diuretic agents. Amiloride interferes with the mechanism involved in the exchange of sodium for potassium in the distal convoluted tubule and collecting duct of the nephron. An increase in sodium and a decrease in potassium and hydrogen ion excretion are induced in the presence or absence of aldosterone, thereby suggesting a direct tubular action of the drug. Chloride excretion may remain unchanged or increase slowly with continued therapy.

Amiloride, when administered with hydrochlorothiazide, has been shown to result in less excretion of magnesium than thiazide or loop diuretics used alone.

Approximately 50% of an oral dose is absorbed. Amiloride usually begins to act within 2 hours after an oral dose. Its effect on electrolyte excretion reaches a peak between 6 and 10 hours and lasts about 24 hours. Peak plasma levels are obtained in 3 to 4 hours and plasma half-life varies from 6 to 9 hours.

Amiloride is not metabolized by the liver. About 50% of a 20 mg dose is excreted unchanged in the urine and 40% is excreted in the stool within 72 hours. In clinical studies amiloride was found to have little effect on glomerular filtration rate or renal blood flow.

Indications: For use alone or concomitantly with thiazide diuretics or other kaliuretic-diuretic agents in the treatment of patients with cirrhosis of the liver with ascites and edema.

Amiloride is indicated as an adjunct to the treatment with thiazide diuretics or other kaliuretic-diuretic agents in those patients with edema of cardiac origin or hypertension who: have hypokalemia, or in whom maintenance of normal serum potassium levels is considered to be clinically important, e.g., digitalized patients, patients in whom adequate dietary intake of potassium is not feasible or patients with cardiac arrhythmias.

Use in hepatic cirrhosis with ascites and edema: Amiloride used alone may provide satisfactory diuresis with diminished potassium loss and with a reduced risk of metabolic alkalosis. In resistant cases amiloride may be used with kaliuretic diuretic agents to help produce satisfactory diuresis, while maintaining a more balanced serum electrolyte pattern. As with all therapy for the ascites of hepatic cirrhosis, gradual weight loss and avoidance of electrolyte imbalance are the chief objectives (see Precautions).

Contraindications: Hyperkalemia: Should not be used in the presence of elevated serum potassium levels (see Warnings).

Antikaliuretic Therapy or Potassium Salts: Other antikaliuretic agents and potassium supplements are contraindicated in patients receiving amiloride (such combination therapy is commonly associated with rapid increases in plasma potassium levels).

Impaired Renal Function: Anuria, acute renal failure, severe or progressive renal disease, and diabetic nephropathy (see Warnings).

Hypersensitivity to any component of this product.

Warnings: Hyperkalemia: Hyperkalemia, e.g., serum potassium levels over 5.5 mEq/L, has been observed in some patients who received amiloride either alone or with diuretics. This has been noted particularly in elderly patients, in diabetic patients, and in hospitalized patients with hepatic cirrhosis or cardiac edema who had known renal impairment, were seriously ill, or were receiving vigorous diuretic therapy. Since fatalities have occurred, patients should be monitored carefully for clinical, laboratory, and ECG evidence of hyperkalemia and for acidosis. Monitoring of the serum potassium level is important because hyperkalemia is not always associated with an abnormal ECG.

Warning signs or symptoms of hyperkalemia include paresthesias, muscular weakness, fatigue, flaccid paralysis of the extremities, bradycardia, shock, and ECG abnormalities.

When abnormal, the ECG in hyperkalemia is characterized primarily by tall, peaked T waves or elevations from previous tracings. There may also be lowering of the R wave and increased depth of the S wave, widening and even disappearance of the P wave, progressive widening of the QRS complex, prolongation of the PR interval, and ST depression.

If hyperkalemia occurs in patients taking amiloride, the drug should be discontinued immediately. If the serum potassium level exceeds 6.5 mEq/L, active measures should be taken to reduce it. Such measures include the i.v. administration of sodium bicarbonate solution or oral or parenteral glucose with a rapid-acting insulin preparation. If needed, a cation exchange resin such as sodium polystyrene sulfonate may be given orally or by enema. Patients with persistent hyperkalemia may require dialysis.

Diabetes Mellitus: In diabetic patients, hyperkalemia has been commonly reported with the use of amiloride, particularly if they have chronic renal disease or prerenal azotemia. Some deaths occurred in this last group of patients. Therefore, if therapy with amiloride is considered essential, the drug should be used with caution in diabetic or suspected diabetic patients and only after first determining the status of renal function.

Careful monitoring of serum potassium levels is required throughout the therapy.

One patient with poorly controlled diabetes mellitus who became severely hyperkalemic while on amiloride died following 2 repeated i.v. glucose tolerance tests. Therefore, amiloride should be discontinued at least 3 days before glucose tolerance testing.

Metabolic or Respiratory Acidosis: Antikaliuretic therapy should be instituted only with caution in patients in whom respiratory or metabolic acidosis may occur, such as patients with cardiopulmonary disease or diabetes. If amiloride is given to these patients, frequent monitoring of acid-base balance is necessary. Shifts in acid-base balance alter the ratio of extracellular/intracellular potassium, and the development of acidosis may be associated with rapid increases in serum potassium levels.

Impaired Renal Function: Patients with impaired renal function other than those listed under Contraindications and who have BUN levels over 30 mg/100 mL, serum creatinine levels over 1.5 mg/100 mL, or with whole blood urea values over 60 mg/100 mL, or with diabetes mellitus, should not receive the drug without careful, frequent monitoring of serum electrolytes, creatinine, and BUN levels. Potassium retention associated with the use of amiloride is accentuated in the presence of renal impairment and may result in the rapid development of hyperkalemia. Prolongation of amiloride excretion was observed in patients with renal impairment.

Precautions: Electrolyte Imbalance and BUN Increases: Hyponatremia and hypochloremia may occur when used with other diuretics. Increases in BUN levels have been reported. These increases usually have accompanied vigorous fluid elimination, especially when diuretic therapy was used in seriously ill patients, such as those who had hepatic cirrhosis with ascites and metabolic alkalosis, or those with resistant edema. Therefore, careful monitoring of serum electrolytes and BUN levels is important when using amiloride.

Effects Related to Diuresis in Cirrhotic Patients: Patients with hepatic cirrhosis and ascites are intolerant of acute shifts in electrolyte balance and often have pre-existing hypokalemia as a result of associated secondary hyperaldosteronism. When oral diuretic therapy is used, these patients should be carefully monitored and diuresis should be gradual.

Hepatic encephalopathy, manifested by tremors, confusion, and coma, has been reported in association with amiloride therapy.

In a few cirrhotic patients, pre-existing jaundice increased, but the relationship to drug is uncertain.

Obstetrics: Teratologic studies with amiloride in rabbits and mice revealed no evidence of harm to the fetus. Reproduction studies in rats showed no evidence of impaired fertility. At approximately 5 or more times the expected maximum daily dose for humans, some toxicity was seen in adult rats and rabbits and a decrease in rat pup growth and survival occurred.

In rats a trace of drug crossed the placental barrier.

Pregnancy: Because clinical experience is limited, amiloride is not recommended for use during pregnancy. The potential benefits of the drug must be weighed against possible hazards to the fetus if it is administered to a woman of childbearing age.

Lactation: It is not known whether amiloride is excreted in human milk. In rats secretion of amiloride in milk has been demonstrated. Because many drugs are excreted in human milk and because of the potential for serious adverse reactions, a decision should be made whether to discontinue nursing or to discontinue the drug taking into account the importance of the drug to the mother.

Children: Safety in children has not been established; therefore amiloride is not recommended in the pediatric age group.

Drug Interactions: Lithium should generally not be given with diuretics because they reduce the renal clearance of lithium and add to the high risk of lithium toxicity.

When amiloride is administered concomitantly with an angiotensin-converting enzyme inhibitor, the risk of hyperkalemia may be increased. Therefore, if concomitant use of these agents is indicated because of demonstrated hypokalemia, they should be used with caution and with frequent monitoring of serum potassium.

Concomitant administration of non-steroidal anti-inflammatory drugs (NSAIDs) and potassium-sparing agents, including amiloride, may cause hyperkalemia and renal failure, particularly in elderly patients. Therefore, when amiloride is used concomitantly with NSAIDs, renal function and serum potassium levels should be carefully monitored.

Adverse Effects: While rare, the most serious adverse effect of amiloride is symptomatic hyperkalemia (symptoms of hyperkalemia may include paresthesias, muscular weakness, fatigue, flaccid paralysis of the extremities, bradycardia, shock and ECG abnormalities) (see Contraindications and Warnings).

The following incidence of adverse reactions was determined from clinical trials (837 patients treated with amiloride). See Table I.

A causal relationship could not be established with other reactions which have been reported rarely. However, the possibility could not be excluded. These were: Activation of probable pre-existing peptic ulcer, aplastic anemia, neutropenia, abnormalities of liver function tests.

In cirrhotic patients, jaundice associated with the underlying disease process has deepened in a few instances, but the relationship to drug is uncertain.

In patients with pre-existing severe liver disease, hepatic encephalopathy, manifested by tremors, confusion, and coma, and increased jaundice, have been reported in association with diuretics, including amiloride.

Overdose: Symptoms: No data are available in regard to overdosage in humans.

Treatment: It is not known whether the drug is dialyzable.

If hyperkalemia occurs, active measures should be taken to reduce the serum potassium levels (see Warnings). The most likely signs and symptoms to be expected with overdosage are dehydration and electrolyte imbalance. These can be treated by established procedures. Therapy with amiloride should be discontinued and the patient observed closely. There is no specific antidote. Emesis should be induced or gastric lavage performed. Treatment is symptomatic and supportive.

Dosage: The incidence of hyperkalemia is dose-related and this should be considered especially when daily doses over 10 mg are used.

Hepatic cirrhosis with ascites and edema: Treatment should be started with a small dose of amiloride, i.e., one 5 mg daily, plus a small dose of a diuretic agent (other than antikaliuretics). If necessary, dosages of both drugs may be increased gradually until effective diuresis is obtained. The dosage of amiloride should not exceed 4 tablets (20 mg) a day. Maintenance doses may be lower than those required to initiate diuresis; therefore, reduction in the daily dosage should be attempted when the patient's weight is stabilized. In cirrhotic patients, gradual weight reduction is especially desirable to reduce the likelihood of untoward reactions associated with diuretic therapy.

In those instances where amiloride is used alone, the initial daily dosage should be two 5 mg tablets (as a single dose or one tablet twice a day). Dosage may be increased depending on the need. The total daily dosage should not exceed 4 tablets (20 mg). After diuresis has been achieved the dosage may be reduced by decrements of 1 tablet to the least amount required.

Table I—Midamor

Adverse Effects

	Incidence $\geq 3\%$	Incidence $>1\%$-$<3\%$	Incidence $\leq 1\%$
Gastrointestinal (in 12.1% of patients)	Nausea/anorexia (6.1%) Diarrhea (3.8%) Vomiting (3.3%)	Abdominal pain Gas pain Appetite changes Constipation	Jaundice Gastrointestinal bleeding Abdominal fullness Gastrointestinal disturbance Thirst Heartburn Flatulence Dyspepsia Dryness of the mouth
CNS (in 9.6% of patients)	Headache (7.6%)	Dizziness Encephalopathy	Paresthesia Tremors Vertigo Nervousness Mental confusion Insomnia Decreased libido Depression Somnolence
Metabolic (in 8% of patients)	Asymptomatic hyperkalemia (8.0%)		Symptomatic hyperkalemia Hyponatremia
Musculoskeletal (in 6.1% of patients)		Muscle cramps Weakness Fatigability	Joint pain Leg ache Back pain Chest pain Neck/shoulder ache Pain extremities
Respiratory (in 2% of patients)		Cough Dyspnea	Shortness of breath
Urogenital (in 3.8% of patients)		Impotence	Polyuria Dysuria Urinary frequency Bladder spasms
Cardiovascular (in 1.5% of patients)			Angina pectoris Orthostatic hypotension Arrhythmia Palpitation One patient with a partial heart block developed complete heart block
Dermatologic (in 1.9% of patients)			Skin rash Pruritus Alopecia
Special Senses (in 2.0% of patients)			Visual disturbances Nasal congestion Increased intraocular pressure Tinnitus

Midamor (cont'd)

Edema of cardiac origin: Amiloride, one or two 5 mg tablets daily, may be given with the usual doses of a diuretic agent (other than antikaliuretics). This dose is sufficient in most cases. If potassium levels remain low, the dosage of amiloride may be increased gradually. The dosage of amiloride should not exceed 4 tablets (20 mg) a day.

The optimal dosage is determined by the serum potassium level. Reduction in dosage should be attempted for maintenance therapy. Maintenance therapy may be on an intermittent basis.

Hypertension: Amiloride, one or two 5 mg tablets daily, is given with the usual antihypertensive dosage of a diuretic agent (other than antikaliuretics). The dosage may be adjusted if necessary. More than two 5 mg tablets of amiloride daily usually is not needed; in any event, the maximum dosage is 4 tablets (20 mg) a day.

Supplied: Each yellow, diamond shaped, compressed tablet, coded MSD 92 contains: amiloride HCl 5 mg. Nonmedicinal ingredients: calcium phosphate, cornstarch, D&C Yellow No. 10, iron oxides, magnesium stearate and quinoline yellow WS. Gluten- and tartrazine-free. Bottles of 100.

(Shown in Product Recognition Section)

MIDAZOLAM

General Monograph, CPhA

see BENZODIAZEPINES

MIDOL®

Bayer Consumer

ASA—Caffeine

Dysmenorrhea Therapy

Supplied: Regular: Each white caplet, engraved MIDOL on one side of the caplet, contains: ASA 325 mg and caffeine anhydrous 65 mg. Nonmedicinal ingredients: cornstarch, hydrogenated castor oil, microcrystalline cellulose and sodium lauryl sulfate. Lactose-, paraben-, sulfite- and sucrose-free. Blister packages of 24.

Traditional: Each white caplet, engraved MIDOL on both sides of the caplet, contains: ASA 500 mg and caffeine anhydrous 32.4 mg. Nonmedicinal ingredients: cornstarch, hydrogenated vegetable oil, microcrystalline cellulose and sodium lauryl sulfate. Lactose-, paraben-, sulfite- and sucrose-free. Blister packages of 12 and 24.

(Shown in Product Recognition Section)

MIDOL® EXTRA STRENGTH

Bayer Consumer

Acetaminophen—Caffeine—Pyrilamine Maleate

Dysmenorrhea Therapy

Supplied: Caplets: Each film-coated, white caplet printed in blue ink on one face with MIDOL with a score on each end, contains: acetaminophen 500 mg, caffeine 60 mg and pyrilamine maleate 15 mg. Nonmedicinal ingredients: ammonium hydroxide, carnauba wax, cornstarch, croscarmellose sodium, ethyl alcohol, FD&C Blue No. 2, hydroxypropyl methylcellulose, isopropyl alcohol, magnesium stearate, microcrystalline cellulose, n-butyl alcohol, propylene glycol, titanium hydroxide and triacetin. Lactose-, sulfite- and tartrazine-free. Blister packages of 16. Bottles of 32.

Gelcaps: Each gelatin coated caplet, light blue on one face, dark blue on the other, imprinted MIDOL in black ink on one side, contains: acetaminophen 500 mg, caffeine 60 mg and pyrilamine maleate 15 mg. Nonmedicinal ingredients: carnauba wax, cornstarch, croscarmellose sodium, D&C Red No. 33, EDTA, FD&C Blue No. 1, gelatin, glycerin, hydroxypropyl methylcellulose, lecithin, magnesium stearate, microcrystalline cellulose, pharmaceutical glaze, simethicone, stearic acid, synthetic black & brown iron oxides, titanium dioxide and triacetin. Lactose- and tartrazine-free. Blister packages of 12.

MIDOL® PMS EXTRA STRENGTH

Bayer Consumer

Acetaminophen—Pamabrom—Pyrilamine Maleate

Premenstrual Syndrome Therapy

Supplied: Each white caplet, with MIDOL in orange on one side, contains: acetaminophen 500 mg, pamabrom 25 mg and pyrilamine maleate 15 mg. Nonmedicinal ingredients: carnauba wax, cornstarch, croscarmellose sodium, D&C Red No. 30, D&C Yellow No. 10, hydroxypropyl methylcellulose, magnesium stearate, microcrystalline cellulose, titanium dioxide and triacetin. Energy: 0.53 kJ (0.126 kcal). Lactose-, paraben-, sulfite- and sucrose-free. Blister packages of 16 and 32.

(Shown in Product Recognition Section)

MIGRANAL®

Novartis Pharmaceuticals

Dihydroergotamine Mesylate

Migraine Therapy

Pharmacology: Dihydroergotamine displays agonist activity at the 5-HT_{1D} receptor, which, by reducing 5-HT neuronal function and/or contracting elements of the cranial vasculature and/or suppressing neurogenic inflammation, is believed to underlie its antimigraine efficacy. It also displays affinity for the 5-HT_{1C} receptor and antagonistic activity at the 5-HT_2 subtype. Dihydroergotamine displays blocking actions at alpha adrenoreceptors, with a direct stimulating effect on the smooth muscle of peripheral blood vessels. Its tonic effect on capacitance vessels (veins) is particularly pronounced, compared to its effects on resistance vessels (arterioles). Dihydroergotamine differs from ergotamine by being more potent with respect to its adrenergic blocking actions and less potent with respect to its capacity to produce arterial vasoconstriction, but it maintains a marked venoconstrictor effect. Dihydroergotamine reduces the incidence and degree of nausea, photophobia, and phonophobia.

Intranasally administered dihydroergotamine is rapidly absorbed in a dose-independent manner (t_{max}=approximately 45 minutes). Significant relief of migraine begins within approximately 30 minutes following administration of dihydroergotamine nasal spray. Once pain is relieved, the incidence of return of pain within 24 hours is low. The bioavailability of dihydroergotamine administered intranasally is 43%.

Dihydroergotamine is 93% bound to plasma proteins and has a steady-state volume of distribution of about 800 L. The parent drug constitutes 70 to 80% of plasma concentrations of drug-related materials. The nasal spray form of dihydroergotamine, like most parenteral dose routes, is not subject to first-pass hepatic metabolism. The total body clearance is about 1.5 L/min, reflecting mainly a hepatic clearance. Plasma elimination of dihydroergotamine is biphasic with a mean terminal half-life of 10 hours. The major route of excretion is via the bile in the feces. After intranasal administration, the urinary recovery of parent drug amounts to about 2% of the dose.

Indications: For the treatment of migraine headaches, with or without aura in adults.

Dihydroergotamine nasal spray is not indicated for prophylactic therapy or for the management of hemiplegic or basilar migraine.

Contraindications: Patients who have previously shown hypersensitivity to ergot alkaloids, or to any of the components of dihydroergotamine nasal spray.

Dihydroergotamine nasal spray is contraindicated in patients having conditions predisposing to vasospastic reactions such as known peripheral arterial disease, coronary heart disease (in particular unstable or vasospastic angina), septic conditions and shock, vascular surgery, obliterative vascular disease, inadequately controlled hypertension, and severely impaired hepatic function.

Pregnancy and *Lactation:* Dihydroergotamine possesses oxytocic properties and, therefore, should not be administered during pregnancy. It is likely that dihydroergotamine is excreted in breast milk. Dihydroergotamine nasal spray is therefore contraindicated for nursing mothers.

Warnings: Dihydroergotamine could cause vasospastic reactions, including angina, although it seems to do so less frequently than ergotamine. This action appears to be dose-related. These reactions are manifested by intense arterial vasoconstriction, producing signs and symptoms of peripheral vascular ischemia (e.g., muscle pains, numbness, coldness and pallor or cyanosis of the digits), angina or unusual syndromes, such as mesenteric ischemia. Consequently, dihydroergotamine nasal spray should be discontinued immediately if signs or symptoms of vasoconstriction develop.

The solution used in Migranal was especially developed for intranasal administration and **must not be injected.**

Precautions: Children: Safety and effectiveness of dihydroergotamine nasal spray in children have not been established.

Geriatrics: Experience with the use of dihydroergotamine nasal spray in patients aged over 65 years is limited.

<u>*Drug Interactions:*</u> The concomitant use of oral contraceptives by female patients does not appear to influence the disposition of dihydroergotamine nasal spray.

Dihydroergotamine nasal spray should not be used with vasoconstrictors because the combination may cause a further elevation of blood pressure.

Concurrent use of vasoconstrictor agents including ergotamine, sumatriptan and nicotine may enhance the risk of vasoconstriction. Twenty four hours should elapse before taking sumatriptan following administration of dihydroergotamine nasal spray. This will avoid additive vasospastic effects. Conversely, dihydroergotamine nasal spray can be taken 6 hours following the administration of sumatriptan.

Although there have been reports that propranolol may potentiate the vasoconstrictive action of ergotamine by synergism upon β-blockade, the results of a limited clinical study (n=8) did not indicate a safety problem associated with the administration of dihydroergotamine nasal spray in subjects already receiving propranolol.

The concomitant use of macrolide antibiotics such as erythromycin, troleandomycin or josamycin with dihydroergotamine nasal spray should be avoided since these antibiotics may increase the plasma level of dihydroergotamine.

Lactation: It is likely that dihydroergotamine is excreted in human milk, although it is not known at which concentration, while it is known that ergotamine is excreted in breast milk and may cause vomiting, diarrhea, weak pulse and unstable blood pressure in breast-fed infants. Because of the potential for these serious adverse events in breast-fed infants, nursing mothers should not use dihydroergotamine nasal spray.

Information for the Patient: Currently available data have not demonstrated drug abuse and psychological dependence with dihydroergotamine nasal spray. However, due to the chronicity of migraines, patients should be advised not to exceed recommended dosages.

Patients should be advised to report immediately to the physician any of the following: numbness or tingling in the fingers and toes, muscle pain in the arms and legs, weakness in the legs, pain in the chest, temporary speeding or slowing of the heart rate, swelling, or itching.

Patients should be advised of the importance of priming the applicator (pump 4 times) prior to administration to ensure correct dosage. No more than 4 sprays should be administered for any single migraine headache attack. No more than 8 sprays should be administered during any 24 hour period. The maximum weekly dosage is 24 sprays (see Dosage).

Adverse Effects: The most commonly reported adverse events associated with the use of dihydroergotamine nasal spray in placebo-controlled, double-blind studies for the treatment of migraine headaches, and not reported at an equivalent incidence by placebo-treated patients, were rhinitis (which includes reports of all nasal-related adverse reactions), nausea, taste disturbance and application site reaction. In clinical trials these events were transient and self-limiting, and generally did not result in patient drop-out. Table I (on following page) lists the adverse events experienced at incidences greater than 1%.

In a few patients who have taken oral dihydroergotamine continuously over years, development of fibrotic changes, in particular of the pleura and the retroperitoneum, has been observed.

Chest tightness/pain was seen in earlier studies although the incidence was less than 1%, and a causal relationship was not established.

In rare cases, vascular spasms may occur, particularly in the lower extremities. If signs of vascular spasms are observed, dihydroergotamine nasal spray should be discontinued and treatment with a peripheral vasodilator initiated (see Overdose: Symptoms and Treatment).

Table I—Migranal

Adverse Events Reported in Double-Blind Placebo Controlled Studies for the Treatment of Migraine Headaches (Reported at Incidences ≥1%)

Adverse Reactions According to Body System	Rate of Occurrence (%) Migranal (N=642)	Rate of Occurrence (%) Placebo (N=632)
CNS		
Dizziness	2	2
Somnolence	2	1
Fatigue	1	1
Confusion	1	<1
Nervousness	1	<1
Asthenia	1	<1
Gastrointestinal System		
Nausea	9	4
Taste disturbance	7	1
Vomiting	4	2
Diarrhea	2	<1
Dysphagia	1	0
Respiratory System		
Rhinitis*	25	7
Application site reaction	4	1
Pharyngitis	3	1
Nasal discharge	1	<1
Sinusitis	1	<1
Musculoskeletal System		
Myalgia	1	<1
Stiffness	1	0
Autonomic Nervous System		
Hot Flushes	1	<1
Sweating increased	1	0
Dry mouth	1	1

* Rhinitis includes reports of nasal/nose congestion, nose dryness, nose edema, rhinitis, rhinorrhea and excessive sneezing.

Overdose: Symptoms and Treatment: There have been no reports of acute overdosage with dihydroergotamine nasal spray. The symptoms of an acute oral dihydroergotamine overdose are similar to those of an ergotamine overdose, although there is less pronounced nausea and vomiting with dihydroergotamine. These symptoms include the following: peripheral signs and symptoms of vasospasm (e.g., numbness, tingling, pain and cyanosis of the extremities associated with diminished or absent peripheral pulses); respiratory depression; an increase and/or decrease in blood pressure usually in that order; confusion, delirium, convulsions and coma; and/or some degree of nausea, vomiting and abdominal pain.

The treatment of an overdosage is symptomatic under close monitoring of the cardiovascular and respiratory systems. Treatment includes discontinuation of the drug, local application of warmth to the affected area and nursing care to prevent tissue damage; in case of severe vasospasms, vasodilators should be administered (e.g., sodium nitroprusside, phentolamine or dihydralazine). In the case of coronary constriction, appropriate treatment such as nitroglycerin should be initiated.

Dosage: Prior to administration of dihydroergotamine nasal spray the sprayer must be primed (pumped 4 times in the air) (See Blue Section—Information for the Patient "Migranal").

For best results, treatment should be initiated at the first symptom or sign of an attack. However, dihydroergotamine nasal spray can be used at any stage of a migraine attack.

The usual dosage required to obtain optimal efficacy and lasting relief is a total dosage of four sprays (corresponding to 1 bottle) of dihydroergotamine nasal spray. At the first sign or symptoms of a migraine headache, or as early as possible after the onset of headache pain, 1 spray of dihydroergotamine nasal spray should be administered into each nostril (total of 2 sprays). If the condition has not sufficiently improved approximately 15 minutes later, or to obtain optimal efficacy, an additional spray of dihydroergotamine nasal spray should be administered to each nostril (total of additional 2 sprays). **Once the sprayer has been prepared, it must be discarded with any remaining drug after 8 hours.**

In order to let the drug be absorbed through the skin in the nose, patients should not inhale deeply through the nose while spraying or immediately after spraying.

Dihydroergotamine nasal spray is exclusively indicated for the symptomatic treatment of migraine attacks. **Dihydroergotamine nasal spray should not be used as a prophylactic therapy.**

Significant relief of migraine begins within approximately 30 minutes following nasal administration of dihydroergotamine nasal spray.

No more than 1 bottle (4 sprays) should be administered for any single migraine attack. An interval of at least 6 to 8 hours should be observed before treating another migraine attack with dihydroergotamine nasal spray or any drug containing dihydroergotamine or ergotamine. No more than 2 bottles (8 sprays) should be administered during any 24-hour period. The maximum weekly dosage is 6 bottles (24 sprays) of dihydroergotamine nasal spray. Once pain is relieved, the incidence of pain return within 24 hours (migraine recurrence) is low.

Dihydroergotamine nasal spray does not need to be administered with an antiemetic, as is recommended with the parenteral form of dihydroergotamine mesylate, since the administration of the nasal spray form is not associated with nausea and vomiting to the same extent as the parenteral form.

Information for the Patient: See Blue Section—Information for the Patient "Migranal".

Supplied: Each mL of clear, colorless to faintly yellow solution contains: dihydroergotamine mesylate USP 4 mg. Nonmedicinal ingredients: anhydrous caffeine, anhydrous dextrose, carbon dioxide and water. Packages of 3 units, each unit consisting of 1 bottle and a sprayer. Store at room temperature (15 to 25°C).

(Shown in Product Recognition Section)

Reviewed 1999

MINESTRIN™ 1/20 Ⓟ

Parke-Davis

Norethindrone Acetate—Ethinyl Estradiol

Oral Contraceptive

Pharmacology: Minestrin 1/20 achieves its contraceptive effect primarily by inhibition of ovulation through gonadotrophin suppression.

It is well-established that oral contraceptives containing estrogen and progestogen affect hypothalamic, pituitary and ovarian functions. They may alter many other physiological systems. Although the exact mechanisms of action are incompletely understood, there is universal agreement that the inhibition of the ovulatory peak of luteinizing hormone (LH) is a constant and contributing factor. Oral contraceptives may exert their contraceptive action in at least 4 ways: alteration of the physical and chemical properties of the cervical mucus, thereby inhibiting sperm penetration; endometrial changes hindering implantation; inhibition of ovulation; subtle changes in the hypothalamic-pituitary-ovarian axis with possible altered corpus luteum function. The steroid profiles quite often indicate either an absence of or insufficient luteal activity, or a significant and gradual decrease in several of the indices of luteal function.

Probably none of these factors alone accounts for the high degree of antifertility effect of any oral contraceptive. They may all play a part in the production of effective contraception.

Indication: Conception control.

Contraindications: Thrombophlebitis, thromboembolic disorders or a history of these conditions; history of/or actual cerebrovascular disorders; history of/or actual myocardial infarction or coronary arterial disease; active liver disease; history of/or actual benign or malignant liver tumors; known or suspected carcinoma of the breast; known or suspected estrogen-dependent neoplasia; undiagnosed abnormal vaginal bleeding; any ocular lesion arising from ophthalmic vascular disease, such as partial or complete loss of vision or defect in visual fields; when pregnancy is suspected or diagnosed.

Warnings: Predisposing Factors for Coronary Artery Disease: Cigarette smoking increases the risk of serious cardiovascular side effects and mortality. Birth control pills increase this risk, especially with increasing age. Convincing data are available to support an upper age limit of 35 years for oral contraceptive use in women who smoke.

Other women who are independently at high risk for cardiovascular disease include those with diabetes, hypertension, abnormal lipid profile, or a family history of these. Whether oral contraceptives accentuate this risk is unclear.

In low risk, nonsmoking women of any age, the benefits of oral contraceptive use outweigh the possible cardiovascular risks associated with low dose formulations. Consequently, oral contraceptives may be prescribed for these women up to the age of menopause.

> Cigarette smoking increases the risk of serious adverse effects on the heart and blood vessels. This risk increases with age and becomes significant in oral contraceptive users over 35 years of age. Women should be counselled not to smoke.

Discontinue medication at the earliest manifestation of:

A. Thromboembolic and cardiovascular disorders such as: thrombophlebitis, pulmonary embolism, cerebrovascular disorders, myocardial ischemia, mesenteric thrombosis and retinal thrombosis.

B. Conditions which predispose to venous stasis and to vascular thrombosis, e.g., immobilization after accidents or confinement to bed during long-term illness. Other nonhormonal methods of contraception should be used until regular activities are resumed. For use of oral contraceptives when surgery is contemplated, see Precautions.

C. Visual defects, partial or complete.

D. Papilledema, or ophthalmic vascular lesions.

E. Severe headache of unknown etiology or worsening of pre-existing migraine headache.

Precautions: Physical Examination and Follow-up: Before oral contraceptives are used, a thorough history and physical examination should be performed, including a blood pressure determination. Breasts, liver, extremities and pelvic organs should be examined. A Papanicolaou smear should be taken if the patient has been sexually active.

The first follow-up visit should be done 3 months after oral contraceptives are prescribed. Thereafter, examinations should be performed at least once a year or more frequently if indicated. At each annual visit, examination should include those procedures that were done at the initial visit as outlined above or per recommendations of the Canadian Workshop on Screening for Cancer of the Cervix. For women who had 2 consecutive negative Pap Smears, screening could be continued every 3 years up to the age of 69.

Pregnancy: Oral contraceptives should not be taken by pregnant women. However, if conception accidently occurs while taking the pill, there is no conclusive evidence that the estrogen and progestin contained in the oral contraceptive will damage the developing child.

Lactation: In breast-feeding women, the use of oral contraceptives results in the hormonal components being excreted in breast milk and may reduce its quantity and quality. If the use of oral contraceptives is initiated after the establishment of lactation, there does not appear to be any effect on the quantity and quality of the milk. There is no evidence that low dose oral contraceptives are harmful to the nursing infant.

Hepatic Function: Patients who have had jaundice including a history of cholestatic jaundice during pregnancy should be given oral contraceptives with great care and under close observation.

The development of severe generalized pruritus or icterus requires that the medication be withdrawn until the problem is resolved.

If a patient develops jaundice which proves to be cholestatic in type, the use of oral contraceptives should not be resumed. In patients taking oral contraceptives, changes in the composition of the bile may occur and an increased incidence of gallstones has been reported.

Hepatic nodules (adenoma and focal nodular hyperplasia) have been reported, particularly in long-term users of oral contraceptives. Although these lesions are extremely rare, they have caused fatal intra-abdominal hemorrhage and should be considered in women presenting with an abdominal mass, acute abdominal pain, or evidence of intra-abdominal bleeding.

Hypertension: Patients with essential hypertension whose blood pressure is well-controlled may be given oral contraceptives but only under close supervision. If a significant elevation of blood pressure in previously normotensive or hypertensive subjects occurs at any time during the administration of the drug, cessation of medication is necessary.

Migraine and Headache: The onset or exacerbation of migraine or the development of headache of a new pattern which is recurrent, persistent or severe, requires discontinuation of oral contraceptives and evaluation of the cause.

Diabetes: Current low dose oral contraceptives exert minimal impact on glucose metabolism. Diabetic patients, or those with a family history of diabetes, should be observed closely to detect any worsening of carbohydrate metabolism. Patients predisposed to diabetes who can be kept under close supervision may be given oral contraceptives. Young diabetic patients whose disease is of recent origin, well-controlled, and not

Minestrin 1/20 (cont'd)

associated with hypertension or other signs of vascular disease such as ocular fundal changes, should be monitored more frequently while using oral contraceptives.

Ocular Disease: Patients who are pregnant or are taking oral contraceptives, may experience corneal edema that may cause visual disturbances and changes in tolerance to contact lenses, especially of the rigid type. Soft contact lenses usually do not cause disturbances. If visual changes or alterations in tolerance to contact lenses occur, temporary or permanent cessation of wear may be advised.

Breasts: Increasing age and a strong family history are the most significant risk factors for the development of breast cancer. Other established risk factors include obesity, nulliparity and late age at first full-term pregnancy. The identified groups of women that may be at increased risk of developing breast cancer before menopause are long-term users of oral contraceptives (more than 8 years) and starters at early age. In a few women, the use of oral contraceptives may accelerate the growth of an existing but undiagnosed breast cancer. Since any potential increased risk related to oral contraceptive use is small, there is no reason to change prescribing habits at present.

Women receiving oral contraceptives should be instructed in self-examination of their breasts. Their physicians should be notified whenever any masses are detected. A yearly clinical breast examination is also recommended because, if a breast cancer should develop, estrogen-containing drugs may cause a rapid progression.

Vaginal Bleeding: Persistent irregular vaginal bleeding requires assessment to exclude underlying pathology.

Fibroids: Patients with fibroids (leiomyomata) should be carefully observed. Sudden enlargement, pain, or tenderness requires discontinuance of the use of oral contraceptives.

Emotional Disorders: Patients with a history of emotional disturbances, especially the depressive type, may be more prone to have a recurrence of depression while taking oral contraceptives. In cases of a serious recurrence, a trial of an alternate method of contraception should be made which may help to clarify the possible relationship. Women with premenstrual syndrome (PMS) may have a varied response to oral contraceptives, ranging from symptomatic improvement to worsening of the condition.

Laboratory Tests: Results of laboratory tests should be interpreted in the light that the patient is on oral contraceptives. The following laboratory tests are modified.

A. Liver function tests: Aspartate serum transaminase (AST): variously reported elevations. Alkaline phosphatase and gamma glutamine transaminase (GGT): slightly elevated.

B. Coagulation tests: Minimal elevation of test values reported for such parameters as Factors VII, VIII, IX and X.

C. Thyroid function tests: Protein binding of thyroxine is increased as indicated by increased total serum thyroxine concentrations and decreased T_3 resin uptake.

D. Lipoproteins: Small changes of unproven clinical significance may occur in lipoprotein cholesterol fractions.

E. Gonadotropins: LH and FSH levels are suppressed by the use of oral contraceptives. Wait 2 weeks after discontinuing the use of oral contraceptives before measurements are made.

Tissue Specimens: Pathologists should be advised of oral contraceptive therapy when specimens obtained from surgical procedures and Pap smears are submitted for examination.

Return to Fertility: After discontinuing oral contraceptive therapy, the patient should delay pregnancy until at least 1 normal spontaneous cycle has occurred in order to date the pregnancy. An alternative contraceptive method should be used during this time.

Amenorrhea: Women having a history of oligomenorrhea, secondary amenorrhea, or irregular cycles may remain anovulatory or become amenorrheic following discontinuation of estrogen-progestin combination therapy.

Amenorrhea, especially if associated with breast secretion, that continues for 6 months or more after withdrawal, warrants a careful assessment of hypothalamic-pituitary function.

Thromboembolic Complications—Post-surgery: There is an increased risk of post-surgery thromboembolic complications in oral contraceptive users, after major surgery. If feasible, oral contraceptives should be discontinued and an alternative method substituted at least 1 month prior to **major** elective surgery. Oral contraceptives should not be resumed until the first menstrual period after hospital discharge following surgery.

<u>*Drug Interactions:*</u> The concurrent administration of oral contraceptives with other drugs may result in an altered response to either agent. Reduced effectiveness of the oral contraceptive, should it occur, is more likely with the low dose formulations. It is important to ascertain all drugs that a patient is taking, both prescription and nonprescription, before oral contraceptives are prescribed.

Refer to the revised 1994 Report on Oral Contraceptives, Health and Welfare Canada, for possible drug interactions with oral contraceptives.

Noncontraceptive Benefits of Oral Contraceptives: Several health advantages other than contraception have been reported.

1. Combination oral contraceptives reduce the incidence of cancer of the endometrium and ovaries.
2. Oral contraceptives reduce the likelihood of developing benign breast disease.
3. Oral contraceptives reduce the likelihood of development of functional ovarian cysts.
4. Pill-users have less menstrual blood loss and have more regular cycles, thereby reducing the chance of developing iron-deficiency anemia.
5. The use of oral contraceptives may decrease the severity of dysmenorrhea and premenstrual syndrome, and may improve acne vulgaris, hirsutism, and other androgen-mediated disorders.
6. Other noncontraceptive benefits are outlined in the revised 1994 Report on Oral Contraceptives, Health and Welfare Canada.

> Oral contraceptives **do not protect** against sexually transmitted diseases (STDs) including HIV/AIDS. For protection against STDs, it is advisable to use latex condoms **in combination with** oral contraceptives.

Adverse Effects: An increased risk of the following serious adverse reactions has been associated with the use of oral contraceptives: thrombophlebitis; pulmonary embolism; mesenteric thrombosis; neuro-ocular lesions, e.g., retinal thrombosis; myocardial infarction; cerebral thrombosis; cerebral hemorrhage; hypertension; benign hepatic tumors; gallbladder disease.

The following adverse reactions also have been reported in patients receiving oral contraceptives: nausea and vomiting, usually the most common adverse reaction, occurs in approximately 10% or less of patients during the first cycle. Other reactions, as a general rule, are seen less frequently or only occasionally.

Other reactions, as a general rule, are seen less frequently or only occasionally: gastrointestinal symptoms (such as abdominal cramps and bloating); breakthrough bleeding; spotting; change in menstrual flow; dysmenorrhea; amenorrhea during and after treatment; temporary infertility after discontinuance of treatment; edema; chloasma or melasma which may persist; breast changes: tenderness, enlargement, and secretion; change in weight (increase or decrease); endocervical hyperplasias; possible diminution in lactation when given immediately postpartum; cholestatic jaundice; migraine; increase in size of uterine leiomyomata; rash (allergic); mental depression; reduced tolerance to carbohydrates; vaginal candidiasis; premenstrual-like syndrome; intolerance to contact lenses; change in corneal curvature (steepening); cataracts; optic neuritis; retinal thrombosis; changes in libido; chorea; changes in appetite; cystitis-like syndrome; rhinitis; headache; nervousness; dizziness; hirsutism; loss of scalp hair; erythema multiforme; erythema nodosum; hemorrhagic eruption; vaginitis; porphyria; impaired renal function; Raynaud's phenomenon; auditory disturbances; hemolytic uremic syndrome; pancreatitis.

Overdose: Symptoms and Treatment: In case of overdosage or accidental ingestion by children, the physician should observe the patient closely although no medication is required. Gastric lavage should be given if considered necessary.

Dosage: Information for the Patient on How to Take the Birth Control Pill:

1. **Read these directions:**
   - before you start taking your pills, and
   - any time you are not sure what to do.
2. **Look at your pill pack** to see if it has 21 or 28 pills:
   - 21-Pill Pack: 21 active pills (with hormones) taken daily for 3 weeks, and then take no pills for 1 week

   or
   - 28-Pill Pack: 21 active pills (with hormones) taken daily for 3 weeks, and then 7 "reminder" pills (no hormones) taken daily for 1 week.

   Also check (1) **where to start and** (2) **direction to take pills in.**
3. You may wish to use a second method of birth control (e.g., latex condoms and spermicidal foam or gel) for the first 7 days of the first cycle of pill use. This will provide a back-up in case pills are forgotten while you are getting used to taking them.
4. When receiving any medical treatment, be sure to tell your doctor that you are using birth control pills.
5. **Many women have spotting or light bleeding or may feel sick to their stomach during the first 3 months on the pill.** If you do feel sick, do not stop taking the pill. The problem will usually go away. If it does not go away, check with your doctor or clinic.
6. **Missing pills also can cause some spotting or light bleeding,** even if you make up the missed pills. You also could feel a little sick to your stomach on the days you take 2 pills to make up for missed pills.
7. **If you miss pills at any time, you could get pregnant. The greatest risks for pregnancy are:**
   - when you start a pack late, or
   - when you miss pills at the beginning or at the very end of the pack.
8. **Always be sure you have ready:**
   - **another kind of birth control** (such as latex condoms and spermicidal foam or gel) to use as a back-up in case you miss pills, and
   - **an extra, full pack of pills.**
9. **If you have vomiting or diarrhea, or if you take certain medicines,** such as antibiotics, your pills may not work as well. Use a back-up method, such as latex condoms and spermicidal foam or gel, until you can check with your doctor or clinic.
10. **If you forget more than 1 pill 2 months in a row,** talk to your doctor or clinic about how to make pill-taking easier or about using another method of birth control.
11. **If your questions are not answered here, call your doctor or clinic.**

When to start the first pack of pills: Be sure to read these instructions:

- before you start taking your pills, and
- any time you are not sure what to do.

Decide with your doctor or clinic what is the best day for you to start taking your first pack of pills. Your pills may be either a 21-day or a 28-day type.

A. 21-Day Combination: With this type of birth control pill, you are 21 days on pills with 7 days off pills. You must not be off the pills for more than 7 days in a row.

1. **The first day of your menstrual period (bleeding) is Day 1 of your cycle.** Your doctor may advise you to start taking the pills on Day 1, on Day 5, or on the first Sunday after your period begins. If your period starts on Sunday, start that same day.

   Minestrin 1/20 (21's) is recommended for a Day 1 start.
   - Label the pack by selecting the appropriate day label strip that starts with Day 1 of your menstrual period (counting the first day of menstrual flow as Day 1. Place the strip in the space where you see the words "Place Day Label Here." Having the compact dispenser labelled with the correct day of the week will help remind you to take your tablet every day.
   - On Day 1 of your menstrual cycle, take your first tablet, beginning with the first tablet in the top row (where you see the word "start"). This tablet should correspond to the day of the week that you are taking your first tablet. To remove the tablet, push it through the back of the compact dispenser.
   - On the following day, take the next tablet in the row, always proceeding from left to right. Each new row will always begin on the same day of the week.
2. Take 1 pill at approximately the same time every day for 21 days; **Then take no pills for 7 days.** Start a new pack on the eighth day. You will probably have a period during the seven days off the pill. (This bleeding may be lighter and shorter than your usual period.) Always have a new compact ready to start each cycle (refills may be obtained by giving a pharmacist the number on the prescription label).

B. 28-Day Combination: With this type of birth control pill, you take 21 pills which contain hormones and 7 pills which contain no hormones.

1. **The first day of your menstrual period (bleeding) is Day 1 of your cycle.** Your doctor may advise you to start taking the pills on Day 1, on Day 5, or on the first Sunday after your period begins. If your period starts on Sunday, start that same day.

   Minestrin 1/20 (28's) is recommended for a Day 1 start.
   - Label the pack by selecting the appropriate day label strip that starts with Day 1 of your menstrual period (counting

the first day of menstrual flow as Day 1). Place the strip in the space where you see the words "Place Day Label Here." Having the compact dispenser labelled with the correct day of the week will help remind you to take your tablet every day.

- On Day 1 of your menstrual cycle, take your first tablet, beginning with the first tablet in the top row (where you see the word "start"). This tablet should correspond to the day of the week that you are taking your first tablet. To remove the tablet, push it through the back of the compact dispenser.
- On the following day, take the next tablet in the row, always proceeding from left to right. Each new row will always begin on the same day of the week.

2. Take one pill at approximately the same time every day for 28 days. Begin a new pack the next day, **not missing any days on the pills.** Your period should occur during the last 7 days of using that pill pack. Always have a new compact ready to start each new cycle (refills may be obtained by giving a pharmacist the number on the prescription label).

What to do during the month:

1. **Take a pill at approximately the same time every day until the pack is empty.**
   - Try to associate taking your pill with some regular activity like eating a meal or going to bed.
   - Do not skip pills even if you have bleeding between monthly periods or feel sick to your stomach (nausea).
   - Do not skip pills even if you do not have sex very often.
2. **When you finish a pack:**
   - **21 pills: Wait 7 days** to start the next pack. You will have your period during that week.
   - **28 pills:** Start the next pack **on the next day.** Take 1 pill every day. Do not wait any days between packs.

What to do if you miss pills: Table I outlines the actions you should take if you miss 1 or more of your birth control pills on a Day 1 start. If you are not using a Day 1 start, check with your doctor or clinic.

Table I—Minestrin 1/20

What to Do If You Miss Pills

Day 1 Start

Miss 1 pill

Take it as soon as you remember, and take the next pill at the usual time. This means that you might take 2 pills in one day.

Miss 2 pills in a row

First 2 Weeks:

1. Take 2 pills the day you remember and 2 pills the next day.
2. Then take 1 pill a day until you finish the pack.
3. Use a back-up method of birth control if you have sex in the 7 days after you miss the pills.

Third Week:

1. Safely dispose of the rest of the pill pack and start a new pack that same day.
2. Use a back-up method of birth control if you have sex in 7 days after you miss the pills.
3. You may not have a period this month.

If you miss 2 periods in a row, call your doctor or clinic.

Miss 3 or more pills in a row

Anytime in the Cycle:

1. Safely dispose of the rest of the pill pack and start a new pack that same day.
2. Use a back-up method of birth control if you have sex in the 7 days after you miss the pills.
3. You may not have a period this month.

If you miss 2 periods in a row, call your doctor or clinic.

Note: 28-Day Pack: If you forget any of the 7 "reminder" pills (without hormones) in Week 4, just safely dispose of the pills you missed. Then keep taking 1 pill each day until the pack is empty. You do not need to use a back-up method.

Always be sure you have on hand:

- a back-up method of birth control (such as latex condoms and spermicidal foam or gel) in case you miss pills, and
- an extra, full pack of pills.

If you forget more than 1 pill 2 months in a row, talk to your doctor or clinic. Talk about ways to make pill-taking easier or about using another method of birth control.

Information for the Patient: See Blue Section—Information for the Patient "Oral Contraceptives".

Supplied: Each white tablet contains: norethindrone acetate 1 mg and ethinyl estradiol 20 μg. Nonmedicinal ingredients (white tablets): acacia, lactose, magnesium stearate, starch, sugar and talc; (lilac tablets): acacia, FD&C Blue No. 1, FD&C Red No. 3, FD&C Red No. 40, lactose, magnesium stearate, starch, sugar and talc. Energy: 1 kJ (0.24 kcal). Gluten-, sodium-, sulfite-, paraben- and tartrazine-free. Credit-card dispensers of 21 tablets (white) and 28 tablets (21 white tablets and 7 lilac inert tablets). Packages of 5.

(Shown in Product Recognition Section)

MINIMS®
Ophtapharma

Sterile single dose disposable eye drops

Supplied: Artificial Tears, Atropine 1% Ⓟ, Benoxinate 0.4%, Chloramphenicol 0.5% Ⓟ, Cyclopentolate 0.5% Ⓟ and 1% Ⓟ, Fluorescein 2%, Lignocaine 4%/Fluorescein 0.25%, Gentamicin 0.3% Ⓟ, Homatropine 2%, Phenylephrine 2.5% Ⓟ and 10% Ⓟ, Pilocarpine 2% Ⓟ and 4% Ⓟ, Prednisolone 0.5% Ⓟ, Sodium chloride 0.9%, Tetracaine 0.5% Ⓟ and 1% Ⓟ and Tropicamide 1% Ⓟ. Nonmedicinal ingredients: borax (Artificial Tears, Chloramphenicol 0.5%, Gentamicin 0.3%), boric acid (Chloramphenicol 0.5%), disodium edetate (Phenylephrine 2.5% and 10%), polyvinyl pyrrolidone (Lignocaine 4%/Fluorescein 0.25%), sodium chloride (Artificial Tears, Gentamicin 0.3%, Prednisolone 0.5%), sodium dihydrogen phosphate (Prednisolone 0.5%), sodium edetate (Prenisolone 0.5%), sodium hydroxide (Tropicamide 1%) and sodium metabisulfite (Phenylephrine 2.5% and 10%). Each single dose plastic applicator contains 0.3 mL of solution. Boxes of 20.

MINIPRESS™ Ⓟ
Pfizer

Prazosin HCl

Antihypertensive

Pharmacology: Prazosin causes a decrease in total peripheral resistance. Animal studies suggest that the vasodilator effect of prazosin is related to selective blockade of post-synaptic $alpha_1$-adrenoceptors. The results of dog forelimb experiments demonstrate that the peripheral vasodilator effect is confined mainly to the level of the resistance vessels (arterioles). Hemodynamic studies have been carried out in man following acute single dose administration and during the course of long-term maintenance therapy. The results confirm that the therapeutic effect is a fall in blood pressure unaccompanied by a clinically significant change in heart rate, renal blood flow and glomerular filtration rate. In patients with hypertension there is little change in cardiac output. In addition, clinical pharmacology studies have shown that prazosin antagonizes the vasopressor effect of i.v. phenylephrine, an $alpha_1$-agonist.

In man blood pressure is lowered in both the supine and standing positions. The hypotensive effect of prazosin is greater when the patient is standing, and a mild reflex tachycardia can result. Tolerance has not been observed to develop in long-term hypertensive therapy. Rebound elevation of blood pressure does not seem to occur following abrupt cessation of therapy with prazosin.

Following oral administration in normal volunteers and hypertensive patients, plasma concentrations reach a peak at about 3 hours with a plasma half-life of 2 to 3 hours. The drug is highly bound to plasma protein (97%). After chronic administration, no apparent drug accumulation was observed nor were any obvious decreases in plasma concentrations noted. Secondary plasma drug peaks and shoulders suggested probable enterohepatic circulation. Animal studies indicate that prazosin is extensively metabolized, primarily by demethylation and conjugation, and excreted (primarily as glucuronide conjugates) mainly via bile and feces. Similar metabolism and excretion has been documented in human studies.

Most clinical studies indicate that chronic therapy with prazosin has little effect on plasma renin activity. However one report suggests a transient increase in plasma renin activity following the initial dose, as well as attenuated transient increase with subsequent doses.

Hypotensive Action: The nature of the hypotensive action of prazosin was studied both by in vitro and in vivo methodology. I.V. administered prazosin in dogs caused prolonged hypotension and reduction in total peripheral resistance. Cardiac output, heart rate, and blood flow in the femoral, renal, and splanchnic vascular beds were increased transiently. Cardiac responses to electrical stimulation of cardioaccelerator nerves were not depressed, nor was there sympathetic ganglion or adrenergic neurone blockade. Although prazosin reversed the epinephrine pressor response in intact animals, vasodilator activity was only slightly diminished when the vessels were deprived of sympathetic tone by ganglionic blockade.

Physiologic and direct radioligand binding data from studies in experimental animals indicates that the hypotensive effect of prazosin ascribed to peripheral vasodilation is achieved primarily by competitive blockade of the vascular postsynaptic $alpha_1$-adrenergic receptors. As prazosin acts preferentially on postsynaptic $alpha_1$-adrenergic receptors, the feedback control of neuronal norepinephrine release by presynaptic $alpha_2$-receptors remains unchanged.

In the dog, the hypotensive effect of prazosin i.v. was reversed by metaraminol and norepinephrine given by i.v. infusion.

Miscellaneous Actions: At doses considerably higher than those required for antihypertensive activity, prazosin has mild CNS depressant activity, decreases heart norepinephrine and adrenal epinephrine in rats, causes diuresis in anesthetized dogs, but fluid retention in conscious dogs and mice and is hyperglycemic in rats.

In clinical studies in which lipid profiles were followed, there were generally no adverse changes noted between pre- and post-treatment lipids levels.

Indications: The treatment of hypertension. As an antihypertensive drug it is mild to moderate in activity. It is employed in a general treatment program in conjunction with a diuretic and/or other antihypertensive drugs as needed for proper patient response. Prazosin may be tried as a sole therapy in those patients in whom treatment with other agents caused adverse effects or is inappropriate.

Contraindications: Known sensitivity to quinazolines.

Warnings: Prazosin may cause syncope with sudden loss of consciousness. In most cases this is believed to be due to an excessive postural hypotensive effect, although occasionally the syncopal episode has been associated with a bout of severe tachycardia with heart rates of 120 to 160 beats/minute. The incidence of syncopal episodes is approximately 0.8% when the gradual dose build up described under dosage is followed. The incidence is higher if the initial dose exceeds 0.5 mg. Syncopal episodes have occurred within 30 to 90 minutes of the initial dose of the drug. They have also been reported in association with dosage increases or the introduction of prazosin into the regimen of a patient taking another antihypertensive agent or a diuretic.

Physicians are therefore advised to limit the initial dose of the drug to 0.5 mg b.i.d. or t.i.d., to subsequently increase the dosage slowly, and to introduce any additional antihypertensive drugs into the patient's regimen with caution.

Patients whose blood pressure is not adequately controlled by high doses of a β-adrenergic blocking agent such as propranolol may develop acute hypotension when prazosin is added. To minimize the incidence of acute hypotension in such patients, the dose of β-adrenergic blocking agent should be reduced before prazosin is administered. A low initial dose of prazosin is also strongly recommended (see Dosage).

If syncope occurs, place the patient in the recumbent position and institute supportive measures. This adverse effect is self-limiting and in most cases does not recur once a steady maintenance level is initiated. Caution patients to avoid situations where injury could result should syncope occur during prazosin therapy, especially in the initial dose adjustment period.

Occupational Hazards: More common than loss of consciousness are the symptoms often associated with lowering of blood pressure, namely dizziness and light headedness. Caution the patient about these possible adverse effects and advise what measures to take should they develop.

Pregnancy: Although no teratogenic effects were seen in animal testing, there are no adequate and well controlled studies which establish the safety of prazosin in pregnant women. Limited uncontrolled use in the management of hypertension in the later stages of pregnancy suggests that prazosin in combination with a beta-blocker can lower blood pressure in pregnant patients. The drug appears to be less effective in patients with proteinuria in whom the addition of i.v. hydralazine was usually required. Accordingly prazosin should be used during pregnancy only if in the opinion of the physician the potential benefit outweighs potential risk to mother and child.

Lactation: Prazosin has been shown to be excreted in small amounts in human milk. Caution should be exercised when prazosin is administered to nursing mothers.

Minipress (cont'd)

Children: Not recommended for the treatment of children under 12 years of age since safe conditions for its use have not been established in this group.

Precautions: Use in Patients with Moderate to Severe Grades of Renal Impairment: Because some patients with moderate to severe grades of renal impairment have responded to smaller than usual doses of prazosin, it is recommended that therapy be initiated at 0.5 mg daily and that dose increases be instituted cautiously.

Drug Interactions: Prazosin has been administered without any adverse drug interaction in limited clinical experience to date with the following: cardiac glycosides—digitalis and digoxin; hypoglycemics—insulin, chlorpropamide, tolazamide and tolbutamide; tranquilizers and sedatives—chlordiazepoxide, diazepam and phenobarbital; antigout—allopurinol, colchicine and probenecid; antiarrhythmics—procainamide, propranolol (see Warnings), and quinidine; and analgesics, antipyretics and anti-inflammatories—propoxyphene, ASA, indomethacin and phenylbutazone.

Addition of a diuretic or other antihypertensive agent to prazosin has been shown to cause an additive hypotensive effect (see Warnings and Dosage).

Drug/Laboratory Test Interactions: False positive results may occur in screening tests for pheochromocytoma (urinary vanillylmandelic acid [VMA] and methoxyhydroxyphenyl glysol (MHPG) urinary metabolites of norepinephrine in patients who are being treated with prazosin. If an elevated VMA is found, prazosin should be discontinued and the patient retested after a month.

Adverse Effects: The most common reactions associated with prazosin therapy are postural dizziness 11%, nausea 9.5%, drowsiness 8.7%, headache 8.4%, palpitations 6.6%, dry mouth 5.6%, weakness 4.6% and fatigue/malaise 4.5%. In most instances, side effects have disappeared with continued therapy or have been tolerated with no decrease in dose of drug. The following reactions have also been observed during prazosin administration.

Gastrointestinal: vomiting, diarrhea, constipation, abdominal discomfort and/or pain.

Cardiovascular: syncope (see Warnings), orthostatic hypotension, edema, dyspnea, tachycardia, faintness.

CNS: nervousness, vertigo, depression, paresthesia, hallucinations.

Dermatologic: rash, pruritus, alopecia, lichen planus.

Genitourinary: urinary frequency, incontinence, impotence, priapism.

EENT: blurred vision, reddened sclera, epistaxis, tinnitus, nasal congestion.

Hepatic: liver function abnormalities, pancreatitis.

Hematologic: decreased hematocrit/hemoglobin.

Other: diaphoresis, fever, arthralgia, positive ANA titer.

Single reports of pigmentary mottling and serous retinopathy have been reported. In these instances, the exact causal relationship has not been established because the baseline observations were frequently inadequate.

In more specific slit lamp and funduscopic studies, which included adequate baseline examinations, no drug related abnormal ophthalmological findings have been reported.

Literature reports exist associating prazosin therapy with a worsening of pre-existing narcolepsy. A causal relationship is uncertain in these cases.

Overdose: Symptoms: The most frequently observed symptoms of overdose include hypotension and somnolence.

Accidental ingestion of at least 50 mg of prazosin in a 2 year old child resulted in profound drowsiness and depressed reflexes. No decrease in blood pressure was noted. Recovery was uneventful.

Treatment: Should overdosage lead to hypotension, support of the cardiovascular system is of first importance. Restoration of blood pressure and normalization of heart rate may be accomplished by keeping the patient in the supine position. If necessary, vasopressors should be used. If this measure is inadequate, shock should then be treated with volume expanders. Renal function should be monitored and supported as needed. Laboratory data indicate that prazosin is not dialyzable because it is protein bound.

Dosage: Note: When titration is to be undertaken using the tablet formulation it will be necessary to split the 1 mg scored tablet to obtain the 0.5 mg starting dose.

It is recommended that the starting dose of 0.5 mg be given with food, preferably with the evening meal, at least 2 or 3 hours before retiring. The dose should be built up gradually with 0.5 mg being given 2 or 3 times daily for at least 3 days. Unless adverse effects occur and subject to the blood pressure lowering effect, this dose should be increased to 1 mg given 2 or 3 times daily for at least a further 3 days.

Thereafter, as determined by the patient's response to the blood pressure lowering effect, the dose should be increased gradually. Response to prazosin is usually seen within 1 to 14 days if it is to occur at any particular dose. When a response is seen, continue therapy at that dose until the degree of response has reached the optimum before the next dose increment is added. Continue incremental increases until a desired effect is achieved or a maximum daily dose of 20 mg is reached.

The maintenance dose of prazosin may be given as a twice or 3 times daily dosage regimen.

In patients with moderate to severe grades of renal impairment, initiate therapy at 0.5 mg daily and institute dose increases gradually.

Use With Other Drugs: Patients receiving diuretic therapy: The diuretic should be reduced to a maintenance dose level for the particular agent and prazosin initiated at 0.5 mg at bedtime then proceeding to 0.5 mg b.i.d. or t.i.d. After the initial period of observation, gradually increase the prazosin dosage as determined by patient response.

Patients receiving other antihypertensive agents: Because some additive effect is anticipated, reduce the dose of the other agent (e.g. propranolol* or other beta-adrenergic blocking agents*, alpha methyldopa, reserpine, clonidine*) and initiate prazosin at 0.5 mg h.s. then proceeding to 0.5 mg, 2 or 3 times daily. Make subsequent dosage increase depending upon the patient's response.

* Appropriate precautions should be observed when the dosage of these other antihypertensive agents is reduced.

Patients on Prazosin to whom other antihypertensive agents are added: When adding a diuretic or other antihypertensive agent, reduce the dose of prazosin to 1 or 2 mg 2 or 3 times daily and carry out retitration.

Supplied: Each scored tablet contains: prazosin HCl equivalent to 1 mg (orange), 2 mg (white, round) or 5 mg (white, diamond) of prazosin. Nonmedicinal ingredients: calcium phosphate, microcrystalline cellulose, cornstarch, magnesium stearate/sodium lauryl sulfate and dye FD & C Yellow #6 (1 mg tablet only). Tartrazine-free. Bottles (HDPE) of 100 (all tablet strengths) and 500 (1 and 2 mg). Store at room temperature between 15 and 30°C.

(Shown in Product Recognition Section)

Reviewed 1998

MINITRAN™

3M Pharmaceuticals

Nitroglycerin

Antianginal

Pharmacology: The principal pharmacological action of nitroglycerin is relaxation of vascular smooth muscle and consequent dilation of both peripheral arteries and veins, with more prominent effects on the latter. Dilation of the post-capillary vessels, including large veins, promotes peripheral pooling of blood and decreases venous return to the heart, thereby reducing left ventricular end-diastolic pressure (preload). Arteriolar relaxation reduces systemic vascular resistance and arterial pressure (afterload). Dilation of the coronary arteries also occurs. The relative importance of preload reduction, afterload reduction, and coronary dilation remains undefined.

When Minitran is applied to the skin, nitroglycerin is absorbed continuously through the skin into the systemic circulation. Thus, the active drug reaches target sites before inactivation by the liver. Nitroglycerin is rapidly metabolized, principally by a liver reductase, to form glycerol nitrate metabolites and inorganic nitrate. Two active major metabolites, 1,2- and 1,3-dinitroglycerols, the products of hydrolysis, appear to be less potent than nitroglycerin as vasodilators but have longer plasma half-lives. The dinitrates are further metabolized to mononitrates (biologically inactive with respect to cardiovascular effects) and ultimately to glycerol and carbon dioxide. There is extensive first-pass deactivation by the liver following gastrointestinal absorption.

In healthy volunteers, steady-state plasma concentrations of nitroglycerin were reached within 2 hours after application of the patch and were maintained at the same level for the duration of the study (24 hours). Upon removal of the patch, plasma concentrations decline rapidly.

Dosing regimens for most chronically used drugs are designed to provide plasma concentrations that are continuously greater than a minimally effective concentration. This strategy is probably inappropriate for organic nitrates. Some controlled clinical trials using exercise tolerance testing have shown maintenance of effectiveness when patches are worn continuously. The large majority of such controlled trials, however, has shown the development of tolerance (i.e., complete loss of effect as measured by exercise testing) within the first day. Tolerance has occurred even when doses greater than 4 mg/hr were delivered continuously. This dose is far in excess of the effective dose of 0.2 to 0.6 mg/hour delivered intermittently.

Efficacy of organic nitrates is restored after a period of absence of nitrates from the body. Drug-free intervals of 10 to 12 hours are known to be sufficient to restore response. Several studies have demonstrated that when nitroglycerin is administered according to an intermittent regimen, doses of nitroglycerin 0.4 to 0.8 mg/hour (20 to 40 cm^2) have increased exercise capacity for up to 8 hours, with a trend of increased exercise capacity to 12 hours. The results of one controlled clinical trial suggests that the intermittent use of nitrates may be associated with decreased exercise tolerance during the last part of the nitrate-free interval, in comparison to placebo. The clinical relevance of this observation is unknown.

In another clinical trial, there was an increase in nocturnal angina attacks during the drug-free period in some patients treated with nitroglycerin as compared to placebo; therefore, the possibility of increased frequency of severity of angina during the nitrate-free interval should be considered. However, in one controlled clinical study, involving 291 patients with angina, involving exercise tolerance testing at 4 hours duration post-dosing. Minitran did not demonstrate any significant evidence of vascular tolerance or rebound angina attacks during long-term intermittent treatment.

Indications: Used intermittently (see Pharmacology) for the prevention of anginal attacks in patients with stable angina pectoris associated with coronary artery disease. It can be used in conjunction with other antianginal agents such as beta-blockers and/or calcium antagonists.

Minitran is not intended for the immediate relief of acute attacks of angina pectoris. Sublingual nitroglycerin preparations should be used for this purpose.

Contraindications: Known hypersensitivity to nitroglycerin or other nitrates or nitrites. Known or suspected hypersensitivity to components of the patch. Acute circulatory failure associated with marked hypotension (shock and states of collapse). Postural hypotension. Myocardial insufficiency due to obstruction (e.g., in the presence of aortic or mitral stenosis or constrictive pericarditis). Increased intracranial pressure. Increased intraocular pressure. Severe anemia.

Warnings: The benefits and safety of transdermal nitroglycerin in patients with acute myocardial infarction or congestive heart failure have not been established. If one elects to use Minitran in these conditions, careful clinical or hemodynamic monitoring must be used to avoid the hazards of hypotension and tachycardia.

Minitran must be removed before cardioversion or DC defibrillation is attempted, as well as before applying diathermy treatment, since it may be associated with damage to the paddles and burns to the patient.

Precautions: Headaches or symptoms of hypotension, such as weakness or dizziness, particularly when arising suddenly from a recumbent position, may occur. A reduction in dose or discontinuation of treatment may be necessary.

Caution should be exercised when using nitroglycerin in patients prone to, or who might be affected by hypotension. The drug therefore should be used with caution in patients who may have volume depletion from diuretic therapy or in patients who have low systolic blood pressure (e.g., below 90 mmHg). Paradoxical bradycardia and increased angina pectoris may accompany nitroglycerin-induced hypotension.

Nitrate therapy may aggravate the angina caused by hypertrophic cardiomyopathy.

In industrial workers who have had long-term exposure to unknown (presumably high) doses of nitroglycerin, tolerance clearly occurs. There is moreover, physical dependence since chest pain, acute myocardial infarction, and even sudden death have occurred during temporary withdrawal of nitroglycerin from these workers. In clinical trials of angina patients, there are reports of anginal attacks being more easily provoked and of rebound in the hemodynamic effects soon after nitrate withdrawal. The importance of these observations to the routine clinical use of nitroglycerin has not been fully elucidated, but patients should be monitored closely for increased anginal symptoms during drug-free periods.

Caution should be exercised in patients with arterial hypoxemia due to anemia (see Contraindications), because in such patients the biotransformation of nitroglycerin is reduced. Similarly, caution is called for in patients with hypoxemia and a ventilation/perfusion imbalance due to lung disease or ischemic heart failure. Patients with angina pectoris, myocardial infarction, or cerebral ischemia frequently suffer from abnormalities of the small airways (especially alveolar hypoxia). Under these circumstances vasoconstriction occurs within the lung to shift perfusion from areas of alveolar hypoxia to better ventilated regions of the lung. As a potent vasodilator, nitroglycerin could reverse this protective vasoconstriction and thus result in increased perfusion to poorly ventilated areas, worsening of the ventilation/perfusion imbalance, and a further decrease in the arterial partial pressure of oxygen.

Tolerance to nitroglycerin with cross tolerance to other nitrates of nitrites may occur (see Pharmacology). Coadministration of other long-acting nitrates could jeopardize the integrity of the nitrate-free interval and therefore must be avoided. As tolerance to nitroglycerin patches develops, the effect of sublingual nitroglycerin on exercise tolerance, although still observable, is somewhat blunted.

Occupational Hazards: As patients may experience faintness and/or dizziness, reaction time when driving or operating machinery may be impaired, especially at the start of treatment.

Pregnancy: It is not known whether nitroglycerin can cause fetal harm when administered to pregnant women or can affect reproductive capacity. Therefore, use only if the potential benefit justifies the risk to the fetus.

Lactation: It is not known whether nitroglycerin is excreted in human milk. Benefits to the mother must be weighed against the risk to the infant.

Children: Safety and effectiveness of use in children have not been established.

Drug Interactions: Concomitant treatment with other vasodilators, calcium channel blockers, ACE inhibitors, beta-blockers, diuretics, antihypertensives, tricyclic antidepressants and major tranquilizers may potentiate the blood pressure lowering effect of Minitran. Dose adjustment may be necessary.

Alcohol may enhance sensitivity to the hypotensive effects of nitrates.

Marked symptomatic orthostatic hypotension has been reported when calcium channel blockers and organic nitrates were used in combination. Dosage adjustments of either class of agents may be necessary.

Concurrent administration of Minitran with dihydroergotamine may increase the bioavailability of dihydroergotamine. Special attention should be paid to this point in patients with coronary artery disease, because dihydroergotamine antagonizes the effect of nitroglycerin and may lead to coronary vasoconstriction.

The possibility that the ingestion of ASA and nonsteroidal anti-inflammatory drugs might diminish the therapeutic response to nitrates and nitroglycerin cannot be excluded.

Information for the Patient: Daily headaches sometimes accompany treatment with nitroglycerin. In patients who get these headaches, the headaches may be a marker of the activity of the drug. Patients should resist the temptation to avoid headaches by altering the schedule of their treatment with nitroglycerin, since loss of headache may be associated with simultaneous loss of antianginal efficacy.

Treatment with nitroglycerin may be associated with lightheadedness on standing, especially just after rising from a recumbent or seated position. This effect may be more frequent in patients who have also consumed alcohol.

After normal use, there is enough residual nitroglycerin in discarded patches that they are a potential hazard to children and pets.

A patient leaflet is supplied with the patches (see Blue Section—Information for the Patient).

Adverse Effects: Headache, which may be severe, is the most commonly reported side effect. Headache may be recurrent with each daily dose, especially at high doses of nitroglycerin. Headaches may be treated with concomitant administration of mild analgesics. If such headaches are unresponsive to treatment, the nitroglycerin dosage should be reduced or the product discontinued. Transient episodes of lightheadedness, occasionally related to blood pressure changes, may also occur. Hypotension occurs infrequently, but in some patients it may be severe enough to warrant discontinuation of therapy.

Reddening of the skin, with or without a mild local itching or burning sensation, as well as allergic contact dermatitis may occasionally occur. Upon removal of the patch, any slight reddening of the skin will usually disappear within a few hours. The application site should be changed regularly to prevent local irritation.

Less frequently reported adverse reactions include dizziness, faintness, facial flushing and postural hypotension which may be associated with reflex tachycardia. Syncope, crescendo angina and rebound hypertension have been reported but are uncommon. Nausea and vomiting have been reported rarely.

Overdose: Symptoms: Nitroglycerin overdose may result in severe hypotension, persistent throbbing headache, vertigo, palpitations, visual disturbances, flushing, and perspiring skin (later becoming cold and cyanotic), nausea and vomiting (possibly with colic and even bloody diarrhea), syncope (especially in the upright posture), methemoglobinemia with cyanosis, initial hyperpnea, dyspnea, and slow breathing, slow pulse (dicrotic and intermittent), heart block, and bradycardia, increased intracranial pressure with cerebral symptoms of fever, confusion and coma possibly followed by paralysis, clonic convulsions and death due to circulatory collapse.

Treatment: Keep the patient recumbent in a shock position and comfortably warm. Remove all nitroglycerin patches. Passive movement of the extremities may aid venous return. Administer oxygen and artificially ventilate if necessary. Epinephrine is ineffective in reversing the severe hypotensive events associated with overdose; it and related compounds are contraindicated in this situation.

I.V. infusion of normal saline or similar fluid may also be required to produce sufficient central volume expansion. However, in patients with renal disease or congestive heart failure, therapy resulting in central volume expansion is not without hazard. Treatment of nitroglycerin overdose in these patients may be subtle and difficult, and invasive monitoring may be required.

Methemoglobinemia: Case reports of clinically significant methemoglobinemia are rare at conventional doses of nitroglycerin. The formation of methemoglobin is dose-related, and in the case of genetic abnormalities of hemoglobin that favor methemoglobin formation, even conventional doses of organic nitrates can produce harmful concentrations of methemoglobin. Methemoglobin levels are available from most clinical laboratories. The diagnosis should be suspected in patients who exhibit signs of impaired oxygen delivery despite adequate cardiac output and adequate arterial pO_2. Classically, methemoglobinemic blood is described as chocolate brown, without color change on exposure to air. If methemoglobinemia is present, i.v. administration of 1 to 2 mg/kg methylene blue 1% solution for injection may be required.

Dosage: Daily Dosage Schedule: The daily dosage schedule is based on intermittent therapy to prevent the development of tolerance to nitroglycerin. The optimal dose should be selected based upon the clinical response, side effects and the effects of therapy on blood pressure.

The suggested starting dose is between 0.2 and 0.4 mg/hour. Doses between 0.2 and 0.8 mg/hour have shown continued effectiveness for 12 hours daily for at least 1 month (the longest period of studies) of intermittent administration. Although the minimum nitrate-free interval has not been defined, data show that a nitrate-free interval of 10 to 12 hours is sufficient (see Pharmacology). Thus, an appropriate dosing schedule for nitroglycerin patches would include a daily patch-on period of 12 to 14 hours during waking hours and a patch-off period of 10 to 12 hours, usually overnight.

Prevention of Tolerance: Although some controlled clinical trials using exercise tolerance testing have shown maintenance of effectiveness when patches are worn continuously, the large majority of such controlled trials have shown the development of tolerance (i.e., complete loss of effect) within the first 24 hours after therapy was initiated. Dose adjustments even to levels much higher than generally used did not prevent the development of tolerance.

Tolerance can be prevented or attenuated by use of an intermittent dosage schedule. Although the minimum nitrate-free interval has not been defined, clinical trials have demonstrated that an appropriate dosing schedule for nitroglycerin patches would provide for a daily patch-on period of 12 to 14 hours and a daily patch-off period of 10 to 12 hours. The patch-free time should coincide with the period in which angina pectoris is least likely to occur (usually at night). Patients should be watched carefully for an increase of angina pectoris during the patch-free period. Adjustment of background medication may be required.

The dose of Minitran should be periodically reviewed in relation to continuing antianginal control.

Site of Application: Minitran should be applied to the chest, shoulders, upper arm or back and should not be applied to the distal extremities. The skin area should be free of hair in order to provide direct contact of the patch to the skin. If hair is likely to interfere with adhesion of the patch, the area may be lightly shaved. The skin area should be clean, dry and free of irritation or cuts. A different skin site should be used each time a new Minitran patch is applied. It may be necessary to apply more than one patch in order to achieve the optimal dose level. Following use, the patch should be discarded in a manner that prevents accidental application or ingestion by curious children or others.

Information for the Patient: See Blue Section—Information for the Patient "Minitran".

Supplied: The Minitran transdermal delivery system is a unit designed to provide continuous controlled release of nitroglycerin through intact skin. The rate of release of nitroglycerin is linearly dependent upon the area of the applied system; each cm^2 of applied system delivers approximately 0.03 mg of nitroglycerin per hour. Thus, the 6.7, 13.3, and 20 cm^2 systems deliver approximately 0.2, 0.4, and 0.6 mg of nitroglycerin per hour, respectively (see Table I).

The remainder of the nitroglycerin in each system serves as a reservoir and is not delivered in normal use. After 12 hours, for example, each system has delivered about 14% of its original content of nitroglycerin.

The Minitran transdermal delivery system contains nitroglycerin in a hypoallergenic, medical grade, acrylate-based polymer adhesive. Each patch is packaged in foil/polymer film laminate. Cartons of 30 and 100.

Store at controlled room temperature 15 to 30°C. Extremes of temperature and/or humidity should be avoided.

Table I—Minitran

Minitran Systems

Related Release in vivo (mg/hr)	System Size (cm^2)	Nitroglycerin in System (mg)
0.2	6.7	18
0.4	13.3	36
0.6	20.0	54

(Shown in Product Recognition Section)

MINOCIN® Pr

Wyeth-Ayerst

Minocycline HCl

Antibiotic

Pharmacology: Minocycline is a tetracycline with antibacterial activity against some Gram-negative and Gram-positive organisms. The action is primarily bacteriostatic and it is thought to exert its antimicrobial effect by the inhibition of protein synthesis.

Indications: For the treatment of the following infections due to susceptible strains of the designated organisms: gallbladder infections caused by E. coli.

Urinary Tract Infections: cystitis, gonorrhea, pyelonephritis caused by E. coli, Proteus species, Klebsiella species, E. aerogenes, N. gonorrhea.

When penicillin is contraindicated, minocycline may be employed as an alternative drug in the treatment of anal and pharyngeal gonorrhea and syphilis.

Skin and Soft Tissue Infections: abscess, cellulitis, furunculosis, impetigo and pyoderma caused by: S. epidermidis, S. aureus, S. pyogenes, Proteus species, E. coli. Although tetracyclines are not the drugs of choice in any staphylococcal or streptococcal infection, minocycline could be useful in circumstances where these organisms are shown to be resistant to other agents but sensitive to minocycline. Bacterial evaluation of clinical cases involving proteus suggests a relatively lower success rate may be expected where these organisms are concerned.

Respiratory Tract Infections: Bronchitis, pharyngitis, pneumonia, bronchopneumonia, sinusitis and tonsillitis caused by: H. influenzae, Klebsiella species, Enterobacter species. Tetracyclines should not be prescribed for acute throat infections.

Contraindications: History of hypersensitivity to minocycline or any other tetracycline.

Warnings: Newborns, Infants and Children: The use of tetracyclines, including minocycline, during tooth development (last half of pregnancy, infancy and childhood under the age of 13 years) has been shown to cause permanent tooth discoloration (yellow-grey-brown). This is more common during long-term use, but has been observed following short-term courses. Enamel hypoplasia has also been reported. All tetracyclines including minocycline form a stable calcium complex in any bone-forming tissue. A decrease in the fibula growth rate has been observed in prematures given oral tetracycline in doses of 25 mg/kg every 6 hours. This appeared to be reversible when the drug was discontinued. Minocycline

Minocin (cont'd)

should not be used in such patients unless other drugs are ineffective or are contraindicated.

Pregnancy and *Lactation:* Tetracyclines, including minocycline, are not recommended during pregnancy and lactation because of possible adverse effects on developing bones and teeth of the fetus and neonate. Results of animal studies indicate that tetracyclines cross the placenta, are found in fetal tissues and can have toxic effects on the developing fetus (often related to retardation of skeletal development).

Evidence of embryotoxicity has also been noted in animals treated early in pregnancy. The safety for use during pregnancy has not been established.

Tetracyclines, including minocycline, are excreted in the milk of lactating women.

It is advisable to avoid giving minocycline in conjunction with penicillin since some bacteriostatic drugs may interfere with the bactericidal action of penicillin.

Minocycline should not be used for the treatment of streptococcal diseases unless the organism is demonstrated to be sensitive, since most streptococci have been found to be resistant to tetracycline drugs. If it is deemed necessary that infection due to Group A beta-hemolytic streptococci be treated with minocycline, then such treatment should be continued for at least 10 days.

In the presence of significant renal impairment, usual oral doses may lead to excessive systemic accumulations of minocycline and possible liver toxicity. Under such conditions, lower than usual doses may be indicated. After initial therapy, and if therapy is prolonged, serum level determinations of the drug are advisable.

The anti-anabolic action of tetracyclines can also produce dose-related increases in BUN; consequently, in patients with significant renal impairment, elevated serum minocycline levels can lead to azotemia, hypophosphatemia and acidosis.

Renal failure, including interstitial nephritis has been reported rarely.

Minocycline is capable of aggravating the symptoms associated with lupus erythematosus. Therefore, caution should be taken when administering the drug to patients with this disease.

Minocycline has been shown to depress plasma prothrombin activity. Therefore, patients who are on anticoagulant therapy should be monitored regularly and may require downward adjustment of their anticoagulant dosage. Interference with vitamin K synthesis by microorganisms in the gut has been reported.

Cross-sensitization among the various tetracyclines is extremely common.

Pigmentation of skin, thyroid, bone and teeth have been reported occasionally in persons receiving minocycline usually for extended periods of time. The pigmentation may be irreversible.

Reduced efficacy and increased incidence of breakthrough bleeding has been suggested with concomitant use of tetracycline and oral contraceptive preparations.

Precautions: The administration of minocycline to children under 13 years of age is not recommended.

Bulging fontanels have been reported in young infants following full therapeutic dosage of tetracyclines including minocycline. Pseudotumor cerebri has very rarely been reported in adults (see Adverse Effects).

Patients should be warned to avoid exposure to direct sunlight and/or ultraviolet light while under treatment with minocycline or other tetracycline drugs, and treatment should be discontinued at the first evidence of skin erythema or discomfort. Photosensitivity manifested by an exaggerated sunburn reaction has been observed in some individuals taking tetracyclines. Studies to date indicate that photosensitivity is rarely reported with minocycline.

Occupational Hazards: Patients treated with minocycline may suffer from headaches, light-headedness, dizziness or vertigo. Decreased hearing has been rarely reported in patients on minocycline. Administration in excess of the recommended dosage can increase the frequency and severity of these CNS symptoms. Patients should be cautioned about driving vehicles or using hazardous machinery while on drug therapy. These symptoms may disappear during therapy and usually disappear rapidly when the drug is discontinued.

As with other antibiotics, therapy may result in overgrowth of non-susceptible organisms (including fungi). If superinfection occurs, minocycline should be discontinued and appropriate therapy instituted.

The development of cross-resistance to many antibiotics can develop rapidly in several species of microorganisms. The clinician should bear this in mind if minocycline is not achieving expected results.

The frequency of resistance to minocycline in hemolytic streptococci is highest in strains from infections of the ear, wounds and skin. Culture and sensitivity studies should be performed whenever feasible and routinely in suspected streptoccal infections.

Since sensitivity reactions are more likely to occur in persons with a history of allergy, asthma, hay fever, or urticaria, minocycline should be used with caution in such individuals.

Before treating patients with gonorrhea, a darkfield examination should be made from any lesion suggestive of concurrent syphilis. Serological tests for syphilis should be repeated monthly for at least 4 months.

Minocycline should be used with caution in patients with hepatic dysfunction and in conjunction with alcohol or other hepatotoxic drugs.

In long-term therapy, periodic laboratory evaluation of organ systems, including hematopoietic, renal and hepatic studies, should be performed.

Minocycline has been shown to depress plasma prothrombin activity. Therefore, patients who are on anticoagulant therapy should be monitored regularly and may require downward adjustment of their anticoagulant dosage. Interference with vitamin K synthesis by microorganisms in the gut has been reported.

Antacids containing aluminum, calcium or magnesium and oral iron preparations impair absorption and should not be given to patients taking oral minocycline.

Food and/or milk reduce the absorption of tetracycline. Minocycline is not affected to the same extent.

In a study by Leyden, the absorption of a single 100 mg dose of minocycline was inhibited by the ingestion of solid food by 13% (as measured by a reduction in mean serum concentration), and the absorption of a single 250 mg dose of tetracycline was inhibited by 46% when that antibiotic was administered with solid food. When administered with milk, the mean serum concentration of minocycline was reduced by 27% and that tetracycline, by 67%. The clinical significance of such declines in serum levels is not known.

Adverse Effects: The following adverse reactions have been reported with the tetracycline analogues including minocycline: CNS: increased intracranial pressure, light-headedness, dizziness or vertigo and, rarely, fainting spells have been reported with a variable but overall incidence of approximately 7% in patients treated. These symptoms usually disappear rapidly when the drug is discontinued. Headache, alone, has also been reported.

Gastrointestinal: anorexia, nausea, vomiting, diarrhea, stomatitis, glossitis, enterocolitis, pancreatitis, pruritus ani, constipation, dysphagia, inflammatory lesions (with monilial overgrowth) in the anogenital region, increases in liver enzymes, and rarely hepatitis and acute liver failure have been reported. Rare instances of esophagitis and esophageal ulcerations have been reported in patients taking the tetracycline-class antibiotics in capsule and tablet form. Most of these patients took the medication immediately before going to bed.

Teeth and Bone: Dental staining (yellow-gray-brown) has been reported in children of mothers given tetracyclines, including minocycline, during the latter half of pregnancy, and in children given the drug during the neonatal period, infancy and childhood to age of 13 years. Enamel hypoplasia has also been reported. Discoloration of bones and teeth has been documented to occur rarely in adolescents and adults upon extended treatment. The effects may be irreversible. At present the mechanism of staining, although not completely elucidated, appears to be mediated by the formation of a stable iron complex.

Renal: Rise in BUN has been reported and is apparently dose-related. Increased excretion of nitrogen and sodium has also been reported. Renal failure, including interstitial nephritis has been reported rarely.

Skin: maculopapular and erythematous rashes. Rarely reported–exfoliative dermatitis, onycholysis, discoloration of the nails, pigmentation of the skin and mucous membrane, erythema multiforme, Stevens-Johnson syndrome. Lesions occurring on the glans penis have caused balanitis.

Hypersensitivity: urticaria, angioneurotic edema, polyarthralgia, anaphylaxis, anaphylactoid purpura, pericarditis and exacerbation of systemic lupus erythematosus.

Pseudotumor cerebri (benign intracranial hypertension) in adults has been associated with the use of tetracyclines. The usual clinical manifestations are headache and blurred vision. Bulging fontanels have been associated with the use of tetracyclines in infants. While both of these conditions and related symptoms usually resolve soon after discontinuation of the tetracycline, the possibility for permanent sequelae exists.

Other: elevated AST or ALT values, hepatic cholestasis, hemolytic anemia, neutropenia, thrombocytopenia and eosinophilia. When given over prolonged periods, minocycline, like other tetracyclines, has been reported to produce brown-black microscopic discoloration of the thyroid gland. Abnormalities of thyroid function have not been shown to date. If adverse reactions or idiosyncrasy occur, the administration should be discontinued and appropriate alternate therapy instituted.

Overdose: Symptoms: dizziness, nausea, vomiting, abdominal pain, intestinal hemorrhage, hypotension, lethargy, coma, acidosis, azotemia without a concomitant rise in creatinine.

Treatment: Specific antidote: None. General antidotes: Antacids (e.g., calcium carbonate or lactate, milk of magnesia, aluminum hydroxide) which form relatively insoluble complexes with minocycline. (Calcium Solution 5%: 50 g calcium carbonate or lactate dissolved in 1 000 mL water, yields a 5% solution). Gastric lavage, if necessary.

Dosage: Children (13 years and over): The usual dosage is 4 mg/kg initially followed by 2 mg/kg every 12 hours. Tetracyclines are not recommended in children under 13 years of age (see Warnings).

Adults: The usual oral dosage is 100 or 200 mg initially, followed by 100 mg every 12 hours. Alternatively, if more frequent doses are preferred, 2 or 4 doses of 50 mg may be given initially, followed by one 50 mg dose every 6 hours. Therapy should be continued for 1 or 2 days beyond the time when characteristic symptoms or fever have subsided.

For treatment of syphilis, therapy should be administered over a period of 10 or 15 days. Close follow-up, including laboratory tests, is recommended.

Concomitant Therapy: Antacids containing aluminum, calcium or magnesium and/or iron preparations impair absorption and should not be given to patients taking minocycline.

Supplied: 50 mg: Each orange hard shell capsule, printed "Lederle M2" and "MINOCIN 50 mg", contains: minocycline HCl equivalent to minocycline 50 mg. Nonmedicinal ingredients: magnesium stearate, mineral oil and starch; empty capsule: FD&C Yellow 6, gelatin, silicon dioxide, sodium lauryl sulfate and titanium dioxide. Energy: <4.2 kJ (1 kcal). Tartrazine-free. Bottles of 100 and 500.

100 mg: Each orange-purple hard shell capsule, printed "Lederle M4" and "MINOCIN 100 mg", contains: minocycline HCl equivalent to minocycline 100 mg. Nonmedicinal ingredients: magnesium stearate, mineral oil and starch; empty capsule: FD&C Blue 1, FD&C Red 3, FD&C Yellow 6, gelatin, silicon dioxide, sodium lauryl sulfate and titanium dioxide. Energy: <4.2 kJ (1 kcal). Tartrazine-free. Bottles of 50, 100 and 500.

Reviewed 1998

MINOCYCLINE Ⓟ

General Monograph, CPhA

see TETRACYCLINES

MIN-OVRAL® 21 Ⓟ
MIN-OVRAL® 28 Ⓟ

Wyeth-Ayerst

Levonorgestrel—Ethinyl Estradiol

Oral Contraceptive

Pharmacology: Although the primary mechanism of action is inhibition of ovulation, the effectiveness of Min-Ovral may also result from other mechanisms of action, such as hostility of the cervical mucus to sperm penetration and migration.

Indications: Conception control.

Contraindications: History of/or actual thrombophlebitis or thromboembolic disorders; history of/or actual cerebrovascular disorders; history of/or actual myocardial infarction or coronary arterial disease; active liver disease or history of/or actual benign or malignant liver tumors; known or suspected carcinoma of the breast; known or suspected estrogen-dependent neoplasia; undiagnosed abnormal vaginal bleeding; any ocular lesion arising from ophthalmic vascular disease, such as partial or complete loss of vision or defect in visual fields; when pregnancy is suspected or diagnosed.

Warnings: Predisposing Factors for Coronary Artery Disease: Cigarette smoking increases the risk of serious cardiovascular side effects and mortality. Birth control pills increase this risk, especially with increasing age. Convincing data are available to support an upper age limit of 35 years for oral contraceptive use by women who smoke.

Other women who are independently at high risk for cardiovascular disease include those with diabetes, hypertension, abnormal lipid profile, or a family history of these. Whether oral contraceptives accentuate this risk is unclear.

In low-risk, nonsmoking women of any age, the benefits of oral contraceptive use outweigh the possible cardiovascular risks associated with low-dose formulations. Consequently, oral contraceptives may be prescribed for these women up to the age of menopause.

> Cigarette smoking increases the risk of serious adverse effects on the heart and blood vessels. This risk increases with age and becomes significant in oral contraceptive users older than 35 years of age. Women should be counselled not to smoke.

Discontinue medication at the earliest manifestation of the following:

A. Thromboembolic and cardiovascular disorders such as: thrombophlebitis, pulmonary embolism, cerebrovascular disorders, myocardial ischemia, mesenteric thrombosis, and retinal thrombosis.

B. Conditions that predispose to venous stasis and to vascular thrombosis, (e.g., immobilization after accidents or confinement to bed during long-term illness). Other nonhormonal methods of contraception should be used until regular activities are resumed. For use of oral contraceptives when surgery is contemplated, see Precautions.

C. Visual defects, partial or complete.

D. Papilledema, or ophthalmic vascular lesions.

E. Severe headache of unknown etiology or worsening of pre-existing migraine headache.

A meta-analysis from 54 epidemiological studies reported that there is a slightly increased relative risk (RR=1.24) of having breast cancer diagnosed in women who are currently using combined oral contraceptives. The increased risk gradually disappears during the course of the 10 years after cessation of combined oral contraceptive use. Because breast cancer is rare in women under 40 years of age, the excess number of breast cancer diagnoses in current and recent combined oral contraceptive use is small in relation to the lifetime risk of breast cancer. These studies do not provide evidence for causation. The observed pattern of increased risk may be due to an earlier diagnosis of breast cancer in combined oral contraceptive users, the biological effects of combined oral contraceptives or a combination of both. The breast cancers diagnosed in ever-users tend to be less advanced clinically than the cancers diagnosed in the never-users.

Precautions: Physical Examination and Follow-up: Before oral contraceptives are used, a thorough history and physical examination should be performed, including a blood pressure determination. Breasts, liver, extremities and pelvic organs should be examined and a Papanicolaou smear should be taken if the patient has been sexually active.

The first follow-up visit should be 3 months after oral contraceptives are prescribed. Thereafter, examinations should be performed at least once a year or more frequently if indicated. At each annual visit, examination should include those procedures that were done at the initial visit as outlined above or per recommendations of the Canadian Workshop on Screening for Cancer of the Cervix. Their suggestion was that, for women who had 2 consecutive negative Pap smears, screening could be continued every 3 years to the age of 69.

Pregnancy: Oral contraceptives should not be taken by pregnant women. However, if conception accidently occurs while taking the pill, there is no conclusive evidence that the estrogen and progestin contained in the oral contraceptive will damage the developing child.

Lactation: In breast-feeding women, the use of oral contraceptives results in the hormonal components being excreted in breast milk and may reduce its quantity and quality. If the use of oral contraceptives is initiated after the establishment of lactation, there does not appear to be any effect on the quantity and quality of the milk. There is no evidence that low-dose oral contraceptives are harmful to the nursing infant.

Hepatic Function: Patients who have had jaundice, including a history of cholestatic jaundice during pregnancy, should be given oral contraceptives with great care and under close observation.

The development of severe generalized pruritus or icterus requires that the medication be withdrawn until the problem is resolved.

If a patient develops jaundice that proves to be cholestatic in type, the use of oral contraceptives should not be resumed.

In patients taking oral contraceptives, changes in the composition of the bile may occur and an increased incidence of gallstones has been reported.

Hepatic nodules (adenoma and focal nodular hyperplasia) have been reported, particularly in long-term users of oral contraceptives. Although these lesions are extremely rare, they have caused fatal intra-abdominal hemorrhage and should be considered in women presenting with an abdominal mass, acute abdominal pain, or evidence of intra-abdominal bleeding.

Hypertension: Patients with essential hypertension whose blood pressure is well-controlled may be given oral contraceptives but only under close supervision. If a significant elevation of blood pressure in previously normotensive or hypertensive subjects occurs at any time during the administration of the drug, cessation of medication is necessary.

Migraine and Headache: The onset or exacerbation of migraine or the development of headache of a new pattern that is recurrent, persistent or severe, requires discontinuation of oral contraceptives and evaluation of the cause.

Diabetes: Current low-dose oral contraceptives exert minimal impact on glucose metabolism. Diabetic patients, or those with a family history of diabetes, should be observed closely to detect any worsening of carbohydrate metabolism. Patients predisposed to diabetes who can be kept under close supervision may be given oral contraceptives. Young diabetic patients whose disease is of recent origin, well-controlled, and not associated with hypertension or other signs of vascular disease such as ocular fundal changes, should be monitored more frequently while using oral contraceptives.

Ocular Disease: Patients who are pregnant or are taking oral contraceptives, may experience corneal edema that may cause visual disturbances and changes in tolerance to contact lenses, especially of the rigid type. Soft contact lenses usually do not cause disturbances. If visual changes or alterations in tolerance to contact lenses occur, temporary or permanent cessation of wear may be advised.

Breasts: Increasing age and a strong family history are the most significant risk factors for the development of breast cancer. Other established risk factors include obesity, nulliparity and late age at first full-term pregnancy. The identified groups of women that may be at increased risk of developing breast cancer before menopause are long-term users of oral contraceptives (more than 8 years) and starters at early age. In a few women, the use of oral contraceptives may accelerate the growth of an existing but undiagnosed breast cancer. Since any potential increased risk related to oral contraceptive use is small, there is no reason to change prescribing habits at present.

Women receiving oral contraceptives should be instructed in self-examination of their breasts. Their physicians should be notified whenever any masses are detected. A yearly clinical breast examination is also recommended because, if a breast cancer should develop, drugs that contain estrogen may cause a rapid progression.

Vaginal Bleeding: Persistent irregular vaginal bleeding requires assessment to exclude underlying pathology.

Fibroids: Patients with fibroids (leiomyomata) should be carefully observed. Sudden enlargement, pain, or tenderness require discontinuation of the use of oral contraceptives.

Emotional Disorders: Patients with a history of emotional disturbances, especially the depressive type, may be more prone to have a recurrence of depression while taking oral contraceptives. In cases of a serious recurrence, a trial of an alternate method of contraception should be made which, may help to clarify the possible relationship. Women with premenstrual syndrome (PMS) may have a varied response to oral contraceptives, ranging from symptomatic improvement to worsening of the condition.

Table I*—Min-Ovral

Drugs that May Decrease the Efficacy of Oral Contraceptives

Class of Compound	Drug	Proposed Mechanism	Suggested Management
Anticonvulsants	Carbamazepine Ethosuximide Phenobarbital Phenytoin Primidone	Induction of hepatic microsomal enzymes. Rapid metabolism of estrogen and increased binding of progestin and ethinyl estradiol to SHBG.	Use higher-dose OCs (50 μg ethinyl estradiol), another drug or another method.
Antibiotics	Ampicillin Cotrimoxazole Penicillin	Enterohepatic circulation disturbance, intestinal hurry.	For short course, use additional method or use another drug. For long course, use another method.
	Rifampin	Increased metabolism of progestins. Suspected acceleration of estrogen metabolism.	Use another method.
	Chloramphenicol Metronidazole Neomycin Nitrofurantoin Sulfonamides Tetracyclines	Induction of hepatic microsomal enzymes. Also disturbance of enterohepatic circulation.	For short course, use additional method or use another drug. For long course, use another method.
	Troleandomycin	May retard metabolism of OCs, increasing the risk of cholestatic jaundice.	
Antifungals	Griseofulvin	Stimulation of hepatic metabolism of contraceptive steroids may occur.	Use another method.
Cholesterol-lowering Agents	Clofibrate	Reduces elevated serum triglycerides and cholesterol; this reduces OC efficacy.	Use another method.
Sedatives and Hypnotics	Benzodiazepines Barbiturates Chloral hydrate Glutethimide Meprobamate	Induction of hepatic microsomal enzymes.	For short course, use additional method or another drug. For long course, use another method or higher-dose OCs.
Antacids		Decreased intestinal absorption of progestins.	Dose 2 hours apart.
Other Drugs	Phenylbutazone** Antihistamines** Analgesics** Antimigraine preparations** Vitamin E	Reduced OC efficacy has been reported. Remains to be confirmed.	

*Adapted from Dickey, RP, ed.: Managing Contraceptive Pill Patients, 5th edition Creative Informatics Inc., Durant, OK, 1987.

**Refer to Oral Contraceptives 1994, A Report by the Special Advisory Committee on Reproductive Physiology to the Drugs Directorate, Health Protection Branch, Health Canada.

Min-Ovral (cont'd)

Laboratory Tests: Results of laboratory tests should be interpreted in the light that the patient is on oral contraceptives. The following laboratory tests are modified.
A. Liver Function Tests: Bromsulphthalein Retention Test (BSP): moderate increase. AST and GGT: minor increase. Alkaline phosphatase: variable increase. Serum bilirubin: increased, particularly in conditions predisposing to or associated with hyperbilirubinemia.
B. Coagulation Tests: Factors II, VII, IX, X, XII, and XIII: increased. Factor VIII: mild increase. Platelet aggregation and adhesiveness: mild increase in response to common aggregating agents. Fibrinogen: increased. Plasminogen: mild increase. Antithrombin III: mild decrease. Prothrombin Time: increased.
C. Thyroid Function Tests: Protein-bound Iodine (PBI): increased. Total Serum Thyroxine (T_4): increased. Thyroid Stimulating Hormone (TSH): unchanged.
D. Adrenocortical Function Tests: Plasma Cortisol: increased.
E. Miscellaneous Tests: Serum Folate: occasionally decreased. Glucose Tolerance Test: variable increase with return to normal after 6 to 12 months. Insulin Response: mild to moderate increase. c-Peptide Response: mild to moderate increase.
Tissue Specimens: Pathologists should be advised of oral contraceptive therapy when specimens obtained from surgical procedures and Pap smears are submitted for examination.
Return to Fertility: After discontinuing oral contraceptive therapy, the patient should delay pregnancy until at least 1 normal spontaneous cycle has occurred in order to date the pregnancy. An alternate contraceptive method should be used during this time.
Amenorrhea: Women having a history of oligomenorrhea, secondary amenorrhea, or irregular cycles may remain anovulatory or become amenorrheic following discontinuation of estrogen-progestin combination therapy.

Amenorrhea, especially if associated with breast secretion, that continues for 6 months or more after withdrawal, warrants a careful assessment of hypothalamic-pituitary function.
Thromboembolic Complications—Postsurgery: There is an increased risk of thromboembolic complications in oral contraceptive users, after major surgery. If feasible, oral contraceptives should be discontinued and an alternative method substituted at least 1 month prior to **major** elective surgery. Oral contraceptives should not be resumed until the first menstrual period after hospital discharge following surgery.
Drug Interactions: The concurrent administration of oral contraceptives with other drugs may result in an altered response to either agent. Reduced effectiveness of the oral contraceptive, should it occur, is more likely with the low dose formulations. It is important to ascertain all drugs that a patient is taking, both prescription and nonprescription, before oral contraceptives are prescribed.

For possible drug interactions with oral contraceptives see Table I (on previous page) and Table II.
Noncontraceptive Benefits of Oral Contraceptives: Several health advantages other than contraception have been reported.
1. Combination oral contraceptives reduce the incidence of cancer of the endometrium and ovaries.
2. Oral contraceptives reduce the likelihood of developing benign breast disease.
3. Oral contraceptives reduce the likelihood of development of functional ovarian cysts.
4. Pill users have less menstrual blood loss and have more regular cycles, thereby reducing the chance of developing iron-deficiency anemia.
5. The use of oral contraceptives may decrease the severity of dysmenorrhea and premenstrual syndrome, and may improve acne vulgaris, hirsutism, and other androgen-mediated disorders.
6. Other noncontraceptive benefits are outlined in Oral Contraceptives 1994, Health Canada.

Oral contraceptives **do not protect** against sexually transmitted diseases including HIV/AIDS. For protection against STDs, it is advisable to use latex condoms **in combination with** oral contraceptives.

Adverse Effects: An increased risk of the following serious adverse reactions has been associated with the use of oral contraceptives: thrombophlebitis; pulmonary embolism; mesenteric thrombosis; neuro-ocular lesions, e.g., retinal thrombosis; myocardial infarction; cerebral thrombosis; cerebral hemorrhage; hypertension; benign hepatic tumors; gallbladder disease.

The following adverse reactions also have been reported in patients receiving oral contraceptives: nausea and vomiting, usually the most common adverse reaction, occurs in approximately 10% or fewer of patients during the first cycle. Other reactions, as a general rule, are seen less frequently or only occasionally.
Other Adverse Reactions: The following adverse reactions have been reported in patients receiving oral contraceptives and are believed to be drug related: gastrointestinal symptoms (such as abdominal cramps and bloating); breakthrough bleeding; spotting; change in menstrual flow; amenorrhea; temporary infertility after discontinuance of treatment; edema; melasma which may persist; breast changes: tenderness, enlargement, and secretion; change in weight (increase or decrease); change in cervical erosion and secretion; diminution in lactation when given immediately postpartum; cholestatic jaundice; migraine; rash (allergic); depression; reduced tolerance to carbohydrates; vaginal candidiasis; change in corneal curvature (steepening); intolerance to contact lenses.

The following adverse reactions have been reported in users of oral contraceptives, and the association has been neither confirmed nor refuted: congenital anomalies, premenstrual syndrome, cataracts, optic neuritis, changes in appetite, cystitis-like syndrome, headache, nervousness, dizziness, hirsutism, loss of scalp hair, erythema multiforme, erythema nodosum, hemorrhagic eruption, vaginitis, porphyria, impaired renal function, hemolytic uremic syndrome, Budd-Chiari syndrome, acne, changes in libido, colitis, sickle-cell disease, cerebral-vascular disease with mitral valve prolapse, lupus-like syndromes.

Table II*—Min-Ovral

Modification of Other Drug Action by Oral Contraceptives

Class of Compound	Drug	Modification of Other Drug Action	Suggested Management
Alcohol		Possible increased levels of ethanol or acetaldehyde.	Use with caution.
Alpha-II Adrenoreceptor Agents	Clonidine	Sedation effect increased.	Use with caution.
Anticoagulants	All	OCs increase clotting factors, decrease efficacy. However, OCs may potentiate action in some patients.	Use another method.
Anticonvulsants	All	Fluid retention may increase risk of seizures.	Use another method.
Antidiabetic Drugs	Oral hypoglycemics and insulin	OCs may impair glucose tolerance and increase blood glucose.	Use low-dose estrogen and progestin OC or another method. Monitor blood glucose.
Antihypertensive Agents	Guanethidine and methyldopa	Estrogen component causes sodium retention, progestin has no effect.	Use low-dose estrogen OC or use another method.
	Beta-blockers	Increased drug effect (decreased metabolism).	Adjust dose of drug if necessary. Monitor cardiovascular status.
Antipyretics	Acetaminophen	Increased metabolism and renal clearance.	Dose of drug may have to be increased.
	Antipyrine	Impaired metabolism.	Decrease dose of drug.
	ASA	Effects of ASA may be decreased by the short-term use of OCs.	Patients on chronic ASA therapy may require an increase in ASA dosage.
Aminocaproic Acid		Theoretically, a hypercoagulable state may occur because OCs augment clotting factors.	Avoid concomitant use.
Betamimetic Agents	Isoproterenol	Estrogen causes decreased response to these drugs.	Adjust dose of drug as necessary. Discontinuing OCs can result in excessive drug activity.
Caffeine		The actions of caffeine may be enhanced as OCs may impair the hepatic metabolism of caffeine.	Use with caution.
Cholesterol-lowering Agents	Clofibrate	Their action may be antagonized by OCs. OCs may also increase metabolism of clofibrate.	May need to increase dose of clofibrate.
Corticosteroids	Prednisone	Markedly increased serum levels.	Possible need for decrease in dose.
Cyclosporine		May lead to an increase in cyclosporine levels and hepatotoxicity.	Monitor hepatic function. The cyclosporine dose may have to be decreased.
Folic Acid		OCs have been reported to impair folate metabolism.	May need to increase dietary intake, or supplement.
Meperidine		Possible increased analgesia and CNS depression due to decreased metabolism of meperidine.	Use combination with caution.
Phenothiazine Tranquilizers	All phenothiazines, reserpine and similar drugs	Estrogen potentiates the hyperprolactinemia effect of these drugs.	Use other drugs or lower dose OCs. If galactorrhea or hyperprolactinemia occurs, use other method.
Sedatives and Hypnotics	Chlordiazepoxide Lorazepam Oxazepam Diazepam	Increased effect (increased metabolism).	Use with caution.
Theophylline	All	Decreased oxidation, leading to possible toxicity.	Use with caution. Monitor theophylline levels.
Tricyclic Antidepressants	Clomipramine (possibly others)	Increased side effects; i.e., depression.	Use with caution.
Vitamin B_{12}		OCs have been reported to reduce serum levels of Vitamin B_{12}.	May need to increase dietary intake, or supplement.

*Adapted from Dickey, R.P., ed.: Managing Contraceptive Pill Patients, 5th edition Creative Informatics Inc., Durant, OK, 1987.

Overdose: Symptoms: With norgestrel and ethinyl estradiol, acute doses in excess of clinical levels, when administered to experimental animals, have been shown to have a minimal deleterious effect. The LD_{50} values for the combination of norgestrel and ethinyl estradiol in acute oral administration approximates 500 000 times the equivalent human oral dose. In humans, however, the extent of ill effects to be expected following accidental ingestion of a large dose of any oral contraceptive has not been firmly established.

Depending upon the amount ingested, liver toxicity, temporary interference with the function of the seminiferous tubules, or in the case of females, possible withdrawal bleeding within a few days of consumption, are theoretically possible. However, case histories of both male and female children, some of whom ingested more than half a month's supply of oral contraceptive tablets, indicate that the effects are asymptomatic and without immediate consequence. Despite the frequency of nausea and vomiting in adult females during the first few cycles of use, none of these children presented such symptoms.

Treatment: Although the physiologic effects of oral contraceptives may be theoretically offset by concomitant administration of gonadotropin preparations, there are no known chemotherapeutic agents which will neutralize their effects subsequent to accidental ingestion. In the practical management of acute overdosage, gastric lavage may be of value if the offending agent has recently been swallowed. The general rules for observation and symptomatic resolution should be followed. Liver function tests should be conducted, particularly transaminase levels, 2 to 3 weeks after consumption.

Dosage: Min-Ovral 21: Each cycle consists of 21 days on medication and a 7-day interval without medication (3 weeks on, 1 week off).

The dosage is 1 tablet daily for 21 consecutive days per menstrual cycle, according to prescribed schedule.

For the first cycle of medication, the patient is instructed to take 1 tablet daily for 21 consecutive days beginning on Day 1 of her menstrual cycle, on Day 5, or on the first Sunday after her period begins. (For the first cycle only, the first day of menstrual flow is considered Day 1.) The tablets are then discontinued for 7 days (1 week). Withdrawal bleeding should usually occur within 3 days following discontinuation of Min-Ovral.

The patient begins her next and all subsequent 21-day courses of tablets (following the same 21 days on, 7 days off) on the same day of the week that she began her first course. She begins taking her tablets 7 days after discontinuation, regardless of whether or not withdrawal bleeding is still in progress.

Min-Ovral 28: Each cycle consists of 21 days of white Min-Ovral tablets followed by 7 days of pink inert tablets (3 weeks on Min-Ovral, 1 week on inert tablets).

The dosage of Min-Ovral tablets is 1 tablet daily for 21 consecutive days per menstrual cycle, according to prescribed schedule, followed by 1 inert tablet daily for 7 consecutive days according to prescribed schedule.

For the first cycle of medication, the patient is instructed to take 1 white tablet daily for 21 consecutive days beginning on Day 1 of her menstrual cycle, on Day 5, or on the first Sunday after her period begins. (For the first cycle only, the first day of menstrual flow is considered Day 1.) One pink tablet is taken daily for the following 7 consecutive days. Withdrawal bleeding should usually occur within 3 days following the discontinuation of white Min-Ovral tablets, i.e., during the week the patient is taking the pink inert tablets. The patient begins her next and all subsequent 28-day courses of tablets on the same day of the week that she began her first course. She continues her next course of 28 tablets immediately after the last course, regardless of whether or not a period of withdrawal bleeding is still in progress. There is no need for the patient to count days between cycles because there are no "off-tablet days".

Special Notes on Administration: It is recommended that Min-Ovral tablets be taken at the same time each day, preferably after the evening meal or at bedtime.

Min-Ovral is effective from the first day of therapy if the tablets are begun as described under Dosage.

If Min-Ovral administration is initiated later than the fifth day of the first menstrual cycle of medication or postpartum, contraceptive reliance should not be placed on Min-Ovral until after the first 7 consecutive days of administration. The possibility of ovulation and conception prior to initiation of medication should be considered. In the nonlactating mother, Min-Ovral may be prescribed in the postpartum period either immediately or at the first postpartum examination, whether or not menstruation has resumed.

If spotting or breakthrough bleeding occurs, the patient is instructed to continue on the same regimen. This type of bleeding usually is transient and without significance; however, if the bleeding is persistent or prolonged, the patient is advised to consult her physician.

The patient should be instructed to use Table III if she misses one or more of her birth control pills. She should be told to match the number of pills with the appropriate starting time for her type of pill.

Information for the Patient: See Blue Section—Information for the Patient "Oral Contraceptives".

Supplied: Min-Ovral 21: Each white tablet, imprinted "W" on one face and "M-0" on the other, contains: levonorgestrel 150 μg and ethinyl estradiol 30 μg. Nonmedicinal ingredients: lactose, magnesium stearate, microcrystalline cellulose and polacralin potassium. Energy: 1.67 kJ (0.40 kcal). Gluten- and tartrazine-free. Compacts and compact refills of 21 tablets.

Min-Ovral 28: Each white tablet, imprinted "W" on one face and "M-0" on the other, contains: levonorgestrel 150 μg and ethinyl estradiol 30 μg. Nonmedicinal ingredients: lactose, magnesium stearate, microcrystalline cellulose and polacralin potassium. In addition, inert tablets contain FD&C Red No. 3 Lake. Energy: 1.67 kJ (0.40 kcal). Gluten- and tartrazine-free. Compacts and compact refills of 28 tablets (21 white Min-Ovral tablets and 7 pink inert tablets).

(Shown in Product Recognition Section)

Reviewed 1997

Table III—Min-Ovral

What To Do If You Miss Pills

Sunday Start	**Other Than Sunday Start**
Miss 1 pill	**Miss 1 pill**
Take it as soon as you remember, and take the next pill at the usual time. This means that you might take 2 pills in one day.	Take it as soon as you remember, and take the next pill at the usual time. This means that you might take 2 pills in one day.
Miss 2 pills in a row	**Miss 2 pills in a row**
First 2 Weeks: 1. Take 2 pills the day you remember and 2 pills the next day. 2. Then take 1 pill a day until you finish the pack. 3. Use a back-up method of birth control if you have sex in the 7 days after you miss the pills.	**First 2 Weeks:** 1. Take 2 pills the day you remember and 2 pills the next day. 2. Then take 1 pill a day until you finish the pack. 3. Use a back-up method of birth control if you have sex in the 7 days after you miss the pills.
Third Week: 1. Keep taking 1 pill a day until Sunday. 2. On Sunday, safely discard the rest of the pack and start a new pack that day. 3. Use a back-up method of birth control if you have sex in the 7 days after you miss the pills. 4. You may not have a period this month. **If you miss 2 periods in a row, call your doctor or clinic.**	**Third Week:** 1. Safely dispose of the rest of the pill pack and start a new pack that same day. 2. Use a back-up method of birth control if you have sex in the 7 days after you miss the pills. 3. You may not have a period this month. **If you miss 2 periods in a row, call your doctor or clinic.**
Miss 3 or more pills in a row	**Miss 3 or more pills in a row**
Anytime in the Cycle: 1. Keep taking 1 pill a day until Sunday. 2. On Sunday, safely discard the rest of the pack and start a new pack that day. 3. Use a back-up method of birth control if you have sex in the 7 days after you miss the pills. 4. You may not have a period this month. **If you miss 2 periods in a row, call your doctor or clinic.**	**Anytime in the Cycle:** 1. Safely dispose of the rest of the pill pack and start a new pack that same day. 2. Use a back-up method of birth control if you have sex in the 7 days after you miss the pills. 3. You may not have a period this month. **If you miss 2 periods in a row, call your doctor or clinic.**

MINOX ℞

Riva

Minoxidil

Hair Growth Stimulant

Supplied: Each mL of topical solution contains: minoxidil 20 mg (2%). Nonmedicinal ingredients: alcohol, propylene glycol and water. Bottles of 60 mL with a metered disposable pump spray applicator. An extended spray tip and a rub-on applicator are also available. For external use only. Keep container tightly closed. Store at controlled room temperature between 15 and 30°C.

MINTEZOL® ℞

MSD

Thiabendazole

Anthelmintic

Pharmacology: Thiabendazole is an anthelmintic for the treatment of various nematode infections of man.

Thiabendazole provides systemic treatment for cutaneous larva migrans. It causes worms to be eliminated spontaneously from the cutaneous blister or it eases their manual removal. In some instances the devitalized worm is not expelled and encystment with lysis occurs.

In some patients, the drug has been useful in the treatment of trichinosis.

Thiabendazole is vermicidal/vermifugal against Ascaris lumbricoides (roundworm), Strongylоides stercoralis (threadworm), Necator americanus and Ancylostoma duodenale (hookworm), Trichuris trichiura (whipworm), and Enterobius vermicularis (pinworm). It also possesses ovicidal effects (roundworm, hookworm, pinworm), and interferes with the embryonation and development of larval stages (threadworm). It may inhibit the subsequent development of those eggs or larvae which are passed in the feces.

Indications: Intestinal parasitosis (whether encountered singly or in combintaion), Strongyloidiasis, Ascariasis (large roundworm disease), Uncinariasis (hookworm disease-both Necator americanus and Ancylostoma duodenale), Trichuriasis (whipworm disease).

Cutaneous larva migrans (creeping eruption).

Trichinosis: In trichinosis, relief of symptoms and fever and reduction of eosinophilia have followed use of thiabendazole during the invasion stage of the disease. However, the effect of thiabendazole on the viability of the larvae which have migrated to muscle is incompletely defined, and not all patients respond to the recommended dosage of the drug.

Although not indicated as primary therapy, when Enterobiasis (pinworm) occurs with any of the conditions listed under Indications, additional therapy is not required for most patients.

Thiabendazole should be used only in the following infestations when more specific therapy is not available, or cannot be used, or when further therapy with a second agent is desirable: uncinariasis (hookworm: Necator americanus and Ancylostoma duodenale); trichuriasis (whipworm); ascariasis (large roundworm).

Contraindications: History of hypersensitivity reaction to thiabendazole.

Warnings: Occupational Hazards: Thiabendazole may impair the alertness in some patients: operation of automobiles and other activities made hazardous by diminished alertness should be avoided.

If hypersensitivity reactions occur, the drug should be discontinued immediately and not resumed. Erythema multiforme has been associated with thiabendazole therapy: In severe cases (Stevens-Johnson syndrome) fatalities have occurred.

Mintezol (cont'd)

Pregnancy and *Lactation:* Safety for the use of this drug in pregnancy and lactation has not been established.

Reproduction studies of successive generations of mice, rats, swine, rabbits, cattle and sheep have shown no fetal abnormalities that could be related directly to thiabendazole (see Pharmacology).

Thiabendazole is excreted in the milk of cattle.

Precautions: Ideally, supportive therapy is indicated for anemic, dehydrated or malnourished patients prior to initiation of the anthelmintic therapy.

Thiabendazole is not suitable for the treatment of mixed infections with ascaris because it may cause these worms to migrate.

Thiabendazole should be used only in patients in whom susceptible worm infestation has been diagnosed and should not be used prophylactically.

Since thiabendazole is metabolized in the liver and excreted by the kidneys, hepatic and renal function should be carefully monitored in patients with dysfunction of these organs.

Thiabendazole may compete with other drugs, such as theophylline, for sites of metabolism in the liver, thus elevating the serum levels of such compounds to potentially toxic levels. Therefore, when concomitant use of thiabendazole and xanthine derivatives is anticipated, it may be necessary to monitor blood levels and/or reduce the dosage of such compounds. Such concomitant use should be administered under careful medical supervision.

Adverse Effects: Side effects most frequently encountered are anorexia, nausea, vomiting and dizziness. Less frequently, diarrhea, epigastric distress, pruritus, weariness, drowsiness, giddiness and headache have occurred.

Side effects which have occurred rarely, include: tinnitus, collapse, abnormal sensation in eyes, blurring of vision, hyperirritability, numbness, hyperglycemia, proteinuria, xanthopsia, enuresis, decrease in pulse rate, hypotension, jaundice, cholestasis and parenchymal liver damage and a transient rise in cephalin flocculation and AST.

Hypersensitivity reactions include: fever, facial flush, chills, conjunctival injection, angioneurotic edema, anaphylaxis, lymphadenopathy, erythema multiforme including Stevens-Johnson syndrome, perianal rash and skin rash.

Appearance of live Ascaris in the mouth and nose has been reported on rare occasions.

Some patients may excrete a metabolite which imparts an odor to urine. This is much like that which occurs after ingestion of asparagus and is noted during therapy and for about 24 hours after completion of therapy.

Crystalluria with or without hematuria has been reported on occasion as having occurred during treatment with thiabendazole. The crystalluria promptly subsides with discontinuation of therapy.

Transient leukopenia has been reported in a few patients while receiving thiabendazole therapy. The cause and effect relationship in these cases has not been established.

Overdose: Symptoms and Treatment: No specific antidote. Induce emesis or perform gastric lavage. Treatment is symptomatic and supportive.

Dosage: Thiabendazole should be given with meals, where possible and should be chewed before swallowing. Dietary restriction, complementary medications and cleansing enemas are not needed.

The usual dosage schedule for all conditions is 2 doses/day. The size of the dose is determined by the patient's weight (see Table I). Patients weighing less than 60 kg—25 mg/kg/dose. Patients weighing 60 kg and over—1.5 g/dose. **The maximum daily dose for adults weighing more than 60 kg is 3 g.**

Table I—Mintezol

Weight—Dose Chart

Weight (kg)	Each Dose g	Each Dose Tablets (0.5 g each)
10	0.25	½
20	0.50	1
30	0.75	1½
40	1.00	2
50	1.25	2½
60 (or over)	1.50	3

In certain patients, a twice daily dose may lead to a higher incidence of side effects. In these circumstances 25 mg/kg may be given after the largest meal on the first day and repeated 24 hours later after a similar meal on the second day.

The regimen for each indication is shown in Table II.

Table II—Mintezol

Therapeutic Regimens

Indications	Regimen	Comments
Strongyloidiasis*	2 doses per day for 2 successive days.	A single dose of 50 mg/kg may be employed as an alternative schedule, but a higher incidence of side effects should be expected.
Cutaneous Larva Migrans (Creeping Eruption)	2 doses per day for 2 successive days.	If active lesions are still present 2 days after completion of therapy, a second course is recommended.
Trichinosis*	2 doses per day for 2–4 successive days according to the response of the patient.	The optimal dosage for the treatment of trichinosis has not been established.
Other indications: Intestinal roundworms* (including Ascariasis, Uncinariasis and Trichuriasis)	2 doses per day for 2 successive days.	A single dose of 50 mg/kg may be employed as an alternative schedule, but a higher incidence of side effects should be expected.

*Clinical experience with thiabendazole for treatment of each of these conditions in children weighing less than 15 kg has been limited.

Supplied: Each orange (peach) colored, 1.90 cm in diameter, beveled edge, compressed chewable tablet, scored on one side with MSD 907 engraved on the other, contains: thiabendazole 500 mg. Units of 6.

(Shown in Product Recognition Section)

MIOCARPINE® Ⓟ

CIBA Vision

Pilocarpine HCl

Miotic—Cholinergic

Supplied: Each 15 mL plastic squeeze bottle with dropper tip contains: pilocarpine hydrochloride 1%, 2%, 4% or 6% (w/v). Nonmedicinal ingredients: benzalkonium chloride 0.01% w/v (preservative), boric acid, disodium edetate, hydroxypropyl methylcellulose, potassium chloride, purified water, sodium carbonate. Store at 15 to 30°C. Keep bottle tightly closed when not in use.

MIOCHOL®-E Ⓟ

CIBA Vision

Acetylcholine Chloride—Electrolytes

Miotic

Pharmacology: Acetylcholine is a naturally occurring neurohormone which mediates nerve impulse transmission at all cholinergic sites involving somatic and autonomic nerves. After release from the nerve ending, acetylcholine is rapidly inactivated by the enzyme acetylcholinesterase by hydrolysis to acetic acid and choline.

Direct application of acetylcholine to the iris will cause rapid miosis of short duration. Topical ocular instillation of acetylcholine to the intact eye causes no discernible response as cholinesterase destroys the molecule more rapidly than it can penetrate the cornea.

Indications: To obtain miosis of the iris in seconds after delivery of the lens in cataract surgery, in penetrating keratoplasty, iridectomy and other anterior segment surgery where rapid miosis may be required.

Contraindications: None known.

Warnings: Do not gas sterilize. If blister or peelable backing is damaged or broken, sterility of the enclosed bottle cannot be assured. Open under aseptic conditions only.

Precautions: General: In the reconstitution of the solution, as described under Directions for Using Univial, if the centre rubber plug seal in the univial does not go down or is down, do not use the vial.

If miosis is to be obtained quickly with Miochol-E, anatomical hindrances to miosis, such as anterior or posterior synechiae, must be released prior to administration. During cataract surgery, use Miochol-E only after delivery of the lens.

Aqueous solutions of acetylcholine are unstable. Prepare solution immediately before use. Do not use solution which is not clear and colorless. Discard any solution that has not been used.

Drug Interactions: Although clinical studies with acetylcholine and animal studies with acetylcholine or carbachol revealed no interference, and there is no known pharmacological basis for an interaction, there have been reports that acetylcholine and carbachol have been ineffective when used in patients treated with topical nonsteroidal anti-inflammatory agents.

Children: Safety and effectiveness in children have not been established.

Adverse Effects: Infrequent cases of corneal edema, corneal clouding and corneal decompensation have been reported with the use of intraocular acetylcholine.

Adverse reactions have been reported rarely which are indicative of systemic absorption. These include bradycardia, hypotension, flushing, breathing difficulties and sweating.

Overdose: Symptoms and Treatment: Atropine sulfate (0.5 to 1 mg) should be given i.m. or i.v. and should be readily available to counteract possible overdosage. Epinephrine (0.1 to 1 mg s.c.) is also of value in overcoming severe cardiovascular or bronchoconstrictor responses.

Dosage: With a new needle of sturdy gauge, 18 to 20, draw all the solution into a dry, sterile syringe. Replace needle with a suitable atraumatic cannulae for intraocular irrigation.

The Miochol-E solution is instilled into the anterior chamber before or after securing one or more sutures. Instillation should be gentle and parallel to the iris face and tangential to pupil border.

If there are no mechanical hindrances, the pupil starts to constrict in seconds and the peripheral iris is drawn away from the angle of the anterior chamber. Any anatomical hindrance to miosis must be released to permit the desired effect of the drug. In most cases, 0.5 to 2 mL produces satisfactory miosis.

In cataract surgery, use Miochol-E only after delivery of the lens.

Aqueous solutions of acetylcholine are unstable. Prepare solution immediately before use. Do not use solution which is not clear and colorless. Discard any solution that has not been used.

Directions for using the univial: **Sterile unless package open or broken.**

1. Inspect univial while inside unopened blister. Diluent must be in upper chamber.
2. Peel open blister.
3. Aseptically transfer univial to sterile field. Maintain sterility of outer container during preparation of solution.
4. Immediately before use, give plunger-stopper a quarter turn and press to force diluent and centre plug into lower chamber.
5. Shake gently to dissolve drug.
6. Discard univial and any unused solution.

Supplied: Each univial (two chamber vial) contains: acetylcholine chloride 20 mg and mannitol 56 mg (lower chamber) and electrolyte diluent 2 mL (upper chamber). The reconstituted solution provides acetylcholine chloride 10 mg/mL. Nonmedicinal ingredients: calcium chloride dihydrate, magnesium chloride hexahydrate, mannitol, potassium chloride, sodium chloride and sterile water for injection. Store at controlled room temperature 15 to 30°C. **Keep from freezing.**

MIOSTAT® Ⓟ

Alcon

Carbachol

Miotic

Supplied: Each glass vial contains: a sterile buffered solution of carbachol 0.01%. Contains no preservative. Nonmedicinal ingredients: calcium chloride, hydrochloric acid, magnesium chloride, potassium chloride, purified water, sodium acetate, sodium chloride, sodium citrate and sodium hydroxide. Glass vials of 1.5 mL, cartons of 12.

MIRAPEX® Ⓟ

Boehringer Ingelheim

Pramipexole Dihydrochloride

Antiparkinsonian Agent—Dopamine Agonist

Pharmacology: Pramipexole is a non ergot dopamine agonist with high in vitro specificity at the D_2 subfamily of dopamine receptors. Pramipexole is a full agonist and exhibits higher affinity to the D_3 receptor subtypes (which are in prominent distribution within the mesolimbic area) than to D_2 or D_4 receptor subtypes. While pramipexole exhibits high affinity for the dopamine D2 receptor subfamily, it has low affinity for α_2-adrenergic receptors and negligible or undetectable affinity for other dopaminergic, adrenergic, histaminergic, adenosine and benzodiazepine receptors.

The ability of pramipexole to alleviate the signs and symptoms of Parkinson's disease is believed to be related to its ability to stimulate dopamine receptors in the striatum. This assumption is supported by a dose-dependent antagonism of Parkinsonian symptoms in rhesus monkeys pretreated with the neurotoxin N-methyl-4-phenyl-1,2,3,6-tetrahydropyridine (MPTP) which destroys dopamine cell bodies in the substantia nigra.

Pharmacokinetics: Absorption: Following oral administration, pramipexole is rapidly absorbed reaching peak concentrations between 1 and 3 hours. The absolute bioavailability of pramipexole is greater than 90%. Pramipexole can be administered with or without food. A high-fat meal did not affect the extent of pramipexole absorption (AUC and C_{max}) in healthy volunteers, although the time to maximal plasma concentration (T_{max}) was increased by about 1 hour.

Pramipexole displays linear pharmacokinetics over the range of doses that are recommended for patients with Parkinson's disease.

Distribution: Pramipexole is extensively distributed, having a volume of distribution of about 500 L. Protein binding is less than 20% in plasma; with albumin accounting for most of the protein binding in human serum. Pramipexole distributes into red blood cells as indicated by an erythrocyte to plasma ratio of approximately 2.0 and a blood to plasma ratio of approximately 1.5. Consistent with the large volume of distribution in humans, whole body autoradiography and brain tissue levels in rats indicated that pramipexole was widely distributed throughout the body, including the brain.

Metabolism and Elimination: Urinary excretion is the major route of pramipexole elimination. Approximately 88% of a ^{14}C-labeled dose was recovered in the urine and less than 2% in the feces following single i.v. and oral doses in healthy volunteers. The terminal elimination half-life was about 8.5 hours in young volunteers (mean age 30 years) and about 12 hours in elderly volunteers (mean age 70 years). Approximately 90% of the recovered ^{14}C-labeled dose was unchanged drug; with no specific metabolites having been identified in the remaining 10% of the recovered radiolabeled dose. Pramipexole is the levorotational (-) enantiomer, and no measurable chiral inversion or racemization occurs in vivo.

The renal clearance of pramipexole is approximately 400 mL/min, approximately 3 times higher than the glomerular filtration rate. Thus, pramipexole is secreted by the renal tubules, probably by the organic cation transport system.

Pharmacokinetics in Special Populations: Because therapy with pramipexole is initiated at a subtherapeutic dose and gradually titrated according to clinical tolerability to obtain optimal therapeutic effect, adjustment of the initial dose based on gender, weight, or age is not necessary. However, renal insufficiency, which can cause a large decrease in the ability to eliminate pramipexole, may necessitate dosage adjustment.

Parkinson's Disease Patients: The pharmacokinetics of pramipexole were comparable between early and advanced Parkinson's disease patients.

Age: Renal function declines with age. Since pramipexole clearance is correlated with renal function, the drug's total oral clearance was approximately 25 to 30% lower in elderly (aged 65 years or older) compared with young healthy volunteers (aged less than 40 years). The decline in clearance resulted in an increase in elimination half-life from approximately 8.5 hours in young volunteers (mean age 30 years) to 12 hours in elderly volunteers (mean age 70 years).

Gender: Pramipexole renal clearance is about 30% lower in women than in men, most of this difference can be accounted for by differences in body weight. The reduced clearance resulted in a 16 to 42% increase in AUC and a 2 to 10% increase in C_{max}. The differences remained constant over the age range of 20 to 80 years. The difference in pramipexole half-life between males and females was less than 10%.

Race: The potential influence of race on pramipexole pharmacokinetics has not been evaluated.

Children: The pharmacokinetics of pramipexole in the pediatric population have not been evaluated.

Renal Insufficiency: The clearance of pramipexole was about 75% lower in patients with severe renal impairment (creatinine clearance approximately 20 mL/min) and about 60% lower in patients with moderate impairment (creatinine clearance approximately 40 mL/min) compared with healthy volunteers.

A lower starting and maintenance dose is recommended in patients with renal impairment (see Dosage). In patients with varying degrees of renal impairment, pramipexole clearance correlates well with creatinine clearance. Therefore, creatinine clearance can be used as a predictor of the extent of decrease in pramipexole clearance. As pramipexole clearance is reduced even more in dialysis patients (N=7), than in patients with severe renal impairment, the administration of pramipexole to patients with end stage renal disease is not recommended.

Hepatic Insufficiency: The potential influence of hepatic insufficiency on pramipexole pharmacokinetics has not been evaluated; however, it is considered to be small. Since approximately 90% of the recovered ^{14}C-labeled dose was excreted in the urine as unchanged drug, hepatic impairment would not be expected to have a significant effect on pramipexole elimination.

Clinical Studies: Up to February 29, 1996, 1 715 patients have been exposed to pramipexole, with 669 patients being exposed for over 1 year and 222 patients being exposed for over 2 years.

The effectiveness of pramipexole in the treatment of Parkinson's disease was evaluated in a multinational drug development program consisting of 7 randomized controlled trials. Three were conducted in patients with early Parkinson's disease who were not receiving concomitant levodopa, and 4 were conducted in patients with advanced Parkinson's disease who were receiving concomitant levodopa. Among these 7 studies, 3 Phase 3 studies provide the most persuasive evidence of pramipexole's effectiveness in the management of patients with Parkinson's disease who were or were not receiving concomitant levodopa. Two of the trials enrolled patients with early Parkinson's disease (not receiving levodopa), and 1 enrolled patients with advanced Parkinson's disease who were receiving maximally tolerated doses of levodopa.

In all studies, the Unified Parkinson's Disease Rating Scale (UPDRS), or one or more of its subscales, served as the primary outcome assessment measure.

Studies in Patients with Early Parkinson's Disease: Patients in the 2 studies with early Parkinson's disease had a mean disease duration of 2 years, limited or no prior exposure to levodopa, and were not experiencing the ''on-off'' phenomenon and dyskinesia characteristics of later stages of the disease.

One of the trials was a double-blind, placebo-controlled, parallel study in which patients were randomized to pramipexole (N=164) or placebo (N=171). The trial consisted of a 7-week dose escalation period and a 6-month maintenance period. Patients could be on selegiline and/or anticholinergics but not on levodopa products. Patients treated with pramipexole had a starting dose of 0.375 mg/day and were titrated to a maximally tolerated dose, but no higher than 4.5 mg/day, administered in three divided doses. At the end of the 6-month maintenance period, the mean improvement from baseline on the UPDRS Part II (activities of daily living [ADL] subscale) score was 1.9 in the pramipexole group and −0.4 in the placebo group. The mean improvement from baseline on the UPDRS part III (motor subscale) was 5 in the pramipexole group and −0.8 in the placebo group. Both differences were statistically significant. The mean daily dose of pramipexole during the maintenance period was 3.8 mg/day.

The difference in mean daily dose between males and females was less than 10%. Patients >75 years (N=26) received the same mean daily dose as younger patients.

The second early Parkinson's disease study was a double-blind, placebo-controlled parallel trial which evaluated dose-response relationships. It consisted of a 6-week dose escalation period and a 4-week maintenance period. A total of 264 patients were enrolled. Patients could be on selegiline, anticholinergics, amantadine, or any combination of these, but not on levodopa products. Patients were randomized to 1 of 4 fixed doses of pramipexole (1.5 mg, 3 mg, 4.5 mg, or 6 mg/day) or placebo. No dose-response relationship was demonstrated. The between treatment differences on both parts of the UPDRS were statistically significant in favor of pramipexole at all doses.

In both studies in early Parkinson's disease patients, no differences in effectiveness were detected based upon age or gender. Patients receiving selegiline or anticholinergics had responses similar to patients not receiving these drugs.

To date, results comparing pramipexole to levodopa are not available.

Studies in Patients with Advanced Parkinson's Disease: In the advanced Parkinson's disease study, the primary assessments were the UPDRS and daily diaries that quantified amounts of on and off times.

Patients (N=181 on pramipexole, N=179 on placebo) had a mean disease duration of 9 years, had been exposed to levodopa for a mean of 8 years, received concomitant levodopa during the trial and had ''on-off'' periods. Patients could additionally be on selegiline, anticholinergics, amantadine, or any combination of these. The study consisted of a 7-week dose-escalation period and a 6-month maintenance period. Patients treated with pramipexole had a starting dose of 0.375 mg/day and were titrated to a maximally tolerated dose but no higher than 4.5 mg/day, administered in 3 divided doses. At the end of the 6-month maintenance period, the mean improvement from baseline on the UPDRS part II (ADL) score was 2.7 in the pramipexole group and 0.5 in the placebo group. The mean improvement from baseline on the UPDRS part III (motor) score was 5.6 in the pramipexole group and 2.8 in the placebo group. Both differences were statistically significant. The mean daily dose of pramipexole during the maintenance period was 3.5 mg/day.

The dose of levodopa could be reduced if dyskinesia or hallucinations developed. Levodopa dose reduction occurred in 76% and 54% of pramipexole and placebo-treated patients, respectively. On average, the percent decrease was 27% in the pramipexole group and 5% in the placebo group.

In females the mean daily dose was approximately 10% lower than in male patients. Patients aged over 75 years (N=24) had approximately a 10% lower dose than younger patients.

The mean number of ''off'' hours per day during baseline was approximately 6 hours for both groups. Throughout the trial, patients treated with pramipexole had a mean ''off'' period of approximately 4 hours, while the duration of ''off'' periods remained essentially unchanged in the placebo-treated subjects.

No differences in effectiveness were detected based upon age or gender.

Indications: In the treatment of the signs and symptoms of idiopathic Parkinson's disease.

Pramipexole may be used both as early therapy, without concomitant levodopa and as an adjunct to levodopa.

Contraindications: In patients who have demonstrated hypersensitivity to pramipexole or the excipients of the drug product (see Supplied).

Warnings: Hypotension: Dopamine agonists appear to impair the systemic regulation of blood pressure with resulting postural (orthostatic) hypotension specially during dose escalation. Postural (orthostatic) hypotension has been observed in patients treated with pramipexole. Therefore, patients should be carefully monitored for signs and symptoms of orthostatic hypotension especially during dose escalation (see Dosage) and should be informed of this risk (see Blue Section—Information for the Patient).

In clinical trials of pramipexole, however, and despite clear orthostatic effects in normal volunteers, the reported incidence of clinically significant orthostatic hypotension was not greater among those assigned to pramipexole than among those assigned to placebo. This result is clearly unexpected in light of the previous experience with the risks of dopamine agonist therapy.

While this finding could reflect a unique property of pramipexole, it might also be explained by the conditions of the study and the nature of the population enrolled in the clinical trials. Patients were very carefully titrated, and patients with active cardiovascular disease or significant orthostatic hypotension at baseline were excluded.

Hallucinations: In the double-blind, placebo-controlled trials in early Parkinson's disease, hallucinations were observed in 9% (35 of 388) of patients receiving pramipexole, compared with 2.6% (6 of 235) of patients receiving placebo. In the double-blind, placebo-controlled trials in advanced Parkinson's disease, where patients received pramipexole and concomitant levodopa, hallucinations were observed in 16.5% (43 of 260) of patients receiving pramipexole compared with 3.8% (10 of 264) of patients receiving placebo. Hallucinations were of sufficient severity to cause discontinuation of treatment in 3.1% of the early Parkinson's disease patients and 2.7% of the advanced Parkinson's disease patients compared with about 0.4% of placebo patients in both populations.

Age appears to increase the risk of hallucinations. In patients with early Parkinson's disease, the risk of hallucinations was

Mirapex (cont'd)

1.9 times and 6.8 times greater in pramipexole patients than placebo patients <65 years old, and >65 years old, respectively. In patients with advanced Parkinson's disease, the risk of hallucinations was 3.5 times and 5.2 times greater in pramipexole patients than placebo patients <65 years old, and >65 years old, respectively.

Precautions: Renal: Since pramipexole is eliminated through the kidneys, caution should be exercised when prescribing pramipexole to patients with renal insufficiency (see Pharmacology—Pharmacokinetics and Dosage).

Dyskinesia: Pramipexole may potentiate the dopaminergic side effects of levodopa and may cause or exacerbate preexisting dyskinesia. Decreasing the dose of levodopa may ameliorate this side effect.

Retinal Pathology in Albino Rats: Pathologic changes (degeneration and loss of photoreceptor cells) were observed in the retina of albino rats in the 2-year carcinogenicity study with pramipexole. These findings were first observed during week 76 and were dose-dependant in animals receiving 2 mg/kg/day (25/50 male rats, 10/50 female rats) and 8 mg/kg/day (44/50 male rats, 37/50 female rats). Plasma AUCs at these doses were 2.5 and 12.5 times the AUC seen in humans at the maximal recommended dose of 4.5 mg/day. Similar findings were not present in either control rats, or in rats receiving 0.3 mg/kg/day of pramipexole (0.3 times the AUC seen in humans at the 4.5 mg/day dose).

Studies demonstrated that pramipexole at very high dose (25 mg/kg/day) reduced the rate of disk shedding from the photoreceptor rod cells of the retina in albino rats; this reduction was associated with enhanced sensitivity to the damaging effects of light. In a comparative study, degeneration and loss of photoreceptor cells occurred in albino rats after 13 weeks of treatment with 25 mg/kg/day of pramipexole (54 times the highest clinical dose on a mg/m² basis) and constant light (100 lux) but not in Brown-Norway rats exposed to the same dose but higher light intensities (500 lux).

The albino rats seem to be more susceptible than pigmented rats to the damaging effect of pramipexole and light. While the potential significance of this effect on humans has not been established, it cannot be excluded that human albinos (or people who suffer from albinismus oculi) might have an increased susceptibility to pramipexole compared to normally pigmented people. Therefore, such patients should take pramipexole only under ophthalmological control.

Rhabdomyolysis: A single case of rhabdomyolysis occurred in a 49-year old male with advanced Parkinson's disease treated with pramipexole. The patient was hospitalized with an elevated CPK (10.631 IU/L). The symptoms resolved with discontinuation of the medication.

Geriatrics: Pramipexole total oral clearance was approximately 25 to 30% lower in the elderly (aged 65 years and older) as a result of a decline in pramipexole renal clearance due to an age-related reduction in renal function. This resulted in an increase in elimination half-life from approximately 8.5 hours to 12 hours (see Pharmacology, Pharmacokinetics).

In clinical studies, 40.8% (699 of 1 715) of patients were between the ages of 65 and 75 years, and 6.5% (112 of 1 715) of patients were >75 years old. There were no apparent differences in efficacy or safety between older and younger patients, except that the relative risk of hallucination associated with the use of pramipexole was increased in the elderly.

Children: The safety of pramipexole in pediatric patients has not been established.

Carcinogenesis, Mutagenesis, Impairment of Fertility: Two-year carcinogenicity studies have been conducted with pramipexole in mice and rats. In rats, pramipexole was administered in the diet, at doses of 0.3, 2 and 8 mg/kg/day. The highest dose corresponded to 12.5 times the highest recommended clinical dose (1.5 mg t.i.d.) based on comparative AUC values. No significant increases in tumors occurred.

Testicular Leydig cell adenomas were found in male rats as follows: 13 of 50 control group A males, 9 of 60 control group B males, 17 of 50 males given 0.3 mg/kg/day, 22 of 50 males given 2 mg/kg/day, and 22 of 50 males given 8 mg/kg/day. Leydig cell hyperplasia and increased numbers of adenomas are attributed to pramipexole-induced decreases in serum prolactin levels, causing a down-regulation of Leydig cell luteinizing hormone (LH) receptors and a compensatory elevation of LH secretion by the pituitary gland. The endocrine mechanisms believed to be involved in rats are not relevant to humans.

In mice, pramipexole was administered in the diet, at doses of 0.3, 2 and 10 mg/kg/day. The highest dose corresponded to 11 times the highest recommended clinical dose on a mg/m² basis. No significant increases in tumors occurred.

Pramipexole was not mutagenic in a battery of in vitro and in vivo assays including the Ames assay and the in vivo mouse micronucleus assay.

In rat fertility studies, pramipexole at a dose of 2.5 mg/kg/day, prolonged the estrus cycle and inhibited implantation. These effects were associated with a reduction in serum levels of prolactin, a hormone necessary for implantation and maintenance of early pregnancy in rats.

Pregnancy: There are no studies of pramipexole in pregnant women. Because animal reproduction studies are not always predictive of human response, pramipexole should be used during pregnancy only if the potential benefit outweighs the potential risk to the fetus.

Pramipexole, at a dose of 2.5 mg/kg/day inhibited implantation. Pramipexole, at a dose of 1.5 mg/kg/day (4.3 times the AUC observed in humans at the maximal recommended clinical dose of 1.5 mg t.i.d.) resulted in a high incidence of total resorption of embryos. This finding is thought to be due to the prolactin lowering effect of pramipexole. Prolactin is necessary for implantation and maintenance of early pregnancy in rats, but not in rabbits and humans. Because of pregnancy disruption and early embryonic loss, the teratogenic potential of pramipexole could not be assessed adequately. In pregnant rabbits which received doses up to 10 mg/kg/day during organogenesis (plasma AUC 71 times that seen in humans at the 1.5 mg t.i.d. dose), there was no evidence of adverse effects on embryo-fetal development. Postnatal growth was inhibited in the offspring of rats treated with a 0.5 mg/kg/day dose of pramipexole during the latter part of pregnancy and throughout lactation.

Lactation: The excretion of pramipexole into breast milk has not been studied in women. Since pramipexole suppresses lactation, it should not be administered to mothers who wish to breast-feed infants.

A single-dose, radiolabeled study showed that drug-related materials were excreted into the breast milk of lactating rats. Concentrations of radioactivity in milk were 3 to 6 times higher than concentrations in plasma at equivalent time points.

Laboratory Tests: There are no specific laboratory tests recommended for the management of patients receiving pramipexole.

Drug Interactions: Antiparkinsonian Drugs: In volunteers (N=11), selegiline did not influence the pharmacokinetics of pramipexole.

Population pharmacokinetic analysis suggests that amantadine is unlikely to alter the oral clearance of pramipexole (N=54). Levodopa/carbidopa did not influence the pharmacokinetics of pramipexole in volunteers (N=10). Pramipexole did not alter the extent of absorption (AUC) or elimination of levodopa/carbidopa, although it increased levodopa C_{max} by about 40%, and decreased T_{max} from 2.5 to 0.5 hours.

Cimetidine: Cimetidine, a known inhibitor of renal tubular secretion of organic bases via the cationic transport system, increased pramipexole AUC by 50% and increased its half-life by 40% in volunteers (N=12).

Probenecid: Probenecid, a known inhibitor of renal tubular secretion of organic acids via the anionic transport system, did not influence the pharmacokinetics of pramipexole in volunteers (N=12).

Other Drugs Eliminated via Renal Secretion: Concomitant therapy with drugs secreted by the renal cationic transport system (e.g., cimetidine, ranitidine, diltiazem, triamterene, verapamil, quinidine and quinine), will decrease the oral clearance of pramipexole and thus, necessitate a reduction in the dosage of pramipexole. Concomitant therapy with drugs secreted by the renal anionic transport system (e.g., cephalosporins, penicillins, indomethacin, hydrochlorothiazide and chlorpropamide) are not likely to have any effect on the oral clearance of pramipexole.

CYP Interactions: Inhibitors of cytochrome P450 enzymes would not be expected to affect pramipexole elimination because pramipexole is not appreciably metabolized by these enzymes in vivo or in vitro. Pramipexole does not inhibit CYP1A2, CYP2C9, CYP2C19, CYP2E1, and CYP3A4. Inhibition of CYP2D6 was observed with an apparent Ki of 30 μM, indicating that pramipexole will not inhibit CYP enzymes at plasma concentrations observed following the highest recommended clinical dose (1.5 mg t.i.d.).

Dopamine Antagonists: Since pramipexole is a dopamine agonist, dopamine antagonists such as the neuroleptics (phenothiazines, butyrophenones, thioxanthines) or metoclopramide may diminish the effectiveness of pramipexole and should ordinarily not be administered concurrently.

Drug-Laboratory Test Interactions: There are no known interactions between pramipexole and laboratory tests.

Occupational Hazards: Psychomotor Activities: Patients should be cautioned not to drive a motor vehicle or operate potentially hazardous machinery until they are reasonably certain that pramipexole does not affect their ability to engage in such activities.

Dependence Liability: Pramipexole has not been systematically studied in animals or humans for its potential for abuse, tolerance, or physical dependence. However, in a rat model on cocaine self-administration, pramipexole had little or no effect.

Adverse Effects: During the premarketing development of pramipexole, patients enrolled in clinical trials had either early or advanced Parkinson's disease. Apart from the severity and duration of their disease, the 2 populations differed in their use of concomitant levodopa therapy. Namely, patients with early disease did not receive concomitant levodopa therapy during treatment with pramipexole, while those with advanced Parkinson's disease did. Because these 2 populations may have differential risk for various adverse events, adverse event data will be presented for both populations.

All controlled clinical trials performed during premarketing development (except one fixed dose study) used a titration design. Consequently, it was impossible to adequately evaluate the effects of a given dose on the incidence of adverse events.

Adverse Reactions Associated with Discontinuation of Treatment: Early Parkinson's Disease: Approximately 12% of 388 patients treated with pramipexole and 11% of 235 patients treated with placebo discontinued treatment due to adverse events. The events most commonly causing discontinuation of treatment were related to the nervous system, namely hallucinations (3.1% on pramipexole vs 0.4% on placebo), dizziness (2.1% on pramipexole vs 1.0% on placebo), somnolence (1.6% on pramipexole vs 0% on placebo), headache and confusion (1.3% and 1%, respectively, on pramipexole vs 0% on placebo), and to the gastrointestinal system (nausea 12.1% on pramipexole vs 0.4% on placebo).

Advanced Parkinson's Disease: Approximately 12% of 260 patients treated with pramipexole and 16% of 264 patients treated with placebo discontinued treatment due to adverse events. The events most commonly causing discontinuation of treatment were related to the nervous system, namely hallucinations (2.7% on pramipexole vs 0.4% on placebo), dyskinesia (1.9% on pramipexole vs 0.8% on placebo), dizziness (1.2% on pramipexole vs 1.5% on placebo), confusion (1.2% on pramipexole vs 2.3% on placebo), and to the cardiovascular system (postural [orthostatic] hypotension 2.3% on pramipexole vs 1.1% on placebo).

Most Frequent Adverse Events: Adverse events occurring with an incidence of greater than, or equal to, 10% and listed in decreasing order of frequency, were as follows:

Early Parkinson's Disease: nausea, dizziness, somnolence, insomnia, asthenia and constipation.

Advanced Parkinson's Disease: postural [orthostatic] hypotension, dyskinesia, insomnia, dizziness, hallucinations, accidental injury, dream abnormalities, constipation and confusion.

Incidence of Adverse Events in Placebo Controlled Trials: Table I (on following page) lists treatment-emergent adverse events that were reported in the double-blind, placebo-controlled studies by ≥1% of patients treated with pramipexole and were numerically more frequent than in the placebo group. Adverse events were usually mild or moderate in intensity.

The prescriber should be aware that these figures cannot be used to predict the incidence of adverse events in the course of usual medical practice where patient characteristics and other factors differ from those that prevailed in the clinical studies. Similarly, the cited frequencies cannot be compared with figures obtained from other clinical investigations involving different treatments, uses, and investigators. However, the cited figures do provide the prescribing physician with some basis for estimating the relative contribution of drug and nondrug factors to the adverse-event incidence rate in the population studied.

Other events reported by 1% or more of patients treated with pramipexole but reported equally or more frequently in the placebo group were as follows:

Early Parkinson's Disease: infection, accidental injury, headache, pain, tremor, back pain, syncope, postural hypotension, hypertonia, diarrhea, rash, ataxia, dry mouth, leg cramps, twitching, pharyngitis, sinusitis, sweating, rhinitis, urinary tract infection, vasodilation, flu syndrome, increased saliva, tooth disease, dyspnea, increased cough, gait abnormalities, urinary frequency, vomiting, allergic reaction, hypertension, pruritus, hypokinesia, increased creatine PK, nervousness, dream abnormalities, chest pain, neck pain, paresthesia, tachycardia, vertigo, voice alteration, conjunctivitis, paralysis,

Table I—Mirapex

Adverse Events from Placebo-controlled Early and Adjunct Therapy Studies (Incidence of Events ≥ 1% in Patients[a] Treated with Mirapex and Numerically More Frequent than in Patients Treated with Placebo)

	Early Therapy		Advanced Therapy	
Body System/ Adverse Event	**Mirapex N=388 % occurrence**	**Placebo N=235 % occurrence**	**Mirapex[b] N=260 % occurrence**	**Placebo[b] N=264 % occurrence**
Body as a Whole				
Asthenia	14	12	10	8
General Edema	5	3	4	3
Malaise	2	1	3	2
Reaction Unevaluable	2	1	—	—
Fever	1	0	—	—
Chest pain	—	—	3	2
Accidental Injury	—	—	17	15
Digestive				
Nausea	28	18	—	—
Constipation	14	6	10	9
Anorexia	4	2	—	—
Dysphagia	2	0	—	—
Dry Mouth	—	—	7	3
Metabolic and Nutritional				
Peripheral Edema	5	4	2	1
Decreased Weight	2	0	—	—
Increased Creatine PK	—	—	1	0
Cardiovascular				
Postural Hypotension	—	—	53	48
Nervous				
Dizziness	25	24	26	25
Somnolence	22	9	9	6
Insomnia	17	12	27	22
Hallucinations	9	3	17	4
Confusion	4	1	10	7
Amnesia	4	2	6	4
Hyperesthesia	3	1	—	—
Dystonia	2	1	8	7
Thinking Abnormalities	2	0	3	2
Decreased Libido	1	0	—	—
Myoclonus	1	0	—	—
Hypertonia	—	—	7	6
Paranoid Reaction	—	—	2	0
Delusions	—	—	1	0
Sleep Disorders	—	—	1	0
Dyskinesia	—	—	47	31
Gait Abnormalities	—	—	7	5
Dream Abnormalities	—	—	11	10
Special Senses				
Vision Abnormalities	3	0	3	1
Accommodation Abnormalities	—	—	4	2
Diplopia	—	—	1	0
Urogenital				
Impotence	2	1	—	—
Urinary Frequency	—	—	6	3
Urinary Tract Infection	—	—	4	3
Urinary Incontinence	—	—	2	1
Musculoskeletal				
Arthritis	—	—	3	1
Twitching	—	—	2	0
Bursitis	—	—	2	0
Myasthenia	—	—	1	0
Respiratory				
Dyspnea	—	—	4	3
Rhinitis	—	—	3	1
Pneumonia	—	—	2	0
Skin and Appendages				
Skin Disorders	—	—	2	1

[a] Patients may have reported multiple adverse experiences during the study or at discontinuation, thus, patients may be included in more than one category.
[b] Patients received concomitant levodopa.

accommodation abnormalities, tinnitus, diplopia and taste perversiono.

Advanced Parkinson's Disease: nausea, pain, infection, headache, depression, tremor, hypokinesia, anorexia, back pain, dyspepsia, flatulence, ataxia, flu syndrome, sinusitis, diarrhea, myalgia, abdominal pain, anxiety, rash, paresthesia, hypertension, increased saliva, tooth disorder, apathy, hypotension, sweating, vasodilation, vomiting, increased cough, nervousness, pruritus, hyperesthesia, neck pain, syncope, arthralgia, dysphagia, palpitations, pharyngitis, vertigo, leg cramps, conjunctivitis and lacrimation.

Adverse Events: Relationship to age, Gender and Race: Among the treatment-emergent adverse events in patients treated with pramipexole, hallucinations appeared to exhibit a positive relationohip to age. No gender-related differences were observed. Only a small percentage (4%) of patients enrolled were noncaucasian, therefore, an evaluation of adverse events related to race is not possible.

Other Adverse Events Observed During all Phase 2 and 3 Clinical Trials: Pramipexole has been administered to 1 715 subjects during the premarketing development program, 782 of whom participated in double-blind, controlled studies. During these trials, all adverse events were recorded by the clinical investigators using terminology of their own choosing. To provide a meaningful estimate of the proportion of individuals having adverse events, similar types of events were grouped into a smaller number of standardized categories using modified COSTART dictionary terminology. These categories are used in the listing below. The events listed below occurred in less than 1% of the 1 715 subjects exposed to pramipexole. All reported events, except those already listed above, are included, without regard to determination of a causal relationship to pramipexole.

Events are listed within body system categories in order of decreasing frequency.

Body as a Whole: fever, enlarged abdomen, rigid neck, no drug effect.

Cardiovascular: palpitations, angina pectoris, atrial arrhythmia, peripheral vascular disease.

Digestive: tongue discoloration, gastrointestinal hemorrhage, fecal incontinence.

Endocrine: diabetes mellitus.

Hemic and Lymphatic: ecchymosis.

Metabolic and Nutritional: gout.

Musculoskeletal: bursitis, myasthenia.

Nervous: apathy, libido decrease, paranoid reaction, akinesia, coordination abnormalities, speech disorder, hyperkinesia, neuralgia.

Respiratory: voice alteration, asthma, hemoptysis.

Skin and Appendages: skin disorder, herpes simplex.

Special Senses: tinnitus, taste perversion, otitis media, dry eye, ear disorder, hemianopia.

Urogenital: urinary incontinence, dysuria, prostate disorder, kidney calculus.

Overdose: Symptoms: There is no clinical experience with massive overdosage. One patient with a 10-year history of schizophrenia (who participated in a schizophrenia study) took 11 mg/day of pramipexole for 2 days; this was 2 to 3 times the daily dose recommended in the protocol. No adverse events were reported related to the increased dose. The blood pressure remained stable although pulse rates increased to between 100 and 120 beats/minute. The patient withdrew from the study at the end of week 2 due to lack of efficacy.

Treatment: There is no known antidote for overdosage of a dopamine agonist. If signs of CNS stimulation are present, a phenothiazine or other butyrophenone neuroleptic agent may be indicated; the efficacy of such drugs in reversing the effects of overdosage has not been assessed. Management of the overdose may require general supportive measures along with gastric lavage, i.v. fluids, and ECG monitoring.

Dosage: Pramipexole should be taken three times daily.

In all clinical studies, dosage was initiated at a subtherapeutic level to avoid orthostatic hypotension and severe adverse effects. Pramipexole should be titrated gradually in all patients. The dosage should be increased to achieve maximal therapeutic effect, balanced against the principal adverse reactions of dyskinesia, nausea, dizziness and hallucinations.

Initial Treatment: Dosages should be increased gradually from a starting dose of 0.375 mg/day given in 3 divided doses and should not be increased more frequently than every 5 to 7 days. A suggested ascending dosage schedule that was used in clinical studies is shown in Table II.

Table II—Mirapex

Ascending-Dose Schedule of Mirapex

Week	Dosage (mg)	Total Daily Dose (mg)
1	0.125 t.i.d.	0.375
2	0.25 t.i.d.	0.75
3	0.50 t.i.d.	1.50
4	0.75 t.i.d.	2.25
5	1.00 t.i.d.	3.00
6	1.25 t.i.d.	3.75
7	1.50 t.i.d.	4.50

The maximal recommended dose is 4.5 mg/day. Pramipexole is not recommended at the 6 mg/day dose since the incidence of some adverse reactions is higher.

Maintenance Treatment: Pramipexole was effective and well tolerated over a dosage range of 1.5 to 4.5 mg/day, administered in equally divided doses 3 times/day, as monotherapy or in combination with levodopa (approximately 800 mg/day). In a fixed-dose study in patients with early Parkinson's disease, pramipexole at doses of 3, 4.5 and 6 mg/day was not shown to provide any significant benefit beyond that achieved at a daily dose of 1.5 mg/day. For individual patients who have not achieved efficacy at 1.5 mg/day, higher doses can result in additional therapeutic benefit.

When pramipexole is used in combination with levodopa, a reduction of the levodopa dosage should be considered. In the controlled study in advanced Parkinson's disease, the dosage of levodopa was reduced by an average of 27% from baseline.

Mirapex (cont'd)

Patients with Renal Impairment: Since the clearance of pramipexole is reduced in patients with renal impairment (see Pharmacology, Pharmacokinetics), the following dosage recommendation should be considered (see Table III).

Table III—Mirapex

Mirapex Dosage in Renal Impairment

Renal Status	Starting Dose (mg)	Maximum Dose (mg)
Mild Impairment (Creatinine Cl >60 mL/min)	0.125 t.i.d.	1.5 t.i.d.
Moderate Impairment (Creatinine Cl=35 to 59 mL/min	0.125 b.i.d.	1.5 b.i.d.
Severe Impairment (Creatinine Cl=15 to 34 mL/min	0.125 daily	1.5 daily
Very Severe Impairment (Creatinine Cl <15 mL/min and Hemodialysis Patients	Mirapex has not been adequately studied in this group and its administration to patients with end stage renal disease is not recommended.	

Discontinuation of Treatment: It is recommended that pramipexole be discontinued over a period of 1 week. However, in some studies, abrupt discontinuation was uneventful.

Information for the Patient: See Blue Section—Information for the Patient "Mirapex".

Supplied: 0.25 mg: Each white, oval, scored tablet, with "U" twice on one side and "4" twice on the reverse side, contains: pramipexole dihydrochloride 0.25 mg as pramipexole dihydrochloride monohydrate. Nonmedicinal ingredients: colloidal silicon dioxide, cornstarch, magnesium stearate, mannitol and povidone. Bottles of 90.

1 mg: Each white, round, scored tablet, with "U" twice on one side and "6" twice on the reverse side, contains: pramipexole dihydrochloride 1 mg as pramipexole dihydrochloride monohydrate. Nonmedicinal ingredients: colloidal silicon dioxide, cornstarch, magnesium stearate, mannitol and povidone. Bottles of 90.

1.5 mg: Each white, round, scored tablet, with "U" twice on one side and "37" twice on the reverse side, contains: pramipexole dihydrochloride 1.5 mg as pramipexole dihydrochloride monohydrate. Nonmedicinal ingredients: colloidal silicon dioxide, cornstarch, magnesium stearate, mannitol and povidone. Bottles of 90.

Dispense in the original container. Store at controlled room temperature of 15 to 30°C. Protect from light.

(Shown in Product Recognition Section)

New Product 1998

MIREZE® 🅿
Allergan

Nedocromil Sodium

Antiallergic—Anti-inflammatory

Pharmacology: Nedocromil displays specific antiallergic and anti-inflammatory properties.

The pharmacological actions of nedocromil in many respects resemble those of sodium cromoglycate, a compound which has been shown to have effects on both the symptoms of ocular allergic inflammation and the level of inflammatory mediators present in the tears. Nedocromil is not only an inhibitor of the immunological release of inflammatory mediators, but also extends this activity to mucosal mast cells, which are thought to play an important role in allergic inflammatory diseases. The conclusion that nedocromil sodium is an anti-inflammatory agent is supported by in vivo observations of its capacity to inhibit the late response to antigen challenge, microvascular leakage and platelet activating factor (PAF) induced bronchoconstriction and hyper-responsiveness. In the dog and guinea-pig, nedocromil sodium has been shown to modify sensory nerve responses, a possible mechanism for its observed inhibitory effects on reflex bronchoconstriction and cough.

When administered as 2% ophthalmic solution in human volunteers, up to 4% of a dose of nedocromil sodium is absorbed; absorption occurs primarily through the nasal mucosa since much of the dose of an ophthalmic solution will drain from the eye via the nasolacrimal duct. Approximately 4 to 8% of an intranasal dose and 2 to 3% of an oral dose of nedocromil sodium is absorbed.

Nedocromil is bound reversibly (up to 89%) to human proteins and to a lesser extent in animals. It is not metabolized in man or animals. In man it is excreted unchanged in the urine (approximately 70%) and in feces (approximately 30%). While the plasma concentration falls rapidly (i.e., 10% of peak levels in 8 hours) and urinary excretion is 90% within 12 hours, fecal eliminations may take up to 3 days to be completed.

Indications: For the treatment of seasonal allergic conjunctivitis.

It must be used regularly to ensure optimal control of symptoms.

Treatment should be initiated as closely as possible to the start of the symptoms.

Nedocromil may be used in conjunction with other antiallergic therapies, including topical ophthalmics, (xylometazoline, naphazoline, sodium cromoglycate) topical nasal solutions (xylometazoline, flunisolide, pseudoephedrine) and systemic therapies (e.g., oral antihistamine) as no interactions have been reported.

Contraindications: Known hypersensitivity to nedocromil, disodium edetate or benzalkonium chloride.

Warnings: Patients who use soft contact lenses must not wear them during the treatment period with Mireze ophthalmic solution. Benzalkonium chloride, a constituent of the formulation, may accumulate in soft contact lenses. This preservative, when slowly released, could possibly irritate the cornea.

In patients who continue to wear hard or gas permeable contact lenses during nedocromil treatment, the lenses should be taken out of the eye prior to instillation of the drops. They should be inserted again not earlier than 5 minutes after administration, in order to allow an even conjunctival distribution of the solution.

To avoid contamination of the contents, patients should not touch the tip of the container or allow the tip of the bottle to come into contact with the eye.

Discard any remaining contents 4 weeks after first opening the bottle.

Precautions: Geriatrics: There is no evidence to suggest that a dose reduction in the elderly is required, as 2% nedocromil sodium ophthalmic solution appears to have a similar activity and safety profile in all groups of patient studied with allergic conjunctivitis. However there is limited clinical trial experience with nedocromil sodium ophthalmic solution, in the elderly.
Children: The safety and efficacy of nedocromil in children under 6 years of age has not yet been established.
Pregnancy: Safety in human pregnancy and the absence of adverse effects on the human reproductive process have not been established. Small amounts of nedocromil are known to cross the placenta but without effect in animals. In fact, in reproductive studies, nedocromil at dosage levels up to 100 mg/kg (more than 800 times the human maintenance dose) has shown no teratogenic or embryotoxic effects, nor has it been observed to interfere with reproductive performance, gestation, parturition, or lactation. Nedocromil has not affected male or female fertility nor has it altered the development of progeny.

Although there is no reason to suspect that nedocromil affects the fetus or mother, as with any drug caution must be exercised, especially during the first trimester. The benefits of treatment to the mother must be weighed against the potential risk to the fetus before proposing its use.
Lactation: Safety in breast-fed infants has not been established. Animal studies have indicated no toxicity of nedocromil in suckling newborns receiving drug from the parent or directly by injection. The concentrations of nedocromil in milk of animals were very low but have not been measured in human milk. The benefits of treating a nursing mother must be weighed against potential risk to the infant.
Drug Interactions: Nedocromil has been given to man in conjunction with other drugs with no apparent ill-effects. These included ophthalmic solutions such as xylometazoline, antazoline and naphazoline, pheniramine, sodium cromoglycate and dexamethasone; topical nasal therapies, such as xylometazoline, flunisolide, pseudoephedrine, chlorpheniramine and beclomethasone diproprionate, and oral antihistamines such as clemastine, astemizole, diphenhydramine, terfenadine, brompheniramine and promethazine.

Nedocromil by inhalation has also been used with inhaled and oral β_2-adrenergic agonists, inhaled and oral corticosteroids, theophylline and other methylxanthines and ipratropium bromide. No drug-drug interactions have been observed in humans or in animals.

Adverse Effects: No major adverse events associated with nedocromil ophthalmic solution have been reported in any of the clinical trials. Only minor adverse effects were reported which were mostly mild and self-limiting.

Those adverse events reported with a frequency ≥1% in patients who received nedocromil in controlled therapeutic trials are displayed in Table I.

Table I—Mireze

Percentage of Patients Reporting Common Adverse Events in Controlled Therapeutic Trials (AEs reported with a frequency of ≥1% for the Total Nedocromil Sodium 2% Group)

Adverse Event	Total Nedocromil Sodium 2% (n=1 552)	Total Placebo (n=1 353)
Headache	10.9	9.3
Eye Burning	7.4*	4.2
Eye Stinging	6.0*	3.1
Taste Perversion	5.4*	0.6
Eye Redness	2.3	1.8
Eye Itching	2.2	3.4
Rhinitis	1.9	2.3
Eye Watering	1.7	1.6
Eye Soreness	1.7	0.9
Pharyngitis	1.7	1.2
URI	1.7	1.1
Photophobia	1.2	1.1

* $p < 0.01$.

Overdose: Symptoms and Treatment: There have been no reported cases of overdosage in humans. Animal studies have not shown evidence of toxic effects of nedocromil sodium even at high dosage. If overdosage is suspected, treatment should be supportive and directed to the control of the relevant symptoms.

Dosage: The ophthalmic solution must be used regularly to ensure optimal control of symptoms.

Treatment should be initiated as closely as possible to the start of the symptoms.
Adults and Children (over 6 years of age): Seasonal Allergic Conjunctivitis: 1 drop into each eye twice daily. Dosage can be increased when necessary to 4 times daily.
Important: Soft contact lenses must not be worn during the treatment period. Benzalkonium chloride, a constituent of the formulation, may accumulate in soft contact lenses. This preservative, when slowly released, could possibly irritate the cornea.

In patients who continue to wear hard or gas permeable contact lenses during treatment, the lenses should be taken out of the eye prior to instillation of the drops. They should be inserted again not earlier than 5 minutes after administration, in order to allow an even conjunctival distribution of the solution.

To avoid contamination of the contents, do not touch any surface with the tip of the container.

Discard any remaining contents 28 days after opening the bottle.

Information for the Patient: See Blue Section—Information for the Patient "Mireze".

Supplied: Each mL of sterile, aqueous, isotonic, preserved, stabilized, clear pale yellow ophthalmic solution, contains: nedocromil sodium 2% w/v. Nonmedicinal ingredients: benzalkonium chloride, disodium edetate (EDTA), purified water and sodium chloride. White opaque or translucent polyethylene dropper bottles of 2.5, 5 and 10 mL. Drop size is a nominal 0.04 mL, delivering 0.8 mg nedocromil sodium to the eye. Store between 4 and 25°C. Protect from direct sunlight.

Reviewed 1998

New drugs require close post-marketing surveillance. Report suspected adverse reactions and interactions to the Health Protection Branch using the form provided in the CLIN-INFO SECTION.

MITOMYCIN FOR INJECTION, USP ℞

Faulding

Antineoplastic

Caution: Mitomycin is a potent drug and should be used only by physicians experienced with cancer chemotherapeutic drugs (see Warnings and Precautions). Blood counts should be taken weekly. Mitomycin must be discontinued or dosage reduced upon evidence of abnormal depression of the bone marrow or the development of significant renal or pulmonary toxicity.

Pharmacology: Mitomycin was investigated at first as an antibiotic in Japan. It was then found to be active as an antineoplastic agent. It selectively inhibits the synthesis of deoxyribonucleic acid (DNA) secondary to alkylation. The molecular site of DNA binding has been identified as the guanine-N^2 link in the minor groove of B-DNA. At high concentrations of the drug, cellular RNA and protein synthesis are also suppressed.

In humans, mitomycin is rapidly cleared from the plasma after i.v. administration with a biphasic plasma elimination curve. Time required to reduce the serum concentration by 50% after a 30 mg bolus injection is 17 minutes. After injection of 30 mg, 20 mg or 10 mg i.v., the maximal serum concentrations were 2.4 µg/mL, 1.7 µg/mL and 0.52 µg/mL respectively. In general, the smaller the dose, the more rapidly blood levels of mitomycin decreased. Clearance is effected primarily by metabolism in the liver, but metabolism occurs in other tissues as well.

Approximately 10% of a dose of mitomycin is excreted unchanged in the urine. Since metabolic pathways are saturated at relatively low doses, the percent of a dose excreted in urine increases with increasing doses. In children, excretion of i.v. administered mitomycin is similar.

Mitomycin is not appreciably absorbed from the urinary bladder, following intravesical administration. Serial plasma samples from 55 patients treated with doses of 20 to 40 mg of mitomycin by intravesical instillation were assayed. There was no mitomycin detectable (assay limit 10 to 100 ng/mL) in any plasma samples collected during and 30 minutes post-therapy at any dose.

Indications: In the palliative treatment as an adjunct to surgery, radiation or chemotherapy for adenocarcinoma of the stomach and colon.

Mitomycin as a single agent is indicated as topical therapy for superficial (no invasion beyond the lamina propria) transitional cell carcinoma of the urinary bladder. Efficacy has been demonstrated both in patients who have had no prior intravesical chemotherapy and in those who have failed such therapy with thiotepa or other antineoplastic agents.

Contraindications: Patients who have demonstrated a hypersensitivity to it in the past.

In patients with thrombocytopenia, leukopenia, coagulation disorder or an increased bleeding tendency due to other causes.

For intravesical administration in patients who have demonstrated a hypersensitive or idiosyncratic reaction to it in the past.

Warnings: It is recommended that mitomycin be administered under the supervision of a qualified physician experienced in the use of cancer chemotherapeutic agents. Since facilities for necessary laboratory studies must be available, hospitalization of patients is recommended.

Mitomycin should not be administered to any patient with a white blood cell count below 4 000 mm³ and a platelet count below 150 000 mm³ or to those with potentially serious infections.

Bone marrow depression, notably thrombocytopenia and leukopenia, is the most severe toxicity (see Adverse Effects). This may contribute to overwhelming infection in an already compromised, poor risk patient and may result in death.

In the treatment of each patient, the physician must weigh carefully the possibility of achieving therapeutic benefit versus the risk of toxicity. Studies have shown that mitomycin is carcinogenic in animals.

Pregnancy: Safe use of mitomycin in pregnant women has not been established. Mitomycin has known teratogenic properties in animals, therefore, the benefits derived from the use of mitomycin in pregnancy must be weighed against the hazards involved.

Precautions: Mitomycin should be administered, preferably, to patients who are hospitalized and who can be observed carefully and frequently during and after therapy.

It should be used with extreme caution in patients with significant impairment of renal function.

Since mitomycin has a high incidence of bone marrow depression, particularly thrombocytopenia and leukopenia, the following studies should be obtained frequently during therapy and for at least 7 weeks following therapy: platelet count, prothrombin time, bleeding time, white blood count and differential. The persistence of thrombocytopenia below 150 000/mm³ or a significant prolongation of prothrombin time or bleeding time or a WBC below 4 000/mm³ is an indication for the termination of therapy.

Patients should be advised of the potential toxicity of this drug, particularly bone marrow depression. A low incidence of septicemic deaths, as a result of leukopenia attributable to the drug, have been reported. Patients receiving mitomycin should be observed for evidence of renal toxicity. Mitomycin should not be given to patients with a serum creatinine greater than 1.7 mg %.

Mitomycin-associated pulmonary toxicity has been reported. Cases have been reported with both single-agent therapy and combination chemotherapy. Dyspnea and nonproductive cough are the usual presenting symptoms. Radiographic evidence of interstitial infiltrates may or may not be present. If other etiologies have been eliminated, a diagnosis of mitomycin-related pulmonary toxicity may be made.

Signs and symptoms of pneumonitis associated with mitomycin may be reversed if appropriate therapy is instituted early. The use of mitomycin should be discontinued. Corticosteroids have been reported by several authors to expedite symptomatic relief.

Acute shortness of breath and severe bronchospasm have been reported following the administration of vinca alkaloids in patients who had previously or simultaneously received mitomycin. The onset of this acute respiratory distress occurred within minutes or hours after the vinca alkaloid injection. The total number of doses for each drug has varied considerably. Bronchodilators, steroids and/or oxygen have produced symptomatic relief.

A few cases of adult respiratory distress syndrome have been reported in patients receiving mitomycin, in combination with other chemotherapy, and maintained at FiO_2 concentrations greater than 50% preoperatively. Therefore, caution should be exercised using only enough oxygen to provide adequate arterial saturation, since oxygen itself is toxic to the lungs. Careful attention should be paid to fluid balance and overhydration should be avoided.

Adverse Effects: Bone Marrow Toxicity: The most serious and most common toxicity of mitomycin is thrombocytopenia and leukopenia which occur anytime within 8 weeks after onset of therapy. In a recent study, at a dose of 20 mg/m² every 6 to 8 weeks, by itself or in combination with 5-fluorouracil, leukopenia occurred in 74 of 94 patients, with 10 being in the life-threatening category; and thrombocytopenia occurred in 68 of 94 patients, with 18 being in the life-threatening category. In a previous study, at doses of 0.5 mg/kg/day for 5 days and repeating once monthly, or 0.25 mg/kg every two weeks, leukopenia and/or thrombocytopenia occurred in 605 of 937 patients. The return to normal counts after cessation of therapy was within 10 weeks. Mitomycin produces cumulative myelosuppression.

Integument and Mucous Membrane Toxicity: This has occurred in approximately 4% of patients treated with mitomycin. Cellulitis at the injection site has been reported and is occasionally severe. Stomatitis and alopecia also occur frequently. Rashes are rarely reported. The most important dermatological problem with this drug, however, is the necrosis and consequent sloughing of tissue which results if the drug is extravasated during injection.

Extravasation may occur with or without an accompanying stinging or burning sensation and even if there is adequate blood return when the injection needle is aspirated. There have been reports of delayed erythema and/or ulceration occurring either at or distant from the injection site, weeks to months after mitomycin, even when no obvious evidence of extravasation was observed during administration. Skin grafting has been required in some of the cases.

Pulmonary Toxicity: Refer to section on pulmonary toxicity in Precautions.

Renal Toxicity: A small number of patients demonstrated a significant rise in BUN from a baseline pretherapy. There appeared to be no correlation between total dose administered or duration of therapy and renal toxicity. Seventy-five percent of the patients with a definite renal toxicity had evidence of metastatic disease. The data, to date, are inconclusive as far as a direct relationship of mitomycin to renal toxicity.

Hemolytic Uremic Syndrome (HUS): A serious and often fatal syndrome consisting of microangiopathic hemolytic anemia, thrombocytopenia, renal failure and hypertension has been reported in patients receiving mitomycin. Most of these patients received long-term therapy (6 to 12 months) with mitomycin in combination with fluorouracil and doxorubicin; however, some patients received mitomycin in combination with other drugs or were treated for less than 6 months.

Acute Side Effects: fever, hemolytic anemia, anorexia, stomatitis, hypoglycemia, mucositis and diarrhea have occurred.

Other Undesirable Side Effects: headache, blurring of vision, confusion, drowsiness, syncope, fatigue, weakness, edema, thrombophlebitis, hematemesis, nausea, vomiting, weight loss, ataxia and pain. These do not appear to be dose-related and it was difficult to determine whether these were dose-related or due to the primary or metastatic disease process.

Genitourinary irritation following intravesical administration indicated dysuria, cystitis, nocturia and increased frequency of micturition, hematuria and other symptoms of local irritation. Approximately 25% of the patients treated experienced irritative symptoms, but not all were unequivocally drug-related and may have been symptoms of the disease.

Dermatitis occurred in approximately 10% of the patients treated. It was commonly manifested as palmar rash with desquamation, generally appearing on the extremities and less often on the trunk, and also as genital rash. Topical steroids have been employed but their therapeutic value has not been determined.

Overdose: Symptoms and Treatment: No specific antidote for mitomycin is known. Management of overdosage would include general supportive measures to sustain the patient through any period of toxicity that might occur.

Dosage: Mitomycin should be given with care to avoid extravasation of the compound into the tissue. If extravasation occurs, cellulitis, ulceration and slough may result.

I.V. Use: After full hematological recovery from any previous chemotherapy, either of the following dosage schedules may be used at 6- to 8-week intervals. Because of cumulative myelosuppression, patients should be re-evaluated after each course of mitomycin and the dose reduced if the patient has experienced any toxicities (see Guide to Dosage Adjustment).

Doses greater than 20 mg/m² do not demonstrate increased effectiveness and are more toxic than lower doses. (1) 20 mg/m² i.v. as a single dose via a functioning i.v. catheter. (2) 2 mg/m²/day i.v for 5 days. After a drug-free interval of 2 days, 2 mg/m²/day for 5 days, thus making the total initial dose of 20 mg/m² given over 10 days.

Intravesical Use: 20 to 40 mg intravesically once per week for 8 weeks. Patients are advised to abstain from liquids for 12 hours prior to therapy. The patient is catheterized, bladder drained and mitomycin instilled. The solution should be retained for 2 hours. If desired, the patient may rotate positions every 15 minutes, for maximum-area contact.

The following schedule is suggested as a guide to dosage adjustment: see Table I.

Table I—Mitomycin for Injection, USP

Guide to Dosage Adjustment

Nadir After Prior Dose		Percentage of Prior Dose to be Given
Leukocytes	**Platelets**	
>4 000	>100 000	100%
3 000-3 999	75 000-99 999	100%
2 000-2 999	25 000-74 999	70%
<2 000	<25 000	50%

No repeat dosage should be given until leukocyte count has returned to 3 000 and platelet count to 75 000.

When mitomycin is used in combination with other myelosuppressive agents, the doses should be adjusted accordingly. If the disease continues to progress after 2 courses of mitomycin, the drug should be stopped since chances of response are minimal.

Reconstitution: Solutions for Reconstitution: Sterile Water for Injection.

To reconstitute a vial of 5 mg of mitomycin, add 10 mL of Sterile Water for Injection to obtain an approximate concentration of 0.5 mg/mL.

To reconstitute a vial of 20 mg of mitomycin, add 40 mL of Water for Injection to obtain an approximate concentration of 0.5 mg/mL.

Stability and Storage: Mitomycin vials should be stored between 15 and 25°C and protected from light.

Mitomycin for Injection, USP (cont'd)

Reconstituted with Sterile Water for Injection to a concentration of 0.5 mg/mL, mitomycin is stable for 72 hours refrigerated (2 to 8°C), or 24 hours at controlled room temperature (15 to 25°C). Protect from light.

Diluted in various i.v. fluids at controlled room temperature (15 to 25°C), to a concentration of 20 to 40 µg/mL: see Table II.

Table II—Mitomycin for Injection, USP

Dilution Stability

I.V. Fluid	Stability
0.9% Sodium Chloride Injection	11 hours
Sodium Lactate Injection	24 hours

The **combination** of mitomycin (5 to 15 mg) and heparin (1 000 to 10 000 units) in 30 mL of 0.9% Sodium Chloride Injection is stable for 24 hours at controlled room temperature (15 to 25°C).

Warning: The reconstituted and diluted solutions should be inspected visually for discoloration, haziness, precipitation, particulate matter and leakage prior to administration. Discard unused portion.

Handling and Disposal: 1. Preparation of mitomycin should be done in a vertical laminar flow hood (Biological Safety Cabinet—Class II). 2. Personnel preparing mitomycin should wear PVC gloves, safety glasses, disposable gowns and masks. 3. All needles, syringes, vials and other materials which have come in contact with mitomycin should be segregated and incinerated at 1 000°C or more. Sealed containers may explode sealed. Intact vials should be returned to the manufacturer for destruction. Proper precautions should be taken in packaging these materials for transport. 4. Personnel regularly involved in the preparation and handling of mitomycin should have biannual blood examinations.

Supplied: 5 mg: Each vial of sterile lyophilized powder contains: mitomycin 5 mg. Nonmedicinal ingredients: mannitol. Preservative-free. Single use vials, boxes of 1.

20 mg: Each vial of sterile lyophilized powder contains: mitomycin 20 mg. Nonmedicinal ingredients: mannitol. Preservative-free. Single use vials, boxes of 1.

Store between 15 and 25°C and protected from light.

New Product 1998

MITOMYCIN FOR INJECTION USP ℞

Novopharm

Antineoplastic

Pharmacology: Mitomycin was first investigated as an antibiotic in Japan. It was then found to be active as an antineoplastic agent. It selectively inhibits the synthesis of deoxyribonucleic acid (DNA). The exact point of mitomycin attachment to DNA remains unknown. There is a correlation between the guanine and cytosine content of DNA and the degree of mitomycin-induced cross-linking. At high concentrations of the drug, cellular RNA and protein synthesis are also suppressed.

Pharmacokinetics: In humans, mitomycin is rapidly cleared from the plasma after i.v. administration with a biphasic plasma elimination curve. Time required to reduce the serum concentration by 50% after a 30 mg bolus injection is 17 minutes. After injection of 30 mg, 20 mg or 10 mg i.v., the maximal serum concentrations were 2.4 µg/mL, 1.7 µg/mL and 0.52 µg/mL, respectively.

In general, the smaller the dose, the more rapidly blood levels of mitomycin decreased. Clearance is effected primarily by metabolism in the liver, but metabolism occurs in other tissues as well.

Approximately 10% of a dose of mitomycin is excreted unchanged in the urine. Since metabolic pathways are saturated at relatively low doses, the percent of a dose excreted in urine increases with increasing doses. In children, excretion of i.v. administered mitomycin is similar.

Mitomycin is not appreciably absorbed from the urinary bladder, following intravesical administration. Serial plasma samples from 55 patients treated with doses of 20 to 40 mg of mitomycin by intravesical instillation were assayed. There was no mitomycin detectable (assay limit 10 to 100 ng/mL) in any plasma samples collected during and 30 minutes post-therapy at any dose.

Indications: In the palliative treatment as an adjunct to surgery, radiation or chemotherapy for adenocarcinoma of the stomach and colon.

Mitomycin as a single agent is indicated as topical therapy for superficial (no invasion beyond the lamina propria) transitional cell carcinoma of the urinary bladder. Efficacy has been demonstrated both in patients who have had no prior intravesical chemotherapy and in those who have failed such therapy with thiotepa or other antineoplastic agents.

Contraindications: Patients who have demonstrated a hypersensitivity to it in the past; Patients with thrombocytopenia, leukopenia, coagulation disorder, or an increased bleeding tendency due to other causes.

Mitomycin is contraindicated for intravesical administration in patients who have demonstrated a hypersensitive or idiosyncratic reaction to it in the past.

Warnings: Caution: Mitomycin is a potent drug and should be used only by physicians experienced with cancer chemotherapeutic drugs (see Precautions). Blood counts should be taken weekly. Mitomycin must be discontinued or dosage reduced upon evidence of abnormal depression of the bone marrow or the development of significant renal or pulmonary toxicity.

It is recommended that mitomycin be administered under the supervision of a qualified physician experienced in the use of cancer chemotherapeutic agents. Since facilities for necessary laboratory studies must be available, hospitalization of patients is recommended.

Mitomycin should not be administered to any patient with a white blood cell count below 4 000 mm³ and a platelet count below 150 000 mm³, or to those with potentially serious infections.

Bone marrow depression, notably thrombocytopenia and leukopenia, is the most severe toxicity (see Adverse Effects). This may contribute to overwhelming infection in an already compromised, poor risk patient and may result in death.

In the treatment of each patient, the physician must weigh carefully the possibility of achieving therapeutic benefit versus the risk of toxicity. Studies have shown that mitomycin is carcinogenic in animals.

Pregnancy: Safe use of mitomycin in pregnant women has not been established. Mitomycin has known teratogenic properties in animals, therefore, the benefits derived from the use of mitomycin in pregnancy must be weighed against the hazards involved.

Precautions: Mitomycin should be administered, preferably, to patients who are hospitalized and who can be observed carefully and frequently during and after therapy.

It should be used with extreme caution in patients with significant impairment of renal function.

Since mitomycin has a high incidence of bone marrow depression, particularly thrombocytopenia and leukopenia, the following studies should be obtained frequently during therapy and for at least 7 weeks following therapy: platelet count, prothrombin time, bleeding time, white blood count and differential. The persistence of thrombocytopenia below 150 000 mm³ or a significant prolongation of prothrombin time or bleeding time, or a white blood cell count below 4 000 mm³ is an indication for the termination of therapy.

Patients should be advised of the potential toxicity of this drug, particularly bone marrow depression. A low incidence of septicemic deaths, as a result of leukopenia attributable to the drug, have been reported. Patients receiving mitomycin should be observed for evidence of renal toxicity. Mitomycin should not be given to patients with a serum creatinine greater than 1.7 mg %.

Mitomycin-associated pulmonary toxicity has been reported. Cases have been reported with both single-agent therapy and combination chemotherapy. Dyspnea and nonproductive cough are the usual presenting symptoms. Radiographic evidence of interstitial infiltrates may or may not be present. If other etiologies have been eliminated, a diagnosis of mitomycin-related pulmonary toxicity may be made.

Signs and symptoms of pneumonitis associated with mitomycin may be reversed if appropriate therapy is instituted early and mitomycin is discontinued. Corticosteroids have been reported by several authors to expedite symptomatic relief.

Acute shortness of breath and severe bronchospasm have been reported following the administration of vinca alkaloids in patients who had previously or simultaneously received mitomycin. The onset of this acute respiratory distress occurred within minutes to hours after the vinca alkaloid injection. The total number of doses for each drug has varied considerably. Bronchodilators, steroids and/or oxygen have produced symptomatic relief.

A few cases of adult respiratory distress syndrome have been reported in patients receiving mitomycin, in combination with other chemotherapy, and maintained at FiO_2 concentrations greater than 50% perioperatively. Therefore, caution should be exercised using only enough oxygen to provide adequate arterial saturation, since oxygen itself is toxic to the lungs. Careful attention should be paid to fluid balance and overhydration should be avoided.

Adverse Effects: Bone Marrow Toxicity: The most serious and most common toxicity of mitomycin is thrombocytopenia and leukopenia which occur anytime within 8 weeks after onset of therapy. In a recent study, at a dose of 20 mg/m² every 6 to 8 weeks, by itself or in combination with 5-fluorouracil, leukopenia occurred in 74 of 94 patients, with 10 being in the life-threatening category; and thrombocytopenia occurred in 68 of 94 patients, with 18 being in the life-threatening category. In a previous study, at doses of 0.5 mg/kg/day for 5 days and repeating once monthly, or 0.25 mg/kg every 2 weeks, leukopenia and/or thrombocytopenia occurred in 605 of 937 patients. The return to normal counts after cessation of therapy was within 10 weeks. Mitomycin produces cumulative myelosuppression.

Integument and Mucous Membrane Toxicity: This has occurred in approximately 4% of patients treated with mitomycin. Cellulitis at the injection site has been reported and is occasionally severe. Stomatitis and alopecia also occur frequently. Rashes are rarely reported.

The most important dermatological problem with this drug, however, is the necrosis and consequent sloughing of tissue which results if the drug is extravasated during injection.

Extravasation may occur with or without an accompanying stinging or burning sensation and even if there is adequate blood return when the injection needle is aspirated. There have been reports of delayed erythema and/or ulceration occurring either at or distant from the injection site, weeks to months after mitomycin, even when no obvious evidence of extravasation was observed during administration. Skin grafting has been required in some of the cases.

Pulmonary Toxicity: Refer to section on pulmonary toxicity under Precautions.

Renal Toxicity: A small number of patients demonstrated a significant rise in BUN from a baseline pretherapy. There appeared to be no correlation between total dose administered or duration of therapy and renal toxicity. Seventy-five percent of the patients with a definite renal toxicity had evidence of metastatic disease. The data, to date, are inconclusive as far as a direct relationship of mitomycin to renal toxicity.

Hemolytic Uremic Syndrome (HUS): A serious and often fatal syndrome consisting of microangiopathic hemolytic anemia, thrombocytopenia, renal failure, and hypertension has been reported in patients receiving mitomycin. Most of these patients received long-term therapy (6 to 12 months) with mitomycin in combination with fluorouracil and doxorubicin; however, some patients received mitomycin in combination with other drugs or were treated for less than 6 months.

Acute Side Effects: Fever, hemolytic anemia, anorexia, stomatitis, hypoglycemia, mucositis and diarrhea have occurred.

Other Undesirable Side Effects: headache, blurring of vision, confusion, drowsiness, syncope, fatigue, weakness, edema, thrombophlebitis, hematemesis, nausea, vomiting, weight loss, ataxia and pain. It is difficult to determine whether these side effects are dose-related or due to the primary or metastatic disease process.

Genitourinary Irritation: Genitourinary irritation following intravesical administration indicated dysuria, cystitis, nocturia and increased frequency of micturition, hematuria, and other symptoms of local irritation. Approximately 25% of the patients treated experienced irritative symptoms, but not all were unequivocally drug-related and may have been symptoms of the disease.

Dermatitis: Dermatitis occurred in approximately 10% of the patients treated. It was commonly manifested as palmar rash with desquamation, generally appearing on the extremities and less often on the trunk, and also as genital rash. Topical steroids have been employed but their therapeutic value has not been determined.

Overdose: Symptoms and Treatment: No specific antidote for mitomycin is known. Management of overdosage would include general supportive measures to sustain the patient through any period of toxicity that might occur.

Dosage: Mitomycin should be given with care to avoid extravasation of the compound into the tissue. If extravasation occurs, cellulitis, ulceration and slough may result.

To reconstitute a vial, add Sterile Water for Injection as listed in the Reconstitution Table I.

Table I—Mitomycin for Injection USP

Reconstitution

Vial Size	Diluent Added to Vial (mL)	Approximate Available Volume (mL)	Approximate Concentration (mg/mL)
5 mg	10	9.5	0.5
20 mg	40	39	0.5

Shake well until dissolved. If the product does not dissolve immediately, shake under warm tap water for approximately 2 minutes until a solution is obtained.

I.V.: After full hematological recovery from any previous chemotherapy, either of the following Dosage Schedules may be used at 6- to 8-week intervals. Because of cumulative myelosuppression, patients should be re-evaluated after each course of mitomycin and the dose reduced if the patient has experienced any toxicities (see Table II, Guide to Dosage Adjustment).

Doses greater than 20 mg/m² do not demonstrate increased effectiveness and are more toxic than lower doses. (1) 20 mg/m² i.v. as a single dose via a functioning i.v. catheter. (2) 2 mg/m²/day i.v. for 5 days. After a drug-free interval of 2 days, 2 mg/m²/day for 5 days, thus making the total initial dose of 20 mg/m² given over 10 days.

Intravesical: A dose of 20 to 40 mg intravesically once per week for 8 weeks. Patients are advised to abstain from liquids for 12 hours prior to therapy. The patient is catheterized, the bladder is drained and mitomycin is instilled. The solution should be retained for 2 hours. If desired, the patient may rotate positions every 15 minutes, for maximum area contact.

The schedule in Table II is suggested as a Guide to Dosage Adjustment.

Table II—Mitomycin for Injection USP

Guide to Dosage Adjustment

Nadir After Prior Dose: Leukocytes	Platelets	Percentage of Prior Dose to be Given
>4 000	>100 000	100%
3 000-3 999	75 000-99 999	100%
2 000-2 999	25 000-74 999	70%
<2 000	<25 000	50%

No repeat dosage should be given until leukocyte count has returned to 3 000 and platelet count to 75 000.

When mitomycin is used in combination with other myelosuppressive agents, the doses should be adjusted accordingly. If the disease continues to progress after 2 courses of mitomycin, the drug should be stopped since chances of response are minimal.

Reconstituted Solutions: Solutions for Reconstitution: Sterile Water for Injection. For more information, refer to the Reconstitution Table (see Table I).

Stability: Reconstituted with Sterile Water for Injection to a concentration of 0.5 mg/mL, mitomycin is stable for 14 days refrigerated or 7 days at controlled room temperature (15 to 30°C), protected from light.

Parenteral Products: Reconstituted solutions may be further diluted at controlled room temperature (15 to 30°C) with one of the following diluents to a concentration of 20 to 40 μg/mL (see Table III).

Table III—Mitomycin for Injection USP

Dilution

I.V. Fluid	Stability
5% Dextrose Injection	3 hours
0.9% Sodium Chloride Injection	12 hours
Sodium Lactate Injection	24 hours

The combination of mitomycin (5 to 15 mg) and heparin (1 000 to 10 000 units) in 30 mL of 0.9% Sodium Chloride Injection is stable for 48 hours at room temperature.

The reconstituted and diluted solutions should be inspected for discoloration, haziness, particulate matter and leakage prior to administration. Discard unused portion.

Handling and Disposal: Preparation of mitomycin should be done in a vertical laminar flow hood (Biological Safety Cabinet-Class II). Personnel preparing mitomycin should wear PVC gloves, safety glasses, disposal gowns and masks. All needles, syringes, vials and other materials which have come in contact with mitomycin should be segregated and incinerated at 1 000°C or more. Sealed containers may explode. Intact vials should be returned to the manufacturer for destruction. Proper precautions should be taken in packaging these materials for transport. Personnel regularly involved in the preparation and handling of mitomycin should have biannual blood examinations.

Supplied: 5 mg: Each vial contains: mitomycin 5 mg. Nonmedicinal ingredients: mannitol, sodium hydroxide and/or hydrochloric acid for pH adjustment. Single use vials packaged individually.

20 mg: Each vial contains: mitomycin 20 mg. Nonmedicinal ingredients: mannitol, sodium hydroxide and/or hydrochloric acid for pH adjustment. Single use vials packaged individually.

Store at controlled room temperature (15 to 30°C) protected from light.

Reviewed 1998

MIVACRON® Ⓟ

Glaxo Wellcome

Mivacurium Chloride

Nondepolarizing Skeletal Neuromuscular Blocking Agent

Pharmacology: Mivacurium is a short-acting, nondepolarizing skeletal neuromuscular blocking agent which is hydrolyzed by plasma cholinesterase. Mivacurium results in a blockade of neuromuscular transmission by binding competitively with cholinergic receptors on the motor end-plate to antagonize the action of acetylcholine.

Pharmacodynamics: The time to maximum neuromuscular block is similar for mivacurium and intermediate-acting agents (e.g., atracurium), but longer than for the ultra-short-acting agent, succinylcholine. The clinically effective duration of action of mivacurium is one-third to one-half that of intermediate-acting agents and 2 to 2.5 times that of succinylcholine.

The average ED_{95} (dose required to produce 95% suppression of the adductor pollicis muscle response to ulnar nerve stimulation) of mivacurium is 0.07 mg/kg (range: 0.06 to 0.09 mg/kg) in adults receiving opioid/nitrous oxide/oxygen anesthesia. The pharmacodynamics of various doses of $\geq ED_{95}$ administered over 5 to 15 seconds during stable-state opioid/nitrous oxide/oxygen anesthesia are summarized in Table I. Administration of mivacurium over 60 seconds does not alter the time to maximum neuromuscular block or the duration of action.

When administered during the induction of adequate anesthesia using thiopental or propofol, nitrous oxide/oxygen, and co-induction agents such as fentanyl and/or midazolam, doses of 0.15 mg/kg ($2\times ED_{95}$) mivacurium administered over 5 to 15 seconds or 0.2 mg/kg mivacurium administered over 30 seconds produced generally good-to-excellent tracheal intubation conditions in 2.5 to 3 and 2 to 2.5 minutes, respectively. A dose of 0.25 mg/kg mivacurium administered as a divided dose (0.15 mg/kg followed 30 seconds later by 0.10 mg/kg) produced generally good-to-excellent intubation conditions in 1.5 to 2 minutes after initiating the dosing regimen. Rapid bolus administration of mivacurium at doses of 0.20 and 0.25 mg/kg should be avoided, as these doses may be associated with transient decreases in mean arterial blood pressure (MAP) and increases in heart rate (HR) in some patients (see Hemodynamics and Dosage).

Tachyphylaxis or cumulative neuromuscular blocking effects are not observed when mivacurium is administered as repeated maintenance doses or as a continuous infusion for up to 2.5 hours in ASA Physical Status I-II patients. Spontaneous recovery after infusion is independent of the duration of infusion and comparable to recovery reported for single doses (see Table I). Limited data are available from patients receiving infusions of mivacurium for longer than 2.5 hours.

Mivacurium has a higher ED_{95} (0.1 mg/kg), faster onset, shorter duration of action, and more rapid recovery time in 2 to 12 year-old children than in adults (see Table I). Under conditions of opioid/nitrous oxide/oxygen anesthesia, the time to maximum neuromuscular block for 0.2 mg/kg mivacurium in children is approximately 80 seconds faster than the time for an equipotent dose (0.15 mg/kg) in adults. Recovery following reversal is faster in children than in adults. In children, the mean time for spontaneous recovery of the twitch response from 25 to 75% of control amplitude is about 5 minutes (n=4) following an initial dose of 0.2 mg/kg mivacurium.

Antagonism: The neuromuscular block produced by mivacurium is readily antagonized by anticholinesterase agents. The deeper the level of neuromuscular block at reversal, the longer the time required for recovery of neuromuscular function and the greater the dose of anticholinesterase agent required.

Table I—Mivacron

The Pharmacodynamic Dose-Response of Mivacron ($\geq ED_{95}$) During Stable-State Opioid/Nitrous Oxide/Oxygen Anesthesia in ASA Physical Status I-II Patients

Initial Mivacron Dose (mg/kg)	Maximum Twitch Suppression[a] %	Time to Maximum Block[a] (min)	Time to Spontaneous Recovery[a]: 5% Recovery (min)	25% Recovery[b] (min)	95% Recovery[c] (min)	T_4/T_1 Ratio ≥75%[c] (min)	25–75% Recovery Index (min)
Adults: Dose administered over 5 to 15 s							
0.07–0.08 (n=18)	91.2 (68–100)	4.9 (3.5–7.3)	8 (7–9)	12 (10–16)	21 (10–32)	21 (10–28)	6 (4.5–9.0)
0.10 (n=18)	97.3 (80–100)	3.9 (2.0–6.7)	12 (8–19)	14 (8–24)	25 (14–36)	24 (16–36)	6 (2.8–9.0)
0.15 (n=50)	99.6 (53–100)	3.3 (1.5–8.8)	13 (6–31)	16 (9–38)	26 (16–41)	26 (15–45)	6 (3.3–9.2)
0.20[d] (n=50)	99.9 (93–100)	2.5 (1.2–6.0)	16 (10–29)	20 (10–36)	31 (15–51)	34 (19–56)	7 (3.6–15.5)
0.25[d] (n=48)	100 (97–100)	2.3 (1.0–4.8)	19 (11–29)	23 (14–38)	34 (22–64)	43 (26–75)	8 (3.5–24.3)
Adults: Dose administered over 30 s (0.20 mg/kg) and 60 s (0.25 mg/kg)							
0.20 (n=27)	100 (95–100)	2.9 (1.5–4.3)	16 (10–25)	19 (8–29)	31 (15–43)	35 (29–46)	7 (4.0–10.0)
0.25 (n=18)	100 (100–100)	1.8 (1.10–2.5)	17 (10–26)	21 (12–31)	30 (18–47)	33 (28–38)	6 (3.4–10.8)
Children							
2 to 12 years: Dose administered over 5 to 15 s							
0.11–0.12 (n=17)	98.3 (89–100)	2.0 (1.2–4.6)	5 (3–9)	7 (4–10)	—	—	—
0.20 (n=18)	99.5 (95–100)	1.9 (1.3–3.3)	7 (3–12)	10 (6–15)	19 (14–26)	16 (12–23)	5 (3.8–5.4)
0.25 (n=9)	100 (100–100)	1.6 (1.0–2.2)	7 (4–9)	9 (5–12)	—	—	—

[a]Values shown are medians of means from individual studies (range of individual patient values).
[b]Duration of clinically effective neuromuscular block.
[c]Data available for as few as 40% of adults in specific dose groups and for 22% of children in the 0.20 mg/kg dose group due to administration of reversal agents or additional doses of mivacurium prior to 95% recovery or T_4/T_1 ratio recovery to ≥75%.
[d]Rapid administration not recommended due to possibility of decreased blood pressure. Administer 0.20 mg/kg over 30 seconds; administer 0.25 mg/kg as divided dose (0.15 mg/kg followed 30 seconds later by 0.10 mg/kg). See Dosage. When mivacurium was administered as a divided dose of 0.15 mg/kg followed 30 seconds later by 0.1 mg/kg, the maximum reduction in train-of-four count was observed at 4.6 minutes after the initial mivacurium dose.

Mivacron (cont'd)

Because spontaneous recovery after mivacurium is rapid, routine reversal may not always result in a clinical benefit.

Histamine Release: Like certain other benzylisoquinoline compounds, mivacurium has a tendency to release histamine, particularly at higher doses. Plasma histamine levels generally peak within the first few minutes following the initial mivacurium bolus injection and return toward baseline by 5 minutes post-injection. In clinical trials, the histamine release response was reduced when 0.2 and 0.25 mg/kg doses were administered slowly over 30 or 60 seconds. Administration of the 0.15 mg/kg dose at injection rates slower than 5 to 15 seconds has not been studied for effects on histamine release, but may be expected to result in a diminished occurrence of this reaction. See Table II.

Table II—Mivacron

Histamine Release Responses Following the Administration of Mivacron at Various Doses and Delivery Rates

Parameters: Dose (mg/kg)	Delivery Rate (s)	Post-Injection Sample Time (min)	Plasma Histamine Concentration (pg/mL): n	Mean	Range	% Pts ≥ 2-fold Increase
0.15	5–15	0	11	549	109–2 138	
		2	11	877	101–2 902	27
		5	11	429	93–1 484	18
0.20	5–15	0	30	466	113–2 279	
		2	30	2 270	103–14 999	63
		5	30	950	63–3 419	53
0.20	30	0	18	757	153–2 524	
		2	18	1 209	231–8 548	39
		5	18	657	211–3 239	22
0.25	5–15	0	30	534	137–2 121	
		2	30	6 341	321–57 257	77
		5	30	1 710	91–18 103	37
0.25	30	0	9	667	252–2 039	
		2	9	1 453	178–4 275	44
		5	9	911	126–2 521	11
0.25	60	0	18	560	79–5 076	
		2	18	518	128–2 507	33
		5	18	372	88–1 020	17

Hemodynamics: Mivacurium-induced histamine release is sometimes associated with decreases in mean arterial blood pressure (MAP) and increases in heart rate (HR). For patients receiving bolus doses of 0.15 mg/kg mivacurium over 5 to 15 seconds during clinical trials, average mean arterial blood pressure values at the time of maximal change during the first 5 minutes post-injection were in the range of 88 to 102% of pre-injection values. At higher doses of 0.2 to 0.3 mg/kg delivered over 5 to 15 seconds, transient decreases in mean arterial blood pressure of 20% or more were reported in 45 to 85% of patients (see Adverse Effects, Table V on following page). These decreases in mean arterial pressure were usually maximal within 1 to 3 minutes following the dose and typically resolved without treatment in an additional 1 to 3 minutes, although pharmacological intervention was occasionally necessary. Owing to the increased incidence of decreases in mean arterial blood pressure at doses of 0.2 to 0.3 mg/kg, rapid bolus administration of these doses in routine clinical practice should be avoided. Decreases in mean arterial pressure are diminished by administering mivacurium slowly over 30 to 60 seconds (see Dosage).

Children experience minimal changes in MAP or HR after administration of ≤0.2 mg/kg mivacurium over 5 to 15 seconds. Higher doses (≥0.25 mg/kg) may be associated with transient decreases in MAP in some children (see Table V on following page).

In patients with cardiovascular disease undergoing coronary artery bypass grafting or valve replacement procedures, mivacurium was associated with few changes in MAP or HR when administered as a 0.15 mg/kg dose over 60 seconds. Higher doses (0.2 to 0.25 mg/kg) administered over 60 seconds were associated with transient decreases in MAP in some patients. More rapid administrations of mivacurium have not been studied in this patient population.

Pharmacokinetics: The mean elimination half-life of mivacurium ranges from 1.7 to 2.6 minutes in healthy, young adults administered 0.1 to 0.25 mg/kg mivacurium. Mean plasma clearance rates range from 40 to 70 mL/min/kg and mean steady-state volume of distribution values range from 0.08 to 0.11 L/kg. The short elimination half-life and high clearance are consistent with the short duration of action of mivacurium.

Geriatrics: Pharmacokinetic parameters in 9 healthy elderly patients (68 to 77 years) administered 0.1 mg/kg mivacurium were not significantly different from those of 9 healthy young adults (21 to 47 years). However, the onset of maximum twitch suppression was delayed by approximately 1 to 2 minutes (n=8). The clinically effective duration of action of 0.1 mg/kg mivacurium averaged 3 to 4 minutes longer in elderly patients than in young adults (see Table III).

Renal Impairment: Pharmacokinetic parameters were not significantly different in 9 patients with end-stage kidney disease undergoing kidney transplant surgery and 8 control patients with normal renal function. However, average times from injection of 0.15 mg/kg mivacurium to 25 and 95% recovery were longer in patients with end-stage kidney disease than in patients with normal renal function (see Table III).

Hepatic Impairment: In 9 patients with end-stage liver disease undergoing liver transplant surgery, plasma clearance was approximately 50% lower than that in 8 control patients with normal hepatic function, while the elimination half-life increased to 4.4 minutes from the 1.8 minute control value. Average times from injection of 0.15 mg/kg mivacurium to 25 and 95% recovery were longer in patients with end-stage liver disease (n=8) than in patients with normal hepatic function (see Table III). The longer duration of action in patients with end-stage liver disease is likely related to the markedly decreased plasma cholinesterase activity (30% of healthy patient values).

Stereochemistry: Mivacurium is a mixture of three stereoisomers: the trans-trans diester, the cis-trans diester, and the cis-cis diester. These isomers do not interconvert in vivo. The two more potent isomers, cis-trans (36% of the mixture) and trans-trans (57% of the mixture), have very high clearance rates that exceed cardiac output, reflecting the extensive metabolism by plasma cholinesterase. The volume of distribution is relatively small, reflecting limited tissue distribution secondary to the polarity and large molecular weight of mivacurium. The combination of high metabolic clearance and low distribution volume results in a short elimination half-life of approximately 2 minutes for the two active isomers. These findings are consistent with the short duration of action of mivacurium. Table IV presents the results from a study in which 9 ASA physical status I-II patients received a 5 μg/kg/min mivacurium infusion for a 60-minute period followed by a 10 μg/kg/min infusion for an additional 60 minutes. The pharmacokinetics of these isomers appeared to be dose-proportional as the steady-state concentrations of the cis-trans and trans-trans isomers doubled when the infusion rate was increased from 5 to 10 μg/kg/min.

Table IV—Mivacron

Stereoisomer Pharmacokinetic Parameters[a] of Mivacron in ASA Physical Status I-II Adult Patients[b] [n=9] During Opioid/Nitrous Oxide/Oxygen Anesthesia

Parameter	trans-trans isomer	cis-trans isomer	cis-cis isomer
t½ (min)	2.3 (1.4–3.6)	2.1 (0.8–4.8)	55[c] (32–102)
Volume of Distribution (L/kg)	0.15 (0.06–0.24)	0.27 (0.08–0.56)	0.31 (0.18–0.46)
Plasma Clearance (mL/min/kg)	53 (32–105)	99 (52–230)	4.2 (2.4-5.4)

[a]Values shown are mean (range).
[b]Ages 31 to 48 years.
[c]n=8.

In cats, the cis-cis isomer (6% of the mixture) has approximately one-tenth the neuromuscular blocking potency of the trans-trans and cis-trans isomers. The neuromuscular blocking potency of the cis-cis isomer in humans has not been established; however, modeling of clinical pharmacokinetic/pharmacodynamic data suggests that the cis-cis isomer produces minimal (<5%) neuromuscular block during a 2-hour infusion. In studies in which infusions of up to 2.5 hours were administered to ASA Physical Status I-II patients, the 25 to 75% recovery times were independent of the duration of infusion, suggesting that the cis-cis isomer does not contribute significant neuromuscular block during use for up to 2.5 hours. Limited data are available from infusions of longer duration or from patients with compromised elimination capacities (hepatic or renal failure).

Metabolism and Excretion: Hydrolysis by plasma cholinesterase is the primary mechanism for inactivation of mivacurium and yields a quaternary monoester, a quaternary alcohol and a dicarboxylic acid. Tests in which these metabolites were administered to cats and dogs suggest that each metabolite is unlikely to produce significant neuromuscular, autonomic, or cardiovascular effects following administration of mivacurium. Little mivacurium is excreted unchanged in urine and bile, but urine and bile are important elimination pathways for the metabolites. In young adults, approximately 40 to 50% of an administered dose is excreted in the urine within 5 to 6 hours, while in the elderly approximately 30% of the total dose is excreted within this time span. High metabolite concentrations (412 to 1 832 times the simultaneously determined plasma concentration) were found in samples of bile approximately 70 to 90 minutes after an initial dose of mivacurium in patients undergoing cholecystectomy.

Indications: As an adjunct to general anesthesia, to facilitate non-emergency tracheal intubation and to provide skeletal muscle relaxation during surgery.

Contraindications: Patients with a known hypersensitivity to this or other benzylisoquinolinium compounds or with a history

Table III—Mivacron

Pharmacodynamic Parameters[a] of Mivacron in Different Patient Groups During Isoflurane/Nitrous Oxide/Oxygen Anesthesia

Parameter	ASA Physical Status I-II: Young Adult Patients (21-47 years) (n=9)	Young Adult Patients (20-36 years) (n=8)	Elderly Patients (68-77 years) (n=8)	Kidney Transplant Patients (27-41 years) (n=9)	Liver Transplant Patients[b] (22-59 years) (n=8)
Initial Dose[c]	0.10 mg/kg	0.15 mg/kg	0.10 mg/kg	0.15 mg/kg	0.15 mg/kg
Maximum Block (%)	98 (83–100)	99.8 (98–100)	99 (95–100)	100 (100–100)	100 (100-100)
Time to Maximum Block (min)	3.2 (2.0–6.0)	1.9 (0.8–3.5)	4.8 (3.0–7.0)	2.6 (1.0–4.5)	2.1 (1.0–4.0)
Clinically Effective Duration of Block[d] (min)	17 (9–29)	19 (12–30)	20 (14–28)	30 (19–58)	57 (29–80)

[a]Values shown are mean (range).
[b]Liver transplant patients received isoflurane without nitrous oxide.
[c]Doses administered over 5–15 seconds.
[d]Time from injection to 25% recovery of the control twitch height.

(e.g., severe anaphylactoid reactions or asthma) suggesting the risk of serious adverse reactions in response to histamine release. Multiple-dose vials of Mivacron contain benzyl alcohol, while single-dose vials do not. Use from multiple-dose vials is contraindicated in patients with a known hypersensitivity to benzyl alcohol.

In newborn infants (children less than 1 month in age), benzyl alcohol has been associated with an increased incidence of neurological and other complications which are sometimes fatal. I.V. preparations containing benzyl alcohol should not be used in newborns.

Warnings: Mivacurium should be used only by those trained in airway management and respiratory support. Equipment and personnel must be immediately available for tracheal intubation and support of ventilation, including administration of positive pressure oxygen. Adequacy of respiration must be assured through assisted or controlled ventilation. Reversal agents should be immediately available. A peripheral nerve stimulator should be employed to monitor drug response, need for additional relaxant, and adequacy of spontaneous recovery or anticholinesterase antagonism.

General: Mivacurium has no known effect on consciousness, pain threshold, or cerebration. To avoid distress to the patient, neuromuscular block should not be induced before unconsciousness.

Histamine Release: The possibility of substantial histamine release with consequent bronchospasm or anaphylaxis in sensitive individuals must be considered. Particular caution should be observed when considering the use of mivacurium in patients for whom substantial histamine release would be especially hazardous (e.g., patients with clinically significant cardiovascular disease) or in patients with any history suggesting a greater than normal sensitivity to histamine release. Release of histamine is related to the dose and speed of injection. If mivacurium is to be administered to these patients, an initial dose not exceeding 0.15 mg/kg should be administered slowly over 1 minute. Hemodynamic status should be monitored and adequate hydration assured.

Homozygotes for Atypical Plasma Cholinesterase: Mivacurium is not recommended for patients who are known or suspected to be homozygotes for the atypical plasma cholinesterase gene.

Other Diseases and Disorders: In patients who have neuromuscular diseases such as myasthenia gravis or the myasthenic (Eaton-Lambert) syndrome, small doses of neuromuscular blocking agents may have profound effects. For patients having conditions in which prolonged neuromuscular blockade is a possibility (e.g., neuromuscular disease, carcinomatosis, severe cachexia or debilitation), a peripheral nerve stimulator and use of a small test dose (0.015 to 0.02 mg/kg) may be of particular value in monitoring the response to the administration of muscle relaxants.

Mivacurium has not been studied in patients with bronchial asthma or burns or during vaginal delivery or cesarean section. The use of mivacurium in these situations is, therefore, not recommended.

Long-Term Use in the Intensive Care Unit: To reduce the possibility of prolonged neuromuscular blockade and other complications that might occur following long-term use in the ICU, mivacurium or any other neuromuscular blocking agent should be administered in carefully adjusted doses by or under the supervision of experienced clinicians who are familiar with its actions and with appropriate peripheral nerve stimulator muscle monitoring techniques.

Reversal of Neuromuscular Blockade: Evidence of spontaneous recovery from neuromuscular blockade should be observed prior to administration of reversal agents (e.g., neostigmine). The use of a peripheral nerve stimulator to evaluate recovery prior to and during reversal of neuromuscular blockade is strongly recommended.

Compatibility: Mivacurium injection is acidic (pH 3.5 to 5.5) and should not be mixed in the same syringe with highly alkaline solutions having a pH greater than 8.5 (e.g., barbiturate solutions) or administered simultaneously through the same needle during i.v. infusion. In the presence of an alkaline solution, there is a risk that mivacurium may be inactivated and a free acid precipitated.

Precautions: Cardiovascular Disease: Caution should be exercised in administering mivacurium to patients with clinically significant cardiovascular disease for whom transient decreases in blood pressure would be especially hazardous. In clinical trials, mivacurium has been administered to 106 ASA III and IV patients undergoing coronary artery bypass graft (CABG) and valve replacement procedures during narcotic anesthesia. When administered as a 0.15 mg/kg bolus dose, delivered over 60 seconds, mivacurium did not result in major fluctuations in mean arterial pressure in these patients (mean values 98 to 101% of baseline at 2 minutes post-injection, range 84 to 110%). However, when mivacurium was administered at 0.2 or 0.25 mg/kg doses over 60 seconds, individual patients experienced transient episodes of marked hypotension (see Adverse Effects, Table V). More rapid rates of bolus delivery have not been tested in patients with cardiovascular disease.

In clinical trials in ASA I and II patients, a 0.15 mg/kg dose of mivacurium delivered over 5 to 15 seconds was associated with transient decreases in mean arterial pressure of 20% or more in 21% of patients.

Mivacurium has no clinically significant effect on heart rate at recommended doses and will not counteract the bradycardia produced by many anesthetic agents or by vagal stimulation.

Long-Term Use in the Intensive Care Unit: No information is available concerning the efficacy and safety of long-term (days to weeks) i.v. mivacurium infusion to facilitate mechanical ventilation in the intensive care unit (ICU).

In rare cases, long-term use of other neuromuscular blocking drugs to facilitate mechanical ventilation in ICU settings has been associated with prolonged paralysis and/or skeletal muscle weakness that is first noted during attempts to wean patients from the ventilator. In such patients, neuromuscular blockade may have been enhanced by acid-base or electrolyte imbalances, hypoxic episodes of varying duration, extreme debilitation, and/or concurrent treatment with broad spectrum antibiotics, narcotics and/or steroids. Additionally, patients immobilized for extended periods frequently develop symptoms consistent with disuse muscle atrophy. The recovery picture may vary from regaining movement and strength in all muscles to initial recovery of movement of the facial muscles and small muscles of the extremities then to the remaining muscles. In rare cases recovery may require an extended period of time or even rehabilitation. Therefore, when long-term mechanical ventilation is indicated, the risk-benefit ratio of neuromuscular blockade must be considered.

Whenever the use of mivacurium or any neuromuscular blocking agent is contemplated in the ICU, it is recommended that a peripheral nerve stimulator be used to continuously monitor neuromuscular transmission during administration and recovery. Additional doses of mivacurium or any other neuromuscular blocking agent should not be given before there is a definite response to T_1 or to the first twitch. If no response is elicited, the infusion should be discontinued until a response returns.

Burns: Resistance to nondepolarizing neuromuscular blocking agents may develop in patients with burns, depending upon the time elapsed since the injury and the size of the burn. Patients with burns may have reduced pseudocholinesterase activity which may offset this resistance. Mivacurium has not been studied in patients with burns, but use of a test dose (0.015 to 0.02 mg/kg) is recommended.

Acid-Base or Electrolyte Abnormalities: Acid-base and/or electrolyte abnormalities may antagonize or potentiate the action of neuromuscular blocking agents. For example, hyperkalemia has been reported to antagonize nondepolarizing agents while hypokalemia has been associated with an enhancement of their activity.

Histamine Release: In 11 patients administered a 0.15 mg/kg bolus dose of mivacurium over 5 to 15 seconds, mean plasma histamine levels were increased 1.6-fold (range: 0.5 to 4-fold) at 2 minutes post-injection and returned to near baseline levels at 5 minutes post-injection. At a dose of 0.2 mg/kg delivered over 5 to 15 seconds, mean histamine levels were typically increased 3- to 6-fold at 2 minutes post-injection. When administration of the drug was slowed to 30 seconds, the 0.2 mg/kg dose typically resulted in a 2-fold increase in histamine levels. Slow bolus injections should be considered whenever the risk of histamine release is to be minimized.

I.M. Use: No data are available to support the use of mivacurium by i.m. injection.

Renal and Hepatic Disease: The effects of renal and hepatic dysfunction on the action of mivacurium have been studied in a small number of patients with end-stage kidney (n=9) or liver disease (n=8) undergoing transplantation surgery. For kidney transplant patients, the mean 25 and 95% recovery times were increased by 1.6 and 1.9 times, respectively, over the values obtained in elective surgery patients (n=8). For liver transplant patients, both of these recovery times were tripled. The possibility of prolonged neuromuscular block must be considered when mivacurium is used in patients with renal or hepatic disease. Chronic hepatic diseases such as hepatitis, liver abscess, and cirrhosis of the liver are commonly associated with pronounced reductions in plasma cholinesterase activity. Acute or chronic renal disease may also be associated with reduced plasma cholinesterase activity.

Plasma Cholinesterase Deficiency: The possibility of prolonged neuromuscular block following the administration of mivacurium must be considered in patients with reduced plasma cholinesterase (pseudocholinesterase: PsChE) activity.

PsChE activity may be diminished in the presence of genetic abnormalities of PsChE (e.g., patients heterozygous or homozygous for atypical PsChE), pregnancy, liver or kidney disease, malignant tumors, infections, burns, anemia, decompensated heart disease, peptic ulcer or myxedema. PsChE activity may also be diminished by chronic administration of oral contraceptives, glucocorticoids, or certain MAO inhibitors and by irreversible inhibitors of PsChE (e.g., organophosphate insecticides, echothiophate, and certain antineoplastic drugs). Consideration should be given to administration of a test dose of mivacurium in patients suspected of having a clinically significant reduction of PsChE activity.

Mivacurium has been used safely in patients heterozygous for the atypical plasma cholinesterase gene. In patients with the heterozygous genotype (1 in 40 patients), the mean clinically effective duration of action of 0.1 and 0.2 mg/kg doses is increased by approximately 50%.

As with succinylcholine, patients homozygous for atypical PsChE (1 in 2 500 patients) are extremely sensitive to the neuromuscular blocking effect of mivacurium. In 4 of these patients, a small dose of 0.03 mg/kg produced complete neuromuscular block for 26 to 128 minutes. Once spontaneous recovery had begun, neuromuscular block produced by mivacurium in patients homozygous for atypical PsChE could be antagonized with conventional doses of neostigmine. In 1 adult patient who was homozygous for the atypical plasma cholinesterase gene, a 0.18 mg/kg dose of mivacurium produced complete neuromuscular blockade for about 4 hours. Recovery of all 4 responses to train-of-four stimulation occurred after 6 hours and extubation was performed after 8 hours.

Malignant Hyperthermia: Multiple factors in anesthesia practice are suspected of triggering malignant hyperthermia (MH), a potentially fatal hypermetabolic state of skeletal muscle. Halogenated anesthetic agents and succinylcholine are recognized as the principal pharmacologic triggering agents in MH-susceptible patients; however, since MH can develop in the absence of established triggering agents, the clinician should be prepared to recognize and treat MH in any patient scheduled for general anesthesia. In a study of 8 MH-susceptible pigs, mivacurium did not trigger MH. Mivacurium has not been studied in MH-susceptible patients.

Drug Interactions: Mivacurium has been administered safely following succinylcholine-facilitated tracheal intubation. Prior administration of succinylcholine can potentiate the neuromuscular blocking effects of nondepolarizing agents. Evidence of spontaneous recovery from succinylcholine should be observed before the administration of mivacurium. No information is available on the administration of mivacurium, prior to succinylcholine, to attenuate some of the side effects of succinylcholine (e.g., muscle pain and fasciculations). The administration of mivacurium in conjunction with other nondepolarizing neuromuscular blocking agents, simultaneously or consecutively, has been reported to produce neuromuscular blockade of a degree and duration exceeding that which might be expected from an equipotent total dose of mivacurium. Any synergistic effect may vary between different drug combinations.

A depolarizing muscle relaxant such as succinylcholine should not be administered to prolong the neuromuscular blocking effects of nondepolarizing agents, as this may result in a prolonged and complex block which can be difficult to reverse with anticholinesterase drugs.

Based on data from 2 studies of adult patients receiving isoflurane (n=34) or enflurane (n=32) anesthesia, these agents may decrease the ED_{50} doses of mivacurium by as much as 25%. Mivacurium bolus doses in the recommended therapeutic range are not potentiated by halogenated anesthetics in a consistent or clinically significant manner. In some clinical studies, infusion requirements were approximately 30% lower during steady-state anesthesia with enflurane or isoflurane than during opioid/nitrous oxide/oxygen anesthesia. Halothane has little or no effect on the ED_{50} of mivacurium, but may prolong its duration of action and decrease the average infusion requirement in adult patients.

Drugs that may enhance the neuromuscular blocking action of nondepolarizing agents such as mivacurium include certain antibiotics (e.g., aminoglycosides, tetracyclines, bacitracin, polymyxins, lincomycin, clindamycin, colistin and sodium colistimethate), magnesium salts, lithium salts, local anesthetics, procainamide and quinidine. The neuromuscular blocking effects of mivacurium may also be enhanced by drugs that reduce plasma cholinesterase activity (e.g., chronically administered oral contraceptives, glucocorticoids, pancuronium or

Mivacron (cont'd)

certain MAO inhibitors) or by drugs that irreversibly inhibit plasma cholinesterase (e.g., organophosphate insecticides, echothiophate, and certain antineoplastic drugs).

Pregnancy: (Teratogenic Effects): Teratology testing in non-ventilated pregnant rats and mice revealed no maternal or fetal toxicity or teratogenic effects. However, as mivacurium was administered by the s.c. route at sub-paralyzing doses, the relevance of these studies to the clinical use of the drug cannot be assessed. Because animal reproduction studies have not been performed under conditions that would approximate those of clinical use, mivacurium should be used during pregnancy only if the potential benefit justifies the potential risk to the fetus. There are no studies of mivacurium in pregnant women.

Labor and Delivery: The use of mivacurium during labor, vaginal delivery or cesarean section has not been studied in humans. Doses of 0.08 and 0.2 mg/kg mivacurium given to 3 female beagles undergoing cesarean section resulted in negligible levels of mivacurium in umbilical vessel blood of neonates and no deleterious effects on the puppies. In humans, it is not known whether mivacurium administered to the mother has effects on the fetus. The possibility that a forceps delivery will be necessary may increase. The possibility of respiratory depression in the neonate should be considered following deliveries during which a neuromuscular blocking agent has been administered. The action of neuromuscular blocking agents may be enhanced by magnesium salts administered for the management of toxemia of pregnancy.

Lactation: It is not known whether mivacurium is excreted in human milk. Because many drugs are excreted in human milk, caution should be exercised when mivacurium is administered to a nursing woman.

Children: For children 2 to 12 years of age, see Pharmacology and Dosage. The safety and efficacy of mivacurium in children below the age of 2 years have not been established.

Geriatrics: Mivacurium has been administered to elderly patients ≥65 years of age (n=64), including patients with significant cardiovascular disease (n=31) (see Cardiovascular Disease). The duration of neuromuscular block may be slightly longer in elderly patients (see Pharmacology).

Obesity: Ideal body weight should be considered in dosage calculations for obese patients with appropriate attention to the attendant risk of underdosing. Severe obesity may pose airway or ventilatory problems before, during, or after the use of nondepolarizing neuromuscular blockers.

Increased Volume of Distribution: The onset of action of neuromuscular blocking agents may be delayed in patients in whom the volume of distribution is increased as a result of old age, edematous states, or cardiovascular disease. In these patients, more time should be permitted for the drug to achieve its maximal effect.

Hypothermia: Hypothermia (25 to 28°C) has been associated with a decreased requirement for nondepolarizing neuromuscular blocking agents.

Adverse Effects: Mivacurium was well tolerated during extensive clinical trials. Prolonged neuromuscular block, which is an important adverse experience associated with neuromuscular blocking agents as a class, was reported as an adverse experience in 3 of 2 074 patients administered mivacurium. In 2 074 patients administered mivacurium in clinical trials, the following adverse experiences were reported (all events judged by investigators during the clinical trials to have a possible causal relationship): incidence >1%: Cardiovascular: flushing (15%). Incidence <1%: Cardiovascular: hypotension, tachycardia, bradycardia, cardiac arrhythmia, phlebitis; Respiratory: bronchospasm, wheezing, hypoxemia. Dermatological: rash, urticaria, erythema, injection site reaction. Neurologic: dizziness. Musculoskeletal: muscle spasms. Nonspecific: prolonged drug effect.

Skin flushing, erythema, urticaria, hypotension, tachycardia, wheezing, or bronchospasm associated with the use of mivacurium have been attributed to histamine release. Histamine release is dose related and more common following the rapid administration of initial doses of 0.2 mg/kg or more and can be reduced by injecting mivacurium slowly over 30 to 60 seconds or in divided doses over 30 seconds.

The most commonly reported adverse experience was transient, dose-related cutaneous flushing about the face, neck and/or chest. In clinical trials, flushing was reported in approximately 25% of adult patients who received 0.15 mg/kg over 5 to 15 seconds. Flushing reactions typically had an onset time of 1 to 2 minutes and a duration of 3 to 5 minutes.

Hypotension was infrequently reported as an adverse experience in the clinical trials of mivacurium. One of 332 (0.3%) healthy adults who received 0.15 mg/kg mivacurium over 5 to 15 seconds and none of 37 cardiac surgery patients who received 0.15 mg/kg mivacurium over 60 seconds were treated for a decrease in blood pressure in association with the administration of mivacurium. Treatment for a decrease in blood pressure was reported in 1 to 2% of healthy adults given ≥0.2 mg/kg mivacurium over 5 to 15 seconds, 2 to 3% of healthy adults given 0.2 mg/kg over 30 seconds, none of 100 healthy adults given 0.25 mg/kg as a divided dose (0.15 mg/kg followed 30 seconds later by 0.1 mg/kg), and 2 to 4% of cardiac surgery patients given ≥0.2 mg/kg over 60 seconds. None of 63 children who received the recommended dose of 0.2 mg/kg mivacurium was treated for a decrease in blood pressure in association with the administration of mivacurium.

Observed During Clinical Practice: General: allergic reactions, anaphylactoid reactions (very rarely, severe anaphylactic or anaphylactoid reactions) have been reported. Musculoskeletal: diminished drug effect, prolonged drug effect, re-paralysis following initial cholinesterase-induced reversal. Cardiovascular: hypotension, flushing, edema, angioedema, tachycardia, bradycardia, cardiovascular collapse, cardiac arrest, arrhythmias. Respiratory: bronchospasm, laryngospasm, wheezing. Integumentary: rash, erythema, urticaria.

Overdose: Symptoms and Treatment: The possibility of iatrogenic overdosage can be minimized by carefully monitoring the muscle twitch response to peripheral nerve stimulation. Overdosage with neuromuscular blocking agents may result in neuromuscular block beyond the time needed for surgery and anesthesia. The primary treatment is maintenance of a patent airway and controlled ventilation until recovery of normal respiration is assured. Once evidence of spontaneous recovery from neuromuscular block is observed, further recovery may be facilitated by administration of an anticholinesterase agent (e.g., neostigmine or edrophonium) in conjunction with an appropriate anticholinergic agent. Overdosage may increase the risk of histamine release and hemodynamic side effects, especially decreases in blood pressure. If needed, cardiovascular support may be provided by proper positioning of the patient, fluid administration and/or vasopressor agent administration. A peripheral nerve stimulator should be used to monitor recovery.

Antagonism of Neuromuscular Blockade: Anticholinesterase agents should be used to antagonize neuromuscular blockade only after spontaneous recovery of the muscle twitch response has begun. Antagonists should not be administered if complete neuromuscular blockade is evident or suspected. Owing to the rapid spontaneous recovery from mivacurium-induced neuromuscular blockade, the use of anticholinesterase reversal agents may not always represent a clinically significant advantage in terms of recovery time. However, mivacurium-induced neuromuscular blockade can be antagonized by anticholinesterase agents once spontaneous recovery has begun. As with other nondepolarizing neuromuscular blocking agents, the time required for anticholinesterase-mediated recovery is longer for reversals attempted at deeper levels of blockade.

Administration of 0.03 to 0.064 mg/kg neostigmine or 0.5 mg/kg edrophonium to adults at approximately 10% recovery from neuromuscular block (range: 1 to 15%) produced 95% recovery of the muscle twitch response and a T_4/T_1 ratio of ≥75% in about 10 minutes. The time from 25% recovery of the muscle twitch response to T_4/T_1 ratios of ≥75% under these conditions of antagonism averaged about 7 to 9 minutes. In comparison, average times for spontaneous recovery from 25% to a T_4/T_1 ratio of ≥75% were 12 to 13 minutes.

Patients should be evaluated for adequate clinical evidence of antagonism, e.g., 5-second head lift and grip strength. Ventilation must be supported until no longer required. Conditions that may be associated with delayed antagonism include debilitation, carcinomatosis, concomitant use of certain broad spectrum antibiotics, or use of anesthetic agents or other drugs that enhance neuromuscular blockade or depress respiration.

Dosage: To avoid distress to the patient, mivacurium should not be administered before unconsciousness has been induced. It should not be mixed in the same syringe, or administered simultaneously through the same needle, with alkaline solutions (e.g., barbiturate solutions).

Mivacurium should be administered i.v. only. Do not administer mivacurium by the i.m. route. The dosage information provided below is intended as a guide only. The use

Table V—Mivacron

Frequency of Maximum Changes in Mean Arterial Pressure (MAP) and Heart Rate (HR) Following Doses of Mivacron Administered Over 5 to 15 Seconds to Healthy Adult and Pediatric Patients and Over 60 Seconds to Adult Patients with Cardiovascular Disease During Opioid/Nitrous Oxide/Oxygen Anesthesia

Initial Mivacron Dose (mg/kg)		Maximum Change[a] MAP (mm Hg)	Maximum Change[a] HR (beats/min)	Patients with 20–29% Dec or Inc: MAP Dec %	MAP Inc %	HR Dec %	HR Inc %	Patients with 30–39% Dec or Inc: MAP Dec %	MAP Inc %	HR Dec %	HR Inc %	Patients with ≥40% Dec or Inc: MAP Dec %	MAP Inc %	HR Dec %	HR Inc %
Adults (ASA Physical Status I-II)															
0.07	(n=14)	0.7 (−18 to 23)	−2.4 (−14 to 23)	7	14	0	0	0	0	0	0	0	0	0	0
0.10	(n=16)	0 (−14 to 4.1)	−5.8 (−25 to 8)	0	0	0	0	0	6	0	0	0	1	0	0
0.15	(n=53)	−4.1 (−42 to 32)	−2.6 (−43 to 19)	19	2	3	8	4	4	4	2	1	1	0	1
0.20[b]	(n=53)	−14.1 (−41 to 16)	4.1 (−33 to 33)	14	4	5	7	30	0	0	8	13	0	0	7
0.25[b]	(n=44)	−14.2 (−48 to 59)	5.6 (−36 to 61)	14	3	2	18	39	2	0	14	14	2	0	8
Children 2-12 years (ASA Physical Status I-II)															
0.11-0.12	(n=17)	0.8 (−14 to 17)	−0.7 (−18 to 17)	0	9	0	0	0	6	0	0	0	0	0	0
0.20	(n=17)	−0.2 (−17 to 17)	−2.4 (−32 to 17)	6	21	3	0	0	0	0	0	0	0	0	0
0.25	(n=8)	−10.4 (−24 to 9)	−6.1 (−18 to 5)	19	0	0	0	13	0	0	0	0	0	0	0
Adults (ASA Physical Status III-IV)[c]															
0.15	(n=36)	−1.3 (−3.8 to 0.7)	−3.4 (−4.7 to −2.7)	0	3	0	0	0	0	0	0	0	0	0	0
0.20	(n=43)	0.9 (0.0 to 3.6)	−2.7 (−3.2 to 0)	0	2	0	2	2	7	0	0	0	2	0	0
0.25	(n=23)	0.7 (−0.9 to 2.6)	−3.7 (−5.5 to −1.9)	4	4	4	4	4	4	0	0	4	0	0	0

[a] Values shown are medians of means from individual studies (range of individual patient values).
[b] Rapid administration not recommended due to possibility of decreased blood pressure. Administer 0.2 mg/kg over 30 seconds; administer 0.25 mg/kg as divided dose (0.15 mg/kg followed 30 seconds later by 0.1 mg/kg). See Dosage.
[c] For recommended dosage in patients with cardiovascular disease, see Dosage.

of a peripheral nerve stimulator will permit the most advantageous use of mivacurium, minimize the possibility of overdosage or underdosage, and assist in the evaluation of recovery. Dosage requirements may vary and dosage should be individualized. The duration of action of mivacurium may be increased in elderly patients or in patients with renal or hepatic disease. In patients known or suspected of having a significant reduction in plasma cholinesterase activity, consideration should be given to the administration of a small test dose of mivacurium (see Precautions).

When using mivacurium or other neuromuscular blocking agents to facilitate tracheal intubation, it is important to recognize that the most important factors affecting intubation are the depth of general anesthesia and the level of neuromuscular block. Satisfactory intubating conditions can usually be achieved before complete neuromuscular block is attained if there is adequate anesthesia.

When using a stimulator to monitor onset of neuromuscular block, clinical studies have shown that all 4 twitches of the train-of-four response may be present, with little or no fade, at the times recommended for intubation. Therefore, as with other neuromuscular blocking agents, it is important to use other criteria, such as clinical evaluation of the status of relaxation of jaw muscles and vocal cords, in conjunction with peripheral muscle twitch monitoring, to guide the appropriate time of intubation.

The onset of conditions suitable for tracheal intubation occurs earlier after a conventional intubating dose of succinylcholine than after recommended doses of mivacurium.

Parenteral drug products should be inspected visually for particulate matter and discoloration prior to administration whenever solution and container permit.

Adults: Initial Bolus Doses: Doses of 0.15 mg/kg administered over 5 to 15 seconds, 0.2 mg/kg administered over 30 seconds, or 0.25 mg/kg administered in divided doses (0.15 mg/kg followed 30 seconds later by 0.1 mg/kg) are recommended for facilitation of non-emergency tracheal intubation for most patients (see Table VI).

The purpose of slowed or divided dosing of mivacurium at doses above 0.15 mg/kg is to minimize the transient decreases in blood pressure, and other symptoms of histamine release, observed in some patients given these doses over 5 to 15 seconds (see Pharmacology, Precautions and Adverse Effects). The quality of intubation conditions does not significantly differ for the times and doses of mivacurium recommended in Table VI, but the onset of suitable intubation conditions may be reached earlier with higher doses. The choice of a particular dose and regimen should be based on individual circumstances and patient requirements (see Precautions).

In patients for whom a sudden decrease in blood pressure may prove hazardous (e.g., patients with significant cardiovascular disease) or with any history suggesting a greater sensitivity to histamine release, the dose of mivacurium should be ≤0.15 mg/kg administered over 60 seconds (see Precautions). No data are available on the use of doses of mivacurium above 0.15 mg/kg in patients with clinically significant kidney or liver disease.

In patients receiving opioid/nitrous oxide/oxygen anesthesia, 0.15 mg/kg mivacurium typically produces 96 to 100% maximal twitch suppression (range: 53 to 100%) in 3 to 7 minutes (range: 2 to 11 min). Clinically effective neuromuscular block generally lasts for 15 to 20 minutes (range: 8 to 38 min) and spontaneous recovery may be expected to be 95% complete in 25 to 30 minutes (range: 14 to 74 min).

Table VI—Mivacron

Recommended Initial Dosing Regimens for Adults

Dosing Paradigm*	Anesthetic Induction Technique Studied	Time to Generally Good-to-Excellent Intubating Conditions
0.15 mg/kg, i.v. (over 5 to 15 s)	Thiopental/opioid/N_2O/O_2 or propofol/opioid	2.5–3 min after completion of dose
0.20 mg/kg, i.v. (over 30 s)	Thiopental/opioid/N_2O/O_2 or propofol/opioid	2–2.5 min after completion of dose
0.25 mg/kg, i.v. (0.15 mg/kg followed 30 s later by 0.10 mg/kg)	Propofol/opioid	1.5–2 min after completion of 0.15 mg/kg dose

*Dosing instituted after induction of adequate general anesthesia.

Table VII—Mivacron

Infusion Rates for Maintenance of Neuromuscular Blockade During Opioid/Nitrous Oxide/Oxygen Anesthesia Using Mivacron Injection (2 mg/mL)–mL/h

Patient Weight (kg)	Mivacron Delivery Rate (μg/kg/min) / Infusion Delivery Rate (mL/h): 4	5	6	7	8	10	14	16	18	20
10	1.2	1.5	1.8	2.1	2.4	3.0	4.2	4.8	5.4	6.0
15	1.8	2.3	2.7	3.2	3.6	4.5	6.3	7.2	8.1	9.0
20	2.4	3.0	3.6	4.2	4.8	6.0	8.4	9.6	10.8	12.0
25	3.0	3.8	4.5	5.3	6.0	7.5	10.5	12.0	13.5	15.0
35	4.2	5.3	6.3	7.4	8.4	10.5	14.7	16.8	18.9	21.0
50	6.0	7.5	9.0	10.5	12.0	15.0	21.0	24.0	27.0	30.0
60	7.2	9.0	10.8	12.6	14.4	18.0	25.2	28.8	32.4	36.0
70	8.4	10.5	12.6	14.7	16.8	21.0	29.4	33.6	37.8	42.0
80	9.6	12.0	14.4	16.8	19.2	24.0	33.6	38.4	43.2	48.0
90	10.8	13.5	16.2	18.9	21.6	27.0	37.8	43.2	48.6	54.0
100	12.0	15.0	18.0	21.0	24.0	30.0	42.0	48.0	54.0	60.0

Table VIII—Mivacron

Infusion Rates for Maintenance of Neuromuscular Blockade During Opioid/Nitrous Oxide/Oxygen Anesthesia Using Mivacron Admixture (0.5 mg/mL)–mL/h

Patient Weight (kg)	Mivacron Delivery Rate (μg/kg/min) / Infusion Delivery Rate (mL/h): 4	5	6	7	8	10	14	16	18	20
10	5	6	7	8	10	12	17	19	22	24
15	7	9	11	13	14	18	25	29	32	36
20	10	12	15	17	19	24	34	38	43	48
25	12	15	18	21	24	30	42	48	54	60
35	17	21	26	29	34	42	59	67	76	84
50	24	30	36	42	48	60	84	96	108	120
60	29	36	43	50	58	72	101	115	130	144
70	34	42	50	59	67	84	118	134	151	168
80	39	48	58	67	77	96	134	154	173	192
90	44	54	65	76	86	108	151	173	194	216
100	48	60	72	84	96	120	168	192	216	240

A dose of 0.1 mg/kg produces a mean 96 to 100% maximal twitch suppression in about 4 minutes during balanced anesthesia with a mean clinically effective duration of action of approximately 15 minutes (range: 8 to 24 min).

The expected duration of clinically effective block and the time to 95% spontaneous recovery following 0.2 mg/kg mivacurium are approximately 20 and 30 minutes, respectively, and following 0.25 mg/kg mivacurium are approximately 25 and 35 minutes. Initiation of maintenance dosing during opioid/nitrous oxide/oxygen anesthesia is generally required approximately 15, 20, and 25 minutes following initial mivacurium doses of 0.15, 0.20, and 0.25 mg/kg, respectively (see Table I on previous page). Maintenance doses of 0.1 mg/kg administered to patients at approximately 10% twitch recovery each provide approximately 13 minutes (range: 10 to 19 min) of ≥95% twitch suppression. For a shorter or longer duration of action, smaller or larger maintenance doses may be administered. Repeated administration of maintenance doses or continuous infusion of mivacurium for up to 2.5 hours is not associated with development of tachyphylaxis or cumulative neuromuscular blocking effects in ASA Physical Status I-II patients (see Pharmacology).

Continuous Infusion: Continuous infusion of mivacurium may be used to maintain neuromuscular block. Upon early evidence of spontaneous recovery from the intial dose, an infusion rate of 9 to 10 μg/kg/min counteracts the rapid spontaneous recovery of neuromuscular function in most patients (Tables VII and VIII). If continuous infusion is initiated simultaneously with the administration of an initial bolus dose, a lower initial infusion rate should be used (e.g., 4 μg/kg/min). In either case, the initial infusion rate should be adjusted according to the response to peripheral nerve stimulation and to clinical criteria. On average, an infusion rate of 6 to 7 μg/kg/min (range: 1 to 15 μg/kg/min) may be expected to maintain neuromuscular block within the range of 89 to 99% for extended periods in adults receiving opioid/nitrous oxide/oxygen anesthesia. Upon cessation of infusions delivered at these rates, 25% recovery can generally be expected in about 6 to 9 minutes (range: 2 to 45 min) and 95% recovery in 16 to 24 minutes (range: 8 to 34 min).

Children: Mivacurium has not been studied in children under 2 years of age.

Initial Bolus Doses: Dosage requirements for mivacurium on a mg/kg basis are higher in children than in adults. Onset and recovery of neuromuscular block occur more rapidly in children than in adults (see Pharmacology).

The recommended initial dose of mivacurium in children 2 to 12 years of age is 0.2 mg/kg. The use of mivacurium to facilitate endotracheal intubation in children has not been studied. In 18 pediatric patients, an initial dose of 0.2 mg/kg produced maximum block of 95 to 100% in an average of 1.9 minutes (range: 1 to 3 min) and clinically effective block for 10 minutes (range: 6 to 15 min) during stable opioid/nitrous oxide/oxygen anesthesia. Under the same anesthetic conditions, doses of 0.11 to 0.12 mg/kg produced maximum neuromuscular block of 89 to 100% in an average of 2.8 minutes (range 1 to 5 min) and clinically effective block for an average of 7 minutes (range: 4 to 10 min) in 17 pediatric patients. Maintenance doses may be required more frequently in children than in adults. Administration of mivacurium doses above the recommended range (>0.2 mg/kg) is associated with transient decreases in MAP in some children.

Continuous Infusion: Children require higher mivacurium infusion rates than adults. During opioid/nitrous oxide/oxygen anesthesia the infusion rate required to maintain 89 to 99% neuromuscular block averages 14 μg/kg/min (range: 5 to 31 μg/kg/min). Following cessation of infusion, 25% recovery can typically be expected in 3 to 4 minutes (range: 2 to 11 min) and 95% recovery in 11 to 12 minutes (range 6 to 17 min). The principles for infusion of mivacurium in adults (see above) are also applicable to children.

Infusion Rate Tables: For adults and children the amount of infusion solution required per hour depends upon the clinical requirements of the patient, the concentration of mivacurium in the infusion solution, and the patient's weight. The contribution of the infusion solution to the fluid requirements of the patient must be considered. Table VII provides guidelines for delivery in mL/h (equivalent to microdrops/min when 60 microdrops=1 mL) of Mivacron Injection (2 mg/mL). Table VIII gives similar guidelines when admixtures of Mivacron are to be used (see Parenteral Products).

Parenteral Products: Mivacron injection should not be mixed with highly alkaline solutions (e.g., barbiturate solutions).

Mivacron injection is compatible with: 5% Dextrose Injection USP, 0.9% Sodium Chloride Injection USP, 5% Dextrose and 0.9% Sodium Chloride Injection USP, Lactated Ringer's Injection USP and 5% Dextrose in Lactated Ringer's Injection.

Mivacron (cont'd)

These solutions may be administered simultaneously with Mivacron injection or used to prepare admixtures of Mivacron injection (e.g., 0.5 mg/mL). Compatibility studies with other parenteral products have not been done.

Dilution Stability: Mivacron injection diluted to 0.5 mg mivacurium per mL in the above mentioned diluents is physically and chemically stable when stored in PVC (polyvinyl chloride) bags at room temperature for up to 24 hours. All solutions should be visually inspected for particulate matter and discoloration prior to i.v. administration whenever solution and container permit. Solutions that are not clear and colorless should not be used. Aseptic techniques should be used to avoid microbial contamination of the admixture. Admixtures of Mivacron injection should be prepared for single-patient use only and used within 24 hours of preparation. The unused portion of the admixture should be discarded.

Supplied: Each mL of sterile, nonpyrogenic solution contains: mivacurium chloride equivalent to mivacurium 2 mg in water for injection, pH 3.5 to 5.5. Hydrochloric acid may have been added to adjust pH. Multiple dose vials contain benzyl alcohol 0.9% w/v. Single dose vials of 10 mL, trays of 10. Multiple dose vials of 20 mL, trays of 10. Multiple dose vials of 50 mL, boxes of 1. Store at room temperature of 15 to 25°C. **Do not freeze.**

Reviewed 1997

M-M-R® II
MSD

Measles, Mumps and Rubella Virus Vaccine, Live, Attenuated, MSD Std

Pharmacology: M-M-R II is for immunization against measles (rubeola), mumps, and rubella (German measles). One injection of M-M-R II consists of Attenuvax (Measles Virus Vaccine, Live, Attenuated, MSD Std), Mumpsvax (Mumps Virus Vaccine, Live, Attenuated, MSD Std) and Meruvax II (Rubella Virus Vaccine, Live, Attenuated, MSD Std).

Clinical studies of 279 triple seronegative children, 11 months to 7 years of age, demonstrated that M-M-R II is highly immunogenic and generally well tolerated. In these studies, a single injection of the vaccine induced measles hemagglutination-inhibition (HI) antibodies in 95%, mumps neutralizing antibodies in 96%, and rubella HI antibodies in 99% of susceptible persons.

The RA 27/3 rubella strain in M-M-R II elicits higher immediate postvaccination HI, complement-fixing and neutralizing antibody levels than other strains of rubella vaccine and has been shown to induce a broader profile of circulating antibodies including anti-theta and anti-iota precipitating antibodies. The RA 27/3 rubella strain immunologically simulates natural infection more closely than other rubella vaccine viruses. The increased levels and broader profile of antibodies produced by RA 27/3 strain rubella virus vaccine appear to correlate with greater resistance to subclinical reinfection with the wild virus, and provide greater confidence for lasting immunity.

Vaccine-induced antibody levels following administration of M-M-R II have been shown to persist for over 11 years.

Indications: For the simultaneous immunization against measles, mumps and rubella in persons from 1 year of age or older. A second dose of M-M-R II or monovalent measles vaccine is recommended (see Revaccination).

Infants who are less than 12 months of age may fail to respond to the measles component of the vaccine due to presence in the circulation of residual measles antibody of maternal origin; the younger the infant, the lower the likelihood of seroconversion. In geographically isolated or other relatively inaccessible populations for whom immunization programs are logistically difficult, and in population groups in which natural measles infection may occur in a significant proportion of infants before one year of age, it may be desirable to give the vaccine to infants during their first year of life. Infants vaccinated under these conditions at less than 12 months of age should be revaccinated after reaching 15 months of age. There is some evidence to suggest that infants immunized at less than 1 year of age may not develop sustained antibody levels when later reimmunized. The advantage of early protection must be weighed against the chance for failure to respond adequately on reimmunization.

Previously unimmunized children of susceptible pregnant women should receive live attenuated rubella vaccine, because an immunized child will be less likely to acquire natural rubella and introduce the virus into the household.

Individuals planning travel abroad, if not immune, can acquire measles, mumps, or rubella and import these diseases to their country. Therefore, prior to international travel, individuals known to be susceptible to one or more of these diseases can receive either a single antigen vaccine (measles, mumps or rubella), or a combined antigen vaccine as appropriate. However, M-M-R II is preferred for persons likely to be susceptible to mumps and rubella as well as measles; and if single-antigen measles vaccine is not readily available, travelers should receive M-M-R II regardless of their immune status to mumps or rubella.

Passively acquired antibody can interfere with the response to live, attenuated-virus vaccines. Therefore, administration of M-M-R II should be deferred until approximately 3 months after passive immunization.

Revaccination: Children vaccinated when younger than 12 months of age should be revaccinated at 15 months of age. Based on available evidence, there is no reason to routinely revaccinate persons who were vaccinated originally when 12 months of age or older. However, persons should be revaccinated if there is evidence to suggest that initial immunization was ineffective.

A number of national, governmental vaccine authorities, the American Academy of Pediatrics (AAP), the Immunization Practices Advisory Committee (ACIP) and the National Advisory Committee on Immunization (NACI) have recommended guidelines for routine measles revaccination and to help control measles outbreaks.

A second dose of measles-containing vaccine should be deferred for HIV-infected persons with moderate or advanced immunodeficiency. Measles revaccination may still be appropriate for HIV-infected persons with moderate immunodeficiency if there is a high risk of wild strain measles in the local community, or travel to an area where measles is endemic.

Note: A primary difference among these recommendations is the timing of revaccination: The NACI recommends routine revaccination at least 1 month after the first dose or at 18 months, or with entry into daycare or school. The ACIP recommends routine revaccination at entry into kindergarten or first grade (4 to 6 years), whereas the AAP recommends routine revaccination at entrance to middle school or junior high school. In addition, some public health jurisdictions mandate the age for revaccination. The complete text of applicable guidelines should be consulted.

Vaccines available for revaccination include monovalent measles vaccine and polyvalent vaccines containing measles (e.g., M-M-R II). If the prevention of sporadic measles outbreaks is the sole objective, revaccination with a monovalent measles vaccine should be considered. If concern also exists about immune status regarding mumps or rubella, revaccination with appropriate monovalent or polyvalent vaccine should be considered after consulting the appropriate Product Monographs. Unnecessary doses of a vaccine are best avoided by ensuring that written documentation of vaccination is preserved and a copy given to each vaccinee's parent or guardian.

Nonpregnant Adolescent and Adult Females: Immunization of susceptible nonpregnant adolescent and adult females of childbearing age with live attenuated rubella virus vaccine is indicated if certain precautions are observed (see Precautions). In view of the importance of protecting this age group against rubella, reasonable precautions in a rubella immunization program include asking females if they are pregnant, excluding those who say they are, and explaining the theoretical risks to the others. Vaccinating susceptible postpubertal females confers individual protection against subsequently acquiring rubella infection during pregnancy, which in turn prevents infection of the fetus and consequent congenital rubella injury.

Women of childbearing age should be advised not to become pregnant for 3 months after vaccination and should be informed on the reasons for this precaution.

It is recommended, when feasible, that rubella susceptibility be determined by serologic testing prior to immunization. Since serologic testing is expensive and not always accurate, rubella vaccination of a woman who is not known to be pregnant and has no history of vaccination is justifiable without serologic testing. If immune, as evidenced by a specific rubella antibody titer of 1:8 or greater (hemagglutination-inhibition test), vaccination is unnecessary. Congenital malformations do occur in up to 7% of all live births. Their chance appearance after vaccination could lead to misinterpretation of the cause, particularly if the prior rubella-immune status of vaccinees is unknown.

Postpubertal females should be informed of the frequent occurrence of generally self-limited arthralgia and/or possible arthritis beginning 2 to 4 weeks after vaccination (see Adverse Effects).

Postpartum Women: It has been found convenient in many instances to vaccinate rubella-susceptible women in the immediate postpartum period (see Precautions, Lactation).

Use with other Vaccines: M-M-R II should be given 1 month before or after administration of other vaccines.

However, other schedules have been used. For example, the AAP has noted that when the patient may not return, some practitioners prefer to administer DTP, OPV, and M-M-R II on a single day. If done, separate sites and syringes should be used for DTP and M-M-R II. The ACIP recommends routine simultaneous administration of M-M-R II, DTP and OPV or inactivated polio vaccine (IPV) to all children ≥15 months who are eligible to receive these vaccines on the basis that there are equivalent antibody responses and no clinically significant increases in the frequency of adverse events when DTP, M-M-R II and OPV or IPV are administered either simultaneously at different sites or separately. Administration of M-M-R II at 15 months followed by DTP and OPV (or IPV) at 18 months remains an acceptable alternative, especially for children with caregivers known to be generally compliant with other health-care recommendations. According to NACI, most of the commonly used antigens can safely be given simultaneously. DPT, M-M-R II and OPV vaccines can all be given simultaneously without increased side effects. Inactivated vaccines can be given simultaneously, but at separate sites, bearing in mind the precautions that apply to each individual vaccine.

Note: The ACIP recommends administering M-M-R II concomitantly with the fourth dose of DTP and the third dose of OPV to children 15 months of age or older providing that 6 months have elapsed since DTP-3; or, if fewer than 3 DTPs have been received, at least 6 weeks have elapsed since the last dose of DTP and OPV.

Contraindications: *Pregnancy:* Do not give M-M-R II to pregnant females; the possible effects of the vaccine on fetal development are unknown at this time. If vaccination of postpubertal females is undertaken, pregnancy must be avoided by medically acceptable methods for 3 months following vaccination (see Precautions, Pregnancy).

Histologic changes, similar to those seen in gestational rubella, have been observed and rubella virus has been recovered from decidua following vaccination of pregnant women with live attenuated rubella vaccine. These vaccines may thus constitute a risk to the fetus.

Anaphylactic or anaphylactoid reactions to neomycin. Each dose of reconstituted vaccine contains approximately 17.5 μg neomycin base (present as sulfate).

Any febrile respiratory illness or other active febrile infection.

Active untreated tuberculosis.

Patients receiving immunosuppressive therapy with ACTH, corticosteroids, irradiation, alkylating agents or antimetabolites. This contraindication does not apply to patients who are receiving corticosteroids as replacement therapy, e.g., for Addison's disease.

Individuals with blood dyscrasias, leukemia, lymphomas of any type, or other malignant neoplasms affecting the bone marrow or lymphatic systems.

Primary immunodeficiency states, including cellular immune deficiencies, hypogammaglobulinemic and dysgammaglobulinemic states. M-M-R II is recommended for asymptomatic HIV-infected individuals. M-M-R II is not normally recommended for symptomatic HIV-infected individuals because safety and immunogenicity data are not yet available. If there is a known exposure to measles, measles-immune globulin (IG) should be given within 6 days whether or not the individual has been vaccinated, although the efficacy of IG for passive immunoprophylaxis of measles in HIV-infected individuals is uncertain.

Individuals with a family history of congenital or hereditary immunodeficiency, until the immune competence of the potential vaccine recipient is demonstrated.

Hypersensitivity to Eggs: Live measles vaccine and live mumps vaccine are produced in chick embryo cell culture. Persons with a history of anaphylactic, anaphylactoid or other immediate reactions (e.g., hives, swelling of the mouth and throat, difficulty breathing, hypotension, or shock) subsequent to egg ingestion should not be vaccinated. Evidence indicates that persons are not at increased risk if they have egg allergies that are not anaphylactic or anaphylactoid in nature. Such persons may be vaccinated in the usual manner. There is no evidence to indicate that persons with allergies to chickens or feathers are at increased risk of reaction to the vaccine.

Note: NACI has revised its recommendations for measles-mumps-rubella immunization of individuals allergic to eggs as follows: "Egg allergy is not a contraindication to immunization with measles-mumps-rubella vaccine. In individuals with histories of anaphylactic hypersensitivity to hens' eggs (urticaria, swelling of the mouth and throat, difficulty breathing or hypotension), measles immunization can be administered in the routine manner without prior skin testing. However, immunization should take place where adequate facilities are available to manage anaphylaxis. Persons at risk should be observed for 30 minutes after immunization for any signs of allergic reaction."

Precautions: Administer M-M-R II s.c.; **do not give i.v.**

Adequate treatment provisions including epinephrine should be available for immediate use in case an anaphylactic or anaphylactoid reaction occurs.

Due caution should be employed in administration of M-M-R II to persons with individual or family histories of convulsions, a history of cerebral injury or any other condition in which stress due to fever should be avoided. The physician should be alert to the temperature elevation which may occur 5 to 12 days following vaccination (see Adverse Effects).

Children and young adults who are known to be infected with human immunodeficiency viruses but without overt clinical manifestations of immunosuppression may be vaccinated; however, the vaccinees should be monitored closely for exposure to vaccine-preventable diseases because immunization may be less effective than for uninfected persons. In selected cases confirmation of circulating antibody levels may be indicated to help guide appropriate protective measures, including immunoprophylaxis if immunity has waned to nonprotective levels.

Vaccination should be deferred for at least 3 months following blood or plasma transfusions, or administration of human immune serum globulin.

Excretion of small amounts of the live attenuated rubella virus from the nose or throat has occurred in the majority of susceptible individuals 7 to 28 days after vaccination. There is no confirmed evidence to indicate that such virus is transmitted to susceptible persons who are in contact with the vaccinated individuals. Consequently, transmission, while accepted as a theoretical possibility, is not regarded as a significant risk. However, transmission of the rubella vaccine virus to infants via breast milk has been documented (see Lactation).

There are no reports of transmission of live attenuated measles or mumps viruses from vaccinees to susceptible contacts.

It has been reported that live attenuated measles, mumps and rubella virus vaccines given individually may result in a temporary depression of tuberculin skin sensitivity. Therefore, if a tuberculin test is to be done, it should be administered either before or simultaneously with M-M-R II.

Children under treatment for tuberculosis have not experienced exacerbation of the disease when immunized with live measles virus vaccine; no studies have been reported to date of the effect of measles virus vaccines on untreated tuberculous children.

As for any vaccine, vaccination with M-M-R II may not result in seroconversion in 100% of susceptible subjects given the vaccine.

Pregnancy: Animal reproduction studies have not been conducted with M-M-R II. It is also not known whether M-M-R II can cause fetal harm when administered to a pregnant woman or can affect reproduction capacity. Therefore, the vaccine should not be administered to pregnant females; furthermore, pregnancy should be avoided for 3 months following vaccination (see Contraindications).

In counselling women who are inadvertently vaccinated when pregnant or who become pregnant within 3 months of vaccination, the physician should be aware of the following: In a 10 year survey involving over 700 pregnant women who received rubella vaccine within 3 months before or after conception (of whom 189 received the Wistar RA 27/3 strain), none of the newborns had abnormalities compatible with congenital rubella syndrome; although mumps virus is capable of infecting the placenta and fetus, there is no good evidence that it causes congenital malformations in humans. Mumps vaccine virus has been shown to infect the placenta, but the virus has not been isolated from the fetal tissues from susceptible women who were vaccinated and underwent elective abortions; and reports have indicated that contracting of natural measles during pregnancy enhances fetal risk. Increased rates of spontaneous abortion, stillbirth, congenital defects and prematurity have been observed subsequent to natural measles during pregnancy. There are no adequate studies of the attenuated (vaccine) strain of measles virus in pregnancy. However, it would be prudent to assume that the vaccine strain of virus is also capable of inducing adverse fetal effects.

Lactation: It is not known whether measles or mumps vaccine virus is secreted in human milk. Recent studies have shown that lactating postpartum women immunized with live attenuated rubella vaccine may secrete the virus in breast milk and transmit it to breast-fed infants. In the infants with serological evidence of rubella infection, none exhibited severe disease; however, one exhibited mild clinical illness typical of acquired rubella. Caution should be exercised when M-M-R II is administered to a nursing woman.

Adverse Effects: The adverse reactions associated with the use of M-M-R II are those which have been reported following administration of the monovalent vaccines.

Common: burning and/or stinging of short duration at the injection site.

Occasional: Body as a whole: fever (38.3°C or higher).

Skin: rash, usually minimal but may be generalized. Generally, fever, rash, or both appear between the 5th and the 12th days.

Rare: Body as a whole: mild local reactions such as erythema, induration and tenderness; sore throat, malaise.

Digestive: parotitis, nausea, vomiting, diarrhea.

Hematologic/Lymphatic: regional lymphadenopathy, thrombocytopenia, purpura.

Hypersensitivity: allergic reactions such as wheal and flare at injection site, anaphylaxis and anaphylactoid reactions, urticaria.

Musculoskeletal: arthralgia and/or arthritis (usually transient and rarely chronic [see below]), myalgia.

Nervous/Psychiatric: febrile convulsions in children, afebrile convulsions or seizures, headache, dizziness, paresthesia, polyneuritis, Guillain-Barré syndrome, ataxia. Encephalitis/encephalopathy have been reported approximately once for every three million doses. In no case has it been shown that reactions were actually caused by vaccine. The risk of such serious neurological disorders following live measles virus vaccine administration remains far less than that for encephalitis and encephalopathy with natural measles (1 per 2 000 reported cases).

Skin: erythema multiforme.

Special Senses: forms of optic neuritis, including retrobulbar neuritis, papillitis, and retinitis; ocular palsies, otitis media, nerve deafness, conjunctivitis.

Urogenital: orchitis.

There have been reports of subacute sclerosing panencephalitis (SSPE) in children who did not have a history of natural measles but did receive measles vaccine. Some of these cases may have resulted from unrecognized measles in the first year of life or possibly from the measles vaccination. Based on estimated nationwide measles vaccine distribution, the association of SSPE cases to measles vaccination is about one case per million vaccine doses distributed. This is far less than the association with natural measles, 6 to 22 cases of SSPE per 1 000 000 cases of measles. The results of a retrospective case-controlled study conducted by the Centers for Disease Control suggest that the overall effect of measles vaccine has been to protect against SSPE by preventing measles with its inherent higher risk of SSPE.

Local reactions characterized by marked swelling, redness and vesiculation at the injection site of attenuated live measles virus vaccines and systemic reactions including atypical measles have occurred in persons who received killed measles vaccine previously. M-M-R II was not given under this condition in clinical trials. Rarely, more severe reactions that require hospitalization, including prolonged high fevers and extensive local reactions, have been reported. Panniculitis has been reported rarely following administration of measles vaccine.

Arthralgia and/or arthritis (usually transient and rarely chronic), and polyneuritis are features of natural rubella and vary in frequency and severity with age and sex, being greatest in adult females and least in prepubertal children.

Chronic arthritis has been associated with natural rubella infection and has been related to persistent virus and/or viral antigen isolated from body tissues. Only rarely have vaccine recipients developed chronic joint symptoms.

Following vaccination in children, reactions in joints are uncommon and generally of brief duration. In women, incidence rates for arthritis and arthralgia are generally higher than those seen in children (children: 0 to 3%, women: 12 to 20%), and the reactions tend to be more marked and of longer duration. Symptoms may persist for a matter of months or on rare occasions for years. In adolescent girls, the reactions appear to be intermediate in incidence between those seen in children and in adult women. Even in older women (35 to 45 years), these reactions are generally well tolerated and rarely interfere with normal activities. Such reactions occur much less frequently after revaccination than primary vaccination.

Dosage: The dosage of M-M-R II vaccine is the same for all persons.

After suitably cleansing the immunization site, inject the total volume of the single dose (about 0.5 mL) of reconstituted vaccine s.c., preferably into the outer aspect of the upper arm. Do not inject M-M-R II i.v. **Do not give immune globulin (IG) concurrently with M-M-R II.**

Caution: A sterile syringe free of preservatives, antiseptics, and detergents should be used for each injection and/or reconstitution of the vaccine because these substances may inactivate the live virus vaccine. A 25 gauge, 15 mm needle is recommended.

Reconstitution: Prior to Reconstitution: Check the appearance of the content of each vial of vaccine. The content should be a white to off-white solid mass ("plug") of powder which fills the bottom of each vial.

To reconstitute, use only the diluent supplied, since it is free of preservatives or other antiviral substances which might inactivate the vaccine.

First withdraw the entire volume of diluent (0.7 mL) into the syringe to be used for reconstitution. Inject all the diluent in the syringe into the vial of lyophilized vaccine, and agitate to mix thoroughly. Withdraw the entire contents into a syringe and inject the total volume of restored vaccine s.c.

Prior to Administration: Inspect the reconstituted solution for particulate matter and discoloration. The reconstituted solution should be **clear yellow.** Should complete dissolution not occur within 2 minutes, do not use and return for reimbursement.

It is important to use a separate sterile syringe and needle for each individual patient to prevent transmission of hepatitis B and other infectious agents from one person to another.

Stability and Storage Recommendations: Store unreconstituted M-M-R II at 2 to 8°C. **Protect from light.**

To conserve refrigerator space, the diluent may be stored separately at room temperature.

Unreconstituted M-M-R II retains at least 8 times the minimum immunizing dose even after 6 weeks at 22°C or 1 week at 37°C. Storage at temperatures above 2 to 8°C cannot be recommended due to the difficulty in monitoring the exact temperature and monitoring repeated exposures to time out of refrigeration.

Shipment: During shipment, to insure that there is no loss of potency, the vaccine must be maintained at a temperature of 10°C or less.

Reconstituted Solutions: **To maintain the potency, it is imperative that only the sterile diluent for Merck Sharp and Dohme live, attenuated virus vaccines (Sterile Water) be used for reconstitution and injection (see Table I).**

Table I—M-M-R II

Reconstitution

Vial Size	Volume of Diluent to be Added to Vial	Number of Doses Available
Single dose	0.7 mL	1 (0.5 mL/dose)

Use **as soon as possible** after reconstitution. Protect vaccine from light at all times since such exposure may inactivate the viruses. Store the reconstituted vaccine in a dark place at 2 to 8°C. Discard if not used **within 8 hours.**

Supplied: When reconstituted as directed, the dose for injection (0.5 mL) contains: not less than the equivalent of 1 000 $CCID_{50}$ (50% cell culture infective dose) of measles virus; 5 000 $CCID_{50}$ of mumps virus; and 1 000 $CCID_{50}$ of rubella virus. Preservative-free. Each dose contains approximately 17.5 μg of neomycin base (present as sulfate). Sorbitol and hydrolysed gelatin are added as stabilizers. Boxes of 10 single dose vials of sterile lyophilized vaccine with boxes of 10 vials (0.7 mL) of diluent.

Reviewed 1999

MOBIFLEX® Ⓟ

Roche

Tenoxicam

Anti-inflammatory—Analgesic

Pharmacology: Tenoxicam is a nonsteroidal anti-inflammatory agent with analgesic and antipyretic properties. Its mechanism of action, as with other nonsteroidal anti-inflammatory agents, is not yet completely known. Tenoxicam is an inhibitor of prostaglandin biosynthesis both in vitro and in vivo (protects mice against arachidonic acid induced toxicity). In vitro tests

Mobiflex (cont'd)

of leukocyte peroxidase also suggest that tenoxicam may act as a scavenger for active oxygen at the site of inflammation. These effects probably explain in part, the activity of tenoxicam in the treatment of painful inflammatory and degenerative diseases of the musculoskeletal system. Tenoxicam does not act by pituitary-adrenal stimulation.

After 4, 7, 10 or 14 days of culture with tenoxicam (2.4, 12, 48 μg/mL), there was no significant effect on the amount of cartilage proteoglycans synthesized and released into the culture medium of human chondrocytes, as compared to untreated cultures.

In vitro studies have also shown that tenoxican inhibits the activity of both proteoglycanase and collagenase enzymes obtained from human osteoarthritic cartilage. These in vitro results suggest a positive effect of tenoxicam on the joint cartilage under experimental conditions by slowing down the enhanced catabolism of the osteoarthritic cartilage matrix. The clinical significance of these findings is not yet known and is being investigated.

Pharmacokinetics: Tenoxicam is extensively absorbed following oral administration with an absolute bioavailability of approximately 100%. Following a single oral dose of the 20 mg tablet, peak plasma concentrations (1.46 to 3.31 μg/mL) were reached within 0.5 to 6 hours (median: 1.25 hours), and the mean half-life was 72±28 hours (range: 32 to 110 hours) in 8 fasted healthy males. When taken with a meal, tenoxicam is absorbed to the same extent but at a slower rate (peak plasma concentration is attained after 4 hours).

Approximately two thirds of a single 40 mg oral dose of tenoxicam is excreted in the urine, mainly as inactive 5′hydroxy-tenoxicam (20 to 30%). Only small amounts of the unchanged drug (0.5%) were found in the urine.

Following multiple doses of 20 mg once daily, steady state conditions are reached within 10 to 15 days. Maximum steady state plasma concentrations fall within the range of 10 to 15 μg/mL.

An average of 17% (4.8 to 45.3%) of a 20 mg oral dose is found in the bile as the C-7 or C-8 0-glucuronide of tenoxicam.

In 14 elderly patients suffering from osteoarthritis or rheumatoid arthritis, the mean peak plasma concentration after a single 20 mg dose of tenoxicam was 2.6 μg/mL, and the mean maximum steady state plasma concentration after multiple dosing was 12.4 μg/mL.

In 8 male and 4 female patients with renal insufficiency (creatinine clearance 6 to 57 mL/min), peak plasma concentrations were in the range of 1.2 to 5.2 μg/mL and the half-life of elimination ranged from 30 to 110 hours after a single 20 mg dose of tenoxicam. Pharmacokinetic parameters in patients with renal insufficiency were not significantly different from those in healthy volunteers.

In 4 male and 2 female patients with liver cirrhosis, the mean peak plasma concentration was 2.6 μg/mL and the half-life of elimination ranged between 26 to 84 hours after a single 20 mg dose of tenoxicam.

Tenoxicam is highly bound to the albumin component of plasma proteins (98 to 99%).

The sex-dependent difference in the disposition of tenoxicam was investigated. There was no difference in the maximum plasma concentrations, whereas a difference, at the 0.10 level of significance, was seen for the time to reach maximum drug concentrations, (3.6 hours for males, 1.52 hours for females) and for the half-life of elimination (72.4 hours for males and 61.8 hours for females).

Total tenoxicam concentrations in synovial fluid were determined in 6 patients (3 male, 3 female) after receiving a single 40 mg oral dose of tenoxicam. Peak synovial concentrations (1.82 μg/mL) were reached after 10 hours. The area under the synovial fluid tenoxicam concentration-time curve was 40 to 50% of the area under the plasma tenoxicam concentration-time curve.

Over a 2-week period of observation 6 healthy volunteers, taking tenoxicam 20 mg daily in a single dose, showed significantly less mean daily fecal blood loss (5.71 mL/week) than they did when taking 1.2 to 3 g of ASA daily (9.41 mL/week).

Indications: For the symptomatic treatment of rheumatoid arthritis, osteoarthritis, ankylosing spondylitis and extra-articular inflammations such as tendinitis, bursitis and periarthritis of the shoulders or hips.

Contraindications: Tenoxicam should not be administered to patients with active peptic ulcer or active inflammatory diseases of the gastrointestinal tract. Tenoxicam is contraindicated in patients who have shown hypersensitivity to the drug. It should not be used in patients in whom acute asthmatic attacks, urticaria, rhinitis or other allergic manifestations are precipitated by ASA or other nonsteroidal anti-inflammatory agents. Fatal anaphylactoid reactions have occurred in such individuals.

Before anesthesia or surgery, tenoxicam should not be given to elderly patients, to patients at risk of renal failure, or to patients with increased risk of bleeding, because of an increased risk of acute renal failure and possibility of impaired hemostasis.

Warnings: Peptic ulceration, perforation and gastrointestinal bleeding, sometimes severe and occasionally fatal have been reported during therapy with nonsteroidal anti-inflammatory drugs (NSAIDs) including tenoxicam.

Caution should be exercised when a NSAID such as tenoxicam is used in patients with a history suggestive of peptic ulcer, melena or any gastrointestinal disease. In these cases, the physician must weigh the benefits of treatment against the possible hazards.

Patients taking any NSAID including this drug should be instructed to contact a physician immediately if they experience symptoms or signs suggestive of peptic ulceration or gastrointestinal bleeding. These reactions can occur without warning symptoms or signs and at any time during the treatment.

Elderly, frail and debilitated patients appear to be at higher risk from a variety of adverse reactions from nonsteroidal anti-inflammatory drugs (NSAIDs). As with other nonsteroidal anti-inflammatory drugs, tenoxicam should be used with special caution in these patients.

Pregnancy and *Lactation:* The safety of tenoxicam during pregnancy and lactation has not been established and therefore its use during pregnancy and lactation is not recommended.

No teratogenic effects were observed in animal reproductive studies. Rats receiving tenoxicam during pregnancy showed delayed delivery. Tenoxicam readily passes into the milk of lactating rats.

Children: Tenoxicam is not recommended for use in patients under 16 years of age as the dose and indications in this population have not been established.

Precautions: Gastrointestinal: If peptic ulceration or gastrointestinal bleeding occur in patients under treatment with tenoxicam, the drug should be immediately withdrawn.

There is no definitive evidence that the concomitant administration of histamine H_2-receptor antagonists and/or antacids will either prevent the occurrence of gastrointestinal side effects or allow continuation of tenoxicam therapy when and if these adverse reactions appear.

Renal Function: As with other nonsteroidal anti-inflammatory drugs, long-term administration of tenoxicam to animals has resulted in renal papillary necrosis and other abnormal renal pathology. In humans, there have been reports of acute interstitial nephritis with hematuria, proteinuria and occasionally nephrotic syndrome.

A second form of renal toxicity has been seen in patients with prerenal conditions leading to the reduction in renal blood flow or blood volume, where the renal prostaglandins have a supportive role in the maintenance of renal perfusion. In these patients, administration of a nonsteroidal anti-inflammatory drug may cause a dose-dependent reduction in prostaglandin formation and may precipitate overt renal decompensation. Patients at greatest risk of this reaction are those with impaired renal function, heart failure, liver dysfunction, those taking diuretics, and the elderly. Discontinuation of nonsteroidal anti-inflammatory therapy is usually followed by recovery to the pre-treatment state.

Reversible elevation of BUN and serum creatinine have been reported with tenoxicam. The effect is thought to result from inhibition of renal prostaglandin synthesis resulting in changes in medullary and deep cortical blood flow with an attendant effect on renal function. Patients with impaired renal function or on diuretics, as well as elderly patients and those with congestive heart failure or liver ascites, are more at risk.

During long-term therapy, kidney function should be monitored periodically.

Hepatic Function: As with other nonsteroidal anti-inflammatory drugs, borderline elevations of one or more liver tests may occur. These abnormalities may progress, may remain essentially unchanged, or may be transient with continued therapy. A patient with symptoms and/or signs suggesting liver dysfunction, or in whom an abnormal liver test has occurred, should be evaluated for evidence of the development of more severe hepatic reactions while on therapy with this drug. Severe hepatic reactions including jaundice and cases of fatal hepatitis have been reported with this drug as with other nonsteroidal anti-inflammatory drugs. Although such reactions are rare, if abnormal liver tests persist or worsen, if clinical signs and symptoms consistent with liver disease develop, or if systemic manifestations occur (e.g. eosinophilia, rash, etc.), this drug should be discontinued.

During long-term therapy, liver function tests should be monitored periodically.

Fluid and Electrolyte Balance: Fluid retention and edema have been observed in patients treated with tenoxicam. Therefore, as with many other nonsteroidal anti-inflammatory drugs, the possibility of precipitating congestive heart-failure in elderly patients or those with compromised cardiac function should be born in mind. Tenoxicam should be used with caution in patients with heart failure, hypertension or other conditions predisposing to fluid retention.

With NSAID treatment, there is a potential risk of hyperkalemia particularly in patients with conditions such as diabetes mellitus or renal failure; elderly patients and patients receiving concomitant therapy with β-adrenergic blockers, angiotensin converting enzyme inhibitors or some diuretics. Serum electrolytes should be monitored periodically during long-term therapy, especially in those patients at risk.

Hematology: Drugs inhibiting prostaglandin biosynthesis do interfere, with platelet function to some degree; therefore, patients who may be adversely affected by such an action should be carefully observed when tenoxicam is administered.

Blood dyscrasias associated with the use of nonsteroidal anti-inflammatory drugs is rare, but could be with severe consequences.

Infection: In common with other anti-inflammatory drugs, tenoxicam may mask the usual signs of infection.

Ophthalmology: Blurred and/or diminished vision has been reported with the use of tenoxicam and other nonsteroidal anti-inflammatory drugs. If such symptoms develop this drug should be discontinued and an ophthalmologic examination performed, ophthalmic examination should be carried out at periodic intervals in any patient receiving this drug for an extended period of time.

Hypersensitivity Reactions: As with other NSAIDs, allergic reactions may occur. Manifestation of allergic reactions include urticaria, bronchospasm and anaphylaxis and in rare instances, severe skin reactions such as Stevens-Johnson syndrome and Lyell Syndrome.

Drug Interactions: ASA or Other NSAIDs: Plasma concentrations of tenoxicam are reduced to approximately 80% of their normal concentrations when single doses of tenoxicam are administered in conjunction with ASA (2 600 to 3 900 mg/day). At steady state, simultaneous administration of ASA does not appear to have a significant effect on the plasma concentration of tenoxicam. The use of tenoxicam in conjunction with ASA or another nonsteroidal anti-inflammatory agent is not recommended since data are not available demonstrating that the combination produces greater improvement than that achieved with either drug alone, and the potential for adverse reactions is increased.

Protein-Bound Drugs: As with other NSAIDs, tenoxicam is highly protein-bound, and therefore, might be expected to displace other protein-bound drugs, such as anticoagulants, oral hypoglycemics (sulfonylureas), phenytoin and sulfonamides.

Short-term pharmacodynamic studies have demonstrated that tenoxicam does not potentiate the anticoagulant effect of coumarin-type anticoagulants nor the hypoglycemic effect of sulfonylurea drugs. However, when a NSAID such as tenoxicam is administered concomitantly with anticoagulants, oral hypoglycemics or other highly protein bound drugs, the patients should be monitored and dosage adjustments made, if necessary.

Diuretics/Antihypertensives: As with other nonsteroidal anti-inflammatory drugs, tenoxicam can attenuate the blood pressure lowering effect of hydrochlorothiazide and the peak excretion rates of Na^+ and Cl^- in patients with hypertension. Therefore, close monitoring of patients on this drug combination is advisable. The excretion of electrolytes was not significantly affected when tenoxicam (two-day loading dose of 40 mg daily, followed by 20 mg daily) was administered to normotensive patients receiving furosemide therapy (40 mg daily).

Some NSAIDs have been reported to reduce the antihypertensive effects of certain beta-blockers. The interaction between tenoxicam and beta-blockers has not been studied.

Digoxin: In elderly patients, with normal plasma creatinine levels, plasma digoxin levels were not altered by the concomitant administration of tenoxicam (30 mg daily).

Antacids: The administration of 15 mL of an aluminum hydroxide or an aluminum and magnesium hydroxide antacid just prior to a single 20 mg oral dose of tenoxicam did not affect the bioavailability of tenoxicam.

Cholestyramine: The average half-life of tenoxicam, after a single 20 mg i.v. dose, was reduced from 67.4 hours to

31.9 hours following the administration of cholestyramine (4 g in 200 mL water orally t.i.d.). The apparent drug clearance of tenoxicam increased by 105%.

Lithium: Nonsteroidal anti-inflammatory agents have been reported to increase steady state plasma lithium concentrations. It is recommended that these concentrations be monitored when initiating, adjusting and discontinuing tenoxicam treatment.

Methotrexate: The co-administration of some NSAIDs and methotrexate has been associated with reduced renal tubular secretion of methotrexate, higher plasma concentrations and severe methotrexate toxicity. Therefore, caution should be exercised when NSAIDs such as tenoxicam, are administered concurrently with methotrexate. The interaction between tenoxicam and methotrexate has not been studied.

Adverse Effects: The most common adverse reactions encountered with nonsteroidal anti-inflammatory drugs are gastrointestinal, of which peptic ulcer, with or without bleeding, is the most severe. Fatalities have occurred on occasion, particularly in the elderly.

In approximately 12 000 patients administered tenoxicam 10 to 40 mg/day, (approximately four/fifths receiving 20 mg/day), the incidence of peptic ulceration and the incidence of gastrointestinal bleeding (including hematemesis and melena) was 0.1 to 0.6%.

The approximate incidences of other adverse effects listed by systems are summarized below.

Gastrointestinal (10.4 to 23.0%): dyspepsia (0.1 to 9.7%), nausea (2.0 to 6.7%), constipation (0.5 to 2.9%), abdominal pain (0.7 to 3.3%), diarrhea (0.5 to 2.3%), flatulence (0.04 to 1.9%), vomiting (0.2 to 1.1%), ulcerative stomatitis (0.1 to 0.7%), gastritis (0.1 to 0.8%), esophagitis (0.2%), abdominal discomfort (1.4 to 2.2%), pyrosis (1.3 to 1.9%), epigastric discomfort (0.2 to 0.4%), epigastric pain (1.8 to 2.5%), hyperacidity (0.02 to 0.4%), anorexia (0.05 to 0.4%), indigestion (0.1 to 0.2%), meteorism (0.2 to 0.4%), gastric pressure (0.5 to 1.0%), mouth dryness (0.1 to 0.3%). Glossitis, stomatitis, dysphagia and reflux esophagitis were each reported in less than 0.1% of the patients.

Dermatologic (1.6 to 3.9%): rash (0.2 to 1.4%), pruritus (0.3 to 1.3%), sweating (0.06 to 0.3%), exanthema (0.2 to 0.3%), itching (0.05 to 0.4%). Photosensitivity reaction, seborrhea, urticaria, eczema and nail disorder were each reported in 0.1% or less of the patients. One case of angioedema was also reported.

CNS (2.0 to 9.1%): headache (0.9 to 4.3%), dizziness (0.8 to 3.3%), malaise (0.04 to 0.8%), paresthesia (0.02 to 0.5%), somnolence (0.1 to 0.7%), vertigo (0.2 to 0.4%), confusion (0.2%), fatigue (0.1 to 0.9%), depression (0.6%), insomnia (0.1 to 0.2%). Leg cramps, nervousness, fever and paresis were each reported in 0.1% of the patients.

Cardiovascular: hypertension (0.02 to 0.3%), palpitations (0.02 to 0.2%), flushing (0.02 to 0.03%), purpura (0.02 to 0.2%). Tachycardia was reported in less than 0.1% of the patients.

Hematologic: anemia (0.04 to 0.3%), leukopenia (0.04 to 0.4%). Thrombocytopenia was reported in 0.1% or less of the patients.

Renal: hematuria (0.02 to 0.2%), edema (0.2 to 1.3%), micturition frequency (0.02 to 0.3%), polyuria (0.03 to 0.1%). Dysuria, cystitis, increased BUN, increased creatinine and albuminuria were each reported in less than 0.1% of the patients. Isolated cases of abnormal renal function and one case of renal failure were reported.

Hepatic (0.06 to 0.4%): abnormal hepatic function (0.3%). Jaundice, increased AST (SGOT), ALT (SGPT), gamma GT and bilirubin were each reported in less than 0.1% of the patients. Hepatitis, hepatic coma and hepatic failure were each reported once.

Respiratory (0.02 to 0.65%): dyspnea (0.2%), bronchospasm (0.1%).

Eyes, Ears, Nose, Throat: vision abnormal (0.02 to 0.3%). Diplopia, conjunctivitis, tinnitus, deafness, epistaxis and abnormal lacrimation were each reported in 0.1% or less of the patients.

Overdose: Symptoms and Treatment: Cases of overdose with tenoxicam have not been reported. In the event of overdosage, supportive and symptomatic therapy is indicated.

Dosage: A single daily dose of 20 mg should be taken orally at the same time each day. Higher doses should be avoided as they do not usually achieve a significantly greater therapeutic effect, but may be associated with a higher risk of adverse events.

In some patients a 10 mg daily dose may be sufficient. The smallest effective dose should be prescribed.

Geriatrics: As with other NSAIDs, tenoxicam should be used with special caution in elderly patients since they may be less able to tolerate side effects than younger patients. They are also more likely to be receiving concomitant medication or to have impaired hepatic, renal or cardiovascular function.

Information for the Patient: See Blue Section—Information for the Patient "Mobiflex".

Supplied: Each yellow, film-coated, oblong tablet, single scored on one side, imprinted ROCHE, contains: tenoxicam 20 mg. Nonmedicinal ingredients: cornstarch, hydroxypropyl methylcellulose, iron oxide, lactose, magnesium stearate, talc and titanium dioxide. White, opaque high density polyethylene bottles of 100. Store at 15 to 30°C.

(Shown in Product Recognition Section)

MODECATE® Ⓟ
MODECATE® CONCENTRATE Ⓟ

Squibb

Fluphenazine Decanoate

Antipsychotic

Pharmacology: The effects of fluphenazine decanoate are the same as those of fluphenazine HCl; however, the slow release of the decanoate derivative of fluphenazine from the site of injection results in a prolonged duration of action. Once released in the blood, fluphenazine decanoate is rapidly hydrolyzed by blood esterases with no attenuation of its antipsychotic action. The onset of action generally appears between 24 to 72 hours after injection, and the effects of the drug on psychotic symptoms become significant within 48 to 96 hours. Amelioration of symptoms then continues for 1 to 8 weeks with an average duration of 3 to 4 weeks. There is considerable variation in the individual response of patients to this depot fluphenazine and its use for maintenance therapy requires careful supervision.

Like other phenothiazines fluphenazine exerts activity at various levels of the CNS as well as on peripheral organ systems which accounts for its antipsychotic action and side effects common to this class of drugs. Indirect evidence indicates that the antipsychotic effects of phenothiazines are linked to their effect in blocking dopamine and other catecholamine receptor sites.

Fluphenazine differs from some phenothiazine derivatives in several respects: it has less potentiating effect on CNS depressants and anesthetics than do some of the phenothiazines and appears to be less sedating. While hypotension may occur less frequently than with other phenothiazines, appropriate precautions should be observed when using fluphenazine decanoate (see Precautions). Fluphenazine however, is among the group of phenothiazines which exhibit a greater propensity for producing extrapyramidal reactions.

Indications: Long-acting parenteral preparations for the management of manifestations of schizophrenia (see Dosage).

Contraindications: In patients with marked cerebral atherosclerosis, suspected or established subcortical brain damage, with or without hypothalamic damage, since a hyperthermic reaction with temperatures above 40°C may occur, sometimes not until 14 to 16 hours after drug administration.

Phenothiazines should not be used in patients receiving large doses of hypnotics, due to the possibility of potentiation. In comatose or severely depressed patients, and in the presence of blood dyscrasias, liver damage, renal insufficiency, pheochromocytoma or in patients with severe cardiovascular disorders. Patients who have shown hypersensitivity to other phenothiazines, including fluphenazine, should not be given fluphenazine decanoate as cross-sensitivity reactions may occur.

Fluphenazine decanoate is not indicated for the management of severely agitated psychotic patients, psychoneurotic patients or geriatric patients with confusion and/or agitation.

It is not intended for use in children under 12 years of age.

Warnings: Severe adverse reactions requiring immediate medical attention may occur and are difficult to predict. Therefore, the evaluation of tolerance and response, and establishment of adequate maintenance therapy, require careful stabilization of each patient under continuous, close medical observation and supervision.

Occupational Hazards: Mental and physical abilities required for driving a car or operating heavy machinery may be impaired. Potentiation of the effects of alcohol may also occur.

Pregnancy: Safety during pregnancy has not been established. The drug should not be administered to women of childbearing potential, particularly during the first trimester, unless, in the opinion of the physician, the expected benefits outweigh the potential risks to the fetus.

Children: Safety and efficacy of fluphenazine decanoate in children have not been established. Therefore, it is not indicated for use in the pediatric age group.

Tardive Dyskinesia: Tardive dyskinesia (TD) is a syndrome of involuntary hyperkinetic abnormal movements that occur in predisposed individuals during or following the cessation of long-term neuroleptic drug therapy. TD is characterized by involuntary, repetitive, purposeless hyperkinetic movements that involve the tongue, face, mouth, lips or jaw, trunk and extremities. The prevalence of TD greatly varies; when the mildest symptoms are included, prevalence can be 70%, whereas severe symptom rates are around 2.5%. The frequency and severity of TD increases with age, particularly in females.

Whether neuroleptic drugs differ in their potential to cause TD is unknown. The cautious interpretation is that any neuroleptic drug that suppresses TD, has the capacity to produce it. The mechanism of TD is not known; though dopamine dysfunction is believed to underlie TD, it may be necessary but not sufficient to explain this complex disorder.

There is no known treatment for established cases of TD, although the syndrome may remit, partially or completely, if neuroleptic treatment is withdrawn. However, neuroleptic treatment itself suppresses the signs and symptoms of the syndrome thereby masking the underlying disease process.

Given these considerations, neuroleptic drugs should be prescribed in a manner that is most likely to minimize the occurrence of TD. Reducing the dose to the lowest effective level or discontinuing the drug for as long as possible continues to be the most rational approach. In patients who require chronic treatment, the smallest dose and the shortest duration of treatment producing a satisfactory clinical response should be sought. The need for continued treatment should be reassessed periodically.

Precautions: Phenothiazines, particularly those with a long duration of action, should be used with caution in patients with a history of convulsive disorders since grand mal seizures have been known to occur.

Because of the possibility of cross sensitivity, fluphenazine decanoate should be used with caution in patients who have developed cholestatic jaundice, and dermatoses or other allergic reactions to phenothiazine derivatives.

Hypotensive phenomena may develop in phenothiazine-treated patients who are undergoing surgery. Careful observation is necessary and anesthetic or CNS depressant dosages may have to be reduced.

During the first months of therapy routine blood counts and hepatic function tests are advised as blood dyscrasias and liver damage, manifested by cholestatic jaundice, may occur. In patients on long-term therapy renal function should be monitored; if BUN becomes abnormal, treatment should be discontinued.

The effects of atropine or other drugs with similar action may be potentiated in patients receiving phenothiazines because of added anticholinergic effects. Paralytic ileus, even resulting in death, may occur especially in the elderly. Fluphenazine decanoate should be used cautiously in patients exposed to extreme heat or phosphorus insecticides.

As with other antipsychotic agents, the physician should be alert to the possible development of silent pneumonias in patients under treatment with phenothiazines.

The possibility of liver damage, lenticular and corneal deposits, pigmentary retinopathy and the development of irreversible dyskinesia should be borne in mind when patients are on prolonged therapy.

Since hypotension and ECG changes suggestive of myocardial ischemia have been associated with the administration of phenothiazines, fluphenazine decanoate should be used with caution in patients with compensated cardiovascular or cerebrovascular disorders.

Alterations in cephalin flocculation, alkaline phosphatase, sometimes accompanied by abnormalities in other liver function tests, have been reported in patients receiving esterified fluphenazine who have had no clinical evidence of liver damage. This, however, is not uncommon with phenothiazine therapy.

Neuroleptic drugs elevate prolactin levels; the elevation persists during chronic administration. Tissue culture experiments indicate that approximately one-third of human breast cancers are prolactin dependent in vitro, a factor of potential importance if the prescription of these drugs is contemplated in a patient with a previously detected breast cancer. Although disturbances such as galactorrhea, amenorrhea, gynecomastia, and impotence have been reported, the clinical significance of elevated serum prolactin levels is unknown for most patients. An increase in mammary neoplasms has been found in rodents after chronic administration of neuroleptic drugs.

Modecate (cont'd)

Neither clinical studies nor epidemiologic studies conducted to date, however, have shown an association between chronic administration of these drugs and mammary tumorigenesis; the available evidence is considered too limited to be conclusive at this time.

Adverse Effects: CNS: Extrapyramidal Symptoms: The side effects most frequently reported with phenothiazine compounds are extrapyramidal symptoms including pseudoparkinsonism (tremor, rigidity, etc.), dystonia, dyskinesia, akathisia, oculogyric crises, opisthotonos, and hyperreflexia. Fluphenazine decanoate produces a higher incidence of extrapyramidal reactions than the less potent piperazine derivatives or the straight-chain phenothiazines such as chlorpromazine. Extrapyramidal reactions tend to occur in the first few days after an injection. Caution should be exercised in those who have marked extrapyramidal reactions to oral phenothiazines or similar drugs, particularly elderly females. Extrapyramidal reactions may be alarming, and the patient should be forewarned and reassured. These reactions are often dose related and tend to subside when the dose is reduced or the drug temporarily withdrawn. However, antiparkinsonian medication may be required to control serious reactions.

The use of prophylactic antiparkinson medication may be considered, although its therapeutic value has not yet been established.

Tardive Dyskinesia: (see Warnings). The syndrome is characterized by rhythmical involuntary movements of the tongue, face, mouth, or jaw (e.g., protrusion of tongue, puffing of cheeks, puckering of mouth, chewing movements). These may be accompanied by involuntary movements of the trunk and the extremities.

As with all antipsychotic agents, tardive dyskinesia may appear in some patients on long-term therapy or may occur upon dosage reduction or after drug therapy has been discontinued. The risk seems to be greater in elderly patients on high dose therapy, especially females. The symptoms are persistent and in some patients appear to be irreversible.

There is no known effective treatment for tardive dyskinesia; antiparkinsonian agents usually do not alleviate the symptoms of this syndrome.

Neuroleptic drugs should be prescribed in a manner that is most likely to minimize the occurrence of tardive dyskinesia. Reducing the dose to the lowest effective level or discontinuing the drug for as long as possible continues to be the most rational approach. In patients who require chronic treatment, the smallest dose and the shortest duration of treatment producing a satisfactory clinical response should be sought. The need for continued treatment should be reassessed periodically.

Other CNS Effects: Drowsiness or lethargy, if they occur, may necessitate a reduction in dosage; the induction of a catatonic-like state has been known to occur with high dosages of fluphenazine. As with other phenothiazine compounds, reactivation or aggravation of psychotic processes may be encountered.

In some patients, phenothiazine derivatives have been known to cause restlessness, excitement, or bizarre dreams.

Rare occurrences of neuroleptic malignant syndrome (NMS) have been reported in patients on neuroleptic therapy. The syndrome is characterized by hyperthermia, muscular rigidity, autonomic instability (labile blood pressure, tachycardia, diaphoresis), akinesia, and altered consciousness, sometimes progressing to stupor or coma. Leukocytosis, elevated CPK, liver function abnormalities, and acute renal failure may also occur. Neuroleptic therapy should be discontinued immediately and vigorous symptomatic treatment implemented since the syndrome is potentially fatal.

Autonomic Nervous System: Hypotension, hypertension and fluctuations in blood pressure have been reported with fluphenazine.

Patients with pheochromocytoma, cerebral vascular or renal insufficiency, or a severe cardiac reserve deficiency such as mitral insufficiency, appear to be particularly prone to hypotensive reactions with phenothiazine compounds and should therefore be observed closely when the drug is administered. If severe hypotension should occur, supportive measures including the use of i.v. vasopressor drugs should be instituted immediately. Levarterenol bitartrate injection, USP is the most suitable drug for this purpose; **epinephrine should not be used** since phenothiazine derivatives can reverse its action, resulting in a further lowering of blood pressure.

Autonomic reactions including nausea and loss of appetite, salivation, polyuria, perspiration, dry mouth, headache, and constipation may occur. Autonomic effects can usually be controlled by reducing or temporarily discontinuing dosage.

In some patients, phenothiazine derivatives have caused blurred vision, glaucoma, bladder paralysis, fecal impaction, paralytic ileus, tachycardia, or nasal congestion.

Metabolic and Endocrine: Weight change, peripheral edema, abnormal lactation, gynecomastia, menstrual irregularities, false pregnancy test results, impotency in men and increased libido in women have all been known to occur in some patients on phenothiazine therapy.

Allergic Reactions: Skin disorders such as itching, erythema, urticaria, seborrhea, photosensitivity, eczema and exfoliative dermatitis have been reported with phenothiazine derivatives. The possibility of anaphylactoid reactions should be borne in mind.

Hematologic: Leukopenia, agranulocytosis, thrombocytopenic or nonthrombocytopenic purpura, eosinophilia, and pancytopenia have been observed with phenothiazine derivatives. If any soreness of the mouth, gums or throat or any symptoms of upper respiratory infection occur and confirmatory leukocyte count indicates cellular depression, therapy should be discontinued and other appropriate measures instituted immediately.

Hepatic: Liver damage as manifested by cholestatic jaundice may be encountered, particularly during the first months of therapy; treatment should be discontinued if this occurs. An increase in cephalin flocculation, sometimes accompanied by alterations in other liver function tests, has been reported in patients receiving the enanthate ester of fluphenazine (a closely related compound) who have had no clinical evidence of liver damage.

Others: Sudden, unexpected and unexplained deaths have been reported in hospitalized psychotic patients receiving phenothiazines. Previous brain damage or seizures may be predisposing factors; high doses should be avoided in known seizure patients. Several patients have shown flare-ups of psychotic behaviour patterns shortly before death. Autopsy findings have usually revealed acute fulminating pneumonia or pneumonitis, aspiration of gastric contents or intramyocardial lesions.

Potentiation of CNS depressants (opiates, analgesics, antihistamines, barbiturates, alcohol) may occur.

The following adverse reactions have also occurred with phenothiazine derivatives: systemic lupus erythematosus like syndrome, hypotension severe enough to cause fatal cardiac arrest, altered ECG and EEG tracings, altered CSF proteins, cerebral edema, asthma, disturbances of body temperature (hypo- or hyperthermia), laryngeal edema, and angioneurotic edema. Skin pigmentation, and lenticular and corneal opacities have been seen with long-term use.

Injections of fluphenazine decanoate are well tolerated, local tissue reactions occur only rarely.

Overdose: Symptoms: Will likely be manifested as extrapyramidal signs, hypotension and sedation. Initial hospitalization may be required in cases of large overdose and close medical supervision should be maintained throughout the duration of drug action.

Treatment: Supportive and symptomatic: no further injections should be given until the patient shows signs of relapse and the dosage then should be decreased. An airway should be maintained. Severe hypotension calls for the immediate use of an i.v. vasopressor drug, such as levarterenol bitartrate USP. Epinephrine should **not** be used, as a further lowering of blood pressure may result. Extrapyramidal symptoms may be treated with antiparkinsonian agents.

Dosage: Fluphenazine decanoate is given i.m. preferably in the gluteus maximus, or s.c. It is not for i.v. use.

As a long-acting depot fluphenazine, fluphenazine decanoate has been found useful in the maintenance treatment of non-agitated, chronic schizophrenic patients who when stabilized with short-acting neuroleptics, might benefit from transfer to longer-acting injectable medication. The changeover of medication should aim at maintaining a clinical outcome similar to, or better than, that obtained with the previous therapy. To achieve and maintain the optimum dose, the changeover from other neuroleptic medication should proceed gradually and constant supervision is required during the period of dosage adjustment in order to minimize the risk of overdosage or insufficient suppression of psychotic symptoms before the next injection.

The initial recommended dose is 2.5 mg to 12.5 mg. An initial dose of 12.5 mg is usually well tolerated. However, an initial test dose of 2.5 mg is recommended in patients: over the age of 50 or with disorders that predispose to undue reactions; whose individual or family history suggests a predisposition to extrapyramidal reactions; who have not previously received a long acting depot neuroleptic.

The onset of action generally appears between 24 to 72 hours after injection, and the effects of the drug on psychotic symptoms become significant within 48 to 96 hours.

Discontinuation of oral neuroleptic medication has been recommended for up to 1 week prior to initiation of depot fluphenazine therapy.

Subsequent doses and frequency of administration must be determined for each patient. There is no reliable dosage comparability between a short-acting neuroleptic and depot fluphenazine and, therefore, the dosage of the long-acting drug must be individualized. Except in particularly sensitive patients, a second dose of 12.5 mg or 25 mg can be given 4 to 10 days after the initial injection. Subsequent dosage adjustments are made in accordance with the clinical circumstances and the response of the patient. Patients can usually be controlled with 25 mg or less, every 2 to 3 weeks. Although doses greater than 50 mg are usually not necessary, doses up to 100 mg have been used in some patients. If doses greater than 50 mg are necessary, the next dose and succeeding doses should be increased in increments of 12.5 mg. While the response to a single injection lasts usually 2 to 3 weeks, it may last for 4 weeks or more.

After an appropriate dosage adjustment is achieved, regular and continuous supervision and reassessment is considered essential in order to permit any further dosage adjustments that might be required to ensure use of the lowest effective individual dose and avoid troublesome side effects.

Since higher doses increase the incidence of extrapyramidal reactions and other adverse effects, the amount of drug used should not be increased in order to prolong the intervals between injections. With higher doses, there is also more variability in the action of depot fluphenazine.

Modecate Concentrate 100 mg/mL may be administered in preference to Modecate 25 mg/mL in patients who complain of discomfort with a large injection volume or when smaller injection volume is desirable.

A dry syringe with a needle of at least 21 gauge should be used. A wet needle or syringe may cause the solution to become cloudy.

Supplied: Modecate: Each mL of injectable solution contains: fluphenazine decanoate 25 mg. Nonmedicinal ingredients: benzyl alcohol 1.5% w/v (preservative) and sesame oil. Vials of 5 mL. Store at room temperature and protect from light.

Modecate Concentrate: Each mL of injectable solution contains: fluphenazine decanoate 100 mg. Nonmedicinal ingredients: benzyl alcohol 1.5% w/v (preservative) and sesame oil. Ampuls of 1 mL. Store at room temperature and protect from light.

MODITEN® ENANTHATE Ⓟ

Squibb

Fluphenazine Enanthate

Antipsychotic

Pharmacology: The esterification of fluphenazine markedly prolongs its duration of effect without unduly attenuating its beneficial action. The onset of action generally appears 24 to 72 hours after injection, and the antipsychotic effects become significant within 48 to 96 hours. Amelioration of symptoms continues for 1 to 3 weeks or longer, with an average duration of effect of about 2 weeks.

Indications: A long acting parenteral antipsychotic agent indicated in the maintenance therapy of schizophrenia. There is considerable individual variability in the response and duration of action of Moditen Enanthate Injectable and, frequently, the need to control with oral medication the extrapyramidal reactions which are produced by this long acting preparation.

Depot fluphenazines are not indicated in the management of severely agitated psychotic patients, psychoneurotic patients or geriatric patients with confusion and/or agitation.

Children: The safety and efficacy of fluphenazine enanthate in children has not been established; therefore, the drug is not indicated for use in the pediatric age group.

Contraindications, Precautions and Adverse Effects: See Moditen HCl. Some adverse effects may be severe. The evaluation of tolerance and response requires stabilization of each patient under continuous and close medical observation. Local tissue reactions to the injection occur infrequently.

Depot fluphenazines produce a higher incidence of extrapyramidal reactions than the less potent piperazine derivatives or the straight chain phenothiazines such as chlorpromazine. Extrapyramidal reactions tend to occur in the first few days after injection of depot fluphenazines. Extrapyramidal reactions may be alarming, and the patient should be forewarned and reassured. These reactions are often dose related and tend to subside when the dose is reduced or the drug temporarily withdrawn. However, antiparkinsonian medication may be required to control serious reactions. The evidence available tends to indicate that persistent tardive dyskinesias result from heavy drug overloading of the extrapyramidal system. Therefore, avoid overdosing of depot fluphenazines and do not exceed the optimum dosage in an attempt to decrease the frequency of injections, since this will tend to elicit marked extrapyramidal reactions.

An increase in cephalin flocculation, sometimes accompanied by alterations in other liver function tests, has been reported in patients who have had no clinical evidence of liver damage.

Dosage: Usual adult dosage is 25 mg injected every 2 weeks by the i.m. route only, not by the i.v. route. Requirements vary and may range from 12.5 to 100 mg given at intervals of 1 to 3 weeks. Doses of 75 mg or even less have caused severe reactions in some patients; therefore, a gradual increase in dosage is recommended.

It may be advisable to start with a short acting form of fluphenazine before giving the enanthate in patients who have had no history of taking phenothiazines, severely agitated patients and poor risk patients.

Supplied: Each mL of injectable solution contains: fluphenazine enanthate USP 25 mg in sesame oil with benzyl alcohol 1.5% as preservative. Nonmedicinal ingredients: benzyl alcohol 1.5% w/v (preservative) and sesame oil. Vials of 5 mL.

MODITEN® HCl ℞

Squibb

Fluphenazine HCl

Antipsychotic

Pharmacology: Fluphenazine hydrochloride exerts activity at various levels of the CNS as well as on peripheral organ systems, which accounts for its antipsychotic action and side effects. Indirect evidence indicates that the antipsychotic effects of phenothiazines are linked to their effect in blocking dopamine and other catecholamine receptor sites.

Fluphenazine has less potentiating effect on CNS depressants and anesthetics and appears to be less sedating than some other phenothiazines. While hypotension may occur less frequently than with other phenothiazines, appropriate precautions should be observed when using fluphenazine hydrochloride (see Precautions). Fluphenazine, however, is among the group of phenothiazines which exhibits a greater propensity for producing extrapyramidal reactions.

Indications: For the management of manifestations of psychotic disorders not associated with mental retardation.

Contraindications: In patients with suspected or established subcortical brain damage with or without hypothalamic damage, since hyperthermic reactions with temperatures above 40°C may occur, sometimes not until 14 to 16 hours after drug administration; patients receiving large doses of hypnotics, due to the possibility of potentiation; comatose or severely depressed states, and in the presence of blood dyscrasias, bone marrow depression or liver damage; patients who have shown hypersensitivity to fluphenazine. Cross-sensitivity reactions to other phenothiazine derivatives may occur; patients with pheochromocytoma, cerebrovascular or renal insufficiency, or severe cardiac reserve deficiency, such as mitral insufficiency, or in patients who have exhibited idiosyncrasy to other centrally-acting drugs, as these patients may experience severe reactions to phenothiazine compounds and are particularly prone to hypotensive reactions.

Warnings: Insidious severe adverse reactions requiring immediate medical attention may occur. Therefore, the evaluation of tolerance and response, and establishment of adequate maintenance therapy require careful stabilization of each patient under continuous, close medical observation and supervision.

Potentiation of CNS depressants (opiates, analgesics, antihistamines, barbiturates, alcohol) may occur.

The antiemetic effect of phenothiazines can obscure signs of toxicity due to overdosage of other drugs, or mask the symptoms of disease such as brain tumor or intestinal obstruction.

Occupational Hazards: Mental and physical abilities required for driving a car or operating heavy machinery may be impaired.

Pregnancy: Safety during pregnancy has not been established. The drug should not be administered to women of childbearing potential, and particularly during the first trimester unless, in the opinion of the physician, the expected benefits outweigh the potential risks to the fetus.

Children: Safety and efficacy of fluphenazine hydrochloride in children have not been established, therefore it is not recommended for use in the pediatric age group.

Precautions: Phenothiazines should be used with caution in patients with a history of convulsive disorders since grand mal seizures have been known to occur.

During the first months of therapy, routine blood counts, renal and hepatic function tests are advised as blood dyscrasias and liver damage, manifested by cholestatic jaundice, may occur. Renal function should be monitored in patients on long term therapy; if BUN becomes abnormal, treatment should be discontinued.

Because of the possibility of cross-sensitivity, fluphenazine hydrochloride should be used with caution in patients who have developed cholestatic jaundice, dermatoses or other allergic reactions to phenothiazine derivatives.

Neuroleptic drugs elevate prolactin levels; the elevation persists during chronic administration. Tissue culture experiments indicate that approximately one-third of human breast cancers are prolactin dependent in vitro, a factor of potential importance if the prescription of these drugs is contemplated in a patient with a previously detected breast cancer. Although disturbances such as galactorrhea, amenorrhea, gynecomastia, and impotence have been reported, the clinical significance of elevated serum prolactin levels is unknown for most patients. An increase in mammary neoplasms has been found in rodents after chronic administration of neuroleptic drugs. Neither clinical studies nor epidemiologic studies conducted to date, however, have shown an association between chronic administration of these drugs and mammary tumorigenesis; the available evidence is considered too limited to be conclusive at this time.

Hypotensive phenomena may develop in psychotic patients treated with large doses of phenothiazines who are undergoing surgery. Careful observation is necessary and it should be remembered that the dosage of anesthetics and CNS depressants may have to be reduced.

Hypotension, which is typically orthostatic, may occur especially in elderly and alcoholic patients. This effect may be additive with other agents that cause a lowering of blood pressure. Fluphenazine hydrochloride may also block the antihypertensive action of guanethidine and similar compounds. Avoid epinephrine in the treatment of phenothiazine induced hypotension because phenothiazines may reverse the action of epinephrine and thereby cause a further decrease in blood pressure.

Hypotension and ECG changes have been associated with the administration of phenothiazines, therefore fluphenazine hydrochloride should be used with caution in patients with cardiovascular or cerebrovascular disorders.

Exercise caution in patients with special medical disorders, such as mitral insufficiency or pheochromocytoma.

Agranulocytosis has been observed with phenothiazines, usually between the fourth and tenth week of treatment. Patients on long-term therapy should be observed with particular care during this period and the drug should be discontinued and WBC and differential counts obtained if the patient develops sore throat, fever, and/or weakness.

The effects of atropine or other drugs with similar action may be potentiated in patients receiving phenothiazines because of added anticholinergic effects.

Paralytic ileus, even resulting in death, may occur, especially in the elderly. This possibility should be kept in mind and appropriate measures should be taken if constipation develops.

Exercise caution in patients exposed to extreme heat or phosphorus insecticides, or with a history of ulcer disease.

The possibility of liver damage, pigmentary retinopathy, lenticular and corneal deposits and the development of irreversible dyskinesia should be borne in mind when patients are on prolonged therapy.

Phenothiazines do not produce psychic dependence; however, gastritis, nausea and vomiting, dizziness and tremulousness have been reported following abrupt cessation of high dose therapy. Reports suggest that these symptoms can be reduced if concomitant antiparkinsonian agents are continued for several weeks after the phenothiazine is withdrawn.

The physician should be alert to the possible development of silent pneumonias in patients under treatment with phenothiazines.

The occasional increase in activity resulting from treatment may augment the severity of pain in angina pectoris patients. Such patients should be observed carefully and the drug withdrawn if necessary.

Adverse Effects: CNS: Most frequently reported are extrapyramidal symptoms including pseudo-parkinsonism, dystonia, dyskinesia, akathisia, oculogyric crises, opisthotonos, and hyperreflexia. Fluphenazine produces a higher incidence of extrapyramidal reactions than the less potent piperazine derivatives or the straight chain phenothiazines, such as chlorpromazine. Extrapyramidal reactions tend to occur in the first few days following an injection and the patient should be forewarned and reassured. These reactions are often dose related and tend to subside when the dose is reduced or the drug temporarily withdrawn. Antiparkinsonian medication (such as benztropine mesylate, USP or i.v. caffeine and sodium benzoate injection, USP) may be required to control serious reactions. Drowsiness or lethargy, if they occur, may necessitate a reduction in dosage; the induction of a catatonic like state has been known to occur with dosages in excess of the recommended amounts. Reactivation or aggravation of psychotic processes may be encountered. In some patients phenothiazine derivatives have been known to cause restlessness, excitement, or bizarre dreams.

Persistent Tardive Dyskinesia: May appear in some patients on long-term therapy or after drug therapy has been discontinued. The risk seems to be greater in elderly patients on high dose therapy, especially females. The symptoms are persistent and in some patients appear to be irreversible. The syndrome is characterized by rhythmical involuntary movements of the tongue, face, mouth, or jaw (e.g., protrusion of tongue, puffing of cheeks, puckering of mouth, chewing movements). These may be accompanied by involuntary movements of the extremities. Evidence indicates that persistent tardive dyskinesias result from heavy drug overloading of the extrapyramidal system. The lowest effective dose should be used. There is no known effective treatment for tardive dyskinesia; antiparkinsonian agents usually do not alleviate the symptoms of this syndrome. It is suggested that all antipsychotic agents be discontinued if these symptoms appear. If it is necessary to reinstitute treatment, increase the dosage of the agent, or change the antipsychotic agent, the syndrome may be masked. The physician may lessen the risk of the syndrome's occurrence by restricting the use of neuroleptic drugs, reducing the dose, or discontinuing the drug, when possible, particularly in patients over the age of fifty. Fine vermicular movements of the tongue may be an early sign of the syndrome and if the medication is stopped at that time, the syndrome may not develop.

Autonomic Nervous System: Hypotension, hypertension and fluctuations in blood pressure have been reported with phenothiazines. Patients with pheochromocytoma, cerebrovascular or renal insufficiency, or a severe cardiac reserve deficiency such as mitral insufficiency, are prone to hypotensive reactions with phenothiazine compounds, and should therefore be observed closely when the drug is administered. If severe hypotension should occur, supportive measures, including the use of i.v. vasopressor drugs, should be instituted immediately. Levarterenol bitartrate injection, USP, is the drug of choice; **epinephrine should not be used** since phenothiazine derivatives can reverse its action, resulting in a further lowering of blood pressure.

Nausea, anorexia, salivation, polyuria, perspiration, dry mouth, headache, and constipation may occur. Autonomic effects can usually be controlled by reducing dosage or temporarily discontinuing treatment.

In some patients, blurred vision, glaucoma, bladder paralysis, fecal impaction, paralytic ileus, tachycardia, or nasal congestion have occurred.

Metabolic and Endocrine: Weight change, peripheral edema, abnormal lactation, gynecomastia, menstrual irregularities, false pregnancy test results, impotency in men and increased libido in women have all been known to occur in some patients on phenothiazine therapy.

Allergic: Skin disorders such as itching, hypertrophic papillae of the tongue, angioneurotic edema, contact dermatitis, allergic purpura, erythema, urticaria, seborrhea, photosensitivity, eczema and exfoliative dermatitis have been reported. Fevers, laryngeal edema, and asthma have also been reported. The possibility of anaphylactoid reactions, occurring in some patients, should be borne in mind.

Hematologic: Leukopenia, agranulocytosis, thrombocytopenic or non-thrombocytopenic purpura, eosinophilia, anemia, granulocytopenia and pancytopenia have been observed. If any soreness of the mouth, gums, or throat or any symptoms of upper respiratory infection occur and confirmatory leukocyte count indicates cellular depression, therapy should be discontinued and other appropriate measures instituted immediately.

Hepatic: Treatment should be discontinued if liver damage (as manifested by cholestatic jaundice) occurs, particularly during

Moditen HCl (cont'd)

the first months of therapy. An increase in cephalin flocculation, sometimes accompanied by alterations in other liver function tests, has been reported in patients receiving the enanthate ester of fluphenazine (a closely related compound). They have had no clinical evidence of liver damage.

Others: Sudden, unexpected and unexplained deaths have been reported in hospitalized psychotic patients receiving phenothiazines. Previous brain damage or seizures may be predisposing factors; high doses should be avoided in known seizure patients. Several patients have shown flareup of psychotic behaviour patterns shortly before death. Autopsy findings have usually revealed acute fulminating pneumonia or pneumonitis, aspiration of gastric contents or intramyocardial lesions.

The following adverse reactions have also occurred with phenothiazine derivatives: systemic lupus erythematosus-like syndrome, hypotension severe enough to cause fatal cardiac arrest, altered ECG and EEG tracings, altered CSF proteins, cerebral edema. Skin pigmentation, and lenticular and corneal opacities have been seen with long-term use.

Overdose: Symptoms: Manifested as extrapyramidal signs, hypotension and sedation. Initial hospitalization may be required in cases of large overdose and close medical supervision should be maintained throughout the duration of drug action.

Treatment: Supportive and symptomatic: the drug should be discontinued until the patient shows signs of relapse and treatment may be reinstituted at lower doses. In severe cases of oral overdosing vomiting should be induced or gastric lavage instituted if the patient is conscious. An airway should be maintained. Severe hypotension calls for the immediate use of an i.v. vasopressor drug, such as levarterenol bitartrate U.S.P. **Epinephrine should not be used,** as a further lowering of blood pressure may result. Extrapyramidal symptoms may be treated with antiparkinsonian agents.

Dosage: The smallest amount of drug that will produce the desired results must be carefully determined for each individual since optimal dosage levels of this potent drug vary from patient to patient.

Adults: Depending on severity and duration of symptoms, total daily oral dose for psychotic patients may range initially from 2.5 to 10 mg, administered in divided doses every 6 to 8 hours. Treatment is best instituted with a low initial dosage, which may be increased, if necessary, until the desired clinical effects are achieved. Oral doses exceeding 20 mg daily should be used with caution.

When symptoms are controlled, dosage can generally be reduced gradually to daily oral maintenance doses of 1.0 or 5.0 mg, often given as a single daily dose. Continued treatment is needed to achieve maximum therapeutic benefits; further adjustments in dosage may be necessary during the course of therapy to meet the patient's requirements.

Geriatrics: The suggested starting dose is 1.0 to 2.5 mg orally/day, adjusted according to the response of the patient. Fluphenazine enanthate or fluphenazine decanoate, both long acting injectables may be a better alternative to oral fluphenazine hydrochloride when patients are unable or unwilling to take oral therapy.

Supplied: Each sugar-coated, coral tablet contains: fluphenazine hydrochloride 10 mg. Nonmedicinal ingredients: acacia, calcium carbonate, castor oil, cornstarch, D&C red No. 27, ethyl cellulose, FD&C yellow No. 5, gelatin, lactose, magnesium carbonate, magnesium stearate, pharmaceutical glaze, povidone, printing ink, sodium benzoate, sucrose, talc and titanium dioxide. Bottles of 100. Store at room temperature, keep tightly closed, protect from light, and avoid excessive heat.

(Shown in Product Recognition Section)

MODULON® ℞

Axcan Pharma

Trimebutine Maleate

Lower Gastrointestinal Tract Motility Regulator

Pharmacology: Trimebutine is a noncompetitive spasmolytic agent. It possesses moderate opiate receptor affinity and has a marked antiserotonin activity especially on "mu" receptors. It induces regulation of spontaneous activity and increases synchronization between electrophysiological spikes and contractions in isolated guinea pig taenia coli and ileum. However, it does not alter normal motility, but regulates abnormal intestinal activity.

Indications: For the treatment and relief of symptoms associated with the irritable bowel syndrome (spastic colon). In postoperative paralytic ileus in order to accelerate the resumption of the intestinal transit following abdominal surgery.

Contraindications: Known hypersensitivity to trimebutine or any of the excipients.

In addition to the above, trimebutine injectable is contraindicated in neonates.

No other contraindications have been identified at this time.

Warnings: *Pregnancy:* Although teratological studies have not shown any drug related adverse effects on the course and outcome of pregnancy in laboratory animals by both oral and parenteral routes, the use of trimebutine in pregnant women is not recommended.

Caution should be exercised when administering trimebutine parenterally to patients under antihypertensive therapy.

Children: Not recommended for use in children under 12 years of age.

Precautions: Drug Interactions: Animal studies have shown that trimebutine increases the duration of d-tubocurarine-induced curarization. No other drug interactions have been observed during clinical trials or otherwise reported.

Adverse Effects: In clinical studies, adverse effects of mild to moderate nature occurred in 7% of the patients treated with trimebutine. No single side effect occurred in more than 1.8% of the patients and some of these might have been related to the patients' conditions rather than the medication. The commonly reported adverse effects are as follows:

Oral: Gastrointestinal: Dry mouth, foul taste, diarrhea, dyspepsia, epigastric pain, nausea and constipation were reported in a total of 3.1% of the patient population.

CNS: Drowsiness, fatigue, dizziness, hot/cold sensations and headaches were reported in 3.3%.

Allergic Reactions: Rash in 0.4% of the patients.

Miscellaneous effects: Menstrual problems, painful enlargement of breasts, anxiety, urine retention and slight deafness were also infrequently reported.

Injectable: The most frequently reported side effects were dizziness (1.8%), hypotension/vagal episode (1.0%), diarrhea (0.6%) and lightheadedness (0.5%). Isolated cases of convulsions, nausea, vomiting, malaise, lipothymic reaction, confusion, sweating, bradycardia, cramps and reaction at injection site were also reported.

Overdose: Symptoms and Treatment: No evidence of overdosage have been reported to date. However, if overdosage should occur following oral administration of trimebutine, gastric lavage is recommended. Treatment should be made according to the symptoms observed.

Dosage: Tablets: The adult recommended dose is up to 600 mg daily in divided doses. It may be administered as two 100 mg tablets 3 times daily before meals or one 200 mg tablet 3 times daily before meals.

Parenteral Solution: Dosage should be individually tailored according to response, but the total parenteral daily dose should not exceed 300 mg. The usual adult dose is 50 to 100 mg 3 times daily, administered as an i.m. injection, as a 3 minute i.v. injection or as a 60 minute i.v. infusion (in dextrose 5% injection or in sodium chloride injection), until resumption of intestinal motility.

Supplied: Tablets: 100 mg: Each white, round, biconvex tablet, bisected on one side and embossed "J" on the other side, contains: trimebutine maleate 100 mg. Nonmedicinal ingredients: cornstarch, gelatin, lactose spray, magnesium stearate, manitol, polyethylene glycol and sucrose. Bottles of 250. Store at room temperature.

200 mg: Each white, round, biconvex tablet, bisected on one side and embossed "J" on the other side, contains: trimebutine maleate 200 mg. Nonmedicinal ingredients: lactose, magnesium stearate, microcrystalline cellulose, polyvidone, silica gel and sodium carboxymethyl ether. Bottles of 100. Store at room temperature.

Parenteral Solution: Each 5 mL ampul contains: trimebutine maleate 50 mg. Nonmedicinal ingredients: benzyl alcohol, sodium chloride and water for injection. Boxes of 5. Store in refrigerated place (5°C). At room temperature it should be used within 48 hours.

(Shown in Product Recognition Section)

MODURET® ℞

MSD

Hydrochlorothiazide—Amiloride HCl

Diuretic—Antihypertensive

Pharmacology: Moduret is a diuretic/antihypertensive combining the potent natriuretic action of hydrochlorothiazide with the potassium conserving property of amiloride. The mild diuretic and antihypertensive actions of amiloride are additive to the natriuretic, diuretic and antihypertensive activity of the thiazide while minimizing the loss of potassium and lessening the likelihood of acid base imbalance. The onset of the diuretic action is within 1 to 2 hours and this action appears to be sustained for approximately 24 hours.

Hydrochlorothiazide: Hydrochlorothiazide is a diuretic and antihypertensive agent. It affects the renal tubular mechanism of electrolyte reabsorption.

Hydrochlorothiazide increases excretion of sodium and chloride in approximately equivalent amounts, and may cause a simultaneous, usually mimimal, loss of bicarbonate. Natriuresis is usually accompanied by some loss of potassium.

The mechanism of the antihypertensive effect of thiazides may be related to the excretion and redistribution of body sodium. Hydrochlorothiazide usually does not decrease normal blood pressure.

The onset of the diuretic action of hydrochlorothiazide occurs in 2 hours and the peak action in about 4 hours. Diuretic activity lasts about 6 to 12 hours. Hydrochlorothiazide is eliminated rapidly by the kidney.

Amiloride: Amiloride is an antikaliuretic drug with mild natriuretic diuretic and antihypertensive activity. These activities may be additive to the effects of thiazides or other saluretic-diuretic agents. The principal use of amiloride is to conserve potassium in selected patients receiving kaliuretic-diuretic agents. The action is not related to the level of aldosterone excretion. Amiloride is not an aldosterone antagonist. The drug acts directly on the distal portion of the nephron. Amiloride causes an increase in sodium excretion and a decrease in potassium and hydrogen ion excretion. Chloride excretion may remain unchanged or increase slowly with continued therapy.

Approximately 50% of an oral dose is absorbed. Amiloride usually begins to act within 2 hours after an oral dose. Its effect on electrolyte excretion reaches a peak between 6 and 10 hours and lasts about 24 hours. Peak plasma levels are obtained in 3 to 4 hours and plasma half-life varies from 6 to 9 hours.

Amiloride is not metabolized by the liver. About 50% of a 20 mg dose of amiloride is excreted unchanged in the urine and 40% is excreted in the stool within 72 hours. In clinical studies amiloride was found to have litle effect on glomerular filtration rate or renal blood flow.

Indications: Fixed dose combination drugs are not indicated for initial therapy. Patients should be titrated on the individual drugs. If the fixed combination represents the dosage so determined, its use may be more convenient in patient management. If during maintenance therapy dosage adjustment is necessary it is advisable to use the individual drugs.

Moduret is indicated in the maintenance therapy of patients with hepatic cirrhosis with ascites and edema. In those patients with edema of cardiac origin or with arterial hypertension who are hypokalemic or in whom maintenance of normal potassium levels is considered to be clinically important e.g., digitalized patients, patients in whom adequate dietary intake of potassium is not feasible or patients with cardiac arrhythmias.

Hepatic Cirrhosis with Ascites and Edema: Amiloride used alone may provide satisfactory diuresis with diminished potassium loss and with a reduced risk of metabolic alkalosis. In resistant cases amiloride may be used with kaliuretic diuretic agents to help produce satisfactory diuresis, while maintaining a more balanced serum electrolyte pattern. As with all therapy for the ascites of hepatic cirrhosis, gradual weight loss and avoidance of electrolyte imbalance are the chief objectives (see Precautions).

Contraindications: Hyperkalemia: Moduret should not be used in the presence of elevated serum potasssium levels (see Warnings).

Antikaliuretic Therapy or Potassium Salts: Other antikaliuretic agents and potassium supplements are contraindicated in patients receiving Moduret (such combination therapy is commonly associated with rapid increases in plasma potassium levels).

Impaired Renal Function: Anuria, acute renal failure, severe or progressive renal disease, and diabetic nephropathy are contraindications to the use of Moduret (see Warnings).

Hypersensitivity: in patients who are hypersensitive to either component, or to other sulfonamide-derived drugs.

Warnings: Hyperkalemia: Hyperkalemia, i.e., serum potassium levels over 5.5 mEq/L, has been observed in some patients who received amiloride either alone or with diuretics. This has been noted particularly in elderly patients, in diabetic patients, and in hospitalized patients with hepatic cirrhosis or cardiac edema who had known renal impairment, were seriously ill, or were receiving vigorous diuretic therapy. Since fatalities have occurred in such patients, they should be monitored carefully for clinical, laboratory, and electrocardiographic (ECG) evidence of hyperkalemia and for acidosis. Monitoring of the serum potassium level is important because hyperkalemia is not always associated with an abnormal ECG.

Warning signs and symptoms of hyperkalemia include paresthesias, muscular weakness, fatigue, flaccid paralysis of the extremities, bradycardia, shock and ECG abnormalities.

When abnormal, the ECG in hyperkalemia is characterized primarily by tall, peaked T waves or elevations from previous tracings. There may also be lowering of the R wave and increased depth of the S wave, widening and even disappearance of the P wave, progressive widening of the QRS complex, prolongation of the PR interval, and ST depression.

If hyperkalemia occurs in patients taking Moduret the drug should be discontinued immediately. If the serum potassium level exceeds 6.5 mEq/L, active measures should be taken to reduce it. Such measures include the intravenous administration of sodium bicarbonate solution or oral or parenteral glucose with a rapid-acting insulin preparation. If needed, a cation exchange resin such as sodium polystyrene sulfonate may be given orally or by enema. Patients with persistent hyperkalemia may require dialysis.

Diabetes Mellitus: In diabetic patients, hyperkalemia has been commonly reported with the use of amiloride, particularly if they have chronic renal disease or prerenal azotemia. Some deaths occurred in this last group of patients. Therefore, if therapy with amiloride is considered essential, the drug should be used with caution in diabetic or suspected diabetic patients and only after first determining the status of renal function.

Careful monitoring of serum potassium levels is required throughout the therapy.

One patient with poorly controlled diabetes mellitus who became severely hyperkalemic while on amiloride died following 2 repeated i.v. glucose tolerance tests. Therefore, amiloride should be discontinued at least 3 days before glucose tolerance testing.

In diabetic patients, insulin requirements may be increased, decreased, or unchanged due to the hydrochlorothiazide component. Diabetes mellitus which has been latent may become manifest during administration of thiazide diuretics.

Metabolic or Respiratory Acidosis: Antikaliuretic therapy should be instituted only with caution in patients in whom respiratory or metabolic acidosis may occur, such as patients with cardiopulmonary disease or diabetes. If Moduret is given to the patients, frequent monitoring of acid-base balance is necessary. Shifts in acid-base balance alter the ratio of extracellular/intracellular potassium, and the development of acidosis may be associated with rapid increases in serum potassium levels.

Impaired Renal Function: Patients with impaired renal function other than those listed under Contraindications and who have BUN levels over 30 mg/100 mL, serum creatinine levels over 1.5 mg/100 mL, or blood urea values over 60 mg/100 mL should not receive the drug without careful, frequent monitoring of serum electrolytes, creatinine, and BUN levels. Potassium retention associated with the use of Moduret is accentuated in the presence of renal impairment and may result in the rapid development of hyperkalemia. Prolongation of amiloride hydrochloride excretion was observed in patients with renal impairment.

Table I—Moduret

Other Adverse Reactions

	Incidence ≥3%	Incidence >1%–<3%	Incidence ≤1%
Gastrointestinal (7.1% of patients)	Nausea/Anorexia (3.7%)	Diarrhea Gastrointestinal pain Abdominal pain	Constipation Gastrointestinal bleeding Gastrointestinal disturbance Appetite changes Abdominal fullness Hiccups Thirst Vomiting Anorexia Flatulence Bad taste
CNS (13.9% of patients)	Headache (7.8%) Dizziness (6.1%) Weakness (4.0%)		Paresthesia/numbness Stupor Vertigo Insomnia Nervousness Depression Sleepiness Mental confusion Visual disturbance
Dermatologic (5.2% of patients)	Rash (3.4%)	Pruritus	Flushing
Cardiovascular (4.3% of patients)		Arrhythmia	Tachycardia Digitalis toxicity Orthostatic hypotension Angina pectoris
Musculoskeletal (3.7% of patients)		Leg ache	Muscle cramps/spasm Joint pain Chest pain Back pain
Respiratory (2.6% of patients)		Dyspnea	Nasal congestion
Urogenital (1.7% of patients)			Impotence Nocturia Dysuria Incontinence
Endocrine (0.9% of patients)			Gout Dehydration
Other (2.6% of patients)		Fatigue/tiredness	Malaise

Precautions: Electrolyte Imbalance and BUN Increases: Hyponatremia and hypochloremia may occur during the use of Moduret. Hypokalemia may also occur although the incidence is less than with thiazides alone. Any chloride deficit is usually mild and may be corrected by the use of ammonium chloride (except in patients with hepatic disease) and largely prevented by a near normal salt intake. Increases in BUN levels have been reported and have usually accompanied vigorous fluid elimination, especially when diuretic combinations were used in seriously ill patients, such as those who have hepatic cirrhosis with ascites and metabolic alkalosis, or those with resistant edema. Therefore, careful monitoring of serum electrolytes and BUN levels is important when using Moduret.

In patients with impaired renal function azotemia may be precipitated or increased by hydrochlorothiazide. Careful monitoring of such patients is therefore necessary. If increasing azotemia and oliguria occur during treatment Moduret should be discontinued.

Effects Related to Diuresis in Cirrhotic Patients: Patients with hepatic cirrhosis and ascites are intolerant of acute shifts in electrolyte balance and often have pre-existing hypokalemia as a result of associated secondary hyperaldosteronism. When oral diuretic therapy is used, these patients should be carefully monitored and diuresis should be gradual.

Hepatic encephalopathy, manifested by tremors, confusion, and coma, has been reported in association with amiloride therapy.

In cirrhotic patients receiving amiloride alone, jaundice associated with the underlying disease process has deepened in a few instances, but the relationship to the drug is uncertain.

Other Precautions: Thiazides may decrease serum PBI levels without signs of thyroid disturbance.

Calcium excretion is decreased by hydrochlorothiazide and magnesium excretion is increased.

Pathological changes in the parathyroid glands with hypercalcemia and hypophosphatemia have been observed in a few patients on prolonged thiazide therapy. The common complications of hyperparathyroidism such as renal lithiasis, bone resorption and peptic ulceration have not been seen. Thiazides should be discontinued before carrying out tests for parathyroid function.

Hyperuricemia may occur or gout may be precipitated.

Patients should be observed regularly for the possible occurrence of liver dysfunction, idiosyncratic reactions, or blood dyscrasias.

Sensitivity reactions to thiazides may occur in patients with or without a history of allergy or bonchial asthma.

The possibility of exacerbation or activation of systemic lupus erythematosus has been reported with the thiazides.

Pregnancy: Because clinical experience is limited, Moduret is not recommended for use during pregnancy.

Teratologic studies with amiloride in rabbits and mice revealed no evidence of harm to the fetus. Reproduction studies in rats showed no evidence of impaired fertility. At approximately 5 or more times the expected maximum daily dose for humans, some toxicity was seen in adult rats and rabbits and a decrease in rat pup growth and survival occurred.

In rats a trace of drug crossed the placental barrier.

Thiazides cross the placental barrier and appear in the cord blood. Therefore, the use of Moduret when pregnancy is present or suspected requires that the benefits of the drug be weighed against possible hazards to the fetus. These hazards include fetal or neonatal jaundice, thrombocytopenia and possibly other side effects that have occurred in the adult.

Lactation: It is not known whether amiloride is excreted in human milk. In rats secretion of amiloride in milk has been demonstrated. Thiazides appear in breast milk. Because of the potential for serious adverse reactions in nursing infants, if the use of Moduret is deemed essential, the patient should stop nursing.

Children: The safety for use of amiloride in children has not been established; therefore, Moduret is not recommended in the pediatric age group.

Drug Interactions: Hydrochlorothiazide potentiates the action of other antihypertensive drugs. Therefore, the dosage of these agents, especially the ganglion blockers, may need to be reduced when Moduret is added to the regimen.

Moduret (cont'd)

Lithium should generally not be given to patients receiving diuretics, since the risk of lithium toxicity is very high in such patients.

Thiazide-containing drugs may increase the responsiveness to tubocurarine. The antihypertensive effect of the drug may be enhanced in the postsympathectomy patient.

Hydrochlorothiazide may decrease arterial responsiveness to norepinephrine. This diminution is not sufficient to preclude the effectiveness of the pressor agent for therapeutic use.

Orthostatic hypotension may occur and may be potentiated by alcohol, barbiturates, or narcotics.

Adverse Effects: While rare, the most serious adverse effect is symptomatic hyperkalemia. Other metabolic changes that occur are asymptomatic hyperkalemia, hypokalemia and hypochloremia.

The following incidence of other adverse reactions was determined from clinical trials (607 patients treated with Moduret (see Table I on previous page)).

Other adverse reactions that have been reported with the individual components are listed below:

Cardiovascular: necrotizing angiitis (vasculitis, cutaneous vasculitis).

Gastrointestinal: abnormal liver function, jaundice (intrahepatic cholestatic jaundice), activation of pre-existing peptic ulcer, cramping, gastric irritation, pancreatitis, dry mouth, sialadenitis.

Endocrine: glycosuria, hyperglycemia, hyperuricemia.

Hypersensitivity: urticaria, anaphylactic reactions.

Respiratory: respiratory distress including pneumonitis.

Special senses: photosensitivity, transient blurred vision, xanthopsia.

Hematologic: agranulocytosis, aplastic anemia, hemolytic anemia, leukopenia, purpura, thrombocytopenia, neutropenia.

Others: restlessness, fever.

Overdose: Symptoms: No data are available in regard to overdosage in humans with Moduret or with the amiloride component.

The most common signs and symptoms to be expected from overdosage are dehydration and electrolyte imbalance. Serum electrolytes should be carefully monitored with special attention to potassium levels.

Cardiac arrhythmias may be caused by abnormal potassium levels. Digitalized patients are especially prone to arrhythmias.

Treatment: No specific information is available on the treatment of overdosage and no specific antidote is available. Treatment is symptomatic and supportive. Therapy with Moduret should be discontinued and the patient observed closely. Suggested measures include induction of emesis and/or gastric lavage.

It is not known whether the drug is dialyzable.

Dosage: Optimal dosage should be established by the individual titration of the components.

Maintenance doses may be lower than those required to initiate diuresis; therefore, reduction in the daily dosage should be attempted when the patient's weight is stabilized. In cirrhotic patients, gradual weight reduction is especially desirable to reduce the likelihood of untoward reactions associated with diuretic therapy.

Hepatic Cirrhosis with Ascites and Edema: Maintenance: 1 tablet once daily. The dosage should not exceed 4 tablets a day in single or divided doses.

Edema of Cardiac Origin: Maintenance: 1 or 2 tablets given once daily or in divided doses. The dosage should not exceed 4 tablets a day. Therapy may be on an intermittent basis.

Hypertension: Maintenance: 1 or 2 tablets once daily or in divided doses. The dosage should not exceed 4 tablets a day.

Supplied: Each peach colored, diamond-shaped, compressed tablet, scored on one side with code MSD 917, and tradename MODURET on other, contains: hydrochlorothiazide 50 mg and amiloride hydrochloride 5 mg. Also contains lactose. Gluten- and tartrazine-free. Bottles of 100 and 1 000.

(Shown in Product Recognition Section)

MOGADON® ℞

Roche

Nitrazepam

Hypnotic—Anticonvulsant

Pharmacology: Nitrazepam is a benzodiazepine with hypnotic and anticonvulsant properties.

In sleep laboratory studies, nitrazepam decreased sleep latency, increased total sleep time and decreased awake time. There is delay in the onset, and decrease in the duration of REM sleep. Nitrazepam is reported to significantly decrease stage 1, 3 and 4 sleep and to increase stage 2. Following discontinuation of the drug, REM sleep rebound has been reported in some studies.

Nitrazepam has been shown to raise the seizure threshold.

General Benzodiazepine: The duration of hypnotic effect and the profile of unwanted effects may be influenced by the alpha (distribution) and beta (elimination) half-lives of the administered drug and any active metabolites formed. When half-lives are long, the drug or metabolite may accumulate during periods of nightly administration and be associated with impairments of cognitive and motor performance during waking hours. If half-lives are short, the drug and metabolites will be cleared before the next dose is ingested, and carryover effects related to sedation or CNS depression should be minimal or absent. However, during nightly use and for an extended period, pharmacodynamic tolerance or adaptation to some effects of benzodiazepine hypnotics may develop. If the drug has a very short elimination half-life it is possible that a relative deficiency (i.e., in relation to the receptor site) may occur at some point in the interval between each night's use. This sequence of events may account for two clinical findings reported to occur after several weeks of nightly use of rapidly eliminated benzodiazepine hypnotics: 1) increased wakefulness during the last third of the night; and 2) the appearance of increased daytime anxiety (see Warnings).

Nitrazepam has an intermediate half-life.

Rebound Insomnia: A transient syndrome whereby the symptoms that led to treatment with a benzodiazepine recur in an enhanced form may occur on withdrawal of hypnotic treatment.

Pharmacokinetics: Nitrazepam is rapidly absorbed from the gastrointestinal tract. Bioavailability after an oral dose averages about 80%. Peak blood concentrations after oral administration are observed in approximately 3 hours.

Following the administration of single oral doses of 5 or 10 mg nitrazepam to healthy volunteers, mean peak plasma concentrations ranged between 23 to 66 ng/mL and 55 to 107 ng/mL, respectively. In elderly patients suffering from various debilitating diseases, a mean peak plasma concentration of 22 ng/mL was observed after a single dose of 5 mg nitrazepam. Steady-state plasma concentrations following administration of 5 mg nitrazepam once daily were reached after approximately 4 days. Steady-state plasma concentrations of nitrazepam were approximately 40 ng/mL.

Nitrazepam is a lipophilic drug and crosses the membrane barriers of the body readily. The concentrations in cerebrospinal fluid, about 10% of the total plasma level, are similar to the protein free fraction of plasma. Following oral administration, mean volumes of distribution were greater in elderly patients than in young volunteers (4.8 ± 1.7 vs 2.4 ± 0.8 L/kg, respectively). Total clearance was not significantly different in the two groups (78 ± 25 and 68 ± 33 mL/min, respectively).

Nitrazepam has no clinically active metabolites. The drug is excreted in human urine mainly as conjugated and nonconjugated aminonitrazepam and aceta-midonitrazepam. When given orally, 65 to 71% of the dose eventually appears in the urine and 14 to 20% in the feces. Only about 1% of the administered dose is excreted in the urine as unchanged nitrazepam. The major pathway involves hepatic nitroreduction.

The half-life of nitrazepam in healthy young volunteers is approximately 30 hours (range 18 to 57 hours). Elderly, ill patients showed a prolonged half-life of approximately 40 hours. Due to its slow elimination, nitrazepam accumulates when taken every night.

Approximately 87% of unchanged nitrazepam is bound to plasma proteins. In patients with liver cirrhosis, protein binding was significantly less than in healthy subjects (19 vs 14% unbound). In patients with mild to moderate renal insufficiency, protein binding was somewhat less than in healthy volunteers (16.8 vs 15.0% unbound).

Nitrazepam crosses the placental barrier and is excreted in maternal milk. Milk nitrazepam concentrations increased significantly from the first (30 nmol/L) to the fifth morning (48 nmol/L) in nursing mothers receiving 5 mg nitrazepam at night. The milk to plasma ratio of nitrazepam was 0.27 after 7 hours and did not vary from day 1 to day 5.

Indications: Sleep disturbance may be the presenting manifestation of a physical and/or psychiatric disorder. Consequently, a decision to initiate symptomatic treatment of insomnia should only be made after the patient has been carefully evaluated.

Nitrazepam is indicated for the symptomatic relief of transient and short-term insomnia characterized by difficulty in falling asleep, frequent nocturnal awakenings, and/or early morning awakenings.

Treatment with nitrazepam should usually not exceed 7 to 10 consecutive days. Use for more than 2 to 3 consecutive weeks requires complete re-evaluation of the patient. Prescriptions for nitrazepam should be written for short-term use (7 to 10 days) and it should not be prescribed in quantities exceeding a 1-month supply.

The use of hypnotics should be restricted for insomnia where disturbed sleep results in impaired daytime functioning.

Nitrazepam is also useful for the management of myoclonic seizures.

Contraindications: In patients with known hypersensitivity to the drug, any component to its formulation, or to other benzodiazepines; myasthenia gravis; sleep apnea syndrome.

Nitrazepam is contraindicated in patients who in the past manifested paradoxical reactions to alcohol and/or sedative medications.

Warnings: General: Benzodiazepines should be used with extreme caution in patients with a history of substance or alcohol abuse.

Geriatrics: The smallest possible effective dose should be prescribed for elderly patients. Inappropriate, heavy sedation in the elderly, may result in accidental events/falls.

The failure of insomnia to remit after 7 to 10 days of treatment may indicate the presence of a primary psychiatric and/or medical illness or the presence of sleep state misperception.

Worsening of insomnia or the emergence of new abnormalities of thinking or behavior may be the consequence of an unrecognized psychiatric or physical disorder. These have also been reported to occur in association with the use of drugs that act at the benzodiazepine receptors.

Pregnancy: The use of nitrazepam during pregnancy is not recommended. Benzodiazepines may cause fetal damage when administered during pregnancy. During the first trimester of pregnancy, several studies have suggested an increased risk of congenital malformations associated with the use of benzodiazepines. During the last weeks of pregnancy, ingestion of therapeutic doses of a benzodiazepine hypnotic has resulted in neonatal CNS depression due to transplacental ditribution. If nitrazepam is prescribed to women of childbearing potential, the patient should be warned of the potential risk to a fetus and advised to consult her physician regarding the discontinuation of the drug if she intends to become pregnant or suspects that she might be pregnant.

Memory Disturbance: Anterograde amnesia of varying severity has been reported following therapeutic doses of benzodiazepines. The event is rare with nitrazepam. Anterograde amnesia is a dose-related phenomenon and elderly subjects may be at particular risk.

Cases of transient global amnesia and ''traveller's amnesia'' have also been reported in association with benzodiazepines, the latter in individuals who have taken benzodiazepines, often in the middle of the night, to induce sleep while travelling. Transient global amnesia and traveller's amnesia are unpredictable and not necessarily dose-related phenomena. Patients should be warned not to take nitrazepam under circumstances in which a full night's sleep and clearance of the drug from the body are not possible before they need again to resume full activity.

Abnormal thinking and psychotic behavioral changes have been reported to occur in association with the use of benzodiazepines, including nitrazepam, although rarely. Some of the changes may be characterized by decreased inhibition, e.g., aggressiveness or extroversion that seem excessive, similar to that seen with alcohol and other CNS depressants (e.g., sedative/hypnotics). Particular caution is warranted in patients with a history of violent behavior and a history of unusual reactions to sedatives including alcohol and the benzodiazepines. Psychotic behavioral changes that have been reported with benzodiazepines include bizarre behavior, hallucinations, and depersonalization. Abnormal behavior associated with the use of benzodiazepines have been reported more with chronic use and/or high doses but they may occur during the acute, maintenance or withdrawal phases of treatment.

It can rarely be determined with certainty whether a particular instance of abnormal behavior listed above is drug induced, spontaneous in origin, or a result of an underlying psychiatric disorder. Nevertheless, the emergence of any new behavioral sign or symptom of concern requires careful and immediate evaluation.

Confusion: The benzodiazepines affect mental efficiency, e.g., concentration, attention and vigilance. The risk of confusion is greater in the elderly and in patients with cerebral impairment.

Anxiety, Restlessness: An increase in daytime anxiety and/or restlessness have been observed during treatment with short half-life benzodiazepines although the syndrome can apply on occasion to drugs with longer elimination half-lives as well. Nitrazepam has an intermediate half-life.

Depression: Caution should be exercised if nitrazepam is prescribed to patients with signs or symptoms of depression that could be intensified by hypnotic drugs. The potential for self-harm (e.g., intentional overdose) is high in patients with depression and thus, the least amount of drug that is feasible should be available to them at any one time.

Precautions: *Drug Interactions:* Nitrazepam may produce additive CNS depressant effects when coadministered with alcohol, sedative antihistamines, narcotic analgesics, anticonvulsants, or psychotropic medications which themselves can produce CNS depression.

Compounds which inhibit certain hepatic enzymes (particularly cytochrome P450) may enhance the activity of benzodiazepines. Examples include cimetidine or erythromycin.

Drug Abuse, Dependence and Withdrawal: Withdrawal symptoms, similar in character to those noted with barbiturates and alcohol (convulsions, tremor, abdominal and muscle cramps, vomiting, sweating, dysphoria, perceptual disturbances and insomnia) have occurred following abrupt discontinuation of benzodiazepines, and may follow the discontinuation of nitrazepam. The more severe symptoms are usually associated with higher dosages and longer usage, although patients given therapeutic dosages for as few as 1 to 2 weeks can also have withdrawal symptoms including daytime anxiety between nightly doses. Consequently, abrupt discontinuation should be avoided and a gradual dosage tapering schedule is recommended in any patient taking more than the lowest dose for more than a few weeks. The recommendation for tapering is particularly important in patients with a history of seizures.

The risk of dependence is increased in patients with a history of alcoholism, drug abuse, or in patients with marked personality disorders. Caution must be exercised if it is at all necessary to administer nitrazepam to these individuals.

As with all hypnotics, repeat prescriptions should be limited to those who are under medical supervision.

Patients with Specific Conditions: Nitrazepam should be given with caution to patients with impaired hepatic or renal function, or severe pulmonary insufficiency. Respiratory depression has been reported in patients with compromised respiratory function.

Occupational Hazards: Because of nitrazepam CNS depressant effect, patients receiving the drug should be cautioned against engaging in hazardous occupations requiring complete mental alertness such as operating machinery or driving a motor vehicle. For the same reason, patients should be warned against the concomitant ingestion of nitrazepam and alcohol or CNS depressant drugs.

Bronchial Hypersecretion, Excessive Salivation: In infants and young children, as well as elderly, bedridden patients, bronchial hypersecretion and excessive salivation leading to aspiration/pneumonia may occur on rare occasions.

Pregnancy: Nitrazepam is not recommended for use during pregnancy. For teratogenic effects see Warnings. Nonteratogenic effects: a child born to a mother who is on benzodiazepines may be at risk for withdrawal symptoms from the drug during the postnatal period. Also, neonatal flaccidity has been reported in an infant born to a mother who had been receiving benzodiazepines.

Lactation: Since nitrazepam is excreted in maternal milk, nursing should not be undertaken while the patient is taking nitrazepam.

Children: The safety and effectiveness of nitrazepam as a hypnotic in children below the age of 18 have not been established.

Geriatrics: Elderly patients are especially susceptible to dose-related adverse effects, such as drowsiness, dizziness, or impaired coordination. Inappropriate, heavy sedation may result in accidental events/falls. Therefore, the lowest possible dose should be used in these subjects.

Adverse Effects: The most common adverse reactions are fatigue, dizziness, lightheadedness, drowsiness, lethargy, mental confusion, staggering, ataxia and falling.

Depressed dreaming and nightmares have also been reported.

Sedative effects can often be decreased by a reduction in dosage. Elderly and/or debilitated patients are more susceptible to sedative effects and paradoxical reactions. Therefore, these patients should be carefully screened before they are given hypnotics and the lowest effective dose should be used.

Paradoxical reactions such as agitation, hyperactivity, excitement, hallucinations, increased muscle spasticity, aggressiveness, irritability, rages, psychoses and violent behavior have been reported in rare instances when using drugs that act at the benzodiazepine receptors. Should these occur, the drug should be discontinued.

Hangover, disorientation, severe sedation, hypotension, signs and symptoms of withdrawal including delirium tremens, and cutaneous reactions have been reported. Headache, heartburn, upset stomach, diarrhea, constipation, nausea, vomiting, weakness, faintness, palpitations, blurred vision, dyspnea, nervousness, apprehension, depression, numbed emotions, changes in libido, inappropriate behavior, altered hepatic function tests and, in rare instances, leukopenia and granulocytopenia have been reported with this drug or other drugs of this class.

Overdose: Symptoms: The cardinal manifestations are drowsiness, confusion, reduced reflexes, increasing sedation, and coma. Effects on respiration, pulse and blood pressure are noticed with large overdoses. Patients exhibit some jitteriness and overstimulation usually when the effects of the drug begin to wear off.

Treatment: Immediate gastric lavage may be beneficial if performed soon after ingestion of nitrazepam. If respiratory depression and/or coma are observed, the presence of other CNS depressants should be suspected. Respirations, pulse and blood pressure should be monitored. General supportive measures aimed at maintaining cardiopulmonary function should be instituted and administration of i.v. fluids started. Hypotension and CNS depression are managed by the usual means. Dialysis is usually of little value.

Reversal Agent: The benzodiazepine antagonist, flumazenil is a specific antidote in known or suspected benzodiazepine overdose. (For conditions of use see Anexate Product Monograph.)

The use of flumazenil **is not** recommended in epileptic patients who have been treated with nitrazepam (or any other benzodiazepine). The reversal of the benzodiazepine effect could induce convulsions in such patients.

Dosage: The lowest effective dose should be used. Treatment should be as short as possible, and should usually not exceed 7 to 10 consecutive days. Use for more than 2 to 3 consecutive weeks requires complete re-evaluation of the patient.

Dosage should be individualized for maximal beneficial effect.

Insomnia: Adults: The usual adult dose is 5 or 10 mg before retiring.

Elderly and/or Debilitated Patients: It is recommended that in these patients therapy be initiated with 2.5 mg until individual responses are determined. Doses higher than 5 mg are not usually recommended in the elderly.

Myoclonic seizures: Children: (up to 30 kg of body weight) between 0.3 and 1.0 mg/kg/day given in 3 divided doses. Treatment should be initiated with a lower dose than the usual recommended dosage range in order to determine tolerance and response. If a dose within the recommended dosage range does not control the condition, a higher dosage may be gradually attempted. Higher doses may cause excessive drowsiness. Whenever possible the daily dosage should be divided into 3 equal doses. If doses are not equally divided, the larger dose should be given before retiring. In some patients tolerance develops to the effects of nitrazepam.

The use of multiple anticonvulsants may result in an increase of CNS depressant adverse effects. This should be borne in mind whenever nitrazepam is added to an already existing anticonvulsant regimen.

Information for the Patient: See Blue Section—Information for the Patient "Mogadon".

Supplied: 5 mg: Each white cylindrical, bi-plane scored tablet, contains: nitrazepam 5 mg. Energy: 1.68 kJ (0.4 kcal). Nonmedicinal ingredients: cornstarch, lactose and magnesium stearate. Bottles of 100 and 500.

10 mg: Each white, cylindrical, bi-plane, scored tablet, contains: nitrazepam 10 mg. Energy: 3.2 kJ (0.8 kcal). Nonmedicinal ingredients: cornstarch, lactose and magnesium stearate. Bottles of 100 and 500.

Gluten-, paraben-, sodium-, sulfite- and tartrazine-free. Protect from light. Store at 15 to 30°C.

(Shown in Product Recognition Section)

MOISTUREL®
Westwood-Squibb

Petrolatum—Dimethicone

Emollient—Moisturizer

Indications: Heals and protects dry sensitive skin. Relieves associated itching.

Contraindications: The presence of acute inflammation or a known sensitivity to any of its components.

Dosage: Apply to skin as often as needed, preferably after bathing, to soften and smooth dry skin and relieve itching.

Supplied: Cream: Each jar contains: petrolatum 30% and dimethicone 1% in a fragrance-free, paraben-free vehicle. Nonmedicinal ingredients: carbomer 934, cetyl alcohol, diazolidinyl urea, glycerin, Kathon CG, laureth-23, magnesium aluminum silicate, PVP hexadecene copolymer, PG dioctanoate, sodium hydroxide, steareth-2 and water. Jars of 120 and 450 g.

Lotion: Each bottle of fragrance-free, paraben-free, non-greasy moisturizer contains: white petrolatum 6% and dimethicone 3%. Nonmedicinal ingredients: benzyl alcohol, carbomer-934, cetyl alcohol, glycerin, laureth-23, magnesium aluminum silicate, potassium sorbate, sodium hydroxide, steareth-2 and water. Flip top bottles of 225 mL. Pump top bottles of 400 mL.

MOMETASONE Ⓟ
General Monograph, CPhA

see CORTICOSTEROIDS: TOPICAL
see CORTICOSTEROIDS: EYE EAR NOSE

MONAZOLE® 7
Technilab

Miconazole Nitrate

Antifungal

Supplied: Each g of vaginal cream contains: miconazole nitrate 20 mg (2%). Nonmedicinal ingredients: benzoic acid, ceteareth-12, cetyl alcohol, ethylene glycol monostearate, glycerin, light mineral oil, PEG-20 glyceryl stearate and purified water. Fifty g of miconazole are sufficient for 7 intravaginal applications with additional cream for external use (vulva) if required. Aluminum tubes of 50 g in a carton containing 7 disposable, 5 g capacity applicators and patient instructions. Store between 15 to 30°C. Protect from freezing.

MONISTAT® 7 Cream
MONISTAT® 7 Vaginal Suppositories
MONISTAT® 7 DUAL-PAK® Package (Also known as Combination Packs)
MONISTAT® DERM Cream
MONISTAT® 3 DUAL-PAK® Package (Also known as Combination Packs)
MONISTAT® 3 Vaginal Ovules
McNeil Consumer Products

Miconazole Nitrate

Antifungal

Pharmacology: Depending upon concentration, miconazole exhibits broad spectrum in vitro fungistatic or fungicidal activity against species of the genus Candida. Miconazole also inhibits several other genera of fungi, including dermatophytes and yeasts, as well as Gram-positive bacteria.

Miconazole inhibits the biosynthesis of ergosterol or other sterols, damaging the fungal cell wall membrane and altering its permeability. In fungi, it also inhibits biosynthesis of triglycerides and phospholipids as well as oxidative and peroxidative enzymes. The latter action results in intracellular buildup of toxic concentrations of hydrogen peroxide, which may contribute to deterioration of subcellular organelles and cellular necrosis.

C. albicans cells have been observed to exhibit progressive cytoplasmic deterioration and prominent shape changes resulting in complete cell necrosis depending on the dose and duration of exposure to miconazole. The sequence of morphologic alterations induced by miconazole at fungistatic doses (10^{-6} M) are lysis of cytoplasmic organelles, focal to complete loss of cell plasmalemma and irregular thickening of the cell wall containing multiple inclusions. Administration of

Monistat (cont'd)

fungicidal doses (10^{-4} M) induces a completely necrotic cell interior with an unaltered cell wall.

In C. albicans, miconazole inhibits the transformation of blastospores into invasive mycelial form. Not all species or strains of a particular organism may be susceptible to miconazole.

Miconazole has been clinically effective in treating tinea pedis (athlete's foot), tinea cruris, tinea corporis, and tinea versicolor caused by dermatophytes. Monistat Derm Cream is also effective in cutaneous candidiasis. Among the organisms against which Monistat Derm Cream has been found effective are T. rubrum, T. mentagrophytes, T. interdigitale, E. floccosum, M. canis, M. gypseum, species of Candida including C. albicans, and M. furfur.

To date, no wild strains or fungal mutants with substantial acquired resistance to miconazole have been reported; however, miconazole resistant C. albicans has been isolated from an infant following bladder irrigation with miconazole for the treatment of urinary candidiasis.

Indications: Monistat 7 Vaginal Cream, Monistat 7 Vaginal Suppositories and Monistat 3 Vaginal Ovules: For the local treatment of vulvovaginal candidiasis (moniliasis).

Monistat 7 Dual-pak and Monistat 3 Dual-pak: For the local treatment of vulvovaginal candidiasis (moniliasis) and for the relief of particularly severe external itching and irritation associated with vulvovaginal candidiasis.

Although vulvovaginal candidiasis may be more difficult to cure during pregnancy, pregnant patients can be treated with the same regimen as nonpregnant patients. The 3-day regimen is preferred, with the 7-day regimen providing an effective alternative.

No significant difference in therapeutic cure rate (therapeutic cure includes both symptomatic and microbiological cure) was reported between the pregnant and nonpregnant patient groups who participated in clinical evaluations of the 3-day (ovules) or 7-day (suppositories+cream) treatment regimens.

Similarly, users and non-users of oral contraceptives who participated in these clinical evaluations experienced therapeutic cure rates which did not differ significantly.

In addition, no statistically significant differences in therapeutic cure rates were noted between patients undergoing dosage regimens of varying duration (3, 7, 10 and 14 day).

Monistat Derm Cream: Used clinically in conjunction with vaginal ovules or suppositories in Monistat 3 and Monistat 7 Dual-paks, respectively, when symptoms of vulvovaginal candidiasis are particularly extensive. Also effective for other Candida infections, dermatophytes and lesions caused by mixed infections involving susceptible fungi.

Contraindications: Hypersensitivity to any of the components.

Precautions: Discontinue medication if sensitization or other signs of irritation (rash, burning, blistering, redness), not present before therapy, occur from intravaginal or topical use. Avoid contact with the eyes.

Patients should not use vaginal preparations for self-medication if vaginal pruritus or discomfort is occurring for the first time. In this instance, a physician must be consulted to establish the diagnosis of vulvovaginal candidiasis.

Patients should not use vaginal preparations for self-medication if they experience unusual pain in the back or lower abdomen, fever or a malodorous vaginal discharge is present, as a condition more serious than vulvovaginal candidiasis may exist.

Intractable candidiasis may be the presenting symptom of unrecognized diabetes; thus appropriate urine/blood studies may be indicated in patients not responding to treatment. In any case unresponsive to therapy, repeat appropriate microbiological studies to confirm the diagnosis of vulvovaginal candidiasis and to rule out other pathogens.

During vaginal therapy it may be advisable to instruct the patient to abstain from intercourse.

Pregnancy and *Lactation:* Advise pregnant patients either to exercise caution in the insertion of the applicator during vaginal therapy or to insert the suppository or ovule digitally.

Follow up reports on infants born to 167 of 263 pregnant patients (some follow-up reports are not yet available) who participated in North American clinical evaluations of miconazole nitrate 2% cream administered in a 14-day regimen, and infants born to 26 pregnant patients who participated in European and North American clinical evaluations of miconazole nitrate 100 mg suppositories, described no complications or adverse effects attributed to this therapeutic agent. Nevertheless, since miconazole nitrate is absorbed in small amounts from the human vagina, Monistat vaginal preparations should not be used by pregnant or nursing women unless the physician considers it essential to the welfare of the patient.

Concurrent use of the suppository, ovule or cream prefilled applicator with natural rubber products, such as vaginal diaphrams or condoms, is not recommended.

Adverse Effects: In general, the complaints reported with miconazole therapy concerned vulvovaginal burning, itching, irritation, pelvic cramping, edema as well as hives and rash.

A total of 1 089 patients participated in clinical evaluations of miconazole nitrate 2% vaginal cream administered in dosage regimens of varying duration. Of these, 59 patients reported reactions which were possibly drug related but not severe enough to cause discontinuation of therapy, 4 patients discontinued therapy due to vulvovaginal burning and itching, and 1 patient discontinued therapy due to hives.

A total of 1 724 patients participated in clinical evaluations of miconazole nitrate 100 mg vaginal suppositories administered in dosage regimens of varying duration. Of these, 3 patients reported reactions which were interpreted as minor treatment emergent signs and symptoms (burning, itching, edema) and considered by the investigators to be nontherapy related. No patients were reported to have discontinued therapy due to drug related reasons.

The 3-day treatment with miconazole nitrate 400 mg vaginal ovules was exceptionally well tolerated by a total of 410 patients in 3 clinical studies, without any related side effects. However, the generally reported complaints referred to above could be expected with this dosage form and regimen as well.

The combination pack products combine a small amount (9 g) of miconazole nitrate 2% cream to be applied externally during a course of therapy with miconazole nitrate vaginal suppositories or ovules so a similar safety and efficacy profile, as with each individually, could be expected.

Dosage: Monistat 7 Cream: Administer one 5 g applicatorful intravaginally once daily at bedtime for 7 consecutive days. The course of therapy may be repeated if the patient remains symptomatic and it has been determined by appropriate smears and cultures that the infecting organism is still miconazole susceptible Candida.

Monistat 7 Vaginal Suppositories: Administer 1 suppository intravaginally once daily at bedtime for 7 consecutive days. The course of therapy may be repeated if the patient remains symptomatic and it has been determined by appropriate smears and cultures that the infecting organism is still miconazole susceptible Candida.

Monistat Derm Cream: Apply a thin layer of cream topically to cover the affected area twice daily. Massage gently until cream disappears.

Early clinical improvement (1 to 2 weeks) has been seen in the treatment of infections caused by dermatophytes and Candida species and in mixed fungal infections, but resistant lesions may take longer to clear. Candida infections should be treated for 2 weeks and dermatophyte infections for 1 month in order to reduce the possibility of recurrence. If a patient shows no clinical improvement after 30 days of treatment, the diagnosis should be reconsidered.

Monistat 3 Vaginal Ovules: Administer 1 ovule intravaginally once daily at bedtime for 3 consecutive days. The course of therapy may be repeated if the patient remains symptomatic and it has been determined by appropriate smears and cultures that the infecting organism is still miconazole susceptible Candida.

Monistat 7 and Monistat 3 Dual-paks (to be used when symptoms are particularly extensive): One 100 mg suppository or one 400 mg ovule administered intravaginally once daily at bedtime for 7 (Monistat 7) or 3 (Monistat 3) consecutive days, respectively. Apply a thin layer of cream to external areas twice daily, in the morning and evening. Massage gently until cream disappears.

Supplied: Monistat 7 Cream: Each package contains: 7 prefilled disposable applicators of white, water miscible cream containing miconazole nitrate 2%, sufficient for one 7-day course of therapy, and a consumer information leaflet. Nonmedicinal ingredients: benzoic acid, cetyl alcohol, isopropyl myristate, polysorbate 60, potassium hydroxide, propylene glycol, purified water and stearyl alcohol.

Monistat 7 Vaginal Suppositories: Each white, egg shaped vaginal suppository contains: miconazole nitrate 100 mg. Boxes of 7 suppositories individually sealed in opaque polyvinylchloride moulds, 1 vaginal suppository applicator, and a consumer information leaflet. Nonmedicinal ingredients: hydrogenated vegetable oil base.

Monistat 7 Dual-Pak Package: Each package contains: 7 Monistat 7 vaginal suppositories sufficient for one 7-day course of therapy, a vaginal applicator and a 9 g tube of Monistat Derm Cream, along with a consumer information leaflet. Also known as Combination Packs.

Monistat Derm Cream: Each tube contains: miconazole nitrate 2%. Tubes of 15 and 30 g. Nonmedicinal ingredients: benzoic acid, butylated hydroxyanisole, mineral oil, peglicol 5 oleate, pegoxol 7 stearate, purified water.

Monistat 3 Vaginal Ovules: Each package contains: 3 soft, gelatin ovules filled with a suspension of miconazole nitrate 400 mg, sufficient for one 3-day course of therapy, 1 vaginal applicator and a consumer information leaflet. Nonmedicinal ingredients: gelatin, glycerin, mineral oil, sodium ethylparaben, sodium propylparaben, titanium dioxide and white petrolatum.

Monistat 3 Dual-Pak Package: Each package contains: 3 Monistat 3 vaginal ovules sufficient for one 3-day course of therapy, a vaginal applicator and a 9 g tube of Monistat Derm Cream, along with a consumer information leaflet. Also known as Combination Packs.

(Shown in Product Recognition Section)

Reviewed 1999

MONITAN® Ⓟ
Wyeth-Ayerst

Acebutolol HCl
Antihypertensive—Antianginal Agent

Pharmacology: Acebutolol is a beta-adrenergic receptor blocking agent. In vitro and in vivo animal studies have shown that it has a preferential effect on beta$_1$-adrenoreceptors, chiefly located in cardiac muscle. This preferential effect is not absolute, however, and at higher doses acebutolol also inhibits beta$_2$-adrenoreceptors, chiefly located in the bronchial and vascular musculature. It possesses some partial agonist activity (or intrinsic sympathomimetic activity—ISA). It is used in the treatment of hypertension and/or prophylaxis of angina pectoris.

The mechanism of the antihypertensive effect has not been established. Among the factors that may be involved are: competitive ability to antagonize catecholamine-induced tachycardia at the beta-receptor sites in the heart, thus decreasing cardiac output; inhibition of renin release by the kidneys; inhibition of the vasomotor centres.

Pharmacokinetics: The mechanism of the anti-anginal effects is also uncertain. An important factor may be the reduction of myocardial oxygen requirements by blocking catecholamine-induced increases in heart rate, systolic blood pressure, and the velocity and extent of myocardial contraction.

Acebutolol is well absorbed from the gastrointestinal tract. It undergoes extensive first-pass hepatic biotransformation, with an absolute bioavailability of approximately 40% for the parent compound. The major metabolite, an N-acetyl derivative (diacetolol), is pharmacologically active. This metabolite is equipotent to acebutolol and, in cats, is more cardioselective; therefore, this first-pass phenomenon does not attenuate the therapeutic effect of acebutolol. Food intake does not have a significant effect on the area under the plasma concentration time curve (AUC) of acebutolol although the rate of absorption and peak concentration decreased slightly.

The plasma elimination half-life of acebutolol is approximately 3 to 4 hours, while that of its metabolite, diacetolol, is 8 to 13 hours. The time to reach peak concentration for acebutolol is 2.5 hours and for diacetolol, after oral administration of acebutolol, 3.5 hours.

Within the single oral dose range of 200 to 400 mg, the kinetics are dose proportional. However, this linearity is not seen at higher doses, probably due to saturation of hepatic biotransformation sites. In addition, after multiple dosing the lack of linearity is also seen by AUC increases of approximately 100% as compared to single oral dosing. Elimination via renal excretion is approximately 30 to 40% and by nonrenal mechanisms 50 to 60%, which includes excretion into the bile and direct passage through the intestinal wall.

Acebutolol has a low binding affinity for plasma proteins (about 26%). Acebutolol and its metabolite, diacetolol, are relatively hydrophilic and therefore only minimal quantities have been detected in the cerebrospinal fluid.

Indications: Hypertension: In patients with mild to moderate hypertension. It is usually used in combination with other drugs, particularly a thiazide diuretic. However, it may be tried alone as an initial agent in those patients in whom, in the judgment of the physician, treatment should be started with a beta-blocker rather than a diuretic.

In patients with severe hypertension a beta-adrenergic blocking agent may be used as part of a multiple drug regimen which would normally include a diuretic and a vasodilator.

The combination of acebutolol with a diuretic or peripheral vasodilator has been found to be compatible and generally more effective than acebutolol alone. Limited experience with other antihypertensive agents has not shown evidence of incompatibility.

Acebutolol is not indicated in the emergency treatment of hypertensive crises.

Angina Pectoris: In the long-term management of patients with angina pectoris due to ischemic heart disease.

Contraindications: Acebutolol should not be used in the presence of: sinus bradycardia, second- and third-degree AV block, right ventricular failure secondary to pulmonary hypertension, congestive heart failure, cardiogenic shock, anesthesia with agents that produce myocardial depression, e.g., ether.

Warnings: Increase in antinuclear antibody (ANA) titre was observed in approximately 12.5% of patients on chronic acebutolol therapy. Rare instances ($<1\%$) of a syndrome resembling lupus erythematosus have been reported with maintenance therapy. Similar symptoms were occasionally observed with some other beta-blockers. In addition to increased ANA titres, polyarthralgia, myalgia and pleuritic pain were the main presenting symptoms. Symptoms and ANA titres appear reversible upon discontinuation of acebutolol therapy. The drug should be withdrawn if symptoms appear or if the results of ANA testing are significantly positive. Patients should be followed up both clinically and serologically until resolution of symptoms.

Cardiac Failure: Special caution should be exercised when administering acebutolol to patients with a history of heart failure. Sympathetic stimulation is a vital component supporting circulatory function in congestive heart failure, and inhibition with beta-blockade always carries the potential hazard of further depressing myocardial contractility and precipitating cardiac failure. Acebutolol acts selectively without abolishing the inotropic action of digitalis on the heart muscle. However, the positive inotropic action of digitalis may be reduced by the negative inotropic effect of acebutolol when the 2 drugs are used concomitantly.

The effects of beta-blockers and digitalis are additive in depressing AV conduction.

In patients without a history of cardiac failure, continued depression of myocardium over a period of time can, in some cases, lead to cardiac failure. Therefore, at the first sign or symptom of impending cardiac failure, patients should be fully digitalized and/or given a diuretic and the response observed closely. If cardiac failure continues despite adequate digitalization and diuretic therapy, acebutolol should be immediately withdrawn.

Abrupt Cessation of Therapy: Patients with angina should be warned against abrupt discontinuation of acebutolol. There have been reports of severe exacerbation of angina, and of myocardial infarction or ventricular arrhythmias occurring in patients with angina pectoris, following abrupt discontinuation of beta-blocker therapy. The last 2 complications may occur with or without preceding exacerbation of angina pectoris. Therefore, when discontinuation is planned in patients with angina pectoris, the dosage should be gradually reduced over a period of about 2 weeks and the patient should be carefully observed. The same frequency of administration should be maintained. In situations of greater urgency, acebutolol therapy should be discontinued stepwise and under conditions of closer observation. If angina markedly worsens or acute coronary insufficiency develops, it is recommended that treatment with acebutolol be reinstituted promptly, at least temporarily.

Various skin rashes and conjunctival xerosis have been reported with beta-blockers, including acebutolol. A severe syndrome (oculo-muco-cutaneous syndrome) whose signs include conjunctivitis sicca and psoriasiform rashes, otitis, and sclerosing serositis has occurred with the chronic use of one beta-adrenergic-blocking agent (practolol). This syndrome has not been observed with acebutolol or any other such agent. However, physicians should be alert to the possibility of such reactions and should discontinue treatment in the event that they occur.

Severe sinus bradycardia may occur with the use of acebutolol from unopposed vagal activity remaining after blockade of $beta_1$-adrenergic receptors; in such cases, dosage should be reduced.

In patients with thyrotoxicosis, the possible deleterious effects from long-term use of acebutolol have not been adequately appraised. It may give a false impression of improvement by masking the clinical signs of continuing hyperthyroidism or its complications. Therefore, abrupt withdrawal of acebutolol may be followed by an exacerbation of the symptoms of hyperthyroidism, including thyroid storm.

Pregnancy: Reproduction studies have been performed with acebutolol in rats and rabbits at doses of up to 60 mg/kg/day by the oral route and 18 mg/kg/day by the i.v. route. In one rabbit study where acebutolol was administered by the i.v. route, the following malformations were observed: rib defects, gastroschisis, ventricular septal defect, dysplasia of urogenital system and umbilical hernia. These results could not be confirmed in a repeat i.v. study and were not seen in a study using the oral route.

Studies have also been performed with diacetolol (the major metabolite) at doses of up to 450 mg/kg/day orally in rabbits and 1 800 mg/kg/day orally in rats. There was a significant elevation of postimplantation loss in rabbit dams receiving 450 mg/kg/day, a level at which food consumption and body weight gain were reduced; a nonstatistically significant increase in incidence of bilateral cataracts was also noticed in rat fetuses from dams treated with 1 800 mg/kg/day.

There has been no experience with the use of acebutolol in pregnant women; however, studies have shown that both acebutolol and diacetolol cross the placenta. Acebutolol should not be given to pregnant patients. Its use in women with childbearing potential requires that the anticipated benefit be cautiously weighed against possible hazards.

Lactation: Acebutolol and diacetolol appear in breast milk with a milk:plasma ratio of 7.1 and 12.2 respectively. Use in nursing mothers is not recommended.

Precautions: Patients with bronchospastic disease should, in general, not receive a beta-blocker. Because of its relative $beta_1$-selectivity, however, low doses of acebutolol may be used with caution in patients with bronchospastic disease who do not respond to, or who cannot tolerate, alternative treatment. Since $beta_1$-selectivity is not absolute and is dose-dependent, a $beta_2$-stimulating agent should be administered concomitantly and the lowest possible dose of acebutolol should be used initially, preferably in divided doses to avoid the higher plasma levels associated with the longer dose-interval.

There may be increased difficulty in treating an allergic type reaction in patients on beta-blockers. In these patients, the reaction may be more severe due to pharmacological effects of beta-blockers and problems with fluid changes. Epinephrine should be administered with caution since it may not have its usual effects in the treatment of anaphylaxis. On the one hand, larger doses of epinephrine may be needed to overcome the bronchospasm, while on the other, these doses can be associated with excessive alpha-adrenergic stimulation with consequent hypertension, reflex bradycardia and heart-block and possible potentiation of bronchospasm. Alternatives to the use of large doses of epinephrine include vigorous supportive care such as fluids and the use of beta-agonists including parenteral salbutamol or isoproterenol to overcome bronchospasm, and norepinephrine to overcome hypotension.

Acebutolol should be administered with caution to patients subject to spontaneous hypoglycemia, or to diabetic patients (especially those with labile diabetes) who are receiving insulin or oral hypoglycemic agents. Beta-adrenergic blockers may mask the premonitory signs and symptoms of acute hypoglycemia.

Acebutolol should be administered with caution to patients with impaired renal function. Acebutolol is excreted through the gastrointestinal tract, but the active metabolite diacetolol, is eliminated predominantly by the kidney. There is a linear relationship between renal clearance of diacetolol and creatinine clearance. The daily dose should be reduced in patients with a creatinine clearance less than 50 mL/min.

Geriatrics: Acebutolol has been used in the elderly without specific adjustment of dosage. However, this patient population may require lower maintenance doses because the bioavailability of both acebutolol and its metabolite are approximately doubled in this age group. This increased bioavailability is probably due to decreases in first-pass metabolism and renal function in the elderly.

Acebutolol dosage should be individually adjusted when used concomitantly with other antihypertensive agents (see Dosage).

Liver function tests should be performed at regular intervals during long-term treatment.

Elective or Emergency Surgery: The management of patients being treated with beta-blockers and undergoing elective or emergency surgery is controversial. Although beta-adrenergic-receptor blockade impairs the ability of the heart to respond to beta-adrenergically-mediated reflex stimuli, abrupt discontinuation of therapy with acebutolol may be followed by severe complications (see Warnings). Some patients receiving beta-adrenergic-blocking agents have been subject to protracted severe hypotension during anesthesia. Difficulty in restarting and maintaining the heartbeat has also been reported. For these reasons, in patients with angina undergoing elective surgery, acebutolol should be withdrawn gradually following the recommendation given under Abrupt Cessation of Therapy (see Warnings). According to available evidence, all clinical and physiological effects of beta-blockade are no longer present 72 hours after cessation of medication.

In emergency surgery, since acebutolol is a competitive inhibitor of beta-adrenergic-receptor agonists, its effects may be reversed, if necessary, by sufficient doses of such agonists as isoproterenol.

Children: There is no experience with acebutolol in the treatment of pediatric age groups and therefore use in children is not recommended.

<u>*Drug Interactions:*</u> Catecholamine-depleting drugs, such as reserpine, may have an additive effect when given with β-blocking agents. Patients treated with acebutolol plus catecholamine depletors should, therefore be observed closely for evidence of marked bradycardia or hypotension which may present as vertigo, syncope/presyncope, or orthostatic changes in blood pressure without compensatory tachycardia.

Exaggerated hypertensive responses have been reported from the combined use of β-adrenergic antagonists and α-adrenergic stimulants, including those contained in proprietary cold remedies and vasoconstrictive nasal drops. Patients receiving β-blockers should be warned of this potential hazard.

No significant interactions with digoxin, hydrochlorothiazide, hydralazine, sulfinpyrazone, oral contraceptives, tolbutamide or warfarin have been observed.

Should it be decided to discontinue therapy in patients receiving beta-blockers and clonidine concurrently, the beta-blocker should be discontinued several days before the gradual withdrawal of clonidine. It has been suggested that withdrawal of clonidine in the presence of beta-blockade may exaggerate the clonidine withdrawal syndrome (see also prescribing information for clonidine).

Adverse Effects: The incidence of treatment-related side effects is derived from clinical trials in 3 090 patients with hypertension, angina pectoris or arrhythmia.

The most serious adverse reactions encountered with acebutolol are congestive heart failure, severe bradycardia and bronchospasm occurring in less than 1% of patients.

The most common adverse reactions reported are fatigue (4%), dyspnea (2.5%), nausea (2%), dizziness (2%), hypotension (1%) and rashes (1%).

Adverse reactions grouped by systems are as follows: Cardiovascular: congestive heart failure (see Warnings); secondary effects of decreased cardiac output which include: syncope, vertigo, lightheadedness and postural hypotension; severe bradycardia; lengthening of PR interval; second- and third-degree AV block; sinus arrest; palpitation; chest pain; cold extremities; Raynaud's phenomenon; hot flushes; pain in legs; edema.

CNS: headache, dizziness, mental depression, tiredness, drowsiness or somnolence, lightheadedness, anxiety, tinnitus, weakness, confusion, vivid dreams, paresthesia, insomnia.

Gastrointestinal: nausea and vomiting, heartburn, indigestion, flatulence, abdominal pain, diarrhea, constipation.

Respiratory: dyspnea, cough, shortness of breath, wheezing, bronchospasm.

Allergic-Dermatological (see Warnings): urticaria; pruritus; sweating; exfoliative dermatitis; psoriasiform rash; lupus-like syndrome with arthralgia, myalgia, dyspnea and pleuritic pain, reversible upon cessation of the drug.

EENT: blurred vision and nonspecific visual disturbances, itching eyes, conjunctivitis.

Miscellaneous: weight gain, loss of appetite, decrease in libido, shivering, micturition (frequency), nocturia.

Laboratory Tests: Occasional reports of increased transaminase, alkaline phosphatase and lactic dehydrogenase values. Positive antinuclear antibodies (see Warnings).

Overdose: Symptoms: The most common signs to be expected with a beta-adrenergic blocking agent are bradycardia, congestive heart failure, hypotension, bronchospasm and hypoglycemia.

Treatment: If overdosage occurs, in all cases therapy with acebutolol should be discontinued and the patient observed closely. In addition, if required, the following therapeutic measures are suggested: 1. Bradycardia: atropine or another anticholinergic drug.

2. Heart block (second- or third-degree): isoproterenol or transvenous cardiac pacemaker.

3. Congestive heart failure: conventional therapy.

Monitan (cont'd)

4. Hypotension (depending on associated factors): epinephrine rather than isoproterenol or norepinephrine may be useful in addition to atropine and digitalis (see Precaution concerning the use of epinephrine in β-blocked patients).
5. Bronchospasm: aminophylline or isoproterenol.
6. Hypoglycemia: i.v. glucose.

Acebutolol and its major metabolite are dialyzable.

It should be remembered that acebutolol is a competitive antagonist of isoproterenol and hence large doses of isoproterenol can be expected to reverse many of the effects of excessive doses of acebutolol. However, the complications of excess isoproterenol should not be overlooked.

Dosage: The dose of acebutolol must always be adjusted to the individual requirements of the patient in accordance with the following guidelines:

Hypertension: Acebutolol is usually used in conjunction with other antihypertensive agents, particularly thiazide diuretics but may be used alone (see Indications).

Treatment should be initiated with doses of 100 mg twice daily. If an adequate response is not seen after 1 week, the dosage should be increased to 200 mg twice daily. In some cases, the daily dosage may need further increments of 100 mg twice daily at intervals of not less than 2 weeks, up to the maximum of 400 mg twice daily.

The maintenance dose is within the range of 400 to 800 mg daily. Patients who show a satisfactory response at a daily dose of 400 mg or less may be given the total dose once daily in the morning. Daily doses above this should be divided into 2 equal doses.

Angina Pectoris: The initial dose is 200 mg twice daily. If after 2 weeks a satisfactory response has not been obtained, the dosage should be increased to a maximum of 300 mg twice daily.

The usual maintenance dose in angina pectoris is in the range of 200 to 600 mg daily administered in 2 divided doses.

In patients adequately controlled on 400 mg daily, a lower maintenance dose of 100 mg twice a day may be tried.

Geriatrics: Older patients have an approximately 2-fold increase in bioavailability and are likely to require lower maintenance doses.

Impaired Renal Function: The daily dose of acebutolol should be reduced by 50% when creatinine clearance is less than 50 mL/min and by 75% when it is less than 25 mL/min (see Precautions).

Supplied: 100 mg: Each white, film-coated, scored, round, biconvex tablet, marked "100" on one side and "WYETH" on the other, contains: acebutolol HCl 100 mg. Nonmedicinal ingredients: cornstarch, hydroxypropyl methylcellulose, lactose hydrous, magnesium stearate, methylcellulose, polyethylene glycol, propylene glycol, talc and titanium dioxide. Energy: 0.41 kJ (0.10 kcal). Gluten- and tartrazine-free. Bottles of 100 and 500.

200 mg: Each white, film-coated, oval, biconvex tablet, scored and marked "200" on one side and "WYETH" on the other, contains: acebutolol HCl 200 mg. Nonmedicinal ingredients: cornstarch, hydroxypropyl methylcellulose, lactose hydrous, magnesium stearate, methylcellulose, polyethylene glycol, propylene glycol, talc and titanium dioxide. Energy: 0.82 kJ (0.20 kcal). Gluten- and tartrazine-free. Bottles of 100 and 500.

400 mg: Each white to off-white, film-coated, capsule-shaped, biconvex, scored tablet, marked "400" on one side and "MONITAN" on the other, contains: acebutolol HCl 400 mg. Nonmedicinal ingredients: cornstarch, hydroxypropyl methylcellulose, lactose hydrous, magnesium stearate, methylcellulose, polyethylene glycol, propylene glycol, talc and titanium dioxide. Energy: 1.63 kJ (0.39 kcal). Gluten- and tartrazine-free. Bottles of 100 and 500.

Store at 15 to 30°C. Protect from light.

(Shown in Product Recognition Section)

MONOPRIL™ Ⓟ

Bristol-Myers Squibb

Fosinopril Sodium

Angiotensin Converting Enzyme Inhibitor

Pharmacology: Fosinopril is an angiotensin converting enzyme (ACE) inhibitor which is used in the treatment of mild to moderate essential hypertension and in the management of symptomatic congestive heart failure.

Following oral administration, fosinopril is rapidly hydrolyzed to fosinoprilat, its principal active metabolite.

ACE is a peptidyl dipeptidase that catalyzes the conversion of angiotensin I to the vasoconstrictor substance, angiotensin II. Angiotensin II also stimulates aldosterone secretion by the adrenal cortex. Inhibition of ACE activity leads to decreased levels of angiotensin II thereby resulting in decreased vasoconstriction and decreased aldosterone secretion. The latter decrease may result in a small increase in serum potassium. Decreased levels of angiotensin II and the accompanying lack of negative feedback on renal renin secretion results in increases in plasma renin activity.

ACE is identical to kininase II. Thus, fosinopril may interfere with the degradation of bradykinin, a potent peptide vasodilator. However, it is not known whether this contributes to the therapeutic effects of fosinopril.

While the mechanism through which fosinopril lowers blood pressure appears to result primarily from suppression of the renin-angiotensin-aldosterone system, fosinopril has an antihypertensive effect even in patients with low-renin hypertension.

The antihypertensive effect of angiotensin converting enzyme inhibitors is generally lower in black patients than in nonblacks.

Pharmacokinetics: Following oral administration, fosinopril (the prodrug) is absorbed slowly. The absolute absorption of fosinopril averaged 36% of an oral dose. The primary site of absorption is the proximal small intestine (duodenum/jejunum). While the rate of absorption may be slowed by the presence of food in the gastrointestinal tract, the extent of absorption of fosinopril is essentially unaffected. The bioavailability of fosinoprilat is reduced by about 20%.

Hydrolysis of fosinopril to the active fosinoprilat is rapid and complete. This biotransformation probably occurs in the gastrointestinal mucosa and liver.

After an oral dose of radiolabeled fosinopril to healthy subjects, 75% of radioactivity in plasma was present as active fosinoprilat, 20 to 30% as a glucuronide conjugate of fosinoprilat, and 1 to 5% as a p-hydroxy metabolite of fosinoprilat. In urine, 75% of the drug excreted was fosinoprilat, the remainder consisted primarily of the glucuronide conjugate of fosinoprilat. In rats, the para-hydroxy metabolite of fosinoprilat is as potent an inhibitor of ACE as fosinoprilat; the glucuronide conjugate of fosinoprilat is devoid of ACE inhibitor activity.

After single and repeated doses, areas under serum concentration-time curves (AUCs) and peak concentrations (C_{max}) were directly proportional to the dose of fosinopril. The time to reach peak concentrations (T_{max}) was independent of dose and achieved in approximately 3 hours. In patients with congestive heart failure, the effective half-life was about 14 hours.

In hypertensive patients with normal renal and hepatic function, who received repeated doses of fosinopril, the effective half-life for accumulation of fosinoprilat averaged 11.5 hours, while in patients with heart failure, the effective half-life was 14 hours. Fosinoprilat is highly protein-bound (≥95%), has a relatively small volume of distribution, and negligible binding to cellular components in blood.

After i.v. administration, elimination of fosinoprilat was shared equally by the liver and kidney. After an oral dose of radiolabeled fosinopril, approximately half of the absorbed dose was excreted in urine and the remainder was excreted in the feces. In normal subjects, the mean body clearance of i.v. fosinoprilat was between 26 and 39 mL/min.

In patients with renal insufficiency, pharmacokinetic parameters (including absorption, bioavailability, protein binding, and biotransformation/metabolism) were not appreciably altered by reduced renal function. The total body clearance of fosinoprilat in patients with impaired renal function (creatinine clearance < 80 mL/min/1.73 m²) was approximately 50% slower than in patients with normal renal function. Since hepatobiliary elimination partially compensates for diminished renal elimination, the body clearance of fosinoprilat does not appreciably differ with any degree of renal insufficiency including end-stage renal failure (creatinine clearance values < 10 mL/min/1.73 m²). A modest increase in plasma AUC levels (< 2 times that in normals) was observed in patients with various degrees of renal insufficiency, including end stage renal failure (see Dosage).

Clearance of fosinoprilat by hemodialysis and peritoneal dialysis averages 2% and 7%, respectively, of urea clearances.

In patients with hepatic insufficiency (alcoholic or biliary cirrhosis), the extent of absorption was not affected. In single and multiple dose pharmacokinetic studies, the mean AUC for fosinoprilat were markedly increased (50 to 100%) as compared to those of patients with normal liver functions. The extent of hydrolysis of fosinopril was not appreciably reduced although the rate may be slowed. Patients with hepatic insufficiency could develop elevated plasma levels of unchanged fosinopril.

In elderly (male) subjects (65 to 74 years old) with clinically normal renal and hepatic function, there were no significant differences in the pharmacokinetic parameters of fosinoprilat as compared to those in younger subjects (20 to 35 years old).

Fosinoprilat was found to cross the placenta of pregnant animals.

Studies in animals indicate that fosinopril and fosinoprilat do not cross the blood-brain barrier.

Pharmacodynamics: Administration of fosinopril to patients with mild to moderate essential hypertension has reduced both supine and standing blood pressures with minimal effect on heart rate. Following administration of a single dose, the onset of an antihypertensive effect is seen within 1 hour with peak blood pressure reduction usually achieved by 3 to 6 hours after dosing. Achievement of maximum blood pressure lowering effect may require several weeks of therapy in some patients. At the recommended doses, antihypertensive effects are maintained throughout the 24-hour dosing interval in most patients. The effectiveness of fosinopril appears to be similar in the elderly (over 65 years of age) and younger adult patients given the same daily dosages.

The antihypertensive effect of fosinopril and thiazide diuretics used concurrently is greater than that seen with either agent alone.

Abrupt withdrawal of fosinopril has not resulted in rapid increase in blood pressure.

In hemodynamic study involving patients with mild to moderate hypertension, after 3 months of therapy, responses (changes in blood pressure, heart rate, cardiac index and peripheral vascular resistance) to various stimuli (e.g., isometric exercise, 45 degree head-up tilt and mental challenge) were unchanged compared to baseline, suggesting that fosinopril does not affect the activity of the sympathetic nervous system. Reduction in systemic blood pressure appears to have been mediated by a decrease in peripheral vascular resistance without reflex cardiac effects. Similarly, renal, splanchnic, cerebral and skeletal muscle blood flow were unchanged compared to baseline, as was glomerular filtration rate.

Administration of fosinopril to patients with congestive heart failure reduces afterload and preload of the heart, resulting in an increase in cardiac output, without reflex tachycardia. At the recommended doses, the hemodynamic effects are maintained throughout the 24-hour dosing interval in most patients.

Indications: In the treatment of mild to moderate essential hypertension. It may be used alone or in association with thiazide diuretics.

In using fosinopril consideration should be given to the risk of angioedema (see Warnings).

Fosinopril should normally be used in those patients in whom treatment with a diuretic or a beta-blocker was found ineffective or has been associated with unacceptable adverse effects.

Fosinopril can also be tried as an initial agent in those patients in whom use of diuretics and/or beta-blockers is contraindicated or in patients with medical conditions in which these drugs frequently cause serious adverse effects.

The safety and efficacy of fosinopril in renovascular hypertension have not been established and therefore, its use in this condition is not recommended.

The safety and efficacy of concurrent use of fosinopril with antihypertensive agents other than thiazide diuretics have not been established.

In the management of symptomatic congestive heart failure as adjunctive treatment with diuretics, and where appropriate, digoxin. Treatment with fosinopril should be initiated under medical supervision.

Pregnancy: **When used in pregnancy during the second and third trimesters, ACE inhibitors can cause injury or even death of the developing fetus. When pregnancy is detected fosinopril should be discontinued as soon as possible (see Warnings, Pregnancy and Precautions, Information for the Patient).**

Contraindications: Patients who are hypersensitive to this product and in patients with a history of angioedema related to previous treatment with an angiotensin converting enzyme inhibitor.

Warnings: Angioedema: Angioedema has been reported in patients treated with ACE inhibitors, including fosinopril. Angioedema associated with laryngeal involvement may be fatal. If laryngeal stridor or angioedema of the face, tongue, or glottis occurs, fosinopril should be discontinued immediately, the patient treated appropriately in accordance with accepted medical care, and carefully observed until the swelling disappears. In instances where swelling is confined to the face and lips, the condition generally resolves without treatment, although antihistamines may be useful in relieving symptoms. Where there is involvement of the tongue, glottis or larynx, likely to cause airway obstruction, appropriate therapy (including but not limited to 0.3 to 0.5 mL of s.c. epinephrine solution 1:1 000) should be administered promptly (see Adverse Effects).

The incidence of angioedema during ACE inhibitor therapy has been reported to be higher in black than in nonblack patients.

Patients with a history of angioedema unrelated to ACE inhibitor therapy may be at increased risk of angioedema while receiving an ACE inhibitor (see Contraindications).

Hypotension: Symptomatic hypotension has occurred after administration of fosinopril, usually after the first or second dose or when the dose was increased. It is more likely to occur in patients who are volume depleted by diuretic therapy, dietary salt restriction, dialysis, diarrhea or vomiting. Volume and/or salt depletion should be corrected before initiating therapy with fosinopril.

In patients with severe congestive heart failure, with or without associated renal insufficiency, ACE inhibitor therapy may cause excessive hypotension and has been associated with oliguria and/or progressive azotemia, and rarely, with acute renal failure and/or death. In patients with ischemic heart or cerebrovascular disease, an excessive fall in blood pressure could result in a myocardial infarction or cerebrovascular accident (see Adverse Effects). Because of the potential fall in blood pressure in these patients, therapy with fosinopril should be started under close medical supervision. Such patients should be followed closely for the first weeks of treatment and whenever the dose of fosinopril or diuretic is increased. Consideration should be given to reducing the diuretic dose in patients with normal or low blood pressure who have been treated vigorously with diuretics or who are hyponatremic.

If hypotension occurs, the patient should be placed in a supine position, and, if necessary, receive an i.v. infusion of 0.9% sodium chloride. A transient hypotensive response is not a contraindication to further doses which usually can be given without difficulty once the blood pressure has increased after volume expansion. However, lower doses of fosinopril and/or reduced concomitant diuretic therapy should be considered.

Neutropenia/Agranulocytosis: Agranulocytosis and bone marrow depression have been caused by ACE inhibitors. Current experience with fosinopril shows the incidence to be rare and a causal relationship to the administration of fosinopril has not been established. Periodic monitoring of white blood cell counts should be considered, especially in patients with collagen vascular disease and/or renal disease.

Pregnancy: ACE inhibitors can cause fetal and neonatal morbidity and mortality when administered to pregnant women. Several dozen cases have been reported in the world literature. When pregnancy is detected, fosinopril should be discontinued as soon as possible.

In rare cases (probably less than once in every thousand of pregnancies) in which no alternative to ACE inhibitors therapy will be found, the mothers should be apprised of the potential hazards to their fetuses. Serial ultrasound examinations should be performed to assess fetal development and well-being and the volume of amniotic fluid.

If oligohydramnios is observed, fosinopril should be discontinued unless it is considered life-saving for the mother. A nonstress test (NST), and/or a biophysical profiling (BPP) may be appropriate, depending upon the week of pregnancy. If concerns regarding fetal well-being still persist, a contraction stress testing (CST) should be considered. Patients and physicians should be aware, however, that oligohydramnios may not appear until after the fetus has sustained irreversible injury.

Infants with a history of in utero exposure to ACE inhibitors should be closely observed for hypotension, oliguria, and hyperkalemia. If oliguria occurs, attention should be directed toward support of blood pressure and renal perfusion. Exchange transfusion or dialysis may be required as a means of reversing hypotension and/or substituting for impaired renal function, however, limited experience with those procedures has not been associated with significant clinical benefit. Clearance of fosinoprilat by hemodialysis and peritoneal dialysis averages 2% and 7%, respectively of urea clearance.

Human Data: It is not known whether exposure limited to the first trimester of pregnancy can adversely affect fetal outcome. The use of ACE inhibitors during the second and third trimesters of pregnancy has been associated with fetal and neonatal injury including hypotension, neonatal skull hypoplasia, anuria, reversible or irreversible renal failure and death. Oligohydramnios has also been reported, presumably resulting from decreased fetal renal function; oligohydramnios in this setting has been associated with fetal limb contractures, craniofacial deformation, and hypoplastic lung development. Prematurity and patent ductus arteriosus have also been reported, although it is not clear whether these occurrences were due to the ACE-inhibitor exposure.

Animal Data: In pregnant rabbits, maternal toxicity was evident at doses ranging from 2.5 to 40 mg/kg/day (approximately 3 to 50 times the maximum human dose). Fosinopril was embryocidal in rabbits at 10 and 40 mg/kg/day (approximately 12 and 50 times the maximum human dose). These effects were probably due to marked decreases in blood pressure caused by ACE inhibition in this species. There were no teratogenic effects in rabbits at any dose level tested.

In pregnant rats, there was evidence of maternal toxicity at all dose levels tested, i.e. 25 to 400 mg/kg/day (about 30 to 500 times the maximum human dose). Slight reductions in placental weights and degree of skeletal ossification were observed at all dose levels, and fetal body weights were reduced in the high-dose group. Three similar orofacial malformations and one fetus with situs inversus occurred in fosinopril-treated animals. The association of these anomalies with treatment is uncertain.

Precautions: Renal Impairment: As a consequence of inhibiting the renin-angiotensin-aldosterone system, changes in renal function have been seen in susceptible individuals. In patients whose renal function may depend on the activity of the renin-angiotensin-aldosterone system, such as patients with bilateral renal artery stenosis, unilateral renal artery stenosis to a solitary kidney, or severe congestive heart failure, treatment with agents that inhibit this system has been associated with oliguria, progressive azotemia, and rarely, acute renal failure and/or death. In susceptible patients, concomitant diuretic use may further increase risk.

Use of fosinopril should include appropriate assessment of renal function.

Surgery/Anesthesia: ACE inhibitors may augment the hypotensive effects of anesthetics and analgesics. In patients undergoing surgery or during anesthesia with agents that produce hypotension, fosinopril will block the angiotensin II formation that could otherwise occur secondary to compensatory renin release. Hypotension that occurs as a result of this mechanism can be corrected by volume expansion.

Hyperkalemia and Potassium-Sparing Diuretics: In clinical trials, elevated serum potassium (greater than 5.5 mEq/L) was observed in approximately 2.6% of hypertensive patients receiving fosinopril. In most cases these were isolated values which resolved despite continued therapy. Hyperkalemia was a cause of discontinuation of therapy in less than 0.1% of hypertensive patients. Risk factors for the development of hyperkalemia may include renal insufficiency, diabetes mellitus, and the concomitant use of agents to treat hypokalemia or other drugs associated with increases in serum potassium (e.g., heparin) (see Precautions, Drug Interactions and Adverse Effects).

Anaphylactoid Reactions During Membrane Exposure: Anaphylactoid reactions have been reported in patients dialysed with high-flux membranes (e.g., polyacrylonitrile (PAN) and treated concomitantly with an ACE inhibitor. Dialysis should be stopped immediately if symptoms such as nausea, abdominal cramps, burning, angioedema, shortness of breath and severe hypotension occur. Symptoms are not relieved by antihistamines. In these patients consideration should be given to using a different type of dialysis membrane or a different class of antihypertensive agents.

Anaphylactoid Reactions During Desensitization: There have been isolated reports of patients experiencing sustained life threatening anaphylactoid reactions while receiving ACE inhibitors during desensitizing treatment with hymenoptera (bees, wasps) venom. In the same patients, these reactions have been avoided when ACE inhibitors were temporarily withheld for at least 24 hours, but they have reappeared upon inadvertent rechallenge.

Valvular Stenosis: There is concern on theoretical grounds that patients with aortic stenosis might be at particular risk of decreased coronary perfusion when treated with vasodilators because they do not develop as much afterload reduction.

Patients with Impaired Liver Function: Hepatitis (hepatocellular and/or cholestatic), elevations of liver enzymes and/or serum bilirubin have occurred during therapy with ACE inhibitors including fosinopril, in patients with or without pre-existing liver abnormalities (see Adverse Effects). Fosinopril therapy was discontinued because of serum transaminase elevations in 0.7% of patients. In most cases the changes were reversed on discontinuation of the drug.

Should the patients receiving fosinopril experience any unexplained symptoms particularly during the first weeks or months of treatment, it is recommended that a full set of liver function tests and any other necessary investigation be carried out. Discontinuation of fosinopril should be considered when appropriate.

Fosinopril should be used with particular caution in patients with pre-existing liver abnormalities. In such patients baseline liver function tests should be obtained before administration of the drug and close monitoring of response and metabolic effects should apply.

Cough: Cough has been reported with the use of fosinopril. Characteristically, ACE-inhibitor induced cough is non productive, persistent and resolves after discontinuation of therapy or lowering of the dose. Fosinopril induced cough should be considered as part of the differential diagnosis of the cough.

Lactation: Ingestion of 20 mg daily for 3 days resulted in detectable levels of fosinoprilat in breast milk. Fosinopril should not be administered to nursing mothers.

Children: The safety and effectiveness of fosinopril in children have not been established; therefore, its use in this age group is not recommended.

Geriatrics: Although clinical experience has not identified differences in response between the elderly and younger patients, greater sensitivity of some older individuals cannot be ruled out.

Drug Interactions: Concomitant Diuretic Therapy: Patients concomitantly taking ACE inhibitors and diuretics, and especially those in whom diuretic therapy was recently instituted, may occasionally experience an excessive reduction of blood pressure after initiation of therapy. The possibility of hypotensive effects after the first dose of fosinopril can be minimized by either discontinuing the diuretic or increasing the salt intake prior to initiation of treatment with fosinopril. If it is not possible to discontinue the diuretic, the starting dose can be reduced, and the patient should be closely observed for several hours following an initial dose and until blood pressure has stabilized (see Warnings and Dosage).

Decreases in serum sodium and increases in serum creatinine occurred more frequently in patients on concomitant diuretics than in those treated with fosinopril alone (see Adverse Effects, Laboratory Test Abnormalities).

Agents Increasing Serum Potassium: Since fosinopril decreases aldosterone production, elevation of serum potassium may occur. Potassium sparing diuretics such as spironolactone, triamterene or amiloride, or potassium supplements should be given only for documented hypokalemia and with caution and frequent monitoring of serum potassium, since they may lead to a significant increase in serum potassium. Salt substitutes which contain potassium should also be used with caution.

Agents Causing Renin Release: The antihypertensive effect of fosinopril is augmented by antihypertensive agents that cause renin release (e.g., diuretics).

With Lithium: Increased serum lithium levels and symptoms of lithium toxicity have been reported in patients receiving concomitant lithium and ACE inhibitor therapy. These drugs should be coadministered with caution and frequent monitoring of serum lithium levels is recommended. If a diuretic is also used, it may increase the risk of lithium toxicity.

With Antacids: In a clinical pharmacology study, coadministration of an antacid (aluminum hydroxide, magnesium hydroxide and simethicone) with fosinopril reduced serum levels and urinary excretion of fosinoprilat as compared with fosinopril administered alone, suggesting that antacids may impair absorption of fosinopril. Therefore, if concomitant administration of these agents is indicated, dosing should be separated by 2 hours.

With ASA: In a study with concomitant administration of ASA and fosinopril the bioavailability of unbound fosinoprilat was not altered. Since it is believed that it is free fosinoprilat that inhibits ACE, the reduced bioavailability (30 to 40%) of bound fosinoprilat would not be expected to have a significant effect on the antihypertensive effects of fosinopril.

With Digoxin: In a study with concomitant administration of digoxin and fosinopril, the bioavailability of fosinoprilat was not altered. The bioavailability of digoxin (i.e. AUC and C_{max}) appeared to be reduced slightly in the presence of fosinopril. This reduction, of less than 20%, is considered to have little or no clinical relevance.

With Furosemide: In a steady-state pharmacokinetic study, coadministration of furosemide with fosinopril increased the AUC of fosinoprilat by 26% and C_{max} by 25%. Furosemide levels were decreased.

With Warfarin: In a pharmacokinetic interaction study with warfarin, bioavailability parameters, the degree of protein

Monopril (cont'd)

binding and the anticoagulant effect (measured by prothrombin time) of warfarin were not significantly changed. The bioavailability of fosinoprilat was not altered by coadministration of fosinopril with warfarin.

Other: In separate single or multiple dose pharmacokinetic interaction studies with chlorthalidone, nifedipine, propranolol, hydrochlorothiazide, cimetidine, metoclopramide and propantheline, the bioavailability of fosinoprilat was not altered by coadministration of fosinopril with any one of these drugs.

Drug/Laboratory Test Interactions: Fosinopril may cause a false low measurement of serum digoxin levels with the Digi-Tab RIA kit for digoxin. Other kits such as the Coat-A-Count RIA kit may be used.

Information for the Patient: Angioedema: Angioedema, including laryngeal edema, may occur especially following the first dose of fosinopril. Patients should be so advised and told to report immediately any signs or symptoms suggesting angioedema (swelling of face, eyes, lips, tongue, difficulty in swallowing or breathing); they should immediately stop taking fosinopril and consult with their physician (see Warnings).

Hypotension: Patients should be cautioned to report lightheadedness, especially during the first few days of fosinopril therapy. If actual syncope occurs, the patients should be told to discontinue the drug and consult with their physician.

All patients should be cautioned that excessive perspiration and dehydration may lead to an excessive fall in blood pressure because of reduction in fluid volume. Other causes of volume depletion such as vomiting or diarrhea may also lead to a fall in blood pressure; patients should be advised to consult with their physician.

Neutropenia: Patients should be advised to report promptly any signs or symptoms of infection (e.g., pharyngitis, fever) since these may be an early indicator of neutropenia (see Warnings and Adverse Effects).

Impaired Liver Function: Patients should be advised to return to the physician if he/she experiences any symptoms possibly related to liver dysfunction. This would include "viral-like symptoms" in the first weeks to months of therapy (such as fever, malaise, muscle pain, rash or adenopathy which are possible indicators of hypersensitivity reactions), or if abdominal pain, nausea or vomiting, loss of appetite, jaundice, itching or any other unexplained symptoms occur during therapy.

Hyperkalemia: Patients should be advised not to use potassium supplements or salt substitutes containing potassium without consulting their physician (see Precautions and Adverse Effects).

Pregnancy: **Since the use of fosinopril during pregnancy can cause injury and even death of the developing fetus, patients should be advised to report promptly to their physician if they become pregnant.**

Adverse Effects: Fosinopril has been evaluated for safety in hypertension trials in 1 548 patients. Of these, 1 479 patients including 1 048 who were treated with fosinopril monotherapy. In heart failure trials, 516 patients were treated with fosinopril including 316 who participated in placebo-controlled trials. Fosinopril has been evaluated for long-term safety in approximately 519 patients treated for 1 year or more.

Severe adverse reactions occurring in hypertensive patients treated with fosinopril were: angioedema (1 case) and orthostatic hypotension (2.7%). Myocardial infarction (2 cases) and cerebrovascular accident (4 cases) occurred, possibly secondary to excessive hypotension in high risk patients (see Warnings). In 516 heart failure patients, the severe adverse reaction occurring with the highest frequency was angina pectoris (1.6%).

In placebo-controlled hypertensive trials, the most frequent adverse experiences were: nausea/vomiting, diarrhea, fatigue, musculoskeletal pain, headache, dizziness and cough. Discontinuation of therapy due to adverse events was required in 4.1% of the 688 patients. Cough was the cause for discontinuation of therapy in 0.4% of these patients.

In placebo-controlled heart failure trials, the most frequent adverse reactions were: dizziness, cough, headache and fatigue. Significant hypotension after the first dose of fosinopril occurred in 2.4% of patients, while 0.8% discontinued due to first dose hypotension (see Warnings, Hypotension). Discontinuation of therapy due to adverse events was required in 7.8% of the 361 patients. Cough was the cause for discontinuation of therapy in 0.8% of these patients.

Adverse reactions occurring in 1% or more of the 1 048 hypertensive and 361 congestive heart failure patients in controlled clinical trials who were treated with fosinopril monotherapy are listed in Table I.

Table I—Monopril

Adverse Reactions

Body System/Reaction	Hypertension[a] N=1 048 %	Heart Failure[b] N=361 %
Cardiovascular		
Hypotension	–	4.4
Orthostatic hypotension	1.4	1.9
Palpitation	–	1.4
Angina pectoris	–	1.1
Edema	–	1.1
Dermatologic		
Rash	1.0	1.4
Endocrine/Metabolic		
Sexual dysfunction	1.7	–
Gastrointestinal		
Nausea/Vomiting	1.4	2.2
Diarrhea	1.4	2.2
Pyrosis	1.0	–
Dry mouth	1.0	–
Abdominal pain	–	1.4
General		
Fatigue	2.8	4.7
Chest pain (noncardiac)	–	2.2
Weakness	–	1.4
Musculoskeletal/ Connective Tissue		
Musculoskeletal pain	–	3.3
Muscle cramp	–	1.4
Nervous System		
Headache	4.6	3.6
Dizziness	3.8	11.9
Insomnia	–	1.1
Respiratory		
Cough	4.0	9.7
Dyspnea	–	4.4
Upper respiratory infection	–	2.2

[a]Placebo and active controlled trials.
[b]Placebo controlled trials.

Clinical adverse reactions occurring in less than 1% of the 1 479 hypertensive patients and 516 heart failure patients treated with fosinopril in controlled clinical trials are listed below by body system:

Cardiovascular: angina/myocardial infarction, cerebrovascular accidents, palpitations, syncope, edema, tachycardia, flushing, cardiac chest pain, hypertension, rhythm disturbances, heart failure, peripheral vascular disease of arteries, cardiac tamponade, coronary artery disease, hypertensive crisis, sudden death, cardiorespiratory arrest, shock, atrial rhythm disturbance, nonanginal chest pain, edema lower extremity, conduction disorder and bradycardia.

Dermatologic: pemphigus, Stevens-Johnson syndrome pruritus, dermatitis, skin induration, skin dryness, urticaria, skin eschar, photosensitivity, pruritic rash and nail abnormality.

Endocrine/Metabolic: gout, libido change, breast disorder and menstrual disorder.

Gastrointestinal: upper abdominal pain, abdominal distention, appetite change, constipation, flatulence, dysphagia, pancreatitis, hepatitis, tongue lesion and hepatomegaly.

General: chest pain, excess sweating, change in weight, volume depletion, influenza, fever, hyperhidrosis and sensation of cold.

Hematologic: lymphadenopathy, leukopenia, neutropenia (see Warnings), eosinophilia and hemolytic anemia.

Immunology/Sensitivity Disorders: angioedema.

Musculoskeletal/Connective Tissue: arthralgia, muscle/ache, swelling extremity, and weakness extremity.

Nervous System: sleep disturbance, stress, paresthesia, mood change, equilibrium disturbance, drowsiness, tremor, cerebrovascular accident, mental activity disorder, memory disturbance, cranial nerve disorder, confusion, vertigo, cerebral infarction, transient ischemic attack, depression, numbness and behavior change.

Renal/Genitourinary: renal insufficiency, change in urinary frequency, abnormal urination and kidney pain.

Respiratory: sinus abnormality, pharyngitis, rhinitis, epistaxis, hoarseness, laryngitis, breathing abnormality, asthma, bronchospasm, sinusitis, abnormal vocalization, tracheobronchitis and pleuritic chest pain. A symptom-complex of cough, bronchospasm and eosinophilia has been observed in 2 hypertensive patients treated with fosinopril.

Special Senses: eye irritation, vision disturbance, tinnitus, taste disturbance, ear pain, abnormal visual field and abnormal intraocular pressure.

As with other ACE inhibitors, a syndrome has been reported which includes: fever, myalgia, arthralgia, rash or other dermatologic manifestations, eosinophilia and an elevated ESR. Findings have usually resolved with discontinuation of treatment.

Laboratory Test Findings: Serum Electrolytes: hyperkalemia (see Precautions), hyponatremia (see Precautions, Drug Interactions-with Diuretics).

BUN/Serum Creatinine: Elevations, usually transient and minor, of BUN or serum creatinine have been observed. In placebo-controlled clinical trials, there were no significant differences in the number of patients experiencing increases in serum creatinine (outside the normal range or 1.33 times the pretreatment value) between the fosinopril and placebo treatment groups.

Urinary Albumin: In placebo-controlled trials, a urinary albumin (2 consecutive dip-stick values greater than 3+ or ≥2 times the pretreatment value) unassociated with a rise in serum creatinine was seen in 0.4% of fosinopril-treatment patients without pre-existing renal disease. Increases in urinary albumin usually developed in patients with pre-existing proteinuria or diabetes mellitus. In the majority of these patients, values returned to baseline despite continuation of therapy.

Hematology: In controlled trials, a mean hemoglobin decrease of 0.1 g/dL was observed in fosinopril-treated patients. In individual patients decreases in hemoglobin or hematocrit were usually transient, small, and not associated with symptoms. No patient was discontinued from therapy due to the development of anemia.

Liver Function Tests: Elevations of transaminases, LDH, alkaline phosphatase and serum bilirubin have been reported.

Overdose: Symptoms and Treatment: No data are available regarding overdosage of fosinopril in humans. The most likely clinical manifestation would be symptoms attributable to severe hypotension, which should be normally treated by i.v. volume expansion with 0.9% sodium chloride. Hemodialysis and peritoneal dialysis have little effect on the elimination of fosinoprilat.

Dosage: Dosage must be individualized.

Hypertension: Initiation of therapy requires consideration of recent antihypertensive drug treatment, the extent of blood pressure elevation and salt restriction. The dosage of other antihypertensive agents being used with fosinopril may need to be adjusted.

Monotherapy: The recommended initial dose is 10 mg once daily. Dosage should be adjusted according to blood pressure response, generally, at intervals of at least 2 weeks. The usual maintenance dose is 20 mg daily administered in a single daily dose. No additional blood pressure lowering effects were achieved with doses greater than 40 mg daily. A dose of 40 mg daily should not be exceeded.

In most patients, the antihypertensive effect of fosinopril is maintained with a once daily dosage regimen. In some patients treated once daily, the antihypertensive effect may diminish towards the end of the dosing interval. This can be evaluated by measuring blood pressure just prior to dosing to determine whether satisfactory control is being maintained for 24 hours. If it is not, either twice daily administration with the same total daily dose, or an increase in dose should be considered. If blood pressure is not controlled with fosinopril alone, a diuretic may be added. After the addition of a diuretic, it may be possible to reduce the dose of fosinopril.

Concomitant Diuretic Therapy: Symptomatic hypotension occasionally may occur following the initial dose of fosinopril and is more likely in patients who are currently being treated with a diuretic. The diuretic should, if possible, be discontinued for 2 to 3 days before beginning therapy with fosinopril to reduce the likelihood of hypotension (see Warnings). If the diuretic cannot be discontinued, an initial dose of 10 mg fosinopril should be used with careful medical supervision for several hours and until blood pressure has stabilized. The dosage of fosinopril should subsequently be titrated to the optimal response.

Heart Failure: Fosinopril is generally used in conjunction with a diuretic, with or without digoxin. Blood pressure and renal function should be monitored, both before and during treatment with fosinopril, because severe hypotension, and more rarely renal failure, have been reported (see Warnings, Hypotension and Precautions, Renal Impairment).

Initiation of therapy requires consideration of recent diuretic therapy, and the possibility of severe salt/volume depletion. If possible, the dose of diuretic should be reduced before beginning treatment to reduce the likelihood of hypotension (see Precautions, Drug Interactions).

In patients with heart failure, the recommended initial dose is 10 mg once daily, initiated under close medical supervision. If the initial dose is well tolerated, the dose should be titrated over 1 to 3 weeks to 20 to 40 mg once daily. The occurrence of hypotension after the initial dose may not preclude careful dose titration following effective management of hypotension.

In patients with severe congestive heart failure with or without renal insufficiency, therapy should be initiated with caution (see Warnings, Hypotension). A lower starting dose should be considered.

Renal Impairment: In hypertensive patients with renal impairment and normal liver function no dosage adjustment is necessary. The recommended initial dose is 10 mg once daily. Depending on the response, the dose should then be titrated, to achieve the optimal response (see Pharmacology, Pharmacokinetics and Precautions, Hemodialysis Patients). In such patients with heart failure, therapy should be initiated with caution.

Hepatic Impairment: In hypertensive patients with hepatic impairment and normal renal function no dosage adjustment is necessary. The recommended initial dose is 10 mg once daily. Depending on the response, the dose should then be titrated to achieve the optimal response (see Pharmacology, Pharmacokinetics). In such patients with heart failure, therapy should be initiated with caution.

Supplied: 10 mg: Each white to off-white, flat end diamond-shaped, compressed tablet, with a partial bisect bar engraved with BMS on one side and MONOPRIL 10 on the other, contains: fosinopril sodium 10 mg. Nonmedicinal ingredients: crospovidone, lactose, microcrystalline cellulose, povidone and sodium stearyl fumarate. Bottles of 100.

20 mg: Each white to off-white, oval-shaped, compressed tablet, engraved with BMS on one side and MONOPRIL 20 on the other, contains: fosinopril sodium 20 mg. Nonmedicinal ingredients: crospovidone, lactose, microcrystalline cellulose, povidone and sodium stearyl fumarate. Bottles of 100.

Store at room temperature (15 to 30°C). Keep container tightly closed. Protect from high humidity.

(Shown in Product Recognition Section)

Reviewed 1998

MORPHINE Ⓝ
General Monograph, CPhA

see OPIOID ANALGESICS

MORPHINE HP® Ⓝ
Sabex

Morphine Sulfate

Opioid Analgesic

Supplied: 25 mg/mL: Each mL contains: morphine sulfate 25 mg. Nonmedicinal ingredients: sodium chloride, sulfuric acid and/or sodium hydroxide (to adjust pH) and water for injection. Preservative-free. Single use amber vials of 1 mL, boxes of 10. Single use amber vials of 4 mL, boxes of 5.

50 mg/mL: Each mL contains: morphine sulfate 50 mg. Nonmedicinal ingredients: sodium chloride, sulfuric acid and/or sodium hydroxide (to adjust pH) and water for injection. Preservative-free. Single use amber vials of 1 mL, boxes of 10. Single use amber vials of 5 and 10 mL, boxes of 5. Single use amber vials of 50 mL, boxes of 1.

Store between 15 and 30°C. Protect from light. Discard unused portion. Do not autoclave.

Geriatric patients may experience unique drug-induced effects. Be aware of potential side effects and drug interactions. For more information, refer to the CLIN-INFO SECTION.

MORPHINE SULFATE Ⓝ
Abbott

Opioid Analgesic

Supplied: Ampuls: Each mL contains: morphine sulfate 2 mg, 10 mg or 15 mg, sodium metabisulfite and water for injection. Ampuls of 1 mL. Boxes of 100.

Cartridges: Each mL contains: morphine sulfate 1, 2 or 5 mg and sodium metabisulfite. Also contains citric acid, sodium chloride, sodium citrate and water for injection. Cartridges (single dose vials) of 30 mL for Patient-Controlled-Analgesia infusor (PCA).

Morphine Forte: Each mL contains: morphine sulfate pentahydrate 25 mg in water for injection. Ampuls of 1 and 4 mL. Sleeves of 5.

Morphine Extra-Forte: Each mL contains: morphine sulfate pentahydrate 50 mg in water for injection. Ampuls of 1 mL. Sleeves of 5.

Morphine-EPD Preservative-free: 0.5 mg: Each mL contains: morphine sulfate injection USP 0.5 mg. Also contains hydrochloric acid, sodium chloride, sodium hydroxide and water for injection. Ampuls of 10 mL, vials of 20 mL. Cartons of 5.

1 mg: Each mL contains: morphine sulfate injection USP 1 mg. Also contains hydrochloric acid, sodium chloride, sodium hydroxide and water for injection. Ampuls of 5 mL. Cartons of 5.

MORPHINE SULFATE INJECTION BP (1 mg/mL and 2 mg/mL) Ⓝ
Faulding

Opioid Analgesic

Pharmacology: Morphine exerts its main actions by acting as an agonist at specific receptor sites in the CNS.

Morphine produces many effects including analgesia, decreased gastrointestinal motility, respiratory depression, nausea, vomiting, drowsiness, changes in mood and alterations of the endocrine and autonomic nervous systems.

Maximum analgesia occurs within 50 to 90 minutes after s.c. administration, and 20 minutes after i.v. administration. Analgesia persists for 2.5 to 7 hours.

Morphine is rapidly metabolized by the liver and excreted in the urine primarily as the active metabolite, morphine-6-glucuronide. The half-life of morphine in young adults is about 2 hours; the half-life of morphine-6-glucuronide is somewhat longer. In older patients, the volume of distribution is considerably smaller and initial concentrations of morphine are correspondingly higher.

Indications: For the symptomatic relief of severe pain of various categories.

Contraindications: Hypersensitivity to any of the components of the drug product. The Rapiject syringe formulation contains sodium metabisulfite which may cause allergic-type reactions, including anaphylaxis and life-threatening or less severe asthmatic episodes, in certain susceptible individuals. The overall prevalence of sulfite sensitivity in the general population is unknown but probably low; such sensitivity appears to occur more frequently in asthmatic than in non-asthmatic individuals.

Respiratory insufficiency or depression; severe CNS depression, attack of bronchial asthma; heart failure secondary to chronic lung disease; cardiac arrhythmias; increased intracranial or cerebrospinal pressure; head injuries, brain tumor; acute alcoholism; delirium tremens; convulsive disorders; after biliary tract surgery; suspected surgical abdomen; surgical anastomosis; concomitantly with MAO inhibitors or within 14 days of such treatment.

Warnings: Morphine can produce dependence and therefore has the potential for being abused. Psychic dependence, physical dependence and tolerance may develop upon repeated administration of morphine.

Morphine should be used with caution and in reduced dosage in patients who are concurrently receiving other opioid analgesics, general anesthetics, phenothiazines, other tranquilizers, sedative-hypnotics, tricyclic antidepressants and other CNS depressants (including alcohol). Respiratory depression, hypotension and profound sedation or coma may result.

The respiratory depressant effects of morphine and its capacity to elevate cerebrospinal fluid pressure may be markedly exaggerated in the presence of head injury, other intracranial lesions, or a pre-existing increase in intracranial pressure. Furthermore, opioids produce adverse reactions which may obscure the clinical course of patients with head injuries. In such patients, morphine must be used with extreme caution and only if its use is deemed essential.

Morphine should be used with extreme caution in patients having an acute asthmatic attack, patients with chronic obstructive pulmonary disease or cor pulmonale, patients having a substantially decreased respiratory reserve, and patients with pre-existing respiratory depression, hypoxia or hypercapnia. In such patients, even usual therapeutic doses of opioids may decrease respiratory drive while simultaneously increasing airway resistance to the point of apnea.

Precautions: Acute Abdominal Condition: The administration of morphine or other opioids may obscure the diagnosis or clinical course in patients with acute abdominal conditions.

Hypotensive Effect: The administration of morphine may result in severe hypotension in the postoperative patient or any individual whose ability to maintain blood pressure has been compromised by a depleted blood volume or the administration of such drugs as the phenothiazines or certain anesthetics.

Supraventricular Tachycardias: Because of possible vagolytic action that may produce a significant increase in the ventricular response rate, morphine should be used with caution in patients with atrial flutter and other supraventricular tachycardias.

Convulsions: Morphine may aggravate pre-existing convulsions in patients with convulsive disorders. If dosage is escalated substantially above recommended levels because of tolerance development, convulsions may occur in individuals without a history of convulsive disorders.

Other Special Risk Patients: Morphine should be given with caution to certain patients, such as the elderly or debilitated and those with severe impairment of hepatic or renal function, hypothyroidism, Addison's disease, prostatic hypertrophy or urethral stricture.

Morphine should be used with extreme caution in patients with disorders characterized by hypoxia, since even usual therapeutic doses of opioids may decrease respiratory drive to the point of apnea while simultaneously increasing airway resistance.

Morphine may have a prolonged duration and cumulative effect in patients with kidney or liver dysfunction. In these patients, analgesia may last for 6, 8 or even up to 24 hours following a standard dose. Continuous infusions should be avoided.

In patients with shock, impaired perfusion may prevent complete absorption following s.c. or i.m. injection of morphine. Repeated administration may result in overdosage due to an excessive amount of morphine suddenly being absorbed when circulation is restored.

Information for the Patient: Occupational Hazards: Morphine may impair the mental and/or physical abilities required for the performance of potentially hazardous tasks, such as driving a car or operating machinery. Morphine in combination with other opioid analgesics, phenothiazines, sedative-hypnotics or alcohol has additive depressant effects. The patient should be cautioned accordingly.

Drug Interactions: Morphine in combination with other opioid analgesics, general anesthetics, phenothiazines, tranquilizers, sedative-hypnotics or other CNS depressants (including alcohol) has additive depressant effects. Dosage reduction of one or both agents is required.

Pregnancy: Animal reproduction studies have not been conducted with morphine. It is not known whether it can cause fetal harm when administered to a pregnant woman or whether it can affect reproduction capacity. On the basis of the historical use of morphine during all stages of pregnancy, there is no known risk of fetal abnormality. Morphine should be given to a pregnant woman only if clearly needed.

Labor and Delivery: The use of morphine in obstetrics may prolong labor. It passes the placental barrier and may produce respiratory depression in the newborn. In resuscitation and severe depression, the administration of an opioid antagonist such as naloxone or nalorphine may be required.

Lactation: Morphine appears in the milk of nursing mothers. Breast-feeding should be discontinued if morphine is required.

Children: Safety and efficacy of morphine in neonates and children have not been established.

Morphine Sulfate Injection BP (cont'd)

Adverse Effects: The major hazards of morphine, as with other opioid analgesics, are respiratory depression and, to a lesser degree, circulatory depression; respiratory arrest, shock and cardiac arrest have occurred. The most frequently observed adverse reactions include lightheadedness, dizziness, sedation, nausea, vomiting and sweating. These effects seem to be more prominent in ambulatory patients and in those who are not experiencing severe pain. In such individuals, lower doses are advisable. Some adverse reactions in ambulatory patients may be alleviated if the patient lies down.

Rapid i.v. injection of the drug may result in an increased frequency of opiate-induced adverse effects; severe respiratory depression, apnea, hypotension, peripheral circulatory collapse, chest wall rigidity, cardiac arrest and possible anaphylactoid reactions.

Other adverse reactions include: CNS: euphoria, dysphoria, weakness, headache, agitation, tremor, uncoordinated muscle movements, transient hallucinations and disorientation, visual disturbances.

Gastrointestinal: dry mouth, constipation, biliary tract spasm.

Cardiovascular: flushing of the face, tachycardia, bradycardia, palpitation, faintness, syncope.

Genitourinary: urinary retention.

Allergic: pruritus, urticaria, other skin rashes, wheal and flare over the vein with i.v. injection.

Other: pain at injection site; local tissue irritation and induration following s.c. injection, particularly when repeated; antidiuretic effect.

Overdose: Symptoms: Overdosage with morphine is characterized by respiratory depression (a decrease in respiratory rate and/or tidal volume, Cheyne-Stokes respiration, cyanosis), extreme somnolence progressing to stupor or coma, skeletal muscle flaccidity, cold and clammy skin, and sometimes bradycardia and hypotension. In severe overdosage, apnea, circulatory collapse, cardiac arrest and death may occur.

Treatment: Immediate attention should be given to the re-establishment of adequate respiratory exchange through provision of a patent airway and institution of assisted or controlled ventilation.

Oxygen, i.v. fluids, vasopressors and other supportive measures should be employed as indicated.

The opioid antagonist naloxone is a specific antidote against respiratory depression which may result from overdosage or unusual sensitivity to opioids. The recommended adult dose of naloxone is 0.4 to 2 mg i.v. every 2 to 3 minutes as necessary, simultaneously with assisted respiration.

An antagonist should only be administered in cases of clinically significant respiratory or cardiovascular depression.

In an individual physically dependent on opioids, the administration of the usual dose of opioid antagonist will precipitate an acute withdrawal syndrome. The severity of this syndrome will depend on the degree of physical dependence and the dose of antagonist administered. The use of opioid antagonists in such individuals should be avoided if possible. If an opioid antagonist must be used to treat serious respiratory depression in the physically dependent patient, the antagonist should be administered with extreme care at about 10 to 20% the usual initial dose administered.

Dosage: Morphine sulfate should be given in the smallest effective dose and as infrequently as possible in order to minimize the development of tolerance and physical dependence. Following successful relief of severe pain, periodic attempts to reduce the opioid dose should be made. Lower doses or complete discontinuation of the opioid analgesic may become feasible due to physiological change or improved mental state of the patient.

Reduced dosage is indicated in patients with renal dysfunction or with respiratory problems, in very young or elderly patients, and in patients receiving CNS depressants. Wide patient variability exists. Titrate dosage individually. In patients with severe chronic pain, adjust dosage according to the severity of the pain and the response and tolerance of the patient. In patients with exceptionally severe chronic pain and/or in those who have become tolerant to the analgesic effect of opiate agonists, it may be necessary to exceed the usual dosage.

In cases of chronic pain of malignant disease, it is important that the analgesic be given regularly around the clock, day and night, and not on a when needed basis.

Morphine sulfate injection B.P. 1 or 2 mg/mL may be administered by s.c. or slow i.v. injection or by i.v. infusion. Alternatively s.c. infusion using a portable pump is suggested.

S.C. or Slow I.V. Injection: For i.v. administration, 2.5 to 15 mg of morphine may be diluted in 4 to 5 mL of sterile water for injection and injected i.v. slowly over 4 to 5 minutes in adults; it is preferable for the patient to be in the recumbent position.

Children may receive a s.c. morphine dose of 0.1 to 0.2 mg/kg every 4 hours as necessary; a single pediatric dose should not exceed 15 mg.

To relieve pain of myocardial infarction in adults, 8 to 15 mg of morphine may be administered parenterally. For very severe pain, additional smaller doses may be given every 3 to 4 hours.

Continuous I.V. or S.C. Infusion: Useful in patients who are not able to tolerate oral or rectal routes and require frequent s.c., i.m. or i.v. injections; have poor pain control with intermittent injections; require high doses of intermittent injections; and in cachectic or thrombocytopenic patients and those with coagulation disorders.

If a patient is presently in pain and was previously poorly controlled on analgesics, start loading dose of 1 to 2 mg/min until pain is relieved. Administer loading dose in 4 to 5 mL of i.v. fluid slowly over 1 minute. Check vital signs. If diastolic blood pressure decreases more than 10% or if respiration rate is less than 10/min, postpone further dosing until vital signs are acceptable.

If the patient's pain is presently controlled, calculate previous day's 24-hour opioid requirement (keeping route and analgesic equivalents in mind) and calculate hourly dose.

When morphine is administered by continuous i.v. or s.c. infusion for relief of severe chronic pain associated with cancer, the dosage of the drug must be individualized according to the response and tolerance of the patient. Continuous i.v. infusions of the drug have been initiated at 0.8 to 10 mg/hour in adults and then increased to an effective dosage as necessary; an i.v. loading dose of 15 mg or more can be administered for initial relief of pain prior to initiating continuous i.v. infusion of the drug. In adults with severe chronic pain, maintenance dosages usually have ranged from 0.8 to 80 mg/hour infused i.v., although higher (e.g., 150 mg/hour) maintenance dosages occasionally have been required. In addition, relatively high dosages (e.g., 275 to 440 mg/hour) occasionally have been infused i.v. for several hours or days to provide relief of exacerbations of chronic pain in adults previously stabilized on lower dosages or whose dosage had been gradually titrated to relatively high levels; subsequent dosage reductions according to patient response generally were possible.

When morphine is administered by multiple, slow i.v. injections for patient-controlled analgesia (PCA), dosage is adjusted according to the severity of the pain and response of the patient; the operator's manual for the patient-controlled infusion device should be consulted for directions on administering the drug at the desired rate of infusion. Care must be exercised to avoid overdosage, which could result in respiratory depression, or abrupt cessation of therapy with the drug, which could precipitate opiate withdrawal.

If a patient has low muscle mass or is cachectic or has no accessible peripheral veins, s.c. infusion using a portable pump may be indicated. When switching from i.v. to s.c. infusion, use the same dose and monitor the same parameters. The maximum dose that can be safely given has not been defined but doses as high as 480 mg/24 hours have been given. Erythema around the injection site may occur. Change needle site periodically (every 7 to 10 days although some clinicians prefer every 48 hours).

Opioid Analgesics: Approximate Analgesic Equivalences: See Table I.

Stability and Storage: Store at room temperature below 25°C. Protect from light. Do not autoclave.

Morphine sulfate injection 1 mg/mL and 2 mg/mL and dilutions of morphine sulfate injection in dextrose 5% injection or sodium chloride 0.9% injection may be stored in portable infusion pump cassettes, syringes and PVC infusion bags. Protected from light, they will stay stable for 24 hours at room temperature or for 72 hours if kept refrigerated. Proper aseptic technique must be used in order to minimize contamination of the solution.

Table I—Morphine Sulfate Injection BP (1 mg/mL and 2 mg/mL)

Opioid Analgesics: Approximate Analgesic Equivalences

Drug	Equivalent Dose (mg)[a] (compared to morphine 10 mg i.m.) Parenteral	Oral	Duration of Action (hours)
Strong Opioid Agonists			
Morphine (single dose)	10	60	3-4
(chronic dose)	10	20-30[b]	3-4
Hydromorphone	1.5-2	6-7.5	2-4
Anileridine	25	75	2-3
Levorphanol	2	4	4-8
Meperidine[c]	75	300	1-3
Oxymorphone	1.5	5 (rectal)	3-4
Methadone[d]			
Heroin	5-8	10-15	3-4
Weak Opioid Agonists			
Codeine	120	200	3-4
Oxycodone	5-10	10-15	2-4
Propoxyphene	50	100	2-4
Mixed Agonist-Antagonists[e]			
Pentazocine	60	180	3-4
Nalbuphine	10		3-6
Butorphanol	2		3-4

[a] Most of these data were derived from single-dose, acute pain studies and should be considered an approximation for selection of doses when treating chronic pain.

[b] For acute pain, the oral dose of morphine is 6 times the injectable dose. However, for chronic dosing, this ratio becomes 2 or 3:1, possibly due to the accumulation of active metabolites.

[c] These drugs are not recommended for the management of chronic pain.

[d] Extremely variable equianalgesic dose. Patients should undergo personalized titration starting at an equivalent to 1/10 of the morphine dose.

[e] Mixed agonist-antagonists can precipitate withdrawal in patients on pure opioid agonists.

Warning: As with all parenteral drug products, i.v. admixtures should be inspected visually for clarity, particulate matter, precipitate and leakage prior to administration, whenever solution and container permit. Solutions showing haziness, particulate matter, precipitate or leakage should not be used. Development of a yellow color in morphine solutions does not indicate toxicity nor loss of potency or efficacy.

Supplied: Each mL of clear, colorless or pale yellow, sterile solution contains: morphine sulfate BP 1 mg or 2 mg, with 0.9 mg sodium metabisulfite, sodium chloride 7.6 mg, citric acid 0.4 mg, sodium citrate 0.2 mg, in sterile water for injection. Sodium hydroxide or citric acid may be added for pH adjustment. Rapiject prefilled, single dose syringes of 50 mL.

Medication, needle and fluid pathway are sterile in the unopened, intact Rapiject system with caps in place.

These products contain no bacteriostat or antimicrobial agents and are intended as single dose units. When the dosing requirement is completed, the unused portion should be discarded in an appropriate manner.

Directions for Use of Rapiject Prefilled Syringe: 1. Remove protective caps from vial and injector. 2. Insert vial into injector. 3. Rotate vial 3 turns in a clockwise direction until some resistance occurs. Then rotate vial another turn or two. The needle will then be in contact with the morphine solution. 4. Remove the needle cap and expel air. 5. The Rapiject is now ready for use.

MORPHINE SULFATE INJECTION BP (50 mg/mL) Ⓝ

Faulding

Opioid Analgesic

Pharmacology: Morphine exerts its main actions by acting as an agonist at specific receptor sites in the CNS.

Morphine produces many effects including analgesia, decreased gastrointestinal motility, respiratory depression, nausea, vomiting, drowsiness, changes in mood and alterations of the endocrine and autonomic nervous systems.

Maximum analgesia occurs within 50 to 90 minutes after s.c. administration, 30 to 60 minutes after i.m. administration and 20 minutes after i.v. administration. Analgesia persists for 2.5 to 7 hours.

Morphine is rapidly metabolized by the liver and excreted in the urine primarily as the active metabolite, morphine-6-glucuronide. The half-life of morphine in young adults is about 2 hours; the half-life of morphine-6-glucuronide is somewhat longer. In older patients, the volume of distribution is considerably smaller and initial concentrations of morphine are correspondingly higher.

Indications: Morphine sulfate injection 50 mg/mL used without dilution is indicated for the relief of severe pain in patients who require opioids in doses higher than those usually needed.

Morphine sulfate injection 50 mg/mL provides a smaller injection volume, thus reducing the discomfort associated with large volume s.c. or i.m. injection. Morphine sulfate injection 50 mg/mL may also be diluted for i.v. infusion (see Dosage, I.V. Infusion with Dilution).

Contraindications: Hypersensitivity to morphine; respiratory insufficiency or depression; severe CNS depression; attack of bronchial asthma; heart failure secondary to chronic lung disease; cardiac arrhythmias; increased intracranial or cerebrospinal pressure; head injuries, brain tumor; acute alcoholism; delirium tremens; convulsive disorders; after biliary tract surgery; suspected surgical abdomen; surgical anastomosis; concomitantly with MAO inhibitors or within 14 days of such treatment.

Warnings: Morphine sulfate injection 50 mg/mL used without dilution should be used specifically for patients who are already receiving large doses of opioids. This strength of morphine undiluted is indicated for the relief of severe pain in opioid-tolerant patients. The inadvertant administration of this strength of morphine to patients requiring standard dosage strengths may lead to overdose or death.

Morphine can produce drug dependence and therefore has the potential for being abused. Psychic dependence, physical dependence and tolerance may develop upon repeated administration of morphine. However it should be noted that clinically significant respiratory depression, addiction, rapid tolerance and euphoria rarely develop when doses of morphine are carefully titrated against the pain in patients with terminal disease and severe pain.

Drug dependence does not develop if morphine is administered regularly at individually optimized doses to the cancer patient with severe pain. While a certain degree of physical dependence occurs, psychological dependence does not occur. If a cancer patient no longer requires an opioid for pain control, a gradual reduction in dose will prevent any withdrawal symptoms, although these are usually mild or absent even after abrupt discontinuance. Clinically significant tolerance to morphine is unusual in the cancer patient being treated for severe pain. In most cases, a plateauing of dose requirements is seen and a need to increase morphine dose means an increase in pain and not tolerance.

Morphine should be used with caution and in reduced dosage in patients who are concurrently receiving other opioid analgesics, general anesthetics, phenothiazines, other tranquilizers, sedative-hypnotics, tricyclic antidepressants and other CNS depressants (including alcohol). Respiratory depression, hypotension and profound sedation or coma may result.

The respiratory depressant effects of morphine and its capacity to elevate cerebrospinal fluid pressure may be markedly exaggerated in the presence of head injury, other intracranial lesions or a pre-existing increase in intracranial pressure. Furthermore, opioids produce adverse reactions which may obscure the clinical course of patients with head injuries.

Morphine should be used with extreme caution in patients having an acute asthmatic attack, patients with chronic obstructive pulmonary disease or cor pulmonale, patients having a substantially decreased respiratory reserve, and patients with pre-existing respiratory depression, hypoxia or hypercapnia. In such patients, even usual therapeutic doses of opioids may decrease respiratory drive while simultaneously increasing airway resistance to the point of apnea.

Precautions: Acute Abdominal Condition: The administration of morphine or other opioids may obscure the diagnosis or clinical course in patients with acute abdominal conditions.

Hypotensive Effect: The administration of morphine may result in severe hypotension in the postoperative patient or any individual whose ability to maintain blood pressure has been compromised by a depleted blood volume or the administration of such drugs as the phenothiazines or certain anesthetics.

Supraventricular Tachycardias: Because of possible vagolytic action that may produce a significant increase in the ventricular response rate, morphine should be used with caution in patients with atrial flutter and other supraventricular tachycardias.

Convulsions: Morphine may aggravate pre-existing convulsions in patients with convulsive disorders. If dosage is escalated substantially above recommended levels because of tolerance development, convulsions may occur in individuals without a history of convulsive disorders.

Other Special Risk Patients: Morphine should be given with caution to certain patients, such as the elderly or debilitated and those with severe impairment of hepatic or renal function, hypothyroidism, Addison's disease, prostatic hypertrophy or urethral stricture.

Morphine should be used with extreme caution in patients with disorders characterized by hypoxia, since even usual therapeutic doses of opioids may decrease respiratory drive to the point of apnea while simultaneously increasing airway resistance.

Morphine may have a prolonged duration and cumulative effect in patients with kidney or liver dysfunction. In these patients, analgesia may last for 6, 8 or even up to 24 hours following a standard dose. Continuous infusions should be avoided.

In patients with shock, impaired perfusion may prevent complete absorption following s.c. or i.m. injection of morphine. Repeated administration may result in overdosage due to an excessive amount of morphine suddenly being absorbed when circulation is restored.

Information for the Patient: Occupational Hazards: Morphine may impair the mental and/or physical abilities required for the performance of potentially hazardous tasks, such as driving a car or operating machinery. Morphine in combination with other opioid analgesics, phenothiazines, sedative-hypnotics or alcohol has additive depressant effects. The patient should be cautioned accordingly.

Drug Interactions: Morphine in combination with other opioid analgesics, general anesthetics, phenothiazines, tranquilizers, sedative-hypnotics or other CNS depressants (including alcohol) has additive depressant effects. Dosage reduction of one or both agents is required.

Pregnancy: Animal reproduction studies have not been conducted with morphine. It is not known whether it can cause fetal harm when administered to a pregnant woman or whether it can affect reproduction capacity. On the basis of the historical use of morphine during all stages of pregnancy, there is no known risk of fetal abnormality. Morphine should be given to a pregnant woman only if clearly needed.

Labor and Delivery: The use of morphine in obstetrics may prolong labor. It passes the placental barrier and may produce respiratory depression in the newborn. In resuscitation and severe depression, the administration of an opioid antagonist such as naloxone or nalorphine may be required.

Lactation: Morphine appears in the milk of nursing mothers. Breast-feeding should be discontinued if morphine is required.

Children: Safety and efficacy of morphine in neonates and children have not been established.

Adverse Effects: The major hazards of morphine, as with other opioid analgesics, are respiratory depression and, to a lesser degree, circulatory depression; respiratory arrest, shock and cardiac arrest have occurred. The most frequently observed adverse reactions include lightheadedness, dizziness, sedation, nausea, vomiting and sweating. These effects seem to be more prominent in ambulatory patients and in those who are not experiencing severe pain. In such individuals, lower doses are advisable. Some adverse reactions in ambulatory patients may be alleviated if the patient lies down.

Rapid i.v. injection of the drug may result in an increased frequency of opiate-induced adverse effects; severe respiratory depression, apnea, hypotension, peripheral circulatory collapse, chest wall rigidity, cardiac arrest and possible anaphylactoid reactions.

Other adverse reactions include: CNS: euphoria, dysphoria, weakness, headache, agitation, tremor, uncoordinated muscle movements, transient hallucinations and disorientation, visual disturbances.

Gastrointestinal: dry mouth, constipation, biliary tract spasm.

Cardiovascular: flushing of the face, tachycardia, bradycardia, palpitation, faintness, syncope.

Genitourinary: urinary retention.

Allergic: pruritus, urticaria, other skin rashes, wheal and flare over the vein with i.v. injection.

Other: pain at injection site; local tissue irritation and induration following s.c. injection, particularly when repeated; antidiuretic effect.

Overdose: Symptoms: Overdosage with morphine is characterized by respiratory depression (a decrease in respiratory rate and/or tidal volume, Cheyne-Stokes respiration, cyanosis), extreme somnolence progressing to stupor or coma, skeletal muscle flaccidity, cold and clammy skin, and sometimes bradycardia and hypotension. In severe overdosage, apnea, circulatory collapse, cardiac arrest and death may occur.

Treatment: Immediate attention should be given to the re-establishment of adequate respiratory exchange through provision of a patent airway and institution of assisted or controlled ventilation.

Oxygen, i.v. fluids, vasopressors and other supportive measures should be employed as indicated.

The opioid antagonist naloxone is a specific antidote against respiratory depression which may result from overdosage or unusual sensitivity to opioids. The recommended adult dose of naloxone is 0.4 to 2 mg i.v. every 2 to 3 minutes as necessary, simultaneously with assisted respiration.

An antagonist should only be administered in cases of clinically significant respiratory or cardiovascular depression.

In an individual physically dependent on opioids, the administration of the usual dose of opioid antagonist will precipitate an acute withdrawal syndrome. The severity of this syndrome will depend on the degree of physical dependence and the dose of antagonist administered. The use of opioid antagonists in such individuals should be avoided if possible. If an opioid antagonist must be used to treat serious respiratory depression in the physically dependent patient, the antagonist should be administered with extreme care at about 10 to 20% the usual initial dose administered.

Dosage: General Information: The dosage range for morphine is wide; there is no "normal" range. This is due to individual patient pharmacokinetic differences, disease type and increasing pain with advancing disease.

Orally administered morphine should be used in preference to parenteral morphine whenever adequate pain control can be achieved by this route. However oral morphine is often inadequate or impractical in the terminally ill patient.

Patients being converted from oral morphine to concentrated morphine sulfate injection require dosage reduction (about half), since about 66% of oral morphine is metabolized in first pass metabolism. If the patient has been treated previously with a lower strength of parenteral morphine, similar doses should be given initially, and then titrated according to the patient's clinical response.

Morphine sulfate injection should be given regularly around the clock, in most instances every 4 hours. The basis of pain control with morphine sulfate injection should be regular scheduling rather than on an "as required" or PRN opioid order. Patients requiring high doses of morphine usually need to be awakened for medication during the night to prevent morning pain.

Morphine Dosage Reduction: During the first 2 to 3 days of effective pain relief, the patient may sleep for many hours. This can be misinterpreted as the effect of excessive analgesic dosing rather than the first sign of relief in a pain-exhausted patient. The dose, therefore, should be maintained for about 3 days before reduction, if respiratory activity and other vital signs are adequate. Following successful relief of severe pain, periodic attempts to reduce the opioid dose should be made. Lower doses or complete discontinuation of the opioid analgesic may become feasible due to a physiological change or the improved mental state of the patient.

Morphine Dosage Increase: Dosage increases should not be made more frequently than every 24 hours, since it will take approximately 4 to 5 morphine half-lives to attain a new steady state concentration in a patient with normal liver and kidney function.

Following all dosage increases, the patient must be monitored closely for side effects, the most common being sedation, nausea, vomiting, constipation and hypotension.

S.C. or I.M. Injection: **Morphine sulfate injection 50 mg/mL used without dilution, is not to be given to patients who are not already receiving large doses of opioids.** These strengths of morphine are indicated exclusively for the relief of severe pain in opioid-tolerant patients.

The s.c. route of injection is preferred over the I.m. route in terminal cancer patients. **In any case, i.v. or s.c. infusion is preferred over injection because of the risks of accidental overdose with direct injection.**

I.V. Infusion with Dilution: Morphine sulfate injection may be diluted in a parenteral solution (Dextrose 5% in Water or Sodium Chloride Injection) to the desired concentration (usually 0.1 to 0.5 mg/mL) and administered by i.v. infusion. **It is recommended that an opioid antagonist and equipment for artificial ventilation be available.**

S.C. Infusion: Morphine sulfate injection may be given by s.c. infusion using a portable pump. When switching from i.v. to s.c. infusion, use the same dose and monitor the same parameters.

Morphine Sulfate Injection BP (50 mg/mL) (cont'd)

The maximum dose that can be safely given has not been defined, but doses as high as 480 mg/24 hours have been administered. The infusion rate tolerated by patients is variable. Most patients can tolerate 10 mL/hour s.c. and some may tolerate higher infusion rates. When an infusion rate is excessive there may be leakage at the infusion site. This is most likely to occur at lower infusion rates in severely cachectic patients who have minimal s.c. tissue. In such cases, higher strength solutions or potent opioids will permit lower infusion rates and minimize the chance of leakage.

Erythema, bruising, induration or tenderness around the injection site may occur. The injection site must be inspected daily for these effects, and for injection or leakage of medication. The needle site should be rotated at least every 7 to 10 days.

Opioid Analgesics: Approximate Analgesic Equivalences: See Table I.

Table I—Morphine Sulfate Injection BP (50 mg/mL)

Opioid Analgesics: Approximate Analgesic Equivalences

Drug	Equivalent Dose (mg)[a] (compared to morphine 10 mg i.m.)		Duration of Action (hours)
	Parenteral	Oral	
Strong Opioid Agonists:			
Morphine (single dose)	10	60	3-4
(chronic dose)	10	20-30[b]	3-4
Hydromorphone	1.5-2	6-7.5	2-4
Anileridine	25	75	2-3
Levorphanol	2	4	4-8
Meperidine[c]	75	300	1-3
Oxymorphone	1.5	5 (rectal)	3-4
Methadone[d]			
Heroin	5-8	10-15	3-4
Weak Opioid Agonists:			
Codeine	120	200	3-4
Oxycodone	5-10	10-15	2-4
Propoxyphene	50	100	2-4
Mixed Agonist-Antagonists[e]			
Pentazocine	60	180	3-4
Nalbuphine	10		3-6
Butorphanol	2		3-4

[a] Most of these data were derived from single-dose, acute pain studies and should be considered an approximation for selection of doses when treating chronic pain.

[b] For acute pain, the oral dose of morphine is 6 times the injectable dose. However, for chronic dosing, this ratio becomes 2 or 3:1, possibly due to the accumulation of active metabolites.

[c] These drugs are not recommended for the management of chronic pain.

[d] Extremely variable equianalgesic dose. Patients should undergo personalized titration starting at an equivalent to 1/10 of the morphine dose.

[e] Mixed agonist-antagonists can precipitate withdrawal in patients on pure opioid agonists.

Stability and Storage: Store morphine sulfate injection at room temperature below 25°C, protected from light. Do not autoclave.

Morphine sulfate injection diluted to concentrations of 0.1 to 0.5 mg/mL in PVC bags containing Dextrose 5% Injection or Sterile Water for Injection should be used within 24 hours after dilution, when stored at room temperature, in order to avoid the risk of microbial contamination.

Morphine sulfate injection 50 mg/mL and dilutions of morphine sulfate injection in Dextrose 5% Injection or Sodium Chloride 0.9% Injection may be stored in portable infusion pump cassettes, syringes and PVC infusion bags. When protected from light, these dilutions are stable for 24 hours at room temperature or for 72 hours refrigerated. Proper aseptic technique should be used in order to minimize contamination of the solution.

Warning: As with all parenteral drug products, i.v. admixtures should be inspected visually for clarity, particulate matter, precipitate and leakage prior to administration, whenever solution and container permit. Solutions showing haziness, particulate matter, precipitate or leakage should not be used. Development of a yellow color in morphine solutions does not indicate toxicity nor loss of potency or efficacy.

Supplied: Each mL of clear, colorless or pale yellow, sterile solution contains: morphine sulfate 50 mg, with sodium chloride 4.5 mg, in sterile water for injection. Sodium hydroxide or sulfuric acid may be added for pH adjustment. Contains no preservative or antioxidant. Sulfite-free. Rapiject prefilled, single dose syringes of 50 mL.

Medication, needle and fluid pathway are sterile in the unopened, intact Rapiject system with caps in place.

This product contains no antibacterial agent and is intended as single dose units. When the dosing requirement is completed, the unused portion should be discarded in an appropriate manner.

Directions for use of Rapiject prefilled syringe: 1. Remove protective caps from vial and injector. 2. Insert vial into injector. 3. Rotate vial 3 turns in a clockwise direction until some resistance occurs. Then rotate vial another turn or two. The needle will then be in contact with the morphine solution. 4. Remove the needle cap and expel air. 5. The Rapiject is now ready for use.

MORPHITEC®-1 Ⓝ
MORPHITEC®-5 Ⓝ
MORPHITEC®-10 Ⓝ
MORPHITEC®-20 Ⓝ

Technilab

Morphine HCl

Opioid Analgesic

Supplied: Morphitec-1: Each mL of orange-flavored, yellow syrup, contains: morphine HCl 1 mg. Nonmedicinal ingredients: artificial flavoring, calcium cyclamate, FD&C Yellow #5, glycerin, methylparaben, propylparaben, purified water and sorbitol. Energy: 12.6 kJ (2.23 kcal)/mL. Alcohol- and sucrose-free. Plastic bottles of 200 and 450 mL.

Morphitec-5: Each mL of orange-flavored, yellow syrup, contains: morphine HCl 5 mg. Nonmedicinal ingredients: artificial flavoring, calcium cyclamate, FD&C Yellow #5, glycerin, methylparaben, propylparaben, purified water and sorbitol. Energy: 12.6 kJ (2.23 kcal)/mL. Alcohol- and sucrose-free. Plastic bottles of 200 and 450 mL.

Morphitec-10: Each mL of orange-flavored, yellow syrup, contains: morphine HCl 10 mg. Nonmedicinal ingredients: artificial flavoring, calcium cyclamate, FD&C Yellow #5, glycerin, methylparaben, propylparaben, purified water and sorbitol. Energy: 12.6 kJ (2.23 kcal)/mL. Alcohol- and sucrose-free. Plastic bottles of 200 mL.

Morphitec-20: Each mL of unflavored, yellow syrup, contains: morphine HCl 20 mg. Nonmedicinal ingredients: calcium cyclamate, FD&C Yellow #5, glycerin, methylparaben, propylparaben, purified water and sorbitol. Energy: 12.6 kJ (2.23 kcal)/mL. Alcohol- and sucrose-free. Plastic bottles of 50 mL with calibrated glass dropper.

Store at room temperature. Protect from freezing and light.

MoRu-Viraten BERNA™

Berna Products

Measles and Rubella Virus Vaccine, Live, Attenuated

Active Immunizing Agent

Pharmacology: MoRu-Viraten Berna is a live virus vaccine for immunization against measles (rubeola) and rubella (German measles).

A single dose of MoRu-Viraten Berna vaccine was administered to 26 children, 15 months to 9 years of age, who were seronegative [a rubella hemagglutination-inhibition (HI) titer of <10 and a measles plaque reduction (PR) titer of <8] to both vaccine components. Approximately 6 to 8 weeks later all seronegative children possessed a rubella HI titer of ≥10 (geometric mean titer of 161, range 40 to 320) and a measles PR titer of ≥8 (geometric mean titer of 130, range 12 to >256). The viral vaccine strains that comprise MoRu-Viraten Berna vaccine have also been administered to children 15 months to 14 years of age, together with a live attenuated mumps virus vaccine in the form of a trivalent vaccine, Triviraten Berna vaccine. In comparative studies involving 349 seronegative children, the seroconversion rate was 97% for measles and 100% for rubella. In noncomparative studies in 529 seronegative children, the seroconversion rate was 98% for measles and 99% for rubella. The persistence of vaccine-induced antibodies is unknown.

Indications: Children: For the simultaneous immunization against measles and rubella in individuals 12 to 15 months of age or older. A booster dose of either MoRu-Viraten Berna vaccine, monovalent measles vaccine or trivalent measles, mumps and rubella vaccine is recommended (see Reimmunization).

It is recommended that children less than 12 to 15 months of age not be immunized as they may not mount a protective immune response to the measles component. This is due to the inhibitory activity of persisting antimeasles maternal antibodies. In general, the younger the child is at the time of immunization the less likely they are to mount a protective immune response. In certain circumstances it may be desirable to vaccinate children less than 12 months of age. This would include groups with a high risk of acquiring measles at an age less than 12 months or populations difficult to vaccinate due to geographical isolation. Children falling into these categories who are vaccinated at less than 12 months of age should be revaccinated after reaching their 15th month of life. Data exist to indicate that children vaccinated at less than 12 months of age may not adequately respond to a booster dose of vaccine administered subsequent to their 15th month of life. Therefore, the potential advantages of vaccination at an early age must be weighed against the possibility of an inadequate immune response upon revaccination.

Children with no history of immunization against rubella residing with a susceptible pregnant woman should be immunized with a live attenuated rubella vaccine in an effort to reduce the risk of introducing wild-type rubella virus into the household.

Nonpregnant Adolescent and Adult Females: Susceptible nonpregnant adolescent and adult females of childbearing age should be immunized with a vaccine containing live attenuated rubella virus as long as certain precautions are observed (see Precautions). Immunization of this susceptible population is warranted due to the fact that protection is conferred against rubella infection during pregnancy, which prevents fetal infection with attendant congenital rubella syndrome.

Women of childbearing age who are immunized with a vaccine containing live attenuated rubella vaccine should be counseled and be advised not to become pregnant for at least 3 months following vaccination (see Contraindications).

Postpubertal females should be informed of the frequent occurrence of self-limiting arthralgia, arthritis or both syndromes with an onset 2 to 4 weeks postvaccination (see Adverse Effects).

Postpartum Women: Rubella-susceptible women may also be vaccinated with a live attenuated rubella vaccine immediately postpartum (see Precautions, Lactation).

Reimmunization: Children younger than 12 months of age when first vaccinated should be revaccinated at 15 months of age followed by another at 4 to 6 years of age. Revaccination may be accomplished by the administration of the following vaccines: monovalent measles vaccine when the sole concern is to augment protection against measles; bivalent measles and rubella vaccine where enhanced protection is desired against both measles and rubella; and trivalent measles, mumps and rubella vaccine when there is concern relating to the immune status against all 3 viral pathogens.

Children vaccinated at 12 to 15 months of age are recommended for revaccination at the age of 4 to 6 years or at the age of 11 to 12 years when a combined measles, mumps, rubella vaccine is usually administered.

Use in Combination with Other Vaccines and Immune Globulin: The simultaneous administration of diphtheria, tetanus and pertussis vaccines and/or oral polio vaccine with MoRu-Viraten Berna vaccine is not recommended due to insufficent data on the effect of such a combined administration on the immune response to the individual vaccine antigens. MoRu-Viraten Berna vaccine should be administered no sooner than 30 days before or after the receipt of other viral vaccines.

Antibodies present in immune globulin preparations, blood or plasma may suppress the immune response to live attenuated measles and rubella vaccines. Vaccination should be delayed for at least 3 months after the receipt of such products. If such preparations are administered within 2 weeks of vaccination it is recommended that the immune status to measles and rubella be determined by appropriate serological tests 3 months after vaccination or, if not feasible, to repeat the vaccination with MoRu-Viraten Berna vaccine.

Contraindications: Hypersensitivity to any component of the vaccine.

Pregnancy: MoRu-Viraten Berna vaccine should not be administered to pregnant women as its effects on fetal development have not been studied. Following vaccination, women of childbearing age should avoid becoming pregnant for 3 months (see Precautions, Pregnancy).

Vaccination should be delayed in the face of a febrile illness or in persons with active tuberculosis. Congenital or acquired humoral or cellular immunodeficiency states, including patients receiving treatment with immunosuppressvive or antimitotic drugs, hypogammaglobulinemia and dysgammaglobulinemia. Patients with leukemia, lymphoma, malignant neoplasia of the bone marrow or lymphatic systems. This contraindication does not extend to patients receiving corticosteroids as replacement therapy such as for Addison's disease.

Precautions: General: The vaccine should not be administered in the face of an acute febrile illness or to persons with active tuberculosis. MoRu-Viraten Berna vaccine should not be administered to persons with a known hypersensitivity to any vaccine component. Appropriate therapy, such as epinephrine, should be available to treat any anaphylactic or anaphylactoid reaction.

Caution should be exercised when MoRu-Viraten Berna vaccine is to be administered to individuals with a known or suspected cerebral injury, individual or familial history of convulsions or seizures or any other conditions known to be aggravated by elevated fever. The attending physician should be aware of the fact that an elevation in body temperature often follows immunization (see Adverse Effects).

Individuals known to be infected with human immunodeficiency viruses without overt symptoms associated with immunosuppression may be vaccinated. However, such individuals may fail to mount a protective immune response at a higher rate than noninfected subjects.

Immunization should be delayed for at least 3 months following the receipt of immune globulin, blood or plasma.

The majority of vaccinated individuals will secrete live attenuated rubella virus in nasal or throat secretions for up to 1 month postimmunization. Although the possibility exists that transmission to susceptible close contacts may occur, this has yet to be conclusively demonstrated and is therefore considered a minimal risk. Transmission of rubella virus to nursing infants via breast milk has been documented (see Lactation).

There have been no confirmed reports of transmission of measles virus from vaccinated individuals to seronegative contacts.

Vaccination with measles and/or rubella viruses can temporarily suppress tuberculin skin reactivity. If a tuberculin skin test is to be performed, it should be done before or concurrently with vaccination. Immunization with MoRu-Viraten Berna vaccine may not engender a 100% seroconversion rate in susceptible individuals.

Carcinogenesis, Mutagenesis, Impairment of Fertility: Long-term studies in animals with MoRu-Viraten Berna vaccine have not been performed to evaluate carcinogenic potential, mutagenic potential or impairment of fertility.

Pregnancy: Category C: Animal reproductive studies have not been conducted with MoRu-Viraten Berna vaccine. It is not known whether this vaccine can cause fetal harm when administered to pregnant women or can affect reproduction capacity. Therefore, the vaccine should not be administered to pregnant women. In addition, pregnancy should be avoided for a period of 3 months following vaccination (see Contraindications).

Lactation: It is not known if measles virus is excreted in human milk. Studies have shown that lactating women who have been immunized with live rubella virus vaccine can secrete the virus in breast milk and transmit it to breast-feeding infants. Therefore, caution should be exercised when MoRu-Viraten Berna vaccine is administered to nursing mothers.

Adverse Effects: The adverse events reported with the administration of MoRu-Viraten Berna vaccine are similar to those associated with the use of the individual vaccine components, or with the use of a combined measles, mumps and rubella vaccine.

Local: Local reactions reported include tenderness at the injection site, erythema, swelling, induration, a wheal and flare reaction or urticaria at the injection site. Rash is an infrequent reaction and is usually localized but can be generalized in rare cases.

Systemic: Systemic reactions are characterized by moderate fever (38.3 to 39.4°C), which is an occasional occurrence. High fever (>39.4°C) is a far less common reaction. Rarely will children who develop fever present with convulsions. Malaise, headache, nausea, runny nose, conjunctivitis, sore throat, respiratory tract symptoms, localized lymphadenopathy, rash, deafness, purpura and thrombocytopenia have also been associated with MoRu-Viraten Berna vaccine, the individual vaccine components or similar vaccines.

Natural rubella infection is characterized by transient or intermittent arthritis, arthralgia and polyneuritis. The appearance and severity of such symptoms are dependent upon both age and sex, being most pronounced in adult females and least severe in prepubertal children. A similar syndrome, which also includes myalgia and paresthesia, has been reported following the administration of live attenuated rubella virus vaccine. Chronic arthritis is often associated with natural rubella infection. Similar symptomatology is rarely observed in recipients of live attenuated rubella virus vaccines.

Children: Immunized children infrequently present with joint symptomatology, which is usually transient.

The incidence of joint symptoms, such as arthralgia and arthritis, is higher among women than children. In general, such reactions are more severe and of a longer duration in women than in children. The severity and persistence of such symptoms appear to be intermediate in adolescent girls. In all age groups of females, joint symptoms are rarely debilitating.

CNS Involvement: Optic neuritis, papillitis and retinitis may be associated with naturally acquired viral infections. These symptoms have also been reported approximately 1 to 4 weeks following immunization with some types of live attenuated viral vaccines.

Encephalitis, in addition to other CNS reactions, has been reported as a very rare occurrence associated with the use of live attenuated measles and rubella vaccine. Such reactions may also occur following immunization with MoRu-Viraten Berna vaccine.

Clinical experience in the U.S. through 1975, involving more than 80 million doses of live attenuated measles vaccine, has shown that a single case of significant CNS involvement occurring within 30 days of vaccination has been temporally associated with the administration of 1 million doses of vaccine. In no instance was the cause of such reactions identified as the vaccine. The U.S. Centers for Disease Control has stated that "a certain number of cases of encephalitis may be expected to occur in a large childhood population in a defined period of time even when no vaccines are administered." However, there are data to indicate that 1 or more of these cases may have been caused by measles vaccines. The risk of such serious CNS disorders associated with the use of live attenuated measles vaccines is much less than for encephalitis and encephalopathy associated with natural measles (1/1 000 cases reported). Cases of subacute sclerosing panencephalopathy (SSPE) have been reported in children who have received measles vaccine. These children had no history of having had naturally acquired measles. The association of SSPE to measles vaccination is approximately 1 case/million doses of measles vaccine distributed in the U.S. Following natural measles infection, it is estimated that 6 to 22 cases of SSPE will occur per million cases of measles. The U.S. Centers for Disease Control has reported that data from a retrospective case-controlled study has shown that the use of measles vaccine has reduced the overall risk of SSPE by preventing natural measles infections with their inherent higher risk of subsequent SSPE.

Dosage: The dose for all ages is the same, being 0.5 mL of reconstituted vaccine.

Prior to administration, the skin at the injection site should be cleansed with a suitable germicide. The vaccine is to be administered s.c. preferably at the deltoid region of the upper arm. After insertion of the needle, aspirate to prevent accidental injection into a blood vessel. Do not administer by either the i.m. or intradermal route.

Do not administer immune globulin simultaneously with MoRu-Viraten Berna vaccine.

A separate sterile needle and syringe should be used to administer each dose of vaccine to prevent the spread of adventitious infectious agents.

Stability and Storage Recommendations: Store refrigerated at 2 to 8°C away from freezer compartment. Do not freeze. Protect from light.

Reconstitution: Prior to reconstitution the appearance of each vial of vaccine and diluent (sterile water for injection, USP) should be checked. The vaccine should appear as a white to off-white powder, while the diluent should appear as a clear liquid. Only the diluent supplied should be used for reconstitution of the vaccine. The cap of the vaccine and diluent vials should be removed and the top cleaned with a suitable germicide. The entire contents of the diluent vial should be transferred to the vaccine vial using a sterile needle and syringe. The vaccine vial should then be gently rotated to dissolve the lyophilized vaccine. The reconstituted vaccine should be red to yellow-reddish in color and clear. Discard if it appears otherwise.

Immediately prior to use, the vial should be inspected for particulate matter and discoloration. The entire contents of the vial should be used within 1 hour of reconstitution since no preservative is included.

Supplied: Each sterile, lyophilized preparation, contains: 31 000 TCID50 (tissue culture infectious dose) of each vaccine virus. Antibiotic-, avian protein- and preservative-free. Single dose vials of 0.5 mL. Boxes of 1, 10 and 50, together with 1, 10 and 50 vials of diluent respectively. Each diluent vial contains 0.5 mL of sterile water for injection, USP.

Reviewed 1998

M.O.S.™ Ⓝ
M.O.S.-SR™ Ⓝ

ICN

Morphine HCl

Opioid Analgesic

Supplied: M.O.S.: Concentrate: M.O.S.—20: Each mL of clear, yellow-colored, unflavored, syrupy liquid contains: morphine HCl BP 20 mg. Nonmedicinal ingredients: propylene glycol, sodium benzoate, sodium metabisulfite and sorbitol. Alcohol-free. Graduated, opaque brown glass bottles of 50 mL with calibrated glass dropper.

M.O.S.—50: Each mL of clear, yellow-colored, unflavored, syrupy liquid contains: morphine HCl BP 50 mg. Nonmedicinal ingredients: propylene glycol, sodium benzoate, sodium metabisulfite and sorbitol. Alcohol-free. Graduated, opaque brown glass bottles of 50 mL with calibrated glass dropper.

Suppositories: M.O.S.—10: Each suppository, unit dosed, torpedo-shaped, mold-imprinted M.O.S.—10, contains: morphine HCl BP 10 mg in a bland, white vegetable oil base. Packages of 24.

M.O.S.—20: Each suppository, unit dosed, torpedo-shaped, mold-imprinted M.O.S.—20, contains: morphine HCl BP 20 mg in a bland, yellow vegetable oil base. Packages of 24.

M.O.S.—30: Each suppository, unit dosed, torpedo-shaped, mold-imprinted M.O.S.—30, contains: morphine HCl BP 30 mg in a bland, pink vegetable oil base. Packages of 24.

Syrup: M.O.S.—1: Each mL of clear, yellow-colored, orange-flavored (alcohol 5%) or unflavored (alcohol-free) syrupy liquid contains: morphine HCl BP 1 mg. Nonmedicinal ingredients: citric acid, ethyl alcohol, fructose, propylene glycol, sodium benzoate, sodium cyclamate, sodium metabisulfite and sorbitol. Graduated, opaque brown glass bottles of 250 and 500 mL.

M.O.S.—5: Each mL of clear, yellow-colored, orange-flavored (alcohol 5%) syrupy liquid contains: morphine HCl BP 5 mg. Nonmedicinal ingredients: citric acid, ethyl alcohol, fructose, propylene glycol, sodium benzoate, sodium cyclamate, sodium metabisulfite and sorbitol. Graduated, opaque brown glass bottles of 250 and 500 mL.

M.O.S.—10: Each mL of clear, yellow-colored, orange-flavored, syrupy liquid (alcohol 5%) contains: morphine HCl BP 10 mg. Nonmedicinal ingredients: citric acid, ethyl alcohol, fructose, propylene glycol, sodium benzoate, sodium cyclamate, sodium metabisulfite and sorbitol. Graduated, opaque brown glass bottles of 250 mL.

Tablets: M.O.S.—10: Each round, beige, film-coated tablet, contains: morphine HCl BP 10 mg. Nonmedicinal ingredients: croscarmellose sodium, isopropyl alcohol, lactose, microcrystalline cellulose, magnesium stearate, povidone, starch and talc. Bottles of 100.

M.O.S.—20: Each round, salmon-pink, film-coated tablet, contains: morphine HCl BP 20 mg. Nonmedicinal ingredients: croscarmellose sodium, isopropyl alcohol, lactose, microcrystalline cellulose, magnesium stearate, povidone, starch and talc. Bottles of 100.

M.O.S.—40: Each round, blue, film-coated tablet, contains: morphine HCl BP 40 mg. Nonmedicinal ingredients: croscarmellose sodium, isopropyl alcohol, lactose, microcrystalline cellulose, magnesium stearate, povidone, starch and talc. Bottles of 100.

M.O.S.—60: Each round, yellow, film-coated tablet, contains: morphine HCl BP 60 mg. Nonmedicinal ingredients: croscarmellose sodium, isopropyl alcohol, lactose, microcrystalline cellulose, magnesium stearate, povidone, starch and talc. Bottles of 100.

M.O.S.-SR: Tablets: M.O.S.-SR—30: Each blue, round, biconvex, film-coated, slow release tablet printed M.O.S.-SR on one side, 30 on the other, contains: morphine HCl 30 mg. Nonmedicinal ingredients: microcrystalline cellulose, magnesium stearate, simetry and talc. Bottles of 50. Store below 30°C. Protect from light.

M.O.S.-SR—60: Each red, round, biconvex film-coated, slow release tablet printed M.O.S.-SR on one side, 60 on the

M.O.S. (cont'd)

other, contains: morphine HCl 60 mg. Nonmedicinal ingredients: microcrystalline cellulose, magnesium stearate, simetry and talc. Bottles of 50. Store below 30°C. Protect from light.

M.O.S.-SULFATE Ⓝ
ICN
Morphine Sulfate
Opioid Analgesic

Supplied: M.O.S.-Sulfate 5: Each round, green tablet contains: morphine sulfate, USP (pentahydrate) 5 mg. Nonmedicinal ingredients: cornstarch, croscarmellose sodium, D&C Yellow #10, FD&C Blue #1, isopropyl alcohol, lactose, magnesium stearate, microcrystalline cellulose, povidone and talc. Bottles of 100.

M.O.S.-Sulfate 10: Each round, blue tablet contains: morphine sulfate, USP (pentahydrate) 10 mg. Nonmedicinal ingredients: as in 5 mg tablets, but FD&C Blue #1 only. Bottles of 100.

M.O.S.-Sulfate 25: Each round, pink tablet contains: morphine sulfate, USP (pentahydrate) 25 mg. Nonmedicinal ingredients: as in 5 and 10 mg tablets, but FD&C Red #40 only. Bottles of 100.

M.O.S.-Sulfate 50: Each round, orange tablet contains: morphine sulfate, USP (pentahydrate) 50 mg. Nonmedicinal ingredients: as in 5, 10 and 25 mg tablets, but FD&C Yellow #6 only. Bottles of 100.

Store below 30°C. Keep containers well closed. Protect from light. Keep out of reach of children.

MOTILIDONE Ⓟ
Technilab
Domperidone Maleate
Modifier of Upper Gastrointestinal Motility

Supplied: Each white to faintly cream film-coated tablet contains: domperidone maleate 12.72 mg (equivalent to domperidone 10 mg). Nonmedicinal ingredients: cornstarch, hydroxypropylcellulose, lactose, magnesium stearate, microcrystalline cellulose, polyethylene glycol, povidone, sodium benzoate, sodium croscarmellose, sodium docusate, sorbitol and titanium dioxide. HDPE bottles of 100 and 500. Store at room temperature between 15 and 30°C. Protect from light and moisture.

MOTILIUM® Ⓟ
Janssen-Ortho
Domperidone Maleate
Upper Gastrointestinal Motility Modifier

Pharmacology: Domperidone is a peripheral dopamine antagonist structurally related to the butyrophenones with antiemetic and gastroprokinetic properties.

Domperidone effectively increases esophageal peristalsis and lower esophageal sphincter pressure (LESP), increases gastric motility and peristalsis, enhances gastroduodenal coordination and consequently facilitates gastric emptying and decreases small bowel transit time.

The mechanism of action of domperidone is related to its peripheral dopamine receptor blocking properties. Emesis induced by apomorphine, hydergine, morphine or levodopa through stimulation of the chemoreceptor trigger zone (situated outside the blood-brain barrier) can be blocked by domperidone. There is indirect evidence that emesis is also inhibited at the gastric level, since domperidone also inhibits emesis induced by oral levodopa, and local gastric wall concentrations following oral domperidone are much greater than those of the plasma and other organs. Domperidone does not readily cross the blood-brain barrier and therefore is not expected to have central effects.

Domperidone elevates serum prolactin levels but has no effect on circulating aldosterone levels.

Pharmacokinetics: In man, peak plasma levels of domperidone occur within 10 to 30 minutes following i.m. injection and 30 minutes after oral (fasted) administration. Plasma concentrations 2 hours after oral administration are lower than following i.m. injection, and this is likely the result of hepatic first-pass and gut wall metabolism. Peak plasma concentrations are 40 ng/mL following an i.m. injection of 10 mg, 20 ng/mL after a single 10 mg tablet, and 70 to 100 ng/mL after oral doses of 60 mg (tablets or oral drops). The half-life was calculated as approximately 7.0 hours in each case. The degree of human plasma protein binding was calculated from tritiated domperidone concentrations of 10 and 100 ng/mL as 91.7 and 93.0%, respectively.

The major metabolic pathways for domperidone in man are hydroxylation and oxidative N-dealkylation, the products of which are hydroxydomperidone and 2,3-dihydro-2-oxo-1-H-benzimidazol-1-propionic acid, respectively. After oral administration of 40 mg ^{14}C-domperidone to healthy volunteers, 31% of the radioactivity is excreted in the urine and 66% in the feces over a period of 4 days.

Indications: In the symptomatic management of upper gastrointestinal motility disorders associated with chronic and subacute gastritis and diabetic gastroparesis. Domperidone may also be used to prevent gastrointestinal symptoms associated with the use of dopamine agonist antiparkinsonian agents.

Contraindications: In patients with known sensitivity or intolerance to the drug.

Domperidone should not be used whenever gastrointestinal stimulation might be dangerous, i.e., gastrointestinal hemorrhage, mechanical obstruction or perforation.

Also contraindicated in patients with a prolactin-releasing pituitary tumor (prolactinoma).

Warnings: Dopamine receptor blocking agents elevate prolactin levels; the elevation persists during chronic administration. Tissue culture experiments indicate that approximately one-third of human breast cancers are prolactin dependent in vitro, a factor of potential importance if the prescription of these drugs is contemplated in a patient with previously detected breast cancer. Although disturbances such as galactorrhea, amenorrhea, gynecomastia, and impotence have been reported, the clinical significance of elevated serum prolactin levels is unknown for most patients. An increase in mammary neoplasms has been found in rodents after chronic administration of dopamine receptor blocking agents. Neither clinical studies nor epidemiologic studies conducted to date, however, have shown an association between chronic administration of these drugs and mammary tumorigenesis. The available evidence is considered too limited to be conclusive at this time.

Pregnancy: While animal studies have not shown drug-related teratogenic or primary embryotoxic effect on animal fetuses, comparable studies have not been performed in pregnant women. For this reason, domperidone should not be used in pregnant women unless the benefit outweighs the potential hazard.

Lactation: Domperidone is excreted in breast milk in very low concentrations. Therefore, nursing is not recommended for mothers taking domperidone unless the expected benefits outweigh any potential risk.

Children: Safety and efficacy in children have not been established, therefore, domperidone should not be used in children.

Precautions: In the event that the patient develops galactorrhea and/or gynecomastia, withdrawal of the drug will result in alleviation of these symptoms.

Drug Interactions: The concomitant administration of anticholinergic drugs may compromise the beneficial effects of domperidone.

Since domperidone enhances gastric and small intestinal motility, it may accelerate absorption of drugs from the small bowel while slowing absorption of drugs taken up from the stomach, particularly those with sustained-release or enteric-coated formulations.

Care should be exercised when domperidone is administered in combination with MAO inhibitors.

The concomitant administration of domperidone maleate with antacids or H_2-receptor blockers does not decrease the absorption of domperidone.

Hepatic Impairment: Since domperidone is highly metabolized in the liver, it should be used with caution in patients with hepatic impairment.

Adverse Effects: In clinical studies with oral domperidone the overall incidence of side effects with domperidone was <7%. Some of these side effects are an extension of its dopamine antagonist properties of domperidone. Most side effects resolve spontaneously during continued therapy or are easily tolerated. The more serious or troublesome side effects (galactorrhea, gynecomastia, menstrual irregularities) are dose-related and gradually resolve after lowering the dose or discontinuing therapy.

CNS (4.6%): dry mouth (1.9%), headache/migraine (1.2%), insomnia, nervousness, dizziness, thirst, lethargy, irritability (all <1%).

Gastrointestinal (2.4%): abdominal cramps, diarrhea, regurgitation, changes in appetite, nausea, heartburn, constipation (all <1%).

Endocrinological (1.3%): hot flushes, mastalgia, galactorrhea, gynecomastia, menstrual irregularities.

Mucocutaneous (1.1%): rash, pruritus, urticaria, stomatitis, conjunctivitis.

Urinary (0.8%): urinary frequency, dysuria.

Cardiovascular (0.5%): edema, palpitations.

Musculoskeletal (0.1%): leg cramps, asthenia.

Miscellaneous (0.1%): drug intolerance.

Laboratory parameters: elevated serum prolactin, elevation of AST, ALT and cholesterol (all <1%).

Extrapyramidal phenomena are rare in adults; they reverse spontaneously as soon as treatment is stopped. When the blood-brain barrier is immature (as in infants) or impaired, the possible occurrence of neurological side effects cannot be excluded.

Overdose: Symptoms: Based on the pharmacological properties of domperidone, symptoms of overdosage may include CNS effects (such as drowsiness, disorientation and extrapyramidal reactions, especially in children) and cardiovascular effects (arrhythmia, hypotension) might possibly occur.

Treatment: Anticholinergic, anti-parkinsonian drugs or antihistamines with anticholinergic properties may be helpful in controlling the extrapyramidal reactions. There is no specific antidote to domperidone but in the event of overdosage, gastric lavage as well as the administration of activated charcoal may be useful. Close observation and supportive therapy are recommended. Symptoms are self-limiting and usually disappear within 24 hours.

Dosage: Upper Gastrointestinal Motility Disorders: The usual dosage in adults is 10 mg orally 3 to 4 times a day, 15 to 30 minutes before meals and at bedtime if required. In severe or resistant cases the dose may be increased to a maximum of 20 mg 3 to 4 times a day.

Nausea and Vomiting Associated with Dopamine Agonist Antiparkinsonian Agents: The usual dosage in adults is 20 mg orally 3 to 4 times a day. Higher doses may be required to achieve symptom control while titration of the antiparkinsonian medication is occurring.

Supplied: Each white to faintly cream, film-coated tablet contains: domperidone maleate 12.72 mg (equivalent to domperidone 10 mg). Nonmedicinal ingredients: cornstarch, hydroxypropyl methylcellulose, lactose, magnesium stearate, microcrystalline cellulose, polysorbate, povidone, pregelatinized starch, propylene glycol and silicone dioxide. Bisulfite-, gluten- and tartrazine-free. HDPE bottles of 500. Store at room temperature between 15 and 30°C, protected from light and moisture.

Reviewed 1999

MOTRIN® Ⓟ
Pharmacia & Upjohn
Ibuprofen
Anti-inflammatory—Analgesic—Antipyretic

Pharmacology: Ibuprofen has demonstrated anti-inflammatory, analgesic and antipyretic activity in animal studies designed to specifically demonstrate these effects. Its mode of action, like that of other nonsteroidal anti-inflammatory agents, is not completely understood, but may be related to prostaglandin synthetase inhibition. Ibuprofen does not alter the course of the underlying disease. Ibuprofen has no demonstrable glucocorticoid effect.

Ibuprofen has been found to be less likely to cause gastrointestinal bleeding in doses usually used than is ASA.

Clinical trials in man have shown that a daily dose of 1 200 to 1 800 mg of ibuprofen is comparable in activity, to a daily dose of 3.6 g of ASA.

Pharmacokinetics: Following a single 200 mg dose of ibuprofen in humans, blood levels were demonstrable in 45 minutes and still present in 6 hours but at barely detectable levels. Peak serum iduprofen levels are generally attained 1 to 1.5 hours after administration of an ibuprofen tablet.

When ibuprofen is administered immediately after a meal, there is a reduction in the rate of absorption but no appreciable decrease in the extent of absorption.

Ibuprofen is extensively bound (99%) to human serum albumin. Approximately 15% of the primary binding sites were estimated to be occupied at therapeutic drug concentrations. Studies suggest that ibuprofen binds to a single binding site on the albumin molecule.

Ibuprofen is rapidly metabolized and eliminated in the urine. The excretion of ibuprofen is virtually complete in 24 hours after the last dose. The serum half-life is 1.8 to 2.0 hours. There is no evidence of drug accumulation or enzyme induction.

Table I—Motrin

Table of Representative Pharmacokinetic Parameters

Motrin Dose mg	T_{max} (h)	C_{max} (µg/mL)	AUC (µg·h/mL)
200	1.2	22.4	69.5
300	1.2	25.1	85.1
400	1.5	35.7	117.9
600	1.6	53.7	163.3

Dose = single oral dose.
T_{max} = time to reach peak serum concentration.
C_{max} =peak serum concentration.
AUC = area under the curve.

The pharmacokinetic parameters presented in Table I are representative of parameters obtained in bioavailability studies using ibuprofen tablets.

Pharmacokinetics in the Elderly: Studies have shown no statistically significant differences in pharmacokinetic parameters between elderly and young women treated with ibuprofen. In elderly males, however, a significant prolongation of ibuprofen half-life and a decrease in weight corrected total metabolic clearance has been reported. The clinical significance of these findings has not been established since the half-life of ibuprofen exceeded 3 hours in only 1 individual.

Indications: The treatment of rheumatoid arthritis and osteoarthritis.

The relief of mild to moderate pain accompanied by inflammation, in conditions such as musculoskeletal trauma and post dental extraction.

The relief of pain associated with dysmenorrhea.

Contraindications: Should not be used in patients who have peptic ulcer or active inflammatory disease of the gastrointestinal system. Should not be used in patients who have previously exhibited hypersensitivity to the drug, or in individuals with the syndrome of nasal polyps, bronchospastic reactivity and angioedema to ASA, ibuprofen or other NSAIDs. Fatal anaphylactoid reactions have occurred in such individuals.

Warnings: Ulceration, perforation and bleeding of the stomach, small intestine or large intestine, sometimes severe and occasionally fatal have been reported during therapy with nonsteroidal anti-inflammatory drugs (NSAIDs) including ibuprofen.

Should be given under close medical supervision to patients prone to gastrointestinal tract irritation particularly those with a history of peptic ulcer, diverticulosis or other inflammatory disease of the gastrointestinal tract. In these cases the physician must weigh the benefits of treatment against the possible hazards.

Patients taking any NSAID including ibuprofen should be instructed to contact a physician immediately if they experience symptoms or signs suggestive of peptic ulceration or gastrointestinal bleeding. These reactions can occur without warning symptoms or signs and at any time during the treatment.

Elderly, frail and debilitated patients appear to be at higher risk from a variety of adverse reactions from NSAIDs. For such patients, consideration should be given to a starting dose lower than usual, with individual adjustment when necessary and under close supervision (see Precautions).

Pregnancy: Reproductive studies conducted in rats and rabbits at doses somewhat less than the maximal clinical dose did not demonstrate evidence of developmental abnormalities. As there are no adequate data concerning use in pregnant women, and because of the known effects of NSAIDs on the fetal cardiovascular system (closure of ductus arteriosus), use during late pregnancy should be avoided. As with other drugs known to inhibit prostaglandin synthesis, an increased incidence of dystocia and delayed parturition occurred in rats. Administration of ibuprofen is not recommended during pregnancy.

Lactation: In limited studies, an assay capable of detecting 1 µg/mL did not demonstrate ibuprofen in the milk of lactating mothers. However, because of the limited nature of the studies, and the possible adverse effects of prostaglandin-inhibiting drugs on neonates, ibuprofen is not recommended for use in nursing mothers.

Children: Controlled clinical trials to establish the safety and efficacy of ibuprofen in children have not been conducted; therefore, the use of ibuprofen is not recommended in children under 12 years of age.

Pre-existing Asthma: About 10% of patients with asthma may have ASA-sensitive asthma. The use of ASA in patients with ASA-sensitive asthma has been associated with severe bronchospasm which can be fatal. Since cross-reactivity, including bronchospasm, between ASA and other NSAIDs has been reported in such ASA-sensitive patients, ibuprofen should not be administered to patients with this form of ASA-sensitivity and should be used with caution in all patients with pre-existing asthma.

Precautions: Gastrointestinal: If peptic ulceration is suspected or confirmed, or if gastrointestinal bleeding or perforation occurs, ibuprofen should be discontinued, an appropriate treatment instituted and the patient closely monitored.

There is no definitive evidence that the concomitant administration of histamine H_2-receptor antagonists and/or antacids will either prevent the occurrence of gastrointestinal side effects or allow continuation of therapy when and if these adverse reactions appear.

Renal Function: Long-term administration of ibuprofen to animals has resulted in renal papillary necrosis and other abnormal renal pathology. In humans, there have been reports of acute interstitial nephritis with hematuria, proteinuria, and occasionally nephrotic syndrome.

A second form of renal toxicity has been seen in patients with pre-renal conditions leading to a reduction in renal blood flow or volume, where the renal prostaglandins have a supportive role in the maintenance of renal perfusion. In these patients administration of NSAIDs may cause a dose dependent reduction in prostaglandin formation and may precipitate overt renal decompensation. Patients at greatest risk of this reaction are those with impaired renal function, heart failure, liver dysfunction, those taking diuretics and the elderly. Discontinuation of NSAID therapy is usually followed by recovery to the pretreatment state.

Glomerular filtration rate and renal blood flow decreased in patients with mild impairment of renal function who took 1 200 mg of ibuprofen for 1 week.

Since ibuprofen is eliminated primarily by the kidneys, patients with significantly impaired renal function should be closely monitored and a reduction in dosage should be anticipated to avoid drug accumulation.

During long-term therapy, kidney function should be monitored periodically, particularly in those patients at high risk for developing renal dysfunction.

Hepatic: As with other NSAIDs, borderline elevations of one or more liver tests may occur. These abnormalities may progress, may remain essentially unchanged, or may be transient with continued therapy. A patient with symptoms and/or signs suggesting liver dysfunction, or in whom an abnormal liver test has occurred, should be evaluated for evidence of the development of more severe hepatic reaction while on therapy with this drug. Severe hepatic reactions including jaundice and cases of fatal hepatitis have been reported with this drug as with other NSAIDs. Although such reactions are rare, if abnormal liver tests persist or worsen, if clinical signs and symptoms consistent with liver disease develop, or if systemic manifestations occur (e.g., eosinophilia, rash, etc.) ibuprofen should be discontinued.

During long-term therapy, liver function tests should be monitored periodically. If ibuprofen is to be used in the presence of impaired liver function, it must be done under strict observation.

Fluid and Electrolyte Balance: Fluid retention and edema have been observed in association with ibuprofen. Therefore, as with many other NSAIDs the possibility of precipitating congestive heart failure in elderly patients or those with compromised cardiac function should be borne in mind. Ibuprofen should be used with caution in patients with heart failure, hypertension or other conditions predisposing to fluid retention.

Serum electrolytes should be monitored periodically during long-term therapy, especially in those patients at risk.

Hematology: Ibuprofen, (like other nonsteroidal anti-inflammatory agents), can inhibit platelet aggregation but the effect is quantitatively less and of shorter duration than that seen with ASA. Ibuprofen has been shown to prolong bleeding time (but within the normal range) in normal subjects. This prolonged bleeding effect may be exaggerated in patients with underlying hemostatic defects. The safety of ibuprofen in combination with anticoagulants has not been established, and if such use is necessary, special caution should be used.

Blood dyscrasias associated with the use of NSAIDs are rare, but could be with severe consequences.

Infection: The anti-inflammatory, antipyretic and analgesic effects may mask the usual signs of infection and the physician should be alert to the development of infection in patients receiving the drug. Aseptic meningitis has been reported in connection with ibuprofen therapy in patients with systemic lupus erythematosus. Such patients may also develop a hypersensitivity reaction to ibuprofen such as fever, rash or abnormal liver function more often than those with other disorders. Caution should therefore be exercised when considering ibuprofen therapy for patients with systemic lupus erythematosus.

When ibuprofen is added to the treatment program of patients who have been on prolonged corticosteroid therapy, and it is decided to discontinue this therapy, the corticosteroid should be tapered slowly to avoid exacerbation of the disease or adrenal insufficiency.

Ophthalmology: Blurred and/or diminished vision, scotomata, and/or changes in color vision have been reported. Any patient who develops eye complaints while receiving ibuprofen should discontinue the drug and have an ophthalmologic examination. Ophthalmic examinations should be carried out at periodic intervals in any patient receiving this drug for an extended period of time.

Elderly: Should be used with caution in the elderly, and the dosage should be adjusted individually.

Drug Interactions: ASA: Animal studies show that ASA given with nonsteroidal anti-inflammatory agents including ibuprofen yield a net decrease in anti-inflammatory activity with lowered blood levels of the non-ASA drug. Although correlative clinical studies have not been done, the use of ASA as an analgesic in patients stabilized on ibuprofen is questioned on pharmacokinetic grounds. While single dose bioavailability studies in normal volunteers have failed to show an effect of ASA on ibuprofen blood levels, multiple dose studies show that ibuprofen serum levels are decreased by 50% when given in conjunction with ASA.

Coumarin-type Anticoagulants: Several short-term controlled studies failed to show that ibuprofen significantly affected prothrombin times or a variety of other clotting factors when administered to individuals on coumarin-type anticoagulants. However, because bleeding has been reported when ibuprofen and other nonsteroidal anti-inflammatory agents have been administered to patients on coumarin-type anticoagulants, the physician should be cautious when administering the drug to patients on anticoagulants.

Furosemide: Ibuprofen antagonizes the action of i.v. or oral furosemide.

Antihypertensives: In 12 patients with essential hypertension taking at least 2 antihypertensive drugs and ibuprofen 400 mg every 8 hours, a mean increase in blood pressure after 3 weeks' treatment was noted as compared to placebo. Ibuprofen could interfere with blood pressure control in certain patients with treated mild-to-moderate hypertension.

Antacids: A bioavailability study has shown that there was no interference with the absorption of ibuprofen when given in conjunction with an antacid containing both aluminum hydroxide and magnesium hydroxide.

Methotrexate: Ibuprofen and other NSAIDs have been reported to reduce renal tubular secretion of methotrexate in vitro. This may enhance the toxicity of methotrexate. Caution should be used if ibuprofen is administered concomitantly with methotrexate.

Lithium: Plasma lithium levels should be carefully monitored in patients taking combination therapy of ibuprofen and lithium. Ibuprofen has been shown to increase plasma lithium levels and to decrease renal lithium clearance.

Gold Salts/Corticosteroids: Ibuprofen can be used in combination with gold salts and/or corticosteroids.

Protein Binding: Ibuprofen is extensively bound (99%) to human serum albumin. Approximately 15% of the primary binding sites were estimated to be occupied at therapeutic drug concentrations. Studies suggest that ibuprofen binds to a single binding site on the albumin molecule. Although drugs such as anticoagulants, sulfonamides and phenytoin do not bind to this site on albumin, patients receiving such combination therapy should be monitored.

Adverse Effects: The most frequently encountered adverse reactions ocurring with NSAIDs are gastrointestinal, of which peptic ulcer, with or without bleeding, is the most severe. Fatalities have occurred on occasion, particularly in the elderly. In controlled clinical trials the percentage of patients reporting one or more gastrointestinal complaints ranged from 4 to 16%.

Motrin (cont'd)

In 2 postmarketing clinical studies, the incidence of a decreased hemoglobin level was greater than previously reported. Decrease in hemoglobin of 1 g or more was observed in 17.1% of 193 patients on 1 600 mg ibuprofen daily (osteoarthritis), and in 22.8% of 189 patients taking 2 400 mg of ibuprofen daily (rheumatoid arthritis). Positive stool occult blood tests, anemia, and elevated serum creatinine levels were also observed in these studies.

The occurrence rates for adverse reactions are as follows: Gastrointestinal (4 to 16%): 3 to 9%: nausea, epigastric pain, heartburn; 1 to 3%: diarrhea, abdominal cramps or pain, fullness of the gastrointestinal tract (bloating or flatulence); Less than 1%: gastric or duodenal ulcers with bleeding and/or perforation, gastritis, gastrointestinal hemorrhage, melena (see Warnings).
Allergic (less than 1%): anaphylaxis, (see Contraindications) syndrome of abdominal pain, fever, chills, nausea, vomiting, bronchospasm, serum sickness, lupus erythematosus syndrome and Henoch-Schölein vasculitis.
CNS (4 to 13%): 3 to 9%: dizziness; 1 to 3%: headache, nervousness; less than 1%: depression, insomnia, confusion, emotional lability, somnolence, aseptic meningitis with fever and coma (probably more common in patients with systemic lupus erythematosus and related connective tissue disease). Causal relationship unknown: paresthesia, hallucinations, dream abnormalities and pseudo-tumor cerebri.
Dermatologic (4 to 13%): 3 to 9%: rash (including maculopapular type); 1 to 3%: pruritus; less than 1%: vesiculobullous eruptions, urticaria, erythema multiforme, alopecia, Stevens-Johnson syndrome, toxic epidermal necrolysis and photoallergic skin reactions.
Cardiovascular (less than 1%): congestive heart failure in patients with marginal cardiac function, elevated blood pressure and palpitations. Causal relationship unknown: arrhythmias (sinus tachycardia, sinus bradycardia).
Special Senses (2 to 4%): 1 to 3%: tinnitus; less than 1%: amblyopia (blurred and/or diminished vision, scotomata and/or changes in color vision) (see Precautions) and hearing loss; causal relationship unknown: conjunctivitis, diplopia, optic neuritis.
Hematologic (1 to 20%): 1 to 20%: decrease in hemoglobin (by 1 g or more) and hematocrit; 3 to 9%: anemia; less than 1%: leukopenia, hemolytic anemia (sometimes coombs positive), thrombocytopenia (with or without purpura), neutropenia, agranulocytosis, aplastic anemia and eosinophilia; causal relationship unknown: bleeding episodes (e.g., epistaxis, menorrhagia).
Renal (1 to 9%): 3 to 9%: decreased creatinine clearance; less than 1%: acute renal failure in patients with pre-existing significantly impaired renal function, cystitis, hematuria, polyuria, azotemia and interstitial nephritis, nephrotic syndrome and renal papillary necrosis.
Hepatic (less than 1%): hepatitis, jaundice, abnormal liver function [AST, serum bilirubin and alkaline phosphatase].
Metabolic (1 to 3%): decreased appetite, edema, fluid retention (see Precautions).
Endocrine (less than 1%): Causal relationship unknown: gynecomastia, hypoglycemic reaction.
Miscellaneous (less than 1%): dry eyes and mouth, gingival ulcer and rhinitis. Causal relationship unknown: pancreatitis.

Rare events are derived principally from worldwide marketing experience and the literature. Accurate rate estimates are generally impossible. These include the following: colitis, exacerbation of inflammatory bowel disease, perforation of the colon, inflammation of the small intestine with loss of blood and protein, collagenous colitis, small bowel perforation, ulcer or stricture, complications of colonic diverticula (perforation, fistula).

Overdose: Symptoms: A nineteen-month-old child weighing 12 kg ingested from 2 800 to 4 000 mg and presented with apnea, cyanosis and responded only to painful stimuli. Oxygen and parenteral fluids were given and at 12 hours she appeared completely recovered. Two other children (10 kg each) ingested 1 200 mg of ibuprofen each and there were no signs of acute intoxication or late sequelae. A 19-year-old male who had ingested 8 000 mg of ibuprofen reported dizziness, and nystagmus was noted. He recovered with no reported sequelae after parenteral hydration and 3 days' bed rest.

Treatment: In cases of acute overdosage, the stomach should be emptied by vomiting or lavage, though little drug will likely be recovered if more than an hour has elapsed since ingestion. Because the drug is acidic and is excreted in the urine, it is theoretically beneficial to administer alkali and induce diuresis.

Dosage: Rheumatoid arthritis and osteoarthritis: The initial daily dosage in adults is 1 200 mg divided into 3 or 4 equal doses. Depending on the therapeutic response, the dose may be adjusted downward or upward. The daily dosage should not exceed 2 400 mg.

Maintenance therapy, once maximum response is obtained, will range from 800 to 1 200 mg per day.

Mild to moderate pain accompanied by inflammation or dysmenorrhea: 400 mg repeated as required every 4 to 6 hours. The daily dosage should not exceed 2 400 mg.
Children: Due to the lack of clinical experience, ibuprofen is not indicated for use in children under 12 years of age.

Information for the Patient: See Blue Section—Information for the Patient "Motrin".

Supplied: 300 mg: Each white, film-coated tablet contains: ibuprofen 300 mg. Nonmedicinal ingredients: branding ink, carnauba wax, cornstarch, hydroxymethylcellulose, pregelatinized starch, propylene glycol, silicon dioxide and stearic acid. Gluten- and lactose-free. Bottles of 100.

400 mg: Each orange, film-coated tablet, branded "MOTRIN 400 MG" contains: ibuprofen 400 mg. Nonmedicinal ingredients: carnauba wax, cornstarch, hydroxymethylcellulose, pregelatinized starch, opaspray dark orange, propylene glycol, silicon dioxide and stearic acid. Gluten- and lactose-free. Bottles of 100 and 1 000.

600 mg: Each peach, film-coated tablet, branded "MOTRIN 600 MG" contains: ibuprofen 600 mg. Nonmedicinal ingredients: carnauba wax, cornstarch, hydroxymethylcellulose, pregelatinized starch, opaspray orange, propylene glycol, silicon dioxide and stearic acid. Gluten- and lactose-free. Bottles of 100 and 1 000.

(Shown in Product Recognition Section)

MOTRIN® (CHILDREN'S)

McNeil Consumer Products

Ibuprofen

Analgesic—Antipyretic

Pharmacology: Ibuprofen is a member of the class of agents commonly known as nonsteroidal anti-inflammatory drugs (NSAIDs). Consistent with this classification, ibuprofen exhibits anti-inflammatory activity at higher dosage ranges. At lower adult single doses (200 to 400 mg) relevant to the nonprescription analgesic/antipyretic indications and dosage strength, ibuprofen relieves pain of mild to moderate intensity and reduces fever. Clinical studies have also confirmed the antipyretic and analgesic effects of ibuprofen in children. Analogous to ASA, the prototype of this class, this analgesic/antipyretic activity of ibuprofen occurs at lower doses than necessary for anti-inflammatory effects which are thought to require sustained administration of higher individual doses.

Ibuprofen is rapidly absorbed after oral administration. As is true with most tablet and suspension formulations, Children's Motrin suspension is absorbed somewhat faster than a tablet. For example, peak serum ibuprofen levels are generally attained 1 to 2 hours after administration of ibuprofen tablets and within about 1 hour after ibuprofen suspension. Oral absorption is estimated to be 80% of the dose. Both the rate of ibuprofen absorption and peak plasma concentrations are reduced when the drug is taken with food, but, bioavailability as measured by total area under the concentration-time curve is minimally altered. Ibuprofen has an elimination half-life of approximately 2 hours. It is rapidly metabolized through oxidation and glucuronic acid conjugation with urinary excretion of the inactive metabolites usually complete within 24 hours. Less than 10% is excreted unchanged in the urine. Clinical studies indicate a duration of clinical effect for up to 8 hours for fever and 6+ hours for pain.

Studies demonstrate no significant alterations in ibuprofen pharmacokinetics in the elderly or in children. Ibuprofen pharmacokinetics have also been studied in patients with alcoholic liver disease who have been assessed to have fair to poor hepatic function. Results suggest that, despite the liver being the primary organ of metabolism of ibuprofen, its kinetic parameters are not substantially altered by this condition.

The basic mechanism of the pharmacological actions of ibuprofen, like other NSAIDs, has not been precisely determined. It is generally thought to be related to the inhibition of prostaglandin synthesis (Cox I and II).

Indications: For the temporary relief of minor aches and pains in muscles, bones and joints, headache, fever, the aches and fever due to the common cold or flu, immunizations, toothache (dental pain), sore throat, earache.

Contraindications: In patients who have previously exhibited hypersensitivity to ibuprofen or in individuals who are known to have a sensitivity (manifested as asthma, bronchospasm, hypotension, angioedema, laryngeal edema, swelling, shock or urticaria) to ASA or other nonsteroidal anti-inflammatory drugs.

Ibuprofen should not be used during pregnancy. Ibuprofen levels in breast milk are extremely low and are unlikely to affect a nursing infant; however, because its safety under these conditions has not been established, consult a doctor before use in nursing mothers.

Ibuprofen is contraindicated in patients with systemic lupus erythematosus as an anaphylaxis-like reaction with fever may occur, particularly when ibuprofen has been administered previously. Aseptic meningitis has also been reported.

Ibuprofen should not be used in patients with acute peptic ulcer or gastrointestinal bleeding.

Warnings: Anaphylactoid reactions have occurred after administration of ibuprofen to patients with known ASA or other NSAID sensitivity manifested as asthma, swelling, shock or hives.

Gastrointestinal side effects to ibuprofen have been reported including dyspepsia, heartburn, nausea, vomiting, anorexia, diarrhea, constipation, stomatitis, flatulence, bloating, epigastric pain, abdominal pain. Peptic ulceration with gastrointestinal bleeding or perforation has been reported and has been associated with a fatal outcome. Ibuprofen should therefore be given only under close supervision to patients with a history of upper gastrointestinal tract disease.

Precautions: Occasionally, serious gastrointestinal side effects have been associated with the anti-inflammatory uses of ibuprofen (see Warnings). Minor gastrointestinal complaints have also been reported during the clinical use of ibuprofen at analgesic doses. The administration of ibuprofen with food or milk is recommended since occasional and mild heartburn, upset stomach or stomach pain may occur with its use. Patients should be advised to seek the consultation of a physician if gastrointestinal side effects occur consistently, persist, or appear to worsen.

Ibuprofen, like other nonsteroidal anti-inflammatory agents, can inhibit platelet aggregation but the effect is quantitatively less than that seen with ASA. Ibuprofen has been shown to prolong bleeding time (but within the normal range) in normal subjects. Because this prolonged bleeding effect may be exaggerated in patients with underlying hemostatic defects, ibuprofen should be avoided by persons with intrinsic coagulation defects and by those on anticoagulant therapy.

Tinnitus, blurred and/or diminished vision, scotoma, and/or changes in color vision have been reported. If a patient develops such complaints while taking ibuprofen, the drug should be discontinued. Patients with any visual disturbances should have an ophthalmologic examination.

Advanced age, hypertension, use of diuretics, diabetes, atherosclerotic cardiovascular disease, chronic renal failure, cirrhosis, and conditions that may be associated with dehydration appear to increase the risk of renal toxicity. Ibuprofen should therefore be used with caution when these risk factors are present. In children, dehydration would more commonly follow acute diarrhea, vomiting or lack of fluid intake, so ibuprofen should not be used under those circumstances.

Patients taking ibuprofen should be cautioned to report to their physician unusual signs or symptoms which might be a manifestation of gastrointestinal intolerance and/or bleeding, blurred vision or other ocular symptoms, skin rash, tinnitus, dizziness, weight gain, edema, or respiratory difficulties.

If ibuprofen is taken in conjunction with prolonged corticosteroid therapy, and it is decided to discontinue steroid therapy, the corticosteroid should be tapered slowly to avoid exacerbation of disease or adrenal insufficiency.

Although Children's Motrin is labeled specifically for children, particular caution should be observed should it be administered to elderly patients, as they are more likely to be taking other medications or have pre-existing disease states that can increase the likelihood of the complications that have been associated with ibuprofen. Elderly patients appear to be more susceptible to the CNS reactions; cognitive dysfunction (forgetfulness, inability to concentrate, a feeling of separation from the surroundings) in such patients has been reported.
Pregnancy: No evidence specifically identifies exposure to analgesic doses of ibuprofen as a cause of harm to either mother or fetus during pregnancy. Nonsteroidal anti-inflammatory drugs in general, however, are known to affect the action of prostaglandin synthetase which could alter a variety of the physiological functions of prostaglandins or platelets during delivery such as facilitating uterine contraction in the mother, closure of the ductus arteriosus in the fetus, and platelet-related hemostasis. Patients should therefore be advised not

to use ibuprofen during pregnancy without the advice of a physician, particularly during the last trimester. Clinical information is limited on the effects of ibuprofen in pregnancy.

Lactation: Pharmacokinetic studies indicated that following oral administration of ibuprofen 400 mg, the level of drug that appeared in breast milk was below detection levels of 1 μg/mL. The amount of ibuprofen to which an infant would be exposed through this source was considered negligible. However, since the absolute safety of ibuprofen ingested under these circumstances has not been determined, nursing mothers should be advised to consult a physician before using ibuprofen.

Patients with Special Diseases and Conditions: Several medical conditions that can predispose patients to the adverse effects of nonsteroidal anti-inflammatory drugs in general may be applicable to ibuprofen.

Ibuprofen should be used with caution in patients with a history of cardiac failure or kidney disease because of the possibility of aggravating pre-existing states of fluid retention or edema. Mild impairment of renal function (decreased renal blood flow and glomerular filtration rate) can occur at maximal doses of ibuprofen. Renal papillary necrosis has been reported.

Also, patients with underlying medical or pharmacologically induced hemostatic defects could experience further prolongation of bleeding time through the inhibition of platelet aggregation induced to varying degrees by this class of drugs.

Long-term ingestion of combinations of analgesics has been associated with the condition analgesic nephropathy. It is therefore appropriate that patients be discouraged from long-term, unsupervised consumption of analgesics, particularly in combination. Patients should therefore be directed to consult a physician if their underlying condition requires administration of ibuprofen for more than 3 days for fever or 5 days for pain. Ibuprofen usually should not be administered along with acetaminophen or ASA.

Patients with any serious medical condition should consult a physician before using ibuprofen as an analgesic or antipyretic.

Drug Interactions: The platelet inhibiting effects of ibuprofen, although less potent and of shorter duration than those induced by ASA, warrant cautionary supervision by a physician before co-administration of ibuprofen and anticoagulants.

Coumarin-type Anticoagulants: Several short-term controlled studies failed to show that ibuprofen significantly affected prothrombin time or a variety of other clotting factors when administered to individuals on coumarin-type anticoagulants. However, bleeding has been reported when ibuprofen and other NSAID agents have been administered to patients on coumarin-type anticoagulants. The use of ibuprofen in patients who are taking anticoagulants should therefore be avoided because of the possibility of enhanced gastrointestinal bleeding or an additive anticoagulant effect due to ibuprofen's reversible antiplatelet action.

ASA: Animal studies show that ASA given with NSAID agents, including ibuprofen, yields a net decrease in anti-inflammatory activity with lowered blood levels of the non-ASA drug. Single dose bioavailability studies in normal volunteers have failed to show an effect of ASA on ibuprofen blood levels. Correlative clinical studies have not been done.

Since there have been no controlled trials to demonstrate whether there is any beneficial or harmful interaction with the use of ibuprofen in conjunction with ASA, the combination cannot be recommended.

Other Anti-inflammatory Agents (NSAIDs): The addition of ibuprofen to a pre-existent prescribed NSAID regimen in patients with a condition such as rheumatoid arthritis may result in increased risk of adverse effects.

Diuretics: Ibuprofen, because of its fluid retention properties, can decrease the diuretic and antihypertensive effects of diuretics, and increased diuretic dosage may be needed. Patients with impaired renal function taking potassium-sparing diuretics who develop ibuprofen-induced renal insufficiency might be in serious danger of fatal hyperkalemia.

Acetaminophen: Although interactions have not been reported, concurrent use with ibuprofen is not advisable.

Other Drugs: Although ibuprofen binds to a significant extent to plasma proteins, interactions with other protein-bound drugs occur uncommonly. Nevertheless, caution should be observed when other drugs also having a high affinity for protein binding sites are used concurrently. Some observations have suggested a potential for ibuprofen to interact with digoxin, methotrexate, phenytoin and lithium salts. However, the mechanisms and clinical significance of these observations are presently not known.

Patients taking other prescribed medications should consult a physician before using ibuprofen to assure its compatibility with the other medications.

Table I—Motrin (Children's)

Adverse Effects

Adverse Effect	Incidence 3-9%	Incidence 1-3%	Incidence Less than 1%
Gastrointestinal	nausea epigastric pain heartburn	diarrhea abdominal distress nausea and vomiting indigestion constipation abdominal cramps and pain gastrointestinal tract fullness (bloating or flatulence)	gastric or duodenal ulcer with bleeding and/or perforation gastrointestinal hemorrhage melena hepatitis jaundice abnormal liver function (AST, serum bilirubin and alkaline phosphatase)
	The generally modest elevations of serum transaminase activity that has been observed are usually without clinical sequelae but severe, potentially fatal toxic hepatitis can occur.		
CNS	dizziness	headache nervousness	depression insomnia
	Also reported but with unknown causal relationship: paresthesias hallucinations dream abnormalities aseptic meningitis in patients with systemic lupus erythematosus or other connective tissue disease. aseptic meningitis and meningoencephalitis, in 1 case accompanied by eosinophilia in the cerebrospinal fluids, in patients who took ibuprofen intermittently and did not have any connective tissue disease cognitive dysfunction has been observed in elderly patients who took ibuprofen		
Dermatologic	rash (including maculopapular type)	pruritus	vesiculobullous eruptions urticaria erythema multiforme
	Also reported but with unknown causal relationship: alopecia Stevens-Johnson syndrome		
Special Senses		tinnitus	amblyopia (blurred and/or diminished vision, scotomata and/or changes in color vision) Any patient with eye complaints during ibuprofen therapy should have an ophthalmological examination.
	Also reported but with unknown causal relationship: conjunctivitis diplopia optic neuritis		
Metabolic		decreased appetite edema fluid retention	
	Fluid retention generally responds promptly to drug discontinuation.		
Hematologic			leukopenia and decreases in hemoglobin and hematocrit
	Also reported but with unknown causal relationship, rare cases of: hemolytic anemia thrombocytopenia granulocytopenia bleeding episodes (e.g., purpura, epistaxis, hematuria, menorrhagia) autoimmune hematological anemia occurred in 1 patient who took 600 mg/day for 8 months.		
Cardiovascular			congestive heart failure in patients with marginal cardiac function elevated blood pressure Conditions such as congestive heart failure and hypertension may be aggravated by sodium retention and edema caused by ibuprofen in such patients.
	Also reported but with unknown causal relationship, rare cases of: arrhythmias (sinus tachycardia, sinus bradycardia, palpitations)		
Allergic			anaphylaxis (see Contraindications)
	Also reported but with unknown causal relationship, rarely: fever serum sickness lupus erythematosus syndrome		
Endocrine	Reported but with unknown causal relationship, rare cases of: gynecomastia hypoglycemic reaction menstrual delays of up to 2 weeks and dysfunctional uterine bleeding in 9 patients taking ibuprofen 400 mg 3 times a day for 3 days before menses		

Motrin (Children's) (cont'd)

Table I—Motrin (Children's) *(cont'd)*

Adverse Effects	
	Reported but with unknown causal relationship: decreased creatine clearance; polyuria; azotemia. Like other nonsteroidal anti-inflammatory agents, ibuprofen inhibits renal prostaglandin synthesis which may decrease renal function and cause sodium retention. Renal blood flow glomerular filtration rate decreased in patients with mild impairment of renal functions who took 1 200 mg/day of ibuprofen for 1 week. Renal papillary necrosis
Renal	A number of factors appear to increase the risk of renal toxicity (see Precautions).

Table II—Motrin (Children's)

Prescribed vs OTC Dosage and Administration

	Prescription		**OTC (Self-medication)**
Indications	**Fever Reduction:** Children: 6 months to 12 years	**Analgesia (mild to moderate pain):** Children: 6 months to 12 years	**For mild to moderate pain or fever:** Children: 6 months to 12 years
Single Dose Recommendation	Baseline Temperature <39.2°C: 5 mg/kg; Baseline Temperature ≥39.2°C: 10 mg/kg	10 mg/kg	Based on a single dose of approximately 7.5 mg/kg†
Dosing Frequency	every 6-8 hours	every 6-8 hours	Single dose may be given every 6-8 hours, as needed
Recommended Daily Dose	40 mg/kg	40 mg/kg	Do not exceed 4 doses unless advised by a doctor
Additional Comments	Dosage may be adjusted on the basis of the initial temperature level as indicated above.	Doses should be given so as not to disturb the child's sleep pattern.	†Refer to Table III for detailed dosing information for children based on age and weight.
	Individualization of Dosage: The dose of ibuprofen should be tailored to each child, and may be lowered or raised from the suggested doses depending on the severity of symptoms either at the time of initiating drug therapy or as the child responds or fails to respond. Limited data suggests that, after the initial dose of ibuprofen, subsequent doses may be lowered and still provide adequate fever control. In a situation when lower fever would require the ibuprofen 5 mg/kg dose in a child with pain, the dose that will effectively treat the predominant symptom should be chosen.		Adults and Children over 12 years of age: The equivalent adult dosage of Children's Motrin suspension is 200 to 400 mg (10 to 20 mL) as required every 4 to 6 hours, not to exceed 1 200 mg (60 mL) in 24 hours unless directed by a physician.

Adverse Effects: Experience reported with prescription use of ibuprofen has included the adverse reactions listed in Table I (on previous page).

Note: Reactions listed in Table I (on previous page) as unknown causal relationship are those where a causal relationship could not be established; however, in these rarely reported events, the possibility of a relationship to ibuprofen also cannot be excluded.

Overdose: Symptoms: A clear pattern of clinical features associated with accidental or intentional overdose of ibuprofen has not been established. Reported cases of overdose have often been complicated by co-ingestions or additional suicidal gestures. The range of symptoms observed has included nausea, vomiting, abdominal pain, drowsiness, nystagmus, diplopia, headache, tinnitus, impaired renal function, coma and hypotension. A review of 4 fatalities associated with ibuprofen overdose indicates other contributing factors co-existed so it would be difficult to identify the toxicity of ibuprofen as a specific cause of death.

Postingestion blood levels may be useful to confirm a diagnosis and to quantify the degree of exposure but otherwise have not been helpful in predicting clinical outcome. Generally, full recovery can be expected with appropriate symptomatic management.

The following cases of overdose have been reported. A 19-month-old-child, 1½ hours after the ingestion of seven to ten 400 mg tablets of ibuprofen presented apnea, cyanosis and responded only to painful stimuli. After treatment with O_2, $NaHCO_3$, infusion of dextrose and normal saline, the child was responsive and 12 hours after ingestion appeared completely recovered. Blood levels of ibuprofen reached 102.9 µg/mL, 8½ hours after the accident. Two other children weighing approximately 10 kg had taken an estimated 120 mg/kg. There were no signs of acute intoxication or late sequelae. In 1 child the ibuprofen blood level at 90 minutes after ingestion was approximately 700 µg/mL. A 19-year-old-male who ingested 8 000 mg of ibuprofen reported dizziness, and nystagmus was noted. He recovered with no reported sequelae after parenteral hydration and 3 days of bed rest.

For perspective, therapeutic doses (200 to 400 mg) in adults results in average peak serum levels of 22.4 to 35.7 µg/mL.

Table III—Motrin (Children's)

OTC Dosing for Children

	Weight	**Single Dose**[a]	
Age	**kg**	**mL**	**mg**
6 to 11 months[b]	6 to 7.9	2.5	50
12 to 23 months[b]	8 to 10.9	3.75	75
2 to 3 years	11 to 15.9	5	100
4 to 5 years	16 to 21.9	7.5	150
6 to 8 years	22 to 26.9	10	200
9 to 10 years	27 to 31.9	12.5	250
11 years	32 to 43.9	15	300

[a]Single dose may be given every 6 to 8 hours as needed but do not exceed 4 doses per day unless advised by your doctor.
[b]Consumer labeling for Children's Motrin brand of ibuprofen does not offer dosing information for children under 2 years of age; therefore, these doses are provided as a guide for professional recommendations to consumers.

Treatment: Appropriate interventions to decontaminate the gastrointestinal tract may be beneficial within the first 4 hours after ingestion. Routine symptomatic and supportive treatment is then recommended. Physicians should contact the Regional Poison Control Centre for additional guidance about ibuprofen overdose management.

Dosage: See Tables II and III.

Clinical experience with ibuprofen to date is insufficient for labeling Children's Motrin for use in children under 6 months of age. Do not take for fever for more than 3 days or pain for more than 5 days unless directed by a physician. If the painful area is red or swollen, if condition deteriorates or new symptoms occur, consult a physician.

Supplied: Each 5 mL of pale orange-colored liquid suspension contains: ibuprofen 100 mg. Nonmedicinal ingredients: citric acid, cornstarch, D&C yellow no. 10, FD&C red no. 40, flavor, glycerin, polysorbate 80, purified water, sodium benzoate, sucrose and xanthan gum. Gluten-, lactose-, paraben-, sulfite-, and tartrazine-free. Bottles of 30†, 60† and 120 mL†. Store at room temperature; avoid high humidity and excessive heat (40°C). Keep out of the reach of children.
†Containers provided with a child-resistant closure. All packages are safety sealed.

(Shown in Product Recognition Section)

New Product 1998

MOTRIN® IB

McNeil Consumer Products

Ibuprofen

Analgesic—Antipyretic—Anti-inflammatory

Pharmacology: Ibuprofen is a member of the class of agents commonly known as nonsteroidal anti-inflammatory drugs (NSAIDs). Consistent with this classification, ibuprofen exhibits anti-inflammatory activity at higher dosage ranges. At lower adult single doses relevant to a 200 mg dosage strength (200 to 400 mg) ibuprofen relieves pain of mild to moderate intensity and reduces fever. Analogous to ASA, the prototype of this class, this analgesic/antipyretic activity of ibuprofen occurs at lower doses than necessary for anti-inflammatory effects which are thought to require sustained administration of higher individual doses.

Pharmacokinetics: Ibuprofen is rapidly absorbed after oral administration, with peak serum or plasma levels generally appearing within 1.5 to 2 hours. Oral absorption is estimated to be 80% of the dose. Both the rate of absorption and peak plasma concentrations are reduced when the drug is taken with food, but, bioavailability as measured by total area under the concentration-time curve is minimally altered. Ibuprofen has an elimination half-life of approximately 2 hours. It is rapidly metabolized through oxidation and glucuronic acid conjugation with urinary excretion of the inactive metabolites usually complete within 24 hours. Less than 10% is excreted unchanged in the urine. Clinical studies indicate a duration of clinical effect for up to 8 hours for fever and 6+ hours for pain.

Studies demonstrate no significant alterations in ibuprofen pharmacokinetics in the elderly. Ibuprofen pharmacokinetics has also been studied in patients with alcoholic liver disease who have been assessed to have fair to poor hepatic function. Results suggest that, despite the liver being the primary organ of metabolism of ibuprofen, its kinetic parameters are not substantially altered by this condition.

The basic mechanism of the pharmacological actions of ibuprofen, like other NSAIDs, has not been precisely determined. It is generally thought to be related to the inhibition of prostaglandin synthesis (Cox I & II).

Indications: Adults: For fast and effective relief of headaches, menstrual pain, toothache (dental pain), pain due to arthritis, minor aches and pains in muscles, bones and joints, such as sprains or strains, backache, the aches and fever due to the common cold and for the reduction of fever.

Contraindications: Ibuprofen should not be used in patients who have previously exhibited hypersensitivity to it or in individuals who are known to have a sensitivity (manifested as asthma, bronchospasm, hypotension, angioedema, laryngeal edema, swelling, shock or urticaria) to ASA or other NSAIDs.

Pregnancy and *Lactation:* Ibuprofen should not be used during pregnancy. Ibuprofen levels in breast milk are extremely low and are unlikely to affect a nursing infant, however because its safety under these conditions has not been established, consult a doctor before use in nursing mothers.

Ibuprofen is contraindicated in patients with systemic lupus erythematosus as an anaphylaxis like reaction with fever may occur, particularly when ibuprofen has been administered previously. Aseptic meningitis has also been reported.

Ibuprofen should not be used in patients with acute peptic ulcer or gastrointestinal bleeding.

Warnings: Anaphylactoid reactions have occurred after administration of ibuprofen to patients with known ASA or other NSAID sensitivity manifested as asthma, swelling, shock or hives.

Gastrointestinal side effects to ibuprofen have been reported including dyspepsia, heartburn, nausea, vomiting, anorexia, diarrhea, constipation, stomatitis, flatulence, bloating, epigastric pain, abdominal pain. Peptic ulceration with gastrointestinal bleeding or perforation has been reported and has been associated with a fatal outcome. Ibuprofen should therefore be given only under close supervision to patients with a history of upper gastrointestinal tract disease.

Precautions: Occasionally serious gastrointestinal side effects have been associated with the anti-inflammatory uses of ibuprofen (see Warnings). Minor gastrointestinal complaints have also been reported during the clinical use of ibuprofen at analgesic doses. The administration of ibuprofen with food or milk is recommended since occasional and mild heartburn, upset stomach or stomach pain may occur with its use. Patients should be advised to seek the consultation of a physician if gastrointestinal side effects occur consistently, persist or appear to worsen.

Ibuprofen, like other NSAIDs, can inhibit platelet aggregation but the effect is quantitatively less than that seen with ASA. Ibuprofen has been shown to prolong bleeding time (but within the normal range) in normal subjects. Because this prolonged bleeding effect may be exaggerated in patients with underlying hemostatic defects, ibuprofen should be avoided by persons with intrinsic coagulation defects and by those on anticoagulant therapy.

Tinnitus, blurred and/or diminished vision, scotoma, and/or changes in color vision have been reported. If a patient develops such complaints while taking ibuprofen, the drug should be discontinued. Patients with any visual disturbances should have an ophthalmologic examination.

Advanced age, hypertension, use of diuretics, diabetes, atherosclerotic cardiovascular disease, chronic renal failure, cirrhosis and conditions which may be associated with dehydration appear to increase the risk of renal toxicity. Ibuprofen should therefore be used with caution when these risk factors are present.

Patients taking ibuprofen should be cautioned to report to their physician signs or symptoms of gastrointestinal intolerance and/or bleeding, blurred vision or other ocular symptoms, skin rash, tinnitus, dizziness, weight gain, edema or respiratory difficulties.

If ibuprofen is taken in conjunction with prolonged corticosteroid therapy and it is decided to discontinue steroid therapy, the corticosteroid should be tapered slowly to avoid exacerbation of disease or adrenal insufficiency.

Geriatrics: Particular caution should be observed in elderly patients taking ibuprofen, as they are more likely to be taking other medications or have pre-existing disease states which can increase the likelihood of the complications that have been associated with ibuprofen. Elderly patients appear to be more susceptible to the CNS reactions; cognitive dysfunction (forgetfulness, inability to concentrate, a feeling of separation from the surroundings) in such patients has been reported.

Pregnancy: No evidence specifically identifies exposure to analgesic doses of ibuprofen as a cause of harm to either mother or fetus during pregnancy. NSAIDs in general, however, are known to affect the action of prostaglandin synthetase which could alter a variety of the physiological functions of prostaglandins or platelets during delivery such as facilitating uterine contraction in the mother, closure of the ductus arteriosus in the fetus, and platelet-related hemostasis. Patients should therefore be advised not to use ibuprofen during pregnancy without the advice of a physician, particularly during the last trimester. Clinical information is limited on the effects of ibuprofen in pregnancy.

Lactation: Pharmacokinetic studies indicated that following oral administration of ibuprofen 400 mg the level of drug which appeared in breast milk was below detection levels of 1 μg/mL. The amount of ibuprofen to which an infant would be exposed through this source was considered negligible. However, since the absolute safety of ibuprofen ingested under these circumstances has not been determined, nursing mothers should be advised to consult a physician before using ibuprofen.

Patients with Special Diseases and Conditions: Several medical conditions which can predispose patients to the adverse effects of NSAIDs in general may be applicable to ibuprofen.

Ibuprofen should be used with caution in patients with a history of cardiac failure or kidney disease because of the possibility of aggravating pre-existing states of fluid-retention or edema. Mild impairment of renal function (decreased renal

Table I—Motrin IB

Adverse Effects

Adverse Effect	Incidence 3-9%	Incidence 1-3%	Incidence Less than 1%
Gastrointestinal	nausea epigastric pain heartburn	diarrhea abdominal distress nausea and vomiting indigestion constipation abdominal cramps and pain gastrointestinal tract fullness (bloating or flatulence)	gastric or duodenal ulcer with bleeding and/or perforation gastrointestinal hemorrhage melena hepatitis jaundice abnormal liver function (AST, serum bilirubin and alkaline phosphatase)
	The generally modest elevations of serum transaminase activity that has been observed are usually without clinical sequelae but severe, potentially fatal toxic hepatitis can occur.		
CNS	dizziness	headache nervousness	depression insomnia
	Also reported but with unknown causal relationship: paresthesias hallucinations dream abnormalities aseptic meningitis in patients with systemic lupus erythematosus or other connective tissue disease. aseptic meningitis and meningioencephalitis, in one case accompanied by eosinophilia in the cerebrospinal fluids, in patients who took ibuprofen intermittently and did not have any connective tissue disease. cognitive dysfunction has been observed in elderly patients who took ibuprofen.		
Dermatologic	rash (including maculopapular type)	pruritus	vesiculobullous eruptions urticaria erythema multiforme
	Also reported but with unknown causal relationship: alopecia Stevens-Johnson syndrome		
Special Senses		tinnitus	amblyopia (blurred and/or diminished vision, scotomata and/or changes in color vision) Any patient with eye complaints during ibuprofen therapy should have an ophthalmological examination.
	Also reported but with unknown causal relationship: conjunctivitis diplopia optic neuritis		
Metabolic		decreased appetite edema fluid retention	
	Fluid retention generally responds promptly to drug discontinuation.		
Hematologic			leukopenia and decreases in hemoglobin and hematocrit
	Also reported but with unknown causal relationship, rare cases of: hemolytic anemia thrombocytopenia granulocytopenia bleeding episodes (e.g., purpura, epistaxis, hematuria, menorrhagia) autoimmune hematological anemia occurred in 1 patient who took 600 mg/day for 8 months.		
Cardiovascular			congestive heart failure in patients with marginal cardiac function elevated blood pressure Conditions such as congestive heart failure and hypertension may be aggravated by sodium retention and edema caused by ibuprofen in such patients.
	Also reported but with unknown causal relationship, rare cases of: arrhythmias (sinus tachycardia, sinus bradycardia, palpitations)		
Allergic			anaphylaxis (see Contraindications)
	Also reported but with unknown causal relationship, rarely: fever		
Endocrine	Reported but with unknown causal relationship, rare cases of: gynecomastia hypoglycemic reaction menstrual delays of up to 2 weeks and dysfunctional uterine bleeding in 9 patients taking ibuprofen 400 mg 3 times a day for 3 days before menses.		
Renal	Reported but with unknown causal relationship: decreased creatinine clearance polyuria azotemia Like other NSAIDs, ibuprofen inhibits renal prostaglandin synthesis which may decrease renal function and cause sodium retention. Renal blood flow glomerular filtration rate decreased in patients with mild impairment of renal functions who took 1 200 mg/day of ibuprofen for 1 week. Renal papillary necrosis A number of factors appear to increase the risk of renal toxicity (see Precautions).		

Motrin IB (cont'd)

blood flow and glomerular filtration rate) can occur at maximal doses of ibuprofen. Renal papillary necrosis has been reported.

Also, patients with underlying medical or pharmacologically-induced hemostatic defects could experience further prolongation of bleeding time through the inhibition of platelet aggregation induced to varying degrees by this class of drugs.

Long-term ingestion of combinations of analgesics has been associated with analgesic nephropathy. It is therefore appropriate that patients be discouraged from long-term, unsupervised consumption of analgesics, particularly in combination. Patients should therefore be directed to consult a physician if their underlying condition requires administration of ibuprofen for more than 5 days. Ibuprofen usually should not be administered along with acetaminophen or ASA.

Patients with any serious medical condition should consult a physician before using ibuprofen as an analgesic or antipyretic.

Drug Interactions: The platelet inhibiting effects of ibuprofen, although less potent and of shorter duration than those induced by ASA, warrant cautionary supervision by a physician before coadministration of ibuprofen and anticoagulants.

Coumarin Type Anticoagulants: Several short-term controlled studies failed to show that ibuprofen significantly affected prothrombin time or a variety of other clotting factors when administered to individuals on coumarin-type anticoagulants. However, bleeding has been reported when ibuprofen and other NSAID agents have been administered to patients on coumarin-type anticoagulants. The use of ibuprofen in patients who are taking anticoagulants should therefore be avoided because of the possibility of enhanced gastrointestinal bleeding or an additive anticoagulant effect due to ibuprofen's reversible antiplatelet actions.

ASA: Animal studies show that ASA given with NSAIDs, including ibuprofen, yields a net decrease in anti-inflammatory activity with lowered blood levels of the non-ASA drug. Single dose bioavailability studies in normal volunteers have failed to show an effect of ASA on ibuprofen blood levels. Correlative clinical studies have not been done.

Other NSAIDs: The addition of ibuprofen to a pre-existent prescribed NSAID regimen in patients with a condition such as rheumatoid arthritis may result in increased risk of adverse effects.

Diuretics: Ibuprofen, because of its fluid retention properties, can decrease the diuretic and antihypertensive effects of diuretics, and increased diuretic dosage may be needed. Patients with impaired renal function taking potassium-sparing diuretics who develop ibuprofen-induced renal insufficiency might be in serious danger of fatal hyperkalemia.

Acetaminophen: Although interactions have not been reported, concurrent use with ibuprofen is not advisable.

Other Drugs: Although ibuprofen binds to a significant extent to plasma proteins, interactions with other protein-bound drugs occur uncommonly. Nevertheless, caution should be observed when other drugs also having a high affinity for protein binding sites are used concurrently. Some observations have suggested a potential for ibuprofen to interact with digoxin, methotrexate, phenytoin and lithium salts. However, the mechanisms and clinical significance of these observations are presently not known.

Patients taking other prescribed medications should consult a physician before using ibuprofen to assure its compatibility with the other medications.

Adverse Effects: Experience reported with prescription use of ibuprofen has included the following adverse reactions. Note: Reactions listed in Table I as unknown causal relationship are those where a causal relationship could not be established; however, in these rarely reported events, the possibility of a relationship to ibuprofen also cannot be excluded. The adverse reactions most frequently seen with ibuprofen therapy involve the gastrointestinal system.

Overdose: Symptoms: A clear pattern of clinical features associated with accidental or intentional overdose of ibuprofen has not been established. Reported cases of overdose have often been complicated by coingestion or additional suicidal gestures. The range of symptoms observed has included nausea, vomiting, abdominal pain, drowsiness, nystagmus, diplopia, headache, tinnitus, impaired renal function, coma and hypotension. Overview of 4 fatalities associated with ibuprofen overdose indicates other contributing factors coexisted so it would be difficult to identify the toxicity of ibuprofen as a specific cause of death.

Postingestion blood levels may be useful to confirm a diagnosis and to quantify the degree of exposure but otherwise have not been helpful in predicting clinical outcome. Generally, full recovery can be expected with appropriate symptomatic management.

The following cases of overdose have been reported. A 19-month-old child, 1.5 hours after the ingestion of seven to ten 400 mg tablets of ibuprofen presented apnea, cyanosis and responded only to painful stimuli. After treatment with $NaHCO_3$, O_2, infusion of dextrose and normal saline, the child was responsive and 12 hours after ingestion appeared completely recovered. Blood levels of ibuprofen reached 102.9 μg/mL, 8.5 hours after the accident. Two other children weighing approximately 10 kg, had taken an estimated 120 mg/kg. There were no signs of acute intoxication or late sequelae. In 1 child the ibuprofen blood level at 90 minutes after ingestion was approximately 700 μg/mL. A 19-year-old male who ingested 8 000 mg of ibuprofen reported dizziness and nystagmus. He recovered with no reported sequelae after parenteral hydration and 3 days of bed rest.

For perspective, therapeutic doses (200 to 400 mg) in adults result in average peak serum levels of 22.4 to 35.7 μg/mL.

Treatment: Appropriate interventions to decontaminate the gastrointestinal tract may be beneficial within the first 4 hours after ingestion. Routine symptomatic and supportive treatment is then recommended. Physicians should contact the Regional Poison Control Centre for additional guidance about ibuprofen overdose management.

Dosage: For mild to moderate pain or fever.

Adults: 200 to 400 mg (1 to 2 tablets, caplets or gelcaps) as required every 4 hours, not to exceed 1 200 mg (6 tablets, caplets or gelcaps) in 24 hours unless directed by a physician.

Children: Refer to Motrin (Children's) monograph for use and dosing instruction for children under 12 years of age.

Do not take for pain for more than 5 consecutive days or fever for more than 3 days unless directed by a physician. If the painful area is red or swollen, if condition deteriorates or new symptoms occur, consult a physician.

Supplied: Caplets: Each white, film-coated, capsule-shaped tablet, with "Motrin IB" printed in black ink, contains: ibuprofen 200 mg. Nonmedicinal ingredients: carbon black, carnauba wax, colloidal silicon dioxide, cornstarch, hydroxypropyl methylcellulose, pharmaceutical glaze, propylene glycol, stearic acid and titanium dioxide. Gluten-, lactose-, paraben-, sulfite- and tartrazine-free. Bottles of 24† and 50†. Store away from heat and direct light.

Gelcaps: Each solid capsule-shaped tablet, coated with white gelatin on one end and orange gelatin on the other with "Motrin IB" printed in grey ink, contains: ibuprofen 200 mg. Nonmedicinal ingredients: calcium disodium EDTA, castor oil, cellulose, colloidal silicon dioxide, cornstarch, FD&C yellow no. 6, gelatin, hydroxypropyl methylcellulose, magnesium stearate, parabens, povidone, propylene glycol, sodium lauryl sulfate, sodium propionate, sodium starch glycolate, synthetic black iron oxide and titanium dioxide. Gluten-, lactose-, sulfite- and tartrazine-free. Bottles of 20† and 40†. Store at room temperature; avoid high humidity and excessive heat (40°C).

Tablets: Each white, film-coated tablet, with "Motrin IB" printed in red ink, contains: ibuprofen 200 mg. Nonmedicinal ingredients: carnauba wax, cellulose, colloidal silicon dioxide, cornstarch, FD&C red no. 40, glycerol triacetate, hydroxypropyl methylcellulose, sodium lauryl sulfate, sodium starch glycolate and titanium dioxide. Gluten-, lactose-, paraben-, sulfite- and tartrazine-free. Bottles of 24†, 50† and 100†. Store away from heat and direct light.

For all preparations, keep out of the reach of children.

†Containers provided with a child-resistant closure.

All packages are safety sealed.

(Shown in Product Recognition Section)

MS CONTIN® Ⓝ

Purdue Frederick

Morphine Sulfate

Opioid Analgesic

Pharmacology: Morphine is an opioid analgesic which exerts an agonist effect at specific, saturable opioid receptors in the CNS and other tissues. In man, morphine produces a variety of effects including analgesia, constipation from decreased gastrointestinal motility, suppression of the cough reflex, respiratory depression from reduced responsiveness of the respiratory centre to CO_2, nausea and vomiting via stimulation of the CTZ, changes in mood including euphoria and dysphoria, sedation, mental clouding, and alterations of the endocrine and autonomic nervous systems.

Morphine is readily absorbed when given orally, rectally or by s.c. or i.m. injection. Due to "first-pass" metabolism in the liver, the effect of an oral dose is less than after parenteral administration. With repeated regular dosing, oral morphine is about 1/3 as potent as when given by i.m. injection and rectal sustained-release suppositories have approximately 40% the potency of s.c. morphine. The rectal dose of the sustained-release suppositories is approximately equivalent to the oral dose of the sustained-release tablets after repeated dosing. Morphine is primarily excreted in the urine as morphine-3-glucuronide. Formation of glucuronidated metabolites is less following rectal administration compared to oral administration. About 7 to 10% of a dose of morphine is excreted in the feces via the bile.

When administered every 12 hours, the sustained-release tablets provide equivalent analgesia to morphine oral solution given 4-hourly. In most cases, administration on a 12-hourly schedule produces equivalent pain control to 8-hourly administration. The sustained-release suppositories given 12-hourly provide equivalent pain control to the sustained-release tablets given orally at the same dose and frequency, or to morphine administered s.c. at a dose approximately 40% of the daily rectal dose.

Absorption of the sustained-release tablets is equivalent to that of immediate-release tablet or liquid formulations and is not significantly affected by administration with food. At steady-state, the sustained-release tablets produce peak morphine levels approximately 4 to 5 hours post-dose and therapeutic levels persist for a 12-hourly period. Comparison of the sustained-release suppositories and tablets indicate attainment of peak concentrations at 4.1 and 4.3 hours post-dose respectively. The extent of absorption of sustained-release suppositories at steady-state is equivalent to that of the sustained-release tablets and approximately 40% of that of s.c. morphine.

The relationship between mean plasma concentration and dose has been shown to be linear over a dosage range of 60 to 600 mg/day in the case of the sustained-release tablets and 60 to 1 200 mg/day in the case of the sustained-release suppositories.

Indications: For the relief of severe pain requiring the prolonged use of an opioid analgesic preparation.

Contraindications: Should not be given to patients with: hypersensitivity to opioid analgesics; acute asthma or other obstructive airway disease and acute respiratory depression; cor pulmonale; cardiac arrhythmias; acute alcoholism; delirium tremens; severe CNS depression; convulsive disorders; increased cerebrospinal or intracranial pressure; head injury; brain tumor; suspected surgical abdomen; concomitant MAO inhibitors (or within 14 days of such therapy).

Warnings: Drug Dependence: As with other opioids, tolerance and physical dependence tend to develop upon repeated administration of morphine and there is potential for abuse of the drug and for development of strong psychological dependence. The sustained-release tablets should therefore be prescribed and handled with the high degree of caution appropriate to the use of a drug with strong abuse potential. Drug abuse is not a problem in patients with severe pain in which morphine is appropriately indicated. However, in the absence of a clear indication for a strong opioid analgesic, drug-seeking behavior must be suspected and resisted, particularly in individuals with a history of, or propensity for drug abuse. Withdrawal symptoms may occur following abrupt discontinuation of morphine therapy or upon administration of an opioid antagonist. Therefore, patients on prolonged therapy should be withdrawn gradually from the drug if it is no longer required for pain control.

CNS Depression: Morphine should be used only with caution and in reduced dosage during concomitant administration of other opioid analgesics, general anesthetics, phenothiazines and other tranquilizers, sedative-hypnotics, tricyclic antidepressants and other CNS depressants (including alcohol). Respiratory depression, hypotension and profound sedation or coma may result.

Severe pain antagonizes the subjective and respiratory depressant actions of morphine. Should pain suddenly subside, these effects may rapidly become manifest. Patients who are scheduled for cordotomy or other interruption of pain transmission pathways should not receive morphine sulfate sustained release tablets within 24 hours of the procedure.

Pregnancy: Animal studies with morphine and other opioids have indicated the possibility of teratogenic effect. In humans, it is not known whether morphine can cause fetal harm when administered during pregnancy or can affect reproductive capacity. The sustained-release morphine should be given to pregnant patients only if clearly needed and when the anticipated benefits outweigh the risks to the fetus.

Precautions: General: The respiratory depressant effects of morphine, and the capacity to elevate cerebrospinal fluid pressure, may be greatly increased in the presence of an already elevated intracranial pressure produced by trauma. Also, morphine may produce confusion, miosis, vomiting and other side effects which obscure the clinical course of patients with head injury. In such patients, morphine must be used with extreme caution and only if it is judged essential.

Morphine should be used with extreme caution in patients with substantially decreased respiratory reserve, pre-existing respiratory depression, hypoxia or hypercapnia. Such patients are often less sensitive to the stimulatory effects of carbon dioxide on the respiratory centre and the respiratory depressant effects of morphine may reduce respiratory drive to the point of apnea.

Morphine administration may result in severe hypotension in patients whose ability to maintain adequate blood pressure is compromised by reduced blood volume, or concurrent administration of such drugs as phenothiazines or certain anesthetics. Morphine may obscure the diagnosis or clinical course of patients with acute abdominal conditions.

Special Risk Groups: Morphine should be administered with caution, and in reduced dosages, to elderly or debilitated patients, to patients with severely reduced hepatic or renal function, and in patients with Addison's disease, hypothyroidism, prostatic hypertrophy or urethral stricture.

Labor/Delivery and *Lactation:* Morphine crosses the placental barrier and its administration during labor can produce respiratory depression in the neonate. Morphine has been detected in human breast milk. Caution should be exercised if morphine is administered to a nursing mother.

Occupational Hazards: Morphine may impair the mental and/or physical abilities needed for certain potentially hazardous activities such as driving a car or operating machinery. Patients should be cautioned accordingly. Patients should also be cautioned about the combined effects of morphine with other CNS depressants, including other opioids, phenothiazines, sedative/hypnotics and alcohol.

Drug Interactions: Generally, the effects of morphine may be antagonized by acidifying agents and potentiated by alkalizing agents.

The analgesic effect of morphine is potentiated by amphetamines, chlorpromazine and methocarbamol. CNS depressants, such as other opioids, anesthetics, sedatives, hypnotics, barbiturates, phenothiazines, chloral hydrate and glutethimide may enhance the depressant effects of morphine. Monoamine oxidase inhibitors (including procarbazine), pyrazolidone antihistamines, beta-blockers and alcohol may also enhance the depressant effect of morphine.

Morphine may increase the anticoagulant activity of coumarin and other anticoagulants.

Adverse Effects: The major hazards associated with morphine, as with other opioid analgesics, are respiratory depression and, to a lesser degree, circulatory depression. Respiratory arrest, shock and cardiac arrest have occurred following oral or parenteral use of morphine.

Most Common Adverse Effects Requiring Medical Attention: The most frequently observed side effects of opioid analgesics such as morphine are sedation, nausea, vomiting, constipation, lightheadedness, dizziness and sweating.

Sedation: Some degree of sedation is experienced by most patients upon initiation of therapy. This may be at least partly because patients often recuperate from prolonged fatigue after the relief of persistent pain. Drowsiness usually clears in 3 to 5 days and is usually not a reason for concern providing that it is not excessive, or associated with unsteadiness or confusion. If excessive sedation persists the reason for it must be sought. Some of these are: concomitant sedative medications, hepatic or renal failure, exacerbated respiratory failure, higher doses than tolerated in an older patient, or the patient is actually more severely ill than realized. If it is necessary to reduce the dose, it can be carefully increased again after 3 or 4 days if it is obvious that the pain is not being well controlled. Dizziness and unsteadiness may be caused by postural hypotension particularly in elderly or debilitated patients. It can be alleviated if the patient lies down. Because of the slower clearance in patients over 50 years of age, an appropriate dose in this age group may be as low as half or less the usual dose in the younger age group.

Nausea and Vomiting: Nausea and vomiting occur frequently after single doses of opioids or as an early unwanted effect of regular narcotic therapy. When instituting prolonged therapy for chronic pain the routine prescription of an antiemetic should be considered. Patients taking the equivalent of 20 mg or more of oral morphine every 4 hours (60 mg every 12 hours of MS Contin) usually require an antiemetic during early therapy. Small doses of prochlorperazine or haloperidol are the most frequently prescribed antiemetics. Nausea and vomiting tend to lessen in a week or so but may persist due to opioid-induced gastric stasis. In such patients, metoclopramide is often useful.

Constipation: Practically all patients become constipated while taking opioids on a persistent basis. In some patients, particularly the elderly or bedridden, fecal impaction may result. It is essential to caution the patients in this regard and to institute an appropriate regimen of bowel management at the start of prolonged narcotic therapy. Stool softeners, stimulant laxatives and other appropriate measures should be used as required.

Other adverse reactions include: Cardiovascular: supraventricular tachycardia, postural hypotension, palpitations, faintness and syncope.

CNS: euphoria, dysphoria, weakness, insomnia, dizziness, confusion symptoms and occasionally hallucinations.

Gastrointestinal: dry mouth, anorexia, constipation, cramps, taste alterations and biliary tract spasm.

Genitourinary: urinary retention or hesitance, reduced libido or potency.

Endocrine: A syndrome of inappropriate antidiuretic hormone secretion characterized by hyponatremia secondary to decreased free-water excretion may be prominent (monitoring of electrolytes may be necessary).

Allergic: pruritus, urticaria, other skin rashes and edema.

Withdrawal (Abstinence) Syndrome: Physical dependence with or without psychological dependence tend to occur on chronic administration. An abstinence syndrome may be precipitated when opioid administration is discontinued or opioid antagonists administered. The following withdrawal symptoms may be observed after opioids are discontinued: body aches, diarrhea, gooseflesh, loss of appetite, nervousness or restlessness, runny nose, sneezing, tremors or shivering, stomach cramps, nausea, trouble with sleeping, unusual increase in sweating and yawning, weakness, tachycardia and unexplained fever. With appropriate medical use of opioids and gradual withdrawal from the drug, these symptoms are usually mild.

Overdose: Symptoms: Serious morphine overdosage is characterized by respiratory depression (reduced respiratory rate and/or tidal volume; Cheyne-Stokes respiration; cyanosis), extreme somnolence progressing to stupor or coma, flaccidity of skeletal muscle, cold or clammy skin, and sometimes hypotension and bradycardia. Severe overdosage may result in apnea, circulatory collapse, cardiac arrest and death.

Treatment: Primary attention should be given to the establishment of adequate respiratory exchange through the provision of a patent airway and controlled or assisted ventilation. The opioid antagonist naloxone HCl is a specific antidote against respiratory depression due to overdosage or as a result of unusual sensitivity to morphine. An appropriate dose of one of the antagonists should therefore be administered, preferably by the i.v. route. The usual initial i.v. adult dose of naloxone is 0.4 mg or higher. Concomitant efforts at respiratory resuscitation should be carried out. Since the duration of action of morphine, particularly sustained release formulations, may exceed that of the antagonist, the patient should be under continued surveillance and doses of the antagonist should be repeated as needed to maintain adequate respiration.

An antagonist should not be administered in the absence of clinically significant respiratory or cardiovascular depression. Oxygen, i.v. fluids, vasopressors and other supportive measures should be used as indicated. In an individual physically dependent on opioids, the administration of the usual dose of opioid antagonist will precipitate an acute withdrawal syndrome. The severity of this syndrome will depend on the degree of physical dependence and the dose of antagonist administered. The use of opioid antagonists in such individuals should be avoided if possible. If an opioid antagonist must be used to treat serious respiratory depression in the physically dependent patient, the antagonist should be administered with extreme care by using dosage titration, commencing with 10 to 20% of the usual recommended initial dose. Evacuation of gastric contents may be useful in removing unabsorbed drug, particularly when a sustained release formulation has been taken.

Dosage: Administration and dosing of morphine should be individualized bearing in mind the properties of the drug. In addition, the nature and severity of the pain or pains experienced, and the total condition of the patient must be taken into account. Of special importance is other medication given previously or concurrently.

As with other strong opioid analgesics, use of morphine for the management of persistent pain should be preceded by a thorough assessment of the patient and diagnosis of the specific pain or pains and their causes. Use of opioids for the relief of chronic pain, including cancer pain, all important as it may be, should be only one part of a comprehensive approach to pain control including other treatment modalities or drug therapy, nondrug measures and psychosocial support.

References on the important details of cancer pain management may be obtained from the manufacturer.

Initial Adult Dose: Individual dosing requirements vary considerably based on each patient's age, weight, severity of pain, and medical and analgesic history.

The most frequent initial dose is 30 mg orally or rectally every 12 hours.

The suppository may be used in situations where the patient cannot tolerate oral dosing. Up to 2 suppositories of the same or varying strengths may be used at one time, to achieve the required dose for 12-hourly administration.

Suppository administration is achieved by finger length insertion into the rectum, with the patient in a reclining position. Where appropriate, patients should be encouraged to attempt a bowel movement prior to insertion of the suppository. When a bowel movement occurs after insertion of a suppository, loss of a portion of the dose is possible. In such cases, the dose of the suppositories should not be repeated until the next scheduled administration. In the intervening period, breakthrough pain should be managed with appropriate rescue analgesics.

Patients over the age of 50 tend to require much lower doses of morphine than in the younger age group. In elderly and debilitated patients and those with impaired respiratory function or significantly decreased renal function, the initial dose should be one-half the usual recommended dose.

Patients currently receiving other oral morphine formulations may be transferred to MS Contin at the same total daily morphine dosage, equally divided into two 12-hourly MS Contin doses.

For patients who are receiving an alternate opioid, the "oral morphine sulfate equivalent" of the analgesic presently being used should be determined. Having determined the total daily dosage of the present analgesic, Table I (on following page) can be used to calculate the approximate daily oral morphine sulfate dosage that should provide equivalent analgesia. This total daily oral morphine dosage should then be equally divided into two 12-hourly MS Contin doses. Some patients may require a lower dose on initial conversion, followed by further titration during chronic dosing, to maintain optimal analgesia.

Dose Titration: Dose titration is the key to success with morphine therapy. **Proper optimization of doses scaled to the relief of the individual's pain should aim at the regular administration of the lowest dose of morphine which will maintain the patient free of pain at all times.**

Dose adjustments should be based on the patient's clinical response. Higher doses at certain times may be justified in some patients to cover periods of physical activity.

Because of the sustained release properties of MS Contin, dosage adjustments should generally be separated by 48 hours. If dose increments turn out to be required, they should be proportionately greater at the lower dose level (in terms of percentage of previous dose), than when adjusting a higher dose. The usual recommended dose (every 12 hours) increments for the tablets are 15, 30, 45, 60, 90, 120, 150, 180 and 200 mg. The usual recommended dose (q12h) increments for the suppositories are 30, 60, 90, 120, 160 and 200 mg. Above the 200 mg/dose (400 mg/day) increments should be by 30 to 60 mg/dose.

MS Contin is designed to allow 12-hourly dosing. If "breakthrough" pain repeatedly occurs at the end of a dose interval, it is generally an indication for a dosage increase, **not** more frequent administration. However, where judged necessary for optimization of drug effects, the product may be administered every 8 hours. More frequent (than every 8 hours) administration is not recommended.

MS Contin (cont'd)

Table I—MS Contin

Opioid Analgesics: Approximate Analgesic Equivalences[a]

Drug	Equivalent Dose (mg)[b] (compared to morphine 10 mg i.m.) Parenteral	Oral	Duration of Action (hours)
Strong Opioid Agonists			
Morphine	10[c]	60[c]	3-4
Hydromorphone	1.5	7.5	2-4
Anileridine	25	75	2-3
Levorphanol	2	4	4-8
Meperidine[d]	75	300	1-3
Oxymorphone	1.5	5(rectal)	3-4
Methadone[e]			
Heroin	5-8	10-15	3-4
Weak Opioid Agonists			
Codeine	120	200	3-4
Oxycodone		10-15[f]	2-4
Propoxyphene	50	100	2-4
Mixed Agonist-Antagonists[g]			
Pentazocine[d]	60	180	3-4
Nalbuphine	10		3-6
Butorphanol	2		3-4

[a] References: Cancer Pain: A monograph on the Management of Cancer Pain, Health and Welfare Canada 1984. Foley, K.M., New Engl. J.Med. 313: 84-95, 1985. Aronoff, G.M. and Evans, W.O., In Evaluation and Treatment of Chronic Pain, 2nd Ed, G.M. Aronoff (Ed.), Williams and Wilkins, Baltimore, pp. 359-368, 1992. Cherny, N.I. and Portenoy, R.K., In: Textbook of Pain, 3rd Ed., P.D. Wall and R. Melzack (Eds.), Churchill Livingstone, London, pp. 1437-1467, 1994.

[b] **Most of this data was derived from single-dose, acute pain studies and should be considered an approximation for selection of doses when treating chronic pain.**

[c] **For acute pain, the oral or rectal dose of morphine is 6 times the injectable dose. However, for chronic dosing, clinical experience indicated that this ratio is 2-3:1 (i.e., 20 to 30 mg of oral or rectal morphine is equivalent to 10 mg of parenteral morphine). The potency ratio for MS Contin suppositories and MS Contin tablets is approximately 1:1, with repeated dosing.**

[d] These drugs are not recommended for the management of chronic pain.

[e] Extremely variable equianalgesic dose. Patients should undergo individualized titration starting at an equivalent to 1/10 of the morphine dose.

[f] In combination with acetaminophen or ASA. For acute pain, single entity oral oxycodone is twice as potent as oral morphine.

[g] Mixed agonist-antagonists can precipitate withdrawal in patients on pure opioid agonists.

Adjustment or Reduction of Dosage: During the first 2 or 3 days of effective pain relief, the patient may exhibit drowsiness or sleep for prolonged periods. This can be misinterpreted as the effect of excessive analgesic dosing rather than the first sign of relief in a pain-exhausted patient. The dose, therefore, should be maintained for at least 3 days before reduction, provided the sedation is not excessive or associated with unsteadiness and confusion, and respiratory activity and other vital signs are adequate. If excessive sedation persists, the reason(s) for such an effect must be sought. Some of these are: concomitant sedative medications, hepatic or renal failure, exacerbated respiratory failure, higher doses than tolerated by an older patient, or the patient is actually more severely ill than realized. If it is necessary to reduce the dose, it can be carefully increased again after 3 or 4 days if it is obvious that the pain is not being well controlled.

Following successful relief of severe pain, periodic attempts to reduce the narcotic dose should be made. Smaller doses or complete discontinuation may become feasible due to a change in the patient's condition or improved mental state.

The tablets should be swallowed intact, not chewed or crushed. The 200 mg tablet (only) is scored and may be broken in half. The half tablet should also be swallowed intact.

Opioid analgesics may only be partially effective in relieving dysesthetic pain, post-herpetic neuralgia, stabbing pains, activity-related pain, and some forms of headache. This is not to say that patients with advanced cancer suffering from some of these forms of pain should not be given an adequate trial of opioid analgesics, but it may be necessary to refer such patients at an early time for other forms of pain therapy.

Information for the Patient: See Blue Section—Information for the Patient "MS Contin".

Supplied: Suppositories: 30 mg: Each sustained-release suppository contains: morphine sulfate 30 mg. Nonmedicinal ingredients: calcium phosphate, glycerol tricocoate and sodium alginate. Alcohol-, gluten-, lactose-, sulfite- and tartrazine-free. Strips of 6; cartons of 4 strips.

60 mg: Each sustained-release suppository contains: morphine sulfate 60 mg. Nonmedicinal ingredients: calcium phosphate, glycerol tricocoate and sodium alginate. Alcohol-, gluten-, lactose-, sulfite- and tartrazine-free. Strips of 6; cartons of 4 strips.

100 mg: Each sustained-release suppository contains: morphine sulfate 100 mg. Nonmedicinal ingredients: calcium phosphate, glycerol, tricocoate and sodium alginate. Alcohol-, gluten-, lactose-, sulfite- and tartrazine-free. Strips of 6; cartons of 4 strips.

200 mg: Each sustained-release suppository contains: morphine sulfate 200 mg. Nonmedicinal ingredients: calcium phosphate, glycerol tricocoate and sodium alginate. Alcohol-, gluten-, lactose-, sulfite- and tartrazine-free. Strips of 6; cartons of 4 strips.

Tablets: 15 mg: Each green, round, sustained-release, film-coated, bi-convex tablet, imprinted with PF on one side and 15 mg on the other, contains: morphine sulfate 15 mg. Nonmedicinal ingredients: cetostearyl alcohol, D&C Yellow #10 aluminum lake, FD&C Blue #1 aluminum lake, hydroxyethyl cellulose, lactose, magnesium stearate, methylcellulose, polyethylene glycol, talc and titanium dioxide. Alcohol-, gluten-, sulfite- and tartrazine-free. Plastic, opaque bottles of 50; blister packs of 25.

30 mg: Each violet, round, sustained-release, film-coated, bi-convex tablet, imprinted with PF on one side and 30 mg on the other, contains: morphine sulfate 30 mg. Nonmedicinal ingredients: cetostearyl alcohol, D&C Red #7 calcium lake, FD&C Blue #1 aluminum lake, hydroxyethyl cellulose, hydroxypropyl methylcellulose, lactose, magnesium stearate, polyethylene glycol, polysorbate 80, talc and titanium dioxide. Alcohol-, gluten-, sulfite- and tartrazine-free. Plastic, opaque bottles of 50; blister packs of 25.

60 mg: Each orange, round, sustained-release, film-coated, bi-convex tablet, imprinted with PF on one side and 60 mg on the other, contains: morphine sulfate 60 mg. Nonmedicinal ingredients: cetostearyl alcohol, D&C Yellow #10 aluminum lake, FD&C Red #3 aluminum lake, FD&C Yellow #6 aluminum lake, hydroxyethyl cellulose, hydroxylpropyl methylcellulose, lactose, magnesium stearate, polyethylene glycol, talc and titanium dioxide. Alcohol-, gluten-, sulfite- and tartrazine-free. Plastic, opaque bottles of 50; blister packs of 25.

100 mg: Each grey, round, sustained-release, film-coated, bi-convex tablet, imprinted with PF on one side and 100 mg on the other, contains: morphine sulfate 100 mg. Nonmedicinal ingredients: cetostearyl alcohol, FD&C Blue #2 aluminum lake, iron oxide, hydroxyethyl cellulose, hydroxylpropyl methylcellulose, magnesium stearate, polyethylene glycol, talc and titanium dioxide. Alcohol-, gluten-, lactose-, sulfite- and tartrazine-free. Plastic, opaque bottles of 50; blister packs of 25.

200 mg: Each red, scored, caplet-shaped, sustained-release, film-coated, bi-convex tablet, imprinted with PF on one side and 200 mg on the other, contains: morphine sulfate 200 mg. Nonmedicinal ingredients: cetostearyl alcohol, FD&C Blue #2,, FD&C Red #3, FD&C Yellow #6 aluminum lake, hydroxyethyl cellulose, hydroxylpropyl methylcellulose, magnesium stearate, polyethylene glycol, talc and titanium dioxide. May be broken in half. Alcohol-, gluten-, lactose-, sulfite- and tartrazine-free. Plastic, opaque bottles of 50; blister packs of 25.

Store tablets and suppositories 15 to 30 °C. The suppositories may also be refrigerated.

(Shown in Product Recognition Section)

MSD® ENTERIC COATED ASA

Johnson & Johnson • Merck

ASA

Nonsteroidal Anti-inflammatory—Analgesic—Platelet Aggregation Inhibitor

Pharmacology: ASA has analgesic, antipyretic and anti-inflammatory properties.

In rheumatic diseases, although the analgesic and antipyretic effects are useful, the major purpose for which ASA is used is to reduce the intensity of the inflammatory process. Inhibition of prostaglandin synthesis may be involved in the anti-inflammatory action of ASA.

ASA also alters platelet aggregation and release reaction by inhibiting prostaglandin synthesis. Thromboxane A_2 is an essential step in platelet aggregation. ASA prevents thromboxane A_2 formation by acetylation of platelet cyclooxygenase. This inhibition of prostaglandin synthesis is irreversible and affects platelet function for the life of the platelet.

The enteric coating substantially resists disintegration in aqueous fluids having a pH lower than 3.5 for a period of at least 2 hours and is capable of disintegrating in aqueous fluids having a pH of at least 5.5 in from 10 to 30 minutes. Thus, enteric coating effectively inhibits the release of ASA in the stomach, while allowing the tablet to dissolve in the upper portion of the small intestine for absorption from the duodenal area.

Clinical experience has shown that enteric-coated ASA diminishes or eliminates gastric distress during long-term treatment with high doses of ASA.

Pharmacokinetics: Since this product is enteric-coated, the pharmacological effects are not immediate. Peak serum salicylate concentrations are reached 6 to 8 hours after single oral administration. This means that MSD Enteric Coated ASA tablets are more useful for chronic administration as in arthritis, than for providing prompt relief of pain and fever.

The plasma half-life of salicylate concentrations is dose-dependent being 3 to 6 hours at low doses (325 mg to 1.3 g) and 15 to 30 hours at high doses.

Indications: Whenever gastric intolerance to ASA is of concern.

For the relief of signs and symptoms of the following: osteoarthritis, rheumatoid arthritis, spondylitis, bursitis and other forms of rheumatism, musculoskeletal disorders and rheumatic fever, however, penicillin and other appropriate therapy should be administered concomitantly. ASA is generally considered to be the primary therapy for most forms of arthritis.

Also indicated for reducing the risk of recurrent transient ischemic attacks or stroke in men who have had transient ischemia of the brain due to fibrin platelet emboli. At present, there is no evidence that ASA is effective in reducing transient ischemic attacks in women, or is of benefit in the treatment of completed strokes in men or women.

Contraindications: Sensitivity to the ingredients; active peptic ulcer; patients who had a bronchospastic reaction to ASA or nonsteroidal anti-inflammatory drugs.

Warnings: ASA is one of the most frequent causes of accidental poisoning in toddlers and infants. ASA should, therefore, be kept well out of the reach of all children.

Precautions: Salicylates should be administered with caution to patients with asthma and other allergic conditions, with a history of gastrointestinal ulcerations, with bleeding tendencies, with significant anemia or with hypoprothrombinemia.

Salicylates can produce changes in thyroid function tests.

Acute hepatitis has been reported rarely in patients with systemic lupus erythematosus and juvenile rheumatoid arthritis with plasma salicylate concentrations above 25 mg/100 mL. Patients have recovered upon cessation of therapy.

Pregnancy: ASA does not appear to have any teratogenic effects. ASA has been found to delay parturition in rats. This effect has also been described with nonsteroidal anti-inflammatory agents which inhibit prostaglandin synthesis.

High doses (3 g daily) of ASA during pregnancy may lengthen the gestation and parturition time.

Because of possible adverse effects on the neonate and the potential for increased maternal blood loss, ASA should be avoided during the last three months of pregnancy.

Children: Recent studies have suggested that ASA usage may cause the development of Reye's syndrome in children and teenagers with acute febrile illnesses, especially influenza and varicella. Although a direct causal relationship has not been established, it is recommended that salicylates be avoided when possible, in children and teenagers with influenza or varicella.

Drug Interactions: Caution is necessary when ASA and anticoagulants are prescribed concurrently, as ASA may potentiate the action of anticoagulants.

Salicylates may potentiate sulfonylurea hypoglycemic agents. Large doses of salicylates may have a hypoglycemic action, and thus, affect the insulin requirements of diabetics.

Although salicylates in large doses are uricosuric agents, smaller amounts may depress uric acid clearance, and thus decrease the uricosuric effects of probenecid, sulfinpyrazone and phenylbutazone.

Sodium excretion produced by spironolactone may be decreased in the presence of salicylates.

Salicylates also retard the renal elimination of methotrexate.

Adverse Effects: Gastrointestinal: nausea, vomiting, diarrhea, gastrointestinal bleeding and/or ulceration.
Ear: tinnitus, vertigo, hearing loss.
Hematologic: leukopenia, thrombocytopenia, purpura.
Dermatologic and Hypersensitivity: urticaria, angioedema, pruritus, various skin eruptions, asthma and anaphylaxis.
Miscellaneous: acute reversible hepatotoxicity, mental confusion, drowsiness, sweating and thirst.

Overdose: Symptoms: In mild overdosage, these may include rapid and deep breathing, nausea, vomiting (leading to alkalosis), hyperpnea, vertigo, tinnitus, flushing, sweating, thirst and tachycardia. (High blood levels of ASA lead to acidosis.) Severe cases may show fever, hemorrhage, excitement, confusion, convulsions or coma and respiratory failure.

Treatment: Treatment is essentially symptomatic and supportive. Administer water, universal antidote and remove by gastric lavage or emesis. Force fluids (e.g., salty broth) to replace sodium loss. If the patient is unable to retain fluids orally, the alkalosis can be treated by hypertonic saline i.v. If salicylism acidosis is present, sodium bicarbonate i.v. is preferred because it increases the renal excretion of salicylates. Vitamin K is indicated if there is evidence of hemorrhage. Hemodialysis has been used with success.

Respiratory depression may require artificial ventilation with oxygen. Convulsions may best be treated by the administration of succinylcholine and artificial ventilation with oxygen. CNS depressant agents should not be used.

Hyperthermia and dehydration are immediate threats to life and initial therapy must be directed to their correction and to the maintenance of adequate renal function. External cooling with cool water or alcohol should be provided quickly to any child who has a rectal temperature over 40°C.

Dosage: Analgesic/Antipyretic: Patients should be advised not to exceed 4 g daily. Single doses should not be administered more frequently than every 4 hours.
Adults: Single dose should not exceed 650 mg, to be repeated every 4 to 6 hours; the total daily dosage should not exceed 4 000 mg ASA unless otherwise advised by a physician, i.e., 12 tablets 325 mg, or 6 tablets 650 mg. If the underlying condition requires continued use of ASA for more than 5 days, a physician should be consulted.
Children: **Only** as directed by a physician.
Anti-inflammatory: Because the suppression of inflammation increases with the dose of salicylate even beyond the point of toxicity, the therapeutic objective is to employ as large a dose as possible short of toxicity. Most patients will tolerate blood salicylate levels in the range of 20 to 25 mg %. The most common reason for failing to obtain a therapeutic response to ASA is the administration of inadequate doses.

The generally accepted way to achieve effective "anti-inflammatory" salicylate blood levels of 20 to 25 mg% is to titrate the dosage by starting with 2.6 to 3.9 g daily, according to the size, age and sex of the patient. If necessary, the dosage is then gradually adjusted by daily increments of 0.65 g. Optimally, salicylate therapy should be monitored by periodic blood salicylate level determinations. If this is not practical, the appearance of auditory symptoms in the form of tinnitus or deafness are acceptable as an indication of the maximum tolerated salicylate dose.

In adults, the median dose at which tinnitus develops is 4.5 g/day, but the range extends from 2.6 to 6 g/day.

Intermittent administration is ineffective. Patients should be advised not to vary the dose from day to day depending on the level of pain because that often fluctuates independently of the intensity of the inflammation. A continuous regimen of 0.65 g 4 times daily is considered to be minimum therapy for adults. ASA should be administered 4 times daily. For nighttime and early morning benefits, the last dose should be given at bedtime.

There is an inverse relation between blood salicylate levels at which auditory symptoms appear and the age of the patient. In the young adult, this is usually in the range of 20 to 30 mg%. In children, however, the level may be much higher, or the effect apparently absent. Because salicylate toxicity may appear without such warning in children, the usual practice is to give ASA in a daily dose of 50 to 80 mg/kg of body weight and to follow blood levels aiming for a concentration of about 30 mg%.
Rheumatic Fever: A total daily dosage of 80 mg/kg of body weight administered in divided doses to allay the pain, swelling and fever.
Cerebral Ischemic Attacks (Men): The recommended dosage is 1 300 mg/day (650 mg twice a day or 325 mg 4 times a day).

Information for the Patient: See Blue Section—Information for the Patient "MSD Enteric Coated ASA".

Supplied: 325 mg: Each round, brown, film-coated, unprinted, enteric-coated tablet contains: ASA 325 mg. Nonmedicinal ingredients: cellulose acetate phthalate, cornstarch, dictyl phthalate, guar gum, hydrogenated vegetable oil, hydroxypropyl methylcellulose, microcrystalline cellulose, polyvinyl acetate phthalate, red ferric oxide, sodium lauryl sulfate and sucrose. Bottles of 1 000 (for dispensing use only).
650 mg: Each oval, orange, film-coated, unprinted, enteric-coated tablet contains: ASA 650 mg. Nonmedicinal ingredients: cellulose acetate phthalate, cornstarch, dietyl phthalate, guar gum, hydrogenated vegetable oil, hydroxypropyl cellulose, hydroxypropyl methylcellulose, microcrystalline cellulose, sodium lauryl sulfate, sunset yellow aluminum lake and titanium dioxide. Bottles of 1 000 (for dispensing use only).

Store at 15 to 30°C. Protect from moisture.

(Shown in Product Recognition Section)

MS•IR® Ⓝ
Purdue Frederick

Morphine Sulfate
Opioid Analgesic

Pharmacology: Morphine is an opioid analgesic which exerts an agonist effect at specific, saturable opioid receptors in the CNS and other tissues. In man, morphine produces a variety of effects including analgesia, constipation from decreased gastrointestinal motility, suppression of the cough reflex, respiratory depression from reduced responsiveness of the respiratory centre to CO_2, nausea and vomiting via stimulation of the CTZ, changes in mood including euphoria and dysphoria, sedation, mental clouding, and alterations of the endocrine and autonomic nervous systems.

Morphine is readily absorbed when given orally, rectally or by s.c. or i.m. injection. Due to first-pass metabolism in the liver, the effect of an oral dose is less than after parenteral administration. With repeated regular dosing, oral morphine is about 1/3 as potent as when given by i.m. injection. Morphine is primarily excreted in the urine as morphine-3-glucuronide. Formation of glucuronidated metabolites is less following rectal administration compared to oral administration. About 7 to 10% of a dose of morphine is excreted in the feces via the bile.

Indications: For the symptomatic relief of severe pain.

Contraindications: Should not be given to patients with: hypersensitivity to opiate analgesics; acute asthma or other obstructive airway disease and acute respiratory depression; cor pulmonale; cardiac arrhythmias; acute alcoholism; delirium tremens; severe CNS depression; convulsive disorders; increased cerebrospinal or intracranial pressure; head injury; brain tumor; suspected surgical abdomen; concomitant MAO inhibitors (or within 14 days of such therapy).

Warnings: Drug Dependence: As with other opioids, tolerance and physical dependence tend to develop upon repeated administration of morphine and there is potential for abuse of the drug and for development of strong psychological dependence. Morphine should therefore be prescribed and handled with the high degree of caution appropriate to the use of a drug with strong abuse potential. Drug abuse is not, however, a problem in patients with severe pain in which morphine is appropriately indicated. However, in the absence of a clear indication for a strong opioid analgesic, drug-seeking behavior must be suspected and resisted, particularly in individuals with a history of, or propensity for drug abuse. Withdrawal symptoms may occur following abrupt discontinuation of morphine therapy or upon administration of an opioid antagonist. Therefore, patients on prolonged therapy should be withdrawn gradually from the drug if it is no longer required for pain control.
CNS Depression: Morphine should be used only with caution and in reduced dosage during concomitant administration of other opioid analgesics, general anesthetics, phenothiazines and other tranquilizers, sedative-hypnotics, tricyclic antidepressants and other CNS depressants (including alcohol). Respiratory depression, hypotension and profound sedation or coma may result.

Severe pain antagonizes the subjective and respiratory depressant actions of morphine. Should pain suddenly subside, these effects may rapidly become manifest. Patients who are scheduled for cordotomy or other interruption of pain transmission pathways should not receive morphine within 24 hours of the procedure.
Pregnancy: Animal studies with morphine and other opioids have indicated the possibility of teratogenic effect. In humans, it is not known whether morphine can cause fetal harm when administered during pregnancy or can affect reproductive capacity. Morphine should be given to pregnant patients only if clearly needed and when the anticipated benefits outweigh the risks to the fetus.

Precautions: General: The respiratory depressant effects of morphine, and the capacity to elevate cerebrospinal fluid pressure, may be greatly increased in the presence of an already elevated intracranial pressure produced by trauma. Also, morphine may produce confusion, miosis, vomiting and other side effects which obscure the clinical course of patients with head injury. In such patients, morphine must be used with extreme caution and only if it is judged essential.

Morphine should be used with extreme caution in patients with substantially decreased respiratory reserve, pre-existing respiratory depression, hypoxia or hypercapnia. Such patients are often less sensitive to the stimulatory effects of carbon dioxide on the respiratory centre and the respiratory depressant effects of morphine may reduce respiratory drive to the point of apnea.

Morphine administration may result in severe hypotension in patients whose ability to maintain adequate blood pressure is compromised by reduced blood volume, or concurrent administration of such drugs as phenothiazines or certain anesthetics.

Morphine may obscure the diagnosis or clinical course of patients with acute abdominal conditions.
Special Risk Groups: Morphine should be administered with caution, and in reduced dosages, to elderly or debilitated patients, to patients with severely reduced hepatic or renal function, and to patients with Addison's disease, hypothyroidism, prostatic hypertrophy or urethral stricture.
Labor/Delivery and *Lactation:* Morphine crosses the placental barrier and its administration during labor can produce respiratory depression in the neonate. Morphine has been detected in human breast milk. Caution should be exercised if morphine is administered to a nursing mother.
Occupational Hazards: Morphine may impair the mental and/or physical abilities needed for certain potentially hazardous activities such as driving a car or operating machinery. Patients should be cautioned accordingly.

Patients should also be cautioned about the combined effects of morphine with other CNS depressants, including other opioids, phenothiazines, sedative/hypnotics and alcohol.
Drug Interactions: Generally, the effects of morphine may be antagonized by acidifying agents and potentiated by alkalizing agents.

The analgesic effect of morphine is potentiated by amphetamines, chlorpromazine and methocarbamol. CNS depressants, such as other opioids, anesthetics, sedatives, hypnotics, barbiturates, phenothiazines, chloral hydrate and glutethimide may enhance the depressant effects of morphine. MAO inhibitors (including procarbazine HCl), pyrazolidone antihistamines, beta-blockers and alcohol may also enhance the depressant effect of morphine.

Morphine may increase the anticoagulant activity of coumarin and other anticoagulants.

Adverse Effects: The major hazards with morphine, as with other narcotic analgesics, are respiratory depression and, to a lesser degree, circulatory depression. Respiratory arrest, shock and cardiac arrest have occurred following oral or parenteral use of morphine.
Most Common Adverse Effects Requiring Medical Attention: The most frequently observed side effects of narcotic analgesics such as morphine are sedation, nausea and vomiting, constipation, lightheadedness, dizziness and sweating.
Sedation: Some degree of sedation is experienced by most patients upon initiation of therapy. This may be a least partly because patients often recuperate from prolonged fatigue after the relief of persistent pain. Drowsiness usually clears in 3 to 5 days and is usually not a reason for concern providing that it is not excessive, or associated with unsteadiness or confusion. If excessive sedation persists, the reason for it must be sought. Some of these are: concomitant sedative medications, hepatic or renal failure, exacerbated respiratory failure, higher doses than tolerated in an older patient, or the patient is actually more severely ill than realized. If it is necessary to reduce the dose, it can be carefully increased again after 3 or 4 days if it is obvious that the pain is not being well controlled. Dizziness and unsteadiness may be caused by postural hypotension particularly in elderly or debilitated patients. It can be alleviated if the patient lies down. Because of the slower clearance in patients over 50 years of age, an

MS•IR (cont'd)

appropriate dose in this age group may be as low as half or less the usual dose in the younger age group.

Nausea and Vomiting: Nausea and vomiting occur frequently after single doses of opioids or as an early unwanted effect of regular opioid therapy. When instituting prolonged therapy for chronic pain the routine prescription of an antiemetic should be considered. Patients taking a single dose of 20 mg or more of oral morphine every 4 hours usually require an antiemetic during early therapy. Small doses of prochlorperazine or haloperidol are the most frequently prescribed antiemetics. Nausea and vomiting tend to lessen in a week or so but may persist due to opioid-induced gastric stasis. In such patients, metoclopramide is often useful.

Constipation: Practically all patients become constipated while taking opioids on a persistent basis. In some instances, particularly the elderly or bedridden, fecal impaction may result. It is essential to caution the patients in this regard and to institute an appropriate regimen of bowel management at the start of prolonged opioid therapy. Stool softeners, stimulant laxatives and other appropriate measures should be used as required.

Other adverse reactions include: Cardiovascular: supraventricular tachycardia, postural hypotension, palpitations, faintness and syncope.

CNS: euphoria, dysphoria, weakness, insomnia, dizziness, confusion and occasionally hallucinations.

Gastrointestinal: dry mouth, anorexia, constipation, cramps, taste alterations and biliary tract cramps.

Genitourinary: urinary retention or hesitance, reduced libido or potency.

Endocrine: A syndrome of inappropriate antidiuretic hormone secretion characterized by hyponatremia secondary to decreased free-water excretion may be prominent (monitoring of electrolytes may be necessary).

Allergic: pruritus, urticaria, other skin rashes and edema.

Withdrawal (Abstinence) Syndrome: Physical dependence with or without psychological dependence tends to occur on chronic administration. An abstinence syndrome may be precipitated when opioid administration is discontinued or opioid antagonists administered. The following withdrawal symptoms may be observed after opioids are discontinued: body aches, diarrhea, gooseflesh, loss of appetite, nervousness or restlessness, runny nose, sneezing, tremors or shivering, stomach cramps, nausea, trouble with sleeping, unusual increase in sweating and yawning, weakness, tachycardia and unexplained fever. With appropriate medical use of opioids and gradual withdrawal from the drug, these symptoms are usually mild.

Overdose: Symptoms: Serious morphine overdosage is characterized by respiratory depression (reduced respiratory rate and/or tidal volume; Cheyne-Stokes respiration; cyanosis), extreme somnolence progressing to stupor or coma, flaccidity of skeletal muscle, cold or clammy skin, and sometimes hypotension and bradycardia. Severe overdosage may result in apnea, circulatory collapse, cardiac arrest and death.

Treatment: Primary attention should be given to the establishment of adequate respiratory exchange through the provision of a patent airway and controlled or assisted ventilation. The opioid antagonist naloxone HCl is a specific antidote against respiratory depression due to overdosage or as a result of unusual sensitivity to morphine. An appropriate dose should therefore be administered, preferably by the i.v. route. The usual initial i.v. adult dose of naloxone is 0.4 mg or higher. Concomitant efforts at respiratory resuscitation should be carried out. Since the duration of action of morphine may exceed that of the antagonist, the patient should be under continued surveillance and doses of the antagonist should be repeated as needed to maintain adequate respiration.

An antagonist should not be administered in the absence of clinically significant respiratory or cardiovascular depression. Oxygen, i.v. fluids, vasopressors and other supportive measures should be used as indicated.

In an individual physically dependent on opioids, the administration of the usual dose of opioid antagonist will precipitate an acute withdrawal syndrome. The severity of this syndrome will depend on the degree of physical dependence and the dose of antagonist administered. The use of opioid antagonists in such individuals should be avoided if possible. If an opioid antagonist must be used to treat serious respiratory depression in the physically dependent patient, the antagonist should be administered with extreme care by using dosage titration, commencing with 10 to 20% of the usual recommended initial dose.

Evacuation of gastric contents may be useful in removing unabsorbed drug.

Dosage: Administration and dosing of morphine should be individualized bearing in mind the properties of the drug. In addition, the nature and severity of the pain or pains experienced, and the total condition of the patient must be taken into account. Of special importance is other medication given previously or concurrently.

As with other strong opioid analgesics, use of morphine for the management of persistent pain should be preceded by a thorough assessment of the patient and diagnosis of the specific pain or pains and their causes. Use of opioids for the relief of chronic pain, including cancer pain, all important as it may be, should be only one part of a comprehensive approach to pain control including other treatment modalities or drug therapy, nondrug measures and psychosocial support.

Initial Adult Dose: Individual dosing requirements vary considerably based on each patient's age, weight, severity of pain, and medical and analgesic history.

The most frequent initial dose is 10 mg every 4 hours as needed for acute pain and every 4 hours around the clock for chronic pain, or as directed by a physician. The suppository may be used in situations where the patient cannot tolerate oral dosing, at the same dosage and frequency.

Patients over the age of 50 tend to require much lower doses of morphine than in the younger age group. In elderly and debilitated patients and those with impaired respiratory function or significantly decreased renal function, the initial dose should be one half the usual recommended dose.

For patients who are receiving an alternate opioid, the "oral morphine sulfate equivalent" of the analgesic presently being used should be determined. Having determined the total daily dosage of the present analgesic, Table I can be used to calculate the approximate daily oral morphine sulfate dosage that should provide equivalent analgesia.

Table I—MS•IR

Opioids: Approximate Analgesic Equivalences[a]

Drug	Equivalent Dose (mg)[b] (compared to morphine 10 mg i.m.)		Duration of Action (hours)
	Parenteral	**Oral**	
Strong Opioid Agonists			
Morphine	10	60[c]	3-4
Oxycodone[d]	15	30	2-4
Hydromorphone	1.5	7.5	2-4
Anileridine	25	75	2-3
Levorphanol	2	4	4-8
Meperidine[f]	75	300	1-3
Oxymorphone	1.5	5 (rectal)	3-4
Methadone[e]	—	—	—
Heroin	5-8	10-15	3-4
Weak Opioid Agonists			
Codeine	120	200	3-4
Propoxyphene	50	100	2-4
Mixed Agonist-Antagonists[g]			
Pentazocine[f]	60	180	3-4
Nalbuphine	10	—	3-6
Butorphanol	2	—	3-4

[a]References: Cancer Pain: A Monograph on the Management of Cancer Pain, Health and Welfare Canada 1984.
Foley, K.M., New Engl. J. Med. 313: 84-95, 1985.
Aronoff, G.M. and Evans, W.O., In Evaluation and Treatment of Chronic Pain, 2nd Ed, G.M. Aronoff (Ed.), Williams and Wilkins, Baltimore, pp. 359-368, 1992.
Cherny, N.I. and Portenoy, R.K., In: Textbook of Pain, 3rd Ed., P.D. Wall and R. Melzack (Eds.), Churchill Livingstone, London, pp. 1437-1467, 1994.

[b]**Most of the data were derived from single-dose, acute pain studies and should be considered an approximation for selection of doses when treating chronic pain.**

[c]**For acute pain, the oral or rectal dose of morphine is 6 times the injectable dose. However, for chronic dosing, clinical experience indicates that this ratio is 2-3: 1 (i.e., 20 to 30 mg of oral or rectal morphine is equivalent to 10 mg of parenteral morphine).**

[d]Based on single entity oral oxycodone in acute pain.

[e]Extremely variable equianalgesic dose. Patients should undergo individualized titration starting at an equivalent to 1/10 of the morphine dose.

[f]Not recommended for the management of chronic pain.

[g]Mixed agonist-antagonists can precipitate withdrawal in patients on pure opioid agonists.

Dose Titration: Dose titration is the key to success with morphine therapy. Proper optimization of doses scaled to the relief of the individual's pain should aim at the **regular** administration of the lowest dose of morphine which will maintain the patient free of pain at all times.

Dose adjustments should be based on the patient's clinical response. Higher doses may be justified in some patients to cover periods of physical activity.

Adjustment or Reduction of Dosage: During the first 2 or 3 days of effective pain relief, the patient with chronic pain may exhibit drowsiness or sleep for prolonged periods. This can be misinterpreted as the effect of excessive analgesic dosing rather than the first sign of relief in a pain-exhausted patient. The dose, therefore, should be maintained for at least 3 days before reduction, provided the sedation is not excessive or associated with unsteadiness and confusional symptoms, and respiratory activity and other vital signs are adequate. If excessive sedation persists, the reason(s) for such an effect must be sought. Some of these are: concomitant sedative medications, hepatic or renal failure, exacerbated respiratory failure, higher doses than tolerated by an older patient, or the patient is actually more severely ill than realized. If it is necessary to reduce the dose, it can be carefully increased again after 3 or 4 days if it is obvious that the pain is not being well controlled.

Following successful relief of severe pain, periodic attempts to reduce the opioid dose should be made. Smaller doses or complete discontinuation may become feasible due to a change in the patient's condition or improved mental state.

Opioid analgesics may only be partially effective in relieving dysesthetic pain, postherpetic neuralgia, stabbing pains, activity-related pain, and some forms of headache. This is not to say that patients with advanced cancer suffering from some of these forms of pain should not be given an adequate trial of opiate analgesics, but it may be necessary to refer such patients at an early time for other forms of pain therapy. Pain without nociception is usually not narcotic-responsive.

Supplied: Suppositories: 10 mg: Each smooth, white, immediate-release, rectal suppository contains: morphine sulfate pentahydrate 10 mg. Nonmedicinal ingredients: glycerol tricocoate. Boxes of 4 strips of 6. Store at room temperature.

20 mg: Each smooth, white, immediate-release, rectal suppository contains: morphine sulfate pentahydrate 20 mg. Nonmedicinal ingredients: glycerol tricocoate. Boxes of 4 strips of 6. Store at room temperature.

30 mg: Each smooth, white, immediate-release, rectal suppository contains: morphine sulfate pentahydrate 30 mg. Nonmedicinal ingredients: glycerol tricocoate. Boxes of 4 strips of 6. Store at room temperature.

Tablets: 5 mg: Each round, white, film-coated, immediate-release tablet, scored with "5" engraved on one side and "PF" on the other, contains: morphine sulfate pentahydrate 5 mg. Nonmedicinal ingredients: croscarmellose sodium, hydroxypropyl methylcellulose, lactose, magnesium stearate, microcrystalline cellulose and polyethylene glycol 400.

10 mg: Each round, white, film-coated, immediate-release tablet, scored with "10" engraved on one side and "PF" on the other, contains: morphine sulfate pentahydrate 10 mg. Nonmedicinal ingredients: croscarmellose sodium, hydroxypropyl methylcellulose, lactose, magnesium stearate, microcrystalline cellulose and polyethylene glycol 400.

20 mg: Each caplet-shaped, white, film-coated, immediate-release tablet, scored with "20" engraved on one side and "PF" on the other, contains: morphine sulfate pentahydrate 20 mg. Nonmedicinal ingredients: croscarmellose sodium, hydroxypropyl methylcellulose, lactose, magnesium stearate, microcrystalline cellulose and polyethylene glycol 400.

30 mg: Each caplet-shaped, white, film-coated, immediate-release tablet, scored with "30" engraved on one side and "PF" on the other, contains: morphine sulfate pentahydrate 30 mg. Nonmedicinal ingredients: croscarmellose sodium, hydroxypropyl methylcellulose, lactose, magnesium stearate, microcrystalline cellulose and polyethylene glycol 400.

Plastic opaque bottles of 50 and control packs of 4×25. Store at room temperature.

(Shown in Product Recognition Section)

Reviewed 1997

Many medications require special consideration when administered to geriatric patients. Refer to Drugs and Older Individuals found within the CLIN-INFO SECTION.

MUCAINE®
Axcan Pharma

Oxethazaine—Aluminum Hydroxide—Magnesium Hydroxide

Antacid—Mucosal Anesthetic

Pharmacology: Alumina gel and magnesium hydroxide react chemically to neutralize or buffer existing quantities of stomach acid but have no direct effect on its production. This action increases gastric pH, providing symptomatic relief of hyperacidity.

Gastroscopic observations reveal that alumina gel, especially when swallowed undiluted, forms a diffuse coating over the inflamed gastric mucosa for a variable period of time. Because of this adherent vehicle, oxethazaine exerts a prolonged topical anesthetic action.

Oxethazaine is a topical anesthetic which when applied to the mucous membranes produces a more potent anesthesia of longer duration than either cocaine or lidocaine. An ultra-dilute solution of 0.0005% oxethazaine induces the same duration of anesthesia of rabbit cornea as does the more concentrated 0.25% solution of cocaine; as a 1% solution of lidocaine; or as a 2% solution of procaine.

The higher order of potency of oxethazaine permits clinical use of dilute solutions; a 0.2% concentration of oxethazaine in alumina gel is therapeutically effective. In vitro, oxethazaine produces antispasmodic action on smooth muscle. It antagonizes the action of serotonin on smooth muscle as demonstrated on isolated rabbit jejunum strips.

A wide margin of safety exists between the effective dose of oxethazaine in alumina gel and the oral toxic dose of the compound. In mice, the oral LD50 of oxethazaine is approximately 400 mg of base/kg; when suspended in alumina gel as a vehicle the oral LD50 in mice is 1 012 mg of base/kg. The effective dose, 5 to 10 mL, contains 10 or 20 mg of oxethazaine respectively; this is only 0.2 or 0.4 mg/kg of body weight for a human weighing 50 kg. In humans, toxic effects have not been observed on continued ingestion of recommended therapeutic doses.

Pharmacokinetics: Studies have shown that a small amount of aluminum from aluminum hydroxide is absorbed from the intestine. Approximately 10% of the magnesium in magnesium hydroxide is absorbed from the intestine.

After oral administration of 20 mg oxethazaine contained in 10 mL of alumina gel with magnesium hydroxide, the peak oxethazaine plasma level was approximately 20 ng/mL and occurred about 1 hour after dosing.

Oxethazaine undergoes rapid and extensive biotransformation resulting in a short plasma half-life of approximately one hour. Less than 0.1% unchanged oxethazaine was recovered in the urine within 24 hours. Major metabolites were β-hydroxy-mephentermine and β-hydroxy-phentermine. Mephentermine and phentermine appeared in the plasma in pharmacologically insignificant amounts and their cumulative 24-hour urinary excretion was less than 0.1% of the dose administered.

Indications: For the symptomatic relief of peptic ulcer, gastritis, and esophagitis. Symptoms of esophageal irritation are usually relieved in patients who do not respond to antacid therapy alone.

Contraindications: This product should not be given to any patient who has demonstrated a sensitivity to it.

The use of aluminum- or magnesium-containing antacids is contraindicated in patients with symptoms of appendicitis since these products may increase the danger of perforation or rupture due to their constipating or laxative effects.

The use of aluminum-containing antacids (except those containing aluminum phosphate) is contraindicated in patients with hypophosphatemia due to the phosphate binding properties of aluminum salts.

The use of magnesium-containing antacids is contraindicated in patients with severe renal function impairment due to increased danger of occurrence of hypermagnesemia.

Warnings: Adequate diagnostic studies are recommended. The possibility of gastrointestinal carcinoma should be considered in patients with protracted or recurrent indigestion.

Precautions: The use of magnesium-containing antacids in patients with mild to moderate renal impairment should be carefully monitored due to a possible increased danger of hypermagnesemia.

In patients with chronic renal failure, hyperaluminemia may occur.

Hypophosphatemia may occur with prolonged administration or large doses of aluminum-containing antacids (except aluminum phosphate) especially in patients with an inadequate dietary intake of phosphorus.

Laboratory Tests: Serum phosphate levels should be monitored at monthly or bi-monthly intervals in patients on maintenance hemodialysis who are receiving chronic antacid therapy.

Carcinogenesis, Mutagenesis, and Impairment of Fertility: Long-term animal studies have not been performed to evaluate the carcinogenic or mutagenic potential of Mucaine. No evidence of impaired fertility was revealed during a breeding experiment with male and female rats fed Mucaine orally throughout the experiment. The effect on human fertility is not known.

Pregnancy: A reproduction study performed in rabbits revealed no evidence of harm to the fetus. There are, however, no adequate or well-controlled studies in pregnant women. Use during pregnancy if the benefits outweigh the potential risks.

Lactation: It is not known if Mucaine is excreted in breast milk. Because many drugs are excreted in breast milk, a decision should be made whether to discontinue nursing or to discontinue Mucaine, taking into account the importance of the drug to the mother and the potential risk to the infant.

Children: The safety and effectiveness of Mucaine in children have not been established. Therefore this product is recommended for adult use only.

Adverse Effects: Hypersensitivity reactions including skin eruptions (dermatitis, urticaria), pruritus, glossitis, angioedema, and collapse have been reported in occasional cases.

If the dose of this product exceeds 60 mL/day, some patients may experience dizziness, faintness, or drowsiness.

Magnesium-containing antacids may cause diarrhea. Aluminum-containing antacids may cause constipation.

Drug Interactions: The rate and/or extent of absorption of many drugs may be increased or decreased when they are used concurrently with aluminum-magnesium hydroxide-containing antacids. Therefore, as a general rule, medication should not be taken within 1 to 2 hours of an antacid, if possible.

An incomplete list of substances for which the above statement has been shown to apply includes; tetracycline, iron salts, chlorpromazine, levodopa, isoniazid, digoxin, H_2-antagonists, indomethacin, nitrofurantoin, and dicumarol.

An increase in the plasma level of quinidine and possible toxicity may result if alkalization of the urine occurs during antacid therapy.

Overdose: Symptoms and Treatment: Patients should be observed with symptomatic therapy instituted as indicated by the clinical situation.

Dosage: The recommended dose is 5 to 10 mL taken 4 times daily, 15 minutes before meals and at bedtime. Do not exceed recommended dosage.

The maximum dose recommended may be decreased following adequate control of the symptoms. The suspension should preferably be taken undiluted; however, if desired, it may be followed by a sip of water.

Supplied: Each 5 mL of oral suspension contains: oxethazaine 10 mg, aluminum hydroxide 300 mg and magnesium hydroxide 100 mg. Nonmedicinal ingredients: artificial flavor, glycerin, methocel, methylparaben, peppermint oil, propylparaben, sodium benzoate, sodium cyclamate and sorbitol solution. Energy: 10 kJ (2.4 kcal). Tartrazine-free. Bottles of 350 and 500 mL. Shake well before use. Keep tightly closed. Store in a cool area. Protect from freezing.

MUCOMYST®
Roberts

Acetylcysteine

Mucolytic—Antidote for Acetaminophen Poisoning

Pharmacology: The viscosity of pulmonary mucous secretions depends on the concentrations of mucoprotein and to a lesser extent deoxyribonucleic acid (DNA). The latter increases with increasing purulence owing to cellular debris. The mucolytic action of acetylcysteine is related to the sulfhydryl group in the molecule. This group probably "opens" disulfide linkages in mucus thereby lowering the viscosity. The mucolytic activity of acetylcysteine is unaltered by the presence of DNA, and increases with increasing pH. Significant mucolysis occurs between pH 7 and 9.

Acetaminophen is rapidly absorbed from the upper gastrointestinal tract with peak plasma levels occurring between 30 and 60 minutes after therapeutic doses and usually within 4 hours following an overdose. The parent compound, which is non-toxic, is extensively metabolized in the liver to form principally the sulfate and glucuronide conjugates which are also non-toxic and are rapidly excreted in the urine.

A small fraction of the ingested dose is metabolized in the liver by the cytochrome P-450 mixed function oxidase enzyme system to form a reactive, potentially toxic, intermediate metabolite which preferentially conjugates with hepatic glutathione to form the non-toxic cysteine and mercapturic acid derivatives which are then excreted by the kidney.

Therapeutic doses of acetaminophen do not saturate the glucuronide and sulfate conjugation pathways and do not result in formation of sufficient reactive metabolite to deplete glutathione stores.

However, following ingestion of a large overdose (150 mg/kg or greater) the glucuronide and sulfate conjugation pathways are saturated resulting in a larger fraction of the drug being metabolized via the P-450 pathway. The increased formation of reactive metabolite may deplete the hepatic stores of glutathione with subsequent binding of the metabolite to protein molecules within the hepatocyte resulting in cellular necrosis. Acetylcysteine probably protects the liver by maintaining or restoring the glutathione levels, or by acting as an alternate substrate for conjugation with and thus detoxification of the reactive metabolite.

Indications: As adjuvant therapy for patients with abnormal, viscid, or inspissated mucous secretions in such conditions as: chronic bronchopulmonary disease (chronic emphysema, emphysema with bronchitis, chronic asthmatic bronchitis, tuberculosis, bronchiectasis and primary amyloidosis of the lung); acute bronchopulmonary disease (pneumonia, bronchitis, tracheobronchitis); pulmonary complications of cystic fibrosis; post-tracheostomy care; pulmonary complications associated with surgery; use during anesthesia; post-traumatic chest conditions; atelectasis due to mucous obstruction; diagnostic bronchial studies (bronchograms, bronchospirometry and bronchial wedge catheterization).

Administered orally or i.v., as an antidote to prevent or lessen hepatic injury which may occur following the ingestion of a potentially hepatotoxic quantity of acetaminophen.

Contraindications: In those patients who are sensitive or who have developed a sensitivity to it.

There are no contraindications to oral or i.v. administration of acetylcysteine in the treatment of acetaminophen overdose.

Warnings: After proper administration of acetylcysteine, an increased volume of liquefied bronchial secretions may occur. When cough is inadequate, the open airway must be maintained by mechanical suction if necessary. When there is a large mechanical block due to foreign body or local accumulation, the airway should be cleared by endotracheal aspiration, with or without bronchoscopy.

Asthmatics under treatment with acetylcysteine should be watched carefully. If bronchospasm progresses, this medication should be immediately discontinued.

Generalized urticaria has been observed rarely in patients receiving oral acetylcysteine for acetaminophen overdose. If this occurs and other allergic symptoms appear, treatment with acetylcysteine should be discontinued unless it is deemed essential and the allergic symptoms cannot be otherwise controlled.

If encephalopathy due to hepatic failure is evident, acetylcysteine treatment should be discontinued to avoid further administration of nitrogenous substances. There are no data indicating acetylcysteine adversely influences hepatic failure; however, this remains a theoretical possibility.

Precautions: With the administration of acetylcysteine as a mucolytic agent, the patient may initially notice a slight disagreeable odor which soon is not noticeable. With a face mask, there may be a stickiness on the face after nebulization which is easily removed by washing with water.

Acetylcysteine is not compatible with rubber and metals, particularly iron, copper and nickel. Silicone and lacquered rubber and plastic are satisfactory for use with acetylcysteine.

Under certain conditions, a color change may take place in the solution of acetylcysteine in the open vial. The light purple color is the result of a chemical reaction which does not significantly impair the safety or mucolytic efficacy of acetylcysteine.

Continued nebulization of an acetylcysteine solution with a dry gas will result in an increased concentration of the drug in the nebulizer because of evaporation of the solvent. Extreme concentration may impede nebulization and efficient delivery of the drug. Dilution of the nebulizing solution with Sterile Water for Injection USP, as concentration occurs, will obviate this problem.

Occasionally severe and persistent vomiting occurs as a symptom of acute acetaminophen overdose. Treatment with oral acetylcysteine may aggravate the vomiting. Patients at risk of gastric hemorrhage (e.g., esophageal varices, peptic

Mucomyst (cont'd)

ulcers, etc.) should be evaluated concerning the risk of upper gastrointestinal hemorrhage versus the risk of developing hepatic toxicity, and treatment with acetylcysteine given accordingly. Dilution of the acetylcysteine with cola drinks minimizes the propensity of oral acetylcysteine to aggravate vomiting.

Drug/Laboratory Interaction: Acetylcysteine may cause a false-positive reaction with reagent dipstick tests for urinary ketones.

Adverse Effects: Adverse reactions have been included in order of frequency: stomatitis, nausea and rhinorrhea. Sensitivity and sensitization to acetylcysteine have been reported very rarely. A few susceptible patients, particularly asthmatics (see Warnings), may experience varying degrees of bronchospasm associated with the administration of nebulized acetylcysteine. Most patients with such bronchospasm are quickly relieved by the use of a bronchodilator given by nebulization.

Oral or i.v. administration of acetylcysteine, especially in the large doses needed to treat acetaminophen overdose, in order of frequency may result in nausea, vomiting and other gastrointestinal symptoms. Hypersensitivity reactions following the i.v. administration of acetylcysteine have been reported. Symptoms include rashes, facial edema, urticaria, hypotension and bronchospasm.

Compatibility: The physical and chemical compatibility of acetylcysteine solutions with other drugs commonly administered by nebulization, direct instillation, or topical application, has been studied.

Acetylcysteine should not be mixed with all antibiotics. For example, the antibiotics tetracycline HCl, oxytetracycline HCl and erythromycin lactobionate were found to be incompatible when mixed in the same solution. These agents may be administered from separate solutions if administration of these agents is desirable.

Dosage: As a Mucolytic Agent: The 20% solution may be diluted to a lesser concentration with either sterile normal saline or Sterile Water for Injection, USP. Any unused portion of a vial should be refrigerated and used within 96 hours.

Nebulization-face mask, mouth piece, tracheostomy: When nebulized into a face mask, mouth piece or tracheostomy, 1 to 10 mL of the 20% solution may be given every 2 to 6 hours; the recommended dose for most patients is 3 to 5 mL of the 20% solution 3 to 4 times daily.

Nebulization-tent, croupette: In special circumstances it may be necessary to nebulize into a tent or croupette, and this method of use must be individualized to take into account the available equipment and the patient's particular needs. This form of administration requires very large volumes of the solution, occasionally as much as 300 mL during a single treatment period. If a tent or croupette must be used, the recommended dose is the volume of solution that will maintain a very heavy mist in the tent or croupette for the desired period. Administration for intermittent or continuous prolonged periods, including overnight, may be desirable.

Direct instillation: When used by direct instillation, 1 to 2 mL of a 10 to 20% solution may be given as often as every hour.

When used for the routine nursing care of patients with tracheostomy, 1 to 2 mL of a 10 to 20% solution may be given every 1 to 4 hours by instillation into the tracheostomy.

Acetylcysteine may be introduced directly into a particular segment of the bronchopulmonary tree by inserting (under local anesthesia and direct vision) a small plastic catheter into the trachea. Two to 5 mL of the 20% solution may then be instilled by means of a syringe connected to the catheter.

Acetylcysteine may also be given through a percutaneous intratracheal catheter. One to 2 mL of the 20% solution may be given every 1 to 4 hours by a syringe attached to the catheter.

Diagnostic Bronchograms: For diagnostic bronchial studies, 2 or 3 administrations of 1 to 2 mL of the 20% solution should be given by nebulization or by instillation intratracheally, prior to the procedure.

Administration of Aerosol: Materials: Acetylcysteine may be administered using conventional nebulizers made of plastic or glass. Certain materials used in nebulization equipment react with acetylcysteine. The most reactive of these are certain metals (notably iron and copper), and rubber. Where materials may come into contact with acetylcysteine solution, parts made of the following acceptable materials should be used: glass, plastic, aluminum, anodized aluminum, chromed metal, tantalum, sterling silver or stainless steel. Silver may become tarnished after exposure, but this is not harmful to the drug action or the patient.

Nebulizing Gases: Compressed tank gas (air) or an air compressor should be used to provide pressure for nebulizing the solution. Oxygen may also be used but should be used with usual caution in patients with severe respiratory disease and CO_2 retention.

As an Antidote for Acetaminophen Poisoning: In the case of an overdosage of acetaminophen, acetylcysteine should be administered immediately if 24 hours or less have elapsed from the reported time of ingestion. To be effective in protecting against severe liver damage, therapy with acetylcysteine must be started within 10 hours of acetaminophen ingestion. There is some evidence of progressively diminished efficacy thereafter, possibly lasting up to 24 hours.

It should be borne in mind that after a fatal dose of acetaminophen, the patient may appear relatively well initially and may even continue normal activities for a day or two before the onset of hepatic failure.

The following procedure is recommended: 1. The stomach should be emptied promptly by lavage or by inducing emesis with syrup of ipecac. Syrup of ipecac should be given in a dose of 15 to 30 mL for children and 30 to 45 mL for adults accompanied by drinking copious quantities of water. The dose should be repeated if emesis does not occur in 20 minutes.

2. In the case of a mixed drug overdose activated charcoal may be indicated. However, if activated charcoal has been administered, perform gastric lavage before administering oral acetylcysteine treatment. Activated charcoal will absorb acetylcysteine and reduce its effectiveness.

3. Draw blood for acetaminophen plasma assay and for baseline AST, ALT, bilirubin, prothrombin time, creatinine, BUN, blood sugar and electrolytes. The acetaminophen assay provides a reliable prognostic indication of potential hepatotoxicity and serves as a basis for determining the need for continuing with the maintenance doses of acetylcysteine treatment. The laboratory measurements are used to monitor hepatic and renal function and electrolyte fluid balance.

4. Administer the loading dose of acetylcysteine as outlined in Table I or II according to route of administration employed.

5. For information regarding oral and i.v. maintenance doses, see Tables I and II.

6. If the patient vomits the oral loading dose or any oral maintenance dose within 1 hour of administration, repeat that dose.

7. If the patient is unable to retain the orally administered acetylcysteine, the antidote may be administered by duodenal intubation or by the i.v. route.

8. Repeat AST, ALT, bilirubin, prothrombin time, creatinine, BUN, blood sugar and electrolytes daily if acetaminophen plasma level is in the potentially toxic range.

Preparation of solution for oral administration: Oral administration requires dilution of the 20% solution with cola drinks, or other soft drinks, to a final concentration of 5% (see Table I). If administered via gastric tube or Miller-Abbott tube, water may be used as the diluent. The dilutions should be freshly

Table I—Mucomyst

Dosage Guide and Preparation for Oral Administration

Body Weight (kg)	Dose of acetylcysteine: Grams acetylcysteine	mLs of 20% acetylcysteine	mLs of diluent	Total mLs of 5% solution
Loading Dose*				
100–110	15	75	225	300
90–100	14	70	210	280
80–90	13	65	195	260
70–80	11	55	165	220
60–70	10	50	150	200
50–60	8	40	120	160
40–50	7	35	105	140
30–40	6	30	90	120
20–30	4	20	60	80
Maintenance Dose*				
100–110	7.5	37	113	150
90–100	7.0	35	105	140
80–90	6.5	33	97	130
70–80	5.5	28	82	110
60–70	5.0	25	75	100
50–60	4.0	20	60	80
40–50	3.5	18	52	70
30–40	3.0	15	45	60
20–30	2.0	10	30	40

4 hours after the loading dose, administer the first maintenance dose (70 mg of acetylcysteine/kg). The maintenance dose is then repeated at 4 hour intervals for a total of 17 doses unless the acetaminophen assay reveals a non-toxic level as discussed above.

* If patient weighs less than 20 kg, usually patients younger than 6 years, calculate the dose of acetylcysteine. Each mL of 20% solution contains 200 mg of acetylcysteine. The loading dose is 140 mg/kg of body weight. The maintenance dose is 70 mg/kg. Three mLs of diluent are added to each mL of 20% solution. Do not decrease the proportion of diluent. Increased gastrointestinal irritation is associated with increased concentrations of acetylcysteine.

Table II—Mucomyst

Dosage Guide and Preparation for I.V. Administration

Body Weight (kg)	Initial Infusion (in 5% dextrose over 15 minutes): Acetylcysteine (mL)	5% Dextrose (mL)	2nd Infusion (in 500 mL 5% dextrose over 4 hours): Acetylcysteine (mL)	3rd Infusion (in 1 L 5% dextrose over 16 hours): Acetylcysteine (mL)
10–15	11.25	40	3.75	7.50
15–20	15.00	50	5.00	10.00
20–25	18.75	75	6.25	12.50
25–30	22.50	75	7.50	15.00
30–40	30.00	100	10.00	20.00
40–50	37.50	200	12.50	25.00
50–60	45.00	200	15.00	30.00
60–70	52.50	200	17.50	35.00
70–80	60.00	200	20.00	40.00
80–90	67.50	200	22.50	45.00
90–100	75.00	200	25.00	50.00
100–110	82.50	200	27.50	55.00

The volumes and rates of infusion for children suggested above must be adjusted according to the medical circumstances and restrictions in the volumes of parenteral fluids administered as they apply to each individual patient.

prepared and utilized within 1 hour. Remaining undiluted solutions in opened vials can be stored in the refrigerator up to 96 hours.
Preparation of solution for i.v. administration: Acetylcysteine may be used for i.v. administration following acetaminophen overdose according to Dosage Guidelines in Table II. Dilutions recommended should be prepared with 5% Dextrose and Water, as appropriate. Acetylcysteine for i.v. use should be considered as a single-dose container. Solutions recommended under each column in Table II should be freshly prepared and used only over times stated.

Supportive treatment of acetaminophen overdose: Maintain fluid and electrolyte balance based on clinical evaluation of state of hydration and serum electrolytes. Treat as necessary for hypoglycemia. Administer vitamin K_1 if prothrombin time ratio exceeds 1.5 or fresh frozen plasma if the prothrombin time ratio exceeds 3.0. Diuretics and forced diuresis should be avoided.

Hemodialysis or peritoneal dialysis have not been found helpful.

Supplied: Each rubber-stoppered, glass vial contains: a sterile 20% solution of acetylcysteine. Vials of 10 and 30 mL.

MULTIPAX® Ⓟ
Rhône-Poulenc Rorer
Hydroxyzine HCl
Anxiolytic—Antihistaminic

Supplied: Each opaque soft gelatin green capsule contains: hydroxyzine HCl 25 mg. Nonmedicinal ingredients: bleached lecithin, D&C Yellow No 10, FD&C Blue No 1, gelatin, glycerin, hydrogenated vegetable oil, methylparaben, propylparaben, soy bean oil, titanium dioxide, vegetable shortening and wax. Tartrazine-free. Bottles of 100 and 500.

(Shown in Product Recognition Section)

MULTI-TAR PLUS
ICN
Tar—Zinc Pyrithione
Antidandruff—Antiseborrheic

Supplied: Multi-Tar Plus and Multi-Tar Plus Herbal: Each mL of shampoo contains: a 1% blend of equal parts of juniper tar USP, pine tar USP, and coal tar solution USP plus 1% zinc pyrithione in a soap-free vehicle. Nonmedicinal ingredients: bentonite, edetate disodium, hexylene glycol, lauramide D.E.A., oleyl alcohol, PEG-40-castor oil, perfume herbal, phosphoric acid, polysorbate 80 and T.E.A. lauryl sulfate. Multi-Tar Plus, plastic bottles of 150 and 300 mL. Multi-Tar Plus Herbal, plastic bottles of 150 mL.

Multi-Tar Plus Mild: Each mL of shampoo contains: 0.5% blend of equal parts of juniper tar USP, pine tar USP, and coal tar solution USP plus 1% zinc pyrithione in a soap-free vehicle. Nonmedicinal ingredients: bentonite, edetate disodium, hexylene glycol, lauramide D.E.A., oleyl alcohol, PEG-40-castor oil, perfume herbal, phosphoric acid, polysorbate 80 and T.E.A. lauryl sulfate. Plastic bottles of 150 mL.

MULTITEST® CMI
Connaught
Skin Test Antigens for Cell-Mediated Immunity
Diagnostic Aid

Pharmacology: The delayed cutaneous responses associated with the ubiquitous antigens in the Multitest battery appear to be typical cellular hypersensitivity reactions. A relatively small amount of soluble antigen is introduced into the epidermia and superficial dermal tissue by puncture. Circulating T-cells (lymphocytes), sensitized to the antigen from prior contact, react with the antigens in the skin and induce a specific immune response which includes mitosis (blastogenesis) and the release of numerous soluble mediators (lymphokines). Specific lymphokines initiate inflammation (vasculitis and edema) that is manifest after several hours.

The intensity of the overall dermal inflammation reaches its peak 24 to 72 hours after antigen application and is resolved within days or weeks.

Delayed hypersensitivity skin testing may be useful in evaluating individuals suspected of having primary or acquired immune deficiency disorders in which cell-mediated immunity is decreased or absent.

An assessment of cellular hypersensitivity reactions has been shown to be useful in many conditions with other products. Protein calorie malnutrition often complicated by the increasing frequency and severity of infection. Malnutrition of moderate or severe degree (weight for height less than 70% of standard) is almost invariably associated with impaired immune response. Delayed hypersensitivity is one of the immunocompetence response criteria in moderate to severe protein calorie malnutrition. Even marginal malnutrition may be associated with alterations in immunocompetence.

Delayed hypersensitivity tests again have been shown to be a comparative immunocompetence parameter. Marginal malnutrition has been shown to have a predictive value for morbidity and mortality. The presence of deficiencies of minerals, other trace elements and certain vitamin such as ascorbic acid has been associated with decreased delayed hypersensitivity response. Other factors such as diabetes mellitus, uremia, and certain acquired immune deficiency disorders can decrease delayed hypersensitivity. Skin testing at periodic intervals may be useful to determine if a state of immunodepression persists or if delayed hypersensitivity skin test responsiveness returns to normal. Delayed hypersensitivity testing has been useful to assess nutritional and immunocompetence criteria in pre- and postsurgical evaluations to detect high risk groups and adopt improved nutritional support and therapeutic programs.

Indications: For detection of anergy (nonresponsiveness to antigens) by means of delayed hypersensitivity skin testing.

Cutaneous anergy may indicate functional impairment of, or abnormalities in, the cellular immune system. Delayed cellular hypersensitivity is a valuable measure of immune response because it involves a complex series of immunologic, cellular, mediator-associated, and vascular effects.

Numerous investigators have shown a positive correlation between defective cell-mediated immunity, as indicated by anergy to multiple skin test antigens, and disseminated cancer. The occurrence of anergy may be correlated to some extent with advanced stage disease. The demonstration of anergy can be a negative prognostic factor in certain malignant diseases since diminished cutaneous reactivity has been associated with poor prognosis.

In general, patients capable of displaying normal delayed hypersensitivity skin test reactions to standard skin test antigens may have a better prognosis, whereas those who remain anergic or who exhibit significantly impaired reactivity, tend to experience a poor response to therapy, an increased incidence of recurrences and a shortened survival.

Table I summarizes data obtained from studies with the Multitest CMI antigens in France, in a normal population and in cancer patients. Table I illustrates differences in skin test responses between the sexes and between healthy persons compared to those with cancer. Clinical studies conducted in Canada and the U.S. using similar products manufactured by Institut Merieux show comparable results to those obtained in France.

Delayed hypersensitivity skin testing is not an absolute determinant of immune system dysfunction, and any such interpretation must be avoided. Delayed cutaneous hypersensitivity may be diminished or absent when there is in vitro evidence that T-lymphocyte function remains intact, and when antibody associated immunity and phagocytic function appear normal.

Until data are available for infants and children (to age 16), skin testing with Multitest CMI is recommended only for subjects 17 years of age or greater.

Contraindications: Do not apply at sites involving acneiform, infected or inflamed skin. Although severe systemic reactions to diphtheria and tetanus antigens are rare, persons known to have a history of such reactions should be tested with Multitest CMI only after the test heads containing these antigens have been removed.

Warnings: Epinephrine should be available in case of severe reactions.

Precautions: Discard the applicator after use. **Do not reuse.** The sterility is guaranteed only when the seals on the individual test heads are intact. Do not attempt to resterilize or reuse the applicator.

If periodic testing is done more frequently than every 2 months, then the test sites should be rotated so that retesting is not conducted at the same site sooner than 2 months.

Reactivity to delayed hypersensitivity skin test antigens may decrease or disappear temporarily as a result of: febrile illness; measles and other viral infections; live virus vaccination including measles, mumps, rubella, and poliomyelitis vaccines.

Individuals may acquire skin testing sensitivity resulting from either immunization or infection.

Epinephrine should be available in case of severe reactions.
Information for the Patient: Patients should be informed of the types of test site reactions that may be expected.
Drug Interactions: It is possible to observe loss of reactivity in patients undergoing treatment with drugs or procedures that suppress immunity, such as: corticosteroids, chemotherapeutic agents, antilymphocyte globulin and irradiation.
Drug Laboratory Test Interactions: The effect of repeated skin testing on specific antibody levels is not yet known, consequently those doing in vitro testing must be cognizant of the fact that repeated skin testing may alter antibody levels.
Pregnancy: Animal reproduction studies have not been conducted with Multitest CMI. It is also not known whether Multitest CMI can cause fetal harm when administered to a pregnant woman or can affect reproduction capacity. The skin test should be given to a pregnant woman only if clearly needed. Pregnancy may result in a decreased level of sensitivity to the test antigens.
Children: The safety and effectiveness in children below the age of 17 have not been established.

Adverse Effects: Vesiculation, ulceration or necrosis may occur in highly sensitive subjects at the test site. Pain or pruritus at the test site may be relieved by topical glucocorticoids or ice pack.

Systemic reactions may occur in those persons sensitive to allergenic media components.

Dosage: Carefully follow each step of instructions below. Preparation of the Site and Multitest CMI: 1. Remove the skin test from refrigeration approximately 1 hour before use.
2. Select only test sites that permit sufficient surface area and s.c. tissue to allow adequate penetration of all points on all 8 test heads. Preferred sites are the volar surfaces of the arms and the back. Skin of the posterior thighs may be used if necessary. If several tests are planned, alternating forearms is desirable. Avoid hairy areas when possible because interpretation of reactions will be more difficult.
3. Cleanse test site with alcohol and allow to dry completely before testing. Ether or acetone may also be used.
4. Tear off the foil strip covering the test heads.
5. Tap the device on a hard surface, foil side up, to release antigen from top of cap.
6. Remove the protective plastic cap on each preloaded test head by twisting cap clockwise and counterclockwise. Carefully lift cap away from points.
Application of Multitest CMI: 1. Point "T-bar" end toward a constant reference point such as the elbow or head of the subject being tested to eliminate later identification problems with antigens or the control. The antigens and control are numbered clockwise, beginning top right through 8 on the round plastic platform supporting each test head.
2. Keep the skin at test site taut.
3. Press loaded unit into the skin with sufficient pressure to puncture the skin and allow adequate penetration of all points. Maintain firm contact for at least 5 seconds. During application the device should be "rocked" back and forth and side to side without removing any of the test heads from the skin sites. Bleeding rarely occurs with proper pressure.

Table I—Multitest CMI

Result with 7 Antigens*

	Normal Volunteers		Localized Cancer		Disseminated Cancer	
	Male	Female	Male	Female	Male	Female
Total Subjects Tested	315	299	393	296	229	164
% Anergic	1.2	4.3	14.8	24.7	22.3	33.5
Geometric Mean Scores (mm)	18.3	12.2	12.1	9.6	9.8	7.5
Mean No. Antigens Positive	4.5	3.5	3.3	2.8	2.8	2.3

*Induration ≥2 mm at 48 hours is considered a positive reaction.

Multitest CMI (cont'd)

4. If adequate pressure is applied it will be possible to observe: a. The puncture marks of the 9 tines on each of the 8 test heads. b. An imprint of the circular platform surrounding each test head. c. Residual antigen and glycerin at each of the 8 sites. If any of the above 3 criteria are not fully followed, the test results may not be reliable.
5. Identify the area of test sites by drawing one line above test sites No. 8 and No. 1, and another below test sites No. 5 and No. 4. The lines should be drawn about ¼ inch from the puncture patterns and made with an indelible marker so that they will remain clearly visible on the skin for at least 48 hours.
6. Allow residual antigens and glycerin to remain on the skin surface for at least 3 minutes then gently dab with a gauze pad so as not to cross-contaminate test sites with antigen.
7. Discard applicator after use. Do not reuse.

Reading and Recording Results: 1. Reading should be done in good light. Read the test sites at both 24 and 48 hours, if possible. The largest reaction recorded from the 2 readings at each test site should be used. If 2 readings are not possible, a single 48 hour reading is recommended. The time for maximal reactivity to the various antigens may vary in different people. This may depend on the presence of antibodies.
2. A positive reaction from any of the 7 delayed hypersensitivity skin test antigens is induration of 2 mm or greater providing there is no induration at the negative control site. Fewer than 2% of healthy volunteers tested during clinical studies exhibited detectable induration from the glycerin negative control solution. Should induration occur at the negative control site, then indurated reactions from individual antigens must exceed the size of induration from the negative control solution by 2 mm or greater to be considered positive. Erythema without induration is of no significance. **The size of the induration reactions with Multitest CMI may be smaller than those obtained with other intradermal procedures.**
3. Determine the size of an indurated area at any test site by inspection, palpation with gentle finger stroking, and measurements across 2 diameters at right angles. Record the average diameter of induration (a+b)÷2.

Scoring: Periodic testing with Multitest CMI can be conducted to determine if a state of anergy persists, or if skin test reactivity returns. A 2 part scoring system has been developed for the test battery that consists of the number of positive antigens and the total induration resulting from all positive antigen test sites. Whenever positive skin test reactions occur, the scoring system can be used to assist in determining the degree of skin test reactivity and whether there is a trend over a period of time toward greater or lesser skin test responsiveness. The scoring system can be illustrated by this hypothetical example: Three of the 7 delayed hypersensitivity skin test antigens administered simultaneously produce indurated reactions measuring 3 mm and 5 mm respectively. The resulting score in this hypothetical case is 3/10 mm. The figure 3 represents the number of antigens positive, while 10 mm represents the sum total of induration from all three positive test sites. If a patient is anergic, the score is 0/0 mm, signifying no reaction to any antigen and no resulting induration.

Occasionally, a small and diffused reaction (2 to 3 mm) may be present at one time of testing and not at another. The disappearance or recurrence of such a reaction is probably not significant, providing positive reaction sizes to other antigens remain relatively constant. However, the disappearance or substantial reduction in size of a larger, well defined reaction may be significant, even though the total score is not appreciably affected.

Supplied: Multitest CMI is a disposable, plastic applicator consisting of 8 sterile test heads preloaded with the following 7 delayed hypersensitivity skin test antigens and glycerin negative control for percutaneous administration: Tetanus Toxoid Antigen, Diphtheria Toxoid Antigen, Streptococcus Antigen, Tuberculin Old, Candida Antigen, Trichophyton Antigen, and Proteus Antigen. The test provides a quick, convenient and uniform procedure for delayed cutaneous hypersensitivity testing.

The 8 test heads of the Multitest CMI applicator are numbered 1 through 8 and are preloaded with the following test substances: (see manufacturer's package insert for illustration).

Test Head No. 1—Tetanus Toxoid Antigen: Tetanus Toxoid Antigen is a sterile, glycerinated solution containing tetanus toxoid prepared from the culture filtrate of C. tetani, inactivated and detoxified with formaldehyde. Residual formaldehyde does not exceed 0.02%. The potency of each lot is determined by a comparison of responses obtained by the intradermal injection of the lot and a reference Tetanus Toxoid into sensitized guinea pigs. Each mL of Tetanus Toxoid Antigen in 70% W/V glycerin is biologically equivalent to 550 000 Merieux Tetanus Units.

Test Head No. 2—Diphtheria Toxoid Antigen: Diphtheria Toxoid Antigen is a sterile glycerinated solution containing diphtheria toxoid prepared from the culture filtrate of C. diptheriae, inactivated and detoxified with formaldehyde. Residual formaldehyde does not exceed 0.02%. The potency of each lot is determined by a comparison of responses obtained by the intradermal injection of the lot and a reference Diphtheria Toxoid into sensitized guinea pigs. Each mL of Diphtheria Toxoid Antigen in 70% W/V glycerin is biologically equivalent to 1 100 000 Mérieux Diphtheria Units.

Test Head No. 3—Streptococcus Antigen: Streptococcus Antigen is a sterile, glycerinated solution containing culture filtrate of Streptococcus (Group C) inactived with phenol. Residual phenol does not exceed 0.5%. The potency of each lot is determined by a comparison of responses obtained by the intradermal injection of the lot and a reference Streptococcus preparation into sensitized guinea pigs. Each mL of Streptococcus Antigen in 70% W/V glycerin is biologically equivalent to 2 000 Merieux Streptococcus Units.

Test Head No. 4—Tuberculin, Old: Tuberculin, Old is a sterile glycerinated solution containing standardized culture filtrates of M. tuberculosis (C, D and PN) and M. bovis (Vallee). The potency of each lot is standardized by a comparison of responses obtained by the intradermal injection of the lot and the U.S. Standard Tuberculin, Old into sensitized guinea pigs. Each mL of Tuberculin, Old in 70% W/V glycerin is biologically equivalent to 300 000 U.S. Tuberculin Units (T.U.).

Test Head No. 5—Glycerin Negative Control: Glycerin Negative Control is a 70% W/V sterile glycerin solution identical to the glycerin solution that serves as a vehicle for the skin test antigens.

Test Head No. 6—Candida Antigen: Candida Antigen is a sterile glycerinated solution containing culture filtrate of C. albicans inactivated with phenol. Residual phenol does not exceed 0.5%. The potency of each lot is determined by a comparison of responses obtained by the intradermal injection of the lot and a reference Candida preparation into sensitized guinea pigs. Each mL of Candida Antigen in 70% W/V glycerin is biologically equivalent to 2 000 Merieux Candida Units.

Test Head No. 7—Trichophyton Antigen: Trichophyton Antigen is a sterile glycerinated solution containing culture filtrate of Trichophyton mentagrophytes inactivated by the addition of phenol. Residual phenol does not exceed 0.5%. The potency of each lot is determined by a comparison of responses obtained by the intradermal injection of the lot and a reference Trychophyton preparation into sensitized guinea pigs. Each mL of Trichophyton Antigen in 70% W/V glycerin is biologically equivalent to 150 Merieux Trichophyton Units.

Test Head No. 8—Proteus Antigen: Proteus Antigen is a sterile glycerinated solution containing culture filtrate of P. mirabilis inactivated by the addition of phenol. Residual phenol does not exceed 0.5%. The potency of each lot is determined by a comparison of responses obtained by the intradermal injection of the lot and a reference Proteus preparation into sensitized guinea pigs. Each mL of Proteus Antigen in 70% W/V glycerin is biologically equivalent to 150 Mérieux Proteus Units.

Each individual carton contains 1 preloaded Skin Test Antigens for Cell-Mediated Immunity. Boxes of 12. Store at room temperature not exceeding 25°C. Avoid the proximity of any heat sources.

Reviewed 1998

MUMPSVAX®
MSD

Mumps Virus Vaccine, Live, Attenuated
Mumps Prophylaxis

Description: This vaccine is prepared from the Jeryl Lynn (B Level) strain, named after the patient from whom the virus was initially recovered.

Mumpsvax is a sterile lyophilized preparation of the Jeryl Lynn (B level) strain of mumps virus. The virus was adapted to and propagated in cell cultures of chick embryo, free of avian leukosis, virus and other adventitious agents according to the general procedures used to prepare Enders' measles virus vaccine, live, attenuated. The vaccine is tested for safety and efficacy.

The reconstituted vaccine is for s.c. administration. When reconstituted as directed, the dose of injection contains not less than the equivalent of 5 000 $TCID_{50}$ (tissue culture infectious doses) of the US Reference Mumps Virus. Each dose contains approximately 17.5 μg of neomycin base (present as sulfate). The product contains no preservative. Sorbitol and hydrolized gelatin are added as stabilizers.

Pharmacology: Usually, mumps is a mild disease. However, it may occasionally be severe and produce serious complications. For example, meningoencephalitis has been estimated to occur in about 10% of patients, and unilateral orchitis in about 20 to 30% of postpubertal males.

Postinfectious encephalitis, oophoritis, pancreatitis, muscular weakness, myelitis, myocarditis, facial neuritis, arthritis, hepatitis, and deafness may also occur. The relationship of endocardial fibroelastosis in infants, and mumps in the mother during pregnancy, has not been conclusively established.

Mumpsvax produces a modified, non-communicable mumps infection in susceptible persons. Extensive clinical trials have demonstrated that the vaccine is highly immunogenic and well tolerated. A single injection has been shown to induce mumps neutralizing antibodies in approximately 97% of susceptible children and approximately 93% of susceptible adults. The pattern of antibody response closely resembles that observed for natural mumps. Although the antibody level is significantly lower than that following natural infection, it is protective and long lasting. Vaccine-induced antibody levels have been shown to persist for at least 15 years with a rate of decline comparable to that seen in natural infection. If the present pattern continues, it will provide a basis for the expectation that immunity following vaccination will be permanent. However, continued surveillance will be required to demonstrate this point.

Indications: Mumpsvax induces protective antibodies in essentially all nonimmune recipients, provides protection against natural mumps in most cases and has not been shown to cause significant systemic or local reactions. Evidence indicates that the mumps virus infection initiated by the vaccine is not contagious.

For immunization against mumps in children 12 months of age or older, and adults. It is not recommended for infants less than a year old because they may retain maternal mumps neutralizing antibodies which may interfere with the immune response.

Mumps vaccine is recommended for asymptomatic HIV infected children.

Evidence indicates that the vaccine will not offer protection when given after exposure to natural mumps. Passively acquired antibody can interfere with the response to live, attenuated virus vaccines. Therefore, administration of mumps virus vaccine should be deferred until approximately 3 months after passive immunization.

Revaccination: Based on available evidence, there is no reason to routinely revaccinate children vaccinated originally when 12 months of age or older. However, persons should be revaccinated if there is evidence to suggest that initial immunization was ineffective.

Use with other vaccines: There are no data available concerning simultaneous use of Mumpsvax with monovalent or trivalent poliovirus vaccine, live, oral or with killed poliovirus vaccines. However, serologic evidence shows that when M-M-R containing the HPV-77 rubella strain is given simultaneously with trivalent poliovirus vaccine, live, oral, antibody responses can be expected to be comparable to those which follow administration of the vaccines at different times. From this it follows that when Mumpsvax is given simultaneously with either monovalent or trivalent poliovirus vaccine, live, oral, Attenuvax and/or Meruvax II, antibody responses can be expected to be comparable to those which follow administration of the vaccines at different times.

Contraindications: Hypersensitivity to neomycin. Each dose of reconstituted vaccine contains approximately 17.5 μg of neomycin base (present as sulfate).

Any febrile respiratory illness or other active febrile infection.

Active untreated tuberculosis.

Patients receiving therapy with ACTH, corticosteroids, irradiation, alkylating agents or antimetabolites. This contraindication does not apply to patients who are receiving corticosteroids as replacement therapy, e.g., for Addison's disease.

Individuals with blood dyscrasias, leukemia, lymphomas of any type, or other malignant neoplasms affecting the bone marrow or lymphatic systems.

Primary immunodeficiency states, including cellular immune deficiencies, hypogammaglobulinemic and dysgammaglobulinemic states. Also, individuals with symptomatic AIDS.

Individuals with a family history of congenital or hereditary immunodeficiency, until the immune competence of the potential vaccine recipient is demonstrated.

Hypersensitivity to eggs, chicken or chicken feathers: This vaccine is essentially devoid of potentially allergenic substances derived from host tissues (chick embryo). However, because the attenuated virus in this vaccine is propagated in cell cultures of chick embryo, there is a potential risk of hypersensitivity reactions in patients allergic to eggs, chicken or chicken feathers. Widespread use of the vaccine for more than a decade has resulted in only rare, isolated reports of minor allergic reactions attributed to allergens of this kind, possibly related to the vaccine. Significantly, when children with known allergies to eggs, chicken and chicken feathers were given a similarly prepared vaccine in a clinical study, none experienced reactions other than those reactions previously observed in nonallergic children.

Pregnancy: Do not give Mumpsvax to pregnant females; the possible effects of the vaccine on fetal development are unknown at this time. When vaccination of postpubertal females is undertaken, pregnancy at the time of vaccination must be ruled out and in addition, the possibility of pregnancy occurring in the 3 months following vaccination must be eliminated by medically acceptable methods.

Precautions: For s.c. use; do not give i.v. Mumpsvax may be given simultaneously with monovalent or trivalent poliovirus vaccine, live, oral, with Attenuvax and/or Meruvax II. Mumpsvax should not be given less than 1 month before or after administration of other live virus vaccines.

Adequate treatment provisions including epinephrine, should be available for immediate use should an anaphylactoid reaction occur.

Vaccination should be deferred for at least 3 months following blood or plasma transfusions, or administration of human immune serum globulin.

It has been reported that attenuated live mumps virus vaccine may result in a temporary depression of tuberculin skin sensitivity. Therefore, if a tuberculin test is to be done, it should be administered either before or simultaneously with Mumpsvax.

As for any vaccine, vaccination with Mumpsvax may not result in seroconversion in 100% of susceptible persons given the vaccine.

Adverse Effects: Because of the slightly acidic pH (6.2 to 6.6) of the vaccine, patients may complain of burning and/or stinging of short duration at the injection site.

Mild fever occurs occasionally. Fever above 39.4°C is uncommon.

Parotitis has been reported to occur in very low incidence, and orchitis rarely in persons who were vaccinated. In most instances investigated, prior exposure to natural mumps was established. In other instances, whether or not this was due to vaccine or to prior natural mumps exposure or to other causes has not been established.

Reports of purpura and allergic reactions such as wheal and flare at the injection site or urticaria have been extremely rare.

Forms of optic neuritis, including retrobular neuritis and papillitis may infrequently follow viral infections, and have been reported to occur 1 to 3 weeks following inoculation with some live virus vaccines.

Very rarely encephalitis, febrile seizures, deafness and other nervous system reactions have occurred in vaccinees. A cause-effect relationship has not been established.

Clinical experience with the vaccine thus far indicates that CNS reactions such as meningoencephalitis, facial paresis, aphasia, ataxia and dystonia have occurred rarely within 4 days to 4 weeks following vaccine administration. A cause-effect relationship has not been established.

In patients who have previously received killed mumps vaccine, it is possible that local reactions may occur at the site of injection with live mumps vaccine. This has not been reported with Mumpsvax.

Shipment, Storage and Reconstitution: During shipment, to insure that there is no loss of potency, maintain the vaccine at 10°C or less.

Prior to reconstitution, store the vaccine in a refrigerator at 2 to 8°C. **Protect from light.**

To reconstitute, use only the diluent supplied, since it is free of preservatives or other antiviral substances which might inactivate the vaccine.

First withdraw the entire volume of diluent into the syringe to be used for reconstitution. Inject all the diluent in the syringe into the vial of lyophilized vaccine, and agitate to mix thoroughly. Withdraw the entire contents into a syringe and inject the total volume of restored vaccine s.c.

It is important to use a separate sterile syringe and needle for each individual patient to prevent transmission of hepatitis B and other infectious agents from one person to another.

Use only the diluent supplied and reconstitute the vaccine just before using. Use the vaccine as soon as possible after reconstitution. Protect the vaccine from light at all times since such exposure may inactivate the virus. Store the reconstituted vaccine in a dark place at 2 to 8°C and discard if not used within 8 hours.

Parenteral drug products should be inspected visually for particulate matter and discoloration prior to administration.

The vaccine's color when reconstituted is clear yellow.

Dosage: The dosage of vaccine is the same for all persons. After suitably cleansing the immunization site, inject total volume (about 0.5 mL) of reconstituted vaccine s.c., preferably into the outer aspect of the upper arm. **Do not inject i.v.**

Do not give immune globulin concurrently with Mumpsvax.

Caution: A sterile syringe free of preservatives, antiseptics, and detergents should be used for each injection of the vaccine because these substances may inactivate the live virus vaccine. A 25 gauge, 15 mm needle is recommended.

Supplied: Boxes of 10 single-dose vials of vaccine and boxes of 10 vials of diluent. Diluent may be stored at room temperature.

MUSTARGEN® ℞

MSD

Mechlorethamine HCl

Alkylating Agent

Pharmacology: Mechlorethamine, a biologic alkylating agent, has a cytotoxic action which inhibits rapidly proliferating cells.

Indications: Before using mechlorethamine see Contraindications, Warnings, Precautions, Adverse Effects and Dosage.

Administered i.v., mechlorethamine is indicated for the palliative treatment of Hodgkin's disease (Stages III and IV), lymphosarcoma, chronic myelocytic or chronic lymphocytic leukemia, polycythemia vera, mycosis fungoides and bronchogenic carcinoma.

Mechlorethamine, administered intrapleurally, intraperitoneally or intrapericardially, is indicated for the palliative treatment of metastatic carcinoma resulting in effusion.

Contraindications: Because of the toxicity of mechlorethamine, and the unpleasant side effects following its use, the potential risk and discomfort from the use of mechlorethamine in patients with inoperable neoplasms or in the terminal stage of the disease must be balanced against the limited gain obtainable. These gains will vary with the nature and the status of the disease under treatment. Routine use in all cases of widely disseminated neoplasms is to be discouraged.

The use of mechlorethamine in patients with leukopenia, thrombocytopenia, and anemia, due to invasion of the bone marrow by tumor carries a greater risk. In such patients a good response to treatment with disappearance of the tumor from the bone marrow may be associated with improvement of bone marrow function. However, in the absence of a good response or in patients who have been previously treated with chemotherapeutic agents, hematopoiesis may be further compromised, and leukopenia, thrombocytopenia and anemia may become more severe and lead to the demise of the patient.

Tumors of bone and nervous tissue have responded poorly to therapy. Its use is contraindicated in the presence of known infectious diseases. Results are unpredictable in disseminated and malignant tumors of different types.

Warnings: Extravasation of the drug into s.c. tissues results in a painful inflammation. The area usually becomes indurated and sloughing may occur. If leakage of drug is obvious, prompt infiltration of the area with sterile isotonic sodium thiosulfate (1/6 molar) and application of an ice compress for 6 to 12 hours may minimize the local reaction. For a 1/6 molar solution of sodium thiosulfate use 4.14 g of sodium thiosulfate/100 mL of Sterile Water for Injection or 2.64 g of anhydrous sodium thiosulfate/100 mL or dilute 4 mL of Sodium Thiosulfate Injection USP (10%) with 6 mL of Sterile Water for Injection USP.

Before using mechlorethamine, an accurate histologic diagnosis of the disease, a knowledge of its natural course, and an adequate clinical history are important. The hematologic status of the patient must first be determined. It is essential to understand the hazards and therapeutic effects to be expected. Careful clinical judgment must be exercised in selecting patients. If the indication for its use is not clear, the drug should not be used.

As nitrogen mustard therapy may contribute to extensive and rapid development of amyloidosis, it should be used only if foci of acute and chronic suppurative inflammation are absent.

Precautions: Mechlorethamine is highly toxic and both powder and solution must be handled and administered with care. Since this product is a powerful vesicant, it is intended primarily for i.v. use, and in most instances is given by this route. Inhalation of dust or vapors and contact with skin or mucous membranes, especially that of the eyes, must be avoided. Should accidental eye contact occur, copious irrigation with normal saline or a balanced salt ophthalmic irrigating solution should be instituted immediately, followed by prompt ophthalmologic consultation. Should accidental skin contact occur, the affected part must be irrigated immediately with copious amounts of water, for at least 15 minutes, followed by 2% sodium thiosulfate solution (see Warnings).

Do not use if the solution is discolored or if droplets of water are visible within the vial. Prepare fresh solution for injection and dispose of the unused portion after neutralization (see Dosage).

Precautions must be observed with the use of mechlorethamine and x-ray therapy or other chemotherapy in alternating courses. Hematopoietic function is characteristically depressed by either form of therapy, and neither mechlorethamine following x-ray therapy nor x-ray therapy subsequent to the drug should be given until bone marrow function has recovered. In particular, irradiation of such areas as sternum, ribs, and vertebrae shortly after a course of nitrogen mustard may lead to hematologic complications.

Therapy with alkylating agents such as mechlorethamine may be associated with an increased incidence of a second malignant tumor, especially when such therapy is combined with other antineoplastic agent or radiation therapy.

Hyperuricemia may develop during therapy. The problem of urate precipitation should be anticipated, particularly in the treatment of the lymphomas, and adequate methods for control of hyperuricemia should be instituted and careful attention directed toward adequate fluid intake before treatment.

Since drug toxicity, especially sensitivity to bone marrow failure, seems to be more common in chronic lymphatic leukemia than in other conditions, mechlorethamine should be given in this condition with great caution, if at all.

Pregnancy: There is evidence that the nitrogen mustards have induced fetal abnormalities particularly when used early in pregnancy. The possible benefits of administration in women of childbearing potential must be weighed against the considered risks; patients should be apprised of the risks involved. In pregnant patients requiring treatment for a life-threatening progressive tumor, use of mechlorethamine should be avoided at least until the third trimester.

Adverse Effects: Clinical use usually is accompanied by toxic manifestations.

Local: Thrombosis and thrombophlebitis may result from direct contact of the drug with the intima of the injected vein. Avoid high concentration and prolonged contact with the drug, especially in cases of elevated pressure in the antebrachial vein (e.g. in mediastinal tumor compression from severe vena cava syndrome).

Systemic: Nausea, vomiting and depression of formed elements in the circulating blood are dose-limiting side effects and usually occur with the use of full doses of mechlorethamine. Jaundice, alopecia, vertigo, tinnitus and diminished hearing may occur infrequently.

Rarely, hemolytic anemia associated with such diseases as the lymphomas and chronic lymphocytic leukemia may be precipitated by treatment with alkylating agents including mechlorethamine. Also, various chromosomal abnormalities have been reported in association with nitrogen mustard therapy.

Mechlorethamine is given preferably at night in case sedation for adverse effects is required. Nausea and vomiting usually occur 1 to 3 hours after use of the drug. Emesis may disappear in the first 8 hours, but nausea may persist for 24 hours. Nausea and vomiting may be so severe as to precipitate vascular accidents in patients with a hemorrhagic tendency. Premedication with antiemetics, in addition to sedatives, may help control severe nausea and vomiting. Anorexia, weakness and diarrhea, may also occur.

The usual course of mechlorethamine (total dose of 0.4 mg/kg either given as a single i.v. dose or divided into 2 or 4 daily doses of 0.2 or 0.1 mg/kg respectively) generally produces a lymphocytopenia within 24 hours after the first injection; significant granulocytopenia occurs within 6 to 8 days and lasts for 10 days to 3 weeks. Agranulocytosis

Mustargen (cont'd)

appears to be relatively infrequent and recovery from leukopenia in most cases is complete within 2 weeks of the maximum reduction. Thrombocytopenia is variable but the time course of the appearance and recovery from reduced platelet counts generally parallels the sequence of granulocyte levels. In some cases, severe thrombocytopenia may lead to bleeding from the gums and gastrointestinal tract, petechiae, and small s.c. hemorrhages; these symptoms appear to be transient and in most cases disappear with return to a normal platelet count. However, a severe and even uncontrollable depression of the hematopoietic system occasionally may follow the usual dose of mechlorethamine, particularly in patients with widespread disease and debility and in patients previously treated with other antineoplastic agents or x-ray. Persistent pancytopenia has been reported. In rare instances, hemorrhagic complications may be due to hyperheparinemia. Erythrocyte and hemoglobin levels may decline during the first 2 weeks after therapy but rarely significantly. Depression of the hematopoietic system may be found up to 50 days or more after starting therapy. Renal damage manifested by azotemia and oliguria has been reported.

Mechlorethamine has been reported to have immunosuppressive activity. Therefore, it should be borne in mind that use of the drug may predispose the patient to bacterial, viral or fungal infection. This is more likely to occur when concomitant steroid therapy is employed.

Occasionally, a maculopapular skin eruption occurs, but this may be idiosyncratic and does not necessarily recur with subsequent courses of the drug. In one patient erythema multiforme has been observed. Herpes zoster, a common complicating infection in patients with lymphomas, may first appear after therapy is instituted and on occasion may be precipitated by treatment. Further treatment should be discontinued during the acute phase of this illness to avoid progression to generalized herpes zoster.

Since the gonads are susceptible to mechlorethamine, treatment may be followed by delayed catamenia, oligomenorrhea, or temporary or permanent amenorrhea. Impaired spermatogenesis, azoospermia, and total germinal aplasia have been reported in male patients treated with alkylating agents, especially in combination with other drugs. In some instances spermatogenesis may return in patients in remission, but this may occur only several years after intensive chemotherapy has been discontinued. Patients should be warned of the potential risk to their reproductive capacity.

With total doses exceeding 0.4 mg/kg body weight for a single course, severe leukopenia, anemia, thrombocytopenia and a hemorrhagic diathesis with subsequent delayed bleeding may develop. Death may follow. The only treatment in instances of excessive dosage appears to be repeated blood product transfusions, antibiotic treatment of complicating infections and general supportive measures. **Extreme caution must be used in exceeding the average recommended dose.**

Dosage: I.V. Administration: The dosage varies with the clinical situation, the therapeutic response and the magnitude of hematologic depression. A total dose of 0.4 mg/kg of body weight for each course usually is given either as a single dose or in divided doses of 0.1 to 0.2 mg/kg/day. Dosage should be based on ideal dry body weight. The presence of edema or ascites must be considered so that dosage will be based on actual weight unaugmented by these conditions.

Within a few minutes after i.v. injection, mechlorethamine undergoes chemical transformation, combines with reactive compounds, and is no longer present in its active form in the blood stream.

Subsequent courses should not be given until the patient has recovered hematologically from the previous course; this is best determined by repeated studies of the peripheral blood elements awaiting their return to normal levels. It is often possible to give repeated courses of mechlorethamine as early as 3 weeks after treatment.

The margin of safety in therapy with mechlorethamine is narrow and considerable care must be exercised in the matter of dosage. Repeated examinations of blood are mandatory as a guide to subsequent therapy.

Preparation of Solution and I.V. Administration: Each vial contains 10 mg of mechlorethamine HCl triturated with sodium chloride q.s. 100 mg. In neutral or alkaline aqueous solution it undergoes rapid chemical transformation and is highly unstable. Although solutions prepared according to instructions are acidic and do not decompose as rapidly, they should be prepared immediately before each injection since they will decompose on standing.

Using a sterile 10 mL syringe, inject 10 mL of Sterile Water for Injection or 10 mL Sodium Chloride Injection into a vial of mechlorethamine. With the needle still in the rubber stopper, shake the vial several times to dissolve the drug completely. The resultant solution contains 1 mg of mechlorethamine HCl/mL.

Withdraw into the syringe the calculated volume of solution required for a single injection. **Dispose of any remaining solution after neutralization.** Although the drug may be injected directly into any suitable vein, it is injected preferably into the rubber or plastic tubing of a flowing i.v. infusion set. This reduces the possibility of severe local reactions due to extravasation or high concentration of the drug. Injecting the drug into the tubing rather than adding it to the entire volume of the infusion fluid minimizes a chemical reaction between the drug and the solution. The rate of injection apparently is not critical provided it is completed within a few minutes.

Intracavitary Administration: Nitrogen mustard has been used by intracavitary administration with varying success in certain malignant conditions for control of pleural, peritoneal, and pericardial effusions caused by malignant cells.

The technic and the dose used by any of these routes varies. Therefore, if mechlorethamine is given by the intracavitary route, the published articles concerning such use should be consulted. **Because of the inherent risks involved, the physician should be experienced in the appropriate injection technics, and be thoroughly aware of the indications, dosages, hazards and precautions as set forth in the published literature. When using mechlorethamine by the intracavitary route, the general precautions concerning this agent should be borne in mind.**

As a general guide, reference is made especially to the technics of Weisberger et al. Intracavitary use is indicated in the presence of pleural, peritoneal, or pericardial effusion due to metastatic tumors. Local therapy with nitrogen mustard is used only when malignant cells are demonstrated in the effusion. Intracavitary injection is not recommended when the accumulated fluid is chylous in nature, since results are likely to be poor.

Paracentesis is first performed with most of the fluid being removed from the pleural or peritoneal cavity. The intracavitary use may exert at least some of its effect through production of a chemical poudrage. Therefore, the removal of excess fluid allows the drug to more easily contact the peritoneal and pleural linings. For intrapleural or intrapericardial injection nitrogen mustard is introduced directly through the thoracentesis needle. For intraperitoneal injection it is given through a rubber catheter inserted into the trocar used for paracentesis or through a No. 18 gauge needle inserted at another site. This drug should be injected slowly, with frequent aspiration to ensure that a free flow of fluid is present. If fluid cannot be aspirated, pain and necrosis due to injection of solution outside the cavity may occur. Free flow of fluid also is necessary to prevent injection into a loculated pocket and to ensure adequate dissemination of nitrogen mustard.

The usual dose of nitrogen mustard for intracavitary injection is 0.4 mg/kg of body weight, though 0.2 mg/kg (or 10 to 20 mg) has been used by the intrapericardial route. The solution is prepared, as previously described for i.v. injection, by adding 10 mL of Sterile Water for Injection or 10 mL of Sodium Chloride Injection to the vial containing 10 mg of mechlorethamine (Amounts of diluent of 50 to 100 mL of normal saline have also been used). The position of the patient should be changed every 5 to 10 minutes for an hour after injection to obtain more uniform distribution of the drug throughout the serous cavity. The remaining fluid may be removed from the pleural or peritoneal cavity by paracentesis 24 to 36 hours later. The patient should be followed carefully by a clinical and x-ray examination to detect reaccumulation of fluid.

Pain occurs rarely with intrapleural use; it is common with intraperitoneal injection and is often associated with nausea, vomiting and diarrhea of 2 to 3 days duration. Transient cardiac irregularities may occur with intrapericardial injection. Death, possibly accelerated by mechlorethamine, has been reported following the use of this agent by the intracavitary route. Although absorption of mechlorethamine when given by the intracavitary route is probably not complete because of its rapid deactivation by body fluids, the systemic effect is unpredictable. The acute side effects such as nausea and vomiting are usually mild. Bone marrow depression is generally milder than when the drug is given i.v. Care should be taken to avoid use by the intracavitary route when other agents which may suppress bone marrow function are being used systemically.

To clean rubber gloves, tubing, glassware, etc., after giving mechlorethamine, soak them in an aqueous solution containing equal volumes of sodium thiosulfate (5%) and sodium bicarbonate (5%) for 45 minutes. Excess reagents and reaction products are washed away easily with water. Any unused injection solution should be neutralized by mixing with an equal volume of sodium thiosulfate/sodium bicarbonate solution. Allow the mixture to stand for 45 minutes. Vials that have contained mechlorethamine should be treated in the same way with thiosulfate/bicarbonate solution before disposal.

Supplied: Each vial of light yellow/brown powder contains: mechlorethamine HCl 10 mg triturated with sodium chloride q.s. 100 mg.

MUTACOL BERNA®

Berna Products

Cholera Vaccine Live Oral CVD 103-HgR

Cholera Prophylaxis

Pharmacology: V. cholerae is the etiological agent of cholera, an acute diarrheal disease. This vaccine will not afford protection against species of vibrio other than 01 V. cholerae or against other bacteria that cause enteric disease. Mutacol Berna vaccine will not afford protection against 0139 V. cholerae.

There are less than 30 cases of cholera diagnosed per year in the U.S. while 8 cases were identified in Canada during 1995. All of these cases were contracted during travel outside of Canada. A small number of cholera cases have been contracted in the U.S. following the consumption of contaminated foodstuffs. No secondary spread of the disease was observed. Cholera is now considered to be endemic in most of Central and South America, sub-Saharan Africa and Southeast Asia. Antibiotics and oral rehydration solutions are used to treat cholera. Death associated with cholera among European or North American travelers is rare.

Upon ingestion, virulent strains of V. cholerae are able to pass through the stomach acid barrier and colonize the intestinal tract. V. cholerae present in the intestinal tract secrete cholera toxin which acts to stimulate fluid secretion, thereby resulting in the diarrhea characteristic of cholera. Possible mechanisms whereby disease may be prevented include evoking a local antibacterial and/or antitoxin immune response in the intestinal tract. Such local immunity may be induced by oral ingestion of a live attenuated strain of V. cholerae undergoing an aborted infection.

The ability of V. cholerae to cause disease and to induce a protective immune response is dependent upon colonization of the intestinal tract and secretion of cholera toxin. The V. cholerae CVD 103-HgR vaccine strain was attenuated by deletion of the enzymatically active portion of the cholera toxin molecule from the bacterial chromosome. The nonactive portion of the cholera toxin molecule is still synthesized. In addition, the insertion of a mercury-resistance marker into hlyA gene appears to have diminished the ability of CVD 103-HgR to colonize the intestinal tract. Oral administration of the V. cholerae CVD 103-HgR strain is able to elicit a local intestinal and serum antibody response which recognizes native cholera toxin and wild type V. cholerae. Due to the inability of V. cholerae CVD 103-HgR to synthesize active cholera toxin, disease symptoms normally associated with V. cholerae infection are absent.

The efficacy of CVD 103-HgR has been evaluated in a series of studies in which volunteers received either vaccine or placebo and subsequently ingested an amount of wild type V. cholerae sufficient to cause disease symptoms. The results of these studies are summarized in Table I (on following page).

The degree of protection was influenced by the biotype and serotype of the challenge strain. Immunization with V. cholerae CVD 103-HgR conferred complete protection against a challenge strain of the same biotype/serotype (Classical/Inaba). Protection was evident 8 days after immunization. An undiminished level of protection was maintained for up to 6 months postimmunization. A lower level of protection was observed when a challenge strain with a heterologous biotype and/or serotype was used. It should be noted that immunization with V. cholerae CVD 103-HgR conferred 94% protection against moderate to severe diarrhea (≥2 L of total stool volume purged).

Additional challenge studies were performed with V. cholerae CVD 103, which is identical to V. cholerae CVD 103-HgR with the exception that it does not contain a mercury-resistance marker. The protection afforded following immunization with V. cholerae CVD 103 and challenge approximately 1 month later with a Classical/Inaba, Classical/Ogawa or El Tor/Inaba strain was 87%, 82% and 67%, respectively. While V. cholerae CVD 103-HgR is excreted in the stool at a lower

Table I—Mutacol Berna

Protection Against Experimental Cholera Conferred Following Immunization With V. cholerae CVD 103-HgR

Biotype/Serotype of challenge strain[a]	Number of subjects	Day of challenge[b]	% protection against diarrhea[c]	p
Classical/Inaba	22	8	100	<0.01
	27	30	100	<0.01
	29	180	100	<0.01
El Tor/Inaba	14	30	62	0.06
El Tor/Ogawa	27	10	54	0.038
El Tor/Ogawa	19	30	64	<0.01

[a]V. cholerae CVD 103-HgR is a Classical/Inaba strain.
[b]Represents the number of days after immunization at which the challenge was performed.
[c]Diarrhea was defined as the passage of 2 or more loose stools within 48 hours and at least 200 mL in volume, or a single loose stool of ≥300 mL in volume.

rate than V. cholerae CVD 103, the level of protection conferred when identical challenge strains were used was comparable (100% versus 87% for V. cholerae CVD 103-HgR and V. cholerae CVD 103, respectively, against a Classical/Inaba challenge, and 62 vs 67% against an El Tor/Inaba challenge).

The efficacy of CVD 103-HgR vaccine strain has not been evaluated in cholera endemic areas. However, the above observations support the expectation that this vaccine will provide protection to recipients from noncholera endemic areas such as Canada who travel to cholera endemic areas.

Indications: For immunization of adults and children 2 years of age and older against disease caused by V. cholerae. Results from clinical studies indicate that adults and children 2 years of age and older may be protected against cholera following the oral ingestion of 1 dose of this vaccine. Immunization should be completed at least 1 week prior to potential exposure to V. cholerae.

Routine immunization against cholera is not recommended in Canada. Selective immunization against cholera is recommended for travelers to areas of the world with a risk of exposure to cholera and for travelers to countries requiring evidence of cholera vaccination for entry.

Not all recipients of Mutacol Berna Vaccine will be fully protected against cholera. Travelers should take all necessary precautions to avoid contact with or ingestion of potentially contaminated sources of food or water.

There is no evidence to support the use of cholera vaccine to control common source outbreaks or in the management of household contacts.

Mutacol Berna vaccine will not afford protection against enteric organisms other than V. cholerae. An optimal booster dose has not yet been established. However, it is recommended that a booster dose be taken every 6 months under conditions of repeated or continued exposure to cholera (see Dosage).

Cholera is present in many parts of the world. Travelers entering such areas are at risk of contracting cholera following the ingestion of contaminated food or water. Parenterally administered cholera vaccine has been shown to be effective at reducing the incidence of disease in such endemic areas. However, immunization with such vaccines is frequently accompanied by adverse reactions such as pain and/or swelling at the injection site, fever, malaise and headache.

Contraindications: Hypersensitivity to any component of the vaccine or the buffer.

Safety of Mutacol Berna vaccine has not been demonstrated in persons deficient in their ability to mount a humoral or cell-mediated immune response, due to either a congenital or acquired immunodeficient state including treatment with immunosuppressive or antimitotic drugs. The vaccine should not be administered to these persons regardless of the benefits.

Warnings: Mutacol Berna vaccine is not to be taken during an acute febrile illness or in the face of an acute gastrointestinal illness. Postpone taking the vaccine if persistent diarrhea or vomiting is occurring (see Precautions, General).

Phenylketonurics: Contains 17 mg of phenylalanine per double-chambered sachet. This is due to the fact that Mutacol Berna vaccine is sweetened by aspartame (a phenylalanine derivative).

Precautions: General: Mutacol Berna vaccine should not be administered to persons during an acute febrile illness or acute gastrointestinal illness. The vaccine should not be administered to individuals receiving sulfonamides or antibiotics since these agents may be active against the vaccine strain and prevent a sufficient degree of multiplication to occur. Antimalarial prophylaxis with chloroquine should begin no sooner than 1 week after administration of Mutacol Berna vaccine since concomitant use of this drug has been shown to decrease the immune response to the vaccine. The simultaneous administration of mefloquine or proguanil with Mutacol Berna vaccine has been shown not to significantly decrease the seroconversion rate. The concomitant administration of oral polio vaccine or yellow fever vaccine did not suppress the immune response elicited by Mutacol Berna vaccine. There is no reason to believe that simultaneous administration of parenteral vaccines or immunoglobulins with Mutacol Berna vaccine will decrease vaccine efficacy. The administration of Mutacol Berna vaccine and Vivotif Berna vaccine, enteric coated capsules, should be separated by at least 8 hours due to the fact that the buffer administered with Mutacol Berna vaccine may affect the transit of enteric coated capsules through the gastrointestinal tract.

Information for the Patient: Vaccine potency is dependent upon storage under refrigeration (between 2 and 8°C). The vaccine should be stored under refrigeration at all times. The vaccine should be ingested approximately 1 hour before a meal. It is essential that the buffer and vaccine be resuspended in cold or lukewarm water (temperature not to exceed body temperature, e.g., 37°C). Do not resuspend in milk, juice or in a carbonated beverage. It is essential that the buffer (Chamber A) and vaccine (Chamber B) be added to the liquid (approximately 100 mL) at the same time and mixed for 5 to 10 seconds to yield a homogeneous suspension. The reconstituted vaccine should be swallowed as soon after reconstitution and mixing as possible.

Phenylketonurics: Contains 17 mg of phenylalanine per double-chambered sachet. This is due to the fact that Mutacol Berna vaccine is sweetened by aspartame (a phenylalanine derivative).

Carcinogenesis, Mutagenesis, Impairment of Fertility: Long-term studies in animals with Mutacol Berna vaccine have not been performed as to carcinogenic potential, mutagenic potential or impairment of fertility.

Pregnancy: Animal reproduction studies have not been conducted with Mutacol Berna vaccine. It is not known whether Mutacol Berna vaccine can cause fetal harm when administered to pregnant women or can affect reproduction capacity. Mutacol Berna vaccine should be given to a pregnant woman only if clearly needed.

Lactation: There are no data to warrant the use of this product in nursing mothers. It is not known if Mutacol Berna vaccine is excreted in human milk.

Children: The safety of Mutacol Berna vaccine has not been established in children under 2 years of age. This product is therefore not recommended for use in children under 2 years of age.

Adverse Effects: Several lots of Mutacol Berna vaccine have been evaluated in controlled clinical studies involving adults and children 2 to 9 years of age. Objectively monitored side effects, e.g., abdominal pain, diarrhea, nausea, vomiting, fever, headache and skin rash, did not appear at a statistically higher frequency in the vaccinated group as compared with a placebo group. Reported adverse reactions include nausea, abdominal cramps and diarrhea.

Overdose: Symptoms and Treatment: Mutacol Berna vaccine containing between 5×10^9–1×10^{10} viable vaccine organisms has been administered to several hundred adults and children 2 years of age and older. This dosage was, at a minimum, 5-fold higher than the currently recommended dose. Objectively monitored adverse reactions, e.g., abdominal pain, diarrhea, nausea, vomiting, fever, headache and skin rash, did not occur at a statistically higher rate among the vaccine recipients as compared with a placebo group.

Dosage: The sachet containing the buffer (Chamber A) and vaccine (Chamber B) should be inspected to ensure that the foil is intact. The vaccine is to be swallowed approximately 1 hour before a meal.

The vaccine is to be reconstituted in the following manner (see diagram on sachet). The sachet is to be folded along the solid black line and cut along the dotted line after ensuring that the contents have been displaced to the bottom to prevent spillage. The contents of both chambers are to be emptied simultaneously into 100 mL of cold or lukewarm water (temperature not to exceed body temperature, e.g., 37°C). Do not resuspend in milk, juice or in a carbonated beverage. Resuspend the sachet contents by gently mixing for 5 to 10 seconds. The vaccine should be swallowed as soon after mixing as possible. Not all recipients of Mutacol Berna vaccine will be fully protected against cholera.

Travelers should take all necessary precautions to avoid contact with or ingestion of potentially contaminated food or water.

Booster: The optimum booster schedule for Mutacol Berna vaccine has not been determined. Efficacy has been shown to persist for at least 6 months. Further, there is no experience with Mutacol Berna vaccine as a booster in persons previously immunized with parenteral cholera vaccine. Despite these limitations, it is recommended that a booster dose be given every 6 months under conditions of repeated or continued exposure to cholera.

Supplied: Mutacol Berna vaccine is a live attenuated vaccine for oral administration. The vaccine contains the attenuated strain V. cholerae CVD 103-HgR and is manufactured by the Swiss Serum and Vaccine Institute Berne. The vaccine strain is grown under controlled conditions in a medium containing casamino acids, yeast extract and mineral salts. The bacteria are collected by filtration, mixed with a stabilizer containing sucrose, ascorbic acid and amino acids, and lyophilized. The lyophilized bacteria are mixed with lactose and aspartame and filled into 1 chamber of an aluminum foil sachet. Mutacol Berna vaccine is sweetened by aspartame (a phenylalanine derivative) and therefore contains 17 mg of phenylalanine. The other chamber of the sachet contains a sodium bicarbonate ascorbic acid buffer which serves to neutralize gastric acid.

The contents of the vaccine and buffer chamber are: Buffer Chamber (A): sodium bicarbonate 2.4 to 2.9 g; ascorbic acid 1.5 to 1.8 g; lactose 0.18 to 0.22 g. Vaccine Chamber (B): viable V. cholerae CVD 103-HgR $2\text{-}10\times10^8$ colony-forming units; non-viable V. cholerae CVD 103-HgR $20\text{-}100\times10^8$ bacterial cells; sucrose 1.4 to 30 mg; amino acid mixture 0.15 to 3 mg; ascorbic acid 0.06 to 1 mg; aspartame 20 to 30 mg; lactose 1.8 to 2.1 g. Packages of 1 single double-chambered aluminum foil sachet containing 1 dose of vaccine.

The contents of each chamber (chamber A and B) require simultaneous reconstitution prior to oral administration. Mutacol Berna is not stable when exposed to ambient temperatures. The vaccine should therefore be shipped and stored between 2 and 8°C. Each package of vaccine shows an expiration date. This expiration date is valid only if the product has been maintained at 2 to 8°C. Store in a dry place and protect from light.

Reviewed 1998

MUTAMYCIN® Ⓟ

Bristol

Mitomycin

Antineoplastic

Pharmacology: Mitomycin was investigated at first as an antibiotic in Japan. It was then found to be active as an antineoplastic agent. It selectively inhibits the synthesis of deoxyribonucleic acid (DNA). The exact point of mitomycin attachment to DNA remains unknown. At high concentrations of the drug, cellular RNA and protein synthesis are also suppressed.

Mitomycin is rapidly cleared from the plasma after i.v. administration with a biphasic plasma elimination curve. Mitomycin is widely distributed but does not appear to cross the blood brain barrier. After i.v. injection of 30, 20 or 10 mg of mitomycin, the maximal serum concentrations were 2.4, 1.7 and 0.52 µg/mL respectively. Serum half-life after a 30 mg bolus injection is 17 minutes. Clearance is effected primarily by metabolism in the liver, but metabolism occurs in other tissues as well. In general, the smaller the dose, the more rapidly blood levels of mitomycin decreased.

Approximately 10% of a dose of mitomycin is excreted unchanged in the urine. Since metabolic pathways are saturated at relatively low doses, the percent of a dose excreted in urine increases with increasing doses. In children, excretion of i.v. administered mitomycin is similar.

Mutamycin (cont'd)

Mitomycin is not appreciably absorbed from the urinary bladder following intravesical administration. Serial plasma samples from 55 patients treated with doses of 20 and 40 mg of mitomycin by intravesical instillation were assayed. There was no mitomycin detectable (assay limit 10 and 100 ng/mL) in any plasma samples collected during and 30 minutes post-therapy at any dose.

Indications: In the palliative treatment as an adjunct to surgery, radiation, or chemotherapy for adenocarcinoma of the stomach and colon.

Mitomycin as a single agent is indicated as topical therapy for superficial (no invasion beyond the lamina propria) transitional cell carcinoma of the urinary bladder. Efficacy has been demonstrated both in patients who have had no prior intravesical chemotherapy and in those who have failed such therapy with thiotepa or other antineoplastic agents.

Contraindications: Patients who have demonstrated hypersensitivity or an idiosyncratic reaction to it, or any component of its formulation, in the past.

Mitomycin is contraindicated in patients with thrombocytopenia, leukopenia, coagulation disorder, or an increased bleeding tendency due to other causes.

Mitomycin is contraindicated for intravesical administration in patients who have demonstrated a hypersensitive or idiosyncratic reaction to it in the past.

Warnings: Caution: Mitomycin is a potent drug and should be used only by physicians experienced with cancer chemotherapeutic drugs (see Precautions). Blood counts should be taken weekly. Mitomycin must be discontinued or dosage reduced upon evidence of abnormal depression of the bone marrow, or the development of significant renal or pulmonary toxicity.

It is recommended that mitomycin be administered under the supervision of a qualified physician experienced in the use of cancer chemotherapeutic agents. Since facilities for necessary laboratory studies must be available, hospitalization of patients is recommended.

Mitomycin should not be administered to any patient with a white blood cell count below 4 000 mm^3 or a platelet count below 150 000 mm^3, or those with potentially serious infections.

Bone marrow depression, notably thrombocytopenia and leukopenia is the most severe toxicity (see Adverse Effects). Thrombocytopenia may contribute to hemorrhage and leukopenia to overwhelming infection in an already compromised, poor risk patient and may result in death.

In the treatment of each patient, the physician must weigh carefully the possibility of achieving therapeutic benefit versus the risk of toxicity. Studies have shown that mitomycin is carcinogenic in animals.

Pregnancy: Safe use of mitomycin in pregnant women has not been established. Mitomycin has known teratogenic properties in animals, therefore, the benefits derived from the use of mitomycin must be weighed against the hazards involved.

Lactation: It is not known if mitomycin is excreted in human milk. It is recommended that women receiving mitomycin not breast-feed because of the potential for serious adverse reactions from mitomycin in nursing infants.

Precautions: Mitomycin should be administered, preferably, to patients who are hospitalized.

It should be used with extreme caution in patients with significant impairment of renal function.

Since mitomycin has a high incidence of bone marrow depression, particularly thrombocytopenia and leukopenia, dose adjustment according to nadir count may be required. The following studies should be obtained repeatedly during therapy and for at least 8 weeks following therapy: platelet count, prothrombin time, bleeding time, white blood count and differential. The persistence of thrombocytopenia below 150 000/mm^3 or a significant prolongation of prothrombin time or bleeding time or a WBC below 4 000/mm^3 is an indication for the termination of therapy.

Hemolytic Uremic Syndrome (HUS), a serious complication of chemotherapy, consisting primarily of microangiopathic hemolytic anemia, thrombocytopenia and irreversible renal failure has been reported in patients receiving mitomycin. The syndrome may occur at any time during systemic therapy with mitomycin as a single agent or in combination with other cytotoxic drugs, however, most cases occur at doses $\geq$60 mg of mitomycin. Blood product transfusion may exacerbate the symptoms associated with this syndrome. The incidence of the syndrome has not been defined (see Adverse Effects).

Patients should be advised of the potential toxicity of this drug, particularly bone marrow depression. A low incidence of septicemic deaths, as a result of leukopenia attributable to the drug, have been reported. Patients should be instructed of the relevant symptomatology and advised of the importance of promptly notifying their physicians of the development of these symptoms.

Patients receiving mitomycin should be observed for evidence of renal toxicity. Mitomycin should not be given to patients with a serum creatinine greater than 1.7 mg/dL (150 μmol/L).

Mitomycin-associated pulmonary events have occurred infrequently but can be severe and life-threatening. Cases have been reported with both single-agent therapy and combination chemotherapy. Dyspnea and nonproductive cough are the usual presenting symptoms. Radiographic evidence of interstitial infiltrates may or may not be present. If other etiologies have been eliminated, a diagnosis of mitomycin-related pulmonary toxicity may be made. Corticosteroids have been employed in treatment, but their therapeutic value has not been determined.

Signs and symptoms of pneumonitis associated with mitomycin may be reversed if appropriate therapy is instituted early. The use of mitomycin should be discontinued. Corticosteroids have been reported by several authors to expedite symptomatic relief.

Acute shortness of breath and severe bronchospasm have been reported following the administration of vinca alkaloids in patients who had previously or simultaneously received mitomycin. The onset of this acute respiratory distress has occurred within minutes to hours after the vinca alkaloid injection. The total number of doses for each drug has varied considerably. Bronchodilators, corticosteroids and/or oxygen have produced symptomatic relief.

A few cases of adult respiratory distress syndrome have been reported in patients receiving mitomycin in combination with other chemotherapeutic agents who were being maintained perioperatively at FiO_2 concentrations greater than 50%. Therefore, caution should be exercised, and only enough oxygen to provide adequate arterial saturation should be used since oxygen itself can be toxic to the lungs. Careful attention should be paid to fluid balance and overhydration should be avoided.

Adverse Effects: Hematologic: The most serious and most common toxicity of mitomycin is bone marrow suppression. Thrombocytopenia and/or leukopenia may occur anytime within 8 weeks after initiation of therapy, with an average time of 4 weeks. The return to normal counts after cessation of therapy was within 10 weeks. In a recent study, at a dose of 20 mg/m^2 every 6 to 8 weeks, by itself or in combination with 5-fluorouracil, leukopenia occurred in 74 of 94 patients, with 10 being in the life-threatening category and thrombocytopenia occurring in 68 of 94 patients, with 18 being in the life-threatening category. In a previous study, at doses of 0.5 mg/kg/day for 5 days and repeating once monthly, or 0.25 mg/kg every 2 weeks, leukopenia and/or thrombocytopenia occurred in 605 of 937 patients. About 25% of the leukopenic or thrombocytopenic episodes did not resolve. Mitomycin produces cumulative myelosuppression.

Skin and Mucous Membrane: Cellulitis at the injection site has been reported and is occasionally severe. Stomatitis and alopecia also occur frequently. Rashes are rarely reported. The most important dermatological event is necrosis and consequent sloughing of tissue which results if the drug is extravasated during injection.

Extravasation may occur with or without an accompanying stinging or burning sensation and even if there is adequate blood return when the injection needle is aspirated. There have been reports of delayed erythema and/or ulceration occurring either at or distant from the injection site, weeks to months after mitomycin, even when no obvious evidence of extravasation was observed during administration. Skin grafting has been required in some of the cases.

Pulmonary Toxicity: Refer to section on pulmonary toxicity in Precautions.

Renal: A small number of patients in clinical trials demonstrated a significant rise in BUN from a baseline pretherapy. There appeared to be no correlation between total dose administered or duration of therapy and renal toxicity. Seventy-five percent of the patients with a definite renal toxicity had evidence of metastatic disease. The data, to date, are inconclusive as far as a direct relationship of mitomycin to renal toxicity.

Hemolytic Uremic Syndrome (HUS): This serious complication of chemotherapy consisting of microangiopathic hemolytic anemia (hematocrit $\leq$25%), thrombocytopenia ($\leq$100 000/mm^3), and irreversible renal failure (serum creatinine $\geq$1.6 mg/dL or $\geq$140 μmol/L) has been reported in patients receiving systemic mitomycin. Most of these patients received long-term therapy (6 to 12 months) with mitomycin in combination with fluorouracil and doxorubicin; however, some patients received mitomycin in combination with other drugs or were treated for less than 6 months. Microangiopathic hemolysis with fragmented red blood cells seen on peripheral blood smears has occurred in 98% of the patients with the syndrome. Other less frequent complications of the syndrome may include pulmonary edema (65%), neurologic abnormalities (16%), and hypertension. Exacerbation of the symptoms associated with HUS has been reported in some patients receiving blood product transfusions. The incidence of the syndrome has not been defined. A high mortality rate (52%) has been associated with this syndrome (see Precautions).

The syndrome may occur at any time during systemic therapy with mitomycin as a single agent or in combination with other cytotoxic drugs. Less frequently, HUS has also been reported in patients receiving combinations of cytotoxic drugs not including mitomycin. Of 83 patients studied, 72 developed the syndrome at total doses exceeding 60 mg of mitomycin. Consequently, patients receiving $\geq$60 mg of mitomycin should be monitored closely for unexplained anemia with fragmented cells on peripheral blood smear, thrombocytopenia, and decreased renal function.

Acute Adverse Effects: Fever, hemolytic anemia, anorexia, stomatitis, hypoglycemia, mucositis, and diarrhea have occurred.

Other adverse effects that have been reported during mitomycin therapy have been: headache, blurring of vision, confusion, drowsiness, syncope, fatigue, weakness, edema, thrombophlebitis, hematemesis, nausea, vomiting, weight loss, ataxia and pain. These do not appear to be dose-related and it was unclear whether they were drug-related or due to the primary or metastatic disease process.

Genitourinary irritation following intravesical administration indicated dysuria, cystitis, nocturia and increased frequency of micturition, hematuria and other symptoms of local irritation. Approximately 25% of the patients treated experienced irritative symptoms, but not all were unequivocally drug-related and may have been symptoms of the disease.

Dermatitis occurred in approximately 10% of the patients treated. It was commonly manifested as palmar rash with desquamation, generally appearing on the extremities and less often on the trunk, and also as genital rash. Topical steroids have been employed, but their therapeutic value has not been determined.

Overdose: Symptoms and Treatment: No specific antidote for mitomycin is known. Management of overdosage would include general supportive measures to sustain the patient through any period of toxicity that might occur.

Dosage: Mitomycin should be given with care to avoid extravasation of the compound into the tissue. If extravasation occurs, cellulitis, ulceration and sloughing may result.

To reconstitute a vial, add Sterile Water for Injection as listed in the Reconstitution Table (see Table I).

Table I—Mutamycin

Reconstitution Table

Vial Size	Diluent Added to Vial (mL)	Approximate Available Volume (mL)	Approximate Concentration (mg/mL)
5 mg	10	9.5	0.5
20 mg	40	39.0	0.5

Shake well until dissolved. If the product does not dissolve immediately, shake under warm tap water for approximately 2 minutes until a solution is obtained.

I.V.: After full hematological recovery from any previous chemotherapy, either of the following Dosage Schedules may be used at 6- to 8-week intervals. Because of cumulative myelosuppression, patients should be re-evaluated after each course of mitomycin and the dose reduced if the patient has experienced any toxicities (see Guide to Dosage Adjustment). Doses greater than 20 mg/m^2 do not demonstrate increased effectiveness and are more toxic than lower doses.

(1) 20 mg/m^2 i.v. as a single dose via a functioning i.v. catheter.

(2) 2 mg/m^2/day i.v. for 5 days. After a drug-free interval of 2 days, 2 mg/m^2/day for 5 days, thus making the total initial dose of 20 mg/m^2 given over 10 days.

Intravesicle: 20 to 40 mg intravesically at a concentration of 1 mg/mL in sterile water once per week for 8 weeks. Patients are advised to abstain from liquids for 12 hours prior to

therapy. The patient is catheterized, bladder drained and mitomycin instilled. The solution should be retained for 2 hours. If desired, the patient may rotate positions every 15 minutes, for maximum area-contact.
Guide to Dosage Adjustment: The schedule in Table II is suggested as a guide to dosage adjustment.

Table II—Mutamycin

Guide to Dosage Adjustment

Nadir After Prior Dose Leukocytes (mm³)	Platelets (mm³)	Percentage of Prior Dose to be Given (%)
>4 000	>100 000	100
3 000–3 999	75 000–99 999	100
2 000–2 999	25 000–74 999	70
<2 000	<25 000	50

No repeat dosage should be given until leukocyte count has returned to 3 000 and platelet count to 75 000/mm³.

When mitomycin is used in combination with other myelosuppressive agents, the doses should be adjusted accordingly. If the disease continues to progress after 2 courses of mitomycin, the drug should be stopped since chances of response are minimal.
Stability: Store mitomycin at room temperature (15 to 30°C) and protect from light.

When reconstituted with Sterile Water for Injection to a concentration of 0.5 mg/mL, mitomycin is stable for 14 days when refrigerated (2 to 8°C), or for 7 days at room temperature (15 to 30°C). Protect from light.

When reconstituted with Sterile Water for Injection to a concentration of 1 mg/mL, mitomycin is stable for 7 days at room temperature (25°C). If undissolved particles appear after reconstitution, warm the vial slightly with shaking. Solutions of mitomycin at a concentration of 1 mg/mL, should not be stored under refrigeration since precipitation may occur.

When diluted in various i.v. fluids at room temperature (15 to 30°C), to a concentration of 20 to 40 µg/mL, mitomycin is stable as shown in Table III.

Table III—Mutamycin

Dilution

I.V. Fluid	Stability (Hours)
5% Dextrose Injection	3
0.9% Sodium Chloride Injection	12
Sodium Lactate Injection	24

The combination of mitomycin (5 to 15 mg) and heparin (1 000 to 10 000 units) in 30 mL of 0.9% Sodium Chloride Injection is stable for 48 hours at room temperature (15 to 30°C).
Handling and Disposal: Preparation of Mutamycin should be done in a vertical laminar flow hood (Biological Safety Cabinet-Class II).

Personnel preparing Mutamycin should wear PVC gloves, safety glasses, disposable gowns and masks.

All needles, syringes, vials and other materials which have come in contact with Mutamycin should be segregated and incinerated at 1 000°C or more. Sealed containers may explode sealed. Intact vials should be returned to the Manufacturer for destruction. Proper precautions should be taken in packaging these materials for transport.

Personnel regularly involved in the preparation and handling of Mutamycin should have bi-annual blood examinations.

Supplied: Each vial contains: mitomycin 5 mg and 20 mg as sterile lyophilized powder. Nonmedicinal ingredients: mannitol. Store at room temperature (15 to 30°C) and protect from light.

Reviewed 1998

M.V.I.®-12 (MULTIVITAMIN INFUSION)

Rhône-Poulenc Rorer

Multivitamins

Vitamin Supplement

Indications: This formulation is indicated as daily multivitamin maintenance dosage for adults and children aged 11 and above receiving parenteral nutrition.

It is also indicated in other situations where administration by the i.v. route is required.

Such situations include surgery, (including pre- and postoperative parenteral nutrition), extensive burns, fractures and other trauma, severe infectious diseases and comatose states, which may provoke a stress situation with profound alterations in the body's metabolic demands and consequent tissue depletion of nutrients.

The physician should not await the development of clinical signs of vitamin deficiency before initiating vitamin therapy. The use of multivitamin product eliminates the need to speculate on the status of individual vitamin levels.

M.V.I.-12 (administered in i.v. fluids after proper dilution) contributes to the intake of these necessary vitamins toward maintaining the body's normal resistance and repair processes.

Patients with multiple vitamin deficiencies or with markedly increased requirements may be given multiples of the daily dosage for 2 or more days as indicated by the clinical status.

M.V.I.-12 does not contain vitamin K, which may have to be administered separately.

Clinical testing indicates that some patients do not maintain adequate levels of certain vitamins when this formulation in recommended amounts is the sole source of vitamins. No vitamin deficiencies were clinically evident, but blood levels of vitamins A, C, D and folic acid declined in a number of subjects who received this formulation as the only vitamin source for 4 to 6 months. Therefore, in patients for whom total parenteral nutrition will be continued for long periods of time, these vitamins should be monitored. If deficiencies appear to be developing, multiples of the formulation (1.5 to 3 times) may be needed for a period of time. When multiples of the formulation are used for more than a few weeks, vitamins A and D should be monitored occasionally to be certain that an excess accumulation of these vitamins is not occurring.

Contraindications: Known hypersensitivity to any of the vitamins contained in this product or pre-existing hypervitaminosis.

Precautions: Drug Interactions: M.V.I.-12 is not physically compatible with acetazolamide 500 mg, i.v. sodium chlorothiazide 500 mg, or moderately alkaline solutions. Tetracycline 500 mg may not be physically compatible with M.V.I.-12. It has been reported that folic acid is unstable in the presence of calcium salts such as calcium gluconate. Some of the vitamins in M.V.I.-12 may react with vitamin K bisulfite. Direct addition of M.V.I.-12 to i.v. fat emulsions is not recommended.

Adverse Effects: There have been rare reports of anaphylactoid reactions following large i.v. doses of thiamine. The risk, however, is negligible if thiamine is co-administered with other vitamins in the B group. There have been no reports of fatal anaphylactoid reactions associated with M.V.I.-12.

There have been rare reports of the following types of reactions: Dermatologic: rash, erythema, pruritus.
CNS: headache, dizziness, agitation, anxiety.
Ophthalmic: diplopia.
Allergic: urticaria, periorbital and digital edema.

Dosage: M.V.I.-12 in the two-vial package is ready for immediate use in the adults and children aged 11 and above, when added to i.v. infusion fluids.

M.V.I.-12 should not be given as a direct, undiluted i.v. injection as it may give rise to dizziness, faintness, and possible tissue irritation.

For i.v. feeding, 1 daily dose of M.V.I.-12 (5 mL of vial 1 plus 5 mL of vial 2) should be added directly to not less than 500 mL, preferably 1 000 mL, of i.v. dextrose, saline or similar infusion solutions.

Parenteral drug products should be inspected visually for particulate matter and discoloration prior to administration, whenever solution and container permit.
Storage: Keep the unopened vials in the refrigerator (2 to 8°C).

After M.V.I.-12 is diluted in an i.v. infusion, the resulting solution should be refrigerated unless it is to be administered immediately, and in any event should be stored in glass and administered within 48 hours. Some of the vitamins in this product, particularly vitamins A, D and riboflavin, are light-sensitive, and exposure to light should be minimized.

Supplied: Each sterile, single dose package contains: one 5 mL vial (labelled **Vial 1**) and one 5 mL vial (labelled **Vial 2**) which after mixing, provide 1 dose of 10 mL. Boxes of 10.

Vial 1: Each mL provides ascorbic acid 20 mg, vitamin A 660 IU, vitamin D 40 IU, thiamine (as HCl) 0.6 mg, riboflavin (as phosphate) 0.72 mg, pyridoxine HCl 0.8 mg, niacinamide 8 mg, d-pantothenic acid (as d-panthenol) 3 mg and vitamin E 2.0 IU. Nonmedicinal ingredients: alkali oil, gentisic acid ethanolamide, polysorbate 80, propylene glycol and water for injection.

Vial 2: Each mL provides biotin 12 µg, folic acid 0.08 mg and vitamin B_{12} 1 µg. Nonmedicinal ingredients: alkali oil, citric acid, propylene glycol, sodium citrate and water for injection.

MYAMBUTOL® Ⓟ

Wyeth-Ayerst

Ethambutol HCl

Tuberculostatic Agent

Supplied: Each round, white, scored, film-coated tablet, engraved "LL" and "M7", contains: ethambutol HCl 400 mg. Nonmedicinal ingredients: alcohol, ethylcellulose, FD&C Blue No. 2 aluminum lake, gelatin, hydroxypropyl cellulose, hydroxypropyl methylcellulose, magnesium stearate, methyl alcohol, methylene chloride technical, mineral oil, sorbitol solution, stearic acid, sucrose granulated, sucrose extra ground starch-free and titanium dioxide. Energy: <4.2 kJ (1 kcal). Tartrazine-free. Bottles of 100.

MYCIFRADIN® Ⓟ

Pharmacia & Upjohn

Neomycin Sulfate

Antibiotic

Pharmacology: Neomycin is an aminoglycoside antibiotic, active against many strains of Gram-negative bacteria. Neomycin is poorly absorbed from the normal gastrointestinal tract. The small absorbed fraction is rapidly distributed in the tissues and is excreted by the kidney in keeping with the degree of kidney function. The unabsorbed portion of the drug (approximately 97%) is eliminated unchanged in the feces.

Growth of most intestinal bacteria is rapidly suppressed following oral administration of neomycin, with the suppression persisting for 48 to 72 hours. Nonpathogenic yeasts and occasionally resistant strains of E. aerogenes (formerly A. aerogenes) replace the intestinal bacteria.

As with other aminoglycosides, the amount of systemically absorbed neomycin transferred to the tissues increases cumulatively with each repeated dose administered until a steady state is achieved. The kidney functions as the primary excretory path as well as the tissue binding site with the highest concentration found in the renal cortex. With repeated dosings, progressive accumulation also occurs in the inner ear. Release of tissue bound neomycin occurs slowly over a period of several weeks after dosing has been discontinued.

Protein binding studies have shown that the degree of aminoglycoside protein binding is low and depending upon the methods used for testing, this may be between 1 and 30%.

Indications: For adjunctive therapy in the preoperative preparation of the bowel prior to abdominal or perineal surgery involving the lower intestinal tract. Neomycin has also proved a valuable adjunct in the management of hepatic coma by reducing the ammonia-forming bacteria in the intestinal tract.

Contraindications: In the presence of intestinal obstruction and in individuals with a history of hypersensitivity to the drug.

Patients with a history of hypersensitivity or serious toxic reaction to other aminoglycosides may have a cross-sensitivity to neomycin.

Also contraindicated in patients with inflammatory or ulcerative gastrointestinal disease because of the potential for enhanced gastrointestinal absorption of neomycin.

Warnings: Systemic absorption of neomycin occurs following oral administration, and toxic reactions may occur. Patients treated with neomycin should be under close clinical observation because of the potential toxicity associated with their use.

Neurotoxicity (including ototoxicity) and nephrotoxicity following the oral use of neomycin have been reported, even when used in recommended doses. The potential for nephrotoxicity, permanent bilateral auditory ototoxicity and sometimes vestibular toxicity is present in patients with normal renal function when treated with higher doses of neomycin and/or for longer periods than recommended.

Serial, vestibular, and audiometric tests, as well as tests of renal function, should be performed (especially in high risk patients). The risk of nephrotoxicity and ototoxicity is greater in patients with impaired renal function.

Ototoxicity is often delayed in onset and patients developing cochlear damage will not have symptoms during therapy to warn them of developing eighth nerve destruction and total or partial deafness may occur long after neomycin has been discontinued.

Neuromuscular blockade and respiratory paralysis have been reported following the oral use of neomycin. The possibility of the occurrence of neuromuscular blockage and respiratory paralysis should be considered if neomycin is

Mycifradin (cont'd)

administered, especially to patients receiving anesthetics, neuromuscular blocking agents such as tubocurarine, succinylcholine, decamethonium, or in patients receiving massive transfusions of citrate anticoagulated blood. If blockage occurs, calcium salts may reverse these phenomena but mechanical respiratory assistance may be necessary.

Concurrent and/or sequential systemic, oral, or topical use of other aminoglycosides including paromomycin and other potentially nephrotoxic and/or neurotoxic drugs such as bacitracin, cisplatin, vancomycin, amphotericin B, polymyxin B, colistin, and viomycin should be avoided because the toxicity may be additive.

Other factors which increase the risk of toxicity are advanced age and dehydration.

The concurrent use of neomycin with potent diuretics such as ethacrynic acid or furosemide should be avoided since certain diuretics by themselves may cause ototoxicity. In addition, when administered i.v., diuretics may enhance neomycin toxicity by altering the antibiotic concentration in serum and tissue.

Additional manifestations of neurotoxicity may include numbness, skin tingling, muscle twitching, and convulsions.

The risk of hearing loss continues after drug withdrawal.

Pregnancy: Aminoglycosides can cause fetal harm when administered to a pregnant woman. Aminoglycoside antibiotics cross the placenta and there have been several reports of total irreversible bilateral congenital deafness in children whose mothers received streptomycin during pregnancy. Although serious side effects to fetus or newborn have not been reported in the treatment of pregnant women with other aminoglycosides, the potential for harm exists. Animal reproduction studies of neomycin have not been conducted. If neomycin is used during pregnancy, or if the patient becomes pregnant while taking this drug, the patient should be apprised of the potential hazard to the fetus.

Precautions: General: As with other antibiotics, use of oral neomycin may result in overgrowth of nonsusceptible organisms, particularly fungi. If this occurs, appropriate therapy should be instituted.

Neomycin is quickly and almost totally absorbed from body surfaces (except the urinary bladder) after local irrigation and when applied topically in association with surgical procedures. Delayed-onset, irreversible deafness, renal failure, and death due to neuromuscular blockade (regardless of the status of renal function) have been reported following irrigation of both small and large surgical fields with minute quantities of neomycin.

Aminoglycosides should be used with caution in patients with muscular disorders such as myasthenia gravis or parkinsonism since these drugs may aggravate muscle weakness because of their potential curare-like effect on the neuromuscular junction.

Small amounts of orally administered neomycin are absorbed through intact intestinal mucosa. The drug may be absorbed from ulcerated or denuded areas.

There have been many reports in the literature of nephrotoxicity and/or ototoxicity with the oral use of neomycin. If renal insufficiency develops during oral therapy, consideration should be given to reducing the drug dosage or discontinuing therapy.

An oral neomycin dose of 12 g/day produces a malabsorption syndrome for a variety of substances including fat, nitrogen, cholesterol, carotene, glucose, xylose, lactose, sodium, calcium, cyanocobalamin and iron.

Orally administered neomycin increases fecal bile acid excretion and reduces intestinal lactase activity.

Laboratory Tests: Patients with renal insufficiency may develop toxic neomycin blood levels unless doses are properly regulated. If renal insufficiency develops during treatment, the dosage should be reduced or the antibiotic discontinued. To avoid nephrotoxicity and eighth nerve damage associated with high doses and prolonged treatment, the following should be performed prior to and periodically during therapy: urinalysis for increased excretion of protein, decreased specific gravity, casts and cells; renal function tests such as serum creatinine, BUN or creatinine clearance; tests of the vestibulocochlearis nerve (eighth cranial nerve) function.

Serial, vestibular and audiometric tests should be performed (especially in high risk patients). Since elderly patients may have reduced renal function which may not be evident in the results of routine screening tests such as BUN or serum creatinine, a creatinine clearance determination may be more useful.

Drug Interactions: Caution should be taken in concurrent or serial use of other neurotoxic and/or nephrotoxic drugs because of possible enhancement of the nephrotoxicity and/or ototoxicity of neomycin (see Warnings).

Caution should also be taken in concurrent or serial use of other aminoglycosides and polymyxins because they may enhance neomycin's nephrotoxicity and/or ototoxicity and potentiate neomycin's neuromuscular blocking effects.

Oral neomycin inhibits the gastrointestinal absorption of penicillin V, oral vitamin B_{12}, methotrexate and 5-fluorouracil. The gastrointestinal absorption of digoxin also appears to be inhibited. Therefore, digoxin serum levels should be monitored.

Oral neomycin may enhance the effect of coumarin anticoagulants by decreasing vitamin K availability.

Carcinogenesis, Mutagenesis, Impairment of Fertility: No long-term animal studies have been performed with neomycin to evaluate carcinogenic or mutagenic potential or impairment of fertility.

Lactation: It is not known whether neomycin is excreted in human milk but it has been shown to be excreted in cow milk following a single i.m. injection. Other aminoglycosides have been shown to be excreted in human milk. Because of the potential for serious adverse reactions from the aminoglycosides in nursing infants, a decision should be made whether to discontinue nursing or to discontinue the drug, taking into account the importance of the drug to the mother.

Children: The safety and efficacy of oral neomycin in patients less than 18 years of age have not been established. If treatment of a patient less than 18 years of age is necessary, neomycin should be used with caution and the period of treatment should not exceed 2 weeks because of absorption from the gastrointestinal tract.

Adverse Effects: The most common adverse reactions to oral neomycin are nausea, vomiting and diarrhea. The "Malabsorption Syndrome" characterized by increased fecal fat, decreased serum carotene and fall in xylose absorption has been reported with prolonged therapy.

Nephrotoxicity, ototoxicity, and neuromuscular blockage have been reported (see Warnings and Precautions).

Overdose: Symptoms and Treatment: Because of low absorption, it is unlikely that acute overdosage would occur with oral neomycin. However, prolonged administration could result in sufficient systemic drug levels to produce neurotoxicity, ototoxicity, and/or nephrotoxicity.

Hemodialysis will remove neomycin from the blood.

Dosage: To minimize the risk of toxicity use the lowest possible dose and the shortest possible treatment period to control the condition. Treatment for periods longer than 2 weeks is not recommended.

Bowel Preparation Prior to Surgery: Where there is no contraindication to the use of neomycin, the following regimen is recommended. 1. Low-residue diet. 2. One gram of neomycin (2 tablets) immediately following a cathartic. Repeat dose every 4 hours to a total of 6 g. **Preoperative treatment should ordinarily be carried out for 24 hours, and should not extend beyond 72 hours in any case.**

Note: Neomycin is usually used in combination with erythromycin or metronidazole.

Hepatic Coma: For use as an adjunct in the management of hepatic coma, the recommended dose is 4 to 12 g/day given in the following regimen: 1. Withdraw protein from diet. Avoid use of diuretic agents. 2. Give supportive therapy including blood products, as indicated. 3. Give neomycin Oral Solution in doses of 4 to 12 g of neomycin/day in divided doses. Treatment should be continued over a period of 5 to 6 days during which time protein should be returned incrementally to the diet. 4. If less potentially toxic drugs cannot be used for chronic hepatic insufficiency, neomycin in doses of up to 4 g daily may be necessary. The risks for the development of neomycin induced toxicity progressively increase when treatment must be extended to preserve the life of a patient with hepatic encephalopathy who has failed to fully respond. Frequent periodic monitoring of these patients to ascertain the presence of drug toxicity is mandatory (see Precautions). Also, neomycin serum concentrations should be monitored to avoid potentially toxic levels. The benefits to the patient should be weighed against the risks of nephrotoxicity, permanent ototoxicity and neuromuscular blockade following the accumulation of neomycin in the tissues.

Supplied: Oral Solution: Each 5 mL of clear red, cherry-flavored solution contains: neomycin sulfate 125 mg. Nonmedicinal ingredients: benzoic acid, cherry flavor, FD&C Red No. 4, glycerin, methylparaben, propylparaben, purified water, sodium cyclamate and sodium phosphate, standard supercel and sulfuric acid. Bottles of 100 mL.

Tablets: Each ivory, full oval, compressed tablet contains: neomycin sulfate 0.5 g. Nonmedicinal ingredients: alcohol, calcium stearate and povidone. Bottles of 100.

Store at controlled room temperature 15 to 30°C in tight, light-resistant containers.

(Shown in Product Recognition Section)

MYCIGUENT® Ⓟ
Pharmacia & Upjohn

Neomycin Sulfate

Topical Antibiotic

Indications: The prevention and treatment of infection in minor skin breaks caused by cuts, scratches, burns and other injuries.

Contraindications: Neomycin sensitivity.

Precautions: Articles in current medical literature indicate an increase in the incidence of patients sensitive to neomycin. The possibility of such a reaction should be borne in mind. Discontinue use if sensitization occurs. As with any antibiotic product, overgrowth by resistant organisms may occur, particularly monilia. If this occurs, discontinue treatment and institute appropriate measures.

Dosage: Apply to affected area once or twice daily.

Supplied: Each g of ointment contains: neomycin sulfate 5 mg (0.5%) (equivalent to 3.5 mg neomycin base) in wool fat, mineral oil and white petrolatum. Tubes of 25 g.

MYCIL®
Roberts

Chlorphenesin

Fungicide

Supplied: Each g of cream contains: chlorphenesin 1%. Cartoned tubes of 30 g.

MYCOBUTIN® Ⓟ
Pharmacia & Upjohn

Rifabutin

Antibacterial Agent

Pharmacology: Rifabutin is a derivative of rifamycin S, belonging to the class of ansamycins. The rifamycins owe their antimycobacterial efficacy to their ability to penetrate the cell wall and to their ability to complex with and to inhibit DNA-dependent RNA polymerase. Rifabutin has been found to interact with and to penetrate the outer layers of the mycobacterial envelope.

Rifabutin inhibits DNA-dependent RNA polymerase in susceptible strains of E. coli and B. subtilis but not in mammalian cells. In resistant strains of E. coli, rifabutin, like rifampin, did not inhibit this enzyme. It is not known whether rifabutin inhibits DNA-dependent RNA polymerase in M. avium or in M. intracellulare which constitutes M. avium complex (MAC). Rifabutin inhibited incorporation of thymidine into DNA of rifampin-resistant M. tuberculosis suggesting that rifabutin may also inhibit DNA synthesis which may explain its activity against rifampin-resistant organisms.

Pharmacokinetics: Following oral administration, at least 53% of rifabutin dose is rapidly absorbed with rifabutin peak plasma concentrations attained in 2 to 4 hours. High-fat meals slow the rate without influencing the extent of absorption of rifabutin from the capsule dosage form.

The mean (±SD) absolute bioavailability assessed in HIV positive patients in a multiple dose study was 20% (±16%, n=5) on day 1 and 12% (±5%, n=7) on day 28.

In healthy adult volunteers administered a single oral dose of 300 mg of rifabutin, the mean (±SD) peak plasma concentration (C_{max}) was 375 (±267) ng/mL (range: 141 to 1 033 ng/mL). Mean rifabutin steady-state trough levels (C_p, min^{ss}, 24-hour post dose) ranged from 50 to 65 ng/mL in HIV positive patients and in healthy normal volunteers. Pharmacokinetic dose-proportionality over the 300 to 900 mg single dose range has been demonstrated in early symptomatic HIV positive patients and in healthy normal volunteers over the 300 to 600 mg single dose range.

Rifabutin appears to be widely distributed throughout the body and has been detected in all tissues and body fluids examined. Several times higher concentrations than those achieved in plasma have been observed in lung parenchyma, gallbladder and the small intestinal wall. The apparent volume of distribution at steady-state (V_{ss}) estimated in early symptomatic HIV positive male patients following i.v. dosing was large (8 to 9 L/kg), suggesting extensive distribution of rifabutin into the tissues. About 85% of the drug is bound to plasma proteins over a concentration range of 50 to 1 000 ng/mL. Binding is predominantly to human serum albumin, is concentration independent and does not appear to be influenced by renal or hepatic dysfunction.

Rifabutin undergoes extensive oxidative metabolism. Of the 5 metabolites that have been identified, 25-O-deacetyl and 31-hydroxy are the most predominant and show a plasma metabolite:parent area under the curve ratio of 0.10 for 25-O-deacetyl and 0.07 for 31-hydroxy metabolite. The 25-O-deacetyl metabolite has antimycobacterial activity equal to the parent drug and contributes up to 10% to the total antimicrobial activity. The 31-hydroxy metabolite has some antimicrobial activity (1/16 that of parent drug), but, considering its concentration in plasma, it is probably not contributing significantly to the therapeutic activity of rifabutin. Rifabutin can induce its own metabolism on multiple dosing. The area under the plasma concentration-time curve (AUC) following multiple dosing decreased by 38%, but its terminal half-life remained unchanged.

The plasma elimination profile of rifabutin is biphasic with an initial half-life of approximately 4 hours followed by a mean terminal half-life 45 (±17) hours (range: 16 to 69 hours). Mean systemic clearance in healthy adult volunteers following a single oral dose was 0.69 (±0.32) L/hour/kg (range: 0.46 to 1.34 L/hour/kg). Rifabutin is mainly excreted in the urine, primarily as metabolites and to a lesser extent in the feces. Fifty-three percent (53%) of the oral dose of ^{14}C-labelled drug was recovered in the urine by 5 days post-dose and 30% was recovered in the feces over the same period. Renal and biliary excretion of unchanged drug each contribute approximately 5% to the systemic clearance.

The pharmacokinetic profile of rifabutin is not significantly modified by age or by hepatic dysfunction, although the inter-individual variability in elderly subjects (71 to 80 years) was slightly higher. Rifabutin steady-state pharmacokinetics in early symptomatic HIV positive patients are similar to those in healthy normal volunteers but the variability between individuals is higher in the HIV positive patients. Renal insufficiency was correlated to a decrease in rifabutin urinary excretion. Other pharmacokinetic parameters did not appear to differ in a clinically relevant way between patients with various degrees of renal insufficiency and patients with normal renal function. Care is recommended when treating patients with severe renal insufficiency. No rifabutin disposition information is currently available in children or adolescents under 18 years of age.

Indications: For the prevention of disseminated M. avium complex (MAC) disease in patients with advanced HIV infection (CD4+ cell count ≤200/mm³ with an AIDS defining diagnosis, or CD4+ cell count ≤100/mm³ without an AIDS defining diagnosis).

Contraindications: In patients who have had clinically significant hypersensitivity to this drug, or to any other rifamycins.

Warnings: Rifabutin prophylaxis must not be administered to patients with **active** tuberculosis. Among HIV positive patients, tuberculosis is common and may present with atypical or extrapulmonary findings. Patients are likely to have a nonreactive purified protein derivative (PPD) test despite active disease. In addition to chest x-ray and sputum culture, the following studies may be useful in the diagnosis of tuberculosis in the HIV positive patient: blood culture, urine culture, or biopsy of a suspicious lymph node.

Patients who develop signs and symptoms consistent with active tuberculosis while on rifabutin prophylaxis should be evaluated immediately, so that those with active disease may be given an effective combination regimen of antituberculosis medications. Administration of rifabutin, as a single-agent, to patients with active tuberculosis is likely to lead to the development of tuberculosis which is resistant both to rifabutin and to rifampin.

There is no evidence that rifabutin provides effective prophylaxis against M. tuberculosis infections. Patients requiring prophylaxis against both M. tuberculosis and M. avium complex may be given isoniazid and rifabutin concurrently.

Precautions: General: Because rifabutin may be associated with neutropenia, and more rarely thrombocytopenia, physicians should consider obtaining hematologic studies periodically in patients receiving rifabutin prophylaxis.

Geriatrics: Rifabutin administered as a single dose has been evaluated in 24 healthy, elderly (71 to 80 years) volunteers. The pharmacokinetic profile of rifabutin is not significantly modified by age, although the inter-individual variability in this age group was slightly higher when compared to younger (25 to 37 years) volunteers.

Children: The safety and effectiveness of rifabutin for prophylaxis of MAC disease in children and adolescents under 18 years of age have not been established. However, limited safety data are available from 22 HIV positive children who received rifabutin as treatment for disseminated MAC disease, in combination with at least 2 other antimycobacterials for periods ranging from 1 to 183 weeks.

The mean daily doses (mg/kg) for these children were: infants 1 year of age, 18.5 (range 15.0 to 25.0); children 2 to 10 years, 8.6 (range 4.4 to 18.8); adolescents 14 to 16 years, 4.0 (range 2.8 to 5.4). Rifabutin was generally safe in this treatment group. Adverse experiences were similar to those observed in the adult population, and included leukopenia, neutropenia and skin rash. Doses of rifabutin may be administered mixed with foods such as applesauce.

Pregnancy: There are no adequate and well-controlled studies of rifabutin use in pregnant women. No teratogenic effects were observed in reproduction studies carried out in rats and rabbits. Because animal reproduction studies are not always predictive of human response, rifabutin should be used in pregnant women only if the potential benefit justifies the potential risk to the fetus.

Lactation: It is not known whether rifabutin is excreted in human milk. Because many drugs are excreted in human milk and given the potential for serious adverse reactions in nursing infants, a decision should be made whether to discontinue nursing or discontinue the drug, taking into account the importance of the drug to the nursing mother.

Renal Impairment: In a study of 18 patients with increasing degrees of renal insufficiency, rifabutin was administered as a single 300 mg dose. Renal insufficiency was correlated to a decrease in rifabutin urinary excretion. Other pharmacokinetic parameters did not appear to differ in a clinically relevant way between patients with various degrees of renal insufficiency and patients with normal renal function. Care is recommended when treating patients with severe renal insufficiency.

Hepatic Impairment: The pharmacokinetics of single dose rifabutin have been studied in 12 patients with alcoholic liver disease. Hepatic impairment did not significantly modify the overall pharmacokinetic profile of rifabutin.

Drug Interactions: In 10 healthy adult volunteers and 8 HIV positive patients, steady-state plasma levels of zidovudine (ZDV), an antiretroviral agent which is metabolized mainly through glucuronidation, were decreased after repeated rifabutin dosing. The mean zidovudine decrease in C_{max} was 48% and in the AUC, 32%. In vitro studies have demonstrated that rifabutin does not affect the inhibition of HIV by ZDV.

Steady-state kinetics in 12 HIV positive patients show that both the rate and extent of systemic availability of didanosine (ddI), was not altered after repeated dosing of rifabutin.

Possible drug-drug interaction between rifabutin and fluconazole was also evaluated in HIV positive patients. Preliminary results from the Phase I study did not show any alterations in the steady-state fluconazole plasma kinetics following multiple rifabutin dosing.

Rifabutin has liver enzyme-inducing properties. The related drug rifampin is known to reduce the activity of a number of drugs, including dapsone, narcotics (including methadone), anticoagulants, corticosteroids, cyclosporine, cardiac glycoside preparations, quinidine, oral contraceptives, oral hypoglycemic agents (sulfonylureas), and analgesics. Rifampin has also been reported to decrease the effects of concurrently administered ketoconazole, barbiturates, diazepam, verapamil, beta-adrenergic blockers, clofibrate, progestins, disopyramide, mexiletine, theophylline, chloramphenicol and anticonvulsants. Because of the structural similarity of rifabutin and rifampin, rifabutin may be expected to have some effect on these drugs as well. However, unlike rifampin, rifabutin appears not to affect the acetylation of isoniazid. When the effects of rifabutin on hepatic microsomal enzyme activity were compared to those of rifampin in a study with 8 healthy normal volunteers, rifabutin appeared to be a less potent enzyme inducer than rifampin. The significance of this finding for clinical drug interactions is not known. **Dosage adjustment of drugs listed above may be necessary if they are given concurrently with rifabutin.**

Patients using oral contraceptives should consider changing to nonhormonal methods of birth control.

Information for the Patient: Mycobutin is used for the prevention of serious disease caused by M. avium complex (MAC) organisms in patients with advanced HIV infection. Mycobutin should not be given to patients with active tuberculosis. Patients should ask their physicians to advise them of the signs and symptoms of both MAC disease and tuberculosis. Patients should consult their physician if they develop new complaints suggestive of either MAC disease or tuberculosis.

Mycobutin should be taken as a single dose (two 150 mg capsules) once daily with or without food. For those patients who experience nausea, vomiting or other stomach upsets, it may be useful to split the Mycobutin dose in half (one 150 mg capsule) twice a day with food.

The most common side effect of Mycobutin is that urine may be colored brown-orange. Similar discoloration may affect stools, saliva, sputum, perspiration, tears or the skin. Contact lenses may be permanently stained.

Other side effects associated with Mycobutin include: a reduction in the number of white blood cells which fight infections, skin rashes, and gastrointestinal complaints such as indigestion, belching, flatulence, nausea, vomiting and abdominal pain. Very rarely, Mycobutin may cause muscle aches, inflammation of the inside of the eye (uveitis), and generalized joint pains.

Adverse Effects: Rifabutin was generally well tolerated in the controlled clinical trials involving 566 patients treated with rifabutin and 580 patients treated with placebo. The most serious adverse reaction to rifabutin was neutropenia.

The most common adverse events, reported more frequently in the rifabutin treated patients than in the placebo group were: urine discoloration, neutropenia, skin rash, nausea and/or vomiting, and abdominal pain (see Table I). The incidence of urine discoloration and neutropenia in patients treated with rifabutin were significantly greater than in patients treated with placebo (Fisher's Test, $p<0.01$ and $p=0.03$ respectively).

Sixteen percent (16%) of rifabutin treated patients discontinued therapy due to an adverse event as compared to 8% of placebo-treated patients. The primary reasons for discontinuation of rifabutin were: skin rash (4%), gastrointestinal intolerance (3%) and neutropenia (2%).

Table I enumerates adverse experiences that occurred at a frequency of 1% or greater among the patients treated with rifabutin and those treated with placebo in the Phase III clinical trials.

Table I—Mycobutin

Clinical Adverse Experiences Reported in ≥1% of Patients Treated with Mycobutin

Adverse Event	Mycobutin (n=566)%	Placebo (n=580)%
Body as a Whole		
Abdominal Pain	4	3
Headache	3	5
Fever	2	1
Asthenia	1	1
Chest Pain	1	1
Pain	1	2
Digestive System		
Nausea	6	5
Nausea and Vomiting	3	2
Vomiting	1	1
Diarrhea	3	3
Dyspepsia	3	1
Eructation	3	1
Anorexia	2	2
Flatulence	2	1
Musculoskeletal System		
Myalgia	2	1
Nervous System		
Insomnia	1	1
Skin and Appendages		
Rash	11	8
Pruritus	1	1
Special Senses		
Taste Perversion	3	1
Urogenital System		
Discolored Urine	30	6

Considering data from the Phase III clinical trials, and from other clinical studies, rifabutin appears to be a likely cause of the following adverse events which occurred in less than 1% of the treated patients: arthralgia, chest pressure or pain with dyspnea, hemolysis, hepatitis, myositis, and skin discoloration.

The following adverse events have occurred in more than 1 patient receiving rifabutin, but an etiologic role for rifabutin has not been established: aphasia, confusion, non-specific T wave changes on the ECG, and seizures.

Mycobutin (cont'd)

When rifabutin was administered at doses from 1 050 mg/day to 2 400 mg/day, generalized arthralgia and uveitis were reported. These adverse experiences abated when rifabutin was discontinued.

Laboratory Test Abnormalities: Table II enumerates the changes in laboratory values that were considered as laboratory test abnormalities in the Phase III clinical trials.

Table II—Mycobutin

Percentage of Patients with Laboratory Abnormalities

Laboratory Test Abnormalities	Mycobutin (n=566)%	Placebo (n=580)%
Chemistry:		
Increased ALT (>150 U/L)	9	11
Increased AST (>150 U/L)	7	12
Increased Alkaline Phosphatase (>450 U/L)	<1	3
Hematology:		
Neutropenia (ANC <750/mm³)	25	20
Leukopenia (WBC <1 500/mm³)	17	16
Anemia (Hemoglobin <8.0 g/dL)	6	7
Thrombocytopenia (Platelet count <50 000/mm³)	5	4
Eosinophilia	1	1

Although thrombocytopenia was not significantly more common among rifabutin treated patients in the Phase III trials, rifabutin has been clearly linked to thrombocytopenia in rare cases. One patient in the Phase III trials developed thrombotic thrombocytopenic purpura which was attributed to rifabutin.

Overdose: Symptoms: No information is available on accidental overdosage in humans.

Treatment: While there is no experience in the treatment of overdose with rifabutin, clinical experience with rifamycins suggest that gastric lavage to evacuate gastric contents (within a few hours of overdose), followed by instillation of an activated charcoal slurry into the stomach, may help absorb any remaining drug from the gastrointestinal tract.

Rifabutin is 85% protein bound, and distributed extensively into tissues (V_{ss}:8 to 9 L/kg). As unchanged drug, rifabutin is not primarily excreted via the urinary route (less than 10%), therefore, neither hemodialysis nor forced diuresis is expected to enhance the systemic elimination of unchanged rifabutin from the body in a patient with rifabutin overdose.

Dosage: It is recommended that 300 mg of rifabutin be administered once daily with or without food. For those patients who experience nausea, vomiting or other gastrointestinal upsets, it may be useful to split the rifabutin dose in half (one 150 mg capsule) twice a day with food.

Supplied: Each hard gelatin capsule having an opaque red-brown cap and body, imprinted with PHARMACIA/MYCOBUTIN, in white ink, contains: rifabutin 150 mg. Nonmedicinal ingredients: microcrystalline cellulose, magnesium stearate, red iron oxide, silica gel, sodium lauryl sulfate, titanium dioxide and edible white ink. Bottles of 60, 100 and 250. Store at controlled room temperature, 15 to 30°C. Keep container tightly closed.

MYCOSTATIN® Preparations

Squibb

Nystatin

Antifungal Antibiotic

Indications: Oral: Prevention and treatment of candidal infections of the oral cavity and esophagus, for intestinal candidiasis and for protection against candidal overgrowth during antimicrobial or corticosteroid therapy.

Topical: Treatment of cutaneous or mucocutaneous mycotic infections caused by Candida (Monilia) species.

Vaginal: Local treatment of vaginal mycotic infections caused by C. albicans (Monilia) and other Candida species and treatment of pregnant patients to prevent thrush in the newborn.

Contraindications: Hypersensitivity to nystatin or any components of Mycostatin products.

Precautions: Nystatin oral preparations are not indicated for the treatment of systemic mycoses.

It is recommended that appropriate microbiological studies (e.g. KOH smears and/or cultures) be used to confirm the diagnosis of candidiasis and rule out other pathogens. If there is a lack of therapeutic response, appropriate microbiological studies should be repeated. Discontinue medication if irritation occurs with topical or intravaginal use.

Pregnancy: Use of the vaginal applicator may not be considered desirable during pregnancy. Appropriate measures should be taken to avoid possible reinfection during sexual intercourse.

Animal reproduction studies have not been conducted with nystatin oral preparations. It is also not known whether these preparations can cause fetal harm when administered to a pregnant woman or can affect reproductive capacity. Nystatin oral preparations should be administered to a pregnant woman only if the potential benefit to the mother outweighs the potential risk to the fetus.

Lactation: It is not known whether nystatin is excreted in human milk. Caution should be exercised when nystatin is prescribed to a nursing woman.

Mycostatin oral tablets contain tartrazine which may cause allergic-type reactions (including bronchial asthma) in certain susceptible individuals. Although the overall incidence of tartrazine sensitivity in the general population is low, it is frequently seen in patients who also have aspirin hypersensitivity.

Information for the Patient: Patients taking the oral medication should receive the following information and instructions:
1. The patient should be instructed to use the medication as directed (including the replacement of missed doses). The medication is not for any disorder other than that for which it is prescribed. 2. Even if symptomatic relief occurs within the first few days of treatment, the patient should be advised not to interrupt or discontinue the medication until the prescribed course of treatment is completed. 3. If symptoms of irritation develop, the patient should be advised to notify the physician promptly. 4. When prescribing nystatin oral suspension, advise the patient of the importance of good oral hygiene, including the proper care (where applicable) of dentures.

Adverse Effects: Nystatin is well tolerated by all age groups including debilitated infants, even on prolonged administration. Rarely, oral irritation or sensitization may occur.

The following adverse reactions have been reported with nystatin oral dosage forms: Gastrointestinal: diarrhea (including one case of bloody diarrhea), nausea, vomiting, gastrointestinal upset/disturbances.

Dermatologic: rash

In addition, rarely reported cases of: tachycardia, bronchospasm, facial swelling, urticaria and nonspecific myalgia.

Stevens-Johnson syndrome has been reported very rarely.

There have been no reports of serious toxic effects or superinfections.

Local or intravaginal irritation occurs rarely.

Overdose: Symptoms and Treatment: Large oral doses (in excess of 5 million units daily) have caused nausea and gastrointestinal upset.

Dosage: Oral Suspension: Infants: Usual prophylactic and therapeutic dosage is 100 000 units 4 times daily, dropped into the side of the mouth and swallowed. Dosage may be increased if necessary.

For prophylaxis in the newborn, 100 000 units once daily may be given by dropper directly into the mouth.

Children and adults: Usual therapeutic dose is 100 000 units 4 times daily, dropped into the mouth and held for some time before swallowing. Dosage may be doubled for those occasional infections which are severe or difficult to treat, if necessary.

Note: When candidal lesions of the skin and/or nasal, vaginal or rectal mucosae are present in addition to intestinal infection, these should be treated concomitantly with a topical anticandidal preparation.

Oral Tablets: Usual prophylactic and therapeutic dose is 500 000 units 3 times daily. Dosage may be increased to 1 000 000 units 3 times daily if intestinal fungi are not adequately suppressed.

Topical: Apply cream or ointment liberally to affected areas 1 to 4 times daily or as indicated until healing is complete. The cream is usually preferred to the ointment in candidiasis involving intertriginous areas. Apply powder to candidal lesions 2 or 3 times daily until lesions have healed. For fungal infection of the feet caused by Candida species, dust the powder freely on the feet and in the shoes and socks.

Vaginal Cream: Usual dosage is 4 g (100 000 units) once or twice (100 000 or 200 000 units) daily deposited high in the vagina by means of the applicator.

In most cases, 2 weeks of therapy will be sufficient, but more prolonged treatment may be necessary. Administration should generally be continued for at least 48 hours after clinical cure to prevent relapse. It is important that therapy be continued during menstruation. Adjunctive measures such as therapeutic douches are unnecessary and sometimes inadvisable. Cleansing douches may be used by nonpregnant women, if desired, for esthetic purposes.

Pregnant patients with monilial infections should receive a dosage of 4 g vaginal cream once or twice daily for 3 to 6 weeks before term to prevent thrush in the newborn.

Nystatin therapeutic administration should generally be continued for at least 48 hours after clinical cure to prevent relapse. If signs and symptoms worsen or persist beyond 14 days of treatment, the patient should be reevaluated, and alternate therapy considered. When oral nystatin is given concomitantly with an oral antibacterial agent, oral nystatin should be continued at least as long as the antibacterial agent. Local treatment of chronic or resistant vaginal, oral or cutaneous moniliasis with nystatin may be supplemented with oral nystatin administration.

Supplied: Oral Suspension Pr: Each mL of pale yellow, cherry-mint-flavored suspension contains: nystatin 100 000 units. Nonmedicinal ingredients: carboxymethylcellulose, cinnamaldehyde, dibasic sodium phosphate, ethyl alcohol 1% (v/v), flavor, glycerin, methylparaben, propylparaben, sodium saccharin, sucrose and water. Hydrochloric acid and sodium hydroxide for pH adjustments. Bottles of 24 and 48 mL with calibrated dropper. Store at room temperature. Avoid freezing.

Oral Tablets Pr: Each brown, coated tablet contains: nystatin 500 000 units. Nonmedicinal ingredients: cornstarch, FD&C red No. 3, blue No. 2 and yellow No. 6, hydroxypropyl methylcellulose, lactose, magnesium stearate, microcrystalline cellulose, povidone, printing ink, stearic acid, talc, tartrazine and titanium dioxide and triacetin. Bottles of 100. Store at room temperature.

Topical Cream: Each g of aqueous, perfumed vanishing cream base contains: nystatin 100 000 units. Nonmedicinal ingredients: aluminum hydroxide gel, glyceryl monostearate, perfume, polyethylene glycol monostearate, polyoxyethylene fatty alcohol ether, propylene glycol, simethicone, sorbic acid, sorbitol solution, titanium dioxide, water and white petrolatum. Tubes of 15 and 30 g.

Topical Ointment: Each g contains: nystatin 100 000 units in Plastibase (plasticized hydrocarbon gel), a polyethylene and mineral oil gel base. Nonmedicinal ingredients: mineral oil heavy and polyethylene. Tubes of 30 g.

Topical Powder: Each g contains: nystatin 100 000 units dispersed in talc. Nonmedicinal ingredients: talc. Bottles of 15 g.

Vaginal Cream Pr: Each g contains: nystatin 25 000 units in a cream base. Nonmedicinal ingredients: aluminum hydroxide gel, methylparaben, polyoxyethylene fatty alcohol ether, propylene glycol, propylparaben, simethicone, water and white petrolatum. Hydrochloric acid or sodium hydroxide (for pH adjustments). Tubes of 120 g with applicator designed to deliver a 4 g dose (100 000 units).

(Shown in Product Recognition Section)

MYDFRIN®

Alcon

Phenylephrine HCl

Vasoconstrictor—Mydriatic

Supplied: Each plastic Drop-Tainer dispenser contains: a sterile, buffered, isotonic 2.5% solution of phenylephrine HCl USP. Preservative: benzalkonium chloride. Nonmedicinal ingredients: boric acid, edetate disodium, hydrochloric acid, purified water, sodium bisulfite and sodium hydroxide. Protect from light and excessive heat. Plastic Drop-Tainer dispensers of 5 mL.

MYDRIACYL® Pr

Alcon

Tropicamide

Mydriatic—Cycloplegic—Anticholinergic

Supplied: Each Drop-Tainer dispenser contains: a sterile, buffered, isotonic solution of tropicamide 0.5% or 1%. Preservatives: benzalkonium chloride. Nonmedicinal ingredients: edetate disodium, hydrochloric acid, purified water, sodium chloride and sodium hydroxide. Drop-Tainer dispensers of 15 mL.

MYLANTA™ Preparations

Warner-Lambert Consumer Healthcare

Aluminum Hydroxide—Magnesium Hydroxide Compound

Antacid—Antiflatulent

Indications: The treatment and relief of symptoms of peptic ulcer, gastritis, hiatus hernia, hyperacidity, and the management of gastrointestinal disorders accompanied by excessive gas or flatus.

Contraindications: Alkalosis, hypermagnesemia, where distention may be due to partial or complete intestinal obstruction. Not recommended for severely debilitated patients or those with impaired renal function.

Precautions: Do not take maximum dose for more than 2 weeks unless recommended by physician. Since magnesium salts may cause CNS depression, Mylanta preparations should be given with caution to patients with any degree of renal insufficiency. Aluminum hydroxide, may, by reacting with phosphates to form insoluble aluminum phosphate, cause phosphorus deficiency in those patients whose diet is low in phosphorus.

Antacids can interfere with the absorption of iron preparations, tetracyclines or other antibiotics.

Should not be taken within 2 hours of another medication because the effectiveness of the other medication may be altered.

Dosage: Mylanta Regular Strength: Liquid: 10 to 20 mL, 4 times a day between meals and at bedtime.

Tablets: 2 to 4 tablets, 4 times a day between meals and at bedtime. Tablets should be chewed well.

Mylanta Double Strength: Take 2 to 4 tablets, 4 times a day between meals and at bedtime. Chew well.

Mylanta Double Strength Plain: 5 to 10 mL 4 times a day between meals and at bedtime.

Mylanta Extra Strength: 5 to 10 mL, 4 times daily between meals and at bedtime. May be taken with milk or water.

Supplied: Mylanta Regular Strength: Liquid: Each 5 mL of sugar-free, lemon- and mint-flavored suspension contains: dried aluminum hydroxide gel 200 mg (equivalent to 153 mg aluminum hydroxide), magnesium hydroxide 200 mg and simethicone 20 mg. Nonmedicinal ingredients: carbomer, citric acid, hydroxypropyl methylcellulose, flavors, parabens, sorbitol and water. Energy: 10.1 kJ (2.42 kcal)/5 mL. Sodium: <1 mmol (3.2 mg)/5 mL. Gluten-, lactose-, sucrose-, sulfite- and tartrazine-free. Bottles of 350 mL.

Tablets: Each white, lemon- and mint-flavored chewable tablet contains: dried aluminum hydroxide gel 200 mg (equivalent to 153 mg aluminum hydroxide), magnesium hydroxide 200 mg and simethicone 20 mg. Nonmedicinal ingredients: lemon flavor, magnesium stearate, mannitol, sorbitol, spearmint oil and sugar. Energy: 11.6 kJ (2.78 kcal). Sodium: <1 mmol (0.9 mg). Gluten-, lactose-, paraben-, sulfite- and tartrazine-free. Boxes of 50 tablets in blister packages.

Mylanta Double Strength: Each tablet contains: dried aluminum hydroxide gel 400 mg (equivalent to 306 mg aluminum hydroxide), magnesium hydroxide 400 mg and simethicone 30 mg. Nonmedicinal ingredients: lemon flavor, magnesium stearate, sorbitol, spearmint oil and sugar. Energy: 14.0 kJ (3.35 kcal). Sodium: <1 mmol (1.5 mg). Gluten-, lactose-, paraben-, sulfite- and tartrazine-free. Boxes of 50 in blister packages.

Mylanta Double Strength Plain: Each 5 mL of sugar-free, lemon- and mint-flavored suspension contains: dried aluminum hydroxide gel 400 mg (equivalent to 306 mg aluminum hydroxide) and magnesium hydroxide 400 mg. Nonmedicinal ingredients: citric acid, flavors, parabens, sorbitol and water. Energy: 11.2 kJ (2.68 kcal)/5 mL. Sodium: <1 mmol (10 mg)/5 mL. Gluten-, lactose-, sucrose-, sulfite- and tartrazine-free. Bottles of 350 mL.

Mylanta Extra Strength: Each 5 mL of sugar-free, lemon- and mint-flavored suspension contains: dried aluminum hydroxide gel 650 mg (equivalent to 497 mg aluminum hydroxide), magnesium hydroxide 350 mg and simethicone 30 mg. Nonmedicinal ingredients: calcium cyclamate, citric acid, flavors, parabens, sorbitol and water. Energy: 6.1 kJ (1.45 kcal)/5 mL. Sodium: <1 mmol (1.8 mg)/5 mL. Gluten-, lactose-, sucrose-, sulfite- and tartrazine-free. Bottles of 350 mL.

MYLERAN® Ⓟ

Glaxo Wellcome

Busulfan

Antileukemic

Pharmacology: Busulfan is a bifunctional alkylating agent. Binding to DNA is believed to play a role in its mode of action, and di-guanyl derivatives have been isolated, but interstrand crosslinking has not been conclusively demonstrated.

The basis for the uniquely selective effect of busulfan on granulocytopoiesis is not fully understood.

Pharmacokinetics: Early pharmacokinetic studies were carried out with radioactively labelled busulfan. More recently, gas liquid chromatography with selected ion monitoring has been used to quantitate busulfan in biological fluids. Busulfan doses of 2 to 6 mg were well absorbed and the kinetic data could be fitted to a zero-order absorption, 1 compartment open model. The mean half-life for drug elimination was 2.57 hours.

The pharmacokinetics of busulfan have also been studied in patients following high-dose administration (1 mg/kg administered orally every 6 hours for 4 days). The mean elimination half-life was found to be 2.3 hours after the final busulfan dose, but 3.4 hours after the first dose. This suggests that busulfan may increase its own metabolic rate on repeated administration. The mean steady-state plasma concentration was 1.1 μg/mL after dosing. Due to the variable absorption kinetics observed, it was not possible to evaluate the order of kinetics.

The primary mode of elimination of busulfan is through extensive metabolism and approximately 1% of the drug is excreted unchanged in the urine. In humans, busulfan is at least partly metabolized via the glutathione route. The urinary metabolites of busulfan have been identified as 3-hydroxysulpholane, tetrahydrothiophene 1-oxide and sulpholane, in patients treated with high-dose busulfan. The clinical activity of these compounds, however, remains unclear.

Busulfan given in high doses has recently been shown to enter the cerebrospinal fluid (CSF) in concentrations comparable to those found in plasma, with a mean CSF:plasma ratio of 1.3: 1. The saliva:plasma distribution of busulfan was found to be 1.1: 1.

The level of busulfan bound reversibly to plasma proteins has been variably reported to range from insignificant to approximately 55%. Irreversible binding of drug to blood cells and plasma proteins has been reported to be 47% and 32%, respectively.

Indications: Chronic granulocytic (myelocytic, myeloid) leukemia for the production of remissions. May be used with extreme caution in patients with prior radiation or P_{32} therapy and in those untreated by any other means.

Contraindications: Busulfan should not be given if neutrophil or platelet counts are depressed.

Busulfan should not be used in patients whose disease has demonstrated resistance to busulfan. Busulfan should not be given to patients with previous hypersensitivity reaction to the drug or any of its components.

Warnings: Caution: Busulfan is a potent cytotoxic drug and should be used only by physicians experienced in the administration of cancer chemotherapeutic drugs. Blood counts should be taken at frequent intervals and not less than weekly. Therapy should be discontinued or the dosage reduced at the first signs of abnormal depression of bone marrow.

The most frequent, serious side effect of treatment with busulfan is the induction of bone marrow failure (which may or may not be anatomically hypoplastic) resulting in severe pancytopenia. The pancytopenia caused by busulfan may be more prolonged than that induced with other alkylating agents. It is generally felt that the usual cause of busulfan-induced pancytopenia is the failure to stop administration of the drug soon enough; individual idiosyncrasy to the drug does not seem to be an important factor. **Busulfan should be used with extreme caution and exceptional vigilance in patients whose bone marrow reserve may have been compromised by prior irradiation or chemotherapy, or whose marrow function is recovering from previous cytotoxic therapy.** Although recovery from busulfan-induced pancytopenia may take from 1 month to 2 years, this complication is potentially reversible and the patient should be vigorously supported through any period of severe pancytopenia.

A rare, important complication of busulfan therapy is the development of bronchopulmonary dysplasia with pulmonary fibrosis. Symptoms have been reported to occur within 8 months to 10 years after initiation of therapy—the average duration of therapy being 4 years. The histologic findings associated with busulfan lung mimic those seen following pulmonary irradiation. Clinically, patients have reported the insidious onset of cough, dyspnea, and low-grade fever. Pulmonary function studies have revealed diminished diffusion capacity and decreased pulmonary compliance. It is important to exclude more common conditions (such as opportunistic infections or leukemic infiltration of the lungs) with appropriate diagnostic techniques. If measures such as sputum cultures, virologic studies and exfoliative cytology fail to establish an etiology for the pulmonary infiltrates, lung biopsy may be necessary to establish the diagnosis. Treatment of established busulfan-induced pulmonary fibrosis is unsatisfactory; in most cases the patients have died within 6 months after the diagnosis was established. There is no specific therapy for this complication other than the immediate discontinuation of busulfan. The administration of corticosteroids has been suggested, but the results have not been impressive or uniformly successful.

If anesthesia is required in patients with possible pulmonary toxicity, the concentration of inspired oxygen should be kept as low as safely possible and careful attention given to postoperative respiratory care.

Busulfan may cause cellular dysplasia in many organs in addition to the lung. Cytologic abnormalities characterized by giant, hyperchromatic nuclei have been reported in lymph nodes, pancreas, thyroid, adrenal glands, liver, and bone marrow. This cytologic dysplasia may be severe enough to cause difficulty in interpretation of exfoliative cytologic examinations from the lung, bladder, breast and the uterine cervix.

In addition to the widespread epithelial dysplasia that has been observed during busulfan therapy, chromosome aberrations have been reported in cells from patients receiving busulfan.

Busulfan is mutagenic in mice and, possibly in man.

A number of malignant tumors have been reported in patients on busulfan therapy and this drug may be a human carcinogen. Four cases of acute leukemia occurred among 243 patients treated with busulfan as adjuvant chemotherapy following surgical resection of bronchogenic carcinoma. All 4 cases were from a subgroup of 19 of these 243 patients who developed pancytopenia while taking busulfan 5 to 8 years before leukemia became clinically apparent. These findings suggest that busulfan is leukemogenic, although its mode of action is uncertain.

Hepatic veno-occlusive disease, which may be life-threatening, has been reported following the investigational use of very high doses of busulfan in combination with cyclophosphamide or other chemotherapeutic agents prior to bone marrow transplantation. Possible risk factors for the development of hepatic veno-occlusive disease include: total busulfan dose exceeding 16 mg/kg based on the ideal body weight, and concurrent use of multiple alkylating agents. A clear cause and effect relationship with busulfan has not been demonstrated. Periodic measurement of serum transaminases, alkaline phosphatase, and bilirubin is indicated for early detection of hepatotoxicity.

Cardiac tamponade has been reported in a small number of patients with thalassemia (2% in one series) who received high doses of busulfan and cyclophosphamide as the preparatory regimen for bone marrow transplantation. In this series, the cardiac tamponade was often fatal. Abdominal pain and vomiting preceded the tamponade in most patients.

If high dose busulfan is prescribed, patients should be given prophylactic anticonvulsant therapy preferably with a benzodiazepine rather than enzyme inducing anticonvulsants (e.g. phenytoin) (see Precautions, Drug Interactions).

Pregnancy: Busulfan may cause fetal harm when administered to a pregnant woman. Although there have been a number of cases reported where apparently normal children have been born after busulfan treatment during pregnancy, 1 case has been cited where a malformed baby was delivered by a mother treated with busulfan. During the pregnancy that resulted in the malformed infant, the mother received x-ray therapy early in the first trimester, mercaptopurine until the third month, then busulfan until delivery. When cytotoxic drugs are used in pregnancy, the possible teratogenic effect on the fetus should be kept in mind. Delay treatment as long as possible and certainly until after the first 3 months of pregnancy. Women of childbearing potential should be advised to avoid becoming pregnant.

In pregnant rats, busulfan produces sterility in both male and female offspring due to the absence of germinal cells in testes and ovaries. Germinal cell aplasia or sterility in offspring of mothers receiving busulfan during pregnancy has not been reported in humans.

Myleran (cont'd)

Effects on Fertility: Ovarian suppression and amenorrhea with menopausal symptoms commonly occur during busulfan therapy in premenopausal patients. Busulfan interferes with spermatogenesis in experimental animals and there have been clinical reports of sterility, azoospermia and testicular atrophy in male patients.

Precautions: General: Use of busulfan should be restricted to patients for whom complete blood counts are available at intervals of at least 1 week. The most careful hematological control is essential since large doses may produce irreversible depression of the bone marrow which may not be obvious for 4 to 6 months.

The most consistent, dose-related toxicity is bone marrow suppression. This may be manifested by anemia, leukopenia, thrombocytopenia or any combination of these. It is imperative that patients be instructed to report promptly the development of fever, sore throat, signs of local infection, bleeding from any site or symptoms suggestive of anemia. Any one of these findings may indicate busulfan toxicity; however, they may also indicate transformation of the disease to an acute blastic form. Since busulfan may have a delayed effect on the bone marrow, it is important to withdraw the medication temporarily at the first sign of an abnormally large or exceptionally rapid fall in any of the formed elements of the blood.

Seizures have been reported in patients receiving very high, investigational doses of busulfan. As with any potentially epileptogenic drug, caution should be exercised when administering very high doses of busulfan to patients with a history of seizure disorder, head trauma, or receiving other potentially epileptogenic drugs. Some investigators have used prophylactic anticonvulsivant therapy in this setting.

Pregnancy: Teratogenic Effects: see Warnings.

Nonteratogenic Effects: There have been reports in the literature of small infants being born after the mothers received busulfan during pregnancy, in particular, during the third trimester. One case was reported where an infant had mild anemia and neutropenia at birth after busulfan was administered to the mother from the eighth week of pregnancy to term.

As with all cytotoxic chemotherapy, adequate contraceptive precautions should be used when either partner is receiving busulfan.

Lactation: It is not known whether busulfan or its metabolites are excreted in human milk. Because of the potential for tumorigenicity shown in animal and human studies, a decision should be made whether to discontinue nursing or to discontinue the drug, taking into account the importance of the drug to the mother.

Drug Interactions: Busulfan may cause additive pulmonary toxicity when administered with other cytotoxic drugs.

Busulfan may cause additive myelosuppression when used with other myelosuppressive drugs.

The administration of phenytoin to patients receiving high-dose busulfan may result in a decrease in the myeloblative effect due to increased busulfan clearance.

In one study, 12 of approximately 330 patients receiving continuous busulfan and thioguanine therapy for treatment of chronic myelogenous leukemia were found to have esophageal varices associated with abnormal liver function tests. Subsequent liver biopsies were performed in 4 of these patients, all of which showed evidence of nodular regenerative hyperplasia. Duration of combination therapy prior to the appearance of esophageal varices ranged from 6 to 45 months. With the present analysis of the data, no cases of hepatotoxicity have appeared in the busulfan alone arm of the study. Long-term continuous therapy with thioguanine and busulfan should be used with caution.

Laboratory Tests: It is recommended that evaluation of the hemoglobin or hematocrit, total white blood cell count and differential count, and quantitative platelet count be obtained weekly while the patient is on busulfan therapy. In cases where the cause of fluctuation in the formed elements of the peripheral blood is obscure, bone marrow examination may be useful for evaluation of marrow status. A decision to increase, decrease, continue, or discontinue a given dose of busulfan should be based not only on the absolute hematologic values, but also on the rapidity with which changes are occurring. The dosage of busulfan may need to be reduced if combined with other drugs whose primary toxicity is myelosuppression. Occasionally patients may be unusually sensitive to busulfan administered at standard dosages and suffer neutropenia or thrombocytopenia after a relatively short exposure to the drug. Busulfan should not be used where facilities for complete blood counts, including quantitative platelet counts, are not available at weekly (or more frequent) intervals.

Adverse Reactions: Hematologic: The chief toxic effect is a dosage-related myelosuppression which may cause thrombocytopenia (hemorrhage) and eventually lead to pancytopenia.

Pulmonary: Interstitial pulmonary fibrosis has been reported rarely, but it is a clinically significant adverse effect when observed and calls for immediate discontinuation of further administration of the drug. The role of corticosteroids in arresting or reversing the fibrosis has been reported to be beneficial in some cases and without effect in others.

The lung pathology may be complicated by superimposed infections.

Pulmonary ossification and dystrophic calcification have also been reported.

Metabolic: Hyperuricemia and/or hyperuricosuria are not uncommon in patients with chronic myelogenous leukemia. Additional rapid destruction of granulocytes may accompany the initiation of chemotherapy and increase the urate pool. The risk of uric acid nephropathy can be minimized by increased hydration, urine alkalinization, and the prophylactic administration of an xanthine oxidase inhibitor such as allopurinol.

In a few cases, a clinical syndrome closely resembling adrenal insufficiency and characterized by weakness, severe fatigue, anorexia, weight loss, nausea and vomiting, and melanoderma has developed after prolonged busulfan therapy. The symptoms have sometimes been reversible when busulfan was withdrawn.

Cardiac: Cardiac tamponade has been reported in a small number of patients with thalassemia who received high doses of busulfan and cyclophosphamide as the preparatory regimen for bone marrow transplantation (see Warnings).

One case of endocardial fibrosis has been reported in a 79-year-old woman who received a total dose of 7 200 mg over a period of 9 years for the management of chronic myelogenous leukemia. At autopsy, she was found to have endocardial fibrosis of the left ventricle in addition to interstitial pulmonary fibrosis.

Ocular: Busulfan is capable of inducing cataracts in rats and there have been several reports indicating that this is a rare complication in humans. In the few cases reported in humans, cataracts have occurred only after prolonged administration of busulfan.

Corneal thinning has been reported with the investigational use of high-dose busulfan prior to bone marrow transplantation.

Dermatologic: Hyperpigmentation is the most common adverse skin reaction and occurs in 5 to 10% of patients, particularly those with a dark complexion. It is often most marked on the neck, upper trunk, nipples, abdomen and palmar creases.

Gastrointestinal and Hepatic: Esophageal varices have been reported in patients receiving continuous busulfan and thioguanine therapy for treatment of chronic myelogenous leukemia (see Precautions, Drug Interactions).

Hepatic veno-occlusive disease has been observed in patients receiving higher than recommended doses of busulfan (see Warnings).

Miscellaneous: Other complications of therapy include instances of nausea, vomiting, diarrhea, dryness of the oral mucous membranes and cheilosis, glossitis, urticaria, erythema multiforme, erythema nodosum, porphyria cutanea tarda, myasthenia gravis, cholestatic jaundice, impotence, sterility, amenorrhea, gynecomastia, excessive dryness and fragility of the skin with anhidrosis, alopecia and, hemorrhagic cystitis. Seizures have been observed in patients receiving higher than recommended doses of busulfan (see Precautions, General).

Overdose: There is no known antidote to busulfan. The principal toxic effect is on the bone marrow. Survival after a single dose of 140 mg has been reported in an 18 kg 4-year-old child, but hematological toxicity is likely to be more profound with chronic overdosage.

Symptoms: Purpuric hemorrhages.

Treatment: The hematologic status should be closely monitored and vigorous supportive measures instituted if necessary. Induction of vomiting or gastric lavage followed by administration of charcoal would be indicated if ingestion were recent. It is not known whether busulfan is dialyzable.

Dosage: Busulfan is administered orally at a dosage of 0.06 mg/kg (1.8 mg/m² body surface area) to a total maximum dose of 4 mg daily, until maximum hematological and clinical improvement is obtained or symptoms of toxicity supervene. During remission the patient is examined at monthly intervals and the treatment is resumed when the white cell count reaches 50 000/mm³. When remission is shorter than 3 months, maintenance therapy of 1 to 3 mg daily may be advisable in order to keep the hematological status under control and prevent rapid relapse. Discontinue drug or reduce dosage at the first sign of abnormal depression of platelets, hemoglobin, or low white blood cell count.

Special Instructions: All materials which have come in contact with cytotoxic drugs should be segregated and incinerated at 1 000°C or more.

Tablets should be returned to the manufacturer for destruction. Proper precautions should be taken in packaging these materials for transport.

Personnel regularly involved in the preparation and handling of cytotoxic agents should have biannual blood examinations.

Care should be taken when handling or halving the tablets so as not to contaminate hands or to inhale the drug.

Information for the Patient: See Blue Section—Information for the Patient ''Myleran''.

Supplied: Each white, biconvex tablet, with code number MYLERAN K2A on same side as score mark, contains: busulfan 2 mg. Nonmedicinal ingredients: magnesium stearate and sodium chloride. Bottles of 25. Store between 15 and 30°C in a dry place.

(Shown in Product Recognition Section)

Reviewed 1999

MYOCHRYSINE® Ⓟ

Rhône-Poulenc Rorer

Sodium Aurothiomalate

Antirheumatic Agent

Pharmacology: Sodium aurothiomalate exhibits anti-inflammatory, antiarthritic and immunomodulating effects. The predominant clinical effect of sodium aurothiomalate appears to be suppression of the synovitis in the active stage of the rheumatoid disease. The precise mechanism of action is unknown but it has been suggested that the drug may act by inhibiting cell-mediated and humoral immune mechanisms. Additional modes of action include alteration or inhibition of various enzyme systems, suppression of phagocytic activity of macrophage and polymorphonuclear leukocytes, and alteration of collagen biosynthesis.

The metabolic fate of sodium aurothiomalate in humans is unknown but it is believed not to be broken down to elemental gold. It is very highly bound to plasma proteins. Sixty to 90% is excreted very slowly by the renal route while 10 to 40% is eliminated in the feces mostly via biliary secretion. The biologic half-life of gold following a single 50 mg dose of parenteral gold has been reported to range from 6 to 25 days. It increases following successive weekly doses.

The appearance of clinical effect is slow. It may take at least 8 weeks to become significant and the maximum benefits may not be achieved for at least 6 months.

Indications: In the treatment of both adult and juvenile rheumatoid arthritis.

It may also be of benefit in the treatment of patients with psoriatic arthritis or Felty's syndrome.

It is usually used for treating patients who show evidence of continued or additional disease activity despite conservative drug therapy, e.g., with salicylates or other anti-inflammatory agents. Sodium aurothiomalate may induce partial or complete remission of rheumatoid arthritis. In chronic advanced rheumatoid arthritis, it may prevent further damage to affected joints; however, it does not reverse existing damage.

Contraindications: In patients with known hypersensitivity to gold.

It is also contraindicated in patients who have experienced the following serious adverse effects with previous gold therapy; bone marrow aplasia or other hematological disorders, exfoliative dermatitis, necrotizing enterocolitis or pulmonary fibrosis.

Pregnancy: While reassuring, the information concerning the administration of gold during pregnancy is sparse and largely anecdotal; there have been no controlled prospective studies of the effect of sodium aurothiomalate on human fetal development.

In rats, gold compounds have been shown to cause hydrocephalus and microphthalmia when administered at a dose of 25 mg/kg per day from day 6 through day 15 of gestation; in rabbits, they caused gastroschisis, umbilical hernia, anomalies of the brain, heart, lung and skeleton, microphthalmia and limb defects when given at 20 to 45 mg/kg per day from day 6 through day 18 of gestation.

Gold is known to cross the placenta and it can reach significant concentrations in the fetus.

Gold therapy is seldom needed during pregnancy. If its use is nevertheless contemplated, the risk/benefit ratio should be considered keeping in mind the potential of sodium aurothiomalate for teratogenicity.

Lactation: Parenterally administered gold is excreted in human breast milk and has been detected in the blood of a nursing infant. Although problems in humans have not been documented, the use of sodium aurothiomalate in nursing mothers is not usually recommended because of the potential for serious adverse effects in the infant.

Warnings: The following conditions may aggravate or precipitate adverse reactions to sodium aurothiomalate, or their symptoms may mask the forewarning signs of gold toxicity: blood dyscrasias or a history of agranulocytosis, hemorrhagic diathesis or drug induced granulocytopenia or anemia; renal disease; hepatic dysfunction; systemic lupus erythematosus; significant dermatitis including urticaria or eczema.

Any of the above conditions should be considered as a relative contraindication to the use of sodium aurothiomalate. In such cases, treatment should be initiated with extreme caution and only after careful assessment of expected benefits versus the potential risks.

Rarely, anaphylactic shock, syncope, bradycardia, thickening of the tongue, difficulty in swallowing and breathing, and angioedema may occur in the minutes that follow the injection of sodium aurothiomalate. If an anaphylactic reaction occurs, treatment should be discontinued. A vasomotor (nitritoid) reaction may occur within several minutes of a sodium aurothiomalate injection. The nitritoid reaction is characterized by flushing, tachycardia and faintness. When it occurs, caution should be exercised before resuming therapy in patients with compromised cardiovascular status.

Carcinogenicity/Tumorigenicity: Renal adenoma and adenocarcinoma have been reported in rats after prolonged administration of frequent, high doses of parenteral gold compounds (2 mg/kg/week for 45 weeks followed by 6 mg/kg/day for 47 weeks in one study; 3 mg/kg or 6 mg/kg/day for up to 2 years in a second study). The adenomas were similar to those produced in rats by chronic administration of other heavy metals such as lead or nickel. The relevance of these findings to man is unknown. Renal adenomas have not been reported in humans receiving therapeutic doses of sodium aurothiomalate.

Precautions: Sodium aurothiomalate should be administered only to selected patients who are under the supervision of a physician experienced with chrysotherapy and thoroughly familiar with the toxicity and benefits of the drug.

Patient monitoring: Toxic reactions to sodium aurothiomalate are relatively frequent and, in certain cases, may be quite severe. Thus emphasis should be placed on careful clinical and laboratory monitoring and early detection of adverse reactions.

Baseline evaluation should include a biochemical profile to identify any preexisting conditions. Before receiving gold, patients should also have a complete blood cell count with differential, platelet count, hemoglobin determination and urinalysis for protein, white cells, red cells and casts; these tests should be repeated before each injection and patients should have an examination of the skin and buccal mucosa for skin rash, bruising or mouth ulcers. They should be questioned for the presence of pruritus, rash, stomatitis or metallic taste.

Dermatitis and lesions of the mucous membranes are common and may be serious; pruritus may precede the early development of a skin reaction. Renal toxicity ranges from mild proteinuria to the nephrotic syndrome; prognosis is usually good. Hematologic reactions have been observed rarely but fatalities have ensued. Other severe toxic manifestations include cholestatic jaundice, enterocolitis and interstitial lung disease.

If toxicity develops, sodium aurothiomalate should be discontinued immediately and symptomatic treatment be given as required.

If the reaction to gold therapy is not of a serious type, injections may be cautiously resumed 2 or 3 weeks after the toxic reaction has subsided. In these circumstances, from 5 to 10 mg of gold is administered; if the challenge dose is tolerated, sodium aurothiomalate may be administered cautiously in larger doses on subsequent injections.

Severe reactions are a contraindication to further gold therapy.

Drug Interactions: The concurrent use of D-penicillamine or other drugs with potential bone marrow toxicity may increase the potential for serious hematologic and/or renal adverse reactions.

Adverse Effects: The most frequent adverse reactions with sodium aurothiomalate involve the skin (ranging from simple rash to severe exfoliative dermatitis) and mucous membranes (ulcers) and may affect 30% of patients. Renal effects are next in frequency with proteinuria being observed in 10 to 15% of patients.

The severe adverse reactions are those affecting the bone marrow (agranulocytosis, thrombocytopenia and aplastic anemia), exfoliative dermatitis, enterocolitis, liver failure, anaphylactoid reactions and nephropathy; these are rare but may be fatal. It has been proposed that serious reactions may be the result of failure to discontinue therapy when earlier less serious symptoms occur. Close patient monitoring will not eliminate untoward effects but may help reduce their severity (see Precautions).

The following adverse reactions have been reported: Skin and Mucus Membranes: pruritus and rash (30%) ranging from simple erythema to exfoliative dermatitis, and mucus membrane lesions (20%) including stomatitis.

Hematological: leukopenia (2%), thrombocytopenia (1 to 3%), eosinophilia, agranulocytosis and aplastic anemia.

Renal: proteinuria (10 to 15%), nephrotic syndrome, acute renal failure.

Allergic: anaphylactoid and vasomotor (nitritoid) reactions.

Digestive: metallic taste, diarrhea, enterocolitis, cholestatic jaundice.

Miscellaneous: Other very rare reactions include encephalitis, peripheral neurophathy and pulmonary infiltrates.

Chrysiasis (affecting the skin and mucus membranes) and corneal gold deposits have been noted in some patients.

A transient flare of articular inflammation appearing within 24 hours of injection and lasting 2 or 3 days has also been reported.

Overdose: Symptoms: Heavy metal toxicity includes: pruritus, dermatitis, stomatitis, vague gastrointestinal discomfort, albuminuria with or without a nephrotic syndrome, hematuria, agranulocytosis, thrombocytopenic purpura, and aplastic anemia.

Treatment: Gold therapy should be discontinued promptly and supportive treatments should be given as required for specific complications.

Patients with severe dermatitis may benefit from oral antihistamines, topical corticosteroids or emollients.

For the management of severe renal, hematologic, pulmonary enterocolic or generalized pruritic reactions, moderate to high dose corticosteroid therapy (e.g. prednisone 20 to 100 mg daily in divided doses) reportedly is beneficial.

When high-dose corticosteroid therapy is ineffective or substantial adverse reactions to steroids occur, a chelating agent (e.g. dimercaprol) or a drug such as N-acetylcysteine may be used to enhance the elimination of gold.

Dosage: Should be administered by the **i.m. route only,** preferably in the gluteal muscle.

Do not use a darkened solution (more than pale yellow).

Because of the possibility of anaphylactic reaction, it is recommended that patients be kept under medical observation for a period of 30 minutes after the administration of the drug.

Adults: Initial 10 mg i.m. the first week, 25 mg the second week, then 25 to 50 mg weekly for the next 20 weeks or until toxicity occurs.

At this stage the response to therapy should dictate the future course of treatment. Patients with good to excellent response can go to maintenance therapy. In those with modest improvement a prolonged period of weekly injections may be maintained.

Maintenance: 50 mg i.m. tapered progressively to every 2 to 4 weeks according to clinical response and tolerance, and maintained indefinitely.

Pediatrics: 10 mg i.m. the first week followed by 1 mg/kg of body weight/week; do not exceed 50 mg/dose. See adult dosage for intervals between injections.

Note: To reinstitute therapy following mild adverse reactions, see Precautions, Patient monitoring.

Supplied: Each mL of aqueous solution contains: 10, 25 or 50 mg of sodium aurothiomalate. Nonmedicinal ingredients: chlorocresol and water for injection. Ampuls of 1 mL, boxes of 3. Store between 15 and 25°C. Protect from light or discoloration may occur.

Do not use a darkened solution (more than pale yellow).

...The health care professional should carefully weigh the anticipated therapeutic benefit from any drug against all potential adverse effects.

MYOFLEX®

Bayer Consumer

Triethanolamine Salicylate

Topical Analgesic

Indications: Analgesic rub for the temporary relief of aches and pains of muscles and joints associated with backache, lumbago, neck ache, arthritic or rheumatic pain, strains, sprains, pain of tendons and ligaments.

Contraindications: Salicylate hypersensitivity.

Warnings: For external use only. Use only as directed. Keep this and all other drugs out of the reach of children.

Precautions: If rash or irritation occurs, discontinue use. Do not apply to wounds or damaged skin. Avoid contact with eyes and mucous membranes. If pain persists for more than 7 days or redness is present, consult a physician. In case of accidental ingestion, seek professional assistance or contact the Poison Control Centre immediately. The application of external heat, such as an electric heating pad, may result in excessive skin irritation or skin burn. Protect from excessive heat or freezing.

Dosage: Apply to area of soreness with gentle massage, 3 or 4 times daily. Children (under 2 years): consult a physician.

Supplied: Extra Strength: Each g contains: triethanolamine salicylate 15% w/w in a greaseless, nonstaining, odorless, vanishing cream base. Nonmedicinal ingredients: cetyl alcohol, EDTA, lavender oil, propylene glycol, sodium lauryl sulfate, stearyl alcohol and white wax. Tubes of 50 and 100 g. Plastic tubs of 175g.

Regular: Each g contains: triethanolamine salicylate 10% w/w in a greaseless, nonstaining, odorless, vanishing cream base. Nonmedicinal ingredients: cetyl alcohol, EDTA, lavender oil, propylene glycol, sodium lauryl sulfate, stearyl alcohol and white wax. Tubes of 100 g.

Ultra: Each g contains: triethanolamine salicylate 20 % w/w in a greaseless, nonstaining, odorless, vanishing cream base. Nonmedicinal ingredients: carbomer ultrez, EDTA, lavender oil, propylene glycol, silicon dioxide and titanium dioxide. Tubes of 50 and 100 g.

(Shown in Product Recognition Section)

MYOFLEX® ICE PLUS

Bayer Consumer

Triethanolamine Salicylate—Menthol

Topical Analgesic

Supplied: Each g of ice plus gel contains: triethanolamine salicylate 15% w/w and menthol 3% w/w. Nonmedicinal ingredients: carboxypolymethylene, colloidal silicon dioxide, deionized water, EDTA, FD&C Blue #1, isopropyl alcohol, lavender oil, propylene glycol and triethanolamine. Tubes of 100 g.

MYOTONACHOL® Ⓟ

Glenwood

Bethanechol Chloride

Parasympathomimetic Agent

Pharmacology: Bethanechol acts principally by producing the effects of stimulation of the parasympathetic nervous system. It increases the tone of the detrusor urinae muscle, usually producing a contraction sufficiently strong to initiate micturition and empty the bladder. It stimulates gastric motility, increases gastric tone, and often restores rhythmic peristalsis. Stimulation of the parasympathetic nervous system releases acetylcholine at the nerve endings. When spontaneous stimulation is reduced and therapeutic intervention is required, acetylcholine can be given, but it is rapidly hydrolyzed by cholinesterase, and its effects are transient. Bethanechol is not destroyed by cholinesterase and its effects are more prolonged and predictable than those of acetylcholine.

It has predominant muscarinic action and only feeble nicotinic action. Doses that stimulate micturition and defecation and increase peristalsis do not ordinarily stimulate ganglia or voluntary muscles. Therapeutic test doses in normal human subjects have little effect on the heart rate, blood pressure, or peripheral circulation.

Myotonachol (cont'd)

Indications: The treatment of acute postoperative and postpartum nonobstructive (functional) urinary retention and for neurogenic atony of the urinary bladder with retention.

As adjunctive therapy in the treatment of gastro-esophageal reflux with pyrosis unresponsive to conventional therapy.

Contraindications: Hyperthyroidism, *pregnancy*, *lactation*, peptic ulcer, latent or active bronchial asthma, pronounced bradycardia or hypotension, vasomotor instability, coronary artery disease, epilepsy and parkinsonism.

Should not be employed when the strength or integrity of the gastrointestinal or bladder wall is in question, or in the presence of mechanical obstruction; when increased muscular activity of the gastrointestinal tract or urinary bladder might prove harmful, as following recent urinary bladder surgery, gastrointestinal resection and anastomosis, or when there is possible gastrointestinal obstruction; in bladder neck obstruction, spastic gastrointestinal disturbances, acute inflammatory lesions of the gastrointestinal tract, or peritonitis; or in marked vagotonia.

Precautions: Drug Interactions: Special care and consideration are required when bethanechol is administered to patients being treated concomitantly with other drugs with which pharmacological interactions may occur. Examples of drugs with potentials for such interactions are: quinidine and procainamide, which may antagonize cholinergic effects: cholinergic drugs, particularly cholinesterase inhibitors, where additive effects may occur.

Special care is required when bethanechol is given to patients receiving ganglionic blocking compounds because a critical fall in blood pressure may occur. Usually, severe abdominal symptoms appear before there is a fall in the blood pressure.

In urinary retention, if the sphincter fails to relax as bethanechol contracts the bladder, urine may be forced up the ureter into the kidney pelvis. If there is bacteriuria, this may cause reflux infection.

Adverse Effects: Abdominal discomfort, salivation, flushing of the skin ("hot feeling") and sweating.

Large doses more commonly result in effects of parasympathetic stimulation, such as malaise, headache, sensation of heat about the face, flushing, colicky pain, diarrhea, nausea and belching, abdominal cramps, borborygmi, asthmatic attacks and fall in blood pressure.

Overdose: Symptoms: Symptoms of an overdose are an extension of the adverse effects. In rare instances violent symptoms of cholinergic over-stimulation including fall in blood pressure, circulatory collapse, cardiac arrest, shock, severe abdominal cramps with bloody diarrhea and possibly severe bronchospasm.

Treatment: Adults: 600 μg atropine s.c. (i.v. emergencies); children: proportionately smaller doses s.c.

Administer the atropine first followed by standard treatment for cardiac arrest, circulatory collapse, shock and/or bronchospasm. Bloody diarrhea and other symptoms of violent cholinergic over-stimulation rarely require any additional treatment following adequate doses of atropine.

Dosage: Must be individualized, depending on the type and severity of the condition to be treated. Preferably the drug is given when the stomach is empty. If taken soon after eating, nausea and vomiting may occur. The usual adult dosage is 10 to 50 mg 3 or 4 times a day. The minimum effective dose is determined by giving 5 to 10 mg initially and repeating the same amount at hourly intervals until a satisfactory response occurs or a maximum of 50 mg has been given.

The effects of the drug sometimes appear within 30 minutes and usually within 60 to 90 minutes. They persist for up to 6 hours. Individual doses should therefore be spaced at least 6 hours apart.

Supplied: 10 mg: Each white, flat beveled edge with single score tablet contains: bethanechol chloride 10 mg. Nonmedicinal ingredients: calcium sulfate dihydrate, magnesium stearate BP, maize starch BP and talc BP (iron-free). Bottles of 100.

25 mg: Each white, flat beveled edge with cross score tablet contains: bethanechol chloride 25 mg. Nonmedicinal ingredients: calcium sulfate dihydrate, magnesium stearate BP, maize starch BP and talc BP (iron-free). Bottles of 100.

MYSOLINE® Ⓟ
Wyeth-Ayerst

Primidone

Anticonvulsant

Supplied: Tablets: Each white, round, flat, beveled-edge tablet, embossed AYERST on one side with a double score line on other side, contains: primidone USP 250 mg. Nonmedicinal ingredients: lactose, magnesium stearate, methylcellulose, microcrystalline cellulose, sodium lauryl sulfate, sodium starch glycolate and talc. Energy: 0.96 kJ (0.23 kcal). Alcohol-, gluten-, parabens-, sulfites- and tartrazine-free. Bottles of 100.

Pediatric Chewable Tablets: Chew tablets before swallowing. Each white, banana-flavored, round, flat, beveled-edge, chewable tablet, embossed AYERST on one side with a score line on other side, contains: primidone USP 125 mg. Nonmedicinal ingredients: flavor banana, lactose, magnesium stearate, methylcellulose, microcrystalline cellulose, sodium lauryl sulfate, sodium starch glycolate, sodium cyclamate and talc. Energy: 0.50 kJ (0.12 kcal). Sodium: <1 mmol (2.50 mg). Alcohol-, gluten-, parabens-, sulfites- and tartrazine-free. Bottles of 100. Store at room temperature (15 to 30°C), in well-closed containers.

(Shown in Product Recognition Section)

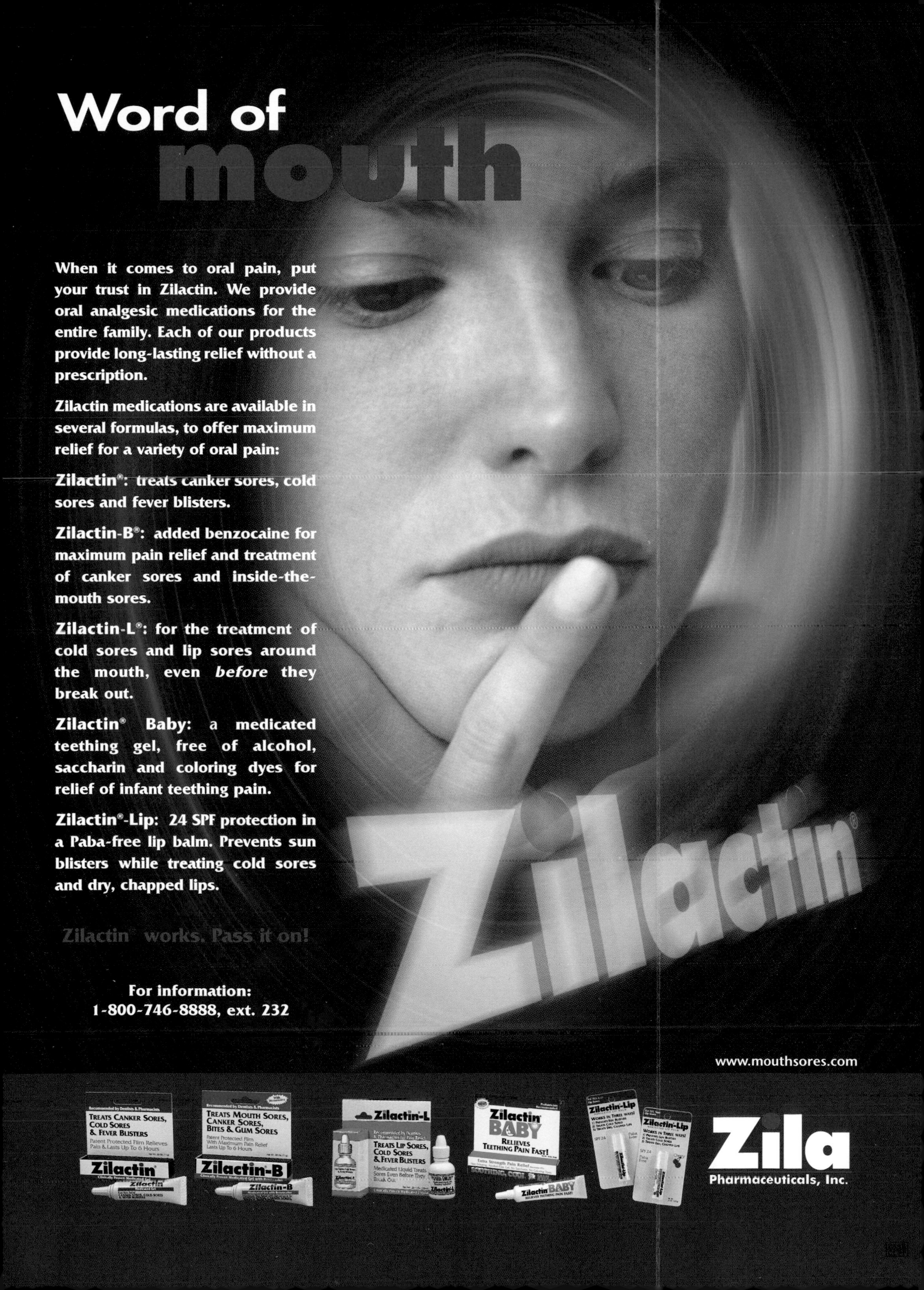
Word of
mouth
When it comes to oral pain, put your trust in Zilactin. We provide oral analgesic medications for the entire family. Each of our products provide long-lasting relief without a prescription.
Zilactin medications are available in several formulas, to offer maximum relief for a variety of oral pain:
Zilactin®: treats canker sores, cold sores and fever blisters.
Zilactin-B®: added benzocaine for maximum pain relief and treatment of canker sores and inside-the-mouth sores.
Zilactin-L®: for the treatment of cold sores and lip sores around the mouth, even before they break out.
Zilactin® Baby: a medicated teething gel, free of alcohol, saccharin and coloring dyes for relief of infant teething pain.
Zilactin®-Lip: 24 SPF protection in a Paba-free lip balm. Prevents sun blisters while treating cold sores and dry, chapped lips.
Zilactin® works. Pass it on!
For information:
1-800-746-8888, ext. 232
Zilactin®
www.mouthsores.com
Treats Canker Sores, Cold Sores & Fever Blisters
Zilactin
Treats Mouth Sores, Canker Sores, Bites & Gum Sores
Zilactin-B
Zilactin-L
Treats Lip Sores, Cold Sores & Fever Blisters
Zilactin Baby
Relieves Teething Pain Fast!
Zilactin-Lip
Works in Three Ways!
Zila
Pharmaceuticals, Inc.

BP CONTROL THAT END
FROM ONE DAY

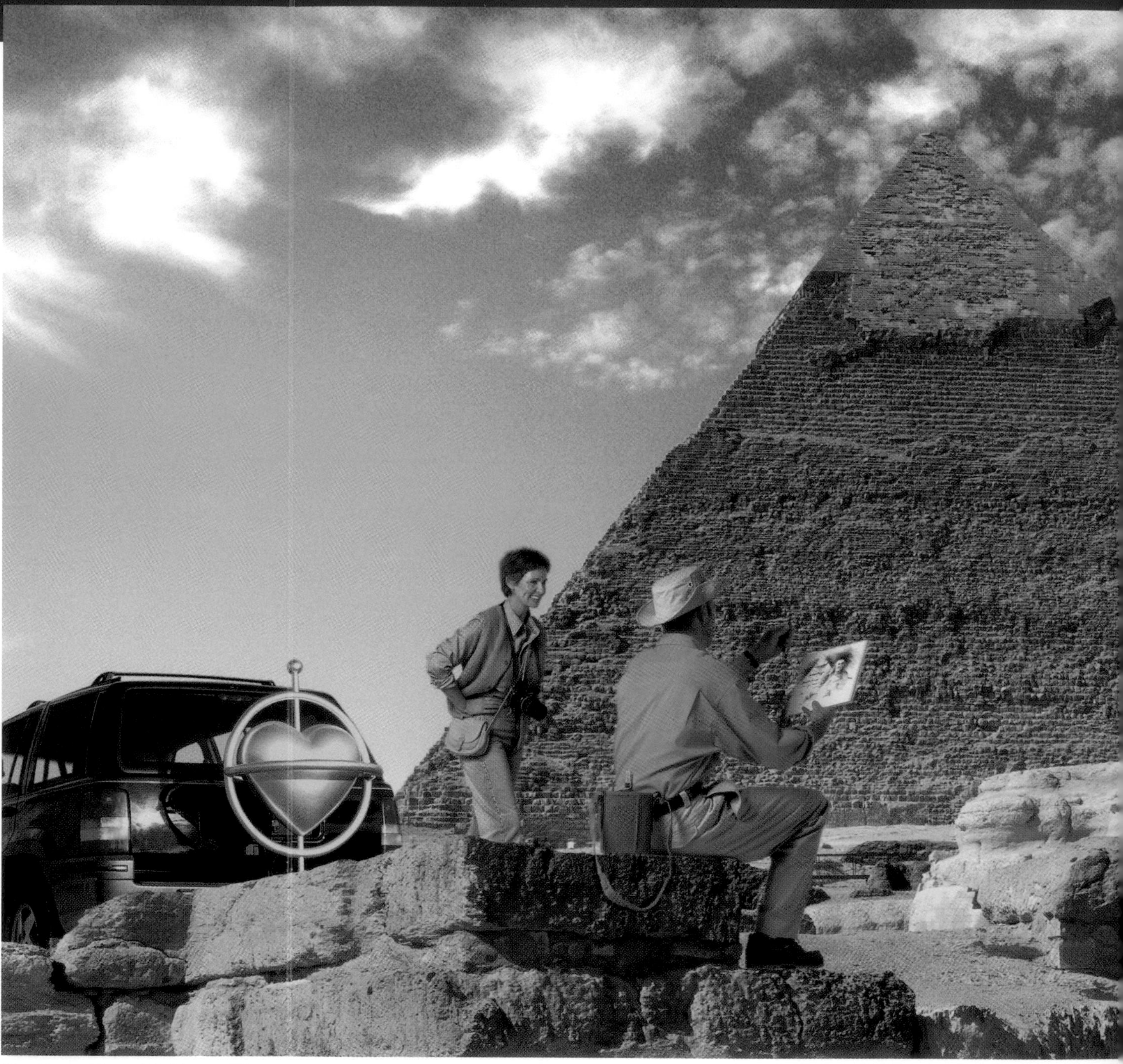

The Pyramids and Sphinx at Giza

H E R E T O D A Y.

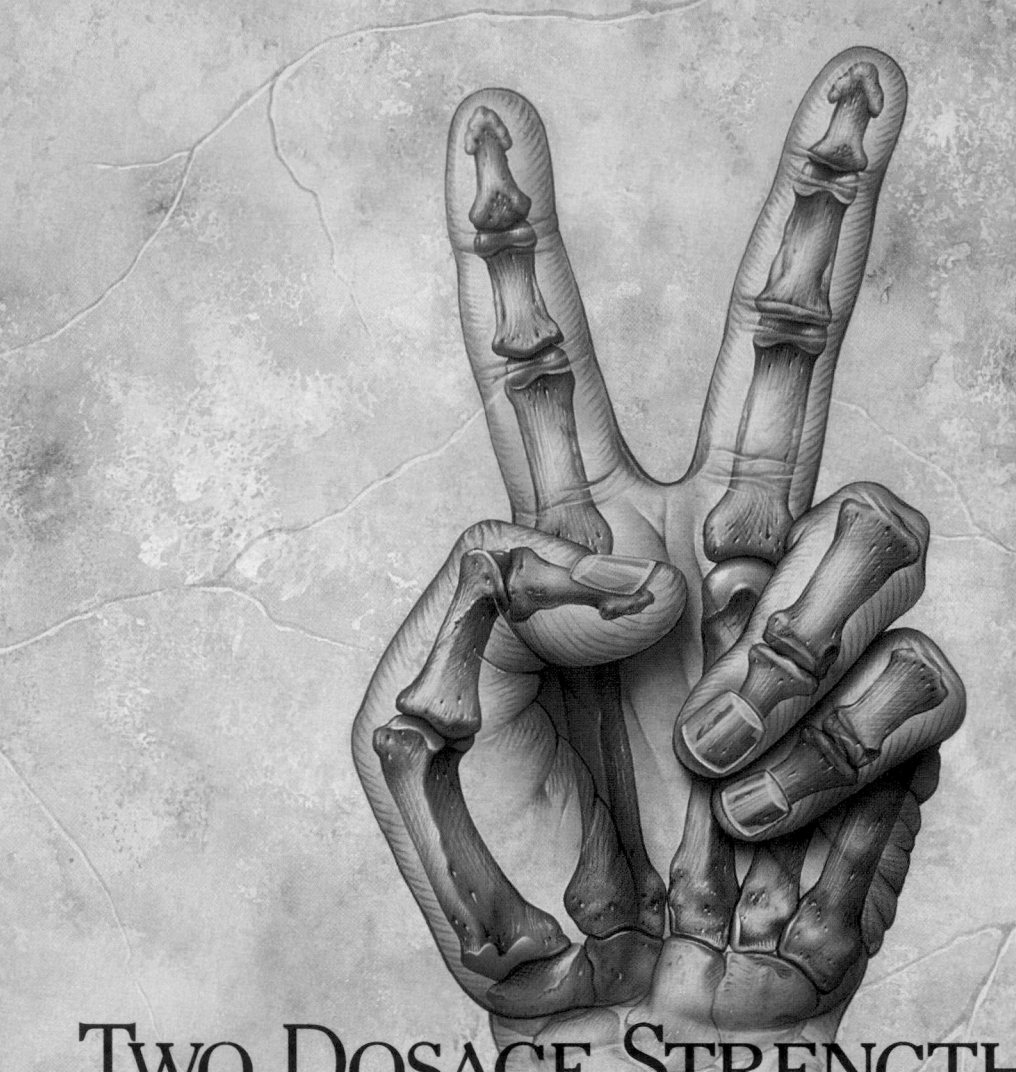

References: 1. Arthrotec® Product Monograph 2. De Melo Gomes JA. The safety of Arthrotec® in patients with rheumatoid arthritis or osteoarthritis: An assessment of the upper gastrointestinal tract by endoscopy. Scand J Rheumatol 1992;Suppl. 96:23-31. 3. Melo Gomes JA., et al. Double-blind comparison of efficacy and gastroduodenal safety of diclofenac/misoprostol, piroxicam and naproxen in the treatment of osteoarthritis. Annals of the Rheum Dis. 1993;52(12):881-885.

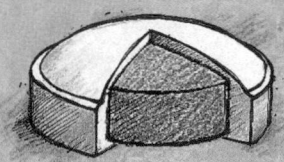

N

NADOPEN-V® ℗
Nadeau

Penicillin V Potassium

Antibiotic

Indications: Mild to moderately severe infections caused by penicillin V sensitive microorganisms including streptococcal pharyngitis, staphylococcal infection without bacteremia and pneumococcal infections. Therapy should be guided by bacteriologic sensitivity tests and clinical response.

For prophylaxis following rheumatic fever and/or chorea. (Prophylaxis with oral penicillin on a continuing basis has proved effective in preventing recurrences of these conditions.) To prevent bacterial endocarditis in patients with congenital and/or rheumatic heart lesions before dental procedures, minor upper respiratory tract surgery or instrumentation. Prophylaxis should be instituted the day of the procedure and continued for 2 or more postoperative days. Patients with a past history of rheumatic fever who are receiving continuous antibiotic prophylaxis may harbour increased numbers of penicillin resistant organisms; use of another anti-infective agent should be considered. If penicillin is to be used in these patients during surgery, the regular rheumatic fever program should be interrupted 1 week before the procedure. At the time of surgery, penicillin may be reinstituted prophylactically.

For the prevention of bacteremia following tooth extraction.

Contraindications: Oral penicillin should not be used as adjunctive prophylaxis for genitourinary instrumentation or surgery, lower intestinal tract surgery, sigmoidoscopy and childbirth; in patients with a history of penicillin or cephalosporin allergy; against beta lactamase (penicillinase) producing organisms; the active treatment of syphilis; subacute bacterial endocarditis, diphtheria, gas gangrene, or other severe infections due to penicillin-susceptible organisms.

Precautions: Serious and occasionally fatal hypersensitivity (anaphylactoid) reactions have been reported in patients receiving penicillin therapy. Although anaphylaxis is more frequent following parenteral therapy, it has occurred with oral penicillins. These reactions are more apt to occur in individuals with a history of sensitivity to multiple allergens.

Careful inquiry should be made concerning previous hypersensitivity reactions to penicillins, cephalosporins and other allergens. Effective and safe skin tests which will predict an anaphylactic reaction are not generally available. Cross sensitivity between penicillin and cephalosporins is well documented.

Penicillin should be used with caution in individuals with histories of allergies and/or asthma.

Oral administration should not be relied on in patients with severe illness, with nausea, vomiting, gastric dilatation, cardiospasm, or intestinal hypermotility.

Occasional patients will not absorb therapeutic amounts of oral penicillin.

In streptococcal infections, therapy should be given for 10 days minimum. Cultures should be taken following treatment to assure eradication of streptococci.

Prolonged use of antibiotics may promote overgrowth of nonsusceptible organisms, including fungi. Should superinfection occur, take appropriate measures.

Adverse Effects: Although the incidence of reactions to oral penicillins is much lower than to parenteral therapy, all degrees of hypersensitivity including fatal anaphylaxis have been reported.

The most common reactions to oral penicillin are nausea, vomiting, epigastric distress, diarrhea, and black hairy tongue. The hypersensitivity reactions reported are skin eruptions (maculopapular to exfoliative dermatitis), urticaria; reactions resembling serum sickness, including chills, fever, edema, and anaphylaxis. Fever and eosinophilia may frequently be the only reactions observed. Hemolytic anemia, leukopenia, thrombocytopenia, neuropathy, and nephropathy may occur but are usually associated with high doses of parenteral penicillin.

Overdose: Symptoms and Treatment: Anaphylactic shock must be treated with epinephrine 0.3 mL of 1:1 000 solution given by the i.v. or i.m. route in repeated doses until relief of bronchospasm and hypotension has occurred or excessive tachycardia has been induced. Mild hypersensitivity reactions may respond to antihistamines.

Dosage: The dosage should be determined according to the sensitivity of the causative microorganisms and the severity of infection and adjusted to the clinical response of the patient.

The usual dosage recommendations for adults and children 12 years and over are as follows:

Beta hemolytic streptococcal infections—mild to moderately severe (without associated bacteremia) of the upper respiratory tract including scarlet fever and mild erysipelas: 200 000 to 500 000 units 3 times a day for a minimum of 10 days to prevent development of rheumatic fever. Dosage for routine prophylaxis against streptococcal infection in patients with a history of rheumatic fever or congenital heart disease may be 200 000 units once or twice daily. When such patients undergo tonsillectomy, tooth extraction or other minor surgery the prophylactic dose should be 500 000 units every 6 hours 2 days before surgery and 2 days postoperatively. If oral medication is not feasible on the day of surgery, parenteral therapy should be given.

Pneumococcal infections—mild to moderately severe infections of the respiratory tract including otitis media: 400 000 to 500 000 units every 6 hours until the patient has been afebrile for at least 2 days.

Staphylococcal infections—mild infections of the skin and soft tissue (culture and sensitivity tests should be performed): 400 000 to 500 000 units every 6 to 8 hours in conjunction with the indicated surgical procedure.

Fusospirochetosis (Vincent's Angina) of the oropharynx, mild to moderately severe infections: 400 000 to 500 000 units every 6 to 8 hours.

Prophylaxis in the following conditions—to prevent recurrence following rheumatic fever and/or chorea: 200 000 to 250 000 units twice daily on a continuing basis.

To prevent bacterial endocarditis in patients with rheumatic or congenital heart lesions before dental or upper respiratory tract surgery or instrumentation: i.m. penicillin is more reliable. However, if oral penicillin is preferred, penicillin V 2 g, one hour prior to the surgical procedure, then 1.0 g six hours later is recommended by the American Heart Association (1984). For practical purposes, 7 tablets of 300 mg (3.5 million units), one hour prior to surgery, then 3½ tablets of 300 mg (1.75 million units) could be given.

Pediatric doses: penicillin V full adult dose if greater than 27 kg (60 lb); one-half adult dose if less than 27 kg (60 lb).

Supplied: Oral Solution: Nadopen-V 200: After reconstitution, each 5 mL of red, strawberry flavored solution contains: penicillin V potassium 125 mg (200 000 IU). Energy: 57.9 kJ (13.64 kcal). Sodium: trace. Bottles of 100 mL.

Nadopen-V 400: After reconstitution, each 5 mL of red, strawberry flavored solution contains: penicillin V potassium 250 mg (400 000 IU). Energy: 55.25 kJ (13.0 kcal). Sodium: trace. Bottles of 100 mL.

Tablets: Each peach colored, round, scored tablet, engraved with the Nadeau logo and the figure 300, contains: penicillin V potassium 300 mg (500 000 IU). Sodium: trace. Bottles of 100, 500 and 1 000.

NADOSTINE® Preparations
Nadeau

Nystatin

Antifungal—Antibiotic

Indications: Oral Suspension: Prevention and treatment of candidal infections of the mouth (thrush) and intestinal candidiasis in infants and children.

Oral Tablets: Prevention and treatment of oral, esophageal and intestinal candidiasis. Protection against candidal overgrowth during antibiotic and/or corticosteroid therapy.

Topical Products: Treatment of mucocutaneous candidiasis. The cream is usually used to treat intertriginous areas.

Vaginal Products: Local treatment of vaginal candidiasis.

Contraindications: Hypersensitivity to nystatin or any other components of these preparations.

Precautions: Nystatin exhibits no appreciable activity against bacteria, protozoa or viruses. Discontinue medication if irritation occurs with topical or intravaginal use.

Take appropriate measures to avoid possible reinfection during sexual intercourse.

Pregnancy: Use of the vaginal applicator may not be considered desirable during pregnancy.

Adverse Effects: Large oral doses have occasionally produced diarrhea, gastrointestinal disorders, nausea or vomiting. Local or intravaginal irritation occurs rarely.

Dosage: Oral Suspension: Infants: Usual prophylactic and therapeutic dose is 100 000 units 4 times daily. May be dropped directly on the tongue by means of the calibrated dropper, or may be mixed with milk, lukewarm formula or other non acid vehicles. Thrush prevention in infants: 100 000 units daily. Children and adults: Usual therapeutic dose is 100 000 units 4 times daily, dropped into the mouth by means of the calibrated dropper, and held for some time before swallowing.

Oral Tablets: Usual prophylactic and therapeutic dose is 500 000 units 3 times a day. Double dosage if necessary for adults.

Ointment and Topical Cream: Apply to affected area 1 to 4 times daily as required.

Vaginal Tablets and Vaginal Cream: Insert deeply into the vagina 1 tablet (100 000 units) or 4 g (100 000 units) of cream once or twice daily by means of the applicator. Continue treatment for 2 weeks or more if necessary. Continue administration during menstruation.

Adjunctive measures such as therapeutic douches are unnecessary and sometimes inadvisable. Cleansing douches may be used by nonpregnant women, if desired, for esthetic purposes.

Pregnant patients with monilial infections should receive a dosage of 1 vaginal tablet or 4 g of vaginal cream once or twice daily for 3 to 6 weeks before term to prevent thrush in the newborn.

Nystatin therapeutic administration should generally be continued for at least 48 hours after clinical cure to prevent relapse. Oral nystatin should be prescribed at least as long as the oral antibacterial agent when these two medications are given concomitantly. Local treatment of chronic or resistant vaginal, oral or cutaneous candidiasis may be supplemented with oral nystatin administration.

Supplied: Oral Suspension ℗: Each mL of banana flavored yellow suspension contains: nystatin 100 000 units. Energy: 55.25 kJ (13.0 kcal)/5 mL. Bottles of 25, 50 and 100 mL with calibrated dropper. Bottles of 500 mL.

Oral Suspension (sucrose-free) ℗: Each mL of cherry flavored yellow suspension contains: nystatin 100 000 units. Energy: 8.9 kJ (2.1 kcal)/5 mL. Sweetening agents: sorbitol and sodium saccharine. Bottles of 50 and 100 mL with calibrated dropper.

Oral Tablets ℗: Each round, brown, film coated tablet contains: nystatin 500 000 units. Energy: 1.81 kJ (0.43 kcal). Bottles of 100.

Topical Cream: Each g of homogeneous, yellow, water soluble cream contains: nystatin 100 000 units. Tubes of 15 and 30 g. Jars of 500 g.

Topical Ointment: Each g of homogeneous, yellow ointment contains: nystatin 100 000 units. Tubes of 15 g.

Vaginal Cream ℗: Each g of homogeneous, yellow, water soluble cream contains: nystatin 25 000 units. Tubes 120 g with calibrated applicator.

Vaginal Tablets ℗: Each yellow, diamond shaped tablet contains: nystatin 100 000 units. Boxes of 15 and 30 in aluminum foil with applicator.

NAFTIN® Preparations
Allergan

Naftifine HCl

Topical Antifungal

Supplied: Cream: Each tube of cream contains: naftifine HCl 1% w/w. Nonmedicinal ingredients: benzyl alcohol, cetyl alcohol, cetyl esters wax, isopropyl myristate, polysorbate 60, purified water, sodium hydroxide, sorbitan monostearate and stearyl alcohol. Collapsible tubes of 2, 15 and 30 g. Store below 25°C.

Gel: Each tube of gel contains: naftifine HCl 1% w/w. Nonmedicinal ingredients: alcohol (52%), carbomer 934P, diisopropanolamine, edetate disodium, polysorbate 80 and purified water. Tubes of 2, 20 and 40 g. Store below 25°C.

NALBUPHINE ®
General Monograph, CPhA
see OPIOID ANALGESICS

NALCROM® ℞
Rhône-Poulenc Rorer
Sodium Cromoglycate
Antiallergic Agent

Pharmacology: Sodium cromoglycate seems to exert a stabilizing effect upon mast cells capable of releasing mediators. In gastrointestinal disease, the release of mediators causes a local inflammation which can either result in gastrointestinal symptoms or may allow absorption of antigenic material leading to systemic allergic reactions. It is most effective when given prior to antigen challenge.

Sodium cromoglycate has no antihistaminic or anti-inflammatory activity.

In humans, oral administration of sodium cromoglycate was followed by a low rate of urinary excretion. The mean urinary excretion of the administered dose over 24 hours was only 0.5%. This indicates that little of the compound is absorbed from the gastrointestinal tract.

Indications: Gastrointestinal allergy.

Contraindications: Hypersensitivity to sodium cromoglycate. Possible immunologic changes resulting in reactions such as, polymyositis, pneumonitis and heart failure, urticaria and anaphylaxis have been reported in conjunction with inhalation of sodium cromoglycate and are being actively investigated.

Warnings: *Pregnancy* and Children: Safety in pregnancy, and for the treatment of children under two years, has not yet been established.

The drug should not be used in such patients unless, in the opinion of the prescribing physician, the potential benefits outweigh the possible hazards.

Patients should be warned against suddenly discontinuing therapy when symptoms have been partially or completely controlled. Particular care should be taken where steroid and/or salazopyrine dosage has been reduced during sodium cromoglycate treatment.

The optimum dose required to maintain remission will need to be determined for each patient, but it is probably not less than 2 capsules 4 times daily.

Precautions: Clinical experience is limited and patients should be carefully observed while undergoing treatment.

The effect of sodium cromoglycate has been studied with those antibody systems concerned with immunity. To date, no effect was observed.

Adverse Effects: Nausea, headache, insomnia, skin rashes and joint pains have been reported in a few cases with oral dosing.

The most frequently reported adverse reactions attributed to sodium cromoglycate on inhalation (on the basis of recurrence following readministration) involve the respiratory tract and include bronchospasm, cough, laryngeal edema (rare), nasal congestion, pharyngeal irritation and wheezing.

Cases of erythema, urticaria or maculopapular rash have been reported and these have cleared within a few days on withdrawal of the drug. Occasional headache, sneezing, cough and unpleasant taste in the mouth have been reported.

Overdose: Symptoms and Treatment: There have been no reported cases in humans of overdosage of the drug.

As sodium cromoglycate is absorbed to a very limited extent, no action other than medical observation should be necessary. If any symptoms appear, symptomatic treatment is recommended.

Dosage: For optimal results, dissolve the contents of the capsule in warm water and take as a solution.

Chronic inflammatory bowel disease: Initial dose: Adults: 200 mg 4 times daily 15 to 20 minutes before meals.
Initial dose: Children from 2 to 14 years: 100 mg 4 times daily 15 to 20 minutes before meals.
Maintenance dose: To prevent relapses dosage should be maintained indefinitely at 200 mg 4 times daily in adults and 100 mg 4 times daily in children.

Food allergy: Initial dose: Adults: 200 mg 4 times daily 15 to 20 minutes before meals.
Initial dose: Children from 2 to 14 years: 100 mg 4 times daily 15 to 20 minutes before meals. If satisfactory control of symptoms is not achieved within 2 to 3 weeks the dosage may be doubled but should not exceed 40 mg/kg/day.
Maintenance dose: Once a therapeutic response has been achieved the dose may be reduced to the minimum required to maintain the patient free of symptoms. Patients unable to avoid allergenic foods under certain circumstances may be able to protect themselves against the effect of these foods by taking a single dose 15 minutes before the meal. The optimum dosage will need to be determined for each patient. A suitable starting dose would be 200 mg in adults and 100 mg in children.

Supplied: Each clear, hard gelatin capsule for oral use, imprinted Fisons 101 in black, contains: sodium cromoglycate 100 mg as a white powder. Nonmedicinal ingredients: iron oxide and gelatin. Sodium: <1 mmol (9.0 mg). Tartrazine-free. Bottles of 100.

(Shown in Product Recognition Section)

NALFON® ℞
Lilly
Fenoprofen Calcium
Anti-inflammatory—Analgesic

Pharmacology: Fenoprofen has demonstrated anti-inflammatory, analgesic and antipyretic activities in animal studies. Although fenoprofen's modes of action are unknown, in vitro tests have shown that it inhibits synthesis and/or release of prostaglandins; stabilizes lysosomes; inhibits platelet aggregation and platelet adhesiveness, and enhances fibrinolytic activity. All of these activities may have a role in the amelioration of inflammation, pain and fever. Animal studies indicate that fenoprofen does not stimulate the pituitary or adrenal glands; therefore, its effects are not mediated by secretions from these glands. In clinical trials 2.4 g of fenoprofen produced approximately the same clinical activity as 3.9 g of ASA.

Under fasting conditions, fenoprofen is rapidly absorbed, and peak plasma levels of 50 μg/L are achieved within 2 hours after oral administration of 600 mg doses. Good dose proportionality was observed between 200 and 600 mg doses in fasting male volunteers. The plasma half-life is approximately 3 hours. About 90% of a single oral dose is eliminated within 24 hours as fenoprofen glucuronide and 4′-hydroxyfenoprofen glucuronide, the major urinary metabolites of fenoprofen. Fenoprofen is highly bound (99%) to albumin. Peak plasma levels of fenoprofen in normal elderly volunteers were similar to those observed in normal young volunteers. Elderly volunteers had a mean plasma clearance of 2.2 L/hour while plasma clearance of fenoprofen in normal young volunteers ranged from 3 to 3.5 L/hour. The overall elimination rate constant, plasma half-life and ratio of renal to nonrenal clearance of fenoprofen was the same in elderly and young volunteers. The 30 to 60% decrease in plasma clearance is due to a decrease in the volume of distribution in the body. The concomitant administration of antacid (containing both aluminum and magnesium hydroxide) does not interfere with absorption of fenoprofen. There is less suppression of collagen-induced platelet aggregation with single doses of fenoprofen than there is with ASA.

Indications: Treatment of rheumatoid arthritis and osteoarthritis.

Contraindications: Peptic ulcer or any inflammatory gastrointestinal tract disease. Hypersensitivity to fenoprofen.

Fenoprofen should not be used in patients in whom acute asthmatic attacks, urticaria, rhinitis or other allergic manifestations are precipitated by ASA or other nonsteroidal anti-inflammatory agents. Fatal anaphylactoid reactions have occurred in such individuals. Fenoprofen should not be administered to patients with a history of significantly impaired renal function.

Data to establish safety and a dosage regimen in the pediatric age group are not available at this time, and use in children under 14 years of age is contraindicated.

Warnings: Peptic ulceration, perforation and gastrointestinal bleeding, sometimes severe and occasionally fatal have been reported during therapy with nonsteroidal anti-inflammatory drugs (NSAIDs) including fenoprofen. Fenoprofen should be given under close medical supervision to patients prone to gastrointestinal tract irritation particularly those with a history of peptic ulcer, diverticulosis or other inflammatory disease of the gastrointestinal tract. Patients taking any NSAID including fenoprofen should be instructed to contact a physician immediately if they experience symptoms or signs suggestive of peptic ulceration or gastrointestinal bleeding. These reactions can occur without warning symptoms or signs and at any time during treatment. Elderly, frail and debilitated patients appear to be at higher risk from a variety of adverse reactions from NSAIDs. For such patients, consideration should be given to a starting dose lower than usual, with individual adjustments when necessary and under close supervision. Since fenoprofen has been marketed, there have been reports of genitourinary tract problems in patients taking it. The most frequent reported problems have been episodes of dysuria, cystitis, hematuria, interstitial nephritis, and nephrotic syndrome. This syndrome may be preceded by the appearance of fever, rash, arthralgia, oliguria, and azotemia and may progress to anuria. There may also be substantial proteinuria, and, on renal biopsy, electron microscopy has shown foot process fusion and T-lymphocyte infiltration in the renal interstitium. Early recognition of the syndrome and withdrawal of the drug have been followed by rapid recovery. Administration of steroids and the use of dialysis have also been included in the treatment. Because a syndrome with some of these characteristics has also been reported with other NSAIDs, it is recommended that patients who have had these reactions with other such drugs not be treated with fenoprofen. In patients with possibly compromised renal function, periodic renal function examinations should be done.

Precautions: Gastrointestinal: If peptic ulceration is suspected or confirmed, or if gastrointestinal bleeding or perforation occurs fenoprofen should be discontinued, an appropriate treatment instituted and patient closely monitored. There is no definitive evidence that the concomitant administration of histamine H2-receptor antagonists and/or antacids will either prevent the occurrence of gastrointestinal side effects or allow continuation of fenoprofen calcium therapy when and if these adverse reactions appear.

Renal: As with nonsteroidal anti-inflammatory drugs, long-term administration of fenoprofen to animals has resulted in renal papillary necrosis and other abnormal renal pathology. In humans, there have been reports of acute interstitial nephritis with hematuria, proteinuria and occasionally nephrotic syndrome. A second form of renal toxicity has been seen in patients with prerenal conditions leading to the reduction in renal blood flow or blood volume, where the renal prostaglandins have a supportive role in the maintenance of renal perfusion. In these patients, administration of a nonsteroidal anti-inflammatory drug may cause a dose-dependent reduction in prostaglandin formation and may precipitate overt renal decompensation. Patients at greatest risk of this reaction are those with impaired renal function, heart failure, liver dysfunction, those taking diuretics, and the elderly. Discontinuation of nonsteroidal anti-inflammatory therapy is usually followed by recovery to the pretreatment state. Fenoprofen and its metabolites are eliminated primarily by the kidneys, therefore the drug should be used with great caution in patients with impaired renal function, especially the elderly. In these cases, lower doses of fenoprofen should be anticipated and patients carefully monitored. During long-term therapy, kidney function should be monitored periodically.

Hepatic: As with other nonsteroidal anti-inflammatory drugs, borderline elevations in 1 or more liver tests may occur. These abnormalities may progress, may remain essentially unchanged, or may be transient with continued therapy. A patient with symptoms and/or signs suggesting liver dysfunction, or in whom an abnormal liver test has occurred, should be evaluated for evidence of the development of more severe hepatic reactions while on therapy with this drug. Severe hepatic reactions, including jaundice and cases of fatal hepatitis, have been reported with this drug, as with other nonsteroidal anti-inflammatory drugs. Although such reactions are rare, if abnormal liver tests persist or worsen, if clinical signs and symptoms consistent with liver disease develop, or if systemic manifestations occur (e.g., eosinophilia and rash), this drug should be discontinued. During long-term therapy, liver function should be monitored periodically. If this drug is to be used in the presence of impaired liver function, it must be done under strict supervision.

Fluid and Electrolyte Balance: Fluid retention and edema have been observed in patients treated with fenoprofen. Therefore, as with many other nonsteroidal anti-inflammatory drugs, the possibility of precipitating congestive heart failure in elderly patients or those with compromised cardiac function should be borne in mind. Fenoprofen should be used with caution in patients with heart failure, hypertension or other conditions predisposing to fluid retention. Serum electrolytes should be monitored periodically during long-term therapy, especially in those patients at risk.

Hematology: Drugs inhibiting prostaglandin biosynthesis do interfere with platelet function to some degree; therefore, patients who may be adversely affected by such an action should be carefully observed when fenoprofen is administered.

Blood dyscrasias associated with the use of nonsteroidal anti-inflammatory drugs are rare, but could be with severe consequences.
Infection: In common with other anti-inflammatory drugs, fenoprofen may mask the usual signs of infection.
Ophthalmology: Blurred and/or diminished vision has been reported with the use of fenoprofen and other nonsteroidal anti-inflammatory drugs. If such symptoms develop, this drug should be discontinued and an ophthalmologic examination performed; ophthalmic examination should be carried out at periodic intervals in any patient receiving this drug for an extended period of time.
CNS: Caution should be exercised by patients whose activities require alertness if they experience CNS side effects while taking fenoprofen. Peripheral edema has been observed in some patients taking fenoprofen; therefore, fenoprofen should be used with caution in patients with compromised cardiac function or hypertension. The possibility of renal involvement should be considered.
Pregnancy: Fenoprofen's safety in human pregnancy has not been established. Therefore, it should be used in pregnancy only when possible benefits to the patient outweigh possible risks to the fetus. Animal reproductive studies with fenoprofen have not revealed teratogenic or embryocidal effects. Animal experiments indicate that the drug interferes with parturition and therefore its use during labor is not recommended.
Drug Interactions: The coadministration of ASA decreases the biologic half-life of fenoprofen because of an increase in metabolic clearance that results in a greater amount of hydroxylated fenoprofen in the urine. Although the mechanism of interaction between fenoprofen and ASA is not totally known, enzyme induction and displacement of fenoprofen from plasma albumin binding sites are possibilities. Because fenoprofen has not been shown to produce any additional effect beyond that obtained with ASA alone and because ASA increases the rate of excretion of fenoprofen, the concomitant use of fenoprofen and salicylates is not recommended. Chronic administration of phenobarbital, a known enzyme inducer, may be associated with a decrease in the plasma half-life of fenoprofen. When phenobarbital is added to or withdrawn from treatment, dosage adjustment of fenoprofen may be required. In vitro studies have shown that fenoprofen, because of its affinity for albumin, may displace from their binding sites other drugs that are also albumin bound, and this may lead to drug interaction. Theoretically, fenoprofen could likewise be displaced. Patients receiving hydantoin, sulfonamides or sulfonylureas should be observed for increased activity of these drugs and, therefore, signs of toxicity from these drugs. In patients receiving coumarin-type anticoagulants, the addition of fenoprofen to therapy could prolong the prothrombin time. Patients receiving both drugs should be under careful observation. Patients treated with fenoprofen may be resistant to the effects of loop diuretics.
Laboratory Test Interactions: Amerlex-M kit assay values of total and free triiodothyronine in patients receiving fenoprofen calcium have been reported as falsely elevated on the basis of a chemical cross-reaction that directly interferes with the assay. Thyroid-stimulating hormone, total thyroxine, and thyrotropin-releasing hormone response are not affected.

Adverse Effects: The potential for adverse reactions was assessed in 6 786 patients. The most common adverse reactions encountered with NSAIDs are gastrointestinal, of which peptic ulcer, with or without bleeding, is the most severe. Fatalities have occurred on occasion, particularly in the elderly.
Gastrointestinal: During clinical trials with fenoprofen, the most common adverse reactions were gastrointestinal in nature and occurred in about 20.8% of patients. In descending order of frequency, these reactions included dyspepsia (10.3%), nausea (7.7%), constipation (7%), vomiting (2.6%), abdominal pain (2%) and diarrhea (1.8%). Anorexia, occult blood in the stool, flatulence and dry mouth occurred at a frequency of < 1%. The drug was discontinued because of adverse gastrointestinal reactions in less than 2% of patients.
Allergic: 2 instances of hypersensitivity were reported. Angioedema (angioneurotic edema).
CNS: The most frequent adverse neurologic reactions were headache (8.7%) and somnolence (8.5%). Dizziness (6.5%), tremor (2.2%), confusion (1.4%) and insomnia were noted less frequently. Fenoprofen was discontinued in less than 0.5% of patients because of these side effects.
Dermatologic: pruritus (4.2%), rash (3.7%), increased sweating (4.6%) and urticaria were observed. Exfoliative dermatitis, toxic epidermal necrolysis, Stevens-Johnson syndrome and alopecia have also been reported.
Cardiovascular: palpitations (2.5%), atrial fibrillation, pulmonary edema, ECG changes and supraventricular tachycardia.
Special Senses: tinnitus (4.5%), blurred vision (2.2%), and decreased hearing (1.6%). Burning tongue, diplopia and optic neuritis were reported.
Hematologic: purpura, bruising, hemorrhage, thrombocytopenia, hemolytic anemia, aplastic anemia, agranulocytosis and pancytopenia have been reported to occur at a frequency of < 1%.
Renal: azotemia, interstitial nephritis, nephrosis, papillary necrosis, dysuria, cystitis, hematuria, oliguria and anuria have been observed at a frequency of < 1%.
Hepatic: jaundice, cholestatic hepatitis, increase in alkaline phosphatase, LDH and AST.
Respiratory: dyspnea (2.8%), upper respiratory infection (1.5%) and nasopharyngitis (1.2%) were reported.
Other: nervousness (5.7%), asthenia (5.4%), fatigue (1.7%) and peripheral edema (5%). Malaise, anaphylaxis, urticaria and insomnia were seen < 1% of the time.

Overdose: Symptoms: Symptoms of overdose appear within several hours and generally involve the gastrointestinal and central nervous systems. They include dyspepsia, nausea, vomiting, abdominal pain, dizziness, headache, ataxia, tinnitus, tremor, drowsiness and confusion. Hyperpyrexia, tachycardia, hypotension and acute renal failure may occur rarely following overdose. Respiratory depression and metabolic acidosis have also been reported following overdose with certain NSAIDs.

Treatment: In managing overdosage, consider the possibility of multiple drug overdoses, interaction among drugs and unusual drug kinetics in your patient. Protect the patient's airway and support ventilation and perfusion. Meticulously monitor and maintain, within acceptable limits, the patient's vital signs, blood gases, serum electrolytes, etc. Absorption of drugs from the gastrointestinal tract may be decreased by giving activated charcoal, which, in many cases, is more effective than emesis or lavage; consider charcoal instead of or in addition to gastric emptying. Repeated doses of charcoal over time may hasten elimination of some drugs that have been absorbed. Safeguard the patient's airway when employing gastric emptying or charcoal. Alkalinization of the urine, forced diuresis, peritoneal dialysis, hemodialysis and charcoal hemoperfusion do not enhance systemic drug elimination.

Dosage: Rheumatoid Arthritis: Initiate the treatment of active rheumatoid arthritis with 600 mg 3 or 4 times a day. Once a satisfactory response has been obtained, decrease the daily dose in increments of 300 mg until the minimum effective dose has been established. Doses as low as 600 mg daily have been shown to control mild disease activity in the occasional patient. In the event of inadequate response, increase the dosage in increments of 300 mg. Maximum fenoprofen daily dose should not exceed 3.0 g.
Osteoarthritis: Patients with degenerative joint disease in general require less medication than those with rheumatoid arthritis. Doses of 300 to 600 mg may be given 3 to 4 times a day to alleviate pain and increase mobility. Adjust the dose to the patient's need. Only infrequently will it be necessary to increase the daily dose to 2.4 g.

Supplied: Each para capsule shaped, scored, yellow film-coated tablet, marked "Lilly" and "NALFON", contains: fenoprofen calcium equivalent to fenoprofen 600 mg. Tartrazine-free. Nonmedicinal ingredients: cornstarch, dibasic calcium phosphate, magnesium stearate, polacrilin potassium and stearic acid; coating: benzyl alcohol, hydroxypropyl methylcellulose, polyethylene glycol, propylene glycol, titanium dioxide and yellow orange S Aluminum Lake. Bottles of 100.

NAPHCON®-A
Alcon
Naphazoline HCl—Pheniramine Maleate
Ocular Decongestant—Antihistamine

Supplied: Each Drop-Tainer dispenser contains: a sterile buffered solution of naphazoline HCl 0.025% and pheniramine maleate 0.3%; preserved with benzalkonium chloride. Nonmedicinal ingredients: boric acid, edetate disodium, hydrochloric acid, purified water, sodium borate, sodium chloride and sodium hydroxide. Drop-Tainer dispensers of 15 mL.

Refer to the BLUE SECTION for a review of patient information which should be provided to women taking oral contraceptives.

NAPHCON® FORTE
Alcon
Naphazoline HCl
Ophthalmic Vasoconstrictor

Supplied: Each Drop-Tainer dispenser contains: a sterile, buffered solution of naphazoline HCl 0.1% preserved with benzalkonium chloride. Nonmedicinal ingredients: boric acid, edetate disodium, hydrochloric acid, potassium chloride, purified water, sodium carbonate and sodium chloride. Drop-Tainer dispensers of 15 mL.

NAPROSYN® Ⓟ
Roche
Naproxen
Anti-inflammatory—Analgesic

Pharmacology: Naproxen has demonstrated anti-inflammatory, analgesic and antipyretic properties in classical animal test systems. In patients with rheumatoid arthritis, the anti-inflammatory action has been shown by a reduction in joint swelling, pain, and duration of morning stiffness, and by enhanced grip strength and increased mobility. It exhibits an anti-inflammatory effect even in adrenalectomized animals, and therefore its action is not mediated through the pituitary-adrenal axis. It is not a corticosteroid.

During clinical trials, naproxen has been found to be less likely to cause gastrointestinal bleeding in doses usually used than is ASA.

Human clinical trials have shown the clinical activity of 500 mg of naproxen daily to be similar to that of 3.6 g of ASA daily.

From clinical trials, it appears that naproxen enteric-coated tablets have reduced potential for severe complaints when compared to standard naproxen.

Naproxen is rapidly and completely absorbed from the gastrointestinal tract. After oral administration of naproxen, peak plasma levels of naproxen anion are attained in 2 to 4 hours, with steady-state conditions normally achieved after 4 to 5 doses. Plasma naproxen levels and areas under plasma concentration vs. time curves increased linearly with dose increments up to 500 mg twice a day, but larger doses resulted in a plateau effect. The time to reach peak plasma concentration following rectal administration of naproxen 500 mg suppository relative to the oral tablet was not significantly different. 0 to 24 hour areas under the plasma concentration versus time curves for the 500 mg dose of either naproxen tablets or suppository were similar. The mean biological half-life of the anion in humans is approximately 13 hours, and at therapeutic levels it is greater than 99% albumin bound. Approximately 95% of the dose is excreted in the urine, primarily as naproxen, 6-0-desmethyl naproxen or their conjugates. The rate of excretion has been found to coincide closely with the rate of drug disappearance from the plasma. The drug does not induce metabolizing enzymes.

In children with rheumatic diseases aged between 5 to 16 years, naproxen reached peak plasma levels 2 to 4 hours following oral dosing and the mean plasma half-life was 11.5 to 14.1 hours. Naproxen suspension was found to have similar bioavailability to the naproxen tablets in 2 single dose studies done in 24 healthy male volunteers. No clinically significant differences in tolerance were reported between the 2 dosage forms.

When naproxen is administered in the sustained release form (Naprosyn SR), the peak plasma levels are delayed and the maximum plasma concentrations are reduced compared to those seen with standard release formulations of naproxen. The minimum plasma concentrations, at steady state, are equivalent between naproxen sustained release given once a day and the corresponding standard dosage given twice a day. The peak to trough plasma concentration ratio of 2.2 and 2.6 observed with the standard tablet formulation (375 mg b.i.d. and 500 mg b.i.d. respectively) is reduced to 1.6 and 1.8 with 750 and 1 000 mg sustained release tablets respectively, resulting in smaller fluctuations in plasma concentrations of naproxen with the sustained release tablets. The average T_{max} of naproxen in subjects receiving the 1 000 mg sustained release tablet immediately after a high fat meal did not differ significantly when compared to the fasting state (7.7 hours postprandial; 9.7 hours fasting). The average C_{max} increased significantly from 63.1 μg/mL (fasting) to 86.1 μg/mL (postprandial). This increase in C_{max} was still lower than that observed with the 1000 mg dose of standard naproxen tablets.

Naprosyn (cont'd)

Based upon the 95% confidence interval, the AUC's were equivalent when the SR tablet was administered under fasting and nonfasting conditions. A 28 day study of chromium-51-labeled red blood cell loss in feces was conducted with the 750 mg sustained release naproxen tablets in 20 patients. There was no statistically significant differences in red blood cell loss between patients 60 years of age or younger and those over 60.

Naproxen enteric-coated tablets are designed to be dispersed and dissolved in the small bowel rather than the stomach, so the absorption is delayed until the stomach is emptied. Naproxen enteric-coated tablets were bioequivalent to the standard 375 and 500 mg tablets, except for a substantially increased time to peak plasma concentration (T_{max}). The average maximum plasma concentration (C_{max}) following the 375 mg, 2×250 mg and 500 mg enteric-coated tablets were 47.9, 58.2 and 60.7 μg/mL, while the C_{max} following the 375 and 500 mg standard immediate release tablets were 46.6 and 63.1 μg/mL, respectively. The T_{max}'s were 4.5, 4.2 and 4.2 hours for the respective enteric-coated formulations as compared to 2.3 and 2.6 hours after standard naproxen tablets. At steady state (multiple dosing) naproxen enteric coated and the standard naproxen were equivalent to each other with respect to C_{max}, C_{ave}, C_{max}/C_{ave}, 0 to 12 hours. AUC and half-life. In addition, fluctuation in plasma levels about C_{ave} were considerably less with naproxen enteric-coated tablets as compared to the standard naproxen (49.3 vs 85.3%). Administration of 500 mg enteric-coated naproxen tablets with food and antacid did not alter the extent of absorption of naproxen as compared to the fasting condition. However, antacid treatment resulted in a higher C_{max} (70.7 vs 58.5 μg/mL) and earlier T_{max} (5.2 vs 8.7 hours) in comparison to the fasting condition. Relative to the fasting state, the average T_{max} was delayed following a high fat meal (5.6 to 8.7 hours fasting, 9.2 to 10.8 hours post-prandial) while the average C_{max} and AUC were bioequivalent.

Indications: Treatment of osteoarthritis, rheumatoid arthritis, ankylosing spondylitis and juvenile rheumatoid arthritis.

Naproxen is also indicated for the relief of minor aches and pains in muscles, bones and joints, mild to moderate pain accompanied by inflammation in musculoskeletal injuries (sprains and strains) and primary dysmenorrhea.

Modified release formulations of naproxen (i.e., enteric-coated and sustained release) are not recommended for initial treatment of acute pain because the absorption of naproxen is delayed.

Contraindications: In patients with active peptic ulcers or active inflammatory diseases of the gastrointestinal tract. Known hypersensitivity to naproxen or to naproxen sodium. Since cross sensitivity has been demonstrated, do not give naproxen to patients in whom ASA or other nonsteroidal anti-inflammatory drugs induce the syndrome of asthma, rhinitis or urticaria. Sometimes severe and occasionally fatal anaphylactoid reactions have occurred in such individuals.

Naproxen suppositories are contraindicated in children under 12 years of age. The suppositories are also contraindicated in patients with any inflammatory lesions of rectum or anus and in patients with recent history of rectal or anal bleeding.

Warnings: Peptic ulceration, perforation and gastrointestinal bleeding, sometimes severe and occasionally fatal, have been reported during therapy with nonsteroidal anti-inflammatory drugs (NSAIDs) including naproxen. Naproxen should be given under close supervision to patients prone to gastrointestinal tract irritation; particularly those with a history of peptic ulcer, diverticulosis, or other inflammatory disease of the gastrointestinal tract. In these cases the physician must weigh the benefits of treatment against the possible hazards.

Patients taking any NSAID including this drug should be instructed to contact a physician immediately if they experience symptoms or signs suggestive of peptic ulceration or gastrointestinal bleeding. These reactions can occur without warning symptoms or signs and at any time during the treatment.

Elderly, frail and debilitated patients appear to be at higher risk from a variety of adverse reactions from NSAIDs. For such patients, consideration should be given to a starting dose lower than usual, with individual adjustment when necessary and under close supervision. See Precautions for further advice.

Pregnancy and *Lactation:* Naproxen's safety in pregnancy and lactation has not been established, and its use is therefore not recommended. Reproduction studies have been performed in rats, rabbits and mice. In rats, pregnancy was prolonged when naproxen was given before the onset of labour, and when given after the delivery process had begun, labour was protracted. Similar results have been found with other nonsteroidal anti-inflammatory agents, and the evidence suggests that this may be due to decreased uterine contractility resulting from the inhibition of prostaglandin synthesis. Moreover, because of the known effect of drugs of this class on the human fetal cardiovascular system (closure of ductus arteriosus), use during late pregnancy should be avoided. Naproxen readily crosses the placental barrier. It has also been found in the milk of lactating women at a concentration approximately 1% of that found in the plasma.

Precautions: Naproxen should not be used concomitantly with the related drug naproxen sodium since they both circulate in plasma as the naproxen anion.

Gastrointestinal: If peptic ulceration is suspected or confirmed, or gastrointestinal bleeding or perforation occurs naproxen should be discontinued, and appropriate treatment instituted and patient closely monitored.

There is no definitive evidence that the concomitant administration of a H_2-receptor antagonist and/or antacids will either prevent the occurrence of gastrointestinal side effects or allow continuation of naproxen therapy when and if these adverse reactions appear.

Naproxen suppositories should be given under close supervision in patients with any rectal or anal pathology (see Contraindications).

Renal Effects: As with other nonsteroidal anti-inflammatory drugs, long-term administration of naproxen to animals has resulted in renal papillary necrosis and other abnormal renal pathology. In humans, there have been reports of acute interstitial nephritis with hematuria, proteinuria, and occasionally nephrotic syndrome.

A second form of renal toxicity has been seen in patients with prerenal conditions leading to the reduction in renal blood flow or blood volume, where the renal prostaglandins have a supportive role in the maintenance of renal perfusion. In these patients, administration of a nonsteroidal anti-inflammatory drug may cause a dose-dependent reduction in prostaglandin formation and may precipitate overt renal decompensation. Patients at greatest risk of this reaction are those with impaired renal function, extracellular volume depletion, sodium restrictions, heart failure, liver dysfunction, those taking diuretics, and the elderly. Assessment of renal function in these patients before and during therapy with naproxen is recommended. Discontinuation of nonsteroidal anti-inflammatory therapy is typically followed by recovery to the pretreatment state.

Naproxen and its metabolites are eliminated primarily by the kidneys, therefore, the drug should be used with great caution in patients with significantly impaired renal function and the monitoring of serum creatinine and/or creatinine clearance is advised in these patients. A reduction in daily dosage should be anticipated to avoid the possibility of excessive drug accumulation.

Naproxen should not be used chronically in patients having baseline creatinine clearance less than 20 mL/min. During long-term therapy, kidney function should be monitored periodically.

Peripheral edema has been observed in some patients receiving naproxen. Therefore, as with many other NSAIDs, the possibility of precipitating congestive heart failure in elderly patients or those with compromised cardiac function should be borne in mind. Although sodium retention has not been reported in metabolic studies, the drug should be used with caution in patients with fluid retention, hypertension or heart failure.

Naproxen formulated as a suspension (25 mg/mL) contains sodium chloride (20 mg/mL). This should be considered in patients whose overall intake of sodium must be restricted.

With NSAID treatment, there is a potential risk of hyperkalemia particularly in patients with conditions such as diabetes mellitus or renal failure; elderly patients; and patients receiving concomitant therapy and other beta adrenergic blockers, angiotensin converting enzyme inhibitors or some diuretics. Serum electrolytes should be monitored periodically during long-term therapy, especially those patients at risk.

Anaphylactoid reactions to naproxen or naproxen sodium, whether of the true allergic type or the pharmacologic idiosyncratic (e.g., ASA syndrome) type, usually but not always occur in patients with a known history of such reactions. Therefore, careful questioning of patients for such things as asthma, nasal polyps, urticaria, and hypotension associated to nonsteroidal anti-inflammatory drugs before starting therapy is important. In addition, if such symptoms occur during therapy, treatment should be discontinued.

Geriatrics: One study indicated that although total plasma concentration of naproxen is unchanged, the unbound plasma fraction of naproxen is increased in the elderly. The implication of this finding for naproxen dosing is unknown, but caution is advised when high doses are required. As with other drugs used in the elderly, it is prudent to use the lowest effective dose.

Patients with Impaired Liver Function: As with other nonsteroidal anti-inflammatory drugs, borderline elevations of one or more liver tests may occur in up to 15% of patients. These abnormalities may progress, may remain essentially unchanged, or may be transient with continued therapy. A patient with symptoms and/or signs suggesting liver dysfunction, or in whom an abnormal liver test has occurred, should be evaluated for evidence of the development of more severe hepatic reaction while on therapy with this drug. Severe hepatic reactions including jaundice and cases of fatal hepatitis have been reported with this drug as with other nonsteroidal anti-inflammatory drugs. Although such reactions are rare, if abnormal liver tests persist or worsen, if clinical signs and symptoms consistent with liver disease develop, or if systemic manifestations occur (e.g. eosinophilia, rash, etc.), this drug should be discontinued. During long-term therapy, liver function tests should be monitored periodically. If this drug is to be used in the presence of impaired liver function, it must be done under strict observation.

Chronic alcoholic liver disease and probably also other forms of cirrhosis reduce the total plasma concentration of naproxen, but the plasma concentration of unbound naproxen is increased. The implication of this finding for naproxen dosing is unknown, but caution is advised when high doses are required. It is prudent to use the lowest effective dose.

Hematology: Drugs inhibiting prostaglandin biosynthesis do interfere with platelet function to some degree; therefore, patients who may be adversely affected by such an action should be carefully observed when naproxen is administered. Blood dyscrasias associated with the use of NSAIDs are rare but could be with severe consequences.

Patients with initial hemoglobin values of 10 g or less who are to receive long-term therapy should have hemoglobin values determined frequently.

Infection: The anti-inflammatory, antipyretic and analgesic effects of naproxen may mask the usual signs of infection and the physician should be alert for development of infection in patients receiving naproxen.

Ophthalmology: Because of adverse eye findings in animal studies with drugs of this class it is recommended that ophthalmic studies be carried out within a reasonable period of time after starting therapy and at periodic intervals thereafter if the drug is to be used for an extended period of time.

Occupational Hazards: Caution should be exercised by patients whose activities require alertness if they experience drowsiness, dizziness, vertigo or depression during therapy with the drug.

Drug Interactions: Naproxen may displace from their binding sites other drugs which are also albumin-bound and may lead to drug interactions. For example, in a patient receiving bishydroxycoumarin or warfarin, the addition of naproxen to therapy could prolong the prothrombin time. Patients receiving both drugs should be under careful observation. Similarly, patients receiving naproxen and a hydantoin, sulfonamide or sulfonylurea should be observed for signs of toxicity.

The natriuretic effect of furosemide has been reported to be inhibited by some drugs of this class. Inhibition of renal lithium clearance leading to increases in plasma lithium concentrations have also been reported.

Naproxen and other nonsteroidal anti-inflammatory drugs can reduce the anti-hypertensive effect of propranolol and other beta blockers as well as other antihypertensive agents.

The rate of absorption of naproxen is altered by concomitant administration of antacids but is not adversely influenced by the presence of food. Probenecid given concurrently increases naproxen anion plasma levels and extends its plasma half-life significantly.

Caution is advised in the concomitant administration of naproxen and methotrexate since naproxen and other nonsteroidal anti-inflammatory agents have been reported to reduce the tubular secretion of methotrexate in an animal model, thereby possibly enhancing its toxicity.

Laboratory Tests: Naproxen decreases platelet aggregation and prolongs bleeding time. This effect should be kept in mind when bleeding times are determined. Other laboratory tests in patients on naproxen therapy have shown sporadic abnormalities but no definite trend was seen that would indicate potential toxicity.

The administration of naproxen may result in increased urinary values for 17-ketogenic steroids because of an interaction between the drug and/or its metabolites with m-dinitrobenzene used in this assay. Although 17-hydroxy corticosteroid measurements (Porter-Silber test) do not appear to be artifactually altered, it is suggested that Naprosyn therapy be temporarily discontinued 48 hours before adrenal function tests are performed.

The drug may interfere with some urinary assays of 5-hydroxy indoleacetic acid (5HIAA).

Adverse Effects: The most common adverse reactions encountered with NSAIDs are gastrointestinal, of which peptic ulcer, with or without bleeding, is the most severe. Fatalities have occurred on occasion, particularly in the elderly.

A clinical study found gastrointestinal reactions to be more frequent and more severe in rheumatoid arthritis patients taking daily doses of 1 500 mg naproxen compared to those taking 750 mg naproxen.

Adverse reactions reported in controlled clinical trials in 960 patients treated for rheumatoid arthritis or osteoarthritis with the naproxen standard tablets are listed below. (1) Denotes incidence of reported reaction between 3% and 9%. (2) Denotes incidence of reported reactions between 1% and 3%. Reactions occurring in less than 1% of the patients are unmarked.

Gastrointestinal: heartburn (1), constipation (1), abdominal pain (1), nausea (1), diarrhea (2), dyspepsia (2), stomatitis (2), diverticulitis (2), gastrointestinal bleeding, hematemesis, melena, peptic ulceration with or without bleeding and/or perforation, vomiting, ulcerative stomatitis.

In addition to the above, rectal burning (1) has been reported occasionally and rectal bleeding rarely, with the use of naproxen suppositories.

CNS: headache (1), dizziness (1), drowsiness (1), lightheadedness (2), vertigo (2), depression (2) and fatigue (2). Occasionally patients had to discontinue treatment because of the severity of some of these complaints (headache and dizziness). Other adverse effects were inability to concentrate, malaise, myalgia, insomnia and cognitive dysfunction (i.e. decreased attention span, loss of short-term memory, difficulty with calculations).

Skin: pruritus (1), ecchymoses (1), skin eruptions (1), sweating (2), purpura (2), alopecia, urticaria, skin rash, erythema multiforme, Stevens-Johnson syndrome, epidermal necrolysis, photosensitive dermatitis, exfoliative dermatitis and erythema nodosum.

Hepatic: abnormal liver function tests, jaundice, cholestasis and hepatitis.

Cardiovascular: dyspnea (1), peripheral edema (1), palpitations (2), congestive heart failure and vasculitis.

Renal: glomerular nephritis, hematuria, interstitial nephritis, nephrotic syndrome, nephropathy and tubular necrosis.

Hematologic: eosinophilia, granulocytopenia, leukopenia, thrombocytopenia, agranulocytosis, aplastic anemia and hemolytic anemia.

Special Senses: tinnitus (1), hearing disturbances (2), hearing impairment and visual disturbances.

Others: thirst (2), muscle weakness, anaphylactoid reactions, menstrual disorders, pyrexia (chills and fever), angioneurotic edema, hyperglycemia, hypoglycemia, hematuria and eosinophilic pneumonitis.

The adverse reactions reported on both the standard tablets and the sustained release tablets were similar.

Overdose: Symptoms and Treatment: Significant overdosage may be characterized by drowsiness, heartburn, indigestion, nausea or vomiting. No evidence of toxicity or late sequelae have been reported 5 to 15 months after ingestion for 3 to 7 days of doses up to 3 000 mg of naproxen. One patient ingested a single dose of 25 g of naproxen and experienced mild nausea and indigestion. It is not known what dose of the drug would be life threatening. The oral LD_{50} of the drug is 543 mg/kg in rats, 1 234 mg/kg in mice, 4 110 mg/kg in hamsters and greater than 1 000 mg/kg in dogs.

Should the patient ingest a large number of naproxen tablets, the stomach may be emptied and usual supportive measures employed. Animal studies suggest that the prompt administration of 5 g of activated charcoal would tend to reduce markedly the absorption of the drug. In dogs 0.5 g/kg of charcoal was effective in reducing the plasma levels of naproxen. Hemodialysis does not decrease the plasma concentration of naproxen because of the high degree of its protein binding. However, hemodialysis may still be appropriate in the management of renal failure.

Dosage: Oral: Adults: The usual total daily dosage for osteoarthritis, rheumatoid arthritis, and ankylosing spondylitis is 500 mg (20 mL) a day in divided doses. It may be increased gradually to 750 or 1 000 mg or decreased, depending on the patient's response.

Studies have not shown any clinically significant benefit in using doses higher than 1 000 mg/day. In patients who tolerate lower doses of naproxen well and who exhibit only a partial response to 1 000 mg/day, the dose may be increased to 1 500 mg/day for **limited periods.** Experience with 1 500 mg/day naproxen is limited to using the standard tablets. Naproxen tablets should be swallowed with food or milk.

When treating such patients with naproxen 1 500 mg/day, the physician should observe sufficient increased clinical benefit to offset the potential increased risk (see Adverse Effects).

In addition, patients on 1 500 mg/day need to be followed closely for the development of any adverse events.

During long-term administration the dose of naproxen may be adjusted up or down depending on the clinical response of the patient. A lower dose may suffice for long-term administration.

Patients with rheumatoid arthritis or osteoarthritis maintained on a dose of 750 or 1 000 mg/day in divided doses can be switched to a once daily dose of naproxen sustained release 750 mg or 1 000 mg respectively. The single daily dose of naproxen sustained release should not be exceeded and can be administered in the morning or evening. Naproxen sustained release tablets should be swallowed whole.

Rectal: Adults: 500 mg suppositories can replace one of the oral doses in patients receiving 1 000 mg/day. **Suppositories are not indicated in children under 12 years of age.**

Naprosyn E and Naprosyn SR have not been studied in subjects under the age of 18.

Juvenile Rheumatoid Arthritis: The recommended total daily dose is approximately 10 mg/kg in 2 divided doses at 12 hour intervals. Table I may be used as a guide.

Table I—Naprosyn

Dosage—Juvenile Rheumatoid Arthritis

Child's Weight	Dose
13 kg	2.5 mL b.i.d.
25 kg	5.0 mL b.i.d.
38 kg	7.5 mL b.i.d.

Administration of naproxen more frequently than twice daily is not necessary. Clinical experience has shown that steroids can often be decreased, and sometimes eliminated, when naproxen is administered. Bottles of naproxen suspension should be shaken gently before use.

Analgesia/Musculoskeletal Injuries: Oral: The recommended dose is 750 mg/day divided into either 2 or 3 doses/day. This may be increased to 1 000 mg/day if needed. The lowest effective dose should be used.

Modified release formulations of naproxen (i.e., enteric-coated and sustained release) are not recommended for initial treatment of acute pain because the absorption of naproxen is delayed.

Dysmenorrhea: Oral: The recommended starting dose is two 250 mg tablets, followed by one 250 mg tablet every 6 to 8 hours, as required. The total daily dose should not exceed 5 tablets (1 250 mg). Alternatively, one 500 mg tablet given twice daily may be used.

Modified release formulations of naproxen (i.e., enteric-coated and sustained release) are not recommended for initial treatment of acute pain because the absorption of naproxen is delayed.

Information for the Patient: See Blue Section—Information for the Patient "Naprosyn".

Supplied: Suppositories: Each white, opaque suppository contains: naproxen 500 mg. Nonmedicinal ingredients: witepsol H15. Boxes of 30, packed in polyethylene lined white polyvinyl shells in perforated strips of 5 suppositories. Store at room temperature.

Suspension: Each 5 mL contains: naproxen 125 mg. Nonmedicinal ingredients: FD&C Yellow #6, fumaric acid, imitation orange flavor, imitation pineapple flavor, magnesium aluminum silicate, methylparaben, sodium chloride, sorbitol solution and sucrose. Lactose-free. Bottles of 474 mL. Store at room temperature not exceeding 25°C, with protection from light.

Tablets: 250 mg: Each round, yellow tablet, engraved NPR LE 250 on one side and single score on the other, contains: naproxen 250 mg. Nonmedicinal ingredients: croscarmellose sodium, iron oxide, magnesium stearate and povidone. Tartrazine-free. Bottles of 100. Store at room temperature.

375 mg: Each pink, oval tablet, engraved NPR LE 375 on one side, contains: naproxen 375 mg. Nonmedicinal ingredients: croscarmellose sodium, iron oxide, magnesium stearate and povidone. Tartrazine-free. Bottles of 100. Store at room temperature.

500 mg: Each yellow, scored, capsule-shaped tablet, engraved NPR LE 500, contains: naproxen 500 mg. Nonmedicinal ingredients: croscarmellose sodium, iron oxide, magnesium stearate and povidone. Tartrazine-free. Bottles of 50 and 500. Store at room temperature.

Enteric-coated Tablets: 250 mg: Each round, biconvex, enteric-coated tablet, with one side printed in black NPR EC 250, contains: naproxen 250 mg. Nonmedicinal ingredients: croscarmellose sodium, ferric iron, magnesium stearate, methacrylic acid copolymer, povidone, sodium hydroxide, talc and triethyl citrate. Bottles of 100. Store at room temperature.

375 mg: Each oval-shaped, enteric-coated tablet, with one side printed in black NPR EC 375, contains: naproxen 375 mg. Nonmedicinal ingredients: croscarmellose sodium, ferric iron, magnesium stearate, methacrylic acid copolymer, povidone, sodium hydroxide, talc and triethyl citrate. Bottles of 100 and 500. Store at room temperature.

500 mg: Each oblong-shaped, enteric-coated tablet, with one side printed in black NPR EC 500, contains: naproxen 500 mg. Nonmedicinal ingredients: croscarmellose sodium, ferric iron, magnesium stearate, methacrylic acid copolymer, povidone, sodium hydroxide, talc and triethyl citrate. Bottles of 100 and 500. Store at room temperature.

Sustained-release Tablets: Each peach, oval-shaped tablet, NPR SR 750 engraved on one side, contains: naproxen 750 mg. Nonmedicinal ingredients: croscarmellose sodium, FD&C Yellow #6, ferric iron, hydroxypropyl methylcellulose, magnesium stearate, methacrylic acid copolymer, povidone, sodium hydroxide, talc and triethyl citrate. Lactose- and tartrazine-free. Bottles of 100 and 500. Store at room temperature.

With the exception of the suspension which contains sorbitol, all preparations are bisulfite-, erythrosine-, gluten-, sorbitol- and xylitol-free.

(Shown in Product Recognition Section)

Reviewed 1998

NARCAN® Ⓟ

DuPont Pharma

Naloxone HCl

Narcotic Antagonist

Pharmacology: Naloxone prevents or reverses the effects of opioids including respiratory depression, sedation and hypotension.

Naloxone is an essentially pure narcotic antagonist which does not possess the 'agonistic' or morphine-like properties characteristic of other narcotic antagonists. It does not produce respiratory depression, psychotomimetic effects or pupillary constriction. In the absence of narcotic or agonistic effects of other narcotic antagonists, it exhibits essentially no pharmacologic activity.

In the presence of narcotic addiction, naloxone will produce withdrawal symptoms; it has not been shown to cause addiction.

Narcan (cont'd)

Mechanism of Action: While the mechanism of action is not fully understood, the preponderance of evidence suggests that naloxone antagonizes the opioid effects by competing for the same receptor sites.

When naloxone is administered i.v. the onset of action is generally apparent within 2 minutes; the onset of action is only slightly less rapid when it is administered s.c. or i.m. The duration of action is dependent on the dose and route of administration of naloxone. I.M. administration produces a more prolonged effect than i.v. administration. The requirement for repeat doses of naloxone, however, will also be dependent upon the amount, type and route of administration of the narcotic being antagonized (see Warnings).

Following parenteral administration, naloxone is rapidly distributed in the body. It is metabolized in the liver, primarily by glucuronide conjugation, and excreted in urine. In one study the serum half-life in adults ranged from 30 to 81 (mean 64±12) minutes. In a neonatal study the mean plasma half-life was observed to be 3.1±0.5 hours.

Single s.c. doses of naloxone as high as 24 mg/70 kg (0.343 mg/kg) and multiple doses of 90 mg daily for 2 weeks administered to normal volunteers produced no behavioral or physiologic changes, yet its antagonistic activity to subsequent morphine challenge persisted.

Indications: The complete or partial reversal of narcotic depression, including respiratory depression, induced by opioids including natural and synthetic narcotics, propoxyphene, methadone and the agonist-antagonist analgesics such as pentazocine, butorphanol and nalbuphine.

Also indicated for the diagnosis of suspected acute opioid overdosage.

Contraindications: Known hypersensitivity to naloxone.

Warnings: Naloxone should be administered cautiously to persons, including newborns of mothers, who are known or suspected to be physically dependent on opioids. In such cases, an abrupt and complete reversal of narcotic effects may precipitate an acute abstinence syndrome. The severity of such a syndrome will depend on the degree of physical dependence and the dose of antagonist administered. In the presence of serious respiratory depression in a physically dependent individual, the antagonist, when indicated, should be administered with extreme care, under close monitoring, by using appropriate titration with smaller doses than usual. The patient who has satisfactorily responded to naloxone should be kept under surveillance and repeated doses should be administered, as necessary, since the duration of action of some narcotics may exceed that of naloxone.

Naloxone is not effective in counteracting depression due to barbiturates, tranquilizers, or other non-narcotic anesthetics or sedatives. It has been safely administered to patients who received both narcotic and non-narcotic drugs.

Reversal of buprenorphine induced respiratory depression may be incomplete. If an incomplete response occurs, respirations should be mechanically assisted.

Pregnancy: Safe use during pregnancy (other than labor) has not been established. Although animal reproduction studies have not demonstrated teratogenic or other embryotoxic effects, naloxone should be administered to pregnant patients only when, in the judgement of the physician, potential benefits outweigh possible hazards.

Lactation: It is not known whether naloxone is excreted in human milk. Because many drugs are excreted in human milk, caution should be exercised when naloxone is administered to a nursing woman.

Precautions: Other resuscitative measures such as maintenance of a free airway, artificial ventilation, cardiac massage and vasopressor agents should be available and employed when necessary to counteract acute narcotic poisoning.

Several instances of hypotension, hypertension, ventricular tachycardia and fibrillation, and pulmonary edema have been reported. These have occurred in postoperative patients in whom pre-existing cardiovascular disorders or other drugs may have contributed to the adverse cardiovascular effects. Although a direct cause and effect relationship has not been established, naloxone should be administered very cautiously for postoperative narcotic reversal, particularly in patients with pre-existing cardiac disease or patients who have received potentially cardiotoxic drugs. The clinical course should be monitored by ECG (see Dosage).

Adverse Effects: Abrupt reversal of narcotic depression may result in nausea, vomiting, sweating, tachycardia, increased blood pressure, tremulousness and cardiac arrest. In postoperative patients, excessive dosage of naloxone may result in excitement and significant reversal of analgesia. Hypotension, hypertension, ventricular tachycardia and fibrillation, and pulmonary edema have been associated with naloxone use postoperatively (see Precautions and Dosage, Postoperative Narcotic Depression). Seizures have been reported to occur infrequently after the administration of naloxone; however, a causal relationship has not been established.

Overdose: Symptoms and Treatment: There have been no experiences of overdosage.

Dosage: See Table I.

Naloxone may be administered i.v., i.m. or s.c. The most rapid onset of action is achieved by i.v. administration and it is recommended in emergency situations.

Since the duration of action of some narcotics may exceed that of naloxone, the patient should be kept under continued surveillance and repeated doses of naloxone should be administered as necessary.

Parenteral drug products should be inspected visually for particulate matter and discoloration prior to administration whenever solution and container permit. Naloxone should not be mixed with preparations containing bisulfite, metabisulfite, long-chain or high molecular weight anions, or any solution having an alkaline pH. No drug or chemical agent should be added to naloxone unless its effect on the chemical and physical stability of the solution has first been established.

Adults: Narcotic overdose, known or suspected: The usual initial dose is 0.4 to 2 mg administered i.v. If the desired degree of counteraction and improvement in respiratory function is not obtained it may be repeated at 2 to 3 minute intervals. If no response is observed after 10 mg, the diagnosis of narcotic- induced or partial narcotic-induced toxicity should be questioned. I.M. or s.c. administration may be necessary if i.v. route is not available.

I.V. infusion: Naloxone may be diluted for i.v. infusion in normal saline or 5% dextrose solutions. The addition of 2 mg in 500 mL of either solution provides a concentration of 4 µg (0.004 mg)/mL. Mixtures should be used within 24 hours. After 24 hours, the remaining unused solution must be discarded.

Infusion may be useful in cases of overdose with long-acting drugs such as methadone and propoxyphene. The infusion rate for adults is approximately 100 mL/hr (0.4 mg/hr). Infusion rate and concentration should be individually adjusted to obtain the desired antagonist effect without fluid overload or production of withdrawal.

Postoperative Narcotic Depression: For the partial reversal of narcotic depression following the use of narcotics during surgery, smaller doses of naloxone are usually sufficient. The dose should be titrated according to the patient's response. For the initial reversal of respiratory depression, inject naloxone slowly in increments of 100 to 200 µg (0.1 to 0.2 mg) i.v. at 2 to 3 minute intervals to the desired degree of reversal, i.e., adequate ventilation and alertness without significant pain or discomfort. Larger than necessary dosage of naloxone may result in significant reversal of analgesia and increase in blood pressure. Similarly, too rapid reversal may induce nausea, vomiting, sweating or circulatory stress (see Precautions).

Repeat doses of naloxone may be required within 1 to 2 hour intervals depending upon the amount, type (i.e., short or long-acting) and time interval since last administration of narcotic. Supplemental i.m. doses have been shown to produce a longer lasting effect.

Children: Narcotic Overdose–known or suspected: The usual initial dose is 10 µg (0.01 mg)/kg body weight given i.v. If this dose does not result in the desired degree of clinical improvement, a subsequent dose of 100 µg (0.1 mg)/kg body weight may be administered. If an i.v. route of administration is not available, naloxone may be administered i.m. or s.c. in divided doses. If necessary, naloxone can be diluted with sterile water for injection.

I.V. Infusion: I.V. Infusion may be useful in cases of overdose with long-acting drugs such as methadone and propoxyphene (see Adults). The infusion rate for children should be suitably adjusted according to the patient's weight and response.

Postoperative Narcotic Depression: Follow the recommendations and cautions under Adult Postoperative Depression. For the initial reversal of respiratory depression naloxone should be injected in increments of 5 to 10 µg (0.005 mg to 0.01 mg) i.v. at 2 to 3 minute intervals to the desired degree of reversal.

Neonates: Narcotic-induced Depression: The usual initial dose is 10 µg (0.01 mg)/kg body weight administered by i.v., i.m., or s.c. routes. This dose may be repeated in accordance with adult administration guidelines for postoperative narcotic depression.

Table I—Narcan

Summary of Dosages

	Dosage Form	Indication and Dosage Range
Adults	Narcan (any strength)	Narcotic Overdose 0.4 to 2 mg i.v. repeated if necessary at 2 to 3 minute intervals Postoperative Narcotic Depression 0.1 to 0.2 mg i.v. repeated if necessary at 2 to 3 minute intervals.
Children	Narcan (any strength)	Narcotic Overdose 0.01 mg/kg of body weight i.v. If desired degree of improvement is not obtained, 0.1 mg/kg i.v. may be administered. Naloxone may be diluted with sterile water for injection. Postoperative Narcotic Depression 0.005 to 0.01 mg i.v. repeated if necessary at 2 to 3 minute intervals.
Neonates	Narcan (20 µg/mL) (0.02 mg/mL)	Narcotic-induced Depression 0.01 mg/kg of body weight i.v., i.m., or s.c. repeated if necessary at 2 to 3 minute intervals.

Note: The patient should be kept under continuous surveillance and repeated doses of naloxone should be administered as necessary for adequate reversal.

Supplied: 0.02 mg/mL: Each mL of aqueous injectable solution contains: naloxone HCl 20 µg. Also contains sodium chloride. pH is adjusted to 3.5±0.5 with hydrochloric acid. Ampuls of 2 mL, boxes of 10. Labels are blue coded.

0.4 mg/mL: Each mL of aqueous injectable solution contains: naloxone HCl 400 µg. Also contains methyl- and propylparaben (vial format only) and sodium chloride. Ampuls of 1 mL, boxes of 10. Vials of 10 mL. Labels are orange coded.

1 mg/mL: Each mL of aqueous injectable contains: naloxone HCl 1 000 µg. Also contains sodium chloride. pH is adjusted to 3.5±0.5 with hydrochloric acid. Ampuls of 2 mL, boxes of 10. Labels are red and white color coded.

NARCOTIC ANALGESICS Ⓝ

General Monograph, CPhA

See OPIOID ANALGESICS

NARDIL® Ⓟ

Parke-Davis

Phenelzine Sulfate

Antidepressant

Pharmacology: Phenelzine is a potent monoamine oxidase (MAO) inhibitor. Monoamine oxidase is a complex enzyme system, widely distributed throughout the body. Drugs that inhibit monoamine oxidase in the laboratory are associated with a number of clinical effects. Thus, it is unknown whether MAO inhibition per se, other pharmacologic actions, or an interaction of both is responsible for the clinical effects observed.

All the currently employed MAO inhibitors are readily absorbed after oral administration. They are not given parenterally. These drugs produce maximal inhibition of MAO in biopsy samples from man within 5 to 10 days. However, although their biological activity is prolonged due to the characteristics of their interaction with the enzyme, their clinical efficacy appears to be reduced when given less frequently than once daily. In chronically treated phenelzine patients on 60 mg/day, steady-state trough and peak levels are between 1 and 10 ng/mL.

Indications: In the treatment of depressed patients clinically characterized as "atypical", "nonendogenous" or "neurotic". These patients often have mixed anxiety and depression and phobic or hypochondriacal features. There is less conclusive evidence of its usefulness for severely depressed patients with endogenous features. Phenelzine is indicated for patients who have failed to respond to the drugs more commonly used for these conditions.

Contraindications: Known hypersensitivity to the drug or its ingredients, pheochromocytoma, congestive heart failure, history of liver disease or abnormal liver function tests.

The potentiation of sympathomimetic substances and related compounds by MAO inhibitors may result in hypertensive crises (see Warnings). Therefore, patients taking phenelzine should not be given sympathomimetic drugs (including amphetamines, cocaine, methylphenidate, dopamine, epinephrine and norepinephrine), or related compounds (including methyldopa, L-dopa, L-tryptophan, L-tyrosine and phenylalanine). Hypertensive crises during phenelzine therapy may also be caused by ingestion of foods with a high concentration of tyramine or dopamine. Therefore patients being treated with phenelzine should avoid high protein food that has undergone protein breakdown by aging, fermentation, pickling, smoking or bacterial contamination; patients should also avoid cheeses (especially aged varieties), pickled herring, beer, wine, liver, yeast extract (including brewer's yeast in large quantities), dry sausage (including Genoa salami, hard salami, pepperoni and Lebanon bologna), pods of broad beans (fava beans) and yogurt. Excessive amounts of caffeine or chocolate can also potentiate hypertensive reactions.

Phenelzine should not be used in combination with dextromethorphan or with CNS depressants such as alcohol and certain narcotics. Excitation, seizures, delirium, hyperpyrexia, circulatory collapse, coma and death have been reported in patients receiving MAO inhibitor therapy, who have been given a single dose of meperidine. Phenelzine should not be administered together with or in rapid succession to other MAO inhibitors (see Table I) or dibenzazepine derivative drugs (see below), because **hypertensive crises** and convulsive seizures, fever, marked sweating, excitation, delirium, tremor, coma and circulatory collapse may occur.

Table I—Nardil

List of Other MAO Inhibitors

Generic Name	Trademark	Manufacturer
Moclobemide	Manerix	Roche
Procarbazine	Natulan	Roche
Tranylcypromine	Parnate	SmithKline Beecham

Dibenzazepine Derivative Drugs: amitriptyline, amitriptyline and perphenazine, amoxapine, carbamazepine, clomipramine, cyclobenzaprine, desipramine, doxepin, imipramine, maprotiline, nortriptyline, protriptyline, trimipramine.

At least 10 days should elapse between the discontinuation of another MAO inhibitor and the institution of phenelzine therapy.

Phenelzine should not be used in combination with buspirone HCl, since several cases of elevated blood pressure have been reported in patients taking MAO inhibitors who were then given buspirone HCl. At least 10 days should elapse between the discontinuation of phenelzine and the institution of another antidepressant or buspirone HCl, or the discontinuation of another MAO inhibitor and the institution of phenelzine therapy.

The concurrent administration of an MAO inhibitor and bupropion HCl is contraindicated.

There have been reports of serious reactions (including hyperthermia, rigidity, myoclonic movements and death) when serotonin re-uptake inhibitors or venlafaxine have been combined with an MAO inhibitor. Therefore, phenelzine should not be used in combination with venlafaxine or serotonin re-uptake inhibitors. Allow at least 5 weeks between discontinuation of fluoxetine and initiation of phenelzine, and at least 10 days between discontinuation of phenelzine and initiation of fluoxetine or other serotonin re-uptake inhibitors. Before initiating phenelzine treatment, after having used other serotonin re-uptake inhibitors, a sufficient amount of time must be allowed for clearance of the serotonin re-uptake inhibitor and its active metabolites.

The combination of MAO inhibitors and tryptophan has been reported to cause behavioral and neurologic symptoms including disorientation, confusion, amnesia, delirium, agitation, hypomanic signs, ataxia, myoclonus, hyperflexia, shivering, ocular oscillations and Babinski signs.

Patients taking phenelzine should not undergo elective surgery requiring general anesthesia. Also, they should not be given cocaine or local anesthesia containing sympathomimetic vasoconstrictors. The possible combined hypotensive effects of phenelzine and spinal anesthesia should be kept in mind. Phenelzine should be discontinued at least 10 days prior to elective surgery.

MAO inhibitors including phenelzine are contraindicated in patients receiving guanethidine.

Warnings: The most serious reactions to phenelzine involve changes in blood pressure.

Hypertensive Crises: The most important reaction associated with phenelzine administration is the occurrence of hypertensive crises, which have sometimes been fatal. These crises are characterized by some or all of the following symptoms: occipital headache which may radiate frontally, palpitation, neck stiffness or soreness, nausea, vomiting, sweating (sometimes with fever and sometimes with cold, clammy skin), dilated pupils and photophobia. Either tachycardia or bradycardia may be present and can be associated with constricting chest pain.

Note: Intracranial bleeding has been reported in association with the increase in blood pressure.

Blood pressure should be observed frequently to detect evidence of any pressor response in patients receiving phenelzine. Therapy should be discontinued immediately upon the occurrence of palpitation or frequent headaches during therapy.

Recommended Treatment in Hypertensive Crises: If a hypertensive crises occurs, phenelzine should be discontinued immediately and therapy to lower blood pressure instituted immediately. On the basis of present evidence, phentolamine is recommended. (The dosage reported for phentolamine is 5 mg i.v..) Care should be taken to administer this drug slowly in order to avoid producing an excessive hypotensive effect. Fever should be managed by means of external cooling.

Information for the Patient: All patients, should be warned that the following foods, beverages and medications (Tables II and III) must be avoided while taking phenelzine, and for 2 weeks after discontinuing use.

Table II—Nardil

Foods and Beverages to Avoid During Phenelzine Therapy

Meat and Fish:	Pickled herring, liver, dry sausage (including Genoa salami, hard salami, pepperoni, and Lebanon bologna)
Vegetables:	Broad bean pods (fava beans) and sauerkraut
Dairy Products:	Cheese (cottage cheese and cream cheese are allowed), yogurt
Beverages:	Beer and wine, alcohol-free and reduced-alcohol beer and wine products
Miscellaneous:	Yeast extract (including brewer's yeast in large quantities), meat extract, excessive amounts of chocolate or caffeine

Patients being treated with phenelzine should also avoid any spoiled or improperly refrigerated, handled or stored protein-rich foods such as meats, fish and dairy products, including foods that may have undergone protein breakdown by aging, pickling, fermentation, or smoking to improve flavor.

Table III—Nardil

OTC Medications to Avoid During Phenelzine Therapy

1. Cold and cough preparations (including those containing dextromethorphan)
2. Nasal decongestants (tablets, drops or spray)
3. Hay-fever medications
4. Sinus medications
5. Asthma inhalant medications
6. Anti-appetite medicines
7. Weight-reducing preparations
8. L-tryptophan containing preparations

Certain prescription drugs should be avoided. Therefore, patients under the care of another physician or dentist, should inform him/her they are taking phenelzine.

Patients should be warned that the use of the above foods, beverages or medicines may cause a reaction characterized by headache and other serious symptoms due to a rise in blood pressure, with the exception of dextromethorphan, which may cause reactions similar to those seen with meperidine.

Patients should be instructed to report promptly the occurrence of headache or other unusual symptoms.

Precautions: General: In depressed patients, the possibility of suicide should always be considered and adequate precautions taken. It is recommended that careful observation of patients undergoing phenelzine treatment should be maintained until control of depression is achieved. If necessary, additional measures (ECT, hospitalization, etc.) should be instituted.

All patients undergoing treatment with phenelzine should be closely followed for symptoms of postural hypotension. Hypotensive side effects have occurred in hypertensive as well as normal and hypotensive patients. Blood pressure usually returns to pretreatment levels rapidly when the drug is discontinued or the dosage is reduced.

Because the effect of phenelzine on the convulsive threshold may be variable, adequate precautions should be taken when treating epileptic patients.

Of the more severe side effects that have been reported with any consistency, hypomania has been the most common. This reaction has been largely limited to patients in whom disorders characterized by hyperkinetic symptoms coexist with, but are obscured by, depressive effect; hypomania usually appears as depression improves. If agitation is present, it may be increased with phenelzine. Hypomania and agitation have been reported at higher than recommended doses, or following long-term therapy.

Phenelzine may cause excessive stimulation in schizophrenic patients; in manic-depressive states it may result in a swing from a depressive to a manic phase.

MAO inhibitors, including phenelzine, potentiate hexobarbital hypnosis in animals. Therefore, barbiturates should be given at a reduced dose with phenelzine.

MAO inhibitors inhibit the destruction of serotonin and norepinephrine, which are believed to be released from tissue stores by rauwolfia alkaloids. Accordingly, caution should be exercised when rauwolfia is used concomitantly with an MAO inhibitor, including phenelzine.

There is conflicting evidence as to whether or not MAO inhibitors affect glucose metabolism or potentiate the effect of hypoglycemic agents. This should be kept in mind if phenelzine is administered to diabetic patients.

Phenelzine as with other hydrazine derivatives has been reported to induce pulmonary and vascular tumors in an uncontrolled lifetime study in mice.

Drug Interactions: Phenelzine should be used with caution in combination with antihypertensive drugs, including thiazide diuretics and β-blockers, since exaggerated hypotensive effects may result. See Contraindications and Warnings for additional drug interactions.

Pregnancy: The safe use of phenelzine during pregnancy or lactation has not been established. The potential benefit of this drug, if used during pregnancy, lactation, or in women of childbearing age, should be weighed against the possible hazard to the mother or fetus.

Doses of phenelzine in pregnant mice well exceeding the maximum recommended human dose have caused a significant decrease in the number of viable offspring per mouse. In addition, the growth of young dogs and rats has been retarded by doses exceeding the maximum human dose.

Lactation: The safe use of phenelzine sulfate during lactation has not been established. There are insufficient adequate and well-controlled studies in lactating women. Therefore, phenelzine should be used in lactating women only if clearly needed. It is not known whether this drug is excreted in human milk. Because many drugs are excreted in human milk and because of the potential for serious adverse reactions in nursing infants to phenelzine, a decision should be made whether to discontinue the drug, taking into account the importance of the drug to the mother, or to discontinue nursing.

Children: Phenelzine is not recommended for patients under 16 years of age since there are no controlled studies of safety in this age group.

Adverse Effects: Phenelzine is a potent inhibitor of monoamine oxidase. Because this enzyme is widely distributed throughout the body, diverse pharmacologic effects may be expected to occur. When they occur, such effects tend to be mild to moderate in severity (see below), often subside with continuing treatment, and may be minimized by adjusting dosage; rarely is it necessary to institute counteracting measures or to discontinue phenelzine.

Common side effects include: Nervous System: dizziness, headache, drowsiness, sleep disturbances (including insomnia and hypersomnia), weakness and fatigue, tremors, twitching, myoclonic movements and hyperreflexia.

Gastrointestinal: constipation, dry mouth, gastrointestinal disturbances, elevated serum transaminases (without accompanying signs and symptoms).

Metabolic: weight gain.

Cardiovascular: postural hypotension, edema.

Genitourinary: sexual disturbances, i.e., anorgasmic, ejaculatory disturbances and impotence.

Less common mild to moderate side effects, some of which have been reported in a single patient or by a single physician,

Nardil (cont'd)

include: Nervous System: jitteriness, palilalia, euphoria, nystagmus, paresthesias.
Genitourinary: urinary retention.
Metabolic: hypernatremia.
Dermatologic: pruritus, skin rash, sweating.
Special Senses: blurred vision, glaucoma.

Although reported less frequently, and sometimes only once, additional severe side effects include: Nervous System: ataxia, shock-like coma, toxic delirium, manic reaction, convulsions, acute anxiety reaction, precipitation of schizophrenia, transient respiratory and cardiovascular depression following ECT.
Gastrointestinal: To date, fatal progressive necrotizing hepatocellular damage has been reported in a very few patients. Reversible jaundice.
Hematologic: leukopenia.
Immunologic: lupus-like syndrome.
Metabolic: hypermetabolic syndrome (which may include, but is not limited to, hyperpyrexia, tachycardia, tachypnea, muscular rigidity, elevated CK levels, metabolic acidosis, hypoxia, coma, and may resemble an overdose).
Respiratory: edema of the glottis.
Other: fever associated with increased muscle tone.

Withdrawal may be associated with nausea, vomiting and malaise.

An uncommon withdrawal syndrome following abrupt withdrawal of phenelzine has been infrequently reported. Signs and symptoms of this syndrome generally commence 24 to 72 hours after drug discontinuation and may range from vivid nightmares with agitation to frank psychosis and convulsions. This syndrome generally responds to reinstitution of low-dose phenelzine therapy followed by cautious downward titration and discontinuation.

Overdose: Symptoms: Note: For management of hypertensive crises, see Warnings. Accidental or intentional overdosage may be more common in patients who are depressed. It should be remembered that multiple drugs and/or alcohol may have been ingested.

Depending on the amount of overdosage with phenelzine, a varying and mixed clinical picture may develop, involving signs and symptoms of CNS and cardiovascular stimulation and/or depression. Signs and symptoms may be absent or minimal during the initial 12-hour period following ingestion and may develop slowly thereafter, reaching a maximum in 24 to 48 hours. Death has been reported following overdosage. Therefore, immediate hospitalization, with continuous patient observation and monitoring throughout this period, is essential.

Signs and symptoms of overdosage may include, alone or in combination, any of the following: drowsiness, dizziness, faintness, irritability, hyperactivity, agitation, severe headache, hallucinations, trismus, opisthotonos, rigidity, convulsions and coma, rapid and irregular pulse, hypertension, hypotension and vascular collapse, precordial pain, respiratory depression and failure, hyperpyrexia, diaphoresis, and cool, clammy skin.

Treatment: Intensive symptomatic and supportive treatment may be required. Induction of emesis or gastric lavage with instillation of charcoal slurry may be helpful in early poisoning, provided the airway has been protected against aspiration. Signs and symptoms of CNS stimulation, including convulsions, should be treated with diazepam, given slowly i.v. Phenothiazine derivatives and CNS stimulants should be avoided. Hypotension and vascular collapse should be treated with i.v. fluids, and if necessary, blood pressure titration with an i.v. infusion of dilute pressor agent. It should be noted that adrenergic agents may produce a markedly increased pressor response.

Respiration should be supported by appropriate measures, including management of the airway, use of supplemental oxygen, and mechanical ventilatory assistance, as required. Body temperature should be monitored closely. Intensive management of hyperpyrexia may be required. Maintenance of fluid and electrolyte balance is essential.

There are no data on the lethal dose in man. The pathophysiologic effects of massive overdosage may persist for several days, since the drug acts by inhibiting physiologic enzyme systems. With symptomatic and supportive measures, recovery from mild overdosage may be expected within 3 to 4 days.

Hemodialysis, peritoneal dialysis, and charcoal hemoperfusion may be of value in massive overdosage, but sufficient data are not available to recommend their routine use in these cases.

Toxic blood levels of phenelzine have not been established, and assay methods are not practical for clinical or toxicological use.

Dosage: Initial Dose: The usual starting dose is 1 tablet (15 mg) 3 times/day.
Early Phase Treatment: Dosage should be increased to at least 60 mg/day at a fairly rapid pace consistent with patient tolerance. It may be necessary to increase dosage up to 90 mg/day to obtain sufficient MAO inhibition. Many patients do not show a clinical response until treatment at 60 mg has been continued for at least 4 weeks.
Maintenance Dose: After maximum benefit from phenelzine is achieved, dosage should be reduced slowly over several weeks. Maintenance dose may be as low as 1 tablet, 15 mg/day or every other day, and should be continued for as long as is required.

Supplied: Each orange, biconvex glossy, sugar-coated tablet contains: phenelzine sulfate, equivalent to phenelzine base 15 mg. Nonmedicinal ingredients: acacia, calcium carbonate, candelilla wax, cornstarch, FD&C Yellow No. 6, gelatin, kaolin, magnesium stearate, mannitol, pharmaceutical glaze, povidone, sucrose and talc. Energy: 3.1 kJ (0.75 kcal). Gluten-, lactose-, paraben-, sodium-, sulfite- and tartrazine-free. Bottles of 100 and 500. Store between 15 and 30°C.

(Shown in Product Recognition Section)

Reviewed 1998

NAROPIN®
Astra

Ropivacaine HCl
Local Anesthetic

Pharmacology: Mechanism of Action: Ropivacaine, a local anesthetic of the amino amide class, is supplied as the pure S-(-)-enantiomer. Ropivacaine, like other local anesthetics, causes reversible blockade of impulse propagation along nerve fibres by preventing the inward movement of sodium ions through the cell membrane of the nerve fibres.

Ropivacaine has both anesthetic and analgesic effects. At high doses, surgical anesthesia is achieved. At lower doses, ropivacaine produces sensory block (analgesia) with limited and nonprogressive motor block.

After epidural infusion of ropivacaine, the spread of sensory block and the degree of motor block, as well as their subsequent regression, are dose-dependent.

The duration of action of local anesthetics depends on the injection site, the route of administration, and the concentration and volume of the drug. The duration and intensity of ropivacaine block are not improved by the addition of epinephrine.

Pharmacodynamics: In 2 clinical pharmacology studies (total N=24) ropivacaine and bupivacaine were infused (10 mg/min) in human volunteers until the appearance of CNS symptoms, e.g., visual or hearing disturbances, perioral numbness, tingling and others. Similar symptoms were seen with both drugs. In one study, the mean$\pm$SD maximum tolerated i.v. dose of ropivacaine infused (124$\pm$38 mg) was significantly higher than that of bupivacaine (99$\pm$30 mg), while in the other study the doses were not different (115$\pm$29 mg of ropivacaine and 103$\pm$30 mg of bupivacaine). In the latter study, the number of subjects reporting each symptom was similar for both drugs with the exception of muscle twitching, which was reported by more subjects with bupivacaine than ropivacaine at comparable i.v. doses. At the end of the infusion, ropivacaine in both studies caused significantly less depression of cardiac conductivity (less QRS widening) than bupivacaine. Ropivacaine and bupivacaine caused evidence of depression of cardiac contractility, but there were no changes in cardiac output.

Hemodynamics: Ropivacaine, like other local anesthetics, can also have effects on the central nervous and cardiovascular systems. If excessive amounts of drug reach the systemic circulation rapidly, symptoms and signs of CNS toxicity and cardiotoxicity may appear.

Signs and symptoms of CNS toxicity (see Overdose: Symptoms and Treatment) generally occur at lower plasma concentrations than do those of cardiotoxicity. Following systemic absorption, local anesthetics can produce CNS stimulation, depression or both. Apparent central stimulation is usually manifested as restlessness, tremors, and shivering, progressing to convulsions, followed by depression and coma, leading ultimately to respiratory arrest. However, the local anesthetics have a primary depressant effect on the medulla and on higher centres. The depressed stage may occur without a prior excited stage. High blood concentrations of local anesthetics resulting from systemic absorption or intravascular injection can depress cardiac conduction and excitability. At toxic levels, atrioventricular block, ventricular arrhythmias, cardiac arrest, and death are possibilities.

Indirect cardiovascular effects (hypotension, bradycardia) may occur after epidural administration, depending on the extent of the concomitant sympathetic block.

Pharmacokinetics: Absorption: The systemic concentration of local anesthetics is dependent upon the total dose and the concentration administered, the route of administration, the patient's hemodynamic/circulatory condition and the vascularity of the injection site. Ropivacaine follows linear pharmacokinetics and the maximum plasma concentration is proportional to the dose.

Ropivacaine shows complete and biphasic absorption from the epidural space. The mean half-lives of the 2 phases are in the order of 14 min and 4 h. The slow absorption is the rate-limiting factor in the elimination of ropivacaine, which explains why the apparent elimination half-life is longer after epidural than after i.v. administration. Ropivacaine shows dose proportionality at epidural doses up to 250 mg and i.v. doses up to 80 mg.

Distribution: Following i.v. administration, the volume of distribution of ropivacaine is approximately 40 L. Ropivacaine is extensively bound to alpha$_1$-acid glycoprotein in plasma with an unbound, i.e., pharmacologically active, fraction of about 6%. An increase in total plasma concentration during continuous epidural infusion has been observed in postoperative patients and is related to the postoperative increase of alpha$_1$-acid glycoprotein. Variations in unbound concentration have been much less than in total plasma concentration.

Ropivacaine readily crosses the placenta and equilibrium, in regard to unbound concentration, is rapidly reached. The degree of plasma protein binding in the fetus is less than in the mother, which results in lower total plasma concentrations in the fetus than in the mother. The ratios of umbilical vein to maternal vein total and free concentrations are 0.31 and 0.74, respectively.

Metabolism: Ropivacaine is extensively metabolized in the liver predominantly to 3-OH-ropivacaine by an aromatic hydroxylation process mediated by cytochrome P4501A. Conjugated and unconjugated 3-hydroxy-ropivacaine represent the major urinary metabolites. Urinary excretion of the 4-hydroxy and both the 3-hydroxy and 4-hydroxy N-dealkylated metabolites accounts for less than 3% of the dose. An additional metabolite, 2-hydroxy-methyl-ropivacaine has been identified, but not quantified in urine. 3-Hydroxy- and 4-hydroxy-ropivacaine have local anesthetic activity in animal models although less than that of ropivacaine.

There is no evidence of in vivo racemization of ropivacaine.

Elimination: After intravascular administration, 86% of the total dose of ropivacaine is excreted in the urine of which approximately 1% is the parent compound and 36% is 3-OH ropivacaine. Ropivacaine has a total plasma clearance in the order of 300 to 400 mL/min, an unbound plasma clearance of 8 L/min, and a renal clearance of 1 mL/min. Ropivacaine has an intermediate hepatic extraction ratio of about 0.4. The terminal elimination half-life is 1.6 to 1.8 hours after i.v. administration, 4.1 to 6.5 hours after epidural administration, and 5.7 to 8.0 hours after brachial plexus block. The total and unbound clearance of epidural ropivacaine at term in pregnancy (223 to 256 mL/min and 2.8 to 3.3 L/min, respectively), are lower than that observed in nonpregnant patients.

Clinical Trials: Epidural Administration in Surgery: The use of ropivacaine for epidural anesthesia in general surgery was investigated in 25 clinical studies performed in 942 patients. Ropivacaine was administered in doses ranging from 75 to 250 mg. The intensity and duration of sensory and motor block were dose-dependent. At doses ranging from 100 to 200 mg, the median time to achieve a T10 sensory block was 10 (5 to 13) minutes, while the median duration of anesthesia at this dermatome was 4 (3 to 5) hours. For 20 mL volumes of 5, 7.5 and 10 mg/mL solutions, the median duration of motor block was 3, 4 and 5 hours, respectively.

Epidural Administration in Cesarean Section: Seven studies of epidural anesthesia with ropivacaine have been performed in a total of 194 women undergoing Cesarean section. In these studies, ropivacaine 5 mg/mL was administered at mean total doses ranging from 110 to 150 mg. The median onset of sensory block at T6 ranged from 11 to 26 minutes, while the median duration of sensory block at this dermatome ranged from 1.7 to 3.2 hours. The duration of motor block ranged from 1.4 to 2.9 hours. The quality of analgesia was considered to be satisfactory in 73 to 100% of patients, while the quality of muscle relaxation was rated as satisfactory in 100% of patients.

Major Nerve Block: Eight studies have been performed to investigate the efficacy of ropivacaine in a single instance of major nerve block, brachial plexus block. In studies in which the 5 mg/mL solution (total doses of 175 to 190 mg) was administered by the supraclavicular approach, anesthesia at dermatomes T1 to C5 was achieved in 83 to 100% of patients. Following median onset times ranging from 10 to 25 minutes, the median duration of anesthesia at these dermatomes ranged from 8 to 12 hours. The quality of brachial plexus block was rated as satisfactory in 91 to 100% of these patients.

Success rates were lower with axillary blocks than with supraclavicular blocks. In patients receiving 175 to 275 mg of ropivacaine 5 mg/mL by the axillary approach, satisfactory analgesia was achieved in 62 to 72% of patients. The frequency of anesthesia at the nerves studied ranged from 52 to 90%. The mean onset time ranged from 10 to 45 min with a duration of anesthesia in the range of 3.7 to 8.7 hours.

Epidural Administration in Labor and Delivery: Nine studies have been performed to investigate the use of epidural ropivacaine for pain relief during labor in pregnant females with full term singleton fetuses in the vertex presentation. Loading doses of approximately 25 mg were administered as fractionated doses. In 4 clinical trials in which continuous infusions were administered, the total infusion dose ranged from 3 to 30 mg/h with median values of 22 to 25 mg/h. Infusion times up to 13 hours have been studied. In the remaining studies, supplementary analgesia was provided by up to 8 top up doses of ropivacaine at median doses ranging from 14 to 18 mg/h. In these studies, the median values for the onset of pain relief after the main dose ranged from 9 to 18 min. Median upper spread of sensory block ranged from T5 to T10.

Epidural Administration in Postoperative Pain Management: Eight clinical trials have been performed to investigate the epidural use of ropivacaine in postoperative pain management following orthopedic or upper or lower abdominal surgery. All patients had received epidural anesthesia with ropivacaine intraoperatively prior to the initiation of postoperative epidural infusion. A total of 421 patients received ropivacaine in these studies. Of these, 382 were eligible for efficacy analyses. The infusion of ropivacaine at doses ranging from 10 to 30 mg/h was associated with decreases in pain scores and morphine requirement. The frequency and intensity of motor block tended to decrease during the 21 hour period. Motor block was dose-dependent. In 2 dose-controlled studies, infusion rates of 12 to 20 mg/h provided satisfactory analgesia (85 to 100% rated good or excellent) with relatively slight motor block. At the end of the infusion, 14 to 24% of patients exhibited motor block at 20 mg/h as compared with 41% at 24 mg/h and 50 to 67% at 28 mg/h. Infusion times up to 21 hours have been studied.

Infiltration: Pre- and postoperative wound infiltration with ropivacaine for postoperative pain relief have been studied in 6 clinical trials. An additional study examined local infiltration with ropivacaine for operation upon benign nevi. Of the 308 patients studied, 297 were evaluable for efficacy. In the wound infiltration studies, ropivacaine at doses of 100 to 200 mg resulted in lower pain scores and/or a decreased analgesia requirement in the immediate postoperative period in 3 of 4 studies which contained inactive control groups. In the study of nevus excision, doses of 5 to 20 mg were considered to provide adequate analgesia in the 30 patients studied.

Indications: Analgesia: Acute pain management in connection with: continuous epidural infusion or intermittent bolus administration e.g., postoperative or labor pain; field block e.g., infiltration.

Anesthesia: Surgical anesthesia in connection with: epidural block for surgery, including Cesarean section; major nerve block e.g., brachial plexus block; field block e.g., infiltration.

Contraindications: In patients with a known hypersensitivity to ropivacaine or any other local anesthetic agent of the amide type.

The use of ropivacaine is contraindicated for i.v. regional anesthesia (Bier block).

Ropivacaine should not be used in obstetric paracervical block anesthesia. Use of other local anesthetics in this technique has resulted in fetal bradycardia and death.

Warnings: Local anesthetics should only be employed by clinicians who are well versed in the diagnosis and management of dose-related toxicity and other acute emergencies which might arise from the block to be employed. For management of toxic reactions and related emergencies, cardiopulmonary resuscitative equipment, oxygen, resuscitative drugs, and personnel resources should be immediately available when any local anesthetic is used. Delay in proper management of dose-related toxicity, underventilation from any cause and/or altered sensitivity may lead to the development of acidosis, cardiac arrest and, possibly, death (see Adverse Effects and Overdose).

For Cesarean section, the 5 mg/mL ropivacaine solution in doses up to 150 mg is recommended. The 7.5 and 10 mg/mL solutions should not be used for this indication. As with all local anesthetics, ropivacaine should be administered in incremental doses. Since ropivacaine should not be injected rapidly in large doses, it is not recommended for emergency situations where a fast onset of surgical anesthesia is necessary. Historically, pregnant patients were reported to have a high risk for cardiac arrhythmias, cardiac/circulatory arrest and death when bupivacaine was inadvertently administered by rapid i.v. injection.

Solutions of ropivacaine should not be used for the production of retrobulbar block or spinal anesthesia (subarachnoid block) due to insufficient data to support such use.

It is essential that aspiration for blood and cerebrospinal fluid be done prior to injecting any local anesthetic, both for the original dose and all subsequent doses, to avoid intravascular or subarachnoid injection. However, a negative aspiration does not ensure against an intravascular or subarachnoid injection.

A well known risk of epidural anesthesia is unintentional subarachnoid injection of the local anesthetic. Two clinical studies have been performed to verify the safety of ropivacaine injected into the subarachnoid space at a volume of 3 mL, selected to be representative of an incremental epidural volume that could be unintentionally injected. The 15 and 22.5 mg doses injected resulted in sensory block levels as high as T5 and T4, respectively. Sensory block started in the sacral dermatomes in 2 to 3 minutes, extended to the T10 level in 10 to 13 minutes and lasted for approximately 2 hours. The results of these 2 clinical studies showed that a 3 mL dose did not produce any serious adverse events when spinal anesthesia was achieved.

Epidural anesthesia or analgesia may lead to hypotension and bradycardia. This risk can be reduced either by preloading the circulation or by injecting a vasopressor such as ephedrine 20 to 40 mg i.m. Hypotension should be treated promptly with e.g., ephedrine 5 to 10 mg i.v. and repeated as necessary.

Ropivacaine should be used with caution in patients receiving other local anesthetics or agents structurally related to amide-type local anesthetics, since the toxic effects are additive.

Precautions: The safe and effective use of local anesthetics depends on proper dosage, correct technique, adequate precautions and readiness for emergencies. Resuscitative equipment, oxygen and resuscitative drugs should be available for immediate use (see Adverse Effects and Overdose). During major regional nerve blocks, the patients should have i.v. fluids running via an indwelling catheter to assure a functioning i.v. pathway. The lowest dosage of local anesthetic that results in effective anesthesia should be used. Injections should be made slowly and incrementally, with frequent aspirations before and during the injection to avoid intravascular injection. When a continuous catheter technique is used, syringe aspirations should be performed before and during each supplemental injection.

Epidural Anesthesia and Analgesia: During epidural administration, it is recommended that a test dose of a local anesthetic with a fast onset of action be administered initially. The patient should be monitored for CNS and cardiovascular toxicity, as well as for signs of unintended intrathecal administration, before proceeding. When clinical conditions permit, test doses of local anesthetic solutions which contain epinephrine should be considered because circulatory changes compatible with epinephrine may also serve as a warning sign of unintended intravascular injection. If injected into a blood vessel, this amount of epinephrine is likely to produce a transient "epinephrine response" within 45 seconds, consisting of an increase in heart rate and systolic blood pressure, circumoral pallor, palpitations and nervousness in the unsedated patient. The sedated patient may exhibit only a pulse rate increase of 20 or more beats/minute for 15 or more seconds. Therefore, following the test dose, the heart rate should be continuously monitored. Patients on beta-blockers may not manifest changes in heart rate, but blood pressure monitoring can detect a rise in systolic blood pressure. A test dose of a short-acting amide anesthetic such as lidocaine (30 to 40 mg) is recommended to detect an unintentional intrathecal administration. This will be manifested within a few minutes by signs of spinal block (e.g., decreased sensation of the buttocks, paresis of the legs, or, in the sedated patient, absent knee jerk). An intravascular or subarachnoid injection is still possible even if results of the test dose are negative. The test dose itself may produce a systemic toxic reaction, high spinal or epinephrine-induced cardiovascular effects.

During epidural administration, ropivacaine should be administered in incremental doses of 3 to 5 mL with sufficient time between doses to detect toxic manifestations of unintentional intravascular or subarachnoid injection. Frequent aspirations for blood or cerebrospinal fluid (where applicable, i.e., when using a "continuous" intermittent catheter technique) should be performed before and during each supplemental injection because plastic tubing in the epidural space can migrate into a blood vessel or through the dura. A negative aspiration, however, does not ensure against an intravascular or intrathecal injection.

If blood is aspirated, relocate the needle. Inadvertent intravascular injection may cause serious consequences. Absorption is more rapid when injections are made into highly vascular tissues. Administration of higher than recommended doses of ropivacaine to achieve greater motor blockade or increased duration of sensory blockade may pose a particular risk in the event that an inadvertent intravascular injection occurs. In epidural administration, the procedure should be discontinued and re-initiated if the subarachnoid space has been entered, as shown by aspiration of spinal fluid.

Careful and constant monitoring of cardiovascular and respiratory vital signs (adequacy of ventilation) and the patient's state of consciousness should be performed during the anesthetic procedure. It should be kept in mind at such times that restlessness, anxiety, incoherent speech, lightheadedness, numbness and tingling of the mouth and lips, metallic taste, tinnitus, dizziness, blurred vision, tremors, twitching, depression, or drowsiness may be early warning signs of CNS toxicity.

High Risk Populations: Local anesthetics should be used with caution in patients in poor general condition due to advanced age, debilitation, or other compromising factors such as partial or complete heart conduction block, advanced liver disease, or severe renal dysfunction. To reduce the risk of potentially serious adverse reactions, attempts should be made to optimize the patient's condition before major blocks are performed. Dosage should be adjusted accordingly.

Hepatic or Renal Impairment: Because amide-type local anesthetics such as ropivacaine are metabolized by the liver, these drugs, especially repeat doses, should be used cautiously in patients with hepatic disease. Patients with severe hepatic disease, because of their inability to metabolize local anesthetics normally, are at an increased risk of developing toxic plasma concentrations.

Normally there is no need to modify the dose of ropivacaine when used for single dose or short-term treatment in patients with impaired renal function. Acidosis and reduced plasma protein concentration, frequently seen in patients with chronic renal failure, may increase the risk of systemic toxicity.

Inflammation: Local anesthetic procedures should be performed with care in inflamed regions. Injections should not be performed through inflamed tissue nor when there is sepsis at or near the injection site.

Psychomotor Effects: Local anesthetics may have a dose-dependent effect on mental function and coordination, causing temporary impairment of locomotion and alertness, even in the absence of overt CNS toxicity.

Head and Neck Area: Small doses of local anesthetics injected into the head and neck area, including dental and stellate ganglion blocks, may produce adverse reactions as a result of inadvertent intra-arterial injection and subsequent retrograde flow to the cerebral circulation. These adverse reactions may be similar to systemic toxicity seen with unintentional intravascular injections of larger doses. Confusion, convulsions, respiratory depression, and/or respiratory arrest, and cardiovascular stimulation or depression have been reported. Patients receiving these blocks should have their circulation and respiration monitored and be constantly observed.

Naropin (cont'd)

Resuscitative equipment and personnel for treating adverse reactions should be immediately available. Dosage recommendations should not be exceeded.

Geriatrics: The risk of hypotension and bradycardia in patients receiving epidural anesthesia with ropivacaine increases in an age-dependent manner (see Adverse Effects, Table V).

Cardiovascular Disease: Local anesthetics should also be used with caution in patients with impaired cardiovascular function who may be less able to compensate for functional changes associated with prolongation of AV conduction produced by these drugs. Hypotension, hypovolemia, or heart block represent risk factors.

Ophthalmic Surgery: The use of ropivacaine in retrobulbar blocks for ophthalmic surgery has not been studied. Until appropriate experience is gained, the use of ropivacaine for such surgery is not recommended.

Pregnancy: Reproduction studies have been performed in rats and rabbits.

No effects on fertility and general reproductive performance were seen in rats over 2 generations. At the highest dose level, increased pup loss was seen during the first 3 days post partum, which was considered to be secondary to impaired maternal care of the newborn, due to maternal toxicity.

Teratogenicity studies in rats and rabbits did not show evidence of any adverse effects of ropivacaine on organogenesis or early fetal development. There were no treatment-related effects on late fetal development, parturition, lactation, neonatal viability or growth of the offspring in a perinatal and postnatal study in rats using the maximum tolerated dose.

An additional perinatal and postnatal study in rats, in which ropivacaine was compared with bupivacaine, showed that maternal toxicity was observed at much lower dose levels and at lower unbound plasma concentrations of bupivacaine than of ropivacaine.

There are no clinical studies in preterm pregnant women on the effects of ropivacaine on the developing fetus. Ropivacaine should be used during pregnancy only if the potential benefit justifies the potential risk to the fetus. The use of ropivacaine at term for obstetric anesthesia or analgesia is well documented.

Labor and Delivery: Local anesthetics, including ropivacaine, rapidly cross the placenta, and when used for an epidural block, can cause varying degrees of maternal, fetal and neonatal toxicity. The incidence and degree of toxicity depend upon the procedure performed, the type and amount of drug used, and the technique of drug administration. Adverse reactions in the parturient, fetus and neonate involve alterations of the CNS, peripheral vascular tone and cardiac function. Maternal hypotension has resulted from epidural analgesia with ropivacaine for obstetrical pain relief. Elevating the patient's legs and positioning her on her left side will help prevent decreases in blood pressure. The fetal heart rate also should be monitored continuously, and electronic fetal monitoring is highly advisable.

It is extremely important to avoid aorto-caval compression by the gravid uterus during administration of regional block to parturients. The patient should be maintained in the left lateral decubitus position if possible, or manual displacement of the uterus off the great vessels should be accomplished.

Lactation: The excretion of ropivacaine or its metabolites in human milk has not been studied. Based on the milk/plasma concentration ratio in rats, the estimated daily dose to a pup will be about 4% of the dose given to the mother. Caution should be exercised when ropivacaine is administered to a nursing woman. Assuming that the milk/plasma concentration ratio in humans is of the same order, the total ropivacaine dose to which the baby is exposed by breast-feeding is far lower than by exposure in utero in pregnant women at term.

Children: As the safety and efficacy of ropivacaine have not been investigated in children under 18 years of age, no dosage recommendations can be provided.

Drug Interactions: Ropivacaine should be used with caution in patients receiving other local anesthetics or agents structurally related to amide-type local anesthetics, since the toxic effects are additive.

If sedatives are employed to reduce patient apprehension, they should be used in reduced doses, since local anesthetic agents, like sedatives, are CNS depressants which in combination may have an additive effect.

In vitro studies indicate that cytochrome P4501A is involved in the formation of 3-hydroxy ropivacaine, the major metabolite. Thus, agents administered concomitantly with ropivacaine which are also metabolized by this isozyme family may potentially interact with ropivacaine. Such interactions might occur with drugs known to be metabolized by P4501A2 such as theophylline or imipramine or with potent inhibitors such as fluvoxamine and verapamil.

Adverse Effects: Reactions to ropivacaine are characteristic of those associated with other long-acting local anesthetics of the amide type.

Most Common Adverse Events: In clinical trials, the great majority of adverse events reported with ropivacaine were related to the expected effects of the block and to the clinical situation, rather than reactions to the drug. When all clinical studies were pooled (Total n=2 250), hypotension and nausea were registered in 39% (n=872) and 25% (n=556) of the patients, respectively. Similar incidences were reported for bupivacaine in the double-blind comparisons.

Adverse reactions to local anesthetics are very rare in the absence of overdose or inadvertent intravascular injection. The effects of systemic overdose and unintentional intravascular injections can be serious, but should be distinguished from the physiological effects of the nerve block itself e.g., a decrease in blood pressure and bradycardia during epidural anesthesia.

Acute systemic toxicity from local anesthetics is generally dose-related and due to high plasma levels which may result from overdosage, rapid absorption from the injection site, diminished tolerance, or from inadvertent intravascular injection. Most commonly, the acute adverse experiences originate from the central nervous and cardiovascular systems.

See Tables I, II, III, IV and V.

Table I—Naropin

Adverse Events Reported in ≥1% of Adult Patients Receiving Regional or Local Anesthesia (Surgery, Labor, Cesarean Section, Peripheral Nerve Block and Local Infiltration)

	Total n=742	
Adverse Reaction	**n**	**(%)**
Hypotension	237	(31.9)
Nausea	92	(12.4)
Paresthesia	51	(6.9)
Vomiting	48	(6.5)
Pain	39	(5.3)
Back pain	36	(4.9)
Bradycardia	32	(4.3)
Fever	25	(3.4)
Headache	23	(3.1)
Dizziness	18	(2.4)
Chills	16	(2.2)
Pruritus	16	(2.2)
Urinary Retention	10	(1.3)
Hypoesthesia	8	(1.1)

Table II—Naropin

Adverse Events Reported in ≥1% of Fetuses or Neonates of Mothers Who Received Regional Anesthesia (Cesarean Section and Labor Studies)

	Total n=337	
Adverse Reaction	**n**	**(%)**
Fetal bradycardia	58	(17.2)
Neonatal jaundice	12	(3.6)
Neonatal tachypnea	8	(2.4)
Fetal tachycardia	7	(2.1)
Neonatal fever	6	(1.8)
Neonatal respiratory distress	5	(1.5)
Neonatal vomiting	5	(1.5)
Fetal distress	4	(1.2)

Table IV—Naropin

Most Common Adverse Events by Gender (Epidural Administration)
Total n: female=405, males=355

	Female		Male	
Adverse Reaction	**n**	**(%)**	**n**	**(%)**
Hypotension	220	(54.3)	138	(38.9)
Nausea	119	(29.4)	23	(6.5)
Bradycardia	65	(16.0)	56	(15.8)
Vomiting	59	(14.6)	8	(2.3)
Back Pain	41	(10.1)	23	(6.5)
Headache	33	(8.1)	17	(4.8)
Chills	18	(4.4)	5	(1.4)
Fever	16	(4.0)	3	(0.8)
Pruritus	16	(4.0)	1	(0.3)

Table V—Naropin

Effects of Age on Hypotension (Epidural Administration)
Total n: Naropin=760

	5 mg/mL		7.5 mg/mL		10 mg/mL	
Age	**n**	**(%)**	**n**	**(%)**	**n**	**(%)**
<65	68	(32.2)	99	(43.2)	87	(51.5)
≥65	31	(68.9)	47	(69.1)	26	(68.4)

CNS: These are characterized by excitation and/or depression. Restlessness, anxiety, dizziness, tinnitus, blurred vision or tremors may occur, possibly proceeding to convulsions. However, excitement may be transient or absent, with depression being the first manifestation of an adverse reaction. This may quickly be followed by drowsiness merging into unconsciousness and respiratory arrest. Other CNS effects may be nausea, vomiting, chills, and constriction of the pupils.

The incidence of convulsions associated with the use of local anesthetics varies with the procedure used and the total dose administered. One case of convulsions has been observed after an unintended intravascular injection occurred while attempting a brachial plexus block with 200 mg ropivacaine. The patient was treated with a standard regimen of drugs and recovered completely.

Cardiovascular System: High doses or unintentional intravascular injection may lead to high plasma levels and related depression of the myocardium, decreased cardiac output, heart block, hypotension, bradycardia, ventricular arrhythmias, including ventricular tachycardia and ventricular fibrillation, and cardiac arrest. Reactions due to systemic absorption may be either slow or rapid in onset. Cardiovascular collapse and cardiac arrest can occur rapidly (see Overdose: Symptoms and Treatment).

Allergic: Allergic type reactions are rare and may occur as a result of sensitivity to local anesthetics of the amide-type. These reactions are characterized by signs such as urticaria, pruritus, erythema, angioneurotic edema (including laryngeal edema), tachycardia, sneezing, nausea, vomiting, dizziness, syncope, excessive sweating, elevated temperature, and in the most severe instances, anaphylactic shock.

Neurologic: The incidence of adverse neurologic reactions may be related to the total dose of local anesthetic administered but is also dependent upon the particular drug used, the route of administration and the physical status of the patient. Neuropathy and spinal cord dysfunction (e.g., anterior spinal artery syndrome, arachnoiditis, cauda equina syndrome), have been associated with regional anesthesia. Neurological effects may be related to local anesthetic techniques, with or without a contribution from the drug.

In the practice of lumbar epidural block, occasional unintentional penetration of the subarachnoid space by the catheter or needle may occur. For example, a high spinal is characterized by paralysis of the legs, loss of consciousness, respiratory paralysis and bradycardia.

Table III—Naropin

Common Events (Epidural Administration)

	5 mg/mL Total n=256		7.5 mg/mL Total n=297		10 mg/mL Total n=207	
Adverse Reaction	**n**	**(%)**	**n**	**(%)**	**n**	**(%)**
Hypotension	99	(38.7)	146	(49.2)	113	(54.6)
Nausea	34	(13.3)	68	(22.9)	–	–
Bradycardia	29	(11.3)	58	(19.5)	40	(19.3)
Back pain	18	(7.0)	23	(7.7)	34	(16.4)
Vomiting	18	(7.0)	33	(11.1)	23	(11.1)
Headache	12	(4.7)	20	(6.7)	16	(7.7)
Fever	8	(3.1)	5	(1.7)	18	(8.7)

Neurologic effects following unintentional subarachnoid administration during epidural anesthesia may include spinal block of varying magnitude (including total or high spinal block), hypotension secondary to spinal block, urinary retention, fecal and urinary incontinence, loss of perineal sensation and sexual function, persistent anesthesia, paresthesia, weakness, paralysis of the lower extremities and loss of sphincter control, all of which may have slow, incomplete or no recovery; headache, backache, septic meningitis, meningismus, slowing of labor, increased incidence of forceps delivery, or cranial nerve palsies due to traction on nerves from loss of cerebrospinal fluid.

Elevation of Body Temperature: Epidural infusion of ropivacaine has, in some cases, been associated with transient elevations in body temperature to >38.5°C. This has occurred more frequently at doses greater than 16 mg/hour.

Overdose: In clinical trials, 1 patient experienced a life-threatening generalized aclonic convulsion, and another, grand mal convulsions, following the inadvertent intravascular injection of 200 and 225 mg ropivacaine, respectively. These patients recovered completely following treatment.

Acute systemic toxicity from local anesthetics is generally related to high plasma levels encountered during therapeutic use or to unintended intravascular or subarachnoid injection (see Adverse Effects, Warnings and Precautions).

Symptoms: Accidental intravascular injections may cause immediate toxic effects. In the event of overdose, peak plasma concentrations may not be reached for 1 to 2 hours, depending on the site of injection, with signs of toxicity thus being delayed.

CNS toxicity is a graded response with symptoms and signs of escalating severity. Initially symptoms such as visual or hearing disturbances, perioral numbness, dizziness, lightheadedness, tingling and paresthesia are seen. Dysarthria, muscular rigidity and muscular twitching are more serious and may precede the onset of generalized convulsions. These signs must not be mistaken for a neurotic behavior. Unconsciousness and grand mal convulsions may follow which may last from a few seconds to several minutes. Hypoxia and hypercarbia occur rapidly following convulsions due to the increased muscular activity, together with the interference with normal respiration and loss of the airway. In severe cases apnea may occur. The respiratory and metabolic acidosis increases the toxic effects of local anesthetics.

Recovery is due to redistribution and metabolism of the local anesthetic drug. Recovery may be rapid unless large amounts of the drug have been administered.

Cardiovascular toxicity indicates a more severe situation. Hypotension, bradycardia, arrhythmia and cardiac arrest may occur as a result of high systemic concentrations of local anesthetic. In volunteers, the i.v. infusion of ropivacaine resulted in signs of depression of conductivity and contractility.

Cardiovascular toxic effects are generally preceded by signs of toxicity in the CNS, unless the patient is receiving a general anesthetic or is heavily sedated with drugs such as a benzodiazepine or barbiturate.

Treatment: The first consideration is prevention, best accomplished by incremental injection of ropivacaine, careful and constant monitoring of cardiovascular and respiratory vital signs and the patient's state of consciousness after each local anesthetic injection and during continuous infusion. At the first sign of change, oxygen should be administered. If signs of acute systemic toxicity appear, injection of the local anesthetic should be immediately stopped.

The first step in the management of systemic toxic reactions, as well as underventilation or apnea due to unintentional subarachnoid injection of drug solution, consists of immediate attention to the establishment and maintenance of a patent airway and assisted or controlled ventilation with oxygen and a delivery system capable of permitting immediate positive airway pressure by mask. This may prevent convulsions if they have not already occurred.

If necessary, use drugs to control the convulsions. An anticonvulsant should be given i.v. if the convulsions do not stop spontaneously in 15 to 20 seconds. Thiopental 100 to 150 mg i.v. will abort the convulsions rapidly. Alternatively diazepam 5 to 10 mg i.v. may be used, although its action is slower. Both these drugs, however, depress the CNS, respiratory and cardiac function, add to postictal depression, and may result in apnea. Succinylcholine will stop the muscle convulsions rapidly, but will require tracheal intubation and controlled ventilation.

If cardiovascular depression is evident (hypotension, bradycardia) administration of i.v. fluids or a vasopressor such as ephedrine or epinephrine may be required.

Should circulatory arrest occur, immediate cardiopulmonary resuscitation should be instituted. Optimal oxygenation and ventilation and circulatory support as well as treatment of acidosis are of vital importance.

Clinical data from patients experiencing local anesthetic-induced convulsions demonstrated rapid development of hypoxia, hypercarbia, and acidosis within a minute of the onset of convulsions. These observations suggest that oxygen consumption and carbon dioxide production are greatly increased during local anesthetic convulsions and emphasize the importance of immediate and effective ventilation with oxygen which may avoid cardiac arrest.

The supine position is dangerous in pregnant women at term because of aorto-caval compression by the gravid uterus. Therefore, during treatment of systemic toxicity, maternal hypotension or fetal bradycardia following regional block, the parturient should be maintained in the left lateral decubitus position if possible, or manual displacement of the uterus off the great vessels should be accomplished. Resuscitation of obstetrical patients may take longer than resuscitation of non-pregnant patients and closed-chest cardiac compression may be ineffective. Rapid delivery of the fetus may improve the response to resuscitative efforts.

In human volunteers given i.v. ropivacaine, the mean maximum tolerated total and free arterial plasma concentrations were 4.3 and 0.6 µg/mL respectively, at which time moderate CNS symptoms (muscle twitching) were noted.

Dosage: Ropivacaine should only be used by or under the supervision of clinicians experienced in regional anesthesia.

It is recommended that hospitals using local anesthetic infusions have a treatment protocol in place for nursing to follow in order to safely monitor the level of the block and for the proper management of complications and/or toxic reactions. If toxic reactions occur, the infusion should be stopped immediately.

Adults: The dosages in Table VI are recommended as a guide for use in the average adult for the more commonly used blocks. The clinician's experience and knowledge of the patient's physical status are of importance in calculating the required dose.

Ropivacaine should be administered at the smallest dose and the lowest concentration which are consistent with the necessary degree of anesthesia or analgesia. The rapid injection of a large volume of local anesthetic solution should be avoided and fractional doses should always be used. In general, surgical anesthesia, e.g., epidural administration, requires the use of higher concentrations and doses. For analgesia, e.g., epidural administration for acute pain management, lower concentrations and doses are recommended.

The dose of any local anesthetic administered varies with the anesthetic procedure, the area to be anesthetized, the vascularity of the tissues, the number of neuronal segments to be blocked, the depth of anesthesia and degree of muscle relaxation required, the duration of anesthesia desired, individual tolerance, and the physical condition of the patient.

Patients in poor general condition due to advanced age or other compromising factors such as partial or complete heart conduction block, advanced liver disease or severe renal dysfunction require special attention although regional anesthesia is frequently indicated in these patients. To reduce the risk of potentially serious adverse reactions, attempts should be made to optimize the patient's condition before major blocks are performed, and the dosage should be adjusted accordingly.

Parenteral drug products should be inspected visually for particulate matter and discoloration prior to administration, whenever solution and container permit. Solutions which are discolored or which contain particulate matter should not be administered. For specific techniques and procedures, refer to standard contemporary textbooks.

Careful aspiration before and during injection is recommended to prevent intravascular injection. When employing an epidural block, a test dose of 3 to 5 mL lidocaine 1.5% with epinephrine is recommended. An inadvertent intravascular injection may be recognized by a temporary increase in heart rate and an accidental subarachnoid injection by signs of a spinal block. Aspiration should be repeated prior to and during administration of the main dose, which should be injected slowly or in incremental doses, at a rate of 25 to 50 mg/min, while closely observing the patient's vital functions and maintaining verbal contact. If toxic symptoms occur, the injection should be stopped immediately. The test dose should be repeated if the patient is moved in such a fashion as to have displaced the epidural catheter.

In epidural block for surgery, single doses of up to 250 mg ropivacaine have been used and are well tolerated.

When prolonged blocks are used, either through continuous infusion or through repeated bolus administration, the risks of reaching a toxic plasma concentration or inducing local neural injury must be considered. Experience to date indicates that a cumulative dose of up to 770 mg ropivacaine administered over 24 hours is well tolerated in adults when used for postoperative pain management.

For treatment of postoperative pain, the following technique is recommended: Unless preoperatively instituted, an epidural block with ropivacaine 5 to 7.5 mg/mL is induced via an epidural catheter. Analgesia is maintained with ropivacaine 2 mg/mL infusion. Clinical studies have demonstrated that infusion rates of 6 to 10 mL (12 to 20 mg)/h provide adequate analgesia with only slight and nonprogressive motor block in most cases of moderate to severe postoperative pain. With this technique, a significant reduction in the need for opioids has been observed. Clinical studies also show, however, that some patients require higher doses. Infusion rates of 12 to 14 mL (24 to 28 mg)/h have been well tolerated. Clinical experience supports the use of ropivacaine epidural infusions for up to 21 hours.

As the safety and efficacy of ropivacaine have not been investigated in children under 18 years of age, no dosage recommendations can be provided.

Table VI—Naropin

Adult Dosage Recommendations for Naropin

Type of Block	Conc. (mg/mL)	Volume (mL)	Dose (mg)
Acute Pain Management			
Lumbar epidural			
Bolus	2	10-20	20-40
intermittent injections (top-up) e.g., labor pain management	2	10-15 (minimum interval 30 minutes)	20-30
Continuous infusion e.g., labor pain and postoperative pain management	2	6-14 mL/h	12-28 mg/h
Field block			
e.g., infiltration	2	1-100	2-200
	5	1-40	5-200
Surgical Anesthesia			
Lumbar epidural			
Surgery	5	15-30	75-150
	7.5	15-25	113-188
	10	15-20	150-200
Cesarean Section	5	20-25	100-150
Major nerve block			
e.g., brachial plexus block	5	35-50	175-250
Field block			
e.g., infiltration	5	1-40	5-200

The doses in the table are those considered to be necessary to produce a successful block and should be regarded as guidelines for use in adults. The figures reflect the expected average dose range needed. For other local anesthetic techniques standard textbooks should be consulted.

Naropin (cont'd)

The duration and intensity of ropivacaine block are not improved by the addition of epinephrine.

Alkalinization may lead to precipitation since ropivacaine is poorly soluble above pH 6.0.

Ropivacaine solutions are sterile, without preservative and are for single use only. Discard unused portion.

Parenteral products should be visually inspected for precipitation, haziness, particulate matter and leakage prior to use.

Supplied: 2 mg/mL: Each mL of sterile isotonic solution contains: ropivacaine HCl 2 mg. Nonmedicinal ingredients: sodium chloride, sodium hydroxide and/or hydrochloric acid to adjust pH to 4.0 to 6.0 and water for injection. Polybag (plastic infusion bags) of 100 and 200 mL packed in a sterile pack. Polyamp Duofit (plastic ampuls suitable for Luer lock and Luer fit syringes) of 10 and 20 mL packed in sterile blister packs.

5 mg/mL: Each mL of sterile isotonic solution contains: ropivacaine HCl 5 mg. Nonmedicinal ingredients: sodium chloride, sodium hydroxide and/or hydrochloric acid to adjust pH to 4.0 to 6.0 and water for injection. Polyamp Duofit (plastic ampuls suitable for Luer lock and Luer fit syringes) of 10 and 20 mL packed in sterile blister packs.

7.5 mg/mL: Each mL of sterile isotonic solution contains: ropivacaine HCl 7.5 mg. Nonmedicinal ingredients: sodium chloride, sodium hydroxide and/or hydrochloric acid to adjust pH to 4.0 to 6.0 and water for injection. Polyamp Duofit (plastic ampuls suitable for Luer lock and Luer fit syringes) of 10 and 20 mL packed in sterile blister packs.

10 mg/mL: Each mL of sterile isotonic solution contains: ropivacaine HCl 10 mg. Nonmedicinal ingredients: sodium chloride, sodium hydroxide and/or hydrochloric acid to adjust pH to 4.0 to 6.0 and water for injection. Polyamp Duofit (plastic ampuls suitable for Luer lock and Luer fit syringes) of 10 and 20 mL packed in sterile blister packs.

Store solutions at 15 to 30°C. Do not autoclave.

Reviewed 1998

NASACORT™ Pr

Rhône-Poulenc Rorer

Triamcinolone Acetonide

Corticosteroid

Pharmacology: Triamcinolone is a potent anti-inflammatory steroid with strong topical and weak systemic activity. When administered intranasally in therapeutic doses, it has a direct anti-inflammatory action on the nasal mucosa, the mechanism of which is not yet completely defined. The minute amount absorbed in therapeutic doses has not been shown to exert any apparent clinical systemic effects.

Indications: For the topical treatment of the symptoms of perennial and seasonal allergic rhinitis unresponsive to conventional treatment.

Contraindications: Active or quiescent tuberculosis or untreated fungal, bacterial and viral infection. Hypersensitivity to any of the ingredients.

Warnings: In patients previously on prolonged periods or high doses of systemic steroids, the replacement with a topical corticosteroid can be accompanied by symptoms of withdrawal, e.g., joint and/or muscular pain, lassitude and depression; in severe cases, adrenal insufficiency may occur, necessitating the temporary resumption of systemic steroid therapy. Careful attention must be given to patients with asthma or other clinical conditions in whom a rapid decrease in systemic steroids may cause a severe exacerbation of their symptoms.

Pregnancy: See Precautions.

Precautions: The replacement of a systemic steroid with Nasacort has to be gradual and carefully supervised by the physician. The guidelines under Dosage should be followed in all such cases.

During long-term therapy pituitary-adrenal function and hematological status should be assessed.

Patients should be informed that the full effect of triamcinolone therapy is not achieved until 2 to 3 days of treatment have been completed. Treatment of seasonal rhinitis should, if possible, start before the exposure to allergens.

Treatment should not be stopped abruptly but tapered off gradually.

Corticosteroids may mask some signs of infection and new infections may appear. A decreased resistance to localized infections has been observed during corticosteroid therapy; this may require treatment with appropriate therapy or stopping the administration of triamcinolone.

The long-term effects of triamcinolone are still unknown, in particular, its local effects; the possibility of atrophic rhinitis and/or pharyngeal candidiasis should be kept in mind.

There is an enhanced effect of corticosteroids on patients with hypothyroidism and in those with cirrhosis. ASA should be used cautiously in conjunction with corticosteroids in hypothrombinemia.

Because of the inhibitory effect of corticosteroids on wound healing, in patients who have had recent nasal surgery or trauma, a nasal corticosteroid should be used with caution until healing has occurred. As with other nasally inhaled corticosteroids, nasal septal perforations have been reported in rare instances.

Patients should be advised to inform subsequent physicians of prior use of corticosteroids.

Until greater clinical experience has been gained, the continuous, long-term treatment of children under age 12 is not recommended.

Pregnancy: The safety of triamcinolone in pregnancy has not been established. If used, the expected benefits should be weighed against the potential hazard to the fetus, particularly during the first trimester of pregnancy.

Like other glucocorticosteroids, triamcinolone is teratogenic to rodents and nonhuman primates. The relevance of these findings to humans has not yet been established. Infants born of mothers who have received substantial doses of glucocorticosteroids during pregnancy should be carefully observed for hypoadrenalism.

Lactation: Glucocorticosteroids are secreted in human milk. It is not known whether triamcinolone would be secreted in human milk, but it is suspected to be likely. Its use in nursing mothers, requires that the possible benefits of the drug be weighed against the potential hazards to the infant.

Children: Triamcinolone is not presently recommended for children younger than 12 years of age due to limited clinical data in this age group.

Fluorocarbon propellants may be hazardous if they are deliberately abused. Inhalation of high concentrations of aerosol sprays has brought about cardiovascular toxic effects and even death, especially under conditions of hypoxia. Aerosols are safe when used properly and with adequate ventilation, but excessive use should be avoided.

To ensure the proper dosage and administration of the drug, the patient should be instructed by a physician or other health professional in the use of Nasacort (see Information for the Patient).

Adverse Effects: Adverse reactions reported in both controlled and uncontrolled studies involving 1 148 patients who received intranasal triamcinolone are provided in Table I.

Table I—Nasacort

Adverse Reactions

Adverse Experience	Nasacort % (n=1 077)	Placebo % (n=545)
Headache	20.4	19.4
Upper Respiratory Infection	5.3	8.1
Nasal Irritation	5.1	4.2
Throat Discomfort	4.6	3.3
Dry Mucous Membranes	3.5	2.2
Epistaxis	4.6	6.6
Sneezing	3.1	5.5
Sinusitis	2.1	3.7

When patients are transferred to Nasacort from a systemic steroid, allergic conditions such as asthma or eczema may be unmasked (see Warnings).

Overdose: Symptoms and Treatment: Like any other nasally administered corticosteroid, acute overdosing is unlikely in view of the total amount of active ingredient present. However when used chronically in excessive doses or in conjunction with other corticosteroid formulations, systemic corticosteroid effects such as hypercorticism and adrenal suppression may appear. If such changes recur, the dosage of triamcinolone should be discontinued slowly consistent with accepted procedures for discontinuation of chronic steroid therapy.

The restoration of hypothalamic-pituitary axis may be slow; during periods of pronounced physical stress (i.e., severe infections, trauma, surgery) a supplement with systemic steroids may be advisable.

Dosage: See Warnings.

Nasacort is not recommended for children under 12 years of age.

Careful attention must be given to patients previously treated for prolonged periods with systemic corticosteroids when transferred to Nasacort. Initially, Nasacort and the systemic corticosteroid must be given concomitantly, while the dose of the latter is gradually decreased. The usual rate of withdrawal of the systemic steroid is the equivalent of 2.5 mg of prednisone every 4 days if the patient is under close supervision. If continuous supervision is not feasible, the withdrawal of the systemic steroid should be slower, approximately 2.5 mg of prednisone (or equivalent) every 10 days. If withdrawal symptoms appear, the previous dose of the systemic steroid should be resumed for a week before further decrease is attempted.

The therapeutic effects of corticosteroids, unlike those of decongestants, are not immediate. Since the effect of Nasacort depends on its regular use, patients must be instructed to take the nasal inhalations at regular intervals and not as with other nasal sprays, as they feel necessary.

In the presence of excessive nasal mucus secretion or edema of the nasal mucosa, the drug may fail to reach the site of action. In such cases it is advisable to use a nasal vasoconstrictor for 2 to 3 days prior to Nasacort therapy. Patients should be instructed on the correct method of use, which is to blow the nose, then insert the nozzle firmly into the nostril, compress the opposite nostril and actuate the spray while inspiring through the nose, with the mouth closed.

An improvement of symptoms usually becomes apparent within a few days after the start of therapy. However, symptomatic relief may not occur in some patients for as long as 2 weeks. Nasacort should not be continued beyond 3 weeks in the absence of significant symptomatic improvement.

Adults and Children 12 Years of Age and Older: The recommended starting dose is 400 μg/day given as 2 sprays (100 μg/spray) in each nostril once a day. If needed, the dose may be increased to 800 μg/day (100 μg/spray) either as once a day dosage or divided up to 4 times a day, i.e., twice a day (2 sprays/nostril), or 4 times a day (1 spray/nostril).

After the desired effect is obtained, patients may be maintained on a dose of 1 spray (100 μg) in each nostril once a day (total daily dose: 200 μg/day).

Information for the Patient: See Blue Section—Information for the Patient "Nasacort".

Supplied: Each metered-dose aerosol unit contains a microcrystalline suspension of triamcinolone acetonide. Each canister contains: triamcinolone acetonide 15 mg. Each actuation releases approximately 100 μg triamcinolone acetonide of which approximately 55 μg are delivered from the nasal actuator to the patient (estimated from in vitro testing). Nonmedicinal ingredients: alcohol and dichlorodifluoromethane. There are at least 100 actuations in one canister. The device should not be used after 100 nasal inhalations, since the amount delivered thereafter per actuation may not be consistent. Boxes of 1 with a nasal adapter and patient instructions.

(Shown in Product Recognition Section)

NASACORT® AQ Pr

Rhône-Poulenc Rorer

Triamcinolone Acetonide

Corticosteroid

Pharmacology: Triamcinolone acetonide is a potent anti-inflammatory steroid with strong topical and weak systemic activity. Triamcinolone acetonide is a more potent derivative of triamcinolone. Although triamcinolone itself is approximately 1 to 2 times as potent as prednisone in animal models of inflammation, triamcinolone acetonide is approximately 8 times more potent than prednisone.

When administered intranasally in therapeutic doses, it has a direct anti-inflammatory action on the nasal mucosa, the mechanism of which is not yet completely defined. The minute amount absorbed in therapeutic doses has not been shown to exert any apparent clinical systemic effects.

Corticosteroids are very effective. However, when allergic symptoms are very severe, local treatment with recommended doses (μg) of any available topical corticosteroid are not as effective as treatment with larger doses (mg) of oral or parenteral formulations. Corticosteroids do not have an immediate effect on allergic signs and symptoms. An improvement of symptoms may be seen as early as the first day after initiation of treatment and full benefit may be expected in 3 to 4 days. However, symptomatic relief may not occur in some patients for as long as 2 weeks. Triamcinolone aqueous should not be continued beyond 3 weeks in the absence of significant symptomatic improvement.

Pharmacokinetics: Based upon i.v. dosing of triamcinolone acetonide phosphate ester, the half-life of triamcinolone acetonide was reported to be 88 minutes. The volume of distribution (Vd) reported was 99.5 L (SD±27.5) and clearance was 45.2 L/hour (SD±9.1) for triamcinolone acetonide. The plasma half-life of corticosteroids does not correlate well with the biologic half-life.

Pharmacokinetic characterization of the triamcinolone aqueous nasal spray formulation was determined in both normal subjects and in patients with allergic rhinitis. Single dose intranasal administration of 220 μg of triamcinolone aqueous in normal adult subjects and patients demonstrated minimal absorption of triamcinolone. The mean peak plasma concentration was approximately 0.5 ng/mL (range: 0.1 to 1 ng/mL) and occurred at 1.5 hours post dose. The mean plasma drug concentration was less than 0.06 ng/mL at 12 hours, and below the assay detection limit at 24 hours. The average terminal half-life was 3.1 hours. Dose proportionality was demonstrated in normal subjects and in patients following a single intranasal dose of 110 μg or 220 μg triamcinolone aqueous. Following multiple doses in pediatric patients ages 6 to 12 years old receiving 440 μg/day, plasma drug concentration, AUC, C_{max} and T_{max} were similar to those values observed in adult patients.

Triamcinolone aqueous administered intranasally has been shown to be minimally absorbed into the systemic circulation in humans. Patients with active rhinitis showed absorption similar to that found in normal volunteers.

In order to determine if systemic absorption plays a role in triamcinolone aqueous treatment of allergic rhinitis symptoms, a 2 week double-blind placebo-controlled clinical study was conducted comparing Nasacort AQ, orally ingested triamcinolone acetonide, and placebo in 297 patients with seasonal allergic rhinitis. The study demonstrated that the therapeutic efficacy of Nasacort AQ can be attributed to the topical effects of triamcinolone.

In order to evaluate the effects of systemic absorption on the Hypothalamic-Pituitary-Adrenal (HPA) axis, a clinical study was performed comparing 220 μg or 440 μg Nasacort AQ, or 10 mg prednisone to placebo for 42 days. Adrenal response to a 6-hour cosyntropin stimulation test clearly indicated that Nasacort AQ administered at doses of 220 μg and 440 μg had no effect on HPA activity versus placebo. Conversely, oral prednisone at 10 mg/day significantly reduced the response to ACTH.

A 6-week study was conducted in 80 pediatric patients to evaluate the effect of 220 μg or 440 μg of Nasacort AQ versus placebo on HPA function. No evidence of adrenal axis suppression was observed in the pediatric patients exposed to systemic levels of triamcinolone acetonide higher than the systemic levels observed following administration of the maximum recommended dose of Nasacort AQ Nasal Spray.

Clinical Trials: The safety and efficacy of triamcinolone aqueous nasal spray has been evaluated in 10 double-blind, placebo-controlled clinical trials in adults and children 12 years and older with seasonal or perennial allergic rhinitis. The number of patients treated with the triamcinolone aqueous nasal spray in these studies was 1 204; of these patients, 668 were males and 536 were females.

Overall, in double-blind clinical trials of 2 to 4 weeks duration, analysis of the clinical studies has demonstrated that triamcinolone aqueous nasal spray 220 μg once daily (2 sprays in each nostril) when compared to placebo provides statistically significant relief of nasal symptoms including sneezing, stuffiness, discharge, and itching.

The safety and efficacy of triamcinolone aqueous nasal spray, at doses of 110 or 220 μg once daily, has also been studied in 2 double blind placebo controlled trials of 2 and 12 weeks duration in children ages 4 through 12 years with seasonal and perennial allergic rhinitis. These trials included 355 males and 183 females. Triamcinolone aqueous administered at either dose resulted in statistically significant reductions of allergic rhinitis symptoms.

Indications: For the topical treatment of the symptoms of perennial and seasonal allergic rhinitis unresponsive to conventional treatment.

Regular usage is essential since maximum relief may not be obtained until after 2 to 3 days of treatment.

Contraindications: Hypersensitivity to any of the ingredients of the triamcinolone aqueous nasal spray, and patients with active or quiescent tuberculosis, or untreated fungal, bacterial and viral infection.

Warnings: In patients previously on prolonged periods or high doses of systemic steroids, the replacement with a topical corticosteroid can be accompanied by symptoms of withdrawal, e.g. joint and/or muscular pain, lassitude, and depression; in severe cases, adrenal insufficiency may occur, necessitating the temporary resumption of systemic steroid therapy. These patients should be carefully monitored for acute adrenal insufficiency in response to stress. Careful attention must be given to patients with asthma or other clinical conditions in whom a rapid decrease in systemic steroids may cause a severe exacerbation of their symptoms.

The use of triamcinolone aqueous nasal spray with alternate day systemic prednisone could increase the likelihood of hypothalamic-pituitary-adrenal (HPA) suppression compared to a therapeutic dose of either one alone. Therefore, triamcinolone aqueous nasal spray should be used with caution in patients already receiving alternate-day prednisone treatment for any disease.

Patients who are on immunosuppressant drugs are more susceptible to infections than healthy individuals. Chickenpox and measles, for example, can have a more serious or even fatal course in children or adults on immunosuppressant doses of corticosteroids. In such children, or in adults who have not had these diseases, particular care should be taken to avoid exposure. If exposed, therapy with varicella zoster immune globulin (VZIG) or pooled i.v. immunoglobulin (IVIG), as appropriate, may be indicated. If chickenpox develops, treatment with antiviral agents may be considered.

Pregnancy: See Precautions.

Precautions: The replacement of a systemic steroid with triamcinolone aqueous nasal spray has to be gradual and carefully supervised by the physician. The guidelines under Dosage should be followed in all such cases.

During long-term therapy pituitary-adrenal function and hematological status should be assessed.

Patients should be informed that the full effect of triamcinolone aqueous nasal spray therapy is not achieved until 2 to 3 days of treatment have been completed. Treatment of seasonal rhinitis should, if possible, start before the exposure to allergens.

Treatment with triamcinolone aqueous nasal spray should not be stopped abruptly but tapered off gradually.

Corticosteroids may mask some signs of infection and new infections may appear. A decreased resistance to localized infections has been observed during corticosteroid therapy; this may require treatment with appropriate therapy or stopping the administration of triamcinolone aqueous nasal spray.

Glaucoma and osteoporosis are possible adverse effects associated with a long-term use of large doses of corticosteroids. The possibility of atrophic rhinitis and/or pharyngeal candidiasis should be kept in mind.

There is an enhanced effect of corticosteroids on patients with hypothyroidism and in those with cirrhosis. ASA should be used cautiously in conjunction with corticosteroids in hypothrombinemia.

Because of the inhibitory effect of corticosteroids on wound healing, in patients who have had recent nasal surgery or trauma, a nasal corticosteroid should be used with caution until healing has occurred. As with other nasally inhaled corticosteroids, nasal septal perforations have been reported in rare instances.

Patients should be advised to inform subsequent physicians of prior use of corticosteroids.

Until greater clinical experience has been gained, the continuous, long-term treatment of children under age 4 is not recommended.

Pregnancy: The safety of triamcinolone aqueous nasal spray in pregnancy has not been established. If used, the expected benefits should be weighed against the potential hazard to the fetus, particularly during the first trimester of pregnancy.

Like other glucocorticosteroids, triamcinolone acetonide is teratogenic to rodents and non-human primates. The relevance of these findings to humans has not yet been established. Infants born of mothers who have received substantial doses of glucocorticosteroids during pregnancy should be carefully observed for hypoadrenalism.

Lactation: Glucocorticosteroids are excreted in human milk. It is not known whether triamcinolone would be secreted in human milk, but it is suspected to be likely. The use of triamcinolone aqueous nasal spray in nursing mothers, requires that the possible benefits of the drug be weighed against the potential hazards to the infant.

Children: Triamcinolone aqueous nasal spray is not presently recommended for children younger than 4 years of age due to limited clinical data in this age group. Oral corticosteroids have been shown to cause growth suppression in children and teenagers, particularly with higher doses over extended periods. If a child or teenager on any corticosteroids appears to have growth suppression, the possibility that they are particularly sensitive to this effect of steroids should be considered.

To ensure the proper dosage and administration of the drug, the patient should be instructed by a physician or other health professional in the use of triamcinolone aqueous nasal spray (see Information for the Patient).

Adverse Effects: In placebo-controlled, double-blind and open-label clinical studies, 1 483 adults and children 12 years and older received treatment with triamcinolone acetonide aqueous nasal spray. These patients were treated for an average duration of 50.7 days. In the controlled, seasonal trials (2 to 5 weeks duration) from which the following adverse reaction data is derived, 1 394 patients were treated with triamcinolone aqueous nasal spray for an average of 18.7 days. In the long-term, open-label study, the 172 patients enrolled received treatment for an average of 286 days duration.

The most commonly reported adverse reactions included those involving mucous membranes of the nose and throat. The 3 most prevalent adverse reactions considered to be at least possibly drug-related in adults and children 12 years and older were rhinitis (1.5%), headache (0.7%), and pharyngitis (0.3%) and in children 4 to 12 years were epistaxis (3.1%), rhinitis (1.4%) and headache (1.2%).

Children 4 to 12 years of age (n=622) were studied in 3 controlled clinical trials. Of these, 179 received 110 μg/day and 215 received 220 μg/day of triamcinolone aqueous nasal spray in 2-, 6-, or 12-week trials. The longest average duration of treatment for patients receiving 110 μg/day was 76.3 days and 79.6 days for those receiving 220 μg/day.

The incidence of specific nasopharyngeal-related adverse reactions considered drug related is summarized in Table I.

These adverse reactions, with the exception of epistaxis (in adults), and the exception of nasal congestion and sneezing (in children) were reported at approximately the same or lower incidence as placebo treated patients. Only 1% of the patients in the controlled trials discontinued treatment (e.g. pharyngitis, headache). In children, no patient receiving 110 μg/day discontinued due to a serious adverse event and 1 patient receiving 220 μg/day discontinued due to a serious event that was considered not drug-related. Overall, these studies found the adverse experience profile for triamcinolone aqueous nasal spray to be similar to placebo.

Table II (on following page) summarizes the adverse events (% of patients) present in at least 5% of patients in the double-blind and open label phase studies in adults and in controlled studies in children 4 to 12 years of age.

In the event of accidental overdose, an increased potential for these adverse experiences may be expected, but systemic adverse experiences are unlikely (see Overdose).

Hypersensitivity reactions including skin rash and edema of the face or tongue have been reported with other intranasal corticosteroids.

When patients are transferred to triamcinolone aqueous nasal spray from a systemic steroid, allergic conditions such as asthma or eczema may be unmasked (see Warnings).

Overdose: Symptoms and Treatment: Like any other nasally administered corticosteroid, acute overdosing is unlikely in

Table I—Nasacort AQ

Nasopharyngeal-Related Adverse Reactions

Variables	Placebo (N=176)	Nasacort AQ 110 μg (N=179)	Nasacort AQ 220 μg (N=187)	Placebo (N=626)	Nasacort AQ 27.5-440 μg (N=1 068)
Nasal AEs (overall)	15 (8.5%)	8 (4.5%)	12 (6.4%)	20 (3.2%)	31 (2.9%)
Dry mucous membranes	0	0	0	2 (0.3%)	3 (0.3%)
Epistaxis	9 (5.1%)	6 (3.4%)	6 (3.2%)	3 (0.5%)	17 (1.6%)
Nasal irritation	5 (2.8%)	0	2 (1.1%)	3 (0.5%)	9 (0.8%)
Naso-sinus congestion	0	1 (0.6%)	1 (0.5%)	1 (0.2%)	2 (0.2%)
Sneezing	1 (0.6%)	0	2 (1.1%)	6 (1.0%)	2 (0.2%)
Throat discomfort	1 (0.6%)	1 (0.6%)	1 (0.5%)	6 (1.0%)	3 (0.3%)

Nasacort AQ (cont'd)

Table II—Nasacort AQ

Adverse Events

	Studies in Adults		
	Double-Blind		Open-Label
Variables	**Placebo N=90**	**Nasacort AQ 220 µg N=88**	**Nasacort AQ 220/110 µg N=172**
Flu Syndrome	5 (5.6%)	5 (5.7%)	17 (9.9%)
Headache	12 (13.3%)	6 (6.8%)	38 (22.1%)
Epistaxis	1 (1.1%)	6 (6.8%)	31 (18.0%)
Pharyngitis	5 (5.6%)	13 (14.8%)	55 (32.0%)
Rhinitis	5 (5.6%)	6 (6.8%)	49 (28.5%)
Injury Accident	–	–	20 (11.6%)
Back Pain	–	–	13 (7.6%)
Cough Increased	–	–	14 (8.1%)
Sinusitis	–	–	27 (15.7%)
Pain	–	–	10 (5.8%)
Diarrhea	–	–	10 (5.8%)

Adverse Events

Variables	**Placebo N=202**	**Nasacort AQ 110 µg N=179**	**Nasacort AQ 220 µg N=215**	**Nasacort AQ 440 µg N=26**
Fever	11 (5.4%)	8 (4.5%)	12 (5.6%)	2 (7.7%)
Flu Syndrome	15 (7.4%)	16 (8.9%)	4 (1.9%)	0
Headache	22 (10.9%)	18 (10.1%)	16 (7.4%)	4 (15.4%)
Infection	15 (7.4%)	13 (7.3%)	16 (7.4%)	0
Injury Accidental	3 (1.5%)	3 (1.7%)	4 (1.9%)	2 (7.7%)
Cough Increased	13 (6.4%)	15 (8.4%)	15 (7.0%)	0
Epistaxis	14 (6.9%)	8 (4.5%)	10 (4.7%)	1 (3.8%)
Pharyngitis	13 (6.4%)	14 (7.8%)	16 (7.4%)	2 (7.7%)
Rhinitis	18 (8.9%)	18 (10.1%)	18 (8.4%)	0
Sinusitis	16 (6.4%)	7 (3.9%)	7 (3.3%)	0

view of the total amount of active ingredient present. In the event that the entire contents of the bottle were administered all at once, via either oral or nasal application, clinically significant systemic adverse events would most likely not result. The patient may experience some gastrointestinal upset.

However when used chronically in excessive doses or in conjunction with other corticosteroid formulations, systemic corticosteroid effects such as hypercorticism and adrenal suppression may appear. If such changes occur, the dosage of triamcinolone aqueous nasal spray should be discontinued slowly consistent with accepted procedures for discontinuation of chronic steroid therapy (see Dosage).

The restoration of hypothalamic-pituitary axis may be slow; during periods of pronounced physical stress (i.e. severe infections, trauma, surgery) a supplement with systemic steroids may be advisable.

Dosage: See Warnings.

Not recommended for children under 4 years of age.

Careful attention must be given to patients previously treated for prolonged periods with systemic corticosteroids when transferred to triamcinolone aqueous nasal spray. Initially, triamcinolone aqueous nasal spray and the systemic corticosteroid must be given concomitantly, while the dose of the latter is gradually decreased. The usual rate of withdrawal of the systemic steroid is the equivalent of 2.5 mg of prednisone every 4 days if the patient is under close supervision. If continuous supervision is not feasible, the withdrawal of the systemic steroid should be slower, approximately 2.5 mg of prednisone (or equivalent) every 10 days. If withdrawal symptoms appear, the previous dose of the systemic steroid should be resumed for a week before further decrease is attempted.

The therapeutic effects of corticosteroids, unlike those of decongestants, are not immediate. Since the effect of triamcinolone aqueous nasal spray depends on its regular use, patients must be instructed to take the nasal inhalations at regular intervals and not as with other nasal sprays, as they feel necessary.

In the presence of excessive nasal mucus secretion or edema of the nasal mucosa, the drug may fail to reach the site of action. In such cases it is advisable to use a nasal vasoconstrictor for 2 to 3 days prior to triamcinolone aqueous nasal spray therapy. Patients should be instructed on the correct method of use, which is to blow the nose, then insert the nozzle firmly into the nostril, compress the opposite nostril and actuate the spray while inspiring through the nose, with the mouth closed.

An improvement of symptoms usually becomes apparent within a few days after the start of therapy. However symptomatic relief may not occur in some patients for as long as 2 weeks. The triamcinolone aqueous nasal spray should not be continued beyond 3 weeks in the absence of significant symptomatic improvement.

Adults and Children 12 years of age and older: The recommended starting dose is 220 µg as 2 sprays in each nostril once daily.

It is always desirable to titrate an individual patient to the minimum effective dose to reduce the possibility of side effects. Therefore, when the maximum benefit has been achieved and symptoms have been controlled, reducing the dose to 110 µg (1 spray in each nostril once/day) has been shown to be effective in maintaining control of the allergic rhinitis symptoms in patients who were initially controlled at 220 µg/day (see Precautions, Warnings, Information for the Patient, and Adverse Effects).

Children 4 to 12 years of age: The recommended starting dose is 110 µg/day given as 1 spray in each nostril once a day. Patients who do not achieve maximum symptom control may benefit from a dose of 220 µg given as 2 sprays in each nostril once a day. Once symptoms are controlled, patients can be maintained on 110 µg (1 spray in each nostril) once daily.

Information for the Patient: See Blue Section—Information for the Patient "Nasacort AQ"

Supplied: Each actuation releases approximately triamcinolone acetonide 55 µg from the nasal actuator to the patient (estimated from in vitro testing) in an unscented, thixotrophic, water-based formulation. Nonmedicinal ingredients: benzalkonium chloride, carboxymethylcellulose, dextrose, disodium EDTA, hydrochloric acid, microcrystalline cellulose, polysorbate 80, purified water and sodium hydroxide. Non-chlorofluorocarbon (CFC) containing-metered dose pump spray which will provide 120 actuations. After 120 actuations, the amount delivered per actuation may not be consistent and the unit should be discarded. It is supplied with a nasal adapter and patient instructions including a check-off form to track usage. Each bottle contains triamcinolone acetonide 9.075 mg. Store at controlled room temperature (15 to 30°C).

(Shown in Product Recognition Section)

Reviewed 1998

NATAVITE™
Schein Pharmaceutical
Multivitamins—Minerals
Prenatal Supplement

Supplied: Each coated tablet contains: vitamin A (as palmitate) 2 000 IU, beta-carotene 4 000 IU, vitamin D_3 400 IU, thiamine (as mononitrate) 5 mg, riboflavin 3 mg, pyridoxine HCl 3 mg, niacinamide 20 mg, folic acid 1 mg, vitamin B_{12} 5 µg, ascorbic acid 100 mg, iron (as fumarate) 60 mg and calcium (as carbonate) 160 mg. Bottles of 100. Security seal on the cap. Do not use if seal is broken. Keep out of reach of children.

NAVANE™ Ⓟ
Pfizer
Thiothixene
Antipsychotic

Pharmacology: Thiothixene is an antipsychotic agent of the thioxanthene series. It possesses certain chemical and pharmacologic similarities to the piperazine phenothiazines and differences from the aliphatic group of phenothiazines. Thiothixene's mode of action has not been clearly established.

Indications: An antipsychotic agent useful in the management of schizophrenia and other psychotic disorders.

As with other antipsychotic agents, some patients resistant to previous medication have responded favorably to thiothixene. It may also be of value in the management of withdrawn, apathetic schizophrenic patients.

Thiothixene is not recommended for the treatment of nonpsychotic mental and emotional disorders.

Contraindications: Children: Safety for use in children under 12 years of age has not yet been established.

Circulatory collapse, comatose states, CNS depression due to any cause and blood dyscrasias.

Known hypersensitivity to the drug. It is not known whether a cross sensitivity between the thioxanthenes and the phenothiazines exists, but this possibility should be considered.

Warnings: Occupational Hazards: As is true with many CNS drugs, thiothixene may impair the mental and/or physical abilities required for the performance of potentially hazardous tasks such as driving a car or operating machinery, especially during the first few days of therapy. Therefore, the patient should be cautioned accordingly.

As in the case of other CNS-acting drugs, patients should be cautioned about the possible additive effects (which may include hypotension) with CNS depressants and with alcohol. Potentiation of CNS depressants (sedatives, tranquilizers, narcotic analgesics, antihistamines, anesthetics, alcohol), atropine and organophosphorus insecticides, and reversal of epinephrine effect, have been observed with related drugs.

Pregnancy: Safe use in pregnancy has not been established. It should, therefore, not be used in women of childbearing potential unless, in the opinion of the physician, the expected benefits of the drug outweigh the potential hazard to the fetus.

Precautions: In consideration of the known capability of thiothixene and certain other antipsycotic drugs to precipitate convulsions, extreme caution should be used in patients with a history of convulsive disorders or those in a state of alcohol withdrawal, since it may lower the convulsive threshold. Although the drug potentiates the actions of the barbiturates, the dosage of the anticonvulsant therapy should not be reduced when it is administered concurrently.

Production or aggravation of ECG changes has occurred with thiothixene and therefore caution should be observed when there is increased risk to the patient (see Adverse Effects).

Though exhibiting rather weak anticholinergic properties, thiothixene should be used with caution in patients who are known or are suspected to have glaucoma, and in those who might be exposed to extreme heat or who are receiving atropine or related drugs. Undue exposure to sunlight should be avoided. Photosensitive reactions have been reported in patients.

Careful observation should be made for pigmentary retinopathy, and lenticular pigmentation (fine lenticular pigmentation has been noted in a small number of patients treated with thiothixene for prolonged periods). Blood dyscrasias (agranulocytosis, pancytopenia, thrombocytopenic purpura), and liver damage (jaundice, biliary stasis), have been reported with related drugs.

Caution as well as careful adjustment of the dosages is indicated when thiothixene is used in conjunction with other CNS depressants.

An antiemetic effect observed in animal studies may also occur in man; therefore, it is possible that thiothixene may mask signs of overdosage of toxic drugs and it may obscure conditions such as intestinal obstruction and brain tumor.

To lessen the likelihood of adverse reactions related to drug accumulation, patients on long-term therapy, particularly on high doses, should be evaluated periodically to decide whether the maintenance dosage could be lowered or drug therapy discontinued. Periodic blood counts and liver function tests should be performed. Sudden onset of severe CNS or vasomotor symptoms should be kept in mind.

Adverse Effects: Since thiothixene has pharmacologic properties similar to those of the phenothiazines, all the known adverse reactions of that class of drugs should be borne in mind when it is used.

Behavioral: The most common side effects are initial and transient drowsiness, restlessness and agitation and insomnia. (The incidence of sedation appears to be similar to that of the piperazine group of phenothiazines, but less than that of certain aliphatic phenothiazines.)

Other adverse reactions reported less frequently are weakness or fatigue, excitement, depression and headache.

Psychic and motor hyperactivity may be desirable, except in an already agitated and excited patient. Activation of psychotic symptomatology has been observed, but it usually responds to reduction of dosage or temporary discontinuation of the drug. Toxic confusional states may occur on rare occasions.

Neurological: The incidence and nature of extrapyramidal symptoms, including akathisia, pseudo-parkinsonism and dystonic reactions, are similar to those encountered with the piperazine phenothiazines, but thiothixene is more likely to produce akathisia. They are usually controlled by reduction of dosage and/or administration of antiparkinson drugs depending on the type and severity of symptoms. Cerebral seizures have been reported (see Precautions). Phenothiazine derivatives have been associated with cerebral edema and cerebrospinal fluid abnormalities.

Hyperreflexia has been reported in infants delivered from mothers having received structurally related drugs.

Tardive Dyskinesias: As with all antipsychotic agents, tardive dyskinesia may appear in some patients on long-term therapy or may appear after drug therapy has been discontinued. The risk appears to be greater in elderly patients on high dose therapy, especially females. The symptoms are persistent and in some patients appear to be irreversible. The syndrome is characterized by rhythmical involuntary movements of the tongue, face, mouth or jaw (e.g., protrusion of tongue, puffing of cheeks, puckering of mouth, chewing movements). Sometimes these may be accompanied by involuntary movements of extremities.

There is no known effective treatment for tardive dyskinesia; antiparkinsonian agents usually do not alleviate the symptoms of this syndrome. All antipsychotic agents should be discontinued if these symptoms appear. Should it be necessary to reinstitute treatment, or increase the dosage of the agent, or switch to a different antipsychotic agent, the syndrome may be masked. The physician may be able to reduce the risk of this syndrome by minimizing the unnecessary use of neuroleptics and reducing the dose or discontinuing the drug, if possible, when manifestations of this syndrome are recognized, particularly in patients over the age of 50. Fine vermicular movements of the tongue may be an early sign of the syndrome. If the medication is stopped at that time, the syndrome may not develop.

Autonomic: Dry mouth, blurred vision, nasal congestion, constipation, increased salivation and sweating, and impotence have occurred infrequently. Phenothiazines have been associated with miosis, mydriasis and adynamic ileus.

Cardiovascular: tachycardia, hypotension, lightheadedness, and syncope. (In the event hypotension occurs, epinephrine should **not** be used as a pressor agent since a paradoxical further lowering of blood pressure may result.) Nonspecific ECG changes have been observed in some patients receiving thiothixene. These changes are usually reversible and frequently disappear on continued therapy. The clinical significance of these changes is not known. Cardiac arrhythmias, including AV block, paroxysmal tachycardia and ventricular fibrillation have been observed with some phenothiazines.

Note: Sudden deaths have occasionally been reported in patients who have received certain phenothiazine derivatives. In some cases the cause of death was apparently cardiac arrest or asphyxia due to failure of the cough reflex. In others, the cause could not be determined nor could it be established that death was due to phenothiazine administration.

Endocrine: Lactation, moderate breast enlargement and amenorrhea have occurred in a small percentage of females receiving thiothixene. If persistent, this may necessitate a reduction in dosage or the discontinuation of therapy. Phenothiazines have been associated with false positive pregnancy tests, gynecomastia, hypoglycemia, hyperglycemia, and glycosuria.

Allergic: Rash, pruritus, urticaria, and rare cases of anaphylaxis have been reported. Undue exposure to sunlight should be avoided. Although not experienced with thiothixene, exfoliative dermatitis, contact dermatitis (in nursing personnel), have been reported with certain phenothiazines.

Hematologic: As is true with certain other antipsychotic drugs, leukopenia and leukocytosis, which are usually transient, can occur occasionally. Other antipsychotic drugs have been associated with agranulocytosis, eosinophilia, hemolytic anemia, thrombocytopenia and pancytopenia.

Hepatic: Elevations of serum transaminase and alkaline phosphatase, usually transient, have been infrequently observed in some patients. No clinically confirmed cases of jaundice attributable to the drug have been reported.

Ophthalmological: fine lenticular pigmentation after prolonged therapy.

Miscellaneous: hyperpyrexia, anorexia, nausea, vomiting, diarrhea, increase in appetite and weight, weakness or fatigue, polydipsia and peripheral edema. Although not reported with thiothixene, evidence indicates there is a relationship between phenothiazine therapy and the occurrence of a systemic lupus erythematosus-like syndrome.

Overdose: Symptoms: Manifestations include muscular twitching, drowsiness, and dizziness. Symptoms of gross overdosage may include CNS depression, rigidity, weakness, torticollis, tremor, salivation, dysphagia, hypotension, disturbances of gait, or coma.

Treatment: Essentially symptomatic and supportive. Early gastric lavage may be helpful. Keep patient under careful observation and maintain an open airway, since involvement of the extrapyramidal system may produce dysphagia and respiratory difficulty in severe overdosage. If hypotension occurs, the standard measures for managing circulatory shock should be used (i.v. fluids and/or vasoconstrictors).

If a vasoconstrictor is needed, norepinephrine and phenylephrine are the most suitable drugs. Other pressor agents, including epinephrine, are **not** recommended, since phenothiazine derivatives may reverse the usual pressor elevating action of these agents and cause further lowering of blood pressure.

If CNS depression is present, recommended stimulants include caffeine and sodium benzoate. Picrotoxin or pentylenetetrazol should be avoided. Extrapyramidal symptoms may be treated with antiparkinson drugs.

There are no data on the use of peritoneal or hemodialysis, but they are known to be of little value in phenothiazine intoxication.

Dosage: The usual optimal dosage of thiothixene is in the range of 15 to 30 mg daily. In most conditions, the initial dosage should be 5 to 10 mg daily. The dosage should be gradually increased to the optimally effective level based on patient response. An increase to 60 mg/day may be necessary; however, exceeding a total daily dosage of 60 mg/day rarely increases beneficial response. Patients on the average therapeutic dosage may be maintained on once a day therapy. Higher dosage can be given in 2 or 3 equally divided doses. The dosage should be reduced to the lowest possible maintenance level as soon as possible.

Supplied: 2 mg: Each white, hard gelatin capsule contains: thiothixene 2 mg. Nonmedicinal ingredients: cornstarch, lactose, magnesium stearate and sodium lauryl sulfate; capsule shell: gelatin, silicon dioxide, sodium lauryl sulfate and titanium dioxide. Tartrazine-free. Bottles of 100.

5 mg: Each orange and white, hard gelatin capsule contains: thiothixene 5 mg. Nonmedicinal ingredients: cornstarch, lactose, magnesium stearate and sodium lauryl sulfate; capsule shell: FD&C Red No. 3, FD&C Yellow No. 6, gelatin, silicon dioxide, sodium lauryl sulfate and titanium dioxide. Tartrazine-free. Bottles of 100.

10 mg: Each orange, hard gelatin capsule contains: thiothixene 10 mg. Nonmedicinal ingredients: cornstarch, lactose, magnesium stearate and sodium lauryl sulfate; capsule shell: FD&C Red No. 3, FD&C Yellow No. 6, gelatin, silicon dioxide, sodium lauryl sulfate and titanium dioxide. Tartrazine-free. Bottles of 100.

Store between 15 and 30°C.

(Shown in Product Recognition Section)

NAVELBINE® Ⓟ

Glaxo Wellcome

Vinorelbine Tartrate

Antineoplastic

Pharmacology: Vinorelbine is a novel vinca alkaloid which interferes with microtubule assembly. Vinca alkaloids are structurally similar compounds comprising two multiringed units, vindoline and catharanthine. Vinorelbine is a vinca alkaloid in which the catharanthine unit is the site of structural modification. This structural change imparts unique pharmacologic properties which may translate into clinical benefits for patients with various malignancies. The antitumor activity of vinorelbine is thought to be due primarily to inhibition of mitosis at metaphase through its interaction with tubulin. Vinorelbine may also interfere with amino acid, cyclic AMP, and glutathione metabolism; calmodulin-dependent Ca^{++}-transport ATPase activity; cellular respiration; and nucleic acid and lipid biosynthesis.

Pharmacokinetics: Following i.v. administration, vinorelbine concentration in plasma decays in a triphasic manner. The initial rapid decline represents distribution of drug to peripheral compartments and metabolism of the drug. The prolonged terminal phase is due to relatively slow efflux of vinorelbine from peripheral compartments. The terminal phase half-life averaged 27.7 to 43.6 hours; the mean plasma clearances ranged from 0.97 to 1.26 L/hr/kg; and steady state volume of distribution (V_{ss}) values ranged from 25.4 to 40.1 L/kg.

The disposition of radiolabeled vinorelbine has been studied in a limited number of patients. Approximately 18% of the administered dose was recovered in the urine and 46% in the feces. Incomplete recovery in humans is consistent with results in animals. A separate study of the urinary excretion of vinorelbine showed that $10.9\% \pm 0.7\%$ of a 30 mg/m² i.v. dose was excreted unchanged in the urine.

One metabolite of vinorelbine, deacetylvinorelbine, has been shown to possess antitumor activity. This metabolite has been detected but not quantified in human plasma. The effects of renal or hepatic dysfunction on the disposition of vinorelbine have not been assessed.

The pharmacokinetics of vinorelbine are not influenced by the concurrent administration of cisplatin with vinorelbine (see Precautions, Drug Interactions).

Indications: In the treatment of advanced non-small cell lung cancer (NSCLC), as a single agent or in combination.

Also indicated for the treatment of patients with metastatic breast cancer who have failed standard first-line chemotherapy for metastatic disease. In addition, vinorelbine is indicated for the treatment of patients with metastatic breast cancer who have relapsed within 6 months of anthracycline-based adjuvant therapy.

Contraindications: In patients with known hypersensitivity to vinorelbine.

As with other vinca alkaloids, vinorelbine is contraindicated in patients who have drug-induced severe granulocytopenia or severe thrombocytopenia.

Warnings: Vinorelbine is a cytotoxic drug and should be used only by physicians experienced with cancer chemotherapeutic drugs. Blood counts should be taken prior to each dose. The dosage should be reduced or the drug discontinued upon evidence of abnormal depression of the bone marrow.

This preparation is for i.v. administration only. Intrathecal administration of other vinca alkaloids has resulted in death. Syringes containing this product should be labelled "Warning—For Intravenous use only". Fatal if given intrathecally.

Vinorelbine is for i.v. use only. Vinorelbine is a moderate vesicant and can produce phlebitis or extravasation injury. Inadequate flushing of the vein after peripheral administration may increase the risk of phlebitis.

It is extremely important that the needle be properly positioned in the vein before this product is injected. If leakage into surrounding tissue should occur during i.v. administration of vinorelbine, it may cause severe irritation. The injection should be discontinued immediately, and any remaining portion of the dose should then be introduced into another vein.

A low incidence of death (1%) due to neutropenic sepsis has been reported (see Adverse Effects). Bone marrow toxicity, specifically granulocytopenia, is dose-limiting. Complete blood counts with differentials should be performed and results reviewed prior to each dose of vinorelbine. Vinorelbine should not be administered to patients with granulocyte counts

Navelbine (cont'd)

<1 000 cells/mm³. Patients developing severe granulocytopenia should be monitored carefully for evidence of infection and/or fever (see Dosage).

Pregnancy: There are no studies in pregnant women. Vinorelbine has been shown to be embryotoxic and/or fetotoxic in animals. Vinorelbine should not be used in pregnancy.

Lactation: It is not known whether the drug is excreted in human milk. Because many drugs are excreted in human milk and because of its potential for serious adverse reactions in nursing infants, it is recommended that nursing be discontinued in women who are receiving therapy with vinorelbine.

Children: Safety and effectiveness in children have not been established.

Precautions: General: In all instances where the use of vinorelbine is considered for chemotherapy, the physician must evaluate the need and usefulness of the drug against the risk of adverse events. Most drug-related adverse reactions are reversible. If severe adverse events occur, the drug should be reduced in dosage or discontinued and appropriate corrective measures should be taken based on the clinical judgment of the physician. Reinstitution of therapy with vinorelbine should be carried out with caution and alertness as to possible recurrence of toxicity.

Vinorelbine should be used with extreme caution in patients whose bone marrow reserve may have been compromised by prior irradiation or chemotherapy, or whose marrow function is recovering from previous chemotherapy.

Administration of vinorelbine to patients with prior radiation therapy may result in radiation recall reactions (see Adverse Effects and Drug Interactions).

Patients with a prior history or pre-existing neuropathy, regardless of etiology, should be monitored for new or worsening signs and symptoms of neuropathy while receiving vinorelbine.

Acute shortness of breath and severe bronchospasm have been reported infrequently following the administration of vinorelbine and of other vinca alkaloids. These events have been encountered most commonly when the vinca alkaloid was used in combination with mitomycin and may require aggressive treatment, particularly when there is pre-existing pulmonary dysfunction. Bronchodilators, steroids and/or oxygen have produced symptomatic relief.

Care must be exercised to avoid contamination of the eye with vinorelbine. Accidental exposure should be treated immediately with a large volume of irrigation solution (water or sodium chloride).

Hematologic: Since dose-limiting clinical toxicity is the result of depression of the white blood cell count, it is imperative that complete blood counts with differentials be obtained prior to each dose of vinorelbine (see Adverse Effects, Hematologic).

Hepatic: There is no evidence that the toxicity of vinorelbine is enhanced in patients with elevated liver enzymes; no data are available for patients with severe baseline cholestasis. However, pharmacologic evidence suggests that the liver plays an important role in the metabolism of vinorelbine. Although there are no data available from patients with severe liver disease, caution should be exercised when administering vinorelbine to patients with severe hepatic injury or impairment.

Drug Interactions: Acute pulmonary reactions have been reported with vinorelbine and other vinca alkaloids used in conjunction with mitomycin (see Precautions, General). Vinorelbine should be administered with caution in combination with mitomycin. Although the pharmacokinetics of vinorelbine are not influenced by the concurrent administration of cisplatin, the incidence of toxicities, specifically granulocytopenia, with the combination of vinorelbine and cisplatin is significantly higher than with single-agent vinorelbine.

Patients who receive vinorelbine and paclitaxel, either concomitantly or sequentially, should be monitored for signs and symptoms of neuropathy. Administration of vinorelbine to patients with prior or concomitant radiation therapy may result in radiosensitizing effects.

Pregnancy: See Warnings.

Geriatrics: Of the total number of patients in North American clinical studies of i.v. vinorelbine, approximately one-third were 65 years of age or greater. No overall differences in effectiveness or safety were observed between these patients and younger patients. Other reported clinical experience has not identified differences in responses between the elderly and younger patients, but greater sensitivity of some older individuals cannot be ruled out.

Information for the Patient: Patients should be informed that vinorelbine is a vesicant and can produce phlebitis or extravasation injury, and that the major acute toxicities of vinorelbine are related to bone marrow toxicity, specifically granulocytopenia with increased susceptibility to infection, and neuropathy. They should also be advised to report fever or chills immediately. Vinorelbine should not be used in pregnancy unless the physician feels the potential benefit justifies the risk of potential harm to the fetus.

Adverse Effects: Data in Tables I and II are based on the experience of 365 patients (143 patients with NSCLC; 222 patients with advanced breast cancer) for whom a complete safety database was available and who were treated with vinorelbine as a single agent in 3 North American trials (1 NSCLC trial and 2 advanced breast cancer trials). Patients treated for breast cancer were allowed to have received adjuvant chemotherapy in both trials, and in one, up to two prior regimens for advanced disease. The dosing schedule was 30 mg/m² i.v. vinorelbine on a weekly basis.

Hematologic: Granulocytopenia was the major dose-limiting toxicity with vinorelbine; it was generally reversible and not cumulative over time. Granulocyte nadirs occurred 7 to 10 days after the dose and usually recovered within the following 7 to 14 days. Granulocytopenia resulted in hospitalizations for fever and/or sepsis in 8% of NSCLC and 9% of breast cancer patients. Septic deaths occurred in approximately 1% of patients.

Table I—Navelbine

Hematologic Adverse Events and Clinical Chemistry Elevations in 365 Patients Receiving Single-Agent Navelbine that are Possibly Attributable to the Study Medication[a,b]

Hematology		ABC (%)	NSCLC (%)
Granulocytopenia	<2 000 cells/mm³	96	80
	<500 cells/mm³	41	28
Leukopenia	<4 000 cells/mm³	99	81
	<1 000 cells/mm³	16	12
Thrombocytopenia	<100 000 cells/mm³	6	4
	<50 000 cells/mm³	<1	1
Anemia	<11 g/dL Hgb	87	77
	<8 g/dL Hgb	14	1
Hospitalizations due to granulocytopenic complications		9	8

	% Incidence All Grades		% Incidence Grade 3		% Incidence Grade 4	
Clinical Chemistry Elevations	**ABC**	**NSCLC**	**ABC**	**NSCLC**	**ABC**	**NSCLC**
Total Bilirubin NSCLC: n=137 ABC: n=214	14	9	4	3	3	2
AST NSCLC: n=133 ABC: n=213	74	54	7	2	<1	1

Legend: ABC=Advanced Breast Cancer.
NSCLC=Non-Small Cell Lung Cancer.

[a]Grade based on modified criteria of the National Cancer Institute.

[b]Patients with NSCLC had not received prior chemotherapy. The majority of patients with advanced breast cancer had received prior chemotherapy.

Table II—Navelbine

Summary of Adverse Events Occurring in ≥5% of 365 Patients Receiving Single-Agent Navelbine that are Possibly Attributable to the Study Medication[a,b]

	% Incidence All Grades		% Incidence Grade 3		% Incidence Grade 4	
Adverse Event	**ABC n=222**	**NSCLC n=143**	**ABC n=222**	**NSCLC n=143**	**ABC n=222**	**NSCLC n=143**
General						
Injection site reaction	21	38	1	5	0	0
Asthenia	41	25	8	5	0	0
Pain	16	15	3	2	0	0
Pain injection site	18	13	3	1	0	0
Fever	19	10	1	0	0	1
Pain Abdomen	12	6	1	1	0	0
Pain Chest	8	5	1	2	0	0
Phlebitis	5	10	0	1	0	0
Digestive						
Nausea	50	33	3	1	0	0
Constipation	38	28	3	2	0	0
Anorexia	19	16	<1	2	0	0
Stomatitis	16	15	0	0	0	0
Vomiting	23	14	2	1	0	0
Diarrhea	20	13	<1	1	0	0
Musculoskeletal						
Myasthenia	9	5	2	1	<1	0
Nervous System						
Paresthesia	20	11	0	1	0	0
Hypesthesia	11	10	<1	0	<1	0
Respiratory						
Dyspnea	9	3	1	2	1	0
Skin and Appendages						
Alopecia	12	12	0	1	0	0
Rash	5	5	0	0	0	0

Legend: ABC=Advanced Breast Cancer.
NSCLC=Non-Small Cell Lung Cancer.

[a]Grade based on modified criteria of the National Cancer Institute.

[b]Patients with NSCLC had not received prior chemotherapy. The majority of patients with advanced breast cancer had received prior chemotherapy.

Grade 3 or 4 anemia occurred in 1% of lung cancer and 14% of breast cancer patients. Blood products were administered to 18% of patients who received vinorelbine. The incidence of Grade 3 and 4 thrombocytopenia was less than 1%.

Neurologic: Mild to moderate peripheral neuropathy manifested by paresthesia and hypesthesia were the most frequently reported neurologic toxicities (10% to 20%, see Table II). Loss of deep tendon reflexes occurred in less than 5% of patients. The development of severe peripheral neuropathy was unusual.

Dermatologic: Alopecia was reported in only 12% of patients and was usually mild.

Vinorelbine is a moderate vesicant. Injection site reactions, including erythema, pain at injection site, and vein discoloration occurred in approximately one-third of all patients; 2% were severe. Chemical phlebitis along the vein proximal to the site of injection was reported.

Gastrointestinal: Mild or moderate nausea occurred in 32% of NSCLC and 47% of breast cancer patients treated with vinorelbine. Severe nausea was infrequent (1% and 3% in NSCLC and breast cancer patients, respectively). Prophylactic administration of antiemetics was not routine in patients treated with single-agent vinorelbine. Constipation occurred in approximately 28% of NSCLC and 38% of breast cancer patients, with paralytic ileus occurring in less than 2% of patients. Vomiting, diarrhea, anorexia and stomatitis were usually mild or moderate and occurred in less than 20% of patients.

Hepatic: Transient elevations of liver enzymes were reported without clinical symptoms.

Cardiovascular: Chest pain was reported in 5% of NSCLC and 8% of breast cancer patients. Most reports of chest pain were in patients who had either a history of cardiovascular disease or tumor within the chest. There have been rare reports of myocardial infarction; however, these have not been shown definitely attributable to vinorelbine.

Pulmonary: Shortness of breath was reported in 3% of NSCLC and 9% of breast cancer patients and was severe in 2% of each patient population. Interstitial pulmonary changes have been documented in a few patients.

Other: Asthenia occurred in approximately 25% of patients with NSCLC and 41% of patients with breast cancer. It was usually mild or moderate but tended to increase with cumulative dosing.

Other toxicities that have been reported in ≤5% of patients include jaw pain, myalgia, arthralgia, headache, dysphagia and rash. Hemorrhagic cystitis and the syndrome of inappropriate ADH secretion were reported in <1% of patients. The treatment of these entities are mainly symptomatic. The treatment of hemorrhagic cystitis is i.v. fluids for forced diuresis and/or irrigation of bladder. For the treatment of SIADH, please refer to the major textbooks of medicine.

Observed During Clinical Practice: In a randomized study in NSCLC patients, 206 patients received treatment with vinorelbine plus cisplatin and 206 patients received single-agent vinorelbine. The incidence of severe nausea and vomiting was 30% for vinorelbine/cisplatin compared to <2% for single-agent vinorelbine. Cisplatin did not appear to increase the incidence of neurotoxicity observed with single-agent vinorelbine. However, myelosuppression, specifically Grade 3 and 4 granulocytopenia, was greater with the combination of vinorelbine/cisplatin (79%) than with single-agent vinorelbine (53%). The incidence of fever and infection may be increased with the combination.

In addition to adverse events reported from clinical trials, the following events have been identified during postmarketing use of vinorelbine. Because they are reported voluntarily from a population of unknown size, estimates of frequency cannot be made. These events have been chosen for inclusion due to combination of their seriousness, frequency of reporting, or potential causal connection to vinorelbine or a combination of these factors.

Body as a Whole: Systemic allergic reactions reported as anaphylaxis, pruritus, urticaria and angioedema, flushing and radiation recall events such as dermatitis and esophagitis (see Precautions) have been reported.

Hematologic: Thromboembolic events including pulmonary embolus and deep venous thrombosis have been reported primarily in seriously ill and debilitated patients with known predisposing risk factors for these events.

Neurologic: Peripheral neurotoxicities such as, but not limited to, muscle weakness and disturbance of gait have been observed in patients with and without prior symptoms. Vestibular and auditory deficits have been observed with vinorelbine, usually when used in combination with cisplatin. There may be increased potential for neurotoxicity in patients with preexisting neuropathy, regardless of etiology, who receive vinorelbine. Patients who receive vinorelbine and paclitaxel, either concomitantly or sequentially, should be monitored for signs and symptoms of neuropathy (see Precautions).

Skin: Injection site reactions, including localized rash and urticaria, blister formation and skin sloughing have been observed in clinical practice. Some of these reactions may be delayed in appearance.

Gastrointestinal: Dysphagia and mucositis have been reported.

Cardiovascular: Hypertension, hypotension, vasodilation, tachycardia and pulmonary edema have been reported.

Pulmonary: Pneumonia has been reported.

Vinorelbine can produce acute and subacute pulmonary reactions. The acute reaction usually resembles an allergic event and may respond to bronchodilators. Subacute pulmonary reactions occur shortly after drug administration and may be characterized by cough, dyspnea, hypoxemia, and interstitial infiltration. Subacute pulmonary reactions may respond to corticosteroid therapy.

Musculoskeletal: Heachache has been reported with and without other musculoskeletal aches and pains.

Other: Pain in tumor-containing tissue, back pain and abdominal pain have been reported. Electrolyte abnormalities including hyponatremia consistent with the syndrome of inappropriate ADH secretion, have been reported in seriously ill and debilitated patients.

Combination Use: Patients with prior exposure to paclitaxel and who have demonstrated neuropathy should be monitored closely for new or worsening neuropathy. Patients who have experienced neuropathy with previous drug regimens should be monitored for symptoms of neuropathy while receiving vinorelbine. Vinorelbine may result in radiosensitizing effects with prior or concomitant radiation therapy (see Precautions).

Overdose: Symptoms and Treatment: The primary anticipated complications of overdosage would consist of bone marrow suppression and peripheral neurotoxicity.

There is no known antidote for vinorelbine overdosage. Overdoses involving quantities up to 10 times the recommended dose (30 mg/m²) have been reported. The toxicities described were consistent with those listed in the Adverse Effects section including paralytic ileus, stomatitis, and esophagitis. Bone marrow aplasia, sepsis, and paresis have also been reported. Fatalities have occurred following overdose of vinorelbine. If overdosage occurs, general supportive measures together with appropriate blood transfusions, growth factors and antibiotics should be instituted as deemed necessary by the physician.

Dosage: This preparation is for i.v. administration only. It should be administered by individuals experienced in the administration of cancer chemotherapeutic drugs.

The usual initial dose is 30 mg/m² administered weekly. The recommended method of administration is an i.v. injection over 6 to 10 minutes.

No dose adjustments are required for renal insufficiency. If moderate or severe neurotoxicity develops, vinorelbine should be discontinued. The dosage should be adjusted according to hematologic toxicity or hepatic insufficiency.

Dose Modifications for Hematologic Toxicity: Granulocyte counts shoud be ≥1 000 cells/mm³ prior to the administration of vinorelbine. In the referenced North American trial, in which hematologic adverse events were observed, the dose adjustment scheme in Table III was employed and should be followed in patients receiving vinorelbine.

Table III—Navelbine

Dose Adjustments Based on Granulocyte Counts

Granulocytes (cells/mm³) on days of Treatment	Dose of Navelbine (mg/m²)
≥1 500	30
1 000 to 1 499	15
<1 000	Do not administer. Repeat granulocyte count in 1 week. If granulocyte count is <1 000 cells/mm³ for >3 weeks, discontinue Navelbine.

Note: For patients who, during treatment with vinorelbine, have experienced fever and/or sepsis while granulocytopenic or required a delay in dosing of up to 3 weeks due to granulocytopenia, the dose of vinorelbine should be: 22.5 mg/m² for granulocytes ≥1 500 cells/m³ and 11.25 mg/m² for granulocytes 1 000 to 1 499 cells/m³.

Vinorelbine should be administered with caution to patients with hepatic insufficiency. In patients who develop hyperbilirubinemia during treatment with vinorelbine, the dose should be adjusted for total bilirubin.

Administration Precautions: Vinorelbine must be administered i.v. It is extremely important that the i.v. needle or catheter be properly positioned before any vinorelbine is injected. Leakage into surrounding tissue during i.v. administration of vinorelbine may cause considerable irritation, local tissue necrosis and/or thrombophlebitis. If extravasation occurs, the injection should be discontinued immediately, and any remaining portion of the dose should then be introduced into another vein. Local injection of hyaluronidase and the application of moderate heat to the area of leakage has been reported to help disperse drug and minimize discomfort associated with the extravasation of other vinca alkaloids.

As with other toxic compounds, caution should be exercised in handling and preparing the solution of vinorelbine. Skin reactions may occur with accidental exposure. The use of gloves is recommended. If the solution of vinorelbine contacts the skin or mucosa, immediately wash the skin or mucosa thoroughly with soap and water. Severe irritation of the eye has been reported with accidental contamination of the eye with another vinca alkaloid. If this happens with vinorelbine, the eye should be washed with water immediately and thoroughly.

Preparation for Administration: Vinorelbine injection must be diluted in either a syringe or i.v. bag using one of the recommended solutions. The diluted vinorelbine should be administered over 6 to 10 minutes into the side port of a free-flowing i.v. followed by flushing with at least 75 to 125 mL of one of the solutions. For diluents that may be used, see Reconstituted Solutions.

Syringe: The calculated dose of vinorelbine should be diluted to a concentration between 1.5 and 3 mg/mL.

I.V. Bag: The calculated dose of vinorelbine should be diluted to a concentration between 0.5 and 2 mg/mL.

Reconstituted Solutions: Syringe: Vinorelbine diluted to a concentration between 1.5 and 3 mg/mL may be used for up to 24 hours when stored in polypropylene syringes at 5 to 30°C. The following solutions may be used for dilution: 5% Dextrose Injection, USP; 0.9% Sodium Chloride Injection, USP.

I.V. Bag: Vinorelbine diluted to a concentration between 0.5 and 2 mg/mL may be used for up to 24 hours when stored in polyvinylchloride bags at 5 to 30°C. The following solutions may be used for dilution: 5% Dextrose Injection, USP; 0.9% Sodium Chloride Injection, USP; 0.45% Sodium Chloride Injection, USP; 5% Dextrose and 0.45% Sodium Chloride Injection, USP; Ringer's Injection, USP; Lactated Ringer's Injection, USP.

Potassium chloride injection solutions are found to be compatible with vinorelbine.

As with all the parenteral drug products, i.v. admixtures should be inspected visually for clarity, particulate matter, discoloration and leakage prior to administration, whenever solution and container permit. Any unused portion should be discarded.

Special Instructions: Since vinorelbine is a cytostatic agent, established procedures specific to the handling and use of such agents must be followed.

Vinorelbine injection is initially clear and colorless to pale yellow, but may develop a slightly darker yellow to light amber color in time. This does not indicate a change which should preclude its use. Parenteral drug products should be visually inspected for particulate matter and discoloration prior to administration whenever solution and container permit. If particulate matter is seen, vinorelbine should not be administered.

Supplied: Each mL of clear, colorless to pale yellow aqueous solution contains: vinorelbine tartrate equivalent to vinorelbine base 10 mg. Additive- and preservative-free. Single-dose clear flint glass vials of 1 and 5 mL. Store vials under refrigeration (2 to 8°C) in the original package to protect from light. This product should not be frozen.

Reviewed 1999

NAXEN® Ⓟ

AltiMed

Naproxen

Analgesic—Anti-inflammatory

Supplied: Suppositories: Each white, opaque suppository contains: naproxen 500 mg. Nonmedicinal ingredients: witepsol H15. Boxes of 30, packed in polyethylene-lined white polyvinyl shells in perforated strips of 5 suppositories.

Naxen (cont'd)

Tablets: 250 mg: Each yellow, round beveled-edge tablet, with scoreline on one side and NAXEN 250 on the other, contains: naproxen 250 mg. Nonmedicinal ingredients: croscarmellose sodium, magnesium stearate, povidone and iron oxide. Tartrazine-free. Bottles of 100 and 1 000.

375 mg: Each pink, oval tablet, plain on one side and NAXEN 375 on the other, contains: naproxen 375 mg. Nonmedicinal ingredients: croscarmellose sodium, magnesium stearate, povidone and iron oxide. Tartrazine-free. Bottles of 100 and 500.

500 mg: Each yellow, capsule-shaped tablet, with scoreline on one side and NAXEN 500 on the other, contains: naproxen 500 mg. Nonmedicinal ingredients: croscarmellose sodium, magnesium stearate, povidone and iron oxide. Tartrazine-free. Bottles of 100 and 500.

Store at room temperature.

NEBCIN® Ⓟ

Lilly

Tobramycin Sulfate

Antibiotic

Pharmacology: Like other aminoglycosides, the bactericidal activity of tobramycin is accomplished by specific inhibition of normal protein synthesis in susceptible bacteria, but at the present time, very little is known about this action. It is thought that inhibition of synthesis is due to an action on ribosomes that, in turn, causes bacterial misreading of messenger RNA.

Peak serum concentrations of tobramycin occur between 30 and 130 minutes after i.m. administration.

In patients with normal renal function, tobramycin administered every 8 hours does not accumulate in the serum. A serum half-life of about 2 hours was reported for patients with normal renal function while in patients with impaired renal function serum half-life of the drug ranged from 5 to 47 hours.

Dosage for such patients must, therefore, be adjusted accordingly (see Dosage).

After i.v. administration, serum concentrations are similar to those following i.m. injection, and are dose-related.

Pediatric studies indicate that although the serum half-life in neonates was found to be 2 or 3 times longer than in adults, no accumulation of tobramycin occurred even after multiple doses of 4 mg/kg/day.

Tobramycin is eliminated almost exclusively by glomerular filtration; renal clearance is similar to that of endogenous creatinine. Ultrafiltration studies demonstrate that practically no serum protein binding occurs. In patients with normal renal function, up to 84% of the dose is recoverable from the urine in 8 hours and up to 93% in 24 hours.

Peak urine concentrations up to 100 μg/mL have been observed after the i.m. injection of a single dose of 1 mg/kg. After several days of treatment, the amount of tobramycin excreted in the urine approaches the daily dose administered.

An inverse relationship exists between half-life and creatinine clearance, and the dosage schedule should be adjusted according to the degree of renal impairment. In patients undergoing hemodialysis, 25 to 70% of the administered dose may be removed, depending upon the duration of hemodialysis. Peritoneal dialysis was considered to be less efficient.

Tobramycin can be detected in tissues and body fluids after parenteral administration. Concentrations in bile ordinarily have been low, which suggests minimum biliary excretion. Tobramycin has been found in low and unpredictable concentrations in the cerebrospinal fluid following parenteral administration and would be inadequate against many gram negative organisms causing meningitis. It has also been found in sputum and in abscess fluids though possibly in nontherapeutic concentrations. Tobramycin crosses the placental membranes producing in 1 study a fetal serum half-life of 3.2 hours and a peak serum concentration of 1.2 μg/mL.

Indications: Tobramycin may be indicated for the treatment of the following infections when caused by susceptible organisms: septicemia, complicated and recurrent urinary tract infections, lower respiratory infections, serious skin and soft tissue infections including burns and peritonitis and CNS infections caused by organisms resistant to antibiotics usually considered efficacious in these infections.

Nebcin is usually active against most strains of the following organisms in vitro and in clinical infections: P. aeruginosa; Proteus sp. (indole-positive and indole-negative), including P. mirabilis, M. morganii, P. rettgeri, and P. vulgaris; E. coli; Klebsiella-Enterobacter-Serratia group; Citrobacter sp.; Providencia sp.; Staphylococci, including S. aureus (coagulase-positive and coagulase-negative).

Tobramycin may be considered in serious staphylococcal infections when penicillin or other potentially less toxic drugs are contraindicated and when bacterial susceptibility testing and clinical judgment indicate its use.

Appropriate sensitivity studies should be performed to determine the susceptibility of the causative organism to tobramycin. Clinical judgement and anticipated bacteriological findings may permit the start of therapy before results of susceptibility studies are obtained.

Note: If susceptibility tests show that the causative organism is resistant to tobramycin, other appropriate therapy should be instituted.

Contraindications: Known hypersensitivity to tobramycin or any other aminoglycoside. Cross-allergenicity to other aminoglycosides has been established.

Warnings: Patients treated with tobramycin or other aminoglycosides should be under close clinical observation because these drugs have an inherent potential for causing ototoxicity and nephrotoxicity.

Both vestibular and auditory toxicity can occur. Impairment of eighth nerve function is most likely in patients with preexisting renal damage, especially if the drug is administered for longer periods or in higher doses than those recommended.

Patients with known or suspected impairment of renal function should be under close clinical observation, and renal and eighth nerve function should be monitored during therapy.

Such monitoring is also recommended during the treatment of patients in whom renal function is initially normal, but in whom oliguria or evidence of nitrogen retention (increasing BUN, NPN, or creatinine) develops during therapy. Evidence of developing impairment in renal, vestibular, and/or auditory function requires careful observance of dosage adjustments (see dosage chart). Discontinuation of the drug may be indicated.

Peak and trough serum concentrations of aminoglycosides should be monitored periodically during therapy to assure adequate levels and to avoid potentially toxic levels. Prolonged serum concentrations above 12 mg/L should be avoided. Rising trough levels (above 2 mg/L) may indicate tissue accumulation. Such accumulation, excessive peak concentrations, advanced age, and cumulative dose may contribute to ototoxicity and nephrotoxicity.

Concurrent and/or sequential use of other potentially neurotoxic and/or nephrotoxic drugs, particularly other aminoglycosides (e.g., amikacin, streptomycin, neomycin, kanamycin, gentamicin, and paromomycin), amphotericin B, cephaloridine, viomycin, polymyxin B, colistin, cisplatin, and vancomycin, requires careful monitoring. Other factors that may increase patient risk are advanced age and dehydration.

Tobramycin should not be used concurrently with potent diuretics because some diuretics themselves cause ototoxicity.

Tobramycin sulfate contains sodium bisulfite, a sulfite that may cause allergic-type reactions, including anaphylactic symptoms and life-threatening or less severe asthmatic episodes, in certain susceptible people.

Pregnancy: Safety for use in pregnancy has not been established. Animal and human studies have demonstrated that there is a maternal-fetal transfer of tobramycin. No reports to date have revealed teratogenic effects in humans. However, one study in guinea pigs using high doses (50 to 100 mg/kg) in the last 4 weeks of pregnancy revealed a low incidence of ototoxicity in the newborn.

Precautions: Neuromuscular block and respiratory paralysis have been reported in cats receiving very high doses of tobramycin (40 mg/kg). The possibility that these phenomena may occur in man should be considered if tobramycin is administered to patients who are also receiving general anesthesia and/or neuromuscular blocking agents such as succinylcholine and tubocurarine, or in patients with myasthenia gravis or Parkinson's disease.

Tobramycin should be used with caution in premature and neonatal infants because of their renal immaturity and the resulting prolongation of serum half-life of the drug.

If overgrowth of nonsusceptible organisms occurs, appropriate therapy should be initiated, and if necessary, withdraw the drug.

Although not indicated for intraocular and/or subconjunctival use, there have been reports of macular necrosis following this type of injection of aminoglycosides, including tobramycin.

Adverse Effects: Nephrotoxicity: Renal function changes, as shown by rising BUN, NPN, and serum creatinine and by oliguria, have been reported, especially in patients with a history of renal impairment who were treated for longer periods or with doses higher than those recommended.

Neurotoxicity: Adverse effects on both vestibular and auditory branches of the eighth-nerve have been reported, especially in patients on high dosage and/or prolonged therapy. Symptoms include dizziness, vertigo, tinnitus, roaring in the ears and high frequency hearing loss.

Other adverse reactions that have been reported, and may be associated with tobramycin therapy, include increased serum transaminases (AST, ALT), increased alkaline phosphatase and increased serum bilirubin; anemia, granulocytopenia, and thrombocytopenia; fever, rash, exfoliative dermatitis, itching, urticaria, nausea, vomiting, diarrhea, headache and lethargy. Local reaction at the injection site has been reported.

Overdose: Symptoms: The severity of the signs and symptoms following a tobramycin overdose are dependent on the dose administered, the patient's renal function, state of hydration, and age and whether or not other medications with similar toxicities are being administered concurrently. Toxicity may occur in patients treated more than 10 days, given more than 5 mg/kg/day, children given more than 7.5 mg/kg/day, or patients with reduced renal function whose dose has not been appropriately adjusted.

Nephrotoxicity following the parenteral administration of an aminoglycoside is most closely related to the area under the curve of the serum concentration versus time graph. Nephrotoxicity is more likely if trough blood concentrations fail to fall below 2 mg/L and is also proportional to the average blood concentration. Patients who are elderly, have abnormal renal function, are receiving other nephrotoxic drugs, or are volume depleted are at greater risk for developing acute tubular necrosis. Auditory and vestibular toxicities have been associated with aminoglycoside overdose. These toxicities occur in patients treated longer than 10 days, in patients with abnormal renal function, in dehydrated patients, or in patients receiving medications with additive auditory toxicities. These patients may not have signs or symptoms or may experience dizziness, tinnitus, vertigo, and a loss of high-tone acuity as ototoxicity progresses. Ototoxicity signs and symptoms may not begin to occur until long after the drug has been discontinued.

Neuromuscular blockade or respiratory paralysis may occur following administration of aminoglycosides. Neuromuscular blockade, prolonged respiratory paralysis, and respiratory failure may occur more commonly in patients with myasthenia gravis or Parkinson's disease. Prolonged respiratory paralysis may also occur in patients receiving decamethonium, tubocurarine, or succinylcholine. If neuromuscular blockade occurs, it may be reversed by the administration of calcium salts but mechanical assistance may be necessary.

If tobramycin were ingested, toxicity would be less likely because aminoglycosides are poorly absorbed from an intact gastrointestinal tract.

Treatment: The initial management in a tobramycin overdose is to assess respiration and if necessary to establish an airway and ensure oxygenation and ventilation. Resuscitative measures should be initiated promptly if respiratory paralysis occurs.

Patients that have received an overdose of tobramycin and have normal renal function should be carefully hydrated to maintain a urine output of 3 to 5 mL/kg/hour. Fluid balance, creatinine clearance, and tobramycin plasma levels should be carefully monitored until the serum tobramycin level falls below 2 μg/mL.

Patients in whom the elimination half-life is greater than 2 hours or whose renal function is abnormal may require more aggressive therapy. In such patients, hemodialysis may be beneficial.

Dosage: Tobramycin may be given i.m. or i.v. The i.v. dose is the same as the i.m. dose.

Adults: Patients with normal renal function: 1 mg/kg every 8 hours, for a total of 3 mg/kg/day. Mild to moderate infections of the lower urinary tract have responded to doses of 2 to 3 mg/kg/day administered once daily. When renal tissue is involved or in serious infections, especially when there are signs of systemic involvement, 2 or 3 equally divided doses are recommended.

The usual dosage for patients weighing more than 60 kg is 80 mg (2 mL) every 8 hours. For patients weighing 60 kg or less, the usual dosage is 60 mg (1.5 mL) every 8 hours.

In patients with life threatening infections, dosages up to 5 mg/kg/day may be administered in 3 or 4 equal doses. This dosage should be reduced to 3 mg/kg/day as soon as clinically indicated. To prevent increased toxicity due to excessive blood levels, dosage should not exceed 5 mg/kg/day unless serum levels are monitored.

Children: 6 to 7.5 mg/kg/day in 3 or 4 equally divided doses.

Neonates (1 week of age or less): Dosage up to 4 mg/kg/day may be administered in 2 equal doses every 12 hours (see Precautions).

The usual duration of treatment is 7 to 10 days. A longer course of therapy may be necessary in difficult and complicated infections. Monitoring of renal, auditory, and vestibular functions is advisable in these cases because neurotoxicity is more likely to occur when treatment is extended for longer than 10 days.

Patients with Impaired Renal Function: Serum tobramycin concentrations should be monitored during therapy.

Following a loading dose of 1 mg/kg, subsequent dosage in these patients must be adjusted, either with lower doses administered at 8 hour intervals or with normal doses at prolonged intervals (see Table I). Both regimens should be based on the BUN, the serum creatinine or the creatinine clearance of the patient, because these values correlate with the half-life of tobramycin.

Adjusted dose at 8-hour intervals (Regimen I): An appropriately reduced dosage range can be found in Table I for any patient for whom the BUN, creatinine clearance or serum creatinine values are known. The choice of dose within the indicated range should be based on the severity of the infection, the sensitivity of the pathogen, and individual patient considerations, especially renal function.

Adjusted intervals between fixed doses (Regimen II): Recommended intervals between doses are given in Table I. As a general rule, the interval in hours can be determined by multiplying the patient's serum creatinine level by 6.

Both of these regimens are suggested as guides to be used when serum levels of tobramycin cannot be measured directly. The appropriate dosage schedules derived from either regimen should be used in conjunction with careful clinical and laboratory observations of the patient and should be modified as necessary.

Dosage in Moderate to Marked Obesity: The appropriate dose may be calculated by using the patient's estimated lean body weight plus 40% of the excess as the basic weight on which to figure mg/kg.

I.V. Administration: This route is recommended when the i.m. route is not feasible, e.g. in the presence of shock, hematologic disorders, severe burns or reduced muscle mass.

The concentration of Nebcin in solution should not normally exceed 1 mg/mL for either adults or children. The solution should be infused over a period of 20 to 60 minutes. When it is necessary to restrict the volume of solution infused, a more concentrated solution may be used; however, it is important that the infusion time exceed 5 minutes to prevent excessively high serum concentrations. A volume control set is recommended for this administration.

Table I—Nebcin

Two Maintenance Tobramycin Regimens based on Renal Function and Body Weight following a Loading Dose of 1 mg/kg[a]

Renal Function[b]		Regimen I — Adjusted Doses at 8-Hour Intervals — Weight		OR Regimen II — Adjusted Intervals Between Fixed Doses
Serum Creatinine µmol/L	Creatinine Clearance mL/s	50–60 kg	60–80 kg	Weight: Dose 50–60 kg: 60 mg 60–80 kg: 80 mg
≤115	≥1.17	60 mg	80 mg	q. 8 h
125–170	1.15–0.67	30–60 mg	50–80 mg	q. 12 h
175–290	0.65–0.33	20–25 mg	30–45 mg	q. 18 h
300–470	0.32–0.17	10–18 mg	15–24 mg	q. 24 h
475–660	0.15 0.08	5–9 mg	7–12 mg	q. 36 h
≥670	≤0.07	2.5–4.5 mg	3.5–6 mg	q. 48 h[c]

[a] For life-threatening infections, dosages 50% above those recommended may be used. The dosage should be reduced as soon as possible after improvement is noted.

[b] If used to estimate degree of renal impairment, serum creatinine concentrations should reflect a steady state of renal azotemia.

[c] When dialysis is not being performed.

Note: Nebcin should not be physically premixed with other drugs but should be administered separately according to the recommended dose and route.

Reconstitution (see Table II): Solutions for reconstitution: Sterile Water for Injection.

Table II—Nebcin

Reconstitution Table for Pharmacy Bulk Vial

Vial Size	Volume to be added to vial	Approximate Available volume	Approximate Average Conc.
1.2 g Powder (Bulk Pharmacy Vial)	30 mL	31.0 mL	40 mg/mL

Shake well until dissolved.

The Pharmacy Bulk Vial is intended only for i.v. infusion (by single puncture for multiple dispensing).

Solutions for I.V. Infusion: 5% Dextrose in water; 10% Dextrose in water; 0.9% Sodium Chloride Injection; 5% Dextrose and 0.9% Sodium Chloride; Ringer's Solution; Lactated Ringer's Solution.

Stability of solution: Storage: Nebcin diluted with any of the solutions for i.v. infusion listed above in a concentration range of 1 mg/mL to 0.2 mg/mL should be used within 24 hours if kept at room temperature and 36 hours if stored under refrigeration. The Pharmacy Bulk Vial is intended for multiple dispensing for i.v. use employing a single puncture. Following reconstitution, the solution should be dispensed and diluted for use within 8 hours. Any unused reconstituted solution should be discarded after 8 hours.

Nebcin should be stored at controlled room temperatures below 30°C. Nebcin injection requires no refrigeration.

Special Instructions: Pharmacy Bulk Vials: Pharmacy Bulk Vials contain no preservatives. Care must be taken to minimize the potential for inadvertent introduction of microorganisms during manipulation in the hospital environment. The availability of the Pharmacy Bulk Vial is restricted to hospitals with a recognized i.v. admixture program.

Supplied: Injection: 10 mg: Each mL of solution contains: tobramycin sulfate equivalent to tobramycin 10 mg (pediatric). Rubber stoppered vials of 2 mL.

40 mg: Each mL of solution contains: tobramycin sulfate equivalent to tobramycin 40 mg. Rubber stoppered vials of 2 mL.

Pharmacy Bulk Vials: Pharmacy Bulk Vial (7040), equivalent to sterile tobramycin 1.2 g powder, and equivalent to tobramycin 1.2 g in 30 mL of solution at a concentration of 40 mg/mL, for single puncture multiple dispensing. Rubber stoppered vials of 30 mL.

Pharmacy Bulk Vial (7090), equivalent to 1.2 g liquid for multiple puncture and dispensing. Rubber stoppered vials of 30 mL.

Nonmedicinal ingredients: edetate disodium, phenol, sodium bisulfite and water for injection.

...How to obtain emergency drugs—refer to the CLIN-INFO SECTION.

NegGram® Ⓟ

Sanofi

Nalidixic Acid

Urinary Antibacterial

Pharmacology: Nalidixic acid has bactericidal activity against gram-negative rods such as Escherichia, Klebsiella, Aerobacter and Proteus. It is relatively inactive against gram-positive bacteria. The mode of action is believed to be interference with the replication of genetic information by the blocking of the synthesis of bacterial DNA.

Bacterial cross-resistance between nalidixic acid and other quinolone antimicrobials has been observed only with oxolinic acid. Even in patients treated for prolonged periods, no fungal overgrowth has been reported during therapy with nalidixic acid.

Following oral administration, nalidixic acid is rapidly absorbed from the gastrointestinal tract, partially metabolized in the liver, and rapidly excreted through the kidneys. Unchanged nalidixic acid appears in the urine along with an active metabolite, hydroxynalidixic acid, which has antibacterial activity similar to that of nalidixic acid. Other metabolites include glucuronic acid conjugates of nalidixic acid and hydroxynalidixic acid, and the dicarboxylic acid derivative.

The hydroxy metabolite represents 30% of the biologically active drug in the blood and 85% in the urine. Peak serum levels of active drug average approximately 20 to 40 µg/mL (90% protein bound), 1 to 2 hours after administration of a 1 g dose to a fasting normal individual, with a half-life of about 90 minutes. Peak urine levels of active drug average approximately 150 to 200 µg/mL, 3 to 4 hours after administration with a half-life of about 6 hours.

Approximately 4% of nalidixic acid is excreted in the feces.

Indications: Acute or chronic urinary tract infections due to one or more species of nalidixic acid-sensitive gram-negative pathogenic organisms, in particular Proteus species, E. coli, Aerobacter and Klebsiella (disc sensitivity testing with the 30 µg disc is recommended). It is useful in mixed urinary tract infection when the nalidixic acid-sensitive gram-negative rods predominate.

When urinary tract pathogens which are resistant to other types of antibacterial drugs are found to be sensitive to nalidixic acid, the use of nalidixic acid should be considered.

Contraindications: Known hypersensitivity to nalidixic acid and in patients with a history of convulsive disorders. Until further experience is gained, the drug should not be administered to infants under 3 months of age.

Warnings: CNS effects, including brief convulsions, increased intracranial pressure, and toxic psychosis, have been reported with nalidixic acid therapy. Convulsive seizures have been reported with other drugs in this class. Therefore, nalidixic acid should be used with caution in patients with known or suspected CNS disorders such as cerebral arteriosclerosis or other factors which predispose to seizures (see Adverse Effects). Quinolones may also cause CNS stimulation which may lead to tremor, restlessness, lightheadedness, confusion and hallucinations. If these reactions occur in patients receiving nalidixic acid, the drug should be discontinued and appropriate measures instituted.

Serious and occasionally fatal hypersensitivity (anaphylactoid) reactions, some following the first dose, have been reported in patients receiving quinolone therapy. Some reactions were accompanied by cardiovascular collapse, loss of consciousness, tingling, pharyngeal or facial edema, dyspnea, urticaria and itching. Serious anaphylactoid reactions required immediate emergency treatment with epinephrine. Oxygen, i.v. steroids, and airway management, including intubation, should be administered as indicated.

Precautions: Although prolonged treatment with nalidixic acid has been generally well tolerated, it is advisable to carry out blood counts and renal and liver function tests periodically if treatment is continued for more than 2 weeks.

Nalidixic acid should only be used with caution in patients with liver disease. While caution should be used in patients with severe renal failure, therapeutic concentrations of nalidixic acid in the urine, without increased toxicity due to drug accumulation in the blood, have been observed in patients on full dosage, with creatinine clearances as low as 2 to 8 mL/min. However, it has been recommended that nalidixic acid not be used if the creatinine clearance is < 10 mL/min.

Microorganisms may develop resistance to nalidixic acid. It is also possible that resistant bacteria, not previously present or identified, may emerge. Conventional chromosomal resistance to nalidixic acid taken in full dosage has been reported

NegGram (cont'd)

to emerge in approximately 2 to 14% of patients during treatment; however, bacterial resistance to nalidixic acid has not been shown to be transferable via R factor. If bacterial resistance to nalidixic acid emerges during treatment, it usually does so within 48 hours, necessitating change to another antimicrobial. Therefore, if the clinical response is unsatisfactory or if relapse occurs, cultures and sensitivity tests should be repeated. Underdosage with nalidixic acid during initial treatment (with less than 4 g/day for adults) or during maintenance treatment (with less than 2 g/day for adults), may predispose a patient to emergence of bacterial resistance. It should be recognized that apparent relapse or bacterial resistance may frequently be due to obstruction of the urinary tract.

Drug Interactions: Active proliferation of the organism is a necessary condition for the antibacterial action of nalidixic acid and it is possible that the presence of bacteriostatic substances may inhibit its action. Such an effect has been demonstrated in vitro with nitrofurantoin, tetracycline and chloramphenicol.

Quinolones, including nalidixic acid may enhance the effect of oral anticoagulants, warfarin or bishydroxycoumarin, by displacing significant amounts from serum albumin binding sites. When concomitant administration of these products cannot be avoided, daily measurements of prothrombin time or other suitable coagulation tests are essential.

Elevated plasma levels of theophylline have been reported with concomitant quinolone use. There have been reports of theophylline-related side effects in patients on concomitant therapy with quinolones and theophylline. Therefore, monitoring of theophylline and plasma levels should be considered and dosage of theophylline adjusted, as required.

Interference with Laboratory Tests: When Benedict's or Fehling's solutions or Clinitest Reagent tablets are used to test the urine of patients taking nalidixic acid, a false-positive reaction for glucose may be obtained, due to the liberation of glucuronic acid from the metabolites excreted. However, a colorimetric test for glucose based on an enzyme reaction (e.g. with Clinistix Reagent Strips or Tes-Tape) does not give a false-positive reaction to the liberated glucuronic acid.

Incorrect values may be obtained for urinary 17-keto and ketogenic steroids in patients receiving nalidixic acid, because of an interaction between the drug and the m-dinitrobenzene used in the assay method. In such cases, the Porter-Silber test for 17-hydroxy-corticoids may be used.

Children: Recent toxicological studies have shown that high doses of nalidixic acid or other chemically related antibacterial agents can produce erosions of the cartilage in weight-bearing joints and other signs of arthropathy in immature animals of most species tested. No such joint lesions have been reported in man to date. Nevertheless, until the significance of this finding is clarified, it should be carefully considered before prescribing this product for prepubertal children.

Pregnancy: There are no adequate and well controlled studies in pregnant women. Nalidixic acid should be used during pregnancy only if the potential benefit justifies the potential risk to the fetus.

Caution should be used in administering nalidixic acid in the days prior to delivery because of the theoretical risk that exposure to maternal nalidixic acid in utero may lead to significant blood levels of nalidixic acid in the neonate immediately after birth. Patients using nalidixic acid during pregnancy should be advised to discontinue use at the first sign of labor.

Lactation: When treating women who are breast feeding, consideration should be given to the fact that traces of nalidixic acid are excreted in the milk. Because other drugs are excreted in human milk and because of the potential for serious adverse reactions in nursing infants from nalidixic acid, a decision should be made whether to discontinue nursing or to discontinue the drug, taking into account the importance of the drug to the mother.

Information for the Patient: Patients should be advised that nalidixic acid may be taken with or without meals. Patients should be advised to drink fluids liberally and not take antacids within 2 hours of taking nalidixic acid, as antacids may interfere with its absorption. Patients should be advised that quinolones may be associated with hypersensitivity reactions, even following a single dose, and to discontinue the drug at the first sign of a skin rash or other allergic reactions.

Since reversible photosensitivity reactions have been reported in a small number of cases, patients should be cautioned to avoid direct sunlight while on nalidixic acid therapy. Therapy should be discontinued if photosensitivity occurs.

Quinolones may cause dizziness and lightheadedness; therefore, patients should know how they react to nalidixic acid before they operate an automobile or machinery or engage in activities requiring mental alertness or coordination.

Patients should be advised to avoid excessive caffeine intake, as quinolones may increase the effects of caffeine containing compounds.

Adverse Effects: Nalidixic acid is usually well tolerated. It is seldom necessary to discontinue treatment or to reduce the dosage. Gastrointestinal: abdominal pain, nausea, vomiting and diarrhea.

Hypensensitivity: rash, pruritus, urticaria, angioedema, arthralgia with joint stiffness and swelling and, rarely, anaphylactoid reactions. Photosensitivity reactions consisting of erythema and bullae on exposed skin surfaces, usually resolve completely in 2 weeks to 2 months after nalidixic acid is discontinued; however, bullae may continue to appear with successive exposures to sunlight or with mild skin trauma for up to 3 months after discontinuation of drug (see Precautions).

CNS: drowsiness, weakness, headache, dizziness, vertigo and, rarely, paresthesia.

Toxic psychosis or brief convulsions have been reported rarely, usually following excessive doses. In general, the convulsions have occurred in patients with predisposing factors such as epilepsy or cerebral arteriosclerosis (see Dosage).

In infants and children receiving therapeutic doses of nalidixic acid, increased intracranial pressure with bulging anterior fontanel, papilledema, and headache has occasionally been observed. A few cases of 6th cranial nerve palsy have been reported. Although the mechanisms of these reactions are unknown, the signs and symptoms usually disappeared rapidly with no sequelae when treatment was discontinued.

Hemotological: Eosinophilia, thrombocytopenia, leukopenia and hemolytic anemia (rare; observed in patients with and those without a deficiency in glucose-6-phosphate dehydrogenase activity). A single case of fatal acute immune hemolytic anemia has been reported, without a deficiency in glucose-6-phosphate dehydrogenase activity.

Ocular: Overbrightness of lights, change in color perception, difficulty in focusing, decrease in visual acuity and double vision. These visual disturbances were subjective and without objective findings, occurred infrequently (generally with each dose during the first few days of treatment), and were reversible (usually disappearing promptly when dosage was reduced or therapy was discontinued).

Other: rarely, cholestasis and metabolic acidosis. Erythema multiforme and Stevens-Johnson syndrome have been reported with nalidixic acid and other drugs in this class. A single case of non fatal pulmonary hypersensitivity to nalidixic acid has been reported in the literature.

Overdose: Symptoms: Toxic psychosis, convulsions, increased intracranial pressure, or metabolic acidosis may occur in patients taking more than the recommended dosage. Vomiting, nausea and lethargy may also occur following overdosage.

Treatment: Reactions are generally short-lived (2 to 3 hours) because the drug is rapidly excreted. If overdosage is noted early, gastric lavage is indicated. If absorption has occurred, increased fluid administration is advisable and supportive measures such as oxygen and means of artificial respiration should be available. Although anticonvulsant therapy has not been used in the few instances of overdosage reported, it may be indicated in a severe case.

Dosage: Adults: Initial therapy: 1 g administered 4 times daily for 1 or 2 weeks (total daily dose 4 g). For prolonged therapy, the total daily dose may be reduced to 2 g after the initial treatment period. Underdosage during initial treatment may predispose to emergence of bacterial resistance. Adjustment of urinary pH is not necessary.

Children: Dosage in children 12 years of age and under should be calculated on the basis of body weight. The recommended total daily dosage for initial therapy is 55 mg/kg/day, administered in 4 equally divided doses. For prolonged therapy, the total daily dose may be reduced to 33 mg/kg/day.

Note: In light of potential neurologic reactions, the recommended dose should not be increased except under the careful supervision of a physician. Until further experience is gained, the drug should not be administered to infants under 3 months of age.

Supplied: Each scored, yellow caplet with "N" on one side of the score and "22" on the other, with the flying W on the reverse, contains: nalidixic acid 500 mg. Nonmedicinal ingredients: cellulose (microcrystalline), methylcellulose, sodium lauryl sulfate, vegetable oil (hydrogenated) and yellow iron oxide. Gluten-, lactose-, starch-, sucrose-, sulfite- and tartrazine-free. Bottles of 56 and 500.

(Shown in Product Recognition Section)

NEMASOL SODIUM®—ICN ℞

ICN

Aminosalicylate Sodium

Tuberculostatic Agent

Supplied: Each white, compressed tablet, imprinted ICN N11, contains: aminosalicylate sodium, USP 500 mg. Nonmedicinal ingredients: alcohol, microcrystalline cellulose, povidone, starch and stearic acid. Bottles of 1 000.

NEMBUTAL® SODIUM

Abbott

Pentobarbital Sodium

Sedative—Hypnotic

Supplied: Capsules: Each yellow capsule contains: pentobarbital sodium 100 mg. Also contains cornstarch and tartrazine. Alcohol-, gluten-, lactose-, paraben-, sodium-, sucrose- and sulfite-free. Bottles of 100.

Injection: Each mL contains: pentobarbital sodium 50 mg. Nonmedicinal ingredients: alcohol, hydrochloric acid, propylene glycol, sodium hydroxide and water for injection. Alcohol: 10%. Ampuls of 2 mL, boxes of 50.

NEOCITRAN Preparations

Novartis Consumer Health

Acetaminophen—Chlorpheniramine Maleate—Dextromethorphan HBr—Phenylephrine HCl—Pheniramine Maleate—Pseudoephedrine HCl Compound

Analgesic—Antihistamine—Antitussive—Decongestant Preparations

Supplied: NeoCitran A (Allergies & Colds): Each pouch contains: phenylephrine HCl 10 mg and pheniramine maleate 20 mg. Nonmedicinal ingredients: calcium phosphate, citric acid, FD&C Yellow No. 5, FD&C Yellow No. 6, malic acid, natural lemon flavor, sodium citrate, sucrose, titanium dioxide and vitamin C. Boxes of 10.

NeoCitran Adult (Colds & Flu): Each pouch contains: pheniramine maleate 20 mg, phenylephrine HCl 10 mg and acetaminophen 325 mg. Nonmedicinal ingredients: calcium phosphate, citric acid, D&C Yellow No. 10, FD&C Yellow No. 6, malic acid, natural lemon flavor, sodium citrate, sucrose, titanium dioxide and vitamin C. Boxes of 10 and 20.

NeoCitran DM (Coughs & Colds): Each pouch contains: phenylephrine HCl 10 mg, pheniramine maleate 20 mg and dextromethorphan HBr 30 mg. Nonmedicinal ingredients: calcium phosphate, citric acid, FD&C Yellow No. 5, FD&C Yellow No. 6, malic acid, natural lemon flavor, sodium citrate, sucrose, titanium dioxide and vitamin C. Boxes of 10.

NeoCitran Extra Strength (Colds & Flu)-Apple Cinnamon: Each pouch contains: pheniramine maleate 20 mg, phenylephrine HCl 10 mg and acetaminophen 650 mg. Nonmedicinal ingredients: apple and cinnamon flavors, calcium phosphate, caramel, citric acid, ethyl maltol, malic acid, sodium citrate, sucrose, titanium dioxide and vitamin C. Boxes of 10.

NeoCitran Extra Strength (Colds & Flu)-Lemon: Each pouch contains: pheniramine maleate 20 mg, phenylephrine HCl 10 mg and acetaminophen 650 mg. Nonmedicinal ingredients: calcium phosphate, citric acid, citrus favor, D&C Yellow No. 10, FD&C Red No. 3, malic acid, sodium citrate, sucrose, titanium dioxide and vitamin C. Boxes of 10 and 20.

NeoCitran Extra Strength (Cough Cold & Flu): Each pouch contains: acetaminophen 650 mg, chlorpheniramine maleate 4 mg, pseudoephedrine HCl 60 mg, dextromethorphan HBr 20 mg. Nonmedicinal ingredients: calcium phosphate, citric acid, D&C Yellow No. 10, flavor, silicon dioxide, sodium citrate, starch, sucrose, titanium dioxide and vitamin C. Boxes of 10.

NeoCitran Extra Strength Daycaps: Each caplet contains: acetaminophen 500 mg, dextromethorphan HBr 15 mg and pseudoephedrine HCl 30 mg. Nonmedicinal ingredients: carnauba wax, croscarmellose sodium, D&C Yellow No. 10, hydroxypropyl cellulose, lactose, magnesium stearate, methylparaben, silicon dioxide, starch and titanium dioxide. Boxes of 12.

NeoCitran Calorie Reduced: Each pouch contains: pheniramine maleate 20 mg, phenylephrine HCl 10 mg and acetaminophen 325 mg. Nonmedicinal ingredients: aspartame, calcium phosphate, citric acid, maltodextrin, D&C Yellow No. 10, FD&C Red No. 3, malic acid, natural lemon flavor, sodium citrate, titanium dioxide and vitamin C. Boxes of 10.

NeoCitran Sinus Extra Strength: Each pouch contains: phenylephrine HCl 10 mg and acetaminophen 650 mg. Nonmedicinal ingredients: calcium phosphate, citric acid, citrus flavor, D&C Yellow No. 10, FD&C Yellow No. 6, sodium citrate, sucrose, titanium dioxide and vitamin C. Boxes of 10.

NEO-CORTEF® Preparations ℞

Pharmacia & Upjohn

Neomycin Sulfate—Hydrocortisone Acetate

Antibiotic—Corticosteroid

Indications: These preparations are indicated in the following conditions when threatened with or complicated by infection due to neomycin sensitive organisms.
Eye Drops: phlyctenular kerato-conjunctivitis, nonspecific superficial keratitis, acne rosacea keratitis, allergic conjunctivitis, sclerokeratitis, episcleritis, traumatic keratitis. In generalized uveitis and inflammatory diseases of the posterior segment, systemic corticosteroid therapy should be employed.
Ointment: allergic, atopic and seborrheic dermatitis, pruritus ani and vulvae, and neurodermatitis.

Contraindications: Viral diseases of the cornea, conjunctiva, or skin. Tuberculosis of the eye or skin, fungal diseases of the eye or skin, active purulent untreated infections of the eye, which like other diseases caused by microorganisms may be masked or enhanced by the presence of the steroid. Cutaneous infections which do not respond to neomycin. Individuals with a history of hypersensitivity to any of the components.

Precautions: Extended ophthalmic use of corticosteroid drugs may cause increased intraocular pressure in certain patients and in those diseases causing thinning of the cornea, perforation has been known to occur. As with any antibiotic containing product, overgrowth by resistant organisms may occur, particularly monilia. If this occurs, discontinue treatment and institute appropriate measures.

Articles in current medical literature indicate an increase in the incidence of patients allergic to neomycin. The possibility of such a reaction should be borne in mind.

Ototoxicity and nephrotoxicity have been reported following absorption of topically applied neomycin.

Although untoward effects associated with the use of topical corticosteroids are uncommon and not to be expected from ordinary use, sensitization, irritation and failure of therapeutic response have been noted in rare instances. Application to extensive areas, too-frequent application, or application under occlusive dressings may result in systemic absorption with symptoms of adrenal suppression, localized atrophy and striae. If secondary bacterial infection exists or supervenes, concomitant antimicrobial therapy is indicated.
Pregnancy: Although topical steroids have not been reported to have an adverse effect on pregnancy, the safety of their use has not absolutely been established. Therefore, use with care during pregnancy.

Adverse Effects: The following local adverse reactions have been reported with topical corticosteroids, either with or without occlusive dressings: burning sensation, itching, irritation, dryness, folliculitis, secondary infection, skin atrophy, striae, miliaria, hypertrichosis, acneiform eruptions, laceration of the skin and hypopigmentation.

Dosage: Eye Drops: Ocular–1 or 2 drops in conjunctival sac every hour during day and every 2 hours at night. After improvement occurs this may be reduced to 1 or 2 drops 3 or 4 times daily. Duration of therapy should be determined by the judgment of the physician and the response of the patient to the medication.
Ointment: A small amount rubbed gently into the area 1 to 3 times daily.

Supplied: Eye Drops: Each mL contains: hydrocortisone acetate 15 mg (1.5%), neomycin sulfate 5 mg in sterile, aqueous suspension. Nonmedicinal ingredients: myristyl-gamma-picolinium chloride, polyethylene glycol, povidone and sodium citrate. Sodium hydroxide or hydrochloric acid may be used to adjust pH. Dropper bottles of 5 mL.

Ointment: Each g contains: hydrocortisone acetate 5 mg (0.5%) or 10 mg (1%) and neomycin sulfate 5 mg (equivalent to 3.5 mg neomycin base). Nonmedicinal ingredients: butylparaben and methylparaben in a bland base composed of cholesterol, microcrystalline wax, mineral oil and white petrolatum. Tubes of 25 g.

NEO-LARYNGOBIS®

Technilab

Bismuth Dipropylacetate

Sore Throat—Loss of Voice Treatment

Supplied: Each adult rectal suppository contains: bismuth dipropylacetate 135 mg. Nonmedicinal ingredients: semisynthetic glycerides. Boxes of 2.

NEO-MEDROL® Acne Lotion ℞

Pharmacia & Upjohn

Methylprednisolone—Neomycin Compound

Acne Therapy

Indications: For control of acne vulgaris in the adolescent and young adult. Also in some cases of acne rosacea and seborrheic dermatitis.

Contraindications: In tuberculosis of the skin, herpes simplex, vaccinia, varicella and in other cutaneous infections which do not respond to neomycin. Known hypersensitivity to any of the components.

Precautions: Avoid contact with eyes. If signs of irritation or sensitivity develop, application should be discontinued. As with any antibiotic containing product, overgrowth by resistant organisms may occur, particularly monilia. If this occurs, discontinue treatment and institute appropriate measures. Articles in current medical literature indicate an increase in the incidence of patients allergic to neomycin. The possibility of such a reaction should be borne in mind.

If extensive areas are treated or if the occlusion technique is used, the possibility exists of increased absorption of the corticosteroid and suitable precautions should be taken. The prolonged use of antibiotic-containing preparations may result in overgrowth of nonsusceptible organisms, particularly fungi. If new infections appear during treatment, appropriate therapy should be instituted.

Convulsions have been reported with concurrent use of methylprednisolone and cyclosporine. Since concurrent administration of these agents results in a mutual inhibition of metabolism, it is possible that convulsions and other adverse events associated with the individual use of either drug may be more apt to occur.

Ototoxicity and nephrotoxicity have been reported following absorption of topically applied neomycin.
Pregnancy: Although topical steroids have not been reported to have an adverse effect on pregnancy, the safety of their use has not absolutely been established. Therefore, use with care during pregnancy.
Children: When topical corticosteroids are applied for a prolonged period of time, sufficient systemic absorption can suppress the hypothalamic-pituitary-adrenal axis. Growth suppression may also occur.

Adverse Effects: The following local adverse reactions have been reported with topical corticosteroids, either with or without occlusive dressings: burning sensation, itching, irritation, dryness, folliculitis, secondary infection, skin atrophy, striae, hypertrichosis, acneiform eruptions, allergic contact dermatitis, laceration of the skin and hypopigmentation.

Dosage: After careful cleansing of the affected skin to minimize the possibility of introducing infection, Neo-Medrol Acne Lotion should be applied sparingly to the affected areas once or twice a day initially. Care should be taken to avoid contact with the eyes. The frequency of application will vary from patient to patient, depending on their susceptibility to the drying effect of the lotion, and may have to be reduced to every other day in some patients.

Supplied: Each mL contains: methylprednisolone acetate 2.5 mg, neomycin sulfate 2.5 mg, aluminum chlorhydroxide complex 100 mg and colloidal sulfur 50 mg. Nonmedicinal ingredients: butylparaben, cetyl palmitate, lexemul ar, methylcellulose, methylparaben, perfume oil, polyethylene glycol, polysorbate 80, polysorbate 85 and propylene glycol. Plastic squeeze bottles of 25 and 75 mL.

NEO-MEDROL® VERIDERM® Cream ℞

Pharmacia & Upjohn

Methylprednisolone—Neomycin Sulfate

Glucocorticoid—Antibiotic

Indications: An adjunct in the treatment of contact, atopic and seborrheic dermatitis, pruritus ani and vulvae, and neurodermatitis when complicated by infection caused by organisms sensitive to neomycin.

Contraindications: Tuberculosis of the skin, chickenpox, herpes simplex, vaccinia, superficial fungus or yeast infections. Not for use in the eye. Known hypersensitivity to any of the components.

Precautions: Although untoward effects associated with the use of topical corticosteroids are uncommon and not to be expected from ordinary use, sensitization, irritation and failure of therapeutic response have been noted in rare instances. Application to extensive areas, too frequent application, or application under occlusive dressings may result in systemic absorption with symptoms of adrenal suppression, localized atrophy and striae. If secondary bacterial infection exists or supervenes, concomitant antimicrobial therapy is indicated.

Articles in current medical literature indicate an increase in the incidence of patients allergic to neomycin. The possibility of such a reaction should be borne in mind.

Ototoxicity and nephrotoxicity have been reported following absorption of topically applied neomycin.

Convulsions have been reported with concurrent use of methylprednisolone and cyclosporine. Since concurrent administration of these agents results in a mutual inhibition of metabolism, it is possible that convulsions and other adverse events associated with the individual use of either drug may be more apt to occur.
Pregnancy: The safety of the use of topical corticosteroid preparations during pregnancy has not been fully established. Therefore, corticosteroids should not be used unnecessarily during pregnancy or for prolonged periods of time.

Adverse Effects: Burning, itching, irritation, dryness, folliculitis, hypertrichosis, acneiform eruptions and hypopigmentation have been reported with topical corticosteroids.

With the use of occlusive dressings, the occurrence of miliaria, folliculitis, pyodermas, and localized atrophy is a possibility. Contact sensitivity to a particular dressing material or adhesive may occur occasionally. When corticosteroid preparations are used for long periods in intertriginous areas or under occlusive dressings, striae may occur.

Dosage: Apply a small amount after careful cleansing of the affected skin. Initially, application may be made 1 to 3 times daily. After control has been achieved, the frequency of application may be reduced.

Supplied: Each g contains: methylprednisolone acetate 2.5 mg (0.25%), neomycin sulfate 5 mg (equivalent to 3.5 mg neomycin base), in a synthetic skin lipid base. Nonmedicinal ingredients: butydhydroxyan, butydhydrolytol, butylparaben, cetyl palmitate, cetyl alcohol, cholesterol, corn oil, glycerin, lexemul ar, methylparaben, mineral oil, oleic acid, oleyl alcohol, perfume oil, polyoxyl 40 stearate, sorbitan monooleate, squalene, stearic acid, stearyl alcohol and tocopherol. Tubes of 25 and 50 g.

NEORAL® ℞
SANDIMMUNE® I.V. ℞

Novartis Pharmaceuticals

Cyclosporine

Immunosuppressant

Caution: Transplantation: Only physicians experienced in immunosuppressive therapy and management of organ transplant patients should prescribe Neoral and Sandimmune I.V. Patients receiving the drug should be managed in centres staffed with professionals experienced in transplantation and the use of immunosuppressants and equipped with adequate laboratory facilities to monitor cyclosporine levels. The ability to measure cyclosporine blood levels facilitates the management of the patient. The radioimmunoassay (RIA) method has been used most often in clinical trials.

For long-term follow-up, the attending physician should receive complete information from the transplant centre on the patient, to include: recommended Neoral dosage, target trough levels of cyclosporine and frequency of determination of these levels. The attending physician should consult with the transplant centre when making dose adjustments to ensure that toxicity is minimized while maintaining adequate immunosuppression.

Sandimmune and Neoral, which are different in formulation, should not be used interchangeably.

Following initiation of treatment with Neoral, due to the different bioavailabilities of the different oral cyclosporine formulations, patients should not be converted to any other oral formulation of cyclosporine without appropriate monitoring of cyclosporine blood concentrations, serum creatinine levels and blood pressure. This does not apply to the conversion between Neoral soft gelatin capsules and Neoral oral solution as these two dosage forms are bioequivalent.

It is therefore important that prescribers, pharmacists and patients be aware that substitution of Neoral with any other oral formulation of cyclosporine is not recommended as this may lead to alterations in cyclosporine blood concentrations. For this reason, it might be appropriate to prescribe by brand.

Psoriasis/Rheumatoid Arthritis/Nephrotic Syndrome: Careful monitoring of Neoral treated patients is mandatory. Neoral should only be prescribed for psoriasis, rheumatoid arthritis or nephrotic syndrome by physicians experienced with its use. Neoral is indicated: In patients with severe psoriasis in whom conventional therapy is ineffective or inappropriate and when the psoriasis is of such severity that the risks inherent in treatment with cyclosporine are justified for that patient; for the treatment of severe, active rheumatoid arthritis in patients for whom classical slow-acting antirheumatic agents are inappropriate or ineffective; in patients with steroid dependent and steroid resistant nephrotic syndrome.

Pharmacology: Cyclosporine is a potent immunosuppressive agent with a narrow therapeutic range which has been shown in man to prolong the survival of allogenic transplants.

Neoral capsules and oral solution include a microemulsion formulation of cyclosporine. When compared to Sandimmune capsules and oral solution, Neoral provides a more complete and consistent absorption profile and is less influenced by concomitant food intake or by diurnal rhythm than is Sandimmune. These properties combined yield a lower intra-patient variability, as well as in some cases, a lower inter-patient variability in pharmacokinetics of cyclosporine and a stronger correlation between trough concentration and total exposure (AUC_B) for a more accurate targeting of the level of immunosuppression.

As a consequence of these properties, the time schedule of Neoral administration does not require that meals be considered. In addition, Neoral produces a more even exposure to cyclosporine throughout the day and from day to day on a maintenance regimen, thereby helping to avoid periods of either under-immunosuppression or over-exposure to the drug.

The data available indicate that following a 1:1 conversion from Sandimmune oral formulations to Neoral the following differences are observed: see Table I.

Table I—Neoral

Switch from Sandimmune Oral Formulations to Neoral

Parameter	Difference following 1:1 Switch from Sandimmune Oral Formulations to Neoral
C_{min} in whole blood	comparable*
T_{max}	1 hour earlier for Neoral
C_{max}	59% higher for Neoral
Absolute bioavailability (AUC)	29% higher for Neoral

* Varies from patient to patient. See Dosage, Switch from Sandimmune oral formulations to Neoral.

Because of these differences in bioavailability parameters, caution is advised in switching patients from Sandimmune oral formulations to Neoral. The two should not be used interchangeably.

Cyclosporine is distributed largely outside the blood volume. In the blood, 33 to 47% is present in plasma, 4 to 9% in lymphocytes, and 41 to 58% in erythrocytes. In plasma, approximately 90% is bound to proteins, mostly lipoproteins.

Cyclosporine is extensively biotransformed to approximately 15 metabolites. There is no single major metabolic pathway. Elimination is primarily biliary, with only 6% of the oral dose excreted in the urine; only 0.1% is excreted in the urine as unchanged drug. The distribution of cyclosporine appears to conform to a multicompartmental model in which continued administration leads to eventual saturation of the peripheral compartment.

The half-life of cyclosporine is approximately 18 hours (range 7.7 to 26.9). However there is a high variability in the data reported on the terminal half-life of cyclosporine depending on the assay applied and on the target population. For example, the terminal half-life ranged from 6.3 hours in healthy volunteers to 20.4 hours in patients with severe liver disease.

Indications: Solid Organ Transplantation: Neoral capsules and oral solution and Sandimmune I.V. are indicated in the prevention of graft rejection following solid organ transplantation and treatment of transplant rejection in patients previously receiving other immunosuppressive agents.

Bone Marrow Transplantation: Neoral capsules and oral solution and Sandimmune I.V. are indicated in the prevention of graft rejection following bone marrow transplantation and prevention or treatment of graft-versus-host disease (GVHD).

Psoriasis: Neoral capsules and oral solution are indicated for the treatment of severe psoriasis in patients for whom conventional therapy is ineffective or inappropriate.

Rheumatoid Arthritis: Neoral capsules and oral solution are also indicated for the treatment of severe active rheumatoid arthritis in patients for whom classical slow-acting antirheumatic agents are inappropriate or ineffective.

Nephrotic Syndrome: Neoral capsules and oral solution are indicated in adults and children for steroid dependent and steroid resistant nephrotic syndrome due to glomerular diseases such as minimal change nephropathy; focal and segmental glomerulosclerosis, or membranous glomerulonephritis. Neoral can be used to induce remissions and to maintain them. It can also be used for maintenance of steroid induced remissions, allowing withdrawal of, or reduction in the dosage of steroids.

Contraindications: Patients with a hypersensitivity to cyclosporine, or any of its excipients.

Neoral is also contraindicated in the treatment of psoriasis and rheumatoid arthritis patients under the following circumstances: abnormal renal function; uncontrolled hypertension; malignancy (except nonmelanoma skin cancer); uncontrolled infection; primary or secondary immunodeficiency excluding autoimmune disease.

Warnings: Transplantation: Neoral capsules and oral solution and Sandimmune I.V. should be prescribed only by physicians who are experienced in immunosuppressive therapy and management of transplant patients and can provide adequate follow-up, including regular full physical examination, measurement of blood pressure and control of laboratory safety parameters. Patients receiving the drug should be managed in facilities with adequate laboratory and supportive medical resources.

The concentrate for i.v. infusion contains polyoxyethylated castor oil which has been reported to cause anaphylactoid reactions. Patients receiving Sandimmune I.V. should be observed continuously for at least 30 minutes following the start of the infusion and at frequent intervals thereafter (see Precautions, Patient Management Transplants).

Psoriasis: Neoral should only be prescribed for psoriatic patients by physicians experienced with its use. All patients to be treated with Neoral for psoriasis must have a pretreatment physical examination to include blood pressure, renal function and careful examination for tumors, particularly of the skin, to establish accurate baseline values and clinical status.

Skin lesions not typical of psoriasis should be biopsied to exclude skin cancers, mycosis fungoides or other premalignant conditions.

Rheumatoid Arthritis: Patients with abnormal renal function, abnormal liver function, uncontrolled hypertension, uncontrolled infections or any kind of malignancy should not receive Neoral. Discontinuation of the drug is recommended if hypertension developing during Neoral therapy cannot be controlled with appropriate antihypertensive therapy. As with other long-term immunosuppressive treatments, an increased risk of lymphoproliferative disorders must be borne in mind.

Nephrotic Syndrome: Neoral should only be prescribed by physicians experienced with its use. All patients to be treated with Neoral for nephrotic syndrome must have a pretreatment physical examination to include blood pressure, renal function (see Dosage) and screening for malignancies.

For All Patients: Appropriate patient and laboratory monitoring is essential to prevent, reverse or minimize the following adverse events: nephrotoxicity; hypertension; the development of malignancies and lymphoproliferative disorders; increased risk of infections; hepatotoxicity; lipoprotein abnormalities; neurotoxicity (see Precautions).

Pregnancy: Cyclosporine is not teratogenic in animals but was shown to be both embryo- and feto-toxic in rats and rabbits at 2 to 5 times the human dose.

To date, information has been received on 514 pregnancies with exposure to Sandimmune. In most patients, the indication for cyclosporine therapy was organ transplantation.

Most patients who became pregnant continued cyclosporine therapy throughout pregnancy, usually in combination with other immunosuppressive drugs and further medication.

Fetal loss occurred in 9.1% of the patients, which is within the range found in a normal population. In 4.9% of the patients, the pregnancy was interrupted, either for medical considerations or at the wish of the patient. The course of pregnancy was often complicated by disorders specific to pregnancy, in particular in renal transplant patients, or by disorders relating to the underlying disease. A large proportion of the pregnancies ended in preterm delivery. Accordingly, the main problems seen in the neonates relate to prematurity, best exemplified by the short median gestation duration of 35.7 weeks in the 439 pregnancies completed, and the low median birth weight, 2 291 g, of the 446 babies delivered, including 10 twins.

It appears that premature delivery and the delivery of infants small for their age occur more often in patients who have undergone a renal transplantation.

Out of 102 babies born to mothers treated with Sandimmune, 5 were born with malformations. It is not clear what role cyclosporine has played in the complications of pregnancy.

Males treated with cyclosporine have fathered normal children.

Neoral or Sandimmune I.V. should be used during pregnancy only if the potential benefit justifies the potential risk to the fetus.

Lactation: As cyclosporine is transferred into breast milk of lactating females, mothers receiving treatment with Neoral or Sandimmune I.V. should not breast-feed.

Children: Experience with Neoral in children is still limited. Experience in children is almost entirely based on Sandimmune. In several studies pediatric patients required and tolerated higher doses of Sandimmune per kg body weight than those used in adults.

Precautions: For All Patients: Because of the difference in bioavailability parameters, caution is advised in switching patients from Sandimmune oral formulations to Neoral. The two should not be used interchangeably.

Nephrotoxicity: Cyclosporine may cause increases in serum creatinine and urea levels, even at recommended doses as a result of reduced glomerular filtration rate (GFR). The mechanism leading to these increases is not fully understood. These functional changes are dose dependent and reversible, and usually respond to dose reduction. Although less frequent, some patients may develop structural changes in the kidney (e.g., interstitial fibrosis) during long-term treatment. Although these renal changes are less common, they may be irreversible. In renal transplant patients, structural changes in the kidney must be differentiated from organ rejection.

Close monitoring of parameters that assess renal function is required. Abnormal values may necessitate dose reduction.

In patients who are treated with cyclosporine for nontransplant indications, the risk of renal structural changes is greater if the serum creatinine level increases more than 30% from the patient's own baseline value. Thus regular measurements of serum creatinine levels must be made.

Hepatotoxicity: Cyclosporine may also cause dose-dependent, reversible increases in serum bilirubin and, occasionally, in liver enzymes.

Close monitoring of parameters that assess hepatic function is required. Abnormal values may necessitate dose reduction.

Hypertension: Patients receiving cyclosporine may develop hypertension, and regular monitoring of blood pressure is required. Caution is advised in choosing an agent to treat this hypertension. Diuretics are not recommended (see Drug Interactions).

In addition, in psoriasis patients; beta-blockers are not generally recommended due to their propensity to exacerbate psoriasis. Only calcium channel blockers which do not interfere with cyclosporine pharmacokinetics are recommended (see Drug Interactions).

Lipoprotein Abnormalities: Many transplant patients have hyperlipidemia and cyclosporine may contribute to the genesis of this problem. It is advisable to perform lipid determination before treatment and after the first month of therapy. If lipids are increased, restriction of dietary fat should be considered. (If the risk benefit ratio warrants, a reduction of Neoral capsules and oral solution dose may also be considered.) Caution is advised in the coadministration of Neoral or Sandimmune I.V. and the HMG-CoA reductase inhibitor, lovastatin, due to the risk of myocyte necrosis. The potential for interaction with other drugs in this class should be considered (see Drug Interactions and Adverse Effects).

Neurotoxicity: Cyclosporine has the potential to induce tremor, convulsions and paresthesia in post-transplant recipients. Rarely, more complex neurological abnormalities including motor spinal cord and cerebellar syndromes have been reported in post-transplant patients.

Malignancy: Malignancy and lymphoproliferative disorders have developed, but their incidence and distribution are similar to those in patients on conventional immunosuppressive therapy.

In psoriatic patients on cyclosporine therapy, development of malignancies (in particular of the skin) has been reported. Skin lesions, not typical of psoriasis, but suspected to be malignant or premalignant should be biopsied before starting cyclosporine treatment. Patients with malignant or premalignant alterations of the skin should be treated with cyclosporine only after appropriate treatment of such lesions and if no other option for successful therapy exists. Cyclosporine should be discontinued if malignancy occurs.

Infection/Immunization: Since cyclosporine is an immunosuppressive drug, patients will be at increased risk for infections. Vaccination may be less effective and the use of live attenuated vaccines should be avoided.

Hyperkalemia/Hyperuricemia: Since cyclosporine occasionally causes hyperkalemia or may aggravate pre-existing hyperkalemia, monitoring of serum potassium is recommended, especially in patients with marked renal dysfunction.

Patients receiving cyclosporine should avoid high dietary potassium intake and the use of potassium-containing medications or potassium-sparing diuretics is not recommended.

Caution is required in treating patients with hyperuricemia (see Drug Interactions).

Geriatrics: Experience with cyclosporine in the elderly is limited, but no particular problems have been reported following the use of the drug at the recommended dose. However, factors sometimes associated with aging, in particular impaired renal function, necessitate careful supervision and may necessitate dosage adjustment.

Drug Interactions: See Table II. Caution should be exercised in patients receiving drug treatment with: nephrotoxic drugs; cytotoxic drugs; immunosuppressants or radiation (including PUVA or UVB); drug affecting metabolism/absorption of cyclosporine.

If combined administration is unavoidable, careful monitoring of blood cyclosporine concentration and appropriate modification of Neoral or Sandimmune I.V. dosage are essential.

Nonsteroidal Anti-inflammatory Drugs: NSAID therapy should be discontinued where possible. As nonsteroidal anti-inflammatory drugs alone can have an adverse effect on renal function, addition of these drugs to Neoral or Sandimmune I.V. therapy or an increase in their dosage should be accompanied by particular close monitoring of renal function.

Miscellaneous Interactions: see Table III.

Table II—Neoral/Sandimmune I.V.

Summary of Drug Interactions

	Drugs Increasing the Serum Concentration of Cyclosporine	Drugs Decreasing the Serum Concentration of Cyclosporine	Drugs Causing Additive Nephrotoxicity
Substantiated Interactions	Ketoconazole Erythromycin Josamycin Corticosteroids Oral contraceptives Norethisterone or danazol Doxycycline Calcium channel blockers -Diltiazem -Verapamil -Nicardipine Propafenone Metoclopramide Imipenem Methylprednisolone	Phenytoin or phenobarbital Rifampin i.v. Sulfadimine i.v. and trimethoprim i.v. Nafcillin Carbamazepine Octreotide Barbiturates Metamizole	Amphotericin B Aminoglycerides Melphalan Cotrimoxazole or trimethoprim Ciprofloxacin Colchicine
Suspected or Potential Interactions	H_2-antagonists Cephalosporins Thiazide diuretics Furosemide Androgenic steroids Acyclovir Warfarin	Sulfinpyrazone Anticonvulsants	Nonsteroidal anti-inflammatory drugs

Table III—Neoral/Sandimmune I.V.

Miscellaneous Interactions

Alteration of Immunosuppressive Effect	Interactions with Alcohol Content	Others
Propranolol	Disulfiram	Digoxin
Verapamil	Chlorpropamide	Captopril
Etoposide	Metronidazole	Toxoids or vaccines
		Nifedipine*
		HMG-CoA reductase inhibitors
		Prednisolone
		Colchicine

*Should be avoided in patients who develop gingival hypertrophy.

Grapefruit juice should be avoided owing to its possible interference with the P450 enzyme system which may result in an increase in the bioavailability of Neoral.

HMG-CoA Reductase Inhibitors: In transplant patients who received the HMG-CoA reductase inhibitor lovastatin in combination with cyclosporine and other immunosuppressive drugs, there have been reports of severe rhabdomyolysis that precipitated acute renal failure. The potential for Neoral or Sandimmune I.V. to interact with drugs in this class should be considered.

Cyclosporine may also enhance the potential of lovastatin and colchicine to induce muscular toxicity including muscle pain and weakness. The concomitant use of these drugs with Neoral capsules and oral solution or Sandimmune I.V. should be carefully considered.

Prednisolone and Methylprednisolone: It has been noted that cyclosporine reduces the clearance of prednisolone and conversely, high dose therapy with methylprednisolone can increase the blood concentration of cyclosporine.

Transplant Patient Management: Clinical: The concentrate for i.v. infusion contains polyoxyethylated castor oil which has been reported to cause anaphylactoid reactions. These reactions consist of flushing of the face and upper thorax, acute respiratory distress with dyspnea and wheezing, blood pressure changes and tachycardia.

Special caution is therefore necessary in patients who have previously received, by i.v. injection or infusion, preparations containing polyoxyethylated castor oil, or in patients with an allergic predisposition. Thus, patients receiving Sandimmune I.V. should be observed continuously for at least the first 30 minutes following the start of the infusion and at frequent intervals therafter. If anaphylaxis occurs, the infusion should be discontinued. An aqueous solution of epinephrine 1:1 000 and a source of oxygen should be available at the bedside. Prophylactic administration of an antihistamine (H_1+H_2 blocker) prior to Sandimmune I.V. has also been successfully employed to reduce the severity and prevent the occurrence of anaphylactoid reactions. The oral forms of Neoral do not contain polyoxyethylated castor oil.

Laboratory: Accurate and regular monitoring of cyclosporine blood levels in conjunction with other laboratory and clinical parameters is regarded as an essential aid to maintain the trough concentrations within the relatively narrow therapeutic window between efficacy and toxicity.

During the immediate postoperative period, levels should be monitored every 2 to 3 days.

Monitoring schedules should continue until the patient's clinical condition and Neoral or Sandimmune I.V. dosage are stable. Following discharge from hospital, cyclosporine levels are determined at each clinic visit, which is usually twice weekly for the first 2 months, weekly until 4 months and monthly thereafter for the first year.

The reported therapeutic range for 12-hour trough levels from whole blood which appear to minimize side effects and rejection episodes are between 100 to 400 ng/mL as measured by the RIA method using specific monoclonal antibody (see Dosage).

Two methods are available for the specific assay of cyclosporine parent compound: radioimmunoassay (RIA) and high-performance liquid chromatography (HPLC). Comparative findings for the analysis of blood samples by both the RIA method (based on specific monoclonal antibody) and the HPLC method has established that the specific antibody gives a selective measure of the cyclosporine parent compound without significant interference from drug metabolites. Therefore, 12-hour trough levels of the cyclosporine parent compound should routinely be measured using the radioimmunoassay (RIA) kit for cyclosporine based on the specific monoclonal antibody.

Because there is a temperature and time-dependent uptake of cyclosporine by erythrocytes, the concentration of cyclosporine in plasma separated at room temperature and 37°C will differ substantially, the latter being higher. For this reason, it is not recommended to use plasma or serum as the matrix of choice. However, if plasma or serum are used, a standard separation protocol (time and temperature) should be followed.

Whole blood is the matrix of choice. Specimens should be collected into tubes containing ethylene diamine tetraacetic acid (EDTA) anticoagulant. Heparin anticoagulation is not recommended because of the tendency to form clots on storage. Samples which are not to be analyzed immediately should be stored in a refrigerator (4°C) and assayed within 7 days; if the samples are to be kept longer they should be deep frozen (−20°C) for up to 6 months.

Psoriasis/Rheumatoid Arthritis/Nephrotic Syndrome Patient Management: Prior to initiation of Neoral Therapy: Clinical: Before treatment, the patient should undergo a history and physical examination with investigations as warranted. An initial blood pressure reading should be made on at least 2 occasions within 2 weeks to establish a baseline. As Neoral is immunosuppressive, a search should be made for tumors of all kinds, particularly of the skin. Any persistent previously undiagnosed skin lesion should be biopsied for a confirmed diagnosis prior to starting therapy. Female patients should have an examination of the cervix within the first 6 months of therapy, and periodically thereafter, to exclude malignancy.

Neoral/Sandimmune I.V. (cont'd)

Laboratory: Prior to therapy, a 12-hour fasting serum creatinine should be measured on at least 3 occasions within 2 weeks to give an accurate baseline value. A baseline creatinine clearance is also suggested, if possible. It is recommended that initial investigations should include urinalysis, complete blood count, liver function tests, serum uric acid and serum potassium.

Follow-up during Neoral Therapy: Clinical: Regular clinical examinations are necessary during treatment with Neoral. Follow-up assessment of blood pressure should be performed every 2 weeks during the initial 3 months and every month thereafter. Should hypertension occur, in the majority of patients, elevated blood pressure can be adequately controlled by dose reduction. Should antihypertensive therapy be necessary, diuretics are not recommended. In addition, in **psoriasis** patients, beta-blockers are not generally recommended due to their propensity to exacerbate psoriasis. Only calcium channel blockers which do not interfere with Neoral pharmacokinetics are recommended (see Drug Interactions). If hypertension is uncontrolled with antihypertensive treatment, Neoral should be discontinued. When Neoral is discontinued, blood pressure returns to normal within 3 months. Development of malignancies has been reported in patients when treated with cyclosporine. In patients with **nephrotic syndrome** treated with immunosuppressants (including cyclosporine) the occurrence of malignancies (including Hodgkin's lymphoma) has occasionally been reported. Careful physical examination should thus be made for malignancies, notably of skin, oral mucosa, major lymph nodes. Psoriatic patients should avoid direct sun exposure as this will increase the risk of skin cancer.

Laboratory: Psoriasis and Rheumatoid Arthritis: A complete blood count including, differential WBC, platelet counts, liver function tests, urinalysis, serum potassium, uric acid should be measured periodically during treatment with Neoral. Serum creatinine should be measured every 2 weeks for the initial 3 months (see Dosage). Thereafter, if creatinine levels remain stable, measurements should be made every 2 months in patients who are receiving up to 2.5 mg/kg/day and every 4 weeks in patients who are receiving higher doses.

More frequent checks are necessary when the Neoral dose is increased or concomitant treatment with an NSAID is initiated or the dosage is increased. The same precaution applies to the introduction of any drug known to increase cyclosporine blood levels.

Routine measurements of cyclosporine blood levels are not necessary because of their poor predictive value, but may be useful in special cases where drug interactions or altered bioavailability are suspected.

Nephrotic Syndrome: Since cyclosporine can impair renal function, it is necessary to assess renal function frequently and, if the serum creatinine remains increased by more than 30% above baseline at more than one measurement the dosage of Neoral must be reduced by 25 to 50%.

In some patients it may be difficult to detect cyclosporine-induced renal dysfunction because of changes in renal function related to the nephrotic syndrome itself. This may explain why, in rare cases, cyclosporine-associated structural kidney alterations have been observed without changes in serum creatinine. Renal biopsy should be considered for patients with steroid-dependent minimal change nephropathy in whom cyclosporine therapy has been maintained for more than 1 year.

Periodic monitoring of cyclosporine trough levels is recommended.

Adverse Effects: Despite the increase in C_{max} and AUC seen in patients who are treated with Neoral capsules and oral solution, a similar safety profile to the conventional formulation of cyclosporine (Sandimmune capsules and oral solution) has been observed. Studies have reported no significant difference between the 2 formulations in terms of renal safety, risk of adverse events, or laboratory parameters (e.g., blood pressure, creatinine clearance, serum levels of urea, creatinine, potassium, cholesterol, triglycerides). Furthermore, there is no indication of a correlation between peak cyclosporine concentration (C_{max}) and changes in renal function.

The following adverse reactions observed with Sandimmune are also likely to occur with Neoral. In some cases, adverse reactions are dose-dependent and responsive to dose reduction. See Table IV.

Especially in liver transplant patients, signs of encephalopathy, vision and movement disturbances, and impaired consciousness are described. Whether these alterations are caused by cyclosporine, the underlying disease or other conditions remains to be established.

Table IV—Neoral/Sandimmune I.V.

Adverse Reactions

Body System	Frequency of Occurrence: Common	Occasional	Rare
Cardiovascular/Circulatory	Hypertension (particularly in heart transplant patients)	Edema	Muscle cramps Muscle weakness
Gastrointestinal	Abdominal pain Nausea Vomiting Anorexia Gingival hypertrophy Diarrhea		
Skin	Hypertrichosis	Rash (of possible allergic origin)	
Liver	Hepatic dysfunction		
Nervous System	Tremor Burning sensation in hands and feet	Headache Convulsions Paresthesia	
Genitourinary	Impaired renal function	Hyperuricemia Reversible dysmenorrhea or amenorrhea	
Blood		Mild anemia	
Metabolic		Weight gain Hyperkalemia	
Other	Fatigue Burning sensation in hands and feet	Hypomagnesemia Pancreatitis	Myopathy

In rare instances, thrombocytopenia, in some patients associated with micro-angiopathic hemolytic anemia and renal failure (hemolytic uremic syndrome), has been observed.

Malignancies and lymphoproliferative disorders have developed, but their incidence and distribution are similar to those in patients on conventional immunosuppressive therapy.

Transplantation: The adverse events shown in Table V occurred in patients involved in 2 clinical trials with Neoral. The first column reports on a study in which stable renal transplant patients were switched to Neoral; in the second, de novo renal transplant patients were treated with Neoral.

Table V—Neoral

Adverse Events with Neoral

Adverse Event	Stable Renal Transplant Patients (n=372) (%)	New Renal Transplant Patients (n=45) (%)
Gingival hyperplasia	29 (7.8)	3 (6.7)
Hypertrichosis	24 (6.5)	17 (37.8)
Edema	32 (8.6)	14 (31.1)
Tremor	31 (8.3)	19 (42.2)
Loss of muscle strength	3 (0.8)	8 (17.8)
Change in vegetative functions	24 (6.5)	8 (17.8)
Nausea, vomiting, epigastrical pain	30 (8.1)	7 (15.6)
Headache	37 (10)	10 (22.2)
Paresthesia	16 (4.3)	5 (11.1)
Heat Sensations	28 (7.5)	5 (11.1)
Others	62 (16.7)	11 (27.5)

Psoriasis: In clinical trials, the most frequent side effects associated with the use of cyclosporine in psoriasis were renal dysfunction, hypertension, gastrointestinal disorders, hypertrichosis, paresthesia, headache, influenza-like symptoms, upper respiratory tract infections, gum hyperplasia, fatigue, hyperuricemia, hypomagnesemia and increase in plasma liquids.

The adverse events (excluding renal dysfunction, hypertension and malignancies) shown in Table VI occurred in 3% or greater of 631 psoriatic patients involved in clinical trials.

In psoriasis in 1 439 patients treated with Sandimmune the following were reported: 21 cases of skin cancer, 17 cases of solid malignant tumors and 6 cases of lymphoproliferative disorders (2 lymphomas). There is an increased risk of malignancies, particularly skin cancer in psoriasis patients especially when the psoriasis has been previously treated with carcinogens, such as PUVA treatment.

Rheumatoid Arthritis: In clinical trials, the most frequent side effects associated with the use of cyclosporine in rheumatoid arthritis were hypertrichosis; hypertension; nausea; abdominal pain; paresthesia; headache and gum disorders (see Table VII on following page).

Table VI—Neoral

Adverse Events (Excluding Renal Dysfunction, Hypertension and Malignancies) Occurring in Psoriatic Patients Involved in Clinical Trials

Body System Adverse Event	%
Skin and Appendages	
Hypertrichosis	14.6
Central and Peripheral Nervous System	
Paresthesia	11.4
Headache	9.4
Gastrointestinal	
Nausea	4.8
Gingival overgrowth	4.6
Gastrointestinal disorder	3.3
General Disorders	
Fatigue	4.0
E.N.T. and Respiratory	
Influenza-like symptoms	5.5
Upper respiratory tract infection	4.6

Nephrotic Syndrome: In clinical trials, the most frequent side effects associated with the use of cyclosporine in nephrotic syndrome were: renal dysfunction, hypertrichosis, gingival hyperplasia, hypertension, tremor and paresthesia, and gastrointestinal symptoms.

The following events (see Table VIII on following page) occurred in 3% or greater of nephrotic syndrome patients involved in clinical trials.

In nephrotic syndrome of 660 patients treated with Sandimmune, malignancies occurred in 5 patients (3 carcinomas, 2 Hodgkin's lymphomas).

Overdose: Symptoms and Treatment: No experience of acute overdosage of Neoral capsules and oral solution is available. Documented cases include both single and multiple overdoses of Sandimmune capsules and oral solution to a maximum overdose of 25 000 mg. High blood levels of cyclosporine result in acute toxic symptoms which may include: nausea, headache, hyperesthesia in the hands and feet, flushing of face, gum soreness and bleeding, and sensation of increased abdominal girth. Although high levels may cause transient hepato- and nephrotoxicity, no permanent residual or long-term sequelae have been reported. If indicated, general supportive measures should follow. Elimination can be achieved only by nonspecific measures including gastric lavage, as cyclosporine is not dialyzable to any great extent nor is it cleared well by charcoal hemoperfusion.

Dosage: The dose ranges of Neoral capsules and oral solution and Sandimmune I.V. given below are intended to serve as a guideline only. Routine monitoring of cyclosporine blood levels is required; this can be carried out by means of RIA method

Table VII—Neoral

Adverse Events Associated with the Use of Cyclosporine in Rheumatoid Arthritis in Clinical Trials

Body System Adverse Event	Sandimmune Patients Initial Dose <6 mg/kg/day (n=378) (%)	Placebo-Treated Patients (n=176) (%)
Skin Appendages		
Alopecia	3.4	2.3
Hypertrichosis	33.9	5.1
Rash	3.4	6.3
Central and Peripheral Nervous System		
Cramps	4.0	0.6
Dizziness	4.5	4.5
Headache	15.6	9.7
Paresthesia	15.9	6.3
Tremor	13.5	3.4
Autonomic Nervous		
Flushing	5.0	1.7
Gastrointestinal		
Abdominal pain	18.8	10.2
Diarrhea	6.1	6.3
Dyspepsia	9.5	5.7
Gum Disorders	11.6	0.6
Nausea	27.2	13.6
Vomiting	8.2	2.3
Body as a Whole		
Fatigue	4.2	4.0
Fever	3.2	2.3
Edema	4.8	2.8
Resistance Change		
Pharyngitis	3.2	2.3

Table VIII—Neoral

Adverse Events Occurring in ≥3% of Nephrotic Syndrome Patients Involved in Clinical Trials

Body System Adverse Event	Sandimmune Patients (n=270) (%)
Skin/Appendages	
Hypertrichosis	31.5
Hypotrichosis	3.0
Musculoskeletal	
Muscle Contraction	4.1
Central and Peripheral Nervous System	
Paresthesia	12.2
Headache	5.6
Tremor	5.6
Psychiatric Disorders	
Weakness	4.8
Gastrointestinal	
Gingival Hyperplasia	27.0
Nausea	4.4
Gastric Pain	3.7
Diarrhea	3.3
Abdominal Pain	3.1
Liver and Biliary System	
Liver Enzyme Increase	3.3
Metabolic and Nutritional	
Hypomagnesemia	5.2
Cardiovascular	
Hypertension	13.7
Urinary System	
Renal Dysfunction	7.0

based on monoclonal antibodies. The results obtained will serve as a guide for determining the actual dosage required to achieve the desired target concentration in individual patients.

Solid Organ Transplantation: Treatment with Neoral may be initiated within 12 hours prior to surgery at a dose of 10 to 15 mg/kg given in 2 divided doses. This dose should be maintained as the daily dose for 1 to 2 weeks post-operatively before being gradually reduced in accordance with blood levels until a maintenance dose of about 2 to 6 mg/kg given in 2 divided doses is reached. Table IX outlines the recommended steady-state therapeutic ranges of cyclosporine 12-hour trough levels (the level immediately before the next dose).

Table IX—Neoral/Sandimmune I.V.

Target Trough Levels

RIA Method	Blood ng/mL	Plasma/ Serum ng/mL
Monoclonal specific[a]	100-400	50-200
Polyclonal nonspecific[b]	150-1 500	50-300

[a]Values are based on HPLC data and the results of a multicentre comparison of the monoclonal specific RIA with the polyclonal RIA kit. Plasma serum values are based on separation at 37°C. These values will be lower if plasma/serum is separated at room temperature.

[b]Whole blood values are based on a multiplication factor of 3–5x concentration obtained using plasma/serum values. Plasma/serum values are based on separation at 22°C.

When Neoral is given with other immunosuppressants (e.g., with corticosteroids or as part of a triple or quadruple drug therapy), lower doses (e.g., 3 to 6 mg/kg given in 2 divided doses for the initial treatment) may be used.

Recommended Dosage of Concentrate for I.V. Infusion: Patients unable to take Neoral soft gelatin capsules or oral solution pre- or postoperatively, may be treated with the Sandimmune I.V. at one-third the oral dose.

The initial dose of Sandimmune I.V. is 3 to 5 mg/kg/day. This daily dose is continued postoperatively for up to 2 weeks until the patient can tolerate the Neoral soft gelatin capsules or oral solution. Patients should be switched to Neoral as soon as possible after surgery. In pediatric usage, the adult dose and dosing regimen have been used initially and adjusted to target blood levels (see Precautions).

Bone Marrow Transplantation: The initial dose should be given on the day before transplantation. In most cases i.v. infusion of Sandimmune is preferred for this purpose (see previous section). Maintenance treatment with Neoral is at a daily dose of about 12.5 mg/kg given in 2 divided doses and should be continued for at least 3 months (and preferably for 6 months) before the dose is gradually decreased to zero by 1 year after transplantation. If Neoral is used to initiate therapy, the recommended daily dose is 12.5 to 15 mg/kg given in 2 divided doses, starting on the day before transplantation.

Higher doses of Neoral, or the use of i.v. therapy, may be necessary in the presence of gastrointestinal disturbances which might decrease drug absorption.

In some patients, GVHD occurs after discontinuation of cyclosporine treatment, but usually responds favorably to re-introduction of therapy. Low doses of Neoral should be used to treat mild, chronic GVHD.

Psoriasis: Recommended Dosage: Dose Titration for Induction of Remission: The recommended initial dose is 2.0 mg/kg/day given in 2 divided oral doses. If there is no improvement after 1 month, the daily dose may be gradually increased. Dose adjustments should be made in increments of 0.5 to 1.0 mg/kg/day body weight/month and total daily dose, depending on monitoring of drug tolerance, should not exceed 5 mg/kg/day.

Treatment Discontinuation: Treatment should be discontinued in patients in whom psoriatic lesions do not respond sufficiently within 6 weeks on 5.0 mg/kg/day, **or in whom the effective dose is not compatible with the safety guidelines given below under Monitoring.** As skin lesions improve the dose should be reduced in increments of 0.5 to 1 mg/kg/day/month.

Long-term Goals of Therapy: Psoriasis generally recurs when Neoral treatment is stopped. The goal of maintenance therapy is to optimize therapy and achieve sustained improvement. That is, to keep the patient's disease controlled with the minimal dose of Neoral in order to avoid adverse effects. Total clearing of the skin should not always be the ultimate goal.

Maintenance Dose: After reaching a relatively disease-free state, the patient should be given the minimum effective maintenance dose. For maintenance treatment, **doses should be titrated individually to the lowest effective level,** and, depending on monitoring of drug tolerance, should not exceed 5.0 mg/kg/day.

If a patient experienced a worsening of the condition during maintenance, therapy can be changed to a dose that is sufficient to control psoriasis while **remaining compatible with the safety guidelines,** i.e., maximum 5.0 mg/kg/day. An attempt should then be made to reduce the dose to the lowest effective level. Dosage adjustments should follow the guidelines for inducing remission. If no relapse occurs within 6 months, an attempt should be made to wean the patient off Neoral.

Monitoring for Psoriasis Patients: Since Neoral can impair renal function, serum creatinine should be measured every 2 weeks for the first 3 months of therapy. Thereafter, if creatinine remains stable, measurements should be done every 2 months in patients who are on up to 2.5 mg/kg/day, and at monthly intervals in patients who require higher doses. The dose must be reduced by 25 to 50% when serum creatinine increases by more than 30% above the patient's own baseline, even if the values are still within the normal range. If dose reduction is not successful within 1 month, Neoral treatment should be discontinued.

Discontinuation of Neoral therapy is also recommended if hypertension developing during Neoral therapy cannot be controlled with appropriate therapy.

As cyclosporine is an immunosuppressive agent, search should be made for tumors of all kinds, in particular the skin, oral mucosa and major lymph nodes. This physical examination should be made initially at least every 3 months and any skin lesion not typical for psoriasis should be biopsied. Neoral treatment should be discontinued if a malignancy occurs, and appropriate treatment of the malignancy instituted.

Rheumatoid Arthritis: Recommended Dosage: For the first 6 weeks of treatment, the recommended initial dose is 2.0 mg/kg/day orally given in 2 divided doses. If necessary, the daily dose may then be increased gradually as **tolerability permits** (see Warnings) but, depending on monitoring of drug tolerance, should not exceed 5 mg/kg/day. Up to 12 weeks of Neoral therapy may be required before full effectiveness is achieved.

For maintenance therapy, the dose must be titrated individually according to tolerability.

Neoral may be given in combination with low-dose corticosteroids and/or nonsteroidal anti-inflammatory drugs (see Precautions).

Monitoring for Rheumatoid Arthritis Patients: Since cyclosporine can impair renal function, a reliable baseline level of serum creatinine should be established by at least 2 measurements prior to treatment, and serum creatinine should be monitored every 2 weeks during the first 3 months of therapy. Thereafter, if creatinine remains stable, measurements can be made every 4 weeks. More frequent checks are necessary when the dose of Neoral is increased or concomitant treatment with a nonsteroidal anti-inflammatory drug is initiated or its dosage increased. The same precaution applies to the introduction of any drug known to increase cyclosporine blood levels.

Dose adjustment based on creatinine values: If serum creatinine remains increased by more than 30% above baseline at more than 1 measurement, the dosage of Neoral should be reduced. If serum creatinine increases by more than 50%, a dosage reduction by 50% is mandatory. These recommendations apply even if the patient's values still lie within the laboratory normal range. If dose reduction is not successful in reducing levels within 1 month, Neoral treatment should be discontinued.

Nephrotic Syndrome: Recommended Dosage: Dose Titration for Induction of Remission: The recommended initial daily dose, given in 2 divided oral doses, is 3.5 mg/kg for adults and 4.2 mg/kg for children if, except for proteinuria, renal function is normal. In patients with impaired renal function, the initial dose should not exceed 2.5 mg/kg/day.

The combination of Neoral with low doses of oral corticosteroids is recommended if the effect of Sandimmune Neoral is not satisfactory, especially in steroid-resistant patients.

Treatment Discontinuation: Treatment should be discontinued if no improvement has been observed after 3 months of Neoral therapy.

Maintenance Dose: The dose must be adjusted individually according to efficacy (proteinuria) and safety (primarily serum creatinine), but, depending on monitoring of drug tolerance, should not exceed 5 mg/kg a day in adults and 6 mg/kg a day in children.

For maintenance treatment, the dose should be slowly reduced to the lowest effective level.

Monitoring for Nephrotic Syndrome Patients: Since Neoral can impair renal function, it is necessary to assess renal function frequently and if serum creatinine remains increased by more than 30% above baseline at more than 1 measurement, the dosage of Sandimmune Neoral must be reduced by 25 to 50%.

In some patients it may be difficult to detect cyclosporine-induced renal dysfunction because of changes in renal function related to the nephrotic syndrome itself. Renal biopsy should be considered for patients with steroid-dependent minimal change nephropathy in whom Neoral therapy has been maintained for more than 1 year.

Periodic monitoring of cyclosporine trough levels is recommended.

Neoral/Sandimmune I.V. (cont'd)

Switch from Sandimmune oral formulations to Neoral: Caution is advised in switching patients from Sandimmune oral formulations to Neoral. The two should not be used interchangeably.

The available data indicate that after a 1:1 switch from Sandimmune oral formulations to Neoral, the following differences are observed (see Table X).

Table X—Neoral

Switch from Sandimmune Oral Formulations to Neoral

Parameter	Difference following 1:1 Switch from Sandimmune Oral Formulations to Neoral
C_{min} in whole blood	comparable*
T_{max}	1 hour earlier for Neoral
C_{max}	59% higher for Neoral
Absolute bioavailability (AUC)	29% higher for Neoral

*Varies from patient to patient.

Transplant Indications: For converting patients from Sandimmune oral formulations to Neoral, an initial mg for mg conversion from Sandimmune to Neoral is recommended, with subsequent dose titration if required. Available data confirm that following this initial mg for mg conversion, comparable trough concentrations of cyclosporine in whole blood are achieved, maintaining in most patients adequate immunosuppression. In many patients, higher peak concentrations (C_{max}) and an increased exposure to the drug (AUC) may occur. No additional adverse events, including renal dysfunction were observed due to these changes in pharmacokinetic parameters during long-term treatment. In a small percentage of patients, these changes may be more marked and of clinical significance. Their magnitude depends largely on the individual ability to absorb cyclosporine from the originally used Sandimmune oral formulations. (For example, in specific clinical situations like early after transplantation, in recipients of liver grafts or patients who were transplanted for cystic fibrosis, the absorption of cyclosporine from Sandimmune is even more markedly variable). In these patients, dose reduction should be undertaken to achieve the appropriate trough concentration range.

Clinical data in renal transplant patients have demonstrated that a large proportion of patients previously on Sandimmune therapy can be maintained at the same dose of Neoral as with Sandimmune oral formulations.

Moreover, all patients should be monitored according to the following recommendations: a) Preconversion (i.e., on Sandimmune): Measure cyclosporine trough concentration, serum creatinine and blood pressure. b) Day 1: Convert the patient to the same daily dose of Neoral as was previously used with oral Sandimmune (i.e., on a mg to mg basis). c) Days 4 to 7 post conversion: Follow-up visit to measure cyclosporine trough concentration, serum creatinine and blood pressure. d) Subsequent follow-up: Depending on the findings on review at days 4 to 7, subsequent follow-up visits may need to be arranged (e.g., week 2 and week 4) in the first 2-month period after conversion to Neoral. During these visits, cyclosporine trough concentrations, serum creatinine and blood pressure should be measured and dependent on these measurements the dose of Neoral adjusted accordingly.

Caution is advised in switching patients from Sandimmune oral formulations to Neoral. The two should not be used interchangeably.

Nontransplant Indications: In psoriasis, rheumatoid arthritis or nephrotic syndrome patients, the clinical status of each patient should be assessed prior to initiating Neoral therapy. Initial conversion from Sandimmune oral formulations to Neoral should be conducted on a 1:0.7 basis with monitoring for dose-dependent side effects as outlined below. The dose of Neoral should be subsequently adjusted according to each patient's response.

If, on more than 1 measurement, the serum creatinine increases more than 30% above the pre-Sandimmune (oral formulations) baseline, the dose of Neoral should be decreased (see Precautions).

All patients should be monitored according to the following recommendations: a) Preconversion: Measure serum creatinine and blood pressure prior to conversion from oral Sandimmune to Neoral. b) Day 1: Initiate Neoral therapy. c) Week 2, 4 and 8: Measure serum creatinine and blood pressure. If serum creatinine levels increase to more than 30% above the pre-Sandimmune baseline level at more than one measurement, the dose of Neoral should be reduced. In addition, if either parameter exceeds the level at the time of conversion, consider reducing the dose of Neoral. d) For nephrotic syndrome patients, monitoring of cyclosporine trough levels is recommended.

Administration: Neoral should always be given in 2 divided doses.

Neoral Soft Gelatin Capsules: When the blister package is opened, a characteristic smell is noticeable. This is normal and does not mean that there is anything wrong with the capsule.

Capsules should be swallowed whole.

Neoral Solution should be diluted with preferably orange juice or apple juice. Grapefruit juice should be avoided for dilution owing to its possible interference with the P450 enzyme system. Immediately before taking the solution, it should be stirred well. Other drinks such as soft drinks can be used according to individual taste.

The syringe should not come into contact with the diluent. If the syringe is to be cleaned, do not rinse it but wipe the outside with a dry tissue.

Sandimmune I.V. (50 mg/mL Concentrate for I.V. Infusion) is diluted to 1:20 to 1:100, immediately prior to use, with 5% glucose or normal saline and administered by slow i.v. infusion over a period of 2 to 6 hours (see Precautions).

If available, glass containers should be used. Plastic bottles should only be used if they conform to the requirements for "plastic containers for blood" of the European pharmacopoeia, since polyoxyethylated castor oil contained in the concentrate can cause phthalate stripping from PVC. Containers and stoppers should be free of silicon oil and fatty substances.

Information for the Patient: See Blue Section—Information for the Patient "Neoral".

Supplied: Sandimmune I.V. (concentrate for i.v. infusion): Each mL of sterile ampul in a polyoxyethylated castor oil/ethanol vehicle contains: cyclosporine 50 mg. Ampuls of 1 and 5 mL. Dilution: The concentrate for i.v. infusion should be diluted to between 1:20 and 1:100 in 5% glucose or normal saline only, immediately prior to use (see Dosage).

Store the i.v. product, protected from light, at temperatures not exceeding 30°C. Do not store in the refrigerator and protect from freezing.

Neoral: Capsules: 10 mg: Each soft gelatin capsule contains: cyclosporine for microemulsion 10 mg. Nonmedicinal ingredients: dl-α-tocopherol, ethanol, hydrogenated castor oil, maize oil and propylene glycol; shell: gelatin, glycerol and propylene glycol; coloring agents: aluminum chloride, hydroxypropyl methylcellulose, sodium hydroxide and titanium dioxide. Packs of 60 (6 full aluminum blister strips of 10 capsules each).

25 mg: Each soft gelatin capsule contains: cyclosporine for microemulsion 25 mg. Nonmedicinal ingredients: dl-α-tocopherol, ethanol, hydrogenated castor oil, maize oil and propylene glycol; shell: gelatin, glycerol and propylene glycol; coloring agents: aluminum chloride, carmimic acid, hydroxypropyl methylcellulose, iron oxide black, sodium hydroxide and titanium dioxide. Packs of 30 (6 full aluminum blister strips of 5 capsules each).

50 mg: Each soft gelatin capsule contains: cyclosporine for microemulsion 50 mg. Nonmedicinal ingredients: dl-α-tocopherol, ethanol, hydrogenated castor oil, maize oil and propylene glycol; shell: gelatin, glycerol and propylene glycol; coloring agents: aluminum chloride, hydroxypropyl methylcellulose, sodium hydroxide and titanium dioxide. Packs of 30 (6 full aluminum blister strips of 5 capsules each).

100 mg: Each soft gelatin capsule contains: cyclosporine for microemulsion 100 mg. Nonmedicinal ingredients: dl-α-tocopherol, ethanol, hydrogenated castor oil, maize oil and propylene glycol; shell: gelatin, glycerol and propylene glycol; coloring agents: aluminum chloride, carmimic acid, hydroxypropyl methylcellulose, iron oxide black, sodium hydroxide and titanium dioxide. Packs of 30 (6 full aluminum blister strips of 5 capsules each).

The capsules should be stored at temperatures between 15 and 25°C and should not be removed from the blister packs until required for use. Occasional increases in temperature up to 30°C do not affect the quality of the product.

Solution: Each mL contains: cyclosporine for microemulsion 100 mg dissolved. Nonmedicinal ingredients: dl-α-tocopherol, ethanol, hydrogenated castor oil, maize oil and propylene glycol. Bottles of 50 mL. A graduated syringe for dispensing is provided.

Once opened, the contents must be used within 2 months. Store and dispense in the original container. Store between 15 and 30°C, preferably not below 20°C for prolonged periods, as it contains oily components of natural origin which tend to solidify at low temperatures. Do not store in the refrigerator and protect from freezing.

A jelly-like formation may occur below 20°C, which is however reversible at temperatures up to 30°C. Minor flakes or a slight sediment may still be observed. These phenomena do not affect the efficacy and safety of the product, and the dosing by means of the syringe remains accurate.

(Shown in Product Recognition Section)

Reviewed 1997

NEOSPORIN® Preparations Ⓟ

Glaxo Wellcome

Polymyxin B—Neomycin Compound

Antibiotic

Indications: Cream: Infection in dermatologic disorders particularly where the lesions are moist or weeping. Prophylactically, against bacterial contamination in burns, skin grafts, incisions and other clean lesions. For abrasions, minor cuts and wounds, the cream may prevent infection and permit normal healing.

Irrigating Solution: To be diluted and used as a continuous irrigant or rinse for short-term use in the urinary bladder of abacteriuric patients to help prevent bacteriuria and gram-negative rod bacteremia associated with the use of indwelling catheters.

Ointment: For all lesions which are infected or likely to become infected by bacteria.

Sterile Ophthalmic Ointment: Infections of eyes and external ear.

Eye and Ear Solution: For prophylaxis and treatment of eye and ear infections.

Contraindications: Hypersensitivity to any of the components.

The presence of preexisting nerve deafness is a contraindication to the use of any topical aminoglycoside in circumstances where significant systemic absorption could occur.

Neosporin cream and Neosporin ointment should not be used in the eyes or in the external ear canal if the eardrum is perforated.

A possibility of increased neomycin absorption exists in neonates and infants, thus Neosporin is not recommended for use in neonates, and should be used at reduced dosages in infants.

Warnings: In neonates and infants, absorption by immature skin may be enhanced. Immaturity of renal function may predispose these patients to decreased elimination and increased blood levels.

Irrigating Solution: Prophylactic bladder care with Neosporin irrigant should not be given where there is a possibility of systemic absorption. Neosporin should not be used for irrigation other than for the urinary bladder. Systemic absorption after topical application of neomycin to open wounds, burns and granulating surfaces is significant and serum concentrations comparable to and often higher than those attained following oral and parenteral therapy have been reported. Absorption of neomycin from the denuded bladder surface has been reported.

However, the likelihood of toxicity following topical irrigation of the intact urinary bladder with Neosporin is low since no appreciable amounts of these antibiotics enter the systemic circulation by this route if irrigation does not exceed 10 days.

Neosporin irrigant is intended for continuous prophylactic irrigation of the lumen of the intact urinary bladder of patients with indwelling catheters. Patients should be under constant supervision by a physician. Irrigation should be avoided in patients with defects in the bladder mucosa or bladder wall, such as vesical rupture, or in association with operative procedures on the bladder wall, because of the risk of toxicity due to systemic absorption following diffusion into absorptive tissues and spaces. When absorbed, neomycin and polymyxin B are nephrotoxic antibiotics, and the nephrotoxic potentials are additive. In addition, both antibiotics, when absorbed, are neurotoxins: neomycin can destroy fibers of the acoustic nerve causing permanent bilateral deafness; neomycin and polymyxin B are additive in their neuromuscular blocking effects, not only in terms of potency and duration but also in terms of characteristics of the blocks produced.

Eye and Ear Solution: The manifestations of sensitization to neomycin are usually itching, reddening and edema of the conjunctiva and eyelid. It may be manifest simply as a failure to heal. During long-term use of neomycin-containing products, periodic examination for such signs is advisable, and the patient should be told to discontinue the product if they are observed. These symptoms subside quickly on withdrawing the medication. Neomycin-containing applications should be avoided for the patient thereafter.

Precautions: Articles in current medical literature indicate an increase in the incidence of allergies to neomycin in patients with stasis ulcers or eczema. The possibility of an allergic reaction to neomycin should be borne in mind. As with other antibiotic preparations, prolonged use may result in overgrowth of nonsusceptible organisms, including fungi. Appropriate measures should be taken if this occurs.

Because of the potential hazard of nephrotoxicity and ototoxicity due to neomycin, care should be exercised when treating extensive burns, trophic ulceration and other extensive conditions where absorption of neomycin is possible.

After a maximal course, treatment should **not** be repeated for at least 3 months.

Pregnancy and *Lactation:* There is little information to demonstrate the possible effect of topically applied neomycin in pregnancy and lactation. However, neomycin present in maternal blood can cross the placenta and may give rise to a theoretical risk of fetal toxicity, thus use of Neosporin is not recommended in pregnancy and lactation.

Children: Dosage in children should be reduced in proportion to body weight.

Geriatrics: No specific information is available regarding the use of Neosporin in the elderly; however, the maximum dosage should be reduced in cases where a decrease in renal function may exist.

Irrigating Solution: Care should be taken to prevent reflux of the solution up the ureters, since the concentration of neomycin may cause renal toxicity. Ototoxicity, nephrotoxicity, and neuromuscular blockade may occur if the components of the preparation are systemically absorbed (see Warnings). Absorption of neomycin from the denuded bladder surface has been reported. Patients with impaired renal function, infants, dehydrated patients, elderly patients, and patients receiving high doses of prolonged treatment are especially at risk for the development of the toxicity.

The safety and effectiveness of the preparation for use in the care of patients with recent lower urinary tract surgery have not been established.

Urine specimens should be collected during prophylactic bladder care for urinalysis, culture, and susceptibility testing. Positive culture suggest the presence of organisms which are resistant to the bladder rinse antibiotics.

Eye and Ear Solution: Should not be given subconjunctivally or intraocularly, nor should it be used for the irrigation of fistulous tracts in or about the eye or its socket. Treatment should be continued until at least 48 hours after the eye has apparently recovered. In patients with perforated ear drums or long-standing otitis media, treatment should be restricted to 10 days.

Adverse Effects: Neomycin occasionally causes skin sensitization. Ototoxicity and nephrotoxicity have also been reported (see Warnings). Adverse reactions have occurred with topical use of antibiotic combinations including neomycin and polymyxin B. Exact incidence figures are not available since no denominator of treated patients is available. The reaction occurring most often is allergic sensitization. In 1 clinical study, using a 20% neomycin patch, neomycin-induced allergic skin reactions occurred in two of 2 175 (0.09%) individuals in the general population. In another study the incidence was found to be approximately 1%.

Irrigating Solution: Irritation of the urinary bladder mucosa has been reported.

Overdose: Symptoms and Treatment: Gastric lavage.

Dosage: Cream: Apply a small quantity 2 to 5 times daily, as required, rub in gently if condition permits.

Irrigating Solution: For use with 3-way catheters or with other catheter systems permitting continuous irrigation of bladder. Under sterile conditions add 1 mL to 1 000 mL bottle of isotonic saline solution. Connect this bottle to inflow lumen of the three way catheter which has been inserted with aseptic precautions. Outflow lumen is connected via sterile disposable plastic hose, to a sterile disposable collection bag. In-flow rate, for most patients, should be adjusted to a slow drip to deliver about 1 000 mL every 24 hours. If the patient's urine output exceeds 2 L/day, it is recommended that the in-flow rate should be adjusted to deliver 2 000 mL of the solution in a 24-hour period.

Ointment: Apply 2 to 5 times daily over the affected area. Cover with dressing or leave exposed. **Do not use in the eyes.**

Sterile Ophthalmic Ointment: Apply 2 to 5 times daily over the affected area. Cover with dressing or leave exposed.

Eye and Ear Solution: The suggested dose is 1 or 2 drops in the affected eye or ear, 2 to 4 times a day, or more frequently as required.

Children and Infants: Neosporin is suitable for use in children at the same dose as adults, but the doses should be reduced for use in infants. Neosporin is not recommended for use in neonates (see Warnings).

Information for the Patient: See Blue Section—Information for the Patient "Neosporin Preparations".

Supplied: Cream: Each g contains: polymyxin B sulfate 10 000 units, neomycin sulfate (equiv. to 3.5 mg neomycin base) 5 mg, gramicidin 250 µg in a white vanishing cream base, pH approximately 5.0. Nonmedicinal ingredients: emulsifying wax, methylparaben, mineral oil, poloxamer, propylene glycol, purified water and white petrolatum. Tubes of 15 g. Store at 15 to 25°C.

Irrigating Solution: Each mL of sterile, aqueous solution contains: neomycin (as sulfate, 57 mg) 40 mg, polymyxin B (as sulfate) 200 000 units. Nonmedicinal ingredients: methylparaben and water for injection in 20 mL vials. Not for injection. Ampuls of 1 mL. Vials of 20 mL. Store at 2 to 8°C.

Ointment: Each g contains: polymyxin B sulfate 5 000 units, zinc bacitracin 400 units and neomycin sulfate 5 mg, in a low melting point petrolatum base. Tubes of 15 and 30 g. Store at 15 to 25°C.

Sterile Ophthalmic Ointment: Each g contains: polymyxin B sulfate 10 000 units, zinc bacitracin 400 units and neomycin sulfate 5 mg, in a low melting point petrolatum base. Tubes of 3.5 g. Store at 15 to 25°C.

Eye and Ear Solution: Each mL contains: polymyxin B sulfate 10 000 units, 2.5 mg neomycin sulfate, 25 µg gramicidin. Nonmedicinal ingredients: alcohol, benzalkonium chloride, poloxamer, propylene glycol and water for injection. Plastic dropper bottles of 10 mL. Store at 15 to 25°C.

Reviewed 1998

NEOSTRATA™ AHA Preparations

Canderm Pharma

Glycolic Acid and Gluconolactone

Supplied: Astringent Acne Treatment: Each mL contains: salicylic acid 2% in a base containing an alpha hydroxy acid. Bottles of 50 mL.

Blemish Spot Gel: Each mL contains: salicylic acid USP 2% in a base containing glycolic acid 5% (40% ethanol). Bottles of 15 mL.

Cleansing Lotion: Each bottle contains: gluconolactone 4%. Bottles of 110 mL.

Conditioner: Lip and Lip Contour Conditioner: Each stick contains: gluconolactone 8%. Sticks of 4 g.

Cream: Each jar contains: glycolic acid 8% in an opalescent water washable cream. Jars of 70 g.

Eye Contour Cream: Each jar contains: gluconolactone 4%. Jars of 15 mL.

HQ Gel: Each g of gel contains: hydroquinone USP 2% w/w in a nonmedicinal gel base containing glycolic acid 10%. Tubes of 45 g.

Light Textured Smoothing Cream Ultra Moisturizing Formula SPF 15: Each mL contains: octyl methoxycinnamate 7.5% and oxybenzone 5% in a base containing gluconolactone 4%. Tubes of 50 mL.

Lotion: Each bottle contains: glycolic acid 10% in an opalescent water washable lotion. Bottles of 175 mL.

Oil-Free Smoothing & Moisturizing Hydragel: Each mL contains: a hygragel moisturizer in a base containing gluconolactone 4%. Bottles of 50 mL.

Sensitive Skin Cream: Each jar contains: glycolic acid 4%. Jars of 70 g.

Smoothing and Moisturizing Lotion Sensitive Skin Formula SPF 15: Each mL contains: octyl methoxycinnamate 7.5% and oxybenzone 5% in a base containing glycolic acid 4%. Tubes of 50 mL.

Smoothing and Moisturizing Formula SPF 15: Each mL contains: octyl methoxycinnamate 7.5% and oxybenzone 5% in a base containing glycolic acid 8%. Tubes of 50 mL.

Solution: Each bottle contains: glycolic acid 8%. Bottles of 110 mL.

Ultra Moisturizing Cream: Each jar contains: gluconolactone 4%. Jars of 50 mL.

NEO-SYNEPHRINE® Parenteral

Sanofi

Phenylephrine HCl

Vasopressor

Pharmacology: When applied topically or infiltrated into the tissues, phenylephrine produces vasoconstriction that lasts longer than that of epinephrine and ephedrine. Its action on the heart contrasts sharply with that of epinephrine and ephedrine, in that it slows the heart rate and increases the stroke output, inducing no disturbance in the rhythm of the pulse.

In therapeutic doses, it produces little if any stimulation of either the spinal cord or cerebrum. A singular advantage of this drug is the fact that repeated injections produce comparable effects.

Indications: For the maintenance of blood pressure during spinal and inhalation anesthesia, and also for overcoming vascular failure in shock and shock-like states, drug-induced hypotension or hypersensitivity. Employed to overcome paroxysmal supraventricular tachycardia, to prolong spinal anesthesia and as a vasoconstrictor in regional anesthesia.

Precautions: Should not be administered with MAO inhibitors, halothane anesthesia, with oxytocic drugs in obstetrics, in the presence of severe hypertension, ventricular tachycardia or hypersensitivity to phenylephrine.

Use with caution in elderly patients or those with hyperthyroidism, bradycardia, partial heart block, myocardial disease or severe arteriosclerosis. MAO inhibitors and tricyclic antidepressants may potentiate pressor response.

Pregnancy: Animal reproduction studies have not been conducted with phenylephrine. It is also not known whether phenylephrine can cause fetal harm when administered to a pregnant woman or can affect reproduction capacity. Phenylephrine should be given to a pregnant woman only if clearly needed.

Lactation: It is not known whether this drug is excreted in human milk. Because many are excreted in human milk, caution should be exercised when phenylephrine is administered to a nursing woman.

Adverse Effects: Headache, reflex bradycardia, excitability, restlessness and rarely arrhythmias.

Overdose: Symptoms: Overdosage may induce ventricular extrasystoles and short paroxysms of ventricular tachycardia, sensations of fullness in the head and tingling of the extremities.

Treatment: An excessive elevation of blood pressure may be immediately relieved by an α-adrenergic blocking agent.

Dosage: Phenylephrine is generally injected s.c., i.m., slowly i.v., or in dilute solution as a continuous i.v. infusion. In patients with paroxysmal supraventricular tachycardia and, if indicated, in case of emergency, phenylephrine is administered directly i.v. The dose should be adjusted according to the pressor response.

Mild or Moderate Hypotension: S.C. or I.M.: Usual dose, from 2 to 5 mg. Range, from 1 to 10 mg. Initial dose should not exceed 5 mg.

I.V.: Usual dose, 0.2 mg. Range, from 0.1 to 0.5 mg. Initial dose should not exceed 0.5 mg.

Injections should not be repeated more often than every 10 to 15 minutes. A 5 mg i.m. dose should raise blood presssure for 1 to 2 hours. A 0.5 mg i.v. dose should elevate the pressure for about 15 minutes.

Severe Hypotension and Shock: Blood volume depletion should always be corrected as fully as possible before any vasopressor is administered. When, as an emergency measure, intraaortic pressures must be maintained to prevent cerebral or coronary artery ischemia, phenylephrine can be administered before and concurrently with blood volume replacement.

Higher initial and maintenance doses of phenylephrine are required in patients with persistent or untreated severe hypotension or shock. Hypotension produced by powerful peripheral adrenergic blocking agents, chlorpromazine, or pheochromocytomectomy may also require more intensive therapy.

Continuous Infusion: Add 10 mg of the drug (1 mL of 1% solution) to 500 mL of Dextrose Injection, USP, or Sodium Chloride Injection, USP (providing a 1:50 000 solution). To raise the blood pressure rapidly, start the infusion at about 100 to 180 µg/minute (based on 20 drops/mL, this would be 100 to 180 drops/minute). When the blood pressure is stabilized (at a low normal level for the individual), a maintenance rate of 40 to 60 µg/minute usually suffices (based on 20 drops/

Neo-Synephrine Parenteral (cont'd)

mL, this would be 40 to 60 drops/minute). If the drop size of the infusion system varies from 20 drops/mL, the dose must be adjusted accordingly. If a prompt initial pressor response is not obtained, additional increments of phenylephrine (10 mg or more) are added to the infusion bottle. The rate of flow is then adjusted until the desired blood pressure level is obtained. (In some cases, a more potent vasopressor, such as norepinephrine, may be required.) Hypertension should be avoided. The blood pressure should be checked frequently. Headache and/or bradycardia may indicate hypertension. Arrhythmias are rare.

Spinal Anesthesia—Hypotension: Routine parenteral use of phenylephrine has been recommended by many investigators for the prophylaxis and treatment of hypotension during spinal anesthesia. It is best administered s.c. or i.m. 3 or 4 minutes before injection of the spinal anesthetic. The total requirement for high anesthetic levels is usually 3 mg and for lower levels, 2 mg. For hypotensive emergencies during spinal anesthesia, phenylephrine may be injected i.v. beginning with a dose of 0.2 mg. Any subsequent dose should not exceed the previous dose by more than 0.1 to 0.2 mg and should not be more than 0.5 mg. To combat hypotension during spinal anesthesia in children, a dose of 0.5 to 1 mg/11.3 kg of body weight, administered s.c. or i.m., is recommended.

Prolongation of Spinal Anesthesia: The addition of 2 to 5 mg of phenylephrine to the anesthetic solution increases the duration of motor block as much as approximately 50% without any increase in the incidence of complications such as nausea, vomiting, or blood pressure disturbances.

Vasoconstrictor for Regional Analgesia: Concentrations about 10 times those of epinephrine are recommended. The optimum strength is 1:20 000 (made by adding 1 mg of phenylephrine to every 20 mL of local anesthetic solution). Some pressor responses can be expected when 2 mg or more are injected.

Paroxysmal Supraventricular Tachycardia: **Rapid i.v.** injection (within 20 to 30 seconds) is recommended; the initial dose should not exceed 0.5 mg, and subsequent doses, which are determined by the initial blood pressure response, should not exceed the preceding dose by more than 0.1 to 0.2 mg, and should never exceed 1 mg.

Drug-Induced Reactions: Hypotension and occasionally severe shock may result from overdosage or idiosyncrasy following the administration of certain drugs, especially adrenergic and ganglionic blocking agents, rauwolfia and veratrum alkaloids, and phenothiazine tranquilizers. Patients who receive a phenothiazine derivative as a preoperative medication are especially susceptible to these reactions. As an adjunct in the management of such episodes, phenylephrine is a suitable agent for restoring blood pressure.

Supplied: Each mL of 1% solution contains: phenylephrine HCl 10 mg in water for injection. Nonmedicinal ingredients: citric acid monohydrate, sodium chloride, sodium citrate dihydrate and sodium metabisulfite. Ampuls of 1 mL, boxes of 10.

NEOTOPIC ℞

Technilab

Polymyxin B Sulfate—Neomycin Sulfate—Bacitracin Zinc

Antibiotic

Supplied: Each g of ointment contains: polymyxin B sulfate 5 000 units, bacitracin zinc 400 units and neomycin sulfate 5 mg. Nonmedicinal ingredients: light mineral oil and petrolatum. Tubes of 15 and 30 g. Store between 15 and 30°C.

NEPTAZANE® ℞

Wyeth-Ayerst

Methazolamide

Carbonic Anhydrase Inhibitor

Supplied: 25 mg: Each white, square tablet, engraved LL on one side and N2 on the other, contains: methazolamide 25 mg. Nonmedicinal ingredients: acacia, alginic acid, dibasic calcium phosphate, gelatin, magnesium stearate, starch and water purified. Tartrazine-free. Bottles of 100.

50 mg: Each white, round, scored tablet, engraved LL on one side and N above 1 below the score on the other side, contains: methazolamide 50 mg. Nonmedicinal ingredients: acacia, alginic acid, dibasic calcium phosphate, gelatin, magnesium stearate, starch and water purified. Tartrazine-free. Bottles of 100.

Store at 15 to 30°C.

(Shown in Product Recognition Section)

NERISALIC® ℞

Stiefel

Diflucortolone Valerate—Salicylic Acid

Topical Corticosteroid—Keratolytic

Pharmacology: Nerisalic combines the anti-inflammatory, antipruritic and vasoconstrictive activity of diflucortolone valerate and the keratolytic effects of salicylic acid.

Both diflucortolone valerate and its split ester are topically active.

Indications: The topical treatment of chronic eczema, psoriasis vulgaris, neuro-dermatitis and scaly crusty dermatoses which respond to corticosteroid therapy.

Nerisalic is not suitable for the treatment of perioral dermatitis and rosacea.

Contraindications: In patients who have shown hypersensitivity, allergy or intolerance to diflucortolone valerate or other corticosteroids or salicylic acid or to any excipients in the preparation. Nerisalic should not be applied to skin areas with fissures, erosions, scratches or excoriations.

Topical steroids are contraindicated in untreated bacterial and/or fungal skin infections. Topical steroids should not be applied in cases of tuberculosis of the skin, or syphilitic skin infections, chickenpox, eruptions following vaccinations and viral diseases of the skin in general.

Warnings: Nerisalic is not for ophthalmic use and, consequently, should not be used in or near the eyes.

Nerisalic should not be applied in rhagades and ulcerations (e.g. lower leg ulcers). Inclusion of salicylic acid in this preparation increases steroid penetration into the viable epidermis thereby increasing the potential for skin atrophy.

Pregnancy: The safety of Nerisalic during pregnancy has not been established. Teratogenic and embryotoxic effects of diflucortolone valerate have been reported following dermal application in animal studies. Nerisalic should be used during pregnancy only if the potential benefits justify the potential risks to the fetus.

Lactation: Systemically administered corticosteroids can appear in human milk and can suppress growth, interfere with endogenous corticosteroid production or cause adverse effects. Caution should be exercised when Nerisalic is administered to a nursing woman since it is not known whether the ingredients of Nerisalic are excreted in human milk.

Precautions: Systemic absorption of topical corticosteroids has produced reversible hypothalamic-pituitary-adrenal (HPA) axis suppression, manifestations of Cushing's syndrome, hyperglycemia and glucosuria in some patients.

Significant systemic absorption may occur when steroids are applied over large areas of the body or if used under an occlusive dressing. To minimize this possibility when long-term therapy is anticipated, interrupt treatment periodically or treat one area of the body at a time. It is recommended that patients receiving a large dose of a potent topical steroid applied over a large surface area be evaluated periodically for evidence of HPA axis suppression by using the urinary free cortisol and ACTH stimulation tests. If HPA axis inhibition is observed, an attempt should be made to withdraw the drug, to reduce the frequency of application or substitute a less potent steroid. Recovery of HPA axis function is generally prompt and complete upon discontinuation of the drug. Infrequently, signs and symptoms of steroid withdrawal may occur, requiring supplemental systemic corticosteroids.

If irritation or hypersensitivity reactions develop, Nerisalic should be discontinued and appropriate therapy initiated.

Prolonged use of topical corticosteroid products may produce atrophy of the skin and of s.c. tissues, particularly on flexor surfaces and on the face, telangiectasias, hirsutism and steroid induced acne. If this is noted, discontinue use of the product. Long-term therapy with Nerisalic should be avoided.

In cases of bacterial or fungal skin infections, appropriate antibacterial agents should be used as primary therapy. If it is considered necessary, Nerisalic may be used as an adjunct to control inflammation, erythema and itching.

Nerisalic should be used with caution in patients with stasis dermatitis and other skin diseases associated with impaired circulation, on extremities of diabetics with impaired circulation or on patients with inherent compromised cardiovascular circulatory problems.

Patients should be advised to inform subsequent physicians of the prior use of corticosteroids.

Systemic absorption of the corticosteroid and salicylic acid may be increased with elevated body temperature or occlusive dressings. Patients with elevated temperatures should be monitored for HPA axis effects and occlusive dressings should not be used.

Occlusive dressings should not be applied if there is an elevation of body temperature.

Because of the risk of salicylate intoxication, long term or large area and occlusive use of Nerisalic should be avoided in patients with impaired renal function.

Since salicylic acid is absorbed almost completely, the simultaneous topical or internal use of other preparations containing salicylic acid or salicylate is inadvisable. The concentration of salicylic acid contained in the preparation is not high enough for the treatment of secondary skin diseases caused by bacteria or fungi. Additional antibacterial or antimycotic therapy is recommended in these cases.

Children: Due to their larger skin surface area to body weight ratio, children may demonstrate a greater susceptibility to the topical corticosteroid-induced HPA axis suppression and Cushing's syndrome than mature patients.

Suppression of the HPA axis, Cushing's syndrome and intracranial hypertension have been reported in children receiving topical corticosteroids. Manifestations of adrenal suppression in children include linear growth retardation, delayed weight gain, low plasma cortisol levels and absence of response to ACTH stimulation. Manifestations of intracranial hypertension include bulging fontanelles, headaches and bilateral papilledema.

Administration of topical corticosteroid to children should be limited to the least amount compatible with an effective therapeutic regimen. Chronic corticosteroid therapy may interfere with the growth and development of the children.

The following tests may be helpful in evaluating HPA axis suppression due to corticosteroid component: urinary free cortisol test and ACTH stimulation test.

Because of the risk, of salicylate intoxication, long term or large area and occlusive use of Nerisalic should be avoided in babies, infants and in children.

Adverse Effects: The following local adverse reactions are reported when topical corticosteroids are used as recommended. These reactions are listed in an approximate decreasing order of occurrence: burning, itching, irritation, dryness folliculitis, hypertrichosis, acneiform eruptions, hypopigmentation, perioral dermatitis, allergic contact dermatitis, maceration of the skin, secondary infection, skin atrophy, telangiectasia, striae and miliaria. Hypothalamic-pituitary-adrenal axis suppression have also been reported following topical corticosteroid therapy.

Posterior sub-capsular cataracts have been reported following systemic use of corticosteroids.

In addition, the salicylic acid contained in the preparation may produce some desquamation, local reddening of the skin, pruritus, burning, pain and stinging. Hypersensitivity to salicylic acid may occur. If this occurs, discontinue use

Overdose: No specific antidote is available. Treatment should be symptomatic.

Symptoms: Percutaneous absorption of corticosteroids can occur when large amounts of corticosteroids are applied. Toxic effects may include ecchymosis of skin, peptic ulceration, hypertension, aggravation of infection, hirsutism, acne, edema and muscle weakness due to protein depletion.

High levels of salicylates may cause temporary hearing or visual disturbance, drowsiness and nausea.

Treatment: Appropriate symptomatic treatment of corticosteroid and/or salicylic acid overdosage is indicated. Acute hypercorticoid symptoms are usually reversible. Treat electrolyte imbalance, if necessary. In cases of chronic toxicity, slow withdrawal of corticosteroid is advised.

Dosage: Nerisalic should be applied as a thin film to diseased areas 2 to 3 times daily in the first week of treatment. During subsequent weeks, 1 or 2 applications/day are sufficient. The duration of the treatment should not exceed a total of 4 weeks.

The total dose applied weekly should not exceed 100 g.

If improvement is not noted within a few days to a week, the local application of Nerisalic should be discontinued and the patient re-evaluated.

Supplied: Each g of oily cream contains: diflucortolone-21-valerate 0.1% and salicylic acid 3% in a water-in-oil emulsion. Nonmedicinal ingredients: hydrocarbons (white petrolatum, paraffin), white wax and dehymuls E. There is no preservative. Tubes of 30 g. Store at 15 to 30°C. Avoid freezing.

NERISONE® Ⓟ
Stiefel
Diflucortolone Valerate
Topical Corticosteroid

Supplied: Cream: Each g of oil-in-water emulsion contains: diflucortolone valerate 1 mg (0.1%). Nonmedicinal ingredients: carbomer 934 NF, edetate disodium, methyl paraben, mineral oil, polyoxyl 40 stearate, propyl paraben, purified water USP, sodium hydroxide, stearyl alcohol NF and white petrolatum. Tubes of 30 g.

Oily Cream: Each g of water-in-oil emulsion contains: diflucortolone valerate 1 mg (0.1%). Nonmedicinal ingredients: mineral oil, penta. eryth. F.A.E. comp., purified water USP, white petrolatum and white wax. There is no preservative. Tubes of 30 g.

Ointment: Each g of single-phase fatty ointment contains: diflucortolone valerate 1 mg (0.1%). Nonmedicinal ingredients: ceresin, hydrogenated castor oil, mineral oil and white petrolatum. There is no preservative. Tubes of 30 g.

Store between 15 and 30°C.

NESACAINE®-CE
Astra
Chloroprocaine HCl
Local Anesthetic

Pharmacology: Chloroprocaine stabilizes the neuronal membrane and prevents the initiation and transmission of nerve impulses, thereby effecting local anesthetic action.

The onset of action is rapid (usually within 6 to 12 minutes). The duration of anesthesia depends on the procedure and the amount used, but could last up to 60 minutes.

Chloroprocaine is rapidly hydrolyzed in plasma by pseudocholinesterase. This hydrolysis results in the formation of β-diethylaminoethanol and 2-chloro-4-aminobenzoic acid which inhibits the action of sulfonamides (see Precautions).

Solutions of chloroprocaine do not injure nervous tissue and are not irritating to other tissues in the recommended concentrations.

Indications: For the production of local anesthesia by infiltration and regional nerve block, including caudal and epidural blocks. Any unused portion should be discarded. Chloroprocaine should not be used for spinal anesthesia.

Contraindications: Hypersensitive (allergic) to drugs of the PABA ester group.

Although CNS disease is generally considered a contraindication to caudal or epidural nerve block, it is not a contraindication to peripheral nerve block. Pathologic changes of the vertebral column may make epidural puncture impossible or inadvisable.

Warnings: Local anesthetics should only be employed by clinicians who are well versed in diagnosis and management of dose related toxicity and other acute emergencies which might arise from the block to be employed, and then only after ensuring the immediate availability of oxygen, other resuscitative drugs, cardiopulmonary resuscitative equipment, and the personnel resources needed for proper management of toxic reactions and related emergencies (see also Adverse Effects and Precautions). Delay in proper management of dose related toxicity, underventilation from any cause and/or altered sensitivity may lead to the development of acidosis, cardiac arrest and possibly, death.

Vasopressors should not be used in the presence of ergot-type oxytocic drugs, since a severe persistent hypertension may occur. To avoid intravascular injection, aspiration should be performed before the anesthetic solution is injected. The needle must be repositioned until no blood return can be elicited. However, the absence of blood in the syringe does not guarantee that intravascular injection has been avoided.

There are no data concerning use of chloroprocaine for obstetrical paracervical block when toxemia of pregnancy is present or when fetal distress or prematurity is anticipated in advance of the block; such use is, therefore, not recommended.

The following information should be considered by clinicians who select chloroprocaine for obstetrical paracervical block anesthesia: Fetal bradycardia (generally a heart rate of less than 120 per minute for more than 2 minutes) has been noted by electronic monitoring in about 5% to 10% of the cases (various studies) where initial total doses of 120 mg to 400 mg of chloroprocaine were employed. The incidence of bradycardia, within this dose range, might not be dose related. Fetal acidosis has not been demonstrated by blood gas monitoring around the time of bradycardia or afterwards. These data are limited and are generally restricted to non-toxemic cases where fetal distress or prematurity was not anticipated in advance of the block. No intact chloroprocaine and only trace quantities of a hydrolysis product, 2-chloro-4-aminobenzoic acid have been demonstrated in umbilical cord arterial or venous plasma following properly administered paracervical block with chloroprocaine. The role of drug factors and non-drug factors associated with fetal bradycardia following paracervical block are unexplained at this time.

Precautions: The safety and effectiveness of chloroprocaine injections depend upon proper dosage, correct technique, adequate precautions and readiness for emergencies.

The lowest dosage that results in effective anesthesia should be used to avoid high plasma levels and serious undesirable systemic side effects. Tolerance varies with the status of the patient. Debilitated patients, elderly patients, acutely ill patients and children should be given reduced doses commensurate with their age and physical status. Solutions containing vasoconstrictors should be used cautiously in the presence of disease which may adversely affect the patient's cardiovascular system.

Since ester-type local anesthetics are hydrolyzed by plasma cholinesterase produced by the liver, chloroprocaine should be used cautiously in patients with hepatic disease.

Injections should always be made slowly and with frequent aspirations to avoid inadvertent rapid intravascular administration which can produce systemic toxicity.

Chloroprocaine should be employed cautiously in persons with known drug allergies or sensitivities.

Injections of solutions containing epinephrine (see Dosage) in areas where the blood supply is limited (i.e., ears, nose, digits, etc.) or when peripheral vascular disease is present should be used cautiously.

Drug Interactions: Serious cardiac arrhythmias may occur if preparations containing a vasopressor are employed in patients during or following the administration of choloroform, halothane, cyclopropane, trichloroethylene, or other related agents. The para-aminobenzoic acid metabolite of chloroprocaine inhibits the action of sulfonamides. Therefore, chloroprocaine should not be used in any condition in which a sulfonamide drug is being employed.

In obstetrics, if vasoconstrictor drugs are used either to correct hypotension or are added to the local anesthetic solution, the obstetrician should be warned that some oxytocic drugs may cause severe persistent hypertension and even rupture of a cerebral blood vessel may occur during the postpartum period.

Solutions containing vasoconstrictors, particularly epinephrine and norepinephrine, should be used with extreme caution in patients receiving certain antidepressants, such as MAO inhibitors and tricyclic compounds, since severe prolonged hypertension may occur.

Carcinogenesis, Mutagenesis and Impairment of Fertility: Long-term studies in animals to evaluate carcinogenic potential and reproduction studies to evaluate mutagenesis or impairment of fertility have not been conducted with chloroprocaine.

Pregnancy: Safe use of chloroprocaine has not been established with respect to adverse effects upon fetal development. This fact should be carefully considered before administering this drug to women of childbearing potential, particularly during early pregnancy. This does not preclude the use of the drug at term for obstetrical analgesia. Adverse effects on the fetus, course of labor, or delivery have rarely been observed when proper dosage and proper technique have been employed.

Labor and Delivery: Local anesthetics rapidly cross the placenta, and when used for epidural, paracervical, pudendal or caudal block anesthesia, can cause varying degrees of maternal, fetal and neonatal toxicity.

The incidence and degree of toxicity depend upon the procedure performed, the type and amount of drug used, and the technique of drug administration. Adverse reactions in the parturient, fetus and neonate involve alterations of the CNS, peripheral vascular tone and cardiac function.

Maternal hypotension has resulted from regional anesthesia. Local anesthetics produce vasodilation by blocking sympathetic nerves. Elevating the patient's legs and positioning her on her left side will help prevent decreases in blood pressure. The fetal heart rate should also be monitored continuously, and electronic fetal monitoring is highly advisable.

Lactation: It is not known whether this drug is excreted in human milk. Because many drugs are excreted in human milk, caution should be exercised when chloroprocaine is administered to a nursing mother.

Adverse Effects: Systemic: Systemic adverse reactions result from high plasma levels due to rapid absorption, inadvertent intravascular injection or excessive dosage. Hypersensitivity, idiosyncrasy, or diminished tolerance (as in patients with plasma cholinesterase deficiency) are other causes of reactions. Reactions due to overdosage (high plasma levels) are systemic and involve the CNS and the cardiovascular system.

CNS: These are characterized by excitation and/or depression. Restlessness, anxiety, dizziness, tinnitus, blurred vision or tremors may occur, possibly proceeding to convulsions. However, excitement may be transient or absent, with depression the first manifestation of an adverse reaction. This may quickly be followed by drowsiness merging into unconsciousness and respiratory arrest.

Cardiovascular: High doses or unintended intravascular injection may cause depression of the myocardium manifested by an initial episode of hypotension and bradycardia and even cardiac arrest.

Allergic: Allergic reactions are rare and may occur as a result of sensitivity to chloroprocaine and are characterized by cutaneous lesions, urticaria, edema and anaphylactoid type symptomatology. These allergic reactions should be managed by conventional means. The detection of potential sensitivity by skin testing has not been fully established.

Neurologic: In the practice of epidural block, occasional inadvertent penetration of the subarachnoid space by the catheter may occur. The subsequent reactions depend on the amount of drug administered subdurally and may include, among others, spinal block of varying magnitude, loss of bowel and bladder control, loss of perineal sensation and sexual function. Persistent neurological deficit of some lower spinal segments with slow recovery (several months) has been reported in rare instances (see Dosage, Caudal and Epidural Block). Backache and headache have also been noted following lumbar epidural or caudal block.

Other: There have been reports of back pain following the use of chloroprocaine 3% for epidural anesthesia. In general, these experiences have occurred in healthy young to middle aged adults undergoing minor surgery as outpatients.

In all cases, the syndrome has resolved within 72 hours of the start of epidural analgesia, and there have been no reports of permanent or persistent sequelae.

Most of these experiences have been associated with the use of larger volumes of chloroprocaine than recommended and/or its use for skin and needle track infiltration prior to epidural puncture (see Dosage for recommended doses).

Overdose: Symptoms and Treatment: Acute emergencies from local anesthetics are generally related to high plasma levels encountered during therapeutic use of local anesthetics or to unintended subarachnoid injection of local anesthetic solution (see Adverse Effects, Warnings, and Precautions).

Treatment of a patient with toxic manifestations consists of assuring and maintaining a patent airway and supporting ventilation with oxygen and assisted or controlled ventilation (respiration) as required. This usually will be sufficient in the management of most reactions. Should a convulsion persist despite ventilatory therapy, small increments of anticonvulsive agents may be given i.v. such as a benzodiazepine (e.g. diazepam), or an ultra-short acting barbiturate (e.g. thiopental or thiamylal) or a short-acting barbiturate (e.g. pentobarbital or secobarbital). Cardiovascular depression may require circulatory assistance with i.v. fluids and/or vasopressors (e.g. ephedrine) as dictated by the clinical situation.

If not treated immediately, both convulsions and cardiovascular depression can result in hypoxia, acidosis, bradycardia, arrhythmias and cardiac arrest. If cardiac arrest should occur, standard cardiopulmonary resuscitative measures should be instituted. Recovery has been reported after prolonged resuscitative efforts.

Dosage: The lowest dose needed to provide effective anesthesia should be administered. As with all local anesthetics, the dosage varies and depends upon the area to be anesthetized, vascularity of the tissues, number of neuronal segments to be blocked, individual tolerance and the technique employed.

Dosages should be reduced for children, elderly or debilitated patients, and in patients with cardiac and/or liver disease. For specific techniques and procedures, refer to standard textbooks.

Preparation of Epinephrine Solution: To prepare a 1:200 000 epinephrine-chloroprocaine HCl solution add 0.15 mL of a 1:1 000 epinephrine injection USP to 30 mL of Nesacaine CE. Please consult package insert text for epinephrine for Contraindications, Warnings and Precautions.

Nesacaine-CE (cont'd)

As a guide for some routine procedures, suggested doses are given below:
1. Infiltration and Nerve Block: Local Infiltration: Quantity depends on the concentration of chloroprocaine, the site to be infiltrated and the discretion of the operator (see Table I).

Table I—Nesacaine-CE

Nerve Blocks

Type of Block	Volume (mL)	Concentration	Total Dose (mg)
Mandibular	2 to 3	2%	40–60
Infraorbital	0.5 to 1	2%	10–20
Brachial Plexus	30 to 40	2%	600–800
Pudendal Block for obstetrics	10 mL each side	2%	400

2. Caudal and Epidural Block: Caudal Anesthesia: The initial dose is 15 to 25 mL of a 2% or 3% solution. This volume should not be exceeded. Repeated doses may be given at 40 to 60 minute intervals.
Epidural Anesthesia: The recommended total volume of chloroprocaine for the main dose in epidural anesthesia is 15 to 25 mL, and this volume should not be exceeded. Furthermore, a local anesthetic agent other than chloroprocaine, such as Xylocaine Parenteral Solution for infiltration and nerve block, should be used for skin and needle tract infiltration. Repeated doses 2 to 6 mL less than the original dose may be given at 40 to 50 minute intervals.

In order to guard against possible adverse reactions resulting from inadvertent penetration of the subarachnoid space, the following procedures are recommended:
1. Use of an adequate (in the case of Nesacaine-CE, approximately 3 mL of 3% or 5 mL of 2%) test dose prior to induction of complete block. This test dose should be repeated if the patient is moved in such a fashion as to have displaced the epidural catheter. At least 5 minutes should elapse after each test dose prior to proceeding further.
2. Injection of a large, single therapeutic dose through a catheter should be avoided; instead, repeated fractional doses are advocated.
3. In the event of the known injection of a large volume of Nesacaine-CE into the subarachnoid space, an appropriate amount of cerebrospinal fluid (such as 10 mL) should be withdrawn through the catheter or by separate lumbar puncture.
Maximum Dosage: Adults: The maximum single recommended doses of chloroprocaine in adults are: without epinephrine, 11 mg/kg body weight, not to exceed 800 mg; and with epinephrine (1:200 000), 14 mg/kg body weight, not to exceed 1 000 mg. For caudal and lumbar epidural anesthesia, a total of 25 mL of solution should not be exceeded.
Sterilization, Storage and Technical Procedures: As with other anesthetics having a free aromatic amino group, Nesacaine-CE solutions are slightly photosensitive and may become discolored after prolonged exposure to light. It is recommended that these vials be stored in the original outer containers, protected from direct sunlight. Discolored solution should not be administered. If exposed to low temperatures, Nesacaine-CE may deposit crystals of chloroprocaine HCl, which will redissolve with shaking when returned to room temperature. The product should not be used if it contains undissolved material.

While Nesacaine-CE solutions are sterile, the vials may be autoclaved once for terminal sterilization with no significant decrease in potency. Sterilization of vials with ethylene oxide is not recommended, since absorption through the closure may occur.

Chloroprocaine is incompatible with caustic alkalis and their carbonates, soaps, silver salts, iodine and iodides.

Supplied: Nesacaine-CE 2%: Each mL contains: chloroprocaine HCl 20 mg. Also contains sodium chloride, sodium bisulfite and calcium disodium edetate. Single use vials of 30 mL, packages of 10.

Nesacaine-CE 3%: Each mL contains: chloroprocaine HCl 30 mg. Also contains sodium chloride, sodium bisulfite and calcium disodium edetate. Single use vials of 30 mL, packages of 10.

Keep from freezing. Protect from light. Store at controlled room temperature 15 to 30°C.

***...CPS* is also available in a French language edition.**

NETROMYCIN®

Schering

Netilmicin Sulfate

Antibiotic

Pharmacology: Netilmicin is a semisynthetic, aminocyclitol, aminoglycoside antibiotic prepared from a dehydrogenated analog of gentamicin C_{1a}.

Netilmicin is a bactericidal antibiotic which acts by inhibiting normal protein synthesis in susceptible bacteria. It is thought to prevent amino acid polymerization by binding to the 30S ribosomal subunit.

Netilmicin is rapidly and completely absorbed after i.m. administration. In adult subjects with normal renal function, mean peak serum levels of 5.5 and 8.8 µ/mL were obtained 30 to 60 minutes after a single i.m. administration of 2 and 3 mg/kg, respectively.

When 2 mg/kg or 3 mg/kg was given as a 30 minute infusion in normal saline, the average maximum serum concentrations, occurring at the end of infusion, were 11.8 and 15.6 µg/mL, respectively. An infusion of 2 mg/kg over 60 minutes resulted in a peak concentration of 10.8 µg/mL.

Netilmicin can also be administered by bolus injection over a 2 to 5 minute interval. A single dose of 2 mg/kg given in this manner resulted in a peak serum concentration of 17 to 20 µg/mL at 5 minutes post injection.

Netilmicin is not metabolized and is excreted in the urine by glomerular filtration. In adult patients with normal renal function, 60 to 70% of a 2 mg/kg dose was recovered in the urine during the first 6 hours and 80 to 90% in the first 24 hours. Renal clearance was about 80 mL/minute per 1.73m², i.e. 60% of the creatinine clearance.

For infants receiving 3 mg/kg doses, the average concentrations of netilmicin in urine were 46 µg/mL (range 11 to 98 µg/mL) during the first 3 hours post injection and 29 µg/mL (range 10 to 66 µg/mL) during the subsequent 3 hour collection period. On the average, 18% of a 2.5 mg/kg i.m. dose was excreted in the urine during the first 8 hours.

Renal insufficiency: In patients with chronic renal insufficiency, plasma levels increased with greater renal impairment. The increase in the elimination half life was particularly pronounced when the creatinine clearance fell below 30 mL/min per 1.73 m². Renal insufficiency did not significantly modify the apparent volume of distribution. Urinary elimination was inversely related to the degree of renal impairment as only 7.1 to 15.7% of an injected dose was recovered in the urine of severely uremic patients during the first 24 hours.

In patients with renal failure undergoing hemodialysis, the amount of netilmicin removed from the blood will depend upon several factors such as plasma flow rate, length of procedure and dialysis equipment used. A 7 to 8 hour dialysis session showed a mean serum concentration decrease to 63.3±9% of the initial concentration and a mean half life of 5.49±0.72 hours.

Indications: The treatment of infections caused by susceptible strains of E. coli, Proteus species, (indole negative and some indole positive), Klebsiella, Enterobacter, Citrobacter and Staphylococcus species.

Clinical studies have shown netilmicin to be effective in some serious infections caused by P. aeruginosa and Serratia species.

Netilmicin may be indicated in the treatment of the following when caused by susceptible organisms: septicemia, lower respiratory tract infections, urinary tract infections, peritonitis, endometritis.

Limited clinical studies have shown netilmicin may also be effective in the treatment of serious bone and soft tissue infections.

Appropriate sensitivity studies should be performed to determine the susceptibility of the causative organism to netilmicin. On the basis of clinical judgment and anticipated bacteriological findings, therapy may be instituted before results of these tests are obtained. If susceptibility tests show that the causative organism is resistant to netilmicin, treatment should be replaced by other appropriate therapy.

Although netilmicin may be indicated for the treatment of serious staphylococcal infections, its use should be reserved for those staphylococcal infections also involving susceptible strains of gram-negative bacteria and then only when penicillin or other potentially less nephrotoxic drugs are inappropriate, (e.g. patients allergic to penicillin).

Contraindications: History of hypersensitivity to aminoglycosides.

Warnings: Netilmicin has the potential to cause disturbances in balance and a hearing loss. At greater risk are those patients with compromised renal function, those who have been treated previously with ototoxic drugs, or those who are receiving higher doses of netilmicin than recommended. Reversal of developing ototoxicity is contingent on early recognition of the signs and symptoms such as tinnitus, dizziness or hearing loss.

In patients with impaired renal function, the dose and/or frequency of administration of netilmicin must be reduced (see Administration and Dosage) and renal, vestibular and auditory function, as well as serum levels of netilmicin should be monitored frequently.

Netilmicin should not be administered concomitantly with potent loop diuretics such as furosemide and ethacrynic acid as the potential for ototoxicity is enhanced by the combination. Diuretics may enhance aminoglycoside toxicity either by altering the antibiotic concentration in serum and tissues or by a direct action on the auditory apparatus.

The administration of other potentially nephrotoxic drugs prior to or in conjunction with netilmicin is likely to increase the risk of nephrotoxicity.

Nephrotoxicity manifested by an increase in the level of blood urea nitrogen or serum creatinine, a decrease in creatinine clearance, or the presence of casts, cells or protein in the urine has been observed in patients administered netilmicin. These have been observed more frequently in the elderly, in patients with a history of decreased renal function and in patients treated with larger doses of netilmicin than those recommended. In most cases, these changes have been mild and were reversible on discontinuing the administration of netilmicin. Other risk factors include duration of therapy and concomitant administration of anticoagulants or furosemide. Patients with diabetes mellitus appeared to have a slightly higher incidence of renal reactions.

Pregnancy: The safety of netilmicin for use during pregnancy has not been established. Aminoglycoside antibiotics cross the placenta and may cause harm when administered to pregnant women. Irreversible bilateral congenital deafness in children whose mothers received streptomycin during pregnancy has been reported. Serious side effects to mother, fetus, or newborn have not been reported following treatment of pregnant women with other aminoglycosides, however, the potential for fetal toxicity exists. It is not known whether netilmicin can cause fetal harm when administered to pregnant women or can affect reproductive capacity. Netilmicin should be used during pregnancy only in life threatening situations or severe infections, bearing in mind the possible adverse effects on the fetus.

Lactation: Studies in nursing mothers indicate that small amounts of the drug are excreted in breast milk. Because of the potential for serious adverse reactions from aminoglycosides in nursing infants, a decision should be made whether to discontinue nursing, or to discontinue netilmicin therapy, taking into account the importance of the drug to the mother.

Precautions: Treatment with netilmicin may result in the overgrowth of nonsusceptible organisms. If superinfection occurs, appropriate therapeutic measures should be instituted.

Netilmicin, at doses considerably above those clinically recommended (i.e. greater than 10 times), has been shown to cause neuromuscular blockade and respiratory arrest in rats and mice. The injection of calcium chloride elicited a complete and rapid antagonistic effect whereas neostigmine was ineffective.

The possibility of neuromuscular blockade and respiratory arrest occurring in man should be considered, particularly if netilmicin is administered to patients receiving anesthetics, neuromuscular blocking agents (e.g. succinylcholine or tubocurarine) or massive transfusions of citrate anticoagulated blood. Thiazide diuretics have been reported to aggravate tubocurarine induced neuromuscular block.

Patients with neuromuscular disorders, such as myasthenia gravis, Parkinson's disease or infant botulism, are at particular risk, since netilmicin could aggravate muscular weakness.

Netilmicin should be used with caution in premature and neonatal infants because of renal immaturity and the resulting prolongation of serum half life of the drug.

In patients with renal or pre-existing 8th nerve dysfunction, pre-treatment audiograms should be performed and repeated during the course of therapy. If tinnitus or subjective hearing loss should occur, the administration of netilmicin should be discontinued.

It is recommended that peak serum concentrations of netilmicin be monitored where feasible. Peak concentrations in excess of 16 µg/mL for prolonged periods as well as trough concentrations greater than 4 µg/mL should be avoided.

The possibility of development of resistance during prolonged therapy with netilmicin should be kept in mind.

Concurrent and/or sequential systemic or topical use of other potentially neurotoxic and/or nephrotoxic drugs, such as cisplatin, bacitracin, polymyxin B, colistin, cephaloridine, amphotericin B, kanamycin, acyclovir, gentamicin, amikacin, sisomicin, tobramycin, neomycin, streptomycin, paromomycin, viomycin and vancomycin should be avoided. Advanced age and dehydration may increase patient risk of toxicity.

A Fanconi-like syndrome, with aminoaciduria and metabolic acidosis, has been reported in some adults and infants treated with netilmicin.

In vitro mixing of an aminoglycoside with beta-lactam type antibiotics (penicillins or cephalosporins) may result in a significant mutual inactivation. Even when an aminoglycoside and a penicillin-type drug are administered separately by different routes, a reduction in aminoglycoside serum half-life or serum levels has been reported in patients with normal renal function. Usually such inactivation of the aminoglycoside is clinically significant only in patients with severely impaired renal function.

Netromycin contains sodium metabisulfite and sodium sulfite; these may cause allergic-type reactions including anaphylactic symptoms and life-threatening or less severe asthmatic episodes in certain susceptible people. Sulfite sensitivity is observed more frequently in asthmatic than in non-asthmatic people.

Netromycin ranges in color from water white to pale yellow. Dark yellow solutions should not be used.

Adverse Effects: In addition to the ototoxicity and nephrotoxicity, other rarely reported adverse reactions possibly related to netilmicin include: headache, malaise, visual disturbances, disorientation, tachycardia, hypotension, palpitations, thrombocytosis, paresthesia, rash, chills, fever, fluid retention, vomiting and diarrhea. Very rarely, anaphylaxis has been reported.

Laboratory abnormalities possibly related to netilmicin include: increased blood sugar; increased alkaline phosphatase; increased AST or ALT, bilirubin; increased potassium; other abnormal liver function tests; decreased hemoglobin, WBCs and platelets; eosinophilia, anemia and increase in prothrombin time.

Overdose: Symptoms and Treatment: In the event of overdose or toxic reaction, hemodialysis will aid in the removal of netilmicin from the blood. Appropriate supportive therapy should be instituted to maintain respiratory and kidney function.

Dosage: Netilmicin deep i.m. injection or i.v. The recommended dose for i.m. and i.v. administration is identical. Dosage should be calculated on the basis of body weight but in obese patients or emaciated patients with low volumes of distribution, dosage should be based on an estimate of lean body mass.

It is desirable to measure peak and trough netilmicin serum concentrations to assure adequate but not excessive levels. With the administration of netilmicin in 2 or 3 daily doses, the peak concentration, measured 30 minutes to 1 hour after administration, is expected to be in the range of 4 to 12 μg/mL; the dosage should be adjusted to avoid prolonged peak serum concentrations above 16 μg/mL. Trough concentrations above 4 μg/mL, measured just before the next dose is given, should be avoided. Generally, desirable peak and trough concentrations should be in the range of 6 to 10 and 0.5 to 2 μg/mL, respectively.

The usual duration of treatment is 7 to 14 days. In complicated infections, a longer course of therapy may be necessary. Patients treated beyond the usual period should be carefully monitored for changes in renal, auditory and vestibular function.

Patients with normal renal function: Adults: Patients with uncomplicated urinary tract infections: 4.0 mg/kg/day divided into 2 equal doses and administered every 12 hours for 7 to 10 days. For the average adult (50 to 80 kg) 150 mg may be given every 12 hours.

Patients with systemic infections: 4.0 to 6.0 mg/kg/day divided into 2 or 3 equal doses and administered every 12 or 8 hours, respectively. For the average adult (50 to 80 kg), depending on the severity of infection, the usual dose is 100 mg to 150 mg administered every 8 hours or 150 mg to 200 mg every 12 hours for 7 to 14 days.

Patients with serious systemic infections (life threatening), i.v. dosages up to 7.5 mg/kg/day divided into 3 equal doses. This dosage should be reduced to 6.0 mg/kg/day as soon as clinically indicated, usually within 48 hours.

Concomitant administration of a penicillin type antibiotic with netilmicin should be considered as initial therapy in certain cases of sepsis, particularly in immunosuppressed patients, while awaiting culture and susceptibility results. Treatment should be adjusted when these results become available.

Children: 6.0 to 7.5 mg/kg/day divided into 3 equal doses and administered every 8 hours. This should be reduced to 6.0 mg/kg/day as soon as clinically indicated.

Infants and Neonates: (Greater than 1 week of age): 7.5 to 9.0 mg/kg/day divided into 3 equal doses and administered every 8 hours.

Premature and Full Term Neonates: (Less than 1 week of age): 6 mg/kg/day divided into 2 equal doses and administered every 12 hours (see Precautions).

Patients with impaired renal function: Adults: The initial dose is the same as that recommended for patients with normal renal function. Dosage must be adjusted in patients with impaired renal function and when possible, serum concentrations of netilmicin should be monitored. If serum concentrations cannot be monitored, serum creatinine or preferably, creatinine clearance values can be used as a guide for dosage adjustments. Adjustments in dosage can be made by either lengthening the interval between doses or by a reduction in dose administered at 8 hour intervals as follows. In the elderly or debilitated patients, it is suggested that creatinine clearance values be used:

Adjusted Intervals: Normal Dosage: If the patient's serum creatinine is known, the interval between the usual single dose given at 8 hourly intervals can be calculated by multiplying the patient's serum creatinine by a factor of 8. Thus, a patient with a serum creatinine of 3 mg/100 mL would be given 2 mg/kg every 24 hours (i.e. 3 x 8=24) rather than the usual dose of 2 mg/kg every 8 hours.

Adjusted Dosage; Fixed Interval: Table I can be used as a rough guide for determining the appropriate reduced dosage at 8 hour intervals. The dosage can also be calculated using the following formula:

$$\text{Reduced maintenance dose} = \frac{\text{observed creatinine clearance} \times \text{usual dose}}{\text{normal creatinine clearance}}$$

Table I—Netromycin

Dosage Adjustment Guide for Patients with Renal Impairment (Dosage at 8-Hour Intervals after the Usual Initial Dose)

Approximate Creatinine Clearance Rate (mL/min/1.73 m²)	**% of Usual Dose**
>100	100
70–100	80
55– 70	65
45– 55	55
40– 45	50
35– 40	40
30– 35	35
25– 30	30
20– 25	25
15– 20	20
10– 15	15
<10	10

For patients requiring dialysis, as approximately 50% of the initial dose may be removed during standardized hemodialysis, at least 50% of the initial loading dose would be required after dialysis. In these patients serum concentrations of netilmicin should be monitored.

Children: At present there is insufficient data to recommend a specific dosage for children with impaired renal function.

Administration: I.M.: Netilmicin should be given by deep i.m. injection.

I.V.: I.V. administration of netilmicin is recommended when the i.m. route is not advisable, e.g. patients in shock or with severe burns, hematological bleeding disorders or a reduced muscle mass.

Adults: A single dose of netilmicin may be diluted in 50 to 200 mL of one of the compatible sterile solutions listed below and administered over a 30 to 60 minute period. A single 2.0 mg/kg dose may also be given directly into a vein or sidearm of an i.v. tubing, provided that it is administered over a 3 to 5 minute period.

Infants and Children: The volume of diluent should be proportionally less, according to the fluid requirements of the patient.

I.V. Solution: Netilmicin has been shown to be compatible with the following solutions: sterile water for injection, normal saline, 5% dextrose in water, 10% dextrose in water, Ringer's solution and lactated Ringer's solution. When diluted to a concentration of 3 mg/mL the prepared solutions should not be stored for longer than 24 hours at room temperature or 48 hours under refrigeration.

Netromycin should not be physically premixed with other drugs but should be administered separately in accordance with the recommended dosage schedule.

Supplied: 100 mg/mL: Each mL of clear, sterile aqueous solution contains: netilmicin (as sulfate USP) 100 mg. Nonmedicinal ingredients: benzyl alcohol, edetate disodium, sodium metabisulfite and sodium sulfite. Vials of 2 mL and pharmacy bulk vials of 20 mL.

50 mg/mL: Each mL of clear, sterile aqueous solution contains: netilmicin (as sulfate USP) 50 mg. Nonmedicinal ingredients: edetate disodium, methylparaben, propylparaben, sodium metabisulfite, sodium sulfate and sodium sulfite. Vials of 2 mL.

Store at 2 to 30°C. Protect from freezing.

NEULEPTIL® Ⓟ

Rhône-Poulenc Rorer

Pericyazine

Psychotropic Agent

Pharmacology: Pericyazine is a phenothiazine of the piperidine group. It has been shown to reduce pathologic arousal and affective tension in some psychotic patients, while the symptoms of abnormal mental integration are relatively unaffected.

It is a sedative phenothiazine with weak antipsychotic properties. It also has adrenolytic, anticholinergic, metabolic and endocrine effects, and an action on the extrapyramidal system. Like other phenothiazines, it is presumed to act principally in the subcortical areas, by producing what has been described as a central adrenergic blockade.

A group of 12 healthy human volunteers were administered two 10 mg pericyazine capsules. A peak concentration of 150 ng/mL (410 nmol/L) was achieved 2 hours after drug administration and the half-life was approximately 12 hours. In some subjects, detectable amounts of pericyazine were still present in the blood after 36 hours.

Indications: As adjunctive medication in some psychotic patients, for the control of residual prevailing hostility, impulsiveness and aggressiveness.

Contraindications: Circulatory collapse, altered states of consciousness or comatose states, particularly when they are due to intoxication with CNS depressants; history of blood dyscrasias, liver disease or hypersensitivity to phenothiazines; should not be administered in association with spinal or regional anesthetics.

Warnings: Geriatrics and Debilitated Patients: Particular care should be exercised when pericyazine is given to elderly or debilitated patients as some appear to be unduly sensitive to the effects of the drug.

Occupational Hazards: Because drowsiness, slowing of reaction time or impaired judgment may occur, patients should generally not operate a motor vehicle or engage in dangerous activities while under the action of the drug.

Pregnancy: Since the safety of use of pericyazine during pregnancy has not been established, it should not be used in women of childbearing potential unless the expected benefits outweigh the possible risks to the fetus.

Patients who have demonstrated a hypersensitivity reaction (e.g., blood dyscrasias, jaundice) with a phenothiazine should not be re-exposed to any phenothiazine unless, in the judgment of the physician, the potential benefits of treatment outweigh the possible hazards.

It should not be used in patients with convulsive disorders that are not receiving appropriate anticonvulsive medication.

Tardive Dyskinesias: As with all antipsychotic agents, tardive dyskinesia may appear in some patients on long-term therapy or may appear after drug therapy has been discontinued. The risk appears to be greater in elderly patients on high-dose therapy, especially females. The symptoms are persistent and in some patients appear to be irreversible. The syndrome is characterized by rhythmical involuntary movements of the tongue, face, mouth or jaw (e.g., protrusion of tongue, puffing of cheeks, puckering of mouth, chewing movements). Sometimes these may be accompanied by involuntary movements of extremities.

There is no known effective treatment for tardive dyskinesia; antiparkinsonism agents usually do not alleviate the symptoms of this syndrome. It is suggested that all antipsychotic agents be discontinued if these symptoms appear. Should it be necessary to reinstitute treatment, or increase the dosage of the agent, or switch to a different antipsychotic agent, the syndrome may be masked. The physician may be able to reduce the risk of this syndrome by minimizing the unnecessary use

Neuleptil (cont'd)

of neuroleptic drugs and reducing the dose or discontinuing the drug, if possible, when manifestations of this syndrome are recognized, particularly in patients over the age of 50. It has been reported that fine vermicular movements of the tongue may be an early sign of the syndrome and if the medication is stopped at that time the syndrome may not develop.

Precautions: Pericyazine may potentiate the action of other drugs; caution should therefore be exercised when it is prescribed with other phenothiazine derivatives or CNS depressants such as barbiturates, analgesics, narcotics or antihistamines, and the usual doses of these compounds should be reduced by at least half while the new treatment is being gradually introduced. Patients should also be advised against ingesting alcohol while under treatment.

Therapy should be initiated at low doses and caution used in patients with arteriosclerosis, cardiovascular disease, or other conditions where sudden hypotension is undesirable. Careful adjustments of dosage may be necessary if other drugs likely to cause postural hypotension are being administered concurrently. If hypotension should occur and a pressor agent is required, norepinephrine or phenylephrine may be used. Epinephrine should **not** be used since it may further lower blood pressure.

Because of its anticholinergic action, pericyazine should be used with great caution in patients with glaucoma or prostatic hypertrophy. Paralytic ileus has occurred in patients, particularly in the elderly, taking one or more drugs with anticholinergic action for extended periods. In such patients caution should be observed if constipation develops.

Retinal changes and abnormal skin pigmentation have been observed with phenothiazines and may occur after prolonged therapy. Discontinue therapy if these changes are observed.

It is generally advisable to perform periodic liver function tests during prolonged medication with pericyazine. Periodic blood counts should also be performed, particularly during the first 2 or 3 months of therapy and patients should be observed for any signs or symptoms suggestive of blood dyscrasia.

To lessen the likelihood of adverse reactions related to drug accumulation, patients on long-term therapy, particularly on high doses, should be evaluated periodically to decide whether the maintenance dosage could be lowered or drug therapy discontinued. Sudden onset of severe CNS or vasomotor symptoms should be kept in mind.

Adverse Effects: Drowsiness, hypotension and extrapyramidal symptoms are the more frequently reported adverse reactions. Autonomic and psychomotor effects are usually observed at the beginning of treatment and frequently resolve while therapy is being continued or subside upon adjustment of dosage. Extrapyramidal reactions usually occur somewhat later and are mainly observed with higher dosages.

Adverse reactions with different phenothiazines vary in type, frequency, and mechanism of occurrence, i.e., some are dose-related, while others involve individual patient sensitivity. Some adverse reactions may be more likely to occur, or occur with greater intensity, in patients with special medical problem e.g., patients with mitral insufficiency or pheochromocytoma have experienced severe hypotension following recommended doses of certain phenothiazines.

Not all of the following adverse reactions have been observed with every phenothiazine derivative, but they have been reported with one or more and should be borne in mind when drugs of this class are administered:

Behavioral: Drowsiness and impaired psychomotor activity are the most frequent initial untoward reactions but tend to subside within 1 to 3 weeks. Small initial doses will test tolerance to the drug. If a toxic-confusional state appears the medication should be stopped immediately. Paradoxical effects, such as agitation, insomnia, inversion of sleep, increased aggressiveness and activation of psychotic symptoms, have been occasionally observed.

Autonomic Nervous System: Postural hypotension and acute hypotensive crisis have been observed, particularly in the elderly, and occur more often at the beginning of treatment or when initial high dosages are used. These reactions may be avoided by testing the patient's tolerance with initial low doses. ECG changes and cardiac arrhythmias, including AV block paroxysmal tachycardia, and ventricular fibrillation, although not reported with pericyazine, have been observed with some phenothiazines.

Predominant anticholinergic effects or sympathetic depression may be responsible for following adverse reactions: tachycardia, blurred vision, aggravation of glaucoma, dry mouth (sometimes with oral infections and dental caries), nausea, vomiting, constipation, fecal impactation, paralytic ileus, perspiration, diarrhea, and nasal congestion. Changes in body temperature and hyperglycemia have been known to occur with phenothiazines.

CNS: The extrapyramidal reactions include: **Parkinsonism, dystonic reactions and akathisia.**

Parkinsonism occurs more frequently in patients receiving high doses and can usually be controlled by reducing the dose or temporarily discontinuing medication and, when necessary, by administering an antiparkinson drug. The dystonic reactions consist mainly of protrusion of the tongue, hyperextension of the neck and trunk, contraction of muscles of the neck and face, oculogyric crises, myolonic twitches and carpopedal spasm. Dystonic reactions are usually not dose-related but may be quite dramatic and require urgent treatment. Dystonic reactions have been reported with pericyazine.

Tardive persistent dyskinesia resistant to treatment has been reported in connection with phenothiazine drugs (for detailed description see Warnings).

EEG changes, disturbed temperature regulation and seizures have also been reported. Pericyazine is generally well tolerated by epileptics maintained on anticonvulsive therapy. However, epileptic attacks have been reported and it has not been established that pericyazine effectively controls arousal or affective tension in these patients.

Allergic or Toxic Reactions: Agranulocytosis and other blood dyscrasias are among the more serious adverse reactions to phenothiazines. They may occur suddenly or follow a fall in blood count, usually during the first 2 or 3 months of treatment. Cholestatic jaundice occurs uncommonly.

Skin reactions, photosensitivity, asthma, laryngeal edema, angioneurotic edema, hyperpyrexia and other allergic reactions may also occur. Abnormal pigmentation, including corneal and lens deposits have been observed, usually when high doses of phenothiazines are given for prolonged periods.

Endocrine System: Endocrine effects from phenothiazines such as delayed ovulation, menstrual irregularities, lactation, gynecomastia, changes in libido, inhibition of ejaculation, false positive pregnancy tests, weight gain and edemas, have been known to occur. Voracious appetite and weight gain have been reported in some patients on pericyazine therapy.

Miscellaneous: Unexpected sudden deaths, hypostatic pneumonia, and potentiation of other drugs have occurred during phenothiazine therapy. In some unexpected deaths, myocardial lesions have been observed. Previous brain damage or seizures may also be predisposing factors; high doses should be avoided in known seizure patients. Several patients have shown sudden exacerbations of psychotic behavior patterns shortly before death. Autopsy findings have also revealed acute fulminating pneumonia or pneumonitis and aspiration of gastric contents. The physician should therefore be alerted to the possible development of ''silent pneumonias''.

Overdose: Symptoms: In milder cases of phenothiazine overdosage the patient may be agitated, delirious and confused. Frequently he is lethargic or in a comatose state. Twitching, dystonic movements or convulsions may be present and hypotension, cardiovascular collapse, arrhythmias and hypothermia might be observed.

Treatment: Symptomatic (no specific antidote). Careful supportive management is required until the patient is well out of drug-induced CNS depression. Shock, arrhythmia, respiratory failure and hypothermia are the main management problems. Induce gastric lavage when indicated. Treat hypotension with levarterenol or phenylephrine. Epinephrine should **not** be used because it may cause further hypotension. Centrally acting emetic drugs to induce emesis are ineffective due to the antiapomorphine effect of pericyazine. Extrapyramidal symptoms may be treated with benztropine mesylate.

Dosage: Adults: 5 to 20 mg in the morning and 10 to 40 mg in the evening. For maintenance therapy, the dosage should be reduced to the minimum effective dose. Lower doses of 2.5 to 15 mg in the morning, and 5 to 30 mg in the evening have been suggested.

For elderly patients the initial total daily dosage should be in the order of 5 mg and increased gradually as tolerated, until an adequate response is obtained. A daily dosage of more than 30 mg will rarely be needed.

Children and adolescents (5 years of age and over): 2.5 to 10 mg in the morning and 5 to 30 mg in the evening. These dosages approximate a daily dosage range of 1 to 3 mg/year of age.

In general, for both children and adults, the lower doses should not be exceeded initially. Subsequently, dosage may be gradually increased until the most effective level is reached. Caution is required when these dosages are exceeded.

Troublesome initial drowsiness has often been observed following pericyazine administration. This may be obviated by giving the drug twice daily and reserving the major portion of the daily dosage for the evening.

Pericyazine is not recommended in children under 5 years of age, since limited clinical experience is available.

Supplied: Capsules: 5 mg: Each capsule, blue cap and body, imprinted 5 mg, contains: pericyazine 5 mg. Nonmedicinal ingredients: calcium phosphate, croscarmellose sodium, FD&C Blue No 1, FD&C Red No 3, gelatin, magnesium stearate and titanium oxide. Tartrazine-free. Bottles of 100.

10 mg: Each capsule, blue cap and body, imprinted 10 mg, contains: pericyazine 10 mg. Nonmedicinal ingredients: calcium phosphate, croscarmellose sodium, FD&C Blue No 1, FD&C Red No 3, gelatin, magnesium stearate and titanium oxide. Tartrazine-free. Bottles of 100 and 500.

20 mg: Each capsule, blue cap and body, imprinted 20 mg, contains: pericyazine 20 mg. Nonmedicinal ingredients: calcium phosphate, croscarmellose sodium, FD&C Blue No 1, FD&C Red No 3, gelatin, magnesium stearate and titanium oxide. Tartrazine-free. Bottles of 100.

Oral Drops: Each mL of liquid contains: pericyazine 10 mg. Nonmedicinal ingredients: alcohol, ascorbic acid, caramel, glycerin, peppermint oil, purified water, sucrose and tartaric acid. Energy: 4.3 kJ (1.0 kcal)/mL. Tartrazine-free. Bottles of 100 mL with calibrated dropper.

(Shown in Product Recognition Section)

NEUPOGEN® Ⓟ

Amgen

Filgrastim

Granulocyte Colony Stimulating Factor—Hematopoietic Agent

Pharmacology: Filgrastim is a human granulocyte colony stimulating factor (G-CSF) produced by recombinant DNA technology. G-CSF regulates the production of neutrophils within the bone marrow; endogenous G-CSF is a glycoprotein produced by monocytes, fibroblasts, and endothelial cells. G-CSF is a colony stimulating factor which has been shown to have minimal direct in vivo or in vitro effects on the production of other hematopoietic cell types. Filgrastim is the name for recombinant methionyl human granulocyte colony stimulating factor (r-metHuG-CSF).

Filgrastim is a 175 amino acid protein manufactured by recombinant DNA technology. Filgrastim is produced by E. coli bacteria into which has been inserted the human granulocyte colony stimulating factor gene. Filgrastim has a molecular weight of 18 800 daltons. The protein has an amino acid sequence that is identical to the natural sequence predicted from human DNA sequence analysis, except for the addition of an N-terminal methionine necessary for expression in E. coli. Because filgrastim is produced in E. coli, the product is non-glycosylated and thus differs from G-CSF isolated from a human cell.

Pre-clinical Studies: The results of all pre-clinical studies indicate that the pharmacologic effects are consistent with its role as a specific regulator of neutrophil production and function.

Colony Stimulating Factors: Colony stimulating factors are glycoproteins which act on hematopoietic cells by binding to specific cell surface receptors and stimulating proliferation, differentiation commitment, and some end-cell functional activation.

Endogenous G-CSF is a lineage-specific colony stimulating factor with selectivity for the neutrophil lineage. G-CSF is not species specific and has been shown to primarily affect neutrophil progenitor proliferation, differentiation, and selected end-cell functional activation (including enhanced phagocytic ability, priming of the cellular metabolism associated with respiratory burst, antibody dependent killing, and the increased expression of some functions associated with cell surface antigens).

Pharmacologic Effects of Filgrastim: In Phase I studies involving 96 patients with various non-myeloid malignancies, filgrastim administration resulted in a dose-dependent increase in neutrophil counts over the dose range of 1 to 70 μg/kg/day. This increase in neutrophil counts was observed whether filgrastim was administered i.v. (1 to 70 μg/kg twice daily), s.c. (1 to 3 μg/kg once daily), or by continuous s.c. infusion (3 to 11 μg/kg/day). With discontinuation of filgrastim therapy, neutrophil counts returned to baseline, in most cases within 4 days. Isolated neutrophils displayed normal phagocytic (measured by zymosan-stimulated chemoluminescence) and chemotactic [measured by migration under agarose using

N-formyl-methionyl-leucyl-phenylalanine (fMLP) as the chemotaxin] activity in vitro.

The absolute monocyte count was reported to increase in a dose-dependent manner in most patients receiving filgrastim, however, the percentage of monocytes in the differential count remained within the normal range. In all studies to date, absolute counts of both eosinophils and basophils did not change and were within the normal range following administration of filgrastim. Increases in lymphocyte counts following filgrastim administration have been reported in some normal subjects and cancer patients.

White blood cell differentials obtained during clinical trials have demonstrated a shift towards granulocyte progenitor cells (left shift), including the appearance of promyelocytes and myeloblasts, usually during neutrophil recovery following the chemotherapy-induced nadir. In addition, Döhle bodies, increased granulocyte granulation, as well as hypersegmented neutrophils have been observed. Such changes were transient, and were not associated with clinical sequelae nor were they necessarily associated with infection.

Pharmacokinetics: Absorption and clearance of filgrastim follows first-order pharmacokinetic modeling without apparent concentration dependence. A positive linear correlation occurred between the parenteral dose and both the serum concentration and area under the concentration-time curves. Continuous i.v. infusion of 20 µg/kg of filgrastim over 24 hours resulted in mean and median serum concentrations of approximately 48 and 56 ng/mL, respectively.

S.C. administration of 3.45 µg/kg and 11.5 µg/kg resulted in maximum serum concentrations of 4 and 49 ng/mL, respectively, within 2 to 8 hours. The volume of distribution averaged 150 mL/kg in normal subjects and cancer patients. The elimination half-life, in both normal subjects and cancer patients, was approximately 3.5 hours. Clearance rates of filgrastim were approximately 0.5 to 0.7 mL/min/kg. Single parenteral doses or daily i.v. doses, over a 14 day period, resulted in comparable half-lives. The half-lives were similar for i.v. administration (231 minutes, following filgrastim doses of 34.5 µg/kg) and for s.c. administration (210 minutes, following filgrastim doses of 3.45 µg/kg). Continuous 24-hour i.v. infusions of 20 µg/kg over an 11 to 20 day period produced steady-state serum concentrations of filgrastim with no evidence of drug accumulation over the time period investigated.

Clinical Experience: Response to Filgrastim: Cancer Patients Receiving Myelosuppressive Chemotherapy: Filgrastim has been shown to be safe and effective in accelerating the recovery of neutrophil counts following a variety of chemotherapy regimens for a number of cancer types. In a Phase III clinical trial in small cell lung cancer, patients received s.c. administration of filgrastim (4 to 8 µg/kg/day, days 4 to 17) or placebo. In this study, the benefits of filgrastim therapy were shown to be prevention of infection as manifested by febrile neutropenia, decreased hospitalization, and decreased antibiotic usage.

In the Phase III, randomized, double-blind placebo-controlled trial conducted in patients with small cell lung cancer, patients were randomized to receive filgrastim (n=101) or placebo (n=110). Of the 211 patients enrolled, 207 patients were evaluable for safety (filgrastim, n=98; placebo, n=109) and 199 patients were evaluable for efficacy (filgrastim, n=95; placebo, n=104). Filgrastim was started on day 4, after patients received standard dose chemotherapy with cyclophosphamide, doxorubicin and etoposide.

The incidence of febrile neutropenia during Cycle I was significantly reduced by 51% in the filgrastim group as compared to the placebo group (28% versus 57%, respectively; $p<0.001$). The difference in the cumulative incidence of febrile neutropenia over all 6 cycles between the placebo group (77%) and the filgrastim group (40%) was statistically significant ($p<0.001$). The incidence of culture confirmed infections was reduced by 50% from 13 to 6.5%.

The absolute neutrophil nadir (severity) and duration of severe neutropenia [days with absolute neutrophil count (ANC) $<0.5\times10^9/L$] were significantly reduced in all 6 cycles for patients receiving filgrastim compared to placebo ($p<0.005$). For all treatment cycles combined, the median duration of severe neutropenia was 6 days per cycle in the placebo group compared to 1 day per cycle in the filgrastim group.

Thus, treatment with filgrastim resulted in a clinically and statistically significant reduction in the incidence of infection, as manifested by febrile neutropenia, as well as the severity and duration of severe neutropenia following chemotherapy.

In-patient hospitalization and antibiotic use were evaluated as secondary endpoints (clinical sequelae) to neutropenia. The incidence of febrile neutropenia with hospitalization during Cycle 1 was significantly reduced by 50% in the filgrastim group compared to the placebo group (26% versus 55%; $p<0.001$). Over all 6 cycles there was a 45% reduction in the mean number of days of hospitalization in the filgrastim group compared to the placebo group. Furthermore, there was an overall 47% reduction in the mean number of days of i.v. antibiotic use.

Administration of filgrastim resulted in an earlier ANC nadir following chemotherapy than was experienced by patients receiving placebo (day 10 versus day 12). Filgrastim was well tolerated when given s.c. daily at doses of 4 to 8 µg/kg for up to 14 consecutive days following each cycle of chemotherapy (see Adverse Effects).

In 36 patients receiving M-VAC (methotrexate, vinblastine, doxorubicin, and cisplatin) for treatment of transitional cell carcinoma of the urothelium, both the severity ($p=0.0001$) and the duration of granulocytopenia (absolute granulocyte count $<1.0\times10^9/L$) ($p=0.0001$) were reduced during cycles of chemotherapy in which filgrastim was administered, when compared to cycles of chemotherapy without filgrastim. The accelerated recovery of granulocyte counts during M-VAC cycles when filgrastim was administered resulted in clinically and statistically significant increases in the number of patients eligible to receive planned doses of methotrexate and vinblastine on schedule on cycle day 14 ($p=0.0001$). Filgrastim was generally well tolerated at all doses treated (up to 115 µg/kg/day) when administered as a 15 to 30 minute i.v. infusion on days 4 to 11 of the 21-day M-VAC cycle.

In 45 patients treated with melphalan for a variety of advanced malignancies, patients were treated with filgrastim at several doses and using 3 routes of administration (s.c. bolus, i.v. and s.c. infusion). This was a dose finding study without controls. A dose-dependent effect on maximum ANC was demonstrated in this study [$p=0.004$ (nonparametric test of ordered responses)]. Descriptive analysis showed that the period of severe neutropenia (ANC $<0.5\times10^9/L$) was reduced by filgrastim treatment independent of route.

The effect of filgrastim has also been studied in 12 patients receiving chemotherapy (doxorubicin, ifosfamide with Mesna, and etoposide) for small cell lung cancer. Chemotherapy cycles without filgrastim were alternated with cycles in which filgrastim was administered following chemotherapy. There was a statistically significant reduction in the duration of both severe (ANC $<0.5\times10^9/L$) and moderate (ANC $<1.0\times10^9/L$) neutropenia between the filgrastim and no filgrastim groups for cycles 1 and 2 [$p=0.01$ in each case (Wilcoxon signed-ranks test)]. The duration of febrile neutropenia and hospitalization was also reduced. Filgrastim was well tolerated at doses of 1 to 45 µg/kg/day, given as a continuous infusion on days 4 through 17 of a 21-day chemotherapy cycle.

Cancer Patients Receiving Myeloablative Chemotherapy followed by Bone Marrow Transplantation: In 2 separate randomized, controlled trials, patients with Hodgkin's and non-Hodgkin's lymphoma were treated with myeloablative chemotherapy and autologous bone marrow transplantation (ABMT). In one study (n=54), filgrastim was administered at doses of 10 or 30 µg/kg/day; a third treatment group in this study received no filgrastim. A statistically significant reduction in the median number of days of severe neutropenia (ANC $<0.5\times10^9/L$) occurred in the filgrastim-treated group versus the control group [23 days in the control group, 11 days in the 10 µg/kg/day group, and 14 days in the 30 µg/kg/day group, (11 days in the combined treatment groups, $p=0.004$)].

In the second study (n=44, 43 patients evaluable), filgrastim was administered at doses of 10 or 20 µg/kg/day; a third treatment group in this study received no filgrastim. A statistically significant reduction in the median number of days of severe neutropenia occurred in the filgrastim-treated group versus the control group (21.5 days in the control group and 10 days in both treatment groups, $p<0.001$). The number of days of febrile neutropenia was also reduced significantly in this study [13.5 days in the control group, 5 days in the 10 µg/kg/day group, and 5.5 days in the 20 µg/kg/day group, (5 days in the combined treatment groups, $p<0.0001$)]. Reductions in the number of days of hospitalization and antibiotic use were also seen, although these reductions were not statistically significant. There were no effects on red blood cell or platelet levels.

In a randomized, placebo-controlled trial, 70 patients with myeloid and nonmyeloid malignancies were treated with myeloablative therapy and allogeneic bone marrow transplant followed by 300 µg/m²/day of filgrastim. A statistically significant reduction in the median number of days of severe neutropenia occurred in the treated group versus the control group (19 days in the control group and 15 days in the treatment group, $p<0.001$) and time to recovery of ANC to $\geq0.5\times10^9/L$ (21 days in the control group and 16 days in the treatment group, $p<0.001$).

In three nonrandomized studies (n=119), patients received ABMT and treatment with filgrastim. One study (n=45) involved patients with breast cancer and malignant melanoma. A second study (n=39) involved patients with Hodgkin's disease. The third study (n=35) involved patients with non-Hodgkin's lymphoma, acute lymphoblastic leukemia (ALL), and germ cell tumor. In these studies, the recovery of the ANC to $\geq0.5\times10^9/L$ ranged from a median of 11.5 to 13 days.

Cancer Patients Undergoing Peripheral Blood Progenitor Cell (PBPC) Collection and Therapy: Use of filgrastim either alone, or after chemotherapy, mobilizes hematopoietic progenitor cells into the peripheral blood. These autologous peripheral blood progenitor cells may be harvested and infused after high dose chemotherapy, either in place of, or in addition to bone marrow transplantation. Infusion of peripheral blood progenitor cells accelerates the rate of neutrophil and platelet recovery reducing the risk of hemorrhagic complications and the need for platelet transfusions.

Filgrastim Mobilized PBPC Collection: In 4 studies (n=126), patients with NHL, HD, ALL, and breast cancer received filgrastim for 6 to 7 days to mobilize hematopoietic progenitor cells into the circulating blood pool where they were collected by 3 aphereses on days 5, 6, and 7 (except for 13 patients in 1 study who where pheresed on days 4, 6, and 8). In 2 studies, the tested doses and schedules of filgrastim resulted in a greater number of PBPC in the pheresis product compared to the baseline leukapheresis product.

Filgrastim Mobilized PBPC Therapy Followed by Filgrastim: In a randomized study of patients with HD or NHL undergoing myeloablative chemotherapy, 27 patients received filgrastim mobilized PBPC followed by filgrastim and 31 patients received ABMT plus filgrastim. Patients randomized to the filgrastim mobilized PBPC group compared to the ABMT group had significantly fewer median days of platelet transfusions, (6 vs 10 days, $p<0.001$), a significantly shorter median time to a sustained platelet count $>20\times10^9/L$, (16 vs 23 days, $p=0.02$), a significantly shorter median time to recovery of a sustained ANC $\geq0.5\times10^9/L$ (11 vs 14 days, $p=0.005$), and a significantly shorter duration of hospitalization (17 vs 23 days, $p=0.002$).

Overall, therapy with filgrastim mobilized peripheral blood progenitor cells provided rapid and sustained hematologic recovery. Long-term (limited to 100 days) follow up hematology data from patients treated with PBPCT alone or in combination with bone marrow, was compared to historical data from patients treated with ABMT alone (1 study only). This retrospective analysis indicated that engraftment is durable.

Patients with Severe Chronic Neutropenia: In the Phase III trial in patients with severe chronic neutropenia (SCN), patients with diagnoses of congenital, cyclic and idiopathic neutropenia were evaluated. Untreated patients had a median absolute neutrophil count (ANC) of $0.210\times10^9/L$. Filgrastim therapy was adjusted to maintain the median ANC between $1.5\times10^9/L$ and $10\times10^9/L$. A complete response was seen in 88% of patients (defined as a median ANC $\geq1.5\times10^9/L$ over 5 months of filgrastim therapy). Overall, complete response to filgrastim was observed in 1 to 2 weeks. The median ANC after 5 months of filgrastim therapy for all patients was $7.46\times10^9/L$ (range 0.03 to $30.88\times10^9/L$). In general, patients with congenital neutropenia responded to filgrastim therapy with a lower median ANC than patients with idiopathic or cyclic neutropenia.

Dosing requirements were generally higher for patients with congenital neutropenia (2.3 to 40 µg/kg/day) than for patients with idiopathic (0.6 to 11.5 µg/kg/day) or cyclic (0.5 to 6 µg/kg/day) neutropenia.

Overall, daily treatment with filgrastim resulted in clinically and statistically significant reductions in the incidence and duration of fever, infection, and oropharyngeal ulcers. As a result, there also were decreases in requirements for antibiotic use and hospitalization. Additionally, patients treated with filgrastim reported fewer episodes of diarrhea, nausea, fatigue and sore throat. These clinical findings may translate into improvements in the quality of life in these patients.

Patients with HIV Infection: Filgrastim has been shown to be safe and effective in preventing and treating neutropenia in patients with HIV infection. In a randomized, controlled, multicenter trial of 258 patients, a statistically significant reduction was observed in the incidence of grade 4 neutropenia (ANC <500 cells/µL, $p<0.0001$) in filgrastim-treated patients. Three of 172 (1.7%) filgrastim-treated patients and 19 of 86 (22.1%) untreated patients experienced confirmed grade 4 neutropenia.

In this randomized study, 85 patients had a total of 128 new or worsening bacterial infections, during the 168 day study period. Of these, a total of 26 events were graded as severe bacterial infections (WHO toxicity grade 3 or higher).

Neupogen (cont'd)

The incidence of bacterial infections was decreased by 31% (p=0.07, p=0.03 [adjusted for number of prior opportunistic infections and baseline CD4 count]) and the incidence of severe bacterial infections was decreased by 54% (p=0.005, p=0.002 [adjusted]) in filgrastim-treated patients when compared with untreated patients. In addition, the total number of hospitalizations or prolonged hospitalizations due to a bacterial infection for all groups in this study, was 24 events in 21 patients, for a total duration of 392 days. Days of hospitalization for bacterial infection were decreased by 45% (p=0.05, p=0.03 [adjusted]). A 28% decrease in the number of days of IV antibacterial medications was seen in filgrastim-treated patients (p=0.17, p=0.08 [adjusted]).

In three open-label nonrandomized clinical studies, the response to filgrastim (ANC >2 000 cells/µL) was observed in a median of 2 to 9 days with either daily or intermittent dosing (see Dosage). Filgrastim therapy was titrated to maintain ANCs between 2 000 and 10 000 cells/µL.

In the randomized controlled trial, there was a 12% increase in the number of days patients were able to receive full or high-dose myelosuppressive medications. In a multicentre, noncomparative study of 200 patients, filgrastim allowed more than 80% of patients to increase or maintain dosing of ganciclovir, zidovudine, trimethoprim/sulfamethoxazole and pyrimethamine, or to add one or more medications to their therapy. The number of these four medications received per patient increased by approximately 20% during filgrastim therapy.

In an open-label study to evaluate neutrophil function by in vitro chemiluminescence measurement, filgrastim-treated patients had increased oxidase-myeloperoxidase activity and potentially greater microbial killing capacity.

In the randomized controlled study, 13 deaths (5%) were reported on-study. There were 13 additional deaths within 30 days of study completion. The leading causes of death were HIV-associated complications and AIDS progression. There were no other patterns observed for cause of death. In three uncontrolled studies, 16 of the 32 deaths were reported as AIDS progression, the other 16 deaths were attributed to HIV-associated complications. In these clinical studies, all deaths were reported by the investigator as not related or unlikely to be related to filgrastim.

In clinical trials, changes in HIV viral load were evaluated by a quantitative HIV-1 RNA RT- Polymerase Chain Reaction (PCR) analyses and by measurement of HIV-1 p24 antigen levels. These studies did not show any evidence of increased HIV replication associated with filgrastim administration.

Indications: Cancer Patients Receiving Myelosuppressive Chemotherapy: To decrease the incidence of infection, as manifested by febrile neutropenia, in patients with nonmyeloid malignancies receiving myelosuppressive antineoplastic drugs.

A complete blood count and platelet count should be obtained prior to chemotherapy, and twice per week (see Precautions, Laboratory Monitoring) during filgrastim therapy to avoid leukocytosis and to monitor the neutrophil count. In Phase III clinical studies, filgrastim therapy was discontinued when the absolute neutrophil count (ANC) was $>10\times10^9$/L after expected chemotherapy-induced nadir.

Cancer Patients Receiving Myeloablative Chemotherapy followed by Bone Marrow Transplantation: To reduce the duration of neutropenia and neutropenia-related clinical sequelae, e.g., febrile neutropenia, in patients undergoing myeloablative therapy followed by bone marrow transplantation.

A complete blood count and platelet count should be obtained at a minimum of 3 times per week following marrow infusion to monitor marrow reconstitution (see Precautions, Laboratory Monitoring).

Cancer Patients Undergoing Peripheral Blood Progenitor Cell (PBPC) Collection and Therapy: For the mobilization of autologous peripheral blood progenitor cells in order to accelerate hematopoietic recovery by infusion of such cells, supported by filgrastim, after myelosuppressive or myeloablative chemotherapy (see Pharmacology, Clinical Experience).

Patients with Severe Chronic Neutropenia: For chronic administration to increase neutrophil counts and to reduce the incidence and duration of infection in patients with a diagnosis of congenital, cyclic or idiopathic neutropenia (see Pharmacology, Clinical Experience).

Patients with HIV Infection: Filgrastim is indicated in patients with HIV infection for the prevention and treatment of neutropenia, to maintain a normal ANC (e.g., between 2 000 and 10 000 cells/µL). Filgrastim therapy reduces the clinical sequelae associated with neutropenia (e.g., bacterial infections) and increases the ability to deliver myelosuppressive medications used for the treatment of HIV and its associated complications (see Pharmacology, Clinical Experience). It is recommended that complete blood counts and platelet counts be monitored at regular intervals (e.g., initially twice weekly for 2 weeks, once weekly for an additional 2 weeks, then once monthly thereafter, or as clinically indicated) during filgrastim therapy (see Precautions, Laboratory Monitoring).

Contraindications: Patients with known hypersensitivity to E. coli derived products or to any constituent of the product.

Precautions: General: Simultaneous Use with Chemotherapy: The safety and efficacy of filgrastim given simultaneously with cytotoxic chemotherapy have not been established. Because of the potential sensitivity of rapidly dividing myeloid cells to cytotoxic chemotherapy, do not use filgrastim in the period 24 hours before through 24 hours after the administration of cytotoxic chemotherapy (see Dosage).

The efficacy of filgrastim has not been evaluated in patients receiving chemotherapy associated with delayed myelosuppression (e.g., nitrosoureas) or with mitomycin C or with myelosuppressive doses of antimetabolites such as 5-fluorouracil or cytosine arabinoside.

The safety and efficacy of filgrastim have not been evaluated in patients receiving concurrent radiation therapy. Simultaneous use of filgrastim with chemotherapy and radiation therapy should be avoided.

Growth Factor Potential: Filgrastim is a growth factor that primarily stimulates production of neutrophils. However, the possibility that filgrastim can act as a growth factor for certain tumor types, particularly myeloid malignancies, cannot be excluded. Therefore, because of the possibility of tumor growth, precaution should be exercised in using this drug in patients with myelodysplasia or in any malignancy with myeloid characteristics.

Tumor cells may be collected in the leukapheresis product, following PBPC mobilization by filgrastim. The clinical significance and the effect of reinfusion of tumor cells with the leukapheresis product is still unknown and the possible contribution of clonogenic tumor cells to an eventual relapse has not been determined.

Acute myeloid leukemia (AML) has been reported to occur in the natural history of severe chronic neutropenia without cytokine therapy. It is not known what, if any, additional risk may be imposed by filgrastim therapy.

Cancer Patients Receiving Myelosuppressive Chemotherapy: Leukocytosis: In all studies, including Phase I/II dose ranging studies, white blood cell counts of 100×10^9/L or greater were observed in approximately 2% of patients receiving filgrastim at doses above 5 and up to 115 µg/kg/day. There were no reports of adverse events associated with this degree of leukocytosis. In order to avoid the potential complications of excessive leukocytosis, a complete blood count (CBC) is recommended twice per week during filgrastim therapy (see Laboratory Monitoring).

Premature Discontinuation of Filgrastim Therapy: A transient increase in neutrophil counts is typically seen 1 to 2 days after initiation of filgrastim therapy. However, for a sustained therapeutic response, filgrastim therapy should be continued following chemotherapy until the post nadir ANC reaches 10×10^9/L. Therefore, the premature discontinuation of filgrastim therapy, prior to the time of recovery from the expected neutrophil nadir, is generally not recommended (see Dosage).

Patients with Severe Chronic Neutropenia: Diagnosis of Congenital, Cyclic or Idiopathic Neutropenia: Care should be taken to confirm the diagnosis of congenital, cyclic or idiopathic neutropenia, which may be difficult to distinguish from myelodysplasia, before initiating filgrastim therapy. The safety and efficacy of filgrastim in the treatment of neutropenia or pancytopenia due to other hematopoietic disorders (e.g., myelodysplastic disorders or myeloid leukemia) have not been established.

It is, therefore, essential that serial complete blood counts with differential and platelet counts, and an evaluation of bone marrow morphology and karyotype, be performed prior to initiation of filgrastim therapy.

Acute myeloid leukemia (AML) or abnormal cytogenetics have been reported to occur in the natural history of severe chronic neutropenia without cytokine therapy. Abnormal cytogenetics have been associated with the eventual development of myeloid leukemia. The effect of continued filgrastim administration in patients with abnormal cytogenetics is unknown. If a patient with severe chronic neutropenia (SCN) develops abnormal cytogenetics, the risks and benefits of continuing filgrastim should be carefully considered (see Adverse Effects).

Chronic Administration: The safety and efficacy of chronic daily administration of filgrastim in patients with SCN have been established in Phase I/II clinical trials of 74 patients treated for up to 4.5 years, and in a Phase III trial of 123 patients treated for up to 3.5 years.

Although the relationship to filgrastim is unclear, osteoporosis has been reported in approximately 7% of patients receiving filgrastim therapy for up to 4.5 years in clinical trials in patients with SCN. Patients with SCN, particularly those with congenital neutropenia and those with underlying osteoperotic bone disease, should be monitored for the possible occurrence of bone density changes while on long-term filgrastim therapy. Other infrequently observed adverse events included exacerbation of some preexisting skin disorders (e.g., psoriasis), cutaneous vasculitis (leukocytoclastic), alopecia, hematuria/proteinuria, thrombocytopenia (platelets less than 50×10^9/L).

Patients with HIV Infection: Risks Associated with Increased Doses of Myelosuppressive Medications: Treatment with filgrastim alone does not preclude thrombocytopenia and anemia due to myelosuppressive medications. As a result of the potential to receive higher doses or a greater number of these medications with filgrastim therapy, the patient may be at higher risk of developing thrombocytopenia (see Adverse Effects) and anemia. Regular monitoring of blood counts is recommended.

Infections Causing Myelosuppression: Neutropenia may be due to bone marrow infiltrating opportunistic infections such as M. avium complex or malignancies such as lymphoma. In patients with known bone marrow infiltrating infection or malignancy, consideration should be given to appropriate therapy for treatment of the underlying condition, in addition to administration of filgrastim for treatment of neutropenia.

Other: The response to filgrastim may be diminished in patients with reduced neutrophil precursors such as those previously treated with extensive dose chemotherapy or radiotherapy.

In studies of filgrastim administration following chemotherapy, most reported side effects were consistent with those usually seen as a result of cytotoxic chemotherapy (see Adverse Effects). As a result of the potential of receiving higher doses of chemotherapy (i.e., full doses on the prescribed schedule), the patient may be at greater risk of thrombocytopenia, anemia, and nonhematological consequences of increased chemotherapy doses (please refer to the prescribing information of the specific chemotherapy agents used). Regular monitoring of the hematocrit and platelet count is recommended.

In septic patients receiving filgrastim, the physician should be alert to the theoretical possibility of adult respiratory distress syndrome, due to the possible influx of neutrophils at the site of inflammation.

Cardiac events (myocardial infarctions, arrhythmias) have been reported in 11 of 375 cancer patients receiving filgrastim in clinical studies; the relationship to filgrastim therapy is unknown. However, patients with preexisting cardiac conditions receiving filgrastim should be monitored closely.

Information for the Patient: In those situations in which the physician determines that the patient can safely and effectively self-administer filgrastim, the patient should be instructed as to the proper dosage and administration. Patients should also be instructed that filgrastim should be refrigerated, but not allowed to freeze. The most common adverse experience occurring with filgrastim therapy is bone pain. Patients should also be instructed about the rare possibility of an allergic-type reaction, possibly manifested as shortness of breath, faintness, or rash. If any of these symptoms occur, patients should contact their physician immediately (see Adverse Effects). If home use is prescribed, patients should be thoroughly instructed in the importance of proper disposal and cautioned against the reuse of needles, syringes, or drug product. A puncture-resistant container for the disposal of used syringes and needles should be available to the patient. The full container should be disposed of according to the directions provided by the physician.

Laboratory Monitoring: Cancer Patients Receiving Myelosuppressive Chemotherapy: A CBC and platelet count should be obtained prior to chemotherapy, and at regular intervals (twice per week) during filgrastim therapy. Following cytotoxic chemotherapy, the neutrophil nadir occurred earlier during cycles when filgrastim was administered, and white blood cell differentials demonstrated a left shift, including the appearance of promyelocytes and myeloblasts. In addition, the duration of severe neutropenia was reduced, and was followed by an accelerated recovery in the neutrophil counts. Therefore, regular monitoring of white blood cell counts, particularly at the time of the recovery from the post chemotherapy nadir, is recommended in order to avoid excessive leukocytosis.

Cancer Patients Receiving Myeloablative Chemotherapy followed by Bone Marrow Transplantation: A CBC and platelet count should be obtained at regular intervals (3 times/week during filgrastim therapy) following marrow infusion.

Cancer Patients Undergoing Peripheral Blood Progenitor Cell (PBPC) Collection and Therapy: After 4 days of filgrastim treatment for PBPC mobilization, neutrophil counts should be monitored. Monitoring of platelet and red blood cell counts is recommended during the leukapheresis period. Frequent complete blood counts and platelet counts are recommended (at least 3 times/week) following PBPC reinfusion.

Patients with Severe Chronic Neutropenia: During the initial 4 weeks of filgrastim therapy, and for 2 weeks following any dose adjustment, a complete blood count (CBC) with differential and platelet determination should be performed twice weekly. Once a patient is clinically stable, a CBC with differential and platelet determination should be performed monthly.

In clinical trials, the following laboratory results were observed: Cyclic fluctuations in the neutrophil counts were frequently observed in patients with congenital or idiopathic neutropenia after initiation of filgrastim therapy.

Platelet counts were generally at the upper limits of normal prior to filgrastim therapy. With filgrastim therapy, platelet counts decreased but generally remained within normal limits (see Adverse Effects).

Early myeloid forms were noted in the peripheral blood in most patients, including the appearance of metamyelocytes and myelocytes. Promyelocytes and myeloblasts were noted in some patients.

Relative increases were occasionally noted in the number of circulating eosinophils and basophils. No consistent increases were observed with filgrastim therapy.

As in other trials, increases were observed in serum uric acid, lactic dehydrogenase, and serum alkaline phosphatase.

Patients with HIV Infection: A CBC and platelet count should be obtained prior to starting filgrastim therapy and at regular intervals (e.g., initially twice weekly for 2 weeks, once weekly for an additional 2 weeks, then once monthly thereafter, or as clinically indicated) during filgrastim therapy. Some patients may respond very rapidly and with a considerable increase in neutrophil count to the initial doses of filgrastim. It is recommended that blood samples be drawn for ANC measurement prior to any scheduled dosing with filgrastim.

Drug Interactions: Interactions of filgrastim with other cytokines, including hematopoietic growth factors, have been observed in animal studies. The safety, efficacy, and possible interactions of filgrastim used in combination with other cytokines have not been characterized in clinical trials. Drugs which may potentiate the release of neutrophils, such as lithium, should be used with caution.

Carcinogenesis, Mutagenesis, Impairment of Fertility: The carcinogenic potential of filgrastim has not been studied. Filgrastim failed to induce bacterial gene mutations in either the presence or absence of a drug metabolizing enzyme system. Filgrastim had no observed effect on the fertility of male or female rats, or on gestation at doses up to 500 µg/kg.

Pregnancy: Filgrastim has been shown to cause adverse effects in pregnant rabbits when given in doses 2 to 10 times the human dose.

In rabbits, increased abortion and embryolethality were observed in animals treated with filgrastim at 80 µg/kg/day. Filgrastim administered to pregnant rabbits at doses of 80 µg/kg/day during the period of organogenesis was associated with increased fetal resorption, genitourinary bleeding, developmental abnormalities, and decreased body weight, live births, and food consumption. External abnormalities were not observed in the fetuses of dams treated at 80 µg/kg/day. Reproductive studies in pregnant rats have shown that filgrastim was not associated with lethal, teratogenic, or behavioral effects on fetuses when administered by daily i.v. injection during the period of organogenesis at dose levels up to 575 µg/kg/day.

In Segment III studies in rats, offspring of dams treated at greater than 20 µg/kg/day exhibited a delay in external differentiation (detachment of auricles and descent of testes) and slight growth retardation, possibly due to lower body weight of females during rearing and nursing. Offspring of dams treated at 100 µg/kg/day exhibited decreased body weights at birth, and a slightly reduced 4 day survival rate.

There are no adequate, well controlled studies in pregnant women, therefore, filgrastim is not recommended for use in pregnant women.

Lactation: It is not known whether filgrastim is excreted in human milk, therefore, filgrastim is not recommended for use in nursing women.

Children: Cancer Patients Receiving Myelosuppressive Chemotherapy: Twelve pediatric patients with neuroblastoma have received up to 6 cycles of cyclophosphamide, cisplatin, doxorubicin, and etoposide chemotherapy concurrently with filgrastim, in this population, filgrastim was well tolerated. There was one report of palpable splenomegaly associated with filgrastim therapy; however, the only consistently reported adverse event was musculoskeletal pain, which is no different from the experience in the adult population.

Patients with Severe Chronic Neutropenia: Serious long-term risks of daily treatment with filgrastim have been rarely observed in clinical trials. Potential effects of long-term treatment with this hematopoietic growth factor, such as alterations of growth and development, sexual maturation, or endocrine function, have not been observed.

The safety and efficacy in neonates and patients with autoimmune neutropenia of infancy have not been established.

Adverse Effects: Cancer Patients Receiving Myelosuppressive Chemotherapy: In clinical trials involving over 350 patients receiving filgrastim following cytotoxic chemotherapy, most adverse experiences were the sequelae of the underlying malignancy or cytotoxic chemotherapy. In all Phase II and III trials, medullary bone pain, reported in 24% of patients, was the only consistently observed adverse reaction attributed to filgrastim therapy. This bone pain was generally reported to be of mild-to-moderate severity, and could be controlled in most patients with nonopioid analgesics; infrequently, bone pain was severe enough to require opioid analgesics. Bone pain was reported more frequently in patients treated with higher doses (20 to 100 µg/kg/day) administered i.v., and less frequently in patients treated with lower s.c. doses (3 to 10 µg/kg/day).

In the randomized, double-blind, placebo-controlled trial of filgrastim therapy following combination chemotherapy in patients (n=207) with small cell lung cancer, the adverse events in Table I were reported during blinded cycles of study medication (placebo or filgrastim at 4 to 8 µg/kg/day). Events are reported as exposure adjusted since patients remained on double-blind filgrastim a median of 3 cycles versus 1 cycle for placebo.

Table I—Neupogen Adverse Effects

	% of Blinded Cycles with Events	
Event	**Neupogen N=384 Patient Cycles**	**Placebo N=257 Patient Cycles**
Nausea/Vomiting	57	64
Skeletal Pain	22	11
Alopecia	18	27
Diarrhea	14	23
Neutropenic Fever	13	35
Mucositis	12	20
Fever	12	11
Fatigue	11	16
Anorexia	9	11
Dyspnea	9	11
Headache	7	9
Cough	6	8
Skin Rash	6	9
Chest Pain	5	6
Generalized Weakness	4	7
Sore Throat	4	9
Stomatitis	5	10
Constipation	5	10
Pain (Unspecified)	2	7

In this study, there were no serious, life-threatening, or fatal adverse reactions attributed to filgrastim therapy. Specifically, there were no reports of flu-like symptoms, pleuritis, pericarditis, or other major systemic reactions.

Spontaneously reversible elevations in uric acid, lactate dehydrogenase, and alkaline phosphatase occurred in 27 to 58% of 98 patients receiving blinded filgrastim therapy following cytotoxic chemotherapy; increases were generally mild to moderate. Transient decreases in blood pressure (<90/60 mmHg) which did not require clinical treatment, were reported in 7 of 176 patients in Phase III clinical studies following administration of filgrastim. No evidence of interaction of filgrastim with other drugs was observed in the course of clinical trials (see Precautions, Simultaneous Use with Chemotherapy).

Since commercial introduction, there have been rare reports (<1 in 4 000 patients) of allergic-type reactions in patients treated with filgrastim. These have generally been characterized by systemic symptoms involving at least 2 body systems, most often skin (rash, urticaria, facial edema), respiratory (wheezing, dyspnea), and cardiovascular (hypotension, tachycardia). Some reactions occurred on initial exposure. Reactions tended to occur within the first 30 minutes after administration and appeared to occur more frequently in patients receiving filgrastim i.v. Rapid resolution of symptoms occurred in most cases after administration of antihistamines, steroids, bronchodilators, and/or epinephrine. Symptoms recurred in more than half the patients who were rechallenged. There has been no evidence of the development of antibodies to filgrastim or of a blunted or diminished response over time in patients who have received filgrastim daily for almost 2 years.

Cancer Patients Receiving Myeloablative Chemotherapy followed by Bone Marrow Transplantation: In clinical trials, the reported adverse effects were those typically seen in patients receiving intensive chemotherapy followed by bone marrow transplantation. The most common events reported in both control and treatment groups included stomatitis and nausea and vomiting, generally of mild to moderate severity and were considered unrelated to filgrastim. In the randomized studies of BMT involving 167 patients who received study drug, the following events occurred more frequently in patients treated with filgrastim than in controls; nausea (10% vs. 4%), vomiting (7% vs. 3%), hypertension (4% vs. 0%), rash (12% vs. 10%), and peritonitis (2% vs. 0%). None of these events were reported by the investigator to be related to filgrastim. One event of erythema nodosum was reported moderate in severity and possibly related to filgrastim.

Cancer Patients Undergoing Peripheral Blood Progenitor Cell (PBPC) Collection and Therapy: Filgrastim: Mobilized PBPC Collection: In clinical trials, 126 patients have received filgrastim for mobilization of PBPC. During the mobilization period, adverse events related to filgrastim consisted primarily of mild to moderate musculoskeletal symptoms, reported in 44% of patients. These symptoms were predominantly events of medullary bone pain (38%). Headache was reported related to filgrastim in 7% of patients. Mild to moderate transient increases in alkaline phosphatase levels were reported related to filgrastim in 21% of the patients who had serum chemistries evaluated during the mobilization phase.

All patients had increases in neutrophil counts consistent with the biological effects of filgrastim. Two patients had a white blood cell count greater than 100×10^9/L with white blood cell count increases during the mobilization period ranging from 16.7×10^9/L to 138×10^9/L above baseline. Eighty eight percent of patients had an increase in white blood cell count between 10×10^9/L and 70×10^9/L above baseline. No clinical sequelae were associated with any grade of leukocytosis.

Sixty five percent of patients had mild to moderate anemia and 97% of patients had decreases in platelet counts possibly related to the leukapheresis procedure. Only 5 patients had platelet counts $<50\times10^9$/L.

PBPC Transplantation followed by Filgrastim: During the period of filgrastim administration post PBPC transplant, filgrastim was administered to 110 patients as supportive therapy and adverse events were consistent with those expected after high dose chemotherapy. Mild to moderate musculoskeletal pain was the most frequently reported adverse event related to filgrastim, reported in 15% of patients.

Patients with Severe Chronic Neutropenia: Mild to moderate bone pain was reported in approximately 33% of patients in clinical trials. This symptom was usually readily controlled with mild analgesics. General musculoskeletal pain was also noted in higher frequency in patients treated with filgrastim. Palpable splenomegaly was observed in approximately 30% of patients. Abdominal or flank pain was seen infrequently and thrombocytopenia ($<50\times10^9$/L) was noted in 12% of patients with palpable spleens. Less than 3% of all patients underwent splenectomy, and most of these had a pre-study history of splenomegaly. Approximately 7% of patients had thrombocytopenia ($<50\times10^9$/L) during filgrastim therapy, most of whom had a pre-study history. In most cases, thrombocytopenia was managed by filgrastim dose reduction or interruption. There were no associated serious hemorrhagic sequelae in these patients. Epistaxis was noted in 15% of patients treated with filgrastim, but was associated with thrombocytopenia in only 2% of patients. Anemia was reported in approximately 10% of patients, but in most cases appeared to be related to frequent diagnostic phlebotomy, chronic illness or concomitant medications. Myelodysplasia or myeloid leukemia was reported to have developed during filgrastim therapy in approximately 2% (5 of 316) of the patients (see Precautions, Diagnosis of Congenital, Cyclic or Idiopathic Neutropenia).

Eight patients from a subset of 94 who had normal cytogenetic evaluations at baseline were subsequently found to have

Neupogen (cont'd)

abnormalities, including monosomy 7, on routine repeat evaluation conducted 18 to 52 months of filgrastim therapy. It is unknown whether the development of these findings is related to chronic daily filgrastim administration or reflects the natural history of SCN.

There have been rare reports (<1 in 7 000 patients) of cutaneous vasculitis in patients treated with filgrastim. In most cases the severity of the cutaneous vasculitis was moderate or severe. Most of the reports involved patients with severe chronic neutropenia receiving long-term filgrastim therapy. Symptoms of vasculitis generally developed simultaneously with an increase in the ANC and abated when the ANC decreased. Many patients were able to continue filgrastim at a reduced dose.

Other adverse events infrequently observed and possibly related to filgrastim therapy were: injection site reaction, headache, hepatomegaly, arthralgia, osteoporosis, rash, alopecia and hematuria/proteinuria.

Patients with HIV Infection: In the multicenter, randomized, controlled trial, 172 of 258 patients were treated with filgrastim. Filgrastim was generally well-tolerated. The most frequently reported treatment-related adverse events in the 24-week treatment period were skeletal pain (14.5%), headache (6.4%), back pain and myalgia (5.8% each), and increased alkaline phosphatase (5.2%).

There were no new or unexpected treatment-related events seen in filgrastim-treated patients. Adverse events observed in clinical trials were consistent with progression of HIV disease or events observed in other clinical settings.

There was no apparent increase or decrease in HIV replication and viral load as measured by quantitative reverse transcriptase polymerase chain reaction (RT-PCR). Although prior in vitro and in vivo studies have not shown any increase in viral load following use of filgrastim in HIV-infected patients, the randomized study was not powered to address this issue and possibility of an effect due to filgrastim on HIV replication cannot be entirely excluded.

As of 31 January 1996, an estimated 1.2 million patients worldwide have received filgrastim therapy across all indications. Of an estimated 150 000 HIV-infected patients receiving filgrastim to date, there have been 106 spontaneous adverse event reports received worldwide. No new adverse event patterns were identified in adults or children receiving filgrastim for neutropenia associated with HIV infection. Five deaths were reported in 106 postmarketing reports in patients receiving filgrastim for HIV infection. Three of five deaths were attributed to various manifestations of HIV disease progression. In the fourth case, the cause of death was not reported. In the fifth case, the physician reported that death in the context of ARDS occurred in the absence of fever and microbiological cause and was typical of bleomycin pulmonary toxicity; however, the physician reported that this may have been enhanced by filgrastim. It is notable, however, that randomized trials, and non-randomized trials demonstrated no increase in the known pulmonary toxicity of bleomycin when filgrastim was added to treatment.

In the randomized controlled study, the overall incidence of thrombocytopenia was 9.9% in the filgrastim-treated groups compared with 8.1% in the control group. Severe thrombocytopenia occurred in 7% of the filgrastim-treated patients and 3.5% of control patients in the controlled, randomized study. During this study, mean platelet count decreased at week 2 in the filgrastim-treated patients, but returned to baseline by week 3 and remained stable thereafter. In the post-marketing experience of HIV-infected patients which includes an estimated 150 000 patients worldwide, 10 of 106 spontaneous reports of adverse reactions were for thrombocytopenia. Of these, 3 cases were reported as serious.

Because adverse events of thrombocytopenia in HIV-infected individuals are multifactorial and may be attributed to the natural progression of HIV disease and associated infections, and because of the inconsistent occurrence of thrombocytopenia in a small number of patients in the aforementioned clinical trials, no definitive relationship between filgrastim therapy in HIV-infected patients and thrombocytopenia can be established.

In one study, 16 of 24 patients (66.7%) were reported to have splenomegaly during an observation period of 49 to 701 days. However, no baseline measurements of spleen size were made for comparison to on-study values. In three other uncontrolled clinical trials, only one of 297 patients (0.3%) had a report of splenomegaly. Since splenomegaly is a common clinical finding in 72% of patients with AIDS sometime during the course of their disease, it is likely that the observed splenomegaly was associated with HIV disease and not related to filgrastim.

Overdose: Symptoms and Treatment: The maximum tolerated dose of filgrastim has not been determined. In dose ranging studies, 5 of 16 patients given ≥69 µg/kg/day were withdrawn due to adverse experiences. In these and other clinical trials, only 2 of 253 patients on lower doses were withdrawn due to adverse events.

In filgrastim clinical trials of cancer patients receiving myelosuppressive chemotherapy, white blood cell counts $>100\times10^9$/L have been reported in less than 2% of patients and were not associated with any reported adverse clinical effects.

It is recommended, to avoid the potential risks of excessive leukocytosis, that filgrastim therapy should be discontinued if the ANC surpass 10×10^9/L after the chemotherapy-induced ANC nadir has occurred.

In cancer patients receiving myelosuppressive chemotherapy, discontinuation of filgrastim therapy usually results in a 50% decrease in circulating neutrophils within 1 to 2 days, with a return to pretreatment levels in 1 to 7 days.

Dosage: Cancer Patients Receiving Myelosuppressive Chemotherapy: The recommended starting dose is 5 µg/kg/day, administered as a single daily injection by s.c. bolus injection, by short i.v. infusion (15 to 30 minutes), or by continuous s.c. or continuous i.v. infusion. A CBC and platelet count should be obtained before instituting filgrastim therapy, and monitored twice weekly during therapy. Doses may be increased in increments of 5 µg/kg for each chemotherapy cycle, according to the duration and severity of the ANC nadir. Therapy should be discontinued if the ANC surpasses 10×10^9/L after the ANC nadir has occurred.

Filgrastim should be administered no earlier than 24 hours after the administration of cytotoxic chemotherapy. Filgrastim should not be administered in the period 24 hours before the administration of chemotherapy (see Precautions). Filgrastim should be administered daily for up to 2 weeks, until the ANC has reached 10×10^9/L following the expected chemotherapy-induced neutrophil nadir. The duration of therapy needed to attenuate chemotherapy-induced neutropenia may be dependent on the myelosuppressive potential of the chemotherapy regimen employed. Filgrastim therapy should be discontinued if the ANC surpasses 10×10^9/L after the expected chemotherapy-induced neutrophil nadir (see Precautions). In Phase III trials, efficacy was observed at doses of 4 to 8 µg/kg/day.

Cancer Patients Receiving Myeloablative Chemotherapy followed by Bone Marrow Transplantation: The recommended dose following bone marrow transplant is 10 µg/kg/day given as an i.v. infusion of 4 or 24 hours, or as a continuous 24-hour s.c. infusion. Filgrastim should be administered no earlier than 24 hours after the administration of cytotoxic chemotherapy and at least 24 hours after bone marrow infusion.

During the period of neutrophil recovery, the daily dose of filgrastim should be titrated against the neutrophil response as shown in Table II.

Table II—Neupogen

Dose Adjustment

Absolute Neutrophil Count	Neupogen Dose Adjustment
When ANC $>1.0\times10^9$/L for 3 consecutive days	Reduce to 5 µg/kg/day*
then:	
If ANC remains $>1.0\times10^9$/L for 3 more consecutive days	Discontinue Neupogen
If ANC decreases to $<1.0\times10^9$/L	Resume at 5 µg/kg/day

*If ANC decreases to $<1.0\times10^9$/L at any time during the 5 µg/kg/day administration, Neupogen should be increased to 10 µg/kg/day, and the above steps should then be followed.

Cancer Patients Undergoing Peripheral Blood Progenitor Cell (PBPC) Collection and Therapy: The recommended dose of filgrastim for peripheral blood progenitor cell mobilization is 10 µg/kg/day given as a single daily s.c. injection or a continuous 24 hour infusion. Filgrastim therapy should be given for at least 4 days before the first leukapheresis procedure, and should be continued through to the day of the last leukapheresis procedure. Collections should be commenced on day 5 and continued on consecutive days until the desired yield of haematopoietic progenitor cells is obtained. For peripheral blood progenitor cells mobilized with filgrastim, a schedule of leukapheresis collections on days 5, 6, and 7 of a 7 day treatment regimen has been found to be effective.

The target number of progenitor cells to be collected and reinfused is to be determined by the treating physician. The following should be considered: 1. A minimum or optimal number of progenitor cells in the leukapheresis product, needed for adequate haematopoietic reconstitution, has not been determined. However, studies indicate that the infusion of higher numbers of progenitor cells appears to be associated with a shorter time to neutrophil and platelet recovery, 2. Tests for quantifying the number of progenitor cells, measured as CD34+ or GM-CFU, are not standardized and variations may exist between laboratories, and 3. Factors other than filgrastim dosage, such as prior cytotoxic chemo-or radio-therapy, may affect the number and quality of progenitor cells mobilized and collected by leukapheresis.

The recommended dose of filgrastim following PBPC transplant is 5 µg/kg/day given either s.c. or as an i.v. infusion. The first dose should be administered at least 24 hours after cytotoxic chemotherapy and at least 24 hours after PBPC infusion. The daily dose of filgrastim should be titrated according to the schedule provided above (Cancer patients receiving BMT).

Patients with HIV Infection: The recommended starting dose of filgrastim is 1 µg/kg/day or 300 µg 3 times/week by s.c. injection until a normal neutrophil count is reached and can be maintained (ANC ≥2 000 cells/µL). Dose adjustments may be necessary as determined by the patient's ANC to maintain the ANC between 2 000 and 10 000 cells/µL.

When reversal of neutropenia has been achieved, the minimal effective dose to maintain a normal neutrophil count should be established. An initial dose of 300 µg 3 times/week by s.c. injection is recommended. A further dose adjustment may be necessary to maintain the ANC between 2 000 and 10 000 cells/µL.

In clinical trials, the maximum filgrastim dose did not exceed 10 µg/kg/day.

Patients with Severe Chronic Neutropenia: Starting Dose: Congenital Neutropenia: The recommended daily starting dose is 12 µg/kg s.c. (single or divided dose).

Idiopathic or Cyclic Neutropenia: The recommended daily starting dose is 5 µg/kg s.c. (single or divided dose).

Dose Adjustments: Filgrastim may be administered s.c. as a single daily injection to increase and sustain the absolute neutrophil count above 1.5×10^9/L. Chronic daily administration is required to maintain an adequate neutrophil count. After 1 to 2 weeks of therapy, the initial dose may be doubled or halved. Subsequently, the dose may be individually adjusted not more than every 1 to 2 weeks to maintain the absolute neutrophil count between 1.5×10^9/L and 10×10^9/L. WBC/ANC monitoring should be done more frequently (e.g., every other day) if the ANC reaches values above 25×10^9/L, and the dose reduced if the ANC remains greater than 25×10^9/L for 1 week.

In clinical trials in patients with severe chronic neutropenia (SCN), 91% of patients who responded to filgrastim therapy responded at doses of less than or equal to 12 µg/kg/day. Ninety-seven percent of patients responded at doses of less than or equal to 24 µg/kg/day. Therefore, patients with SCN who do not respond to the recommended starting dose should be treated with up to 24 µg/kg/day in order to determine if they will respond. In some cases, where higher doses were tried, an improvement in the ANC and the clinical condition was seen with a few patients only.

Dilution: If required, filgrastim may be diluted in 5% dextrose. Filgrastim diluted to a concentration between 5 and 15 µg/mL should be protected from adsorption to plastic materials by the addition of Albumin (Human) at a concentration of 2 mg/mL. When diluted in 5% dextrose or 5% dextrose plus Albumin (Human), filgrastim is compatible with glass bottles, PVC and polyolefin i.v. bags and polypropylene syringes.

Dilution of filgrastim to a final concentration of less than 5 µg/mL even in the presence of Albumin (Human) is not recommended at any time. **Do not dilute with saline at any time: product may precipitate.**

Stability and Storage: Store in the refrigerator at 2 to 8°C. Avoid vigorous shaking. Accidental exposure to room temperature (up to 30°C) or exposure to freezing temperatures does not adversely effect the stability of the product. Prior to injection Neupogen may be allowed to reach room temperature for a maximum of 24 hours. Any vial left at room temperature for greater than 24 hours should be discarded.

Parenteral drug products should be inspected visually for particulate matter and discoloration prior to administration, whenever solution and container permit.

Supplied: Each mL of sterile, clear, colorless, preservative-free liquid for parenteral administration contains: filgrastim 0.30 mg (3×10^7 units/mL) formulated in a 10 mM sodium acetate buffer at pH 4.0 with sorbitol 5% and 0.004% Tween

80. Single use, preservative-free vials of 1 mL (filgrastim 300 µg) and 1.6 mL (filgrastim 480 µg). Boxes of 10.

Use only one dose per vial; do not reenter the vial. Discard unused portions. Do not save unused drug for later administration.

Reviewed 1998

NEURONTIN™ Ⓟ

Parke-Davis

Gabapentin

Antiepileptic

Pharmacology: Gabapentin exhibits antiseizure activity in mice and rats both in the maximal electroshock and in the pentylenetetrazol seizure models.

Gabapentin is structurally related to the neurotransmitter GABA (gamma-aminobutyric acid) but does not interact with GABA receptors, it is not metabolized to GABA or to GABA agonists, and it is not an inhibitor of GABA uptake or degradation. Gabapentin at concentrations up to 100 µM did not demonstrate affinity for other receptor sites such as benzodiazepine, glutamate, glycine or N-methyl-D-aspartate receptors nor does it interact with neuronal sodium channels or L-type calcium channels.

The mechanism of action of gabapentin has not yet been established; however, it is unlike that of the commonly used anticonvulsant drugs.

In vitro studies with radiolabeled gabapentin have revealed a gabapentin binding site in rat brain tissues including neocortex and hippocampus. The identity and function of this binding site remain to be elucidated.

Pharmacokinetics: Adults: Following oral administration of gabapentin, peak plasma concentrations are observed within 2 to 3 hours. Absolute bioavailability of a 300 mg dose of Neurontin capsules is approximately 59%. At doses of 300 and 400 mg, gabapentin bioavailability is unchanged following multiple dose administration. Gabapentin elimination from plasma is best described by linear pharmacokinetics. The elimination half-life of gabapentin is independent of dose and averages 5 to 7 hours in subjects with normal renal function.

Plasma gabapentin concentrations are dose-proportional at doses of 300 to 400 mg q8h, ranging between 1 µg/mL and 10 µg/mL, but are less than dose-proportional above the clinical range (>600 mg q8h). There is no correlation between plasma levels and efficacy. Gabapentin pharmacokinetics are not affected by repeated administration, and steady-state plasma concentrations are predictable from single-dose data.

Gabapentin is not appreciably metabolized in humans, is eliminated solely by renal excretion, and can be removed from plasma by hemodialysis.

Gabapentin does not induce or inhibit hepatic mixed function oxidase enzymes responsible for drug metabolism, does not interfere with the metabolism of commonly coadministered antiepileptic drugs, and is minimally bound to plasma proteins.

Food has no effect on the rate or extent of absorption of gabapentin.

Table I summarizes the mean steady-state pharmacokinetic parameters of Neurontin capsules.

Table I—Neurontin

Summary of Neurontin Mean Steady-State Pharmacokinetic Parameters in Adults Following q8h Administration

Pharmacokinetic Parameter	300 mg (n=7)	400 mg (n=11)
C_{max} (µg/mL)	4.02	5.50
t_{max} (hr)	2.7	2.1
t½ (hr)	5.2	6.1
AUC ($_{0-\infty}$) (µg•hr/mL)	24.8	33.3
AE%*	NA	63.6

* Amount excreted in urine (% of dose).
Legend: NA=Not available.

In patients with epilepsy, gabapentin concentrations in cerebrospinal fluid are approximately 20% of corresponding steady-state trough plasma concentrations.

Geriatrics: Apparent oral clearance (CL/F) of gabapentin decreased as age increased, from about 225 mL/min in subjects under 30 years of age to about 125 ml /min in subjects over 70 years of age. Renal clearance (CLr) of gabapentin also declined with age; however, this decrease can largely be explained by the decline in renal function. Reduction of gabapentin dose may be required in patients who have age-related compromised renal function (see Dosage).

Renal Impairment: In patients with impaired renal function, gabapentin clearance is markedly reduced and dosage adjustment is necessary (see Dosage, Table V).

Hemodialysis: In a study in anuric subjects (n=11), the apparent elimination half-life of gabapentin on nondialysis days was about 132 hours; dialysis 3 times a week (4 hours duration) lowered the apparent half-life of gabapentin by about 60%, from 132 hours to 51 hours. Hemodialysis thus has a significant effect on gabapentin elimination in anuric subjects.

Dosage adjustment in patients undergoing hemodialysis is necessary (see Dosage, Table V).

Children: There are no pharmacokinetic data available in children under 18 years of age.

Hepatic Impairment: Because gabapentin is not appreciably metabolized in humans, no study was performed in patients with hepatic impairment.

Clinical Trials: In placebo-controlled trials in patients not satisfactorily controlled with current antiepileptic drugs, gabapentin, when added to current antiepileptic therapy, was superior to placebo in reducing the frequency of both simple and complex partial seizures and secondarily generalized tonic-clonic seizures. Further analysis of data indicated a higher efficacy for complex partial seizures and secondarily generalized tonic-clonic seizures as compared to all seizure types. Doses ranged from 900 to 1 800 mg/day, with a median dose of 1 200 mg/day.

Long-term, open, uncontrolled studies in drug-resistant patients for periods of up to 18 months demonstrated that doses up to 2 400 mg/day did not result in anything unusual in the type or frequency of adverse events.

Indications: As adjunctive therapy for the management of patients with epilepsy who are not satisfactorily controlled by conventional therapy.

Contraindications: Patients who have demonstrated hypersensitivity to the drug or to any of the components of the formulation.

Precautions: General: Gabapentin is not considered effective in the treatment of absence seizures and should therefore be used with caution in patients who have mixed seizure disorders that include absence seizures.

Tumorigenic Potential: Gabapentin produced an increased incidence of acinar cell adenomas and carcinomas in the pancreas of male rates, but not female rats or in mice, in oncogenic studies with doses of 2 000 mg/kg which resulted in plasma concentrations 14 times higher than those occurring in humans at the maximum recommended dose of 2 400 mg/day. The relevance of these pancreatic acinar cell tumors in male rats to humans is unknown, particularly since tumors of ductal rather than acinar cell origin are the predominant form of human pancreatic cancer.

Drug Discontinuation: As with other anticonvulsant agents, abrupt withdrawal is not recommended because of the possibility of increased seizure frequency. When in the judgment of the clinician there is a need for dose reduction, discontinuation or substitution with alternative medication, this should be done gradually over a minimum of one week.

Occupational Hazards: Patients with uncontrolled epilepsy should not drive or handle potentially dangerous machinery. During clinical trials, the most common adverse reactions observed were somnolence, ataxia, fatigue and nystagmus. Patients should be advised to refrain from activities requiring mental alertness or physical coordination until they are sure that gabapentin does not affect them adversely.

Drug Interactions: **Antiepileptic Agents: There is no interaction between gabapentin and phenytoin, valproic acid, carbamazepine, or phenobarbital. Consequently, Neurontin may be used in combination with other commonly used antiepileptic drugs without concern for alteration of the plasma concentrations of gabapentin or the other antiepileptic drugs.**

Gabapentin steady-state pharmacokinetics are similar for healthy subjects and patients with epilepsy receiving antiepileptic agents.

Oral Contraceptives: Coadministration of gabapentin with the oral contraceptive NorlEstrin does not influence the steady-state pharmacokinetics of norethindrone or ethinyl estradiol.

Antacids: Coadministration of gabapentin with an aluminum and magnesium-based antacid reduces gabapentin bioavailability by up to 24%. Although the clinical significance of this decrease is not known, coadministration of similar antacids and gabapentin is not recommended.

Probenecid: Renal excretion of gabapentin is unaltered by probenecid.

Cimetidine: A slight decrease in renal excretion of gabapentin observed when it is coadministered with cimetidine is not expected to be of clinical importance.

Pregnancy: No evidence of impaired fertility or harm to the fetus due to gabapentin administration was revealed in reproduction studies in mice at doses up to 62 times, and in rats and rabbits at doses up to 31 times the human dose of 2 400 mg/day.

There are, however, no adequate and well-controlled studies in pregnant women. Because animal reproduction studies are not always predictive of human response, this drug should only be used during pregnancy if the potential benefit to the mother justifies the potential risk to the fetus.

Lactation: It is not known if gabapentin is excreted in human milk, and the effect on the nursing infant is unknown. However, because many drugs are excreted in human milk, and because of the potential for serious adverse reactions in nursing infants from gabapentin, breast-feeding is only recommended if the potential benefit outweighs the potential risks.

Children: Systematic studies to establish safety and efficacy in children have not been performed. Data in 39 patients between the ages of 12 and 18 years included in the double-blind, placebo-controlled trials showed that gabapentin was superior to placebo in reducing seizure frequency. Safety data showed that the incidence of adverse events in this group of patients were similar to those observed in older individuals.

Geriatrics: Systematic studies in geriatric patients have not been conducted. Adverse clinical events reported among 59 patients over the age of 65 years treated with gabapentin did not differ from those reported for younger individuals. The small number of individuals evaluated and the limited duration of exposure limits the strength of any conclusions reached about the influence of age, if any, on the kind and incidence of adverse events associated with the use of gabapentin.

As gabapentin is eliminated primarily by renal excretion, dosage adjustment may be required in elderly patients because of declining renal function (see Dosage).

Renal Impairment: Gabapentin clearance is markedly reduced in this patient population and dosage reduction is necessary (see Dosage, Table V on following page).

Laboratory Tests: Clinical trials data do not indicate that routine monitoring of clinical laboratory parameters is necessary for the safe use of gabapentin. Gabapentin may be used in combination with other commonly used antiepileptic drugs without concern for alteration of the blood concentrations of gabapentin or other antiepileptic drugs.

For urinary protein determination the sulfosalicylic acid precipitation procedure is recommended, as false positive readings were reported with the Ames N-Multistix SG dipstick test, when gabapentin or placebo was added to other anticonvulsant drugs.

Adverse Effects: Incidence in Controlled Clinical Trials: Table II (on following page) lists treatment-emergent signs and symptoms that occurred in at least 1% of patients with partial seizures participating in placebo-controlled studies. In these studies, either gabapentin (at doses of 600, 900, 1 200 or 1 800 mg/day) or placebo were added to the patient's current antiepileptic drug therapy.

The most commonly observed adverse events associated with the use of gabapentin in combination with other antiepileptic drugs, not seen at an equivalent frequency in placebo-treated patients, were somnolence, dizziness, ataxia, fatigue, nystagmus and tremor.

Among the treatment-emergent adverse events occurring in gabapentin-treated patients, somnolence and ataxia appeared to exhibit a positive dose-response relationship. Patients treated with 1 800 mg/day (n=54, from one controlled study) experienced approximately a 2-fold increase, as compared to patients on lower doses of 600 to 1 200 mg/day (n=489, from several controlled studies), in the incidence of nystagmus (20.4%), tremor (14.8%), rhinitis (13%), peripheral edema (7.4%), abnormal coordination, depression and myalgia (all at 5.6%). Adverse events were usually mild to moderate in intensity, with a median time to resolution of 2 weeks.

Since gabapentin was administered most often in combination with other antiepileptic agents, it was not possible to determine which agent(s) was associated with adverse events.

Data from long-term, open, uncontrolled studies shows that gabapentin treatment does not result in any new or unusual adverse events.

Neurontin (cont'd)

Table II—Neurontin

Treatment-Emergent Adverse Event Incidence in Placebo-Controlled Add-on Trials (Events in at Least 1% of Neurontin Patients and Numerically More Frequent than in the Placebo Group)

Body System/ Adverse Event (AE)	Neurontin* n=543 %	Placebo* n=378 %
Body as a Whole		
Fatigue	11.0	5.0
Weight Increase	2.9	1.6
Back Pain	1.8	0.5
Peripheral Edema	1.7	0.5
Cardiovascular		
Vasodilatation	1.1	0.3
Digestive System		
Dyspepsia	2.2	0.5
Dry Mouth or Throat	1.7	0.5
Constipation	1.5	0.8
Dental Abnormalities	1.5	0.3
Increased Appetite	1.1	0.8
Hematologic and Lymphatic Systems		
Leukopenia	1.1	0.5
Musculoskeletal System		
Myalgia	2.0	1.9
Fracture	1.1	0.8
Nervous System		
Somnolence	19.3	8.7
Dizziness	17.1	6.9
Ataxia	12.5	5.6
Nystagmus	8.3	4.0
Tremor	6.8	3.2
Nervousness	2.4	1.9
Dysarthria	2.4	0.5
Amnesia	2.2	0.0
Depression	1.8	1.8
Abnormal Thinking	1.7	1.3
Twitching	1.3	0.5
Abnormal Coordination	1.1	0.3
Respiratory System		
Rhinitis	4.1	3.7
Pharyngitis	2.8	1.6
Coughing	1.8	1.3
Skin and Appendages		
Abrasion	1.3	0.0
Pruritus	1.3	0.5
Urogenital System		
Impotence	1.5	1.1
Special Senses		
Diplopia	5.9	1.9
Amblyopia	4.2	1.1
Laboratory Deviations		
WBC Decreased	1.1	0.5

* Plus background antiepileptic drug therapy.

Withdrawal from Treatment Due to Adverse Events: Approximately 6.4% of the 543 patients who received gabapentin in the placebo-controlled studies withdrew due to adverse events. In comparison, approximately 4.5% of the 378 placebo-controlled participants withdrew due to adverse events during these studies. The adverse events most commonly associated with withdrawal were somnolence (1.2%), ataxia (0.8%), fatigue, nausea and/or vomiting and dizziness (all at 0.6%).

Other Adverse Events Observed in All Clinical Trials: Adverse events that occurred in at least 1% of the 2 074 individuals who participated in all clinical trials are described below, except those already listed in Table II.

Body as a Whole: asthenia, malaise, facial edema.

Cardiovascular: hypertension.

Digestive: anorexia, flatulence, gingivitis.

Hematologic and Lymphatic: purpura; most often described as bruises resulting from physical trauma.

Musculoskeletal: arthralgia.

CNS: vertigo, hyperkinesia, paresthesia, anxiety, hostility, decreased or absent reflexes.

Respiratory: pneumonia.

Special Senses: abnormal vision.

Overdose: Symptoms and Treatment: Acute, life-threatening toxicity has not been observed with gabapentin overdoses of up to 49 g ingested at one time. In these cases, double vision, slurred speech, drowsiness, lethargy and diarrhea were observed. All patients recovered with supportive care.

Gabapentin can be removed by hemodialysis. Although hemodialysis has not been performed in the few overdose cases reported, it may be indicated by the patients clinical state or in patients with significant renal impairment.

Reduced absorption of gabapentin at higher doses may limit drug absorption at the time of overdosing and, hence, reduce toxicity from overdoses.

An oral lethal dose of gabapentin was not identified in mice and rats given doses as high as 8 000 mg/kg. Signs of acute toxicity in animals included ataxia, labored breathing, ptosis, hypoactivity, or excitation.

Dosage: Adults: The usual effective maintenance dose is 900 to 1 200 mg/day. Treatment should be initiated with 300 to 400 mg/day. Titration to an effective dose, in increments of 300 or 400 mg/day, can progress rapidly and can be accomplished over 3 days (see Table III). Gabapentin is given orally with or without food.

Table III—Neurontin

Titration Schedule

Dose	Day 1	Day 2	Day 3
900 mg/day	300 mg od	300 mg b.i.d.	300 mg t.i.d.
1 200 mg/day	400 mg od	400 mg b.i.d.	400 mg t.i.d.

Data from clinical trials suggest that doses higher than 1 200 mg/day may have increased efficacy in some patients; however, higher doses may also increase the incidence of adverse events (see Adverse Effects).

Daily maintenance doses should be given in 3 equally divided doses (see Table IV), and the maximum time between doses in a 3 times daily schedule should not exceed 12 hours. It is not necessary to monitor gabapentin plasma concentrations in order to optimize gabapentin therapy. Further, as there are no drug interactions with commonly used antiepileptic drugs, Neurontin may be used in combination with these drugs without concern for alteration of plasma concentrations of either gabapentin or other antiepileptic drugs.

Table IV—Neurontin

Maintenance Dosage Schedule

Total Daily Dose (mg/day)	Schedule
900	300 mg t.i.d.
1 200	400 mg t.i.d.
1 800	2 × 300 mg t.i.d.
2 400	2 × 400 mg t.i.d.

Dosage adjustment in elderly patients due to declining renal function and in patients with renal impairment or undergoing hemodialysis is recommended as shown in Table V.

Table V—Neurontin

Maintenance Dosage of Neurontin in Adults with Reduced Renal Function

Renal Function Creatinine Clearance (mL/min)	Total Daily Dose (mg/day)	Dose Regimen (mg)
>60	1 200	400 t.i.d.
30-60	600	300 b.i.d.
15-30	300	300 od
<15	150	300 od every other day
Hemodialysis[a]	—	200-300[b]

[a]Loading dose of 300 to 400 mg.

[b]Maintenance dose of 200 to 300 mg Neurontin following each 4 hours of hemodialysis.

Children over 12 years of age: The dosage used in a limited number of patients in this age group was 900 to 1 200 mg/day. Doses above 1 200 mg/day have not been investigated.

Information for the Patient: See Blue Section—Information for the Patient "Neurontin".

Supplied: 100 mg: Each hard gelatin capsule, with white opaque body and cap printed with "PD" on one side and "Neurontin/100 mg" on the other, contains: gabapentin 100 mg. Nonmedicinal ingredients: cornstarch, lactose and talc; capsule shells may contain FD&C blue No. 2, gelatin, red iron oxide, silicon dioxide, sodium lauryl sulfate, titanium dioxide and yellow iron oxide. Bottles of 100.

300 mg: Each hard gelatin capsule, with yellow opaque body and cap printed with "PD" on one side and "Neurontin/300 mg" on the other, contains: gabapentin 300 mg. Nonmedicinal ingredients: cornstarch, lactose and talc; capsule shells may contain FD&C blue No. 2, gelatin, red iron oxide, silicon dioxide, sodium lauryl sulfate, titanium dioxide and yellow iron oxide. Bottles of 100.

400 mg: Each hard gelatin capsule, with orange opaque body and cap printed with "PD" on one side and "Neurontin/400 mg" on the other, contains: gabapentin 400 mg. Nonmedicinal ingredients: cornstarch, lactose and talc; capsule shells may contain FD&C blue No. 2, gelatin, red iron oxide, silicon dioxide, sodium lauryl sulfate, titanium dioxide and yellow iron oxide. Bottles of 100.

Store at controlled room temperature 15 to 30°C.

(Shown in Product Recognition Section)

NEUTREXIN® Pr

Lilly

Trimetrexate Glucuronate

Antiprotozoal Agent

Pharmacology: In vitro studies have shown that trimetrexate is a competitive inhibitor of dihydrofolate reductase (DHFR) from bacterial, protozoan and mammalian sources. DHFR catalyzes the reduction of intracellular dihydrofolate to the active coenzyme tetrahydrofolate. Inhibition of DHFR results in the depletion of this coenzyme, leading directly to interference with thymidylate biosynthesis, as well as inhibition of folate-dependent formyltransferases, and indirectly to inhibition of purine biosynthesis. The end result is disruption of DNA, RNA and protein synthesis, with consequent cell death.

Leucovorin (folinic acid) is readily transported into mammalian cells by an active carrier-mediated process and can be assimilated into cellular folate pools following its metabolism. In vitro studies have shown that leucovorin provides a source of reduced folates necessary for normal cellular biosynthetic processes. Because the P. carinii organism lacks the reduced folate carrier-mediated transport system, leucovorin is prevented from entering the organism. Therefore, at concentrations achieved with therapeutic doses of trimetrexate plus leucovorin, the selective transport of trimetrexate, but not leucovorin, into the P. carinii organism allows the concurrent administration of leucovorin to protect normal host cells from the cytotoxicity of trimetrexate without inhibiting the antifolate's inhibition of P. carinii. It is not known if considerably higher doses of leucovorin would affect trimetrexate's effect on P. carinii.

Pharmacokinetics: The pharmacokinetics of trimetrexate were assessed in 6 patients with acquired immunodeficiency syndrome (AIDS) who had P. carinii pneumonia (4 patients) or toxoplasmosis (2 patients). Trimetrexate was administered i.v. as a bolus injection at a dose of 30 mg/m^2/day along with leucovorin 20 mg/m^2 every 6 hours for 21 days. Trimetrexate clearance (mean±SD) was 38 ± 15 mL/min/m^2 and volume of distribution at steady state (Vd_{ss}) was 20 ± 8 L/m^2. The plasma concentration time profile declined in a biphasic manner over 24 hours with a terminal half-life of 11 ± 4 hours.

Indications: Trimetrexate with concurrent leucovorin administration (leucovorin protection) is indicated as an alternative therapy for the treatment of moderate-to-severe P. carinii pneumonia (PCP) in immunocompromised patients, including patients with the acquired immunodeficiency syndrome (AIDS), who are intolerant of, or are refractory to trimethoprim-sulfamethoxazole therapy or for whom trimethoprim-sulfamethoxazole is contraindicated.

This indication is based on the results of a randomized, controlled double-blind trial comparing trimetrexate with concurrent leucovorin protection (TMTX/LV) to trimethoprim-sulfamethoxazole (TMP/SMX) in patients with moderate-to-severe P. carinii pneumonia, defined as (A-a) baseline gradient >30 mmHg, as well as results of a Treatment IND. A detailed description of these clinical studies is available.

Contraindications: Patients with clinically significant sensitivity to trimetrexate, leucovorin or methotrexate.

Warnings: Trimetrexate must be used with concurrent leucovorin to avoid potentially serious or life-threatening complications including bone marrow suppression, oral and gastrointestinal mucosal ulceration, and renal and hepatic dysfunction. Leucovorin therapy must extend for 72 hours past the last dose of trimetrexate. Patients should be informed that failure to take the recommended dose and duration of leucovorin can lead to fatal toxicity. Patients should be closely monitored for the development of serious hematologic adverse reactions (see Precautions and Dosage).

Precautions: General: Patients receiving trimetrexate may experience severe hematologic, hepatic, renal and gastrointestinal toxicities. Caution should be used in treating patients with impaired hematologic, renal or hepatic function. Patients who require concomitant therapy with nephrotoxic, myelosuppressive, or hepatotoxic drugs should be treated with trimetrexate at the discretion of the physician and be monitored carefully. To allow for full therapeutic doses of trimetrexate, treatment with zidovudine should be discontinued during trimetrexate therapy.

Trimetrexate-associated myelosuppression, stomatitis and gastrointestinal toxicities can generally be ameliorated by adjusting the dose of leucovorin. Mild elevations in transaminases and alkaline phosphatase have been observed with trimetrexate administration and are usually not cause for modification of trimetrexate therapy (see Dosage). Seizures have been reported rarely (<1%) in AIDS patients receiving trimetrexate; however, a causal relationship has not been established. An anaphylactoid reaction has been reported in a cancer patient receiving trimetrexate as a bolus injection.

Trimetrexate has not been evaluated clinically for the treatment of concurrent pulmonary conditions such as bacterial, viral or fungal pneumonia or mycobacterial diseases. In vitro activity has been observed against T. gondii, M. avium complex, gram-positive cocci and gram-negative rods. If clinical deterioration is observed in patients, they should be carefully evaluated for other possible causes of pulmonary disease and treated with additional agents as appropriate.

Laboratory Tests: Patients receiving trimetrexate with leucovorin protection should be seen frequently by a physician. Blood tests to assess the following parameters should be performed at least twice a week during therapy: hematology (absolute neutrophil counts [ANC], platelets), renal function (serum creatinine, BUN), and hepatic function (ALT, AST, alkaline phosphatase).

Drug Interactions: Since trimetrexate is metabolized by a P450 enzyme system, drugs that induce or inhibit this drug metabolizing enzyme system may elicit important drug-drug interactions that may alter trimetrexate plasma concentrations. Agents that might be coadministered with trimetrexate in AIDS patients for other indications that could elicit this activity include erythromycin, rifampin, rifabutin, ketoconazole and fluconazole. In vitro perfusion of isolated rat liver has shown that cimetidine caused a significant reduction in trimetrexate metabolism and that acetaminophen altered the relative concentration of trimetrexate metabolites possibly by competing for sulfate metabolites. Based on an in vitro rat liver model, nitrogen substituted imidazole drugs (clotrimazole, ketoconazole, miconazole) were potent, non-competitive inhibitors of trimetrexate metabolism. Patients medicated with these drugs and trimetrexate should be carefully monitored.

Pregnancy: Trimetrexate can cause fetal harm when administered to a pregnant woman. Trimetrexate has been shown to be fetotoxic and teratogenic in rats and rabbits. If trimetrexate is used during pregnancy, or if the patient becomes pregnant while taking this drug, the patient should be apprised of the potential hazard to the fetus. Women of childbearing potential should be advised to avoid becoming pregnant.

Lactation: It is not known if trimetrexate is excreted in human milk. Because many drugs are excreted in human milk and because of the potential for serious adverse reactions in nursing infants from trimetrexate, it is recommended that breast-feeding be discontinued if the mother is treated with trimetrexate.

Children: The safety and effectiveness of trimetrexate for the treatment of histologically confirmed PCP has not been established for patients under 18 years of age. Under the Compassionate Use Protocol (maintained by U.S. Bioscience), 2 children, ages 15 months and 9 months, were treated with trimetrexate and leucovorin using a dose of 45 mg/m² of trimetrexate per day for 21 days and 20 mg/m² of leucovorin every 6 hours for 24 days. There were no serious or unexpected adverse effects.

Information for the Patient: **Patients should be informed that failure to take the recommended dose and duration of leucovorin can lead to fatal toxicity.**

Adverse Effects: Because many patients who participated in clinical trials of trimetrexate had complications of advanced HIV disease, it is difficult to distinguish adverse events caused by trimetrexate from those resulting from underlying medical conditions.

Table I lists the adverse events that occurred in ≥1% of the patients who participated in the Comparative Study of Neutrexin plus leucovorin versus TMP/SMX.

Laboratory toxicities were generally manageable with dose modification of trimetrexate/leucovorin (see Dosage).

Table II lists the adverse events resulting in discontinuation of study therapy in the Neutrexin Comparative Study with TMP/SMX. Twenty-nine percent of the patients on the TMP/SMX arm discontinued therapy due to adverse events compared to 10% of the patients treated with TMTX/LV ($p < 0.001$).

Hematologic toxicity was the principal dose-limiting side effect. An anaphylactoid reaction has been reported in a cancer patient receiving trimetrexate as a bolus injection.

Overdose: Symptoms and Treatment: Trimetrexate administered without concurrent leucovorin can cause lethal complications. There has been no extensive experience in humans receiving single i.v. doses of trimetrexate greater than 90 mg/m²/day with concurrent leucovorin. The toxicities seen at this dose were primarily hematologic. In the event of overdose, trimetrexate should be stopped and leucovorin should be administered at a dose of 40 mg/m² every 6 hours for 3 days.

Dosage: Caution: Trimetrexate must be administered with concurrent leucovorin (leucovorin protection) to avoid potentially serious or life-threatening toxicities. Leucovorin therapy must extend for 72 hours past the last dose of trimetrexate.

Trimetrexate is administered at a dose of 45 mg/m² once daily by i.v. infusion over 60 to 90 minutes. Leucovorin must be administered daily during treatment with trimetrexate and for 72 hours past the last dose of trimetrexate. Leucovorin may be administered i.v. at a dose of 20 mg/m² over 5 to 10 minutes every 6 hours for a total daily dose of 80 mg/m², or orally as 4 doses of 20 mg/m² spaced equally throughout the day. The oral dose should be rounded up to the next higher 25 mg increment. The recommended course of therapy is 21 days of trimetrexate and 24 days of leucovorin.

Dosage Modifications: Hematologic Toxicity: Trimetrexate and leucovorin doses should be modified based on the worst hematologic toxicity according to Table III (on following page). If leucovorin is given orally, doses should be rounded up to the next higher 25 mg increment.

Hepatic Toxicity: Transient elevations of transaminases and alkaline phosphatase have been observed in patients treated with trimetrexate. Interruption of treatment is advisable if transaminase levels or alkaline phosphatase levels increase to >5 times the upper limit of normal range.

Renal Toxicity: Interruption of trimetrexate is advisable if serum creatinine levels increase to >2.5 mg/dL and the elevation is considered to be secondary to trimetrexate.

Other Toxicities: Interruption of treatment is advisable in patients who experience severe mucosal toxicity which interferes with oral intake. Treatment should be discontinued for fever (oral temperature ≥40.5°C) that cannot be controlled with antipyretics.

Table I—Neutrexin

Neutrexin Comparative Trial Comparison of Adverse Events Reported for ≥1% of Patients

Adverse Events	Number and Percent (%) of Patients with Adverse Events TMTX/LV (n=109)		TMP/SMX (n=111)	
Non-Laboratory Adverse Events:				
Fever	9	(8.3)	14	(12.6)
Rash/Pruritus	6	(5.5)	14	(12.6)
Nausea/Vomiting	5	(4.6)[a]	15	(13.5)[a]
Confusion	3	(2.8)	3	(2.7)
Fatigue	2	(1.8)	0	(0.0)
Hematologic Toxicity:				
Neutropenia (≤1 000/mm³)	33	(30.3)	37	(33.3)
Thrombocytopenia (≤75 000/mm³)	11	(10.1)	17	(15.3)
Anemia (Hgb <8 g/dL)	8	(7.3)	10	(9.0)
Hepatotoxicity:				
Increased AST (>5×ULN[b])	15	(13.8)	10	(9.0)
Increased ALT (>5×ULN)	12	(11.0)	13	(11.7)
Increased Alkaline Phosphatase (>5×ULN)	5	(4.6)	3	(2.7)
Increased Bilirubin (2.5×ULN)	2	(1.8)	1	(0.9)
Renal:				
Increased Serum Creatinine (>3×ULN)	1	(0.9)	2	(1.8)
Electrolyte Imbalance:				
Hyponatremia	5	(4.6)	10	(9.0)
Hypocalcemia	2	(1.8)	0	(0.0)
No. of Patients with at Least One Adverse Event[c]	**58**	**(53.2)**	**60**	**(54.1)**

[a] Statistically significant difference between treatment groups (Chi-square: $p=0.022$).
[b] ULN=Upper limit of normal range.
[c] Patients could have reported more than one adverse event; therefore, the sum of adverse events exceeds the number of patients.

Table II—Neutrexin

Neutrexin Comparative Trial Adverse Events Resulting in Discontinuation of Therapy

Adverse Experiences	Number and Percent of Patients Discontinued for Adverse Events[b] TMTX/LV (n=109)		TMP/SMX (n=111)	
Non-Laboratory Adverse Events:				
Rash/Pruritus	3	(2.8)	5	(4.5)
Fever	2	(1.8)	4	(3.6)
Nausea/Vomiting	1	(0.9)	8	(7.2)
Neurologic Toxicity	1	(0.9)[c]	2	(1.8)
Hematologic Toxicity:				
Neutropenia (≤1 000/mm³)	4	(3.7)	6	(5.4)
Thrombocytopenia (≤75 000/mm³)	0	(0.0)	4	(3.6)
Anemia (Hgb <8 g/dL)	0	(0.0)	4	(3.6)
Hepatotoxicity:				
Increased AST (>5×ULN[a])	3	(2.8)	9	(8.1)
Increased ALT (>5×ULN)	1	(0.9)	4	(3.6)
Increased Alkaline Phosphatase (>5×ULN)	0	(0.0)	1	(0.9)
Electrolyte Imbalance:				
Hyponatremia	0	(0.0)	3	(2.7)
No. of Patients Discontinuing Therapy Due to an Adverse Event[b]	**11**	**(10.1)[d]**	**32**	**(28.8)[d]**

[a] ULN=Upper limit of normal range.
[b] Patients could discontinue therapy due to more than one toxicity; therefore, the sum exceeds number of patients who discontinued due to toxicity.
[c] Patient discontinued TMTX/LV due to seizure, though causal relationship could not be established.
[d] Statistically significant difference between treatment groups (Chi-square: $p < 0.001$).

Neutrexin (cont'd)

Table III—Neutrexin

Dose Modifications for Hematologic Toxicity

Toxicity Grade	Neutrophils (Polys and Bands)	Platelets	Recommended Dosages of Neutrexin	Recommended Dosages of Leucovorin
1	>1 000/mm³	>75 000/mm³	45 mg/m² once daily	20 mg/m² every 6 hours
2	750–1 000/mm³	50 000–75 000/mm³	45 mg/m² once daily	40 mg/m² every 6 hours
3	500–749/mm³	25 000–49 999/mm³	22 mg/m² once daily	40 mg/m² every 6 hours
4	<500/mm³	<25 000/mm³	Day 1–9 Discontinue; Day 10–21 Interrupt up to 96 hours*	40 mg/m² every 6 hours

* If Grade 4 hematologic toxicity occurs prior to Day 10, trimetrexate should be discontinued. Leucovorin (40 mg/m², q6h) should be administered for an additional 72 hours. If Grade 4 hematologic toxicity occurs at Day 10 or later, trimetrexate may be held up to 96 hours to allow counts to recover. If counts recover to Grade 3 within 96 hours, trimetrexate should be administered at a dose of 22 mg/m² and leucovorin maintained at 40 mg/m², q6h. When counts recover to Grade 2 toxicity, trimetrexate dose may be increased to 45 mg/m², but the leucovorin dose should be maintained at 40 mg/m² for the duration of treatment. If counts do not improve to ≤Grade 3 toxicity within 96 hours, trimetrexate should be discontinued. Leucovorin at a dose of 40 mg/m², q6h should be administered for 72 hours following the last dose of trimetrexate.

Leucovorin therapy must extend for 72 hours past the last dose of trimetrexate.

Administration: Reconstituted solution should be further diluted with 5% Dextrose Injection, USP to yield a final concentration of 0.25 to 2 mg of trimetrexate per mL. The diluted solution should be administered by i.v. infusion over 60 to 90 minutes. Neutrexin should not be mixed with solutions containing either chloride ion or leucovorin, since precipitation occurs instantly. It is stable under refrigeration or at room temperature for up to 24 hours. Do not freeze. Discard the unused portions after 24 hours after initial reconstitution. The i.v. line must be flushed thoroughly with 10 mL of 5% Dextrose Injection, USP before and after administering trimetrexate.

Leucovorin protection may be administered prior to or following trimetrexate. In either case the i.v. line must be flushed thoroughly with at least 10 mL of 5% Dextrose Injection USP. Leucovorin Calcium for injection is diluted with 5 mL of Sterile Water for Injection, USP and administered over 5 to 10 minutes every 6 hours.

Caution: Parenteral products should be inspected visually for particulate matter and discoloration prior to administration whenever solution and container permit. Neutrexin forms a precipitate instantly upon contact with chloride ion or leucovorin; therefore, it should not be added to solutions containing sodium chloride or other anions. Trimetrexate and leucovorin solutions must be administered separately. I.V. lines should be flushed with at least 10 mL of 5% Dextrose Injection, USP between trimetrexate and leucovorin infusions.

Special Instructions: If trimetrexate contacts the skin or mucosa, immediately wash thoroughly with soap and water. Procedures for proper disposal of cytotoxic drugs should be considered. Several guidelines on this subject have been published.

Reconstituted Solutions: See Table IV. Trimetrexate is supplied as a sterile lyophilized powder in 5 mL, single-dose vials. Each 5 mL vial contains trimetrexate glucuronate equivalent to 25 mg of trimetrexate. The vials should be reconstituted with **Sterile Water for Injection, USP or 5% Dextrose Injection, USP.** When reconstituted with 2 mL of Sterile Water for Injection, USP or 5% Dextrose Injection, USP, each mL contains 12.5 mg trimetrexate. Do not use if cloudiness or precipitation is observed. This solution should be filtered (0.22 μm) prior to further dilution. Reconstituted solutions should be further diluted with 5% Dextrose Injection, USP to yield a final concentration of 0.25 to 2 mg of trimetrexate per mL. The diluted solution should be administered by i.v. infusion over 60 to 90 minutes.

Stability and Storage Recommendations: Trimetrexate vials as lyophilized powder should be stored at controlled room temperature (15 to 30°C). Protect from exposure to light. When reconstituted with Sterile Water for Injection, USP or 5% Dextrose Injection, USP, the solution is stable for 24 hours at room temperature or under refrigeration. The further diluted solution of trimetrexate in 5% Dextrose Injection, USP should be used within 24 hours.

Supplied: Each 5 mL single-dose vial of sterile, lyophilized powder contains: trimetrexate glucuronate equivalent to trimetrexate 25 mg. Nonmedicinal Ingredients: D-glucuronic acid, nitrogen (NF) and water for injection, USP. Chipboard cartons of 10 (10 Pack).

Table IV—Neutrexin

Reconstitution Table

Vial Size	Volume of Sterile Water for Injection, USP or 5% Dextrose Injection, USP To Be Added to Vial	Approximate Available Volume	Nominal Concentration per mL
5 mL	2 mL	1.9–2.0 mL	12.5 mg

NIACIN
NIACINAMIDE
General Monograph, CPhA

Nicotinic Acid, Vitamin B₃
Nicotinamide

Vitamin

This monograph has been compiled by CPhA. It may contain information different from that approved by Therapeutic Products Programme, Health Canada, and the pharmaceutical manufacturers' approval has not been requested.

Pharmacology: Niacin and niacinamide are water-soluble B complex vitamins. In vivo, niacin is converted to niacinamide, a constituent of nicotinamide adenine dinucleotide (NAD) and nicotinamide adenine dinucleotide phosphate (NADP), which are coenzymes involved in glycogenolysis, tissue respiration and lipid metabolism. Niacin deficiency results in pellagra, a chronic wasting disease characterized by dermatitis, dementia and diarrhea.

Niacin produces peripheral vasodilation, a process believed to be mediated by prostacyclin, which affects the cutaneous vessels of the upper body. Tolerance to this effect usually develops after about 2 weeks of treatment.

Niacin has been reported to stimulate histamine release resulting in increased gastric motility and acid production which may activate peptic ulcer. Reports have also indicated that large doses of niacin may decrease uric acid excretion and impair glucose tolerance. These effects may result in precipitation of an episode of gout in susceptible patients and may necessitate adjustment of diet and antihyperglycemic therapy in diabetic patients.

Niacin decreases the rate of hepatic synthesis of very low-density lipoprotein (VLDL) and low-density lipoprotein (LDL) while raising high-density lipoprotein in serum, both in normal individuals and patients with type II, III, IV or V hyperlipoproteinemia. This has led to a lowering of serum cholesterol by 10 to 15% and triglycerides by 20 to 30%. Niacinamide is not effective in lowering serum cholesterol.

Pharmacokinetics: Niacin and niacinamide are readily absorbed from the gastrointestinal tract. Following oral administration, niacin-induced vasodilation occurs within 20 minutes and persists for about 20 to 60 minutes. These effects are manifested by symptoms of flushing, itching and tingling sensations, and are accompanied by an increase in skin temperature.

Niacin is metabolized in the liver to niacinamide when taken in physiologic doses. When therapeutic doses are taken, only a portion is converted to niacinamide. The remainder is eventually excreted unchanged in the urine. Niacinamide is widely distributed in the body and is further metabolized in the liver before being excreted in the urine.

Dietary tryptophan is converted to niacin at a rate of 1 mg niacin for every 60 mg tryptophan.

Indications: Niacin and niacinamide are used in the prophylaxis and treatment of pellagra. Niacin is used as adjunctive therapy in addition to diet and other measures to lower elevated serum cholesterol and triglycerides in patients with type II, III, IV or V hyperlipoproteinemia. Niacinamide is not effective for the reduction of serum cholesterol levels.

Contraindications: Hypersensitivity to niacin or niacinamide. At larger doses used to treat pellagra and lower cholesterol, niacin is contraindicated in individuals with hepatic dysfunction, active peptic ulcer, diabetes mellitus, severe hypotension, hyperuricemia with a history of gouty arthritis.

Precautions: Patients with gallbladder disease or history of jaundice, liver disease or peptic ulcer should be monitored closely while taking niacin. Liver function tests should be conducted frequently in the initial stages of therapy and periodically thereafter.

Niacin and niacinamide may cause hyperglycemia. Periodic blood glucose monitoring is advised, especially in the early phase of therapy.

Elevated uric acid levels have occurred; therefore, niacin must be used with caution in patients predisposed to gout (see Contraindications).

Niacin may cause false elevation in fluorometric determinations of urinary catecholamines and false-positive results may be obtained for urinary glucose when Benedict's reagent is used. Niacin has also been reported to give false-positive results for blood bilirubin tests.

Drug Interactions: Due to an additive vasodilating effect, postural hypotension may occur when niacin is added to the therapeutic regimen of patients taking adrenergic blocking agents.

Niacin appears to increase the risk of myopathy when used in antihyperlipidemic doses concurrently with fluvastatin, lovastatin, pravastatin or simvastatin. Patients should be advised to report any pain, tenderness or muscle weakness to their physician.

Because niacin can cause hyperglycemia, dosage adjustment of insulin or oral antihyperglycemic therapy may be required in diabetic patients.

Pregnancy: Safety has not been established. Although fetal abnormalities have not been reported with niacin, its use in lowering elevated serum cholesterol requires high dosages, and animal reproduction or teratology studies have not been done.

Lactation: Niacin is distributed into breast milk. Problems have not been reported with intake of normal daily requirements, but there is no information pertaining to higher doses used in the treatment of hyperlipidemia.

Children: Studies on use in children are insufficient.

Adverse Effects: The more common adverse effects of niacin therapy are dose related and generally seen with high doses used to treat hyperlipidemia. Severe generalized flushing (due to peripheral cutaneous vasodilation) that may be accompanied by burning, stinging or tingling sensations, gastrointestinal symptoms (nausea, vomiting, bloating, flatulence, heartburn, diarrhea), pruritus and hypotension. The severity of these effects can be decreased by starting therapy at lower doses and gradually tapering upward. Flushing usually subsides over several weeks, despite continuation of niacin therapy.

Long term use of large doses of niacin has also been associated with rash, hyperpigmentation, dry skin, xerostomia, hyperuricemia which may precipitate gout, activation of peptic ulcer, blurred vision, hyperglycemia and abnormal liver function test results.

Niacinamide lacks vasodilating effects but is not effective in the lowering of serum cholesterol levels. Parenteral solutions of B complex vitamins containing niacinamide may cause flushing, itching or burning of the skin in patients susceptible to the effects of niacinamide. Niacinamide has also caused hyperhidrosis, nausea and abdominal cramps.

Dosage: To prevent deficiency, adequate dietary intake is preferred over supplementation whenever possible. For information on dietary sources of niacin see Vitamin Food Sources in the Clin-Info section. For a listing of recommended daily intake of niacin for different patient groups, see Recommended Nutrient Intake in the Clin-Info section. Dosage of niacin and niacinamide must be carefully adjusted according to the patient's response and tolerance. In the treatment and prophylaxis of pellagra, niacin and niacinamide can be administered in equivalent doses.

Treatment of Pellagra: Adults: 300 to 500 mg daily in divided doses.

Children: 100 to 300 mg daily in divided doses.

Antihyperlipidemic (niacin only): Efforts should initially be made to lower serum cholesterol through dietary and weight control measures. Many clinicians recommend 1.5 to 6 g daily, given in 2 to 4 divided doses. Some patients may require up to 9 g daily to achieve the desired reductions in serum cholesterol and triglyceride concentrations. Some clinicians recommend beginning with 100 mg orally 3 times daily with meals, increasing the daily dose by 300 mg at 4 to 7-day intervals as necessary.

Usual antihyperlipidemic maintenance dose: 1 to 2 g 3 times daily (maximum 6 g/day). To minimize flushing, administration of 325 mg ASA 1 hour prior to niacin has been recommended.

Serum cholesterol and triglyceride concentrations should be determined prior to initiation of therapy and regularly (every 3 to 6 months) during treatment.

Reviewed 1998

NIACIN SUSTAINED RELEASE
Stanley

Nicotinic Acid

Vitamin

Pharmacology: Nicotinic acid, when released, is readily absorbed from the gastrointestinal tract following oral administration and widely distributed in the body fluids and tissues, even in the breast milk. The main route of metabolism in the liver is conversion first to nicotinamide then to N-methyl nicotinamide, the 2-pyridone and 4-pyridone derivatives and nicotinuric acid formed which are excreted in the urine. Small amounts of nicotinic acid and nicotinamide are excreted unchanged in the urine following therapeutic doses; however, the amount excreted unchanged is increased with larger doses.

Both nicotinic acid and nicotinamide have vitamin activity but only nicotinic acid induces vasodilation resulting in flushing, a sensatiokn of heat, faintness and a pounding of the head. This vasodilation occurs within 20 minutes of oral administration and persists for about 20 to 60 minutes. Tolerance usually develops after 2 weeks of treatment. Sustained release niacin tablets induce less vasodilation than unmodified-release forms.

Nicotinic acid is converted to nicotinamide which is a constituent of nicotinamide adenine dinucleotide (NAD) and nicotinamide adenine dinucleotide phosphate (NADP) which are co-enzymes involved in glycogenolysis, lipid metabolism and tissue respiration for electron transfer reactions. Deficiency results in pellagra, characterized by skin lesions, gastrointestinal, neurological and mental distrubances. Hence use as prophylactic and therapeutic vitamin.

Nicotinic acid also lowers both total serum cholesterol and triglyceride concentrations probably by reducing the synthesis of very low-density lipoprotein (VLDL) and low-density lipoprotein (LDL). It also elevates the high-density lipoprotein cholesterol (HDL). This effect on the plasma lipids occurs at daily dosages exceeding 1 g.

Niacin may also increase gastric motility and acid secretion via the release of histamine, therein may aggravate or initiate peptic ulcer. High dosages of niacin may decrease uric acid excretion or impair glucose tolerance thereby precipitating a bout of gout or hypoglycemia. Postural hypotension may occur in patients already hypotensive due to the additional vasodilative effect.

Indications: For the prophylaxis and treatment of vitamin B_3 deficiency states such as pellagra; and supplementation due to increased requirements in conditions such as diabetes mellitus; malignancy; inborn errors of metabolism (Hartup disease); malabsorption syndromes associated with pancreatic incufficiency; diseases of the small intestines (e.g. celiac and tropical sprue); hyperthyroidism and others.

Niacin has also been used in the treatment of primary hyperlipidemia (Type IIa & b, III, IV or V hyperlipoproteinemia) as a drug of first choice for initiating therapy to redule LDL-cholesterol concentrations and triglycerides and to increase HDL-cholesterol concentrations. Slow release niacin has particularly been used where it was desirable to minimize flushing and associated symptoms which occur at initiation of therapy; but therapy must be carefully monitored by a physician particularly for liver enzymes.

Contraindications: Contraindication is not absolute but careful risk-benefit consideration must be given when treating patients with a history of gout, diabetes mellitus, peptic ulcer, liver dysfunction, sever hypotension or arterial bleeding or hemorrhage. Not recommended for persons hypersensitive to niacin and children below the age of 12.

Precautions: *Pregnancy, Lactation,* Children and Geriatrics: Problems during pregnancy and breastfeeding, when treating pediatrics and geriatrics have not been well documented; therefore, appropriate monitoring should be observed particularly during initiation of therapy.

Isoniazid may cause deficiency by inhibiting niacin incorporation into nicotinamide adenine dinucleotide (NAD). Also chenodiol's effect may be reduced because of the resulting increase in cholesterol in the bile.

Urinary catecholamine concentration measurements by fluorimetric methods may be falsely elevated by niacin, while a positive urine glucose determination using Benedict's reagent (cupric sulfate) may be falsely produced by niacin.

All subjects should be monitored for liver function during niacin therapy.

Adverse Effects: Water soluble vitamins seldom cause toxicity in persons with normal renal function. However, flushing or redness of the skin, especially on face and neck; feeling of warmth, headache or an allergic reaction may occur but usually subside in 2 weeks.

At higher doses, diarrhea, dizziness or faintness, dryness of skin or eyes; nausea or vomiting; aggravation of peptic ulcer causing stomach pain; pruritus; hyperglycemia; hyperuricemia; cardiac arrhythmias and hepatotoxicity are more likely to occur.

Dosage: Vitamin: Use up to 500 mg a day taken with milk or meals. Swallow whole without crushing or chewing but tablet may be broken in half if a smaller dose is desired.

Antihyperlipidemic: 1 g 2 or 3 times a day, the dosage being increased in increments of 500 mg a day every 2 to 4 weeks as needed and tolerated. Maintenance dosages range from 1 to 2 g 2 or 3 times a day to a maximum of 6 g a day. Tablets may be broken but not crushed or chewed before swallowing. Flushing may be reduced by taking a 325 mg ASA tablet, 1 hour prior to the niacin tablet.

Supplied: Each elongated, oval, sustained release tablet contains: nicotinic acid (niacin) 500 mg. Nonmedicinal ingredients: carnauba wax, glyceryl behenate and magnesium stearate. Bottles of 100.

NICODERM®
Hoechst Marion Roussel

Nicotine

Smoking Cessation Aid

Pharmacology: Nicoderm is a multilayered rectangular film containing nicotine as the active ingredient. It provides 24 hour rate-controlled delivery of nicotine following its application to intact skin. Nicoderm reduces the withdrawal symptoms associated with smoking cessation and thus increases the success rate of smoking cessation programs.

Indications: As an aid to smoking cessation for partial relief of nicotine withdrawal symptoms. This treatment should be used as part of a comprehensive behavioral smoking-cessation program.

Contraindications: Patients with hypersensitivity or allergy to nicotine or the components of the transdermal system. Patients with acute hypersensitivity reactions should discontinue use of Nicoderm and should be advised of the possibility of acute hypersensitivity reactions to other forms of nicotine, including cigarettes.

Nonsmokers or occasional smokers.

In children under 18 years of age (see Precautions).

In patients during the immediate post-myocardial infarction period, in patients with life-threatening arrhythmias, in patients with severe or worsening angina pectoris, in patients who have had a recent cerebral vascular accident (see Warnings), in pregnant women (see Precautions: Pregnancy), in nursing mothers, and in patients with generalized skin disorders.

Warnings: Nicotine from any source can be toxic and addictive. The amounts of nicotine that are tolerated by adult smokers can produce symptoms of poisoning and could prove fatal if the Nicoderm system is applied or ingested by children or pets. Used Nicoderm systems contain approximately 70% of their initial drug content. Therefore, patients should be cautioned to keep both the used and unused Nicoderm systems out of the reach of children and pets.

Cardiovascular or Peripheral Vascular Disease: The risks of nicotine replacement in patients with certain cardiovascular and peripheral vascular diseases should be weighed against the benefits of including nicotine replacement in a smoking-cessation program for them. Specifically, patients with coronary heart disease (history of myocardial infarction and/or angina pectoris), serious cardiac arrhythmias, or vasospastic diseases (Buerger's disease, Prinzmetal's variant angina) should be carefully screened and evaluated before nicotine replacement is prescribed.

Tachycardia occurring in association with the use of Nicoderm therapy has been reported occasionally. If serious cardiovascular symptoms occur with the use of Nicoderm therapy, it should be discontinued.

Precautions: General: The patient should be urged to stop smoking completely when initiating Nicoderm therapy (see Dosage). Patients should be informed that if they continue to smoke while using Nicoderm systems, they may experience adverse effects due to peak nicotine levels higher than those experienced from smoking alone. If there is a clinically significant increase in cardiovascular or other effects attributable to nicotine, the Nicoderm dose should be reduced or Nicoderm treatment discontinued (see Warnings). The use of Nicoderm systems beyond 3 months by patients who stop smoking should be discouraged. If the patient continues to smoke, treatment should be discontinued after 4 weeks.

Pregnancy: Women of childbearing age should be advised to take adequate precautions to avoid becoming pregnant while using Nicoderm. Nicoderm therapy should be discontinued if pregnancy is suspected (see Contraindications).

Drug Interactions: Physicians should anticipate that the pharmacokinetics of certain concomitant medications may be altered by smoking cessation with or without nicotine replacement. Therefore the dosage of certain concomitant medications may require adjustment (see Table I).

Table I—Nicoderm

Dose Adjustment of Concomitant Medications

May require a decrease in dose at cessation of smoking	**Possible Mechanism**
Acetaminophen, caffeine, imipramine, oxazepam, pentazocine, propranolol, theophylline	Deinduction of hepatic enzymes on smoking cessation
Insulin	Increase in s.c. insulin absorption with smoking cessation
Adrenergic antagonists (e.g. prazosin, labetalol)	Decrease in circulating catecholamines with smoking cessation
May require an increase in dose at cessation of smoking	**Possible Mechanism**
Adrenergic agonists (e.g. isoproterenol, phenylephrine)	Decrease in circulating catecholamines with smoking cessation

Allergic Reactions: Patients should be instructed to promptly discontinue the use of Nicoderm systems and contact their physicians if they experience severe or persistent local skin reactions (e.g., severe erythema, pruritus, or edema) at the site of application or a generalized skin reaction (e.g., urticaria, hives, or generalized rash). Patients using Nicoderm therapy concurrently with other transdermal systems may exhibit local reactions at both application sites. In such patients use of one or both systems may have to be discontinued.

Skin Disease: Nicoderm systems are usually well tolerated by patients with normal skin, but may be irritating for patients with some skin disorders (atopic or eczematous dermatitis).

Renal or Hepatic Insufficiency: The pharmacokinetics of nicotine have not been studied in the elderly or in patients with renal or hepatic impairment; however, given that nicotine is

Nicoderm (cont'd)

extensively metabolized and that its total system clearance is dependent on liver blood flow, some influence of hepatic impairment on drug kinetics (reduced clearance) should be anticipated. Only severe renal impairment would be expected to affect the clearance of nicotine or its metabolites from the circulation.

Endocrine Diseases: Nicoderm therapy should be used with caution in patients with hyperthyroidism, pheochromocytoma, or insulin-dependent diabetes since nicotine causes the release of catecholamines by the adrenal medulla.

Peptic Ulcer Disease: Nicotine delays healing in peptic ulcer disease; therefore, Nicoderm therapy should be used with caution in patients with active peptic ulcers and only when the benefits of including nicotine replacement in a smoking-cessation program outweigh the risks.

Accelerated Hypertension: Nicotine therapy constitutes a risk factor for development of malignant hypertension in patients with accelerated hypertension; therefore, Nicoderm therapy should be used with caution in these patients and only when the benefits of including nicotine replacement in a smoking-cessation program outweigh the risks.

Children and Geriatrics: Nicoderm therapy is not recommended for use in children under 18 years of age, because its safety and effectiveness in children and adolescents who smoke has not been evaluated. In clinical trials Nicoderm therapy appeared to be as effective in the over 60 age group as in younger adult smokers. However, asthenia, various body aches and dizziness occurred slightly more often in patients over 60 years of age.

Drug Dependency: Nicoderm therapy is likely to have a low abuse potential based on differences between it and cigarettes in 4 characteristics commonly considered important in contributing to abuse: much slower absorption, much smaller fluctuations in blood levels, lower blood levels of nicotine, and less frequent use (i.e., once daily).

Dependence on nicotine polacrilex chewing gum replacement therapy has been reported. Such dependence might also occur from transference to Nicoderm systems of tobacco-based nicotine dependence. The use of the system beyond 3 months has not been evaluated and should be discouraged. To minimize the risk of dependence, patients should be encouraged to withdraw gradually from Nicoderm treatment after 4 to 8 weeks of use. Recommended dose reduction is to progressively decrease the dose every 2 to 4 weeks (see Dosage).

Strenuous Exercise: Preliminary evidence suggests that wearing a nicotine transdermal patch during periods of strenuous exercise may lead to nicotine toxicity as a result of increased absorption of nicotine from the depot of nicotine in the skin under the patch, due to increased skin temperature and increased cutaneous vasodilation and perfusion from exercising. Three cases illustrating this phenomenon were described in Health Canada Adverse Reaction Newsletter, Volume 6, Number 1, January, 1996. Advise to remove the nicotine patch before engaging in strenuous exercise was recommended by W. Dafoe and P. Huston. Until definitive studies have been undertaken to clarify this hazard, it is advisable to remove the nicotine patch prior to engaging in prolonged strenuous activity.

Adverse Effects: Assessment of adverse events in patients who participated in controlled clinical trials is complicated by the occurrence of gastrointestinal and CNS effects of nicotine withdrawal as well as nicotine excess. The actual incidence of both are confounded by concurrent smoking by many of the patients. When reporting adverse events in the clinical trials, the clinical investigators did not attempt to identify the cause of the symptom.

The most common adverse event associated with Nicoderm is a short-lived erythema, pruritus and/or burning at the application site, which was seen at least once in 47% of patients on the Nicoderm system in the clinical trials. Local erythema after system removal was noted at least once in 14% of patients and local edema in 3%. Erythema generally resolved within 24 hours. Cutaneous hypersensitivity (contact sensitization) occurred in 2% of patients on Nicoderm systems (see Precautions).

Table II presents the number of patients reporting adverse events at a frequency greater than 1% in placebo-controlled clinical trials.

Table II—Nicoderm

Number (%) of Patients Reporting Adverse Events (Patient-Treatment N=1 080*) (Patient N=1 061)

Adverse Event	Nicoderm (n=744)	Placebo (n=336)
Body as a Whole		
headache	118 (15.9%)	52 (15.5%)
asthenia	38 (5.1%)	15 (4.5%)
flu syndrome	26 (3.5%)	10 (3.0%)
pain	21 (2.8%)	6 (1.8%)
abdominal pain	13 (1.7%)	4 (1.2%)
Cardiovascular		
palpitations	11 (1.5%)	3 (0.9%)
tachycardia	9 (1.2%)	1 (0.3%)
Digestive		
dyspepsia	43 (5.8%)	10 (3.0%)
nausea	40 (5.4%)	18 (5.4%)
diarrhea	17 (2.3%)	9 (2.7%)
constipation	16 (2.2%)	5 (1.5%)
dry mouth	13 (1.7%)	2 (0.6%)
nausea and vomiting	10 (1.3%)	3 (0.9%)
flatulence	10 (1.3%)	4 (1.2%)
stomatitis	8 (1.1%)	5 (1.5%)
Musculoskeletal		
myalgia	26 (3.5%)	3 (0.9%)
Nervous System		
insomnia	117 (15.7%)	38 (11.3%)
dizziness	53 (7.1%)	25 (7.4%)
abnormal dreams	47 (6.3%)	4 (1.2%)
nervousness	23 (3.1%)	8 (2.4%)
depression	23 (3.1%)	15 (4.5%)
hypertonia	11 (1.5%)	3 (0.9%)
somnolence	11 (1.5%)	13 (3.9%)
paresthesia	10 (1.3%)	4 (1.2%)
Respiratory		
cough increased	21 (2.8%)	4 (1.2%)
pharyngitis	19 (2.6%)	4 (1.2%)
rhinitis	10 (1.3%)	3 (0.9%)
dyspnea	8 (1.1%)	7 (2.1%)
Skin and Appendages		
rash	15 (2.0%)	5 (1.5%)
sweating	12 (1.6%)	3 (0.9%)
Special Senses		
taste perversion	23 (3.1%)	10 (3.0%)

*19 patients were in more than one Nicoderm treatment group.

Overdose: Symptoms and Treatment: Treatment of overdosage generally involves symptomatic and supportive care; there is no specific antidote for nicotine intoxication. Signs and symptoms of an overdose from a Nicoderm system are generally the same as those of acute nicotine poisoning, including pallor, cold sweat, nausea, salivation, vomiting, abdominal pain, diarrhea, headache, dizziness, disturbed hearing and vision, tremor, mental confusion and weakness. Prostration, hypotension and respiratory failure may ensue with large overdoses. Lethal doses of nicotine produce convulsions quickly and death follows as a result of peripheral or central respiratory paralysis or, less frequently, cardiac failure. The oral minimum single acute lethal dose for nicotine in human adults is reported to be 40 to 60 mg (<1 mg/kg). Much lower doses have been reported to be toxic in children.

The Nicoderm system should be removed immediately if the patient shows signs of overdosage, and the patient should seek immediate medical care, by contacting a physician or local poison control centre. The skin surface should be flushed with water and dried. Soap must not be used since it may increase nicotine absorption. Nicotine will continue to be delivered into the bloodstream for several hours after removal of the system because of a depot of nicotine in the skin.

Persons ingesting Nicoderm systems should be referred to a health care facility for management. Due to the possibility of nicotine-induced seizures, activated charcoal should be administered. In unconscious patients with a secure airway, instill activated charcoal via a nasogastric tube. Repeated doses of activated charcoal should be administered as long as the system remains in the gastrointestinal tract since it will continue to release nicotine for many hours. A saline cathartic or sorbitol added to the first dose of activated charcoal may speed gastrointestinal passage of the system.

Other supportive measures include diazepam or barbiturates for seizures, atropine for excessive bronchial secretions or diarrhea, respiratory support for respiratory failure, and vigorous fluid support for hypotension and cardiovascular collapse.

Dosage: Patients must desire to stop smoking and should be instructed to stop smoking immediately as they begin using Nicoderm therapy. The patient should read the patient instruction sheet on Nicoderm therapy and be encouraged to ask questions.

Therapy should begin with the Nicoderm 21 mg/day system and continue for 6 weeks. The patient should stop smoking cigarettes completely during this period. If the patient is unable to stop smoking within 4 weeks, Nicoderm therapy should be stopped, since few additional patients in clinical trials were able to quit after this time. Patients who have successfully abstained from smoking should have their dose of Nicoderm reduced after 6 weeks of treatment. Treatment with Nicoderm 14 mg/day should then be initiated for 2 weeks followed by 2 weeks on Nicoderm 7 mg/day. For patients who have cardiovascular disease, who weigh less than 45 kg or who smoke less than ½ pack of cigarettes a day, treatment should be started with Nicoderm 14 mg/day for 6 weeks. The dose should then be decreased to Nicoderm 7 mg/day for the final 2 to 4 weeks of treatment.

In all patients the need for dosage adjustment should be assessed during the first 2 weeks of therapy. The entire course of nicotine replacement and gradual withdrawal should take 8 to 12 weeks, depending on the size of the initial dose.

As the use of Nicoderm beyond 3 months has not been studied, this duration of treatment should not be exceeded.

The Nicoderm system should be applied promptly upon its removal from the protective pouch to prevent evaporative loss of nicotine from the system. Nicoderm systems should be used only when the pouch is intact to assure that the product has not been tampered with.

Nicoderm systems should be applied only once a day to a non-hairy, clean, dry skin site on the upper body or outer upper arm. After 24 hours, the used Nicoderm system should be removed and a new system applied to an alternate skin site. Skin sites should not be reused for at least a week. Patients should be cautioned not to continue to use the same system for more than 24 hours.

Safety and Handling: The Nicoderm system can be a dermal irritant and can cause contact sensitization. Patients should be instructed in the proper use of Nicoderm systems by using demonstration systems. Although exposure of health care workers to nicotine from Nicoderm systems should be minimal, care should be taken to avoid unnecessary contact with active systems. When handling active systems, wash with water alone, since soap may increase nicotine absorption. Do not touch the eyes.

Disposal: **When the used system is removed from the skin, it should be folded over and placed in the protective pouch that contained the new system. The used system should be immediately disposed of in such a way as to prevent its access by children or pets. See Information for the Patient for further directions on handling and disposal.**

Information for the Patient: See Blue Section—Information for the Patient "Nicoderm".

Supplied: Each Nicoderm (nicotine transdermal system) contains nicotine base in an ethylene-vinyl acetate copolymer matrix. Proceeding from the visible surface toward the surface attached to the skin are (1) an occlusive backing (polyethylene/aluminum/polyester/ethylene-vinyl acetate copolymer); (2) a drug reservoir containing nicotine (in an ethylene-vinyl acetate copolymer matrix); (3) a rate-controlling membrane (polyethylene); (4) a polyisobutylene adhesive; and (5) a protective liner that covers the adhesive layer and which must be removed before application to the skin.

Nicoderm 21 mg/day: Each rectangular 22 cm² system contains: nicotine 114 mg and provides 24 hour rate-controlled delivery of 21 mg/day to the patient. Boxes of 7 and 14 with user's guide.

Nicoderm 14 mg/day: Each rectangular 15 cm² system contains: nicotine 78 mg and provides 24 hour rate-controlled delivery of 14 mg/day to the patient. Boxes of 7 with user's guide.

Nicoderm 7 mg/day: Each rectangular 7 cm² system contains: nicotine 36 mg and provides 24 hour rate-controlled delivery of 7 mg/day to the patient. Boxes of 7 with user's guide.

Store at room temperature, between 15 and 30°C. Apply immediately upon removal from pouch, and do not store after the pouch has been opened.

Reviewed 1999

NICORETTE®

Hoechst Marion Roussel

Nicotine Polacrilex

Smoking Cessation Aid

Pharmacology: The active component of Nicorette is nicotine in the form of a natural extract from the tobacco plant.

In small doses, nicotine stimulates autonomic ganglia. Larger doses of the drug result in a blockage of the ganglia. The effects on autonomic ganglia vary according to the degree of tolerance to nicotine. The major cardiovascular effects of nicotine are vasoconstriction, tachycardia and elevated blood pressure resulting from stimulation of sympathetic ganglia and the adrenal medulla as well as from the activation of chemoreceptors of aortic and carotid bodies.

The pharmacokinetics of nicotine favor buccal (rather than gastrointestinal) absorption. Absorption from the mouth is more rapid than from the stomach and the absorbed nicotine avoids immediate and rapid inactivation by the liver (first pass effect).

Nicorette is formulated to provide blood nicotine levels via buccal absorption that will approximate those produced by the inhalation of tobacco smoke. The nicotine in Nicorette is bound to an ion exchange resin and is released only during chewing. The rate of release of nicotine and, as a consequence, nicotine blood levels, are related to the rate and vigor with which Nicorette is chewed. The chewing of a Nicorette piece over a 30-minute period on a one-time-only basis produces peak blood nicotine levels of 5 ng/mL. This peak is reached by about the 25th minute and compares with a peak of 16 to 35 ng/mL reached within 5 minutes from smoking a cigarette of mild to moderate nicotine content. Blood nicotine levels increase and stabilize at 25 ng/mL, following repeated administration at half-hourly intervals. Thus, with Nicorette, it is possible to produce nicotine blood levels of the same order as those produced by smoking cigarettes.

The elimination half-life of nicotine in plasma is 120 minutes. Both nicotine and its metabolites are rapidly eliminated by the kidney. The rate of urinary excretion is dependent on the pH of the urine; excretion diminishes when the urine is alkaline.

Indications: Nicorette is designed to provide partial substitution for the nicotine in cigarette smoke and is intended as a temporary aid in cushioning the patient against the psychopharmacological effects of the withdrawal symptoms of smoking cessation.

Before initiating treatment with Nicorette 2 mg, the physician or pharmacist should determine the patient's level of nicotine dependence using the Fagerström Nicotine Tolerance Scale shown in Table I.

Instructions for Use of the Fagerström Scale: Assign the appropriate score indicated in each column according to the patient's answer to the questions (note that not all questions have an answer in Column C). The highest possible score is 11.

If the score is 6 or less, Nicorette 2 mg is recommended for use. If the score is 7 or greater, Nicorette Plus (4 mg) should be used.

Contraindications: In patients during the immediate postmyocardial infarction period, patients with life-threatening arrhythmias, and in patients with severe or worsening angina pectoris; in patients with active temporomandibular joint disease; in pregnant women; in breast-feeding mothers, as nicotine is excreted in breast milk, and in nonsmokers and children under 18 years of age (see Warnings).

Warnings: The amounts of nicotine that are tolerated by adult smokers can produce symptoms of poisoning and could prove fatal if ingested by children or pets. Patients should be warned to keep Nicorette out of the reach of children and pets.

Simultaneous smoking and chewing of Nicorette should be avoided.

In patients with certain cardiovascular and endocrine diseases, the risks of using nicotine should be carefully weighed against the benefits of including Nicorette in a smoking cessation program. Patients with coronary heart disease (history of myocardial infarction and/or angina pectoris), serious cardiac arrhythmias, or vasospastic diseases (Buerger's disease, Prinzmetal's variant angina) should be carefully screened and evaluated before Nicorette is used. Occasional reports of tachyarrhythmias occurring in association with the use of Nicorette have been reported; therefore, if an increase in cardiovascular symptoms occurs with the use of Nicorette it should be discontinued.

As the action of nicotine on the adrenal medulla (release of catecholamines) does not appear to be affected by tolerance,

Table I—Nicorette

The Fagerström Tolerance Scale

	A=0 points	B=1 point	C=2 points	Score
How soon after you wake do you smoke your first cigarette?	After 30 minutes	Within 30 minutes		
How many cigarettes a day do you smoke?	1–15	16–25	more than 26	
Does the brand you smoke have a low, medium or high nicotine content?	Low, less than 0.4 mg	Medium, between 0.5 and 0.8 mg	High, greater than 0.9 mg	
Which of all the cigarettes you smoke a day is the most satisfying one?	Any other than the first one in the morning	The first one in the morning		
Do you smoke more during the morning than during the rest of the day?	No	Yes		
Do you smoke when you are so ill that you are in bed most of the day?	No	Yes		
Do you find it difficult to refrain from smoking in places where it is forbidden, such as the library, theatre, doctor's office?	No	Yes		
How often do you inhale smoke from your cigarette?	Never	Sometimes	Always	
			Score	

Nicorette should be used with caution in patients with hyperthyroidism, pheochromocytoma or insulin-dependent diabetes.

Cigarette smoking is felt to play a perpetuating role in hypertension and peptic ulcer disease. Therefore, Nicorette should be used in patients with systemic hypertension or peptic ulcer (active or inactive) only when the benefits of including Nicorette in a smoking cessation program outweigh the risks.

Pregnancy: Women of childbearing age should be advised to take adequate precautions to avoid becoming pregnant while using Nicorette. Nicorette therapy should be discontinued if pregnancy is suspected (see Contraindications).

Lactation: Nicotine passes freely into the breast milk. Because of the potential for adverse reactions in nursing infants from nicotine, a decision should be made whether to discontinue nursing or to discontinue the drug, taking into account the importance of the drug to the mother (see Contraindications).

Children: Safety and effectiveness in children and adolescents who smoke has not been evaluated. The use of Nicorette is not recommended in smokers under 18 years of age (see Contraindications).

Precautions: General: Nicorette should be used with caution in patients with oral or pharyngeal inflammation and in patients with a history of esophagitis or peptic ulcer.

The Nicorette dosage form dictates that it be used with caution in patients whose dental problems might be exacerbated by chewing gum. In such patients, prior dental evaluation may be advisable.

Nicorette is sugar-free and has been formulated to minimize stickiness. As with other gums, however, the degree to which Nicorette may stick to dentures, dental caps or partial dentures may depend on the materials from which they are made and other factors such as amount of saliva produced, possible interaction with denture adhesives, denture cleaning compounds, dryness of mouth due to other causes and salivary constituents. Should an excessive degree of adherence to dental work occur, there is the possibility that, as with other gums, Nicorette may damage dental work. If this should occur, the patient should discontinue its use and consult a physician or dentist.

The sustained use of Nicorette by former smokers is not to be encouraged because the chronic consumption of nicotine is addicting. The relative risks of a possible return to smoking should be weighed against the long-term use of Nicorette.

Nicotine was not mutagenic in the Ames Salmonella test. Literature reports indicate that nicotine is neither an initiator nor a tumor-promoter in mice. There is inconclusive evidence to suggest that cotinine, an oxidized metabolite of nicotine, may be carcinogenic in rats. Cotinine was not mutagenic in the Ames Salmonella test.

Studies have shown a decrease of litter size in rats treated with nicotine during the time of fertilization.

Drug Interactions: Physicians should anticipate that the pharmacokinetics of certain concomitant medications may be altered by smoking cessation, with or without nicotine replacement. Therefore, the dosage of certain concomitant medications may require adjustment (see Table II).

Table II—Nicorette

Drug Interactions

May require a decrease in dose at cessation of smoking	Possible Mechanism
Acetaminophen, caffeine, imipramine, oxazepam, pentazocine, propranolol, theophylline	Deinduction of hepatic enzymes on smoking cessation
Insulin	Increase in subcutaneous insulin absorption with smoking cessation
Adrenergic antagonists (e.g., prazosin, labetalol)	Decrease in circulating catecholamines with smoking cessation
Propoxyphene	"First Pass" metabolism decreased
Adrenergic agonist (e.g., isoproterenol, phenylephrine)	Decrease in circulating catecholamines with smoking cessation
Glutethimide	Absorption may be decreased

Other reported effects of smoking, which do not involve enzyme induction, include reduced diuretic effects of furosemide and decreased cardiac output, and reduced efect on blood pressure with propranolol, which may also relate to the hormonal effects of nicotine. Smoking cessation may reverse these actions.

Weight Gain: Weight gain is commonly associated with abstention from smoking. The mechanism for this is believed to be a combination of the abstention from the oral habit of cigarette smoking and its replacement by increased intake of food and reduced GI motility due to the absence of the stimulant nicotine. Patients who quit smoking should always be monitored for weight gain.

Liquid Consumption: Patients should be advised not to consume liquids while chewing Nicorette, as the pH of the oral cavity may be reduced and interfere with absorption of nicotine.

Adverse Effects: Adverse reactions reported in association with the use of Nicorette include both local effects and systemic effects representing the pharmacological action of nicotine.

Local Side Effects: Mechanical effects of gum chewing include traumatic injury to oral mucosa or teeth, jaw ache, and eructation secondary to air swallowing. These side effects may be minimized by modifying chewing technique. Oral mucosa changes such as stomatitis, glossitis, gingivitis, pharyngitis, and aphthous ulcers, in addition to changes in taste

Nicorette (cont'd)

perception, can occur during smoking cessation efforts with or without the use of Nicorette.
Systemic Side Effects: Although the type of systemic adverse drug effects seen in clinical trials are similar from one trial to the other, the incidence of individual effects vary considerably from trial to trial. In 2 well-controlled clinical trials (1 performed in the United States and 1 in England) designed to evaluate the safety and efficacy of Nicorette this variation was evident (see Table III).

Table III—Nicorette

Adverse Event Incidence

Body System / Event	Number of Subjects: U.S. Trial 94	British Trial 58
Autonomic		
Excessive salivation	2.1	—
CNS		
Insomnia	1.1	—
Dizziness/Lightheadedness	2.1	19.0
Irritable/Fussy	1.1	—
Headache	1.1	24.1
Gastrointestinal		
Nonspecific gastrointestinal distress	9.6	—
Eructation	6.4	—
Indigestion	—	41.4
Nausea/Vomiting	18.1	31.0
Reactions Referable to Mouth, Jaw or Teeth		
Mouth or throat soreness	37.2	56.9
Jaw muscle ache	18.1	44.8
Others		
Anorexia	1.1	—
Hiccups	14.9	22.4

Due to its inherent variability, the list of adverse event incidences can be used only as an indication of the relative frequency of adverse events reported in representative clinical trials. It cannot predict expected incidences of these effects during the course of usual medical practice.

In addition to the reported effects in clinical trials, the following events have been reported: Cardiovascular: edema, flushing, hypertension, palpitations, tachyarrhythmias, tachycardia, chest pain; CNS: confusion, convulsions, depression, euphoria, numbness, paresthesia, syncope, tinnitus, weakness; Dermatologic: erythema, itching, rash, urticaria; Gastrointestinal: alteration of liver function tests, constipation, diarrhea; Respiratory: breathing difficulty, cough, hoarseness, sneezing, wheezing; Other: dry mouth, systemic nicotine intoxication.

Reports of myocardial infarction, congestive heart failure, cerebrovascular accident and cardiac arrest, including death have been received. A cause and effect relationship between these reports and the use of Nicorette has not been established.

Rare reports of miscarriage have been received and a relationship to drug therapy as a contributing factor cannot be excluded.

In addition, rare reports of an apparent severe allergic reaction have been received.

Overdose: Overdosage could occur if many pieces were chewed simultaneously or in rapid succession. The risk of poisoning by swallowing the gum is small because absorption in the absence of chewing is slow and incomplete. The consequences of overdosage will most likely be minimized by the early nausea and vomiting known to occur with excessive nicotine intake. Should an overdosage occur the symptoms would be those of acute nicotine poisoning.

Symptoms: Mild to moderate poisoning causes nausea, salivation, abdominal pain, vomiting, diarrhea, cold sweat, headache, dizziness, disturbed hearing and vision, mental confusion, and marked weakness. Faintness and prostration will likely ensue and hypotension may occur; breathing is difficult; the pulse may be rapid, weak, and irregular; circulatory collapse may be followed by terminal convulsions. Death may result within a few minutes from respiratory failure caused by paralysis of the respiratory muscles.

The oral minimum acute lethal dose for nicotine in human adults is 40 to 60 mg. In human volunteer studies, ten 4 mg nicotine polacrilex pieces were deliberately swallowed and blood nicotine levels followed over a 24-hour period. At no time did the blood nicotine level exceed 5 ng/mL in that period, a level that is considerably less than that produced by smoking a mild cigarette. An analysis of the Nicorette pieces recovered from the feces of the volunteers showed that only 32% of the original nicotine content had been released.

Treatment: In a conscious, alert patient, prompt evacuation of the stomach should be performed. When evacuation is complete, activated charcoal may be administered by mouth, if necessary.

In comatose patients, a clear airway must be established immediately and ventilatory support may be required. Other therapeutic measures are purely symptomatic and should be conducted according to the attending physician's assessment of the patient. When the patient's clinical status stabilizes, consideration may be given to gastric lavage and administration of activated charcoal. Hypotension and/or cardiovascular collapse may occur and should be treated vigorously.

Dosage: Nicorette should be regarded as an adjunct to, and a pharmaceutical and psychological reinforcer of a program to quit smoking, and not as a long-term nicotine substitute. Nicorette consumption should be terminated once the patient has successfully broken the smoking habit. This can take up to 6 months in some smokers. It is strongly recommended that Nicorette pieces be carried by the patient for up to 3 months following cigarette abstention in case a sudden overpowering urge to smoke occurs.

For optimum results, the initial treatment should be based on the patient's level of nicotine dependence, which can be determined by using the Fagerström Nicotine Tolerance Scale (see Indications).

If the score is 6 or less, Nicorette 2 mg is recommended for use. If the score is 7 or greater, Nicorette Plus (4 mg) should be used.

Most patients require approximately 10 pieces of Nicorette 2 mg/day during the first month of treatment. **Patients should be instructed not to exceed 20 pieces of Nicorette 2 mg/day.** One piece should be chewed for up to half an hour when the desire to smoke arises.

Information for the Patient: See Blue Section—Information for the Patient "Nicorette".

Supplied: Each off-white, mint- or fruit-flavored square, buffered to maintain a pH of 8.5 in the mouth, contains: nicotine 2 mg. Nonmedicinal ingredients: gum, menthol, magnesium oxide, peppermint oil, sodium bicarbonate, sodium carbonate and xylitol. Blister packs of 30 pieces and 105 pieces. Store at room temperature, between 15 and 30°C. Protect from light.

Reviewed 1999

NICORETTE® PLUS

Hoechst Marion Roussel

Nicotine Polacrilex

Smoking Cessation Aid

Pharmacology: The active component of Nicorette Plus is nicotine in the form of a natural extract from the tobacco plant.

In small doses, nicotine stimulates autonomic ganglia. Larger doses of the drug result in a blockage of the ganglia. The effects on autonomic ganglia vary according to the degree of tolerance to nicotine. The major cardiovascular effects of nicotine are vasoconstriction, tachycardia and elevated blood pressure resulting from stimulation of sympathetic ganglia and the adrenal medulla as well as from the activation of chemoreceptors of aortic and carotid bodies.

The pharmacokinetics of nicotine favour buccal (rather than gastrointestinal) absorption. Absorption from the mouth is more rapid than from the stomach and the absorbed nicotine avoids immediate and rapid inactivation by the liver (first pass effect).

Nicorette Plus is formulated to provide blood nicotine levels via buccal absorption that will approximate those produced by the inhalation of tobacco smoke. The nicotine in Nicorette Plus is bound to an ion exchange resin and is released only during chewing. The rate of release of nicotine and, as a consequence, nicotine blood levels, are related to the rate and vigor with which the gum is chewed. The chewing of a Nicorette Plus piece over a 30-minute period on a one-time-only basis produces peak blood nicotine levels of 10 ng/mL. This peak is reached by about the 25th minute and compares with a peak of 16 to 35 ng/mL reached within 5 minutes from smoking a cigarette of mild to moderate nicotine content. Blood nicotine levels increase and stabilize at 50 ng/mL, following repeated administration of Nicorette Plus at half-hourly intervals. Thus, with Nicorette Plus, it is possible to produce nicotine blood levels of the same order as those produced by smoking cigarettes.

The elimination half-life of nicotine in plasma is 120 minutes. Both nicotine and its metabolites are rapidly eliminated by the kidney. The rate of urinary excretion is dependent on the pH of the urine; excretion diminishes when the urine is alkaline.

Indications: Nicorette Plus is designed to provide partial substitution for the nicotine in cigarette smoke and is intended as a temporary aid in cushioning the patient against the psychopharmacological effects of the withdrawal symptoms of smoking cessation.

Before initiating treatment with Nicorette Plus, the physician or pharmacist should determine the patient's level of nicotine dependence using the Fagerström Nicotine Tolerance Scale shown in Table I (on following page).

Instructions for Use of the Fagerström Scale: Assign the appropriate score indicated in each column according to the patient's answer to the questions (note that not all questions have an answer in Column C). The highest possible score is 11.

If the score is 6 or less, Nicorette 2 mg is recommended for use. If the score is 7 or greater, Nicorette Plus (4 mg) should be used.

Contraindications: In patients during the immediate postmyocardial infarction period, patients with life-threatening arrhythmias, and in patients with severe or worsening angina pectoris; in patients with active temporomandibular joint disease; in pregnant women (see Warnings); in breast-feeding mothers, as nicotine is excreted in breast milk (see Warnings), and in nonsmokers and children under 18 years of age (see Warnings).

Warnings: The amounts of nicotine that are tolerated by adult smokers can produce symptoms of poisoning and could prove fatal if ingested by children or pets. Patients should be warned to keep Nicorette Plus out of the reach of children and pets.

Simultaneous smoking and chewing of Nicorette Plus should be avoided.

In patients with certain cardiovascular and endocrine diseases, the risks of using nicotine should be carefully weighed against the benefits of including Nicorette Plus in a smoking cessation program. Patients with coronary heart disease (history of myocardial infarction and/or angina pectoris), serious cardiac arrhythmias, or vasospastic diseases (Buerger's disease, Prinzmetal's variant angina) should be carefully screened and evaluated before Nicorette Plus is used. Occasional reports of tachyarrhythmias occurring in association with the use of Nicorette Plus have been reported; therefore, if an increase in cardiovascular symptoms occurs with the use of Nicorette Plus it should be discontinued.

As the action of nicotine on the adrenal medulla (release of catecholamines) does not appear to be affected by tolerance, Nicorette Plus should be used with caution in patients with hyperthyroidism, pheochromocytoma or insulin-dependent diabetes.

Cigarette smoking is felt to play a perpetuating role in hypertension and peptic ulcer disease. Therefore, Nicorette Plus should be used in patients with systemic hypertension or peptic ulcer (active or inactive) only when the benefits of including Nicorette Plus in a smoking cessation program outweigh the risks.

Pregnancy: Women of childbearing age should be advised to take adequate precautions to avoid becoming pregnant while using Nicorette Plus. Nicorette Plus therapy should be discontinued if pregnancy is suspected (see Contraindications).

Lactation: Nicotine passes freely into the breast milk. Because of the potential for adverse reactions in nursing infants from nicotine, a decision should be made whether to discontinue nursing or to discontinue the drug, taking into account the importance of the drug to the mother (see Contraindications).

Children: Safety and effectiveness in children and adolescents who smoke has not been evaluated. The use of Nicorette Plus is not recommended in smokers under 18 years of age (see Contraindications).

Precautions: General: Nicorette Plus should be used with caution in patients with oral or pharyngeal inflammation and in patients with a history of esophagitis or peptic ulcer.

The Nicorette Plus dosage form dictates that it be used with caution in patients whose dental problems might be exacerbated by chewing gum. In such patients, prior dental evaluation may be advisable.

Nicorette Plus is sugar-free and has been formulated to minimize stickiness. As with other gums, however, the degree to which Nicorette Plus may stick to dentures, dental caps or partial dentures may depend on the materials from which they

Table I—Nicorette Plus

The Fagerström Nicotine Tolerance Scale

	A=0 points	B=1 point	C=2 points	Score
How soon after you wake do you smoke your first cigarette?	After 30 minutes	Within 30 minutes		
How many cigarettes a day do you smoke?	1–15	16–25	more than 26	
Does the brand you smoke have a low, medium or high nicotine content?	Low, less than 0.4 mg	Medium, between 0.5 and 0.8 mg	High, greater than 0.9 mg	
Which of all the cigarettes you smoke a day is the most satisfying one?	Any other than the first one in the morning	The first one in the morning		
Do you smoke more during the morning than during the rest of the day?	No	Yes		
Do you smoke when you are so ill that you are in bed most of the day?	No	Yes		
Do you find it difficult to refrain from smoking in places where it is forbidden, such as the library, theatre, doctor's office?	No	Yes		
How often do you inhale smoke from your cigarette?	Never	Sometimes	Always	
			Score	

are made and other factors such as amount of saliva produced, possible interaction with denture adhesives, denture cleaning compounds, dryness of mouth due to other causes and salivary constituents. Should an excessive degree of adherence to dental work occur, there is the possibility that, as with other gums, Nicorette Plus may damage dental work. If this should occur, the patient should discontinue its use and consult a physician or dentist.

The sustained use of Nicorette Plus by former smokers is not to be encouraged because the chronic consumption of nicotine is addicting. The relative risks of a possible return to smoking should be weighed against the long-term use of Nicorette Plus.

Nicotine was not mutagenic in the Ames Salmonella test. Literature reports indicate that nicotine is neither an initiator nor a tumor-promoter in mice. There is inconclusive evidence to suggest that cotinine, an oxidized metabolite of nicotine, may be carcinogenic in rats. Cotinine was not mutagenic in the Ames Salmonella test.

Studies have shown a decrease of litter size in rats treated with nicotine during the time of fertilization.

Drug Interactions: Physicians should anticipate that the pharmacokinetics of certain concomitant medications may be altered by smoking cessation with or without nicotine replacement. Therefore the dosage of certain concomitant medications may require adjustment (see Table II).

Table II—Nicorette Plus

Dose Adjustment of Concomitant Medications

May require a decrease in dose at cessation of smoking	Possible Mechanism
Acetaminophen, caffeine, imipramine, oxazepam, pentazocine, propranolol, theophylline	Deinduction of hepatic enzymes on smoking cessation
Insulin	Increase in s.c. insulin absorption with smoking cessation
Adrenergic antagonists (e.g., prazosin, labetalol)	Decrease in circulating catecholamines with smoking cessation
Propoxyphene	"First pass" metabolism decreased
May require an increase in dose at cessation of smoking	**Possible Mechanism**
Adrenergic agonist (e.g., isoproterenol, phenylephrine)	Decrease in circulating catecholamines with smoking cessation
Glutethimide	Absorption may be decreased

Other reported effects of smoking, which do not involve enzyme induction, include reduced diuretic effects of furosemide and decreased cardiac output, and reduced effect on blood pressure with propranolol, which may also relate to the hormonal effects of nicotine. Smoking cessation may reverse these actions.

Weight Gain: Weight gain is commonly associated with abstention from smoking. The mechanism for this is believed to be a combination of the abstention from the oral habit of cigarette smoking and its replacement by increased intake of food and reduced gastrointestinal motility due to the absence of the stimulant nicotine. Patients who quit smoking should always be monitored for weight gain.

Liquid Consumption: Patients should be advised not to consume liquids while chewing Nicorette Plus, as the pH of the oral cavity may be reduced and interfere with absorption of nicotine.

Adverse Effects: Adverse reactions reported in association with the use of Nicorette Plus include both local effects and systemic effects representing the pharmacological action of nicotine.

Local Side Effects: Mechanical effects of gum chewing include traumatic injury to oral mucosa or teeth, jaw ache, and eructation secondary to air swallowing. These side effects may be minimized by modifying chewing technique. Changes in the oral mucosa such as stomatitis, glossitis, gingivitis, pharyngitis, and aphthous ulcers, in addition to changes in taste perception, can occur spontaneously during smoking cessation efforts and may not be related to the use of Nicorette Plus.

Oral adverse events occurring with a frequency of 1% or greater in 1 801 patients using Nicorette Plus in 2 clinical trials were throat irritation 5%, stomatitis (excluding aphthous and ulcerative stomatitis) 4%, taste perversion 3%, tooth disorder (e.g., occlusal stress as a result of chewing, loosening of fillings, gum sticking to dentures etc.) 2%, aphthous stomatitis 2%, gingivitis 1% and glossitis 1%.

Other oral events reported were gingival bleeding, taste loss, tongue discoloration and tongue ulceration.

Systemic Side Effects: Adverse events which occurred in 1 801 patients who participated in 2 clinical trials of Nicorette Plus are listed by body system. Incidences of 1% or greater are shown in brackets. The list also includes other events which have been reported, including events reported postmarketing.

Cardiovascular: chest pain (1%), edema, flushing, hypertension, palpitations, tachyarrhythmias, tachycardia.

CNS: headache (11%), dizziness (4%), insomnia (2%), fatigue (1%), abnormal dreaming, agitation, anxiety, apathy, confusion, convulsions, depersonalization, depression, drug dependence, emotional lability, euphoria, hypoesthesia, impaired concentration, irritability, lightheadedness, migraine, nervousness, nightmare, numbness, paresthesia, sleep disorder, syncope, tinnitus, tremor.

Dermatologic: acne, erythema, itching, pruritus, rash, urticaria.

Gastrointestinal: dyspepsia (9%), nausea (9%), abdominal pain (1%), diarrhea (1%), eructation (1%), flatulence (1%), vomiting (1%), abdominal distention, alteration of liver function tests, colitis, constipation, diarrhea, diverticulitis, gastritis, gastroesophageal reflux, increased salivation, nonspecific gastrointestinal distress, peptic ulcer, ulcer.

Respiratory: cough (1%), breathing difficulty, bronchitis, bronchospasm, congestion, epistaxis, hoarseness, laryngitis, nasal irritation, rhinitis, rhinorrhea, sinusitis, sneezing.

Other: hiccups (10%), pain (2%), dry mouth (1%), malaise (1%), abnormal lacrimation, abnormal serum folate test, allergic reaction, anorexia, arthralgia, back pain, dehydration, dysmenorrhea, dysphagia, dysphonia, earache, ear disorder, fever, halitosis, hot flushes, hypothyroidism, leg cramps, lymphadenopathy, malaise, mucus membrane disorder, myalgia, nail disorder, oliguria, sweating, systemic nicotine intoxication, thirst, vision abnormality, weakness.

Reports of myocardial infarction, congestive heart failure, cerebrovascular accident and cardiac arrest, including death have been received. Although a cause and effect relationship between these reports and the use of Nicorette Plus has not been established, the possibility that nicotine was involved cannot be ruled out.

Rare reports of miscarriage have been received and a relationship to drug therapy as a contributing factor cannot be excluded.

Rare reports of severe allergic reactions have been received.

Overdose: Overdosage could occur if many pieces were chewed simultaneously or in rapid succession. The risk of poisoning by swallowing the gum is small because absorption in the absence of chewing is slow and incomplete. The consequences of overdosage will most likely be minimized by the early nausea and vomiting known to occur with excessive nicotine intake. Should an overdosage occur the symptoms would be those of acute nicotine poisoning.

Symptoms: Mild to moderate poisoning causes nausea, salivation, abdominal pain, vomiting, diarrhea, cold sweat, headache, dizziness, disturbed hearing and vision, mental confusion, and marked weakness. Faintness and prostration will likely ensue and hypotension may occur; breathing is difficult; the pulse may be rapid, weak, and irregular; circulatory collapse may be followed by terminal convulsions. Death may result within a few minutes from respiratory failure caused by paralysis of the respiratory muscles.

The oral minimum acute lethal dose for nicotine in human adults is 40 to 60 mg. In human volunteer studies, ten 4 mg nicotine polacrilex pieces were deliberately swallowed and blood nicotine levels followed over a 24-hour period. At no time did the blood nicotine level exceed 5 ng/mL in that period, a level that is considerably less than that produced by smoking a mild cigarette. An analysis of the Nicorette Plus pieces recovered from the feces of the volunteers showed that only 32% of the original nicotine content had been released.

Treatment: In a conscious, alert patient, prompt evacuation of the stomach should be performed. When evacuation is complete, activated charcoal may be administered by mouth, if necessary.

In comatose patients, a clear airway must be established immediately and ventilatory support may be required. Other therapeutic measures are purely symptomatic and should be conducted according to the attending physician's assessment of the patient. When the patient's clinical status stabilizes, consideration may be given to gastric lavage and administration of activated charcoal. Hypotension and/or cardiovascular collapse may occur and should be treated vigorously.

Dosage: Nicorette Plus should be regarded as an adjunct to, and a pharmaceutical and psychological reinforcer of a program to quit smoking, and not as a long-term nicotine substitute. Nicorette Plus consumption should be terminated once the patient has successfully broken the smoking habit. This can take up to 6 months in some smokers. It is strongly recommended that Nicorette Plus pieces be carried by the patient for up to 3 months following cigarette abstention in case a sudden overpowering urge to smoke occurs.

For optimum results, the initial treatment should be based on the patient's level of nicotine dependence, which can be determined by using the Fagerström Nicotine Tolerance Scale (see Indications).

If the score is 6 or less, Nicorette 2 mg is recommended for use. If the score is 7 or greater, Nicorette Plus (4 mg) should be used.

Most patients require approximately 10 pieces of Nicorette Plus/day during the first month of treatment. **Patients should be instructed not to exceed 20 pieces of Nicorette Plus/day.**

Nicorette Plus (cont'd)

One piece should be chewed for up to half an hour when the desire to smoke arises.

Information for the Patient: See Blue Section—Information for the Patient "Nicorette Plus".

Supplied: Each off-white, mint- or fruit-flavored square, buffered to maintain a pH of 8.5 in the mouth, contains: nicotine 4 mg. Nonmedicinal ingredients: gum, magnesium oxide, menthol, peppermint oil, sodium carbonate, xylitol and yellow D&C #10. Blister packs of 30 and 105 pieces. Store at room temperature, between 15 and 30°C. Protect from light.

Reviewed 1999

NICOTINAMIDE
General Monograph, CPhA
see NIACIN/NIACINAMIDE

NICOTINIC ACID
General Monograph, CPhA
see NIACIN/NIACINAMIDE

NICOTROL®
Johnson & Johnson • Merck
Nicotine
Stop Smoking Aid

Pharmacology: Nicotrol is a multilayered, laminated, flexible thin film containing nicotine as the active ingredient. Nicotrol has been specifically designed to provide a 16-hour rate controlled delivery of nicotine following its application to intact skin. It is intended to be applied during the day and removed at night prior to sleeping, thus minimizing the potential for any sleep disturbances. The Nicotrol system provides nicotine without the other ingredients in tobacco smoke (e.g. tar, carbon monoxide, hydrogen cyanide) thereby attenuating abstinence symptoms associated with nicotine withdrawal during the cessation of smoking. Nicotrol increases the success rate of cessation in smokers who are motivated to quit.

Indications: Nicotrol, applied while patients are awake, is indicated as a temporary aid to facilitate smoking cessation in smokers with a strong desire to quit and to provide partial substitution for the nicotine in cigarettes in order to lessen withdrawal symptoms of smoking cessation. Nicotrol treatment should be used as part of a comprehensive behavioral smoking-cessation program.

Contraindications: Patients with hypersensitivity or allergy to nicotine or the components of the transdermal system. Patients with acute hypersensitivity reactions should discontinue use of Nicotrol and should be advised of the possibility of acute hypersensitivity reactions to other forms of nicotine, including cigarettes.

Patients with generalized skin disorders.
Nonsmokers or occasional smokers.
Persons under 18 years of age (see Warnings).
Pregnant women or nursing mothers (see Warnings).

Patients during the immediate postmyocardial infarction period, patients with life-threatening arrhythmias, patients with severe or worsening angina pectoris and patients who have had a recent cerebral vascular accident (see Warnings).

Warnings: General: Nicotine from any source can be toxic and addictive. For any smoker, with or without concomitant disease, the risk of nicotine replacement in a smoking cessation program should be weighed against the hazard of continued smoking.

Safety Note Concerning Children and Pets: The amounts of nicotine that are tolerated by adult smokers can cause severe poisoning and even prove fatal if the Nicotrol system is applied or ingested by children or pets. Used Nicotrol systems contain approximately 40% of their initial nicotine content. Therefore, patients should be cautioned to keep both the used and unused Nicotrol systems out of the reach of children and pets.

Children: Nicotrol is not to be used by persons under 18 years of age. The use of Nicotrol in children and adolescents who smoke has not been evaluated (see Contraindications).

Pregnancy and *Lactation:* Tobacco smoke (containing nicotine, hydrogen cyanide and carbon monoxide) has been shown to be harmful to the fetus. Nicotine has been shown in animal studies to cause fetal harm. It is therefore presumed that nicotine from Nicotrol systems can cause fetal harm when administered to a pregnant woman. Women of childbearing potential should be advised to take adequate precautions to avoid becoming pregnant while using Nicotrol (see Contraindications).

Pregnant smokers should be encouraged to attempt cessation using educational and behavioral interventions before using pharmacological approaches.

The safety of Nicotrol therapy in nursing infants has not been examined. Nicotine passes freely into breast milk; the milk to plasma ratio averages 2.9. Nicotine is absorbed orally (see Contraindications).

Cardiovascular or Peripheral Vascular Disease: The risks of nicotine replacement in patients with certain cardiovascular and peripheral vascular diseases should be weighed against the benefits of including nicotine replacement in a smoking-cessation program for them. Specifically, patients with coronary heart disease (history of myocardial infarction and/or angina pectoris), serious cardiac arrhythmias, or vasospastic diseases (Buerger's disease, Prinzmetal's variant angina) should be carefully screened and evaluated before nicotine replacement is recommended.

Palpitations occurring in association with the use of Nicotrol therapy have been reported occasionally. If serious cardiovascular symptoms occur with the use of Nicotrol therapy, it should be discontinued.

Accelerated Hypertension: Nicotrol therapy should be used with caution in these patients and only when the benefits of including nicotine replacement in a smoking-cessation program outweigh the risks.

Peptic Ulcer Disease: Nicotine delays healing in peptic ulcer disease; therefore, Nicotrol therapy should be used with caution in patients with active peptic ulcers and only when the benefits of including nicotine replacement in a smoking-cessation program are considered to outweigh the risks.

Precautions: General: The patient should stop smoking completely when initiating Nicotrol therapy (see Dosage). Patients should be informed that they should not continue to smoke while using Nicotrol systems, because they may experience adverse effects due to peak nicotine levels higher than those experienced from smoking alone. If there is a clinically significant increase in cardiovascular or other effects attributable to nicotine, the Nicotrol dose should be reduced or Nicotrol treatment discontinued (see Warnings). The use of Nicotrol systems beyond 10 weeks by patients who stop smoking should be discouraged because the chronic consumption of nicotine by any route can be harmful and addicting. If the patient continues to smoke, treatment should be discontinued.

Allergic Reactions: Patients should be instructed to discontinue promptly the use of Nicotrol systems and contact their physician if they experience severe or persistent local skin reactions (e.g., urticaria, hives, or generalized rash). Patients using Nicotrol therapy concurrently with other transdermal systems may exhibit local reactions at both application sites. In such patients use of one or both systems may have to be discontinued. Serious allergic reactions may occur rarely. About 1% of patients dropped out of clinical trials due to skin reactions; none had classical contact sensitization.

Skin Disease: Nicotrol systems are usually well tolerated by patients with normal skin, but may be irritating for patients with some skin disorders (atopic or eczematous dermatitis).

Strenuous Exercise: Preliminary evidence suggests that wearing a nicotine transdermal patch during periods of strenuous exercise may lead to nicotine toxicity as a result of increased absorption of nicotine from the depot of nicotine in the skin under the patch, due to increased skin temperature and increased cutaneous vasodilation and perfusion from exercising. Three cases illustrating this phenomenon were described in Health Canada Adverse Reaction Newsletter, Volume 6, Number 1, January, 1996. Advice to remove the nicotine patch before engaging in strenuous exercise was recommended by; W. Dafoe and P. Huston, Current Trends in Cardiac Rehabilitation, Canadian Medical Association Journal, February 15, 1997; 156(4) 527-532. Until definitive studies have been undertaken to clarify this hazard, it is advisable to remove the nicotine patch prior to engaging in strenuous activity.

Geriatrics: Seventy-nine patients over the age of 60 participated in clinical trials of Nicotrol therapy. Nicotrol therapy appeared to be as effective in this age group as in younger smokers. The initial dose in elderly patients may have to be adjusted because their concomitant diseases may increase risk.

Endocrine Diseases: Nicotrol therapy should be used with caution in patients with hyperthyroidism, pheochromocytoma, or insulin-dependent diabetes since nicotine causes the release of catecholamines by the adrenal medulla.

Renal or Hepatic Insufficiency: The pharmacokinetics of nicotine have not been studied in the elderly or in patients with renal or hepatic impairment; however, given that nicotine is extensively metabolized and that its total system clearance is dependent on liver blood flow, some influence of hepatic impairment on drug kinetics (reduced clearance) should be anticipated. Only severe renal impairment would be expected to affect the clearance of nicotine or its metabolites from the circulation.

Drug Interactions: Physicians should anticipate that the pharmacokinetics of certain concomitant medications may be altered by smoking cessation with or without nicotine replacement. Therefore the dosage of certain concomitant medications may require adjustment (see Table I).

Table I—Nicotrol

Dose Adjustment of Concomitant Medications

May Require a Decrease in Dose at Cessation of Smoking	Possible Mechanism
Acetaminophen, caffeine, imipramine, oxazepam, pentazocine, propranolol, theophylline	Deinduction of hepatic enzymes on smoking cessation
Insulin	Increase in s.c. insulin absorption with smoking cessation
Adrenergic antagonists (e.g. prazosin, labetalol)	Decrease in circulating catecholamines with smoking cessation
May Require an Increase in Dose at Cessation of Smoking	**Possible Mechanism**
Adrenergic agonists (e.g. isoproterenol, phenylephrine)	Decrease in circulating catecholamines with smoking cessation

Drug Dependency: Nicotrol therapy is likely to have a low abuse potential based on differences between it and cigarettes in 4 characteristics commonly considered important in contributing to abuse: much slower absorption, much smaller fluctuations in blood levels, lower blood levels of nicotine, and less frequent use (i.e., once daily). Dependency on Nicotrol has not been reported.

To minimize the risk of dependence, therapy should not exceed 10 weeks (see Dosage).

Information for Patients: A separate Patient Instruction Leaflet is included in the package of Nicotrol systems (see Blue Section—Information for the Patient). It contains important information on how to use and dispose of Nicotrol systems, properly. Patients should be encouraged to ask questions to ensure they understand the instructions. **Patients must be advised to keep both used and unused Nicotrol systems out of the reach of children and pets.**

Adverse Effects: Assessment of adverse events in patients who participated in controlled clinical trials is complicated by the occurrence of gastrointestinal and CNS effects of nicotine withdrawal as well as nicotine excess. The actual incidence of both are confounded by concurrent smoking by many of the patients. When reporting adverse events in the clinical trials, the clinical investigators did not attempt to identify the cause of the symptom.

The most common adverse event associated with Nicotrol is a mild, short-lived erythema and/or pruritus at the application site, which was seen at least once in 47% of patients on the Nicotrol system (versus 45% of patients on placebo) in the clinical efficacy trials. These signs were not considered clinically relevant and usually disappeared within 1 hour. After removal of the system, local erythema was noted at least once in 7% of patients and local edema in 3% of patients. Erythema generally resolved within 24 hours. About 1% of patients dropped out of the clinical trials due to skin reactions. None of these were classified as contact sensitization reactions. In the prescription to OTC switch trials approximately 32% of reported events were skin reactions.

Table II summarizes the adverse events with an incidence of greater than 1% in 2 placebo-controlled clinical trials and 2 prescription to nonprescription switch trials.

Table II—Nicotrol

Adverse Reactions with an Incidence of >1% in Placebo-Controlled Clinical Trials and Prescription to OTC Switch Trials

	Prescription Treatment Groups		Prescription to OTC Switch
Body System/Adverse Event	**Nicotrol % (n=258)**	**Placebo % (n=251)**	**Nicotrol % (n=3 885)**
CNS			
Headache	5.4	4.0	3.3
Vertigo	3.1	0.8	–
Digestive			
Nausea	3.5	4.0	2.4
Flatulence	2.7	2.4	–
Diarrhea	1.9	1.6	–
Taste Perversion	1.9	1.6	–
Mouth Ulceration	1.6	0.4	–
Heartburn/Indigestion	1.2	2.4	–
Tongue Disorder	1.2	0.4	–
Musculoskeletal			
Myalgia	3.1	3.1	–
Skin (Not Application Site			
Rash/Pruritus/Tingling/ Edema	1.9	1.2	–
Acne	1.2	0.0	–
Body as a whole			
Pain	–	–	2.1

Overdose: Symptoms: There have been 2 reported cases of applying several nicotine patches simultaneously. Both people were attempting suicide and combined several nicotine patches, 21 mg, with other drugs. No serious effects resulted from either attempt.

Signs and symptoms of an overdose from a Nicotrol system are expected to be the same as those of acute nicotine poisoning, including: pallor, cold sweat, nausea, salivation, vomiting, abdominal pain, diarrhea, headache, dizziness, disturbed hearing and vision, tremor, mental confusion and weakness. Prostration, hypotension, and respiratory failure may ensue with large overdoses. Lethal doses of nicotine produce convulsions quickly and death follows as a result of peripheral or central respiratory paralysis or, less frequently, cardiac failure. The acute, minimal, oral lethal dose of nicotine in human adults is reported to be 40 to 60 mg (<1 mg/kg). Much lower doses have been reported to be toxic in children.

Treatment: The Nicotrol system should be removed immediately if the patient shows signs of overdosage and the patient should seek immediate medical care by contacting a physician or local poison control centre. The skin surface should be flushed with water and dried. **Soap must not be used since it may increase nicotine absorption.** Nicotine will continue to be delivered into the bloodstream for several hours after removal of the system because of a depot of nicotine in the skin.

Persons ingesting Nicotrol systems should be referred to a health care facility for management. Due to the possibility of nicotine-induced seizures, activated charcoal should be administered. In unconscious patients with a secure airway, instill activated charcoal via a nasogastric tube. Repeated doses of activated charcoal should be administered as long as the system remains in the gastrointestinal tract since it will continue to release nicotine for many hours. A saline cathartic or sorbitol added to the first dose of activated charcoal may speed gastrointestinal passage of the system.

Other supportive measures include diazepam or barbiturates for seizures, atropine for excessive bronchial secretions or diarrhea, respiratory support for respiratory failure, and vigorous fluid support for hypotension and cardiovascular collapse.

Dosage: Patients must desire to stop smoking and should be instructed to stop smoking immediately as they begin using Nicotrol therapy.

If the patient is unable to avoid cigarette smoking within 2 weeks of starting treatment, Nicotrol therapy should be stopped, since few additional patients in clinical trials were able to quit after this time. The duration of treatment should not exceed 10 weeks.

The patient should be told to read the patient instruction leaflet on Nicotrol therapy and should be encouraged to ask questions.

Dosage: One patch daily for 6 weeks. For patients who wish to wean themselves rather than abruptly stop, follow the regimen outlined in Table III.

Table III—Nicotrol

Dosing Schedule in Adults

Dose	**Duration**
Nicotrol 15 mg/16 hours	First 6 weeks
Nicotrol 10 mg/16 hours	Next 2 weeks
Nicotrol 5 mg/16 hours	Last 2 weeks

Smoking cessation should be accompanied by a behavioral support program.

Administration: The Nicotrol system should be applied promptly upon its removal from the protective pouch to prevent loss of nicotine from the system. A Nicotrol system should be applied only once a day to a nonhairy, clean, and dry skin site on the upper arm or the hip. A different site of application should be chosen each day. Each day a new Nicotrol system should be applied upon waking and removed at bedtime. It should not be worn for more than 16 hours/day.

Safety and Handling: Nicotrol systems can be a dermal irritant and can cause contact sensitization. Care should be taken to avoid unnecessary contact with active systems. If you do handle active systems, wash with water alone since soap may increase nicotine absorption. Do not touch your eyes.

Disposal: When the used system is removed from the skin, it should be folded over and placed in its pouch. The used system should be disposed of immediately in such a way as to prevent its access by children or pets (see Information for the Patient for further directions on handling and disposal).

Information for the Patient: See Blue Section—Information for the Patient "Nicotrol".

Supplied: The Nicotrol system is a multilayered, rectangular-shaped, laminated thin film containing nicotine as the active ingredient. Proceeding from the visible surface toward the surface attached to the skin, there are 3 distinct layers: 1. An outer backing layer composed of a laminated polyester film. 2. A middle layer containing an adhesive, a structural nonwoven material and nicotine. The adhesive controls the rate of delivery of nicotine to the skin. 3. A disposable liner that protects the systems; the liner is removed prior to use.

Nicotrol systems are labeled with the average amount of nicotine absorbed by the patient over 16 hours. Nicotrol systems are available in 3 strengths as follows:

Nicotrol 15 mg/16 hours System: Each 30 cm² system contains: nicotine 24.9 mg and provides a rate-controlled delivery of 15 mg/16 hours. The Backing Layer of each patch is imprinted with the phrase "Nicotrol 15 mg". Boxes of 7 and 14.

Nicotrol 10 mg/16 hours System: Each 20 cm² system contains: nicotine 16.6 mg and provides a rate-controlled delivery of 10 mg/16 hours. The Backing Layer of each patch is imprinted with the phrase "Nicotrol 10 mg". Boxes of 7 and 14.

Nicotrol 5 mg/16 hours System: Each 10 cm² system contains: nicotine 8.3 mg and provides a rate-controlled delivery of 5 mg/16 hours. The Backing Layer of each patch is imprinted with the phrase "Nicotrol 5 mg". Boxes of 7 and 14.

Store at room temperature below 30°C. Once removed from the protective pouch, Nicotrol systems should be applied promptly since nicotine is volatile and the system may lose strength.

(Shown in Product Recognition Section)

Reviewed 1999

NIDAGEL™ Ⓟ

3M Pharmaceuticals

Metronidazole

Antibacterial

Pharmacology: Metronidazole demonstrates antibacterial activity against bacteria classified as obligate anaerobes including Bacteroides and to a lesser extent against anaerobic gram-positive rods. The nitro group of the drug is thought to be reduced in the target cell leading to the production of cytotoxic metabolites.

Bioavailability studies on the administration of a single 5 g dose of NidaGel into the vaginas of 12 normal subjects showed a mean maximum serum concentration of 237 ng/mL. This is approximately 2% of the mean maximum serum concentration afforded by a single 500 mg tablet of metronidazole taken orally (mean C_{max} = 12 785 ng/mL). Therefore, under normal usage levels, the formulation affords minimal serum concentrations of metronidazole.

Indications: For the treatment of bacterial vaginosis (formerly called nonspecific vaginitis, G. vaginalis or Haemophilus vaginitis).

A clinical diagnosis of bacterial vaginosis is usually defined by the presence of a homogenous vaginal discharge that: has a pH of greater than 4.5; emits a fishy amine odor when mixed with a 10% KOH solution; contains clue cells on microscopic examination.

Other pathogens commonly associated with vulvovaginitis, e.g., T. vaginalis, C. trachomatis, N. gonorrhoeae, C. albicans and herpes simplex virus should be ruled out.

Use of metronidazole during menses is not recommended.

Contraindications: Patients with a prior history of hypersensitivity to metronidazole, parabens, other ingredients of the formulation or other nitroimidazole derivatives.

Pregnancy: Metronidazole is contraindicated during the first trimester of pregnancy (see Precautions).

Warnings: Convulsive seizures and peripheral neuropathy, the latter characterized mainly by numbness or paresthesia of an extremity, have been reported in patients treated with oral metronidazole. The appearance of abnormal neurologic signs demands the prompt discontinuation of metronidazole therapy. It should be administered with caution to patients with CNS diseases. Psychotic reactions to oral metronidazole have been reported in alcoholic patients who are using metronidazole and disulfiram concurrently.

Precautions: NidaGel affords minimal serum levels of metronidazole compared to oral metronidazole therapy. Although these lower serum levels are less likely to produce the common reactions seen with oral metronidazole, the possibility of these and other reactions cannot be excluded.

General: Patients with severe hepatic disease metabolize metronidazole slowly, with resultant accumulation of metronidazole and its metabolites in the plasma. Accordingly, for such patients, metronidazole should be administered cautiously.

Known or previously unrecognized candidiasis may present more prominent symptoms during therapy with metronidazole and requires treatment with a candicidal agent.

No reports of alcohol interaction were received during clinical studies with metronidazole. Despite the relatively low serum levels of metronidazole afforded by NidaGel, the possibility of a disulfiram-like reaction to alcohol while on metronidazole therapy cannot be excluded. Patients should be advised to abstain from alcohol during therapy and for 1 day following therapy.

Hematologic Effects: Metronidazole is a nitroimidazole and should be used with care in patients with evidence of or history of blood dyscrasia. A mild transient leukopenia has been observed during oral metronidazole administration.

In clinical studies with 0.75% metronidazole vaginal gel a mild, clinically insignificant leukopenia was observed in some patients. Relationship to therapy could not be determined.

Drug Interactions: Oral metronidazole has been reported to potentiate the anticoagulant effect of warfarin and other coumarin anticoagulants, resulting in a prolongation of prothrombin time. This possible drug interaction should be considered when metronidazole is prescribed for patients on this type of anticoagulant therapy.

Laboratory Test Interactions: Metronidazole may interfere with certain types of determinations of serum chemistry values, such as aspartate aminotransferase (AST), alanine aminotransferase (ALT), lactate dehydrogenase (LDH), triglycerides and hexokinase glucose. These determinations are based on the decrease in ultraviolet absorbance which occurs when NADH is oxidized to NAD. Metronidazole causes an increase in absorbance at the peak of NADH (340 nm) resulting in falsely decreased values.

Carcinogenicity: Metronidazole has shown evidence of carcinogenic activity following chronic oral administration in mice and rats. Pulmonary tumorigenesis has been reported in mice, and significant increases in the incidence of mammary and hepatic tumors have been found in female rats. Lifetime tumorigenicity studies in hamsters have given negative results.

These studies were conducted with orally administered metronidazole which results in significantly higher systemic blood levels than those obtained after use of 0.75% metronidazole vaginal gel.

Pregnancy: There has been no experience to date with the use of NidaGel in pregnant patients. Metronidazole crosses the placental barrier and enters the fetal circulation rapidly. It should not be used during the first trimester of pregnancy. Use of metronidazole for bacterial vaginosis in the second and

Nidagel (cont'd)

third trimesters should be restricted to those patients in whom local palliative treatment has been inadequate to control symptoms. No fetotoxicity was observed after oral metronidazole in pregnant rats or mice. Because animal reproduction studies are not always predictive of human response, this drug should be used during pregnancy only if clearly needed (see Contraindications).

Lactation: NidaGel blood levels are significantly lower than those achieved with oral metronidazole. After oral administration metronidazole has been shown to be secreted in breast milk in concentrations similar to those found in plasma. If the use of metronidazole is considered to be necessary in nursing mothers, the potential benefits must be weighed against the possible risks to the infant.

Children: Safety and effectiveness in children have not been established.

Adverse Effects: Based on a multicenter clinical trial involving 505 patients, comparing NidaGel twice-daily dosing to once-daily dosing, adverse event experiences are listed below, in descending order of frequency: vaginal discharge, descriptions of which varied in both color and consistency (12%), yeast infection (9%), vulva/vaginal irritative symptoms (9%), gastrointestinal discomfort which included patient descriptions of abdominal or stomach cramping, pain and discomfort (7%), headache (5%), nausea and vomiting (4%), pelvic discomfort (3%). The following reactions were seen at a frequency of 2%: unusual taste, dizziness, cramping, undocumented or self-diagnosed yeast infections. The following reactions were seen at a frequency of 1%: decreased appetite, diarrhea/loose stools, fatigue, medication leakage, urinary tract infection symptoms. The following reactions were seen at a frequency of <1%: abdominal bloating/gas, constipation, thirst/dry mouth, depression, irritability, menstrual discomfort, menstrual irregularities, vaginal numbness, vaginal spotting/bleeding, itching, darkened urine.

Other reactions noted with oral metronidazole therapy include anorexia, epigastric distress, nausea, vomiting, furry tongue, dry mouth, metallic taste, transient eosinophilia or neutropenia, convulsive seizures, peripheral neuropathy, vertigo, incoordination, ataxia, confusion, insomnia, flushing, headache, dryness of the vagina, dysuria, darkened urine, modification of taste of alcoholic beverages, rash, pruritus, palpitation and chest pain.

Overdose: Symptoms and Treatment: There is no human experience with overdosage of metronidazole. Massive ingestion may produce vomiting and slight disorientation. There is no specific antidote. Early gastric lavage may remove a large amount of the drug; otherwise, treatment should be symptomatic.

Dosage: One applicator full (approximately 5 g) of vaginal gel should be inserted into the vagina once daily at bedtime for 5 days, or twice daily at morning and bedtime for 5 days. Controlled studies with alternate dosage schedules have not been conducted. If patients do not respond to initial therapy, it is recommended that appropriate laboratory measures be used to rule out other conditions before retreating with metronidazole.

Pregnancy: Pregnant patients should not be treated during the first trimester of pregnancy (see Contraindications and Precautions).

Use during menses is not recommended.

Information for the Patient: See Blue Section—Information for the Patient "NidaGel".

Supplied: Each g of colorless to straw-colored, slightly hazy gel contains: metronidazole 7.5 mg. Nonmedicinal ingredients: carbomer 934P, edetate disodium, methylparaben, propylene glycol, propylparaben, purified water and sodium hydroxide to adjust the pH to 4. Aluminum tubes of 40 and 70 g, packaged with a 5 g vaginal applicator. Store between 15 and 25°C.

Reviewed 1999

NIFEDIPINE PA 10 ℞
NIFEDIPINE PA 20 ℞

Schein Pharmaceutical

Nifedipine

Antihypertensive

Pharmacology: Nifedipine is a calcium ion influx inhibitor (calcium channel blocker or calcium ion antagonist).

The antihypertensive action of this group of drugs is believed to be related to their specific cellular action of selectively inhibiting transmembrane influx of calcium ions into vascular smooth muscles. The contractile processes of vascular smooth muscle are dependent upon the movement of extracellular calcium into the cells through specific ion channels. Nifedipine selectively inhibits the transmembrane influx of calcium through the slow channel without affecting to any significant degree the transmembrane influx of sodium through the fast channel. This results in a reduction of free calcium ions available within the muscle cells and an inhibition of the contractile processes. Nifedipine does not alter total serum calcium.

The specific mechanisms by which nifedipine reduces blood pressure have not been fully determined but are believed to be brought about largely by its vasodilatory action on peripheral blood vessels which, thereby reduces peripheral vascular resistance.

The negative inotropic effect of nifedipine is usually not of major clinical significance because at therapeutic doses, nifedipine's vasodilatory property evokes a baroreceptor mediated reflex tachycardia which tends to counterbalance this negative inotropic effect. Continued administration of nifedipine to hypertensive patients has shown no significant increase in heart rate.

Although nifedipine causes a slight depression of sinoatrial node function and atrioventricular conduction in isolated myocardial preparations, such effects have not been seen in studies in intact animals or in man. In formal electrophysiologic studies, predominantly in patients with normal conduction systems, nifedipine has had no tendency to prolong atrioventricular conduction or sinus node recovery time, or to slow sinus rate.

Pharmacokinetics: In man, after oral administration of a single tablet of Nifedipine PA 20, nifedipine was detected in plasma after about 30 minutes and peak plasma concentrations (approximately 26 ng/mL) were reached in about 4 hours. The subsequent decline in concentrations was slow, with a terminal (absorption) half-life of 10 hours, such that concentration of 10 to 15 ng/mL were still present after 12 hours. The absorption and disposition data were not dose dependent nor did the pharmacokinetic character of the tablet vary after prolonged administration (2 tablets daily for 7 days).

The absolute bioavailability of nifedipine from Nifedipine PA 10 or 20 is between 50 and 70%. The extent of absorption does not change in the presence of food.

Nifedipine is transformed into 2 pharmacologically inactive metabolites. The main metabolite (95%) is the hydroxycarboxylic acid derivative which is mainly excreted in the urine; the other (5%) is the corresponding lactone. Protein binding of circulating nifedipine exceeds 90%.

Pharmacokinetic studies in patients with hepatic cirrhosis showed a clinically significant alteration in the kinetics of nifedipine (prolonged elimination half-life and decreased total clearance). In these patients, there is a considerable risk of accumulation (see Precautions).

In a grapefruit juice-nifedipine interaction study in healthy male volunteers pharmacokinetics of nifedipine showed significant alteration. Following administration of a single dose of nifedipine 10 mg with 250 mL of grapefruit juice, the mean value of nifedipine AUC increased by 34% and the t_{max} increased from 0.8 to 1.2 hours, as compared to water (see Precautions).

Indications: Treatment of essential hypertension. Nifedipine should normally be used in those patients in whom treatment with diuretics or beta-blockers has been ineffective, or has been associated with unacceptable adverse effects.

Nifedipine can be tried as an initial agent in those patients in whom the use of diuretics and/or beta-blockers is contraindicated, or in patients with medical conditions in which these drugs frequently cause serious adverse effects.

Combination of nifedipine with a diuretic or beta-blocker has been found to be compatible, and has shown added antihypertensive effect (see Precautions).

Contraindications: *Pregnancy* and *Lactation:* Nifedipine is contraindicated in pregnancy, during lactation and in women of childbearing potential. Fetal malformations and adverse effects on pregnancy have been reported in animals.

An increase in the number of fetal mortalities and resorptions occurred after the administration of 30 and 100 mg/kg nifedipine to pregnant mice, rats and rabbits. Fetal malformations occurred after the administration of 30 and 100 mg/kg nifedipine to pregnant mice and 100 mg/kg to pregnant rats.

Patients with hypersensitivity to nifedipine.

Patients with cardiovascular shock.

Warnings: Increased Angina and/or Myocardial Infarction: Rarely, patients, particularly those who have severe obstructive coronary artery disease have developed well-documented increased frequency, duration and/or severity of angina or acute myocardial infarction on starting nifedipine or at the time of dosage increase. The mechanism of this effect is not established.

Beta-Blocker Withdrawal: Patients with angina recently withdrawn from beta-blockers may develop a withdrawal syndrome with increased angina, probably related to increased sensitivity to catecholamines. Initiation of nifedipine treatment will not prevent this occurrence and might be expected to exacerbate it by provoking reflex catecholamine release. There have been occasional reports of increased angina in a setting of beta-blocker withdrawal and initiation of nifedipine. If a beta-blocker has to be discontinued, it must be tapered off gradually rather than stopped abruptly.

Patients with Heart Failure: There have been isolated reports of severe hypotension and lowering of cardiac output following administration of nifedipine to patients with severe heart failure. Rarely, patients, usually receiving a beta-blocker, have developed heart failure after beginning nifedipine therapy.

In patients with severe aortic stenosis, nifedipine will not produce its usual afterload reducing effects and there is a possibility that an unopposed negative inotropic action of the drug may produce heart failure if the end-diastolic pressure is raised.

Caution should therefore be exercised when using nifedipine in patients with these conditions.

Precautions: Heart Rate: Because nifedipine is an arterial and arteriolar vasodilator, a compensatory increase in heart rate may occur in some patients. Thus, heart rate should be monitored carefully during nifedipine therapy.

Peripheral Edema: Mild to moderate peripheral edema, typically associated with arterial vasodilation and not due to left ventricular dysfunction, has been reported to occur in patients treated with nifedipine (see Adverse Effects.) This edema occurs primarily in the lower extremities and usually responds to diuretic therapy. With patients whose hypertension is complicated by congestive heart failure, care should be taken to differentiate this peripheral edema from the effects of increasing left ventricular dysfunction.

Hypotension: Symptomatic hypotension may occasionally occur in hypertensive patients treated with nifedipine. Careful monitoring of blood pressure during the initial administration and titration of the drug is recommended, especially in patients with a history of cerebrovascular insufficiency, and those who are taking medications known to lower blood pressure.

Geriatrics: Nifedipine should be administered cautiously to the elderly since the incidence of adverse reactions reported in these patients is approximately 10% higher than in patients below 65 years of age. The adverse reactions occurring more frequently in this group include syncope, peripheral edema and palpitations (see Dosage).

Diabetics: The use of nifedipine in diabetic patients may require adjustment of their control.

Impaired Liver Function: Nifedipine should be used with caution in patients with impaired liver function (see Pharmacology). A dose reduction, particularly in severe cases, may be required. Close monitoring of response and metabolic effect should apply.

Interaction with Grapefruit Juice: Published data indicate that through inhibition of cytochrome P-450, flavonoids present in the grapefruit juice can increase plasma levels and augment pharmacodynamic effects of some dihydropyridine calcium channel blockers, including nifedipine (see Pharmacology). Therefore, the administration of nifedipine with grapefruit juice should be avoided.

Drug Interactions: Nifedipine may potentiate the effects of other agents having antihypertensive activity. The concomitant administration of nifedipine with beta-blockers warrants caution and careful monitoring of blood pressure and pulmonary signs and symptoms of congestive failure (see Warnings).

Concomitant use of nifedipine with short-acting nitrates, furosemide and anticoagulants has shown no interaction or unusual toxic effects. There have been no controlled studies to evaluate the concurrent use of long-acting nitrates and nifedipine.

Administration of nifedipine with digoxin may lead to reduced digoxin clearance, and therefore, an increase in the plasma digoxin level. It is recommended that digoxin levels be monitored when initiating, adjusting and discontinuing nifedipine to avoid possible under- or over- dosing with digitalis.

The addition of nifedipine to a stable quinidine regimen may reduce the quinidine concentration by 50%; an enhanced response to nifedipine may also occur. The addition of quinidine to a stable nifedipine regimen may result in elevated nifedipine concentrations and a reduced response to quinidine. Some patients have experienced elevated quinidine levels when nifedipine was discontinued. Therefore patients receiving concomitant therapy of nifedipine and quinidine, or those who had their nifedipine discontinued while still receiving quinidine, should be closely monitored, including determination of plasma levels of quinidine. Consideration should be given to dosage adjustment.

Pharmacokinetic studies have shown that concurrent administration of cimetidine or ranitidine with nifedipine results in significant increases in nifedipine plasma levels (approximately 80% with cimetidine and 70% with ranitidine). Patients receiving either of these drugs concomitantly with nifedipine should be monitored carefully for the possible exacerbation of effects of nifedipine, such as hypotension. Adjustment of nifedipine dosage may be necessary.

Adverse Effects: Safety evaluations of controlled and open studies have been carried out for nifedipine.

In 814 hypertensive patients treated with nifedipine, either alone or in combination with other antihypertensive agents, adverse effects were reported in 32.3% of patients and required discontinuation of therapy in 3.8% of patients. The most common adverse effects were: flushing and heat sensation (13.9%), headache (7.9%), peripheral edema (4.7%), tiredness/weakness (4.7%), dizziness/light-headedness (4.5%).

The following percentage adverse effects, divided by system, were reported: Cardiovascular: flushing, heat sensation or reddening of skin (13.9%), peripheral edema, fluid retention or swelling (4.7%), palpitation or tachycardia (1.2%), hypotension (0.5%), syncope (0.2%).

In patients with angina, rarely, and possibly due to tachycardia, nifedipine has been reported to have precipitated an angina pectoris attack. In addition, more serious events were occasionally observed, not readily distinguishable from the natural history of the disease in these patients. It remains possible, however, that some or many of these events were drug related. These events include myocardial infarction, congestive heart failure or pulmonary edema, and ventricular arrhythmias or conduction disturbances.

CNS: headache (7.9%), tiredness or weakness (4.7%), dizziness, light-headedness or giddiness (4.5%), shakiness, nervousness or jitteriness (0.6%).

Gastrointestinal: nausea or vomiting (2.2%), abdominal discomfort or heartburn (3.3%), constipation (0.6%).

Musculoskeletal: joint stiffness, muscle pain or cramps (2.2%).

Others: pruritus, dermatitis, uticaria or rash (1.4%), polyuria (1.6%).

The following additional adverse effects have occurred in an incidence of less than 0.5% in clinical trials: insomnia, hypokalemia, numbness/tingling, paresthesia, dry mouth, dyspnea on effort, extrasystole, chest pain, vision disturbance, nightmares, neuralgia, diminished concentration, impotence, decreased libido.

Two cases of hypersensitivity have been reported following nifedipine administration, resulting in allergic hepatitis, which resolved when the drug was discontinued. In one case, recurrence was observed on rechallenge.

In a small number of patients, nifedipine has been reported to cause gingival hyperplasia similar to that caused by phenytoin. The lesions usually regressed on discontinuation of the drug. However, on occasion, gingivectomy was necessary.

Gynecomastia has been observed rarely in older men on long term therapy, but has so far always regressed completely on discontinuation of the drug.

Laboratory Tests: Rarely, mild to moderate transient elevations of enzymes such as alkaline phosphatase, CPK, LDH, AST and ALT have been noted after treatment with nifedipine. These laboratory abnormalities have rarely been associated with clinical symptoms, however, cholestasis with or without jaundice has been reported. Infrequent reversible elevations in BUN and serum creatinine have been reported in patients with pre-existing chronic renal insufficiency taking nifedipine.

Overdose: Symptoms and Treatment: Although there is no well-documented experience with nifedipine overdosage, available data suggests that gross overdosage could result in excessive peripheral vasodilation with subsequent marked, and probably prolonged, systemic hypotension. Clinically significant hypotension due to overdosage requires active cardiovascular support, including monitoring of cardiac and respiratory function, elevation of extremities, and attention to circulating fluid volume and urine output. A vasoconstrictor (such as norepinephrine) may be helpful in restoring vascular tone and blood pressure, provided that there is no contraindication to its use. Clearance of nifedipine would be expected to be prolonged in patients with impaired liver function. Since nifedipine is highly protein-bound, dialysis is not likely to be of benefit.

Dosage: Dosage should be individualized depending on patient's tolerance and responsiveness to nifedipine and to concurrent antihypertensive medications (see Indications and Precautions).

The recommended initial dose is 10 to 20 mg twice daily. The usual adult dose is 20 mg twice daily. If required, the dose may be increased to 40 mg twice daily. A maximum daily dose of 80 mg should not be exceeded.

At a given dosage regimen of nifedipine, the full reduction in blood pressure may take at least 3 weeks. Therefore, in order to assess adequately the response to a particular dose level, there should be an interval of at least 3 weeks between increases in dose.

Supplied: Nifedipine PA 10: Each dusty rose, round, biconvex, prolonged action tablet, marked "10" on one side, contains: nifedipine 10 mg. Blister packs in units of 6 strips of 10.

Nifedipine PA 20: Each dusty rose, round, biconvex prolonged action tablet, marked "20" on one side, contains: nifedipine 20 mg. Blister packs in units of 6 strips of 10.

Store below 30°C. Avoid freezing. Protect from light. Broken tablets should not be used.

Reviewed 1997

NILSTAT®
Technilab

Nystatin
Antifungal Antibiotic

Indications: Oral Drops: Monilial infections of the mouth (thrush) and intestinal moniliasis in infants and children.

Oral Tablets: Prevention and treatment of intestinal moniliasis. Prevention or treatment of lower intestinal and anal infections caused by Candida albicans (monilia).

Powder: For the treatment of infections of the oral cavity by C. albicans (monilia).

Cream and Ointment: Treatment of cutaneous or mucocutaneous mycotic infections caused by Candida (monilia) species.

Vaginal Cream, Tablets: Local treatment of vaginal mycotic infections caused by Candida albicans.

Precautions: Little activity against bacteria, protozoa and viruses. Discontinue medication if irritation should occur from topical or intravaginal use.

Pregnancy: During pregnancy, the vaginal applicators should be used only on the advice of a physician.

Appropriate measures should be taken to avoid reinfection during sexual intercourse.

Adverse Effects: High oral dosage may produce nausea, vomiting and diarrhea.

Tachycardia, bronchospasm, facial swelling, urticaria and nonspecific myalgia have been reported rarely.

Dosage: Therapy should generally be continued for at least 48 hours after clinical cure to prevent relapse. When oral nystatin is given concomitantly with an oral antibacterial agent, oral nystatin should be continued at least as long as the antibacterial agent. Local treatment of chronic or resistant vaginal, oral or cutaneous moniliasis with nystatin may be supplemented with oral nystatin administration.

Oral Drops: Infants and children: 100 000 units 3 to 4 times daily for oral (thrush) and intestinal moniliasis. For treatment of infections of the oral cavity, the medication should be dropped directly on the tongue by means of the calibrated dropper and retained in the mouth for as long as possible before swallowing. For treatment of intestinal infections, may be dropped directly on the tongue by means of the calibrated dropper, or may be mixed with milk, lukewarm formula, or other nonacid vehicles, or incorporated in honey, jelly or peanut butter.

Oral Tablets: 500 000 units 3 times daily. Double dosage, if necessary, for adults.

Powder: Children and adults: Oral suspension: 400 000 to 600 000 units 4 times daily.

Topical Cream and Ointment: Apply cream or ointment liberally to affected areas twice daily or as prescribed by the physician.

Vaginal Cream: 1 applicatorful (500 000 units) daily. In cases of severe infection, repeat application every 12 hours. Generally 2 weeks therapy will be sufficient; however, more prolonged therapy may be necessary. Therapy should be continued during menstruation.

Vaginal Tablets: 1 tablet inserted high in the vagina by means of the applicator once or twice daily for 2 weeks or as required. Therapy should be continued during menstruation.

Supplied: Oral: Drops ℞: Each mL contains: nystatin 100 000 units. Nonmedicinal ingredients: artificial flavoring, calcium disodium EDTA, D&C Yellow #10, magnesium aluminum silicate, methylparaben, polysorbate 80, propylparaben, purified water and sucrose. Energy: <12.6 kJ (3 kcal)/mL. Bottles of 24, 48 and 100 mL with calibrated dropper.

Tablets ℞: Each round, film-coated, pink tablet, engraved "LL" and "N5", contains: nystatin 500 000 units. Nonmedicinal ingredients: cornstarch, ethylcellulose, hydroxypropyl methylcellulose, isopropyl alcohol, light mineral oil, magnesium stearate, stearic acid and titanium dioxide. Bottles of 100.

Powder: For use only in extemporaneous prescription compounding of oral and topical preparations. Nonmedicinal ingredients: talc. Bottles of 1 billion units.

Topical: Cream: Each g contains: nystatin 100 000 units. Nonmedicinal ingredients: emulsifying wax, glycerin, isopropyl myristate, lactic acid, purified water, sodium hydroxide and sorbic acid. Tubes of 15 and 30 g. Jars of 450 mg.

Ointment: Each g contains: nystatin 100 000 units. Nonmedicinal ingredients: light mineral oil and polyethylene. Tubes of 30 g.

Vaginal: Cream ℞: Each g contains: nystatin 100 000 units. Nonmedicinal ingredients: emulsifying wax, glycerin, isopropyl myristate, lactic acid, purified water, sodium hydroxide and sorbic acid. Tubes of 75 g with re-usable applicator.

Tablets ℞: Each oval, pale yellow tablet, engraved "LL" and "N6", contains: nystatin 100 000 units. Nonmedicinal ingredients: isopropyl alcohol, lactose, magnesium stearate, povidone, sorbitol and starch. Boxes of 15 with applicator.

NIMBEX® ℞
Glaxo Wellcome

Cisatracurium Besylate
Nondepolarizing Skeletal Neuromuscular Blocking Agent

Pharmacology: Cisatracurium is an intermediate-acting, nondepolarizing neuromuscular blocking agent for i.v. administration. Cisatracurium, 1 of 10 isomers of atracurium besylate, constitutes approximately 15% of that mixture. Cisatracurium binds competitively to cholinergic receptors on the motor endplate to antagonize the action of acetylcholine, resulting in block of neuromuscular transmission. This action is antagonized by acetylcholinesterase inhibitors such as neostigmine and edrophonium.

Pharmacodynamics: The average ED_{95} (dose required to produce 95% suppression of the adductor pollices muscle twitch response to ulnar nerve stimulation) of cisatracurium is 0.05 mg/kg (range: 0.048 to 0.053 mg/kg) in adults receiving opioid/nitrous oxide/oxygen anesthesia. For comparison, the average ED_{95} for atracurium when also expressed as the parent biscation is 0.17 mg/kg under similar anesthetic conditions. When the dose of cisatracurium is doubled, the clinically effective duration of block increased by approximately 25 to 35 minutes. Once recovery begins, the rate of recovery is independent of dose.

The pharmacodynamics of 2 to 8 times the ED_{95} (0.1 to 0.4 mg/kg) of cisatracurium administered over 5 to 10 seconds during opioid/nitrous oxide/oxygen anesthesia are summarized in Table I.

The neuromuscular blocking potency of cisatracurium is approximately 3-fold that of atracurium besylate. At equipotent doses, the time to maximum block of cisatracurium is up to 2 minutes longer than that of atracurium besylate. The clinically effective duration of action and rate of spontaneous recovery from equipotent doses of cisatracurium and atracurium besylate are similar.

The neuromuscular blocking effect of cisatracurium administered by infusion is potentiated by potent inhalation anesthetics. Isoflurane or enflurane administered with nitrous oxide/oxygen to achieve 1.25 MAC [Minimum Alveolar Concentration] may prolong the clinically effective duration of action of initial and maintenance doses, and decrease the average infusion rate requirement of cisatracurium. The magnitude of these effects may depend on the duration of administration of the volatile agents. Fifteen to 30 minutes of exposure to 1.25 MAC isoflurane or enflurane had minimal effects on the duration of action of initial doses of cisatracurium and

Nimbex (cont'd)

therefore, no adjustment to the initial dose should be necessary when cisatracurium is administered shortly after initiation of volatile agents. In long surgical procedures during enflurane or isoflurane anesthesia, less frequent maintenance dosing, lower maintenance doses, or reduced infusion rates of cisatracurium may be necessary. As for atracurium, the average infusion rate requirement for cisatracurium may be decreased under these circumstances by as much as 30 to 40%.

The onset, duration of action, and recovery profiles of cisatracurium during propofol/oxygen or propofol/nitrous oxide/oxygen anesthesia are similar to those during opioid/nitrous oxide/oxygen anesthesia.

oxygen anesthesia). At 0.1 mg/kg during opioid anesthesia, cisatracurium had a faster onset and shorter duration of action in children than in adults (see Table I). Recovery following reversal is faster in children than in adults.

Hemodynamics Profile: Cisatracurium had no dose-related effects on mean arterial blood pressure (MAP) or heart rate (HR) in healthy adult ASA class 1 or 2 patients, after administration over 5 to 10 seconds at the following doses: $2\times ED_{95}$ (0.10 mg/kg), n=153; $4\times ED_{95}$ (0.20 mg/kg), n=15; $5\times ED_{95}$ (0.25 mg/kg), n=14 or $8\times ED_{95}$ (0.40 mg/kg), n=15.

The safety of $2\times ED_{95}$ (0.1 mg/kg) cisatracurium, administered over 5 to 10 seconds, was evaluated in the following number of patients with cardiovascular disease: New York Heart Association(NYHA) Class I-III: n=45; (NYHA) Class IV: n=16.

Table I—Nimbex

Pharmacodynamic Dose Response[a] of Nimbex Administered Over 5 to 10 Seconds During Opioid/Nitrous Oxide/Oxygen Anesthesia

Initial Dose of Nimbex (mg/kg)	Time to 90% Block (min)	Time to Maximum Block (min)	Time to Spontaneous Recovery[g] 5% Recovery (min)	25% Recovery[b] (min)	95% Recovery (min)	T_4:T_1 Ratio[c] ≥70% (min)	25-75% Recovery Index (min)
Adults							
0.1 ($2\times ED_{95}$) n[d]=98	3.3 (1.0-8.7)	5.0 (1.2-17.2)	33 (15-51)	42 (22-63)	64 (25-93)	64 (32-91)	13 (5-30)
0.15[e] ($3\times ED_{95}$) n= 39	2.6 (1.0-4.4)	3.5 (1.6-6.8)	46 (28-65)	55 (44-74)	76 (60-103)	75 (63-98)	13 (11-16)
0.2 ($4\times ED_{95}$) n=30	2.4 (1.5-4.5)	2.9 (1.9-5.2)	59 (31-103)	65 (43-103)	81 (53-114)	85 (55-114)	12 (2-30)
0.25 ($5\times ED_{95}$) n=15	1.6 (0.8-3.3)	2.0 (1.2-3.7)	70 (58-85)	78 (66-86)	91 (76-109)	97 (82-113)	8 (5-12)
0.4 ($8\times ED_{95}$) n=15	1.5 (1.3-1.8)	1.9 (1.4-2.3)	83 (37-103)	91 (59-107)	121 (110-134)	126 (115-137)	14 (10-18)
Children (2-12 years)							
0.08[f] ($2\times ED_{95}$) n=60	2.2 (1.2-6.8)	3.3 (1.7-9.7)	22 (11-38)	29 (20-46)	52 (37-64)	50 (37-62)	11 (7-15)
0.1 n=16	1.7 (1.3-2.7)	2.8 (1.8-6.7)	21 (13-31)	28 (21-38)	46 (37-58)	44 (36-58)	10 (7-12)

[a]Values shown are medians of means from individual studies. Values in parentheses are ranges of individual patient values.
[b]Clinically effective duration of block.
[c]Train-of-four ratio.
[d]n=the number of patients with Time to Maximum Block data.
[e]Propofol anesthesia.
[f]Halothane anesthesia.
[g]Not all patients (~50%) were evaluated for spontaneous recovery parameters.

Intubation Conditions: When administered during the induction of adequate anesthesia using propofol, nitrous oxide/oxygen, and coinduction agents (e.g., fentanyl, midazolam), good or excellent conditions for tracheal intubation occurred in 67/71 (94%) patients in 1.5 to 2.0 minutes following 0.15 mg/kg ($3\times ED_{95}$) cisatracurium and in 69/80 (87%) patients in 1.5 minutes following 0.2 mg/kg ($4\times ED_{95}$) cisatracurium. Favorable intubation conditions, within 2 minutes, were achieved less frequently with a cisatracurium dose of 0.1 mg/kg ($2\times ED_{95}$).

Maintenance Doses: Repeated administration of maintenance doses or a continuous infusion of cisatracurium for up to 3 hours is not associated with development of tachyphylaxis or cumulative neuromuscular blocking effects. The time needed to recover from successive maintenance doses does not change with the number of doses administered as long as partial recovery is allowed to occur between doses. Maintenance doses can therefore be administered at relatively regular intervals with predictable results. The rate of spontaneous recovery of neuromuscular function after infusion is independent of the duration of infusion and comparable to the rate of recovery following initial doses (see Table I).

Anticholinesterase Antagonism: The neuromuscular block produced by cisatracurium is readily antagonized by anticholinesterase agents once recovery has started. As with other nondepolarizing neuromuscular blocking agents, the more profound the neuromuscular block at the time of reversal, the longer the time required for recovery of neuromuscular function.

Children: In children (2 to 12 years) cisatracurium has a lower ED_{95} than in adults (0.04 mg/kg, halothane/nitrous oxide/

No clinically significant effects on MAP or HR were noted in this patient population at this dose. However, the number of NYHA Class IV patients contributing data was limited.

In a double-blind comparative study involving patients undergoing coronary artery bypass grafting (CABG), there were no clinically significant differences in the hemodynamic effects following equipotent doses of up to 0.3 mg/kg cisatracurium (NYHA Class I-III, n=37) or vecuronium (NYHA Class I-III, n=31; NYHA Class IV, n=1). There is no information regarding the safety of cisatracurium doses above 0.1 mg/kg ($2\times ED_{95}$) in NYHA class IV patients.

Doses greater than $6\times ED_{95}$ have not been studied in patients with cardiovascular disease.

Cisatracurium, at therapeutic doses of 2 to 4 times the ED_{95} (0.1 to 0.2 mg/kg), administered over 5 to 10 seconds, does not cause dose-related elevations in mean plasma histamine concentration. Clinical experience with initial bolus doses greater than 0.2 mg/kg is limited in this regard (0.25 mg/kg, n=15; 0.40 mg/kg, n=15).

No clinically significant changes in MAP or HR were observed following administration of doses up to 0.1 mg/kg cisatracurium over 5 to 10 seconds in children (2 to 12 years) receiving either halothane/nitrous oxide/oxygen or opioid/nitrous oxide/oxygen anesthesia.

Pharmacokinetics: Following i.v. administration of cisatracurium, plasma concentrations of cisatracurium are best described by a 2-compartment open model. Cisatracurium undergoes degradation in the body at physiological pH and temperature by organ-independent Hofmann elimination to form laudanosine and the monoquaternary acrylate metabolite. Laudanosine is further metabolized to many components which are eliminated in the urine. The monoquaternary acrylate metabolite undergoes hydrolysis by nonspecific plasma esterases to form the monoquaternary alcohol metabolite. Cisatracurium does not appear to undergo direct hydrolysis by nonspecific plasma esterases. Organ-independent Hofmann elimination appears to be the predominant pathway for the elimination of cisatracurium. The liver and the kidney play a minor role in the elimination of cisatracurium but are primary routes for elimination of the metabolites.

Tests in which the monoquaternary alcohol metabolite or the monoquaternary acrylate was administered to cats suggest that metabolites are unlikely to produce clinically significant neuromuscular, autonomic, or cardiovascular effects following administration of cisatracurium. Laudanosine, a biologically active metabolite of cisatracurium without neuromuscular blocking activity, produces transient hypotension and, in higher concentrations, cerebral excitatory effects when administered in several species of animals. The relationship between CNS excitation and laudanosine concentrations in humans has not been established. Because cisatracurium is 3 times more potent than atracurium and lower doses are required, maximum concentrations of laudanosine following infusions of cisatracurium to surgical patients were lower (5-to 8-fold) than following atracurium besylate. After adjusting for differences in doses, the AUC for laudanosine was significantly lower following cisatracurium administration than following atracurium besylate administration (i.e., less laudanosine may be formed following cisatracurium than following atracurium besylate). The clinical relevance of this finding is unknown.

Plasma cisatracurium concentrations and neuromuscular block data from 261 patients in 6 studies were combined to develop population estimates of the pharmacokinetic/pharmacodynamic parameters for cisatracurium in healthy adult patients. The plasma clearance was 4.6 mL/min/kg and the volume of distribution at steady-state was 145 mL/kg in healthy adult patients receiving opioid/nitrous oxide/oxygen anesthesia. Results from population pharmacokinetic/pharmacodynamic analyses and from conventional pharmacokinetic analyses of cisatracurium in healthy adult patients and in patient subpopulations (e.g., geriatric, pediatric, obese) are described below.

Dose Proportionality: Conventional pharmacokinetic analysis from a study of 10 healthy adult patients receiving 0.1 mg/kg ($2\times ED_{95}$) cisatracurium and 10 healthy adult patients receiving 0.2 mg/kg ($4\times ED_{95}$) cisatracurium indicated no statistically significant differences in the pharmacokinetic parameters between the 2 groups (see Table II on following page). In addition, population pharmacokinetic/pharmacodynamic analyses revealed no statistically significant effect of dose on plasma clearance between 0.1 mg/kg and 0.4 mg/kg (2× to $8\times ED_{95}$) doses of cisatracurium. The pharmacokinetics are linear between these doses of cisatracurium (i.e., plasma concentrations are approximately proportional to dose).

Geriatrics: The results of conventional pharmacokinetic analysis from a study of 12 healthy elderly patients (≥65 years) and 12 healthy young adult patients (18 to 50 years) receiving a single i.v. dose of 0.1 mg/kg ($2\times ED_{95}$) cisatracurium are summarized in Table III (on following page). Plasma clearance of cisatracurium was not affected by age; however, the volume of distribution was slightly larger in elderly patients than in young patients, resulting in a slightly longer half-life for cisatracurium. The time to maximum block was approximately 1 minute slower in elderly patients than in young patients. These minor differences in pharmacokinetics of cisatracurium between elderly and young adult patients were not associated with clinically significant differences in the recovery profile of cisatracurium.

Hepatic Diseases: Organ-independent Hofmann elimination is the predominant pathway for the elimination of cisatracurium. Table IV (on following page) summarizes the conventional pharmacokinetic analysis from a study of 13 patients with end-stage liver disease undergoing liver transplantation and 11 healthy adult patients undergoing elective surgery. The slightly larger volume of distribution in liver transplant patients was associated with slightly higher plasma clearance of cisatracurium. The parallel changes in these parameters resulted in no difference in half-life.

The time to maximum block was approximately 1 minute faster in liver transplant patients than in healthy adult patients. These minor differences in pharmacokinetics were not associated with clinically significant changes in the recovery profile of cisatracurium.

The time to maximum block was approximately 1 minute faster in liver transplant patients than in healthy adult patients receiving 0.1 mg/kg cisatracurium. These minor differences in pharmacokinetics were not associated with clinically significant changes in the recovery profile of cisatracurium.

Table II—Nimbex

Pharmacokinetic Parameters* of Cisatracurium in Healthy Adult Patients (Opioid/Nitrous Oxide/Oxygen Anesthesia)

Parameter	Initial Dose of Nimbex (mg/kg) 0.1 (2×ED_{95}) n=10	0.2 (4×ED_{95}) n=10
Elimination Half-life ($t_{1/2\beta}$, min)	22.4±2.7	25.5±4.1
Volume of Distribution at Steady-State (mL/kg)	144±34	121±22
Plasma Clearance (mL/min/kg)	5.3±1.2	4.7±0.7

*Values presented are mean±S.D.

Table III—Nimbex

Pharmacokinetic Parameters[a] of Cisatracurium in Healthy Elderly and Young Adult Patients Following 0.1 mg/kg (2×ED_{95}) Nimbex (Isoflurane/Nitrous Oxide/Oxygen Anesthesia)

Parameter	Elderly Patients n=12	Young Adult Patients n=12
Elimination Half-life ($t_{1/2\beta}$, min)	25.8±3.6[b]	22.1±2.5
Volume of Distribution at Steady-State (mL/kg)	156±17[b]	133±15
Plasma Clearance (mL/min/kg)	5.7±1.0	5.3±0.9

[a]Values presented are mean±S.D.
[b]$p<0.05$ for comparisons between the 2 groups.

Table IV—Nimbex

Pharmacokinetic Parameters[a] of Cisatracurium in Healthy Adult Patients and in Patients Undergoing Liver Transplantation Following 0.1 mg/kg (2×ED_{95}) Nimbex (Isoflurane/Nitrous Oxide/Oxygen Anesthesia)

Parameter	Healthy Adult Patients	Liver Transplant Patients
Elimination Half-life ($t_{1/2\beta}$, min)	23.5±3.5	24.4±2.9
Volume of Distribution at Steady-State (mL/kg)	161±23	195±38[b]
Plasma Clearance (mL/min/kg)	5.7±0.8	6.6±1.1[b]

[a]Values presented are mean±S.D.
[b]$p<0.05$ for comparisons between liver transplant patients and healthy adult patients.

The $t_{1/2\beta}$ values of metabolites are longer in patients with hepatic disease and concentrations may be higher after long-term administration.

Renal Disease: Results from a conventional pharmacokinetic study of 13 healthy adult patients and 15 patients with end-stage renal disease (ESRD) undergoing elective surgery are summarized in Table V. The pharmacokinetics of cisatracurium were similar in healthy adult patients and ESRD patients.

The time to 90% block was approximately 1 minute slower in ESRD patients following 0.1 mg/kg cisatracurium. There was no difference in the duration or rate of recovery between ESRD and healthy adult patients.

The $t_{1/2\beta}$ values of metabolites are longer in patients with renal failure and concentrations may be higher after long-term administration.

Population pharmacokinetic analysis revealed that patients with creatinine clearances ≤70 mL/min had a slower rate of equilibration between plasma concentrations and neuromuscular block than patients with normal renal function; therefore, the predicted time to 90% T_1 suppression may be slightly slower in patients with renal dysfunction. There was no clinically significant alteration in the recovery profile of cisatracurium in patients with renal dysfunction. The recovery profile of cisatracurium is unchanged in the presence of renal or hepatic failure, which is consistent with predominantly organ-independent elimination.

Children: Population pharmacokinetic analysis of cisatracurium revealed a plasma clearance of 5.9 mL/kg/min and a volume of distribution at steady-state of 125 mL/kg in 20 healthy pediatric patients during halothane anesthesia. These minor differences were associated with a faster time to onset and a shorter duration of cisatracurium-induced neuromuscular block in pediatric patients.

Other Patient Factors: Population pharmacokinetic/pharmacodynamic analysis revealed that gender and obesity were associated with statistically significant effects on the pharmacokinetics and/or pharmacodynamics of cisatracurium; these factors were not associated with clinically significant alterations in the predicted onset or recovery profile of cisatracurium. The use of inhalation anesthesia (i.e., enflurane or isoflurane) was associated with statistically significant effects on the pharmacokinetics and pharmacodynamics of cisatracurium. These changes were associated with a slightly faster predicted time to 90% suppression for patients under inhalation anesthesia, but there were no clinically significant alterations in the predicted recovery profile of cisatracurium.

Indications: As an adjunct to general anesthesia, to facilitate nonemergency endotracheal intubation, and to provide skeletal muscle relaxation during surgery or mechanical ventilation.

Contraindications: Patients known to have an allergic hypersensitivity to cisatracurium, atracurium besylate or other bis-benzylisoquinolinium agents. Use of cisatracurium from vials containing preservative is contraindicated in patients with a known hypersensitivity to benzyl alcohol.

Warnings: Cisatracurium should be administered in carefully adjusted dosage by or under the supervision of experienced clinicians who are familiar with the drug's actions and the possible complications of its use. The drug should not be administered unless personnel and facilities for resuscitation and life support (tracheal intubation, artificial ventilation, oxygen therapy), and an antagonist of cisatracurium are immediately available. It is recommended that a peripheral nerve stimulator be used to measure neuromuscular function during the administration of cisatracurium in order to monitor drug effect, determine the need for additional doses, and confirm recovery from neuromuscular block.

Cisatracurium has no known effect on consciousness, pain threshold, or cerebration. To avoid distress to the patient, neuromuscular block should not be induced before unconsciousness.

Cisatracurium injection is acidic (pH 3.25 to 3.65) and should not be mixed with alkaline solutions having a pH greater than 8.5 (e.g., barbiturate solutions). Cisatracurium is also hypotonic and must not be administered into the infusion line of a blood transfusion.

The 10 mL multiple dose vials of cisatracurium contain benzyl alcohol. In newborn infants, benzyl alcohol has been associated with an increased incidence of neurological and other complications which are sometimes fatal. Single use vials (20 mL) of cisatracurium do not contain benzyl alcohol. **Cisatracurium has not been studied in children less than 2 years old.**

Intensive Care Unit: To reduce the possibility of prolonged neuromuscular blockade and other complications that might occur following long-term use in the ICU, cisatracurium or any other neuromuscular relaxant should be administered in carefully adjusted doses by or under the supervision of experienced clinicians who are familiar with its actions and with appropriate peripheral nerve stimulator muscle monitoring techniques.

In patients with neuromuscular disease such as myasthenia gravis or myasthenic (Eaton-Lambert) syndrome, small doses of nondepolarizing neuromuscular blocking agents may have profound effects. In these patients, and patients with conditions in which prolonged neuromuscular blockade is a possibility (e.g., neuromuscular disease, carcinomatosis, severe cachexia or debilitation), the use of a peripheral nerve stimulator and a first dose of not more than 0.02 mg/kg cisatracurium is recommended to assess the level of neuromuscular block and to monitor dosage requirements.

Precautions: General: Because of its intermediate onset of action, cisatracurium is not recommended for rapid sequence endotracheal intubation.

Recommended doses of cisatracurium have no clinically significant effects on heart rate; therefore, cisatracurium will not counteract the bradycardia produced by many anesthetic agents or by vagal stimulation.

Patients with burns have been shown to develop resistance to nondepolarizing neuromuscular blocking agents, including atracurium. The extent of altered response depends upon the size of the burn and the time elapsed since the burn injury. Cisatracurium has not been studied in patients with burns; however, based on its structural similarity to atracurium, the possibility of increased dosing requirements and shortened duration of action must be considered if cisatracurium is administered to burn patients.

Patients subjected to hypothermia may necessitate a reduction in the rate of infusion of cisatracurium (see Dosage).

Patients with hemiparesis or paraparesis also may demonstrate resistance to nondepolarizing neuromuscular blocking agents in affected limbs. To avoid inaccurate dosing, neuromuscular monitoring should be performed on the nonparetic limb.

Acid-base and/or serum electrolyte abnormalities may potentiate or antagonize the action of neuromuscular blocking agents. The action of neuromuscular blocking agents may be enhanced by magnesium salts administered for the management of toxemia of pregnancy.

As cisatracurium has not been studied in patients with asthma or a history of severe anaphylactic reactions, it should be administered with caution to these patient groups.

No data are available to support the use of cisatracurium by i.m. injection.

Malignant Hyperthermia (MH): In a study of MH-susceptible pigs, cisatracurium besylate did not trigger MH. Cisatracurium has not been studied in MH-susceptible patients. Because MH can develop in the absence of established triggering agents, the clinician should be prepared to recognize and treat MH in any patient undergoing general anesthesia.

Long-Term Use in the Intensive Care Unit (ICU): There is limited information regarding the safety and efficacy of long-term infusion of cisatracurium during mechanical ventilation in the ICU (up to 2 days n=37, 2 to 4 days n=19, 4 to 6 days n=12) and no information on its use beyond 6 days. Thus dosage recommendations cannot be made at this time. In rare cases, long-term use of neuromuscular blocking drugs to facilitate mechanical ventilation in ICU settings has been associated with prolonged paralysis and/or skeletal muscle weakness that is first noted during attempts to wean patients from the ventilator. In these patients, the actions of the neuromuscular blocking agent may be enhanced by other drugs (e.g., broad spectrum antibiotics, narcotics and/or steroids) or by conditions such as acid-base or electrolyte imbalance, hypoxic episodes of varying duration, or extreme debilitation. Additionally patients immobilized for extended periods frequently develop symptoms consistent with disuse muscle atrophy. The recovery picture may vary from regaining movement and strength in all muscles to initial recovery of movement of the facial muscles and small muscles of the extremities then to the remaining muscles. In rare cases, recovery may involve an extended period of time or even require rehabilitation. Therefore, when there is a need for long-term mechanical ventilation, the benefits to risk ratio of neuromuscular blockade must be considered. The syndrome of critical illness polyneuropathy associated with sepsis and multiorgan failure may be associated with prolonged muscle paralysis, but can also occur without the use of muscle relaxants. Thus, the role of muscle relaxants in the etiology of prolonged paralysis in the ICU is not known with certainty. Continuous infusion or intermittent bolus dosing to support

Table V—Nimbex

Pharmacokinetic Parameters* for Cisatracurium in Healthy Adult Patients and in Patients with End-Stage Renal Disease (ESRD) Receiving 0.1 mg/kg (2×ED_{95}) Nimbex (Opioid/Nitrous Oxide/Oxygen Anesthesia)

Parameter	Healthy Adult Patients	ESRD Patients
Elimination Half-life ($t_{1/2\beta}$, min)	29.4±4.1	32.3±6.3
Volume of distribution at Steady-State (mL/kg)	149±35	160±32
Plasma Clearance (mL/min/kg)	4.66±0.86	4.26±0.62

*Values presented are mean±S.D.

Nimbex (cont'd)

long-term mechanical ventilation has not been studied sufficiently to support dosage recommendations.

Whenever the use of cisatracurium or any neuromuscular blocking agent is contemplated in the ICU, it is recommended that a peripheral nerve stimulator be used to continuously monitor neuromuscular transmission during administration and recovery. Additional doses of cisatracurium or any other neuromuscular blocking agent should not be given before there is evidence of the return of the first twitch response to peripheral nerve stimulation. If no response is elicited, the infusion should be discontinued until a response returns.

Renal and Hepatic Disease: No clinically significant alterations in the recovery profile were observed in patients with renal dysfunction or in patients with end-stage liver disease following a 0.1 mg/kg (2×ED_{95}) dose of cisatracurium. The onset time was approximately 1 minute faster in patients with end-stage liver disease and approximately 1 minute slower in patients with renal dysfunction than in healthy adult control patients.

Pregnancy: Teratogenic Effects: Teratology testing in rats revealed no maternal or fetal toxicity or teratogenic effects. There are no adequate and well-controlled studies of cisatracurium in pregnant women. Because animal studies are not always predictive of human response, cisatracurium should be used during pregnancy only if clearly needed.

Labor and Delivery: The use of cisatracurium during labor, vaginal delivery, or cesarean section has not been studied in humans and it is not known whether cisatracurium administered to the mother has effects on the fetus. Doses of 0.2 or 0.4 mg/kg (4 or 8× human ED_{95}) cisatracurium given to female beagles undergoing cesarean section resulted in negligible levels of cisatracurium in umbilical vessel blood of neonates and no deleterious effects on the pups.

Lactation: It is not known whether cisatracurium besylate is excreted in human milk. Because many drugs are excreted in human milk, caution should be exercised following administration of cisatracurium to a nursing woman.

Children: Cisatracurium has not been studied in children under 2 years of age (see Pharmacology for clinical experience and Dosage for recommendations for use in children 2 to 12 years of age).

Geriatrics: Cisatracurium was safely administered during clinical trials to 130 elderly (≥65 years) patients, including a subset of patients with significant cardiovascular disease (see Precautions, General).

Minor differences in the pharmacokinetics of cisatracurium between elderly and young adult patients are not associated with clinically significant differences in the recovery profile of cisatracurium following a single 0.1 mg/kg (2×ED_{95}) dose; the time to maximum block is approximately 1 minute slower in elderly patients (see Pharmacology, Pharmacokinetics).

The effects of hemofiltration, hemodialysis, and hemoperfusion on plasma levels of cisatracurium and its metabolites are unknown.

<u>*Drug Interactions*</u>: Succinylcholine: The use of cisatracurium prior to succinylcholine, for the purpose of attenuating succinylcholine-induced side effects, has not been studied.

The use of cisatracurium following varying degrees of recovery from succinylcholine-induced neuromuscular block has been assessed in a limited number of patients. Administration of 0.1 mg/kg (2×ED_{95}) cisatracurium at 10% (n=15) or 95% recovery (n=15) following an intubating dose of succinylcholine (1 mg/kg) produced ≥95% neuromuscular block. The time of onset of maximum block following cisatracurium is approximately 2 minutes faster with prior administration of succinylcholine. Prior administration of succinylcholine had no effect on the duration of neuromuscular block following initial or maintenance bolus doses of cisatracurium. Cisatracurium infusion requirements were comparable or slightly greater in patients who received succinylcholine prior to the cisatracurium infusions, in contrast to patients who did not receive succinylcholine.

Other nondepolarizing Muscle Relaxants: Although not studied systematically in clinical trials, no drug interactions were observed when vecuronium, pancuronium, or atracurium were administered following varying degrees of recovery from single doses or infusions of cisatracurium.

Inhalation Anesthetics: Isoflurane or enflurane administered with nitrous oxide/oxygen to achieve 1.25 MAC [Minimum Alveolar Concentration] may prolong the clinically effective duration of action of initial and maintenance doses of cisatracurium, and decrease the average infusion rate of cisatracurium. The magnitude of these effects may depend on the duration of administration of the volatile agents. Fifteen to 30 minutes of exposure to 1.25 MAC isoflurane or enflurane had minimal effects on the duration of action of initial doses of cisatracurium. Hence, no adjustment to the initial dose should be necessary when cisatracurium is administered shortly after initiation of volatile agents. In long surgical procedures during enflurane or isoflurane anesthesia, less frequent maintenance dosing, lower maintenance doses, or reduced infusion rates of cisatracurium may be necessary. The average infusion rate requirement may be decreased by as much as 30 to 40%.

I.V. Anesthetics: In clinical studies, propofol had no effect on the duration of action or dosing requirements for cisatracurium.

Anticonvulsants: Resistance to the neuromuscular blocking action of nondepolarizing neuromuscular blocking agents has been demonstrated in patients chronically administered phenytoin or carbamazepine. While the effects of chronic phenytoin or carbamazepine therapy on the action of cisatracurium are unknown, slightly shorter durations of neuromuscular block may be anticipated and infusion rate requirements may be higher.

Other drugs: The neuromuscular blocking action of nondepolarizing agents such as cisatracurium may be enhanced by certain antibiotics (e.g., aminoglycosides, tetracyclines, bacitracin, polymyxins, lincomycin, clindamycin, colistin, and sodium colistemethate), magnesium salts, lithium, local anesthetics, procainamide, and quinidine.

Drug/Laboratory Test Interactions: None known.

Adverse Effects: Observed in Clinical Trials of Surgical Patients: Adverse experiences were uncommon among the 908 surgical patients who received cisatracurium in conjunction with other drugs in U.S. and European clinical studies in the course of a wide variety of procedures in patients receiving opioid, propofol, or inhalation anesthesia. The following adverse experiences were judged by investigators during the clinical trials to have a possible causal relationship to cisatracurium. (incidence less than 1%): Cardiovascular: flushing (0.2%), hypotension (0.2%) and bradycardia (0.4%).

Respiratory: bronchospasm (0.2%).

Dermatological: rash (0.1%).

Observed During Clinical Practice: In addition to events reported from clinical trials, the following events have been identified during post-approval use of cisatracurium besylate in conjunction with one or more anesthetic agents in clinical practice. Because they are reported voluntarily from a population of unknown size, estimates of frequency cannot be made. These events are reported due to their seriousness, frequency of reporting, or potential causal relationship to cisatracurium besylate.

General: Hypersensitivity reactions including anaphylactic or anaphylactoid responses which, in some cases were severe.

Musculoskeletal: Prolonged neuromuscular block, inadequate neuromuscular block.

Overdose: Symptoms: Overdosage with neuromuscular blocking agents may result in neuromuscular block beyond the time needed for surgery and anesthesia.

Treatment: The primary treatment is maintenance of a patent airway and controlled ventilation until recovery of normal neuromuscular function is assured. Once recovery from neuromuscular block begins, further recovery may be facilitated by administration of an anticholinesterase agent (e.g., neostigmine, edrophonium) in conjunction with an appropriate anticholinergic agent (see Antagonism of Neuromuscular Block below). A peripheral nerve stimulator should be used to monitor recovery.

Antagonism of Neuromuscular Block: **Antagonists (such as neostigmine and edrophonium) should not be administered when complete neuromuscular block is evident or suspected. The use of a peripheral nerve stimulator to evaluate recovery and antagonism of neuromuscular block is recommended. The time required for anticholinesterase-mediated recovery is longer for reversals attempted at deeper levels of blockade.**

Administration of 0.04 to 0.07 mg/kg neostigmine at approximately 10% recovery from neuromuscular block (range: 0 to 15%) produced 95% recovery of the muscle twitch response and a T_4:T_1 ratio ≥70% in an average of 9 to 10 minutes. The time from 25% recovery of the muscle twitch response to a T_4:T_1 ratio ≥70% following these doses of neostigmine averaged 7 minutes. The mean 25 to 75% recovery index following reversal was 3 to 4 minutes.

Administration of 1.0 mg/kg edrophonium at approximately 25% recovery from neuromuscular block (range: 16 to 30%) produced 95% recovery and a T_4:T_1 ratio ≥70% in an average of 3 to 5 minutes.

Patients administered antagonists should be evaluated for evidence of adequate clinical recovery (e.g., 5-second head lift and grip strength). Ventilation must be supported until no longer required.

The onset of antagonism may be delayed in the presence of debilitation, cachexia, carcinomatosis, and the concomitant use of certain broad spectrum antibiotics, or anesthetic agents and other drugs which enhance neuromuscular block or separately cause respiratory depression (see Precautions, Drug Interactions). Under such circumstances the management is the same as that of prolonged neuromuscular block (see Overdose).

Dosage: Should be administered only by i.v. route. This drug should be administered by or under the supervision of experienced clinicians familiar with the use of neuromuscular blocking agents. Dosage must be individualized in each case.

To avoid patient distress, cisatracurium should **not** be administered prior to the induction of unconsciousness. It should **not** be mixed in the same syringe or administered simultaneously through the same needle with alkaline solutions (e.g., barbiturate solutions).

Individualization of Dosages: **The dosage information provided below is intended as a guide only. Doses should be individualized and a peripheral nerve stimulator should be used to measure neuromuscular function during administration in order to monitor drug effect, to determine the need for additional doses, and to confirm recovery from neuromuscular block.** The use of a peripheral nerve stimulator will permit the most advantageous use of cisatracurium, minimize the possibility of overdosage or underdosage, and assist in the evaluation of recovery.

Adults: Initial Doses: One of 2 intubating doses may be chosen, based on the desired time to intubation and the anticipated length of surgery. Doses of 0.15 mg/kg (3×ED_{95}) and 0.20 mg/kg (4×ED_{95}), as components of a propofol/nitrous oxide/oxygen induction-intubation technique, each may produce generally good or excellent conditions for tracheal intubation in 1.5 to 2 minutes. The clinically effective durations of action for 0.15 and 0.20 mg/kg of cisatracurium during propofol anesthesia are 55 minutes (range: 44 to 74 minutes) and 61 minutes (range: 41 to 81 minutes), respectively. Lower doses may result in a longer time for the development of satisfactory intubation conditions. In addition to the dose of the neuromuscular blocking agent, the presence of coinduction agents (e.g., fentanyl and midazolam) and the depth of anesthesia are factors that can influence intubation conditions. Doses of cisatracurium up to 8 times the ED_{95} (0.40 mg/kg) have been administered to a limited number of healthy adult patients (n=15) and the larger doses are associated with a longer clinically effective duration of action (see Pharmacology).

Cardiovascular Disease: Doses of up to 0.3 mg/kg (6×ED_{95}) were found to have no significant hemodynamic effects in patients with cardiovascular disease (NYHA Class I-III)(see Pharmacology). However, doses higher than 0.1 mg/kg (2×ED_{95}) have not been studies in NYHA Class IV patients. At a dose of 0.1 mg/kg an extension of the interval between administration of cisatracurium and the intubation attempt may be required to achieve satisfactory intubation conditions.

Geriatrics and Renal Failure Patients: Because a slower time to onset of complete neuromuscular block was observed in elderly patients and in patients with renal failure, extending the interval between administration of cisatracurium and the intubation attempt for these patients may be required to achieve adequate intubation conditions.

Maintenance Doses: A dose of 0.03 mg/kg is recommended for maintenance of neuromuscular block during prolonged surgical procedures. Maintenance doses of 0.03 mg/kg each sustain neuromuscular block for approximately 20 minutes. Although maintenance dosing is generally required 40 to 50 minutes following an initial dose of 0.15 mg/kg (3×ED_{95}), and 50 to 60 minutes following an initial dose of 0.20 mg/kg (4×ED_{95}), the need for maintenance doses should be determined by clinical criteria. For a shorter or longer duration of action, smaller or larger maintenance doses may be administered.

Isoflurane or enflurane administered with nitrous oxide/oxygen to achieve 1.25 MAC [Minimum Alveolar Concentration] may prolong the clinically effective duration of action of initial and maintenance doses. The magnitude of these effects may depend on the duration of administration of the volatile agents. Fifteen to 30 minutes of exposure to 1.25 MAC isoflurane or enflurane had minimal effects on the duration of action of initial doses of cisatracurium; therefore, no adjustment to the initial dose should be necessary when cisatracurium is administered shortly after initiation of volatile agents. In long surgical procedures during enflurane or isoflurane anesthesia, less frequent maintenance dosing or lower maintenance doses of cisatracurium may be necessary.

No adjustments to the initial dose of cisatracurium are required when used in patients receiving propofol anesthesia.

Children: Initial Doses: The recommended dose for children 2 to 12 years of age is 0.10 mg/kg administered over 5 to 10 seconds during either halothane or opioid anesthesia. When administered during stable opioid/nitrous oxide/oxygen anesthesia, 0.10 mg/kg produces maximum neuromuscular block in an average of 2.8 minutes (range: 1.8 to 6.7 minutes) and clinically effective block for an average of 28 minutes (range: 21 to 38 minutes). Cisatracurium has not been studied in children under 2 years of age.

Special Conditions: Based on the known action of cisatracurium and other neuromuscular blocking agents, the following factors should be considered when administering cisatracurium.

Renal and Hepatic Disease: Doses for patients with renal disease or hepatic disease are as recommended for healthy adult patients. However, see Precautions.

Drugs or Conditions Causing Potentiation of, or Resistance to, Neuromuscular Block: Persons with certain pre-existing conditions or receiving certain drugs may require individualization of dosing (see Precautions).

Burns: Patients with burns have been shown to develop resistance to nondepolarizing neuromuscular blocking agents, and may require individualization of dosing (see Precautions).

Hypothermia: The rate of infusion of atracurium required to maintain adequate surgical relaxation in patients undergoing coronary artery bypass surgery with induced hypothermia (25 to 28°C) is approximately half the rate required during normothermia. Based on the structural similarity between cisatracurium and atracurium, a similar effect on the infusion rate of cisatracurium may be expected.

Use by Continuous Infusion: Infusion in the Operating Room (OR): After administration of an initial bolus dose, a diluted solution can be administered by continuous infusion to adults and children (≥ 2 years of age) for maintenance of neuromuscular block during extended surgical procedures. Infusion should be individualized for each patient. The rate of administration should be adjusted according to the patient's response as determined by peripheral nerve stimulation. Accurate dosing is best achieved using a precision infusion device.

Infusion should be initiated only after early evidence of spontaneous recovery from the initial bolus dose. An initial infusion rate of 3 μg/kg/min may be required to rapidly counteract the spontaneous recovery of neuromuscular function. Thereafter, a rate of 1 to 2 μg/kg/min should be adequate to maintain continuous neuromuscular block in the range of 89 to 99% in most pediatric and adult patients under opioid/nitrous oxide/oxygen anesthesia.

Reduction of the infusion rate by up to 30 to 40% should be considered when cisatracurium is administered during stable isoflurane or enflurane anesthesia (administered with nitrous oxide/oxygen to achieve 1.25 MAC). Greater reductions in the infusion rate of cisatracurium may be required with longer durations of administration of isoflurane or enflurane.

Spontaneous recovery from neuromuscular block following discontinuation of cisatracurium infusion may be expected to proceed at a rate comparable to that following administration of a single bolus dose.

Infusion Rate Tables: The amount of infusion solution required per minute will depend upon the concentration of cisatracurium in the infusion solution, the desired dose and the patient's weight. The contribution of the infusion solution to the fluid requirements of the patient also must be considered. Tables VI and VII provide guidelines for delivery in mL/h (equivalent to microdrops/min when 60 microdrops=1 mL) of solutions in concentrations of 0.1 mg/mL (10 mg/100 mL) or 0.4 mg/mL (40 mg/100 mL).

Stability and Storage Recommendation: Cisatracurium slowly loses potency with time at a rate of approximately 5% per year under refrigeration (5°C). **Cisatracurium should be stored under refrigeration (2 to 8°C)** and protected from light to preserve potency. **Protect from freezing.**

The rate of loss in potency increases to approximately 5% per month at 25°C. If removed from refrigeration to room temperature storage (25°C), cisatracurium must be used within 21 days, even if rerefrigerated.

Parenteral Products: Y-site Administration: Cisatracurium Injection is acidic (pH=3.25 to 3.65) and may not be compatible with alkaline solution having a pH greater than 8.5 (e.g., barbiturate solutions).

Studies have shown that cisatracurium injection is compatible with: 5% Dextrose Injection USP; 0.9% Sodium Chloride Injection USP; 5% Dextrose and 0.9% Sodium Chloride Injection USP; Sufenta Injection, diluted as directed; Alfenta Injection, diluted as directed; Sublimaze Injection, diluted as directed; Versed Injection, diluted as directed; Droperidol Injection USP, diluted as directed.

Cisatracurium Injection is not compatible with Diprivan Injection or Toradol Injection for Y-site administration. Studies of other parenteral products have not been conducted.

Dilution Stability: Cisatracurium Injection diluted to 0.1 mg/mL in 5% Dextrose Injection USP, 0.9% Sodium Chloride Injection USP, or 5% Dextrose and 0.9% Sodium Chloride Injection USP, may be stored either under refrigeration or at room temperature for 24 hours without significant loss of potency. Dilutions to 0.1 mg/mL in 5% Dextrose and Lactated Ringer's Injection may be stored under refrigeration for 24 hours.

Cisatracurium Injection should not be diluted in Lactated Ringer's Injection USP due to chemical instability.

Parenteral drug products should be inspected visually for particulate matter and discoloration prior to administration whenever solution and container permit. Solutions which are not clear, or contain visible particulates, should not be used.

Supplied: 2 mg/mL: Each mL of a sterile, nonpyrogenic, aqueous solution, colorless to slightly yellow or greenish-yellow, contains: cisatracurium 2 mg (as besylate). Nonmedicinal ingredients: benzyl alcohol (see Warnings concerning newborn infants) and water for injection. Multidose vials of 10 mL.

10 mg/mL: Each mL of a sterile, nonpyrogenic, aqueous solution, colorless to slightly yellow or greenish-yellow, contains: cisatracurium 10 mg (as besylate). Nonmedicinal ingredients: water for injection. Benzyl alcohol-free. Single dose vials of 20 mL.

Store under refrigeration (2 to 8°) and protect fom light to preserve potency. Protect from freezing.

Reviewed 1998

Table VI—Nimbex

Nimbex Infusion Rates for Maintenance of Neuromuscular Block During Opioid/Nitrous Oxide/Oxygen Anesthesia Using Nimbex Injection at a Concentration of 0.1 mg/mL

Patient Weight (kg)	Drug Delivery Rate (μg/kg/min) 1.0	1.5	2.0	3.0	5.0
	Infusion Delivery Rate (mL/h)				
10	6	9	12	18	30
45	27	41	54	81	135
70	42	63	84	126	210
100	60	90	120	180	300

Table VII—Nimbex

Nimbex Infusion Rates for Maintenance of Neuromuscular Block During Opioid/Nitrous Oxide/Oxygen Anesthesia Using Nimbex Injection at a Concentration of 0.4 mg/mL

Patient Weight (kg)	Drug Delivery Rate (μg/kg/min) 1.0	1.5	2.0	3.0	5.0
	Infusion Delivery Rate (mL/h)				
10	1.5	2.3	3.0	4.5	7.5
45	6.8	10.1	13.5	20.3	33.8
70	10.5	15.8	21.0	31.5	52.5
100	15.0	22.5	30.0	45.0	75.0

NIMOTOP® Ⓟ
NIMOTOP® I.V. Ⓟ

Bayer

Nimodipine

Adjunct in the Management of Subarachnoid Hemorrhage—Calcium Channel Blocking Agent

Pharmacology: Delayed neurologic deterioration secondary to cerebral ischemic deficits is believed to be a major determinant of outcome in patients who survive their initial subarachnoid hemorrhage (SAH). Nimodipine is a calcium channel blocker of the dihydropyridine group. It appears to have a more marked effect on the cerebral circulation than on the peripheral circulation. Since it acts on the vascular smooth muscle tone by modifying the contractile process which is dependent upon the movement of extracellular calcium into the cells during depolarization, it was tested in patients with SAH in an effort to improve the neurologic outcome in these patients. Clinical studies with nimodipine support its usefulness as an adjunct in the management of some patients with SAH from ruptured aneurysm by improving their neurologic outcome, particularly in Hunt and Hess grades 1 to 3 patients (consult the manufacturer for further information).

A prospective, multicentre, randomized, double-blind placebo-controlled study was conducted with nimodipine in patients with traumatic head injuries in which traumatic subarachnoid hemorrhage (tSAH) was confirmed by computer tomography (CT) scanning. Within 12 hours of head injury, patients received either a sequential course of i.v. nimodipine (2 mg/hour) for 7 to 10 days followed by oral nimodipine (60 mg q4h) until day 21 or matching placebo. The majority of the patients (approximately 80%) in both nimodipine and placebo groups did not receive cytochrome P450 enzyme-inducing anticonvulsants (i.e., phenytoin or carbamazepine) as a concomitant medication. The incidence of unfavorable outcomes (death, severe disability, vegetative state as defined by the Glasgow Outcome Scale) at 6 months was 25% in nimodipine treated patients (n=60) vs 46% in placebo treated patients (p=0.02, n=61). The incidence of favorable outcomes (good recovery or moderate disability) in the nimodipine group was 75% vs 54% in placebo treated patients (p=0.02) (consult the manufacturer for further information). Due to the small number of patients in this study, the results can only be considered to be preliminary.

The actual mechanism of the possible beneficial effect of nimodipine is, however, unknown. The original rationale for using nimodipine after SAH was to reduce cerebral arterial spasm, but available evidence indicates that nimodipine does not reduce the incidence or severity of cerebral spasm as seen on angiography.

Pharmacokinetics: Nimodipine is rapidly and completely absorbed after oral administration of the capsule. Because of a strong first-pass metabolism in the liver, only about 10% of the unchanged drug enters the systemic circulation. The drug is detectable in plasma 15 minutes after oral administration, and peak levels occur within 90 minutes. The earlier elimination half-life is approximately 2 hours indicating the need for frequent dosing, although the terminal elimination half-life is 8 to 9 hours. The absolute bioavailability of nimodipine capsule is approximately 13%. No change in the average maximum and minimum plasma concentration occurred after a repeated oral dosage regimen of 3 times a day for 7 days in volunteers.

Nimodipine injection exhibits a terminal elimination half-life of about 1 hour and a plasma clearance of approximately 125 L/hour.

Nimodipine is metabolized through the cytochrome P450 system, mainly by the CYP 3A4 isoenzyme.

Nimodipine is 99% bound to serum proteins. Approximately 80% is excreted in the bile, and 20% by the kidney.The metabolites of nimodipine are believed to be either inactive or considerably less active than the parent compound.

Indications: Nimodipine may be useful as an adjunct to improve the neurologic outcome following subarachnoid hemorrhage (SAH) from ruptured intracranial aneurysm.

Contraindications: Hypersensitivity to nimodipine.

Nimotop (cont'd)

Warnings: Intestinal pseudo-obstruction (paralytic ileus) has been reported rarely. A causal relationship to nimodipine cannot be ruled out. In 3 cases, the condition responded to conservative management, but a fourth patient required surgical decompression of the extremely distended colon.

Management of Patients with SAH: In view of the potential usefulness of nimodipine in improving the neurologic outcome in some patients with SAH, an early decision (whenever possible within 4 days of the ictus) should be made regarding the use of the drug. Since nimodipine is an adjunct in the management of SAH, an early assessment and a complete management program for the individual patient, including the possible indication of neurosurgery, are imperative.

Blood Pressure: Nimodipine has the hemodynamic effects of a calcium channel blocker. In the course of clinical studies in patients with SAH, hypotension was reported in 6.6% of patients with Hunt and Hess grades III to V given 90 mg doses (n=91), and in 7.5% of patients with grades I and II using 30 to 60 mg doses (n=255). A fall in blood pressure requiring discontinuation of the drug was reported in 2.2% of the patients in the former group. Hypertensive patients may be more susceptible to a lowering of the blood pressure. Blood pressure should, nevertheless, always be carefully monitored during treatment with nimodipine. The use of nimodipine is, however, not generally recommended in patients taking antihypertensive drugs, including other calcium channel blockers, since it may potentiate the effects of these medications.

Simultaneous i.v. administration of beta blockers can lead to mutual potentiation of negative inotropic effects and even to decompensated heart failure.

Patients with Myocardial Infarction: Since there has not been a study of nimodipine in acute myocardial infarction reported, similar effects of nimodipine to that of immediate-release nifedipine cannot be excluded in acute myocardial infarction. Immediate-release nifedipine is contraindicated in acute myocardial infarction.

Patients with Unstable Angina: Some clinical trials have shown that treatment with the immediate-release formulation of the dihydropyridine, nifedipine, in this setting increases the risk of myocardial infarction and recurrent ischemia.

Cerebral Edema or Severely Raised Intracranial Pressure: Nimodipine should be used only with great caution under these conditions.

Pregnancy: Nimodipine has been shown to have a teratogenic effect in rabbits and to be embryotoxic, causing resorption, stunted growth, and higher incidence of skeletal variations, in rats. The safety of nimodipine with respect to adverse effects on human fetal development has not been established. Nimodipine should, therefore, not be used during pregnancy unless the potential benefits are considered to justify the potential risk to the fetus.

Precautions: *Lactation:* Nimodipine and/or its metabolites have been shown to appear in rat milk at concentrations much higher than those in maternal plasma although it is not known whether the drug is excreted in human milk. Nursing mothers are advised not to breast-feed their babies when taking the drug.

Children: Safety and effectiveness in children have not been established.

Hepatic Dysfunction: The metabolism of nimodipine is decreased in patients with impaired hepatic function. Such patients should be given lower doses of the drug and their blood pressure and pulse should be closely monitored.

Renal Dysfunction: There are insufficient data on patients with impaired renal function. Patients with known renal disease and/or receiving nephrotoxic drugs should have renal function closely monitored during i.v. treatment with nimodipine.

Administration with Food: A pharmacokinetic study has shown that the bioavailability of nimodipine capsule is reduced in the presence of an American standard breakfast to about two thirds of its value in the fasted condition. Patients should be advised to be consistent in the timing of nimodipine capsule administration with or without food.

Interaction with Grapefruit Juice: Published data indicate that through inhibition of cytochrome P450, grapefruit juice can increase plasma levels and augment pharmacodynamic effects of some dihydropyridine calcium channel blockers. Therefore, consumption of grapefruit juice prior to or during treatment with nimodipine should be avoided.

Drug Interactions: General: As with all drugs, care should be exercised when treating patients with multiple medications. Dihydropyridine calcium channel blockers undergo biotransformation by the cytochrome P450 system, mainly via the CYP 3A4 isoenzyme. Coadministration of nimodipine with other drugs which follow the same route of biotransformation may result in altered bioavailability.

Dosages of similarly metabolized drugs, particularly those of low therapeutic ratio, and especially in patients with renal and/or hepatic impairment, may require adjustment when starting or stopping concomitantly administered nimodipine to maintain optimum therapeutic blood levels.

Drugs known to be inhibitors of the cytochrome P450 system include: azole antifungals, cimetidine, cyclosporine, erythromycin, quinidine, terfenadine, warfarin.

Drugs known to be inducers of the cytochrome P450 system include: phenobarbital, phenytoin, rifampin.

Drugs known to be biotransformed via P450 include: benzodiazepines, flecainide, imipramine, propafenone, theophylline.

Cimetidine: A pharmacokinetic study has shown that concurrent administration of cimetidine and oral nimodipine results in an almost doubling of the area under the nimodipine plasma concentration curve and about a 50% increase in the peak nimodipine plasma concentration. Patients receiving the 2 drugs concomitantly should be watched carefully for the possible exaggeration of the effects of nimodipine. It may be necessary to adjust the dosage of nimodipine.

Warfarin: An interaction study with nimodipine and warfarin has shown no clinically significant interactions between these drugs.

Diazepam: An interaction study with nimodipine and diazepam has shown no clinically significant interactions between these drugs.

Antiepileptic Drugs: A pharmacokinetic study in epileptic patients receiving long-term treatment has shown that concurrent administration of oral nimodipine and antiepileptic drugs (phenobarbital, phenytoin and/or carbamazepine) reduces the bioavailability of nimodipine by about 80%. In those patients receiving sodium valproate and oral nimodipine, the bioavailability of the nimodipine increased by about 50%. Therefore, the concomitant use of oral nimodipine and these antiepileptic drugs requires close monitoring and appropriate adjustment of the dosage of nimodipine.

Rifampin: From experience with the calcium antagonist nifedipine it is to be expected that rifampin accelerates the metabolism of nimodipine capsules due to enzyme induction. Thus, efficacy of nimodipine capsules could be reduced when concomitantly administered with rifampin.

Ethanol: Since ethanol is a solvent in nimodipine for injection, interactions with alcohol-incompatible drugs may occur.

Adverse Effects: Capsules: The most commonly reported adverse events in double-blind clinical studies for patients receiving 60 or 90 mg every 4 hours (n=666) were decreased blood pressure (5.0%), nausea (1.1%), bradycardia (0.9%), rash (0.8%), edema (0.6%), and diarrhea (0.5%). Adverse events reported with a frequency greater than 1% are shown in Table I (by dose).

Adverse events for the 60 and 90 mg q4h doses with an incidence of less than 1% at all dosages were hepatitis, itching, diaphoresis, gastrointestinal hemorrhage, vomiting, thrombocytopenia, anemia, jaundice, hematoma, hyponatremia, decreased platelet count, disseminated intravascular coagulation, deep vein thrombosis, palpitation, hypertension, congestive heart failure, light headedness, dizziness, rebound vasospasm, neurological deterioration, wheezing, and phenytoin toxicity.

In severely ill patients, there was overall increased mortality in the nimodipine group using the 90 mg q4h dose as compared to placebo.

Table I—Nimotop

Frequency of Adverse Events

	Nimodipine (dose q4h)					Placebo
Sign/Symptom	**0.35 mg/kg n=82 (%)**	**30 mg n=71 (%)**	**60 mg n=494 (%)**	**90 mg n=172 (%)**	**120 mg n=4 (%)**	**n=479 (%)**
Decreased Blood Pressure	1 (1.2)	0	19 (3.8)	14 (8.1)	2 (50.0)	6 (1.2)
Abnormal Liver Function Test	1 (1.2)	0	2 (0.4)	1 (0.6)	0	7 (1.5)
Edema	0	0	2 (0.4)	2 (1.2)	0	3 (0.6)
Diarrhea	0	3 (4.2)	0	3 (1.7)	0	3 (0.6)
Rash	2 (2.4)	0	3 (0.6)	2 (1.2)	0	3 (0.6)
Headache	0	1 (1.4)	6 (1.2)	0	0	1 (0.2)
Gastrointestinal Symptoms	2 (2.4)	0	0	2 (1.2)	0	0
Nausea	1 (1.2)	1 (1.4)	6 (1.2)	1 (0.6)	0	0
Dyspnea	1 (1.2)	0	0	0	0	0
EKG Abnormalities	0	1 (1.4)	0	1 (0.6)	0	0
Tachycardia	0	1 (1.4)	0	0	0	0
Bradycardia	0	0	5 (1.0)	1 (0.6)	0	0
Muscle Pain/Cramp	0	1 (1.4)	1 (0.2)	1 (0.6)	0	0
Acne	0	1 (1.4)	0	0	0	0
Depression	0	1 (1.4)	0	0	0	0

Laboratory Values: Isolated cases of nonfasting elevated serum glucose levels (0.8%), elevated LDH levels (0.4%), decreased platelet counts (0.3%), elevated BUN (0.3%), elevated alkaline phosphatase levels (0.2%) and elevated ALT levels (0.2%) have been reported.

I.V.: The most commonly reported adverse events in patients receiving nimodipine injection (n=1 306) classified as possibly/probably related to the drug were predominantly mild to moderate decreases in blood pressure (3.4%), abnormal liver function test (1.9%), headache (1.2%), and extrasystoles (0.6%). Discontinuation of therapy was required in 21 patients (1.6%) because of adverse events.

Other adverse events reported were hypertension (0.3%), hyperglycemia (0.3%), diaphoresis (0.2%), thrombophlebitis (0.2%), and vomiting (0.2%). Adverse events with an incidence of less than 0.1% were agitation, hypernatremia, hypokalemia, injection site pain, paraesthesia, vasodilation, anxiety, asthma, depression, diabetes mellitus, dizziness, atrial fibrillation, heart arrest, laboratory test abnormalities (increased AST and ALT), liver damage, abdominal pain, phlebitis, and rash. Electrocardiographic (ECG) abnormalities, such as bradycardia (1.5%), extrasystoles (0.8%), tachycardia (0.6%), and arrhythmias (0.2%), were reported in 39/1 306 patients (3.0%). Since the association of ECG abnormalities with SAH is well known, it is likely that some or all of these abnormalities occurred as a result of the natural course of the disease due to stimulation of the parasympathetic/sympathetic system by hemorrhage.

In one study, there were more deaths caused by re-bleeding in the nimodipine group (8 patients) compared to 4 deaths in the placebo group.

Adverse events known to be associated with calcium channel blockers should be appropriately monitored.

Overdose: Symptoms and Treatment: There have been no reports of overdosage from the administration of nimodipine. Symptoms of overdosage would be expected to be related to cardiovascular effects and the patients may experience peripheral vasodilation with flushing, headache, and marked systemic hypotension.

Clinically significant hypotension due to overdosage may require active cardiovascular support and should include close monitoring of cardiac and respiratory function. Since nimodipine is 99% bound to serum protein, dialysis is not likely to be of benefit.

Dosage: For the management of neurological deficits following subarachnoid hemorrhage (SAH), nimodipine therapy should commence as soon as possible or within 4 days of the diagnosis of SAH. Sequential administration (see below) provides an opportunity to obtain therapeutic concentrations as rapidly as possible and/or to provide the drug to patients unable to swallow.

Sequential Administration: Nimodipine injection must be administered by co-infusion via 3-way stop cock to the central catheter. The initial dosage is 5 mL i.v. (equivalent to 1 mg nimodipine)/hour infused continuously for the first 2 hours; this is approximately 15 μg/kg body weight/hour. Co-infusion solution must be administered at a rate of 20 mL/hour with this initial dosage. If this dosage is tolerated, particularly if there is no severe reduction in blood pressure, the dosage should then be increased to 10 mL i.v. solution/hour with a corresponding increase in rate of co-infusion solution to 40 mL/hour. Infusion should continue for 7 to 10 days after diagnosis of SAH.

Rates of administration of recommended co-infusion solutions must be followed due to the possibility of crystal formation as seen in in vitro tests with nimodipine i.v. at higher dilutions.

I.V. lines must be changed every 24 hours.

Thereafter, the recommended dosage of nimodipine capsule is 60 mg (2 capsules of 30 mg) administered orally every 4 hours up to 21 days after diagnosis of SAH. Doses of up to 90 mg every 4 hours have been used in some patients, although the safety of higher doses in severely ill patients has not been well established.

Patients weighing considerably less than 70 kg or those having labile blood pressure should receive an initial dosage of 2.5 mL nimodipine i.v./hour with corresponding reduction in rate of co-infusion solution and, if at all possible, the dosage should not be raised above 5 mL i.v./hour.

Patients with hepatic insufficiency may have substantially reduced clearance and approximately doubled maximum plasma concentration; dosage should be reduced to 2.5 mL/hour and/or one 30 mg nimodipine capsule every 4 hours in these patients.

Nimodipine may be used during anaesthesia or surgical procedures. In the event of surgical intervention, administration of nimodipine should be continued, with dosages as above, for at least 5 days in the case of nimodipine i.v. to complete the 21 day period in the case of nimodipine capsules.

Due to the possibility of hydrolysis in high alkaline pH, alkaline mixtures should not be given for 2 hours before or after administering nimodipine capsules.

Drug effects should be carefully monitored in all patients, particularly if higher doses are used.

Oral Administration: The recommended dosage is 60 mg (2 capsules of 30 mg) administered orally every 4 hours for 21 consecutive days after diagnosis of SAH. Doses of up to 90 mg every 4 hours have been used in some patients, although the safety of higher doses in severely ill patients has not been well established.

If the patient is unable to swallow, the capsule contents may be aspirated into a syringe, emptied into the patients' in-situ naso-gastric tube and washed down the tube with 30 mL normal saline.

Patients with hepatic insufficiency may have substantially reduced clearance and approximately doubled maximum plasma concentration; accordingly, dosage should be reduced to one 30 mg capsule every 4 hours in these patients.

Nimodipine may be used during anesthesia or surgical procedures. In the event of surgical intervention, administration of nimodipine should be continued, with dosages as above, to complete the 21 day period.

Due to the possibility of hydrolysis in high alkaline pH, alkaline mixtures should not be given for 2 hours before or after administering nimodipine capsules.

Drug effects should be carefully monitored in all patients, particularly if higher doses are used.

Parenteral Products: Continuous I.V. Infusion: Should be administered by means of an infusion pump in the bypass together with the recommended infusion solution via 3-way stop cock to the central catheter.

The ratio of nimodipine solution to concomitant infusion solution should be maintained at 1 to 4 by volume to ensure appropriate dilution of nimodipine i.v. This avoids the possibility of precipitating nimodipine with resulting crystal formation seen in in vitro tests at higher dilutions.

The following i.v. infusion fluids were found to be compatible at recommended administration rates: glucose 5%, Ringer's Lactate, dextran 40, saline.

Other common infusion solutions must not be used.

I.V. lines must be changed every 24 hours.

Since the nimodipine is absorbed by polyvinylchloride (PVC) only polyethylene (PE) infusion tubing, and polyethylene (PE) or polypropylene (PPE) extensions, taps, connectors may be used.

Nimodipine is slightly light-sensitive such that its use in direct sunlight should be avoided. No special protective measures need to be taken for up to 10 hours if nimodipine i.v. is being administered in diffuse daylight or in artificial light.

The simultaneous use of nimodipine with other calcium antagonists, beta-receptor-blockers or methyldopa should be avoided, especially during continuous i.v. infusion of the drug.

Nimodipine i.v. contains 20% ethanol and 17% polyethylene glycol 400; this should be taken into account during treatment.

Nimodipine i.v. must not be added to an infusion bag or bottle.

Nimodipine capsules and nimodipine i.v. may be used during anaesthesia or surgical procedures.

Supplied: Capsules: Each ivory-colored, soft gelatin capsule, imprinted with the word NIMOTOP, contains: nimodipine 30 mg. Nonmedicinal ingredients: gelatin, glycerin, peppermint oil, polyethylene glycol and titanium dioxide. Individually packed in foil strips, cartons of 100.

I.V.: Each mL of solution contains: nimodipine 0.2 mg. Nonmedicinal ingredients: citric acid, ethanol, polyethylene glycol and sodium citrate. Brown glass bottles of 250 mL, packages of 1.

Nimodipine is light sensitive and therefore the i.v. solution and capsule should be **stored only in the manufacturer's light-protective container** below 25°C. **Protect from freezing.**

(Shown in Product Recognition Section)

Reviewed 1999

NIPRIDE® Ⓟ
Roche

Sodium Nitroprusside
Antihypertensive

Pharmacology: Nitroprusside is a potent, rapid acting i.v. antihypertensive agent. The antihypertensive action of nitroprusside is probably due to the nitroso (NO) group. Its effect is almost immediate and usually ends when the i.v. infusion is stopped. The brief duration of the drug's action is due to its rapid biotransformation. The hypotensive effect is augmented by ganglionic blocking agents. The hypotensive effects of nitroprusside are caused by peripheral vasodilation as a result of a direct action on the blood vessels, independent of autonomic innervation. No relaxation is seen in the smooth muscle of the uterus or duodenum in situ in animals.

Nitroprusside administered i.v. to hypertensive and normotensive patients produced a marked lowering of the arterial blood pressure, a slight increase in heart rate, a mild decrease in cardiac output, and a moderate diminution in calculated total peripheral vascular resistance.

The decrease in calculated total peripheral vascular resistance suggests arteriolar vasodilation. The decreases in cardiac and stroke index noted may be due to the peripheral vascular pooling of blood.

Indications: Treatment of acute hypertension refractory to standard therapeutic measures.

Nitroprusside is also indicated for producing controlled hypotension during anesthesia in order to reduce bleeding in surgical procedures where surgeon and anesthesiologist deem it appropriate. In each case, the benefit-risk ratio should be carefully considered on an individual basis.

Contraindications: Nitroprusside should not be used in the treatment of compensatory hypertension, e.g., arteriovenous shunt or coarctation of the aorta. It is also contraindicated in physically poor risk patients (ASA Risk 5), in patients with uncorrected anemia or hypovolemia or in those with known inadequate cerebral circulation.

Controlled hypotension during anesthesia induced by nitroprusside is contraindicated in patients with liver disease, severe renal disease, Leber's optic atrophy, tobacco amblyopia and disease states associated with vitamin B_{12} deficiency.

Warnings: Nitroprusside is only to be used as an infusion with sterile 5% dextrose in water. Not for direct injection.

Nitroprusside can cause precipitous decreases in blood pressure. In patients not properly monitored, these decreases can lead to irreversible ischemic injuries or death. Nitroprusside should be used only when available equipment and personnel allow blood pressure to be continuously monitored.

Except when used briefly or at low (<2 μg/kg/min) infusion rates, nitroprusside injection gives rise to important quantities of cyanide ion, which can reach toxic, potentially lethal levels. The usual dose rate is 0.5 to 8 μg/kg/min, but infusion at the upper dose rate should never last more than 10 minutes. If blood pressure has not been adequately controlled after 10 minutes of infusion at 8 μg/kg/min, administration of nitroprusside should be terminated immediately. Infusion rates greater than 8 μg/kg/min are virtually never required.

Although acid-base balance and venous oxygen concentration should be monitored and may indicate cyanide toxicity, these laboratory tests provide imperfect guidance.

Fatalities due to cyanide poisoning have occurred following nitroprusside administration. One factor is common to all known cases, namely that large amounts of nitroprusside were infused at high rates. Since detoxification relies upon enzymatic action, the rare possibility of deficient or atypical enzymes occurring in humans should always be considered. Patients most apt to run into difficulty are those who are resistant to the hypotensive effect or those in whom maintenance at the selected blood pressure level is difficult or impossible.

Constant attention to the patient's dose-response characteristics is mandatory. If infusion rates are in excess of 8 μg/kg/min. determine the nature of the response (effective constant response at higher dose; tachyphylactic; resistant—none or less than the expected). As soon as either tachyphylaxis or resistance is determined, the infusion of nitroprusside should be discontinued immediately. In abnormal responders, acid-base balance should be monitored since metabolic acidosis is evidence of cyanide toxicity.

Nitroprusside infusions at rates above 2 μg/kg/min generate cyanide ion (CN^-) faster than the body can normally dispose of it. (When sodium thiosulfate is given, the body's capacity for CN^- elimination is greatly increased.) Methemoglobin normally present in the body can buffer a certain amount of CN^-, but the capacity of this system is exhausted by the CN^- produced from about 500 μg/kg of nitroprusside (see Pharmacology). This amount of nitroprusside is administered in approximately 1 hour when the drug is administered at 8 μg/kg/min.

Nitroprusside is metabolized to cyanide and then to thiocyanate, which in turn is excreted by the kidney (see Pharmacology). If excessive amounts of nitroprusside are used, thiocyanate toxicity (e.g., tinnitus, blurred vision (miosis), delirium hyperreflexia) may occur. Estimating the thiocyanate blood levels will help to determine thiocyanate toxicity but may not reflect cyanide toxicity. Thiocyanate is mildly neurotoxic at serum levels of 60 mg/L (1 mmol/L). Thiocyanate toxicity is life-threatening when levels are 3 or 4 times higher (200 mg/L).

Since thiocyanate inhibits both the uptake and binding of iodine, caution should be exercised in using nitroprusside in patients with hypothyroidism and patients with severe renal impairment.

Blood levels of thiocyanate should be determined if treatment is to be extended. This monitoring is critical in patients with severe renal dysfunction. Although nitroprusside i.v. infusions are not intended for long-term use, as long as blood thiocyanate levels are measured daily and do not exceed 100 mg/L, it is probably safe to continue with the infusion until the patient can be safely treated with oral antihypertensive medications. Peritoneal dialysis can be helpful if too high levels of thiocyanate are found.

Hypertensive patients are more sensitive to the i.v. effect of nitroprusside than are normotensive subjects. Patients who are also receiving concomitant antihypertensive medications (specifically, hydralazine or hexamethonium) are more sensitive to the hypotensive effect of nitroprusside; the dosage of nitroprusside should be adjusted downward accordingly.

Signs of cerebral underperfusion, such as confusion and somnolence, may occur if blood pressure is reduced too rapidly, especially in hypertensive patients with encephalopathy.

There is marked variation in individual sensitivity to the antihypertensive action of nitroprusside.

The following warnings apply to the use of nitroprusside for controlled hypotension during anesthesia: 1. Extreme caution should be exercised in patients who are especially poor surgical risks (ASA class 4 and 4E). 2. Tolerance to blood loss, anemia and hypovolemia may be diminished. If possible, preexisting anemia and hypovolemia should be corrected prior to employing controlled hypotension. 3. Hypotensive anesthetic techniques may alter pulmonary ventilation perfusion ratio. Patients intolerant of additional dead air space at ordinary oxygen partial pressure may benefit from higher oxygen partial pressure. 4. Resistance and tachyphylaxis occur more frequently in normotensive patients infused with nitroprusside. Induction of deliberate hypotension in healthy young individuals may prove to be more difficult than in other segments of the population. 5. Upon discontinuation of the nitroprusside infusion for the purpose of controlled hypotension during anesthesia a rebound hypertension has been observed on rare occasions.

Pregnancy: The safety of nitroprusside in women who are or who may become pregnant has not been established; hence, it should be given only when the potential benefits have been weighed against possible hazard to mother and child.

Precautions: Adequate facilities, equipment and trained personnel should be available for frequent and vigilant monitoring of blood pressure. The hypotensive effects of nitroprusside occur rapidly, and blood pressure usually begins to rise immediately and returns to pretreatment values within 1 to 10 minutes when the infusion is slowed or stopped. It should

Nipride (cont'd)

be used with caution and initially in low doses in elderly patients, since they may be more sensitive to the drug's hypotensive effects.

Because of the rapid onset of action and potency of nitroprusside, it should be administered with the use of an infusion pump, micro-drip regulator, or any similar device that would allow precise measurement of the flow rate.

If, in the clinical situation, stress, induced by pain or manipulation, is reduced or eliminated during nitroprusside infusion, the patient could experience a greater than expected reduction in blood pressure unless the rate of infusion is adjusted downward as required.

Several authors have reported tachyphylaxis in young male patients during hypotensive anesthesia. However, tachyphylaxis has not been reported to date with nitroprusside in the treatment of hypertensive emergencies.

Once dissolved in solution, nitroprusside tends to deteriorate in the presence of light. It should be protected from light by wrapping the container of the prepared solution with aluminum foil or other opaque materials. Solutions of nitroprusside should not be kept or used longer than 12 hours. Nitroprusside in aqueous solution yields the nitroprusside ion, which reacts with even minute quantities of a wide variety of inorganic and organic substances to form usually highly colored reaction products (blue, green or dark red). If this occurs, the infusion should be replaced as quickly as possible.

Adverse Effects: Fatalities due to cyanide poisoning have occurred following nitroprusside administration (see Warnings).

Nausea, retching, emesis, diaphoresis, apprehension, headache, restlessness, agitation, muscle twitching, retrosternal discomfort and chest pain, palpitations, dizziness, faintness, weakness, rash, abdominal pain, confusion and somnolence have been noted with too rapid reduction in blood pressure, but these symptoms rapidly disappeared with slowing of the rate of infusion or temporary discontinuation of infusion and did not reappear with continued slower rate of administration.

Irritation of the injection site may occur.

One case of hypothyroidism following prolonged therapy with i.v. nitroprusside has been reported. Thiocyanate blood levels were 95 µg/mL after 21 days of nitroprusside administration to this patient with severe hypertension and renal disease.

Methemoglobinemia has been reported in the literature. Nitroprusside infusions can cause sequestration of hemoglobin as methemoglobin (see Pharmacology). Clinically significant methemoglobinemia (>10%) is seen only rarely in patients receiving nitroprusside. Methemoglobinemia should be suspected in patients who have received >10 mg/kg of nitroprusside and who exhibit signs of impaired oxygen delivery.

Overdose: Symptoms: Overdosage of nitroprusside can be manifested as excessive hypotension or cyanide toxicity or as thiocyanate toxicity. In moderate cases, the signs are dyspnea, headache, vomiting, dizziness, ataxia and loss of consciousness. Massive overdosage produces coma with imperceptible pulse, absent reflexes, widely dilated pupils, pink color, distant heart sounds, hypotension and very shallow breathing. Relief with oxygen alone is not seen. Death may result. High overdosage also results in the occurrence of hyperkalemia and metabolic acidosis which will require appropriate corrective measures.

Treatment of cyanide toxicity: Cyanide levels can be measured by many laboratories, and blood-gas studies that can detect venous hyperoxemia or acidosis are widely available. Acidosis may not appear until more than an hour after the appearance of dangerous cyanide levels, and laboratory tests should not be awaited. Reasonable suspicion of cyanide toxicity is adequate grounds for initiation of treatment.

The treatment of cyanide toxicity consists of: discontinuing the administration of nitroprusside, providing a buffer for cyanide by using sodium nitrite to convert as much hemoglobin into methemoglobin as the patient can safely tolerate; and then infusing sodium thiosulfate in sufficient quantity to convert the cyanide into thiocyanate.

Treatment: (a) Discontinue immediately nitroprusside infusion or any other medication. (b) If the patient is conscious, administer amyl nitrite ampuls immediately by inhalation, 1 for 30 seconds every 2 minutes, unless pressure is below 80 mm Hg. If there is a delay in obtaining 3% sodium nitrite solution, amyl nitrite may be repeated as indicated. (c) Follow as soon as possible (but not together with amyl nitrite) with i.v. injection of 10 mL of 3% sodium nitrite over a 3 minute period (i.v. infusion of noradrenaline may be necessary to maintain blood pressure during this injection). (d) Administer 50 mL of 25% sodium thiosulfate i.v. over a 10 minute period following the sodium nitrite administration. (e) Institute supportive measures as soon as possible, e.g. artificial respiration with 100% oxygen. (f) Administration of sodium nitrite and sodium thiosulfate may have to be repeated if symptoms reappear, with a 50% dosage reduction. (g) Peritoneal dialysis may be helpful in reducing thiocyanate concentrations. (h) Undertake constant monitoring for cyanide and thiocyanate blood levels. (i) If a severe and prolonged hypoxemia results due to excessive methemoglobinemia inhalation of pure oxygen or a blood transfusion may be required. (j) Further treatment should be symptomatic.

A cyanide antidote kit is available from Eli Lilly Canada Inc.

Dosage: Use of nitroprusside in anesthetized normotensive patients undergoing deliberate hypotensive surgery must be restricted to carefully selected cases. There is a possibility of an abnormal response occurring in normotensive patients. In the event of an abnormal response, the infusion of nitroprusside should be discontinued immediately (see Warnings).

Dissolve the contents of the 50 mg vial in 3 mL of sterile 5% dextrose in water without preservatives. **No other diluents should be used.** Depending on the desired concentration, dilute all of the prepared stock solution in 500 to 1 000 mL of sterile 5% dextrose in water and promptly wrap container in aluminum foil or other opaque material to protect from light. Both the stock solution and the infusion solution should be freshly prepared and any unused portion discarded. The freshly prepared solution for infusion has a very faint brownish tint. Discard if highly colored (see Precautions).

Once prepared, the solution should not be kept or used longer than 12 hours. Do not employ the infusion fluid used for nitroprusside administration as a vehicle for simultaneous administration of any other drug.

Administer the i.v. infusion by an infusion pump, micro-drip regulator or any similar device that will allow precise measurement of the flow rate (see Table I). Care should be taken to avoid extravasation.

Table I—Nipride

I.V. Infusion

50 mg Nipride in 1 000 mL 5% DW (50 µg/mL)		
Dose/kg	**µg/kg/min**	**mL/kg/min**
Average	3.0	0.06
Range	0.5 to 8.0	0.01 to 0.16
50 mg Nipride in 500 mL 5% DW (100 µg/mL)		
Dose	**µg/kg/min**	**mL/kg/min**
Average	3.0	0.03
Range	0.5 to 8.0	0.005 to 0.08

In patients who are not receiving antihypertensive drugs, the average dose of nitroprusside for both adults and children, is 3 µg/kg/minute (range of 0.5 to 8 µg/kg/minute). Usually, at 3 µg/kg/minute, blood pressure can be lowered by about 30 to 40% below the pretreatment diastolic levels and maintained.

In hypertensive patients receiving concomitant antihypertensive medications, smaller doses are required.

In order to avoid excessive thiocyanate levels and to lessen the possibility of a precipitous drop in blood pressure, infusion rates greater than 8 µg/kg/minute should rarely be used. If, at this rate, an adequate blood pressure reduction is not obtained within 10 minutes, administration of nitroprusside should be stopped.

Nitroprusside dosage varies considerably from patient to patient; hence the need for individual titration. Start the infusion at the lower dosage range, 0.5 µg/kg/min. and adjust in increments of 0.2 µg/kg/min., usually every 5 minutes, until the desired blood pressure reduction is obtained. Continuous, careful blood pressure monitoring on a minute to minute basis is necessary. Adjustments in the rate of infusion may be required to keep the blood pressure smoothly controlled and prevent extremes of hypotension and hypertension.

The blood pressure usually starts to drop immediately or at least within a few minutes. It is recommended that the blood pressure should not be allowed to drop at a too rapid rate and that the systolic pressure should not be lowered below 60 mm Hg. Too rapid a reduction in blood pressure may result in retching or vomiting, muscular twitching, diaphoresis and agitation. These symptoms subside promptly when the rate of infusion is slowed or temporarily stopped.

In hypertensive emergencies nitroprusside infusion may be continued until the patient can safely be treated with oral antihypertensive medications alone.

Supplied: Each 5 mL amber colored ampul contains: sodium nitroprusside USP 50 mg. Reconstitute with 3 mL of sterile 5% dextrose in water only and dilute with sterile 5% dextrose in water only. Sodium: <1 mmol (9.2 mg)/ampul. Alcohol-, paraben- and sulfite-free. Packs of 10. Store powder at 15 to 30°C. Protect the reconstituted powder and i.v. infusion fluid from light.

NITOMAN® Ⓟ

Roche

Tetrabenazine

Monoamine Depleting Agent

Pharmacology: The central effects of tetrabenazine closely resemble those of reserpine, but it differs from the latter in having less peripheral activity and in being much shorter acting. In laboratory animals, tetrabenazine interferes with vesicular storage of biogenic amines, including dopamine as well as serotonin and norepinephrine; this effect is mainly limited to the brain.

Hydroxytetrabenazine is believed to be the principle active moiety, and it is thought that its clinical activity in movement disorders results from its action on monoamine storage in the brain. The duration of action of tetrabenazine ranges from 16 to 24 hours.

Tetrabenazine also has dopamine antagonistic effects, such as displacing ^{3}H-spiperone from striatal binding sites in vitro, and blocking dopaminergic inhibition of prolactin release in vitro and in vivo.

Pharmacokinetics: Tetrabenazine has a low and erratic bioavailability. It is extensively metabolised by first-pass metabolism. Little to no unchanged tetrabenazine can be detected in the urine. The major metabolite, hydroxytetrabenazine, is formed by reduction. Following i.v. administration of radiolabelled tetrabenazine to humans, the radioactivity decreased to minimal levels within 10 hours and could not be detected 3 days later. Forty percent of total activity was found in the urine within 24 hours and 2.5% in the feces. Fifty four percent of the total activity was excreted after 48 hours.

Indications: In the treatment of hyperkinetic movement disorders such as Huntington's chorea, Hemiballismus, Senile Chorea, Tic and Gille's de la Tourette Syndrome and Tardive Dyskinesia.

Tetrabenazine is not indicated for the treatment of levodopa-induced dyskinetic/choreiform movements (see Warnings).

Tetrabenazine should only be used by (or in consultation with) physicians who are experienced in the treatment of hyperkinetic movement disorders.

Contraindications: Patients with a known hypersensitivity to the drug or to any of the components of the formulation.

Tetrabenazine is contraindicated in patients with a current episode or a history of clinical depression (see Warnings).

Tetrabenazine should not be administered together with a MAO inhibitor. At least 14 days should elapse between the discontinuation of an MAO inhibitor and initiation of treatment with tetrabenazine, as well as between the discontinuation of tetrabenazine and the initiation of treatment with an MAO inhibitor (see Precautions, Drug Interactions).

Warnings: Depression: Tetrabenazine may cause depression. Recognition of depression may be difficult because this condition may often be disguised by somatic complaints. The drug should be stopped immediately at the first signs or symptoms of depression. The depression can be profound, and the possibility of suicide should be kept in mind until the depression clears. There is no information on the safety or efficacy of antidepressant drug treatment in tetrabenazine-induced depression.

Parkinsonism: Tetrabenazine can induce symptoms of parkinsonism, which are seen more frequently in the elderly and at relatively low doses. Tetrabenazine dosage should be adjusted as tolerated and needed. Levodopa-induced dyskinetic/choreiform movements should be treated by reducing the dose of levodopa, and not by giving tetrabenazine, since the latter exacerbates parkinsonian symptoms.

Precautions: General: Occupational Hazards: Tetrabenazine may cause drowsiness and orthostatic hypotension. Therefore caution is recommended when driving, operating machinery, or performing other skilled tasks until the effect of tetrabenazine is known.

Pregnancy: Animal reproductive studies have not been performed with tetrabenazine. There is no information on the safety of the drug in human pregnancy. However, tetrabenazine has been used for many years and no cases of malformation have been reported.

Lactation: Limited information indicates that tetrabenazine is excreted in milk, therefore it should be avoided in breast-feeding mothers.

Drug Interactions: Levodopa: Tetrabenazine exacerbates Parkinsonian symptoms, and thereby attenuates the effect of levodopa (see Warnings).

Antidepressants and MAO Inhibitors: Central excitation and possibly hypertension have occurred when tetrabenazine was added to existing therapy with desipramine or MAO inhibitors.

There is no information on the safety and efficacy of antidepressant drugs, including MAO inhibitors, in the treatment of tetrabenazine-induced depression (see Contraindications).

Neuroleptic Agents: There is a potential for severe manifestations of dopamine deficiency, when administering tetrabenazine concomitantly with neuroleptic agents (e.g., haloperidol, chlorpromazine, metoclopramide, etc.).

Adverse Effects: The most commonly observed adverse reactions with tetrabenazine include, in decreasing order of frequency and observed during clinical use of the drug: signs and symptoms of Parkinsonism; drowsiness, fatigue, weakness; depression; anxiety, nervousness; insomnia; restlessness, akathisia; drooling; irritability, agitation; nausea, vomiting, epigastric pain; confusion, disorientation; hypotension; dizziness.

Although tetrabenazine has been in clinical use for a number of years, controlled clinical trials with the drug are limited.

Overdose: Symptoms Signs and symptoms of overdosage may include drowsiness, sweating, hypotension and hypothermia.

Treatment: Treatment is symptomatic.

Dosage: General: The initial dose should be low, and dosage should be titrated slowly according to the tolerance and responsiveness of the individual patient.

Adults: An initial starting dose of 12.5 mg 2 to 3 times a day is recommended. This can be increased by 12.5 mg a day every 3 to 5 days until the maximal tolerated and effective dose is reached for the individual, and may have to be up/down titrated depending on individual tolerance. In most cases the maximal tolerated dose will be 25 mg t.i.d. In very rare cases, a 200 mg dose has been reached (the maximum recommended dose in some publications).

If there is no improvement at the maximal tolerated dose in 7 days, it is unlikely that tetrabenazine will be of benefit to the patient, either by increasing the dose or by extending the duration of treatment.

Geriatrics and Debilitated Patients: No adequately controlled clinical studies have been performed in the elderly and/or debilitated patients. Clinical experience suggests that a reduced initial and maintenance dose should be used. Parkinsonian-like adverse reactions are relatively common in these patients and may be dose-limiting.

Children: No adequately controlled clinical studies have been performed in children. Limited clinical experience suggests that treatment should be started at approximately half the adult dose, and titrated slowly and carefully according to tolerance and individual response.

Information for the Patient: See Blue Section—Information for the Patient "Nitoman".

Supplied: Each round, yellowish-buff tablet, with ROCHE imprinted across one face and a single break bar on the other, contains: tetrabenazine 25 mg. Nonmedicinal ingredients: iron oxide, lactose, magnesium stearate, starch maize white and talc. Bottles of 120. Store in well-closed containers. Store at 15 to 30°C.

Reviewed 1998

NITRAZADON ℞

ICN

Nitrazepam

Hypnotic—Anticonvulsant

Supplied: 5 mg: Each white, round, scored tablet, imprinted "N21", contains: nitrazepam BP 5 mg. Nonmedicinal ingredients: croscarmellose sodium, lactose, magnesium stearate and microcrystalline cellulose. Bottles of 100 and 500.

10 mg: Each white, round, scored tablet, imprinted "N22", contains: nitrazepam BP 10 mg. Nonmedicinal ingredients: croscarmellose sodium, lactose, magnesium stearate and microcrystalline cellulose. Bottles of 100 and 500.

NITRAZEPAM ℞

General Monograph, CPhA

see BENZODIAZEPINES

NITRO-DUR®

Key

Nitroglycerin

Antianginal

Pharmacology: The principal pharmacological action of nitroglycerin is relaxation of vascular smooth muscle and consequent dilation of both peripheral arteries and veins, with more prominent effects on the latter. Dilation of the post-capillary vessels, including large veins, promotes peripheral pooling of blood and decreases venous return to the heart, thereby reducing left ventricular end-diastolic pressure (preload). Arteriolar relaxation reduces systemic vascular resistance and arterial pressure (afterload). Dilation of the coronary arteries also occurs. The relative importance of preload reduction, afterload reduction, and coronary dilation remains undefined.

When Nitro-Dur is applied to the skin, nitroglycerin is absorbed continuously through the skin into the systemic circulation. Thus, the active drug reaches target sites before inactivation by the liver. Nitroglycerin is rapidly metabolized, principally by a liver reductase, to form glycerol nitrate metabolites and inorganic nitrate. Two active major metabolites, the 1,2- and 1,3- dinitroglycerols, the products of hydrolysis, appear to be less potent than nitroglycerin as vasodilators but have longer plasma half-lives. The dinitrates are further metabolized to mononitrates (biologically inactive with respect to cardiovascular effects) and ultimately to glycerol and carbon dioxide. There is extensive first-pass deactivation by the liver following gastrointestinal absorption.

In healthy volunteers, steady-state plasma concentrations of nitroglycerin were reached within 2 hours after application of the patch and were maintained at the same level for the duration of the study (24 hours). Between 2 and 24 hours, the mean steady-state concentration was 0.224 ng/mL (20 cm² patch); the total amount of nitroglycerin delivered in 24 hours was 5.11 ± 1.69 mg, 10.67 ± 4.78 mg and 17.85 ± 7.40 mg from 10 cm², 20 cm², and 40 cm² patches, respectively, indicating that the dose delivered is proportional to the surface area of the patch. Within 1 hour of removal of the patch, the plasma concentration declines to about 50% of steady-state concentration and to undetectable concentrations by 2 hours.

Dosing regimens for most chronically used drugs are designed to provide plasma concentrations that are continuously greater than a minimally effective concentration. This strategy is probably inappropriate for organic nitrates. Some well-controlled clinical trials using exercise tolerance testing have shown maintenance of effectiveness when patches are worn continuously. The large majority of such controlled trials, however, have shown the development of tolerance (i.e. complete loss of effect as measured by exercise testing) within the first day. Tolerance has occurred even when doses greater than 4 mg/hour were delivered continuously. This dose is far in excess of the effective dose of 0.2 to 0.8 mg/hour delivered intermittently.

Efficacy of organic nitrates is restored after a period of absence of nitrates from the body. Drug-free intervals of 10 to 12 hours are known to be sufficient to restore response. Several studies have demonstrated that when nitroglycerin is administered according to an intermittent regimen, doses of nitroglycerin 0.4 to 0.8 mg/hour (20 to 40 cm²) have increased exercise capacity for up to 8 hours, with a trend of increased exercise capacity for up to 12 hours. One controlled clinical trial suggested that the intermittent use of nitrates may be associated with a decreased, in comparison to placebo, exercise tolerance during the last part of the nitrate-free interval; the clinical relevance of this observation is unknown. In another clinical trial there was an increase in nocturnal angina attacks during the drug-free period in some patients treated with nitroglycerin as compared to placebo. Therefore the possibility of increased frequency or severity of angina during the nitrate-free interval should be considered.

Indications: Nitroglycerin used intermittently (see Pharmacology), for the prevention of anginal attacks in patients with stable angina pectoris associated with coronary artery disease. It can be used in conjunction with other antianginal agents such as beta-blockers and/or calcium antagonists.

Nitroglycerin is not intended for the immediate relief of acute attacks of angina pectoris. Sublingual nitroglycerin preparations should be used for this purpose.

Contraindications: Known hypersensitivity or idiosyncrasy to nitroglycerin or other nitrates or nitrites. Allergy to the adhesive used in nitroglycerin patches has been reported and constitutes a contraindication to the use of this product. Acute circulatory failure associated with marked hypotension (shock and states of collapse). Postural hypotension. Myocardial insufficiency due to obstruction (e.g. in the presence of aortic or mitral stenosis or of constrictive pericarditis). Increased intracranial pressure. Increased intraocular pressure. Severe anemia.

Warnings: The benefits and safety of transdermal nitroglycerin in patients with acute myocardial infarction or congestive heart failure have not been established. If one elects to use Nitro-Dur in these conditions, careful clinical or hemodynamic monitoring must be used to avoid the hazards of hypotension and tachycardia.

Nitro-Dur must be removed before cardioversion or DC defibrillation is attempted, as well as before applying diathermy treatment, since it may be associated with damage to the paddles and burns to the patient.

Precautions: Headaches or symptoms of hypotension, such as weakness or dizziness, particularly when arising suddenly from a recumbent position, may occur. A reduction in dose or discontinuation of treatment may be necessary.

Caution should be exercised when using nitroglycerin in patients prone to, or who might be affected by hypotension. The drug therefore should be used with caution in patients who may have volume depletion from diuretic therapy or in patients who have low systolic blood pressure (e.g. below 90 mmHg). Paradoxical bradycardia and increased angina pectoris may accompany nitroglycerin-induced hypotension.

Nitrate therapy may aggravate the angina caused by hypertrophic cardiomyopathy.

In industrial workers who have had long-term exposure to unknown (presumably high) doses of nitroglycerin, tolerance clearly occurs. There is moreover, physical dependence since chest pain, acute myocardial infarction, and even sudden death have occurred during temporary withdrawal of nitroglycerin from these workers. In clinical trials of angina patients, there are reports of anginal attacks being more easily provoked and of rebound in the hemodynamic effects soon after nitrate withdrawal.

The importance of these observations to the routine clinical use of nitroglycerin has not been fully elucidated, but patients should be monitored closely for increased anginal symptoms during drug-free periods.

Caution should be exercised in patients with arterial hypoxemia due to anemia (see Contraindications), because in such patients the biotransformation of nitroglycerin is reduced. Similarly, caution is called for in patients with hypoxemia and a ventilation/perfusion imbalance due to lung disease or ischemic heart failure. Patients with angina pectoris, myocardial infarction, or cerebral ischemia frequently suffer from abnormalities of the small airways (especially alveolar hypoxia). Under these circumstances vasoconstriction occurs within the lung to shift perfusion from areas of alveolar hypoxia to better ventilated regions of the lung. As a potent vasodilator, nitroglycerin could reverse this protective vasoconstriction and thus result in increased perfusion to poorly ventilated areas, worsening of the ventilation/perfusion imbalance, and a further decrease in the arterial partial pressure of oxygen.

Tolerance to nitroglycerin with cross tolerance to other nitrates or nitrites may occur (see Pharmacology). As tolerance to nitroglycerin patches develops, the effect of sublingual nitroglycerin on exercise tolerance, although still observable, is somewhat blunted.

Occupational Hazards: As patients may experience faintness and/or dizziness, reaction time when driving or operating machinery may be impaired, especially at the start of treatment.

Pregnancy and *Lactation:* It is not known whether nitroglycerin can cause fetal harm when administered to pregnant women or can affect reproductive capacity. Therefore, use nitroglycerin only if the potential benefit justifies the risk to the fetus.

It is not known whether nitroglycerin is excreted in human milk. Benefits to the mother must be weighed against the risk to the infant.

Children: Safety and effectiveness in children have not been established.

Drug Interactions: Concomitant treatment with other vasodilators, calcium antagonists, ACE inhibitors, beta blockers, diuretics, antihypertensives, tricyclic antidepressants and major tranquilizers may potentiate the blood pressure lowering effect of nitroglycerin. Dose adjustment may be necessary.

Nitro-Dur (cont'd)

Alcohol may enhance sensitivity to the hypotensive effects of nitrates.

Concurrent administration of nitroglycerin with dihydroergotamine may increase the bioavailability of dihydroergotamine. Special attention should be paid to this point in patients with coronary artery disease, because dihydroergotamine antagonizes the effect of nitroglycerin and may lead to coronary vasconstriction.

The possibility that the ingestion of ASA and nonsteroidal anti-inflammatory drugs might diminish the therapeutic response to nitrates and nitroglycerin cannot be excluded.

Adverse Effects: Headache, which may be severe, is the most commonly reported side effect. Headache may be recurrent with each daily dose, especially at higher doses of nitroglycerin. Headaches may be treated with concomitant administration of mild analgesics. If such headaches are unresponsive to treatment, the nitroglycerin dosage should be reduced or the product discontinued. Transient episodes of lightheadedness, occasionally related to blood pressure changes, may also occur. Hypotension occurs infrequently, but in some patients it may be severe enough to warrant discontinuation of therapy.

Reddening of the skin, with or without a mild local itching or burning sensation, as well as allergic contact dermatitis may occasionally occur. Upon removal of the patch, any slight reddening of the skin will usually disappear within a few hours. The application site should be changed regularly to prevent local irritation.

Less frequently reported adverse reactions include dizziness, faintness, facial flushing, postural hypotension which may be associated with reflex tachycardia. Syncope, crescendo angina and rebound hypertension have been reported but are uncommon. Nausea and vomiting have been reported rarely.

Overdose: Symptoms: Nitroglycerin overdose may result in severe hypotension, persistent throbbing headache, vertigo, palpitations, visual disturbances, flushing and perspiring skin (later becoming cold and cyanotic), nausea and vomiting (possibly with colic and even bloody diarrhea), syncope (especially in the upright posture), methemoglobinemia with cyanosis, initial hyperpnea, dyspnea, and slow breathing, slow pulse (dicrotic and intermittent), heart block, increased intracranial pressure with cerebral symptoms of confusion and moderate fever, paralysis, coma, clonic convulsions and death due to circulatory collapse.

Treatment: Keep the patient recumbent in a shock position and comfortably warm. Remove the Nitro-Dur patch. Passive movement of the extremities may aid venous return. Administer oxygen and artificial ventilation if necessary. Epinephrine is ineffective in reversing the severe hypotensive events associated with overdose; it and related compounds are contraindicated in this situation.

Methemoglobinemia: Case reports of clinically significant methemoglobinemia are rare at conventional doses of nitroglycerin. The formation of methemoglobin is dose-related, and in the case of genetic abnormalities of hemoglobin that favor methemoglobin formation, even conventional doses of organic nitrates can produce harmful concentrations of methemoglobin. If methemoglobinemia is present, i.v. administration of 1 to 2 mg/kg of methylene blue 1% solution for injection may be required.

Dosage: Daily Dosage Schedule: The daily dosage schedule is based on intermittent therapy to prevent the development of tolerance to nitroglycerin. The optimal dose should be selected based upon the clinical response, side effects, and the effects of therapy on blood pressure.

Starting dose is 1 Nitro-Dur 0.2 patch (10 cm²), usually applied in the morning. If 0.2 mg/hour (10 cm²) is well tolerated, the dose can be increased to 0.4 mg/hour (20 cm²) if required. A maximum of 0.8 mg/hour (40 cm²) may be used.

Prevention of Tolerance: Although some controlled clinical trials using exercise tolerance testing have shown maintenance of effectiveness when patches are worn continuously, the large majority of such controlled trials have shown the development of tolerance (i.e. complete loss of effect) within the first 24 hours after therapy was initiated. Dose adjustments even to levels much higher than generally used did not prevent the development of tolerance.

Tolerance can be prevented or attenuated by use of an intermittent dosage schedule. Although the minimum nitrate-free interval has not been defined, clinical trials have demonstrated that an appropriate dosing schedule for nitroglycerin patches would provide for a daily patch-on period of 12 to 14 hours and a daily patch-off period of 10 to 12 hours. The patch-free time should coincide with the period in which angina pectoris is least likely to occur (usually at night). Patients should be watched carefully for an increase of angina pectoris during the patch-free period. Adjustment of background medication may be required.

The dose of Nitro-Dur should be periodically reviewed in relation to continuing antianginal control.

Site of Application: The Nitro-Dur nitroglycerin transdermal system may be applied to any convenient skin area; a recommended site of application is the arm or chest. Application sites should be rotated. A suitable area may be shaved if necessary. Do not apply Nitro-Dur to the distal part of the extremities. Hands should be washed thoroughly after application. Following use, the patch should be discarded in a manner that prevents accidental application or ingestion by curious children or others.

Information for the Patient: See Blue Section—Information for the Patient "Nitro-Dur".

Supplied: The Nitro-Dur nitroglycerin transdermal system is a flat unit designed to provide continuous controlled release of nitroglycerin through intact skin. The rate of release of nitroglycerin is linearly dependent upon the area of the applied system; each cm² of applied system delivers approximately 0.02 mg of nitroglycerin per hour. Thus, the 10-, 15-, 20-, 30- and 40-cm² systems deliver approximately 0.2, 0.3, 0.4, 0.6 and 0.8 mg of nitroglycerin per hour, respectively. The remainder of the nitroglycerin in each system serves as a reservoir and is not delivered in normal use.

The Nitro-Dur transdermal system contains nitroglycerin in acrylic-based polymer adhesives with a resinous cross-linking agent to provide a continuous source of active ingredient.

Nitro-Dur 0.2 (0.2 mg/hour): Each 10 cm² patch contains: nitroglycerin 40 mg.

Nitro-Dur 0.3 (0.3 mg/hour): Each 15 cm² patch contains: nitroglycerin 60 mg.

Nitro-Dur 0.4 (0.4 mg/hour): Each 20 cm² patch contains: nitroglycerin 80 mg.

Nitro-Dur 0.6 (0.6 mg/hour): Each 30 cm² patch contains: nitroglycerin 120 mg.

Nitro-Dur 0.8 (0.8 mg/hour): Each 40 cm² patch contains: nitroglycerin 160 mg.

Each unit is sealed in a paper polyethylene-foil pouch. Retail unit dose boxes of 30. Hospital unit dose boxes of 100. Store between 15 to 30°C. Do not refrigerate.

(Shown in Product Recognition Section)

NITROGLYCERIN

General Monograph, CPhA

Glyceryl Trinitrate

Antianginal—Antihypertensive

This monograph has been compiled by CPhA. It may contain information different from that approved by Therapeutic Products Programme, Health Canada, and the pharmaceutical manufacturers' approval has not been requested.

Pharmacology: Nitroglycerin, in common with other nitrates, produces generalized vasodilation, thereby decreasing venous return and workload on the heart. Both arterial and venous dilation occur, although venous effects predominate. Coronary vasodilation also occurs even in the presence of atherosclerosis. Relaxation of vascular smooth muscle is a result of stimulation of cyclic guanosine monophosphate (GMP) production as well as inhibition of thromboxane synthetase, permitting preferential formation of prostacyclin. Left ventricular end-diastolic pressure and volume are decreased, resulting in reduction of ventricular size and wall tension. Therapeutic doses reduce systolic, diastolic and mean arterial blood pressure; reflex tachycardia may occur, presumably in response to these effects.

Tolerance to the antianginal and hemodynamic effects of nitrates develops and is more likely to occur at higher doses and with formulations which have longer half-lives. It is common in patients being treated with topical, transdermal or continuous i.v. infusions and is not as likely to develop with the use of short-acting preparations.

Efficacy of organic nitrates is restored after a drug-free interval of 10 to 12 hours. The intermittent use of nitrates may be associated with decreased exercise tolerance during the last part of the nitrate-free interval; the clinical relevance of this observation is unknown. There may also be an increase in nocturnal angina attacks during the drug-free period in some patients. Therefore, the possibility of increased frequency or severity of angina during the nitrate-free interval should be considered.

Pharmacokinetics: Nitroglycerin is widely distributed in the body with an apparent volume of distribution of approximately 200 L in adult male subjects (only 1% present in the plasma). Half-life is estimated at 1 to 4 minutes. Nitroglycerin is rapidly metabolized in the liver by hepatic enzymes to dinitrates and mononitrates. The 2 active major metabolites are the hydrolysis products, 1,3- and 1,2-dinitroglycerols. There are also 2 inactive minor metabolites. Nitroglycerin is approximately 60% protein bound while the metabolites 1,2 dinitroglycerol and 1,3 dinitroglycerol are 60 and 30% protein bound, respectively. Extensive first-pass deactivation follows gastrointestinal absorption. Nitroglycerin is excreted by the renal route, primarily as the 2 dinitrometabolites, which have an excretion half-life of approximately 3 to 4 hours.

Table I provides information on the pharmacokinetics of specific dosage forms.

Indications: Acute symptomatic relief of angina pectoris; prophylactic management in situations likely to provoke angina attacks; long-term prophylactic management of angina pectoris.

I.V.: Congestive heart failure associated with acute MI, control of blood pressure during surgical procedures, especially cardiovascular; treatment of angina unresponsive to oral nitrates or β-blockers.

Contraindications: Nitroglycerin should not be administered to individuals with: a known hypersensitivity to nitroglycerin or a known idiosyncratic reaction to organic nitrates; severe anemia because of potential for reduced hemoglobin level and impaired oxygen delivery; early MI (long-acting forms of nitroglycerin); hypotension or uncorrected hypovolemia, as the use of nitroglycerin in such states could produce severe hypotension or shock; open- or closed-angle glaucoma, although pressure is at most increased only briefly and drainage of aqueous humor is not impeded; head trauma or cerebral hemorrhage (to avoid increased intracranial pressure); constrictive pericarditis and pericardial tamponade.

Warnings: The use of nitroglycerin in acute myocardial infarction or congestive heart failure requires careful clinical and/or hemodynamic monitoring.

Nitrate dependence may occur in patients with chronic use. In industry workers continuously exposed to nitrates, chest pain, acute myocardial infarction and even sudden death have occurred during temporary withdrawal of nitrate exposure. To avoid possible withdrawal effects, the administration of nitroglycerin should be reduced gradually.

Precautions: Nitroglycerin ointment, transdermal or oral tablets are not intended for immediate relief of acute attacks of angina pectoris. Sublingual, metered dose spray, or buccal nitroglycerin preparations should be used for this purpose.

Caution should be exercised in using the drug in patients who are volume depleted or have low systolic blood pressure. Severe hypotension, especially postural, may occur. Nitroglycerin can act as a physiological antagonist to norepinephrine, acetylcholine and histamine. Alcohol may accentuate cerebral ischemic symptoms.

Table I—Nitroglycerin

Pharmacokinetics of Various Dosage Forms

Dosage Form	Onset of Action	Duration of Action
I.V. injection	1 to 2 minutes	3 to 5 minutes*
Sublingual tablets	1 to 3 minutes	10 to 30 minutes
Translingual spray	2 to 4 minutes	10 to 30 minutes
Buccal or transmucosal extended-release tablets	2 to 5 minutes	3 to 5 hours
Oral extended-release tablets	20 to 45 minutes	3 to 6 hours
Topical ointment or transdermal patch	30 to 60 minutes	4 to 8 hours

*After infusion discontinued.

Nitroglycerin should be used with caution in patients with severe liver or renal disease. In patients with gastrointestinal hypermotility or malabsorption syndrome, avoid extended release preparations.

Headaches or symptoms of hypotension, such as weakness or dizziness, particularly when arising suddenly from a recumbent position, may be due to overdosage. If this occurs the dose should be reduced or the frequency of topical application should be reduced.

Nitroglycerin can cause sudden severe hypotension. Excessive hypotension, especially for prolonged periods of time, must be avoided because of possible deleterious effects on the brain, heart, liver and kidneys from poor perfusion and attendant risk of ischemia, thrombosis, and altered function of these organs. Paradoxical bradycardia and increased angina pectoris may accompany nitroglycerin-induced hypotension. Patients with normal or low pulmonary capillary wedge pressure are especially sensitive to the hypotensive effects of nitroglycerin. A fall in pulmonary capillary wedge pressure precedes the onset of arterial hypotension and is thus a useful guide to safe titration of the drug.

The smallest dose required for effective relief of the acute anginal attack should be taken. Excessive use may lead to the development of tolerance. Tolerance to nitroglycerin (especially with transdermal, sustained-release and i.v. preparations) and cross tolerance to other nitrates may occur. A minimum interval of 10 to 12 hours per day without the transdermal patch in place is required for continued effectiveness when using this dosage form. With the chronic use of nitrates, there have been reports of anginal attacks being more easily provoked as well as reports of rebound in hemodynamic effects, occurring soon after nitrate withdrawal.

Cardioversion: Remove nitroglycerin patches prior to cardioversion to avoid formation of electrical arc.

Carcinogenesis, Mutagenesis, Impairment of Fertility: No long-term studies in animals were performed to evaluate the carcinogenic potential of nitroglycerin.

Drug Interactions: Alcohol: Alcohol and nitroglycerin may have additive vasodilatory effects possibly resulting in hypotension. Caution with this combination is advised.

Hypotensive Agents: Patients receiving hypotensive agents and nitroglycerin should be observed for possible additive hypotensive effect.

Heparin: Heparin resistance has been encountered with i.v. nitroglycerin. It is suggested to monitor the APTT when nitroglycerin is added or discontinued in patients receiving heparin. The dose of heparin may need to be adjusted.

Salicylates: Analgesic doses of ASA (>500 mg) may reduce the metabolism of nitroglycerin by decreasing hepatic blood flow. Patients may be more susceptible to headache or hypotension with this combination.

Ergot Alkaloids: The effect of nitroglycerin is antagonized by ergot alkaloids, which may precipitate angina. As well, nitroglycerin can reduce the metabolism of dihydroergotamine.

Pregnancy: Animal reproduction studies have not been conducted with nitroglycerin. It is not known whether nitroglycerin can cause fetal harm when administered to a pregnant woman or whether it can affect reproduction capacity. Nitroglycerin should be given to a pregnant woman only if clearly needed.

Lactation: It is not known whether nitroglycerin is excreted in human milk. Because many drugs are excreted in human milk, caution should be exercised when nitroglycerin is administered to a nursing woman.

Children: Safety and effectiveness in children have not been established.

Adverse Effects: The most frequent adverse reaction to nitroglycerin is headache which occurs in up to 50% of patients at the beginning of therapy and is a result of dilation of cerebral vessels. Headache usually disappears within several days with continued treatment. Acetaminophen may be used to treat nitrate headaches.

Other adverse reactions occurring in less than 1% of patients are: Allergic: itching, wheezing, tracheobronchitis, contact dermatitis with topical dosage forms.

Cardiovascular: hypotension, reflex tachycardia, paradoxical increase of anginal pain, palpitations and bradycardia. Syncope due to nitrate vasodilation, although rare, has been reported.

CNS: headache, weakness, dizziness, apprehension and restlessness.

Dermatologic: exfoliative dermatitis, cutaneous vasodilation, crusty skin lesions, pruritus, rash.

Gastrointestinal: nausea, vomiting, diarrhea and abdominal pain.

Genitourinary: dysuria, urinary frequency, impotence.

Metabolic: methemoglobinemia, especially in the presence of methemoglobin reductase deficiencies or in congenital hemoglobin variants.

Musculoskeletal: arthralgia, muscle twitching.

Ophthalmologic: blurred vision.

Respiratory: bronchitis, pneumonia, upper respiratory infection.

Overdose: Symptoms: Symptoms of overdosage are primarily related to vasodilation: cutaneous flushing, headache, nausea, dizziness, hypotension and tachycardia. Methemoglobinemia is also possible with extremely large doses.

Treatment: Most of these effects can be obviated by discontinuing the drug immediately.

Treatment should primarily be symptomatic and supportive. If nitroglycerin has been ingested, empty stomach by using ipecac syrup or gastric lavage. Follow with activated charcoal and a saline cathartic. However, nitrates are usually rapidly absorbed.

Severe hypotension and tachycardia can be treated by elevating the legs and administering i.v. fluids. Since the duration of the hemodynamic effects following nitroglycerin administration is brief, additional corrective measures are usually not required. However, if further therapy is indicated, administration of an i.v. adrenergic agonist (e.g., phenylephrine) should be considered. Oxygen and artificial ventilation may be necessary. If methemoglobinemia occurs, methylene blue should be administered.

Dosage: Prevention of Tolerance: Tolerance can be prevented or attenuated by the use of an intermittent dosage schedule. An appropriate dosing schedule for nitroglycerin should provide for a nitrate-free period of 10 to 12 hours daily. The drug-free time should coincide with the period in which angina pectoris is least likely to occur (usually at night). Patients should be watched carefully for an increase of angina pectoris during the nitrate-free period. Adjustment of other cardiovascular medication may be required.

Buccal: Initial dose is 1 mg every 5 hours during waking hours, adjusted to control symptoms. Tablets should be placed between the lip and gum, above the incisors, and should not be swallowed.

I.V.: Not for direct i.v. injection. Nitroglycerin must be diluted in dextrose 5% injection USP or sodium chloride 0.9% injection USP, prior to infusion. Nitroglycerin should not be mixed with other drugs.

Caution: Several preparations of nitroglycerin for injection are available which differ in concentration and/or volume/vial. When switching from one product to another, attention must be paid to the dilution, dosage and administration instructions.

Because of alterations to the amount of nitroglycerin delivered to the patient caused by variations in administration sets, pumps, and the great variations in responsiveness of individual patients to nitroglycerin, there is no fixed optimum dose of nitroglycerin. Each patient must be titrated to the desired level of hemodynamic function.

Initial dosage should be 5 to 10 µg/min delivered through an infusion pump capable of exact and constant delivery of the drug. Subsequent titration must be adjusted to the clinical situation, with dose increments becoming more cautious as partial response is seen. Initial titration should be in 5 µg/min increments with increases every 3 to 5 minutes until some response is noted. If no response is seen at 20 µg/min, increments of 10 to 20 µg/min can be used. Once a partial blood pressure response is observed, the dose increase should be reduced and the interval between increments should be lengthened. Some patients with normal or low left ventricular filling pressure or pulmonary capillary wedge pressure (e.g., angina patients without other complications) may respond fully to doses as small as 5 µg/min. These patients require especially careful titration and monitoring.

Ointment: May be applied every 4 to 8 hours if necessary. May be wiped off at bedtime to provide a nitrate-free interval. The usual dose is 2.5 to 5 cm as squeezed from the tube. The optimal dose is determined by starting with an application of 1.25 cm and increasing the dose by 1.25 cm increments until side effects (usually headache) occur or satisfactory response is obtained. Some patients may require as much as 10 to 12.5 cm and/or application every 4 hours.

Any nonhairy skin area may be used; some patients psychologically prefer the chest.

The dose and frequency of application should be adjusted to meet the individual patient's needs.

Methods of Application: Apply ointment using specially designed dose-determining applicator. The ointment is spread over at least 2 x 3 inch (50 x 75 mm) area in a thin uniform layer using the applicator. The dose-determining applicator serves the dual purpose of measuring the amount of ointment and preventing absorption of the ointment through the fingers while it is being applied. The dose/area ratio should be kept constant.

Oral Sustained-release Tablets: Recommended initial dosage is 1 tablet (2.6 mg) 3 times daily, before breakfast, late afternoon before a meal and before retiring. Dosage may be increased progressively up to 2 tablets 3 times a day.

Spray: For an acute attack of angina pectoris or for prophylaxis before planned exercise: 1 or 2 metered doses (0.4 or 0.8 mg) of nitroglycerin administered onto or under the tongue, **without inhaling.** The mouth must be closed immediately after each dose. May be repeated twice at 5- to 10-minute intervals.

Sublingual: Usual adult dosage range: 0.3 to 0.6 mg. One tablet should be dissolved under the tongue or in the buccal pouch immediately upon indication of an acute anginal attack. This dose may be repeated every 5 minutes until relief is obtained. If pain persists after a total of 3 tablets over a 15-minute period, the physician should be contacted. For prophylactic use, 1 sublingual tablet can be taken 5 to 10 minutes before engaging in activities which may precipitate an anginal event.

Storage: Store at room temperature, below 30°C. To prevent loss of potency, the tablets should be dispensed and kept in tight amber glass containers. The container should be closed tightly immediately after each use. No more than 100 tablets should be packaged in a container.

Repeated opening of the container may shorten the period of potency of sublingual tablets. Replacement of tablet stock is recommended 6 months after opening the bottle. Specific manufacturers may have different recommendations. The stabilized sublingual tablets are designed to provide potency for longer periods, but must still receive proper storage. Whether the tablet stings or tingles when placed under the tongue is not an indication of potency and should not be used to assess whether the tablets will work or not.

Transdermal: Patient instructions provided with the product should be consulted for each individual product. Generally a patch is applied to a hairless, clean area of skin that is not subject to excessive movement (i.e., trunk). Do not apply to areas with cuts, burns or abrasions or use on distal parts of extremities (i.e., forearms). Each successive application should be placed on a different site. Patch is applied once daily (usually in the morning) and left on for 12 to 14 hours, then removed. The starting dose is usually 0.2 mg/hour (10 cm²). Maximum dose is 0.8 mg/hour (40 cm²).

Reviewed 1997

NITROGLYCERIN INJECTION USP
Faulding

Vasodilator

Supplied: Each mL of solution contains: nitroglycerin USP 5 mg. Ampuls of 10 mL. Packs of 5. Store between 15 and 30°C. Protect from freezing. Protect from light.

NITROGLYCERIN IN 5% DEXTROSE INJECTION
Baxter

Vasodilator

Supplied: Each mL of clear, practically colorless, sterile, nonpyrogenic solution contains: nitroglycerin in 5% dextrose. Nonmedicinal ingredients: alcohol USP, citric acid hydrous USP, hydrochloric acid, propylene glycol, sodium hydroxide and water for injection USP. pH 4.0 (3.0 to 5.0). Osmolarity: 428, 440 and 465 mOsmol/L (calc), respectively. Glass, single dose bottles in the following sizes and concentrations: see Table I.

Table I—Nitroglycerin in 5% Dextrose Injection

Supplied		
Total Volume (mL)	Total Nitroglycerin Content (mg)	Nitroglycerin Concentration (mg/mL)
250	25	0.1
250	50	0.2
250	100	0.4

Store between 15 and 25°C. Protect from light and freezing. Do not use unless vacuum is present and solution is clear.

NITROL®

Rhône-Poulenc Rorer

Nitroglycerin

Antianginal—Vasodilator

Pharmacology: The principal action of nitroglycerin is that of all nitrates, namely relaxation of vascular smooth muscle. Nitrates act primarily by reducing myocardial oxygen demands rather than increasing its oxygen supply. This effect is thought to be brought about predominantly by peripheral action. Although venous effects predominate, nitroglycerin produces, in a dose-related manner, dilation of both arterial and venous beds. Dilation of the post-capillary vessels, including large veins, promotes peripheral pooling of blood and decreases venous return to the heart, reducing left ventricular end-diastolic pressure (pre-load). Arteriolar relaxation reduces systemic vascular resistance and arterial pressure (after-load). Left ventricular end-diastolic pressure and volume are decreased, resulting in reduction of ventricular size and wall tension. The reduction in ventricular wall tension results in a net decrease in myocardial oxygen consumption and a favorable net balance between myocardial oxygen supply and demand.

When the ointment is spread on the skin, nitroglycerin is continuously absorbed through the skin into the systemic circulation, bypassing portal circulation. Therapeutic effect can be anticipated 15 minutes after application. The duration of action of the ointment has been shown to be approximately 3 to 8 hours.

Indications: For the prevention of attacks of angina pectoris associated with chronic angina of effort.

Contraindications: Patients with severe anemia, increased intraocular pressure, increased intracranial pressure and hypotension. Also, patients with known idiosyncrasy to organic nitrates.

Warnings: Data on the safe use of nitroglycerin ointment during the early phase of myocardial infarction (the period during which clinical and laboratory findings are unstable) are insufficient to establish safety.

The use of this ointment in patients with congestive heart failure requires careful clinical and/or hemodynamic monitoring.

Nitrate dependence may occur in patients with chronic use. To avoid possible withdrawal effects, the administration of nitroglycerin ointment should gradually be reduced over 4 to 6 weeks. In industry workers continuously exposed to nitrates, chest pain, acute myocardial infarction and even sudden death have occurred during temporary withdrawal of nitrate exposure.

Precautions: Headaches or symptoms of hypotension, such as weakness or dizziness, particularly when arising suddenly from a recumbent position, may be due to overdosage. When they occur, the dose should be reduced or use of nitroglycerin ointment discontinued.

Nitroglycerin is a potent vasodilator and causes a slight decrease in mean blood pressure (approximately 10 to 15 mm Hg) in some patients when used in therapeutic dosages. Caution should be exercised in using the drug in patients who are prone to, or who might be affected by hypotension.

Nitroglycerin ointment is not intended for immediate relief or acute attacks of angina pectoris. Sublingual nitroglycerin preparations should be used for this purpose.

Tolerance to this drug and cross tolerance to other nitrates or nitrites may occur.

Adverse Effects: Headache is the most common side effect, especially when higher dosages of the ointment are used. Headache may be treated with concomitant administration of mild analgesics. If headache is unresponsive to such treatment, the dose of nitroglycerin ointment should be reduced or the use of the product discontinued.

Less frequently, postural hypotension, an increase in heart rate, faintness, flushing, dizziness, nausea and dermatitis have been reported.

Overdose: Symptoms: Symptoms of overdosage are primarily related to vasodilation, including cutaneous flushing, headache, nausea, dizziness and hypotension. Methemoglobinemia is also possible.

Treatment: No specific antidote is available. Ointment should be wiped off immediately, followed by symptomatic and supportive treatment.

Dosage: Angina Pectoris: Ointment may be applied every 3 to 8 hours if necessary, but one application at bedtime frequently suffices for the entire night. The usual dose is 2.5 to 5 cm as squeezed from the tube. The optimal dose is determined by starting with an application of 1.25 cm and increasing the dose by 1.25 cm at a time until side effects (usually headache) occur or satisfactory response is obtained. Some patients may require as much as 10 to 12.5 cm, and/or application every 4 hours.

Nitroglycerin ointment is effective in the control of angina pectoris regardless of the site of application on the skin. Therefore, any convenient skin area may be used, but many patients prefer the chest because anginal pain originates in this area. Method of application: **Using Appli-ruler:** In applying the ointment, the specially designed Appli-ruler (supplied in each package) is placed printed-side down, and the necessary amount of ointment is squeezed from the tube onto the applicator. Then, the applicator is placed with the ointment-side down onto the desired area of the skin, usually the chest (although other areas can be used). The ointment is spread over at least 50×75 mm area in a thin uniform layer using the Appli-ruler that serves the dual purpose of measuring the amount of ointment and preventing absorption of the ointment through the fingers while it is being applied. The ointment should be covered with the Appli-ruler paper, plastic kitchen wrap or other suitable material. This can be held in place with adhesive or transparent tape.

Supplied: Each tube of ointment contains: 2% nitroglycerin. Nonmedicinal ingredients: lactose, lanolin, petrolatum and purified water. Tubes of 30 and 60 g. Keep tube tightly closed and store at room temperature (15 to 30°C).

NITROLINGUAL® PUMPSPRAY

Rhône-Poulenc Rorer

Nitroglycerin

Antianginal

Pharmacology: The principal action of nitroglycerin is that of all nitrates, namely, relaxation of vascular smooth muscle. Nitrates act primarily by reducing myocardial oxygen demand rather than increasing its oxygen supply. This effect is thought to be brought about predominantly by peripheral action. Although venous effects predominate, nitroglycerin produces, in a dose-related manner, dilation of both arterial and venous beds. Dilation of the post capillary vessels, including large veins, promotes peripheral pooling of blood and decreases venous return to the heart, reducing left ventricular end-diastolic pressure (pre-load). Arteriolar relaxation reduces systemic vascular resistance and arterial pressure (after-load). Left ventricular end-diastolic pressure and volume are decreased, resulting in reduction of ventricular size and wall tension. The reduction in ventricular wall tension results in a net decrease in myocardial oxygen consumption and a favourable net balance between myocardial oxygen supply and demand.

Pharmacokinetics: In a pharmacokinetic study when a single 0.8 mg dose of nitroglycerin Pumpspray was administered to 24 healthy volunteers, the mean C_{max} and t_{max} were 1.04 pg/mL.min and 7.5 min, respectively. Additionally, in these subjects the mean AUC was 12.8 pg/mL.min.

Nitroglycerin is rapidly metabolized in the liver by hepatic enzymes. The 2 active major metabolites are the hydrolysis products, 1,3-and 1,2-dinitro-glycerols. There are also two inactive minor metabolites, the 1- and 2-mononitroglycerols which are considered biologically inactive. Nitroglycerin and its major metabolites are approximately 60% protein bound.

Nitroglycerin is excreted by the renal route primarily as the 2 dinitro-metabolites, which have an excretion half-life of approximately 3 to 4 hours.

Indications: For the management and treatment of acute attacks of angina pectoris.

Contraindications: Severe anemia, closed angle glaucoma, increased intracranial pressure, myocardial infarction, hypotension or uncorrected hypovolemia, known hypersensitivity to nitroglycerin or previous idiosyncratic reaction to organic nitrates.

Warnings: The use of nitroglycerin in patients with congestive heart failure or with acute myocardial infarction requires careful clinical and/or hemodynamic monitoring.

Precautions: Headaches or symptoms of hypotension, such as weakness or dizziness, particularly when arising suddenly from a recumbent position, may be due to overdosage. When they occur, the dose or frequency of application of nitroglycerin should be reduced.

Nitroglycerin is a potent vasodilator and causes a slight decrease in mean blood pressure (approximately 10 to 15 mmHg) in some patients when used in therapeutic dosages. Caution should be exercised in using the drug in patients who are prone to, or who might be affected by hypotension. Alcohol may enhance sensitivity to the hypotensive effects of nitrates.

Tolerance to this drug and cross-tolerance to other nitrates or nitrites may occur. Physical dependence has also been described. With the chronic use of nitrates, there have been reports of anginal attacks being more easily provoked as well as reports of rebound in hemodynamic effects, occurring soon after nitrate withdrawal.

Pregnancy: Animal reproduction studies have not been done with nitroglycerin Pumpspray. As with all medication, nitroglycerin should only be given to a pregnant woman if clearly indicated.

Lactation: Because it is not known if nitroglycerin is excreted in human milk, caution should be exercised when the nitroglycerin Pumpspray is administered to a nursing mother.

Children: The safety and effectiveness of nitroglycerin in children have not been established.

Adverse Effects: Adverse reactions to nitroglycerin are generally dose-related. In a clinical trial studying patients with chronic stable angina, the following adverse events were reported during the use of the nitroglycerin Pumpspray: headache, dizziness, paresthesia and dyspnea. All adverse events were mild to moderate.

In clinical trials at various doses of nitroglycerin, the following adverse effects have been observed: headache, which may be severe and persistent, is the most commonly reported side effect of nitroglycerin. Cutaneous vasodilation with flushing, transient dizziness and weakness, as well as other signs associated with postural hypotension, such as tachycardia, may occasionally develop. Occasionally, an individual may exhibit marked sensitivity to the hypotensive effects of nitrates and severe responses (nausea, vomiting, weakness, restlessness, pallor, retrosternal discomfort, perspiration and collapse) may occur even with therapeutic doses. Nausea and vomiting appear to be uncommon. Drug rash and/or exfoliative dermatitis have been reported in patients receiving nitrate therapy. Clinically significant methemoglobinemia is rare at conventional doses, but may occur especially in patients with genetic hemoglobin abnormalities.

Overdose: Symptoms and Treatment: Symptoms of overdosage are primarily related to vasodilation, and include cutaneous flushing, headache, nausea, dizziness, and hypotension. Methemoglobinemia is also possible.

No specific antidote is available. Treatment should be symptomatic and supportive.

Dosage: The spray should not be inhaled and should be kept away from eyes. This spray formulation is intended to be applied and absorbed on or under the tongue.

Upon initiating therapy with the nitroglycerin Pumpspray, especially when changing from another form of nitroglycerin administration, patients should be followed closely by their physicians in order to determine the minimal effective dose for each patient.

Each metered dose contains 0.4 mg nitroglycerin. With the onset of an acute attack of angina pectoris, 1 or 2 metered doses (0.4 or 0.8 mg of nitroglycerin), as determined by experience, may be administered on or under the tongue, **without inhaling**. The optimal dose may be repeated twice at 5 to 10 minute intervals. Dosage must be individualized and should be sufficient to provide relief without producing untoward reactions.

During administration the patient should be at rest, ideally in the sitting position, and the container kept vertical with the nozzle head up. The opening in the nozzle head should be kept as close to the mouth as possible. Patients should familiarize themselves with the position of the spray orifice, identified by the finger rest on top of the valve, in order to facilitate administration at night.

Information for the Patient: See Blue Section—Information for the Patient "Nitrolingual Pumpspray".

Supplied: Each metered dose contains: nitroglycerin 0.4 mg in an aromatized oily solution. Nonmedicinal ingredients: dehydrated alcohol, medium chained partial glycerides, medium chained triglycerides and peppermint oil. Spray bottles delivering 200 metered doses. Store at room temperature (15 to 30°C). Do not place in hot water or near radiators, stoves or other sources of heat. Do not open forcefully or incinerate container or expose to temperature over 40°C.

New Product 1998

NITROLINGUAL® Spray
Rhône-Poulenc Rorer

Nitroglycerin

Antianginal

Pharmacology: The principal action of nitroglycerin is that of all nitrates, namely relaxation of vascular smooth muscle. Nitrates act primarily by reducing myocardial oxygen demand rather than increasing its oxygen supply. This effect is thought to be brought about predominantly by peripheral action. Although venous effects predominate, nitroglycerin produces, in a dose-related manner, dilation of both arterial and venous beds. Dilation of the post capillary vessels, including large veins, promotes peripheral pooling of blood and decreases venous return to the heart, reducing left ventricular end-diastolic pressure (pre-load). Arteriolar relaxation reduces systemic vascular resistance and arterial pressure (after-load). Left ventricular end-diastolic pressure and volume are decreased, resulting in reduction of ventricular size and wall tension. The reduction in ventricular wall tension results in a net decrease in myocardial oxygen consumption and a favorable net balance between myocardial oxygen supply and demand.

Pharmacokinetics: In one study of 13 healthy males, nitroglycerin was shown to have an apparent volume of distribution of approximately 250 L. No statistically significant differences were demonstrated between the mean values of maximum plasma concentration (C_{max}) and time to achieve C_{max} (T_{max}) with equal doses (0.8 mg) of Nitrolingual Spray and sublingual nitroglycerin tablets.

C_{max} after 0.8 mg of nitroglycerin by spray administration occurred on average within 5 minutes and the apparent plasma elimination half-life was approximately 5 minutes.

Nitroglycerin is rapidly metabolized in the liver by hepatic enzymes. The two active major metabolites are the hydrolysis products, 1,3- and 1,2-dinitroglycerols. There are also 2 inactive minor metabolites, the 1- and 2-mononitroglycerols which are considered biologically inactive. Nitroglycerin and its major metabolites are approximately 60% protein bound. Nitroglycerin is excreted by the renal route primarily as the 2 dinitrometabolites, which have an excretion half-life of approximately 3 to 4 hours.

Indications: For the management and treatment of acute attacks of angina pectoris.

Contraindications: Severe anemia, glaucoma, increased intracranial pressure, myocardial infarction, hypotension, known hypersensitivity to nitroglycerin or previous idiosyncratic reaction to organic nitrates.

Warnings: The use of nitroglycerin in patients with congestive heart failure or with acute myocardial infarction requires careful clinical and/or hemodynamic monitoring.

Precautions: Headaches or symptoms of hypotension, such as weakness or dizziness, particularly when arising suddenly from a recumbent position, may be due to overdosage. When they occur, the dose or frequency of application should be reduced.

Nitroglycerin is a potent vasodilator and causes a slight decrease in mean blood pressure (approximately 10 to 15 mmHg) in some patients when used in therapeutic dosages. Caution should be exercised in using the drug in patients who are prone to, or who might be affected by hypotension. Alcohol may enhance sensitivity to the hypotensive effects of nitrates.

Tolerance to this drug and cross tolerance to other nitrates or nitrites may occur. Physical dependence has also been described. With the chronic use of nitrates, there have been reports of anginal attacks being more easily provoked as well as reports of rebound in hemodynamic effects, occurring soon after nitrate withdrawal.

Pregnancy: Animal reproduction studies have not been done with nitroglycerin sublingual spray. As with all medication, nitroglycerin should only be given to a pregnant woman if clearly indicated.

Lactation: Because it is not known if nitroglycerin is excreted in human milk, caution should be exercised when this spray is administered to a nursing mother.

Children: The safety and effectiveness of nitroglycerin in children has not been established.

Adverse Effects: The use of nitroglycerin has been associated with headache, faintness, giddiness, lightheadedness, pallor, feeling cold, numbness of the legs. Nitroglycerin may also cause flushing, tachycardia, nausea, vomiting, restlessness, retrosternal discomfort, postural hypotension or dermatitis. An occasional individual may exhibit marked sensitivity to the hypotensive effects of nitrates. Clinically significant methemoglobinemia is rare at conventional doses, but may occur especially in patients with genetic hemoglobin abnormalities.

Overdose: Symptoms: Symptoms of overdosage are primarily related to vasodilation, and include cutaneous flushing, headache, nausea, dizziness, and hypotension. Methemoglobinemia is also possible.

Treatment: No specific antidote is available. Treatment should be symptomatic and supportive.

Dosage: Do not shake canister. Not for inhalation.

Upon initiating therapy with Nitrolingual Spray, especially when changing from another form of nitroglycerin administration, patients should be followed closely by their physicians in order to determine the minimal effective dose for each patient.

With the onset of an acute attack of angina pectoris, 1 or 2 metered doses (0.4 or 0.8 mg) of nitroglycerin, as determined by experience, may be administered onto or under the tongue, **without inhaling.** The optimal dose may be repeated twice at 5 to 10 minute intervals. Dosage must be individualized and should be sufficient to provide relief without producing untoward reactions.

During administration, the patient should be at rest, ideally in the sitting position, and the canister kept vertical with the nozzle head up. The opening in the nozzle head should be kept as close to the mouth as possible. Patients should familiarize themselves with the position of the spray orifice, identified by the finger rest on top of the valve, in order to facilitate administration at night.

Supplied: Each metered dose contains: nitroglycerin 0.4 mg in an aromatized oily solution. Nonmedicinal ingredients: dichlorodifluoromethane, dichlorotetrafluoroethane, ether, menthol, peppermint oil and vegetable oil. Nonflammable nontoxic propellant. Aerosol bottles delivering 200 metered doses. Do not expose the aerosol unit to temperatures above 50°C and do not open.

(Shown in Product Recognition Section)

NITRONG® SR
Rhône-Poulenc Rorer

Nitroglycerin

Antianginal

Pharmacology: The principal action of Nitrong (nitroglycerin) is that of all nitrates, namely relaxation of vascular smooth muscle. Nitrates act primarily by reducing myocardial oxygen demands rather than increasing its oxygen supply. This effect is thought to be brought about predominantly by peripheral action. Although venous effects predominate, nitroglycerin produces, in a dose-related manner, dilation of both arterial and venous beds. Dilatation of postcapillary vessels, including large veins, promotes peripheral pooling of blood, decreases venous return to the heart, reducing left ventricular end-diastolic pressure (preload). Arteriolar relaxation reduces systemic vascular resistance and arterial pressure (afterload). Left ventricular end-diastolic pressure and volume are decreased, resulting in reduction of ventricular size and wall tension. The reduction in ventricular wall tension results in a net decrease in myocardial oxygen consumption and a favorable net balance between myocardial oxygen supply and demand.

Studies in patients with angina have demonstrated that when given orally in adequate dosage, nitroglycerin has significant vasodilator activity (lasting approximately 8 hours) and improves exercise tolerance. Additional evidence that nitroglycerin is absorbed when given orally is provided by studies in which this agent improved cardiac performance for several hours in patients with severe intractable chronic congestive heart failure.

Indications: For the prevention of attacks of angina pectoris associated with chronic angina of effort.

Contraindications: Patients with severe anemia, increased intraocular pressure, increased intracranial pressure and hypotension. Known idiosyncrasy to organic nitrates.

Warnings: Data on the safe use of nitroglycerin during the early phase of myocardial infarction (the period during which clinical and laboratory findings are unstable) are insufficient to establish safety. The use of nitroglycerin in patients with congestive heart failure requires careful clinical and/or hemodynamic monitoring. Nitrate dependence may occur in patients with chronic use. To avoid possible withdrawal effect, which is a characteristic of vasodilators of the nitrate class, the administration of nitroglycerin should be gradually reduced over a period of 4 to 6 weeks. In industry workers continuously exposed to nitrates, chest pain, acute myocardial infarction and even sudden death have occurred during temporary withdrawal of nitrate exposure.

Precautions: Headaches or symptoms of hypotension, such as weakness or dizziness, particularly when arising suddenly from a recumbent position may be due to overdosage. When they occur, the dose should be reduced or the use discontinued.

Nitroglycerin is a potent vasodilator and causes a slight decrease in mean blood pressure (approximately 10 to 15 mmHg) in some patients when used in therapeutic dosages. Caution should be used in dispensing nitroglycerin in patients who are prone to, or who might be affected by hypotension. Nitrong-SR tablets are not intended for immediate relief of acute attacks of angina pectoris. Sublingual nitroglycerin preparations should be used for this purpose.

Tolerance to this drug and cross tolerance to other nitrates or nitrites may occur.

Adverse Effects: Headache is the most common side effect which can be treated with mild analgesics. If headache is unresponsive to such treatment, the dose should be reduced or its use discontinued.

Less frequently, postural hypotension, an increase in heart rate, faintness, flushing, dizziness, nausea, vomiting and dermatitis have been reported.

Overdose: Symptoms: Primarily related to vasodilation including cutaneous flushing, headache, nausea, dizziness and hypotension; methemoglobinemia is also possible.

Treatment: No specific antidote is available. Treatment should be symptomatic and supportive.

Dosage: Adults: Recommended initial dosage is 1 tablet 3 times a day before breakfast, late afternoon before a meal and before retiring. Dosage may be increased progressively up to 2 tablets 3 times a day.

Supplied: Each oral sustained-release tablet contains: nitroglycerin 2.6 mg. Nonmedicinal ingredients: alcohol, calcium stearate, D&C Yellow No. 10 aluminum lake, dicalcium phosphate, iron oxide, shellac, starch, sucrose and talc. Bottles of 100 and 1 000.

(Shown in Product Recognition Section)

NITROSTAT™
Parke-Davis

Nitroglycerin

Coronary Vasodilator

Indications: For the prophylaxis, treatment and management of patients with angina pectoris.

Contraindications: In patients with early myocardial infarction, severe anemia, increased intracranial pressure and those with a known hypersensitivity to nitroglycerin.

Warnings: The use of nitroglycerin during the early course of acute myocardial infarction requires particular attention to hemodynamic monitoring and clinical status because of the possibility of hypotension.

Precautions: Only the smallest dose required for effective relief of the acute anginal attack should be used. Excessive use may lead to the development of tolerance. Nitrostat tablets are intended for sublingual or buccal administration and should not be swallowed. The drug should be discontinued if blurring of vision or drying of the mouth occurs. Excessive dosage of nitroglycerin may produce severe headaches.

Severe hypotension particularly with upright posture, may occur even with small doses of nitroglycerin. The drug should be used cautiously in patients with volume depletion or low systolic blood pressure.

Paradoxical bradycardia and increased angina pectoris may accompany nitroglycerin-induced hypotension.

Nitratre therapy may aggravate angina caused by hypertrophic cardiomyopathy.

Tolerance to the vascular and antianginal effects of nitroglycerin and cross-tolerance to other nitrates and nitrites may occur.

Drug Interactions: Concomitant use of nitrates and alcohol may cause hypotension. Patients receiving antihypertensive drugs, beta-adrenergic blockers or phenothiazines and nitrates should be observed for possible additive hypotensive effects.

Marked orthostatic hypotension has been reported when calcium channel blockers and organic nitrates were used concomitantly. Dose adjustment of either drug may be necessary.

ASA may decrease the clearance and enhance the hemodynamic effects of sublingual nitroglycerin.

Nitrostat (cont'd)

A decrease in the therapeutic effect of sublingual nitroglycerin may result from use of long-acting nitrates.

Drug/Laboratory Test Interactions: Nitrates may interfere with the Zlatkis-Zak color reaction, causing a false report of decreased serum cholesterol.

Pregnancy: Nitroglycerin should be given to a pregnant woman only if clearly needed.

Lactation: Caution should be exercised when nitroglycerin is administered to a nursing woman.

Children: Safety and effectiveness in children have not been established.

Information for the Patient: If possible, patients should sit down when taking Nitrostat tablets. This eliminates the possibility of falling due to lightheadedness or dizziness.

Nitroglycerin may produce a burning or tingling sensation when administered sublingually; however, the ability to produce a burning or tingling sensation should not be considered a reliable method for determining the potency of the tablets.

Nitrostat should be kept in the original glass container, tightly capped. The cotton should be discarded once the bottle is opened.

Adverse Effects: Headache, which may be severe and persistent, may occur immediately after use. Vertigo, weakness, palpitation and other manifestations of postural hypotension may develop occasionally, particularly in erect, immobile patients. Marked sensitivity to the hypotensive effects of nitrates (manifested by nausea, vomiting, weakness, diaphoresis, pallor and collapse) may occur at therapeutic doses. Syncope due to nitrate vasodilation has been reported. Flushing, drug rash and exfoliative dermatitis have been reported in patients receiving nitrate therapy.

Overdose: Symptoms and Treatment: Nitrate overdose may result in severe hypotension, tachycardia, bradycardia, heart block, palpitation, death due to circulatory collapse, syncope, persistent throbbing headache, vertigo, visual disturbance, increased intracranial pressure, paralysis and coma. These may be followed by convulsions, flushing and diaphoresis, nausea and vomiting, colic and diarrhea, dyspnea and methemoglobinemia.

Since hypotension from nitroglycerin overdose results from venodilation and arterial hypovolemia, therapy should be directed towards central volume expansion. Elevation of extremities may be sufficient, but i.v. infusion may also be necessary. Use of arterial vasoconstrictors may do more harm than good. Management of nitroglycerin overdose in patients with renal disease or congestive heart failure may require invasive monitoring.

If methemoglobinemia is present, i.v. administration of methylene blue (1 to 2 mg/kg) may be required.

No specific antidote is available. Treatment should be symptomatic and supportive.

Dosage: Usual adult dosage range 0.3 to 0.6 mg. One tablet should be dissolved under the tongue or in the buccal pouch at the first sign of an acute anginal attack. The dose may be repeated approximately every 5 minutes until relief is obtained. If the pain persists after a total of 3 tablets in a 15-minute period, prompt medical attention is recommended. Nitrostat may be used prophylactically 5 to 10 minutes prior to engaging in activities that might precipitate an acute attack.

No dosage adjustment is required in patients with renal failure.

Supplied: 0.3 mg: Each sublingual tablet contains: nitroglycerin 0.3 mg. Nonmedicinal ingredients: alcohol, lactose, polyethylene glycol and sucrose. Energy: 0.13 kJ (0.54 kcal). Gluten-, paraben-, sodium-, sulfite- and tartrazine-free. Bottles of 100.

0.6 mg: Each sublingual tablet contains: nitroglycerin 0.6 mg. Nonmedicinal ingredients: alcohol, lactose, polyethylene glycol and sucrose. Energy: 0.13 kJ (0.54 kcal). Gluten-, paraben-, sodium-, sulfite- and tartrazine-free. Bottles of 100.

(Shown in Product Recognition Section)

Reviewed 1997

NIX® Creme Rinse

Warner-Lambert Consumer Healthcare

Permethrin

Topical Pediculicide—Ovicide

Pharmacology: Permethrin is a synthetic pyrethroid, active against a broad range of pests including lice, ticks, fleas, mites, and other arthropods. It acts on the nerve cell membrane to disrupt the sodium channel current by which the polarization of the membrane is regulated. Delayed repolarization and paralysis of the pests are the consequences of this disturbance.

In vitro data indicate that permethrin has excellent pediculicidal and ovicidal activity against Pediculus humanus var. capitis. The high cure rate of permethrin in patients with head lice following a single application is attributable to a combination of its pediculicidal and ovicidal activities and its residual persistence on the hair which may also prevent reinfestation.

Permethrin is rapidly metabolized by ester hydrolysis to inactive metabolites which are excreted primarily in the urine. Although the amount of permethrin absorbed after a single application of the 1% cream rinse has not been determined precisely, preliminary data suggest it is less than 2% of the amount applied. Residual persistence of permethrin is detectable on the hair for at least 10 days following a single application.

Indications: For the single-application treatment of infestation with Pediculus humanus var. capitis (the head louse) and its nits (eggs). Retreatment for recurrences is required in less than 1% of patients since the ovicidal activity may be supplemented by residual persistence of permethrin in the hair. If live lice are observed after at least 7 days following the initial application, a second application can be given.

Contraindications: In patients with known hypersensitivity to any of its components, to any synthetic pyrethroid or pyrethrin, or to chrysanthemums.

Warnings: If hypersensitivity to permethrin occurs, discontinue use.

Precautions: Head lice infestation is often accompanied by pruritus, erythema and edema. Treatment with permethrin may temporarily exacerbate these conditions.

Pregnancy: Reproduction studies have been performed in mice, rats and rabbits and have revealed no evidence of impaired fertility or harm to the fetus due to permethrin. There are, however, no adequate and well-controlled studies in pregnant women. Because animal reproduction studies are not always predictive of human response, this drug should be used during pregnancy only if clearly needed.

Lactation: It is not known whether this drug is excreted in human milk. Because many drugs are excreted in human milk, and because of the evidence for tumorigenic potential of permethrin in animal studies, consideration should be given to discontinuing nursing temporarily or withholding the drug while the mother is nursing.

Children: Permethrin is safe and effective in children 2 years of age and older. Safety and effectiveness in children less than 2 years of age have not been established.

Adverse Effects: The most frequent adverse reaction to permethrin is pruritus. This is usually a consequence of head lice infestation itself, but may be temporarily aggravated following treatment with permethrin. Mild temporary itching was experienced by 5.9% of patients enrolled in clinical studies; 3.4% experienced mild transient burning/stinging, tingling, numbness or scalp discomfort; and 2.1% experienced mild transient erythema, edema or rash of the scalp.

Overdose: Symptoms and Treatment: No instance of accidental ingestion has been reported. If ingested, gastric lavage and general supportive measures should be employed.

Dosage: Adults and Children: For use after the hair has been washed with conditioner-free shampoo, rinsed with water and towel dried. Apply a sufficient volume of permethrin to saturate the hair and scalp. It should remain on the hair for 10 minutes before being rinsed off with water. A single treatment is sufficient to eliminate head lice infestation. Remove nits using a fine toothed (nit) comb.

Shake well before using.

Information for the Patient: See Blue Section—Information for the Patient "Nix Creme Rinse".

Supplied: Each g of creme rinse contains: permethrin 1% w/w. Nonmedicinal ingredients: balsam Canada, cetyl alcohol, citric acid, FD&C Yellow No. 6, hydrolyzed animal protein, hydroxyethylcellulose, isopropyl alcohol, methylparaben , perfume, polyoxyethylene 10 cetyl ether, propylene glycol, propylparaben and stearalkonium chloride. Plastic squeeze bottles of 56 g (59 mL). Store at 15 to 25°C.

For comparative information on Tetracyclines, see the CPhA General Monograph in the WHITE SECTION.

NIX® Dermal Cream

Glaxo Wellcome

Permethrin

Topical Scabicide

Pharmacology: Permethrin is a synthetic pyrethroid, which is active against a broad range of pests including lice, ticks, fleas, mites, and other arthropods. It acts on the nerve cell membrane to disrupt the sodium channel current by which the polarization of the membrane is regulated. Delayed repolarization and paralysis of the pests are the consequences of this disturbance.

A very small amount (<2%) of topically administered permethrin is absorbed through the skin. This contrasts to the 32% absorption seen after ingestion. The maximum absorption occurs during the first 48 hours following application. Permethrin is metabolized by ester hydrolysis to dichlorovinyl acid derivatives (DCVAs). Blood levels of metabolites were still quantifiable after 28 days in one-third of test samples. The main route of excretion is via the kidneys.

Lag time for penetration of permethrin through the skin ranged from 1.3 to 4 hours for cis-permethrin and 2.6 to 4.8 hours for trans-permethrin. Male patients excreted more DCVA than female patients. Excretion of trans-DCVA in the urine was 4 to 5 times faster than cis-DCVA reflecting its greater concentration and more rapid rate of metabolism. Presence of esterase in skin could account for observed differences in the amount of DCVA excreted in urine of male and female patients.

There was no evidence of contact sensitization to permethrin during induction or challenge phases of maximization testing. No reactions were observed during phototoxicity testing.

Indications: For the treatment of infestation with Sarcoptes scabiei (scabies). If live mites or new lesions appear, a second treatment may be necessary 7 to 10 days after the first treatment.

Contraindications: Patients with known hypersensitivity to any of its components, to any synthetic pyrethroid or pyrethrin, or to chrysanthemums.

Warnings: If hypersensitivity to the dermal cream occurs, discontinue use.

Precautions: General: Scabies infestation is often accompanied by pruritus, edema and erythema. Treatment with permethrin may temporarily exacerbate these conditions. Pruritus caused by an acquired sensitivity to mites and their products frequently persists for one to several weeks following treatment; this reaction does not indicate treatment failure.

Information for the Patient: Patients with scabies should be advised that itching, mild burning and/or stinging may occur after application of permethrin. In clinical trials, approximately 75% of patients treated with permethrin who continued to manifest pruritus at 2 weeks had cessation by 4 weeks. If irritation persists, they should consult their physician. Permethrin may be very mildly irritating to the eyes. Patients should be advised to avoid contact with eyes during application and to flush with water immediately if the cream gets in the eyes.

Pregnancy: Teratogenic Effects: Reproduction studies have been performed in mice, rats, and rabbits (200 to 400 mg/kg/day orally) and have revealed no evidence of impaired fertility or harm to the fetus due to permethrin. There are, however, no adequate and well-controlled studies in pregnant women. Because animal reproduction studies are not always predictive of human response, this drug should be used during pregnancy only if clearly needed.

Lactation: It is not known whether this drug is excreted in human milk. Because many drugs are excreted in human milk and because of the evidence for tumorigenic potential of permethrin in some animal species, consideration should be given to discontinuing nursing temporarily or withholding the drug while the mother is nursing.

Children: Permethrin is safe and effective in children 2 years of age and older. Safety and effectiveness in children between 2 and 23 months of age are limited. This product should therefore only be used in this age group on the advice and supervision of a physician.

Adverse Effects: Ten percent of patients in clinical trials experienced generally mild and transient burning and stinging following application of the dermal cream. This was associated with the severity of infestation. Pruritus was reported in 7% of patients at various times post-application. Erythema, numbness, tingling and rash were reported in up to 2% of patients.

Overdose: Symptoms and Treatment: No instance of accidental ingestion has been reported. If ingested, gastric lavage and general supportive measures should be employed.

Dosage: Adults and Children over 12 Years: Approximately one 30 g tube/½ of a 60 g tube. 5 to 12 years: Approximately ½ of a 30 g tube/¼ of a 60 g tube. 2 to 5 years: Approximately ¼ of a 30 g tube/⅛ of a 60 g tube.

Usually 30 g is sufficient for an average adult. A few adults may need to use an additional 30 g.

It is recommended that family members and close contacts, including sexual partners, be treated with permethrin to reduce the risk of transmission or eliminate reinfestation.

Administration: Thoroughly massage the dermal cream into the skin from the head to the soles of the feet paying particular attention to the areas between the fingers and toes, wrists, axillae (arm pits), external genitalia (external sexual organs) and buttocks. Reapply to the hands if washed off with soap and water within 8 hours of application. It is **not necessary** to apply a thick visible layer of cream into the skin as it disappears on application. Scabies rarely infests the scalp of adults, although the hairline, neck, temple and forehead may be infested in geriatric patients. Children should be supervised by an adult.

The dermal cream should be removed by washing (shower or bath) after 12 to 14 hours.

In the majority of individuals, the scabies infestation is cleared with a single application of the cream. If necessary, a second application may be given 7 to 10 days after the first, but only if live mites can be demonstrated or new lesions appear.

To prevent reinfestations all clothing and bed linens used within 2 days prior to treatment should be machine-washed in hot water and dried in the dryer for at least 20 minutes, or dry cleaned.

Persistent pruritus after treatment is not an indication for retreatment (see Precautions).

Children Aged 2 to 23 Months: Children aged between 2 and 23 months should be treated only under medical supervision. The dose required is usually between ⅛ and ¼ of a 30 g tube. The cream should be massaged thoroughly into the skin from the head to the soles of the feet, as directed for adults and older children. Infants should also be treated on the scalp, temples and forehead.

Information for the Patient: See Blue Section—Information for the Patient "Nix Dermal Cream".

Supplied: Each g of dermal cream contains: permethrin 5%. Nonmedicinal ingredients: butylated hydroxytoluene, carbomer 934P, coconut oil, glycerin, glyceryl monostearate, isopropyl myristate, lanolin alcohols, mineral oil, polyoxyethylene cetyl ethers, purified water and sodium hydroxide. Formaldehyde 1 mg (0.1%) added as preservative. Tubes of 30 and 60 g. Store between 15 and 25°C.

NIZORAL® Cream ℞

Janssen-Ortho

Ketoconazole

Topical Antifungal

Pharmacology: In vitro studies suggest that the antifungal properties of ketoconazole may be related to its ability to impair the synthesis of ergosterol, a component of fungal and yeast cell membranes. Without the availability of this essential sterol, there are morphological alterations of the fungal and yeast cell membranes manifested as abnormal membranous inclusions between the cell wall and the plasma membrane. The inhibition of ergosterol synthesis has been attributed to interference with the reactions involved in the removal of the 14-α-methyl group of the precursor of ergosterol, lanosterol.

Indications: For the topical treatment of tinea pedis, tinea corporis and tinea cruris caused by T. rubrum, T. mentagrophytes and E. floccosum; and in the treatment of tinea versicolor (pityriasis) caused by M. furfur (P. orbiculare); and in the treatment of seborrheic dermatitis caused by P. ovale; and in the treatment of cutaneous candidiasis caused by C. albicans.

Contraindications: In persons who have shown hypersensitivity to the active or excipient ingredients of this formulation.

Warnings: Ketoconazole cream should never be employed for the treatment of infections of the eye.

To prevent a rebound effect after stopping a prolonged treatment with topical corticosteroids, it is recommended to continue applying a mild topical corticosteroid in the morning and to apply ketoconazole cream in the evening, and to subsequently and gradually withdraw the steroid therapy over a period of 2 to 3 weeks.

Precautions: If a reaction suggesting sensitivity or chemical irritation should occur, use of ketoconazole cream should be promptly discontinued.

Pregnancy and *Lactation:* Limited short-term studies in animals and in human volunteers on whom limited quantities of ketoconazole cream were tested have failed to demonstrate absorption of ketoconazole in detectable amounts. Due to the teratogenic nature of the active ingredient, ketoconazole, caution should be exercised when ketoconazole cream is administered to pregnant or nursing women.

Cross sensitivity with miconazole and other imidazoles may exist and caution is suggested when ketoconazole cream is employed in patients with known sensitivities to imidazoles.

Adverse Effects: Short-term studies indicate that ketoconazole cream is well tolerated by the skin. During clinical trials, 43 (5.0%) of 867 patients treated with the cream and 3 (1.8%) of 167 patients treated with placebo reported side effects consisting mainly of severe irritation, pruritus and stinging. One of the patients treated with ketoconazole cream 2% developed a painful allergic reaction (swelling of the foot).

In rare circumstances, allergic local skin phenomena such as contact dermatitis have been associated with ketoconazole cream or one of its components, namely sodium sulfite or propylene glycol.

Overdose: Symptoms and Treatment: There has been no experience with overdosage of ketoconazole cream. Treatment should include general supportive measures.

Dosage: When clinically warranted, therapy with ketoconazole cream may be initiated while results of culture and susceptibility tests are pending. Treatment should be adjusted according to the findings.

Ketoconazole cream should be applied to the affected and immediate surrounding area in patients with the following conditions: (see Table I).

Table I—Nizoral Cream

Dosage		
Conditions	**Frequency**	**Duration**
Tinea pedis	once daily	4 to 6 weeks
Tinea corporis	once daily	3 to 4 weeks
Tinea cruris	once daily	2 to 4 weeks
Tinea versicolor	once daily	2 to 3 weeks
Cutaneous candidiasis	once daily	2 to 3 weeks

More resistant cases may be treated twice daily depending on patient response.

Seborrheic dermatitis: Use twice daily for 4 weeks.

The full course of therapy should be followed to reduce the possibility of recurrence. If however, there is no response within the recommended treatment period, the diagnosis should be re-evaluated.

The safety of ketoconazole cream has not been established with treatment periods exceeding those recommended; therefore, treatment must not exceed the recommended duration of therapy indicated above.

Supplied: Each g of white, odorless cream contains: ketoconazole 20 mg (2%). Nonmedicinal ingredients: cetyl alcohol, isopropyl myristate, polysorbate 60, polysorbate 80, propylene glycol, purified water, sodium bisulfite, sorbitan monostearate and stearyl alcohol. Tubes of 30 g. Store at room temperature, below 25°C. Keep from freezing.

(Shown in Product Recognition Section)

Reviewed 1999

NIZORAL® Shampoo

McNeil Consumer Products

Ketoconazole

Topical Antifungal

Pharmacology: In vitro studies suggest that the antifungal properties of ketoconazole may be related to its ability to impair the synthesis of ergosterol, a component of fungal and yeast cell membranes. Without the availability of this essential sterol, there are morphological alterations of the fungal and yeast cell membranes manifested as abnormal membranous inclusions between the cell wall and the plasma membrane. The inhibition of ergosterol synthesis has been attributed to interference with the reactions involved in the removal of the 14-α-methyl group of the precursor of ergosterol, lanosterol.

Except for its specific pharmacologic effect, i.e., a sporocidal or fungicidal activity, ketoconazole when formulated in a 2% shampoo is not expected to exert any other pharmacodynamic effect when applied topically on the skin or hair.

Indications: For the topical treatment and prophylaxis of conditions in which the yeast Pityrosporum is involved, such as pityriasis capitis (dandruff). Also for seborrheic dermatitis.

Contraindications: In persons who have shown hypersensitivity to the active or excipient ingredients of this formulation.

Warnings: Irritation may occur when the shampoo is used immediately after prolonged treatment with topical corticosteroids. To prevent a rebound effect after stopping a prolonged treatment with topical corticosteroids, it is recommended to continue applying a mild topical corticosteroid at the onset of treatment with ketoconazole shampoo, and to subsequently and gradually withdraw the steroid therapy over a period of 2 to 3 weeks.

Precautions: If a reaction suggesting sensitivity or chemical irritation should occur, use of the shampoo should be discontinued.

Pregnancy and *Lactation:* Ketoconazole shampoo does not produce detectable blood levels after topical application. However due to the teratogenic nature of the active ingredient, ketoconazole, the use of the shampoo is not recommended in pregnant or nursing women except under the advice of a physician.

Children: Clinical data on the use of ketoconazole shampoo in children under 12 are not available; therefore, such use is not recommended except under the advice of a physician.

Adverse Effects: Ketoconazole 2% shampoo causes minimal skin and scalp irritation. During clinical trials, 33 (3.7%) of 892 patients treated with the shampoo and 12 (3.6%) of 330 patients treated with placebo reported side effects. The adverse effects reported by patients treated with ketoconazole 2% shampoo consisted mainly of: greasy hair or scalp (1.2%); dry (brittle) hair or scalp (0.9%); irritation (0.5%); burning sensation and dryness (eyebrows) (0.2%). All other adverse experiences were reported with an incidence of 0.1%: exfoliative dermatitis; dandruff; irritation around mouth (acne perioralis); contact allergy; worsening of acne; burning sensation or pruritus (scalp); cosmetological disorder; hair loss; tiny pustules on scalp; dryness and itching of forehead and cheeks.

In rare circumstances, mainly in patients with chemically damaged hair or gray hair, a discoloration of the hair has been observed.

Overdose: Symptoms and Treatment: Ingestion is usually followed by nausea and vomiting due to the detergent. In the event of accidental ingestion, only supportive measures should be carried out. In order to avoid aspiration, neither emesis nor gastric lavage should be performed. It has been reported that ketoconazole cannot be removed by hemodialysis.

Dosage: Adults and children over 12 years of age: Shampoo (5 to 10 mL) should be applied to the wet scalp, worked into a lather and left on for 3 to 5 minutes before rinsing with water. As with other shampoos, care should be taken to keep the shampoo out of the eyes and off the eyelids.

Treatment: Twice weekly for 2 to 4 weeks.

Prophylaxis: Once every 1 or 2 weeks.

Supplied: Each mL of orange viscous shampoo contains: ketoconazole 2% (20 mg/g). Nonmedicinal ingredients: coconut fatty acid diethanolamide, disodium monolaureth sulphosuccinate, erythrosin, hydrochloric acid, imidurea, laurdimonium hydrolyzed animal collagen, macrogol 120 methyl glucose dioleate, perfume bouquet, sodium chloride, sodium hydroxide, sodium laureth sulfate and purified water. HDPE flasks of 120 mL. Store at or below 25°C.

(Shown in Product Recognition Section)

NIZORAL® Tablets ℞

Janssen-Ortho

Ketoconazole

Antifungal

Pharmacology: In vitro studies suggest that the antifungal properties of ketoconazole may be related to its ability to impair the synthesis of ergosterol, a component of fungal and yeast cell membranes. Without the availability of this essential sterol, there are morphological alterations of the fungal and yeast cell membranes manifested as abnormal membranous inclusions between the cell wall and the plasma membrane. The inhibition of ergosterol synthesis has been attributed to interference with the reactions involved in the removal of the 14-α-methyl group of the precursor of ergosterol, lanosterol.

Nizoral Tablets (cont'd)

Indications: For the treatment of serious or life-threatening systemic fungal infections in normal, predisposed or immunocompromised patients where alternate therapy is considered inappropriate or has been unsuccessful: systemic candidiasis, chronic mucocutaneous candidiasis, coccidioidomycosis and paracoccidioidomycosis, histoplasmosis and chromomycosis.

The use of ketoconazole may also be considered in the treatment of severe, recalcitrant dermatophytoses unresponsive to other forms of therapy.

The type of organism responsible for the infection should be identified; however, therapy may be initiated prior to obtaining these results, when clinically warranted.

Note: The treatment of fungal infections of the CNS is not recommended; ketoconazole penetrates poorly into the CNS.

Contraindications: In patients with known hypersensitivity to the drug and in patients with hepatic dysfunction. Ketoconazole is contraindicated in women of childbearing potential unless effective forms of contraception are employed.

Concurrent therapy of ketoconazole tablets together with terfenadine is contraindicated. Ketoconazole may inhibit the metabolism of terfenadine, causing increased plasma levels of terfenadine. Increased plasma levels of terfenadine can result in prolonged QT intervals. Cases of severe cardiovascular events including death, cardiac arrest, torsades de pointes and other ventricular dysrhythmias have been reported in patients taking terfenadine in combination with ketoconazole.

Concurrent therapy of astemizole with oral ketoconazole is contraindicated. Pharmacokinetic data indicate that oral ketoconazole inhibits the metabolism of astemizole, resulting in elevated plasma levels of astemizole and its active metabolite desmethylastemizole which may prolong QT intervals.

Concomitant administration of oral ketoconazole and cisapride is contraindicated because it has resulted in markedly elevated cisapride plasma concentrations and prolonged QT intervals. This interaction has been rarely associated with ventricular arrhythmia and torsades de pointes.

Oral midazolam and triazolam should not be used by patients treated with ketoconazole tablets. Pharmacokinetic data revealed higher and prolonged midazolam concentrations when oral midazolam was administered concomitantly with oral ketoconazole versus placebo. A more pronounced and prolonged hypnotic effect of midazolam was also observed. Metabolism of both ketoconazole and midazolam by the same cytochrome P450 3A isozyme may explain this interaction. Similar pharmacokinetic and pharmacodynamic effects have been observed with triazolam which is primarily metabolized by the same P450 3A isozyme (see Precautions, Drug Interactions).

Pharmacokinetics data indicate that another oral antifungal, itraconazole inhibits the metabolism of HMG-CoA reductase inhibitors such as lovastatin. Coadministration of itraconazole and lovastatin resulted in elevated and prolonged plasma concentrations of lovastatin and its active metabolite, lovastatin acid, which may increase the risk of diffuse myalgia and rhabdomyolysis. Based on the chemical resemblance of itraconazole and ketoconazole, HMG-CoA reductase inhibitors that are metabolized by the P450 3A enzyme system, such as lovastatin should not be used during treatment with ketoconazole.

Warnings: Cases of idiosyncratic hepatocellular dysfunction have been reported during ketoconazole treatment. It is important to recognize that liver disorders can occur during therapy with ketoconazole. The occurrence of liver disorders while on ketoconazole could be fatal unless properly recognized and managed. Liver function tests such as SGGT, alkaline phosphatase, AST, ALT and bilirubin should be performed before treatment after 2 weeks and at periodic intervals during treatment (monthly or more frequently) particularly in patients who are expected to be on prolonged therapy (>2 weeks) or who have a history of significant alcohol consumption. The concurrent use of ketoconazole with potentially hepatotoxic drugs should be most carefully monitored, especially in patients who are expected to be on prolonged therapy or who have a history of significant alcohol consumption. Other factors increasing the risk of hepatitis are: women over 50, history of liver disease and known drug intolerance.

A mild transient asymptomatic increase of transaminases or alkaline phosphatase sometimes occurs. This asymptomatic reaction is harmless and does not necessarily require a discontinuation of the therapy but these patients should be monitored.

However, it should be emphasized that the occurrence of symptoms of hepatotoxicity, even with minor elevations of liver enzymes, is an indication for termination of therapy. Deaths have been reported with therapeutic doses of ketoconazole associated with evidence of hepatotoxicity.

Clinical studies in men have shown that single doses of ketoconazole at 200, 400 and 600 mg caused a dose-related decrease in serum testosterone levels, which returned to baseline values 8 to 24 hours later. During chronic administration (12 months) of 200 mg ketoconazole daily, testosterone levels were not significantly suppressed. However, at high doses (1 200 mg a day), administration of ketoconazole resulted in a reduction of serum testosterone to the castrate level (24 ng/dL) within 24 hours; this reduction was maintained for the duration of therapy (3 to 10 months). Oligospermia and azoospermia have been reported at therapeutic doses and above. In 6 healthy females receiving 400 mg once in the late follicular phase and once in the luteal phase, ketoconazole produced a 38% drop in 17-β-estradiol along with a 50% increase in progesterone during the follicular phase as well as a 61% drop in 17-β-estradiol and a 94% increase in progesterone during the luteal phase. Since ketoconazole influences steroid synthesis, the potential for a deleterious effect on puberty and/or fertility must be carefully considered when long-term therapy is contemplated in children.

A single 200 mg oral dose of ketoconazole had no effect on human cortisol levels. After a single dose of 400 or 600 mg, ketoconazole caused a slight nonsignificant fall in basal cortisol levels from 11.7 to 9.3 and 8.1 μg/dL respectively. There was a significant blunting of cortisol response to ACTH which was reversible; following a single dose of 400 or 600 mg ketoconazole, cortisol levels fell from 25.4 to 15.7 and 13.5 μg/dL respectively. Chronic (1 to 34 months) administration of 800 or 1 200 mg ketoconazole impaired the ability of the adrenal gland to produce cortisol, although evidence of frank adrenal insufficiency was not observed. In patients predisposed to adrenal insufficiency, in those having marginal adrenal function or during periods of prolonged stress, such as in the intensive care unit, cortisol levels should be monitored regularly. Administration of ketoconazole to males at a dose of 1 200 mg/day resulted in a rapid and significant decline in adrenal androgens (androstenedione and dehydroepiandrosterone).

Because the effects of ketoconazole on hormonal pathways are incompletely understood, judicious consideration is recommended before ketoconazole is prescribed on a long-term basis.

Toxicity studies in rats receiving ketoconazole admixed in the diet at doses of 160 mg/kg have indicated that ketoconazole leads to increased bone fragility in females. Therefore, therapeutic doses (400 mg/day) should not be exceeded in patients such as postmenopausal women and elderly patients, susceptible to increased bone fragility. In view of the ability of ketoconazole to interfere with steroid synthesis and vitamin D metabolism, careful consideration should be given prior to the use of ketoconazole in children. During long-term treatment, calcium and phosphorus serum levels should be monitored.

Studies in pregnant rats and in guinea pigs with ^{3}H-ketoconazole indicate that ketoconazole crosses the placental barrier. Whereas in the rat, fetal levels of total radioactivity were 6 times lower than those of the placenta, unchanged drug levels were 3.5 times lower in the fetuses. Concentrations of radioactivity in the fetal membrane indicate that ketoconazole is only very slowly eliminated from this membrane. In the pregnant patient the implications of placental transfer of ketoconazole must be carefully considered.

Precautions: Patients should be instructed to report any signs and symptoms which may suggest liver dysfunction so that appropriate biochemical testing can be done. Such signs and symptoms would include unusual fatigue, anorexia, nausea and/or vomiting, jaundice, dark urine or pale stools. Patients who receive ketoconazole concomitantly with potentially hepatotoxic drugs, those who are expected to be on long-term therapy (>2 weeks) as well as those with a history of significant alcohol intake or suspicion of liver disorder should have liver function tests performed before and during the initial days of treatment and at periodic intervals during treatment [monthly or more frequently (see Warnings)].

Since ketoconazole influences steroid synthesis, the potential for a deleterious effect on puberty and/or fertility must be carefully considered when long-term therapy is contemplated in children.

Anaphylactic reactions to ketoconazole with severe angioedema have been reported in 2 cases. Cross-sensitivity with miconazole may exist and caution is suggested when ketoconazole is administered to patients with a known sensitivity to miconazole.

Patients with Decreased Gastric Acidity: Absorption of ketoconazole is impaired when gastric acidity is decreased. In patients also receiving acid neutralizing medicines (e.g., aluminium hydroxide) these should be administered at least 2 hours after the intake of ketoconazole. In patients with achlorhydria such as certain AIDS patients and patients on acid secretion suppressors (e.g., H_2-antagonists, proton pump inhibitors) it is advisable to administer ketoconazole with a cola beverage.

Women of Childbearing Age: In women of childbearing potential, an effective form of contraception must be used during therapy with ketoconazole.

Pregnancy: Ketoconazole has been shown to be teratogenic (syndactyly, oligodactyly, abnormal head and leg formation) in the rat when given at 80 mg/kg administered in the diet. When ketoconazole was given to rats by gavage, evidence of maternal toxicity and embryotoxicity was seen with doses as low as 10 mg/kg. There is no experience with the use of ketoconazole in pregnant women, but animal experiments in pregnant rats and guinea pigs indicate that ketoconazole crosses the placental barrier and that ketoconazole is only very slowly eliminated from fetal membranes.

Very careful consideration should be given to the implications for both mother and fetus before using ketoconazole in pregnant patients.

Lactation: Ketoconazole is excreted in the milk. When treatment with the drug is deemed necessary for the lactating patient, nursing should be stopped before therapy with ketoconazole is initiated.

Children: Although ketoconazole has been used in children under 2 years of age, the number of instances is limited and monitoring was not comprehensive. Caution should be exercised when ketoconazole is administered to children and careful hepatic and hematological monitoring is indicated. In view of the ability of ketoconazole to interfere with steroid synthesis and vitamin D metabolism, careful consideration should be given prior to the use of ketoconazole in children. There has been a report of hypoparathyroidism developing in a 6 year old during long-term therapy with ketoconazole. During long-term treatment, calcium and phosphorus serum levels should be monitored.

Drug Interactions: Since ketoconazole inhibits certain hepatic P450 enzymes, especially of the CYP 3A family, it may decrease the elimination of coadministered drugs whose metabolism depends on such enzymes. Increased levels of such drugs, when used together with ketoconazole, have been associated with an increase and/or a prolongation of their effects, including side effects. Known examples of potentially serious interactions are:

Ketoconazole has been reported to increase plasma concentrations of cyclosporine. When ketoconazole and cyclosporine are used concomitantly, the dose requirement for cyclosporine may be substantially reduced in order to achieve appropriate plasma trough levels. Blood levels of cyclosporine should be monitored when the 2 drugs are given concomitantly.

Ketoconazole (tablets or suspension) inhibits the metabolism of terfenadine, resulting in an increased plasma concentration of terfenadine and a delay in the elimination of its acid metabolite. The increased plasma concentration of terfenadine or its metabolite may result in prolonged QT intervals (see Contraindications).

Pharmacokinetic data indicate that oral ketoconazole inhibits the metabolism of astemizole, resulting in elevated plasma levels of astemizole and its active metabolite desmethylastemizole which may prolong QT intervals (see Contraindications).

Human pharmacokinetic data indicate that oral ketoconazole potently inhibits the metabolism of cisapride, increasing its half-life and plasma concentration and resulting in a mean 8-fold increase in its AUC. Data suggest that coadministration of oral ketoconazole and cisapride can result in prolongation of the QT interval on the ECG (see Contraindications).

After the coadministration of 200 mg oral ketoconazole twice daily and one 20 mg dose of loratadine to 11 subjects, the AUC and C_{max} of loratadine averaged 302% (±142 S.D.) and 251% (±68 S.D.), respectively, of those obtained after cotreatment with placebo. The AUC and C_{max} of descarboethoxyloratadine, an active metabolite, averaged 155% (±27 S.D.) and 141% (±35 S.D.), respectively. However, no related changes were noted in the QT_c on ECG taken at 2, 6, and 24 hours after the coadministration. Also, there were no clinically significant differences in adverse events when loratadine was administered with or without ketoconazole.

Pharmacokinetic data suggest that oral ketoconazole may inhibit the metabolism of oral midazolam. In 9 subjects, pretreatment with 400 mg ketoconazole once daily for 4 days resulted in a 15-fold increase in midazolam $AUC_{0-\infty}$, an approximate 4-fold increase in C_{max}, and an approximate 3-fold increase in $t^1/_2$. Enhanced and prolonged sedative effects were also observed. Similar pharmacokinetic and pharmacodynamic effects have been observed for triazolam which is primarily metabolized by the same P450 3A isozyme. In 9 subjects, pretreatment with 400 mg ketoconazole for 4 days resulted in a 22-fold increase in triazolam $AUC_{0-\infty}$, a 3-fold increase in C_{max} and a 6-fold increase in $t½$. Midazolam and triazolam should not be used by patients treated with ketoconazole (see Contraindications). If midazolam is administered i.v., special precaution is required since the sedative effect may be prolonged.

Pharmacokinetic data demonstrate that when coadministered, another oral antifungal, itraconazole inhibits the metabolism of lovastatin, resulting in increased plasma concentrations of lovastatin, and its active metabolite lovastatin acid, and a 20-fold increase in AUC for both compounds. These increased plasma levels potentially elevate the risk of skeletal muscle toxicity such as diffuse myalgia and rhabdomyolysis. Based on the chemical resemblance of itraconazole and ketoconazole, concomitant administration of ketoconazole with HMG-CoA reductase inhibitors such as lovastatin is contraindicated (see Contraindications).

There has been a report of potentiation of the action of warfarin by ketoconazole. In patients, the possibility of a sharp drop in the prothrombin level during concomitant administration of ketoconazole with antivitamin-K type oral anticoagulants should be considered and more careful monitoring of anticoagulant effect is necessary, with an appropriate adjustment of the warfarin dose.

Ketoconazole may increase the plasma levels of methylprednisolone and possibly busulphane and tacrolimus. The dosage of such drugs, if coadministered with ketoconazole, should be reduced if necessary.

There have also been reports of decreased insulin needs in diabetic patients treated with ketoconazole. Because of a possible insulin-sparing effect of ketoconazole, insulin requirements should be assessed more frequently when ketoconazole is used concomitantly with insulin.

Since administration of rifampicin and/or enzyme inducers such as isoniazid in conjunction with ketoconazole reduces the blood levels of the latter, these drugs should not be administered concomitantly.

There has been a report of an interaction between ketoconazole and phenytoin in a patient receiving concomitant therapy. This interaction is complex and is a result of the opposing actions of both agents on cytochrome P450 enzymes: while ketoconazole tends to inhibit this enzymatic system, phenytoin induces it, resulting in a decrease or an increase of either drug in the plasma.

Rare cases of a disulfiram-like reaction to alcohol, characterized by flushing, rash, peripheral edema, nausea and headache have been reported. All symptoms completely resolved within a few hours.

Adverse Effects: Some deaths have occurred during clinical trials with ketoconazole. These may or may not be drug-related.
Gastrointestinal: dyspepsia, nausea and vomiting (3%), GI hemorrhage (<1%), abdominal pain (1.2%), diarrhea (<1%).
Dermatological: pruritus (1.5%), alopecia (<1%), purpura (<1%), rash (<1%), dermatitis (<1%).
CNS: headache, dizziness, somnolence, tremors, nervousness, paresthesias (<1% in all cases).
Endocrinological: gynecomastia (<1%), dose-dependent decrease in testosterone serum levels, decrease in basal and ACTH-induced cortisol levels, increased serum levels of 17-OH progesterone and decreased urinary levels of 17-ketosteroids, hypoparathyroidism.
Genitourinary: oligospermia and azoospermia, impotence, loss of libido, menstrual irregularities.
Hematological: thrombocytopenia, eosinophilia, decreased hematocrit, anemia, leukopenia, neutropenia (<1%).
Hepatic: idiosyncratic hepatocellular dysfunction (<0.01%; see Warnings); transient increases in liver enzymes. Three patients have died in hepatic coma; 2 when ketoconazole therapy was continued despite icteric symptoms, and the third despite discontinuation of therapy.
Miscellaneous: fever and chills, photophobia, idiosyncratic allergic reactions, anaphylactic shock, pronounced dyspnea, arthralgia, sensation of detachment (at 800 mg/day), corneal deposits, cataract enlargement (<1%).
Postmarketing: In rare instances, cases of exanthema, urticaria and reversible increased intracranial pressure (e.g., papiloedema, bulging fontanelle in infants) have been reported in association with ketoconazole treatment.

Overdose: Symptoms and Treatment: In the event of accidental overdosage with ketoconazole, supportive measures, including gastric lavage (within the first hour) with sodium bicarbonate, may be employed. Activated charcoal may be given if considered appropriate. It has been reported that ketoconazole cannot be removed by hemodialysis.

Dosage: When ketoconazole therapy may be indicated, the type of organism responsible for the infection should be identified, although therapy may be initiated prior to obtaining these results, when clinically warranted.

General guidelines for the duration of ketoconazole treatment in patients with severe or recalcitrant fungal infections: See Table I.
Note: See Warnings and Precautions.

Table I—Nizoral

Duration of Treatment

Condition	Recommended Treatment[a]	Response Time[b]
Dermal and Cutaneous Mycoses		
Dermatomycoses	4–8 weeks	4 weeks
Hair or scalp mycoses	4–8 weeks	4 weeks
Pityriasis versicolor	3–6 weeks	3 weeks
Oral thrush	1–2 weeks	1 week
Chronic mucocutaneous candidiasis	6–12 months	4 months
Onychomycosis	6–12 months	3 months
Deep Mycoses[c]		
Systemic candidiasis	2–4 weeks	4 weeks
Paracoccidioidomycosis	2–4 months	2 months
Coccidioidomycosis	>6 months	6 months
Histoplasmosis	2–4 months	2 months
Chromomycosis	>6 months	3 months

[a]The final decision on length of therapy in individual patients should be based on clinical and mycological response whenever possible.
[b]If no response is seen during this period, dosage can be increased up to the maximum recommended dose.
[c]In deep mycoses treatment should continue for at least 1 week after apparent eradication of the infecting fungus.

Adults: Ketoconazole should be administered at a dose of 200 mg once a day. Patients who fail to show a response (see Table I) may have inadequate blood levels (<1 μg/mL) as determined by bioassay and the dose may be increased to 400 mg. Ketoconazole blood levels can also be determined by an HPLC assay.

A maximum daily dose of 400 mg should not be exceeded.
Children: 20 kg or less: 50 mg once daily; 20 to 40 kg: 100 mg once daily; over 40 kg: 200 mg once daily.

A maximum daily dose of 100 to 400 mg should not be exceeded.

Ketoconazole should be taken once daily with a meal. Concomitant administration of agents which inhibit gastric secretion should be avoided since ketoconazole requires adequate gastric acidity for dissolution. In patients also receiving acid neutralizing medicines (e.g., aluminium hydroxide) these should be administered at least 2 hours after the intake of ketoconazole. In patients with achlorhydria such as certain AIDS patients and patients on acid secretion suppressors (e.g. H_2-antagonists, proton pump inhibitors) it is advisable to administer ketoconazole with a cola beverage.

Supplied: Each white to slightly grey, half-scored tablet, imprinted JANSSEN on one face and NIZORAL on the other, contains: ketoconazole 200 mg. Nonmedicinal ingredients: colloidal silicone dioxide, cornstarch, lactose, magnesium stearate, microcrystalline cellulose and povidone. Bisulfites-, gluten- and tartrazine-free. HDPE bottles of 30 and 100. Store at room temperature (15 to 30°C).

(Shown in Product Recognition Section)

Reviewed 1999

NOLVADEX®
NOLVADEX®-D

Zeneca

Tamoxifen Citrate

Antineoplastic

Pharmacology: Tamoxifen, the active ingredient, is a nonsteroidal agent which has demonstrated potent antiestrogenic properties in animal test systems. The antiestrogenic effects are related to its ability to compete with estrogen for binding sites in target tissues such as breast and uterus. Tamoxifen inhibits the induction of rat mammary carcinoma induced by dimethylbenzanthracene (DMBA), and causes the regression of already established DMBA-induced tumors. In this rat model, tamoxifen appears to exert its antitumor effects by binding to estrogen receptors.

In cytosols derived from human endometrium and human breast and uterine adenocarcinomas, tamoxifen competes with estradiol for estrogen receptor protein.

Reports of advanced breast cancer trials conducted worldwide, however, indicate that, using established criteria, there is an objective response rate (complete and partial remission) to tamoxifen of approximately 10% in patients with estrogen receptor negative tumors which may indicate other mechanisms of action. A further small percentage of patients show positive benefit in that they are reported to fall into the disease stabilization category. This may be explained by the shortcomings of the assay procedure or by actions of tamoxifen at loci other than the estrogen receptor.

Ranges as large as 0 to 300 fmol/mg protein have been reported in histologically comparable portions of the same tumor. In addition, the collection, transport and storage of tumor specimens can affect the validity of current estrogen receptor assays.

The apparent discrepancy in correlation between estrogen receptor status and clinical response may also be explained by recent in vitro evidence indicating that not all of the growth inhibiting effects of tamoxifen are mediated through the estrogen receptor. Tamoxifen has been shown to have a low affinity for the androgen receptor and on a binding site distinct from the estrogen receptor. The possibility also exists that tamoxifen interferes with the action of hormonal steroids on cell growth, that it could modulate the action of peptide hormones at their receptors by effects on cell membranes, and that it inhibits prostaglandin synthetase thereby having the potential to limit tumor growth. It is recognized that tamoxifen also displays estrogenic-like effects on several body systems including the endometrium, bone and blood lipids.

Therefore, although evidence suggests that patients with estrogen receptor positive tumors are more likely to respond, tamoxifen therapy may be considered in patients whose estrogen receptor status is unknown, in doubt or negative.

Pharmacokinetics: Preliminary pharmacokinetics in women using radiolabeled tamoxifen have shown that most of the radioactivity is slowly excreted in the feces, with only small amounts appearing in urine. The drug is excreted mainly as conjugates, with unchanged drug and hydroxylated metabolites accounting for 30% of the total. Blood levels of total radioactivity following single oral doses of approximately 0.3 mg/kg reached peak values of 0.06 to 0.14 μg/mL at 3 to 7 hours after dosing, with only 20 to 30% of the drug present as tamoxifen. There was an initial half-life of 7 to 14 hours with secondary peaks 4 or more days later. The prolongation of blood levels and fecal excretion is believed to be due to enterohepatic circulation.

Indications: In the treatment of breast cancer in estrogen receptor positive tumors.

Contraindications: In persons hypersensitive to this product.
Pregnancy: Tamoxifen must not be given during pregnancy. There have been a small number of reports of spontaneous abortions, birth defects and fetal deaths after women have taken tamoxifen, although no causal relationship has been established.

Reproductive toxicology studies in rats, rabbits and monkeys have shown no teratogenic potential.

In rodent models of fetal reproductive tract development, tamoxifen was associated with changes similar to those caused by estradiol, ethynylestradiol, clomiphene and diethylstilbestrol (DES). Although the clinical relevance of these changes is unknown, some of them, especially vaginal adenosis, are similar to those seen in young women who were exposed to DES in utero and who have a 1 in 1 000 risk of developing clear-cell carcinoma of the vagina or cervix. Only a small number of pregnant women have been exposed to tamoxifen. Such exposure has not been reported to cause subsequent vaginal adenosis or clear-cell carcinoma of the vagina or cervix in young women exposed in utero to tamoxifen.

Women should be advised not to become pregnant while taking tamoxifen and should use barrier or other nonhormonal contraceptive methods if sexually active. Premenopausal patients must be carefully examined before treatment to exclude the possibility of pregnancy. Women should be informed of the potential risks to the fetus, should they become pregnant while taking tamoxifen or within 2 months of cessation of therapy.

Warnings: Tamoxifen should be used only for the conditions listed under the Indications section.

Disturbances of menstrual function, including oligomenorrhea and amenorrhea, have been reported in a proportion of premenopausal women receiving tamoxifen for the treatment

Nolvadex (cont'd)

of breast cancer. Available information indicates that in those women receiving tamoxifen for up to 2 years for the treatment of early breast cancer who develop disturbances of menstrual function on treatment, a proportion return to normal cyclical bleeding on cessation of therapy.

Hepatocellular carcinomas as well as cataracts have been reported in the 2-year oncogenicity study in rats receiving tamoxifen. Gonadal tumors have been reported in mice receiving tamoxifen in long-term studies. The clinical relevance of these findings has not been established.

A number of second primary tumors, occurring at sites other than the endometrium and the opposite breast, have been reported in clinical trials, following the treatment of breast cancer patients with tamoxifen. No causal link has been established and the clinical significance of these observations remains unclear.

Precautions: Tamoxifen should be used cautiously in patients with existing thrombocytopenia or leukopenia. Decreases in platelet counts, usually to 50 000 to 100 000/mm^3, infrequently lower, have been observed occasionally during treatment with tamoxifen. However, no hemorrhagic tendency has been reported, and the platelet counts returned to normal levels even though treatment with tamoxifen was continued.

Transient decreases in leukocytes also have been observed occasionally during treatment. Although it was uncertain if these occasional incidences of leukopenia and thrombocytopenia were due to tamoxifen therapy, complete blood counts, including platelet counts, should be obtained periodically.

As with other additive hormonal therapy (estrogens and androgens), hypercalcemia has been reported in some breast cancer patients with bone metastases within a few weeks of starting treatment with tamoxifen. Any symptoms suggestive of hypercalcemia should be evaluated promptly. Patients who have metastatic bone disease should have periodic serum calcium determinations during the first few weeks of tamoxifen therapy. If hypercalcemia is present, appropriate measures should be taken and, if severe, tamoxifen should be discontinued.

The first patient follow-up should be done within 1 month following initiation of treatment. Thereafter, examinations may be performed at 1- to 2-month intervals. If adverse reactions such as hot flashes, nausea or vomiting occur, and are severe, they may be controlled in some patients by a reduction of dosage (within the recommended dose range) without loss of effect on the disease.

Bone pain, if it should occur, may require the use of analgesics.

An increased incidence of endometrial cancer has been reported in association with tamoxifen treatment. The incidence and pattern of this increase suggest that the underlying mechanism may be related to estrogenic properties of tamoxifen. Any patients receiving tamoxifen or having previously received tamoxifen who report abnormal gynecological symptoms, especially vaginal bleeding, should be promptly investigated. Ovarian cysts have been observed in a small number of premenopausal patients with advanced breast cancer who have been treated with tamoxifen.

In clinical studies, the median duration of treatment before the onset of a definite objective response has been 2 months. However, approximately 25% of patients who eventually responded were treated for 4 or more months before a definite objective response was recorded.

The duration of treatment with tamoxifen will depend on the patient's response. The drug should be continued as long as there is a favorable response.

With obvious disease progression, the drug should be discontinued. However, because an occasional patient will have a local disease flare (see Adverse Effects) or an increase in bone pain shortly after starting tamoxifen, it is sometimes difficult during the first few weeks of treatment to determine whether the patient's disease is progressing or whether it will stabilize or respond to continued treatment. There are data to suggest that, if possible, treatment should not be discontinued before a minimum of 3 to 4 weeks.

Drug Interactions: When tamoxifen is used in combination with coumarin-type anticoagulants, a significant increase in anticoagulant effect may occur. Where such coadministration exists, careful monitoring of the patient's prothrombin time is recommended.

When tamoxifen is used in combination with cytotoxic agents, there is increased risk of thromboembolic events occurring.

Lactation: It is not known if tamoxifen is excreted in human milk and, therefore, the drug is not recommended during lactation. The decision either to discontinue nursing or discontinue tamoxifen should take into account the importance of the drug to the mother.

Adverse Effects: The most frequent adverse reactions to tamoxifen are hot flashes, nausea and vomiting. These may occur in up to 25% of all patients and are rarely severe enough to require discontinuation of treatment.

Less frequently reported adverse reactions are vaginal bleeding, vaginal discharge and skin rash. Usually these have not been of sufficient severity to require dosage reduction or discontinuation of treatment.

Increased bone and tumor pain and also local disease flare have occurred. These are sometimes associated with a good tumor response. Patients with soft tissue disease may have sudden increases in the size of pre-existing lesions, sometimes associated with marked erythema within and surrounding the lesions, and/or the development of new lesions. When they occur, the bone pain or disease flare are seen shortly after starting tamoxifen and generally subside rapidly.

Other adverse reactions which are seen infrequently are hypercalcemia, peripheral edema, distaste for food, pruritus vulvae, depression, dizziness, light-headedness, headache and alopecia. Isolated cases of erythema multiforme, Stevens-Johnson syndrome and bullous pemphigoid, have also been reported.

Elevation of ALT, AST and GGT levels has been reported infrequently during tamoxifen therapy. Overt cholestasis has occurred less frequently and, in addition, there have been rare reports of benign, symptomatic hepatic cyst, peliosis hepatitis and fatty liver.

Ocular changes have been reported in a few breast cancer patients who, as part of a clinical trial, were treated for periods longer than 1 year with doses of tamoxifen that were at least 4 times the highest recommended daily dose of 40 mg. In each instance, the total amount of drug exceeded 100 g. These changes were a retinopathy and, in a few patients, corneal changes and decreased visual acuity. There were multiple light refractile opacities in the paramacular area, and macular edema. The corneal lesions consist of whorl-like superficial opacities. Ophthalmologic examinations of selected patients who received long-term therapy with tamoxifen at recommended doses did not detect any ocular pathology attributable to the drug.

In addition, a number of cases of ocular changes including visual disturbance, cataracts, and/or corneal changes and/or retinopathy have been reported in patients treated with tamoxifen at recommended doses. It is uncertain if these effects are due to tamoxifen, however, cataracts have been seen in the 2-year oncogenicity study in rats.

Uterine fibroids and endometrial changes including hyperplasia and polyps have been reported.

Leukopenia has been observed following the administration of tamoxifen, sometimes in association with anemia and/or thrombocytopenia. Neutropenia has been reported on rare occasions; this can sometimes be severe.

There have been infrequent reports of thromboembolic events occurring during tamoxifen therapy. There is some evidence of an increased incidence of these events during tamoxifen therapy, although a causal relationship with tamoxifen has not been established.

Overdose: Symptoms: Acute overdosage in humans has not been reported. Possible overdosage effects might include hot flashes, nausea, vomiting and vaginal bleeding.

Treatment: No specific treatment for overdosage is known and treatment must be symptomatic. In the case of accidental ingestion by a child, gastric emptying is suggested.

Dosage: The recommended daily dose is 20 to 40 mg in a single or 2 divided doses. The lowest effective dose should be used.

Information for the Patient: See Blue Section—Information for the Patient "Nolvadex/Nolvadex-D".

Supplied: Nolvadex: Each off-white to white, round, film-coated, biconvex tablet, intagliated with NOLVADEX 10 on one face and plain on the reverse, contains: tamoxifen citrate 15.2 mg, equivalent to 10 mg of tamoxifen. Nonmedicinal ingredients: cornstarch, croscarmellose sodium, gelatin, lactose, macrogol, magnesium stearate, methylhydroxypropylcellulose, and titanium dioxide. Energy: 1.68 kJ (0.4 kcal)/tablet. Alcohol-, sodium- and tartrazine-free. Containers of 250. Plain and unit dose packs of 60.

Nolvadex-D: Each off-white to white, octagonal, film-coated, biconvex tablet, intagliated with NOLVADEX D on one face and plain on the reverse, contains: tamoxifen citrate 30.4 mg equivalent to 20 mg tamoxifen. Nonmedicinal ingredients: cornstarch, croscarmellose sodium, gelatin, lactose, macrogol, magnesium stearate, methylhydroxypropylcellulose, and titanium dioxide. Energy: 3.36 kJ (0.8 kcal)/tablet. Alcohol-, sodium- and tartrazine-free. Plain and unit dose packs of 30 and 60.

Store at room temperature protected from light.

Reviewed 1999

NORCURON® Ⓟ

Organon

Vecuronium Bromide

Nondepolarizing Neuromuscular Blocking Agent

Pharmacology: Vecuronium is a nondepolarizing neuromuscular blocking agent possessing all of the characteristic curariform pharmacological actions of this class of drugs. It acts by competing for cholinergic receptors at the motor end-plate. The antagonism to acetylcholine is inhibited and neuromuscular block is reversed by acetylcholinesterase inhibitors such as neostigmine, edrophonium, and pyridostigmine. Vecuronium is about a third more potent than pancuronium; the duration of neuromuscular blockade produced by vecuronium is shorter than that of pancuronium at initially equipotent doses. The time to onset of paralysis decreases and the duration of maximum effect increases with increasing vecuronium doses. The use of a peripheral nerve stimulator is of benefit in assessing the degree of muscular relaxation.

The ED_{90} (dose required to produce 90% suppression of the muscle twitch response while under balanced anesthesia) has averaged 0.057 mg/kg (0.049 to 0.062 mg/kg in various studies). An initial vecuronium dose of 0.08 to 0.10 mg/kg generally produces first depression of twitch in approximately 1 minute, good or excellent intubation conditions within 2.5 to 3.0 minutes, and maximum neuromuscular blockade within 3 to 5 minutes of injection in most patients. Under balanced anesthesia, the time to 25% recovery of the control twitch response (clinical duration) is approximately 25 to 40 minutes after injection and recovery is usually 95% complete approximately 45 to 65 minutes after injection of an intubating dose.

The neuromuscular blocking action of vecuronium is slightly enhanced in the presence of potent inhalation anesthetics. If vecuronium is first administered more than 5 minutes after the start of the inhalation of enflurane, isoflurane, or halothane, or when steady state has been achieved, the intubating dose of vecuronium may be decreased by approximately 15% (see Dosage).

Prior administration of succinylcholine may enhance the neuromuscular blocking effect of vecuronium and its duration of action. With succinylcholine as the intubating agent, initial doses of 0.04 to 0.06 mg/kg of vecuronium will produce complete neuromuscular block with clinical duration of action of 25 to 30 minutes. If succinylcholine is used prior to vecuronium, the administration of vecuronium should be delayed until the patient starts recovering from succinylcholine-induced neuromuscular blockade. The effect of prior use of other nondepolarizing neuromuscular blocking agents on the activity of vecuronium has not been studied (see Precautions, Drug Interactions).

Repeated administration of maintenance doses of vecuronium has little or no cumulative effect on the duration of neuromuscular blockade. Therefore, repeat doses can be administered at relatively regular intervals with predictable results. After an initial dose of 0.08 to 0.10 mg/kg under balanced anesthesia, the first maintenance dose of 0.010 to 0.015 mg/kg is generally required within 25 to 40 minutes; subsequent maintenance doses, if required, may be administered at approximately 12 to 15 minute intervals. Halothane anesthesia increases the clinical duration of the maintenance dose only slightly. Under enflurane, a maintenance dose of 0.010 mg/kg is approximately equal to a 0.015 mg/kg dose under balanced anesthesia.

The recovery index (time from 25% to 75% recovery) is approximately 15 to 25 minutes under balanced or halothane anesthesia. When recovery from vecuronium neuromuscular blocking effect begins, it proceeds more rapidly than recovery from pancuronium. Once spontaneous recovery has started, the neuromuscular block produced by vecuronium is readily reversed with various anticholinesterase agents, e.g., pyridostigmine, neostigmine, or edrophonium in conjunction with an anticholinergic agent such as atropine or glycopyrrolate. There have been no reports of recurarization following satisfactory reversal of vecuronium induced neuromuscular blockade;

rapid recovery is a finding consistent with its short elimination half-life.

Pharmacokinetics: At clinical doses of 0.04 to 0.10 mg/kg, 60 to 80% of vecuronium is usually bound to plasma protein. The distribution half-life following a single i.v. dose (range 0.025 to 0.280 mg/kg) is approximately 4 minutes. Elimination half-life over this same dosage range is approximately 65 to 75 minutes in healthy surgical patients and in renal failure patients undergoing transplant surgery. In late pregnancy, elimination half-life may be shortened to approximately 35 to 40 minutes. The volume of distribution at steady state is approximately 300 to 400 mL/kg; systemic rate of clearance is approximately 3 to 4.5 mL/minute/kg. In man, urinary recovery of vecuronium varies from 3 to 35% within 24 hours. Data derived from patients requiring insertion of a T-tube in the common bile duct suggest that 25 to 50% of a total i.v. dose of vecuronium may be excreted in bile within 42 hours. Only unchanged vecuronium has been detected in human plasma following clinical use. One metabolite, 3-deacetyl vecuronium, has been recovered in the urine of some patients in quantities that account for up to 10% of the injected dose; 3-deacetyl vecuronium has also been recovered by T-tube in some patients accounting for up to 25% of the injected dose. This metabolite has been judged by animal screening (dogs and cats) to have 50% or more the potency of vecuronium, equipotent doses are of approximately the same duration as vecuronium in dogs and cats.

Limited data derived from the patients with cirrhosis or cholestasis and in the elderly, suggest that some measurements of recovery may be doubled in such patients. In patients with renal failure, measurements of recovery do not differ significantly from similar measurements in healthy patients. Studies involving routine hemodynamic monitoring in good risk surgical patients reveal that the administration of vecuronium in doses up to 3 times that needed to produce clinical relaxation (0.15 mg/kg) did not produce clinically significant changes in systolic, diastolic or mean arterial blood pressure. The heart rate remained unchanged in some studies and was lowered by a mean of up to 8% in other studies. A large dose of 0.28 mg/kg administered during a period of no stimulation, while patients were being prepared for coronary artery bypass grafting, was not associated with alterations in rate pressure product or pulmonary-capillary-wedge pressure. Systemic vascular resistance was lowered slightly and cardiac ouput was increased insignificantly. (The drug has not been studied in patients with hemodynamic dysfunction secondary to cardiac valvular disease).

Limited clinical experience in 3 patients with pheochromocytoma has shown that administration of this drug during surgery is not associated with changes in blood pressure or heart rate. Unlike other nondepolarizing skeletal muscle relaxants, vecuronium has no clinically significant effects on hemodynamic parameters and will not counteract those hemodynamic changes or known side effects produced by or associated with anesthetic agents.

In one clinical study, the duration of action of vecuronium was increased 5-fold during hypothermic cardiopulmonary bypass.

Preliminary data on histamine assay in 16 patients and available clinical experience in more than 600 patients indicate that hypersensitivity reactions such as bronchospasm, flushing, redness, hypotension, tachycardia, and other reactions commonly associated with histamine release are unlikely to occur.

Indications: As an adjunct to general anesthesia, to facilitate endotracheal intubation and to provide skeletal muscle relaxation during surgery or mechanical ventilation.

Contraindications: Hypersensitivity to the drug. Pregnant and lactating women, since reproductive studies in animals have not yet been performed (see Warnings).

Warnings: General: Vecuronium should be administered in carefully adjusted dosage by or under the supervision of experienced clinicians who are familiar with its actions and the possible complications that might occur following its use. The drug should not be administered unless facilities for intubation, artificial respiration, oxygen therapy, and reversal agents are immediately available. The clinician must be prepared to assist or control respiration. A peripheral nerve stimulator should be employed to monitor drug response, need for additional relaxant, and adequacy of spontaneous recovery or anticholinesterase antagonism.

Intensive Care Unit: To reduce the possibility of prolonged neuromuscular blockade and other complications that might occur following long-term use in the ICU, vecuronium or any other neuromuscular blocking agent should be administered in carefully adjusted doses by or under the supervision of experienced clinicians who are familiar with its actions and with appropriate peripheral nerve stimulator muscle monitoring techniques.

Neuromuscular Disease: In patients who are known to have myasthenia gravis or the myasthenic (Eaton-Lambert) syndrome, small doses of vecuronium may have profound effects. In such patients, a peripheral nerve stimulator and use of a small test dose may be of particular value in assessing and monitoring dosage requirements.

Precautions: General: Limited data on histamine assay and available clinical experience indicate that hypersensitivity reactions such as bronchospasm, flushing, redness, hypotension, tachycardia and other reactions commonly associated with histamine release are unlikely to occur.

Cardiovascular: As vecuronium has no significant effects on heart rate in the recommended dosage range, it will not counteract the bradycardia produced by many anesthetic agents or vagal stimulation.

Renal Failure: Vecuronium is well-tolerated without clinically significant prolongation of neuromuscular blocking effect in patients with renal failure who have been optimally prepared for surgery by dialysis. Under emergency conditions in anephric patients some prolongation of neuromuscular blockade may occur; therefore, if anephric patients cannot be prepared for non-elective surgery, a lower initial dose of vecuronium should be considered.

Hepatic Disease: Limited experience in patients with cirrhosis or cholestasis has revealed prolonged recovery time in keeping with the role the liver plays in vecuronium metabolism and excretion (see Pharmacology, Pharmacokinetics). Data currently available do not permit dosage recommendations in patients with impaired liver function.

Increased Volume of Distribution: The onset of action of neuromuscular blocking agents may be delayed in patients who have increased volumes of distribution as a result of old age, edematous states, or cardiovascular disease. More time should be permitted for the drug to achieve its maximal effect in these patients. Dosage should not be increased.

Long-term Use in ICU: Limited information if available concerning the efficacy and safety of long-term (days to weeks) i.v. vecuronium infusion to facilitate mechanical ventilation in the intensive care unit. In rare cases, long-term use of neuromuscular blocking drugs to facilitate mechanical ventilation in ICU settings may be associated with prolonged paralysis and/or skeletal muscle weakness, that may be first noted during attempts to wean patients from ventilator. Typically, such patients have received other drugs such as broad spectrum antibiotics, narcotics and/or steroids and may have electrolyte imbalances and diseases which lead to electrolyte imbalances, hypoxic episodes of varying duration, acid-base imbalance and extreme debilitation any of which may enhance the actions of a neuromuscular blocking agent. Additionally, patients immobilized for extended periods frequently develop symptoms consistent with disuse muscle atrophy. The recovery picture may vary from regaining movement and strength in all muscles to initial recovery of movement of the facial and small muscles of the extremities then to the remaining muscles. In rare cases recovery may be over an extended period of time and may even, on occasion, involve rehabilitation. Therefore, when there is a need for long-term mechanical ventilation the benefits-to-risk ratio of neuromuscular blockade must be considered.

Continuous infusion or intermittent bolus dosing to support mechanical ventilation, has not been studied sufficiently to support dosage recommendations.

Whenever the use of vecuronium or any neuromuscular blocking agent is contemplated in the ICU, it is recommended that neuromuscular transmission be monitored continuously during administration and recovery with the help of a nerve stimulator. Additional doses of vecuronium or any other neuromuscular blocking agent should not be given before there is a definite response to T_1 or to the first twitch. If no response is elicited, infusion administration should be discontinued until a response returns.

Severe Obesity or Neuromuscular Disease: Patients with severe obesity or neuromuscular disease may pose airway and/or ventilatory problems requiring special care before, during and after the use of neuromuscular blocking agents such as vecuronium.

Malignant Hyperthermia: Many drugs used in anesthetic practice are suspected of being capable of triggering a potentially fatal hypermetabolism of skeletal muscle known as malignant hyperthermia. There are insufficient data derived from screening in susceptible animals (swine) to establish whether or not vecuronium is capable of triggering malignant hyperthermia.

CNS: Vecuronium has no known effect on consciousness, pain threshold or cerebration. Administration must be accompanied by adequate anesthesia or sedation.

Hypothermia: Hypothermia (25 to 28°C) has been associated with a decreased requirement for nondepolarizing neuromuscular blocking agents.

Burns: Resistance to nondepolarizing neuromuscular blocking agents may develop in patients with burns, depending upon the time elapsed since the injury and the size of the burn.

Pregnancy and *Lactation:* Animal studies have not been conducted with vecuronium. It is not known whether vecuronium can cause fetal harm when administered to a pregnant woman, or if it can affect reproductive capacity. It is not known whether vecuronium is secreted in breast milk and therefore is not recommended in lactating women.

Obstetrics: It is not known whether muscle relaxants administered during vaginal delivery have immediate or delayed adverse effects on the fetus, or increase the likelihood that resuscitation of the newborn will be necessary. The possibility that a forceps delivery will be necessary may increase.

The possibility of respiratory depression in the newborn infant should always be considered following cesarean section during which a neuromuscular blocking agent has been administered.

Children: Infants under 1 year of age but older than 7 weeks also tested under halothane anesthesia, are moderately more sensitive to vecuronium on a mg/kg basis than adults and take about 1 ½ times as long to recover. Information presently available does not permit recommendations for usage of vecuronium in neonates.

Carcinogenesis, Mutagenesis, Impairment of Fertility: Long-term studies in animals have not been performed to evaluate carcinogenic or mutagenic potential or impairment of fertility.

Drug Interactions: Succinylcholine: Prior administration of succinylcholine may enhance the neuromuscular blocking effect of vecuronium and its duration of action. If succinylcholine is used before vecuronium, the administration of vecuronium should be delayed until the succinylcholine effect shows signs of wearing off. With succinylcholine as the intubating agent, initial doses of 0.04 to 0.06 mg/kg of vecuronium may be administered to produce complete neuromuscular block with clinical duration of action of 25 to 30 minutes (see Pharmacology).

The use of vecuronium before succinylcholine, in order to attenuate some of the side effects of succinylcholine, has not been sufficiently studied. Other nondepolarizing neuromuscular blocking agents (pancuronium, d-tubocurarine, metocurine and gallamine) act in the same fashion as does vecuronium; therefore, these drugs and vecuronium may manifest an additive effect when used together. There are insufficient data to support concomitant use of vecuronium and other competitive muscle relaxants in the same patient.

Inhalation Anesthetics: Use of volatile inhalational anesthetics such as enflurane, isoflurane, and halothane with vecuronium will enhance neuromuscular blockade. Potentiation is most prominent with the use of enflurane and isoflurane.

With the above agents the initial doses of vecuronium may be the same as with balanced anesthesia unless the inhalational anesthetic has been administered for a sufficient time at a sufficient dose to have reached clinical equilibrium (see Pharmacology).

Antibiotics: Parenteral/intraperitoneal administration of high doses of certain antibiotics may intensify or produce a neuromuscular block on their own. The following antibiotics have been associated with various degrees of paralysis: aminoglycosides (such as neomycin, streptomycin, kanamycin, gentamicin, and dihydrostreptomycin); tetracyclines; bacitracin; polymyxin B; colistin; and sodium colistimethate. If these or other newly introduced antibiotics are used in conjunction with vecuronium during surgery, unexpected prolongation of neuromuscular block should be considered a possibility.

Other: Experience concerning injection of quinidine during recovery from use of other muscle relaxants suggests that recurrent paralysis may occur. This possibility must also be considered for vecuronium. Vecuronium induced neuromuscular blockade has been counteracted by alkalosis and enhanced by acidosis in experimental animals (cat). Electrolyte imbalance and diseases which lead to electrolyte imbalance, such as adrenal cortical insufficiency, have been shown to alter neuromuscular blockade. Depending on the nature of the imbalance, either enhancement or inhibition may be expected. Magnesium salts, administered for the management of toxemia of pregnancy, may enhance neuromuscular blockade.

Adverse Effects: The most frequent adverse reaction to non depolarizing blocking agents as a class consists of an extension of the drug's pharmacological action beyond the time period needed for surgery and anesthesia. This may vary from

Norcuron (cont'd)

skeletal muscle weakness to profound and prolonged skeletal muscle paralysis resulting in respiratory insufficiency or apnea.

Inadequate reversal of the neuromuscular blockade, although not yet reported, is possible with vecuronium as with all curariform drugs. These adverse reactions are managed by manual or mechanical ventilation until recovery is judged adequate. Little or no increase in intensity of blockade or duration of action of vecuronium is noted from the use of thiobarbiturates, narcotic analgesics, nitrous oxide, or droperidol. See Overdose for discussion of other drugs used in anesthetic practice which also cause respiratory depression.

Overdose: Symptoms and Treatment: There has been no experience with vecuronium overdosage. The possibility of iatrogenic overdosage can be minimized by carefully monitoring muscle twitch response to peripheral nerve stimulation.

Excessive doses of vecuronium can be expected to produce enhanced pharmacological effects. Residual neuromuscular blockade beyond the time period needed for surgery and anesthesia may occur with vecuronium as with other neuromuscular blockers. This may be manifested by skeletal muscle weakness, decreased respiratory reserve, low tidal volume, or apnea. A peripheral nerve stimulator may be used to assess the degree of residual neuromuscular blockade and help to differentiate residual neuromuscular blockade from other causes of decreased respiratory reserve.

Respiratory depression may be due either wholly or in part to other drugs used during the conduct of general anesthesia such as narcotics, thiobarbiturates and other CNS depressants. Under such circumstances the primary treatment is maintenance of a patent airway and manual or mechanical ventilation until complete recovery of normal respiration is assured.

Pyridostigmine, neostigmine, or edrophonium, in conjunction with atropine or glycopyrrolate will usually antagonize the skeletal muscle relaxant action of vecuronium. Satisfactory reversal can be judged by adequacy of skeletal muscle tone and by adequacy of respiration. A peripheral nerve stimulator may also be used to monitor restoration of twitch height.

Failure of prompt reversal (within 30 minutes) may occur in the presence of extreme debilitation, carcinomatosis, and with concomitant use of certain broad spectrum antibiotics, or anesthetic agents and other drugs which enhance neuromuscular blockade or cause respiratory depression on their own. Under such circumstances the management is the same as that of prolonged neuromuscular blockade. Ventilation must be supported by artificial means until the patient has resumed control of his respiration. Prior to the use of reversal agents, reference should be made to the specific package insert of the reversal agent.

Dosage: Vecuronium is for i.v. use only. This drug should be administered by or under the supervision of experienced clinicians familiar with the use of neuromuscular blocking agents. Dosage must be individualized in each case.

The dosage information which follows is derived from studies based upon units of drug per unit of body weight and is intended to serve as a guide only, especially regarding enhancement of neuromuscular blockade of vecuronium by volatile anesthetics and by prior use of succinylcholine (see Precautions, Drug Interactions).

To obtain the maximum clinical benefits of vecuronium and to minimize the possibility of overdosage, the monitoring of muscle twitch response to peripheral nerve stimulation is advised.

The recommended initial dose of vecuronium is 0.08 to 0.10 mg/kg (1.4 to 1.75 times the ED_{90}) given as an i.v. bolus injection. This dose can be expected to produce good or excellent non-emergency intubation conditions in 2.5 to 3.0 minutes after injection. Under balanced anesthesia, clinically required neuromuscular blockade lasts approximately 25 to 30 minutes, with recovery to 25% of control achieved approximately 25 to 40 minutes after injection and recovery to 95% of control achieved approximately 45 to 65 minutes after injection. In the presence of potent inhalation anesthetics, the neuromuscular blocking effect of vecuronium is enhanced. If vecuronium is first administered more than 5 minutes after the start of administration of an inhalation agent, or when steady state has been achieved, the initial vecuronium dose may be reduced by approximately 15%, to 0.060 to 0.085 mg/kg.

Prior administration of succinylcholine may enhance the neuromuscular blocking effect and duration of action of vecuronium. If intubation is performed using succinylcholine, a reduction of the initial dose of vecuronium to 0.04 to 0.06 mg/kg with inhalation anesthesia and 0.05 to 0.06 mg/kg with balanced anesthesia may be required. The administration of vecuronium should be delayed until the succinylcholine effect shows signs of wearing off.

During prolonged surgical procedures, maintenance doses of 0.010 to 0.015 mg/kg of vecuronium are recommended. After the initial vecuronium injection, the first maintenance dose will generally be required within 25 to 40 minutes. However, clinical criteria should be used to determine the need for maintenance doses. Since vecuronium lacks clinically important cumulative effects, subsequent maintenance doses, if required, may be administered at relatively regular intervals for each patient, ranging approximately from 12 to 15 minutes under balanced anesthesia, slightly longer under inhalation agents. (If less frequent administration is desired, higher maintenance doses may be administered.)

Should there be reason for the selection of larger doses in individual patients, initial doses ranging from 0.15 mg/kg up to 0.28 mg/kg have been administered during surgery under halothane anesthesia without ill effects to the cardiovascular system being noted as long as ventilation is properly maintained (see Pharmacology).

The recovery index (time from 25% to 75% recovery) is approximately 15 to 25 minutes under balanced or halothane anesthesia. When recovery from vecuronium neuromuscular blocking effect begins, it proceeds more rapidly than recovery from pancuronium. Once spontaneous recovery has started, the neuromuscular block produced by vecuronium is readily reversed with various anticholinesterase agents, e.g., pyridostigmine, neostigmine, or edrophonium in conjunction with an anticholinergic agent such as atropine or glycopyrrolate.

Use by Infusion: Following the administration of a recommended initial bolus dose of vecuronium, a diluted solution of vecuronium can be administered by continuous infusion to adults for maintenance of neuromuscular blockade during extended surgical procedures. Long-term i.v. infusion to support mechanical ventilation in the intensive care unit has not been studied sufficiently to support dosage recommendations (see Precautions).

Infusion of vecuronium should be individualized for each patient. The rate of administration should be adjusted according to the patient's response as determined by peripheral nerve stimulation.

Infusion of vecuronium should be initiated only after early evidence of spontaneous recovery from the bolus dose (typically 10 to 20% recovery of the initial twitch response). During balanced anesthesia, an initial infusion rate of 1 µg/kg/min is recommended with subsequent rate adjustments to maintain a 90% suppression of the twitch response.

Individual infusion rates may range from 0.6 to 1.8 µg/kg/min.

Inhalation anesthetics, particularly enflurane and isoflurane may enhance the neuromuscular blocking action of nondepolarizing muscle relaxants. In the presence of steady-state concentrations of enflurane or isoflurane, it may be necessary to use infusion rates which are 25 to 60% lower than those recommended during balanced anesthesia. Reduced infusion rates may not be required during halothane anesthesia.

Spontaneous recovery and reversal of neuromuscular blockade following discontinuation of vecuronium infusion may be expected to proceed at rates comparable to those following single bolus doses (see Pharmacology).

Infusion solutions of vecuronium can be prepared by mixing vecuronium with an appropriate infusion solution such as 5% dextrose injection, USP; 0.9% sodium chloride injection, USP; 5% dextrose and 0.9% sodium chloride injection, USP; or lactated Ringer's injection, USP. Use within 24 hours of mixing with the above solutions. Unused portions of infusion solutions should be discarded.

Infusion rates of vecuronium can be individualized for each patient using Table I.

Table I—Norcuron

Norcuron Infusion Rates

Drug Delivery Rate (µg/kg/min)	Infusion Delivery Rate (mL/kg/min)	
	0.1 mg/mL[a]	0.2 mg/mL[b]
0.7	0.007	0.0035
0.8	0.008	0.0040
0.9	0.009	0.0045
1.0	0.010	0.0050
1.1	0.011	0.0055
1.2	0.012	0.0060
1.3	0.013	0.0065

[a]10 mg of Norcuron* in 100 mL solution.
[b]20 mg of Norcuron* in 100 mL solution.

Table II is a guideline for mL/min delivery for a solution of 0.1 mg/mL (10 mg in 100 mL) with an infusion pump.

Table II—Norcuron

Norcuron Infusion Rate—mL/min

Amount of Drug (µg/kg/min)	Patient Weight—kg 40	50	60	70	80	90	100
0.7	0.28	0.35	0.42	0.49	0.56	0.63	0.70
0.8	0.32	0.40	0.48	0.56	0.64	0.72	0.80
0.9	0.365	0.45	0.54	0.63	0.72	0.81	0.90
1.0	0.40	0.50	0.60	0.70	0.80	0.90	1.00
1.1	0.44	0.55	0.66	0.77	0.88	0.99	1.10
1.2	0.48	0.60	0.72	0.84	0.96	1.08	1.20
1.3	0.52	0.65	0.78	0.91	1.04	1.17	1.30

Note: If a concentration of 0.2 mg/mL is used (20 mg in 100 mL), the rate should be decreased by one-half.

Children: Older children (10 to 17 years of age) have approximately the same dosage requirements (mg/kg) as adults and may be managed the same way. Younger children (1 to 10 years of age) may require a slightly higher initial dose and may also require supplementation slightly more often than adults. Infants under 1 year of age but older than 7 weeks are moderately more sensitive to vecuronium on a mg/kg basis than adults and take about 1 ½ times as long to recover. See also subsection of Precautions titled Children. Information presently available does not permit recommendation on usage in neonates (see Precautions).

Reconstitution: Reconstitute each vial with 10 mL of bacteriostatic water for injection or 10 mL of compatible diluent to obtain a solution containing 1 mg/mL vecuronium bromide. Compatible diluents include: 0.9% sodium chloride injection, USP, 5% dextrose injection, USP, 5% dextrose and 0.9% sodium chloride injection, USP, sterile water for injection, USP and lactated Ringer's injection, USP. Parenteral drug products should be inspected visually for particulate matter and discoloration prior to administration, whenever solution and container permit.

When reconstituted with bacteriostatic water for injection, use within 5 days. When reconstituted with recommended diluents, use within 24 hours. Single dose vial. Discard unused portion.

Supplied: Sterile freeze-dried buffered cake of very fine microscopic crystalline particles for i.v. injection only. Nonmedicinal ingredients: citric acid, mannitol, phosphoric acid, sodium hydroxide and sodium phosphate dibasic. Vials of 10 mL. Boxes of 10. Protect from light. Store at 15 to 30°C.

NORFLEX™

3M Pharmaceuticals

Orphenadrine Citrate

Skeletal Muscle Relaxant

Pharmacology: The mode of therapeutic action has not been clearly identified but may be related to its analgesic properties. Orphenadrine citrate also possesses anticholinergic actions. Norflex is an extended release formulation that gives a peak level of 60 ng/mL at 8 hours following a 100 mg dose, as opposed to an immediate release product that gives a peak of 100 ng/mL at 3 hours following the same dose. The apparent half-life of Norflex is 18 hours.

Indications: Acute skeletal muscle spasm.

Contraindications: Stenosing peptic ulcers, prostatic hypertrophy, glaucoma, pyloric or duodenal obstruction, bladder neck obstruction, cardiospasm and myasthenia gravis. Hypersensitivity to orphenadrine.

Precautions: Use with caution in patients with cardiac decompensation, coronary insufficiency, cardiac arrhythmias and tachycardia. The concurrent use of orphenadrine and propoxyphene need not be avoided when indicated. If toxic CNS effects occur, they are probably due to either drug alone and require a reduction in the dose or discontinuation of one or both agents.

Safety of continuous long-term therapy with orphenadrine has not been established. Therefore, if orphenadrine is prescribed for prolonged use, periodic monitoring of blood, urine and liver values is recommended.

Occupational Hazards: Some patients may experience transient episodes of light-headedness, dizziness or syncope. Orphenadrine may impair the ability of the patient to engage in potentially hazardous activities such as operating machinery or driving a motor vehicle; ambulatory patients should therefore be cautioned accordingly.

Pregnancy: Safe use of orphenadrine has not been established with respect to adverse effects upon fetal development. Therefore, orphenadrine should be used in women of childbearing potential and particularly during early pregnancy only when the potential benefits outweigh the possible hazards.

Children: Safety and effectiveness in children have not been established; therefore, this drug is not recommended for use in the pediatric age group.

Adverse Effects: Mainly due to the mild anticholinergic action of orphenadrine, and are usually associated with higher dosage. Dryness of the mouth is the first untoward effect to appear. When the daily dose is increased, possible adverse effects include: tachycardia, palpitation, urinary hesitancy or retention, blurred vision, dilatation of the pupil, increased ocular tension, weakness, nausea, vomiting, headache, dizziness, constipation and drowsiness and rarely, urticaria and other dermatoses. Infrequently, an elderly patient may experience some degree of mental confusion. These adverse effects can usually be eliminated by reduction in the dosage. Two cases of aplastic anemia associated with the use of orphenadrine citrate tablets have been reported. No causal relationship has been established.

Dosage: Average adult dose, 60 mg i.v. or i.m. Orally, 100 mg twice daily.

Supplied: Ampuls: Each 2 mL ampul contains: orphenadrine citrate 60 mg. Nonmedicinal ingredients: sodium bisulfite, sodium chloride, sodium hydroxide and water for injection, USP. Ampuls of 2 mL, boxes of 6.

Tablets: Each white, unscored tablet, imprinted with "3M" on one side and "221" imprinted on the other side, contains: orphenadrine citrate 100 mg in an extended release formulation. Nonmedicinal ingredients: calcium stearate, ethylcellulose and lactose. Tartrazine-free. Bottles of 100 and 500.

Store at controlled room temperature (15 to 30°C).

Reviewed 1997

NORGESIC™
NORGESIC™ FORTE

3M Pharmaceuticals

Orphenadrine Citrate—ASA—Caffeine

Analgesic—Skeletal Muscle Relaxant

Indications: Symptomatic relief of mild to moderate pain.

Contraindications, Precautions and Adverse Effects: See Norflex and ASA. Do not exceed the recommended dose without consulting a physician.

Reye's Syndrome may develop in individuals who have chickenpox, influenza, or flu symptoms. Some studies suggest a possible association between the development of Reye's Syndrome and the use of medicines containing salicylate or ASA. Norgesic and Norgesic Forte contain ASA and therefore are not recommended for use in patients with chickenpox, influenza or flu symptoms.

Dosage: Norgesic: Adults, 1 to 2 tablets 3 or 4 times a day. Norgesic Forte: Adults: 1 tablet 3 or 4 times daily.

Supplied: Norgesic: Each white and yellow tablet, "3M" imprint on yellow face, "NORGESIC" imprint on white face, contains: orphenadrine citrate 25 mg, ASA 385 mg, caffeine 30 mg. Nonmedicinal ingredients: D&C yellow #10, lactose, polyethylene glycol, povidone, starch, sucrose and zinc stearate. Tartrazine-free. Bottles of 100.

Norgesic Forte: Each white and yellow capsule-shaped tablet, "3M" imprint on yellow face, "NORGESIC FORTE" imprint/bisect score on white face, contains: orphenadrine citrate 50 mg, ASA 770 mg, caffeine 60 mg. Nonmedicinal ingredients: D&C yellow #10, lactose, polyethylene glycol, povidone, starch, sucrose and zinc stearate. Tartrazine-free. Bottles of 100.

NORINYL® 1/50 Ⓟ

Searle

Norethindrone—Mestranol

Oral Contraceptive

Pharmacology: Estrogen-progestogen combinations act primarily through the mechanism of gonadotropin suppression due to the estrogenic and progestational activity of their components. Although the primary mechanism of action is inhibition of ovulation, alterations in the cervical mucus and the endometrium may also contribute to effectiveness.

Indications: Prevention of pregnancy.

Contraindications: History of or actual thrombophlebitis or thromboembolic disorders; history of or actual cerebrovascular disorders; history of or actual myocardial infarction or coronary arterial disease; active liver disease or history of or actual benign or malignant liver tumors; history of or known or suspected carcinoma of the breast; history of or known or suspected estrogen-dependent neoplasia; undiagnosed abnormal vaginal bleeding; any ocular lesion arising from ophthalmic vascular disease, such as partial or complete loss of vision or defect in visual fields; when pregnancy is suspected or diagnosed.

Warnings: Predisposing Factors for Coronary Artery Disease: Cigarette smoking increases the risk of serious cardiovascular side effects and mortality. Birth control pills increase this risk, especially with increasing age. Convincing data are available to support an upper age limit of 35 years for oral contraceptive use in women who smoke.

Other women who are independently at high risk for cardiovascular disease include those with diabetes, hypertension, abnormal lipid profile, or a family history of these. Whether oral contraceptives accentuate this risk is unclear.

In low risk, nonsmoking women of any age, the benefits of oral contraceptive use outweigh the possible cardiovascular risks associated with low-dose formulations. Consequently, oral contraceptives may be prescribed for these women up to the age of menopause.

> Cigarette smoking increases the risk of serious adverse effects on the heart and blood vessels. This risk increases with age and becomes significant in oral contraceptive users over 35 years of age. Women should be counselled not to smoke.

Discontinue Medication at the Earliest Manifestation of the Following:

A. Thromboembolic and cardiovascular disorders such as: thrombophlebitis, pulmonary embolism, cerebrovascular disorders, myocardial ischemia, mesenteric thrombosis and retinal thrombosis.

B. Conditions that predispose to venous stasis and to vascular thrombosis, e.g., immobilization after accidents or confinement to bed during long-term illness. Other nonhormonal methods of contraception should be used until regular activities are resumed. For use of oral contraceptives when surgery is contemplated, see Precautions.

C. Visual defects, partial or complete.

D. Papilledema or ophthalmic vascular lesions.

E. Severe headache of unknown etiology or worsening of pre-existing migraine headache.

Precautions: Physical Examination and Followup: Before oral contraceptives are used, a thorough history and physical examination should be performed, including a blood pressure determination. Breasts, liver, extremities and pelvic organs should be examined and a Papanicolaou smear should be taken if the patient has been sexually active.

The first followup visit should be done 3 months after oral contraceptives are prescribed. Thereafter, examinations should be performed at least once a year or more frequently if indicated. At each annual visit, examination should include those procedures that were done at the initial visit as outlined above or per recommendations of the Canadian Workshop on Screening for Cancer of the Cervix. Their suggestion was that, for women who had 2 consecutive negative Pap smears, screening could be continued every 3 years up to the age of 69.

Pregnancy: Fetal abnormalities have been reported to occur in the offspring of women who have taken estrogen-progestogen combinations in early pregnancy. Rule out pregnancy as soon as it is suspected.

Lactation: The use of oral contraceptives during the period a mother is breast feeding her infant may not be advisable. The hormonal components are excreted in breast milk and may reduce its quantity and quality. The long-term effects on the developing child are not known.

Hepatic Function: Patients who have had jaundice including a history of cholestatic jaundice during pregnancy should be given oral contraceptives with great care and under close observation.

The development of severe generalized pruritus or icterus requires that the medication be withdrawn until the problem is resolved.

If a patient develops jaundice that proves to be cholestatic in type, the use of oral contraceptives should not be resumed. In patients taking oral contraceptives, changes in the composition of the bile may occur and an increased incidence of gallstones has been reported.

Hepatic nodules have been reported to be associated with use of oral contraceptives, particularly in long-term users of oral contraceptives. These nodules include benign hepatic adenomas, focal nodular hyperplasia and other hepatic lesions. In addition, hepatocellular carcinoma has been reported. Although these lesions are extremely rare, they have caused fatal intra-abdominal hemorrhage and should be considered in women presenting with an abdominal mass, acute abdominal pain, or evidence of intra-abdominal bleeding.

Hypertension: Patients with essential hypertension whose blood pressure is well-controlled may be given oral contraceptives but only under close supervision. If a significant elevation of blood pressure in previously normotensive or hypertensive subjects occurs at any time during the administration of the drug, cessation of medication is necessary.

Migraine and Headache: The onset or exacerbation of migraine or the development of headache of a new pattern which is recurrent, persistent or severe, requires discontinuation of oral contraceptives and evaluation of the cause.

Diabetes: Current low dose oral contraceptives exert minimal impact on glucose metabolism. Diabetic patients, or those with a family history of diabetes, should be observed closely to detect any worsening of carbohydrate metabolism. Patients predisposed to diabetes who can be kept under close supervision may be given oral contraceptives. Young diabetic patients whose disease is of recent origin, well-controlled, and not associated with hypertension or other signs of vascular disease such as ocular fundal changes should be monitored more frequently while using oral contraceptives.

Ocular Disorders: Patients who are pregnant or are taking oral contraceptives may experience corneal edema that may cause visual disturbances and changes in tolerance to contact lenses, especially of the rigid type. Soft contact lenses usually do not cause disturbances. If visual changes or alterations in tolerance to contact lenses occur, temporary or permanent cessation of wear may be advised.

Breasts: Increasing age and a strong family history are the most significant risk factors for the development of breast cancer. Other established risk factors include obesity, nulliparity and late age at first full-term pregnancy. The identified groups of women that may be at increased risk of developing breast cancer before menopause are long-term users of oral contraceptives (more than 8 years) and starters at early age. In a few women, the use of oral contraceptives may accelerate the growth of an existing but undiagnosed breast cancer. Since any potential increased risk related to oral contraceptive use is small, there is no reason to change prescribing habits at present.

Women receiving oral contraceptives should be instructed in self-examination of their breasts. Their physicians should be notified whenever any masses are detected. A yearly clinical breast examination is also recommended because, if a breast cancer should develop, drugs that contain estrogen may cause a rapid progression.

Vaginal Bleeding: Persistent irregular vaginal bleeding requires assessment to exclude underlying pathology.

Fibroids: Patients with fibroids (leiomyomata) should be carefully observed. Sudden enlargement, pain, or tenderness requires discontinuance of the use of oral contraceptives.

Emotional Disorders: Patients with a history of emotional disturbances, especially the depressive type, may be more prone to have a recurrence of depression while taking oral contraceptives. In cases of a serious recurrence, a trial of an alternate method of contraception should be made which may help to clarify the possible relationship. Women with premenstrual syndrome (PMS) may have a varied response to oral contraceptives, ranging from symptomatic improvement to worsening of the condition.

Metabolic and Endocrine Diseases: In metabolic or endocrine diseases and when metabolism of calcium and phosphorus is abnormal, careful clinical evaluation should precede medication and a regular followup is recommended.

Connective Tissue Disease: The use of oral contraceptives in some women has been associated with positive lupus erythematous cell tests and with clinical lupus erythematous. In some instances, exacerbation of rheumatoid arthritis and synovitis have been observed.

Laboratory Tests: Results of laboratory tests should be interpreted in the light of the fact that the patient is on oral contraceptives. The laboratory tests listed below are modified.

Norinyl 1/50 (cont'd)

A. Liver function tests: Aspartate serum transaminase (AST): variously reported elevations. Alkaline phosphatase and gamma glutamine transaminase (GGT): slightly elevated.
B. Coagulation tests: Minimal elevation of test values reported for such parameters as Factors VII, VIII, IX and X. Increased platelet aggregation. Decreased antithrombin III.
C. Thyroid function tests: Protein binding of thyroxine is increased as indicated by increased total serum thyroxine concentrations and decreased T_3 resin uptake.
D. Lipoproteins: Small changes of unproven clinical significance may occur in lipoprotein cholesterol fractions.
E. Gonadotropins: LH and FSH levels are suppressed by the use of oral contraceptives. Wait 2 weeks after discontinuing the use of oral contraceptives before measurements are made.
Tissue Specimens: Pathologists should be advised of oral contraceptive therapy when specimens obtained from surgical procedures and Pap smears are submitted for examination.
Return to Fertility: After discontinuing oral contraceptive therapy, the patient should delay pregnancy until at least 1 normal spontaneous cycle has occurred in order to date the pregnancy. An alternative contraceptive method should be used during this time.
Amenorrhea: Women having a history of oligomenorrhea, secondary amenorrhea, or irregular cycles may remain anovulatory or become amenorrheic following discontinuation of estrogen-progestin combination therapy.

Amenorrhea, especially if associated with breast secretion, that continues for 6 months or more after withdrawal, warrants a careful assessment of hypothalamic-pituitary function.
Thromboembolic Complications—Postsurgery: There is an increased risk of postsurgery thromboembolic complications in oral contraceptive users, after major surgery. If feasible, oral contraceptives should be discontinued and an alternative method substituted at least 1 month prior to **major** elective surgery. Oral contraceptives should not be resumed until the first menstrual period after hospital discharge following surgery.
Drug Interactions: The concurrent administration of oral contraceptives with other drugs may result in an altered response to either agent. Reduced effectiveness of the oral contraceptive, should it occur, is more likely with the low dose formulations. It is important to ascertain all drugs that a patient is taking, both prescription and nonprescription, before oral contraceptives are prescribed.

Refer to the revised 1994 Report on Oral Contraceptives, Health Canada, for possible drug interactions with oral contraceptives.
Noncontraceptive Benefits of Oral Contraceptives: Several health advantages other than contraception have been reported.
Effects on menses: Increased menstrual cycle regularity; decreased menstrual blood loss; decreased incidence of iron deficiency anemia secondary to reduced menstrual blood loss; decreased incidence of dysmenorrhea.
Effects related to ovulation inhibition: Decreased incidence of functional ovarian cysts; decreased incidence of ectopic pregnancy.
Effects on other organs of the reproductive tract: Decreased incidence of acute salpingitis; decreased incidence of endometrial cancer (50%); decreased incidence of ovarian cancer (40%); potential beneficial effects on endometriosis; improvement of acne vulgaris, hirsutism, and other androgen-mediated disorders.
Effects on breasts: Decreased incidence of benign breast disease (fibroadenomas and fibrocystic breast disease); decreased incidence of breast biopsies.

The noncontraceptive benefits of oral contraceptives should be considered in addition to the efficacy of these preparations when counselling patients regarding contraceptive method selection.

Oral contraceptives **do not protect** against sexually transmitted diseases (STDs) including HIV/AIDS. For protection against STDs, it is advisable to use latex condoms **in combination with** oral contraceptives.

Adverse Effects: An increased risk of the following serious adverse reactions has been associated with the use of oral contraceptives: thrombophlebitis; pulmonary embolism; mesenteric thrombosis; neuro-ocular lesions, e.g., retinal thrombosis; myocardial infarction; cerebral thrombosis; cerebral hemorrhage; hypertension; benign hepatic tumors; gallbladder disease.

The following adverse reactions also have been reported in patients receiving oral contraceptives: Nausea and vomiting, usually the most common adverse reactions, occur in approximately 10% or less of patients during the first cycle. Other reactions, as a general rule, are seen less frequently or only occasionally.
Other Adverse Reactions: gastrointestinal symptoms (such as abdominal cramps and bloating); breakthrough bleeding; spotting; change in menstrual flow; dysmenorrhea; amenorrhea during and after treatment; infertility after discontinuance of treatment; edema; chloasma or melasma which may persist; breast changes: tenderness, enlargement, and secretion; change in weight (increase or decrease); endocervical hyperplasias; possible diminution in lactation when given immediately post-partum; cholestatic jaundice; migraine; increase in size of uterine leiomyomata; rash (allergic); mental depression; reduced tolerance to carbohydrates; vaginal candidiasis; premenstrual-like syndrome; intolerance to contact lenses; change in corneal curvature (steepening); cataracts; optic neuritis; retinal thrombosis; changes in libido; chorea; changes in appetite; cystitis-like syndrome; rhinitis; headache; nervousness; dizziness; hirsutism; loss of scalp hair; erythema multiforme; erythema nodosum; hemorrhagic eruption; vaginitis; porphyria; impaired renal function; Raynaud's phenomenon; auditory disturbances; hemolytic uremic syndrome; pancreatitis; arterial thromboembolism.

Overdose: Symptoms and Treatment: Numerous cases of the ingestion by children of estrogen-progestogen combinations have been reported. Although mild nausea may occur, there appears to be no other reaction. Treatment should be limited to a laxative such as citrate of magnesia with the aim of removing unabsorbed material as rapidly as possible.

Dosage: Information for the Patient on How to Take the Birth Control Pill:

1. **Read these directions:**
   - before you start taking your pills, and
   - any time you are not sure what to do.
2. **Look at your pill pack** to see if it has 21 or 28 pills:
   - 21-Pill Pack: 21 active pills (with hormones) taken daily for 3 weeks, and then take no pills for 1 week

   or
   - 28-Pill Pack: 21 active pills (with hormones) taken daily for 3 weeks, and then 7 "reminder" pills (no hormones) taken daily for 1 week.

Also check the pill pack for instructions on (1) where to start and (2) directions to take pills (see package insert for illustrations).

3. It is recommended that you use a second method of birth control (e.g., latex condoms and spermicidal foam or gel) for the first 7 days of the first cycle of pill use. This will provide a back-up in case pills are forgotten while you are getting used to taking them.
4. **When receiving any medical treatment, be sure to tell your doctor that you are using birth control pills.**
5. **Many women have spotting or light bleeding or may feel sick to their stomach during the first 3 months on the pill.** If you do feel sick, do not stop taking the pill. The problem will usually go away. If it does not go away, check with your doctor or clinic.
6. **Missing pills also can cause some spotting or light bleeding,** even if you make up the missed pills. You also could feel a little sick to your stomach on the days you take 2 pills to make up for missed pills.
7. **If you miss pills at any time, you could get pregnant. The greatest risks for pregnancy are:**
   - when you start a pack late, or
   - when you miss pills at the beginning or at the very end of the pack.
8. **Always be sure you have ready:**
   - **another kind of birth control** (such as latex condoms and spermicidal foam or gel) to use as a backup in case you miss pills, and
   - **an extra, full pack of pills.**
9. **If you experience vomiting or diarrhea, or if you take certain medicines,** such as antibiotics, your pills may not work as well. Use a backup method, such as latex condoms and spermicidal foam or gel, until you can check with your doctor or clinic.
10. **If you forget more than 1 pill 2 months in a row,** talk to your doctor or clinic about how to make pill-taking easier or about using another method of birth control.
11. **If your questions are not answered here, call your doctor or clinic.**

When to start the first pack of pills: Be sure to read these instructions:
- before you start taking your pills, and
- any time you are not sure what to do.

Decide with your doctor or clinic what is the best day for you to start taking your first pack of pills. Your pills may be either a 21-day or a 28-day type.

A. 21-Day Combination: With this type of birth control pill, you are on pills for 21 days and off pills for 7 days. You must not be off the pills for more than 7 days in a row.
1. **The first day of your menstrual period (bleeding) is Day 1 of your cycle.** Your doctor may advise you to start taking the pills on Day 1, on Day 5, or on the first Sunday after your period begins. If your period starts on Sunday, start that same day.
2. Take 1 pill at approximately the same time every day for 21 days; **then take no pills for 7 days.** Start a new pack on the 8th day. You will probably have a period during the

Table I—Norinyl 1/50

What to Do if You Miss Pills

Sunday Start	**Other Than Sunday Start**
Miss 1 pill	**Miss 1 pill**
Take it as soon as you remember, and take the next pill at the usual time. This means that you might take 2 pills in one day.	Take it as soon as you remember, and take the next pill at the usual time. This means that you might take 2 pills in one day.
Miss 2 pills in a row	**Miss 2 pills in a row**
First 2 Weeks: 1. Take 2 pills the day you remember and 2 pills the next day. 2. Then take 1 pill a day until you finish the pack. 3. Use a backup method of birth control if you have sex in the 7 days after you miss the pills.	**First 2 Weeks:** 1. Take 2 pills the day you remember and 2 pills the next day. 2. Then take 1 pill a day until you finish the pack. 3. Use a backup method of birth control if you have sex in the 7 days after you miss the pills.
Third Week: 1. Keep taking 1 pill a day until Sunday. 2. On Sunday, safely discard the rest of the pack and start a new pack that day. 3. Use a backup method of birth control if you have sex in the 7 days after you miss the pills. 4. You may not have a period this month.	**Third Week:** 1. Safely dispose of the rest of the pill pack and start a new pack that same day. 2. Use a backup method of birth control if you have sex in the 7 days after you miss the pills. 3. You may not have a period this month.
If you miss 2 periods in a row, call your doctor or clinic.	**If you miss 2 periods in a row, call your doctor or clinic.**
Miss 3 or more pills in a row	**Miss 3 or more pills in a row**
Anytime in the Cycle: 1. Keep taking 1 pill a day until Sunday. 2. On Sunday, safely discard the rest of the pack and start a new pack that day. 3. Use a backup method of birth control if you have sex in the 7 days after you miss the pills. 4. You may not have a period this month.	**Anytime in the Cycle:** 1. Safely dispose of the rest of the pill pack and start a new pack that same day. 2. Use a backup method of birth control if you have sex in the 7 days after you miss the pills. 3. You may not have a period this month.
If you miss 2 periods in a row, call your doctor or clinic.	**If you miss 2 periods in a row, call your doctor or clinic.**

7 days off the pill. (This bleeding may be lighter and shorter than your usual period.)

B. 28-Day Combination: With this type of birth control pill, you take 21 pills which contain hormones and 7 pills which contain no hormones.

1. **The first day of your menstrual period (bleeding) is Day 1 of your cycle.** Your doctor may advise you to start taking the pills on Day 1, on Day 5, or on the first Sunday after your period begins. If your period starts on Sunday, start that same day.
2. Take 1 pill at approximately the same time every day for 28 days. Begin a new pack the next day, **not missing any days on the pills.** Your period should occur during the last 7 days of using that pill pack.

What to do during the month:

1. **Take a pill at approximately the same time every day until the pack is empty.**
   - Try to associate taking your pill with some regular activity like eating a meal or going to bed.
   - Do not skip pills even if you have bleeding between monthly periods or feel sick to your stomach (nausea).
   - Do not skip pills even if you do not have sex very often.
2. **When you finish a pack:**
   - **21 pills: Wait 7 days** to start the next pack. You will have your period during that week.
   - **28 pills:** Start the next pack **on the next day.** Take 1 pill every day. Do not wait any days between packs.

What to do if you miss pills: Table I (on previous page) outlines the actions you should take if you miss 1 or more of your birth control pills. Match the number of pills missed with the appropriate starting time for your type of pill pack.

Note: 28-Day Pack: If you forget any of the 7 orange "reminder" pills (without hormones) in Week 4, just safely dispose of the pills you missed. Then keep taking 1 pill each day until the pack is empty. You do not need to use a backup method.

Always be sure you have on hand:

- a backup method of birth control (such as latex condoms and spermicidal foam or gel) in case you miss pills, and
- an extra, full pack of pills.

If you forget more than 1 pill 2 months in a row, talk to your doctor or clinic about ways to make pill-taking easier or about using another method of birth control.

Dosage: **A. 21-Day Pack:** With this type of birth control pill, the patient is 21 days on pills with 7 days off pills. The patient must not be off the pills for more than 7 days in a row.

1. **The first day of the patient's menstrual period (bleeding) is day 1 of a cycle.** The doctor may advise the patient to start taking the pills on Day 1, on Day 5, or on the first Sunday after a period begins. If a period starts on Sunday, the patient starts that same day.
2. The pack must be labelled correctly before starting. The pack is pre-printed with a Sunday starting day. If the patient is starting on a day other than a Sunday, she should use the Flexi-start sticker labels provided. The patient peels off the label with the chosen starting day and applies it over the pre-printed days on top of the card.
3. The patient takes 1 pill at approximately the same time every day for 21 days; **then she takes no pills for 7 days.** She starts a new pack on the 8th day. She will probably have a period during the 7 days off the pill. (This bleeding may be lighter and shorter than a usual period.)

B. 28-Day Pack: With this type of birth control pill, the patient takes 21 pills which contain hormones and 7 pills which contain no hormones.

1. **The first day of the patient's menstrual period (bleeding) is day 1 of a cycle.** The doctor may advise the patient to start taking the pills on Day 1, on Day 5, or on the first Sunday after a period begins. If a period starts on Sunday, the patient starts that same day.
2. The pack must be labelled correctly before starting. The pack is pre-printed with a Sunday starting day. If the patient is starting on a day other than a Sunday, she should use the Flexi-start sticker labels provided. The patient peels off the label with the chosen starting day and applies it over the pre-printed days on top of the card.
3. The patient takes 1 pill at approximately the same time every day for 28 days. She begins a new pack the next day, **not missing any days on the pills.** The patient's period should occur during the last 7 days of using that pill pack.

What to do during the month:

1. **The patient takes a pill at approximately the same time every day until the pack is empty.**
   - The patient should try to associate taking the pill with some regular activity like eating a meal or going to bed.
   - The patient must not skip pills even if she has bleeding between monthly periods or feels sick to her stomach (nausea).
   - The patient must not skip pills even if she does not have sex very often.
2. **When a pack is finished:**
   - **21 Pills: The patient must wait 7 days** to start the next pack. A period will begin during that week.
   - **28 Pills:** The patient starts the next pack **on the next day.** She takes 1 pill every day. She does not wait any days between packs.

Information for the Patient: See Blue Section—Information for the Patient "Oral Contraceptives".

Supplied: Norinyl 1/50 (21's): Each white circular tablet, impressed "SEARLE" on one side and "1" on one other, contains: norethindrone 1 mg and mestranol 0.05 mg. Nonmedicinal ingredients: Active tablets: cornstarch, lactose hydrous, magnesium stearate and polyvidone. Tartrazine-free. Dispensers of 21 tablets.

Norinyl 1/50 (28's): Each dispenser contains the same tablets as Norinyl 1/50 (21) plus 7 plain orange-colored tablets, impressed "SEARLE" on one side and P on the other, containing inert ingredients. Nonmedicinal ingredients: placebo tablets: FD&C Yellow No. 6 Lake, lactose, lactose monohydrate, magnesium stearate and microcrystalline cellulose. Tartrazine-free. Dispensers of 28 tablets.

(Shown in Product Recognition Section)

Reviewed 1998

NORITATE® Ⓟ

Dermik Laboratories Canada

Metronidazole

Antirosacea Agent

Pharmacology: Metronidazole topical cream is particularly effective against the inflammatory papulopustular component of rosacea. The mechanisms by which metronidazole act in reducing inflammatory lesions of rosacea are unknown, but may include an antibacterial and/or an anti-inflammatory effect.

Indications: For topical application in the treatment of inflammatory papules, pustules and erythema of rosacea.

Contraindications: In individuals with a history of hypersensitivity to metronidazole, parabens or other ingredients of the formulation.

Warnings: Avoid contact with eyes.

Studies in rats and mice have provided some evidence that metronidazole may cause tumors in these species when administered orally for a long period at high doses. The relevance of these findings in humans undergoing topical treatment with metronidazole is not known.

The mutagenic potential of metronidazole was tested in two ways: the dominant lethal test in mammalian germ cells, which yielded negative results, and a test using a bacterial indicator strain, which yielded positive results. The inherent antimicrobial property of metronidazole complicates the interpretation of this result with respect to any possible risk to humans.

Children: Safety and effectiveness in children have not been established.

Pregnancy: There has been no experience to date with the use of Noritate in pregnant patients. Systemically administered metronidazole crosses the placental barrier and enters the fetal circulation rapidly. No fetotoxicity was observed after oral metronidazole in rats or mice. However, because animal reproduction studies are not always predictive of the human response, this drug should be used during pregnancy only after careful assessment of the risk/benefit ratio.

Lactation: Even though metronidazole blood levels are significantly lower after topical than after oral administration, a decision should be made whether to discontinue nursing or to discontinue the drug, taking into account the importance of the drug to the mother. After oral administration, metronidazole is secreted in breast milk in concentrations similar to those found in plasma.

Precautions: Because of the minimal absorption of metronidazole and consequently its insignificant plasma concentration after topical administration, the adverse experiences reported with the oral form of the drug have not been reported with Noritate.

General: Metronidazole has been reported to cause tearing of the eyes. Therefore, contact with the eyes should be avoided. If a reaction suggesting local irritation occurs, patients should be directed to use the medication less frequently, discontinue use temporarily or discontinue use until further instructions. Metronidazole is a nitromidazole and should be used with care in patients with evidence of, or a history of, blood dyscrasia. Although rosacea is a chronic disease, data on the long-term use of metronidazole in rosacca are not available. In controlled clinical trials, patients were treated for a maximum 2 months (see Dosage).

Drug Interactions: Drug interactions are less likely with topical administration, but should be kept in mind when metronidazole is prescribed for patients who are receiving anticoagulant treatment. Oral metronidazole has been reported to potentiate the anticoagulant effect of coumarin and warfarin resulting in a prolongation of prothrombin time. Oral metronidazole also interacts with alcohol, producing a disulfiram-like reaction. Although this response has never been reported with topically applied metronidazole, an interaction with alcohol may be a possibility.

Dermatological Sensitivity: During clinical trials, there were 3 reports of possible contact dermatitis during treatment with metronidazole. Sensitivity to metronidazole was confirmed in only 1 of these patients by re-challenging with the product. In the other patients, a clear causal relationship could not be established. Nevertheless, physicians should be aware of the possibility of skin sensitivity reactions to metronidazole and/or of cross-sensitization with other imidazole preparations, such as clotrimazole and tioconazole.

Adverse Effects: Adverse conditions reported included transient skin irritation, dryness and stinging, as well as three cases of possible contact dermatitis. The incidence of these dermatological effects was about 3 to 4% during clinical trials.

Watering or tearing eyes may also occur if metronidazole is applied too closely to this area.

Gastrointestinal side effects (nausea, constipation, gastrointestinal upset) were reported in 7 patients (less than 2% of the total clinical experience with Noritate).

Table I provides specific information about the adverse effects observed during the two controlled clinical trials in which a total of 99 patients received metronidazole.

Table I—Noritate

Adverse Effects Observed During Controlled Clinical Trials

Body System/ Adverse Effect	Severity	Incidence (No. of Patients)	Course of Action Taken
Skin			
Burning Sensation	Mild	1	None required
	Moderate	1	None required
Pruritus	Mild	2	None required
Pruritus/Erythema/ Burning	Mild/ Moderate	1	None required
Erythema	Mild	1	None required
Oily Skin	Mild	1	None required
Photosensitivity	Moderate	1	None required
Papular Rash	Mild	1	Drug discontinued
Contact Dermatitis	Moderate	1	Drug discontinued
	Severe	2	Drug discontinued
Gastrointestinal			
Nausea	Mild	1	None required
	Moderate	1	None required
Burping	Mild	1	None required
Gastrointestinal Upset	Mild	1	None required
	Severe	2	Drug discontinued[a]
Gastrointestinal Cramps/Anorexia	Moderate/ Severe	1	Drug discontinued[b]

[a] One of these patients likely received an oral antibiotic.
[b] Patient predisposed to stomach ailments.

Overdose: There is no human experience with overdosage of topically applied metronidazole cream.

Symptoms: Massive ingestion may produce vomiting and slight disorientation.

Treatment: There is no specific antidote. Ipecac syrup or gastric lavage; then activated charcoal followed by a saline cathartic is suggested. Treatment should include symptomatic and supportive therapy.

Dosage: Cleanse all affected areas of the skin. Then, squeeze out approximately ½ cm of metronidazole cream and apply to the entire affected areas twice daily, morning and evening. Rub in lightly.

Significant therapeutic results should be evident within the first month of treatment and controlled clinical studies have

Noritate (cont'd)

demonstrated continuing improvement through 8 weeks of therapy. The dosage required for long-term administration is uncertain (see Precautions).

Patients may use cosmetics after application of metronidazole.

Supplied: Each g of white to slightly off-white soft cream, contains: metronidazole 10 mg (1% w/w). Nonmedicinal ingredients: glycerin, glyceryl monostearate, methylparaben, propylparaben, purified water, stearic acid and triethanolamine. Aluminum tubes of 30 g. Store at room temperature (15 to 30°C).

Reviewed 1997

NORLUTATE® ℞
Parke-Davis

Norethindrone Acetate

Progestational Agent

Pharmacology: Norethindrone acetate differs from norethindrone only in potency; the acetate is approximately twice as potent.

Transforms proliferative endometrium into secretory endometrium. Inhibits (at the usual dose range) the secretion of pituitary gonadotropins, which in turn prevents follicular maturation and ovulation. May also demonstrate some estrogenic, anabolic or androgenic activity but should not be relied upon.

Indications: Amenorrhea; in abnormal uterine bleeding due to hormonal imbalance in the absence of organic pathology, such as submucous fibroids or uterine cancer; and in endometriosis.

Contraindications: Thrombophlebitis, thromboembolic disorders, cerebral apoplexy or patients with a past history of these conditions; markedly impaired liver function or disease; known or suspected carcinoma of the breast; undiagnosed vaginal bleeding; missed abortion.

Warnings: The use of progestational agents during the first 4 months of pregnancy is not recommended. Progestational agents have been used beginning with the first trimester of pregnancy in an attempt to prevent habitual abortion or to treat threatened abortion. There is no adequate evidence that such use is effective and there is evidence of potential harm to the fetus when such drugs are given during the first 4 months of pregnancy. Furthermore, in the vast majority of women, the cause of abortion is a defective ovum, which progestational agents could not be expected to influence. In addition, the use of progestational agents, with their uterine-relaxant properties, in patients with fertilized defective ova may cause a delay in spontaneous abortion. Therefore, the use of such drugs during the first 4 months of pregnancy is not recommended. Several reports suggest an association between intrauterine exposure to female sex hormones and congenital anomalies, including congenital heart defects and limb reduction defects. One study estimated a 4.7 fold increased risk of limb reduction defects in infants exposed in utero to sex hormones (oral contraceptives, hormone withdrawal test for pregnancy, or attempted treatment for threatened abortion). Some of these exposures were very short and involved only a few days of treatment. The data suggest that the risk of limb reduction defects in exposed fetuses is somewhat less than 1 in 1 000.

If the patient is exposed to Norlutate during the first 4 months of pregnancy or if she becomes pregnant while taking this drug, she should be appraised of the potential risk to the fetus.

Precautions: Discontinue medication pending examination if there is a sudden partial or complete loss of vision, or if there is a sudden onset of proptosis, diplopia or migraine. If examination reveals papilledema or retinal vascular lesions, withdraw the medication.

Lactation: Detectable amounts of progestogens have been identified in the milk of mothers receiving them. The effect of this on the nursing infant has not been determined.

Because of the occasional occurrence of thrombophlebitis and pulmonary embolism in patients taking progestogens, the physician should be alert for the earliest manifestations of the disease.

Pregnancy: Masculinization of the female fetus has occurred when progestogens have been used in pregnant women. Birth defects have been reported in the newborns of women who had received progestogens during the first trimester of pregnancy.

Some beagle dogs treated with medroxyprogesterone acetate developed mammary nodules. Although nodules occasionally appeared in control animals they were intermittent in nature, whereas nodules in treated animals were larger and more numerous, and they persisted. There is no general agreement as to whether the nodules are benign or malignant. Their significance with respect to man has not been established.

The pretreatment physical examination should include special reference to breasts and pelvic organs, as well as a Papanicolaou smear.

Because this drug may cause some degree of fluid retention, particular caution is indicated in epilepsy, migraine, asthma, cardiac or renal dysfunction.

In cases of breakthrough bleeding, as in all cases of irregular bleeding per vaginam, nonfunctional causes should be borne in mind. In cases of undiagnosed vaginal bleeding, adequate diagnostic measures are indicated.

Patients who have a history of psychic depression should be carefully observed and the drug discontinued if the depression recurs to a serious degree.

Any possible influence of prolonged progestogen therapy on pituitary, ovarian, adrenal, hepatic or uterine functions awaits further study.

A decrease in glucose tolerance has been observed in a small percentage of patients on estrogen/progestogen combination drugs. The mechanism of this decrease is obscure. For this reason, diabetic patients should be carefully observed while receiving progestogen therapy.

The age of the patient constitutes no absolute limiting factor although treatment with progestogens may mask the onset of the climacteric.

Advise the pathologist of progestagen therapy when relevant specimens are submitted.

Steroid hormones are metabolized by the liver; therefore, these drugs should be administered with caution in patients with impaired liver function.

Adverse Effects: The following adverse reactions have been observed in women taking progestogens: breakthrough bleeding, spotting, change in menstrual flow, amenorrhea, edema, changes in weight (increase or decrease), changes in cervical erosion and cervical secretions, cholestatic jaundice, rash (allergic) with and without pruritus, melasma or chloasma, mental depression.

The pregnanediol determination may be altered by the use of progestogens. In addition, the following laboratory results may be altered by the concomitant use of estrogens with progestogens: hepatic function; coagulation tests: increase in prothrombin, Factors VII, VIII, IX and X; increase in PBI, BEI and a decrease in T3 uptake; metyrapone test.

A statistically significant association has been demonstrated between use of estrogen/progestogen combination drugs and the following serious adverse reactions: thrombophlebitis; pulmonary embolism and cerebral thrombosis and embolism. For this reason, patients on progestogen therapy should be carefully observed.

Although available evidence is suggestive of an association, such a relationship has been neither confirmed nor refuted for the following serious adverse reactions: neuro-ocular lesions, e.g., retinal thrombosis and optic neuritis.

The following adverse reactions have been observed in patients receiving estrogen/progestogen combination drugs: rise in blood pressure in susceptible individuals, premenstrual like syndrome, changes in libido, changes in appetite, cystitis like syndrome, headache, nervousness, dizziness, fatigue, backache, hirsutism, loss of scalp hair, erythema multiforme, erythema nodosum, hemorrhagic eruption, itching. In view of these observations, patients on progestogen therapy should be carefully observed for their occurrence.

Dosage: Adapt dosage to the specific indications and therapeutic response of the individual patient. This dosage schedule assumes the interval between menses to be 28 days. Amenorrhea, abnormal uterine bleeding due to hormonal imbalance in the absence of organic pathology: 2.5 to 10 mg starting with the fifth day of the menstrual cycle and ending on the 25th day. Endometriosis: Initial daily dose of 5 mg for 2 weeks with increments of 2.5 mg/day every 2 weeks until 15 mg/day is reached. Therapy may be held at this level for from 6 to 9 months or until annoying breakthrough bleeding demands temporary termination.

Supplied: Each grooved, salmon-colored, slightly mottled tablet, debossed "PD" on one side, contains: norethindrone acetate 5 mg. Nonmedicinal ingredients: cornstarch, FD&C Red No. 3, FD&C Yellow No. 5, lactose, magnesium stearate, sugar and talc. Energy: 1.4 kJ (0.34 kcal). Sodium: 0.30 mg. Gluten-, paraben-, sulfite- and tartrazine-free. Bottles of 30.

(Shown in Product Recognition Section)

NORMACOL®
Rivex Pharma

Sterculia

Bulk Laxative

Indications: Sterculia is used as a bulk laxative, since by taking up moisture it increases the volume of the feces and promotes peristalsis. Ten mL of sterculia provide dietary bulk equivalent to 2 kg of fresh vegetables. It provides gentle relief of occasional constipation. Produces bowel movement in 12 to 72 hours.

Precautions: As with all hygroscopic laxatives, it is important to stress the need to ingest adequate quantities of water immediately with the preparation. It may be unwise if the patient is elderly or debilitated, to suggest taking the preparation prior to retiring.

Do not use in the presence of abdominal pain, nausea, fever or vomiting.

Do not take within 2 hours of any other medication as the desired effect of the other medicine may be reduced.

Dosage: Adults: 1 or 2 sachets, once or twice daily or as directed by the physician. Children: Consult the physician for children under 12 years of age.

Place the dry granules on the tongue, in small quantities if necessary. Swallow the granules with a full glass (250 mL) of water or other liquid, without chewing.

Supplied: Each sachet (1 dose) of granules contains: sterculia gum equivalent to sterculia BP 62% w/w. Nonmedicinal ingredients: gum arabic, paraffin, sodium bicarbonate, sucrose, talc, titanium dioxide and vanillin. Sucrose: 1.54 g. Boxes of 30. Store in a cool dry place below 25°C.

NOROXIN® ℞
MSD

Norfloxacin

Antibacterial Agent

Pharmacology: Norfloxacin inhibits bacterial deoxyribonucleic acid synthesis and is bactericidal.

At the molecular level 3 specific actions have been attributed to norfloxacin in the inhibition of E. coli cells: inhibition of the ATP-dependent DNA supercoiling reaction catalyzed by DNA gyrase, inhibition of the relaxation of supercoiled DNA, promotion of double-stranded DNA breakage.

Pharmacokinetics: Mean peak serum concentrations were 0.8 and 1.5 mg/L occurring within 1 to 1.5 hours of oral administration of 200 and 400 mg doses respectively to 15 healthy fasting male volunteers.

The mean elimination half-life was approximately 3 hours. Therefore, as was noted in another group of 26 healthy male and 3 female volunteers aged 19 to 50 years, norfloxacin regimens of 400 mg given every 12 hours produced slight accumulation.

Theoretically it could be expected that steady-state concentrations will be attained after 2 days of recommended dosage.

Following oral administration to 15 healthy fasting male volunteers, aged 22 to 52 years, 25 to 30% of a dose was recovered unchanged in urine within 48 hours.

During the same period of time, an additional 8 to 10% of the dose was recovered as 6 metabolites with modifications on the piperazine ring. The 2 major metabolites are the 3-oxo-piperazinyl derivative and the 7-ethylenediamine derivative. The 3-oxo-piperazinyl predominates and no glucuronide conjugates were detected. Norfloxacin and these metabolites were detected in bile. The concentration of norfloxacin in bile was 5 μg/mL collected 1 to 2 hours after oral administration of a 200 mg dose to 1 patient with choledocholithiasis. A similar distribution ratio of the same 6 metabolites was in both bile and urine. These data suggest that 30 to 40% of an oral dose is absorbed. After a single 400 mg dose, mean antimicrobial activities equivalent to 164, 338, 632, and 126 μg of norfloxacin/g of feces were recovered over 0 to 12, 12 to 24, and 24 to 36, and 36 to 48 hours, respectively.

Renal excretion of norfloxacin occurs by both glomerular filtration and tubular secretion as evidenced by the high rate of renal clearance 275 mL/min, (4.58 mL/s). Two to three hours after a single 400 mg dose, mean urinary concentrations of 200 mg/L or more were obtained in the urine. In healthy volunteers, mean urinary concentrations of norfloxacin remain above 30 mg/L for at least 12 hours following a 400 mg dose.

Factors influencing the pharmacokinetics: Food: Food slightly reduces the absorption of norfloxacin as evidenced by a reduction of approximately 30% in peak serum concentration and of approximately 35% in peak urine concentration.

Geriatrics: In 4 females and 2 males, 67- to 74-year-old patients with normal renal function for their age i.e., creatinine clearance 91 mL/min/1.73 m², norfloxacin was eliminated more slowly because of their slightly decreased renal function causing a small increase in plasma concentrations of drug.

Approximately 22% of the dose was recovered unchanged in urine. The renal clearance of drug was 154 mL/min (2.57 mL/s). The maximum plasma concentration was approximately 2 mg/L, occurring 1.3 hours after drug administration. The plasma half-life of norfloxacin in these individuals was 4 hours (see Table I).

Table I—Noroxin

Comparison of Pharmacokinetic Parameters Between Healthy Elderly Volunteers and Healthy Younger Volunteers Following a Single 400 mg Oral Dose

Parameter	Elderly Volunteers	Younger Volunteers
C_{max}, mg/L	2.0	1.5
T_{max}, h	1.3	1.0
Half-life, h*	3.9	3.2
Total (AUC), mg• h/L	9.8	6.6
Renal clearance, mL/min	154.0	299.0
Renal clearance, mL/s	2.57	4.98
%-Dose Urinary Recovery	22.0	27.0

*Harmonic mean.

Impaired Renal Function: Excretion of norfloxacin in patients with creatinine clearance (C_{cr}) greater than 30 mL/min/1.73 m² (0.50 mL/s/1.73 m²), was similar to that of healthy volunteers. In patients with C_{cr} less than 30 mL/min/1.73 m² (0.50 mL/s/1.73 m²) but greater than 6.6 mL/min/1.73 m² (0.11 mL/s/1.73 m²), less than 10% of an oral dose was excreted in urine. The mean elimination half-life of norfloxacin in serum increased to 6.5 hours in these patients (see Table II).

Table II—Noroxin

Mean Pharmacokinetic Parameters for Norfloxacin Following a Single 400 mg Oral Dose in Healthy Volunteers and in Patients with Varying Degrees of Renal Insufficiency

Group	Creatinine Clearance (mL/min/1.73 m²) [mL/s/1.73 m²]	C_{max} (mg/L)	T_{max} (h)	Half-Life* (h)	Total (AUC) (mg•h/L)	Renal Clearance (mL/min)	%-Dose Urinary Recovery
I	≥90 [≥1.5]	1.51	1.4	3.47	6.94	297.2	28.2
II	31–89 [0.52–1.48]	1.91	1.3	3.38	9.53	264.5	35.3
III	10–30 [0.17–0.50]	1.70	1.8	6.57	24.01	17.8	6.7
IV	6.6–9 [0.11–0.15]	1.70	1.8	6.40	16.46	14.7	2.4

*Harmonic mean.

Probenecid: The 12-hour urinary excretion of norfloxacin following a 200 mg dose was diminished from 28% of the dose to 14% of the dose by the coadministration of probenecid.

Serum protein binding: At a serum concentration of 2.5 mg/L the human serum protein binding is 10 to 15%.

Norfloxacin is found in the liver, gallbladder, gallbladder bile, bile in common bile duct, bile, prostate, kidney.

Indications: The treatment of upper and lower urinary tract infections, specifically complicated and uncomplicated cystitis, pyelitis and pyelonephritis caused by susceptible strains of the following microorganisms: E. coli, K. pneumoniae, unspecified Klebsiella spp., unspecified Enterobacter spp., unspecified Citrobacter spp., P. mirabilis, S. aureus, S. faecalis, P. aeruginosa.

The treatment of adults with gonococcal urethritis, or cervicitis due to penicillinase-producing and nonpenicillinase-producing N. gonorrhea.

Appropriate culture and susceptibility studies should be carried out prior to initiation of therapy with norfloxacin and if clinically indicated during treatment. Therapy may be initiated before obtaining results of these tests, however, modification of such treatment may be required once the results become available.

Contraindications: In patients with known hypersensitivity to norfloxacin, to any component of this product or other quinolone antibacterial agents.

Warnings: Children: Safety in children is unknown. Adults: Norfloxacin should not be given to patients in whom epiphyseal closure has not occurred. In 2 animal species (dogs and rabbits) in which norfloxacin was administered to young animals, lameness and lesions (i.e., blister formation and eventual erosion) of the articular cartilage of the weight-bearing joints were observed. In young dogs this occurred following a single dose several times the recommended human dose. These changes were not observed in dogs 6 months of age or older. Similar changes in animals have been observed with other structurally related drugs.

Norfloxacin should be used with caution in individuals with a history of convulsions or known factors that predispose to seizures. Convulsions have been reported rarely in patients receiving norfloxacin; however, a causal relationship to norfloxacin has not been established.

Pregnancy: Safety in the treatment of infections in pregnant women is not established.

Precautions: General: Norfloxacin should be used with caution in patients with a history of convulsions.

During therapy, patients should be reminded to drink sufficient amounts of fluids to maintain adequate hydration in order to avoid possible development of crystalluria.

As with other quinolones, tendinitis and/or tendon rupture have been observed rarely in patients taking norfloxacin, especially when corticosteroids are taken concomitantly. If a patient develops symptoms of tendinitis and/or tendon rupture, norfloxacin should be discontinued immediately and the patient advised to seek appropriate medical management.

Rarely, hemolytic reactions have been reported in patients with latent or actual defects in glucose-6-phosphate dehydrogenase activity who take quinolone antibacterial agents, including norfloxacin (see Adverse Effects).

Photosensitivity reactions have been observed in patients exposed to sunlight while receiving quinolone antibiotics. While taking norfloxacin, excessive exposure to sunlight should be avoided and therapy discontinued if photosensitivity should occur.

Pregnancy: Safety in the treatment of infections in pregnant women is not established; consider its use only if the anticipated benefits to the mother justifies the potential risks to the fetus. Following a single dose of 200 mg norfloxacin concentrations in umbilical cord serum ranged from nondetectable levels to 0.5 mg/L and in amniotic fluid from nondetectable levels to 0.92 mg/L. The pharmacokinetics of norfloxacin in pregnant patients have not been investigated.

Reproduction studies have been carried out in the mouse, rat, rabbit and monkey. Norfloxacin did not show any teratogenic effects in these studies. In the monkey, however, an increased incidence of embryonic loss has been observed at a dosage of 10 times the human dose which results in peak plasma levels approximately 2 to 3 times that in humans. In the rabbit, embryonic loss was observed when norfloxacin was given by the oral route but not by the s.c. route. The clinical significance of the study results observed in rabbits and monkeys is not known.

Lactation: Norfloxacin was not detected in human milk following a single 200 mg dose. However, because this dose was low (half the recommended single dose) and as many drugs are secreted in human milk, caution should be exercised if it is to be administered to a nursing woman.

Geriatrics: Alterations in dosage are not recommended (see Dosage and Pharmacology). When norfloxacin was administered to 4 females and 2 males, 67 to 74 years old, with normal renal function for their age, i.e., creatinine clearance 91±14 mL/min/1.73 m² (1.52 mL/s/1.73 m²), the plasma half-life of the drug was only slightly prolonged.

Drug Interactions: Since urinary excretion of norfloxacin is diminished by concomitant administration of probenecid, norfloxacin should not be administered concomitantly with probenecid.

Elevated plasma levels of theophylline have been reported with concomitant quinolone use. There have been rare reports of theophylline-related adverse reactions in patients on concomitant therapy with norfloxacin and theophylline. Therefore, monitoring of theophylline plasma levels should be considered and dosage of theophylline adjusted as required.

Elevated serum levels of cyclosporine have been reported with concomitant use with norfloxacin. Therefore, cyclosporine serum levels should be monitored and appropriate cyclosporine dosage adjustments made when these drugs are used concomitantly.

Norfloxacin may enhance the effects of the oral anticoagulant warfarin or its derivatives. When these products are administered concomitantly, prothrombin time or other suitable coagulation tests should be closely monitored.

Multivitamins, products containing iron or zinc, antacids or sucralfate should not be administered concomitantly with, or within 2 hours of, the administration of norfloxacin because they may interfere with absorption resulting in lower serum and urine levels of norfloxacin.

Norfloxacin has been shown to interfere with the metabolism of caffeine. This may lead to reduced clearance of caffeine and a prolongation of its plasma half-life.

Antagonism has been demonstrated in vitro between norfloxacin and nitrofurantoin.

Renal Impairment: Since norfloxacin is eliminated primarily by the kidney, it should be used with caution and at a reduced dosage in patients with impaired renal function (see Dosage). Norfloxacin is not recommended for anuric patients.

There is insufficient data on which to have a dosage recommendation for the treatment of gonorrhea in patients with a creatinine clearance of 30 mL/min/1.73 m² (0.5 mL/s/1.73 m²) or less.

Adverse Effects: Norfloxacin is generally well tolerated. In controlled clinical trials involving 1 528 patients, the overall incidence of drug-related adverse reactions was approximately 3%. The following adverse reactions were reported: Gastrointestinal: nausea 2%, dyspepsia 0.3%, flatulence 0.3%, heartburn 0.3%, abdominal pain 0.3%, vomiting 0.2%, diarrhea 0.2%, anorexia 0.1%.

Nervous System: headache 1.6%; dizziness/lightheadedness 1.2%; drowsiness<1%; mood alterations<1% (anxiety disorders, 2 cases; depression, 4 cases; disorientation, 1 case; dream abnormalities, 1 case; euphoria, 2 cases; explosive personality disorder, 1 case; hallucinations, 1 case; irritability, 1 case; nervousness, 2 cases); paresthesia<1%; visual disturbances<0.1% (epiphora, 1 case); insomnia<0.4%.

Musculoskeletal: tendinitis 0.1%, arthralgia 0.1%.

Hypersensitivity: rash 0.4%; erythema 0.2%; urticaria 0.1%; pruritus 0.1%.

The following additional adverse reactions have been reported since the drug was marketed: Musculoskeletal: tendon rupture, possible exacerbation of myasthenia gravis.

Body as a Whole/Site Unspecific: asthenia/fatigue.

Hypersensitivity: anaphylaxis, interstitial nephritis, angioedema, vasculitis, urticaria, arthritis, myalgia.

Ocular: conjunctivitis, eye pain/irritation.

Skin: photosensitivity, Stevens-Johnson syndrome, toxic epidermal necrolysis, exfoliative dermatitis, erythema multiforme, pruritus.

Gastrointestinal: constipation, flatulence, pseudomembranous colitis, pancreatitis (rare), hepatitis.

Nervous System/Psychiatric: convulsions, confusion, paresthesia, polyneuropathy including Guillain-Barré syndrome, psychic disturbances including psychotic reactions, somnolence.

Hematologic: hemolytic anemia, thrombocytopenia.

Special Senses: tinnitus.

Genitourinary: vaginal candidiasis.

Laboratory: Abnormal adverse reactions observed rarely in clinical trials include leukopenia, eosinophilia, neutropenia, proteinuria and elevation of ALT, AST, alkaline phosphatase,

Noroxin (cont'd)

bilirubin, increased BUN, serum creatinine, and LDH, and decreased hematocrit.

On very rare occasions, the following have been reported: hypertonia, renal failure, dyspnea, ataxia, dysarthria, dysphasia, hemophthalmia, nystagmus, periorbital erythema, fever, dry mouth, transient hearing loss.

Others: Although the following adverse reactions were not observed in these clinical trials, they have been reported following treatment with other quinolone antibacterial agents: hemolytic anemia in patients with latent or actual defects in glucose-6-phosphate dehydrogenase (G6PD) activity; overbrightness of light, change in color perception, difficulty in focusing, decrease in visual acuity and double vision; restlessness; bullae; palpitation; soreness of the gums; joint stiffness; swelling of the extremities; metallic taste; toxic psychosis (rare); perineal burning; vertigo; edema; cholestasis; metabolic acidosis; (signs and symptoms of increased intracranial pressure in infants and children which usually disappeared rapidly with no sequelae when treatment was discontinued).

Overdose: Symptoms and Treatment: There has not been any case of overdose with norfloxacin reported to date; consequently, neither the signs nor the symptoms of overdosage have been identified.

In the event of recent acute overdose, the stomach should be emptied by inducing vomiting or by gastric lavage, and the patient carefully observed and given symptomatic and supportive treatment. Adequate hydration should be maintained to avoid the possible development of crystalluria. Norfloxacin is not dialyzable.

Dosage: Adults: For urinary tract infections, 400 mg twice a day taken with a glass of water at least 1 hour before, or 2 hours after a meal or milk ingestion for 7 to 10 days.

For women with uncomplicated acute cystitis, the duration of therapy can be reduced to 3 days.

For adults with gonococcal urethritis or cervicitis, the recommended dosage of norfloxacin is two 400 mg tablets (800 mg) given as a single dose.

Geriatrics: The recommended dosage of norfloxacin in elderly patients with normal renal function for their age is the same as given for adults above.

Impaired Renal Function: Norfloxacin may be used in the treatment of patients with renal insufficiency who do not require hemodialysis.

In patients with a glomerular filtration rate of less than 30 mL/min/1.73 m^2 (0.50 mL/s/1.73 m^2) but greater than 6.6 mL/min/1.73 m^2 (0.11 mL/s/1.73 m^2) the recommended dose is 400 mg once daily (see Precautions).

When only the serum creatinine level is available, the following formula (based on sex, weight, and age of the patient) may be used to convert this value into creatinine clearance. The serum creatinine should represent a steady state of renal function:

$$\text{Males: } \frac{\text{Weight (kg)} \times (140\text{–age})}{72 \times \text{serum creatinine (mg/100 mL)}}$$

Females: 0.85×above value

To convert to international units multiply results by 0.01667.

The administration to anuric patients is not recommended.

Children: Safety and efficacy of norfloxacin in prepubertal children have not been established. Norfloxacin should not be used in patients in whom epiphyseal closure has not occurred (see Warnings).

Supplied: Each oval-shaped, white, film-coated compressed tablet, scored on one side and engraved MSD 705 on the other, contains: norfloxacin 400 mg. Nonmedicinal ingredients: carnauba wax, croscarmellose sodium, hydroxypropyl cellulose, hydroxypropyl methylcellulose, magnesium stearate, microcrystalline cellulose and titanium dioxide. Gluten- and tartrazine-free. Bottles of 30 and 100. Store at 15 to 30°C in tightly closed containers, protected from heat, moisture and direct light.

(Shown in Product Recognition Section)

Reviewed 1999

Did you know that the *CPS* provides information on certain drugs or drug classes in the shaded monographs in the WHITE SECTION? Check out the index at the beginning of the section.

NOROXIN® Ophthalmic Solution ℞

MSD

Norfloxacin

Antibacterial

Pharmacology: Norfloxacin ophthalmic solution is a fluoroquinolone carboxylic acid antibacterial agent for ocular administration. Norfloxacin inhibits bacterial deoxyribonucleic acid synthesis and is bactericidal.

At the molecular level 3 specific actions have been attributed to norfloxacin in the inhibition of E. coli cells: inhibition of the ATP-dependent DNA supercoiling reaction catalyzed by DNA gyrase, inhibition of the relaxation of supercoiled DNA and promotion of double-stranded DNA breakage.

Indications: For the treatment of acute superficial infections of the eye and its adnexae (conjunctivitis, blepharoconjunctivitis and blepharitis) when caused by susceptible bacteria in adults and children.

Contraindications: Patients with known hypersensitivity to any component of this product or any chemically related quinolone antibacterial agent.

Precautions: General: As with other antibacterial preparations, prolonged use may result in overgrowth of non-susceptible bacteria including fungi. If superinfection or resistance should develop, treatment with norfloxacin ophthalmic solution should be discontinued and appropriate therapy instituted.

Information for the Patient: Patients should be instructed of the following: how to properly use this ophthalmic solution as this is a sterile solution; to avoid contaminating the solution by preventing the dropper tip from touching any surface; to consult a physician, a) unless otherwise informed, if there has been no improvement after 4 days of continuous treatment or if the infection seems to get worse, b) if irritation or sensitization develops, c) before wearing contact lenses.

The preservative (benzalkonium chloride) in Noroxin ophthalmic solution may deposit in soft contact lenses. The lenses should be removed before application of the drops and not be reinserted earlier than 15 minutes after use. Ideally, patients with an eye infection should not wear their contact lenses until their treatment is finished.

Pregnancy: Norfloxacin has not been studied in human pregnancy. Therefore, the ophthalmic solution should be given to a pregnant woman only if clearly needed.

Lactation: It is not known whether norfloxacin is excreted in human milk following ocular administration.

Adverse Effects: The most frequently reported side effect was local burning or smarting (5.4%). Other drug related side effects were conjunctival hyperemia (0.5%), chemosis (0.3%), photophobia (0.5%) and a bitter taste following instillation.

Dosage: The recommended dose is 1 or 2 drops of ophthalmic solution in the affected eye(s) 4 times daily. Depending on the severity of the infection, the dosage for the first day of therapy may be increased to 1 or 2 drops every 2 hours during the waking hours.

The usual course of treatment is 7 days.

Supplied: Each mL of sterile, clear, colorless to light yellow ophthalmic solution contains: norfloxacin 3 mg. White, opaque, plastic Ocumeter ophthalmic dispensers of 5 mL with a controlled drop tip. Protect from light. Store at room temperature, below 30°C.

NORPLANT® ℞

Wyeth-Ayerst

Levonorgestrel

Contraceptive Implant

Pharmacology: Norplant consists of levonorgestrel implants, a set of 6 flexible closed capsules made of Silastic (dimethylsiloxane/methylvinylsiloxane copolymer) each containing 36 mg of the progestin levonorgestrel. Levonorgestrel, 18,19-Dinorpregn-4-en-20-yn-3-one,13-ethyl-17-hydroxy-,(17α)-(-)-, is a totally synthetic and biologically-active progestin which exhibits no significant estrogenic activity and is highly progestational. The absolute configuration conforms to that of D-natural steroids. Levonorgestrel is not subjected to a "first-pass" effect and is virtually 100% bioavailable. Plasma concentrations average 0.30 ng/mL over 5 years and are variable as a function of individual metabolism and body weight.

Diffusion of levonorgestrel through the wall of each capsule provides a continuous low dose of the progestin. Resulting blood levels are substantially below those generally observed among users of combination oral contraceptives containing the progestins, norgestrel or levonorgestrel. Because of the range of variability in blood levels and variation in individual response, blood levels are not predictive of the risk of pregnancy in an individual woman.

At least two mechanisms are active in preventing pregnancy: ovulation inhibition and thickening of the cervical mucus. Other mechanisms may add to these contraceptive effects.

Mean plasma levonorgestrel levels decrease below 0.1 ng/mL by 96 hours after removal of the implants and below the level of assay sensitivity (0.05 ng/mL) by 5 to 14 days. Once the implants are removed, the contraceptive effects cease quickly and women can become pregnant as rapidly as women who have not used the method. Circulating concentrations can be used to forecast the risk of pregnancy only in a general statistical sense.

No statistically significant increases have been reported in the ratio of total cholesterol to HDL-cholesterol

Indications: For the prevention of pregnancy and is a long-term (up to 5 years) reversible contraceptive product. Norplant should be removed by the end of the 5th year. A new Norplant may be inserted at that time if continuing contraceptive protection is desired.

Norplant is particularly suited for women who are seeking long-term (up to 5 years) reversible contraception, want to avoid daily contraceptive use or cannot use estrogen-containing contraceptives, or, do not want to undergo permanent sterilization.

In multiclinic trials, 402 subjects on Norplant were evaluated. In the first 5 years, a total of 1 271 woman-years of experience was accumulated. The annual and 5-year cumulative pregnancy rate per 100 women on Norplant is shown in Table I. Pregnancy rates did not differ appreciably by age, weight, or by parity of the women who participated in clinical trials comprised of 402 subjects.

The overall safety experience with Norplant is derived from evaluations on 2 470 subjects.

Table I—Norplant

Annual and 5-Year Cumulative Pregnancy Rates per 100 Continuing Norplant Users

Pregnancy Rates	Year 1	Year 2	Year 3	Year 4	Year 5
Annual Rate	0.2	0.0	0.4	0.5	0.0
Cumulative Rate	0.2	0.2	0.6	1.1	1.1
Pregnancies	1	0	1	1	0

Norplant gross annual discontinuation and continuation rates are summarized in Table II.

Table II—Norplant

Annual Rates per 100 Users

	Year 1	Year 2	Year 3	Year 4	Year 5
Pregnancy	0.2	0.0	0.4	0.5	0.0
Bleeding Irregularities	9.0	8.9	4.3	5.0	2.4
Medical (excl. bleeding irreg.)	5.2	3.5	3.9	2.0	3.2
Personal	2.8	4.5	9.9	13.3	17.4
Continuation	83.7	83.9	82.5	79.9	74.6

Contraindications: Active thrombophlebitis or thromboembolic disorders; undiagnosed abnormal genital bleeding; known or suspected pregnancy; acute liver disease; benign or malignant liver tumors; known or suspected carcinoma of the breast; history of idiopathic intracranial hypertension; hypersensitivity to levonorgestrel or any of the other components of Norplant.

Warnings: Warnings based on experience with Norplant:

Bleeding Irregularities: Most women can expect some variation in menstrual bleeding patterns. Irregular bleeding, intermenstrual spotting, prolonged episodes of bleeding and spotting, and amenorrhea occur in some women. Irregular bleeding patterns associated with the Norplant implant could mask symptoms of cervical or endometrial cancer. Overall, these irregularities diminish with continuing use. Since some Norplant users experience periods of amenorrhea, missed menstrual periods cannot serve as the only means of identifying early pregnancy. Pregnancy tests should be performed whenever a pregnancy is suspected. Six weeks or more of amenorrhea after a pattern of regular menses may signal pregnancy. If pregnancy occurs, the implants must be removed.

Although bleeding irregularities have occurred in clinical trials, proportionately more women had increases rather than decreases in hemoglobin concentrations, a difference that was highly statistically significant. This finding generally indicates that reduced menstrual blood loss is associated with the use of Norplant. In rare instances, blood loss did result in hemoglobin values consistent with anemia.

Ovarian Cysts (Delayed Follicular Atresia): If follicular development occurs with Norplant, atresia of the follicle is sometimes delayed and the follicle may continue to grow beyond the size it would attain in a normal cycle. These enlarged follicles cannot be distinguished clinically from ovarian cysts. In the majority of women, enlarged follicles will spontaneously disappear and should not require surgery. Rarely, they may twist or rupture, sometimes causing abdominal pain, and surgical intervention may be required.

Pregnancy: Ectopic Pregnancies: Clinical studies have demonstrated that ectopic pregnancies have occurred among Norplant users, at similar rates as with users of no method or of IUDs. The incidence among Norplant users was 1.3 per 1 000 woman-years. The risk of ectopic pregnancy may increase with the duration of Norplant use and possibly with increased weight of the user. Physicians should be alert to the possibility of an ectopic pregnancy among women using Norplant who become pregnant or complain of lower abdominal pain. The risk of ectopic pregnancies increases as the risk of pregnancy increases. Therefore, any patient who presents with lower abdominal pain must be evaluated to rule out ectopic pregnancy.

Use Before or During Pregnancy: There have been rare reports of congenital anomalies in offspring of women who were using Norplant inadvertently during early pregnancy. A cause and effect relationship is not believed to exist.

Breast-feeding: Steroids are not considered the contraceptives of first choice for breast-feeding women. Levonorgestrel has been identified in the breast milk. The health of breast-fed infants whose mothers began using the Norplant during the 5th to 7th week postpartum was evaluated: no significant effects were observed on the growth or development of infants who were followed to 12 months of age. No data are available on use in breast-feeding mothers earlier than this after parturition.

Foreign Body Carcinogenesis: Rarely, cancers have occurred at the site of foreign body intrusions or old scars. None has been reported in Norplant clinical trials. In rodents, which are highly susceptible to such cancers, the incidence decreases with decreasing size of the foreign body. Because of the resistance of human beings to these cancers and because of the small size of the implants, the risk to users of Norplant is judged to be minimal.

Thromboembolic Disorders: Patients who develop active thrombophlebitis or thromboembolic disease should have Norplant removed. Physicians should therefore be alert to the early manifestations of thromboembolic disorders (e.g., pulmonary embolism, stroke, retinal thrombosis, etc.). Norplant removal should also be considered in women who will be subjected to prolonged immobilization due to surgery or other illnesses.

Idiopathic Intracranial Hypertension: Idiopathic intracranial hypertension (pseudotumor cerebri, benign intracranial hypertension) is a disorder of unknown etiology which is seen most commonly in obese females of reproductive age. There have been reports of idiopathic intracranial hypertension in Norplant users. A cardinal sign of idiopathic intracranial hypertension is papilledema; early symptoms may include headache (associated with a change in frequency, pattern, severity, or persistence; of particular importance are those headaches that are unremitting in nature) and visual disturbances. Patients with these symptoms, particularly obese patients or those with recent weight gain, should be screened for papilledema and, if present, the patient should be referred to a neurologist for further diagnosis and care. Norplant should be removed from patients experiencing this disorder.

Precautions: General: Physical Examination and Followup: A complete medical history and physical examination should be taken prior to the implantation or re-implantation of Norplant and at least annually during its use. At each annual visit, examination should include those procedures that were done at the initial visit. These physical examinations should include special reference to the implant site, blood pressure, breasts, liver, abdomen, extremities and pelvic organs, including cervical cytology and relevant laboratory tests. In case of undiagnosed, persistent or recurrent abnormal vaginal bleeding, appropriate diagnostic measures should be conducted to rule out malignancy. Women with a strong family history of breast cancer or who have benign breast nodules should be monitored with particular care.

Sexually Transmitted Diseases: Norplant does not protect against sexually transmitted diseases (STDs) including HIV/AIDS. For protection against STDs, it is advisable to use latex condoms along with Norplant.

Autoimmune Diseases: Autoimmune diseases such as scleroderma, systemic lupus erythematosus and rheumatoid arthritis occur in the general population and more frequently among women of childbearing age. There have been rare reports of various autoimmune diseases, including the above, in Norplant users; however the rate of reporting is significantly less than the expected incidence for these diseases. Studies have raised the possibility of developing antibodies against silicone-containing devices; however, the specificity and clinical relevance of these antibodies are unknown. While it is believed that the occurrence of autoimmune disease among Norplant users is coincidental, healthcare providers should be alert to the earliest manifestations.

Carbohydrate and Lipid Metabolism: An altered glucose tolerance characterized by decreased insulin sensitivity following glucose loading has been found in some users of combination and progestin-only oral contraceptives. Diabetic patients, or those with a family history of diabetes, should be observed closely to detect any alterations in carbohydrate metabolism. Young diabetic patients whose disease is of recent origin, well-controlled, and not associated with hypertension or other signs of vascular disease such as ocular fundal changes, should be closely observed. The effects of Norplant on carbohydrate metabolism appear to be minimal. In a study in which pretreatment serum glucose levels were compared with levels after 1 and 2 years of Norplant use, no statistically significant differences in mean serum glucose levels were evident 2 hours after glucose loading. The clinical significance of these findings is unknown but diabetic and prediabetic patients should be carefully observed while using Norplant.

Women who are being treated for hyperlipidemias should be followed closely if they elect to use Norplant. Some progestins may elevate LDL levels and may render the control of hyperlipidemias more difficult.

Liver Function: If jaundice develops in any women while using Norplant, consideration should be given to removing the implants. Steroid hormones may be poorly metabolized in patients with impaired liver function.

Fluid Retention: Steroid contraceptives may cause some degree of fluid retention. They should be prescribed with caution, and only with careful monitoring, in patients with conditions which might be aggravated by fluid retention.

Emotional Disorders: Consideration should be given to removing Norplant in women who become significantly depressed since the symptom may be drug related. Women with a history of depression should be carefully observed and Norplant removal considered if depression recurs to a serious degree.

Contact Lenses: Contact lens wearers who develop visual changes or changes in lens tolerance should be assessed by an ophthalmologist. Temporary or permanent cessation of wear may be advised.

Insertion and Removal: To be sure that the woman is not pregnant at the time of implant placement and to assure contraceptive effectiveness during the first cycle of use, it is advisable that the Norplant insertion be done during the first 7 days of the cycle or immediately following an abortion. However, Norplant capsules may be inserted at any time during the cycle provided pregnancy has been excluded and a nonhormonal contraceptive method is used for the remainder of that cycle following insertion. Insertion is not recommended before 6 weeks postpartum in breast-feeding women.

Insertion and removal are not difficult procedures but instructions must be followed closely. It is strongly advised that all healthcare professionals who insert and remove Norplant be instructed in the procedures before they attempt them. A proper insertion just under the skin will facilitate removals. Proper Norplant insertion and removal should result in minimal scarring. If the implants are placed too deeply, they can be harder to remove. There have been infrequent reports of the use of general anesthesia during the removal procedure; it is generally not required. Before initiating the removal procedure, all Norplant capsules should be localized via palpation. If all 6 capsules cannot be palpated, they may be localized via ultrasound (7 MHz) or X-ray (soft tissue). If all implants cannot be removed at the first attempt, removal should be attempted later when the site has healed. Bruising may occur at the implant site during insertion or removal. Other cutaneous reactions that have been reported include blistering, ulcerations and sloughing. There have been reports of arm pain, numbness and tingling following these procedures. In some women, hyperpigmentation occurs over the implantation site but is usually reversible following removal. See Dosage for Insertion and Removal Instructions.

Infections: Infection at the implant site, including cellulitis, has been uncommon. Attention to aseptic technique and proper insertion and removal of the Norplant implants reduces the possibility of infection. If infection occurs, suitable treatment should be instituted. If infection persists, the implants should be removed.

Capsule Expulsion and Displacement: Expulsion of implants was uncommon. It occurred more frequently when placement of the implants was extremely shallow, too close to the incision, or when infection was present. Replacement of an expelled implant must be accomplished using a new sterile implant. Contraceptive efficacy may be inadequate with fewer than 6 implants. If infection is present, it should be treated and cured before replacement.

There have been reports of capsule displacement (i.e., movement) most of which involve minor changes in the positioning of the capsules. However, infrequent reports of significant displacement (a few to several inches) have been received. Some reports have been associated with pain or discomfort. In the event that capsule movement occurs, the removal technique may need to be modified, such as additional incisions or visits.

Provisions for Removal: Women should be counselled that they can request removal of the implants at any time for medical or personal reasons. The removal should be done on request or at the end of 5 years of usage by personnel instructed in the removal technique.

Drug Interactions: Reduced efficacy (pregnancy) has been reported for Norplant users taking phenytoin and carbamazepine. These drugs may increase the metabolism of levonorgestrel through induction of microsomal liver enzymes. Norplant users should be warned of the possibility of decreased efficacy with use of drugs exhibiting enzyme-inducing activity such as those noted above and rifampicin. For women receiving long-term therapy with hepatic enzyme inducers, another method of contraception should be considered.

Drug/Laboratory Test Interactions: Certain endocrine tests may be affected by Norplant use: sex hormone binding globulin concentrations are decreased, thyroxine concentrations may be slightly decreased and triiodothyronine uptake increased.

Adverse Effects: The following adverse reactions have been associated with Norplant and a slightly different version (more inert filler) subdermal levonorgestrel implant during the first year of use (combined database of 2 470 women): many bleeding days or prolonged bleeding 27.6%, spotting 17.1%, amenorrhea 9.4%, irregular (onsets of) bleeding 7.6%, frequent bleeding onsets 7%, scanty bleeding 5.2%, pain or itching near implant site (usually transient) 3.7%, infection at implant site 0.7%, removal difficulties including damage to capsules 13.2%.

In interpreting the frequency, one should remember that users may have employed several descriptors for the same condition. This means that frequencies for related descriptions cannot simply be added to obtain total rates.

Controlled clinical studies suggest that the following adverse reactions occurring during the first year are **probably** associated with Norplant use. These adverse reactions have also been reported postmarketing: headache, nervousness/anxiety, nausea/vomiting, dizziness, adnexal enlargement, dermatitis/rash, acne, change of appetite, mastalgia, weight gain, hirsutism, hypertrichosis and scalp hair loss.

In addition, the following adverse reactions have been reported with a frequency of 5% or greater during the first year and are **possibly** related to Norplant use: breast discharge, cervicitis, musculoskeletal pain, abdominal discomfort, leukorrhea, vaginitis.

The following adverse reactions have been reported postmarketing with an incidence of less than 1% and are possibly related to Norplant use: emotional lability, idiopathic intracranial hypertension (IIH, pseudotumor cerebri, benign intracranial hypertension), dysmenorrhea, migraine, arm pain, numbness, tingling, depression.

The following adverse reactions have been reported postmarketing with an incidence of less than 1%. These events occurred under circumstances where a causal relationship to Norplant is unknown. These reactions are listed as information for physicians: congenital anomalies, pulmonary embolism, superficial venous thrombosis, deep-vein thrombosis, myocardial infarction, thrombotic thrombocytopenic purpura (TTP), stroke, pruritus, urticaria, asthenia (fatigue/weakness).

Overdose: Symptoms and Treatment: Overdosage can result if more than 6 capsules of Norplant are in situ. All implanted Norplant capsules should be removed before inserting a new

Norplant (cont'd)

set. Overdosage may cause fluid retention with its associated effects and uterine bleeding irregularities.

Dosage: Norplant implants consist of 6 Silastic capsules each containing 36 mg of the progestin levonorgestrel. Thus, the total administered (implanted) dose is 216 mg. Implantation of all 6 capsules should be performed during the first 7 days of the onset of menses by a healthcare professional instructed in the Norplant insertion technique. Insertion is subdermal, through a 2 mm incision, in the mid-portion of the upper arm about 8 to 10 cm above the elbow crease. Distribution should be in a fanlike pattern, about 15° apart, for a total of 75°. Proper insertion will facilitate later removal.

Instructions for Insertion and Removal: Norplant consists of 6 levonorgestrel-releasing capsules that are inserted subdermally in the medial aspect of the upper arm.

Norplant provides up to 5 years of effective contraceptive protection.

The basis for successful use and subsequent removal of Norplant capsules is a correct and carefully performed subdermal insertion of the 6 capsules. It is recommended that healthcare professionals performing insertions or removals of Norplant capsules avail themselves of instruction and supervision in the proper technique prior to attempting these procedures. During insertion, special attention should be given to the following: asepsis, correct subdermal placement of the capsules, careful technique to minimize tissue trauma.

This will help to avoid infections and excessive scarring at the insertion area and will help keep the capsules from being inserted too deeply in the tissue. If the capsules are placed too deeply, they will be more difficult to remove than correctly placed subdermal capsules.

Insertion Procedure: Insertion should be performed within 7 days from the onset of menses. However, Norplant capsules may be inserted at any time during the cycle provided pregnancy has been excluded and a nonhormonal contraceptive method is used for the remainder of that cycle following insertion. It is recommended that a complete history and physical examination, including a gynecologic examination be performed before the insertion of the Norplant capsules. Determine if the subject has any allergies to the antiseptic or anesthetic to be used or contraindications to progestin-only contraception. If none are found, the capsules are inserted using the procedure outlined below.

Norplant consists of 6 capsules in a sterile pouch. The insertion is performed under aseptic conditions using a trocar to place the capsules under the skin. See package insert for illustrations.

Fig. 1: The following equipment is recommended for the insertion: an examining table for the patient to lie on; sterile surgical drapes, sterile gloves (free of talc), antiseptic solution; local anesthetic, needles and syringe; #11 scalpel, #10 trocar, forceps; skin closure, sterile gauze and compresses.

The plastic cover and tray are **not sterile.**

Fig. 2: Have the patient lie on her back on the examination table with her left arm (if the patient is left-handed, the right arm) flexed at the elbow and externally rotated such that her hand is lying by her head. The capsules will be inserted subdermally through a small 2 mm incision, and positioned in a fanlike manner with the fan opening towards the shoulder.

Fig. 3: Prep the patient's upper arm with antiseptic solution; cover the arm above and below the insertion area with a sterile cloth. The optimal insertion area is in the inside of the upper arm about 8 to 10 cm above the elbow crease.

Fig. 4: Open the sterile Norplant package carefully by pulling apart the sheets of the pouch, allowing the capsules to fall onto a sterile cloth. Count the 6 capsules.

Fig. 5: After determining the absence of known allergies to the anesthetic agent or related drugs, fill a 5 mL syringe with the local anesthetic. Since blood loss is minimal with this procedure, use of epinephrine-containing anesthetics is not considered necessary. Anesthetize the insertion area by first inserting the needle under the skin and releasing a small amount of anesthetic. Then anesthetize 6 areas about 4 to 4.5 cm long, to mimic the fanlike position of the implanted capsules.

Fig. 6: Use the scalpel to make a small, shallow incision (about 2 mm) just through the dermis of the skin. Alternatively, the trocar may be inserted directly through the skin without making an incision with the scalpel. The bevel of the trocar should always face up during the insertion.

Fig. 7: The trocar has 2 marks on it. The first mark is closer to the hub and indicates how far the trocar should be introduced under the skin before the loading of each capsule. The second mark is close to the tip and indicates how much of the trocar should remain under the skin following the insertion of each implant.

Fig. 8: Insert the tip of the trocar through the incision beneath the skin at a shallow angle. Once the trocar is inserted, it should be oriented with the bevel up toward the skin to keep the capsules in a superficial plane. It is important to keep the trocar subdermal by tenting the skin with the trocar as failure to do so may result in deep placement of the capsules and could make removal more difficult.

Advance the trocar gently under the skin to the first mark near the hub of the trocar. The tip of the trocar is now at a distance of about 4 to 4.5 cm from the incision.

Do not force the trocar. If resistance is felt, try another direction.

Fig. 9: When the trocar has been inserted the appropriate distance, remove the obturator and load the first capsule into the trocar using the thumb and forefinger.

Fig. 10: Gently advance the capsule with the obturator towards the tip of the trocar until you feel resistance. Never force the obturator.

Fig. 11: Hold the obturator steady and bring the trocar back until it touches the handle of the obturator.

Fig. 12: The capsule should have been released under the skin when the mark close to the tip of the trocar is visible in the incision. Release of the capsule can be checked by palpation. It is important to keep the obturator steady and not to push the capsule into the tissue.

Fig. 13: Do not remove the trocar from the incision until all 6 capsules have been inserted. The trocar is withdrawn only to the mark close to its tip. Each succeeding capsule is always inserted next to the previous one, to form a fanlike shape. Fix the position of the previous capsule with the forefinger and middle finger of the free hand and advance the trocar along the tips of the fingers. This will ensure a suitable distance of about 15° between capsules and keep the trocar from puncturing any of the previously inserted capsules.

Leave a distance of about 5 mm between the incision and the tips of the capsules. This will help avoid spontaneous expulsions. The correct position of the capsules can be ensured by feeling them with the fingers after the insertion has been completed.

Fig. 14: After placement of the sixth capsule, a sterile gauze may be used to apply pressure briefly to the insertion site to ensure hemostasis. Palpate the distal ends of the capsules to make sure that all 6 have been properly placed.

Fig. 15: Press the edges of the incision together and close the incision with a skin closure. Suturing the incision should not be necessary.

Fig. 16: Cover the insertion area with a dry compress and wrap gauze around the arm to ensure hemostasis.

Observe the patient for a few minutes for signs of syncope or bleeding from the incision before she is discharged.

Advise the patient to keep the insertion area dry and avoid heavy lifting for 2 to 3 days. The gauze may be removed after 1 day, and the butterfly bandage as soon as the incision has healed, i.e., normally in 3 days.

Removal Procedure: Described below is a removal procedure which was developed and used during the clinical trials for Norplant. As with many surgical procedures, variations of the technique have appeared and some have been published. No one particular procedure routinely appears to have any advantage over another.

It is recommended that removals be prescheduled so that preparations for carrying out the procedure can be facilitated.

Removal of the capsules should be performed very gently and will take more time than insertion. Capsules are sometimes nicked, cut, or broken during removal. The incidence of overall removal difficulties, including damage to capsules, has been 13.2%. Less than half of these removal difficulties have caused inconvenience to the patient. If the removal of some of the capsules proves difficult have the patient return for a second visit. The remaining capsule(s) will be easier to remove after the area is healed. It may be appropriate to seek consultation or provide referral for patients in whom initial attempts at capsule removal prove difficult. If contraception is still desired, a barrier method should be advised until all capsules are removed.

The position of the patient and the asepsis are the same as for insertion.

Fig. 17: The following equipment is needed for the removal: an examining table for the patient to lie on; sterile surgical drapes, sterile gloves (free of talc), antiseptic solution; local anesthetic, needles and syringe; #11 scalpel, forceps (straight and curved mosquito); skin closure, sterile gauze and compresses.

Fig. 18: Locate the implanted capsules by palpation, possibly marking their position with a sterile skin marker. If all 6 capsules cannot be palpated, they may be localized via ultrasound (7 MHz) or X-ray (soft tissue).

Fig. 19: Once all 6 capsules are located, apply a small amount of local anesthetic **under** the capsule ends nearest the original incision site. This will serve to raise the ends of the capsules. Anesthetic injected over the capsules will obscure them and make removal more difficult. Additional small amounts of the anesthetic can be used for the removal of each of the capsules, if required.

Fig. 20: Make a 4 mm incision with the scalpel close to the ends of the capsules. Do not make a large incision.

Fig. 21: Push each capsule gently towards the incision with the fingers. When the tip is visible or near to the incision, grasp it with a mosquito forceps.

Fig. 22: Use the scalpel, forceps, or gauze to very gently open the tissue sheath that has formed around the capsule.

Fig. 23 and 24: Remove the capsule from the incision with the second forceps.

Fig. 25 and 26: After the procedure is completed, the incision is closed and bandaged as with insertion. The upper arm should be kept dry for a few days.

Following removal, a return to the previous level of fertility is usually prompt and a pregnancy may occur at any time.

If the patient wishes to continue using the method, a new Norplant can be inserted through the same incision in the same or opposite direction.

Hints: Insertion: Counselling of the patient on the benefits and side-effects of the method prior to insertion will greatly increase patient satisfaction.

Correct subdermal placement of the capsules will facilitate removal.

Before insertion, apply the anaesthetic just beneath the skin so as to raise the dermis above the underlying tissue.

Never force the trocar.

To ensure subdermal placement, the trocar with bevel up should be supported by the index finger and should visibly raise the skin at all times during insertion.

To avoid damaging the previous implanted capsule, stabilize the capsule with your forefinger and middle finger and advance the trocar alongside the finger tips at an angle of 15°.

After insertion, make a drawing for the patient's file showing the location of the 6 capsules and describe any variations in placement. This will greatly aid removal.

Removal: Alternate removal techniques have been developed.

The removal of the implanted capsules will take a little more time than the insertion.

Before initiating removal, all capsules should be located by palpation. If all 6 capsules cannot be palpated, they may be localized via ultrasound (7 MHz) or X-ray (soft tissue).

Before removal, apply the anesthetic **under** the capsule ends nearest the original incision site.

If one of the capsules has moved away from the incision, in order to facilitate finding it, use the straight mosquito clamp first to pull the capsule closer to the incision. Then change to the curved mosquito forceps to make the tip of the capsule visible and remove the surrounding connective tissue. When the capsule has been freed this way, re-grasp it with the straight forceps and pull it out gently.

It may facilitate removal of the capsule if you grasp the proximal tip with the straight mosquito clamp which is then turned 180° with the handle facing the patient's shoulder.

It is usually not helpful to enlarge the incision for easier removal.

If the removal of some of the capsules proves difficult, interrupt the procedure and have the patient return for another visit. The remaining capsule(s) will be easier to remove after the area is healed.

It may be appropriate to seek consultation or provide referral for patients in whom initial attempts at capsule removal prove difficult.

Fig. 27: Occasionally, a Norplant capsule may have a U or V shape due to faulty insertion. To remove such a disfigured insert, one may have to make a second incision at the tip of the capsule (see Fig. 27). Grasp the tip with the curved forceps, clean the connective tissue and remove the capsule with the straight forceps in the usual fashion.

If extreme force is applied on the capsule when grasping during removal, it may break. If this happens, the capsule fragments can be removed by pushing them with a finger towards the incision or by making a second incision at the opposite end of the capsule.

It is important to line up all the fragments after removal and compare them with an intact capsule to ensure that all the pieces have been removed.

If the removal of some of the capsules proves difficult, interrupt the procedure and have the patient return for a second visit 4 to 6 weeks later. The remaining capsule(s) will be easier to remove after the area is healed.

Information for the Patient: See Blue Section—Information for the Patient "Norplant".

Supplied: Each subdermal implant contains: levonorgestrel 36 mg. Each Norplant system consists of 6 capsules and is available as a Norplant System Kit.

Each Norplant System Kit contains: 1 Norplant System (subdermal 36 mg levonorgestrel implants), a set of 6 implants; 1 Norplant System Trocar (10G×2.75"); 1 scalpel; 1 forceps; 1 syringe (6 cc); 1 syringe needle (22G×1.5"); 1 syringe needle (18G×1"); 1 package of skin closures; 3 packages of gauze sponges; 1 stretch bandage; 1 surgical drape (fenestrated); 2 surgical drapes; 1 patient labelling leaflet; 1 patient folder; 1 prescribing information leaflet. Nonmedicinal ingredients: polydimethylsiloxane. Store between 15 and 30°C. Protect from excess heat and moisture.

Reviewed 1998

NORPRAMIN® Ⓟ

Hoechst Marion Roussel

Desipramine HCl

Antidepressant

Pharmacology: Desipramine displays an antidepressant property similar to that of other tricyclic antidepressants. It is the active "in vivo" metabolite of imipramine and as such, shares many of imipramine's pharmacologic effects.

The anticholinergic actions of desipramine are responsible for many of the commonly observed side effects of the drug. Desipramine causes ECG changes such as prolongation of the P-R interval and a decreased magnitude with an increased width of the T wave. These ECG changes are seen most frequently in elderly patients as is postural hypotension. Desipramine is known to lower the convulsive threshold.

Desipramine increases the percentage of Stage 4 sleep (deep sleep) and decreases the percentage of REM sleep. A partial recovery of REM sleep is seen after 3 to 5 weeks of drug administration. However, in spite of this recovery, a REM rebound occurs following rapid drug withdrawal, which is experienced as an increase in dreaming. The significance of these effects on the sleep cycle remains to be clarified.

An increase in psychomotor activity is observed as an early manifestation of the effects of desipramine; however, a significant antidepressant effect should not be expected before the end of the second week.

Desipramine is easily absorbed from the gastrointestinal tract following oral administration and is extensively bound to tissue and plasma proteins in the order of 90 to 95%. It is inactivated by hydroxylation and by further demethylation in the liver. Desipramine is excreted as a glucuronide largely in the urine (approximately 70%) and partly in the bile.

Therapeutic actions of tricyclic antidepressants seem to be related to their plasma steady state which, given the same oral dosages, can vary considerably from one individual to another. The largest influence on steady state levels seems to be genetic; however, the influence of concomitant drug administration is also of some practical clinical significance (see Dosage).

Indications: Treatment of endogenous depressive illness, including the depressed phase of manic depressive illness, involutional melancholia and psychotic depression. It may also be indicated in the management of depression of a nonpsychotic degree such as in selected cases of depressive neurosis. Patients with transient mood disturbances or normal grief reaction are not expected to benefit from tricyclic antidepressants.

Contraindications: Desipramine should not be given in conjunction with, or within 2 weeks of, treatment with a MAO inhibitor; hyperpyretic crises, severe convulsions and death have occurred in patients receiving MAO inhibitors and tricyclic antidepressants. When desipramine is substituted for an MAO inhibitor, at least 2 weeks should elapse between the treatments; administration of desipramine should then be started cautiously and should be increased gradually.

The drug is contraindicated in the acute recovery period following myocardial infarction or in cases of poorly controlled cardiac decompensation. It should not be used in those who have shown prior hypersensitivity to the drug. Cross-sensitivity between this and other dibenzazepines is a possibility.

Warnings: Extreme caution should be used when desipramine is given in the following situations: (1) In patients with cardiovascular disease, because of the possibility of conduction defects, arrhythmias, tachycardias, strokes and acute myocardial infarction. (2) In patients with a history of urinary retention or glaucoma, because of the anticholinergic properties of the drug. (3) In patients with thyroid disease or those taking thyroid medication, because of the possibility of cardiovascular toxicity, including arrhythmias. (4) In patients with a history of seizure disorder, because this drug has been shown to lower the seizure threshold.

Occupational Hazards: Desipramine may impair the mental and/or physical abilities required for the performance of potentially hazardous tasks such as driving a car or operating machinery; therefore, the patient should be cautioned accordingly.

Pregnancy and *Lactation:* Safe use of desipramine during pregnancy and lactation has not been established; therefore, if it is to be administered to pregnant patients, nursing mothers, or women of childbearing potential, the possible benefits must be weighed against the possible hazards to mother and child. Animal reproductive studies have been inconclusive.

Children: Not recommended for use in children since safety and effectiveness in the pediatric age group have not been established (see Adverse Effects, Cardiovascular).

Precautions: It is important that this drug be dispensed in the least possible quantities to depressed outpatients, since suicide has been accomplished with this class of drug. Ordinary prudence requires that children not have access to this drug, or to potent drugs of any kind; if possible, this drug should be dispensed in containers with child-resistant safety closures.

Storage of this drug in the home must be supervised responsibly. If serious adverse effects occur, dosage should be reduced or treatment altered.

Desipramine therapy in patients with manic-depressive illness may induce a hypomanic state after the depressive phase terminates.

The drug may cause exacerbation of psychosis in schizophrenic patients.

There is limited clinical experience in the concurrent administration of ECT and antidepressant drugs. Thus, if such treatment is essential, the possibility of increased risk relative to benefits should be considered.

Both elevation and lowering of blood sugar levels have been reported.

Leukocyte and differential counts should be performed in any patient who develops fever and sore throat during therapy; the drug should be discontinued if there is evidence of pathological neutrophil depression.

Drug Interactions: Norpramin may potentiate the effect of a variety of drugs. Close supervision and careful adjustment of dosage are required when this drug is administered concomitantly with anticholinergic or sympathomimetic drugs. Patients should be warned that, while taking desipramine, their response to alcoholic beverages or other CNS depressants may be exaggerated. This drug should be discontinued as soon as possible prior to elective surgery because of possible cardiovascular effects. Hypertensive episodes have been observed during surgery in patients on desipramine. The contraindication regarding its concomitant use with MAO inhibitors should be noted, as well as the warning regarding patients taking thyroid medication.

Desipramine, on the other hand, may decrease the action of other drugs; it is capable of blocking the antihypertensive effect of guanethidine and similarly acting compounds by blocking their uptake into adrenergic neurones.

There have been greater than twofold increases of previously stable plasma levels of tricyclic antidepressants when fluoxetine has been administered in combination with these agents.

Adverse Effects: The more common adverse reactions involve anticholinergic effects such as dry mouth, disturbances of visual accommodation, constipation and mild urinary retention. Also commonly seen are light headedness, drowsiness, increased perspiration and mild tremors as well as insomnia. Adverse reactions of the cardiovascular system may be much more serious, however, these occur less frequently.

Note: Included in the listing that follows are a few adverse reactions that have not been reported with desipramine. However, the pharmacological similarities among the tricyclic antidepressant drugs require that each of the reactions be considered when desipramine is administered.

Cardiovascular: hypotension, hypertension, tachycardia, palpitation, arrhythmias, heart block, myocardial infarction, stroke, premature ventricular contractions, ventricular tachycardia, ventricular fibrillation, sudden death.

There has been a report of an acute collapse and sudden death in an 8-year-old (18 kg) male, treated for 2 years for hyperactivity. There have been additional reports of sudden death in children.

Psychiatric: confusional states (especially in the elderly) with hallucinations, disorientation, delusions; anxiety, restlessness, agitation; insomnia and nightmares; hypomania; exacerbation of psychosis.

Neurological: numbness, tingling, paresthesias of extremities; incoordination, ataxia, tremors; peripheral neuropathy; extrapyramidal symptoms; seizures; alteration in EEG patterns; tinnitus.

Anticholinergic: dry mouth, and rarely associated sublingual adenitis; blurred vision, disturbance of accommodation, mydriasis; constipation, paralytic ileus; urinary retention, delayed micturition, dilatation of urinary tract.

Allergic: skin rash, petechiae, urticaria, itching, photosensitization (excessive exposure to sunlight should be avoided), edema (of face and tongue or general), drug fever, cross-sensitivity with other tricyclic drugs.

Hematologic: bone marrow depressions including agranulocytosis, eosinophilia, purpura, thrombocytopenia.

Gastrointestinal: anorexia, nausea and vomiting, epigastric distress, peculiar taste, abdominal cramps, diarrhea, stomatitis, black tongue, hepatitis, jaundice (simulating obstructive), altered liver function, elevated liver function tests, increased pancreatic enzymes.

Endocrine: gynecomastia in the male, breast enlargement and galactorrhea in the female; increased or decreased libido, impotence, painful ejaculation, testicular swelling; elevation or depression of blood sugar levels; syndrome of inappropriate antidiuretic hormone secretion (SIADH).

Other: jaundice (simulating obstructive), altered liver function; weight gain or loss; perspiration, flushing, urinary frequency, nocturia; parotid swelling; drowsiness, dizziness, weakness and fatigue, headache; alopecia; elevated alkaline phosphatase.

Withdrawal Symptoms: Though not indicative of addiction, abrupt cessation of treatment after prolonged therapy may produce nausea, headache, malaise and abdominal cramping.

Overdose: Symptoms: In patients presenting with signs of peripheral atropine effects, agitation and cardiac arrhythmias, the possibility of tricyclic antidepressant overdosage should be entertained. In view of the extensive tissue and protein binding of these drugs, blood and urine levels may not accurately reflect the extent of intoxication but may be helpful in identifying the presence of the drug.

The following signs and symptoms of overdosage may occur; reflecting CNS intoxication, the patient may exhibit pressure of speech, agitation, hallucinations, hyperacusia, choreoathetoid movements and myoclonus which may be mistaken for seizures, increased tendon reflexes, Babinski reflex, grand mal seizures and hyperactive coma progressing to flaccid coma; the cardiovascular complications are the most life threatening and may involve arrhythmias including tachycardia, nodal tachycardia, atrioventricular block, intraventricular conduction delays and asystole as well as myocardial damage, congestive heart failure and shock; in general, other signs of intoxication would also resemble those of atropine poisoning and would include flushed skin, dry mouth, dilated pupils, pyrexia, urinary retention with distended bladder and rarely, adynamic ileus.

Treatment: General management measures as in other cases of coma and shock would be applicable including bladder catheterization, cardiac monitoring, etc. Early appropriate evacuation of the ingested material and/or the use of activated charcoal is indicated.

Injectable physostigmine salicylate is presently considered the treatment of choice in the reversal of the more severe CNS and cardiovascular complications of poisoning from tricyclic antidepressants. However, in uncomplicated cases the use of this drug may not be indicated, or, may be used as a therapeutic trial only, in a reduced dosage of 1 mg injected slowly i.v. In adults, the usual dosage of physostigmine in severe cases of poisoning would be 1 to 2 mg injected i.v. over a

Norpramin (cont'd)

period of about 2 minutes. The therapeutic response may be seen, often dramatically, within 5 minutes of the injection. Since physostigmine is a short-acting drug, repeat injections in more severe, responsive, cases may be needed at 30- to 60-minute intervals, provided there are no serious signs of cholinergic effects. According to one author the initial pediatric dose should be 0.5 mg administered slowly i.v. in cases of acute tricyclic antidepressant poisoning. If toxic signs persist and no serious cholinergic effects are produced, the drug can be re-administered at 5-minute intervals until a maximum dose of 2 mg is obtained.

If physostigmine salicylate is used, atropine sulfate should be available to reverse excessive cholinergic effects such as bradycardia, marked salivation, emesis and bronchospasm. In the event of such a cholinergic crisis, atropine sulfate in a dosage equal to one-half of the physostigmine dosage may be given in order to control the muscarinic effects of the physostigmine.

Other measures of the value in tricyclic antidepressant overdose may include: diazepam for the control of persistent seizures; and careful management of electrolyte and acid-base balance.

The various dialysis techniques are relatively ineffective in reversing signs of overdosage because of the low free plasma levels and the firm tissue and protein binding of these drugs. Forced diuresis is of limited value. Digitalis, if possible, should be avoided due to its tendency to aggravate cardiac conduction problems.

Prolonged observation of at least a week is strongly recommended since deaths attributed to arrhythmias have been reported many days following an apparent recovery from a tricyclic antidepressant overdose.

Dosage: Not recommended for use in children.

Lower dosages are recommended for elderly and debilitated patients. Lower dosages are also recommended for outpatients compared to hospitalized patients, who are closely supervised. Dosage should be initiated at a low level and increased according to clinical response and any evidence of intolerance. Following remission, maintenance medication may be required for a period of time and should be at the lowest dose that will maintain remission.

Adults: The usual adult dose is 100 to 200 mg/day. In more severely ill patients, dosage may be further increased gradually to 300 mg/day if necessary. Dosages above 300 mg/day are not recommended.

Dosages should be initiated at a lower level and increased according to tolerance and clinical response.

Treatment of patients requiring as much as 300 mg should generally be initiated in hospitals, where regular visits by the physician, skilled nursing care and frequent ECGs are available.

The best available evidence of impending toxicity from very high doses of desipramine is prolongation of the QRS or QT intervals on the ECG. Prolongation of the PR interval is also significant, but less closely correlated with plasma levels. Clinical symptoms of intolerance, especially drowsiness, dizziness, and postural hypotension, should also alert the physician to the need for reduction in dosage. Plasma desipramine measurement would constitute the optimal guide to dosage monitoring.

Initial therapy may be administered in divided doses or a single daily dose. Maintenance therapy may be given on a once-daily schedule for patient convenience and compliance.

Geriatrics and Debilitated Patient dose: The usual elderly and debilitated patient dose is 25 to 100 mg daily. Dosage should be initiated at a lower level and increased according to tolerance and clinical response to a usual maximum of 100 mg daily. In more severely ill patients, dosage may be further increased to 150 mg/day. Doses above 150 mg/day are not recommended in these patients.

Initial therapy may be administered in divided doses or a single daily dose. Maintenance therapy may be given on a once-daily schedule for patient convenience and compliance.

Supplied: 10 mg: Each blue, round, biconvex, sugar-coated tablet, imprinted 68-7 in black, contains: desipramine HCl 10 mg. Nonmedicinal ingredients: acacia, calcium carbonate, cornstarch, gelatin, hydrogenated vegetable oil, magnesium stearate, mannitol, mineral oil, Opalux blue AS-4021, polishing waxes, polyethylene glycol, sucrose and titanium dioxide. Energy: <2.5 kJ (0.6 kcal). Tartrazine-free. Plastic bottles of 100.

25 mg: Each yellow, round, biconvex, film-coated tablet, imprinted NORPRAMIN 25 in black, contains: desipramine HCl 25 mg. Nonmedicinal ingredients: cornstarch, hydrogenated vegetable oil, hydroxypropyl methylcellulose, magnesium stearate, mannitol, microcrystalline cellulose, polyethylene glycol, polysorbate, starch pregelatinized, titanium dioxide, yellow D&C No. 10 and yellow FD&C No. 6. Energy: <2.5 kJ (0.6 kcal). Tartrazine-free. Plastic bottles of 100 and 500.

50 mg: Each green, round, biconvex, film-coated tablet, imprinted NORPRAMIN 50 in black, contains: desipramine 50 mg. Nonmedicinal ingredients: lactose monohydrate, magnesium stearate, microcrystalline cellulose, Opadry Green YS-1-3131, pregelatinized starch, starch and talc. Energy: <2.5 kJ (0.6 kcal). Tartrazine-free. Plastic bottles of 100.

75 mg: Each orange, round, biconvex, sugar-coated tablet, imprinted NORPRAMIN 75 in black, contains: desipramine HCl 75 mg. Nonmedicinal ingredients: acacia, calcium carbonate, cornstarch, gelatin, hydrogenated vegetable oil, magnesium stearate, mannitol, mineral oil, Opalux orange AS-2574, polish waxes, polyethylene glycol, sucrose, talc and titanium dioxide. Energy: <2.5 kJ (0.6 kcal). Tartrazine-free. Plastic bottles of 50.

100 mg: Each peach, round, biconvex, sugar-coated tablet, imprinted NORPRAMIN 100 in black, contains: desipramine HCl 100 mg. Nonmedicinal ingredients: acacia, calcium carbonate, cornstarch, D&C Red No. 30, D&C Yellow No. 10, gelatin, hydrogenated vegetable oil, magnesium stearate, mannitol, methylparaben, mineral oil, polish waxes, polyethylene glycol, povidone, propylparaben, sodium benzoate, sucrose, talc and titanium dioxide. Energy: <2.5 kJ (0.6 kcal). Tartrazine-free. Plastic bottles of 50.

Store at room temperature in a tightly closed container. Avoid extreme heat.

(Shown in Product Recognition Section)

NORVASC™ Ⓟ

Pfizer

Amlodipine Besylate

Antihypertensive—Antianginal

Pharmacology: Amlodipine is a calcium ion influx inhibitor (calcium entry blocker or calcium ion antagonist). Amlodipine is a member of the dihydropyridine class of calcium antagonists.

Mechanism of Action: The therapeutic effect of this group of drugs is believed to be related to their specific cellular action of selectively inhibiting transmembrane influx of calcium ions into vascular smooth muscle and cardiac muscle. The contractile processes of these tissues are dependent upon the movement of extracellular calcium ions into these cells through specific ion channels. Amlodipine inhibits calcium ion influx across cell membranes selectively, with a greater effect on vascular smooth muscle cells than on cardiac muscle cells. Serum calcium concentration is not affected by amlodipine. Within the physiologic pH range, amlodipine is an ionized compound and its kinetic interaction with the calcium channel receptor is characterized by the gradual association and dissociation with the receptor binding site. Experimental data suggest that amlodipine binds to both dihydropyridine and nondihydropyridine binding sites.

Hypertension: The mechanism by which amlodipine reduces arterial blood pressure involves direct peripheral arterial vasodilation and reduction in peripheral vascular resistance.

Angina: The precise mechanism by which amlodipine relieves angina has not been fully delineated. Amlodipine is a dilator of peripheral arteries and arterioles which reduces the total peripheral resistance and, therefore, reduces the workload of the heart (afterload). The unloading of the heart is thought to decrease ischemia and relieve effort angina by reducing myocardial energy oxygen consumption and oxygen requirements.

Pharmacokinetics and Metabolism: After oral administration of therapeutic doses of amlodipine, absorption occurs gradually with peak plasma concentration reached between 6 and 12 hours. Absolute bioavailability has been estimated to be between 64 and 90%. The bioavailability of amlodipine is not altered by the presence of food.

Amlodipine is metabolized through the cytochrome P450 system, mainly via CYP 3A4 isoenzyme.

Amlodipine is extensively (about 90%) converted to inactive metabolites (via hepatic metabolism) with 10% of the parent compound and 60% of the metabolites excreted in the urine. Ex vivo studies have shown that approximately 93% of the circulating drug is bound to plasma proteins in hypertensive patients. Elimination from the plasma is biphasic with a terminal elimination half-life of about 35 to 50 hours. Steady state plasma levels of amlodipine are reached after 7 to 8 days of consecutive daily dosing.

The pharmacokinetics of amlodipine are not significantly influenced by renal impairment. Plasma concentrations in the patients with moderate to severe renal failure were higher than in the normal subjects. Accumulation and mean elimination half-life in all patients were within the range of those observed in other pharmacokinetic studies with amlodipine in normal subjects.

In elderly hypertensive patients (mean age 69 years) there was a decrease in clearance of amlodipine from plasma as compared to young volunteers (mean age 36 years) with a resulting increase in the area under the curve (AUC) of about 60%.

Following single oral administration of 5 mg of amlodipine, patients with chronic mild-moderate hepatic insufficiency showed about 40% increase in AUC of amlodipine as compared to normal volunteers. This was presumably due to a reduction in clearance of amlodipine as the terminal elimination half-life was prolonged from 34 hours in young normal subjects to 56 hours in the elderly patients with hepatic insufficiency.

Following oral administration of 10 mg amlodipine to 20 male volunteers, pharmacokinetics of amlodipine were similar when amlodipine was administered with and without grapefruit juice. Geometric mean C_{max} of amlodipine was 6.2 ng/mL when the drug was administered with grapefruit juice and 5.8 ng/mL when administered with water. Mean T_{max} of amlodipine was 7.6 hours with grapefruit juice and 7.9 hours with water. Geometric mean $AUC_{0-\infty}$ was 315 ng/hr/mL with grapefruit juice and 293 ng/hr/mL with water. Geometric mean bioavailability of amlodipine was 85% when administered with grapefruit juice and 81% when administered with water.

Pharmacodynamics: Hemodynamics: Following administration of recommended doses to patients with hypertension, amlodipine produces vasodilation resulting in a reduction of supine and standing blood pressures. These decreases in blood pressure are not accompanied by any significant change in heart rate or plasma catecholamine levels with chronic dosing. With chronic once daily oral administration (5 and 10 mg once daily), antihypertensive effectiveness is maintained throughout the 24 hours dose interval with minimal peak to trough differences in blood pressure reduction. Since the vasodilation induced by amlodipine is gradual in onset, acute hypotension has rarely been reported after oral administration of amlodipine. In normotensive patients with angina amlodipine has not been associated with any clinically significant reductions in blood pressure or changes in heart rate.

Negative inotropic effects have not been observed when amlodipine was administered at the recommended doses to man, but has been demonstrated in animal models. Hemodynamic measurements of cardiac function at rest and during exercise (or pacing) in angina patients with normal ventricular function have generally demonstrated a small increase in cardiac index without significant influence on dP/dt or on left ventricular end diastolic pressure or volume.

In hypertensive patients with normal renal function, therapeutic doses of amlodipine resulted in a decrease in renal vascular resistance and an increase in glomerular filtration rate and effective renal plasma flow without change in filtration fraction.

Electrophysiologic Effects: Amlodipine does not change sinoatrial nodal function or atrioventricular conduction in intact animals, or man. In patients with chronic stable angina, i.v. administration of 10 mg of amlodipine and a further 10 mg of amlodipine after a 30 minute interval produced peripheral vasodilation and afterload reduction, but did not significantly alter A-H and H-V conduction and sinus node recovery time after pacing. Similar results were obtained in patients receiving amlodipine and concomitant beta-blockers. In clinical studies in which amlodipine was administered in combination with beta-blockers to patients with either hypertension or angina, no adverse effects on electrocardiographic parameters were observed. In clinical trials with angina patients, amlodipine as monotherapy did not alter electrocardiographic intervals.

Indications: Hypertension: The treatment of mild to moderate essential hypertension. Amlodipine should normally be used in those patients in whom treatment with diuretics or beta-blockers was found ineffective or has been associated with unacceptable adverse effects.

Amlodipine can be tried as an initial agent in those patients in whom the use of diuretics and/or beta-blockers is contraindicated or in patients with medical conditions in which these drugs frequently cause serious adverse effects.

Combination of amlodipine with a diuretic, a beta-blocking agent or an angiotensin converting enzyme inhibitor has been found to be compatible and showed additive antihypertensive effect.

Chronic Stable Angina: For the management of chronic stable angina (effort-associated angina) in patients who remain symptomatic despite adequate doses of beta-blockers and/or organic nitrates or who cannot tolerate those agents.

Amlodipine may be tried in combination with beta-blockers in chronic stable angina in patients with normal ventricular function. When such concomitant therapy is introduced, care must be taken to monitor blood pressure closely since hypotension can occur from the combined effects of the drugs.

Contraindications: Patients with hypersensitivity to the drug or other dihydropyridines and in patients with severe hypotension (less than 90 mmHg systolic).

Warnings: Increased Angina and/or Myocardial Infarction: Rarely, patients, particularly those with severe obstructive coronary artery disease, have developed documented increased frequency, duration and/or severity of angina or acute myocardial infarction on starting calcium channel blocker therapy or at the time of dosage increase. The mechanism of this effect has not been elucidated.

Outflow Obstruction (Aortic Stenosis): Amlodipine should be used with caution in a presence of fixed left ventricular outflow obstruction (aortic stenosis).

Patients with Impaired Hepatic Function: There are no adequate studies in patients with liver dysfunction and dosage recommendations have not been established. In a small number of patients with mild to moderate hepatic impairment given single dose of 5 mg, amlodipine half-life has been prolonged (see Pharmacology, Pharmacokinetics and Metabolism). Amlodipine should, therefore, be administered with caution in these patients and careful monitoring should be performed. A lower starting dose may be required (see Dosage).

Beta-blocker Withdrawal: Amlodipine gives no protection against the dangers of abrupt beta-blocker withdrawal and such withdrawal should be done by the gradual reduction of the dose of beta-blocker.

Precautions: Patients With Congestive Heart Failure: Although generally calcium channel blockers should only be used with caution in patients with heart failure, it has been observed that amlodipine had no overall deleterious effect on survival and cardiovascular morbidity in both short-term and long-term clinical trials in these patients. While a significant proportion of the patients in these studies had a history of ischemic heart disease, angina or hypertension, the studies were not designed to evaluate the treatment of angina or hypertension in patients with concomitant heart failure.

Hypotension: Amlodipine may occasionally precipitate symptomatic hypotension. Careful monitoring of blood pressure is recommended, especially in patients with a history of cerebrovascular insufficiency, and those taking medications known to lower blood pressure.

Peripheral Edema: Mild to moderate peripheral edema was the most common adverse event in the clinical trials (see Adverse Effects). The incidence of peripheral edema was dose-dependent and ranged in frequency from 3.0 to 10.8% in 5 to 10 mg dose range. Care should be taken to differentiate this peripheral edema from the effects of increasing left ventricular dysfunction.

Pregnancy: Although amlodipine was not teratogenic in the rat and rabbit some dihydropyridine compounds have been found to be teratogenic in animals. In rats, amlodipine has been shown to prolong both the gestation period and the duration of labor. There is no clinical experience with amlodipine in pregnant women. Amlodipine should be used during pregnancy only if the potential benefit outweighs the potential risk to the mother and fetus.

Lactation: It is not known whether amlodipine is excreted in human milk. Since amlodipine safety in newborns has not been established, amlodipine should not be given to nursing mothers.

Children: The use of amlodipine is not recommended in children since safety and efficacy have not been established in that population.

Geriatrics: In elderly patients (≥65 years) clearance of amlodipine is decreased with a resulting increase in AUC (see Pharmacology, Pharmacokinetics and Metabolism). In clinical trials the incidence of adverse reactions in elderly patients was approximately 6% higher than that of younger population (<65 years). Adverse reactions include edema, muscle cramps and dizziness. Amlodipine should be used cautiously in elderly patients. Dosage adjustment is advisable (see Dosage).

Interaction With Grapefruit Juice: Published data indicate that through inhibition of the cytochrome P450 system, grapefruit juice can increase plasma levels and augment pharmacodynamic effects of some dihydropyridine calcium channel blockers. Following oral administration of 10 mg amlodipine to 20 male volunteers, pharmacokinetics of amlodipine were similar when amlodipine was administered with and without grapefruit juice (see Pharmacology, Pharmacokinetics).

Drug Interactions: As with all drugs, care should be exercised when treating patients with multiple medications. Dihydropyridine calcium channel blockers undergo biotransformation by the cytochrome P450 system, mainly via CYP 3A4 isoenzyme. Coadministration of amlodipine with other drugs which follow the same route of biotransformation may result in altered bioavailability of amlodipine or these drugs. Dosages of similarly metabolized drugs, particularly those of low therapeutic ratio, and especially in patients with renal and/or hepatic impairment, may require adjustment when starting or stopping concomitantly administered amlodipine to maintain optimum therapeutic blood levels.

Drugs known to be inhibitors of the cytochrome P450 system include: azole antifungals, cimetidine, cyclosporine, erythromycin, quinidine, terfenadine, warfarin.

Drugs known to be inducers of the cytochrome P450 system include: phenobarbital, phenytoin, rifampin.

Drugs known to be biotransformed via P450 include: benzodiazepines, flecainide, imipramine, propafenone, theophylline.

Amlodipine has a low (rate of first-pass) hepatic clearance and consequent high bioavailability, and thus, may be expected to have a low potential for clinically relevant effects associated with elevation of amlodipine plasma levels when used concomitantly with drugs that compete for or inhibit the cytochrome P450 system.

Cimetidine, Warfarin, Cyclosporin, Digoxin: Pharmacokinetic interaction studies with amlodipine in healthy volunteers have indicated: cimetidine did not alter the pharmacokinetics of amlodipine; amlodipine did not change warfarin-induced prothrombin response time; amlodipine does not significantly alter the pharmacokinetics of cyclosporin; amlodipine did not change serum digoxin levels or digoxin renal clearance.

Antacids: Concomitant administration of Maalox had no effect on the disposition of a single 5 mg dose of amlodipine in 24 subjects.

Beta-blockers: When beta-adrenergic receptor blocking drugs are administered concomitantly with amlodipine, patients should be carefully monitored since blood pressure lowering effect of beta-blockers may be augmented by amlodipine's reduction in peripheral vascular resistance.

Adverse Effects: Amlodipine has been administered to 1 714 patients (805 hypertensive and 909 angina patients) in controlled clinical trials (vs placebo alone and with active comparative agents). Most adverse reactions reported during therapy were of mild to moderate severity.

Hypertension: In the 805 hypertensive patients treated with amlodipine in controlled clinical trials, adverse effects were reported in 29.9% of patients and required discontinuation of therapy due to side effects in 1.9% of patients. The most common adverse reactions in controlled clinical trials were: edema (8.9%) and headache (8.3%).

The following adverse reactions were reported with an incidence of ≥0.5% in the controlled clinical trials program (n=805): Cardiovascular: edema (8.9%), palpitations (2.0%), tachycardia (0.7%), postural dizziness (0.5%).

Skin and Appendages: pruritus (0.7%).

Musculoskeletal: muscle cramps (0.5%).

Central and Peripheral Nervous System: headache (8.3%), dizziness (3.0%), paresthesia (0.5%).

Autonomic Nervous System: flushing (3.1%), increased sweating (0.9%), dry mouth (0.7%).

Psychiatric: somnolence (1.4%).

Gastrointestinal: nausea (2.4%), abdominal pain (1.1%), dyspepsia (0.6%), constipation (0.5%).

General: fatigue (4.1%), pain (0.5%).

Angina: In the controlled clinical trials in 909 angina patients treated with amlodipine, adverse effects were reported in 30.5% of patients and required discontinuation of therapy due to side effects in 0.6% of patients. The most common adverse reactions reported in controlled clinical trials were: edema (9.9%) and headache (7.8%).

The following adverse reactions occurred at an incidence of ≥0.5% in the controlled clinical trials program (n=909): Cardiovascular: edema (9.9%), palpitations (2.0%), postural dizziness (0.6%).

Skin and Appendages: rash (1.0%), pruritus (0.8%).

Musculoskeletal: muscle cramps (1.0%).

Central and Peripheral Nervous System: headache (7.8%), dizziness (4.5%), paresthesia (1.0%), hypoesthesia (0.9%).

Autonomic Nervous System: flushing (1.9%).

Psychiatric: somnolence (1.2%), insomnia (0.9%), nervousness (0.7%).

Gastrointestinal: nausea (4.2%), abdominal pain (2.2%), dyspepsia (1.4%), diarrhea (1.1%), flatulence (1.0%), constipation (0.9%).

Respiratory: dyspnea (1.1%).

Special Senses: vision abnormal (1.3%), tinnitus (0.6%).

General: fatigue (4.8%), pain (1.0%), asthenia (1.0%).

Amlodipine has been evaluated for safety in about 11 000 patients with hypertension and angina. The following events occurred in <1% but >0.1% of patients in comparative clinical trials (double-blind comparative vs placebo or active agents; n=2 615) or under conditions of open trials or marketing experience where a causal relationship is uncertain.

Cardiovascular: arrhythmia (including ventricular tachycardia and atrial fibrillation), bradycardia, hypotension, peripheral ischemia, syncope, tachycardia, postural dizziness, postural hypotension.

Central and Peripheral Nervous System: hypoesthesia, tremor, vertigo.

Gastrointestinal: anorexia, constipation, dysphagia, vomiting, gingival hyperplasia.

General: asthenia+, back pain, hot flushes, malaise, rigors, weight gain.

Musculoskeletal: arthralgia, arthrosis, myalgia.

Psychiatric: sexual dysfunction (male+ and female), insomnia, nervousness, depression, abnormal dreams, anxiety, depersonalization.

Respiratory: epistaxis.

Skin and Appendages: pruritus+, rash erythematous, rash maculopapular, erythema multiforme.

Special Senses: conjunctivitis, diplopia, eye pain, tinnitus.

Urinary: micturition frequency, micturition disorder, nocturia.

Autonomic Nervous System: dry mouth, sweating increased.

Metabolic and Nutritional: thirst.

Hemopoietic: purpura.

+These events occurred in less than 1% in placebo controlled trials, but the incidence of these side effects was between 1 and 2% in all multiple dose studies.

The following events occurred in ≤0.1% of patients: cardiac failure, skin discoloration, urticaria, skin dryness, Stevens-Johnson syndrome, alopecia, twitching, ataxia, hypertonia, migraine, apathy, amnesia, gastritis, pancreatitis, increased appetite, coughing, rhinitis, parosmia, taste perversion, and xerophthalmia.

Isolated cases of angioedema have been reported. Angioedema may be accompanied by breathing difficulty.

In postmarketing experience, jaundice and hepatic enzyme elevations (mostly consistent with cholestasis) in some cases severe enough to require hospitalization have been reported in association with use of amlodipine.

Overdose: Symptoms: Overdosage can cause excessive peripheral vasodilation with marked and probably prolonged hypotension and possibly a reflex tachycardia. In humans, experience with overdosage of amlodipine is limited. When amlodipine was ingested at doses of 105 to 250 mg some patients remained normotensive with or without gastric lavage while another patient experienced hypotension (90/50 mmHg) which normalized following plasma expansion. A patient who took 70 mg of amlodipine with benzodiazepine developed shock which was refractory to treatment and died. In a 19 month old child who ingested 30 mg of amlodipine (about 2 mg/kg) there was no evidence of hypotension but tachycardia (180 bpm) was observed. Ipecac was administered 3.5 hours after ingestion and on subsequent observation (overnight) no sequelae were noted.

Treatment: Clinically significant hypotension due to overdosage requires active cardiovascular support including monitoring of cardiac and respiratory function, elevation of extremities, and attention to circulating fluid volume and urine output. A vasoconstrictor (such as nonrepinephrine) may be helpful in restoring vascular tone and blood pressure, provided that there is no contraindication to its use. As amlodipine is highly protein bound, hemodialysis is not likely to be of benefit. I.V. calcium gluconate may be beneficial in reversing the effects of calcium channel blockade. Clearance of amlodipine is prolonged in elderly patients and in patients with impaired

Norvasc (cont'd)

liver function. Since amlodipine absorption is slow, gastric lavage may be worthwhile in some cases.

Dosage: Dosage should be individualized depending on patient's tolerance and responsiveness.

For both hypertension and angina, the recommended initial dose is 5 mg once daily. If necessary, dose can be increased after 1 to 2 weeks to a maximum dose of 10 mg once daily.

Geriatrics or Patients with Impaired Renal Function: The recommended initial dose in patients over 65 years of age or patients with impaired renal function is 5 mg once daily. If required, increasing in the dose should be done gradually and with caution (see Precautions).

Patients with Impaired Hepatic Function: Dosage requirements have not been established in patients with impaired hepatic function. When amlodipine is used in these patients, the dosage should be carefully and gradually adjusted depending on patients tolerance and response. A lower starting dose of 2.5 mg once daily should be considered (see Warnings).

Supplied: 5 mg: Each white, octagonal tablet, scored, debossed on one face as NRV 5 with Pfizer on the opposite face, contains: amlodipine besylate equivalent to amlodipine 5 mg. Nonmedicinal ingredients: dibasic calcium phosphate anhydrous, magnesium stearate, microcrystalline cellulose and sodium starch glycolate. White plastic (high density polyethylene) bottles of 100 and 250.

10 mg: Each white, octagonal tablet, debossed on one face as NRV 10 with Pfizer on the opposite face, contains: amlodipine besylate equivalent to amlodipine 10 mg. Nonmedicinal ingredients: dibasic calcium phosphate anhydrous, magnesium stearate, microcrystalline cellulose and sodium starch glycolate. White plastic (high density polyethylene) bottles of 100 and 250.

Store at 15 to 30°C. Protect from light.

(Shown in Product Recognition Section)

Reviewed 1999

NORVENTYL ℞

ICN

Nortriptyline HCl

Antidepressant

Supplied: 10 mg: Each capsule with white opaque body and yellow opaque cap, imprinted with ICN N31, contains: nortriptyline HCl USP 10 mg. Nonmedicinal ingredients: colloidal silicon dioxide, cornstarch, gelatin, sodium lauryl sulfate NF and titanium dioxide. Bottles of 100 and 500.

25 mg: Each capsule with white opaque body and yellow opaque cap, imprinted with ICN N32, contains: nortriptyline HCl USP 25 mg. Nonmedicinal ingredients: colloidal silicon dioxide, cornstarch, gelatin, sodium lauryl sulfate NF and titanium dioxide. Bottles of 100 and 500.

NORVIR® ℞

Abbott

Ritonavir

Human Immunodeficiency Virus (HIV) Protease Inhibitor

Pharmacology: Ritonavir is an inhibitor of HIV protease with activity against the Human Immunodeficiency Virus (HIV).

Pharmacodynamics: Ritonavir is an orally active peptidomimetic inhibitor of both the HIV-1 and HIV-2 proteases. Inhibition of HIV protease renders the enzyme incapable of processing the gag-pol polyprotein precursor which leads to the production of HIV particles with immature morphology that are unable to initiate new rounds of infection. Ritonavir has selective affinity for the HIV protease and has little inhibitory activity against human aspartyl proteases.

In vitro data indicate that ritonavir is active against all strains of HIV tested in a variety of transformed and primary human cell lines. The concentration of drug that inhibits 50% and 90% (EC_{50}, EC_{90}) of viral replication is approximately 0.02 and 0.11 µM, respectively. Studies which measured direct cell toxicity of ritonavir on several cell lines showed no direct toxicity at concentrations up to 25 µM, with a resulting in vitro therapeutic index of at least 1 000.

Pharmacokinetics: The pharmacokinetics of ritonavir have been studied in healthy volunteers and HIV-infected patients (CD_4 ≥50 cells/µL). See Table I for ritonavir pharmacokinetic characteristics.

Table I—Norvir

Ritonavir Pharmacokinetic Characteristics

Parameter	n	Values (Mean±SD)
C_{max} SS[a]	10	11.2±3.6 µg/mL
C_{trough} SS[a]	10	3.7±2.6 µg/mL
Vβ/F[b]	91	0.41±0.25 L/kg
$t_{1/2}$	—	3-5 h
CL/F[a]	10	8.8±3.2 L/h
CL/F[b]	91	4.6±1.6 L/h
CL_R	62	<0.1 L/h
RBC/Plasma Ratio	—	0.14
Percent bound[c]	—	98-99%

[a]SS=steady-state; patients taking ritonavir 600 mg q12h.
[b]Single ritonavir 600 mg dose.
[c]Primarily bound to human serum albumin and α_1-acid glycoprotein over the range 0.01 to 30 µg/mL of ritonavir.

The absolute bioavailability of ritonavir has not been determined. After a 600 mg dose of oral solution, peak concentrations of ritonavir were achieved approximately 2 and 4 hours after dosing under fasting and nonfasting (514 kcal; 9% fat, 12% protein, and 79% carbohydrate) conditions, respectively. When the oral solution was given under nonfasting conditions, peak ritonavir concentrations decreased 23% and the extent of absorption decreased 7% relative to fasting conditions. Dilution of oral solution, within 1 hour of administration, with 240 mL of chocolate milk, Advera or Ensure did not significantly affect the extent and rate of ritonavir absorption. After a single 600 mg dose under nonfasting conditions, in 2 separate studies, the capsule (n=21) and oral solution (n=18) formulations yielded mean±SD areas under the plasma concentration-time curve (AUCs) of 129.5±47.1 and 129±39.3 µg.h/mL, respectively. Relative to fasting conditions, the extent of absorption of ritonavir from the capsule formulation was 15% higher when administered with a meal (771 kcal; 46% fat, 18% protein and 37% carbohydrate).

Nearly all of the plasma radioactivity after a single oral 600 mg dose of ^{14}C-ritonavir oral solution (n=5) was attributed to unchanged ritonavir. Five ritonavir metabolites have been identified in human urine and feces. The isopropyl thiazole oxidation metabolite (M-2) is the major metabolite and has antiviral activity similar to that of parent drug; however, the concentrations of this metabolite in plasma are low. Studies utilizing human liver microsomes have demonstrated that cytochrome P450 3A (CYP3A) is the major isoform involved in ritonavir metabolism, although CYP2D6 also contributes to the formation of M-2.

In a study of 5 subjects receiving a 600 mg dose of ^{14}C-ritonavir oral solution, 11.3±2.8% of the dose was excreted into the urine, with 3.5±1.8% of the dose excreted as unchanged parent drug. In that study, 86.4±2.9% of the dose was excreted in the feces with 33.8±10.8% of the dose excreted as unchanged parent drug. Upon multiple dosing, ritonavir accumulation is less than predicted from a single dose possibly due to a time and dose-related increase in clearance.

Special Populations: Gender, Race and Age: No age-related pharmacokinetic differences have been observed in adult patients (18 to 63 years). Ritonavir pharmacokinetics have not been studied in older patients. A study of ritonavir pharmacokinetics in healthy males and females showed no statistically significant differences in the pharmacokinetics of ritonavir. Pharmacokinetic differences due to race have not been identified.

Renal Insufficiency: Ritonavir pharmacokinetics have not been studied in patients with renal insufficiency, however, since renal clearance is negligible, a decrease in total body clearance is not expected in patients with renal insufficiency.

Because ritonavir is highly protein bound it is unlikely that ritonavir will be significantly removed by dialysis (see Overdose: Symptoms and Treatment).

Hepatic Insufficiency: Ritonavir pharmacokinetics have not been studied in subjects with hepatic insufficiency (see Precautions).

<u>*Drug Interactions:*</u> Table II summarizes the effects on AUC and C_{max} with 95% confidence intervals (95% CI) around the mean differences, of coadministration of ritonavir with a variety of drugs. For information about clinical recommendations, see Precautions, Drug Interactions.

Indications: In combination with reverse-transcriptase inhibitor (RTI) nucleoside analogues for the treatment of HIV-infection when therapy is warranted. For patients with advanced HIV disease, this indication is based on the results from a study that showed a reduction in both mortality and AIDS-defining clinical events for patients who received ritonavir. Median duration of follow-up in this study was 6 months. The clinical benefit from ritonavir therapy for longer periods of treatment is unknown.

For patients with less advanced disease, this indication is based on changes in surrogate markers in studies evaluating

Table II—Norvir

Effects on AUC and C_{max} of Coadministration of Ritonavir with Other Drugs

Drug	Ritonavir Dosage	n	AUC % (95% CI)	C_{max} % (95% CI)
Effect on Ritonavir				
Clarithromycin 500 mg q12h 4 days	200 mg q8h 4 days	22	↑ 12% (2, 23%)	↑ 15% (2, 28%)
Didanosine 200 mg q12h 4 days, about 2.5 h before ritonavir	600 mg q12h 4 days	12	↔	↔
Fluconazole 400 mg day 1, 200 mg daily 4 days	200 mg q6h 4 days	8	↑ 12% (5, 20%)	↑ 15% (7, 22%)
Fluoxetine 30 mg q12h 8 days	600 mg single dose	16	↑ 19% (7, 34%)	↔
Rifampin 600 mg or 300 mg daily 10 days[a]	500 mg q12h 20 days	7,9[c]	↓ 35% (7, 55%)	↓ 25% (−5, 46%)
Zidovudine 200 mg q8h 4 days	300 mg q6h 4 days	10	↔	↔
Effect on Coadministered Drug				
Drug	**Ritonavir Dosage**	**n**	**AUC % (95% CI)**	**C_{max} % (95% CI)**
Clarithromycin 500 mg q12h 4 days	200 mg q8h 4 days	22	↑ 77% (56, 103%)	↑ 31% (15, 51%)
14-OH clarithromycin metabolite			↓ 100%	↓ 99%
Desipramine 100 mg single dose	500 mg q12h 12 days	14	↑ 145% (103, 211%)	↑ 22% (12, 35%)
2-OH desipramine metabolite			↓ 15% (3, 26%)	↓ 67% (62, 72%)
Didanosine 200 mg q12h 4 days, about 2.5 h before ritonavir	600 mg q12h 4 days	12	↓ 13% (0, 23%)	↓ 16% (5, 26%)
Ethinyl estradiol 50 µg single dose	500 mg q12h 16 days	23	↓ 40% (31, 49%)	↓ 32% (24, 39%)
Rifabutin 150 mg daily 16 days	500 mg q12h 10 days	5,11[c]	↑ 4-fold (2.8, 6.1X)	↑ 2.5-fold (1.9, 3.4X)
25-O-desacetyl rifabutin metabolite			↑ 35-fold (25, 78X)	↑ 16-fold (14, 20X)
Sulfamethoxazole 800 mg single dose[b]	500 mg q12h 12 days	15	↓ 20% (16, 23%)	↔
Theophylline 3 mg/kg q8h 15 days	500 mg q12h 10 days	13,11[c]	↓ 43% (42, 45%)	↓ 32% (29, 34%)
Trimethoprim 160 mg single dose[b]	500 mg q12h 12 days	15	↑ 20% (3, 43%)	↔
Zidovudine 200 mg q8h 4 days	300 mg q6h 4 days	9	↓ 25% (15, 34%)	↓ 27% (4, 45%)

[a]Preliminary data.
[b]Sulfamethoxazole and trimethoprim taken as single combination tablet.
[c]Parallel group design; entries are subjects receiving combination and control regimens, respectively.
Legend: ↑ Indicates increase; ↓ Indicates decrease; ↔ Indicates no change.

patients who received ritonavir alone or in combination with other antiretroviral agents.

Contraindications: In patients with known hypersensitivity to ritonavir or any of its ingredients.

Ritonavir is expected to produce large increases in the plasma concentrations of the following drugs: amiodarone, astemizole, bepridil, bupropion, cisapride, clozapine, dihydroergotamine, encainide, ergotamine, flecainide, meperidine, pimozide, piroxicam, propafenone, propoxyphene, quinidine, rifabutin, and terfenadine. These agents have recognized risks of arrhythmias, hematologic abnormalities, seizures, or other potentially serious adverse effects. These drugs should not be coadministered with ritonavir. Ritonavir coadministration is likely to produce large increases in these highly metabolized sedatives and hypnotics: alprazolam, clorazepate, diazepam, estazolam, flurazepam, midazolam, triazolam, and zolpidem. Due to the potential for extreme sedation and respiratory depression from these agents, they should not be coadministered with ritonavir.

Postmarketing reports of acute ergot toxicity characterized by peripheral vasospasm and ischemia of the extremities have been associated with coadministration of ritonavir and ergotamine or dihydroergotamine.

Warnings: Coadministration of ritonavir with certain nonsedating antihistamines, sedative hypnotics, or antiarrhythmics may result in potentially serious and/or life-threatening adverse events due to possible effects of ritonavir on the hepatic metabolism of certain drugs (see Contraindications and Precautions).

Allergic reactions including urticaria, mild skin eruptions, bronchospasm, and angioedema have been reported. Rare cases of anaphylaxis and Stevens-Johnson syndrome have also been reported.

Hepatic transaminase elevations exceeding 5 times the upper limit of normal, clinical hepatitis, and jaundice have occurred in patients receiving ritonavir alone or in combination with other antiretroviral drugs (see Table V on following pages). There may be an increased risk for transaminase elevations in patients with underlying hepatitis B or C. Therefore, caution should be exercised when administering ritonavir to patients with pre-existing liver disease, liver enzyme abnormalities, or hepatitis.

There have been postmarketing reports of hepatic dysfunction, including some fatalities. These have generally occurred in patients taking multiple concomitant medications and/or with advanced AIDS. A definitive causal relationship has not been established.

New onset diabetes mellitus, exacerbation of pre-existing diabetes mellitus and hyperglycemia have been reported during postmarketing surveillance in HIV-infected patients receiving protease inhibitor therapy. Some patients required either initiation or dose adjustments of insulin or oral hypoglycemic agents for treatment of these events. In some cases diabetic ketoacidosis has occurred. In those patients who discontinue protease inhibitor therapy, hyperglycemia persisted in some cases. Because these events have been reported voluntarily during clinical practice, estimates of frequency cannot be made and a causal relationship between protease inhibitor therapy and these events has not been established.

Precautions: General: Toxicological studies in laboratory animals identified various organs as targets for toxicity at drug exposures below or approaching those achieved in patients participating in clinical trials with ritonavir. Because no safety margin or a small safety margin has been demonstrated in long-term studies, these organs should be assessed periodically or if clinical signs and symptoms occur during therapy.

Bleeding in Hemophiliacs: There have been reports of increased bleeding including spontaneous skin hematomas and hemarthrosis in patients with Hemophilia Type A and Type B treated with protease inhibitors. In some patients, additional Factor VIII was given. In more than half of the reported cases, treatment with protease inhibitors was continued or reintroduced. There is no proven relationship between protease inhibitors and such bleeding, however, the frequency of bleeding episodes should be closely monitored in patients on ritonavir.

Drug Interactions: See Contraindications. Agents which increase CYP3A activity (e.g., phenobarbital, carbamazepine, dexamethasone, phenytoin, rifampin, and rifabutin) would be expected to increase the clearance of ritonavir resulting in decreased ritonavir plasma concentrations. Tobacco use is associated with an 18% decrease in the AUC of ritonavir.

Ritonavir can produce large increases in plasma concentrations of certain highly metabolized drugs. Ritonavir has a high affinity for several cytochrome P450 (CYP) isoforms with the following rank order: CYP3A > CYP2D6 > CYP2C9, CYP2C19 >> CYP2A6, CYP1A2, CYP2E1. There is some evidence that ritonavir may increase the activity of glucuronosyltransferases; thus, loss of therapeutic effects from directly glucuronidated agents during ritonavir therapy may signify the need for dosage alteration of these agents.

A systematic review of over 200 medications prescribed to HIV-infected patients was performed to identify potential drug interactions with ritonavir. In addition to the drugs listed in the Contraindications section, Table III summarizes some commonly prescribed drugs, categorized by the predicted magnitude of interaction that could result if coadministered with ritonavir. It is advised that concomitant use of any of these agents with ritonavir should be accompanied by therapeutic drug concentration monitoring and/or increased monitoring of therapeutic and adverse effects, especially for agents with narrow therapeutic margins (e.g., oral anticoagulants, immunosuppressants). Large dosage reductions (>50% reduction) may be required for those agents extensively metabolized by CYP3A.

The following list provides information based on studies of the coadministration of ritonavir with the pharmacokinetic properties of several commonly prescribed medications.

Clarithromycin: The mean increase in the AUC of clarithromycin in the presence of ritonavir was 77%. Clarithromycin may be administered without dosage adjustment to patients with normal renal function. However, for patients with renal impairment the following dosage adjustments should be considered. For patients with CL_{CR} 30 to 60 mL/min the dose of clarithromycin should be reduced by 50%. For patients with CL_{CR} <30 mL/min the dose of clarithromycin should be decreased by 75%. Doses of clarithromycin greater than 1 g/ day should not be coadministered with ritonavir.

Desipramine: Coadministration of ritonavir resulted in a 145% mean increase in the AUC of desipramine. Dosage reduction of desipramine should be considered in patients taking the combination.

Disulfiram/Metronidazole: Ritonavir formulations contain alcohol, which can produce reactions when coadministered

Table III—Norvir

Predicted Effects on Drugs Coadministered with Ritonavir

Drug Category	Representative Drugs by Theoretical Prediction of Interaction Category					
	Contraindicated Medications	**Large[a] ↑ AUC[b]**	**Moderate[a] ↑ AUC[b]**	**Moderate[a] ↑ or ↓ AUC[b]**	**Unknown**	**Possible ↓ AUC[b]**
Analgesics, narcotic	Meperidine Propoxyphene	Alfentanil Fentanyl Methadone	Hydrocodone Oxycodone Tramadol		Levomethadyl (LAAM)	Codeine Hydromorphone Morphine
Analgesics, nonsteroidal	Piroxicam			Diclofenac Flurbiprofen Ibuprofen Indomethacin	Nabumetone Sulindac	Ketoprofen Ketorolac Naproxen
Antiarrhythmics	Amiodarone Encainide Flecainide Propafenone Quinidine	Lidocaine	Disopyramide Mexiletine		Tocainide[d] Digoxin	
Antiasthmatic						Theophylline[e]
Antibiotics, macrolides		Erythromycin	Clarithromycin[e]			
Anticoagulants			R-warfarin	S-warfarin		
Anticonvulsants		Carbamazepine	Clonazepam Ethosuximide	Phenytoin	Phenobarbital	Divalproex Lamotrigine
Antidepressants, tricyclic			Amitriptyline Clomipramine Desipramine[e] Imipramine Maprotiline Nortriptyline Trimipramine		Doxepin[d]	
Antidepressants, other (SSRIs and nontricyclics)	Bupropion	Nefazodone Sertraline	Fluoxetine Paroxetine Trazodone Venlafaxine		Fluvoxamine	
Antidiarrheal						Diphenoxylate Loperamide
Antiemetics, Prokinetics	Cisapride		Dronabinol Ondansetron		Prochlorperazine[d] Promethazine[d]	Metoclopramide
Antifungal Agents		Itraconazole Ketoconazole Miconazole				
Antihistamine	Astemizole Terfenadine	Loratadine				
Antihypertensives				Losartan	Doxazosin[d] Prazosin[d] Terazosin[d]	
Antimycobacterial	Rifabutin				Ethionamide Rifampin	
Antiparasitics		Quinine		Proguanil	Albendazole Chloroquine Metronidazole Primaquine Pyrimethamine Trimetrexate	Atovaquone
Antiulcer Agents				Lansoprazole Omeprazole		
β-blockers			Metoprolol Penbutolol Pindolol Timolol	Propranolol	Betaxolol[d]	

Norvir (cont'd)

Table III (Cont'd)—Norvir

Predicted Effects on Drugs Coadministered with Ritonavir

Drug Category	Representative Drugs by Theoretical Prediction of Interaction Category					
	Contraindicated Medications	Large[a] ↑ AUC[b]	Moderate[a] ↑ AUC[b]	Moderate[a] ↑ or ↓ AUC[b]	Unknown	Possible ↓ AUC[b]
Calcium Channel Blockers	Bepridil	Amlodipine Diltiazem Felodipine Isradipine Nicardipine Nifedipine Nimodipine Nisoldipine Nitrendipine Verapamil				
Cancer Chemotherapeutic Agents		Tamoxifen	Etoposide Paclitaxel Vinblastine Vincristine	Cyclophosphamide[c] Ifosfamide[c]	Daunorubicin[d] Doxorubicin[d]	
Ergot Alkaloids and Derivatives	Dihydroergotamine Ergotamine	Bromocriptine			Ergonovine[d] Methylergonovine[d] Methysergide[d]	
Hemorrheologic Agent					Pentoxifylline	
HIV Antivirals		Indinavir Saquinavir[e]			Nevirapine[d]	
Hypoglycemics				Glimepiride Glipizide Glyburide Tolbutamide		
Hypolipidemics		Fluvastatin Lovastatin Simvastatin	Pravastatin		Gemfibrozil	Clofibrate
Immuno-suppressants		Cyclosporine Tacrolimus				
Neuroleptics	Clozapine Pimozide		Chlorpromazine Haloperidol Perphenazine Risperidone Thioridazine			
Sedative/ Hypnotics	Alprazolam Clorazepate Diazepam Estazolam Flurazepam Midazolam Triazolam Zolpidem					Lorazepam Oxazepam Propofol Temazepam
Steroids		Dexamethasone	Prednisone			Ethinyl Estradiol
Stimulants			Dexfenfluramine Methamphetamine		Methylphenidate	

[a] Large= >3X; Moderate=1.5-3X.
[b] AUC=area under the plasma concentration-time curve, a measure of drug exposure.
[c] An increase in the AUC of cyclophosphamide and ifosfamide, both activated by CYP, may correspond to a decrease in the AUC of the active metabolite(s) and a possible decrease in efficacy of these drugs.
[d] A possible increase in concentration is more likely when combined with ritonavir.
[e] Clinical drug interaction study has been performed.

with disulfiram or other drugs that produce disulfiram-like reactions (e.g., metronidazole).

Oral Contraceptives: The mean AUC of a single dose of ethinyl estradiol, a component in oral contraceptives, was reduced 40% during concomitant dosing with ritonavir 500 mg q12h; dosage increase or alternative contraceptive measures should be considered.

Saquinavir: Ritonavir extensively inhibits the metabolism of saquinavir resulting in greatly increased saquinavir plasma concentrations. Coadministration of ritonavir 400 or 600 mg b.i.d. regimens produced greater than 20-fold increases in steady-state dose-normalized saquinavir concentrations in healthy subjects. The appropriate dosing for this combination has not been established.

Theophylline: The average AUC of theophylline was reduced by 43% when coadministered with ritonavir. Increased dosage of theophylline may be required.

DDI: A pharmacokinetic study demonstrated that the concomitant administration of ritonavir 600 mg q12h and didanosine (DDI) 200mg q12h resulted in a reduction of the DDI steady-state C_{max} and AUC of 16% and 13%, respectively. In contrast, little if any effect was noted on ritonavir pharmacokinetics. Dose alteration of DDI during concomitant ritonavir therapy should not be necessary; however, dosing of the 2 drugs should be separated by 2.5 hours to avoid formulation incompatibility.

Rifabutin: Do not coadminister with ritonavir due to observed 4-fold increase in AUC of rifabutin and 35-fold increase in AUC of active desacetyl metabolite and documented significant increase in uveitis/arthralgia/leukopenia when administered with ritonavir.

Sulfamethoxazole/Trimethoprim: A pharmacokinetic study demonstrated that the concomitant administration of ritonavir 500 mg q12h and sulfamethoxazole/trimethoprim resulted in a 20% reduction of the sulfamethoxazole AUC and a 20% increase of trimethoprim AUC. Dose alteration of sulfamethoxazole/trimethoprim during concomitant ritonavir therapy should not be necessary.

Zidovudine: A pharmacokinetic study demonstrated that the concomitant administration of ritonavir 300 mg q6h and zidovudine (ZDV) 200 mg q8h resulted in a reduction of the zidovudine C_{max} and AUC of 27 and 25% respectively. In contrast, little if any effect was noted on ritonavir pharmacokinetics. Dose alteration of ZDV during concomitant ritonavir therapy should not be necessary.

Disopyramide, Mexiletine, Nefazodone or Fluoxetine: Postmarketing Experience: Cardiac and neurologic events have been reported when ritonavir has been coadministered with disopyramide, mexiletine, nefazodone, or fluoxetine. The possibility of drug interaction cannot be excluded.

Laboratory Tests: Ritonavir has been associated with alterations in cholesterol, triglycerides, AST, ALT, GGT, CPK, and uric acid. Appropriate laboratory testing should be performed prior to initiating ritonavir therapy and at periodic intervals or if any clinical signs or symptoms occur during therapy. For comprehensive information concerning laboratory test alterations associated with nucleoside analogues, physicians should refer to the complete product information for each of these drugs.

Impaired Hepatic Function: Ritonavir is principally metabolized by the liver. Preclinical studies have identified the liver as a toxicity target. Therefore, appropriate tests should be performed at treatment initiation and at periodic intervals to assess hepatic function.

Resistance/Cross-resistance: HIV-1 isolates with reduced susceptibility to ritonavir have been selected in vitro and have been isolated from patients in clinical trials.

The potential for HIV cross-resistance between protease inhibitors has not been fully explored. Therefore, it is unknown what effect ritonavir therapy will have on the activity of subsequent protease inhibitors.

CNS Penetration: CNS penetration of ritonavir has not been established.

Pregnancy: There are no adequate and well-controlled studies in pregnant women. Because animal reproduction studies are not always predictive of human response, this drug should be used during pregnancy only if clearly needed.

In rat fertility studies, hepatic toxicity precluded drug exposures equal to those achieved with the proposed human therapeutic dose. No effects on fertility in rats were produced at drug exposures approximately 40% (male) and 60% (female) of that achieved with the proposed human therapeutic dose.

No treatment-related malformations were observed when ritonavir was administered to pregnant rats or rabbits. Developmental toxicity observed in rats (early resorptions, decreased fetal body weight and ossification delays and developmental variations) occurred at a maternally toxic dosage at an exposure equivalent to approximately 30% of that achieved with the proposed therapeutic dose. A slight increase in the incidence of cryptorchidism was also noted in rats at an exposure approximately 22% of that achieved with the proposed therapeutic dose.

Developmental toxicity observed in rabbits (resorptions, decreased litter size and decreased fetal weights) also occurred at a maternally toxic dosage equivalent to 1.8 times the proposed therapeutic dose based on a body surface area conversion factor.

Lactation: It is not known whether this drug is excreted in human milk. Because many drugs are excreted in human milk, caution should be exercised when ritonavir is administered to a nursing woman. However, it is advisable for HIV-infected women not to breast-feed to avoid postnatal transmission of HIV to a child who may not be infected.

Pediatric: The safety and effectiveness of ritonavir in children below the age of 12 have not been established.

Information for the Patient: Patients should be informed that ritonavir is not a cure for HIV infection and that they may continue to acquire illnesses associated with advanced HIV infection, including opportunistic infections.

Patients should be told that the long-term effects of ritonavir are unknown at this time. They should be informed that ritonavir therapy has not been shown to reduce the risk of transmitting HIV to others through sexual contact or blood contamination.

Patients should be advised to take ritonavir with food, if possible.

Patients should be informed to take ritonavir every day as prescribed. Patients should not alter the dose or discontinue ritonavir without consulting their doctor. If a dose is missed, patients should take the next dose as soon as possible. However, if a dose is skipped, the patient should not double the next dose.

Since ritonavir interacts with a number of drugs when taken together, patients should be advised to report to their doctor the use of any other medications, including prescription and nonprescription drugs.

Patients should be advised of the likelihood of experiencing muscle weakness, nausea, diarrhea, vomiting, abdominal pain, loss of appetite, numbness and tingling, and/or taste perversion while taking ritonavir.

Storage: Store capsules under refrigeration between 2 and 8°C. Protect from light. Store oral solution at room temperature, between 20 and 25°C. Do not refrigerate. **Shake well before each use.** Product should be stored in the original container. Avoid exposure to excessive heat. Keep cap tightly closed.

The ritonavir oral solution dosage cup should be cleaned immediately with hot water and dish soap after use. When cleaned immediately, drug residue is removed. The dosage cup must be dry prior to use.

Adverse Effects: The safety of ritonavir alone and in combination with nucleoside analogues was studied in 1 140 patients. Table IV lists treatment-emergent adverse events (at least possibly related and of at least moderate intensity) that occurred in 2% or greater of patients receiving ritonavir alone or in combination with nucleosides in Study 245 or Study 247. At the time of this safety assessment, the median duration of treatment in Study 245 and Study 247 was 3.7 and 2.4 months, respectively. However, safety data was collected on patients for greater than 6 months of treatment. The most frequently reported clinical adverse events, other than asthenia, among patients receiving ritonavir were gastrointestinal and neurological disturbances including nausea, diarrhea, vomiting, anorexia, abdominal pain, taste perversion, and circumoral and peripheral paresthesias. Similar adverse event profiles were reported in patients receiving ritonavir in other trials.

Adverse events occurring in less than 2% of patients receiving ritonavir in all phase II/phase III studies and considered at least possibly related or of unknown relationship to treatment and of at least moderate intensity are listed below by body system.

Body as a Whole: abdomen enlarged, accidental injury, allergic reaction, back pain, cachexia, chest pain, chills, facial edema, facial pain, flu syndrome, hormone level altered, hypothermia, kidney pain, neck pain, neck rigidity, pain (unspecified), substernal chest pain, and photosensitivity reaction.

Cardiovascular: hemorrhage, hypotension, migraine, palpitation, peripheral vascular disorder, postural hypotension, syncope and tachycardia.

Digestive: abnormal stools, bloody diarrhea, cheilitis, cholangitis, colitis, dry mouth, dysphagia, eructation, esophagitis, gastritis, gastroenteritis, gastrointestinal disorder, gastrointestinal hemorrhage, gingivitis, hepatitis, hepatomegaly, ileitis, liver damage, liver function tests abnormal, mouth ulcer, oral moniliasis, pancreatitis, periodontal abscess, rectal disorder, tenesmus and thirst.

Endocrine: diabetes mellitus.

Hemic and Lymphatic: anemia, ecchymosis, leukopenia, lymphadenopathy, lymphocytosis and thrombocytopenia.

Metabolic and Nutritional Disorders: avitaminosis, dehydration, edema, glycosuria, gout, hypercholesteremia, peripheral edema and weight loss.

Musculoskeletal: arthralgia, arthrosis, joint disorder, muscle cramps, muscle weakness, myositis and twitching.

Nervous: abnormal dreams, abnormal gait, agitation, amnesia, anxiety, aphasia, ataxia, confusion, convulsion, depression, diplopia, emotional lability, euphoria, grand mal convulsion, hallucinations, hyperesthesia, incoordination, decreased libido, nervousness, neuralgia, neuropathy, paralysis, peripheral neuropathy, peripheral sensory neuropathy, personality disorder, tremor, urinary retention and vertigo.

Respiratory: asthma, dyspnea, epistaxis, hiccup, hypoventilation, increased cough, interstitial pneumonia, lung disorder and rhinitis.

Skin and Appendages: acne, contact dermatitis, dry skin, eczema, folliculitis, maculopapular rash, molluscum contagiosum, pruritus, psoriasis, seborrhea, urticaria and vesiculobullous rash.

Special Senses: abnormal electro-oculogram, abnormal electroretinogram, abnormal vision, amblyopia/blurred vision, blepharitis, ear pain, eye pain, hearing impairment, increased cerumen, iritis, parosmia, photophobia, taste loss, tinnitus, uveitis and visual field defect.

Urogenital: dysuria, hematuria, impotence, kidney calculus, kidney failure, nocturia, penis disorder, polyuria, pyelonephritis, urethritis and urinary frequency.

Postmarketing Experience: There have been postmarketing reports of seizure. Hyperglycemia has been reported in individuals with and without a known history of diabetes. Cause and effect relationship has not been established.

Dehydration, usually associated with gastrointestinal symptoms, and sometimes resulting in hypotension, syncope, or renal insufficiency has been reported. Syncope, orthostatic hypotension and renal insufficiency have also been reported without known dehydration.

Extreme Laboratory Determinations: Table V (on following page) shows the percentage of patients who developed marked laboratory abnormalities.

Overdose: Symptoms: Acute Overdosage: Human Overdose Experience: Human experience of acute overdose with ritonavir is limited. One patient in clinical trials took ritonavir 1 500 mg/day for 2 days. The patient reported paresthesias which resolved after the dose was decreased.

A postmarketing case of renal failure with eosinophilia has been reported with ritonavir overdose.

Treatment: Treatment of overdose with ritonavir consists of general supportive measures including monitoring of vital signs and observation of the clinical status of the patient. There is no specific antidote for overdose with ritonavir. Administration of activated charcoal may be used to aid in removal of unabsorbed drug. Since ritonavir is extensively metabolized by the liver and is highly protein bound, dialysis is unlikely to be beneficial in significant removal of the drug. A Certified Poison Control Centre should be consulted for up-to-date information on the management of overdose with ritonavir.

Dosage: Ritonavir is administered orally. It is recommended that it be taken with meals if possible. Patients may improve the taste of oral solution by mixing with chocolate milk, Ensure, or Advera within 1 hour of dosing. The effects of antacids on the absorption of ritonavir have not been studied.

The recommended dosage is 600 mg twice daily orally. Some patients experience nausea upon initiation of 600 mg twice daily dosing. Use of a dose titration schedule may help to reduce treatment-emergent adverse events while maintaining appropriate ritonavir plasma levels. Ritonavir should be started at no less than 300 mg twice daily and increased by 100 mg twice daily increments up to 600 mg twice daily not to exceed a period of 14 days. Patients should be aware that frequently observed adverse events, such as mild to moderate gastrointestinal disturbances and paresthesias, may diminish as therapy is continued. In addition, patients initiating combination regimens with ritonavir and nucleosides may improve gastrointestinal tolerance by initiating ritonavir alone and subsequently adding nucleosides before completing 2 weeks of ritonavir monotherapy. The long-term effect of dose escalation on efficacy have not been established.

Table IV—Norvir

Percentage of Patients with Treatment-Emergent* Adverse Events of Moderate or Severe Intensity Occurring in ≥2% of Patients Receiving Norvir

	Study 245 Naive Patients			Study 247 Advanced Patients	
Adverse Event	**Norvir+ZDV n=116**	**Norvir n=117**	**ZDV n=119**	**Norvir n=541**	**Placebo n=547**
Body as a Whole					
Abdominal Pain	4.3	3.4	4.2	7.0	3.1
Asthenia	27.6	9.4	10.1	14.2	5.3
Fever	1.7	0.9	1.7	4.4	2.2
Headache	7.8	5.1	7.6	6.3	4.0
Malaise	4.3	1.7	3.4	0.7	0.2
Cardiovascular					
Vasodilation	2.6	1.7	0.8	1.3	0.0
Digestive					
Anorexia	7.8	0.9	3.4	6.1	2.0
Constipation	2.6	0.0	0.8	0.0	0.4
Diarrhea	21.6	12.8	0.0	18.3	6.1
Dyspepsia	1.7	0.0	1.7	4.8	0.7
Flatulence	2.6	0.9	0.8	0.9	0.6
Local Throat Irritation	1.7	1.7	0.8	2.6	0.2
Nausea	46.6	23.1	24.4	26.2	5.7
Vomiting	22.4	12.8	12.6	15.2	2.6
Metabolic and Nutritional					
Creatine Phosphokinase Increased	1.7	3.4	3.4	0.9	0.2
Hyperlipidemia	1.7	1.7	0.0	4.1	0.0
Musculoskeletal					
Myalgia	1.7	1.7	0.8	2.2	0.9
Nervous					
Circumoral Paresthesia	5.2	2.6	0.0	5.9	0.2
Dizziness	5.2	2.6	1.7	3.3	1.1
Insomnia	3.4	2.6	0.8	1.3	0.6
Paresthesia	5.2	2.6	0.0	2.0	0.2
Peripheral Paresthesia	0.0	6.0	0.0	5.0	0.7
Somnolence	2.6	2.6	0.0	2.0	0.2
Thinking Abnormal	2.6	0.0	0.8	0.7	0.2
Respiratory					
Pharyngitis	0.9	2.6	0.0	0.4	0.4
Skin and Appendages					
Rash	0.9	0.0	0.8	2.6	0.9
Sweating	3.4	2.6	1.7	1.3	0.6
Special Senses					
Taste Perversion	15.5	10.3	7.6	5.4	1.7

* Includes those adverse events at least possibly related to study drug or of unknown relationship and excludes concurrent HIV conditions.

Norvir (cont'd)

Table V—Norvir

Percentage of Patients, by Study and Treatment Group, with Marked Chemistry and Hematology Laboratory Value Abnormalities

Variable	Limit	Norvir+ZDV	Study 245 Naive Patients Norvir	ZDV	Study 247 Advanced Patients Norvir	Placebo
Chemistry	**High**					
Glucose	(>250 mg/dL)	2.0	—	0.9	0.4	1.1
Uric Acid	(>12 mg/dL)	—	—	—	3.6	0.2
Creatinine	(>3.6 mg/dL)	—	—	—	0.2	0.2
Potassium	(>6.0 mEq/L)	—	—	—	0.4	0.2
Chloride	(>122 mEq/L)	—	0.9	—	—	—
Total Bilirubin	(>3.6 mg/dL)	—	—	—	1.2	0.2
Alkaline Phosphatase	(>550 IU/L)	—	0.9	—	1.4	1.7
AST	(>180 IU/L)	2.9	6.5	1.7	3.8	4.3
ALT	(>215 IU/L)	3.9	5.6	2.6	6.1	2.6
GGT	(>300 IU/L)	2.0	2.8	0.9	14.7	6.7
LDH	(>1 170 IU/L)	—	—	—	1.0	0.2
Triglycerides	(>1 500 mg/dL)	1.0	2.8	—	10.1	0.2
Triglycerides Fasting	(>1 500 mg/dL)	2.1	1.4	—	7.9	0.4
CPK	(>1 000 IU/L)	7.0	7.5	7.1	8.6	4.5
Amylase	(>2×ULN)	—	0.9	—	0.2	—
Chemistry	**Low**					
Albumin	(<2.0 g/dL)	—	—	—	0.2	0.6
Sodium	(<123 mEq/L)	—	—	—	0.2	—
Potassium	(<3.0 mEq/L)	—	0.9	—	2.0	1.1
Chloride	(<84 mEq/L)	—	0.9	—	—	0.4
Magnesium	(<1.0 mEq/L)	—		—	0.4	0.4
Calcium	(<6.9 mEq/L)	—	—	—	1.2	0.9
Hematology	**Low**					
Hemoglobin	(<8.0 g/dL)	—	—	—	2.8	2.4
Hematocrit	(<30%)	2.0	—	—	11.7	16.0
RBC	(<3.0 x 10^{12}/L)	1.0	—	1.7	14.9	19.7
WBC	(<2.5 x 10^{9}/L)	—	—	3.5	25.1	51.4
Platelet Count	(<20 x 10^{9}/L)	—	—	—	0.4	0.6
Neutrophils	(≤0.5 x 10^{9}/L)	—	—	—	4.0	6.9
Hematology	**High**					
WBC	(>25 x 10^{9}/L)	—	—	—	1.6	0.7
Neutrophils	(>20 x 10^{9}/L)	—	—	—	1.8	0.9
Eosinophils	(>1.0 x 10^{9}/L)	—	1.9	0.9	1.8	2.6
Prothrombin Time	(>1.5 x ULN[1])	1.0	—	—	1.0	1.3

Legend: ULN=Upper limit of the normal range.
— Indicates no events reported.

Information for the Patient: See Blue Section—Information for the Patient "Norvir".

Supplied: Capsules: Each white capsule, imprinted with Abbott logo, 100 mg and Abbo-code PI, contains: ritonavir 100 mg. Nonmedicinal ingredients: caprylic/capric triglycerides, citric acid, ethanol, gelatin, polyglycolyzed glycerides, propylene glycol, polyoxyl 35 castor oil and polysorbate 80. Bottles of 84, cartons of 2. Store under refrigeration between 2 and 8°C. Protect from light.

Oral Solution: Each mL of orange-colored oral solution, in a peppermint and caramel-flavored vehicule, contains: ritonavir 80 mg. Nonmedicinal ingredients: anhydrous citric acid (to adjust pH), creamy caramel flavoring, ethanol, FD&C Yellow No. 6, peppermint oil, polyoxyl 35 castor oil, propylene glycol and saccharin sodium. Amber-colored, multidose bottles of 240 mL with marked dosage cup of 7.5 mL (600 mg/7.5 mL). Store at room temperature, between 20 and 25°C. Do not refrigerate. **Shake well before each use.** Product should be stored in the original container. Avoid exposure to excessive heat. Keep cap tightly closed.

Reviewed 1999

NOVAHISTEX® C Ⓝ

Hoechst Marion Roussel

Codeine Phosphate—Phenylephrine HCl

Antitussive—Decongestant

Indications: The treatment of adults with cough associated with inflamed mucosa, which does not respond to products of lesser potency.

Contraindications, Precautions, Adverse Effects and Overdose: See Novahistex DH.

Dosage: Adults: 5 mL every 4 to 6 hours. Children: 6 to 12 years, one-half adult dosage; not recommended for children under 6 years.

Supplied: Each 5 mL of red, raspberry flavored liquid contains: codeine phosphate 15 mg and phenylephrine HCl 20 mg. Nonmedicinal ingredients: artificial flavors (raspberry and others), citric acid, FD&C Blue No. 1, glucose, glycerin, purified water, red No. 2, sodium benzoate, sodium chloride, sodium citrate, sodium cyclamate, sorbitol and xylitol. Alcohol- and sucrose-free. Bottles of 100 mL.

NOVAHISTEX® DH Ⓝ

Hoechst Marion Roussel

Hydrocodone Bitartrate—Phenylephrine HCl

Antitussive—Decongestant

Indications: The treatment of adults with cough associated with inflamed mucosa, which does not respond to products of lesser potency.

Contraindications: Patients undergoing therapy with MAO inhibitors, hypersensitivity to any of the components.

Precautions: Before prescribing medication to suppress or modify cough, it is important to ascertain that the underlying cause of the cough is identified, that modification of the cough does not increase the risk of clinical or physiologic complications and that appropriate therapy for the primary disease is provided.

Continuous dosage over extended periods of time may cause a hydrocodone bitartrate dependent state.

In young children the respiratory centre is especially susceptible to the depressant action of narcotic cough suppressants. Benefit to risk ratio should be carefully considered, especially in children with respiratory embarrassment, e.g., croup. Estimation of dosage relative to the child's age and weight is of great importance.

Pregnancy: Since hydrocodone crosses the placental barrier, its use in pregnancy is not recommended.

As hydrocodone may inhibit peristalsis, patients with chronic constipation should be given the drug only after weighing the potential therapeutic benefit against the hazards involved.

Administer with caution to patients hypersensitive to sympathomimetic preparations, patients with severe hypertension, hyperthyroidism, diabetes mellitus, glaucoma, cardiac or peripheral vascular disease.

Occupational Hazards: Patients should be cautioned not to operate vehicles or hazardous machinery until their response to the drug has been determined.

Since the depressant effects of antihistamines are additive to those of other drugs affecting the CNS, patients should be cautioned against drinking alcoholic beverages or taking hypnotics, sedatives, psychotherapeutic agents or other drugs with CNS depressant effects during antihistaminic therapy.

Adverse Effects: Occasional drowsiness, dry mouth, dizziness, blurred vision, mild mental stimulation and gastric irritation may occur rarely.

Overdose: Symptoms: Symptoms are similar to those caused by overdosage of hydrocodone. Narcosis is usually present, sometimes associated with convulsions. Tachycardia, pupillary constriction, nausea and vomiting or respiratory depression can occur.

Treatment: If respiration is severely depressed, administer the narcotic antagonist, naloxone. Adults: 400 µg by i.v., i.m. or s.c. routes and repeated at 2 to 3 minute intervals if necessary. Children: 10 µg/kg by i.v., i.m. or s.c. routes. Dosage may be repeated as for the adult administration. Failure to obtain significant improvement after 2 to 3 doses suggests that causes other than narcotic overdosage may be responsible for the patient's condition.

If naloxone is unsuccessful, institute intubation and respiratory support or conduct gastric lavage in the unconscious patient.

Dosage: Adults and children over 12 years, 5 mL every 4 hours.

Supplied: Each 5 mL of red, raspberry flavored liquid contains: hydrocodone bitartrate 5 mg and phenylephrine HCl 20 mg. Nonmedicinal ingredients: artificial flavor (raspberry and others), citric acid, glucose, glycerin, menthol, propylene glycol, purified water, Red #2, sodium benzoate, sodium chloride, sodium citrate, sodium cyclamate and xylitol. Alcohol- and sucrose-free. Bottles of 100 mL and 2 L.

NOVAHISTEX® DH EXPECTORANT Ⓝ

Hoechst Marion Roussel

Hydrocodone Bitartrate—Guaifenesin—Phenylephrine HCl

Antitussive—Expectorant—Decongestant

Indications: In adults, to facilitate expectoration and control cough associated with inflamed mucosa and tenacious sputum which does not respond to products of lesser potency.

Contraindications, Precautions, Adverse Effects and Overdose: See Novahistex DH.

Guaifenesin has been shown to produce a color interference with certain clinical laboratory determinations of 5-hydroxyindoleacetic acid (5-HIAA) and vanillylmandelic acid (VMA).

Dosage: Adults and children over 12 years: 5 mL every 4 hours.

Supplied: Each 5 mL of amber, mixed fruit flavored liquid contains: phenylephrine HCl 20 mg, hydrocodone bitartrate 5 mg and guaifenesin 200 mg. Nonmedicinal ingredients: artificial flavor, citric acid, FD&C Blue #1, FD&C Yellow #6, glucose, glycerin, menthol, natural cherry flavor, propylene glycol, purified water, Red #2, sodium benzoate, sodium chloride, sodium citrate and sodium cyclamate. Alcohol- and sucrose-free. Bottles of 100 mL.

Do not refrigerate. Crystals of guaifenesin may form if product is subjected to cold temperatures. On warming, crystals will slowly dissolve.

NOVAHISTEX® DM
NOVAHISTEX® DM Decongestant
NOVAHISTEX® DM Decongestant Expectorant
NOVAHISTINE® DM
NOVAHISTINE® DM Decongestant
NOVAHISTINE® DM Decongestant Expectorant

Hoechst Marion Roussel

Dextromethorphan HBr
Dextromethorphan HBr—Pseudoephedrine HCl
Dextromethorphan HBr—Pseudoephedrine HCl—Guaifenesin
Dextromethorphan HBr
Dextromethorphan HBr—Pseudoephedrine HCl
Dextromethorphan HBr—Pseudoephedrine HCl—Guaifenesin

Antitussive
Antitussive—Decongestant
Antitussive—Decongestant—Expectorant
Antitussive
Antitussive—Decongestant
Antitussive—Decongestant—Expectorant

Pharmacology: Dextromethorphan (DM) suppresses the cough reflex by a direct effect on the cough centre in the medulla of the brain. The drug acts centrally to elevate the threshold for coughing. Although it is chemically related to morphine, it has no analgesic or addictive properties. Its antitussive activity is about equal to that of codeine.

Pseudoephedrine is a stereoisomer of ephedrine that is less potent than ephedrine in producing tachycardia, increased blood pressure and CNS stimulation. The medication shrinks swollen nasal mucous membranes; reduces tissue hyperemia, edema and nasal congestion; and increases nasal airway patency.

It is a sympathomimetic amine with peripheral effects similar to ephedrine and central effects similar to, but less intense than amphetamines. Patients taking pseudoephedrine orally have not been reported to experience the rebound congestion sometimes experienced with frequent, repeated use of topical decongestants. Pseudoephedrine is not known to produce drowsiness.

Guaifenesin acts as an expectorant by increasing the volume of respiratory tract fluid excreted from the bronchial airways, which reduces the viscosity of tenacious secretions, making expectoration of sputum (phlegm) and bronchial secretions easier.

Indications: DM: For the symptomatic relief of nonproductive coughs associated with colds.

DM Decongestant: For the symptomatic relief of nonproductive coughs and nasal sinus congestion associated with colds, bronchitis, influenza, and sinusitis.

DM Decongestant Expectorant: For the symptomatic relief of nonproductive coughs, nasal sinus congestion, and to facilitate the expectoration of mucus/phlegm associated with colds, bronchitis, influenza, and sinusitis.

Contraindications: Novahistex: DM: In patients with hypersensitivity to dextromethorphan. Dextromethorphan preparations should not be used in patients receiving monoamine oxidase (MAO) inhibitors.

DM Decongestant and DM Decongestant Expectorant: In patients with severe hypertension, severe coronary artery disease, and in patients on MAO inhibitor therapy.

Hypersensitivity: This product is contraindicated in patients with hypersensitivity to dextromethorphan and in patients with hypersensitivity or idiosyncrasy to sympathomimetic amines. Patient idiosyncrasy to adrenergic agents may be manifested by insomnia, dizziness, weakness, tremor or arrhythmias.

Lactation: Pseudoephedrine is excreted in breast milk and therefore use by nursing mothers is not recommended because of the risk of side effects to the nursing child.

Novahistine: DM: In patients with hypersensitivity to dextromethorphan. Dextromethorphan preparations should not be used in patients receiving monoamine oxidase (MAO) inhibitors.

DM Decongestant and DM Decongestant Expectorant: In patients with severe hypertension, severe coronary artery disease, and in patients on MAO inhibitor therapy.

Hypersensitivity: This product is contraindicated in patients with hypersensitivity to dextromethorphan. In patients with hypersensitivity or idiosyncrasy to sympathomimetic amines. Patient idiosyncrasy to adrenergic agents may be manifested by insomnia, dizziness, weakness, tremor or arrhythmias.

Warnings: DM: If cough persists after medication has been used for 7 days or if high fever, skin rash, or continuing headache is present with cough, consult a physician.

DM Decongestant and DM Decongestant Expectorant: If cough persists after medication has been used for 7 days or if high fever, skin rash, or continuing headache is present with cough, consult a physician. At dosages higher than the recommended dose, nervousness, dizziness, sleeplessness, nausea, or headache may occur.

Precautions: Novahistex: DM: Dextromethorphan should not be taken for persistent or chronic cough (e.g., with smoking, emphysema, asthma) or when coughing is accompanied by excessive secretions, unless directed by a physician. Concurrent use of CNS depressant medications may potentiate the CNS depressant effect of these medications or dextromethorphan. This product should not be used by patients taking a prescription drug for depression without the advice of a physician. *Pregnancy* and *Lactation:* Pregnant or nursing patients, consult a physician before using this product. Diabetes: Diabetic patients should take note of the presence of glucose in this preparation (see Supplied for glucose and energy contents).

DM Decongestant: Dextromethorphan should not be taken for persistent or chronic cough (e.g., with smoking, emphysema, asthma) or when coughing is accompanied by excessive secretions, unless directed by a physician. Concurrent use of CNS depressant medications may potentiate the CNS depressant effect of these medications or dextromethorphan. Pseudoephedrine should be used with caution in patients with diabetes mellitus, hypertension, cardiovascular disease, coronary artery disease (severe), glaucoma, hyperthyroidism, prostatic hypertrophy, severe organic disease, asthma, urinary retention and hypersensitivity to ephedrine. MAO inhibitors and beta-adrenergic blockers potentiate the sympathomimetic effect of pseudoephedrine. This product should not be used by patients taking a prescription drug for hypertension or depression without the advice of a physician. *Pregnancy* and *Lactation:* Pregnant or nursing patients, consult a physician before using this product. Diabetes: Diabetic patients should take note of the presence of glucose in this preparation (see Supplied for glucose and energy contents).

DM Decongestant Expectorant: Dextromethorphan should not be taken for persistent or chronic cough (e.g., with smoking, emphysema, asthma) or when coughing is accompanied by excessive secretions, unless directed by a physician. Concurrent use of CNS depressant medications may potentiate the CNS depressant effect of these medications or dextromethorphan. Pseudoephedrine should be used with caution in patients with diabetes mellitus, hypertension, cardiovascular disease, coronary artery disease (severe), glaucoma, hyperthyroidism, prostatic hypertrophy, severe organic disease, asthma, urinary retention and hypersensitivity to ephedrine. MAO inhibitors and beta-adrenergic blockers potentiate the sympathomimetic effect of pseudoephedrine. Guaifenesin interferes with the colorimetric determination of 5-hydroxyindoleacetic acid (5-HIAA) and vanillylmandelic acid (VMA). This product should not be used by patients taking a prescription drug for hypertension or depression without the advice of a physician. *Pregnancy* and *Lactation:* Pregnant or nursing patients, consult a physician before using this product. Diabetes: Diabetic patients should take note of the presence of glucose in this preparation (see Supplied for glucose and energy contents)

Novahistine: DM: Dextromethorphan should not be taken for persistent or chronic cough (e.g., with smoking, emphysema, asthma) or when coughing is accompanied by excessive secretions, unless directed by a physician. Concurrent use of CNS depressant medications may potentiate the CNS depressant effect of these medications or dextromethorphan. This product should not be used by patients taking a prescription drug for depression without the advice of a physician. Diabetes: Diabetic patients should take note of the presence of glucose in this preparation (see Supplied for glucose and energy contents).

DM Decongestant: Dextromethorphan should not be taken for persistent or chronic cough (e.g., with smoking, emphysema, asthma) or when coughing is accompanied by excessive secretions, unless directed by a physician. Concurrent use of CNS depressant medications may potentiate the CNS depressant effect of these medications or dextromethorphan. Pseudoephedrine should be used with caution in patients with diabetes mellitus, hypertension, cardiovascular disease, coronary artery disease (severe), glaucoma, hyperthyroidism, severe organic disease, asthma, urinary retention and hypersensitivity to ephedrine. MAO inhibitors and beta-adrenergic blockers potentiate the sympathomimetic effect of pseudoephedrine. This product should not be used by patients taking a prescription drug for hypertension or depression without the advice of a physician. Diabetes: Diabetic patients should take note of the presence of glucose in this preparation (see Supplied for glucose and energy contents).

DM Decongestant Expectorant: Dextromethorphan should not be taken for persistent or chronic cough (e.g., with smoking, emphysema, asthma) or when coughing is accompanied by excessive secretions, unless directed by a physician. Concurrent use of CNS depressant medications may potentiate the CNS depressant effect of these medications or dextromethorphan. Pseudoephedrine should be used with caution in patients with diabetes mellitus, hypertension, cardiovascular disease, coronary artery disease (severe), glaucoma, hyperthyroidism, severe organic disease, asthma, urinary retention and hypersensitivity to ephedrine. MAO inhibitors and beta-adrenergic blockers potentiate the sympathomimetic effect of pseudoephedrine. Guaifenesin interferes with the colorimetric determination of 5-hydroxyindoleacetic acid (5-HIAA) and vanillylmandelic acid (VMA). This product should not be used by patients taking a prescription drug for hypertension or depression without the advice of a physician. Diabetes: Diabetic patients should take note of the presence of glucose in this preparation (see Supplied for glucose and energy contents).

Adverse Effects: DM: Adverse effects with dextromethorphan are rare, but nausea and/or other gastrointestinal disturbances, slight drowsiness, and dizziness sometimes occur.

DM Decongestant and DM Decongestant Expectorant: Adverse effects with dextromethorphan are rare, but nausea and/or other gastrointestinal disturbances, slight drowsiness, and dizziness sometimes occur.

Adverse effects with pseudoephedrine: Individuals may display ephedrine-like reactions such as tachycardia, palpitations, headache, dizziness or nausea. Sympathomimetic drugs have been associated with reactions such as confusion, fear, anxiety, tenseness, restlessness, tremor, weakness, pallor, respiratory difficulty, dysuria, insomnia, hallucinations, convulsions, CNS stimulation, arrhythmias and cardiovascular collapse with hypotension. Children and the elderly may be more susceptible to systemic effects of the drug than are adults.

Overdose: Symptoms: Manifestations of Acute Overdosage: DM: Dextromethorphan has a low order of toxicity with the potential for toxic effects following acute overdosage being extremely low. Drowsiness or dizziness; nausea or vomiting; blurred vision; shallow respiration; urinary retention; stupor; toxic psychosis; coma. Consult with a physician as soon as possible if any of these symptoms occur.

DM Decongestant and DM Decongestant Expectorant: Dextromethorphan has a low order of toxicity with the potential for toxic effects following acute overdosage being extremely low. Drowsiness or dizziness; nausea or vomiting; blurred vision; shallow respiration; urinary retention; stupor; toxic psychosis; coma. Pseudoephedrine may cause convulsions, hallucinations, increase in blood pressure, irregular heartbeat, troubled breathing, nervousness, restlessness, excitement, following acute overdosage. Consult with a physician as soon as possible if any of these symptoms occur.

Treatment: Treatment of Acute Overdosage: DM Decongestant and DM Decongestant Expectorant: Treatment is symptomatic and directed towards supporting the various bodily systems. Gastric lavage should be performed at the discretion of the attending physician. Assisted respiration may be required. Acidify the urine to enhance elimination and institute general supportive measures. If CNS stimulation is prominent, an anticonvulsant may be administered. Heart signs and electrolytes should be monitored.

Dosage: Novahistex: Adults and Children over 12 years: DM: 10 mL every 6 to 8 hours. Maximum 4 doses in 24 hours.

DM Decongestant and DM Decongestant Expectorant: 10 mL every 4 to 6 hours. Maximum 4 doses in 24 hours.

Do not exceed recommended dose.

Novahistine: DM: Children 6 to 12 years: 10 mL every 6 to 8 hours. Maximum 4 doses in 24 hours; 2 to 5 years: 5 mL every 6 to 8 hours. Maximum 4 doses in 24 hours; under 2 years: consult a physician.

DM Decongestant and DM Decongestant Expectorant: Children 6 to 12 years: 10 mL every 4 to 6 hours. Maximum 4 doses

Novahistex DM (cont'd)

in 24 hours; 2 to 5 years: 5 mL every 4 to 6 hours. Maximum 4 doses in 24 hours; under 2 years: consult a physician.

Do not exceed recommended dose.

Supplied: Novahistex: DM: Each 5 mL of red-colored, raspberry-flavored liquid contains: dextromethorphan HBr 15 mg. Nonmedicinal ingredients: artificial raspberry flavor, citric acid, FD&C blue No. 1, FD&C red No. 2, FD&C yellow No. 6, glucose, glycerin, purified water, sodium benzoate, sodium chloride, sodium citrate, sodium cyclamate, sorbitol and xylitol. Energy: 16.7 kJ (4 kcal)/5 mL. Glucose: 975 mg. Bottles of 100 mL.

DM Decongestant: Each 5 mL of red-colored, raspberry-flavored liquid contains: dextromethorphan HBr 15 mg and pseudoephedrine HCl 30 mg. Nonmedicinal ingredients: artificial raspberry flavor, citric acid, FD&C blue No. 1, FD&C red No. 2, FD&C yellow No. 6, glucose, glycerin, purified water, sodium benzoate, sodium chloride, sodium citrate, sodium cyclamate, sorbitol and xylitol. Energy: 16.7 kJ (4 kcal)/5 mL. Glucose: 975 mg. Bottles of 100 mL.

DM Decongestant Expectorant: Each 5 mL of red-colored, cherry-flavored liquid contains: dextromethorphan HBr 15 mg, pseudoephedrine HCl 30 mg and guaifenesin 100 mg. Nonmedicinal ingredients: artificial and natural cherry flavors, citric acid, FD&C blue No. 1, FD&C red No. 2, FD&C yellow No. 6, glucose, menthol, propylene glycol, purified water, sodium benzoate, sodium chloride, sodium citrate, sodium cyclamate and xylitol. Energy : 46 kJ (11 kcal)/5 mL. Glucose: 2 750 mg. Bottles of 100 mL.

Novahistine: DM: Each 5 mL of purple-colored, grape-flavored liquid contains: dextromethorphan HBr 7.5 mg. Nonmedicinal ingredients: artificial and natural grape flavors, citric acid, FD&C blue No. 1, FD&C red No. 2, glucose, glycerin, purified water, sodium benzoate, sodium chloride, sodium citrate, sodium cyclamate, sorbitol and xylitol. Energy: 16.7 kJ (4 kcal)/5 mL. Glucose: 975 mg. Bottles of 100 mL.

DM Decongestant: Each 5 mL of purple-colored, grape-flavored liquid contains: dextromethorphan HBr 7.5 mg and pseudoephedrine HCl 15 mg. Nonmedicinal ingredients: artificial and natural grape flavors, citric acid, FD&C blue No. 1, FD&C red No. 2, glucose, glycerin, purified water, sodium benzoate, sodium chloride, sodium citrate, sodium cyclamate, sorbitol and xylitol. Energy: 16.7 kJ (4 kcal)/5 mL. Glucose: 975 mg. Bottles of 100 mL.

DM Decongestant Expectorant: Each 5 mL of red-colored, raspberry-flavored liquid contains: dextromethorphan HBr 7.5 mg, pseudoephedrine HCl 15 mg and guaifenesin 50 mg. Nonmedicinal ingredients: artificial raspberry flavor, citric acid, FD&C red No. 2, glucose, glycerin, purified water, sodium benzoate, sodium citrate, sodium cyclamate, sorbitol and xylitol. Energy: 16.7 kJ (4 kcal)/5 mL. Glucose: 1 000 mg. Bottles of 100 mL.

All preparations are alcohol-, gluten-, lactose-, sulfite- and tartrazine-free. Store between 15 and 30°C.

Reviewed 1998

NOVAHISTINE® DH Ⓝ

Hoechst Marion Roussel

Hydrocodone Bitartrate—Phenylephrine HCl

Antitussive—Decongestant

Indications: The treatment of children with cough associated with inflamed mucosa, which does not respond to products of lesser potency.

Contraindications, Precautions, Adverse Effects and Overdose: See Novahistex DH.

Dosage: Children 1 to 12 years, 2.5 to 5 mL every 4 hours; 12 years and over, 10 mL every 4 hours. Infants 6 months to 1 year, 1.25 to 2.5 mL every 4 hours.

Supplied: Each 5 mL of purple, grape-flavored liquid contains: hydrocodone bitartrate 1.7 mg and phenylephrine HCl 10 mg. Nonmedicinal ingredients: artificial and natural grape flavor, citric acid, D&C Green #5, D&C Red #33, glucose, purified water, sodium benzoate, sodium chloride, sodium citrate, sodium cyclamate and xylitol. Alcohol- and sucrose-free. Bottles of 100 mL and 2 L.

NOVAMILOR Ⓟ

Novopharm

Amiloride HCl—Hydrochlorothiazide

Antihypertensive—Diuretic

Supplied: Each peach-colored, diamond-shaped, compressed tablet, engraved 5/50 on one side and N/N on the other side, contains: amiloride HCl 5 mg and hydrochlorothiazide 50 mg. Gluten- and tartrazine-free. Bottles of 100 and 1 000.

NOVAMOXIN® Ⓟ

Novopharm

Amoxicillin Trihydrate

Antibiotic

Pharmacology: Amoxicillin exerts its bactericidal action by interfering with bacterial cell wall synthesis.

Indications: The treatment of infections due to susceptible strains of the following microorganisms: Gram-negative organisms: H. influenzae, P. mirabilis and N. gonorrhea. Gram-positive organisms: streptococci (including S. faecalis and S. pneumoniae).

Amoxicillin is not active against P. aeruginosa, indole-positive Proteus species, S. marcescens, Klebsiella and Enterobacter species.

In emergency cases, where the causative organism is not yet identified, therapy may be initiated with amoxicillin on the basis of clinical judgment while awaiting bacteriologic tests to determine its antimicrobial sensitivity.

Amoxicillin may be indicated as a prophylaxis against alpha-hemolytic (Viridan's group) Streptococci before dental, oral or upper respiratory tract surgery or instrumentation.

It may be also indicated as a prophylaxis of bacterial endocarditis in patients with any of the following conditions: congenital cardiac malformations, rheumatic and other acquired valvular lesions, prosthetic heart valves, previous history of bacterial endocarditis, hypertrophic cardiomyopathy, surgically constructed systemic pulmonary shunts, mitral valve prolapse with valvular regurgitation of mitral valve prolapse without valvular regurgitation but associated with thickening and/or redundancy of the valve leaflets.

Contraindications: A history of a previous hypersensitivity reaction to any of the penicillins or cephalosporins is a contraindication.

Amoxicillin is also contraindicated in cases where infectious mononucleosis is either suspected or confirmed.

Warnings: Serious and occasionally fatal hypersensitivity (anaphylactoid) reactions have been reported in patients on penicillin therapy. Although anaphylaxis is more frequent following parenteral therapy, it has occurred in patients following oral dosing of penicillins. These reactions are more apt to occur in individuals with a history of sensitivity to multiple allergens. There have been well-documented reports of individuals with a history of penicillin hypersensitivity reactions who have experienced severe hypersensitivity reactions when treated with cephalosporins. Before initiating therapy with a penicillin, careful inquiry should be made concerning previous hypersensitivity reactions to penicillins, cephalosporins and other allergens. If an allergic reaction occurs, administration of amoxicillin should be discontinued and appropriate therapy instituted.

Serious anaphylactoid reactions require immediate emergency treatment with epinephrine. Oxygen, i.v. steroids and airway management, including intubation, should also be administered as indicated.

Precautions: Periodic assessment of renal, hepatic and hematopoietic functions should be made during prolonged therapy with amoxicillin.

Because amoxicillin is excreted mostly by the kidney, the dosage for patients with renal impairment should be reduced in proportion to the degree of loss of renal function.

Geriatrics: There are no known specific precautions for the use of amoxicillin in the elderly.

If superinfections with mycotic or bacterial pathogens occur (usually involving Aerobacter, Pseudomonas or Candida) treatment with amoxicillin should be discontinued and appropriate therapy instituted.

Pregnancy: The safety of amoxicillin in the treatment of infections during pregnancy has not been established. If the administration of amoxicillin to pregnant patients is considered to be necessary, its use requires that the potential benefits be weighed against the possible hazards to the fetus.

A morbilliform rash following the use of ampicillin in patients with infectious mononucleosis has been well documented and has also been reported to occur following the use of amoxicillin.

Adverse Effects: As with other penicillins, it may be expected that untoward reactions will be related to sensitivity phenomena. They are more likely to occur in individuals who have previously demonstrated hypersensitivity to penicillins and cephalosporins and in those with a history of allergy, asthma, hay fever or urticaria.

The following adverse reactions have been reported as associated with the use of Novamoxin.

Gastrointestinal: nausea, vomiting and diarrhea.

Hypersensitivity Reactions: Skin rashes and urticaria have been reported frequently. A few cases of exfoliative dermatitis and erythema multiforme have been reported. Anaphylaxis is the most serious reaction experienced and has usually been associated with the parenteral dosage form.

Note: Urticaria, other skin rashes, and serum sickness-like reactions may be controlled with antihistamines and if necessary, systemic corticosteroids. Whenever such reactions occur, amoxicillin should be discontinued unless, in the opinion of the physician, the condition being treated is life-threatening and amenable only to amoxicillin therapy. Serious anaphylactic reactions require the immediate use of epinephrine, oxygen and i.v. steroids.

Liver: A moderate rise in AST has been noted, particularly in infants, but the significance of this finding is not known. Transient increases in serum alkaline phosphatase and lactic dehydrogenase levels have also been observed but they returned to normal on discontinuation of amoxicillin.

Hemic and Lymphatic: Anemia thrombocytopenia, thrombocytopenic purpura, eosinophilia, leukopenia, neutropenia and agranulocytosis have been reported during therapy with the penicillins. These reactions are usually reversible on discontinuation of therapy and are believed to be a hypersensitivity phenomena.

Oral: glossitis, black "hairy" tongue and stomatitis.

CNS: As with other penicillins, acute and chronic toxicity is not a clinical problem. At extremely high doses, convulsions can occur. When penicillin reaches a high concentration in the cerebrospinal fluid, neurotoxic symptoms consisting of myoclonia, convulsive seizures and depressed consciousness may occur. Unless administration of the drug is stopped or its dosage reduced, the syndrome may progress to coma and death. Although penicillins do not normally cross the blood-brain barrier to any substantial extent, if massive doses are given (several grams per day) to elderly patients, patients with inflamed meninges or patients with impaired renal function, the above toxic reactions are likely to occur.

Overdose: Symptoms and Treatment: Treatment of overdosage would likely be needed only in patients with severely impaired renal function, since patients with normal kidneys excrete penicillins at a fast rate. Hemodialysis would, therefore, represent the main form of treatment.

Dosage: Infections of the upper respiratory tract (ear, nose and throat) due to susceptible strains of streptococci (beta-hemolytic and S. pneumoniae), nonpenicillinase-producing staphylococci and H. influenzae; infections of the urinary tract due to P. mirabilis and S. faecalis; infections of the skin and soft-tissues due to streptococci and staphylococci (nonpenicillinase producing): Adults: 250 mg every 8 hours.

Children <20 kg: 20 mg/kg/day in divided doses every 8 hours. This dosage should not exceed the recommended adult dosage.

Children weighing 20 kg or more should be dosed according to the adult recommendations.

In severe infections or infections associated with organisms where sensitivity determinations require higher blood concentrations: 500 mg every 8 hours for adults and 40 mg/kg/day in divided doses every 8 hours for children less than 20 kg may be needed.

Infections of the lower respiratory tract, due to susceptible strains of the causative organism and acute otitis media: Adults: 500 mg every 8 hours.

Children <20 kg: 40 mg/kg/day in divided doses every 8 hours. This dosage should not exceed the recommended adult dosage.

Children weighing 20 kg or more should be dosed according to the adult recommendations.

Urethritis due to nonpenicillinase producing N. gonorrhea acquired in area with active monitoring for resistance to penicillin and where the percentage of penicillin-resistant isolates is <3%: Adults and children >45 kg: (3 g as a single oral dose); 1 g of oral probenecid should be administered concomitantly as well as appropriate therapy for presumptive or proven infection with C. trachomatis.
Children <45 kg: a single 50 mg/kg dose (maximum 3 g) given with a single 25 mg/kg (up to 1 g) dose of probenecid. However, probenecid is not recommended in children under 2 years of age. Appropriate therapy of presumptive or proven infection with C. trachomatis should be included as well. Cases of gonorrhea with a suspected lesion of syphilis should have darkfield examinations before receiving amoxicillin, and monthly serological tests for a minimum of 4 months.

For prevention of endocarditis: Adults: 3 g orally 1 hour before procedure; then 1.5 g 6 hours after the initial dose. Children: 50 mg/kg (not to exceed adult dose) orally 1 hour before procedure; then 25 mg/kg 6 hours after the initial dose.

It should be recognized that in the treatment of chronic urinary tract infections, frequent bacteriological and clinical appraisals are necessary. Smaller doses than those recommended above should not be used. Even higher doses may be needed at times and in stubborn infections therapy may be required for several weeks. It may be necessary to continue clinical and/or bacteriological follow-up for several months after cessation of therapy. Except for gonorrhoea, treatment should be continued for a minimum of 48 to 72 hours beyond the time that the patient becomes asymptomatic or evidence of bacterial eradication has been obtained. It is recommended that there be at least 10 days treatment for any infection caused by beta-hemolytic streptococci to prevent the occurrence of acute rheumatic fever or glomerulonephritis.

In order to obtain optimal absorption of drug from Novamoxin capsules they should be administered between meals with a glass of water (250 mL).
Directions for Dispensing Oral Suspension: Prepare these formulations at the time of dispensing. For ease in preparation, add water to the bottle in 2 portions and shake well after each addition. Add the total amount of water as directed on the labeling of the package being dispensed.

Supplied: Capsules: 250 mg: Each hard gelatin capsule with opaque scarlet cap and yellow body imprinted NOVO 250 contains: amoxicillin BP (as the trihydrate) 250 mg (#2 capsules). Gluten-, sodium- and tartrazine-free. Bottles of 100, 500 and 1 000. Unit dose strips of 100.

500 mg: Each hard gelatin capsule with opaque scarlet cap and yellow body imprinted NOVO 500 contains: amoxicillin BP (as the trihydrate) 500 mg (#0 capsules). Gluten-, sodium- and tartrazine-free. Bottles of 100, 250, 500 and 1 000. Unit dose strips of 100.

Store between 15 and 30°C. Unit dose strips should be stored between 15 and 25°C and protected from high humidity.

Chewable Tablets: 125 mg: Each chewable, cherry-flavored, rose-colored, mottled, oval-shaped, single-scored, compressed tablet, engraved NOVO with scoreline on one side and 125 on the other side, contains: amoxicillin 125 mg as the trihydrate. Gluten- and tartrazine-free. Bottles of 100.

250 mg: Each chewable, cherry-flavored, rose-colored, mottled, oval-shaped, single-scored, compressed tablet, engraved NOVO with scoreline on one side and 250 on the other side, contains: amoxicillin 250 mg as the trihydrate. Bottles of 100 and 500. Gluten- and tartrazine-free.

Store between 15 and 30°C.

Suspension: 125 mg: Following reconstitution, each 5 mL of strawberry-flavored suspension contains: amoxicillin trihydrate equivalent to amoxicillin 125 mg. Energy: 48.5 kJ (11.6 kcal)/5 mL. Sodium: <1 mmol (3 mg)/5 mL. Gluten- and tartrazine-free. Bottles of 75, 100 and 150 mL.

250 mg: Following reconstitution, each 5 mL of orange/banana-flavored suspension contains: amoxicillin trihydrate equivalent to 250 mg amoxicillin. Energy: 46 kJ (11 kcal)/5 mL. Sodium: <1 mmol (3 mg)/5 mL. Gluten- and tartrazine-free. Bottles of 75, 100 and 150 mL.

Sugar-Reduced Suspension: 125 mg: Following reconstitution, each 5 mL of strawberry-flavored suspension contains: amoxicillin trihydrate equivalent to amoxicillin 125 mg. Gluten- and tartrazine-free. Bottles of 75, 100 and 150 mL.

250 mg: Following reconstitution, each 5 mL of orange/banana-flavored suspension contains: amoxicillin trihydrate equivalent to 250 mg amoxicillin. Gluten- and tartrazine-free. Bottles of 75, 100 and 150 mL.

Store granules for oral suspension at room temperature (between 15 and 30°C). Keep bottle tightly closed. The reconstituted formulation is stable for 14 days under refrigeration (between 2 and 8°C) or 7 days at room temperature (between 15 and 30°C).

NOVANTRONE® Ⓟ
Wyeth-Ayerst

Mitoxantrone HCl
Antineoplastic

Pharmacology: Although its mechanism of action has not been determined, mitoxantrone is a DNA-reactive agent. It induces nuclear aberrations with chromosome scattering in cell cultures (human colon carcinoma line) and is a potent inhibitor of RNA and DNA synthesis.

Compared on an equimolar basis, mitoxantrone is 7 times more potent than doxorubicin in inhibiting the uptake of ^{3}H-uridine and 4 times more potent in inhibiting the uptake of ^{3}H-thymidine by mouse lymphoma L5178Y cells in vitro.

Indications: For chemotherapy in patients with carcinoma of the breast, including locally advanced and metastatic disease. Also for relapsed adult leukemia, lymphoma patients and patients with hepatoma.

Mitoxantrone in combination with other drug(s) is indicated in the initial therapy of acute nonlymphocytic leukemia (ANLL) in adults. The category includes myelogenous, promyelocytic, monocytic and erythroid acute leukemias.

Contraindications: In patients who have demonstrated prior hypersensitivity to anthracyclines.

Warnings: Caution: Mitoxantrone is a potent drug and should be used only by physicians experienced with cancer chemotherapeutic drugs (see Precautions). Blood counts should be taken at frequent intervals prior, during, and post-therapy. Cardiac monitoring is advised in those patients who have received prior anthracyclines, prior mediastinal radiotherapy, or with pre-existing cardiac disease.

Since mitoxantrone produces myelosuppression (see Adverse Effects), it should be used with caution in patients in poor general condition or with pre-existing myelosuppression.

Cases of functional cardiac changes, including congestive heart failure and decreases in left ventricular ejection fraction (LVEF) have been reported. These cardiac events may be more common in patients who have had prior treatment with anthracyclines, prior mediastinal radiotherapy or with pre-existing heart disease. Cardiac monitoring of LVEF is advisable in such patients from the initiation of therapy. It is suggested that cardiac monitoring also be performed in all other patients before initiation of therapy and during therapy exceeding 140 mg/m² (after approximately 10 courses of mitoxantrone).

Mitoxantrone may impart a blue-green coloration to the urine for 24 hours after administration, and patients should be advised to expect this during active therapy. A reversible blue coloration in the sclerae has been reported in 2 cases.
Pregnancy and *Lactation:* Mitoxantrone may cause fetal harm when administered to a pregnant woman.

In rats treated at doses of ≥0.1 mg/kg (0.05 times the recommended human dose on a mg/m² basis), low fetal weight and retarded development of the fetal kidney were seen in greater frequency. In treated rabbits, an increased incidence of premature delivery was observed at doses ≥0.01 mg/kg (0.01 times the recommended human dose on a mg/m² basis). Mitoxantrone was not teratogenic in rabbits.

There are no adequate and well-controlled studies in pregnant women. If this drug is used during pregnancy, or if the patient becomes pregnant while taking this drug, the patient should apprised of the potential hazard to the fetus. Women of childbearing potential should be advised to avoid becoming pregnant.

Mitoxantrone is excreted in human milk and significant concentrations (18 ng/mL) have been reported for 28 days after the last administration. Because of the potential for serious adverse reactions in infants from mitoxantrone, breast-feeding should be discontinued before starting treatment.
Hepatic Impairment: Mitoxantrone should not be used in patients with severe hepatic dysfunction and poor performance status. If performance status is favorable, mitoxantrone in reduced dosage may be used, with careful supervision.

Precautions: Full blood counts should be undertaken serially during a course of treatment. Dosage adjustments may be necessary based on these counts (see Dosage).

It is recommended that mitoxantrone not be mixed in the same infusion with other drugs. Mitoxantrone should not be mixed in the same infusion with heparin since a precipitate may form.

Topoisomerase II inhibitors, including mitoxantrone, in combination with other antineoplastic agents, have been associated with the development of acute leukemia.

Adverse Effects: Some degree of leukopenia is to be expected following recommended doses of mitoxantrone. With dosing every 21 days, suppression of WBC counts below 1 000/mm³ is infrequent. Leukopenia is usually transient, reaching its nadir at about 10 days after dosing, with recovery usually occurring by the 21st day. Thrombocytopenia can occur, and anemia occurs less frequently. Myelosuppression may be more severe and prolonged in patients having had extensive prior chemotherapy or radiotherapy or in debilitated patients.

The most commonly encountered side effects are nausea and vomiting, although in the majority of cases these are mild (WHO Grade 1) and transient. Alopecia may occur, but is most frequently of minimal severity and reversible on cessation of therapy.

Other side effects which have occasionally been reported include allergic reactions (one with anaphylaxis), abdominal pain, amenorrhea, constipation, anorexia, diarrhea, dyspnea, fatigue, weakness, fever, gastrointestinal bleeding, stomatitis/mucositis, and nonspecific neurological side effects. Tissue necrosis following extravasation has been reported rarely.

Changes in laboratory test values have been observed infrequently, e.g., increased liver enzyme levels, elevated serum creatinine and blood urea nitrogen levels (with occasional reports of severe impairment of hepatic function in patients with leukemia).

Cardiovascular effects, which have only occasionally been of clinical significance, include decreased left ventricular ejection fraction (determined by ECHO or MUGA scan), ECG changes and acute arrhythmia. Congestive heart failure has been reported. Such cases generally responded well to treatment with digitalis and/or diuretics.

In patients with leukemia there is an increase in the frequency of cardiac events, the direct role of mitoxantrone in these cases is difficult to assess, since most patients had received prior therapy with anthracyclines and since their course is frequently complicated by anemia, fever, sepsis, and i.v. fluid therapy.

In leukemia patients treated with a single course of 12 mg/m² i.v. daily for 5 days, the following drug-related toxicities occurred: moderate or severe jaundice or hepatitis (8%), moderate nausea or vomiting (8%), moderate or severe stomatitis/mucositis (9 to 29%), diarrhea (9 to 13%), and moderate or severe alopecia (11%).
Clinical Results: Introduction: Clinical trials experience has established the dosage range, efficacy and safety profile of mitoxantrone.

A single dose can be given intermittently every 3 or 4 weeks. The recommended initial treatment dose in good risk patients is 14 mg/m².

The following efficacy and safety results were generated from analyses of all data during January, 1985. The database, by its nature, is dynamic and there has been no change in benefit to risk noted to date.
Efficacy: Breast: Efficacy data are available on 349 patients with locally advanced or metastatic breast carcinoma. Results are dependent on many predisposing factors including prior chemotherapy and/or radiotherapy, the health of the patients, sites of metastases, and dose of the agent employed. In a European multicenter, first-line, single-agent trial using an initial dose of 14 mg/m², the overall response rate was 39%, which compared favorably to doxorubicin therapy at a dose of 60 to 75 mg/m² when given to patients with 9 similar stage disease. In an ongoing study of a direct comparison with doxorubicin, given as second-line therapy to breast cancer patients who failed a standard first line combination, response rates are 27% for mitoxantrone and 23% for doxorubicin. The mean duration of response observed after mitoxantrone was greater than those reported after doxorubicin. Responses have been seen in all major sites of metastases including lymph nodes, lung, bone, skin and viscera, in patients both with and without prior hormonal therapy. Available data suggest that mitoxantrone is comparable in efficacy with doxorubicin in the treatment of advanced breast cancer. Myelosuppression with 21-day treatment intervals is comparable with that observed with doxorubicin. Multiple courses of single-agent mitoxantrone therapy, in some cases for longer than 12 cycles, have been administered with excellent tolerance and a good

Novantrone (cont'd)

response. Mitoxantrone showed incomplete cross-resistance with doxorubicin since responses have been observed in patients in whom doxorubicin had failed or who relapsed after response to that drug. A continuing large-scale clinical trials program with combination therapy also demonstrated early positive results for efficacy and safety. In seven studies, over 100 cycles of combination therapy have been given to 77 patients.

Additional Indications: A total of 966 patients have been treated with mitoxantrone for 3 other indications of which 259 patients had non-Hodgkin's lymphoma (NHL), 546 had leukemia, and 161 had hepatocellular carcinoma (HCC). Table I summarizes the accrual of these 966 patients:

Table I—Novantrone

Accrual of Patients

Indication	Lederle-Sponsored Studies (No. Treated)	Independent Studies Reported in the Literature (No. Treated)
NHL	186	73
Leukemia (including pediatric cases)	282	264
HCC	75	86
Totals	543	423

Non-Hodgkin's Lymphoma: Three key studies evaluated single agent mitoxantrone in 148 patients with relapsed or refractory advanced NHL at a dose of 14 mg/m², i.v., every 3 weeks. Of 127 patients evaluable for response in 2 trials, there were 10 complete responses (CR) and 42 partial responses (PR) producing an overall therapeutic response rate of 41%. The median duration of responses in the multicenter study (122 evaluable patients) was 195 days. Many patients' responses lasted in excess of 1 year. Responses were seen in all histological subtypes of NHL. Response to mitoxantrone was independent of prior chemotherapy and independent of whether the patient received prior doxorubicin. This demonstrated a lack of complete cross-resistance between mitoxantrone and other drugs including anthracyclines.

Mitoxantrone was evaluated in combination with other agents for the treatment of NHL. A total of 28 patients were treated with different regimens. A first-line comparative trial of the combination of intermediate dose methotrexate with leucovorin rescue + bleomycin + doxorubicin + cyclophosphamide + vincristine + dexamethasone (m-BACOD) versus the same combination with 10 mg/m² mitoxantrone replacing doxorubicin (m-BNCOD) has shown activity: 4 PR's in 6 evaluable patients with m-BNCOD and 3 PR's in 6 with m-BACOD. The combination of mitoxantrone at 10 mg/m², daily for 3 days, + vincristine + dexamethasone (NOD) produced 3 PR's in 5 evaluable patients. A first-line comparative trial of the combination of cyclophosphamide + vincristine + prednisone + doxorubicin (CHOP) versus the same combinations with 10 mg/m² mitoxantrone replacing doxorubicin (CNOP) has only recently begun.

Mitoxantrone at 5 mg/m², daily for 3 days every 3 weeks produced one CR and 2 PR's in 8 evaluable patients with NHL; 10 patients were enrolled. Several other studies reported in the literature and not sponsored by Lederle support the activity of mitoxantrone in the treatment of NHL.

Leukemia: Four key studies sponsored by Lederle evaluated single agent mitoxantrone in 181 adult patients with refractory or relapsed acute non-lymphocytic leukemia (ANLL) or chronic myelogenous leukemia in blast crisis (B-CML) at doses ranging from 8 to 12 mg/m², i.v., daily for 5 days, every 3 weeks. A dose response effect was evident. Optimal activity was seen at a dose of 12 mg/m², daily for 5 days. At this dose level, there were 19 CR's in 49 evaluable adult patients with ANLL in relapse producing an overall response rate of 39%. The median duration of complete response in the largest (121 patients) single agent study was 98 days. Several patients had remissions lasting in excess of 1 year.

There were 4 studies comprising 63 patients in which mitoxantrone was evaluated in combination with other agents in the treatment of leukemia. The highest complete remission rate of 49% (11 CR's in 23 evaluable patients with ANLL) was obtained when mitoxantrone at 10 to 12 mg/m², daily for 3 days, was combined with cytosine arabinoside at 100 mg/m² daily for 7 days. When mitoxantrone at 10 mg/m², daily for 5 days was combined with the same dose of cytosine arabinoside, it produced 2 CR's in 8 evaluable patients. Treatment of patients with acute lymphoblastic leukemia using 10 mg/m² mitoxantrone, daily for 3 days, + vincristine + prednisone produced 10 responses in 16 evaluable patients, for a response rate of 62.5%.

Activity was also seen in B-CML. Since no standard therapy exists for this disease and bone marrow is never truly normal in this disorder, both CR's and PR's were considered evidence of efficacy. The optimal dose of mitoxantrone was 12 mg/m², daily for 5 days, producing 6 responses in 17 evaluable patients.

Experience in pediatric leukemia patients is limited. Twenty-four patients were treated with 6 to 8 mg/m² mitoxantrone, daily for 5 days. There were 3 responses in 24 evaluable children.

Fourteen adult leukemia patients received 20 to 37 mg/m² mitoxantrone once every 2 weeks. No therapeutic responses were observed using this schedule.

Several other studies reported in the literature and not sponsored by Lederle support the activity of mitoxantrone in the treatment of ANLL and B-CML.

Hepatocellular Carcinoma: Three clinical trials sponsored by Lederle have been conducted using mitoxantrone in the therapy of HCC. Mitoxantrone was administered to 65 patients i.v. at 12 mg/m² every 3 weeks in 2 studies, and in 1 study with 10 patients at 6 to 10 mg/m²/day by continuous hepatic artery infusion for 3 consecutive days, every 3 weeks. Considering the short life span of patients presenting with HCC, a response of stable disease was included along with PR's and CR's in assessing efficacy. In these 3 studies, the overall therapeutic response rate was 46.7% (11 CR's and PR's + 10 stable disease in 45 evaluable patients). Activity was confirmed in other studies not sponsored by Lederle. Duration of response was variable among these studies and ranged between 3 and 52 weeks.

Safety: Data on the overall safety profile of mitoxantrone (based on 989 patients) demonstrated advantages of mitoxantrone compared to the anthracyclines with respect to both the quality of life and the long-term safety of patients. The majority of side effects with mitoxantrone are mild in nature. Removal of patients from mitoxantrone treatment for reasons of toxicity has been rare in clinical studies. A number of patients have reported no side effects at all. In addition, the relatively low risk of serious side effects has permitted treatment of patients on an out-patient basis. The most common acute effects were nausea and/or vomiting (only 3.5% severe or very severe with mitoxantrone, compared to 10 to 15% reported with doxorubicin), stomatitis/mucositis (only 0.3% severe or very severe with mitoxantrone) and alopecia (only 0.9% severe or very severe, and 15% overall with mitoxantrone compared with 85% severe or very severe and 100% overall reported with doxorubicin). Serious local reactions have been reported rarely following extravasation of mitoxantrone at the infusion site.

With respect to myelosuppression, initial mitoxantrone doses of 14 mg/m² every 3 weeks are well-tolerated in good-risk patients. Severe degrees of myelosuppression have been rare. The median white cell nadir in a European second-line study was 2.5×10³; in a European first-line study only 4.8% (2/42) of patients experienced a nadir of less than 1 000. The nadir usually occurs around day 10 or 11 and returns to normal baseline value by day 21, in time for the next course of treatment. After multiple courses of mitoxantrone, white blood cell and platelet nadirs show no further decrease beyond those observed in the first few cycles, indicating no cumulative or permanent effects of mitoxantrone on marrow reserves.

Mitoxantrone had an exceptional safety profile and was well tolerated by patients treated for NHL, leukemia and hepatoma, as well as for breast cancer. However, due to the pathophysiology of leukemia and the higher doses of mitoxantrone employed, the safety profile differed from that seen in NHL and in hepatoma (see Adverse Effects). The most severe and life-threatening events, i.e. bleeding and infection, are well described morbid complications of acute leukemia. Many of the episodes of hepatic dysfunction were probably related to the increased bilirubin load and increased exposure to hepatitis viruses as a result of the multiple transfusions of blood products necessary in the proper treatment of this disorder.

Cardiotoxicity: In investigational trials of intermittent single doses, patients who received up to the cumulative dose of 140 mg/m² had a cumulative 2.6% probability of clinical congestive heart failure. The overall cumulative probability rate of moderate or serious decreases in LVEF at this dose was 13% in comparative trials. In contrast, doxorubicin has been reported to produce chronic cardiomyopathy and irreversible congestive heart failure in up to 11% of patients given 9 or more courses of that drug at the usual dose schedule (60 mg/m² every 3 weeks).

Overdose: Symptoms and Treatment: There is no known specific antidote for mitoxantrone. Accidental overdoses have been reported. Some patients receiving 140 to 180 mg/m² as a single bolus injection died as a result of severe leukopenia with infection. Hematologic support and antimicrobial therapy may be required during prolonged periods of medullary hypoplasia. Although patients with severe renal failure have been studied, mitoxantrone is extensively tissue bound and it is unlikely that the therapeutic effect or toxicity would be mitigated by peritoneal or hemodialysis (see Warnings, Precautions and Adverse Effects).

Dosage: Breast Cancer, Lymphoma, Hepatoma: The recommended initial dosage for use as a single agent is 14 mg/m² of body surface area, given as a single i.v. dose, which may be repeated at 21-day intervals. A lower initial dose (12 mg/m² or less) is recommended in patients with inadequate marrow reserves due to prior therapy or poor general condition.

Dosage modification and timing of subsequent dosing should be determined by clinical judgment depending on the degree and duration of myelosuppression. If 21-day white blood cell and platelet counts have returned to adequate levels, prior doses can usually be repeated. Table II indicates a guide to dosing based on myelosuppression.

Table II—Novantrone

Guide to Dosing Based on Myelosuppression

WBC and Platelet Nadir	Time to Recovery	Subsequent Dosing
If WBC Nadir > 1 500 **and** Platelet Nadir > 50 000	Recovery ≤21 days	Repeat prior dose or increase by 2 mg/m² if myelosuppression not considered adequate.
If WBC Nadir > 1 500 **and** Platelet Nadir > 50 000	Recovery >21 days	Withhold until recovery then repeat prior dose
If WBC Nadir < 1 500 **or** Platelet Nadir < 50 000	Any duration	Decrease by 2 mg/m² from prior dose after recovery
If WBC Nadir < 1 000 **or** Platelet Nadir < 25 000	Any duration	Decrease by 4 mg/m² from prior dose after recovery

Combination Therapy for Breast Cancer, Lymphoma: Mitoxantrone has been given in various combination regimens with the following cytotoxic agents for the treatment of breast cancer and lymphomas: cyclophosphamide, fluorouracil, vincristine, vinblastine, bleomycin, methotrexate (standard dose or 200 mg/m² with leucovorin rescue) and glucocorticoids.

As a guide, the initial dose of mitoxantrone when used with other myelosuppressive agents should be reduced by 2 to 4 mg/m² below the doses recommended for single agent usage; subsequent dosing depends on the degree and duration of myelosuppression.

Dosage for Patients With Acute Leukemia in Relapse: The recommended dosage for induction is 12 mg/m² of body surface area, given as a single i.v. dose daily for 5 consecutive days (total of 60 mg/m²).

In clinical studies, with a dosage of 12 mg/m² daily for 5 days, patients who achieved a complete remission did so as a result of the first induction course.

Re-induction upon relapse may be attempted with mitoxantrone and again the recommended dosage is 12 mg/m² daily for 5 days.

Combination Therapy for Leukemia: Mitoxantrone, together with cytosine arabinoside, has been used successfully for the treatment of both first line and second line patients with acute nonlymphocytic leukemia.

For induction, the recommended dosage is 10 to 12 mg/m² of mitoxantrone for 3 days and 100 mg/m² of cytosine arabinoside for 7 days (the latter given as a continuous 24-hour infusion).

If a second course is indicated, then the second course is recommended with the same combination at the same daily dosage levels but with mitoxantrone given for only 2 days and cytosine arabinoside for only 5 days.

If severe or life-threatening nonhematological toxicity is observed during the first induction course, the second induction course should be withheld until the toxicity clears.
Children: Experience in pediatric patients is limited; however, complete remissions have been observed with mitoxantrone as single agent therapy at a dosage of 8 mg/m² daily for 5 days.

Administration of Solution: Mitoxantrone solution should be diluted to at least 50 mL with either Sodium Chloride for Injection USP or 5% Dextrose for Injection USP. This solution should be introduced slowly into the tubing of a freely running i.v. infusion of Sodium Chloride for Injection USP or 5% Dextrose for Injection USP administered over not less than 3 to 5 minutes i.v. If extravasation occurs, the administration should be stopped immediately and restarted in another vein. The nonvessicant properties of mitoxantrone minimize the possibility of severe reactions following extravasation, however, tissue necrosis has been reported rarely.

Mitoxantrone should be administered by individuals experienced in the use of antineoplastic therapy.

A 20 gauge or smaller needle size is recommended as the optimal needle size. Doses should be removed using slightly negative pressure.

Caution in the handling and preparation of mitoxantrone solutions must be exercised and the use of protective eyeglasses, gloves and other protective clothing is recommended. See Guidelines for Safe Use by Hospital Personnel.
Storage: Store at 15 to 25°C.

Following preparation of the infusion, the diluted solution should be stored at room temperature and used within 24 hours. Any original solution which remains in the vial should be discarded.

Note: Like the original solutions, the dilutions should also not be frozen.

Guidelines for Safe Use by Hospital Personnel: Handling: 1. Preparation of antineoplastic solutions should be done in a vertical laminar flow hood (Biological Safety Cabinet-Class II). 2. Personnel preparing mitoxantrone solutions should wear PVC gloves, safety glasses and protective clothing such as disposable gowns and masks. 3. Personnel regularly involved in the preparation and handling of antineoplastics should have bi-annual blood examinations.
Disposal: 1. Avoid contact with skin and inhalation of airborne particles by use of PVC gloves and disposable gowns and masks. 2. All needles, syringes, vials, ampuls and other materials which have come in contact with mitoxantrone should be segregated in plastic bags, sealed and marked as hazardous waste. Incinerate at 1 000°C or higher. Sealed containers may explode if a tight seal exists. 3. If incineration is not available, mitoxantrone HCl may be detoxified by adding 5.5 parts by weight of calcium hypochlorite to each 1 part by weight of mitoxantrone HCl in 13 parts by weight of water. The calcium hypochlorite should be added **gradually** and the procedure carried out with adequate ventilation since chlorine gas is liberated.
Vials: Prepare an adequate quantity of calcium hypochlorite solution (e.g., Add 43.5 g calcium hypochlorite to 100 mL of water*). Withdraw any mitoxantrone remaining in the vial with the aid of a hypodermic syringe. Add to the prepared calcium hypochlorite solution slowly, preferably in chemical fume hood or biological safety cabinet-Class II. Add an appropriate quantity of the calcium hypochlorite solution to the vial to detoxify any remaining drug.
*Appropriate safety equipment such as goggles and gloves should be worn while working with calcium hypochlorite solution since it is corrosive.

Withdraw the solution and discard in the sewer system with running water. Dispose of the detoxified vials in a safe manner.
Needles, Syringes, Disposable and Nondisposable Equipment: Rinse equipment with an appropriate quantity of calcium hypochlorite solution (43.5 g/100 mL of water*). Discard the solution in the sewer system with running water and discard disposable equipment in a safe manner. Thoroughly wash nondisposable equipment in soap and water.
*Appropriate safety equipment such as goggles and gloves should be worn while working with calcium hypochlorite solution since it is corrosive.
Spillage/Contamination: Wear gloves, mask, protective clothing. Place spilled material in an appropriate container (i.e., cardboard for broken glass) and then in a polyethylene bag; absorb remains with gauze pads or towels; wash area with water and absorb with gauze or towels again and place in bag; seal, double bag and mark as a hazardous waste. Dispose of waste by incineration or by other methods approved for hazardous materials. Personnel involved in cleanup should wash with soap and water.

Supplied: 20 mg: Each mL of clear, dark blue, sterile aqueous solution for injection contains: mitoxantrone HCl equivalent to mitoxantrone (free base) 2 mg. Nonmedicinal ingredients: acetic acid, sodium acetate, sodium chloride and water for injection. Preservative- and tartrazine-free. Vials of 10 mL.

25 mg: Each mL of clear, dark blue, sterile aqueous solution for injection contains: mitoxantrone HCl equivalent to mitoxantrone (free base) 2 mg. Nonmedicinal ingredients: acetic acid, sodium acetate, sodium chloride and water for injection. Preservative- and tartrazine-free. Vials of 12.5 mL.

Reviewed 1999

NOVA RECTAL® ⊕
Sabex
Sodium Pentobarbital
Hypnotic—Sedative

Supplied: Each suppository contains: sodium pentobarbital 50 mg in a polyethylene glycol base. Nonmedicinal ingredients: polyethylene glycol. Boxes of 12. Store in a cool place.

NOVASEN
Novopharm
ASA
Anti-inflammatory—Analgesic

Supplied: 325 mg: Each brown, round, enteric, film-coated tablet, embossed N on one side, plain on reverse, contains: ASA 325 mg. Bottles of 100, 500 and 1 000. Unit dose strips of 100.

650 mg: Each orange, oval, enteric, film-coated tablet, embossed N on one side, plain on reverse, contains: ASA 650 mg. Bottles of 100, 500 and 1 000. Unit dose strips of 100.

NOVASOURCE™ RENAL
Novartis Nutrition
Therapeutic Nutrient

Indications: A nutritionally complete, calorically dense, moderate protein formula with a vitamin/mineral profile designed for dialysis patients with acute and chronic renal failure. Appropriate for both oral and tube feeding use.

Precautions: Not for parenteral administration.

Dosage: 1 000 mL or 8 360 kJ (4.2 Tetra Brik Paks or 2 000 kcal) provides at least 100% of the Canadian RNI (adult males, 25 to 49) for protein and essential vitamins and minerals except for vitamin D, phosphorus and magnesium. NovaSource Renal is ready to use and does not require dilution with water. It may be fed at room temperature or chilled.
Tube Feeding: Follow a physician's or dietitian's instructions for tube feedings. When initiating feeding, the flow rate, volume and dilution are dependent on patient condition and tolerance. Care should be taken to avoid contamination of this product during preparation and administration. Additional fluid requirements should be met by giving water orally with or after feedings, or when flushing the feeding tube.
Oral: For oral feeding, it may be used as a sole source of nutrition or as a supplement with and between meals for added nutritional support.

Supplied: Each 237 mL Tetra Brik Pak contains: ⓤ-D water, corn syrup, sodium and calcium caseinates, high oleic sunflower oil, corn oil, medium-chain triglycerides, fructose, L-arginine, lactic acid, calcium carbonate, artificial flavor, soy lecithin, potassium chloride, hydrolyzed cornstarch, magnesium carbonate, cellulose gel, choline chloride, calcium phosphate tribasic, L-carnitine, sodium ascorbate, taurine, cellulose gum, high selenium yeast, zinc sulfate, alpha tocopheryl acetate, ferrous sulfate, niacinamide, calcium pantothenate, manganese sulfate, copper gluconate, pyridoxine HCl, thiamine HCl, riboflavin, beta carotene, folic acid, vitamin A palmitate, biotin, potassium iodide, phytonadione (vitamin K_1), cyanocobalamin (vitamin B_{12}), cholecalciferol (vitamin D_3). See Table I.

Energy Distribution: protein 15%, fat 45%, carbohydrate 40%; 836 kJ (200 kcal)/100 mL.

Table I—NovaSource Renal

Analysis	100 mL	
Energy	836 (200)	kJ (kcal)
Proteins[a]	7.4	g
Carbohydrate	20	g
Fat	10.2	g
Linoleic Acid	1.2	g
Sodium	100	mg
Potassium	81	mg
Vitamin A[b]	333	mg
Vitamin C	8.0	mg
Thiamine	0.25	mg
Riboflavin	0.29	mg
Niacin	3.4	mg
Calcium	130	mg
Iron	1.8	mg
Vitamin D	8.0	mg
Vitamin E	4.5	mg
Vitamin B_6	0.8	mg
Folic Acid	0.1	mg
Vitamin B_{12}	0.001	mg
Phosphorus	65	mg
Iodine	0.016	mg
Magnesium	20	mg
Zinc	2.5	mg
Copper	0.2	mg
Biotin	0.05	mg
Pantothenic Acid	1.6	mg
Vitamin K	0.008	mg
Choline	33	mg
Chloride	84	mg
Manganese	0.5	mg
Selenium	0.01	mg
Carnitine	26.5	mg
Taurine	15	mg
Osmolality	700	mOsm/kg water

[a]Includes protein from caseinates and L-arginine.
[b]Includes vitamin A activity from beta carotene.

NovaSource Renal is a calorically dense, moderate protein, low residue formula. Designed for dialysis patients with acute or chronic renal failure it is low in: vitamin D, phosphorus, magnesium, sodium and potassium. Citrate-, gluten- and lactose-free. Contains only 10% of total calories from saturated fat and contains medium-chain triglycerides to facilitate rapid, effective fat absorption.

Aseptic Tetra Brik Paks of 237 mL (vanilla), cases of 27. Store unopened at room temperature. Once opened, store covered in refrigerator and use within 24 hours.

New Product 1998

NOVA-T
Berlex Canada
Intrauterine Copper
Intrauterine Contraceptive

Description: Nova-T is an intrauterine device made of plastic (polyethylene) approximately in the shape of a T. Polyethylene threads are attached to the lower portion. The horizontal and vertical arms of the T are 32 mm in length and 1.2 mm in diameter; a loop 2.6 mm wide is found at the tip of the vertical arm; and a thin copper wire (107-141 mg Cu, surface area of 200 mm²) stablized with a silver core (11-29 mg Ag) is coiled onto the vertical portion of the T. The silver core prevents fragmentation of the wire and prolongs the lifespan of the device.

Indications: For intrauterine contraception in gynecologically normal women of childbearing age. The reported annual pregnancy rate for intrauterine devices is less than 1 to 6 per 100 women.
Duration of Use: Nova-T can be left inserted for a maximum of 30 months. If continued contraception is desired by the patient, a new Nova-T should be inserted at once.

Contraindications: Nova-T should not be used in the presence or suspicion of: pregnancy, malignant tumor in the genital area; acute, subacute and chronic pelvic inflammatory disease (including a history of such infections), profuse menstrual bleeding; congenital or acquired anatomical changes of the uterus or cervix; endometriosis; hypoplasia or extreme positional anomalies of the uterus; genital bleeding of unknown origin; clotting disorders; conditions which can lead

Nova-T (cont'd)

to or promote bacteremia (e.g., valvular defects, congenital heart disease); severe anemia; conditions associated with a weakened immune defense; Wilson's disease; copper allergy; a history of ectopic pregnancy.

Warnings: The risk/benefit ratio of inserting an intrauterine device must be carefully weighed following surgery on the uterine body or in the pelvic and abdominal cavity, and particularly on the fallopian tubes, since there have been isolated reports of an increased risk of ectopic pregnancy and uterine perforation.

The rate of expulsion may be increased when insertions are made before normal uterine involution occurs following delivery or abortion. It is recommended that Nova-T be inserted 1 month postpartum or postabortion. Current data indicate that slightly higher expulsion and pregnancy rates may be anticipated with earlier insertion.

In young and nulliparous women, the risk/benefit ratio must be carefully appraised because of reports of higher failure rates and complications. Some epidemiological surveys suggest that nulliparous patients using an intrauterine device may be at a greater risk of pelvic inflammatory disease and subsequent infertility. Women with multiple sexual partners also seem to be more affected in this respect.

Patients should be examined for the presence of pelvic inflammatory disease before inserting Nova-T. In cases of infection (e.g., subsequent to a septic abortion or a sexually transmitted disease) appropriate treatment should be given before inserting the IUD.

Nova-T, as other intrauterine devices, is not effective in preventing ectopic pregnancies. There is therefore a risk of an ectopic pregnancy occurring with an intrauterine device in situ.

Nova-T should be removed for the following reasons: Perforation of the uterus which places the device outside the uterine cavity (usually occurs during insertion).

Excessive and persistent bleeding and cramping, and inflammation in the region of the uterus or pelvis minor, to prevent worsening of these symptoms or possible infertility. Note: In patients with inflammation or mild symptoms indicative of inflammatory changes (e.g., discharge), bacteriological examinations and antibiotic therapy, where applicable, are indicated. If actinomycetes are found in cytological smears, consideration must be given to removing the intrauterine device as a precaution—particularly after it has been in situ for a long time—even in asymptomatic patients and to giving appropriate treatment.

Partial or total downward displacement of Nova-T within the cervical canal (in some cases the tip of the "T" device can be palpated). Note: Nova-T should be removed by gentle traction on the threads or on the tip of the "T". When Nova-T is in the cervical canal, protection against pregnancy may be reduced or absent.

Pregnancy occurring with Nova-T in situ. Note: Nova-T should be removed by pulling on the threads to reduce the increased risk of secondary symptoms (e.g. abortion, general bacterial infection); however, if Nova-T cannot be withdrawn, termination of pregnancy should be considered.

Important: If there is any suspicion that Nova-T is incorrectly positioned, it must be removed and replaced by another sterile Nova-T.

Precautions: Prior to inserting Nova-T, the physical examination should include a complete pelvic examination and a Papanicolaou smear. Pregnancy must be ruled out.

It is advisable to insert Nova-T at the end of the menstrual period since at this time the patient is unlikely to be pregnant and the cervical canal is still dilated.

Nova-T must be placed as high as possible within the uterine cavity, to help avoid downward displacement, expulsion or accidental pregnancy.

As a general principle, Nova-T should be inserted under aseptic conditions.

The patient should be informed that she may have some spotting, light bleeding or cramps during the first few days after insertion. If these events continue or are severe, they should be reported to the physician.

If there is complaint of discomfort during intercourse, the possibility of displacement or cervical perforation should be ruled out.

Should the patient become aware that Nova-T has been expelled, she should contact her physician because she is no longer protected from pregnancy.

The patient should contact her physician immediately if she misses a menstrual period or thinks she may be pregnant.

After insertion the threads remain outside the cervical canal in the vagina. At weekly intervals or at least after each menstrual period, the patient should be instructed to verify with a finger whether the threads of Nova-T can be felt in the vagina. If the patient cannot feel the threads or sense the device, she should see her physician. If the threads are not visible, they may have been drawn up into the cervical canal or Nova-T may have been expelled unnoticed. In exceptional cases Nova-T may be lying outside the uterus as a result of perforation. An x-ray examination should be performed to assess the situation. The plastic component of Nova-T contains barium sulfate and therefore gives good contrast. The position of Nova-T can also be ascertained by ultrasound. Normally, Nova-T can be removed by simply pulling on the threads. If Nova-T is inside the uterus, the device or the threads can be gripped through the cervical canal by a slender, slightly convex forcep. If the position of the device is extrauterine, surgical removal is essential, using laparoscopy if possible.

Patients should be followed up at 1, 3, 6 and 12 months after insertion, and thereafter at approximately yearly intervals. A Papanicolaou smear should be done at least once a year.

Ectopic pregnancy must be considered in the presence of vague lower abdominal complaints associated with irregular cycles (especially amenorrhea after persistent bleeding).

Women who are taking anticoagulants should inform their physician because of the increased tendency to hemorrhage.

Reports have been published indicating that the contraceptive effect of intrauterine devices appears to be diminished in patients receiving chronic treatment with NSAIDs (particularly ASA) and with corticoids; however, experience has shown that contraceptive protection is not reduced during short-term treatment of dysmenorrhea with NSAIDs.

Caution should be exercised when performing diathermy (short-wave or microwave), of the sacral or abdominal region since heating of the copper can subsequently damage Nova-T.

Adverse Effects: In extremely rare cases, a brief loss of consciousness or decelerated pulse rate may occur during insertion or removal of intrauterine devices. Perforation of the uterus or the cervix may occur. Initially, Nova-T can cause persistent pain in the lower abdomen or sacral area, but this usually subsides.

Menstrual bleeding is sometimes stronger and of longer duration than normal, or is more painful. Iron-deficiency anemia may then occur in individual cases. Slight intermenstrual bleeding, often in the form of spotting, may occur but it usually subsides spontaneously (the physician should be informed if intermenstrual bleeding persists).

Lower abdominal infections, with the risk of subsequent infertility, occur more frequently in patients using an IUD device than in other women.

Isolated cases of skin reactions have been described in the literature which may be attributable to copper allergy, since they disappeared when the copper device was removed.

Dosage: Insertion Technique: Prior to Insertion: Prior to the insertion of Nova-T the patient should be given a thorough gynecological examination. The size and position of the uterus should be established and pregnancy or other contraindications should be ruled out (see Contraindications).

Insertion: Nova-T can be inserted on any day of the cycle; however, the last days of menses are recommended since at this time the patient is unlikely to be pregnant and the cervical canal is still dilated, thus facilitating insertion. Given its small diameter, the insertion tube is easy to introduce and usually does not call for further dilation.

As a general principle, Nova-T should be inserted under aseptic conditions using sterile gloves. The following steps should be followed when inserting Nova-T: 1. Insert a speculum to visualize the external os uteri and disinfect the vagina and cervix. 2. Use a tenaculum forcep to stretch the neck of the uterus. The forceps should be left in position until Nova-T has been inserted. 3. Utilize a sound to determine the position and length of the uterine lumen. 4. Prepare Nova-T: Open the plastic covering far enough to expose the lower end of the insertion tube; however, Nova-T and the insertion tube are not to be withdrawn. While holding the tube firmly with one hand, expose the threads and draw the device into the insertion tube.

Steadying the yellow ring with one hand, move the insertion tube until the yellow ring's **lower** rim indicates the previously sounded length on the scale. Holding the threads slightly stretched with one hand, place the plunger into the tube with the free hand. This will ensure that the threads are lying straight in the tube and are not disarranged by the plunger. If necessary, the insertion tube can be bent so that it is better adapted to the position of the uterus.

Remove Nova-T from the plastic covering. Gently insert Nova-T into the cervical canal and advance it until the yellow ring touches the cervix. The broad sides of the yellow ring must be horizontal to ensure subsequent correct unfolding of the arms.

Hold the plunger firmly with one hand and draw the tube back until it reaches the ribbed part of the plunger, thereby, removing the yellow ring from the cervix (distance approximately 1.5 cm). The arms of Nova-T are now unfolded.

Advance the insertion tube until the yellow ring touches the cervix again. Nova-T is then in contact with the fundus uteri.

To release Nova-T entirely from the insertion tube, hold the plunger firmly and draw the tube back as far as the backstop. To avoid entangling the threads between the tube and the plunger, carefully remove the plunger **first** and then the insertion tube. Cut the threads about 3 cm from the cervix. See manufacturer's package insert for illustration of the above steps.

Supplied: Individual sterile package units, with an insertion tube imprinted with a centimetre scale, and a plunger.

(Shown in Product Recognition Section)

Reviewed 1997

NOVO-ACEBUTOLOL ℞

Novopharm

Acebutolol HCl

Antihypertensive—Antianginal

Supplied: 100 mg: Each off-white, round, biconvex, film-coated tablet, engraved N/100 on one side, contains: acebutolol HCl equivalent to acebutolol 100 mg. Gluten- and tartrazine-free. Bottles of 100, 500 and 1 000. Unit dose strips of 100.

200 mg: Each off-white, oval, biconvex, film-coated tablet, scored and engraved novo on one side and 200 on the other, contains: acebutolol HCl equivalent to acebutolol 200 mg. Gluten- and tartrazine-free. Bottles of 100, 500 and 1 000. Unit dose strips of 100.

400 mg: Each off-white, oval, biconvex, film-coated tablet, scored and engraved novo on one side and 400 on the other, contains: acebutolol HCl equivalent to acebutolol 400 mg. Gluten- and tartrazine-free. Bottles of 100, 500 and 1 000. Unit dose strips of 100.

NOVO-ALPRAZOL ℞

Novopharm

Alprazolam

Anxiolytic—Sedative

Supplied: 0.25 mg: Each white, oval, compressed tablet, engraved no/vo on one side, and 0.25 on the reverse, contains: alprazolam 0.25 mg. Gluten- and tartrazine-free. Bottles of 100 and 1 000. Unit dose strips of 100.

0.5 mg: Each peach-colored, oval, compressed tablet, engraved no/vo on one side, and 0.5 on the reverse, contains: alprazolam 0.5 mg. Gluten- and tartrazine-free. Bottles of 100 and 1 000. Unit dose strips of 100.

NOVO-AMPICILLIN ℞

Novopharm

Ampicillin

Antibiotic

Supplied: Capsules: 250 mg: Each red and black no. 2 capsule, imprinted NOVO 250 contains: ampicillin 250 mg. Bottles of 100, 500 and 1 000.

500 mg: Each red and black no. 0 capsule, imprinted NOVO 500 contains: ampicillin 500 mg. Bottles of 100, 500 and 1 000.

Suspensions: 125 mg: After reconstitution each 5 mL of cherry-flavored suspension contains: ampicillin 125 mg. Energy: 49 kJ (11.7 kcal)/5 mL. Bottles of 100 and 150 mL.

250 mg: After reconstitution each 5 mL of cherry-flavored suspension contains: ampicillin 250 mg. Energy: 46.4 kJ (11.1 kcal)/5 mL. Bottles of 100 and 150 mL.

NOVO-ATENOL ℞

Novopharm

Atenolol

Antihypertensive—Antianginal

Supplied: 50 mg: Each white, round, scored tablet, embossed arched NOVO/50 on one side and plain on reverse side, contains: atenolol 50 mg. Gluten- and tartrazine-free. Patient packs of 30. Bottles of 100 and 500. Unit dose strips of 100.

100 mg: Each white, round, scored tablet, embossed no/vo and 100 on opposite sides, contains: atenolol 100 mg. Gluten- and tartrazine-free. Patient packs of 30. Bottles of 100 and 500. Unit dose strips of 100.

NOVO-AZT ℞

Novopharm

Zidovudine

Antiretroviral Agent

Pharmacology: Zidovudine is a potent inhibitor of the in vitro replication of certain retroviruses including human immunodeficiency virus, HIV (formerly known as HTLV III, LAV or ARV). Zidovudine is a thymidine analogue whereby the 3-hydroxy (−OH) group is replaced by an azido ($-N_3$) group. Zidovudine is transformed into zidovudine monophosphate by cellular thymidine kinase. The monophosphate is then converted to the diphosphate and to the triphosphate by cellular thymidylate kinase and other cellular enzymes, respectively. Zidovudine triphosphate interferes with the HIV viral RNA dependent DNA polymerase (reverse transcriptase) and therefore viral replication is inhibited. At concentrations 100 times higher than those required to inhibit reverse transcriptase zidovudine triphosphate also inhibits cellular α-DNA polymerase. Zidovudine triphosphate has been shown to be incorporated into growing chains of DNA by viral reverse transcriptase in in vitro studies. Once incorporation by the viral enzyme has occurred, the DNA chain is terminated. Cell culture studies have shown that zidovudine incorporation by cellular α-DNA polymerase may occur, but only to a very small degree and not in all test systems. No chain termination has been demonstrated with cellular α-DNA polymerase.

I.V. dosing of zidovudine in adults has shown dose-independent kinetics over the range of 1 to 5 mg/kg with a mean half-life of 1.1 hours. Zidovudine is rapidly metabolized to 3'-azido-3'-deoxy-5'-O-β-D-glucopyranuronosylthymidine (GAZT). Both are rapidly eliminated by the kidney. After oral doses of zidovudine, it is rapidly absorbed from the gastrointestinal tract with peak serum concentrations occurring within 0.5 to 1.5 hours, with an average oral bioavailability of 65%. Studies in pediatric patients older than 3 months have shown pharmacokinetics of zidovudine similar to those in adult patients.

Indications: For the management of adult patients with HIV infection who demonstrate evidence of impaired immunity (CD_4 cell count of approximately 500/mm³ or less) before therapy is begun.

For HIV-infected children over 3 months of age who have advanced symptomatic HIV disease (pediatric AIDS or advanced ARC). It may also be of value to children who are asymptomatic with abnormal laboratory values indicating significant HIV-related immunosuppression.

These indications are based on results obtained from randomized, double-blind, placebo-controlled trials in adult patients with varying severity of HIV infection. Separate studies were conducted to evaluate zidovudine therapy in asymptomatic HIV-infected individuals, in patients with early HIV disease and in patients with advanced HIV disease, including AIDS, and in children with advanced symptomatic HIV disease (pediatric AIDS or advanced ARC). Progression of disease was delayed by zidovudine in asymptomatic and early symptomatic patients for approximately 1 year. Zidovudine prolonged survival and decreased the incidence of opportunistic infections in patients with advanced HIV disease treated for up to 24 weeks.

Contraindications: In patients who have potentially life-threatening allergic reactions to any of the components of the formulations.

Warnings: In patients who have bone marrow compromise evidenced by granulocyte count <1 000/mm³ or hemoglobin <9.5 g/dL, zidovudine should be used with extreme caution. Anemia and granulocytopenia were the most significant adverse events observed in all of the placebo-controlled studies, but most frequently in patients with advanced symptomatic disease. Incidences of pancytopenia have been reported with the use of zidovudine, however, in most instances this was reversible after discontinuation of the drug.

In individuals receiving zidovudine therapy, sensitization reactions, including anaphylaxis, have been reported. Patients experiencing a rash should undergo medical evaluation.

Concomitant administration of zidovudine with other drugs metabolized by glucuronidation should be avoided since the toxicity of either drug may be potentiated (see Precautions, Drug Interactions).

Controlled trials of zidovudine have been conducted in significant numbers of asymptomatic and symptomatic HIV infected patients, but only for limited periods of time. Therefore, the full safety and efficacy profile of zidovudine has not been clearly established, particularly in regard to prolonged use and especially in HIV-infected individuals who have less advanced disease.

Precautions: Zidovudine is eliminated from the body primarily via renal excretion following metabolism in the liver (glucuronidation). Currently, very little information is available regarding the use of zidovudine in patients with impaired renal function and no data in those with impaired hepatic function. There may be a greater risk of toxicity for these patients from zidovudine.

Infants and Young Children: Overall, the pharmacokinetics of zidovudine in pediatric patients greater than 3 months of age and adult patients is similar. There is insufficient clinical experience to recommend a dosing regimen in infants under 3 months of age. Preliminary evidence suggests that zidovudine clearance may be reduced in children less than 1 month of age.

In children under 15 months of age, a positive test for HIV-antibody may represent passively acquired maternal antibodies, rather than an active antibody response to infection in the infant. Therefore, in a child less than 15 months of age, the presence of HIV-antibody must be interpreted with caution, especially in the asymptomatic infant. In such children, auxillary diagnostic tests may be required to confirm infection.

Pregnancy: Whether or not zidovudine can cause fetal harm when administered to a pregnant woman or can affect reproductive capacity is unknown. The risk of withholding treatment of the mother must be weighed against the unknown risks of the drug to the fetus.

Lactation: It is not known whether zidovudine is excreted in human milk. It is advisable to caution mothers against breast feeding because of uncertainties related to the transmission of virus and to excretion of zidovudine in breast milk.

Drug Interactions: Concomitant administration of zidovudine with drugs that are nephrotoxic, cytotoxic or which interfere with RBC/WBC number or function (e.g., dapsone, pentamidine, amphotericin B, flucytosine, vincristine, vinblastine, doxorubicin or interferon) may increase the risk of toxicity.

Some nucleoside analogues (e.g., ganciclovir) which are being studied in AIDS and ARC patients may affect RBC/WBC number or function and may increase the potential for hematologic toxicity of zidovudine. Other nucleoside analogues (e.g., ribavirin) affecting DNA replication antagonize the in vitro antiviral activity of zidovudine against HIV, and therefore, concomitant use of such drugs should be avoided.

Administration of trimethoprim-sulfamethoxazole, pyrimethamine and acyclovir may be necessary for the management or prevention of opportunistic infections. In a controlled trial, with limited exposure to these drugs, increased toxicity was not detected. There is, however, one published report of neurotoxicity (profound lethargy) associated with concomitant use of zidovudine and acyclovir.

There is some limited data which suggests that probenecid may inhibit glucuronidation and/or reduce renal excretion of zidovudine. Other drugs, (e.g., acetaminophen, ASA or indomethacin) may competitively inhibit glucuronidation as well (see Warnings).

In some patients receiving zidovudine, phenytoin levels have been reported to be low, while in one case a high level was documented. These observations suggest that in patients receiving concomitant zidovudine, phenytoin levels should be carefully monitored.

Adverse Effects: Adults: The frequency and severity of adverse events associated with the use of zidovudine in adults are greater in those patients with more advanced infection at the time of initiation of therapy.

Anemia and Granulocytopenia: Anemia and granulocytopenia were the most significant adverse events observed in all of the placebo-controlled studies, but most frequently in patients with advanced symptomatic HIV disease.

Significant anemia may occur as early as 2 weeks, however, it most commonly occurred after 4 to 6 weeks. In many cases dose adjustment, discontinuation of zidovudine, and/or blood transfusions were necessary. In patients with advanced HIV disease receiving zidovudine, frequent blood counts are strongly recommended. Blood counts may be obtained less frequently for asymptomatic HIV-infected individuals and patients with early HIV disease, most of whom have better marrow reserve, depending upon the patient's overall status. Dosage adjustments may be necessary if anemia or granulocytopenia develops (see Dosage).

Tables I, II and III summarize the relative incidence of hematologic adverse events reported in the placebo-controlled clinical studies by degree of HIV disease present at the start of treatment.

Other Adverse Events (Advanced HIV Disease): The HIV-infected adults who participated in these clinical trials often had baseline symptoms and signs of HIV disease and/or experienced adverse events at some point during the study. Distinguishing adverse events possibly associated with zidovudine administration from underlying signs of HIV disease or intercurrent illness was often difficult.

Table IV (on following page) summarizes clinical adverse events or symptoms reported by at least 5% of all patients with advanced HIV disease treated with zidovudine in the original placebo-controlled study. Of the items listed in the table, only severe headache, nausea, insomnia and myalgia were reported at a significantly greater rate in zidovudine recipients.

Table I—Novo-AZT

Relative Incidence of Hematologic Adverse Events in an Asymptomatic HIV Infection Study

Asymptomatic HIV Infection Study (n=1 338)	Granulocytopenia (<750/mm³) Zidovudine[a] 1 500 mg[b]	500 mg	Placebo	Anemia (Hgb<8 g/dL) Zidovudine[a] 1 500 mg[b]	500 mg	Placebo
CD4≤500	6.4% (n=457)	1.8% (n=453)	1.6% (n=428)	6.4% (n=457)	1.1% (n=453)	0.2% (n=428)

Table II—Novo-AZT

Relative Incidence of Hematologic Adverse Events in an Early HIV Disease Study

Early HIV Disease Study (n=713)	Granulocytopenia (<750/mm³) Zidovudine[a] 1 200 mg	Placebo	Anemia (Hgb<8g/dL) Zidovudine[a] 1 200 mg	Placebo
CD4>200	4% (n=361)	1% (n=352)	4% (n=361)	0% (n=352)

Table III—Novo-AZT

Relative Incidence of Hematologic Adverse Events in an Advanced HIV Disease Study

Advanced HIV Disease Study (n=281)	Granulocytopenia (<750/mm³) Zidovudine[a] 1 500 mg	Placebo	Anemia (Hgb<7.5g/dL) Zidovudine[a] 1 500 mg	Placebo
CD4>200	10% (n=30)	3% (n=30)	3% (n=30)	0% (n=30)
CD4<200	47% (n=114)	10% (n=107)	29% (n=114)	5% (n=107)

[a] Total daily dose.
[b] Three times the recommended dose in asymptomatic patients.

Novo-AZT (cont'd)

Table IV—Novo-AZT

Percentage (%) of Patients with Clinical Events in the Advanced HIV Disease Study

Adverse Event	Zidovudine (n=144)%	Placebo (n=137)%
Body as a Whole		
Asthenia	19	18
Diaphoresis	5	4
Fever	16	12
Headache	42	37
Malaise	8	7
Gastrointestinal		
Anorexia	11	8
Diarrhea	12	18
Dyspepsia	5	4
GI pain	20	19
Nausea	46	18
Vomiting	6	3
Musculoskeletal		
Myalgia	8	2
Nervous		
Dizziness	6	4
Insomnia	5	1
Paresthesia	6	3
Somnolence	8	9
Respiratory		
Dyspnea	5	3
Skin		
Rash	17	15
Special Senses		
Taste Perversion	5	8

Listed below are clinical adverse events which occurred in less than 5% of all adult patients treated with zidovudine in the advanced HIV study. Since many of these adverse reactions were noted in placebo-treated patients as well as zidovudine recipients, their possible relationship to the drug is unknown.

Body as a whole: body odor, chills, edema of the lip, flu syndrome, hyperalgesia, back pain, chest pain, lymphadenopathy.

Cardiovascular: vasodilation.

Gastrointestinal: constipation, dysphagia, edema of the tongue, eructation, flatulence, bleeding gums, rectal hemorrhage, mouth ulcer.

Muscoskeletal: arthralgia, muscle spasm, tremor, twitch.

CNS: anxiety, confusion, depression, emotional lability, nervousness, syncope, loss of mental activity, vertigo.

Respiratory: cough, epistaxis, pharyngitis, rhinitis, sinusitis, hoarseness.

Skin: acne, pruritus, urticaria.

Special Senses: amblyopia, hearing loss, photophobia.

Urogenital: dysuria, polyuria, urinary frequency, urinary hesitancy.

In a few adults receiving zidovudine therapy, subsequent to the initial trial, myopathy and sensitization reactions, including anaphylaxis, have been reported.

Other Adverse Events (Early Symptomatic/Asymptomatic HIV Disease): In the placebo controlled studies in adults with early HIV disease and asymptomatic HIV infection all unexpected events and events of a severe or life-threatening nature were monitored. Information regarding the occurrence of additional signs or symptoms was also collected. There was no distinction made between events possibly associated with the administration of the study medication and those due to the underlying disease. Tables V and VI summarize those events reported significantly more often by zidovudine recipients in these studies.

The following events, which may occur as part of the underlying disease process have been reported in adult patients receiving zidovudine therapy: seizures, nail pigmentation, changes in liver function tests. The relationship between these events and the use of zidovudine is uncertain.

Children: Anemia and Granulocytopenia: The incidences of anemia and granulocytopenia among children with advanced HIV disease receiving zidovudine were similar to those reported for adults with AIDS or advanced ARC (see above). Table VII summarizes the occurrence of anemia (Hgb<7.5 g/dL) and granulocytopenia (<750/mm³) in 124 children receiving zidovudine for an average of 267 days (range 3 to 855 days).

Table V—Novo-AZT

Percentage (%) of Patients with Clinical Events in the Early HIV Disease Study

Adverse Event	1 200 mg Zidovudine (n=361) %	Placebo (n=352) %
Body as a Whole		
Asthenia	69	62
Gastrointestinal		
Dyspepsia	6	1
Nausea	61	41
Vomiting	25	13

Table VI—Novo-AZT

Percentage (%) of Patients with Clinical Events[a] in an Asymptomatic HIV Infection Study

Adverse Event	1 500 mg[c] Zidovudine (n=457) %	500 mg Zidovudine (n=453) %	Placebo (n=428) %
Body as a Whole			
Asthenia	10.1	8.6[b]	5.8
Headache	58.0[b]	62.5	52.6
Malaise	55.6	53.2	44.9
Gastrointestinal			
Anorexia	19.3	20.1	10.5
Constipation	8.1	6.4[b]	3.5
Nausea	57.3	51.4	29.9
Vomiting	16.4	17.2	9.8
Nervous			
Dizziness	20.8	17.9[b]	15.2

[a]Reported >5% of study population.
[b]Not statistically significant versus placebo.
[c]Three times the recommended dose in asymptomatic patients.

Table VII—Novo-AZT

Occurrence of Anemia and Granulocytopenia

	Granulocytopenia (<750/mm³)		Anemia (Hgb<7.5 g/dL)	
	N	%	N	%
Advanced Pediatric HIV disease (N=124)	48	39	28*	23

*Twenty-two children received one or more transfusions due to a decline in hemoglobin to <7.5 g/dL; an additional 15 children were transfused for hemoglobin levels >7.5 g/dL. Fifty-nine percent of the patients transfused had a pre-study history of anemia or transfusion requirements.

Management of neutropenia and anemia included dose modification and/or blood product transfusions in some cases. In the open-label studies, 17% had their dose modified (generally a reduction in dose by 30%) due to anemia, and 25% had their dose modified (temporary discontinuation or reduction by 30%) for neutropenia.

An increase in MCV (macrocytosis) was seen among the majority participating in the studies.

Other Adverse Events (Children): The clinical adverse reactions reported among adult zidovudine recipients may also occur in children.

In the open-label studies conducted in 124 children, 16 different clinical adverse reactions were reported by 24 children. There was no event which was reported by more than 5.6% of the study populations. It was difficult to determine possible zidovudine-related versus disease-related events due to the open-label design of the studies. Therefore, all clinical events reported as associated with zidovudine therapy or of unknown relationship to zidovudine therapy are presented in Table VIII.

Overdose: Symptoms and Treatment: There have been cases of acute overdose in both children and adults reported. None of these were fatal. The maximum dose reported with recovery is 50 g in adults while in children the dose was 400 mg/m².

Spontaneous or induced nausea and vomiting was the only consistent finding in these cases of overdose. There have been no significant hematological changes reported due to acute overdose. Lethargy and drowsiness were other less-consistent signs and symptoms. Three hours after ingestion of 36 g of zidovudine, a grand mal seizure occurred in 1 adult male. All patients recovered without permanent sequelae. Management of overdose included supportive measures, induction of emesis and administration of activated charcoal. Hemodialysis appears to have a negligible effect on removal of zidovudine while elimination of its primary metabolite, GAZT, is enhanced.

Table VIII—Novo-AZT

Percentage (%) of Pediatric Patients with Clinical Events in Open Label Studies

Adverse Event	N	%
Body as a Whole		
Fever	4	3.2
Phlebitis*/Bacteremia	2	1.6
Headache	2	1.6
Gastrointestinal		
Nausea	1	0.8
Vomiting	6	4.8
Abdominal Pain	4	3.2
Diarrhea	1	0.8
Weight Loss	1	0.8
CNS		
Insomnia	3	2.4
Nervousness/Irritability	2	1.6
Decreased Reflexes	7	5.6
Seizure	1	0.8
Cardiovascular		
Left Ventricular Dilation	1	0.8
Cardiomyopathy	1	0.8
S_3 Gallop	1	0.8
Congestive Heart Failure	1	0.8
Generalized Edema	1	0.8
ECG Abnormality	3	2.4
Urogenital		
Hematuria/Viral Cystitis	1	0.8

*Peripheral vein i.v. catheter site.

Dosage: Adults: Asymptomatic HIV Infection: The recommended dose for adults is 100 mg administered orally every 4 hours while awake for a total daily dose of 500 mg.

Symptomatic HIV Disease: The recommended dose for adults is 100 mg of zidovudine administered every 4 hours around the clock for a total daily dose of 600 mg. In advanced disease consideration should be given to an initial dose of 1 200 mg/day for 4 weeks (see Explanatory Note).

Children: Currently limited data suggest an oral dose in children 3 months to 12 years of age of 180 mg/m²/day every 6 hours (720 mg/m²/day). This dose is equivalent to 1 200 mg/day in adults. Do not exceed 200 mg for any individual dose.

Explanatory Note for Symptomatic HIV Disease Dosage Recommendations: The study upon which the dose recommendation is based used an initial dose of 1 200 mg/day for 4 weeks. Therefore, strictly interpreted, data are lacking to support a starting dose of 600 mg/day in symptomatic HIV disease. However, since the frequency of adverse effects is known to be lower at this dosage, a starting dose of 600 mg/day is widely used.

Consideration could be given to an initial dose of 1 200 mg/day for the first 4 weeks of treatment, for advanced HIV disease, if tolerated. The effectiveness of 600 mg/day of zidovudine in decreasing the neurologic dysfunction associated with HIV infection is unknown.

Monitoring of Patients: It appears that hematologic toxicities appear to be related to pretreatment bone marrow reserve and to dose and duration of therapy. Frequent monitoring of hematologic indices is recommended in patients with poor bone marrow reserve, particularly in patients with advanced symptomatic disease, to detect serious anemia or granulocytopenia (see Adverse Effects). Reduction in hemoglobin may occur as early as 2 to 4 weeks, and granulocytopenia usually occurs after 6 to 8 weeks, in patients who experience hematologic toxicity.

In order to manage potential opportunistic infections associated with HIV disease, patients treated with zidovudine should be under close clinical observation. Prompt recognition of infection or toxicities and appropriate management is necessary.

Dose Adjustment: If significant anemia (hemoglobin of <7.5 g/dL or reduction of >25% of baseline) and/or significant granulocytopenia (granulocyte count of <750/mm³ or reduction of >50% from baseline) a dose interruption may be required until some evidence of marrow recovery is observed (see Adverse Effects). Dose modification does not necessarily eliminate the need for transfusion in patients who develop significant anemia.

A reduction in daily dose may be adequate for less severe anemia or granulocytopenia. Gradual increases in dose may be appropriate if marrow recovery occurs, depending on hematologic indices and patient tolerance.

In patients with impaired renal or hepatic function, there is insufficient information to make recommendations about dose adjustment of zidovudine.

Supplied: Each white capsule with blue band, imprinted novo 100, contains: zidovudine 100 mg as a white to off-white powder. Gluten- and tartrazine-free. Bottles of 100.

NOVO-BACLOFEN
Novopharm

Baclofen

Muscle Relaxant—Antispastic

Supplied: 10 mg: Each white, oval-shaped tablet, engraved 10 on scored side and N on the other side, contains: baclofen 10 mg. Gluten- and tartrazine-free. Bottles of 100 and 1 000. Unit dose strips of 100.

20 mg: Each white, capsule-shaped tablet, engraved 20 on scored side and N on the other side, contains: baclofen 20 mg. Gluten- and tartrazine-free. Bottles of 100. Unit dose strips of 100.

NOVO-BENZYDAMINE
Novopharm

Benzydamine HCl

Local Analgesic

Supplied: Each mL of clear yellow-green liquid oral rinse contains: benzydamine HCl 0.15%. Nonmedicinal ingredients: ethanol, FD&C Blue #1, FD&C Yellow #10, flavor natural mint, glycerin, methylparaben, polysorbate 80, propylparaben and water. Bottles of 100, 250 and 1 000 mL.

NOVO-BROMAZEPAM
Novopharm

Bromazepam

Anxiolytic—Sedative

Supplied: 3 mg: Each pink, round tablet, engraved with "novo" on one side and "3" on the other, contains: bromazepam 3 mg. Gluten- and tartrazine-free. Bottles of 100 and 500.

6 mg: Each pale-green, round tablet, engraved with "novo" on one side and "6" on the other, contains: bromazepam 6 mg. Gluten- and tartrazine-free. Bottles of 100 and 500.

NOVO-BUSPIRONE
Novopharm

Buspirone HCl

Anxiolytic

Supplied: Each white, barrel-shaped, compressed single-scored tablet, engraved "N" on one side and "1l0" on the other side, contains: buspirone HCl 10 mg. Nonmedicinal ingredients: colloidal silicon dioxide, dextrin, lactose, magnesium stearate, microcrystalline cellulose and sodium starch glycolate. Gluten- and tartrazine-free. Bottles of 100 and 500.

NOVOCAIN®
Sanofi

Procaine HCl

Local Anesthetic

Pharmacology: Local anesthetics block the generation and the conduction of nerve impulses, presumably by increasing the threshold for electrical excitation in the nerve, by slowing the propagation of the nerve impulse and by reducing the rate of rise of the action potential. In general, the progression of anesthesia is related to the diameter, myelination, and conduction velocity of affected nerve fibres. Clinically, the order of loss of nerve function is as follows: pain, temperature, touch, proprioception, and skeletal muscle tone. Procaine lacks topical anesthetic activity.

The rate of systemic absorption of local anesthetics is dependent upon the total dose and concentration of drug administered, the route of administration, the vascularity of the administration site, and the presence or absence of epinephrine in the anesthetic solution. A dilute concentration of epinephrine (1:200 000 or 5 μg/mL) usually reduces the rate of absorption and plasma concentration of procaine. It also will promote local hemostasis and increase the duration of anesthesia.

Onset of anesthesia with procaine is rapid, the time of onset for sensory block ranging from about 2 to 5 minutes depending upon such factors as the anesthetic technique, the type of block, the concentration of the solution, and the individual patient. The degree of motor blockade produced is dependent on the concentration of the solution.

The duration of anesthesia also varies depending upon the technique and type of block, the concentration, and the individual. Procaine will normally provide anesthesia which is adequate for 1 hour.

Local anesthetics are bound to plasma proteins in varying degrees. Generally, the lower the plasma concentration of drug, the higher the percentage of drug bound to plasma.

Local anesthetics appear to cross the placenta by passive diffusion. The rate and degree of diffusion is governed by the degree of plasma protein binding, the degree of ionization, and the degree of lipid solubility. Fetal/maternal ratios of local anesthetics appear to be inversely related to the degree of plasma protein binding, because only the free, unbound drug is available for placental transfer. The extent of placental transfer is also determined by the degree of ionization and lipid solubility of the drug. Lipid, soluble nonionized drugs readily enter the fetal blood from the maternal circulation.

Depending upon the route of administration, local anesthetics are distributed to some extent to all body tissues, with high concentrations found in highly perfused organs such as the liver, lungs, heart, and brain. Various pharmacokinetic parameters of the local anesthetics can be significantly altered by the presence of hepatic or renal disease, addition of epinephrine, factors affecting urinary pH, renal blood flow, the route of drug administration, and the age of the patient. The in vitro plasma half-life of procaine in adults is 40 ± 9 seconds and in neonates 84 ± 30 seconds.

Procaine is readily absorbed following parenteral administration and is rapidly hydrolyzed by plasma cholinesterase to para-aminobenzoic acid and diethylaminoethanol.

The para-aminobenzoic acid metabolite inhibits the action of the sulfonamides (see Precautions).

For procaine, approximately 90% of the para-aminobenzoic acid metabolite and its conjugates and 33% of the dimethylaminoethanol metabolite are recovered in the urine, while less than 2% of the administered dose is recovered unchanged in the urine.

Indications: Local infiltration and peripheral nerve block.

Contraindications: Sensitivity to PABA esters; sensitivity to procaine.

Warnings: Local anesthetics should only be employed by clinicians who are well versed in diagnosis and management of dose-related toxicity and other acute emergencies which might arise from the block to be employed, and then only after insuring the immediate availability of oxygen, other resuscitative drugs, cardiopulmonary resuscitative equipment, and the personnel resources needed for proper management of toxic reactions and related emergencies. Delay in proper management of dose-related toxicity, underventilation from any cause, and/or altered sensitivity may lead to the development of acidosis, cardiac arrest, and, possibly, death.

Precautions: In general, reactions and complications are best averted by using the minimal effective dosage and lowest concentration of the anesthetic agent. Injections should always be made slowly and with frequent aspiration. When procaine is used with epinephrine, the caution required by any vasopressor drug is in order, especially in cases of patients with hypertension, diabetes mellitus and thyrotoxicosis.

Pregnancy: Animal reproduction studies have not been conducted with procaine. It is not known whether procaine can cause fetal harm when administered to a pregnant woman or can affect reproduction capacity. Procaine should be given to a pregnant woman only if clearly needed and the potential benefits outweigh the risk. This does not exclude the use of procaine at term for obstetrical anesthesia or analgesia.

Labor and Delivery: Local anesthetics rapidly cross the placenta, and when used for paracervical or pudendal block anesthesia, can cause varying degrees of maternal, fetal, and neonatal toxicity. The incidence and degree of toxicity depend upon the procedure performed, the type and amount of drug used, and the technique of drug administration. Adverse reactions in the parturient, fetus, and neonate involve alterations of the CNS, peripheral vascular tone, and cardiac function.

Paracervical or pudendal anesthesia may alter the forces of parturition through changes in uterine contractility or maternal expulsive efforts.

Fetal bradycardia which frequently follows paracervical block may be indicative of high fetal blood concentrations of procaine with resultant fetal acidosis.

Added risk appears to be present in prematurity, toxemia of pregnancy, and fetal distress.

Cases compatible with unintended fetal intracranial injection of local anesthetic solution have been reported following intended paracervical or pudendal block or both. Babies so affected present with unexplained neonatal depression at birth, which correlates with high local anesthetic serum levels, and usually manifest seizures within 6 hours. Prompt use of supportive measures combined with forced urinary excretion of the local anesthetic has been used successfully to manage this complication.

Adverse Effects: Characteristic of those associated with other ester-type local anesthetics. CNS stimulation followed by depression. Cardiac depression. Allergic skin rashes or urticaria may occur.

Dosage: For infiltration anesthesia: 0.25 or 0.5% solution, 350 to 600 mg is generally a safe total single dose. 15 mL of 2% solution diluted with 45 mL of sterile saline make up 60 mL of 0.5% solution (5 mg/mL). 0.5 mL to 1 mL of epinephrine 1:1 000 per 100 mL anesthesia solution may be added for vasoconstrictive effect (1:200 000 to 1:100 000). Peripheral nerve block: 0.5% (up to 200 mL), 1% (up to 100 mL) or 2% solution (up to 50 mL) may be employed. Dilutions may be prepared by taking appropriate volumes of 2% solutions and saline as diluent (see infiltration anesthesia for dilution procedure). Use should usually be limited to cases requiring a small amount (200 to 500 mg) of anesthetic in solution. Epinephrine 1:1 000 (0.5 to 1 mL/100 mL) may be added for vasoconstrictive effect. The usual total dose should not exceed 1 000 mg.

Supplied: Each mL of 2% solution contains: procaine HCl 20 mg in water for injection. Nonmedicinal ingredients: acetone, chlorobutanol anhydrous, sodium bisulfite and sodium chloride. Vials of 30 mL, boxes of 5.

NOVO-CAPTORIL
Novopharm

Captopril

Angiotensin Converting Enzyme Inhibitor

Pharmacology: Captopril is an angiotensin converting enzyme inhibitor which is used in the treatment of hypertension and heart failure.

The mechanism responsible for the action of captopril is not yet fully understood. It appears to lower blood pressure and improve cardiac output in heart failure patients primarily through the suppression of the renin angiotensin-aldosterone system; however, no definite correlation between renin levels and response to the drug has been found. Renin is an enzyme which is synthesized by the kidneys and released into the circulation where it acts on a plasma globulin substrate to produce angiotensin I, a relatively inactive decapeptide. Angiotensin converting enzyme (ACE) then converts angiotensin I to angiotensin II which is a potent endogenous vasoconstrictor substance. Angiotensin II also contributes to sodium and fluid retention by stimulating aldosterone secretion from the adrenal cortex.

The conversion of angiotensin I to angiotensin II is prevented by captopril through the competitive inhibition of ACE, a peptidyldipeptide carboxyhydrolase.

Captopril may also interfere with the degradation of the vasodepressor peptide bradykinin since ACE is identical to bradykininase, the enzyme responsible for its degradation. However, at therapeutic doses the effectiveness of captopril appears to be unrelated to the potentiation of the actions of bradykinin. The higher bradykinin or prostaglandin E_2 levels may play a part in producing the therapeutic effect of captopril, especially in low-renin hypertension.

The inhibition of ACE causes a decrease in plasma angiotensin II which leads to a reduction in aldosterone secretion with subsequent sodium and fluid loss accompanied by small increases in serum potassium. Also, plasma renin activity (PRA) is increased as a result of the loss of negative feedback on renin release caused by reduction in angiotensin II levels.

Novo-Captoril (cont'd)

The antihypertensive effects of captopril persist longer than the demonstrable inhibition of circulating ACE. It is not known if ACE in the vascular endothelium is inhibited for a longer period of time than ACE present in circulating blood.

In hypertensive patients, captopril administration reduces peripheral arterial resistance with either no change or an increase in cardiac output. Captopril administration is followed by an increase in renal blood flow. Glomerular filtration rate usually remains unchanged. In cases where there is rapid decrease of long-standing or severe high blood pressure, the glomerular filtration rate might be transiently reduced.

Maximal reductions of blood pressure are often reached 60 to 90 minutes after oral administration of an individual dose of captopril and the duration of effect appears to be dose related. The reduction in blood pressure may be progressive, therefore several weeks of therapy may be required before the maximum therapeutic effect is achieved. The blood pressure lowering effects of captopril appear to be additive with those of thiazide-type diuretics. However, captopril and beta-blockers have a less than additive effect.

Blood pressure is lowered to approximately the same degree in both standing and supine positions. Orthostatic effects and tachycardia are infrequent, but may occur in volume depleted patients. Rapid increases in blood pressure have not been associated with abrupt withdrawal of captopril.

Captopril significantly decreased systemic vascular resistance (afterload), reduced pulmonary capillary wedge pressure (preload) and pulmonary vascular resistance, increased cardiac output (stroke index) and increased exercise tolerance time (ETT) in patients with heart failure. Clinical improvement has been observed in some patients where the acute hemodynamic effects were minimal.

Studies in rats and cats indicate that captopril does not cross the blood-brain barrier to any significant degree.

Pharmacokinetics: Captopril is rapidly absorbed following oral administration of therapeutic doses and peak blood levels are attained at about 1 hour. Absorption is decreased by 30 to 40% if food is present in the gastrointestinal tract. The average minimal absorption based on carbon-14 labeling is approximately 75%. Over 95% of the absorbed dose is eliminated in the urine in a 24 hour period; 40 to 50% of this is unchanged drug (may be less in patients with congestive heart failure) and most of the remainder is the disulfide dimer of captopril and captopril-cysteine disulfide.

The plasma protein binding of captopril is approximately 30%. The apparent elimination half-life for total radioactivity in the blood is 4.3 ± 0.2 hours. At present an accurate determination of the half-life of unchanged captopril is not possible, however, it is probably about 2 hours.

In patients with normal kidney function, absorption and disposition of a labeled dose are not changed after 7 days of captopril therapy. In patients with impaired kidney function, however, retention of captopril occurs (see Dosage).

The absorption and disposition of a labeled dose of captopril are not altered after 10 days of administration in patients with normal renal function. However, retention of captopril does occur in patients with renal impairment (see dosage).

Indications: In the treatment of essential or renovascular hypertension. It is normally given in combination with other drugs, especially thiazide diuretics. The antihypertensive actions of captopril and thiazides are approximately additive. Consideration should be given to the risk of neutropenia/agranulocytosis whenever captopril is prescribed (see Warnings).

Patients with Normal Renal Function: For the treatment of moderate hypertension, captopril should normally only be prescribed in patients who have not responded to drugs such as thiazides or beta-adrenergic receptor blocking agents or where these agents have produced unacceptable adverse effects. Captopril may be used as an initial agent in patients with severe hypertension or in patients with medical conditions that make them more susceptible to frequent adverse effects of diuretics and/or beta-blockers or in whom these agents are contraindicated.

Patients with Impaired Renal Function: In these patients, particularly those with collagen vascular disease, captopril should only be used in those hypertensive patients who have either developed unacceptable side effects to other drugs or have failed to respond satisfactorily to combination regimens (see Warnings).

Captopril is effective alone; however, it is usually combined with other antihypertensive agents, especially thiazide-type diuretics. The blood pressure lowering effects of captopril appear to be additive with thiazides.

Also indicated in patients with heart failure who have not responded adequately or who cannot be controlled by conventional therapy with diuretics and digitalis. Captopril is intended to be used in conjunction with diuretics and digitalis.

Contraindications: Patients with a history of captopril hypersensitivity.

Warnings: Proteinuria: Total urinary proteins in excess of 1 g/day were observed in approximately 1.2% of the patients receiving captopril. These have primarily occurred in patients with prior renal disease, in patients receiving relatively high doses (more than 150 mg/day), or both. The incidence of proteinuria was 0.5% in patients without evidence of prior renal disease. The parameters of renal function (BUN, serum creatinine) are seldom altered. Proteinuria subsides or clears within 6 months in most cases regardless of whether or not captopril is continued. However, in some patients proteinuria persists. The nephrotic syndrome occurs in approximately one fourth of the proteinuric patients.

Most cases of proteinuria occurred by the eighth month of therapy with captopril, therefore, patients receiving captopril should have urinary protein estimates (dipstick on first morning urine or quantitative 24 hour urine) prior to therapy, at approximately monthly intervals for the first 9 months of treatment, and periodically thereafter. Twenty-four hour quantitative determinations provide greater precision when proteinuria is persistent and/or at low levels. The benefits and risks of continuing captopril should be evaluated for patients in whom proteinuria is increasing or is in excess of 1 g/day.

Membranous glomerulopathy, which may have been drug related, was found in biopsies from proteinuric patients. The patients were not biopsied before treatment, and membranous glomerulopathy has also been associated with hypertension in the absence of captopril treatment; therefore, a causal relationship has not been established.

Neutropenia/Agranulocytosis: Neutropenia (<1 000/mm^3) associated with myeloid hyperplasia has resulted from captopril use. Approximately half of the neutropenic patients developed systemic oral cavity infections or other features of the agranulocytosis syndrome. The risk of neutropenia is dependent on the clinical status of the patient. In clinical trials, the frequency of neutropenia in patients with normal renal function (serum creatinine less than 1.6 mg/dL) and no collagen decrease was 0.02%. In patients with some degree of renal failure (serum creatinine at least 2 mg/dL) but no collagen vascular disease, the risk of neutropenia was 0.20% in clinical trials. In patients with impaired renal function and collagen vascular disease (such as systemic lupus erythematosus or scleroderma), the risk of neutropenia was increased to 3.7%. The use of allopurinol concomitantly with captopril in patients with renal failure has been associated with neutropenia.

Neutropenia has also occurred during clinical experience in patients with heart failure. Approximately half of the reported cases had serum creatinine greater than 1.6 mg/dL and more than 75% of the affected patients were receiving procainamide concomitantly. It appears that the same risk factors for neutropenia are present in heart failure.

The neutropenia was usually detected within the first 3 months after captopril treatment was initiated. In patients with neutropenia, bone marrow examinations consistently showed myeloid hypoplasia, which was frequently accompanied by erythroid hypoplasia and decreased numbers of megakaryocytes (hypoplasic bone marrow and pancytopenia). Anemia and thrombocytopenia were also occasionally observed.

Neutrophils generally returned to normal approximately 2 weeks after captopril was discontinued and serious infections were limited to clinically complex patients. Neutropenia has ended fatally in approximately 13% of the cases; however, almost all of the fatalities occurred in seriously ill patients having collagen vascular disease, renal failure, heart failure or who were receiving immunosuppressant therapy, or a combination of these factors.

Assessment of renal function should always be included in the evaluation of hypertensive or heart failure patients.

White blood cell and differential counts should be performed in patients with impaired renal function prior to the onset of treatment, at approximately 2-week intervals during the first 3 months of treatment, and periodically thereafter.

Captopril should be prescribed only after an assessment of benefit and risk (particularly when there is impaired renal function), and then only with caution in patients with collagen vascular disease or those who are exposed to other drugs which are known to affect white blood cells or the immune response.

All patients receiving captopril treatment should be told to report any signs of infection (for example; sore throat, fever) and if infection is suspected, white blood cell counts should be performed immediately.

Discontinuation of captopril and other drugs has generally resulted in the prompt return of normal white counts. Therefore, upon confirmation of neutropenia (neutrophil count <1 000/mm^3), the physician should withdraw captopril treatment and follow the patient's course closely. Captopril decreases aldosterone production; therefore, in rare cases, serum potassium may be elevated, especially in patients with renal failure (see Precautions, Drug Interactions).

Hypotension: Excessive hypotension, which may have been a consequence of captopril, has been observed in patients with severe salt or volume depletion, such as those treated vigorously with diuretics (i.e. those with severe heart failure) (see Precautions, Drug Interactions).

Transient decreases in mean blood pressure greater than 20% were observed in approximately 50% of the heart failure patients with either normal or low blood pressure. This transient hypotension may occur after any of the first few doses and may result in either no symptoms or brief mild lightheadedness. In rare instances, this hypotension has been associated with arrhythmia or defects in conduction. In 3 to 5% of patients with heart failure, hypotension was the reason for the discontinuation of captopril treatment.

In light of the potential for decrease in blood pressure, captopril treatment should be initiated under close medical supervision in these patients. The hypotensive effect may be minimized with a low starting dose (see Dosage). Close supervision is recommended for the first 2 weeks of treatment and whenever the dose of captopril or diuretic is increased. These considerations can also be applied to patients with ischemic heart disease or cerebrovascular disease in whom a drastic reduction of blood pressure may precipitate myocardial infarction or cerebrovascular accident. The hypotension itself is not an indication to withdraw captopril therapy. Persistant or troublesome associated symptoms are usually relieved by a reduction in the captopril or diuretic dose.

Precautions: Impaired Renal Function: Following reduction of blood pressure with captopril, some hypertensive patients with renal disease, particularly those with severe renal artery stenosis, have developed increases in BUN and serum creatinine. A reduction in the captopril dosage and/or discontinuation of the diuretic may be required. For some of these patients, normalizing the blood pressure and maintenance of adequate renal perfusion may not be possible.

During long-term therapy with captopril, approximately 20% of the heart failure patients develop stable elevations of BUN and serum creatinine of more than 20% above normal or baseline levels. Less than 5% of patients, generally those with severe pre-existing renal disease, have had to terminate captopril treatment because of progressively increasing creatinine. Subsequent improvement is probably dependent on the severity of the underlying renal disease (see Pharmacology, Dosage and Adverse Effects).

Impaired Liver Function: Increases in liver enzymes and/or serum bilirubin, incidences of cholestatic jaundice and hepatocellular injury with or without secondary cholestasis have been reported in patients without pre-existing liver abnormalities while on captopril treatment.

Usually, the changes were reversible upon termination of treatment. If a patient has any unaccountable symptoms while taking captopril, especially in the first weeks or months of therapy, a full set of liver enzyme tests and other required tests should be performed. Withdrawal of captopril should be considered when felt to be necessary.

No proper investigations have been carried out in patients with cirrhosis and/or liver dysfunction. Captopril should be used with particular care in patients with pre-existent liver abnormalities. In these patients, a baseline liver function test should be performed prior to the administration of captopril. Response and metabolic effects of these patients should be watched closely.

Valvular Stenosis: Patients with aortic stenosis may theoretically be at particular risk of decreased coronary perfusion when treated with vasodilators since they do not develop as much reduction in afterload.

Surgery/Anesthesia: Captopril will block angiotensin II formation secondary to compensatory renin release in patients undergoing major surgery or during anesthesia with agents that produce hypotension. If hypotension occurs and is considered to be due to this mechanism, it can be corrected by volume expansion.

Pregnancy: In rabbits, captopril was embryocidal at doses 2 to 70 times (on a mg/kg basis) the maximum recommended human dose and had a low frequency of craniofacial malformations. The particularly marked decrease in blood pressure caused by captopril in this species was most probably responsible for the embryocidal effect in rabbits.

Captopril was also embryocidal in sheep at doses similar to those administered to humans.

Neonatal survival was reduced when captopril was administered continuously to pregnant rats during gestation and lactation at 400 times the recommended human dose.

In hamsters, rats and rabbits, no teratogenic effects (malformations) have been observed following large doses of captopril.

Since captopril crosses the placenta and there are no adequate and well controlled studies in pregnant women, it should only be used during pregnancy if the potential benefit justifies the potential risk to the fetus. Captopril has been found in cord blood.

Post-marketing experience with ACE inhibitors indicates that there is a danger of fetal hypotension, reduced birth weight, reduced renal perfusion or anuria in the fetus exposed in utero to ACE inhibitors in the second or third trimesters of pregnancy. Oligohydramnios in the mother has occurred, probably as a manifestation of reduced renal function in the fetus. Complications related to prematurity such as patent ductus arteriosus have occurred in relation to the use of ACE inhibitors by the mother, but it has not been determined whether they are caused by ACE inhibition, maternal hypertension or the underlying prematurity.

Any neonate exposed to captopril in utero should be kept under close supervision and monitored for oliguria, hypotension and hyperkalemia. If necessary, appropriate medical measures should be taken in terms of supporting blood pressure and renal perfusion and should include administration of fluids and vasopressors. Captopril can be removed from the circulation of the newborn by peritoneal dialysis and theoretically by exchange transfusion although the latter procedure has never been performed.

Lactation: The concentrations of captopril present in human milk are about 1% of the maternal blood concentrations after oral administration. Since the effect of low levels of captopril on nursing infants has not been determined, caution should be exercised whenever captopril is administered to nursing women and, in general, nursing should be interrupted.

Children: The safety and effectiveness of captopril have not been established in children. However, there is limited experience with captopril in children aged 2 months to 15 years with secondary hypertension and varying degrees of renal insufficiency. The dosage on a weight basis was comparable to those used in adults. Captopril should only be used in children if other measures for controlling blood pressure have failed to be effective.

Information for the Patient: All patients receiving captopril treatment should be told to report any sign of infection (for example; sore throat, fever) which may be indicative of neutropenia or of progressive edema which may be associated with proteinuria and nephrotic syndrome.

All patients should also be cautioned that because of the reduction in fluid volume, excessive perspiration and dehydration may lead to an excessive fall in blood pressure. Other causes of volume depletion, such as diarrhea or vomiting may also lead to a drop in blood pressure; patients should be advised to consult with their physician.

Patients should be advised to immediately contact their doctor if they experience any symptoms that could be associated with liver dysfunction. These include viral-like symptoms during the first weeks to months of therapy (e.g. fever, malaise, muscle pain, rash or adenopathy which are possible signs of hypersensitivity reactions) or abdominal pain, nausea, vomiting, loss of appetite, jaundice, itching or any other unaccountable symptom which may occur while the patient is receiving treatment.

Patients should be warned against interrupting or discontinuing captopril therapy without the advice of their physician.

Patients being treated for severe congestive heart failure should be cautioned to increase their physical activity slowly.

Patients should be told that captopril should be taken 1 hour before meals (see Dosage).

Drug Interactions: Patients on Diuretic Therapy: Patients who are receiving diuretics and especially those in whom diuretic therapy was recently instituted, as well as those on severe dietary salt restriction or dialysis, may experience a precipitous reduction of blood pressure within the first hour of the intial dose of captopril (see Warnings).

The possibility of hypotensive effects can be minimized by either discontinuing diuretic treatment or increasing salt intake approximately 1 week prior to the start of captopril treatment. Alternatively, medical supervision should be provided for at least 1 hour after the initial dose. If hypotension does occur, the patient should be placed in a supine position and if necessary should receive an i.v infusion of normal saline. This transient hypotensive response is not a contraindication to further doses which can be given without difficulty once the blood pressure has increased following volume expansion.

Agents Having Vasodilator Activity: No data are available on the effect of the concomitant use of other vasodilators in patients with heart failure receiving captopril. Therefore, nitroglycerin or other nitrates (such as those used in the treatment of angina) or other drugs having vasodilator activity should be discontinued, if possible, before captopril treatment is initiated. If these agents are resumed during captopril treatment, they should be administered cautiously and possibly at a lower dosage.

Agents Causing Renin Release: Antihypertensive agents that cause the release of renin will augment the effects of captopril. Diuretics (such as thiazides), for example may activate the renin-angiotensin-aldosterone system.

Agents Affecting Sympathetic Activity: In patients receiving captopril alone or with diruretics, the sympathetic nervous system may be especially important in supporting blood pressure. Therefore, caution should be exercised when using agents which affect sympathetic activity (such as ganglionic blocking agents or adrenergic neuron blocking agents). Beta-adrenergic blocking agents enhance the antihypertensive effect of captopril, however, the overall response is less than additive.

Special caution is necessary in patients with heart failure since sympathetic stimulation is a vital component supporting circulatory function and with beta-blockade inhibition there is always the potential risk of further depression of myocardial contractility.

Agents Increasing Serum Potassium: Since captopril decreases aldosterone production, serum potassium levels may be elevated. Potassium-sparing diuretics, such as spironolactone, triamterene, amiloride, or potassium supplements may significantly increase serum potassium and should therefore be given with caution and only for documented hypokalemia. Salt substitutes containing potassium should be used cautiously also.

Inhibitors of Endogenous Prostaglandin Synthesis: The antihypertensive effect of captopril may be reduced by indomethacin, especially in cases of low renin hypertension. Other nonsteroidal anti-inflammatory agents, such as ASA, may also produce this effect.

The blood pressure lowering effect of captopril and beta-blockers are less than additive.

The use of allopurinol concomitantly with captopril in patients with renal failure has been associated with neutropenia.

The concomitant use of procainamide and captopril in patients with heart failure has also been associated with neutropenia.

Drug/Laboratory Test Interactions: Captopril may cause false-positive urine tests for acetone, dipstick tests and ketones.

Adverse Effects: Reported incidences are based on clinical trials involving approximately 7 000 treated patients.

Renal: Approximately 1% of patients developed proteinuria (see Warnings).

Each of the following has been reported in approximately 1 to 2 of 1 000 patients and are of uncertain relationship to drug use: renal insufficiency, renal failure, polyuria, oliguria and urinary frequency.

Hematologic: Neutropenia/agranulocytosis has occurred (see Warnings). Anemia, thrombocytopenia and pancytopenia have also been reported.

Dermatologic: Rash, often with pruritus, and sometimes with fever and eosinophilia, occurred in approximately 8.5% of patients with normal renal function and 13% of patients with prior evidence of renal impairment, usually during the first 4 weeks of therapy. It was also found to be dose related since it occurred in 7% of patients at doses of 150 mg or less per day. It is usually maculopapular but rarely urticarial. The rash is usually mild and disappears within a few days of dosage reduction, short-term treatment with an antihistaminic agent and/or discontinuing therapy; remission may occur even if captopril is continued. Pruritus, without rash occurs in about 2 of 100 patients. Between 7 and 10% of patients with skin rash have shown an eosinophilia and/or positive ANA titers. A reversible associated pemphigoid-like lesion and photosensitivity have also been reported.

Allergic: Angioedema of the face, mucous membranes of the mouth, or of the extremities has been observed in approximately 1 of 1 000 patients and is reversible on discontinuance of captopril therapy. Serum sickness and bronchospasm have been reported. One case of laryngeal edema has also been reported.

Cardiovascular: Hypotension may occur (see Precautions, Drug Interactions for discussion of hypotension on initiation of captopril therapy).

Tachycardia, chest pain and palpitations have each been observed in approximately 1 of 100 patients.

Angina pectoris, myocardial infarction, Raynaud's syndrome and congestive heart failure have each occurred in 2 to 3 of 1 000 patients. Flushing or pallor has been reported in 0.2 to 0.5% of the patients.

Alterations in Taste: Approximately 2% of patients receiving 150 mg or less per day and 7% of patients receiving an excess of 150 mg/day developed a diminution or loss of taste perception. Taste impairment is reversible and usually self-limited to 2 or 3 months, even with continued drug administration. Weight loss may be associated with the loss of taste.

The following adverse effects have been reported in 0.5 to 2% of patients:

Gastrointestinal: gastric irritation, abdominal pain, nausea, vomiting, diarrhea, anorexia and constipation, aphthous ulcers and peptic ulcer.

Nervous System: dizziness, headache, malaise, fatigue, insomnia and paresthesia.

Other: dry mouth, dyspnea, cough, alopecia, impotence, loss of libido, disturbed vision and itching and/or dry eyes.

Other adverse reactions have occurred since marketing of the drug. In many instances, the effect cannot be directly linked to captopril use with certainty.

General: asthenia, gynecomastia.

Cardiovascular: cardiac arrest, cerebrovascular accident, syncope.

Dermatologic: bullous pemphigus.

Gastrointestinal: pancreatitis, glossitis.

Hematologic: anemia, including aplastic and hemolytic.

Hepatobiliary: hepatitis, including rare incidences of necrosis, cholestasis (see Precautions).

Metabolic: symptomatic hyponatremia.

Musculoskeletal: myalgia, myasthenia.

Nervous/Psychiatric: ataxia, confusion, depression, nervousness, somnolence.

Respiratory: bronchospasm, eosinophilic pneumonitis, rhinitis.

Special Senses: blurred vision.

As with other ACE inhibitors, a syndrome has occurred which includes: fever, myalgia, arthralgia, rash or other dermatologic manifestations, eosinophilia and an elevated ESR. These symptoms have usually disappeared upon withdrawal of the drug.

Altered Laboratory Findings: Elevations of liver enzymes and/or serum bilirubin have been noted in a few patients (see Precautions) but no causal relationship to captopril use has been established. Rare cases of cholestatic jaundice and hepatocellular injury with or without secondary cholestasis have been reported in association with captopril administration.

A transient elevation of BUN and serum creatinine may occur, especially in patients who are volume-depleted or who have renovascular hypertension. In instances of rapid reduction of longstanding or severely elevated blood pressure, the glomerular filtration rate may decrease transiently, also resulting in transient rises in serum creatinine and BUN.

Small increases in the serum potassium concentration frequently occur, especially in patients with renal impairment (see Precautions).

Overdose: Symptoms and Treatment: In the event of overdosage, treatment should be symptomatic.

The primary concern should be the correction of hypotension. The treatment of choice for the restoration of blood pressure is volume expansion with an i.v. infusion of normal saline.

Hemodialysis may be used to remove captopril from the general circulation.

Dosage: Captopril should be taken 1 hour before meals. Dosage must be individualized.

Hypertension: Initiation of therapy requires consideration of recent antihypertensive drug treatment, the extent of blood pressure elevation, salt restriction and other clinical circumstances. If possible, the patient's previous antihypertensive drug regimen should be discontinued 1 week before treatment with captopril is initiated. If this is not possible, particularly in severe hypertension, the diuretic should be continued.

The initial dose is 25 mg b.i.d. or t.i.d. The dosage may be increased to 50 mg b.i.d. or t.i.d. if satisfactory reduction of blood pressure is not achieved after 1 to 2 weeks.

The dose should not usually exceed 50 mg t.i.d.; therefore, a modest dose of thiazide-type diuretic (such as hydrochlorothiazide 25 mg daily) should be added if the blood pressure is not satisfactorily controlled after another 1 or 2 weeks of therapy (and the patient is not already taking a diuretic). The

Novo-Captoril (cont'd)

dose of diuretic may be increased at 1 to 2 week intervals until its highest usual antihypertensive dose is reached.

Captopril therapy should be initiated under close medical supervision in patients already receiving a diuretic (see Warnings and Precautions regarding hypotension). The dosage and titration of captopril should be as outlined above.

In patients with severe hypertension, the dose of captopril may be increased to 100 mg b.i.d. or t.i.d. and then if necessary to 150 mg b.i.d. or t.i.d. (while continuing diuretic therapy) if further reductions in blood pressure are required. The usual dose range is 25 to 150 mg b.i.d. or t.i.d. The maximum daily dose should not exceed 450 mg.

For patients with accelerated or malignant hypertension, when temporary discontinuation of current antihypertensive therapy is not practical or desirable, or when prompt titration to more normotensive blood pressure levels is indicated, diuretic should be continued but other concurrent antihypertensive medication stopped and captopril dosage promptly initiated at 25 mg t.i.d., under close medical supervision. The daily dose of captopril may be increased every 24 hours under continuous medical supervision when necessitated by the patient's condition until a satisfactory blood pressure response is obtained or until the maximum dose is reached. The addition of a more potent diuretic, such as furosemide may also be indicated in this regimen.

Beta-blockers may also be used in conjunction with captopril therapy (see Precautions, Drug Interactions), however, the effects of these 2 drugs are less than additive.

Heart Failure: Initiation of therapy requires consideration of recent diuretic therapy and the possibility of severe salt or volume depletion. A starting dose of 6.25 or 12.5 mg t.i.d. may minimize the magnitude or duration of the hypotensive effect in patients with either normal or low blood pressure who have been vigorously treated with diuretics and who may be hyponatremic and/or hypovolemic. Titration to the usual daily dosage can then occur over the next several days in these patients.

The usual initial daily dosage is 25 mg t.i.d. for most patients. After a dose of 50 mg t.i.d. is reached, further increases in dosage should be delayed for at least 2 weeks where possible in order to determine if a satisfactory response has occurred. A satisfactory clinical improvement has occurred in most patients at 50 or 100 mg t.i.d. A maximum dose of 450 mg daily should not be exceeded.

Captopril is to be used in conjunction with a diuretic and digitalis. Therapy must be initiated under very close medical supervision.

Dosage Adjustments in Renal Impairment: Captopril is excreted primarily by the kidneys. Therefore, the excretion rate of this drug is reduced in patients with impaired renal function. These patients require longer to reach steady-state levels and will attain higher steady-state levels for a given daily dose than patients with normal renal function. These patients may therefore respond to smaller or less frequent doses.

Accordingly, the initial dosage of captopril should be reduced for patients with significant renal impairment. Titration should be quite slow (1 to 2 week intervals) in these patients and smaller increments should be used. Once the desired therapeutic effect has been achieved, the dose should be back-titrated slowly in order to determine the minimum effective dose. When concomitant diuretic therapy is required in patients with severe renal impairment, a loop diuretic (such as furosemide) is preferred over a thiazide diuretic.

Table I based on theoretical considerations may be useful as a guide to minimize drug accumulation.

Table I—Novo-Captoril

Dosage Adjustments in Renal Impairment

Creatinine Clearance (mL/min/1.73 m²)	Dosage Interval (Hours)
5-7	72-108 (3 to 4.5 days)
8-19	48-72
20-34	24-48
35-75	12-24
>75	8

Captopril is removed by hemodialysis.

Supplied: 12.5 mg: Each white, caplet-shaped, single scored, compressed tablet, engraved novo on one side, 12.5 on the opposite side, contains: captopril 12.5 mg. Gluten- and tartrazine-free. Bottles of 100 and 500. Unit dose strips of 100.

25 mg: Each white, square-shaped, compressed tablet, quadrisect scored on one side, engraved novo over 25 contains: captopril 25 mg. Gluten- and tartrazine-free. Bottles of 100 and 1 000. Unit dose strips of 100.

50 mg: Each white, oval-shaped, bi-convex, single scored, compressed tablet, engraved novo on one side, 50 on the other, contains: captopril 50 mg. Gluten- and tartrazine-free. Bottles of 100 and 500. Unit dose strips of 100.

100 mg: Each white, oval-shaped, bi-convex, single scored, compressed tablet, engraved novo on one side, 100 on the other side, contains: captopril 100 mg. Gluten- and tartrazine-free. Bottles of 100.

Store between 15 to 30°C in tightly closed bottles. Protect product from moisture. Store unit dose packages between 15 to 25°C and protect from high humidity.

NOVO-CARBAMAZ ℞

Novopharm

Carbamazepine

Anticonvulsant

Supplied: Each white, round, flat tablet, quadrisect on one side and engraved N on the other side, contains: carbamazepine 200 mg. Gluten- and tartrazine-free. Bottles of 100 and 500. Unit dose strips of 100. Protect from heat and humidity.

NOVO-CHOLAMINE ℞
NOVO-CHOLAMINE LIGHT ℞

Novopharm

Cholestyramine Resin

Antidiarrheal—Antihypercholesterolemic

Pharmacology: Cholesterol is believed to be the sole precursor of bile acids which are secreted into the intestines during normal digestion. A major portion of the bile acids is absorbed from the intestinal tract and, via the enterohepatic circulation, is then returned to the liver. In normal serum only very small amounts of bile acids are found.

Cholestyramine resin absorbs and combines with the bile acids in the intestine to form an insoluble complex. This is then excreted in the feces. As a result, bile acids are partially removed from the enterohepatic circulation by preventing their absorption.

Due to cholestyramine resin administration, the increased fecal loss of bile acids leads to an increased oxidation of cholesterol to bile acids, a decrease in beta lipoprotein or low density lipoprotein plasma levels and a decrease in serum cholesterol levels. Although cholestyramine resin causes an increase in hepatic synthesis of cholesterol in man, plasma, cholesterol levels fall.

Indications: As adjunctive therapy to diet and exercise for the reduction of elevated serum cholesterol in patients with primary hypercholesterolemia (elevated low density lipoproteins). Such a reduction of serum cholesterol may reduce the risks of atherosclerotic coronary artery disease and myocardial infarction. In patients with combined hypercholesterolemia and hypertriglyceridemia, cholestyramine resin may be useful to lower elevated cholesterol but it is not indicated where hypertriglyceridemia is the abnormality of most concern.

Cholestyramine resin is indicated as a symptomatic control of bile acid induced diarrhea as a result of short bowel syndrome.

Cholestyramine resin is also indicated for the relief of pruritus which accompanies partial biliary obstruction.

Patients should be placed on a standard cholesterol-lowering diet at least equivalent to the American Heart Association (AHA) step 1 Diet, which should be continued during treatment. If appropriate, a program of weight control and physical exercise should be implemented.

Contraindications: In patients with complete biliary obstruction where bile is not excreted into the intestine. It is also contraindicated in those individuals who have shown hypersensitivity to any of its components and in those individuals who have phenylketonuria (sensitivity to phenylalanine in aspartame, which is a sweetener in both Novo-Cholamine and Novo-Cholamine Light).

Warnings: Cholestyramine resin should never be ingested in its dry form. Before taking, always admix with water or other fluids.

Since cholestyramine resin may bind other drugs given concurrently, to avoid impeding their absorption, patients should take other drugs at least 1 hour before or 4 to 6 hours after cholestyramine resin (or at as great an interval as possible).

Pregnancy: Cholestyramine resin is not expected to cause fetal harm when administered during pregnancy in recommended dosages since it is not absorbed systemically. There are, however, no adequate and well-controlled studies in pregnant women and, the known interference with absorption of fat-soluble vitamins may be harmful to the fetus even in the presence of supplementation.

Lactation: When administering cholestyramine resin to a nursing mother, caution should be exercised. Poor vitamin absorption as described in the Pregnancy section may have an effect on nursing infants.

Children: The effect of cholestyramine resin in maintaining lowered cholesterol levels in pediatric patients and long-term effects of drug administration has not yet been determined. A dosage schedule in children has not yet been established.

Geriatrics: Appropriate studies on the relationship of age to the effects of cholestyramine have not been performed in the geriatric population. However, patients over 60 years of age may be more likely to experience gastrointestinal side effects, as well as adverse nutritional effects.

Carcinogenesis and Mutagenesis: Cholestyramine resin was used as a tool in studies conducted in rats to determine the role of various intestinal factors (e.g., fat, bile salts and microbial flora). In cholestyramine treated rats, the incidence of intestinal tumors induced by potent carcinogens was greater than in control rats. The significance of this observation is not evident, as the results in one study indicated a statistically insignificant increase in tumor incidence whereas a more recent study did not demonstrate any presence of tumors following cholestyramine administration. Therefore, the relevance of these studies conducted in rats to clinical use of cholestyramine resin has not been determined.

Precautions: An attempt should be made to control serum cholesterol by appropriate dietary regimen, weight reduction, and the treatment of any underlying disorder which might be the cause of hypercholesterolemia before instituting therapy with cholestyramine resin. Serum cholesterol and triglyceride concentration should be determined prior to and regularly during cholestyramine therapy. During the first month of cholestyramine resin therapy a favorable trend in cholesterol should occur. In order to sustain cholesterol reduction, therapy should be continued.

With chronic use of cholestyramine resin a tendency of increased bleeding due to hypoprothrombinemia associated with vitamin K deficiency may occur. Parenteral vitamin K_1 will usually promptly rectify this and recurrences can be prevented by oral administration of vitamin K_1. Long-term administration of cholestyramine resin has been reported to cause a reduction of serum or red cell folate. In these cases, supplementation of folic acid should be considered.

Since cholestyramine resin is a chloride form of anion exchange resin there is a possibility that prolonged use may produce hyperchloremic acidosis. In younger and smaller patients where the relative dosage may be higher, this would especially be true.

Pre-existing constipation may occur or be worsened with use of cholestyramine resin. In such cases, dosage should be reduced or discontinued. Aggravation of hemorrhoids and fecal impaction may occur. In those patients with clinically symptomatic coronary artery disease, every effort should be made to avert severe constipation and its inherent problems.

Studies have suggested that control of elevated cholesterol and triglycerides may not lessen the danger of cardiovascular disease and mortality, although incidence of nonfatal myocardial infarctions may be decreased.

Laboratory Tests: Serum cholesterol and serum triglyceride determinations should be made prior to initiation of therapy with cholestyramine and at periodic intervals during therapy to confirm efficacy and to determine that a positive response is maintained.

Drug Interactions: **Because cholestyramine resin may bind other drugs given concurrently, patients should take other drugs at least 1 hour before or 4 to 6 hours after cholestyramine resin (or at as great an interval as possible) to avoid impeding their absorption.**

Since cholestyramine is the chloride form of anion-exchange resin, it is capable of binding to a number of drugs in the gastrointestinal tract and may delay or reduce their absorption. Acidic drugs are strongly absorbed to cholestyramine, neutral and basic drugs may be nonspecifically bound.

Patients should be instructed to allow as long a time interval as possible between ingestion of other drugs and cholestyramine resin, however separation of doses may not prevent interaction with drugs that undergo enterohepatic circulation (see Warnings).

Drug Interactions with Other Lipid-Lowering Drugs: Concomitant therapy with other lipid-lowering agents should be approached with caution as information from controlled clinical trials is limited.

HMG-CoA Reductase Inhibitors: The cholesterol-lowering effects of cholestyramine and HMG-CoA reductase inhibitors (i.e., lovastatin, simvastatin, pravastatin, etc.) are additive. Cholestyramine significantly reduced the bioavailability of fluvastatin and pravastatin when the HMG-CoA reductase inhibitor was given 1 hour before and up to 4 hours after the cholestyramine dose.

When fluvastatin was administered concomitantly 2 to 4 hours after cholestyramine, fluvastatin decreases of more than 50% for the fluvastatin AUC and 50 to 80% for the fluvastatin C_{max} occurred. However, administration of fluvastatin 4 hours after cholestyramine resulted in a clinically significant additive effect in reducing total-cholesterol and LDL-cholesterol compared with that achieved with either component drug.

Fibric Acid Derivatives and Niacin: Cholestyramine had little effect on the bioavailability of gemfibrozil, clofibrate, fenofibrate and niacin.

Probucol: The combination of cholestyramine and probucol demonstrated an additive effect with no additional side effects.

Drug Interactions with Other Drugs: Antibiotics: Concurrent use with cholestyramine may result in binding of medications such as oral tetracyclines and oral penicillin G, thus decreasing their absorption; an interval of several hours between administration of cholestyramine and any of these medications is recommended.

Cholestyramine has been shown to bind oral vancomycin significantly when used concurrently, resulting in decreased stool concentrations and marked reduction in antibacterial activity of vancomycin. Concurrent use is not recommended; patients should be advised to take oral vancomycin and cholestyramine several hours apart.

Anticoagulants: Concurrent use may significantly increase the anticoagulant effect as a result of depletion of vitamin K, but cholestyramine may also bind with oral anticoagulants in the gastrointestinal tract and reduce their effects; administration at least 6 hours before cholestyramine and adjustment of anticoagulant dosage based on frequent prothrombin-time determinations are recommended.

Antihypertensives and Cardiac Glycosides: Antihypertensives (i.e., propranolol) concomitantly administered with cholestyramine may interact depending on the amounts of each component drug administered.

Cholestyramine may reduce the half-life of these medications by decreasing intestinal reabsorption and enterohepatic circulation; caution is recommended, especially when cholestyramine is withdrawn from a patient who was stabilized on the digitalis glycoside while receiving cholestyramine, because of the potential for serious toxicity; some clinicians recommend administration of cholestyramine approximately 8 hours after the digitalis glycoside.

Anti-inflammatory Agents: Concurrent use of anti-inflammatory agents such as phenylbutazone or ASA with cholestyramine may retard or reduce absorption of the anti-inflammatory agents, depending on the amount of each component drug administered.

Chenodiol or Ursodiol: The effect may be decreased when chenodiol or ursodiol is used concurrently with cholestyramine, which binds these medications and decreases their absorption and also tends to increase cholesterol saturation of bile.

Diuretics: Depending on the amounts of cholestyramine or diuretic (i.e., thiazides) administered, concomitant administration may reduce plasma thiazide levels.

Fat-Soluble Vitamins: Cholestyramine may interfere with absorption of fat-soluble vitamins as result of its interference with fat absorption; supplemental vitamin A and D in water-miscible or parenteral form are recommended in patients receiving cholestyramine for prolonged periods; supplemental vitamin K may be required in some patients who develop bleeding tendencies.

Folic Acid: Concurrent use with cholestyramine may interfere with absorption of folic acid; folic acid supplementation is recommended in patients receiving cholestyramine for prolonged periods.

Thyroid Hormones: Concurrent use with cholestyramine may decrease the effects of thyroid hormones by binding and delaying or preventing absorption; an interval of 4 to 5 hours between administration of the two medications and regular monitoring of thyroid function tests are recommended.

Adverse Effects: Constipation is the most common adverse reaction. Predisposing factors for most complaints of constipation are high dose and increased age (more than 60 years old), when cholestyramine is used as a cholesterol lowering agent. Conventional therapy controls most instances of constipation which are usually mild and transient. A temporary decrease in dosage or discontinuance of therapy may be required by some patients.

Less frequently reported adverse reactions: abdominal discomfort, flatulence, nausea, vomiting, diarrhea, heartburn, anorexia, indigestive feeling and steatorrhea, bleeding tendencies due to hypoprothrombinemia (vitamin K deficiency) as well as vitamin A (one case of night blindness reported) and D deficiencies, hyperchloremic acidosis in children, osteoporosis, rash and irritation of the skin, tongue and perianal area.

In patients to whom cholestyramine resin has been given, occasional calcified material has been observed in the biliary tree, including calcification of the gallbladder. This may be a manifestation of the liver disease and not related to drug therapy.

Other adverse reactions (not necessarily drug related) include: Gastrointestinal: gastrointestinal-rectal bleeding, black stools, hemorrhoidal bleeding, bleeding from known duodenal ulcer, dysphagia, hiccups, ulcer attack, sour taste, pancreatitis, rectal pain, diverticulitis.

Hematologic: increased prothrombin time, ecchymosis, anemia, dental bleeding.

Hypersensitivity: urticaria, asthma, wheezing, shortness of breath.

Metabolic and Electrolyte Effects: Hyperchloremic acidoses and increased urinary calcium excretion have been seen with high doses or usual doses in small patients or children. Increased urinary excretion of calcium may lead to osteoporosis.

Musculoskeletal: backache, muscle and joint pains, arthritis.

Neurologic: headache, anxiety, vertigo, dizziness, fatigue, tinnitus, syncope, drowsiness, femoral nerve pain, paresthesia.

Eye: uveitis.

Renal: hematuria, dysuria, burnt odor of urine, diuresis.

Overdose: Symptoms and Treatment: There have been no reported overdosages with cholestyramine resin. Should overdosage occur the chief potential problem would be obstruction of the gastrointestinal tract. Treatment would be determined by the location of such potential obstruction, the degree of obstruction, and the presence or absence of normal gut motility.

Dosage: Cholestyramine resin should not be taken in its dry form. To avoid accidental inhalation or esophageal distress or intestinal blockage, the drug should be mixed with at least 120 or 180 mL of water or other fluids before being ingested. See Preparation instructions. Patients should be placed on a standard cholesterol-lowering diet at least equivalent to the American Heart Association (AHA) step 1 Diet, which should be continued during treatment. If appropriate, a program of weight control and physical exercise should be implemented.

It is desirable to begin all therapy with one dose of cholestyramine resin daily, in order to familiarize the patient with cholestyramine resin and to minimize gastrointestinal side effects. Dosage is then increased within 1 day or 2 to the desired level for effective control.

Motivation of the patient to continue the prescribed regimen in spite of gastrointestinal problems is important. Physician encouragement and supervision are essential for successful management.

The recommended adult dose is 4 g of cholestyramine resin, 1 to 6 times daily. Dosage may be adjusted as required to meet the patient's needs. A pediatric dosage schedule has not been established.

Cholesterol levels should be monitored periodically and consideration should be given to reducing the dosage of cholestyramine resin if cholesterol levels fall below the targeted range, such as that recommended by the Second Report of the U.S. National Cholesterol Education Program (NCEP).

Preparation: Place the contents of 1 packet (4 g of anhydrous cholestyramine) or 1 level scoop (4 g of anhydrous cholestyramine) of Novo-Cholamine Powder on the surface of 120 to 180 mL of water or noncarbonated beverage such as milk or fruit juice. After 1 to 2 minutes mix thoroughly by stirring.

Novo-Cholamine may also be mixed in thin soups or pulpy fruits with a high moisture content.

In calculating dosages, 1 packet or level scoop of Novo-Cholamine (sweetening agents; sucrose and aspartame) contains 9 g of powder which is equivalent to 4 g of anhydrous cholestyramine resin or 1 packet of Novo-Cholamine Light (sweetening agent, aspartame) contains 5.5 g of powder which is equivalent to 4 g of anhydrous cholestyramine resin.

Supplied: Novo-Cholamine: Each packet (1 dose) of oral suspension powder contains: anhydrous cholestyramine resin 4 g. Nonmedicinal ingredients: aspartame and sucrose. Boxes of 30 packets and in cans of 378 g.

Novo-Cholamine Light: Each packet (1 dose) of oral suspension powder contains: anhydrous cholestyramine resin 4 g. Nonmedicinal ingredients: aspartame. Boxes of 30 packets and in cans of 231 g.

Store between 15 and 30°C.

NOVO-CIMETINE Ⓟ

Novopharm

Cimetidine

Histamine H_2 Receptor Antagonist

Supplied: 200 mg: Each pale green, round, scored, film-coated tablet, engraved novo over 200, contains: cimetidine 200 mg. Gluten- and tartrazine-free. Bottles of 100 and 500.

300 mg: Each pale green, round, scored, film-coated tablet, engraved novo over 300, contains: cimetidine 300 mg. Gluten- and tartrazine-free. Bottles of 100, 500 and 1 000. Unit dose strips of 100.

400 mg: Each pale green, oval, scored, film-coated tablet, engraved novo and 400 on opposite sides, contains: cimetidine 400 mg. Gluten- and tartrazine-free. Bottles of 100, 500 and 1 000. Unit dose strips of 100.

600 mg: Each pale green, oval, scored, film-coated tablet, engraved novo and 600 on opposite sides, contains: cimetidine 600 mg. Gluten- and tartrazine-free. Bottles of 100 and 500. Unit dose strips of 100.

800 mg: Each pale green, oval, scored, film-coated tablet, engraved novo and 800 on opposite sides, contains: cimetidine 800 mg. Gluten- and tartrazine-free. Bottles of 100 and 500.

NOVO-CLOBAZAM Ⓟ

Novopharm

Clobazam

Anticonvulsant

Supplied: Each white to off-white, round, scored tablet, engraved N on one side and 1/0 on the other side, contains: clobazam 10 mg. Nonmedicinal ingredients: colloidal silicon dioxide, lactose, magnesium stearate, sodium starch glycolate, starch and talc. Blister packs of 30.

New Product 1998

NOVO-CLOBETASOL Ⓟ

Novopharm

Clobetasol Propionate

Topical Anti-inflammatory Steroid

Supplied: Cream: Each g of white cream contains: clobetasol propionate 0.05% w/w. Tubes of 15 and 50 g.

Ointment: Each g of white ointment contains: clobetasol propionate 0.05% w/w. Tubes of 15 and 50 g.

NOVO-CLONIDINE Ⓟ

Novopharm

Clonidine HCl

Antihypertensive

Supplied: 0.1 mg: Each round, scored, white tablet, engraved no/vo on one side and 0.1 on the other side, contains: clonidine HCl 0.1 mg. Gluten- and tartrazine-free. Bottles of 100 and 500.

0.2 mg: Each round, scored, orange tablet, engraved no/vo on one side and 0.2 on the other side, contains: clonidine HCl 0.2 mg. Gluten- and tartrazine-free. Bottles of 100 and 500.

NOVO-CLOPAMINE ℞
Novopharm

Clomipramine HCl

Antidepressant—Antiobsessional

Supplied: 10 mg: Each sugar-coated, cream, triangle-shaped tablet, contains: clomipramine HCl 10 mg. Nonmedicinal ingredients: 2A alcohol, chroma-kote yellow T-2892-Y, colloidal silicon dioxide, heavy syrup, lactose, magnesium stearate, microcrystalline cellulose, polishing solution, purified water and talc. Bottles of 100 and 500.

25 mg: Each sugar-coated, cream, round tablet, printed in black ink N on one side and 25 on the other side, contains: clomipramine HCl 25 mg. Nonmedicinal ingredients: 2A alcohol, chroma-kote yellow T-2892-Y, colloidal silicon dioxide, croscarmellose sodium, heavy syrup, magnesium stearate, microcrystalline cellulose, polishing solution, purified water and talc. Bottles of 100 and 500.

50 mg: Each round, white, shallow convex, film-coated tablet, engraved novo on one side and 50 on the other side, contains: clomipramine HCl 50 mg. Nonmedicinal ingredients: 2A alcohol, carnauba wax, clear finishing solution, colloidal silicon dioxide, color coating suspension, croscarmellose sodium, magnesium stearate, microcrystalline cellulose, opadry white YS-5-7419, opadry clear YS-3-7413 and purified water. Bottles of 100 and 500.

NOVO-CLOPATE ℞
Novopharm

Clorazepate Dipotassium

Anxiolytic—Sedative

Supplied: 3.75 mg: Each white and grey capsule, imprinted NOVO 3.75, contains: clorazepate dipotassium 3.75 mg. Gluten- and tartrazine-free. Bottles of 100 and 500.

7.5 mg: Each scarlet and grey capsule, imprinted NOVO 7.5, contains: clorazepate dipotassium 7.5 mg. Gluten- and tartrazine-free. Bottles of 100, 500 and 1 000.

15 mg: Each grey capsule, imprinted NOVO 15, contains: clorazepate dipotassium 15 mg. Gluten- and tartrazine-free. Bottles of 100 and 500.

NOVO-CLOXIN ℞
Novopharm

Cloxacillin Sodium

Antibiotic

Supplied: Capsules: Each orange body and black cap capsule contains: cloxacillin sodium equivalent to 250 or 500 mg cloxacillin. Sodium: 250 mg: <1 mmol (13.6 mg), 500 mg: 1.2 mmol (27 mg). Gluten- and tartrazine-free. Bottles of 100, 500 and 1 000. Unit dose strips of 100.

Solution: Following reconstitution, each 5 mL of cherry-flavored solution contains: cloxacillin sodium equivalent to 125 mg cloxacillin. Energy: 39 kJ (9.3 kcal)/5 mL. Gluten- and tartrazine-free. Sodium: 1.4 mmol (34.5 mg)/5 mL. Bottles of 60, 100 and 200 mL. Reconstituted solution is stable for 7 days at room temperature (25°C) or 14 days refrigerated (6°C).

NOVO-CROMOLYN ℞
Novopharm

Sodium Cromoglycate

Asthma Prophylaxis

Supplied: Each mL of sterile nebulizer solution contains: sodium cromoglycate 1% in water. Ampuls of 2 mL, cartons of 48. Store at room temperature. Protect from direct sunlight.

...The GREEN SECTION lists the brand and generic names of products available in Canada.

NOVO-CYCLOPRINE ℞
Novopharm

Cyclobenzaprine HCl

Skeletal Muscle Relaxant

Pharmacology: Cyclobenzaprine relieves skeletal muscle spasm of local origin without interfering with muscle function. It is not effective in muscle spasm caused by CNS disease.

Cyclobenzaprine has been shown to improve the signs and symptoms of skeletal muscle spasm in controlled clinical studies.

Pharmacokinetics: In man, cyclobenzaprine is well absorbed. Plasma levels of radioactivity were comparable following the administration of oral or i.v. doses (10 mg) of ^{14}C-labelled cyclobenzaprine to human subjects. Similar excretion of radioactivity was also found after both routes (38 to 51% in the urine and 14 to 15% in the feces) which suggested almost complete absorption orally. The half-life varies from 1 to 3 days. In 14 human subjects, coadministration of cyclobenzaprine and multiple doses of ASA had no effect on plasma levels or bioavailability.

In man, the metabolism of cyclobenzaprine is extensive. Approximately 1.8% of the dose was excreted in the urine as unchanged cyclobenzaprine in the study with ^{14}C-labelled drug. The metabolites, probably glucuronides, were excreted as water-soluble conjugates. In 2 subjects, only 0.2 to 1.5% of the dose was excreted within 24 hours as unchanged drug in the urine following the administration of oral or i.v. doses of 40 mg of unlabelled cyclobenzaprine.

Indications: As an adjunct to rest and physical therapy for relief of muscle spasm associated with acute, painful musculoskeletal conditions.

Adequate evidence for the prolonged use of cyclobenzaprine is not available and because muscle spasm associated with acute, painful musculoskeletal conditions is generally of short duration and specific therapy for longer periods is seldom warranted, the drug should be used only for short periods of up to 2 or 3 weeks.

Cyclobenzaprine has not been proven effective in treating spasticity associated with cerebral or spinal cord disease, or in children with cerebral palsy.

Contraindications: In patients who have exhibited hypersensitivity to the drug, in patients with arrhythmias, heart block or conduction disturbances, congestive heart failure or during the acute recovery phase of myocardial infarction, in patients with hyperthyroidism and during the concomitant use of MAO inhibitors (or within 14 days after their discontinuation).

Warnings: Cyclobenzaprine should not be used for periods longer than 2 or 3 weeks (see Indications).

Cyclobenzaprine is closely related to the tricyclic antidepressants, e.g., amitriptyline and imipramine. Some of the more serious reactions of the CNS that have been noted with the tricyclic antidepressants have occurred with cyclobenzaprine in short-term studies for indications other than muscle spasm related to acute musculoskeletal conditions (and usually at somewhat higher than recommended doses for skeletal muscle spasm) (see Warnings and Adverse Effects).

Interactions may occur between cyclobenzaprine and MAO inhibitors. In patients receiving tricyclic antidepressants and MAO inhibitors, hyperpyretic crises, severe convulsions and death have occurred.

Arrhythmias, sinus tachycardia, prolongation of the conduction time leading to myocardial infarction and stroke have been produced by tricyclic antidepressants.

The effects of alcohol, barbiturates and other CNS depressants may be enhanced by cyclobenzaprine.

Precautions: Occupational Hazards: Mental and/or physical abilities required for performance of hazardous tasks, such as operating machinery or driving a motor vehicle may be impaired by cyclobenzaprine.

Caution should be exercised when using cyclobenzaprine in patients with a history of urinary retention, angle-closure glaucoma, increased intraocular pressure and in patients taking anticholinergic medication due to the drugs atropine-like action.

The antihypertensive action of guanethidine and similarly acting compounds may be blocked by tricyclic antidepressants.

Pregnancy: The safety of cyclobenzaprine administration in pregnant women has yet to be established. Therefore, it should not be used in women who are, or may become pregnant, unless, in the opinion of a physician, the potential risk to the fetus is outweighed by the expected benefits for the mother.

Lactation: Cyclobenzaprine is not recommended for use in nursing mothers since it is likely that the drug is excreted in milk.

Children: Safety and effectiveness of cyclobenzaprine have not been established in children below the age of 15.

Adverse Effects: Most frequent: drowsiness (39%), dry mouth (27%), dizziness (11%).

Less frequent: increased heart rate (and several cases of tachycardia), weakness, fatigue, dyspepsia, nausea, paresthesia, unpleasant taste, blurred vision, insomnia.

Rare: sweating, myalgia, dyspnea, abdominal pain, constipation, tongue discoloration, tremors, dysarthria, nervousness, disorientation, confusion, headache, urinary retention, ataxia, depressed mood, hallucinations, allergic reaction (including rash, urticaria and edema of the face and tongue).

The following adverse reactions have not been reported with cyclobenzaprine when used for muscle spasm of peripheral origin in short-term studies but have been reported with tricyclic compounds. However, when cyclobenzaprine was studied for other indications, and usually at a higher dosage, some of these reactions were noted. Each of the reactions should be considered when cyclobenzaprine is administered due to pharmacologic similarities among the tricyclic drugs.

Cardiovascular: hypotension, hypertension, palpitation, myocardial infarction, arrhythmias, heart block, stroke.

CNS and Neuromuscular: confusional states, disturbed concentration, delusions, excitement, anxiety, restlessness, nightmares, numbness and tingling of the extremities, peripheral neuropathy, incoordination, seizures, alteration in EEG patterns, extrapyramidal symptoms, tinnitus, syndrome of inappropriate ADH (antidiuretic hormone) secretion.

Anticholinergic: disturbance of accommodation, paralytic ileus, dilatation of the urinary tract.

Allergic: skin rash, urticaria, photosensitization, edema of the face and tongue.

Hematologic: bone marrow depression including agranulocytosis, leukopenia, eosinophilia, purpura, thrombocytopenia.

Gastrointestinal: epigastric distress, vomiting, anorexia, stomatitis, diarrhea, parotid swelling, black tongue. Rarely hepatitis (including altered liver function and jaundice).

Endocrine: testicular swelling and gynecomastia in the male, breast enlargement and galactorrhea in the female, increased or decreased libido, elevation and lowering of blood sugar levels.

Other: weight gain or loss, urinary frequency, mydriasis, jaundice, alopecia.

Withdrawal Symptoms: Nausea, headache and malaise may be caused by the abrupt cessation of treatment after prolonged administration: however, these are not indicative of addiction.

Overdose: Symptoms: Temporary confusion, disturbed concentration, transient visual hallucinations, agitation, hyperactive reflexes, muscle rigidity, vomiting, hyperpyrexia and anything listed under Adverse Effects may be caused by high doses of cyclobenzaprine. Drowsiness, hypothermia, tachycardia and other cardiac rhythm abnormalities such as bundle branch block, ECG evidence of impaired conduction and congestive heart failure may be caused by overdosage, on the basis of the known pharmacologic actions of the drug. Dilated pupils, convulsions, severe hypotension, stupor and coma may be other manifestations.

Treatment: Treatment is symptomatic and supportive. The stomach should be emptied as quickly as possible by emesis, followed by gastric lavage. Activated charcoal may be administered following gastric lavage. If there is any evidence of dysrhythmia, an ECG should be taken and cardiac function must be carefully monitored. An open airway must be maintained and it is necessary to regulate body temperature and provide adequate fluid intake.

It may be helpful to use physostigmine for treating cyclobenzaprine overdose. When life-threatening signs such as arrhythmias, convulsions and deep coma recur or persist, the dosage of physostigmine should be repeated as often as required due to its rapid metabolism.

Circulatory shock and metabolic acidosis should be managed by standard medical measures. Phenytoin, lidocaine or propranolol may be used to treat cardiac arrhythmias. A short acting digitalis preparation should be considered for use when signs of cardiac failure occur. It is advisable to closely monitor cardiac function.

Seizures may be controlled by anticonvulsants.

Due to low plasma concentrations of cyclobenzaprine, dialysis is probably of no value.

During the recovery phase, patients may attempt suicide by other means, since overdosage is often deliberate.

Dosage: The usual dosage is 10 mg 3 times a day, with a range of 20 to 40 mg/day in divided doses. Dosage should not exceed 60 mg/day. Use of cyclobenzaprine is not indicated or recommended for periods longer than 2 or 3 weeks.

Supplied: Each yellow, film-coated, D-shaped tablet, embossed novo and 10, on opposite sides, contains: cyclobenzaprine HCl 10 mg. Gluten- and tartrazine-free. Bottles of 100 and 500.

NOVO-CYPROTERONE ℞

Novopharm

Cyproterone Acetate

Antiandrogen

Pharmacology: Cyproterone is a steroid which clinically demonstrates 2 distinct properties: Antiandrogenic: Cyproterone blocks the binding of dihydrotestosterone – the active metabolite of testosterone – to the specific receptors in the prostatic carcinoma cell. Progestogenic/Antigonadotrophic: Cyproterone exerts a negative feed-back on the hypothalamo-pituitary axis, by inhibiting the secretion of LH leading to diminished production of testicular testosterone.

Pharmacokinetics: The absorption of cyproterone following oral administration is complete. Peak plasma levels are reached 3 to 4 hours after administration. Plasma levels fall rapidly during the first 24 hours as a result of tissue distribution and excretion, and plasma half-life was 38 ± 5 hours.

Most of the cyproterone is excreted unchanged in the feces (60%) or urine (33%) within 72 hours.

Cyproterone is eliminated with the urine mainly in the form of unconjugated metabolites and with the bile (feces) in the form of glucuronidized metabolites.

The principal metabolite identified was 15β-hydroxy-cyproterone acetate.

Indications: For the palliative treatment of patients with advanced prostatic carcinoma.

Contraindications: Known hypersensitivity to the drug. Active liver disease and hepatic dysfunction. Renal insufficiency.

Warnings: Liver Function: Direct hepatic toxicity, including jaundice, hepatitis and hepatic failure, which has been fatal in some cases, has been reported in patients treated with 200 to 300 mg cyproterone. Most reported cases are in men with prostatic cancer. Toxicity is dose-related and develops usually, several months after treatment has begun. Liver function tests should be performed before treatment and whenever any symptoms or signs suggestive of hepatotoxicity occur. If hepatotoxicity is confirmed, cyproterone should normally be withdrawn, unless the hepatotoxicity can be explained by another cause, e.g., metastatic disease, in which case cyproterone should be continued only if the perceived benefit outweighs the risk.

Inhibition of Spermatogenesis: The sperm count and the volume of ejaculate are reduced at oral doses of 50 to 300 mg/day. Infertility is usual, and there may be azoospermia after 8 weeks of therapy, which is associated with atrophy of seminiferous tubules.

Followup examinations on discontinuation of therapy have shown these changes to be reversible.

Spermatogenesis usually reverts to its previous level about 3 to 5 months after stopping cyproterone acetate, or in some patients, after up to 20 months. Production of abnormal spermatozoa during cyproterone therapy has been observed; their relationship to abnormal fertilization or malformed embryos is not known.

Gynecomastia: Benign nodules (hyperplasia) of the breast have been reported, these generally subside 1 to 3 months after discontinuation of therapy and/or after a reduction of dosage. The reduction of dosage should be weighed against the risk of inadequate tumor control.

Depression: Cyproterone acetate therapy has occasionally been associated with an increased incidence of depressive mood changes, especially during the first 6 to 8 weeks of therapy. Similar mood changes have also been seen following surgical castration and are considered to be due to androgen deprivation. Patients with tendencies to depressive reaction should be carefully observed.

Precautions: Thromboembolism: Clinical investigations have shown that when cyproterone is used alone it has minor effect on blood clotting factors. However, when cyproterone was combined with ethinyl estradiol, changes were found in increased coagulation capability. There is an inherent risk for those patients with a history of thrombophlebitis or thromboembolism for recurrence of the disease. Cyproterone should be discontinued at the first sign of thrombophlebitis or thromboembolism. And, the patient should be carefully re-evaluated if manifestations of thrombotic disorders: thrombophlebitis, cerebrovascular complications, retinal thrombosis or pulmonary embolism occur.

Adrenocortical Function: Suppression of adrenocortical function tests have occurred in patients receiving high doses (100 mg/m²) of cyproterone.

Reduced response to endogenous ACTH was noted by metyrapone test; furthermore, reduced ACTH and cortisol blood levels determined by Mattingly method were also found.

It is therefore recommended that adrenocortical function tests should be monitored periodically by serum cortisol assay.

Diabetes: Cyproterone may impair carbohydrate metabolism. Parameters of carbohydrate metabolism, fasting blood glucose and glucose tolerance test, should be examined carefully in all patients and particularly in all diabetics before and regularly during therapy with cyproterone.

Hematology: Hypochromic anemia has been observed rarely during therapy with cyproterone. Regular hematological assessment is recommended.

Nitrogen Balance: A negative nitrogen balance is usual at the start of therapy, but does generally correct itself within 3 months of continued therapy.

Metabolic Effects: Fluid retention, hypercalcemia and changes in plasma lipid profile may occur. Accordingly, cyproterone should be used with caution in patients with cardiac disease.

Skin: Cyproterone therapy may cause a reduction of sebum production leading to dryness of the skin, and transient patchy loss of body hair.

Concomitant Alcohol: Alcohol may reduce the antiandrogenic effect of cyproterone in hypersexuality. The relevance of this in prostatic carcinoma is not known, however, it would be prudent to inform the patients that the use of alcohol during cyproterone therapy is not advisable.

Occupational Hazards: Patients should be informed that fatigue and lassitude are common in the first few weeks of therapy, but usually becomes much less pronounced from the third month on. Marked lassitude and asthenia necessitate special care when driving or operating machinery.

Adverse Effects: The adverse events associated most frequently with the use of cyproterone are those related to the hormonal effects of the drug. These reactions usually disappear upon discontinuation of therapy or reduction of dose: increased libido, breast enlargement, breast tenderness, benign nodular hyperplasia of the breast, galactorrhea, gynecomastia, abnormal spermatozoa, impotence, inhibition of spermatogenesis.

Other adverse events which have been reported are listed below: Cardiovascular: hypotension, tachycardia, heart failure, syncope, myocardial infarct, hemorrhage, cerebrovascular accident, cardiovascular disorder, retinal vascular disorder, embolus, pulmonary embolism, superficial and deep thrombophlebitis, thrombosis, retinal vein thrombosis, phlebitis, vascular headache and shock.

Gastrointestinal: constipation, diarrhea, indigestion, anorexia, nausea, vomiting, cholestatic jaundice, cirrhosis of liver, hepatic coma, hepatitis, hepatoma, hepatomegaly, jaundice, liver carcinoma, liver failure, abnormal liver function test, liver necrosis, pancreatitis and glossitis.

Hematology: increased fibrinogen, decreased prothrombin, thrombocytopenia, anemia, hemolytic anemia, hypochromic anemia, normocytic anemia, leukopenia and leukocytosis.

Metabolism: negative nitrogen balance, decreased response to ACTH, hyperglycemia, lowered cortisol, hypercalcemia, increased AST, increased ALT, increased creatinine, hypernatremia, edema, weight gain, weight loss and diabetes mellitus.

Musculoskeletal: myasthenia and osteoporosis.

Nervous system: fatigue, lassitude, weakness, hot flashes, increased sweating, aphasia, coma, depression, dizziness, encephalopathy, hemiplegia, personality disorder, psychotic depression, abnormal gait and headache.

Respiratory: asthma, increased cough, dyspnea, hyperventilation, respiratory disorder, shortness of breath on effort and lung fibrosis.

Skin: eczema, urticaria, erythema nodosum, exfoliative dermatitis, rash, maculopapular rash, dryness of the skin, pruritus, alopecia, hirsutism, skin discoloration, photosensitivity reactions and scleroderma.

Sensory: ear disorder, optic atrophy, optic neuritis, abnormality of accommodation, abnormal vision, blindness and retinal disorder.

Urogenital: enlarged uterine fibroids, uterine hemorrhage, increased urinary frequency, bladder carcinoma, kidney failure, hematuria, urate crystalluria and urine abnormality.

Other: ascites, allergic reaction, asthenia, chills, fetal chromosome abnormality, death, fever, hernia, malaise and injection site reaction.

Adverse reactions are rarely of sufficient severity to require dosage reduction or discontinuation of treatment.

If reactions are severe, it may be beneficial to reduce the dosage.

Overdose: Symptoms and Treatment: There have been no reports of fatal overdosage in man with cyproterone. There are no specific antidotes and treatment should be symptomatic. If oral overdosage is discovered within 2 to 3 hours, gastric lavage can safely be used if indicated.

Dosage: The usual daily initial and maintenance dose is 200 to 300 mg (4 to 6 tablets) divided into 2 to 3 doses and taken after meals.

After orchiectomy a lower daily dose of 100 to 200 mg (2 to 4 tablets) is recommended.

Therapy should not be discontinued when remission or improvement occurs.

Supplied: Each white, round, flat-sided tablet with beveled edges, engraved 50 on the scored side and N on the other side, contains: cyproterone acetate 50 mg. Nonmedicinal ingredients: cornstarch, lactose monohydrate, magnesium stearate, pregelatinized starch and sodium starch glycolate. Bottles of 100, 500 and 1 000. Store between 15 and 30°C.

New Product 1998

NOVO-DESIPRAMINE ℞

Novopharm

Desipramine HCl

Antidepressant

Supplied: 10 mg SC: Each blue, round, biconvex, sugar-coated tablet, printed "novo" arched over "10" in black, contains: desipramine HCl 10 mg. Gluten- and tartrazine-free. Bottles of 100 and 500. Unit dose strips of 100.

25 mg SC: Each yellow, round, biconvex, sugar-coated tablet, printed "novo" arched over "25" in black, contains: desipramine HCl 25 mg. Gluten- and tartrazine-free. Bottles of 100 and 500. Unit dose strips of 100.

50 mg FC: Each green, round, biconvex, film-coated tablet, printed "novo" arched over "50" in black, contains: desipramine HCl 50 mg. Gluten- and tartrazine-free. Bottles of 100 and 500. Unit dose strips of 100.

75 mg SC: Each orange, round, biconvex, sugar-coated tablet, printed "novo" arched over "75" in black, contains: desipramine HCl 75 mg. Gluten- and tartrazine-free. Bottles of 100 and 500. Unit dose strips of 100.

NOVO-DIFENAC® ℞
NOVO-DIFENAC® SR ℞

Novopharm

Diclofenac Sodium

Anti-inflammatory—Analgesic

Pharmacology: Diclofenac is a nonsteroidal anti-inflammatory agent possessing both analgesic and antipyretic properties. Diclofenac does not act through the pituitary-adrenal axis; however, the specific mode of action is not fully known. It inhibits prostaglandin synthesis by interfering with the action of prostaglandin synthetase, which may explain, in part, its actions.

Clinically, a daily dose of 75 to 150 mg diclofenac is comparable in efficacy to 3 to 5 g daily of ASA.

Diclofenac is similar in activity to equivalent dosages of indomethacin (75 to 150 mg daily), and causes less central nervous side effects at these doses.

The use of diclofenac in arthritic patients does not affect the progressive course of the disease but it has been shown to be effective with respect to pain relief, decreased joint tenderness and swelling and increased mobility.

Diclofenac is rapidly and efficiently absorbed following oral administration. Food delays absorption and time to peak concentration. With the enteric coated preparation, peak concentrations are attained after 1.5 to 2.5 hours. Like other nonsteroidal anti-inflammatory drugs, diclofenac is highly (≥99%) bound to plasma protein and has a plasma half-life of approximately 1.2 to 1.8 hours. The plasma clearance is 263 ± 56 mL/min.

Age and renal or hepatic impairment do not appear to have any significant effect on plasma levels of unchanged diclofenac, although metabolite concentrations may be increased by severe renal impairment.

Novo-Difenac (cont'd)

C_{max} is reached at approximately 4 hours or later following administration of slow-release diclofenac. A significant concentration of drug remains in plasma for a longer period of time. No accumulation of diclofenac was found following repeated once daily administration of diclofenac 100 mg slow release tablets.

Indications: For the treatment of symptoms related to rheumatoid arthritis and osteoarthritis, including degenerative joint disease of the hip.

Contraindications: Patients with active, or recent history of, inflammatory diseases of the gastrointestinal tract such as peptic ulcer, gastritis, regional enteritis, or ulcerative colitis.

Known or suspected hypersensitivity to the drug. Diclofenac should not be used in patients in whom acute asthmatic attacks, urticaria, rhinitis or other allergic manifestations are precipitated by ASA or other nonsteroidal anti-inflammatory agents. Fatal anaphylactoid reactions have occurred in such individuals.

Warnings: Peptic ulceration, perforation and gastrointestinal bleeding, sometimes severe and occasionally fatal have been reported during therapy with nonsteroidal anti-inflammatory drugs (NSAIDs) including diclofenac.

Diclofenac should be given under close medical supervision to patients prone to gastrointestinal tract irritation, particularly those with a history of peptic ulcer, melena diverticulosis or other inflammatory disease of the gastrointestinal tract (such as ulcerative colitis or Crohn's disease). In these cases, the physician must weigh the benefits of treatment against the possible hazards (see Contraindications and Adverse Effects).

Patients taking any NSAID including this drug should be instructed to contact a physician immediately if they experience symptoms or signs suggestive of peptic ulceration or gastrointestinal bleeding. These reactions can occur without warning symptoms or signs and at any time during the treatment.

Pregnancy and *Lactation:* The safety of diclofenac has not been established in these conditions and therefore its use is not recommended during pregnancy or lactation. When diclofenac was administered before or after the delivery process had begun in rats, rabbits and mice, a prolonged pregnancy and protracted labor was observed. Other nonsteroidal anti-inflammatory agents have shown similar results, and the evidence suggests that this may be due to decreased uterine contractility resulting from the inhibition of prostaglandin synthesis. The inhibition of prostaglandins may also cause premature closure of the ductus arteriosus.

Diclofenac readily crosses the placenta. A level of 100 ng/mL was measured in the breast milk of a patient on long-term treatment with a daily dosage of 150 mg diclofenac. Extrapolation suggests that an infant of 4 to 5 kg, consuming 1 L of breast milk/day would receive less than 0.03 mg/kg/day of diclofenac.

Geriatrics: Elderly, frail, and debilitated patients should be started with the lowest dosage that will provide control of symptoms and dosage adjusted when necessary and closely supervised.

Children: Diclofenac is not recommended for use in children under 16 years of age because safety and dosage ranges have not been established for pediatric patients.

Occupational Hazards: Headache, dizziness, lightheadedness and mental confusion have been reported by patients following therapy with diclofenac. Patients should be cautioned against operating machinery or motor vehicles if they are experiencing these symptoms (see Adverse Effects).

Precautions: Gastrointestinal: If peptic ulceration is suspected or confirmed, or if gastrointestinal bleeding or perforation occurs, diclofenac should be discontinued, an appropriate treatment instituted and the patient closely monitored.

There is no definitive evidence that the concomitant administration of histamine H_2-receptor antagonists and/or antacids will either prevent the occurrence of gastrointestinal side effects or allow continuation of diclofenac therapy when and if these adverse reactions appear.

Because abnormalities of bone marrow function have occurred, patients being treated with diclofenac should have periodic evaluations of their hemopoietic system. Anemia secondary to gastrointestinal tract toxicity can occur, therefore periodic hemoglobin estimations are advised.

Renal Function: As with other nonsteroidal anti-inflammatory drugs, long-term administration of diclofenac to animals has resulted in renal papillary necrosis and other abnormal renal pathology. In humans, there have been reports of acute interstitial nephritis with hematuria, proteinuria, and occasionally nephrotic syndrome.

A second form of renal toxicity has been seen in patients with prerenal conditions leading to the reduction in renal blood flow or blood volume, where the renal prostaglandins have a supportive role in the maintenance of renal perfusion. In these patients, administration of a nonsteroidal anti-inflammatory drug may cause a dose-dependent reduction in prostaglandin formation and may precipitate overt renal decompensation. Patients at greatest risk of this reaction are those with impaired renal function, heart failure, liver dysfunction, those taking diuretics, and the elderly. Discontinuation of nonsteroidal anti-inflammatory therapy is usually followed by recovery to the pre-treatment state.

Diclofenac and its metabolites are eliminated primarily by the kidneys; therefore, the drug should be used with great caution in patients with impaired renal function. In these cases lower doses should be anticipated and patients carefully monitored.

During long-term therapy, kidney function should be monitored periodically.

Hepatic Function: As with other nonsteroidal anti-inflammatory drugs, borderline elevations of one or more liver tests may occur. These abnormalities may progress, may remain essentially unchanged, or may be transient with continued therapy. A patient with symptoms and/or signs suggesting liver dysfunction, or in whom an abnormal liver test has occurred, should be evaluated for evidence of the development of more severe hepatic reaction while on therapy with this drug. Severe hepatic reactions including jaundice and cases of fatal hepatitis have been reported with this drug as with other nonsteroidal anti-inflammatory drugs. Although such reactions are rare, if abnormal liver tests persist or worsen, if clinical signs and symptoms consistent with liver disease develop, or if systemic manifestations occur (e.g., eosinophilia, rash, etc.), this drug should be discontinued.

During long-term therapy, liver function tests should be monitored periodically. If this drug is to be used in the presence of impaired liver function, it must be done under strict observation.

Diclofenac should be used with caution in patients with hepatic porphyria, since it may trigger an attack.

Fluid and Electrolyte Balance: Fluid retention and edema have been observed in patients treated with diclofenac. Therefore, as with many other nonsteroidal anti-inflammatory drugs, the possibility of precipitating congestive heart failure in elderly patients or those with compromised cardiac function should be borne in mind. Diclofenac should be used with caution in patients with hypertension, cardiac decompensation and renal diseases and in those recovering from surgical operations under general anesthesia and other conditions predisposing to fluid retention.

Serum electrolytes should be monitored periodically during long-term therapy, especially in those patients at risk.

Hematology: Drugs inhibiting prostaglandin biosynthesis do interfere with platelet function to some degree; therefore, patients who may be adversely affected by such an action should be carefully observed when diclofenac is administered.

Blood dyscrasias associated with the use of nonsteroidal anti-inflammatory drugs are rare, but could be with severe consequences.

Infection: The anti-inflammatory, antipyretic and analgesic effects of diclofenac may mask the usual signs of infection; therefore, the physician should be alert to the development of infection in patients receiving the drug.

Ophthalmology: Blurred and/or diminished vision has been reported with the use of diclofenac and other nonsteroidal anti-inflammatory drugs. If such symptoms develop, this drug should be discontinued and an ophthalmologic examination performed; ophthalmic examination should be carried out at periodic intervals in any patient receiving this drug for an extended period of time.

Hypersensitivity: As with other nonsteroidal anti-inflammatory drugs, hypersensitivity reactions including anaphylactic/anaphylactoid reactions, can occur without prior exposure to the drug; therefore, careful questioning of patients for a history of asthma, nasal polyps, urticaria, and hypotension associated with nonsteroidal anti-inflammatory drugs, before starting therapy is important. Patients should be told to immediately report occurrence of symptoms such as skin rash, swelling, hives or itching as well as shortness of breath, wheezing, troubled breathing or tightness in the chest.

Drug Interactions: In man, the plasma levels and bioavailability of diclofenac are reduced when taken simultaneously with ASA.

Concurrent use of lithium and diclofenac has been reported to impair lithium clearance and to increase steady state plasma lithium concentration. Monitoring of plasma lithium levels is therefore advised and reduction of lithium dosage may be required in order to prevent lithium intoxication.

Digoxin plasma concentration may be increased by simultaneous administration of diclofenac and hence, adjustment of digoxin dosage may be required.

Pharmacodynamic studies have not shown potentiation of oral hypoglycemic or anticoagulant drugs during concomitant diclofenac administration; however, caution with concurrent use is recommended as isolated reports of both hypoglycemic and hyperglycemic effects in the presence of diclofenac have been reported.

Isolated cases of an increased risk of hemorrhage with the combined use of diclofenac and acenocoumarol therapy have been reported. Special caution is therefore recommended and frequent laboratory tests should be performed in order to check that the desired response to the anticoagulant is being maintained. At usual therapeutic dosages diclofenac has little effect on spontaneous platelet aggregation even though it is an inhibitor of induced platelet aggregation in vitro or in vivo.

Nonsteroidal anti-inflammatory drugs have been reported to inhibit the activity of diuretics. Increased serum potassium levels may be associated with concomitant treatment with potassium-sparing diuretics.

The antihypertensive effect of hydrochlorothiazide may be decreased by diclofenac in patients with essential hypertension.

Concurrent administration of glucocorticoids may increase the risk of side effects including ulceration or hemorrhage; however, concurrent use with glucocorticoids in the treatment of arthritis may provide additional therapeutic benefit and permit reduction of glucocorticoid dosage.

Simultaneous oral therapy with 2 or more nonsteroidal anti-inflammatory drugs may increase the risk of side effects.

Methotrexate plasma concentrations may be increased due to the effects of diclofenac on renal prostaglandins. Patients should not receive this combination since severe and sometimes fatal toxicity has been reported.

The concomitant administration of aluminum hydroxide or magnesium hydroxide antacids may delay the absorption of diclofenac but does not affect the total amount of drug absorbed.

Increased nephrotoxicity of cyclosporin may occur through effects of nonsteroidal anti-inflammatory drugs on renal prostaglandins.

Laboratory Tests: Changes in laboratory test values may occur during diclofenac therapy. Diclofenac increases platelet aggregation time but does not affect bleeding time, plasma thrombin clotting time, plasma fibrinogen or Factors V and VII to XII. Statistically significant changes in prothrombin and partial thromboplastin times have been reported in normal volunteers. The mean changes were observed to be less than 1 second in both instances, however, and are unlikely to be clinically important. Persistently abnormal or worsening renal, hepatic or hematological test values should be followed up carefully as with any drug, since they may, in rare cases, be related to therapy.

Adverse Effects: The most common adverse reactions encountered with nonsteroidal anti-inflammatory drugs are gastrointestinal, dermatological and CNS adverse reactions. The most severe gastrointestinal adverse reactions observed were ulceration and bleeding. The most severe dermatological reactions observed were erythema multiforme (Stevens-Johnson Syndrome and Lyell Syndrome). Fatalities have occurred on rare occasion, particularly in the elderly. The following adverse reactions with approximate incidences have been reported: Gastrointestinal: The approximate incidence of gastrointestinal side effects is 15.2%. Epigastric or abdominal discomfort, pressure, heaviness or distention was the most frequently seen gastrointestinal adverse reaction (6%). Additional gastrointestinal adverse reactions with approximate incidence include: epigastric, gastric or abdominal pain (5%); nausea (2%); anorexia (1%); diarrhea, vomiting, flatulence, constipation or eructation (1%); and gastric and duodenal ulcerations and bleeding (0.2%). Rare (<1%): peptic ulcer with perforation, bloody diarrhea, melena, hematemesis.

In isolated cases (<0.001%): lower gut disorders (e.g. nonspecific hemorrhagic colitis and exacerbation of ulcerative colitis or Crohn's protocolitis), hyperacidity, stomatitis, glossitis, coated tongue, esophageal lesions.

CNS: The total incidence of CNS adverse reactions is approximately 9%. Dizziness (5%) was the most common CNS adverse reaction followed by headache (3%). Other CNS adverse reactions with an approximate incidence of 1% included vertigo, malaise, insomnia, drowsiness, impaired

concentration and tiredness. In isolated cases (<0.001%): irritability, sweating, disturbances of sensation including paresthesia, impaired hearing, tinnitus, convulsions, memory disturbance, disorientation, depression, anxiety, nightmares, tremor, psychotic reactions, taste alteration disorders.
Cardiovascular: Cardiovascular system adverse reactions had an approximate incidence of 4.5% consisting of palpitations (2.5%), angina and arrhythmias (2.0%).

In isolated cases (<0.001%): exacerbation of cardiac failure, hypertension.
Dermatologic: The approximate incidence of dermatologic side effects was 4% including rash (2%) and pruritus (1.5%). Skin eruption, eczema and urticaria, erythema occurred less frequently than 0.5%. In isolated cases (<0.001%): photosensitivity reactions; loss of hair; erythema multiforme and variants (Stevens-Johnson syndrome; Lyell's syndrome); erythroderma, purpura including allergic purpura.
Edema and Water Retention: Facial edema had an approximate incidence of 2% and general edema was reported less frequently (0.5%). Peripheral edema.
Renal: In isolated cases (<0.001%): renal failure, nephrotic syndrome, urinary abnormalities (e.g. hematuria), interstitial nephritis, papillary necrosis.
Respiratory: Asthma in patients sensitive to ASA.
Hepatic: Occasional (<10%): elevation of serum aminotransferase enzymes (AST, ALT). Rare (<1%): liver function disorders including hepatitis with or without jaundice. In isolated cases (<0.001%): fulminant hepatitis.
Ophthalmological: In isolated cases (<0.001%): disturbances of vision (blurred vision, diplopia).
Allergic: Rare (<1%): hypersensitivity reactions (e.g. bronchospasm, analphylactic/anaphylactoid systemic reactions including hypotension).
Other: In isolated cases (<0.001%): impotence (association with diclofenac intake doubtful), pancreatitis.

Overdose: Symptoms and Treatment: Experience with diclofenac overdosage is limited and there is no specific antidote. In the event of overdosage, absorption should be prevented by induction of vomiting, gastric aspiration and lavage or treatment with activated charcoal. Supportive and symptomatic treatment should be given for complications such as hypotension, renal failure, convulsions, gastrointestinal irritation and respiratory depression. Measures to accelerate elimination (forced diuresis, hemoperfusion, dialysis) may be considered, but may be of limited use because of the high protein-binding and extensive metabolism.

Dosage: Novo-Difenac: In the symptomatic treatment of rheumatoid arthritis, the recommended starting dose is 75 to 150 mg daily in 3 divided doses, depending on the severity of the condition. For maintenance, the dose should be reduced to the minimum amount that will provide continuous control of symptoms, usually 75 to 100 mg daily in 3 divided doses.

In osteoarthritis, the recommended starting dose and maintenance dose is usually 75 mg/day in 3 divided doses. The dose should be adjusted individually to the minimum dose which will provide control of symptoms.

The maximum recommended daily dose is 150 mg.

Diclofenac should be taken with food and the tablets should be swallowed whole.

Novo-Difenac SR: Treatment should be initiated and individual titration carried out using the enteric coated tablets. Patients with rheumatoid arthritis or osteoarthritis on a maintenance dose of 75 mg/day may be changed to a once daily dose of the SR 75 mg tablet, administered morning or evening.

Patients with rheumatoid arthritis or osteoarthritis on a maintenance dose of 100 mg/day may be changed to a once daily dose of the SR 100 mg tablets, administered morning or evening.

Patients on a maintenance dose of 150 mg/day may be changed to a twice daily dose of one SR 75 mg tablet administered morning and evening.

The maximum daily dose should not exceed 150 mg.

The SR tablets should be swallowed whole, with liquid, preferably at mealtime.

Suppositories: 50 or 100 mg suppositories, may be given as substitute for the 100 or 150 mg/day oral daily doses, to a total daily dose not greater than 150 mg.

Information for the Patient: See Blue Section—Information for the Patient "Novo-Difenac/Novo-Difenac SR".

Supplied: Tablets: Novo-Difenac: 25 mg: Each yellow, round, enteric-coated tablet, printed $\frac{N}{25}$ on one side, plain on the reverse, contains: diclofenac sodium 25 mg. Bottles of 100 and 500.

50 mg: Each light brown, round, enteric-coated tablet, printed $\frac{N}{50}$ on one side, plain on the reverse, contains: diclofenac sodium 50 mg. Bottles of 100 and 500.

Novo-Difenac SR: 75 mg: Each white, triangular, biconvex, beveled-edged, film-coated, slow-release tablet, printed novo on one side and $\frac{SR}{75}$ on the other side, contains: diclofenac sodium 75 mg. Bottles of 100 and 250.

100 mg: Each white, round, film-coated, slow-release tablet, printed novo on one side and $\frac{SR}{100}$ on the other side, contains: diclofenac sodium 100 mg. Bottles of 100 and 250.

Suppositories: 50 mg: Each white, torpedo-shaped, foil-wrapped suppository contains: diclofenac sodium 50 mg. Gluten- and tartrazine-free. Boxes of 30.

100 mg: Each white, torpedo-shaped, foil-wrapped suppository contains: diclofenac sodium 100 mg. Gluten- and tartrazine-free. Boxes of 30.

Store between 15 and 30°C. Protect from high humidity.

NOVO-DIFLUNISAL 🄿

Novopharm

Diflunisal

Analgesic—Anti-inflammatory

Supplied: 250 mg: Each peach, oblong, film-coated tablet, engraved novo on one side and 250 on the other side, contains: diflunisal 250 mg. Gluten- and tartrazine-free. Bottles of 60.

500 mg: Each orange, oblong, film-coated tablet, engraved novo on one side and 500 on the other side, contains: diflunisal 500 mg. Gluten- and tartrazine-free. Bottles of 60 and 500.

NOVO-DILTAZEM 🄿
NOVO-DILTAZEM SR 🄿

Novopharm

Diltiazem HCl

Antianginal

Antihypertensive—Antianginal

Pharmacology: Novo-Diltazem tablets and Novo-Diltazem SR capsules are formulations of diltiazem HCl, which is a calcium ion influx inhibitor (calcium entry blocker or calcium ion antagonist).
Mechanism of Action: The therapeutic effect of this group of drugs is believed to be related to their specific cellular action of selectively inhibiting transmembrane influx of calcium ions into cardiac muscle and vascular smooth muscle. The contractile processes of these tissues are dependent upon the movement of extracellular calcium into the cells through specific ion channels. Diltiazem blocks transmembrane influx of calcium through the slow channel without affecting to any significant degree the transmembrane influx of sodium through the fast channel. This results in a reduction of free calcium ions available within cells of the above tissues. Diltiazem does not alter total serum calcium.
Angina: The precise mechanism by which diltiazem relieves angina has not been fully determined but it is believed to be brought about largely by its vasodilator action. In angina due to coronary spasm, diltiazem increases myocardial oxygen delivery by dilating both large and small coronary arteries and by inhibiting coronary spasm at drug levels which cause little negative inotropic effect. The resultant increases in coronary blood flow are accompanied by dose dependent decreases in systemic blood pressure and decreases in peripheral resistance.

In angina of effort it appears that the action of diltiazem is related to the reduction of myocardial oxygen demand. This is probably caused by a decrease in blood pressure brought about by the reduction of peripheral resistance and of heart rate.
Hypertension: The antihypertensive effect of diltiazem is believed to be brought about largely by its vasodilatory action on peripheral blood vessels with resultant decrease in peripheral vascular resistance.
Hemodynamic and Electrophysiologic Effects: Diltiazem produces antihypertensive effects both in the supine and standing positions. Resting heart rate is usually slightly reduced. During dynamic exercise, increases in diastolic pressure are inhibited while maximum achievable systolic pressure is usually unaffected. Heart rate at maximum exercise is reduced.

Studies to date, primarily in patients with normal ventricular function, have shown that cardiac output, ejection fraction and left ventricular end-diastolic pressure have not been affected.

Chronic therapy with diltiazem produces no change, or an increase, in circulating plasma catecholamines. However, no increased activity of the renin-angiotensin-aldosterone axis has been observed. Diltiazem inhibits the renal and peripheral effects of angiotensin II.

In man i.v. diltiazem in doses of 20 mg prolongs AH conduction time and AV node functional and effective refractory periods by approximately 20%. Chronic oral administration of diltiazem in doses up to 540 mg/day has resulted in small increases in PR interval. Second-degree and third-degree AV block have been observed (see Warnings). In patients with sick sinus syndrome, diltiazem significantly prolongs sinus cycle length (up to 50% in some cases).
Pharmacokinetics: Diltiazem is well absorbed from the gastrointestinal tract and is subject to an extensive first-pass effect giving absolute bioavailability (compared to i.v. dosing) of about 40%. Therapeutic blood levels appear to be in the 50 to 200 ng/mL range and the plasma elimination half-life (beta-phase) following single or multiple drug administration is approximately 3.5 to 6 hours. In vitro human serum binding studies revealed that 70 to 80% of diltiazem is bound to plasma proteins. Diltiazem undergoes extensive hepatic metabolism in which only 2 to 4% of the drug appears unchanged in the urine and 6 to 7% appears as metabolites. The metabolic pathways of diltiazem include N-and O-demethylation (via cytochrome P450), deacetylation (via plasma and tissue esterases), in addition to conjugation (via sulfation and glucuronidation). In vitro studies have demonstrated that CYP 3A4 is the principal CYP isoenzyme involved in N-demethylation. The major metabolite, desacetyl diltiazem, is present in the plasma at levels 10 to 20% of the parent drug and is 25 to 50% as potent as diltiazem in terms of coronary vasodilation.
Diltiazem Tablets: Single oral doses of 30 to 120 mg of diltiazem tablets result in detectable plasma levels within 30 to 60 minutes and peak plasma levels 2 to 4 hours after drug administration. There is a departure from linearity of accumulation of diltiazem when diltiazem tablets are administered to steady-state in normal subjects. A 240 mg daily dose (60 mg q.i.d.) gave plasma levels 2.3 times higher than a 120 mg daily dose (30 mg q.i.d.) and a 360 mg daily dose (90 mg q.i.d.) had levels 1.7 times higher than the 240 mg daily dose.
Diltiazem SR (Twice-a-day) Capsules: Diltiazem is absorbed from the sustained release (SR) capsule formulation to about 93% of the tablet form at steady-state. A single 120 mg dose of the capsule resulted in detectable plasma levels within 2 to 3 hours and peak plasma levels at 7 to 11 hours. The apparent elimination half-life after single or multiple dosing is 5 to 7 hours. A departure from linearity similar to that observed with the diltiazem tablet is observed. As the dose of diltiazem SR capsules is increased from a daily dose of 120 mg (60 mg b.i.d.) to 240 mg (120 mg b.i.d.) daily, there is an increase in bioavailability of 2.6 times. When the dose is increased from 240 mg to 360 mg daily there is an increase in bioavailability of 1.8 times. The average plasma levels of the capsule dosed twice daily at steady-state are equivalent to the tablet dosed 4 times daily when the same total daily dose is administered.

A study which compared patients with normal hepatic function to liver cirrhosis patients noted an increase in half-life and a 69% increase in bioavailability in the hepatically impaired patients. A single dose study in patients with severely impaired renal function showed no difference in the half-life of diltiazem as compared to patients with normal renal function (see Precautions and Dosage).

Indications: Novo-Diltazem: Angina: In the management of angina resulting from coronary artery spasm.

For the management of chronic stable angina (effort-associated angina) without evidence of vasospasm in patients who remain symptomatic despite adequate doses of beta-blockers and/or organic nitrates or who cannot tolerate those agents.

Novo-Diltazem tablets may be useful in unstable angina when spasm of the coronary vessels is definitely a contributing factor (e.g., ST segment elevation). In the absence of objective evidence of a spastic component, nitrates or nitrates plus a beta-blocker are at present the treatment of choice. If, in the view of a cardiologist, the addition of Novo-Diltazem to this regimen is considered necessary and safe, then the use of Novo-Diltazem tablets might be considered. Generally, the patient should be hospitalized and treatment initiated under the supervision of a cardiologist.

Novo-Diltazem tablets may be tried in combination with beta-blockers in chronic stable angina in patients with normal

Novo-Diltazem (cont'd)

ventricular function. When such concomitant therapy is introduced, patients must be monitored closely (See Warnings).

Novo-Diltazem SR (Twice-a-day): Angina: For maintenance therapy in the management of chronic stable angina. Treatment should be initiated and individual titration of dosage carried out using the regular tablets. The sustained release formulation may be substituted as maintenance, provided the dosage requirement is suitable (see also Pharmacology). When patients who have been stabilized on tablets are switched to SR capsules for maintenance, close medical supervision is recommended since in some patients the dosage of the SR formulation may require adjustment.

Since the safety and efficacy of SR capsules in the management of unstable or vasospastic angina have not been substantiated, use of this formulation for these indications is not recommended.

Hypertension: In the treatment of mild to moderate essential hypertension. Novo-Diltazem SR should normally be used in those patients in whom treatment with diuretics or beta-blockers has been associated with unacceptable adverse effects.

Novo-Diltazem SR can be tried as initial agent in those patients in whom the use of diuretics and/or beta-blockers is contraindicated or in patients with medical conditions in which these drugs frequently cause serious adverse effects.

Combination of Novo-Diltazem SR with a diuretic has been found to be compatible and showed additive antihypertensive effect. In a single clinical study, the concomitant use of Novo-Diltazem SR with captopril was also found to be compatible.

Safety of concurrent use of Novo-Diltazem SR with other antihypertensive agents has not been established.

Contraindications: Patients with sick sinus syndrome except in the presence of a functioning ventricular pacemaker; patients with second- or third-degree AV block; patients with known hypersensitivity to diltiazem; patients with severe hypotension (less than 90 mmHg systolic); myocardial infarction patients who have left ventricular failure manifested by pulmonary congestion.

Pregnancy: In pregnancy and in women of childbearing potential. Fetal malformations and adverse effects on pregnancy have been reported in animals. In repeated dose studies a high incidence of vertebral column malformations were present in the offspring of mice receiving more than 50 mg/kg of diltiazem HCl orally.

In the offspring of mice receiving a single oral dose of 50 or 100 mg/kg on day 12 of gestation, the incidence of cleft palate and malformed extremities was significantly higher. Vertebral malformations were most prevalent when they received the drug on day 9. In rats, a significantly higher fetal death rate was present when 200 and 400 mg/kg were given orally on days 9 to 14 of gestation. Single oral dose studies in rats resulted in a significant incidence of skeletal malformations in the offspring of the group receiving 400 mg/kg on day 11. In rabbits, all pregnant dams receiving 70 mg/kg orally from day 6 to 18 of gestation aborted; at 35 mg/kg, a significant increase in skeletal malformations was recorded in the offspring.

Warnings: Cardiac Conduction: Diltiazem prolongs AV node refractory periods without significantly prolonging sinus node recovery time, except in patients with sick sinus syndrome. This effect may rarely result in abnormally slow heart rates (particularly in patients with sick sinus syndrome) or second- or third-degree AV block (6 of 1 208 patients or 0.5%).

Concomitant use of diltiazem with beta-blockers or digitalis may result in additive effects on cardiac conduction.

Congestive Heart Failure: Because diltiazem has a negative inotropic effect in vitro and it affects cardiac conduction, the drug should only be used with caution and under careful medical supervision in patients with congestive cardiac failure (see also Contraindications).

Use with Beta-blockers: The combination of diltiazem and beta-blockers warrants caution since in some patients additive effects on heart rate, AV conduction, blood pressure or left ventricular function have been observed. Close medical supervision is recommended.

Generally, diltiazem should not be given to patients with impaired left ventricular function while they receive beta-blockers. However, in exceptional cases when, in the opinion of the physician, concomitant use is considered essential, such use should be instituted gradually in a hospital setting.

Diltiazem gives no protection against the dangers of abrupt beta-blocker withdrawal and such withdrawal should be done by the gradual reduction of the dose of beta-blocker.

Hypotension: Since diltiazem lowers peripheral vascular resistance, decreases in blood pressure may occasionally result in symptomatic hypotension. In patients with angina or arrhythmias using antihypertensive drugs, the additional hypotensive effect of diltiazem should be taken into consideration.

Patients with Myocardial Infarction: Use of immediate release diltiazem at 240 mg/day started 3 to 15 days after a myocardial infarction was associated with an increase in cardiac events in patients with pulmonary congestion, and no overall effect on mortality. Although there has not been a study of diltiazem in acute myocardial infarction reported, their use may have effects similar to those of immediate release diltiazem in acute myocardial infarction.

Acute Hepatic Injury: In rare instances, significant elevations in alkaline phosphatase, CPK, LDH, AST, ALT and symptoms consistent with acute hepatic injury have been observed. These reactions have been reversible upon discontinuation of drug therapy. Although a causal relationship to diltiazem has not been established in all cases, a drug induced hypersensitivity reaction is suspected (see Adverse Effects). As with any drug given over prolonged periods, laboratory parameters should be monitored at regular intervals.

Precautions: Impaired Hepatic or Renal Function: Because diltiazem is extensively metabolized by the liver and excreted by the kidney and in bile, monitoring of laboratory parameters and cautious dosage titration are recommended in patients with impaired hepatic or renal function (see Adverse Effects).

Children: The safety of diltiazem in children has not yet been established.

Lactation: Diltiazem has been reported to be excreted in human milk. One report suggests that concentrations in breast milk may approximate serum levels. Since diltiazem safety in newborns has not been established, it should not be given to nursing mothers.

Geriatrics: Administration of diltiazem to elderly patients (over or equal to 65 years of age) requires caution. The incidence of adverse reactions is approximately 13% higher in this group. Those adverse reactions which occur more frequently include: peripheral edema, bradycardia, palpitation, dizziness, rash and polyuria. Therefore, particular care in titration is advisable (see Dosage).

Drug Interactions: As with all drugs, care should be exercised when treating patients with multiple medications. Calcium channel blockers undergo biotransformation by the cytochrome P450 system. Coadministration of diltiazem with other drugs which follow the same route of biotransformation may result in altered bioavailability. Dosages of similarly metabolized drugs, particularly those of low therapeutic ratio, and especially in patients with renal and/or hepatic impairment, may require adjustment when starting or stopping concomitantly administered diltiazem to maintain optimum therapeutic blood levels.

Drugs known to be inhibitors of the cytochrome P450 system include: azole antifungals, cimetidine, cyclosporine, erythromycin, quinidine, terfenadine, warfarin.

Drugs known to be inducers of the cytochrome P450 system include: phenobarbital, phenytoin, rifampin.

Drugs known to be biotransformed via P450 include: benzodiazepines, flecainide, imipramine, propafenone, theophylline.

Anesthetics: The depression of cardiac contractility, conductivity, and automaticity as well as the vascular dilation associated with anesthetics may be potentiated by calcium channel blockers. When used concomitantly, anesthetics and calcium channel blockers should be titrated carefully.

Benzodiazepines: Diltiazem significantly increases peak plasma levels and the elimination half-life of triazolam and midazolam.

Beta-blockers: The concomitant administration of diltiazem with beta adrenergic blocking drugs warrants caution and careful monitoring. Such an association may have an additive effect on heart rate, on AV conduction or on blood pressure (See Warnings). Appropriate dosage adjustments may be necessary. A study in 5 normal subjects showed that diltiazem increased propranolol bioavailability by approximately 50%.

Carbamazepine: Concomitant administration of diltiazem with carbamazepine has been reported to result in elevated serum levels of carbamazepine (40 to 72% increase) resulting in toxicity in some cases. Patients receiving these drugs concurrently should be monitored for a potential drug interaction.

Cimetidine: A study in 6 healthy volunteers has shown a significant increase in peak diltiazem plasma levels (58%) and AUC (53%) after a 1-week course of cimetidine at 1 200 mg/day and a single dose of oral diltiazem 60 mg. Ranitidine produced smaller, nonsignificant increases. The effect may be mediated by cimetidine's known inhibition of hepatic cytochrome P450, the enzyme system responsible for the first-pass metabolism of diltiazem. Patients currently receiving diltiazem therapy should be carefully monitored for a change in pharmacological effect when initiating and discontinuing therapy with cimetidine. An adjustment in the diltiazem dose may be warranted.

Cyclosporine: A pharmacokinetic interaction between diltiazem and cyclosporine has been observed during studies involving renal and cardiac transplant patients. In renal and cardiac transplant recipients, a reduction of cyclosporine dose ranging from 15 to 48% was necessary to maintain cyclosporine trough concentrations similar to those seen prior to the addition of diltiazem. If these agents are to be administered concurrently, cyclosporine concentrations should be monitored, especially when diltiazem therapy is initiated, adjusted or discontinued. The effect of cyclosporine on diltiazem plasma concentrations has not been evaluated.

Digitalis: Diltiazem and digitalis glycosides may have an additive effect in prolonging AV conduction. In clinical trials, concurrent administration of diltiazem and digoxin have resulted in increases in serum digoxin levels with prolongation of AV conduction. This increase may result from a decrease in renal clearance of digoxin. Patients on concomitant therapy, especially those with renal impairment, should be carefully monitored. The dose of digoxin may need downward adjustment.

Rifampin: Administration of diltiazem with rifampin markedly reduced plasma diltiazem concentrations and the therapeutic effect of diltiazem.

Short and Long-acting Nitrates: Diltiazem may be safely coadministered with nitrates, but there have been few controlled studies to evaluate the antianginal effectiveness of this combination.

Other Calcium Antagonists: Limited clinical experience suggests that in certain severe conditions not responding adequately to verapamil or to nifedipine, using diltiazem in conjunction with either of these drugs may be beneficial.

Adverse Effects: See also Overall Diltiazem Safety Profile.

Diltiazem Tablets: A safety evaluation was carried out in controlled clinical trials with 1 208 North American angina patients, some of whom were severely ill and were receiving multiple concomitant therapy. Adverse effects were reported in 19.6% of patients and required discontinuation of treatment in 7.2%.

The most common occurrences and their frequency are: nausea (2.7%), swelling/edema (2.4%), arrhythmia (2%) (AV block, bradycardia, tachycardia and sinus arrest), headache (2%), rash (1.8%) and asthenia (1.1%).

In addition, the following events were reported in less than 1% of cases: Cardiovascular: angina, bradycardia, congestive heart failure, flushing, hypotension, palpitations, syncope. A patient with Prinzmetal's angina experiencing episodes of vasospastic angina developed periods of transient asymptomatic asystole approximately 5 hours after receiving a single 60 mg dose of diltiazem.

Nervous System: amnesia, confusion, depression, dizziness, drowsiness, gait abnormality, hallucinations, insomnia, nervousness, paresthesia, personality change, tremor, weakness.

Gastrointestinal: anorexia, constipation, diarrhea, dyspepsia, vomiting.

Dermatologic: petechiae, pruritus, urticaria.

Other: amblyopia, decreased sexual performance, dysgeusia, dyspnea, epistaxis, eye irritation, hyperglycemia, nocturia, osteo-articular pain, paresthesia, photosensitivity, polyuria, thirst, tinnitus, weight increase.

Rarely, reports of extremely elevated liver enzymes, cholestasis, hyperbilirubinemia, jaundice, epigastric pain, anorexia, nausea, vomiting, stool discoloration, dark urine and weight loss have been reported. The symptoms and laboratory test abnormalities have been reversible on drug discontinuation (see Warnings).

Two incidents of marked hyperglycemia, hyperkalemia, bradycardia, asthenia, hypotension and gastrointestinal disturbances have been reported in diabetic patients receiving diltiazem, glyburide and a beta-blocker along with several other medications. Drugs were discontinued and supportive measures were administered which resulted in the patients fully recovering within a few days.

Laboratory Tests: In rare instances, mild to moderate transient elevations of alkaline phosphatase, AST, ALT, LDH and CPK, have been noted during diltiazem therapy.

Diltiazem SR (Twice-a-day) Capsules: A safety evaluation was carried out in controlled and open-label studies in 611 hypertensive patients treated with diltiazem SR capsules either alone or in combination with other antihypertensive agents. Adverse effects were reported in 34.2% of patients and required discontinuation of therapy in 7.2%.

The most common adverse effects were: peripheral edema (8.3%); headache (4.9%); dizziness (4.7%); asthenia (3.9%), vasodilation (flushing) (2.3%) and bradycardia (2.1%).

The following percentage of adverse effects, divided by system, was reported: Cardiovascular: peripheral edema

(8.3%), vasodilation (flushing) (2.3%), bradycardia (2.1%), AV block (first degree) (1.6%), palpitations (1.3%), arrhythmia (1%), heart failure right (0.5%).
CNS: headache (4.9%), dizziness (4.7%), asthenia (3.9%), somnolence (1%), nervousness (anxiety) (0.8%), paresthesia (0.7%), insomnia (0.5%), depression (0.5%), dream abnormality (0.5%), tinnitus (0.5%).
Gastrointestinal: dyspepsia (1.1%), nausea (1.1%), constipation (0.7%).
Dermatological: rash (1.6%).
Laboratory Tests: increased alkaline phosphatase (0.7%).
Other: impotence (1.6%), musculoskeletal pain (1.5%), nocturia (1.1%), polyuria (1%), rhinitis (0.5%).

The following additional adverse effects have occurred with an incidence of less than 0.5% in clinical trials: syncope, AV block, postural hypotension, chest pain, dyspnea, tremor, gait abnormality, vertigo, taste alteration, anorexia, increased appetite, dry mouth, vomiting, diarrhea, increased saliva, acute hepatic injury, pruritus, urticaria, conjunctivitis, amblyopia, ejaculation abnormality, malaise, fever.

The following abnormal laboratory findings have been rarely reported: increased AST/ALT, bilirubinemia, hyperproteinemia, hypercholesteremia, hyperlipidemia, hyperglycemia, hypokalemia, urine abnormality (see Precautions).

Overall Diltiazem Safety Profile: In clinical trials of diltiazem tablets, and diltiazem SR capsules involving over 3 300 patients, the most common adverse reactions were headache (4.6%), edema (4.6%), dizziness (3.5%), asthenia (2.7%), first-degree AV block (2.4%), bradycardia (1.7%), flushing (1.5%), nausea (1.4%), rash (1.2%), and dyspepsia (1.0%).

In addition, the following events were reported with a frequency of less than 1%: Cardiovascular: angina, arrhythmia, bundle branch block, tachycardia, ventricular extrasystoles, congestive heart failure, syncope, palpitations, AV block (second-or third-degree), hypotension, ECG abnormalities.
Nervous System: amnesia, depression, gait abnormality, nervousness, somnolence, hallucinations, paresthesia, personality change, tinnitus, tremor, abnormal dreams, insomnia.
Gastrointestinal: anorexia, diarrhea, dysgeusia, mild elevations of AST, ALT, LDH, and alkaline phosphatase (see Warnings), vomiting, weight increase, thirst, constipation.
Dermatological: petechiae, pruritus, photosensitivity, urticaria.
Other: amblyopia, CPK increase, dyspnea, epistaxis, eye irritation, hyperglycemia, sexual difficulties, nasal congestion, nocturia, osteoarticular pain, impotence, dry mouth, polyuria, hyperuricemia.

The following postmarketing events have been reported infrequently in patients receiving diltiazem: allergic reactions, alopecia, asystole, erythema multiforme (including Stevens-Johnson syndrome, toxic epidermal necrolysis), exfoliative dermatitis, extrapyramidal symptoms, gingival hyperplasia, hemolytic anemia, detached retina, increased bleeding time, leukopenia, purpura, retinopathy, and thrombocytopenia. Isolated cases of angioedema have been reported. Angioedema may be accompanied by breathing difficulty. In addition, events such as myocardial infarction have been observed which are not readily distinguishable from the natural history of the disease in these patients. A number of well-documented cases of generalized rash, some characterized as leukocytoclastic vasculitis, have been reported. However, a definitive cause and effect relationship between these events and diltiazem therapy is yet to be established.

Overdose: Symptoms and Treatment: There have been reports of diltiazem overdose in amounts ranging from <1 to 18 g. In cases with a fatal outcome, the majority involved multiple drug ingestion.

Events observed following diltiazem overdose included bradycardia, hypotension, heart block and cardiac failure. Most reports of overdose described some supportive medical measure and/or drug treatment. Bradycardia frequently responded favorably to atropine as did heart block, although cardiac pacing was also frequently utilized to treat heart block. Fluids and vasopressors were used to maintain blood pressure, and in cases of cardiac failure, inotropic agents were administered. In addition, some patients received treatment with ventilatory support, gastric lavage, activated charcoal, and i.v. calcium.

The effectiveness of i.v. calcium administration to reverse the pharmacological effects of diltiazem overdose has been inconsistent. In a few reported cases, overdose with calcium channel blockers associated with hypotension and bradycardia that was initially refractory to atropine became more responsive to atropine after the patients received i.v. calcium. In some cases i.v. calcium has been administered (1 g calcium chloride or 3 g calcium gluconate) over 5 minutes, and repeated every 10 to 20 minutes as necessary. Calcium gluconate has also been administrated as a continous infusion at a rate of 2 g/hour for 10 hours. Infusions of calcium for 24 hours or more may be required. Patients should be monitored for signs of hypercalcemia.

In the event of overdosage or exaggerated response, appropriate supportive measures should be employed in addition to gastric lavage. Limited data suggest that plasmapheresis or charcoal hemoperfusion may hasten diltiazem elimination. The following measures may be considered:
Bradycardia: Administer atropine. If there is no response to vagal blockade, administer isoproterenol cautiously.
High-degree AV Block: Treat as for bradycardia above. Fixed high-degree AV block should be treated with cardiac pacing.
Cardiac Failure: Administer inotropic agents (isoproterenol, dopamine or dobutamine) and diuretics.
Hypotension: Vasopressors (e.g., dopamine or norepinephrine bitartrate).

Actual treatment and dosage should depend on the severity of the clinical situation.

Dosage: Novo-Diltiazem: Angina: Chronic Stable Angina or Vasospastic Angina: Dosage must be adjusted to each patient's needs. Starting with 30 mg 4 times daily, before meals and at bedtime, dosage may be increased gradually to 240 mg a day (given in 3 to 4 equally divided doses) at 1- to 2-day intervals, until optimum response is obtained. Limited clinical experience in rare resistant cases suggests that dosage of up to 360 mg a day in 3 to 4 equally divided doses may be tried under careful supervision.

In patients with vasospastic angina, the last dose of the day may be given at bedtime to help minimize angina pain which in such patients frequently occurs in early morning.

Unstable Angina Pectoris: Dosage of Novo-Diltiazem tablets should be carefully titrated in the Intensive Care Unit, up to 360 mg/day given in 3 to 4 equally divided doses. The titration should be done as rapidly as possible with consideration of concomitant therapy (see Precautions, Drug Interactions).

Geriatrics: Pharmacokinetics of diltiazem in elderly patients has not been fully elucidated. Preliminary results in elderly patients (over 65 years old) suggest that a lower dosage might be required in this age group (see Precautions).

There are few available data concerning dosage requirements in patients with impaired renal or hepatic function. If diltiazem must be used in these patients, the dosage should be carefully and gradually adjusted depending on patient tolerance and response (see Precautions).

Novo-Diltiazem SR (Twice-a-day): Angina: Novo-Diltiazem SR is intended for maintenance therapy in chronic stable angina patients requiring doses within the range of 120 to 360 mg/day. **Initiation of treatment and individual titration of dosage should be carried out using the conventional tablets.** Novo-Diltazem SR may be preferred for maintenance because of the convenience of twice daily dosage. Patients stabilized on a maintenance regimen between 120 and 360 mg of regular tablets may be changed to the same daily dose of Novo-Diltazem SR capsules divided into 2 equal doses and taken every 12 hours. **When patients are switched to SR capsules, close medical supervision is recommended since in some patients the dosage of the SR formulation may require adjustment.**

Hypertension: Dosage should be individualized depending on patient's tolerance and responsiveness to Novo-Diltiazem SR capsules and to concurrent antihypertensive medications (see Indications and Precautions).

The adult dose range is 120 to 360 mg/day administered in 2 equally divided doses. Although individual patients may respond to any dosage level, the average optimum dosage range in clinical trials is between 240 and 360 mg/day. Maximum antihypertensive effect is usually observed by the second to fourth week of chronic therapy; therefore, dosage adjustments should be scheduled accordingly.

A maximum daily dose of 360 mg should not be exceeded.

Geriatrics: There is evidence that the effective dose in the elderly (over 65 years of age) is somewhat lower than in younger patients (average dose: 255 mg vs 288 mg respectively); therefore, Novo-Diltiazem SR should be administered cautiously to elderly patients and the dosage should be carefully and gradually adjusted depending on patient tolerance and response (see Precautions).

Novo-Diltazem SR has an additive antihypertensive effect when used concomitantly with other antihypertensive agents. Therefore, it may be necessary to decrease the dose of Novo-Diltazem SR and/or the dose of the concomitant antihypertensive drug when adding one to the other (see Indications and Warnings).

Novo Diltazem SR should not be used in severe hepatic or renal dysfunction.

Novo-Diltazem tablets or Novo-Diltazem SR capsules should not be chewed or crushed.

Supplied: Novo-Diltazem: 30 mg: Each green, unscored tablet contains: diltiazem HCl 30 mg. Bottles of 100 and 500. Unit dose strips of 100.

60 mg: Each yellow, scored tablet contains: diltiazem HCl 60 mg. Bottles of 100 and 500. Unit dose strips of 100.

Novo-Diltazem SR (Twice-a-day): 60 mg: Each ivory/brown, sustained-release capsule, with n and 60 imprinted on the capsule, contains: diltiazem HCl 60 mg. Bottles of 100 and 300.

90 mg: Each gold/brown, sustained-release capsule, with n and 90 imprinted on the capsule, contains: diltiazem HCl 90 mg. Bottles of 100 and 300.

120 mg: Each caramel/brown, sustained-release capsule, with n and 120 imprinted on the capsule, contains: diltiazem HCl 120 mg. Bottles of 100 and 300.

Keep between 15 and 30°C.

Reviewed 1998

NOVO-DIPIRADOL ℞

Novopharm

Dipyridamole

Coronary Vasodilator—Platelet Inhibitor

Supplied: 25 mg: Each orange, round, sugar-coated tablet, engraved N over 25 on same side, contains: dipyridamole 25 mg. Bottles of 100 and 500.

50 mg: Each brown, round, sugar-coated tablet, engraved N over 50 on same side, contains: dipyridamole 50 mg. Bottles of 100 and 1 000.

75 mg: Each deep orange, round, sugar-coated tablet, engraved N over 75 on same side, contains: dipyridamole 75 mg. Bottles of 100 and 500.

NOVO-DOMPERIDONE ℞

Novopharm

Domperidone Maleate

Modifier of Upper Gastrointestinal Motility

Pharmacology: Domperidone is a peripheral dopamine antagonist structurally related to the butyrophenones with antiemetic and gastroprokinetic properties.

Domperidone effectively increases esophageal peristalsis and lower esophageal sphincter pressure (LESP), increases gastric motility and peristalsis, enhances gastroduodenal coordination and consequently facilitates gastric emptying and decreases small bowel transit time.

The mechanism of action of domperidone is related to its peripheral dopamine receptor blocking properties. Domperidone can block emesis induced by apomorphine, hydergine, morphine or levodopa through stimulation of the chemoreceptor trigger zone (situated outside the blood brain barrier). There is indirect evidence that emesis is also inhibited at the gastric level, since domperidone also inhibits emesis induced by oral levodopa, and local gastric wall concentrations following oral domperidone are much greater than those of the plasma and other organs. Domperidone does not readily cross the blood-brain barrier and, therefore, is not expected to have central effects.

Domperidone elevates serum prolactin levels, but has no effect on circulating aldosterone levels.

Pharmacokinetics: Peak plasma levels of domperidone, in man, occur within 10 to 30 minutes following i.m. injection and 30 minutes after oral (fasted) administration. Plasma concentrations 2 hours after oral administration are lower than following i.m. injection, and this is likely the result of hepatic first-pass and gut wall metabolism. Peak plasma concentrations are 40 ng/mL following an i.m. injection of 10 mg, 20 ng/mL after a single 10 mg tablet, and 70 to 100 ng/mL after oral doses of 60 mg (tablets or oral drops). In each case, the half-life was calculated as approximately 7.0 hours. The degree of human plasma protein binding was calculated from tritiated domperidone concentrations of 10 and 100 ng/mL as 91.7 and 93.0%, respectively. In man, the major metabolic pathways for domperidone are hydroxydomperidone and 2,3-dihydro-2-oxo-1-H-benzimidazol-1-propionic acid, respectively. After oral administration of 40 mg ^{14}C-domperidone to healthy volunteers, 31% of the radioactivity is excreted in the urine and 66% in the feces over a period of 4 days.

Novo-Domperidone (cont'd)

Indications: In the symptomatic management of upper gastrointestinal motility disorders associated with chronic and subacute gastritis and diabetic gastroparesis. Domperidone may also be used to prevent gastrointestinal symptoms associated with the use of dopamine agonist antiparkinsonian agents.

Contraindications: In patients with known sensitivity or intolerance to the drug. Domperidone should not be used whenever gastrointestinal stimulation might be dangerous, i.e., gastrointestinal hemorrhage or mechanical obstruction.

Warnings: Prolactin levels are elevated by dopamine receptor blocking agents; the elevation persists during chronic administration. Tissue culture experiments indicate that approximately one-third of human breast cancers are prolactin dependent in vitro, a factor of potential importance if the prescription of these drugs is contemplated in a patient with a previously detected breast cancer. Although disturbances such as galactorrhea, amenorrhea, gynecomastia and impotence have been reported, the clinical significance of elevated serum prolactin levels is unknown for most patients. After chronic administration of dopamine receptor blocking agents, an increase in mammary neoplasms has been found in rodents. Neither clinical studies nor epidemiologic studies conducted to date, however, have shown an association between chronic administration of these drugs and mammary tumorigenesis. The available evidence is considered too limited to be conclusive at this time.

Pregnancy: While animal studies have not shown drug related teratogenic or primary embryo toxic effect on animal fetuses, comparable studies have not been performed in pregnant women. Therefore, domperidone should not be used in pregnant women unless the expected benefit outweighs the potential hazard.

Lactation: Domperidone is excreted in breast milk in very low concentrations. Caution should be exercised when domperidone is administered to nursing mothers.

Children: As the safety and efficacy of domperidone in children have not been established, domperidone should not be used in children.

Precautions: In the event that the patient develops galactorrhea and/or gynecomastia, withdrawal of the drug will result in alleviation of these symptoms.

Drug Interactions: The beneficial effects of domperidone may be compromised by the concomitant administration of anticholinergic drugs.

Since domperidone enhances gastric and small intestinal motility, it may accelerate absorption of drugs taken up from the stomach.

When domperidone is administered in combination with MAO inhibitors, care should be exercised.

Domperidone absorption requires some gastric acidity, therefore, concomitant administration of high doses of antacids and H_2-receptor blockers should be avoided.

Adverse Effects: The overall incidence of side effects was <7% in clinical studies with oral domperidone. Some of these side effects are an extension of the dopamine antagonist properties of domperidone. During continued therapy, most side effects resolve spontaneously or are easily tolerated. The more serious or troublesome side effects (galactorrhea, gynecomastia, menstrual irregularities) are dose-related and gradually resolve after lowering the dose or discontinuing of therapy.

CNS: 4.6%: dry mouth (1.9%), headache/migraine (1.2%), insomnia, nervousness, dizziness, thirst, lethargy, irritability (all <1%).

Gastrointestinal: 2.4%: abdominal cramps, diarrhea, regurgitation, nausea, changes in appetite, heartburn, constipation (all <1%).

Endocrinological: 1.3%: hot flushes, mastalgia, galactorrhea, gynecomastia, menstrual irregularities.

Urinary: 0.8%: urinary frequency, dysuria.

Mucocutaneous: 1.1%: rash, pruritus, urticaria, stomatitis, conjunctivitis.

Cardiovascular: 0.5%: edema, palpitations.

Musculoskeletal: 0.1%: leg cramps, asthenia.

Miscellaneous: 0.1%: drug intolerance.

Laboratory Parameters: elevated serum prolactin, elevation of AST, ALT and cholesterol (all <1.0%).

Overdose: Symptoms: There has been no experience with overdosage of domperidone maleate, however, based on the pharmacological properties of domperidone, CNS effects (dyskinesias) and cardiovascular effects (arrhythmia, hypotension) might possibly occur.

Treatment: Treatment is gastric lavage with close observation and supportive therapy.

Dosage: Upper Gastrointestinal Motility Disorders: The usual dosage in adults is 10 mg orally 3 to 4 times a day, 15 to 30 minutes before meals and at bedtime if required. In severe or resistant cases the dose may be increased to a maximum of 20 mg 3 to 4 times a day.

Nausea and Vomiting Associated with Dopamine Agonist Antiparkinsonian Agents: The usual dosage in adults is 20 mg orally 3 to 4 times a day. Higher doses may be required to achieve symptom control while titration of the antiparkinsonian medication is occurring.

Supplied: Each white to off-white colored, round, film-coated tablet engraved 'N' over '10' on one side and plain on the other, contains: domperidone maleate 12.72 mg equivalent to domperidone 10 mg. Nonmedicinal ingredients: 2A alcohol, carnauba wax, colloidal silicon dioxide, lactose, magnesium stearate, microcrystalline cellulose, Opadry clear YS-3-7413, povidone, polysorbate 80, pregelatinized starch, purified water, starch and wax. Bottles of 100 and 500. Boxes of 100 as unit dose strips. Store between 15 to 30°C. Protect from light. Unit dose strips should be stored between 15 and 25°C and protected from high humidity and light.

New Product 1998

NOVO-DOXEPIN Ⓟ

Novopharm

Doxepin HCl

Antidepressant

Supplied: 25 mg: Each #4 size capsule with pink body/blue cap, imprinted with novo 25, contains: doxepin HCl 25 mg. Gluten- and tartrazine-free. Bottles of 100 and 500.

50 mg: Each #2 size capsule with pale pink body/pink cap, imprinted with novo 50, contains: doxepin HCl 50 mg. Gluten- and tartrazine-free. Bottles of 100 and 500.

75 mg: Each #2 size capsule with pale pink body/pink cap, imprinted with novo 75, contains: doxepin HCl 75 mg. Gluten- and tartrazine-free. Bottles of 100.

100 mg: Each #1 size capsule with pale pink body/blue cap, imprinted with novo 100, contains: doxepin HCl 100 mg. Gluten- and tartrazine-free. Bottles of 100.

150 mg: Each #0 size capsule with pink body/pink cap, imprinted with novo 150, contains: doxepin HCl 150 mg. Gluten- and tartrazine-free. Bottles of 100.

NOVO-DOXYLIN Ⓟ

Novopharm

Doxycycline Hyclate

Antibiotic

Supplied: Capsules: Each blue, hard gelatin capsule, imprinted NOVO 100, contains: doxycycline hyclate equivalent to doxycycline 100 mg. Gluten- and tartrazine-free. Bottles of 50, 100 and 200. Protect from light. Dispense in a light-resistant container. Store at room temperature.

Tablets: Each coral, round, film-coated tablet contains: doxycycline 100 mg. Gluten- and tartrazine-free. Bottles of 100.

NOVO-FAMOTIDINE Ⓟ

Novopharm

Famotidine

Histamine H_2-Receptor Antagonist

Pharmacology: Famotidine is a competitive inhibitor of histamine H_2-receptors. The primary clinically important pharmacologic activity is inhibition of gastric juice secretion. Famotidine reduces the acid and pepsin content, as well as the volume of basal, nocturnal, and stimulated gastric secretion.

Indications: The treatment of the following conditions where a controlled reduction of gastric secretion is required: treatment of acute duodenal ulcer; prophylactic use in duodenal ulcer; treatment of acute benign gastric ulcer; treatment of pathological hypersecretory conditions (e.g., Zollinger-Ellison syndrome); treatment of gastroesophageal reflux disease (GERD).

Contraindications: Hypersensitivity to any component of this medication.

Precautions: Patients with Severe Renal Insufficiency: Dosing intervals may need to be prolonged in patients with advanced renal insufficiency (creatinine clearance <10 mL/min) to adjust for the longer elimination half-life of famotidine (see Dosage).

Drug Interactions: Studies with famotidine in man, in animal models, and in vitro have shown no significant interference with the disposition of compounds metabolized by the hepatic microsomal enzymes, e.g., cytochrome P450 system. Compounds tested in man have included warfarin, theophylline, phenytoin, diazepam, aminopyrine and antipyrine. Indocyanine green as an index of hepatic blood flow and/or hepatic drug extraction has been tested and no significant effects have been found.

Gastric Ulcer: Gastric malignancy should be excluded prior to initiation of therapy of gastric ulcer with famotidine. Symptomatic response of gastric ulcer to famotidine therapy does not preclude the presence of gastric malignancy.

Pregnancy: Reproductive studies have been performed in rats and rabbits at oral doses of up to 2 000 and 500 mg/kg/day, respectively (approximately 2 500 and 625 times the maximum recommended human dose, respectively), and have revealed no evidence of impaired fertility or harm to the fetus due to famotidine. There are, however, no adequate or well-controlled studies in pregnant women.

Since the safe use of famotidine in pregnant women has not been established, the benefits of treatment should be weighed against potential risks.

Lactation: Famotidine is detectable in human milk. Nursing mothers should either stop this drug or should stop nursing.

Children: Safety and effectiveness in children have not been established.

Geriatrics: No dosage adjustment is required based on age.

Adverse Effects: Famotidine is usually well tolerated; most adverse effects have been mild and transient. The adverse effects listed below have been reported during clinical trials in 2 333 patients. In those controlled clinical trials in which famotidine was compared to placebo, the overall incidence of adverse experiences in the group which received famotidine 40 mg at bedtime, was similar to the placebo group. No antiandrogenic or other adverse hormonal effects have been observed.

The following adverse effects have been reported at a rate of greater than 1% in patients on therapy with famotidine in controlled clinical trials, and may be causally related to the drug: headache (4.6%), dizziness (1.2%), constipation (1.2%) and diarrhea (1.6%).

Other reactions have been reported in clinical trials but occurred under circumstances where a causal relationship could not be established. However, in these rarely reported events, that possibility cannot be excluded. Therefore, these observations are listed to serve as alerting information to physicians.

Gastrointestinal (8.0%): nausea 1.6%, vomiting 0.9%, anorexia 0.5%, abdominal discomfort 0.3%, dry mouth 0.2%.

CNS/Psychiatric (7.3%): insomnia 0.6%, somnolence 0.4%, anxiety 0.3%, paresthesia 0.3%, depression 0.2%, libido decreased 0.1%.

Respiratory (4.4%): bronchospasm <0.1%.

Body as a Whole (3.0%): fatigue 0.6%, asthenia 0.3%, fever 0.2%.

Musculoskeletal (1.7%): musculoskeletal pain 0.1%, arthralgia 0.1%.

Skin (1.7%): pruritus 0.4%, rash 0.3%, alopecia 0.2%, flushing 0.2%, acne 0.1%, dry skin 0.1%.

Cardiovascular (1.0%): palpitations 0.2%.

Special Senses (0.9%): taste disorder 0.1%, tinnitus 0.1%, orbital edema <0.1%.

Urogenital (0.9%).

The following additional adverse reactions have been reported since the drug was marketed: urticaria, liver enzymes abnormalities, cholestatic jaundice, anaphylaxis and angioedema.

The following adverse reactions have been reported; however, a causal relationship to therapy with famotidine has not been established: agitation, confusion, hallucinations, grand mal seizures, rare cases of impotence, thrombocytopenia, pancytopenia, leukopenia and agranulocytosis.

Laboratory Abnormalities: Laboratory parameters may be affected during treatment with famotidine, but the changes are usually not considered serious. Among the laboratory changes that were reported during clinical trials were increases in AST, ALT, BUN, and serum creatinine. These changes were rarely of clinical significance.

Only 3 patients had to be discontinued from therapy because of laboratory adverse experiences, however laboratory abnormalities were present at baseline.

Overdose: Symptoms and Treatment: There is no experience to date with deliberate overdosage. Doses of up to 800 mg/day have been employed in patients with pathological hypersecretory conditions with no serious adverse effects. In the event of overdosage, treatment should be symptomatic and supportive. Unabsorbed material should be removed from the gastrointestinal tract, the patient should be monitored, and supportive therapy should be employed.

The oral LD_{50} of famotidine in male and female rats and mice was > 5 000 mg/kg.

Dosage: Duodenal Ulcer: Acute Therapy: The recommended adult oral dosage of famotidine for acute duodenal ulcer is 40 mg once a day at bedtime. Treatment should be given for 4 to 8 weeks, but the duration of treatment may be shortened if healing can be documented. Healing occurs within 4 weeks in most cases of duodenal ulcer.

Maintenance Therapy: For the prevention of recurrence of duodenal ulcer, it is recommended that therapy be continued with a dose of 20 mg once a day at bedtime, for a duration of up to 6 to 12 months depending on the severity of the condition.

Benign Gastric Ulcer: Acute Therapy: The recommended adult oral dosage for acute benign gastric ulcer is 40 mg once a day at bedtime. Treatment should be given for 4 to 8 weeks, but the duration of treatment may be shortened if healing can be documented.

Pathological Hypersecretory Conditions (such as Zollinger-Ellison Syndrome): The dosage of famotidine in patients with pathological hypersecretory conditions varies with the individual patient. The recommended adult oral starting dose for pathological hypersecretory conditions is 20 mg every 6 hours. In some patients, a higher starting dose may be required. Doses should be adjusted to individual patient needs and should continue as long as clinically indicated. Doses up to 800 mg/day have been administered to some patients with severe Zollinger-Ellison syndrome.

Gastroesophageal Reflux Disease: The recommended dosage for the symptomatic relief of gastroesophageal reflux disease is 20 mg of famotidine twice a day.

For the treatment of esophageal erosion or ulceration associated with gastroesophageal reflux disease, the recommended dosage is 40 mg of famotidine twice a day.

Concomitant Use with Antacids: Antacids may be given concomitantly if needed.

Dosage Adjustment for Patients with Severe Renal Insufficiency: In patients with advanced renal insufficiency, i.e., with a creatinine clearance less than 10 mL/min, the elimination half-life of famotidine may exceed 20 hours reaching approximately 24 hours in anuric patients.

To avoid excess accumulation of the drug, the dosing interval of famotidine may be prolonged to 36 to 48 hours as indicated by the patient's clinical response.

Supplied: 20 mg: Each beige, D-shaped, film-coated tablet, imprinted novo on one side and 20 on the other, contains: famotidine 20 mg. Bottles of 100 and 500. Unit dose strips of 100. Patient paks of 30.

40 mg: Each light brownish orange, D-shaped, film-coated tablet, imprinted novo on one side and 40 on the other, contains: famotidine 40 mg. Bottles of 100 and 500. Unit dose strips of 100. Patient paks of 30.

NOVOFINE® 28G
NOVOFINE® 30G

Novo Nordisk

Disposable Needles

Insulin Delivery Device

Supplied: NovoFine® 28G (0.36×12 mm) and NovoFine® 30G (0.3×8 mm) needles are intended for single use. Sterile, nontoxic, nonpyrogenic, sterilized with ethylene oxide. NovoFine® needles should not be used after the expiry date printed on the protective tab. Sterility is guaranteed until expiry date if needle seal is unbroken.

Use once and destroy. Do not use needles where the protective tab is missing or damaged.

NovoFine® needles are specifically designed for use with Novolin-Pen® 1.5 and Novolin-Pen® 3 (see Novo Nordisk Insulin Delivery Devices). NovoFine® needles offer the added safety of Function Check capability when used with Novo Nordisk injection devices.

The NovoFine® needles should be removed from the Novolin-Pen® 1.5/Novolin-Pen® 3 after each injection. If the needle is not removed, changes in ambient temperature can result in some liquid being expelled from the cartridge. In the case of insulin suspensions, removal of supernatant liquid can cause an increase in insulin concentration (i.e., strength) remaining in the cartridge.

Consult Insulin Delivery System Instruction Manual for information on assembly; injection and Function Check capability.

(Shown in Product Recognition Section)

NOVO-5 ASA ℞

Novopharm

5-Aminosalicylic Acid

Lower Gastrointestinal Anti-inflammatory

Supplied: Each brown-red, capsule-shaped, enteric-coated tablet contains: 5-aminosalicylic acid 400 mg, coated with an acrylic-based resin. Gluten- and tartrazine-free. Bottles of 100 and 500.

NOVO-FLUOXETINE ℞

Novopharm

Fluoxetine HCl

Antidepressant—Antiobsessional—Antibulimic

Pharmacology: The antidepressant, antiobsessional, and antibulimic actions of fluoxetine are presumed to be linked to its ability to selectively inhibit the neuronal reuptake of serotonin. At clinically relevant doses fluoxetine blocks the uptake of serotonin into human platelets. Antagonism of muscarinic, histaminergic and α_1-adrenergic receptors has been hypothesized to be associated with various anticholinergic, sedative and cardiovascular effects of classical tricyclic antidepressant drugs. In vitro receptor binding studies have demonstrated that fluoxetine binds to these and other membrane receptors [opiate, serotonergic ($5\text{-}HT_1$, $5\text{-}HT_2$) adrenergic (α_1, α_2, ß) and dopaminergic] much less potently than do the tricyclic drugs.

Pharmacokinetics: Fluoxetine is well absorbed after oral administration. In man, following a single oral 40 mg dose, peak plasma concentrations of fluoxetine from 15 to 55 ng/mL are observed after 6 to 8 hours. Food does not appear to affect the systemic bioavailability of fluoxetine, although it may delay its absorption inconsequentially. Thus fluoxetine may be administered with or without food.

Fluoxetine is extensively metabolized in the liver to norfluoxetine, and other unidentified metabolites. The pharmacological activity of norfluoxetine, which is formed by demethylation of fluoxetine appears to be similar to that of the parent drug. Norfluoxetine contributes to the long duration of action of fluoxetine. The primary route of elimination appears to be hepatic metabolism to inactive metabolites excreted by the kidney.

Clinical Issues Related to Metabolism/Elimination: The complexity of the metabolism of fluoxetine has several consequences that may potentially affect its clinical use.

Accumulation and Slow Elimination: The relatively slow elimination of fluoxetine (elimination half-life of 1 to 3 days after acute administration and 4 to 6 days after chronic administration) and its active metabolite, norfluoxetine (elimination half-life 4 to 16 days after acute and chronic administration) results in significant accumulation during chronic use. After 30 days of dosing at 20 mg/day, mean plasma concentrations of fluoxetine 79.1 ± 33.4 ng/mL and of norfluoxetine 129 ± 42.0 ng/mL have been observed. Plasma concentrations of fluoxetine were higher than those predicted by single-dose studies, presumably because fluoxetine's metabolism is not proportional to dose. Norfluoxetine, however, appears to have linear pharmacokinetics. Its mean terminal half-life after a single dose was 8.6 days and after multiple dosing was 9.3 days.

Steady state plasma levels are attained after 4 to 5 weeks of continuous drug administration. Patients receiving fluoxetine at doses of 40 to 80 mg/day over periods as long as 3 years exhibited, on average, plasma concentrations similar to those seen among patients treated for 4 to 5 weeks.

Similarly, because of the long half-lives of fluoxetine and norfluoxetine, it may take up to 1 to 2 months for the active drug substance to disappear from the body. This is of potential consequence in the withdrawal of fluoxetine (see Warnings).

Age: The disposition of single doses of fluoxetine in healthy elderly subjects (greater than 65 years of age) did not differ significantly from that in younger normal subjects. However, given the long half-life and nonlinear disposition of the drug, a single-dose study is not adequate to rule out the possibility of altered pharmacokinetics in the elderly, particularly if they have systemic illness or are receiving multiple drugs for concomitant diseases.

The effects of age upon the metabolism of fluoxetine have been investigated in a subset of 260 elderly, but otherwise healthy, depressed patients (mean age: 67.4 years, range 60 to 85 years) who received 20 mg fluoxetine for 6 weeks. Mean plasma concentrations were found to be 89.5 ± 53.6 ng/mL for fluoxetine and 119 ± 51.3 ng/mL for norfluoxetine.

Protein Binding: Approximately 94% of fluoxetine is protein bound. The interaction between fluoxetine and other highly protein bound drugs has not been fully evaluated, but may be important (see Precautions).

Liver Disease: As might be predicted from its primary site of metabolism, liver impairment can affect the elimination of fluoxetine. In patients with cirrhosis, the elimination half-life of fluoxetine was prolonged, with a mean of 7.6 days compared to the range of 2 to 3 days seen in subjects without liver disease; norfluoxetine elimination half-life was also delayed, with a mean duration of 12 days for cirrhotic patients compared to the range of 7 to 9 days in normal subjects. This suggests that the use of fluoxetine in patients with liver disease must be approached with caution (see Precautions and Dosage).

Renal Disease: In single dose studies, the pharmacokinetics of fluoxetine and norfluoxetine were similar among subjects with all levels of impaired renal function including anephric patients on chronic hemodialysis. However, with chronic administration, additional accumulation of fluoxetine or its metabolites (possibly including some not yet identified) may occur in patients with severely impaired renal function and use of a lower or less frequent dose is advised (see Precautions).

Clinical Trials: The efficacy of fluoxetine was established in 5 and 6 week placebo controlled clinical trials in depressed outpatients (≥ 18 yrs of age), who meet the DSM-III criteria for major depressive disorder.

Two, 6 week, placebo controlled clinical trials in depressed elderly patients, who met the DSM-III-R criteria for major depressive disorder (mean age 67.4 years, range 60 to 85 years) have shown fluoxetine, 20 mg/day to be effective.

Indications: Depression: Fluoxetine is indicated for the symptomatic relief of depressive illness.

Bulimia Nervosa: Fluoxetine has been shown to significantly reduce binge-eating and purging activity when compared with placebo treatment.

Obsessive-Compulsive Disorder: Fluoxetine has been shown to significantly reduce the symptoms of obsessive-compulsive disorder in double-blind, placebo-controlled clinical trials. The obsessions or compulsions must be experienced as intrusive, markedly distressing, time consuming, or interfering significantly with the person's social or occupational functioning.

The efficacy of fluoxetine in hospitalized patients has not been adequately studied.

The effectiveness of fluoxetine in long-term use (i.e. for more than 5 to 6 weeks in depression, for more than 16 weeks in bulimia nervosa, or for more than 13 weeks in obsessive compulsive disorder), has not been systematically evaluated in controlled trials. Therefore, the physician who elects to use fluoxetine for extended periods should periodically re-evaluate the long-term usefulness of the drug for the individual patient.

Contraindications: Patients with known hypersensitivity to the drug.

MAO Inhibitors: There have been reports of serious, sometimes fatal, reactions (including hyperthermia, rigidity, myoclonus, autonomic instability with possible rapid fluctuations of vital signs, and mental status changes that include extreme agitation progressing to delirium and coma) in patients receiving fluoxetine in combination with an MAO inhibitor, and in patients who have recently discontinued fluoxetine and then started on an MAO inhibitor. Some cases presented with features resembling neuroleptic malignant syndrome. Therefore, fluoxetine should not be used in combination with an MAO inhibitor, or within 14 days of discontinuing therapy with an MAO inhibitor. Since fluoxetine and its major metabolite have very long elimination half-lives, at least 5 weeks should be allowed after stopping fluoxetine before starting an MAO inhibitor. Limited reports suggest that i.v. administered dantrolene or orally administered cyproheptadine may benefit patients experiencing such reactions.

Warnings: Allergic Reactions (Rash and Accompanying Events): During premarketing testing of more than 5 600 patients given fluoxetine, about 4% developed rash and/or urticaria. Among these cases, almost a third were withdrawn from treatment because of the rash and/or systemic signs or symptoms associated with the rash. Other symptoms reported in association with these allergic reactions were

Novo-Fluoxetine (cont'd)

fever, leukocytosis, arthralgias, edema, carpal tunnel syndrome, respiratory distress, lymphadenopathy, proteinuria, and a mild increase in transaminase. Most patients improved promptly with discontinuation of fluoxetine and/or adjunctive therapy with antihistamines or steroids, and all patients experiencing these events were reported to recover completely.

Two patients involved in these premarketing trials developed a serious cutaneous systemic illness. In neither case was there an unequivocal diagnosis, but one was considered to have a leukocytoclastic vasculitis, and the other, severe desquamation that was considered variously to be a vasculitis or erythema multiforme. Other patients have had systemic manifestations suggestive of serum sickness.

Since the introduction of fluoxetine, systemic effects which are possibly related to vasculitis have developed in patients with rash. Although these events occur rarely, they could be serious and involve the lung, kidney or liver. Death has been reported to occur in association with these systemic events.

Anaphylactoid events including bronchospasm, angioedema, and urticaria alone and in combination have been reported. Pulmonary events such as inflammatory processes of varying histopathology and/or fibrosis, have been reported rarely. These events have occurred with dyspnea as the only preceding symptom.

It is not known whether these systemic events and rash have a common underlying cause or are due to different etiologies or pathogenic processes. In addition, a specific underlying immunologic cause for these events has not been found. If a rash or other possibly allergic phenomena appear for which there is no alternative explanation, fluoxetine should be discontinued. Particular caution should be exercised in patients with a history of allergic reactions.

Implications of the Long Elimination Half-Life of Fluoxetine: Due to the long elimination half-lives of fluoxetine and its major active metabolite, norfluoxetine, alterations in dosage will not be fully reflected in plasma for several weeks, affecting both strategies for titration to final dose and discontinuation of therapy (see Pharmacology and Dosage). Even when treatment is withdrawn, the active drug will remain in the body for weeks because of the long elimination half-lives of fluoxetine and norfluoxetine. This is of potential consequence when discontinuation is desired or when drugs are to be administered which may interact with either fluoxetine or the active metabolite following discontinuation of fluoxetine.

Precautions: Anxiety and Insomnia: In premarketing investigations, anxiety, nervousness and insomnia occurred in 10 to 15% of the patients treated with fluoxetine. These effects required discontinuation of the drug in 5% of the patients.

Weight Change: Significant weight loss, especially in underweight depressed patients and the elderly, may be an undesirable result of treatment with fluoxetine.

Mania/Hypomania: In the premarketing trials carried out in a patient population composed mainly of unipolar depressives, hypomania or mania occurred in about 1% of patients given fluoxetine. The frequency of these events in a general patient population which might include bipolar depressives is unknown. The possibility of hypomanic or manic episodes may be greater with higher doses. Such reactions require a reduction in dosage or discontinuation of the drug.

Seizures: Fluoxetine should be used with caution in patients with a history of convulsive disorders. The frequency of seizures occurring during clinical trials of fluoxetine was not different from that reported with other marketed antidepressants; however, patients with a history of convulsive disorders were excluded from these trials.

Simultaneous administration of fluoxetine with electroshock therapy should be avoided due to the lack of experience in this area. Prolonged seizures have occurred rarely in patients taking fluoxetine and receiving ECT treatment.

Hypokalemia: Self-induced vomiting often leads to hypokalemia which may lower seizure threshold and/or may lead to cardiac conduction abnormalities. Electrolyte levels of bulimic patients should be assessed prior to initiation of treatment.

Suicide: The possibility of a suicide attempt is inherent in depression and may persist until significant remission occurs. Thus, those patients with a greater probability for attempting suicide should be watched closely while on therapy and the possible requirement for hospitalization should be considered. In order to minimize the opportunity for overdosage, the smallest amount of drug necessary for good patient management should be prescribed at any one time.

Concomitant Illness: Fluoxetine should be used cautiously in patients with systemic illness especially those with diseases or conditions affecting metabolism or hemodynamic responses since clinical data regarding these patients is limited.

Fluoxetine has not been tested or used to any appreciable extent in patients with a recent history of myocardial infarction or unstable heart disease. Such patients were systematically excluded from premarketing clinical trials. Retrospective analysis of EKG's in some of these trials found no conduction abnormalities that resulted in heart block. The mean heart rate was lowered by about 3 beats/minute.

Fluoxetine should be given with caution to patients suffering from anorexia nervosa and only if the expected benefits (e.g., co-morbid depression) markedly outweigh the potential weight reducing effect of the drug.

In diabetic patients, fluoxetine could affect glycemic control. Hypoglycemia has been reported during fluoxetine treatment and hyperglycemia has developed following termination of treatment. As with many other types of drugs, insulin and/or oral hypoglycemic dosage adjustment may be necessary in diabetic patients when fluoxetine therapy is begun or terminated.

Fluoxetine is extensively metabolized, excretion of unchanged drug in urine is a minor route of elimination. Until sufficient data has been collected from patients with severe renal impairment receiving chronic fluoxetine therapy, the drug should be used cautiously in such patients.

Since clearances of fluoxetine and norfluoxetine may be decreased in patients with impaired liver function including cirrhosis, a lower or less frequent dose should be used in such patients.

Hyponatremia: Several instances of hyponatremia have occurred (some with serum sodium levels less than 110 mmol/L). The hyponatremia appears to be reversible upon termination of fluoxetine treatment. Although these cases were complex with many different possible etiologies, it is possible that some were due to the syndrome of inappropriate antidiuretic hormone secretion (SIADH). Most of these cases have been in older patients and in patients receiving diuretics or who were otherwise volume depleted.

In a placebo-controlled, double-blind trial in elderly patients, 10 of 313 fluoxetine-treated patients and 6 of 320 placebo-treated patients had a lowering of serum sodium below the reference range. The lowest observed concentration of sodium in a fluoxetine treated patient was 129 mmol/L.

Platelet Function: Rare cases of altered platelet function and/or abnormal results from laboratory studies have been reported in patients receiving fluoxetine. Though abnormal bleeding has been reported in several patients taking fluoxetine it is not certain whether this was due to fluoxetine.

Occupational Hazards: Patients should be advised against driving automobiles or performing hazardous tasks until they are quite sure that fluoxetine does not cause any adverse effects.

Pregnancy and *Lactation:* The safe use of fluoxetine in pregnant or lactating women has not been determined. Thus, fluoxetine should be avoided by women of childbearing potential or nursing mothers unless, in the opinion of the treating physician, the expected benefits to the patient markedly outweigh the possible hazards to the fetus or child.

In a sample of breast milk, the concentration of fluoxetine plus norfluoxetine was measured to be 70.4 ng/mL. The concentration in the mother's plasma was 295 ng/mL. No adverse effects on the infant were noted. In another case, a 6 week infant, nursed by a mother on fluoxetine, developed crying, decreased sleep, vomiting and watery stools. The breast milk showed concentrations of 69 ng/mL for fluoxetine and 90 ng/mL for norfluoxetine. In the infant's plasma, the concentrations of fluoxetine and norfluoxetine were 340 and 208 ng/mL, respectively.

Children: The safe and effective use of fluoxetine in patients under 18 years of age has not been determined.

Geriatrics: Evaluation of patients over the age of 60 who received fluoxetine 20 mg daily revealed no unusual pattern of adverse events relative to the clinical experience in younger patients. These data are however insufficient to rule out possible age-related differences during chronic use, particularly in elderly patients who have concomitant systemic illnesses or who are receiving concomitant drugs.

Drug Interactions: The concomitant use of fluoxetine and MAO inhibitors is **contraindicated** (see Contraindications).

There have been greater than 2 fold increases of previously stable plasma levels of other antidepressants when fluoxetine has been administered in combination with these agents.

There have been reports of both increased and decreased lithium levels when lithium was used concomitantly with fluoxetine. Cases of lithium toxicity have been reported. Lithium levels should be monitored when these drugs are administered concomitantly.

Five patients receiving fluoxetine in combination with tryptophan experienced adverse reactions including agitation, restlessness and gastrointestinal distress.

The half-life of concurrently administered diazepam may be prolonged in some patients. Experience with the use of fluoxetine in combination with other CNS-active drugs is limited and caution is advised if such concomitant medication is required (see Warnings).

Phenytoin: In patients on stable, maintenance doses of phenytoin, plasma phenytoin concentrations increased substantially and symptoms of phenytoin toxicity appeared (nystagmus, diplopia, ataxia and CNS depression) following initiation of concomitant fluoxetine treatment.

Drugs tightly bound to plasma protein: Fluoxetine is highly plasma protein bound and thus the concomitant use of fluoxetine with another drug which is tightly bound to protein (e.g., warfarin, digitoxin) may cause a shift in plasma concentrations potentially resulting in an adverse effect. Conversely, adverse effects may result from displacement of protein bound fluoxetine by other tightly bound drugs.

P_{450} Isozyme (IID6): Like other selective serotonin reuptake inhibitors, fluoxetine inhibits the specific hepatic cytochrome P_{450} isozyme (IID6) which is responsible for the metabolism of debrisoquine and sparteine. Although the clinical significance of this effect has not been established, inhibition of IID6 may lead to elevated plasma levels of co-administered drugs which are metabolized by this isozyme. Drugs metabolized by cytochrome P_{450} IID6 include the tricyclic antidepressants (e.g., nortriptyline, amitriptyline, imipramine and desipramine), phenothiazine neuroleptics (e.g., perphenazine and thioridazine), and Type IC antiarrhythmics (e.g., propafenone and flecainide).

Dependence Liability: The potential for abuse, tolerance or physical dependence to fluoxetine has not been investigated in animals or humans. Therefore, physicians should carefully evaluate patients for history of drug abuse and monitor these patients closely, checking for signs of misuse or abuse (e.g., development of tolerance, incrementation of dose, drug-seeking behavior).

Adverse Effects: In clinical trials, the most frequently observed adverse effects related to the use of fluoxetine and occurring at a higher incidence than with the use of placebo were: CNS effects such as headache, nervousness, insomnia, drowsiness, fatigue or asthenia, anxiety, tremor, and dizziness or lightheadedness; gastrointestinal effects such as nausea, diarrhea, dry mouth and anorexia; and excessive sweating. Fluoxetine treatment had to be terminated in 15% of about 4 000 patients in North American clinical trials because of adverse effects. The most common causes for withdrawing treatment were: psychiatric (5.3%), mainly nervousness, anxiety, and insomnia; digestive (3.0%), mainly nausea; nervous system (1.6%), mainly dizziness, asthenia, and headaches; skin (1.4%), mainly rash and pruritus.

In obsessive compulsive disorder studies, 12.1% of fluoxetine treated patients discontinued treatment early because of adverse events. Anxiety, and rash, at incidences of less than 2%, were the most frequently reported events. In bulimia nervosa studies, 10.2% of fluoxetine treated patients discontinued treatment early because of adverse events. Insomnia, anxiety and rash, at incidences of less than 2%, were the most frequently reported events.

Serious Adverse Reactions: Suicidal thoughts and acts are far more common among depressed patients than in the general population. It is estimated that suicide is 22 to 36 times more prevalent in depressed persons than in the general population. A comprehensive meta-analysis of pooled data from 17 double blind clinical trials in patients with major depressive disorder compared fluoxetine (n=1 765) with a tricyclic antidepressant (n=731) or placebo (n=569), or both. The pooled incidence of emergence of substantial suicidal ideation was 1.2% for fluoxetine, 2.6% for placebo and 3.6% for tricyclic antidepressants.

In countries where the drug is presently marketed, the following potentially serious adverse effects have been observed; interactions with MAO inhibitors and possibly other drugs, allergic reactions, cardiovascular reactions, syndrome of inappropriate ADH secretion, and grand mal seizure. Death and life threatening effects have been linked to some of these reactions, though a definite association with fluoxetine has not been determined.

Adverse Experience Reports: The pattern of treatment-emergent adverse experience incidence (≥5%) for both fluoxetine and placebo was somewhat different in bulimia and obsessive compulsive disorder (OCD) trials than in the adult and elderly depression studies, and is summarized in Table I.

The following adverse reactions, were reported on at least 1 occasion by patients during treatment with fluoxetine either during clinical trials or after marketing. All reported events are included except those where a drug cause was remote or the event term so general as to be unhelpful. Multiple events may have been reported by a single patient and related to a single condition, which may have pre-existed. Therefore, while the following events occurred during treatment with fluoxetine, they were not necessarily caused by it.

Events are further classified within body system categories and enumerated in order of decreasing frequency using the following definitions: frequent adverse events are defined as those occurring on 1 or more occasions in at least 1/100 patients; infrequent adverse events are those occurring in less than 1/100 but at least 1/1 000 patients, rare events are those occurring in less than 1/1 000 patients.

Allergic or Toxic: Frequent: rash, pruritus. Infrequent: chills and fever, urticaria, maculopapular rash. Rare: allergic reaction, erythema multiforme, vesiculobullous rash, serum sickness, contact dermatitis, erythema nodosum, purpuric rash, leukocytoclastic vasculitis, leukopenia, thrombocytopenia, arthralgia, angioedema, bronchospasm, lung fibrosis, allergic alveolitis, larynx edema, respiratory distress.

Neurologic: Frequent: headache, tremor, dizziness or lightheadedness, asthenia. Infrequent: abnormal gait, ataxia, akathisia, buccoglossal syndrome, hyperkinesia, hypertonia, incoordination, neck rigidity, extrapyramidal syndrome, convulsions, photophobia, myoclonus, vertigo, migraine, tinnitus, hypesthesia, neuralgia, neuropathy, acute brain syndrome. Rare: dysarthria, dystonia, torticollis, decreased reflexes, nystagmus, paralysis, paresthesia, carpal tunnel syndrome, stupor, coma, abnormal electroencephalogram, chronic brain syndrome, dyskinesia and other movement disorders [including worsening of pre-existing conditions or appearance in patients with risk factors (e.g., Parkinson's disease, treatment with neuroleptics or other drugs known to be associated with movement disorders)], neuroleptic malignant syndrome-like events.

Behavioral: Frequent: insomnia, anxiety, nervousness, agitation, abnormal dreams, drowsiness and fatigue. Infrequent: confusion, delusions, hallucinations, manic reaction, paranoid reaction, psychosis, depersonalization, apathy, emotional lability, euphoria, hostility, amnesia, increased libido. Rare: antisocial reaction, hysteria, suicidal ideation, violent behaviors.

Autonomic: Frequent: excessive sweating. Infrequent: dry mouth, constipation, urinary retention, vision disturbance, diplopia, mydriasis, hot flushes.

Cardiovascular: Infrequent: chest pain, hypertension, syncope, hypotension (including postural hypotension), angina pectoris, arrhythmia, tachycardia. Rare: bradycardia, ventricular arrhythmia, first degree AV block, bundle branch block, myocardial infarct, cerebral ischemia, cerebral vascular accident, thrombophlebitis.

Gastrointestinal: Frequent: nausea, disturbances of appetite, diarrhea. Infrequent: vomiting, stomatitis, dysphagia, eructation, esophagitis, gastritis, gingivitis, glossitis, melena, thirst, abnormal liver function tests. Rare: bloody diarrhea, hematemesis, gastrointestinal, hemorrhage, duodenal ulcer, stomach ulcer, mouth ulceration, hyperchlorhydria, colitis, enteritis, cholecystitis, cholelithiasis, hepatitis, hepatomegaly, liver tenderness, jaundice, increased salivation, salivary gland enlargement, tongue discoloration, fecal incontinence, pancreatitis.

Table I—Novo-Fluoxetine

Adverse Experience Reports

Body System/ Adverse Event	Depression (Adults) Fluoxetine (N=1 730)	Depression (Adults) Placebo (N=799)	Depression (Elderly) Fluoxetine (N=335)	Depression (Elderly) Placebo (N=336)	Obsessive Compulsive Disorder Fluoxetine (N=264)	Obsessive Compulsive Disorder Placebo (N=89)	Bulimia Fluoxetine (N=418)	Bulimia Placebo (N=210)
Nervous								
Headache	20.3	15.5	27.5	23.8	32.6	23.6	30.1	26.9
Nervousness	14.9	8.5	12.2	7.4	14. 4	14.6	10.8	5.2
Insomnia	13.8	7.1	18.2	12.5	29.6	22.5	33.1	15.0
Somnolence	11.6	6.3	9.3	5.7	17.1	6.7	12.7	7.1
Anxiety	9.4	5.5	13.1	8.0	13.6	6.7	16.3	1 1.1
Tremor	7.9	2.4	7.8	3.9	9.1	1.1	13.7	2.0
Dizziness	5.7	3.3	11.0	10.1	13. 3	11.2	11.4	5.4
Libido, Decreased	1.6	—	—	—	11.4	2.3	5.9	0.9
Depression	—	—	—	—	8.0	14.6	10.1	16.4
Emotional Lability	—	—	—	—	—	—	2.7	7.8
Digestive								
Nausea	21.1	10.1	16.7	7.4	26.5	13.5	29.7	13.5
Diarrhea	12.3	7.0	14.3	8.9	18.2	13.5	7.5	6.7
Dry Mouth	9.5	6.0	6.6	4.8	12.1	3.4	9.9	8.6
Anorexia	8.7	1.5	10.7	1.8	16.7	10.1	8. 8	4.4
Dyspepsia	6.4	4.3	11.0	5.1	9.9	4.5	10.7	6.7
Gastrointestinal Disorder	—	—	—	—	5.7	1.1	5.7	5.9
Constipation	—	—	6.9	6.3	4.2	6.7	4 .8	4.6
Flatulence	—	—	7.2	2.4	3.4	5.6	—	—
Skin and Appendages								
Sweating, Excessive	8.4	3.8	7.2	3.3	7.2	—	8.9	1.6
Rash	—	—	—	—	6.4	3.4	5.1	4.9
Body as a Whole								
Asthenia	4.4	1.9	12.8	10.1	15.2	10.1	21.7	9.6
Flu Syndrome	—	—	—	—	9.9	6.7	10.1	5.9
Back Pain	—	—	6.9	8.6	2.7	5.6	3.9	7.0
Infection	—	—	—	—	—	—	6.2	6.2
Abdominal Pain	—	—	6.0	5.7	4.9	11.2	9.6	6.5
Myalgia	—	—	3.3	5.4	—	—	4.7	9.4
Respiratory								
Upper Respiratory Infection	7.6	6.0	—	—	—	—	—	—
Rhinitis	—	—	9.0	14.3	22.7	23.6	23.0	29.1
Pharyngitis	—	—	—	—	10.6	9.0	11.1	5.5
Sinusitis	—	—	3.3	6.8	—	—	5.7	6.9
Yawn	—	—	—	—	7.2	—	11.1	0.8
Cardiovascular								
Vasodilatation	—	—	—	—	5.3	—	—	—
Urogenital								
Menstrual Disorder	—	—	—	—	3.4	5.6	8.3	4.8
Dysmenorrhea	—	—	—	—	3.4	5.6	6.1	7.8
Urinary Frequency	—	—	—	—	—	—	6.2	1.6
Urinary Tract Infection	—	—	—	—	—	—	5.1	2.0

Respiratory: Frequent: bronchitis, rhinitis, yawn. Infrequent: asthma, dyspnea, hyperventilation, pneumonia, hiccups, epistaxis. Rare: apnea, lung edema, hypoxia, pleural effusion, hemoptysis.

Endocrine: Frequent: weight loss. Infrequent: generalized edema, peripheral edema, face edema, tongue edema, hypoglycemia, hypothyroidism, weight gain. Rare: dehydration, gout, goitre, hyperthyroidism, hypercholesterolemia, hyperglycemia, hyperlipidemia, hyperprolactinemia, hypokalemia, hyponatremia, iron deficiency anemia, syndrome of inappropriate ADH secretion.

Hematologic: Infrequent: anemia, lymphadenopathy, hemorrhage. Rare: bleeding time increased, leukocytosis, lymphocytosis, thrombocytopenia, thrombocytopenic purpura, thrombocythemia, retinal hemorrhage, petechia, purpura, sedimentation rate increased, aplastic anemia, pancytopenia, immune-related hemolytic anemia.

Dermatologic: Infrequent: acne, alopecia, dry skin, herpes simplex. Rare: excema, psoriasis, seborrhea, skin hypertrophy, skin discoloration, herpes zoster, fungal dermatitis, hirsutism, ecchymoses.

Musculoskeletal: Frequent: muscle pain, back pain, joint pain. Infrequent: arthritis, bone pain, bursitis, tenosynovitis, twitching. Rare: bone necrosis, osteoporosis, pathological fracture, chondrodystrophy, myositis, rheumatoid arthritis, muscle hemorrhage.

Urogenital: Frequent: painful menstruation, sexual dysfunction, impotence, urinary tract infection, frequent micturition. Infrequent: abnormal ejaculation, menopause, amenorrhea, menorrhagia, ovarian disorder, vaginitis, leukorrhea, fibrocystic breast, breast pain, cystitis, dysuria, urinary urgency, urinary incontinence. Rare: breast enlargement, galactorrhea, abortion, dyspareunia, uterine spasm, vaginal hemorrhage, metrorrhagia, hematuria, albuminuria, polyuria, pyuria, epididymitis, orchitis, pyelonephritis, salpingitis, urethritis, kidney calculus, urethral pain, urolithiasis.

Miscellaneous: Frequent: chills, abnormal vision. Infrequent: amblyopia, conjunctivitis, cyst, ear pain, eye pain, jaw pain, neck pain, pelvic pain, hangover effect, malaise. Rare: abdomen enlarged, blepharitis, cataract, corneal lesion, glaucoma, iritis, ptosis, strabismus, deafness, taste loss, moniliasis, hydrocephalus, LE syndrome.

Overdose: During clinical trials, there were 2 deaths among approximately 38 reports of acute overdose with fluoxetine, either alone or in combination with other drugs and/or alcohol. One death involved a combined overdose with approximately 1 800 mg of fluoxetine and an undetermined amount of maprotiline. Plasma concentrations of fluoxetine and maprotiline were 4.57 mg/L and 4.18 mg/L, respectively.

A second death involved 3 drugs yielding plasma concentrations as follows: fluoxetine, 1.93 mg/L; norfluoxetine, 1.10 mg/L; codeine, 1.80 mg/L; temazepam, 3.80 mg/L.

One other patient who reportedly took up to 3 000 mg of fluoxetine experienced 2 grand mal seizures that remitted spontaneously without specific treatment. Since vomiting occurred, the amount of drug absorbed may have been less than that ingested.

In the postmarketing phase, there have been 16 confirmed reports of overdose of fluoxetine taken alone. The amount of drug ingested has varied from 80 to 2 000 mg and the patients have ranged in age from 13 to 51 years. There have been no deaths in this group of patients, some of whom were treated vigorously with activated charcoal in the acute phase. Furthermore, patient recoveries were remarkable in the absence of serious adverse events with the exception of a 13 year old male who ingested 1 880 mg and experienced 2 brief seizures but thereafter had an uneventful recovery.

Since introduction, reports of death attributed to overdosage of fluoxetine alone have been rare.

Symptoms: Nausea and vomiting were prominent in overdoses involving higher fluoxetine doses. Other prominent symptoms of overdose included agitation, restlessness, hypomania, and other signs of CNS excitation, including seizures.

Treatment: Establish and maintain an airway; insure adequate oxygenation and ventilation. Activated charcoal, which may be used with sorbitol, may be as or more

Novo-Fluoxetine (cont'd)

effective than emesis or lavage, and should be considered in treating overdose.

Cardiac and vital signs monitoring is recommended, along with general symptomatic and supportive measures. Based on experience in animals, which may not be relevant to humans, fluoxetine-induced seizures which fail to remit spontaneously may respond to diazepam.

There are no specific antidotes for fluoxetine.

Due to large volume of distribution of fluoxetine, forced diuresis, dialysis, hemoperfusion, and exchange transfusion are unlikely to be of benefit. In managing overdosage, consider the possibility of multiple drug involvement. The physician should consider contacting a poison control centre on the treatment of any overdosage.

Dosage: Since it may take up to 4 or 5 weeks to reach steady-state plasma levels of fluoxetine, sufficient time should be allowed to elapse before dosage is gradually increased. Higher dosages are usually associated with an increased incidence of adverse reactions.

Depression: Initial Adult Dosage: The usual initial dosage is 20 mg administered once daily in the morning. A gradual dose increase should be considered only after a trial period of several weeks if the expected clinical improvement does not occur. Dosage should not exceed a maximum of 80 mg per day since clinical experience with doses above 80 mg per day is very limited.

Geriatrics: Fluoxetine was evaluated in depressed elderly patients only at a dosage of 20 mg/day. A lower or less frequent dosage may be effective and should be considered in elderly patients with concurrent disease or on multiple medications.

Children: The safety and effectiveness of fluoxetine in patients below the age of 18 years have not been established.

Bulimia Nervosa: Adult Dosage: The recommended dosage is 60 mg/day, although studies show that lower doses may also be efficacious. Electrolyte levels should be assessed prior to initiation of treatment.

Obsessive-Compulsive Disorder: A dose range of 20 to 60 mg/day is recommended for the treatment of obsessive compulsive disorder.

For any indication, the total fluoxetine dosage should not exceed a maximum of 80 mg/day since clinical experience with doses above 80 mg/day is very limited. During maintenance therapy, the dosage should be kept at the lowest effective level.

A lower or less frequent dosage should be used in patients with renal and/or hepatic impairment and in those on multiple medications.

Supplied: 10 mg: Each hard gelatin capsule with opaque green cap and opaque grey body, imprinted with black ink novo on cap and 10 on body contains: fluoxetine HCl equivalent to fluoxetine 10 mg. Nonmedicinal ingredients: colloidal silicon dioxide, magnesium stearate, sodium carboxymethyl starch and starch. Capsule shell: FD&C blue #1, FD&C yellow #6, D&C yellow #10, gelatin, silicon dioxide, sodium lauryl sulfate and titanium dioxide. Bottles of 100, 500 and 1 000. Boxes of 100 as unit dose strips.

20 mg: Each hard gelatin capsule with opaque green cap and opaque ivory body, imprinted with black ink novo on cap, 20 on body, contains: fluoxetine HCl equivalent to fluoxetine 20 mg. Nonmedicinal ingredients: colloidal silicon dioxide, magnesium stearate, sodium carboxymethyl starch and starch. Capsule shell: D&C yellow #10, FD&C blue #1, FD&C yellow #6, gelatin, silicon dioxide, sodium lauryl sulfate and titanium dioxide. Bottles of 30, 100, 500 and 1 000. Boxes of 100 as unit dose strips.

Store bottles between 15 to 30°C. Protect from light. Unit dose boxes should be kept between 15 to 25°C. Protect from high humidity and light.

Reviewed 1997

NOVO-FLURPROFEN ℞

Novopharm

Flurbiprofen

Anti-inflammatory—Analgesic

Supplied: 50 mg: Each white, oval-shaped, film-coated tablet, printed black N over 50 on one side and plain on the other side, contains: flurbiprofen 50 mg. Gluten- and tartrazine-free. Bottles of 100 and 500.

100 mg: Each blue, oval-shaped, film-coated tablet, printed black N over 100 on one side and plain on the other side, contains: flurbiprofen 100 mg. Gluten- and tartrazine-free. Bottles of 100 and 500.

NOVO-FLUTAMIDE ℞

Novopharm

Flutamide

Nonsteroidal Antiandrogen

Pharmacology: Flutamide demonstrates potent antiandrogenic effects by inhibiting androgen uptake and/or inhibiting nuclear binding of androgen in target tissues. In adult male rats, ventral prostrate weights and seminal vesicle weights were markedly reduced by daily administration of flutamide.

Indications: For use in combination with LHRH agonistic analogues (such as leuprolide acetate) for the treatment of metastatic prostatic carcinoma (stage D_2). To achieve the benefit of the adjunctive therapy with flutamide, treatment must be started simultaneously using both drugs. Also as an adjunctive therapy to orchiectomy, in order to achieve complete androgen blockade.

Contraindications: Patients who have shown hypersensitivity to flutamide or any component of this preparation.

Warnings: Gynecomastia occurred in 9% of patients receiving flutamide together with medical castration. Physicians must familiarize themselves with the proper use of LHRH before combination medication is contemplated.

Pregnancy: Flutamide may cause fetal harm when administered to a pregnant woman. There was decreased 24-hour survival in the offspring of rats treated with flutamide at doses of 30, 100, or 200 mg/kg/day (approximately 3, 9, and 19 times the human dose) during pregnancy. A slight increase in minor variations in the development of the sternebra and vertebra was seen in fetuses of rats at the two higher doses. Feminization of the males also occurred at the two higher dose levels. There was a decreased survival rate in the offspring of rabbits receiving the highest dose (15 mg/kg/day; equal to 1.4 times the human dose).

Precautions: Periodic liver function tests and sperm count determinations must be performed in patients on long-term treatment with flutamide.

Since flutamide tends to elevate plasma testosterone and estradiol levels, fluid retention may occur. Accordingly, flutamide should be used with caution in those patients with cardiac disease.

Hepatic Injury: Since transaminase abnormalities, cholestatic jaundice, hepatic necrosis and hepatic encephalopathy have been reported with the use of flutamide, periodic liver function tests should be considered. **Appropriate laboratory testing should be done at the first symptom/sign of liver dysfunction (e.g., pruritus, dark urine, persistent anorexia, jaundice, right upper quadrant tenderness or unexplained "flu-like" symptoms). If the patient has laboratory evidence of liver injury or jaundice, in the absence of biopsy-confirmed liver metastases, flutamide therapy should be discontinued or the dosage reduced. The hepatic injury is usually reversible after discontinuation of therapy and in some patients, after dosage reduction.** However, there have been reports of death following severe hepatic injury associated with use of flutamide.

Information for the Patient: Patients should be informed that flutamide and the drug used for medical castration should be administered concomitantly, and that they should not interrupt their dosing or stop taking these medications without consulting their physician.

Drug Interactions: In patients receiving long-term warfarin therapy, increases in prothrombin time have been reported after flutamide monotherapy was initiated. Adjustment of the anticoagulant dose may be necessary when flutamide tablets are administered concomitantly with warfarin.

Adverse Effects: The most frequently reported adverse reactions to flutamide **monotherapy** are gynecomastia and/or breast tenderness, sometimes accompanied by galactorrhea. These reactions usually disappear upon discontinuation of treatment or reduction in dosage. **The incidence of gynecomastia is reduced greatly when flutamide tablets are administered concomitantly with an LHRH agonist.**

The most frequently reported (greater than 5%) adverse experiences during treatment with flutamide in combination with a LHRH agonist are listed in Table I. For comparison, adverse experiences seen with a LHRH agonist and placebo are also listed in Table I.

Table I—Novo-Flutamide

Adverse Effects	(n=294) Flutamide+ LHRH-Agonist % All	(n=285) Placebo+ LHRH-Agonist % All
Hot Flashes	61	57
Loss of Libido	36	31
Impotence	33	29
Diarrhea	12	4
Nausea/Vomiting	11	10
Gynecomastia	9	11
Other	7	9
Other Gastrointestinal Effects	6	4

As shown in Table I, for both treatment groups, the most frequently occurring adverse experiences (hot flashes, impotence, loss of libido) were those known to be associated with low serum androgen levels and known to occur with LHRH-agonists alone.

The only notable difference was the higher incidence of diarrhea in the flutamide+LHRH agonist opposed to the placebo+LHRH-agonist (4%), which was severe in less than 1%. In addition, the following adverse reactions were reported during treatment with flutamide+LHRH-agonist. No causal relatedness of these reactions to drug treatment has been made, and some of the adverse experiences reported are those that commonly occur in elderly patients.

Cardiovascular: Hypertension in 1% of patients. Rarely thrombophlebitis, pulmonary embolism, myocardial infarction.

CNS: CNS (drowsiness/confusion/depression/anxiety/nervousness) reactions occurred in 1% of patients. Rarely insomnia, tiredness, headache, weakness, blurred vision and decreased libido have been reported.

Endocrine: Gynecomastia in 9% of patients. Rarely breast tenderness sometimes accompanied by galactorrhea.

Gastrointestinal: Nausea/vomiting occurred in 11%; diarrhea 12%, anorexia 4%, and other gastrointestinal disorders occurred in 6% of patients. Increased appetite, indigestion and constipation have also been reported.

Hematopoietic: Anemia occurred in 6% of patients, leukopenia 3%, thrombocytopenia 1%.

Liver and Biliary: Clinically evident hepatitis and jaundice occurred in $<1\%$ of patients.

Skin: Irritation at the injection site and rash occurred in 3% of patients. Photosensitivity reactions have been reported in 5 patients.

Other: pruritus, ecchymosis, herpes zoster, thirst, lymphoedema, lupus-like syndrome, hematuria. Reduced sperm counts have been reported rarely in long-term treatment. Edema occurred in 4% of patients; neuromuscular, genitourinary symptoms occurred in 2% of patients. Pulmonary symptoms occurred in $<1\%$ of patients.

Laboratory Values: Abnormal laboratory test results reported include elevated AST, ALT; elevated blood urea nitrogen (BUN) and bilirubin levels; less frequently, elevated serum creatinine levels and elevated gamma-glutamyl transferase levels have been reported.

In addition, the following adverse experiences have been reported during world-wide marketing of flutamide: hemolytic anemia, macrocytic anemia, methemoglobinemia, photosensitivity reactions (including erythema, ulcerations, bullous eruptions and epidermal necrolysis), and change in urine color to an amber or yellow-green appearance, which can be attributed to flutamide and/or its metabolites. Also observed were cholestatic jaundice, hepatic encephalopathy and hepatic necrosis. The hepatic conditions were usually reversible after discontinuing therapy; however, there have been reports of death following severe hepatic injury associated with the use of flutamide.

Overdose: Symptoms: In animal studies with flutamide alone, signs of overdose included hypoactivity, piloerection, slow respiration, ataxia, and/or lacrimation, anorexia, tranquillization and emesis.

Clinical trials have been conducted with flutamide in doses up to 1 500 mg/day for periods up to 36 weeks with no serious adverse effects reported. Those adverse reactions reported included gynecomastia, breast tenderness and some increases in AST. The single dose of flutamide ordinarily associated with symptoms of overdose or considered to be life-threatening has not been established.

Treatment: Since flutamide is highly protein bound, dialysis may not be of any use as treatment for overdose. As in the management of overdosage with any drug, it should be borne in mind that multiple agents may have been taken. If vomiting does not occur spontaneously, it should be induced if the patient is alert. General supportive care, including frequent monitoring of the vital signs and close observation of the patient, is indicated.

Dosage: The recommended dose is one 250 mg tablet 3 times/day.

Supplied: Each light yellow colored, round, standard convex compressed tablet, engraved novo on the scored side and 250 on the other side, contains: flutamide 250 mg. Bottles of 100. Boxes of 100 as unit dose strips. Store at room temperature (15 to 30°C).

Reviewed 1998

NOVO-FURANTOIN Ⓟ
Novopharm

Nitrofurantoin

Urinary Tract Antibacterial

Supplied: 50 mg: Each yellow/white capsule, imprinted with N 50 in black ink, contains: nitrofurantoin 50 mg. Gluten- and tartrazine-free. Bottles of 100 and 500.

100 mg: Each yellow/yellow capsule, imprinted with N and 100 on opposing cap and body in black ink, contains: nitrofurantoin 100 mg. Gluten- and tartrazine-free. Bottles of 100 and 500.

NOVO-GEMFIBROZIL Ⓟ
Novopharm

Gemfibrozil

Antihyperlipidemic Agent

Supplied: Each white, oval-shaped, film-coated tablet, engraved novo and 600 on opposite sides, contains: gemfibrozil 600 mg. Gluten- and tartrazine-free. Bottles of 100 and 500.

NOVO-GESIC C8 Ⓝ
NOVO-GESIC C15 Ⓝ
NOVO-GESIC C30 Ⓝ
Novopharm

Acetaminophen—Caffeine—Codeine Phosphate

Analgesic—Antipyretic

Supplied: Novo-Gesic C8: Each white, round, biconvex, compressed tablet, engraved N and 1 on opposite sides, contains: acetaminophen 300 mg, caffeine 15 mg and codeine phosphate 8 mg. Bottles of 100 and 200.

Novo-Gesic C15: Each white, round, biconvex, scored, compressed tablet, engraved N and 2 on opposite sides, contains: acetaminophen 300 mg, caffeine 15 mg and codeine phosphate 15 mg. Bottles of 100 and 500. Unit dose strips of 100.

Novo-Gesic C30: Each white, round, biconvex, compressed tablet, engraved N and 3 on opposite sides, contains: acetaminophen 300 mg, caffeine 15 mg and codeine phosphate 30 mg. Bottles of 500. Unit dose strips of 100.

NOVO-GLICLAZIDE Ⓟ
Novopharm

Gliclazide

Oral Hypoglycemic

Supplied: Each white to off-white, round, beveled-edged compressed tablet, quadrisect (+) on one side and engraved N on the other side, contains: gliclazide 80 mg. Nonmedicinal ingredients: glyceryl behenate, lactose monohydrate, microcrystalline cellulose, povidone, purified water and sodium starch. Bottles of 100.

New Product 1998

NOVO-GLYBURIDE Ⓟ
Novopharm

Glyburide

Oral Hypoglycemic

Supplied: 2.5 mg: Each white, round, scored tablet, engraved no/vo and 2.5 on opposite sides, contains: glyburide 2.5 mg. Gluten- and tartrazine-free. Bottles of 100 and 500. Unit dose strips of 100 and patient packs of 30.

5 mg: Each white, capsule-shaped, scored tablet, engraved N/N and 5 on opposite sides, contains: glyburide 5 mg. Gluten- and tartrazine-free. Bottles of 100 and 500. Unit dose strips of 100 and patient packs of 30.

NOVO-HYDROXYZIN Ⓟ
Novopharm

Hydroxyzine HCl

Antihistamine—Anxiolytic

Supplied: 10 mg: Each oval, soft gelatin, orange capsule, contains: hydroxyzine HCl 10 mg. Bottles of 100 and 500.

25 mg: Each oval, soft gelatin, green capsule, contains: hydroxyzine HCl 25 mg. Bottles of 100 and 500.

50 mg: Each oval, soft gelatin, red capsule, contains: hydroxyzine HCl 50 mg. Bottles of 100.

NOVO-HYLAZIN Ⓟ
Novopharm

Hydralazine HCl

Antihypertensive

Supplied: 10 mg: Each yellow, round, broken scored tablet, engraved N and 10 on same side, contains: hydralazine HCl 10 mg. Bottles of 100 and 500.

25 mg: Each blue, round, sugar-coated tablet, engraved N over 25 on same side, contains: hydralazine HCl 25 mg. Bottles of 100 and 500.

50 mg: Each pink, round, sugar-coated tablet, engraved N over 50 on same side, contains: hydralazine HCl 50 mg. Bottles of 100 and 500.

NOVO-INDAPAMIDE Ⓟ
Novopharm

Indapamide

Diuretic—Antihypertensive

Supplied: Each pink, sugar-coated tablet contains: indapamide 2.5 mg. Nonmedicinal ingredients: acacia, carnauba wax, colloidal silicon dioxide, D&C red No. 30 aluminum lake, FD&C yellow No. 6 aluminum lake, lactose, magnesium stearate, microcrystalline cellulose, povidone, pregelatinized starch, sodium benzoate, sodium lauryl sulfate, sodium starch glycolate, sucrose, talc and titanium dioxide. Gluten- and tartrazine-free. Bottles of 100. Blister packs of 30.

NOVO-IPRAMIDE Ⓟ
Novopharm

Ipratropium Bromide

Bronchodilator

Supplied: Each bottle of clear, colorless or almost colorless solution contains: ipratropium bromide 250 µg/mL (0.025%) in isotonic solution. Preserved with benzalkonium chloride 250 µg/mL and EDTA-disodium 500 µg/mL at a pH of 3.4. Amber glass bottles of 20 mL with screw cap.

NOVO-KETO Ⓟ
NOVO-KETO-EC Ⓟ
Novopharm

Ketoprofen

Analgesic—Anti-inflammatory

Supplied: Novo-Keto: Each off-white suppository contains: ketoprofen 100 mg. Gluten- and tartrazine-free. Boxes of 30.

Novo-Keto-EC: 50 mg: Each yellow, round, enteric-coated tablet, engraved 50 on one side and novo on the other side, contains: ketoprofen 50 mg. Gluten- and tartrazine-free. Bottles of 100 and 500.

100 mg: Each yellow, round, enteric-coated tablet, engraved 100 on one side and novo on the other side, contains: ketoprofen 100 mg Gluten- and tartrazine-free. Bottles of 100 and 500.

NOVO-KETOROLAC Ⓟ
Novopharm

Ketorolac Tromethamine

NSAID Analgesic

Supplied: Each white, plain, round, biconvex film-coated tablet, printed in black ink N on one side and 10 on the other, contains: ketorolac tromethamine 10 mg. Nonmedicinal ingredients: colloidal silicon dioxide, lactose, magnesium stearate, microcrystalline and purified water. Bottles of 100, 500 and 1 000. Boxes of 100 as unit dose strips.

New Product 1998

NOVO-KETOTIFEN Ⓟ
Novopharm

Ketotifen Fumarate

Pediatric Asthma Prophylactic—Antiallergic Agent

Supplied: Syrup: Each 5 mL of clear syrup contains: ketotifen 1 mg. Nonmedicinal ingredients: alcohol, citric acid, flavor strawberry, methyl p-hydroxybenzoate, propyl-p-hydroxybenzoate, sodium phosphate, sorbitol solution, sucrose and water. Gluten- and tartrazine-free. Bottles of 250 mL.

Tablets: Each white, round, tablet engraved N/N on one side and 1 on the other, contains: ketotifen fumarate 1.38 mg equivalent to ketotifen 1 mg. Nonmedicinal ingredients: cornstarch, lactose, magnesium stearate and water. Gluten- and tartrazine-free. Bottles of 56.

NOVO-LEVAMISOLE Ⓟ
Novopharm

Levamisole HCl

Immunomodulator

Supplied: Each white, film-coated, biconvex tablet, with Novo inscribed on one side and 50 on the other contains: levamisole 50 mg as levamisole HCl. Nonmedicinal ingredients: carnauba wax, colloidal silicon dioxide, hydrogenated vegetable oil, hydroxypropylcellulose, hydroxypropyl methylcellulose, lactose, microcrystalline cellulose, polyethylene glycol, talc, titanium dioxide and triethyl citrate. Blister packs, boxes of 36.

NOVO-LEVOBUNOLOL Ⓟ
Novopharm

Levobunolol HCl

Glaucoma Therapy

Pharmacology: Levobunolol is a noncardioselective beta-adrenoceptor antagonist which is equipotent at both $beta_1$ and $beta_2$ receptors. Levobunolol is approximately 60 times more potent than the dextro isomer of bunolol in its beta-blocking activity, yet it is equipotent in its potential for direct myocardial depression. Accordingly, levobunolol, the levo isomer, is used. Levobunolol does not possess a significant local anesthetic (membrane stabilizing) effect or intrinsic sympathomimetic activity.

Novo-Levobunolol (cont'd)

Beta-adrenergic receptor blockade decreases cardiac output in both healthy subjects and patients with heart disease. In patients with severe impairment of myocardial function, beta-adrenergic receptor blockade may inhibit the stimulatory effect of the sympathetic nervous system necessary to maintain adequate cardiac function.

Beta-adrenergic receptor blockade in the bronchi and bronchioles results in increased airway resistance from unopposed parasympathetic activity. This effect is potentially dangerous in patients with asthma or other bronchospastic conditions.

When instilled into the eye, levobunolol will lower elevated intraocular pressure (IOP) as well as normal (IOP), whether or not accompanied by glaucoma. Elevated IOP is a major risk factor in the pathogenesis of glaucomatous visual field loss. The higher the level of intraocular pressure, the greater the likelihood of optic nerve damage and visual field loss.

With 1 drop of levobunolol, the onset of action can be detected within 1 hour after treatment, with maximum effect seen between 2 and 6 hours. A significant decrease in IOP can be maintained for up to 24 hours with once daily dosing of levobunolol 0.5%.

Measurements of aqueous flow and total outflow facility suggest that levobunolol lowers IOP primarily by decreasing aqueous humor production. Levobunolol decreases IOP with little or no effect on pupil size or accommodation, in contrast to the miosis which cholinergic agents are known to produce. The blurred vision and night blindness often associated with miotics would not be expected. In patients with central lens opacities who would experience decreased visual acuity with pupillary constriction this is particularly important.

Levobunolol has been demonstrated to be as effective as timolol in lowering intraocular pressure.

In controlled clinical studies lasting up to 2 years, intraocular pressure was well controlled in approximately 80% of subjects treated with levobunolol 0.5% b.i.d. The mean IOP decreases from baseline were between 6.87 mm Hg and 7.81 mm Hg. There were no significant effects on pupil size, tear production or corneal sensitivity observed. At concentrations of 0.5 and 1% topically applied levobunol decreased heart rate and blood pressure in some patients. Over the course of these studies, the IOP-lowering effect of levobunolol was well maintained. In a 3-month controlled clinical study, once-daily application of levobunolol 0.5% controlled the IOP of 72% of subjects, resulting in an overall mean decrease in IOP of 7.0 mm Hg. Once-daily application of timolol 0.5% controlled the IOP of 64% of subjects, resulting in a mean decrease of IOP of 4.5 mm Hg. The difference in overall mean reduction of IOP was statistically significant.

In 2 subsequent 3-month trials comparing levobunolol 0.5% with timolol 0.5% administered once daily, overall differences between the 2 drugs were not found to be statistically significant. A greater percentage of subjects in both the levobunolol groups and the timolol groups maintained adequately lowered intraocular pressure in the latter 2 studies, most likely because subjects with severe ocular hypertension, unlikely to be controlled by therapy with a beta-blocker alone, were excluded from the study.

In one 3-month study and one 1-year study, levobunolol 0.25% administered twice daily controlled the IOP of approximately 63 and 70% of the subjects, respectively. The overall mean decreases from baseline were 5.4 and 5.1 mm Hg, respectively.

In another 3-month clinical study, the mean reduction in IOP was significantly greater (more than 2 mm Hg) in the 0.25 and 0.5% levobunolol twice daily treatment groups than in the betaxolol 0.5% twice-daily treatment group.

In a controlled study, the prophylactic effect of topical 0.5% levobunolol on IOP elevations after neodymium: YAG laser posterior capsulotomies was investigated. Thirty to 120 minutes prior to the capsulotomy, 1 drop was administered. Eight subjects (38%) in the vehicle treatment group and none in the levobunolol group experienced increases from baseline in IOP of 10 mm HG or greater. Mean reductions in IOP from baseline ranged from 2.1 to 2.9 mm Hg in the levobunolol group, while in the vehicle treatment group, IOP increases (4.4 to 6.4 mm Hg) were observed at hours 1, 2, and 3 following capsulotomy.

In a controlled study, immediately after a unilateral extracapsular cataract extraction and implantation of a posterior chamber intraocular lens, 0.5% levobunolol or placebo were administered. Treatment continued on a once-daily basis for 7 days. The incidence of IOP elevations from baseline ≥10 mm Hg was 8 subjects (40%) in the vehicle group and 4 subjects (19%) in the levobunolol group. At 24 hours, mean IOP increased from baseline up to 8.6 mm Hg in the vehicle group and up to 2 mm Hg in the levobunolol group.

In another controlled study, levobunolol 0.5% was shown to be significantly more effective than betaxolol 0.5% or placebo in preventing increased IOP after cataract extraction and posterior chamber lens placement. After surgery, 2 drops of the assigned medication were administered to the study eye. A significant mean increase in intraocular pressure from the preoperative to the early postoperative period was noted in the groups treated with betaxolol (6.73 mm Hg), placebo (5.35 mm Hg) and timolol (3.83 mm Hg). A mean decrease in pressure of 0.43 mm Hg was noted in levobunolol-treated eyes.

An IOP of 30 mm Hg or greater was found in 3 placebo-treated eyes (15%), 4 betaxolol-treated eyes (20%), 1 timolol-treated eye (5%) and none of the levobunolol-treated eyes. Five placebo-treated eyes (25%), 6 betaxolol-treated eyes (30%), 5 timolol-treated eyes (25%), and 1 lebovunolol-treated eye (5%) experienced a pressure rise of 10 mm Hg or greater.

Indications: For the control of intraocular pressure in patients with chronic open-angle glaucoma or mild to moderate ocular hypertension.

Contraindications: Those individuals with bronchial asthma or with a history of bronchial asthma, or severe chronic obstructive pulmonary disease; sinus bradycardia; second and third degree atrioventricular block; overt cardiac failure; cardiogenic shock; or hypersensitivity to any component of this product.

Warnings: As with other topically applied ophthalmic drugs, levobunolol may be absorbed systemically. The same adverse reactions found with systemic administration of beta-adrenergic blocking agents may occur with topical administration.

This product contains sodium metabisulfite, a sulfite which may cause allergic-type reactions including anaphylactic symptoms and life-threatening or less severe asthmatic episodes in certain susceptible people. The overall prevalence of sulfite sensitivity in the general population is not known and probably low. Sulfite sensitivity is seen more frequently in asthmatic than in nonasthmatic people.

Keep out of reach of children. For external use only. Do not touch dropper tip to any surface, since this may cause contamination of the solution. Protect from light and excessive heat. Discard any unused solution after end of treatment period.

Precautions: General: Should be used with caution in patients with known contraindications to systemic use of beta-adrenoceptor blocking agents. These include abnormal low heart rate and heart block more severe than first degree. Before beginning therapy with levobunolol, congestive heart failure should be adequately controlled. In patients with a history of cardiac disease, especially arrhythmia and bradycardia, pulse rates should be monitored.

In patients with known hypersensitivity to other beta-adrenoceptor blocking agents, levobunolol should be used with caution.

Use with caution in patients with known diminished pulmonary function.

Lactation: It is unknown whether this drug is excreted in human breast milk. It is known that systemic beta-blockers and topical timolol maleate are excreted in human breast milk. Caution should be exercised when levobunolol is administered to a nursing woman.

Children: Safety and effectiveness in children have not been established.

Drug Interactions: Levobunolol may demonstrate additive effects in patients taking systemic antihypertensive drugs. These possible additive effects may include hypotension, including orthostatic hypotension, bradycardia, dizziness, and/or syncope. Conversely, systemic beta-adrenoceptor blocking agents may potentiate the ocular hypotensive effect of levobunolol.

Close observation of the patient is recommended when a beta-blocker is administered to patients receiving catecholamine-depleting drugs such as reserpine due to possible additive effects and the development of hypotension and/or marked bradycardia, which may produce vertigo, syncope, or postural hypotension.

Adverse Effects: Transient burning, stinging or itching, blepharoconjunctivitis and decreases in heart rate and blood pressure have been reported occasionally with the use of levobunolol. Iridocyclitis, headache, transient ataxia, dizziness, lethargy, urticaria and pruritus have been reported rarely with the use of levobunolol. Decreased corneal sensitivity has been noted in a small number of patients. The following additional adverse reactions have been reported with ophthalmic use of $beta_1$ and $beta_2$ (nonselective) adrenergic receptor blocking agents: Body as a Whole: headache.
Cardiovascular: arrhythmia, syncope, heart block, cerebral vascular accident, cerebral ischemia, congestive heart failure, palpitation.
Digestive: nausea.
Psychiatric: depression.
Skin: hypersensitivity, including localized and generalized rash.
Respiratory: bronchospasm (predominantly in patients with pre-existing bronchospastic disease), respiratory failure.
Endocrine: masked symptoms of hypoglycemia in insulin-dependent diabetics.
Special Senses: signs and symptoms of keratitis, blepharoptosis, visual disturbances including refractive changes (due to withdrawal of miotic therapy in some cases), diplopia, ptosis.

Other reactions associated with the oral use of nonselective adrenergic receptor blocking agents should be considered potential effects with ophthalmic use of these agents.

Overdose: Symptoms and Treatment: Overdosage with levobunolol has not been reported to date. Should accidental ocular overdosage occur, flush eye(s) with water or normal saline. If accidentally ingested, efforts to decrease further absorption may be appropriate (gastric lavage). The most common signs and symptoms to be expected with overdosage of a systemic beta-adrenergic blocking agent are symptomatic bradycardia, hypotension, bronchospasm, and acute cardiac failure. Should these symptoms occur, discontinue levobunolol therapy and initiate appropriate supportive therapy.

Dosage: The recommended starting dose is 1 drop of levobunolol 0.25% twice a day in the affected eye(s). If the clinical response is not adequate, the dosage may be changed to 1 drop of levobunolol 0.5% twice a day in the affected eye(s). Levobunolol 0.5% once a day has been found to be effective in controlling IOP in many patients with mild to moderate open-angle glaucoma and ocular hypertension. As with any new medication, careful monitoring of patients is advised.

Dosages above 1 drop of levobunolol 0.5% b.i.d. are generally not more effective. If the patient's IOP is not at a satisfactory level on this regimen, concomitant therapy with dipivefrin and/or epinephrine, and/or pilocarpine and other miotics, and/or systemically administered carbonic anhydrase inhibitors, such as acetazolamide, can be instituted.

Supplied: Each mL of clear colorless to slightly amber colored solution, contains: levobunolol HCl 2.5 mg (0.25%) or 5 mg (0.5%)/mL. Dropper bottles of 5, 10 and 15 mL.

Reviewed 1997

NOVO-LEXIN® Ⓟ

Novopharm

Cephalexin

Antibiotic

Supplied: Tablets: 250 mg: Each oblong, orange, film-coated tablet, engraved N 250 with partial bisect on one side and plain on the reverse, contains: cephalexin 250 mg. Gluten- and tartrazine-free. Bottles of 100, 250, 500 and 1 000. Unit dose strips of 100.

500 mg: Each oblong, orange, film-coated tablet, engraved N 550 with partial bisect on one side and plain on the reverse, contains: cephalexin 500 mg. Gluten- and tartrazine-free. Bottles of 100, 250 and 500. Unit dose strips of 100.

Capsules: 250 mg: Each hard gelatin orange capsule, imprinted NOVO 250, contains: cephalexin 250 mg. Gluten- and tartrazine-free. Bottles of 100 and 500. Unit dose strips of 100.

500 mg: Each hard gelatin, grey and orange capsule, imprinted NOVO 500, contains: cephalexin 500 mg. Gluten- and tartrazine-free. Bottles of 100, 250 and 500. Unit dose strips of 100.

Granules: Each 5 mL of reconstituted suspension contains: cephalexin equivalent to 125 (orange/banana-flavored) or 250 mg cherry-flavored cephalexin. Sodium: <1 mmol (4.3 mg). Gluten- and tartrazine-free. Bottles of 100 and 150 mL. The reconstituted formulation is stable for 14 days under refrigeration (6°C).

NOVOLIN®ge

Novo Nordisk

see INSULIN HUMAN (Biosynthetic) Preparations

NOVOLIN-PEN® 1.5

Novo Nordisk

Insulin Delivery Device

Supplied: In appearance Novolin-Pen® 1.5 resembles a cartridge pen. The device is loaded with a Penfill® cartridge containing 1.5 mL of U100 human insulin (Novolin®**ge** Toronto; NPH; or 30/70, an insulin mixture containing Novolin®**ge** Toronto and Novolin®**ge** NPH, respectively, in the proportion indicated by the ratio). Novolin-Pen® 1.5 is a dial-a-dose injection device capable of delivering 2 to 40 units of insulin, delivered in increments of 1 unit, with a single depression of the push button.

The product is designed for use with Novolin®**ge** Penfill® insulin preparations and NovoFine® needles. See Insulin Human Biosynthetic Preparations.

The NovoFine® needle should be removed after each injection. If the needle is not removed, changes in ambient temperature can result in some liquid being expelled from the cartridge. In the case of insulin suspensions, removal of supernatant liquid can cause an increase in insulin concentration (i.e., strength) remaining in the cartridge.

Novo Nordisk cannot be held responsible for malfunctions occurring as a consequence of using Novolin-Pen® 1.5 in combination with products that do not meet the same specifications or quality standards as Novolin®**ge** Penfill® 1.5 mL insulin preparations and NovoFine® needles.

Consult the manufacturer for instructions for use.

NOVOLIN-PEN® 3

Novo Nordisk

Insulin Delivery Device

Supplied: In appearance Novolin-Pen® 3 resembles a cartridge pen. The device is loaded with a Penfill® cartridge containing 3 mL of U100 human insulin (Novolin®**ge** Toronto, NPH, 10/90, 20/80, 30/70, 40/60, or 50/50). Novolin-Pen® 3 is a dial-a-dose injection device capable of delivering 2 to 70 units of insulin, delivered in increments of 1 unit, with a single depression of the push button.

The product is designed for use with Novolin®**ge** Penfill® insulin preparations and NovoFine® needles. See Insulin Human Biosynthetic Preparations.

The NovoFine® needle should be removed after each injection. If the needle is not removed, changes in ambient temperature can result in some liquid being expelled from the cartridge. In the case of insulin suspensions, removal of supernatant liquid can cause an increase in insulin concentration (i.e., strength) remaining in the cartridge.

Novo Nordisk cannot be held responsible for malfunctions as a consequence of using Novolin-Pen® 3 in combination with products that do not meet the same specifications or quality standards as Novolin®**ge** Penfill® 3 mL insulin preparations and NovoFine® needles.

Consult the manufacturer for instructions for use.

(Shown in Product Recognition Section)

NOVO-LOPERAMIDE

Novopharm

Loperamide HCl

Antidiarrheal

Pharmacology: Diarrhea is the failure or imbalance of one or a combination of activities in the gut including secretion, absorption and motility. In man, an increase in intestinal transit time and a reduction of intestinal motility occurs by a direct effect of loperamide on the nerve endings of the intestinal wall. Although loperamide has been shown not to alter the rate of absorption, there is some evidence that it can directly inhibit fluid and electrolyte secretion.

In clinical studies, a single 4 mg dose of loperamide has been shown to effectively reduce fecal output and frequency, improve stool consistency and relieve symptoms of abdominal cramping and fecal incontinence.

Pharmacokinetics: In man, peak plasma concentrations of unchanged loperamide were attained in 4 hours after administration of 2 mg ^{3}H-loperamide. The maximum concentration was 2 ng/mL corresponding to about 0.3% of the administered dose. Approximately 1% of the administered dose was excreted unchanged in the urine and 6% as nonvolatile metabolites. Approximately 40% of the administered dose was excreted with the feces primarily within the first 4 days of this. Only 30% was due to unchanged loperamide. The elimination half-life of loperamide has been shown to range from 7 to 15 hours. The elimination rate was not significantly altered when the dose was increased from 18 to 54 mg.

Indications: As an adjunct to rehydration therapy for the symptomatic control of acute nonspecific diarrhea, for chronic diarrhea associated with inflammatory bowel disease and for the reduction of the discharge volume for ileostomies, colostomies and other intestinal resections.

Contraindications: In children less than 2 years of age. In patients with a known hypersensitivity to the drug and in those patients in whom constipation must be avoided.

Warnings: Loperamide should not be used in cases of acute dysentery characterized by blood in the stools and elevated temperature. Fluid and electrolyte depletion may occur in patients who have diarrhea and the use of loperamide does not preclude the administration of appropriate fluid and electrolyte therapy.

Agents which inhibit intestinal motility or delay intestinal transit time have been reported to induce toxic megacolon in some patients with acute ulcerative colitis or pseudomembranous colitis associated with broad spectrum antibiotics. Loperamide should not be used in acute diarrhea associated with organisms that penetrate the intestinal mucosa (e.g., toxigenic E. coli, Salmonella and Shigella). If abdominal distension occurs or if other untoward symptoms develop, loperamide therapy should be discontinued promptly.

Children: Loperamide administration is not recommended in children less than 12 years of age except on the advice of a physician (see Dosage). Administration of loperamide has been reported to cause poisoning and death in infants.

Special caution should be exercised when loperamide is administered in young children and patients with compromised blood brain barrier (e.g., those with meningitis) since there is a greater variability of response in these groups. Dehydration may further influence the variability of response to loperamide, particularly in young children.

In case of accidental ingestion of loperamide by children, see Overdose: Symptoms and Treatment.

Precautions: *Pregnancy* and *Lactation:* The safety of loperamide usage during pregnancy and lactation has yet to be established. Reproduction studies in the rat and in the rabbit failed to reveal any evidence of impaired fertility or detrimental effects on the fetus with dosage levels up to 30 times the human therapeutic dose.

Due to the extensive first pass metabolism of loperamide in the liver, patients with hepatic dysfunction should be monitored for signs of CNS toxicity.

The use of loperamide should be discontinued if no improvement in symptoms of acute diarrhea is observed within 48 hours.

Dependence Liability: Physical dependence to loperamide has not been observed in humans although in studies with morphine dependent monkeys, loperamide prevented signs of morphine withdrawal at doses above those recommended for humans. When the naloxone challenge pupil test was performed on humans after a single high dose and after more than 2 years of therapeutic use, the results were negative (a positive result indicates opiate-like effects).

Adverse Effects: The adverse reactions reported in adults during clinical trials were difficult to distinguish from the symptoms associated with the diarrheal syndrome. The adverse reactions in adults were generally minor and self-limiting and included: abdominal pain, distention or discomfort, constipation, drowsiness or dizziness, dry mouth, nausea and vomiting and hypersensitivity including skin rash. The most frequently reported side effect is constipation which may be as a result of the therapeutic action of the drug. Children may be more sensitive to adverse CNS effects of the drug than adults. Opiate-like effects have been observed in children under 3 years of age. Paralytic ileus has been reported in infants.

Overdose: Symptoms and Treatment: Clinical trials have shown that a slurry of activated charcoal can reduce the amount of loperamide which is absorbed into the systemic circulation by as much as 9-fold if administered promptly after ingestion of the drug. If vomiting occurs spontaneously upon ingestion of loperamide, a slurry of 100 g of activated charcoal should be administered orally as soon as fluids can be retained.

Following overdosage these symptoms may be observed: nausea, vomiting, constipation, respiratory depression, bradycardia, CNS depression, miosis, apnea and hypoxia.

If vomiting has not occurred, gastric lavage should be performed followed by 100 g of the activated charcoal slurry administered through the gastric tube.

In the event of overdosage, patients should be monitored for signs of CNS depression for at least 24 hours. Naloxone may be administered if CNS depression is observed. If the patient is responsive to naloxone, vital signs must be monitored carefully for the recurrence of symptoms of overdose for at least 24 hours after the last dose of naloxone.

The patient must be monitored closely and treated repeatedly with naloxone as indicated since loperamide has a prolonged duration of action and naloxone has a relatively short duration of action (1 to 3 hours). Forced diuresis is not expected to be effective for loperamide overdosage since relatively little of the drug is excreted in the urine.

In clinical trials, an adult who took three 20 mg doses within a 24-hour period was nauseated after the second dose and vomited after the third. In studies which were designed to examine the potential for side effects, the intentional ingestion of up to 60 mg of loperamide in a single dose by healthy subjects did not result in any significant adverse effects.

Dosage: Adults: Acute Diarrhea: The recommended initial dose is 4 mg followed by 2 mg after each unformed stool. A maximum daily dosage of 16 mg should not be exceeded.

Chronic Diarrhea: The recommended initial dose is 4 mg followed by 2 mg after each unformed stool until diarrhea is controlled; thereafter, the dosage of loperamide should be reduced to meet the needs of the individual patient. Once the optimal daily dosage has been established, it may be administered as a single dose or in divided doses.

The average maintenance dosage used in clinical trials was 4 to 8 mg daily. If improvement is not observed after 10 days of treatment with 16 mg/day, the symptoms are not likely to be controlled by further administration of loperamide.

Children: Acute or Chronic Diarrhea: Loperamide should be administered to children only on the advice of a physician. Loperamide caplets are not recommended for use in children 2 to 5 years of age. Caplets may be administered to children 6 to 12 years of age (10 to 20 kg). The following schedule of administration will usually fulfill the initial dosage requirements in children 6 to 12 years of age: See Table I.

Table I—Novo-Loperamide

Recommended First-Day Dosage Schedule	
6 to 8 years: (20 to 30 kg)	2 mg b.i.d. (4 mg/day)
8 to 12 years: (over 30 kg)	2 mg t.i.d. (6 mg/day)

Following the first treatment day, it is recommended that subsequent loperamide doses (1 mg/10 kg body weight) be administered only after a loose stool.

Duration of Treatment: Loperamide may be administered for prolonged periods of time. No tolerance to the antidiarrheal effects has been observed. Blood, urine, liver and kidney function, ECG and ophthalmological examinations did not reveal any significant abnormalities after several years of loperamide administration. In patients with chronic diarrhea who received loperamide orally for prolonged periods, naloxone pupil challenge studies indicated a lack of CNS effects.

Supplied: Each light green, capsule-shaped tablet, engraved LOP on one side, 2/MG on the opposite side, contains: loperamide HCl 2 mg. Bottles of 50, 100 and 500 and boxes of 6, 12 and 18 as blister pack strips.

NOVO-LORAZEM® Ⓟ

Novopharm

Lorazepam

Anxiolytic—Sedative

Supplied: 0.5 mg: Each small, white, round, unscored, compressed tablet, embossed N on one side and .5 on the other, contains: lorazepam 0.5 mg. Bottles of 100, 500 and 1 000.

1 mg: Each small, white, oblong, embossed N1 on one side, single scored tablet contains: lorazepam 1 mg. Bottles of 100, 500, 1 000 and 3 000. Unit dose strips of 100.

2 mg: Each small, white, oval embossed N2 on one side, single scored tablet contains: lorazepam 2 mg. Bottles of 100, 500, 1 000 and 3 000. Unit dose strips of 100.

NOVO-MAPROTILINE [P]

Novopharm

Maprotiline HCl

Antidepressant

Supplied: 10 mg: Each round, cream-colored, film-coated tablet, engraved $\frac{N}{10}$ on one side, plain on the reverse, contains: maprotiline HCl 10 mg. Gluten- and tartrazine-free. Bottles of 100.

25 mg: Each round, orange-colored, slightly beveled-edged, film-coated tablet, engraved $\frac{N}{25}$ on one side, plain on the reverse, contains: maprotiline HCl 25 mg. Gluten- and tartrazine-free. Bottles of 100.

50 mg: Each round, orange-colored, slightly beveled-edged, film-coated tablet, engraved $\frac{N}{50}$ on one side, plain on the reverse, contains: maprotiline HCl 50 mg. Gluten- and tartrazine-free. Bottles of 100.

75 mg: Each round, red-colored, shallow, single-scored, film-coated tablet, engraved $\frac{N}{75}$ on one side, plain on the reverse, contains: maprotiline HCl 75 mg. Gluten- and tartrazine-free. Bottles of 100.

NOVO-MEDOPA® [P]

Novopharm

Methyldopa

Antihypertensive

Supplied: 125 mg: Each yellow, round, film-coated tablet, embossed novo and 125 on opposite sides, contains: methyldopa 125 mg. Gluten- and tartrazine-free. Bottles of 100 and 500.

250 mg: Each yellow, round, film-coated tablet, embossed novo and 250 on opposite sides, contains: methyldopa 250 mg. Gluten- and tartrazine-free. Bottles of 100, 500 and 1 000.

500 mg: Each yellow, round, film-coated tablet, embossed novo and 500 on opposite sides, contains: methyldopa 500 mg. Gluten- and tartrazine-free. Bottles of 100 and 500.

NOVO-MEDRONE [P]

Novopharm

Medroxyprogesterone Acetate

Progestagen

Pharmacology: Medroxyprogesterone is an orally active progestational steroid which, when taken by women with adequate endogenous estrogen, converts a proliferative endometrium into a secretory endometrium. Medroxyprogesterone blocks the secretion of pituitary gonadotropin resulting in the prevention of follicular maturation and ovulation in women of reproductive age.

Pharmacokinetics: Medroxyprogesterone has an apparent half-life of approximately 30 hours.

Medroxyprogesterone is rapidly absorbed from the gastrointestinal tract and metabolized in the liver to several progestin metabolites. The major metabolite of medroxyprogesterone acetate is a 6 alpha-methyl-6 beta, 17 alpha, 21-trihydroxy-4-pregnene-3, 20-dione-17-acetate, which is eliminated in the urine. This accounts for approximately 8% of an oral dose, and is found to be excreted as a glucuronide conjugate.

Medroxyprogesterone is primarily eliminated via fecal excretion, to which biliary secretion may contribute. Approximately 44% of an oral dose is eliminated through urinary excretion in the form of metabolites.

Indications: For the treatment of functional menstrual disorders caused by hormonal imbalance in non-pregnant women, in the absence of organic pathology; for hormonal replacement therapy, to oppose the effects of estrogen on the endometrium.

Contraindications: Thrombophlebitis, thromboembolic disorders, cerebral apoplexy or in patients with a history of these conditions. Known sensitivity to medroxyprogesterone. Undiagnosed vaginal bleeding. Undiagnosed urinary tract bleeding. Undiagnosed breast pathology. Pregnancy whether the use is for diagnosis or for therapy (see Warnings).

Warnings: Liver function tests should be carried out periodically in patients who have or are suspected of having hepatic disease. The doctor should watch for the earliest signs of impaired liver function. If these occur or are suspected, treatment should be terminated and the patient's condition re-evaluated.

Before prescribing medroxyprogesterone the doctor should be aware and watch for the earliest signs of thrombotic disorders, such as thrombophlebitis, cerebrovascular disorders, pulmonary embolism and retinal thrombosis. If any of these symptoms occur, treatment should be withdrawn immediately. The patient's status and need for treatment should be carefully assessed before continuing therapy.

Pregnancy: Usage in pregnancy is not advised. Progestational agents should also not be used as a diagnostic test for pregnancy. If the patient is exposed to medroxyprogesterone during pregnancy or if she becomes pregnant while taking the drug, she should be apprised of the potential risk to the fetus.

If there is a sudden loss of vision, whether partial or complete, or sudden onset of proptosis, diplopia or migraine, an examination should be carried out. Upon examination, if papilledema or retinal vascular lesions are found, the drug should be discontinued.

Clinical suppression of adrenocortical function has not been observed at low dose levels. However, the high doses of medroxyprogesterone used in the treatment of certain cancers, in some cases, produce Cushingoid symptoms (e.g., "moon" facies, fluid retention, glucose intolerance and blood pressure elevation).

Lactation: Detectable amounts of progestin have been identified in the milk of mothers receiving the drug. Infants exposed to medroxyprogesterone via breast milk have been studied for developmental and behavioral effects through puberty. No adverse effects have been noted.

Anaphylactic and anaphylactoid reactions have occurred at times in people taking medroxyprogesterone.

Precautions: Prior to administering medroxyprogesterone, a thorough examination should be performed with special reference to breast and pelvic organs, and should include a Papanicolaou smear. This evaluation should exclude the presence of genital or breast neoplasia before considering the use of this drug.

Since this drug might cause some degree of fluid retention, patients with conditions which may be affected by this factor, e.g., epilepsy, migraine, asthma, cardiac or renal dysfunction, should remain under close supervision.

In cases of breakthrough bleeding, as in all cases of irregular bleeding per vagina, organic causes should be considered. In cases of undiagnosed vaginal bleeding, adequate diagnostic measures are indicated.

Patients should be advised of the menstrual bleeding patterns expected with the sequential regimen (see Dosage).

Upon sequential administration of medroxyprogesterone to women with adequate levels of estrogen (endogenous or exogenous), withdrawal bleeding usually occurs within 7 days after stopping this drug. Bleeding that occurs during medroxyprogesterone administration indicates a need for a longer duration, or a higher dose.

Patients with a history of psychic depression should be carefully monitored while receiving therapy with medroxyprogesterone. Some patients may complain of premenstrual like depression while on this medication.

A reduction in glucose tolerance has been reported in some patients on progestins. The mechanism of this reduction is not fully understood. Therefore, diabetic patients should be kept under close supervision while taking medroxyprogesterone.

The patient's age does not present an absolute limiting factor although progestin therapy could hide the onset of the climacteric.

The pathologist should be made aware of any progestin therapy when relevant specimens are submitted.

Drug Interactions: Aminoglutethimide administered concomitantly with medroxyprogesterone may significantly depress the bioavailability of medroxyprogesterone.

Rifampin can increase the metabolism of exogenously administered progestational agents. The extent to which rifampin may alter the metabolism of medroxyprogesterone remains to be determined; the possibility of an interaction should be considered.

Adverse Effects: The following adverse reactions have been associated with the use of medroxyprogesterone:

Breast: Tenderness or galactorrhea have occasionally been reported.

Reproductive System: breakthrough bleeding, spotting, alterations in menstrual flow, amenorrhea, alterations in cervical erosion and cervical secretions.

CNS: headache, nervousness, dizziness, depression, insomnia, somnolence, fatigue, premenstrual syndrome-like symptoms.

Thromboembolic Phenomena: including thrombophlebitis and pulmonary embolism.

Skin and Mucous Membranes: Sensitivity reactions such as pruritus, urticaria, angioneurotic edema, generalized rash and anaphylaxis; acne, alopecia, hirsutism.

Gastrointestinal: abdominal discomfort, nausea, bloating.

Miscellaneous: pyrexia, increase in weight , peripheral edema, "moon" facies.

Laboratory Results: The following laboratory tests could be influenced by the use of medroxyprogesterone: levels of gonadotropin, plasma progesterone, urinary pregnanediol, plasma testosterone (in males), plasma estrogen (in females), plasma cortisol, glucose tolerance test, metyrapone test.

Overdose: Symptoms: In females, an overdose could cause a period of amenorrhea of a variable length and could be followed by irregular menses for several cycles.

There have been no overdoses reported in males. If overdose were to occur in males however, there would probably be no symptoms.

Treatment: There is no specific treatment for overdose with medroxyprogesterone. Doses as high as 1 000 mg have been taken for the treatment of endometrial carcinoma without any adverse reaction.

Dosage: Functional Menstrual Disorders: Secondary Amenorrhea: After ruling out pregnancy, medroxyprogesterone can be used in doses ranging from 5 to 10 mg daily depending on the amount of endometrial stimulation required. The dose should be given daily for 12 to 14 days every month.

Note: In patients with underdeveloped endometria, standard estrogen therapy should be administered in combination with medroxyprogesterone. Withdrawal bleeding normally occurs within 3 days of commencement of combination therapy of estrogen and medroxyprogesterone.

Dysfunctional Uterine Bleeding: Medroxyprogesterone can be administered in doses ranging from 5 to 10 mg for 10 to 14 days commencing on the assumed or calculated 12 to 16th day of the cycle. This regimen should be repeated for 2 subsequent cycles or longer if necessary.

When bleeding is caused by a lack of both ovarian hormones, as evidenced by an underdeveloped proliferative endometrium, estrogens should be given in combination with medroxyprogesterone. If this controls the bleeding satisfactorily, treatment should be maintained for at least 2 subsequent cycles.

If dysfunctional uterine bleeding is not controlled by hormone therapy, appropriate diagnostic measures should be undertaken to rule out uterine pathology.

Hormone Replacement Therapy: Progestin Challenge Test: Subsequent to the diagnosis of menopause, the progestin challenge test is recommended for amenorrheic women with an intact uterus. Medroxyprogesterone 10 mg daily should be administered for 10 days.

A negative test is identified by the absence of withdrawal bleeding, and implies the absence of endometrial stimulation due to insufficient estrogen secretion. In these women, hormone replacement therapy consisting of estrogen therapy, and concurrent medroxyprogesterone, should be considered.

A positive test is indicated by the presence of withdrawal bleeding which occurs within 7 days after stopping medroxyprogesterone treatment. Withdrawal bleeding implies the presence of sufficient endogenous estrogen to stimulate the endometrium. Therapy should be administered, as above, until withdrawal bleeding no longer occurs. This cessation of withdrawal bleeding indicates the absence of endometrial stimulation due to a decline in estrogen secretion. In these women, hormone replacement therapy consisting of estrogen therapy, and concurrent medroxyprogesterone, should be considered.

Sequential Therapy: see Table I (on following page).

In women with an intact uterus receiving estrogen replacement therapy, medroxyprogesterone may be given in a dosage of 5 to 10 mg daily for 12 to 14 days. The recommended starting dose should be 10 mg/day, administered for 12 to 14 days. A dose of 5 mg/day for 12 to 14 days may be appropriate for some women.

Table I—Novo-Medrone

Sequential Therapy

Days of the Month 1–11	12	13 14 15 16 17 18 19 20 21 22 23 24 25	26 27 28 29 30 31
Sequential Estrogen–25 days			
	Start	Novo-Medrone 5–10 mg/day	
Continuous Estrogen–Everyday			
Novo-Medrone 5–10 mg/day	Stop		

Note: The lowest dose required to protect the endometrium from estrogenic-hyperstimulation should be used. A good indicator is the lowest dose that will consistently result in withdrawal bleeding within 7 days after stopping the treatment. Bleeding that occurs during the treatment indicates a need for a longer duration, or higher dose.

Supplied: 2.5 mg: Each peach colored, round tablet, scored and engraved with "novo" on one side and "2.5" on the other contains: medroxyprogesterone acetate 2.5 mg. Bottles of 100, 500 and 1 000.

5 mg: Each blue, round tablet, engraved with "novo" on the scored side and "5" on the other side contains: medroxyprogesterone acetate 5 mg. Bottles of 100, 500 and 1 000.

10 mg: Each white, round tablet, engraved with "novo" on the scored side and "10" on the other side contains: medroxyprogesterone acetate 10 mg. Bottles of 100, 500 and 1 000.

Reviewed 1998

NOVO-MEPRAZINE ℞

Novopharm

Methotrimeprazine Maleate

Neuroleptic

Pharmacology: Methotrimeprazine possesses antipsychotic, tranquilizing, anxiolytic, sedative and analgesic properties and it is also a potent potentiator of anesthetics.

Methotrimeprazine possesses strong sedative properties. It potentiates ether and hexobarbital anesthesia as well as morphine analgesia. It also exerts a potent anti-apomorphine effect, a hypothermic action 3 times more potent than that of chlorpromazine and strong antispasmodic and antihistaminic effects. Methotrimeprazine is capable of reversing epinephrine-induced hypertension but has practically no effect against norepinephrine and acetylcholine. It readily protects rats against traumatic shock and produces deep local anesthesia following parasciatic injections.

Indications: Psychotic disturbances: acute and chronic schizophrenias, senile psychoses, manic-depressive syndromes.

Conditions associated with anxiety and tension: autonomic disturbances, personality disturbances, emotional troubles secondary to such physical conditions as resistant pruritus, etc.

Methotrimeprazine is also employed: As an analgesic: in pain due to cancer, zona, trigeminal neuralgia and neurocostal neuralgia and in phantom limb pains and muscular discomforts.

As a potentiator of anesthetics: in general anesthesia where it can be used as both a pre- and post-operative sedative and analgesic.

As an antiemetic: for the treatment of nausea and vomiting of central origin.

As a sedative: for the management of insomnia.

Contraindications: In cases of coma or CNS depression due to alcohol, hypnotics, analgesics or narcotics.

It is also contraindicated in patients with blood dyscrasia, hepatic troubles or a sensitivity to phenothiazines.

Warnings: Occupational Hazards: Methotrimeprazine can reduce psychomotor activity especially during the first few days of treatment. Patients should therefore be cautioned not to drive a motor vehicle or to participate in activities requiring total mental alertness.

Pregnancy: The drug should be used with caution in pregnant women, particularly during the first trimester, unless the benefit to the patient outweighs any possible risk to the fetus.

Precautions: In high oral or parenteral doses, orthostatic hypotension may be encountered at the start of treatment. Patients whose treatment is started by the parenteral route should be kept in bed during the first few days.

Methotrimeprazine therapy should be initiated at low doses in patients with arteriosclerosis or cardiovascular problems.

Methotrimeprazine potentiates the action of other phenothiazines and CNS depressants (barbiturates, analgesics, narcotics and antihistaminics). The usual doses of these agents should be reduced by half if they are to be given concomitantly with methotrimeprazine until the dosage of the latter has been established.

Because of its anticholinergic effects, methotrimeprazine must be administered with caution in patients with glaucoma or prostatic hypertrophy.

During long-term therapy, periodic liver function tests should be performed. In addition, blood counts should be conducted regularly, particularly during the first 2 or 3 months of treatment, and physicians should watch for any signs of blood dyscrasia.

Methotrimeprazine does not alter EEG activity. Nevertheless, since phenothiazines can lower the threshold of cortical excitation, it is advisable to administer an appropriate anticonvulsant medication to epileptic patients receiving methotrimeprazine therapy.

Adverse Effects: May be classified as follows: CNS: drowsiness may appear early in treatment but will gradually disappear during the first weeks or with an adjustment in the dosage.

Extrapyramidal effects are rare and usually appear only after prolonged therapy at high doses. These reactions may be corrected either by reducing the dose of methotrimeprazine or by administering an antiparkinsonian agent.

Autonomic Nervous System: dryness of the mouth and, in older patients, occasional urinary retention, constipation and tachycardia.

Cardiovascular: orthostatic hypotension may be encountered at the start of treatment by the parenteral route or with high oral doses.

Blood: rare instances of agranulocytosis have been reported.

Endocrine: weight gain has been occasionally reported in patients during prolonged treatment with high doses.

Gastrointestinal: rare cases of cholostatic jaundice without liver damage have been observed.

Skin Reactions: skin reactions due to photosensitivity or allergies are extremely rare.

Additional adverse effects were observed during clinical trials. These adverse reactions include: feeling faint/fainting, lightheadedness/dizziness, nausea, nasal congestion, headache, restlessness/anxiousness, feeling hot/sweaty, tremor/twitches, swollen eyelids, dry lips/nose, sensitivity to light, ocular redness and decreased alertness.

Overdose: Symptoms: Symptoms of acute intoxication may include: simple CNS depression, spasms, tremor or tonic and clonic convulsions, coma accompanied by hypotension and respiratory depression.

Treatment: There is no specific antidote. After gastric lavage, treatment is symptomatic. Centrally acting emetics are ineffective because of the antiemetic action of methotrimeprazine.

Hypotension: A 5% glucose solution may be administered. If a hypertensive agent is required, norepinephrine or phenylephrine may be used, but not epinephrine which can aggravate hypotension.

Respiratory Depression: Oxygen by inhalation or controlled respiration after tracheal intubation.

Respiratory Infection: Wide spectrum antibiotics.

Extrapyramidal Reactions: An antiparkinsonian agent or chloral hydrate, however, the latter must be used with caution because of its depressant effect on respiration.

Any CNS stimulant should be used with caution.

Dosage: Dosage must be adjusted according to the indication and individual needs of the patient. If sedation during the day is too pronounced, lower doses may be given during the day and higher doses at night.

Adults: Oral: Minor conditions in which methotrimeprazine may be given in low doses as a tranquilizer, anxiolytic, analgesic or sedative: begin treatment with 6 to 25 mg/day in 3 divided doses at mealtimes. Increase the dosage until the optimum level has been reached. As a sedative, a single nighttime dose of 10 to 25 mg is usually sufficient.

Severe Conditions: Such as psychoses or intense pain in which methotrimeprazine is employed at higher doses: begin treatment with 50 to 75 mg/day divided into 2 or 3 daily doses; increase the dosage until the desired effect is obtained. In certain psychotics doses may reach 1 g or more/day. If it is necessary to start therapy with higher doses, i.e., 100 to 200 mg/day, administer the drug in divided daily doses and keep the patient in bed for the first few days.

Children: Oral: The initial dose has been established at 0.25 mg/kg daily given in 2 or 3 divided doses. This dosage may be increased gradually until an effective level is reached which should not surpass 40 mg/day for a child less than 12 years of age.

Supplied: 5 mg: Each yellow tablet contains: methotrimeprazine 5 mg (as the maleate). Tartrazine-free. Bottles of 100 and 500.

25 mg: Each yellow tablet contains: methotrimeprazine 25 mg (as the maleate). Tartrazine-free. Bottles of 100 and 500.

50 mg: Each yellow tablet contains: methotrimeprazine 50 mg (as the maleate). Tartrazine-free. Bottles of 100 and 500.

Store between 15 and 30°C. Protect from light.

Reviewed 1997

NOVO-METFORMIN ℞

Novopharm

Metformin HCl

Antihyperglycemic Agent

Pharmacology: Metformin is a biguanide derivative producing an antihyperglycemic effect which can only be observed in man or in the diabetic animal and only when there is insulin secretion. Metformin, at therapeutic doses, does not cause hypoglycemia when used alone in man or in the nondiabetic animal, except when using a near lethal dose. Metformin has no effects on the pancreatic beta cells. The mode of action of metformin is not fully understood. It has been postulated that metformin might potentiate the effect of insulin or that it might enhance the effect of insulin on peripheral receptor sites. This increased sensitivity seems to follow an increase in the number of insulin receptors on cell surface membranes.

Pharmacokinetics: Metformin absorption is relatively slow and may extend over about 6 hours. The drug is excreted in urine at a high renal clearance rate of about 450 mL/min. The initial elimination of metformin is rapid with a half-life varying between 1.7 and 3 hours. The terminal elimination phase accounting for about 4 to 5% of the absorbed dose is slow with a half-life between 9 and 17 hours. Metformin is not metabolized. Its main sites of concentration are the intestinal mucosa and the salivary glands. The plasma concentration at steady state ranges about 1 to 2 μg/mL. Certain drugs may potentiate the effects of metformin (see Precautions).

Indications: To control hyperglycemia in metformin responsive, stable, mild, nonketosis prone, maturity onset type of diabetes (Type II) which cannot be controlled by proper dietary management, exercise and weight reduction or when insulin therapy is not appropriate. Metformin can be of value for the treatment of obese diabetic patients.

Contraindications: Unstable and/or insulin-dependent (Type I) diabetes mellitus, history of ketoacidosis with or without coma.

In the presence of severe liver disease. In the presence of renal impairment or when renal function is not known, and also in patients with serum creatinine levels above the upper limit of the normal range.

In chronic alcoholism with hepatic damage.

In patients undergoing medical or diagnostic examinations, such as i.v. pyelography or angiography which could lead to a temporary functional oliguria (see Warnings).

In cases of cardiovascular collapse and in disease states associated with hypoxemia such as cardiorespiratory insufficiency, which are often associated with hyperlactacidemia.

In patients suffering from severe dehydration.

During stress conditions, such as severe infections, trauma or surgery and the recovery phase thereafter.

Known sensitivity or allergy to the drug.

In patients with a history of lactic acidosis irrespective of the precipitating factors.

Novo-Metformin (cont'd)

During pregnancy.

Warnings: The use of metformin will not prevent the development of complications peculiar to diabetes mellitus.

Use of metformin must be considered as treatment in addition to proper dietary regimen and not as a substitute for diet.

Care should be taken to ensure that metformin is not given when a contraindication exists. If acidosis of any kind develops, metformin should be discontinued immediately.

The risk of lactic acidosis increases with the degree of renal dysfunction, impairment of creatinine clearance and age of the patient. Patients with serum creatinine above the upper limit of the normal range should not receive metformin.

If during metformin therapy the patient develops acute intercurrent disease such as: clinically significant hepatic dysfunction, cardiovascular collapse, congestive heart failure, acute myocardial infarction, or other conditions complicated by hypoxemia, the drug should be discontinued.

In patients undergoing i.v. pyelography or angiography, metformin should be discontinued 2 days prior to the procedure and therapy may be reinstituted after the renal function has been re-evaluated.

Discontinue metformin 2 days before a surgical intervention. Therapy may be reinstituted following the operation after the renal function has been re-evaluated.

Patients should be warned against using alcohol in excess while on metformin therapy. Alcohol in a diabetic subject may cause an elevation of blood lactate.

Precautions: Patient Selection and Follow-up: Careful selection of patients is important. It is imperative that there be rigid attention to diet and careful adjustment of dosage. When metformin is combined with a sulfonylurea, instruct the patient on hypoglycemic reactions and their control. Regular thorough follow-up examinations are necessary (see Warnings).

If vomiting occurs, withdraw drug temporarily, exclude lactic acidosis, then resume dosage cautiously (see Adverse Effects).

Particular attention should be paid to short and long range complications which are peculiar to diabetes. Periodic cardiovascular, ophthalmic, hematological, hepatic and renal assessments are advisable (see Warnings).

Ascertain that the renal function is within normal range every 6 months while on metformin therapy.

Impairment of vitamin B_{12} and folic acid absorption has been reported in some patients. Therefore, measurements of serum vitamin B_{12} and folic acid are advisable at least every 1 to 2 years in patients on long-term treatment with metformin.

Drug Interactions: Certain drugs may potentiate the effect of metformin, particularly sulfonylurea type of drugs used in the treatment of diabetes. The simultaneous administration of these two types of drugs could produce a hypoglycemic reaction, especially if they are given in patients already receiving other drugs which, themselves, can potentiate the effect of sulfonylureas. These drugs can be: long-acting sulfonamides, tuberculostatics, phenylbutazone, clofibrate, MAO inhibitors, salicylates, probenecid and propranolol.

Other drugs tend to produce hyperglycemia and may lead to a loss of blood sugar control. These include diuretics (thiazides, furosemide), corticosteroids, oral contraceptives (estrogen plus progestogen) and nicotinic acid in pharmacologic doses.

Elimination rate of the anticoagulant, phenprocumon, has been reported to be increased by 20% when used concurrently with metformin. Therefore, patients receiving phenprocumon or other antivitamin K anticoagulants should be watched carefully when both types of drugs are used simultaneously. In such cases, an important increase of prothrombin time may occur upon cessation of metformin therapy, with an increased risk of hemorrhage.

Note: When used as indicated, there has not been a single case of lactic acidosis in Canada. Since its introduction in 1959, an estimated 600 000 patients are taking the drug worldwide. Twenty-eight cases of lactic acidosis have so far been reported and in each case a contraindication existed. Metformin should be immediately discontinued in the presence of acidosis.

Lactic acidosis is a serious and often fatal metabolic complication observed, among other conditions, in diabetic patients. It is characterized by acidosis (decreased blood pH); electrolyte disturbances with an increased anion gap and an increased lactate level with altered lactate-pyruvate ratio; azotemia may also be present. Physicians should instruct their patients to recognize the symptoms which could signal onset of lactic acidosis.

Adverse Effects: The most frequently reported adverse reactions with metformin are: metallic taste in the mouth, epigastric discomfort, nausea and vomiting; rarely, diarrhea and anorexia. Most of these reactions are transient and can be brought under control by reducing the dosage or by discontinuing therapy.

Overdose: Symptoms and Treatment: Available information concerning treatment of a massive overdosage of metformin is very limited. It would be expected that adverse reactions of a more intense character including epigastric discomfort, nausea and vomiting followed by diarrhea, drowsiness, weakness, dizziness, malaise and headache might be seen. Should those symptoms persist, lactic acidosis should be excluded. The drug should be discontinued and proper supportive therapy instituted.

Dosage: In diabetic patients, individual determination of the minimum dose that will lower blood glucose adequately should be made.

In patients where on initial trial the maximal recommended dose fails to lower the blood glucose adequately, the drug should be discontinued. Deterioration of the patient's condition can occur during the treatment of diabetes. It is advisable to ascertain the contribution of the drug in the control of blood glucose by discontinuing the medication semi-annually or at least annually with careful monitoring of the patient. If the need for the drug is not evident, the drug should not be resumed. In some diabetic subjects, short-term administration of the drug may be sufficient during periods of transient loss of blood sugar control.

The usual starting dose is 500 mg, 3 or 4 times a day, or 850 mg 2 or 3 times a day. Maximal dose should not exceed 2.5 g a day. To minimize gastric intolerance such as nausea and vomiting, metformin should be taken with food whenever possible.

Supplied: 500 mg: Each white, round, biconvex tablet, scored on one side, engraved novo on the reverse, contains: metformin HCl 500 mg. Gluten- and tartrazine-free. Bottles of 100 and 500.

850 mg: Each white, oval tablet contains: metformin HCl 850 mg. Gluten- and tartrazine-free. Bottles of 100 and 500.

NOVO-METHACIN Ⓟ

Novopharm

Indomethacin

Nonsteroidal Anti-inflammatory—Analgesic

Supplied: Capsules: 25 mg: Each hard gelatin capsule with opaque white body and light blue cap, engraved NOVO 25 contains: indomethacin 25 mg (capsule size #3). Gluten- and tartrazine-free. Bottles of 100, 500 and 1 000. Unit dose strips of 100.

50 mg: Each hard gelatin, light blue/white capsule engraved NOVO 50 contains: indomethacin 50 mg (capsule size #1). Gluten- and tartrazine-free. Bottles of 100, 500 and 1 000. Unit dose strips of 100.

Suppositories: 50 mg: Each white opaque suppository contains: indomethacin 50 mg. Gluten- and tartrazine-free. Boxes of 30. Keep suppositories away from excessive heat.

100 mg: Each white opaque suppository contains: indomethacin 100 mg. Gluten- and tartrazine-free. Boxes of 30. Keep suppositories away from excessive heat.

NOVO-METOPROL Ⓟ

Novopharm

Metoprolol Tartrate

Antihypertensive—Antianginal

Supplied: 50 mg: Coated: Each pink, capsule-shaped, film-coated tablet, embossed N/50, contains: metoprolol tartrate 50 mg. Gluten- and tartrazine-free. Bottles of 100, 500 and 1 000. Unit dose strips of 100.

Uncoated: Each white, round, biconvex tablet, embossed N over 50 on the scored side, contains: metoprolol tartrate 50 mg. Gluten- and tartrazine-free. Bottles of 100, 500 and 1 000.

100 mg: Coated: Each light blue, capsule-shaped, film-coated tablet, embossed N/100, contains: metoprolol tartrate 100 mg. Gluten- and tartrazine-free. Bottles of 100, 500 and 1 000. Unit dose strips of 100.

Uncoated: Each white, round, biconvex tablet, embossed N over 100 on the scored side, contains: metoprolol tartrate 100 mg. Gluten- and tartrazine-free. Bottles of 100, 500 and 1 000.

NOVO-MEXILETINE Ⓟ

Novopharm

Mexiletine HCl

Antiarrhythmic

Supplied: 100 mg: Each orange/scarlet, hard gelatin capsule, with N imprinted in white on the cap and "100" on the body, contains: mexiletine HCl 100 mg. Gluten- and tartrazine-free. Bottles of 100, 500 and 1 000. Boxes of 100 as unit dose strips.

200 mg: Each scarlet, hard gelatin capsule, with N imprinted in white on the cap and "200" on the body, contains: mexiletine HCl 200 mg. Gluten- and tartrazine-free. Bottles of 100, 500 and 1 000. Boxes of 100 as unit dose strips.

NOVO-MINOCYCLINE Ⓟ

Novopharm

Minocycline HCl

Antibiotic

Pharmacology: Minocycline, a tetracycline antibiotic, has activity against some gram-negative and gram-positive organisms. The antibacterial effect of minocycline is primarily bacteriostatic and is thought to act by inhibiting protein synthesis.

Indications: For the treatment of the following infections due to susceptible strains of the following organisms: gallbladder infections caused by E. coli.

Urinary Tract Infections: cystitis, gonorrhea, pyelonephritis caused by E. coli, Proteus species, E. aerogenes, N. gonorrhea, Klebsiella species.

Minocycline may be employed as an alternative drug in the treatment of anal and pharyngeal gonorrhea and syphilis when penicillin is contraindicated.

Skin and Soft Tissue Infections: abscess, cellulitis, furunculosis, impetigo and pyoderma caused by: S. epidermidis, S. aureus, S. pyogenes, Proteus species, E. coli. Minocycline could be useful in circumstances where staphylococcal or streptococcal organisms are shown to be resistant to other agents but sensitive to minocycline, even though tetracyclines are not the drugs of choice in these infections. Bacterial evaluation suggests that a relatively lower success rate may be expected in clinical cases involving proteus organisms.

Respiratory Tract Infections: pharyngitis, bronchitis, pneumonia, bronchopneumonia, sinusitis and tonsillitis caused by H. influenzae, Klebsiella species, Enterobacter species. For acute throat infections, tetracyclines should not be prescribed.

Contraindications: In patients with a hypersensitivity to minocycline or any other tetracycline.

Warnings: Newborns, Infants and Children: Permanent tooth discoloration (yellow-gray-brown) has resulted from the use of tetracyclines, including minocycline, during tooth development (last half of pregnancy, infancy and childhood under the age of 13 years). Although it has been observed following short-term courses, it is more common during long-term use. There have also been reports of enamel hypoplasia. A stable calcium complex is formed by all tetracyclines, including minocycline, in any bone forming tissue. The fibula growth rate has been observed to decrease in prematures given oral tetracycline in doses of 25 mg/kg every 6 hours. Upon discontinuation of the drug, this appeared to be reversible. Unless other drugs are ineffective or are contraindicated, minocycline should not be used in such patients.

Pregnancy and *Lactation:* Because of possible adverse effects on developing bones and teeth of the fetus and neonate, tetracyclines, including minocycline, are not recommended during pregnancy and lactation. Animal study results have indicated that tetracyclines cross the placenta, are found in fetal tissues and can have toxic effects on the developing fetus (often related to retardation of skeletal development).

Animals treated early in pregnancy have shown evidence of embryotoxicity. It has not been established if minocycline is safe for use during pregnancy.

Minocycline and other tetracyclines are excreted in the milk of lactating women.

Since some bacteriostatic drugs may interfere with the bactericidal action of penicillin, it is advisable to avoid giving minocycline in conjunction with penicillin.

As most streptococci have been found to be resistant to tetracycline drugs, minocycline should not be used for the treatment of streptococcal diseases unless the organism is demonstrated to be sensitive. Treatment of infections due to Group A beta-hemolytic streptococci should be continued for at least 10 days if it is deemed necessary to treat such infections with minocycline. Usual oral doses may lead to excessive systemic accumulations of minocycline and possible liver toxicity when significant renal impairment exists. Lower than usual doses may be indicated under such conditions. Serum level determinations of the drug are advisable after initial therapy and if therapy is prolonged.

The anti-anabolic action of tetracyclines also produce dose related increases in BUN; therefore, in patients with significant renal impairment, higher serum minocycline levels can lead to azotemia, hypophosphatemia and acidosis.

The symptoms associated with lupus erythematosus may be aggravated by minocycline. Therefore, when administering the drug to patients with this disease, caution should be taken.

Depressed plasma prothrombin activity has occurred with minocycline use. Therefore, patients should be monitored regularly if they receive anticoagulant therapy. Their anticoagulant dosage may require downward adjustment. There have been reports of interference with vitamin K synthesis by microorganisms in the gut.

It is extremely common to have cross-sensitization among the various tetracyclines.

In persons receiving minocycline, usually for extended periods of time, there have been occasional reports of pigmentation of skin, thyroid, bone and teeth which may be irreversible.

Reduced efficacy and increased incidence of breakthrough bleeding has been suggested with concomitant use of tetracycline and oral contraceptives.

Precautions: It is recommended that minocycline not be administered to children under 13 years of age.

Following full therapeutic dosage of tetracyclines, including minocycline, bulging fontanels have been reported in young infants. Very rarely, pseudotumor cerebri have been reported in adults. Upon discontinuation of the drug, these signs disappeared rapidly (see Adverse Effects).

While under treatment with minocycline or other tetracycline drugs, patients should be warned to avoid exposure to direct sunlight and/or ultraviolet light. Treatment should be discontinued at the first evidence of skin erythema or discomfort. In some individuals taking tetracyclines, photosensitivity manifested by an exaggerated sunburn reaction has been observed. Studies to date have rarely reported photosensitivity in association with minocycline.

Occupational Hazards: Headaches, lightheadedness, dizziness or vertigo may occur in patients treated with minocycline. The frequency and severity of these CNS symptoms can be increased when minocycline is administered in excess of the recommended dosage. While on minocycline therapy, patients should be cautioned about driving vehicles or using hazardous machinery. These symptoms usually disappear when the drug is discontinued, but may disappear during therapy.

Minocycline therapy may result in overgrowth of non-susceptible organisms (including fungi), as with other antibiotics. Minocycline should be discontinued if superinfection occurs, and appropriate therapy instituted.

Cross-resistance to many antibiotics can develop rapidly in several species of microorganisms. The clinician should consider this if therapy with minocycline is not achieving the expected results.

Strains of hemolytic streptococci from infections of the ear, wounds and skin have the highest frequency of resistance to minocycline. Whenever feasible, culture and sensitivity studies should be performed. In suspected streptococcal infections, these studies should be performed routinely.

Minocycline should be used with caution in patients with a history of allergy, asthma, hay fever or urticaria since sensitivity reactions are more likely to occur in such individuals.

A darkfield examination should be made from any lesion suggestive of concurrent syphilis before treating patients with gonorrhea. Monthly serological tests for syphilis should be repeated for at least 4 months.

Minocycline should be used cautiously in patients with hepatic dysfunction and when used in conjunction with alcohol or other hepatotoxic drugs.

Periodic laboratory evaluation of organ systems, including hematopoietic, renal and hepatic studies, should be performed when minocycline is used in long-term therapy.

Plasma prothrombin activity has been depressed with minocycline. Patients on anticoagulant therapy should, therefore, be monitored regularly. Their anticoagulant dosage may require downward adjustment. The interference of vitamin K synthesis by microorganisms in the gut has been reported.

Patients taking oral minocycline should not be given oral iron preparations and antacids containing aluminum, calcium or magnesium since they impair absorption.

Absorption can be delayed by dairy products. However, studies to date have not indicated that food notably influences minocycline absorption.

Adverse Effects: Adverse reactions which have been reported with tetracycline analogues, including minocycline, follow: CNS: increased intracranial pressure, headaches, lightheadedness, dizziness or vertigo and fainting spells (rare) have been reported with an overall incidence of approximately 7% in patients treated with minocycline. This is variable, however. When the drug is discontinued, these symptoms usually disappear rapidly.

Gastrointestinal System: nausea, vomiting, anorexia, diarrhea, stomatitis, glossitis, enterocolitis, pruritus ani, constipation, dysphagia and inflammatory lesions (with monilial overgrowth) in the anogenital region.

Teeth and Bone: There have been reports of dental staining (yellow-gray-brown) in children of mothers given tetracyclines, including minocycline, during the latter half of pregnancy and in children given the drug during the neonatal period, infancy and childhood to the age of 13 years. Enamel hypoplasia has been reported also. Rarely, upon extended treatment with minocycline, discoloration of bones and teeth has been documented to occur. The mechanism of staining, although not completely elucidated at present, appears to be mediated by the formation of a stable iron complex. The effects may be irreversible.

Renal: An apparently dose related rise in BUN has been reported. There have also been reports of increased excretion of nitrogen and sodium.

Skin: maculopapular and erythematous rashes. Exfoliative dermatitis, onycholysis, discoloration of the nails, pigmentation of the skin and mucous membrane, erythema multiforme and Stevens-Johnson syndrome.

Hypersensitivity Reactions: urticaria, angioneurotic edema, anaphylaxis, anaphylactoid purpura, pericarditis, polyarthralgia and exacerbation of systemic lupus erythematosus.

Pseudotumor cerebri (benign intracranial hypertension) in adults has been associated with the use of tetracyclines. The usual clinical manifestations are headache and blurred vision. Bulging fontanels have been associated with the use of tetracyclines in infants. While both of these conditions and related symptoms usually resolve soon after stoppage of the tetracycline, the possibility for permanent consequences exists.

Other: elevated AST or ALT values, hepatic cholestasis, hemolytic anemia, neutropenia, thrombocytopenia and eosinophilia. Minocycline, like other tetracyclines, has been reported to produce brown-black microscopic discoloration of the thyroid gland when given over prolonged periods. Abnormalities of thyroid function in humans, however, have not been shown to date. The administration of minocycline should be discontinued and appropriate alternate therapy instituted if adverse reactions or idiosyncrasy occur.

Overdose: Symptoms: Dizziness, nausea, vomiting, abdominal pain, intestinal hemorrhage, hypotension, lethargy, coma, acidosis, azotemia without a concomitant rise in creatinine.

Treatment: There is no specific antidote. Antacids (e.g., calcium carbonate or lactate, milk of magnesia, aluminum hydroxide) are general antidotes as they form relatively insoluble complexes with minocycline. (Calcium solution 5%: 50 g calcium carbonate or lactate dissolved in 1 000 mL water yields a 5% solution). Gastric lavage may be used, if necessary.

Dosage: Children 13 years of Age or Older: Minocycline should usually be initiated at 4 mg/kg, followed by 2 mg/kg every 12 hours. The administration of tetracyclines to children under 13 years of age is not recommended (see Warnings).

Adults: Initially, the usual oral dosage of minocycline is 100 or 200 mg, followed by 100 mg every 12 hours. If more frequent doses are preferred, two or four 50 mg doses may be given initially, followed by one 50 mg dose every 6 hours. Minocycline therapy should be continued for 1 or 2 days beyond the time when characteristic symptoms or fever have subsided.

Minocycline should be administered over a period of 10 or 15 days for the treatment of syphilis. In these patients, close follow-up, including laboratory tests, is recommended.

Concomitant therapy: Patients taking minocycline should not be given antacids containing aluminum, calcium or magnesium and/or iron preparations because they impair absorption.

Supplied: 50 mg: Each orange, hard gelatin capsule, imprinted NOVO and 50, contains: minocycline 50 mg. Bottles of 100.

100 mg: Each orange and purple, hard gelatin capsule, imprinted NOVO and 100, contains: minocycline 100 mg. Bottles of 100.

Store bottles between 15 and 30°C in tight, light-resistant containers. Unit dose boxes should be stored between 15 to 25°C and protected from light and high humidity.

NOVO-MUCILAX
Novopharm

Psyllium Hydrophilic Mucilloid

Laxative

Supplied: Novo-Mucilax contains dietary fibre (a natural, gluten-free substance) derived from the refined husk of the psyllium seed (Plantago ovata).

Unflavored Powder: Each rounded teaspoonful of light buff-colored, coarse powder (approximately 6.2 g) contains: approximately 3 g psyllium hydrophilic mucilloid and 3.19 g dextrose (no sucrose). Energy: 53 kJ (13 kcal). Bottles of 300 and 530 g.

Orange Flavored Powder: Each rounded teaspoonful of orange colored, sweet tasting, coarse powder (approximately 6.2 g) contains: 3 g psyllium hydrophilic mucilloid and 2 563 mg dextrose (no sucrose). Energy: 43 kJ (10 kcal). Bottles of 300 g.

Sugar-Free Powder: Each rounded teaspoonful of buff-colored, coarse powder contains: approximately 3 g psyllium hydrophilic mucilloid. Containers of 225 g.

All formulations are gluten- and tartrazine-free.

NOVO-NADOLOL Ⓟ
Novopharm

Nadolol

Antianginal—Antihypertensive

Supplied: 40 mg: Each white to off-white, round, standard convex, single-scored, compressed tablet, engraved with novo on scored side and 40 on the other side, contains: nadolol 40 mg. Gluten- and tartrazine-free. Bottles of 100.

80 mg: Each white to off-white, round, standard convex, single-scored, compressed tablet, engraved with novo on scored side and 80 on the other side, contains: nadolol 80 mg. Gluten- and tartrazine-free. Bottles of 100.

NOVO-NAPROX Ⓟ
Novopharm

Naproxen

Anti-inflammatory—Analgesic

Supplied: 125 mg: Each green, oval, unscored tablet with NOVO on one side and 125 on the other side, contains: naproxen USP 125 mg. Gluten- and tartrazine-free. Bottles of 100 and 500.

250 mg: Each yellow, oval, unscored tablet with NOVO on one side and 250 on the other side, contains: naproxen USP 250 mg. Gluten- and tartrazine-free. Bottles of 100, 500 and 1 000. Unit dose strips of 100.

375 mg: Each peach, oblong, scored tablet with NOVO and 375 on opposite sides, contains: naproxen USP 375 mg. Gluten- and tartrazine-free. Bottles of 100 and 500. Unit dose strips of 100.

500 mg: Each yellow, oblong, scored tablet with NOVO and 500 on one side contains: naproxen USP 500 mg. Gluten- and tartrazine-free. Bottles of 100 and 500.

NOVO-NAPROX SODIUM ℞
NOVO-NAPROX SODIUM DS ℞

Novopharm

Naproxen Sodium

Analgesic—Anti-inflammatory Agent

Supplied: Novo-Naprox Sodium: Each blue, elliptical, film-coated tablet, engraved novo on one side and 275 on the other, contains: naproxen sodium 275 mg. Gluten- and tartrazine-free. Bottles of 100 and 500.

Novo-Naprox Sodium DS: Each blue, elliptical, film-coated tablet, engraved novo on one side and 550 on the other, contains: naproxen sodium 550 mg. Gluten- and tartrazine-free. Bottles of 100 and 500.

NOVO-NIDAZOL ℞

Novopharm

Metronidazole

Trichomonacide

Supplied: Each white, scored, film-coated tablet, engraved N and 250 on same side, contains: metronidazole 250 mg. Sodium: <1 mmol (2.2 mg). Tartrazine-free. Bottles of 100, 500 and 1 000. Unit dose strips of 100.

NOVO-NIFEDIN ℞

Novopharm

Nifedipine

Antianginal

Supplied: 5 mg: Each tan, oval, soft gelatin capsule, imprinted N5, contains: nifedipine 5 mg. Gluten- and tartrazine-free. Bottles of 100 and 500.

10 mg: Each tan, oblong, soft gelatin capsule, imprinted NOVO 10, contains: nifedipine 10 mg. Gluten- and tartrazine-free. Bottles of 100 and 500.

NOVO-NORTRIPTYLINE ℞

Novopharm

Nortriptyline HCl

Antidepressant

Supplied: 10 mg: Each white opaque body and yellow opaque cap, imprinted with black ink N and 10 on opposing cap and body portion of the capsule, contains: nortriptyline 10 mg. Nonmedicinal ingredients: colloidal silicon dioxide, lactose hydrous, magnesium stearate, starch, talc and white dextrin. Bottles of 100, 500 and 1 000.

25 mg: Each white opaque body and yellow opaque cap, imprinted with black ink N and 25 on opposing cap and body portion of the capsule, contains: nortriptyline 25 mg. Nonmedicinal ingredients: colloidal silicon dioxide, lactose hydrous, magnesium stearate, starch, talc and white dextrin. Bottles of 100, 500 and 1 000.

Store between 15 to 30°C.

New Product 1998

NOVO-OXYBUTYNIN ℞

Novopharm

Oxybutynin Chloride

Anticholinergic—Antispasmodic

Supplied: Each blue, round tablet, engraved with N/N on the scored side and 5 on the opposite side, contains: oxybutynin chloride 5 mg. Gluten- and tartrazine-free. Bottles of 100 and 500. Unit dose boxes of 100.

NOVO-PEN-VK® ℞

Novopharm

Potassium Phenoxymethyl Penicillin

Antibiotic

Supplied: Suspension: After reconstitution, each 5 mL of light pink, fruity-flavored suspension contains: penicillin V potassium 300 mg. Sodium: <1 mmol (8.4 mg)/5 mL. Gluten- and tartrazine-free. Bottles of 100 mL.

Tablets: Each orange, round, film-coated tablet, engraved novo on one side, contains: penicillin V potassium 300 mg. Gluten-, sodium- and tartrazine-free. Bottles of 100, 500 and 1 000. Unit dose strips of 100.

NOVO-PERIDOL ℞

Novopharm

Haloperidol

Antipsychotic

Supplied: Tablets: Each round tablet contains: haloperidol 0.5 mg (white), 1 mg (yellow), 2 mg (pink), 5 mg (green), 10 mg (aqua) or 20 mg (salmon). Gluten- and tartrazine-free. Bottles of 100, 500 and 1 000 (0.5 mg, 1 mg, 2 mg, 5 mg, 10 mg). Bottles of 100 (20 mg).

Oral Solution: Each mL of colorless, odorless, and tasteless solution contains: haloperidol 2 mg. Dropper bottles of 100 mL.

NOVO-PINDOL ℞

Novopharm

Pindolol

Antihypertensive—Antianginal

Supplied: 5 mg: Each white, round, single-scored, compressed tablet, engraved novo and 5 on same side, contains: pindolol 5 mg. Gluten- and tartrazine-free. Bottles of 100 and 500.

10 mg: Each white, round, single-scored, compressed tablet, engraved novo and 10 on same side, contains: pindolol 10 mg. Gluten- and tartrazine-free. Bottles of 100 and 500.

15 mg: Each white, round, single-scored, compressed tablet, engraved novo and 15 on same side, contains: pindolol 15 mg. Gluten- and tartrazine-free. Bottles of 100.

Protect from light and store in well closed containers.

NOVO-PIROCAM® ℞

Novopharm

Piroxicam

Anti-inflammatory—Analgesic

Supplied: 10 mg: Each no. 2 maroon/blue opaque hard gelatin capsule, engraved NOVO 10, contains: piroxicam 10 mg. Gluten- and tartrazine-free. Bottles of 100 and 500.

20 mg: Each no. 2 maroon opaque hard gelatin capsule, engraved NOVO 20, contains: piroxicam 20 mg. Gluten- and tartrazine-free. Bottles of 100 and 500.

NOVO-POXIDE ℞

Novopharm

Chlordiazepoxide HCl

Anxiolytic

Supplied: 5 mg: Each green and yellow capsule, imprinted NOVO and 5 on opposing cap and body, contains: chlordiazepoxide HCl 5 mg. Nonmedicinal ingredients: lactose, starch and talc. Gluten- and tartrazine-free. Bottles of 100 and 1 000.

10 mg: Each black and green capsule, imprinted NOVO and 10 on opposing cap and body, contains: chlordiazepoxide HCl 10 mg. Nonmedicinal ingredients: lactose, starch and talc. Gluten- and tartrazine-free. Bottles of 100 and 1 000.

25 mg: Each green and white capsule, imprinted NOVO and 25 on opposing cap and body, contains: chlordiazepoxide HCl 25 mg. Nonmedicinal ingredients: lactose, starch and talc. Gluten- and tartrazine-free. Bottles of 100 and 1 000.

New Product 1998

NOVO-PRAZIN ℞

Novopharm

Prazosin HCl

Antihypertensive

Supplied: 1 mg: Each peach, capsule-shaped, single-scored, compressed tablet, engraved novo on one side and 1 on the other side, contains: prazosin HCl 1 mg. Gluten- and tartrazine-free. Bottles of 100 and 500.

2 mg: Each white, round, biconvex, broken-scored, compressed tablet, engraved novo on one side and 2 on the other side, contains: prazosin HCl 2 mg. Gluten- and tartrazine-free. Bottles of 100 and 500.

5 mg: Each white, diamond-shaped, biconvex, single-scored, compressed tablet, engraved novo on one side and 5 on the other side, contains: prazosin HCl 5 mg. Gluten- and tartrazine-free. Bottles of 100.

NOVO-PROFEN® ℞*

Novopharm

Ibuprofen

Anti-inflammatory—Analgesic

Supplied: Each tablet contains: ibuprofen 200 mg (yellow, film-coated), 300 mg (white, sugar-coated), 300 mg (white, film-coated), 400 mg (orange, sugar-coated), 400 mg (orange, film-coated) and 600 mg (peach, film-coated). Gluten- and tartrazine-free. Bottles of 24, 50 and 100 (200 mg FCT). Bottles of 100, 500 and 1 000 (300 mg SCT, 400 mg SCT and FCT, 600 mg FCT). Bottles of 100, 500 and 1 000 and unit dose boxes of 100 (400 mg FCT). Bottles of 100 and 1 000 and unit dose boxes of 100 (300 mg FCT).

*200 mg strength available without prescription.

NOVO-RANIDINE ℞

Novopharm

Ranitidine HCl

Histamine H_2-Receptor Antagonist

Pharmacology: Ranitidine is a selective antagonist of histamine at gastric H_2-receptor sites. Both basal gastric secretions and gastric acid secretion induced by histamine, pentagastrin and other secretagogues are inhibited by ranitidine. On a weight basis, ranitidine is between 4 and 10 times more potent than cimetidine. Following i.v., intraduodenal and oral administration of ranitidine, a dose-related inhibition of gastric acid secretion has been observed with a maximum response being achieved at an oral dose of 150 mg.

Pepsin secretion is also inhibited but secretion of gastric mucus is not affected. The secretion of bicarbonate or enzymes from the pancreas in response to secretin and pancreozymin is not altered by ranitidine.

Ranitidine is rapidly absorbed after oral administration. Although reports from the literature indicate that peak plasma concentrations are achieved within 1 to 3 hours, data from 2 comparative bioavailability studies of Novo-Ranidine and Zantac tablets shows that peak concentrations in plasma are achieved within 2 to 3 hours. The presence of food in the stomach at the time of oral administration or the presence of antacids does not significantly influence these plasma concentrations.

Bioavailability of ranitidine is approximately 50%. In man, serum protein binding of ranitidine is in the range of 10 to 19%. The elimination half-life is approximately 3 hours and the principal route of excretion is the urine (40% recovery of free and metabolized drug in 24 hours).

A significant linear correlation exists between the dose administered and the inhibitory effect upon gastric acid secretion for doses up to 150 mg. A plasma ranitidine concentration of 50 ng/mL has an inhibitory effect of approximately 50% upon stimulated gastric acid secretion. Reported IC_{50} values ranged from 36 to 94 ng/mL. Following the oral administration of 150 mg ranitidine, plasma concentrations in excess of this lasted for more than 8 hours, and after 12 hours, the plasma concentrations were sufficiently high to have a significant inhibitory effect upon gastric acid secretion. In patients with duodenal ulcer, the mean 24 hour hydrogen ion activity was significantly reduced by 69% and nocturnal gastric acid output was reduced by 90% following the oral administration of 150 mg ranitidine every 12 hours. Ranitidine 150 mg twice daily was superior to cimetidine 200 mg 3 times daily and 400 mg at night with respect to both 24 hour acidity and nocturnal acid output ($p < 0.001$ and $p < 0.05$ respectively). Blood levels of ranitidine remain effective over a 24-hour period whether given in a single 300 mg dose at night or as 150 mg given twice daily.

No significant gastrointestinal or CNS side effects have been reported by volunteers treated with ranitidine. Furthermore, pulse rate, blood pressure, ECG and EEG were not significantly affected in man following ranitidine administration.

Ranitidine did not influence plasma levels of the following hormones in healthy human volunteers and patients: cortisol, testosterone, estrogens, growth hormone, follicle stimulating hormone, luteinizing hormone, thyroid stimulating hormone, aldosterone or gastrin. Ranitidine, like cimetidine, reduced vasopressin output. Oral treatment with ranitidine 150 mg twice daily for up to 6 weeks did not affect the human hypothalamic-pituitary-testicular-ovarian or adrenal axes.

I.V. administration of 20 to 100 mg ranitidine had no effect on prolactin levels. At the 300 mg i.v. dose level, an increase in prolactin secretion equivalent to that produced by 200 mg of cimetidine i.v. was observed.

Reported laboratory studies have shown that ranitidine has negligible affinity for the cytochrome P450-linked hepatic mixed function oxidase system. In man, the metabolism of antipyrine, aminopyrine, warfarin and diazepam was not impaired by ranitidine treatment.

Indications: For the treatment of all conditions where a controlled reduction of gastric acid secretion is required for the rapid relief of pain and/or ulcer healing. These include duodenal ulcer, benign gastric ulcer and reflux esophagitis.

Contraindications: In patients with a known hypersensitivity to the drug.

Warnings: Treatment with a histamine H_2-antagonist may mask symptoms associated with carcinoma of the stomach and therefore may delay diagnosis of the condition. Therefore, when gastric ulcer is suspected, the possibility of malignancy should be excluded before therapy with ranitidine is instituted.

Precautions: *Pregnancy* and *Lactation:* The safety of ranitidine in the treatment of conditions where a controlled reduction of gastric secretion is required during pregnancy has not been established. Ranitidine is secreted in the breast milk of lactating women but the clinical significance of this has not been fully evaluated. Reproduction studies performed in rats and rabbits have revealed no evidence of impaired fertility or harm to the fetus due to ranitidine. If the administration of ranitidine is considered to be necessary in pregnant women, the potential benefits should be weighed against possible hazards to the patient and to the fetus.

Impaired Renal Function: Since ranitidine is excreted via the kidney, plasma levels of ranitidine are increased and prolonged in the presence of severe renal impairment. Therefore, in these patients, physicians may wish to reduce the dose to one half of the usual dose taken twice daily.

Children: Experience with ranitidine in children is limited and has not been fully evaluated in clinical studies. It has however been used successfully in children between 8 and 18 years of age in doses up to 150 mg twice daily without serious adverse effects.

Drug Interactions: Ranitidine has been reported to bind weakly to cytochrome P450 in vitro; however, at recommended doses ranitidine does not inhibit the action of cytochrome P450-linked oxygenase in the liver. There are conflicting reports in the literature concerning possible interactions between ranitidine and several drugs; however, the clinical significance of these reports has yet to be substantiated. Warfarin, diazepam, metoprolol and propranolol were among the drugs studied.

Adverse Effects: There have been no serious adverse effects reported to date in patients treated with ranitidine. There has been no clinically significant interference with endocrine, gonadal or liver function, nor has the drug adversely affected the CNS even in elderly patients.

Ranitidine was administered orally in doses ranging from 100 to 900 mg/day to 2 322 patients, mainly for the treatment of peptic ulceration, reflux esophagitis and Zollinger-Ellison syndrome. Adverse event monitoring was carried out and the vast majority of reported adverse events were coincidental and not related to treatment. Five adverse events showed a marginally greater incidence when ranitidine treatment was compared to placebo treatment, namely, skin rash (1.20%), headache (0.94%), tiredness (0.79%), constipation (0.39%) and diarrhea (0.24%).

Administration of ranitidine has, in some cases, been associated with increases in serum transaminases and gamma-glutamyl transpeptidase which returned to normal with either continued treatment or cessation of the drug. In placebo-controlled studies with almost 2 500 patients, no difference in the incidence of AST elevation and/or ALT values was seen between the placebo and ranitidine treatment groups. There have been reports of rare cases of hepatitis of a transient nature, although no causal relationship has been established.

Anaphylactoid reactions, such as anaphylaxis, urticaria, angioneurotic edema and bronchospasm have rarely been observed following parenteral and oral administration of ranitidine. Occasionally, these reactions have occurred following a single dose.

In a few patients, decreases in the white blood cell and platelet counts have occurred. No drug-related abnormalities were revealed by other hematological and renal laboratory tests.

There have been no reports of clinically significant interference with endocrine or gonadal function.

Overdose: Symptoms and Treatment: Ranitidine is very specific in action and accordingly no particular problems are expected following overdosage with the drug. The appropriate symptomatic and supportive therapy should be given, and if needed, the drug may be removed from the plasma by hemodialysis.

Dosage: Duodenal Ulcer and Benign Gastric Ulcer: The usual adult dosage is two 150 mg tablets once daily at bedtime or one 300 mg tablet taken at bedtime. It is not necessary to time the dose in relation to meals. In most cases of duodenal ulcer and benign gastric ulcer, healing will occur in 4 weeks. In the small number of patients whose ulcers may not have fully healed, these are likely to respond to a further course of treatment.

Patients who have responded to this short term therapy, particularly those with a history of recurrent ulcer, may usefully have extended maintenance treatment at a reduced dosage of one 150 mg tablet at bedtime.

Gastroesophageal Reflux Disease and Other Acid Related Gastrointestinal Diseases: To help in the management of gastroesophageal reflux disease, the recommended adult course of treatment is one 150 mg tablet twice daily, taken in the morning and before retiring, for up to 8 weeks.

Children: Experience with ranitidine in children is limited and it has not been fully evaluated in clinical studies (see Precautions).

Supplied: 150 mg: Each white, round, film-coated tablet, engraved novo on one side and 150 on the reverse, contains: ranitidine 150 mg (as the hydrochloride). Gluten- and tartrazine-free. Bottles of 100 and 500. Unit dose strips of 500. Patient packs of 60. Course of Treatment Packs of 60.

300 mg: Each white, capsule-shaped, film-coated tablet, engraved novo and 300 on opposing sides, contains: ranitidine 300 mg (as the hydrochloride). Gluten- and tartrazine-free. Bottles of 100 and 500. Patient packs of 30. Course of Treatment Packs of 30.

NOVO-RYTHRO ENCAP Ⓟ

Novopharm

Erythromycin

Antibiotic

Supplied: Each orange/clear capsule imprinted NOVO 250, contains: erythromycin base 250 mg as enteric-coated orange and white pellets. Gluten- and tartrazine-free. Bottles of 100 and 500.

New drugs require close post-marketing surveillance. Report suspected adverse reactions and interactions to the Health Protection Branch using the form provided in the CLIN-INFO SECTION.

NOVO-SALMOL Ⓟ

Novopharm

Salbutamol Sulphate

Bronchodilator

Supplied: 2 mg: Each pink, round tablet with flat beveled edges, scored and imprinted N/2 on one side, contains: salbutamol sulfate 2.4 mg (equivalent to 2 mg salbutamol). Bottles of 100, 500 and 1 000.

4 mg: Each pink, round tablet with flat beveled edges, scored and imprinted N/4 on one side, contains: salbutamol sulfate 4.8 mg (equivalent to 4 mg salbutamol). Bottles of 100, 500 and 1 000.

NOVO-SALMOL INHALER Ⓟ

Novopharm

Salbutamol

Bronchodilator

Pharmacology: Salbutamol produces bronchodilation through stimulation of β_2-adrenergic receptors in bronchial smooth muscle, thereby causing relaxation of muscle fibers. This action results in increased pulmonary function as demonstrated by spirometric measurements.

The onset of improvement in pulmonary function is usually observed 5 to 15 minutes after inhalation of salbutamol as measured by both maximal midexpiratory flow rate (MMEF) and forced expiratory volume in one second (FEV_1). Near maximum improvement in pulmonary function usually occurs within 60 to 90 minutes after 2 inhalations of salbutamol and significant bronchodilation and improvement clinically has been observed for 3 to 4 hours in most patients.

In clinical trials, some patients with asthma showed a therapeutic response (defined by maintaining FEV_1 values 15% or more above baseline) which was still apparent at 6 hours.

Indications: The symptomatic relief of bronchospasm due to bronchial asthma, chronic bronchitis and other chronic bronchopulmonary disorders in which bronchospasm is a complicating factor.

Contraindications: In patients with cardiac tachyarrhythmias and those who have shown hypersensitivity to any of the ingredients.

Warnings: *Pregnancy* and *Lactation:* The safety of salbutamol in pregnancy and lactation has not been established.

Care should be taken with patients suffering from cardiovascular disorders, especially coronary insufficiency, cardiac arrhythmias, hypertension; in patients with convulsive disorders, diabetes mellitus, hyperthyroidism; and in patients who are unusually responsive to sympathomimetic amines.

Special care and supervision are required in patients with idiopathic hypertrophic subvalvular aortic stenosis, in whom an increase in the pressure gradient between the left ventricle and the aorta may occur, causing increased strain on the left ventricle.

Fatalities have been reported following the excessive use of inhaled sympathomimetic amines and the exact cause of these fatalities is unknown. However, cardiac arrest following the unexpected development of a severe acute asthmatic crisis and subsequent hypoxia is suspected. Therefore, it is essential that the physician instruct the patient in the need for further evaluation if the patient's asthma becomes worse. In individual patients, any β_2-adrenergic agonist, including salbutamol, may have a clinically significant cardiac effect.

With repeated excessive use of sympathomimetic inhalation preparations, a few patients have been reported to have developed severe paradoxical bronchospasm. The cause of this refractory state is unknown. In the reported cases, the patients did not respond to other forms of therapy until the initial drug was withdrawn; therefore, it is advisable that in such instances the use of the preparation be discontinued immediately and alternate therapy instituted.

Caution should be exercised when salbutamol is administered to patients being treated with MAOI or tricyclic antidepressants since these drugs may potentiate salbutamol's action on the cardiovascular system.

The action of salbutamol may be antagonized by β-adrenergic blocking drugs, particularly those which are non-cardioselective.

Immediate hypersensitivity reactions may occur after administration of salbutamol, as demonstrated by rare cases

Novo-Salmol Inhaler (cont'd)

of urticaria, angioedema, rash, bronchospasm, anaphylaxis, and oropharyngeal edema.

Large doses of i.v. salbutamol have been reported to aggravate pre-existing diabetes mellitus and ketoacidosis. Additionally, β-agonists, including salbutamol, given i.v. may cause a decrease in serum potassium, possibly through intracellular shunting. The decrease is usually transient, not requiring supplementation. The relevance of these observations to the use of salbutamol inhaler is unknown.

Precautions: General: Salbutamol inhaler should be used with caution in patients sensitive to sympathometic amines. The concomitant use of salbutamol with other sympathomimetic agents is not recommended since such combined use may lead to deleterious cardiovascular effects.

The patient should be instructed in the correct use of the inhaler to ensure optimal delivery of salbutamol to the bronchial tree.

Children: The use of salbutamol inhaler therapy in children should depend on the ability of the individual child to learn the proper use of the inhaler. During inhalation, these children should be assisted or supervised by an adult.

The patients must be informed that the recommended dose of salbutamol inhaler should not be exceeded.

The administration of salbutamol should be stopped in patients in whom salbutamol administration induces cardiac irregularities.

If a reduced response to salbutamol inhaler becomes apparent, the patient should seek medical advice.

Pregnancy: Teratogenic Effects: There are no adequate and well-controlled studies of salbutamol in pregnant women. Salbutamol inhaler should be used during pregnancy only if the potential benefit justifies the potential risk to the fetus. Salbutamol has been shown to be teratogenic in mice when given in doses corresponding to 14 times the human aerosol dose, 5 times the human inhalation dose, the human nebulization dose, 0.2 times the maximum human (child weighing 21 kg) oral dose and 0.4 times the maximum human oral dose.

Labor and Delivery: Although there have been no reports concerning the use of salbutamol during labor and delivery, it has been reported that high doses of salbutamol, administered i.v., inhibit uterine contractions. There are some reports of oral salbutamol delaying pre-term labour. Therefore, cautious use of salbutamol is required in pregnant patients when given for relief of bronchospasm so as to avoid interference with uterine contactility. Use in such patients should be restricted to those patients in whom the benefits clearly outweigh the risks.

Lactation: It is not known if salbutamol is excreted in human milk. Taking into account the importance of the drug to the mother, a decision should be made whether to discontinue nursing or to discontinue the drug because of the potential for tumorigenicity shown for salbutamol in some animal studies. It is not known if salbutamol has harmful effects on the neonate.

Drug Interactions: Salbutamol should not be used concomitantly with other sympathomimetic aerosol bronchodilators. Additional adrenergic drugs, if they are to be administered by any route, should be used with caution to avoid deleterious cardiovascular effects.

Since the action of salbutamol on the vascular system may be potentiated, salbutamol should be administered with extreme caution to patients being treated with MAOI or tricyclic antidepressants.

Salbutamol and β-receptor blocking agents inhibit the effect of each other. It is recommended that a β-blocker with less predominant β_2 blocking effects (e.g., metoprolol) be considered in patients requiring concomitant treatment with a β-blocker. Patients should be monitored carefully for possible deterioration in pulmonary function or the need to adjust the dosage of either drug during concomitant treatment.

Fluorocarbon Propellants: Salbutamol inhaler, like other pressurized aerosol formulations, contains fluorocarbon propellants (trichlorofluoromethane and dichlorodifluoromethane). These propellants may be hazardous if they are deliberately abused. Toxic cardiovascular effects and even death, especially under conditions of hypoxia, have occurred with the inhalation of high concentrations of aerosol sprays. When used properly and with adequate ventilation, however, evidence attests to the relative safety of aerosols.

Adverse Effects: The most frequent adverse reactions are nervousness and tremor. Headache, tachycardia, palpitations, muscle cramps, insomnia, nausea, weakness and dizziness have also been reported. Other reported adverse reactions are: drowsiness, flushing, restlessness, irritability, chest discomfort, difficulty in micturition, hypertension, angina, vomiting, vertigo, central nervous stimulation, unusual taste and drying or irritation of the oropharynx.

Rare cases of urticaria, angioedema, rash, bronchospasm, anaphylaxis and oropharyngeal edema have been reported after the use of salbutamol. With repeated excessive use of sympathomimetic inhalation preparations, a few patients have reportedly developed severe paradoxical bronchospasm. It is advisable that in such instances the use of the drug be discontinued immediately and alternate therapy instituted.

Overdose: Symptoms and Treatment: Overdosage may cause tachycardia, arrhythmia, hypertension and in extreme cases, sudden death. To antagonize the effect of salbutamol the judicious use of a cardioselective B-adrenergic blocking agent (e.g. metoprolol, atenolol), may be considered, bearing in mind the danger of inducing an asthmatic attack.

Dosage: Salbutamol is taken by inhalation at the dose of 1 to 2 puffs up to 4 times daily. More than 8 inhalations/day is not recommended.

Supplied: Each dose of inhalation aerosol contains: salbutamol 100 μg. Tartrazine-free. Canisters of 200 metered doses.

The contents of the inhaler are under pressure. Do not puncture. Do not store or use near heat or open flame. Store container between 15 and 30°C. Bursting may result when exposed to temperatures above 50°C. Never throw container into fire or incinerator. Keep out of reach of children.

NOVO-SELEGILINE Ⓟ

Novopharm

Selegiline HCl

Antiparkinsonian Agent

Pharmacology: Selegiline is an irreversible inhibitor of the enzyme monoamine oxidase (MAO). Because selegiline has greater affinity for type B than type A MAO, it can serve as a selective inhibitor of MAO-B if it is administered at the recommended dose.

Selegiline may have pharmacological effects unrelated to MAO-B inhibition. There is some evidence that it may increase dopaminergic activity by interfering with dopamine re-uptake at the synapse. Effects resulting from selegiline administration may also be mediated through its metabolites. Two of its three principle metabolites, amphetamine and methamphetamine, have pharmacological actions of their own, they interfere with neuronal re-uptake and enhance the release of several neurotransmitters (e.g., norepinephrine, dopamine, serotonin). The extent to which these neurotransmitters contribute to selegiline's effects are unknown.

Rationale for the use of selective MAO-B inhibitors in Parkinson's Disease: Many of the prominent symptoms of Parkinson's Disease are due to a deficiency of striatal dopamine that is the consequence of a progressive degeneration and loss of a population of dopaminergic neurons which originate in the substantia nigra and project to the striatum. Early in the course of the disease, the deficit in the capacity of these neurons to synthesize dopamine can be overcome by the administration of exogenous levodopa. After several years of levodopa therapy, the response to a given dose of levodopa is often accompanied by side effects (dyskinesia, on-off phenomena, freezing).

MAO-B inhibitors may be useful under these conditions because by blocking the catabolism of dopamine, they increase the net amount of dopamine available. In patients with advanced Parkinson's Disease, the addition of selegiline to levodopa (usually with a decarboxylase inhibitor) has been shown to improve the therapeutic effect of levodopa.

Recently, in newly diagnosed patients, selegiline was shown to delay the need to implement levodopa therapy.

The mechanisms of action of selegiline, both in newly diagnosed and in severely incapacitated patients, is unknown.

Hypertensive Crisis ("Cheese Reaction"): MAOs are widely distributed throughout the body; their concentration is especially high in liver, kidney, stomach, intestinal wall and brain. In the intestine, type A is the predominant MAO; it is thought to provide vital protection from exogenous amines (e.g., tyramine) that have the capacity to displace norepinephrine from storage sites and thereby cause a hypertensive crisis. MAO-A catabolizes the exogenous amines which are found in a variety of foods (fermented cheese, red wine, herring) and drugs (over-the-counter cough/cold medications). Since MAO-A in the gut is not inhibited by therapeutic doses of selegiline, in theory, patients may take medications containing pharmacologically active amines and consume tyramine-containing foods without the risk of uncontrolled hypertension.

To date, clinical experience appears to confirm this prediction: hypertensive crises have not been reported in selegiline treated patients. However, until the pathophysiology of the "cheese reaction" is more completely understood, it seems prudent to assume that selegiline can only be used safely without dietary restrictions at doses where it presumably selectively inhibits MAO-B (e.g., 10 mg/day).

Attention to the dose dependent nature of selegiline's selectivity is critical if it is to be used without restrictions being placed on diet and concomitant drug use (see Warnings and Precautions).

Pharmacokinetics: The extremely short half-life of selegiline (<0.15 hours following a 10 mg i.v. dose) is consistent with the inability to detect unchanged selegiline in the serum and urine following oral administration.

Only preliminary information about the details of the pharmacokinetics of selegiline and its metabolites is available. In a 7-day study undertaken to investigate the effect of selegiline on the kinetics of an oral hypoglycemic agent, subjects were given a 10 mg dose of selegiline for 7 consecutive days. Serum levels of intact selegiline were below the limit of detection (<10 ng/mL). Trough levels of the 3 metabolites were as follows: N-desmethyldeprenyl, the major metabolite, was not detectable; the levels of amphetamine and methamphetamine were 3.5 ng/mL and 8.0 ng/mL, respectively.

The rate of MAO-B regeneration following discontinuation of treatment has not been quantified. It is this rate, dependent upon de novo protein synthesis, which seems likely to determine how fast normal MAO-B activity can be restored.

Indications: May be of value as an adjunct to levodopa (with or without a decarboxylase inhibitor) in the management of the signs and symptoms of Parkinson's disease; in newly diagnosed patients before symptoms begin to affect the patient's social or professional life, at which time more efficacious treatment becomes necessary.

Contraindications: In patients with known hypersensitivity to this drug.

Selegiline should not be used in patients with other extrapyramidal disorders such as excessive tremor or tardive dyskinesia, or in patients with severe psychosis or profound dementia.

Selegiline is contraindicated in combination with meperidine, (see Precautions, Drug Interactions). This contraindication is often extended to other opioids as well.

Selegiline should not be used in patients with active peptic ulcer.

Warnings: Selegiline should not be used at daily doses exceeding those recommended (10 mg/day) because of the risks associated with nonselective inhibition of MAO (see Pharmacology).

The selectivity of selegiline for MAO-B may not be absolute at the recommended daily dose of 10 mg/day, and selectivity is further diminished with increasing daily doses. The precise dose at which selegiline becomes a nonselective inhibitor of all MAO is unknown but may be in the range of 30 to 40 mg/day.

Clinical data on the concomitant use of selegiline and fluoxetine hydrochloride are not available. Death has been reported to occur following the initiation of therapy with nonselective MAO inhibitors (phenelzine, tranylcypromine) shortly after discontinuation of fluoxetine. To date, this reaction has not been reported with selegiline; however, since the mechanism of this reaction is not fully understood it seems prudent, in general, to avoid this combination. Because of the long half-lives of fluoxetine and its active metabolite, at least 5 weeks (approximately 5 half-lives) should elapse between discontinuation of fluoxetine and initiation of MAO inhibitor therapy. Based on experience with the combined use of MAO inhibitors and tricyclic antidepressants, at least 14 days should elapse between discontinuation of a MAO inhibitor and initiation of treatment with fluoxetine.

Precautions: General: Some patients given selegiline may experience an exacerbation of levodopa-associated side effects, presumably due to the increased amounts of dopamine reacting with supersensitive postsynaptic receptors. These effects may often be mitigated by reducing the dose of levodopa by approximately 10 to 30%.

The decision to prescribe selegiline should take into consideration that the MAO system of enzymes is complex and incompletely understood and there is only a limited amount of carefully documented clinical experience with selegiline.

Consequently the full spectrum of possible responses to selegiline may not have been observed in the premarketing evaluation of the drug. It is advisable, therefore, to observe the patients closely for atypical responses.

Information for the Patient: Patients should be advised of the possible need to reduce levodopa dosage after initiation of selegiline therapy. The patients (or their families if the patient is incompetent) should be advised not to exceed the recommended daily dose of 10 mg. The risk of using higher daily doses of selegiline should be explained, and a brief description of the hypertensive crisis ("cheese reaction") provided. While hypertensive reactions with selegiline have not been reported, documented experience is limited. Consequently, it may be useful to inform patients (or their families) about the signs and symptoms associated with MAO inhibitors induced hypertensive reactions. In particular, patients should be urged to report, immediately, any severe headache or other atypical or unusual symptoms not previously experienced.

Laboratory Tests: Transient or continuing abnormalities with a tendency for elevated levels of liver enzymes have been described during long-term therapy. Although serious hepatic toxicity has not been observed, caution is recommended in patients with a history of hepatic dysfunction. Periodic routine evaluation of all patients however, is appropriate.

Drug Interactions: The occurrence of stupor, muscular rigidity, severe agitation and elevated temperature has been reported in a man receiving selegiline and meperidine, as well as other medications. Symptoms resolved over days when the combination was discontinued. This case is typical of the interaction of meperidine and MAO inhibitors.

Other serious reactions (including severe agitation, hallucinations, and death) have been reported in patients receiving this combination. While it cannot be said definitively that all of these reactions were caused by this combination, they are all compatible with this well recognized interaction.

Although the database of documented clinical experience is limited, MAO inhibitors are ordinarily contraindicated for use with meperidine. This warning is often extended to other opioids (see Contraindications).

It is also prudent to avoid the concomitant use of selegiline and fluoxetine (see Warnings).

Other than the possible exacerbation of side effects in patients receiving levodopa therapy, no interactions attributed to the combined use of selegiline and other drugs have been reported. However, because the database of documented clinical experience is limited, the level of reassurance provided by this lack of adverse reporting is uncertain (see Warnings and Precautions).

Carcinogenesis: Studies have not been performed to date to evaluate the carcinogenic potential of selegiline.

Pregnancy: Insufficient animal reproduction studies have been done with selegiline to conclude that selegiline poses no teratogenic potential. However, one rat study carried out at doses as much as 180 fold the recommended human dose revealed no evidence of a teratogenic effect. It is not known whether selegiline can cause fetal harm when administered to a pregnant woman or can affect reproductive capacity. Selegiline should be given to a pregnant woman only if clearly needed.

Lactation: It is not known whether selegiline is excreted in human milk. Because many drugs are excreted in human milk, consideration should be given to discontinuing the use of all but absolutely essential drug treatments in nursing women.

Children: The effects of selegiline in children under 18 have not been evaluated.

Adverse Effects: The side effects of selegiline are usually those associated with excessive dopaminergic stimulation. The drug may potentiate the side effects of levodopa, therefore, adjustment of drug dosages may be required. Some of the most serious adverse reactions reported with the combination of selegiline and levodopa were hallucinations and confusion, particularly visual hallucinations.

Although a cause and effect relationship has not been established, a tendency to a progressive rise in several liver enzymes has been reported after long-term therapy.

In prospective clinical trials, the following adverse effects, (listed in decreasing order of frequency), led to the **discontinuation** of selegiline: nausea, hallucinations, confusion, depression, loss of balance, insomnia, orthostatic hypotension, increased akinetic involuntary movements, agitation, arrhythmia, bradykinesia, chorea, delusions, hypertension, new or increased angina pectoris and syncope.

Events reported only rarely as a cause of discontinuation of treatment include anxiety, drowsiness/lethargy, nervousness, dystonia, increased episodes of freezing, increased tremor, weakness, excessive perspiration, constipation, weight loss, burning lips/mouth, ankle edema, gastrointestinal bleeding and hair loss.

In controlled clinical trials involving a very limited number of patients (n=49 receiving Novo-Selegiline in combination with levodopa; n=50 receiving placebo) the following adverse reactions were reported (see Table I).

Table I—Novo-Selegiline

Incidence* of Treatment-emergent Adverse Events in Clinical Trials

	Number of Patients Reporting Events	
Adverse Event	**Novo-Selegiline n=49**	**Placebo n=50**
Nausea	10	3
Dizziness/lightheaded/fainting	7	1
Abdominal pain	4	2
Confusion	3	0
Hallucinations	3	1
Dry mouth	3	1
Vivid dreams	2	0
Dyskinesia	2	5
Headache	2	1
The following events were reported once in either or both groups:		
Ache, generalized	1	0
Anxiety/tension	1	1
Anemia	0	1
Diarrhea	1	0
Hair loss	0	1
Insomnia	1	1
Lethargy	1	0
Leg pain	1	0
Low back pain	1	0
Malaise	0	1
Palpitations	1	0
Urinary retention	1	0
Weight loss	1	0

*Incidences are devoid of practical statistical significance.

In Monotherapy: The incidence of adverse reactions occurring in trials using selegiline as monotherapy has not been fully reported to date. Serious adverse reactions were as follows: depression, chest pain, myopathy and diarrhea. Other reported adverse reactions included insomnia, headache, nausea, dizziness and vertigo.

In all prospectively monitored clinical investigations, enroling approximately 920 patients, the following adverse events, classified by body system, were reported.

CNS: Motor/Coordination/Extrapyramidal: increased tremor, chorea, loss of balance, restlessness, blepharospasm, increased bradykinesia, facial grimace, falling down, heavy leg, muscle twitch, myoclonic jerks, stiff neck, tardive dyskinesia, dystonic symptoms, dyskinesia, involuntary movements, freezing, festination, increased apraxia, muscle cramps.

Mental Status/Behavioral/Psychiatric: hallucinations, dizziness, confusion, anxiety, depression, drowsiness, behavior/mood change, dreams/nightmares, tiredness, delusions, disorientation, lightheadedness, impaired memory, increased energy, transient high, hollow feeling, lethargy/malaise, apathy, overstimulation, vertigo, personality change, sleep disturbance, restlessness, weakness, transient irritability.

Pain/Altered Sensation: headache, back pain, leg pain, tinnitus, migraine, supraorbital pain, throat burning, generalized ache, chills, numbness of toes/fingers, taste disturbance.

Autonomic Nervous System: dry mouth, blurred vision, sexual dysfunction.

Cardiovascular: orthostatic hypotension, hypertension, arrhythmia, palpitations, new or increased angina pectoris, hypotension, tachycardia, peripheral edema, sinus bradycardia, syncope.

Gastrointestinal: nausea/vomiting, constipation, weight loss, anorexia, poor appetite, dysphagia, diarrhea, heartburn, rectal bleeding, bruxism.

Genitourinary/Gynecologic/Endocrine: transient anorgasmia, nocturia, prostatic hypertrophy, urinary hesitancy, urinary retention, decreased penile sensation, urinary frequency.

Skin and Appendages: increased sweating, diaphoresis, facial hair, hair loss, hematoma, rash, photosensitivity.

Miscellaneous: asthma, diplopia, shortness of breath, speech affected.

Toxic delirium has also been reported with selegiline when used as adjunctive therapy to levodopa treatment.

Overdose: Symptoms: No specific information is available about clinically significant overdoses with selegiline. However, experience gained during the development of selegiline reveals that some individuals exposed to doses of 600 mg/day of selegiline suffered severe hypotension and psychomotor agitation.

Since the selective inhibition of MAO-B by selegiline is achieved only at doses recommended for the treatment of Parkinson's Disease (i.e., 10 mg/day), overdoses are likely to cause significant inhibition of both MAO-A and MAO-B. Consequently, the signs and symptoms of overdose may resemble those observed with marketed nonselective MAO inhibitors (e.g., tranylcypromine and phenelzine).

Overdose with Nonselective MAO Inhibitors: Note: This section is provided for reference; it dose not describe events that have actually been observed with selegiline in overdose.

Characteristically, signs and symptoms of nonselective MAO inhibitor overdose may not appear immediately. Delays of up to 12 hours between ingestion of the drug and the appearance of signs may occur. Importantly, the peak intensity of the syndrome may not be reached for upwards of a day following the overdose. Death has been reported following overdose. Therefore, immediate hospitalization, with continuous patient observation and monitoring for a period of at least 2 days following the ingestion of such drugs in overdose is strongly recommended.

The clinical picture of MAO inhibitor overdose varies considerably; its severity may be a function of the amount of drug consumed. The CNS and cardiovascular systems are prominently involved.

Signs and symptoms of overdosage may include, alone or in combination, any of the following: drowsiness, dizziness, faintness, irritability, hyperactivity, agitation, severe headache, hallucinations, trismus, opisthotonos, convulsions and coma; rapid and irregular pulse, hypertension, hypotension and vascular collapse; precordial pain, respiratory depression and failure, hyperpyrexia, diaphoresis, and cool, clammy skin.

Treatment: Because there is no recorded experience with selegiline overdose, the following suggestions, based on the management of nonselective MAO inhibitor poisoning, might be applicable.

Treatment of overdose with nonselective MAO inhibitors is symptomatic and supportive. Induction of emesis or gastric lavage with instillation of charcoal slurry may be helpful in early poisoning, provided the airway has been protected against aspiration. Signs and symptoms of CNS stimulation, including convulsions, should be treated with diazepam, given slowly i.v. Phenothiazine derivatives and CNS stimulants should be avoided. Hypotension and vascular collapse should be treated with i.v. fluids and, if necessary, blood pressure titration with an i.v. infusion of a dilute pressor agent. It should be noted that adrenergic agents may produce a markedly increased pressor response. Respiration should be supported by appropriate measures, including management of the airway, use of supplemental oxygen and mechanically supported ventilatory assistance, as required. Body temperature should be monitored closely. Intensive management of hyperpyrexia may be required. Maintenance of fluid and electrolyte balance is essential.

Dosage: The recommended dosage of selegiline as monotherapy in newly diagnosed patients, or as an adjunct to levodopa (usually with a decarboxylase inhibitor) is 10 mg/day administered as divided doses of 5 mg each taken at breakfast and lunch.

When selegiline adjunctive therapy is added to the existing levodopa therapeutic regime, a reduction, usually of 10 to 30% in the dose of levodopa (in some instances a reduction of the dose of selegiline to 5 mg/day) may be required during the period of adjustment of therapy or in case of exacerbation of adverse effects.

Doses higher than 10 mg/day should not be used. There is no evidence that additional benefit will be obtained from the administration of higher doses. Furthermore, higher doses will result in a loss of selectivity of selegiline towards MAO-B with an increase in the inhibition of type MAO-A. There is an increased risk of adverse reactions with higher doses as well as an increased risk of hypertensive episode ("cheese reaction").

Supplied: Each almost white, flat tablet, scored on one side with the other face engraved with n, contains: 5 mg of the l-isomer of selegiline HCl (formerly l-deprenyl HCl). Nonmedicinal ingredients: citric acid, lactose, magnesium stearate and microcrystalline cellulose. Gluten- and tartrazine-free. Bottles of 60 and 300. Store between 15 and 30°C.

NOVO-SOTALOL ℞

Novopharm

Sotalol HCl

Antiarrhythmic

Supplied: 80 mg: Each light blue, capsule-shaped, scored tablet, embossed "N/N" on the scored side and "80" on the other, contains: sotalol HCl 80 mg. Nonmedicinal ingredients: FD&C blue #2, lactose, magnesium stearate and pregelatinized starch. Bottles of 100 and 500.

160 mg: Each light blue, round, scored tablet, embossed "N/N" on the scored side and "160" on the other, contains: sotalol HCl 160 mg. Nonmedicinal ingredients: FD&C blue #2, lactose, magnesium stearate and pregelatinized starch. Bottles of 100 and 500.

NOVO-SPIROTON ℞

Novopharm

Spironolactone

Aldosterone Antagonist

Supplied: 25 mg: Each cream-colored, round, standard convex tablet, single scored, and with a peppermint aroma, embossed novo on one side and 25 on the other side, contains: spironolactone 25 mg. Gluten- and tartrazine-free. Bottles of 100 and 500. Unit dose strips of 100.

100 mg: Each cream-colored, round, standard convex tablet, single scored, and with a peppermint aroma, embossed N contains: spironolactone 100 mg. Tartrazine-free. Bottles of 100, 500 and 1 000. Unit dose strips of 100.

NOVO-SPIROZINE ℞

Novopharm

Hydrochlorothiazide—Spironolactone

Diuretic—Aldosterone Antagonist

Supplied: 25 mg: Each round, standard convex, ivory tablet, single scored with a peppermint aroma, embossed 25/25 on one side and novo on the other side, contains: spironolactone 25 mg and hydrochlorothiazide 25 mg. Gluten- and tartrazine-free. Bottles of 100, 500 and 1 000.

50 mg: Each round, standard convex, white tablet, single scored with a peppermint aroma, embossed 50/50 on one side and novo on the other side, contains: spironolactone 50 mg and hydrochlorothiazide 50 mg. Gluten- and tartrazine-free. Bottles of 100 and 250.

NOVO-SUCRALATE ℞

Novopharm

Sucralfate

Gastroduodenal Cytoprotective Agent

Pharmacology: Sucralfate exerts a generalized gastric cytoprotective effect by enhancing natural mucosal defence mechanisms. Studies conducted in animals and clinical trials in humans have demonstrated that sucralfate can protect the gastric mucosa against various irritants such as alcohol, ASA, hydrochloric acid, sodium hydroxide or sodium taurocholate.

In addition, sucralfate has been demonstrated to have a greater affinity for ulcerated gastric or duodenal mucosa than for non-ulcerated mucosa.

Sucralfate produces an adherent and cytoprotective barrier at the ulcer site. This barrier protects the ulcer site from the potential ulcerogenic properties of acid, pepsin and bile. Furthermore, sucralfate blocks acid diffusion across the sucralfate protein barrier and also complexes directly with pepsin and bile.

The action of sucralfate is non-systemic as the drug is only minimally absorbed from the gastrointestinal tract. The minute amounts of the sulfated disaccharide which are absorbed are primarily excreted in the urine.

Each g of sucralfate contains approximately 200 mg of aluminum. The aluminum moiety can dissociate at low pH and aluminum release in the stomach can be expected; however, aluminum is poorly absorbed from the intact gastrointestinal tract. Following administration of 1 g of sucralfate 4 times a day to individuals with normal renal function, approximately 0.001% to 0.017% of sucralfate's aluminum content is absorbed and excreted in the urine. The results in an aluminum load of between 0.008 mg and 0.136 mg following a 4 g daily dose. Individuals with normal renal function excrete absorbed aluminum and can respond to an increased aluminum load by increasing urinary excretion. These values were determined in individuals with intact gastrointestinal mucosa. Available evidence does not indicate that absorption of aluminum would be different in individuals with ulcerated gastrointestinal mucosa. Experiments have shown that sucralfate is not an antacid.

Indications: For the treatment of duodenal and non-malignant gastric ulcer.

Also indicated for the prophylaxis of duodenal ulcer recurrence.

Contraindications: There are no known contraindications to the use of sucralfate. However, the physician should read the Warnings section when considering the use of this drug in pregnant or pediatric patients, or patients of childbearing potential.

Warnings: *Pregnancy:* There has been no experience to date with the use of sucralfate in pregnant women. Therefore, sucralfate should not be used in pregnant women or women of childbearing potential unless, in the judgment of the physician, the anticipated benefits outweigh the potential risk.

Children: Clinical experience in children is limited. Therefore, sucralfate therapy cannot be recommended for children under 18 unless, in the judgment of the physician, anticipated benefits outweigh the potential risk.

Precautions: General: The following should be taken into account before treating patients with sucralfate: Recurrence may be observed in patients after a successful course of treatment for gastric or duodenal ulcers. While the treatment with sucralfate can result in complete healing of the ulcer, a successful course of treatment with sucralfate should not be expected to alter the underlying cause of ulcer disease.

Proper diagnosis is important since symptomatic response to sucralfate therapy does not rule out the presence of a gastric malignancy.

Drug Interactions: Antacids should not be taken within half an hour before or after sucralfate intake because of the possibility of decreased binding of sucralfate with the gastroduodenal mucosa as a consequence of a change of intragastric pH.

Animal studies have shown that simultaneous administration of sucralfate with tetracycline, phenytoin or cimetidine results in a statistically significant reduction in the bioavailability of these agents. Cimetidine absorption was not reduced in humans. In clinical trials, the concomitant administration of sucralfate reduced the bioavailability of digoxin.

These interactions appear to be non-systemic and to result from the binding of sucralfate to the concomitantly administered drug in the gastrointestinal tract. In all cases, complete bioavailability was restored by separating the administration of sucralfate from that of the other agent by 2 hours.

Sucralfate, administered respectively 30 and 60 minutes before ASA or ibuprofen did not alter the bioavailability of these agents. In a study comparing the prior administration of a single dose of sucralfate tablets on the bioavailability of naproxen, indomethacin or ketoprofen versus administration in the absence of sucralfate, it was shown that the total amount of these drugs absorbed was not altered; however, the peak concentration of each was reduced, and the time to reach peak concentration was delayed.

The physician should consider the possible clinical implications of these interactions. It is recommended to separate the administration of any drug from that of sucralfate when the potential for altered bioavailability is felt to be critical to the effectiveness of that drug.

Chronic Renal Failure: Dialyzed Patients: Sucralfate should be used with caution in patients with chronic renal failure. When sucralfate is administered orally, small amounts of aluminum are absorbed from the gastrointestinal tract (see Pharmacology). Existing evidence indicates that patients with normal renal function receiving the recommended doses of sucralfate adequately excrete aluminum in the urine; however, patients with chronic renal failure or those receiving dialysis have impaired excretion of absorbed aluminum, and in these individuals, aluminum is known to accumulate in serum and in tissues. In particular, dialysis patients are at greater risk as aluminum does not cross dialysis membranes of the dialysis machine since it is bound to plasma proteins, most notably albumin and transferrin.

In patients with chronic renal failure undergoing dialysis, aluminum-related toxicity (encephalopathy and aluminum-related bone disease), associated with administration of sucralfate and/or other sources of aluminum has been reported. Consideration should therefore be given to the total daily load of aluminum before administering sucralfate in combination with other aluminum-containing medications, such as aluminum-containing antacids.

Nondialyzed Patients: In a study of 6 nondialyzed chronic renal failure patients with glomerular filtration rates ranging from approximately 10 to 40% of normal, sucralfate administered at a dose of 1 g 4 times daily for 3 weeks resulted in elevated serum aluminum concentrations which plateaued at approximately 23 μg/L after 1 week of treatment from a pretreatment level of 3 μg/L. Renal aluminum clearance increased in relation to the increase in serum levels and returned to baseline within 2 weeks following discontinuation of sucralfate as did serum aluminum concentrations. No adverse events were reported in these patients.

These data indicate that the use of sucralfate in nondialyzed chronic renal failure patients requires physician discretion since the excretion of absorbed aluminum may be impaired in these individuals.

Adverse Effects: Very few side effects have been reported with sucralfate. They are mild in nature and have only exceptionally led to discontinuation of therapy.

The main complaint has been constipation ranging from 1.7 to 3.3% of patients.

Other side effects reported included diarrhea, nausea, gastric discomfort, indigestion, dry mouth, skin rash, pruritus, back pain, dizziness, sleepiness and vertigo.

See the Precautions section for information on the potential for aluminum toxicity in dialyzed chronic renal failure patients.

Overdose: Symptoms and Treatment: Overdosage has never been observed with sucralfate and appears to be unlikely since, using maximal doses of up to 12 g/kg/body weight in a variety of animal species, a lethal dose could not be established.

Overdosage is likely to be associated with symptoms similar to those described in the Adverse Effects section, such as constipation. These should be treated symptomatically.

Dosage: Duodenal and Gastric Ulcer: The recommended adult oral dosage for duodenal and gastric ulcer is 1 tablet of 1 g 4 times a day, 1 hour before meals and at bedtime, on a empty stomach. For duodenal ulcer, sucralfate may also be administered as two 1 g tablets twice daily, on waking and at bedtime on an empty stomach.

In duodenal ulcers, while healing with sucralfate often occurs within 2 to 4 weeks, treatment should be continued for a maximum of 8 to 12 weeks unless healing has been demonstrated by x-ray and/or endoscopic examination.

In the case of gastric ulcers, an alternative treatment should be considered if no objective improvement is observed following 6 weeks of sucralfate therapy. However, patients with a large gastric ulcer that has demonstrated a progressive healing tendency may require an additional 6 weeks of treatment. For the prophylaxis of duodenal ulcer recurrence, the recommended dosage is 1 tablet of 1 g twice daily, on an empty stomach. Treatment may be continued for up to 1 year.

For relief of pain, antacids may be added to the treatment. However, antacids should not be taken within ½ hour before or after sucralfate intake.

Duration of continuous treatment in patients with chronic renal failure receiving dialysis should be evaluated by periodic monitoring of serum aluminum levels, due to the possibility of aluminum accumulation in these patients (see Precautions). According to information widely available in the literature, patients with serum aluminum concentrations that approach 100 μg/L should be carefully monitored for symptoms of aluminum toxicity and treatment should be discontinued if such symptoms appear.

There is no evidence to indicate that patients with chronic renal failure, who do not require dialysis, are at risk of developing aluminum toxicity while receiving the recommended doses of sucralfate. Physician discretion should be exercised when considering the duration of treatment (see Precautions).

Supplied: Each white, capsule-shaped, partially scored, compressed tablet, embossed novo inside a raised border on one side, plain on reverse, contains: sucralfate 1 g. Gluten- and tartrazine-free. Bottles of 100 and 500.

Let your network of health care professionals know that there is information on chronic medication management before surgery in the CLIN-INFO SECTION.

NOVO-SUNDAC

Novopharm

Sulindac

Anti-inflammatory—Analgesic

Supplied: 150 mg: Each yellow, hexagonal-shaped, broken scored tablet, embossed N and 150 on opposite sides, contains: sulindac 150 mg. Gluten- and tartrazine-free. Bottles of 100 and 500.

200 mg: Each yellow, hexagonal-shaped, broken scored tablet, embossed N and 200 on opposite sides, contains: sulindac 200 mg. Gluten- and tartrazine-free. Bottles of 100 and 500.

NOVO-TAMOXIFEN

Novopharm

Tamoxifen Citrate

Antineoplastic

Supplied: 10 mg: Each white, round, biconvex, film-coated tablet embossed N over 10 on same side, contains: tamoxifen citrate equivalent to tamoxifen 10 mg. Gluten- and tartrazine-free. Bottles of 100 and 250. Patient packages of 60.

20 mg: Each white, round, biconvex, film-coated tablet embossed N over 20 on same side, contains: tamoxifen citrate equivalent to tamoxifen 20 mg. Gluten- and tartrazine-free. Bottles of 100. Patient packages of 30.

Store at room temperature. Protect from heat and light.

NOVO-TEMAZEPAM

Novopharm

Temazepam

Hypnotic

Supplied: 15 mg: Each maroon and flesh-colored capsule, imprinted with N and 15 on opposing cap and body portions of the capsule, contains: temazepam 15 mg. Gluten- and tartrazine-free. Bottles of 100 and 500.

30 mg: Each maroon and blue-colored capsule, imprinted with N and 30 on opposing cap and body portions of the capsule, contains: temazepam 30 mg. Gluten- and tartrazine-free. Bottles of 100 and 500.

NOVO-TENOXICAM

Novopharm

Tenoxicam

Anti-inflammatory—Analgesic

Supplied: Each yellow, oval-shaped, biconvex, film-coated tablet, engraved "N" on one side and "20" on the scored side, contains: tenoxicam 20 mg. Nonmedicinal ingredients: carnauba wax, cornstarch, dibutyl sebacate, ethylcellulose, hydroxypropyl methylcellulose, lactose, magnesium stearate, polydextrose, pregelatinized starch, sodium lauryl sulfate, synthetic yellow, iron oxide, talc, titanium dioxide and triacetin. Gluten- and tartrazine-free. Bottles of 100.

NOVO-TERAZOSIN

Novopharm

Terazosin HCl

Antihypertensive—Symptomatic Treatment of Benign Prostatic Hyperplasia (BPH)

Pharmacology: Hypertension: The antihypertensive effect of terazosin is believed to be a direct result of peripheral vasodilation. Although the exact mechanism by which the lowering of blood pressure is achieved is not known, the relaxation of vessels appears to be produced mainly by selective blockade of alpha-1-adrenoceptors.

Benign Prostatic Hyperplasia (BPH): The reduction in the symptoms associated with BPH following administration of terazosin may be related to the changes in muscle tone produced by a blockade of alpha-1-adrenoceptors in the smooth muscle of the bladder neck and prostate.

Pharmacodynamics: Hypertension: Systolic and diastolic blood pressure is lowered in both supine and standing positions. In clinical trials, blood pressure responses were measured at the end of the dosing interval (24 hours) with the usual supine response 5 to 10 mmHg systolic and 3.5 to 8 mmHg diastolic. The response in the standing position tended to be larger by 1 to 3 mmHg.

Limited measurements of peak response (2 to 3 hours after dosing) during chronic terazosin administration indicate that this response is somewhat greater than the trough (24-hour) response, suggesting some attenuation of response at 24 hours, presumably due to a fall in blood terazosin concentrations at the end of the dose interval.

The greater blood pressure effect associated with peak plasma concentrations appears to be more position dependent (greater in the standing position) than the effect of terazosin at 24 hours; in the standing position there is also a 6 to 10 beats/min increase in heart rate in the first few hours after dosing. During the first 3 hours after dosing, 12.5% of patients had a decrease in systolic pressure of 30 mmHg or more from supine to standing, or standing systolic pressure below 90 mmHg with a decrease of at least 20 mmHg.

During controlled clinical trials, patients receiving terazosin monotherapy had a small but statistically significant fall (a 3% fall) compared to placebo in total cholesterol and the combined low-density and very-low density lipoprotein fractions. No significant changes were observed in high-density lipoprotein fraction and triglycerides compared to placebo.

Benign Prostatic Hyperplasia (BPH): The symptoms associated with BPH are related to bladder outlet obstruction. The bladder outlet obstruction is comprised of a static obstruction due to the enlarged prostate and a dynamic obstruction which is dependent upon the sympathetically controlled tone of the smooth muscle in the prostate and the bladder neck. Stimulation of alpha-1-adrenoceptors in the smooth muscle of the bladder neck and the prostate causes smooth muscle contraction and an increase in muscle tone.

In 3 placebo-controlled studies in men with symptomatic BPH, symptom evaluation and uroflowmetric measurements were performed approximately 24 hours following dosing. Results from these studies indicated that terazosin significantly improved symptoms and peak urine flow rates over placebo.

In 30 to 70% of patients with symptomatic BPH, placebo has also shown a remarkable and sometimes dramatic effect in controlled short-term studies. The symptoms may subside or fade away without treatment in approximately 20% of patients.

Pharmacokinetics: Orally administered terazosin is essentially completely absorbed in man. Nearly all of the circulating dose is in the form of the parent drug. Food has little or no effect on bioavailability. The plasma levels of the free base peak in about 1 hour and then decline with a half-life of approximately 12 hours. About 90 to 94% of terazosin is bound to plasma proteins and binding is constant over the clinically observed concentration range.

Hepatic metabolism is extensive with major biliary elimination. Approximately 10% of an orally administered dose is excreted as parent drug in the urine and approximately 20% is eliminated in the feces. The remainder is excreted as metabolites. Overall approximately 40% of the administered dose is excreted in the urine and approximately 60% in the feces.

Indications: Hypertension: Terazosin is indicated in the treatment of mild to moderate hypertension. It is employed in a general treatment program in conjunction with a thiazide diuretic and/or other antihypertensive drugs as needed for sufficient patient response. Terazosin can be tried as a sole therapy in those patients in whom other agents caused adverse effects or are inappropriate.

Benign Prostatic Hyperplasia (BPH): Terazosin is also indicated for the treatment of symptoms of benign prostatic hyperplasia (BPH). The onset of effect is rapid, with improvement in peak flow rate and symptoms observed at 2 weeks. The effect on these variables was well maintained throughout the study duration (18 months). Terazosin does not retard or stop the progression of BPH. The long-term effects of terazosin on the incidence of surgery, acute urinary obstruction or other complications of BPH, are yet to be determined.

A number of clinical conditions can mimic symptomatic BPH (i.e., stricture of urethra, stricture of bladder neck, urinary bladder stones, neurogenic bladder dysfunction secondary to diabetes, Parkinsonism, etc.). These conditions should therefore be ruled out before terazosin therapy is initiated.

Contraindications: In individuals who have shown hypersensitivity to terazosin or its analogs.

Warnings: Syncope and First-dose Effect: Terazosin can cause marked hypotension, particularly postural hypotension, and syncope in association with the first dose or first few doses of treatment. A similar effect can occur if therapy is reinstated following interruption for more than a few doses. Syncope has also occurred in association with rapid dosage increases or the introduction of another antihypertensive agent into the regimen of a patient taking high doses of terazosin.

Syncope is believed to be due to an excessive postural hypotensive effect, although occasionally the syncopal episode has been preceded by a bout of severe supraventricular tachycardia with heart rates of 120 to 160 beats/min.

In studies with terazosin the incidence of syncopal episodes was approximately 1% in hypertensive patients and 0.7% in patients with BPH.

The likelihood of syncopal episodes or excessive hypotension can be minimized by limiting the initial dose of the drug to 1 mg of terazosin given at bedtime, by increasing the dosage slowly, and by introducing any additional antihypertensive drugs into the patient's regimen with caution (See Dosage).

Occupational Hazards: Patients should be warned about the possibility of syncopal and orthostatic symptoms, and to avoid driving or hazardous tasks for 12 hours following the initial dose of terazosin, after the dose is increased and after an interruption of therapy when treatment is resumed. They should be cautioned to avoid situations where injury could result should syncope occur.

If syncope occurs, place the patient in the recumbent position and institute supportive measures as necessary.

Patients with a history of micturition syncope should not be given terazosin.

Concomitant administration of terazosin with verapamil in hypertensive patients may result in symptomatic hypotension and in some cases tachycardia (see Precautions).

Anaphylactoid Reactions: Anaphylactoid-like reactions manifested as angioedema of the lips, tongue, pharynx, and/or laryngeal spasm have occurred rarely in patients taking terazosin (see Adverse Effects). In such cases, terazosin should be promptly discontinued and appropriate therapy and monitoring should be provided until complete and sustained disappearance of signs and symptoms has occurred.

Precautions: General: Terazosin therapy does not modify the natural history of benign prostatic hyperplasia (BPH). It does not retard or stop the progression of BPH, nor does it improve urine flow sufficiently to significantly reduce the residual urine volume. However, significant reduction of the mean residual volume have been shown in patients with baseline residual volumes of >50 mL. The patient may continue to be at risk of developing urinary retention and other BPH complications during terazosin therapy.

Prostatic Cancer: Carcinoma of the prostate and BPH cause many of the same symptoms. These two diseases frequently coexist. Therefore, patients thought to have BPH should be examined prior to starting terazosin therapy to rule out the presence of carcinoma of the prostate.

Orthostatic Hypotension: While syncope is the most severe orthostatic effect of terazosin (see Warnings), other symptoms of lowered blood pressure, such as dizziness, lightheadedness, and palpitations are more common with one or more of these occurring in 28% of patients in clinical trials of hypertension. In BPH clinical trials, 21% of the patients experienced one or more of the following: dizziness, hypotension, postural hypotension, syncope and vertigo. Patients should be advised to lie down when these symptoms occur and then wait for a few minutes before standing to prevent their recurrence.

Patients with occupations where such events could result in potential problems should be treated with particular caution.

There is evidence that the orthostatic effect of terazosin is greater, even in chronic use, shortly after dosing.

Concomitant Conditions: Terazosin should not be prescribed to patients with symptomatic BPH who have the following concomitant conditions: chronic urinary retention, high residual urine (over 200 mL), peak urine flow of 5 mL/s or less, history of prior prostatic surgery, chronic fibrous or granulomatous prostatitis, urethral stricture, history of pelvic irradiation, presence of prostatic calculi, presence of large median lobe of prostate, presence of calculi in urinary bladder, recent history of epididymitis, gross hematuria, presence of neurogenic bladder dysfunction (diabetes mellitus, Parkinsonism, uninhibited neurogenic bladder, etc.), hydronephrosis, presence of carcinoma of the prostate, patients with clinically significant renal or hepatic impairment (i.e., serum creatinine >2mg/dL or AST >1.5 times the upper limit of normal (or equivalent level on the international scale).

Novo-Terazosin (cont'd)

Carcinogenesis, Mutagenesis, Impairment of Fertility: Terazosin was devoid of mutagenic potential when evaluated in vivo and in vitro.

Terazosin administered in the feed to rats at doses of 8, 40, and 250 mg/kg/day for 2 years, was associated with a statistically significant increase in benign adrenal medullary tumors of male rats exposed to the 250 mg/kg/day dose. Female rats were unaffected. Terazosin was not oncogenic in mice when administered in feed for 2 years at a maximum tolerated dose of 32 mg/kg/day.

Effect on fertility was assessed in a standard fertility/reproductive performance study in which male and female rats were administered oral doses of 8, 30 and 120 mg/kg/day. Four of 20 male rats given 30 mg/kg and 5 of 19 male rats given 120 mg/kg failed to sire a litter. Testicular weights and morphology were unaffected by treatment.

Vaginal smears at 30 and 120 mg/kg, however, appeared to contain less sperm than smears from control matings and a good correlation was reported between sperm count and subsequent pregnancy.

Oral administration of terazosin for 1 or 2 years resulted in a statistically significant rise in the frequency of testicular atrophy in rats given 40 and 250 mg/kg/day, but not in rats given 8 mg/kg/day. Testicular atrophy also occurred in dogs given 300 mg/kg/day for 3 months but not in those given 20 mg/kg/day for 1 year.

Geriatrics: Terazosin should be used cautiously in the elderly because of the possibility of orthostatic hypotension. There was an age-related trend towards an increased incidence of dizziness, blurred vision, and syncope in elderly patients treated with this drug. Patients over 75 years of age may have limited benefit from terazosin therapy.

Children: The use of terazosin in children is not recommended since the safety and efficacy have not been established.

Patients with Renal Impairment: The use of terazosin in patients with impaired renal function requires careful monitoring. Limited pharmacokinetic studies using low doses (1 mg) showed no difference in the pharmacokinetics of terazosin as compared to patients with normal renal function. Approximately 40% of an oral terazosin dose is excreted by the kidney as parent drug or metabolites.

Patients with Liver Impairment: No information is available on the use of terazosin in patients with impaired liver function.

Peripheral Edema: Fluid retention resulting in weight gain may occur during terazosin therapy. In a placebo-controlled monotherapy trial, male and female patients receiving terazosin gained a mean 0.8 and 1 kg respectively, compared to losses of 0.1 and 0.5 kg, respectively, in the placebo group. Both of these differences are significant.

Pregnancy: The safety of terazosin in pregnancy has not been established. Terazosin is not recommended during pregnancy unless the potential benefits outweigh the risks to the mother and fetus.

In animal studies there was no teratogenic effect. In peri- and postnatal development studies in rats, significantly more pups died in the group dosed with 120 mg/kg/day than in the control group during the 3-week postpartum period.

Lactation: It is not known whether terazosin is eliminated in human milk. Because of possible adverse reactions in nursing infants an alternate method of infant feeding should be considered when the use of drug is essential.

Drug Interactions: In controlled studies, terazosin has been added to diuretics and several beta-adrenergic blockers; except for the additive hypotensive effect, no unexpected interactions were observed. Terazosin has also been used in patients in various concurrent therapies. While these were not formal interaction studies, no interactions were observed. Terazosin has been given concomitantly in at least 50 patients on the following drugs or classes of drugs: analgesic/anti-inflammatory (e.g., acetaminophen, ASA, codeine, ibuprofen, indomethacin); antibiotics (e.g., erythromycin, trimethoprim and sulfamethoxazole); anticholinergic/sympathomimetics (e.g., phenylephrine HCl, phenylpropanolamine HCl, pseudoephedrine HCl); antigout (e.g., allopurinol); antihistamines (e.g., chlorpheniramine); cardiovascular drugs (e.g., atenolol, hydrochlorothiazide, methyclothiazide, propranolol); corticosteroids; gastrointestinal drugs (e.g., antacid); hypoglycemics; sedatives and tranquilizers (e.g., diazepam).

Concomitant treatment of terazosin with verapamil in hypertensive patients resulted in significant increases in AUC, C_{max} and C_{min} of terazosin. The pharmacokinetics of verapamil were not altered. Symptomatic hypotension and in some cases tachycardia, were observed. Caution should therefore be exercised when these drugs are administered concomitantly (see Warnings).

Laboratory Tests: Long-term (6 months or longer) administration of terazosin has produced no pattern of clinically significant changes attributable to the drug in the following clinical laboratory measurements: glucose, uric acid, creatinine, BUN, liver function tests and electrolytes.

Small but statistically significant reductions in hematocrit, hemoglobin, white blood cells, total protein and albumin were observed in controlled clinical studies. These laboratory findings suggested the possibility of hemodilution. Treatment with terazosin for up to 24 months had no significant effect on prostate specific antigen (PSA) levels.

Adverse Effects: Hypertension: The incidence of adverse effects is derived from clinical trials involving 1 986 hypertensive patients on terazosin monotherapy or combination therapy.

The most serious adverse reaction encountered with terazosin is syncope occurring in about 1% of patients.

The most common reactions were dizziness (18.9%), headache (14.1%), asthenia (11%), somnolence (4.8%), nasal congestion (4.6%) and palpitation (4.6%).

The most frequently reported adverse effects which resulted in termination of terazosin were dizziness (3.5%), asthenia (2.1%) and headache (1.8%).

The following events were reported in less than 1% of cases except as indicated in brackets. The order of presentation corresponds within each heading to the relative frequency of occurrence.

Body as a Whole: headache (14.1%), asthenia (11%), peripheral edema (3.6%), chest pain (2.2%), abdominal pain (1.5%), edema (1.3%), facial edema (1.0%), back pain, weight gain, allergic reactions and malaise.

Cardiovascular: palpitation (4.6%), tachycardia (2.9%), syncope (1%), postural hypotension, angina pectoris, arrhythmias, cerebrovascular accident, heart failure, hypotension (at times severe) and migraine.

Digestive: nausea (3.9%), dry mouth (1.7%), diarrhea (1.3%), dyspepsia, vomiting, anorexia, gastritis, liver function abnormality and jaundice.

Nervous System: dizziness (18.9%), somnolence (4.8%), nervousness (2.2%), paresthesia (1.5%), insomnia (1.2%), incoordination, abnormal dreams, confusion, speech disorder, tremor, vertigo, seizure and depression.

Respiratory: nasal congestion (4.6%), dyspnea (2.8%), rhinitis (1.2%), sinusitis, cold symptoms, pharyngitis, asthma, increased cough and laryngeal spasm.

Skin and Appendages: sweating (1.1%), pruritus, rash and photosensitivity.

Special Senses: blurred vision (1.4%), eye disorder (1.2%), tinnitus and taste perversion.

Urogenital: impotence (1.1%), urinary frequency and dysuria.

Miscellanous: pain in extremities (1.8%), hypokalemia, hypophosphatemia and decreased libido.

At least 2 cases of severe anaphylactoid reactions were reported to be associated with administration of terazosin (see Warnings).

Postmarketing Experience: Body as a Whole: fever, neck pain, and shoulder pain.

Cardiovascular: vasodilation, atrial fibrillation has been reported; however, a cause and effect relationship has not been established.

Digestive: constipation and flatulence.

Nervous System: anxiety.

Respiratory: bronchitis, epistaxis and flu symptoms.

Special Senses: conjunctivitis.

Urogenital: priapism, urinary tract infection, and urinary incontinence primarily reported in postmenopausal women.

Musculoskeletal: arthralgia, arthritis, joint disorder and myalgia.

Hematopoietic: thrombocytopenia has been reported.

Metabolic/Nutritional Disorders: gout.

Benign Prostatic Hyperplasia (BPH): In clinical trials involving 1 171 patients with BPH, syncope was reported in 0.7% of patients following treatment with terazosin.

The most common reactions ($\geq 1\%$) were dizziness (14.0%), asthenia (9.0%), headache (6.4%), somnolence (4.5%), postural hypotension (3.8%), impotence (3.5%), urinary tract infection (3.1%), pharyngitis (2.7%), dyspnea (2.5%), rhinitis (2.2%), dysuria (2%), back pain (1.8%), nausea (1.8%), flu syndrome (1.7%), rash (1.7%), sinusitis (1.7%), hypotension (1.5%), chest pain (1.5%), vertigo (1.3%), dyspepsia (1.1%), diarrhea (1%), palpitation (1%), abdominal pain (1%) and amblyopia (1%).

Postmarketing Experience: Thrombocytopenia has been reported. Atrial fibrillation has been reported; however, a cause and effect relationship has not been established. Priapism has also been reported.

Overdose: Symptoms and Treatment: Should administration of terazosin lead to hypotension, support of the cardiovascular system is of first importance. Restoration of blood pressure and normalization of heart rate may be accomplished by keeping the patient in the supine position. If this measure is inadequate, shock should first be treated with volume expanders. If necessary, vasopressors should then be used and the renal function should be monitored and supported as needed. Laboratory data indicate that terazosin is highly protein bound; therefore, dialysis may not be of benefit.

Dosage: Hypertension: The dose and dosing intervals (12 or 24 hours) of terazosin should be adjusted to the patient's individual blood pressure response.

When terazosin is being added to the existing antihypertensive therapy, the patient should be carefully monitored for the occurrence of hypotension. If a diuretic or other antihypertensive agent is being added to terazosin regimen, dosage reduction of terazosin and retitration with careful monitoring may be necessary. The following is a guide to its administration:

Initial Dose: 1 mg of terazosin at bedtime is the starting dose for all patients and this dose should not be exceeded; compliance with this initial dosage recommendation should be strictly observed to minimize the potential for acute hypotensive episodes.

Subsequent Doses: The dose may be slowly increased to achieve the desired blood pressure response. The usual dose range is 1 to 5 mg once a day. Some patients may benefit from doses up to 20 mg/day which is the maximum recommended daily dose.

The blood pressure should be monitored at the end of the dosing interval to ensure that control is maintained. It is also helpful to measure the blood pressure 2 to 3 hours after dosing to see if maximum and minimum responses are similar and to evaluate symptoms.

If response to terazosin is substantially diminished at 24 hours, patients may be tried on a larger dose or twice daily dosage regimen. The latter should also be considered if adverse reactions such as dizziness, palpitations or orthostatic complaints are seen 2 to 3 hours after dosing.

If terazosin administration is discontinued for several days or longer, therapy should be reinstituted using the initial dosage regimen.

Benign Prostatic Hyperplasia (BPH): The dose of terazosin should be adjusted to the patient's individual response.

Initial Dose: 1 mg of terazosin at bedtime is the starting dose for all patients, and this dose should not be exceeded for the first week. Compliance with this initial dosage should be strictly observed to minimize the potential for acute hypotensive episodes.

Subsequent Doses: The dose should be increased in stepwise fashion at weekly intervals to 2, 5 or 10 mg once daily to achieve the desired improvement of symptoms and/or flow rates. Maintenance doses of 5 to 10 mg once daily are generally required for the clinical response. The duration and dosage of treatment should be carefully titrated. Four weeks of terazosin therapy may be required before statistically significant improvement in the objective parameters of flowmetry (peak urine flow) are obtained. Improvement in the symptoms may appear as early as 2 weeks, but may be delayed as late as 6 weeks or more. Some patients may not achieve a clinical response despite appropriate titration. Following 18 months of treatment a complete re-evaluation of the patient's condition should be made.

Following the administration of the maximum recommended dosage, terazosin should be discontinued if improvement in uroflowmetry is not clinically significant from baseline level or improvement in the American Urology Association (AUA) scores are not translated into improvements in quality of life. Terazosin therapy should also be discontinued if terazosin side effects are more bothersome than BPH symptoms or if the patient develops a urinary complication while on terazosin therapy.

If terazosin administration is discontinued for several days or longer, therapy should be reinstituted using the initial dosing regimen.

Supplied: 1 mg: Each white, round, flat-faced, beveled-edged, compressed tablet, engraved with "N" on one side and "1" on the other side, contains: terazosin HCl 1 mg. Nonmedicinal ingredients: cornstarch, lactose, magnesium stearate, povidone and talc. Bottles of 100, 500 and 1 000. Boxes of 100 as unit dose strips.

2 mg: Each orange, round, flat-faced, beveled-edged, compressed tablet, engraved with "N" on one side and "2" on the other side, contains: terazosin HCl 2 mg. Nonmedicinal ingredients: cornstarch, FD&C yellow #6 aluminum lake, lactose, magnesium stearate, povidone and talc. Bottles of 100, 500 and 1 000. Boxes of 100 as unit dose strips.

5 mg: Each tan, round, flat-faced, beveled-edged, compressed tablet, engraved with "N" on one side and "5" on the other side, contains: terazosin HCl 5 mg. Nonmedicinal ingredients: cornstarch, D&C red #30 aluminum lake, FD&C blue #1 aluminum lake, FD&C yellow #6 aluminum lake, lactose, magnesium stearate, povidone and talc. Bottles of 100, 500 and 1 000. Boxes of 100 as unit dose strips.

10 mg: Each green, round, flat-faced, beveled-edged, compressed tablet, engraved with "N" on one side and "10" on the other side, contains: terazosin HCl 10 mg. Nonmedicinal ingredients: cornstarch, D&C yellow #10 aluminum lake, FD&C blue #2 aluminum lake, lactose, magnesium stearate, povidone and talc. Bottles of 100, 500 and 1 000. Boxes of 100 as unit dose strips.

Store between 15 and 30°C and protect from light and high humidity. Store unit dose boxes between 15 and 25°C and protect from light and high humidity.

New Product 1998

NOVO-TETRA ℞
Novopharm
Tetracycline HCl
Antibiotic

Supplied: Capsules: Each yellow and orange capsule, imprinted NOVO 250, contains: tetracycline HCl 250 mg. Sodium: <1 mmol (0.03 mg). Gluten- and tartrazine-free. Bottles of 100, 1 000 and 3 000.

Suspension: Each 5 mL of red, sweet-tasting suspension, contains: tetracycline HCl 125 mg. Sodium: <1 mmol (2 mg)/5 mL. Gluten- and tartrazine-free. Bottles of 500 mL.

NOVO-THEOPHYL SR ℞
Novopharm
Theophylline
Bronchodilator

Supplied: 100 mg: Each white, film-coated, round, biconvex tablet, engraved N/N on one side and 100 on the reverse, contains: theophylline anhydrous 100 mg. Gluten- and tartrazine-free. Bottles of 100 and 500. Unit dose strips of 100.

200 mg: Each white, film-coated, oval-shaped, biconvex tablet, engraved N/N on one side and 200 on the reverse, contains: theophylline anhydrous 200 mg. Gluten- and tartrazine-free. Bottles of 100 and 500. Unit dose strips of 100.

300 mg: Each white, film-coated, capsule-shaped tablet, engraved N/N on one side and 300 on the reverse, contains: theophylline anhydrous 300 mg. Gluten- and tartrazine-free. Bottles of 100 and 500. Unit dose strips of 100.

NOVO-TIAPROFENIC ℞
Novopharm
Tiaprofenic Acid
Anti-inflammatory—Analgesic

Supplied: 200 mg: Each off-white, single-scored, biconvex compressed tablet engraved with novo above and 200 below the scoreline on one side and plain on the other, contains: tiaprofenic acid 200 mg. Gluten- and tartrazine-free. Bottles of 100 and 500. Unit dose boxes of 100.

300 mg: Each off-white, single-scored, biconvex compressed tablet engraved with novo above and 300 below the scoreline on one side and plain on the other, contains: tiaprofenic acid 300 mg. Gluten- and tartrazine-free. Bottles of 100 and 500. Unit dose boxes of 100.

NOVO-TIMOL ℞
Novopharm
Timolol Maleate
Antianginal—Antihypertensive

Supplied: 5 mg: Each white, round, scored tablet, embossed novo and 5 on opposite sides, contains: timolol maleate 5 mg. Gluten- and tartrazine-free. Bottles of 100 and 500.

10 mg: Each light blue, round, scored tablet, embossed novo and 10 on opposite sides, contains: timolol maleate 10 mg. Gluten- and tartrazine-free. Bottles of 100 and 500.

20 mg: Each light blue, capsule-shaped, scored tablet, embossed novo and 20 on opposite sides, contains: timolol maleate 20 mg. Gluten- and tartrazine-free. Bottles of 100.

NOVO-TIMOL Ophthalmic Solution ℞
Novopharm
Timolol Maleate
Glaucoma Therapy

Supplied: 0.25%: Each mL of ophthalmic solution contains: timolol 2.5 mg. White, opaque plastic Ocumeter ophthalmic dispensers of 5, 10 and 15 mL with a controlled drop tip.

0.5%: Each mL of ophthalmic solution contains: timolol 5 mg. White, opaque plastic Ocumeter ophthalmic dispensers of 5, 10 and 15 mL with a controlled drop tip.

Store at room temperature.

NOVO-TOLMETIN ℞
Novopharm
Tolmetin Sodium
Anti-inflammatory—Analgesic—Antipyretic

Supplied: Each orange, opaque, hard gelatin capsule, imprinted novo and 400, contains: tolmetin sodium dihydrate 492 mg equivalent to tolmetin 400 mg. Gluten- and tartrazine-free. Bottles of 100 and 500.

NOVO-TRAZODONE ℞
Novopharm
Trazodone HCl
Antidepressant

Supplied: 50 mg: Each light orange, round, standard convex, film-coated, single-scored tablet, engraved with 50 above scoreline on one side and novo on the other side, contains: trazodone HCl 50 mg. Gluten- and tartrazine-free. Bottles of 100 and 500.

100 mg: Each white, round, standard convex, film-coated, single-scored tablet, engraved with 100 above scoreline on one side and novo on the other side, contains: trazodone HCl 100 mg. Gluten- and tartrazine-free. Bottles of 100 and 500.

150 mg: Each light orange, rectangular-shaped, trisected and bisected, compressed tablet, engraved with 50 on one side of each trisect and n on the other side of each trisect, contains: trazodone HCl 150 mg. Gluten- and tartrazine-free. Bottles of 100 and 500.

NOVO-TRIAMZIDE ℞
Novopharm
Triamterene—Hydrochlorothiazide
Diuretic—Antihypertensive

Supplied: Each peach-colored, round, single scored, flat bevel-edged tablet, imprinted 25/50 on one side and novo on the other side, contains: triamterene 50 mg and hydrochlorothiazide 25 mg. Gluten- and tartrazine-free. Bottles of 100, 500, 1 000 and 3 000. Unit dose strips of 100.

NOVO-TRIMEL ℞
NOVO-TRIMEL D.S. ℞
Novopharm
Sulfamethoxazole—Trimethoprim
Antibacterial

Supplied: Novo-Trimel: Oral Suspension: Each 5 mL of light pink, cherry flavored suspension contains: trimethoprim 40 mg and sulfamethoxazole 200 mg. pH: 5.0 to 6.5. Gluten- and tartrazine-free. Bottles of 100, 400 and 800 mL.

Tablets: Each white, round, scored convex tablet, embossed N over 80, contains: trimethoprim 80 mg and sulfamethoxazole 400 mg. Sodium: <1 mmol (2.6 mg). Gluten- and tartrazine-free. Bottles of 100, 500 and 1 000. Unit dose strips of 100.

Novo-Trimel D.S.: Each white, oval-shaped, scored double strength tablet, embossed N over 160, contains: trimethoprim 160 mg and sulfamethoxazole 800 mg. Sodium: <1 mmol (5.2 mg). Gluten- and tartrazine-free. Bottles of 100 and 500. Unit dose strips of 100.

NOVO-TRIPRAMINE ℞
Novopharm
Trimipramine Maleate
Antidepressant

Supplied: 25 mg: Each pink, round, biconvex tablet with clear film-coat, embossed n and 25 on opposite sides contains: trimipramine maleate equivalent to trimipramine 25 mg. Gluten- and tartrazine-free. Bottles of 100 and 500.

50 mg: Each pink, round, biconvex tablet with clear film-coat, embossed novo and 50 on opposite sides, contains: trimipramine maleate equivalent to trimpramine 50 mg. Gluten- and tartrazine-free. Bottles of 100 and 500.

100 mg: Each pink, round, biconvex tablet with clear film-coat, embossed novo over 100 on same side, contains: trimipramine maleate equivalent to trimipramine 100 mg. Gluten- and tartrazine-free. Bottles of 100 and 500.

NOVO-VALPROIC ℞
Novopharm
Valproic Acid
Anticonvulsant

Pharmacology: Although not yet established, the mechanism of valproic acid's anticonvulsant activity may be related to increased brain concentrations of gamma-aminobutyric acid (GABA). The effect of the drug on the neuronal membrane is unknown.

Valproic acid is rapidly absorbed after oral administration, with peak serum levels occurring approximately 1 to 4 hours after a single oral dose. The half-life of valproic acid in serum is typically in the range of 7 to 16 hours. Usually patients taking other antiepileptic drugs have half-lives in the lower part of this range. When the drug is administered with meals, a slight delay in absorption occurs, but this does not affect the total absorption. Distribution of valproic acid throughout the body is rapid. The drug is strongly bound (95%) to human plasma proteins. Decreases in the extent of protein binding and variable changes in valproic acid clearance and elimination may result with increases in dose. The therapeutic plasma concentration is believed to range from 50 to 100 µg/mL. Occasionally, certain patients may be controlled by serum levels lower or higher than this. A good correlation between daily dose, serum levels and therapeutic effect has not been established.

Valproic acid is primarily metabolized to the glucuronide conjugate in the liver. Only very little unmetabolized parent drug is excreted in the urine. Valproic acid and its metabolites are principally eliminated in the urine, with minor amounts appearing in the feces and expired air.

See statement on fatal hepatic dysfunction in Warnings.

Indications: As sole or adjunctive therapy in the treatment of simple or complex absence seizures, including petit mal, and is useful in primary generalized seizures with tonic clonic manifestations. Valproic acid also may be used adjunctively in patients with multiple seizure types including either absence or tonic clonic seizures.

Simple absence is defined as a very brief loss of consciousness or clouding of the sensorium (lasting usually 2 to 15 seconds) accompanied by certain generalized epileptic discharges without other detectable clinical signs. When other signs are also present, complex absence is the term used.

Contraindications: Patients with hepatic disease or significant dysfunction and those hypersensitive to valproic acid.

Warnings: There have been fatalities due to hepatic failure in patients receiving valproic acid. Usually these incidences have occurred during the first 6 months of treatment with valproic acid.

Children under 2 years of age who received valproic acid as part of multiple anticonvulsant therapy were shown in a recent

Novo-Valproic (cont'd)

survey study of valproate use in the United States in nearly 400 000 patients between 1978 and 1984 to be at the greatest risk (nearly 20-fold increase) of developing fatal hepatotoxicity. In addition to severe seizure disorders, these patients typically had other medical conditions such as congenital metabolic disorders, mental retardation or organic brain disease. In patients receiving valproate as monotherapy, the risk in this age group decreased considerably. Patients aged 3 to 10 years were similarly at somewhat greater risk if they received multiple anticonvulsants than those who received only valproate. Generally, risk declined with increasing age. There have been no reports of death in patients over 10 years of age who received valproate alone.

Valproic acid should be used with **extreme caution** and as a sole agent if it is to be used in children 2 years old or younger. The benefits of control of seizures should be weighted against the risk.

Nonspecific symptoms such as loss of seizure control, malaise, weakness, lethargy, anorexia and vomiting may precede serious or fatal hepatotoxicity. Parents and patients should be instructed to report such symptoms. In patients who become unwell, other than through obvious cause, while taking valproic acid, hepatotoxicity should be suspected because of the nonspecific nature of some of the early signs.

Liver function tests should be performed prior to therapy and, especially during the first 6 months, at frequent intervals. Physicians should not rely totally on serum biochemistry however, since these tests may not be abnormal in all instances, but should also consider the results of careful interim medical history and physical examination. Patients with a prior history of hepatic disease should be administered valproic acid with caution. At particular risk are those patients with various unusual congenital disorders, those with severe seizure disorders accompanied by mental retardation, and those with organic brain disease.

It might also be useful in high risk patients to monitor serum fibrinogen and albumin for decrease in concentrations and serum ammonia for increases in concentration. Valproic acid should be discontinued if changes occur. Dosage should be maintained at the lowest dose found by titration to provide optimal seizure control.

In the presence of significant hepatic dysfunction, suspected or apparent, the drug should be discontinued immediately. Hepatic dysfunction has progressed in spite of discontinuation of the drug in some cases. With increasing doses the frequency of adverse effects, particularly elevated liver enzymes, may increase. Therefore, it is necessary to weigh the benefits gained by improved seizure control by increasing the dosage against the increasing incidence of adverse effects sometimes seen at higher dosages.

Pregnancy: Recent reports in the medical literature indicate that valproic acid may produce teratogenicity in the offspring of human females receiving the drug during pregnancy. The fetus of a mother receiving valproic acid during the first trimester of pregnancy may have an increased incidence of neural tube defects. Based upon a single report, the risk of valproic acid exposed women having children with spina bifida was estimated to be approximately 1.2%. This is similar to the risk which applies to nonepileptic women who have had children with neural tube defects (spina bifida and anencephaly). Teratogenicity has been demonstrated in animal studies, and placental transfer of the drug has been demonstrated in studies in human females.

An association between the use of antiepileptic drugs and an elevated incidence of birth defects in children born to epileptic women taking such medication during pregnancy has been indicated in multiple reports. The incidence in the general population of congenital malformations is regarded to be approximately 2%. In children of treated epileptic women, this incidence may be increased 2 to 3-fold. Specific defects, e.g., congenital malformations of the heart, cleft lip and/or palate and neural tube defects are largely responsible for this increase. Nevertheless, normal infants are delivered to the great majority of mothers receiving anticonvulsant medications.

With respect to phenytoin and phenobarbital, the most commonly prescribed anticonvulsants, data are more extensive. Some reports indicate that a similar association with the use of other antiepileptic drugs, including trimethadione, paramethadione and valproic acid, is possible. However, it is also possible that other factors, e.g., genetic predisposition or the epileptic condition itself, may contribute to, or may be mainly responsible for the higher incidence of birth defects.

Because of the strong possibility of precipitating status epilepticus with attendant hypoxia and risks to both the mother and the unborn child, antiepileptic drugs should not be discontinued in patients to whom the drug is administered to prevent major seizures. It is necessary to weigh the risks of discontinuing drugs given for minor seizures prior to or during pregnancy against the risk of congenital defects in the particular case and with the particular family history.

Epileptic women of childbearing age should be encouraged to seek the counsel of their physician. The onset of pregnancy should be reported promptly. Appropriate consultation might be indicated where the necessity for continued use of antiepileptic medication is in doubt.

Lactation: Valproic acid is secreted in breast milk in concentrations which have been reported to be 1 to 10% of serum concentrations. As a general rule, while a patient is receiving valproic acid, nursing should not be undertaken.

Fertility: Reduced spermatogenesis and testicular atrophy were demonstrated in chronic toxicity studies in juvenile and adult rats and dogs at doses greater than 200 mg/kg/day in rats and 90 mg/kg/day in dogs. Doses up to 350 mg/kg/day for 60 days have been shown to have no effect on fertility in segment 1 fertility studies in rats. In humans, the effect of valproic acid on the development of the testes and on sperm production and fertility is unknown.

A potential carcinogenic risk is indicated in long-term toxicity studies in rats and mice.

Precautions: Hepatic Dysfunction: See Contraindications and Warnings.

General: Platelet counts and bleeding time determination are recommended before instituting therapy and at periodic intervals because of reports of thrombocytopenia and inhibition of platelet aggregation. It is recommended that platelet counts be monitored prior to planned surgery. Pending investigation, clinical evidence of hemorrhage, bruising or a disorder of hemostasis/coagulation is an indication for reduction of dosage or withdrawal of therapy.

Hyperammonemia with or without lethargy or coma has been reported and may be present in the absence of abnormal liver function tests. Valproic acid should be discontinued if elevation occurs.

Periodic serum level determinations of concurrently administered antiepileptics are recommended during the early part of therapy because valproic acid may interact with other antiepileptic drugs (see Drug Interactions). Breakthrough seizures have been reported to occur with the combination of valproic acid and phenytoin.

A false interpretation of the urine ketone test may result as valproic acid is partially eliminated in the urine as a ketone containing metabolite.

Although the clinical significance is unknown, there have been reports of altered thyroid function tests associated with valproic acid.

CNS depression may be produced by valproic acid, especially when combined with another CNS depressant such as alcohol.

Occupational Hazards: Until it is known that they do not become drowsy from the drug, patients should be advised not to engage in potentially hazardous occupations such as driving a car or operating dangerous machinery.

Drug Interactions: The CNS depressant action of alcohol may be potentiated by valproic acid.

There is evidence that valproic acid impairs nonrenal clearance, thereby increasing serum phenobarbital levels. Severe CNS depression may result. Without significantly elevating barbiturate or valproic acid serum levels, the combination of valproic acid and phenobarbital has also been reported to produce CNS depression. Patients should be closely monitored for neurological toxicity when receiving concomitant barbiturate therapy. If possible, serum barbiturate drug levels should be obtained and the barbiturate dosage decreased if indicated.

As primidone is metabolized into a barbiturate, it may also be involved in a similar or identical interaction.

Conflicting evidence regarding the interaction of valproic acid with phenytoin exists (see Precautions). It is not known if there is a change of unbound (free) phenytoin serum levels. Phenytoin dosage should be adjusted as required by the clinical situation.

Absence status may be produced with the concomitant use of valproic acid and clonazepam.

Caution is recommended when drugs affecting coagulation, e.g., ASA and warfarin, are administered with valproic acid (see Adverse Effects).

Adverse Effects: Nausea, vomiting and indigestion are the most commonly reported adverse reactions. In most cases it may not be possible to determine whether the adverse reactions mentioned are due to valproic acid alone or to the combination of drugs since valproic acid has usually been used with other antiepileptics.

Gastrointestinal: At the initiation of therapy, nausea, vomiting and indigestion are the most commonly reported side effects. These effects are usually transient and rarely is discontinuation of therapy required. There are also reports of diarrhea, abdominal cramps and constipation. Increased appetite with some weight gain and anorexia with some weight loss have also been observed.

CNS: Sedative effects, although found most often in patients on combination therapy, have been noted in patients receiving valproic acid alone. Upon reduction of other antiepileptic medications, sedation usually disappears. There have been rare reports of ataxia, headache, nystagmus, diplopia, asterixis, "spots before the eyes", tremor, dysarthria, dizziness and incoordination. In patients receiving valproic acid, alone or in conjunction with phenobarbital, there have been rare cases of coma.

Dermatologic: Hair loss has been observed to increase transiently. Rarely, skin rash and petechiae have been noted.

Endocrine: Patients receiving valproic acid have reported irregular menses and secondary amenorrhea.

There have been reports of abnormal thyroid function tests (see Precautions).

Psychiatric: emotional upset, depression, psychosis, aggression, hyperactivity and behavioral deterioration.

Musculoskeletal: There have been reports of weakness.

Hematopoietic: There have been reports of thrombocytopenia. The second phase of platelet aggregation is inhibited by valproic acid, and this may be reflected in altered bleeding time (see Precautions). There have been reports of bruising, hematoma formation and frank hemorrhage as well as leukopenia, eosinophilia, anemia and bone marrow suppression. Relative lymphocytosis and hypofibrinogenemia have been noted.

Hepatic: Transaminases (e.g., AST and ALT) and LDH frequently undergo mild elevations which appear to be dose related. Increases in serum bilirubin and abnormal changes in other liver function tests are occasionally shown in laboratory tests. These results may reflect potentially serious hepatotoxicity (see Warnings).

Metabolic: Hyperammonemia (see Precautions). Hyperglycinemia in a patient with pre-existing nonketotic hyperglycinemia has been associated with a fatal outcome.

Pancreatic: Valproic acid therapy has been associated with reports of acute pancreatitis.

Other: Edema of the extremities has been noted.

Overdose: Symptoms: A patient reportedly ingested 36 g of valproic acid in combination with phenobarbital and phenytoin. He presented in a deep coma. The diffuse slowing shown by an EEG recording was compatible with the state of consciousness. The patient recovered uneventfully.

Treatment: The CNS depressant effects of valproic acid overdose have reportedly been reversed with naloxone. However, naloxone should be used with caution as it could theoretically also reverse the antiepileptic effects of valproic acid.

Gastric lavage may be of limited value as valproic acid is absorbed very rapidly. General supportive measures are indicated with particular attention to the prevention of hypovolemia and the maintenance of adequate urinary output.

Dosage: Administered orally. An initial dose of 15 mg/kg/day orally is recommended, increasing at 1 week intervals by 5 to 10 mg/kg/day until seizures are controlled or side effects preclude further increases. The maximum recommended dose is 60 mg/kg/day. When the total daily dose of 250 mg is exceeded, it should be given in a divided regimen (see Table I). With increasing dose, the frequency of adverse effects (particularly elevated liver enzymes) may increase. It is therefore necessary to weigh the benefits gained by improved seizure control against the increased incidence of adverse effects.

Table I—Novo-Valproic

Initial Doses by Weight (Based on 15 mg/kg/day)

Weight (kg)	Total daily dose (mg)	Number of 250 mg capsules Dose 1	Dose 2	Dose 3
10–24.9	250	0	0	1
25–39.9	500	1	0	1
40–59.9	750	1	1	1
60–74.9	1 000	1	1	2
75–89.9	1 250	2	1	2

Blood levels of phenobarbital and/or phenytoin may be affected as the valproic acid dosage is raised (see Precautions).

The administration of valproic acid with food or a progressive dosage increase from an initial low level may benefit patients who experience gastrointestinal irritation. To avoid local irritation of the mouth and throat, the capsules should be swallowed without chewing.

Supplied: 250 mg: Each orange, oblong, soft gelatin capsule contains: valproic acid 250 mg as a clear, colorless liquid. Bottles of 100 and 500.

500 mg: Each pale, yellow-colored, oblong, soft gelatin, enteric coated capsule contains: valproic acid 500 mg as a clear, colorless liquid. Bottles of 100 and 500.

Reviewed 1997

NOVO-VERAMIL Ⓟ
NOVO-VERAMIL SR Ⓟ

Novopharm

Verapamil HCl

Antiarrhythmic—Antianginal—Antihypertensive

Antihypertensive

Pharmacology: Angina and Arrhythmia: Verapamil, a calcium ion influx inhibitor (calcium entry blocker or calcium ion antagonist) is believed to exert its antiarrhythmic and antianginal effects by selectively inhibiting transmembrane influx of calcium ions in cardiac muscle, coronary and systemic arteries and in cells of the intracardiac conduction system. Verapamil blocks the transmembrane influx of calcium through the slow channel (calcium ion antagonism) without significantly affecting transmembrane influx of sodium through the fast channel. The result is a reduction of free calcium ions available within the cells of the above tissues.

Verapamil exerts antihypertensive effects by inducing vasodilation and reducing peripheral vascular resistance usually without reflex tachycardia. Verapamil does not blunt hemodynamic response to isometric or dynamic exercise.

Verapamil's action on the sinoatrial and atrioventricular nodes is believed to be responsible for the drug's antiarrhythmic effects. Verapamil slows AV nodal conduction and prolongs functional refractory periods. The normal atrial action potential or intra-ventricular conduction time is not altered by verapamil, but amplitude, velocity of depolarization and conduction in depressed atrial fibers is reduced. It is through this action that verapamil interrupts re-entrant pathways and slows ventricular rate.

Verapamil may shorten the antegrade effective refractory period of the accessory bypass tract. Acceleration of ventricular rate and/or ventricular fibrillation has been reported in patients with atrial flutter or atrial fibrillation and a coexisting accessory AV pathway following administration of verapamil (see Warnings). Verapamil has a local anesthetic action that is 1.6 times that of procaine on an equimolar basis.

Verapamil is a potent smooth muscle relaxant with vasodilator properties, and a depressant of myocardial contractility. These effects are largely independent of autonomic influence. The antianginal action of verapamil in exertional angina is believed to result from a decrease in resistance in the systemic vasculature as well as from a direct effect on myocardial contraction. A decrease in myocardial oxygen consumption is the net pharmacologic effect. Verapamil's effectiveness in vasospastic angina is due to a decrease in coronary vascular tone.

Essential Hypertension: Verapamil induces its antihypertensive effect by peripheral vasodilation and reducing peripheral vascular resistance usually without reflex tachycardia. These effects are brought about by inhibition of calcium ion influx into smooth muscle cells of the arteriolar wall. Verapamil does not affect the hemodynamic response to isometric or dynamic exercise. Verapamil administration did not affect electrolytes, glucose, and creatinine compared to baseline. An increase in sodium intake does not hinder the hypotensive effect of verapamil.

Compared to baseline, verapamil does not affect electrolytes, glucose, and creatinine. The hypotensive effect of verapamil is not blunted by an increase in sodium intake.

In hypertensive normolipidemic patients, verapamil had no effects on plasma lipoprotein fractions.

Pharmacodynamics: In a study in 5 healthy males, the S enantiomer was found to be 8 to 20 times more active than the R enantiomer in slowing AV conduction. In another study using septal strips isolated from the left ventricle of 5 patients with mitral disease, the S enantiomer was 8 times more potent than the R enantiomer in reducing myocardial contractility.

Pharmacokinetics: Verapamil Tablets: Verapamil is rapidly absorbed. From a comparison of the areas under the time concentration curves of total radioactivity, following oral and i.v. administration as well as based on cumulative urinary excretion, absorption has been calculated at approximately 92%. Despite its almost complete absorption, the oral bioavailability of verapamil is only about 10 to 35% due to its extensive first pass metabolism.

Intersubject verapamil plasma concentrations vary after oral administration. Following long-term oral administration of 120 mg conventional tablets every 6 hours to healthy adults, the average steady state plasma concentrations ranged from 125 to 400 ng/mL. The average time to peak plasma concentration (T_{max}) is between 1 and 2 hours and the therapeutic range is considered to be 60 to 70 ng/mL or higher. A nonlinear correlation exists between the dose of verapamil administered and verapamil plasma levels. In the initial dose titration with verapamil, a relationship exists between verapamil plasma concentration and prolongation of the PR interval. Administration with meals slows absorption and decreases the relative bioavailability slightly.

In single dose studies, the elimination half-life of verapamil ranged from 2.8 to 7.4 hours. In these same studies after repetitive dosing, the half-life increased to a range from 4.5 to 12 hours (after less than 10 consecutive doses given 6 hours apart). The half-life of verapamil increases during titration due to saturation of hepatic enzyme systems as plasma verapamil levels rise. Aging affects the pharmacokinetics of verapamil and elimination half-life is prolonged in the elderly. Verapamil and its metabolites are excreted predominantly (70%) in urine and the rest (16% or more) in feces within 5 days. Only 3 to 4% of the amount found in 48 hour pooled urine samples was found to be unchanged verapamil. Twelve metabolites produced by the biotransformation of verapamil have been identified in plasma with the chief one being norverapamil. Norverapamil can reach steady state plasma concentrations approximately equal to those of verapamil itself and appears to have approximately 20% of the cardiovascular activity of verapamil. Metabolism of verapamil is delayed and elimination half-life prolonged up to 14 to 16 hours in patients with hepatic insufficiency (see Warnings and Dosage).

The degree of protein binding of verapamil varied from 88.7 to 92.0%. Verapamil and norverapamil levels were noted in the cerebrospinal fluid after 4 weeks of oral dosing (120 mg q.i.d.). The estimated partition coefficients were 0.06 for verapamil and 0.04 for norverapamil.

Verapamil Sustained Release Tablets: Verapamil sustained release tablets is a racemic mixture consisting of equal portions of the R enantiomer and the S enantiomer. More than 90% of the orally administered dose of verapamil sustained release is absorbed. Upon oral administration, there is rapid stereoselective biotransformation during the first pass of verapamil through the portal circulation. The systemic concentration of R and S enantiomers are dependent upon the route and the rate of administration and the rate and extent of release from the dosage forms.

The following bioavailability information was obtained from healthy volunteers and not from the populations most likely to be treated with verapamil.

In a study in 5 healthy volunteers with oral immediate-release verapamil, the systemic bioavailability varied from 33 to 65% for the R enantiomer and from 13 to 34% for the S enantiomer. The S enantiomer is pharmacologically more active than the R enantiomer (see Pharmacodynamics).

There is a nonlinear correlation between the verapamil dose administered and verapamil plasma levels. In early dose titration with verapamil, a relationship exists between total verapamil (R and S combined) plasma concentration and prolongation of the PR interval. The mean elimination half-life in single dose studies of immediate release verapamil ranged from 2.8 to 7.4 hours. In these same studies, after steady state was reached, the half-life increased to a range from 4.5 to 12 hours (after less than 10 consecutive doses given 6 hours apart). Half-life of verapamil may increase during titration. Aging decreases the clearance and elimination of verapamil.

In a randomized, multiple-dose study in 44 healthy young subjects, administration of verapamil sustained release 240 mg with food produced peak plasma concentrations at approximately 8 hours postdose of 188 and 76 mg/mL and AUC's (0 to 24 hours) of 2 553 and 1 046 ng·h/mL for the R and S enantiomers, respectively. Similar results were demonstrated for plasma norverapamil.

In healthy men, orally administered verapamil undergoes extensive metabolism by the cytochrome P450 system. The particular isoenzyme involved are CYP 3A4, CYP 1A2, and the CYP 2C family. Thirteen metabolites have been identified in urine. Norverapamil can reach steady-state plasma concentrations approximately equal to those of verapamil itself. The cardiovascular activity of norverapamil appears to be approximately 20% that of verapamil. Approximately 70% of an administered dose is excreted as metabolites in the urine and 16% or more in the feces within 5 days. About 3 to 4% is excreted in the urine as unchanged drug. R-verapamil is 94% bound to plasma albumin, while S-verapamil is 88% bound. In addition, R-verapamil is 92% and S-verapamil 86% bound to alpha-1 acid glycoprotein. The degree of biotransformation during the first pass of verapamil may vary according to the status of the liver in different patient populations. In patients with hepatic insufficiency, metabolism is delayed and elimination half-life prolonged up to 14 to 16 hours (see Warnings and Dosage).

Verapamil crosses the placental barrier and can be detected in umbilical vein blood at delivery. Verapamil is excreted in human milk.

A study was conducted in which 240 mg single oral doses of verapamil standard release (fasting) and verapamil sustained release (fed) tablets were given to 12 young, healthy males (19 to 37 years old) in a randomized, crossover (7-day washout) study. Serial blood samples for drug determination were taken over a 48-hour period. The pharmacokinetic data from this study is summarized in Table I.

Table I—Novo-Veramil/Novo-Veramil SR

Pharmacokinetic Data

	Verapamil Standard Release Tablet (240 mg)		Verapamil Sustained Release Tablet (240 mg)	
Parameters	**R-Verapamil**	**S-Verapamil**	**R-Verapamil**	**S-Verapamil**
C_{max} (ng/mL)	258	59.0	60.1	11.3
T_{max} (h)	1.46	1.58	10.8	11.8
AUC_{0-48} (ng·h/mL)	1 250	261	918	150

The steady-state pharmacokinetic data obtained from a single dose comparative study in which 11 volunteers were treated with the sustained release formulation twice daily at 12 hourly intervals and with the standard release formulation three times daily at 8 hourly intervals for 5 days is summarized in Table II.

Table II—Novo-Veramil/Novo-Veramil SR

Steady-state Pharmacokinetic Data from a Single Dose Comparative Study

	Standard Release Tablet[b]	Sustained Release Tablet[b]	Sustained Release Tablet[a]
Parameters	**(360 mg daily)**	**(360 mg daily)**	**(480 mg daily)**
C_{max} (ng/mL)	289.4	250.5	298.4
Cmin (ng/mL)	80.1	110.7	152.0
T_{max} (h)	1.4	4.5	4.4
$T_{1/2}$ (h)	6.1	8.2	8.7
$AUC_{0-\infty}$ (ng/mL/h)	1 850	3 466	4 484
AUC_{0-36} (ng/mL/h)	1 809	3 154	4 116

[a]Last dose = 240 mg.
[b]Last dose = 120 mg.

The data was calculated from samples taken at frequent intervals for 36 hours after the last dose.

Influence of Food: Administration of verapamil SR tablets with food results in a prolongation of T_{max} (45 to 75%), and slight decreases in C_{max} (about 15%) and AUC (1 to 8%). Hence, food produces a slight decrease in bioavailability (AUC), but a narrower peak-to-trough ratio.

Indications: Novo-Veramil: May be used in the treatment of: chronic stable angina of effort; angina resulting from coronary artery spasm; obstructive hypertrophic cardiomyopathy where surgery is not otherwise indicated; atrial fibrillation or flutter

Novo-Veramil (cont'd)

with rapid ventricular response not otherwise controllable with digitalis preparations; follow-up treatment to the use of injectable verapamil in paroxysmal supraventricular tachycardia. Verapamil is indicated in the treatment of mild to moderate essential hypertension. It should be used in those patients in whom treatment with diuretics or beta-blockers produced unacceptable adverse effects.

Verapamil can be used as an initial agent in those patients in whom the use of diuretics and/or beta-blockers is contraindicated or in patients with medical conditions in which these drugs frequently cause serious adverse effects.

Concomitant use of verapamil with a diuretic or an angiotensin converting enzyme inhibitor has been shown to be compatible and to have additive blood pressure lowering effects.

Verapamil should not be concurrently used with beta-blockers in the treatment of hypertension (see Precautions, Drug Interactions).

Safety of concurrent use of verapamil with other antihypertensive agents has not been established and such use cannot be recommended at this time.

Novo-VeramiL SR (Sustained Release) Tablets: Treatment of mild to moderate essential hypertension. Verapamil sustained release tablets should normally be used in those patients in whom treatment with diuretics or beta-blockers has been associated with unacceptable adverse effects.

Verapamil sustained release tablets can be tried as an initial agent in those patients in whom the use of diuretics and/or beta-blockers is contraindicated or in patients with medical conditions in which these drugs frequently cause serious adverse effects.

Combination of verapamil sustained release with a diuretic or an angiotensin converting enzyme inhibitor has been found to be compatible and showed additive antihypertensive effect.

Verapamil sustained release tablets should not be used concurrently with beta-blockers in the treatment of hypertension (see Precautions, Drug Interactions).

Safety of concurrent use of verapamil sustained release tablets with other antihypertensive agents has not been established and such use cannot be recommended at this time.

Contraindications: In patients with: complicated myocardial infarction (patients who have ventricular failure manifested by pulmonary congestion); severe congestive heart failure and/or severe left ventricular dysfunction (unless secondary to a supraventricular tachycardia amendable to verapamil therapy); cardiogenic shock; severe hypotension; second or third degree AV block; sick sinus syndrome (see Warnings); marked bradycardia; hypersensitivity to the drug; atrial flutter or atrial fibrillation and an accessory bypass tract, (e.g., Wolff-Parkinson-White, Lown-Ganong-Levine syndromes) (see Warnings).

Warnings: General: In patients with angina or arrhythmias using antihypertensive drugs, the additional hypotensive effect of verapamil should be taken into consideration.

Heart Failure: Verapamil has a negative inotropic effect and should not be used in patients with poorly compensated congestive heart failure, unless the failure is complicated by or caused by an arrhythmia. If verapamil or verapamil sustained release is to be used in such patients, they must be digitalized prior to treatment and monitored continuously. Digoxin plasma levels may increase significantly with chronic oral verapamil therapy (see Precautions, Drug Interactions).

In the treatment of hypertension, verapamil is not recommended in patients with heart failure caused by systolic dysfunction.

Hypotension: Hypotensive symptoms of lethargy and weakness with faintness have been reported following single oral doses of verapamil and even after some months of treatment. It may be necessary to reduce the dose in these patients.

The additional hypotensive effect of verapamil should be taken into consideration in patients with angina or arrhythmias using antihypertensive drugs.

Conduction Disturbance: Because verapamil slows conduction across the AV node, it rarely may produce second or third degree AV block, bradycardia and in extreme cases asystole. This is more likely to occur in patients with a sick sinus syndrome (SA nodal disease), which is more common in the elderly (see Contraindications).

Verapamil causes dose-related suppression of the SA node. In some patients, sinus bradycardia may occur, especially in patients with a sick sinus syndrome (SA nodal disease), which is more common in the elderly (see Contraindications).

Bradycardia: Bradycardia (ventricular rate less than 50 beats/min) had a total incidence of less than 2% in controlled studies. Asystole in patients other than those with sick sinus syndrome is usually of short duration (few seconds or less), with spontaneous return to AV nodal or normal sinus rhythm. If recovery does not occur promptly, appropriate treatment should be initiated immediately (see Overdose: Symptoms and Treatment).

Accessory Bypass Tract (Wolff-Parkinson-White or Lown-Ganong-Levine): Verapamil may result in significant acceleration of ventricular response during atrial fibrillation or atrial flutter in the Wolff-Parkinson-White (WPW) or Lown-Ganong-Levine syndromes after receiving i.v. verapamil. The safety of verapamil in individual patients with WPW or Lown-Ganong-Levine syndrome should be established by electrophysiologic testing before use. Such patients receiving oral verapamil may be at risk and its use in these patients is contraindicated (see Contraindications).

Concomitant Use with Beta-blockers: The concomitant use of oral verapamil with beta-blockers is not recommended since the depressant effects on myocardial contractility, heart rate and AV conduction may be additive. In general, verapamil and verapamil sustained release tablets should not be given to patients receiving beta-blockers. However, when in the opinion of the physician, concomitant use of verapamil and beta-blockers is considered essential, institute such use gradually in a hospital setting under careful supervision. If combined therapy is used, close surveillance of vital signs and clinical status should be carried out and the need for continued concomitant treatment periodically assessed.

Verapamil provides no protection against the dangers of abrupt beta-blocker withdrawal. When changing patients from beta-blockers to verapamil, withdraw beta-blockers by gradually reducing the dose, then verapamil may be started with the usual dose.

Patients with Hypertrophic Cardiomyopathy: In 120 patients with hypertrophic cardiomyopathy who received therapy with verapamil at doses up to 720 mg/day, a variety of serious adverse effects were seen. Three patients died in pulmonary edema; all had severe left ventricular outflow obstruction and a past history of left ventricular dysfunction. Eight other patients had pulmonary edema and/or severe hypotension, abnormally high (greater than 20 mm Hg) pulmonary wedge pressure and a marked left ventricular outflow obstruction were present in most of these patients. Concomitant administration of quinidine (see Precautions, Drug Interactions) preceded the severe hypotension in 3 of the 8 patients (2 of whom developed pulmonary edema). Sinus bradycardia occurred in 11% of the patients, second-degree AV block in 4%, and sinus arrest in 2%. It must be appreciated that this group of patients had a serious disease with a high mortality rate. Most adverse effects responded well to dose reduction, but in some cases, verapamil use had to be discontinued.

Elevated Liver Enzymes: Elevation of transaminase with and without concomitant elevations in alkaline phosphatase and bilirubin have been reported. Several published cases of hepatocellular injury produced by verapamil have been proven by rechallenge. Clinical symptoms of malaise, fever, and/or right upper quadrant pain, in addition to elevation of AST, ALT and alkaline phosphatase have been reported. Periodic monitoring of liver function in patients receiving verapamil is therefore prudent.

Hepatic Insufficiency: Because verapamil is extensively metabolized by the liver, it should be administered cautiously to patients with impaired hepatic function, since the elimination half-life of verapamil in these patients is prolonged 4-fold (from 3.7 to 14.2 hours). A decreased dosage should be used in patients with hepatic insufficiency and careful monitoring for abnormal prolongation of the PR interval or other signs of excessive pharmacologic effect should be carried out (see Pharmacology, Pharmacokinetics and Dosage).

Renal Insufficiency: About 70% of an administered dose of verapamil is excreted as metabolites in the urine. In 1 study in healthy volunteers, the total body clearance after i.v. administration of verapamil was 12.08 mL/min/kg, while in patients with advanced renal disease it was reduced to 5.33 mL/min/kg. This pharmacokinetic finding suggests that renal clearance of verapamil in patients with renal disease is decreased. In 2 studies with oral verapamil, no difference in pharmacokinetics could be demonstrated. Therefore, until further data is available, verapamil should be used with caution in patients with impaired renal function. These patients should be carefully monitored for abnormal prolongation of the PR interval or other signs of excessive pharmacologic effect (see Dosage).

Precautions: Precautions should be taken when treating any supraventricular arrhythmia on an emergency basis as it may be caused by an undiagnosed sick sinus syndrome (see Contraindications and Warnings).

Although verapamil does not alter serum calcium levels, one report suggested that calcium levels above the normal range may decrease the therapeutic effect of verapamil.

Beagle dogs administered high doses of verapamil were shown to have atypical lens changes and cataracts. This has been concluded to be species specific for the beagle dog. No similar changes have been observed in long-term prospective human ophthalmological trials.

Patients with Attenuated (Decreased) Neuromuscular Transmission: There have been reports that neuromuscular transmission in patients with Duchenne's muscular dystrophy is decreased and recovery from the neuromuscular blocking agent vercuronium is prolonged by verapamil. It may be necessary to decrease the dosage of verapamil when it is administered to patients with attenuated neuromuscular transmission.

Geriatrics: The incidence of adverse reactions is approximately 4% higher in the elderly (≥65 years); therefore, verapamil should be administered with caution to these patients, especially those prone to developing hypotension or those with a history of cerebrovascular insufficiency. Dizziness and constipation are the adverse reactions occurring most frequently.

Pregnancy: Teratology and reproduction studies have been performed in rabbits and rats at oral doses up to 1.5 (15 mg/kg/day) and 6 (60 mg/kg/day) times the human oral daily dose, respectively, and have revealed no evidence of teratogenicity or impaired fertility. In rat, however, this multiple of the human dose was embryocidal and retarded fetal growth and development, probably because of adverse maternal effects reflected in reduced weight gains of the dams. This oral dose has also been shown to cause hypotension in rats.

There are no studies in pregnant women. However, verapamil crosses the placental barrier and can be detected in umbilical vein blood at delivery. Verapamil is not recommended for use in pregnant women unless the potential benefits outweigh potential risks to mother and fetus.

Labor and Delivery: It is not known whether the use of verapamil during labor or delivery has immediate or delayed adverse effects on the fetus, or whether it prolongs the duration of labor or increases the need for forceps delivery or other obstetric intervention.

Lactation: Verapamil is excreted in human milk. Nursing should be discontinued while the drug is administered.

Children: The safety and dosage regimen of oral verapamil in children has not yet been established.

Drug Interactions: As with all drugs, care should be exercised when treating patients with multiple medications. Calcium channel blockers undergo biotransformation by the cytochrome P450 system. Coadministration of verapamil with other drugs which follow the same route of biotransformation may result in altered bioavailability. Dosages of similarly metabolized drugs, particularly those of low therapeutic ratio, and especially in patients with renal and/or hepatic impairment, may require adjustment when starting or stopping concomitantly administered verapamil to maintain optimum therapeutic blood levels.

Drugs known to be inhibitors of the cytochrome P450 system include: azole antifungals, cimetidine, cyclosporine, erythromycin, quinidine, terfenadine, warfarin.

Drugs known to be inducers of the cytochrome P450 system include: phenobarbital, phenytoin, rifampin.

Drugs known to be biotransformed via P450 include: benzodiazepines, flecainide, imipramine, propafenone, theophylline.

Alcohol: Verapamil may increase blood alcohol concentrations and prolong its effects.

Antineoplastic Agents: Verapamil inhibits P-glycoprotein mediated transport of antineoplastic agents out of tumor cells, resulting in their decreased metabolic clearance. Dosage adjustment of antineoplastic agents should be considered when verapamil is administered concomitantly.

Antihypertensive Agents: Verapamil administered concomitantly with other antihypertensive agents such as vasodilators, ACE inhibitors, and diuretics may have an additive effect on lowering blood pressure. In patients with angina or arrhythmias using antihypertensive drugs, this additional hypotensive effect should be taken into consideration. Verapamil should not be combined with beta-blockers for the treatment of hypertension. Concomitant use of verapamil and alpha-adrenoceptors blockers may result in excessive fall in blood pressure in some patients as observed in one study following the concomitant administration of verapamil and prazosin.

ASA: Potential adverse reactions in terms of bleeding due to synergistic antiplatelet effects of the two agents should be taken into consideration in patients taking ASA and verapamil concomitantly.

Beta-Adrenergic Blockers: The concomitant administration of verapamil with beta-blockers can result in severe adverse effects (see Warnings).

Carbamazepine: The concomitant oral administration of verapamil and carbamazepine may potentiate the effects of carbamazepine neurotoxicity. Symptoms include nausea, diplopia, headache, ataxia or dizziness.

Cimetidine: Two clinical trials have shown a lack of significant verapamil interaction with cimetidine. A third study showed cimetidine reduced verapamil clearance and increased elimination half-life.

Cyclosporine: Verapamil therapy may increase serum levels of cyclosporine.

Digoxin: Verapamil treatment increases serum digoxin levels by 50 to 75% during the first week of therapy, and this can result in digitalis toxicity. In patients with hepatic cirrhosis the influence of verapamil on digoxin kinetics is magnified. Verapamil may reduce total body clearance and extrarenal clearance of digitoxin by 27% and 29% respectively. Maintenance and digitalization doses should reduced when verapamil is administered and the patient should be reassessed to avoid over- or underdigitalization. Whenever overdigitalization is suspected, the daily dose of digitalis should be reduced or temporarily discontinued. On discontinuation of verapamil use, the patient should be reassessed to avoid underdigitalization.

Disopyramide: Until data on possible interactions between disopyramide and verapamil are obtained, disopyramide should not be administered within 48 hours before or 24 hours after verapamil.

Flecainide: A study in healthy volunteers showed that the concomitant administration of flecainide and verapamil may have additive effects on myocardial contractility, AV conduction and repolarization. Concomitant therapy with flecainide and verapamil may result in additive negative inotropic effect and prolongation of AV conduction.

Inhalation Anesthetics: When used concomitantly, inhalation anesthetics and calcium antagonists, such as verapamil, should be titrated carefully because additive hemodynamic depressive effects have been observed.

Lithium: Increased sensitivity to the effects of lithium (neurotoxicity) has been reported during concomitant verapamil-lithium therapy with either no change or an increase in serum lithium levels. However, the addition of verapamil has also resulted in the lowering of serum lithium levels in patients receiving chronic stable oral lithium. Patients receiving both drugs must be monitored carefully.

Neuromuscular Blocking Agents: Clinical data and animal studies suggest that verapamil may potentiate the activity of neuromuscular blocking agents (curare-like and depolarizing). It may be necessary to decrease the dose of verapamil and/or the dose of the neuromuscular blocking agent when the drugs are used concomitantly.

Nitrates, Diuretics: No cardiovascular adverse effects have been attributed to any interaction between these agents and verapamil.

Phenobarbital: Phenobarbital therapy may be increase verapamil clearance.

Quinidine: In a small number of patients with hypertrophic cardiomyopathy, concomitant use of verapamil and quinidine resulted in significant hypotension. Until further data are obtained combined therapy of verapamil and quinidine in patients with hypertrophic cardiomyopathy should probably be avoided. The electrophysiologic effects of quinidine and verapamil on AV conduction were studied in 8 patients. Verapamil significantly counteracted the effects of quinidine on AV conduction. There has been a report of increased quinidine levels during verapamil therapy.

Rifampin: Therapy with rifampin may markedly reduce oral bioavailability of verapamil.

Sulfinpyrazone: Increased clearance and decreased bioavailability of verapamil may occur.

Theophylline: Verapamil may inhibit the clearance and increase the plasma levels of theophylline.

Adverse Effects: In 4 826 patients treated with verapamil tablets for arrhythmias, angina or hypertension, the overall adverse reaction rate in these patients was 37.1% and the dropout rate was 10.2%. The majority of these patients were seriously ill and treated under emergency drug regulations.

In controlled pivotal studies with 128 patients treated with verapamil sustained release tablets for hypertension the overall adverse reaction rate was 21.7% and dropout rate was 3.9%.

The most common adverse reactions were: constipation (7.3%), dizziness (3.2%), and nausea (2.7%). In hypertension studies, constipation occurred in 18.5% of patients on verapamil and 4.7% of patients on verapamil sustained release.

The most serious adverse reactions reported with verapamil are heart failure (1.8%), hypotension (2.5%), AV block (1.3%) and rapid ventricular response (see Warnings).

The following reactions to orally administered verapamil were reported from clinical experience in 4 954 patients with angina, arrhythmia or hypertension.

Cardiovascular: hypotension (2.5%), peripheral edema (2.1%), total AV block (1st, 2nd and 3rd degree) (1.2%), AV block (2nd and 3rd degree) (0.8%), bradycardia (HR <50/min) (1.4%), congestive heart failure or pulmonary edema (1.9%).

Nervous System: dizziness (3.2%), headache (2.2%), fatigue (1.7%).

Gastrointestinal: constipation (7.3%), nausea (2.7%).

The following reactions were reported in 1% or less of patients:

Cardiovascular: transient asystole, development of rhythm disturbances including ventricular dysrhythmias, angina pectoris, flushing, atrioventricular dissociation, chest pain, claudication, myocardial infarction, palpitations, purpura, syncope, severe tachycardia, developing or worsening of heart failure, painful coldness and numbness of extremities.

Nervous System: cerebrovascular accident, confusion, equilibrium disorders, insomnia, muscle cramps, paresthesia, psychotic symptoms, shakiness, somnolence, excitation, depression, vertigo, rotary nystagmus, tremor, extrapyramidal disorders, muscle fatigue, hyperkinesis.

Gastrointestinal: vomiting, diarrhea, dry mouth, gastrointestinal distress, gingival hyperplasia.

Hepatic: hepatotoxicity with elevation in enzymes (AST, ALT, alkaline phosphatase) and bilirubin levels, jaundice and associated symptoms of hepatitis with cholestasis have been reported (see Warnings).

Respiratory: bronchospasm and dyspnea.

Urogenital: gynecomastia, increased frequency of urination, spotty menstruation, oligomenorrhea, impotence.

Hematologic and Lymphatic: ecchymosis or bruising.

Skin: arthralgia and rash, exanthema, hair loss, hyperkeratosis, macules, sweating, urticaria, Stevens-Johnson Syndrome, erythema multiforme, pruritus.

Special Senses: blurred vision, diplopia.

In clinical trials related to the control of ventricular response in digitalized patients who had atrial fibrillation or flutter, ventricular rates below 50 at rest occurred in 15% of patients and asymptomatic hypotension occurred in 5% of patients.

Overdose: Symptoms: Transient to severe hypotension; prolonged AV conduction time; AV dissociation, nodal rhythm; ventricular fibrillation and ventricular asystole.

Treatment: Supportive. Beta-adrenergic stimulation or parenteral administration of calcium solutions may increase calcium ion flux across the slow channel. These pharmacologic interventions have been effectively used in treatment of overdosage with oral verapamil. Clinically significant hypotensive reactions should be treated with vasopressor agents and AV block should be treated with atropine and cardiac pacing. Asystole should be handled by the usual Advanced Cardiac Life Support measures including isoproterenol HCl, or other vasopressor agents. Verapamil is not removed by hemodialysis.

In case of overdosage with large amounts of sustained release verapamil, it should be noted that the release of the active drug and the absorption in the intestine may take more than 48 hours. Depending on the time of ingestion, incompletely dissolved tablets may be present along the entire length of the gastrointestinal tract which function as active drug depots. Extensive elimination measures are indicated, such as induced vomiting, removal of the contents of the stomach and the small intestine under endoscopy, intestinal lavage and high enemas.

Table III shows the suggested treatment of acute cardiovascular adverse effects.

Actual treatment and dosage should depend on the severity of the clinical situation and the judgment and experience of the treating physician. Patients with hypertrophic cardiomyopathy treated with verapamil should not be administered positive inotropic agents (marked by asterisks in Table III).

Dosage: Novo-Veramil: Verapamil should be taken with food (see Pharmacology, Pharmacokinetics).

Table III—Novo-Veramil/Novo-Veramil SR

Suggested Treatment of Acute Cardiovascular Adverse Effects

Adverse Reactions	Proven Effective Treatment	Treatment with Good Theoretical Rationale	Supportive Treatment
Shock, cardiac failure, severe hypotension	Calcium salts, e.g., calcium gluconate i.v. Metaraminol* i.v.	Dopamine* i.v. Dobutamine* i.v.	I.V. fluids Trendelenburg position
Bradycardia, AV block, asystole	Isoproterenol HCl* i.v. Atropine sulfate i.v. Cardiac pacing	—	I.V. fluids (slow drip)
Rapid ventricular rate (due to antegrade conduction in flutter/fibrillation with WPW or LGL syndromes)	DC Cardioversion (high energy may be required) Procainamide i.v. Lidocaine HCl i.v.	—	I.V. fluids (slow drip)

*positive inotropic agent.

Angina Pectoris: Usual starting dose in adults is 80 mg of verapamil 3 to 4 times daily. This may be increased to 120 mg 3 to 4 times daily until optimum response is obtained. Do not increase the dose beyond 480 mg/day. In some cases the dose may be decreased following clinical improvement.

Paroxysmal Supraventricular Tachycardias: Replace i.v. therapy with oral treatment as soon as possible. In adults, use the same dosage schedule as for angina pectoris. Duration of treatment will depend on the underlying cause and history of recurrence.

Atrial Fibrillation and Flutter with Rapid Ventricular Response: Verapamil tablets may be administered to adults not completely controlled with digitalis preparations. The same dosage as for angina pectoris can be used but the physician should be aware that digoxin plasma levels may increase with verapamil administration and the reduction of digoxin dose may be necessary (see Precautions, Drug Interactions).

Obstructive Hypertrophic Cardiomyopathy: Usual starting dose is 80 to 120 mg 3 to 4 times daily, and occasionally patients may require up to 600 to 720 mg/day.

Mild to Moderate Essential Hypertension: Verapamil should be individually titrated, depending on patient tolerance and responsiveness.

Initial dose is usually 80 mg 3 times a day. The dose may be increased up to 160 mg 3 times a day. The daily dose should not exceed 480 mg.

Antihypertensive effects will be evident within the first week of therapy. In patients also taking diuretics, the optimal doses should be lower due to additive antihypertensive effects.

Geriatrics: Lower dosages of verapamil may be warranted in elderly patients (i.e. ≥65 years) (see Precautions). The dosage should be carefully and gradually adjusted depending on patient tolerance and response. Elderly patients may be more sensitive to the effects of the usual adult dose. Consideration can be given to beginning titration using one-half of a Novo-Veramil SR Tablet (120 mg) once a day since no suitable strength of standard tablet is available.

Patients with Impaired Hepatic Function: Verapamil should be administered cautiously to patients with impaired hepatic function. The dosage should be carefully and gradually adjusted depending on patient tolerability and response. Careful monitoring for abnormal prolongation of the PR interval or other signs of overdosage should be carried out. At this time, verapamil should not be used in patients with severe hepatic dysfunction (see Warnings).

Patients with Impaired Renal Function: Verapamil should be administered cautiously to patients with impaired renal function. The dosage should be carefully and gradually adjusted depending on patient tolerability and response. These patients should also be monitored carefully for abnormal prolongation of the PR interval or other signs of overdosage.

Novo-Veramil SR: Crushing or chewing Novo-Veramil SR tablets is not recommended since the sustained-release effect will be altered by damage to the tablet structure. The Novo-Veramil SR 240 mg tablet may be split in half.

Novo-Veramil (cont'd)

Mild to Moderate Essential Hypertension (see Indications): Novo-Veramil SR Tablets should be taken with food (see Pharmacology, Pharmacokinetics). The dosage should be individualized by titration depending on patient tolerance and responsiveness to verapamil. Titration should be based on therapeutic efficacy and safety, evaluated weekly and approximately 24 hours after the previous dose.

The usual daily dose of verapamil sustained release is 180 to 240 mg/day. Novo-Veramil SR Tablets are not available as a 180 mg strength but verapamil sustained release tablets are available through other manufacturers. If required, the dose may be increased up to 240 mg twice a day. A maximum daily dose of 480 mg should not be exceeded.

Recommended dosing intervals for specific daily dosages are given in Table IV.

Table IV—Novo-Veramil SR

Recommended Dosing Intervals for Specific Daily Dosages of Novo-Veramil SR

Total Daily Novo-Veramil SR Dose	Recommended Dosing Intervals
180 mg	Once each morning with food
240 mg	Once each morning with food
360 mg	180 mg each morning plus 180 mg each evening, with food or 240 mg each morning plus 120 mg each evening, with food
480 mg	240 mg each morning plus 240 mg each evening, with food

The antihypertensive effects of Novo-Veramil SR are evident within the first week of therapy. Optimal doses are usually lower in patients also receiving diuretics since additive antihypertensive effects can be expected.

Elderly patients (i.e. ≥65 years) should be given a lower dosage of verapamil sustained release. One-half tablet (120 mg) may be given. The dosage should be carefully and gradually adjusted depending on patient tolerability and response.

Patients with Impaired Liver and Renal Function: Verapamil sustained release should be administered cautiously to patients with liver or renal function impairment. Careful titration of dosage is required depending on patient tolerance and response. These patients should be monitored carefully for abnormal prolongation of the PR interval or other signs of overdosage. Verapamil sustained release should not be used in severe hepatic dysfunction (see Warnings).

Switching from Novo-Veramil to Novo-Veramil SR: The total daily dose in mg should be identical when switching from Novo-Veramil to Novo-Veramil SR tablets.

Special Note to Pharmacists: The Novo-Veramil SR 240 mg tablet may be split in half. Crushing Novo-Veramil SR tablets is not recommended since the sustained-release effect will be altered by damage to the tablet structure.

Supplied: Novo-Veramil: 80 mg: Each yellow, round, sugar-coated tablet, imprinted N/80 on one side, plain on the reverse, or unidentified contains: verapamil HCl 80 mg. Imprinted tablets: bottles of 100, 500 and 1 000. Boxes of 100 (as unit dose strips). Unidentified tablets: bottles of 100, 500 and 1 000.

120 mg: Each white, round, sugar-coated tablet, imprinted N/120 on one side, plain on the reverse, or unidentified contains: verapamil HCl 120 mg. Imprinted tablets: bottles of 100, 500 and 1 000. Boxes of 100 (as unit dose strips). Unidentified tablets: bottles of 100, 500 and 1 000.

Novo-Veramil SR: Each pale green, capsule-shaped, biconvex, scored, film-coated tablet, engraved no/vo on one side and 2/40 on the reverse, contains: verapamil HCl 240 mg. Bottles of 100, 500 and 1 000. Boxes of 100 (as unit dose strips).

Store between 15 and 30°C and protect from light. Unit dose strips should be stored between 15 and 25°C, and protected from high humidity and light.

Reviewed 1999

Unfamiliar capsule? Check the color-coded photographs in the PRODUCT RECOGNITION SECTION.

NOZINAN® Ⓟ

Rhône-Poulenc Rorer

Methotrimeprazine Maleate

Neuroleptic

Pharmacology: Methotrimeprazine possesses antipsychotic, tranquilizing, anxiolytic, sedative and analgesic properties and it is also a potent potentiator of anesthetics.

Methotrimeprazine possesses strong sedative properties. It potentiates ether and hexobarbital anesthesia as well as morphine analgesia. It also exerts a potent anti-apomorphine effect, a hypothermic action 3 times more potent than that of chlorpromazine and strong antispasmodic and anti-histaminic effects. Methotrimeprazine is capable of reversing epinephrine-induced hypertension but has practically no effect against norepinephrine and acetylcholine. It readily protects rats against traumatic shock and produces deep local anesthesia following parasciatic injections.

Indications: Psychotic disturbances: acute and chronic schizophrenias, senile psychoses, manic-depressive syndromes.

Conditions associated with anxiety and tension: autonomic disturbances, personality disturbances, emotional troubles secondary to such physical conditions as resistant pruritus, etc.

Methotrimeprazine is also employed: As an analgesic: In pain due to cancer, zona, trigeminal neuralgia and neurocostal neuralgia and in phantom limb pains and muscular discomforts.

As a potentiator of anesthetics: In general anesthesia where it can be used as both a pre- and post-operative sedative and analgesic.

As an antiemetic: For the treatment of nausea and vomiting of central origin.

As a sedative: For the management of insomnia.

Contraindications: In cases of coma or CNS depression due to alcohol, hypnotics, analgesics or narcotics.

It is also contraindicated in patients with blood dyscrasia, hepatic troubles or a sensitivity to phenothiazines.

Warnings: Occupational Hazards: Methotrimeprazine can reduce psychomotor activity especially during the first few days of treatment. Patients should therefore be cautioned not to drive a motor vehicle or to participate in activities requiring total mental alertness.

Pregnancy: The drug should be used with caution in pregnant women, particularly during the first trimester, unless the benefit to the patient outweighs any possible risk to the fetus.

Precautions: In high oral or parenteral doses, orthostatic hypotension may be encountered at the start of treatment. Patients whose treatment is started by the parenteral route should be kept in bed during the first few days.

Methotrimeprazine therapy should be initiated at low doses in patients with arteriosclerosis or cardiovascular problems.

Methotrimeprazine potentiates the action of other phenothiazines and CNS depressants (barbiturates, analgesics, narcotics and antihistaminics). The usual doses of these agents should be reduced by half if they are to be given concomitantly with methotrimeprazine until the dosage of the latter has been established.

Because of its anticholinergic effects, methotrimeprazine must be administered with caution in patients with glaucoma or prostatic hypertrophy.

During long-term therapy, periodic liver function tests should be performed. In addition, blood counts should be conducted regularly, particularly during the first 2 or 3 months of treatment, and physicians should watch for any signs of blood dyscrasia.

Methotrimeprazine does not alter EEG activity. Nevertheless, since phenothiazines can lower the threshold of cortical excitation, it is advisable to administer an appropriate anticonvulsant medication to epileptic patients receiving Nozinan therapy.

Adverse Effects: May be classified as follows: CNS: Drowsiness may appear early in treatment but will gradually disappear during the first weeks or with an adjustment in the dosage.

Extrapyramidal effects are rare and usually appear only after prolonged therapy at high doses. These reactions may be corrected either by reducing the dose of Nozinan or by administering an antiparkinsonian agent.

Autonomic Nervous System: Dryness of the mouth and, in older patients occasional urinary retention, constipation and tachycardia.

Cardiovascular: Orthostatic hypotension may be encountered at the start of treatment by the parenteral route or with high oral doses.

Blood: Rare instances of agranulocytosis have been reported.

Endocrine: Weight gain has been occasionally reported in patients during prolonged treatment with high doses.

Gastrointestinal: Rare cases of cholostatic jaundice without liver damage have been observed.

Skin Reactions: Skin reactions due to photosensitivity or allergies are extremely rare.

Overdose: Symptoms: Symptoms of acute intoxication may include: simple CNS depression, spasms, tremor or tonic and clonic convulsions, coma accompanied by hypotension and respiratory depression.

Treatment: There is no specific antidote. After gastric lavage, treatment is symptomatic. Centrally acting emetics are ineffective because of the anti-emetic action of methotrimeprazine.

Hypotension: A 5% glucose solution may be administered. If a hypertensive agent is required, norepinephrine or phenylephrine may be used, but **not** epinephrine which can aggravate hypotension.

Respiratory depression: Oxygen by inhalation or controlled respiration after tracheal intubation.

Respiratory infection: Wide spectrum antibiotics.

Extrapyramidal reactions: An antiparkinsonian agent or chloral hydrate, however the latter must be used with caution because of its depressant effect on respiration.

Any CNS stimulant should be used with caution.

Dosage: Dosage must be adjusted according to the indication and individual needs of the patient. If sedation during the day is too pronounced, lower doses may be given during the day and higher doses at night.

Adults: Oral: **Minor conditions** in which methotrimeprazine may be given in low doses as a tranquilizer, anxiolytic, analgesic or sedative: begin treatment with 6 to 25 mg/day in 3 divided doses at mealtimes. Increase the dosage until the optimum level has been reached. As a sedative, a single night time dose of 10 to 25 mg is usually sufficient.

Severe conditions: Such as psychoses or intense pain in which methotrimeprazine is employed at higher doses: Begin treatment with 50 to 75 mg/day divided into 2 or 3 daily doses; increase the dosage until the desired effect is obtained. In certain psychotics doses may reach 1 g or more/day. If it is necessary to start therapy with higher doses, i.e., 100 to 200 mg/day, administer the drug in divided daily doses and keep the patient in bed for the first few days.

Parenteral: I.M.: To be used primarily for the initial treatment of psychoses for certain severe pain as a premedication or for the treatment of postoperative pain. In psychoses and pain, doses vary from 75 to 100 mg given as 3 or 4 deep i.m. injections in a large muscle. When given as a premedication or post-operative analgesic, the average dose varies from 10 to 25 mg every 8 hours which is equivalent to 20 to 40 mg given orally. The last dose during premedication, given 1 hour before surgery, can be 25 to 50 mg i.m.

I.V.: To be used primarily as an infusion during surgery or labour. The dose may range from 10 to 25 mg in 500 mL of a 5% glucose solution administered at a rate of 20 to 40 drops/minute. If methotrimeprazine is administered with a barbiturate or narcotic, the doses of the latter must be reduced by at least one-half.

Children: Oral: The initial dose has been established at 1/4 mg/kg daily given in 2 or 3 divided doses. This dosage may be increased gradually until an effective level is reached which should not surpass 40 mg/day for a child less than 12 years of age.

Parenteral: I.M.: A dose of 1/16 to 1/8 mg/kg/day in one or divided among several injections. Oral medication should be substituted as soon as possible.

I.V.: In anesthesia, 1/16 mg/kg in 250 mL of a 5% glucose solution may be administered as a slow infusion (20 to 40 drops per minute) during surgery.

Supplied: Injectable: Each mL contains: methotrimeprazine base 25 mg (as the hydrochloride). Nonmedicinal ingredients: ascorbic acid, sodium chloride, sodium sulfite and water for injection. Ampuls of 1 mL, boxes of 10. Protect from light or discoloration may occur.

Oral Drops: Each mL of brown solution contains: methotrimeprazine base 40 mg (as the hydrochloride). Nonmedicinal ingredients: alcohol 95%, ascorbic acid, caramel, citric acid, ethyl vanillin, glycerin, orange oil deterpine, purified water and sucrose. Alcohol: 16.5% v/v. Energy: 7.3 kJ (1.8 kcal)/mL. Sucrose: 200 mg/mL. Tartrazine-free. Bottles of 100 mL.

Liquid: Each 5 mL of brown liquid contains: methotrimeprazine base 25 mg (as the hydrochloride). Nonmedicinal ingredients: alcohol 95%, apricto essence, ascorbic acid, caramel, citric acid, glycerin, purified water and sucrose. Alcohol:

2.0% v/v. Energy: 62.3 kJ (14.9 kcal)/5 mL. Sucrose: 3.7 g/5 mL. Tartrazine-free. Bottles of 500 mL.

Tablets: Each yellow tablet contains: methotrimeprazine base 2, 5, 25 or 50 mg (as the maleate). Nonmedicinal ingredients: acetic anhydride, carnauba wax, cellulose, D&C Yellow No 10 aluminum lake, dicalcium phosphate, diethyl phthalate, FD&C Yellow No 6 aluminum lake, magnesium stearate, polacrilin potassium, silicon dioxide, sodium oleate, titanium dioxide, and zein. Tartrazine-free. Bottles of 100 and 500.

(Shown in Product Recognition Section)

NU-ACEBUTOLOL Ⓟ
Nu-Pharm

Acebutolol HCl

Antihypertensive—Antianginal

Supplied: 100 mg: Each white, round, biconvex, film-coated tablet, scored and identified NU over 100 on one side, contains: acebutolol HCl equivalent to acebutolol 100 mg. Energy: <1 kJ (0.10 kcal). Gluten-, lactose-, sodium- and tartrazine-free. Bottles of 100.

200 mg: Each white, oval, biconvex, film-coated tablet, scored and identified NU over 200 on one side, contains: acebutolol HCl equivalent to acebutolol 200 mg. Energy: <1 kJ (0.21 kcal). Gluten-, lactose-, sodium- and tartrazine-free. Bottles of 100.

400 mg: Each white, capsule-shaped, biconvex, film-coated tablet, scored and identified NU over 400 on one side, contains: acebutolol HCl equivalent to acebutolol 400 mg. Energy: <1.73 kJ (0.41 kcal). Gluten-, lactose-, sodium- and tartrazine-free. Bottles of 100.

Store at room temperature (15 to 30°C). Protect from light.

New Product 1998

NU-ACYCLOVIR Ⓟ
Nu-Pharm

Acyclovir

Antiviral

Supplied: 200 mg: Each blue, round, flat-faced, beveled-edged tablet, identified NU over 200 on one side, contains: acyclovir 200 mg. Gluten- and tartrazine-free. Bottles of 100.

400 mg: Each pink, round, flat-faced, beveled-edged tablet, identified NU over 400 on one side, contains: acyclovir 400 mg. Gluten-, lactose- and tartrazine-free. Bottles of 100.

800 mg: Each blue, oval, biconvex tablet, scored and identified NU over 800 on one side, contains: acyclovir 800 mg. Gluten-, lactose- and tartrazine-free. Bottles of 100.

Store at room temperature (15 to 30°C).

New Product 1998

NU-ALPRAZ Ⓟ
Nu-Pharm

Alprazolam

Anxiolytic—Sedative

Supplied: 0.25 mg: Each white, oval, biconvex tablet, scored and identified NU over .25 on one side, contains: alprazolam 0.25 mg. Energy: 2.25 kJ (0.54 kcal). Sodium: <1 mmol (0.14 mg). Gluten- and tartrazine-free. Bottles of 100 and 1 000.

0.5 mg: Each peach-colored, oval, biconvex tablet, scored and identified NU over 0.5 on one side, contains: alprazolam 0.5 mg. Energy: 2.33 kJ (0.56 kcal). Sodium: <1 mmol (0.14 mg). Gluten- and tartrazine-free. Bottles of 100 and 1 000.

Store at room temperature (15 to 30°C).

NU-AMILZIDE Ⓟ
Nu-Pharm

Amiloride HCl—Hydrochlorothiazide

Diuretic—Antihypertensive

Supplied: Each peach-colored, diamond-shaped, biconvex tablet, scored and identified NU over 5/50 on one side, contains: hydrochlorothiazide 50 mg and amiloride HCl equivalent to amiloride 5 mg. Energy: 2.9 kJ (0.69 kcal). Sodium: <1 mmol (2.93 mg). Gluten- and tartrazine-free. Bottles of 100 and 1 000.

NU-AMOXI Ⓟ
Nu-Pharm

Amoxicillin Trihydrate

Antibiotic

Supplied: Capsules: 250 mg: Each red and gold No. 2 capsule, identified NU 250, contains: amoxicillin trihydrate equivalent to amoxicillin 250 mg. Energy: <1 kJ (0.21 kcal). Gluten-, lactose- and tartrazine-free. Bottles of 500 and 1 000.

500 mg: Each red and gold No. 0 capsule, identified NU 500, contains: amoxicillin trihydrate equivalent to amoxicillin 500 mg. Energy: 1.52 kJ (0.36 kcal). Gluten-, lactose- and tartrazine-free. Bottles of 500.

Suspensions: 125 mg: After reconstitution each 5 mL of strawberry-flavored suspension contains: amoxicillin trihydrate equivalent to amoxicillin 125 mg. Energy: 38.21 kJ (9.12 kcal)/5 mL. Sodium: <1 mmol (2.18 mg)/5 mL. Paraben-, sulfite- and tartrazine-free. Bottles of 100 and 150 mL.

250 mg: After reconstitution each 5 mL of banana-flavored suspension contains: amoxicillin trihydrate equivalent to amoxicillin 250 mg. Energy: 37.3 kJ (8.91 kcal)/5 mL. Sodium: <1 mmol (2.6 mg)/5 mL. Paraben-, sulfite- and tartrazine-free. Bottles of 100 and 150 mL.

The reconstituted suspension is stable for 7 days at room temperature (15 to 30°C) or 14 days when refrigerated (4.5°C). Keep bottles tightly closed and shake thoroughly to obtain a uniform suspension.

NU-AMPI Ⓟ
Nu-Pharm

Ampicillin Trihydrate

Antibiotic

Supplied: Capsules: 250 mg: Each red and black No. 2 capsule, identified NU 250, contains: ampicillin trihydrate equivalent to ampicillin 250 mg. Energy: <1 kJ (0.22 kcal). Sodium: <1 mmol (0.13 mg). Gluten-, lactose- and tartrazine-free. Bottles of 500 and 1 000.

500 mg: Each red and black No. 0 capsule, identified NU 500, contains: ampicillin trihydrate equivalent to ampicillin 500 mg. Energy: 1.62 kJ (0.39 kcal). Sodium: <1 mmol (0.25 mg). Gluten-, lactose- and tartrazine-free. Bottles of 500.

Oral Suspensions: 125 mg: After reconstitution each 5 mL of cherry-flavored suspension contains: ampicillin trihydrate equivalent to ampicillin 125 mg. Energy: 38.04 kJ (9.09 kcal/5 mL). Sodium: <1 mmol (3.19 mg)/5 mL. Paraben-, sulfite- and tartrazine-free. Bottles of 100 and 150 mL.

250 mg: After reconstitution each 5 mL of cherry-flavored suspension contains: ampicillin trihydrate equivalent to ampicillin 250 mg. Energy: 35.61 kJ (8.5 kcal)/5 mL. Sodium: <1 mmol (6.2 mg)/5 mL. Paraben-, sulfite- and tartrazine-free. Bottles of 100 and 150 mL.

The reconstituted suspension is stable for 7 days at room temperature (15 to 30°C) or 21 days when refrigerated (4.5°C). Keep bottles tightly closed and shake thoroughly to obtain a uniform suspension.

NU-ATENOL Ⓟ
Nu-Pharm

Atenolol

Antihypertensive—Antianginal

Supplied: 50 mg: Each white, round, biconvex tablet, scored and identified NU over 50 on one side, contains: atenolol 50 mg. Energy: 1.91 kJ (0.46 kcal). Sodium: <1 mmol (0.63 mg). Gluten- and tartrazine-free. Bottles of 100 and 500.

100 mg: Each white, round, biconvex tablet, scored and identified NU over 100 on one side, contains: atenolol 100 mg. Energy: 3.82 kJ (0.91 kcal). Sodium: <1 mmol (1.27 mg). Gluten- and tartrazine-free. Bottles of 100 and 500.

Store at room temperature (15 to 30°C). Protect from light and moisture.

NU-BACLO Ⓟ
Nu-Pharm

Baclofen

Muscle Relaxant—Antispastic

Supplied: 10 mg: Each white, oval, flat-faced, beveled-edged tablet, scored and identified NU 10 on one side, contains: baclofen 10 mg. Energy: 3.15 kJ (0.75 kcal). Gluten-, sodium- and tartrazine-free. Bottles of 100 and 500.

20 mg: Each white, capsule-shaped, biconvex tablet, scored and identified NU 20 on one side, contains: baclofen 20 mg. Energy: 6.29 kJ (1.50 kcal). Gluten-, sodium- and tartrazine-free. Bottles of 100.

Store at room temperature (15 to 30°C).

NUBAIN® ⊕
DuPont Pharma

Nalbuphine HCl

Analgesic

Pharmacology: Nalbuphine is a synthetic narcotic agonist-antagonist analgesic for parenteral use, related chemically to the narcotic oxymorphone, and to the narcotic antagonist naloxone.

Nalbuphine has an analgesic (agonist action) potency equivalent to that of morphine on a mg basis, and an antagonist activity (reversal of major effects of opioid drugs) about 25% of that of nalorphine and 10 times that of pentazocine. The analgesic effect of 10 mg of nalbuphine is about equal to that of 10 mg of morphine sulfate. The onset of action begins within 2 to 3 minutes after i.v. administration, and within 15 minutes following s.c. or i.m. injection. The plasma half-life of nalbuphine is 5 hours and the duration of action has ranged from 3 to 6 hours.

At the usual dose of 10 mg, nalbuphine produces respiratory depression equivalent to that of equianalgesic doses of morphine. At much higher doses, above 30 mg i.v. (which produces a respiratory depressant activity equivalent to 20 mg of morphine i.v.), the respiratory depressant effect of nalbuphine does not appear to increase appreciably. Nalbuphine may precipitate abstinence, when administered to individuals taking narcotics chronically or produce withdrawal symptoms when discontinued abruptly after prolonged use. It is reported to have an abuse potential comparable to that of pentazocine. The mechanism of action of nalbuphine has not yet been established.

Indications: For the relief of moderate to severe pain.

Clinical studies indicate that it can also be used for preoperative analgesia, as a supplement to surgical anesthesia, and for obstetrical analgesia during labor.

Contraindications: Hypersensitivity to nalbuphine or its inactive ingredients.

Warnings: In patients physically dependent on opiate drugs, nalbuphine should not be given prior to detoxification since withdrawal symptoms are likely to be produced.

Drug Dependence: On the basis of behavioral substitution, and direct addiction studies in humans, nalbuphine was shown to have low abuse potential which approximates that of pentazocine. Psychological and physical dependence and tolerance may follow the abuse or misuse of nalbuphine. Therefore, caution should be observed in prescribing it for emotionally unstable patients or for individuals with a history of narcotic abuse. Such patients should be closely supervised since increases in dosage or frequency of administration in susceptible individuals might result in physical dependence.

Abrupt discontinuation of nalbuphine following prolonged use has been followed by symptoms of narcotic withdrawal, such as abdominal cramps, nausea and vomiting, rhinorrhea, lacrimation, restlessness, anxiety, elevated temperature and piloerection.

Occupational Hazards: Use in Ambulatory Patients: Nalbuphine may impair the mental or physical abilities required for the performance of potentially dangerous tasks such as driving a car or operating machinery. Administer with caution to ambulatory patients and warn them to avoid such hazards until they recover from the effects of the drug.

Interactions with other CNS Depressants: Although nalbuphine possesses narcotic antagonist activity, there is evidence that in nondependent patients it may not antagonize the analgesic effect of narcotic analgesics. Patients receiving narcotic analgesics, general anesthetics, phenothiazines or other tranquilizers, sedatives, hypnotics or other CNS depressants

Nubain (cont'd)

(including alcohol) concomitantly with nalbuphine may exhibit an additive effect. When such combined therapy is contemplated, the dose of one or both agents should be reduced.

Children: Because clinical experience in children under the age of 12 years is limited, the administration of nalbuphine in this age group is not recommended.

Pregnancy: Safe use in pregnancy (other than labor) has not been established. Although animal reproductive studies have not revealed teratogenic or embryotoxic effects, nalbuphine should only be administered to pregnant women when, in the judgment of the physician, the potential benefits outweigh the possible hazards.

Labor and Delivery: Since nalbuphine can produce respiratory depression in the neonate, it should be administered with caution to women delivering premature infants.

Head Injury and Increased Intracranial Pressure: The possible respiratory depressant effects and the potential of potent analgesics to elevate cerebrospinal fluid pressure (resulting from vasodilation following CO_2 retention) may be markedly exaggerated in the presence of head injury, intracranial lesions, or a pre-existing increase in intracranial pressure. Furthermore, potent analgesics can produce effects which may obscure the clinical course of patients with head injuries. Therefore, nalbuphine should be administered in these circumstances only when essential, and with extreme caution.

Precautions: Impaired Respiration: Caution should be observed when administering nalbuphine to patients with impaired respiration, or who are receiving other medications which produce respiratory depression. In the presence of bronchial asthma, uremia, severe infection, cyanosis, or respiratory obstruction, nalbuphine should be administered only with great caution and in reduced doses. Respiratory depression induced by nalbuphine can be reversed by the administration of naloxone HCl.

Impaired Renal or Hepatic Function: Because nalbuphine is metabolized in the liver and excreted by the kidneys, patients with renal or liver dysfunction may show an exaggerated response to customary doses. Therefore, in these individuals it should be used with caution and administered in reduced amounts.

Myocardial Infarction: As with all potent analgesics, nalbuphine should be used with caution in patients with myocardial infarction who have nausea or vomiting. Hemodynamic studies in patients with severe arteriosclerotic heart changes reveal that nalbuphine has circulatory effects similar to those of morphine, i.e., a minimal decrease in oxygen consumption, cardiac index, left ventricular-end diastolic pressure and cardiac work.

Management of Narcotic Withdrawal Symptoms: If nalbuphine is inadvertently administered to a patient physically dependent on narcotics and unduly troublesome narcotic withdrawal symptoms develop, these symptoms may be controlled by the slow i.v. administration of small increments of morphine until relief occurs.

Adverse Effects: In clinical trials with nalbuphine the most frequently reported side effects were: sedation (36% of 1 066 patients treated), sweaty or clammy (9%), nausea or vomiting (6%), dizziness or vertigo (5%), dry mouth (4%) and headache (3%).

Other adverse reactions which may occur are:

CNS: nervousness, crying, depression, restlessness, euphoria, hostility, confusion, faintness, floating, unusual dreams, numbness, feeling of heaviness, and psychotomimetic effects such as hallucinations, feeling of unreality and dysphoria.

Cardiovascular: hypertension, hypotension, bradycardia, tachycardia.

Gastrointestinal: cramps, dyspepsia, bitter taste.

Respiration: depression, dyspnea, asthma.

Dermatological: itching, burning, urticaria.

Miscellaneous: speech difficulty, urinary urgency, blurred vision, flushing and warmth.

Overdose: Symptoms: These are expected to be similar to those of other drugs of this class. (The administration of single i.m. doses of 72 mg of nalbuphine to 8 normal subjects has been reported to have resulted primarily in symptoms of sleepiness and mild dysphoria).

Treatment: Naloxone HCl administered i.v. is a specific antidote. Since the duration of action of nalbuphine may exceed that of naloxone, the patient should be kept under continued surveillance and repeated doses of naloxone should be administered as necessary. Oxygen, i.v. fluids, vasopressors and other supportive measures should be employed as indicated.

Dosage: Adults: 10 mg/70 kg administered s.c., i.m. or i.v. This dose may be repeated every 3 to 6 hours as required. The recommended dosage range is 10 mg to 20 mg, with a maximum single dose of 20 mg and a maximum total daily dose of 160 mg. Dosage should be adjusted according to the severity of the pain, physical status of the patient, and other medications which the patient may be receiving (see Warnings).

Patients who have been taking narcotics chronically for pain under medical supervision may experience withdrawal symptoms upon the administration of nalbuphine. If nalbuphine is administered to these patients as an analgesic, it should be introduced gradually. Nalbuphine should not be used as a substitute for other narcotics or for withdrawal purposes in individuals dependent on these drugs.

Supplied: 10 mg: Ampuls: Each mL contains: nalbuphine HCl 10 mg, sodium chloride 2 mg, sodium citrate dihydrate 9.41 mg and citric acid 12.62 mg. pH adjusted with hydrochloric acid. Glass ampuls of 1 mL.

Vials: Each mL contains nalbuphine HCl 10 mg, methylparaben 1.8 mg, propylparaben 0.2 mg, sodium chloride 2 mg, sodium citrate dihydrate 9.41 mg and citric acid 12.62 mg. pH adjusted with hydrochloric acid. Vials of 10 mL.

20 mg: Ampuls: Each mL contains: nalbuphine HCl 20 mg, sodium citrate dihydrate 9.41 mg and citric acid 12.62 mg. pH adjusted with hydrochloric acid. Glass ampuls of 1 mL.

Vials: Each mL contains: nalbuphine HCl 20 mg, methylparaben 1.8 mg, propylparaben 0.2 mg, sodium citrate dihydrate 9.41 mg and citric acid 12.62 mg. pH adjusted with hydrochloric aicd. Vials of 10 mL.

Store at controlled room temperature (15 to 30°C). Protect from excessive light.

NU-BROMAZEPAM Ⓟ

Nu-Pharm

Bromazepam

Anxiolytic—Sedative

Supplied: 1.5 mg: Each white, round, flat-faced, beveled-edged tablet, scored and identified NU over B-1.5 on one side, contains: bromazepam 1.5 mg. Gluten- and tartrazine-free. Bottles of 100.

3 mg: Each pink, round, flat-faced, beveled-edged tablet, scored and identified NU over B-3 on one side, contains: bromazepam 3 mg. Gluten- and tartrazine-free. Bottles of 100 and 500.

6 mg: Each green, round, flat-faced, beveled-edged tablet, scored and identified NU over B-6 on one side, contains: bromazepam 6 mg. Gluten- and tartrazine-free. Bottles of 100 and 500.

Store at room temperature (15 to 30°C).

New Product 1998

NU-BUSPIRONE Ⓟ

Nu-Pharm

Buspirone HCl

Anxiolytic

Supplied: Each white, rectangular pillow-shaped, biconvex tablet, identified NU on one side, scored and identified BU 10 on the other, contains: buspirone HCl 10 mg. Gluten- and tartrazine-free. Bottles of 100. Store at room temperature (15 to 30°C) in tightly-closed, light-resistant containers.

New Product 1998

NU-CAL

Odan

Calcium Supplement

Supplied: Each capsule-shaped, light aqua-green, film-coated tablet contains: calcium 500 mg derived from 1 250 mg of oyster shell powder. Nonmedicinal ingredients: magnesium stearate, polyvinyl pyrrolidone, silicon dioxide, sodium starch glycolate, sucrose and starch. Gluten- and tartrazine-free. Bottles of 60, 100, 500 and 1 000.

NU-CAPTO Ⓟ

Nu-Pharm

Captopril

Angiotensin-Converting Enzyme Inhibitor

Supplied: 12.5 mg: Each white, capsule-shaped, flat-faced beveled-edged tablet, partially bisected on both sides, one side identified NU, the other side identified 12.5, contains: captopril 12.5 mg. Energy: <1 kJ (0.14 kcal). Sodium: <1 mmol (0.03 mg). Gluten- and tartrazine-free. Bottles of 100 and 500.

25 mg: Each white, square, biconvex tablet, quadrisected on one side and identified NU over 25 on the other side, contains: captopril 25 mg. Energy: 1.16 kJ (0.27 kcal). Sodium: <1 mmol (0.06 mg). Gluten- and tartrazine-free. Bottles of 100 and 1 000.

50 mg: Each white, oval, biconvex tablet, partially bisected and identified NU-50 on one side, contains: captopril 50 mg. Energy: 2.32 kJ (0.56 kcal). Sodium: <1 mmol (0.13 mg). Gluten- and tartrazine-free. Bottles of 100 and 500.

100 mg: Each white, oval, biconvex tablet, partially bisected and identified NU-100 on one side, contains: captopril 100 mg. Energy: 4.65 kJ (1.11 kcal). Sodium: <1 mmol (0.25 mg). Gluten- and tartrazine-free. Bottles of 100.

Store at room temperature (15 to 30°C) and protect from moisture.

NU-CARBAMAZEPINE Ⓟ

Nu-Pharm

Carbamazepine

Anticonvulsant

Supplied: Each white, round, flat-faced, beveled-edged tablet, cross-scored on one side, identified NU over 200 on the other side, contains: carbamazepine 200 mg. Energy: 1.47 kJ (0.35 kcal). Sodium: <1 mmol (0.25 mg). Gluten-, lactose- and tartrazine-free. Bottles of 100 and 500. Protect from moisture.

NU-CEFACLOR Ⓟ

Nu-Pharm

Cefaclor

Antibiotic

Supplied: 250 mg: Each opaque purple and white, No. 2 capsule, identified NU 250, contains: cefaclor 250 mg. Gluten-, lactose- and tartrazine-free. Bottles of 100 and 500.

500 mg: Each opaque purple and grey, No. 0 capsule, identified NU 500, contains: cefaclor 500 mg. Gluten-, lactose- and tartrazine-free. Bottles of 100.

Store at room temperature (15 to 30°C).

New Product 1998

NU-CEPHALEX Ⓟ

Nu-Pharm

Cephalexin

Antibiotic

Supplied: 250 mg: Each orange, capsule-shaped, biconvex, film-coated tablet, identified NU-250 on one side, contains: cephalexin 250 mg. Energy: 2.14 kJ (0.51 kcal). Gluten-, lactose-, sodium- and tartrazine-free. Bottles of 100 and 1 000.

500 mg: Each orange, capsule-shaped, biconvex, film-coated tablet, scored and identified NU over 500 on one side, contains: cephalexin 500 mg. Energy: 4.18 kJ (1.02 kcal). Gluten-, lactose-, sodium- and tartrazine-free. Bottles of 100 and 500.

Store at room temperature (15 to 30°C).

NU-CIMET Ⓟ

Nu-Pharm

Cimetidine

Histamine H_2-Receptor Inhibitor

Supplied: 200 mg: Each pale green, round, biconvex, film-coated tablet, identified NU over 200 on one side, contains:

cimetidine 200 mg. Energy: 3.11 kJ (0.74 kcal). Sodium: <1 mmol (0.11 mg). Gluten-, lactose- and tartrazine-free. Bottles of 500.

300 mg: Each pale green, round, biconvex, film-coated tablet, identified NU over 300 on one side, contains: cimetidine 300 mg. Energy: 3.59 kJ (0.86 kcal). Sodium: <1 mmol (0.17 mg). Gluten-, lactose- and tartrazine-free. Bottles of 1 000.

400 mg: Each pale green, oblong-shaped, biconvex, film-coated tablet, identified NU over 400 on one side, contains: cimetidine 400 mg. Energy: 4.26 kJ (1.02 kcal). Sodium: <1 mmol (0.23 mg). Gluten-, lactose- and tartrazine-free. Bottles of 100 and 500.

600 mg: Each pale green, oblong-shaped, biconvex, film-coated tablet, identified NU over 600 on one side, contains: cimetidine 600 mg. Energy: 5.85 kJ (1.40 kcal). Sodium: <1 mmol (0.34 mg). Gluten-, lactose- and tartrazine-free. Bottles of 100 and 500.

NU-CLONAZEPAM ℞

Nu-Pharm

Clonazepam

Anticonvulsant

Supplied: 0.5 mg: Each orange, round, flat-faced, beveled-edged tablet, scored and identified NU over C-0.5 on one side, contains: clonazepam 0.5 mg. Gluten- and tartrazine-free. Bottles of 100 and 500.

2 mg: Each white, round, flat-faced, beveled-edged tablet, scored and identified NU over C-2 on one side, contains: clonazepam 2 mg. Gluten- and tartrazine-free. Bottles of 100 and 500.

Store at room temperature (15 to 30°C) in tightly-closed, light-resistant containers.

New Product 1998

NU-CLONIDINE ℞

Nu-Pharm

Clonidine HCl

Antihypertensive

Supplied: 0.1 mg: Each white, round, flat-faced, beveled-edged tablet, scored and identified NU over 0.1 on one side, contains: clonidine HCl 0.1 mg. Energy: 2.46 kJ (0.59 kcal). Gluten-, sodium- and tartrazine-free. Bottles of 100 and 500.

0.2 mg: Each orange, round, flat-faced, beveled-edged tablet, scored and identified NU over 0.2 on one side, contains: clonidine HCl 0.2 mg. Energy: 4.9 kJ (1.17 kcal). Gluten-, sodium- and tartrazine-free. Bottles of 100.

NU-CLOXI ℞

Nu-Pharm

Cloxacillin Sodium

Antibiotic

Supplied: Capsules: 250 mg: Each orange and black No. 2 capsule, identified NU 250, contains: cloxacillin sodium equivalent to cloxacillin 250 mg. Energy: <1 kJ (0.21 kcal). Sodium: <1 mmol (≤13.88 mg). Gluten-, lactose- and tartrazine-free. Bottles of 100 and 1 000.

500 mg: Each orange and black No. 0 capsule, identified NU 500, contains: cloxacillin sodium equivalent to cloxacillin 500 mg. Energy: 1.37 kJ (0.33 kcal). Sodium: ≤1.2 mmol (≤27.76 mg). Gluten-, lactose- and tartrazine-free. Bottles of 100 and 500.

Liquid: After reconstitution each 5 mL of cherry-flavored liquid contains: cloxacillin sodium equivalent to cloxacillin 125 mg. Energy: ≤37.45 kJ (≤8.94 kcal)/5 mL. Sodium: <1 mmol (≤14.08 mg)/5 mL. Paraben-, sulfite- and tartrazine-free. Bottles of 100 mL. The reconstituted liquid is stable for 14 days when refrigerated (4.5°C).

NU-COTRIMOX ℞

Nu-Pharm

Sulfamethoxazole—Trimethoprim

Antibacterial

Supplied: Adult Tablets: Each white, round tablet, one side convex, scored and identified NU over 400-80, other side flat-faced with beveled edges, contains: sulfamethoxazole 400 mg and trimethoprim 80 mg. Energy: <1 kJ (0.15 kcal). Sodium: <1 mmol (0.25 mg). Gluten-, lactose- and tartrazine-free. Bottles of 500 and 1 000.

DS Tablets: Each white, capsule-shaped, biconvex tablet, partially scored and identified NU-DS on one side, contains: sulfamethoxazole 800 mg and trimethoprim 160 mg. Energy: 1.27 kJ (0.3 kcal). Sodium: <1 mmol (0.51 mg). Gluten-, lactose- and tartrazine-free. Bottles of 100 and 500.

Oral Suspension: Each 5 mL of pink, cherry-flavored suspension contains: sulfamethoxazole 200 mg and trimethoprim 40 mg. Energy: 51.67 kJ (12.34 kcal)/5 mL. Sodium: <1 mmol (0.93 mg)/5 mL. Paraben-, sugar-, sulfite- and tartrazine-free. Bottles of 400 mL. Store at room temperature (15 to 30°C).

NU-CROMOLYN ℞

Nu-Pharm

Cromolyn Sodium

Prophylaxis of Symptoms of Bronchial Asthma

Supplied: Each mL of sterile, clear, colorless solution contains: sodium cromoglycate 1% w/v (10 mg/mL). Alcohol-, paraben- and sulfite-free. Plastic ampuls of 2 mL. The ampuls are overwrapped in an aluminum pouch (5×2 mL unit doses), cartons of 50. Store at room temperature (15 to 30°C). Do not refrigerate. Protect from light.

New Product 1998

NU-CYCLOBENZAPRINE ℞

Nu-Pharm

Cyclobenzaprine HCl

Skeletal Muscle Relaxant

Supplied: Each yellow, D-shaped, biconvex, film-coated tablet, identified NU over 10 on one side, contains: cyclobenzaprine HCl 10 mg. Gluten- and tartrazine-free. Bottles of 100 and 500. Store at room temperature (15 to 30°C) in well-closed containers.

New Product 1998

NU-DESIPRAMINE ℞

Nu-Pharm

Desipramine HCl

Antidepressant

Supplied: 10 mg: Each blue, round, biconvex, film-coated tablet contains: desipramine HCl 10 mg. Gluten-, lactose- and tartrazine-free. Bottles of 100.

25 mg: Each yellow-orange, round, biconvex, film-coated tablet, identified 25 on one side, contains: desipramine HCl 25 mg. Gluten-, lactose- and tartrazine-free. Bottles of 100 and 500.

50 mg: Each green, round, biconvex, film-coated tablet, identified 50 on one side, contains: desipramine HCl 50 mg. Gluten-, lactose- and tartrazine-free. Bottles of 100.

75 mg: Each orange, round, biconvex, film-coated tablet, identified 75 on one side, contains: desipramine HCl 75 mg. Gluten-, lactose- and tartrazine-free. Bottles of 50.

100 mg: Each peach-colored, round, biconvex, film-coated tablet, identified 100 on one side, contains: desipramine HCl 100 mg. Gluten-, lactose- and tartrazine-free. Bottles of 100.

Store at room temperature (15 to 30°C).

New Product 1998

NU-DICLO ℞

Nu-Pharm

Diclofenac Sodium

Anti-inflammatory—Analgesic

Supplied: 25 mg: Each yellow, round, biconvex, enteric-coated tablet, identified 25 on one side, contains: diclofenac sodium 25 mg. Energy: 1.99 kJ (0.47 kcal). Sodium: <1 mmol (1.81 mg). Gluten-, lactose- and tartrazine-free. Bottles of 100 and 500.

50 mg: Each light brown, round, biconvex, enteric-coated tablet, identified 50 on one side, contains: diclofenac sodium 50 mg. Energy: 3.97 kJ (0.95 kcal). Sodium: <1 mmol (3.62 mg). Gluten-, lactose- and tartrazine-free. Bottles of 100 and 500.

Store at room temperature (15 to 30°C). Protect from moisture.

NU-DICLO-SR ℞

Nu-Pharm

Diclofenac Sodium

Anti-inflammatory—Analgesic

Supplied: 75 mg: Each light pink, triangular, biconvex, film-coated, slow-release tablet, identified NU over 75 on one side, contains: diclofenac sodium 75 mg. Energy: 2.03 kJ (0.49 kcal). Sodium: <1 mmol (5.43 mg). Gluten-, lactose- and tartrazine-free. Bottles of 100.

100 mg: Each pink, round, biconvex, film-coated, slow-release tablet, identified NU over 100 on one side, contains: diclofenac sodium 100 mg. Energy: 2.71 kJ (0.65 kcal), Sodium: <1 mmol (7.24 mg). Gluten-, lactose- and tartrazine-free. Bottles of 100.

Store at room temperature (15 to 30°C). Protect from light.

New Product 1998

NU-DIFLUNISAL ℞

Nu-Pharm

Diflunisal

Anti-inflammatory—Analgesic

Supplied: 250 mg: Each light orange, capsule-shaped, biconvex, film-coated tablet, identified NU-250 on one side, contains: diflunisal 250 mg. Energy: 2.51 kJ (0.6 kcal). Sodium: <1 mmol (0.51 mg). Gluten-, lactose- and tartrazine-free. Bottles of 100.

500 mg: Each orange, capsule-shaped, biconvex, film-coated tablet, identifed NU 500 on one side, contains: diflunisal 500 mg. Energy: 5.01 kJ (1.20 kcal). Sodium: <1 mmol (1.01 mg). Gluten-, lactose- and tartrazine-free. Bottles of 100 and 500.

Store at room temperature (15 to 30°C). Protect from light and moisture.

NU-DILTIAZ ℞

Nu-Pharm

Diltiazem HCl

Antianginal

Supplied: 30 mg: Each light green, round, biconvex, film-coated tablet, identified NU over 30 on one side, contains: diltiazem HCl 30 mg. Energy: 2.91 kJ (0.69 kcal). Gluten-, sodium- and tartrazine-free. Bottles of 100 and 500.

60 mg: Each yellow, round, biconvex, film-coated tablet, scored and identified NU over 60 on one side, contains: diltiazem HCl 60 mg. Energy: 5.82 kJ (1.39 kcal). Gluten-, sodium- and tartrazine-free. Bottles of 100 and 500.

NU-DOMPERIDONE ℞

Nu-Pharm

Domperidone Maleate

Upper Gastrointestinal Motility Modifier

Supplied: Each white, round, biconvex, film-coated tablet, identified NU on one side and 10 on the other, contains:

Nu-Domperidone (cont'd)

domperidone maleate 12.72 mg (equivalent to domperidone 10 mg). Gluten-, lactose- and tartrazine-free. Bottles of 100 and 500. Store at room temperature (15 to 30°C). Protect from light.

New Product 1998

NU-DOXYCYCLINE Ⓟ
Nu-Pharm

Doxycycline Hyclate

Antibiotic

Supplied: Capsules: Each blue, hard gelatin No. 2 capsule, identified NU 100, contains: doxycycline hyclate equivalent to doxycycline base 100 mg. Energy: 3.09 kJ (0.74 kcal). Sodium: <1 mmol (0.25 mg). Gluten- and tartrazine-free. Bottles of 100.

Tablets: Each orange, round, biconvex, film-coated tablet, identified NU over 100 on one side, contains: doxycycline hyclate equivalent to doxycycline base 100 mg. Energy: 1.86 kJ (0.44 kcal). Sodium: <1 mmol (0.23 mg). Gluten-, lactose- and tartrazine-free. Bottles of 100.

NU-ERYTHROMYCIN-S Ⓟ
Nu-Pharm

Erythromycin Stearate

Antibiotic

Supplied: Each pink, round, biconvex, film-coated tablet, identified NU over 250 on one side, contains: erythromycin stearate equivalent to erythromycin 250 mg. Energy: ≤3.62 kJ (≤0.87 kcal). Sodium: <1 mmol (0.19 mg). Gluten-, lactose- and tartrazine-free. Bottles of 100.

NU-FAMOTIDINE Ⓟ
Nu-Pharm

Famotidine

Histamine H_2-Receptor Antagonist

Supplied: 20 mg: Each beige, D-shaped, film-coated tablet, identified NU over 20 on one side, contains: famotidine 20 mg. Energy: 3.23 kJ (0.77 kcal). Sodium: <1 mmol (0.44 mg). Gluten-, lactose- and tartrazine-free. Bottles of 100 and 500.

40 mg: Each light brown, D-shaped, film-coated tablet, identified NU over 40 on one side, contains: famotidine 40 mg. Energy: 2.9 kJ (0.69 kcal). Sodium: <1 mmol (0.44 mg). Gluten-, lactose- and tartrazine-free. Bottles of 100.

Store at room temperature (15 to 30°C). Protect from light and moisture.

NU-FENOFIBRATE Ⓟ
Nu-Pharm

Fenofibrate

Antihyperlipidemic

Supplied: Each white, opaque, No. 2 capsule, identified NU 100, contains: fenofibrate 100 mg. Gluten- and tartrazine-free. Bottles of 100 and 500. Store at controlled room temperature (15 to 25°C).

New Product 1998

NU-FLUOXETINE Ⓟ
Nu-Pharm

Fluoxetine HCl

Antidepressant—Antiobsessional—Antibulimic

Supplied: 10 mg: Each green and grey, opaque, No. 4 capsule, identified NU 10, contains: fluoxetine HCl equivalent to fluoxetine 10 mg. Gluten- and tartrazine-free. Bottles of 100.

20 mg: Each green and ivory, opaque, No. 3 capsule, identified NU 20, contains: fluoxetine HCl equivalent to fluoxetine 20 mg. Gluten- and tartrazine-free. Bottles of 100 and 500.

Store at room temperature (15 to 30°C) in tightly-closed containers. Protect from light.

New Product 1998

NU-FLURBIPROFEN Ⓟ
Nu-Pharm

Flurbiprofen

Anti-inflammatory—Analgesic

Supplied: 50 mg: Each white, oval, biconvex, film-coated tablet, identified NU over 50 on one side, contains: flurbiprofen 50 mg. Energy: 2.63 kJ (0.63 kcal). Sodium: <1 mmol (1.01 mg). Gluten- and tartrazine-free. Bottles of 100.

100 mg: Each blue, oval, biconvex, film-coated tablet, identified NU over 100 on one side, contains: flurbiprofen 100 mg. Energy: 5.26 kJ (1.26 kcal). Sodium: <1 mmol (2.03 mg). Gluten- and tartrazine-free. Bottles of 100.

Store at room temperature (15 to 30°C).

NU-GEMFIBROZIL Ⓟ
Nu-Pharm

Gemfibrozil

Antihyperlipidemic

Supplied: 300 mg: Each maroon and white No. 1 capsule, identified NU 300, contains: gemfibrozil 300 mg. Energy: 2 kJ (0.48 kcal). Sodium: <1 mmol (0.38 mg). Gluten-, lactose- and tartrazine-free. Bottles of 100. Store at room temperature (15 to 30°C).

600 mg: Each white, oval, biconvex, film-coated tablet, identified NU-600 on one side, contains: gemfibrozil 600 mg. Energy: 1.9 kJ (0.45 kcal). Sodium: <1 mmol (0.76 mg). Gluten-, lactose- and tartrazine-free. Bottles of 100. Store at room temperature (15 to 30°C). Protect from moisture.

NU-GLYBURIDE Ⓟ
Nu-Pharm

Glyburide

Oral Hypoglycemic

Supplied: 2.5 mg: Each white, round, flat-faced, beveled-edged tablet, scored and identified NU over 2.5 on one side, contains: glyburide 2.5 mg. Energy: 1.3 kJ (0.31 kcal). Sodium: <1 mmol (0.13 mg). Gluten- and tartrazine-free. Bottles of 100.

5 mg: Each white, capsule-shaped, flat-faced, beveled edged tablet, scored on one side and identified NU 5 on the other side, contains: glyburide 5 mg. Energy: 2.59 kJ (0.62 kcal). Sodium: <1 mmol (0.25 mg). Gluten- and tartrazine-free. Bottles of 500.

Store at room temperature (15 to 30°C).

NU-HYDRAL Ⓟ
Nu-Pharm

Hydralazine HCl

Antihypertensive

Supplied: 10 mg: Each yellow, round, biconvex tablet, scored and identified NU over 10 on one side, contains: hydralazine HCl 10 mg. Energy: 2.43 kJ (0.58 kcal). Gluten-, lactose-, sodium- and tartrazine-free. Bottles of 100 and 500.

25 mg: Each blue, round, biconvex, film-coated tablet, identified 25 on one side, contains: hydralazine HCl 25 mg. Energy: 1.64 kJ (0.39 kcal). Sodium: <1 mmol (0.02 mg). Gluten-, lactose- and tartrazine-free. Bottles of 100 and 500.

50 mg: Each pink, round, biconvex, film-coated tablet, identified 50 on one side, contains: hydralazine HCl 50 mg. Energy: 1.16 kJ (0.28 kcal). Sodium: <1 mmol (0.03 mg). Gluten-, lactose- and tartrazine-free. Bottles of 100.

NU-IBUPROFEN Ⓟ
Nu-Pharm

Ibuprofen

Anti-inflammatory—Analgesic

Supplied: 300 mg: Each white, round, biconvex, film-coated tablet, identified NU over 300 on one side, contains: ibuprofen 300 mg. Energy: 3.9 kJ (0.93 kcal). Sodium: <1 mmol (0.53 mg). Gluten-, lactose- and tartrazine-free. Bottles of 100.

400 mg: Each orange, round, biconvex, film-coated tablet, identified NU over 400 on one side, contains: ibuprofen 400 mg. Energy: 5.32 kJ (1.27 kcal). Sodium: <1 mmol (0.71 mg). Gluten-, lactose- and tartrazine-free. Bottles of 100.

600 mg: Each light orange, oval, biconvex, film-coated tablet, identified NU-600 on one side, contains: ibuprofen 600 mg. Energy: 7.9 kJ (1.89 kcal). Sodium: <1 mmol (1.07 mg). Gluten-, lactose- and tartrazine-free. Bottles of 100.

NU-INDAPAMIDE Ⓟ
Nu-Pharm

Indapamide Hemihydrate

Diuretic—Antihypertensive

Supplied: Each pink, round, biconvex, film-coated tablet, identified 2.5 on one side, contains: indapamide hemihydrate 2.5 mg. Gluten- and tartrazine-free. Bottles of 100. Store at room temperature (15 to 30°C). Protect from light.

New Product 1998

NU-INDO Ⓟ
Nu-Pharm

Indomethacin

Anti-inflammatory—Analgesic

Supplied: 25 mg: Each blue and white No. 3 capsule, identified NU 25, contains: indomethacin 25 mg. Energy: 3.45 kJ (0.82 kcal). Gluten-, sodium- and tartrazine-free. Bottles of 100 and 1 000.

50 mg: Each blue and white No. 1 capsule, identified NU 50, contains: indomethacin 50 mg. Energy: 7.55 kJ (1.8 kcal). Gluten-, sodium- and tartrazine-free. Bottles of 100 and 500.

NU-IPRATROPIUM Ⓟ
Nu-Pharm

Ipratropium Bromide

Bronchodilator

Supplied: Each ampul of sterile, clear, colorless solution contains: ipratropium bromide 250 µg (0.025%). Alcohol-, paraben- and sulfite-free. Plastic ampuls of 2 mL. The ampuls are overwrapped in an aluminum pouch (10×2 mL unit doses), cartons of 10. Store at room temperature (15 to 30°C). Do not refrigerate. Protect from light.

New Product 1998

NU-KETOPROFEN Ⓟ
NU-KETOPROFEN-E Ⓟ
Nu-Pharm

Ketoprofen

Anti-inflammatory—Analgesic

Supplied: Nu-Ketoprofen: Each dark green and ivory, hard gelatin No. 2 capsule, identified NU-50, contains: ketoprofen 50 mg. Energy: 5.02 kJ (1.2 kcal). Sodium: <1 mmol (0.38 mg). Gluten- and tartrazine-free. Bottles of 100 and 500.

Nu-Ketoprofen-E: 50 mg: Each yellow, round, biconvex, enteric-coated tablet, identified 50 on one side, contains: ketoprofen 50 mg. Energy: 1.7 kJ (0.41 kcal). Sodium: <1 mmol (0.27 mg). Gluten-, lactose- and tartrazine-free. Bottles of 100.

100 mg: Each yellow, round, biconvex, enteric-coated tablet, identified NU over 100 on one side, contains: ketoprofen 100 mg. Energy: 3.39 kJ (0.81 kcal). Sodium: <1 mmol (0.54 mg). Gluten-, lactose- and tartrazine-free. Bottles of 100.

NU-KETOPROFEN-SR Ⓟ

Nu-Pharm

Ketoprofen

Anti-inflammatory—Analgesic

Supplied: Each white, round, biconvex, film-coated, sustained-release tablet, identified NU on one side and 200 on the other, contains: ketoprofen 200 mg. Energy: 2.15 kJ (0.52 kcal). Gluten-, lactose-, sodium- and tartrazine-free. Bottles of 100 and 500. Store at room temperature (15 to 30°C).

New Product 1998

NU-LEVOCARB Ⓟ

Nu-Pharm

Levodopa—Carbidopa

Antiparkinson Agent

Supplied: 100 mg/10 mg: Each blue, oval, biconvex tablet, identified NU on one side, scored and identified 100 over 10 on the other, contains: levodopa 100 mg and carbidopa 10 mg expressed as anhydrous carbidopa. Gluten- and tartrazine-free. Bottles of 100.

100 mg/25 mg: Each yellow, oval, biconvex tablet, identified NU on one side, scored and identified 100 over 25 on the other, contains: levodopa 100 mg and carbidopa 25 mg expressed as anhydrous carbidopa. Gluten- and tartrazine-free. Bottles of 100 and 500.

250 mg/25 mg: Each blue, oval, biconvex tablet, identified NU on one side, scored and identified 250 over 25 on the other, contains: levodopa 250 mg and carbidopa 25 mg expressed as anhydrous carbidopa. Gluten- and tartrazine-free. Bottles of 100.

Store at room temperature (15 to 30°C). Protect from light.

New Product 1998

NU-LORAZ Ⓟ

Nu-Pharm

Lorazepam

Anxiolytic—Sedative

Supplied: 0.5 mg: Each white, round, flat-faced, beveled-edged tablet, identified NU on one side and 0.5 on the other, contains: lorazepam 0.5 mg (500 μg). Energy: <1 kJ (0.19 kcal). Sodium: <1 mmol (0.06 mg). Gluten- and tartrazine-free. Bottles of 100 and 500.

1 mg: Each white, capsule-shaped, flat-faced, beveled edged tablet, scored and identified NU over 1 on one side, contains: lorazepam 1 mg. Energy: 1.57 kJ (0.38 kcal). Sodium: <1 mmol (0.13 mg). Gluten- and tartrazine-free. Bottles of 100 and 1 000.

2 mg: Each white, oval, flat-faced, beveled-edged tablet, scored and identified NU over 2 on one side, contains: lorazepam 2 mg. Energy: 1.96 kJ (0.47 kcal). Sodium: <1 mmol (0.16 mg). Gluten- and tartrazine-free. Bottles of 100 and 1 000.

Store at room temperature (15 to 30°C) and protect from humidity.

NU-LOXAPINE Ⓟ

Nu-Pharm

Loxapine Succinate

Antipsychotic

Supplied: 5 mg: Each yellow, round, biconvex, film-coated tablet, identified NU on one side, scored and identified LOX over 5 on the other, contains: loxapine 5 mg as the succinate salt. Gluten- and tartrazine-free. Bottles of 100.

10 mg: Each green, round, biconvex, film-coated tablet, identified NU on one side, scored and identified LOX over 10 on the other, contains: loxapine 10 mg as the succinate salt. Gluten- and tartrazine-free. Bottles of 100.

25 mg: Each pink, round, biconvex, film-coated tablet, identified NU on one side, scored and identified LOX over 25 on the other side, contains: loxapine 25 mg as the succinate salt. Gluten- and tartrazine-free. Bottles of 100.

50 mg: Each white, round, biconvex, film-coated tablet, identified NU on one side, scored and identified LOX over 50 on the other side, contains: loxapine 50 mg as the succinate salt. Gluten- and tartrazine-free. Bottles of 100.

Store at room temperature (15 to 30°C).

New Product 1998

NU-MEDOPA Ⓟ

Nu-Pharm

Methyldopa

Antihypertensive

Supplied: 125 mg: Each yellow, round, biconvex, film-coated tablet, identified NU over 125 on one side, contains: methyldopa 125 mg. Energy: <1 kJ (0.23 kcal). Sodium: <1 mmol (0.04 mg). Gluten-, lactose- and tartrazine-free. Bottles of 100 and 1 000.

250 mg: Each yellow, round, biconvex, film-coated tablet, identified NU over 250 on one side, contains: methyldopa 250 mg. Energy: 1.91 kJ (0.46 kcal). Sodium: <1 mmol (0.08 mg). Gluten-, lactose- and tartrazine-free. Bottles of 500 and 1 000.

500 mg: Each yellow, round, biconvex, film-coated tablet, identified NU over 500 on one side, contains: methyldopa 500 mg. Energy: 3.82 kJ (0.91 kcal). Sodium: <1 mmol (0.15 mg). Gluten-, lactose- and tartrazine-free. Bottles of 100 and 500.

NU-MEFENAMIC Ⓟ

Nu-Pharm

Mefenamic Acid

Analgesic

Supplied: Each yellow and blue, opaque, No. 1 capsule, identified NU 250, contains: mefenamic acid 250 mg. Gluten- and tartrazine-free. Bottles of 100 and 500. Store at room temperature (15 to 30°C). Protect from moisture.

New Product 1998

NU-MEGESTROL Ⓟ

Nu-Pharm

Megestrol Acetate

Antineoplastic—Oral Progestogen

Supplied: 40 mg: Each light blue, round, flat-faced, beveled-edged tablet, scored and identified NU over 40 on one side, contains: megestrol acetate 40 mg. Gluten- and tartrazine-free. Bottles of 100.

160 mg: Each white, oval, biconvex tablet, scored and identified NU 160 on one side, contains: megestrol acetate 160 mg. Gluten- and tartrazine-free. Bottles of 30.

Store at room temperature (15 to 30°C) in tightly-closed containers.

New Product 1998

NU-METFORMIN Ⓟ

Nu-Pharm

Metformin HCl

Antihyperglycemic

Supplied: 500 mg: Each white, round, flat-faced, beveled-edged tablet, scored and identified NU over M500 on one side, contains: metformin HCl 500 mg. Gluten-, lactose-, sodium- and tartrazine-free. Bottles of 100 and 500.

850 mg: Each white, capsule-shaped, biconvex tablet, identified NU on one side and 850 on the other, contains: metformin HCl 850 mg. Gluten-, lactose-, sodium- and tartrazine-free. Bottles of 100.

Store at room temperature (15 to 30°C) in tightly-closed containers.

New Product 1998

NU-METOCLOPRAMIDE Ⓟ

Nu-Pharm

Metoclopramide HCl

Modifier of Upper Gastrointestinal Motility—Antiemetic

Supplied: 5 mg: Each white, square, biconvex tablet, identified NU over M5 on one side, contains: metoclopramide HCl equivalent to metoclopramide 5 mg. Energy: 1.58 kJ (0.38 kcal). Sodium: <1 mmol (0.06 mg). Gluten- and tartrazine-free. Bottles of 100.

10 mg: Each white, round, biconvex tablet, scored and identified NU over M10 on one side, contains: metoclopramide HCl equivalent to metoclopramide 10 mg. Energy: 3.16 kJ (0.76 kcal). Sodium: <1 mmol (0.11 mg). Gluten- and tartrazine-free. Bottles of 100.

Store at room temperature (15 to 30°C).

NU-METOP Ⓟ

Nu-Pharm

Metoprolol Tartrate

Antianginal—Antihypertensive

Supplied: 50 mg: Each pink, capsule-shaped, biconvex, film-coated tablet, scored on one side and identified 50 on the other, contains: metoprolol tartrate 50 mg. Energy: 1.74 kJ (0.41 kcal). Sodium: <1 mmol (0.81 mg). Gluten- and tartrazine-free. Bottles of 100 and 1 000.

100 mg: Each blue, capsule-shaped, biconvex, film-coated tablet, scored on one side and identified 100 on the other, contains: metoprolol tartrate 100 mg. Energy: 3.5 kJ (0.84 kcal). Sodium: <1 mmol (1.72 mg). Gluten- and tartrazine-free. Bottles of 100 and 1 000.

NUMORPHAN® Ⓝ

DuPont Pharma

Oxymorphone HCl

Analgesic

Pharmacology: Oxymorphone is a potent narcotic analgesic. When administered parenterally, 1 mg is approximately equivalent in analgesic activity to 10 mg of morphine sulfate. The onset of action of parenterally injected oxymorphone is rapid and the initial effects are usually perceived within 5 to 10 minutes, with analgesia persisting for approximately 3 to 6 hours. Oxymorphone is conjugated with glucuronic acid in the liver and excreted in the urine.

Oxymorphone produces mild sedation and causes little depression of the cough reflex. These properties make it particularly useful in postoperative patients.

Indications: For the relief of moderate to severe pain. Parenterally for preoperative medication, for support of anesthesia, for obstetrical analgesia, and for relief of anxiety in patients with dyspnea associated with acute left-ventricular failure and pulmonary edema.

Oxymorphone suppositories are useful in situations requiring a potent, rapid acting analgesic, i.e., in older or debilitated patients unable to tolerate injectable analgesics; for the control of pain in neoplastic disorders (terminal cancer including bone metastases); as an analgesic postoperatively for relief of moderate to severe pain.

Contraindications: Children: Safe use in children under 12 years of age has not been established.

Do not use in patients known to be hypersensitive to morphine analogs or with pre-existing respiratory depression or convulsive states.

Warnings: May be habit forming. As with other narcotic drugs, tolerance and addiction may develop. The addicting potential of the drug appears to be about the same as for morphine.

Drug Interactions: Interaction With Other CNS Depressants: Patients receiving other narcotic analgesics, general

Numorphan (cont'd)

anesthetics, phenothiazines, other tranquilizers sedatives, hypnotics or other CNS depressants (including alcohol) concomitantly with oxymorphone may exhibit an additive CNS depression. When such combined therapy is contemplated, the dose of one or both agents should be reduced.

Pregnancy and *Lactation:* Safe use in pregnancy has not been established (relative to possible adverse effects on fetal development). As with other analgesics, the use of oxymorphone in pregnancy, in nursing mothers, or in women of childbearing potential requires that the possible benefits of the drug be weighed against the possible hazards to the mother and child.

Precautions: The same care and caution should be taken when administering oxymorphone as when other potent analgesics are used. It should be borne in mind that some respiratory depression may occur as with all potent narcotics, especially when other analgesic and/or anesthetic drugs with depressant action have been given shortly before administration of oxymorphone.

The respiratory depressant effects of narcotics and their capacity to elevate CSF pressure may be markedly exaggerated in the presence of head injury, other intracranial lesions or a pre-existing increase in intracranial pressure. Furthermore, narcotics produce adverse reactions which may obscure the clinical course of patients with head injuries.

Caution must also be exercised in elderly and debilitated patients and in patients who are known to be sensitive to CNS depressants, such as those with cardiovascular, pulmonary, or hepatic disease, in hypothyroidism (myxedema), acute alcoholism, delirium tremens, convulsive disorders, bronchial asthma and kyphoscoliosis. Debilitated and elderly patients and those with severe liver diseases should receive smaller doses.

Adverse Effects: Include respiratory depression, drowsiness, nausea, vomiting, miosis, itching, dysphoria, lightheadedness, and headache.

Overdose: Symptoms: Respiratory depression (a decrease in respiratory rate and/or tidal volume, Cheyne-Stokes respiration, cyanosis), extreme somnolence progressing to stupor or coma, skeletal muscle flaccidity, cold and clammy skin, and sometimes bradycardia and hypotension. In severe overdosage, apnea, circulatory collapse, cardiac arrest and death may occur.

Treatment: Primary attention should be given to the reestablishment of adequate respiratory exchange through provision of a patent airway and the institution of assisted or controlled ventilation.

Naloxone is a specific antidote against respiratory depression which may result from overdosage or unusual sensitivity to narcotics, including oxymorphone. Administer appropriate dose, [usual initial adult dose: 400 µg (0.4 mg)] preferably i.v. and simultaneously with efforts at respiratory resuscitation. Since the duration of action of oxymorphone may exceed that of the antagonist, the patient should be kept under continued surveillance. Administer repeated doses as needed to maintain adequate respiration. Oxygen, i.v. fluids, vasopressors and other supportive measures should be employed as indicated.

Dosage: Injection: Usual adult dose: s.c. or i.m. administration: 1 to 1.5 mg initially and every 4 to 6 hours thereafter, as needed. I.V.: 0.5 mg initially. In nondebilitated patients, the dose can be cautiously increased until satisfactory pain relief is obtained. For analgesia during labor: 0.5 to 1 mg i.m.

Suppositories: Adults: One suppository (5 mg), every 4 to 6 hours. In nondebilitated patients the dose can be cautiously increased until satisfactory pain relief is obtained.

Supplied: Injection: Each mL of solution contains: 1.5 mg of oxymorphone HCl. Nonmedicinal ingredients: methylparaben, propylparaben, sodium chloride, sodium dithionite, sodium hydroxide solution and water for injection. Ampuls of 1 mL, boxes of 10. Store at 15 to 30°C. Protect from light.

Suppositories: Each suppository contains: oxymorphone HCl 5 mg in a base of polyethylene glycol 1 000 and 3 350. Gluten-, lactose-, sodium-, sulfite- and tartrazine-free. Boxes of 6. Store in refrigerator (2 to 8°C). Protect from light.

For a list of Canadian manufacturers who do not use tartrazine in their products, see the CLIN-INFO SECTION.

NU-NAPROX ℞
Nu-Pharm

Naproxen

Anti-inflammatory—Analgesic

Supplied: 125 mg: Each green, oval, biconvex tablet, identified NU-125 on one side, contains: naproxen 125 mg. Energy: <1 kJ (0.19 kcal). Sodium: <1 mmol (0.17 mg). Gluten-, lactose- and tartrazine-free. Bottles of 500.

250 mg: Each yellow, oval, biconvex tablet, identified NU-250 on one side, contains: naproxen 250 mg. Energy: 1.6 kJ (0.38 kcal). Sodium: <1 mmol (0.34 mg). Gluten-, lactose- and tartrazine-free. Bottles of 100 and 1 000.

375 mg: Each peach-colored, capsule-shaped, biconvex tablet, scored and identified NU over 375 on one side, contains: naproxen 375 mg. Energy: 2.43 kJ (0.58 kcal). Sodium: <1 mmol (0.51 mg). Gluten-, lactose- and tartrazine-free. Bottles of 100 and 500.

500 mg: Each yellow, capsule-shaped, biconvex tablet, scored and identified NU over 500 on one side, contains: naproxen 500 mg. Energy: 3.2 kJ (0.76 kcal). Sodium: <1 mmol (0.68 mg). Gluten-, lactose- and tartrazine-free. Bottles of 100 and 500.

NU-NIFED ℞
Nu-Pharm

Nifedipine

Antianginal

Supplied: Each mustard-colored, soft gelatin capsule, identified NU 10, contains: nifedipine 10 mg. Energy: 7.64 kJ (1.82 kcal). Gluten-, sodium- and tartrazine-free. Bottles of 100. Store at room temperature (15 to 30°C). Protect from light. Avoid freezing.

NU-NIFEDIPINE-PA ℞
Nu-Pharm

Nifedipine

Antihypertensive

Supplied: 10 mg: Each grey-pink, round, biconvex, film-coated, prolonged-action tablet, identified NU on one side and 10 on the other, contains: nifedipine 10 mg. Gluten-, lactose-, sodium- and tartrazine-free. Bottles of 100.

20 mg: Each grey-pink, round, biconvex, film-coated, prolonged-action tablet, identified NU on one side and 20 on the other, contains: nifedipine 20 mg. Gluten-, lactose-, sodium- and tartrazine-free. Bottles of 100.

Store at room temperature (15 to 30°C). Protect from light.

New Product 1998

NU-NORTRIPTYLINE ℞
Nu-Pharm

Nortriptyline HCl

Antidepressant

Supplied: 10 mg: Each white and yellow, opaque, No. 4 capsule, identified NU 10, contains: nortriptyline HCl 10 mg. Gluten- and tartrazine-free. Bottles of 100.

25 mg: Each white and yellow, opaque, No. 2 capsule, identified NU 25, contains: nortriptyline HCl 25 mg. Gluten- and tartrazine-free. Bottles of 100 and 500.

Store at room temperature (15 to 30°C) in tightly-closed containers.

New Product 1998

NU-OXYBUTYN ℞
Nu-Pharm

Oxybutynin Chloride

Anticholinergic—Antispasmodic

Supplied: Each blue, round, biconvex tablet, scored and identified NU over 5 on one side, contains: oxybutynin chloride 5 mg. Gluten- and tartrazine-free. Bottles of 100 and 500. Store at room temperature (15 to 30°C) in tightly-closed, light-resistant containers.

New Product 1998

NU-PENTOXIFYLLINE-SR ℞
Nu-Pharm

Pentoxifylline

Vasoactive Agent

Supplied: Each pink, capsule-shaped, biconvex, film-coated, sustained-release tablet, identified NU on one side and 400 on the other, contains: pentoxifylline 400 mg. Gluten-, lactose-, sodium- and tartrazine-free. Bottles of 100 and 500. Store at room temperature (15 to 30°C).

New Product 1998

NU-PEN-VK ℞
Nu-Pharm

Phenoxymethyl Penicillin Potassium

Antibiotic

Supplied: Each white, round, flat-faced, beveled-edged tablet, scored and identified NU over 300 on one side, contains: penicillin potassium V 300 mg (500 000 IU). Energy: 1 kJ (0.09 kcal). Sodium: <1 mmol (0.19 mg). Gluten-, lactose- and tartrazine-free. Bottles of 100 and 1 000.

NUPERCAINAL® Cream
NUPERCAINAL® Ointment
Novartis Consumer Health

Dibucaine—Domiphen Bromide

Dibucaine

Topical Anesthetic

Indications: For the relief of pain and itching in hemorrhoids, anal fissure, abrasions, minor burns, sunburn, chapping, herpes simplex, herpes zoster, insect bites, pruritus. The cream is also indicated for local antisepsis.

Precautions: Not more than 2 tubes of the cream, or 1 tube of the ointment, should be applied within 24 hours to an adult, or one half tube of cream or one quarter tube of ointment to a very young child.

Rectal bleeding may indicate a serious condition. Local medication should not be used until a physician has been consulted. Severe or extensive sunburn can be serious. In such cases, consult a physician promptly.

Adverse Effects: Increased irritation and sensitivity to dibucaine have been reported in rare instances.

Dosage: Cream: Apply 3 or 4 times daily.

Ointment: Apply on light dressing or by means of applicator.

Supplied: Cream: Each tube contains: dibucaine 0.5% and domiphen bromide 0.05% in a water washable base. Nonmedicinal ingredients: acetone sodium bisulfite, fragrance, glycerin, potassium hydroxide, stearic acid, triethanolamine and water. Parabens-free. Tubes of 30 g.

Ointment: Each g of ointment contains: dibucaine 1% in a lanolin and petrolatum base. Nonmedicinal ingredients: acetone sodium bisulfite, lanolin, petrolatum and water. Parabens-free. Tubes of 30 g.

NU-PINDOL ℞
Nu-Pharm

Pindolol

Antihypertensive—Antianginal

Supplied: 5 mg: Each white, round, flat-faced, beveled-edged tablet, scored and identified NU over 5 on one side, contains: pindolol 5 mg. Energy: 1.25 kJ (0.3 kcal). Sodium: <1 mmol (0.09 mg). Gluten- and tartrazine-free. Bottles of 100.

10 mg: Each white, round, biconvex tablet, scored and identified NU over 10 on one side, contains: pindolol 10 mg. Energy: 2.49 kJ (0.6 kcal). Sodium: <1 mmol (0.07 mg). Gluten- and tartrazine-free. Bottles of 100.

15 mg: Each white, round, flat-faced, beveled-edged tablet, scored and identified NU over 15 on one side, contains: pindolol 15 mg. Energy: 3.74 kJ (0.89 kcal). Sodium: <1 mmol (0.27 mg). Gluten- and tartrazine-free. Bottles of 100.

NU-PIROX ℞
Nu-Pharm

Piroxicam

Anti-inflammatory—Analgesic

Supplied: 10 mg: Each maroon and blue No. 2 capsule, identified NU 10, contains: piroxicam 10 mg. Energy: 4.66 kJ (1.11 kcal). Gluten-, sodium- and tartrazine-free. Bottles of 100 and 500.

20 mg: Each maroon No. 2 capsule, identified NU 20, contains: piroxicam 20 mg. Energy: 4.49 kJ (1.07 kcal). Gluten-, sodium- and tartrazine-free. Bottles of 100.

NU-PRAZO ℞
Nu-Pharm

Prazosin HCl

Antihypertensive

Supplied: 1 mg: Each peach-colored, capsule-shaped, flat-faced, beveled-edged tablet, scored and identified NU over 1 on one side, contains: prazosin HCl equivalent to prazosin 1 mg. Energy: 2.31 kJ (0.55 kcal). Sodium: <1 mmol (0.16 mg). Gluten- and tartrazine-free. Bottles of 100.

2 mg: Each white, round, biconvex tablet, scored and identified NU over 2 on one side, contains: prazosin HCl equivalent to prazosin 2 mg. Energy: 2.63 kJ (0.63 kcal). Sodium: <1 mmol (0.19 mg). Gluten- and tartrazine-free. Bottles of 100.

5 mg: Each white, diamond-shaped, biconvex tablet, scored and identified NU over 5 on one side, contains: prazosin HCl equivalent to prazosin 5 mg. Energy: 6.57 kJ (1.57 kcal). Sodium: <1 mmol (0.48 mg). Gluten- and tartrazine-free. Bottles of 100.

Store at room temperature (15 to 30°C).

NU-PROCHLOR ℞
Nu-Pharm

Prochlorperazine Bimaleate

Antipsychotic—Antiemetic

Supplied: 5 mg: Each peach-colored, round, biconvex, film-coated tablet, identified NU over 5 on one side, contains: prochlorperazine base 5 mg (as the bimaleate). Gluten-, lactose- and tartrazine-free. Bottles of 100 and 500.

10 mg: Each peach-colored, round, biconvex, film-coated tablet, identified NU over 10 on one side, contains: prochlorperazine base 10 mg (as the bimaleate). Gluten-, lactose- and tartrazine-free. Bottles of 100 and 500.

NU-PROPRANOLOL ℞
Nu-Pharm

Propranolol HCl

Beta-adrenergic Receptor Blocking Agent

Supplied: 10 mg: Each orange, round, biconvex tablet, scored and identified NU over 10 on one side, contains: propranolol HCl 10 mg. Energy: 2.41 kJ (0.58 kcal). Gluten-, sodium- and tartrazine-free. Bottles of 1 000.

20 mg: Each blue, hexagonal-shaped, biconvex tablet, scored and identified NU over 20 on one side, contains: propranolol HCl 20 mg. Energy: 2.65 kJ (0.63 kcal). Gluten-, sodium- and tartrazine-free. Bottles of 100 and 1 000.

40 mg: Each green, round, biconvex tablet, scored and identified NU over 40 on one side, contains: propranolol HCl 40 mg. Energy: 2.8 kJ (0.67 kcal). Sodium: <1 mmol (0.03 mg). Gluten- and tartrazine-free. Bottles of 1 000.

80 mg: Each yellow, round, biconvex tablet, scored and identified NU over 80 on one side, contains: propranolol HCl 80 mg. Energy: 3.93 kJ (0.94 kcal). Sodium: <1 mmol (0.07 mg). Gluten- and tartrazine-free. Bottles of 100 and 1 000.

120 mg: Each rose-colored, round, biconvex tablet, scored and identified NU over 120 on one side, contains: propranolol HCl 120 mg. Energy: 5.44 kJ (1.3 kcal). Sodium: <1 mmol (0.03 mg). Gluten- and tartrazine-free. Bottles of 100 and 500.

NU-RANIT ℞
Nu-Pharm

Ranitidine HCl

Histamine H_2-Receptor Antagonist

Supplied: 150 mg: Each white, round, biconvex, film-coated tablet, identified NU over 150 on one side, contains: ranitidine 150 mg (as the HCl). Energy: 2.54 kJ (0.61 kcal). Sodium: <1 mmol (0.37 mg). Gluten-, lactose- and tartrazine-free. Bottles of 100 and 500.

300 mg: Each white, capsule-shaped, biconvex, film-coated tablet, identified NU 300 on one side, contains: ranitidine 300 mg (as the HCl). Energy: 5.07 kJ (1.21 kcal). Sodium <1 mmol (0.73 mg). Gluten-, lactose- and tartrazine-free. Bottles of 100 and 500.

NUROMAX™ ℞
Glaxo Wellcome

Doxacurium Chloride

Nondepolarizing Skeletal Neuromuscular Blocking Agent

Pharmacology: Doxacurium is a long-acting, nondepolarizing, skeletal neuromuscular blocking agent for i.v. administration. Nondepolarizing agents antagonize the neurotransmitter action of acetylcholine by binding competitively with cholinergic receptor sites on the motor end-plates. This antagonism is inhibited, and neuromuscular block reversed, by acetylcholinesterase inhibitors such as neostigmine.

Pharmacodynamics: Doxacurium is approximately 2.5 to 3 times more potent than pancuronium and 10 to 12 times more potent than metocurine. Doxacurium in doses of 1.5 to 2×ED_{95} has a clinical duration of action (range and variability) similar to that of equipotent doses of pancuronium and metocurine (historic data and limited comparison).

The average ED_{95} (dose required to produce 95% suppression of the adductor pollicis muscle twitch response to ulnar nerve stimulation) of doxacurium is 0.025 mg/kg (range: 0.020 to 0.033 mg/kg) in adults receiving balanced anesthesia.

An initial doxacurium dose of 0.025 mg/kg (ED_{95}) administered after 10 to 100% recovery from an intubating dose of 1 mg/kg succinylcholine is followed by maximum block in about 9 to 10 minutes (range: 5 to 16 minutes). The duration of clinically effective neuromuscular block (i.e., time from injection to 25% recovery) is approximately 55 minutes (range: 9 to 145 minutes) during balanced anesthesia (see Table IV under Dosage).

An initial dose of 0.05 mg/kg (2×ED_{95}) in patients receiving balanced anesthesia, generally produces sufficient block for intubation within 4 to 5 minutes. Neuromuscular block reaches a maximum in 5 to 6 minutes (range: 2.5 to 13 minutes), and has a clinically effective duration of approximately 100 minutes (range: 39 to 232 minutes) (see Table IV under Dosage).

Intubation is generally possible 3 to 4 minutes after administration of a 0.08 mg/kg (3×ED_{95}) dose. The time to onset of the maximum neuromuscular blocking effect averages 3.5 minutes (range: 2.4 to 5 minutes). Clinically effective block lasts for approximately 160 minutes (range: 110 to 338 minutes) (see Table IV under Dosage).

As with other long-acting agents, the duration of neuromuscular block associated with doxacurium shows considerable interpatient variability. An analysis of 390 cases in U.S. clinical trials utilizing a variety of premedications, varying lengths of surgery and various anesthetic agents, indicates that approximately two-thirds of the patients had clinical durations within 30 minutes of the duration predicted by dose (based on mg/kg actual body weight). Patients ≥60 years old were approximately twice as likely to experience prolonged clinical duration (30 minutes longer than predicted) as patients <60 years old; thus, care should be used in these patients when prolonged recovery is undesirable (see Precautions, Geriatrics and Dosage, Individualization of Dosages). In addition, obese patients (patients weighing ≥30% more than ideal body weight for height) were almost twice as likely to experience prolonged clinical duration as non-obese patients. Dosing for obese patients should therefore be based on ideal body weight (see Dosage, Individualization of Dosages).

Most patients receiving doxacurium in clinical trials required pharmacologic reversal prior to full spontaneous recovery from neuromuscular block; therefore, relatively few data are available on the time from injection to 95% recovery of the twitch response. As a class, long-acting neuromuscular blocking agents may be associated with prolonged times to full spontaneous recovery. Some patients may require as long as 3 to 4 hours to exhibit full spontaneous recovery following initial doses of 0.025 to 0.05 mg/kg doxacurium and even longer following an initial dose of 0.08 mg/kg.

Cumulative neuromuscular blocking effects are not associated with the repeated administration of maintenance doses of doxacurium at 25% twitch recovery. Therefore, in a particular patient, maintenance doses can be administered at relatively regular intervals with predictable results. As with initial doses, however, the duration of action following maintenance doses of doxacurium may vary considerably between patients.

To achieve comparable levels of block, children require higher doxacurium doses on a mg/kg basis than do adults. The doxacurium ED_{95} for children 2 to 12 years of age receiving halothane anesthesia is approximately 0.03 mg/kg. The onset time and duration of block are shorter in children than in adults. During halothane anesthesia, doses of 0.03 mg/kg and 0.05 mg/kg doxacurium produce maximal block in approximately 7 and 4 minutes, respectively. The duration of clinically effective block is approximately 30 minutes after an initial dose of 0.03 mg/kg and approximately 45 minutes after 0.05 mg/kg. Doxacurium has not been studied in children under 2 years of age.

The neuromuscular block produced by doxacurium may be antagonized by anticholinesterase agents. As with other nondepolarizing neuromuscular blocking agents, the deeper the level of neuromuscular block at reversal, the longer is the time required for recovery of neuromuscular function.

Hemodynamics: Administration of doxacurium doses up to and including 0.08 mg/kg (approximately 3×ED_{95}) over 5 to 15 seconds revealed no dose-related effects on mean arterial blood pressure (MAP) or heart rate (HR) in healthy adult patients during steady state balanced anesthesia or in patients with serious cardiovascular disease undergoing coronary artery bypass grafting, cardiac valvular repair or vascular repair. In 2 to 12 year old children receiving halothane anesthesia, no dose-related changes in MAP or HR were observed following the administration of up to 0.05 mg/kg doxacurium over 5 to 15 seconds.

Doxacurium doses of 0.03 to 0.08 mg/kg (1.2 to 3×ED_{95}) were not associated with dose-dependent changes in mean plasma histamine concentration. Clinical experience with more than 1 000 patients indicates that adverse reactions typically associated with histamine release (e.g., bronchospasm, hypotension, tachycardia, cutaneous flushing, urticaria, etc.) are infrequent following the administration of doxacurium (see Adverse Effects).

Pharmacokinetics: Pharmacokinetic and pharmacodynamic results from a study of 24 healthy young adult patients and 8 healthy elderly patients are summarized in Table I (on following page). The pharmacokinetics are linear over the dosage range tested (i.e., plasma concentrations are approximately proportional to dose). The pharmacokinetics of doxacurium are similar in healthy young adult and elderly patients. Some healthy elderly patients tend to be more sensitive to the neuromuscular blocking effects than healthy young adult patients receiving the same dose. The time to maximum block is longer in elderly patients than in young adult patients (11.2 minutes vs 7.7 minutes at 0.025 mg/kg doxacurium). In addition, the clinically effective durations of block are more variable and tend to be longer in some healthy elderly patients than in healthy young adult patients receiving the same dose.

Table II (on following page) summarizes the pharmacokinetic and pharmacodynamic results from a study of 9 healthy young adult patients, 8 patients with end-stage kidney disease undergoing kidney transplantation and 7 patients with end-stage liver disease undergoing liver transplantation. The results suggest that a longer $t_{1/2}$ can be expected in patients with end-stage kidney disease; in addition, these patients may be more sensitive to the neuromuscular blocking effects of doxacurium. The time to maximum block was slightly longer and the clinically effective duration of block was prolonged in patients with end-stage kidney disease.

The pharmacokinetics of doxacurium are not significantly altered in liver transplant patients. Sensitivity to the neuromuscular blocking effects of Nuromax was highly variable in patients undergoing liver transplantation. Three of 7 patients developed ≤50% block, suggesting that these patients may have a reduced sensitivity to this drug. In those patients who developed >50% neuromuscular block, the time to maximum block and the clinically effective duration of action tended to

Nuromax (cont'd)

Table I—Nuromax

Pharmacokinetic and Pharmacodynamic Parameters[a] of Nuromax in Young Adult and Elderly Patients (Isoflurane Anesthesia)

Parameter	Healthy Young Adult Patients (22 to 49 yrs) 0.025 mg/kg (n=8)	0.05 mg/kg (n=8)	0.08 mg/kg (n=8)	Healthy Elderly Patients (67 to 72 yrs) 0.025 mg/kg (n=8)
t½ elimination (min)	86 (25-171)	123 (51-163)	98 (47-163)	96 (50-114)
Volume of Distribution at Steady State (L/kg)	0.15 (0.10-0.21)	0.24 (0.13-0.30)	0.22 (0.16-0.33)	0.22 (0.14-0.40)
Plasma Clearance (mL/min/kg)	2.22 (1.02-3.95)	2.62 (1.21-5.70)	2.53 (1.88-3.38)	2.47 (1.58-3.60)
Maximum Block (%)	97 (88-100)	100 (100-100)	100 (100-100)	96 (90-100)
Clinically Effective Duration of Block[b] (min)	68 (35-90)	91 (47-132)	177 (74-268)	97 (36-179)

[a]Values shown are mean (range).
[b]Time from injection to 25% recovery of the control twitch height.

Table II—Nuromax

Pharmacokinetic and Pharmacodynamic Parameters[a] of Nuromax in Healthy Patients and in Patients with End-Stage Kidney or Liver Disease (Isoflurane Anesthesia)

Parameter	Healthy Young Adult Patients 0.015 mg/kg (n=9)	Kidney Transplant Patients 0.015 mg/kg (n=8)	Liver Transplant Patients 0.015 mg/kg (n=7)
t½ elimination (min)	99 (48-193)	221 (84-592)	115 (69-148)
Volume of Distribution at Steady State (L/kg)	0.22 (0.11-0.43)	0.27 (0.17-0.55)	0.29 (0.17-0.35)
Plasma Clearance (mL/min/kg)	2.66 (1.35-6.66)	1.23 (0.48-2.40)	2.30 (1.96-3.05)
Maximum Block %	86 (59-100)	98 (95-100)	70 (0-100)
Clinically Effective Duration of Block[b] (min)	36 (19-80)	80 (29-133)	52 (20-91)

[a]Values shown are mean (range).
[b]Time from injection to 25% recovery of the control twitch height.

be longer than in healthy young adult patients (see Dosage, Individualization of Dosages). No data are available from patients with liver disease not requiring transplantation.

Consecutively administered maintenance doses of 0.005 mg/kg doxacurium, each given at a 25% T_1 recovery following the preceding dose, do not result in a progressive increase in the plasma concentration of doxacurium or a progressive increase in the depth or duration of block produced by each dose.

Doxacurium is not metabolized in vitro in fresh human plasma. Plasma protein binding of doxacurium is approximately 30% in human plasma.

In vivo data from humans suggest that doxacurium is not metabolized and that the major elimination pathway is excretion of the unchanged drug in urine and bile. In studies of healthy adult patients, 24 to 38% of an administered dose was recovered as parent drug in the urine over 6 to 12 hours after dosing. High bile concentrations of doxacurium (relative to plasma) have been found 35 to 90 minutes after administration in patients undergoing cholecystectomy. The overall extent of biliary excretion is unknown. The data derived from analysis of human urine and bile are consistent with data from in vivo studies in the rat, cat and dog, which indicate that all of an administered dose of doxacurium is recovered as parent drug in the urine and bile of these species.

Indications: As an adjunct to general anesthesia to provide skeletal muscle relaxation during surgery or mechanical ventilation. Doxacurium may also be used for non-emergency tracheal intubation.

Contraindications: Patients who have a known hypersensitivity to it.

Nuromax contains benzyl alcohol and is not indicated for use in newborns (children less than 1 month of age). In newborn infants, benzyl alcohol has been associated with an increased incidence of neurological and other complications which are sometimes fatal.

Warnings: Doxacurium should be used only by those trained in airway management and respiratory support. Equipment and personnel must be immediately available for tracheal intubation and support of ventilation, including administration of positive pressure oxygen. Adequacy of respiration must be assured through assisted or controlled ventilation. Reversal agents should be immediately available.

Clinicians administering long-acting neuromuscular blocking agents such as doxacurium should employ a peripheral nerve stimulator to monitor drug response, need for additional relaxant and adequacy of spontaneous recovery or anticholinesterase antagonism.

Doxacurium has no known effect on consciousness, pain threshold or cerebration. To avoid distress to the patient, neuromuscular block should not be induced before unconsciousness.

Doxacurium injection is acidic (pH 4.0 to 5) and should not be mixed with alkaline solutions of pH >8.5 (e.g., barbiturate solutions).

Neuromuscular blocking agents may have a profound effect in patients with neuromuscular diseases (e.g., myasthenia gravis, myasthenic [Eaton-Lambert] syndrome). In these and other conditions in which prolonged neuromuscular block is a possibility (e.g., carcinomatosis), the use of a peripheral nerve stimulator and a small test dose of doxacurium may be of value in assessing the level of neuromuscular block and monitoring dosage requirements. Muscle relaxants with a shorter duration of action than doxacurium may be more suitable for these patients.

Precautions: General: Doxacurium has no clinically significant effects on heart rate; therefore, doxacurium will not counteract the bradycardia produced by many anesthetic agents or by vagal stimulation.

No data are available to support the use of doxacurium by i.m. injection.

Burns: Resistance to nondepolarizing neuromuscular blocking agents may develop in patients with burns depending upon the time elapsed since the injury and the size of the burn. Doxacurium has not been studied in patients with burns.

Electrolyte Abnormalities: Acid/base and/or serum electrolyte abnormalities may antagonize or potentiate the action of neuromuscular blocking agents. For example, hyperkalemia has been reported to antagonize nondepolarizing neuromuscular blockers, while hypokalemia has been associated with an enhancement of their activity.

Asthma: As doxacurium has not been studied in patients with asthma or a history of severe anaphylactoid reactions, it should be administered with caution to these patient groups.

Renal and Hepatic Disease: The effects of renal and hepatic dysfunction on the action of doxacurium have been studied in patients with end-stage kidney (n=8) or liver (n=7) disease undergoing kidney and liver transplantation (see Pharmacology). The possibility of prolonged neuromuscular block in patients undergoing renal transplantation, and the possibility of a variable onset and duration of action in patients undergoing liver transplantation, must be considered when doxacurium is used in such patients.

Obesity: In obese patients, administration of doxacurium on the basis of actual body weight is associated with prolonged neuromuscular blockade. Ideal body weight should be considered in dosage calculations for obese patients, and appropriate attention paid to the attendant risk of underdosing. Severe obesity may pose airway or ventilatory problems requiring special care before, during or after the use of nondepolarizing neuromuscular blockers such as doxacurium.

Malignant Hyperthermia (MH): Doxacurium has not been studied in MH-susceptible patients. In a study of MH-susceptible Pietrain pigs (n=8) doxacurium did not trigger MH. Since MH can develop in the absence of established triggering agents, the clinician should be prepared to recognize and treat MH in any patient scheduled for general anesthesia.

Hypothermia: Hypothermia (25 to 28°C) has been associated with a decreased requirement for nondepolarizing neuromuscular blocking agents.

Long-Term Use in the Intensive Care Unit (ICU): The long-term use of doxacurium in patients undergoing mechanical ventilation in the intensive care unit has not been studied. When there is a need for long-term mechanical ventilation, the relative benefits and risks of inducing neuromuscular block with doxacurium must be considered.

Drug Interactions: Doxacurium has been administered following succinylcholine-facilitated tracheal intubation. Prior administration of succinylcholine has no clinically important effect on the neuromuscular blocking action of doxacurium. The depth, onset and duration of neuromuscular block produced by an ED_{95} dose of doxacurium given in the absence of prior administration of succinylcholine was not consistently altered when the same dose was given after complete (95%) or partial (10%) recovery from an intubating dose of succinylcholine. The administration of doxacurium before succinylcholine to attenuate succinylcholine-induced side effects (e.g., muscle fasciculations, postoperative myalgia) has not been studied.

There are no clinical data on the concomitant use of doxacurium and other nondepolarizing neuromuscular blocking agents.

Isoflurane, enflurane and halothane reduce the ED_{50} of doxacurium by 30 to 45%.

Other drugs which may enhance the neuromuscular blocking action of nondepolarizing agents such as doxacurium include certain antibiotics (e.g., aminoglycosides, tetracyclines, bacitracin, polymyxins, lincomycin, clindamycin, colistin and sodium colistimethate), magnesium salts, lithium, local anesthetics, procainamide and quinidine.

Concomitant phenytoin and carbamazepine treatment may be associated with an increase in the onset time of doxacurium and a decrease in its duration of block. Similar interactions have been reported for other nondepolarizing neuromuscular relaxants.

Carcinogenesis, Mutagenesis, Impairment of Fertility: Carcinogenesis and fertility studies have not been performed. Doxacurium was evaluated in a battery of 4 short-term mutagenicity tests. It was non-mutagenic in the Ames Salmonella assay, in the mouse lymphoma assay and in the human lymphocyte assay. In the in vivo rat bone marrow cytogenetic assay, statistically significant increases in the incidence of structural abnormalities, relative to vehicle controls, were observed in male rats dosed with 0.1 mg/kg (0.625 mg/m²) doxacurium and sacrificed at 6 hours, but not at 24 or 48 hours, and in female rats dosed with 0.2 mg/kg (1.25 mg/m²) doxacurium and sacrificed at 24 hours, but not at 6 or 48 hours. There was no increase in structural abnormalities in either male or female rats given 0.3 mg/kg (1.875 mg/m²) doxacurium and sacrificed at 6, 24 or 48 hours. Thus, the incidence of abnormalities in the in vivo rat bone marrow cytogenetic assay was not dose-dependent and, therefore, the likelihood that the observed abnormalities were treatment-related or clinically significant is low.

Pregnancy: Doxacurium was not shown to be teratogenic when given to nonventilated pregnant rats and mice by the s.c. route at sub-paralyzing doses. Studies at paralyzing doses have not been performed. There are no studies in pregnant women. Because animal reproduction studies have not been performed under conditions that would approximate those of clinical use, doxacurium should not be used during pregnancy unless, in the opinion of the physician, the potential benefits outweigh the unknown hazards. The action of neuromuscular blocking agents may be enhanced by magnesium salts administered for the management of toxemia of pregnancy.

Labor and Delivery: As the duration of action of doxacurium exceeds that of operative obstetrics, this drug is not recommended for use in patients undergoing cesarean section. The use of doxacurium during labor or during vaginal delivery or cesarean section has not been studied. It is not known whether doxacurium administered to the mother has immediate or delayed effects on the fetus.

Lactation: It is not known whether doxacurium is excreted in human milk. Because many drugs are excreted in human milk, caution should be exercised when doxacurium is administered to a nursing woman.

Children: For children 2 to 12 years of age, see Pharmacology and Dosage. The safety and efficacy of doxacurium in children less than 2 years of age have not been studied.

Geriatrics: Doxacurium has been used in elderly patients, including patients with significant cardiovascular disease. In elderly patients, the onset of maximum block is slower and the duration of neuromuscular block produced by doxacurium is more variable, and in some cases longer, than in young adult patients (see Pharmacology and Dosage). As with other long-acting neuromuscular blocking agents, the possibility of prolonged block must be considered when doxacurium is administered to elderly patients, especially those known to have reduced liver or kidney function.

Increased Volume of Distribution: The onset of action of neuromuscular blocking agents may be delayed in patients who have increased volumes of distribution as a result of old age, edematous states or cardiovascular disease. In these patients, more time should be permitted for the drug to achieve its maximum effect. Increased doses should be avoided, owing to the possibility of a markedly prolonged duration of action.

Adverse Effects: The most frequent adverse reaction to nondepolarizing blocking agents as a class consists of an extension of the pharmacological action beyond the time needed for surgery and anesthesia. This effect may vary from skeletal muscle weakness to profound and prolonged skeletal muscle paralysis resulting in respiratory insufficiency or apnea which require manual or mechanical ventilation until recovery is judged to be clinically adequate (see Overdose: Symptoms and Treatment). Inadequate reversal of neuromuscular block is possible with doxacurium, as with all nondepolarizing agents. Prolonged neuromuscular block and inadequate reversal may lead to postoperative complications.

Observed in Clinical Trials: Adverse experiences were uncommon among the 1 034 surgical patients and volunteers who received doxacurium and other drugs in U.S. clinical studies in the course of a wide variety of procedures conducted during balanced or inhalational anesthesia. The following adverse experiences were reported in patients administered doxacurium (all events judged by investigators during the clinical trials to have a possible causal relationship):

Incidence greater than 1%: none.

Incidence less than 1%: Cardiovascular*: hypotension†, flushing†, ventricular fibrillation, myocardial infarction.

Respiratory: bronchospasm, wheezing.

Dermatological: urticaria, injection site reaction.

Special Senses: diplopia.

Nonspecific: difficult neuromuscular block reversal, prolonged drug effect, fever.

* Reports of ventricular fibrillation (n=1) and myocardial infarction (n=1) were limited to ASA Class 3-4 patients undergoing cardiac surgery (n=142).

† 0.3% incidence. All other reactions unmarked were ≤0.1%.

Overdose: Symptoms and Treatment: The possibility of iatrogenic overdose can be minimized by carefully monitoring muscle twitch response to peripheral nerve stimulation. Because a long duration of neuromuscular block may result from overdose, a peripheral nerve stimulator should be used to monitor recovery. Residual neuromuscular block beyond the time needed for surgery and anesthesia may occur with doxacurium as with other neuromuscular blocking agents. This may be manifested by skeletal muscle weakness, low tidal volume or apnea. A nerve stimulator may be used to differentiate residual neuromuscular block from other causes of apnea or decreased tidal volume, such as narcotics, barbiturates or other CNS depressants. The primary treatment of overdose with nondepolarizing neuromuscular blocking agents is maintenance of a patent airway and manual or mechanical ventilation until recovery of normal respiration is assured. Recovery may be facilitated by administration of an anticholinesterase agent such as neostigmine in conjunction with an appropriate anticholinergic agent. In general, as with other nondepolarizing neuromuscular blocking agents, reversal should not be attempted until evidence of spontaneous recovery from neuromuscular block is present (see Dosage, Reversal).

Dosage: Doxacurium should be administered only i.v.

Parenteral drug products should be inspected visually for particulate matter and discoloration prior to administration whenever solution and container permit.

Like other long-acting neuromuscular blocking agents, doxacurium displays variability in the duration of its effect and has the potential for prolonged clinical duration. The dosage information provided below is intended as a guide only. Doses should be individualized (see Individualization of Dosage). Factors that may warrant dosage adjustment include: advanced age, concomitant drug treatment, type of surgical procedure or general anesthetic, the presence of kidney or liver disease or obesity (patients weighing ≥30% more than ideal body weight for height). The use of a peripheral nerve stimulator will permit the most advantageous use of doxacurium and minimize the possibility of overdosage or underdosage and assist in the evaluation of recovery.

Adults: The recommended dosage range in adults receiving balanced anesthesia is 0.025 to 0.08 mg/kg (1 to 3 times the ED_{95} value). The potency of doxacurium is enhanced by halogenated anesthetics. If doxacurium is administered during steady-state isoflurane, enflurane or halothane anesthesia, initial and maintenance doses should be reduced by approximately one-third.

In North American clinical trials performed in ASA 1 and 2 adults, the ED_{95} values in Table III were obtained for doxacurium in the presence of different anesthetic agents.

Table III—Nuromax

ED_{95} Values

Anesthetic	Nuromax ED_{95} (mg/kg)
Thiopental-Narcotic	0.02-0.03
Enflurane	0.014-0.015
Isoflurane	0.015-0.016
Halothane	0.014-0.025

Table IV and the information provided below are intended as a guide only. Doses should be individualized (see Individualization of Dosages subsection below).

Initial Doses: See Table IV. An initial 0.025 mg/kg (ED_{95}) dose of doxacurium administered during balanced anesthesia should be preceded by pre-intubation with succinylcholine. Doxacurium may be given as soon as recovery from the effects of succinylcholine becomes evident. An initial dose of 0.025 mg/kg doxacurium provides approximately 60 minutes of clinically effective neuromuscular block for surgery.

When administered as a component of a thiopental/narcotic induction-intubation paradigm with the intention to produce a long duration of neuromuscular block during surgery, an initial 0.05 mg/kg ($2\times ED_{95}$) dose of doxacurium generally produces good-to-excellent conditions for tracheal intubation in approximately 4 to 5 minutes. Clinically effective neuromuscular block following a dose of 0.05 mg/kg doxacurium may be expected to last approximately 100 minutes in patients receiving balanced anesthesia.

An initial dose of 0.08 mg/kg ($3\times ED_{95}$) doxacurium should be reserved for instances in which a need for very prolonged neuromuscular block is anticipated. Good-to-excellent intubation conditions may generally be expected approximately 3 to 4 minutes after administration of this dose. Clinically effective block may be expected to persist for 160 minutes or more.

Maintenance Doses: The need for maintenance dosing should be based on use of a peripheral nerve stimulator and/or clinical criteria. Maintenance doses will generally be required about 60 minutes after an initial dose of 0.025 mg/kg doxacurium or 100 minutes after an initial dose of 0.05 mg/kg doxacurium during balanced anesthesia. Repeated maintenance doses administered at 25% twitch recovery may be expected to be required at relatively regular intervals in individual patients. The interval may vary considerably between patients. Maintenance doses of 0.005 and 0.01 mg/kg doxacurium provide an average 30 minutes (range: 9 to 57 minutes) and 45 minutes (range: 14 to 108 minutes) respectively, of additional clinically effective neuromuscular block. For shorter and longer desired durations, smaller or larger maintenance doses may be administered.

If doxacurium is administered during steady-state isoflurane, enflurane or halothane anesthesia, maintenance doses should be reduced by approximately 30 to 40%.

Children: Dose-response studies in children 2 to 12 years of age indicate that the dose requirements for doxacurium on a mg/kg basis are higher in children than in adults and that recovery from neuromuscular block induced by doxacurium occurs more rapidly. In children anesthetized with halothane, an initial doxacurium dose of 0.03 mg/kg (ED_{95}) produces maximal block in about 7 minutes (range: 5 to 11 minutes), and clinically effective block persists for approximately 30 minutes (range: 12 to 54 minutes). An initial dose of 0.05 mg/kg produces maximal block in about 4 minutes (range: 2 to 10 minutes) and clinically effective block persists for approximately 45 minutes (range: 30 to 80 minutes). Maintenance doses of doxacurium may be required with slightly greater frequency in children than in adults. Because of the potentiating effect of halothane, a higher dose of doxacurium may be required in children receiving balanced anesthesia than in children receiving halothane anesthesia to achieve a comparable onset and duration of neuromuscular block. Doxacurium has not been studied in children under 2 years of age.

Reversal: Once spontaneous recovery is evident, reversal of the neuromuscular block produced by doxacurium can be achieved with various anticholinesterase agents such as neostigmine in conjunction with an appropriate anticholinergic agent. As with other nondepolarizing neuromuscular blocking agents, the time required for anticholinesterase-mediated recovery may be lengthened if reversal is attempted at a deep level of block or if inadequate doses of reversal agent are employed.

In clinical trials, a dose of 1 mg/kg edrophonium was not as effective as a dose of 0.06 mg/kg neostigmine in antagonizing moderate to deep levels of neuromuscular block (i.e., <60% T_1 recovery). Therefore, the use of 1 mg/kg edrophonium is not recommended for reversal of moderate to deep levels of block. The use of pyridostigmine has not been studied.

Patients should be evaluated for adequate clinical evidence of antagonism, e.g., 5-second head lift and grip strength. Ventilation must be supported until no longer required. As with other neuromuscular blocking agents, physicians should be alert to the possibility that the action of the drugs used to antagonize neuromuscular block may wear off before the effects of doxacurium on the neuromuscular junction have declined sufficiently.

Antagonism may be delayed in the presence of debilitation or carcinomatosis, and during the concomitant use of certain broad spectrum antibiotics, or anesthetic agents and other drugs which enhance neuromuscular block or cause respiratory depression (see Precautions, Drug Interactions). Under

Table IV—Nuromax

Pharmacodynamic Characteristics[a] of Nuromax Administered at Recommended Initial Dosages to Adult Surgical Patients (ASA 1 and 2) in Clinical Trials (Balanced Anesthesia)

Dose	0.025 mg/kg (ED_{95}) n=34	0.05 mg/kg ($2\times ED_{95}$) n=27	0.08 mg/kg ($3\times ED_{95}$) n=9
Time to intubation (min)	Pre-intubation with succinylcholine required[b]	4–5	3–4
Time to Maximum Twitch Suppression (min)	9.3 (5.4–16)	5.2 (2.5–13)	3.5 (2.4–5)
Time to 25% Recovery (i.e., effective clinical duration)[a] (min)	55 (9–145)	100 (39–232)	160 (110–338)

[a] Values shown are means followed by the range of individual values in parentheses.

[b] Doxacurium was administered after 10 to 100% recovery from an intubating dose of succinylcholine.

Nuromax (cont'd)

such circumstances the management is the same as that of prolonged neuromuscular block.

Individualization of Dosages: Recommended doses of doxacurium are more likely to be associated with a prolonged duration of clinically effective block in the elderly or in patients with obesity or renal impairment than in healthy young adult patients of normal body weight (see Pharmacology). In elderly patients or patients who have kidney disease, the potential for a prolongation of block may be reduced by decreasing the initial doxacurium dose and by titrating the dose to achieve the desired depth of block. For obese patients (i.e., patients weighing ≥30% more than ideal body weight for height), ideal body weight should be used when determining the dose.

Dosage requirements for patients with serious liver disease are variable; some patients may require a higher than normal initial doxacurium dose to achieve clinically effective block. Once adequate block is established, the clinical duration of block may be prolonged relative to patients with normal liver function.

As is the case with pancuronium, metocurine and vecuronium, resistance to doxacurium, manifested by a reduced intensity and/or shortened duration of block, must be considered when doxacurium is selected for use in patients receiving phenytoin or carbamazepine (see Precautions, Drug Interactions). Similarly, a reduction in dosage of doxacurium must be considered in cachectic or debilitated patients, in patients with neuromuscular diseases, severe electrolyte abnormalities, or carcinomatosis, and in other patients in whom potentiation of neuromuscular block or difficulty with reversal is anticipated. Increased doses of doxacurium may be required in burn patients (see Precautions).

Stability and Storage: The injection should be stored at room temperature between 15 and 25°C. **Do not freeze.**

Parenteral Products: Doxacurium injection may not be compatible with alkaline solutions with a pH greater than 8.5 (e.g., barbiturate solutions).

When administered through a y-site during i.v. infusion, doxacurium is physically and chemically compatible with the following diluents: 5% Dextrose Injection, USP; 0.9% Sodium Chloride Injection, USP; 5% Dextrose and 0.9% Sodium Chloride Injection, USP; Lactated Ringer's Injection, USP; 5% Dextrose and Lactated Ringer's Injection.

Doxacurium diluted up to 1:10 in 5% Dextrose Injection USP or 0.9% Sodium Chloride Injection, USP is physically and chemically stable stored in polypropylene syringes at room temperature, 15 to 25°C for up to 24 hours. Since dilution diminishes the preservative effectiveness of benzyl alcohol, aseptic techniques should be used to prepare the diluted product. Immediate use of the diluted product is preferred; any unused portion of diluted doxacurium should be discarded after 8 hours.

Supplied: Each mL of injection contains: doxacurium chloride 1 mg. Multiple-dose vials of 5 mL containing 0.9% w/v benzyl alcohol as a preservative. May also contain hydrochloric acid as a pH adjuster and water for injection. Store at room temperature between 15 and 25°C. **Does not require refrigeration. Do not freeze.**

NURSOY®

Wyeth-Ayerst

Soy Protein Isolate

Hypoallergenic Infant Formula

Indications: A nutritionally complete soy-based and milk- and lactose-free formula for common infant feeding problems associated with lactose intolerance or cow's-milk protein sensitivity or allergy. Symptoms that may require a milk-free formula include diarrhea, vomiting, spitting up, feeding difficulties, gas, bloating, colic, and fussiness. Iron-fortified Nursoy contains vitamin A in the form of beta-carotene and has a fat blend patterned after breast milk.

Supplied: Protein: soy protein isolate 100%. Carbohydrate: glucose polymers 75%, sucrose 25%. Fat: polyunsaturated 15%, monounsaturated 40%, saturated 45%. Vitamins and Minerals: at recommended levels.

Nursoy Concentrated Liquid contains (by descending order): water; corn syrup solids; soy protein isolate sucrose; oleo (beef), coconut and soybean oils; high monounsaturate safflower or sunflower oil; potassium citrate; monobasic sodium phosphate; magnesium chloride; calcium carbonate; calcium chloride; calcium hydroxide; soy lecithin; L-methionine; dibasic calcium phosphate; ascorbic acid; choline chloride; calcium carrageenan; taurine; potassium bicarbonate; ferrous sulfate; sodium chloride; zinc sulfate; alpha-tocopheryl acetate; L-carnitine; niacinamide; calcium pantothenate; vitamin A palmitate; riboflavin; cupric sulfate; thiamine and pyridoxine hydrochlorides; beta-carotene; phytonadione; potassium iodide; folic acid; biotin; cholecalciferol; cyanocobalamin. Note: Composition of powder, ready-to-serve and ready-to-feed formulas may vary slightly. See Table I.

Table I—Nursoy

Nursoy Concentrated Liquid

Analysis	Normal dilution 100 mL	
Energy:		
Calories	67	kcal
kJ	280	kJ
Carbohydrate	6.9	g
Fat	3.6	g
Linoleic acid	0.33	g
Protein	1.8	g
Ash	0.35	g
Vitamin A	200	IU
Vitamin D	40	IU
Vitamin E	0.95	IU
Vitamin K_1	0.010	mg
Vitamin C	5.5	mg
Thiamine	0.067	mg
Riboflavin	0.1	mg
Niacin	0.5	mg
Vitamin B_6	0.042	mg
Folic acid	0.005	mg
Vitamin B_{12}	0.0002	mg
Biotin	0.0035	mg
d-pantothenic acid	0.3	mg
Calcium	60	mg
Phosphorus	42	mg
Magnesium	6.7	mg
Iron	1.2	mg
Iodine	0.006	mg
Zinc	0.5	mg
Copper	0.047	mg
Manganese	0.02	mg
Sodium	20	mg
Potassium	70	mg
Chloride	37.5	mg
Choline	8.5	mg
Taurine	3.76	mg
Inositol	2.7	mg

Concentrated Liquid: Normal dilution: equal amounts of liquid and water. Cans of 385 mL, cases of 12.

Powder: Normal dilution: 1 scoop powder and 60 mL water. Scoop provided in each can. Cans of 450 g, cases of 6.

Ready-to-Serve: No dilution required. 20 kcal/30 mL (280 kJ/100 mL). Cans of 385 mL, cases of 12.

Ready-to-Feed: No dilution required. For hospital use only. Presterilized, disposable bottles of 20 kcal/30 mL (280 kJ/100 mL). Bottles of 100 mL, cases of 48.

Reviewed 1997

NU-SALBUTAMOL Solution ℞

Nu-Pharm

Salbutamol Sulfate

Bronchodilator—β_2-adrenergic Stimulant

Supplied: Each ampul of sterile, clear, colorless solution contains: salbutamol sulfate equivalent to salbutamol base 2.5 mg (1 mg/mL) or 5 mg (2 mg/mL). Alcohol-, paraben- and sulfite-free. Plastic ampuls of 2.5 mL. The ampuls are overwrapped in an aluminum pouch (20×2.5 mL unit doses), cartons of 20. Store at room temperature (15 to 30°C). Do not refrigerate. Protect from light.

New Product 1998

Look for CPhA general monographs to provide additional drug information. These are shaded gray and listed in the WHITE SECTION of the *CPS.*

NU-SALBUTAMOL Tablets ℞

Nu-Pharm

Salbutamol Sulfate

Bronchodilator

Supplied: 2 mg: Each light-purple, round, flat-faced, beveled-edged tablet, scored and identified NU over 2 on one side, contains: salbutamol sulfate equivalent to salbutamol 2 mg. Energy: 1.45 kJ (0.35 kcal). Gluten-, sodium- and tartrazine-free. Bottles of 100.

4 mg: Each light-purple, round, flat-faced, beveled-edged tablet, scored and identified NU over 4 on one side, contains: salbutamol sulfate equivalent to salbutamol 4 mg. Energy: 2.90 kJ (0.69 kcal). Gluten-, sodium- and tartrazine-free. Bottles of 100.

Store at room temperature (15 to 30°C).

NU-SELEGILINE ℞

Nu-Pharm

Selegiline HCl

Antiparkinsonian Agent

Supplied: Each white, round, flat-faced, beveled-edged tablet, identified S5 on one side, contains: 5 mg of the l-isomer of selegiline HCl. Gluten-, sodium- and tartrazine-free. Bottles of 100. Store at room temperature (15 to 30°C). Protect from light.

New Product 1998

NU-SOTALOL ℞

Nu-Pharm

Sotalol HCl

Antiarrhythmic

Supplied: 80 mg: Each blue, capsule-shaped, biconvex tablet, scored on one side, identified NU-80 on the other, contains: sotalol HCl 80 mg. Gluten-, lactose- and tartrazine-free. Bottles of 100.

160 mg: Each blue, capsule-shaped, biconvex tablet, scored on one side, identified NU-160 on the other, contains: sotalol HCl 160 mg. Gluten-, lactose- and tartrazine-free. Bottles of 100.

Store at room temperature (15 to 30°C). Protect from light.

New Product 1998

NU-SUCRALFATE ℞

Nu-Pharm

Sucralfate

Gastroduodenal Cytoprotective Agent

Supplied: Each white, capsule-shaped tablet, partially scored on both sides, one side convex, other side flat-faced, scored and identified NU-1g, contains: sucralfate 1 g. Energy: <1 kJ (0.05 kcal). Sodium: <1 mmol (0.76 mg). Gluten-, lactose- and tartrazine-free. Bottles of 100 and 500. Store at room temperature (15 to 30°C).

NU-SULFINPYRAZONE ℞

Nu-Pharm

Sulfinpyrazone

Platelet Inhibitor—Uricosuric

Supplied: 100 mg: Each white, round, flat-faced, beveled-edged tablet, scored and identified NU over 100 on one side, contains: sulfinpyrazone 100 mg. Energy: 3.62 kJ (0.86 kcal). Sodium: <1 mmol (0.19 mg). Gluten- and tartrazine-free. Bottles of 100.

200 mg: Each white, round, biconvex, film-coated tablet, identified NU over 200 on one side, contains: sulfinpyrazone 200 mg. Energy: 3.22 kJ (0.77 kcal). Gluten-, lactose-, sodium- and tartrazine-free. Bottles of 100.

NU-SULINDAC ℞
Nu-Pharm

Sulindac

Anti-inflammatory—Analgesic

Supplied: 150 mg: Each yellow, hexagonal, biconvex tablet, scored and identified NU over 150 on one side, contains: sulindac 150 mg. Energy: 1.19 kJ (0.28 kcal). Sodium: <1 mmol (0.04 mg). Gluten- and tartrazine-free. Bottles of 100 and 500.

200 mg: Each yellow, hexagonal, biconvex tablet, scored and identified NU over 200 on one side, contains: sulindac 200 mg. Energy: 1.59 kJ (0.38 kcal). Sodium: <1 mmol (0.05 mg). Gluten- and tartrazine-free. Bottles of 100.

Store at room temperature (15 to 30°C).

NU-TEMAZEPAM ℞
Nu-Pharm

Temazepam

Hypnotic

Supplied: 15 mg: Each maroon and pink, opaque, No. 3 capsule, identified NU 15, contains: temazepam 15 mg. Gluten- and tartrazine-free. Bottles of 100 and 500.

30 mg: Each maroon and light blue, opaque, No. 3 capsule, identified NU 30, contains: temazepam 30 mg. Gluten- and tartrazine-free. Bottles of 100 and 500.

Store at room temperature (15 to 30°C) in well-closed, light-resistant containers.

New Product 1998

NU-TERAZOSIN ℞
Nu-Pharm

Terazosin HCl

Antihypertensive—Symptomatic Treatment of Benign Prostatic Hyperplasia (BPH)

Supplied: 1 mg: Each white, round, flat-faced, beveled-edged tablet, identified NU on one side and T1 on the other, contains: terazosin 1 mg (as terazosin HCl dihydrate). Gluten-, sodium- and tartrazine-free. Bottles of 100.

2 mg: Each orange, round, flat-faced, beveled-edged tablet, identified NU on one side and T2 on the other, contains: terazosin 2 mg (as terazosin HCl dihydrate). Gluten-, sodium- and tartrazine-free. Bottles of 100.

5 mg: Each tan, round, flat-faced, beveled-edged tablet, identified NU on one side and T5 on the other, contains: terazosin 5 mg (as terazosin HCl dihydrate). Gluten-, sodium- and tartrazine-free. Bottles of 100.

10 mg: Each green, round, flat-faced, beveled-edged tablet, identified NU on one side and T10 on the other, contains: terazosin 10 mg (as terazosin HCl dihydrate). Gluten-, sodium- and tartrazine-free. Bottles of 100.

Store at room temperature (15 to 30°C).

New Product 1998

NU-TETRA ℞
Nu-Pharm

Tetracycline HCl

Antibiotic

Supplied: Each yellow and orange No. 2 capsule, identified NU 250, contains: tetracycline HCl 250 mg. Energy: <1 kJ (0.21 kcal). Gluten-, lactose-, sodium- and tartrazine-free. Bottles of 1 000.

NU-TIAPROFENIC ℞
Nu-Pharm

Tiaprofenic Acid

Anti-inflammatory—Analgesic

Supplied: 200 mg: Each white, round, biconvex, film-coated tablet, scored and identified NU over 200 on one side, contains: tiaprofenic acid 200 mg. Gluten-, lactose- and tartrazine-free. Bottles of 100.

300 mg: Each white, round, biconvex, film-coated tablet, scored and identified NU over 300 on one side, contains: tiaprofenic acid 300 mg. Gluten-, lactose- and tartrazine-free. Bottles of 100.

Store at room temperature (15 to 30°C). Protect from excessive heat, light and humidity.

New Product 1998

NU-TICLOPIDINE ℞
Nu-Pharm

Ticlopidine HCl

Inhibitor of Platelet Function

Supplied: Each white, oval-shaped, biconvex, film-coated tablet, identified NU on one side and 250 on the other, contains: ticlopidine HCl 250 mg. Gluten-, Lactose- and tartrazine-free. Bottles of 100. Store at room temperature (15 to 30°C).

New Product 1998

NU-TIMOLOL ℞
Nu-Pharm

Timolol Maleate

Antihypertensive—Antianginal

Supplied: 5 mg: Each white, round, flat-faced, beveled-edged tablet, scored and identified NU over T5 on one side, contains: timolol maleate 5 mg. Energy: 1.58 kJ (0.38 kcal). Sodium: <1 mmol (0.06 mg). Gluten- and tartrazine-free. Bottles of 100.

10 mg: Each light blue, round, flat-faced, beveled edged tablet, scored and identified NU over 10 on one side, contains: timolol maleate 10 mg. Energy: 3.16 kJ (0.75 kcal). Sodium: <1 mmol (0.13 mg). Gluten- and tartrazine-free. Bottles of 100.

20 mg: Each light blue, capsule-shaped, biconvex tablet, scored and identified NU over 20 on one side, contains: timolol maleate 20 mg. Energy: 6.32 kJ (1.51 kcal). Sodium: <1 mmol (0.25 mg). Gluten- and tartrazine-free. Bottles of 100.

NU-TRAZODONE ℞
NU-TRAZODONE-D ℞
Nu-Pharm

Trazodone HCl

Antidepressant

Supplied: Nu-Trazodone: 50 mg: Each pale orange, round, biconvex tablet, scored and identified NU over T50 on one side, contains: trazodone HCl 50 mg. Energy: 1.62 kJ (0.39 kcal). Sodium: <1 mmol (<0.26 mg). Gluten-, lactose- and tartrazine-free. Bottles of 100.

100 mg: Each white, round, biconvex tablet, scored and identified NU over T100 on one side, contains: trazodone HCl 100 mg. Energy: 3.23 kJ (0.77 kcal). Sodium: <1 mmol (<0.53 mg). Gluten-, lactose- and tartrazine-free. Bottles of 100.

Nu-Trazodone-D: 150 mg: Each pale orange, rectangular, flat-faced, beveled-edged tablet, bisected (grooved) on the edges and trisected (scored) on both sides, identified NU NU NU on one side and 50 50 50 on the other side, contains: trazodone HCl 150 mg. Energy: 4.85 kJ (1.16 kcal). Sodium: <1 mmol (<0.79 mg). Gluten-, lactose- and tartrazine-free. Bottles of 100.

Store at room temperature (15 to 30°C).

NU-TRIAZIDE ℞
Nu-Pharm

Triamterene—Hydrochlorothiazide

Diuretic—Antihypertensive

Supplied: Each yellow-orange, round, flat-faced, beveled-edged tablet, scored and identified NU over T on one side, contains: triamterene 50 mg and hydrochlorothiazide 25 mg. Energy: 3.69 kJ (0.88 kcal). Sodium: <1 mmol (1.52 mg). Gluten- and tartrazine-free. Bottles of 1 000.

NU-TRIMIPRAMINE ℞
Nu-Pharm

Trimipramine Maleate

Antidepressant

Supplied: 12.5 mg: Each pink, round, biconvex, film-coated tablet, contains: trimipramine maleate equivalent to trimipramine 12.5 mg. Energy: <1 kJ (0.03 kcal). Sodium: <1 mmol (<0.01 mg). Gluten-, lactose- and tartrazine-free. Bottles of 100.

25 mg: Each pink, round, biconvex, film-coated tablet, identified 25 on one side, contains: trimipramine maleate equivalent to trimipramine 25 mg. Energy: <1 kJ (0.05 kcal). Sodium: <1 mmol (0.02 mg). Gluten-, lactose- and tartrazine-free. Bottles of 100.

50 mg: Each pink, round, biconvex, film-coated tablet, identified NU over 50 on one side, contains: trimipramine maleate equivalent to trimipramine 50 mg. Energy: <1 kJ (0.1 kcal). Sodium: <1 mmol (0.04 mg). Gluten-, lactose- and tartrazine-free. Bottles of 100 and 500.

100 mg: Each pink, round, biconvex, film-coated tablet, scored and identified NU over 100 on one side, contains: trimipramine maleate equivalent to trimipramine 100 mg. Energy: <1 kJ (0.21 kcal). Sodium: <1 mmol (0.07 mg). Gluten-, lactose- and tartrazine-free. Bottles of 100 and 500.

NUTRINEAL™ PD4
Baxter

Amino Acids—Electrolytes

Peritoneal Dialysis Solution

Supplied: Nutrineal PD4 contains: 1.1 g of amino acids per 100 mL (or 11 g/L), approximately 170 mg total nitrogen per 100 mL, and is formulated at a pH of 6.6. Nutrineal PD4 is for intraperitoneal administration only and contains no bacteriostatic or antimicrobial agents. Each 100 mL of Nutrineal PD4 contains:

Total Amino Acids 1.1 g; total nitrogen (approximately) 170 mg; pH 6.6 (5.7 to 6.8) (pH adjusted with hydrochloric acid).

Essential Amino Acids: valine 139.3 mg; leucine 102 mg; isoleucine 85 mg; methionine 85 mg; lysine (added as lysine HCl) 95.5 mg; histidine 71.4 mg; threonine 64.6 mg; phenylalanine 57 mg and tryptophan 27 mg.

Nonessential Amino Acids: arginine 107.1 mg; alanine 95.1 mg; proline 59.5 mg; glycine 51 mg; serine 51 mg and tyrosine 30 mg.

Electrolytes: sodium chloride 538 mg; sodium lactate 448 mg; calcium chloride dihydrate 18.4 mg; magnesium chloride hexahydrate 5.1 mg and water for injection qs.

Concentration of ions: calcium 1.25 mmol/L, chloride 105 mmol/L, lactate 40 mmol/L, magnesium 0.25 mmol/L and sodium 132 mmol/L. Calculated osmolarity: approx. 365 mOsm/L.

TWIN BAG containers of 2 000 and 2 500 mL. Protect from light until ready to use. Exposure of pharmaceutical products to heat should be minimized. It is recommended the product be stored at room temperature (15 to 30°C). Do not remove from carton until ready to use. The plastic TWIN BAG solution container system is fabricated from polyvinyl chloride (PL146 Plastic). Exposure to temperatures above 30°C during transport and storage will lead to minor losses in moisture content. Higher temperatures lead to greater losses. It is unlikely that these minor losses will lead to clinically significant changes within the expiration period. The amount of water that can permeate from inside the solution container into the overpouch is insufficient to affect the solution significantly. Solutions in contact with the plastic container may leach out certain chemical components from the plastic in very small amounts; however, biological testing was supportive of the safety of the plastic container materials.

NUTRISOURCE®
Novartis Nutrition

Therapeutic Nutrient

Indications: A standard, fibre containing tube feeding (nasogastric, nasoduodenal or jejunal) for patients with normal gastrointestinal function.

Nutrisource (cont'd)

Recommended for both short-term and long-term tube feeding.

Not recommended when a low residue tube feeding is required.

Precautions: Not for parenteral administration.

Dosage: 6 cans [1 500 mL or 7 520 kJ (1 800 kcal)] provides at least 100% of the Canadian RNI (adult males, 25 to 49) for protein and essential vitamins and minerals.

Ready-to-use: Feed at room temperature. Follow a physician's or dietitian's directions. When initiating feedings, the flow rate, volume and dilution are dependent on the patient's condition and tolerance. Care should be taken to avoid contamination of the product during preparation and administration. Additional fluid requirements should be met by giving water orally with or after feedings or when flushing the feeding tube.

Feeding should be initiated at a slow rate. Rate and volume of feeding can be increased gradually over 48 hours if well tolerated. If intolerance develops, return to previously tolerated rate, or dilute formula to half strength until desired rate is achieved, then switch to full strength. Do not alter strength and volume at the same time. Rinse the tube with 20 to 30 mL water after each intermittent feeding or every 3 to 4 hours during continuous feeding to avoid clogging and provide additional water.

Supplied: Each 250 mL ready-to-use can contains: Ⓓ-D water, maltodextrin, corn syrup solids, sodium and calcium caseinates, modified coconut oil (medium chain triglycerides), canola oil, soy cotyledon, potassium citrate, sodium citrate, calcium phosphate tribasic, magnesium chloride, sodium ascorbate, polyglycerol esters of fatty acids, choline chloride, potassium chloride, molybdenum yeast, selenium yeast, *artificial flavor, chromium yeast, niacinamide, zinc sulfate, alpha tocopheryl acetate, ferrous sulfate, D-calcium pantothenate, copper gluconate, manganese sulfate, thiamine hydrochloride, pyridoxine hydrochloride, riboflavin, vitamin A palmitate, biotin, folic acid, potassium iodide, vitamin K_1, maltol, cyanocobalamin and vitamin D_3. See Table I.

*This ingredient does not appear in bottled products.

Energy Distribution: protein 14%, fat 30%, carbohydrate 56%; 500 kJ (120 kcal)/100 mL. Contains 2.5 g/250 mL of dietary fibre (from soy cotyledon).

Table I—Nutrisource

Analysis	100 mL	
Energy	500 (120)	kJ (kcal)
Protein	4.3	g
Carbohydrate	16.9	g
Fat	4.2	g
Linoleic Acid	0.4	g
Dietary Fibre	1.0	g
Sodium	113	mg
Potassium	180	mg
Vitamin A	333	IU
Vitamin C	20	mg
Thiamine	0.2	mg
Riboflavin	0.23	mg
Niacin	2.67	mg
Calcium	66.8	mg
Iron	1.2	mg
Vitamin D	26.7	IU
Vitamin E	3.0	IU
Vitamin B_6	0.27	mg
Folic Acid	0.027	mg
Vitamin B_{12}	0.0008	mg
Phosphorus	66.8	mg
Iodine	0.013	mg
Magnesium	26.7	mg
Zinc	1.67	mg
Copper	0.13	mg
Biotin	0.04	mg
Pantothenic Acid	1.33	mg
Vitamin K	0.006	mg
Choline	33.3	mg
Chloride	113	mg
Manganese	0.33	mg
Selenium	0.01	mg
Chromium	0.01	mg
Molybdenum	0.02	mg
Osmolality	390	mOsm/kg water

Cans of 250 mL, cases of 24. Store unopened at room temperature. Once opened, store covered in refrigerator and use within 24 hours.

NUTRISOURCE® HN

Novartis Nutrition

Therapeutic Nutrient

Indications: A high nitrogen, complete fibre containing tube feeding (nasogastric, nasoduodenal or jejunal) for patients with normal gastrointestinal function.

Recommended for both short-term and long-term tube feeding.

Not recommended when a low residue tube feeding is required.

Precautions: Not for parenteral administration.

Dosage: 6 cans [1 500 mL or 7 520 kJ (1 800 kcal)] provides at least 100% of the Canadian RNI (adult males, 25 to 49) for protein and essential vitamins and minerals.

Ready-to-use: Feed at room temperature. Follow a physician's or dietitian's directions. When initiating feedings, the flow rate, volume and dilution are dependent on the patient's condition and tolerance. Care should be taken to avoid contamination of the product during preparation and administration. Additional fluid requirements should be met by giving water orally with or after feedings or when flushing the feeding tube.

Feeding should be initiated at a slow rate. Rate and volume of feeding can be increased gradually over 48 hours if well tolerated. If intolerance develops, return to previously tolerated rate, or dilute formula to half strength until desired rate is achieved, then switch to full strength. Do not alter strength and volume at the same time. Rinse the tube with 20 to 30 mL water after each intermittent feeding or every 3 to 4 hours during continuous feeding to avoid clogging and provide additional water.

Supplied: Each 250 mL ready-to-use can or 1 000 mL closed system bottle contains: Ⓓ-D water, maltodextrin, corn syrup solids, sodium and calcium caseinates, modified coconut oil (medium chain triglycerides) canola oil, soy cotyledon, potassium citrate, calcium phosphate tribasic, sodium citrate, magnesium chloride, sodium ascorbate, polyglycerol esters of fatty acids, choline chloride, potassium chloride, molybdenum yeast, selenium yeast, *artificial flavor, chromium yeast, niacinamide, zinc sulfate, alpha tocopheryl acetate, ferrous sulfate, d-calcium pantothenate, copper gluconate, manganese sulfate, thiamine hydrochloride, pyridoxine hydrochloride, riboflavin, vitamin A palmitate, biotin, folic acid, potassium iodide, vitamin K_1, maltol, cyanocobalamin and vitamin D_3. See Table I.

*This ingredient does not appear in bottled products.

Table I—Nutrisource HN

Analysis	100 mL	
Energy	500 (120)	kJ (kcal)
Protein	5.3	g
Carbohydrate	15.9	g
Fat	4.2	g
Linoleic Acid	0.4	g
Dietary Fibre	0.67	g
Sodium	113	mg
Potassium	180	mg
Vitamin A	333	IU
Vitamin C	20	mg
Thiamine	0.2	mg
Riboflavin	0.23	mg
Niacin	2.67	mg
Calcium	66.8	mg
Iron	1.2	mg
Vitamin D	26.7	IU
Vitamin E	3.0	IU
Vitamin B_6	0.27	mg
Folic Acid	0.027	mg
Vitamin B_{12}	0.0008	mg
Phosphorus	66.8	mg
Iodine	0.013	mg
Magnesium	26.7	mg
Zinc	1.67	mg
Copper	0.13	mg
Biotin	0.04	mg
Pantothenic Acid	1.33	mg
Vitamin K	0.006	mg
Choline	33.3	mg
Chloride	113	mg
Manganese	0.33	mg
Selenium	0.01	mg
Chromium	0.01	mg
Molybdenum	0.02	mg
Osmolality	390	mOsm/kg water

Energy Distribution: protein 18%, fat 30%, carbohydrate 52%; 500 kJ (120 kcal)/100 mL. Contains 1.7 g/250 mL of dietary fibre (from soy cotyledon).

Cans of 250 mL, cases of 24. Closed system bottles of 1 L, cases of 6. Store unopened at room temperature. Once opened, store covered in refrigerator and use within 24 hours.

NUTROPIN® Ⓟ
NUTROPIN® AQ Ⓟ

Roche

Somatropin

Growth Hormone

Pharmacology: General: Somatropin is a human growth hormone (hGH) produced by recombinant DNA technology. The amino acid sequence of the somatropin protein is identical to that of pituitary-derived human growth hormone. In vitro and in vivo preclinical testing, and clinical testing have demonstrated that somatropin is therapeutically equivalent to pituitary-derived human growth hormone in pharmacokinetics, in stimulation of linear growth and in other actions.

Treatment of children who lack adequate secretion of endogenous growth hormone with somatropin results in an increase in growth rate and an increase in insulin-like growth factor-I, similar to that seen with pituitary-derived human growth hormone.

Somatropin treatment of children with chronic renal insufficiency results in improved growth rate and height standard deviation and an overall increase in cumulative growth, as compared to placebo-treated children with chronic renal insufficiency.

Actions that have been demonstrated for somatropin, somatrem (methionyl human growth hormone), and/or pituitary-derived human growth hormone include:

Tissue Growth: Skeletal Growth: Somatropin stimulates skeletal growth in children with growth failure due to a lack of adequate secretion of endogenous growth hormone and in children with growth failure secondary to chronic renal insufficiency. Skeletal growth is accomplished at the epiphyseal plates at the ends of a growing long bone. Growth and metabolism of epiphyseal plate cells are directly stimulated by growth hormone and one of its mediators, insulin-like growth factor-I. Serum levels of insulin-like growth factor-I are low in children and adolescents who are growth hormone deficient, but increase during treatment with somatropin. New bone is formed at the epiphyses in response to growth hormone. This results in linear growth until these growth plates fuse at the end of puberty.

The clinical effect of the skeletal growth action of somatropin has been observed in well-controlled clinical trials with somatropin in the treatment of growth hormone inadequacy and chronic renal insuffiency patients. Limited data regarding the clinical post-transplant growth effect of somatropin treatment administered prior to transplant is available.

Cell Growth: Treatment with pituitary-derived human growth hormone results in an increase in both the number and the size of skeletal muscle cells.

Organ Growth: Growth hormone of human pituitary origin influences the size of internal organs, including kidneys, and increases red cell mass. Treatment of hypophysectomized or genetic dwarf rats with somatropin results in organ growth that is proportional to the overall body growth. In normal rats subjected to nephrectomy-induced uremia, somatropin promoted skeletal and body growth.

Protein Metabolism: Linear growth is facilitated in part by growth hormone-stimulated protein synthesis. This is reflected by nitrogen retention as demonstrated by a decline in urinary nitrogen excretion and blood urea nitrogen (BUN) concentration during growth hormone therapy.

Carbohydrate Metabolism: Growth hormone is a modulator of carbohydrate metabolism. For example, children with inadequate secretion of growth hormone sometimes experience fasting hypoglycemia which is improved by treatment with growth hormone. Growth hormone therapy may decrease glucose tolerance. Administration of somatropin to normal adults, patients who lack adequate secretion of endogenous growth hormone and patients with chronic renal insufficiency resulted in increases in mean serum fasting and postprandial insulin levels. However, mean fasting and postprandial glucose levels and mean hemoglobin A_{1C} levels remained within the normal range. There were no clinically significant persistent abnormalities in any of these measurements of glucose regulation that were related to growth hormone treatment.

Lipid Metabolism: Acute administration of pituitary-derived human growth hormone to humans results in lipid mobilization. Nonesterified fatty acids increase in plasma within 2 hours of pituitary-derived human growth hormone administration. In growth hormone deficient patients, long-term growth hormone administration often decreases body fat. Mean cholesterol levels decreased in patients treated with somatropin.

Mineral Metabolism: The retention of total body potassium in response to growth hormone administration is thought to result from cellular growth. Serum levels of inorganic phosphorus may increase slightly in patients with inadequate secretion of endogenous growth hormone or chronic renal insufficiency after growth hormone therapy due to the metabolic activity associated with bone growth as well as increased tubular reabsorption of phosphate by the kidney. Serum calcium is not significantly altered in these patients. Sodium retention also occurs (see Precautions, Laboratory Tests).

Connective Tissue Metabolism: Growth hormone stimulates the synthesis of chondroitin sulfate and collagen as well as the urinary excretion of hydroxyproline.

Pharmacokinetics: The pharmacokinetics of Nutropin (somatropin lyophilized powder) have been investigated in healthy men after the s.c. administration of 0.1 mg/kg. A mean peak concentration (C_{max}) of 56.1 ng/mL occurred at a mean time of 7.5 hours. The extent of absorption of somatropin, assessed by area under the concentration vs time curve (AUC), was 626 ng·hr/mL and compares with that of somatrem (590 ng·hr/mL). The AUC of somatropin is similar regardless of site of injection.

After s.c. injection of 0.1 mg/kg Nutropin AQ (somatropin injection), a mean peak concentration (C_{max}) of 71.1 ng/mL occurred at a mean time of 3.9 hours. The extent of absorption of Nutropin AQ (AUC) was 673 ng·h/mL and was comparable with that of Nutropin lyophilized powder. Nutropin AQ was bioequivalent to Nutropin lyophilized powder after s.c. administration based on the statistical evaluation of the ratios of the geometric mean of log transformed AUC and C_{max}.

In both normal and growth hormone deficient (GHD) adults and children, the i.m. and s.c. pharmacokinetic profiles of somatropin are similar regardless of growth hormone or dosing regimen used.

Distribution: Growth hormone localizes to highly perfused organs, particularly the liver and kidney. The volume of distribution at steady-state for rhGH in healthy adult males is about 50 mL/kg, approximating the serum volume.

Metabolism: Both the liver and kidney have been shown to be important metabolizing organs for pituitary-derived human growth hormone.

Elimination: Clearance of rhGH after i.v. administration in healthy adults and children is reported to be in the range of 116 to 174 mL/h/kg.

Special Populations: Children: Available literature data suggests that rhGH clearances are similar in adults and children.

Gender: No data is available for rhGH. Available data for methionyl human growth hormone and pituitary-derived human growth hormone suggests that there are no consistent gender-based differences in rhGH clearance.

Race: No data is available.

Growth Hormone Insufficiency (GHI): Reported values for clearance of rhGH in adults and children with GHI range from 138 to 245 mL/h/kg and are similar to those observed in healthy adults and children. Mean terminal $t_{1/2}$ values following i.v. and s.c. administration in GHI patients are also similar to those observed in healthy adult males.

Renal Insufficiency: Children and adults with chronic renal failure (CRF) tend to have decreased clearance as compared to normals. However, no rhGH accumulation has been reported in children with CRF or end-stage renal disease dosed with current regimens.

Hepatic Insufficiency: A reduction in rhGH clearance has been noted in patients with severe liver dysfunction. The clinical significance of this decrease is unknown.

Indications: For the long-term treatment of children who have growth failure due to growth hormone inadequacy.

Somatropin is also indicated for the treatment of children who have growth failure associated with chronic renal insufficiency up to the time of renal transplantation. Somatropin therapy should be used in conjunction with optimal management of chronic renal insufficiency.

Contraindications: Somatropin should not be used in subjects with closed epiphyses.

Somatropin should not be used in patients with active neoplasia. Growth hormone therapy should be discontinued if evidence of neoplasia develops.

Nutropin (somatropin lyophilized powder), when reconstituted with Bacteriostatic Water for Injection, USP (benzyl alcohol preserved), should not be used in newborns or in patients with a known sensitivity to benzyl alcohol (see Warnings).

Warnings: Benzyl alcohol as a preservative in Bacteriostatic Water for Injection, USP has been associated with toxicity in newborns. When administering Nutropin (somatropin lyophilized powder) in newborns or in patients sensitive to benzyl alcohol, reconstitute with Sterile Water for Injection, USP. When Sterile Water for Injection, USP is used, **use only one Nutropin dose per vial and discard the unused portion.**

Precautions: General: Somatropin should be prescribed by physicians experienced in the diagnosis and management of patients with growth failure or chronic renal insufficiency (CRI). No studies have been performed with somatropin in children who have received renal transplants.

Because somatropin may induce a state of **insulin resistance,** patients should be observed for evidence of glucose intolerance.

Patients with a history of an **intracranial lesion** should be examined frequently for progression or recurrence of the lesion.

Intracranial hypertension (IH) with papilledema, visual changes, headache, nausea and/or vomiting has been reported in a small number of patients treated with growth hormone products. Symptoms usually occurred within the first 8 weeks of the initiation of the growth hormone therapy. In all reported cases, IH-associated signs and symptoms resolved after termination of therapy or a reduction of the growth hormone dose. Funduscopic examination of patients is recommended at the initiation and periodically during the course of growth hormone therapy.

Patients with growth failure secondary to chronic renal insufficiency should be examined periodically for evidence of progression of renal **osteodystrophy.** Slipped capital femoral epiphysis or avascular necrosis of the femoral head may be seen in children with advanced renal osteodystrophy, and it is uncertain whether these problems are affected by growth hormone therapy. X-rays of the hips should be obtained prior to initiating therapy for CRI patients.

Slipped capital femoral epiphysis may also occur more frequently in patients with endocrine disorders or in patients undergoing rapid growth. Therefore, physicians and parents should be alert to the development of a limp or complaints of hip or knee pain in both GHI and CRI patients treated with somatropin.

Progression of **scoliosis** can occur in children who experience rapid growth. Because growth hormone increases growth rate, patients with a history of scoliosis who are treated with growth hormone should be monitored for progression of scoliosis. Growth hormone has not been shown to increase the incidence of scoliosis.

Local or systemic **allergic reactions** may occur. Parents/patients should be informed that such reactions are possible and that prompt medical attention should be sought if allergic reactions occur.

Laboratory Tests: Serum levels of **inorganic phosphorous, alkaline phosphatase,** and **parathyroid hormone** may increase with somatropin therapy. Changes in **thyroid hormone** laboratory measurements may develop during growth hormone treatment of children who lack adequate endogenous growth hormone secretion. As untreated hypothyroidism prevents optimal response to somatropin, patients should have periodic thyroid function tests and should be treated with thyroid hormone when indicated.

<u>*Drug Interactions:*</u> Concomitant glucocorticoid therapy may inhibit the growth promoting effect of somatropin. If glucocorticoid replacement is required, the glucocorticoid dose should be carefully adjusted. The use of somatropin in patients with CRI receiving glucocorticoid therapy has not been evaluated.

There was no evidence in the controlled studies of somatropin's interaction with drugs commonly used in patients. However, formal drug interaction studies have not been conducted.

Children: Prudence is indicated for children aged 0 months to 3 years, when administering Nutropin (somatropin lyophilized powder) reconstituted in Bacteriostatic Water for Injection, USP (benzyl alcohol preserved); although there is no information on the toxicity of benzyl alcohol for this age group, the toxic dose for premature neonates is in the range of 100 to 250 mg/kg/day.

Pregnancy: Reproduction studies have not been conducted with somatropin. It is also not known whether somatropin can cause fetal harm when administered to a pregnant woman or can affect reproductive capacity. Somatropin should be given to a pregnant woman only if clearly needed.

Lactation: It is not known whether somatropin is excreted in human milk. Because many drugs are excreted in human milk, caution should be exercised when somatropin is administered to a nursing mother.

Carcinogenicity and Mutagenicity: Carcinogenicity and mutagenicity studies have not been conducted with somatropin. Patients developing neoplasia should be reported to the Health Protection Branch (HPB) by the treating physician.

Information for the Patient/Parent: Patients who are being treated with growth hormone and/or their parents should be informed regarding the potential benefits and risks associated with treatment. If home use is determined to be desirable by the physician, instructions on appropriate use should be given, including a review of the contents of the "Information for the Patient/Parent" insert. This information is intended to aid in the safe and effective administration of the medication. It is not a disclosure of all possible adverse or unintended effects.

If home use is prescribed, a puncture resistant container for the disposal of used syringes and needles should be recommended to the patient. Patients and/or parents should be thoroughly instructed in the importance of proper disposal and cautioned against any reuse of needles and syringes (see Information for the Patient in Blue Section).

Adverse Effects: A small percentage of patients may develop antibodies to the growth hormone protein. Growth hormone antibody binding capacities below 2 mg/L have not been associated with growth attenuation. In some cases when binding capacity exceeds 2 mg/L during growth hormone treatment, growth attenuation has been observed.

In clinical studies of patients treated with Nutropin (somatropin lyophilized powder) for the first time, 0/107 GHI patients and 0/125 CRI patients screened for antibody production developed antibodies with binding capacities >2 mg/L at 6 months.

In a clinical study of naive patients who were treated with Nutropin AQ (somatropin injection), 0/60 GHD patients who were screened for development of antibodies throughout 15 months of treatment, developed antibodies with binding capacities above 2 mg/L.

Short-term immunologic and renal function studies were carried out in a group of patients with chronic renal insufficiency after approximately 1 year of growth hormone treatment to detect potential adverse effects of antibodies to growth hormone. Testing included measurements of Clq, C3, C4, rheumatoid factor, creatinine, creatinine clearance and BUN. No adverse effects of growth hormone antibodies were noted.

In addition to an evaluation of compliance with the treatment program and thyroid status, testing for antibodies to human growth hormone should be carried out in any patient who fails to respond to therapy.

Leukemia has been reported in a small number of growth hormone deficient patients treated with growth hormone. It is uncertain whether this increased risk is related to the pathology of growth hormone deficiency itself, growth hormone therapy or other associated treatments, such as radiation therapy for intracranial tumors. On the basis of current evidence, experts cannot conclude that growth hormone therapy is responsible for these occurrences. The risk to GHI and CRI patients, if any, remains to be established.

In studies of children treated with somatropin, injection site pain was reported infrequently.

Adverse drug reactions which have been reported infrequently (<1%) in growth hormone-treated patients include mild and transient peripheral edema.

Other rare (<0.1%) adverse drug reactions reported in growth hormone-treated patients include the following:

Musculoskeletal: carpal tunnel syndrome.

Skin: increased growth of pre-existing nevi (malignant nevi transformation has not been reported).

Endocrine: gynecomastia and pancreatitis.

Overdose: Symptoms and Treatment: Theoretical risks of long-term human growth hormone treatment with doses exceeding the recommended dosage are signs and symptoms of gigantism and/or acromegaly.

Dosage: Somatropin dosage and administration schedule should be individualized for each patient.

Growth Hormone Inadequacy: A somatropin dose of up to 0.3 mg/kg/week (approximately 0.9 IU/kg/week) administered in divided daily doses by s.c. or i.m. injection is recommended.

The total number of mg per daily dose is calculated as follows: Dose (mg) per injection=Patient weight (kg)×up to 0.043 (mg/kg).

Therapy should not be continued if final height is achieved or epiphyseal fusion occurs. Patients who fail to respond adequately while on somatropin therapy should be evaluated to determine the cause of unresponsiveness.

Nutropin (cont'd)

Chronic Renal Insufficiency: A somatropin dose of up to 0.35 mg/kg/week (approximately 1.05 IU/kg/week) administered in divided daily doses by s.c. or i.m. injection is recommended.

The total number of mg per daily dose is calculated as follows: Dose (mg) per injection=Patient weight (kg)×up to 0.05 (mg/kg).

Therapy may be continued up to the time of renal transplantation. Therapy should not be continued if final height is achieved or epiphyseal fusion occurs. Patients who fail to respond adequately while on somatropin therapy should be evaluated to determine the cause of unresponsiveness.

In order to optimize therapy for CRI patients who require dialysis, the following guidelines for selecting the injection schedule are recommended: 1. Hemodialysis patients should receive their injection at night just prior to going to sleep or at least 3 to 4 hours after their hemodialysis to prevent hematoma formation due to the heparin. 2. Chronic Cycling Peritoneal Dialysis patients should receive their injection in the morning after they have completed dialysis. 3. Chronic Ambulatory Peritoneal Dialysis patients should receive their injection in the evening at the time of the overnight exchange.

Reconstitution of Lyophilized Powder: A 5 mg vial of Nutropin lyophilized powder should be reconstituted with 1 to 5 mL of Bacteriostatic Water for Injection, USP (benzyl alcohol preserved). (Vials are reconstituted to a concentration of 1 mg somatropin/mL with 5 mL of the water.)

A 10 mg vial of Nutropin lyophilized powder should be reconstituted with 1 to 10 mL of Bacteriostatic Water for Injection, USP (benzyl alcohol preserved). (Vials are reconstituted to a concentration of 1 mg somatropin/mL with 10 mL of the water.)

When Nutropin lyophilized powder is reconstituted to 1 mg somatropin/mL, the recommended daily dose of 0.05 mg/kg for treatment of chronic renal insufficiency contains 0.45 mg/kg benzyl alcohol while the recommended daily somatropin dose of 0.043 mg/kg for treatment of growth hormone deficiency contains 0.387 mg/kg benzyl alcohol.

See Warnings for reconstitution of Nutropin lyophilized powder for **use in newborns** and persons sensitive to benzyl alcohol, and see Precautions for use in children aged 6 months to 3 years.

To prepare the Nutropin solution, slowly inject the Bacteriostatic Water for Injection, USP into the vial, aiming the stream of liquid against the glass wall of the vial. Then swirl the vial with a **gentle** rotary motion until the contents are completely dissolved. **Do not shake.** Because somatropin is a protein, shaking can result in a cloudy solution. After reconstitution, the solution should be clear, i.e., it should not have any solid particles floating on the surface. If you notice lumps or solid particles of powder, continue to gently swirl the solution until all of the powder has dissolved. If the solution does not become clear, **do not** inject it. Note also that occasionally, after refrigeration, small colorless particles of protein may be present in the solution. This is not unusual for solutions containing proteins. Allow the vial to come to room temperature and gently swirl until the solution is clear. If the solution remains cloudy or hazy, **do not** inject it.

Nutropin AQ: The vials contain a solution ready for injection. No reconstitution or preparation is required.

Injection: Before needle insertion, wipe the septum of all vials to be used, both the somatropin and diluent vials, with rubbing alcohol or an antiseptic solution to prevent contamination of the contents by microorganisms that may be introduced by repeated needle insertions. Somatropin must be administered using sterile, disposable syringes and needles. The syringes should be of small enough volume that the prescribed dose can be drawn from the vial with reasonable accuracy. If the route of injection selected is i.m., the needle should be of sufficient length (usually 2.5 cm or more) to ensure that the injection reaches the muscular layer. The site of injection should be rotated each time somatropin is administered.

Stability and Storage: Before Reconstitution: Nutropin lyophilized powder and Bacteriostatic Water for Injection, USP (benzyl alcohol preserved) must be refrigerated at 2 to 8°C. **Avoid freezing the vials of Nutropin and Bacteriostatic Water for Injection, USP (benzyl alcohol preserved).** Expiration dates are stated on the labels.

After Reconstitution: Vial contents are stable for 14 days when reconstituted with Bacteriostatic Water for Injection, USP (benzyl alcohol preserved) and refrigerated at 2 to 8°C. Discard the unused portion after 14 days. **Do not freeze the reconstituted vial of Nutropin.**

The remaining Bacteriostatic Water for Injection, USP in the multiple use vial must be refrigerated at 2 to 8°C, and may be used for 14 days after first entry. **Avoid freezing the Bacteriostatic Water for Injection, USP (benzyl alcohol preserved).**

Unusual Handling Conditions: Vials of unreconstituted Nutropin lyophilized powder may be held at ambient temperature (not to exceed 37°C) for a total time not to exceed 7 days. Vials of reconstituted lyophilized powder should not be exposed to temperatures greater than 25°C for more than 24 hours in total.

Nutropin AQ: **Store under refrigeration at 2 to 8°C. Do not freeze.**

Information for the Patient: See Blue Section—Information for the Patient "Nutropin/Nutropin AQ".

Supplied: Nutropin: 5 mg: Each vial of sterile, white, lyophilized powder contains: somatropin 5 mg (approximately 15 IU). Nonmedicinal ingredients: glycine, mannitol, sodium phosphate dibasic and sodium phosphate monobasic; diluent contains: bacteriostatic water for injection and benzyl alcohol. After reconstitution, the resultant solution is nearly isotonic at a concentration of 5 mg growth hormone/mL and has a pH of approximately 7.4. Cartons of 6 Nutropin vials and one 10 mL multiple use diluent vial.

10 mg: Each vial of sterile, white, lyophilized powder contains: somatropin 10 mg (approximately 30 IU). Nonmedicinal ingredients: glycine, mannitol, sodium phosphate dibasic and sodium phosphate monobasic; diluent contains: bacteriostatic water for injection and benzyl alcohol. After reconstitution, the resultant solution is nearly isotonic at a concentration of 5 mg growth hormone/mL and has a pH of approximately 7.4. Cartons of 2 Nutropin vials and two 10 mL multiple use diluent vials.

Nutropin AQ: Each mL of clear, sterile, nearly isotonic solution contains: somatropin 5 mg. Nonmedicinal ingredients: phenol, polysorbate 20, sodium chloride and sodium citrate. The solution has a pH of approximately 6. Vials of 2 mL (10 mg, approximately 30 IU).

Reviewed 1998

NU-VERAP ℗
Nu-Pharm

Verapamil HCl

Antianginal—Antiarrhythmic—Antihypertensive

Supplied: 80 mg: Each yellow, round, biconvex, film-coated tablet, identified NU over 80 on one side, contains: verapamil HCl 80 mg. Energy: 3.07 kJ (0.73 kcal). Sodium: <1 mmol (0.19 mg). Gluten- and tartrazine-free. Bottles of 100 and 500.

120 mg: Each white, round, biconvex, film-coated tablet, identified NU over 120 on one side, contains: verapamil HCl 120 mg. Energy: 4.59 kJ (1.1 kcal). Sodium: <1 mmol (0.29 mg). Gluten- and tartrazine-free. Bottles of 100.

NU-ZOPICLONE ℗
Nu-Pharm

Zopiclone

Hypnotic

Supplied: Each blue, oval, biconvex, film-coated tablet, identified NU over 7.5 on one side, contains: zopiclone 7.5 mg. Gluten-, sodium- and tartrazine-free. Bottles of 100 and 500. Store at room temperature (15 to 30°C). Protect from light.

New Product 1998

NYADERM
Taro

Nystatin

Antifungal—Antibiotic

Supplied: Oral Suspension ℞: Each mL of pale yellow, cherry-mint flavored suspension contains: nystatin 100 000 USP units. Nonmedicinal ingredients: aluminum hydroxide gel, ethanol, glycerin, propylene glycol, purified water, sorbitol solution, sucrose, sodium cyclamate and methylparaben and propylparaben as preservatives. May contain sodium hydroxide or citric acid to adjust pH. Tartrazine-free. Bottles of 24 and 48 mL with a calibrated dropper and bottles of 500 mL.

Topical Cream: Each g of aqueous, perfumed vanishing cream base contains: nystatin USP 100 000 units. Nonmedicinal ingredients: aluminum hydroxide concentrated wet gel, glyceryl monostearate, methylparaben, polyethylene glycol-400 monostearate, polyoxyethylene fatty alcohol ether, propylene glycol, propylparaben, simethicone emulsion, sodium hydroxide, sorbitol solution, titanium dioxide and white petrolatum. Tubes of 15 and 30 g and jars of 454 g.

Topical Ointment: Each g contains: nystatin USP 100 000 units in a soft ointment base of petrolatum with fractionated coconut oil, methylparaben and propylparaben. Tubes of 15 and 30 g and jars of 400 g.

Vaginal Cream ℞: Each g contains: nystatin USP 25 000 units. Nonmedicinal ingredients: aluminum hydroxide gel, methylparaben, polyoxyethylene fatty acid ether, propylene glycol, propylparaben and white petrolatum. Sodium hydroxide and hydrochloric acid to adjust the pH. Tubes of 120 g with applicator designed to deliver a 4 g dose (100 000 units).

NYTOL™
NYTOL™ Extra Strength
Block Drug

Diphenhydramine HCl

Sleep Aid

Pharmacology: The primary action of diphenhydramine is the antagonism of certain effects of histamine such as bronchoconstriction and capillary dilation.

The most frequently encountered secondary effects of diphenhydramine are related to CNS depression. The effects vary from slight drowsiness to deep sleep and have been reported to include the inability to concentrate, lassitude, dizziness, muscular weakness and in-coordination. However, the sedative action of diphenhydramine has been found to be of value for occasional use in the relief of nighttime sleeplessness due to fatigue, over-work or tiredness. The sedative action may last up to 6 hours but often diminishes after a few days as tolerance to this effect develops.

Other actions of diphenhydramine include an antiemetic effect and some anticholinergic activity which can produce blurred vision, dry mouth, and gastrointestinal disturbances (e.g., nausea, vomiting, epigastric pain, diarrhea).

Indications: For the relief of occasional sleeplessness due to fatigue, overwork or tiredness. The use of diphenhydramine, for more than a few consecutive nights at a time is not recommended and more appropriate therapy should be considered in cases of severe and/or chronic insomnia. If pain or other factors appear to be the cause of sleeplessness, sleep-aids should not be considered as primary therapeutic agents.

Contraindications: Patients who are hypersensitive to the drug and in those with the following conditions: asthmatic attack, glaucoma, chronic lung disease, prostatic hypertrophy, stenosing peptic ulcer, pyloroduodenal obstruction, or bladder-neck obstruction. Patients receiving MAO inhibitors should not be given diphenhydramine.

Warnings: Insomnia may be a symptom of serious illness. If it persists for more than 2 weeks the patient should be re-evaluated.

Pregnancy and *Lactation:* Diphenhydramine should not be given to women who are or who are likely to become pregnant, or who are nursing.

Children: Diphenhydramine is not recommended for children under 12 years of age.

Precautions: Diphenhydramine produces additive CNS effects when taken concomitantly with alcohol, hypnotics, anxiolytics, narcotic analgesics and neuroleptic drugs. Similarly significant interactions may occur if the drug is taken concomitantly with anticholinergic agents or tricyclic antidepressants.

Geriatrics: Diphenhydramine should not be used in elderly patients who experience confusion at nighttime. In addition it may produce excitation rather than sedation in the elderly and should therefore not be generally recommended for this age group.

Adverse Effects: The most frequently reported adverse reactions are dizziness, dryness of mouth, inability to concentrate, nausea, nervousness, muscular weakness and coordination.

Other less frequently reported effects are palpitation, blurring of vision, headache, restlessness, insomnia and thickening of bronchial secretions. The following effects may also occur: lassitude, excitement, diplopia, difficulty in urination, constipation, nasal stuffiness, vomiting, drug rash, urticaria, hypotension, photosensitivity, epigastric distress and tightness of the chest and wheezing.

Overdose: Symptoms and Treatment: When diphenhydramine is taken in large doses a toxic syndrome may result. Symptoms may be manifested as an exaggeration of the side effects listed above or may be more severe, but are particularly serious for children. In young children the syndrome may include hallucinations, excitement, ataxia, incoordination, athetosis and convulsions. The convulsions are intermittent, tonic-clonic type and difficult to control. Fixed, dilated pupils with a flushed face and fever are common and may be followed by cardio-respiratory depression and death. The latent period is characteristically short, only mild signs of CNS depression may be observed before the onset of convulsions. In the adult CNS depression is more common. Hyperpyrexia, flushing and convulsions are much less frequently encountered, although excitation may follow depression in a cyclical manner.

There is no specific therapy for diphenhydramine overdose, thus treatment is along general supportive lines and directed towards specific symptoms. If the drug has been taken recently by mouth, and prior to evidence of CNS involvement, gastric lavage is indicated. The patient should be kept quiet to minimize excitation. Convulsions and marked CNS stimulation should be treated preferably with parenteral diazepam, particularly in children. Treatment should include correction of hypoxia, fluid and electrolyte imbalances. Assisted respiration may be necessary, and cooling if hyperpyrexia occurs. Forced diuresis is of little value since antihistamines are rapidly metabolized and only small amounts are recovered in the urine.

Dosage: Regular Strength: The recommended dose is 50 mg taken before retiring. In some individuals 50 mg may produce excessive sedation in which case 25 mg should be recommended.
Extra Strength: The recommended dose is 50 mg taken before retiring. In some individuals 50 mg may produce excessive sedation in which case 25 mg should be recommended.

Information for the Patient: See Blue Section—Information for the Patient ''Nytol/Nytol Extra Strength''.

Supplied: Caplets: Extra Strength: Each blue, coated caplet, imprinted with ''Nytol'' on one side, contains: diphenhydramine HCl 50 mg. Nonmedicinal ingredients: cornstarch, FD&C Blue #1 Aluminum Lake, hydroxypropylmethyl cellulose, lactose, microcrystalline cellulose, polyethylene glycol, polysorbate 80, silicon dioxide, stearic acid and titanium dioxide. Packages of 20.

Tablets: Extra Strength: Each blue, uncoated tablet, imprinted with a ''N'' on one side, contains: diphenhydramine HCl 50 mg. Nonmedicinal ingredients: cornstarch, FD&C Blue #1 Aluminum Lake, lactose, microcrystalline cellulose, silicon dioxide and stearic acid. Packages of 10 and 20.

Regular Strength: Each white, uncoated tablet, imprinted with a ''N'' on one side, contains: diphenhydramine HCl 25 mg. Nonmedicinal ingredients: cornstarch, lactose, microcrystalline cellulose, silicon dioxide and stearic acid. Packages of 20 and 40.

NYTOL™ NATURAL SOURCE

Block Drug

Valerian Root

Sleep Aid

Indications: For the relief of insomnia (restlessness, difficulty in falling asleep) due to overwork, tiredness or fatigue.

Precautions: Keep safely out of reach of children. For occasional use only. Do not use with alcoholic beverages. Insomnia may be a symptom of serious medical illness. Therefore, if sleeplessness persists for more than 2 weeks it is recommended that a physician be consulted.

Dosage: 1 to 2 caplets at bedtime.

Information for the Patient: See Blue Section—Information for the Patient ''Nytol Natural Source''.

Supplied: Each coated, easy to swallow caplet contains: valerian root powdered extract 100 mg (1:4), equivalent to valerian root 400 mg (Valeriana officinalis). Bottles of 20 and 50.

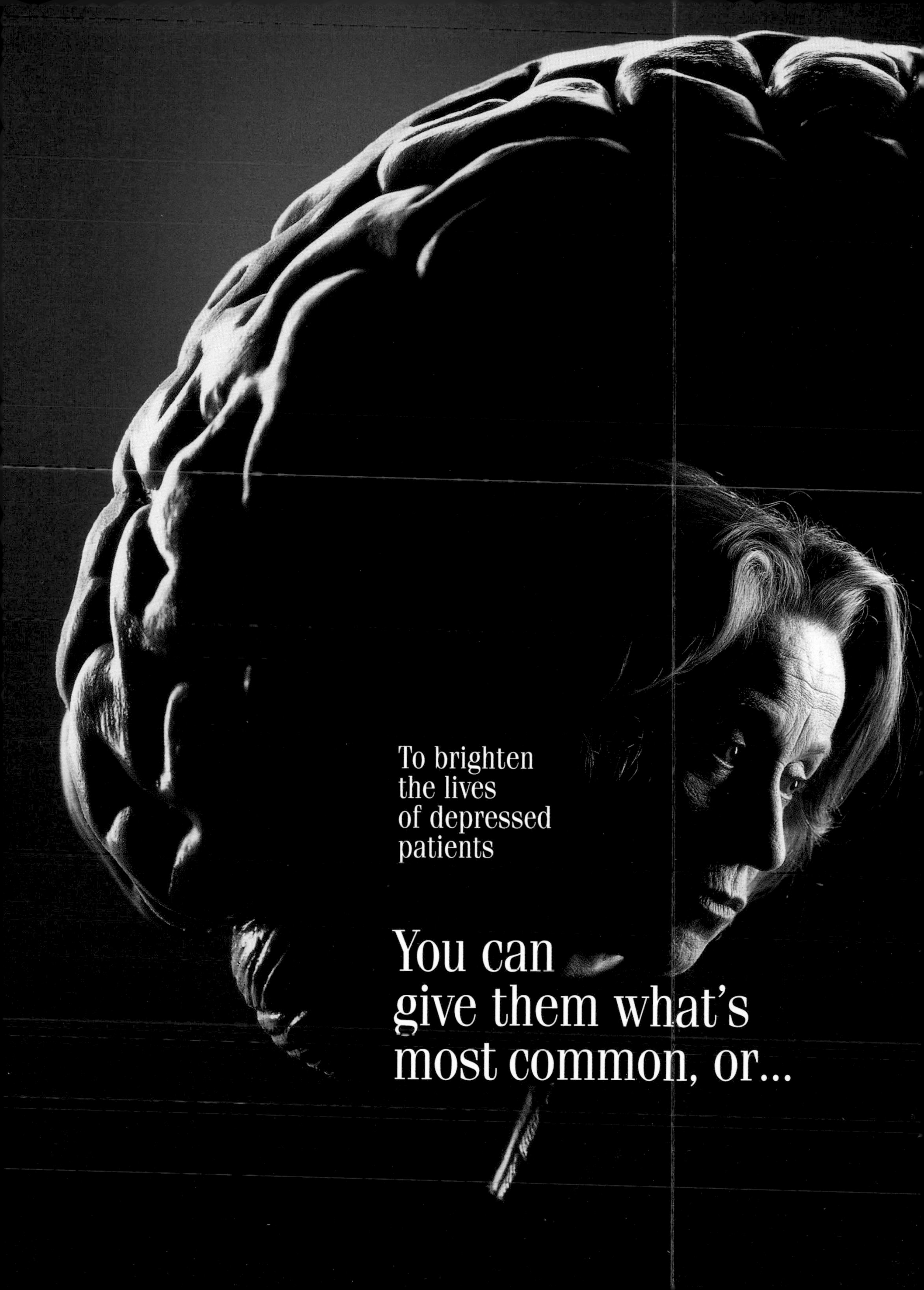
To brighten
the lives
of depressed
patients
You can
give them what's
most common, or...

...what may work best
WYETH-AYERST CANADA INC.
Montreal, Canada
MEMBER PMAC
PAAB
Product Monograph available on request

1. Clinical Study Report Tables Schizophrenia, F1D-MC-HGAJ. Data on file, Eli Lilly and Company, 1995; 2. Tollefson GD *et al.* Olanzapine Versus Haloperidol in the Treatment of Schizophrenia and Schizoaffective and Schizophreniform Disorders: Results of an International Collaborative Trial. *The American Journal of Psychiatry,* 1997; 154:457-465; 3. Tran PV *et al.* Double-Blind Comparison of Olanzapine Versus Risperidone in the Treatment of Schizophrenia and Other Psychotic Disorders. *J Clin Psychopharmacology* 1997; 17:407-418; 4. Dellva MA, Tran PV, Beasley CM, Cousins LM, Krueger JA, Tollefson GD. Clinical Experience with Long-Term Continuation Treatment with Olanzapine. X World Congress of Psychiatry (WPA), Madrid, Spain, August 23-28, 1996; 5. Crawford AMK *et al.* The acute and long-term effect of olanzapine compared with placebo and haloperidol on serum prolactin concentrations. *Schizophrenia Research* 26 (1997);41-54.

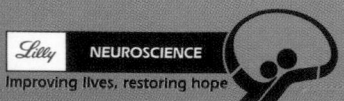

O

OCCLUSAL™
Medicis

Salicylic Acid

Verrucae Therapy

Pharmacology: Although the exact mode of action of salicylic acid in the treatment of warts is not known, its activity appears to be associated with its keratolytic action which results in mechanical removal of epidermal cells infected with wart viruses.

Indications: In the treatment and removal of common warts and plantar warts.

Contraindications: Occlusal should not be used by diabetics or patients with impaired blood circulation. It should not be used on moles, birthmarks, unusual warts with hair growing from them, or warts on the face.

Precautions: For external use only. Do not permit Occlusal to contact eyes or mucous membranes. If contact with eyes or mucous membranes occurs, immediately flush with water for 15 minutes. Salicylic acid should not be allowed to contact normal skin surrounding wart. Treatment should be discontinued if excessive irritation occurs. Occlusal is flammable and should be kept away from fire or flame. Keep bottle tightly capped when not in use.

Adverse Effects: A localized irritant reaction may occur if Occlusal is applied to the normal skin surrounding the wart. Any irritation may normally be controlled by temporarily discontinuing use, and by applying the medication only to the wart site when treatment is resumed.

Dosage: Prior to application, soak wart in warm water for 5 minutes. Remove any loosened tissue by gently rubbing with a brush, wash cloth, or emery board. Dry thoroughly. Using the brush applicator supplied, apply twice to affected area, allowing the first application to dry before applying the second. Treatment should be once a day and should continue as directed by physician. Be careful not to apply to surrounding skin.

Clinically visible improvement will normally occur during the first 2 to 4 weeks of therapy. Maximum resolution may be expected after 6 to 12 weeks of drug use.

Supplied: Each bottle contains: salicylic acid USP 17% in a polyacrylic vehicle of butyl acetate, ethylacetate, isopropyl alcohol 20%, toluene, nitrocellulose, dibutylphthalate, polyester, camphor, acrylates copolymer and benzophenone-1. Bottles of 15 mL with brush applicator.

OCCLUSAL™-HP
Medicis

Salicylic Acid

Verrucae Therapy

Pharmacology: Although the exact mode of action of salicylic acid in the treatment of warts is not known, it activity appears to be associated with its keratolytic action which results in mechanical removal of epidermal cells infected with wart viruses.

Indications: In the treatment and removal of common warts and plantar warts.

Contraindications: Occlusal-HP should not be used by diabetics or patients with impaired blood circulation. It should not be used on moles, birthmarks, unusual warts with hair growing from them, or warts on the face.

Precautions: For external use only. Do not permit Occlusal-HP to contact eyes or mucous membranes. If contact with eyes or mucous membranes occurs, immediately flush with water for 15 minutes. Salicylic acid should not be allowed to contact normal skin surrounding wart. Treatment should be discontinued if excessive irritation occurs. Occlusal-HP is flammable and should be kept away from fire or flame. Keep bottle tightly capped when not in use.

Adverse Effects: A localized irritant reaction may occur if Occlusal-HP is applied to the normal skin surrounding the wart. Any irritation may normally be controlled by temporarily discontinuing use and by applying the medication only to the wart site when treatment is resumed.

Dosage: Prior to application, soak wart in warm water for 5 minutes. Remove any loosened tissue by gently rubbing with a brush, wash cloth, or emery board. Dry thoroughly. Using the brush applicator supplied, apply twice to entire wart surface, allowing the first application to dry before applying the second. Treatment should be once or twice a day and should continue as directed by physician. Be careful not to apply to surrounding skin.

Clinically visible improvement will normally occur during the first or second week of therapy. Maximum resolution may be expected after 4 to 6 weeks of drug use.

Supplied: Each bottle contains: salicylic acid USP 26% in a polyacrylic vehicle of acrylates copolymer, butyl acetate, dibutylphthalate, isopropyl alcohol and polyvinyl butyral. Bottles of 10 mL with brush applicator.

OCTOSTIM® Ⓟ
Ferring

Desmopressin Acetate

Antihemorrhagic

Pharmacology: Desmopressin is a synthetic structural analogue of the natural human hormone, arginine vasopressin.

Desmopressin administration causes a transient increase in all components of the Factor VIII complex (Factor VIII coagulant activity, Factor VIII related antigen, and ristocetin cofactor) and in plasminogen activator. Either directly or indirectly, desmopressin causes these factors to be released very rapidly from their endothelial cell storage sites. In addition, desmopressin may have a direct effect on the vessel wall, with increased platelet spreading and adhesion at injury sites.

A second dose given before endothelial cell stores are replenished will not have as great an effect as the initial dose. Responses as great as the initial one usually are seen if 48 hours or more have elapsed between doses.

The pharmacokinetic and pharmacodynamic profiles after s.c. or i.v. administration to healthy volunteers are equivalent. The plasma half-life ranges from 3.2 to 3.6 hours.

Indications: For prevention of bleeding in patients with mild hemophilia A and mild von Willebrand's disease Type I, and for the prevention or treatment of bleeding in patients with uremia.

Hemophilia A: For patients with hemophilia A with Factor VIII levels greater than 5%.

Desmopressin will often maintain hemostasis in patients with hemophilia A during surgical procedures and postoperatively, when administered 30 minutes prior to the scheduled procedure.

Desmopressin will also stop bleeding in hemophilia A patients with episodes of spontaneous or trauma-induced injuries such as hemarthroses, i.m. hematomas or mucosal bleeding.

In certain clinical situations, it may be justified to try desmopressin in patients with Factor VIII levels between 2 to 5%; however, these patients should be carefully monitored.

von Willebrand's Disease (Type I): For patients with mild to moderate classic von Willebrand's disease (Type I) with Factor VIII levels greater than 5%. Desmopressin will often maintain hemostasis in surgical procedures and postoperatively when administered 30 minutes prior to the scheduled procedure.

Desmopressin will usually stop bleeding in mild to moderate von Willebrand's patients with episodes of spontaneous or trauma-induced injuries such as hemarthroses, i.m. hematomas or mucosal bleeding.

Those von Willebrand's disease patients who are least likely to respond are those with severe homozygous von Willebrand's disease with Factor VIII antigen and von Willebrand's Factor (ristocetin cofactor) activities less than 1%. Other patients may respond in a variable fashion depending on the type of molecular defect they have. Bleeding time and Factor VIII coagulant activity, Factor VIII antigen and von Willebrand's Factor activities should be checked during administration of desmopressin to ensure that adequate levels are being achieved.

Desmopressin is not indicated for the treatment of severe classic Type I von Willebrand's disease and Type IIb and when there is evidence of an abnormal molecular form of Factor VIII antigen (see Contraindications).

Other Hemostatic Disorders: For the treatment of prolonged bleeding time in patients with uremia. It will assist in the maintenance of hemostasis in such patients during surgical procedures and post-operatively when administered prior to the procedure.

Therapeutic efficacy (i.e. normalization of bleeding time) should be established in individual patients at the time of diagnosis of the bleeding disorder, or at least 72 hours prior to an elective treatment, by administration of a test dose of desmopressin (see Precautions, Laboratory Tests).

Contraindications: Hypersensitivity to desmopressin.

Because of the risk of platelet aggregation and thrombocytopenia, desmopressin should not be used in patients with Type IIb or platelet-type (pseudo) von Willebrand's disease.

Warnings: Patients who do not have a need of antidiuretic hormone for its antidiuretic effect, in particular those who are young or elderly, should be cautioned to ingest only enough fluid to satisfy thirst, in order to decrease potential occurrence of water intoxication and hyponatremia. Patients receiving i.v. therapy must have fluid input and output monitored closely to prevent hyponatremia and water intoxication.

Desmopressin must be used with caution in patients prone to vascular headaches, patients with coronary insufficiency and hypertensive cardiovascular diseases, because of possible changes in blood pressure and tachycardia.

Desmopressin has no therapeutic effect in Glazmann's thrombasthenia.

Tachyphylaxis may develop with repeated use.

Lack of therapeutic effect has been noted in patients who have been febrile or otherwise stressed for several days. Whenever possible, therapeutic efficacy (i.e. Factor VIII response in hemophilia and bleeding time correction in other disorders) should be established in individual patients prior to use and followed throughout the course of treatment. The coincident use of antifibrinolytic agents to counteract desmopressin-induced plasminogen activator release has been recommended; however, benefit has not been clearly established.

Precautions: General: The drug should be used with caution in patients with coronary artery insufficiency and/or hypertensive cardiovascular disease, because of possible tachycardia, and changes in blood pressure.

Desmopressin should not be used in patients with hemophilia B because it has no effect on Factor IX levels.

Desmopressin should not be administered to dehydrated patients until water balance has been adequately restored.

Desmopressin has an antidiuretic effect. Patients receiving this drug should be cautioned to reduce their ingestion of fluids for at least 6 hours after receiving the drug. Patients receiving i.v. fluids must be placed on fluid input/output monitoring.

Desmopressin should be used with caution in patients with cystic fibrosis because these patients are prone to hyponatremia. Children and geriatric patients should be closely observed for possible water retention due to over ingestion of fluids.

Children: Use in infants and children will require careful fluid intake restriction to prevent possible hyponatremia and water intoxication.

No controlled trials have been conducted in children with renal insufficiency. No controlled trials have been conducted in infants under 3 months of age with von Willebrand's disease or hemophilia A. The physician should weigh possible therapeutic advantages against potential risks in each case.

Pregnancy: Reproduction studies performed in rats and rabbits have revealed no evidence of harm to the fetus due to desmopressin. The use of desmopressin in pregnant women with no harm to the fetus has been reported; however, no controlled studies have been carried out. Unlike preparations containing the natural hormones, desmopressin in antidiuretic doses has no uterotonic action, but the physician should weigh possible therapeutic advantages against potential risks in each case.

Lactation: There have been no controlled studies in nursing mothers. A single study on a post-partum woman demonstrated a marked change in plasma desmopressin level following an intranasal dose of 10 μg, but little drug was detectable in breast milk.

Drug Interactions: Clofibrate, chlorpropamide and carbamazepine may potentiate the antidiuretic activity of desmopressin while demeclocycline, lithium and norepinephrine may decrease in activity.

Octostim (cont'd)

Although the pressor activity of desmopressin is very low compared with the antidiuretic activity, use of doses of desmopressin as large as 0.3 µg/kg with other pressor agents, should be done only with careful patient monitoring.

Laboratory Tests: Hemophilia A: Laboratory tests for assessing patient status include levels of Factor VIII coagulant, Factor VIII antigen and Factor VIII ristocetin cofactor (von Willebrand factor) as well as activated partial thromboplastin time. Factor VIII coagulant activity should be determined before giving desmopressin for hemostasis. If Factor VIII coagulant activity is present at less than 5% of normal, desmopressin should not be relied upon alone.

von Willebrand's Disease: Laboratory tests for assessing patient status include levels of Factor VIII coagulant, Factor VIII antigen and Factor VIII ristocetin cofactor (von Willebrand factor). The skin bleeding time may be helpful in following these patients and should always be assessed preoperatively.

Uremia: A test dose of desmopressin should be administered at the time of diagnosis of the bleeding disorder, or at least 72 hours prior to an elective treatment. The skin bleeding times should be measured before and 1 hour after desmopressin administration.

Adverse Effects: Infrequently, desmopressin has produced transient headache, mild abdominal cramps and vulvar pain. Facial flushing, tachycardia, mild hypotension and oliguria have also been reported.

Side effects following i.v. administration to 297 patients included transient facial flushing (approximately 18%), fatigue (3%), headache (2%), and oliguria (1%). Other effects reported at a frequency of less than 1% included nausea, dizziness, syncope and abdominal cramping.

Side effect following s.c. administration to 190 subjects included transient facial flushing (7%). Other effects reported at a frequency of less than 1% included hypotension, transient headache, abdominal tension, nausea, tachycardia and discomfort at the injection site.

See Warnings for the possibility of water intoxication and hyponatremia. Very occasionally, i.v. injection of desmopressin has produced local erythema, swelling or burning pain along the course of the vein.

Overdose: Symptoms and Treatment: Excessive doses may cause headaches, abdominal cramps, nausea and facial flushing. In such cases, the dosage should be reduced, frequency of administration decreased, or the drug withdrawn according to the severity of the condition.

There is no known antidote for desmopressin. Water intoxication responds rapidly to diuretic therapy (e.g. furosemide) and appropriate replacement fluid support, without interference with hemostatic effects.

Dosage: Hemophilia A and von Willebrand's Disease Type I and Other Hemostatic Disorders: The injection is administered by s.c. injection or as an i.v. infusion over 20 to 30 minutes.

If desmopressin injection is used preoperatively, it should be administered 30 minutes prior to the scheduled procedure. The peak effect is obtained 1 hour after administration. Response is immediate for bleeding time reduction.

S.C. Injection: 0.3 µg/kg.

Note: The necessity for repeat administration of desmopressin or use of any blood products for hemostasis should be determined by laboratory response as well as the clinical condition of the patient. The tendency toward tachyphylaxis (lessening of response) with repeated administration, given more frequently than every 48 hours should be considered in treating each patient.

I.V. Infusion: Children: 0.3 µg/kg; adults: 0.3 µg/kg (maximum dose 20 µg).

Dilution for Infusion: Dilute in sterile physiological saline and infuse slowly over 20 to 30 minutes. In adults and children weighing more than 10 kg, 50 mL of diluent is used; in children weighing 10 kg or less, 10 mL of diluent is used.

Side effects may be decreased by slow infusion. Blood pressure and pulse rate should be monitored during infusion.

Supplied: Each mL contains: desmopressin acetate 15 µg with sodium chloride and hydrochloric acid to adjust the pH to 3.5, in water for injection. Ampuls of 1 mL, cartons of 5. Unopened ampuls should be kept in the refrigerator at 2 to 8°C (do not freeze). It is recommended that the storage of the diluted solutions at room temperature does not exceed 24 hours.

OCUCLEAR®
Schering
Oxymetazoline HCl
Topical Decongestant

Pharmacology: Oxymetazoline elicits relief of conjunctival hyperemia by causing vasoconstriction of superficial conjunctival blood vessels. The drug's action has been demonstrated in acute allergic conjunctivitis and in chemical (chloride) conjunctivitis. Oxymetazoline has a lesser tendency to dilate the pupils than 0.12% phenylephrine. There are no clinical data available on the degree and rate of systemic absorption of oxymetazoline when used topically in the eye, although no measurable effects are seen in blood pressure.

Indications: For the symptomatic relief of conjunctival hyperemia and edema associated with superficial ocular inflammatory conditions such as acute allergic conjunctivitis and noninfectious conjunctivitis. The usual duration of action is 6 hours.

Contraindications: Hypersensitivity to any of the components, in patients with untreated angle closure glaucoma and in the presence of infection.

Warnings: As with all sympathomimetic amines, oxymetazoline should be used with extreme caution in patients who are receiving MAO inhibitors and β-receptor blocking drugs, as severe hypertensive crises may ensue.

Precautions: Should be used with caution in patients with hypertension, coronary artery disease, hyperthyroidism or diabetes mellitus.

Pregnancy and *Lactation:* The safety of the use of oxymetazoline during pregnancy has not been established. Secretions of oxymetazoline into human breast milk has not been demonstrated, however, because many drugs are excreted in this manner, caution should be exercised when oxymetazoline is administered to a nursing mother.

Children: Safety and effectiveness of oxymetazoline to children below the age of 6 years have not been established.

Adverse Effects: Ocular irritation and eyelid retraction have occasionally been observed. Hypertension, cardiac arrhythmia and hyperglycemia may occur following systemic absorption of large quantities of drugs in this category.

Overdose: Symptoms: Overdosage with oxymetazoline may result in ocular irritation, dryness, mydriasis and increase in intraocular pressure among susceptible individuals. No data are available on the specific dose frequency at which the above signs and symptoms are expected to occur.

Treatment: Discontinue the drug.

Dosage: Adults and children 6 years of age and older: Instill 1 or 2 drops into the conjunctival sac 3 to 4 times daily. The usual duration of treatment is 7 to 10 days. Noticeable improvement should be evident within 3 days and treatment should be continued until the condition is cleared, however, if irritation persists, the diagnosis should be reviewed.

To circumvent bacterial contamination of the solution, do not allow the dropper tip to touch the eye or external surfaces of the dropper bottle. The use of the dispenser by more than one person may contribute to contamination and spread infection. Patients with contact lenses should remove the lenses while using oxymetazoline.

Supplied: Each mL contains oxymetazoline hydrochloride USP, 0.25 mg (0.025%) in a clear, sterile isotonic, buffered aqueous solution. Nonmedicinal ingredients: sodium chloride, disodium edetate, boric acid and benzalkonium chloride. The pH is adjusted to approximately 6.4 with sodium hydroxide or hydrochloric acid. Plastic squeeze bottles of 15 mL with dropper tip. Store between 2 and 30°C.

OCUFEN™ ℞
Allergan
Flurbiprofen Sodium
Topical Nonsteroidal Anti-inflammatory Agent

Supplied: Each mL of sterile ophthalmic solution contains: flurbiprofen sodium 0.03%. Nonmedicinal ingredients: citric acid, edetate disodium, hydrochloric acid and/or sodium hydroxide to adjust the pH, polyvinyl alcohol, potassium chloride, purified water, sodium chloride, sodium citrate and thimerosal. Plastic dropper bottles of 3, 5 and 10 mL. Stable for 18 months when stored at 15 to 25°C.

OCUFLOX™ ℞
Allergan
Ofloxacin
Antibacterial Agent

Pharmacology: The primary mechanism of action of ofloxacin appears to be the specific inhibition of DNA gyrase (topoisomerase II). This enzyme is responsible for the negative supercoiling of bacterial DNA and consequently for its topological configuration, governing functions such as RNA transcription, protein synthesis, DNA replication and repair functions.

Indications: For the treatment of conjunctivitis when caused by susceptible strains of the following bacteria: Gram-positive bacteria: S. aureus, S. epidermidis, S. pneumoniae. Gram-negative bacteria: H. influenzae.

Contraindications: In patients with a history of hypersensitivity to ofloxacin or to any of the components of this medication. A history of hypersensitivity to other quinolones also contraindicates use of ofloxacin.

Warnings: Ofloxacin ophthalmic solution is not for injection into the eye.

Precautions: General: Prolonged use of ofloxacin ophthalmic solution may result in overgrowth of nonsusceptible organisms, including fungi. Whenever clinical judgment dictates, the patient should be examined with the aid of magnification, such as slit lamp biomicroscopy and, where appropriate, fluorescein staining.

In patients receiving systemic quinolone therapy, serious and occasionally fatal hypersensitivity (anaphylatic) reactions, some following the first dose, have been reported. Some reactions were accompanied by cardiovascular collapse, loss of consciousness, tingling, angioedema (including laryngeal, pharyngeal or facial edema), airway obstruction, dyspnea, urticaria, and itching. Only a few patients had a history of hypersensitivity reactions. Serious anaphylatic reactions may require immediate emergency treatment with epinephrine. Oxygen, i.v. steroids and airway management, including intubation, should be administered as clinically indicated.

The systemic administration of quinolones has led to lesions or erosions of the cartilage in weight-bearing joints and other signs of arthropathy in immature animals of various species. Ofloxacin, administered systemically at 10 mg/kg/day in young dogs (equivalent to 150 times the maximum recommended daily **adult ophthalmic** dose), has been associated with these types of effects.

Pregnancy: There have been no adequate and well-controlled studies performed in pregnant women. Since systemic quinolones have been shown to cause arthropathy in immature animals, ofloxacin should be used during pregnancy only if the potential benefit justifies the potential risk to the fetus.

Lactation: Because ofloxacin taken systemically is excreted in breast milk, and there is potential for harm to nursing infants, a decison should be made whether to temporarily discontinue nursing during therapy or not to administer the drug, taking into account the importance of the drug to the mother.

Children: Safety and effectiveness of ofloxacin in children have not been established.

Geriatrics: No comparative data are available with topical ofloxacin therapy in this age category versus other age groups.

Drug Interactions: Specific drug interaction studies have not been conducted with ofloxacin ophthalmic solution. Interactions between ofloxacin and caffeine have not been detected. Systemic use of ofloxacin with nonsteroidal anti-inflammatory drugs has shown that the risk of CNS stimulation and convulsive seizures may increase. A pharmacokinetic study in 15 healthy males has shown that the steady-state peak theophylline concentration increased by an average of approximately 9% and the AUC increased by an average of approximately 13% when oral ofloxacin and theophylline were administered concurrently.

Adverse Effects: Ophthalmic Use of Ofloxacin: The most frequently reported drug-related adverse reaction was transient ocular burning or discomfort. Other reported reactions were ocular redness, stinging, itching, photophobia, tearing and dryness. One report of dizziness, one report of headache and one spontaneous report of toxic epidermal necrolyis have also been received.

Systemic Effects of Ofloxacin: As with all topical ophthalmic drugs, the potential exists for systemic effects. Ofloxacin used systemically has rarely been associated with serious side effects. Serious reactions reported for systemic dosing of ofloxacin include convulsions and increased intracranial pressure. For the oral dosage form of ofloxacin, gastrointestinal symptoms, mainly nausea/vomiting, pain/discomfort, diarrhea and anorexia, were reported most frequently, followed by CNS events (such as dizziness and headaches) and dermatological or hypersensitivity reactions. Photophobia was reported rarely in clinical trials with systemic ofloxacin and phototoxicity has been reported with other drugs in this class.

Overdose: Symptoms and Treatment: In the event of accidental ingestion of 10 mL of ofloxacin ophthalmic solution 0.3%, only 30 mg of ofloxacin would be ingested. Although this amount may not be clinically significant in terms of overdosage, there could be an increased potential for systemic reactions.

A topical overdosage of ofloxacin ophthalmic solution is considered a remote possibility. Discontinue medication if heavy or protracted use is suspected. In the event of a topical overdose, flush the eye with a topical ocular irrigant.

Dosage: 1 to 2 drops every 2 to 4 hours for the first 2 days, and then 4 times daily in the affected eye(s) for 8 days.

If superinfection occurs or if clinical improvement is not noted with 7 days, discontinue use and institute appropriate therapy.

Patients should be advised to avoid contamination of the dropper tip.

Use while wearing contact lenses: The use of ofloxacin ophthalmic solution while wearing contact lenses has not been studied. Therefore, its use is not recommended while the lens is on the eye.

Information for the Patient: See Blue Section—Information for the Patient "Ocuflox".

Supplied: Each bottle contains: ofloxacin 0.3% as a sterile, ophthalmic solution. Nonmedicinal ingredients: benzalkonium chloride 0.005% (as preservative), sodium chloride, hydrochloric acid and/or sodium hydroxide to adjust the pH and purified water. Plastic dropper bottles of 5 and 10 mL. Ofloxacin ophthalmic solution is sterile in the unopened package, and is stable for 24 months when stored at 15 to 25°C.

OGEN® Ⓟ

Pharmacia & Upjohn

Estropipate

Estrogen

Pharmacology: Estropipate is a natural estrogenic substance prepared from purified crystalline estrone, solubilized as the sulfate and stabilized with piperazine. It is appreciably soluble in water and has almost no odor or taste. The amount of piperazine in estropipate is not sufficient to exert a pharmacological action. Its addition ensures solubility, stability and uniform potency of the estrone sulfate.

Estrogens are important in the development and maintenance of the female reproductive system and secondary sex characteristics. They promote growth and development of the vagina, uterus and fallopian tubes, and enlargement of the breasts. Indirectly, they contribute to the shaping of the skeleton, maintenance of tone and elasticity of urogenital structures, changes in the epiphyses of the long bones that allow for the pubertal growth spurt and its termination, growth of axillary and pubic hair, and pigmentation of the nipples and genitals. Along with other hormones such as progesterone, estrogens are intricately involved in the process of menstruation. Estrogens also affect the release of pituitary gonadotropins.

Estropipate owes its therapeutic action to estrone, one of the three principal estrogenic steroid hormones of man: estradiol, estrone and estriol. Estradiol is rapidly hydrolysed in the body to estrone, which in turn may be hydrated to the less active estriol. These transformations occur readily, mainly in the liver, where there is also free interconversion between estrone and estradiol.

A depletion of endogenous estrogens occurs postmenopausally as a result of a decline in ovarian function, and may cause symptomatic vulvovaginal atrophy.

Gastrointestinal absorption of orally administered estrogens is usually prompt and complete. Inactivation of estrogens in the body occurs mainly in the liver. During cyclic passage through the liver, estrogens are degraded to less active estrogenic compounds and conjugated with sulfuric and glucuronic acids. Estrone is 50 to 80% bound to protein as it circulates in the blood, usually as a conjugate with sulfate.

In the normal menstrual cycle, the mean daily excretion of endogenous estrogens at the midovulatory maximum has been found to be 29 μg of estriol, 21 μg of estrone and 8 μg of estradiol (total, 58 μg). In normal women, after menopause, the average daily excretion of these 3 estrogens totals only 6 μg.

In studies of postmenopausal women with low bone density, it has been shown that therapy with estropipate, concomitant with other preventative measures such as an appropriate diet, calcium supplementation and exercise, can prevent further bone loss.

Indications: The treatment of menopausal and postmenopausal symptoms.

Contraindications: Estrogens should not be administered to patients with active hepatic dysfunction or disease, especially of the obstructive type; or a personal history of breast or endometrial cancer, except in special circumstances, or in patients with endometrial hyperplasia unless a progestogen is administered concomitantly.

The drug is also contraindicated in the following situations: undiagnosed vaginal bleeding; a history of cerebrovascular accidents, coronary thrombosis, or in the presence of classical migraine; a history of thrombophlebitis or thromboembolic disease; partial or complete loss of vision or diplopia due to ophthalmic vascular disease, and suspected pregnancy.

Warnings: Before estrogens are administered, the patient should have a complete physical examination including a blood pressure determination. Breasts and pelvic organs should be examined and a Papanicolaou smear should be taken. Baseline tests should include those for blood glucose, calcium, triglycerides and cholesterol, and liver function.

The first follow-up examination should be done preferably within 6 months after initiation of treatment. Thereafter, examinations should be made once a year and should include those procedures outlined above.

If any surgical procedures are performed, the pathologist should be advised of the patient's therapy when specimens are sent for examination. Liver function tests should be made periodically in subjects who have, or are suspected of having, hepatic disease.

An increased risk of endometrial hyperplasia and carcinoma in postmenopausal women exposed to exogenous estrogens for long periods has been reported. The risk appears to depend on both duration of treatment and on estrogen dose. If abnormal vaginal bleeding occurs during therapy, diagnostic aspiration biopsy or curettage should be performed to rule out the possibility of uterine malignancy.

Patients who develop visual disturbances, classical migraine, transient aphasia, paralysis, or loss of consciousness, should discontinue medication.

Although the estrogen content of oral contraceptive therapy have been associated with an increased risk of various thromboembolic, thrombotic and vascular diseases, to date no such increased risk in postmenopausal users of estrogens has been described. Nevertheless, this does not rule out the possibility that such an increase may be present in women who have underlying risk factors or who are receiving relatively large doses of estrogens. Therefore, if the patient develops any sign of phlebitis or thrombotic complications (thrombophlebitis, retinal thrombosis, cerebral embolism and pulmonary embolism), medication should be discontinued immediately.

Precautions: Development or sudden enlargement, pain, or tenderness of uterine fibroids requires discontinuation of medication.

Estrogen may cause fluid retention. Where this may be undesirable such as in cardiac or renal dysfunction, epilepsy or asthma, particular caution is indicated.

Elevation of blood pressure in previously normotensive or hypertensive patients necessitates cessation of medication.

Diabetic patients or those with a predisposition to diabetes should be observed closely to detect any alterations in carbohydrate metabolism.

When liver or endocrine function tests are indicated, the results should not be considered reliable unless therapy has been discontinued for 2 to 4 months.

Adverse Effects: Although not all of the following adverse reactions have been specifically associated with estropipate, they have been reported with estrogens generally and may be encountered when giving any estrogen. Some of these (indicated in brackets) have been documented with oral contraceptives specifically, and have not to now been associated with cyclic menopausal or postmenopausal estrogen therapy.

Gastrointestinal: nausea, (anorexia, vomiting, abdominal cramps, bloating), cholestatic jaundice, increase or decrease in body weight.

Genitourinary: sodium and water retention, breakthrough bleeding, spotting and withdrawal bleeding, increased cervical mucus, endometrial hyperplasia, reactivation of endometriosis, (cystitis-like syndrome).

Endocrine: breast swelling and tenderness, increased blood sugar levels, and decreased glucose tolerance. In males: gynecomastia, reduced potency and feminization.

CNS: headaches, increase or decrease of libido, (nervousness, mental depression, dizziness, fatigue, irritability).

Dermatologic—Hypersensitivity: allergic reactions and rashes, chloasma (loss of scalp hair, hemorrhagic eruption, itching, erythema nodosum, erythema multiforme, pigmentation of the skin).

Cardiovascular: an increase in blood pressure in susceptible individuals, aggravation of migraine headaches.

Hematologic: A statistically significant association has been demonstrated between the use of oral contraceptive preparations containing estrogens and the following serious reactions: thrombophlebitis, pulmonary embolism and cerebral thrombosis. Although available evidence is suggestive of an association, such a relationship has been neither confirmed nor refuted for the following serious reactions: coronary thrombosis and neuro-ocular lesions (e.g., retinal thrombosis and optic neuritis); altered coagulation tests (increase in prothrombin and Factors VII, VIII, IX, X).

Miscellaneous: premenstrual-like syndrome, precipitation or aggravation of porphyria cutanea tarda in predisposed individuals.

Overdose: Symptoms: Excessive doses may result in nausea, vomiting and abdominal cramps, headache, dizziness and general malaise.

Treatment: Remove all of the ingested drug by gastric lavage and give symptomatic treatment.

Dosage: In general, estrogen should be given cyclically (21 to 25 days followed by a 5- to 7-day rest period) and in some cases with progestogen or androgen to avoid overstimulation of breast and endometrial tissues. Withdrawal bleeding commonly occurs toward the end of the rest period. The addition of sufficient progestogen to promote conversion of the endometrium is mandatory in those patients who are receiving sufficient unopposed estrogen to cause vaginal bleeding or endometrial hyperplasia. Obviously, abnormal vaginal bleeding in such patients is an indication for prompt diagnostic measures.

Estropipate is administered orally. As with most drugs, the dosage should be adjusted to the minimum required to control symptoms and the requirement for estrogen therapy should be reassessed periodically.

Estropipate is indicated for a variety of estrogen deficiency states. The usual daily dose is 0.75 to 3.0 mg of estropipate (Ogen 0.625, Ogen 1.25, Ogen 2.5 calculated as sodium estrone sulfate). Titrate dosage as necessary according to the individual patient's clinical response.

Supplied: 0.625 mg: Each yellow-colored, oval, scored tablet, embossed with "U" and "3772" on left and right halves, contains: estropipate 0.75 mg (calculated as sodium estrone sulfate 0.625 mg). Blisters of 20. Cartons of 5 blisters. Bottles of 100.

1.25 mg: Each peach-colored oval, scored tablet, embossed with "U" and "3773" on left and right halves, contains: estropipate 1.5 mg (calculated as sodium estrone sulfate 1.25 mg). Blisters of 20. Cartons of 5 blisters. Bottles of 100.

2.5 mg: Each blue-colored, oval scored tablet, embossed with "U" and "3774" on left and right halves, contains: estropipate 3.0 mg (calculated as sodium estrone sulfate 2.5 mg). Blisters of 20. Cartons of 5 blisters. Bottles of 100.

Nonmedicinal ingredients: blue dye #2 (2.5 mg only), hydrogenated vegetable oil wax, hydroxypropyl cellulose, lactose, magnesium stearate, microcrystalline cellulose, potassium phosphate dibasic, silicon dioxide, sodium starch glycolate, tromethamine, yellow dye #6 (0.625 and 1.25 mg only) and yellow dye #10 (0.625 mg only).

Tablets of all 3 dosage levels are grooved to provide dosage flexibility.

(Shown in Product Recognition Section)

OILATUM® Dermatological Shower and Bath Oil

OILATUM® Soap

Stiefel

Liquid Paraffin

Mineral Oil

Antipruritic—Emollient

Emollient—Cleanser

Supplied: Dermatological Shower and Bath Oil: Each mL of oil contains: light liquid paraffin 63.4%. Nonmedicinal ingredients: fragrance floral-spice, isopropyl palmitate NF, lanolin

Oilatum (cont'd)

alcohol acetylated, PEG 40 sorbitan peroleate and polyethylene glycol 400. Bottles of 250 mL.

Soap: Each g of unscented neutral soap contains: mineral oil 7.5%. Nonmedicinal ingredients: butylated hydroxytoluene, FD&C Orange No. 4, FD&C Red No. 4, hampol 120, purified water, soap chips, tenol 20A, titanium dioxide, octyl hydroxystearate and lecithin. Bars of 75 g.

OLIGOFER®
Sabex

Vitamin and Mineral Supplement

Supplied: Each 10 mL ampul contains: elemental iron 23 mg (as gluconate), vitamin B_{12} 25 μg, manganese 2.5 mg (as gluconate) and cobalt 0.84 mg (as gluconate). Nonmedicinal ingredients: citric acid, copper, flavor, glucose, glycerin, purified water, saccharose sodium benzoate and sodium citrate. Boxes of 20.

OLIGOSOL®, COPPER
Labcatal

Copper Gluconate

Trace Elements

Supplied: Each 2 mL dose contains: copper gluconate 5.18 mg. Nonmedicinal ingredients: glucose and purified water. Sterile, nitrogen-pressurized bottles of 60 mL (30 doses) with a 2 mL metering valve for sublingual use.

OLIGOSOL®, COPPER-GOLD-SILVER
Labcatal

Copper Gluconate—Colloidal Gold—Silver Gluconate

Trace Elements

Supplied: Each 2 mL dose contains: copper gluconate 0.45 mg, colloidal gold 0.0014 mg, silver gluconate 0.06 mg. Nonmedicinal ingredients: glucose and purified water. Plastic bottles of 60 mL (30 doses) with a 2 mL spoon dose for sublingual use.

OLIGOSOL®, MAGNESIUM
Labcatal

Magnesium Gluconate

Trace Elements

Supplied: Each 2 mL dose contains: magnesium gluconate 1.78 mg. Nonmedicinal ingredients: glucose and purified water. Sterile, nitrogen-pressurized bottles of 60 mL (30 doses) with a 2 mL metering valve for sublingual use.

OLIGOSOL®, MANGANESE
Labcatal

Manganese Gluconate

Trace Elements

Supplied: Each 2 mL dose contains: manganese gluconate 0.59 mg. Nonmedicinal ingredients: glucose and purified water. Sterile, nitrogen-pressurized bottles of 60 mL (30 doses) with a 2 mL metering valve for sublingual use.

Geriatric patients may experience unique drug-induced effects. Be aware of potential side effects and drug interactions. For more information, refer to the CLIN-INFO SECTION.

OLIGOSOL®, MANGANESE-COBALT
Labcatal

Manganese Gluconate—Cobalt Gluconate

Trace Elements

Supplied: Each 2 mL dose contains: manganese gluconate 0.59 mg and cobalt gluconate 0.554 mg. Nonmedicinal ingredients: glucose and purified water. Sterile, nitrogen-pressurized bottles of 60 mL (30 doses) with a 2 mL metering valve for sublingual use.

OLIGOSOL®, MANGANESE-COPPER
Labcatal

Manganese Gluconate—Copper Gluconate

Trace Elements

Supplied: Each 2 mL dose contains: manganese gluconate 0.59 mg and copper gluconate 0.518 mg. Nonmedicinal ingredients: glucose and purified water. Sterile, nitrogen-pressurized bottles of 60 mL (30 doses) with a 2 mL metering valve for sublingual use.

OLIGOSOL®, ZINC-NICKEL-COBALT
Labcatal

Zinc Gluconate—Nickel Gluconate—Cobalt Gluconate

Trace Elements

Supplied: Each 2 mL dose contains: zinc gluconate 0.47 mg, nickel gluconate 0.556 mg and cobalt gluconate 0.554 mg. Nonmedicinal ingredients: glucose and purified water. Sterile, nitrogen-pressurized bottles of 60 mL (30 doses) with a 2 mL metering valve for sublingual use.

OMNIPAQUE®
Nycomed Imaging A.S.

Iohexol

Nonionic Radiographic Contrast Medium

Pharmacology: Immediately following rapid intravascular injection, iohexol reaches peak plasma concentration and is then rapidly distributed throughout the extracellular fluid compartment. Iohexol does not normally cross the blood-brain barrier to any significant extent. It is excreted unchanged by the kidneys, mainly by glomerular filtration; tubular secretion plays a minor role, and a very small quantity (1 to 2%) is excreted via the bile. About 80 to 90% of the injected dose is excreted in the first 24 hours, with peak urine concentrations occurring in the first hour.

Pharmacokinetic studies of iohexol following i.v. injection in healthy male volunteers showed, using a 3 compartment open model, that its distribution half-life (alpha phase) is 22 minutes, excretion half-life (beta phase) 2.1 hours, and first-order terminal elimination half-life (gamma phase) 12.6 hours. The volume of distribution of the central compartment is 165-270 mL/kg, the mean renal clearance 120 mL/minute, and the mean total body clearance is 131 mL/minute.

In the presence of impaired renal function, the excretion of iohexol by the kidneys will be delayed and the amount excreted in the bile increases.

Iohexol is not known to be appreciably metabolized in humans. No metabolites have been found in urine. The presence or absence of metabolites in human bile has not been ascertained. (Small quantities of two metabolites were detected in rabbit bile and urine.)

Following its injection into the subarachnoid space, iohexol mixes readily with the cerebrospinal fluid (CSF) and diffuses into root sleeves and upward in the spinal and intracranial subarachnoid spaces. The time it takes iohexol to reach the cervical and intracranial subarachnoid spaces will depend to a large degree on the patient's position and movements. As it diffuses upward, its concentration decreases. Iohexol is eliminated into the systemic circulation via the subarachnoid granulations in the spine and the skull, and is subsequently excreted by the kidneys. Peak plasma concentration following subarachnoid injection of iohexol is reached in 2 to 6 hours. When fitted to a one compartment open model with first order absorption, the mean plasma elimination half-life (beta phase) is 3.4 hours (2.2 to 7.9 hours) and the mean apparent terminal elimination half-life (gamma phase) is 4.5 hours. The mean volume of distribution is 559 mL/kg, the mean renal clearance 111 mL/minute and the total body clearance 119 mL/minute. Within the first 24 hours, about 84% of the injected dose is recovered from the urine.

Subarachnoid: Iohexol, when injected into the lumbar subarachnoid space, will opacify the lumbar subarachnoid spaces and their associated root sleeves to provide contrast for these structures.

Following lumbar subarachnoid injection in conventional radiography, iohexol will continue to provide good diagnostic contrast for at least 30 minutes. After approximately 1 hour, contrast of diagnostic quality will not be available for conventional myelography, due to diffusion throughout the cerebrospinal fluid as well as transfer into the general circulation. If computerized tomography is to follow, it should be deferred for 2 to 6 hours to allow the degree of contrast to decrease. For computerized tomography without conventional radiography, a smaller dose or lower concentration of iohexol would be required.

Computerized tomography shows cerebrospinal fluid contrast enhancement in the thoracic region in about one hour, in the cervical region in about 2 hours, in the basal cisterns in 3 to 4 hours, and in the ventricles and sulci in 5 to 6 hours. Between 8 and 12 hours after lumbar injection, CT scans of the brain may demonstrate contrast medium enhancement of brain tissue in contact with the subarachnoid spaces indicating permeation of the cerebral cortex by the contrast medium; this "blush" effect will normally disappear in 24 hours.

In lumbar myelography studies, iohexol was injected into the lumbar subarachnoid space of 576 adult patients while an additional 208 adult patients received metrizamide under similar dosages and conditions.

Clinically significant, transient individual changes in vital signs, serum chemistry, hematology and neurological tests, when observed, were similar in magnitude and frequency with the two contrast agents used. The electroencephalogram was recorded in 182 patients who received iohexol. EEG changes (mostly theta and delta waves) were recorded in approximately 4% of patients who received iohexol, compared to 35% who received metrizamide. No significant changes in cerebrospinal fluid chemistry obtained by repuncture at either 6 or 24 hours after injection of Omnipaque were evident. Although a few minor increases in cerebrospinal fluid protein, WBC and other laboratory parameters were reported, no effect on IgG, creatinine kinase (CK) or CK-BB band isoenzyme was observed.

Intravascular: Following intravascular injection, iohexol will opacify those vessels in the path of flow of the contrast medium, permitting radiographic visualization of the vasculature of the internal structures and extremities until significant dilution occurs.

After i.v. injection opacification of the renal parenchyma may begin within one minute. Excretion of the contrast material becomes apparent in about 1 to 3 minutes, with optimal contrast in the calyces and collecting system occurring between 5 to 15 minutes. In nephropathic conditions, particularly when excretory capacity has been altered, the rate of excretion varies unpredictably, and opacification may be delayed for up to several hours after injection. Severe renal impairment may result in a lack of diagnostic opacification of the urinary tract, and depending on the degree of renal impairment, prolonged plasma iohexol levels may be anticipated in these patients as well as in infants with immature kidneys.

In comparative clinical trials of the vascular procedures of angiocardiography, cerebral arteriography, peripheral arteriography, urography, peripheral venography and intravenous digital subtraction angiography a total of 885 consenting adult patients received iohexol (523 by arterial injection and 362 by i.v. route) while 724 patients received conventional ionic media (444 intra-arterially and 280 i.v.) for their radiographic examinations.

Statistically significant reductions in patient discomfort, during or shortly after injection, were generally observed with iohexol compared to conventional ionic contrast media. Injection of iohexol was also associated with statistically significant reduction of changes in mean values of some physiological parameters (heart rate, QT interval, ST segment, and systemic pressures), compared to those associated with the use of conventional ionic media in some procedures, especially in angiocardiography. Clinically significant, transient individual changes noted in vital signs and laboratory parameters (increased serum creatinine CK, LDH, AST, ALT, K, decreased creatinine clearance; increased urinary protein, WBC and RBC; and variations in hematology parameters) after administration of Omnipaque were similar in scope to those caused by conventional ionic contrast agents.

In vitro studies done on human basophils from nonallergic, nonatopic, nonreactor subjects showed that iohexol caused a lesser degree of histamine release than diatrizoate, an ionic contrast agent.

As with any iodinated contrast agent, administration of iohexol may lead to changes in thyroid function in some patients, and elevation of thyroxine and/or TSH may be observed.

Since iohexol does not ionize in solution, there is less dilution through hyperosmolar fluid shifts within the renal tubules and hence less osmotic diuresis, compared to conventional ionized contrast media, and a higher iodine concentration in the tubular urine is obtained. Several studies have shown that conventional ionic contrast media caused significantly greater increases in proteinuria, urinary β-hexosaminidase and serum creatinine than did nonionic media at comparable doses. One study, on the other hand, involving 20 pediatric patients, showed that the significant increase in urinary excretion of other renal enzymes (NAG, GGT, MU) following the intravascular administration of iohexol was approximately the same as that caused by conventional ionic contrast media. The clinical relevance of these findings is unclear at the present time.

The lower osmolality of iohexol compared to conventional ionic media of similar iodine concentration can be expected to cause fewer and less severe osmolality-related disturbances. At 350 mg I/mL, the highest concentration used clinically, iohexol has less than half the osmolality of monomeric ionic media of equi-iodine concentration (i.e., approximately 844 mOsm/kg H_2O vs 1 800 mOsm/kg H_2O).

CT Scanning of the Head: In i.v. contrast enhanced computed tomographic head imaging, iohexol does not accumulate in normal brain tissue due to the presence of the normal blood-brain barrier. The increase in x-ray absorption in normal brain is due to the presence of contrast agent within the blood pool. A break in the blood-brain barrier, such as occurs in malignant tumors of the brain, abscesses, vascular accidents, etc. allows for the accumulation of contrast medium within the interstitial tissue of the tumor, and some other lesions. Adjacent normal brain tissue does not contain the contrast medium. The degree of density enhancement is directly related to the iodine content in an administered dose; peak iodine blood levels occur immediately following rapid i.v. injection. Blood levels fall rapidly within 5 to 10 minutes and the vascular compartment half-life is approximately 20 minutes. Maximum contrast enhancement in tissue frequently occurs after peak blood iodine levels are reached. Diagnostic contrast enhancement images of the brain have been obtained up to 1 hour after i.v. bolus administration.

CT Scanning of the Body: In i.v. contrast enhanced computed tomographic body imaging (nonneural tissue), iohexol diffuses rapidly from the vascular into the extravascular space. Increase in x-ray absorption is related to blood flow, concentration of the contrast medium, and extraction of the contrast medium by interstitial tissue of tumors since no barrier exists. Contrast enhancement is thus due to the relative differences in vascularity and extravascular diffusion between normal and abnormal tissue, quite different from that in the brain.

Contrast enhancement appears to be greatest immediately after bolus administration (15 to 120 seconds).

Utilization of a continuous scanning technique (i.e., dynamic CT scanning) may improve enhancement and diagnostic assessment of tumor and other lesions such as abscess, occasionally revealing unsuspected or more extensive disease.

Iohexol may be useful for enhancement of computed tomographic images for detection and evaluation of lesions in the liver, pancreas, kidneys, aorta, mediastinum, pelvic, abdominal cavity and retroperitoneal space.

Indications: Subarachnoid: Omnipaque 180, Omnipaque 240 and Omnipaque 300: For lumbar, thoracic, cervical and total columnar myelography in adults. Omnipaque 180 is indicated for subarachnoid administration in children, by lumbar injection, for lumbar, thoracic, cervical and total columnar myelography and for contrast enhancement in computerized tomography (myelography, cisternography and ventriculography). Delayed CT scans of spinal subarachnoid space and of the intracranial CSF spaces may be obtained at appropriate times following myelography, taking advantage of delayed opacification by the physiological cephalad circulation of the opacified CSF.

Intravascular: Omnipaque 350: In adults for left ventriculography, coronary arteriography, i.v. contrast enhancement for computed tomographic head and body imaging, peripheral arteriography, excretory urography and i.v. digital subtraction arteriography. Omnipaque 350 is indicated in children for angiocardiography.

Omnipaque 300: In adults for cerebral arteriography, peripheral arteriography, i.v. contrast enhancement for computed tomographic head and body imaging, peripheral venography and excretory urography. Omnipaque 300 is indicated in children for excretory urography and may be used in infants for angiocardiography.

Omnipaque 240: In adults for i.v. contrast enhancement in computed tomographic head imaging, and for peripheral venography.

Arthrography: Omnipaque 300 or Omnipaque 240 is recommended in adults for arthrography of the knee joint. Omnipaque 300 is recommended for arthrography of the shoulder joint in adults.

Contraindications: Iohexol should not be administered to patients with known or suspected hypersensitivity to iohexol or in cases of clinically significant impairment of both hepatic and renal function.

Warnings: Use the recommended concentration for the particular procedure to be undertaken.

General: Serious or fatal reactions have been associated with the administration of water-soluble contrast media. It is of utmost importance that a course of action be carefully planned in advance for immediate treatment of serious reactions, and that adequate facilities and appropriate personnel be readily available in case a severe reaction should occur.

Diagnostic procedures which involve the use of radiopaque contrast agents should be carried out only by physicians with the prerequisite training and with a thorough knowledge of the particular procedure to be performed and who are thoroughly familiar with the emergency treatment of all adverse reactions to contrast media.

In addition to the following information, generally accepted contraindications, warnings, precautions and adverse reactions commonly related to the use of radiopaque contrast media should be kept in mind during its administration.

Administration of radiopaque media to patients known or suspected to have pheochromocytoma should be performed with extreme caution. If, in the opinion of the physician, the possible benefits of such procedures outweigh the considered risk, the amount of radiopaque material injected should be kept to a minimum. The blood pressure should be assessed throughout the procedure and measures for treatment of a hypertensive crisis should be available.

Ionic contrast media have been shown to promote the phenomenon of sickling in individuals who are homozygous for sickle cell disease when the material is injected i.v. or intraarterially. Fluid restriction is not advised in these patients.

Some clinicians consider multiple myeloma a contraindication to the use of contrast media because of the possibility of producing transient to fatal renal failure. If a decision to use iohexol is made, the patient should be well hydrated beforehand, since dehydration favors protein precipitation in the renal tubules. A minimal diagnostic dose should be used and renal function and extent of urinary precipitation of the myeloma protein checked for a few days afterwards.

Caution is advised in patients with severe cardiovascular disease, hyperthyroidism, and in patients with a history of bronchial asthma or other allergic manifestations or of sensitivity to iodine. Patients with significant hepatorenal disease should not be examined unless the possibility of benefit clearly outweighs the additional risk. As with other iodinated contrast media, the use of iohexol is not recommended in patients with anuria or severe oliguria.

Elderly patients may present a greater risk (see Precautions, General). Special attention must be paid to dose and concentration of the medium, hydration and technique used.

Subarachnoid: Myelography should not be performed when lumbar puncture is contraindicated as in the presence of local or systemic infection where bacteremia is likely.

Myelography should be performed only in hospitalized patients under close medical observation, which is to be continued for 24 hours following the procedure.

Patients receiving anticonvulsants should be maintained on this therapy. Should a seizure occur, i.v. diazepam or phenobarbital is recommended. In patients with a history of seizure activity who are not on anticonvulsant therapy, premedication with barbiturates should be considered. Iohexol should be used in epileptics only if a water-soluble contrast medium is considered essential.

Prophylactic anticonvulsant treatment with barbiturates should be considered in patients with evidence of inadvertent intracranial entry of a large bolus of contrast medium, since there may be increased risk of seizure in such cases.

Gravitational displacement of a concentrated bolus of iohexol above the level of C1, especially into the intracranial subarachnoid spaces is not recommended.

Vascular: Nonionic iodinated contrast media inhibit blood coagulation less than ionic contrast media. Clotting has been reported when blood remains in contact with syringes, catheters or tubes containing nonionic contrast media. Serious, rarely fatal, thromboembolic events causing myocardial infarction and stroke have been reported during angiographic procedures with nonionic and also with ionic contrast media. Therefore, meticulous intravascular administration technique is necessary, particularly during angiographic procedures, to minimize thromboembolic events. Numerous factors, including length of procedure, number of injections, catheter and syringe material, underlying disease state and concomitant medications may contribute to the development of thromboembolic events. For these reasons, meticulous angiographic techniques are recommended including close attention to keeping guidewires, catheters and all angiographic equipment free of blood, use of manifold systems and/or 3-way stopcocks, frequent catheter flushing with heparinized saline solutions, and minimizing the length of the procedure. Nonionic iodinated contrast media are not recommended as flush solutions. The use of plastic syringes in place of glass syringes has been reported to decrease but not eliminate the likelihood of clotting.

Patients with a serum creatinine level above 3 mg/dL should not be examined unless the possible benefits of the examination clearly outweigh the additional risk.

Extreme caution is advised should the injection of a contrast medium be indicated following the administration of vasopressors since they may strongly potentiate neurologic effects.

General anesthesia may be indicated in some procedures; however, one should be aware of possible increased incidence of adverse reactions in such circumstances.

See Dosage for special warnings and precautions.

Precautions: General: Before any contrast medium is injected, the patient should be questioned for a history of allergy or bronchial asthma. Although a history of allergy may imply a greater than usual risk, it does not arbitrarily contraindicate the use of the medium, but does warrant special precaution. A previous reaction to a contrast medium or a history of iodine sensitivity is not an absolute contraindication to the use of iohexol, however, extreme caution should be exercised in injecting these patients and prophylactic therapy should be considered. Additionally, the possibility of an idiosyncratic reaction in patients who have previously received a contrast medium without ill effect should always be considered.

The i.v. injection of a test dose of 0.5 to 1 mL of the contrast agent before injection of the full dose has been employed in an attempt to predict severe or fatal adverse reactions. The preponderance of recent scientific literature, however, now demonstrates that this provocative test procedure is not reliably predictive of serious or fatal reactions. Severe reactions and fatalities have occurred with the full dose after a nonreactive test dose, and with or without a history of allergy. No conclusive relationship between severe or fatal reactions and antigen-antibody reactions or other manifestations of allergy has been established. A history of allergy may be more useful in predicting reactions, and warrants special attention when administering the drug. Since delayed severe reactions may occur the patient should be kept under close observation following injection (see also Patient Management under Subarachnoid Administration).

It is expected that the results of thyroid function tests will not reflect true function for several weeks following radiopaque examination. Such tests, if indicated, should be performed prior to the administration of this preparation. Tests which directly determine thyroxine levels are less likely to be affected.

Reports of thyroid storm occurring following the intravascular use of iodinated radiopaque agents in patients with hyperthyroidism or with an autonomously functioning thyroid nodule, suggest that this additional risk be evaluated in such patients prior to the use of iohexol.

Preparatory dehydration is unnecessary and usually contraindicated with the use of iohexol for all indications.

Administration of water-soluble contrast media should be deferred for 48 hours in patients with hepatic or biliary disorders who have recently been administered cholecystographic agents, as renal toxicity has been reported in the literature in such patients who received conventional contrast agents.

Omnipaque (cont'd)

Caution should be exercised in performing contrast medium examination in patients with endotoxemia and in those with elevated body temperature.

There have been reports in the literature indicating that patients on adrenergic beta-blockers may be more prone to severe adverse reaction to contrast media. At the same time treatment of allergic-anaphylactoid reactions in these patients is more difficult. Epinephrine should be administered with caution since it may not have its usual effects. On the one hand larger doses of epinephrine may be needed to overcome the bronchospasm, while on the other, these doses can be associated with excessive alpha adrenergic stimulation with consequent hypertension, reflex bradycardia and heart-block and possible potentiation of bronchospasm. Alternatives to the use of large doses of epinephrine include vigorous supportive care such as fluids and the use of beta agonists including parenteral salbutamol or isoproterenol to overcome bronchospasm and norepinephrine to overcome hypotension.

Special precaution is advised in patients with increased intracranial pressure, cerebral thrombosis or embolism, primary or metastatic cerebral lesions, subarachnoid hemorrhage, arterial spasm, transient ischemic attacks, and in any condition when the blood brain barrier is breached or the transit time of the contrast material through the cerebral vasculature is prolonged, since clinical deterioration, convulsions, and serious temporary or permanent neurological complications (including stroke, aphasia, cortical blindness, etc.) may occur following i.v. or intraarterial injection of relatively large doses of contrast media. Such patients, and patients in clinically unstable or critical condition should undergo examinations with intravascular contrast media only if in the opinion of the physician the expected benefits outweigh the potential risks, and the dose should be kept to the absolute minimum.

Caution should be exercised in the administration of contrast media to severely debilitated patients, particularly those with severe hypertension and impaired renal function. Acute renal failure has been reported in patients with diabetic nephropathy and in susceptible nondiabetic patients (often elderly with preexisting renal disease) following administration of iodinated contrast agents. Careful consideration of the potential risks should be given before performing radiographic procedures in these patients.

Pregnancy: There are no studies on the use of iohexol in pregnant women. Reproduction studies have been performed in rats and rabbits with up to 100 times the recommended human dose. No evidence of impaired fertility or definite harm to the fetus has been demonstrated due to iohexol. Animal reproduction studies are not always predictive of human response; therefore, iohexol should be used during pregnancy only if the benefit to the mother clearly outweighs the risk to the fetus.

Lactation: It is not known to what extent iohexol is excreted in human milk. If use of iohexol is considered necessary, it is suggested to discontinue breast feeding for at least 48 hours after administration.

Children: (Indicated for Angiocardiography and Urography) Pediatric patients at higher risk of experiencing adverse events during contrast medium administration may include those having asthma, a sensitivity to medication and/or allergens, congestive heart failure, a serum creatinine >1.5 mg/dL or those less than 12 months of age.

Subarachnoid: Elderly patients may present a greater risk following myelography. The need for the procedure in these patients should be evaluated carefully. Special attention must be given not to exceed the recommended dose of the contrast medium, to see that the patient is sufficiently hydrated and to ensure proper and sterile radiographic technique.

If grossly bloody CSF is encountered, the possible benefits of a myelographic procedure should be considered in terms of the risk to the patient.

Any intrathecally administered medication including nonionic contrast media such as iohexol can enter the brain substance which may increase the risk of adverse effects associated with the procedure. Such adverse reactions may be delayed and, in extremely rare cases, may be life-threatening (see Adverse Effects). Careful patient and dose selection and proper patient management before, during and after the procedure are therefore imperative.

Care is required in patient management to prevent inadvertent intracranial entry of a large bolus of contrast medium. Also, effort should be made to avoid rapid dispersion of the medium (i.e., by active patient movement).

Previous experience with the use of water-soluble contrast media in myelography indicates that in most cases of major motor seizure one or more of the following factors were present, and should therefore, be avoided: deviations from recommended procedure on myelographic management; use in patients with a history of epilepsy; inadvertent overdosage; intracranial entry of a bolus or premature diffusion of a high concentration of the medium; medication with neuroleptic drugs or phenothiazine antinauseants; failure to maintain elevation of the head during and after the procedure; active patient movement or straining.

Repeat procedures: If in the clinical judgment of the physician a repeat examination is required, an interval of 5 days between procedures is recommended.

Drug Interactions: Drugs which lower seizure threshold, especially phenothiazine derivatives including those used for their antihistaminic or antinauseant properties, should not be used with iohexol. Others include MAO inhibitors, tricyclic antidepressants, CNS stimulants, psychoactive drugs described as analeptics, major tranquilizers, or antipsychotic drugs. Such medications should be discontinued at least 48 hours before myelography; should not be used for the control of nausea or vomiting during or after myelography; and should not be resumed for at least 24 hours postprocedure. In nonelective procedures in patients on these drugs, consider prophylactic use of anticonvulsants.

Intravascular: Preparatory dehydration may be dangerous in infants, young children, the elderly, in the presence of multiple myeloma and azotemic patients (especially those with polyuria, oliguria, diabetes, advanced vascular disease or preexisting dehydration). The undesirable dehydration in these patients may be accentuated by the osmotic diuretic action of the medium.

When high doses of contrast media are used, caution should be exercised in patients with congestive heart failure because of the transitory increase in circulatory osmotic load, and such patients should be observed for several hours to detect delayed hemodynamic disturbances.

When considering aortic injection the presence of a vigorous pulsatile flow should be established before using a catheter or pressure injection technique. A small 'pilot' dose (about 2 mL) should be administered to locate the exact site of needle or catheter tip to help prevent injection of the main dose into a branch of the aorta or intramurally.

Avoid entry of a large concentrated bolus into an aortic branch. Mesenteric necrosis, acute pancreatitis, renal shutdown, serious neurologic complications including spinal cord damage and hemiplegia or quadriplegia have been reported following inadvertent injection of a large part of the aortic dose of contrast media into an aortic branch or arterial trunks providing spinal or cerebral artery branches.

Pulsation must be present in the artery to be injected. Extreme caution is advised in considering peripheral angiography in patients suspected of having thromboangiitis obliterans (Buerger's disease) since any procedure (even insertion of a needle or catheter) may induce a severe arterial or venous spasm. Caution is also advisable in patients with severe ischemia associated with ascending infection. Special care is required in patients with suspected thrombosis, ischemic disease, local infection or a significantly obstructed vascular system. Occasional serious neurologic complications, including paraplegia have been reported in patients with aorto-iliac or femoral artery bed obstruction, abdominal compression, hypotension, hypertension and following injection of vasopressors.

When large individual doses are administered an appropriate time interval should be permitted to elapse between injections to allow for subsidence of hemodynamic disturbances.

Following catheter procedures gentle pressure hemostasis is advised followed by immobilization of the limb for several hours to prevent hemorrhage from the site of arterial puncture.

Special precautions, to be observed when performing specific diagnostic procedures, are listed in the Dosage section, under individual paragraphs pertaining to specific procedures.

Adverse Effects: General: Since the reactions which are known to occur upon parenteral administration of iodinated contrast agents are possible with any nonionic agent, the same degree of careful patient observation for adverse reactions, as with the use of conventional contrast media, should be strictly followed. Adequate equipment and appropriate personnel should be readily available in case a severe reaction should occur.

Adverse reactions following the use of iohexol are usually of mild to moderate severity. However, serious, lifethreatening and fatal adverse reactions have been associated with both the intravascular and subarachnoid use of iodinated contrast media, including iohexol.

It should be kept in mind that, although most adverse reactions occur soon after the administration of the contrast medium, some adverse reactions may be delayed and may be of long-lasting nature.

The reported incidence of adverse reactions to contrast media in patients with a history of allergy is twice that of the general population. Patients with a history of previous reactions to a contrast medium are three times more susceptible than other patients. However, sensitivity to contrast media does not appear to increase with repeated examinations.

Reactions Related to Technique: Adverse reactions to specific procedures are dealt with under Dosage. General reactions attributed to technique and/or procedure may include extravasation with burning pain, hematomas, ecchymosis and tissue necrosis, vascular spasm thrombosis, thrombophlebitis, bleeding, perforation, rupture and dissection of blood vessels, dislodgment of atheromatous plaques or thrombi with embolization, subintimal injection, injury to nerves and other structures and general trauma during the procedure.

Subarachnoid: Following subarachnoid administration of iohexol, as with other currently used non-ionic contrast media, the most important adverse reactions involve the CNS and the incidence of such adverse reactions increases when the more cephalad segments of the spinal cord are exposed to the contrast material. The amount and concentration of the contrast material also appear to have a direct relationship to the frequency and severity of such adverse effects.

Adverse reactions known to occur with the subarachnoid use of other nonionic iodinated contrast media may also follow the use of iohexol. Most adverse reactions occur several hours following the procedure necessitating close and prolonged observation.

The most frequently reported adverse reactions are headache, mild to moderate pain including backache, neckache and stiffness, nausea and vomiting. These reactions usually occur 1 to 10 hours after injection, and almost all occur within 24 hours. They are usually mild to moderate in degree, lasting for a few hours, and usually disappearing within 24 hours. Rarely, headaches may be severe or persist for days. Headache is often accompanied by nausea and vomiting and tends to be more frequent and persistent in patients not optimally hydrated.

Transient alterations in vital signs may occur.

Those reactions reported in clinical studies are listed below in decreasing order of occurrence, based on clinical studies of 1 531 patients.

Headache: The most frequently occurring adverse reaction following myelography with iohexol has been headache, with an incidence of approximately 18%. Rarely, headache may be severe, lasting in some cases for several days. In managing the patient, it is considered very important to prevent intracranial entry of contrast medium by postural management (see Patient Management).

Pain: Pain in the back, leg, neck, stiffness and neuralgia occurred following injection with a total incidence of about 8%.

Nausea and vomiting: Mild to severe nausea and vomiting was reported with an incidence of approximately 6% and 3% respectively (see Patient Management). Maintaining normal hydration is very important. The use of phenothiazine antinauseants is not recommended.

Dizziness: Transient dizziness was reported in about 2% of the patients.

The following serious adverse reactions involving the CNS, have been reported with the myelographic use of iohexol (in approximately <0.1%): convulsions, aseptic meningitis syndrome (see below), toxic encephalopathy, myelitis with transient or persistent sensory and motor disturbances of the central and peripheral nervous system; transient or persistent cortical blindness, unilateral or bilateral loss of vision, amblyopia, diplopia, oculomotor weakness, 6th nerve palsy, photophobia, nystagmus, hearing loss, dysphasia, dysarthria, quadriplegia, hemiplegia, spastic paraparesis, paralysis, areflexia, flaccidity, muscle weakness, hyperreflexia, hypertonia, myoclonus, fasciculation, general spasm, muscle spasm, spinal convulsion, cauda equina syndrome, urinary retention, nerve root disturbances, sensory loss, meningismus, neck stiffness, fever, fainting, cerebral edema, cerebral hemorrhage, hydrocephalus, somnolence, stupor, coma, confusion, disorientation, hallucination, decreased concentration, memory dysfunction, amnesia, depersonalization, psychosis, anxiety, agitation, depression, nightmares, elevated WBC and protein in spinal fluid, EEG changes.

An aseptic meningitis syndrome has been reported rarely (<0.01%). It was usually preceded by pronounced headaches, nausea and vomiting. Onset usually occurred about 12 to 18 hours postprocedure.

Prominent features were meningismus, fever, sometimes with oculomotor signs and mental confusion. Lumbar puncture revealed a high white cell count, high protein content often with a low glucose level and with absence of organisms. The condition usually clears spontaneously within a few days.

Profound mental disturbances have also rarely been reported. They have usually consisted of various forms and degrees of aphasia, mental confusion or disorientation. The onset is usually at 8 to 10 hours and lasts for about 24 hours or more. However, occasionally they have been manifest as apprehension, agitation, or progressive withdrawal in several instances to the point of somnolence, stupor and coma. In a few cases these have been accompanied by transitory hearing loss or other auditory symptoms and visual disturbances, including unilateral or bilateral loss of vision which may last for hours. In one case, persistent cortical loss of vision has been reported in association with convulsions. Ventricular block has been reported; amnesia of varying degrees may be present.

Although not previously reported with Omnipaque, as with the injection of any foreign substance into the subarachnoid space, the possibility of the potential of iohexol to produce adhesive arachnoiditis cannot be excluded.

Other reactions occurring with an individual incidence of less than 0.1% include: feelings of heaviness, severe hypotension, vasovagal reactions, bradycardia, cardiorespiratory arrest, sensation of heat, sweating and loss of appetite. Also chills, fever, profuse diaphoresis, pruritus, rash, erythema, periorbital edema, nasal congestion, dyspnea and a case of Guillain-Barré Syndrome.

Children: In controlled clinical trials involving 152 patients for pediatric myelography by lumbar puncture, adverse events following the use of Omnipaque 180 and Omnipaque 210 were as follows: headache 9%, vomiting 6%, backache 1.3%.

Other Reactions: Other reactions occurring with an individual incidence of less than 0.7% (single occurrence in 152 patients) included: fever, hives, stomach ache and visual hallucination.

Intravascular: Adverse reactions following the intravascular use of iohexol are usually of mild to moderate severity. However, as with other iodine-containing contrast media, serious, lifethreatening and fatal reactions have been associated with the intravascular administration of iohexol.

The injection of contrast media is frequently associated with the sensation of warmth and pain, burning sensation, flushing, nausea, vomiting and taste alterations. These relatively minor adverse effects are generally less frequent and less severe with Omnipaque than with conventional ionic contrast media.

Adverse reactions following the intravascular use of iohexol include: Cardiovascular: arrhythmias including PVCs and PACs (2%), angina/chest pain (1%), and severe hypotension (0.8%). Others including cardiac failure, asystole, bradycardia, tachycardia, atrial and ventricular fibrillation, premature beats, bundle branch block, vasovagal reaction, chest pain, coronary thrombosis, dyspnea, pulmonary edema, cyanosis, severe hypertension, hypertensive crisis, hypotension, peripheral vasodilation, acute vascular insufficiency, circulatory collapse, hypotensive and cardiogenic shock, cardiac arrest, and cardiorespiratory arrest were reported with an individual incidence of less than 0.4%.

CNS: vertigo (including dizziness and lightheadedness) (0.7%), pain (3%), photomas (2%), headache (2%) and taste perversion (1%). Others including anxiety, blurred vision, transient or persistent blindness, impairment of memory and coordination, tinnitus, fever, motor and speech dysfunction, convulsion, paresthesia, somnolence, confusion, dizziness, loss of consciousness, coma, apnea, psychotic reaction, stroke, stiff neck, hemiparesis, hemiplegia, nystagmus, restlessness and tremors were reported with an individual incidence of <0.4%.

Renal: occasionally transient proteinuria, hematuria and rarely oliguria, anuria and renal failure.

Allergic anaphylactoid: urticaria (0.3%) and purpura (0.1%). Occasionally asthmatic attacks, nasal and conjunctival symptoms (such as nasal congestion, sneezing, rhinitis, conjunctivitis, lacrimation), dermal reactions (such as urticaria with or without pruritus, erythematous, bullous and pleomorphic rashes), laryngospasm, bronchospasm, wheezing, laryngeal edema, angioneurotic edema, edema of glottis with signs of airway obstruction and rarely, anaphylactic shock leading to cardiorespiratory failure and death.

Other Reactions: Nausea (2%) and vomiting (0.7%), diarrhea, dyspepsia, and dry mouth were reported with an individual incidence of <0.1%, pallor, weakness, sweating, localized areas of edema, especially facial, vein cramps and thrombophlebitis following i.v. injection, rare cases of disseminated intravascular coagulation, neutropenia. Rarely, immediate or delayed rigors can occur, sometimes accompanied by hyperpyrexia. Infrequently, iodism (salivary gland swelling) from organic iodinated compounds appears 2 days after exposure and subsides by the 6th day.

Transient changes in some laboratory parameters are not uncommon.

The occurrence of thyroid storm in patients with hyperthyroidism or with autonomously functioning thyroid nodule have been reported following the use of iodinated contrast media.

Individual adverse reactions which occurred to a significantly greater extent for a specific procedure are also listed under Dosage for that procedure.

Treatment of Adverse Effects: Contrast media should be injected only by physicians thoroughly familiar with the emergency treatment of all adverse reactions to contrast media. The assistance of other trained personnel such as cardiologists, internists and anesthetists is required in the management of severe reactions.

A guideline for the treatment of adverse reactions is presented below. This outline is not intended to be a complete manual on the treatment of adverse reactions to contrast media or on cardiopulmonary resuscitation. The physician should refer to the appropriate texts on the subject.

It is also realized that institutions or individual practitioners will already have appropriate systems in effect and that circumstances may dictate the use of additional or different measures.

For minor allergic reactions: (If considered necessary) The i.v. or i.m. administration of an antihistaminic such as diphenhydramine HCl 25-50 mg is generally sufficient (contraindicated in epileptics). The resulting drowsiness makes it imperative to ensure that outpatients do not drive or go home unaccompanied.

Major or lifethreatening reactions: A major reaction may be manifested by signs and symptoms of cardiovascular collapse, severe respiratory difficulty and nervous system dysfunction. Convulsions, coma and cardio-respiratory arrest may ensue.

The following measures should be considered: Start emergency therapy immediately, carefully monitoring vital signs. Have emergency resuscitation team summoned: do not leave patient unattended. Ensure patent airway: guard against aspiration. Commence artificial respiration if patient is not breathing. Administer oxygen if necessary. Start external cardiac massage in the event of cardiac arrest. Establish route for i.v. medication by starting infusion of appropriate solution (5% dextrose in water). Judiciously administer specific drug therapy as indicated by the type and severity of the reaction. Careful monitoring is mandatory to detect adverse reactions to all drugs administered: soluble hydrocortisone 500 to 1 000 mg, i.v. for all acute allergic-anaphylactic reactions; epinephrine 1:1 000 solution (in the presence of anoxia it may cause ventricular fibrillation—**caution** in patients on adrenergic β-blockers—see Precautions): 0.2 to 0.4 mL s.c. for severe allergic reactions. In extreme emergency 0.1 mL/minute, appropriately diluted, may be given i.v. until desired effect is obtained. Do not exceed 0.4 mL. In case of cardiac arrest 0.1 to 0.2 mL appropriately diluted, may be given intracardially. In hypotension (carefully monitoring blood pressure): phenylephrine HCl 0.1 to 0.5 mg appropriately diluted slowly i.v., or by slow infusion, or norepinephrine bitartrate 4 mL of 0.2% solution in 1 000 mL of 5% dextrose by slow drip infusion; sodium bicarbonate 5% 50 mL i.v., every 10 minutes as needed to combat postarrest acidosis; atropine 0.4 to 0.6 mg i.v., to increase heart rate in sinus bradycardia. May reverse 2nd or 3rd degree block.

To control convulsions: Diazepam 5 to 10 mg slowly i.v., titrating the dose to the response of the patient, or, phenobarbital sodium may be injected i.v., or i.m., at a rate not in excess of 30 to 60 mg/minute. Depending on the patient's response a total dose of 200 to 300 mg may be required. The dose may be repeated in 6 hours if necessary.

Defibrillation, administration of antiarrhythmics and additional emergency measures and drugs may be required. Transfer patient to intensive care unit when feasible for further monitoring and treatment.

Dosage: Before use, the vials should be inspected visually for particulate matter and/or discoloration. If either is present, the vials should be discarded. Iohexol should be injected at or close to body temperature and should be used immediately once the vial seal has been punctured. It should not be transferred from the vial to other delivery systems except immediately prior to use; nor should it be mixed with other drugs. Any unused portion should be discarded. The vials should be protected from exposure to light. Syringes, needles and catheter tips must be kept free of aspirated blood to prevent clotting from prolonged contact.

Subarachnoid: Omnipaque 180, Omnipaque 240 or Omnipaque 300 is recommended for the examination of lumbar, thoracic and cervical regions in adults by lumbar or direct cervical injection. Omnipaque 180 is recommended for the examination of the lumbar, thoracic and cervical regions in children by lumbar injection. Myelography should not be performed in the presence of significant local or systemic infection where bacteremia is likely, or when lumbar or cervical puncture is contraindicated. The volume and concentration of Omnipaque 180, 240 or 300 to be administered will depend on the degree and extent of contrast required within the recommended dose range in the area under examination, and on the equipment and technique employed. Omnipaque solutions are slightly hypertonic to CSF.

Adults: A total dose of 3 060 mg Iodine or a concentration of 300 mg I/mL should not be exceeded in adults in a single myelographic examination.

Children: A total dose of 2 700 mg Iodine or a concentration of 180 mg I/mL should not be exceeded in children in a single myelographic examination. As in all diagnostic procedures, the minimum volume and dose to produce adequate visualization should be used. Most procedures do not require maximum dose.

Anesthesia is not necessary. Patients should be well hydrated. Seizure-prone patients should be maintained on anticonvulsant medication.

Rate of injection: To avoid excessive mixing with CSF and consequent dilution of contrast, injection should be made slowly, over 1 to 2 minutes.

Depending on the estimated volume of iohexol which may be required for the procedure, a small amount of CSF may be removed to minimize distention of the subarachnoid spaces, unless contraindicated.

The spinal puncture needle may be removed immediately following injection since, usually it is not necessary to remove iohexol after injection into the subarachnoid space.

If, in the clinical judgment of the physician, a repeat examination is required, an interval of 5 days between procedures is recommended.

Adults: The usual recommended total dosages of Omnipaque 180, 240 or 300 for use in lumbar, thoracic, cervical and total columnar myelography are in Table I (not to exceed maximum total dose of 3 060 mg iodine).

Table I—Omnipaque

Usual Recommended Total Dosages in Adults

Procedure	Omnipaque Formulations	Concentration (mg I/mL)	Volume (mL)
Lumbar Myelography (via Lumbar Injection)	Omnipaque 180 Omnipaque 240	180 240	10–17 7–12
Thoracic Myelography (via Lumbar or Cervical Injection)	Omnipaque 240 Omnipaque 300	240 300	6–12 6–10
Cervical Myelography (via Lumbar Injection)	Omnipaque 240 Omnipaque 300	240 300	6–12 6–10
Cervical Myelography (via C1-2 Injection)	Omnipaque 180 Omnipaque 240 Omnipaque 300	180 240 300	7–10 6–10 4–10
Total Columnar Myelography (via Lumbar Injection)	Omnipaque 240 Omnipaque 300	240 300	6–12 6–10

Omnipaque (cont'd)

If computerized tomography is to follow, it should be deferred for 2 to 6 hours to allow the degree of contrast to decrease. Computerized tomography shows CSF contrast enhancement in the thoracic region in about 1 hour, in the cervical region in about 2 hours, in the basal cisterns in 3 to 4 hours and in the ventricles and sulci in 5 to 6 hours.

Children: The usual recommended total doses for lumbar, thoracic, cervical and/or total columnar myelography by lumbar puncture in children range from 0.36 to 2.70 g I. Actual volumes administered depend largely on patient age and the following guidelines are recommended (see Table II).

Table II—Omnipaque

Usual Recommended Total Dosages in Children

Age	Concentration (mg I/mL)	Dose (g I)	Volume (mL)
3 to 36 months	180	0.72–1.8	4–10
3 to 7 years	180	0.9 –2.16	5-12
7 to 13 years	180	0.9 –2.34	5-13
13 to 18 years	180	1.08–2.7	6-15

Patient management following subarachnoid administration: Good patient management should be exercised at all times to minimize the potential for complications.

Preprocedure: Discontinue neuroleptic drugs (including phenothiazines, e.g., chlorpromazine, prochlorperazine, and promethazine) at least 48 hours beforehand. Maintain normal diet up to 2 hours before procedure. Ensure hydration with fluids up to procedure. Premedication is not usually considered necessary. Should myelography be necessary in patients with a history of seizures, such patients should be maintained on their anticonvulsant medication.

During procedure: Use minimum dose required for satisfactory contrast (see Dosage). In all positioning techniques keep the patient's head elevated above highest level of spine. Do not lower head of table more than 15° during examination. In patients with excessive lordosis consider lateral position for injection. Inject slowly (over 1 to 2 minutes) to avoid excessive mixing. Move medium within spinal subarachnoid space under fluoroscopic monitoring. Avoid intracranial entry of a bolus. Avoid early and high cephalad dispersion of the medium. Avoid abrupt or active patient movement to minimize excessive mixing with CSF. Instruct patient to remain **passive.** Move patient **slowly** and only as necessary.

Post-procedure: Following myelography move contrast medium to low lumbosacral area by upright positioning of the patient, for a few minutes. Raise head of stretcher to at least 30° before moving patient onto it. Movement onto and off the stretcher should be done slowly with patient completely passive, maintaining **head up** position. Before moving patient onto bed, raise head of bed 30° to 45°. Some clinicians advise patients to remain still in bed, in head up position or in the semi-sitting position, especially in the first few hours. Others have encouraged their patients to be fully ambulatory and have noted a reduction in the incidence of headache, nausea and vomiting. Maintain close observation and head up position for at least 24 hours after myelogram. Obtain visitors' cooperation in keeping the patient quiet and in **head up** position, especially in first few hours. Encourage oral fluids. Diet as tolerated. **If nausea or vomiting** occur, do not use phenothiazine antinauseants. Persistent nausea and vomiting will result in dehydration. Therefore prompt consideration of replacement by i.v. fluids is recommended.

Intravascular: (see Intravascular Dosage tables for recommended indications and dosage for intravascular administration).

Adult Left Ventriculography, Coronary Arteriography and Pediatric Angiocardiography: Omnipaque 350 is recommended in adults for left ventriculography, selective coronary arteriography and aortic root injections.

Omnipaque 350 is recommended in children for angiocardiography. Omnipaque 300 may be used in infants for angiocardiography.

Specific Precautions: During administration of Omnipaque 300 and Omnipaque 350, continuous monitoring of vital signs is desirable and adequate facilities for immediate resuscitation and cardioversion are mandatory. Caution is advised in the administration of large volumes to patients with incipient heart failure because of the possibility of aggravating the preexisting condition. Hypotension should be corrected promptly since it may induce serious arrhythmias.

Special care regarding dosage should be observed in patients with right ventricular failure, pulmonary hypertension or stenotic pulmonary vascular beds because of the hemodynamic changes which may occur.

Injection of contrast media into the cardiac chambers or great vessels causes significant hemodynamic disturbances, especially in right sided injections. Depending on the injection site and the time of recording, significant changes include a drop in cardiac output, elevation or decrease in ventricular pressures (RVSP, LVSP, LVEDP, RVEDP), systemic pressure, peripheral hypotension, brady or tachycardia, ectopic beats and other arrhythmias.

The hemodynamic changes which occur during and after ventricular and coronary injections are, in general, less pronounced with the low-osmolality Omnipaque than those seen with similar concentrations of conventional ionic contrast media, but, serious and life threatening hemodynamic disturbances can occur with the administration of all iodinated contrast media, including iohexol.

If repeat injections are made in rapid succession, all these changes are likely to be more pronounced.

After an initial rise, plasma volume may decrease and continue to fall below control levels, even beyond 30 minutes, probably due to diuresis.

The volume of each individual injection is a more important consideration than the total dose used. When large individual volumes are administered, as in ventriculography, sufficient time should be permitted to elapse between each injection to allow for subsidence of hemodynamic disturbances.

Due to increased risk of adverse reactions following recent acute myocardial infarction, careful patient selection is necessary, and the timing and performance of the examination should be carried out with extreme caution, if invasive radiographic procedures are considered necessary.

Pediatric patients at higher risk of experiencing adverse events during contrast medium administration include those having asthma, a sensitivity to medication and/or allergens, congestive heart failure, preexistent right heart strain, narrowed pulmonary vascular bed, a serum creatinine >1.5 mg/dL or those less than 12 months of age.

Specific Adverse Effects: Transient ECG changes occur frequently during the procedure. The following adverse effects have also occurred following administration of iohexol for this procedure: cardiac arrhythmias (bradycardia, ventricular tachycardia, atrial and ventricular fibrillation, heart block), anginal pain, coronary thrombosis, cardiac arrest, hypotensive shock and death. Apnea, arrhythmias, cerebral effects, convulsions, electrolyte and hemodynamic disturbances are more likely to occur in cyanotic infants.

Procedural complications include dissection of coronary arteries, dislodgment of atheromatous plaques, perforation of heart chambers or coronary arteries, hemorrhage and thrombosis.

Dosage: Adults: Left ventriculography: The usual adult volume of Omnipaque 350 for a single injection is 40 mL with a range of 30 to 60 mL. These doses may be repeated if necessary, but the total procedural dose should be limited to the minimum volume required to achieve a diagnostic examination.

Selective coronary arteriography: The usual adult volume for right or left coronary arteriography is 5 mL (range 3 to 10 mL)/ injection.

Aortic root injection when used alone: The usual adult single injection volume is 35 mL, with a range of 20 to 50 mL.

Children: Weight, a minor consideration in adults, must be considered in infants and young children during the administration of radiographic contrast media.

The usual recommended single injection volume of Omnipaque 350 and Omnipaque 300 for angiographic procedures in children are as follows: Angiocardiography: The usual single injection dose range is 0.5 to 1.5 mL/kg for Omnipaque 300 and 0.5 to 1.2 mL/kg for Omnipaque 350. When multiple injections are given, the total administered dose should not exceed 4 mL/kg or 100 mL, whichever is less.

The inherent risk of angiocardiography in cyanotic infants must be weighed against the necessity for performing this procedure. A dose of 10 to 20 mL may be particularly hazardous in infants weighing less than 7 kg. This risk is probably significantly increased if these infants have preexisting right heart strain, heart failure and effectively decreased or obliterated pulmonary vascular beds.

Apnea, bradycardia and other arrhythmias, cerebral effects, electrolyte and hemodynamic disturbances are more likely to occur in cyanotic infants. Infants are more likely than adults to respond with convulsions, particularly after repeated injections.

Cerebral Arteriography: Omnipaque 300 is recommended in adults for use in cerebral arteriography.

In cerebral arteriography, appropriate patient preparation is indicated. This may include suitable premedication.

Specific Precautions: Cerebral arteriography should be undertaken with extreme care, with special caution in elderly patients, patients in poor clinical condition, advanced arteriosclerosis, severe arterial hypertension, recent cerebral embolism or thrombosis, cardiac decompensation, subarachnoid hemorrhage and following a recent attack of migraine, if the examination is considered to be essential for the welfare of the patient and the patient should be watched for possible untoward reactions.

Specific Adverse Effects: Repeated injections of contrast material, administration of doses in excess of those recommended, the presence of occlusive atherosclerotic vascular disease and the technique and method of injection appear to contribute to the majority of adverse effects attributable to cerebral arteriography.

Normally, adverse effects are mild and transient such as a frequent feeling of warmth in the face and neck and infrequently a more severe burning discomfort is experienced.

Although the degree of pain, flushing and patient movement as the result of the use of iohexol in cerebral arteriography is generally less than that seen with comparable injections of monomeric ionic contrast media, cerebral arteriography has been associated with neurologic complications such as seizures, drowsiness, paresthesia, TIA, cerebral infarct, transient or persistent hemiparesis, and disturbances in speech and vision (slurred speech, blurred vision, nystagmus, photomas). Other adverse effects include hypotension, bradycardia, arrhythmia, vertigo, syncope and ECG and EEG changes. Permanent defects are possible (see Adverse Effects, Intravascular).

Usual Adult Dose: The recommended single dose of Omnipaque 300 for cerebral arteriography is as follows: common carotid artery 6 to 12 mL; internal carotid artery 5 to 10 mL; external carotid artery 4 to 8 mL and vertebral artery 6 to 10 mL. It is advisable to inject at rates approximately equal to the flow rate of the vessel being injected.

Contrast Enhanced Computed Tomography: Omnipaque 240 (iohexol 240 mgI/mL) may be used for i.v. contrast enhanced computed tomography of the head; Omnipaque 300 and Omnipaque 350 are indicated in adults for use in i.v. contrast enhanced computed tomographic head and body imaging by rapid injection or infusion technique.

Specific Warnings: In patients where the blood-brain barrier is known or suspected to be disrupted, the use of any radiographic contrast medium must be assessed on an individual risk to benefit basis, since neurological complications are more likely to occur. Caution is advised in patients with impaired renal function and with congestive heart failure.

Specific Precautions: The decision to employ contrast enhancement should be based upon a careful evaluation of clinical, other radiological and unenhanced CT findings, because unenhanced scanning may provide adequate diagnostic information in the individual patient, and because contrast enhancement may be associated with risk, may obscure certain lesions and increases radiation exposure.

I.V. CT scans of the head performed within 24 hours following myelography may yield false results due to the permeation of the brain by the contrast medium from adjacent CSF spaces. Therefore, if indicated, i.v. CT scan of the brain should be performed either before, or after a period of at least 24 hours following myelography.

Specific Adverse Effects: Following intravascular injection of large doses, transient or persistent neurological changes have been reported.

Usual Adult Dose: The concentration and volume required is influenced by the equipment and imaging technique used. The total procedural dose should be limited to the minimum volume required to achieve a diagnostic examination. The usual adult dose range is: Omnipaque 240: 85 to 150 mL; Omnipaque 300: 60 to 120 mL; Omnipaque 350: 50 to 80 mL.

Peripheral Arteriography: Omnipaque 350 or Omnipaque 300 is recommended in adults for use in peripheral arteriography by aortic (bifurcation) or by femoral artery injection. Sedative premedication may be employed prior to the use of Omnipaque. General anesthesia is not considered necessary.

Specific Precautions: Peripheral arteriography (by aortic injection): Under conditions of slowed aortic circulation there is an increased likelihood for aortic injection to cause muscle spasm. Occasional serious neurologic complications, including paraplegia, have also been reported in patients with aorto-iliac obstruction, femoral artery obstruction, abdominal compression, hypotension, hypertension, spinal anesthesia, injection of vasopressors to increase contrast, and low injection sites (L2-3). Especially in these patients the concentration, volume, and number of repeat injections of the medium should be maintained at a minimum with appropriate intervals between injections. The position of the patient and catheter tip should be carefully monitored.

Entry of a large aortic dose into the renal artery may cause, even in the absence of symptoms, albuminuria, hematuria, elevated creatinine and urea nitrogen and possible renal damage.

Specific Precautions: Peripheral arteriography (by femoral injection): Patient discomfort during and immediately following injection is generally less than that following injection of conventional ionic media. The incidence of discomfort for the second and subsequent injection may be somewhat higher than with the first injection.

Pulsation must be present in the artery to be injected. In thromboangiitis obliterans, severe ischemia with or without ascending infection, severe atherosclerosis or obstruction, arteriography should be performed with extreme caution, if at all.

Specific Adverse Effects: Adverse reactions observed during peripheral arteriography may sometimes be due to trauma during the procedure. Adverse reactions reported with the use of iodinated contrast media include hypotension, soreness in extremities, transient arterial spasm, gangrene, perforation of vessels, extravasation, hemorrhage, hematoma formation with tamponade, injury to nerves and other structures in close proximity to the artery, thrombosis, dissecting aneurysm, arteriovenous fistula, dislodgment of atheromatous plaques, subintimal injection and transient leg pain from contraction of calf muscles in femoral arteriography.

Usual Adult Dose: The volume required will depend on the size, flow rate and disease state of the injected vessel and on the size and condition of the patient, as well as the technique used. Omnipaque dosage recommendations for use in peripheral arteriography are in Table III.

Table III—Omnipaque

Omnipaque Dosage Recommendations for Use in Peripheral Arteriography

Aorto-femoral Runoffs (aortic injection)	20–60 mL Omnipaque 350 or 30–70 mL Omnipaque 300
Selective Arteriograms (femoral/iliac injection)	10–30 mL Omnipaque 350 or 10–40 mL Omnipaque 300

I.V. Digital Subtraction Arteriography: Omnipaque 350 is recommended in adults for use in i.v. digital subtraction arteriography.

It has been demonstrated that arteriograms of diagnostic quality can be obtained following the i.v. administration of contrast media employing digital subtraction and computer imaging enhancement techniques. The i.v. route of administration using these techniques has the advantage of being less invasive than the corresponding selective catheter placement of medium.

The dose is administered into a peripheral vein or the superior vena cava usually by mechanical injection although sometimes by rapid manual injection. Iohexol with this technique has been used to visualize the vessels of the head and neck. Radiographic visualization of these structures is dependent on timing (synchronizing with circulation time).

The solution can be injected i.v. as a rapid bolus to provide arterial visualization using digital subtraction radiography. Preprocedural medications are not considered necessary. Iohexol has provided diagnostic carotid arterial radiographs by i.v. injection in about 92% of patients. In some cases poor arterial visualization has been attributed to patient movement. There is generally less subjective or objective evidence of patient discomfort (general sensation of heat or pain) following injection compared with monomeric ionic media. In about 65% of patients discomfort is either absent or is mild, and is severe in about 2% of patients.

Specific Precautions related to the procedure: Since the dose is usually administered mechanically under high pressure, rupture of venous structures has occurred with extravasation of the contrast medium into the tissues of extremities or the mediastinum. It has been suggested that this is less likely to occur if an i.v. catheter is threaded proximally beyond larger tributaries in the case of the antecubital vein, into the superior vena cava or if the femoral vein is used. However with high pressure injection the catheter tip initially placed in larger venous structures may still recoil into a small tributary resulting in rupture of a small vein with extravasation into the neighboring tissues. In case of mediastinal extravasation severe pain and hypotensive shock have been reported.

Usual Adult Dose: The usual injection volume of Omnipaque 350 for the i.v. digital technique is 30 to 50 mL. This is administered as a bolus at 10 to 30 mL/second either by hand or using a pressure injector. The volume and rate of injection will depend primarily on the type of equipment and technique used, with first exposure made on calculated circulation time.

A dextrose solution may be layered over the contrast medium in the injector with the purpose of delivering the remnant of the bolus forward into the main circulation, and to flush the vein.

The patient is urged not to move or swallow during or immediately after the injection.

Peripheral Venography: Omnipaque 300 or Omnipaque 240 is recommended in adults for peripheral venography.

Specific Precautions: Special care is required when venography is performed in patients with suspected thrombosis, phlebitis, ischemic disease, local infection or significantly obstructed venous system. In the presence of venous stasis, vein irrigation with normal saline should be considered following the procedure.

Specific Adverse Effects: Following venography with iodinated contrast media, especially in the presence of venous stasis, inflammatory changes, thrombosis and gangrene may occur. Thrombosis is rare if the vein is irrigated following the injection.

Usual Adult Dose: The recommended single dose for use in peripheral lower extremity venography is: 20 to 100 mL Omnipaque 240, or 20 to 100 mL Omnipaque 300.

Excretory Urography: Omnipaque 350 or Omnipaque 300 is recommended in adults for excretory urography. Omnipaque 300 is recommended in children for excretory urography.

For pharmacodynamics of excretion in adults see Pharmacology, Intravascular. For adverse effects see Adverse Effects, General and Intravascular.

Patient preparation: Appropriate preparation of the patient is desirable for optimal results. A laxative the night before the examination, unless contraindicated and a low residue diet the day before the examination are recommended.

Specific Precautions: Preparatory dehydration is not recommended, especially in the elderly, infants, young children, diabetic or azotemic patients, or in patients with suspected myelomatosis.

Pediatric patients at higher risk of experiencing adverse events during contrast medium administration may include those having asthma, a sensitivity to medication and/or allergens, congestive heart failure, a serum creatinine >1.5 mg/dL or those less than 12 months of age.

Some clinicians consider multiple myeloma a contraindication to the use of contrast media because of the possibility of producing transient to fatal renal failure. If a decision to use iohexol is made, the patient should be well hydrated beforehand, since dehydration favors protein precipitation in the renal tubules, a minimal diagnostic dose used, and renal function and extent of urinary precipitation of the myeloma protein checked for a few days afterwards.

Caution is advised in patients with congestive heart failure and in cases of impaired renal function. In these patients the patient's clinical status and renal function should be carefully monitored.

Since there is a possibility of temporary suppression of urine formation, it is recommended that an interval of at least 48 hours elapse before excretory urography is repeated in patients with unilateral or bilateral reduction in renal function.

Usual Adult Dose: The usual recommended adult dose range for use in excretory urography is 25 to 50 mL i.v. of Omnipaque 350 or Omnipaque 300.

Children: Excretory Urography: The usual dose of Omnipaque 300 for children is 0.7 to 1.5 mL/kg. Dosage for infants and children should be administered in proportion to age and body weight. The total administered dose in infants should not exceed 3 mL/kg. In older children the maximum dose should not exceed 1.5 mL/kg or 50 mL, whichever is less.

Adult Intravascular Dosage: see Table IV.

Table IV—Omnipaque

Adult Intravascular Dosage

Procedure	Concentration of Solution (mg I/mL)	Usual Recommended Single Dose (mL)
Left Ventriculography	350	30–60
Selective Coronary Arteriography (right or left coronary artery)	350	3–10
Aortic Root	350	20–50
Cerebral Arteriography		
Common Carotid	300	6–12
Internal Carotid	300	5–10
External Carotid	300	4–8
Vertebral	300	6–10
Contrast Enhanced CT		
Head imaging by infusion	240	85–150
Head or body imaging by injection	300	60–120
	350	50–80
I.V. Digital Subtraction Arteriography	350	30–50
Peripheral Arteriography		
Aorto-femoral runoffs (aortic injection)	350	20–60
	300	30–70
Selective Arteriograms (femoral/iliac injection)	350	10–30
	300	10–40
Peripheral Venography	300	20–100
	240	20–100
Excretory Urography	350	25–50
	300	25–50

Pediatric Intravascular Dosage: see Table V.

Table V—Omnipaque

Pediatric Intravascular Dosage

Procedure	Concentration of Solution (mg I/mL)	Usual Recommended Single Dose (mL/kg bodyweight)
Angiocardiography	300	0.5–1.5
	350	0.5–1.2
Excretory Urography	300	0.7–1.5

Arthrography: Omnipaque 300 or Omnipaque 240 is recommended in adults for arthrography of the knee joint. Omnipaque 300 is recommended for arthrography of the shoulder joint in adults.

Specific Precautions: Strict aseptic technique is required to prevent infection. Fluoroscopic control should be used to ensure proper needle placement, prevent extracapsular injection and prevent dilution of contrast medium. Undue pressure should not be exerted during injection.

Specific Adverse Effects: Injection of Omnipaque into the joint is associated with transient discomfort, i.e., pain, swelling. However, delayed severe or persistent discomfort may occur occasionally. Severe pain may often result from undue use of pressure or the injection of large volumes. Joint swelling and effusion may occur. These adverse effects are partly procedurally dependent and of greater frequency when double-contrast technique is employed.

Adverse effects during arthrography included pain (36%), swelling sensation (58%), heat sensation (8%), muscle weakness (0.4%) and hematoma at the injection site (1%). Occasionally, muscle twitching, rash, itching, fatigue, and dry lips, were also observed during clinical studies involving 429 patients who had received iohexol by injection to the knee or shoulder joints. A single case of allergic synovitis associated with the use of Omnipaque has been reported in the literature.

Usual Adult Dose: Arthrography is usually performed under local anesthesia. As much fluid as possible should be aspirated from the joint. Passive or active manipulation is used to disperse the medium throughout the joint space. The amount of Omnipaque injected is largely dependent on the size of the joint to be examined and the technique employed. Contrast is good during the first 5 to 10 minutes following injection and begins to fade at 15 to 20 minutes.

Omnipaque (cont'd)

The following concentrations and volumes are recommended for normal adult knee and shoulder joints but should only serve as guidelines since joints may require more or less contrast medium for optimal visualization.
Knee: 5 to 15 mL Omnipaque 300 or Omnipaque 240.
Shoulder: 5 to 10 mL Omnipaque 300.

Lower volumes of contrast medium are usually injected when performing double-contrast examinations of the knee.

Supplied: Omnipaque is provided as a sterile, pyrogen-free colorless to pale yellow solution, in the following iodine concentrations: 180, 240, 300 and 350 mg I/mL. Each mL iohexol solution contains: tromethamine 1.21 mg and of edetate calcium disodium 0.1 mg in water for injection. pH adjusted between 6.8 and 7.7 with hydrochloric acid or sodium hydroxide. All solutions are sterilized by autoclaving and contain no preservatives. Solutions must be protected from light. Unused portions must be discarded.
Directions for Dispensing from Pharmacy Bulk Vial: The use of Pharmacy Bulk vials is restricted to hospitals with a recognized i.v. admixture program. The Pharmacy Bulk Vial is intended for single puncture, multiple dispensing.

The 4 available concentrations have the following physical properties (see Table VI).

Table VI—Omnipaque

Physical Properties of Omnipaque

Name	Iohexol conc. mg/mL	Iodine conc. mg I/mL	Osmolality mOsm/kg H_2O	Absolute Viscosity (cps) 20°C	Absolute Viscosity (cps) 37°C	Specific gravity (g/mL)
Omnipaque 180	388.3	180	408	3.1	2.0	1.205
Omnipaque 240	517.7	240	520	5.8	3.4	1.276
Omnipaque 300	647.1	300	672	11.8	6.3	1.345
Omnipaque 350	755.0	350	844	20.4	10.4	1.404

Iohexol at recommended concentrations is hypertonic to CSF and blood (300 mOsm/kg).

Normal range for the specific gravity of CSF is 1.005 to 1.009 and for blood, 1.050 to 1.064.

Omnipaque 180: Vials of 10 mL, 180 mg I/mL, boxes of 10. Vials of 15 mL, 180 mg I/mL, boxes of 10.

Omnipaque 240: Vials of 10 mL, 240 mg I/mL, boxes of 10. Vials of 20 mL (with 15 mL fill), 240 mg I/mL, boxes of 10. Vials of 50 mL, 240 mg I/mL, boxes of 10. Bottles of 100 mL, 240 mg I/mL, boxes of 10. Bottles of 200 mL, 240 mg I/mL, boxes of 10. Flexible containers of 100 mL, 240 mg I/mL, boxes of 10. Flexible containers of 200 mL, 240 mg I/mL, boxes of 10.

Omnipaque 300: Vials of 10 mL, 300 mg I/mL, boxes of 10. Vials of 20 mL, 300 mg I/mL, boxes of 10. Vials of 50 mL, 300 mg I/mL, boxes of 10. Bottles of 50 mL, 300 mg I/mL, boxes of 10. Bottles of 100 mL, 300 mg I/mL, boxes of 10. Bottles of 200 mL (with 150 mL fill), 300 mg I/mL, boxes of 10. Bottles of 200 mL, 300 mg I/mL, boxes of 10. Bottles of 500 mL, 300 mg I/mL, boxes of 6. Flexible containers of 100 mL, 300 mg I/mL, boxes of 10. Flexible containers of 150 mL, 300 mg I/mL, boxes of 10.

Omnipaque 350: Vials of 50 mL, 350 mg I/mL, boxes of 10. Bottles of 50 mL, 350 mg I/mL, boxes of 10. Bottles of 100 mL, 350 mg I/mL, boxes of 10. Bottles of 200 mL (with 150 mL fill), 350 mg I/mL, boxes of 10. Bottles of 200 mL, 350 mg I/mL, boxes of 10. Bottles of 500 mL, 350 mg I/mL, boxes of 6. Flexible containers of 100 mL, 350 mg I/mL, boxes of 10. Flexible containers of 150 mL, 350 mg I/mL, boxes of 10. Flexible containers of 200 mL, 350 mg I/mL, boxes of 10.

OMNISCAN® Ⓟ

Nycomed Imaging A.S.

Gadodiamide

Contrast Enhancement Agent for Magnetic Resonance Imaging (MRI)

Pharmacology: Gadodiamide was developed as a contrast agent for diagnostic use in Magnetic Resonance Imaging (MRI). Gadodiamide is a paramagnetic agent with unpaired electron spins which generate a local magnetic field. As water protons move through this local magnetic field, the changes in magnetic field experienced by the protons reorient them with the main magnetic field more quickly than in the absence of a paramagnetic agent.

In magnetic resonance imaging, visualization of normal and pathological brain and spinal tissue depends in part on variations in the radiofrequency signal intensity. These variations occur due to: changes in proton density; alteration of the spin-lattice or longitudinal relaxation time (T_1); and variation of the spin-spin or transverse relaxation time (T_2).

By increasing the relaxation rate, gadodiamide decreases both the T_1 and T_2 relaxation times in tissues where it is distributed. At clinical doses, the effect is primarily on the T_1 relaxation time, and produces an increase in signal intensity.

Gadodiamide does not cross the intact blood-brain barrier and, therefore, does not accumulate in normal brain or in lesions that do not have an abnormal blood-brain barrier e.g., cysts, mature postoperative scars, etc. [Lack of enhancement need not indicate absence of pathology since some types of low grade malignancies or inactive MS-plaques fail to enhance; it can be used for differential diagnosis between different pathologies.] Disruption of the blood-brain barrier or abnormal vascularity allows accumulation of gadodiamide in lesions such as neoplasms, abscesses and subacute infarcts. The extended time for gadodiamide to be accumulated in the lesions is unknown.

Pharmacokinetics: The pharmacokinetics of i.v. administered gadodiamide in normal subjects conforms to an open, 2 compartment model with mean distribution and elimination half-lives (reported as mean±SD) of 3.7±2.7 minutes and 77.8±16 minutes, respectively.

Gadodiamide is eliminated primarily in the urine with 95.4±5.5% (mean±SD) of the administered dose eliminated by 24 hours. There is no detectable biotransformation or decomposition of gadodiamide. The renal and plasma clearance rates of gadodiamide are nearly identical (1.7 and 1.8 mL/min/kg, respectively), and are similar to that of substances excreted primarily by glomerular filtration. The volume of distribution of gadodiamide (200±61 mL/kg) is equivalent to that of extracellular water. No protein binding has been observed.

Plasma clearance and elimination half-life were independent of dose after injection of 0.1 and 0.3 mmol/kg. No metabolites have been detected.
Secondary Pharmacodynamics: There were no clinically significant deviations from preinjection values in hemodynamic, blood and urine laboratory parameters following i.v. injection of gadodiamide in healthy volunteers. However, a minimal transient increase in serum iron levels 8 to 48 hours after gadodiamide injection was observed.

Indications: In adults and the pediatric population for contrast enhancement of Magnetic Resonance Imaging (MRI) of lesions of the CNS with expected abnormal vascularity or those thought to cause abnormalities in the blood-brain barrier. Gadodiamide has been shown to facilitate visualization of CNS lesions including but not limited to tumors.

For i.v. administration for use in MRI in adults to facilitate the visualization of lesions with abnormal vascularity within the thoracic, abdominal, pelvic cavities, breast, retroperitoneal space and musculoskeletal system.

Contraindications: Should not be administered to patients who are known or suspected to be hypersensitive to it or any of its components.

Warnings: As with any contrast agent, the possibility of a reaction, including serious, life-threatening, fatal, anaphylactoid or other idiosyncratic reactions should always be considered (see Adverse Effects), especially in those patients with a known clinical hypersensitivity. In the event of hypersensitive reactions, it is essential that medical personnel be familiar with the practice of emergency measures and that adequate equipment and drugs utilized in these situations be readily available for emergency treatment.

Patients with history of allergy or drug reaction should be observed for several hours after drug administration.

Deoxygenated sickle erythrocytes have been shown in in vitro studies to align perpendicular to a magnetic field which may result in vaso-occlusive complications in vivo. The enhancement of magnetic moment by gadodiamide may possibly potentiate sickle erythrocyte alignment. Gadodiamide injection in patients with sickle cell anemia and other hemoglobinopathies has not been studied.

Patients with other hemolytic anemias have not been adequately evaluated following administration of gadodiamide to exclude the possibility of increased hemolysis.

Precautions: General: Diagnostic procedures involving the use of contrast agents should be conducted under supervision of a physician with the prerequisite training and a thorough knowledge of the procedure to be performed. Gadodiamide should be drawn into the syringe and used immediately. If nondisposable equipment is used, scrupulous care should be taken to prevent residual contamination with traces of cleansing agents.

Since gadodiamide is cleared from the body by glomerular filtration, caution should be exercised in patients with impaired renal function. Gadodiamide can be removed from circulation by hemodialysis.

Adequate time should elapse between administration of iodine containing contrast media and enhanced MRI examination, due to the possibility of inducing reversible renal failure. A single case of reversible renal failure occurred in a clinical study when a patient with previously reported normal kidney function, was administered a high dose of gadodiamide within 24 hours of prior examination with an iodine containing contrast agent.

If, in the clinical judgment of the physician, sequential or repeat examinations are required, a suitable interval of time between administrations should be observed to allow for normal clearance of the drug from the body.
Children: At this time, there is no data in the pediatric population regarding the minimum period of time before a repeat injection of gadodiamide; see Pharmacology for information on pharmacokinetics in adults.
Convulsive States: While there is no evidence suggesting that gadodiamide directly precipitates convulsion, the possibility that it may decrease the convulsive threshold in susceptible patients cannot be ruled out. Appropriate precautionary measures should be taken with patients predisposed to seizure.
Laboratory Test Findings: Asymptomatic transitory changes in serum iron have been observed. The clinical significance is unknown.

Gadodiamide interferes with serum calcium measurements with some colorimetric (complexometric) methods commonly used in hospitals. It may also interfere with determinations of other electrolytes (e.g., iron). Thus it is recommended not to use such methods for 12 to 24 hours after administration of gadodiamide.
Pregnancy: There are no adequate and well-controlled studies in pregnant women. Gadodiamide should be used during pregnancy only if the potential benefit justifies the potential risk to the fetus.

Gadodiamide had no effects on fertility or reproductive performance in rats or in teratology studies in rats and rabbits at doses that did not cause maternal toxicity (1 mmol/kg).
Lactation: It is not known whether this drug is excreted in human milk. Because many drugs are excreted in human milk, caution should be exercised when gadodiamide is administered to a nursing woman.
Children: No studies have been conducted in pediatric patients with severe renal or hepatic dysfunction; clinically unstable hypertension or uncontrolled hypertension; and in premature infants (see Adverse Effects).
Geriatrics: No specific precautions other than those pertinent to MRI and gadodiamide in general are applicable for elderly patients.

Adverse Effects: Adults: The most frequent adverse reactions observed in patients during gadodiamide clinical trials were nausea, headache and dizziness with an incidence of 3% or less. The majority of these adverse reactions were of mild to moderate intensity.

The following adverse reactions occurred in less than 1% of the adult patients: Application Site Disorders: injection site reaction.
Autonomic Nervous System Disorders: vasodilation.
Body as a Whole—General Disorders: anaphylactoid reactions (characterized by cardiovascular, respiratory, and cutaneous symptoms), asthenia, chest pain, fatigue, fever, hot flushes, malaise, pain, rigors, syncope.
Cardiovascular Disorders: cardiac failure, rare arrhythmia and myocardial infarction resulting in death in patients with ischemic heart disease, flushing, deep thrombophlebitis.

Central and Peripheral Nervous System Disorders: aggravated migraine, ataxia, convulsions (including grand mal), abnormal coordination, aggravated multiple sclerosis (characterized by sensory and motor disturbances) paresthesia, tremor.
Gastrointestinal System Disorders: abdominal pain, diarrhea, eructation, melena, dry mouth, vomiting.
Hearing and Vestibular Disorders: tinnitus.
Musculoskeletal System Disorders: arthralgia, myalgia.
Psychiatric Disorders: anorexia, anxiety, personality disorder, somnolence.
Respiratory System Disorders: rhinitis, dyspnea.
Skin and Appendage Disorders: pruritus, rash, erythematous rash, skin discoloration, sweating increased, urticaria.
Special Senses, Other Disorders: taste loss, taste perversion.
Urinary System Disorders: acute reversible renal failure.
Vision Disorders: abnormal vision.
Children: Three adverse events occurred in 3 of 91 (3%) patients during gadodiamide clinical trials in pediatric patients. This includes all adverse events regardless of attribution.
Body as a Whole—General Disorders: fever.
Liver and Biliary System Disorders: abnormal hepatic function.
Skin and Appendage Disorders: rash.

The fever and rash were of mild intensity and the abnormal hepatic function was of severe intensity (although of uncertain relationship to administration of gadodiamide).

Overdose: Symptoms and Treatment: Clinical consequences of overdosage have not been reported and acute symptoms of toxicity are unlikely in patients with normal renal function. Treatment is symptomatic. There is no antidote for this contrast medium. In patients with delayed elimination due to renal insufficiency and in patients who have received excessive doses, the contrast medium may theoretically be eliminated by hemodialysis.

Dosage: Gadodiamide should be drawn into the syringe and used immediately. If nondisposable equipment is used, scrupulous care should be taken to prevent residual contamination with traces of cleansing agents.

Contrast-enhanced MRI should start shortly after administration of the contrast medium. Optimal enhancement is generally observed within 45 minutes after injection of gadodiamide. T_1-weighted scanning sequences are particularly suitable for contrast-enhanced examinations with gadodiamide. In the investigated range of field strengths, from 0.15 Tesla up to 1.5 Tesla, the relative image contrast was found to be independent of the applied field strength.

The recommended dosage of gadodiamide for imaging of the CNS is 0.2 mL/kg (0.1 mmol/kg), administered as a bolus i.v. injection (see Table I). If medically indicated, preprocedural medication (e.g., sedatives) may be administered according to the normal routine for MR examinations. Any unused portion must be discarded.

The recommended dose of gadodiamide for imaging of the body is 0.6 mL/kg (0.3 mmol/kg), administered as a bolus i.v. injection (see Table I).

Table I—Omniscan

Dosage Chart

Body Weight (kg)	Pediatric 0.1 mmol/kg	Adult 0.1 mmol/kg	Adult 0.3 mmol/kg
	Volume (mL)		
5	1.0		
10	2.0		
12	2.4		
14	2.8	—	—
16	3.2	—	—
18	3.6	—	—
20	4.0	—	—
22	4.4	—	—
24	4.8	—	—
26	5.2	—	—
28	5.6	—	—
30	6.0	—	—
40	8.0	8.0	24.0
50	10.0	10.0	30.0
60	12.0	12.0	36.0
70	14.0	14.0	42.0
80	16.0	16.0	48.0
90	—	18.0	54.0
100	—	20.0	60.0
110	—	22.0	66.0
120	—	24.0	72.0
130*	—	26.0	78.0

*The heaviest patient in clinical studies weighed 136 kg.

To ensure complete injection of the contrast medium, the injection should be followed by a 5 mL flush of 0.9% sodium chloride. The imaging procedure should be completed within 1 hour of administration of gadodiamide.

Parenteral products should be inspected visually for particulate matter and discoloration prior to administration, whenever solution and container permit. Do not use the solution if it is discolored or particulate matter is present.

Supplied: Each mL of sterile, clear, colorless to slightly yellow, aqueous solution contains: gadodiamide 287 mg, caldiamide sodium 12 mg and water for injection. The pH is adjusted between 5.5 and 7.0 with hydrochloric acid and/or sodium hydroxide. Vials of 10 mL (5 mL fill); vials of 10 mL; vials of 20 mL (15 mL fill); vials of 20 mL. Boxes of 10 single dose vials.

All solutions are sterilized by autoclaving and contain no preservatives. Unused portions must be discarded. Protect from light. Do not freeze. If inadvertently frozen, do not use gadodiamide solutions, as freezing could cause small cracks in the vials which would compromise the sterility of the product.

Store at controlled room temperature 15 to 30°C.

Reviewed 1999

OMNI-TUSS® Ⓝ

Rhône-Poulenc Rorer

Codeine—Chlorpheniramine—Ephedrine—Phenyltoloxamine (Resin Complex)

Antitussive—Decongestant—Expectorant

Indications: To facilitate expectoration and control cough associated with inflamed mucosa and tenacious sputum which does not respond to products of lesser potency.

Contraindications: Hypertension, cardiac disease, hyper- thyroidism, prostatic hypertrophy, sensitivity to any of the components, patients receiving MAO inhibitors.

Precautions: Before prescribing medication to suppress or modify cough, it is important to ascertain that the underlying cause of the cough is identified, that modification of the cough does not increase the risk of clinical or physiologic complications, and that appropriate therapy for the primary disease is provided.

In young children, the respiratory centre is especially susceptible to the depressant action of narcotic cough suppressants. Benefit to risk ratio should be carefully considered, especially in children with respiratory embarrassment, e.g., croup. Estimation of dosage relative to the child's age and weight is of great importance.

Pregnancy: Since codeine crosses the placental barrier, its use in pregnancy is not recommended.

As codeine may inhibit peristalsis, patients with chronic constipation should be given Omni-Tuss only after weighing the potential therapeutic benefit against the hazards involved.

Omni-Tuss contains codeine: may be habit forming.

Use with caution in patients with glaucoma or diabetes mellitus.

Occupational Hazards: Patients should be cautioned not to operate vehicles or hazardous machinery until their response to the drug has been determined.

Since the depressant effects of antihistamines are additive to those of other drugs affecting the CNS, patients should be cautioned against drinking alcoholic beverages or taking hypnotics, sedatives, psychotherapeutic agents or other drugs with CNS depressant effects during antihistaminic therapy.

See also guaifenesin and codeine phosphate monographs.

Adverse Effects: Rarely: jitteriness, nausea, drying of mouth, insomnia, drowsiness, constipation, which disappear upon adjustment of the dose or discontinuance of treatment.

Overdose: Symptoms: May include nausea, dry mouth, sedation, respiratory depression.

Treatment: Gastric emptying by lavage or emesis, intubation measures aimed at supporting respiration and the administration of a narcotic antagonist, e.g., naloxone. (Adults: 0.4 mg/kg i.v., i.m. or s.c. repeated at 2–3 minute intervals. If no response after 2 or 3 doses, the condition may be due partly or totally to other disease processes or nonopiate drugs. Children: 0.01 mg/kg i.v., im. or s.c. Dose may be repeated as for the adult administration.)

Dosage: Orally, every 12 hours: Adults, 5 mL; children 6 to 12 years, 2.5 mL.

Supplied: Each 5 mL of green, mint-flavored liquid contains: codeine 10 mg, phenyltoloxamine 5 mg, chlorpheniramine 3 mg, ephedrine 25 mg, all as cation exchange resin complexes, and guaiacol carbonate 20 mg. Nonmedicinal ingredients: D&C Yellow No 10, FD&C Blue No 1, flavor of limes, flavor menthol cream, methylparaben, polacrilin potassium, propylparaben, purified water and sorbitol. Energy: 18 kJ (4.4 kcal)/5 mL. Sodium: <1 mmol (20 mg)/5 mL. Alcohol-, gluten-, lactose-, sucrose- and tartrazine-free. Bottles of 500 mL.

ONCASPAR® Ⓟ

Rhône-Poulenc Rorer

Pegaspargase

Antineoplasic

> Caution: Allergic reactions may occur during therapy with pegaspargase, especially in patients with known hypersensitivity to the other forms of L-asparaginase.
>
> In view of the unpredictability of adverse reactions, pegaspargase should be given under the supervision of a physician who is qualified by training and experience to administer cancer chemotherapeutic agents.
>
> Pegaspargase has an adverse effect on liver function in some patients. Therapy with pegaspargase may increase pre-existing liver impairment caused by prior therapy or underlying disease. Because of this, there is a possibility that pegaspargase may increase the toxicity of other concomitant medication.

Pharmacology: In a significant number of patients with acute leukemia, particularly lymphoblastic, the malignant cells are dependent on an exogenous source of L-asparagine for survival. Normal cells, however, are able to synthesize L-asparagine and thus are less affected by its rapid depletion produced by treatment with the enzyme L-asparaginase which hydrolyzes extracellar L-asparagine into L-aspartic acid and ammonia.

Pegaspargase, a pegylated form of the enzyme L-asparaginase derived from E. coli is an oncolytic agent used in combination with chemotherapy for the treatment of patients with acute lymphoblastic leukemia who are hypersensitive to native forms of L-asparaginase.

The disappearance of pegaspargase from plasma is monophasic. The mean half-life, volume of distribution and rate of total clearance were 14.9 days, 2.04 L/m² and 0.13 L/m²·day, respectively, according to a pharmacokinetic study in 25 adult patients with various leukemic disorders who were given 1-hour infusions of pegaspargase 500 to 8 000 IU/m². Plasma enzymatic concentrations were proportional to the dose of pegaspargase. The active enzyme was not detectable in urine. Compared with L-asparaginase, pegaspargase has a longer half-life (6 to 14 days for pegaspargase vs 0.6 to 1.2 days for L-asparaginase) and a slower total clearance but a similar volume of distribution.

Indications: In the treatment of acute lymphoblastic leukemia (ALL) of childhood ($\leq$ 21 years of age at the time of diagnosis), specifically for the patients with known hypersensitivity to other forms of L-asparaginase. Pegaspargase should not be used as the sole induction, consolidation or maintenance agent unless combination therapy is deemed inappropriate.

Contraindications: Patients with pancreatitis or a history of pancreatitis. Acute hemorrhagic pancreatitis has been reported following L-asparaginase administration. Pegaspargase is also contraindicated in patients who have had previous anaphylactic reactions to it and bleeding following L-asparaginase treatment.

Warnings: Allergic reactions may occur during therapy with pegaspargase, especially in patients with known hypersensitivity to the other forms of L-asparaginase.

In view of the unpredictability of adverse reactions, pegaspargase should be given under the supervision of a physician who is qualified by training and experience to administer cancer chemotherapeutic agents.

Pegaspargase has an adverse effect on liver function in some patients. Therapy with pegaspargase may increase pre-existing liver impairment caused by prior therapy or underlying disease. Because of this, there is a possibility that pegaspargase may increase the toxicity of other concomitant medication.

Pegaspargase may cause clinical pancreatitis in some patients.

L-asparaginase has been shown in animals to possess embryotoxic and teratogenic activity. Therefore, it should not be used in pregnant patients unless the clinician considers

Oncaspar (cont'd)

that the benefits to the patient outweigh the possible risks to the patient.

Precautions: General: Pegaspargase is a contact irritant and the solution must be handled and administered with care (see Dosage). Inhalation of vapors and contact with skin or mucous membranes, especially those of the eyes, must be avoided. In case of contact, wash with copious amounts of water for at least 15 minutes.

Patients administered pegaspargase should be observed for 1 hour after administration and all medication for management of anaphylactic reaction should be available on premises. Anaphylactic reactions require the immediate use of epinephrine, oxygen and i.v. steroids.

Patients should be informed of the possibility of allergic reactions to pegaspargase.

Patients administered pegaspargase are prone to infections and bleeding (see Adverse Effects).

Pegaspargase has been reported to have immunosuppressive activity in animal experiments. Accordingly, the possibility that use of the drug in man may predispose to infection should be considered.

Laboratory Tests: The fall in circulating lymphoblasts is often quite marked; normal or below normal leukocyte counts are noted frequently within the first several days after initiating therapy. This may be accompanied by a marked rise in serum uric acid. The development of uric acid nephropathy is possible. Appropriate preventive measures should be taken, e.g., allopurinol, increased fluid intake and alkalization of urine. As a guide to the effects of therapy, the patient's peripheral blood count and bone marrow should be monitored frequently.

Frequent serum amylase determinations should be obtained to detect early evidence of pancreatitis. If pancreatitis occurs, therapy should be stopped and not reinstituted. Blood sugar should be monitored during therapy with pegaspargase because hyperglycemia may occur.

Drug Interactions: Native L-asparaginase has been shown to diminish or abolish the effect of arabinosyl cytosine and methotrexate on malignant cells. This effect lasts as long as L-asparagine levels are suppressed. Since pegaspargase depletes L-asparagine levels for several weeks, clinical use of arabinosyl cytosine or methotrexate may not be optimally effective for a period of time after administration of pegaspargase. Depletion of protein synthesis due to effect of pegaspargase may lead to increased toxicity of protein bound drugs, decreased enzymatic detoxification of other drugs by the liver and prolonged bleeding due to imbalances in coagulation factors. Therefore anticoagulant therapy should be used with caution.

Pregnancy: Animal reproduction studies have not been conducted with pegaspargase. It is also not known whether pegaspargase can cause fetal harm when administered to a pregnant woman or can affect reproduction capacity. Pegaspargase should be given to a pregnant woman only if clearly needed. L-asparaginase has been shown in animals to possess embryotoxic and teratogenic activity. Therefore it should not be used in pregnant patients unless the clinician considers that the benefits to the patient outweigh the possible risks to the patient (see Warnings).

Lactation: It is not known whether pegaspargase is excreted in human milk.

Because many drugs are excreted in human milk, caution should be exercised when pegaspargase is administered to a nursing woman.

Adverse Effects: Like asparaginase, pegaspargase can cause allergic reactions, including anaphylaxis. The incidence of hypersensitivity reactions to pegaspargase in patients who have had reaction to asparaginase is about 30%. Also like asparaginase, pegaspargase can cause pancreatitis, hypoproteinemia, hyperglycemia, bleeding, coagulopathy and hepatic dysfunction. Whether the longer half-life of pegaspargase might aggravate the drug's toxicity is unclear. The i.v. route may be associated with increased toxicity.

Higher proportion of previously hypersensitive patients converted to a high antibody level during therapy than the non-hypersensitive patients. Not all of hypersensitive patients who developed high antibody levels experienced hypersensitivity reactions. Asparaginase specific IgG antibodies appear to correlate better with allergic reactions than do corresponding IgE antibodies and the clinical hypersensitivity reactions appear to be mediated by the complement pathway. While there may be some correlation between clinical hypersensitivity and high anti-asparaginase antibody levels, a causal relationship is not clear. Both of these phenomena may be related to the extent of previous asparaginase exposure. Hypersensitivity due to anti-asparaginase antibody formation may result in less than optimal asparagine depletion and diminished efficacy of asparaginase therapy.

Table I summarizes the overall incidence and incidence of grade 3 and 4 Oncaspar-related toxicities.

Overall, 8% of patients treated with pegaspargase experienced hypersensitivity reactions that resulted in termination from the study. Another 8% experienced nonallergic reactions that resulted in termination from study.

Acute clinical pancreatitis may include symptoms of nausea, vomiting and abdominal pain. Elevation of lipase and amylase concentrations may be present. However, due to the inhibition of protein synthesis, these concentrations may also appear normal. These symptoms usually subside with withdrawal of the drug, but fulminant pancreatitis has resulted in death.

Inhibition of insulin production may lead to clinical hyperglycemia, which requires treatment with insulin, in 2 to 3% of patients treated with pegaspargase. Therefore, patients should be monitored for hyperglycemia as well as alerted to the signs and symptoms of hyperglycemia.

Hemorrhagic events can result from the inhibition of vitamin K-dependent clotting factor synthesis and the prolongation of prothrombin time and partial thromboplastin time. Thromboses can also occur due to inhibition of the synthesis of anticoagulant proteins such as antithrombin III.

Elevations in liver enzymes such as aspartate aminotransferase, alanine aminotransferase, total bilirubin, and alkaline phosphatase are usually seen within the first 2 weeks of treatment and tend to be transient and a function of protein synthesis inhibition.

Gastrointestinal adverse effects may occur with pegaspargase use. Mild to moderate nausea and vomiting may occur in some patients but it can be easily controlled with standard antiemetic therapy. Prophylactic antiemetic therapy is recommended. Other gastrointestinal adverse effects include anorexia and constipation.

CNS changes can occur with the use of pegaspargase. Somnolence, lethargy and generalized weakness have been observed in 33% of patients treated with pegaspargase. More severe CNS changes are rare (2%) but have been observed (e.g., confusion, stupor, coma).

Due to enzyme action of pegaspargase, ammonia may accumulate as an end product in the serum, resulting in the clinical symptomatology. The symptoms tend to disappear when ammonia concentrations return to normal limits and the level of L-asparaginase is depleted in the body.

Overdose: Symptoms and Treatment: Pegaspargase is safe and well tolerated in single doses ranging from 500 to 8 000 IU/m². No consistent, dose-related, dose-limiting toxicity has been observed over this dosage range. Depletion of serum proteins by pegaspargase may increase the toxicity of other drugs that are protein bound.

Dosage: As a component of selected multiple agent regimens, pegaspargase can be administered by either the i.v. or i.m. route. The preferred route of administration, however, is the i.m. route because of a reported lower incidence of toxicity and hypersensitivity reactions (including anaphylaxis) associated with this route of administration. The usual dosage is 2 500 IU/m² (see Recommended Induction Regimens).

When administered i.v., this enzyme should be given over a period of not less than 2 hours through the side arm of an already running infusion of Sodium Chloride Injection or Dextrose Injection 5%. Pegaspargase has little tendency to cause phlebitis when given i.v. Anaphylactic reactions require the immediate use of epinephrine, oxygen and i.v. steroids. The i.v. route may be associated with increased toxicity.

When administering pegaspargase i.m., the volume at a single injection site should be limited to 2 mL. If a volume greater than 2 mL is to be administered, multiple injection sites should be used.

Pegaspargase significantly inhibits cellular protein synthesis, resulting in a number of drug-drug interactions. Methotrexate and cytarabine exhibit schedule-dependent interactions with L-asparaginase and these interactions are expected to occur with pegaspargase as well. Pegaspargase may interfere with the enzymatic detoxification of other drugs, particularly in the liver. It is recommended, therefore, that pegaspargase be used in combination regimens only by physicians familiar with the benefits and risks of a given regimen.

Recommended Induction Regimens: When using chemotherapeutic agents in combination for the induction of remission in patients with acute lymphoblastic leukemia, regimens are sought which provide a maximum chance of success while avoiding excessive cumulative toxicity or drug interactions.

One of the following combination regimens incorporating pegaspargase is recommended for acute lymphoblastic leukemia in patients with known hypersensitivity to other forms of L-asparaginase.

In the regimens below, day 1 is considered to be the first day of induction therapy.

Regimen/I: Administer prednisone, 40 mg/m²/day, orally, in 3 divided doses for 28 days (the total daily dose should be to

Table I—Oncaspar

Incidence of Grade 3 and 4 Toxicity by Route of Administration n(%)

	Overall Toxicities I.V. and I.M. Administration	I.V. Administration (n=48)		I.M. Administration (n=187)	
	(n=235)	Grade 3	Grade 4	Grade 3	Grade 4
Hypersensitivity Reaction	41 (17)				
Anaphylaxis		0 (0)	2 (4.2)	0 (0)	1 (0.5)
Allergic reaction		1 (2.1)	0 (0)	3 (1.6)	0 (0)
Urticaria, rash		1 (2.1)	0 (0)	1 (0.5)	0 (0)
Pancreatitis	15 (6)				
Amylase		0 (0)	0 (0)	1 (0.5)	4 (2.1)
Clinical pancreatitis		0 (0)	0 (0)	1 (0.5)	0 (0)
Hepatotoxicity	173 (74)				
Decreased serum albumin		11 (32.4)	2 (5.9)	20 (18.9)	4 (3.8)
Hepatic failure		0 (0)	1 (2.1)	0 (0)	3 (1.6)
Increased bilirubin		5 (10.4)	10 (20.8)	11 (5.9)	7 (3.7)
Increased AST/ALT		10 (20.8)	0 (0)	27 (14.4)	4 (2.1)
Coagulopathy	123 (52)				
PT		0 (0)	0 (0)	5 (2.7)	3 (1.6)
PTT		2 (4.2)	1 (2.1)	7 (3.7)	9 (4.8)
Fibrinogen		3 (6.2)	2 (4.2)	20 (10.7)	5 (2.7)
Thrombosis		0 (0)	0 (0)	4 (2.1)	1 (0.5)
Gastrointestinal	41 (17)	0 (0)	0 (0)	0 (0)	0 (0)
Hyperglycemia	13 (5)				
Hyperglycemia		4 (8.3)	0 (0)	3 (1.6)	5 (2.7)
Diabetes Mellitus		0 (0)	0 (0)	0 (0)	1 (0.5)
Neurologic Dysfunction	6 (3)				
Convulsion		1 (2.1)	1 (2.1)	1 (0.5)	0 (0)
Renal	81 (34)				
BUN		4 (10.8)	0 (0)	2 (1.9)	0 (0)
Other	–				
Muscle cramp, pain		0 (0)	0 (0)	1 (0.5)	0 (0)

the nearest 2.5 mg). This dosage of prednisone should be tapered gradually over a 7-day period.

Administer vincristine sulfate, 1.5 mg/m²/week, i.v., on days 1, 8, 15 and 22 of the treatment period. The maximum single dose should not exceed 2 mg.

Administer pegaspargase, 2 500 IU/m² i.m. on days 1 and 15 of the treatment period.

Administer Daunorubicin, 25 mg/m² i.v. on days 1, 8, 15 and 22 of treatment.

Regimen/II: Administer prednisone, 40 mg/m²/day, orally, in 3 divided doses for 28 days (the total daily dose should be to the nearest 2.5 mg). This dosage of prednisone should be tapered gradually over a 7-day period.

Administer vincristine sulfate, 1.5 mg/m²/week, i.v., for 4 doses, on days 1, 8, 15, and 22 of the treatment period. The maximum single dose should not exceed 2 mg.

Administer pegaspargase, 2 500 IU/m² i.m. on days 1 and 15 of the treatment period.

When a remission is obtained with either of these regimens, appropriate maintenance therapy must be instituted. Pegaspargase may be used as part of a maintenance regimen. The above regimens do not preclude a need for special therapy directed toward the prevention of CNS leukemia.

It should be noted that pegaspargase has been used in combination regimens other than those recommended above. It is important to keep in mind that pegaspargase administered i.v., concurrently with or immediately before a course of vincristine and prednisone, may be associated with increased toxicity. Use of pegaspargase as the sole induction agent should be undertaken only in an unusual situation when a combined regimen is inappropriate because of toxicity or other specific patient-related factors, or in patients refractory to other therapy. When pegaspargase is to be used as the sole induction agent, the recommended dosage regimen is 2 500 IU/m² every 2 weeks. Physicians using a given regimen should be thoroughly familiar with its benefits and risks.

Patients undergoing induction therapy must be carefully monitored and the therapeutic regimen adjusted according to response and toxicity. Such adjustments should always involve decreasing dosages of one or more agents or discontinuation, depending on the degree of toxicity.

Parenteral drug products should be inspected visually for particulate matter and discoloration prior to administration.

Supplied: Each mL of isotonic, sterile, clear, colorless, phosphate buffered, saline solution contains: pegaspargase 750 IU. Nonmedicinal ingredients: dibasic sodium phosphate, monobasic sodium phosphate, sodium chloride and water for injection. pH 7.3. Single use vials of 5 mL, packages of 1. Store at 2 to 8°C. Avoid excessive agitation. Do not use if cloudy or if precipitate is present. Do not use if stored at room temperature for more than 48 hours. **Do not freeze.** Do not use past the expiration date. Single use vials, discard any unused portion.

New Product 1998

ONCOTICE™

Organon Teknika

Bacillus Calmette-Guérin (BCG), strain TICE

Antineoplastic

Pharmacology: The precise mechanism of OncoTICE's, [Bacillus Calmette-Guérin (BCG), strain TICE], antitumor action is unknown; however, it appears to exert a variety of actions. OncoTICE induces a granulomatous reaction at the local site of administration. Activated histiocytes responding to the BCG are able to kill tumor cells. BCG acts as both a specific and a nonspecific immunopotentiating agent and is able to stimulate, either directly or indirectly, a whole range of immune responses.

In patients with flat urothelial cell carcinoma in situ of the bladder, intravesical instillation of OncoTICE causes cystoscopical and histological remission of the carcinoma in a high percentage of the patients.

In patients with a primary or relapsing superficial urothelial cell carcinoma of the bladder, the intravesical instillation of OncoTICE as an adjuvant to transurethral resection (TUR) of the carcinoma, causes a prolongation of disease-free interval, reduction of the recurrence rate and prevention of progression of the carcinoma to a higher grade and/or stage.

Indications: As a treatment of primary or relapsing flat urothelial cell carcinoma in situ (Tis) of the urinary bladder, and as an adjuvant therapy after TUR of a primary or relapsing superficial urothelial cell carcinoma of the bladder stage T_A (grade 1, 2 or 3) or T_1 (grade 1, 2, or 3).

OncoTICE is not indicated for the treatment of invasive bladder cancer.

Contraindications: OncoTICE should not be used in patients with impaired immune response irrespective whether this impairment is congenital or caused by disease, drugs, or other therapy. OncoTICE should be avoided in patients with a positive HIV serology. OncoTICE is contraindicated during pregnancy and lactation (see Precautions).

OncoTICE should not be used in patients where there is evidence of an active tuberculosis infection or other diseases which need the use of antituberculous agents.

In patients with urinary tract infections, therapy with OncoTICE should be postponed or interrupted until the bacterial culture from urine becomes negative and the therapy with antibiotics and/or urinary antiseptics is stopped.

Warnings: OncoTICE should not be administered i.v., s.c. or i.m. OncoTICE is not for oral or intradermal use.

Before the first intravesical instillation of OncoTICE, a Mantoux test (PPD) should be performed. In the event that this test is positive, the intravesical instillation of OncoTICE is contraindicated only if there is supplementary medical evidence for an active tuberculosis infection.

Traumatic catheterization can promote systemic BCG infection. Delaying OncoTICE administration should be considered in such patients until mucosomal damage has healed.

Precautions: General: OncoTICE contains live, potentially pathogenic bacteria. Reconstitution, preparation of the OncoTICE suspension for instillation and administration should be performed under aseptic conditions. Unused OncoTICE and all equipment, supplies, and receptacles in contact with OncoTICE should be handled and disposed of as biohazardous.

In patients with known risk factors for HIV infection, it is recommended to perform adequate HIV assays prior to therapy.

Care should be taken not to traumatize the urinary tract. Seven to 14 days should elapse before OncoTICE is administered following TUR, biopsy or traumatic catheterization.

Children: Safety and effectiveness for carcinoma of the urinary bladder in children have not been established.

Pregnancy: Animal reproduction studies have not been conducted with OncoTICE. It is also not known whether OncoTICE can cause fetal harm when administered to a pregnant woman or can affect reproductive capacity. OncoTICE should be given to a pregnant woman only if clearly needed. Women should be advised not to become pregnant while on therapy.

Lactation: It is not known whether OncoTICE is excreted in human milk. Because many drugs are excreted in human milk and because of the potential for serious adverse reactions from OncoTICE in nursing infants, a decision should be made whether to discontinue nursing or to discontinue the drug, taking into account the importance of the drug to the mother.

Drug Interactions: OncoTICE is sensitive to the routinely used antituberculous agents, except for pyrazinamide. Studies on the interactions with other drugs have not been performed.

The prior or concomitant use of any immune modulator may interfere with the action of OncoTICE and may also increase risk.

Adverse Effects: Adverse reactions are often localized to the bladder but may be accompanied by systemic manifestations. Symptoms of bladder irritability, related to the inflammatory response induced by intravesical OncoTICE are reported in about 60% of cases. They begin 3 to 4 hours after instillation and last from 24 to 72 hours. The urinary side effects are usually seen after the third treatment and tend to increase in severity after each administration. Generally there are no long-term urinary complications.

Irritative bladder adverse effects associated with OncoTICE administration have been managed symptomatically with pyridium, propantheline bromide or oxybutinin chloride, and acetaminophen or ibuprofen.

Systemic adverse effects such as malaise, fever, and chills may reflect hypersensitivity reactions and can be treated with antihistamines. The "flu-like" syndrome of 1 to 2 day's duration that frequently accompanies OncoTICE administration should be treated symptomatically.

Patients with manifest symptoms of therapy-induced BCG infections should be adequately treated with antituberculous agents following regular treatment schedules used for tuberculosis infections: when systemic infection is present, the triple drug therapy (isoniazid-rifampicin-ethambutol) with or without cycloserine is given first for several weeks and is followed by therapy with isoniazid and rifampicin; rifampicin plus isoniazid are given when there are signs of an active BCG infection without systemic involvement. In these cases, further instillations of OncoTICE are contraindicated.

Deaths have been reported as a result of systemic BCG infections and sepsis. There have been 2 cases of nephrogenic adenoma, a benign lesion of bladder epithelium, associated with intravesical BCG therapy.

In general, the adverse effects of BCG therapy in bladder carcinoma have been of short duration and moderate morbidity.

A summary of the incidence and severity of adverse effects observed in a study of 674 patients with superficial bladder cancer, treated intravesically with OncoTICE is presented in Table I. The adverse events reported in other studies have been similar.

Table I—OncoTICE

Adverse Effects

Local Adverse Effects	Incidence (%)	Severe (%)
Dysuria	59.5	10.7
Urinary Frequency	40.4	7.4
Hematuria	26.0	7.4
Cystitis	5.9	1.9
Urgency	5.8	1.3
Nocturia	4.5	0.6
Cramps/Pain	4.0	0.9
Urinary Incontinence	2.4	–
Urinary Debris	2.2	0.4
Genital Inflammation/Abscess	1.8	0.4
Urinary Tract Infection	1.5	0.9
Urethritis	1.2	–
Pyuria	0.7	0.1
Epididymitis/Prostatitis	0.3	–
Urinary Obstruction	0.3	–
Contracted Bladder	0.2	–
Orchitis	0.2	–
Systemic Adverse Effects	**Incidence (%)**	**Severe (%)**
Fever	19.9	7.6
Malaise/Fatigue	7.4	–
Shaking Chills	3.3	1.0
Nausea/Vomiting	3.0	0.3
Arthritis/Myalgia	2.7	0.4
Headache/Dizziness	2.4	–
Anorexia/Weight Loss	2.2	0.1
Allergic	2.1	0.4
Cardiac	1.9	1.3
Respiratory (Unclassified)	1.6	0.2
Abdominal Pain	1.5	0.6
Anemia	1.3	0.4
Diarrhea	1.2	0.1
Pneumonitis	1.2	0.6
Gastrointestinal (Unclassified)	1.0	–
Neurologic	0.9	0.3
Rash	0.6	0.2
BCG Sepsis	0.4	0.4
Coagulopathy	0.3	0.3
Leukopenia	0.3	–
Thrombocytopenia	0.3	–
Hepatic Granuloma	0.2	0.2
Hepatitis	0.2	0.2

Flu-like syndrome (which includes fever, shaking chills, malaise and myalgia) had an incidence of 33.2% of which 9% were severe. Severe was ECOG Grade 3 or 4.

Overdose: Symptoms and Treatment: Overdosage occurs if more than 1 vial of OncoTICE is administered per instillation. The patient should be closely monitored for signs of systemic BCG infection and treated with antituberculous medication (see Adverse Effects).

Dosage: For each instillation, the contents of 1 vial of OncoTICE reconstituted and diluted as indicated, are instilled into the urinary bladder.

OncoTICE therapy comprises the weekly instillation of OncoTICE for 6 consecutive weeks followed by additional instillations at week 8 and 12 and monthly from months 4 to 12.

Administration: Reconstitution, Preparation and Administration of OncoTICE Suspension for Bladder Instillation: Perform the following procedures under aseptic conditions.

Reconstitution: Add 1 mL of a sterile, pyrogen-free physiological saline solution by means of a sterile syringe and allow to stand for a few minutes. Then gently swirl the vial until a homogeneous suspension is obtained. (Caution: avoid forceful agitation.)

Preparation of the Solution for Instillation: Transfer the suspension from the vial into a sterile 50 mL syringe. Rinse the vial with another 1 mL of sterile physiological saline. Add the rinse fluid to the suspension in the 50 mL syringe. Finally dilute the contents of this syringe (1 mL OncoTICE suspension + 1 mL rinse fluid) by adding sterile physiological saline

OncoTICE (cont'd)

solution up to a total volume of 50 mL. Mix the suspension carefully.

Note: The suspension must **not** be filtered.

The suspension is now ready for instillation; it contains a total of 1 to 8×10⁸ CFU of Tice BCG.

Administration: Insert a catheter via the urethra into the bladder and drain the bladder completely. Connect the 50 mL syringe containing the prepared OncoTICE suspension to the catheter, and instill the suspension into the bladder.

After instillation, remove the catheter.

The instilled OncoTICE suspension must remain in the bladder for a period of 2 hours. During this period care should be taken that the instilled OncoTICE suspension has sufficient contact with the whole mucosal surface of the bladder. Therefore, the patient should not be immobilized or, in case of a bedridden patient, should be turned over from back to prone and vice versa every 15 minutes.

After 2 hours, have the patient void the instilled suspension in a sitting position.

Note: The patient is not allowed to ingest any fluid during a period of 4 hours prior to instillation, or during the time that the OncoTICE suspension remains in the bladder after instillation (2 hours).

If a spill or contamination occurs, sodium hypochlorite (household bleach) or 70% ethanol may be used to decontaminate the area. Wastes should be treated as biohazardous and disposed of accordingly (see Precautions).

Information for the Patient: See Blue Section—Information for the Patient "OncoTICE".

Supplied: Each vial of freeze-dried preparation containing Bacillus Calmette Guérin (BCG), strain TICE which is a live, attenuated strain of Mycobacterium bovis contains: 1 to 8×10⁸ colony forming units (CFU) of Tice BCG. The culture medium from which the freeze-dried cake is prepared has the following relative composition: lactose 150 g, Sauton medium 250 mL and water 750 mL. No preservatives have been added. Vials of 2 mL, boxes of 1 and 6.

Store at 2 to 8°C and protect from light. The expiry date indicated on the label of the ampuls only applies if the vials are stored under these conditions.

The reconstituted solution for bladder instillation can be stored for up to 2 hours when refrigerated at 2 to 8°C and protected from light. Unused solution should be discarded after 2 hours.

Reviewed 1997

ONE A DAY® ADVANCE Preparations

Bayer Consumer

Vitamin—Mineral Supplement

Supplied: One A Day Advance Adults: Each red tablet contains: vitamin A (as acetate) 2 500 IU, beta-carotene 2 500 IU, vitamin B_1 1.5 mg, vitamin B_2 1.7 mg, vitamin B_6 2 mg, vitamin B_{12} 6 μg, biotin 30 μg, vitamin C 60 mg, vitamin D 400 IU, vitamin E (as acetate) 30 IU, folic acid 0.4 mg, niacinamide 20 mg, pantothenic acid 10 mg, calcium (as calcium phosphate dibasic) 130 mg, chloride (as potassium chloride) 34 mg, chromium (as chromium yeast) 10 μg, copper (as cupric sulfate) 2 mg, iodine (as potassium iodide) 0.15 mg, iron (as ferrous fumarate) 18 mg, magnesium (as magnesium hydroxide) 100 mg, manganese (as manganese sulfate), 2.5 mg, molybdenum (as molybdenum yeast) 10 μg, potassium (as potassium chloride) 37.5 mg, selenium (as selenium yeast) 10 μg, zinc (as zinc sulfate) 15 mg. Nonmedicinal ingredients: cellulose, citric acid, croscarmellose sodium, FD&C Blue #2, FD&C Red #40, gelatin, hydroxypropyl cellulose, hydroxypropyl methylcellulose, lecithin, magnesium stearate, microcrystalline cellulose, polyethylene glycol, povidone, silica gel, sodium hexametaphosphate and titanium dioxide. Bottles of 50 and 90.

One A Day Advance Adults 50+: Each red tablet contains: vitamin A (as acetate) 3 000 IU, beta-carotene 3 000 IU, vitamin B_1 4.5 mg, vitamin B_2 3.4 mg, vitamin B_6 6 mg, vitamin B_{12} 25 μg, biotin 30 μg, vitamin C 120 mg, vitamin D 400 IU, vitamin E (as acetate) 60 IU, folic acid 0.4 mg, niacinamide 20 mg, pantothenic acid 20 mg, calcium (as carbonate) 220 mg, chloride (as potassium chloride) 34 mg, chromium (as chromium yeast) 10 μg, copper (as cupric sulfate) 2 mg, iodine (as potassium iodide) 0.15 mg, magnesium (as magnesium hydroxide) 100 mg, manganese (as manganese sulfate) 2.5 mg, molybdenum (as molybdenum yeast) 10 μg, potassium (as potassium chloride) 37.5 mg, selenium (as selenium yeast) 10 μg, zinc (as zinc sulfate) 15 mg. Nonmedicinal ingredients: cellulose, citric acid, croscarmellose sodium, FD&C Yellow #6, hydroxypropyl cellulose, hydroxypropyl methylcellulose, lecithin, magnesium stearate, microcrystalline cellulose, povidone, silica gel, sodium hexametaphosphate and titanium dioxide. Bottles of 90.

One A Day Advance Fem: Each yellow tablet contains: vitamin A (as acetate) 2 500 IU, beta-carotene 2 500 IU, vitamin B_1 1.5 mg, vitamin B_2 1.7 mg, vitamin B_6 2 mg, vitamin B_{12} 6 μg, vitamin C 60 mg, vitamin D 400 IU, vitamin E (as acetate) 30 IU, folic acid 0.4 mg, niacinamide 20 mg, pantothenic acid 10 mg, calcium (as carbonate) 450 mg, iron (as ferrous fumarate) 27 mg, zinc (as zinc oxide) 15 mg. Nonmedicinal ingredients: croscarmellose sodium, hydroxypropyl methylcellulose, lecithin, magnesium stearate, microcrystalline cellulose, sodium hexametaphosphate and tartrazine (FD&C Yellow #5). Bottles of 90.

One A Day Advance High Potency B Complex and C: Each pale orange tablet contains: vitamin A (as acetate) 4 800 IU, beta-carotene 200 IU, vitamin B_1 15 mg, vitamin B_2 10 mg, vitamin B_6 5 mg, vitamin B_{12} 12 μg, vitamin C 600 mg, vitamin D 400 IU, vitamin E (as acetate) 30 IU, folic acid 0.4 mg, niacinamide 100 mg, pantothenic acid 20 mg, copper (as cupric oxide) 2 mg, iron (as ferrous fumarate) 18 mg, zinc (as zinc oxide) 15 mg. Nonmedicinal ingredients: calcium carbonate, calcium silicate, cellulose, FD&C Yellow #6, hydroxypropyl cellulose, hydroxypropyl methylcellulose, lecithin, magnesium stearate, sodium hexametaphosphate and titanium dioxide. Bottles of 90.

(Shown in Product Recognition Section)

ONE-ALPHA® Pr

Leo

Alfacalcidol

Vitamin D₃ Metabolite

Pharmacology: 1α-hydroxyvitamin D_3(1α-OHD_3) stimulates intestinal calcium and phosphorus absorption, the reabsorption of calcium from bone and possibly the renal reabsorption of calcium.

To be effective in disorders resulting from vitamin D deficiency, vitamin D must undergo two metabolic conversions, first in the liver to 25-hydroxyvitamin D and then in the kidney to the physiologically active metabolite, 1,25-dihydroxyvitamin D_3 (1,25-$(OH)_2D_3$). In patients with chronic renal failure, progressive nephron destruction blocks the production of 1,25-$(OH)_2D_3$ by the kidneys resulting in diminished serum levels of this metabolite.

When alfacalcidol is administered in this clinical situation, it is rapidly converted to 1,25-$(OH)_2D_3$ in the liver effectively bypassing the critical renal metabolic conversion. This hepatic conversion of alfacalcidol is accomplished very rapidly, before any stimulation of the intestine or bone occurs.

The biological half-life of alfacalcidol has been shown to be approximately 3 hours in the presence of renal insufficiency. However, serum levels of 1,25-$(OH)_2D_3$ peak approximately 12 hours after a single dose of alfacalcidol and remain measurable for at least 48 hours. The effect of 1 μg of alfacalcidol on intestinal calcium absorption has been observed within 6 hours of ingestion and was maximal at 24 hours.

One of the first abnormalities to be observed in patients with chronic renal failure is the disturbance of calcium metabolism due to increased phosphate retention and impaired production of 1,25-$(OH)_2D_3$. Because calcium metabolism and production of 1,25-$(OH)_2D_3$ is at least partially mediated by the parathyroid glands, hypocalcemia leads to increased parathyroid hormone (PTH) secretion and high plasma PTH levels. Therefore, the patients with renal bone disease most likely to benefit from alfacalcidol therapy are those characterized by abnormally low plasma calcium levels, elevated alkaline phosphatase and PTH levels and histological evidence of osteitic fibrosa and osteomalacia.

In the majority of patients treated with alfacalcidol, clinical symptoms of bone pain and muscle weakness begin to remit promptly, within 2 weeks to 3 months of the start of therapy. Malabsorption of calcium is rapidly corrected. Plasma alkaline phosphatase and PTH levels generally begin to fall within 3 months, but plasma calcium levels may not normalize for several months. This delay should not necessarily be construed as a poor response but may indicate that calcium is being utilized for bone mineralization.

By contrast, hypercalcemia may occur at any stage of treatment, the risk being higher just after treatment is started and later when the plasma alkaline phosphatase level falls towards normal (see Precautions).

Because of a modest action on intestinal phosphorus absorption, alfacalcidol may elevate plasma phosphorus levels even further in patients with renal osteodystrophy and this may require increasing the dose of phosphate binding agents.

Normalization of plasma PTH levels frequently correlates well with healing of osteitis fibrosa, but radiographic improvement can occur without significant changes in plasma PTH concentrations. After 3 to 6 months of treatment, radiological evidence of healing is generally apparent. Histological responses, such as a decrease in the surface of bone undergoing resorption and a decrease in the volume of osteoid, are often much slower.

The beneficial effect of alfacalcidol on the development of renal bone disease in patients with renal failure not yet undergoing dialysis has been demonstrated in a large, randomized, placebo controlled study. Long-term administration of alfacalcidol (maximum dose of 1 μg/day for up to 2 years) improved bone histology and halted the progression of changes in serum alkaline phosphatase activity and parathyroid hormone levels compared to placebo. Long-term administration of alfacalcidol proved to be well tolerated and had no adverse effect on renal function in patients for whom the dose was titrated to prevent persistent hypercalcemia. Although elevation of serum calcium was observed, marked hypercalcemia (>3 mmol/L) was uncommon (4.5% of patients) and readily responded to decreases in drug dosage.

Indications: Management of hypocalcemia and osteodystrophy in patients with chronic renal failure.

Contraindications: Known hypersensitivity to 1α-hydroxyvitamin D_3, vitamin D or any of its analogues and derivatives. Evidence of hypercalcemia, hyperphosphatemia or of vitamin D overdose.

Warnings: Alfacalcidol is a potent cholecalciferol derivative with a profound positive effect on intestinal absorption of dietary calcium. The effect of alfacalcidol on inorganic phosphorus absorption is less marked, although it is important to recognize that the drug may increase plasma phosphorus concentrations, which may increase the requirements for phosphate binding agents.

Alfacalcidol should not be used concomitantly with other vitamin D products or derivatives.

As with all vitamin D preparations and metabolites, hypercalcemia must be anticipated when using alfacalcidol. Regular monitoring of plasma calcium is essential. Indeed, alfacalcidol should only be used when adequate facilities are available for monitoring of blood and urine chemistries on a regular basis.

During treatment with alfacalcidol, progressive hypercalcemia either due to hyperresponsiveness or overdose may become so severe as to require emergency treatment.

Chronic hypercalcemia can lead to generalized vascular calcification, nephrocalcinosis or calcifications of the cornea or other soft tissues. During treatment with alfacalcidol, the total serum calcium (mg/dL) times serum inorganic phosphate (mg/dL) product (Ca×P) should **be maintained at accepted levels.** A dialysate calcium level of 7.0 mg/dL (1.75 mmol/L) or above, in addition to excess dietary calcium supplements may lead to frequent episodes of hypercalcemia.

To control serum inorganic phosphate levels and dietary phosphate absorption, appropriate oral phosphate binding agents in association with a low phosphate diet may be necessary to prevent hyperphosphatemia and extra-skeletal calcifications. Serum phosphate levels were maintained below 2 mmol/L in the study that demonstrated the benefits of alfacalcidol on the development of bone disease in pre-dialysis patients.

Antacids containing magnesium should be avoided as they may contribute towards hypermagnesemia.

In patients on digitalis, hypercalcemia may precipitate cardiac arrhythmias. Use alfacalcidol with extreme caution in these patients.

Pregnancy and *Lactation:* Safety in pregnancy has not been established; use of alfacalcidol in pregnancy may be considered only when the potential benefits have been weighed against possible hazards to mother and fetus. Alfacalcidol may be excreted in human milk, therefore, breast-feeding during treatment should be avoided.

Precautions: The therapeutic margin with alfacalcidol is narrow; the optimal daily dose must be carefully titrated for each individual patient (see Dosage).

The occurrence of hypercalcemia depends on such factors as the degree of bone mineralization, the state of renal function and the dose of alfacalcidol. Excessive doses of the drug induce hypercalcemia and hypercalciuria.

Pre-Dialysis Administration of Alfacalcidol: Serum calcium and phosphate levels should be monitored at monthly intervals or as is considered necessary if hypercalcemia develops.

If hypercalcemia develops at any time during treatment then the dose of alfacalcidol should be reduced by 50% and all calcium supplements stopped until calcium levels return to normal.

Administration of Alfacalcidol to Patients Undergoing Dialysis: Plasma calcium should be measured at weekly intervals depending on the progress of the patient. In early treatment during dosage adjustment, serum calcium should be determined at least twice weekly. In the later stages of treatment when there is evidence of bone healing (e.g., when the plasma alkaline phosphatase level falls toward normal), weekly estimations are recommended.

If hypercalcemia occurs, alfacalcidol should be discontinued immediately. Serum calcium levels generally normalize within a few days to a week. Calcium levels should be rechecked in another week and if still at normal levels, alfacalcidol may be reinstituted at half the previous dose.

Patients with renal bone disease and a relatively high initial plasma calcium and "autonomous" hyperparathyroidism are liable to early hypercalcemia, as are the minority of dialysis patients with low plasma alkaline phosphatase.

Laboratory tests considered essential for adequate patient monitoring include: serum calcium, inorganic phosphorus, magnesium, alkaline phosphatase, creatinine, BUN and protein (for correction of plasma calcium in instances of hypercalcemia). For pre-dialysis patients treated with alfacalcidol serum calcium and phosphate levels should be monitored at monthly intervals or as is considered necessary if hypercalcemia develops. For patients undergoing dialysis serum calcium should be determined at least twice weekly. During maintenance therapy with alfacalcidol, 24-hour urinary calcium and phosphorus should be determined periodically.

Periodic ophthalmological examinations and radiological evaluation of suspected anatomical regions for early detection of ectopic calcifications are advisable.

Drug Interactions: Alfacalcidol should be used with extreme caution in patients on digitalis, as hypercalcemia may trigger cardiac arrhythmias.

Resins such as cholestyramine and mineral oil used as a laxative may interfere with the intestinal absorption of alfacalcidol.

Patients concurrently treated with barbiturates and other anticonvulsant drugs may require higher doses of alfacalcidol, as these drugs may interefere with the action of vitamin D.

Patients and their immediate relatives should be informed about the need for compliance with the dosage instructions, strict adherence to prescribed calcium intake, dietary and supplementary, and avoidance of unapproved nonprescription drugs or medications.

Patients should be made aware of symptoms of hypercalcemia and should be instructed to seek medical attention if such symptoms appear (see Adverse Effects).

Children: The safety and efficacy of alfacalcidol in children have not been established.

Adverse Effects: In general, the adverse effects of alfacalcidol are similar to those encountered with excessive vitamin D intake. a) Early symptoms: Pruritus, weakness, headache, "red-eyes", somnolence, nausea, cardiac arrhythmia, vomiting, excessive thirst, dry mouth, constipation, muscle pain, bone pain and metallic taste. b) Late symptoms: Polyuria, polydipsia, anorexia, weight loss, nocturia, conjunctivitis, corneal calcification, photophobia, rhinorrhea, pancreatitis, pruritus, hyperthermia, decreased libido, elevated BUN, albuminuria, hypercholesterolemia, elevated AST and ALT, ectopic calcification, hypertension, cardiac arrhythmias and, rarely, overt psychosis.

Hypercalcemia and possibly an exacerbation of hyperphosphatemia are the most frequent adverse reactions that have been reported with alfacalcidol in patients with renal osteodystrophy. Elevated levels of calcium and phosphorus increase the risk of metastatic calcification and may accelerate the decline in renal function in some patients with chronic renal failure.

Overdose: Symptoms and Treatment: Hypercalcemia, hypercalciuria and hyperphosphatemia. A high intake of calcium and phosphate concomitantly with therapeutic doses of alfacalcidol may cause similar abnormalities.

Treatment of Hypercalcemia Due to Overdose: General treatment of hypercalcemia (more than 1 mg/dL or 0.25 mmol/L above the upper limit of the normal range (usually 8.0–10.4 mg/dL or 2.2–2.6 mmol/L)) consists of immediate discontinuation of alfacalcidol, institution of a low calcium diet and withdrawal of calcium supplements. Serum calcium levels should be determined daily until the patient achieves normocalcemia. Hypercalcemia frequently resolves in 2 to 7 days. When serum calcium levels have returned to within normal limits, alfacalcidol therapy can be reinstituted at half the previous dose. Serum calcium levels should be carefully monitored (at least twice weekly) during this period of dosage adjustment and subsequent dosage titration. Persistent or markedly elevated serum calcium levels may be corrected by dialysis against a calcium free dialysate.

Treatment of Accidental Overdosage: General supportive measures. If drug ingestion is discovered within a relatively short time, induction of emesis or gastric lavage may be of benefit in preventing further absorption. If the drug has passed through the stomach, the administration of mineral oil may promote its fecal elimination. Serial serum electrolyte determinations (especially calcium ion), rate of urinary calcium excretion and assessment of electrocardiographic abnormalities due to hypercalcemia should be obtained. Such monitoring is critical in patients receiving digitalis. Discontinuation of supplemental calcium and low calcium diet are also indicated in accidental overdosage. Due to the relatively short pharmacological action of alfacalcidol, further measures are probably unnecessary. However, if persistent and markedly elevated serum calcium levels occur, there are a variety of therapeutic alternatives which may be considered depending on the underlying condition of the patient. These include the use of drugs such as phosphates and corticosteroids as well as measures to induce an appropriate forced diuresis. The use of dialysis against a calcium free dialysate has also been reported.

Dosage: The daily dose must be carefully individualized and titrated according to such factors as the state of renal function, degree of bone mineralization and initial plasma calcium and alkaline phosphatase concentrations. Other factors which may be taken into account are urinary calcium excretion, plasma PTH and phosphorus.

The success of alfacalcidol is also based on the assumption that the patient is receiving an adequate daily intake of calcium during treatment. The recommended daily allowance of calcium in adults is about 800 to 1 000 mg (from all sources such as dialysate, diet and calcium supplements). The physician should ensure that each patient receives an adequate daily intake of calcium by prescribing a calcium supplement or instructing the patients in appropriate dietary measures.

Dose Titration: Pre-Dialysis Patients: A dose of alfacalcidol that maintains serum calcium (adjusted for albumin concentration) within the normal range should be selected. An initial dose of 0.25 μg/day is recommended, followed by dose adjustment until an appropriate dose is achieved. Alfacalcidol has been shown to be safe and effective in the prevention of renal bone disease when doses were maintained at or below 1 μg/day. Alfacalcidol is usually administered as a single dose each day taken with food.

The following protocol for dosage adjustment is suggested: An initial dose of 0.25 μg/day should be administered for 2 months, unless hypercalcemia develops. If hypercalcemia occurs then the dose should be reduced to 0.25 μg on alternate days. If serum calcium is below the desired range, the dose may be adjusted in increments of 0.25 μg/day every 2 months. Most patients will be maintained on a dose of 0.5 μg/day. However, doses up to 1 μg/day may be necessary to maintain serum calcium within the desired range. If hypercalcemia develops at any time during treatment then the dose of alfacalcidol should be reduced by 50% and all calcium supplements stopped until calcium levels return to normal.

Serum calcium and phosphate levels should be monitored at monthly intervals or as is considered necessary if hypercalcemia develops. Calcium supplements should not exceed 500 mg of elemental calcium per day.

Dose Titration for Hemodialysis Patients: The recommended initial dose is 1 μg daily. If a satisfactory response in the biochemical parameters and clinical manifestations is not observed within 4 weeks, the daily dose may be increased by 0.5 μg every 2 to 4 weeks. Most patients respond eventually to a dose of between 1 and 2 μg/day. Exceptionally, a dose of 3 μg is required.

Maintenance Therapy: Once serum calcium levels are normalized or only slightly reduced, the dose requirement of alfacalcidol generally decreases. Maintenance doses usually range from 0.25 to 1.0 μg/day. If this small maintenance dose still proves too high, adequate control can usually be achieved by giving the dose on alternate days or even less frequently.

Supplied: Capsules: 0.25 μg: Each white capsule contains: alfacalcidol 0.25 μg. Nonmedicinal ingredients: sesame oil and α-tocopherol; in the shell: gelatin, glycerol (85%), potassium sorbate and titanium dioxide. Amber bottles of 100. Protect from direct sunlight.

1 μg: Each dark brown capsule contains: alfacalcidol 1 μg. Nonmedicinal ingredients: sesame oil and α-tocopherol; in the shell: gelatin, glycerol (85%), potassium sorbate, red iron oxide E172 and black iron oxide E172. Amber bottles of 100. Protect from direct sunlight.

Oral Solution: Each mL of solution contains: alfacalcidol 0.2 μg. Nonmedicinal ingredients: citric acid monohydrate, ethanol, methyl parahydroxybenzoate, polyoxyl 40 hydrogenated castor oil, purified water, sodium citrate, sorbitol and α-tocopherol. Amber bottles of 60 mL. Protect from direct sunlight.

Reviewed 1998

OPHTHETIC®
Allergan

Proparacaine HCl

Ophthalmic Anesthetic

Supplied: Each mL contains: proparacaine HCl 0.5%. Nonmedicinal ingredients: benzalkonium chloride 0.01%, glycerin 2.45%, sodium chloride and purified water. Plastic dropper bottles of 15 mL.

OPHTHO-BUNOLOL® Ⓟ
AltiMed

Levobunolol HCl

Glaucoma Therapy

Supplied: 0.25%: Each mL of sterile, ophthalmic solution contains: levobunolol HCl 2.5 mg. Nonmedicinal ingredients: benzalkonium chloride 0.004% (as preservative), edetate disodium, polyvinyl alcohol (Liquifilm), potassium phosphate monobasic, sodium chloride, sodium metabisulfite, sodium phosphate dibasic and sodium hydroxide or hydrochloric acid to adjust pH. Plastic dropper bottles of 5 and 10 mL.

0.5%: Each mL of sterile, ophthalmic solution contains: levobunolol HCl 5 mg. Nonmedicinal ingredients: benzalkonium chloride 0.004% (as preservative), edetate disodium, polyvinyl alcohol (Liquifilm), potassium phosphate monobasic, sodium chloride, sodium metabisulfite, sodium phosphate dibasic and sodium hydroxide or hydrochloric acid to adjust pH. Plastic dropper bottles of 5, 10 and 15 mL.

Protect from light and excessive heat.

OPHTHO-CHLORAM® Ⓟ
AltiMed

Chloramphenicol

Antibiotic

Supplied: Each mL of sterile, ophthalmic solution contains: chloramphenicol 0.5%. Nonmedicinal ingredients: chlorobutanol 0.5% (as preservative), polyethylene glycol 300 and polyoxyl 40 stearate. Plastic dropper bottles of 10 mL. Refrigerate until dispensed.

OPHTHO-DIPIVEFRIN™ Ⓟ
AltiMed

Dipivefrin HCl

Glaucoma Therapy

Supplied: Each mL of sterile, isotonic, aqueous, ophthalmic solution contains: dipivefrin HCl 1 mg. Nonmedicinal ingredients: benzalkonium chloride 0.005% as preservative and edetate sodium, hydrochloric acid and sodium chloride to adjust pH. Plastic dropper bottles of 10 mL. Do not use if solution is discolored. Not for injection. Store at room temperature. Keep tightly closed. Protect from light and excessive heat.

OPHTHO-TATE® ℞

AltiMed

Prednisolone Acetate

Ophthalmic Corticosteroid

Supplied: Each mL of suspension contains: prednisolone acetate 1%. Nonmedicinal ingredients: benzalkonium chloride, boric acid, disodium edetate, hydroxypropyl methylcellulose, polysorbate 80, purified water, sodium bisulfite, sodium chloride and sodium citrate. Plastic dropper bottles of 5 and 10 mL.

OPHTRIVIN-A®

CIBA Vision

Antazoline—Xylometazoline

Antihistamine—Decongestant

Supplied: Each mL of ophthalmic solution contains: xylometazoline HCl 0.05% and antazoline sulfate 0.5% in a sterile aqueous vehicle with a borate buffer, disodium edetate and preserved with benzalkonium chloride. Plastic squeeze bottles of 10 mL with dropper tips. Store at room temperature and keep tightly closed when not in use.

OPIOIDS Ⓝ

General Monograph, CPhA

Anileridine
Butorphanol
Codeine
Diamorphine
Fentanyl
Hydrocodone
Hydromorphone
Methadone*
Morphine
Nalbuphine
Oxycodone
Oxymorphone
Pentazocine
Pethidine (Meperidine)
Propoxyphene

This monograph has been compiled by CPhA. It may contain information different from that approved by Therapeutic Products Programme, Health Canada, and the pharmaceutical manufacturers' approval has not been requested.

* At present, methadone is not supplied in Canada under a Notice of Compliance and does not have a Drug Identification Number or Product Monograph. The **specific** Canadian regulations pertaining to the importation, distribution, prescribing and dispensing of methadone are contained within the Controlled Drugs and Substances Act and the Narcotic Control Regulations.

Pharmacology: The opioid analgesics act primarily on the CNS. The perception of and emotional response to pain is modified when opioid analgesics bind with stereospecific receptors in the CNS. Five major groups of opioid receptors are known: mu, kappa, sigma, delta and epsilon. Opioid analgesic activity occurs at the mu, kappa and sigma receptors. Opioid agonists such as morphine exert their activity mainly at the mu receptor. Mixed agonist-antagonists such as butorphanol, nalbuphine and pentazocine act primarily at the kappa receptors (thought to mediate analgesic effects) and sigma receptors (may produce subjective and psychotomimetic effects).

In addition to analgesia, opioid agonist activity in the CNS may cause suppression of the cough reflex, respiratory depression, change in mood such as euphoria or dysphoria, mental clouding and EEG changes. Nausea and vomiting, probably caused by stimulation of the chemoreceptor trigger zone, can also occur. Peripheral vasodilation, reduced peripheral resistance and the inhibition of baroreceptors can result in orthostatic hypotension and fainting. The inhibition of peristalsis can lead to constipation while increased bladder sphincter tone may cause urinary retention. Large doses may elicit excitation or seizures. Morphine and its congeners cause miosis. In therapeutic doses they increase accommodation and sensitivity to light reflex and decrease intraocular pressure in both normal patients and those with glaucoma.

Methadone: Methadone is a synthetic diphenylheptane-derivative opioid agonist with pharmacologic properties qualitatively similar to those of morphine. In equianalgesic doses, methadone may produce a similar or slightly higher degree of respiratory depression and less sedation, euphoria and constipation than morphine.

Methadone prevents withdrawal symptoms and reduces opioid cravings in individuals who are opioid-dependent.

Pharmacokinetics: Opioid analgesics are absorbed after administration by many different routes including the oral, rectal, intramuscular, intravenous, epidural, intrathecal, subcutaneous, intranasal and transdermal routes. They are metabolized by the liver and eliminated primarily by the kidney. Dosage adjustment in the presence of renal or hepatic disease is usually indicated. Consult individual product monographs. See Table I for a comparison of pharmacokinetic parameters.

Table I—Opioids

Pharmacokinetics

Drug	Route	Onset of Action (minutes)	Duration of Action (hours)
Agonists			
Anileridine	P.O., parenteral	15	2 to 3
Codeine	P.O., S.C.	15 to 30	4 to 6
	I.M.	10 to 30	4 to 6
Diamorphine	Parenteral	NA[a]	3 to 5
Fentanyl	I.M.	7 to 15	1 to 2
	I.V.		30 to 60[b]
	Transdermal[c]		
Hydrocodone	P.O.	NA[a]	4 to 6[d]
Hydromorphone	P.O.	30	>5
	Parenteral	15	>5
Methadone	P.O.	30 to 60	24 to 48[e]
Morphine	P.O.	10 to 90	1 to 2
	Parenteral	10 to 30	4 to 5
	Epidural	15 to 60	≤24
Oxycodone	P.O.	10 to 15	3 to 6
Oxymorphone	PR	5 to 10	3 to 6
	P.O.	NA[a]	3 to 6
	Parenteral	NA[a]	3 to 6
Pethidine	P.O.	15	2 to 4
	I.M., S.C.	10 to 15	2 to 4
	IV	1	2 to 4
Propoxyphene	P.O.	15 to 60	4 to 6
Agonist-Antagonists			
Butorphanol	Intranasal	30	3 to 4
Nalbuphine	I.V.	2 to 3	3 to 6
	S.C., I.M.	15	3 to 6
Pentazocine	P.O.	15 to 30	≥3
	I.M., S.C.	15 to 20	2
	I.V.	2 to 3	1

[a]No data available.
[b]Minutes.
[c]See product monograph.
[d]Antitussive effect.
[e]With repeated dosing.

Indications: Diamorphine, hydromorphone and morphine are used for the management of severe forms of pain in patients who require a strong opioid analgesic. Codeine and propoxyphene are used for the treatment of mild to moderate pain and the other narcotic analgesics are indicated for moderate to severe pain.

Methadone: In Canada, methadone is used in the detoxification or maintenance treatment of opioid-dependent individuals. Currently, the Therapeutic Products Directorate, Health Canada, is engaged in an extensive review of the policy and regulatory framework controlling the use of methadone. At present, physicians who wish to prescribe or administer methadone must obtain authorization from the Minister of Health (or designate) at the Bureau of Drug Surveillance, (613) 952-8174. In Ontario, the first contact for physicians is the College of Physicians and Surgeons of Ontario. In British Columbia, the Methadone Program is administered by the College of Physicians and Surgeons of BC, but physicians still require authorization by the Federal Minister of Health (or designate). The reader is referred to 2 Health Canada publications (The use of opioids in the management of opioid dependence, 1992; Dispensing Methadone for the Treatment of Opioid Dependence, 1994) for more information. In addition, the following article may be helpful: Help for heroin dependence (what pharmacists need to know about methadone maintenance therapy), Kalvik A., Isaac P., Janecek E. *Pharmacy Practice* 1996; 12 (10): 43-54.

Contraindications: Hypersensitivity to opioid analgesics. Diarrhea caused by poisoning, until the toxic substance has been eliminated from the gastrointestinal tract. Acute respiratory depression, acute asthma attack, and upper airway obstruction.

For Epidural or Intrathecal Use: Infection at or near site of administration, clotting defects due to anticoagulant therapy or hematological disorders.

See individual product monographs for comprehensive information, with attention to the following: Diamorphine, morphine or pethidine should not be used concurrently with MAO inhibitors, or within 2 weeks of such therapy.

Warnings: Opioid analgesics have the potential for abuse. Psychological dependence or physical dependence and tolerance may follow repeated administration. Opioid analgesics should be prescribed and administered with caution, especially in cases of severe hepatic insufficiency, severe CNS depression or coma, in patients with head injuries or conditions in which intracranial pressure is increased, myxedema, Addison's Disease, acute alcohol intoxication, delerium tremens, convulsive disorders and in patients taking MAO inhibitors. Opioid analgesics can cause severe hypotension in individuals whose circulation is already compromised by hypovolemia, shock, drugs producing hypotension or other conditions that interfere with ability to maintain normal blood pressure. These drugs may produce orthostatic hypotension in the ambulatory patient.

Rapid i.v. injection of opioid analgesics increases incidence of adverse reactions such as severe respiratory depression, apnea, hypotension, peripheral circulatory collapse and cardiac arrest. The patient should be lying down during i.v. administration. These drugs should not be administered i.v. unless an opioid antagonist and the facilities for assisted or controlled respiration are immediately available.

Opioid analgesics should be used with extreme caution in patients with chronic obstructive pulmonary disease or cor pulmonale, patients having a substantially decreased respiratory reserve and patients with preexisting respiratory depression, hypoxia or hypercapnia. Refer to individual product monographs for specific warnings with attention to the following:

Nalbuphine: Commercial preparation contains sodium metabisulfite which may cause allergic reactions (e.g., hives, itching, wheezing, anaphylaxis) in susceptible individuals. Prevalence of sensitivity in the general population is probably low; it is seen more frequently in asthmatics or atopic non-asthmatic patients.

Pentazocine: Acute CNS manifestations (e.g., hallucinations, disorientation, confusion) have been reported in patients receiving therapeutic doses.

Methadone: Overdose and death can occur when methadone is ingested by individuals for whom it has not been prescribed, or who are not opioid-dependent. Children are at particular risk for overdose and death due to accidental ingestion.

Precautions: General: Opioid analgesics should be used with caution in elderly and debilitated individuals because of the danger of cardiac or respiratory depression, as well as those patients with hemorrhage and those with severe impairment of hepatic, pulmonary or renal function. Careful consideration should be given before using opioid analgesics in the presence of the following conditions: myxedema or hypothyroidism (increased risk of CNS and respiratory depression); adrenocortical insufficiency; toxic psychosis; CNS depression; prostatic hypertrophy or urethral stricture; kyphoscoliosis; acute alcohol intoxication and delerium tremens; severe inflammatory bowel disease; gallbladder disease. Due to their cholinergic effects, opioid analgesics should be used with caution in patients with cardiac arrhythmias.

Opioid analgesics may obscure the diagnosis or clinical course in patients with acute abdominal conditions and may induce or exacerbate seizures.

Methadone: Patients established on methadone maintenance therapy for opioid dependence develop tolerance to the analgesic, sedative and euphoric effects of methadone. The established maintenance dose of methadone in these patients will consistently prevent withdrawal symptoms, but will not, by itself, meet their analgesic requirements in the event of surgery or pain of another cause. If pain is not severe, nonopioid analgesics such as NSAIDs can be used. For severe pain, pure opioid agonists may be used. The use of agonist-antagonists should be avoided because of the possibility of precipitating withdrawal. See Table I for a list of opioid agonists and agonist-antagonists.

The use of opioid analgesics in patients on methadone maintenance must be closely supervised, with appropriately frequent reassessment of their pain control needs. Similar precautions are recommended for the use of drugs such as benzodiazepines or CNS stimulants in these patients.

Drug Interactions: Serious adverse reactions have been reported in patients who receive MAO inhibitors with pethidine. Other opioid analgesics should be used with extreme caution, if at all, in patients taking MAO inhibitors (including selegiline) or within 14 days of such therapy.

Concomitant administration of other CNS drugs such as sedatives, hypnotics, phenothiazines, anesthetics and alcohol may increase the sedative and depressant effects of opioid analgesics. If the concomitant use of these drugs is considered necessary, their doses should be reduced accordingly.

Opioid analgesics may enhance the effects of neuromuscular blocking agents resulting in increased respiratory depression.

Tricyclic antidepressants may enhance opioid-induced respiratory depression.

Concomitant use of drugs with antimuscarinic activity may increase the risk of severe constipation and/or urinary retention.

Concurrent administration of cimetidine may lead to increased effect or toxicity of opioid analgesics.

Opioid agonists may potentiate the anticoagulant effects of coumarin anticoagulants.

The use of more than one opioid agonist at a time is usually inappropriate; additive CNS depressant, respiratory depressant and hypotensive effects may occur if 2 or more agonists are used concurrently. Potentiation of effects may occur with a previously administered long-acting opioid analgesic.

Agonist-antagonist opioid analgesics (i.e., pentazocine, nalbuphine, butorphanol) should **not** be administered to a patient who has received or is receiving a course of therapy with a pure opioid agonist analgesic. In these patients, mixed agonist-antagonists may reduce the analgesic effect or may precipitate withdrawal symptoms.

Methadone: The use of naltrexone or opioid agonist-antagonists should be avoided in patients on methadone maintenance because of possible withdrawal reactions.

Drug-Laboratory Test Interactions: Opioid analgesics may interfere with certain diagnostic procedures, by increasing plasma amylase and lipase concentrations and by increasing CSF pressure. Gastric emptying is delayed by these drugs so gastric emptying studies will not be valid.

Pregnancy: Safety for use has not been established, although certain opioid analgesics are sometimes used to relieve pain during labor and delivery.

As opioid analgesics cross the placental barrier, potential benefits must be weighed against possible hazards. Babies born to mothers who have been taking opioids regularly prior to delivery will be physically dependent. Withdrawal signs include: irritability and excessive crying, tremors, hyperactive reflexes, increased respiratory rate, increased stools, sneezing, yawning, vomiting and fever.

Methadone: Methadone is sometimes used during pregnancy in opioid-dependent women, even though the fetus will be exposed to the drug and may experience withdrawal after delivery. The use of methadone in pregnancy is often considered to be a safer and more manageable option than the possibility of continued illicit drug use, especially if the mother is likely to engage in high-risk behaviors associated with procuring and using street drugs.

Lactation: Low levels of opioid analgesics have been detected in human milk, and this should be taken into consideration when breast-feeding. Withdrawal symptoms can occur in breast-feeding infants when maternal administration of morphine is stopped.

Methadone: Methadone is distributed into breast milk in small amounts and is generally considered to be compatible with breast-feeding.

Children: The safety and effectiveness have not been adequately evaluated for these drugs. Children up to 2 years of age may be more prone to their adverse pharmacological effects. Paradoxical excitement is particularly likely to occur. Oxycodone should not be used in children, and propoxyphene use is not recommended. See individual product monographs for specific guidelines.

Geriatrics: Elderly patients may be more susceptible to adverse effects, especially respiratory depression and constipation. Caution is advised; the initial dose should be reduced and effects monitored. Elimination and metabolism may be slowed; lower doses or longer dosing intervals may be required.

Occupational Hazards: Patients should be warned against driving or operating machinery if they become drowsy or show impaired mental and/or physical abilities.

Headache: Limited clinical experience appears to suggest patients with migraine headache may be more susceptible to adverse reactions with butorphanol use.

Myocardial Infarction: Opioid analgesics must be used with caution in patients with MI who are experiencing nausea or vomiting.

Adverse Effects: Major: respiratory depression and respiratory arrest. To a lesser degree circulatory depression, shock and cardiac arrest (see Warnings, Precautions).

Most Commonly Requiring Medical Attention: sedation, nausea and vomiting, constipation and sweating. These effects seem to be more prominent in ambulatory patients and in those not experiencing severe pain. In such individuals, lower doses are advisable. Some adverse reactions may be alleviated if the patient lies down.

Cardiovascular: supraventricular tachycardia, bradycardia, palpitations, faintness, syncope, postural hypotension and hypertension, and phlebitis following i.v. injection.

CNS: drowsiness, sedation, euphoria, dysphoria, weakness, headache, agitation, seizures, uncoordinated muscle movements, alterations of mood, dreams, hallucinations and disorientation, visual disturbances, insomnia, miosis, toxic psychoses.

Constipation: Practically all patients become constipated while taking opioid analgesics on a persistent basis. In some instances, particularly the elderly or bedridden, patients may become impacted. It is essential to caution patients in this regard and to institute an appropriate regimen of bowel management at the start of prolonged therapy.

Gastrointestinal: dry mouth, nausea, vomiting, constipation, biliary tract spasm, laryngospasm, anorexia, diarrhea, cramps, dyspepsia, taste alterations.

Genitourinary: urinary retention or hesitance, antidiuretic effect, reduced libido and/or potency.

Hypersensitivity: pruritus, urticaria, other skin rashes, edema, diaphoresis, wheal and flare over the vein with i.v. injection. Because of close structural similarities, patients exhibiting systemic allergy to morphine (e.g., generalized rash, shortness of breath) should **not** receive codeine, diamorphine, hydromorphone, oxycodone or oxymorphone.

Nausea and Vomiting: occur frequently after single doses of narcotics or as an early unwanted effect of regular opioid analgesic therapy.

Withdrawal Syndrome: Physical dependence with or without psychological dependence tends to occur with chronic administration. An abstinence syndrome may be precipitated when an opioid analgesic is abruptly discontinued or opioid antagonists are administered. The following withdrawal symptoms may be observed after abrupt discontinuation of an opioid analgesic: body aches, diarrhea, gooseflesh, loss of appetite, nervousness or restlessness, runny nose, sneezing, tremors or shivering, stomach cramps, nausea, sleep disturbances, unusual increase in sweating and yawning, weakness, tachycardia and unexplained fever. With appropriate medical use and gradual withdrawal from opioid analgesics, these symptoms are usually mild.

Other: abnormal liver function test results (propoxyphene), flushing/warmth, pain at injection site, local tissue irritation and induration following s.c. injection, particularly when repeated.

Overdose: Symptoms: Respiratory depression (reduced respiratory rate and/or tidal volume; Cheyne-Stokes respiration; cyanosis), extreme somnolence progressing to stupor or coma, skeletal muscle flaccidity, cold or clammy skin, and sometimes hypotension and bradycardia. Severe overdosage may result in apnea, circulatory collapse, cardiac arrest and death. Miosis can be one characteristic of morphine derivative overdose. Mydriasis can take place in terminal narcosis, severe hypoxia or as a toxic effect of pethidine or its congeners.

In addition to the effects of opioid analgesic overdose in general, focal and generalized seizures constitute a prominent feature in most cases of severe propoxyphene poisoning. Nephrogenic diabetes insipidus and ECG abnormalities may also occur.

Treatment: Establish adequate respiratory exchange through the provision of a patent airway and institution of assisted or controlled ventilation. Naloxone, a pure opioid antagonist, is used as a specific antidote to reverse the effects of opioid agonists and agonist-antagonists. An appropriate dose of naloxone should be administered, preferably by the i.v. route, simultaneously with efforts at respiratory resuscitation. The usual initial adult dose of naloxone is 0.4 to 2 mg i.v.; children: 0.01 mg/kg i.v. (see product monograph). Since the duration of action of the opioid may exceed that of the antagonist, the patient should be under surveillance and doses of the antagonist should be repeated as needed to maintain adequate respiration. A neuromuscular blocking agent may be required if respiratory depression is related to muscular rigidity. In propoxyphene overdose, in addition to the use of a an opioid antagonist, the patient may require careful titration with an anticonvulsant such as diazepam, bearing in mind the potential additive respiratory depressant effects.

An antagonist should **not** be administered in the absence of clinically significant respiratory or cardiovascular depression. Oxygen, i.v. fluids, vasopressors and other supportive measures should be used as indicated. In an individual physically dependent on opioids, the administration of the usual dose of opioid antagonist will precipitate an acute withdrawal syndrome. The severity of such a syndrome will depend on the degree of physical dependence and the dose of antagonist administered. The use of opioid antagonists in such individuals should be avoided if possible. If an opioid antagonist must be used to treat serious respiratory depression in patients with physical dependence on opioids, the antagonist should be administered with extreme care by using dosage titration, commencing with 10 to 20% of the usual recommended initial dose.

Gastric emptying may be useful in removing unabsorbed drug. Activated charcoal may be of benefit.

Methadone: The relatively long duration of action of methadone compared to that of naloxone may necessitate repeated doses of naloxone to counteract respiratory depression. The possibility of precipitating withdrawal must also be considered. Naloxone should not be used in the absence of clinically significant respiratory or cardiovascular depression.

Dosage: Some basic adult dosing information on morphine is provided in this monograph. Specific product monographs should be consulted for more detailed information. See Table II (on following page) for approximate analgesic equivalences.

Morphine: Oral: 10 to 30 mg every 4 hours; Extended Release: Dose should be individualized in the treatment of cancer pain or chronic pain.

Rectal: 10 to 20 mg every 4 hours.

I.M. or S.C.: 5 to 20 mg every 4 hours.

I.V.: 2.5 to 10 mg every 4 hours, injected over 4 to 5 minutes.

Epidural: Usual initial dose for once daily intermittent injection: 5 mg.

Intrathecal: Initially 0.2 to 1 mg daily.

N.B. Morphine may be administered by i.v., s.c., intrathecal or epidural infusion. Additional references should be consulted for specific information.

Dosing and administration should be individualized for each patient taking into account the following: the nature and severity of pain and medical status of the patient (e.g., renal and hepatic function), daily dose and potency of other opioids or other medication given previously or concurrently, and the degree of tolerance experienced. The use of potent opioid analgesics for the management of persistent pain should be preceded by a thorough assessment of the patient and diagnosis of the pain and its cause.

Methadone: The dosage of methadone in opioid dependence must be individualized, with the aim of controlling abstinence symptoms without causing respiratory depression or excessive sedation. Generally, initial dosage ranges from 15 to 30 mg once daily. Maintenance dosage is usually in the range of 50 to 120 mg daily, but may be higher or lower in some patients.

Opioids (cont'd)

The specific guidelines pertaining to the prescribing and dispensing of methadone are described in the Health Canada publications cited in the Indications section.

Table II—Opioids

Approximate Analgesic Equivalences

Drug	Equivalent Dose mg (compared to standard, Morphine 10 mg i.m.)	
Agonists	**I.M.**	**Oral**
Anileridine	25	75
Codeine	120	200
Diamorphine	5–8	10–15[a]
Fentanyl	0.1–0.2	NA[b]
Hydromorphone	1.5	7.5
Morphine	10	20–30
Oxycodone	NA	10–15[c]
Oxymorphone	1.5	5–15[d]
Pethidine	75	300
Propoxyphene	50	100
Agonist-Antagonists	**I.M.**	**Oral**
Butorphanol	2	NA
Nalbuphine	10	NA
Pentazocine	60	180

[a]Oral use not recommended.
[b]No data available.
[c]This value refers to combinations containing ASA or acetaminophen. For acute pain, single entity oral oxycodone is twice as potent as oral morphine.
[d]Suppository.

The reader is referred to individual product monographs for more specific dosing information.

Reviewed 1999

OPTICROM®

Allergan

Sodium Cromoglycate

Antiallergic

Pharmacology: In the immediate reaction (Type I), the union of antigen with reaginic antibody leads to the formation and release of mediators of the local anaphylactic reaction. The principal effect of sodium cromoglycate is its specific ability to stabilize the membrane of the mast cell and thus prevent the release of mediators of anaphylaxis. The action appears to be specific for reaginic (immediate type) antigen/antibody reactions. No direct effect has been demonstrated on other types of immune reactions (Type II, III, and IV).

Sodium cromoglycate has no vasoconstriction, antihistaminic or anti-inflammatory activity. Within 2 to 3 days of commencing treatment one can expect improvement in the signs and symptoms of seasonal allergic conjunctivitis (itching, tearing, congestion, etc.) in most patients. Continued therapy will usually keep the patient free from ophthalmic allergy symptoms during the challenge period.

Indications: To help relieve and prevent symptoms associated with allergic conjunctivitis or hay fever conjunctivitis.

Contraindications: Those patients who have shown hypersensitivity to sodium cromoglycate or to benzalkonium chloride.

Warnings: The recommended frequency of administration should not be exceeded.

Sodium cromoglycate should only be used for allergic conditions of the eye. In some instances irritation or redness may be due to serious eye conditions such as infection, foreign body in the eye, or other mechanical or chemical corneal trauma requiring the attention of a doctor. If you experience eye pain, changes in vision, pain on exposure to light, acute redness of the eye, excessive discharge, abnormal pupils, if condition worsens or if relief is not obtained within 72 hours consult your doctor immediately.

Any remaining contents should be discarded 4 weeks after opening. Do not touch dropper tip to any surface since this may contaminate the solution.

Precautions: During treatment with sodium cromoglycate solution, soft contact lenses should not be worn.

Children: Safety and effectiveness in children below the age of 5 years has not been established.

Pregnancy: There has been to date, no adequate and well controlled studies in pregnant women.

Lactation: It is not known whether this drug is excreted in human milk. Because many drugs are excreted in human milk, caution should be exercised when sodium cromoglycate is administered to a nursing woman.

Drug Interactions: Sodium cromoglycate has been used in association with other ophthalmic solutions in the rabbit including mydriatrics, antibiotics, steroids, vasoconstrictors and astringents. No drug-drug interactions have been observed in the rabbit eyes.

Adverse Effects: The most frequently reported adverse reaction attributed to the use of sodium cromoglycate on the basis of reoccurrence following administration is transient ocular stinging or burning upon instillation.

The following adverse reactions have been reported as infrequent events; conjunctival injection, watery eyes, itchy eyes, dryness around the eye, puffy eyes, eye irritation and sties. It is unclear whether they are attributable to the drug.

Overdose: Symptoms and Treatment: There have been no reported cases in humans of overdosage of the drug. Symptomatic treatment is suggested should accidental ingestion occur.

Dosage: The effect of therapy is dependent upon its administration at regular intervals as directed in the labelling.

Symptomatic response to treatment (decreased itching, tearing, redness and discharge) is usually evident within 2 to 3 days. Once symptomatic improvement has been established, therapy should be continued for as long as needed to sustain improvement.

Adults and Children Over 5 Years: 2 drops in each eye 4 times daily at regular intervals. One drop contains approximately 0.8 mg of sodium cromoglycate.

Information for the Patient: See Blue Section—Information for the Patient "Opticrom".

Supplied: Each plastic dropper bottle of a clear, colorless to pale yellow sterile solution, contains: sodium cromoglycate 2% w/v. Nonmedicinal ingredients: benzalkonium chloride as a preservative and edetate disodium. Bottles of 10 mL. Store at 15 to 30°C. Protect from direct sunlight. Discard opened bottle after 4 weeks.

Reviewed 1998

OPTIMINE® Ⓟ

Schering

Azatadine Maleate

Antihistamine

Indications: The symptomatic relief of respiratory allergic conditions which include acute and chronic allergic rhinitis, pollenosis (hay fever), and vasomotor rhinitis.

Also indicated in the symptomatic relief of such allergic dermatological conditions as acute and chronic urticaria, angioneurotic edema, allergic eczema, contact dermatitis, insect bites, pruritus vulvae and ani, pruritus of nonspecific origin, drug and serum reactions, dermographism; for anaphylactic reactions, as adjunctive therapy to epinephrine and other standard measures.

Contraindications: Known hypersensitivity to azatadine or its components.

Antihistamines should not be used to treat lower respiratory tract symptoms.

Patients receiving MAO inhibitor therapy or within 10 days of stopping such treatment (see Precautions, Drug Interactions).

Antihistamines should be discontinued approximately 4 days prior to skin testing procedures since these may prevent or diminish otherwise positive reactions to dermal reactivity indicators.

Precautions: Azatadine should be used with caution in patients with narrow angle glaucoma, stenosing peptic ulcer, pyloroduodenal obstruction, prostatic hypertrophy or bladder neck obstruction, cardiovascular disease, hyperthyroidism or those with increased intraocular pressure.

Because of the atropine-like action of antihistamines, this product should be used with caution in patients with a history of bronchial asthma.

Drug Interactions: MAO inhibitors prolong and intensify the effects of antihistamines. Concomitant use of antihistamines with alcohol, tricyclic antidepressants, barbiturates, or other CNS depressants may have an additive effect. The action of oral anticoagulants may be inhibited by antihistamines.

Occupational Hazards: Patients should be warned about engaging in activities requiring mental alertness, such as driving a car or operating appliances, or machinery.

Antihistamines are more likely to cause dizziness, sedation, hypotension in patients over 60 years of age.

Overdosage of antihistamines, particularly in infants and children may produce convulsions and death.

Pregnancy and *Lactation:* The safe use of this product during pregnancy and lactation has not been established and therefore the compound should be used only if the potential benefit justifies the potential risk to the fetus or infant.

Adverse Effects: Adverse effects with antihistamines vary in incidence and severity. Among them are cardiovascular, hematologic (pancytopenia, thrombocytopenia, hemolytic anemia), neurologic (confusion, hallucinations, tremor), gastrointestinal, genitourinary (urinary retention), respiratory adverse reactions and mood changes. The most common include sedation, sleepiness, dizziness, disturbed coordination, epigastric distress, rash, dry mouth and thickening of bronchial secretions.

General side effects such as urticaria, drug rash, anaphylactic shock, photosensitivity, excessive perspiration, chills, dryness of mouth, nose and throat have been reported.

Overdose: Symptoms: Manifestations of overdosage may vary from CNS depression (sedation, apnea, diminished mental alertness, cyanosis, coma, cardiovascular collapse) to stimulation (insomnia, hallucinations, tremors, or convulsions) to death. Other signs and symptoms may be euphoria, excitement, tachycardia, palpitations, thirst, perspiration, nausea, dizziness, tinnitus, ataxia, blurred vision, and hypertension or hypotension. Stimulation is particularly likely in children as are atropine-like signs and symptoms (dry mouth; fixed, dilated pupils; flushing; hyperthermia; and gastrointestinal symptoms).

Treatment: Emergency treatment should be started immediately. The patient should be induced to vomit, even if emesis has occurred spontaneously. Pharmacologically induced vomiting by the administration of ipecac syrup is a preferred method. However, vomiting should not be induced in patients with impaired consciousness. Following emesis, any drug remaining in the stomach may be absorbed by activated charcoal administered as a slurry with water. If vomiting is unsuccessful or contraindicated, gastric lavage should be performed. Dialysis is of little value in antihistamine poisoning. After emergency treatment the patient should continue to be medically monitored.

Treatment of the signs and symptoms of overdosage is symptomatic and supportive. Stimulants (analeptic agents) should not be used. Vasopressors may be used to treat hypotension. Short-acting barbiturates, diazepam, or paraldehyde may be administered to control seizures. Hyperpyrexia, especially in children, may require treatment with tepid water sponge baths or a hypothermic blanket. Apnea is treated with ventilatory support.

Dosage: Adults: 1 mg in the morning and evening. In refractory or more severe cases, 2 mg twice daily may be used. Children 6 to 12 years of age: 0.5 to 1 mg twice daily.

Supplied: Each white, compressed, scored tablet, impressed with the Schering trademark contains: azatadine maleate 1 mg. Nonmedicinal ingredients: cornstarch, lactose, magnesium stearate and povidone. Tartrazine-free. Bottles of 100. Store between 2 and 30°C.

(Shown in Product Recognition Section)

OPTIMYXIN®
OPTIMYXIN PLUS® Ⓟ

Sabex

Polymyxin B Sulfate Compounds

Antibiotic

Supplied: Optimyxin: Ointment: Each g of ophthalmic ointment contains: polymyxin B (as sulfate) 10 000 units and bacitracin (as zinc) 500 units. Nonmedicinal ingredients: mineral oil and petrolatum. Tubes of 3.5 g. Store between 15 and 30°C.

Solution: Each mL of eye/ear solution contains: polymyxin B sulfate 10 000 units and gramicidin 0.025 mg. Nonmedicinal ingredients: benzalkonium chloride, boric acid, ethyl alcohol, poloxamer, purified water and sodium hydroxide (to adjust pH). Thimerosal-free. Plastic dropper bottles of 10 mL. Store between 15 and 30°C.

Optimyxin Plus: Each mL of eye/ear solution contains: polymyxin B sulfate 10 000 units, gramicidin 0.025 mg and neomycin sulfate 2.5 mg. Nonmedicinal ingredients: benzalkonium chloride, boric acid, ethyl alcohol, hydrochloric acid (to adjust pH), poloxamer and purified water. Thimerosal-free. Plastic dropper bottles of 10 mL. Store between 15 and 30°C.

OPTIRAY®

Mallinckrodt

Ioversol

Radiopaque Medium

Pharmacology: General: The pharmacokinetics of ioversol in normal subjects conform to an open 2 compartment model with first order elimination (a rapid alpha phase 6.8 minutes, for drug distribution and a slower beta phase 92 minutes, for drug elimination). Based on the blood clearance curves for 12 healthy volunteers (6 receiving 50 mL and 6 receiving 150 mL of Optiray 320), the biological half-life was 1.5 hours for both dose levels and there was no evidence of any dose related difference in the rate of elimination. The mean half-life for urinary excretion following a 50 mL dose was 118 minutes (105 to 156) and following a 150 mL dose was 105 minutes.

Ioversol is excreted mainly through the kidneys following intravascular administration. Fecal elimination is 3 to 9%. Approximately 50% of the injected dose is excreted at 1.5 hours and 86% at 48 hours; about 1.5% is retained, mostly by the thyroid and liver. In patients with impaired renal function and in infants with immature kidneys, the elimination half-life is prolonged. In patients with severe renal disease, excretion does not occur.

Ioversol does not notably bind to serum or plasma proteins to any marked extent and no significant metabolism, deionization or biotransformation occurs.

Ioversol, like all other contrast media, may induce changes in thyroid function in some patients, and elevation of thyroxine and/or TSH may be observed.

Ioversol, like other nonionic contrast media, has an insignificant effect on blood coagulation (as shown by slightly increased prothrombin time and partial thromboplastin time, and delayed platelet aggregation) and does not possess the anticoagulant properties of ionic contrast media.

Ioversol causes concentration-dependent hemolysis, aggregation and crenation of red blood cells.

Elevations of several laboratory parameters (AST, ALT, LDH, bilirubin, creatinine, BUN) following intravascular administration have been reported in several patients which were not considered clinically significant.

Intravascular: Intravascular injection of ioversol opacifies those vessels in the path of flow of the contract bolus, permitting their radiographic visualization.

Following i.v. contrast medium administration, the increase in density in non-neural tissue is dependent on the presence of iodine in the vascular and extravascular (extra cellular) compartments. This is related to the rate and amount of contrast material administered, blood flow, vascularity, capillary permeability, extravascular effusion and renal filtration.

Peak iodine blood levels occur immediately following rapid i.v. administration, then fall rapidly as the contrast medium is diluted in the plasma volume and diffuses from the vascular into the extravascular spaces. Equilibration between plasma and extravascular iodine concentration occurs within a few minutes.

Contrast enhancement (increase in the **difference** in density between adjacent tissues) is the result of differential vascular and extravascular iodine concentration between normal and abnormal tissues, which may accentuate inherent differences in pre-existent tissue density. With contrast enhancement a pathological lesion may demonstrate increased or decreased density compared to the surrounding normal tissue. Some lesions, however, will remain or become isodense and thus undetectable by attempted contrast enhancement. Contrast enhancement in most cases is greatest immediately after bolus injection.

Ioversol may be visualized in the renal parenchyma within 30 to 60 seconds following rapid i.v. injection. Opacification of the calyces and pelves in patients with normal renal function becomes apparent within 1 to 3 minutes, with optimum contrast occurring within 5 to 15 minutes.

In nephropathic conditions, particularly when excretory capacity has been altered, the rate of excretion varies unpredictably, and opacification may be delayed for up to several hours after injection. Severe renal impairment may result in a lack of diagnostic opacification of the urinary tract, and depending on the degree of renal impairment, prolonged plasma ioversol levels may be anticipated in these patients as well as in infants with immature kidneys.

Ioversol (33%I) was compared in intra-carotid studies in 45 anesthetized rats to iopamidol (32%I) and iohexol (30%I). There was no detectable damage to the blood-brain barrier with any of these substances.

Generally, less warmth and pain are associated with the injection of ioversol than with conventional ionic media. Comparative studies using diatrizoate and iothalamate showed significantly less heat sensation and pain with ioversol. Other non-ionic agents, iohexol and iopamidol, gave results similar to ioversol.

Ioversol had significantly less effect on cardiovascular and ECG parameters than did diatrizoate. For example, it produced significantly less bradycardia, tachycardia, T-wave changes, ST depression, ST elevation and hypotension than were seen with diatrizoate.

Subarachnoid: Following its injection into the subarachnoid space, ioversol mixes readily with the cerebrospinal fluid (CSF) and diffuses into root sleeves and upward in the spinal and intracranial subarachnoid spaces. The time it takes ioversol to reach the cervical and intracranial subarachnoid spaces will depend to a large degree on the patient's position and movements. As it diffuses upward, its concentration decreases.

Following lumbar subarachnoid injection, conventional radiography will continue to provide good diagnostic degree of contrast for at least 30 minutes. At about 1 hour, a diagnostic degree of contrast will usually not be available due to diffusion through the CSF and transfer to the general circulation.

Computerized Tomography: CT Scanning of the Head: In brain scanning, the contrast medium does not accumulate in normal brain tissue due to the presence of the blood brain barrier. The increase in x-ray absorption in the normal brain is due to the presence of the contrast agent within the blood pool. A break in the blood-brain barrier, such as occurs in malignant tumors of the brain, allows accumulation of the contrast medium within the interstitial tumor tissue; adjacent normal brain tissue does not retain the contrast medium.

Rapid infusion of the dose yields peak blood iodine concentrations immediately following infusion (within 15 to 120 seconds), which fall rapidly over the next 5 to 10 minutes.

Diagnostic contrast enhancement images of the brain have been obtained up to 1 hour after i.v. bolus administration.

CT Scanning of the Body: During CT of the body, ioversol diffuses rapidly from the vascular to the extravascular space. Increase in x-ray absorption is related to blood flow, concentration of the contrast medium and extraction of the contrast medium by interstitial tissue. Contrast enhancement is thus due to the relative differences in extravascular diffusion between normal and abnormal tissue—a situation quite different from that in the brain.

Contrast enhancement appears to be greatest immediately after bolus infusion (15 to 120 seconds).

Utilization of a continuous scanning technique (dynamic CT scanning) may improve enhancement of tumor and other lesions, such as an abscess.

Indications: Intravascular: Optiray 160: Adults: For use in adults for intra-arterial digital subtraction angiography.

Optiray 240: Adults: For use in adults for cerebral angiography, venography, excretory urography and for contrast enhanced computed tomographic imaging of the head and body. Optiray 240 may be used in myelography.

Optiray 300: Adults: For use in adults for cerebral angiography, aortography, peripheral and visceral arteriography, i.v. contrast enhancement of computed tomography of the brain and body, excretory urography, i.v. digital subtraction angiography and venography.

Children: In children 1 year of age or over for i.v. excretory urography and intra-arterial digital subtraction angiography.

Optiray 320: Adults: For angiography throughout the cardiovascular system in adults. The uses include cerebral, coronary, peripheral, visceral and renal arteriography, aortography and left ventriculography. Optiray 320 is also recommended for contrast enhanced computed tomographic imaging of the head and in excretory urography.

Children: For angiocardiography, contrast enhanced computed tomography of the head and body, excretory urography.

Optiray 350: Adults: For coronary arteriography and ventriculography, peripheral and visceral arteriography, i.v. contrast enhancement in computed tomography of the head and body, excretory urography, i.v. digital subtraction angiography and venography.

Children: For angiocardiography.

Subarachnoid: Optiray 240: Adults: For subarachnoid administration in adults for lumbar, thoracic and cervical myelography.

Contraindications: Should not be administered to patients with known or suspected hypersensitivity to ioversol or in cases of clinically significant impairment of both hepatic and renal function.

Warnings: General: Serious or fatal reactions have been associated with the administration of all iodine-containing radiopaque media, including ioversol. It is of utmost importance that a course of action be carefully planned in advance for immediate treatment of serious reactions, and that adequate facilities and appropriate personnel be readily available in case a severe reaction should occur.

A previous reaction to a contrast medium of different chemical structure or a history of iodine sensitivity is not an absolute contraindication to the use of ioversol. However, extreme caution should be exercised in injecting these patients and prophylactic therapy (as with corticosteroids, for example) should be considered (see Precautions, General).

There must be a clear indication for performing procedures involving the administration of contrast agents in all patients.

Patients with a history of allergy, bronchial asthma or other allergic manifestations, combined renal and hepatic disease, the elderly, debilitated or severely ill patients, those with homocystinuria, endotoxemia, elevated body temperature, severe hypertension or congestive heart failure, other cardiovascular disease, hyperthyroidism and recent renal transplant recipients, as well as patients sensitive to iodine, present an additional risk and call for careful evaluation of the risks involved against the benefits expected.

Patients with a serum creatinine level above 3 mg/dL should not undergo excretory urography or other radiological procedures unless the benefits clearly outweigh the risks incurred.

In patients with advanced renal disease, iodinated contrast media should be used with caution and only when the examination is essential since excretion of the medium is impaired. Use of ioversol is not recommended in patients with anuria or severe oliguria.

Administration of radiopaque materials to patients known or suspected to have pheochromocytoma should be performed with extreme caution if, in the opinion of the physician, the possible benefits of such procedures outweigh the considered risks. The amount of radiopaque medium injected should be kept to an absolute minimum. The blood pressure should be assessed throughout the procedure, and measures for treatment of a hypertensive crisis should be available.

General anesthesia may be indicated in some procedures; however, one should be aware of possible increased incidence of adverse reactions in such circumstances.

Intravascular: Intravascularly administered iodine-containing contrast media are potentially hazardous.

Non-ionic iodinated contrast media, including ioversol, inhibit blood coagulation less than ionic contrast media. Clotting has been reported when blood remains in contact with syringes, catheters or tubes containing non-ionic contrast media. Serious, rarely fatal, thromboembolic events causing myocardial infarction and stroke have been reported during angiographic procedures with non-ionic and also with ionic contrast media. Therefore, meticulous intravascular administration technique is necessary, particularly during angiographic procedures, to minimize thromboembolic events. Numerous factors, including length of procedure, number of injections, catheter and syringe material, underlying disease state and concomitant medications may contribute to the development of thromboembolic events. For these reasons, meticulous angiographic techniques are recommended including close attention to keeping guidewires, catheters and all angiographic equipment free of blood, use of manifold systems and/or three way stopcocks, frequent catheter flushing with heparinized saline solutions and minimizing the length of the procedure. Non-ionic iodinated contrast media are not recommended as flush solutions. The use of plastic syringes in place of glass syringes has been reported to decrease but not eliminate the likelihood of clotting.

A minimal diagnostic dose should be employed and renal function, as well as extent of urinary precipitation of the myelomatous protein, should be monitored for a few days subsequent to the procedure. The patients should be normally hydrated for the examination since dehydration may predispose to precipitation of myeloma protein in the renal tubules. No form of therapy, including dialysis, has been successful in reversing the effect.

Intravascular administration of contrast media may promote sickling in individuals who are homozygous for sickle cell disease. Fluid restriction is not advised in these patients.

As with any contrast medium, including ioversol, serious neurologic sequelae, including permanent paralysis, can occur following cerebral arteriography and injection into vessels supplying the spinal cord. The injection of a contrast medium

Optiray (cont'd)

should never be made following the administration of vasopressors since they strongly potentiate neurologic effects.

Subarachnoid: Myelography should not be performed when lumbar puncture is contraindicated as in the presence of local or systemic infection where bacteremia is likely.

Myelography should be performed only in hospitalized patients under close medical supervision, which is to be continued for 24 hours following the procedure.

Patients receiving anticonvulsants should be maintained on this therapy. Should a seizure occur, i.v. diazepam or phenobarbital is recommended. In patients with a history of seizure activity who are not on anticonvulsant therapy, premedication with barbiturates should be considered. Ioversol should be used in epileptics only if a water soluble contrast medium is considered essential.

Prophylactic anticonvulsant treatment with barbiturates should be considered in patients with evidence of inadvertent intracranial entry of a large bolus of contrast medium, since there may be increased risk of seizure in such cases.

Gravitational displacement of a concentrated bolus of ioversol above the level of C_1 and especially into the intracranial subarachnoid spaces is to be avoided.

Precautions: General: All procedures utilizing contrast media carry a definite risk of producing severe, life-threatening and fatal reactions. Therefore, the need for the examination should always be carefully assessed and the risk-benefit factor should always be carefully evaluated before such a procedure is undertaken.

At all times a fully equipped emergency cart, or equivalent supplies and equipment, and personnel competent in recognizing and treating adverse reactions of all severity, or situations which may arise as a result of the procedure, should be immediately available. If a serious reaction should occur, immediately discontinue administration and institute appropriate treatment. Since severe delayed reactions have been known to occur, emergency facilities and competent personnel should be available for at least 30 to 60 minutes after administration.

The reported incidences of adverse reactions to contrast media are twice as high in patients with a history of allergy than in the general population. Patients with a history of previous reactions to a contrast medium or iodine are 3 times more susceptible than other patients. Most adverse reactions to intravascularly injected contrast agents appear within 1 to 30 minutes after the start of injection, but delayed reactions may occur.

Before a contrast medium is injected, the patient should be questioned for a history of bronchial asthma or allergy.

Although a history of allergy may imply a greater than usual risk, it does not arbitrarily contraindicate the use of the medium. Premedication with corticosteroids to avoid or minimize possible allergic reactions may be considered.

The possibility of an idiosyncratic reaction in patients who have previously received a contrast medium without ill effect should always be considered. A positive history of bronchial asthma or allergy, a family history of allergy, or a previous reaction of hypersensitivity to another contrast agent warrants special attention. Such a history, by suggesting proneness to reactions, may be more accurate than pretesting in predicting the potential for reaction, although not necessarily the severity or type of reaction in the individual case. A positive history of this type does not arbitrarily contraindicate the use of a contrast agent, when a diagnostic procedure is thought essential, but calls for caution.

The sensitivity test most often performed is the slow injection of 0.5 to 1 mL of the radiopaque medium, administered i.v., prior to injection of the full dose. It should be noted that the absence of a reaction to the test dose does not preclude the possibility of a reaction to the full dose. Severe reactions and fatalities have occurred with the full dose after a nonreactive test dose, and with or without a history of allergy.

Prophylactic therapy with corticosteroids should be considered for patients who present with a strong allergic history, a previous reaction to a contrast medium, or a positive pretest (since in these patients the incidence of reaction is 2 to 3 times that of the general population). Adequate doses of corticosteroids should be started early enough prior to contrast medium injection to be effective and should continue through the time of injection and for 24 hours after injection. Corticosteroids should not be mixed in the same syringe with the contrast medium because of chemical incompatibility.

Renal failure has been reported in patients with liver dysfunction who were given an oral cholecystographic agent followed by an intravascular iodinated radiopaque agent and also in patients with occult renal disease, notably diabetics and hypertensives. Administration of ioversol should be postponed in patients with hepatic or biliary disorder who have recently taken a cholecystographic agent. An interval of at least 48 hours should be allowed between examinations, especially in patients with reduced renal reserve. Especially in these classes of patients there should be no fluid restriction and every attempt made to maintain normal hydration, prior to contrast medium administration, since dehydration is the single most important factor influencing further renal impairment.

Acute renal failure has been reported in patients with diabetic nephropathy and in susceptible nondiabetic patients (often elderly with pre-existing renal disease) following administration of iodinated contrast agents. Careful consideration of the potential risks should be given before performing radiographic procedures with ioversol in these patients.

Intravascular: Diagnostic procedures which involve the use of iodinated intravascular contrast agents should be carried out under the direction of a physician skilled and experienced in the particular procedure to be performed.

Reports of thyroid storm occurring following intravascular use of iodinated radiopaque agents in patients with hyperthyroidism or with an autonomously functioning thyroid nodule suggest that this additional risk be carefully evaluated in such patients before use of ioversol.

Special precaution is advised in patients with increased intracranial pressure, cerebral thrombosis or embolism, primary or metastatic cerebral lesions, subarachnoid hemorrhage, arterial spasm, transient ischemic attacks, and in any condition when the blood-brain barrier is breached or the transit time of the contrast agent material through the cerebral vasculature is prolonged, since clinical deterioration, convulsions and serious temporary or permanent neurological complications (including stroke, aphasia, cortical blindness, etc.) may occur following i.v. or intra-arterial injection of relatively large doses of contrast media. Such patients, and patients in clinically unstable or critical condition, should undergo examinations with intravascular contrast media only if in the opinion of the physician the expected benefits outweigh the potential risks, and the dose should be kept to the absolute minimum.

When considering the use of high doses of contrast media, caution should be exercised in patients with congestive heart failure because of the transitory increase in circulatory osmotic load, and such patients should be kept under surveillance for several hours in order to detect delayed hemodynamic disturbances.

There have been reports in the literature indicating that patients on adrenergic beta-blockers may be more prone to severe adverse reactions to contrast media. At the same time, treatment of allergic-anaphylactoid reactions in these patients is more difficult. Epinephrine should be administered with caution since it may not exert its usual effects. On the one hand larger doses of epinephrine may be needed to overcome the bronchospasm, while on the other, these doses can be associated with excessive alpha adrenergic stimulation with consequent hypertension, reflex bradycardia and heart block and possible potentiation of bronchospasm. Alternatives to the use of large doses of epinephrine include vigorous supportive care such as fluids and the use of beta agonists including parenteral salbutamol or isoproterenol to overcome bronchospasm and norepinephrine to overcome hypotension.

In angiography procedures, the presence of a vigorous pulsatile flow should be established before using a catheter or pressure injection technique. A small pilot dose of about 1 to 2 mL should be administered to locate the exact site of needle or catheter tip to help prevent injection of the main dose into a branch of the aorta or intramurally. Great care should be taken to avoid the entry of a large concentrated bolus into an aortic branch.

Mesenteric necrosis, acute pancreatitis, renal shutdown, and serious neurologic complications including spinal cord damage and hemiplegia or quadriplegia have been reported following inadvertent injection of a large part of the aortic dose of contrast media into an aortic branch or arterial trunks providing spinal or cerebral artery branches.

Pulsation must be present in the artery to be injected. Extreme caution is advised in considering peripheral angiography in patients suspected of having thromboangiitis obliterans (Buerger's disease) since any procedure (even insertion of needle or catheter) may induce a severe arterial or venous spasm. Caution is also advisable in patients with severe ischemia associated with ascending infection. Special care is required in patients with suspected thrombosis, ischemic disease, local infection or a significantly obstructed vascular system. Occasional serious neurologic complications, including paraplegia, have been reported in patients with aorto-iliac or femoral artery bed obstruction, abdominal compression, hypotension, and hypertension and following injection of vasopressors.

When large individual doses are administered, an appropriate time interval should be permitted to elapse between injections to allow for subsidence of hemodynamic disturbances. Angiography should be avoided whenever possible in patients with homocystinuria because of the risk of inducing thrombosis and embolism.

Following catheter procedures, gentle pressure hemostasis is advised followed by immobilization of the limb for several hours to prevent hemorrhage from the site of arterial puncture.

I.V. Contrast Enhancement in Computed Tomography: Following injection of relatively large doses of contrast media used in the procedure, transient or permanent neurological changes have been reported.

Pregnancy: No teratogenic effects attributable to ioversol have been observed to date in studies performed in animals. There are no studies on the use of ioversol in pregnant women. Many injectable contrast media cross the placental barrier in humans and appear to enter fetal tissue passively. Ioversol probably crosses the placental barrier in humans by simple diffusion to reach fetal tissue. Ioversol should be used during pregnancy only if the benefit to the mother clearly outweighs the risk to the fetus. It should be borne in mind that x-ray procedures involve a certain risk related to exposure of the fetus.

Lactation: Because contrast media are secreted in human milk, if the administration of ioversol is considered to be essential, breast-feeding should be discontinued for at least 48 hours following the procedure.

Children: Some pediatric patients have a higher risk of adverse reactions to contrast media. Such patients may include those with sensitivity to allergens, including other drugs, those with asthma, congestive heart failure, a serum creatinine >1.5 mg/dL, or ages under 12 months.

Geriatrics: The tolerance of elderly patients to drugs in general is diminished. These patients may have reduced renal reserve and impaired general health and may be taking medication (e.g., adrenergic B-blockers) which make them more susceptible to the potentially harmful effects of procedures involving the use of contrast media. The need for and the expected benefits of the procedure have to be carefully evaluated and dosage should be very conservative.

Drug Interactions: Drugs which lower seizure threshold, especially phenothiazine derivatives, including those used for their antihistaminic or antinauseant properties, should not be used with ioversol.

Renal toxicity has been reported in a few patients with liver dysfunction who were given oral cholecystographic agents followed by intravascular contrast agents. Therefore administration of a contrast agent should be postponed by at least 48 hours following use of an oral cholecystographic agent.

Subarachnoid: Elderly patients may present a greater risk following myelography. The need for the procedure in these patients should be evaluated carefully. Special attention must be given not to exceed the recommended dose of the contrast medium, to see that the patient is sufficiently hydrated and to ensure proper and sterile radiographic technique.

If grossly bloody CFS is encountered, the possible benefits of a myelographic procedure should be considered in terms of the risk to the patient.

Any intrathecally administered medication including nonionic contrast media such as ioversol can enter the brain substance which may increase the risk of adverse effects associated with the procedure. Such adverse reactions may be delayed and, in extremely rare cases, may be life-threatening. Careful patient and dose selection and proper patient management before, during and after the procedure are therefore imperative. Care is required in patient management to prevent inadvertent intracranial entry of a large bolus of contrast medium. Also, effort should be directed to avoid rapid dispersion of the medium (i.e., by active patient movement).

Experience with the use of water-soluble contrast media in myelography indicates that in most cases of major motor seizure one or more of the following factors were present, and should therefore, be avoided: deviations from recommended procedure on myelographic management; use in patients with a history of epilepsy; inadvertent overdosage; intracranial entry of a bolus or premature diffusion of a high concentration of the medium; medication with neuroleptic drugs or phenothiazine antinauseants; failure to maintain elevation of the head during and after the procedure; active patient movement or straining.

Repeat Procedures: If in the clinical judgment of the physician a repeat examination is required, an interval of 5 days between procedures is recommended.

Special Precautions to be observed with performing specific diagnostic procedures are listed in the Dosage section, under individual paragraphs pertaining to said specific procedures.

Adverse Effects: Since ioversol is an iodinated contrast agent with an adverse reaction profile similar to other non-ionic contrast media, all known adverse effects associated with the use of any contrast agent can occur with ioversol.

Most adverse reactions following the use of ioversol are of mild or moderate intensity, however, serious, life-threatening and fatal adverse reactions, mostly of cardiovascular origin, have been reported.

It should be kept in mind that, although most adverse reactions occur soon after the administration of the contrast medium, some adverse reactions can be delayed and can be of long-lasting nature.

The reported incidence of adverse reactions to contrast media in patients with a history of allergy is twice that of the general population. Patients with a history of previous reactions to a contrast medium are 3 times more susceptible than other patients.

The incidence of serious adverse reactions is higher with coronary arteriography than with other procedures. In those patients only who had coronary arteriography with ioversol, the incidence of angina was 1.2%. Cardiac decompensation, serious arrhythmias, myocardial ischemia or myocardial infarction may occur during coronary arteriography and left ventriculography.

Table I is based upon clinical trials with Optiray formulations in 1 466 patients, regardless of their direct attributability to the drug or the procedure.

Adverse reactions to specific procedures are also dealt with under Dosage.

Table I—Optiray

Adverse Reactions seen with Optiray

System	Adverse Reactions > 1%	Adverse Reactions ≤ 1%
Cardiovascular	none	angina pectoris, hypotension, blood pressure fluctuation, arterial spasm, bradycardia, conduction defect, false aneurysm, hypertension, transient arrhythmia, vascular trauma
Digestive	none	nausea, vomiting
Nervous	none	cerebral infarct, headache, blurred vision, vertigo, lightheadedness, vasovagal reaction, disorientation, paresthesia, dysphasia, muscle spasm, syncope, visual hallucination
Respiratory	none	laryngeal edema, pulmonary edema, sneezing, nasal congestion, coughing, shortness of breath, hypoxia
Skin	none	periorbital edema, urticaria, facial edema, flush, pruritus
Miscellaneous	none	extravasation, hematoma, shaking chills, bad taste, general pain

In addition to the reported reactions in Table I, the following may occur with any contrast agent including ioversol: Cardiovascular: hypoxia, heart block, bundle branch block, coronary thrombosis, cyanosis, hypertensive crisis, peripheral vasodilation, acute vascular insufficiency, circulatory collapse, hypotensive shock and cardiogenic shock.

CNS: photomas, persistent blindness, taste perversion, anxiety, tinnitus, motor dysfunction, convulsion, somnolence, confusion, psychotic reaction, stiff neck, hemiparesis, hemiplegia, nystagmus, restlessness, tremors, aphasia, paralysis, coma and death.

Allergic Type Reaction: purpura, conjunctivitis, lacrimation, erythematous, bullous or pleomorphic rashes, laryngospasm, bronchospasm, apnea, cyanosis, edema of glottis, laryngeal edema, angioneurotic edema, peripheral edema, anaphylactic shock. These allergic type reactions can progress into anaphylaxis, coma and death.

Renal: transient proteinuria, hematuria and rarely oliguria, anuria and renal failure.

Other Reactions: diarrhea, dry mouth, pallor, venous and arterial thrombosis and rarely thrombophlebitis, rare cases of disseminated intravascular coagulation, neutropenia.

Children: In controlled clinical trials involving 128 patients for pediatric angiocardiography, contrast enhanced computed tomography of the head and body and i.v. excretory urography, adverse reactions following the use of Optiray 320 were generally less than with adults. Adverse reactions reported were as follows: fever 1.6%, nausea 0.8%, muscle spasm 0.8%, LV pressure change 0.8%.

Related to Procedure: extravasation, perforation, rupture, dissection of blood vessels, hemorrhage, hematoma, false aneurysm, muscle spasm, arterial spasm, vascular trauma, ecchymosis and tissue necrosis, dislodgment of atheromatous plaques, thrombophlebitis, thrombosis embolization, injury to nerves and neighboring organs, brachial plexus palsy following axillary artery injections.

Treatment of Adverse Effects: Contrast media should be administered only by physicians thoroughly familiar with the emergency treatment of all adverse reactions to contrast media. The assistance of other trained personnel such as cardiologists, internists and anesthetists is required in the management of severe reactions.

A guideline for the treatment of adverse reactions is presented below. This outline is not intended to be a complete manual on the treatment of adverse reactions to contrast media or on cardiopulmonary resuscitation. The physician should refer to the appropriate texts on the subject.

It is also realized that institutions or individual practitioners will already have appropriate systems in effect and that circumstances may dictate the use of additional or different measures.

Minor Allergic Reactions: (if considered necessary). The i.v or i.m. administration of an antihistamine such as diphenhydramine HCl 25 to 50 mg is generally sufficient (contraindicated in epileptics). The resulting drowsiness makes it imperative to ensure that outpatients do not drive or go home unaccompanied.

Major or Life-threatening Reactions: A major reaction may be manifested by signs and symptoms of cardiovascular collapse, severe respiratory difficulty and nervous system dysfunction. Convulsions, coma and cardiorespiratory arrest may ensue.

The following measures should be considered: 1. Start emergency therapy immediately, carefully monitoring vital signs. 2. Have emergency resuscitation team summoned—do not leave patient unattended. 3. Ensure patent airway: guard against aspiration. 4. Commence artificial respiration if patient is not breathing. 5. Administer oxygen, if necessary. 6. Start external cardiac massage in the event of cardiac arrest. 7. Establish route for i.v. medication by starting infusion of appropriate solution (5% dextrose in water). 8. Judiciously administer specific drug therapy as indicated by the type and severity of the reaction. Careful monitoring is mandatory to detect adverse reactions of all drugs administered. (a) Soluble hydrocortisone 500 to 1 000 mg i.v. for all acute allergic-anaphylactic reactions. (b) Epinephrine 1:1 000 solution (in the presence of anoxia it may cause ventricular fibrillation, **caution** in patients on adrenergic beta blockers. See Precautions.) 0.2 to 0.4 mL s.c. for severe allergic reactions; in extreme emergency 0.1 mL/minute, appropriately diluted, may be given i.v. until desired effect is obtained. Do not exceed 0.4 mL; in case of cardiac arrest 0.1 to 0.2 mL, appropriately diluted, may be given intracardially. (c) In hypotension (carefully monitoring blood pressure): phenylephrine HCl 0.1 to 0.5 mg appropriately diluted slowly i.v. or by slow infusion **or** norepinephrine 4 mL of 0.2% solution in 1 000 mL of 5% dextrose by slow drip infusion. (d) Sodium bicarbonate 5%, 50 mL i.v. every 10 minutes as needed to combat post-arrest acidosis. (e) Atropine 0.4 to 0.6 mg i.v. to increase heart rate in sinus bradycardia. May reverse 2nd or 3rd degree block. (f) To control convulsions: pentobarbital sodium 50 mg in fractional doses slowly i.v. (contraindicated if cyanosis is present) **or** diazepam 5 to 10 mg slowly i.v. titrating the dose to the response of the patient. 9. Defibrillation, administration of antiarrhythmics and additional emergency measures and drugs may be required. 10. The patient should be transferred to the intensive care unit when feasible for further monitoring and treatment.

Overdose: Symptoms and Treatment: The adverse effects of overdosage are life-threatening and affect mainly the pulmonary, cardiovascular and central nervous systems. Treatment of an overdosage is directed toward the support of all vital functions, and prompt institution of specific therapy.

Ioversol does not bind to plasma or serum proteins and is therefore dialyzable.

Dosage: Intravascular: Only the lowest dose necessary to obtain adequate visualization should be used.

Use only the recommended concentration for the particular procedure to be undertaken.

Patients should be well hydrated prior to and following administration of ioversol.

Do **not** dehydrate patients for any procedure.

Ioversol should be inspected visually for particulate matter and discoloration prior to administration. If either is present the vial should be discarded.

Ioversol should not be transferred into other delivery systems except immediately before use and should be used immediately once the seal has been punctured.

It is advisable that ioversol be at or close to body temperature when injected.

Under no circumstances should other drugs be administered concomitantly in the same syringe or i.v. administration set as ioversol because of a potential for chemical incompatibility.

Patency of the vessel and the position of the catheter tip or needle should be checked with a small pilot dose of ioversol before injecting the full dose. The catheter tip should be kept free of aspirated blood. Prolonged contact of the contrast medium with blood must be avoided because of potential thromboembolic complications.

The volume of each individual injection is a more important consideration than the total dose used. When large individual volumes are administered, sufficient time should be permitted to elapse between each injection to allow for subsidence of hemodynamic disturbances.

Any unused portion of one container should be discarded.

Cerebral Angiography: Optiray 320, 300 or 240 may be used to visualize the cerebral vasculature.

Patient Preparation: Suitable premedication may be given. Introduction of the catheter or needle is normally performed with local anesthesia. General anesthesia is rarely required (see Precautions, General).

Precautions: In addition to the general precautions previously described, cerebral angiography with ioversol should be performed with special caution in elderly patients, patients in poor clinical condition, patients with advanced arteriosclerosis, severe hypertension, cardiac decompensation, senility, recent cerebral thrombosis, embolism or subarachnoid hemorrhage, following a recent attack of migraine, and in any condition compromising the integrity of the blood brain barrier, and only if the examination is considered to be necessary for the welfare of the patient. The patient should be watched carefully for possible adverse reactions.

Adverse Effects: The major sources of cerebral arteriographic adverse reactions to ioversol appear to be related to repeated injections of the contrast material, administration of doses higher than those recommended, the presence of occlusive atherosclerotic vascular disease and the method and technique of injection.

Since nonionic contrast media have no significant anticoagulant properties, meticulous technique is necessary to avoid thromboembolic complications (see Warnings).

A feeling of warmth in the face and neck is frequently experienced. Infrequently, a more severe burning discomfort is observed. Transient visual hallucinations have been reported.

Serious neurological reactions that have been associated with cerebral angiography include stroke, seizures, amnesia, hemiparesis, visual field loss, cortical blindness, aphasia, confusion, disorientation, hallucination, convulsions, coma and death.

Cardiovascular reactions that may occur with some frequency, but not necessarily with ioversol, are bradycardia, arrhythmia, either an increase or decrease in systemic blood pressure, and ECG changes.

Note: The EEG changes associated with the use of contrast media, including ioversol, for cerebral arteriography are not infrequent: ioversol can be expected to have the same effect on the electrophysiology of the brain, but this has not been systematically assessed.

Usual Adult Dosage: Either Optiray 240, Optiray 300 or Optiray 320 may be used for cerebral angiography. The usual adult dosage of ioversol employed varies with the site and method of injection and the age and condition of the patient. The usual adult dose range for common carotid arteriography is 5 to

Optiray (cont'd)

10 mL; for vertebral arteriography 4 to 8 mL. For aortic arch injection (4 vessel studies) the usual dose for Optiray 320 is 15 to 25 mL, and for Optiray 240 is 15 to 40 mL. Injections should be made at rates approximately equal to the flow rate of the vessel being injected.

These doses may be repeated if indicated. The total dose per procedure should be limited to the smallest volume necessary to achieve a diagnostic examination and should not exceed 200 mL.

Intra-arterial Digital Subtraction Arteriography: Optiray 160 and Optiray 300 are suitable agents for intra-arterial digital subtraction angiography (IA-DSA). With this technique lower iodine concentrations can yield diagnostic images. Other advantages of the procedure are the use of less contrast medium and a decreased need for selective arterial catheterization. However, with aortic injection, visualization of small vessels may be insufficient.

Patient Preparation: No special patient preparation is required for IA-DSA. However, patients should be normally hydrated prior to examination.

Precautions: In addition to the general precautions already described, the risks and adverse reactions associated with IA-DSA are those usually associated with the conventional procedure performed in the area of the specific vessel.

In IA-DSA of the distal aorta great care is necessary to avoid entry of a large aortic bolus into an aortic branch since this could cause deleterious effects on the organs supplied by the branch. Patient motion, including respiration and swallowing, can result in misregistration leading to image degradation and nondiagnostic studies.

Adverse Effects: Adverse reactions seen with IA-DSA are similar to those observed during peripheral arteriography. They may sometimes occur due to trauma during the procedure.

Adverse reactions reported with the use of iodinated contrast media include hypotension, soreness in extremities, transient arterial spasm, gangrene, perforation of vessels, extravasation, hemorrhage, hematoma formation with tamponade, injury to nerves and other structures in close proximity to the artery, thrombosis, dissecting aneurysm, arteriovenous fistula, dislodgment of atheromatous plaques, subintimal injection and transient leg pain from contraction of calf muscles in femoral arteriography.

Usual Adult Dosage Using Optiray 160: As a general rule, the volume and concentration used for IA-DSA are about 50%, or less, of that used for conventional procedures. The actual dosage and flow rate will vary depending on the selectivity of the injection site and the area being examined. The following suggested volumes per injection are intended as a guide (see Table II). Injections may be repeated if necessary. It is advisable to inject at rates approximately equal to the flow rate of the vessel being injected.

Table II—Optiray 160

Usual Adult Dosage	
Carotid Arteries	5–10 mL
Vertebral Arteries	4–8 mL
Aortic Arch	25–50 mL
Distal Aorta	25–50 mL
Iliac Arteries	6–15 mL

Dosage should not usually exceed 250 mL.

Usual Dose in Children Using Optiray 300: The usual dose is 1 to 3 mL/kg, depending on the area to be examined.

Peripheral Arteriography: Optiray 300, Optiray 320 or Optiray 350 may be used for arteriograms of the lower extremities.

Patient Preparation: The procedure is normally performed with local anesthesia. General anesthesia usually is not required (see Precautions, General).

Precautions: In addition to the general precautions previously described, moderate decreases in blood pressure occur frequently with intra-arterial injections. This change is usually transient; however, the blood pressure should be monitored for approximately 10 minutes following injection.

Injection of ioversol in patients with severe arterial disease (e.g., thromboangiitis obliterans, severe atherosclerosis, ischemia, thrombosis, significant obstruction) should be undertaken with extreme caution and only when absolutely necessary.

When injections are being made in the distal aorta for aorto-iliac run-off studies, the possibility of inadvertent injection of a large dose into a branch of the aorta or intramural dissection should be considered.

To prevent extravasation or subintimal injection, the position of the catheter tip or needle should be carefully evaluated. Fluoroscopy is recommended. **Pulsation must be present in the artery to be injected.** A small dose of 1 to 2 mL should be administered to locate the exact site of the needle or catheter tip. Great care is necessary to avoid entry of a large bolus into an aortic branch.

Severe pain, paresthesia or peripheral muscle spasm during injection may require discontinuance of the procedure and a re-evaluation of the catheter tip or needle placement.

Following catheter procedures, gentle pressure hemostasis is advised, followed by observation and immobilization of the limb for several hours to prevent hemorrhage from the site of arterial puncture.

Adverse Effects: Adverse reactions observed during peripheral arteriography may be due to trauma during the procedure or to the injection of the contrast material. Adverse reactions reported with the use of iodinated contrast media include hypotension, soreness in extremities, transient arterial spasm, contrast medium induced thrombosis, embolism, gangrene, perforation of vessels, extravasation, hemorrhage, hematoma formation with tamponade, injury to spinal cord and nerves and other structures in close proximity to the artery; transverse myelitis, thrombosis, dissecting aneurysm, arteriovenous fistula, dislodgment of atheromatous plaques, subintimal injection, leg pain, renal damage including infarction and tubular necrosis due to accidental filling of the renal arteries.

Usual Adult Dosage: The usual single adult dose for aorto-iliac run-off studies is 20 to 50 mL; for iliac and femoral arteries 10 to 30 mL. These doses may be repeated as indicated. The total procedural dose should be limited to the smallest volume required to obtain a diagnostic examination and should not usually exceed 250 mL.

Selective Coronary Arteriography with or without Left Ventriculography: Either Optiray 320 or Optiray 350 is recommended for this procedure.

Precautions: Since the risk in coronary arteriography is increased if the procedure is performed shortly after acute myocardial infarction, some physicians recommend that this procedure should not be performed for approximately 4 weeks following the diagnosis of myocardial infarction. Mandatory prerequisites to the procedure are experienced personnel, ECG monitoring apparatus and adequate facilities for immediate resuscitation and cardioversion.

Patients should be monitored continuously by ECG and vital signs throughout the procedure. The injection of relatively large volumes of hypertonic solutions (e.g., contrast media) into the heart chambers can cause significant hemodynamic disturbances. Caution is advised especially in patients with incipient heart failure because of the possibility of aggravating the pre-existing condition. Hypotension should be corrected promptly since it may induce serious arrhythmias.

Adverse Effects: Most patients will have transient ECG changes during the procedure. The following adverse effects have occurred in conjunction with the administration of iodinated intravascular contrast agents for this purpose: hypotension, shock, anginal pain, coronary thrombosis, myocardial infarction, cardiac arrhythmias (bradycardia, ventricular tachycardia, heart block, ventricular fibrillation), cardiac arrest and death. Severe adverse reactions, especially arrhythmias, are likely to occur with greater frequency following right coronary artery injection. Fatalities have been reported. Complications to the procedures include dissection of coronary arteries, dislodgment of atheromatous plaques, embolization from the catheter, perforation of heart chambers or coronary arteries with cardiac tamponade, hemorrhage and thrombosis.

Usual Adult Dosage: The usual adult dose range with Optiray 320 or Optiray 350 for left coronary arteriography is 2 to 10 mL and for right coronary arteriography is 2 to 6 mL. For left ventriculography, the usual single adult dose is 30 to 40 mL. These doses may be repeated if indicated; however, several minutes should be allowed to elapse between injections to allow for subsidence of hemodynamic disturbance, and the total procedural dose should be limited to the smallest volume necessary to obtain a diagnostic examination. The total procedural dose should not exceed 250 mL.

Children: Optiray 320 or 350 is recommended for this procedure. The usual single dose of Optiray 320 is 1.25 mL/kg body weight with a range of 1 to 1.5 mL/kg. When multiple injections are given, the total administered dose should not exceed 5 mL/kg up to a total of 250 mL.

Aortography and Visceral Arteriography: Optiray 300, 320 or 350 is recommended for this procedure. Great care is necessary to avoid all entry of a large bolus into an aortic branch. Mesenteric necrosis, acute pancreatitis, renal infarction, acute tubular necrosis, renal shutdown and serious neurologic complications, including paraplegia and quadriplegia, have been reported and may be attributable to an excessive dose being injected into an aortic branch or arterial trunks supplying the spinal arteries or to prolonged contact time of the concentrated contrast medium on the CNS tissue. Conditions which can contribute to prolonged contact time include decreased circulation, aortic stenosis or partial occlusions distal to the site of injection, abdominal compression, hypotension, general anesthesia or the administration of vasopressors. When these conditions exist or occur, the necessity of performing or continuing the procedure should be carefully evaluated and the dose and number of repeat injections should be maintained at a minimum with appropriate intervals between injections.

Adverse Effects: With aortic injection, depending on the technique employed, the risks of this procedure also include the following: injury to the aorta and neighboring organs, pleural puncture, renal damage including infarction and acute tubular necrosis with oliguria and anuria due to accidental filling of the renal arteries, retroperitoneal hemorrhage from the translumbar approach and spinal cord injury and pathology associated with the syndrome of transverse myelitis. Occasional serious neurological complications including paraplegia have been reported in patients with aorto-iliac or femoral artery obstruction, abdominal compression, hypotension, hypertension, spinal anesthesia and injection of vasopressor drugs to enhance contrast. In such patients, the concentration, volume and number of injections should be kept to a minimum.

Adult Dosage: Optiray 300, Optiray 320 or Optiray 350 is recommended for this procedure. The usual individual injection volumes are as follows: abdominal aorta 20 to 50 mL, superior mesenteric artery 20 to 40 mL and renal artery 4 to 10 mL.

Total procedural dose should not exceed 250 mL.

I.V. Contrast Enhancement in Computed Tomography (CT): Because unenhanced scanning may provide adequate information in the individual patient and the injection of contrast media may obscure certain lesions visible on the plain scan, contrast enhancement is usually performed only if the unenhanced scan has not provided sufficient information. The decision to employ contrast enhancement, which is associated with additional risk and increased radiation exposure, should be based upon a careful evaluation of the patient's clinical condition, renal and cardiac reserve, the status of the blood-brain barrier and other radiological and unenhanced CT findings.

Warnings: Patients with diabetes mellitus, impaired renal function and congestive heart failure are considered to be at greater risk of developing acute renal failure following injection of large doses of contrast media required for contrast enhancement in CT scanning.

Convulsions and other serious neurologic complications including stroke have occurred in patients with primary or metastatic cerebral lesions or breached blood-brain barrier or slowed cerebral circulation following the administration of iodine-containing radiopaque media for enhancement of CT brain images.

Patient Preparation: No special patient preparation is required for contrast enhancement in computerized tomography. **However, it has to be insured that patients are well hydrated prior to examination.** In patients undergoing abdominal or pelvic examination, opacification of the bowel by dilute oral contrast medium may be valuable in scan interpretation.

Precautions: Patient motion, including respiration, can markedly affect image quality, therefore patient cooperation is essential.

The use of an intravascular contrast medium can obscure some tumors in patients undergoing CT evaluation, resulting in a false negative diagnosis.

Computed Tomography of the Head: Neoplastic Conditions: Optiray 240, Optiray 300, Optiray 320 or Optiray 350 may be used to enhance the demonstration of the presence and extent of certain primary or metastatic malignancies.

The usefulness of contrast enhancement for the investigation of the retrobulbar space and in cases of low grade or infiltrative glioma has not been demonstrated.

In cases where lesions have calcified, there is less likelihood of enhancement. Following therapy, tumors may show decreased or no enhancement. Maximum contrast enhancement of certain tumors may be delayed necessitating delayed scans.

Non-neoplastic Conditions: The use of Optiray 240, Optiray 300, Optiray 320 or Optiray 350 may be beneficial in the image enhancement of non-neoplastic lesions, such as cerebral infarctions of recent onset; however, some infarctions are obscured if contrast media are used.

Arteriovenous malformations and aneurysms will show contrast enhancement. In the case of these vascular lesions, the enhancement is probably dependent on the iodine content of the circulating blood pool.

Hematomas and intraparenchymal bleeders seldom demonstrate any contrast enhancement. However, in cases of intraparenchymal clot, for which there is no obvious clinical explanation, contrast medium administration may be helpful in ruling out the possibility of associated arteriovenous malformation (see Precautions).

The opacification of the inferior vermis following contrast medium administration has resulted in false positive diagnoses in a number of normal studies.

Usual Adult Dosage: For adults the usual dosage of Optiray 300, 320 or 350 is 50 to 100 mL; of Optiray 240, 100 to 250 mL. A maximum dose of 150 mL of Optiray 320 or 350 should not be exceeded. For Optiray 240 the maximum dose is 250 mL. Scanning is usually performed immediately after injection.

Children: The dose recommended for use in children 1 year of age and over is 1 to 3 mL/kg of Optiray 320.

Body Computed Tomography: Optiray 240, 300, 320 or 350 may be administered for contrast enhancement of the organs, tissues and larger blood vessels of the chest, abdomen and pelvis.

Continuous or multiple scans separated by intervals of 1 to 3 seconds during the first 30 to 90 seconds postinjection of the contrast medium (dynamic CT scanning) are required to demonstrate enhanceable lesions not seen with CT alone. Subsets of patients in whom delayed body CT scans might be helpful have not been identified.

Inconsistent results have been reported and abnormal and normal tissues are usually isodense during the time frame used for delayed CT scanning. At present, consistent results have been documented using dynamic CT techniques only.

Usual Adult Dosage: Optiray 240, 300, 320 or 350 may be administered by bolus injection, rapid infusion or by a combination of both. Depending on the area to be examined, the usual dose range is 30 to 100 mL. When prolonged enhancement is required, 25 to 50 mL may be given as a rapid bolus and the remainder as an infusion. The total dose should not exceed 150 mL of Optiray 300, 320 or 350 or 200 mL of Optiray 240. Scanning is usually performed immediately after injection.

Children: The dose recommended for use in children 1 year of age and over is 1 to 3 mL/kg of Optiray 320.

Venography: Optiray 240, 300 or 350 may be used to visualize the peripheral venous circulation. Venograms are obtained by injection or infusion into an appropriate vein in the lower extremity.

Precautions: In addition to the general precautions previously described, specific caution is advised when venography is required in patients with suspected thrombosis, phlebitis, severe ischemic disease, local infection or a significantly obstructed venous system.

Extreme caution is necessary to avoid extravasation and fluoroscopy is recommended. This is especially important in patients with severe venous disease.

Adverse Effects: Complications of the procedure include bleeding, thrombosis, embolism, contrast medium-induced thrombophlebitis, gangrene and major systemic adverse reactions.

Usual Adult Dosage: The usual adult dose of Optiray 240, 300 or 350 will range from 20 to 100 mL for the lower extremity.

Following the procedure, the venous system should be flushed with normal or heparinized saline solution. Massage and elevation of the leg are also helpful for clearing the contrast medium from the extremity to prevent post-procedural thrombophlebitis. The maximum dose should not usually exceed 250 mL.

Excretory Urography: Optiray 240, 300, 320 or 350 may be used for excretory urography. Following i.v. injection in patients with normal renal function, Optiray is excreted mostly by the kidneys. Maximum radiographic density in the calyces and pelves occurs in most instances within 5 to 15 minutes after injection.

In patients with severe renal impairment, contrast visualization may be substantially delayed, or may not occur at all.

Patient Preparation: A low residue diet the day preceding the examination, and a laxative the evening before the examination, may be given unless contraindicated. **Partial dehydration is dangerous and may contribute to acute renal failure.** Maintenance of normal hydration is desirable.

Precautions: Adequate renal function must be present. Dehydration will not improve contrast quality in patients with impaired renal function and will increase the risk of contrast induced renal damage. The examination should not be repeated for at least 72 hours because of the potential of additive renal damage (see Warnings and Precautions).

Adverse Effects: All adverse reactions known to occur with the i.v. use of ioversol can also occur with excretory urography (see Adverse Effects).

Usual Adult Dosage: The usual adult dose of Optiray 300, 320 or 350 is 50 mL in the average normal adult. With Optiray 240 the equivalent dose range is 65 mL in the average normal adult. The dose is injected i.v., usually within 1 to 3 minutes. Maximum doses of 200 mL of Optiray 240, 150 mL of Optiray 300 or 320 and 140 mL of Optiray 350 should not be exceeded.

Children: Optiray 300 and 320 at doses of 0.5 to 3 mL/kg body weight have produced diagnostic opacification of the urinary tract. The usual dose for children is 1 mL/kg.

The total dosage in children should not normally exceed 3 mL/kg.

Subarachnoid: Precautions: Optiray 240 is recommended for the examination of lumbar, thoracic and cervical regions in adults by lumbar injection. Myelography should not be performed in the presence of significant local or systemic infection where bacteremia is likely or when lumbar or cervical puncture is contraindicated.

The volume and concentration of Optiray 240 to be administered will depend on the degree and extent of contrast required within the recommended dose range in the area under examination, and on the equipment and technique employed. Optiray 240 is slightly hypertonic to CSF.

A total dose of 3 600 mg (15 mL) iodine should not be exceeded in adults. As in all diagnostic procedures, the minimum volume and dose to produce adequate visualization should be used. Most procedures do not require the total maximum dose.

Anesthesia is not necessary. Patients should be well hydrated. Seizure-prone patients should be maintained on anticonvulsant medication.

Adverse Reactions: Any adverse reactions known to occur with the i.v. use of ioversol can also occur during myelography, especially those which originate in the CNS. The most commonly observed adverse reaction was headache, which had an incidence of 8.6%.

Rate of injection: To avoid excessive mixing with CSF and consequent dilution of contrast, injection should be made slowly, over 1 to 2 minutes.

Depending on the estimated volume of ioversol which may be required for the procedure, a small amount of CSF may be removed to minimize distension of the subarachnoid spaces, unless contraindicated.

The spinal puncture needle may be removed immediately following injection because it is not usually necessary to remove ioversol after injection into the subarachnoid space.

If, in the clinical judgment of the physician, a repeat examination is required, an interval of 5 days between procedures is recommended.

Adults: Usual Dose: The usual recommended total dose of Optiray 240 for use in lumbar myelography is 10 mL and for thoracic and cervical myelography 15 mL. The following table (see Table III) indicates these dosages.

Table III—Optiray 240

Dosages

Procedure	Optiray Concentration	Concentration (mgI/mL)	Volume (mL)
Lumbar myelography	Optiray 240	240	10
Thoracic myelography	Optiray 240	240	15
Cervical myelography	Optiray 240	240	15

If computerized tomography is to follow, it should be deferred for 2 to 6 hours to allow the amount of contrast to decrease. Computerized tomography shows CSF contrast enhancement in the thoracic region in about one hour.

Patient Management—Subarachnoid Administration: Good patient management should be exercised at all times to minimize the potential for complications.

Pre-procedure: Discontinue neuroleptic drugs (including phenothiazines, e.g., chlorpromazine, prochlorperazine and promethazine) at least 48 hours beforehand. Maintain normal diet up to 2 hours before procedure. Premedication is not usually considered necessary. Should myelography be necessary in patients with a history of seizures, such patients should be maintained on their anticonvulsant medication.

During Procedure: Use minimum dose required for satisfactory contrast (see Dosage). In all positioning techniques keep the patient's head elevated above highest level of spine. Do not lower head of table more than 15° during examination. In patients with excessive lordosis consider lateral position for injection. Inject slowly (over 1 to 2 minutes) to avoid excessive mixing. Move medium within the spinal subarachnoid space under fluoroscopic monitoring. Avoid intracranial entry of a bolus. Avoid early and high cephalad dispersion of the medium. Avoid abrupt or active patient movement to minimize excessive mixing with CSF. Instruct patient to remain **passive**. Move patient **slowly** and only as necessary.

Post-procedure: Following myelography move contrast medium to low lumbosacral area by upright positioning of the patient, for a few minutes. Raise head of stretcher to at least 30° before moving patient onto it. Movement onto and off the stretcher should be done slowly with patient completely passive, maintaining **head-up** position.

Before moving patient onto bed, raise head of bed 30 to 45°. Some clinicians advise patients to remain still in bed, in head up position or in the semi-sitting position, especially in the first few hours. Others have encouraged their patients to be fully ambulatory and have noted a reduction in the incidence of headache, nausea and vomiting. Maintain close observation and head-up position for at least 24 hours after myelogram. Obtain visitors' cooperation in keeping the patient quiet and in **head-up** position, especially in first few hours. Encourage oral fluids. Diet as tolerated. **If nausea or vomiting** occur do not use phenothiazine antinauseants. Persistent nausea and vomiting will result in dehydration. Therefore prompt consideration of replacement by i.v. fluids is recommended.

Supplied: Optiray 160: Each mL of clear, colorless to pale yellow, sterile, nonpyrogenic aqueous solution (ioversol injection 34%) contains: ioversol 339 mg with tromethamine 3.6 mg as a buffer and edetate calcium disodium 0.2 mg as a stabilizer. Optiray 160 provides 16% (160 mg/mL) of organically bound iodine. Osmolality (mOsm/kg water): 355. Viscosity (cps): 2.7 (25°C) and 1.9 (37°C). Vials of 50 mL, boxes of 10 and 25. Bottles of 100 mL fill/150 mL, boxes of 6 and 12.

Optiray 240: Each mL of clear, colorless to pale yellow, sterile, nonpyrogenic aqueous solution (ioversol injection 51%) contains: ioversol 509 mg with tromethamine 3.6 mg as a buffer and edetate calcium disodium 0.2 mg as a stabilizer. Optiray 240 provides 24% (240 mg/mL) organically bound iodine. Osmolality (mOsm/kg water): 502. Viscosity (cps): 4.0 (25°C) and 3.0 (37°C). Vials of 15 mL fill/20 mL, boxes of 10, vials of 50 mL, boxes of 10 and 25. Bottles of 100 mL fill/150 mL, boxes of 6 and 12. Bottles of 200 mL fill/250 mL, boxes of 6 and 12.

Optiray 300: Each mL of clear, colorless to pale yellow, sterile nonpyrogenic aqueous solution (ioversol injection 64%) contains: ioversol 636 mg with tromethamine 3.6 mg as a buffer and edetate calcium disodium 0.2 mg as a stabilizer. Optiray 300 provides 30% (300 mg/mL) organically bound iodine. Osmolality (mOsm/kg water): 651. Viscosity (cps): 8.2 (25°C) and 5.5 (37°C). Vials of 30 mL, boxes of 25. Vials of 50 mL, boxes of 25. Bottles of 100 mL fill/150 mL, boxes of 12. Bottles of 150 mL, boxes of 12. Ultraject prefilled syringes 30 and 50 mL, hand-held 50 mL fill/125 mL power injector, 100 mL fill/125 mL power injector; 125 mL power injector, boxes of 20.

Optiray 320: Each mL of clear, colorless to pale yellow, sterile, nonpyrogenic aqueous solution (ioversol injection 68%) contains: ioversol 678 mg with tromethamine 3.6 mg as a buffer and edetate calcium disodium 0.2 mg as a stabilizer. Optiray 320 provides 32% (320 mg/mL) organically bound iodine. Osmolality (mOsm/kg water): 702. Viscosity (cps): 9.9 (25°C) and 5.8 (37°C). Vials of 20 mL, boxes of 10 and 25. Vials of 30 mL, boxes of 10 and 25. Vials of 50 mL, boxes of 10 and 25. Bottles of 100 mL fill/150 mL, boxes of 6 and 12. Bottles of 150 mL, boxes of 6 and 12. Bottles of 200 mL fill/250 mL, boxes of 6 and 12. Ultraject prefilled syringes 30 mL and 50 mL hand-held, 50 mL fill/125 mL power injector, 75 mL fill/125 mL power injector; 100/125 mL power injector; 125 mL power injector, boxes of 20. Pharmacy Bulk Vial: Multi-dispensing bottles of 500 mL, boxes of 12.

Optiray 350: Each mL of clear, colorless to pale yellow, sterile nonpyrogenic aqueous solution (ioversol injection 74%) contains: ioversol 741 mg with tromethamine 3.6 mg as a buffer and edetate calcium disodium 0.2 mg as a stabilizer. Optiray 350 provides 35% (350 mg/mL) organically bound iodine. Osmolality (mOsm/kg water): 792. Viscosity (cps): 14.3 (25°C) and 9.0 (37°C). Vials of 30 mL, boxes of 25. Vials of 50 mL, boxes of 25. Bottles of 75 mL fill/150 mL, boxes of 12. Bottles of 100 mL fill/150 mL, boxes of 12. Bottles of 150 mL, boxes of 12. Bottles of 200 mL fill 250/mL, boxes of 12. Ultraject prefilled syringes 30 and 50 mL hand-held; 50 mL fill/125 mL power injector, 75 mL fill/125 mL power injector; 100 mL fill/125 mL power injector; 125 mL power injector, boxes of 20.

The pH of the formulations is adjusted between 6.0 and 7.4 with hydrochloric acid or sodium hydroxide. The products do not contain a preservative and are intended for single dose use only. Store between 15 and 30°C. Protect from light. Protect from freezing. Discard unused portion.

Reviewed 1999

ORABASE®
Squibb
Protective—Emollient

Indications: For temporary relief of traumatic lesions of the mouth, including sore spots from new dentures, aphthous ulcers (canker sores), toothbrush injuries, gingivitis.

Contraindications: Not intended for use in the presence of infection.

Dosage: Cover the affected area with a thin film of Orabase. Administration after meals is preferred, and at bedtime to protect against irritation throughout the night.

Supplied: Each 7.5 g tube contains: gelatin, pectin, and sodium carboxymethylcellulose in Plastibase, a mineral oil polyethylene base. Odorless and tasteless, nonirritating and harmless if swallowed.

ORACORT ℞
Taro
Triamcinolone Acetonide
Dental Corticosteroid

Supplied: Each g of dental paste contains: triamcinolone acetonide 1 mg (0.1%) in a protective emollient vehicle containing gelatin, pectin and sodium carboxymethylcellulose in a polyethylene and mineral oil gel base. Tubes of 7.5 g. Keep tightly closed.

ORAFEN® ℞
Technilab
Ketoprofen
Nonsteroidal Anti-inflammatory—Analgesic

Pharmacology: Pharmacological studies in animals have demonstrated that ketoprofen is an NSAID that possesses anti-inflammatory, analgesic and antipyretic properties. The anti-inflammatory action is not mediated through the pituitary adrenal axis.

Ketoprofen, like other nonsteroidal anti-inflammatory analgesics is an inhibitor of prostaglandin synthesis. In vivo studies have demonstrated that ketoprofen is 8 times as potent as indomethacin in inhibiting the synthesis of prostaglandin from arachidonic acid.

Ketoprofen's therapeutic effectiveness has been demonstrated by a reduction in joint swelling, pain and duration of morning stiffness, and by increased grip strength and an improvement in functional capacity.

Clinical trials in rheumatoid arthritis have shown that the antiarthritic activity of ketoprofen 200 mg/day was similar to that of ASA 3.6 g/day and induced less gastrointestinal bleeding.

The effectiveness of ketoprofen as a general purpose analgesic has been studied in standard pain models which have shown the effectiveness of doses of 25 to 150 mg were effective in standard pain models. Doses of 25 mg were superior to placebo. Doses larger than 25 mg generally could not be shown to be significantly more effective, but there was a tendency towards a faster onset and greater duration of action with a 50 mg dose and, in the case of dysmenorrhea, a significantly greater overall effect with 75 mg. Doses greater than 50 to 75 mg did not have an increased analgesic effect.

Pharmacokinetics: In man, ketoprofen is rapidly and almost completely absorbed from the gastrointestinal tract. Maximum plasma levels are reached within 0.5 to 2 hours after administration of capsules or suppositories; however, peak plasma levels are delayed by a further 1 to 2 hours with enteric-coated tablets and by 5 to 6 hours with sustained-release tablets. Pharmacokinetic studies in both young and elderly adults indicated that the T_{max} of ketoprofen is similar for both groups. The $t_{1/2}$ and AUC, however, were significantly increased in the elderly subjects.

When ketoprofen capsules are administered with food, the total bioavailability (AUC) is not altered; however, the rate of absorption is slowed resulting in delayed and reduced peak concentrations (C_{max}). Following a single 50 mg dose of ketoprofen while fasting, the mean C_{max} was 4.1 mg/L (at 1.1 hours); when administered after food, it decreased to 2.4 mg/L (at 2.0 hours).

The composition of the diet slightly but significantly alters the extent of absorption of ketoprofen from sustained-release tablets; a high-fat/high-calorie meal (3 000 calories/day) was associated with lower ketoprofen bioavailability values (about 20%) than a low-fat/low-calorie content (1 200 calories/day). Mean trough ketoprofen plasma concentrations were similar after high or low fat meals.

Following administration of slow-release ketoprofen, absorption is gradual reaching a plateau during which plasma levels remain steady from the 5th to the 12th hour after ingestion and decrease with an apparent half-life of 3 to 4 days. No accumulation of ketoprofen was found following repeated once-daily administration of ketoprofen sustained-release tablets. Repeated administration of the drug, in both animals and man, caused no induction of liver enzymes.

To date, studies of the effects of age and renal-function impairment have been small, generally involving 5 to 8 subjects per group, but they indicate modest decreases in clearance in the elderly and in patients with impaired renal function. In normal elderly volunteers (mean age 73 years), the plasma and renal clearance and protein-binding were reduced while the V_d increased when compared to a younger normal population (mean age 27 years). (Plasma clearance and V_d were 0.05 L/kg/h and 0.4 L/kg in elderly and 0.06 L/kg/h and 0.3 L/kg in young subjects, respectively). The mean half-life of ketoprofen in this normal geriatric population, as well as in a rheumatoid elderly population (mean age 64 years), was about 5 hours as compared to 3 hours in the younger population.

Patients with impaired renal function (mean age 44 years) also demonstrate decreases in plasma clearance (0.04 L/kg/h) of drug, with the mean half-life increasing to about 3.5 hours.

Ketoprofen is rapidly and extensively metabolized in the liver, principally by hydroxylation and conjugation, the latter being the main metabolic pathway in man.

Metabolites as well as the unchanged drug are excreted mainly in the urine; fecal excretion is negligible. Following the administration of capsules or enteric coated tablet in man, 25 to 90% of the drug is excreted in the urine within 24 hours, with the major portion being excreted during the first 6 hours. The elimination half-life is approximately 2 hours and the apparent plasma clearance averages approximately 1 to 1.3 mL/min/kg. Repeated administration of the drug, in both animals and man, caused no induction of liver enzymes.

Indications: In the treatment of rheumatoid arthritis, ankylosing spondylitis and osteoarthritis.

Ketoprofen is also indicated in the treatment of primary dysmenorrhea and the relief of mild to moderate acute pain associated with musculotendinous trauma (sprains and strains), postoperative (including dental surgery) or postpartum pain.

Contraindications: Active peptic ulcer, a history of recurrent ulceration or active inflammatory disease of the gastrointestinal system.

Known or suspected hypersensitivity to the drug or other NSAIDs. The potential for cross-reactivity between different NSAIDs must be kept in mind.

Ketoprofen should not be used in patients with the complete or partial syndrome of nasal polyps, or in whom asthma, anaphylaxis, urticaria, rhinitis or other allergic manifestations are precipitated by ASA or other NSAIDs. Fatal anaphylactoid reactions have occurred in such individuals. As well, individuals with the above medical problems are at risk of a severe reaction even if they have taken NSAIDs in the past without any adverse effects.

Significant hepatic impairment or active liver disease.

Severely impaired or deteriorating renal function (creatinine clearance <30 mL/min). Individuals with lesser degrees of renal impairment are at risk of deterioration of their renal function when prescribed NSAIDs and must be monitored.

Ketoprofen is not recommended for use with other NSAIDs because of the absence of any evidence demonstrating synergistic benefits and the potential for additive side effects.

Ketoprofen suppositories should not be used in patients with any inflammatory lesions of the rectum or anus and in patients with a recent history of rectal or anal bleeding.

Warnings: Gastrointestinal System: Serious gastrointestinal toxicity, such as peptic ulceration, perforation and gastrointestinal bleeding, **sometimes severe and occasionally fatal** can occur at any time, with or without symptoms in patients treated with NSAIDs including ketoprofen.

Minor upper gastrointestinal problems, such as dyspepsia, are common, usually developing early in therapy. Physicians should remain alert for ulceration and bleeding in patients treated with NSAIDs, even in the absence of previous gastrointestinal tract symptoms.

In patients observed in clinical trials of such agents, symptomatic upper gastrointestinal ulcers, gross bleeding, or perforation appear to occur in approximately 1% of patients treated for 3 to 6 months and in about 2 to 4% of patients treated for 1 year. The risk continues beyond 1 year and possibly increases.

The incidence of these complications increases with increasing dose.

Ketoprofen should be given under close medical supervision to patients prone to gastrointestinal tract irritation, particularly those with a history of peptic ulcer, diverticulosis or other inflammatory disease of the gastrointestinal tract such as ulcerative colitis and Crohn's disease. In these cases, the physician must weigh the benefits of treatment against the possible hazards.

Physicians should inform patients about the signs and/or symptoms of serious gastrointestinal toxicity and instruct them to contact a physician immediately if they experience persistent dyspepsia or other symptoms or signs suggestive of gastrointestinal ulceration or bleeding.

Because serious gastrointestinal tract ulceration and bleeding can occur without warning symptoms, physicians should follow chronically treated patients by checking their hemoglobin periodically and by being vigilant for the signs and symptoms of ulceration and bleeding and should inform the patients of the importance of this followup.

If ulceration is suspected or confirmed, or if gastrointestinal bleeding occurs, ketoprofen should be discontinued immediately, appropriate treatment instituted and the patient monitored closely.

No studies, to date, have identified any group of patients **not** at risk of developing ulceration and bleeding. A prior history of serious gastrointestinal events and other factors such as excess alcohol intake, smoking, age, female gender and concomitant oral steroid and anticoagulant use have been associated with increased risk.

Studies to date show that all NSAIDs can cause gastrointestinal tract adverse events. Although existing data does not clearly identify differences in risk between various NSAIDs, this may be shown in the future.

Geriatrics: Patients older than 65 years and frail or debilitated patients are most susceptible to a variety of adverse reactions from NSAIDs: the incidence of these adverse reactions increases with dose and duration of treatment. In addition, these patients are less tolerant to ulceration and bleeding. Most reports of fatal gastrointestinal events are in this population. Older patients are also at risk of lower esophageal ulceration and bleeding.

For such patients, consideration should be given to a starting dose lower than the one usually recommended, with individual adjustment when necessary and under close supervision (see Precautions).

Cross-sensitivity: Patients sensitive to any one of the NSAIDs may also be sensitive to any of the other NSAIDs.

Aseptic Meningitis: In occasional cases, with some NSAIDs, the symptoms of aseptic meningitis (stiff neck, severe headaches, nausea and vomiting, fever or clouding of consciousness) have been observed. Patients with autoimmune disorders (systemic lupus erythematosus, mixed connective tissues diseases, etc.) seem to be predisposed. Therefore, in such patients, the physician must be vigilant to the development of this complication.

Pregnancy, Labor and *Lactation:* The safety of ketoprofen when administered to pregnant or nursing women has not been determined, and therefore such use is not recommended. Pregnant rats who received ketoprofen 6 and 9 mg/kg/day orally from day 15 of gestation, showed dystocia and increased pup mortality.

In rats, ketoprofen did not affect perinatal development at doses of 9 mg/kg (representing approximately 1.5 times the maximum human therapeutic dose). In lactating dogs, ketoprofen concentration in milk was found to be 4 to 5% of the plasma drug level. Data on secretion in human milk after ingestion of ketoprofen do not exist. As with other drugs that are excreted in milk, ketoprofen is not recommended for use in nursing mothers.

Children: The conditions for safe and effective use of ketoprofen in children under 12 years of age have not been established, and the drug is therefore not recommended in this age group.

Precautions: Gastrointestinal System: There is no definitive evidence that the concomitant administration of histamine H_2-receptor antagonists and/or antacids will either prevent the occurrence of gastrointestinal side effects or allow the continuation of ketoprofen therapy when and if these adverse reactions appear.

Suppositories should be given with caution to patients with any rectal or anal pathology.

Renal Function: Long-term administration of NSAIDs to animals has resulted in renal papillary necrosis and other abnormal renal pathology. In humans, there have been reports of acute interstitial nephritis with hematuria, proteinuria, and occasionally nephrotic syndrome.

A second form of renal toxicity has been seen in patients with prerenal conditions leading to the reduction in renal blood flow or blood volume, where the renal prostaglandins have a supportive role in the maintenance of renal perfusion. In these patients, administration of a NSAID may cause a dose-dependent reduction in prostaglandin formation and may precipitate overt renal decompensation. Patients at greatest risk of this reaction are those with impaired renal function, heart failure, liver dysfunction, those taking diuretics, and the elderly. Discontinuation of nonsteroidal anti-inflammatory therapy is usually followed by recovery to the pretreatment state.

Ketoprofen and its metabolites are eliminated primarily by the kidneys; therefore the drug should be used with great caution in patients with impaired renal function. In these cases, utilization of lower doses of ketoprofen should be considered and patients carefully monitored

During long-term therapy kidney function should be monitored periodically.

Genitourinary Tract: Some NSAIDs are known to cause persistent urinary symptoms (bladder pain, dysuria, urinary frequency), hematuria or cystitis. The onset of these symptoms may occur at any time after the initiation of therapy with an NSAID. Some cases have become severe on continued treatment. Should urinary symptoms occur, treatment with ketoprofen **must be stopped immediately** to obtain recovery. This should be done before any urological investigations or treatments are carried out.

Hepatic function: As with other NSAIDs, borderline elevations of one or more liver function tests may occur in up to 15% of patients. These abnormalities may progress, may remain essentially unchanged, or may be transient with continued therapy. Meaningful (3 times the upper limit of normal) elevations of ALT or AST occurred in controlled clinical trials in less than 1% of patients. A patient with symptoms and/or signs suggesting liver dysfunction, or in whom an abnormal liver test has occurred, should be evaluated for evidence of the development of more severe hepatic reaction while on therapy with this drug. Severe hepatic reactions including jaundice and cases of fatal hepatitis have been reported with NSAIDs.

Although such reactions are rare, if abnormal liver tests persist or worsen, if clinical signs and symptoms consistent with liver disease develop, or if systemic manifestations occur (e.g., eosinophilia, rash, etc.), this drug should be discontinued.

During long-term therapy, liver function tests should be monitored periodically. If there is a need to prescribe this drug in the presence of impaired liver function, it must be done under strict observation.

Fluid and Electrolyte Balance: Fluid retention and edema have been observed in patients treated with ketoprofen. Therefore, as with many other NSAIDs, the possibility of precipitating congestive heart failure in elderly patients or those with compromised cardiac function should be borne in mind. Ketoprofen should be used with caution in patients with heart failure, hypertension or other conditions predisposing to fluid retention.

With nonsteroidal anti-inflammatory treatment there is a potential risk of hyperkalemia, particularly in patients with conditions such as diabetes mellitus or renal failure; elderly patients; or in patients receiving concomitant therapy with β-adrenergic blockers, angiotensin converting enzyme inhibitors or some diuretics. Serum electrolytes should be monitored periodically during long-term therapy, especially in those patients who are at risk.

Hematology: Drugs inhibiting prostaglandin biosynthesis do interfere with platelet function to varying degrees; therefore, patients who may be adversely affected by such an action should be carefully observed when ketoprofen is administered.

Blood dyscrasias (such as neutropenia, leukopenia, thrombocytopenia, aplastic anemia and agranulocytosis) associated with the use of NSAIDs are rare, but could occur with severe consequences.

Anemia is commonly observed in rheumatoid arthritis and is sometimes aggravated by NSAIDs, which may produce fluid retention or minor gastrointestinal blood loss in some patients. Therefore, patients with initial hemoglobin values of 10 g/dL or less who are to receive long-term therapy should have hemoglobin values determined frequently.

Infection: In common with other anti-inflammatory drugs, ketoprofen may mask the usual signs of infection.

Ophthalmology: Blurred and/or diminished vision has been reported with the use of ketoprofen and other NSAIDs. If such symptoms develop, this drug should be discontinued and an ophthalmologic examination performed; ophthalmic examination should be carried out at periodic intervals in any patient receiving this drug for an extended period of time.

CNS: Some patients may experience drowsiness, dizziness, vertigo, insomnia or depression with the use of ketoprofen. If patients experience these side effects, they should exercise caution in carrying out activities that require alertness.

Drug interactions: ASA or other NSAIDs: The use of ketoprofen in addition to any other NSAID, including those over the counter drugs (such as ASA and ibuprofen) is not recommended due to the possibility of additive side effects.

Concurrent administration of ASA and ketoprofen reduces protein binding of ketoprofen and increases its plasma clearance. The overall result was a 40% reduction in the AUC of ketoprofen. Ketoprofen does not alter ASA absorption.

Anticoagulants: Numerous studies have shown that the concomitant use of NSAIDs and anticoagulants increases the risk of gastrointestinal adverse events such as ulceration and bleeding.

Because prostaglandins play an important role in hemostasis, and NSAIDs affect platelet function, concurrent therapy of ketoprofen with warfarin requires close monitoring to be certain that no change in anticoagulant dosage is necessary.

Ketoprofen has been shown to depress platelet aggregation and it can prolong bleeding time by approximately 3 to 4 minutes from baseline values. However, a study conducted in 20 patients undergoing therapy with coumarin and simultaneously receiving ketoprofen, failed to demonstrate potentiation of anticoagulant effect. Nevertheless, close monitoring of patients is recommended when ketoprofen is given concomitantly with anticoagulants.

Diuretics: Hydrochlorothiazide, given concomitantly with ketoprofen, produces a reduction in urinary potassium and chloride excretion compared to hydrochlorothiazide alone. Patients taking diuretics are at greater risk of developing renal failure secondary to a decrease in renal blood flow caused by prostaglandin inhibition.

Glucocorticoids: Numerous studies have shown that the concomitant use of NSAIDs and oral glucocorticoids increases the risk of gastrointestinal side effects such as ulceration and bleeding. This is especially the case in older (>65 years of age) individuals.

Antacids: Concomitant administration of magnesium hydroxide and aluminum hydroxide does not interfere with the rate or extent of the absorption of ketoprofen.

Methotrexate: The concomitant administration of ketoprofen and high-dose methotrexate has been associated with prolonged and marked enhancement of serum methotrexate levels resulting in severe methotrexate toxicity. This may also apply to some other NSAIDs. There were no abnormalities in methotrexate kinetics or evidence of toxicity when ketoprofen was given at least 12 hours after completion of high-dose methotrexate infusion. Ketoprofen should not be used in patients receiving high-dose methotrexate.

The potential for severe toxicity should be kept in mind when prescribing ketoprofen and low-dose methotrexate concurrently. Ketoprofen should not be administered within 12 hours of methotrexate infusion.

Lithium: NSAIDs have been reported to increase steady-state plasma lithium levels. It is recommended that plasma lithium levels be monitored when ketoprofen is coadministered with lithium.

Other Drug Interactions: Probenecid: Concurrent administration of probenecid increases both free and bound ketoprofen through reducing the plasma clearance of ketoprofen to about one-third as well as decreasing its protein binding. Ketoprofen is not recommended in association with probenecid.

Ketoprofen is extensively (99%) protein bound to human serum albumin and may compete for binding sites with drugs such as sulfonamides, oral hypoglycemic agents, phenytoin or lithium. Although no significant interaction has been documented, patients with such combination therapy should be monitored.

Clinical Laboratory Tests: The presence of ketoprofen and its metabolites in urine has been shown to interfere with certain tests that are used to detect albumin, bile salts, 17-ketosteroids or 17-hydroxycorticosteroids in urine and which rely upon acid precipitation as an end point or upon color reactions of carbonyl groups. No interference was seen in the tests for proteinuria using Albustix, Hema-Combistix or Labstix Reagent Strips.

Although ketoprofen has been shown to depress platelet adhesion and aggregation and consequently, it can prolong bleeding time by approximately 3 to 4 minutes from baseline values; there has been no observed cases of changes in platelet count, prothrombin time, partial thromboplastin time or thrombin time.

Adverse Effects: The most common adverse reactions encountered with NSAIDs are gastrointestinal, of which peptic ulcer, with or without bleeding, is the most severe. Fatalities have occurred, particularly in the elderly.

In clinical trials involving 1 542 patients treated with ketoprofen, gastrointestinal effects were the most frequently observed adverse reactions and were reported in approximately 22% of patients. Ulceration and gastrointestinal bleeding have been noted in a few patients receiving ketoprofen therapy (less than 1% of 1 076 patients in controlled clinical trials); however, in open label continuation studies in 1 292 patients, the rate was greater than 2%.

A detailed breakdown of side effects with their corresponding frequencies (not indicated when <1%) is presented below. Adverse events have been compiled from foreign reports to manufacturers and regulatory agencies, publications and US clinical trials. See Table I (on following page).

Gastrointestinal (22%): dyspepsia (12.8%), nausea (4%), indigestion and flatulence (2.8%), vomiting (2%), constipation (2%), diarrhea (1.4%), anorexia, ulcer, gastrointestinal bleeding and perforation, melena, hematemesis, stomatitis.

Rectal administration was associated with a lower incidence of upper gastrointestinal reactions (12%) with the exception of ulceration, the incidence of which was the same. However, anorectal reactions presenting as local pain, burning, pruritus, tenesmus and rare instances of rectal bleeding occurred in 16.5% of patients. Five percent of patients discontinued rectal therapy because of these local reactions.

Allergic: These include angioedema, asthma, life-threatening bronchospasm and anaphylaxis.

CNS (3 to 5%): headache (1.7%), fatigue (1%), dizziness, tension, anxiety, depression, drowsiness, impotence, vertigo, migraine, paresthesia.

Dermatologic (<3%): rashes (1.7%), pruritus, flushing, excessive perspiration, alopecia, bullous rash, exfoliative dermatitis, photosensitivity, purpuric rash, urticaria and onycholysis were observed.

Cardiovascular: peripheral edema (2%), palpitation, congestive heart failure, hypertension.

Special Senses: tinnitus, hearing impairment, visual disturbance, conjunctivitis, conjunctivitis sicca, taste perversion.

Hematologic: hypocoagulability, agranulocytosis, anemia, hemolysis, purpura, thrombocytopenia.

Renal: interstitial nephritis, hematuria, nephrotic syndrome, impairment of renal function, acute renal failure.

Hepatic: hepatic dysfunction, jaundice.

Other: Laboratory Tests: abnormal alkaline phosphatase, lactic dehydrogenase, glutamic oxaloacetic transaminase and BUN values were found in some patients receiving ketoprofen therapy. The abnormalities did not lead to discontinuation of treatment and, in some cases, returned to normal while the drug was continued. There have been sporadic reports of decreased hematocrit and hemoglobin values without progressive deterioration on prolonged administration of the drug.

Overdose: Symptoms: Of 20 cases of overdosage (up to 5 000 mg) reported in Great Britain (5 children, 14 adolescents or young adults and 1 elderly), only 4 had mild symptoms (vomiting in 3, drowsiness in 1 child).

Treatment: Administer gastric lavage or an emetic and treat symptomatically: compensate for dehydration, monitor urinary excretion and correct acidosis if present.

The drug is dialyzable; therefore, hemodialysis may be useful to remove circulating drug and to assist in case of renal failure.

Dosage: Adults: Rheumatoid Arthritis and Osteoarthritis: Oral: The usual dosage for ketoprofen capsules or enteric coated tablets is 150 to 200 mg/day in 3 or 4 divided doses.

Once the maintenance dosage has been established, patients may be tried on a twice daily dosing regimen. Clinical trials, however, show that some rheumatoid arthritis patients respond better to more frequent dosing. The usual maintenance dose is 100 mg twice daily.

Rectal: Ketoprofen suppositories offer an alternative route of administration for those patients who prefer it. Administer 1 suppository morning and evening or 1 suppository at bedtime supplemented as needed by divided oral doses.

Use whole suppositories. Do not split or use portions of suppositories. Make sure that the wrapping is fully removed before inserting the suppository into the rectum. Do not take suppositories by mouth.

The total daily dose of ketoprofen capsules, tablets and suppositories should not exceed 200 mg/day. When the patient's response warrants it, the dose may be decreased to the minimum effective level.

Orafen (cont'd)

Table I—Orafen
Frequency of Adverse Reactions
Gastrointestinal
Dyspepsia (12.8%), nausea (4%), indigestion and flatulence (2.8%), vomiting (2%), constipation (2%), diarrhea (1.4%).
(<1%): Anorexia, ulcer, gastrointestinal bleeding and perforation, melena, hematemesis, stomatitis.
Anorectal Reactions*: local pain, burning, pruritus, tenesmus and rare instances of local bleeding (16.5%).
Allergic
(<1%): Angioedema, asthma, life-threatening bronchospasm and anaphylaxis.
CNS
Headache (1.7%), fatigue (1%).
(<1%): Dizziness, tension, anxiety, depression, drowsiness, impotence, vertigo, migraine, paresthesia.
Dermatologic
Rash (1.7%).
(<1%): Pruritus, flushing, excessive perspiration, alopecia, bullous rash, exfoliative dermatitis, photosensitivity, purpuric rash, urticaria and onycholysis.
Cardiovascular
Peripheral edema (2%)
(<1%): Palpitation, congestive heart failure and hypertension.
Special Senses
(<1%): Tinnitus, hearing impairment, visual disturbance, conjunctivitis, conjunctivitis sicca and taste perversion.
Hematologic
(<1%): Hypocoagulability, agranulocytosis, anemia, hemolysis, purpura and thrombocytopenia.
Renal
(<1%): Interstitial nephritis, hematuria, nephrotic syndrome, impairment of renal function and acute renal failure.
Hepatic
(<1%): Hepatic dysfunction, jaundice.

*Five percent of patients discontinued rectal therapy because of these local reactions.

In severe cases, during flare-up of rheumatic activity or if a satisfactory response cannot be obtained with the lower dose, a daily dosage in excess of 200 mg may be used. However, a dose of 300 mg/day should not be exceeded.

Primary Dysmenorrhea and Mild to Moderate Pain: Oral: The usual dose for ketoprofen is 25 to 50 mg 3 or 4 times daily as necessary.

A larger dose may be tried if the patient's response to a previous dose was less than satisfactory, but individual doses above 50 mg have not been shown to give added analgesia. The total daily dose should not exceed 300 mg. In most types of acute pain, a course of 3 to 7 days has been shown to be sufficient.

Elderly and Debilitated Patients: Initial dosage should be reduced by ½ to ⅓ in patients with impaired renal function and the elderly.

Children: Ketoprofen is not indicated in children under 12 years of age because clinical experience in this group of patients is insufficient.

Information for the Patient: See Blue Section—Information for the Patient "Orafen".

Supplied: Each off-white, smooth, torpedo-shaped suppository contains: ketoprofen 100 mg. Nonmedicinal ingredients: semisynthetic glycerides. Boxes of 30. Store below 30°C. Keep away from excessive heat, elevated humidity and light.

Reviewed 1999

ORAHESIVE®

Squibb

Denture Adhesive

Indications: Where a denture adhesive is required.

Dosage: Apply liberally to wet dentures as needed. Patients should be instructed that the use of any adhesive will not remedy the defects of a prosthetically unsatisfactory denture.

Supplied: Each 25 g shaker top bottle contains: a hygroscopic powder formulated with pectin, gelatin and sodium carboxymethylcellulose.

ORAMORPH SR™ Ⓝ

Boehringer Ingelheim

Morphine Sulfate

Narcotic Analgesic

Pharmacology: Morphine is a narcotic analgesic which acts as an agonist at stereospecific and saturable opioid receptors in the CNS and other tissues.

In man, morphine produces a variety of effects including analgesia, sedation, changes in mood including euphoria and dysphoria, mental clouding, respiratory depression from reduced responsiveness of the brain stem respiratory centres to CO_2, suppression of the cough reflex, constipation from decreased gastrointestinal activity, nausea and vomiting via stimulation of the chemoreceptor trigger zone (CTZ), alterations of the endocrine and autonomic nervous system.

Morphine is readily absorbed from the gastrointestinal tract following oral administration. Approximately 40% of the administered dose reaches the central compartment because of presystemic elimination (i.e., metabolism in the gut wall and liver). With repeated regular dosing, oral morphine is about one third as potent as when given by i.m. injection.

Virtually all morphine is converted to glucuronide metabolites, particularly morphine-3-glucuronide. Morphine is primarily excreted in the urine as morphine-3-glucuronide. About 7 to 10% of a dose of morphine is excreted in the feces via the bile.

At steady-state, Oramorph SR tablets produce peak morphine levels approximately 4 to 5 hours post-dose and therapeutic levels tend to persist for a 12 hour period. Steady-state is achieved after about 1 day on a fixed dosing regimen.

Indications: For the relief of moderate to severe chronic pain in patients who require prolonged dosing with an oral narcotic preparation.

Contraindications: Should not be given to patients with: hypersensitivity to opiate narcotics; respiratory depression; acute bronchial asthma or other chronic, obstructive pulmonary diseases or chronic cor pulmonale; cardiac arrhythmias; acute alcoholism; delirium tremens; severe CNS depression; convulsive disorders; increased cerebrospinal or intracranial pressure; head injury; brain tumor; suspected surgical abdomen; biliary tract surgery; concomitantly with MAO inhibitors (or within 14 days of such therapy).

Warnings: Drug Dependence and Abuse: As with other narcotics, morphine may cause physical dependence and tolerance following repeated administration, and there is potential for the development of strong psychological dependence and drug abuse. Morphine should therefore be prescribed and handled with a high degree of caution appropriate to the use of a drug with strong abuse potential. Drug abuse is not, however, a problem in patients with severe pain where morphine is appropriately indicated. On the other hand, in the absence of a clear indication for a strong narcotic analgesic, drug-seeking behavior must be suspected and resisted, particularly in individuals with a history of, or propensity for, drug abuse.

Withdrawal Syndrome: A moderate to severe abstinence syndrome may occur in patients who abruptly discontinue morphine therapy or it may be precipitated through the administration of drugs with narcotic antagonist activity, e.g., naloxone or mixed agonist/antagonist analgesics (pentazocine, etc.). Patients on prolonged therapy who no longer require morphine for pain control should be withdrawn gradually from the drug.

Morphine should be used with caution and in reduced dosage during the concomitant use of other CNS depressants including sedatives or hypnotics, general anesthetics, phenothiazines and other tranquilizers, tricyclic antidepressants and alcohol as these may produce additive depressant effects. Respiratory depression, hypotension and profound sedation or coma may occur. Opioid analgesics, including morphine, may enhance the neuromuscular blocking action of skeletal muscle relaxants and produce an increased degree of respiratory depression.

Severe pain antagonizes the subjective and respiratory depressant actions of morphine. Should pain suddenly subside, these effects may rapidly become manifest. Patients who are scheduled for cordotomy or other interruption of pain transmission pathways should not receive morphine within 24 hours of the procedure.

Pregnancy: Studies of morphine in animals to evaluate the drug's effect on reproduction have not been conducted.

There are no well-controlled studies in pregnant women and it is not known whether morphine can cause fetal harm when administered during pregnancy. Morphine should be given to pregnant patients only if clearly needed and if the anticipated benefits outweigh the risks to the fetus (see Precautions).

Precautions: General: As with any potent opioid, it is critical to adjust the dosing regimen for each patient individually, taking into account the patients prior analgesic treatment experience.

Respiratory depression is the major hazard of all morphine preparations and they should be used with extreme caution in patients with chronic obstructive pulmonary disease or cor pulmonale, and in patients having a substantially decreased respiratory reserve, hypoxia, hypercapnia, or pre-existing respiratory depression. In such patients, even usual therapeutic doses of morphine may decrease respiratory drive while simultaneously increasing airway resistance to the point of apnea.

The respiratory depressant effects of morphine with carbon dioxide retention and secondary elevation of cerebrospinal fluid pressure may be markedly exaggerated in the presence of head injury, other intracranial lesions, or a pre-existing increase in intracranial pressure. Morphine produces effects which may obscure neurologic signs of further increases in pressure in patients with head injuries. In such patients, morphine must be used with extreme caution and only if it is judged essential. Morphine may aggravate pre-existing convulsions in patients with convulsive disorders.

Morphine, like all opioid analgesics, may cause severe hypotension in individuals whose ability to maintain their blood pressure has already been compromised by a depleted blood volume, or a concurrent administration of drugs such as phenothiazines or general anesthetics. It should be administered with caution to patients in circulatory shock, since vasodilation produced by the drug may further reduce cardiac output and blood pressure.

The administration of morphine may obscure the diagnosis or clinical course in patients with acute abdominal conditions. Morphine should be used with caution in patients about to undergo surgery of the biliary tract since it may cause spasm of the sphincter of Oddi. Similarly, morphine should be used with caution in patients with acute pancreatitis secondary to biliary tract disease.

Drug Interactions: In general, the effects of morphine may be antagonized by acidifying agents and potentiated by alkalizing agents. The analgesic effect of morphine is potentiated by amphetamines, chlorpromazine and methocarbamol. CNS depressants, such as other opioids, anesthetics, sedatives, hypnotics, barbiturates, phenothiazines, chloral hydrate and glutethimide may enhance the depressant effects of morphine. MAO inhibitors (including procarbazine hydrochloride), pyrazolidone antihistamines, beta-blockers and alcohol may also enhance the depressant effect of morphine.

Agonist/antagonist opioid analgesics (i.e., pentazocine, nalbuphine, butorphanol or buprenorphine) should **not** be administered to a patient who has received or is receiving a course of therapy with a pure opioid agonist analgesic. In these patients, mixed agonist-antagonists may reduce the analgesic effect or may precipitate withdrawal symptoms.

Morphine may increase the anticoagulant activity of coumarin and other anticoagulants.

Special Risk Groups: Morphine should be administered with caution and in reduced dosages in the following populations: the elderly or debilitated and those with severe impairment of hepatic, pulmonary or renal function; myxoedema or hypothyroidism; adrenocortical insufficiency (e.g., Addison's Disease); CNS depression or coma; toxic psychoses; prostatic hypertrophy or urethral stricture; acute alcoholism; delirium tremens; kyphoscoliosis, or inability to swallow.

Labor and Delivery: Occasionally, opioid analgesics may prolong labor through actions which temporarily reduce the strength, duration and frequency of uterine contractions. However, this effect is not consistent and may be offset by an increased rate of cervical dilation which tends to shorten labor.

Morphine crosses the placental barrier and its administration during labor can produce respiratory depression in the neonate.

Neonates whose mothers received opioid analgesics during labor should be observed closely for signs of respiratory depression. A specific narcotic antagonist, naloxone, should be available for reversal of narcotic-induced respiratory depression in the neonate.

Lactation: Low levels of morphine have been detected in human milk. Withdrawal symptoms can occur in breastfeeding infants when maternal administration of morphine is stopped. Caution should therefore be exercised if morphine is administered to a nursing mother.

Children: The safety and effectiveness of morphine have not been evaluated in children.

Occupational Hazards: Driving and Operating Dangerous Machinery: Morphine may impair the mental and/or physical abilities needed for certain potentially hazardous activities such as driving a car or operating machinery. Patients should be cautioned accordingly.

Patients should also be cautioned about the combined effects of morphine with other CNS depressants, including other opioids, phenothiazines, sedative/hypnotics and alcohol.

Adverse Effects: The adverse reactions caused by morphine are essentially those observed with other opioid analgesics. The major hazards associated with morphine, as with other narcotic analgesics, are respiratory depression and, to a lesser degree, circulatory depression. Respiratory arrest, shock and cardiac arrest have occurred following oral or parenteral use of morphine.

Most Common Adverse Reactions Requiring Medical Attention: The most frequently observed side effects of narcotic analgesics such as morphine are sedation, nausea and vomiting, constipation and sweating.

Sedation: Most patients experience initial drowsiness partly for pharmacokinetic reasons and partly because patients often recuperate from prolonged fatigue after the relief of persistent pain. Drowsiness usually clears in 3 to 5 days and is usually not a reason for concern providing that it is not excessive, or associated with unsteadiness or confusional symptoms. If excessive sedation persists the reason for it must be sought. Some of these are: concomitant sedative medications, hepatic or renal failure, exacerbated respiratory failure, higher doses than tolerated in an older patient, or the patient is actually more severely ill than realized. If it is necessary to reduce the dose, it can be carefully increased again after 3 or 4 days if it is obvious that the pain is not being well controlled. Dizziness and unsteadiness may be caused by postural hypotension particularly in elderly or debilitated patients. It can be alleviated if the patient lies down. Because of the slower clearance in patients over 50 years of age, an appropriate dose in this age group may be as low as half or less the usual dose in the younger age group.

Nausea and Vomiting: Nausea and vomiting occur frequently after single doses of narcotics or as an early unwanted effect of regular narcotic therapy. When instituting prolonged therapy for chronic pain the routine prescription of an antiemetic should be considered. Patients taking the equivalent of a single dose of 20 mg or more of morphine (60 mg every 12 hours of Oramorph SR) usually require an antiemetic during early therapy. Small doses of prochlorperazine or haloperidol are the most frequently prescribed antiemetics. Nausea and vomiting tend to lessen in a week or so but may persist due to narcotic-induced gastric stasis. In such patients, metoclopramide is often useful.

Constipation: Practically all patients become constipated while taking narcotics on a persistent basis. In some instances, particularly the elderly or bedridden, patients may become impacted. It is essential to caution the patients in this regard and to institute an appropriate regimen of bowel management at the start of prolonged narcotic therapy. Softeners, laxatives and other appropriate measures should be used as required.

Less frequently observed side effects include: CNS: weakness, headache, agitation, tremor, uncoordinated muscle movements, seizure, alterations of mood (nervousness, apprehension, depression, floating feeling), dreams, muscle rigidity, transient hallucinations and disorientation, visual disturbances, insomnia and increased intracranial pressure.

Gastrointestinal: dry mouth, constipation, biliary tract spasm, laryngospasm, anorexia, diarrhea, cramps, and taste alterations.

Cardiovascular: supraventricular tachycardia, bradycardia, palpitations, faintness, syncope, postural hypotension and hypertension.

Genitourinary: urinary retention or hesitancy, reduced libido or potency.

Dermatologic: pruritus, urticaria, other skin rashes, edema and diaphoresis.

Endocrine: A syndrome of inappropriate antidiuretic hormone secretion characterized by hyponatremia secondary to decreased free-water excretion may be prominent (monitoring of electrolytes may be necessary).

Other: paresthesia, muscle tremor, blurred vision, nystagmus, diplopia and miosis.

Withdrawal (Abstinence) Syndrome: Physical dependence results in withdrawal symptoms in patients who abruptly discontinue the drug or withdrawal symptoms may be precipitated through the administration of narcotic antagonist drugs. The abstinence syndrome is characterized by some or all of the following; restlessness, lacrimation, rhinorrhea, yawning, perspiration, gooseflesh, restless sleep and mydriasis during the first 24 hours. These symptoms often increase in severity and over the next 72 hours may be accompanied by increasing irritability, anxiety, weakness, twitching and spasms of muscles; kicking movements; severe backache, abdominal and leg pains; abdominal and muscle cramps, hot and cold flashes, insomnia, nausea, anorexia, vomiting, intestinal spasm, diarrhea, coryza and repetitive sneezing; increase in body temperature, blood pressure, respiratory rate and heart rate. Because of excessive loss of fluids through sweating, vomiting and diarrhea, there is usually marked weight loss, dehydration, ketosis, and disturbances in acid-base balance. Cardiovascular collapse can occur. Without treatment most observable symptoms disappear in 5 to 14 days; however, there appears to be a phase of secondary or chronic abstinence which may last for 2 to 6 months characterized by insomnia, irritability and muscular aches. If treatment of physical dependence of patients on morphine is necessary, the patient may be detoxified by gradual reduction of the dosage. Gastrointestinal disturbances or dehydration should be treated accordingly.

Overdose: Symptoms: Serious morphine overdosage is characterized by respiratory depression (reduced respiratory rate and/or tidal volume; Cheyne-Stokes respiration; cyanosis), extreme somnolence progressing to stupor or coma, skeletal muscle flaccidity, cold or clammy skin, and sometimes hypotension and bradycardia. Severe overdosage may result in apnea, circulatory collapse, cardiac arrest and death.

Treatment: Primary attention should be given to the establishment of adequate respiratory exchange through the provision of a patent airway and controlled or assisted ventilation. The narcotic antagonist naloxone HCl is a specific antidote against respiratory depression due to overdosage or as a result of unusual sensitivity to morphine. An appropriate dose of one of the antagonists should therefore be administered, preferably by the i.v. route. The usual initial i.v. adult dose of naloxone is 0.4 mg or higher. Concomitant efforts at respiratory resuscitation should be carried out. Since the duration of action of morphine, particularly extended release formulations, may exceed that of the antagonist, the patient should be under continued surveillance and doses of the antagonist should be repeated as needed to maintain adequate respiration.

An antagonist should **not** be administered in the absence of clinically significant respiratory or cardiovascular depression. Oxygen, i.v. fluids, vasopressors and other supportive measures should be used as indicated.

In an individual physically dependent on narcotics, the administration of the usual dose of narcotic antagonist will precipitate an acute withdrawal syndrome. The severity of this syndrome will depend on the degree of physical dependence and the dose of antagonist administered. The use of narcotic antagonists in such individuals should be avoided if possible. If a narcotic antagonist must be used to treat serious respiratory depression in the physically dependent patient, the antagonist should be administered with extreme care by using dosage titration, commencing with 10 to 20% of the usual recommended initial dose.

Evacuation of gastric contents may be useful in removing unabsorbed drug, particularly when an extended release formulation has been taken.

Dosage: As with any potent opioid product, the administration and dosing of morphine should be individualized for each patient taking into account the following: the properties of morphine; the nature and severity of the pain or pains experienced; the general condition and medical status of the patient; daily dose and potency of opioids or other medication given previously or concurrently and the degree of opioid tolerance, if any.

As with other strong narcotic analgesics, use of morphine for the management of persistent pain should be preceded by a thorough assessment of the patient and diagnosis of the specific pain or pains and their causes. Use of narcotics for the relief of chronic pain, including cancer pain, all important as it may be, should be only one part of a comprehensive approach to pain control including other treatment modalities or drug therapy, non-drug measures and psychosocial support.

Patients over the age of 50 tend to require much lower doses of morphine than in the younger age group. In elderly and debilitated patients and those with impaired respiratory function or significantly decreased renal function, the initial dose should be one half the usual recommended dose.

For essential information on the important details of the management of cancer pain, the reader may wish to consult the following resources:

Cancer Pain: A Monograph on the management of cancer pain. Health and Welfare Canada.

Twycross, R.G. and Lack, S.A. Symptom control in far advanced cancer: Pain relief.

The following dosing recommendations, therefore, can only be considered suggested approaches to what is actually a series of clinical decisions in the management of the pain of an individual patient.

Conversion from Conventional Oral Morphine to Oramorph SR: Patients currently receiving an immediate release oral morphine product (every 4 to 6 hours) may be transferred to Oramorph SR at the same total daily morphine dosage equally divided into two 12 hourly Oramorph SR doses.

For initial conversion, the 30 mg tablet strength is recommended for patients with a daily morphine requirement of 120 mg or less.

Conversion from Parenteral Morphine or Other Opioids (Parenteral or Oral) to Oramorph SR: For patients who are receiving an alternate narcotic, the "oral morphine sulfate equivalent" of the analgesic presently being used should be determined (see Table I).

On the basis of standard equivalence tables, a 1:2 or 1:3 ratio of parenteral to oral morphine equivalence is suggested. The total daily oral morphine dosage should then be equally divided into two 12 hourly Oramorph SR doses.

Estimates of the relative potency of opioids are only approximate and are influenced by route of administration, individual patient differences, and possibly, by an individual's medical condition. Consequently, it is difficult to recommend any fixed rule for converting a patient to Oramorph SR directly. In patients whose daily morphine requirements are expected to be less than or equal to 120 mg/day, the 30 mg tablet strength is recommended for the initial titration period. Once a stable dose regimen is reached, the patient can be converted to the 60 mg or 100 mg tablet strength, as appropriate.

Table I—Oramorph SR

Narcotics: Approximate Analgesic Equivalences[a]

Drug	Equivalent Dose (mg)[b] (compared to standard Morphine 10 mg i.m.)	
Agonists	**i.m.**	**oral**
Morphine sulfate	10	20–30
Codeine phosphate	120	200
Hydromorphone (Dilaudid)	2	4
Levorphanol (Levo-Dromoran)	2	4
Oxycodone (Percodan, Percocet)		10–15
Anileridine (Leritine)	25	75
Meperidine (Demerol)	75	300
Oxymorphone (Numorphan)	1.5	(supp 5 mg)
Methadone	10	20
Heroin	5-8	10–15
Agonist-Antagonist		
Pentazocine (Talwin)	60	180
Nalbuphine (Nubain)	10	
Butorphanol (Stadol)	2	

[a]Adapted from a Monograph on the Management of Cancer Pain, Minister of Supply and Services Canada 1987.

[b]Most of this data was derived from single dose, acute pain studies and should be considered a rough approximation for initial selection of doses when treating chronic cancer pain.

Use of Oramorph SR as the First Opioid Analgesic: There has been no systematic evaluation of Oramorph SR as an initial opioid analgesic in the management of pain. Because it may be more difficult to titrate a patient using extended release morphine, it is ordinarily advisable to begin treatment using an immediate-release formulation.

Dose Titration: Dose titration is the key to success with morphine therapy. **Proper optimization of doses scaled to the relief of the individual's pain should aim at the regular administration of the lowest dose of morphine which will maintain the patient free of pain at all times.** Dose adjustments should be based on the patient's clinical response. Higher doses may be justified in some patients to cover periods of physical activity.

Adjustment in dose should not be attempted by breaking or crushing the tablets. Therefore, in patients with low daily morphine requirements, precise titration may be difficult because the smallest available tablet of Oramorph SR contains 30 mg of morphine. The usual recommended dose (every 12 hours) increments are 15, 30, 45, 60, 90, 120, 150, 180, 200 mg. Above the 200 mg/dose (400 mg/day) increments should be by 30 to 60 mg/dose. Because of the extended release properties of Oramorph SR, dosage adjustments should generally be separated by 48 hours.

Oramorph SR tablets are designed to allow 12 hourly dosing. If "breakthrough" pain repeatedly occurs at the end of a dose interval, it is generally an indication for a dosage increase, **not**

Oramorph SR (cont'd)

more frequent administration. However, where judged necessary for optimization of drug effects, Oramorph SR may be administered every 8 hours. More frequent (than every 8 hours) administration of Oramorph SR is not recommended. Alternatively, a supplemental dose of a short-acting analgesic may be given.

In adjusting dose requirements, it is recommended that the dosing interval **never** be extended beyond 12 hours because the administration of very large single doses may lead to acute overdose.

Adjustment or Reduction of Dosage: During the first 2 or 3 days of effective pain relief, the patient may exhibit drowsiness or sleep for prolonged periods. This can be misinterpreted as the effect of excessive analgesic dosing rather than the first sign of relief in a pain-exhausted patient. The dose, therefore, should be maintained for at least 3 days before reduction, provided the sedation is not excessive or associated with unsteadiness, and symptoms of confusion, and that respiratory activity and other vital signs are adequate. If excessive sedation persists, the reason(s) for such an effect must be sought. Some of these are: concomitant sedative medications, hepatic or renal failure, exacerbated respiratory failure, higher doses than tolerated by an older patient, or the patient is actually more severely ill than realized. If it is necessary to reduce the dose, it can be carefully increased again after 3 or 4 days if it is obvious that the pain is not being well controlled.

Following successful relief of severe pain, periodic attempts to reduce the narcotic dose should be made. Smaller doses or complete discontinuation of the narcotic analgesic may become feasible due to a change in the patient's condition or improved mental state.

Narcotic agents do not relieve effectively dysesthetic pain, post-herpetic neuralgia, stabbing pains, activity-related pain, and some forms of headache. This is not to say that patients with advanced cancer suffering from some of these forms of pain should not be given an adequate trial of opiate analgesics, but it may be necessary to refer such patients at an early time for other forms of pain therapy. Pain without nociception is usually not narcotic-responsive.

Information for the Patient: See Blue Section—Information for the Patient "Oramorph SR".

Supplied: 30 mg: Each off-white compressed biconvex extended release tablet with "30" debossed on one side and product identification "54/090" debossed on the other side, contains: morphine sulfate 30 mg. Nonmedicinal ingredients: colloidal silicon dioxide, hydroxypropyl methylcellulose, lactose and stearic acid. Unit dose, cards of 25; cartons of 4. Opaque plastic bottles of 50.

60 mg: Each off-white compressed biconvex extended release tablet with "60" debossed on one side and product identification "54/933" debossed on the other side, contains: morphine sulfate 60 mg. Nonmedicinal ingredients: colloidal silicon dioxide, hydroxypropyl methylcellulose, lactose and stearic acid. Unit dose, cards of 25; cartons of 4. Opaque plastic bottles of 100.

100 mg: Each off-white compressed biconvex extended release tablet with "100" debossed on one side and product identification "54/862" debossed on the other side, contains: morphine sulfate 100 mg. Nonmedicinal ingredients: colloidal silicon dioxide, hydroxypropyl methylcellulose, lactose and stearic acid. Unit dose, cards of 25; cartons of 4. Opaque plastic bottles of 100.

The tablets should be swallowed intact, not chewed or crushed. Store at 15 to 30°C. Protect from moisture.

ORAP® Ⓟ

Janssen-Ortho

Pimozide

Antipsychotic

Pharmacology: Pimozide is a diphenylbutylpiperidine derivative with neuroleptic properties that has been found to be useful in the management of chronic schizophrenic patients. It is relatively non-sedating and can be administered in a single daily dosage.

It is assumed that the basic mechanism of action of pimozide is related to its action on central aminergic receptors. It appears to have a selective ability to block central dopaminergic receptors, although it affects norepinephrine turnover at higher doses. The extrapyramidal effects typical of other neuroleptic agents are seen also with pimozide, but it appears to have fewer autonomic effects. As with other neuroleptics, endocrine effects and ECG changes have also been reported with pimozide.

Pharmacokinetics: The peak plasma level of pimozide in man occurs between 3 and 8 hours after administration and plasma levels decrease slowly to about 50% of the peak level at 48 to 72 hours after dosing. In a single dose study involving healthy volunteers, the mean plasma half-life of tritiated pimozide (total radioactivity) was found to be 29±10 (S.D.) hours. In a repeat dose study of short duration involving chronic schizophrenics, the mean plasma half-life was 55±20 (S.D.) hours. There was a 13-fold interindividual difference in the area under the serum pimozide concentration-time curve and an equivalent degree of variation in peak serum levels among patients studied. The significance of this is unclear since there are few correlations between plasma levels and clinical findings. In the single dose study, 19% (range 8 to 32%) of the radioactivity was excreted in urine in 24 hours. Approximately 40 to 50% was excreted in urine and 20% in feces within a week. Negligible amounts were excreted after the 7th day, although labelled material was detected up to 14 days after administration. The main metabolite in both urine and feces is 4-bis (p-fluorophenyl) butyric acid. Unchanged pimozide constitutes at least 50% of the fecal radioactivity but only a very small fraction of the plasma and urinary radioactivity.

Indications: The management of the manifestations of chronic schizophrenia in which the main manifestations do not include excitement, agitation or hyperactivity. Pimozide has relatively little sedative action and can be used as a once daily medication.

Pimozide is not indicated in the management of patients with mania or acute schizophrenia.

Contraindications: In CNS depression, comatose states, liver disorders, renal insufficiency, and blood dyscrasias, and in individuals who have previously displayed hypersensitivity to the drug. It should not be used in depressive disorders or Parkinson's syndrome.

Pimozide is contraindicated in patients with congenital long QT syndrome, patients with a history of cardiac arrhythmias, or patients taking other drugs which prolong the QT interval of the ECG (see Precautions, Drug Interactions). A pretreatment ECG is thus recommended to exclude these conditions.

The concomitant use of CYP 3A4-inhibiting drugs such as azole antimycotics, antiviral protease inhibitors and macrolide antibiotics is contraindicated. The concomitant use of CYP 2D6-inhibiting drugs such as quinidine is also contraindicated. The inhibition of either or both cytochrome P450 systems may result in the elevation of pimozide blood concentration and increase the possibility of QT-prolongation.

Warnings: Increased Psychomotor Activity: Clinical trials with pimozide indicate that it is not effective in, and therefore should not be used in, the management of manifestations of chronic schizophrenia in which the main symptoms include agitation, excitement and anxiety.

Cardiac Monitoring: As with other neuroleptics, cases of sudden, unexpected deaths have occurred with pimozide, mainly at doses above 20 mg/day. ECG changes have been reported in association with the use of pimozide (see Adverse Effects), and one possible mechanism for the deaths is prolongation of the QT interval, predisposing patients to ventricular arrhythmia. Periodic assessment of cardiac function, primarily ECG, should be undertaken in those patients receiving pimozide in excess of 16 mg daily. Any indication of repolarization changes, such as prolongation of QT intervals beyond 0.52 seconds in adults, or more than 25% above the patient's original baseline, or T-wave or U-wave changes, should be considered a basis for stopping further increases, possibly lowering the dose, and reviewing the need for pimozide. Caution should be exercised if it is necessary to use pimozide in patients with cardiovascular disorders. Electrolyte imbalance, particularly hypokalemia, should be considered a risk factor.

Liver Disease: Caution is advised in patients with liver disease because pimozide is metabolized in the liver.

Tardive Dyskinesia: As with all antipsychotic agents, tardive dyskinesia may appear in some patients on long-term therapy or after drug discontinuation. The syndrome is mainly characterized by rhythmical involuntary movements of the tongue, face, mouth or jaw. The manifestations may be permanent in some patients. The syndrome may be masked when treatment is reinstituted, when the dosage is increased or when a switch is made to a different antipsychotic drug. Treatment should be discontinued as soon as possible.

Neuroleptic Malignant Syndrome: In common with other antipsychotic drugs, pimozide has been associated with neuroleptic malignant syndrome: an idiosyncratic response characterized by hyperthermia, generalized muscle rigidity, autonomic instability and altered consciousness. Hyperthermia is often an early sign of this syndrome. Antipsychotic treatment should be withdrawn immediately and appropriate supportive therapy and careful monitoring instituted.

Hyperpyrexia, not associated with the above symptom complex, has been reported with other antipsychotic drugs.

Withdrawal Emergent Neurological Signs: Generally, patients receiving short-term therapy experience no problems with abrupt discontinuation of antipsychotic drugs. However, some patients on maintenance treatment experience transient dyskinetic signs after abrupt withdrawal. In certain of these cases the dyskinetic movements are indistinguishable from the syndrome described above under Tardive Dyskinesia except for duration. It is not known whether gradual withdrawal of antipsychotic drugs will reduce the rate of occurrence of withdrawal emergent neurological signs but, until further evidence becomes available, it seems reasonable to gradually withdraw use of antipsychotic drugs.

In schizophrenia, the response to antipsychotic drug treatment may be delayed. If drugs are withdrawn, recurrence of symptoms may not become apparent for several weeks or months. Acute withdrawal symptoms, including nausea, vomiting, transient dyskinetic signs, and insomnia, have very rarely been described after abrupt cessation of high doses of antipsychotic drugs. Gradual withdrawal is advisable.

Potential for Hypotension: Patients receiving pimozide should be observed for evidence of hypotension. Some individuals, especially the elderly or debilitated, have demonstrated transient hypotension for several hours following drug administration.

Precautions: Blood dyscrasia: Leukopenia, granulocytopenia, agranulocytosis and anemia have been reported occasionally following antipsychotic therapy, notably with phenothiazines. Therefore, the possibility of blood dyscrasias cannot be ruled out in patients receiving treatment with pimozide, and they should be observed for any signs or symptoms of blood dyscrasia.

Anticonvulsants: Since pimozide may lower the convulsive threshold, it should be used with caution in epileptic patients and adequate anticonvulsive medication should be maintained.

Antiemetic Effects: As with other antipsychotics, pimozide has a substantial antiemetic effect. Thus, caution should be exercised in cases where the suppression of nausea and vomiting might hinder the diagnosis of an underlying physical disorder.

Pregnancy: The safety of use of pimozide in pregnancy has not been established. Therefore, it should not be administered to women of childbearing potential, particularly during the first trimester of pregnancy, unless, in the opinion of the physician, the expected benefits of the drug to the patient outweigh the potential risk to the fetus or child.

Lactation: Pimozide may be excreted in breast milk. If the use of pimozide is considered essential, breast-feeding should be discontinued.

Children: Safety and effectiveness in children have not been established; therefore, this drug is not recommended for use in the pediatric age group.

Geriatrics: For recommendations for use in elderly see Dosage.

Occupational Hazards: Pimozide may impair alertness, especially at the start of treatment. These effects may be potentiated by alcohol. Patients should be warned of the risks of sedation and advised not to drive or operate machinery during treatment until their susceptibility is known.

Drug Interactions: CNS: Potentiation of the effects of drugs acting on the CNS (anesthetics, opiates, alcohol, etc.) as well as atropine and organophosphorous insecticides may occur with the use of pimozide. Both animal and human data indicate that pimozide may block the action of amphetamines. Therefore, concomitant use of the two medications is not recommended.

Levodopa: Pimozide may in a dose-related way impair the antiparkinson effect of levodopa.

Antihypertensives: Concomitant administration of antihypertensive agents should be undertaken with caution in view of the fact that other antipsychotics, notably the phenothiazines, have blocked the action of these agents.

Drugs that Inhibit Cytochrome P450: Pimozide is metabolized mainly via the cytochrome P450 subtype 3A4 (CYP 3A4) enzyme system and more discreetly via the CYP 2D6 subtype. In vitro data indicate that especially potent inhibitors of CYP 3A4 enzyme system, such as azole antimycotics, antiviral protease inhibitors and macrolide antibiotics will inhibit the metabolism of pimozide, resulting in markedly elevated plasma levels of pimozide. In vitro data also indicate that quinidine diminishes the CYP 2D6-dependent metablism of pimozide. Elevated pimozide levels may enhance the risk of QT prolongation.

Drugs that Prolong QT Interval: Because pimozide prolongs the QT interval of the ECG, an additive effect on QT interval would be anticipated if administered with other drugs, such as phenothiazines (antipsychotics), tricyclic antidepressants or antiarrhythmic agents, which prolong the QT interval. Such concomitant administration should not be undertaken (see Contraindications). Particular care should be taken to avoid toxic plasma levels of lithium when this agent is administered together with pimozide, since such toxic levels have also been associated with QT prolongation.

Adverse Effects: The following adverse reactions have been reported with pimozide or with other antipsychotic agents:

Extrapyramidal symptoms: In common with all neuroleptics, extrapyramidal symptoms may occur, e.g., tremor, rigidity, hypersalivation, bradykinesia, akathisia, acute dystonia. Antiparkinson drugs of the anticholinergic type may be prescribed as required, but should not be prescribed routinely as a preventive measure.

Tardive Dyskinesia: As with all antipsychotic agents, tardive dyskinesia may appear in some patients on long-term therapy or may appear after drug therapy has been discontinued (see Warnings).

Neuroleptic Malignant Syndrome: In common with other antipsychotic drugs, pimozide has been associated with neuroleptic malignant syndrome (see Warnings).

Other CNS Effects: These are occasionally reported and include: insomnia, restlessness, agitation, drowsiness, decreased attention, fatigue and depression have been most commonly observed with pimozide. Irritability, tension, jitteriness, excitement, aggressiveness, anxiety, confusion, nightmares and hallucinations have also been recorded. In some instances, aggravation of the patient's psychotic symptoms has occurred. Toxic confusional states and euphoria have been reported with other antipsychotic therapy.

The most commonly reported neurological adverse reactions are extrapyramidal, including parkinsonism. As with most neuroleptics, reports of parkinsonian side effects, such as tremor, rigidity and sialorrhea, are not uncommon. Akathisia occurs relatively frequently, but can usually be managed by reducing the dosage of pimozide or by the concomitant administration of an antiparkinsonian agent.

Dystonic reactions have been reported, the most common being torticollis, which is generally accompanied by oro-facial symptoms and, in some instances, oculogyric crises, as well as spasms of the face, tongue and jaw. Mouth and throat area dyskinesias, trismus, dysarthria, muscle cramps and athetoid movements have also been observed occasionally. In addition, dizziness or vertigo, weakness, excessive sweating, body temperature disregulation, headache, EEG changes, and an increased incidence of epileptic seizures have been reported, and, in association with other antipsychotics, opisthotonus, hyperreflexia and grand mal convulsions.

Autonomic: Autonomic adverse reactions that have occurred with pimozide are dry mouth, blurred vision, difficulty with accommodation, urinary retention, and urinary and fecal incontinence. Nasal congestion, paralytic ileus and reversed epinephrine effect have been reported with the use of other antipsychotics.

Cardiovascular: Hypotension, tachycardia and fluctuations in blood pressure have been noted with pimozide. Hypertension has occasionally occurred. QT-interval prolongation and/or ventricular arrhythmias have very rarely been reported, and predominantly with high doses and in predisposed patients.

Gastrointestinal: Anorexia, nausea and/or vomiting, constipation, diarrhea, and abdominal cramps or pain have been observed in some patients receiving pimozide.

Endocrine: Hormonal effects of antipsychotic neuroleptic drugs include hyperprolactinemia, which may cause galactorrhea, gynecomastia, oligo- or amenorrhea and impotence. Very rarely, cases of hyponatremia due to either Syndrome of Inappropriate ADH Secretion (SIADH) or psychogenic polydipsia, have been reported.

Miscellaneous: Cases of urticaria and erythematous rash have been reported with pimozide, as well as instances of severe edema, generally limited to the facial area.

Fever, laryngeal edema, angioneurotic edema, asthma, anaphylactoid reactions, hyperpyrexia, obstructive jaundice, biliary stasis, photosensitivity, eczema, exfoliative dermatitis, maculopapular and acneiform reactions, and alopecia have been reported in association with the use of other antipsychotics. Blood dyscrasias (agranulocytosis, leukopenia, granulocytopenia, pancytopenia, thrombocytopenic purpura, eosinophilia, anemia, aplastic anemia) have also occurred.

Cerebral edema, peripheral edema and altered cerebrospinal fluid proteins have been observed with other antipsychotic agents.

Since a peculiar skin-eye syndrome has been recognized as a side effect following long-term treatment with certain phenothiazines, the possibility of this side effect occurring with pimozide cannot be excluded. This reaction is marked by progressive pigmentation of areas of skin or conjunctivae and may be accompanied by discoloration of the exposed sclera and cornea. Opacities of the anterior lens and cornea described as irregular or stellate in shape have also been reported.

Hyperpyrexia: Hyperpyrexia has been reported with other antipsychotic drugs.

Overdose: Symptoms: In general, the signs and symptoms of overdosage with pimozide would be an exaggeration of known pharmacologic effects and adverse reactions, the most prominent of which would be extrapyramidal symptoms. The risk of cardiac arrhythmias, possibly associated with QT-prolongation should be considered. If these arrhythmias are severe, they can be associated with hypotension and circulatory collapse.

Treatment: There is no specific antidote to pimozide. In the event of overdosage, gastric lavage, establishment of a patent airway and, if necessary, mechanically-assisted respiration are advised. Electrocardiographic monitoring should commence immediately and continue until the ECG parameters are within the normal range. Hypotension and circulatory collapse may be counteracted by use of i.v. fluids, plasma, or concentrated albumin, and vasopressor agents such as metaraminol, phenylephrine and norepinephrine. **Epinephrine should not be used.** In case of severe extrapyramidal reactions, antiparkinson medication should be administered. Because of the long half-life of pimozide, patients who take an overdose should be observed for at least 4 days. As with all drugs, the physician should consider contacting a Poison Control Centre for additional information on the treatment of overdose.

Dosage: Adults: The initial recommended dose in patients with chronic schizophrenia for whom pimozide might be indicated is 2 to 4 mg once daily, with weekly increments of 2 to 4 mg until a satisfactory level of therapeutic effect is attained or excessive adverse effects occur. The average maintenance dose is 6 mg daily with the usual range of 2 to 12 mg/day. Daily doses above 20 mg are not recommended.

Geriatrics: The maintenance dose is the same as in adults but it is recommended to start with one half of the adult initial dose.

A single morning dose is recommended for all patients.

Supplied: 2 mg: Each white, uncoated tablet, scored on one side and embossed with McNEIL on the other side, contains: pimozide 2 mg. Nonmedicinal ingredients: calcium stearate, cornstarch, lactose and microcrystalline cellulose. Energy: 1.784 kJ (0.424 kcal). Sodium: <1 mmol (<1 mg). Gluten- and sodium metabisulfite-free. HDPE bottles of 100.

4 mg: Each green, uncoated tablet, scored on one side and embossed with McNEIL on the other side, contains: pimozide 4 mg. Nonmedicinal ingredients: calcium stearate, FD&C Blue No. 1, FD&C Yellow No. 5, lactose, microcrystalline cellulose, starch (corn) and tartrazine. Energy: 1.750 kJ (0.415 kcal). Sodium: <1 mmol (<1 mg). Gluten- and sodium metabisulfite-free. HDPE bottles of 100.

Store at controlled room temperature (15 to 30°C) in well-closed containers.

Reviewed 1999

ORASCAN™

Germiphene

Toluidine Blue O

Oral Cancer Diagnostic System

Indications: As an oral cancer diagnostic and to establish borders for biopsy and surgical site selection.

Precautions: Any use of OraScan must be done after a visual inspection of the oral cavity, and before any instrumentation of soft tissues. OraScan should be used after a complete head and neck cancer exam. Two types of lesions will stain: squamous cell carcinoma and inflamed traumatic. To differentiate, the patient with a positive test is required to be retested in 10 to 14 days to eliminate inflamed traumatic lesions which will have healed in this time. A second positive makes biopsy mandatory.

Pregnancy: At present there have not been controlled clinical studies with OraScan and pregnant women, hence it is not suggested for their use at this time.

Children: Use of OraScan is not recommended for children.

Carcinogenesis: In more than 30 years of use in humans, toluidine blue has not been observed as a cause of any cancer.

Adverse Effects: There is no known allergy or other reactions to the stain materials (toluidine blue has been used i.v. for other applications). There may be a prolonged stain of the vermilion border, dorsum of the tongue and dental plaque, which usually wears off in 4 to 6 hours. Care should be taken to protect clothing as well as equipment and environmental surfaces from being stained. Patients may experience a slight burning sensation. Restorative materials including porcelain, composites and acrylics do not stain permanently.

Dosage: 10 mL solution of 1% toluidine blue O.

Supplied: OraScan is a 3 component system. One component is a flavored 1% toluidine blue O solution. The other two are pre- and post-rinse solutions consisting of flavored 1% acetic acid.

ORCIPREN® Ⓟ

Technilab

Orciprenaline Sulfate

Bronchodilator

Supplied: Each 5 mL of clear, sugar-free, woodruff and honey-flavored syrup contains: orciprenaline sulfate 10 mg. Nonmedicinal ingredients: artificial and natural flavoring, calcium cyclamate, citric acid, methylparaben, propylparaben, purified water, sodium citrate, sorbitol and xanthan gum. PET bottles of 250 mL. Store in its original buffer at controlled room temperature of 15 to 30°C.

ORGARAN® Ⓟ

Organon

Danaparoid Sodium

Antithrombotic

Pharmacology: Danaparoid is a mixture of low molecular weight sulfated glycosaminoglycuronans derived from porcine intestinal mucosa. It consists of heparan sulfate with low affinity for antithrombin III (AT-III) (about 80%), heparan sulfate with high affinity for AT-III (about 4%), dermatan sulfate (8 to 16%) and chondroitin sulfate (<8.5%); but danaparoid is devoid of heparin or heparin fragments. It has been shown both in animal models and in human studies to possess antithrombotic action.

Compared to heparin, danaparoid has a much higher anti-factor Xa/anti-IIa ratio (more than 20:1). Danaparoid exerts a stronger catalytic effect on the inactivation of factor Xa than on the inactivation of thrombin. The anti-Xa activity is mediated by AT-III and is not inactivated by endogenous heparin neutralizing factors. The antithrombin activity is mediated by both AT-III and heparin cofactor II. Danaparoid inhibits thrombus formation with approximately the same potency as heparin, in animal models. In clinical trials, danaparoid showed improved antithrombotic activity when compared to heparin. Both of the heparan sulfate fractions, the high- and low-affinity for AT-III, contribute to the antithrombotic activity. Danaparoid has minimal or no effect on platelet function. It produces less bleeding-enhancing activity than heparin in experimental models. Danaparoid does not inhibit platelet deposition at therapeutic doses and has only minimal effects on platelet degranulation during hemostatic plug formation. In experimental models, the antithrombotic activity of danaparoid is more persistent and the hemorrhagic effects less persistent than those of heparin.

Cross-reactivity between danaparoid and heparin-associated antibody from the plasma of patients with heparin-induced thrombocytopenia (HIT) was less than 10%. Cross-reactivity testing is complex and incompletely understood. The clinical implications are unclear (see Precautions). A negative cross-reactivity test does not necessarily indicate that the patient will not develop danaparoid-induced thrombocytopenia during therapy.

Indications: In the prevention of deep vein thrombosis (DVT) following orthopedic, major abdominal and thoracic surgery. Patients with a positive diagnosis of nonhemorrhagic stroke may also be treated with danaparoid. The prophylactic treatment of patients with danaparoid does not preclude the use of other modalities of prophylaxis (see Precautions, Drug Interactions).

Contraindications: Danaparoid should not be administered i.m. Severe hemorrhagic diathesis, hemorrhagic stroke in the

Organ (cont'd)

acute phase, uncontrollable active bleeding state, hypersensitivity to danaparoid or any of its components including sulfite, active gastric or duodenal ulcer (unless the reason for major abdominal surgery), bacterial endocarditis, major blood clotting disorders, history of thrombocytopenia with danaparoid or in patients in whom an in vitro platelet aggregation test is positive in the presence of danaparoid, severe untreated hypertension, diabetic or hemorrhagic retinopathy, other diseases involving an increased risk of hemorrhage.

Warnings: Danaparoid should be used with care in patients with a history of gastrointestinal ulceration.

Determination of anti-factor Xa levels in plasma is the only method available for monitoring danaparoid activity. Anticoagulant activity is characterized by a very flat dose response curve in clotting assays such as prothrombin time, activated partial thromboplastin time, kaolin cephalin clotting time and thrombin clotting time; therefore, these routine clotting assays are unsuitable for monitoring its anticoagulant activity.

Anti-Xa units of danaparoid have a different relationship to clinical efficacy than those of heparin and low molecular weight heparins.

Protamine is not a neutralizing agent for the activity of danaparoid.

Pregnancy, Lactation and Children: The safety of danaparoid in pregnant women and children has not been established. Animal studies have not demonstrated any teratogenic effects or placental transfer of danaparoid. The use of danaparoid in pregnancy has only been studied incidentally. Observations in pregnant women in the last trimesters have so far given no indication that the use of danaparoid during pregnancy leads to fetal abnormalities or to exacerbation of bleeding in mother or infant during delivery.

There are no data available about danaparoid secretion into breast milk. Mothers receiving danaparoid should avoid breast-feeding.

Precautions: Danaparoid should be used with caution in patients with severely impaired renal function because the main route of elimination is via the kidney. In studies with renal failure patients, it was observed that the individual pharmacokinetics of plasma anti-Xa effect is not readily predictable and may show widely different patterns of interpatient variability. The plasma anti-Xa activity may show accumulation between dialysis periods unless the predialysis bolus is suitably adjusted. The dose of danaparoid for DVT prophylaxis need not be increased for patients on the drug for long-term dialysis.

Danaparoid should be used with caution in patients undergoing epidural anesthesia. In cases of signs of impaired coagulation, it should be discontinued before considering epidural anesthesia.

In stroke patients, hemorrhagic stroke should be excluded by CT scan prior to the administration of danaparoid.

Bleeding Risk: There is a risk of systemic bleeding with danaparoid as with all antithrombotic drugs. Patients should be carefully monitored for bleeding complications. This should include regular physical examination of the patient, close observation of the surgical drain, and periodic hemoglobin determination. Bleeding complications in which hemoglobin has decreased by more than 2 g/dL, or if a transfusion of 2 or more units has been required, may be considered major.

Determination of anti-factor Xa levels in plasma is the only method available for monitoring danaparoid. Routine clotting assays such as prothrombin time (PT), activated partial thromboplastin time (APTT), kaolin cephalin clotting time, and thrombin clotting time are unsuitable because of the very flat dose response curves.

Patient Monitoring: Platelet counts should be determined prior to commencement of treatment with danaparoid and twice weekly thereafter.

Cross-reactivity in Heparin-induced Thrombocytopenia Patients: The clinical implications of cross-reactivity testing in HIT patients are unclear. Danaparoid has been used as an alternative anticoagulant in patients who had developed thrombocytopenia with heparin. In HIT patients tested for initial therapy, the cross-reactivity with danaparoid (<10%) was lower than with LMW heparins (>90%). Data on cross-reactivity development after repeated exposure to danaparoid in HIT patients is limited to 13 patients. The time course and frequency of antibody induction by danaparoid in HIT patients is unknown. Among patients who have not developed detectable cross-reactivity during danaparoid therapy, many have not developed thrombocytopenia, but others have developed life-threatening thrombocytopenia despite negative laboratory results for cross-reactivity.

Although the most certain test for HIT is a positive re-challenge platelet thrombocytopenia, the danger of inducing a serious thromboembolic event prohibits deliberate use in that manner. Reliance upon laboratory demonstration of platelet hypersensitivity with danaparoid is necessary.

Despite limitations with laboratory testing, a negative result should be obtained before beginning danaparoid treatment. The patients must be monitored with particular care, to include platelet counts at least daily. Treatment should be changed immediately if cross-reactivity develops.

The following salient points should be considered with platelet sensitivity testing in HIT patients but are not the only ones: 1. A negative platelet test in an acutely thrombocytopenic patient does not rule out a positive in vivo reaction.
2. Samples taken a few months, or later, after a thrombocytopenic reaction may test negative for cross-reactivity because the antibody has disappeared. However, commencement of danaparoid treatment may induce the production of cross-reaction antibody, with the accompanying risk of thrombocytopenia.
3. Use of a sensitizing agent that resulted in a positive HIT test in the past is not recommended even for a single occasion, because a fatal outcome with danaparoid has been reported.

Drug Interactions: In clinical studies no clinically significant interactions with other medications have been found. Danaparoid may be used together with oral anticoagulants or drugs which interfere with platelet function, such as ASA and nonsteroidal anti-inflammatory drugs, but caution remains necessary. Monitoring of anticoagulant activity of oral anticoagulants by prothrombin time and Thrombotest is unreliable within 5 hours after danaparoid administration.

Danaparoid is intended primarily for s.c. use. When administered as an i.v. bolus, it should be given separately and not mixed with other drugs.

The interaction of danaparoid with the following drugs has been studied. All effects on kinetic parameters mentioned below are considered of no clinical relevance. No clinically relevant effects have been observed on biochemical, hematological and urinary parameters.

ASA: no effects on hemostasis.
Acenocoumarol: slight decrease in anti-Xa clearance.
Cloxacillin: slight increase in elimination half-life of anti-Xa activity.
Ticarcillin: slight increase in anti-Xa clearance.
Digoxin: slight increase in anti-Xa clearance; slight decrease in digoxin area under the curve of plasma concentration versus time.
Chlorthalidone: slight decrease in anti-Xa clearance and central volume of distribution.
Pentobarbital: decrease of anti-IIa clearance.
Antipyrine: no significant effect on cytochrome P-450 system.

Adverse Effects: Most Common Reactions: The most common reported adverse events with danaparoid are related to bleeding. Table I represents all adverse events reported by 2% or more of patients receiving danaparoid and as such represents the most commonly reported adverse events. This type of analysis provides a general picture of the safety profile of danaparoid in comparison to the reference drugs including placebo.

Most serious reactions and deaths: Table II (on following page) summarizes the profile of the more serious adverse events, independent of causality, reported in 1 288 patients during treatment and follow-up for danaparoid and the control treatments according to an organ system classification. Follow-up data were available for more than two thirds of the patients. The individual adverse events reported within each organ system class are also described for danaparoid.

The most common serious adverse events considered to be probably or definitely related to danaparoid were hemorrhages or transient rashes. Three of the rashes were located around the injection site and the other 3 were generalized rashes which disappeared only after stopping treatment. In 2 other cases, generalized rashes occurred in which a relationship with danaparoid was considered to be less likely. Among the 1 288 patients treated with danaparoid in the Phase II and Phase III studies, a total of 59 deaths (4.6%) were registered. This percentage was not significantly different from heparin (4%), dextran (5.4%) or oral anticoagulants (5.1%).

Overdose: Symptoms and Treatment: In the event of serious bleeding, danaparoid should be stopped. Transfusion with fresh frozen plasma may be considered.

Dosage: In general, danaparoid is administered by s.c. injection at a dose of 750 anti-factor Xa units, twice daily up to 14 days for DVT prophylaxis.

Table I—Organ

All Adverse Events (%) Reported in 2% or More of Patients Receiving Orgaran Independent of Causality

Patient Population	Adverse Event	Org 10 172	Placebo	Heparin	Dextran	Coumarin
Operated Patients		**n=1 083**	**n=206**	**n=464**	**n=146**	**n=138**
	Bruise	29.0	21.4	48.5	0.0	0.7
	Hematoma	12.0	1.9	16.4	11.6	0.0
	Hemorrhage NOS	12.3	1.9	21.3	1.4	1.4
	Urinary tract infection	5.4	2.4	6.0	3.4	13.0
	Injection site pain	16.1	11.7	14.4	—	—
	Anemia	2.4	3.4	3.2	0.7	0.7
	Hematuria	3.3	1.0	5.4	0.7	0.7
	Urinary tract bleed microscopic	2.2	0.0	5.2	0.0	0.0
	Peripheral edema	2.5	0.0	1.1	2.1	5.8
	Infection	4.2	1.9	9.1	2.1	4.3
Nonoperated Patients		**n=154**	**n=38**	**n=26**	**not reported**	**not reported**
	Bruise	27.9	0.0	73.1	n.r	n.r
	Urinary tract infection	9.1	2.6	19.2	n.r	n.r
	Urine abnormal	17.5	26.3	0.0	n.r	n.r
	Atrial fibrillation	3.2	0.0	0.0	n.r	n.r
	Unconscious partial	2.6	2.6	0.0	n.r	n.r
	Urine incontinence	2.6	2.6	0.0	n.r	n.r
	Anemia	2.6	0.0	0.0	n.r	n.r
	Pneumonia	2.6	0.0	0.0	n.r	n.r
	Hematoma	2.6	0.0	7.7	n.r	n.r
	Injection site pain	7.1	0.0	0.0	n.r	n.r
	Hematuria	5.2	2.6	7.7	n.r	n.r
Miscellaneous		**n=51**	**n=23**	**n=12**	**n=1**	**n.r**
	Hematoma	2.0	0.0	0.0	0.0	n.r
	Hemorrhage NOS	7.8	0.0	0.0	0.0	n.r
	Hematuria	70.6	56.5	0.0	0.0	n.r
	Involuntary muscle contractions	2.0	0.0	0.0	0.0	n.r
	Tremor	2.0	0.0	0.0	0.0	n.r
	Reduced arterial blood pressure	2.0	0.0	0.0	0.0	n.r
	Marked restlessness	2.0	0.0	0.0	0.0	n.r
	Apnea	2.0	0.0	0.0	0.0	n.r
	Anemia	2.0	0.0	0.0	0.0	n.r
	Urinary tract bleeding	3.9	0.0	0.0	0.0	n.r
	Fatigue	2.0	0.0	0.0	0.0	n.r

Table II—Orgaran

Incidence (%) of Adverse Events Possibly or Probably Related to Orgaran

Adverse Event	Incidence (%)
Dermatologic	
Rash	0.46%
Bullous eruption	0.08%
Musculoskeletal	
Chondrocalcinosis	0.08%
CNS	
Cerebral hemorrhage	0.08%
Gastrointestinal	
Gastrointestinal hemorrhage	0.23%
Gastric dilatation	0.08%
Duodenal ulcer	0.16%
Hepatic	
Jaundice	0.08%
Increased liver enzymes	0.08%
Respiratory	
Hemothorax	0.08%
Pulmonary infarction	0.08%
Hematologic	
Thrombocytopenia	0.08%
Hemorrhage	0.54%
Immunologic	
Allergic reaction	0.08%
Cardiovascular	
Cardiac failure	0.08%
Cerebrovascular disorder	0.16%
Angina pectoris	0.08%
Hemopericardium	0.08%
Urogenital	
Hematuria	0.08%

In surgical patients it is recommended to start prophylaxis preoperatively and to give the last preoperative dose 1 to 4 hours before surgery. In nonhemorrhagic stroke patients the first dose of danaparoid can be given as an i.v. bolus injection of up to 1 000 anti-Xa units.

Plasma anti-Xa activity is linearly related to the dose of danaparoid given. If it is necessary to monitor anticoagulant activity, and for individual dose setting, a functional anti-factor Xa activity assay using a chromogenic peptide substrate should be used. For the results of this assay danaparoid should be used to construct the standard curve.

In patients with severely impaired renal function the second and subsequent doses of danaparoid may have to be reduced. Dosage in the Elderly: Clearance of anti-factor Xa has not been shown to be markedly reduced in the elderly and the usual dosage is recommended.

Supplied: Each glass ampul of sterile, isotonic solution contains: danaparoid sodium 750 anti-Xa units. Each mL contains: danaparoid sodium 1 250 anti-XA units. Nonmedicinal ingredients: hydrochloric acid to pH 7.0, sodium chloride, sodium sulfite and water for injection. The anti-XA unit is derived from the international heparin standard in an antithrombin-III-containing buffer system. Ampuls of 0.6 mL, boxes of 10. Store at 2 to 30°C. Protect from light.

Reviewed 1997

ORIFER® .F

Hoechst Marion Roussel

Vitamins—Minerals

Prenatal Supplement

Indications: Dietary supplement in pregnancy; provides nutritional insurance against the common dietary deficiencies of pregnancy and postpartum.

Precautions: Mild gastrointestinal upset may occur in iron-sensitive patients. The formulation is contraindicated in hemochromatosis, hemosiderosis and hemolytic anemia. Folic acid may obscure pernicious anemia in that the peripheral blood picture may return to normal while neurological manifestations remain progressive.

Dosage: One tablet daily, or as prescribed.

Supplied: Each pink, biconvex, film-coated tablet contains: elemental iron 60 mg (as ferrous sulfate 163 mg), elemental calcium 125 mg (as calcium carbonate 312 mg), elemental zinc 20 mg (as zinc sulfate 49.4 mg), vitamin A acetate 1 600 IU, vitamin D (D_3) 200 IU, vitamin C 50 mg, vitamin B_1 (thiamine mononitrate) 0.75 mg, vitamin B_6 (pyridoxine hydrochloride) 9 mg, riboflavin 1 mg, niacinamide 6 mg, folic acid 0.8 mg. Nonmedicinal ingredients: FD&C red #3, hydrogenated vegetable oil (may contain oil derived from peanut), hydroxypropyl methylcellulose, magnesium stearate, microcrystalline cellulose, polyethylene glycol, polysorbate, sodium carboxymethylcellulose and titanium dioxide. Bottles of 60.

(Shown in Product Recognition Section)

ORO-CLENSE Ⓟ

Germiphene

Chlorhexidine Gluconate

Antigingivitis Oral Rinse

Pharmacology: Chlorhexidine provides antimicrobial activity during oral rinsing which is maintained between rinsings. Microbiologic sampling of plaque has shown a general reduction of both aerobic and anaerobic bacterial counts through 6 months' clinical use. Rinsing with chlorhexidine inhibits the build up and maturation of plaque by reducing certain microbes regarded as gingival pathogens, thereby reducing gingivitis. Chlorhexidine provides antimicrobial activity during rinsing and for several hours thereafter. No significant changes in bacterial sensitivity, overgrowth of potentially opportunistic organisms or other adverse changes in the oral microbial flora were observed following the use of chlorhexidine for 6 months. Three months after discontinued use, the number of bacteria in plaque had returned to pretreatment levels and sensitivity of plaque bacteria to chlorhexidine remained unchanged.

Pharmacokinetics: Studies conducted with human subjects and animals demonstrate that any ingested chlorhexidine is poorly absorbed in the gastrointestinal tract. Excretion of chlorhexidine occurred primarily through the feces (approximately 90%). Less than 1% of the chlorhexidine ingested by these subjects was excreted in the urine.

Indications: For use as part of a professional program for the treatment of moderate to severe gingivitis, and for management of associated gingival bleeding and inflammation according to the recommended dosage and frequency under supervision of a dentist. For patients having coexisting gingivitis and periodontitis, see Precautions.

Contraindications: Should not be used by persons who are known to be hypersensitive to chlorhexidine, chlorhexidine compounds or other ingredients.

Warnings: *Pregnancy:* Reproduction and fertility studies with chlorhexidine have been conducted. No evidence of impaired fertility was observed in male and female rats at doses up to 100 mg/kg/day. No evidence of harm to the fetus was observed in rats and rabbits at doses up to 300 mg/kg/day and 40 mg/kg/day, respectively. These doses are approximately 100, 300, and 40 times that which would result from a person ingesting 30 mL of 0.12% chlorhexidine/day. Reproduction and fertility studies with chlorhexidine in pregnant women have not been conducted, so the benefits of using chlorhexidine should be weighed against possible risk to the fetus.

Lactation: It is not known whether chlorhexidine is excreted in human milk. In parturition and lactation studies with rats, no evidence of impaired parturition or of toxic effects to suckling pups was observed when chlorhexidine was administered at doses over 100 times greater than ingesting the recommended daily dose for rinsing. As many drugs are excreted in human milk, caution should be exercised and the benefits of use weighed against possible risk to the infant being nursed. Children: Clinical effectiveness and safety of chlorhexidine have not been determined in children. The benefits of its use should be weighed against the possible risks.

Precautions: Chlorhexidine can cause staining of tooth surfaces, restorations, and the dorsum of the tongue in some patients especially with prolonged use and in patients who have heavier accumulations of plaque. Staining does not affect the health of oral tissues and can be removed from most tooth surfaces by professional dental prophylaxis. Discretion should be used in prescribing chlorhexidine for patients who have exposed root surfaces or anterior facial restorations with rough surfaces or margins, as stains on this area may be difficult to remove and may require restoration replacement in rare instances. If natural stains cannot be removed from these surfaces by a dental prophylaxis, patients should be excluded from treatment if the risk of permanent discoloration is unacceptable.

Use of chlorhexidine may cause an alteration in taste perception in some patients.

For patients having coexisting gingivitis and periodontitis, the absence of gingival inflammation following treatment with chlorhexidine may not be indicative of the absence of underlying periodontitis. Appropriate treatment of periodontitis is therefore indicated.

For maximum effectiveness the patients should avoid rinsing their mouths, eating or drinking for about 30 minutes after using chlorhexidine.

Adverse Effects: Common side effects occurring from the use of chlorhexidine are staining of teeth and other oral surfaces, a slight and temporary alteration in taste perception, and an increase in supra gingival calculus formation (see Precautions). Epithelial irritation and superficial desquamation of the oral mucosa have been noted in studies of children using chlorhexidine which were reversible upon discontinuation. Parotitis and inflammation of the salivary glands have been reported in some patients using chlorhexidine.

Overdose: Symptoms and Treatment: Ingestion of 30 to 60 mL of chlorhexidine by a small child may result in gastric distress, including nausea, and/or signs of alcohol intoxication. Medical attention should be sought if more than 100 mL is ingested or if signs of alcohol intoxication develop.

Dosage: Use of chlorhexidine should begin immediately following professional dental prophylaxis. Patients should be reexamined at intervals of not more than 6 months and given a thorough prophylaxis. Patient referral for periodontal consultation should be done as necessary.

Rinse with 15 mL of solution for 30 seconds, then expectorate. Use twice daily, after breakfast and before bedtime, or as prescribed. Chlorhexidine is not intended for ingestion and should be expectorated after rinsing.

Do not swallow.

Note: Wait 30 minutes after brushing with conventional toothpastes before using chlorhexidine. Do not rinse the mouth, eat or drink for 30 minutes after using chlorhexidine.

The suggested initial therapy is 3 months, at which time patients should be recalled for evaluation. At the time of the recall visit, the dental professional should: evaluate progress, remove any stain, and reinforce proper home care techniques; discontinue use of chlorhexidine if gingival inflammation and bleeding is controlled and recall the patient in 3 months to assess gingival health; continue use of chlorhexidine for an additional 3 months if gingival inflammation and bleeding persist and schedule a 3-month recall for evaluation; evaluate for evidence of epithelial irritation, desquamation and parotitis.

The generally accepted grading scheme may be of use in evaluating the severity of gingivitis (see Table I).

Table I—ORO-Clense

Loe and Silness Gingival Index (GI)

Grade	Description
1	Normal gingiva, no inflammation, no discoloration, no bleeding.
2	Mild inflammation, slight color change, mild alteration of gingival surface. No bleeding.
3	Moderate inflammation, erythema, swelling, bleeding on probing or when pressure applied.
4	Severe inflammation, severe erythema and swelling, tendency toward spontaneous hemorrhage, some ulceration.

Supplied: Each mL of a near neutral (pH range: 5 to 7), green-colored, spearmint-flavored liquid contains: chlorhexidine gluconate 0.12%. Nonmedicinal ingredients: ethanol, FD&C Blue #1, FD&C Yellow #5, flavor, glycerin, methylparaben, polysorbate 60, propylparaben, purified water, sodium cyclamate and sorbitol. White containers of 227 mL, 480 mL and 4 L. Store between 15 and 25°C.

Reviewed 1997

ORTHO® 1/35 Ⓟ
ORTHO® 0.5/35 Ⓟ
ORTHO® 10/11 Ⓟ
ORTHO® 7/7/7 Ⓟ

Janssen-Ortho

Norethindrone—Ethinyl Estradiol

Oral Contraceptive

Pharmacology: The primary mechanism of action of this product is an inhibition of ovulation. Additionally, other effects

Ortho 1/35, 0.5/35, 10/11, 7/7/7 (cont'd)

caused by the treatment (e.g., alteration of the endometrium and the thickening of the cervical mucus), appear to interfere with implantation and conception.

Indications: Conception control.

Contraindications: History of/or actual thrombophlebitis or thromboembolic disorders; history of/or actual cerebrovascular disorders; history of/or actual myocardial infarction or coronary arterial disease; active liver disease or history of/or actual benign or malignant liver tumors; known or suspected carcinoma of the breast; known or suspected estrogen-dependent neoplasia; undiagnosed abnormal vaginal bleeding; any ocular lesion arising from ophthalmic vascular disease, such as partial or complete loss of vision or defect in visual fields; when pregnancy is suspected or diagnosed.

Warnings: Predisposing Factors For Coronary Artery Disease: Cigarette smoking increases the risk of serious cardiovascular side effects and mortality. Birth control pills increase this risk, especially with increasing age. Convincing data are available to support an upper age limit of 35 years for oral contraceptive use by women who smoke.

Other women who are independently at high risk for cardiovascular disease include those with diabetes, hypertension, abnormal lipid profile, or a family history of these. Whether oral contraceptives accentuate this risk is unclear.

In low risk, non-smoking women of any age, the benefits of oral contraceptive use outweigh the possible cardiovascular risks associated with low dose formulations. Consequently, oral contraceptives may be prescribed for these women up to the age of menopause.

> Cigarette smoking increases the risk of serious adverse effects on the heart and blood vessels. This risk increases with age and becomes significant in oral contraceptive users over 35 years of age. Women should be counselled not to smoke.

Discontinue medication at the earliest manifestation of:

A. Thromboembolic and cardiovascular disorders such as: thrombophlebitis, pulmonary embolism, cerebrovascular disorders, myocardial ischemia, mesenteric thrombosis and retinal thrombosis.

B. Conditions which predispose to venous stasis and to vascular thrombosis, (e.g., immobilization after accidents or confinement to bed during long-term illness). Other non-hormonal methods of contraception should be used until regular activities are resumed. For use of oral contraceptives when surgery is contemplated, see Precautions.

C. Visual defects–partial or complete.

D. Papilledema or ophthalmic vascular lesions.

E. Severe headache of unknown etiology or worsening of pre-existing migraine headache.

Precautions: Physical Examination and Follow-up: Before oral contraceptives are used, a thorough history and physical examination should be performed, including a blood pressure determination. Breasts, liver, extremities and pelvic organs should be examined. A Papanicolaou smear should be taken if the patient has been sexually active.

The first follow-up visit should be 3 months after oral contraceptives are prescribed. Thereafter, examinations should be performed at least once a year or more frequently if indicated. At each annual visit, examination should include those procedures that were done at the initial visit as outlined above or per recommendations of the Canadian Workshop on Screening for Cancer of the Cervix. Their suggestion was that, for women who had 2 consecutive negative Pap smears, screening could be continued every 3 years up to the age of 69.

Pregnancy: Oral contraceptives should not be taken by pregnant women. However, if conception accidentally occurs while taking the pill, there is no conclusive evidence that the estrogen and progestin contained in the oral contraceptive will damage the developing child.

Lactation: In breastfeeding women, the use of oral contraceptives results in the hormonal components being excreted in breast milk and may reduce its quantity and quality. If the use of oral contraceptives is initiated after the establishment of lactation, there does not appear to be any effect on the quantity and quality of the milk. There is no evidence that low dose oral contraceptives are harmful to the nursing infant.

Hepatic Function: Patients who have had jaundice, including a history of cholestatic jaundice during pregnancy, should be given oral contraceptives with great care and under close observation.

> The development of severe generalized pruritus or icterus requires that the medication be withdrawn until the problem is resolved.
>
> If a patient develops jaundice that proves to be cholestatic in type, the use of oral contraceptives should not be resumed. In patients taking oral contraceptives, changes in the composition of the bile may occur and an increased incidence of gallstones has been reported.
>
> Hepatic nodules (adenoma and focal nodular hyperplasia) have been reported, particularly in long-term users of oral contraceptives. Although these lesions are extremely rare, they have caused fatal intra-abdominal hemorrhage and should be considered in women presenting abdominal mass, acute abdominal pain or evidence of intra-abdominal bleeding.
>
> Hypertension: Patients with essential hypertension whose blood pressure is well-controlled may be given oral contraceptives but only under close supervision. If a significant elevation of blood pressure in previously normotensive or hypertensive subjects occurs at any time during the administration of the drug, cessation of medication is necessary.
>
> Migraine and Headache: The onset or exacerbation of migraine or the development of headache of a new pattern, that is recurrent, persistent or severe, requires discontinuation of oral contraceptives and evaluation of the cause.
>
> Diabetes: Current low dose oral contraceptives exert minimal impact on glucose metabolism. Diabetic patients, or those with a family history of diabetes, should be observed closely to detect any worsening of carbohydrate metabolism. Patients predisposed to diabetes who can be kept under close supervision may be given oral contraceptives. Young diabetic patients whose disease is of recent origin, well-controlled, and not associated with hypertension or other signs of vascular disease such as ocular fundal changes, should be monitored more frequently while using oral contraceptives.
>
> Ocular Disease: Patients who are pregnant or are taking oral contraceptives may experience corneal edema that may cause visual disturbances and changes in tolerance to contact lenses, especially of the rigid type. Soft contact lenses usually do not cause disturbances. If visual changes or alterations in tolerance to contact lenses occur, temporary or permanent cessation of wear may be advised.

Breasts: Increasing age and a strong family history are the most significant risk factors for the development of breast cancer. Other established risk factors include obesity, nulliparity and late age at first full-term pregnancy. The identified groups of women that may be at increased risk of developing breast cancer before menopause are long-term users of oral contraceptives (more than 8 years) and starters at early age. In a few women, the use of oral contraceptives may accelerate the growth of an existing but undiagnosed breast cancer. Since any potential increased risk related to oral contraceptive use is small, there is no reason to change prescribing habits at present.

Women receiving oral contraceptives should be instructed in self-examination of their breasts. Their physicians should be notified whenever any masses are detected. A yearly clinical breast examination is also recommended because, if a breast cancer should develop, estrogen-containing drugs may cause a rapid progression.

Vaginal Bleeding: Persistent irregular vaginal bleeding requires assessment to exclude underlying pathology.

Fibroids: Patients with fibroids (leiomyomata) should be carefully observed. Sudden enlargement, pain or tenderness requires discontinuation of the use of oral contraceptives.

Emotional Disorders: Patients with a history of emotional disturbances, especially the depressive type, may be more prone to have a recurrence of depression while taking oral contraceptives. In cases of a serious recurrence, a trial of an alternate method of contraception should be made which may help to clarify the possible relationship. Women with premenstrual syndrome (PMS) may have a varied response to oral contraceptives, ranging from symptomatic improvement to worsening of the condition.

Laboratory Tests: Results of laboratory tests should be interpreted in light of the fact that the patient is on oral contraceptives. The following laboratory tests are modified.

Table I—Ortho 1/35, 0.5/35, 10/11, 7/7/7 Tablets

Drugs Which May Decrease the Efficacy of Oral Contraceptives

Class of Compound	Drug	Proposed Mechanism	Suggested Management
Anticonvulsants	Carbamazepine Ethosuximide Phenobarbital Phenytoin Primidone	Induction of hepatic microsomal enzymes. Rapid metabolism of estrogen and increased binding of progestin and ethinyl estradiol to SHBG.	Use higher dose OCs (50 μg ethinyl estradiol), another drug or another method.
Antibiotics	Ampicillin Cotrimoxazole Penicillin	Enterohepatic circulation disturbance, intestinal hurry.	For short course, use additional method or use another drug. For long course, use another method.
	Rifampin	Increased metabolism of progestins. Suspected acceleration of estrogen metabolism.	Use another method.
	Chloramphenicol Metronidazole Neomycin Nitrofurantoin Sulfonamides Tetracyclines	Induction of hepatic microsomal enzymes. Also disturbance of enterohepatic circulation.	For short course, use additional method or use another drug. For long course, use another method.
	Troleandomycin	May retard metabolism of OCs, increasing the risk of cholestatic jaundice.	
Antifungal	Griseofulvin	Stimulation of hepatic metabolism of contraceptive steroids may occur.	Use another method.
Cholesterol-lowering Agents	Clofibrate	Reduces elevated serum triglycerides and cholesterol; this reduces OC efficacy.	Use another method.
Sedatives and Hypnotics	Benzodiazepines Barbiturates Chloral hydrate Glutethimide Meprobamate	Induction of hepatic microsomal enzymes.	For short course, use additional method or another drug. For long course, use another method or higher dose OCs.
Antacids		Decreased intestinal absorption of progestins.	Dose 2 hours apart.
Other Drugs	Phenylbutazone Antihistamines Analgesics Antimigraine preparations Vitamin E	Reduced OC efficacy has been reported. Remains to be confirmed.	

A. Liver Function Tests: Bromsulphthalein Retention Test (BSP): moderate increase; AST and GGT: minor increase; alkaline phosphatase: variable increase; serum bilirubin: increased, particularly in conditions predisposing to or associated with hyperbilirubinemia.
B. Coagulation Tests: Factors II, VII, IX, X, XII and XIII: increased; Factor VIII: mild increase; platelet aggregation and adhesiveness: mild increase in response to common aggregating agents; fibrinogen: increased; plasminogen: mild increase; antithrombin III: mild decrease; prothrombin time: increased.
C. Thyroid Function Tests: Protein-bound Iodine (PBI): increased; Total Serum Thyroxine (T_4): increased; Thyroid Stimulating Hormone (TSH): unchanged.
D. Adrenocortical Function Tests: plasma cortisol: increased.
E. Miscellaneous Tests: serum folate: occasionally decreased; glucose tolerance test: variable increase with return to normal after 6 to 12 months; insulin response: mild to moderate increase; c-Peptide response: mild to moderate increase.
Tissue Specimens: Pathologists should be advised of oral contraceptive therapy when specimens obtained from surgical procedures and Pap smears are submitted for examination.
Return to Fertility: After discontinuing oral contraceptive therapy, the patient should delay pregnancy until at least 1 spontaneous menstrual cycle has occurred in order to date the pregnancy. An alternative contraceptive method should be used during this time.
Amenorrhea: Women having a history of oligomenorrhea, secondary amenorrhea, or irregular cycles may remain anovulatory or become amenorrheic following discontinuation of estrogen-progestin combination therapy. Amenorrhea, especially if associated with breast secretion, that continues for 6 months or more after withdrawal, warrants a careful assessment of hypothalamic-pituitary function.
Thromboembolic Complications—Post-surgery: There is an increased risk of thromboembolic complications in oral contraceptive users after major surgery. If feasible, oral contraceptives should be discontinued and an alternative method substituted at least 1 month prior to **major** elective surgery. Oral contraceptive use should not be resumed until the first menstrual period after hospital discharge following surgery.
Drug Interactions: The concurrent administration of oral contraceptives with other drugs may result in an altered response to either agent (see Table I on previous page and Table II). Reduced effectiveness of the oral contraceptive, should it occur, is more likely with the low dose formulations. It is important to ascertain all drugs that a patient is taking, both prescription and nonprescription, before oral contraceptives are prescribed.

Refer to Oral Contraceptives 1994 (Chapter 8), Health Canada, for possible drug interactions with OCs.

Non-contraceptive Benefits of Oral Contraceptives: Several health advantages other than contraception have been reported.
1. Combination oral contraceptives reduce the incidence of cancer of the endometrium and ovaries.
2. Oral contraceptives reduce the likelihood of developing benign breast disease and, as a result, decrease the incidence of breast biopsies.
3. Oral contraceptives reduce the likelihood of development of functional ovarian cysts.
4. Pill-users have less menstrual blood loss and have more regular cycles, thereby reducing the chance of developing iron-deficiency anemia.
5. The use of oral contraceptives may decrease the severity of dysmenorrhea and premenstrual syndrome, and may improve acne vulgaris, hirsutism, and other androgen-mediated disorders.
6. Oral contraceptives decrease the incidence of acute pelvic inflammatory disease and, thereby, reduce as well the incidence of ectopic pregnancy.
7. Oral contraceptives have potential beneficial effects on endometriosis.

> Oral contraceptives **do not protect** against sexually transmitted diseases (STDs) including HIV/AIDS. For protection against STDs, it is advisable to use latex condoms **in combination with** oral contraceptives.

Adverse Effects: An increased risk of the following serious adverse reactions has been associated with the use of oral contraceptives: thrombophlebitis; pulmonary embolism; mesenteric thrombosis; neuro-ocular lesions (e.g., retinal thrombosis); myocardial infarction; cerebral thrombosis; cerebral hemorrhage; hypertension; benign hepatic tumors; gallbladder disease.

Table II—Ortho 1/35, 0.5/35, 10/11, 7/7/7 Tablets

Modification of Other Drug Action by Oral Contraceptives

Class of Compound	Drug	Modification of Drug Action	Suggested Management
Alcohol		Possible increased levels of ethanol or acetaldehyde.	Use with caution.
Alpha-II Adrenoreceptor Agents	Clonidine	Sedation effect increased.	Use with caution.
Anticoagulants	All	OCs increase clotting factors, decrease efficacy. However, OCs may potentiate action in some patients.	Use another method.
Anticonvulsants	All	Fluid retention may increase risk of seizures.	Use another method.
Antidiabetic Drugs	Oral hypoglycemics and insulin	OCs may impair glucose tolerance and increase blood glucose.	Use low dose estrogen and progestin OC or another method. Monitor blood glucose.
Antihypertensive Agents	Guanethidine and methyldopa	Estrogen component causes sodium retention, progestin has no effect.	Use low dose estrogen OC or use another method.
	Beta-blockers	Increased drug effect (decreased metabolism).	Adjust dose of drug if necessary. Monitor cardiovascular status.
Antipyretics	Acetaminophen	Increased metabolism and renal clearance.	Dose of drug may have to be increased.
	Antipyrine	Impaired metabolism.	Decrease dose of drug.
	ASA	Effects of ASA may be decreased by the short-term use of OCs.	Patients on chronic ASA therapy may require an increase in ASA dosage.
Aminocaproic Acid		Theoretically, a hypercoagulable state may occur because OCs augment clotting factors.	Avoid concomitant use.
Betamimetic Agents	Isoproterenol	Estrogen causes decreased response to these drugs.	Adjust dose of drug as necessary. Discontinuing OCs can result in excessive drug activity.
Caffeine		The actions of caffeine may be enhanced as OCs may impair the hepatic metabolism of caffeine.	Use with caution.
Cholesterol-lowering Agents	Clofibrate	Their action may be antagonized by OCs. OCs may also increase metabolism of clofibrate.	May need to increase dose of clofibrate.
Corticosteroids	Prednisone	Markedly increased serum levels.	Possible need for decrease in dose.
Cyclosporine		May lead to an increase in cyclosporine levels and hepatotoxicity.	Monitor hepatic function. The cyclosporine dose may have to be decreased.
Folic Acid		OCs have been reported to impair folate metabolism.	May need to increase dietary intake or supplement.
Meperidine		Possible increased analgesia and CNS depression due to decreased metabolism of meperidine.	Use combination with caution.
Phenothiazine Tranquilizers	All phenothiazines, reserpine and similar drugs	Estrogen potentiates the hyperprolactinemia effect of these drugs.	Use other drugs or lower dose OCs. If galactorrhea or hyperprolactinemia occurs, use other method.
Sedatives and Hypnotics	Chlordiazepoxide Lorazepam Oxazepam Diazepam	Increased effect (increased metabolism).	Use with caution.
Theophylline	All	Decreased oxidation, leading to possible toxicity.	Use with caution. Monitor theophylline levels.
Tricyclic Antidepressants	Clomipramine (possibly others)	Increased side effects; i.e., depression.	Use with caution.
Vitamin B_{12}		OCs have been reported to reduce serum levels of Vitamin B_{12}.	May need to increase dietary intake or supplement.

The following adverse reactions also have been reported in patients receiving oral contraceptives: nausea and vomiting, usually the most common adverse reaction, occurs in approximately 10% or less of patients during the first cycle. Other reactions, as a general rule, are seen less frequently or only occasionally, as follows: gastrointestinal symptoms (such as abdominal cramps and bloating); breakthrough bleeding; spotting; change in menstrual flow; dysmenorrhea; amenorrhea during and after treatment; temporary infertility after discontinuance of treatment; edema; chloasma or melasma which may persist; breast changes: tenderness, enlargement, and secretion; change in weight (increase or decrease); endocervical hyperplasias; possible diminution in lactation when given immediately postpartum; cholestatic jaundice; migraine; increase in size of uterine leiomyomata; rash (allergic); mental depression; reduced tolerance to carbohydrates; vaginal candidiasis; premenstrual-like syndrome; intolerance to contact lenses; change in corneal curvature (steepening); cataracts; optic neuritis; retinal thrombosis; changes in libido; chorea; changes in appetite; cystitis-like syndrome; rhinitis; headache; nervousness; dizziness; hirsutism; loss of scalp hair; erythema multiforme; erythema nodosum; hemorrhagic eruption; vaginitis; porphyria; impaired renal function; Raynaud's phenomenon; auditory disturbances; hemolytic uremic syndrome; pancreatitis.

Overdose: Symptoms and Treatment: In case of overdosage or accidental ingestion by children, the physician should observe the patient closely although generally no treatment is required. Gastric lavage may be utilized if considered necessary.

Ortho 1/35, 0.5/35, 10/11, 7/7/7 (cont'd)

Dosage: Information for the Patient on How to Take the Birth Control Pill:

1. **Read these directions:**
   - before you start taking your pills, and
   - any time you are not sure what to do.
2. **Look at your pill pack** to see if it has 21 or 28 pills:
   - 21-Pill Pack: 21 active pills (with hormones) taken daily for 3 weeks, and then take no pills for 1 week

   or
   - 28-Pill Pack: 21 active pills (with hormones) taken daily for 3 weeks, and then 7 "reminder" pills (no hormones) taken daily for 1 week.

Also check the pill pack for instructions on (1) where to start and (2) directions to take pills (see package insert for illustrations).

3. You may wish to use a second method of birth control (e.g., latex condoms and spermicidal foam or gel) for the first 7 days of the first cycle of pill use. This will provide a back-up in case pills are forgotten while you are getting used to taking them.
4. **When receiving any medical treatment, be sure to tell your doctor that you are using birth control pills.**
5. **Many women have spotting or light bleeding or may feel sick to their stomach during the first 3 months on the pill.** If you do feel sick, do not stop taking the pill. The problem will usually go away. If it does not go away, check with your doctor or clinic.
6. **Missing pills also can cause some spotting or light bleeding,** even if you make up the missed pills. You also could feel a little sick to your stomach on the days you take 2 pills to make up for missed pills.
7. **If you miss pills at any time, you could get pregnant. The greatest risks for pregnancy are:**
   - when you start a pack late, or
   - when you miss pills at the beginning or at the very end of the pack.
8. **Always be sure you have ready:**
   - **another kind of birth control** (such as latex condoms and spermicidal foam or gel) to use as a back-up in case you miss pills, and
   - **an extra, full pack of pills.**
9. **If you experience vomiting or diarrhea, or if you take certain medicines,** such as antibiotics, your pills may not work as well. Use a back-up method, such as latex condoms and spermicidal foam or gel, until you can check with your doctor or clinic.
10. **If you forget more than 1 pill 2 months in a row,** talk to your doctor or clinic about how to make pill-taking easier or about using another method of birth control.
11. **If your questions are not answered here, call your doctor or clinic.**

When to start the first pack of pills: Be sure to read these instructions:

- before you start taking your pills, and
- any time you are not sure what to do.

Decide with your doctor or clinic what is the best day for you to start taking your first pack of pills. Your pills may be either a 21-day or a 28-day type.

A. 21-Day Combination: With this type of birth control pill, you are 21 days on pills with 7 days off pills. You must not be off the pills for more than 7 days in a row.

1. **The first day of your menstrual period (bleeding) is Day 1 of your cycle.** The pills may be started up to Day 6 of your cycle. Your starting day will be chosen in discussion with your doctor. You will **always** begin taking your pill on this day of the week. Your doctor may advise you to start taking the pills on Day 1, on Day 5, or on the first Sunday after your period begins. If your period starts on Sunday, start that same day.
2. Take 1 pill at approximately the same time every day for 21 days; **then take no pills for 7 days.** Start a new pack on the 8th day. You will probably have a period during the 7 days off the pill. (This bleeding may be lighter and shorter than your usual period.)

B. 28-Day Combination: With this type of birth control pill, you take 21 pills which contain hormones and 7 pills which contain no hormones.

1. **The first day of your menstrual period (bleeding) is Day 1 of your cycle.** The pills may be started up to Day 6 of your cycle. Your starting day will be chosen in discussion with your doctor. You will **always** begin taking your pill on this day of the week. Your doctor may advise you to start taking the pills on Day 1, on Day 5, or on the first Sunday after your period begins. If your period starts on Sunday, start that same day.
2. Take 1 pill at approximately the same time every day for 28 days. Begin a new pack the next day, **not missing any days on the pills.** Your period should occur during the last 7 days of using that pill pack.

Instructions for Using Your DIALPAK Dispenser: Follow these instructions carefully (see package insert for illustrations):

Ortho 1/35: 21-Day Regimen: Your starting day will be chosen in discussion with your doctor. You should **always** begin taking your tablets on this day of the week. To set the package to the day you and your physician selected, insert a coin into the middle slot and turn the inner wheel counterclockwise until that day appears in the window. The example shown is for a **Sunday** start. Your first peach tablet is below the "V" notch as shown. Ensure that the tab marked "Lift Out" is set over this tablet. Break off the tab and begin tablet taking. To take your second and all subsequent tablets, turn the clear outer cover clockwise to the next available tablet. Take a tablet a day, for 21 days, completing all peach tablets. After you have taken all of your tablets wait 7 days and begin your next package on your chosen starting day whether you have finished menstruating or not. Always remember to set the starting day of each new package to the day chosen by you and your doctor.

Your first pill of each package is always under the "V" notch.

Ortho 1/35: 28-Day Regimen: Always complete the peach tablets before taking the green tablets.

Your starting day will be chosen in discussion with your doctor. You should **always** begin taking your tablets on this day of the week. To set the package to the day you and your physician selected, insert a coin into the middle slot and turn the inner wheel counterclockwise until that day appears in the window. The example shown is for a **Sunday** start. Your first peach tablet is immediately to the right of the green tablets and below the "V" notch as shown. Ensure that the tab marked "Lift Out" is set over this peach tablet. Break off the tab and begin tablet taking. To take your second and all subsequent tablets, turn the clear outer cover clockwise to the next available tablet. Take a tablet a day, every day, first completing all 21 peach tablets, and finally the 7 green tablets. After you have taken all of your tablets, begin your next package the very next day on your chosen starting day, whether you have finished menstruating or not. Always remember to set the starting day of each new package to the day chosen by you and your doctor.

Your first pill of each package is always under the "V" notch.

Ortho 0.5/35: 21-Day Regimen: Your starting day will be chosen in discussion with your doctor. You should **always** begin taking your tablets on this day of the week. To set the package to the day you and your physician selected, insert a coin into the middle slot and turn the inner wheel counterclockwise until that day appears in the window. The example shown is for a **Sunday** start. Your first white tablet is below the "V" notch as shown. Ensure that the tab marked "Lift Out" is set over this tablet. Break off the tab and begin tablet taking. To take your second and all subsequent tablets, turn the clear outer cover clockwise to the next available tablet. Take a tablet a day, for 21 days, completing all white tablets. After you have taken all of your tablets, wait 7 days and begin your next package on your chosen starting day whether you have finished menstruating or not. Always remember to set the starting day of each new package to the day chosen by you and your doctor.

Your first pill of each package is always under the "V" notch.

Ortho 0.5/35: 28-Day Regimen: Always complete the white tablets before taking the green tablets.

Your starting day will be chosen in discussion with your doctor. You should **always** begin taking your tablets on this day of the week. To set the package to the day you and your physician selected, insert a coin into the middle slot and turn the inner wheel counterclockwise until that day appears in the window. The example shown is for a **Sunday** start. Your first white tablet is immediately to the right of the green tablets and below the "V" notch as shown. Ensure that the tab marked "Lift Out" is set over this white tablet. Break off the tab and begin tablet taking. To take your second and all subsequent tablets, turn the clear outer cover clockwise to the next available tablet. Take a tablet a day, every day, first completing all 21 white tablets, and finally the 7 green tablets. After you have taken all of your tablets, begin your next package the very next day on your chosen starting day, whether you have finished menstruating or not. Always remember to set the starting day of each new package to the day chosen by you and your doctor.

Your first pill of each package is always under the "V" notch.

Ortho 10/11: 21-Day Regimen: Always complete white tablets before taking the peach tablets.

Your starting day will be chosen in discussion with your doctor. You should **always** begin taking your tablets on this day of the week. To set the package to the day you and your physician selected, insert a coin into the middle slot and turn the inner wheel counterclockwise until that day appears in the window. The example shown is for a **Sunday** start. Your first white tablet is immediately to the right of the peach tablets and below the "V" notch as shown. Ensure that the tab marked "Lift Out" is set over this white tablet. Break off the tab and begin tablet taking. To take your second and all subsequent tablets, turn the clear outer cover clockwise to the next available tablet. Take 1 tablet every day for 21 days, first completing all 10 white tablets, then all 11 peach tablets. After you have taken all of your tablets, wait 7 days and begin your next package on your chosen starting day, whether you have finished menstruating or not. Always remember to set the starting day of each new package to the day chosen by you and your doctor.

Your first pill of each package is always under the "V" notch.

Ortho 10/11: 28-Day Regimen: Always complete the white and peach tablets before taking the green tablets.

Your starting day will be chosen in discussion with your doctor. You should **always** begin taking your tablets on this day of the week. To set the package to the day you and your physician selected, insert a coin into the middle slot and turn the inner wheel counterclockwise until that day appears in the window. The example shown is for a **Sunday** start. Your first white tablet is immediately to the right of the green tablets and below the "V" notch as shown. Ensure that the tab marked "Lift Out" is set over this white tablet. Break off the tab and begin tablet taking. To take your second and all subsequent tablets, turn the clear outer cover clockwise to the next available tablet. Take 1 tablet every day for 28 days, first completing all 10 white tablets, then all 11 peach tablets and finally the 7 green tablets. After you have taken all of your tablets, begin your next package the very next day, on your chosen starting day, whether you have finished menstruating or not. Always remember to set the starting day of each new package to the day chosen by you and your doctor.

Your first pill of each package is always under the "V" notch.

Ortho 7/7/7: 21-Day Regimen: Always complete white and light peach tablets before taking the dark peach tablets.

Your starting day will be chosen in discussion with your doctor. You should **always** begin taking your tablets on this day of the week. To set the package to the day you and your physician selected, insert a coin into the middle slot and turn the inner wheel counterclockwise until that day appears in the window. The example shown is for a **Sunday** start. Your first white tablet is immediately to the right of the dark peach tablets and below the "V" notch as shown. Ensure that the tab marked "Lift Out" is set over this white tablet. Break off the tab and begin tablet taking. To take your second and all subsequent tablets, turn the clear outer cover clockwise to the next available tablet. Take 1 tablet every day for 21 days, first completing all 7 white tablets, then all 7 light peach tablets, then all 7 dark peach tablets. After you have taken all of your tablets, wait 7 days and begin your next package on your chosen starting day, whether you have finished menstruating or not. Always remember to set the starting day of each new package to the day chosen by you and your doctor.

Your first pill of each package is always under the "V" notch.

Ortho 7/7/7: 28-Day Regimen: Always complete the white, light peach and dark peach tablets before taking the green tablets.

Your starting day will be chosen in discussion with your doctor. You should **always** begin taking your tablets on this day of the week. To set the package to the day you and your physician selected, insert a coin into the middle slot and turn the inner wheel counterclockwise until that day appears in the window. The example shown is for a **Sunday** start. Your first white tablet is immediately to the right of the green tablets and below the "V" notch as shown. Ensure that the tab marked "Lift Out" is set over this white tablet. Break off the tab and begin tablet taking. To take your second and all subsequent tablets, turn the clear outer cover clockwise to the next available tablet. Take 1 tablet every day for 28 days, first completing all 7 white tablets, then all 7 light peach tablets, then all 7 dark peach tablets and finally the 7 green tablets. After you have taken all of your tablets, begin your next package the very next day, on your chosen starting day, whether you have finished menstruating or not. Always remember to set the starting day of each new package to the day chosen by you and your doctor.

Your first pill of each package is always under the "V" notch.

What to do during the month:

1. **Take a pill at approximately the same time every day until the pack is empty.**
   - Try to associate taking your pill with some regular activity like eating a meal or going to bed.
   - Do not skip pills even if you have bleeding between monthly periods or feel sick to your stomach (nausea).
   - Do not skip pills even if you do not have sex very often.
2. **When you finish a pack:**
   - **21 pills: Wait 7 days** to start the next pack. You will have your period during that week.
   - **28 pills:** Start the next pack **on the next day.** Take 1 pill every day. Do not wait any days between packs.

What to do if you miss pills: Table III outlines the actions you should take if you miss 1 or more of your birth control pills. Match the number of pills missed with the appropriate starting time for your type of pill pack.

Table III—Ortho 1/35, 0.5/35, 10/11, 7/7/7 Tablets

What to Do if You Miss Pills

Sunday Start	Other Than Sunday Start
Miss 1 pill	**Miss 1 pill**
Take it as soon as you remember, and take the next pill at the usual time. This means that you might take 2 pills in one day.	Take it as soon as you remember, and take the next pill at the usual time. This means that you might take 2 pills in one day.
Miss 2 pills in a row	**Miss 2 pills in a row**
First 2 Weeks: 1. Take 2 pills the day you remember and 2 pills the next day. 2. Then take 1 pill a day until you finish the pack. 3. Use a back-up method of birth control if you have sex in the 7 days after you miss the pills.	**First 2 Weeks:** 1. Take 2 pills the day you remember and 2 pills the next day. 2. Then take 1 pill a day until you finish the pack. 3. Use a back-up method of birth control if you have sex in the 7 days after you miss the pills.
Third Week: 1. Keep taking 1 pill a day until Sunday. 2. On Sunday, safely discard the rest of the pack and start a new pack that day. 3. Use a back-up method of birth control if you have sex in the 7 days after you miss the pills. 4. You may not have a period this month. **If you miss 2 periods in a row, call your doctor or clinic.**	**Third Week:** 1. Safely dispose of the rest of the pill pack and start a new pack that same day. 2. Use a back-up method of birth control if you have sex in the 7 days after you miss the pills. 3. You may not have a period this month. **If you miss 2 periods in a row, call your doctor or clinic.**
Miss 3 or more pills in a row	**Miss 3 or more pills in a row**
Anytime in the Cycle: 1. Keep taking 1 pill a day until Sunday. 2. On Sunday, safely discard the rest of the pack and start a new pack that day. 3. Use a back-up method of birth control if you have sex in the 7 days after you miss the pills. 4. You may not have a period this month. **If you miss 2 periods in a row, call your doctor or clinic.**	**Anytime in the Cycle:** 1. Safely dispose of the rest of the pill pack and start a new pack that same day. 2. Use a back-up method of birth control if you have sex in the 7 days after you miss the pills. 3. You may not have a period this month. **If you miss 2 periods in a row, call your doctor or clinic.**

Note: 28-Day Pack: If you forget any of the 7 "reminder" pills (without hormones) in Week 4, just safely dispose of the pills you missed. Then keep taking 1 pill each day until the pack is empty. You do not need to use a back-up method.

Always be sure you have on hand:

- a back-up method of birth control (such as latex condoms and spermicidal foam or gel) in case you miss pills, and
- an extra, full pack of pills.

If you forget more than 1 pill 2 months in a row, talk to your doctor or clinic. Talk about ways to make pill-taking easier or about using another method of birth control.

Information for the Patient: See Blue Section—Information for the Patient "Oral Contraceptives".

Supplied: Ortho 1/35: Each peach tablet, unscored with ORTHO 135 engraved on each side, contains: norethindrone 1 mg and ethinyl estradiol 35 µg. Nonmedicinal ingredients: FD&C Yellow No. 6, lactose, magnesium stearate, polyvinylpyrrolidone and starch. In the 28-day regimen the green tablets, embossed on each side with ORTHO, contain inert ingredients. Nonmedicinal ingredients: D&C Yellow No. 10 Lake, FD&C Blue No. 2 Lake, lactose, magnesium stearate, microcrystalline cellulose and starch. Available in 21-day or 28-day VARIDATE DIALPAK Tablet Dispenser Units.

Ortho 0.5/35: Each white tablet, unscored with ORTHO 535 engraved on each side, contains: norethindrone 0.5 mg and ethinyl estradiol 35 µg. Nonmedicinal ingredients: lactose, magnesium stearate, polyvinylpyrrolidone and starch. In the 28-day regimen the green tablets, embossed on each side with ORTHO, contain inert ingredients. Nonmedicinal ingredients: D&C Yellow No. 10 Lake, FD&C Blue No. 2 Lake, lactose, magnesium stearate, microcrystalline cellulose and starch. Available in 21-day or 28-day VARIDATE DIALPAK Tablet Dispenser Units.

Ortho 10/11: Each white tablet, unscored with ORTHO 535 engraved on each side, contains: norethindrone 0.5 mg and ethinyl estradiol 35 µg. Nonmedicinal ingredients: lactose, magnesium stearate, polyvinylpyrrolidone and starch. Each peach tablet, embossed on each side with ORTHO 135, contains: norethindrone 1 mg and ethinyl estradiol 35 µg. Nonmedicinal ingredients: FD&C Yellow No. 6, lactose, magnesium stearate, polyvinylpyrrolidone and starch. In the 28-day regimen the green tablets, embossed on each side with ORTHO, contain inert ingredients. Nonmedicinal ingredients: D&C Yellow No. 10 Lake, FD&C Blue No. 2 Lake, lactose, magnesium stearate, microcrystalline cellulose and starch. Available in 21-day or 28-day VARIDATE DIALPAK Tablet Dispenser Units.

Ortho 7/7/7: Each white tablet, unscored with ORTHO 535 engraved on each side, contains: norethindrone 0.5 mg and ethinyl estradiol 35 µg. Each light peach tablet, embossed on each side with ORTHO 735, contains: norethindrone 0.75 mg and ethinyl estradiol 35 µg. Each dark peach tablet, embossed on each side with ORTHO 135, contains: norethindrone 1 mg and ethinyl estradiol 35 µg. Nonmedicinal ingredients: The white, light peach and dark peach tablets contain lactose, magnesium stearate, polyvinylpyrrolidone and starch. The light and dark peach tablets also contain FD&C Yellow No. 6. In the 28-day regimen the green tablets contain inert ingredients. Nonmedicinal ingredients: D&C Yellow No. 10 Lake, FD&C Blue No. 2 Lake, lactose magnesium stearate, microcrystalline cellulose and starch. Available in 21-day or 28-day VARIDATE DIALPAK Tablet Dispenser Units.

Store between 15 and 30°C. Leave contents in protective packaging until time of use.

(Shown in Product Recognition Section)

Reviewed 1999

ORTHO-CEPT® Ⓟ

Janssen-Ortho

Desogestrel—Ethinyl Estradiol

Oral Contraceptive

Pharmacology: The primary mechanism of action of Ortho-Cept tablets is an inhibition of ovulation. Additionally, other effects caused by the treatment (e.g., alteration of the endometrium and the thickening of the cervical mucus), appear to interfere with implantation and conception.

Indications: Conception control.

Contraindications: History of/or actual thrombophlebitis or thromboembolic disorders. History of/or actual cerebrovascular disorders. History of/or actual myocardial infarction or coronary arterial disease. Active liver disease or history of/or actual benign or malignant liver tumors. Known or suspected carcinoma of the breast. Known or suspected estrogen-dependent neoplasia. Undiagnosed abnormal vaginal bleeding. Any ocular lesion arising from ophthalmic vascular disease, such as partial or complete loss of vision or defect in visual fields. When pregnancy is suspected or diagnosed.

Warnings: Predisposing Factors for Coronary Artery Disease: Cigarette smoking increases the risk of serious cardiovascular side effects and mortality. Birth control pills increase this risk, especially with increasing age. Convincing data are available to support an upper age limit of 35 years for oral contraceptive use by women who smoke.

Other women who are independently at high risk for cardiovascular disease include those with diabetes, hypertension, abnormal lipid profile, or a family history of these. Whether oral contraceptives accentuate this risk is unclear.

In low-risk, nonsmoking women of any age, the benefits of oral contraceptive use outweigh the possible cardiovascular risks associated with low dose formulations. Consequently, oral contraceptives may be prescribed for these women up to the age of menopause.

> Cigarette smoking increases the risk of serious adverse effects on the heart and blood vessels. This risk increases with age and becomes significant in oral contraceptive users over 35 years of age. Women should be counselled not to smoke.

Thromboembolic and Thrombotic Disease: An increased risk of thromboembolic and thrombotic disease associated with the use of oral contraceptives is well established. Data from case control and cohort studies report that oral contraceptives containing desogestrel (Ortho-Cept Tablets contain desogestrel) are associated with a 2-fold increase in the risk of venous thromboembolic disease as compared with other low-dose (containing less than 50 µg of estrogen) pills containing other progestins. According to these studies, this 2-fold risk increases the yearly occurrence of venous thromboembolic disease by about 10 to 15 cases per 100 000 women.

Earlier case control studies on older formulations have found the relative risk of users compared to nonusers to be 3 for the first episode of superficial venous thrombosis, 4 to 11 for deep venous thrombosis or pulmonary embolism, and 1.5 to 6 for women with predisposing conditions for venous thromboembolic disease. Cohort studies have shown the relative risk to be somewhat lower, about 3 for new cases and about 4.5 for new cases requiring hospitalization. The risk of thromboembolic disease associated with oral contraceptives is not related to length of use and disappears after pill use is stopped.

Discontinue medication at the earliest manifestation of:

A. Thromboembolic and cardiovascular disorders such as: thrombophlebitis, pulmonary embolism, cerebrovascular disorders, myocardial ischemia, mesenteric thrombosis and retinal thrombosis.

B. Conditions which predispose to venous stasis and to vascular thrombosis, (e.g., immobilization after accidents or confinement to bed during long-term illness). Other nonhormonal methods of contraception should be used until regular activities are resumed. For use of oral contraceptives when surgery is contemplated, see Precautions.

C. Visual defects, partial or complete.

D. Papilledema, or ophthalmic vascular lesions.

E. Severe headache of unknown etiology or worsening of pre-existing migraine headache.

Precautions: Physical Examination and Follow-up: Before oral contraceptives are used, a thorough history and physical examination should be performed, including a blood pressure determination. Breasts, liver, extremities and pelvic organs

Ortho-Cept (cont'd)

should be examined. A Papanicolaou smear should be taken if the patient has been sexually active.

The first followup visit should be done 3 months after oral contraceptives are prescribed. Thereafter, examinations should be performed at least once a year, or more frequently if indicated. At each annual visit, examination should include those procedures that were done at the initial visit as outlined above or per recommendations of the Canadian Workshop on Screening for Cancer of the Cervix. Their suggestion was that, for women who had 2 consecutive negative Pap smears, screening could be continued every 3 years up to the age of 69.

Pregnancy: Oral contraceptives should not be taken by pregnant women. However, if conception accidentally occurs while taking the pill, there is no conclusive evidence that the estrogen and progestin contained in the oral contraceptive will damage the developing child.

Lactation: In breast-feeding women, the use of oral contraceptives results in the hormonal components being excreted in breast milk and may reduce its quantity and quality. If the use of oral contraceptives is initiated after the establishment of lactation, there does not appear to be any effect on the quantity and quality of the milk. There is no evidence that low dose oral contraceptives are harmful to the nursing infant.

Hepatic Function: Patients who have had jaundice, including a history of cholestatic jaundice during pregnancy, should be given oral contraceptives with great care and under close observation.

The development of severe generalized pruritus or icterus requires that the medication be withdrawn until the problem is resolved.

If a patient develops jaundice that proves to be cholestatic in type, the use of oral contraceptives should not be resumed. In patients taking oral contraceptives, changes in the composition of the bile may occur and an increased incidence of gallstones has been reported.

Hepatic nodules (adenoma and focal nodular hyperplasia) have been reported, particularly in long-term users of oral contraceptives. Although these lesions are extremely rare, they have caused fatal intra-abdominal hemorrhage and should be considered in women with an abdominal mass, acute abdominal pain or evidence of intra-abdominal bleeding.

Hypertension: Patients with essential hypertension whose blood pressure is well controlled may be given oral contraceptives but only under close supervision. If a significant elevation of blood pressure in previously normotensive or hypertensive subjects occurs at any time during the administration of the drug, cessation of medication is necessary.

Migraine and Headache: The onset or exacerbation of migraine or the development of headache of a new pattern, that is recurrent, persistent or severe, requires discontinuation of oral contraceptives and evaluation of the cause.

Diabetes: Current low dose oral contraceptives exert minimal impact on glucose metabolism. Diabetic patients, or those with a family history of diabetes, should be observed closely to detect any worsening of carbohydrate metabolism. Patients predisposed to diabetes who can be kept under close supervision may be given oral contraceptives. Young diabetic patients whose disease is of recent origin, well-controlled and not associated with hypertension or other signs of vascular disease such as ocular fundal changes, should be monitored more frequently while using oral contraceptives.

Ocular Disease: Patients who are pregnant or are taking oral contraceptives may experience corneal edema that may cause visual disturbances and changes in tolerance to contact lenses, especially of the rigid type. Soft contact lenses usually do not cause disturbances. If visual changes or alterations in tolerance to contact lenses occur, temporary or permanent cessation of wear may be advised.

Breasts: Increasing age and a strong family history are the most significant risk factors for the development of breast cancer. Other established risk factors include obesity, nulliparity and late age at first full-term pregnancy. The identified groups of women that may be at increased risk of developing breast cancer before menopause are long-term users of oral contraceptives (more than 8 years) and starters at an early age. In a few women, the use of oral contraceptives may accelerate the growth of an existing but undiagnosed breast cancer. Since any potential increased risk related to oral contraceptive use is small, there is no reason to change prescribing habits at present.

Women receiving oral contraceptives should be instructed in self-examination of their breasts. Their physicians should be notified whenever any masses are detected. A yearly clinical breast examination is also recommended because, if a breast cancer should develop, estrogen-containing drugs may cause a rapid progression.

Vaginal Bleeding: Persistent irregular vaginal bleeding requires assessment to exclude underlying pathology.

Fibroids: Patients with fibroids (leiomyomata) should be carefully observed. Sudden enlargement, pain or tenderness require discontinuation of the use of oral contraceptives.

Emotional Disorders: Patients with a history of emotional disturbances, especially the depressive type, may be more prone to have a recurrence of depression while taking oral contraceptives. In cases of a serious recurrence, a trial of an alternate method of contraception should be made which may help to clarify the possible relationship. Women with premenstrual syndrome (PMS) may have a varied response to oral contraceptives, ranging from symptomatic improvement to worsening of the condition.

Laboratory Tests: Results of laboratory tests should be interpreted in light of the fact that the patient is on oral contraceptives. The following laboratory tests are modified.

A. Liver Function Tests: Bromsulphthalein Retention Test (BSP): moderate increase; AST and GGT: minor increase; alkaline phosphatase: variable increase; serum bilirubin: increased, particularly in conditions predisposing to or associated with hyperbilirubinemia.

B. Coagulation Tests: Factors II, VII, IX, X, XII and XIII: increased; Factor VIII: mild increase; platelet aggregation and adhesiveness: mild increase in response to common aggregating agents; fibrinogen: increased; plasminogen: mild increase; antithrombin III: mild decrease; prothrombin time: increased.

C. Thyroid Function Tests: Protein-bound Iodine (PBI): increased; Total Serum Thyroxine (T_4): increased; Thyroid Stimulating Hormone (TSH): unchanged.

D. Adrenocortical Function Tests: plasma cortisol: increased.

E. Miscellaneous Tests: serum folate: occasionally decreased; glucose tolerance test: variable increase with return to normal after 6 to 12 months; insulin response: mild to moderate increase; c-Peptide response: mild to moderate increase.

Tissue Specimens: Pathologists should be advised of oral contraceptive therapy when specimens obtained from surgical procedures and Pap smears are submitted for examination.

Return to Fertility: After discontinuing oral contraceptive therapy, the patient should delay pregnancy until at least 1 normal spontaneous menstrual cycle has occurred in order to date the pregnancy. An alternative contraceptive method should be used during this time.

Amenorrhea: Women having a history of oligomenorrhea, secondary amenorrhea or irregular cycles may remain anovulatory or become amenorrheic following discontinuation of estrogen-progestin combination therapy.

Amenorrhea, especially if associated with breast secretion, that continues for 6 months or more after withdrawal, warrants a careful assessment of hypothalamic-pituitary function.

Thromboembolic Complications—Postsurgery: There is an increased risk of thromboembolic complications in oral contraceptive users after major surgery. If feasible, oral contraceptives should be discontinued and an alternative method substituted at least 1 month prior to **major** elective surgery. Oral contraceptive use should not be resumed until the first menstrual period after hospital discharge following surgery.

Drug Interactions: The concurrent administration of oral contraceptives with other drugs may result in an altered response to either agent (see Table I and Table II on following page). Reduced effectiveness of the oral contraceptive, should it occur, is more likely with the low-dose formulations. It is important to ascertain all drugs that a patient is taking, both prescription and nonprescription, before oral contraceptives are prescribed.

Refer to Oral Contraceptives 1994 (Chapter 8), Health Canada, for possible drug interactions with OCs.

Non-contraceptive Benefits of Oral Contraceptives: Several health advantages other than contraception have been reported.

Table I—Ortho-Cept

Drugs Which May Decrease the Efficacy of Oral Contraceptives

Class of Compound	Drug	Proposed Mechanism	Suggested Management
Anticonvulsants	Carbamazepine Ethosuximide Phenobarbital Phenytoin Primidone	Induction of hepatic microsomal enzymes: Rapid metabolism of estrogen and increased binding of progestin and ethinyl estradiol to SHBG.	Use higher dose OCs (50 μg ethinyl estradiol), another drug or another method.
Antibiotics	Ampicillin Cotrimoxazole Penicillin	Enterohepatic circulation disturbance, intestinal hurry.	For short course, use additional method or use another drug. For long course, use another method.
	Rifampin	Increased metabolism of progestins. Suspected acceleration of estrogen metabolism.	Use another method.
	Chloramphenicol Metronidazole Neomycin Nitrofurantoin Sulfonamides Tetracyclines	Induction of hepatic microsomal enzymes. Also disturbance of enterohepatic circulation.	For short course, use additional method or use another drug. For long course, use another method.
	Troleandomycin	May retard metabolism of OCs, increasing the risk of cholestatic jaundice.	
Antifungals	Griseofulvin	Stimulation of hepatic metabolism of contraceptive steroids may occur.	Use another method.
Cholesterol-lowering Agents	Clofibrate	Reduces elevated serum triglycerides and cholesterol; this reduces OC efficacy.	Use another method.
Sedatives and Hypnotics	Benzodiazepines Barbiturates Chloral hydrate Glutethimide Meprobamate	Induction of hepatic microsomal enzymes.	For short course, use additional method or another drug. For long course, use another method or higher dose OCs.
Antacids		Decreased intestinal absorption of progestins.	Dose 2 hours apart.
Other Drugs	Phenylbutazone Antihistamines Analgesics Antimigraine preparations Vitamin E	Reduced OC efficacy has been reported. Remains to be confirmed.	

Table II—Ortho-Cept

Modification of Other Drug Action by Oral Contraceptives

Class of Compound	Drug	Modification of Drug Action	Suggested Management
Alcohol		Possible increased levels of ethanol or acetaldehyde.	Use with caution.
Alpha-II Adrenoreceptor Agents	Clonidine	Sedation effect increased.	Use with caution.
Anticoagulants	All	OCs increase clotting factors, decrease efficacy. However, OCs may potentiate action in some patients.	Use another method.
Anticonvulsants	All	Fluid retention may increase risk of seizures.	Use another method.
Antidiabetic Drugs	Oral hypoglycemics and insulin	OCs may impair glucose tolerance and increase blood glucose.	Use low dose estrogen and progestin OC or another method. Monitor blood glucose.
Antihypertensive Agents	Guanethidine and methyldopa	Estrogen component causes sodium retention, progestin has no effect.	Use low dose estrogen OC or use another method.
	Beta-blockers	Increased drug effect (decreased metabolism).	Adjust dose of drug if necessary. Monitor cardiovascular status.
Antipyretics	Acetaminophen	Increased metabolism and renal clearance.	Dose of drug may have to be increased.
	Antipyrine	Impaired metabolism.	Decrease dose of drug.
	ASA	Effects of ASA may be decreased by the short-term use of OCs.	Patients on chronic ASA therapy may require an increase in ASA dosage.
Aminocaproic Acid		Theoretically, a hypercoagulable state may occur because OCs augment clotting factors.	Avoid concomitant use.
Betamimetic Agents	Isoproterenol	Estrogen causes decreased response to these drugs.	Adjust dose of drug as necessary. Discontinuing OCs can result in excessive drug activity.
Caffeine		The actions of caffeine may be enhanced as OCs may impair the hepatic metabolism of caffeine.	Use with caution.
Cholesterol-lowering Agents	Clofibrate	Their action may be antagonized by OCs. OCs may also increase metabolism of clofibrate.	May need to increase dose of clofibrate.
Corticosteroids	Prednisone	Markedly increased serum levels.	Possible need for decrease in dose.
Cyclosporine		May lead to an increase in cyclosporine levels and hepatotoxicity.	Monitor hepatic function. The cyclosporine dose may have to be decreased.
Folic Acid		OCs have been reported to impair folate metabolism.	May need to increase dietary intake or supplement.
Meperidine		Possible increased analgesia and CNS depression due to decreased metabolism of meperidine.	Use combination with caution.
Phenothiazine Tranquilizers	All phenothiazines, reserpine and similar drugs	Estrogen potentiates the hyperprolactinemia effect of these drugs.	Use other drugs or lower dose OCs. If galactorrhea or hyperprolactinemia occurs, use other method.
Sedatives and Hypnotics	Chlordiazepoxide Lorazepam Oxazepam Diazepam	Increased effect (increased metabolism).	Use with caution.
Theophylline	All	Decreased oxidation, leading to possible toxicity.	Use with caution. Monitor theophylline levels.
Tricyclic Antidepressants	Clomipramine (possibly others)	Increased side effects; i.e., depression.	Use with caution.
Vitamin B_{12}		OCs have been reported to reduce serum levels of Vitamin B_{12}.	May need to increase dietary intake or supplement.

1. Combination oral contraceptives reduce the incidence of cancer of the endometrium and ovaries.
2. Oral contraceptives reduce the likelihood of developing benign breast disease and, as a result, decrease the incidence of breast biopsies.
3. Oral contraceptives reduce the likelihood of development of functional ovarian cysts.
4. Pill-users have less menstrual blood loss and have more regular cycles, thereby reducing the chance of developing iron-deficiency anemia.
5. The use of oral contraceptives may decrease the severity of dysmenorrhea and premenstrual syndrome, and may improve acne vulgaris, hirsutism and other androgen-mediated disorders.
6. Oral contraceptives decrease the incidence of acute pelvic inflammatory disease and, thereby, reduce as well the incidence of ectopic pregnancy.
7. Oral contraceptives have potential beneficial effects on endometriosis.

> Oral contraceptives **do not protect** against sexually transmitted diseases (STDs) including HIV/AIDS. For protection against STDs, it is advisable to use latex condoms **in combination with** oral contraceptives.

Adverse Effects: An increased risk of the following serious adverse reactions has been associated with the use of oral contraceptives: thrombophlebitis, pulmonary embolism, mesenteric thrombosis, neuro-ocular lesions, (e.g., retinal thrombosis), myocardial infarction, cerebral thrombosis, cerebral hemorrhage, hypertension, benign hepatic tumors, gallbladder disease.

The following adverse reactions also have been reported in patients receiving oral contraceptives: Nausea and vomiting, usually the most common adverse reaction, occurs in approximately 10% or less of patients during the first cycle. Other reactions, as a general rule, are seen less frequently or only occasionally, as follows: gastrointestinal symptoms (such as abdominal cramps and bloating), breakthrough bleeding, spotting, change in menstrual flow, dysmenorrhea, amenorrhea during and after treatment, temporary infertility after discontinuance of treatment, edema, chloasma or melasma which may persist, breast changes (tenderness, enlargement and secretion), change in weight (increase or decrease), endocervical hyperplasias, possible diminution in lactation when given immediately postpartum, cholestatic jaundice, migraine, increase in size of uterine leiomyomata, rash (allergic), depression, reduced tolerance to carbohydrates, vaginal candidiasis, premenstrual-like syndrome, intolerance to contact lenses, change in corneal curvature (steepening), cataracts, optic neuritis, retinal thrombosis, changes in libido, chorea, changes in appetite, cystitis-like syndrome, rhinitis, headache, nervousness, dizziness, hirsutism, loss of scalp hair, erythema multiforme, erythema nodosum, hemorrhagic eruption, vaginitis, porphyria, impaired renal function, Raynaud's phenomenon, auditory disturbances, hemolytic uremic syndrome, pancreatitis.

Overdose: Symptoms and Treatment: In case of overdose or accidental ingestion by children, the physician should observe the patient closely although generally no treatment is required. Gastric lavage may be utilized if considered necessary.

Dosage: Information for the Patient on How to Take the Birth Control Pill:

1. **Read these directions:**
   - before you start taking your pills, and
   - any time you are not sure what to do.
2. **Look at your pill pack** to see if it has 21 or 28 pills:
   - 21-Pill Pack: 21 active pills (with hormones) taken daily for 3 weeks, and then take no pills for 1 week

   or
   - 28-Pill Pack: 21 active pills (with hormones) taken daily for 3 weeks, and then 7 "reminder" pills (no hormones) taken daily for 1 week.

   Also check the pill pack for instructions on (1) where to start and (2) directions to take pills (see package insert for illustrations).
3. You may wish to use a second method of birth control (e.g., latex condoms and spermicidal foam or gel) for the first 7 days of the first cycle of pill use. This will provide a backup in case pills are forgotten while you are getting used to taking them.
4. **When receiving any medical treatment, be sure to tell your doctor that you are using birth control pills.**
5. **Many women have spotting or light bleeding or may feel sick to their stomach during the first 3 months on the pill.** If you do feel sick, do not stop taking the pill. The problem will usually go away. If it does not go away, check with your doctor or clinic.
6. **Missing pills also can cause some spotting or light bleeding,** even if you make up the missed pills. You also could feel a little sick to your stomach on the days you take 2 pills to make up for missed pills.
7. **If you miss pills at any time, you could get pregnant. The greatest risks for pregnancy are:**
   - when you start a pack late, or
   - when you miss pills at the beginning or at the very end of the pack.
8. **Always be sure you have ready:**
   - **another kind of birth control** (such as latex condoms and spermicidal foam or gel) to use as a backup in case you miss pills, and
   - **an extra, full pack of pills.**
9. **If you experience vomiting or diarrhea, or if you take certain medicines,** such as antibiotics, your pills may not work as well. Use a backup method, such as latex condoms and spermicidal foam or gel, until you can check with your doctor or clinic.
10. **If you forget more than 1 pill 2 months in a row,** talk to your doctor or clinic about how to make pill-taking easier or about using another method of birth control.
11. **If your questions are not answered here, call your doctor or clinic.**

When to start the first pack of pills: Be sure to read these instructions:

- before you start taking your pills, and
- any time you are not sure what to do.

Decide with your doctor or clinic what is the best day for you to start taking your first pack of pills. Your pills may be either a 21-day or a 28-day type.

A. 21-Day Combination: With this type of birth control pill, you are 21 days on pills with 7 days off pills. You must not be off the pills for more than 7 days in a row.

Ortho-Cept (cont'd)

1. **The first day of your menstrual period (bleeding) is Day 1 of your cycle.** The pills may be started up to Day 6 of your cycle. Your starting day will be chosen in discussion with your doctor. You will **always** begin taking your pill on this day of the week. Your doctor may advise you to start taking the pills on Day 1, on Day 5, or on the first Sunday after your period begins. If your period starts on Sunday, start that same day.
2. Take 1 pill at approximately the same time every day for 21 days. **Then take no pills for 7 days.** Start a new pack on the 8th day. You will probably have a period during the 7 days off the pill. (This bleeding may be lighter and shorter than your usual period.)

Instructions for Using Your DIALPAK Tablet Dispenser: Follow these instructions carefully: 21-Day Regimen: (see package insert for illustrations): If you have a refill ring of Ortho-Cept Tablets, you should insert it into your DIALPAK Tablet Dispenser. You do this by removing the empty foil ring and snapping in your new foil ring such that the tab on the side of the foil fits in the notch in the ribbed outer ring of the plastic. You are now ready to align your package.

Note: Be sure that the foil ring is secure in the package before proceeding further.

Please make sure that your DIALPAK Tablet Dispenser is aligned such that the Black Day Arrow in the centre of the plastic points to the Black Day Arrow at the top of the package (towards the cover) as shown in the diagram. To align the Black Day Arrows, turn the ribbed outer ring to the right.

Your starting day will be chosen in discussion with your doctor. You should **always** begin taking your tablets on this day of the week. To set the package to the day you and your doctor selected, a calendar label is enclosed. To put the label in place, identify your correct starting day, locate that day on the label, line that day up with the pill to which the Black Day Arrow is pointing, remove the label from the backing and press the label over the printed calendar on the centre of the plastic. The first orange pill you will take is indicated by the Black Day Arrows. Push down on your first orange tablet with your thumb or forefinger. The tablet will come out through a hole in the back of the package. To take your second and subsequent tablets, turn the ribbed outer ring to the right. Take 1 tablet every day for 21 days, completing all orange tablets. After you have taken all of your tablets, insert your new refill ring as per the above instructions, wait 7 days and begin your next package on your chosen starting day, whether you have finished menstruating or not. Always remember to set the starting day of each new package to the day chosen by you and your doctor.

B. 28-Day Combination: With this type of birth control pill, you take 21 pills which contain hormones and 7 pills which contain no hormones.

1. **The first day of your menstrual period (bleeding) is Day 1 of your cycle.** The pills may be started up to Day 6 of your cycle. Your starting day will be chosen in discussion with your doctor. You will **always** begin taking your pill on this day of the week. Your doctor may advise you to start taking the pills on Day 1, on Day 5, or on the first Sunday after your period begins. If your period starts on Sunday, start that same day.
2. Take 1 pill at approximately the same time every day for 28 days. Begin a new pack the next day, **not missing any days on the pills.** Your period should occur during the last 7 days of using that pill pack.

Instructions for Using Your DIALPAK Tablet Dispenser: Follow these instructions carefully: 28-Day Regimen: (see package insert for illustrations): **Always complete the orange tablets before taking the green tablets.**

If you have a refill ring of Ortho-Cept Tablets, you should insert it into your DIALPAK Tablet Dispenser. You do this by removing the empty foil ring and snapping in your new foil ring such that the tab on the side of the foil fits in the notch in the ribbed outer ring of the plastic. You are now ready to align your package.

Note: Be sure that the foil ring is secure in the package before proceeding further.

Please make sure that your DIALPAK Tablet Dispenser is aligned such that the Black Day Arrow in the center of the plastic points to the Black Day Arrow at the top of the package (towards the cover) as shown in the diagram. To align the Black Day Arrows, turn the ribbed outer ring to the right. The Black Day Arrows should be pointing at the first orange tablet to the left of the green tablets.

Your starting day will be chosen in discussion with your doctor. You should **always** begin taking your tablets on this day of the week. To set the package to the day you and your doctor selected, a calendar label is enclosed. To put the label in place, identify your correct starting day, locate that day on the label, line that day up with the pill to which the Black Day Arrow is pointing, remove the label from the backing and press the label over the printed calendar on the center of the plastic. The first orange tablet you will take is to the left of the green tablets and between the Black Day Arrows. Push down on your first orange tablet with your thumb or forefinger. The tablet will come out through a hole in the back of the package. To take your second and subsequent tablets, turn the ribbed outer ring to the right. Take 1 tablet every day, first completing all 21 orange tablets, and finally the 7 green tablets. After you have taken all of your tablets, insert your new refill ring as per the above instructions. Begin your next package the very next day, your chosen starting day, whether you have finished menstruating or not. Always remember to set the starting day of each new package to the day chosen by you and your doctor.

What to do during the month:

1. **Take a pill at approximately the same time every day until the pack is empty.**
   - Try to associate taking your pill with some regular activity like eating a meal or going to bed.
   - Do not skip pills even if you have bleeding between monthly periods or feel sick to your stomach (nausea).
   - Do not skip pills even if you do not have sex very often.
2. **When you finish a pack:**
   - **21 pills: Wait 7 days** to start the next pack. You will have your period during that week.
   - **28 pills:** Start the next pack **on the next day.** Take 1 pill every day. Do not wait any days between packs.

What to do if you miss pills: Table III outlines the actions you should take if you miss 1 or more of your birth control pills. Match the number of pills missed with the appropriate starting time for your type of pill pack.

Note: 28-Day Pack: If you forgot any of the 7 "reminder" pills (without hormones) in Week 4, just safely dispose of the pills you missed. Then keep taking 1 pill each day until the pack is empty. You do not need to use a backup method.

Always be sure you have on hand:

- a backup method of birth control (such as latex condoms and spermicidal foam or gel) in case you miss pills, and
- an extra, full pack of pills.

If you forget more than 1 pill 2 months in a row, talk to your doctor or clinic about ways to make pill-taking easier or about using another method of birth control.

Information for the Patient: See Blue Section—Information for the Patient "Oral Contraceptives".

Supplied: Each orange tablet, unscored with D 150 engraved on each side, contains: desogestrel 0.15 mg and ethinyl estradiol 0.03 mg. In the 28-day regimen, the green tablet, engraved with ORTHO P on each side, contains: inert ingredients. Nonmedicinal ingredients: Orange tablets: colloidal silicon dioxide, hydroxypropyl methylcellulose, iron oxide (red and yellow), lactose, polyethylene glycol, povidone, starch, stearic acid, talc, titanium dioxide and vitamin E; Green tablets: hydroxypropyl methylcellulose, indigotin blue or FD&C Blue No. 1, iron oxide (red and yellow), lactose, magnesium stearate, polyethylene glycol, starch, talc and titanium dioxide. DIALPAK Tablet Dispenser Units and Refill Packages 21-day (21 active tablets) and 28 days (21 active and 7 inert tablets). Store between 15 and 30°C. Leave contents in protective packaging until time of use.

(Shown in Product Recognition Section)

Reviewed 1999

Table III—Ortho-Cept

What to Do if You Miss Pills

Sunday Start	**Other Than Sunday Start**
Miss 1 pill	**Miss 1 pill**
Take it as soon as you remember, and take the next pill at the usual time. This means that you might take 2 pills in one day.	Take it as soon as you remember, and take the next pill at the usual time. This means that you might take 2 pills in one day.
Miss 2 pills in a row	**Miss 2 pills in a row**
First 2 Weeks: 1. Take 2 pills the day you remember and 2 pills the next day. 2. Then take 1 pill a day until you finish the pack. 3. Use a backup method of birth control if you have sex in the 7 days after you miss the pills.	**First 2 Weeks:** 1. Take 2 pills the day you remember and 2 pills the next day. 2. Then take 1 pill a day until you finish the pack. 3. Use a backup method of birth control if you have sex in the 7 days after you miss the pills.
Third Week: 1. Keep taking 1 pill a day until Sunday. 2. On Sunday, safely discard the rest of the pack and start a new pack that day. 3. Use a backup method of birth control if you have sex in the 7 days after you miss the pills. 4. You may not have a period this month. **If you miss 2 periods in a row, call your doctor or clinic.**	**Third Week:** 1. Safely dispose of the rest of the pill pack and start a new pack that same day. 2. Use a backup method of birth control if you have sex in the 7 days after you miss the pills. 3. You may not have a period this month. **If you miss 2 periods in a row, call your doctor or clinic.**
Miss 3 or more pills in a row	**Miss 3 or more pills in a row**
Anytime in the Cycle: 1. Keep taking 1 pill a day until Sunday. 2. On Sunday, safely discard the rest of the pack and start a new pack that day. 3. Use a backup method of birth control if you have sex in the 7 days after you miss the pills. 4. You may not have a period this month. **If you miss 2 periods in a row, call your doctor or clinic.**	**Anytime in the Cycle:** 1. Safely dispose of the rest of the pill pack and start a new pack that same day. 2. Use a backup method of birth control if you have sex in the 7 days after you miss the pills. 3. You may not have a period this month. **If you miss 2 periods in a row, call your doctor or clinic.**

ORTHOCLONE OKT® 3

Janssen-Ortho

Muromonab-CD3

Immunosuppressant

Pharmacology: Muromonab-CD3 sterile solution is a murine monoclonal antibody to the T3 (CD3) antigen of human T cells which functions as an immunosuppressant. It is for i.v. use only. The antibody is a biochemically purified IgG_{2a} immunoglobulin with a heavy chain of approximately 50 000 daltons and a light chain of approximately 25 000 daltons. It is directed to a glycoprotein with a molecular weight of 20 000 daltons in the human T cell surface which is essential for T cell functions. Because it is a monoclonal antibody preparation, muromonab-CD3 sterile solution is a homogeneous, reproducible antibody product with consistent, measurable reactivity to human T cells.

The proper name, muromonab-CD3, is derived from the descriptive term murine monoclonal antibody. The CD3 designation identifies the specificity of the antibody as the Cell Differentiation (CD) cluster 3 defined by the First International Workshop on Human Leukocyte Differentiation Antigens.

Muromonab-CD3 reverses graft rejection, most probably by blocking the function of all T cells which play a major role in acute allograft rejection. Muromonab-CD3 reacts with and blocks the function of a 20 000 dalton molecule (CD3) in the membrane of human T cells that has been associated in vitro with the antigen recognition structure of T cells and is essential for signal transduction. In in vitro cytolytic assays, muromonab-CD3 blocks both the generation and function of effector cells. It is a potent mitogen in vitro in calf serum, but this mitogenicity is markedly reduced in human serum. Muromonab-CD3 thus blocks all known T cell functions.

In vivo, muromonab-CD3 reacts with most peripheral blood T cells and T cells in body tissues, but has not been found to react with other hematopoietic elements or other tissues of the body.

In all patients studied, a rapid and concomitant decrease in the number of circulating CD3 positive, CD4 positive and CD8 positive T cells was observed within minutes after the administration of muromonab-CD3. Between days 2 and 7 increasing numbers of circulating CD4 positive and CD8 positive cells have been observed in patients, although CD3 positive cells are not detectable. CD3 positive cells reappear rapidly and reach pre-treatment levels within a week after termination of muromonab-CD3 therapy. Increasing numbers of CD3 positive cells have been observed in some patients during the second week of muromonab-CD3 therapy, possibly as a result of the development of neutralizing antibodies to muromonab-CD3.

Antibodies to muromonab-CD3 have been observed, occurring with an incidence of 21% (n=43) for IgM, 86% (n=43) for IgG and 29% (n=35) for IgE. The mean time of appearance of IgG antibodies was 20±2 (mean±SD) days. Early IgG antibodies appeared by the end of the second week of treatment in 3% (n=86) of the patients.

Serum levels of muromonab-CD3 are measurable using an enzyme-linked immunosorbent assay (ELISA). During treatment with 5 mg/day for 14 days, mean serum trough levels of muromonab-CD3 increased during the first 3 days of administration and then remained in a steady state with a mean value of 0.9 μg/mL on days 3 to 14. The levels obtained during therapy have been shown to block T cell effector functions in vitro.

Following administration of muromonab-CD3 in vivo, leukocytes have been observed in cerebrospinal and peritoneal fluids. The mechanism for this effect is not understood.

Indications: For the treatment of acute renal allograft rejection, and acute cardiac and hepatic allograft rejection refractory to conventional antirejection therapy or when conventional therapy is contraindicated.

Controlled Clinical Trials: In a controlled randomized clinical trial, muromonab-CD3 was significantly more effective than conventional high dose steroid therapy in reversing acute renal allograft rejection. In this trial, 122 evaluable patients undergoing acute rejection of cadaveric renal transplants were treated either with muromonab-CD3 daily for a mean of 14 days, with concomitant lowering of the dosage of azathioprine and maintenance steroids (62 patients), or with conventional high dose steroids (60 patients). Muromonab-CD3 reversed 94% of the rejections compared to a 75% reversal rate obtained with conventional high dose steroid treatment (p=0.006). The 1 year Kaplan-Meier (actuarial) estimates of graft survival rates for these patients who had acute rejection were 62% and 45% for muromonab-CD3 and steroid treated patients, respectively (p=0.04). At 2 years the rates were 56% and 42%, respectively (p=0.06).

One- and two-year patient survivals were not significantly different between the 2 groups, being 85% and 75% for muromonab-CD3 treated patients and 90% and 85% for steroid treated patients.

Controlled randomized trials have not been conducted to evaluate the effectiveness of muromonab-CD3 compared to conventional therapy as a first-line treatment for acute cardiac and hepatic allograft rejections.

Open Clinical Trials: In open clinical trials, acute renal allograft rejection was reversed in 92% (n=126) of the patients treated with muromonab-CD3. Muromonab-CD3 also was effective in reversing acute renal, hepatic, and cardiac allograft rejections of cases where steroids and lymphocyte immune globulin preparations were contraindicated or were not successful (rescue) (see Table I).

Table I—Orthoclone OKT 3

Reversal in acute renal, hepatic, and cardiac allograft rejection episodes of cases where steroids and lymphocyte immune globulin preparations were contraindicated or were not successful (rescue).

	Renal Transplant Patients (n=225)	Hepatic Transplant Patients (n=144)	Cardiac Transplant Patients (n=111)
Rate of Reversal	65%	84%	90%

The dosage of other immunosuppressive agents used in conjunction with muromonab-CD3 should be lowered to minimal levels (see Dosage).

Contraindications: In patients who: are hypersensitive to muromonab-CD3, any other product of mouse origin, or any other components of this product; have anti-murine antibody titres ≥1:1 000; are in (uncompensated) heart failure or in fluid overload, as evidenced by chest x-ray or a greater than 3% weight gain within the week prior to planned muromonab-CD3 administration; have a history of seizures or are predisposed to seizures; are pregnant or are suspected to be pregnant or who are breast-feeding (see Precautions, Pregnancy).

Warnings: Only physicians experienced in immunosuppressive therapy and management of organ transplant patients should use muromonab-CD3.

Patients receiving muromonab-CD3 should be managed in facilities equipped and staffed for cardiopulmonary resuscitation.

Patients with fluid overload have developed severe pulmonary edema upon treatment with muromonab-CD3.

Cytokine Release Syndrome: Temporally associated with the administration of the first few doses of muromonab-CD3 (particularly, the first 2 or 3 doses), most patients have developed Cytokine Release Syndrome (CRS), an acute clinical syndrome, that has been attributed to the release of cytokines by activated lymphocytes or monocytes. This clinical syndrome has ranged from a more frequently reported mild, self-limited, "flu-like" illness to a less frequently reported severe, life-threatening shock-like reaction, which may include serious cardiovascular and CNS manifestations.

The syndrome typically begins approximately 30 to 60 minutes after administration of a dose of muromonab-CD3 (but may occur later) and may persist for several hours. The frequency and severity of this symptom complex is usually greatest with the first dose. With each successive dose of muromonab-CD3, both the frequency and severity of the Cytokine Release Syndrome tends to diminish. Increasing the amount of a dose or resuming treatment after a hiatus may result in a reappearance of the CRS.

Common clinical manifestations of the Cytokine Release Syndrome may include: high (often spiking, up to 41.7°C) fever, chills/rigors, headache, tremor, nausea/vomiting, diarrhea, abdominal pain, malaise, and muscle/joint aches and pains, and generalized weakness. Less frequently reported adverse experiences include: minor dermatologic reactions (e.g., rash, pruritus, etc.) and a spectrum of often serious, occasionally fatal, cardiorespiratory and neuropsychiatric adverse experiences.

Cardiorespiratory findings may include: dyspnea/shortness of breath, bronchospasm/wheezing, tachypnea, respiratory arrest/failure/distress, cardiovascular collapse, cardiac arrest, angina/myocardial infarction, chest pain/tightness, tachycardia (including ventricular), hypertension, hemodynamic instability, hypotension including profound shock, heart failure, adult respiratory distress syndrome, hypoxemia, apnea, arrhythmias and pulmonary edema (cardiogenic and noncardiogenic).

Severe pulmonary edema has occurred in patients with volume (fluid) overload and in those who appeared to be euvolemic. The pathogenesis of pulmonary edema may involve all or some of the following: volume overload; increased pulmonary vascular permeability; and/or reduced left ventricular compliance/contractility (i.e., left ventricular dysfunction).

During the first 1 to 3 days of muromonab-CD3 therapy, some patients have experienced an acute and transient decline in the glomerular filtration rate (GFR) and diminished urine output with a resulting increase in the level of serum creatinine. Massive release of cytokines appears to lead to reversible renal functional impairment and/or delayed renal allograft function. Similarly, transient elevations in hepatic transaminases have been reported following administration of the first few doses of muromonab-CD3.

Patients at risk for more serious complications of the Cytokine Release Syndrome may include those with the following conditions: unstable angina; recent myocardial infarction or symptomatic ischemic heart disease; heart failure of any etiology; pulmonary edema of any etiology; any form of chronic obstructive pulmonary disease; intravenous vascular overload or depletion of any etiology (e.g. excessive dialysis, recent intensive diuresis, blood loss, etc.); cerebrovascular disease; patients with advanced symptomatic vascular disease or neuropathy; a history of seizures; and septic shock. Efforts should be made to correct or stabilize background conditions prior to the initiation of therapy.

Prior to administration of muromonab-CD3, the patient's volume (fluid) status should be assessed carefully. It is imperative, especially prior to the first few doses, that there be no clinical evidence of volume overload or uncompensated heart failure, including a chest x-ray free of evidence of heart failure or fluid overload within 24 hours preinjection, and weight restriction of ≤3% above the patient's minimum weight during the week prior to injection. Reactions to the first dose may be minimized by using the recommended steroid regimen (see Dosage).

Management of Cytokine Release Syndrome: Manifestations of the Cytokine Release Syndrome may be prevented or minimized by pretreatment with 8 mg/kg of methylprednisolone (i.e., high dose steroids), given 1 to 4 hours prior to administration of the first dose of muromonab-CD3 therapy, and by closely following recommendations for dosage and treatment duration. Since the CRS may occur following a treatment hiatus and resumption of therapy, similar precautions should be taken in such a case.

If any of the more serious presentations of the Cytokine Release Syndrome occur, intensive treatment including oxygen, i.v. fluids, corticosteroids, pressor amines, antihistamines, intubation, etc., may be required.

Anaphylatic Reactions and other Hypersensitivity Reactions: Anaphylatic or anaphylactoid reactions may occur following administration of any dose or course of muromonab-CD3 therapy.

Serious and occasionally fatal hypersensitivity and/or anaphylactic reactions usually occurring within 10 minutes after administration have been reported in patients treated with muromonab-CD3 therapy. Manifestations of anaphylaxis may appear similar to manifestations of the Cytokine Release Syndrome described above. It may be impossible to determine the mechanism responsible for any systemic reaction(s). Reactions attributed to hypersensitivity have been reported less frequently than those attributed to cytokine release.

Acute hypersensitivity reactions may be characterized by: cardiovascular collapse, cardiorespiratory arrest, loss of consciousness, hypotension, pulmonary edema especially in patients with volume overload, seizures or coma, tachycardia, pruritus, urticaria, tingling, angioedema including laryngeal, pharyngeal or facial edema, dyspnea, bronchospasm, and airway obstruction.

Serious allergic events, including anaphylactic or anaphylactoid reactions, have been reported in patients re-exposed to muromonab-CD3 subsequent to their initial course of therapy. Pretreatment with antihistamines and/or steroids may not reliably prevent anaphylaxis in this setting. Possible allergic hazards of retreatment should be weighed against expected therapeutic benefits and alternatives.

If hypersensitivity is suspected, discontinue the drug immediately. Do not resume therapy or re-expose the patient to muromonab-CD3 therapy.

Severe Cytokine Release Syndrome Versus Anaphylactic Reactions: It may be very difficult, even impossible, to distinguish between an acute hypersensitivity reaction (e.g., anaphylaxis, angioedema, etc.) and the Cytokine Release Syndrome. Potentially serious signs and symptoms having an immediate onset (usually within 10 minutes) following administration of muromonab-CD3 are more likely due to acute hypersensitivity; discontinue the drug immediately. If hypersensitivity is suspected, do not resume therapy or re-expose the patient to muromonab-CD3. Clinical manifestations beginning approximately 30 to 60 minutes (or later) following administration of muromonab-CD3, are more likely cytokine-mediated.

Neuropsychiatric Events: Seizures, encephalopathy, cerebral edema, aseptic meningitis, and headache have been reported, even following the first dose, during therapy with muromonab-CD3, resulting in part from T-cell activation and subsequent systemic release of cytokines.

Headache is frequently seen after any of the first few doses and may occur in any of the following neurological syndromes or by itself.

Seizures, some accompanied by loss of consciousness, cardiorespiratory arrest or death, have occurred independently or in conjunction with any of the neurologic syndromes described below. Patients predisposed to seizures may include those with the following conditions: acute tubular necrosis/uremia, fever, infection, a precipitous fall in serum calcium, fluid overload, hypertension, hypoglycemia, history of seizures, and electrolyte imbalances or those who are taking a medication concomitantly that may, by itself, cause seizures.

Signs and symptoms of the aseptic meningitis syndrome described in association with the use of muromonab-CD3 therapy have included: fever, headache, meningismus (stiff neck), and photophobia. Approximately one-third of the patients with a diagnosis of aseptic meningitis had coexisting signs and symptoms of encephalopathy. Most patients with the aseptic meningitis syndrome had a benign course and recovered without any permanent sequelae during therapy or subsequent to its completion or discontinuation.

Manifestations of encephalopathy may include: impaired cognition, confusion, obtundation, altered mental status, disorientation, auditory/visual hallucinations, psychosis (delirium,

Orthoclone OKT 3 (cont'd)

paranoia), mood changes (e.g., mania, agitation, combativeness, etc.), diffuse hypotonus, hyperreflexia, myclonus, tremor, asterixis, involuntary movements, major motor seizures, lethargy/stupor/coma, and diffuse weakness. Some patients with a diagnosis of encephalopathy also had symptoms of meningismus or headache.

Cerebral edema (and other signs of increased vascular permeability e.g., nasal and ear stuffiness, etc.) has been seen in patients treated with muromonab-CD3 and may accompany some of the other neurologic manifestations.

Patients who may be at greater risk for CNS adverse experiences include those: with known or suspected CNS disorders (e.g., history of seizure disorder, etc.); with cerebrovascular disease (small or large vessel); with conditions having associated neurologic problems (e.g., head trauma, uremia, etc.); with underlying vascular diseases; or who are receiving a medication concomitantly that may, by itself, affect the CNS.

Signs or symptoms of encephalopathy, meningitis, seizures, and cerebral edema, with or without headache, have typically been reversible. Headache, aseptic meningitis, seizures, and less severe forms of encephalopathy resolved in most patients despite continued treatment. Irreversible sequelae associated with serious CNS events (e.g. blindness, deafness, paralysis) have been reported rarely.

Consequences of Immunosuppression: Infection/Viral-Induced Lymphoproliferative Disorders: Infections: Muromonab-CD3 is usually added to immunosuppressive therapeutic regimens, thereby augmenting the degree of immunosuppression. This increase in the total burden of immunosuppression may alter the spectrum of infections observed and increase the risk, the severity, and the potential gravity (morbidity) of infectious complications.

Patients must be observed carefully for any signs and symptoms suggesting infection or viral-induced lymphoproliferative disorders (LPD). Anti-infective prophylaxis should be considered for patients at high risk. If infection or viral-induced LPD occur, cultures should be prepared and a biopsy should be performed as soon as possible. Appropriate anti-infective therapy should be promptly instituted, and if possible, immunosuppressive therapy should be reduced or discontinued.

When using combinations of immunosuppressive agents, the dose of each agent, including muromonab-CD3, should be reduced to the lowest level compatible with an effective therapeutic response so as to reduce the potential for and severity of infections and malignant transformations.

Multiple or intensive courses of any anti-T cell antibody preparation, including muromonab-CD3, which produce profound impairment of cell-mediated immunity, further increase the risk of (opportunistic) infection, especially with the Herpes viruses (HSV, CMV, EBV) and fungi.

Anti-infective prophylaxis may reduce the morbidity associated with certain potential pathogens and should be considered for high-risk patients. It is also possible to reduce the risk of serious CMV or EBV infection by avoiding transplantation of a CMV-seropositive (donor) and/or EBV-seropositive (donor) organ into a seronegative patient.

Neoplasia: As a result of depressed cell-mediated immunity, organ transplant patients have an increased risk of developing malignancies, especially lymphoproliferative disorders (LPD), lymphomas, and skin cancers.

The long-term risk of neoplastic events in patients being treated with muromonab-CD3 has not been determined.

This formulation of Orthoclone OKT 3 contains polysorbate 80 and **must not** be used for the in vitro treatment of bone marrow.

Precautions: Prior to Treatment with muromonab-CD3: Fluid Status: The patient's volume (fluid) status should be assessed carefully. It is imperative, especially prior to the first few doses, that there be no clinical evidence of volume overload, uncontrolled hypertension or uncompensated heart failure. There should be a chest x-ray free of evidence of heart failure or fluid overload and weight restrictions of ≤3% above the patient's minimum weight during the week prior to injection.

Fever: If the temperature of a patient exceeds 37.8°C, it should be lowered by antipyretics before administration of each dose of muromonab-CD3.

Sensitization: Muromonab-CD3 is a murine (immunoglobulin) protein that can induce human antimurine antibody (HAMA) production (i.e., sensitization) in some patients following exposure. Depending upon the HAMA titer, muromonab-CD3 has been used to reverse subsequent rejection episodes in patients without detectable or with weakly positive (≤1:100) antibody titers. Higher antibody titers (>1:100) may preclude successful reuse of muromonab-CD3. If an antibody titer ≥1:1 000 is detected, therapy should not be attempted.

Patients receiving muromonab-CD3 for initial use should be monitored periodically to ensure adequate plasma muromonab-CD3 levels (≥800 ng/mL) or T cell clearance (CD3 positive T cells <25 cells/mm³). Caution should be used if retreatment is considered; anticipated reuse of muromonab-CD3 requires monitoring prior to therapy to determine the HAMA titer. If reuse is deemed appropriate, daily immunologic monitoring is recommended (see Laboratory Tests). Reduced T cell clearance or impaired ability to maintain adequate muromonab-CD3 levels provides a basis for adjusting muromonab-CD3 dosage or for discontinuing therapy (see Intravascular Thrombosis).

Intravascular Thrombosis: As with other immunosuppressive therapies, arterial, venous, and capillary thromboses of allografts and other vascular beds (e.g., heart, lungs, brain, bowel, etc.) have been reported in patients treated with muromonab-CD3. The decision to use muromonab-CD3 therapy in patients with a history of thrombotic events or underlying vascular disease should take into consideration the risks of thrombosis. Concomitant use of prophylactic antithrombotic interventions (e.g., mini-dose heparin, etc.) should be considered.

Use a low protein-binding 0.2 or 0.22 micrometer (μm) filter to prepare the injections (see Dosage, method of administration).

Information for the Patient: Patients should be informed of the expected first dose muromonab-CD3 effects, which are markedly reduced on successive days of muromonab-CD3 treatment. Patients should also be informed regarding the potential benefits and risks of using muromonab-CD3 therapy.

Laboratory Tests: As with many potent drugs, periodic assessment of organ system functions should be performed during treatment with muromonab-CD3.

Prior to and During Muromonab-CD3 Therapy: The following tests should be monitored: Renal: BUN, serum creatinine, etc. Hepatic: transaminases, alkaline phosphatase, bilirubin. Hematopoietic: WBCs and differential, platelet count, etc. Chest x-ray: Within 24 hours before initiating muromonab-CD3 treatment, a chest x-ray should be performed to ensure that there is no evidence of heart failure or fluid overload.

For Initial Use of Muromonab-CD3: One of the following immunologic tests should be monitored during muromonab-CD3 therapy: Plasma muromonab-CD3 levels (as determined by an ELISA); target muromonab-CD3 levels should be ≥800 ng/mL; or quantitative T-lymphocyte surface phenotyping (CD3, CD4, CD8); target CD3 positive T cells <25 cells/mm³.

Prior to Retreatment with muromonab-CD3 therapy: Testing for human antimurine antibody titers is strongly recommended: Human antimurine antibody titers (as determined by an ELISA); a titre >1:100 may preclude successful reuse; a titer ≥1:1 000 is a contraindication for use.

Retreatment requires daily monitoring of either plasma muromonab-CD3 levels or clearance of CD3 positive T cells to achieve the same targets described above for initial use.

Carcinogenesis: Long-term studies have not been conducted in laboratory animals to evaluate the carcinogenic potential of muromonab-CD3 therapy.

Pregnancy and *Lactation:* Muromonab-CD3 is contraindicated in women who are pregnant or are suspected to be pregnant, and those who are breast feeding. Animal reproductive studies have not been conducted with muromonab-CD3. It is not known whether muromonab-CD3 can cause fetal harm when administered to a pregnant woman or whether muromonab-CD3 can affect reproduction.

Children: Safety and effectiveness in children have not been established. No adequately controlled clinical studies have been conducted in children. [Published literature has reported the use of muromonab-CD3 therapy in infants/children. Pediatric recipients are reported to be significantly immunosuppressed for a prolonged period of time and therefore, require close monitoring post-therapy for opportunistic infections, particularly varicella-zoster virus (VZV), which poses an infectious complication unique to this population. Gastrointestinal fluid loss secondary to diarrhea and/or vomiting resulting from the Cytokine Release Syndrome may be significant when treating small children and may require parenteral hydration. It is unknown whether there may be significant long-term sequelae related to the occurrence of seizures, high fever, CNS infections, aseptic meningitis, etc., following muromonab-CD3 treatment. In cases where administration of muromonab-CD3 would be deemed medically appropriate, more vigilant and frequent monitoring is required for children (especially young ones) than in adults.]

Drug Interactions: Concomitant medications (azathioprine, corticosteroids, cyclosporine) may have contributed to the neuropsychiatric, infectious, nephrotoxic, thrombotic, and/or neoplastic events reported in patients treated with muromonab-CD3.

In addition, the use of indomethacin by a few patients who were simultaneously receiving therapy with muromonab-CD3 may have contributed to some encephalopathic and other CNS adverse events (see Adverse Effects).

Adverse Effects: The incidence of adverse experiences reported by patients in clinical trials receiving muromonab-CD3 plus concomitant low dose immunosuppressive therapy (primarily azathioprine and corticosteroids) during the first 2 days of treatment for transplant rejection, was higher than that previously reported by patients receiving conventional therapy. During this period, the majority of patients experienced pyrexia (90%) (of which 19% were 40°C or above) and chills (59%). In addition, other adverse experiences occurring in 8% or more of the patients during the first 2 days of muromonab-CD3 therapy included those listed in Table II.

Table II—Orthoclone OKT 3

Adverse Effects

Event	**Reporting Event**
Dyspnea	21%
Nausea	19%
Vomiting	19%
Chest pain	14%
Diarrhea	14%
Tremor	13%
Wheezing	13%
Headache	11%
Tachycardia	10%
Rigors	8%
Hypertension	8%

Similar adverse effects were observed in the additional open clinical studies.

Additional serious and occasionally fatal cardiorespiratory manifestations have been reported following any of the first few doses (see Warnings, Cytokine Release Syndrome and Adverse Effects, Adverse Events by Body System, Cardiovascular, Respiratory).

Pulmonary Edema: Potentially fatal severe pulmonary edema has been reported following the first 2 doses in less than 2% of renal transplant patients and was always associated with fluid overload. However, post-marketing experience revealed that pulmonary edema has occurred in patients who appeared to be euvolemic, presumably as a consequence of cytokine-mediated increased vascular permeability (''leaky capillaries.'') and/or reduced myocardial contractility/compliance (i.e., left ventricular dysfunction) (see Warnings, Cytokine Release Syndrome and Dosage). It is, therefore, essential that patients receiving muromonab-CD3 not be in fluid overload and remain under close medical supervision for 48 hours after the administration of the first dose. The first dose should be administered as detailed in the Dosage section.

Infections: In the controlled randomized renal rejection trial, the most common infections during the first 45 days of muromonab-CD3 therapy were due to Herpes simplex (27%) and cytomegalovirus (19%). Other severe and life threatening infections were S. epidermidis (4.8%), P. carinii (3.1%), Legionella (1.6%), Cryptococcus (1.6%), Serratia (1.6%), and gram-negative bacteria (1.6%). The incidence of infections was similar in patients treated with muromonab-CD3 and in patients treated with high dose steroids. In a clinical trial of acute hepatic rejection refractory to conventional treatment, the most common infections reported in patients treated with muromonab-CD3 during the first 45 days of the study were cytomegalovirus (15.7% of patients, of which 43% of infections were severe), fungal infections (14.9% of patients, of which 30% were severe), and Herpes simplex (7.5% of patients, of which 10% were severe). Other severe and life-threatening infections were gram-positive infections (9.0% of patients), gram-negative infections (7.5% of patients), viral infections (1.5% of patients), and Legionella (0.7% of patients). In another hepatic rejection trial the incidence of fungal infections was 34% and infections with the Herpes simplex virus was 31%.

In a clinical trial of acute cardiac rejection refractory to conventional treatment, the most common infections reported in the muromonab-CD3 group during the first 45 days of the study were Hepres simplex (5% of patients, of which 20% were severe), fungal infections (4% of patients, of which 75% were severe), and cytomegalovirus (3% of patients, of which 33% were severe). No other severe or life-threatening infections were reported during this period.

Clinically significant infections (e.g., pneumonia, sepsis, etc.) due to the following parthogens have been reported. Bacterial: Clostridium species (including perfringens), Corynebacterium, enterococcus, E. aerogenes, E. coli, Klebsiella species, Lactobacillus, Legionella, L. monocytogenes, Mycobacteria species, N. asteroides, Proteus species, Providencia species, P. aeruginosa, Serratia species, Staphylococcus species, Streptococcus species, Y. enterocolitica, and other gram-negative bacteria.

Fugal:* Aspergillus, Candida, Cryptococcal, Dermatophytes.

Protoza: P. carinii, T. gondii.

Viral: cytomegalovirus* (CMV), Epstein-Barr virus* (EBV), Herpes simplex virus* (HSV), Hepatitis viruses, Varicella zoster virus (VZV).

As a consequence of being a potent immunosuppressive, the incidence and severity of infections with designated(*) pathogens, especially the Herpes family of viruses, may be increased (see Warnings, Infection/Viral-Induced Lymphoproliferative Disorders).

Neoplasia: In patients treated with muromonab-CD3, post-transplant lymphoproliferative disorders (LPD) reported have ranged from lymphadenopathy or benign polyclonal B cell hyperplasias to malignant and often fatal monoclonal B cell lymphomas. In post-marketing experience, approximately one-third of the lymphoproliferations reported were benign and two-thirds were malignant. Classification of these lymphomas has included: B cell, large cell, polyclonal, non-Hodgkin's, lymphocytic, T cell, Burkitt's; the majority have not been classified histologically. When malignant lymphomas have been reported, they have appeared to develop early after transplantation, the majority within the first 4 months post-treatment. Many of these have been rapidly progressive, some fulminant involving the allografted organ, widely disseminated at time of diagnosis, and fatal. Carcinomas of the skin have included: basal cell, squamous cell, Kaposi's sarcoma, melanoma, and keratoacanthoma. Other neoplasms infrequently reported include: multiple myeloma, leukemia, carcinoma of the breast, adenocarcinoma, cholangiocarcinoma, and recurrences of pre-existing hepatoma and renal cell carcinoma.

Hypersensitivity Reactions: Reported adverse reactions resulting from the formation of antibodies to muromonab-CD3 have included antigen-antibody (immune complex) mediated syndromes and IgE-mediated reactions. Reported hypersensitivity reactions have ranged from a mild, self-limited rash or pruritus to severe, life-threatening anaphylactic reactions/shock or angioedema (including: swelling of lips, eyelids, laryngeal spasm and airway obstruction with hypoxia) (see Warnings, Anaphylactic Reactions and other Hypersensitivity Reactions).

Other hypersensitivity reactions have included: ineffectiveness of treatment, serum sickness, arthritis, allergic interstitial nephritis, immune complex deposition resulting in glomerulonephritis, vasculitis, and temporal arteritis, and eosinophilia.

Adverse Events by Body System: Clinical adverse events occurring in clinical trials and post-marketing experience are listed below by body system: Body as a Whole: fever (including, spiking temperatures as high as 41.7°C, chills/rigors, flu-like syndrome, fatigue/malaise, generalized weakness, anorexia.

Cardiovascular: cardiac arrest, hypotension/shock, heart failure, cardiovascular collapse, angina/myocardial infarction, tachycardia, bradycardia, hemodynamic instability, hypertension, left ventricular dysfunction, arrhythmias, chest pain/tightness.

Respiratory: respiratory arrest, adult respiratory distress syndrome (ARDS), respiratory failure, pulmonary edema, (cardiogenic or noncardiogenic), apnea, dyspnea, bronchospasm, wheezing, shortness of breath, hypoxemia, tachypnea/hyperventilation, abnormal chest sounds, and pneumonia/pneumonitis (bacterial, viral, P. carinii, etc.).

Dermatologic: rash, erythema multiforme, urticaria, pruritus, erythema, flushing, diaphoresis.

Gastrointestinal: diarrhea, nausea/vomiting, abdominal pain, bowel infarction, gastrointestinal hemorrhage.

Hematopoietic: pancytopenia, aplastic anemia, neutropenia, leukopenia, thrombocytopenia, lymphopenia, leukocytosis, lymphadenopathy; arterial, venous and capillary thromboses of allografts and other vascular beds (e.g., heart, lung, brain, bowel, etc.); disturbances of coagulation, including disseminated intravascular coagulation; microangiopathic hemolytic anemia.

Hepatobiliary: increases in transaminases (AST, ALT, etc.); hepato/splenomegaly or hepatitis, usually secondary to viral infection or lymphoma.

Neuropsychiatric: seizures, lethargy/stupor/coma, encephalopathy, psychotic reactions (delirium), encephalitis, meningitis, cerebral edema, headache, dizziness, tremor, aphasia, quadri- or paraparesis/plegia, obtundation, confusion, altered mental status (e.g., paranoia, etc.), impaired cognition, disorientation, auditory and visual hallucinations, agitation/combativeness, mood changes (e.g., mania, etc.), hypotonus, hyperreflexia, myoclonus, obnubilation, asterixis, involuntary movements, CNS infections, CNS malignancies, cerebrovascular accident, hemiparesis/ pelgia, transient ischemic attack, subarachnoid hemorrhage.

Musculoskeletal: arthralgia, arthritis, myalgia, stiffness/aches/pains.

Special Senses: blindness, blurred vision, diplopia, hearing loss, otitis media, tinnitus, vertigo, VI cranial nerve palsy, photophobia, conjunctivitis, nasal and ear stuffiness.

Renal: anuria/oliguria; delayed graft function; renal insufficiency/renal failure, usually transient and reversible in association with cytokine release syndrome; abnormal urinary cytology, including exfoliation of damaged lymphocytes, collecting duct cells and cellular casts.

Overdose: Symptoms and Treatment: The maximum amount of muromonab-CD3 that can safely be administered in single or multiple doses has not been determined.

Dosage: The recommended dose of muromonab-CD3 is 5 mg as a single daily (i.v.) dose for 10 to 14 days. The diagnosis of acute allograft rejection should be made prior to administration of muromonab-CD3.

Prior to administration of muromonab-CD3, the patient's volume status should be assessed carefully. It is imperative, especially prior to the first few doses, that there be **no** clinical evidence of volume overload or uncompensated heart failure, including a chest x-ray free of evidence of heart failure or fluid overload and weight restriction of ≤3% above the patient's minimum weight during the week prior to injection. Prior to retreatment with muromonab-CD3, the patient's antimurine antibody titer should be determined.

Patients should be monitored closely for 48 hours after the first dose is administered. I.V. methylprednisolone sodium succinate 8 mg/kg given 1 to 4 hours prior to muromonab-CD3 administration is strongly recommended to decrease the incidence and severity of reactions to the first dose which have been attributed to the muromonab-CD3 mediated Cytokine Release Syndrome. Acetaminophen and antihistamines can be given concomitantly with muromonab-CD3 to reduce early reactions. Patient temperature should not exceed 37.8°C at the administration of each dose of muromonab-CD3 (see Table III).

When using combinations of immunosuppressive agents, the dose of each agent, including muromonab-CD3, should be reduced to the lowest level compatible with an effective therapeutic response so as to reduce the potential for and severity of infections and malignant transformations.

No bacteriostatic agent is present in this product; adherence to aseptic technique is advised. Once the ampul is opened, use immediately and discard the unused portion.

Table III—Orthoclone OKT 3

Suggested Prevention and Treatment of Orthoclone OKT 3 First Dose Effects

Adverse Experience	Effective Prevention or Palliation	Supportive Treatment
Severe pulmonary edema	Clear chest x-ray within 24 h preinjection	Prompt intubation and oxygenation
	Weight restriction to ≤3% gain over 7 days preinjection	24 h close observation
Fever, chills	8 mg/kg methylprednisolone sodium succinate 1–4 h prior to injection	Cooling blanket
	Fever reduction below 37.8°C preinjection	Acetaminophen prn
Respiratory effects	100 mg hydrocortisone sodium succinate 30 min post injection	Additional 100 mg hydrocortisone sodium succinate prn

Method of Administration: Muromonab-CD3 should be inspected visually for particulate matter and discoloration prior to administration. Because muromonab-CD3 is a protein solution, it may develop a few fine translucent particles which have been shown not to affect its potency. **Do not shake.**

Prepare muromonab-CD3 for injection by drawing 5 mL (1 mg/mL) of solution immediately prior to use into a syringe through a sterile low protein-binding 0.2 or 0.22 μm filter. Discard filter and attach needle for i.v. bolus injection.

Administer muromonab-CD3 as an i.v. bolus in less than 1 minute. Do not dilute or administer by i.v. infusion or in conjunction with other drug solutions.

Supplied: Each mL of clear, colorless, sterile solution (which may contain a few fine translucent protein particles) contains: muromonab-CD3 1 mg. Nonmedicinal ingredients: dibasic sodium phosphate, monobasic sodium phosphate, polysorbate 80, sodium chloride and water for injection. Ampuls of 5 mL (muromonab-CD3 5 mg). Packages of 5. Store in refrigerator at 2 to 8°C. **Do not freeze or shake.**

Reviewed 1999

ORTHO® DIENESTROL Ⓟ

Janssen-Ortho

Dienestrol

Vaginitis Therapy

Pharmacology: Dienestrol is a synthetic, nonsteroidal estrogen. The degree of systemic absorption and the mode of action are undetermined. However, one should be aware of the potential for systemic estrogen activity and related risks.

Indications: The treatment of senile or atrophic vaginitis or other vaginal disturbances associated with hypoestrogenic conditions.

Ortho Dienestrol cream is an estrogen product for intravaginal use only.

Contraindications: Known or suspected cancer of the breast; known or suspected estrogen-dependent neoplasia; known or suspected pregnancy (see Warnings); undiagnosed abnormal genital bleeding; active thrombophlebitis or thromboembolic disorders; a history of thrombophlebitis, thrombosis, or thromboembolic disorders; known or suspected hypersensitivity to any of the active or inactive ingredients, e.g., peanut oil.

Warnings: Induction of Malignant Neoplasms: Estrogens have been reported to increase the risk of endometrial carcinoma in postmenopausal women exposed to exogenous estrogens for prolonged periods. The risk appears to depend on both duration of treatment and on estrogen dose.

Long-term continuous administration of natural and synthetic estrogens in certain animal species increases the frequency of carcinomas of the breast, cervix, vagina and liver.

Pregnancy: Estrogens should not be used during pregnancy. Several reports suggest an association between intrauterine exposure to female sex hormones and congenital anomalies.

If the cream is used during pregnancy, or if the patient becomes pregnant while using this drug, she should be apprised of the potential risks to the fetus.

Gallbladder Disease: A 2- to 3-fold increase in the risk of surgically confirmed gallbladder disease in postmenopausal women receiving estrogens has been reported.

The following adverse effects have been associated with the systemic administration of estrogen-containing products: thromboembolic disease, hepatic tumors, hypertension and decreased glucose tolerance.

Precautions: Estrogens may cause fluid retention. Conditions possibly affected by this factor, such as epilepsy, migraine and cardiac or renal dysfunction, require careful observation.

Estrogens should be administered with caution in patients with: metabolic bone diseases that are associated with hypercalcemia; impaired liver function: If jaundice develops in any patient receiving estrogen, the medication should be discontinued while the cause of the jaundice is investigated; a history of mental depression; diabetes and pre-existing uterine leiomyomata (they may increase in size during estrogen use).

Certain patients may develop manifestations of excessive estrogenic stimulation, such as abnormal or excessive uterine bleeding, mastodynia, etc.

Estrogens should be used judiciously in patients in whom bone growth is not complete.

<u>Drug Interactions:</u> Laboratory Tests: Certain endocrine and liver function tests may be affected by estrogen-containing products. These are:

1. Increased sulfobromophthalein retention.

Ortho-Dienestrol (cont'd)

2. Increased prothrombin and factors VII, VIII, IX and X; decreased antithrombin 3; increased norepinephrine-induced platelet aggregability.
3. Increased thyroid-binding globulin (TBG) leading to increased circulating total thyroid hormone, as measured by PBI, T_4 by column or T_4 by radioimmunoassay. Free T_3 resin uptake is decreased, reflecting the elevated TBG; free T_4 is unaltered.
4. Impaired glucose tolerance.
5. Decreased pregnanediol excretion.
6. Reduced response to metapyrone.
7. Reduced serum folate concentration.
8. Increased serum triglyceride and phospholipid concentration.

Adverse Effects: Ortho Dienestrol Cream is generally well tolerated. There have been occasional reports of burning, itching and irritation. The physician should also be aware of those adverse reactions reported to occur with systemic administration of estrogens. (See also Contraindications and Warnings.)

Overdose: Symptoms and Treatment: Overdosage of estrogen may cause nausea and, in females, withdrawal bleeding may occur.

Dosage: The lowest dose that will control symptoms should be chosen and medication should be discontinued as promptly as possible.

Attempts to discontinue or taper medication should be made at 3- to 6-month intervals.

The usual dosage range is 1 or 2 applicatorsful/day for 1 or 2 weeks, then gradually reduced to one-half initial dosage for a similar period. A maintenance dosage of 1 applicatorful, 1 to 3 times a week, may be used after restoration of the vaginal mucosa has been achieved.

Treated patients with an intact uterus should be monitored closely for signs of endometrial cancer and appropriate diagnostic measures should be taken to rule out malignancy in the event of persistent or recurring abnormal vaginal bleeding.

Supplied: The contents of each applicator is 5 g. Each g of water miscible, soft, white cream contains: dienestrol 0.1 mg (0.01%) in a base compounded with glyceryl monostearate, peanut oil, glycerin, benzoic acid, glutamic acid, citric acid, butylated hydroxanisole, sodium hydroxide and water. pH is approximately 4.3. Tubes of 78 g with applicator. Store at controlled room temperature (15 to 30°C).

Reviewed 1999

ORTHO-NOVUM® 1/50 Ⓟ

Janssen-Ortho

Norethindrone—Mestranol

Oral Contraceptive

Pharmacology: Acts through the mechanism of gonadotropin suppression primarily at the pituitary-ovarian axis with secondary pelvic involvement.

Conception Control: The contraceptive efficacy is attributed to suppression of ovulation with a possible contribution from alterations in cervical mucus and in the endometrium.

Amenorrhea: Where normal cycling does not occur, as in amenorrhea, the temporary cyclic administration of Ortho-Novum 1/50 Tablets, which tends to promote shedding of the endometrium during the therapeutic regimen, may result in rhythmic menstruation without exogenous hormonal support when product administration is discontinued.

Dysfunctional Uterine Bleeding: Dysfunctional uterine bleeding in the absence of disease or pathology is generally attributed to endocrine abnormality. Most frequently a disorder or imbalance of the pituitary-ovarian axis is responsible. Again, the temporary cyclic administration of Ortho-Novum 1/50 Tablets may result in rhythmic menstruation without exogenous hormonal support when product administration is discontinued.

Dysmenorrhea: Clinical experience has demonstrated a frequent association between anovulatory cycles and menstruation unaccompanied by dysmenorrhea.

Endometriosis: Signs and symptoms of endometriosis generally regress during administration of the tablets due in part to anovulation brought about by suppression of gonadotropic activity and in part to the transformation of functioning endometrium into decidua-like tissue by increasing levels of estrogen and progestogen.

Indications: For conception control in circumstances where lower dosage estrogen formulations prove to be unacceptable.

Ortho-Novum 1/50 Tablets are also indicated for hormonal therapy, i.e., amenorrhea, dysmenorrhea, endometriosis and dysfunctional uterine bleeding.

Contraindications: History of/or actual thrombophlebitis or thromboembolic disorders; history of/or actual cerebrovascular disorders; history of/or actual myocardial infarction or coronary arterial disease; active liver disease or history of/or actual benign or malignant liver tumors; known or suspected carcinoma of the breast; known or suspected estrogen-dependent neoplasia; undiagnosed abnormal vaginal bleeding; any ocular lesion arising from ophthalmic vascular disease, such as partial or complete loss of vision or defect in visual fields; when pregnancy is suspected or diagnosed.

Warnings: Predisposing Factors For Coronary Artery Disease: Cigarette smoking increases the risk of serious cardiovascular side effects and mortality. Birth control pills increase this risk, especially with increasing age. Convincing data are available to support an upper age limit of 35 years for oral contraceptive use by women who smoke.

Other women who are independently at high risk for cardiovascular disease include those with diabetes, hypertension, abnormal lipid profile, or a family history of these. Whether oral contraceptives accentuate this risk is unclear.

In low-risk, non-smoking women of any age, the benefits of oral contraceptive use outweigh the possible cardiovascular risks associated with low dose formulations. Consequently, oral contraceptives may be prescribed for these women up to the age of menopause.

> Cigarette smoking increases the risk of serious adverse effects on the heart and blood vessels. This risk increases with age and becomes significant in oral contraceptive users over 35 years of age. Women should be counselled not to smoke.

Discontinue medication at the earliest manifestation of:

A. Thromboembolic and cardiovascular disorders such as: thrombophlebitis, pulmonary embolism, cerebrovascular disorders, myocardial ischemia, mesenteric thrombosis and retinal thrombosis.
B. Conditions which predispose to venous stasis and to vascular thrombosis (e.g., immobilization after accidents or confinement to bed during long-term illness). Other non-hormonal methods of contraception should be used until regular activities are resumed. For use of oral contraceptives when surgery is contemplated, see Precautions.
C. Visual defects—partial or complete.
D. Papilledema, or ophthalmic vascular lesions.
E. Severe headache of unknown etiology or worsening of pre-existing migraine headache.

Precautions: Physical Examination and Follow-up: Before oral contraceptives are used, a thorough history and physical examination should be performed, including a blood pressure determination. Breasts, liver, extremities and pelvic organs should be examined. A Papanicolaou smear should be taken if the patient has been sexually active.

The first follow-up visit should be done 3 months after oral contraceptives are prescribed. Thereafter, examinations should be performed at least once a year or more frequently if indicated. At each annual visit, examination should include those procedures that were done at the initial visit as outlined above or per recommendations of the Canadian Workshop on Screening for Cancer of the Cervix. Their suggestion was that, for women who had 2 consecutive negative Pap smears, screening could be continued every 3 years up to the age of 69.

Pregnancy: Oral contraceptives should not be taken by pregnant women. However, if conception accidentally occurs while taking the pill, there is no conclusive evidence that the estrogen and progestin contained in the oral contraceptive will damage the developing child.

Lactation: In breastfeeding women, the use of oral contraceptives results in the hormonal components being excreted in breast milk and may reduce its quantity and quality. If the use

Table I—Ortho-Novum 1/50 Tablets

Drugs Which May Decrease the Efficacy of Oral Contraceptives

Class of Compound	Drug	Proposed Mechanism	Suggested Management
Anticonvulsants	Carbamazepine Ethosuximide Phenobarbital Phenytoin Primidone	Induction of hepatic microsomal enzymes: Rapid metabolism of estrogen and increased binding of progestin and ethinyl estradiol to SHBG.	Use higher dose OCs (50 μg ethinyl estradiol), another drug or another method.
Antibiotics	Ampicillin Cotrimoxazole Penicillin	Enterohepatic circulation disturbance, intestinal hurry.	For short course, use additional method or use another drug. For long course, use another method.
	Rifampin	Increased metabolism of progestins. Suspected acceleration of estrogen metabolism.	Use another method.
	Chloramphenicol Metronidazole Neomycin Nitrofurantoin Sulfonamides Tetracyclines	Induction of hepatic microsomal enzymes. Also disturbance of enterohepatic circulation.	For short course, use additional method or use another drug. For long course, use another method.
	Troleandomycin	May retard metabolism of OCs, increasing the risk of cholestatic jaundice.	
Antifungal	Griseofulvin	Stimulation of hepatic metabolism of contraceptive steroids may occur.	Use another method.
Cholesterol Lowering Agents	Clofibrate	Reduces elevated serum triglycerides and cholesterol; this reduces OC efficacy.	Use another method.
Sedatives and Hypnotics	Benzodiazepines Barbiturates Chloral Hydrate Glutethimide Meprobamate	Induction of hepatic microsomal enzymes.	For short course, use additional method or another drug. For long course, use another method or higher dose OCs.
Antacids		Decreased intestinal absorption of progestins.	Dose 2 hours apart.
Other Drugs	Phenylbutazone Antihistamines Analgesics Antimigraine preparations Vitamin E	Reduced OC efficacy has been reported. Remains to be confirmed.	

of oral contraceptives is initiated after the establishment of lactation, there does not appear to be any effect on the quantity and quality of the milk. There is no evidence that low-dose oral contraceptives are harmful to the nursing infant.

Hepatic Function: Patients who have had jaundice including a history of cholestatic jaundice during pregnancy should be given oral contraceptives with great care and under close observation.

The development of severe generalized pruritus or icterus requires that the medication be withdrawn until the problem is resolved.

If the jaundice should prove to be cholestatic in type, the use of oral contraceptives should not be resumed. In patients taking oral contraceptives, changes in the composition of the bile may occur and an increased incidence of gallstones has been reported.

Hepatic nodules (adenoma and focal nodular hyperplasia) have been reported, particularly in long-term users of oral contraceptives. Although these lesions are extremely rare, they have caused fatal intra-abdominal hemorrhage and should be considered in women with an abdominal mass, acute abdominal pain, or evidence of intra-abdominal bleeding.

Hypertension: Patients with essential hypertension whose blood pressure is well-controlled may be given oral contraceptives but only under close supervision. If a significant elevation of blood pressure in previously normotensive or hypertensive subjects occurs at any time during the administration of the drug, cessation of medication is necessary.

Migraine and Headache: The onset or exacerbation of migraine or the development of headache of a new pattern which is recurrent, persistent or severe, requires discontinuation of oral contraceptives and evaluation of the cause.

Diabetes: Current low-dose oral contraceptives exert minimal impact on glucose metabolism. Diabetic patients, or those with a family history of diabetes, should be observed closely to detect worsening of carbohydrate metabolism. Patients predisposed to diabetes who can be kept under close supervision may be given oral contraceptives. Young diabetic patients whose disease is of recent origin, well-controlled, and not associated with hypertension or other signs of vascular disease such as ocular fundal changes, should be monitored more frequently while using oral contraceptives.

Ocular Disease: Patients who are pregnant or are taking oral contraceptives, may experience corneal edema that may cause visual disturbances and changes in tolerance to contact lenses, especially of the rigid type. Soft contact lenses usually do not cause disturbances. If visual changes or alterations in tolerance to contact lenses occur, temporary or permanent cessation of wear may be advised.

Breasts: Increasing age and a strong family history are the most significant risk factors for the development of breast cancer. Other established risk factors include obesity, nulliparity and late age for first full-term pregnancy. The identified groups of women that may be at increased risk of developing breast cancer before menopause are long-term users of oral contraceptives (more than 8 years) and starters at an early age. In a few women, the use of oral contraceptives may accelerate the growth of an existing but undiagnosed breast cancer. Since any potential increased risk related to oral contraceptive use is small, there is no reason to change prescribing habits at present.

Women receiving oral contraceptives should be instructed in self-examination of their breasts. Their physicians should be notified whenever any masses are detected. A yearly clinical breast examination is also recommended because, if a breast cancer should develop, estrogen-containing drugs may cause a rapid progression.

Vaginal Bleeding: Persistent irregular vaginal bleeding requires assessment to exclude underlying pathology.

Fibroids: Patients with fibroids (leiomyomata) should be carefully observed. Sudden enlargement, pain, or tenderness requires discontinuation of the use of oral contraceptives.

Emotional Disorders: Patients with a history of emotional disturbances, especially the depressive type, may be more prone to have a recurrence of depression while taking oral contraceptives. In cases of a serious recurrence, a trial of an alternate method of contraception should be made which may help to clarify the possible relationship. Women with premenstrual syndrome (PMS) may have a varied response to oral contraceptives, ranging from symptomatic improvement to worsening of the condition.

Laboratory Tests: Results of laboratory tests should be interpreted in the light that the patient is on oral contraceptives. The following laboratory tests are modified.

Liver Function Tests: Bromsulphthalein Retention Test (BSP), moderate increase; AST and GGT, minor increase; alkaline phosphatase, variable increase; serum bilirubin, increased, particularly in conditions predisposing to or associated with hyperbilirubinemia.

Table II—Ortho-Novum 1/50 Tablets

Modification of Drug Action by Oral Contraceptives

Class of Compound	Drug	Modification of Drug Action	Suggested Management
Alcohol		Possible increased levels of ethanol or acetaldehyde.	Use with caution.
Alpha-II Adrenoreceptor Agents	Clonidine	Sedation effect increased.	Use with caution.
Anticoagulants	All	OCs increase clotting factors, decrease efficacy. However, OCs may potentiate action in some patients.	Use another method.
Anticonvulsants	All	Fluid retention may increase risk of seizures.	Use another method.
Antidiabetic Drugs	Oral hypoglycemics and insulin	OCs may impair glucose tolerance and increase blood glucose.	Use low-dose estrogen and progestin OC or another method. Monitor blood glucose.
Antihypertensive Agents	Guanethidine and methyldopa	Estrogen component causes sodium retention, progestin has no effect.	Use low-dose estrogen OC or use another method.
	Beta-blockers	Increased drug effect (decreased metabolism).	Adjust dose of drug if necessary. Monitor cardiovascular status.
Antipyretics	Acetaminophen	Increased metabolism and renal clearance.	Dose of drug may have to be increased.
	Antipyrine	Impaired metabolism.	Decrease dose of drug.
	ASA	Effects of ASA may be decreased by the short-term use of OCs.	Patients on chronic ASA therapy may require an increase in ASA dosage.
Aminocaproic Acid		Theoretically, a hypercoagulable state may occur because OCs augment clotting factors.	Avoid concomitant use.
Betamimetic Agents	Isoproterenol	Estrogen causes decreased response to these drugs.	Adjust dose of drug as necessary. Discontinuing OCs can result in excessive drug activity.
Caffeine		The actions of caffeine may be enhanced as OCs may impair the hepatic metabolism of caffeine.	Use with caution.
Cholesterol Lowering Agents	Clofibrate	Their action may be antagonized by OCs. OCs may also increase metabolism of clofibrate.	May need to increase dose of clofibrate.
Corticosteroids	Prednisone	Markedly increased serum levels.	Possible need for decrease in dose.
Cyclosporine		May lead to an increase in cyclosporine levels and hepatotoxicity.	Monitor hepatic function. The cyclosporine dose may have to be decreased.
Folic Acid		OCs have been reported to impair folate metabolism.	May need to increase dietary intake, or supplement.
Meperidine		Possible increased analgesia and CNS depression due to decreased metabolism of meperidine.	Use combination with caution.
Phenothiazine Tranquilizers	All Phenothiazines, Reserpine and similar drugs	Estrogen potentiates the hyperprolactinemia effect of these drugs.	Use other drugs or lower dose OCs. If galactorrhea or hyperprolactinemia occurs, use other method.
Sedatives and Hypnotics	Chlordiazepoxide Lorazepam Oxazepam Diazepam	Increased effect (increased metabolism).	Use with caution.
Theophylline	All	Decreased oxidation, leading to possible toxicity.	Use with caution. Monitor theophylline levels.
Tricyclic Antidepressants	Clomipramine (possibly others)	Increased side effects; i.e., depression.	Use with caution.
Vitamin B_{12}		OCs have been reported to reduce serum levels of Vitamin B_{12}.	May need to increase dietary intake, or supplement.

Coagulation Tests: Factors II, VII, IX, X, XII and XIII, increased; Factor VIII, mild increase; platelet aggregation and adhesiveness, mild increase in response to common aggregating agents; fibrinogen, increased; plasminogen, mild increase; antithrombin III, mild decrease; prothrombin time, increased.

Thyroid Function Tests: Protein-bound Iodine (PBI), increased; Total Serum Thyroxine (T_4), increased; Thyroid Stimulating Hormone (TSH), unchanged.

Adrenocortical Function Tests: plasma cortisol, increased.

Miscellaneous Tests: serum folate, occasionally decreased; glucose tolerance test, variable increase with return to normal after 6 to 12 months; insulin response, mild to moderate increase; c-peptide response, mild to moderate increase.

Tissue Specimens: Pathologists should be advised of oral contraceptive therapy when specimens obtained from surgical procedures and Pap smears are submitted for examination.

Return to Fertility: After discontinuing oral contraceptive therapy, the patient should delay pregnancy until at least 1 normal spontaneous menstrual cycle has occurred in order to date the pregnancy. An alternative contraceptive method should be used during this time.

Amenorrhea: Women having a history of oligomenorrhea, secondary amenorrhea, or irregular cycles may remain anovulatory or become amenorrheic following discontinuation of estrogen-progestin combination therapy. Amenorrhea, especially if associated with breast secretion, that continues for 6 months or more after withdrawal, warrants a careful assessment of hypothalamic-pituitary function.

Thromboembolic Complications—Post-surgery: There is an increased risk of thromboembolic complications in oral

Ortho-Novum 1/50 (cont'd)

contraceptive users, after major surgery. If feasible, oral contraceptives should be discontinued and an alternative method substituted at least 1 month prior to **major** elective surgery. Oral contraceptives should not be resumed until the first menstrual period after hospital discharge following surgery.

Drug Interactions: The concurrent administration of oral contraceptives with other drugs may result in an altered response to either agent (see Table I (on previous pages) and Table II on previous page). Reduced effectiveness of the oral contraceptive, should it occur, is more likely with the low-dose formulations. It is important to ascertain all drugs that a patient is taking, both prescription and nonprescription, before oral contraceptives are prescribed.

Non-contraceptive Benefits of Oral Contraceptives: Several health advantages other than contraception have been reported.

1. Combination oral contraceptives reduce the incidence of cancer of the endometrium and ovaries.
2. Oral contraceptives reduce the likelihood of developing benign breast disease and, as a result, decrease the incidence of breast biopsies.
3. Oral contraceptives reduce the likelihood of development of functional ovarian cysts.
4. Pill users have less menstrual blood loss and have more regular cycles, thereby reducing the chance of developing iron-deficiency anemia.
5. The use of oral contraceptives may decrease the severity of dysmenorrhea and premenstrual syndrome, and may improve acne vulgaris, hirsutism, and other androgen-mediated disorders.
6. Oral contraceptives decrease the incidence of acute pelvic inflammatory disease and, thereby, reduce as well the incidence of ectopic pregnancy.
7. Oral contraceptives have potential beneficial effects on endometriosis.

> Oral contraceptives **do not protect** against sexually transmitted diseases (STDs) including HIV/AIDS. For protection against STDs, it is advisable to use latex condoms **in combination with** oral contraceptives.

Adverse Effects: An increased risk of the following serious adverse reactions has been associated with the use of oral contraceptives: thrombophlebitis; pulmonary embolism; mesenteric thrombosis; neuro-ocular lesions, e.g., retinal thrombosis; myocardial infarction; cerebral thrombosis; cerebral hemorrhage; hypertension; benign hepatic tumors; gallbladder disease.

The following adverse reactions also have been reported in patients receiving oral contraceptives: nausea and vomiting, usually the most common adverse reaction, occurs in approximately 10% or less of patients during the first cycle. Other reactions, as a general rule, are seen less frequently or only occasionally, as follows: gastrointestinal symptoms (such as abdominal cramps and bloating); breakthrough bleeding; spotting; change in menstrual flow; dysmenorrhea; amenorrhea during and after treatment; temporary infertility after discontinuance of treatment; edema; chloasma or melasma which may persist; breast changes: tenderness, enlargement, and secretion; change in weight (increase or decrease); endocervical hyperplasias; possible diminution in lactation when given immediately postpartum; cholestatic jaundice; migraine; increase in size of uterine leiomyomata; rash (allergic); depression; reduced tolerance to carbohydrates; vaginal candidiasis; premenstrual-like syndrome; intolerance to contact lenses; change in corneal curvature (steepening); cataracts; optic neuritis; retinal thrombosis; changes in libido; chorea; changes in appetite; cystitis-like syndrome; rhinitis; headache; nervousness; dizziness; hirsutism; loss of scalp hair; erythema multiforme; erythema nodosum; hemorrhagic eruption; vaginitis; porphyria; impaired renal function; Raynaud's phenomenon; auditory disturbances; hemolytic uremic syndrome; pancreatitis.

Overdose: Symptoms and Treatment: In case of overdosage or accidental ingestion by children, the physician should observe the patient closely although generally no treatment is required. Gastric lavage may be utilized if considered necessary.

Dosage: Information for the Patient on How to Take the Birth Control Pill:

1. **Read these directions:**
   - before you start taking your pills, and
   - any time you are not sure what to do.
2. **Look at your pill pack** to see if it has 21 or 28 pills:
   - **21-Pill Pack:** 21 active pills (with hormones) taken daily for 3 weeks, and then take no pills taken for 1 week or
   - **28-Pill Pack:** 21 active pills (with hormones) taken daily for 3 weeks, and then 7 "reminder" pills (no hormones) taken daily for 1 week.

Also check the pill pack for instructions on (1) where to start and (2) directions to take pills (see package insert for illustrations).

3. You may wish to use a second method of birth control (e.g., latex condoms and spermicidal foam or gel) for the first 7 days of the first cycle of pill use. This will provide a back-up in case pills are forgotten while you are getting used to taking them.
4. **When receiving any medical treatment, be sure to tell your doctor that you are using birth control pills.**
5. **Many women have spotting or light bleeding, or may feel sick to their stomach during the first 3 months on the pill.** If you do feel sick, do not stop taking the pill. The problem will usually go away. If it does not go away, check with your doctor or clinic.
6. **Missing pills also can cause some spotting or light bleeding,** even if you make up the missed pills. You also could feel a little sick to your stomach on the days you take 2 pills to make up for missed pills.
7. **If you miss pills at any time, you could get pregnant. The greatest risks for pregnancy are:**
   - when you start a pack late, or
   - when you miss pills at the beginning or at the very end of the pack.
8. **Always be sure you have ready:**
   - **another kind of birth control** (such as latex condoms and spermicidal foam or gel) to use as a back-up in case you miss pills, and
   - **an extra, full pack of pills.**
9. **If you experience vomiting or diarrhea, or if you take certain medicines,** such as antibiotics, your pills may not work as well. Use a back-up method, such as latex condoms and spermicidal foam or gel, until you can check with your doctor or clinic.
10. **If you forget more than 1 pill 2 months in a row,** talk to your doctor or clinic about how to make pill-taking easier or about using another method of birth control.
11. **If your questions are not answered here, call your doctor or clinic.**

When to Start the First Pack of Pills: Be sure to read these instructions:

- before you start taking your pills, and
- any time you are not sure what to do.

Decide with your doctor or clinic what is the best day for you to start taking your first pack of pills. Your pills may be either a 21-day or a 28-day type.

A. 21-Day Combination: With this type of birth control pill, you are 21 days on the pill with 7 days off the pill. You must not be off the pills for more than 7 days in a row.

1. **The first day of your menstrual period (bleeding) is Day 1 of your cycle.** The pills may be started up to Day 6 of your cycle. Your starting day will be chosen in discussion with your doctor. You will **always** begin taking your pill on this day of the week. Your doctor may advise you to start taking the pills on Day 1, on Day 5, or on the first Sunday after your period begins. If your period starts on Sunday, start that same day.
2. Take 1 pill at approximately the same time every day for 21 days; **then take no pills for 7 days.** Start a new pack on the 8th day. You will probably have a period during the 7 days off the pill. (This bleeding may be lighter and shorter than your usual period.)

Directions: 21-Day Regimen: **Follow these instructions carefully** (see package insert for illustrations): Your starting day will be chosen in discussion with your doctor. You should **always** begin taking your tablets on this day of the week. To set the package to the day you and your doctor selected, insert a coin into the middle slot and turn the inner wheel counterclockwise until that day appears in the window. The example shown is for a **Sunday** start. Your first yellow tablet is below the "V" notch as shown. Ensure that the tab marked "Lift Out" is set over this tablet. Break off the tab and begin tablet taking. To take your second and all subsequent tablets, turn the clear outer cover clockwise to the next available tablet. Take a tablet a day, for 21 days, completing all yellow tablets. After you have taken all of your tablets wait seven days and begin your next package on your chosen starting day whether you have finished menstruating or not. Always remember to set the starting day of each new package to the day chosen by you and your doctor.

Your first pill of each package is always under the "V" notch.

B. 28-Day Combination: With this type of birth control pill, you take 21 pills which contain hormones and 7 pills which contain no hormones.

1. **The first day of your menstrual period (bleeding) is Day 1 of your cycle.** The pills may be started up to Day 6 of your cycle. Your starting day will be chosen in discussion with your doctor. You will **always** begin taking your pill on this day of the week. Your doctor may advise you to start taking the pills on Day 1, on Day 5, or on the first Sunday after your period begins. If your period starts on Sunday, start that same day.
2. Take 1 pill at approximately the same time every day for 28 days. Begin a new pack the next day, **not missing any**

Table III—Ortho-Novum 1/50 Tablets

What to Do if You Miss Pills

Sunday Start	Other Than Sunday Start
Miss 1 pill	**Miss 1 pill**
Take it as soon as you remember, and take the next pill at the usual time. This means that you might take 2 pills in one day.	Take it as soon as you remember, and take the next pill at the usual time. This means that you might take 2 pills in one day.
Miss 2 pills in a row	**Miss 2 pills in a row**
First 2 Weeks: 1. Take 2 pills the day you remember and 2 pills the next day. 2. Then take 1 pill a day until you finish the pack. 3. Use a back-up method of birth control if you have sex in the 7 days after you miss the pills.	**First 2 Weeks:** 1. Take 2 pills the day you remember and 2 pills the next day. 2. Then take 1 pill a day until you finish the pack. 3. Use a back-up method of birth control if you have sex in the 7 days after you miss the pills.
Third Week: 1. Keep taking 1 pill a day until Sunday. 2. On Sunday, safely discard the rest of the pack and start a new pack that day. 3. Use a back-up method of birth control if you have sex in the 7 days after you miss the pills. 4. You may not have a period this month. **If you miss 2 periods in a row, call your doctor or clinic.**	**Third Week:** 1. Safely dispose of the rest of the pill pack and start a new pack that same day. 2. Use a back-up method of birth control if you have sex in the 7 days after you miss the pills. 3. You may not have a period this month. **If you miss 2 periods in a row, call your doctor or clinic.**
Miss 3 or more pills in a row	**Miss 3 or more pills in a row**
Anytime in the Cycle: 1. Keep taking 1 pill a day until Sunday. 2. On Sunday, safely discard the rest of the pack and start a new pack that day. 3. Use a back-up method of birth control if you have sex in the 7 days after you miss the pills. 4. You may not have a period this month. **If you miss 2 periods in a row, call your doctor or clinic.**	**Anytime in the Cycle:** 1. Safely dispose of the rest of the pill pack and start a new pack that same day. 2. Use a back-up method of birth control if you have sex in the 7 days after you miss the pills. 3. You may not have a period this month. **If you miss 2 periods in a row, call your doctor or clinic.**

days on the pills. Your period should occur during the last 7 days of using that pill pack.

Directions: 28-Day Regimen: **Follow these directions carefully** (see package insert for illustrations): **Always complete the yellow tablets before taking the green tablets.**

Your starting day will be chosen in discussion with your doctor. You should **always** begin taking your tablets on this day of the week. To set the package to the day you and your doctor selected, insert a coin into the middle slot and turn the inner wheel counterclockwise until that day appears in the window. The example shown is for a **Sunday** start. Your first yellow tablet is immediately to the right of the green tablets and below the "V" notch as shown. Ensure that the tab marked "Lift Out" is set over this tablet. Break off the tab and begin tablet taking. To take your second and all subsequent tablets, turn the clear outer cover clockwise to the next available tablet. Take a tablet a day, every day, first completing all 21 yellow tablets, and finally the 7 green tablets. After you have taken all of your tablets, begin your next package the very next day on your chosen starting day, whether you have finished menstruating or not. Always remember to set the starting day of each new package to the day chosen by you and your doctor.

Your first pill of each package is always under the "V" notch.

What to Do During the Month:

1. **Take a pill at approximately the same time every day until the pack is empty.**
   - Try to associate taking your pill with some regular activity such as eating a meal or going to bed.
   - Do not skip pills even if you have bleeding between monthly periods or feel sick to your stomach (nausea).
   - Do not skip pills even if you do not have sex very often.
2. **When you finish a pack:**
   - **21 pills: Wait 7 days** to start the next pack. You will have your period during that week.
   - **28 pills:** Start the next pack **on the next day.** Take 1 pill every day. Do not wait any days between packs.

What to Do if You Miss Pills: Table III (on previous page) outlines the actions you should take if you miss 1 or more of your birth control pills. Match the number of pills missed with the appropriate starting time for your type of pill pack.

Note: 28-Day Pack: If you forget any of the 7 "reminder" pills (without hormones) in Week 4, just safely dispose of the pills you missed. Then keep taking 1 pill each day until the pack is empty. You do not need to use a back-up method.

Always be sure you have on hand:

- a back-up method of birth control (such as latex condoms and spermicidal foam or gel) in case you miss pills, and
- an extra, full pack of pills.

If you forget more than 1 pill 2 months in a row, talk to your doctor or clinic. Talk about ways to make pill-taking easier or about using another method of birth control.

Hormonal Therapy: The requirement for continued therapy should be assessed periodically (see Table IV).

Table IV—Ortho-Novum 1/50 Tablets

Hormonal Therapy		
Indication	**Initial Dosage**	**Duration of Use**
Amenorrhea	1 tablet daily for 3 weeks. Stop for 1 week.	A minimum of 3 months cyclic therapy; thereafter at the discretion of the attending physician.
Dysmenorrhea	1 tablet daily for 3 weeks. Stop for 1 week.	A minimum of 3 months cyclic therapy; thereafter at the discretion of the attending physician.
Endometriosis	**Cyclic Therapy:** 1 tablet daily for 3 weeks. Stop for 1 week.	A minimum of 9 to 12 months; thereafter at the discretion of the attending physician.
	Suppressive Therapy: 1 tablet each day as required.	
Dysfunctional Uterine Bleeding	1 tablet daily for 3 weeks. Stop for 1 week.	A minimum of 3 months cyclic therapy; thereafter at the discretion of the attending physician.

Information for the Patient: See Blue Section—Information for the Patient "Oral Contraceptives".

Supplied: 21-day Regimen: Each yellow, unscored tablet, engraved on each side with "ORTHO 150", contains: norethindrone 1 mg and mestranol 50 μg. Nonmedicinal ingredients: D&C Yellow No. 10 Lake, lactose, magnesium stearate, polyvinylpyrrolidone and starch. Tartrazine-free. Packaged in green VARIDATE DIALPAK Tablet Dispenser Units.

28-day Regimen: Each yellow tablet, engraved on both sides with "ORTHO 150", contains: norethindrone 1 mg and mestranol 50 μg. Nonmedicinal ingredients: D&C Yellow No. 10 Lake, lactose, magnesium stearate, polyvinylpyrrolidone and starch. Each green tablet, embossed on each side with word "ORTHO", contains inert ingredients. Nonmedicinal ingredients: D&C Yellow No. 10 Lake, FD&C Blue No. 2 Lake, lactose, magnesium stearate, microcrystalline cellulose and starch. Tartrazine-free. Packaged in white VARIDATE DIALPAK Tablet Dispenser Units.

Store between 15 and 30°C. Leave contents in protective packaging until time of use.

(Shown in Product Recognition Section)

Reviewed 1999

ORUDIS® Ⓟ
ORUDIS® E Ⓟ
ORUDIS® SR Ⓟ

Rhône-Poulenc Rorer

Ketoprofen

Anti-inflammatory—Analgesic

Pharmacology: Animal pharmacological studies have shown that ketoprofen is a NSAID that possesses anti-inflammatory, analgesic and antipyretic properties. The anti-inflammatory action is not mediated through the pituitary adrenal axis.

Its therapeutic effectiveness has been demonstrated by a reduction in joint swelling, pain and duration of morning stiffness, and by increased grip strength and an improvement in functional capacity.

Clinical trials in rheumatoid arthritis have shown that the antiarthritic activity of ketoprofen 200 mg/day was similar to that of ASA 3.6 g/day.

Ketoprofen 200 mg daily induced less gastrointestinal bleeding than ASA 4 g daily.

The effectiveness of ketoprofen as a general purpose analgesic has been studied in standard pain models which have shown the effectiveness of doses of 25 to 150 mg. Doses of 25 mg were superior to placebo. Larger doses than 25 mg generally could not be shown significantly more effective but there was a tendency toward faster onset and greater duration of action with 50 mg and, in the case of dysmenorrhea, a significantly greater effect overall with 75 mg. Doses greater than 50 to 75 mg did not have increased analgesic effect.

Pharmacokinetics: In man, ketoprofen is rapidly and almost completely absorbed from the gastrointestinal tract. Maximum plasma levels are reached within 0.5 to 2 hours after administration of capsules or suppositories; however, peak plasma levels are delayed by a further 1 to 2 hours with enteric coated tablets and by 5 to 6 hours with sustained-release tablets. The biotransformation of ketoprofen is characterized by 2 main processes: hydroxylation and conjugation, the latter being the main metabolic pathway in man. The drug is 99% bound to plasma proteins, mainly to the albumin fraction. Metabolites as well as the unchanged drug are excreted mainly in the urine. Fecal excretion is negligible.

Following the administration of capsules or enteric coated tablets in man, 25% to 90% of the drug is excreted in the urine within 24 hours, with the major portion being excreted during the first 6 hours. The elimination half-life is approximately 2 hours. Following administration of slow release ketoprofen, absorption is gradual reaching a plateau during which plasma levels remain steady from the fifth to twelfth hour after ingestion and decrease with an apparent half-life of 3 to 4 hours. No accumulation of ketoprofen was found following repeated once daily administration of ketoprofen sustained-release tablets. Repeated administration of the drug, in both animals and man, caused no induction of liver enzymes.

When ketoprofen capsules are administered with food, the total bioavailability (AUC) is not altered; however, the rate of absorption is slowed resulting in delayed and reduced peak concentrations (C_{max}). Following a single 50 mg dose of ketoprofen while fasting, the mean C_{max} was 4.1 mg/L (at 1.1 hours); when administered after food, it decreased to 2.4 mg/L (at 2.0 hours).

The composition of the diet slightly but significantly alters the extent of absorption of ketoprofen from sustained-release tablets: a high-fat/high-calorie meal (3 000 cal/day) was associated with lower ketoprofen bioavailability values (about 20%) than a low low-fat/low-calorie content ($\leq$1 200 cal/day). Mean trough ketoprofen plasma concentrations were similar after high or low fat meals.

To date, studies of the effects of age and renal-function impairment have been small, generally involving 5 to 8 subjects per group, but they indicate modest decrease in clearance in the elderly and in patients with impaired renal function. In normal elderly volunteers (mean age 73 years), the plasma and renal clearance and protein-binding were reduced while the V_d increased when compared to a younger normal population (mean age 27 years). (Plasma clearance and V_d were 0.05 L/kg/h and 0.4 L/kg in elderly and 0.06 L/kg/h and 0.3 L/kg in young subjects, respectively). The mean half-life of ketoprofen in this normal geriatric population, as well as in a rheumatoid elderly population (mean age 64 years), was about 5 hours as compared to 3 hours in the younger population.

Patients with impaired renal function (mean age 44 years) also demonstrate decreases in plasma clearance (0.04 L/kg/h) of drug, with the mean half-life increasing to about 3.5 hours.

Indications: In the treatment of rheumatoid arthritis, ankylosing spondylitis and osteoarthritis.

For the treatment of primary dysmenorrhea as well as for the relief of mild to moderate acute pain associated with musculotendinous trauma (sprains and strains), postoperative (including dental surgery) or postpartum pain.

Contraindications: In patients with active peptic ulcers, a history of recurrent ulceration or active inflammatory diseases of the gastrointestinal tract; suppositories should not be used in patients with any inflammatory lesions of rectum or anus and in patients with a recent history of rectal or anal bleeding.

In patients with known or suspected hypersensitivity to the drug or other NSAIDs. Because of cross-sensitivity, ketoprofen should not be given to patients with the complete or partial syndrome of nasal polyps, or asthma, anaphylaxis, rhinitis or urticaria. Fatal anaphylactoid reactions have occurred in such individuals.

Significant hepatic impairment or active liver disease.

Severely impaired or deteriorating renal function (creatinine clearance <30 mL/min or 0.5 mL/s). Individuals with lesser degrees of renal impairment are at risk of deterioration of their renal function when prescribed NSAIDs and must be monitored.

Ketoprofen is not recommended for use with other NSAIDs because of the absence of any evidence demonstrating synergistic benefits and the potential for additive side effects.

Warnings: Gastrointestinal: Serious gastrointestinal toxicity, such as peptic ulceration, perforation and gastrointestinal bleeding, sometimes severe and occasionally fatal can occur at any time, with or without symptoms in patients treated with NSAIDs including ketoprofen. Unlike most adverse reactions, which usually manifest themselves in the first month if they are going to occur in an individual, new peptic ulcers keep appearing in patients under treatment with ketoprofen at a rate of greater than 1% per year.

Minor upper gastrointestinal problems, such as dyspepsia, are common, usually developing early in therapy. Physicians should remain alert for ulceration and bleeding in patients treated with NSAIDs, even in the absence of previous gastrointestinal tract symptoms.

In patients observed in clinical trials of such agents, symptomatic upper gastrointestinal ulcers, gross bleeding, or perforation appear to occur in approximately 1% of patients treated for 3 to 6 months and in about 2 to 4% of patients treated for 1 year. The risk continues beyond 1 year and possibly increases.

The incidence of these complications increases with increasing dose.

Ketoprofen should be given under close medical supervision to patients prone to gastrointestinal tract irritation particularly those with a history of peptic ulcer, diverticulosis or other inflammatory disease of the gastrointestinal tract such as ulcerative colitis and Crohn's disease. In these cases the physician must weigh the benefits of treatment against the possible hazards.

Physicians should inform patients about the signs and/or symptoms of serious gastrointestinal toxicity and instruct them to contact a physician immediately if they experience persistent dyspepsia or other symptoms or signs suggestive of gastrointestinal ulceration or bleeding.

Orudis (cont'd)

Because serious gastrointestinal tract ulceration and bleeding can occur without warning symptoms, physicians should follow chronically treated patients by checking their hemoglobin periodically and by being vigilant for the signs and symptoms of ulceration and bleeding and should inform the patients of the importance of this follow-up. If ulceration is suspected or confirmed, or if gastrointestinal bleeding occurs, ketoprofen should be discontinued immediately, appropriate treatment instituted and the patients monitored closely.

No studies, to date, have identified any group of patients **not** at risk of developing ulceration and bleeding. A prior history of serious gastrointestinal events and other factors such as excess alcohol intake, smoking, age, female gender and concomitant oral steroid and anticoagulant use have been associated with increased risk.

Studies to date show that all NSAIDs can cause gastrointestinal tract adverse events. Although existing data does not clearly identify differences in risk between various NSAIDs, this may be shown in the future.

Geriatrics: Patients older than 65 years and frail or debilitated patients are most susceptible to a variety of adverse reactions from NSAIDs. The incidence of the adverse reactions increases with dose and duration of treatment. In addition, these patients are less tolerant to ulceration and bleeding. Most reports of fatal gastrointestinal events are in this population. Older patients are also at risk of lower esophageal ulceration and bleeding.

For such patients, consideration should be given to a starting dose lower than the one usually recommended, with individual adjustment when necessary and under close supervision (see Precautions).

Cross-sensitivity: Patients sensitive to any one of the NSAIDs may be sensitive to any of the other NSAIDs also.

Aseptic Meningitis: In occasional cases, with some NSAIDs, the symptoms of aseptic meningitis (stiff neck, severe headaches, nausea and vomiting, fever or clouding of consciousness) have been observed. Patients with autoimmune disorders (systemic lupus erythematosus, mixed connective tissues diseases, etc.) seem to be predisposed. Therefore, in such patients, the physician must be vigilant to the development of this complication.

Pregnancy: The safety of ketoprofen when administered to pregnant or nursing women has not been determined and therefore such use is not recommended. Pregnant rats who received ketoprofen 6 and 9 mg/kg/day orally from day 15 of gestation, showed dystocia and increased pup mortality.

Lactation: In rats, ketoprofen at doses of 9 mg/kg (approximately 1.5 times the maximum human therapeutic dose) did not affect perinatal development. Upon administration to lactating dogs, the milk concentration of ketoprofen was found to be 4 to 5% of the plasma drug level. Data on secretion in human milk after ingestion of ketoprofen do not exist. As with other drugs that are excreted in milk, ketoprofen is not recommended for use in nursing mothers.

Children: The conditions for safe and effective use of ketoprofen in children under 12 years of age have not been established and the drug is therefore not recommended in this age group.

Precautions: Gastrointestinal: There is no definitive evidence that the concomitant administration of histamine H_2-receptor antagonists and/or antacids will either prevent the occurrence of gastrointestinal side effects or allow the continuation of ketoprofen therapy when and if these adverse reactions appear.

Suppositories should be given with caution to patients with any rectal or anal pathology.

Renal Function: Long-term administration of NSAIDs to animals has resulted in renal papillary necrosis and other abnormal renal pathology. In humans, there have been reports of acute interstitial nephritis with hematuria, proteinuria, and occasionally nephrotic syndrome.

A second form of renal toxicity has been seen in patients with prerenal conditions leading to the reduction in renal blood flow or blood volume, where the renal prostaglandins have a supportive role in the maintenance of renal perfusion. In these patients, administration of a NSAID may cause a dose-dependent reduction in prostaglandin formation and may precipitate overt renal decompensation. Patients at greatest risk of this reaction are those with impaired renal function, heart failure, liver dysfunction, those taking diuretics, and the elderly. Discontinuation of nonsteroidal anti-inflammatory therapy is usually followed by recovery to the pretreatment state.

Ketoprofen and its metabolites are eliminated primarily by the kidneys, therefore the drug should be used with great caution in patients with impaired renal function. In these cases, utilization of lower doses of ketoprofen should be considered and patients carefully monitored.

During long-term therapy kidney function should be monitored periodically.

Genitourinary: Some NSAIDs are known to cause persistent urinary symptoms (bladder pain, dysuria, urinary frequency), hematuria or cystitis. The onset of these symptoms may occur at any time after the initiation of therapy with a NSAID. Some cases have become severe on continued treatment. Should urinary symptoms occur, treatment with ketoprofen **must be stopped immediately** to obtain recovery. This should be done before any urological investigations or treatments are carried out.

Hepatic Function: As with other NSAIDs, borderline elevations of one or more liver function tests may occur in up to 15% of patients. These abnormalities may progress, may remain essentially unchanged, or may be transient with continued therapy. Meaningful (3 times the upper limit of normal) elevations of ALT or AST occurred in controlled clinical trials in less than 1% of patients. A patient with symptoms and/or signs suggesting liver dysfunction, or in whom an abnormal liver test has occurred, should be evaluated for evidence of the development of more severe hepatic reaction while on therapy with this drug. Severe hepatic reactions including jaundice and cases of fatal hepatitis have been reported with NSAIDs. Although such reactions are rare, if abnormal liver tests persist or worsen, if clinical signs and symptoms consistent with liver disease develop, or if systemic manifestations occur (e.g., eosinophilia, rash, etc.), this drug should be discontinued.

During long-term therapy, liver function tests should be monitored periodically. If there is a need to prescribe this drug in the presence of impaired liver function, it must be done under strict observation.

Fluid and Electrolyte Balance: Fluid retention and edema have been observed in approximately 2% of patients treated with ketoprofen. Therefore, as with many other NSAIDs, the possibility of precipitating congestive heart failure in elderly patients or those with compromised cardiac function should be borne in mind. Ketoprofen should be used with caution in patients with heart failure, hypertension or other conditions predisposing to fluid retention.

With nonsteroidal anti-inflammatory treatment there is a potential risk of hyperkalemia, particularly in patients with conditions such as diabetes mellitus or renal failure; in elderly patients; or in patients receiving concomitant therapy with β-adrenergic blockers, angiotensin converting enzyme inhibitors or some diuretics. Serum electrolytes should be monitored periodically during long-term therapy, especially in those patients who are at risk.

Hematology: Drugs inhibiting prostaglandin biosynthesis do interfere with platelet function to varying degrees; therefore, patients who may be adversely affected by such an action should be carefully observed when ketoprofen is administered.

Blood dyscrasias (such as neutropenia, leukopenia, thrombocytopenia, aplastic anemia and agranulocytosis) associated with the use of NSAIDs are rare, but could be with severe consequences.

Anemia is commonly observed in rheumatoid arthritis and is sometimes aggravated by NSAIDs, which may produce fluid retention or minor gastrointestinal blood loss in some patients. Therefore, patients with initial hemoglobin values of 10 g/dL or less who are to receive long-term therapy should have hemoglobin values determined frequently.

Infection: In common with other anti-inflammatory drugs, ketoprofen may mask the usual signs of infection.

Ophthalmology: Blurred and/or diminished vision has been reported with the use of ketoprofen and other NSAIDs. If such symptoms develop this drug should be discontinued and an ophthalmologic examination performed; ophthalmic examination should be carried out at periodic intervals in any patient receiving this drug for an extended period of time.

CNS: Some patients may experience drowsiness, dizziness, vertigo, insomnia or depression with the use of ketoprofen. If patients experience these side effects, they should exercise caution in carrying out activities that require alertness.

Drug Interactions: Methotrexate: The concomitant administration of ketoprofen and high-dose methotrexate has been associated with prolonged and marked enhancement of serum methotrexate levels resulting in severe methotrexate toxicity. This may also apply to some other NSAIDs. There were no abnormalities in methotrexate kinetics or evidence of toxicity when ketoprofen was given at least 12 hours after completion of high-dose methotrexate infusion. Ketoprofen should not be used in patients receiving high-dose methotrexate.

The potential for severe toxicity should be kept in mind when prescribing ketoprofen and low-dose methotrexate concurrently. Ketoprofen should not be administered within 12 hours of methotrexate infusion.

ASA or other NSAIDs: Concurrent administration of ASA decreased ketoprofen protein binding and increased its plasma clearance. The overall result was a 40% reduction in the AUC of ketoprofen. Ketoprofen does not alter ASA absorption.

The use of ketoprofen in addition to any other NSAID, including those over-the-counter ones (such as ASA and ibuprofen) is not recommended due to the possibility of additive side effects. Concurrent therapy may increase the risk of gastrointestinal toxicity, including ulceration or hemorrhage, without providing additional symptomatic relief. Concurrent use of ASA with other NSAIDs may also increase the risk of bleeding at sites other than the gastrointestinal tract because of additive inhibition of platelet aggregation.

Oral Anticoagulants: Ketoprofen has been shown to depress platelet aggregation and it can prolong bleeding time by approximately 3 to 4 minutes from baseline values. However, a study conducted in 20 patients undergoing therapy with coumarin and simultaneously receiving ketoprofen, failed to demonstrate potentiation of anticoagulant effect. Nevertheless, close monitoring of patients is recommended when ketoprofen is given concomitantly with anticoagulants.

Numerous studies have shown that the concomitant use of NSAIDs and anticoagulants increases the risk of gastrointestinal adverse events such as ulceration and bleeding.

Diuretics: Hydrochlorothiazide, given concomitantly with ketoprofen, produces a reduction in urinary potassium and chloride excretion compared to hydrochlorothiazide alone. Patients taking diuretics are at greater risk of developing renal failure secondary to a decrease in renal blood flow caused by prostaglandin inhibition. Concurrent use of a potassium-sparing diuretic with some NSAIDs may increase the risk of hyperkalemia.

Glucocorticoids: Numerous studies have shown that the concomitant use of NSAIDs and oral glucocorticoids increases the gastrointestinal side effects such as ulceration and bleeding. This is especially the case in older (>65 years of age) individuals.

Antacids: Concomitant administration of magnesium hydroxide and aluminum hydroxide does not interfere with the rate or extent of the absorption of ketoprofen.

Lithium: NSAIDs have been reported to increase steady-state plasma lithium levels. It is recommended that plasma lithium levels be monitored when ketoprofen is coadministered with lithium.

Probenecid: Concurrent administration of probenecid increases both free and bound ketoprofen through reducing the plasma clearance of ketoprofen to about one-third as well as decreasing its protein binding. Ketoprofen is not recommended in association with probenecid.

Ketoprofen is extensively (99%) protein bound to human serum albumin and may compete for binding sites with drugs such as sulfonamides, oral hypoglycemic agents, phenytoin or lithium. Although no significant interaction has been documented, patients with such combination therapy should be monitored.

Clinical Laboratory Test: The presence of ketoprofen and its metabolites in urine has been shown to interfere with certain tests which are used to detect albumin, bile salts, 17-ketosteroids or 17-hydroxycorticosteroids in urine and which rely upon acid precipitation as an end point or upon color reactions for carbonyl groups. No interference was seen in the tests for proteinuria using Albustix, Hema-Combistix or Labstix Reagent Strips.

Ketoprofen decreases platelet adhesion and aggregation. Therefore, it can prolong bleeding time by approximately 3 to 4 minutes from baseline values. There is no significant change in platelet count, prothrombin time, partial thromboplastin time, or thrombin time.

The following interactions have not been documented with every NSAID. However, they have been reported with several of these medications and should be considered potential precautions to the use of any NSAID, especially with chronic administration.

Acetaminophen: Prolonged concurrent use of acetaminophen with a NSAID may increase the risk of adverse renal effects; it is recommended that patients be under close medical supervision while receiving such combined therapy.

Alcohol: Concurrent use of alcohol with an NSAID may increase the risk of gastrointestinal side effects, including ulceration or hemorrhage.

Colchicine: Concurrent use of colchicine with a NSAID may increase the risk of gastrointestinal ulceration or hemorrhage.

Inhibition of platelet aggregation by NSAIDs, added to colchicine's effects on blood clotting mechanisms, may increase the risk of bleeding at sites other than the gastrointestinal tract.
Cyclosporine: Inhibition of renal prostaglandin by NSAIDs may increase the plasma concentration of cyclosporine and the risk of cyclosporine-induced nephrotoxicity. Patients should be carefully monitored during concurrent use.
Digoxin: The possibility should be considered that some NSAIDs may increase digoxin concentrations, leading to an increased risk of digitalis toxicity. Increased monitoring and dosage adjustments of digoxin may be necessary during and following concurrent NSAID therapy. However, ketoprofen may have no effect on digoxin concentrations.
Oral Antidiabetic Agents: NSAIDs may increase the hypoglycemic effect of oral antidiabetic agents because prostaglandins are directly involved in regulatory mechanisms of glucose metabolism and possibly because of displacement of the oral antidiabetic from serum proteins. Dosage adjustments of the antidiabetic agent may be necessary.
Potassium Supplements: Concurrent use of potassium supplements may increase the risk of gastrointestinal side effects, including ulceration or hemorrhage.
Valproic Acid: Valproic acid may cause hypoprothrombinemia. In addition, it may inhibit platelet aggregation. Concurrent use with a NSAID may increase the risk of bleeding because of additive interference with platelet function and the potential occurrence of NSAID-induced gastrointestinal ulceration or hemorrhage.

Adverse Effects: The most common adverse reactions encountered with NSAIDs are gastrointestinal, of which peptic ulcer, with or without bleeding, is the most severe. Fatalities have occurred on occasion, particularly in the elderly.

In clinical trials involving 1 542 patients, the most common side effects reported were gastrointestinal (22%). The most severe were peptic ulcer or gastrointestinal bleeding which occurred in controlled clinical trials in less than 1% of 1 076 patients; however, in open label continuation studies in 1 292 patients, the rate was greater than 2%.

The detailed breakdown of side effects with their corresponding frequencies (not indicated when < 1%) is given herewith. That includes rare adverse reactions collected from foreign reports to manufacturers and regulatory agencies, publications and US clinical trials.
Gastrointestinal (22%): dyspepsia (12.8%), nausea (4.0%), indigestion and flatulence (2.8%), vomiting (2.0%), constipation (2.0%), diarrhea (1.4%), anorexia, ulcer, gastrointestinal bleeding and perforation, melena, hematemesis, stomatitis.

Rectal administration was associated with a lower incidence of upper gastrointestinal reactions (12%) with the exception of ulceration, the incidence of which was the same. However, ano-rectal reactions presenting as local pain, burning, pruritus, tenesmus and rare instances of rectal bleeding occurred in 16.5% of patients. Five percent of patients discontinued rectal therapy because of these local reactions.
CNS (3 to 5%): headache (1.7%), fatigue (1%), dizziness, tension, anxiety, depression, drowsiness, impotence, vertigo, migraine, paresthesia.
Body as a Whole: angioedema, asthma, life threatening bronchospasm, anaphylaxis.
Dermatologic (< 3%): rashes (1.7%), pruritus, flushing, excessive perspiration, alopecia, bullous rash, exfolliative dermatitis, photosensitivity, purpuric rash, urticaria, onycholysis.
Cardiovascular: peripheral edema (2%), palpitation, congestive heart failure, hypertension.
Special Senses: tinnitus, hearing impairment, visual disturbance, conjunctivitis, conjunctivitis sicca, taste perversion.
Hematologic: hypocoagulability, agranulocytosis, anemia, hemolysis, purpura, thrombocytopenia.
Renal: interstitial nephritis, hematuria, nephrotic syndrome, impairment of renal function, acute renal failure.
Hepatic: hepatic dysfunction, jaundice.
Laboratory Tests: Abnormal alkaline phosphatase, lactic dehydrogenase, AST and BUN values were found in some patients receiving ketoprofen therapy. The abnormalities did not lead to discontinuation of treatment and, in some cases, returned to normal while the drug was continued. There have been sporadic reports of decreased hematocrit and hemoglobin values without progressive deterioration on prolonged administration of the drug.

Overdose: Symptoms: Of 20 cases of overdosage (up to 5 000 mg) reported in Great Britain (5 children, 14 adolescents or young adults, and 1 elderly), only 4 had mild symptoms (vomiting in 3, drowsiness in 1 child).

Treatment: Administer gastric lavage or an emetic and treat symptomatically: compensate for dehydration, monitor urinary excretion and correct acidosis if present.

The drug is dialyzable; therefore, hemodialysis may be useful to remove circulating drug and to assist in case of renal failure.

Dosage: Adults: Rheumatoid arthritis and osteoarthritis: Oral: The usual dosage of ketoprofen capsules or enteric coated tablets is 150 to 200 mg/day in 3 or 4 divided doses.

Once the maintenance dosage has been established, patients may be tried on a twice daily dosing regimen. Clinical trials, however, show that some rheumatoid arthritis patients respond better to more frequent dosing. The usual maintenance dose is 100 mg twice daily.

Patients with rheumatoid arthritis or osteoarthritis on a maintenance dose of 200 mg/day may be changed to a once daily dose of Orudis SR tablets administered in the morning or evening. Orudis SR should be swallowed whole.

Orudis E tablets and Orudis SR provide alternative presentations for those who may prefer these dosage forms. No difference in toxicity profile was documented.
Rectal: Suppositories offer an alternative route of administration for those patients who prefer it. Administer 1 suppository morning and evening or 1 suppository at bedtime supplemented as needed by divided oral doses.

The total daily dose of ketoprofen capsules, tablets and suppositories should not exceed 200 mg/day. When the patient's response warrants it, the dose may be decreased to the minimum effective level.

In severe cases, during a flare-up of rheumatic activity or if a satisfactory response cannot be obtained with the lower dose, a daily dosage in excess of 200 mg may be used. However, a dose of 300 mg/day should not be exceeded.
Primary dysmenorrhea and mild to moderate pain: Oral: The usual dose for ketoprofen is 25 to 50 mg 3 or 4 times daily as necessary.

A larger dose may be tried if the patient's response to a previous dose was less than satisfactory, but individual doses above 50 mg have not been shown to give added analgesia. The total daily dose should not exceed 300 mg. In most types of acute pain, a course of 3 to 7 days has been shown to be sufficient.
Elderly and Debilitated Patients: Initial dosage should be reduced by ½ to ⅓ in patients with impaired renal function and the elderly.
Children: Not indicated in children under 12 years of age because clinical experience in this group of patients is insufficient.

Information for the Patient: See Blue Section—Information for the Patient "Orudis/Orudis E/Orudis SR".

Supplied: Orudis: Capsules: Each ivory and dark green capsule, marked with the logo on one side and identified ORUDIS 50 on the other, contains: ketoprofen 50 mg. Nonmedicinal ingredients: D&C Yellow No 10, FD&C Green No 3, FD&C Yellow No 6, gelatin, lactose, magnesium stearate and titanium dioxide. Tartrazine-free. Bottles of 100 and 500.

Suppositories: Each white to off-white suppository contains: ketoprofen 50 or 100 mg. Nonmedicinal ingredients: colloidal silicon dioxide and hydrogenated vegetable glycerides. Tartrazine-free. Boxes of 30. Store below 30°C.

Orudis E: Each yellow, round, biconvex enteric-coated tablet, marked with on one side and identified 50 or 100 on the other, contains: ketoprofen 50 or 100 mg. Nonmedicinal ingredients: carnauba wax, cornstarch, D&C Yellow No 10 aluminum lake, dextrin, FD&C Yellow No 6 aluminum lake, lactose, magnesium stearate, polyvinyl acetate phthalate, polacrilin potassium, stearic acid, sucrose, talc, titanium dioxide and triethyl citrate. Tartrazine-free. Bottles of 100 and 500.

Orudis SR: Each white, round, biconvex, enteric-coated sustained release tablet, marked with on one side and identified ORUDIS SR 200 on the other, contains: ketoprofen 200 mg. Nonmedicinal ingredients: calcium phosphate dibasic, carnauba wax, cellulose acetate phthalate, diethyl phthalate, ethyl acetate, hydroxyethyl cellulose and magnesium stearate. Tartrazine-free. Bottles of 100 and 500.

(Shown in Product Recognition Section)

Reviewed 1999

ORUVAIL® Ⓟ

May & Baker Pharma

Ketoprofen

Anti-inflammatory—Analgesic

Pharmacology: Animal pharmacological studies have shown that ketoprofen possesses anti-inflammatory, analgesic and antipyretic properties. The anti-inflammatory action is not mediated through the pituitary adrenal axis.

Its therapeutic effectiveness has been demonstrated by a reduction in joint swelling, pain and duration of morning stiffness, and by increased grip strength and an improvement in functional capacity.

Clinical trials in patients with rheumatoid arthritis and osteoarthritis have shown that when given in a dose of 200 mg once daily, the antiarthritic activity of Oruvail is comparable to that of a twice daily administration of ketoprofen (100 mg ketoprofen b.i.d.).

Ketoprofen 200 mg daily induced less gastrointestinal bleeding than ASA 4 g/day.
Pharmacokinetics: Ketoprofen from Oruvail is slowly but almost completely absorbed from the gastrointestinal tract. Mean peak plasma levels of 2.2 and 4.2 mg/L are achieved about 5 hours following single oral doses of Oruvail 100 and 200 mg, respectively. Pharmacokinetics are linear over a dosage range of 100 to 200 mg. The systemic availability of Oruvail is 95% of that of conventional capsules. In a food-effect study, meal composition did not affect the extent of absorption of ketoprofen from Oruvail, although a heavy meal slightly but significantly delayed the absorption of the drug by about 2 hours by comparison to a light meal; in this study, there was no comparison with the fasted state nor with a conventional ketoprofen formulation. Steady-state plasma ketoprofen concentrations are achieved within 4 days with mean peak and trough levels of 4.3 and 0.91 mg/L respectively, after repeated doses of 200 mg once daily.

There is some evidence that C_{max} and bioavailability are increased in the elderly as the result of an age-related reduction in volume of distribution since the apparent elimination half-life of about 8 hours is similar in both young and elderly patients. No or negligible accumulation of ketoprofen was found following repeated once daily dosing of Oruvail 200 mg capsules in either young or aged subjects.

In arthritic patients treated with Oruvail 200 mg once daily for up to 3 months, the steady-state disposition of ketoprofen remains unaltered during chronic administration. When comparing to a group of healthy subjects, no differences with respect to AUC, C_{max}, and elimination half-life were found, indicating that inflammatory joint disease has no influence on the kinetics of Oruvail capsules.

Indications: In the treatment of rheumatoid arthritis, ankylosing spondylitis and osteoarthritis.

Contraindications: In patients with active peptic ulcers, a history of recurrrent ulceration or active inflammatory diseases of the gastrointestinal tract.

In patients with known or suspected hypersensitivity to the drug or other nonsteroidal anti-inflammatory drugs (NSAIDs). Because of cross-sensitivity, ketoprofen should not be given to patients with the complete or partial syndrome of nasal polyps, or asthma, anaphylaxis, rhinitis or urticaria. Fatal anaphylactoid reactions have occurred in such individuals.

Significant hepatic impairment or active liver disease.

Severely impaired or deteriorating renal function (creatinine clearance < 30 mL/min or 0.5 mL/s). Individuals with lesser degrees of renal impairment are at risk of deterioration of their renal function when prescribed NSAIDs and must be monitored.

Ketoprofen is not recommended for use with other NSAIDs because of the absence of any evidence demonstrating synergistic benefits and the potential for additive side effects.

Warnings: Gastrointestinal System: Serious gastrointestinal toxicity, such as peptic ulceration, perforation and gastrointestinal bleeding, sometimes severe and occasionally fatal can occur at any time, with or without symptoms in patients treated with nonsteroidal anti-inflammatory drugs (NSAIDs) including ketoprofen. Unlike most adverse reactions, which usually manifest themselves in the first month if they are going to occur in an individual, new peptic ulcers keep appearing in patients under treatment with ketoprofen at a rate of greater than 1% per year.

Minor upper gastrointestinal problems, such as dyspepsia, are common, usually developing early in therapy. Physicians should remain alert for ulceration and bleeding in patients treated with NSAIDs, even in the absence of previous gastrointestinal tract symptoms.

In patients observed in clinical trials of such agents, symptomatic upper gastrointestinal ulcers, gross bleeding, or perforation appear to occur in approximately 1% of patients treated for 3 to 6 months and in about 2 to 4% of patients treated for 1 year. The risk continues beyond 1 year and possibly increases.

The incidence of these complications increases with increasing dose.

Oruvail (cont'd)

Ketoprofen should be given under close medical supervision to patients prone to gastrointestinal tract irritation particularly those with a history of peptic ulcer, diverticulosis or other inflammatory disease of the gastrointestinal tract such as ulcerative colitis and Crohn's disease. In these cases the physician must weigh the benefits of treatment against the possible hazards.

Physicians should inform patients about the signs and/or symptoms of serious gastrointestinal toxicity and instruct them to contact a physician immediately if they experience persistent dyspepsia or other symptoms or signs suggestive of gastrointestinal ulceration or bleeding.

Because serious gastrointestinal tract ulceration and bleeding can occur without warning symptoms, physicians should follow chronically treated patients by checking their hemoglobin periodically and by being vigilant for the signs and symptoms of ulceration and bleeding and should inform the patients of the importance of this follow-up.

If ulceration is suspected or confirmed, or if gastrointestinal bleeding occurs, ketoprofen should be discontinued immediately, appropriate treatment instituted and the patients monitored closely.

No studies, to date, have identified any group of patients **not** at risk of developing ulceration and bleeding. A prior history of serious gastrointestinal events and other factors such as excess alcohol intake, smoking, age, female gender and concomitant oral steroid and anticoagulant use have been associated with increased risk.

Studies to date show that all NSAIDs can cause gastrointestinal tract adverse events. Although existing data does not clearly identify differences in risk between various NSAIDs, this may be shown in the future.

Geriatrics: Patients older than 65 years and frail or debilitated patients are most susceptible to a variety of adverse reactions from NSAIDs. The incidence of the adverse reactions increases with dose and duration of treatment. In addition, these patients are less tolerant to ulceration and bleeding. Most reports of fatal gastrointestinal events are in this population. Older patients are also at risk of lower esophageal ulceration and bleeding.

For such patients, consideration should be given to a starting dose lower than the one usually recommended, with individual adjustment when necessary and under close supervision (see Precautions)

Cross-sensitivity: Patients sensitive to any one of the NSAIDs may be sensitive to any of the other NSAIDs also.

Aseptic Meningitis: In occasional cases, with some NSAIDs, the symptoms of aseptic meningitis (stiff neck, severe headaches, nausea and vomiting, fever or clouding of consciousness) have been observed. Patients with autoimmune disorders (systemic lupus erythematosus, mixed connective tissues diseases, etc.) seem to be predisposed. Therefore, in such patients, the physician must be vigilant to the development of this complication.

Pregnancy: The safety of ketoprofen when administered to pregnant or nursing women has not been determined and therefore such use is not recommended. Pregnant rats who received ketoprofen 6 and 9 mg/kg/day orally from day 15 of gestation, showed dystocia and increased pup mortality.

Lactation: In rats, ketoprofen at doses of 9 mg/kg (approximately 1.5 times the maximum human therapeutic dose) did not affect perinatal development. Upon administration to lactating dogs, the milk concentration of ketoprofen was found to be 4 to 5% of the plasma drug level. Data on secretion in human milk after ingestion of ketoprofen do not exist. As with other drugs that are excreted in milk, ketoprofen is not recommended for use in nursing mothers.

Children: The conditions for safe and effective use of ketoprofen in children under 12 years of age have not been established and the drug is therefore not recommended in this age group.

Precautions: Gastrointestinal System: There is no definitive evidence that the concomitant administration of histamine H_2-receptor antagonists and/or antacids will either prevent the occurrence of gastrointestinal side effects or allow the continuation of ketoprofen therapy when and if these adverse reactions appear.

Suppositories should be given with caution to patients with any rectal or anal pathology.

Renal function: Long-term administration of nonsteroidal anti-inflammatory drug (NSAID) to animals has resulted in renal papillary necrosis and other abnormal renal pathology. In humans, there have been reports of acute interstitial nephritis with hematuria, proteinuria, and occasionally nephrotic syndrome.

A second form of renal toxicity has been seen in patients with prerenal conditions leading to the reduction in renal blood flow or blood volume, where the renal prostaglandins have a supportive role in the maintenance of renal perfusion. In these patients, administration of a NSAID may cause a dose-dependent reduction in prostaglandin formation and may precipitate overt renal decompensation. Patients at greatest risk of this reaction are those with impaired renal function, heart failure, liver dysfunction, those taking diuretics, and the elderly. Discontinuation of nonsteroidal anti-inflammatory therapy is usually followed by recovery to the pretreatment state.

Ketoprofen and its metabolites are eliminated primarily by the kidneys, therefore the drug should be used with great caution in patients with impaired renal function. In these cases, utilization of lower doses of ketoprofen should be considered and patients carefully monitored.

During long-term therapy kidney function should be monitored periodically.

Genitourinary Tract: Some NSAIDs are known to cause persistent urinary symptoms (bladder pain, dysuria, urinary frequency), hematuria or cystitis. The onset of these symptoms may occur at any time after the initiation of therapy with an NSAID. Some cases have become severe on continued treatment. Should urinary symptoms occur, treatment with ketoprofen **must be stopped immediately** to obtain recovery. This should be done before any urological investigations or treatments are carried out.

Hepatic Function: As with other NSAIDs, borderline elevations of one or more liver function tests may occur in up to 15% of patients. These abnormalities may progress, may remain essentially unchanged, or may be transient with continued therapy. Meaningful (3 times the upper limit of normal) elevations of ALT or AST occurred in controlled clinical trials in less than 1% of patients. A patient with symptoms and/or signs suggesting liver dysfunction, or in whom an abnormal liver test has occurred, should be evaluated for evidence of the development of more severe hepatic reaction while on therapy with this drug. Severe hepatic reactions including jaundice and cases of fatal hepatitis have been reported with NSAIDs. Although such reactions are rare, if abnormal liver tests persist or worsen, if clinical signs and symptoms consistent with liver disease develop, or if systemic manifestations occur (e.g., eosinophilia, rash, etc.), this drug should be discontinued.

During long-term therapy, liver function tests should be monitored periodically. If there is a need to prescribe this drug in the presence of impaired liver function, it must be done under strict observation.

Fluid and Electrolyte Balance: Fluid retention and edema have been observed in approximately 2% of patients treated with ketoprofen. Therefore, as with many other NSAIDs, the possibility of precipitating congestive heart failure in elderly patients or those with compromised cardiac function should be borne in mind. Ketoprofen should be used with caution in patients with heart failure, hypertension or other conditions predisposing to fluid retention.

With nonsteroidal anti-inflammatory treatment there is a potential risk of hyperkalemia, particularly in patients with conditions such as diabetes mellitus or renal failure; elderly patients; or in patients receiving concomitant therapy with β-adrenergic blockers, angiotensin converting enzyme inhibitors or some diuretics. Serum electrolytes should be monitored periodically during long-term therapy, especially in those patients who are at risk.

Hematology: Drugs inhibiting prostaglandin biosynthesis do interfere with platelet function to varying degrees; therefore, patients who may be adversely affected by such an action should be carefully observed when ketoprofen is administered.

Blood dyscrasias (such as neutropenia, leukopenia, thrombocytopenia, aplastic anemia and agranulocytosis) associated with the use of NSAIDs are rare, but could be with severe consequences.

Anemia is commonly observed in rheumatoid arthritis and is sometimes aggravated by NSAIDs, which may produce fluid retention or minor gastrointestinal blood loss in some patients. Therefore, patients with initial hemoglobin values of 10 g/dL or less who are to receive long-term therapy should have hemoglobin values determined frequently.

Infection: In common with other anti-inflammatory drugs, ketoprofen may mask the usual signs of infection.

Ophthalmology: Blurred and/or diminished vision has been reported with the use of ketoprofen and other NSAIDs. If such symptoms develop this drug should be discontinued and an ophthalmologic examination performed; ophthalmic examination should be carried out at periodic intervals in any patient receiving this drug for an extended period of time.

CNS: Some patients may experience drowsiness, dizziness, vertigo, insomnia or depression with the use of ketoprofen. If patients experience these side effects, they should exercise caution in carrying out activities that require alertness.

Drug Interactions: Methotrexate: The concomitant administration of ketoprofen and high-dose methotrexate has been associated with prolonged and marked enhancement of serum methotrexate levels resulting in severe methotrexate toxicity. This may also apply to some other NSAIDs. There were no abnormalities in methotrexate kinetics or evidence of toxicity when ketoprofen was given at least 12 hours after completion of high-dose methotrexate infusion. Ketoprofen should not be used in patients receiving high dose methotrexate.

The potential for severe toxicity should be kept in mind when prescribing ketoprofen and low-dose methotrexate concurrently. Ketoprofen should not be administered within 12 hours of methotrexate infusion.

ASA or other NSAIDs: Concurrent administration of ASA decreased ketoprofen protein binding and increased its plasma clearance. The overall result was a 40% reduction in the AUC of ketoprofen. Ketoprofen does not alter ASA absorption.

The use of ketoprofen in addition to any other NSAID, including those over-the-counter ones (such as ASA and ibuprofen) is not recommended due to the possibility of additive side effects. Concurrent therapy may increase the risk of gastrointestinal toxicity, including ulceration or hemorrhage, without providing additional symptomatic relief. Concurrent use of ASA with other NSAIDs may also increase the risk of bleeding at sites other than the gastrointestinal tract because of additive inhibition of platelet aggregation.

Oral Anticoagulants: Ketoprofen has been shown to depress platelet aggregation and it can prolong bleeding time by approximately 3 to 4 minutes from baseline values. However, a study conducted in 20 patients undergoing therapy with coumarin and simultaneously receiving ketoprofen, failed to demonstrate potentiation of anticoagulant effect. Nevertheless, close monitoring of patients is recommended when ketoprofen is given concomitantly with anticoagulants.

Numerous studies have shown that the concomitant use of NSAIDs and anticoagulants increases the risk of GI adverse events such as ulceration and bleeding.

Diuretics: Hydrochlorothiazide, given concomitantly with ketoprofen, produces a reduction in urinary potassium and chloride excretion compared to hydrochlorothiazide alone. Patients taking diuretics are at greater risk of developing renal failure secondary to a decrease in renal blood flow caused by prostaglandin inhibition. Concurrent use of a potassium-sparing diuretic with some NSAIDs may increase the risk of hyperkalemia.

Glucocorticoids: Numerous studies have shown that the concomitant use of NSAIDs and oral glucocorticoids increases the gastrointestinal side effects such as ulceration and bleeding. This is especially the case in older (>65 years of age) individuals.

Antacids: Concomitant administration of magnesium hydroxide and aluminum hydroxide does not interfere with the rate or extent of the absorption of ketoprofen.

Lithium: NSAIDs have been reported to increase steady-state plasma lithium levels. It is recommended that plasma lithium levels be monitored when ketoprofen is coadministered with lithium.

Probenecid: Concurrent administration of probenecid increases both free and bound ketoprofen through reducing the plasma clearance of ketoprofen to about one-third as well as decreasing its protein binding. Ketoprofen is not recommended in association with probenecid.

Ketoprofen is extensively (99%) protein bound to human serum albumin and may compete for binding sites with drugs such as sulfonamides, oral hypoglycemic agents, phenytoin or lithium. Although no significant interaction has been documented, patients with such combination therapy should be monitored.

Clinical Laboratory Tests: The presence of ketoprofen and its metabolites in urine has been shown to interfere with certain tests which are used to detect albumin, bile salts, 17-ketosteroids or 17-hydroxycorticosteroids in urine and which rely upon acid precipitation as an end point or upon color reactions for carbonyl groups. No interference was seen in the tests for proteinuria using Albustix, Hema-Combistix or Labstix Reagent Strips.

Ketoprofen decreases platelet adhesion and aggregation. Therefore, it can prolong bleeding time by approximately 3 to 4 minutes from baseline values. There is no significant change in platelet count, prothrombin time, partial thromboplastin time, or thrombin time.

The following interactions have not been documented with every NSAID. However, they have been reported with several of these medications and should be considered potential precautions to the use of any NSAID, especially with chronic administration.

Acetaminophen: Prolonged concurrent use of acetaminophen with NSAID may increase the risk of adverse renal effects; it is recommended that patients be under close medical supervision while receiving such combined therapy.

Alcohol: Concurrent use of alcohol with an NSAID may increase the risk of gastrointestinal side effects, including ulceration or hemorrhage.

Colchicine: Concurrent use of colchicine with an NSAID may increase the risk of gastrointestinal ulceration or hemorrhage. Inhibition of platelet aggregation by NSAIDs, added to colchicine's effects on blood clotting mechanisms, may increase the risk of bleeding at sites other than the gastrointestinal tract.

Cyclosporine: Inhibition of renal prostaglandin by NSAIDs may increase the plasma concentration of cyclosporine and the risk of cyclosporine-induced nephrotoxicity. Patients should be carefully monitored during concurrent use.

Digoxin: The possibility should be considered that some NSAIDs may increase digoxin concentrations, leading to an increased risk of digitalis toxicity. Increased monitoring and dosage adjustments of digoxin may be necessary during and following concurrent NSAID therapy. However, ketoprofen may have no effect on digoxin concentrations.

Oral Antidiabetic Agents: NSAIDs may increase the hypoglycemic effect of oral antidiabetic agents because prostaglandins are directly involved in regulatory mechanisms of glucose metabolism and possibly because of displacement of the oral antidiabetic from serum proteins. Dosage adjustments of the antidiabetic agent may be necessary.

Potassium Supplements: Concurrent use of potassium supplements may increase the risk of gastrointestinal side effects, including ulceration or hemorrhage.

Valproic Acid: Valproic acid may cause hypoprothrombinemia. In addition, it may inhibit platelet aggregation. Concurrent use with an NSAID may increase the risk of bleeding because of additive interference with platelet function and the potential occurrence of NSAID-induced gastrointestinal ulceration or hemorrhage.

Adverse Effects: The most common adverse reactions encountered with NSAIDs are gastrointestinal, of which peptic ulcer, with or without bleeding, is the most severe. Fatalities have occurred, particularly in the elderly.

The detailed breakdown of side effects with their corresponding frequencies (not indicated when <1%) is given herewith. That includes rare adverse reactions collected from foreign reports to manufacturers and regulatory agencies, publications and US clinical trials:

Gastrointestinal (22%): dyspepsia (12.8%), nausea (4.0%), indigestion and flatulence (2.8%), vomiting (2.0%), constipation (2.0%), diarrhea (1.4%), anorexia, ulcer, gastrointestinal bleeding and perforation, melena, hematemesis, stomatitis.

Rectal administration was associated with a lower incidence of upper gastrointestinal reactions (12%) with the exception of ulceration, the incidence of which was the same. However, ano-rectal reactions presenting as local pain, burning, pruritus, tenesmus and rare instances of rectal bleeding occurred in 16.5% of subjects. Five percent of patients discontinued rectal therapy because of these local reactions.

CNS (3 to 5%): headache (1.7%), fatigue (1%), dizziness, tension, anxiety, depression, drowsiness, impotence, vertigo, migraine, paresthesia.

Body as a Whole: angioedema, asthma, life threatening bronchospasm, anaphylaxis.

Dermatologic (<3%): rashes (1.7%), pruritus, flushing, excessive perspiration, alopecia, bullous rash, exfoliative dermatitis, photosensitivity, purpuric rash, urticaria, onycholysis.

Cardiovascular: peripheral edema (2%), palpitation, congestive heart failure, hypertension.

Special Senses: tinnitus, hearing impairment, visual disturbance, conjunctivitis, conjunctivitis sicca, taste perversion.

Hematologic: hypocoagulability, agranulocytosis, anemia, hemolysis, purpura, thrombocytopenia.

Renal: interstitial nephritis, hematuria, nephrotic syndrome, impairment of renal function, acute renal failure.

Hepatic: hepatic dysfunction, jaundice.

Laboratory Tests: Abnormal alkaline phosphatase lactic dehydrogenase, AST and BUN values were found in some patients receiving ketoprofen therapy. The abnormalities did not lead to discontinuation of treatment and, in some cases, returned to normal while the drug was continued. There have been sporadic reports of decreased hematocrit and hemoglobin values without progressive deterioration on prolonged administration of the drug.

Overdose: Symptoms: Of 20 cases of overdosage (up to 5 000 mg) reported in Great Britain (5 children, 14 adolescents or young adults, and 1 elderly), only 4 had mild symptoms (vomiting in 3, drowsiness in 1 child).

Treatment: Administer gastric lavage or an emetic and treat symptomatically: compensate for dehydration, monitor urinary excretion and correct acidosis if present.

The drug is dialyzable; therefore, hemodialysis may be useful to remove circulating drug and to assist in case of renal failure.

Dosage: The usual dosage is 150 to 200 mg once daily. The capsules should be taken with food and can be administered in the morning or evening.

Adults: The usual dosage for ketoprofen is 150 to 200 mg/day.

Elderly and Debilitated Patients: The dosage should be reduced in patients with impaired renal function and the elderly. The lower strengths should be used in those cases.

Children: Ketoprofen is not indicated in children under 12 years of age because clinical experience in this age group is insufficient.

Information for the Patient: See Blue Section—Information for the Patient "Oruvail".

Supplied: 150 mg: Each sustained-release, transparent, pink capsule with opaque white cap, each half printed "Oruvail 150" in black, contains: ketoprofen 150 mg as white pellets. Nonmedicinal ingredients: colloidal silicon dioxide, ethylcellulose, erythrosine, gelatin, maize starch, shellac, sucrose, talc and titanium dioxide. Bottles of 100 and 250.

200 mg: Each sustained-release, transparent, pink capsule with opaque blue cap, each half printed "Oruvail 200" in black, contains: ketoprofen 200 mg as white pellets. Nonmedicinal ingredients: brilliant blue, colloidal silicon dioxide, ethylcellulose, erythrosine, gelatin, maize starch, shellac, sucrose, talc and titanium dioxide. Bottles of 100 and 250.

(Shown in Product Recognition Section)

Reviewed 1999

OS-CAL®
Wyeth-Ayerst

Calcium Carbonate

Mineral Supplement

Supplied: 250 mg: Each round, biconvex, pale green tablet embossed OS-CAL on one side contains: elemental calcium 250 mg (12.5 mEq) as 625 mg of calcium carbonate obtained from oyster shell. Nonmedicinal ingredients: calcium stearate, cornstarch, corn syrup solids, D&C Yellow No. 10 Aluminum Lake, FD&C Blue No. 1 Aluminum Lake, flavor ethyl vanillin, hydroxypropyl cellulose, hydroxypropyl methylcellulose, methylparaben, polyethylene glycol, polysorbate 80, propylparaben, sodium starch glycolate, talc and titanium dioxide. Energy: 1.1 kJ (0.27 kcal). Sodium: <4 mg. Alcohol-, gluten-, lactose-, sulfites- and tartrazine-free. Bottles of 100 and 500.

500 mg: Each capsule-shaped, pale green tablet embossed OS-CAL on one side contains: elemental calcium 500 mg (25 mEq) as 1 250 mg of calcium carbonate obtained from oyster shell. Nonmedicinal ingredients: calcium stearate, cornstarch, corn syrup solids, D&C Yellow No. 10 Aluminum Lake, FD&C Blue No. 1 Aluminum Lake, flavor ethyl vanillin, hydroxypropyl cellulose, hydroxypropyl methylcellulose, methylparaben, polyethylene glycol, polysorbate 80, propylparaben, sodium starch glycolate, talc and titanium dioxide. Energy: 2.3 kJ (0.54 kcal). Sodium: <8 mg. Alcohol-, gluten-, lactose-, sulfites- and tartrazine-free. Cartons of 30 push-through blister paks, bottles of 100 and 500.

(Shown in Product Recognition Section)

OS-CAL® D
Wyeth-Ayerst

Calcium Carbonate—Vitamin D

Vitamin and Mineral Supplement

Supplied: Each pale grey, capsule-shaped tablet printed OS-CAL D in black on one side, contains: calcium carbonate 1 250 mg from oyster shells (equivalent to elemental calcium 500 mg), and vitamin D_3 125 I.U. Nonmedicinal ingredients: calcium stearate, cornstarch, corn syrup solids, flavor ethyl vanillin, hydroxypropyl cellulose, hydroxypropyl methylcellulose, methylparaben, polyethylene glycol, polysorbate 80, propylparaben, sodium starch glycolate, synthetic black iron oxide, talc and titanium dioxide. Alcohol-, gluten-, lactose-, sulfite- and tartrazine-free. Blister packs of 30 and bottles of 100. Store at room temperature.

(Shown in Product Recognition Section)

OSMITROL®
Baxter

Mannitol

Osmotic Diuretic

Supplied: Each mL of aqueous solution contains: mannitol 10% or 20%. Viaflex Plus plastic (polyvinyl chloride) containers of 500 mL (20%) and 1 000 mL (10%). Do not store above 30°C. Protect from freezing.

OSMOPAK PLUS
Technilab

Magnesium Sulfate—Benzocaine

Drawing Salve

Supplied: Each g contains: magnesium sulfate equivalent to the hepta-hydrated form 60% and benzocaine 0.5% in a water miscible base. Jars of 50 g.

New Product 1998

OSMOVIST®
Berlex Canada

Iotrolan

Dimeric Nonionic Radiographic Contrast Medium for Myelography

Pharmacology: Iotrolan is a dimeric, nonionic, hexaiodinated radiocontrast medium. The contrast-giving substance, iotrolan, is a dimer of triiodinated isophthalic acid derivatives, in which the firmly bound iodine absorbs the x-rays. Solutions of iotrolan are isotonic to plasma and cerebrospinal fluid at radiologically useful iodine levels.

After intrathecal administration, iotrolan is absorbed from cerebrospinal fluid (CSF) into the blood stream. The mean half-life of the transfer of iotrolan from the spinal fluid to the blood plasma was found to be 5.7±6 hours in adults. The highest concentration of iodine in plasma occurred 3.5±3.1 hours after intrathecal administration. Plasma protein binding at a concentration of 1.2 mg I/mL is 2.4%. The mean elimination half-life of iotrolan in the plasma is 13.6±13.9 hours (median of 9 hours). Approximately 50 to 80% of the administered dose is excreted unmetabolized by the kidneys within 24 hours after administration, and approximately 90% within 72 hours. Only 0.6% of the dose was found in the feces collected up to 72 hours after dosing.

Total and renal clearance following i.v. injection is 93.5±5 mL/min and 90±4 mL/min, respectively.

In patients with renal impairment, depending on the degree of impairment, decreased renal elimination may cause prolonged iotrolan levels in plasma.

After i.v. administration, the blood-chemical parameters—including those in renally impaired patients (creatinine more than 1.5 mg/dL)—did not display any statistically significant changes compared to the baseline values. The fluctuations lay within the circadian range.

There is no evidence of metabolism, deiodination or biotransformation in rats and humans.

Generally, acceptable diagnostic contrast by conventional radiographic techniques can be achieved for at least 30 minutes following intrathecal injection. Computerized tomography may be performed up to 3 to 5 hours after iotrolan administration depending on the level of injection (cervical, thoracic or lumbar).

Contrast enhancement is directly related to the initial dosage of iotrolan administered and patient positioning.

Indications: In adults for lumbar myelography, cervical myelography, total columnar myelography and computerized tomography of spinal and subarachnoid spaces.

Contraindications: Iotrolan should not be administered to patients with known hypersensitivity to the drug or to patients with manifest hyperthyroidism.

Osmovist (cont'd)

Intrathecal administration of corticosteroids with iotrolan is contraindicated.

Lumbar and cervical puncture should not be performed in the presence of significant local or systemic infection where bacteremia is likely.

Warnings: Contrast media which are related chemically to triiodinated benzoic acid derivatives have been associated with serious and fatal reactions. Therefore, clear indication and evaluation of the risk/benefit ratio for every patient should precede each examination with contrast media. Also, it is of utmost importance that adequate facilities and appropriate personnel be readily available and a course of action be planned in advance for the immediate treatment of any serious untoward reaction.

Diagnostic procedures utilizing a radiopaque contrast medium should be conducted only by a physician with the requisite training and a thorough knowledge of the particular procedure to be performed. The physician must also be thoroughly familiar with the emergency treatment of all adverse events.

If grossly bloody CSF is encountered, the possible benefits of a myelographic procedure should be compared in terms of risk to the patient.

Direct intracisternal or ventricular administration for standard radiography is not recommended. Although seizures were not seen in clinical trials of iotrolan, caution should be observed in patients with epilepsy. Patients who are receiving anticonvulsants should be maintained on that therapy. In patients with a history of seizure activity who are not on anticonvulsant therapy, premedication with barbiturates or phenytoin should be considered.

Caution must be exercised in patients with a reduced seizure threshold. Neuroleptics or antidepressants should be discontinued 48 hours before the examination because they reduce the seizure threshold.

Pregnancy: The safe use of iotrolan during pregnancy has not been established. Therefore, it should not be used unless the benefits outweigh the risks.

Lactation: If the use of iotrolan is considered necessary in a nursing mother, it is suggested to discontinue breast feeding for 48 hours.

Children: The safety and effectiveness of iotrolan in myelography for children has not been established.

Geriatrics: Elderly patients may present a special risk in the use of radiographic contrast media. These patients may have compromised renal and cardiac function and may be taking medication (e.g., β-blockers) which may make them more susceptible to the potentially harmful effects of procedures involving the use of contrast media.

Repeat Procedure: A minimal interval of 72 hours should be allowed before repeat examinations with iotrolan; however, a 5 to 7 day interval is recommended (see Dosage).

Precautions: Before any contrast medium is injected, the patient should be questioned for **a history of previous reaction to a contrast medium, a known sensitivity to iodine or known clinical hypersensitivity (bronchial asthma, hay fever and food allergies).** The reported incidence of adverse reactions to contrast media are higher in patients with these conditions. Most adverse reactions to contrast agents appear within 30 minutes after the start of their injection, but a delayed reaction may occur. Premedication with antihistamines (except phenothiazine derivatives, see Drug Interactions) or corticoids may be considered in order to avoid or minimize possible allergic adverse reactions. However, antihistamines or corticosteroids should not be mixed in the same syringe with any contrast medium because of potential chemical incompatibility.

Caution must be exercised in the case of hypersensitivity to iodinated contrast media, latent hyperthyroidism, severe cardiovascular disease and bland nodular goitre. Experience shows that patients with an allergic disposition suffer more frequently from hypersensitivity reactions.

Hypersensitivity reactions to contrast media including shock cannot be ruled out but are expected to be rare in the proposed indications. The susceptible population includes especially patients with a history of a previous reaction to contrast media, with a known sensitivity to iodine, or with known clinical hypersensitivity.

The use of a test dose of the contrast medium before injection of the full dose has been employed to predict severe or fatal reactions. These provocative tests may themselves cause severe, even fatal, reactions and are unreliable in predicting patients at special risk.

Care in patient management should be taken to prevent inadvertent intracranial entry of a large or concentrated bolus of contrast medium, which increases the risk of neurotoxicity. Also, effort should be directed to avoid rapid dispersion of the medium causing inadvertent rise to intracranial levels (e.g., by active patient movement).

Preparatory dehydration is dangerous and may contribute to acute renal failure in patients with advanced vascular disease, diabetic patients and susceptible nondiabetic patients (often elderly patients with pre-existing renal disease). Patients should be well hydrated before and after iotrolan administration.

Assessment of thyroid function may be obscured for several weeks following the administration of iotrolan.

Drug Interactions: Intrathecal administration of corticosteroids with iotrolan is contraindicated.

Many radiopaque contrast agents are incompatible in vitro with some antihistamines and many other drugs; therefore, concurrent drugs should not be physically admixed with contrast agents.

Drugs which lower the seizure threshold, especially phenothiazine derivatives, including those used for their antihistamine properties, should not be used with iotrolan. Other drugs lowering the seizure threshold to be avoided include MAO inhibitors, tricyclic antidepressants, CNS stimulants and psychoactive drugs described as analeptics, or antipsychotic drugs. Such medication should be discontinued at least 48 hours before myelography, should not be used for the control of nausea and vomiting, and should not be resumed for at least 24 hours after the procedure.

Hypersensitivity reactions can be aggravated in patients on β-blockers. The prevalence of delayed reactions (e.g., fever, rash, flu-like symptoms, joint pain and pruritus) to contrast media is higher in patients who have received interleukin.

Adverse Effects: General: Careful patient observation for adverse reactions is recommended in the use of all contrast media. Reactions accompanying use may vary with the dosage, the technique of administration, the procedure and the underlying condition of the patient. Adverse reactions generally occur within 30 minutes after injection and some may be of long-lasting nature. These reactions include: laryngospasm, bronchospasm, wheezing, dyspnea, and status asthmaticus; angioedema, subglottic edema and signs of airway obstruction; anaphylactic shock; cardiovascular collapse with peripheral vasodilation, hypotension, tachycardia, dyspnea, cyanosis, sweating, pallor, ventricular fibrillation and cardiac arrest; CNS stimulation or depression with agitation, convulsions, coma and death. Severe life-threatening reactions to iodinated contrast media require appropriate emergency measures. Temporary renal failure may occur in rare cases. Delayed reactions can occasionally occur.

Many life-threatening reactions begin with only mild symptoms such as nasal congestion, sneezing, watery eyes, skin erythema, or a vague sense of discomfort. It is therefore extremely important that all patients be watched closely until their symptoms have abated. The symptoms, which occur regardless of the amount of contrast medium administered and the mode of administration, can indicate incipient shock. Administration of the contrast medium must then be interrupted immediately and, if necessary, specific therapy initiated i.v. In the case of i.v. administration, use of a flexible indwelling catheter is therefore recommended.

Hypersensitivity reactions to the contrast medium including shock cannot be ruled out, but are expected to be rare in the proposed indications.

As after the use of other myelographic agents, cell count increases can be expected after administration of iotrolan into the CSF. No cases of arachnoiditis have been reported.

The most frequent subjective complaints are headaches, nausea and vomiting; however, experience shows that their incidence is no higher than after the loss of pressure in the subarachnoid space resulting from puncture of the spinal canal. In view of this, an effort should be made to remove only as much fluid as is being replaced by the contrast medium solution. On the other hand, a volume of contrast medium in excess of the amount of fluid removed does not lead to an increase of pressure in the subarachnoid space.

Severe headaches lasting several days may occur.

There have been very rare cases of aseptic meningitis with fever, stiff neck, headaches and an increased cell count in the CSF following administration of hydrosoluble nonionic contrast media for myelography. In most cases, all the symptoms disappeared within a week.

Severe side effects are extremely rare when the contrast medium is administered in the proper manner.

The safety of iotrolan was evaluated in 2 000 patients during clinical trials for myelography. Iotrolan was generally well tolerated. The most frequently reported adverse events were headache (27.5%), neck pain (13.5%), nausea (6.7%), vomiting (3.3%), stiff neck (2.8%), circulatory dysregulation (2.5%), giddiness (2.3%), back pain (2.2%), pain—localized (2.1%), dizziness (1.9%), sweats (1.9%) and tinnitus (1.1%).

Spontaneous Adverse Events having an Incidence of $<1\%$:

Allergic/Cutaneous: allergoid reaction, cellulitis.

CNS: root pain/radicular symptoms, pain—radiating, paresthesia, clouding of sensorium, hyperesthesia, sensation of warmth, disturbed vision, anxiety, sensation of cold, shivering, chills, nystagmus, somnolence, transient change neurobehavior, very brief nonspecific EEG changes, speech disorder.

Gastrointestinal: constipation, abdominal cramps, indigestion, diarrhea, dry mouth.

Musculoskeletal: myoclonia, dystonia/hypertonia, myasthenia.

Other: fever, urinary tract disorder, viral syndrome/URI, hepatitis, crying, bleeding from gums and nose, dyspnea, ear ache, sub-xyphoid pressure.

Treatment of Adverse Effects: Contrast media should be injected only by physicians thoroughly familiar with emergency treatment of all adverse reactions to contrast media. The assistance of other trained personnel such as cardiologists, internists and anesthetists is required in the management of severe reactions.

A guideline for the treatment of adverse reactions is presented below. This outline is not intended to be a complete manual on the treatment of adverse reactions to contrast media or on cardiopulmonary resuscitation. The physician should refer to the appropriate texts on the subject.

It is also realized that institutions or individual practitioners will already have appropriate systems in effect and that circumstances may dictate the use of additional or different measures.

Minor Allergic Reactions: When treatment is considered necessary, the i.v. or i.m. administration of an antihistamine such as diphenhydramine HCl 25 to 50 mg is generally sufficient (contraindicated in epileptics). The resulting drowsiness makes it imperative to ensure that outpatients neither drive nor go home unaccompanied.

Major or Life-threatening Reactions: A major reaction may be manifested by signs and symptoms of cardiovascular collapse, severe respiratory difficulty and nervous system dysfunction. Convulsions, coma and cardiorespiratory arrest may ensue. The following measures should be considered: Start emergency therapy immediately, carefully monitoring vital signs. Have emergency resuscitation team summoned, do not leave patient unattended. Ensure airway is patent, guard against aspiration. Commence artificial respiration if patient is not breathing. Administer oxygen if necessary. Start external cardiac massage in the event of cardiac arrest. Establish route for i.v. medication by starting infusion of appropriate solution (i.e., 5% dextrose in water). Judiciously administer specific drug therapy as indicated by the type and severity of the reaction. Careful monitoring is mandatory to detect adverse reactions of all drugs administered: Acute allergic-anaphylactoid reactions: Soluble hydrocortisone 500 to 1 000 mg i.v. and/or epinephrine injection USP 1:1 000 solution, 0.2 to 0.4 mL s.c. In the presence of anoxia, this may cause ventricular fibrillation. Caution is required in patients on adrenergic beta-blockers. In extreme emergency, 0.1 mL/min, appropriately diluted, may be given i.v. until the desired effect is obtained. Do not exceed 0.4 mL. Cardiac arrest: epinephrine injection USP 1:1 000 solution, 0.1 to 0.2 mL, appropriately diluted, may be given intracardially. Hypotension: Monitor blood pressure carefully. Phenylephrine HCl 0.1 to 0.5 mg appropriately diluted by slow i.v. injection or by slow infusion, or norepinephrine 4 mL of 0.2% solution in 1 000 mL of 5% dextrose by slow drip infusion. Acidosis: Sodium bicarbonate 5%; 50 mL i.v. every 10 minutes as needed to combat post-arrest acidosis. Sinus bradycardia: Atropine 0.4 to 0.6 mg i.v. may also reverse 2nd or 3rd degree block. Convulsions: Phenobarbital sodium 50 mg in fractional doses by slow i.v. injection (contraindicated if cyanosis is present) or diazepam 5 to 10 mg by slow i.v. injection, titrating the dose to the response of the patient. Defibrillation, administration of antiarrhythmics and additional emergency measures and drugs may be required. Transfer patient to intensive care unit when feasible for further monitoring and treatment.

Overdose: Symptoms and Treatment: An overdose of iotrolan should be treated by support of vital functions and prompt institution of symptomatic therapy. On inadvertent overdosage or in greatly limited renal function, iotrolan can be removed from the body by extracorporeal dialysis.

Dosage: Iotrolan is indicated for intrathecal use only.

General Information: As with all radiopaque contrast agents, the minimum concentration and volume to produce adequate visualization should be used. Factors such as age, body size, anticipated pathology and degree and extent of opacification required, structure(s) or area to be examined, disease process, equipment and technique to be employed should be considered. If the equipment available allows films in all necessary projections without having to move the patient and allows instillation under fluoroscopic control, the iodine concentrations and volumes at the lower limit of each specified range are sufficient. Higher concentrations are indicated if it is necessary to reposition the patient since the contrast medium dilutes more quickly due to turbulence.

The dose and concentration used in the spinal area influence the ultimate intracranial concentrations.

After every examination of the subarachnoid space, particularly thoracic/cervical sections, the contrast medium should be drained as far as possible into the lumbar region by sitting the patient up for a few minutes. Then the patient should rest in bed for at least 24 hours, the first 6 hours of which should be spent with the trunk horizontal and the head raised 15°.

Recent evidence suggests that maintaining the patient in an upright position (wheelchair or ambulation) after the myelographic procedure may help minimize adverse effects. The upright position may help to delay dispersion of the medium and to maximize the spinal arachnoid absorption.

Anesthesia is not necessary if thin puncture needles are used, and premedication with sedatives is usually not needed.

The patient should be fasting but adequately hydrated on the day of the examination. Disorders of water and electrolyte balance must be corrected.

Experience has shown that pronounced states of excitement, anxiety and pain can be the cause of side effects or intensified contrast medium-related reactions. They can be counteracted by calm management of the patient and the use of suitable medication.

Solutions of iotrolan, like those of other radiopaque contrast media, should be at or close to body temperature when injected. As with other sterile parenteral products, iotrolan should not be transferred from the vial to other delivery systems except immediately prior to use.

Withdrawal of contrast media from their containers should be accomplished under aseptic conditions with sterile syringes. Spinal puncture must always be performed under sterile conditions.

Parenteral drug products should be inspected visually for particulate matter and discoloration prior to administration. Iotrolan should be used only if particulate free and within the normal colorless to pale yellow range.

Iotrolan should not be drawn into the syringe until immediately before use. Any unused portion should be discarded.

Vials containing contrast medium solutions are not intended for the withdrawal of multiple doses. The rubber stopper should never be pierced more than once. The use of cannulas with a long tip and a maximum diameter of 18 G is recommended for piercing the stopper and drawing up the contrast medium.

Recommended Dosages: The dosage recommendations for conventional radiography or computed tomography are intended as general guidelines (see Table I).

Table I—Osmovist

Dosage Recommendations

	Osmovist 240	Osmovist 300
Radiculography excluding the medullary cone	7–10 mL	7–10 mL
Lumbar Myelography	7–10 mL	7–10 mL
Lumbar Myelography with thoracic transition	7–12 mL	7–12 mL
Thoracic Myelography	10–15 mL	8–12 mL
Total Columnar Myelography	10–15 mL	10–15 mL
Cervical Myelography		
Direct (lateral access between C1/C2)	8–12 mL	7–10 mL
Indirect (instillation in the lumbar region)	15 mL	8–15 mL
Ventriculography		
Indirect (instillation in the lumbar region)	3–5 mL	3–5 mL
Cisternography		
Indirect (instillation in the lumbar region)	4–12 mL	4–10 mL

Rate of Injection: To avoid excessive mixing with CSF and consequent loss of contrast, as well as premature dispersion, injection must be made slowly over 1 to 2 minutes.

Repeat Procedure: A minimal interval of 72 hours should be allowed before repeat examinations with iotrolan; however, a 5 to 7 day interval is recommended.

Note: Higher concentrations are indicated if it will be necessary to reposition the patient during myelographic examination, since the medium becomes diluted more quickly as a result of turbulence, and the clarity of detail deteriorates.

Supplied: Osmovist 240: Each mL of sterile, colorless to slightly yellow, odorless, pyrogen-free, aqueous solution contains: iotrolan 513 mg equivalent to 240 mg of organically bound iodine. Nonmedicinal ingredients: edetate calcium disodium, sodium bicarbonate, sodium chloride and sodium hydroxide to adjust pH and water for injection. pH is adjusted to 6.4 to 8.0. Preservative-free. See Table II. Vials of 10 mL, units of 10.

Osmovist 300: Each mL of sterile, colorless to slightly yellow, odorless, pyrogen-free, aqueous solution contains: iotrolan 641 mg equivalent to 300 mg of organically bound iodine. Nonmedicinal ingredients: edetate calcium disodium, sodium bicarbonate, sodium hydroxide to adjust pH and water for injection. pH is adjusted to 6.4 to 8.0. Preservative-free. See Table II. Vials of 10 mL, units of 10.

Table II—Osmovist

Physical Properties

	Osmovist 240	Osmovist 300
Iodine concentration (mg/mL)	240	300
Iotrolan concentration (mg/mL)	513	641
Viscosity (mPa·s or cp)		
at 20°C	6.8	17.4
at 37°C	3.9	8.4
Osmolarity at 37°C (mOsm/L)	220	208
Osmolality at 37°C (mOsm/kg H_2O)	270	290
pH	6.4–8	6.4–8

Store at room temperature (15 to 30°C). Protect from light. Do not freeze. It should be visually inspected and used only if clear and colorless to slightly yellow and free of particulate matter. Discard unused portions.

Reviewed 1997

OSTAC® 🅿

Roche

Clodronate Disodium

Bone Metabolism Regulator

Pharmacology: Clodronate belongs to the class of bisphosphonates which act primarily on bone. This tissue specificity is due to the high affinity of bisphosphonates for calcium phosphate crystals. Clodronate forms complexes with the hydroxyapatite of bone, altering the crystalline structure in such a way that dissolution of the crystals is inhibited.

The major effect of clodronate is to inhibit osteoclast-mediated bone resorption without an inhibitory effect on mineralization. In responsive patients, inhibition of abnormal bone resorption by clodronate leads to the management of osteolytic bone metastases and, if present, reduction of hypercalcemia.

In patients with bone metastases, clodronate prevents the progression of bone destruction. Prevention of the progression and dissemination of existing metastases, as well as the formation of new skeletal metastases has been demonstrated both by scintigraphy and by radiography. In normocalcemic patients, the anti-osteolytic action of clodronate is also clearly shown in reduced urinary calcium and hydroxyproline excretion. During and also after i.v. administration of clodronate, the elevated serum calcium decreases, in some rare instances to hypocalcemic levels.

Several variables interfere with a precise assessment of the duration of the effect. Variations in the tumor load, in the amount and type of osteolytic mediators produced by the tumor cells, concomitant anticancer therapy and the renal handling of calcium can influence the duration of action.

In hypercalcemic patients, after successful treatment patients remain normocalcemic for some days up to several weeks. In general they become hypercalcemic again within 2 to 3 weeks after termination of therapy with clodronate.

Clodronate is not metabolized and is excreted unchanged by the kidneys. In calcium homeostasis the kidneys have a prominent role. Skeletal osteolysis may be accompanied by the pathogenesis of hypercalcemia and renal dysfunction may occur. At the time of diagnosis most hypercalcemic patients are significantly dehydrated.

The antagonistic effects of calcium on the action of antidiuretic hormone impair the renal concentration mechanisms resulting in polyuria and excessive fluid loss. Hydration status is further compromised by reduction of oral fluid intake due to nausea, vomiting and mental status. Prior to initiation of therapy with clodronate, the state of negative fluid balance requires vigorous and adequate hydration with isotonic saline (0.9% w/v).

Normalization of blood calcium levels by clodronate in adequately hydrated patients may also normalize suppressed plasma parathyroid hormone (PTH) levels and decrease urinary calcium, hydroxyproline and phosphate excretion.

Pharmacokinetics: Clodronate is rapidly cleared from the blood. The mean value for plasma half-life after oral administration of clodronate is 5.6 hours. About 20% of the quantity absorbed is bound to bone. Since no biotransformation occurs, the drug is exclusively cleared by the kidneys at a rate of about 80 mL/min., when kidney function is normal. As with all bisphosphonates, the intestinal absorption and bioavailability of clodronate after oral administration is low (1 to 3%).

After i.v. dose, clodronate exhibits a plasma concentration profile which fits a two-compartment model with a $t_{1/2\alpha}$ approximately 0.3 hours and a $t_{1/2\beta}$ approximately 2 hours, and terminal elimination phase with $t_{1/2}$ approximately 13 hours. The latter accounts for 10 to 15% of renal excretion. Total clearance is about 110 mL/min and renal clearance is approximately 90 mL/min. Volume of distribution is approximately 20 L.

The clinical effect of clodronate is based on its concentration at the site of action, i.e., in bone tissue. Its half-life is dependent on the rate of skeletal turnover. When the bound substance is released from bone tissue during bone resorption, high local concentrations develop at the site of osteolysis, which has a direct action on the bone-resorbing osteoclasts.

Indications: As an adjunct in the management of osteolysis resulting from bone metastases of malignant tumors.

Clodronate is also indicated for the management of hypercalcemia of malignancy.

Prior to treatment with clodronate, renal excretion of excess calcium should be promoted by restoration and maintenance of adequate fluid balance and urine output.

In responsive patients, i.v. infusion of clodronate inhibits osteoclastic activity and bone resorption by decreasing the flux of calcium from the bones and thus reducing the calcium level in the blood.

Clodronate may be administered as a higher single infusion dose or a lower dose for multiple infusion use. Both methods have been shown to be effective.

Treatment with oral clodronate following i.v. infusion has been found to prolong the duration of action (see Dosage).

Contraindications: Renal functional impairment (serum creatinine exceeding 440 μmol/L [5 mg/dL]). Hypersensitivity to clodronate or to other bisphosphonates. Severe inflammation of the gastrointestinal tract. Pregnancy and lactation.

Warnings: Clodronate should not be given as a bolus injection since severe local reactions and thrombophlebitis may occur as the result of high local concentrations. The rapid bolus injection may also precipitate acute renal failure.

The recommended daily dose of clodronate i.v. concentrate for i.v. infusion should always be diluted and administered as a slow i.v. infusion over a minimum 2-hour period (during multiple infusion use) or a minimum 4-hour period (during single infusion use) (see Dosage).

Administration of clodronate may aggravate renal function in some patients. Therefore, appropriate monitoring of renal function during and after i.v. infusion is required. The effect of the drug on the renal function of patients with serum creatinine in excess of 220 μmol/L (2.5 mg/dL) has not been studied in controlled trials. In such situations dose reduction should be considered or the drug should be withheld (see Precautions).

Clodronate should not be given together with other bisphosphonates since the combined effects of these agents are unknown.

Clodronate should not be mixed with calcium-containing i.v. infusions.

If during therapy there is deterioration of renal function, the i.v. infusion must be stopped.

Precautions: Administration of I.V. Infusion: Clodronate i.v. may be administered either as a single infusion or as multiple infusions.

Ostac (cont'd)

Clodronate for infusion is available as a concentrated preparation which must be diluted before use. The only recommended diluents are 0.9% w/v sodium chloride injection, USP or 5% w/v dextrose, USP.

For Single Infusion: Five 10 mL ampuls of clodronate i.v. (concentrate for i.v. infusion) should be added aseptically to 500 mL 0.9% w/v sodium chloride injection, USP or 5% w/v dextrose, USP. No other drugs or nutrients may be added. The diluted solution should be administered by slow i.v. infusion over a period of not less than 4 hours. As with any other highly concentrated i.v. solution there exists a potential for injection site symptoms if extravenous infiltration occurs. The infusion should be monitored closely to avoid infiltration. Prior to infusion of a single 1 500 mg dose, it is important to establish and maintain full hydration with oral or i.v. fluids.

For Multiple Infusions: A single 10 mL ampul of clodronate i.v. should be added aseptically to 500 mL of 0.9% w/v sodium chloride injection, USP or 5% w/v dextrose, USP. No other drugs or nutrients may be added. The diluted injection solution should be administered by slow i.v. infusion over a period of 2 to 6 hours. Slow infusion is important for safety. In patients with hypercalcemia it is recommended that oral or i.v. fluids be administered to establish or maintain full hydration.

Paravenous infiltration should be avoided. Local reactions may occur.

Metabolic and Fluid Balance: Hypercalcemia causes a reversible tubular defect in the kidney that results in the loss of urinary concentrating ability and polyuria, both of which promote dehydration. Hypovolemia in patients with hypercalcemia can diminish glomerular filtration and lead to progressive renal insufficiency.

Most hypercalcemic patients are significantly dehydrated at initial presentation and restoration of intravascular volume is an important initial measure.

The cornerstone of initial treatment is vigorous hydration with isotonic saline (0.9%). It is essential to institute hydration to replenish extracellular fluid volume and restore normal glomerular filtration, as well as sodium diuresis to promote calcium excretion even after hydration status has been corrected.

The rate of administration of isotonic saline should be determined primarily by the severity of the hypercalcemia, the degree of dehydration, and the cardiovascular status of the patient. In general, at least 3 L/day should be administered initially and hydration continued until normocalcemia has been achieved. Urine output must be maintained to avoid possible fluid overload. As many patients with hypercalcemia have other electrolyte abnormalities at presentation, appropriate attention must be given to maintaining electrolyte balance. For example, for hypokalemia, which may be further aggravated by aggressive diuresis, supplementation may be required. The development of hypernatremia during rehydration has been reported, especially in obtunded patients, and may complicate management.

Patient Monitoring: Serum calcium levels should be monitored throughout treatment with clodronate.

Corrected (adjusted) serum calcium values should be calculated using established algorithms, such as:

$Ca_{adj} = Ca_t - 0.71\ (A - A_m)$

Ca_{adj} = adjusted calcium concentration (mg/100 mL)

Ca_t = total calcium concentration (mg/100 mL)

A = albumin concentration (g/100 mL)

A_m = mean normal albumin concentration for the given laboratory (g/100 mL)

Alternative: corrected calcium (mg/dL) = measured calcium + [4.0-albumin (g/dL)] × 0.8

Appropriate monitoring of hepatic function and hematological parameters, including white cell count is advised.

Additionally, serum creatinine and blood urea nitrogen should be monitored in patients with known or suspected renal insufficiency.

Hypocalcemia: Infusion of clodronate may present a risk of hypocalcemia. The drug may chelate blood calcium during therapy, this may contribute to hypocalcemia.

In most cases, plasma calcium concentrations remain within the normal range during the administration of recommended doses of clodronate. When plasma calcium falls into the hypocalcemic range, the patient may remain asymptomatic.

In these cases i.v. administration should be stopped or the oral dose should be decreased. In severe or symptomatic cases of hypocalcemia, oral or parenteral calcium supplementation may be required.

Serum Phosphate: Hyperphosphatemia has not been reported during clodronate therapy in hypercalcemic patients. However, transient hypophosphatemia can occur following therapy with clodronate.

Hyperparathyroidism: Clodronate has not been shown to affect the renal handling of calcium and/or the action of plasma parathyroid hormone (PTH) on this process. A transitory increase in PTH has been reported in certain subjects.

Drug Interactions: The use of clodronate with other agents indicated for reduction of calcium such as corticosteroids, phosphate, calcitonin, mithramycin, loop-diuretics may result in increased hypocalcemic effect depending on tumor type and pathophysiological situation.

Concurrent use of antacids or any drug containing calcium, iron, magnesium or aluminum may prevent absorption of oral clodronate.

Concomitant use of clodronate with mithramycin and thiazides is not recommended.

Concomitant use of i.v. clodronate and aminoglycosides can result in an increased incidence of hypocalcemia.

Concomitant use of clodronate and NSAIDs may promote renal dysfunction. However, a synergistic action has not been established.

Pregnancy: The safety and efficacy of clodronate in pregnancy has not been established (see Contraindications).

Lactation: There is no clinical experience in lactating women and it is not known whether clodronate passes into breast milk (see Contraindications).

Children: The safety and efficacy of clodronate in children has not been established.

Laboratory Examinations: Since clodronate binds to bone, it may interfere with bone scintigraphy examinations.

Retreatment: No formalized studies have been carried out with respect to retreatment. Clinical experience shows that patients with re-increased serum calcium after termination of therapy with clodronate or during oral administration may be retreated either with a higher oral dosage (up to 3 200 mg/day) or with the i.v. infusion preparation as a single infusion (1 500 mg/day) or multiple infusions (300 mg/day). Oral or i.v. treatment should be chosen dependent on the severity of hypercalcemia.

It is recommended that appropriate monitoring of renal function with serum creatinine and/or blood urea nitrogen be carried out during treatment. Serum calcium and phosphate should be monitored periodically. Appropriate monitoring of hepatic function and hematological parameters, including white cell count is advised.

Compatibility with I.V. Solutions: Ostac i.v. is a concentrate for i.v. infusion which **must** be diluted before use. The only recommended diluents are 0.9% w/v sodium chloride injection, USP or 5% w/v dextrose, USP. A single 10 mL ampul (for multiple infusion use) or five 10 mL ampuls (for single infusion use) of Ostac i.v. (300 mg/10 mL) should be added aseptically to 500 mL of 0.9% w/v sodium chloride injection, USP or 5% w/v dextrose, USP. No other drugs or nutrients may be added (see Dosage).

Adverse Effects: Listed in Table I are the crude incidence rates for most common adverse events reported during therapy with the 400 mg capsules and i.v. (concentrate for i.v. infusion).

Table I—Ostac

Incidence Rates for the Most Common Adverse Events Reported During Therapy

Adverse Event	Oral (N=390) %(N)	I.V. (N=188) %(N)
Digestive		
Vomiting	—	3.6 (14)
Nausea	3.1 (12)	1.1 (2)
Diarrhea	1.8 (7)	0.5 (1)
Anorexia	1.0 (4)	—
Metabolic and Nutritional		
Hypocalcemia	1.5 (6)	—
Creatinine Increased	1.3 (5)	—
ALT Increased	0.3 (1)	—
Cardiovascular		
Heart Failure	1.3 (5)	—
Respiratory		
Pneumonia	1.3 (5)	—
Musculoskeletal		
Spontaneous Fracture	1.0 (4)	—

Gastrointestinal symptoms such as nausea, vomiting, anorexia and diarrhea are the most frequent adverse events reported during clodronate therapy, particularly with the oral form. A reduction in dosage, a change to i.v. clodronate or a temporary interruption of therapy may assist in the management of patients where these symptoms are relevant.

Adverse events affecting the calcium homeostasis leading to hypocalcemia were all assessed as possible or probable and reflect the calcium lowering properties of clodronate.

Hypercalcemia of malignancy is frequently associated with abnormal elevation in serum creatinine and BUN. Transient increases in serum creatinine were observed during clodronate therapy. Although in some cases a causal relationship could not be excluded with certainty, the assessment of causality is difficult since in longstanding hypercalcemia, an impairment in renal function, possibly due to the nephrocalcinosis, can reasonably be expected. Careful monitoring of renal function is advised. Transient proteinuria and oliguria have also been reported in few cases immediately following single infusion use of i.v. clodronate.

A causal relationship between clodronate and liver function abnormalities, i.e., increased liver enzymes (ALT, AP, LDH) is also difficult to assess. Pre-existing liver metastases and abnormal liver function values often exist prior to therapy with clodronate. Causal relationship, however, cannot be excluded with certainty in some patients. Careful monitoring of liver function values is advised.

Adverse events affecting the cardiovascular and respiratory systems or reported as spontaneous fractures were all assessed as unrelated to clodronate therapy since alternative causalities were evident (e.g., heart failure prior to clodronate therapy; pneumonia; deficient immune state in patients suffering from advanced malignant diseases).

Patient surveillance encompassing about 2 700 patient-years treated with clodronate detected 5 cases of acute non-lymphocytic leukemia or myelodysplasia in patients without multiple myeloma, and 2 cases in patients with multiple myeloma (2 patients with multiple myeloma also developed non-lymphocytic leukemia while receiving placebo). The causal relationship to clodronate or to the underlying disease has not been established. Appropriate monitoring of hematological parameters, including white cell count is still advised.

A case of bronchospastic reaction in a female patient suffering from an ASA-sensitive asthma bronchiole has been reported after administration of i.v. clodronate.

Hypersensitivity reactions, including angioedema, urticaria, rash and/or pruritus, in association with oral or parenteral clodronate, have been reported in 2 patients.

Overdose: Symptoms and Treatment: There is a lack of documented experience on acute overdosing with clodronate. An overdose of the i.v. preparation could provoke renal damage. Renal function should be monitored. Overdosage may result in hypocalcemia. Careful monitoring for several days for signs and symptoms of hypocalcemia is recommended in cases where the dose given was too high in relation to initial serum calcium (see Precautions). Oral or parenteral calcium supplementation may be required to restore plasma calcium levels.

Gastric lavage may be used to remove unabsorbed drug following acute oral overdosage.

Dosage: I.V.: Single Infusion: Recommended Dosage: The contents of five 10 mL ampuls is administered by slow i.v. infusion over a period of not less than 4 hours.

Administration: Five 10 mL ampuls is diluted with 500 mL of 0.9 % w/v sodium chloride injections, USP or 5% w/v dextrose, USP and administered by slow i.v. infusion over a period of not less than 4 hours.

Note: Other diluents should not be used. No other drugs or nutrients may be added.

Multiple Infusions: Recommended Dosage: The contents of 1 ampul is administered as a single daily dose over a period of 2 to 6 hours.

Administration: 1 ampul is diluted with 500 mL of 0.9% w/v sodium chloride injection, USP or 5% w/v dextrose, USP and administered by slow i.v. infusion over a period of 2 to 6 hours.

Note: Other diluents should not be used. No other drugs or nutrients may be added.

Since the duration of treatment is adjusted in accordance with patient response, daily determination of serum calcium levels must be carried out. Duration of treatment by multiple i.v. infusion should not exceed 10 days.

Response: In most cases, elevated serum calcium levels can be reduced to normal within 2 to 5 days, whichever method of infusion is used. Following normalization, treatment should be continued with clodronate 400 mg capsules in order to maintain normocalcemia. Should the serum calcium level rise again during oral treatment, the i.v. infusion can be reintroduced.

Prior to using clodronate (single or multiple infusions) it is important to establish and maintain full hydration with oral or i.v. fluids.

Oral: Recommended Dosage: The oral recommended daily maintenance dose following i.v. therapy is in the range of

1 600 mg (4 capsules) to 2 400 mg (6 capsules) given in single or 2 divided doses. Maximal recommended daily dose is 3 200 mg (8 capsules).

Oral doses higher than 3 200 mg daily have not been evaluated but would be likely to increase the frequency of adverse intestinal effects.

Dosage should be reduced in patients with severe renal impairment (see Contraindications, Warnings and Precautions).

Administration: Capsules should be administered whole with copious fluids, but not with milk. The patient should not eat 1 hour before or after clodronate intake.

The total daily amount can be given as 1 single dose or, if necessary, in 2 divided doses in order to improve gastrointestinal tolerance. The standard daily dosage generally consists of 4×400 mg capsules (1 600 mg/day). However, in some individual cases, a higher daily dose of up to 8×400 mg capsules (3 200 mg/day) may be necessary.

The duration of treatment is normally 6 months. Treatment, however, can be extended beyond 6 months depending on the course of the disease. Similarly it may be necessary to restart treatment after an interruption.

Reconstitution: The recommended daily dose must be added aseptically to 500 mL of 0.9% w/v sodium chloride injection, USP or 5% w/v dextrose, USP. **Note:** No other diluent should be used and no other drugs or nutrients may be added.

Storage of Diluted Solution: Protect the diluted solution from temperatures below 15°C and above 30°C. The reconstituted solution should be administered within 12 hours of preparation by slow i.v. infusion over a period of 2 to 6 hours.

Information for the Patient: See Blue Section—Information for the Patient "Ostac".

Supplied: Ampuls: Each mL of concentrate for i.v. infusion contains: clodronate disodium 30 mg. Nonmedicinal ingredients: disodium hydrogen carbonate. Ampuls of 10 mL, boxes of 5.

Capsules: Each white, gelatin capsule contains: clodronate disodium 400 mg. Nonmedicinal ingredients: gelatin, iron oxide, magnesium stearate, maize starch, polydimethyl siloxane, shellac, sodium starch glycolate, soya lecithin, talc and titanium oxide. Blister packs of 120.

Store at room temperature (15 to 30°C). Protect from high humidity.

(Shown in Product Recognition Section)

OSTOFORTE® Ⓟ

Frosst

Vitamin D_2 (Ergocalciferol)

Vitamin

Indications: Treatment of refractory rickets (vitamin D-resistant rickets), familial phosphatemia and hypoparathyroidism.

Contraindications: Hypercalcemia, malabsorption syndrome, abnormal sensitivity to the toxic effects of vitamin D, hypervitaminosis D, decreased renal function.

Precautions: Hypersensitivity to vitamin D may be one etiological factor in infants with idiopathic hypercalcemia. In these cases, vitamin D must be severely restricted.

Pregnancy: Safety in excess of 400 IU of vitamin D daily during pregnancy has not been established and animal reproduction studies in several species have shown fetal abnormalities associated with hypervitaminosis D. Avoid the use of vitamin D in excess of the recommended dietary allowance during pregnancy unless the potential benefits outweigh the possible adverse effects.

Vitamin D ingestion from fortified foods, milk with vitamin D added, dietary supplements and other sources should be evaluated.

Readjust therapeutic dosage as soon as there is clinical improvement. Individualize dosage levels and exercise great care to prevent serious toxic effects. In vitamin D-resistant rickets, the range between the therapeutic and toxic doses is narrow. When high therapeutic doses are used, follow progress with frequent serum and urinary calcium (Sulkowitch test), potassium and urea determinations.

In the treatment of hypoparathyroidism, calcium, parathyroid hormone and/or dihydrotachysterol may be required. Mineral oil interferes with the absorption of fat-soluble vitamins.

Overdose: Symptoms: Hypervitaminosis D is characterized by:

Hypercalcemia with anorexia, nausea, weakness, weight loss, vague aches and stiffness, constipation, diarrhea, convulsions, mental retardation, anemia, mild acidosis.

Impairment of renal function with polyuria, nocturia, polydipsia, hypercalcuria, reversible azotemia, hypertension, nephrocalcinosis, generalized vascular calcification, irreversible renal insufficiency, albuminuria, or urinary casts.

Widespread calcification of the soft tissues, including the heart, blood vessels, renal tubules, and lungs. Bone demineralization (osteoporosis) in adults occurs concomitantly.

Decline in the average rate of linear growth and increased mineralization of bones in infants and children (dwarfism).

Treatment: Immediate withdrawal of the vitamin, reduction of calcium intake and increased fluid intake. Hypercalcemic crisis requires more vigorous treatment. Intravenous saline may quickly and significantly increase urinary calcium excretion. Other reported therapeutic measures include dialysis or the administration of citrates, sulfates, phosphates, corticosteroids or EDTA.

Dosage: The recommended total daily intake of vitamin D from all sources is 400 IU. For the correction of vitamin D deficiency, 5 000 IU daily is recommended until a biochemical and radiographic response is apparent.

The range between therapeutic and toxic doses is narrow.

Vitamin D-resistant rickets: 12 000 to 500 000 IU daily.

Hypoparathyroidism: 50 000 to 200 000 IU daily plus 4 g of calcium lactate, administered 6 times per day.

Dosage must be individualized under close medical supervision. Calcium intake should be adequate. Blood calcium, phosphorus and urea determinations must be made every 2 weeks, or more frequently if necessary.

The bones should be x-rayed every month until the condition is corrected and stabilized.

Supplied: Each clear yellow, soft gelatin capsule contains: vitamin D_2 (ergocalciferol) 50 000 IU. Gluten-, lactose- and tartrazine-free. Bottles of 100.

(Shown in Product Recognition Section)

OTRIVIN®

Novartis Consumer Health

Xylometazoline HCl

Nasal Decongestant

Indications: Nasal congestion in colds, rhinitis, sinusitis; also for headache, tubal block and serous otitis media associated with nasal congestion. Xylometazoline facilitates rhinoscopy and is a useful pre- and postoperative adjunct.

Contraindications: Narrow-angle glaucoma. Concurrent therapy with MAO inhibitors. Hypersensitivity to any component. Sensitivity to even small doses of adrenergic substances as manifested by sleeplessness, dizziness, lightheadedness, weakness, tremulousness, or cardiac arrhythmias. Do not use for irrigation or displacement following surgical procedures in which the dura mater may have been entered; e.g. sinus and transnasal operations.

Precautions: Like other topical vasoconstrictors, xylometazoline should not be employed continuously for periods exceeding 2 weeks: prolonged or excessive use may cause rebound congestion. Do not exceed the recommended dose. Systemic effects from the use of topical decongestants can occur due to rapid absorption from the nasal mucous membrane, especially when it is inflamed, and from gastrointestinal absorption if given in excess so that the nasally applied solution is swallowed. Such reactions are most likely to occur in infants, young children and the elderly.

Caution is recommended in patients with hypertension, cardiovascular and thyroid disease.

Pregnancy and *Lactation:* Clinical data are inadequate to establish conditions for safe use in pregnancy and lactation.

Children: Overdosage in children may produce profound sedation.

Adverse Effects: Rarely, rebound congestion, mild tingling, burning sensation in the nose or throat, local irritation or dryness of the nasal mucosa. Intranasal use of xylometazoline may occasionally cause systemic sympathomimetic effects such as hypertension, nervousness, nausea, dizziness, headache, insomnia, palpitation, tachycardia and arrhythmia. In isolated cases, systemic allergic reactions or transient visual disturbances have been reported.

Overdose: Symptoms: In rare instances of accidental poisoning in children, the clinical picture has been marked chiefly by signs such as acceleration and irregularity of the pulse, elevated blood pressure, and sometimes clouding of consciousness.

Treatment: Symptomatic treatment under medical supervision is indicated.

Dosage: May be used every 8 to 10 hours.

Adults: Sprays: With head tilted slightly forward, spray 1 or 2 times into each nostril. Breathe deeply.

Drops: With head tilted back, apply 2 or 3 drops into each nostril.

Measured Dose Pumps: Remove protective cap. Hold bottle upright with thumb under base and nozzle between first and second fingers. With head tilted slightly forward, insert nozzle into nostril, and spray once into each nostril. Breathe deeply. Replace cap after use. Before using Otrivin with M-D Pump for the first time, prime the pump by spraying several times into the air until a fine mist appears.

Children: Sprays: With head tilted slightly forward, spray 1 or 2 times into each nostril. Breathe deeply.

Drops: With head tilted back, apply 2 or 3 drops into each nostril.

Children under 6 years: Sprays: 1 spray into each nostril.

Drops: 1 drop into each nostril.

Supplied: Nasal Drops (Adult): Each bottle contains: xylometazoline HCl 0.1% in aqueous solution. Nonmedicinal ingredients: benzalkonium chloride, edetate disodium, sodium chloride, sodium phosphate and water. Sodium: <1 mmol (3.8 mg)/mL. Bottles of 25 mL.

Nasal Drops (Pediatric): Each bottle contains: xylometazoline HCl 0.05% in aqueous solution. Nonmedicinal ingredients: benzalkonium chloride, edetate disodium, sodium chloride, sodium phosphate and water. Sodium: <1 mmol (3.8 mg)/mL. Bottles of 25 mL.

Nasal Spray (Adult): Each bottle contains: xylometazoline HCl 0.1% in aqueous solution. Nonmedicinal ingredients: benzalkonium chloride, edetate disodium, sodium chloride, sodium phosphate and water. Sodium: <1 mmol (3.8 mg)/mL. Bottles of 20 and 30 mL.

Nasal Spray (Pediatric): Each bottle contains: xylometazoline HCl 0.05% in aqueous solution. Nonmedicinal ingredients: benzalkonium chloride, edetate disodium, sodium chloride, sodium phosphate and water. Sodium: <1 mmol (3.8 mg)/mL. Bottles of 20 mL.

Measured Dose Pump (Adult): Each bottle contains: xylometazoline HCl 0.1% in aqueous solution. Nonmedicinal ingredients: benzalkonium chloride, edetate disodium, sodium chloride, sodium phosphate and water. Sodium: <1 mmol (3.8 mg)/mL. Bottles of 20 mL.

With Menthol Eucalyptol Spray (Adult): Each bottle contains: xylometazoline HCl 0.1% in aqueous solution. Nonmedicinal ingredients: benzalkonium chloride, edetate disodium, eucalyptus oil, hydrogenated castor oil, menthol, sodium chloride, sodium phosphate, sorbitol and water. Bottles of 20 and 30 mL.

With Moisturizers Spray (Adult): Each bottle contains: xylometazoline HCl 0.1% in aqueous solution. Nonmedicinal ingredients: benzalkonium chloride, edetate disodium, polyethylene glycol, propylene glycol, sodium phosphate and water. Bottles of 20 mL.

With Moisturizers Measured Dose Pump (Adult): Each bottle contains: xylometazoline HCl 0.1% in aqueous solution. Nonmedicinal ingredients: benzalkonium chloride, edetate disodium, polyethylene glycol, propylene glycol, sodium phosphate and water. Bottles of 20 mL.

Reviewed 1999

OVOL® Preparations

Carter Horner

Simethicone

Antiflatulent

Indications: Specifically for symptomatic treatment of gastrointestinal discomfort due to entrapped gas. Relief of infant colic.

Overdose: Symptoms and Treatment: Treatment symptomatic.

Dosage: Drops: Infants, 0.25 to 0.50 mL with or after each meal. May be added to formula or given directly from dropper. Maximum: 6 mL/24 hours.

Tablets: Adults: 40 mg (2 tablets, 4 times daily), 80 mg (1 or 2 tablets, 4 times daily); 160 mg (1 tablet, 4 times daily).

Supplied: Drops: Each mL of white, opaque, peppermint flavored suspension with a milky appearance contains: simethicone 40 mg. Nonmedicinal ingredients: aluminum magnesium silicate, cellulose, citric acid, flavor, hydrogen peroxide, parabens, polyoxyl 8 stearate and sucrose. pH: 5.9 to 7.5. Energy:

Ovol Preparations (cont'd)

1.2 kJ (0.3 kcal). Sodium: <1 mmol (0.8 mg). Alcohol-, gluten- and tartrazine-free. Dropper bottles of 15 and 30 mL.

Tablets: Ovol-40: Each white, round, flat, peppermint-flavored chewable tablet with beveled edges, bisected on one side, contains: simethicone 40 mg. Nonmedicinal ingredients: cellulose, flavor, gelatin, magnesium stearate, silicon dioxide, sucrose and talc. Energy: 6.7 kJ (1.6 kcal). Sodium: <1 mmol (0.2 mg). Alcohol-, gluten- and tartrazine-free. Push-through packages of 48.

Ovol-80: Each white, round, flat, peppermint-flavored chewable tablet with beveled edges, quadrisected on both sides, contains: simethicone 80 mg. Nonmedicinal ingredients: cellulose, flavor, gelatin, magnesium stearate, silicon dioxide, sucrose and talc. Energy: 13.4 kJ (3.2 kcal). Sodium: <1 mmol (0.2 mg). Alcohol-, gluten- and tartrazine-free. Push-through packages of 10 and 50.

Ovol-160: Each white, round, flat, cherry-flavored chewable tablet with beveled edges, bisected on one side, engraved Ovol-160 on the other, contains: simethicone 160 mg. Nonmedicinal ingredients: aluminum hydroxide, aspartame, cellulose, citric acid, flavor, gelatin, magnesium stearate, silicon dioxide, sucrose and talc. Energy: 10.3 kJ (2.46 kcal). Sodium: <1 mmol (0.2 mg). Alcohol-, gluten- and tartrazine-free. Push-through packages of 16 and 32.

(Shown in Product Recognition Section)

OVRAL® 21 ℞
OVRAL® 28 ℞
Wyeth-Ayerst

Norgestrel—Ethinyl Estradiol
Oral Contraceptive

Supplied: Ovral 21: Each white tablet, with W in shield on one side and imprinted 23 on the other, contains: 250 μg of d-norgestrel (as 500 μg of the dl-racemate) and 50 μg of ethinyl estradiol. Energy: 1.59 kJ (0.38 kcal). Nonmedicinal ingredients: lactose, magnesium stearate, microcrystalline cellulose and polacrillin potassium. Gluten- and tartrazine-free. Compacts and refill strips of 21 tablets.

Ovral 28: Each compact of 28 tablets contains: 21 white Ovral tablets and 7 pink inert tablets. Nonmedicinal ingredients: (white tablets): lactose, magnesium stearate, microcrystalline cellulose and polacrillin potassium; (pink tablets): FD&C Red No. 3. Energy: 1.59 kJ (0.38 kcal). Gluten- and tartrazine-free.

(Shown in Product Recognition Section)

OXAZEPAM ℞
General Monograph, CPhA

see BENZODIAZEPINES

OXEZE® TURBUHALER® ℞
Astra

Formoterol Fumarate Dihydrate
Bronchodilator

Pharmacology: Pharmacodynamics: Formoterol produces bronchodilation by stimulation of the β_2-adrenergic receptors in bronchial smooth muscle, thereby causing relaxation of smooth muscle fibres.

Following inhalation of formoterol, a marked improvement in pulmonary function is observed within 1 to 3 minutes and lasts for a mean duration of 12 hours after a single dose.

Pharmacokinetics: Absorption: Inhaled formoterol is rapidly absorbed. Peak plasma concentration is reached about 15 minutes after inhalation.

In studies the mean lung deposition of formoterol after inhalation via Turbuhaler ranged from 21 to 37% of the metered dose. The total systemic availability for the higher lung deposition was approximately 46% of the metered dose.

Distribution and Metabolism: Plasma protein-binding is approximately 50%.

Formoterol is metabolized via direct glucuronidation and O-demethylation. The enzyme responsible for O-demethylation has not been identified. Total plasma clearance and volume of distribution has not been determined.

Elimination: The major part of the dose of formoterol is eliminated via metabolism. After inhalation 6 to 10% of the metered dose of formoterol is excreted unmetabolized in the urine. About 20% of an i.v. dose is excreted unchanged in the urine. The terminal half-life after inhalation is estimated to be 8 hours.

Indications: For long-term, twice daily (morning and evening) administration in the maintenance treatment of asthma in patients 12 years of age and older with reversible, obstructive airways disease, including patients with symptoms of nocturnal asthma, who are using optimal corticosteroid treatment and experiencing regular or frequent breakthrough symptoms requiring regular use of a short-acting bronchodilator. Formoterol should not be used in patients whose asthma can be managed by occasional use of short-acting, inhaled β_2-agonists.

Corticosteroids should not be stopped because formoterol is prescribed.

Formoterol is a long-acting β_2-agonist and should not be used as a rescue medication. To relieve acute asthmatic symptoms a short-acting, inhaled bronchodilator (e.g., terbutaline or salbutamol) should be used.

Contraindications: Known hypersensitivity to formoterol or inhaled lactose. Like other sympathomimetic amines, formoterol should not be used in patients with tachyarrhythmias.

Warnings: Acutely Deteriorating Asthma: Formoterol should not be initiated or increased in patients with significantly worsening or acutely deteriorating asthma (see Precautions).

Use of Anti-inflammatory Agents: Patients should be receiving optimal anti-inflammatory therapy with corticosteroids before starting formoterol. Formoterol is not a substitute for inhaled or oral corticosteroids; its use is complementary to them. Corticosteroids should not be stopped when formoterol is initiated. Patients must be advised not to stop or reduce corticosteroid therapy without medical advice (see Precautions).

Treatment of Acute Symptoms: Formoterol should not be used to treat acute symptoms. It is crucial to advise patients accordingly and prescribe a short-acting, inhaled bronchodilator for this purpose. Medical attention should be sought if patients find that short-acting, relief bronchodilator treatment becomes less effective or that they need more inhalations than usual (see Precautions).

Formoterol and the Management of Asthma: The management of asthma should normally follow a stepwise programme, with patient response monitored clinically and by lung function tests. Current asthma management guidelines recommend the following for long-acting β_2-agonists: Oral or inhaled corticosteroids should not be stopped. Adequate education should be provided to the patient regarding the use of long-acting β_2-agonists and the acute treatment of asthma, with close follow-up to ensure compliance. Long-acting β_2-agonists should not be introduced in significantly worsening or acutely deteriorating asthma. Long-acting β_2-agonists should never be used as rescue medication.

Increasing use of short-acting, inhaled β_2-agonists to control symptoms indicates deterioration of asthma control and the need to reassess the patient's therapy.

Sudden or progressive deterioration in asthma control is potentially life-threatening; the treatment plan must be re-evaluated, and consideration be given to increasing corticosteroid therapy. In patients at risk, daily peak flow monitoring with precise instructions for acceptable variation limits should be considered.

Cardiovascular and Hypokalemic Effects: Potentially serious ECG changes (such as increased QTc interval) and hypokalemia may result from β_2-agonist therapy. Although clinically not significant, a small increase in QTc interval and/or decrease in serum potassium has been reported at therapeutic doses of formoterol. Particular caution is advised in severe asthma as these effects may be potentiated by hypoxia and concomitant treatment with xanthine derivatives, steroids and diuretics. Hypokalemia will increase the susceptibility of digitalis patients to cardiac arrhythmias (see Precautions). It is recommended that serum potassium levels be monitored in such situations. Therefore, formoterol, like all sympathomimetic amines, should be used with caution in patients with cardiovascular disorders, arrhythmias and hypertension.

Other Diseases: Sympathomimetic bronchodilators should be administered cautiously to patients who are unusually responsive to sympathomimetic amines, e.g., in patients with hyperthyroidism not yet under adequate control. Since β_2-agonists may increase the blood glucose level, additional blood glucose controls are recommended when asthmatic patients with concomitant diabetes are started on formoterol.

Paradoxical Bronchospasm: As with other inhaled asthma medication, the potential for paradoxical bronchospasm should be kept in mind. If it occurs, treatment with formoterol should be discontinued immediately and alternative therapy instituted.

Postmarketing Experience: The postmarketing experience with Oxeze Turbuhaler is limited. Postmarketing experience with other long-acting β_2-agonists (formoterol and salmeterol) have reported serious exacerbations of asthma including some that have been fatal. In most cases, these have occurred in patients with severe asthma and/or in some patients whose asthma has been acutely deteriorating (see Acutely Deteriorating Asthma), but they have occurred in a few patients with less severe asthma as well. It was not possible from these reports to determine whether long-acting β_2-agonists contributed to these events or simply failed to relieve the deteriorating asthma.

Precautions: Do not introduce formoterol as a treatment for acutely deteriorating asthma. Formoterol is intended for the maintenance treatment of asthma (see Indications) and should not be introduced or increased in acutely deteriorating asthma, which is a potentially life-threatening condition. In patients with worsening asthma, there are no data demonstrating that long-acting β_2-agonists provide greater efficacy than or additional efficacy to short-acting, inhaled β_2-agonists. With other long-acting β_2-agonists, serious acute respiratory events, including fatalities, have been reported, some of which have occurred in patients with severe asthma and/or patients in whom asthma has been acutely deteriorating. Although it is not possible from these reports to determine the causal relationship between long-acting β_2-agonists and these adverse events, the introduction or increased use of a long-acting β_2-agonist in patients with acutely deteriorating asthma is inappropriate.

Do not use formoterol as a substitute for oral or inhaled corticosteroids. Patients who require therapy with formoterol should also receive optimal anti-inflammatory therapy with corticosteroids. Patients must be advised to continue taking their anti-inflammatory therapy after the introduction of formoterol even when symptoms decrease. Any change in corticosteroid dosage should be made **only** after clinical evaluation.

Do not use formoterol to treat acute symptoms. Formoterol should only be used in patients requiring long-term regular bronchodilator therapy and **not** as an alternative to short-acting β_2-agonists used on demand or in the event of an acute attack.

Formoterol should **not** be used to relieve acute asthma symptoms. When prescribing formoterol, the physician must also provide the patient with a short-acting, inhaled β_2-agonist (e.g., terbutaline or salbutamol) for treatment of symptoms that occur acutely, despite regular twice-daily use of formoterol.

Although formoterol has a rapid onset of action (1 to 3 minutes), current asthma management guidelines recommend that long-acting, inhaled bronchodilators should be used only as twice-daily maintenance bronchodilator therapy.

Watch for increased need for short-acting, inhaled β_2-agonists. Bronchodilators of the short-acting, adrenergic stimulant type may be used for relief of breakthrough symptoms while using formoterol. Asthma may deteriorate acutely over a period of hours or slowly over several days or longer. Should symptoms persist, or treatment with short-acting, inhaled β_2-agonist become less effective or a patient needs more inhalations than usual, this indicates a worsening of the underlying condition and warrants reassessment of the treatment regimen and consideration given to increasing corticosteroid therapy. Increasing the daily dosage of formoterol in this situation is not appropriate. Patients requiring increasing doses or inhalations of short-acting β_2-agonists for relief of symptoms should be advised to consult a physician for re-evaluation.

Do not exceed recommended dosage. Formoterol should **not** be used more frequently than twice daily or at higher doses than recommended. Fatalities have been reported in association with excessive use of inhaled sympathomimetic drugs (see below).

Cardiovascular and Other Medical Conditions: Usually no effect on the cardiovascular or central nervous system is seen after the administration of formoterol at recommended doses, but the cardiovascular and central nervous system effects seen with all sympathomimetic drugs (e.g., increased heart rate, cardiac contractility, tremor) can occur while using formoterol. Special care and supervision, with particular emphasis on dosage limits, is required in patients receiving formoterol when the following conditions may exist: ischemic heart disease, cardiac arrhythmias, especially third degree AV block, severe cardiac decompensation, severe hypertension, hypertrophic obstructive cardiomyopathy, thyrotoxicosis or severe heart failure.

Use with caution in patients with idiopathic hypertrophic subvalvular aortic stenosis, in whom an increase in the pressure gradient between the left ventricle and the aorta may occur, causing increased strain on the left ventricle.

Caution should be observed when treating patients with known or suspected prolongation of the QTc-interval. Formoterol itself may induce prolongation of the QTc-interval.

Immediate Hypersensitivity Reactions: Immediate hypersensitivity reactions may occur after administration of formoterol. Oxeze Turbuhaler contains lactose (600 μg/metered dose) and is contraindicated in patients with hypersensitivity to inhaled lactose or formoterol. The amount of lactose in Oxeze Turbuhaler does not normally cause problems in lactose intolerant people (see Contraindications).

Metabolic Effects: Due to the reversible hyperglycemic effect of β_2-agonists, additional blood glucose monitoring is recommended initially in diabetic patients.

Pregnancy: The safety of formoterol during pregnancy has not yet been established (see Labor and Delivery).

Lactation: Formoterol was found to be excreted in the milk of lactating rats after oral administration. Since there is no experience in the use of formoterol in nursing mothers, its use in such circumstances should only be considered if the expected benefit to the mother is greater than the risk to the infant.

Labor and Delivery: There are no well-controlled human studies that have investigated the effects of formoterol on preterm labor or labor at term. Because of the potential for β-agonist interference with uterine contractibility, use of β_2-agonists, such as formoterol during labor should be restricted to those patients in whom the benefits clearly outweigh the risks.

Geriatrics: No adjustment of dose should be required in the elderly, or in patients with renal or hepatic impairment, at the recommended normal doses (see Cardiovascular and Other Medical Conditions and Warnings).

Children: Formoterol is not currently recommended for use in children younger than 12 years of age due to limited clinical data in this age group.

Adolescent Patients and Asthma Severity Reassessment: In adolescent patients the severity of asthma may be variable with age and periodic reassessment should be considered to determine if continued maintenance therapy with formoterol is still indicated. Compliance, especially neglect of anti-inflammatory therapy and overuse of short-acting β_2-agonists, should be carefully followed in adolescents receiving long-acting β_2-agonists.

Drug Interactions: β-Receptor Blocking Agents: β-receptor blocking agents, especially nonselective ones, may partly or totally inhibit the effect of β-stimulants.

Should a patient treated with formoterol also require concomitant treatment with a β-blocker, it is recommended that a β-blocker (e.g., metoprolol) with less predominant β_2-blocking effects be considered. If concomitant treatment is necessary, patients should be monitored carefully for possible deterioration in pulmonary function and the need to adjust the dosage of either drug.

Xanthine Derivatives, Steroids and Diuretics: Concomitant treatment with xanthine derivatives, steroids or diuretics may potentiate a possible hypokalemic effect of β_2-agonists. Hypokalemia may increase the disposition towards arrhythmias in patients who are treated with digitalis glycosides.

Other Drugs: Concomitant treatment with quinidine, disopyramide, procainamide, phenothiazines, antihistamines (terfenadine), MAO inhibitors and tricyclic antidepressants can prolong the QTc-interval and increase the risk of ventricular arrhythmias.

L-dopa, L-thyroxine, oxytocin and alcohol can impair cardiac tolerance towards β_2-sympathomimetics.

Concomitant treatment with MAO inhibitors including agents with similar properties such as furazolidone and procarbazine may precipitate hypertensive reactions.

There is elevated risk of arrhythmias in patients receiving concomitant anesthesia with halogenated hydrocarbons.

Information to be Provided to the Patient: See Blue Section—Information for the Patient. It is important that patients understand how to use formoterol for oral inhalation and how it should be used in relation to other asthma medications they are taking. Patients should be given the following information: The recommended dosage, as follows: Adults: The usual dose is 6 or 12 μg, twice daily, at 12-hour intervals. Some adults may need 24 μg, twice daily. The maximum daily dosage for adults, 48 μg, should not be exceeded. Adolescent Children (12 to 16 years): The usual dose is 6 μg, twice daily, at 12-hour intervals. Some children may need 12 μg, twice daily. The maximum daily dosage for adolescent children, 24 μg, should not be exceeded.

Formoterol is not meant to relieve acute asthma symptoms and extra doses should not be used for that purpose. Acute symptoms should be treated with a short-acting, inhaled β_2-agonist such as terbutaline or salbutamol (the physician should provide the patient with such medication and instruct the patient in how it should be used).

The physician should be notified immediately if any of the following situations occur, which may be a sign of seriously worsening asthma: decreased effectiveness of short-acting, inhaled β_2-agonist; need for more inhalations than usual of short-acting, inhaled β_2-agonist.

Formoterol for oral inhalation should not be used as a substitute for oral or inhaled corticosteroids. Patients must be advised to continue taking their corticosteroid therapy after the introduction of formoterol even when symptoms decrease.

Patients should be cautioned regarding potential adverse cardiovascular effects, such as palpitations or chest pain.

In patients receiving formoterol for oral inhalation, other inhaled medications should be used only as directed by the physician.

Parents/guardians of adolescent children who have been prescribed formoterol should be alerted to the general concern regarding asthma therapy compliance, especially neglect of anti-inflammatory therapy and overuse of short-acting β_2-agonists.

Adverse Effects: Pharmacologically predictable side-effects of β_2-agonist therapy, such as tremor and palpitations, may occur but tend to be transient and reduced with regular therapy. As with other inhalation therapy, paradoxical bronchospasm may occur in very rare cases. The following adverse reactions can be classified as common (i.e., frequency $\geq 1\%$ and $< 10\%$): tremor, palpitations and headache; uncommon (frequency $\geq 0.1\%$ and $< 1\%$): muscle cramps, tachycardia, agitation, restlessness and sleep disturbances; very rare (frequency $< 0.01\%$): bronchospasm, exanthema, urticaria, pruritus and hypokalemia.

The clinical program conducted with formoterol, has involved more than 1 800 patients. The incidence of adverse events, irrespective of causality towards the drug, from 4 controlled trials (duration 1, 3, 3 and 6 months respectively) with formoterol is presented in Table I.

Table I—Oxeze Turbuhaler

Incidence of Adverse Events (Irrespective of Causality) With Frequency Higher Than Placebo in 4 Controlled Trials of Duration 1, 3, 3 and 6 Months Respectively.

	Oxeze Turbuhaler			Placebo Turbuhaler
	Total	6 μg b.i.d.	12 μg b.i.d.	
	N (%)	N (%)	N (%)	N (%)
Total Number of Evaluable Patients	**359**	**190**	**169**	**412**
Headache	66 (18%)	15 (8%)	51 (30%)	84 (20%)
Tremor	11 (3%)	4 (2%)	7 (4%)	2 (0%)
Pharynx Disorder	18 (5%)	3 (2%)	15 (9%)	10 (2%)
Cramps	10 (3%)	3 (2%)	7 (4%)	3 (1%)

Overdose: Symptoms and Treatment: There is no clinical experience on the management of overdose. An overdose would likely lead to effects that are typical of β_2-adrenergic agonists: tremor, headache, palpitations and tachycardia. Hypotension, metabolic acidosis, hypokalemia and hyperglycemia may also occur. Supportive and symptomatic treatment may be indicated.

Dosage: Formoterol should not be initiated or increased in patients with significantly worsening or acutely deteriorating asthma, which may be a life-threatening condition (see Precautions).

Formoterol should only be used in patients requiring long-term regular bronchodilator therapy in addition to optimal corticosteroid therapy and not as an alternative to short-acting β-agonists used on demand or in the event of an acute attack.

Formoterol should not be used to treat acute symptoms. It is crucial to inform patients of this and prescribe a short-acting, inhaled β_2-agonist for this purpose.

Fomoterol should not be used more frequently than twice daily with a 12-hour interval between doses or at higher doses than recommended. Asthma may deteriorate acutely over a period of hours or chronically over several days or longer. If the patient's short-acting, inhaled β_2-agonist becomes less effective or a patient needs more inhalations than usual, this may be a marker of destabilization of asthma. In this setting, the patient requires immediate reassessment of the treatment regimen. Increasing the daily dosage of formoterol in this situation is not appropriate (see Precautions).

Bronchodilators should not be the only or the main treatment in patients with moderate to severe or unstable asthma. Patients with severe asthma may require regular medical assessment. These patients will require high-dose inhaled or oral corticosteroid therapy. Sudden worsening of symptoms may require increased corticosteroids dosage which should be administered under medical supervision.

Since there may be serious adverse effects associated with excessive dosing, the dosage or frequency of administration should not be increased.

As a twice daily regular treatment, formoterol provides 24-hour bronchodilation and can replace regular use of a fast-acting, short-duration, inhaled bronchodilator (e.g., salbutamol or terbutaline), when used concurrently with corticosteroid therapy.

Dosage should be individualized and patient response should be monitored by the prescribing physician on an ongoing basis.

Long-term, Twice Daily Maintenance Therapy: The dose of formoterol should be individualized to the patient's needs and should be the lowest possible dose that keeps the patient symptom-free or fulfills the therapeutic objective.

Adults: The normal dose is 6 or 12 μg twice daily, at 12-hour intervals. Some patients may need 24 μg twice daily. In adults, the maximum recommended daily dose is 48 μg.

Adolescent Children (12 to 16 years): The normal dose is 6 μg twice daily, at 12-hour intervals. Some patients may need 12 μg twice daily. In adolescent children, the maximum recommended daily dose is 24 μg.

In adolescent patients, the severity of asthma may be variable with age and periodic reassessment should be considered to identify the lowest dose required to maintain control and to determine if continued maintenance therapy with formoterol is still indicated (see Precautions).

Oxeze Turbuhaler is available in 2 strengths, 6 or 12 μg/inhalation. Use of the higher strength is recommended for patients requiring 12 μg or more, twice daily. Formoterol is not currently recommended for children younger than 12 years of age due to the limited clinical data in this age group.

It is important to instruct patients to avoid exhaling into the device and to always replace the cover after using Oxeze Turbuhaler.

Note: The medication from Oxeze Turbuhaler is delivered to the lungs as the patient inhales and, therefore, it is important to instruct the patient to breathe in forcefully and deeply through the mouthpiece. The patient may not taste or feel any medication when using Oxeze Turbuhaler due to the small amount of drug dispensed.

Information for the Patient: See Blue Section—Information for the Patient "Oxeze Turbuhaler".

Supplied: 6 μg/metered dose: Each inhalation of a white to off-white or slightly yellow nonhygroscopic crystalline powder contains: formoterol fumarate dihydrate 6 μg. Nonmedicinal ingredients: lactose monohydrate 600 μg/metered dose (this amount does not normally cause problems in lactose-intolerant people). Turbuhalers of 60 doses with a light greenish-blue turning grip.

12 μg/metered dose: Each inhalation of a white to off-white or slightly yellow nonhygroscopic crystalline powder contains: formoterol fumarate dihydrate 12 μg. Nonmedicinal ingredients: lactose monohydrate 600 μg/metered dose (this amount does not normally cause problems in lactose-intolerant people). Turbuhalers of 60 doses with a dark greenish-blue turning grip.

Oxeze Turbuhaler (cont'd)

Oxeze Turbuhaler cannot be refilled and should be discarded when empty. Store at room temperature between 15 and 30°C with the cover tightened, away from moisture.

(Shown in Product Recognition Section)

New Product 1998

OXIZOLE®
Stiefel

Oxiconazole Nitrate
Topical Antifungal

Pharmacology: Oxiconazole nitrate is a broad-spectrum imidazole derivative whose antifungal activity is derived primarily from the inhibition of ergosterol biosynthesis, which is critical for cellular membrane integrity. It has fungicidal or fungistatic activity in vitro against a number of pathogenic fungi including the following dermatophytes, and yeasts: T. rubrum, T. mentagrophytes, T. tonsurans, T. violaceum, E. floccosum, M. canis, M. audouini, M. gypseum, C. albicans, and M. furfur.

Five hours after application of 2.5 mg/cm² of oxiconazole nitrate cream onto human skin, the concentration of oxiconazole nitrate was demonstrated to be 16.2 μmol in the epidermis, 3.64 μmol in the upper corium, and 1.29 μmol in the deeper corium. Systemic absorption of oxiconazole nitrate appears to be low. Less than 0.3% of the applied dose was recovered in the urine of volunteer subjects up to 5 days after application. Feces were not analyzed for the drug, and it is not known whether the absorption is higher than that estimated by recovery of drug in urine.

Indications: For the topical treatment of athlete's foot (tinea pedis) due to T. rubrum, T. mentagrophytes or E. floccosum.

Contraindications: In individuals who have shown hypersensitivity to oxiconazole or any of its components.

Warnings: For external use only, not for ophthalmic or intravaginal use.

Precautions: General: If skin sensitization occurs, discontinue topical administration and institute appropriate therapy as required.

Pregnancy: Reproduction studies have been performed in rabbits, rats and mice at oral doses up to 100, 150 and 200 mg/kg/day, respectively, and revealed no evidence of harm to the fetus due to oxiconazole nitrate. There are, however, no adequate and well-controlled studies in pregnant women. Because animal reproduction studies are not always predictive of human response, oxiconazole preparations should be used during pregnancy only if the potential benefit justifies the potential risk to the fetus.

Lactation: Since oxiconazole is excreted in human milk, caution should be exercised when the drug is administered to a nursing woman. Although human data relating concentrations of oxiconazole in milk were not obtained, after s.c. administration of 5 mg/kg to female rats, the milk: plasma ratio at 1.5 to 12 hours was in the range of 3.0 to 8.0.

Adverse Effects: During clinical trials, 37 (4.2%) of 879 patients treated with oxiconazole cream reported drug-related adverse reactions, including pruritus (1.6%), burning (1.4%), irritation (0.5%), erythema, stinging and allergic contact dermatitis (0.2% each) and folliculitis, fissuring, maceration rash and nodules (0.1% each).

In a controlled, multicenter clinical trial, 7 (2.6%) of 269 patients treated with oxiconazole lotion reported drug-related adverse reactions, including burning and stinging (0.7% each), pruritus, scaling, tingling, pain, and dyshidrotic eczema (0.4% each).

Overdose: Acute overdosage of oxiconazole in humans has not been reported to date.

Symptoms: Animal studies have shown oxiconazole to be a CNS depressant and tissue irritant when administered orally or by injection.

Treatment: In cases of accidental ingestion, gastric lavage should be considered, otherwise, the treatment should be symptomatic.

Dosage: In patients with tinea pedis, oxiconazole cream and lotion should be applied to cover affected and surrounding areas twice daily (in the morning and evening). Medication should be gently massaged into the skin. Tinea pedis should be treated for 1 month to reduce the possibility of recurrence. If a patient shows no clinical improvement after the treatment period, the diagnosis should be reviewed.

Information for the Patient: See Blue Section—Information for the Patient "Oxizole".

Supplied: Cream: Each g of white to off-white, opaque cream base contains: oxiconazole 10 mg as oxiconazole nitrate. Nonmedicinal ingredients: benzoic acid, cetyl alcohol, polysorbate 60, propylene glycol, purified water, stearyl alcohol and white petrolatum. Tubes of 30 g. Store between 15 and 30°C.

Lotion: Each g of white to off-white, opaque lotion base contains: oxiconazole 10 mg as oxiconazole nitrate. Nonmedicinal ingredients: benzoic acid, cetyl alcohol, polysorbate 60, propylene glycol, purified water, stearyl alcohol and white petrolatum. Bottles of 30 mL. Store between 15 and 30°C. Protect from light.

New Product 1998

OXSORALEN™
ICN

Methoxsalen
Melanin Repigmentation—Photochemotherapy of Atopic Dermatitis and Psoriasis

Indications: Repigmentation of vitiliginous lesions, to protect against solar sensitivity. Oral route is preferred if extensive repigmentation is desired, since topical application can only be applied to a small area at a time.

For treatment of psoriasis and atopic dermatitis in combination with high intensity UVA light.

Contraindications: Hepatic insufficiency. Diseases associated with photosensitivity, such as porphyria, acute lupus erythematosus or infectious leukoderma. Safety in those 12 years and under, in people with aphasia, in pregnant women or in women of childbearing age has not been established. In albinism it increases tolerance to sunlight, but has no effect on pigmentation. No preparation with any photosensitizing capacity, internal or external, should be used concomitantly with methoxsalen therapy.

Warnings: Methoxsalen is a potent drug and it is recommended that the entire brochure be read before prescribing or dispensing the information.

Pregnancy and *Lactation:* Safety during pregnancy or lactation has not been demonstrated. Use in these conditions should be undertaken only when in the judgment of the physician, the probable benefits outweigh the possible risks.

All patients should wear goggles and should close their eyes during treatment with UV light.

Precautions: Should be used only by healthy adults, and use solely to produce a cosmetic tan is unwise because of its potential toxicity and equivocal results. When used to increase tolerance to sunlight and accelerate suntan, it should not be given for periods exceeding 2 weeks. When used in patients with vitiligo, liver function tests should be performed monthly for first few months and occasionally thereafter. If impairment of liver function is suspected, give smaller doses or discontinue drug.

There have not been any clinical reports or tests to verify that more severe reactions may result from the concomitant ingestion of food containing furocoumarin while on methoxsalen therapy; but the physician should warn the patient that eating limes, figs, parsley, parsnips, mustard, carrots and celery, might be dangerous. Methoxsalen should be used with caution in patients with defective coagulation or in those patients being treated with anticoagulant drugs.

Adverse Effects: Occasionally, nervousness, insomnia or depression may occur.

Overdose: Symptoms and Treatment: The dosage of this medication must be carefully controlled. Overdosage and/or overexposure may result in serious burning and blistering. To prevent harmful effects, the physician should carefully instruct the patient to adhere to the prescribed dosage schedule and procedure. If an overdose has been taken, emesis should be encouraged. The treatment for severe reactions resulting from overdosage or overexposure should follow accepted procedures for treatment of severe burns.

Dosage: Capsules: Should be taken after meals or with milk. For solar sensitivity and tanning: 20 mg 2 hours before exposure to sunlight. The exposure time during the first 3 or 4 days should be limited to 30 minutes or less. Exposure time, but not dosage may be increased thereafter.

Vitiligo: Adults and children over 12 years: 20 mg 2 to 4 hours before exposure to a source of ultraviolet light. Children 6 to 12 years: 10 to 20 mg daily. Children up to 6 years: 10 mg daily.

For photochemotherapy treatment of psoriasis and atopic dermatitis see product brochure.

Lotion: Apply once weekly to a few depigmented areas and expose to ultraviolet light for a maximum period of 1 minute. When an artificial source of ultraviolet light is used, the initial exposure should be made with 50% of the minimal erythemic dose. Sites of application should be alternated. When oral and topical therapy is used, topically treated areas must be protected from daily exposure to ultraviolet light. Lotion is for use only in vitiligo, not tanning.

Supplied: Capsules: Each light pink capsule, printed ICN 600 contains: methoxsalen USP 10 mg. Bottles of 28 and 100.

Lotion: Each mL contains: methoxsalen USP 1%. Bottles of 30 mL.

OXSORALEN-ULTRA™
ICN

Methoxsalen
Melanin Repigmentation—Tolerance Increase to Solar Exposure—Photochemotherapy of Atopic Dermatitis and Psoriasis

Indications: Repigmentation of idiopathic vitiligo; increasing tolerance to sunlight. Treatment of psoriasis and atopic dermatitis in combination with high intensity UVA light (photochemotherapy).

Contraindications: Hepatic insufficiency and in those diseases associated with photosensitivity; such as porphyria, acute lupus erythematosus, hydroa and polymorphic light eruptions. In leukoderma of infectious origin and in albinism, it increases tolerance to sunlight but has no effect on pigmentation. No preparation with any photosensitizing capacity, internal or external, should be used concomitantly with methoxsalen therapy. To date, the safety in young persons under 12 years of age has not been established and is, therefore, contraindicated.

Warnings: Methoxsalen is a potent drug. Read entire brochure before prescribing or dispensing this medication. Herpes simplex infection may occur during treatment. There is evidence that psoralens enter the eye lens for up to 12 hours after dosing. Patients should be instructed to wear sunglasses (grey or green plastic lenses) on the days they are being treated and should close their eyes during treatment with ultraviolet light.

Pregnancy and *Lactation:* The safety of methoxsalen during pregnancy or lactation has not been demonstrated for the mother or the child. Therefore, methoxsalen should be used during pregnancy only when, in the judgment of the physician, the probable benefits outweigh the possible risks.

Caution: Oxsoralen-Ultra should not be used interchangeably with regular Oxsoralen. This new dosage form of methoxsalen exhibits significantly greater bioavailability and earlier photosensitization onset time than previous methoxsalen dosage forms. Patients should be treated in accordance with the dosimetry specifically recommended for this product. The minimum phototoxic dose (MPD) and phototoxic peak time after drug administration prior to onset of photochemotherapy with this dosage form should be determined.

Precautions: The physician should be familiar with the various characteristics of the drug and its established clinical use. Patients undergoing therapy should be subject to appropriate supervision so that signs or symptoms of possible toxic effects may be detected and evaluated with minimal delay.

There have not been any clinical reports or tests to verify that more severe reactions may result from the concomitant ingestion of furocoumarin-containing food while on methoxsalen therapy; but the physician should warn the patient that taking limes, figs, parsley, parsnips, mustard, carrots and celery, might be dangerous. Methoxsalen should be used with caution in patients with defective coagulation or in those patients being treated with anticoagulant drugs.

Adverse Effects: The most common side effects of methoxsalen in combination with photochemotherapy are excessive erythema, nausea and pruritus. Occasionally, there may occur nervousness, insomnia or depression.

Overdose: Symptoms and Treatment: The dosage of this medication must be carefully controlled. Overdosage and/or overexposure may result in serious burning and blistering. To prevent harmful effects, the physician should carefully instruct the patient to adhere to the prescribed dosage schedule and procedure. If an overdosage of methoxsalen has been taken, emesis should be encouraged. The treatment for severe reactions resulting from overdosage or overexposure should follow accepted procedures for treatment of severe burns.

Dosage: Adults and Children over 12 years of age: Methoxsalen should be taken after meals or with milk.
Vitiligo: 2 capsules daily, taken 1½ to 2 hours before measured period of ultraviolet exposure or fluorescent black light.
Tolerance Increase to Sunlight: 2 capsules daily taken 2 hours before measured periods of exposure to sun or ultraviolet irradiation. Not to be continued for longer than 14 days. The dosage should not be increased as severe burning may occur.
Photochemotherapy Treatment of Psoriasis and Atopic Dermatitis: The dosage of methoxsalen is based upon the patient's weight. The exposure of UVA is carried out in a specially designed system within 1½ to 2 hours after drug ingestion. The initial exposure is based upon the patient's skin type. Following the initial exposure and providing the patient does not develop an erythema greater than Grade 1, subsequent exposures of UVA should follow the recommendations outlined in the product brochure.

Supplied: Each soft green gelatin capsule, printed ICN on one side and 650 on the other contains: methoxsalen USP 10 mg. Nonmedicinal ingredients: polyethylene glycol. Bottles of 50 and 100.

OXTRIPHYLLINE Ⓟ
General Monograph, CPhA
see THEOPHYLLINE and its Salts

OXYBUTYN Ⓟ
ICN
Oxybutynin Chloride
Anticholinergic—Antispasmodic

Supplied: Each blue, round, biconvex tablet, scored on one side and imprinted with ICN 021 on the other side, contains: oxybutynin chloride USP 5 mg. Nonmedicinal ingredients: FD&C blue #1, lactose, magnesium stearate and microcrystalline cellulose. Bottles of 100 and 500.

OXYCOCET® Ⓝ
Technilab
Oxycodone HCl—Acetaminophen
Opioid Analgesic

Supplied: Each white, scored tablet contains: oxycodone HCl 5 mg and acetaminophen 325 mg. Nonmedicinal ingredients: colloidal silicon dioxide, crospovidone, magnesium stearate, microcrystalline cellulose, povidone, pregelatinized starch, sodium starch glycolate and stearic acid. Bottles of 100 and 500. Unit dose push-thru of 100. Store at controlled room temperature (15 to 30°C).

OXYCODAN® Ⓝ
Technilab
Oxycodone HCl—ASA
Opioid Analgesic

Supplied: Each yellow, scored tablet contains: oxycodone HCl 5 mg and ASA 325 mg. Nonmedicinal ingredients: colloidal silicon dioxide, FD&C Yellow #5 aluminum lake, lactose, microcrystalline cellulose, sodium starch glycolate and stearic acid. Bottles of 100 and 500. Store at controlled room temperature (15 to 30°C).

OXYCODONE Ⓝ
General Monograph, CPhA
see OPIOID ANALGESICS

OXYCONTIN® Ⓝ
Purdue Frederick
Oxycodone HCl
Opioid Analgesic

Pharmacology: Oxycodone is a semisynthetic opioid analgesic which exerts an agonist effect at specific, saturable opioid receptors in the CNS and other tissues. In man, oxycodone produces a variety of effects including analgesia, constipation from decreased gastrointestinal motility, suppression of the cough reflex, respiratory depression from reduced responsiveness of the respiratory centre to CO_2, nausea and vomiting via stimulation of the chemoreceptor trigger zone, changes in mood including euphoria and dysphoria, sedation, mental clouding, and alterations of the endocrine and autonomic nervous systems.

Oxycodone retains at least one-half of its analgesic activity when administered orally and with acute dosing is approximately twice as potent as orally administered morphine.

Studies with oxycodone controlled release in normal volunteers and patients demonstrate a consistent relationship between oxycodone dosage and plasma oxycodone concentrations as well as between concentration and pharmacodynamic effects. In a single dose analgesic assay, the peak effect of OxyContin (20 and 30 mg) was greater than that of 10 mg OxyContin and was equivalent to that of 2 tablets of oxycodone (5 mg) plus acetaminophen (325 mg), or 15 mg of immediate release oxycodone, but with a longer duration of action. In patients with cancer pain, OxyContin administered every 12 hours produced equivalent analgesia to immediate release oxycodone administered 4 times per day. In patients with pain due to osteoarthritis, OxyContin every 12 hours was more effective than placebo in decreasing pain and in improving quality of life, mood and sleep. In patients with low back pain, OxyContin every 12 hours was equally effective as immediate release oxycodone given 4 times per day. Titration to analgesic effect was achieved as easily with OxyContin as with immediate release oxycodone.

There is no intrinsic limit to the analgesic effect of oxycodone; like morphine, adequate doses will relieve even the most severe pain. Clinically however, dosage limitations are imposed by the adverse effects, primarily respiratory depression, nausea and vomiting, which can result from high doses.

Pharmacokinetics: After oral administration of oxycodone tablets, the drug is absorbed from the gastrointestinal tract and has a relatively high bioavailability of approximately 60 to 87%. Unlike morphine, oxycodone does not undergo high first pass metabolism, possibly due to the protective effect of a methoxy group in the 3- position which is a site of morphine glucuronidation. Oxycodone is metabolized in the liver by demethylation to noroxycodone and oxymorphone (via CYP2D6), and by conjugation, to a variety of glucuronide metabolites. Oxymorphone is known to possess analgesic activity, but concentrations in the plasma are very low and not as closely correlated to opioid effects as oxycodone concentrations. Although the AUC ratio of noroxycodone to oxycodone is about 0.6 following oral dosing, noroxycodone is reported to be a considerably weaker analgesic than oxycodone and is unlikely to contribute significantly to the analgesic effect of oxycodone. The analgesic activity profile of other metabolites is not known. The terminal elimination half-life after immediate release tablets is approximately 4 hours. The majority of metabolites and unchanged drug (conjugated 2.2%, unconjugated 5.5%) are excreted in the urine.

Pharmacokinetic studies of OxyContin in normal volunteers demonstrate that both AUC and C_{max} increase in a dose proportional manner and that the 4 tablet strengths are bioequivalent. In single dose studies, OxyContin was absorbed to an equivalent extent as immediate release oxycodone but with a reduced maximum concentration (C_{max} ratio approximately 50%) and prolonged (2.4×) time to maximum concentration (t_{max} approximately 2.8 hours).

In steady-state pharmacokinetic studies of OxyContin every 12 hours, maximum plasma concentrations (C_{max}) of oxycodone were equivalent to those obtained with every 6 hours administration of oral immediate release preparations and were achieved approximately 3 hours after administration of OxyContin. Steady-state was achieved within 24 hours of initiation of dosing. The absorption of oxycodone from OxyContin tablets is not significantly influenced when administered in the presence of food.

Plasma concentrations of oxycodone are increased by approximately 15% in elderly subjects receiving OxyContin; by 50 to 60% in patients with moderate degrees of renal impairment; and by approximately 2-fold in patients with hepatic cirrhosis.

Indications: For relief of moderate to severe pain, requiring the prolonged use of an opioid analgesic preparation.

Contraindications: Patients with hypersensitivity to opioid analgesics; acute asthma or other obstructive airway disease and acute respiratory depression; cor pulmonale; acute alcoholism; delirium tremens; severe CNS depression; convulsive disorders; increased cerebrospinal or intracranial pressure; head injury; suspected surgical abdomen; concomitant MAO inhibitors (or within 14 days of such therapy).

Warnings: Drug Dependence: As with other opioids, tolerance and physical dependence may develop upon repeated administration of oxycodone and there is a potential for development of psychological dependence. Oxycodone controlled release should therefore be prescribed and handled with the degree of caution appropriate to the use of a drug with abuse potential. Drug abuse is not a problem in patients with pain in whom oxycodone is appropriately indicated. Withdrawal symptoms may occur following abrupt discontinuation of therapy or upon administration of an opioid antagonist. Therefore, patients on prolonged therapy should be withdrawn gradually from the drug if it is no longer required for pain control.
CNS Depression: Oxycodone should be used with caution and in reduced dosage during concomitant administration of other opioid analgesics, general anesthetics, phenothiazines and other tranquilizers, sedative-hypnotics, tricyclic antidepressants and other CNS depressants, including alcohol. Respiratory depression, hypotension and profound sedation or coma may result.

Severe pain antagonizes the subjective and respiratory depressant actions of opioid analgesics. Should pain suddenly subside, these effects may rapidly become manifest. Patients who are scheduled for cordotomy or other interruption of pain transmission pathways should not receive oxycodone controlled release within 24 hours of the procedure.

Pregnancy: While animal reproduction studies have revealed no evidence of harm to the fetus due to oxycodone, safe use in pregnancy has not been established. Oxycodone controlled release should be given to pregnant patients only when the anticipated benefits outweigh the potential risks to the fetus.

Precautions: General: The respiratory depressant effects of oxycodone, and the capacity to elevate cerebrospinal fluid pressure, may be greatly increased in the presence of an already elevated intracranial pressure produced by trauma. Also, oxycodone may produce confusion, miosis, vomiting and other side effects which obscure the clinical course of patients with head injury. In such patients, oxycodone must be used with extreme caution and only if it is judged essential.

Oxycodone should be used with extreme caution in patients with substantially decreased respiratory reserve, pre-existing respiratory depression, hypoxia or hypercapnia. Such patients are often less sensitive to the stimulatory effects of carbon monoxide on the respiratory centre, and the respiratory depressant effects of oxycodone may reduce respiratory drive to the point of apnea.

Oxycodone administration may result in severe hypotension in patients whose ability to maintain adequate blood pressure is compromised by reduced blood volume, or concurrent administration of such drugs as phenothiazines or certain anesthetics.

Oxycodone may obscure the diagnosis or clinical course of patients with acute abdominal conditions.
Special Risk Groups: Oxycodone should be administered with caution, and in reduced dosages, to debilitated patients, to patients with severely reduced hepatic or renal function, and in patients with Addison's disease, hypothyroidism, prostatic hypertrophy or urethral stricture.
Labor/Delivery and *Lactation:* In view of the potential for opioids to cross the placental barrier and to be excreted in breast milk, oxycodone should be used with caution in nursing mothers. Physical dependence or respiratory depression may occur in the infant if opioids are administered during labor.
Occupational Hazards: Driving and Operating Dangerous Machinery: Oxycodone may impair the mental and/or physical abilities needed for certain potentially hazardous activities such as driving a car or operating machinery. Patients should be cautioned accordingly.

Patients should also be cautioned about the combined effects of oxycodone with other CNS depressants, including other opioids, phenothiazines, sedative/hypnotics and alcohol.
Drug Interactions: CNS depressants, such as other opioids, anesthetics, sedatives, hypnotics, barbiturates, phenothiazines, chloral hydrate and glutethimide may enhance the depressant effects of oxycodone. MAO inhibitors (including procarbazine HCl), pyrazolidone antihistamines, beta-blockers

OxyContin (cont'd)

and alcohol may also enhance the depressant effect of oxycodone.

Adverse Effects: Adverse effects of oxycodone controlled release are similar to those of other opioid analgesics, and represent an extension of pharmacological effects of the drug class. The major hazards of opioids include respiratory and CNS depression and to a lesser degree, circulatory depression, respiratory arrest, shock and cardiac arrest.

The most frequently observed adverse effects are constipation, nausea, somnolence, dizziness, vomiting, pruritus, headache, dry mouth, asthenia and sweating.

Sedation: Sedation is a common side effect of opioid analgesics, especially in opioid naive individuals. Sedation may also occur partly because patients often recuperate from prolonged fatigue after the relief of persistent pain. Most patients develop tolerance to the sedative effects of opioids within 3 to 5 days and, if the sedation is not severe, will not require any treatment except reassurance. If excessive sedation persists beyond a few days, the dose of the opioid should be reduced and alternate causes investigated. Some of these are: concurrent CNS depressant medication, hepatic or renal dysfunction, brain metastases, hypercalcemia and respiratory failure. If it is necessary to reduce the dose, it can be carefully increased again after 3 or 4 days if it is obvious that the pain is not being well controlled. Dizziness and unsteadiness may be caused by postural hypotension, particularly in elderly or debilitated patients, and may be alleviated if the patient lies down.

Nausea and Vomiting: Nausea is a common side effect on initiation of therapy with opioid analgesics and is thought to occur by activation of the chemoreceptor trigger zone, stimulation of the vestibular apparatus and through delayed gastric emptying. The prevalence of nausea declines following continued treatment with opioid analgesics. When instituting therapy with an opioid for chronic pain, the routine prescription of an antiemetic should be considered. In the cancer patient, investigation of nausea should include such causes as constipation, bowel obstruction, uremia, hypercalcemia, hepatomegaly, tumor invasion of celiac plexus and concurrent use of drugs with emetogenic properties. Persistent nausea which does not respond to dosage reduction may be caused by opioid-induced gastric stasis and may be accompanied by other symptoms including anorexia, early satiety, vomiting and abdominal fullness. These symptoms respond to chronic treatment with gastrointestinal prokinetic agents.

Constipation: Practically all patients become constipated while taking opioids on a persistent basis. In some patients, particularly the elderly or bedridden, fecal impaction may result. It is essential to caution the patients in this regard and to institute an appropriate regimen of bowel management at the start of prolonged opioid therapy. Stimulant laxatives, stool softeners, and other appropriate measures should be used as required.

The following adverse effects occur less frequently with opioid analgesics and include those reported in OxyContin clinical trials, whether related or not to oxycodone.

General and CNS: dysphoria, euphoria, anxiety, depression, depersonalization, nervousness, agitation, hyperkinesia, hypotonia, twitching, tremor, speech disorder, vision abnormalities, hypesthesia, paresthesia, thought abnormalities, abnormal dreams, hallucinations, confusion, abnormal gait, insomnia, vertigo and tinnitus.

Cardiovascular: tachycardia, palpitation, faintness, syncope, vasodilation, postural hypotension, chest pain, ST depression and migraine.

Respiratory: bronchospasm, pharyngitis and dyspnea.

Gastrointestinal: dysphagia, anorexia, taste alterations, abdominal pain, diarrhea, dyspepsia, eructation, flatulence, hiccups, gastritis, increased appetite and stomatitis.

Genitourinary: urinary retention or hesitancy, dysuria, polyuria, hematuria, antidiuretic effects and impotence.

Dermatologic: urticaria, exfoliative dermatitis, other skin rashes and edema.

Other: lymphadenopathy, malaise, chills, fever, dehydration and thirst.

Withdrawal (Abstinence) Syndrome: Physical dependence with or without psychological dependence tends to occur on chronic administration. An abstinence syndrome may be precipitated when opioid administration is discontinued or opioid antagonists administered. The following withdrawal symptoms may be observed after opioids are discontinued: body aches, diarrhea, gooseflesh, loss of appetite, nervousness or restlessness, runny nose, sneezing, tremors or shivering, stomach cramps, nausea, trouble with sleeping, unusual increase in sweating and yawning, weakness, tachycardia and unexplained fever. In patients who are appropriately treated with opioid analgesics and who undergo gradual withdrawal from the drug, these symptoms are usually mild.

Overdose: Symptoms: Serious overdosage with oxycodone may be characterized by respiratory depression (a decrease in respiratory rate and/or tidal volume, Cheyne-Stokes respiration, cyanosis), extreme somnolence progressing to stupor or coma, skeletal muscle flaccidity, cold and clammy skin, and sometimes bradycardia and hypotension. Severe overdosage may result in apnea, circulatory collapse, cardiac arrest and death.

Treatment: Primary attention should be given to the establishment of adequate respiratory exchange through the provision of a patent airway and controlled or assisted ventilation. The opioid antagonist naloxone HCl is a specific antidote against respiratory depression due to overdosage or as a result of unusual sensitivity to oxycodone. An appropriate dose of an opioid antagonist should therefore be administered, preferably by the i.v. route. The usual initial i.v. adult dose of naloxone is 0.4 mg or higher. Concomitant efforts at respiratory resuscitation should be carried out. Since the duration of action of oxycodone, particularly sustained release formulations, may exceed that of the antagonist, the patient should be under continued surveillance and doses of the antagonist should be repeated as needed to maintain adequate respiration.

An antagonist should not be administered in the absence of clinically significant respiratory or cardiovascular depression. Oxygen, i.v. fluids, vasopressors and other supportive measures should be used as indicated.

In individuals physically dependent on opioids, the administration of the usual dose of opioid antagonist will precipitate an acute withdrawal syndrome. The severity of this syndrome will depend on the degree of physical dependence and the dose of antagonist administered. The use of opioid antagonists in such individuals should be avoided if possible. If an opioid antagonist must be used to treat serious respiratory depression in the physically dependent patient, the antagonist should be administered with extreme care by using dosage titration, commencing with 10 to 20% of the usual recommended initial dose.

Evacuation of gastric contents may be useful in removing unabsorbed drug, particularly when a sustained release formulation has been taken.

Dosage: Adults: Individual dosing requirements vary considerably based on each patient's age, weight, severity and cause of pain, and medical and analgesic history.

Patients currently receiving other oral oxycodone formulations may be transferred to OxyContin at the same total daily oxycodone dosage, equally divided into two 12 hourly OxyContin doses.

For patients who are receiving an alternate opioid, the "oral oxycodone equivalent" of the analgesic presently being used should be determined. Having determined the total daily dosage of the present analgesic, Table I can be used to calculate the approximate daily oral oxycodone dosage that should provide equivalent analgesia. This total daily oral oxycodone dose should then be equally divided into two 12 hourly OxyContin doses. It is usually appropriate to treat a patient with only one opioid at a time. Patients who are receiving 1 to 5 tablets or capsules/day of a fixed-dose combination opioid/nonopioid containing 5 mg of oxycodone or 30 mg codeine should be started on 10 to 20 mg OxyContin every 12 hours. For patients receiving 6 to 9 tablets or capsules/day of a fixed-dose combination opioid/nonopioid containing 5 mg of oxycodone or 30 mg codeine, a starting dose of 20 to 30 mg every 12 hours should be used and for patients receiving 10 to 12 tablets or capsules/day of a fixed-dose combination opioid/nonopioid containing 5 mg of oxycodone or 30 mg codeine, a starting dose of 30 to 40 mg every 12 hours is suggested. For those receiving >12 tablets or capsules/day of a fixed-dose combination opioid/nonopioid containing 5 mg of oxycodone or 30 mg codeine, conversions should be based on the total daily opioid dose. Patients who have not previously received opioid analgesics should be initiated on OxyContin 10 mg every 12 hours.

If a nonopioid analgesic is being provided, it may be continued. If the nonopioid is discontinued, consideration should be given to increasing the opioid dose to compensate for the nonopioid analgesic. Oxycodone controlled release can be safely used concomitantly with usual doses of other nonopioid analgesics.

OxyContin tablets should not be broken, chewed or crushed.

Dose Titration: Dose titration is the key to success with opioid analgesic therapy. **Proper optimization of doses scaled to the relief of the individual's pain should aim at the regular administration of the lowest dose which will maintain the patient free of pain at all times. Dosage adjustments should be based on the patient's clinical response.** In patients receiving oxycodone controlled release chronically, the dose may be titrated at intervals of 24 hours to that which provides satisfactory pain relief without unmanageable side effects. Oxycodone controlled release is designed to allow 12 hourly dosing. **If breakthrough pain repeatedly occurs at the end of the dosing interval it is generally an indication for a dosage increase rather than more frequent administration.**

Adjustment or Reduction of Dosage: Following successful relief of pain, periodic attempts to re-assess the opioid analgesic requirements should be made. If treatment discontinuation is required, the dose of opioid may be decreased as follows: one-half of the previous daily dose given every 12 hours for the first 2 days, followed thereafter by a 25% reduction every 2 days.

Opioid analgesics may only be partially effective in relieving dysesthetic pain, postherpetic neuralgia, stabbing pains, activity-related pain and some forms of headache. That is not to say that patients with these types of pain should not be given an adequate trial of opioid analgesics, but it may be necessary to refer such patients at an early time to other forms of pain therapy.

Table I—OxyContin

Opioid Analgesics: Approximate Analgesic Equivalences[a]

Drug	**Equivalent Dose (mg)[b] (compared to morphine 10 mg i.m.)**		**Duration of Action (hours)**
	Parenteral	**Oral**	
Strong Opioid Agonists			
Morphine	10	60[c]	3-4
Oxycodone[d]	15	30	2-4
Hydromorphone	1.5	7.5	2-4
Anileridine	25	75	2-3
Levorphanol	2	4	4-8
Meperidine[e]	75	300	1-3
Oxymorphone	1.5	5 (rectal)	3-4
Methadone[f]	—	—	—
Heroin	5-8	10-15	3-4
Weak Opioid Agonists			
Codeine	120	200	3-4
Propoxyphene	50	100	2-4
Mixed Agonist-Antagonists[g]			
Pentazocine[e]	60	180	3-4
Nalbuphine	10	—	3-6
Butorphanol	2	—	3-4

[a] References:

Cancer Pain: A Monograph on the Management of Cancer Pain, Health and Welfare Canada 1984.

Foley, K.M., New Engl. J. Med. 313: 84-95, 1985.

Aronoff, G.M. and Evans, W.O., In Evaluation and Treatment of Chronic Pain, 2nd Ed., G.M. Aronoff (Ed.), Williams and Wilkins, Baltimore, pp. 359-368, 1992.

Cherny, N.I. and Portenoy, R.K., In: Textbook of Pain, 3rd Ed., P.D. Wall and R. Melzack (Eds.), Churchill Livingstone, London, pp. 1437-1467, 1994.

[b] **Most of the data were derived from single-dose, acute pain studies and should be considered an approximation for selection of doses when treating chronic pain.**

[c] **For acute pain, the oral or rectal dose of morphine is 6 times the injectable dose. However, for chronic dosing, clinical experience indicates that this ratio is 2 to 3: 1 (i.e., 20 to 30 mg of oral or rectal morphine is equivalent to 10 mg of parenteral morphine).**

[d] Based on single entity oral oxycodone in acute pain.

[e] Not recommended for the management of chronic pain.

[f] Extremely variable equianalgesic dose. Patients should undergo individualized titration starting at an equivalent to 1/10 of the morphine dose.

[g] Mixed agonist-antagonists can precipitate withdrawal in patients on pure opioid agonists.

Information for the Patient: See Blue Section—Information for the Patient "OxyContin".

Supplied: 10 mg: Each round, unscored, white, biconvex, controlled release tablet, imprinted with OC on one side and the mg strength on the other, contains: oxycodone HCl 10 mg. Nonmedicinal ingredients: hydroxypropyl cellulose, hydroxypropyl methylcellulose, lactose, magnesium stearate, polyethylene glycol, polymethyl acrylate, povidone, stearyl alcohol, talc, triacetin and titanium dioxide. Polyethylene bottles of 50.

20 mg: Each round, unscored, pink, biconvex, controlled release tablet, imprinted with OC on one side and the mg strength on the other, contains: oxycodone HCl 20 mg. Nonmedicinal ingredients: hydroxypropyl methylcellulose, lactose, magnesium stearate, iron oxide, polyethylene glycol, polymethyl acrylate, polysorbate 80, povidone, stearyl alcohol, talc, triacetin and titanium dioxide. Polyethylene bottles of 50.

40 mg: Each round, unscored, yellow, biconvex, controlled release tablet, imprinted with OC on one side and the mg strength on the other, contains: oxycodone HCl 40 mg. Nonmedicinal ingredients: hydroxypropyl methylcellulose, iron oxide, lactose, magnesium stearate, polyethylene glycol, polymethyl acrylate, polysorbate 80, povidone, stearyl alcohol, talc, triacetin and titanium dioxide. Polyethylene bottles of 50.

80 mg: Each round, unscored, green, biconvex, controlled release tablet, imprinted with OC on one side and the mg strength on the other, contains: oxycodone HCl 80 mg. Polyethylene bottles of 50. Nonmedicinal ingredients: FD&C Blue No. 2 aluminum lake, hydroxypropyl methylcellulose, hydroxypropyl cellulose, iron oxide, lactose, magnesium stearate, polyethylene glycol, polymethyl acrylate, povidone, stearyl alcohol, talc, triacetin and titanium dioxide.

Store at 15 to 30°C.

(Shown in Product Recognition Section)

Reviewed 1997

OXYDERM™ 5% OXYDERM™ 10% and 20% Ⓟ

ICN

Benzoyl Peroxide

Keratolytic Agent

Supplied: 5%: Each mL of lotion contains: benzoyl peroxide 5%. Nonmedicinal ingredients: glyceryl monostearate, isopropyl palmitate, methylcellulose, methylparaben, PEG-6-32 stearate, phenoxyethanol, polyethylene glycol, propylparaben, sodium lauryl sulfate, stearic acid and trolamine. Plastic squeeze bottles of 60 mL.

10%: Each mL of lotion contains: benzoyl peroxide 10%. Nonmedicinal ingredients: glyceryl monostearate, isopropyl palmitate, methylcellulose, methylparaben, PEG-6-32 stearate, phenoxyethanol, polyethylene glycol, propylparaben, sodium lauryl sulfate, stearic acid and trolamine. Plastic squeeze bottles of 60 mL.

20%: Each mL of lotion contains: benzoyl peroxide 20%. Nonmedicinal ingredients: glyceryl monostearate, isopropyl palmitate, methylcellulose, methylparaben, PEG-6-32 stearate, phenoxyethanol, polyethylene glycol, propylparaben, sodium lauryl sulfate, stearic acid and trolamine. Plastic squeeze bottles of 60 and 120 mL.

Store in a cool place. Do not freeze.

OXYMORPHONE Ⓝ

General Monograph, CPhA

see OPIOID ANALGESICS

OXYTOCIN INJECTION, USP Ⓟ

Abbott

Oxytocic

Pharmacology: Oxytocin synthetic, acts on the smooth muscle of the uterus to stimulate contractions; response depends on the uterine threshold of excitability. It exerts a selective action on the smooth musculature of the uterus, particularly toward the end of pregnancy, during labor and immediately following delivery. Oxytocin stimulates rhythmic contractions of the uterus, increases the frequency of existing contractions and raises the tone of the uterine musculature. Synthetic oxytocin elicits only slight pressor and antidiuretic activity due to the absence of vasopressin. (Hypertension has been observed resulting from concomitant use of oxytocics and continuous caudal block anesthesia).

Indications: Important Notice: Oxytocin is **not** indicated for the **elective** induction of labor. Elective induction of labor is defined as the initiation of labor for convenience in an individual with a term pregnancy, who is free of medical indications for the initiation of labor.

Oxytocin is indicated in the following: Antepartum: For induction of labor in patients with a medical indication for the initiation of labor, such as Rh problems, maternal diabetes, mild pre-eclampsia at or near term, when delivery is in the best interest of mother and fetus, or when membranes are prematurely ruptured and delivery indicated. For stimulation or reinforcement of labor as in selected cases of uterine inertia. As adjunctive therapy in the management of incomplete or inevitable abortion.

Postpartum: To produce uterine contractions during the third stage of labor and to control postpartum bleeding and hemorrhage.

Contraindications: Significant cephalopelvic disproportion. Severe toxemia. Malpresentation or malposition of the fetus or placenta previa. Prematurity or unripe cervix. Predisposition to uterine rupture (grand multiparity, overdistention of the uterus, previous cesarean section or other surgery involving the uterus). Hypertonic labor patterns. Prolonged use in uterine inertia. Factors predisposing to thromboplastin or amniotic fluid embolism (prolonged retention of dead fetus, abruptio placentae). Serious medical and obstetric conditions and any conditions in which fetal distress already occurs. Inability of physician to be in attendance. Hypersensitivity to oxytocin.

Warnings: Oxytocin, when given for induction or stimulation of labor, must be administered only by the i.v. route and with adequate medical supervision in a hospital (see Precautions).

Precautions: The following should be borne in mind when using oxytocin injection: 1. Use only under close medical/obstetrical supervision. 2. Never administer i.v. undiluted oxytocin, or use in high concentrations. 3. Oxytocin must not be used by more than one route simultaneously, e.g., parenteral and buccal, or parenteral and nasal.

When given for **induction** and **stimulation of labor,** Oxytocin Injection, USP must only be used as **i.v. drip infusion,** and not by i.m., nor by direct i.v. injection.

Careful monitoring (blood pressure, fetal heart rate, possible tocometry) is vital, in order to adjust dosage according to the individual response: if uterine activity interferes at any time with fetal heart rate, the infusion should be discontinued.

In patients with cardiovascular disorders, the infusion volume should be kept low by using a more concentrated solution.

All patients receiving i.v. oxytocin must be under continuous observation by trained personnel with a thorough knowledge of the drug and qualified to identify complications. A physician qualified to manage any complications should be immediately available.

When properly administered, oxytocin should stimulate uterine contractions similar to those seen in normal labor. Overstimulation of the uterus by improper administration can be hazardous to both mother and fetus. Even with proper administration and adequate supervision, hypertonic contractions can occur in patients whose uteri are hypersensitive to oxytocin.

Drug Interactions: Oxytocin should be used with special caution in conjunction with cyclopropane anesthesia since the risk of arrhythmias may be increased. In instances where a vasoconstrictor drug is administered prophylactically in conjunction with continuous caudal block anesthesia, severe hypertension may occur when oxytocin is given within 3 to 6 hours of administration of the vasoconstrictor drug. Sudden, marked elevation of blood pressure occurring under these circumstances has been reported to respond to i.v. administration of chlorpromazine.

Prostaglandin E_2 acts synergistically with oxytocin and the simultaneous parenteral administration of this product usually results in a substantial reduction in the quantity of oxytocin required. When oral prostaglandin E_2 has been employed, the infusion of oxytocin should not be started until at least 1 hour has elapsed following the last dose of prostaglandin E_2. A suitable time period should elapse, usually the following day, before prostaglandin E_2 is to be administered to patients who have previously received oxytocin.

Carcinogenesis, Mutagenesis, Impairment of Fertility: There are no animal or human studies on the carcinogenicity and mutagenicity of this drug, nor is there any information on its effect on fertility.

Pregnancy: Animal reproduction studies have not been conducted with oxytocin. Based on the wide experience with this drug and its chemical structure and pharmacological properties, it would not be expected to present risk of fetal abnormalities when used as indicated.

Adverse Effects: Water intoxication with headaches and nausea has been reported after prolonged or too rapid i.v. infusion of oxytocin (see Overdose: Symptoms and Treatment). Premature ventricular contractions, fetal bradycardia and cardiac arrhythmia have been noted. Hypotension, tachycardia and ECG changes have been observed following i.v. administration of concentrated solutions. Anxiety, dyspnea, precordial pain, edema, cyanosis or reddening of the skin and cardiovascular spasm and collapse have occurred on rare occasions. In very few cases, anaphylactoic reactions (dyspnea, hypotension shock) occurred. Overdosage may give rise to the following complications: slowing of fetal heart, meconium staining of the amniotic fluid and asphyxia; hypertonic contractions, uterine rupture, retention of the placenta, postpartum uterine inertia.

Overdose: I.V. infusion of oxytocin in nonpregnant subjects given at a rate greater than 45 milliunits/minute (4.5 mL/min=90 drops/min using 10 IU/L dilution) has been shown to have an antidiuretic effect comparable to that of vasopressin but of shorter duration.

There are also a number of cases reported in the literature where high i.v. doses of oxytocin administered along with a large volume of electrolyte-free fluid have resulted in the development of water intoxication.

However, high doses of oxytocin can be given without danger of water intoxication provided that the daily fluid intake is limited at this time. Acute overdosage with oxytocin, therefore, is unlikely in any circumstances and adverse effects are to be expected only if the concomitant fluid intake is excessive.

Symptoms: Symptoms of Water Intoxication: Headache, anorexia, nausea, vomiting, abdominal pain, lethargy, drowsiness, unconsciousness, and grand mal type seizures have been reported.

Owing to the excessive retention of water, the serum electrolyte concentration is low.

Treatment: Discontinue oxytocin and restrict all fluid intake. Encourage diuresis by administration of a diuretic such as furosemide. The use of i.v. hypertonic sodium chloride solution should be reserved for severe water intoxication with frank CNS disturbance. Careful supervision and, where necessary, correction of electrolyte imbalance should be undertaken, particularly in the diuretic phase. At the end of the diuretic phase, the hypertonic infusion, if used, should be stopped to avoid water retention due to excessive sodium.

Control convulsions with judicious use of diazepam or barbiturates. Good nursing care is of prime importance, particularly in the comatose patient; it should include regular observation and accurate recording of the vital signs and depth of coma, maintenance of a free airway, frequent turning and other routine measures usually adopted with unconscious patients.

Prophylactic antibiotic therapy in the comatose patient is a matter of individual physician preference.

Dosage: Induction of Labor: I.V. infusion (drip method) is the only acceptable method of administration for the induction or stimulation of labor. Accurate control of the rate of infusion flow is essential. An infusion pump or other such device and frequent monitoring of strength of contractions and fetal heart rate are necessary for the safe administration of oxytocin for the induction or stimulation of labor. If uterine contractions become too powerful, the infusion can be abruptly stopped, and oxytocic stimulation of the uterine musculature will soon wane.

Note: Oxytocin is stable in 0.9% sodium chloride or 5% Dextrose solution for 24 hours. It is unstable in any solution containing preservatives such as bisulfites and metabisulfites. 10 IU of oxytocin are dissolved in 1 L of 5% dextrose solution (=10 milliunits/mL). To ensure the homogeneity of the drip solution, the bottle or bag must be turned upside down at least once before use.

The **initial** dose should be no more than 1 to 4 mU/min=0.1 to 0.4 mL/min=2 to 8 drops/min. The dose may be increased in increments of no more than 1 to 2 mU/min=0.1 to 0.2 mL/min=2 to 4 drops/min., until a contraction pattern has been established, which is similar to normal labor, to a maximum of 20 mU/min=2 mL/min=40 drops/min, provided fetal heart rate, resting uterine tone and the frequency, duration and force of contractions are carefully monitored.

The oxytocin infusion should be discontinued immediately in the event of uterine hyperactivity or fetal distress.

If regular contractions are not established after the infusion of 500 mL (=5 IU oxytocin), the attempt to induce labor

Oxytocin Injection, USP (cont'd)

should be broken off; it can generally be repeated on the following day.

Once labor is initiated, the infusion rate is adjusted (usually reduced) according to need. I.V. infusion should be administered only when strictly medically indicated, rather than for convenience.

Stimulation of Labor: I.V. infusion (as above). Cases must be strictly selected and doses rigidly controlled.

Postpartum Hemorrhage, Postpartum Atony: a) I.V. infusion (see above); b) Administer 5 to 10 IU by **slow** i.v. injection; c) Administer 5 to 10 IU by i.m. injection.

Supplied: Each mL of sterile nonpyrogenic solution prepared by synthesis contains: oxytocin activity 10 IU (10 USP Posterior Pituitary Units), sodium acetate 2 mg, sodium chloride 5.1 mg and chlorobutanol 5 mg (as preservative) in water for injection. pH adjusted with acetic acid to approximately 3.9. Single-dose ampuls of 0.5, 1 and 5 mL. Sleeves of 5 or 10. Use only if solution is clear. Discard unused portion. Store at room temperature (15 to 30°C). Protect from freezing.

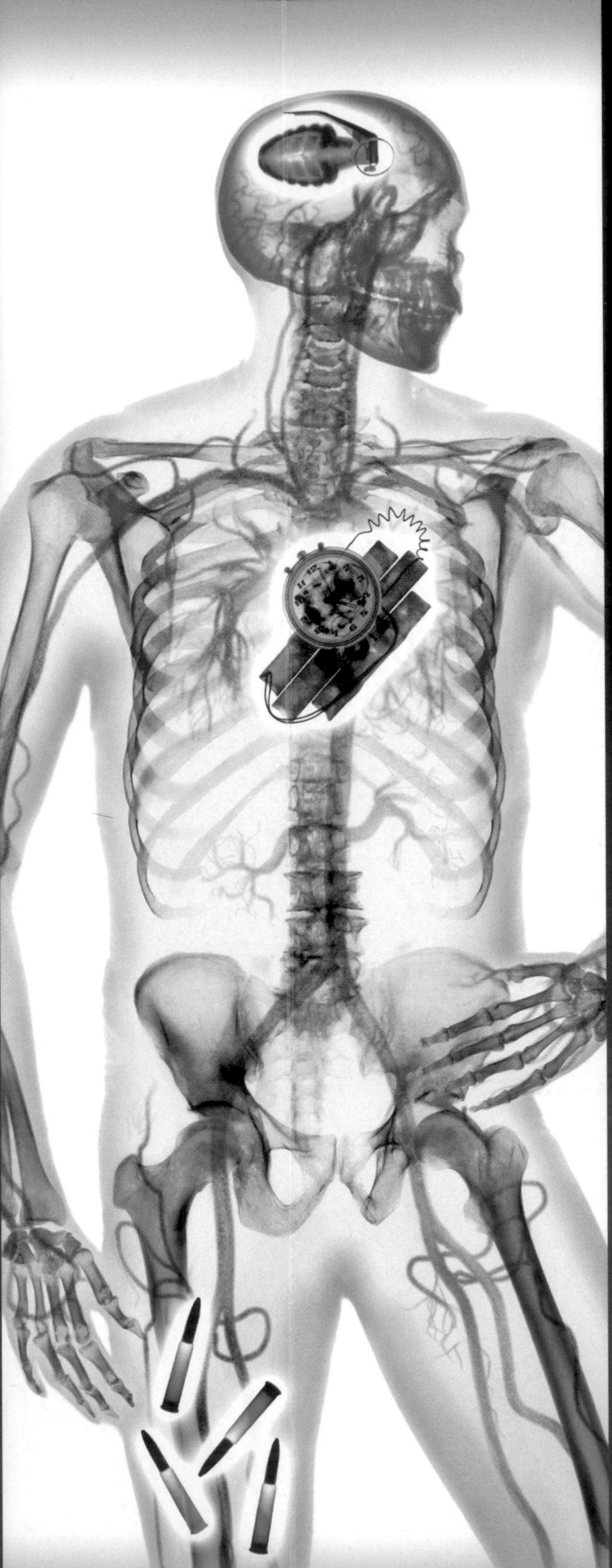

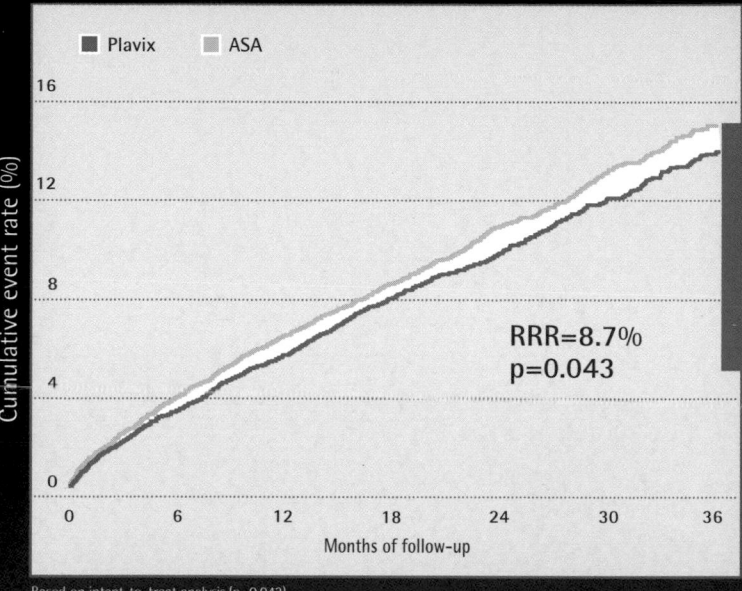

References: 1. CAPRIE Steering Committee. A randomised, blinded trial of clopidogrel versus aspirin in patients at risk of ischaemic events (CAPRIE). *The Lancet* 1996; 348(9038): 1329-1339. 2. Plavix Product Monograph 1998. 3. Antiplatelet Trialists' Collaboration. Collaborative overview of randomised trials of antiplatelet therapy - I: prevention of death, myocardial infarction and stroke by prolonged antiplatelet therapy in various categories of patients. *BMJ* 1994;308: 81-106

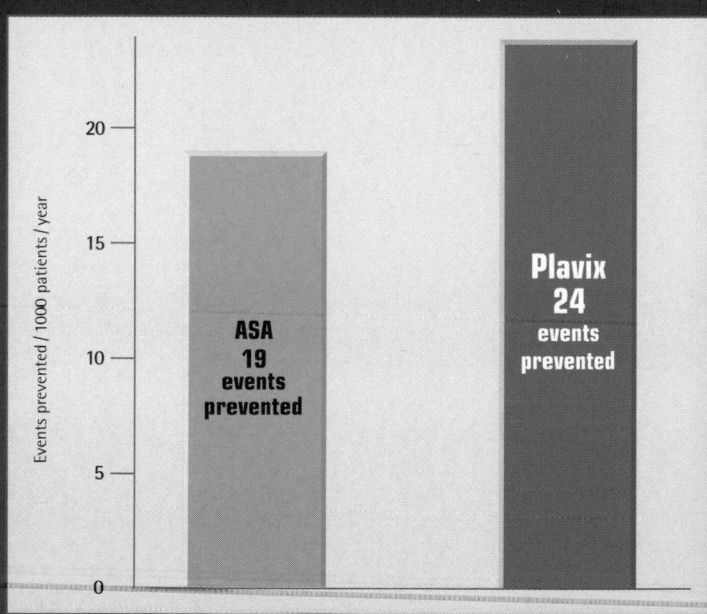

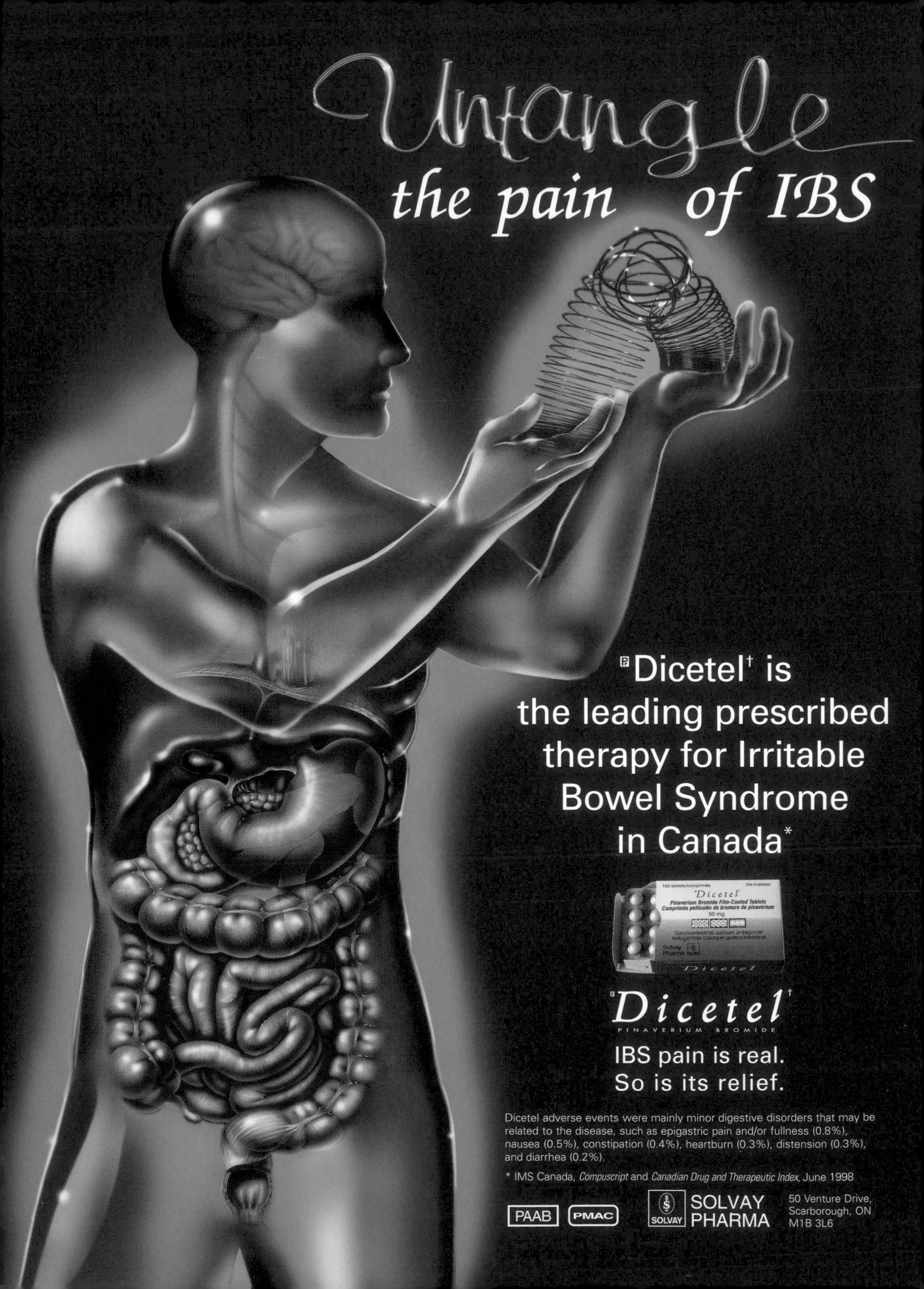

Untangle
the pain of IBS
Dicetel† is the leading prescribed therapy for Irritable Bowel Syndrome in Canada*
Dicetel
Pinaverium Bromide Film-Coated Tablets
Comprimés pelliculés de bromure de pinavérium
50 mg
Dicetel†
PINAVERIUM BROMIDE
IBS pain is real.
So is its relief.
Dicetel adverse events were mainly minor digestive disorders that may be related to the disease, such as epigastric pain and/or fullness (0.8%), nausea (0.5%), constipation (0.4%), heartburn (0.3%), distension (0.3%), and diarrhea (0.2%).
* IMS Canada, *Compuscript* and *Canadian Drug and Therapeutic Index*, June 1998
PAAB
PMAC
SOLVAY PHARMA
50 Venture Drive, Scarborough, ON M1B 3L6

P

PACIS™
Faulding

Bacillus Calmette-Guérin (BCG), substrain Montréal

Antineoplastic

Pharmacology: PACIS (Bacillus Calmette-Guérin (BCG), substrain Montréal) promotes a local inflammatory reaction with histiocytic and leukocytic infiltration in the urinary bladder. The local inflammatory effects are associated with an apparent elimination or reduction of superficial cancerous lesions of the urinary bladder. The exact mechanism by which this is accomplished is unknown.

Indications: For intravesical use in the treatment of initial and recurrent episodes of carcinoma in-situ (CIS), and CIS associated with papillary tumors of the urinary bladder. Also indicated for the treatment of papillary tumors of the urinary bladder following surgical resection and for CIS and/or papillary tumors which have failed to respond to other treatment regimens.

Contraindications: Patients on immunosuppressive therapy or with compromised immune systems should not receive PACIS because of the risk of overwhelming systemic mycobacterial sepsis.

Drug combinations containing bone marrow depressants or immunosuppressants, or radiation, may impair the response to PACIS and may increase the risk of osteomyelitis or disseminated BCG infection.

PACIS should not be administered to patients with fever unless the cause of the fever is determined and evaluated. If the fever is due to an infection, PACIS should be withheld until it subsides.

Patients with urinary tract infection should not receive PACIS treatment because of the risk of disseminated BCG infection or of an increase in the severity of bladder irritation.

Warnings: Administration of intravesical PACIS causes an inflammatory response in the bladder and has been associated with hematuria, urinary frequency, dysuria and bacterial urinary tract infection. Careful monitoring of urinary status is required. Although local irritative symptoms and flu-like symptoms are the most common, other systemic adverse reactions, while rare, have been seen in patients receiving BCG immunotherapy. These have included nausea, diarrhea, anemia and leukopenia, prostatitis and ureteral obstruction, and systemic BCG infection with death. Death has occurred following intravesical administration of BCG. If systemic BCG infection is suspected, the patient should be immediately treated with fast-acting antituberculosis antibiotic therapy following consultations with an infectious disease specialist (see Precautions). PACIS therapy should be withheld upon any suspicion of systemic infection, e.g., granulomatous hepatitis.

Patients undergoing antimicrobial therapy for other infections should be evaluated to assess whether the therapy will obviate the effects of PACIS.

For patients with small bladder capacity, the increased risk of severe local irritation should be considered in decisions to treat with PACIS.

Since intravesical treatment with PACIS may induce a sensitivity to tuberculin, which could complicate future interpretations of skin test reactions to tuberculin in the diagnosis of suspected mycobacterial infections, determination of a patient's reactivity to tuberculin prior to administration of PACIS may be desirable.

Precautions: Contains viable attenuated mycobacteria. Handle as infectious.

All equipment and materials (e.g., syringes, catheters) used for instillation of the product into the bladder should be placed immediately into plastic bags, labelled "Infectious Waste", and disposed of accordingly as biohazardous waste.

Care must be taken during administration of intravesical PACIS, to avoid introducing contaminants into the urinary tract or traumatizing unduly the urinary mucosa.

Because fatalities have been reported with use of BCG after traumatic catheterization, it is recommended that intravesical PACIS not be administered any sooner than 1 week following transurethral resection or other invasive procedures involving the urinary bladder.

If the physician suspects that bladder catherization has been traumatic (e.g., associated with bleeding or possible false passage), then PACIS should not be administered and treatment should be delayed at least 1 week. Subsequent treatment should be resumed as if no interruption in the schedule had occurred; i.e., all remaining doses of PACIS should be administered. Similarly, the full course of treatment should be completed, whenever possible, when interruptions have occurred for other reasons.

If systemic BCG infection is suspected (i.e., if patients have fever over 39°C, or persistent fever above 38°C over 2 days, or severe malaise), fast-acting antituberculosis therapy should be initiated and an infectious disease specialist consulted. It should be noted that presumptive BCG systemic infections can rarely be confirmed by positive cultures.

Concomitant use of ASA may interfere with the attachment of BCG to the bladder mucosa.

Pregnancy: Animal reproduction studies have not been conducted with PACIS. It is also not known whether PACIS can cause fetal harm when administered to a pregnant woman or can affect reproduction capacity. PACIS should be given to a pregnant woman only if clearly needed.

Lactation: A nursing mother with a systemic BCG infection could infect her infant. It is not known whether this drug is excreted in human milk. Therefore, caution should be exercised when PACIS is administered to a nursing mother and nursing should be discontinued.

Children: Safety and effectiveness in children have not been established.

Information for the Patient: Patients must be advised to check with their doctor as soon as possible if there is an increase in their existing symptoms, or if their symptoms persist even after receiving a number of treatments, or if any of the following symptoms develop: More Common: blood in urine, fever and chills, frequent urge to urinate, increased frequency of urination, joint pain, nausea and vomiting, painful urination. Rare: cough, skin rash.

Note: A cough that develops after administration of PACIS could indicate a life-threatening BCG infection. Possible BCG infection should be treated immediately, in consultation with an infectious disease specialist.

Patients should be asked to avoid drinking liquids for the 2 hours prior to and during PACIS therapy.

Ideally, during the first hour following instillation, the patient should lie for 15 minutes each in the prone and supine positions and also on each side. The patient is then allowed to be up but retains the suspension for another 60 minutes for a total of 2 hours. All patients may not be able to retain the suspension for 2 hours and should be instructed to void in less time if necessary. At the end of treatment all patients should void in a seated position for safety reasons. Patients should be instructed to drink enough liquid after treatment to maintain adequate hydration.

Urine voided during the 6 hours after instillation must be disinfected with an equal volume of 5% sodium hypochlorite solution (undiluted household bleach) and allowed to stand for 15 minutes before flushing.

Patients must also be advised that drug combinations containing bone marrow depressants and/or immunosuppressants and/or radiation may impair the response to PACIS or increase the risk of osteomyelitis or disseminated BCG infection. They should also be advised to inform any physicians whom they consult that they are being treated with PACIS.

Adverse Effects: PACIS may affect several organs (or parts) of the body in addition to the cancer cells. The data in Table I have been derived from 2 open studies which were continued for several years.

The following events were also reported in one patient each. Vancouver: contracted bladder, epididymitis, flu like syndrome, arthralgia, increased WBC; Kingston: incontinence, flu-like reaction, lightheadedness, anorexia, arthritis, back pain, sepsis.

The adverse events listed in Table II are taken from a report by Lamm et al (1989) on the complications of treatment with BCG. This report includes data from the use of Montréal (Institut Armand-Frappier), Tice, Connaught, Pasteur and RIVM strains.

This report referred to an earlier publication (Lamm, 1986) in which the incidences of the more common side effects in 1 278 patients were reported. These were: cystitis 91%, hematuria 43%, low grade fever (≤38.5°C) 28%, malaise 24% and nausea 8%.

Table I—PACIS

Adverse Effects

Adverse Event	Vancouver (Total Patients=65) No. Patients (%)	Kingston (Total Patients=94) No. Patients (%)
Cystitis	47 (72.3)	36 (38.3)
Hematuria	3 (4.6)	16 (17.0)
Dysuria	3 (4.6)	12 (12.8)
Frequency	—	4 (4.3)
Urgency	—	5 (5.3)
Urinary tract infection	—	4 (4.3)
Fever	3 (4.6)	9 (9.6)
Malaise	—	4 (4.3)
Chills and fever	—	3 (3.2)

Table II—PACIS

Adverse Effects

Adverse Event	n=2 602 Patients No. of Patients	%
Fever (≥39.5°C)	75	2.9
Granulomatous prostatitis	23	0.9
Pneumonitis/hepatitis	18	0.7
Arthralgia	12	0.5
Hematuria	24	1.0
Rash	8	0.3
Ureteral obstruction	8	0.3
Epididymitis	10	0.4
Contracted bladder	6	0.2
Renal abscess	2	0.1
Sepsis	10	0.4
Cytopenia	2	0.1

Rare complications, several of which have never been seen with intravesical administration of BCG, may include immune-complex glomerulonephritis, choroiditis, nephrogenic adenoma, cardiac toxicity, suppurative lymphadenitis, lupus vulgaris, musculoskeletal lesions and abscesses and fistulae.

Irritative bladder side effects associated with PACIS administration can be managed symptomatically (e.g., with phenazopyridine HCl or propantheline bromide, and acetaminophen).

Systemic side effects (such as malaise, fever and chills) may represent hypersensitivity reactions and can be treated with antihistamines and other appropriate therapy. Systemic infection as a result of the spread of BCG organisms has occasionally occurred with intravesical BCG administration. If systemic BCG infection is suspected (i.e., if patients have fever over 39°C, persistent fever above 38°C over 2 days, or severe malaise), fast-acting antituberculosis therapy should be initiated and an infectious disease specialist consulted.

Dosage: Intravesical treatment should begin between 7 to 14 days after biopsy (or transurethral resection if this procedure is done).

The recommended course of PACIS treatment is a single dose of 120 mg instilled into the bladder once weekly for 6 weeks.

Reconstitute the product according to the further directions: Dilute 1 mL of reconstituted product in 50 mL of sterile physiological saline. Insert a urethral catheter into the bladder under aseptic conditions and drain the bladder. Instill the 50 mL of PACIS suspension into the bladder slowly by gravity. Remove the catheter. Advise the patient (see Precautions, Information for the Patient).

Ideally, during the first hour following instillation, the patient should lie for 15 minutes each in the prone and supine positions and also on each side. The patient is then allowed to be up but retains the suspension for another 60 minutes for a total of 2 hours. All patients may not be able to retain the suspension for 2 hours and should be instructed to void in less time if necessary. At the end of treatment all patients should void in a seated position for safety reasons. Patients should be instructed to drink enough liquid after treatment to maintain adequate hydration.

The induction therapy may be followed by a single instillation given at 3, 6, 12, 18 and 24 months following the initial treatment.

Each person who is immunized should be given a permanent personal immunization record. In addition, it is essential that the physician or nurse record the immunization history in the permanent medical record of each patient. This permanent office record should contain the name of the vaccine, date given, dose, manufacturer and lot number.

PACIS (cont'd)

After use, all equipment should be sterilized or disposed of properly as with any other biohazardous waste (see Precautions).

Reconstitution of Lyophilized Product: Handle as infectious material. Persons handling product should be masked and gloved. PACIS should not be handled by persons with a known immunologic deficiency. Check the expiry date of the product carefully. Note that if stored between 2 and 8°C a new expiry date of 6 months from the start of storage at this temperature supersedes the printed expiry date. Administration of any product past its expiry date is not recommended. Reconstitute and dilute using aseptic technique **immediately prior to use.**

The contents of the PACIS vial should be suspended with a sterile diluent (water for injection, without any preservative). Moisten the surfaces of both rubber stoppers with tampons of sterile cotton wool soaked in a suitable antiseptic and allow the antiseptic to act for a few moments, then wipe dry with sterile dry swabs. With a sterile syringe, remove 1 mL of sterile diluent (water for injection, without any preservative) and add it to the vial containing the PACIS.

Leave them in contact for about 1 minute. Then mix the suspension by withdrawing it into the syringe and expelling it gently back into the ampul 2 or 3 times. Avoid the production of foam; do not shake.

At no time should the reconstituted product be exposed to sunlight, direct or indirect. Exposure to artificial light should be kept to a minimum.

Supplied: Each vacuum-sealed vial of lyophilized preparation of Bacillus Calmette-Guérin (BCG), an attenuated strain of M. bovis, (substrain Montréal) in a 15% (w/v) lactose base contains: a single dose of 120 mg semi-dry weight (2 to 10×10^6 colony-forming units (CFU)/mg) of BCG and is ready to use following reconstitution with the sterile diluent. Neither the BCG nor the sterile diluent contains a preservative.

Store at −30°C wherever possible. May be stored between 2 and 8°C for a maximum of 6 months. At the time of transfer between 2 and 8°C note the new expiry date (i.e., current date plus 6 months) on the carton label in the space provided.

PACIS should **not** be transferred between 2 and 8°C after the expiry date printed on the vial and carton. PACIS should not be used more than 6 months after being transferred between 2 and 8°C, even if this is earlier than the printed expiry date.

At no time should the lyophilized preparation be exposed to sunlight, direct or indirect. The product may be kept at 4 or 25°C, under artificial light for a maximum of 6 hours, while still in the lyophilized state.

PACIS is produced by BioChem Vaccins Inc.

PACLITAXEL INJECTION ℞

Boehringer Ingelheim

Antineoplastic

> Caution: Paclitaxel is a toxic product and should be administered only by or under the supervision of a physician experienced in the use of cancer chemotherapeutic agents.
>
> Patients receiving paclitaxel injection should be pretreated using corticosteroids, antihistamines, and H_2 antagonists (for example dexamethasone, diphenhydramine and cimetidine or ranitidine) to minimize hypersensitivity reactions (see Dosage). All clinical studies referred to in this product monograph were conducted using Taxol (paclitaxel) for injection. Severe hypersensitivity reactions characterized by dyspnea and hypotension requiring treatment, angioedema, and generalized urticaria have occurred in patients receiving paclitaxel. These reactions are probably histamine mediated. One of these reactions was fatal in a patient treated without premedication in a phase 1 study. Patients who experience severe hypersensitivity reactions to paclitaxel injection should not be re-challenged with the product.

Pharmacology: Paclitaxel is an antimicrotubule agent that promotes the assembly of microtubules from tubulin dimers and stabilizes microtubules by the prevention of depolymerization.

In vitro, paclitaxel has cytotoxic activity against a wide variety of both human and rodent tumor cell lines including leukemia, non-small cell lung carcinoma, small cell lung carcinoma, carcinoma of the colon, CNS tumors, melanoma, renal carcinoma, ovarian carcinoma and breast cancer.

Pharmacokinetics: The pharmacokinetics of paclitaxel have been evaluated in doses up to 300 mg/m² infused in a time period ranging from 3 to 24 hours. Following i.v. administration of paclitaxel, the drug exhibited a biphasic decline in plasma concentrations. The initial speedy decline represents distribution to the peripheral compartment and elimination of the drug. The later phase is due, in part, to a relatively slow efflux of paclitaxel from the peripheral compartment. Values for mean terminal phase half-life, total body clearance, and apparent volume of distribution at steady state were determined following doses of 135 and 175 mg/m² administered as 3- and 24-hour infusions. Mean terminal half-life ranged from 3 to 52.7 hours. Total body clearance ranged from 11.6 to 24 L/h/m². The mean steady state volume of distribution ranged from 198 to 688 L/m², indicating extensive extravascular distribution and/or tissue binding of paclitaxel. Mean terminal half-life was estimated at 9.9 hours after 3-hour infusions at 175 mg/m². Mean total body clearance was 12.4 L/h/m². There was no evidence of accumulation of drug with multiple treatment courses. There was minimal variability in systemic drug exposure for successive courses of treatment as measured by $AUC_{0 \to \infty}$.

The pharmacokinetics of paclitaxel are nonlinear; this is most easily seen in patients where high plasma concentrations are achieved and may be due to saturable processes in distribution and elimination/metabolism. There are large disproportional increases in C_{max} and AUC with increased dose and an apparent dose-related decrease in total body clearance.

In vitro studies of binding to human serum proteins, with concentrations of paclitaxel ranging from 0.1 to 50 µg/mL, indicated that, on average, 89% of drug is bound. The presence of cimetidine, ranitidine, dexamethasone, or diphenhydramine did not affect protein binding of paclitaxel.

The disposition of paclitaxel has not been fully determined in humans. After i.v. administration of paclitaxel, mean values for cumulative urinary recovery of unchanged drug ranged from 1.3 to 12.7% of the dose, indicating significant nonrenal clearance. The principal metabolites are hydroxylates isolated from bile. About 20% of an administered dose was recovered in bile as the parent compound and metabolites, in 1 patient in the 24 hours following treatment. Disposition of paclitaxel may be primarily hepatic metabolism and biliary clearance. The effect of renal or hepatic dysfunction on the disposition of paclitaxel has not been investigated.

The clearance of paclitaxel was not affected by cimetidine pre-treatment.

Ketoconazole may inhibit the metabolism of paclitaxel based upon preliminary animal/ex vivo data. Similarly, there are preliminary reports which suggest that plasma levels of doxorubicin and its active metabolite doxorubicinol may be increased when paclitaxel and doxorubicin are used in combination. The mechanism for this interaction is unknown and the pharmacodynamic consequences of this interaction are unclear (see Precautions, Drug Interactions).

Indications: For the treatment of carcinoma of the ovary or breast, alone or in combination.

Ovarian Carcinoma: First line therapy in combination with other chemotherapeutic agents; second line therapy for metastatic carcinoma of the ovary after failure of standard therapy.

Breast Carcinoma: Second line treatment of metastatic carcinoma of the breast after failure of standard therapy.

Contraindications: Patients who have a history of severe hypersensitivity reactions to paclitaxel or other drugs formulated in Cremophor EL (polyethoxylated castor oil). Paclitaxel injection should not be used in patients with severe baseline neutropenia, for example, less than 1 500 cells/mm³.

Warnings: Paclitaxel injection should be administered under the supervision of a physician experienced in the use of cancer chemotherapeutic agents.

Paclitaxel injection should be given as a diluted infusion. Patients receiving the product should be premedicated with corticosteroids, antihistamines, and H_2 antagonists (such as dexamethasone, diphenhydramine, and cimetidine or ranitidine) to minimize hypersensitivity reactions (see Dosage). Severe hypersensitivity reactions including dyspnea, flushing, chest pain, tachycardia, hypotension requiring treatment, angioedema, and generalized urticaria have occurred in patients receiving paclitaxel by i.v. administration. These reactions are probably histamine mediated. One of these reactions resulted in the death of a patient treated without premedication in a Phase I study. Infusion should be discontinued immediately if a patient experiences a severe hypersensitivity reaction to paclitaxel injection. The patient should not be given paclitaxel injection again.

Paclitaxel injection should not be administered to patients with baseline neutrophil counts below 1 500 cells/mm³ . Bone marrow suppression (primarily neutropenia) is dose-dependent and is the dose-limiting toxicity. Neutrophil nadirs occurred at a median of 11 days. Frequent monitoring of blood counts should be instituted during treatment. Patients should not be retreated with subsequent cycles of paclitaxel injection until neutrophils recover to a level above 1 500 cells/mm³ and platelets recover to a level above 100 000 cells/mm³. (See Dosage).

Severe cardiac conduction abnormalities have been rarely reported during therapy with paclitaxel, administered i.v. During administration, if patients develop significant conduction abnormalities, then appropriate therapy should be instituted and continuous ECG monitoring should be performed during subsequent therapy (see Adverse Effects).

Pregnancy: Paclitaxel injection may cause fetal harm when administered to a pregnant woman. Women of childbearing potential should be advised to avoid becoming pregnant during therapy. No studies have been conducted in women who are pregnant. Paclitaxel was shown to be embryo and feto-toxic in rabbits and to decrease fertility in rats.

Lactation: Paclitaxel injection should not be administered to mothers who are nursing.

Precautions: Contact of the undiluted concentrate with plasticized polyvinyl chloride (PVC) equipment or devices used to prepare solutions for infusion is not recommended. To minimize patient exposure to the plasticizer DEHP [di-(2-ethylhexyl)phthalate], which may be leached from PVC infusion bags or sets, diluted paclitaxel injection should preferably be stored in glass or polypropylene bottles, or polypropylene or polyolefin plastic bags and administered through polyethylene-lined administration sets.

Drug Interactions: In a Phase I trial in which paclitaxel (24-hour infusion) and cisplatin (1 mg/min infusion) were administered as sequential infusions, myelosuppression was more profound when paclitaxel was given after cisplatin than with the alternate sequence (that is, paclitaxel before cisplatin). When paclitaxel is administered before cisplatin, then the safety profile of paclitaxel is similar to that for single-agent use. Pharmacokinetic data from these patients demonstrated a decrease in paclitaxel clearance of approximately 33% when paclitaxel was administered following cisplatin. Therefore, when used in combination, paclitaxel injection should be administered before cisplatin.

Preliminary animal/ex vivo data indicate that ketoconazole may inhibit the metabolism of paclitaxel. Caution should be observed in the treatment of patients receiving ketoconazole when undergoing paclitaxel therapy.

There are preliminary reports that suggest that plasma levels of doxorubicin and its active metabolite doxorubicinol may be increased when paclitaxel and doxorubicin are used in combination (see Pharmacology).

Hematology: Paclitaxel injection should not be administered to patients with baseline neutrophil counts of less than 1 500 cells/mm³ (see Warnings and Contraindications). In order to monitor the occurrence of myelotoxicity, it is recommended that frequent peripheral blood cell counts be performed on all patients receiving the drug. Patients should not be retreated with paclitaxel injection until neutrophils recover to a level greater than 1 500 cells/mm³ and platelets recover to a level greater than 100 000 cells/mm³. In the case of severe neutropenia (<500 cells/mm³) during therapy, a 20% reduction in dose for subsequent courses of therapy is recommended (see Dosage).

Hypersensitivity Reactions: Patients with a history of severe hypersensitivity reactions to products containing Cremophor EL should not be treated with paclitaxel injection (see Warnings and Contraindications). Minor symptoms such as flushing, skin reactions, dyspnea, hypotension or tachycardia do not require interruption of therapy. However, severe reactions, such as hypotension requiring treatment, dyspnea requiring bronchodilators, angioedema or generalized urticaria require immediate discontinuation of paclitaxel injection and aggressive symptomatic therapy. Patients who have developed severe hypersensitivity reactions should not be given paclitaxel injection again.

Cardiovascular: Hypotension and bradycardia, usually asymptomatic, can occur during administration of paclitaxel injection but generally do not require treatment. Frequent vital sign monitoring, particularly during the first hour of infusion, is recommended. Continuous cardiac monitoring is not required except for patients who develop serious conduction abnormalities (see Warnings and Adverse Effects).

Nervous System: Although the occurrence of peripheral neuropathy is frequent, the development of severe symptomatology is unusual. Moderate to severe neuropathy requires a dose reduction of 20% for all later courses of paclitaxel injection (see Adverse Effects and Dosage).

Paclitaxel injection contains 396 mg/mL of dehydrated alcohol; the possible CNS and other effects of alcohol should be considered.

Hepatic: There is no evidence of increased toxicity of paclitaxel when administered as a 3-hour infusion to patients with mildly abnormal liver function. No data are available for patients with severe baseline cholestasis (see Adverse Effects).

When paclitaxel is given as a 24-hour infusion to patients with moderate to severe hepatic impairment, increased myelosuppression may be observed compared to patients with mildly elevated liver function tests.

Adverse Effects: The incidence of adverse reactions in Table I are derived from 10 clinical trials in carcinoma of the ovary and of the breast involving 812 patients treated with paclitaxel at doses ranging from 135 to 300 mg/m²/day and schedules of 3 or 24 hours. Data from a subset of 181 patients treated with 175 mg/m² and a 3-hour infusion schedule are also included in Table I.

Table I—Paclitaxel Injection

Summary of Adverse Reactions

		135 to 300 mg/m² % of Patients (N=812)	175 mg/m² % of Patients (N=181)
Bone Marrow			
Neutropenia	<2 000/mm³	90	87
	<500/mm³	52	27
Leukopenia	<4 000/mm³	90	86
	<1 000/mm³	17	4
Thrombocytopenia	<100 000/mm³	20	6
	<50 000/mm³	7	1
Anemia	<11 g/dL	78	62
	<8 g/dL	16	6
Infections		30	18
Bleeding		14	9
Red Cell Transfusions		25	13
Red Cell Transfusions (normal baseline)		12	6
Platelet Transfusions		2	0
Hypersensitivity Reactions			
All		41	40
Severe		2	1
Cardiovascular			
Bradycardia during first 3 hours of infusion		3	3
Hypotension during first 3 hours of infusion		12	11
Severe cardiovascular events		1	2
Abnormal ECG			
All Patients		23	13
Patients with normal baseline		14	8
Peripheral Neuropathy			
Any symptoms		60	64
Severe symptoms		3	4
Myalgia/Arthralgia			
Any symptoms		60	54
Severe symptoms		8	12
Gastrointestinal			
Nausea and vomiting		52	44
Diarrhea		38	25
Mucositis		31	20
Alopecia		87	93
Hepatic (patients with normal baseline)			
Bilirubin elevations		7	4
Alkaline phosphatase elevations		22	18
AST elevation		19	18
Injection Site Reactions		13	4

The safety profile has been evaluated from a large randomized trial (paclitaxel 135 mg/m² over 24 hours with cisplatin 75 mg/m² versus cyclophosphamide/cisplatin) which included 410 patients, 196 of whom received paclitaxel. Use of paclitaxel with platinum agents has not resulted in any clinically significant changes to the safety profile of the product when used at the recommended dosage.

Summary of 3-hour Infusion Data at a Dose of 175 mg/m²: Unless otherwise stated, the following safety data relate to 62 patients with ovarian cancer and 119 patients with breast cancer treated at a dose of 175 mg/m² and a 3-hour infusion schedule, in phase III clinical trials. All patients were premedicated to minimize hypersensitivity reactions. Data from these clinical trials demonstrate that paclitaxel administered at this dose and schedule is well tolerated. Bone marrow suppression and peripheral neuropathy were the principle dose-related adverse reactions. Further, as compared to a 24-hour infusion schedule, the incidence of neutropenia was less common when paclitaxel was administered as a 3-hour infusion. Neutropenia was generally rapidly reversible and did not become worse with cumulative exposure. Repeated exposure increases the frequency of neurologic symptoms.

None of the observed toxicities were influenced by age.

Hematologic: The most frequent notable undesirable effect of paclitaxel was bone marrow suppression. Severe neutropenia (<500 cells/mm³) occurred in 27% of patients, but was not associated with febrile episodes. Only 1% of patients experienced severe neutropenia for 7 days or more. Neutropenia was not more frequent or severe in patients who received prior radiation therapy, nor did it appear to be affected by treatment duration or cumulative exposure. 18% of patients had an infectious episode, all non-fatal. Although severe septic episodes associated with severe neutropenia attributable to paclitaxel were reported in early clinical trials, no severe infections or septic episodes were seen at the recommended dose and infusion schedule. There were 5 fatal septic episodes associated with severe neutropenia attributable to paclitaxel in the overall 812 patient database.

Thrombocytopenia with platelet counts <100 000 cells/mm³ was reported in 6% of patients. Thrombocytopenia with platelet counts <50 000 cells/mm³ was reported in 1% of patients. Severe thrombocytopenia (<50 000 cells/mm³) was observed during the first 2 courses only. Bleeding episodes occurred in 9% of patients; no patient needed platelet transfusion.

Anemia was seen in 62% of patients, but was severe (Hb<8 g/dL) in only 6% of patients. Incidence and severity of anemia are associated with baseline hemoglobin status. Red cell transfusions were required in 13% of patients (6% of those with normal baseline hemoglobin levels).

Hypersensitivity Reactions: Severe hypersensitivity reactions occurred in 1% of patients even with premedication. These reactions occurred generally in early treatment courses and within the first hour of infusion. Dyspnea, flushing, chest pain and tachycardia were the most frequent signs and symptoms.

The dosage and schedule had no effect on the frequency of hypersensitivity reactions which occurred in 21% of courses where patients were given the recommended dose at the recommended schedule. The majority of reactions were minor. The most frequent were flushing (28%), rash (14%), and hypotension (3%).

Cardiovascular: During infusion of paclitaxel, hypotension and bradycardia were experienced by 24% and 4% of patients, respectively, and did not usually occur during the same course; the majority of episodes were asymptomatic and did not require treatment.

One patient experienced transient hypertension during the second paclitaxel cycle. In addition, 2 patients experienced severe cardiovascular events (tachycardia and thrombophlebitis), possibly related to paclitaxel. None of these patients required discontinuation of treatment. In the same studies at a lower dose or longer infusion, 3 severe cardiovascular events (atrioventricular (AV) block, syncope and hypotension associated with coronary stenosis resulting in death) possibly related to paclitaxel administration were reported. Ten severe cardiovascular events occurred which included cardiac rhythm disturbance and syncope among the 812 patients (see Warnings).

An abnormal ECG occurred in 13% of patients during the clinical trials at a dosage of 175 mg/m² and a 3-hour infusion schedule. Some patients (8%) with a normal ECG prior to study entry developed an abnormal tracing during the study. Of the 812 patients, the most frequently reported ECG changes were nonspecific repolarization abnormalities, sinus tachycardia and premature beats. In most cases, there was no clear relationship between the administration of paclitaxel and ECG changes; these changes were of no, or minimal, clinical relevance.

Since the above summary, cases of myocardial infarction have been reported rarely. Congestive heart failure has been reported typically in patients who have received other prior chemotherapy, especially anthracyclines.

Neurologic: Peripheral neuropathy, mainly manifested by paresthesia, affected 64% of patients, but was severe in only 4% of patients. Neurologic symptoms can occur following the first course and can worsen with increased exposure to paclitaxel. Peripheral neuropathy was the cause of drug discontinuation in 3 cases. Sensory symptoms have usually improved or resolved within several months of paclitaxel discontinuation. Pre-existing neuropathies resulting from prior therapies are not a contraindication for paclitaxel therapy. Rare neurologic events include grand mal seizures and encephalopathy. Reports of motor neuropathy with resultant minor distal weakness and autonomic neuropathy resulting in paralytic ileus and orthostatic hypotension have also been observed. Optic nerve and/or visual disturbances (scintillation scotomata) have also been reported, especially in patients who have received higher doses than recommended. These effects have generally been reversible.

Arthralgia/Myalgia: Arthralgia or myalgia affected 54% of patients and was severe in 12% of patients. The symptoms usually were pain in the large joints of the arms and legs and were transient occurring 2 to 3 days after administration and resolving within a few days.

Alopecia: Alopecia was observed in nearly all patients.

Gastrointestinal: Gastrointestinal side effects were usually mild to moderate: nausea/vomiting (44%), diarrhea (25%) and mucositis (20%) were reported. Other gastrointestinal events included anorexia (25%), constipation (18%) and intestinal obstruction (4%). Neutropenic enterocolitis, bowel obstruction/perforation and ischemic colitis and pancreatitis have occurred.

Hepatic: In patients with normal baseline liver function, 4% had elevated bilirubin, 18% had elevated alkaline phosphatase, and 18% had elevated AST. Severe elevations (>5x normal values) of bilirubin, alkaline phosphatase or AST were seen in 1%, 5%, and 5% of patients, respectively. There have been rare reports of hepatic necrosis and hepatic encephalopathy leading to death.

Injection Site Reactions: Phlebitis can occur following the i.v. administration of paclitaxel. Extravasation during i.v. infusion can lead to edema, pain, erythema and induration. Occasionally extravasation can result in cellulitis. Skin discoloration can also occur. Recurrence of skin reactions at a site of previous extravasation following administration at a different site, so called "recall," has been reported rarely. A specific treatment of extravasation reactions is unknown, however treatment with a s.c. injection of hyaluronidase diluted in saline has been shown to be effective in a mouse skin model.

Other: Mild and transient nail and skin changes have been observed. Radiation pneumonitis has been reported in patients who have received concurrent radiotherapy.

Overdose: Symptoms and Treatment: There is not a known antidote for paclitaxel injection overdosage. The primary anticipated complications of overdosage would consist of bone marrow suppression, peripheral neurotoxicity and mucositis.

Dosage: Note: Undiluted concentrate should not come in contact with plasticized PVC equipment. In order to minimize patient exposure to the plasticizer DEHP [di-(2-ethylhexyl)phthalate], which may be leached from PVC infusion bags or sets, diluted paclitaxel injection solutions should preferably be stored in glass or polypropylene bottles, or polypropylene or polyolefin plastic bags and administered through polyethylene-lined administration sets.

Paclitaxel injection should be administered through an in-line filter with a microporous membrane not greater than 0.22 micron. Use of filter devices such as IVEX-2 filters which incorporate short inlet and outlet PVC-coated tubing has not resulted in significant leaching of DEHP.

All patients should be premedicated prior to Paclitaxel Injection administration in order to minimize severe hypersensitivity reactions. Premedication may consist of dexamethasone 20 mg orally (or its equivalent) approximately 12 and 6 hours before paclitaxel injection, diphenhydramine 50 mg i.v. (or its equivalent) 30 to 60 minutes prior to paclitaxel injection, and cimetidine (300 mg) or ranitidine (50 mg) i.v. 30 to 60 minutes preceding paclitaxel injection.

Paclitaxel injection at a dose of 175 mg/m² administered i.v. over 3 hours every 3 weeks has been shown to be effective in patients with metastatic carcinoma of the ovary or breast who have failed standard therapy. Single courses of paclitaxel injection should not be repeated until the neutrophil count is at least 1 500 cells/mm³ and the platelet count is at least 100 000 cells/mm³. Patients who experience severe neutropenia (neutrophil <500 cells/mm³) or moderate to severe peripheral neuropathy during therapy should have the dosage reduced by 20% for subsequent courses.

Preparation and Administration Precautions: Paclitaxel injection is a cytotoxic anticancer drug and, as with other potentially toxic compounds, caution should be used in handling the product. The use of gloves is recommended. Following topical exposure, tingling, burning, and redness have been reported. If Paclitaxel injection solution contacts the skin, wash the skin immediately and thoroughly with soap and water.

Paclitaxel Injection (cont'd)

If paclitaxel injection contacts mucous membranes, the membranes should be flushed thoroughly with water. Upon inhalation, dyspnea, chest pain, burning eyes, sore throat and nausea have been reported.

Paclitaxel injection at a dose of 175 mg/m² administered intravenously over 3 hours every 3 weeks in combination with cisplatin 75 mg/m² is recommended for the primary treatment of patients with advanced carcinoma of the ovary. Paclitaxel injection should be administered before cisplatin when used in combination.

Preparation for I.V. Administration: Paclitaxel injection must be diluted prior to infusion. Paclitaxel injection should be diluted in Sodium Chloride Injection 0.9%, Dextrose Injection 5%, Dextrose 5% and Sodium Chloride 0.9% Injection, or Dextrose 5% in Ringer's Injection to a final concentration of 0.3 to 1.2 mg/mL. The solutions are physically and chemically stable for up to 27 hours at room temperature (15 to 30°C).

Upon preparation, solutions may show haziness, which is attributed to the formulation vehicle. No significant loss in potency has been noted following simulated delivery of the solution through IV tubing which contains an in-line 0.22 micron filter.

Data collected for the presence of the extractable plasticizer DEHP [di-(2-ethylhexyl)phthalate] show that levels increase with time and concentration when dilutions are prepared in PVC (polyvinyl chloride) containers. Consequently, the use of plasticized PVC containers and administration sets is not recommended. Paclitaxel injection solutions should be prepared and stored in glass, polypropylene, or polyolefin containers. Non-PVC containing administration sets, such as those which are polyethylene-lined, should be used.

Preparation for I.V. Administration: Contact of undiluted paclitaxel injection with plasticized PVC equipment or devices used to prepare solutions for infusion is not recommended (see Dosage).

Prior to infusion, paclitaxel injection should be diluted in Sodium Chloride Injection 0.9%, Dextrose Injection 5%, Dextrose 5% and Sodium Chloride 0.9% Injection or Dextrose 5% in Ringer's Injection to a final concentration of 0.3 to 1.2 mg/mL.

As with all parenteral drug products, i.v. admixtures should be inspected visually for clarity, particulate matter, precipitate, discoloration and leakage prior to administration, whenever solution and container permit.

Paclitaxel injection should be administered through an in-line filter with a microporous membrane not greater than 0.22 microns.

Special Instructions: 1. Preparation of paclitaxel injection should be done in a vertical laminar flow hood (Biological Safety Cabinet—Class II). 2. Personnel preparing paclitaxel injection should wear PVC gloves, safety glasses, disposable gowns and masks. 3. All needles, syringes, vials and other materials which have come in contact with paclitaxel injection should be segregated and incinerated at 1 000°C or more. Sealed containers may explode. Intact vials should be returned to the distributor for destruction. Proper precautions should be taken in packaging these materials for transport. 4. Personnel regularly involved in the preparation and handling of paclitaxel injection should have bi-annual blood examinations.

Supplied: Each mL of injection contains: paclitaxel 6 mg. Nonmedicinal ingredients: Cremophor EL (polyethoxylated castor oil) and dehydrated alcohol. Single dose vials of 5 mL. Store under refrigeration (2 to 8°C). Retain in the original package and protect from light. Solutions for infusion prepared as recommended may be stored at room temperature (15 to 30°C) only if necessary. However, the infusion should be initiated within 24 hours of reconstitution.

New Product 1998

PALAFER®

SmithKline Beecham

Ferrous Fumarate

Anemia Therapy

Indications: Increased iron requirements as in childhood, adolescence, and pregnancy; blood losses, overt or occult. Characterized microcytic hypochromic anemia; faulty iron absorption following gastrectomy; iron loss due to menstruation, sub-clinical iron deficiencies in adolescent girls due to precarious iron balance, and geriatrics.

Contraindications: Hemosiderosis, hemochromatosis. Iron compounds are also contraindicated in the treatment of hemolytic anemias unless an iron-deficient state also exists, since storage of iron with a possible exogenous hemosiderosis can result.

Precautions: Where anemia exists, its nature should be established and underlying causes determined.

Prolonged administration of iron should be avoided except in patients with continued bleeding or repeated pregnancies. In infants, large chronic doses of iron may so interfere with the assimilation of phosphorus as to cause severe rickets.

Orally administered iron salts may aggravate existing disorders, such as peptic ulcer, regional enteritis and ulcerative colitis. They may not be absorbed in patients with steatorrhea and those who have had a partial gastrectomy.

Before initiating parenteral iron therapy, it is advisable to give test doses to help detect sensitivity. Iron overload can occur in patients given an excess of parenteral iron, as well as those with hemoglobinopathies or other refractory anemias which might be erroneously diagnosed as iron-deficiency anemia.

Do not administer oral iron preparations concomitantly with parenteral iron.

Iron binds with tetracyclines in equal molecular ratio thus preventing absorption of tetracyclines.

Warn patients that iron is toxic when overdoses are ingested by children. Severe reactions, including fatalities, have resulted.

Concomitant administration of antacids containing aluminum and magnesium salts may impair the absorption of iron.

Adverse Effects: Oral ingestion of iron preparations may be associated with gastrointestinal discomfort (such as nausea) and dose-related bowel effects (such as constipation or diarrhea). Untoward effects usually subside with continuation of therapy or by administration with or after meals.

There is a possibility that liquid dosage forms of iron may stain teeth. To reduce this possibility, mix each dose with water or fruit juice. If staining occurs, remove by brushing with baking soda (sodium bicarbonate).

Parenteral iron administration can cause nausea, vomiting and such acute allergic reactions as chills and fever, arthralgia, urticaria and asthma. Occasional pain and staining of the skin at the site of injection may occur. Severe anaphylactoid reactions with some deaths have been reported in the literature. Although i.m. administration of iron dextran injections have caused sarcoma in laboratory animals, induced malignanacy in man has never been observed.

Overdose: Iron poisoning is rare in adults but serious acute poisoning in children can result from ingestion of doses in excess of 1 g. Doses of 1 g should be considered as toxic in children and therapy instituted as soon as possible. Serum iron levels above 500 μg/100 mL can be taken as presumptive evidence of poisoning; severe poisoning is usually associated with levels well above 1 000 μg/100 mL.

Symptoms: Symptoms may occur within about 30 minutes or may be delayed several hours. They are largely those of gastrointestinal irritation and necrosis with vomiting, diarrhea, tarry stools, hematemesis, fast and weak pulse, lethargy, low blood pressure, coma and signs of peripheral circulatory collapse. There may be a transient period of apparent recovery after 4 to 6 hours, followed by a second crisis characterized by cyanosis, pulmonary edema, circulatory collapse, convulsion and coma may then occur followed by death in 12 to 48 hours.

Treatment: Milk should be given immediately and vomiting induced. Eggs and milk should then be fed (to form iron-protein complexes) until it is possible to perform gastric lavage with 1% sodium bicarbonate solution (to convert the iron to a less soluble form). Gastric lavage should not be performed after the first hour of iron ingestion because of the danger of perforation due to gastric necrosis. If an iron-chelating agent such as deferoxamine mesylate is available, it should be utilized. BAL (dimercaprol) should not be used because it may form a toxic complex. Measures to combat shock, dehydration, blood loss and respiratory failure may be necessary.

Dosage: Capsules: Adults and children over 12 years: 1 capsule daily on an empty stomach preferably at bedtime. Ferrous fumarate is well tolerated by most patients, however for patients sensitive to any form of iron: 1 capsule twice a day with meals is recommended. Characterized iron deficiency anemia: 24 weeks minimum. In pregnancy, 1 capsule daily throughout gestation. Iron supplementation in clinical cases, 12 weeks minimum.

Suspension: Children 0 to 2 years: Preventive: 0 to 6 months: 0.25 mL once daily (5 mg/day of elemental iron). 6 months to 2 years: 0.75 mL once daily (15 mg/day elemental iron). Therapeutic: 0 to 6 months: 0.25 mL t.i.d. (15 mg/day of elemental iron). 6 months to 2 years: 0.75 mL t.i.d. (45 mg/day of elemental iron). Administer between meals with water or fruit juice.

Children 2 to 6 years: 2.5 mL (½ teaspoonful) daily at bedtime. 6 years of age and over: 5 mL (1 teaspoonful) daily at bedtime.

Supplied: Capsules: Each scarlet capsule, printed "PALAFER" in white ink on the body and cap, contains: ferrous fumarate M.D.I. (micro dispersible form) 300 mg representing 100 mg of elemental iron. Nonmedicinal ingredients: D&C yellow No. 10, FD&C red No. 2, FD&C red No. 3, FD&C yellow No. 6, gelatin, lactose, povidone, sucrose, talc, titanium dioxide, silicon dioxide and sodium lauryl sulfate. Energy: 0.2 kJ (0.06 kcal). Cartons of 30 and bottles of 500.

Suspension: Each 5 mL of brown colored suspension contains: ferrous fumarate 300 mg equivalent to 100 mg elemental iron. Nonmedicinal ingredients: artificial cherry flavor, caramel carrageen, glycerin, methylparaben, propylparaben, sorbitol solution, sugar and water. Energy: 28.57 kJ (6.83 kcal)/5 mL. Bottles of 100 mL.

Reviewed 1999

PALAFER® CF

SmithKline Beecham

Ferrous Fumarate Compound

Prenatal Supplement

Indications: For the treatment of hypochromic anemia and avitaminosis C and to prevent megaloblastic anemia of pregnancy due to folic acid depletion.

Contraindications: Hemosiderosis, hemochromatosis. Iron compounds are also contraindicated in the treatment of hemolytic anemias unless an iron-deficient state also exists, since storage of iron with a possible exogenous hemosiderosis can result.

Precautions: Where anemia exists, its nature should be established and underlying causes determined.

Prolonged administration of iron should be avoided except in patients with continued bleeding or repeated pregnancies. In infants, large chronic doses of iron may so interfere with the assimilation of phosphorus as to cause severe rickets.

Orally administered iron salts may aggravate existing disorders, such as peptic ulcer, regional enteritis and ulcerative colitis. They may not be absorbed in patients with steatorrhea and those who have had a partial gastrectomy.

Before initiating parenteral iron therapy, it is advisable to give test doses to help detect sensitivity. Iron overload can occur in patients given an excess of parenteral iron, as well as those with hemoglobinopathies or other refractory anemias which might be erroneously diagnosed as iron-deficiency anemia. Do not administer oral iron preparations concomitantly with parenteral iron.

Iron with tetracyclines binds in equal molecular ratio thus preventing absorption of tetracyclines.

Warn patients that iron is toxic when overdoses are ingested by children. Severe reactions, including fatalities, have resulted.

Concomitant administration of antacids containing aluminum and magnesium salts may impair the absorption of iron.

Adverse Effects: Oral ingestion of iron preparations may be associated with gastrointestinal discomfort (such as nausea) and dose-related bowel effects (such as constipation or diarrhea). Untoward effects usually subside with continuation of therapy or by iron ingestion with or after meals.

Parenteral iron administration can cause nausea, vomiting, and such acute allergic reactions as chills and fever, arthralgia, urticaria, and asthma. Occasional pain and staining of the skin at the site of injection may occur. Severe anaphylactoid reactions with some deaths have been reported in the literature. Although i.m. administration of iron dextran injections has caused sarcoma in laboratory animals, induced malignancy in man has never been observed.

Overdose: Iron poisoning is rare in adults but serious acute poisoning in children can result from ingestion of doses in excess of 1 g. Doses of 1 g should be considered as toxic in children and therapy instituted as soon as possible. Serum iron levels above 500 μg/100 mL can be taken as presumptive evidence of poisoning; severe poisoning is usually associated with levels well above 1 000 μg/100 mL.

Symptoms: Symptoms may occur within about 30 minutes or may be delayed several hours. They are largely those of gastrointestinal irritation and necrosis with vomiting, diarrhea, tarry stools, hematemesis, fast and weak pulse, lethargy, low blood pressure, coma and signs of peripheral circulatory collapse. There may be a transient period of apparent recovery after 4 to 6 hours followed by a second crisis characterized by cyanosis, pulmonary edema, circulatory collapse, convulsion, and coma may then occur followed by death in 12 to 48 hours.

Treatment: Milk should be given immediately and vomiting induced. Eggs and milk should then be fed (to form iron-protein complexes) until it is possible to perform gastric lavage with 1% sodium bicarbonate solution (to convert the iron to a less soluble form). Gastric lavage should not be performed after the first hour of iron ingestion because of the danger of perforation due to gastric necrosis. If an iron-chelating agent such as deferoxamine mesylate is available, it should be utilized. BAL (dimercaprol) should not be used because it may form a toxic complex. Measures to combat shock, dehydration, blood loss and respiratory failure may be necessary.

Dosage: One capsule daily on an empty stomach preferably at bedtime, or as prescribed. Prophylactic administration should be discontinued at term. Iron therapy alone should be administered after parturition.

Supplied: Each pink and red capsule, printed PALAFER CF in white ink on the body and cap, contains: microdispersed ferrous fumarate 300 mg (representing 100 mg of elemental iron), ascorbic acid 200 mg, and folic acid 0.5 mg. Nonmedicinal ingredients: D&C Yellow No. 10, FD&C Blue No. 1, FD&C Red No. 2, FD&C Red No. 3, FD&C Yellow No. 6, gelatin, lactose, magnesium stearate, povidone, silicon dioxide, sodium lauryl sulfate, sugar, talc and titanium dioxide. Energy: 0.6 kJ (0.16 kcal). Cartons of 30 and bottles of 500.

PALUDRINE® ℞

Wyeth-Ayerst

Proguanil HCl

Antimalarial

Pharmacology: Proguanil is metabolized in the body to the antimalarial drug cycloguanil, a triazine derivative, which inhibits plasmodial dihydrofolate reductase thus indirectly inhibiting synthesis of nucleic acids in the parasite. Proguanil, like pyrimethamine, is active against pre-erythrocytic forms and is a slow blood schizontocide. It also has some sporonticidal activity, rendering the gametocytes noninfective to the mosquito vector.

Pharmacokinetics: Proguanil is well absorbed from the gastrointestinal tract and peak plasma concentrations are attained in 3 hours after a single oral dose; about 75% of proguanil in the plasma is bound to proteins and the concentrations of the drug in erythrocytes is approximately 6 times that of plasma. About 50% of the administered dose is excreted in the urine, 60% as unchanged drug and 30% as the active metabolite cycloquanil.

Indications: Causal prophylaxis of falciparum (P. falciparum) malaria; proguanil also supresses other forms of malaria, and it is used to reduce transmission of infection. Proguanil should not be used alone in countries where chloroquine-resistant malaria has been confirmed (see Dosage).

Contraindications: Known or suspected hypersensitivity to proguanil.

A high degree of resistance appears to develop in all species of Plasmodium and in some geographical areas this has limited the usefulness of proguanil. Proguanil alone should not be used if resistance to other antimalarials has been confirmed. Cross-resistance occurs with other antimalarials.

Precautions: It is generaly accepted that all drug treatment should be avoided if possible during the first trimester of pregnancy. A causal connection between the use of proguanil and any adverse effect on mother and fetus has never been established, but the attending physician should carefully weigh the expected benefits against the potential risks.

Use proguanil with caution in patients with severe renal impairment.

Adverse Effects: At normal therapeutic doses, the side effect most commonly encountered is mild gastric intolerance. This usually subsides as treatment is continued. Mouth ulceration has occasionally been reported. Large doses (1 g daily) may cause vomiting, abdominal pain, hematuria and renal irritation. Blood dyscrasias have been reported in patients with renal failure given proguanil.

Selected cases of skin reactions and reversible hair loss have been reported in association with the use of proguanil.

Overdose: Symptoms: The following effects have been reported in cases of overdosage: hematuria, renal irritation, epigastric discomfort and vomiting.

Treatment: There is no specific antidote; symptoms should be treated as they arise. Treatment should be symptomatic and supportive.

Dosage: For prophylaxis of malaria: Adults: Usual dose is 100 mg daily. In highly endemic areas this dose may be safely increased to 200 mg daily. The daily dose is best taken with water after food.

Nonimmune subjects entering a malarious region are advised to begin treatment with proguanil at least 24 hours before arrival. A daily dose of proguanil should be continued for 6 weeks after leaving the area.

Elderly: There are no special dosage recommendations for the elderly, but it may be advisable to monitor elderly patients so that optimum dosage can be individually determined.

Children: Under 1 year: 25 mg daily; 1 to 4 years: 50 mg daily; 5 to 8 years: 75 mg daily; 9 to 12 years: 100 mg daily; over 12 years: adult dose daily.

For a young child, the dose may be administered crushed and mixed with milk, honey or jam.

For all countries with chloroquine-resistant malaria: The dose of proguanil is increased to 200 mg daily with chloroquine (base) given 300 mg once a week, i.e., approximately equivalent to 500 mg chloroquine phosphate.

Note: Although widely used, the safety of this therapeutic regimen has not been formally established.

In Southeast Asia and the Pacific where chloroquine resistance is commonplace, the above regimen is apparently ineffective.

Supplied: Each white, biconvex tablet, embossed P/P on one side with a score line, contains: proguanil HCl 100 mg. Nonmedicinal ingredients: lactose powdered, magnesium stearate, starch corn and starch paste. Energy: 0.6 kJ (0.15 kcal)/tablet. Alcohol-, gluten-, parabens-, sugar-, sulfites- and tartrazine-free. Bottles of 100. Store at temperatures around 25°C.

(Shown in Product Recognition Section)

PAMPRIN®
PAMPRIN® Extra Strength
PAMPRIN® PMS

Chattem

Pamabrom—Pyrilamine Maleate—Acetaminophen

Diuretic—Antihistamine—Analgesic

Indications: For temporary relief of symptoms accompanying premenstrual syndrome such as cramps, headache, irritability, backache and mild to moderate aches and pains. To reduce the temporary excess water frequently associated with the premenstrual period. Pamprin is most effective if taken at the first sign of discomfort, usually a few days before a period.

Contraindications: Hypersensitivity to pamabrom, theophylline derivatives, pyrilamine maleate, or acetaminophen, and in those with the following conditions: asthmatic attacks, narrow-angle glaucoma, bladder-neck obstruction, peptic ulcer or pyloroduodenal obstruction.

Warnings: Individuals with continuing severe or debilitating symptoms accompanying premenstrual syndrome should consult their physician.

Pregnancy and *Lactation:* Should not be given to women who are pregnant or who are nursing.

Children: Not recommended for children less than 12 years old.

Keep safely out of reach of children. This package contains sufficient medication to seriously harm a child.

Precautions: Occupational Hazards: May produce additive CNS effects when taken concomitantly with alcohol, hypnotics, anxiolytics, narcotic analgesics, and neuroleptic drugs. If drowsiness occurs, avoid driving a motor vehicle or operating machinery while taking this product.

Adverse Effects: Side effects are usually mild and may include drowsiness and listlessness. Hypersensitivity reactions are rare but may include urticaria, skin eruptions, pruritus or anaphylaxis.

Overdose: Symptoms: In mild overdosage, symptoms may be manifest as an exaggeration of the adverse effects listed above, but may be more severe, particularly in children. Severe cases may include hallucinations, excitement, ataxia, incoordination, convulsions and cardiovascular depression.

Acetaminophen poisoning can result in severe hepatic damage. The minimum dose of acetaminophen that may cause hepatotoxicity in adults is generally considered to be 10 g, and a dose of 16 g is potentially lethal. However, there have been rare instances of hepatotoxicity and death reported from lower doses, and survival after much larger doses (up to 31 g) is common.

Phenobarbital increases the activity of microsomal enzymes which produce a toxic metabolite which may enhance acetaminophen's hepatotoxicity. Concomitant ingestion of phenobarbital may increase the likelihood of liver necrosis in acetaminophen overdose. The chronic ingestion of alcohol may also increase the potential for hepatic toxicity in acetaminophen overdose.

Early symptoms (nausea, vomiting, weakness) usually occur after ingestion of an acetaminophen overdose large enough to cause hepatic toxicity. However, since some patients may exhibit few or none of these early signs, in cases of suspected acetaminophen overdose, antidotal therapy should begin as soon as possible. A latent period of 24 to 36 hours exists between ingestion and onset of hepatic symptoms. Laboratory evidence usually appears within 24 to 48 hours if severe hepatotoxicity is to occur. In mild cases, clinical evidence of hepatotoxicity may be delayed for as long as 5 days. Patients should be monitored by liver function tests for several days following an overdose. Following the latent period, vomiting, pain in the right hypochondrium and manifestations of hepatic failure may occur. Maximum hepatic necrosis appears 2 to 6 days following overdose. The primary changes in serum chemistries are a gross elevation of hepatic enzymes, an elevation of serum bilirubin, a prolongation of prothrombin time and possible hypoglycemia.

Treatment: Should be supportive and symptomatic. If the product has been taken recently by mouth, gastric lavage or induction of vomiting with ipecac syrup USP is recommended. If activated charcoal is administered, lavage before treatment with oral antidote (acetylcysteine) to prevent absorption of the latter. Plasma levels of acetaminophen should be monitored.

The patient should be kept quiet to minimize excitement. Convulsions and marked CNS stimulation should be treated. Treatment should include correction of hypoxia fluid and electrolyte imbalance. Assisted respiration may be necessary and cooling, if hyperpyrexia occurs. Dialysis has been employed to treat xanthine overdosage.

Dosage: Pamprin: 2 tablets and repeat every 3 to 4 hours as needed. Do not exceed 8 tablets in 24 hours. Do not use for more than 5 consecutive days. Use only as directed by a physician.

Pamprin Extra Strength: 2 caplets and repeat every 3 to 4 hours as needed. Do not exceed 8 caplets in 24 hours. Do not use for more than 5 consecutive days. Use only as directed by a physician.

Pamprin PMS: 2 caplets and repeat every 3 to 4 hours as needed. Do not exceed 8 caplets in 24 hours. Do not use for more than 5 consecutive days. Use only as directed by a physician.

Supplied: Pamprin: Each white, round tablet, embossed with a rosette on one side, contains: pamabrom 25 mg, pyrilamine maleate 12.5 mg and acetaminophen 325 mg. Gluten-, lactose-, sodium- and tartrazine-free. Child-resistant bottles of 24 and 40.

Pamprin Extra Strength: Each white, capsule-shaped tablet, with PAMPRIN embossed on one side, contains: pamabrom 25 mg, pyrilamine maleate 15 mg and acetaminophen 500 mg. Gluten-, lactose-, sodium- and tartrazine-free. Child-resistant bottles of 16 and 32.

Pamprin PMS: Each white, capsule-shaped tablet, with Pamprin PMS embossed on one side, contains: pamabrom 25 mg, pyrilamine maleate 15 mg and acetaminophen 500 mg. Gluten-, lactose-, sodium- and tartrazine-free. Child-resistant bottles of 16 and 32.

Does a pregnant woman require additional vitamin A and D? To answer this and other recommended nutrient intake questions, see the CLIN-INFO SECTION.

PANCREASE®
PANCREASE® MT

Janssen-Ortho

Pancrelipase

Digestant

Pharmacology: The enteric-coated microtablets resist gastric inactivation and deliver predictable, high levels of biologically active pancreatic enzymes (lipase, amylase, and protease) into the duodenum. The enzymes catalyze the hydrolysis of fats into glycerol and fatty acids, proteins into proteoses and derived substances, and starch into dextrins and sugars.

Pharmacokinetics: Absorption: The intestinal bioavailability of Pancrease MT 16 capsules was determined, in vitro, under simulated physiological conditions. The capsules were placed into a test tube containing an incubation medium consisting of 2 g NaCl, 9.2 g NaH_2PO_4 and distilled water ad 1 000 mL. Employing a disintegration tester, the contents of the test tube were shaken at a constant speed of 30 rpm at an incubation temperature of 37°C. The pH of the mixture was adjusted by adding 4N HCl or 4N NaOH.

To simulate the acidic conditions of the stomach during a meal, a pH of 4.0 was initially established and gradually reduced in increments of 0.5 at 30-minute intervals to a pH of 2.5. To simulate the relative alkalinity of the intestine, the preparation was then transferred to a buffer where a pH of 6.6 was maintained. While the preparation was exposed to the buffer, release of pancreatic lipase, the marker enzyme, was measured as a function of time. The lipase content of the incubation medium was determined every 15 minutes for 120 minutes. More than 90% of the enzyme activity of the Pancrease MT capsules was released at 15 minutes with peak levels (97%) occurring at 30 minutes. The results demonstrate that Pancrease MT capsules are nearly 100% bioavailable and rapidly release high levels of pancreatic enzymes.

Excretion: Unused enzymes in the capsules are excreted in the feces. Digested enzymes are absorbed and are subsequently excreted in the urine.

Indications: For patients with exocrine pancreatic enzyme deficiency as in, but not limited to, cystic fibrosis, chronic pancreatitis, post-pancreatectomy, post-gastrointestinal bypass surgery, and ductal obstruction from neoplasm (e.g., of the pancreas or common bile duct).

Contraindications: In patients known to be hypersensitive to pork protein and in patients with acute pancreatitis or with acute exacerbations of chronic pancreatic diseases.

Warnings: Should hypersensitivity occur, discontinue medication and treat the patient symptomatically.

Precautions: To protect the enteric coating, the microtablets should not be crushed or chewed. Where swallowing of capsules is difficult, they may be opened and the contents may be shaken onto a small quantity of a soft food which does not require chewing (e.g., applesauce, dessert gelatin, etc.), and swallowed immediately. Contact of the microtablets with foods having a pH greater than 6.0 (e.g., milk, custard, ice cream and many other dairy products) can dissolve the protective enteric coating.

Cases of fibrotic stricture formation in the ascending colon have been reported in cystic fibrosis patients with the use of high potency enzyme supplements in high doses (6 500 to 50 000 BP lipase units*/kg/meal). If symptoms suggestive of gastrointestinal obstruction occur the possibility of bowel strictures should be considered.

Any change in pancreatic enzyme replacement therapy (e.g., dose or brand of medication) should be made cautiously and only under medical supervision.

*1 BP lipase unit is approximately equal to 1 USP lipase unit.

Pregnancy: Animal reproduction studies have not been conducted with pancrelipase. It is also not known whether enteric coated pancrelipase can cause fetal harm when administered to a pregnant woman or can affect reproduction capacity. The capsules should be given to a pregnant woman only if the potential benefit justifies the potential risk to the fetus.

Adverse Effects: The most frequently reported adverse reactions to pancrelipase-containing products are gastrointestinal in nature such as nausea and diarrhea. Less frequently, allergic-type reactions have also been observed. Extremely high doses of exogenous pancreatic enzymes have been associated with hyperuricemia and hyperuricosuria when the preparations given were pancrelipase in powdered or capsule form or pancreatin in tablet form.

Overdose: Symptoms and Treatment: There have been no reports of accidental or purposeful overdosage with pancrelipase capsules. Pancrelipase microtablets are classified as nontoxic by the Poisindex Information System, and serious toxicity from overdose is unlikely. Should toxicity occur, treat symptomatically.

Dosage: Dosage should be adjusted according to the severity of the exocrine pancreatic enzyme deficiency. The number of capsules or capsule strength given with meals and/or snacks should be estimated by assessing which dose minimizes steatorrhea and maintains good nutritional status. In some patients with pancreatic enzyme deficiency, satisfactory responses have been achieved with dosages (expressed in USP units of lipase) similar to the ones stated below. However, dosages should be adjusted according to the response of the patient.

Dose increases, if required, should be made slowly, with careful monitoring of response and symptomatology. It is important to ensure adequate hydration of patients at all times while administering pancrelipase.

Adults: 4 000 to 16 000 units (more if necessary) with each meal and with snacks.

Children: See Table I.

Table I—Pancrease/Pancrease MT

Dosage in Children

Age	Dosage
7–12 years	4 000 to 12 000 units (more if necessary) with each meal and with snacks.
1–6 years	4 000 to 8 000 units with each meal and 4 000 units with snacks.
6 months –1 year	Children in this age group have responded to 2 000 units of lipase per meal.
Under 6 months	Not established.

The assessment of the end points in children is aided by charting growth curves.

Supplied: Pancrease: Each hard gelatin capsule with a clear or natural cap and opaque, white body, imprinted McNEIL—PANCREASE in synthetic iron oxide with a ring of the same color located around the end of both cap and body and off-white beads visible through the clear end of the capsule contains: No less than lipase 4 000 USP units, capable of liberating a minimum of 4 mEq fatty acid/minute; amylase 20 000 USP units, capable of digesting a minimum of 20 g starch; and, protease 25 000 USP units, capable of digesting a minimum of 25 g protein. Nonmedicinal ingredients: cellulose acetate phthalate, cornstarch, diethyl phthalate, gelatin, povidone, sodium starch glycolate, sugar, talc and titanium dioxide. Energy: 5.887 kJ (1.4 kcal). Bottles of 100 and 250.

Pancrease MT 4: Each yellow opaque, clear hard gelatin capsule, imprinted "PANCREASE MT 4" on clear cap, and "McNEIL" on body, contains: lipase 4 000 USP units, amylase 12 000 USP units and protease 12 000 USP units. Capsules are filled with off-white microtablets. Nonmedicinal ingredients: cellulose, crospovidone, gelatin, iron oxide, magnesium stearate, methacrylic acid copolymer, polydimethylsiloxane, sodium lauryl sulfate, silicon dioxide, talc, titanium dioxide, triethylcitrate, wax and other trace ingredients. Bottles of 100.

Pancrease MT 10: Each pink opaque, clear hard gelatin capsule, imprinted "PANCREASE MT 10" on clear cap, and "McNEIL" on body, contains: lipase 10 000 USP units, amylase 30 000 USP units and protease 30 000 USP units. Capsules are filled with off-white microtablets. Nonmedicinal ingredients: cellulose, crospovidone, gelatin, iron oxide, magnesium stearate, methacrylic acid copolymer, polydimethylsiloxane, sodium lauryl sulfate, silicon dioxide, talc, titanium dioxide, triethylcitrate, wax and other trace ingredients. Bottles of 100.

Pancrease MT 16: Each salmon opaque, clear hard gelatin capsule, imprinted "PANCREASE MT 16" on clear cap, and "McNEIL" on body, contains: lipase 16 000 USP units, amylase 48 000 USP units and protease 48 000 USP units. Capsules are filled with off-white microtablets. Nonmedicinal ingredients: cellulose, crospovidone, gelatin, iron oxide, magnesium stearate, methacrylic acid copolymer, polydimethylsiloxane, sodium lauryl sulfate, silicon dioxide, talc, titanium dioxide, triethylcitrate, wax and other trace ingredients. Bottles of 100.

Keep bottles tightly closed. Store between 10 to 25°C in a dry place. Do not refrigerate. Dispense in tight container.

(Shown in Product Recognition Section)

Reviewed 1999

PANCURONIUM BROMIDE INJECTION

Abbott

Nondepolarizing Neuromuscular Blocking Agent

Supplied: Ampuls: Each mL of solution contains: pancuronium bromide 2 mg. Nonmedicinal ingredients: acid acetic glacial, benzyl alcohol, sodium acetate, sodium chloride, sodium hydroxide and water for injection. Single dose ampuls of 2 and 5 mL, trays of 5 and 10.

Vials: Each mL of solution contains: pancuronium bromide 1 mg. Nonmedicinal ingredients: acid acetic glacial, benzyl alcohol, sodium acetate, sodium chloride, sodium hydroxide and water for injection. Multiple dose fliptop vials of 10 mL, cartons of 5.

PANECTYL® Ⓟ

Rhône-Poulenc Rorer

Trimeprazine Tartrate

Antipruritic—Antihistamine

Pharmacology: Trimeprazine is a propylamino phenothiazine derivative with reduced central activity and enhanced antihistaminic and antipruritic effects.

It is a potent histamine antagonist. Trimeprazine possesses sedative properties, and is active in suppressing apomorphine induced vomiting in the dog. No evidence of teratogenic effect has been demonstrated in animal studies.

Indications: Pruritus regardless of site or etiology. The control of cough of various etiologies and the relief of asthma like dyspnea.

Contraindications: States of CNS depression due to barbiturates, alcohol, narcotics or analgesics. Cases with a history of blood dyscrasias or severe allergic reactions related to trimeprazine or other phenothiazines.

Warnings: Occupational Hazards: Patients should be advised against driving or engaging in activities requiring complete mental alertness or physical coordination, until their response to the drug has been well established.

Pregnancy: Use in pregnant women is not recommended except when in the judgement of the physician it is necessary for the welfare of the patient.

Precautions: Trimeprazine should be used with caution when there is a risk of potentiating CNS depressant drugs such as opiates, analgesics, antihistaminics, barbiturates and alcohol. It should also be used with caution in patients with a history of convulsive disorders or liver disease, and in cases of jaundice.

Since phenothiazines are known to reverse the pressor effect of epinephrine, if hypotension should occur, epinephrine should **not** be used as it may depress further the blood pressure.

The drug should be used cautiously in severely ill or dehydrated children who are more susceptible to seizures associated with phenothiazines.

The antiemetic action of trimeprazine may obscure signs of intestinal obstruction or brain tumor.

Ingestion after meals prolongs absorption of the drug, thus reducing incidence of possible side effects.

Adverse Effects: At recommended therapeutic dosages, trimeprazine is usually well tolerated. Side effects that are likely to occur may be listed as follows:

CNS: Drowsiness is the most common initial untoward reaction but tends to subside within 1 to 3 weeks. It occurs most frequently in older age groups, and often with daily doses of 30 mg or more. Its incidence and intensity can be minimized by starting at a low dosage, gradually increased, or by prescribing the drug after food to promote a more gradual absorption. Should drowsiness persist it can be alleviated by decreasing dosage.

Extrapyramidal symptoms such as tremor, spasticity, painful contractions of skeletal muscles, dystonias have rarely been noted. If a neuromuscular reaction occurs, medication should be stopped and not reinstituted in children or in pregnant patients, while in others it may be resumed later, at a lower dosage. After discontinuation of treatment, extrapyramidal symptoms usually subside gradually within 24 to 48 hours. If a counteractant is necessary, barbiturates or an antiparkinsonian agent may bring rapid relief.

Other infrequent side effects reported include disturbing dreams, elation, depression, and fainting.

Autonomic Nervous System: Dryness of mouth and nasal congestion are rare.
Gastrointestinal: Gastric upset, abdominal discomfort and nausea may occur but usually disappear after a few days of medication. A few cases of cholestatic jaundice have been reported.
Skin: Drug rash and dermatitis have been observed in very few patients.
Allergic or Toxic: Very rare cases of reversible agranulocytosis and leukopenia have been reported. This reaction has responded to immediate withdrawal of trimeprazine and administration of antibiotics and corticosteroids. Since most reported cases of agranulocytosis, associated with the administration of phenothiazines, have occurred within the first 10 weeks of treatment, patients on prolonged therapy should be observed for this reaction particularly during that period.

Overdose: Symptoms: Drowsiness, dizziness, dryness of mucous membranes and gastrointestinal upsets. Massive overdosage may result in oversedation, collapse and coma.

Treatment: There is no specific antidote and treatment should be symptomatic. Gastric lavage should be carried out and the stomach left empty. Centrally acting emetics will not help because of the antiemetic effect of trimeprazine. Keep a clear airway and maintain adequate hydration.

Avoid CNS stimulants which may cause convulsions (e.g. picrotoxin and pentylenetetrazol).

Should collapse occur, put the patient in the head down position; use norepinephrine in an i.v. infusion of dextrose in normal saline, but **not** epinephrine as it may further depress the blood pressure. The infusion must not be stopped abruptly, but the drip rate reduced gradually when the desired blood pressure is reached.

Like other phenothiazine derivatives, trimeprazine is not dialyzable, so that hemodialysis is unlikely to assist recovery from overdosage, unless some other agents (e.g. barbiturate), have been taken concurrently.

Dosage: The dosage may vary with patients. In most cases a low dosage is effective, but it should be adjusted according to the severity of the symptoms and the patient's response. All doses are expressed in terms of trimeprazine base.
Adults: 2.5 or 5 mg twice daily after meals and 5 mg at bedtime. In predominantly nocturnal conditions, a single bedtime dose of 5 to 10 mg may be given.
Children (2 to 12 years): 2.5 mg or 5 mg at bedtime. If necessary, an additional dose of 2.5 mg twice a day after meals may be given. Daily dose should rarely exceed 15 mg.

Supplied: Liquid: Each 5 mL of yellow liquid contains: trimeprazine base 2.5 mg (as the tartrate). Nonmedicinal ingredients: alcohol 95%, artificial chocolate flavor, artificial fruit flavor, ascorbic acid, citric acid, D&C Yellow No 10, purified water and sucrose. Alcohol: 0.6% v/v. Sucrose: 4.2 g/5 mL. Energy: 67.6 kJ (16.1 kcal). Tartrazine-free. Bottles of 500 mL.

Tablets: Each varnished, light pink tablet contains: trimeprazine base 2.5 or 5 mg (as the tartrate). Nonmedicinal ingredients: acetic anhydride, carnauba wax, cellulose, colloidal silicon dioxide, dicalcium phosphate, diethyl phthalate, FD&C Red No 3, FD&C Yellow No 6, magnesium stearate, sodium croscarmellose, sodium oleate, titanium oxide and zein. Tartrazine-free. Bottles of 100 (2.5 and 5 mg) and bottles of 500 (5 mg).

(Shown in Product Recognition Section)

PANOCAINE®

Hoechst Marion Roussel

Benzocaine—Tetracaine HCl

Oral Topical Anesthetic

Pharmacology: Panocaine is a local anesthetic of the ester type which rapidly produces surface anesthesia following application to the mucosa of the oral cavity in clinical dentistry. Panocaine has a short duration of action and is ineffective when applied to intact skin.

Indications: For use in the oral cavity for minimizing the pain associated with needle puncture, deep scaling procedures, application of matrix bands and extraction of primary teeth.

Panocaine is indicated for the reduction of the pharyngeal (gag) reflex associated with the placement into the oral cavity of various dental materials (impression trays, x-ray films, x-ray plate holders).

Contraindications: Patients with a known hypersensitivity to local anesthetics of the ester type or any of the nonmedicinal ingredients (see Precautions).

Panocaine is contraindicated for use outside the oral cavity.

Precautions: Application to severely traumatized areas which are infected or areas of the posterior pharynx that might dull protective reflexes should be avoided.

Local anesthetics should be used with caution in patients with known drug sensitivities, particularly in those known to be allergic to ester-type anesthetics (e.g., benzocaine, procaine, tetracaine).

Repeated and prolonged application may potentiate hypersensitivity.

Dosage: Area where Panocaine is to be applied must be dry prior to application. Removal of excess saliva with cotton rolls of saliva ejector will minimize dilution of the local anesthetic.

Press down on dispenser surface; apply Panocaine to desired area using a cotton swab. Care must be taken to avoid cross-contamination between patients.

When used with new dentures, it is important that patients consult their dentist regularly during the fitting period and that the total dose be limited to no more than 3 applications a day.

Total dose is not to exceed the amount required for anesthesia.

Supplied: Each g of cherry-flavored, topical anesthetic gel contains: benzocaine USP 18% and tetracaine hydrochloride USP 2%. Nonmedicinal ingredients: FD&C Red No. 2 (colorant), flavoring and polyethylene/propylene glycol (base). Plastic containers of 25 g. Store at room temperature, below 25° C.

PANOXYL® AQUAGEL 2.5% and 5%
PANOXYL® AQUAGEL 10% and 20% ℞

Stiefel

Benzoyl Peroxide

Acne Therapy

Supplied: Each g of gel contains: benzoyl peroxide 2.5%, 5%, 10% or 20% in an aqueous gel base (H_2Oxyl formulation). Nonmedicinal ingredients: carbomer 940 NF, ethoxylated lauryl alcohol, imidurea NF, purified water USP and sodium hydroxide. Plastic tubes of 60 g. Keep from heat.

PANOXYL® 5%
PANOXYL® 10%, 15% and 20% ℞

Stiefel

Benzoyl Peroxide

Acne Vulgaris Therapy

Supplied: Gel: Each g of gel contains: benzoyl peroxide 5% (Panoxyl 5), 10% (Panoxyl 10), 15% (Panoxyl 15) or 20% (Panoxyl 20) in an alcohol gel base containing polyoxyethylene lauryl ether. Nonmedicinal ingredients: citric acid anhydrous, ethoxylated lauryl alcohol, ethyl alcohol 65 O.P., hydroxylpropyl methyl cellulose, magnesium aluminum silicate and purified water USP. Plastic tubes of 60 g. Store below 27°C.

Bars: Each g contains: benzoyl peroxide 5% (Panoxyl 5) or 10% (Panoxyl 10). Nonmedicinal ingredients: colloidal silicone dioxide, purified water USP and tensianol base KS-1. Bars of 75 g with plastic storage tray.

PANOXYL® 5% WASH
PANOXYL® 10% WASH ℞

Stiefel

Benzoyl Peroxide

Acne Therapy

Supplied: Each mL contains: benzoyl peroxide 5% or 10% in a lathering base of soapless cleansers (Benoxyl formulation). Nonmedicinal ingredients: citric acid anhydrous, ethoxylated lauryl alcohol, hydroxy propyl methyl cellulose, imidurea/parabens, magnesium aluminum silicate, purified water USP, sodium alkyl aryl polyethylene sulfate, sodium dialkyl octyl sulfate succinate and sodium lauryl sulfoacetate. Plastic flip top bottles of 175 mL. Keep from heat.

PANTOLOC™ ℞

Solvay Pharma/Byk Canada

Pantoprazole

H^+, K^+-ATPase Inhibitor

Pharmacology: Pantoprazole is a specific inhibitor of the gastric H^+, K^+-ATPase enzyme (the proton pump) that is responsible for acid secretion by the parietal cells of the stomach.

Pantoprazole is a substituted benzimidazole that accumulates in the acidic environment of the parietal cells after absorption. Pantoprazole is then converted into the active form, a cyclic sulfenamide, which binds to the H^+, K^+-ATPase, thus inhibiting both the basal and stimulated gastric acid secretion. Pantoprazole exerts its effect in an acidic environment (pH$<$3), and it is mostly inactive at higher pH. Its pharmacological and therapeutic effect is achieved in the acid-secretory parietal cells.

In clinical studies investigating i.v. and oral administration, pantoprazole inhibited pentagastrin-stimulated gastric acid secretion. With a daily oral dose of 40 mg, inhibition was 51% on Day 1 and 85% on Day 7. Basal 24-hour acidity was reduced by 37% and 98% on Days 1 and 7, respectively.

Fasting gastrin values increased during pantoprazole treatment, but in most cases the increase was only moderate.

Pharmacokinetics: Pantoprazole is absorbed rapidly following administration of a 40 mg enteric-coated tablet. Its oral bioavailability compared to the i.v. dosage form is 77% and does not change upon multiple dosing. Following an oral dose of 40 mg, C_{max} is approximately 2.5 mg/L with a t_{max} of 2 to 3 hours. The AUC is approximately 5 mg·h/L. Pantoprazole shows linear pharmacokinetics after both i.v. and oral administration. Therefore, elimination half-life, clearance and volume of distribution are independent of the dose. Concomitant intake of food has no influence on the bioavailability of pantoprazole.

Studies with pantoprazole in humans reveal no inhibition or activation of the cytochrome P450 (CYP 450) system of the liver.

Pantoprazole is 98% bound to serum proteins. It is almost completely metabolized in the liver. Renal elimination represents the major route of excretion (about 82%) for the metabolites of pantoprazole, the remaining metabolites are excreted in feces. The main metabolite in both the serum and urine is desmethylpantoprazole as a sulfate conjugate. The half-life of the main metabolite (about 1.5 hours) is not much longer than that of pantoprazole (approximately 1 hour).

Indications: For the treatment of conditions where a reduction of gastric acid secretion is required, such as the following: duodenal ulcer, gastric ulcer and reflux esophagitis.

Pantoprazole is not indicated for maintenance therapy. Until adequate long-term clinical data are available, pantoprazole should be prescribed only at the recommended dosage regimen (see Dosage).

Contraindications: Patients with a history of hypersensitivity to pantoprazole or to any constituents of the medication (see Supplied). It is also contraindicated in patients with cirrhosis of the liver and in cases of severe liver disease (see Precautions).

Warnings: When gastric ulcer is suspected, the possibility of malignancy should be excluded before therapy with pantoprazole is instituted since treatment with pantoprazole may alleviate symptoms and delay diagnosis.

Pregnancy: There are no adequate or well-controlled studies in pregnant women. Pantoprazole should not be administered to pregnant women unless the expected benefits outweigh the potential risks to the fetus.

Lactation: It is not known whether pantoprazole is secreted in human milk. Pantoprazole should not be given to nursing mothers unless its use is believed to outweigh the potential risks to the infant.

Children: The safety and effectiveness of pantoprazole in children have not yet been established.

Precautions: Carcinogenicity: Effects on long-term treatment relate to hypergastrinemia, possible enterochromaffin-like (ECL) cell hyperplasia and carcinoid formation in the stomach, adenomas and carcinomas in the liver and neoplastic changes in the thyroid.

In a 24 month carcinogenicity study, Sprague-Dawley (SD) rats were treated orally with pantoprazole at 1.5, 5, 50, and 200 mg/kg/day. Pantoprazole produced gastric (ECL) cell hyperplasia and ECL cell carcinoid at doses of 50 mg/kg/day and above in males and at 0.5 mg/kg/day and above in females (first finding after 17 months treatment). The mechanism leading to the formation of gastric carcinoids is considered to be due to the elevated gastrin level occurring in the rat during

Pantoloc (cont'd)

chronic treatment. Similar observations have also been made after administration of other acid secretion inhibitors.

ECL-cell neoplasms were not observed in a 24 month carcinogenicity study in mice which were treated orally with pantoprazole at 5, 25, and 150 mg/kg/day. In clinical studies with treatment of 40 to 80 mg of pantoprazole for 1 year, ECL-cell density remained almost unchanged.

In the liver of the rat and female mouse, hepatocellular tumor formation was seen with pantoprazole. In rats, slightly increased liver tumor incidences were found at 50 mg/kg and above, and in the female mouse at 150 mg/kg. Hepatocellular tumors are common in mice, and the incidence found for the female 150 mg/kg group was within historical control ranges for this strain. The liver tumor incidences in rats treated with 50 mg/kg and in the male rats treated with 200 mg/kg were also within historical control incidences for the SD rat. These tumors occurred late in the life of the animals and were primarily benign. The nongenotoxic mechanism of rodent liver tumor formation after prolonged treatment with pantoprazole is associated with enzyme induction leading to hepatomegaly and centrilobular hypertrophy and is characterized by tumor induction in low incidences at high doses only. Clinical pharmacological studies with pantoprazole show no induction or inhibition of human liver enzymes. Hepatocellular tumors in rodents exposed to high levels of pantoprazole are not indicative of human carcinogenic risk.

A slight increase in neoplastic changes of the thyroid was observed in rats receiving pantoprazole at 200 mg/kg/day. The incidences of these thyroid tumors were within the historical control ranges for this rat strain. The effect of pantoprazole on the thyroid is secondary to the effects on liver enzyme induction, leading to enhanced metabolism of thyroid hormones in the liver. As a consequence, increased TSH is produced, having a trophic effect on the thyroid gland. Clinical studies have demonstrated that neither liver enzyme induction nor changes in thyroid hormonal parameters occur in man after therapeutic doses of pantoprazole.

The clinical implication of the above observations made in animal studies is not known. Until adequate long-term clinical data are available, pantoprazole should not be prescribed beyond the recommended dosage regimens.

Geriatrics: A slight increase in AUC (12%) and C_{max} (7%) for pantoprazole occurs in elderly volunteers when compared to younger volunteers. The daily dose used in elderly patients, as a rule, should not exceed the recommended dosage regimens.

Hepatic Insufficiency: The half-life increased to between 7 and 9 hours, the AUC increased by a factor of 5 to 7, and the C_{max} increased by a factor of 1.5 in patients with liver cirrhosis compared with healthy subjects. Pantoprazole should not be administered to patients with mild to moderate liver impairment unless the expected benefits outweigh the potential risks.

Renal Insufficiency: No dose reduction is required when pantoprazole is administered to patients with impaired kidney function as the difference in AUCs between patients who are dialyzed and those who are not is 4%.

Drug Interactions: Pantoprazole is metabolized in the liver via the CYP 450 system. Pharmacokinetic drug interaction studies in man did not demonstrate the inhibition of the oxidative metabolism of the drug. Pantoprazole does not interact with antipyrine, diazepam, phenytoin, nifedipine, theophylline, warfarin, digoxin, or oral contraceptives. Concomitant use of antacids or consumption of food does not affect the pharmacokinetics of pantoprazole.

Adverse Effects: Pantoprazole is well tolerated. Most adverse events have been mild and transient showing no consistent relationship with treatment. Adverse events have been recorded during controlled clinical investigations in 2 082 patients exposed to pantoprazole.

The following adverse events (at a rate of at least 0.5%) have been reported in individuals receiving pantoprazole therapy (40 mg once daily) in controlled clinical situations: diarrhea (1.5%), headache (1.3%), dizziness (0.7%), pruritus (0.5%) and asthenia (0.3%). No unexpected adverse events have been reported with pantoprazole.

In addition, the following adverse events were reported in clinical trials: Skin: isolated cases of alopecia, acne, edema, maculopapular rash, urticaria, exfoliative dermatitis.

Central and Peripheral Nervous Systems: rare cases of somnolence, insomnia; in isolated cases, depression, vertigo, tremor, tinnitus, paresthesia, nervousness, photophobia.

Sensory Organs: isolated cases of blurred vision.

Gastrointestinal: rare cases of increased appetite, dry mouth, nausea, constipation, dyspeptic symptoms, acid eructation; in one case, gastrointestinal carcinoma.

Urogenital: isolated cases of hematuria and impotence.

Hepatic: in rare cases, increased liver enzymes.

Hematologic: isolated cases of eosinophilia.

Other: in isolated cases, malaise.

An extensive evaluation of clinical laboratory results has not revealed any clinically important changes during pantoprazole treatment (except for gastrin which increased to 1.5-fold after 4 to 8 weeks).

Overdose: Symptoms and Treatment: There are no known reports or experiences of pantoprazole overdosage in man. Doses of up to 240 mg i.v. were administered and were well tolerated.

Treatment should be supportive and symptomatic.

Dosage: Duodenal Ulcer: The recommended adult oral dose is 40 mg given once daily in the morning. Healing usually occurs within 2 weeks. For patients not healed after this initial course of therapy, an additional course of 2 weeks is recommended.

Gastric Ulcer: The recommended adult oral dose is 40 mg given once daily in the morning. Healing usually occurs within 4 weeks. For patients not healed after this initial course of therapy, an additional course of 4 weeks is recommended.

Reflux Esophagitis: The recommended adult oral dose is 40 mg, given once daily in the morning. In most patients, healing usually occurs within 4 weeks. For patients not healed after this initial course of therapy, an additional 4 weeks of treatment is recommended.

Pantoprazole is not indicated for maintenance therapy. Until adequate long-term clinical data are available, pantoprazole should be prescribed only according to the recommended dosage regimens.

Pantoprazole is formulated as an enteric-coated tablet. A whole tablet should not be chewed or crushed, and should be swallowed with water in the morning either before, during or after breakfast.

Information for the Patient: See Blue Section—Information for the Patient "Pantoloc".

Supplied: Each enteric-coated, yellow, oval, biconvex tablet, marked P 40 on one side, contains: pantoprazole 40 mg (pantoprazole sodium sesquihydrate 45.1 mg). Nonmedicinal ingredients: calcium stearate, crospovidone, ferric oxide, mannitol, methylhydroxypropyl cellulose, poly(ethylacrylate, methacrylic acid), polysorbate 80, polyvidone, propylene glycol, anhydrous sodium carbonate, sodium lauryl sulfate, titanium dioxide and triethyl citrate. Bottles of 14 and 28. Store at 15 to 30°C in the recommended packaging.

(Shown in Product Recognition Section)

Reviewed 1998

PANTOTHENIC ACID

General Monograph, CPhA

Vitamin B_5

Vitamin

This monograph has been compiled by CPhA. It may contain information different from that approved by Therapeutic Products Programme, Health Canada, and the pharmaceutical manufacturers' approval has not been requested.

Pharmacology: Pantothenic acid is a water-soluble, B complex vitamin. It is a precursor of coenzyme A and is essential for acetylation reactions in gluconeogenesis, carbohydrate and lipid metabolism, and in the synthesis of steroid hormones, porphyrins, acetylcholine and other compounds.

Pantothenic acid is a required nutrient, but is so widely distributed that deficiency in humans is unlikely. Pantothenic acid deficiency is usually found in combination with deficiency of other B complex vitamins. Requirements may be increased in malabsorption syndromes such as tropical sprue, celiac disease and enteritis.

Only the dextrorotatory isomer of pantothenic acid has vitamin activity.

Pharmacokinetics: Pantothenic acid is readily absorbed from the gastrointestinal tract. It is widely distributed to all body tissues and is not metabolized. About 70% of a dose is excreted unchanged in the urine with the remainder being excreted in the feces. Normal serum concentrations of pantothenic acid are 100 μg/mL or higher.

Indications: Prevention and treatment of deficiency. Pantothenic acid has been used topically in the treatment of minor dermatoses.

Precautions: *Pregnancy:* It is not known whether pantothenic acid can cause fetal harm. It should be used in pregnancy only when clearly needed.

Lactation: No data are available.

Adverse Effects: Pantothenic acid is usually nontoxic, even in large doses.

Dosage: In preventing nutrient deficiency, adequate dietary intake is preferred over supplementation whenever possible. For information on food sources of pantothenic acid and other vitamins, see Vitamin Food Sources in the Clin-Info section. Although there are no official recommendations for pantothenic acid daily intake, the following amounts are generally considered adequate: birth to 3 years, 2 to 3 mg; 4 to 6 years, 3 to 4 mg; 7 to 10 years, 4 to 5 mg; over 10 years, 4 to 7 mg.

In the treatment of deficiency, dosage must be individualized, based on the severity of the deficiency. Each 10 mg calcium pantothenate is equivalent to 9.2 mg pantothenic acid.

Reviewed 1998

PAPAVERINE HCl

Frosst

Smooth Muscle Relaxant

Indications: For the relief of cerebral and peripheral ischemia with arterial spasm.

Adverse Effects: Hepatic hypersensitivity, gastrointestinal disturbances, flushing of face, headache, drowsiness, skin rash, sweating and vertigo. Parenteral administration can cause hypotension and respiratory depression. Contraindicated in presence of heart block.

Dosage: 30 to 65 mg i.m., i.v., or s.c.

Supplied: Each 2 mL ampul contains: papaverine HCl 65 mg and dextrose anhydrous for tonicity adjustment. Tartrazine-free. Boxes of 10.

PARA®

Technilab

Bioallethrin—Piperonyl Butoxide

Pediculicide—Ovicide

Supplied: Shampoo: Each mL of shampoo contains: bioallethrin 1.1% w/v and piperonyl butoxide 4.4% w/v. Plastic bottles of 50 and 250 mL.

Spray: Each g of spray contains: bioallethrin 6.6 mg and piperonyl butoxide 26.4 mg. Bottles of 50 and 90 g.

PARAFON FORTE®

Johnson & Johnson • Merck

Chlorzoxazone—Acetaminophen

Muscle Relaxant—Analgesic

Pharmacology: Parafon Forte tablets combine the muscle-relaxant effect of chlorzoxazone with acetaminophen, a well-known analgesic.

Chlorzoxazone is a centrally acting agent for painful musculoskeletal conditions. Data available from animal experiments, as well as human study, indicate that chlorzoxazone acts primarily at the level of the spinal cord and subcortical areas of the brain where it inhibits multisynaptic reflex arcs involved in producing and maintaining skeletal muscle spasm of varied etiology. The clinical result is a reduction of the skeletal muscle spasm with relief of pain and increased mobility of the involved muscles. Blood levels of chlorzoxazone can be detected in humans during the first 30 minutes after oral administration of Parafon Forte tablets and peak levels may be reached in about 1 to 2 hours. Chlorzoxazone is rapidly metabolized and is excreted in the urine, primarily in a conjugated form as the glucuronide. Less than 1% of a dose of chlorzoxazone is excreted unchanged in the urine in 24 hours.

Acetaminophen provides analgesic action to supplement that which results secondarily from muscle relaxation. Acetaminophen is rapidly absorbed after oral administration, with peak plasma levels occurring in 1 to 2 hours. After 8 hours, only negligible amounts remain in the blood. Only 4% is excreted unchanged; 85% of the ingested dose is recovered in the urine in conjugated form as the glucuronide. Acetaminophen is distributed throughout most tissues of the body. Acetaminophen is metabolized primarily in the liver. Little unchanged drug is excreted in the urine, but most metabolic products appear in the urine within 24 hours.

The mode of action of chlorzoxazone has not been clearly identified, but may be related to its sedative properties. Chlorzoxazone does not directly relax tense skeletal muscles in man.

Following oral administration of chlorzoxazone in combination with acetaminophen, both drugs are rapidly absorbed. Mean drug plasma concentrations reach a peak level in the majority of subjects in 45 to 90 minutes.

The plasma elimination half-life is about 1 hour for chlorzoxazone and ranges from 1.5 to 3.5 hours for acetaminophen.

Metabolism is rapid; the principal metabolites are conjugates of glucuronic acid which are excreted primarily in the urine. Less than 1% of an administered dose of chlorzoxazone and less than 4% of an administered dose of acetaminophen is excreted unchanged in the urine in 24 hours. Only traces of unchanged drug are excreted through the bile into the feces.

Indications: As an adjunct to rest, physical therapy and other measures for the relief of discomfort associated with acute musculoskeletal conditions. Such conditions may include skeletal muscle spasm and pain associated with sprains, strains and other traumatic muscle injuries; myalgias; arthritides; low back pain; tension headache; torticollis; fibrositis; spondylitis; and cervical root and disc syndromes.

Contraindications: Hypersensitivity to the components, hepatic impairment and acute porphyria.

Precautions: Use with caution in patients with known allergies or with a history of allergic reactions to drugs. If a sensitivity reaction occurs such as urticaria, redness, or itching of the skin, the drug should be stopped.

There have been reports of liver damage associated with the use of chlorzoxazone-containing products. If any symptoms suggestive of liver dysfunction are observed, the drug should be discontinued.

Parafon Forte should be used with caution in patients with severe impairment of renal function.

Drowsiness and dizziness can occur with the use of Parafon Forte.

Occupational Hazards: Patients using this drug should be cautioned about driving a car or operating potentially hazardous machinery if they become drowsy, dizzy or show impaired mental or physical abilities while taking this medication.

Drug Interactions: Patients receiving antipsychotics, antianxiety agents or other CNS depressants (including alcohol) concomitantly with this drug may exhibit an additive CNS depression. When such combined therapy is contemplated, the dose of one or both agents should be reduced.

Avoid consumption of alcohol while using this product.

Pregnancy: Should be used during pregnancy only if the potential benefit justifies the potential risk to the fetus.

Lactation: Chlorzoxazone and acetaminophen are not recommended during lactation because safety in nursing mothers has not been established. It is not known if chlorzoxazone is excreted in breast milk. Acetaminophen passes into breast milk but is not likely to have an adverse effect on the infant at therapeutic doses.

Children: Because safety and effectiveness of Parafon Forte have not been established in children such use is not recommended.

Adverse Effects: Regular use of acetaminophen has been shown to produce a slight increase in prothrombin time in patients receiving oral anticoagulants, but the clinical significance of this effect is not clear. As with other nonprescription analgesic drugs, physicians should supervise the use of acetaminophen in patients with alcoholism, serious kidney or serious liver disease. Patients are advised to consult a physician if symptoms do not improve or if new problems such as high fever, rash, or headache occur. A physician should be consulted if the illness lasts more than 5 days despite treatment.

Gastrointestinal: Occasional patients may develop gastrointestinal disturbances and abdominal pain. It is possible in rare instances that chlorzoxazone may have been associated with gastrointestinal bleeding.

CNS: Drowsiness, dizziness, lightheadedness, malaise, or overstimulation may be noted by an occasional patient.

Allergic: Rarely, allergic-type skin rashes, petechiae, or ecchymoses may develop during treatment. Angioneurotic edema or anaphylactic reactions are extremely rare.

Renal Toxicity: There is no evidence that Parafon Forte will cause renal damage. Rarely, a patient may note discoloration of the urine resulting from a phenolic metabolite of chlorzoxazone. This finding is of no known clinical significance.

Hepatotoxicity: Serious, including fatal, hepatocellular toxicity has been reported rarely in patients receiving chlorzoxazone. The mechanism is unknown but appears to be idiosyncratic and unpredictable. Factors predisposing patients to this rare event are not known. Patients should be instructed to report early signs and/or symptoms of hepatotoxicity such as fever, rash, anorexia, nausea, vomiting, fatigue, right upper quadrant pain, dark urine, or jaundice. Chlorzoxazone should be discontinued immediately and a physician consulted if any of these signs or symptoms develop. Chlorzoxazone use should also be discontinued if a patient develops abnormal liver enzymes (e.g., AST, ALT, alkaline phosphatase or bilirubin).

In a controlled multidose clinical trial with chlorzoxazone 500 mg, the following adverse events occurred in $\geq 1\%$ of patients receiving chlorzoxazone or occurred in $< 1\%$ of patients but resulted in patient withdrawal from the study and were considered possibly, probably or definitely related to chlorzoxazone.

Body as a Whole: asthenia (2%), body pain, edema.

CNS: anxiety, dizziness (6%), drowsiness (9%), headache (5%), nervousness, paresthesia, vertigo.

Gastrointestinal: abnormal pain, anorexia, diarrhea (2%), dyspepsia (1%), flatulence, melena, nausea (3%).

Skin: pruritus, rash, skin discoloration.

Urogenital: polyuria.

The following adverse reports occurred with a frequency of $< 1\%$ and the relationship to chlorzoxazone remains undetermined: chills, tachycardia, vasodilation, abnormal thinking, confusion, depression, emotional lability, hypotonia, insomnia, constipation, dry mouth, thirst, vomiting, cough increase, dyspnea, flu symptoms, rhinitis, sweating, increased urinary frequency, menorrhagia.

Overdose: Symptoms: Chlorzoxazone: Initially, gastrointestinal disturbances such as nausea, vomiting, or diarrhea together with drowsiness, dizziness, lightheadedness or headache may occur. Early in the course, there may be malaise or sluggishness followed by marked loss of muscle tone, making voluntary movement impossible. The deep tendon reflexes may be decreased or absent. The sensorium remains intact, and there is no peripheral loss of sensation. Respiratory depression may occur with rapid, irregular respiration and intercostal and substernal retraction. The blood pressure is lowered, but shock has not been observed.

Acetaminophen: In acute acetaminophen overdosage, dose-dependent, potentially fatal hepatic necrosis is the most serious effect. Renal tubular necrosis, hypoglycemia, coma, and thrombocytopenia may also occur. In adults, hepatotoxicity from acetaminophen is unlikely to occur with overdoses of less than 10 g ingested at one time and fatalities are unlikely to occur with overdoses of less than 15 g ingested at one time. Importantly, young children seem to be more resistant than adults to the hepatotoxic effect of an acetaminophen overdose. Despite this, the measures outlined below should be initiated in any adult or child suspected of having ingested an acetaminophen overdose.

Early symptoms following a potentially hepatotoxic overdose may include gastrointestinal irritability, nausea, vomiting, anorexia, diaphoresis and general malaise. However, the early clinical presentation of acetaminophen overdose is nonspecific and symptoms may even be lacking. A high index of suspicion for acetaminophen ingestion is required. Clinical and laboratory evidence of hepatic toxicity may not become evident until 48 to 72 hours post-ingestion.

Treatment: Chlorzoxazone: Appropriate gastrointestinal tract decontamination procedures should be undertaken. Thereafter treatment is entirely supportive. If consciousness is impaired, institute measures to protect the airway. If respiration is impaired, ventilation of the patient may be required. Blood pressure and tissue perfusion should be monitored and maintained by the usual techniques. Cholinergic drugs or analeptic drugs are of no value and should not be used.

Acetaminophen: Appropriate gastrointestinal tract decontamination procedures should be implemented. Patients' estimates of the quantity of drug ingested are notoriously unreliable. Therefore, if an acetaminophen overdose is suspected, a serum acetaminophen assay should be obtained as early as possible, but no sooner than 4 hours following ingestion. Liver function studies should be obtained initially and repeated at 24-hour intervals.

The antidote, N-acetylcysteine, should be administered as early as possible, preferably within 16 hours of ingestion of the overdosage, but in any case, within 24 hours. Following recovery, there are no residual, structural or functional hepatic abnormalities.

Further information on the clinical course of acetaminophen overdose and its treatment with N-acetylcysteine is available from a Regional Poison Control Centre.

Dosage: Adults: 2 tablets 4 times a day. It is hazardous to exceed 8 tablets/day.

Supplied: Each round, hard, flat-faced, beveled, light green tablet, scored on one side and hexabeveled and imprinted "McNEIL" on the other, contains: chlorzoxazone 250 mg and acetaminophen 300 mg. Nonmedicinal ingredients: cellulose, cornstarch, D&C Yellow No. 10, dioctyl sodium succinate, FD&C Blue No. 1 and magnesium stearate. Energy: 1.205 kJ (0.286 kcal). Sodium: <1 mmol (0.14 mg)/tablet. Gluten- and lactose-free. Consumer packs of 20. Bottles of 100.

Protect from light in a tightly closed container. Under normal storage conditions at room temperature, Parafon Forte tablets are stable for 2 years from date of manufacture.

PARAFON FORTE® C8 Ⓝ

Johnson & Johnson • Merck

Chlorzoxazone—Acetaminophen—Codeine Phosphate

Analgesic—Muscle Relaxant

Pharmacology: Parafon Forte C8 combines the muscle-relaxant effect of chlorzoxazone with acetaminophen, a well-known analgesic, and codeine, a centrally-acting narcotic analgesic.

Chlorzoxazone is a centrally acting agent for painful musculoskeletal conditions. Data available from animal experiments, as well as human study, indicate that chlorzoxazone acts primarily at the level of the spinal cord and subcortical areas of the brain where it inhibits multisynaptic reflex arcs involved in producing and maintaining skeletal muscle spasm of varied etiology. The clinical result is a reduction of the skeletal muscle spasm with relief of pain and increased mobility of the involved muscles. Blood levels of chlorzoxazone can be detected in humans during the first 30 minutes after oral administration of Parafon Forte C8 and peak levels may be reached in about 1 to 2 hours. Chlorzoxazone is rapidly metabolized and is excreted in the urine, primarily in a conjugated form as the glucuronide. Less than 1% of a dose of chlorzoxazone is excreted unchanged in the urine in 24 hours.

Acetaminophen provides analgesic action to supplement that which results secondarily from muscle relaxation. Acetaminophen is rapidly absorbed after oral administration, with peak plasma levels occurring in 1 to 2 hours. After 8 hours, only negligible amounts remain in the blood. Only 4% is excreted unchanged; 85% of the ingested dose is recovered in the urine in conjugated form as the glucuronide. Acetaminophen is distributed throughout most tissues of the body. Acetaminophen is metabolized primarily in the liver. Little unchanged drug is excreted in the urine, but most metabolic products appear in the urine within 24 hours.

Codeine supplements the analgesic action of acetaminophen and it retains at least one-half of its analgesic activity when administered orally. A reduced first-pass metabolism of codeine by the liver accounts for the greater oral potency of codeine when compared to most other morphine-like narcotics. Following absorption, codeine is metabolized by the liver and metabolic products are excreted in the urine. Approximately 10% of the administered codeine is demethylated to morphine, which may account for its analgesic activity.

The combination of acetaminophen and codeine provides a pain relieving action to supplement the relief which results secondarily from muscle relaxation. The mode of action of chlorzoxazone has not been clearly identified, but may be related to its sedative properties. Chlorzoxazone does not directly relax tense skeletal muscles in man.

Following oral administration of chlorzoxazone and acetaminophen in combination with codeine, all drugs are rapidly absorbed. Mean drug plasma concentrations reach a peak level in the majority of subjects in 45 to 90 minutes.

The plasma elimination half-life is about 1 hour for chlorzoxazone, ranges from 1.5 to 3.5 hours for acetaminophen and from 1.5 to 4 hours for codeine.

Metabolism is rapid; the principal metabolites are conjugates of glucuronic acid which are excreted primarily in the urine. Less than 1% of an administered dose of chlorzoxazone or codeine, and less than 4% of an administered dose of acetaminophen is excreted unchanged in the urine in 24 hours. Only traces of unchanged drug are excreted through the bile into the feces.

Indications: As an adjunct to rest, physical therapy and other measures for the relief of discomfort associated with acute, painful musculoskeletal conditions. Such conditions may include skeletal muscle spasm and pain associated with sprains, strains and other traumatic muscle injuries; myalgias;

Parafon Forte C8 (cont'd)

arthritides; low back pain; tension headache; torticollis, fibrositis; spondylitis; and cervical root and disc syndromes.

Contraindications: Hypersensitivity to acetaminophen, chlorzoxazone or codeine, hepatic impairment and acute porphyria.

Precautions: Use with caution in patients with known allergies or with a history of allergic reactions to drugs. If a sensitivity reaction occurs such as urticaria, redness, or itching of the skin, the drug should be stopped.

There have been reports of liver damage associated with the use of chlorzoxazone-containing products. If any signs or symptoms suggestive of liver dysfunction are observed, the drug should be stopped.

Head Injury and Increased Intracranial Pressure: The respiratory depressant effects of narcotics and their capacity to elevate cerebrospinal fluid pressure may be markedly exaggerated in the presence of head injury, other intracranial lesions or a pre-existing increase in intracranial pressure. Furthermore, narcotics produce adverse reactions which may obscure the clinical course of patients with head injuries.

Acute Abdominal Conditions: The administration of these drugs or other narcotics may obscure the diagnosis or clinical course of patients with acute abdominal conditions.

Special Risk Patients: These drugs should be given with caution to certain patients such as the elderly or debilitated, and those with severe impairment of hepatic or renal function, hypothyroidism, Addison's disease, and prostatic hypertrophy or urethral stricture.

Occupational Hazards: Drowsiness and dizziness can occur with the use of Parafon Forte C8. Codeine may impair the mental and/or physical abilities required for the performance of potentially hazardous tasks. Patients using this drug should be cautioned about driving a car or operating potentially hazardous machinery if they become drowsy, dizzy or show impaired mental or physical abilities while taking this medication.

The patient should understand the single-dose and 24-hour dose limits, and the time interval between doses. Like other narcotic-containing medications, this drug is subject to the Narcotic Control Act.

Drug Interactions: Patients receiving other narcotic analgesics, antipsychotics, antianxiety agents, or other CNS depressants (including alcohol) concomitantly with this drug may exhibit an additive CNS depression. When such combined therapy is contemplated, the dose of one or both agents should be reduced. Avoid consumption of alcohol while using this product.

The concurrent use of anticholinergics with codeine may produce paralytic ileus.

Pregnancy: Teratogenic Effects: Codeine. A study in rats and rabbits reported no teratogenic effect of codeine administered during the period of organogenesis in doses ranging from 5 to 120 mg/kg. In the rat, doses at the 120 mg/kg level, in the toxic range for the adult animal, were associated with an increase in embryo resorption at the time of implantation. In another study a single 100 mg/kg dose of codeine administered to pregnant mice reportedly resulted in delayed ossification in the offspring.

There are no studies in humans, and the significance of these findings to humans, if any, is not known.

Parafon Forte C8 should be used during pregnancy only if the potential benefit justifies the potential risk to the fetus.

Nonteratogenic Effects: Dependence and withdrawal signs have been reported in newborns whose mothers took opiates regularly during pregnancy. These signs include irritability, excessive crying, tremors, hyperreflexia, fever, vomiting, and diarrhea. Signs usually appear during the first few days of life.

Labor and Delivery: Narcotic analgesics cross the placental barrier. The closer to delivery and the larger the dose used, the greater the possibility of respiratory depression in the newborn. Narcotic analgesics should be avoided during labor if delivery of a premature infant is anticipated. If the mother has received narcotic analgesics during labor, newborn infants should be observed closely for signs of respiratory depression. Resuscitation may be required (see Overdose). The effects of codeine, if any, on the later growth, development, and functional maturation of the child is unknown.

Lactation: Chlorzoxazone and acetaminophen with codeine are not recommended during lactation because safety in nursing mothers has not been established. It is not known if chlorzoxazone is excreted in breast milk. Acetaminophen passes into breast milk but is not likely to have an adverse effect on the infant at therapeutic doses. Some studies, but not others, have reported detectable amounts of codeine in breast milk. The levels are probably not clinically significant after usual therapeutic dosage. The possibility of clinically important amounts being excreted in breast milk in individuals abusing codeine should be considered.

Children: These products contain codeine and should not be administered to children except on the advice of a physician. Because safety and effectiveness of Parafon Forte C8 have not been established in children such use is not recommended.

Drug Abuse and Dependence: Codeine can produce drug dependence of the morphine type and, therefore, has the potential for being abused. Psychic dependence, physical dependence and tolerance may develop upon repeated administration of Parafon Forte C8. This drug should be prescribed and administered with the same degree of caution appropriate to the use of other oral narcotic-containing medications.

Adverse Effects: Regular use of acetaminophen has been shown to produce a slight increase in prothrombin time in patients receiving oral anticoagulants, but the clinical significance of this effect is not clear. As with other nonprescription analgesic drugs, physicians should supervise the use of acetaminophen in patients with alcoholism, serious kidney or serious liver disease. Patients are advised to consult a physician if symptoms do not improve or if new problems such as high fever, rash, or headache occur. A physician should be consulted if the illness lasts more than 5 days despite treatment.

Gastrointestinal: Occasional patients may develop gastrointestinal disturbances and abdominal pain. It is possible in rare instances that chlorzoxazone may have been associated with gastrointestinal bleeding. Codeine has been known to cause constipation after long-term use.

CNS: Drowsiness, dizziness, lightheadedness, sedation, shortness of breath, nausea and vomiting, malaise, or overstimulation may be noted by an occasional patient. These effects seem to be more prominent in ambulatory than nonambulatory patients and some of these adverse effects may be alleviated if the patient lies down.

Allergic: Rarely, allergic-type skin rashes, petechiae, or ecchymoses may develop during treatment. Angioneurotic edema or anaphylactic reactions are extremely rare.

Renal Toxicity: There is no evidence that the drug will cause renal damage. Rarely, a patient may note discoloration of the urine resulting from a phenolic metabolite of chlorzoxazone. This finding is of no known clinical significance.

Hepatotoxicity: Serious, including fatal, hepatocellular toxicity has been reported rarely in patients receiving chlorzoxazone. The mechanism is unknown but appears to be idiosyncratic and unpredictable. Factors predisposing patients to this rare event are not known. Patients should be instructed to report early signs and/or symptoms of hepatotoxicity such as fever, rash, anorexia, nausea, vomiting, fatigue, right upper quadrant pain, dark urine, or jaundice. Chlorzoxazone should be discontinued immediately and a physician consulted if any of these signs or symptoms develop. Chlorzoxazone use should also be discontinued if a patient develops abnormal liver enzymes (e.g., AST, ALT, alkaline phosphatase or bilirubin).

In a controlled multidose clinical trial with chlorzoxazone 500 mg, the following adverse events occurred in $\geq 1\%$ of patients receiving chlorzoxazone or occurred in $< 1\%$ of patients but resulted in patient withdrawal from the study and were considered possibly, probably or definitely related to chlorzoxazone.

Body as a Whole: asthenia (2%), body pain, edema.

CNS: anxiety, dizziness (6%), drowsiness (9%), headache (5%), nervousness, paresthesia, vertigo.

Gastrointestinal: abnormal pain, anorexia, diarrhea (2%), dyspepsia (1%), flatulence, melena, nausea (3%).

Skin: pruritus, rash, skin discoloration.

Urogenital: polyuria.

The following adverse reports occurred with a frequency of $< 1\%$ and the relationship to chlorzoxazone remains undetermined: chills, tachycardia, vasodilation, abnormal thinking, confusion, depression, emotional lability, hypotonia, insomnia, constipation, dry mouth, thirst, vomiting, cough increase, dyspnea, flu symptoms, rhinitis, sweating, increased urinary frequency, menorrhagia.

At higher doses codeine has most of the disadvantages of morphine including respiratory depression.

Overdose: Symptoms: Chlorzoxazone: Initially, gastrointestinal disturbances such as nausea, vomiting, or diarrhea together with drowsiness, dizziness, lightheadedness or headache may occur. Early in the course there may be malaise or sluggishness followed by marked loss of muscle tone, making voluntary movement impossible. The deep tendon reflexes may be decreased or absent. The sensorium remains intact, and there is no peripheral loss of sensation. Respiratory depression may occur with rapid, irregular respiration and intercostal and substernal retraction. The blood pressure is lowered, but shock has not been observed.

Acetaminophen: In acute acetaminophen overdosage, dose-dependent, potentially fatal hepatic necrosis is the most serious effect. Renal tubular necrosis, hypoglycemia, coma, and thrombocytopenia may also occur. In adults, hepatotoxicity from acetaminophen is unlikely to occur with overdoses of less than 10 g ingested at one time and fatalities are unlikely to occur with overdoses of less than 15 g ingested at one time. Importantly, young children seem to be more resistant than adults to the hepatotoxic effect of an acetaminophen overdose. Despite this, the measures outlined below should be initiated in any adult or child suspected of having ingested an acetaminophen overdose.

Early symptoms following a potentially hepatotoxic overdose may include gastrointestinal irritability, nausea, vomiting, anorexia, diaphoresis and general malaise. However, the early clinical presentation of acetaminophen overdose is nonspecific and symptoms may even be lacking. A high index of suspicion for acetaminophen ingestion is required. Clinical and laboratory evidence of hepatic toxicity may not become evident until 48 to 72 hours post-ingestion.

Codeine: Serious overdose with codeine is characterized by respiratory depression (a decrease in respiratory rate and/or tidal volume, Cheyne-Stokes respiration, cyanosis), extreme somnolence progressing to stupor or coma, skeletal muscle flaccidity, cold and clammy skin, and sometimes bradycardia and hypotension. In severe overdosage, apnea, circulatory collapse and death may occur.

Treatment: Chlorzoxazone: Appropriate gastrointestinal tract decontamination procedures should be undertaken. Thereafter treatment is entirely supportive. If consciousness is impaired, institute measures to protect the airway. If respiration is impaired, ventilation of the patient may be required. Blood pressure and tissue perfusion should be monitored and maintained by the usual technique. Cholinergic drugs or analeptic drugs are of no value and should not be used.

Acetaminophen: Appropriate gastrointestinal tract decontamination procedures should be implemented. Patients' estimates of the quantity of drug ingested are notoriously unreliable. Therefore, if an acetaminophen overdose is suspected, a serum acetaminophen assay should be obtained as early as possible, but no sooner than 4 hours following ingestion. Liver function studies should be obtained initially and repeated at 24-hour intervals.

The antidote, N-acetylcysteine, should be administered as early as possible, preferably within 16 hours of ingestion of the overdosage, but in any case, within 24 hours. Following recovery, there are no residual, structural or functional hepatic abnormalities.

Further information on the clinical course of acetaminophen overdose and its treatment with N-acetylcysteine is available from a Regional Poison Control Centre.

Codeine: Primary attention should be given to the re-establishment of adequate respiratory exchange through provision of a patent airway and the institution of assisted or controlled ventilation. The narcotic antagonist naloxone is a specific antidote against respiratory depressions which may result from overdosage or unusual sensitivity to narcotics, including codeine. Therefore, an appropriate dose of naloxone should be administered, preferably by the i.v. route, and simultaneously with efforts at respiratory resuscitation. Since the duration of action of codeine may exceed that of the antagonist, the patient should be kept under continued surveillance and repeated doses of the antagonist should be administered as needed to maintain adequate respiration.

An antagonist should not be administered in the absence of clinically significant respiratory or cardiovascular depression. Oxygen, i.v. fluids, vasopressors and other supportive measures should be employed as indicated.

Dosage: The recommended adult dose is 1 to 2 tablets 4 times daily not to exceed 8 tablets in a 24-hour period.

Supplied: Each round, hard, uncoated, biconvex, pink and white speckled tablet imprinted "PARAFON FORTE C8" on one side and "M" on the reverse, contains: chlorzoxazone 250 mg, acetaminophen 300 mg and codeine phosphate 8 mg. Nonmedicinal ingredients: cornstarch, FD&C Red No. 2, magnesium stearate and sodium lauryl sulfate. Energy: 0.889 kJ (0.211 kcal). Gluten-, lactose- and tartrazine-free. Bottles of 20 and 100. Protect from light in a tightly closed container. Under normal storage conditions at room temperature, tablets are stable for 2 years from date of manufacture.

Reviewed 1997

PARALDEHYDE INJECTION BP ℞

Faulding

Sedative—Anticonvulsant

Supplied: Each mL of sterile solution for parenteral use contains: paraldehyde BP 100% and hydroquinone 100 µg. Ampuls of 5 mL, boxes of 5. Store below 25°C, protect from light. Avoid contact with plastic syringes, cork or rubber components, eyes, skin and clothing.

PARAPLATIN-AQ ℞

Bristol

Carboplatin

Antineoplastic

Pharmacology: Carboplatin has biochemical properties similar to that of cisplatin, thus producing predominantly interstrand DNA crosslinks. In patients with creatinine clearances of 60 mL/min or greater given carboplatin at doses of 300 to 500 mg/m², the plasma concentrations of carboplatin decay in a biphasic manner with mean alpha and beta half-lives of 1.6 h and 3 h, respectively. The total body clearance, apparent volume of distribution, and mean residence time for carboplatin are 73 mL/min, 16 L, and 3.5 h, respectively. The C_{max} value and area under the plasma concentration versus time curve from zero to infinity increase linearly with dose. Therefore, over the range of doses studied, carboplatin exhibits linear, dose-independent pharmacokinetics in patients with creatinine clearances ≥60 mL/min.

Repeated dosing during 4 consecutive days did not produce an accumulation of platinum in plasma. Following administration of carboplatin, reported values for the terminal elimination half-lives of free ultrafilterable platinum and carboplatin in man are approximately 6 hours and 1.5 hours respectively. During the initial phase, most of the free ultrafilterable platinum is present as carboplatin. The terminal half-life for total plasma platinum is 24 hours. Approximately 87% of plasma platinum is protein bound within 24 hours following administration and is slowly eliminated with a minimum half-life of 5 days.

The major route of elimination of carboplatin is renal excretion. Patients with creatinine clearances of about 60 mL/min or greater excrete 70% of the dose of carboplatin in the urine with most of this occurring within 12 to 16 hours. All of the platinum in 24 h urine is present as carboplatin, and only 3 to 5% of the dose is excreted between 24 and 96 hours. Total body and renal clearances of free ultrafilterable platinum correlate with the rate of glomerular filtration, but not tubular secretion.

In patients with creatinine clearances of less than 60 mL/min, carboplatin renal and total body clearances decrease with decreases in creatinine clearance. Doses of carboplatin, therefore, should be reduced in patients with creatinine clearance <60 mL/min (see Dosage).

Indications: For the treatment of advanced ovarian carcinoma of epithelial origin in: first line therapy or second line therapy, after other treatments have failed.

Contraindications: Preexisting severe renal impairment. Do not employ carboplatin in severely myelosuppressed patients and/or in patients with bleeding tumoral localizations. Patients with a history of severe allergic reactions to carboplatin, other platinum containing compounds, or mannitol.

Warnings: Carboplatin is a potent drug and should be used only by physicians experienced with cancer chemotherapeutic drugs. Blood counts as well as renal and hepatic function tests must be done regularly. Discontinue the drug if abnormal depression of bone marrow or abnormal renal or hepatic function is seen.

Myelosuppression is dose dependent and dose limiting and closely related to renal clearance of carboplatin. Patients with abnormal kidney function or receiving concomitant therapy with other drugs with nephrotoxic potential are likely to experience more severe and prolonged myelotoxicity. Myelosuppression may also be more severe and prolonged in patients with extensive prior treatment (in particular with cisplatin) poor performance status and above 65 years of age. Initial dosages in these groups should be appropriately reduced (see Dosage) and renal function parameters should be carefully assessed before and during therapy. Carboplatin courses should not be repeated more frequently than monthly under normal circumstances. Thrombocytopenia, leukopenia and anemia occur after administration of carboplatin. Frequent monitoring of peripheral blood counts is recommended throughout and following therapy (see Precautions). Administration of carboplatin in combination with other myelosuppressive compounds must be planned very carefully with respect to dosages and timing in order to minimize additive effects. Supportive transfusional therapy might be required in patients who suffer severe myelosuppression, particularly in patients receiving prolonged therapy, since anemia is cumulative.

Its carcinogenic potential has not been studied, but compounds with similar mechanisms of action and mutagenicity have been reported to be carcinogenic.

Pregnancy: Carboplatin can cause fetal harm when administered to a pregnant woman. Carboplatin has been shown to be embryotoxic and teratogenic in rats as well as mutagenic in several experimental systems. No controlled studies in pregnant women have been conducted. If this drug is used during pregnancy, or if the patient becomes pregnant while taking this drug, the patient should be apprised of the potential hazard to the fetus. Women with child-bearing potential should be advised to avoid becoming pregnant.

Although carboplatin has limited nephrotoxic potential, concomitant treatment with aminoglycosides has resulted in episodes of increased renal and audiologic toxicity.

As with other platinum compounds, allergic reactions to carboplatin have been reported. These may occur within minutes of administration and should be managed with appropriate supportive therapy.

Visual disturbances, including loss of vision, have been reported rarely after the use of carboplatin, in doses higher than those recommended in patients with renal impairment. Vision appears to recover totally or to a significant extent within weeks of stopping these high doses. Very high dosages of carboplatin (up to 5 times the single agent recommended dose or more) have resulted in severe abnormalities in hepatic and renal function.

Carboplatin can induce nausea and vomiting, which can be more severe in previously treated patients (in particular in patients previously pretreated with cisplatin).

Although peripheral neurologic toxicity is generally rare and mild, its incidence is increased in patients older than 65 years and/or in patients previously treated with cisplatin.

Precautions: Peripheral blood counts, renal and hepatic function tests should be monitored closely. Blood counts are recommended at the beginning of the therapy and weekly to assess hematologic nadir for subsequent dose adjustments. Leukopenia and thrombocytopenia are at their lowest levels between days 14 and 28 and 14 and 21, respectively, after initial therapy. Should the white blood cell count fall below 2 000 cells/mm³ or the platelet count fall below 50 000 cells/mm³, consideration should be given to discontinuation of carboplatin treatment until bone marrow recovery, which usually occurs in 5 to 6 weeks.

Renal toxicity is usually not dose-limiting in patients receiving carboplatin nor does it require preventive measures such as high-volume fluid hydration or forced diuresis. Nevertheless, increasing blood urea or serum creatinine levels can occur in about 6 to 14% of the patients. Renal function impairment, as defined by a decrease in the creatinine clearance below 60 mL/min, may be observed in about 27% of the patients. The incidence and severity of nephrotoxicity may increase in patients who have impaired kidney function before carboplatin treatment. It is not clear whether an appropriate hydration program might overcome such effect. Dosage reduction or discontinuation of therapy is required in the presence of severe alteration of renal function.

Neurotoxicity is usually limited to paresthesias and decreased deep tendon reflexes. The frequency and intensity of this side effect increase in patients previously treated with cisplatin. Thus neurologic evaluations should be performed on a regular basis.

After reconstitution, carboplatin is physically incompatible with any i.v. set, needle and syringe containing aluminum. An interaction will occur between aluminum and platinum from carboplatin causing a black precipitate which is visible in the solution (see Reconstituted Solutions).

Children: Safety and effectiveness in children have not been established.

Lactation: It is not known whether this drug is excreted in human milk. Because many drugs are excreted in human milk and because of the potential for serious adverse reactions in nursing infants from carboplatin, nursing should be discontinued.

Drug Interactions: The use of carboplatin with nephrotoxic compounds is not recommended.

Adverse Effects: The incidences of adverse reactions in Table I are derived from a cumulative database of 1 893 patients receiving single agent carboplatin including post marketing experience.

Table I—Paraplatin

Summary of Adverse Events in 1 893 Patients Receiving Paraplatin

	% Incidence
Bone Marrow in Patients with Normal Baseline Values	
Thrombocytopenia <50 000/mm³	25
Neutropenia <1 000/mm³	18
Leukopenia <2 000/mm³	14
Anemia <11 g/dL	71
Infections	4
Bleeding	5
Transfusions	26
Gastrointestinal	
Vomiting	64
Nausea	15
Pain	17
Diarrhea	6
Constipation	6
Neurologic	
Peripheral Neuropathy	4
CNS Symptoms	5
Clinical Ototoxicity and other sensory disturbances	1
Renal	
↓in Creatinine Clearance (Patients with baseline creatinine clearance, ≥60 mL/min)	27
↑in Serum Creatinine	6
↑in Blood Urea Nitrogen	14
↑in Uric Acid	5
Serum Electrolytes	
↓in Serum Sodium	29
↓in Serum Potassium	20
↓in Serum Calcium	22
↓in Serum Magnesium	29
Hepatic (Patients with normal baseline)	
↑in Alkaline Phosphatase	24
↑in AST	15
↑in Total Bilirubin	5
Hypersensitivity Reaction	
All	2
Other	
Asthenia	8
Alopecia	3

Hematologic: Myelosuppression is the dose-limiting toxicity of carboplatin. In patients with normal baseline values, thrombocytopenia with platelet counts below 50 000/mm³ occurs in 25% of patients, neutropenia with granulocyte counts below 1 000/mm³ in 18% of patients, and leukopenia with WBC counts below 2 000/mm³ in 14% of patients. The nadir usually occurs on day 21 (on day 15 in patients receiving carboplatin in combination). By day 28, recovery of platelet counts above 100 000/mm³ occurs in 90% of patients, recovery of neutrophils above 2 000/mm³ occurs in 74% and recovery of leukocytes above 4 000/mm³ occurs in 67% of patients.

Thrombocytopenia, neutropenia, and leukopenia are more severe in previously treated patients (in particular in patients previously treated with cisplatin) and in patients with impaired kidney function. Patients with poor performance status have also experienced increased leukopenia and thrombocytopenia. These effects, although usually reversible, have resulted in infectious and hemorrhagic complications in 4% and 5% of patients given Paraplatin or Paraplatin-AQ, respectively. These complications have led to death in less than 1% of patients.

Anemia with hemoglobin values below 11 g/dL has been observed in 71% of patients with normal baseline values. The incidence of anemia is increased with increasing exposure to carboplatin. Transfusional support has been administered to 26% of patients given carboplatin. Myelosuppression can be worsened by combination of carboplatin with other myelosuppressive compounds or other forms of treatment.

Gastrointestinal: Vomiting occurs in 64% of patients, and nausea in an additional 15%. About one-third of patients who vomit suffer severe emesis. Previously treated patients (in particular patients previously treated with cisplatin) appear to

Paraplatin (cont'd)

be more prone to vomiting. Nausea and/or vomiting usually disappear within 24 hours after treatment and are usually responsive to (and are prevented by) antiemetic medication. It appears that a prolonged administration time for carboplatin (by continuous infusion or in daily doses administered over 5 consecutive days) can induce less vomiting than the single dose schedule. Emesis is increased when carboplatin is given in combination with other emetogenic compounds. Other gastrointestinal side effects consist of pain, in 17% of patients; diarrhea, in 6% and constipation, in 6% of patients. The actual contribution of carboplatin to these observations is unclear.

Neurologic: Peripheral neuropathies have occurred in 4% of patients administered carboplatin and are evidenced mainly by paresthesias. Patients older than 65 years and patients previously treated with cisplatin, as well as those receiving prolonged treatment with carboplatin, appear to be at increased risk of developing peripheral neuropathies. In one-half of the patients who have pre-existing, cisplatin-induced peripheral neurotoxicity, there is no further worsening of symptoms during therapy with carboplatin. Subclinical decrease in hearing acuity, consisting of high-frequency (4 000–8 000 Hz) hearing loss as determined by audiogram, has been reported in 15% of patients. Clinical ototoxicity, manifested in the majority of cases by tinnitus, and other sensory disturbances (including visual disturbances and taste modifications) have affected only 1% of patients. In patients who have been previously treated with cisplatin and have developed hearing loss related to such treatment, the hearing impairment may persist or worsen. Central nervous symptoms have been reported in 5% of patients and appear frequently to be related to the use of antiemetics.

Although the overall incidence of neurologic side effects seems to be increased in patients receiving carboplatin in combination, this may be related to longer cumulative exposure.

Renal: When given in usual doses, development of abnormal renal function has been uncommon, despite the fact that carboplatin has been administered without high-volume fluid hydration and/or forced diuresis. Elevation of serum creatinine occurs in 6% of patients, elevation of blood urea nitrogen in 14%, and of uric acid in 5% of patients. These are usually mild and are reversible in about one-half of the patients. Creatinine clearance has proven to be the most sensitive parameter of kidney function in patients receiving carboplatin and is useful in correlating drug clearance with myelosuppression. Twenty-seven percent of patients who have a baseline value of 60 mL/min or greater, experience a reduction in creatinine clearance during carboplatin therapy.

Serum Electrolytes: Decreases in serum sodium, potassium, calcium and magnesium occur in 29%, 20%, 22% and 29% of patients respectively. Electrolyte supplementation was not routinely administered together with carboplatin. Combination chemotherapy has not increased the incidence of these electrolyte changes.

Several cases of early hyponatremia have been reported. While the contribution of carboplatin is not clear in light of other contributory factors (diuresis, respiratory dysfunction, malignancy, etc.) the possibility of hyponatremia should be considered especially for patients with other risk factors, such as concurrent diuretic therapy. Sodium replacement or free water restriction generally reversed the hyponatremia.

Hepatic: Modification of liver function in patients with normal baseline values is observed and includes elevation of total bilirubin in 5%, AST in 15% and alkaline phosphatase in 24% of patients. These modifications usually are mild and are reversible in about one-half of the patients. The role of tumor progression in the liver in these patients is unclear. In a limited series of patients receiving very high dosages of carboplatin and autologous bone marrow transplantation, severe elevation of liver function tests has occurred.

Allergy: Hypersensitivity to carboplatin has been reported in 2% of patients. These allergic reactions, comparable in characteristics and outcome to what has been reported in the case of other platinum-containing compounds (rash, urticaria, erythema, fever with no apparent cause, pruritus, rarely bronchospasm and hypotension). Anaphylactic-type reactions have occurred within minutes of administration. Hypersensitivity reactions have been successfully treated with standard epinephrine, corticosteroid and antihistamine therapy.

Other: Respiratory, cardiovascular, mucosal, genitourinary, cutaneous and musculoskeletal side effects have occurred in 5% or less of patients. Fever and chills without evidence of infection or allergic reaction has occurred in 2% of patients. Although death occurred because of cardiovascular events (cardiac failure, embolism, cerebrovascular accident) in less than 1% of patients, it is unclear whether this was related to chemotherapy rather than general patient conditions.

Among miscellaneous side effects, asthenia (8%) and alopecia (3%) were the most frequent. Their incidence is greatly increased in patients receiving carboplatin in combination. Hemolytic-uremic syndrome has been reported rarely.

Overdose: Symptoms and Treatment: No overdosage occurred during clinical trials, but should it occur, symptomatic measures should be taken to sustain the patient through any period of toxicity that might occur. The anticipated complications would be related to myelosuppression as well as impairment of renal and hepatic function. Use of higher than recommended doses of carboplatin has been associated with loss of vision (see Warnings).

Dosage: Needles or i.v. sets containing aluminum parts that may come in contact with carboplatin should not be used for preparation or administration. Aluminum reacts with carboplatin causing precipitate formation and/or loss of potency.

After reconstitution, use carboplatin by the i.v. route only. The recommended dosage in previously untreated adult patients with normal kidney function is 400 mg/m² as a single i.v. dose administered by a short-term (15 to 60 minutes) infusion. Do not repeat therapy until 4 weeks after the previous carboplatin course and/or until the neutrophil count is at least 2 000 cells/mm³ and the platelet count is at least 100 000 cells/mm³.

Reduction of the initial dosage by 20 to 25% is recommended for those patients who present with risk factors such as prior myelosuppressive treatment and low performance status (ECOG-Zubrod 2–4 or Karnofsky below 80). For patients aged 65 and over, dosage adjustment, initially or subsequently, may be necessary depending on the physical condition of the patient.

Determination of the hematologic nadir by weekly blood counts during the initial courses of treatment with carboplatin is recommended for dosage adjustments for subsequent courses of therapy.

Impaired Renal Function: The optimal use of carboplatin in patients presenting with impaired renal function requires adequate dosage adjustments and frequent monitoring of both hematologic nadirs and renal function.

Patients with creatinine clearance values below 60 mL/min are at increased risk of severe myelosuppression. The incidence of severe leukopenia, neutropenia, or thrombocytopenia has been maintained at about 25% with the following dosages: 250 mg/m² i.v. on day 1 in patients with baseline creatinine clearance values between 41 to 59 mL/min; 200 mg/m² i.v. on day 1 in patients with baseline creatinine clearance values between 16 to 40 mL/min.

Insufficient data exist on the use of carboplatin in patients with creatinine clearance of 15 mL/min or less to permit a recommendation for treatment.

All of the above dosing recommendations apply to the initial course of treatment. Subsequent dosages should be adjusted according to the patient's tolerance and to the desired myelosuppressive effect.

Combination Therapy: The optimal use of carboplatin in combination with other myelosuppressive agents requires dosage adjustments according to the regimen and schedule to be adopted.

Reconstituted Solution: Carboplatin may be further diluted with 5% Dextrose in water or 0.9% sodium chloride to concentrations as low as 0.5 mg/mL (500 μg/mL).

The reconstituted solution must be used i.v. only and should be administered by short-term (15 to 60 minutes) i.v. infusion.

Parenteral Products: I.V. needles, syringes or sets having aluminum components should not be employed in preparation or administration of carboplatin solution. An interaction will occur between aluminum and platinum from carboplatin causing a black precipitate which is visible in the reconstituted solution.

Stability and Storage of Solutions: When reconstituted or diluted as directed, carboplatin solution are stable for 8 hours at room temperature. Since no antibacterial preservatives are contained in the present formulation, it is recommended that any carboplatin solution remaining after 8 hours from reconstitution be discarded.

Handling and Disposal: Preparation of carboplatin should be done in a vertical laminar flow hood (Biological Safety Cabinet—Class II).

Personnel preparing carboplatin should wear PVC gloves, safety glasses, disposable gowns and masks.

All needles, syringes, vials and other materials which have come in contact with carboplatin should be segregated and incinerated at 1 000°C or more. Sealed containers may explode. Intact vials should be returned to the manufacturer for destruction. Proper precautions should be taken in packaging these materials for transport.

Personnel regularly involved in the preparation and handling of carboplatin should have bi-annual blood examinations.

Supplied: Each mL contains: carboplatin 10 mg. Nonmedicinal ingredients: water for injection. Clear glass vials of 5, 15 and 45 mL. Store between 15 and 25°C and protect from light.

PARLODEL® Ⓟ

Novartis Pharmaceuticals

Bromocriptine Mesylate

Prolactin Inhibitor—Growth Hormone Suppressant in Acromegaly—Adjunctive Medication in Parkinson's Disease

Pharmacology: Bromocriptine is a dopaminomimetic ergot derivative with D_2 type dopamine receptor agonist activity, which also has D_1 dopamine receptor antagonist properties.

Bromocriptine inhibits the release and synthesis of prolactin by acting directly on the prolactin secreting cells of the anterior pituitary. In patients with acromegaly, in addition to lowering prolactin and elevated levels of growth hormone, bromocriptine has a beneficial effect on clinical symptoms and on glucose tolerance.

The dopaminomimetic activity of bromocriptine in the nigrostriatal pathway is considered responsible for the clinical benefits seen in patients with Parkinson's disease.

The metabolism of dopamine, from exogenous and endogenous origin, is known to involve the formation of peroxides and free radicals. It has been postulated that these agents may in fact contribute to the progression of Parkinson's disease by accelerating the rate at which neuronal cells are lost. Bromocriptine's metabolic pathway does not involve the formation of such peroxides and free radicals. It has been suggested that because bromocriptine attenuates the timing and rate of levodopa dosage increase, early use of the drug may reduce risk of formation of potentially toxic peroxides and free radicals.

In man, bromocriptine is rapidly absorbed after oral administration with an absorption half-life of approximately 0.3 hours. The amount absorbed is about 65 to 95% of the oral dose. About 7% of the dose reaches the systemic circulation unchanged due to a high hepatic extraction rate and first pass metabolism. The plasma protein binding amounts to 96%. Bromocriptine is extensively metabolized by the liver. Only traces of the unchanged compound are found in urine, together with 2 major metabolites. Unchanged drug represents about 10 to 15% of peak levels of radioactivity in plasma measured after single dose of labelled drug. The active parent drug and the metabolites are primarily excreted via the liver, only 6% being eliminated via the kidney. In plasma, the elimination half-life was between 2 to 8 hours for the parent drug and 50 to 70 hours for the metabolites after single oral doses.

The extreme variability in gastrointestinal tract absorption and the extensive and individually variable first-pass metabolism are responsible for the broad variability in plasma concentrations of bromocriptine and, in part, for the variability in dose response.

Indications: Galactorrhea: with or without amenorrhea due to hyperprolactinemia.

Prolactin-dependent menstrual disorders and infertility: e.g., secondary amenorrhea, ovulatory insufficiency and short luteal phase.

Prolactin-secreting adenomas: As a treatment for inoperable macroadenomas or prior to surgery in order to facilitate removal, and as an alternative to surgery in patients with microadenomas.

Prolactin-dependent male hypogonadism.

Acromegaly: The first-line treatment of this condition is by surgery or radiotherapy. Bromocriptine may be a useful adjunct to such treatment, and can be used as monotherapy in special cases.

Parkinson's disease: Bromocriptine is effective when used as adjunct therapy to levodopa in the symptomatic management of Parkinson's disease. Used concomitantly with levodopa, bromocriptine facilitates the use of lower doses of levodopa in early disease and attenuates the rate of increase in the levodopa dosages on long-term usage. In this way the risk of long-term complications such as prominent dyskinesias and/or end-of-dose failure can be reduced.

Contraindications: Hypersensitivity to any of the components of bromocriptine, or other ergot alkaloids. Uncontrolled hypertension, hypertensive disorders of pregnancy (including eclampsia, pre-eclampsia or pregnancy-induced hypertension), hypertension post-partum and in the puerperium. Coronary artery disease and other severe cardiovascular conditions, symptoms and/or a history of serious psychic disorders. For procedure during pregnancy, see Pregnancy under Precautions.

Warnings: In women with nonpuerperal galactorrhea, reduction of prolactin levels may lead to resumption of normal menses. Following discontinuation of medication, galactorrhea returns in some patients and leads to suspicion of pituitary adenomas; a complete investigation at specialized units to identify these patients is advisable.

Treatment with bromocriptine may effectively lower prolactin levels in patients with pituitary tumors but does not obviate the necessity for radiotherapy or surgical intervention where appropriate.

Long-term treatment (6 to 36 months) with bromocriptine in doses ranging from 20 to 100 mg/day has been associated with pulmonary infiltrates, pleural and pulmonary fibrosis, pleural effusion and thickening of the pleura in a few patients. Patients with unexplained pleuropulmonary disorders should be examined thoroughly and discontinuation of bromocriptine should be contemplated. In those instances in which bromocriptine treatment was terminated, the changes slowly reverted toward normal.

In a few patients treated over years with bromocriptine at daily doses higher than 30 mg, retroperitoneal fibrosis has been reported. To ensure recognition of retroperitoneal fibrosis at an early reversible stage, it is recommended that its manifestations (e.g., back pain, edema of the lower limbs or impaired kidney function) should be watched in this category of patients. Bromocriptine medication should be withdrawn immediately if fibrotic changes in the retroperitoneum are diagnosed or suspected.

Particular attention should be paid to patients who have recently been treated or are on concomitant therapy with drugs that can alter blood pressure, e.g., vasoconstrictors such as sympathomimetics or ergot alkaloids including ergometrine or methylergometrine. Although there is no conclusive evidence of an interaction between bromocriptine and these drugs, their concomitant use in the puerperium is not recommended.

Precautions: Bromocriptine may cause hypotension, primarily postural; periodic monitoring of the blood pressure, particularly during the first days of therapy, is advisable.

Occupational Hazards: In some patients, **dizziness** (vertigo) may occur with bromocriptine; patients should therefore be cautioned against activities requiring rapid and precise responses such as driving an automobile or operating dangerous machinery until their response has been determined.

Care should be exercised when administering bromocriptine concomitantly with phenothiazines or with other medications known to lower blood pressure. Dosage should be adjusted accordingly.

In some patients the concomitant use of bromocriptine and alcohol has given rise to alcohol intolerance and the tolerability to bromocriptine may be reduced by alcohol.

In patients being treated with bromocriptine for galactorrhea, prolactin induced amenorrhea, menstrual disorders or acromegaly, infertility might be reversed by restoration of normal menses and ovulation. Women who do not wish to conceive should, therefore, use a reliable method of contraception. Since pregnancy may occur prior to initiation of menses it is recommended that a pregnancy test be conducted at least every 4 weeks during the amenorrheic period, and, once menses are reinitiated, every time a patient misses a menstrual period.

A few cases of gastrointestinal bleeding and gastric ulcer have been reported. If this occurs, bromocriptine should be withdrawn. Patients with a history or evidence of peptic ulceration should be closely monitored when receiving the treatment.

In rare cases, serious adverse events including hypertension, myocardial infarction, seizures and strokes, or psychic disorders have been reported in postpartum women treated with bromocriptine for the inhibition of lactation. In some patients the development of seizures or strokes was preceded by severe headache and/or visual disturbances. Causal relationship of these events to the drug is uncertain.

The use of bromocriptine in the routine inhibition of physiological lactation is not recommended. When the drug is used for the treatment of other conditions, periodic monitoring of blood pressure is advisable. If hypertension, severe, progressive, or unremitting headache (with or without visual disturbances) or evidence of CNS toxicity develop, the administration of bromocriptine should be discontinued and the patient should be evaluated promptly.

Safety and efficacy of bromocriptine have not been established in patients with severe renal or hepatic disease.

Bromocriptine therapy has been demonstrated to be effective in the short-term management of amenorrhea/galactorrhea. Data are not available on the safety or effectiveness of its use in long-term continuous dosage in this indication or in patients given repeated courses of treatment following recurrence of amenorrhea/galactorrhea after initial treatment. Recurrence rates are reportedly very high, ranging from 70 to 80%.

Bromocriptine should always be taken with food. In cases where adverse effects, such as nausea, vomiting and vertigo are severe or persistent, the therapeutic dosage of bromocriptine should be reduced to half of 1 tablet daily (1.25 mg) and increased gradually to that recommended. The dopamine antagonist domperidone may be useful in the control of severe gastrointestinal side effects in Parkinsonian patients receiving bromocriptine (see Drug Interactions).

As with all medication, bromocriptine should be kept safely out of the reach of children.

Prolactin Secreting Adenoma Patients: Since patients with macro-adenomas of the pituitary might have accompanying hypopituitarism due to compression or destruction of pituitary tissue, one should make a complete evaluation of pituitary functions and institute appropriate substitution therapy prior to administration of bromocriptine. In patients with secondary adrenal insufficiency, substitution with corticosteroids is essential. The evolution of tumor size in patients with pituitary macro-adenomas should be carefully monitored and, if evidence of tumor expansion develops, surgical procedures must be considered.

If, in adenoma patients, pregnancy occurs after the administration of bromocriptine, careful observation is mandatory. Prolactin-secreting adenomas may expand during pregnancy. In these patients, treatment with bromocriptine often results in tumor shrinkage and rapid improvement of the visual field defects. In severe cases, compression of the optic or other cranial nerves may necessitate emergency pituitary surgery.

Pregnancy: In patients receiving bromocriptine, immunological confirmation of suspected conception should be performed as soon as possible and bromocriptine treatment stopped unless, in the opinion of the treating physician, the possible benefit to the patient outweighs the potential risk to the fetus. In any event, the patient must be monitored closely throughout pregnancy for signs and symptoms which may develop if a previously undetected prolactin-secreting tumor enlarges.

In human studies with bromocriptine, there were 1 410 reported pregnancies, which yielded 1 236 live and 5 stillborn infants from women who took bromocriptine during early pregnancy. Among the 1 241 infants, 43 cases (31 minor and 12 major) of congenital anomalies were reported. The incidence (3.46%) and type of congenital malformations and the incidence of spontaneous abortions (11.13%) in this group of pregnancies do not exceed that generally reported for such occurrences in the population at large.

Patients with pronounced enlargement of the sella turcica or a visual field defect should, in the first instance, be treated by surgery and/or radiotherapy. If pregnancy occurs in the presence of a pituitary microadenoma, close supervision throughout pregnancy is essential. This includes regular checking of the visual fields.

Lactation: Since bromocriptine inhibits lactation, it should not be administered to mothers who elect to breast-feed.

Parkinson's Disease: Use of bromocriptine, particularly in high doses, may be associated with mental confusion and mental disturbances. Since patients with Parkinson's disease may manifest varying degrees of dementia, caution should be exercised when treating such patients with bromocriptine.

Bromocriptine administered alone or concomitantly with levodopa may cause visual or auditory hallucinations. These usually resolve with dosage reduction but discontinuation of bromocriptine may be required in some cases. Rarely, after high doses, hallucinations have persisted for several weeks following discontinuation of bromocriptine. Caution should be exercised when administering bromocriptine to patients with a history of myocardial infarction, particularly if they have a residual atrial, nodal or ventricular arrhythmia.

Symptomatic hypotension can occur and, therefore, caution should be exercised when administering bromocriptine, particularly in patients receiving antihypertensive medication. Periodic evaluation of hepatic, hematopoietic, cardiovascular and renal function is recommended.

Drug Interactions: The concomitant use of erythromycin, josamycin, other macrolide antibiotics or octreotide may increase bromocriptine plasma levels.

Domperidone, a peripheral dopamine antagonist, may cause increases in serum prolactin. In so doing, domperidone may antagonize the therapeutically relevant prolactin-lowering effect of bromocriptine. It is possible that the anti-tumorigenic effect of bromocriptine in patients with prolactinomas may be partially blocked by domperidone administration.

Adverse Effects: The most frequently observed adverse reactions are nausea, vomiting, headache and gastrointestinal side effects such as abdominal pain, diarrhea and constipation. All these effects may be minimized or even prevented by giving small initial doses of bromocriptine and by taking it with food.

Postural hypotension can, on rare occasions, lead to fainting, and "shock-like" syndromes have been reported in sensitive patients. This is most likely to occur during the first few days of bromocriptine treatment.

In clinical studies to date, the following adverse events were noted: In postpartum women treated with bromocriptine, some rare serious adverse events (about 1 in 100 000) have been reported. These include hypertension, visual disturbances, myocardial infarction, seizures and strokes, or psychic disorders. In some patients the occurrence of seizures or strokes was preceded by severe headache and/or visual disturbances. Causal relationship of these events to the drug is uncertain.

Amenorrhea/Galactorrhea/Female Infertility/Acromegaly: The incidence of side effects in these indications is 68%, and are generally mild to moderate in degree. Therapy was discontinued in approximately 6% of patients because of adverse effects. In decreasing order of frequency these are: nausea 51%, headache 18%, dizziness 16%, fatigue 8%, abdominal cramps 7%, lightheadedness 6%, vomiting 5%, nasal congestion 5%, constipation 3% and diarrhea 3%.

Parkinson's Disease: When bromocriptine is added to levodopa therapy, the incidence of adverse reactions may increase. The most common newly appearing adverse reactions in combination therapy with levodopa are: nausea, abnormal involuntary movements, hallucinations, confusion, "on-off" phenomenon, dizziness, drowsiness, faintness, fainting, vomiting, asthenia, abdominal discomfort, visual disturbance, ataxia, insomnia, depression, hypotension, shortness of breath, constipation and vertigo.

General: Less common adverse reactions include: anorexia, anxiety, blepharospasm, dry mouth, dysphagia, edema of the feet and ankles, erythromelalgia, epileptiform seizures, fatigue, headache, lethargia, mottling of skin, nasal congestion, nervousness, nightmares, paresthesia, skin rash, hair loss, changes in urinary frequency, urinary incontinence and urinary retention. Usually, these side effects are dose dependent and can be controlled by a reduction in dosage. Rarely signs or symptoms of ergotism such as tingling of fingers, cold feet, numbness, muscle cramps of feet and legs or exacerbation of Raynaud's syndrome may occur.

Abnormalities in laboratory tests may include elevation of blood urea nitrogen, AST, ALT, GGPT, CPK, alkaline phosphatase and uric acid, which are usually transient and not of clinical significance.

The occurrence of adverse reactions may be lessened by temporarily reducing dosage to 1.25 mg 2 or 3 times daily.

Overdose: Symptoms: There have been several reports of acute overdosage with bromocriptine in children and adults. All patients who have taken an overdosage of bromocriptine alone have survived; the maximum single dose so far ingested is 325 mg. Symptoms reported could have resulted from overstimulation of dopaminergic receptors; they included nausea, vomiting, dizziness, drowsiness, hypotension and hallucinations.

Treatment: The management of acute intoxication is largely symptomatic. The cardiovascular system should be monitored. Metoclopramide can be used to antagonize the emesis and hallucinations in patients who have taken high doses.

Dosage: Bromocriptine should always be taken with food. In order to establish tolerance, the first dose of 1.25 to 2.5 mg (½ to 1 tablet), depending on the indication, should be given at bedtime with food. Please consult the detailed dosage recommendations for each indication.

Galactorrhea with or without amenorrhea due to hyperprolactinemia: 1.25 to 2.5 mg (½ to 1 tablet) at bedtime with food to establish tolerance; gradually increase after 2 to 3 days to 2.5 mg twice daily with meals. If required the dose may be increased to 2.5 mg 3 times daily. Continue treatment until

Parlodel (cont'd)

milk secretion has ceased completely or, in the case of menstrual dysfunction, until the menstrual cycle has returned to normal.

Prolactin-dependent menstrual disorders and infertility: 1.25 to 2.5 mg (½ to 1 tablet) at bedtime with food to establish tolerance. Gradually increase after 2 to 3 days to 1 tablet twice daily with meals. If required, the dose may be increased to 2.5 mg 3 times daily.

Prolactin-secreting adenomas: 1.25 mg (½ tablet) 2 or 3 times daily, increasing gradually (average maintenance dose: 5 to 7.5 mg daily). If necessary to keep plasma prolactin adequately suppressed, dosage may be increased gradually over a period of several weeks to 10 to 20 mg daily (4 to 8 tablets or 2 to 4 capsules) with meals.

Hyperprolactinemia in men: 1.25 to 2.5 mg (½ to 1 tablet) at bedtime to establish tolerance. Gradually increase after 2 to 3 days to 2.5 mg twice daily with meals or more, as required, to 2.5 mg 3 times/day with meals.

Acromegaly: 1.25 to 2.5 mg (½ to 1 tablet) at bedtime with food to establish tolerance, increasing gradually over a period of 2 to 4 weeks to 10 to 20 mg (4 to 8 tablets or 2 to 4 capsules) daily with meals, depending on clinical response. Daily requirements of 20 mg should be taken in 4 equally divided doses.

For convenience and after titration, some patients may use the 5 mg capsules for maintenance therapy.

The maximum recommended daily dose is 20 mg [8 (2.5 mg) tablets or 4 (5 mg) capsules]. In the event of serious or persistent adverse effects, the dosage should be reduced to 1.25 mg (½ tablet) and increased again gradually to the recommended dose. If reactions such as nausea, vomiting, vertigo or headaches continue to be severe, bromocriptine should be discontinued.

Parkinson's Disease: Bromocriptine should be added to levodopa therapy. It is desirable to combine a slow increase of bromocriptine with a concomitant, limited and gradual reduction of levodopa.

Bromocriptine dosage should be individualized. The initial dose is 1.25 mg (½ tablet) at bedtime to establish tolerance. Thereafter, the recommended dosage is 2.5 mg daily in 2 divided doses, with meals. The dosage may be increased, if necessary, by adding an additional 2.5 mg/day, once every 2 to 4 weeks, taken in 2 or 3 divided doses with meals.

The maximum recommended daily dosage is 40 mg. Clinical assessments are recommended during dosage titration to ensure that the lowest effective dose is employed. Where dose levels permit, use of the 5 mg capsule may be found more convenient by many patients.

Supplied: Tablets: Each easy-to-break white, oval-shaped tablet with parting facilitated score line, upper is sloped face and embossed with double heads, bisect, double heads, with lower flat and embossed "PARLODEL", contains: bromocriptine mesylate 2.87 mg corresponding to bromocriptine base 2.5 mg. Nonmedicinal ingredients: cornstarch, edetate disodium, lactose and maleic acid. Bottles of 100.

Capsules: Each caramel and white, size 3, hard shell capsule, spin printed in black "PARLODEL 5 mg" on the cap with 2 heads, one inside the other, on the body, contains: bromocriptine mesylate 5.74 mg corresponding to bromocriptine base 5 mg. Nonmedicinal ingredients: colloidal silicon dioxide, cornstarch, lactose, magnesium stearate and maleic acid. Bottles of 100.

Protect from light and store between 15 and 25°C.

(Shown in Product Recognition Section)

Reviewed 1998

PARNATE® ℞

SmithKline Beecham

Tranylcypromine Sulfate

Antidepressant

Pharmacology: Tranylcypromine is a nonhydrazine (MAO) inhibitor with a rapid onset of activity. It increases the concentration of epinephrine, norepinephrine and serotonin in storage sites in the nervous system. In theory, the increased concentration of monoamines in the brainstem is the basis for its antidepressant activity.

Tranylcypromine differs from other MAO inhibitors in being a reversible inhibitor. When tranylcypromine is withdrawn, monoamine oxidase activity is generally restored within a week, although the drug is excreted in 24 hours.

Indications: Tranylcypromine has been used successfully to treat psychotic depressive states such as: depressive phase of manic-depressive psychosis, involutional melancholia, reactive depression, psychoneurotic depression of moderate to severe intensity.

In the psychiatric treatment of severe endogenous depression, it is impossible to predict, with presently known data, which patients will respond best to tranylcypromine and which to electroconvulsive therapy (ECT). The drug may be indicated in some reactive depressions in which ECT is not indicated.

Tranylcypromine is not recommended for use in mild depressive states resulting from temporary situational difficulties.

Note: Because tranylcypromine is a potent agent with the capability of producing serious side effects (e.g., hypertensive crises, sometimes complicated by fatal intracranial bleeding), its use should be reserved for patients who can be closely supervised.

Before prescribing tranylcypromine, the physician should be thoroughly familiar with information on its dosage, side effects and contraindications, as well as the principles of MAO inhibitor therapy and the side effects of this class of drugs as reported in the literature. The physician should also be familiar with the symptomatology of mental depression and alternate methods of treatment to aid in the careful selection of patients for tranylcypromine therapy.

Selecting the Patient: Tranylcypromine should be used for the symptomatic treatment of moderate to severe depression. It is not recommended for those mild depressive reactions where more conservative therapy is indicated.

Tranylcypromine should be reserved for those patients who can be followed closely. Blood pressure should be recorded periodically to detect evidence of pressor response to tranylcypromine therapy.

Tranylcypromine should not be used in patients with cerebrovascular or cardiovascular disorders (e.g., arteriosclerosis, hypertension) (see Contraindications).

Tranylcypromine should not be used in patients receiving any other antidepressant medication (see Contraindications).

Tranylcypromine is not recommended for patients with a history of recurring or frequent headaches, especially the tension and vascular types.

Tranylcypromine should not be used alone in patients with marked psychomotor agitation, since it is recognized that antidepressant drugs can aggravate some coexisting symptoms such as agitation or anxiety.

Tranylcypromine Combined With Trifluoperazine: Tranylcypromine has been combined with trifluoperazine in the treatment of coexisting anxiety and depression. Such combined therapy has been found particularly valuable when used to treat depressed patients in whom a persistent disorder of mood is associated with anxiety, moderate agitation, inappropriate mental symptoms (such as unnatural fears or suspicions and phobias) or improper response to single-agent therapy.

Combined tranylcypromine-trifluoperazine therapy has been used successfully in the treatment of psychiatric conditions such as psychoneurotic depression, agitated depression, schizo-affective disorders and pseudoneurotic schizophrenia. If the patient appears to have a pure depression, tranylcypromine should be used alone and, similarly, if the symptoms appear to indicate a pure anxiety state, trifluoperazine should be used first. The combined therapy has frequently displayed striking effectiveness in patients who obtained little benefit from treatment with a succession of single drugs.

For comprehensive prescribing information on trifluoperazine, refer to Prescribing Information on that product.

Contraindications: In patients with cerebrovascular or cardiovascular disorders or a history of recurrent or frequent headaches. As tranylcypromine may cause blood pressure changes, administer with great care to patients with confirmed or suspected cerebrovascular defect, hypertension or cardiac disease. Regulate physical activity in the latter, as tranylcypromine may suppress anginal pain.

The drug should be used with caution in individuals beyond the age of 60 because of the possibility of existing cerebral sclerosis with damaged vessels.

In patients with liver damage or blood dyscrasias. Extensive clinical use and laboratory tests have revealed no evidence of liver toxicity or blood dyscrasias due to tranylcypromine therapy. Because rare cases of hepatitis have been reported, it is recommended that patients with known liver damage or blood dyscrasias should not be treated with tranylcypromine.

In pheochromocytoma. Tranylcypromine should not be used in the presence of known or suspected pheochromocytoma, as such tumors secrete pressor substances.

In combination with certain drugs. Because the effect of many antidepressant drugs may persist for 10 to 20 days, do not commence tranylcypromine therapy within a week of discontinuing treatment with such drugs; then use half the normal dosage for the first week. Similarly, allow 1 week to elapse between the discontinuance of tranylcypromine and the administration of any other drug that is contraindicated with tranylcypromine such as: Other MAO Inhibitors: Other MAO inhibitors such as isocarboxazid and phenelzine sulfate. Dibenzazepine Derivatives: Dibenzazepine derivatives such as amitriptyline, nortriptyline, protriptyline, desipramine, imipramine, doxepin, perphenazine, carbamazepine, cyclobenzaprine, amoxapine, maprotiline and trimipramine, as combination with these drugs may induce hypertensive crises or severe convulsive seizures. Sympathomimetics: Sympathomimetics including amphetamines, ephedrine and over-the-counter preparations for colds, hay fever and weight reduction that contain vasoconstrictors (e.g., phenylephrine, phenylpropanolamine) as well as with methyldopa, dopamine, levodopa and tryptophan, as such combinations may precipitate hypertension, severe headache, hyperpyrexia and rarely even cerebral (subarachnoid) hemorrhage. The combination of MAOI's and tryptophan has been reported to cause behavioral and neurologic syndromes including disorientation, confusion, amnesia, delirium, agitation, hypomanic signs, ataxia, myoclonus, hyperreflexia, shivering, ocular oscillations and Babinski signs. In Combination With Fluoxetine: Although a causal relationship has not been established, death has been reported to occur following the initiation of MAOI inhibitor therapy shortly after discontinuation of fluoxetine. Therefore, tranylcypromine should not be used in combination with fluoxetine. Allow at least 5 weeks between discontinuation of fluoxetine and initiation of tranylcypromine. Other Drugs: dextromethorphan, buspirone HCl.

In combination with cheese or other foods with a high tyramine content. Hypertensive crises have sometimes occurred during tranylcypromine therapy after ingestion of foods with a high tyramine content. Tyramine is normally metabolized by monoamine oxidase in the intestinal and hepatic cells. When monoamine oxidase is inhibited, tyramine absorbed from the gastrointestinal tract passes freely into the circulation. It releases norepinephrine from adrenergic neurones causing exaggerated hypertensive and other effects.

In general, the patient should avoid protein foods in which aging or protein breakdown is used to increase flavor. In particular, patients should be instructed not to take foods such as cheese (exceptions: cream cheese and cottage cheese), sour cream, pickled herring, liver, meat prepared with tenderizers, Bovril, yeast extracts like Marmite, soy sauce, pods of broad beans (fava beans), canned figs, raisins, bananas (peel) or avocados (especially if overripe), chocolate and caviar.

Alcoholic beverages have been known to precipitate a severe reaction. Therefore, the patient should avoid alcoholic drinks, especially red wines (such as chianti), sherry, beer (including nonalcoholic beer), etc.

Patients on tranylcypromine therapy should also be advised not to consume excessive amounts of caffeine in any form (coffee, tea, cola drinks, etc.) because of possible enhanced effects of caffeine on the CNS.

Warnings: Hypertensive Crisis: The most important adverse reaction associated with tranylcypromine is hypertensive crisis which has sometimes been fatal. This response is not usually dose-related. It is associated with a distinctive reaction characterized by some or all of the following symptoms: occipital headache which may radiate frontally, palpitation, neck stiffness or soreness, nausea or vomiting, sweating (sometimes with fever and sometimes with cold, clammy skin) and photophobia. Either tachycardia or bradycardia may be present, sometimes associated with constricting chest pain. Pupillary dilation may occur.

The occipital headache, together with pain and stiffness in the cervical muscles, may mimic subarachnoid hemorrhage, but can equally be associated with actual intracranial bleeding, as in other conditions where a sudden rise in blood pressure occurs. Cases of such bleeding have been reported, some of which have been fatal.

Blood pressure should be followed closely in patients taking tranylcypromine to detect evidence of any pressor response. It is emphasized that full reliance should not be placed on blood pressure readings, but that the patient should also be observed frequently.

Therapy should be discontinued immediately upon the occurrence of palpitation or frequent headache during tranylcypromine therapy. These signs may be prodromal of a hypertensive reaction. Patients should be instructed to report promptly the occurrence of headache or other symptoms.

If a hypertensive reaction occurs, tranylcypromine should be discontinued and therapy to lower blood pressure should be given immediate consideration. Headache tends to abate as blood pressure decreases. On the basis of present evidence, phentolamine is recommended for use in acute cases (the dosage reported for phentolamine is 5 mg i.v. administered slowly). Do not use parenteral reserpine or rauwolfia alkaloids for the treatment of a hypertensive crisis as they may, by releasing catecholamines, exacerbate the condition. For milder reactions, the more moderate adrenolytic action of injectable chlorpromazine may be more appropriate.

Care should be taken to administer these drugs in such a way as to avoid producing an excessive hypotensive effect. Fever should be managed by means of external cooling. Other symptomatic and supportive measures may be desirable in particular cases. Acute distress generally subsides in 24 hours or less.

Hypotension: Hypotension, which may be postural, has been observed during tranylcypromine therapy, particularly at doses above 30 mg daily. It is seen most commonly (but not exclusively) in patients with pre-existing hypertension. In most instances, it affects the systolic readings. Rare instances of syncope have been seen. Dosage increases should be made more gradually in patients showing a tendency toward hypotension at the starting dose. Postural hypotension can usually be relieved by having the patient lie down until blood pressure returns to normal.

This side effect is usually temporary, but if it persists, the drug should be discontinued. Blood pressure usually returns rapidly to pretreatment levels upon discontinuation of the drug.

Also, when tranylcypromine is combined with those phenothiazine derivatives or other compounds known to cause hypotension, the possibility of additive hypotensive effects should be considered.

Precautions: *Drug Interactions* (see also Contraindications): In general, the physician should bear in mind the possibility of a lowered margin of safety when tranylcypromine is administered in combination with potent drugs and should adjust dosage carefully.

A marked potentiating effect has been reported on some CNS depressants such as morphine, meperidine, barbiturates and alcohol. For this reason, narcotics and barbiturates should be used conservatively with tranylcypromine, and patients should be warned that the drug may potentiate the effects of alcoholic beverages.

Caution should be exercised when giving tranylcypromine with hypotensive agents: guanethidine, as its action may be antagonized; reserpine, as hyperactivity may occur; alphamethyldopa, since the combination may give rise to central excitation.

When tranylcypromine is combined with those phenothiazine derivatives or other compounds known to affect blood pressure, patients should be observed more closely because of the possibility of additive hypotensive effects.

Caution should also be exercised when giving tranylcypromine with antiparkinson agents as the combination may result in potentiation, with profuse sweating, tremulousness and rise in body temperature.

Drugs which lower the seizure threshold, including MAO inhibitors, should not be used with Amipaque. As with other MAO inhibitors, tranylcypromine should be discontinued at least 48 hours before myelography and should not be resumed for at least 24 hours after the procedure.

Caution should be exercised when giving tranylcypromine with clomipramine HCl, as this drug, in combination with a MAO inhibitor, has been reported to result in hyperpyrexia, diffuse intravascular coagulation and status epilepticus.

Tranylcypromine should be administered with caution to patients receiving disulfiram. In a single study, rats given high intraperitoneal doses of d-or l-isomers of tranylcypromine plus disulfiram experienced severe toxicity including convulsions and death. Additional studies in rats given high oral doses of racemic tranylcypromine and disulfiram produced no adverse interaction.

Angina: MAO inhibitors may have the capacity to suppress anginal pain that would otherwise serve as a warning of myocardial ischemia.

Depression: Tranylcypromine may aggravate coexisting symptoms in depression, such as anxiety and agitation. In depressed patients, the possibility of suicide should always be considered and adequate precautions taken. Exclusive reliance on drug therapy to prevent suicidal attempts is unwarranted, as there may be a delay in the onset of therapeutic effect or an increase in anxiety and agitation. Also, some patients fail to respond to drug therapy or may respond only temporarily.

Diabetes: Some MAO inhibitors have contributed to hypoglycemic episodes in diabetic patients receiving insulin or oral hypoglycemic agents. Therefore, tranylcypromine should be used with caution in diabetics under treatment with these drugs.

Epilepsy: Because the influence of tranylcypromine on the convulsive threshold is variable in animal experiments, suitable precautions should be taken if epileptic patients are treated.

Hyperthyroidism: Use tranylcypromine with caution in hyperthyroid patients because of their increased sensitivity to pressor amines.

Renal Dysfunction: The usual precautions should be observed in patients with impaired renal function, since there is a possibility of cumulative effects in such patients.

Pregnancy and *Lactation:* Tranylcypromine has been shown to pass through the placental barrier to the fetus of the rat and into the milk of the lactating dog. However, animal reproduction studies and clinical experience in pregnancy to date have not exhibited any teratogenic affect. Nevertheless, as with any potent drug, the physician must assess the definite medical need when prescribing for the pregnant patient, particularly during the first trimester.

Surgery: It is suggested that the drug be discontinued at least 7 days before elective surgery to allow time for recovery of monoamine oxidase activity before anesthetic agents are given.

Drug Dependency: There have been reports of drug dependency in patients using doses of tranylcypromine significantly in excess of the therapeutic range. Some of these patients had a history of previous substance abuse. The following withdrawal symptoms have been reported: restlessness, anxiety, depression, confusion, hallucinations, headache, weakness, diarrhea.

Instructions to the Patient: Patients should be warned against self-medication with proprietary (over-the-counter) drugs such as cold, hay fever or reducing preparations that contain sympathomimetic amines such as phenylpropanolamine and phenylephrine.

Patients should be instructed not to eat cheese, particularly the aged varieties, or those foods listed under Contraindications, nor to drink wines which are high in tyramine content, such as chianti. They should also be advised not to consume excessive amounts of caffeine in any form.

Patients should be warned that tranylcypromine may potentiate the effects of alcoholic beverages.

Patients should be instructed to report the occurrence of headache or other unusual symptoms.

Patients should be encouraged to carry a card or other notification of the fact that they are receiving a MAO inhibitor, so that this fact may be readily ascertained in case of accident, travel or transfer to the care of another physician.

Patients should be instructed to adhere to the above instructions for at least 1 week following discontinuation of tranylcypromine therapy.

Adverse Effects: The most frequently seen side effect is insomnia, which can usually be overcome by giving the last dose of the day not later than 3 p.m., by reducing the dose, or by prescribing a mild hypnotic.

Some of the following unwanted reactions have been reported in the literature; others are possible. They are classified according to their seriousness and probable cause—an arrangement intended to help the physician view them in proper perspective.

Pharmacologic Reactions of a Serious Nature: Hypertensive Crisis: see Warnings.

Hypotension: see Warnings.

Overstimulation: see Warnings. Overstimulation, which may include increased anxiety, agitation and manic symptoms, is usually evidence of excessive therapeutic action. Dosage should be reduced, or a phenothiazine tranquilizer should be administered concomitantly.

Pharmacologic Reactions of a Less Serious Nature: Patients may experience restlessness, insomnia, drowsiness, dizziness, weakness, dry mouth, nausea, abdominal pain, anorexia, diarrhea or constipation. Tachycardia, palpitation, blurred vision, headache without blood pressure elevation, chills, sweating, urinary retention, edema and impotence have each been reported in at least 1 patient.

Toxic or Allergic Reactions: Blood dyscrasias, including anemia, leukopenia, agranulocytosis and thrombocytopenia have been reported. Rare instances of hepatitis (e.g., one case of mild jaundice, not of the serious type associated with hydrazine MAO inhibitors) and skin rash have been reported.

Other Reactions: Tinnitus, muscle spasm and tremors, paresthesia and habituation have been reported so rarely that the role of tranylcypromine cannot be established.

Overdose: Symptoms: The characteristic symptoms that may arise as a result of tranylcypromine overdosage are usually those which have already been described under Warnings and Adverse Effects. However, an intensification of these symptoms and sometimes severe additional manifestations may be seen, depending on the degree of overdosage and on individual susceptibility.

Some patients exhibit insomnia, restlessness and anxiety, progressing in severe cases to agitation, mental confusion and incoherence. Hypotension, dizziness, weakness and drowsiness may occur, progressing in severe cases to extreme dizziness and shock. A few patients have displayed hypertension with severe headache and other symptoms. Rare instances have been reported in which hypertension was accompanied by twitching or myoclonic fibrillation of skeletal muscles with hyperpyrexia, sometimes progressing to generalized rigidity and coma.

Treatment: Treatment normally consists of general supportive measures, close observation of vital signs and steps to counteract specific symptoms as they occur. Gastric lavage is helpful if performed early.

External cooling is recommended if hyperpyrexia occurs. Barbiturates have been reported to help relieve myoclonic reactions, but frequency of administration should be controlled carefully because tranylcypromine may prolong barbiturate activity.

The management of hypertensive reactions is described under Warnings.

When hypotension requires treatment, the standard measures for managing circulatory shock should be initiated. If pressor agents are used, the rate of infusion should be regulated by careful observation of the patient. MAO inhibitors may sometimes increase the pressor response as has been demonstrated with norepinephrine.

Although tranylcypromine is rapidly excreted, its MAO inhibiting action may persist for approximately 1 week.

Dosage: Dosage should be adjusted to the requirements of the individual patient. If the patient responds to therapy, the response is usually seen within 48 hours to 3 weeks after starting medication.

Recommended starting dosage is 20 mg/day (10 mg in the morning and 10 mg in the afternoon).

Continue this dosage for 2 to 3 weeks.

If no signs of a response appear, increase dosage to 30 mg daily (20 mg upon arising and 10 mg in the afternoon).

Continue this dosage for at least 1 week. If no improvement occurs, continued administration is unlikely to be beneficial. Although dosages above 30 mg/day have been used, it should be borne in mind that the incidence and severity of side effects may increase as dosage is raised. Dosage increases should be made in increments of 10 mg/day and ordinarily at intervals of 1 to 3 weeks.

When a satisfactory response is obtained, dosage may be reduced to a maintenance level.

Some patients will be maintained on 20 mg/day; many will need only 10 mg daily.

Reduction from peak to maintenance dosage may be desirable before withdrawal. If withdrawn prematurely, original symptoms will recur. No tendency to produce rebound depressions of greater intensity has been seen, although this is a theoretical possibility in patients treated at high doses. Experimental work indicates that tranylcypromine is rapidly excreted. Inhibition of MAO activity may, however, persist for up to 1 week.

Combined Tranylcypromine-Trifluoperazine Therapy: For those physicians wishing to combine tranylcypromine with trifluoperazine, the usual dosage is tranylcypromine 10 mg plus trifluoperazine 1 mg or 2 mg twice daily (morning and afternoon) depending on the individual patient requirements. After a satisfactory response is secured, medication can often be reduced to one dose daily, usually administered in the morning. Patients displaying marked mental disturbance, especially psychotic manifestations or severe agitation, will usually require larger initial doses of trifluoperazine.

Note: When ECT is being administered concurrently with tranylcypromine, 10 mg b.i.d. can usually be given during the series, then reduced to 10 mg daily for maintenance therapy.

Supplied: Each red, round, biconvex, sugar-coated tablet, monogrammed "SKF N71", contains: tranylcypromine 10 mg, as the sulfate. Nonmedicinal ingredients: acacia, Black Opacode, calcium sulfate, candeilla wax, cellulose, ethylcellulose, FD&C red no. 3, gelatin, glycerin, magnesium stearate, Opaglos, Red Opalux, sodium benzoate, sugar and wheat starch. Sodium: <1 mmol (0.003 mg). Energy: 1.29 kJ (0.31 kcal). Bottles of 100.

(Shown in Product Recognition Section)

Reviewed 1999

PAROXETINE

General Monograph, CPhA

see SELECTIVE SEROTONIN REUPTAKE INHIBITORS

PARSITAN®

Rhône-Poulenc Rorer

Ethopropazine HCl

Antiparkinsonian Agent

Indications: Symptomatic treatment of drug induced extrapyramidal manifestations and of Parkinson's disease of postencephalitic, arteriosclerotic or idiopathic etiology.

Contraindications: Glaucoma and hypersensitivity to phenothiazine drugs.

Precautions: Use with caution in patients with cardiac disease, prostatic hypertrophy or pyloric obstruction.

Adverse Effects: Drowsiness, dizziness, lassitude, blurred vision, dryness of mouth, paresthesia, headache. Very rarely, epigastric distress, confusion and ataxia.

Neuroleptic Malignant Syndrome: As with other neuroleptic drugs, a symptom complex sometimes referred to as neuroleptic malignant syndrome (NMS) may occur. Cardinal features of NMS are hyperpyrexia, muscle rigidity, altered mental status (including catatonic signs), and evidence of autonomic instability (irregular pulse or blood pressure). Additional signs may include elevated CPK, myoglobinuria (rhabdomyolysis), and acute renal failure. NMS is potentially fatal and requires symptomatic treatment and immediate discontinuation of neuroleptic treatment.

Dosage: Must be adapted to each individual. In drug induced extrapyramidal reactions 100 mg twice daily usually brings about good control of symptoms. In post encephalitic, arteriosclerotic or idiopathic parkinsonism, initiate treatment at a low dose of 50 mg 3 times a day and increase from 50 to 100 mg daily every 2 to 3 days until the optimum effect is obtained or the limit of tolerance is attained. Drowsiness and anticholinergic effects which may appear at the beginning of treatment generally subside after a few days. The normal daily dose usually ranges between 100 and 500 mg but it may reach 1 g or more per day in certain patients.

Supplied: Each white, scored tablet contains: ethopropazine base 50 mg (as the hydrochloride). Nonmedicinal ingredients: acetic anhydride, carnauba wax, cellulose, colloidal silicon dioxide, dicalcium phosphate, diethyl phthalate, magnesium stearate, sodium croscarmellose, sodium oleate, titanium oxide and zein. Tartrazine-free. Bottles of 100.

(Shown in Product Recognition Section)

PARVOLEX®

Bioniche

Acetylcysteine

Mucolytic—Antidote for Acetaminophen Poisoning

Pharmacology: The viscosity of respiratory mucous secretions depends primarily on the content of mucoprotein and to a smaller extent on the concentration of desoxyribonucleic acid (DNA). The proportion of DNA is increased with the presence of purulent material, due to cellular debris. The mucolytic action of acetylcysteine is related to the sulphydryl group in the molecule. This group probably opens disulphide bonds in mucus, thereby lowering the viscosity. The mucolytic activity of acetylcysteine is unaltered by the presence of DNA, and increases with increasing pH, with significant mucolysis occurring between pH 7 and 9.

Acetaminophen overdosage causes liver damage due to excessive formation of a highly reactive alkylating metabolite which binds irreversibly to protein molecules within the hepatocyte. After therapeutic doses, acetaminophen is excreted principally as the glucuronide and sulfate conjugates and only approximately 8% of the acetaminophen ingested is transformed into the toxic metabolite. Hepatic-reduced glutathione rapidly activates this metabolite, which is excreted by the kidneys as nontoxic cysteine and mercapturic derivatives. However, after an overdose of acetaminophen, (150 mg/kg or greater) the glucuronide and sulfate conjugation pathways are saturated and a larger fraction of the parent drug is metabolized to form the alkylating metabolite. Hepatic reduced glutathione stores are depleted and the excess metabolite causes hepatic damage and necrosis. Acetylcysteine probably protects the liver by maintaining or restoring the glutathione levels or by acting as an alternative substrate for conjugation with the reactive metabolite.

Indications: As a mucolytic agent: As adjuvant therapy for patients with abnormal, viscid or inspissated mucous secretions in such conditions as: chronic bronchopulmonary disease such as emphysema, chronic bronchitis, lung abscess, tuberculosis, bronchiectasis, and primary amyloidosis of the lung; acute bronchopulmonary disease such as pneumonia, bronchitis and tracheobronchitis; pulmonary complications of cystic fibrosis; tracheostomy care; pulmonary complications associated with surgery; use during anesthesia; post-traumatic chest conditions and pulmonary collapse; diagnostic bronchial studies such as bronchograms, bronchospirometry and bronchial wedge catheterization.

Use in the pathology laboratory: For the digestion of sputum in examinations for M. tuberculosis and for carcinoma cells.

As an antidote for acetaminophen poisoning: As an antidote to prevent or lessen hepatic injury which may occur following the ingestion of a potentially hepatotoxic quantity of acetaminophen.

Contraindications: In those patients who are sensitive or who have developed a sensitivity to acetylcysteine. There are no known contraindications to oral administration of acetylcysteine in the treatment of acetaminophen overdose.

Warnings: After proper administration of acetylcysteine an increased volume of liquefied bronchial secretions may occur. When cough is inadequate the airway must be maintained open by mechanical suction if necessary. When there is a large mechanical block due to foreign body or local accumulation, the airway should be cleared by endotracheal aspiration with or without bronchoscopy. Asthmatics under treatment with acetylcysteine should be watched carefully. If bronchospasm progresses, this medication should be immediately discontinued.

Generalized urticaria has been observed rarely in patients receiving oral acetylcysteine for acetaminophen overdose. If this and other allergic symptoms occur, treatment with acetylcysteine should be discontinued unless it is deemed essential and the allergic symptoms can otherwise be controlled. Although there are no data indicating that acetylcysteine adversely influences hepatic failure, this remains a theoretical possibility. Therefore, in the presence of hepatic failure due to acetaminophen overdose the degree of existing liver damage and the possible risk associated with the administration of acetylcysteine should be considered.

Precautions: After administration of acetylcysteine a slight disagreeable odor may be noticed initially. When a face mask is used, after nebulization, a stickiness on the face may be noticed; this is easily removed by washing with water.

Under certain conditions, acetylcysteine may change its color to a light purple in the open vial. This color change is due to a chemical reaction which does not significantly impair the mucolytic activity or the safety of the drug. After prolonged nebulization, extreme concentration of acetylcysteine in the solvent may occur. This might impede nebulization and efficient delivery of the drug. If this occurs, Sterile Water for Injection USP should be used to dilute the nebulizing solution.

Occasionally severe and persistent vomiting occurs as a symptom of acute acetaminophen overdose. The administration of acetylcysteine may aggravate the vomiting. Patients at risk of gastric hemorrhage (e.g., esophageal varices, peptic ulcers, etc.) should be evaluated concerning the risk of upper gastrointestinal hemorrhage versus the risk of developing hepatic toxicity and treatment with acetylcysteine given accordingly. The propensity of oral acetylcysteine to aggravate vomiting is minimized when it is administered diluted in cola drinks.

Acetylcysteine should be used with caution in asthma or where there is a history of bronchospasm.

Acetylcysteine may cause a false-positive reaction with reagent dipstick tests for urinary ketones.

Acetylcysteine is not compatible with rubber and metals, particularly iron, copper and nickel. Silicone rubber and plastic are satisfactory for use with acetylcysteine.

Adverse Effects: Adverse effects include stomatitis, nausea and rhinorrhea. Sensitivity and sensitization to acetylcysteine have been reported very rarely. Asthmatics and other susceptible patients may experience varying degrees of bronchospasm associated with the administration of nebulized acetylcysteine. In most cases, this is quickly relieved by the use of a bronchodilator given by nebulization.

Rash, asthma and anaphylactoid reactions have been reported with i.v. use. These occur most commonly either during or at the end of the period of an initial high-dose infusion, and may in fact be dose-related. If the anaphylactoid manifestations are mild, and the patient is at high risk of liver toxicity, consideration should be given to continuing the acetylcysteine infusion at a reduced rate. However, this should be given only after discussion with a physician with substantial experience in the treatment of acetaminophen poisoning for a full consideration of possible risks and benefits and with appropriate supportive equipment available.

Oral administration of the large doses needed to treat acetaminophen overdose may result in nausea, vomiting and other gastrointestinal disorders. Rash, with or without mild fever has been reported rarely.

Hypokalemia and ECG changes have been noted in patients with acetaminophen poisoning irrespective of treatment given. Monitoring of plasma potassium is therefore recommended.

Dosage: As a Mucolytic Agent: Parvolex is a 20% solution which may be diluted to a lesser concentration with either sterile normal saline or sterile distilled water.

Nebulization (face mask, mouthpiece, tracheostomy): When nebulized into a face mask, mouthpiece or tracheostomy, 1 to 10 mL of the 20% solution may be given every 2 to 6 hours; the recommended dose for most patients is 3 to 5 mL of the 20% solution 3 to 4 times a day.

Nebulization (tent, croupette): In special circumstances it may be necessary to nebulize into a tent or croupette, and this method must be individualized to take into account the available equipment and the patient's particular needs. This form of administration requires very large volumes of the solution occasionally as much as 300 mL during a single treatment period. If a tent or croupette must be used, the recommended dose is the volume of 20% solution which will maintain a very heavy mist in the tent or croupette for the desired period. Administration for intermittent or continuous prolonged periods, including overnight, may be desirable.

Direct Instillation: When used by direct instillation, 1.5 mL of a 10 to 20% solution may be given as often as every hour. When used for the routine nursing care of patients with tracheostomy, 1 to 2 mL of a 10 to 20% solution may be given every 1 to 4 hours by instillation into the tracheostomy.

Acetylcysteine may be introduced directly into a particular segment of the bronchopulmonary tree by inserting (under local anesthesia and direct vision), a small plastic catheter into the trachea.

Acetylcysteine may also be given through a percutaneous intratracheal catheter.

Diagnostic Bronchograms: For diagnostic bronchial studies, 2 or 3 administrations of 1 to 2 mL of the 20% solution should be given by nebulization or by instillation intratracheally, prior to the procedure.

Administration of Aerosol: Acetylcysteine is usually administered as a fine nebulae for its local effect and the nebulizer used should be capable of providing optimal quantities of a suitable range of particle sizes.

Certain materials used in nebulization equipment react with acetylcysteine. The most reactive are metals (particularly iron and copper) and rubber. Where materials may come into contact with acetylcysteine solutions, parts made of glass or plastic should be used.

The nebulized solution may be breathed directly from the nebulizer. Nebulizers may also be attached to plastic face masks, plastic face tents, plastic mouthpieces, conventional plastic oxygen tents or head tents. Suitable nebulizers may also be fitted for use with the various intermittent positive pressure breathing (IPPB) machines.

The nebulizing equipment should be cleaned immediately after use; the residues may occlude the fine orifices or corrode metal parts.

Prolonged Nebulization: When ¾ of the initial volume of acetylcysteine solution has been nebulized a quantity of Sterile Water for Injection USP (approximately equal to the volume of solution remaining) should be added to the nebulizer. This obviates any concentration of the agent in the residual solvent remaining after prolonged nebulization.

Storage of Open Vials: If only a portion of the solution in the vial is used, to minimize contamination the remainder should be stored in a refrigerator and used within 96 hours.

Compatibility: Acetylcysteine may be mixed with the topical anesthetics lidocaine HCl (4%) and amethocaine HCl (2%); the x-ray contrast media propyliodone and the bronchodilator isoprenaline. It is incompatible with iodized oil (Lipiodol).

Antibiotics which may be mixed with acetylcysteine include polymyxin B sulfate, streptomycin sulfate, methicillin sodium, novobiocin sodium and dihydrostreptomycin sulfate. If it is deemed advisable to prepare an admixture it should be administered immediately after preparation. Do not store mixtures.

Antibiotics found to be incompatible when mixed in solution with acetylcysteine include tetracyclines HCl, oxytetracycline HCl, erythromycin lactobionate and oleandomycin. These agents may be administered by nebulization from separate solutions if necessary.

As An Antidote for Acetaminophen Poisoning: Acetylcysteine should be administered immediately if 24 hours or less have elapsed from the reported time of ingestion of an overdose of acetaminophen, regardless of the quantity reported to have been ingested.

Note: The critical ingestion-treatment interval for complete protection against severe liver damage is 8 hours. Efficacy diminishes progressively thereafter and treatment between 15 and 24 hours post-ingestion of acetaminophen is usually ineffective. However, it does not appear to worsen the condition of patients and it should not be withheld, since the reported time of ingestion may not be correct.

It should be kept in mind that after a fatal dose of acetaminophen, the patient may appear relatively well initially and may even continue normal activities for a day or two before the onset of hepatic failure.

General Management: In the case of patients admitted within 4 hours of ingestion, the stomach should be emptied promptly by lavage or by inducing emesis with syrup of ipecac. Syrup of ipecac should be given in a dose of 15 to 30 mL for children and 30 to 45 mL for adults, accompanied by drinking copious quantities of water. The dose should be repeated if emesis does not occur within 20 minutes. In the case of mixed drug overdose, activated charcoal may be indicated. However, since activated charcoal will absorb acetylcysteine and reduce its effectiveness, gastric aspiration and lavage should be performed before administering acetylcysteine orally.

On admission, blood should be drawn for determination of acetaminophen plasma levels, which will serve as a basis for determining the need for continuation of treatment with acetylcysteine. AST, ALT, bilirubin, prothrombin time, creatinine, BUN, blood sugar and electrolytes also should be determined in order to monitor hepatic and renal function and electrolyte and fluid balance.

I.V. Treatment With Acetylcysteine: Single use vials when used i.v. Discard unused portion. Acetylcysteine should be given i.v. in an initial dose of 150 mg/kg in 5% dextrose (see Table I for volume) over 15 minutes, followed by 50 mg/kg in 500 mL of 5% dextrose over 4 hours and 100 mg/kg in 1 L of 5% dextrose over the next 16 hours (total dose: 300 mg/kg in 20 hours) (See Dosage Guide, Table I). The treatment with acetylcysteine may also be continued if the acetaminophen assay reveals nontoxic plasma levels.

Acetaminophen Assays: Interpretation and Methodology: An overdose of acetaminophen of 150 mg/kg or greater may result in liver damage. However, no reliance can be placed on the number of tablets claimed to have been taken by the patient and early specific clinical manifestations of acetaminophen poisoning. As well, maximal biochemical abnormalities of liver function are usually manifested only 3 to 5 days after ingestion. Therefore, plasma or serum acetaminophen concentrations determined as early as possible, but no sooner than 4 hours following an acute overdose, are essential in assessing the potential risk of hepatotoxicity. Chronic alcohol ingestion and/or concomitant barbiturate therapy may induce a greater formation of the toxic metabolite for any given dose of acetaminophen. This should be kept in mind when therapy is based upon blood levels of acetaminophen.

The following plasma levels of acetaminophen, related to hours post-ingestion, are associated with hepatic toxicity: See Table II.

Table II—Parvolex

Plasma Levels of Acetaminophen Associated with Hepatic Toxicity

Plasma Levels μg/mL	**Hours Post-Ingestion**
150	4
70	8
20	15
4	24

Infusion of acetylcysteine should be continued in patients with these or higher concentrations of acetaminophen in plasma. Acetylcysteine treatment should be initiated immediately regardless of whether or not plasma levels are available on admittance. Acetylcysteine treatment may be discontinued if plasma levels of acetaminophen are below those given in Table II.

The possibility of chronic alcohol ingestion and/or concomitant barbiturate therapy should be considered when evaluating the possibility of discontinuing treatment, since in these instances blood levels of the parent drug may underestimate the true risk of hepatotoxicity.

Oral Treatment With Acetylcysteine: Administer the loading dose of acetylcysteine, 140 mg/kg of body weight. (Prepare acetylcysteine for oral administration as described in Table III). Four hours after the loading dose administer the first maintenance dose (70 mg/kg/body weight) of acetylcysteine. The maintenance dose is then repeated at 4 hour intervals for a total of 17 doses unless the acetaminophen assays reveal a nontoxic level as discussed below.

If the patient vomits the loading dose or any one of the maintenance doses within 1 hour of administration, repeat that dose.

If the patient is unable to retain the orally administered acetylcysteine, the antidote may be administered by duodenal intubation.

Liver function tests should be repeated daily if acetaminophen levels are within the potentially toxic range as discussed below.

Preparation of Acetylcysteine Solution for Oral Administration: The original 20% solution should be diluted to a 5% solution with cola drinks, or other soft drinks. Each diluted solution should be consumed within an hour of preparation. Remaining undiluted solutions in open vials may be stored under refrigeration for up to 96 hours.

If acetylcysteine is to be administered by gastric tube, water may be used as a diluent. The relative amounts of the 20% solution of acetylcysteine and of diluent to be mixed according to body weight of the patient are indicated in Table III.

Table I—Parvolex

Dosage Guide and Preparation for I.V. Administration

	Initial Infusion (in 5% dextrose over 15 minutes)		**2nd Infusion (in 500 mL 5% dextrose over 4 hours)**	**3rd Infusion (in 1 L 5% dextrose over 16 hours)**
Body Weight (kg)	**Parvolex (mL)**	**5% Dextrose (mL)**	**Parvolex (mL)**	**Parvolex (mL)**
10-15	11.25	40	3.75	7.5
15-20	15	60	5	10
20-25	18.75	75	6.25	12.5
25-30	22.5	75	7.5	15
30-40	30	100	10	20
40-50	37.5	200	12.5	25
50-60	45	200	15	30
60-70	52.5	200	17.5	35
70-80	60	200	20	40
80-90	67.5	200	22.5	45
90-100	75	200	25	50
100-110	82.5	200	27.5	55

The volumes and rates of infusion for children suggested above must be adjusted according to the medical circumstances and restrictions in the volume of parenteral fluids administered, as they apply to each individual patient.

Table III—Parvolex

Dosage Guide and Preparation for Oral Administration

Body Weight (kg)	**Grams Parvolex**	**mL of 20%**	**mL of Diluent**	**Total mL of 5% Solution**
		Loading Dose*		
100-110	15	75	225	300
90-100	14	70	210	280
80-90	13	65	195	260
70-80	11	55	165	220
60-70	10	50	150	200
50-60	8	40	120	160
40-50	7	35	105	140
30-40	6	30	90	120
20-30	4	20	60	80
		Maintenance Dose*		
100-110	7.5	37	113	150
90-100	7	35	105	140
80-90	6.5	33	97	130
70-80	5.5	28	82	110
60-70	5	25	75	100
50-60	4	20	60	80
40-50	3.5	18	52	70
30-40	3	15	45	60
20-30	2	10	30	40

*If patient weighs less than 20 kg, usually patients younger than 6 years, calculate the doses of Parvolex. Each mL of 20% Parvolex contains 200 mg of acetylcysteine. The loading dose is 140 mg/kg/body weight. The maintenance dose is 70 mg/kg. Three mL of diluent are added to each mL of 20% Parvolex. Do not decrease the proportion of diluent. Increased gastrointestinal irritation is often associated with increased concentrations of Parvolex.

Supportive Treatment of Acetaminophen Overdose: 1. Maintain fluid and electrolyte balance based on clinical evaluation of state of hydration and serum electrolytes. 2. Treat as necessary for hypoglycemia. 3. Administer vitamin K_1 if prothrombin time ratio exceeds 1.5 or with fresh frozen plasma if the prothrombin time ratio exceeds 3.0. 4. Diuretics and forced diuresis should be avoided. Hemodialysis or peritoneal dialysis have not been found helpful.

Acetaminophen Assays - Interpretation and Methodology: Hepatic toxicity may result from the acute ingestion of 150 mg/kg or more of acetaminophen. The reported quantity of a drug ingested after an overdose is often inaccurate and is not a reliable guide to therapy of the overdose. **Therefore, plasma or serum acetaminophen concentrations, determined as early as possible, but no sooner than 4 hours following ingestion of an acute overdose, are essential in assessing the potential risk of hepatotoxicity.**

Do not wait for assay results to begin acetylcysteine treatment. For any given dose of acetaminophen, a greater formation of toxic metabolite may occur if there is a history of chronic alcohol ingestion and/or concomitant barbiturate therapy. This should be kept in mind when therapy is based on acetaminophen blood levels interpretation of acetaminophen assays: (Refer to manufacturer's package insert for nomogram).

1. Acetaminophen plasma concentrations above the solid line which connects 200 μg/mL at 4 hours with 50 μg/mL at 12 hours are associated with a possibility of hepatic toxicity if an antidote is not administered. 2. Plasma levels above the broken line may be associated with hepatic toxicity; therefore, treatment with acetylcysteine is indicated. 3. If plasma levels of acetaminophen are below the broken line the risk of hepatic toxicity is minimal and acetylcysteine treatment can be discontinued.

When discontinuation of treatment with acetylcysteine is contemplated, the possibility of chronic alcohol ingestion and/or concomitant barbiturate therapy should be kept in mind, since under these circumstances blood levels of the parent compound may underestimate the true risk of hepatotoxicity.

Suitable assay procedures for measuring acetaminophen levels in plasma are listed below. These methods detect only parent acetaminophen and not conjugated.

HPLC:

1. Blair, D. and Rumack, B.H.: Clin. Chem. 23(4); 743-745 (April) 1977.

2. Howie, D., Andriaenssens, P.I. and Prescott, L.F.: Journ. Pharm. and Pharmacol. 9 (4) 235-237; (April) 1977.

GLC:

3. Prescott, L.F.: Journ. Pharm. and Pharmacol. 23 (10); 804-808 (Oct.) 1971.

Colourimetric:

Parvolex (cont'd)

4. Glynn, J.P. and Kendal, S.E.: The Lancet. 1:1147-1148, (17 May) 1975.

Supplied: Each mL of sterile solution contains: acetylcysteine 200 mg, disodium edetate 0.5 mg/mL and sodium hydroxide to adjust pH. Preservative-free, lacquered rubber stoppered glass vials of 10 and 30 mL, trays of 10. Store at room temperature (15 to 30°C) if unopened. Single use vials when used i.v. Discard unused portion. **If previously opened, do not use i.v.** When used for inhalation or oral administration, unused portions should be stored in a refrigerator and used within 96 hours.

PAS SODIUM

General Monograph, CPhA

Aminosalicylate Sodium

Antimycobacterial

This monograph has been compiled by CPhA. It may contain information different from that approved by Therapeutic Products Programme, Health Canada, and the pharmaceutical manufacturers' approval has not been requested.

Pharmacology: Para-aminosalicylate sodium is the sodium salt of para-aminosalicylic acid (PAS).

Note: Aminosalicylate sodium differs from 5-aminosalicylic acid (5-ASA), which is used for the treatment of inflammatory bowel disease.

PAS sodium is a highly specific bacteriostatic agent active only against M. tuberculosis. PAS sodium competitively inhibits the formation of dihydrofolic acid from aminobenzoic acid, thus preventing bacterial synthesis of folic acid required for further growth.

Pharmacokinetics: PAS sodium is readily absorbed from the gastrointestinal tract. Following oral administration of a 4 g dose, peak serum concentration is attained within 0.5 to 1 hour.

The drug is distributed into most tissues and fluids and reaches high concentrations in the lungs, kidneys and liver; however, it does not appear in cerebrospinal fluid in significant amounts except in patients with inflamed meninges, where CSF concentrations are reported to be 10 to 50% of plasma concentration. PAS is 50 to 70% plasma protein bound and has a half-life of about 1 hour. Over 80% is excreted by the kidney in approximately 10 hours with more than 50% in the acetylated form. Excretion is reduced in patients with impaired renal function.

Indications: For use with other antituberculosis agents in the second-line treatment of tuberculosis when caused by susceptible strains of M. tuberculosis.

Contraindications: Severe hypersensitivity to PAS sodium and its congeners.

Precautions: PAS sodium frequently causes gastrointestinal symptoms such as nausea, vomiting, abdominal pain, diarrhea and anorexia. Rarely, peptic ulcer and gastric hemorrhage have occurred. Malabsorption of vitamin B_{12}, folic acid, iron and lipids has also occurred. Supplementation should be considered for patients on long-term therapy.

Hypersensitivity reactions may include fever, rash, vaculitis, blood dyscrasias, hepatitis and jaundice. Patients should be advised to discontinue the drug immediately at the first sign of hypersensitivity. The possibility of cross-sensitivity must be considered in patients who have hypersensitivity to structurally-related compounds such as aminosalicylates, sulfonamides or other salicylates.

PAS sodium should be used with caution in patients with renal or hepatic dysfunction or gastric ulcer.

The sodium load associated with PAS sodium tablets (2.4 mmol/500 mg tablet) should be taken into consideration for patients in whom excess sodium is potentially harmful.

Drug Interactions: There is some evidence that PAS sodium may enhance the hypoprothrombinemic response to warfarin. Dosage adjustment of warfarin may be necessary.

Pregnancy: Safe use of PAS sodium during pregnancy has not been established.

Lactation: PAS is excreted in breast milk; however, effect on the nursing infant is unknown.

Adverse Effects: Gastrointestinal (common): nausea, vomiting, diarrhea, abdominal pain, anorexia. Malabsorption has occurred occasionally. Rarely, PAS sodium has caused peptic ulcer and gastrointestinal hemorrhage.

Hypersensitivity: fever, skin eruptions of various types, infectious mononucleosis-like syndrome, vasculitis, encephalopathy.

Hepatic: jaundice, hepatitis.

Hematological: leukopenia, agranulocytosis, thrombocytopenia, hemolytic anemia (especially in patients with G6PD deficiency), Löffler's eosinophilia.

Other: albuminuria, crystalluria acidosis and goiter with or without myxedema (with high doses of PAS sodium).

Dosage: PAS sodium must not be used alone for treatment of tuberculosis. Adults: 10 to 12 g orally per day in 2 to 4 divided doses.

Children: 150 to 300 mg/kg/day in 3 or 4 divided doses, not to exceed adult dosage.

Dosage reduction in patients with impaired renal function is recommended.

Gastrointestinal disturbances may be minimized by taking the drug with or after meals or with an antacid.

Reviewed 1999

PATANOL™

Alcon

Olopatadine HCl

Antiallergy Agent

Pharmacology: Olopatadine is a mast cell stabilizer and a potent, selective histamine H_1 antagonist that inhibits the in vivo type 1 immediate hypersensitivity reaction. In vitro studies have demonstrated the ability of olopatadine to stabilize rodent basophils and human conjunctival mast cells and inhibit antigen-stimulated release of histamine. In addition, olopatadine inhibits the release of other mast cell inflammatory mediators (i.e., tryptase and prostaglandin D2) as demonstrated in in vitro studies. Olopatadine is a selective histamine H_1 receptor antagonist in vitro and in vivo as demonstrated by its ability to inhibit binding and histamine-stimulated vascular permeability in the conjunctiva following topical ocular administration. Olopatadine is devoid of effects on alpha-adrenergic, dopamine, muscarinic type 1 and 2, and serotonin receptors.

Pharmacokinetics: Following topical ocular administration in man, olopatadine was shown to have low systemic exposure. Two studies in normal volunteers (totalling 24 subjects) dosed bilaterally with olopatadine 0.15% ophthalmic solution once every 12 hours for 2 weeks demonstrated plasma concentrations to be generally below the quantitation limit of the assay (<0.5 ng/mL). Samples in which olopatadine was quantifiable were typically found within 2 hours of dosing and ranged from 0.5 to 1.3 ng/mL. These plasma concentrations were approximately 2 to 3 orders of magnitude below those observed with well-tolerated oral multiple dose regimens. In oral studies, olopatadine was found to be well absorbed. The half-life in plasma was 7 to 14 hours, and elimination was predominantly through renal excretion. Approximately 60 to 70% of the dose was recovered in the urine as parent drug. Two metabolites, the mono-desmethyl and the N-oxide, were detected at low concentrations in the urine.

Indications: For the treatment of allergic conjunctivitis.

Contraindications: Hypersensitivity to any component of this product.

Warnings: For topical use only. Not for injection. Patients should be instructed not to instill olopatadine ophthalmic solution while wearing contact lenses, but to wait for 10 minutes after instillation before inserting contact lenses.

Precautions: Information for the Patient: To prevent contaminating the dropper tip and solution, care should be taken not to touch the eyelids or surrounding areas with the dropper tip of the bottle. Keep bottle tightly closed when not in use.

Carcinogenesis, Mutagenesis, Impairment of Fertility: Olopatadine was not carcinogenic in mice and rats of either sex at doses up to 78 000 and 31 000 times the maximum recommended ocular human use level, respectively. No mutagenic potential was observed when olopatadine was tested in an in vitro bacterial reverse mutation (Ames) test, an in vitro mammalian chromosome aberration assay or an in vivo mouse micronucleus test. Olopatadine administered to male and female rats at oral doses of 62 500 times the maximum recommended ocular human use level resulted in a slight decrease in the fertility index and reduced implantation rate; no effects on reproductive function were observed at doses of 7 800 times the maximum recommended ocular human use level.

Pregnancy: Olopatadine was found not to be teratogenic in rats and rabbits at oral doses >90 000 and >60 000 times the maximum recommended ocular human use level, respectively. There are, however, no adequate and well controlled studies in pregnant women. Because animal studies are not always predictive of human responses, this drug should be used in pregnant women only if the potential benefit to the mother justifies the potential risk to the embryo or fetus.

Lactation: Olopatadine has been identified in the milk of nursing rats following oral administration. Rat pups of mothers administered olopatadine orally at greater than 625 times (but not at 312 times) the maximum recommended ocular human use level demonstrated reduced body weight gain during the nursing period. It is not known whether topical ocular administration could result in sufficient systemic absorption to produce detectable quantities in human breast milk. Nevertheless, caution should be exercised when olopatadine ophthalmic solution is administered to a nursing mother.

Children: Safety and effectiveness in pediatric patients between the ages of 3 and 16 have been established.

Adverse Effects: In clinical studies of olopatadine ophthalmic solution, ocular and nonocular adverse reactions related to therapy were reported at an incidence below 1%.

Ocular: mild transient burning or stinging, pruritus, hyperemia, foreign body sensation, superficial keratitis, lid edema, dry eye, lid dryness, lid spasm, photophobia.

Nonocular: asthenia, headache, taste perversion.

Overdose: Symptoms and Treatment: A topical overdosage may be flushed from the eye(s) with warm tap water.

Dosage: The recommended dose is 1 to 2 drops in each affected eye twice daily.

Supplied: Each mL of ophthalmic solution contains: olopatadine HCl 1.11 mg equivalent to olopatadine 1 mg. Nonmedicinal ingredients: benzalkonium chloride, dibasic sodium phosphate, hydrochloric acid/sodium hydroxide (to adjust pH), purified water and sodium chloride. Plastic Drop-Tainer dispensers of 5 mL. Store at 4 to 30°C.

New Product 1998

PAXIL®

SmithKline Beecham

Paroxetine HCl

Antidepressant—Antiobsessional—Antipanic Agent

Pharmacology: Paroxetine is a potent and selective serotonin (5-hydroxytryptamine, 5-HT) reuptake inhibitor (SSRI). This activity of the drug on brain neurons is thought to be responsible for its antidepressant action as well as its efficacy in the treatment of obsessive-compulsive disorder (OCD) and panic disorder.

Paroxetine is a phenylpiperidine derivative which is chemically unrelated to the tricyclic or tetracyclic antidepressants. In receptor binding studies, paroxetine did not exhibit significant affinity for the adrenergic (α_1, α_2, β), dopaminergic, serotonergic ($5HT_1$, $5HT_2$), or histaminergic receptors of rat brain membrane. A weak affinity for the muscarinic acetylcholine receptor was evident. The predominant metabolites of paroxetine are essentially inactive as 5-HT reuptake inhibitors.

Pharmacokinetics: Paroxetine is well absorbed after oral administration. In healthy volunteers, the absorption of a single 30 mg oral dose of paroxetine was not appreciably affected by the presence or absence of food. Owing to the extensive distribution of paroxetine into the tissues, less than 1% of the total drug in the body is believed to reside in the systemic circulation.

Paroxetine is subject to a biphasic process of metabolic elimination which involves presystemic (first-pass) and systemic pathways. First-pass metabolism is extensive, but may be partially saturable, accounting for the increased bioavailability observed with multiple dosing. As with other selective serotonin reuptake inhibitors, the metabolism of paroxetine is accomplished in part by cytochrome $P450(IID_6)$. Saturation of this enzyme at clinical doses appears to account for the nonlinearity of paroxetine kinetics with increasing dose and increasing duration of treatment. The role of this enzyme in paroxetine metabolism also suggests potential drug-drug interactions (see Precautions). The majority of the dose appears to be oxidized to a catechol intermediate which is converted to highly polar glucuronide and sulfate metabolites through methylation and conjugation reactions. The glucuronide and sulfate conjugates of paroxetine are about >10 000 and

3 000 times less potent, respectively, than the parent compound as inhibitors of 5-HT reuptake in rat brain synaptosomes. Approximately 64% of an administered dose of paroxetine is eliminated by the kidneys and 36% in the feces. Less than 2% of the dose is recovered in the form of the parent compound.

A wide range of interindividual variation is observed for the pharmacokinetic parameters. Following the single or multiple dose administration of paroxetine at doses of 20 to 50 mg, the mean elimination half-life value for healthy subjects appears to be about 24 hours, although a range of 3 to 65 hours has been reported. Both the rate of absorption and the terminal elimination half-life appear to be independent of dose. Steady-state plasma concentrations of paroxetine are generally achieved in 7 to 14 days. No correlation has been established between paroxetine plasma concentrations and therapeutic efficacy or the incidence of adverse reactions.

No clear dose relationship has been demonstrated for the antidepressant effects of paroxetine at doses above 20 mg/day. The results of fixed-dose studies comparing paroxetine and placebo in the treatment of depression and panic disorder revealed the dose dependency for some of the more common adverse events.

In **healthy young volunteers** receiving a 20 mg daily dose of paroxetine for 15 days, the mean maximal plasma concentration was 41 ng/mL at steady-state (see Table I). Peak plasma levels generally occurred within 3 to 7 hours.

In **elderly subjects,** increased steady-state plasma concentrations and prolongation of the elimination half-life were observed relative to younger adult controls (see Table I). Elderly patients should, therefore, be initiated and maintained at the lowest daily dosage of paroxetine which is associated with clinical efficacy.

The results from a multiple dose pharmacokinetic study in subjects with severe **hepatic dysfunction** suggest that the clearance of paroxetine is markedly reduced in this patient group (see Table I). As the elimination of paroxetine is dependent upon extensive hepatic metabolism, its use in patients with hepatic impairment should be undertaken with caution (see Dosage).

In a single dose pharmacokinetic study in patients with mild to severe **renal impairment,** plasma levels of paroxetine tended to increase with deteriorating renal function (see Table II). As multiple-dose pharmacokinetic studies have not been performed in patients with renal disease, paroxetine should be used with caution in such patients.

At therapeutic concentrations, the plasma protein binding of paroxetine is approximately 95%. After the administration of a single 50 mg oral dose to lactating women, the concentrations of paroxetine detected in breast milk were similar to those in plasma.

Table I—Paxil

Steady-state Pharmacokinetics of Paroxetine after Doses of 20 mg Daily (mean and range)

	Young Healthy Subjects [n=22]	Elderly Healthy Subjects [n=22]	Hepatically* Impaired Subjects [n=10]
$C_{max ss}$ (ng/mL)	41 (12–90)	87 (18–154)	87 (11–147)
$T_{max ss}$ (hours)	5.0 (3–7)	5.0 (1–10)	6.4 (2–11)
$C_{min ss}$ (ng/mL)	21 (4–51)	58 (9–127)	66 (7–128)
AUC^{ss} (ng.h/mL)	660 (179–1 436)	1 580 (221–3 286)	1 720 (194–3 283)
T½ (hours)	19 (8–43)	31 (13–92)	66 (17–152)

*Galactose elimination capacity 30 to 70% of normal.

Indications: Depression: Paroxetine is indicated for symptomatic relief of depressive illness.

Clinical trials have provided evidence that continuation treatment with paroxetine in patients with moderate to moderately severe depressive disorder is effective for at least 6 months.

Obsessive-Compulsive Disorder: Paroxetine is indicated for the symptomatic treatment of obsessive-compulsive disorder (OCD). The obsessions or compulsions must be experienced as intrusive, markedly distressing, time-consuming, or interfering significantly with the person's social or occupational functioning.

Table II—Paxil

Pharmacokinetics of Paroxetine after a Single 30 mg Dose in Normal Subjects and Those with Renal Impairment

	[a]Renally Impaired Subjects Severe [n=6]	[b]Renally Impaired Subjects Moderate [n=6]	[c]Healthy Young Subjects [n=6]
C_{max} (ng/mL)	46.2 (35.9–56.7)	36 (3.6–59.4)	19.8 (1.4–54.8)
T_{max} (hours)	6.5 (4.0–11.0)	4.8 (1.5–9.0)	4.3 (1–7)
AUC∞ (ng.h/mL)	2 046 (605–3 695)	1 053 (48–2 087)	574 (21–2 196)
T½ (hours)	29.7 (10.9–54.8)	18.3 (11.2–32.0)	17.3 (9.6–25.1)

[a]Creatinine clearance=13–27 mL/min.
[b]Creatinine clearance=32–46 mL/min.
[c]Creatinine clearance >100 mL/min.
Legend:
C_{max}=maximum plasma concentration.
T_{max}=time to reach C_{max}.
AUC^{ss} =Area under the plasma concentration time curve between dosing intervals (i.e., 24 hours) at steady-state.
AUC∞=Area under the plasma concentration time curve at infinity.
T½=terminal elimination half-life; ss, steady-state.

Panic Disorder: Paroxetine is indicated for the symptomatic treatment of panic disorder, with or without agoraphobia.

The effectiveness in long-term use (i.e., for more than 12 weeks) has not yet been established in controlled trials for OCD and panic disorder. Therefore, the physician who elects to use paroxetine for extended periods in these diseases should periodically re-evaluate the long-term usefulness of the drug for individual patients.

Contraindications: Hypersensitivity: Paroxetine is contraindicated in patients who are known to be hypersensitive to the drug.

MAO Inhibitors: In patients receiving another serotonin reuptake inhibitor drug in combination with a MAO inhibitor, there have been reports of serious, sometimes fatal, reactions including hyperthermia, rigidity, myoclonus, autonomic instability with possible rapid fluctuations of vital signs, and mental status changes that include extreme agitation progressing to delirium and coma. These reactions have also been reported in patients who have recently discontinued that drug and have begun treatment on a MAO inhibitor. Some cases presented with features resembling neuroleptic malignant syndrome. Therefore, paroxetine should not be used in combination with MAO inhibitors or within 2 weeks of terminating treatment with MAO inhibitors. Treatment with paroxetine should then be initiated cautiously and dosage increased gradually until optimal response is reached. MAO inhibitors should not be introduced within 2 weeks of cessation of therapy with paroxetine.

Precautions: Suicide: The possibility of a suicide attempt is inherent in depression and may persist until remission occurs. Therefore, high risk patients should be closely supervised throughout therapy with appropriate consideration to the possible need for hospitalization. In order to minimize the opportunity for overdosage, prescriptions for paroxetine should be written for the smallest quantity of drug consistent with good patient management.

Seizures: During clinical trials, the overall incidence of seizures was 0.15% in patients treated with paroxetine. However, patients with a history of convulsive disorders were excluded from these studies. Caution is recommended when the drug is administered to patients with a history of seizures. The drug should be discontinued in any patient who develops seizures.

Activation of Mania/Hypomania: During clinical testing in depressed patients, approximately 1% of paroxetine-treated patients experienced manic reactions. When bipolar patients were considered as a subgroup the incidence of mania was 2%. As with other Selective Serotonin Reuptake Inhibitors (SSRIs), paroxetine should be used with caution in patients with a history of mania.

Occupational Hazards: Although paroxetine did not cause sedation or interfere with psychomotor performance in placebo-controlled studies in normal subjects, patients should be advised to avoid driving a car or operating hazardous machinery until they are reasonably certain that paroxetine does not affect them adversely.

Cardiac Conditions: Paroxetine does not generally produce clinically significant changes in blood pressure, heart rate or ECG. Paroxetine has not been evaluated or used to any appreciable extent in patients with a recent history of myocardial infarction or unstable heart disease. Hence, the usual precautions should be observed in such patients.

Electroconvulsive Therapy (ECT): The efficacy and safety of the concurrent use of paroxetine and ECT have not been studied.

Geriatrics: Administration of paroxetine to the elderly is associated with increased plasma levels and prolongation of the elimination half-life relative to younger adults (see Pharmacology, Pharmacokinetics). Elderly patients should be initiated and maintained at the lowest daily dose of paroxetine which is associated with clinical efficacy.

Approximately 800 elderly patients (≥65 years) have been treated with paroxetine in worldwide premarketing clinical trials. The pattern of adverse experiences in the elderly was comparable to that in younger patients.

Children: The safety and effectiveness of paroxetine in children under 18 years of age have not been established.

Pregnancy and *Lactation:* Although animal studies have not shown any teratogenic or selective embryotoxic effects, the safety of paroxetine in human pregnancy has not been established. Paroxetine should not be used during pregnancy unless the potential benefit to the patient outweighs the possible risk to the fetus.

The concentrations of paroxetine detected in the breast milk of lactating women are similar to those in plasma. Lactating women should not nurse their infants while receiving paroxetine.

Renal Impairment: Since paroxetine is extensively metabolized by the liver, excretion of unchanged drug in urine is a minor route of elimination. However, single dose pharmacokinetic studies in subjects with clinically significant renal impairment suggest that plasma levels of paroxetine are elevated in such subjects. Paroxetine should therefore be used with caution and the dosage restricted to the lower end of the range in patients with clinically significant renal impairment.

Hepatic Impairment: Pharmacokinetic studies of paroxetine in subjects with clinically significant hepatic impairment suggest that prolongation of the elimination half-life and increased plasma levels can be expected in this patient group. Paroxetine should be used with caution and dosages restricted to the lower end of the range in patients with clinically significant hepatic impairment.

Drug Interactions: MAO Inhibitors: See Contraindications.

Drugs Metabolized by Cytochrome P450(IID_6): Like other selective serotonin reuptake inhibitors, paroxetine inhibits the specific hepatic cytochrome P450 isozyme (IID_6) which is responsible for the metabolism of debrisoquine and sparteine. Poor metabolizers of debrisoquine/sparteine represent approximately 5 to 10% of Caucasians. The median C_{min}(ss) for paroxetine (20 mg daily) at steady-state in poor metabolizers (n=8) was almost triple that reported for extensive metabolizers (n=9).

Although the full clinical significance of this effect has not been established, inhibition of IID_6 can lead to elevated plasma levels of coadministered drugs which are metabolized by this isozyme.

In 2 studies, daily dosing of paroxetine (20 mg daily) under steady-state conditions increased the following mean pharmacokinetic parameters for a single (100 mg) dose of desipramine in extensive metabolizers: C_{max} (2 fold), AUC (6 fold), and t½ (3 to 5 fold). Concomitant steady-state paroxetine treatment did not result in any further impairment of desipramine elimination in poor metabolizers. Insufficient information is available to provide recommendations on the necessary dosage adjustments for tricyclic antidepressants or paroxetine, if these drugs are to be used in combination.

Concomitant use of paroxetine with other drugs metabolized by IID_6 has not been formally studied but may require lower doses that usually prescribed for either paroxetine or the other drug. Drugs metabolized by cytochrome P450 (IID_6) include certain tricyclic antidepressants (e.g., nortriptyline, amitriptyline, imipramine and desipramine), selective serotonin reuptake inhibitors (e.g., fluoxetine), phenothiazine neuroleptics (e.g., perphenazine and thioridazine) and Type IC antiarrhythmics (e.g., propafenone and flecainide).

CNS Drugs: Experience in a limited number of healthy subjects has shown that paroxetine does not increase the sedation and drowsiness associated with haloperidol, amylbarbitone or oxazepam, when given in combination. Since the effects of concomitant administration of paroxetine with neuroleptics have not been studied, the use of paroxetine with these drugs should be approached with caution.

Foods/Antacids: The absorption and pharmacokinetics of paroxetine are not affected by food or antacids.

Paxil (cont'd)

Cardiovascular Drugs: Multiple dose treatment with paroxetine 30 mg/day has little or no effect on the steady-state pharmacokinetics of digoxin (0.25 mg daily) or propanolol (80 mg b.i.d.).

Anticoagulants: Paroxetine should be administered with great caution to patients receiving oral anticoagulants. Preliminary data suggest that a pharmacodynamic interaction between paroxetine and warfarin may result in increased bleeding in the presence of unaltered prothrombin times.

Microsomal Enzyme Inhibition/Induction: The metabolism and pharmacokinetics of paroxetine may be affected by the induction or inhibition of drug metabolizing enzymes.

Steady-state levels of paroxetine (30 mg daily) were elevated by about 50% when cimetidine (300 mg t.i.d.), a known drug metabolizing enzyme inhibitor, was coadministered to steady-state. Consideration should be given to using doses of paroxetine towards the lower end of the range when coadministered with known drug metabolizing enzyme inhibitors.

Coadministration of a single 30 mg dose of paroxetine to subjects receiving chronic daily dosing with 300 mg phenytoin, a known metabolizing enzyme inducer, is associated with decreased plama levels of paroxetine (AUC reduced approximately 30%) and an increased incidence of adverse experiences. When a single 300 mg dose of phenytoin was administered to subjects receiving chronic daily dosing with 30 mg paroxetine the mean AUC of phenytoin was reduced by 12%. No initial dosage adjustment of paroxetine is considered necessary when the drug is to be coadministered with known drug metabolizing enzyme inducers. Any subsequent dosage adjustment should be guided by clinical effect.

Alcohol: The concomitant use of paroxetine and alcohol has not been studied and is not recommended. Patients should be advised to avoid alcohol while taking paroxetine.

Tryptophan can be metabolized to serotonin. As with other serotonin reuptake inhibitors, the use of paroxetine together with tryptophan may result in adverse reactions consisting primarily of headache, nausea, sweating and dizziness. Consequently, concomitant use of paroxetine with tryptophan is not recommended.

Coadministration of paroxetine with anticonvulsants may be associated with an increased incidence of adverse experiences.

Chronic daily dosing with phenobarbital (100 mg q.i.d. for 14 days) decreased the systemic availability of a single 30 mg dose of paroxetine in some subjects. The AUC and $t_{1/2}$ of paroxetine were reduced by an average of 25% and 38% respectively compared to paroxetine administered alone. The effect of paroxetine on phenobarbital pharmacokinetics was not studied. No initial paroxetine dosage adjustment is considered necessary when coadministered with phenobarbital; any subsequent adjustment should be guided by clinical effect.

Paroxetine has been reported to increase the systemic bioavailability of procyclidine. Steady-state plasma levels of procyclidine (5 mg daily) were elevated by about 40% when 30 mg paroxetine was coadministered to steady-state.

Drugs Highly Bound to Plasma Protein: Paroxetine is highly bound to plasma protein, therefore administration of paroxetine to a patient taking another drug that is highly protein bound may cause increased free concentrations of the other drug, potentially resulting in adverse events. Conversely, adverse effects could result from displacement of paroxetine by other highly bound drugs.

In a study of depressed patients stabilized on lithium, no pharmacokinetic interaction between paroxetine and lithium was observed. However, since there is limited experience in patients, the concurrent administration of paroxetine and lithium should be undertaken with caution.

A multiple dose study of the interaction between paroxetine and diazepam showed no alteration in the pharmacokinetics of paroxetine that would warrant changes in the dose of paroxetine for patients receiving both drugs. The effects of paroxetine on the pharmacokinetics of diazepam were not evaluated.

Adverse Effects: Commonly Observed: The most commonly observed adverse experiences associated with the use of paroxetine in clinical trials and not seen at an equivalent incidence among placebo-treated patients were: nausea, somnolence, sweating, tremor, asthenia, dizziness, dry mouth, insomnia, constipation, diarrhea, decreased appetite and male sexual dysfunction.

Adverse Events Leading to Discontinuation of Treatment: 21% of approximately 4 000 patients who received paroxetine in worldwide clinical trials in depression discontinued treatment due to an adverse experience. In obsessive-compulsive and

Table III—Paxil

Treatment-Emergent Adverse Events in Short-Term Flexible Dose Placebo-Controlled Clinical Trials in Depression[a]

Body System	Preferred Term	Paroxetine (n=421) (%)	Placebo (n=421) (%)
Body as a Whole	Headache	17.6	17.3
	Asthenia	15.0	5.9
	Abdominal Pain	3.1	4.0
	Fever	1.7	1.7
	Chest Pain	1.4	2.1
	Trauma	1.4	0.5
	Back Pain	1.2	2.4
Cardiovascular	Palpitation	2.9	1.4
	Vasodilation	2.6	0.7
	Postural Hypotension	1.2	0.5
Dermatological	Sweating	11.2	2.4
	Rash	1.7	0.7
Gastrointestinal	Nausea	25.7	9.3
	Dry Mouth	18.1	12.1
	Constipation	13.8	8.6
	Diarrhea	11.6	7.6
	Decreased Appetite	6.4	1.9
	Flatulence	4.0	1.7
	Vomiting	2.4	1.7
	Oropharynx Disorder[d]	2.1	0.0
	Dyspepsia	1.9	1.0
	Increased Appetite	1.4	0.5
Musculoskeletal	Myopathy	2.4	1.4
	Myalgia	1.7	0.7
	Myasthenia	1.4	0.2
Nervous System	Somnolence	23.3	9.0
	Dizziness	13.3	5.5
	Insomnia	13.3	6.2
	Tremor	8.3	1.9
	Nervousness	5.2	2.6
	Anxiety	5.0	2.9
	Paresthesia	3.8	1.7
	Libido Decreased	3.3	0.0
	Agitation	2.1	1.9
	Drugged Feeling	1.7	0.7
	Myoclonus	1.4	0.7
	CNS Stimulation	1.2	3.6
	Confusion	1.2	0.2
Respiration	Respiratory Disorder[e]	5.9	6.4
	Yawn	3.8	0.0
	Pharyngitis	2.1	2.9
Special Senses	Blurred Vision	3.6	1.4
	Taste Perversion	2.4	0.2
Urogenital System	[b] Abnormal Ejaculation[c]	12.9	0.0
	[b] Male Genital Disorders[f]	8.0	0.0
	Urinary Frequency	3.1	0.7
	Urination Impaired[g]	2.9	0.2
	[b] Impotence	2.5	0.5
	[b] Female Genital Disorders[h]	1.8	0.0

[a] Events reported by at least 1% of patients treated with Paxil are included.
[b] Percentage corrected for gender.
Placebo: male, n=206; female, n=215.
Paroxetine: male, n=201; female, n=220.
[c] Primarily ejaculatory delay. In a trial of fixed doses of paroxetine, the incidence of ejaculatory disturbance in males with 20 mg/day of paroxetine was 6.5% (3/46) vs 0% (0/23) in the placebo group.
[d] Includes mostly lump in throat and tightness in throat.
[e] Includes mostly cold symptoms or URI.
[f] Includes anorgasmia, erectile difficulties, delayed ejaculation/orgasm, sexual dysfunction and impotence.
[g] Includes difficulty with micturition and urinary hesitancy.
[h] Includes anorgasmia and difficulty reaching climax/orgasm.

panic disorder studies, 11.8% (64/542) and 9.4% (44/469) respectively of patients treated with paroxetine discontinued treatment because of adverse events. The most common events leading to discontinuation (reported by 1% or more of subjects) included: asthenia, headache, nausea, somnolence, insomnia, agitation, tremor, dizziness, constipation, impotence and abnormal ejaculation.

Adverse Effects Following Discontinuation of Treatment: Some patients may experience physical symptoms such as dizziness/lightheadedness, gastrointestinal complaints, headache, agitation/restlessness and sleep disturbance during the period following the discontinuation of paroxetine treatment. These events are generally mild and transient.

Adverse Experience Reports: Multiple doses of paroxetine were administered to 4 126 subjects in clinical trials for depression, 542 subjects in clinical trials for OCD and 469 subjects in clinical trials for panic disorder. Untoward experiences associated with this exposure were recorded by clinical investigators using descriptive terminology of their own choosing.

Consequently, it is not possible to provide a meaningful estimate of the proportion of individuals experiencing adverse experiences without first grouping similar types of untoward experiences into a limited (i.e., reduced) number of standardized experience categories.

Table III lists adverse experiences that occurred at an incidence of 1% or higher in short-term (6-week) flexible dose (20 to 50 mg/day) placebo-controlled trials in depression. (An additional 460 patients participated in a fixed-dose placebo-controlled study.)

Table IV (on following page) enumerates adverse events that occurred at a frequency of 2% or more among patients on paroxetine who participated in placebo-controlled OCD trials of 12-weeks duration in which patients were dosed in the range of 20 to 60 mg/day and in placebo-controlled panic disorder trials of 10- to 12-weeks duration in which patients were dosed in the range of 10 to 60 mg/day.

The prescriber should be aware that these figures cannot be used to predict the incidence of side effects in the course of usual medical practice where patient characteristics and other factors differ from those which prevailed in the clinical trials. Similarly the cited incidences cannot be compared with figures obtained from other clinical investigations involving different treatments, uses and investigators. The cited frequencies do however provide the prescribing physician with some basis for estimating the relative contribution of drug and nondrug factors to the side effect incidence rate in the population studied. Reported adverse experiences were classified using a COSTART-based Dictionary terminology for the depression trials and an ADECS (a modified COSTART dictionary) for OCD and panic disorder trials.

In the tabulations which follow, a COSTART or modified COSTART-based Dictionary terminology has been used to classify reported adverse experiences. The frequencies presented therefore represent the portion of the 4 126, 542 and 469 paroxetine-exposed individuals in depression, OCD and panic trials, respectively, who experienced an event of the type cited on at least one occasion while receiving paroxetine. Experiences are further classified within body system categories and enumerated in order of decreasing frequency using the following definitions: frequent experiences are defined as one of those occurring on one or more occasion in at least 1/100 patients; infrequent adverse experiences are those occurring in less than 1/100 but at least 1/1 000 patients; rare experiences are those occurring in less than 1/1 000 patients.

All adverse experiences are included except those already listed in Table III and Table IV, those reported in terms so general as to be uninformative and those experiences for which the drug cause was remote. It is important to emphasize that although the experiences reported did occur during treatment with paroxetine, they were not necessarily caused by it.

Body as a Whole: Frequent: malaise, pain. Infrequent: allergic reaction, chills, face edema, infection, moniliasis, neck pain, overdose. Rare: abnormal laboratory value, abscess, adrenergic syndrome, cellulitis, chills and fever, cyst, hernia, intentional overdose, neck rigidity, pelvic pain, peritonitis, substernal chest pain, ulcer.

Cardiovascular: Frequent: hypertension, syncope, tachycardia. Infrequent: bradycardia, conduction abnormalities, ECG abnormal, hypotension, migraine, ventricular extrasystoles. Rare: angina pectoris, arrhythmia, atrial arrhythmia, atrial fibrillation, bundle branch block, cerebral ischemia, cerebrovascular accident, congestive heart failure, extrasystoles, low cardiac output, myocardial infarct, myocardial ischemia, pallor, phlebitis, pulmonary embolus, supraventricular extrasystoles, thrombosis, varicose vein, vascular headache.

Dermatological: Frequent: pruritus. Infrequent: acne, alopecia, dry skin, ecchymosis, eczema, furunculosis, herpes simplex, urticaria. Rare: angioedema, contact dermatitis, erythema nodosum, herpes zoster, maculopapular rash, photosensitivity, skin discoloration, skin ulcer, skin hypertrophy.

Endocrine: Rare: diabetes mellitus, hyperthyroidism, hypothyroidism, thyroiditis.

Gastrointestinal: Frequent: nausea and vomiting. Infrequent: bruxism, buccal cavity disorders, dysphagia, eructation, gastroenteritis, gastrointestinal flu, glossitis, increased salivation, liver function tests abnormal, mouth ulceration, vomiting and diarrhea, rectal hemorrhage. Rare: aphthous stomatitis, bloody diarrhea, bulimia, colitis, duodenitis, esophagitis, fecal impaction, fecal incontinence, gastritis, gingivitis, hematemesis, hepatitis, ileus, jaundice, melena, peptic ulcer, salivary gland enlargement, stomach ulcer, stomatitis, tongue edema, tooth caries.

Hematologic and Lymphatic: Infrequent: anemia, leukopenia, lymphadenopathy, purpura, WBC abnormality. Rare: eosinophilia, iron deficiency anemia, leukocytosis, lymphedema, lymphocytosis, microcytic anemia, monocytosis, normocytic anemia.

Metabolic and Nutritional: Frequent: weight gain, weight loss. Infrequent: edema, hyperglycemia, peripheral edema, thirst. Rare: alkaline phosphatase increased, bilirubinemia, dehydration, gout, hypercholesteremia, hypocalcemia, hypoglycemia, hypokalemia, hyponatremia, obesity, AST increased, ALT increased.

Musculoskeletal: Infrequent: arthralgia, arthritis, traumatic fracture. Rare: arthrosis, bursitis, cartilage disorder, myositis, osteoporosis, tetany.

Nervous System: Frequent. CNS stimulation, concentration impaired, depression, emotional lability, vertigo. Infrequent: akinesia, alcohol abuse, amnesia, ataxia, convulsion, depersonalization, hallucinations, hyperkinesia, hypertonia, incoordination, lack of emotion, manic reaction, paranoid reaction, thinking abnormal, hypesthesia. Rare: abnormal EEG, abnormal gait, antisocial reaction, choreoathetosis, circumoral paresthesia, delirium, delusions, diplopia, drug dependence, dysarthria, dyskinesia, dystonia, euphoria, fasciculations, grand mal convulsion, hostility, hyperalgesia, hypokinesia, hysteria, libido increased, manic depressive reaction, meningitis, myelitis, neuralgia, neuropathy, nystagmus, psychosis, psychotic depression, reflexes increased, stupor, withdrawal syndrome.

Respiratory: Frequent: cough increased, rhinitis. Infrequent: asthma, bronchitis, dyspnea, epistaxis, hyperventilation, pneumonia, respiratory flu, sinusitis. Rare: hiccup, lung fibrosis, sputum increased, voice alteration.

Special Senses: Infrequent: abnormality of accommodation, conjunctivitis, ear pain, eye pain, mydriasis, otitis media, tinnitus. Rare: amblyopia, cataract specified, conjunctival edema, corneal lesion, corneal ulcer, exophthalmos, eye hemorrhage, glaucoma, hyperacusis, otitis externa, photophobia, retinal hemorrhage, taste loss, anisocoria, deafness, keratoconjunctivitis.

Urogenital: Infrequent: abortion*, amenorrhea*, breast pain*, cystitis, dysmenorrhea*, dysuria, menorrhagia*, nocturia, polyuria, urinary incontinence, urinary retention, urinary tract infection, urinary urgency, vaginitis*. Rare: breast atrophy*, female lactation*, hematuria, kidney calculus, kidney function abnormal, kidney pain, mastitis*, nephritis, oliguria, urethritis, urine abnormality, vaginal moniliasis*.

*Incidence corrected for gender.

Overdose: Symptoms and Treatment: Overdose attempts have been reported with paroxetine; up to 2 000 mg alone and in combination with other agents during premarketing clinical trials. In cases where paroxetine was used alone, no deaths have occurred and recovery was medically uneventful.

Symptoms of overdosage with paroxetine include nausea, vomiting, drowsiness, sinus tachycardia, tremor, dilated pupils, dry mouth and irritability. There are no reports of ECG abnormalities, coma or convulsions following overdosage with paroxetine alone.

Table IV—Paxil

Treatment-Emergent Adverse Experience Incidence in Placebo-Controlled Clinical Trials for Obsessive-Compulsive Disorder and Panic Disorder[a]

		Obsessive-Compulsive Disorder		Panic Disorder	
Body System	**Preferred Term**	**Paroxetine (n=542) (%)**	**Placebo (n=265) (%)**	**Paroxetine (n=469) (%)**	**Placebo (n=324) (%)**
Body as a Whole	Headache	25.3	29.1	25.4	25.3
	Asthenia	21.8	13.6	13.6	4.6
	Infection	5.3	4.9	5.3	6.8
	Abdominal Pain	4.8	4.9	4.3	3.1
	Chest Pain	2.8	1.9	2.3	3.1
	Back Pain	2.4	4.9	3.2	2.2
	Chills	2.0	0.7	2.3	0.6
Cardiovascular	Vasodilation	3.9	1.1	2.1	2.8
	Palpitation	2.0	0.4	2.3	2.5
Dermatologic	Sweating	8.9	3.0	14.3	5.9
	Rash	3.1	1.9	2.3	1.5
Gastrointestinal	Nausea	23.3	9.8	22.8	17.3
	Dry Mouth	18.1	8.7	18.1	10.8
	Constipation	15.7	6.4	7.9	5.2
	Diarrhea	10.3	9.8	11.7	6.5
	Decreased Appetite	9.0	3.4	7.0	2.8
	Increased Appetite	4.2	3.0	2.1	0.6
Nervous System	Somnolence	24.3	7.2	18.8	10.8
	Insomnia	23.8	13.2	17.9	10.2
	Dizziness	12.4	6.0	14.1	9.9
	Tremor	10.5	1.1	8.5	1.2
	Nervousness	8.5	8.3	7.9	8.3
	Libido Decreased	7.2	3.8	8.5	1.2
	Anxiety	4.1	6.8	4.5	4.0
	Abnormal Dreams	3.9	1.1	2.8	3.4
	Myoclonus	3.3	0.4	3.2	1.5
	Concentration Impaired	2.8	1.5	1.1	0.9
	Depersonalization	2.6	0.4	1.7	2.2
	Amnesia	2.2	1.1	0.6	0.0
	Hyperkinesia	2.2	1.5	0.9	0.9
	Agitation	1.7	2.3	4.7	3.7
Respiratory System	Pharyngitis	3.7	4.9	3.2	3.1
	Rhinitis	1.5	3.4	2.6	0.3
	Sinusitis	1.5	4.9	5.8	4.6
	Cough Increased	1.1	1.9	2.3	1.5
Special Senses	Abnormal Vision	3.7	2.3	3.0	2.8
	Taste Perversion	2.0	0.0	1.1	0.6
Urogenital System	Abnormal Ejaculation[b]	23.3	1.3	20.5	0.9
	Impotence[b]	8.2	1.3	5.4	0.0
	Female Genital Disorder[b,c]	3.3	0.0	8.9	0.5
	Urinary Frequency	3.3	1.1	2.1	0.3
	Urination Impaired	3.3	0.4	0.4	0.3
	Urinary Tract Infection	1.5	1.1	2.1	1.2

[a] Events reported by at least 2% of either OCD or Panic Disorder Paxil-treated patients are included, except the following events which had an incidence on placebo ≥ Paxil in both populations: [OCD] trauma, dyspepsia, flatulence, vomiting, myalgia, anxiety, depression; paresthesia, and respiratory disorder. [Panic Disorder] flu syndrome, infection trauma, palpitations, vasodilation, dyspepsia, myalgia, abnormal dreams, depression, nervousness, paresthesia, respiratory disorder, dysmenorrhea.

[b] Incidence is gender-corrected.

OCD: Placebo: male, n=158; female, n=107.

Paroxetine: male, n=330; female, n=212.

Panic: Placebo: male, n=111; female, n=213.

Paroxetine: male, n=166; female, n=303.

[c] Includes anorgasmia and difficulty reaching climax/orgasm.

Paxil (cont'd)

No specific antidote is known. Treatment should consist of those general measures employed in the management of overdose with any antidepressant. Establish and maintain an airway; ensure adequate oxygenation and ventilation. The stomach should be emptied either by the induction of emesis, lavage or both. Following evacuation, 20 to 30 g of activated charcoal may be administered every 4 to 6 hours during the first 24 hours after ingestion. An ECG should be taken and monitoring of cardiac function instituted if there is any evidence of abnormality. Supportive care with frequent monitoring of vital signs and careful observation is indicated. Due to the large volume of distribution of paroxetine, forced diuresis, dialysis, hemoperfusion and exchange transfusions are unlikely to be of benefit.

A specific caution involves patients taking or recently having taken paroxetine who might ingest by accident or intent excessive quantities of a tricyclic antidepressant. In such a case, accumulation of the parent tricyclic and its active metabolite may increase the possibility of clinically significant sequelae and extend the time needed for close medical observation.

In managing overdosage, consider the possibility of multiple drug involvement. The physician should consider contacting a Poison Control Centre for additional information on the treatment of any overdose.

Dosage: General: Paroxetine should be administered once daily in the morning and may be taken with or without food. The tablet should be swallowed rather than chewed.

Dose Adjustments: Based on pharmacokinetic parameters, steady-state paroxetine plasma levels are achieved over a 7 to 14 days interval. Hence, dosage adjustments in 10 mg increments should be made at 1- to 2-week intervals or according to clinician's judgment.

Maintenance: During long-term therapy for any indication, the dosage should be maintained at the lowest effective level.

Discontinuation: Some patients may experience physical symptoms following discontinuation of treatment. **Although it is unknown if gradual discontinuation will reduce or prevent these symptoms, a gradual tapering of dosage should be considered when treatment is to be discontinued** (see Adverse Effects, Adverse Effects Following Discontinuation of Treatment).

Depression: Usual Adult Dose: Administration should be initiated at 20 mg daily. For most patients, 20 mg daily will also be the optimum dose. Therapeutic response may be delayed until the third or fourth week of treatment.

Dose Range: For patients who do not respond adequately to the 20 mg daily dose, a gradual increase of dosage up to 40 mg daily may be considered. Maximum recommended dose is 50 mg.

Obsessive-Compulsive Disorder: Usual Adult Dose: Administration should be initiated at 20 mg/day. The recommended dose of paroxetine in the treatment of OCD is 40 mg daily.

Dose Range: For patients who do not respond adequately to the 40 mg daily dose, a gradual increase in dosage may be considered. Maximum recommended daily dose is 60 mg.

Panic Disorder: Usual Adult Dose: Recommended starting dose is 10 mg/day. The recommended dose of paroxetine in the treatment of panic disorder is 40 mg daily.

Dose Range: For patients who do not respond adequately to the 40 mg daily dose, a gradual increase in dosage may be considered. Maximum recommended daily dose is 60 mg.

Special Patient Populations: For any Indication: Geriatrics: A lower initial dose may be considered for elderly and/or debilitated patients. The dose may be increased if indicated up to a maximum of 40 mg daily.

Children: The use of paroxetine in children under 18 years of age is not recommended as safety and efficacy have not been established in this population.

Renal/Hepatic Impairment: Paroxetine should be used with caution in patients with renal or hepatic impairment. Dosage should be restricted to the lower end of the range in patients with clinically significant renal or hepatic impairment (see Precautions). A maximum dose of 40 mg should not be exceeded.

Information for the Patient: See Blue Section—Information for the Patient "Paxil".

Supplied: 10 mg: Each yellow, film-coated, oval, biconvex tablet, with the product name engraved on one side and strength engraved on the other side, contains: paroxetine HCl equivalent to paroxetine free base 10 mg. Nonmedicinal ingredients: dibasic calcium phosphate dihydrate, hydroxypropyl methylcellulose, magnesium stearate, Opadry yellow, Opadry clear and sodium starch glycolate. HDPE bottles of 30 with polypropylene cap.

20 mg: Each pink, bisected, film-coated, oval, biconvex tablet, with the product name engraved on one side and strength engraved on the other side, contains: paroxetine HCl equivalent to paroxetine free base 20 mg. Nonmedicinal ingredients: dibasic calcium phosphate dihydrate, hydroxypropyl methylcellulose, magnesium stearate, Opadry pink, Opadry clear and sodium starch glycolate. HDPE bottles of 100 with polypropylene cap. "Patient Compliance Pack" blister cards of 30, cartons of 6.

30 mg: Each blue, film-coated, oval, biconvex tablet, with the product name engraved on one side and strength engraved on the other side, contains: paroxetine HCl equivalent to paroxetine free base 30 mg. Nonmedicinal ingredients: dibasic calcium phosphate dihydrate, hydroxypropyl methylcellulose, magnesium stearate, Opadry blue, Opadry clear and sodium starch glycolate. HDPE bottles of 30 with polypropylene cap.

Store at 15 to 30°C.

(Shown in Product Recognition Section)

Reviewed 1999

PCE® ℞

Abbott

Erythromycin Base

Antibiotic

Supplied: Each ovaloid, pink-speckled white Dispertab tablet contains: polymer-coated erythromycin base particles 333 mg. Nonmedicinal ingredients: cellulose microcrystalline, coating solution clear, colloidal silicone, hydrogenated vegetable oil, hydroxypropyl cellulose, lactose monohydrate, magnesium stearate, sodium starch glycolate, stearic acid and wax. Alcohol-, gluten-, paraben-, sodium-, sucrose-, sulfite- and tartrazine-free. Bottles of 100, 250 and 500.

PEDIALYTE®
PEDIALYTE® FREEZER POPS

Abbott

Oral Electrolyte Maintenance Solution

Electrolyte Maintenance

Indications: Prevents dehydration and restores fluids and minerals lost in patients with mild or moderate diarrhea and other conditions causing mild to moderate dehydration; for maintenance of body water and electrolytes and prevention of dehydration secondary to acute diarrhea in infants and children; for oral supplementation and for maintenance following corrective parenteral therapy of severe dehydration; for maintenance and transitional supplementation following surgical procedures and conditions associated with excessive fluid loss or deficient intake.

Precautions: Severe dehydration secondary to diarrhea and other conditions incurring large fluid and electrolyte losses requires parenteral therapy initially. With intractable vomiting, adynamic ileus, intestinal obstruction or perforated bowel, nothing should be administered orally. In the presence of decreased renal function with oliguria and anuria, oral and i.v. solutions should be administered with caution.

Dosage: Administration should be initiated in frequent oral feedings. The dosage of Pedialyte and Pedialyte Freezer Pops should be individualized according to body weight, ongoing extra losses, age of the patient and physician's recommendation. The approximate guidelines for maintenance of body water and electrolytes and the prevention of dehydration secondary to acute diarrhea in infants and children are 100 to 150 mL/kg daily. Children 4 years and older: 2 L or more daily.

Supplied: Pedialyte: Each bottle contains: water, dextrose, potassium citrate, sodium chloride and sodium citrate. Nonmedicinal ingredients: FD&C Blue #1 and Red #40 (grape flavor) and FD&C Red #40 (bubblegum flavor). Bottles of 1 000 mL (unflavored, fruit and bubble-gum flavored). Cases of 8. Do not freeze. For hospital use: glass bottles of 240 mL (unflavored), cases of 24. Protect from heat. After opening, store Pedialyte under refrigeration and use within 48 hours.

Pedialyte Freezer Pops: Each freezer pop contains: water, dextrose, citric acid, sodium chloride, potassium citrate, sodium carboxymethylcellulose and aspartame. Nonmedicinal ingredients: FD&C Blue #1 (blue raspberry flavor), FD&C Red #40 (cherry flavor), FD&C Red #40 and Blue #1 (grape flavor), FD&C Yellow #6 and Red #40 (orange flavor). Cartons of 16 pops of 62.5 mL (1 L), grape, cherry, orange and blue raspberry flavored. Cases of 8. Protect from heat. To freeze, remove from carton. Do not use past expiry date.

Each L provides: sodium 45 mEq or 45 mmol (1 036.5 mg); potassium 20 mEq or 20 mmol (780 mg); chloride 35 mEq or 35 mmol (1 243.5 mg); citrate 30 mEq or 10 mmol (1 890 mg); dextrose 25 g. Energy: 42 kJ (10 kcal)/100 mL.

PEDIAPRED® ℞

Rhône-Poulenc Rorer

Prednisolone Sodium Phosphate

Glucocorticoid—Anti-inflammatory

Pharmacology: Prednisolone sodium phosphate is a synthetic adrenocortical steroid derivative with predominantly glucocorticoid properties possessing anti-inflammatory and immunosuppressive action.

Prednisolone sodium phosphate belongs to the pharmacologic class of glucocorticoid/anti-inflammatory drugs which, following systemic absorption, diffuse across cell membranes and complex with specific cytoplasmic receptors. These complexes may enter the cell nucleus, bind to DNA and stimulate transcription of mRNA. Subsequent cellular responses result in a variety of local and systemic effects. Anti-inflammatory processes such as edema, fibrin deposition, decreased prostaglandin/thromboxane synthesis, capillary dilatation, migration of leukocytes, the phagocytosis stage of wound healing and cicatrization are inhibited. Immune reactions are suppressed. Metabolically, protein catabolism and increased gluconeogenesis along with decreased peripheral utilization of glucose leads to glycogen storage in the liver, increased blood glucose concentration and insulin resistance (diabetogenic effect). During therapy lipolysis is enhanced and abnormal distribution of fat may result (Cushingoid effect). Skeletal calcium is mobilized and lost via renal excretion. Glucocorticoids in general augment renal glomerular filtration and promote urate excretion.

In respect of electrolyte and water balance, sodium tends to be reabsorbed and potassium and hydrogen excreted resulting in water retention and risk of hypokalemic alkalosis.

Pharmacokinetics: Prednisolone is rapidly and well absorbed from the gastrointestinal tract following oral administration. Prednisolone sodium phosphate oral liquid produces a 20% higher peak plasma level of prednisolone which occurs approximately 15 minutes earlier than that seen with tablet formulations. Prednisolone is 70 to 90% protein-bound in the plasma and it is eliminated from the plasma with a half-life of 2 to 4 hours. It is metabolized mainly in the liver and excreted in the urine as sulfate and glucuronide conjugates.

Indications: Management of conditions known to be responsive to prednisone or prednisolone where anti-inflammatory action or immunosuppression or adrenocortical supplementation and replacement is required.

For most indications, glucocorticoid administration provides symptomatic relief, but has no effect on the underlying disease processes. Use of these medications does not eliminate the need for other therapies that may be required.

Prednisolone sodium phosphate oral liquid is appropriate for pediatric usage and for those patients with difficulty swallowing solid oral dosage forms.

Contraindications: Untreated systemic fungal infections. Hypersensitivity to prednisolone sodium phosphate or other corticosteroids, or to any of its ingredients.

Warnings: Glucocorticoid-induced suppression of HPA (Hypothalamic-Pituitary-Adrenal) function is dependent on dose and duration of treatment. Recovery occurs gradually as the steroid dose is reduced and withdrawn. Suppression persists for a period of time after withdrawal depending on dose and length of treatment time.

In patients on corticosteroid therapy subjected to unusual stress, increased dosage of rapidly acting corticosteroids before, during and after the stressful situation is indicated.

Corticosteroids may mask some signs of infection, and new infections may appear during their use. There may be decreased resistance and inability to localize infection when corticosteroids are used.

If corticosteroids have to be used in the presence of fungal or bacterial infections, institute appropriate anti-infective therapy.

Prolonged use of corticosteroids may produce posterior subcapsular cataracts or glaucoma with possible damage to the optic nerves and may enhance the establishment of secondary ocular infections due to fungi or viruses.

Average and large doses of corticosteroids can cause elevation of blood pressure, salt and water retention, and increased excretion of potassium. These effects are less likely to occur with the synthetic derivatives except when used in large doses. Dietary salt restriction and potassium supplementation may be necessary. All corticosteroids increase calcium excretion. While on corticosteroid therapy, patients should not be vaccinated against measles. **Other immunization procedures should not be undertaken in patients who are on corticosteroids, especially on high doses, because of possible hazards of neurological complications and lack of antibody response.**

The use of corticosteroids in active tuberculosis should be restricted to those cases of fulminating or disseminated tuberculosis in which the corticosteroid is used for the management of the disease in conjunction with an appropriate antituberculous regimen.

If corticosteroids are indicated in patients with latent tuberculosis or tuberculin reactivity, close observation is necessary as reactivation of the disease may occur. During prolonged corticosteroid therapy these patients should receive chemoprophylaxis.

Patients who are on drugs which suppress the immune system are more susceptible to infections than healthy individuals. Chickenpox and measles can have a more serious or even fatal course in non-immune children or adults who have not had these diseases and particular care should be taken to avoid exposure. It is not known whether the risk of developing serious cases of these infections is due to prior corticosteroid treatment or to the contribution of the underlying disease which is being treated. If exposed to chickenpox, prophylaxis with varicella zoster immune globulin (VZIG) may be indicated. If exposed to measles, prophylaxis with pooled i.m. immunoglobulin (IG) may be indicated. If chickenpox develops, treatment with antiviral agents may be considered.

Precautions: During prolonged corticosteroid therapy, routine laboratory studies such as urinalysis, 2-hour postprandial blood sugar determinations, blood pressure monitoring, body weight and chest x-ray should be performed at regular intervals. If doses of prednisolone sodium phosphate are high, serum potassium should be monitored regularly. Serious consideration of upper gastrointestinal studies should be contemplated when patients complain of gastric symptoms while on this medication. In general, prolonged therapy above 8 mg/day is associated with increased incidence of adverse effects; mental disorders are associated with doses exceeding 40 mg/day.

Drug-induced secondary adrenocortical insufficiency may be minimized by gradual reduction of dosage. This type of relative insufficiency may persist for months after discontinuation of therapy; therefore, in any situation of stress occurring during that period, hormone therapy should be reinstated. Since mineralocorticoid secretion may be impaired, salt and/or mineralocorticoid should be administered concurrently.

Children: Growth and development of infants and children on prolonged corticosteroid therapy should be carefully observed. Administration of corticosteroids to children should be limited to the least amount compatible with an effective therapeutic regimen.

Pediatric patients demonstrate greater susceptibility to corticosteroid induced HPA axis suppression and Cushing's syndrome than mature patients. HPA axis suppression, Cushing's syndrome and intracranial hypertension have been reported in children taking oral corticosteroids. Manifestations of adrenal suppression in children include linear growth retardation, delayed weight gain, low plasma cortisol levels and absence of response to ACTH stimulation. Manifestations of intracranial hypertension include bulging fontanelles, headaches and bilateral papilloedema.

General Use: There is an enhanced effect of corticosteroids in patients with hypothyroidism and in those with cirrhosis of the liver.

Corticosteroids should be used cautiously in patients with ocular herpes simplex because of possible corneal perforation.

The lowest possible dose of corticosteroid should be used to control the condition under treatment, and when reduction in dosage is possible, the reduction should be gradual.

Psychic derangements may appear when corticosteroids are used, ranging from euphoria, insomnia, mood swings, personality changes, and severe depression, to frank psychotic manifestations. Also, existing emotional instability or psychotic tendencies may be aggravated by corticosteroids.

Following prolonged therapy, psychological and/or physiological dependence may develop. Withdrawal of glucocorticoids may result in symptoms of the glucocorticoid withdrawal syndrome including: fever, myalgia, arthralgia and malaise. This may occur in patients even without evidence of adrenal insufficiency.

ASA and other NSAIDs should be used cautiously in conjunction with corticosteroids in hypoprothrombinemia.

Corticosteroids should be used with caution in the following clinical conditions: nonspecific ulcerative colitis (if there is a probability of impending perforation), abscess or other pyogenic infection, diverticulitis, fresh intestinal anastomoses, active or latent peptic ulcer, renal insufficiency, hypertension, osteoporosis, cardiac disease, thromboembolic disorders and diabetes mellitus.

In myasthenia gravis, hospitalization with careful observation is recommended because transient worsening of symptoms, possibly leading to respiratory distress may precede clinical improvement.

Since complications of treatment with glucocorticoids are dependent on the size of the dose and the duration of treatment, a risk/benefit decision must be made in each individual case as to dose and duration of treatment and as to whether daily or intermittent therapy should be used.

Patients should be warned not to discontinue the use of prednisolone sodium phosphate abruptly or without medical supervision, to advise any medical attendants that they are taking prednisolone sodium phosphate and to seek medical advice at once should they develop fever or other signs of infection (see Information for the Patient).

Persons who are on immunosuppressant doses of corticosteroids should be warned to avoid exposure to chickenpox or measles. Patients should also be advised that if they are exposed, medical advice should be sought without delay (see Warnings).

Steroids may increase or decrease motility and number of spermatozoa in some male patients. However, it is not known whether reproductive capacity in humans is adversely affected.

Carcinogenicity and Mutagenicity: Limited information is available. Glucocorticoids produce cleft palate in the offspring when administered to pregnant mice, rats and hamsters. There are few studies on the carcinogenicity or mutagenicity of prednisolone in animals.

Drug Interactions: Although no unusual drug interactions have been detected during clinical trials, the same precautions should be exercised as for other glucocorticoids. It is recommended to increase the maintenance dose of glucocorticoids if the following drugs are administered at the same time: anticonvulsants (phenobarbital, phenytoin), certain antibiotics (rifampin), anticoagulants (coumadin) and bronchodilators (ephedrine). If the patient receiving glucocorticoids is treated at the same time with some other antibiotics (erythromycin), ketoconazole, estrogens or preparations containing estrogens, a reduction in the dose of prednisolone sodium phosphate is recommended. Since prednisolone sodium phosphate is metabolized in the liver, the possibility remains that concomitant administration of other hepatically metabolized drugs may lead to interactions (e.g., barbiturates).

Anticholinesterase effects may be antagonized in myasthenia gravis. Toxicity may be enhanced when cyclosporin and glucocorticoids are combined in organ transplant patients. Coadministration with digitalis glycosides may enhance the possibility of digitalis toxicity associated with hypocalcemia. Isoniazid and salicylate serum concentrations may be decreased upon coadministration with glucocorticoids.

Potassium-depleting agents (e.g., thiazide diuretics) may enhance hypocalcemia and hypokalemia secondary to glucocorticoid use. Coadministration with nonsteroidal anti-inflammatories may increase the risk of gastrointestinal ulceration. Immunologic response to vaccines and toxoids is reduced by glucocorticoids which may also potentiate the replication of organisms in attenuated vaccines (e.g., measles). Glucocorticoids may alter laboratory or radiological tests for serum T_3 or serum protein-bound iodine, may decrease T_4 minimally or decrease the uptake of ^{131}iodine.

Immunization procedures may be undertaken in patients who are receiving corticosteroids as **replacement** therapy (e.g., Addison's disease).

Pregnancy: Prednisolone sodium phosphate (corticosteroids) have been shown to be teratogenic in various animal species when given in doses equivalent to the human dose. There are no adequate and well-controlled studies in pregnant women. Prednisolone sodium phosphate should be used during pregnancy only if the potential benefit justifies the potential risk to the fetus. Animal studies in which prednisolone sodium phosphate has been given to pregnant rodents and rabbits have yielded an increased incidence of cleft palate in the offspring.

Infants born to mothers who have received substantial doses of corticosteroids during pregnancy, should be carefully observed for signs of hypoadrenalism.

Lactation: Prednisolone sodium phosphate is excreted in breast milk. Caution should be exercised when this drug is administered to a nursing woman.

Adverse Effects: Corticosteroids have a potential for multiple adverse effects. There are essentially 2 types of toxicity observed when administered in therapeutic dosages: withdrawal effects, which could produce life-threatening adrenal insufficiency, and high dosage over long periods, which could produce fluid/electrolyte disturbances, hyperglycemia, increased susceptibility to infections, peptic ulceration, osteoporosis, myopathy, behavioral disturbances, cataracts, or Cushing's habitus. Single doses, or short courses of therapy (over several days) are usually with less harmful effects. The approach to therapy should follow logical and rational sequence of: (i) attempting to control the condition with more conventional mode(s) of management, (ii) weighing the benefits of steroid therapy against the risks, (iii) commencing therapy with high loading dose, reducing to the minimum effective dosage as soon as possible.

Fluid and Electrolyte Disturbances: sodium retention, fluid retention, congestive heart failure in susceptible patients, potassium loss, hypokalemic alkalosis, hypertension.

Musculoskeletal: Muscle weakness, steroid myopathy, loss of muscle mass, osteoporosis, vertebral compression fractures, aseptic necrosis of femoral and humeral heads, pathologic fracture of long bones.

Gastrointestinal: peptic ulcer with possible perforation and hemorrhage, pancreatitis, abdominal distention, ulcerative esophagitis.

Dermatologic: impaired wound healing, thin fragile skin, petechiae and ecchymoses, facial erythema, increased sweating, may suppress reactions to skin tests.

Metabolic: negative nitrogen balance due to protein catabolism.

Neurological: convulsions, increased intracranial pressure with papilledema (pseudotumor cerebri) usually after treatment, vertigo, headache.

Endocrine: menstrual irregularities, development of cushingoid state, secondary adrenocortical and pituitary unresponsiveness, particularly in times of stress, as in trauma, surgery or illness, suppression of growth in children, decreased carbohydrate tolerance, manifestations of latent diabetes mellitus, increased requirements for insulin or oral hypoglycemic agents in diabetics.

Ophthalmic: posterior subcapsular cataracts, increased intraocular pressure, glaucoma, exophthalmos.

Overdose: Symptoms and Treatment: The effects of accidental ingestion of large quantities of prednisolone over a very short period of time have not been reported.

Treatment of acute overdosage is by immediate gastric lavage or emesis. For chronic overdosage in the face of severe disease requiring continuous steroid therapy the dosage of prednisolone may be reduced only temporarily, or alternate day treatment may be introduced.

Dosage: The initial dosage of prednisolone sodium phosphate may vary from 5 to 60 mL (5 to 60 mg prednisolone base)/ day depending on the specific disease entity being treated. In situations of less severity lower doses will generally suffice while in selected patients higher initial doses may be required. The initial dosage should be maintained or adjusted until a satisfactory response is noted. If after a period of time there is a lack of satisfactory clinical response, prednisolone sodium phosphate should be discontinued and the patient transferred to other appropriate therapy (see Table I). **It should be emphasized that dosage requirements are variable and must be individualized on the basis of the disease under treatment and the response of the patient.** Standardized dosing is not available for oral corticosteroids. Therefore, any adjustments in consideration of age or renal function of the patient should be taken into account, along with the patient's weight and severity of the disease when the initial dosage is established. After a favorable response is noted, the proper maintenance dosage should be determined by decreasing the initial drug dosage in small decrements at appropriate time intervals until the lowest dosage which will maintain an adequate clinical response is reached. It should be kept in mind that constant monitoring is needed in regard to drug dosage. Included in the situations which may make dosage adjustments necessary are changes in clinical status secondary to remissions or exacerbations in the disease process, the patient's individual drug responsiveness, and the effect of patient exposure to stressful situations not directly related to the disease entity under treatment; in this latter situation it may be necessary to increase the dosage of prednisolone sodium phosphate for a period of time consistent with the patient's condition. If after long-term therapy the drug is to be stopped, it is recommended that it

Pediapred (cont'd)

be withdrawn gradually rather than abruptly to avoid glucocorticoid withdrawal syndrome.

If on a once daily therapy, prednisolone sodium phosphate should be administered in the morning to simulate the natural circadian rhythm of corticosteroid secretion.

Table I—Pediapred

Equivalent mg Dosage of Glucocorticoids[a,b]

Name	mg/dose
Cortisone	25
Hydrocortisone	20
Prednisolone	5
Prednisone	5
Methylprednisolone	4
Triamcinolone	4
Paramethasone	2
Betamethasone	0.6
Dexamethasone	0.75

[a] These dose relationships apply only to oral or i.v. administration of these compounds.

[b] When these substances or their derivatives are injected i.m. into joint spaces, their relative properties may be greatly altered.

Information for the Patient: See Blue Section—Information for the Patient "Pediapred".

Supplied: Each 5 mL of dye-free, colorless to light straw-colored, raspberry-flavored solution contains: prednisolone 5 mg as prednisolone sodium phosphate USP in a palatable, aqueous vehicle. Nonmedicinal ingredients: disodium edetate, flavor raspberry, methylparaben, purified water, sodium phosphate and sorbitol. Bottles of 120 mL. Store at 15 to 30°C. Do not refrigerate. Keep cap tightly closed.

PEDIASURE™

Abbott

Therapeutic Nutrient

Description: PediaSure liquid nutrition for children is an isotonic enteral nutritional product designed to provide complete balanced nutrition for children 1 to 10 years of age. Fed either by tube or orally, PediaSure can be used as total enteral nutrition support or as a supplement.

Indications: Enteral nutritional support by tube or by mouth for children 1 to 10 years of age. Support for growth. Support recovery from trauma or severe illness. Feed long-term when chronic conditions prevent normal feeding i.e., congenital anomalies or mental retardation, failure to thrive, malnutrition.

Precautions: Not for parenteral administration. Not intended for infants under 1 year of age unless specified by a physician.

Dosage: The nutrient concentrations in 1 100 mL to 1 300 mL of this product meet or exceed 100% of the RNI for proteins, vitamins and minerals for children 1 to 10 years of age.

Oral feeding: As total or supplemental nutrition with or between meals. One to 6 cans daily: 984 kJ to 5 904 kJ (235 kcal to 1 410 kcal). When used as the sole daily feeding: should be administered to meet individual requirements.

Tube feeding: Follow physician's or dietitian's directions. When initiating feeding, the flow-rate, volume and dilution are dependent on patient tolerance; care should be taken to avoid contamination of this product during preparation and administration. Additional fluid requirements should be met by giving water orally with or after feedings, or when flushing the feeding tube.

Special Instructions for Tube feeding: Conservative recommendations for initiating tube feedings are to begin with a formula diluted to hypotonic concentration (¼ to ½ strength). If the patient tolerates the feeding, the volume is advanced over several hours until fluid maintenance is achieved. Once the volume is stabilized, the energy density of the formula is increased. However, children will frequently tolerate feedings initiated with full-strength isotonic or nearly isotonic formulas when the rate is adjusted to promote tolerance. Feedings often are advanced every 4 to 8 hours or, with more conservative management, every 12 hours. If the patient cannot tolerate an adequate volume of formula, supplemental parenteral fluids may be required.

Supplied: Each 235 mL ready-to-use can contains: water, maltodextrin, sucrose, sodium caseinate, high oleic safflower oil, soy oil, fractionated coconut oil, minerals (calcium phosphate tribasic, magnesium chloride, potassium citrate, sodium molybdate, chromium chloride, sodium selenite, potassium phosphate dibasic, potassium chloride, ferrous sulfate, zinc sulfate, manganese sulfate, cupric sulfate, potassium iodine), whey protein concentrate, natural and artificial flavor, mono and diglycerides, soy lecithin, choline chloride, vitamins (ascorbic acid, alpha-tocopheryl acetate, niacinamide, calcium pantothenate, thiamine hydrochloride, pyridoxine hydrochloride, riboflavin, vitamin A palmitate, folic acid, biotin, phylloquinone, vitamin D_3, cyanocobalamin), calcium carrageenan, taurine and L-carnitine. Also contains FD&C Blue #1, FD&C Red #3 and FD&C Yellow #6 (strawberry flavor). See Table I.

Shake well. Dilution not required.

Table I—PediaSure

Analysis	100 mL	
Energy	419 (100)	kJ (kcal)
Water	85.3	g
Carbohydrates	11	g
Proteins	3	g
Fat	5	g
Linoleic Acid	1	g
Choline	30	mg
L-carnitine	1.7	mg
Taurine	7	mg
Vitamin A	259	IU
Vitamin D_3	32.0	IU
Vitamin E	2.3	IU
Vitamin K_1	0.003	mg
Vitamin C	10.2	mg
Thiamine (Vit. B_1)	0.27	mg
Riboflavin (Vit. B_2)	0.21	mg
Niacin	1.7	mg
Vitamin B_6	0.26	mg
Pantothenic Acid	1	mg
Folic Acid	0.037	mg
Biotin	32.3	µg
Vitamin B_{12}	0.60	µg
Sodium	37	mg
Potassium	130	mg
Chloride	101	mg
Calcium	97	mg
Phosphorus	80	mg
Magnesium	19.8	mg
Zinc	1.2	mg
Iron	1.4	mg
Manganese	0.25	mg
Copper	0.10	mg
Iodine	9.7	µg
Molybdenum	3.59	µg
Chromium	3.00	µg
Selenium	2.28	µg
Osmolality	310	mOsm
Dietary Fiber*	0.5	g

* PediaSure with Fiber.

Energy Distribution: Protein 12%; fat 44%; carbohydrate 44% 419 kJ (100 kcal)/100 mL.

Gluten-free. Cans of 235 mL (vanilla, strawberry, chocolate flavor). PediaSure with fibre (vanilla flavor). Cases of 12. Store unopened at room temperature. PediaSure has a calorie to nitrogen ratio of 207:1 which assures protein sparing for tissue restoration and growth. Once opened store covered in refrigerator and use within 48 hours.

PEDIATRIC ELECTROLYTE

Pharmascience

Electrolytes

Electrolyte Maintenance

Indications: Oral administration of required electrolytes and water to patients with mild or moderate diarrhea; for maintenance of body water and electrolyte balance and prevention of dehydration secondary to acute diarrhea in infants and children.

Precautions: Severe dehydration secondary to diarrhea and other conditions incurring large fluid and electrolyte losses requires parenteral therapy initially. With intractable vomiting, adynamic ileus, intestinal obstruction or perforated bowel, nothing should be administered orally. In the presence of decreased renal function with oliguria and anuria, oral and i.v. solutions should be administered with caution.

Dosage: Children under 2 years: Consult physician before using. Children 2 to 10 years: With moderate to severe dehydration, oral dose initially: 15 mL of solution/kg over the first 3 to 4 hours; 100 mL of solution/kg over the next 18 to 24 hours, the amounts and rates being adjusted as needed and tolerated depending on thirst and response to therapy. Not more than 100 mL of fluid should be given during any 20-minute period. The child should drink 1 to 2 L/day while diarrhea continues.

Supplied: Pediatric Electrolyte is prepared from water, dextrose, fructose, potassium citrate, sodium chloride and sodium citrate. Each L of oral electrolyte solution provides: sodium 45 mEq, potassium 20 mEq, chloride 35 mEq, citrate 30 mEq, dextrose 20 g and fructose 5 g (fruit flavor only). Plastic bottles of 1 000 mL (fruit, grape and unflavored), cases of 8. Bottles of 248 mL (fruit, grape and unflavored), cases of 16.

Reviewed 1998

PEDIATRIX

Technilab

Acetaminophen

Antipyretic—Analgesic

Supplied: Drops: Each mL contains: acetaminophen 80 mg. Nonmedicinal ingredients: artificial coloring and flavoring, citric acid, dibasic sodium phosphate, glycerin, methylparaben, polyethylene glycol, propylene glycol, propylparaben, purified water and sodium cyclamate. Alcohol-, gluten-, lactose-, sucrose- and tartrazine-free. Plastic bottles of 24 mL (child resistant cap) with a calibrated dropper. Concentrated, for dropper dosage only.

Oral Solution: Each 5 mL contains: acetaminophen 160 mg. Nonmedicinal ingredients: artificial coloring and flavoring, citric acid, dibasic sodium phosphate, FD&C Yellow #6, glycerin, methylparaben, polyethylene glycol, propylene glycol, propylparaben, purified water, sodium cyclamate and sorbitol. Alcohol-, gluten-, lactose-, sucrose- and tartrazine-free. Amber plastic bottles of 100 mL (child resistant closure) and 500 mL (for pharmacists and hospitals only). All bottles are safety sealed.

Store between 15 and 30°C. Protect from freezing.

PEDIAZOLE® Ⓟ

Abbott

Erythromycin Ethylsuccinate—Sulfisoxazole Acetyl

Antibiotic

Pharmacology: Erythromycin exerts its antibacterial action by binding to the 50 S ribosomal subunit of susceptible bacteria and suppressing protein synthesis. Erythromycin is usually bacteriostatic but may be bactericidal in high concentrations or against highly susceptible organisms.

Sulfisoxazole is a short-acting sulfonamide. Sulfonamides are usually bacteriostatic in action. They interfere with utilization of p-aminobenzoic acid (PABA) in susceptible bacteria, thus inhibiting the biosynthesis of folic acid which is essential for the growth of susceptible organisms. Sulfonamides are structural analogs of PABA and competitively inhibit dihydrofolic acid synthetase which is necessary for the conversion of PABA to folic acid.

A combination of erythromycin and a sulfonamide, as in Pediazole, results in a lowering of the minimal inhibitory concentration (MIC) of each antibacterial as compared with the levels when they are used separately. This combination therefore shows synergism. As a result, the activity against H. influenzae is increased.

Erythromycin: In the presence of normal hepatic function, erythromycin is concentrated in the liver and excreted in the bile; the effect of hepatic dysfunction on excretion of erythromycin by the liver into the bile is not known.

After oral administration, less than 5% of the activity of the administered dose can be recovered in the urine.

Erythromycin diffuses readily into most body fluids. Only low concentrations are normally achieved in the spinal fluid, but passage of the drug across the blood-brain barrier increases in meningitis.

Erythromycin crosses the placental barrier but fetal plasma levels are generally low.

Erythromycin is largely bound to plasma proteins (over 70%). The serum half-life of erythromycin is approximately 2 hours.

Sulfisoxazole: Sulfisoxazole acetyl is absorbed rapidly and completely from the gastrointestinal tract following oral administration. About 70% of the administered dose is deacetylated by enzymatic hydrolysis in the intestine, and both the free drug and the acetylated drug are rapidly eliminated by the kidneys, approximately 80% within 24 hours.

Sulfisoxazole exists in the blood primarily bound to plasma proteins (90%) as well as conjugated and in the active (free) form. Metabolic pathways include N^4-acetylation and oxidation.

The serum half-life of sulfisoxazole is about 6 hours.

Pharmacokinetics: Erythromycin and sulfisoxazole serum levels were determined in 18 adult subjects following oral administration of Pediazole under fasting condition or nonfasting condition. The volunteers received 400 mg of erythromycin as erythromycin ethylsuccinate and 1 200 mg of sulfisoxazole as sulfisoxazole acetyl.

Peak serum levels, C_{max} and AUC for both fasting and nonfasting subjects are shown in Table I.

There have been reports suggesting that erythromycin does not reach the fetus in adequate concentration to prevent congenital syphilis. Infants born to women treated during pregnancy with erythromycin for early syphilis should be treated with an appropriate penicillin regimen.

Sulfonamides: Hypersensitivity reactions, agranulocytosis, aplastic anemia, and other blood dyscrasia have been reported with the administration of sulfonamides. In some instances these complications have been fatal.

During therapy, patients should be carefully evaluated for clinical evidence of serious blood disorders. If signs such as unexplained infection, fever, pallor, bleeding or jaundice appear, discontinue therapy immediately and conduct appropriate hematological investigations.

The frequency of renal complications is considerably lower in patients receiving the most soluble sulfonamides such as sulfisoxazole. Urinalysis with careful microscopic examination should be obtained frequently in patients receiving sulfonamides.

Table I—Pediazole

Mean (±SD) Pharmacokinetic Parameters for Pediazole as a Single Dose in the Fasting and Nonfasting State (18 Adult Males)

	Erythromycin		Sulfisoxazole	
	Fasting	**Nonfasting**	**Fasting**	**Nonfasting**
Dose (mg)	400	400	1 200	1 200
Peak level (mg/L)	0.95±0.56 at 0.5 h	1.2±1.09 at 0.5 h	80.2±20.7 at 2 h	98.1±12.1 at 4.5 h
C_{max} (mg/L)	1.07±0.51	1.31±1.04	84.6±14.7	107.3±11.3
AUC mg·h/L 0-6 h	2.38±1.13	2.76±1.69	383.8±65.6	531.6±55.3

Indications: For the treatment of children with acute otitis media caused by strains of H. influenzae, S. pneumoniae, S. pyogenes or B. catarrhalis susceptible to this combination. Surgical procedures should be performed when indicated.

Contraindications: In patients with known hypersensitivity to either erythromycin, clarithromycin, other macrolide antibacterial agents or sulfonamides.

Patients with a history of hematologic, renal or hepatic dysfunction, allergic drug fever or skin eruptions due to sulfonamide derivatives, including antibacterial sulfonamides, oral hypoglycemics, and thiazides.

Infants less than 2 months of age.

Pregnancy at term and during the nursing period, because sulfonamides pass into the placental circulation and are excreted in human breast milk and may cause kernicterus in the infant.

Uremic patients, and patients with a deficiency of erythrocytic glucose-6-phosphate dehydrogenase (G-6-PD).

Patients with porphyria should not receive sulfonamides, as these drugs have been reported to precipitate an acute attack.

Concurrent therapy with astemizole, terfenadine, cisapride, or pimozide (see Precautions, Drug Interactions).

Warnings: Pseudomembranous colitis has been reported with nearly all antibacterial agents, including Pediazole, and may range in severity from mild to life threatening.

Erythromycin: Erythromycin should be administered with caution to any patient who has demonstrated some form of allergy to drugs.

If an allergic reaction to erythromycin occurs, administration of the drug should be discontinued. Serious hypersensitivity reactions may require epinephrine, antihistamines, or corticosteroids.

Hepatic dysfunction, including increased liver enzymes and hepatocellular and/or cholestatic hepatitis, with or without jaundice, has been infrequently reported with erythromycin. If findings suggestive of significant hepatic dysfunction occur, therapy with erythromycin products should be discontinued.

Pseudomembranous colitis has been occasionally reported to occur in association with erythromycin therapy. Therefore, it is important to consider its diagnosis in patients administered erythromycin who develop diarrhea. Mild cases of colitis may respond to drug discontinuation alone. Moderate to severe cases should be managed with fluid, electrolyte and protein supplementation as indicated. If the colitis is not relieved by discontinuation of erythromycin administration or when it is severe, consideration should be given to the administration of vancomycin or other suitable therapy. Other possible causes of the colitis should also be considered.

Rhabdomyolysis with or without renal impairment has been reported in seriously ill patients receiving erythromycin concomitant with lovastatin.

Cough, shortness of breath, and pulmonary infiltrates are hypersensitivity reactions of the respiratory tract that have been reported in association with sulfonamide treatment.

Pregnancy: The safe use of erythromycin or sulfonamides in pregnancy has not been established (see Contraindications and Precautions).

Precautions: Erythromycin: Prolonged or repeated use of erythromycin may result in an overgrowth of nonsusceptible bacteria or fungi and organisms initially sensitive to erythromycin. If superinfection occurs, erythromycin should be discontinued and appropriate therapy instituted.

Since erythromycin is principally excreted by the liver, caution should be exercised when erythromycin is administered to patients with impaired hepatic function.

There have been reports that erythromycin may aggravate the weakness of patients with myasthenia gravis.

Sulfonamides: Sulfonamides are bacteriostatic. Resistance is frequent in organisms responsible for common infections. Accordingly, sulfonamides should not be used alone in the treatment of meningococcal meningitis unless the organism is known to be sensitive. Sulfonamides should be used only after critical appraisal in patients with liver damage, renal damage, urinary obstruction, blood dyscrasias, allergies or bronchial asthma. Deaths have been reported from hypersensitivity reactions, agranulocytosis, aplastic anemia, and other blood dyscrasias associated with sulfonamide administration.

Although renal complications are rare with modern sulfonamides, weekly urinalysis with careful microscopic examination should be carried out.

Possible overgrowth of nonsusceptible organisms, including fungi, should be looked for when any sulfonamide is administered. Should superinfection occur, treatment should be discontinued and appropriate therapy instituted.

If signs of hypersensitivity (urticaria, drug rash, blood dyscrasias) should occur, therapy should be discontinued.

Adequate fluid intake must be maintained to prevent crystalluria and stone formation. Forcing fluids to ensure a urinary output of 1 500 mL/day or greater should be routine during sulfonamide therapy. Alkalinization of the urine lessens this hazard but also results in lowered blood sulfonamide concentrations. Heavy crystalluria, hematuria, and oliguria are indications for the administration of alkali and cessation of sulfonamide therapy.

Hemolysis may occur in G-6-PD deficient individuals.

Granulocytopenia may occur, rarely, however, after prolonged sulfonamide therapy, and serial blood counts should be done on all patients receiving sulfonamides for longer than 2 weeks.

The sulfonamides are chemically similar to some goitrogens, diuretics (acetazolamide and the thiazides), and oral hypoglycemics. Goiter, diuresis, and hypoglycemia may occur occasionally. Cross-sensitivity may exist with these agents.

Rats appear to be especially susceptible to the goitrogenic effects of sulfonamides, and long-term administration has produced thyroid malignancies in the species.

Drug Interactions: Erythromycin: Theophylline: Recent data from studies of erythromycin in patients reveal that its use in patients who are receiving high doses of theophylline may be associated with an increase in serum theophylline levels and potential theophylline toxicity. In case of theophylline toxicity and/or elevated serum theophylline levels, the dose of theophylline should be reduced while the patient is receiving concomitant erythromycin therapy.

There have been published reports suggesting that when oral erythromycin is given concurrently with theophylline, there is a significant decrease in erythromycin serum concentrations. This decrease could result in subtherapeutic concentrations of erythromycin.

Lincomycin, Clindamycin, Chloramphenicol: In vitro experiments have demonstrated that binding sites for erythromycin, lincomycin, clindamycin and chloramphenicol overlap and competitive inhibition may occur.

Carbamazepine, Cyclosporine, Hexobarbital, Phenytoin, Alfentanil, Disopyramide, Bromocriptine, Valproate, Tacrolimus, Quinidine, Terfenadine, Astemizole: Concomitant administration of erythromycin with drugs metabolized by the cytochrome P450 such as carbamazepine, cyclosporine, hexobarbital, phenytoin, alfentanil, disopyramide, bromocriptine, valproate, tacrolimus, quinidine, terfenadine, and astemizole has been reported to result in elevated plasma levels of these agents, leading to toxicity in some patients.

Serum concentrations of drugs metabolized by the cytochrome P450 system should be monitored closely in patients concurrently receiving erythromycin.

Oral Anticoagulants: Published reports indicate that caution should be observed when some antibiotics, including erythromycin, and oral anticoagulants are used concurrently since prolonged prothrombin time may occur.

Triazolam, Midazolam: Erythromycin has been reported to decrease the clearance of triazolam and midazolam and thus may increase the pharmacologic effect of these benzodiazepines.

Alfentanil: The concomitant use of erythromycin with alfentanil can significantly inhibit the clearance of alfentanil and may increase the risk of prolonged or delayed respiratory depression.

Ergotamine, Dihydroergotamine: There are reports that ischemic reactions may occur when erythromycin is given concurrently with ergotamine-containing drugs.

Concurrent use of erythromycin and ergotamine or dihydroergotamine has been associated in some patients with acute ergot toxicity characterized by severe peripheral vasospasm and dysesthesia.

Digoxin: There have been reports that there is a rise in plasma digoxin levels during concomitant administration of erythromycin.

Lovastatin: Patients receiving concomitant lovastatin and erythromycin should be carefully monitored. Cases of rhabdomyolysis with or without renal impairment have been reported in seriously ill patients receiving erythromycin concomitant with lovastatin.

Terfenadine: Terfenadine undergoes metabolism in the liver by a specific cytochrome P450 isoenzyme. This metabolic pathway may be impaired in patients who are taking erythromycin, an inhibitor of this isoenzyme. Interference with this enzyme can lead to elevated terfenadine plasma levels which may be associated with QT prolongation, and increased risk of ventricular tachyarrythmias (such as torsades de pointes, ventricular tachycardia, and ventricular fibrillation). Erythromycin significantly alters the metabolism of terfenadine when taken concomitantly. Rare cases of serious cardiovascular adverse events, including death, cardiac arrest, torsades de pointes, and other ventricular arrhythmias, have been observed (see Contraindications).

Astemizole: Concomitant administration of astemizole with erythromycin is contraindicated because erythromycin is known to impair the cytochrome P450 enzyme system which also influences astemizole metabolism. Erythromycin significantly alters the metabolism of astemizole when taken concomitantly. Rare cases of serious cardiovascular adverse events including cardiac arrest, torsades de pointes and other ventricular arrhythmias have been observed (see Contraindications and Adverse Effects).

Cisapride/Pimozide: Elevated cisapride levels have been reported in patients receiving erythromycin and cisapride concomitantly. This may result in QT prolongation and cardiac

Pediazole (cont'd)

arrhythmias including ventricular tachycardia, ventricular fibrillation and torsades de pointes. Similar effects have been observed in patients taking pimozide and clarithromycin, another macrolide antibiotic.
Zopiclone: Erythromycin has been reported to decrease the clearance of zopiclone and thus may increase the pharmacodynamic effects of this drug.
Drug/Laboratory Test Interactions: Erythromycin interferes with the fluometric determination of urinary catecholamines.
Sulfonamides: The most important interactions of the sulfonamides involve those with the oral anticoagulants, the sulfonylurea hypoglycemic agents, and the hydantoin anticonvulsants. In each case sulfonamides can potentiate the effects of the other drug by mechanisms that appear to involve primarily inhibition of metabolism and, possibly, displacement from albumin. Dosage adjustment may be necessary when a sulfonamide is given concurrently.

It has been reported that sulfisoxazole may prolong the prothrombin time in patients who are receiving the anticoagulant warfarin.

It has been proposed that sulfisoxazole competes with thiopental for plasma protein binding. It is not known whether chronic oral doses of sulfisoxazole have a similar effect. Until more is known about this interaction, physicians should be aware that patients receiving sulfisoxazole might require less thiopental for anesthesia.

Sulfonamides can displace methotrexate from plasma protein binding sites, thus increasing free methotrexate concentrations.

Sulfisoxazole can also potentiate the blood sugar-lowering activity of sulfonylureas.
Carcinogenesis, Mutagenesis, Impairment of Fertility: Long-term (2-year) oral studies conducted in rats with erythromycin base did not provide evidence of tumorigenicity. Mutagenicity studies have not been conducted. There was no apparent effect on male or female fertility in rats fed erythromycin at levels up to 0.25% of diet.
Pregnancy and *Lactation*: Erythromycin: The safety of erythromycin for use during pregnancy has not been established. Erythromycin crosses the placental barrier. The effect of erythromycin on labor and delivery is unknown. The safety of erythromycin for use during breast-feeding has not been established. Erythromycin is excreted in breast milk.
Sulfonamides: Sulfonamides are contraindicated in pregnancy at term and during the nursing period, because sulfonamides pass into the placental circulation and are excreted in human breast milk and may cause kernicterus in the infant.
Neonates: The safety of erythromycin for use in neonates has not been established. Sulfonamides are contraindicated in infants less than 2 months of age.
Children: See Dosage.

Adverse Effects: Gastrointestinal: The most frequent side effects of oral erythromycin preparations are gastrointestinal and are dose-related. They include abdominal cramping, discomfort. Nausea, vomiting and diarrhea are also observed but less frequently. Anorexia has also been reported. Pseudomembranous colitis has been occasionally reported to occur in association with erythromycin therapy (see Warnings).
Pancreatitis: Recently there has been a report of a case of erythromycin-induced pancreatitis following erythromycin overdose.
Allergic Reactions: urticaria, mild skin eruptions and anaphylaxis. Skin reactions ranging from mild eruptions to erythema multiforme, Stevens-Johnson syndrome and toxic epidermal necrolysis have rarely been reported.
Hepatotoxicity: Symptoms of hepatic dysfunction and/or abnormal liver function test results may occur (see Warnings).
Cardiovascular: Occasional case reports of cardiac arrhythmias such as ventricular tachycardia have been documented in patients receiving erythromycin therapy. Erythromycin has been associated with the production of potentially life-threatening ventricular arrhythmias, including ventricular tachycardia and torsades de pointes, in individuals taking drug that may interact with erythromycin (see Precautions, Drug Interactions).

There have been isolated reports of other cardiovascular symptoms such as chest pain, dizziness, and palpitations; however, a cause and effect relationship has not been established.
Neurological: CNS side effects including seizures, hallucinations, confusion and vertigo have been reported in occasional patients; however, a cause and effect relationship has not been established.
Miscellaneous: During prolonged or repeated therapy, there is a possibility of overgrowth of nonsusceptible bacteria or fungi and organisms initially sensitive to erythromycin (e.g., S. aureus, H. influenzae). If such infections occur, erythromycin should be discontinued and appropriate therapy instituted.

Occasionally there have been reports of reversible hearing loss occurring chiefly in patients with renal insufficiency and in patients receiving high doses of erythromycin.
Sulfonamides: The following untoward effects have been associated with the use of sulfonamides: Hematologic: agranulocytosis, anemia, aplastic anemia, clotting disorders, thrombocytopenia, leukopenia, hemolytic anemia, purpura, hypo-prothrombinemia, methemoglobinemia, hypofibrinogenemia, sulfhemoglobinemia.
Allergic Reactions: anaphylaxis, erythema multiforme (Stevens-Johnson syndrome), generalized skin eruptions, toxic epidermal necrolysis (Lyell's syndrome), angioedema, arteritis, vasculitis, urticaria, rash, serum sickness, pruritus, exfoliative dermatitis, anaphylactoid reactions, periorbital edema, conjunctival and scleral injection, photosensitization, arthralgia and allergic myocarditis.

In addition, periarteritis nodosa and systemic lupus erythematosus have been reported.
Cardiovascular: tachycardia, palpitations, syncope, and cyanosis.
Gastrointestinal: hepatitis, hepatocellular necrosis, jaundice, pseudomembranous colitis, nausea, emesis, anorexia, abdominal pains, diarrhea, gastrointestinal hemorrhage, melena, flatulence, glossitis, stomatitis, salivary gland enlargement, and pancreatitis. Onset of pseudomembranous colitis symptoms may occur during or after treatment with sulfisoxazole, a component of Pediazole (see Warnings).

The sulfisoxazole acetyl component of Pediazole has been reported to cause increased elevation of liver-associated enzymes in patients with hepatitis.
Genitourinary: crystalluria, hematuria, BUN and creatinine elevations, nephritis, and toxic nephrosis with oliguria and/or anuria. Acute renal failure and urinary retention have also been reported.

The frequency of renal complications, commonly associated with some sulfonamides, is lower in patients receiving the more soluble sulfonamides such as sulfisoxazole.
Neurologic: headache, dizziness, peripheral neuritis, paresthesia, convulsions, ataxia, tinnitus, vertigo, insomnia, and intracranial hypertension.
Psychiatric: psychosis, hallucinations, disorientation, mental depression, and anxiety.
Respiratory: cough, shortness of breath, and pulmonary infiltrates (see Warnings).
Vascular: angioedema, arteritis, and vasculitis.
Endocrine: The sulfonamides bear certain chemical similarities to some goitrogens, diuretics (acetazolamide and the thiazides) and oral hypoglycemic agents. Goiter production, diuresis and hypoglycemia have occurred rarely in patients receiving sulfonamides. Cross-sensitivity may exist with these agents.
Miscellaneous: edema (including periorbital), pyrexia, drowsiness, weakness, fatigue, lassitude, rigors, flushing, hearing loss, insomnia, and pneumonitis.

Petechiae, hematuria, drug fever, chills. Periarteritis nodosum and L.E. phenomenon have occurred.

Overdose: Symptoms and Treatment: Erythromycin ethylsuccinate: Similar to those of erythromycin. Symptoms: In oral doses of over 2 g/day, abdominal discomfort, nausea or diarrhea may occur. Recently, there has been a report of a case of erythromycin-induced pancreatitis following erythromycin overdose. Treatment: There is no specific treatment for overdosage. Erythromycin should be discontinued and gastric lavage should be considered; otherwise, the treatment should be symptomatic. Erythromycin is not removed by peritoneal dialysis or hemodialysis.
Sulfisoxazole: Similar to those of any sulfonamide. Symptoms: The most likely symptoms would be gastrointestinal disturbances, hematuria, crystalluria or anuria. Treatment: If poisoning occurs from the ingestion of any overdose, remove the agent from stomach by lavage and/or emesis. If renal function is normal, force fluids orally or parenterally to promote excretion. In extreme overdosage with renal shutdown, consideration should be given to dialysis as a means of both eliminating the sulfonamide and also reducing the risk of uremia. There is no known antidote for sulfonamide poisoning and the patient must be treated symptomatically.

Dosage: Should not be administered to infants under 2 months of age because of contraindications of systemic sulfonamides in this age group (see Contraindications).
Acute Otitis Media in Children: The dose can be calculated based on the erythromycin component (50 mg/kg/day) or the sulfisoxazole component (150 mg/kg/day to a maximum of 6 g/day).

Pediazole is to be given in equally divided doses 3 or 4 times a day for 10 days. It may be administered without regard to meals, but is preferably given immediately after meals.
Reconstitution: Reconstitute by slowly adding the required amount of water (see Table II) to the bottle and shaking moderately until uniformly mixed. When reconstituted, the granules form a white, strawberry-banana flavor suspension.

Table II—Pediazole

Reconstitution Table

Bottle Size (mL)	Volume of Water to be Added (mL)	Concentration (mg/5 mL) Erythromycin	Sulfisoxazole
105	55	200	600
150	75	200	600
200	100	200	600

Stability and Storage: Reconstituted suspensions should be refrigerated and used within 14 days. Unused portion should be discarded after 14 days.

Supplied: After reconstitution, each 5 mL of white, strawberry-banana suspension contains: erythromycin ethylsuccinate equivalent to 200 mg erythromycin activity, and sulfisoxazole acetyl equivalent to 600 mg sulfisoxazole. Nonmedicinal ingredients: ammonium glycyrrhizinate, cane sugar (sucrose), citric acid, flavor, poloxamer, sodium carboxymethyl cellulose, sodium citrate and veegum. Energy: 31.39 kJ (7.5 kcal)/5 mL. Alcohol-, gluten-, lactose-, paraben-, sodium-, sulfite- and tartrazine-free. Bottles of 105, 150 and 200 mL.

Reviewed 1999

PEDI-DENT™
Stanley

Sodium Fluoride
Dental Caries Prophylaxis

Supplied: Drops: Each mL supplies sodium fluoride 6.9 mg (i.e. approx. 1 mg of fluoride ion/8 drops). Nonmedicinal ingredients: diluted phosphoric acid, sodium benzoate and water. Plastic bottles of 2 fl. oz.

Tablets: Each pink, sugar-free, flavored chewable tablet contains: sodium fluoride 2.21 mg equivalent to fluoride ion 1 mg. Nonmedicinal ingredients: colloidal silicon dioxide, D&C Red No. 27, FD&C Red No. 40, flavor, magnesium stearate, mannitol, sodium cyclamate, sorbitol and stearic acid. Bottles of 90.

PedvaxHIB®
MSD

Haemophilus b Conjugate Vaccine (Meningococcal Protein Conjugate)
Vaccine

Pharmacology: Disease Epidemiology: Prior to the introduction of Haemophilus b conjugate vaccines, H. influenzae type b (Haemophilus b) was the most frequent cause of bacterial meningitis and a leading cause of serious systemic bacterial disease in young children worldwide.

Haemophilus b disease occurred primarily in children under 5 years of age in the United States prior to the initiation of a vaccine program and was estimated to account for nearly 20 000 cases of invasive infections annually, approximately 12 000 of which were meningitis. The mortality rate from Haemophilus b meningitis is about 5%. In addition, up to 35% of survivors develop neurological sequelae including convulsions, deafness, and mental retardation. Other invasive diseases caused by this bacterium include cellulitis, epiglottis, sepsis, pneumonia, septic arthritis, osteomyelitis and pericarditis. Since the introduction and widespread use of Haemophilus b conjugate vaccines in the United States, the incidence of invasive Haemophilus b disease has declined 95% among children aged less than 5 years.

Prior to the introduction of the vaccine, it was estimated that 17% of all cases of Haemophilus b disease occurred in infants less than 6 months of age. The peak incidence of Haemophilus b meningitis occurs between 6 and 11 months of age. Forty-seven percent of all cases occur by 1 year of age with the remaining 53% of cases occurring over the next 4 years.

Among children under 5 years of age, the risk of invasive Haemophilus b disease is further increased in certain populations including the following: day-care attendees, lower socioeconomic groups, blacks (especially those who lack the Km(1) immunoglobulin allotype), caucasians who lack the G2m(n or 23) immunoglobulin allotype, native americans, household contacts of cases, individuals with asplenia, sickle cell disease, or antibody deficiency syndromes.

Immunology of Haemophilus B Disease: An important virulence factor of the Haemophilus b bacterium is its polysaccharide capsule (PRP). Antibody to PRP (anti-PRP) has been shown to correlate with protection against Haemophilus b disease. While the anti-PRP level associated with protection using conjugated vaccines has not yet been determined, the level of anti-PRP associated with protection in studies using bacterial polysaccharide immune globulin or nonconjugated PRP vaccines ranged from ≥0.15 to ≥1.0 µg/mL.

PedvaxHIB and Liquid PedvaxHIB are PRP-conjugate vaccines that overcome the deficiencies of nonconjugated PRP vaccines in infants and young children. Conjugation of a carbohydrate to a protein carrier enhances antibody responses to the carbohydrate, a process that is thought to convert the T-independent antigen (PRP alone) into a T-dependent antigen which results in both an enhanced antibody response and immunologic memory.

The protective efficacy, safety, and antibody responses to PedvaxHIB were evaluated in 3 486 Native American (Navajo) infants who completed the primary two-dose regimen in a randomized, double-blind, placebo-controlled study (The Protective Efficacy Study). This population has a much higher incidence of Haemophilus b disease than the United States population as a whole and also has a lower antibody response to Haemophilus b conjugate vaccines, including PedvaxHIB.

Each infant in this study received two doses of either placebo or PedvaxHIB with the first dose administered at a mean of 8 weeks of age and the second administered approximately two months later; DTP and OPV were administered concomitantly. Antibody levels were measured in a subset of each group (see Table I).

In this study, 22 cases of invasive Haemophilus b disease occurred in the placebo group (8 cases after the first dose and 14 cases after the second dose) and only 1 case in the vaccine group (none after the first dose and 1 after the second dose). Following the recommended two-dose regimen, the protective efficacy of PedvaxHIB was calculated to be 93% with a 95% confidence interval of 57 to 98% (p=0.001, two-tailed). In the 2 months between the first and second doses, the difference in number of cases of disease between placebo and vaccine recipients (8 vs 0 cases, respectively) was statistically significant (p=0.008, two-tailed); however, a primary two-dose regimen is required for infants 2 to 14 months of age. A subset of 1 368 infants from this study was followed to 15 months of age with no additional cases of invasive Haemophilus b disease occurring after the primary two-dose regimen of PedvaxHIB (see Dosage, including Booster Dose).

Since protective efficacy with PedvaxHIB was demonstrated in such a high risk population, it would be expected to be predictive of efficacy in other populations.

Clinical Evaluation: The safety and immunogenicity of PedvaxHIB were evaluated in infants and children in other clinical studies that were conducted in various locations throughout the United States. PedvaxHIB was highly immunogenic in all age groups studied.

Antibody responses from these clinical studies (excluding Native Americans) are shown in Table II.

These data were derived by evaluating the sera in one laboratory using a radioimmunoassay which correlated with both the Finnish National Public Health Institute assay and that recommended by the Center for Biologics Evaluation and Research of the FDA (see Tables I and II).

The safety and immunogenicity of Liquid PedvaxHIB were compared with those of PedvaxHIB in a clinical study involving 903 infants 2 to 6 months of age from the general U.S. population. DTP and OPV were administered concomitantly to most subjects. The antibody responses induced by PedvaxHIB and

Table I—PedvaxHIB

Antibody Responses in Navajo Infants

Vaccine	No. of Subjects	Time	% Subjects with >0.15 µg/mL	% Subjects with >1.0 (µg/mL)	Anti-PRP GMT (µg/mL)
PedvaxHIB[a,b]	416	Prevaccination	44	10	0.16
	416	Dose 1	88	52	0.95
	416	Dose 2	91	60	1.43
Placebo[a,b]	461	Prevaccination	44	9	0.16
	461	Dose 1	21	2	0.09
	461	Dose 2	14	1	0.08
PedvaxHIB[c]	27	Prebooster	70	33	0.51
	27	Postbooster[d]	100	89	8.39

[a]Postvaccination values obtained approximately 1 to 3 months after each dose.
[b]The Protective Efficacy Study.
[c]Immunogenicity Trial.
[d]Booster given at 12 months of age; postvaccination values obtained 1 month after administration of booster dose.

Table II—PedvaxHIB

Antibody Responses[a] to PedvaxHIB in Other Clinical Studies

Age (months)	Time	No. of Subjects	% Subjects Responding with >0.15 µg/mL	% Subjects Responding with >1.0 (µg/mL)	Post-Vaccination Anti-PRP GMT (µg/mL)
2-3	Dose 1[b]	113	97	81	2.48
	Dose 2[c]	113	98	88	4.60
4-14	Dose 1[b]	252	98	75	2.53
	Dose 2[c]	252	100	92	6.04
15-17	Single Dose[c]	59	100	83	3.11
18-23	Single Dose[c]	59	98	97	7.43
24-71	Single Dose[c]	52	98	92	10.55

[a]Only subjects with prevaccination anti-PRP 0.15 µg/mL are included in this table (excluding Native Americans).
[b]2 months postvaccination.
[c]1 month postvaccination.

Table III—PedvaxHIB

Antibody Responses to Liquid PedvaxHIB and PedvaxHIB in Infants From the General U.S. Population

Formulation	Age (Months)	Time	No. of Subjects	% Subjects with >0.15 µg/mL	% Subjects with >1.0 µg/mL	Anti-PRP GMT (µg/mL)
		Prevaccination	487	32	7	0.12
Liquid	2-3	Dose 1[a]	480	94	64	1.55
PedvaxHIB		Dose 2[b]	393	97	80	3.22
(7.5 µg PRP)	12-15	Prebooster	284	80	30	0.49
		Postbooster	284	99	95	10.23
	24[c]	Persistence	94	97	55	1.26
		Prevaccination	171	37	6	0.13
PedvaxHIB	2-3	Dose 1[a]	169	97	72	1.88
(15 µg PRP)		Dose 2[b]	133	99	81	2.69
	12-15	Prebooster	87	71	28	0.39
		Postbooster[b]	87	99	91	7.64
	24[c]	Persistence	37	97	54	1.10

[a]Approximately 2 months postvaccination.
[b]Approximately 1 month postvaccination.
[c]Approximately.

Table IV—PedvaxHIB

Antibody Responses[a] After Two Doses of PedvaxHIB Among Infants Initially Vaccinated at 2 to 3 Months of Age by Racial/Ethnic Group

Racial/Ethnic Groups	No. of Subjects	% With Anti-PRP >0.15 µg/mL	% With Anti-PRP >1.0 µg/mL	GMT (µg/mL)
Native American[a]	44	95	68	2.24
Caucasian	155	99	85	4.00
Hispanic	16	100	94	4.60
Black	18	100	94	8.57

[a]Apache and Navajo.
[b]1 month after the second dose.

Liquid PedvaxHIB were similar. Table III shows antibody responses in subjects who received their first dose at 2 to 3 months of age.

Since the magnitude of initial antibody response is lower among younger infants, a booster dose is required in infants who complete the primary two-dose regimen before 12 months of age (see Dosage).

In a multicenter study of immunogenicity and safety in different subpopulations in the United States, antibody responses to PedvaxHIB were evaluated in infants initially vaccinated between the ages of 2 and 3 months (see Table IV).

The antibody responses with PedvaxHIB and Liquid PedvaxHIB were compared in 2 randomized clinical studies. Table V (on following page) shows similar responses in several subgroups of infants vaccinated at 2 to 3 months of age.

PedvaxHIB induced antibody levels greater than 1.0 µg/mL in children who were poor responders to nonconjugated PRP vaccines. In a study involving such a subpopulation, children ranging in age from 27 to 61 months who developed invasive Haemophilus b disease despite previous vaccination with nonconjugated PRP vaccines were assigned randomly to 2 groups. One group (n=14) was immunized with PedvaxHIB and the other group (n=20) with a nonconjugated PRP vaccine at a mean interval of approximately 12 months after recovery from disease. All 14 children immunized with PedvaxHIB but only 6 of 20 children re-immunized with a nonconjugated PRP vaccine achieved an antibody level of

PedvaxHIB (cont'd)

Table V—PedvaxHIB

Antibody Responses After Two Doses of PedvaxHIB and Liquid PedvaxHIB Among Infants Initially Vaccinated at 2 to 3 Months of Age By Racial/Ethnic Group

Racial/Ethnic Groups	No. of Subjects	Liquid % Subjects With Anti-PRP >0.15 µg/mL	Liquid % Subjects With Anti-PRP >1.0 µg/mL	Anti-PRP GMT (µg/mL)
Native American[c]	90	97	78	2.76
Caucasian[b]	143	94	72	2.16
Hispanic[b]	184	98	85	4.34
Black[b]	18	100	94	7.58
Racial/Ethnic Groups	**No. of Subjects**	**Lyophilized[a] % Subjects With Anti-PRP >0.15 µg/mL**	**Lyophilized[a] % Subjects With Anti-PRP >1.0 µg/mL**	**Anti-PRP GMT (µg/mL)**
Native American[a,c]	10	100	80	3.82
Caucasian[b]	46	100	74	2.30
Hispanic[b]	60	98	87	3.30
Black[b]	5	100	100	1.93

[a] 1 month after the second dose.
[b] 1 to 2 months after the second dose.
[c] Apache and Navajo.

>1.0 µg/mL. The 14 children who had not responded to revaccination with the nonconjugated PRP vaccine were then immunized with a single dose of PedvaxHIB and following this vaccination, all achieved antibody levels of >1.0 µg/mL.

In addition, PedvaxHIB has been studied in children 2 to 17 months of age at high risk of Haemophilus b disease because of genetically related deficiencies (Blacks who were Km (1) allotype negative and Caucasians who were G2m (23) allotype negative) and are considered hyporesponsive to nonconjugated PRP vaccines on this basis. The hyporesponsive children had anti-PRP responses comparable to those of allotype positive children of similar age range when vaccinated with PedvaxHIB. All children achieved anti-PRP levels of >1.0 µg/mL.

Antibody Persistence: Persistence of antibody at 36 months of age was studied in 35 children following 3 doses of PedvaxHIB and in 134 children following 3 doses of Liquid PedvaxHIB (last dose [booster] given when 12 to 15 months old). Similar results were observed in children who received either PedvaxHIB or Liquid PedvaxHIB. In those children who received PedvaxHIB or Liquid PedvaxHIB, respectively, 91% and 98% had antibody titres >0.15 µg/mL, and 37% and 58% had antibody titres >1.0 µg/mL. Anti-PRP geometric mean titres (GMTs) in the children who received either PedvaxHIB or Liquid PedvaxHIB, were 0.8 µg/mL and 1.5 µg/mL, respectively.

Postmarket Effectiveness Data: Two post-licensure effectiveness studies using PedvaxHIB were performed: one in the United States with Navajo infants and children, and one in Israel. Both studies demonstrated 95% effectiveness against invasive Hib disease.

Interchangeability of PedvaxHIB and Liquid PedvaxHIB: The immunogenicity of PedvaxHIB (15 µg PRP) and Liquid PedvaxHIB (7.5 µg PRP) in infants and children was compared in a multicenter clinical study and was similar (see Table III on previous page). It is expected that the immune response would be comparable if the two formulations were used interchangeably.

Indications: For routine vaccination against invasive disease caused by H. influenzae type b in infants and children 2 to 59 months of age.

As with other vaccines, several days following administration of PedvaxHIB or Liquid PedvaxHIB are required for protective levels of antibody to be achieved.

PedvaxHIB and Liquid PedvaxHIB will not protect against H. influenzae other than type b or against other microorganisms that cause meningitis or sepsis.

Revaccination: Infants completing the primary two-dose regimen before 12 months of age should receive a booster dose (see Dosage).

Use with Other Vaccines: Studies have been conducted in which PedvaxHIB and Liquid PedvaxHIB have been administered concomitantly with the primary vaccination series and/or booster doses of DTP and OPV, or concomitantly with M-M-R II (using separate sites and syringes). No impairment of immune response to individual tested antigens was demonstrated. The type, frequency and severity of adverse experiences observed in these studies were similar to those seen when the individual vaccines were given alone.

Note: The National Advisory Committee on Immunization (NACI) recommends administration on a single day of all vaccines (i.e., DTP, IPV (or OPV), M-M-R II and H. influenzae type b conjugate vaccine), appropriate to the patient's age and previous vaccination status, if the patient is unlikely to return for further vaccination. If this is done, separate sites and syringes should be used for the injectable vaccines: PedvaxHIB or Liquid PedvaxHIB, M-M-R II, DTP, IPV and DTP-IPV.

Contraindications: Hypersensitivity to any component of the vaccine or the diluent.

Warnings: Use only the aluminum hydroxide diluent supplied to reconstitute the lyophilized vaccine.

The expected immune response may not be obtained when PedvaxHIB or Liquid PedvaxHIB is used in persons with malignancies or those receiving immunosuppressive therapy or who are otherwise immunocompromised.

Precautions: General: Adequate treatment provisions, including epinephrine, should be available for immediate use should an anaphylactoid reaction occur.

As with any vaccine, vaccination with PedvaxHIB or Liquid PedvaxHIB b conjugate vaccine may not result in a protective antibody response in 100% of susceptible persons given the vaccine.

As reported with Haemophilus b polysaccharide vaccine and another Haemophilus b conjugate vaccine, cases of Haemophilus b disease may occur in the week after vaccination, prior to the onset of the protective effects of the vaccines.

There is insufficient evidence showing that PedvaxHIB or Liquid PedvaxHIB given immediately after exposure to natural H. influenzae type b will prevent illness.

Any acute infection or febrile illness is reason for delaying use of PedvaxHIB or Liquid PedvaxHIB except when, in the opinion of the physician, withholding the vaccine entails a greater risk.

An immunogenic response to the carrier protein (N. meningitidis) has been demonstrated but its clinical benefit has not been established.

Pregnancy: Animal reproduction studies have not been conducted with PedvaxHIB or Liquid PedvaxHIB. These products are not recommended for use in individuals 6 years of age or older.

Children: Safety and effectiveness in infants below the age of 2 months and in children 6 years of age and older have not been established.

Carcinogenesis, Mutagenesis, and Impairment of Fertility: PedvaxHIB and Liquid PedvaxHIB have not been evaluated for their carcinogenic or mutagenic potential, or its potential to impair fertility.

Laboratory Tests: Sensitive tests, e.g., Latex Agglutination Kits, may detect PRP derived from the vaccine in the urine of some vaccinees for at least 30 days following vaccination with PedvaxHIB. In clinical studies with PedvaxHIB, children with this antigenuria demonstrated a normal immune response to the vaccine.

Adverse Effects: PedvaxHIB: In clinical studies involving the administration of 8 086 doses of PedvaxHIB alone to 5 027 healthy infants and children 2 months of age to 71 months of age, PedvaxHIB was generally well tolerated. No serious adverse reactions were reported.

In a subset of these infants and children, during a two-day period following vaccination with PedvaxHIB, the most frequently reported adverse reactions, excluding those shown in Table VI, in decreasing order of frequency included irritability, sleepiness, respiratory infection/symptoms, and ear infection/otitis media. Urticaria was reported in 2 children. Thrombocytopenia was seen in one child. A cause and effect relationship between these side effects and the vaccination has not been established.

Summarized in Table VI from early clinical studies are selected objective observations reported by parents over a 48-hour period in infants and children 2 to 71 months of age following primary vaccination with PedvaxHIB.

In later clinical studies with PedvaxHIB, one additional serious adverse reaction (tracheitis, possibly related to the vaccine) was reported.

As with any vaccine, there is the possibility that broad use of PedvaxHIB could reveal adverse reactions not observed in clinical trials. The following additional adverse reactions have been reported with use of the marketed vaccine:

Hemic and Lymphatic System: lymphadenopathy.

Hypersensitivity: rarely, angioedema.

Nervous System: seizures (including febrile seizures).

Skin: sterile injection site abscess; pain at the injection site.

Liquid PedvaxHIB: The type and frequency of adverse reactions reported with Liquid PedvaxHIB were similar to those seen with PedvaxHIB.

In a multicenter clinical study (n=903) comparing the effects of Liquid PedvaxHIB with those of PedvaxHIB, 1 699 doses of Liquid PedvaxHIB were administered to 678 healthy infants 2 to 6 months of age from the general U.S. population. DTP and OPV were administered concomitantly to most subjects. Both PedvaxHIB and Liquid PedvaxHIB were generally well tolerated and no serious vaccine-related adverse reactions were reported.

During a three-day period following primary vaccination with Liquid PedvaxHIB in these infants, the most frequently reported (>1%) adverse reactions, without regard to causality, excluding those shown in Table VII, in decreasing order of frequency, were: irritability, sleepiness, injection site pain/soreness, injection site erythema (≤2.5 cm diameter, see also Table VII), injection site swelling/induration (≤2.5 cm diameter, see also Table VII) unusual high-pitched crying, prolonged crying (>4 hours), diarrhea, vomiting, crying, pain, otitis media, rash, and upper respiratory infection.

Table VI—PedvaxHIB

Fever or Local Reactions in Subjects 2 to 71 Months of Age Vaccinated with PedvaxHIB Alone Early Clinical Studies

Age (Months)	Reaction	No. of Subjects Evaluated	% of Patients Post-Dose 1: 6 h	24 h	48 h	No. of Subjects Evaluated	% of Patients Post-Dose 2: 6 h	24 h	48 h
2-14[a]	Fever >38.3°C (rectal)	532	2.4	3.8	1.9	329	3.0	4.3	3.6
	Erythema >2.5 cm diameter	1 026	0.2	1.0	0.4	585	0.9	1.2	0.7
	Swelling/induration >2.5 cm diameter	1 026	0.6	1.5	1.6	585	0.9	2.8	3.7
15-71[b]	Fever >38.3°C (rectal)	149	4.0	4.0	6.7				
	Erythema >2.5 cm diameter	572	0.0	0.3	0.2				
	Swelling/induration >2.5 cm diameter	572	0.9	2.1	1.4				

[a] Additional complaints reported following vaccination with the first and second dose of PedvaxHIB, respectively, in the indicated number of subjects were: nausea, vomiting and/or diarrhea (101, 41), crying for more than one-half hour (43, 15), rash (16, 17), and unusual high-pitched crying (4, 4).
[b] Additional complaints reported following vaccination with 1 dose of PedvaxHIB in the indicated number of subjects were: nausea, vomiting and/or diarrhea (44), crying for more than one-half hour (19), rash (12), and unusual high-pitched crying (0).

Table VII—PedvaxHIB

Fever or Local Reactions in Subjects First Vaccinated at 2 to 6 Months of Age with PedvaxHIB and Liquid PedvaxHIB[a]

		Liquid Post-Dose 1 (h)				Post-Dose 2 (h)		
Reaction	**No. of Subjects Evaluated**	**6**	**24**	**48**	**No. of Subjects Evaluated**	**6**	**24**	**48**
			%				**%**	
Fever[b] >38.3°C (rectal)	222	18.1	4.4	0.5	206	14.1	9.4	2.8
Erythema >2.5 cm diameter	674	2.2	1.0	0.5	562	1.6	1.1	0.4
Swelling >2.5 cm diameter	674	2.5	1.9	0.9	562	0.9	0.9	1.3
		Lyophilized Post-Dose 1 (h)				Post-Dose 2 (h)		
Reaction	**No. of Subjects Evaluated**	**6**	**24**	**48**	**No. of Subjects Evaluated**	**6**	**24**	**48**
Fever[c] >38.3°C (rectal)	82	16.2	9.6	1.5	67	5.0	4.8	0.0
Erythema >2.5 cm diameter	224	3.1	1.8	1.5	190	1.1	0.0	0.0
Swelling >2.5 cm diameter	224	5.8	1.3	1.0	190	1.1	0.0	0.0

[a] DTP and OPV were administered concomitantly to most subjects.
[b] Fever was also measured by another method or reported as normal for an additional 345 infants after dose 1 and for an additional 249 infants after dose 2: however, these data are not included in this table.
[c] Fever was also measured by another method or reported as normal for an additional 113 infants after dose 1 and for an additional 98 infants after dose 2: these data are not included in this table.

Selected objective observations reported by parents over a 48-hour period in these infants following primary vaccination with Liquid PedvaxHIB are summarized in Table VII.

Adverse reactions reported during a three-day period following primary vaccination were generally similar in type and frequency to those seen following administration of the booster dose.

As with any vaccine, there is the possibility that broad use of Liquid PedvaxHIB could reveal adverse reactions not observed in clinical trials.

Potential Side Effects: The use of Haemophilius b Polysaccharide Vaccines and another Haemophilus b Conjugate Vaccine has been associated with the following additional adverse effects: convulsions, early onset Haemophilus b disease, Guillain Barré syndrome. A cause and effect relationship between these side effects and the vaccination was not established.

Dosage: For i.m. administration. Do not inject i.v. or intradermally.

PedvaxHIB: To reconstitute PedvaxHIB use only the aluminum hydroxide diluent supplied.

First, agitate the diluent vial, then, using sterile technique, withdraw the entire volume of aluminum hydroxide diluent into the syringe to be used for reconstitution. Inject all the aluminum hydroxide diluent in the syringe into the vial of lyophilized vaccine, and agitate to mix thoroughly.

Withdraw the entire contents into a syringe and inject the total volume (about 0.5 mL) of reconstituted vaccine i.m., preferably into the anterolateral thigh or the outer aspect of the upper arm.

It is recommended that the lyophilized vaccine be used as soon as possible after reconstitution. Store reconstituted vaccine in the vaccine vial at 2 to 8°C and discard if not used within 24 hours. Agitate prior to injection.

Liquid PedvaxHIB: The vaccine should be used as supplied; no reconstitution is necessary.

Shake well before withdrawal and use. Thorough agitation is necessary to maintain suspension of the vaccine.

Inject 0.5 mL i.m., preferably into the anterolateral thigh or the outer aspect of the upper arm.

Parenteral drug products should be inspected visually for extraneous particulate matter and discoloration prior to administration. PedvaxHIB (when reconstituted as directed), the aluminum hydroxide diluent and Liquid PedvaxHIB are all slightly opaque white suspensions.

Special care should be taken to ensure that the injection does not enter a blood vessel.

It is important to use a separate sterile syringe and needle for each patient to prevent transmission of hepatitis B or other infectious agents from one person to another.

Children: 2 to 6 months: Infants beginning immunization at 2 to 6 months of age should receive 2 doses of vaccine (0.5 mL/dose) 2 months apart with a booster dose at 12 months of age.

7 to 11 months: Unvaccinated children 7 to 11 months of age should receive 2 doses (0.5 mL/dose) 2 months apart with a booster dose at 15 to 18 months of age (or as soon as possible thereafter) and not less than 2 months after the second dose.

12 to 17 months: Unvaccinated children 12 to 17 months of age should receive a single dose (0.5 mL) of vaccine as soon as possible and an additional dose at, or after 18 months of age, and at least 2 months after the first dose.

18 to 59 months: Children 18 to 59 months of age who have not previously received the vaccine should receive a single dose (0.5 mL) of vaccine.

Supplied: Liquid: Each 0.5 mL dose contains: Haemophilus b PRP 7.5 μg and N. meningitidis OMPC 125 μg. Nonmedicinal ingredients: aluminum as aluminum hydroxide, sodium borate and sodium chloride. Single dose vials of 0.5 mL. Store between 2 and 8°C. **Do not freeze.**

Powder: Each 0.5 mL dose, when reconstituted as directed contains: Haemophilus b PRP 15 μg and N. meningitidis OMPC 250 μg. Nonmedicinal ingredients: aluminum as aluminum hydroxide, lactose, sodium borate, sodium chloride and thimerosal (a mercury derivative) as preservative. Diluent: The aluminum hydroxide diluent is required for the reconstitution of the lyophilized formulation. Boxes of 5 single dose vials (0.5 mL) of lyophilized vaccine and 5 vials (0.7 mL) of aluminum hydroxide as diluent. Before reconstitution, store the lyophilized vaccine and the aluminum hydroxide diluent between 2 and 8°C. Store reconstituted vaccine in the vaccine vial between 2 and 8°C and discard if not used within 24 hours. **Do not freeze** the aluminum hydroxide diluent or the reconstituted vaccine.

The vaccines must be maintained between 2 and 8°C during shipment to ensure that there is no loss of potency.

Reviewed 1999

PEGLYTE™

Pharmascience

PEG-Electrolytes

Gastrointestinal Lavage

Pharmacology: Peglyte cleanses the bowel by induction of diarrhea. The osmotic activity of polyethylene glycol 3350, in combination with the electrolyte concentration, results in virtually no net absorption or secretion of ions or water. Accordingly, large volumes may be administered without significant changes in fluid and electrolyte balance.

Indications: For bowel cleansing prior to colonoscopy or barium enema x-ray examination or surgical procedures requiring a clean colon. PEG lavage solution is also indicated for the treatment of constipation and impaction in the elderly and has been used occasionally in children.

Contraindications: Patients with ileus, gastric retention, bowel perforation, gastrointestinal obstruction, toxic colitis and toxic megacolon.

Warnings: No additional flavorings or ingredients may be added to the solution. Peglyte should be used with caution in patients with severe ulcerative colitis.

Precautions: Patients with impaired gag reflex, unconcious or semiconscious patients and patients prone to regurgitation or aspiration should be observed during the administration of Peglyte, especially if it is administered via nasogastric tube.

If gastrointestinal obstruction or perforation is suspected, appropriate studies should be performed to rule out those conditions before administration of Peglyte.

When it is used in children, caution should be excercised to avoid dehydration.

Drug Interactions: Oral medications administered within 1 hour of the start of administration of Peglyte may be flushed from the gastrointestinal tract and not absorbed.

Carcinogenesis, Mutagenesis, Impairment of Fertility: Long-term carcinogenic and reproductive studies with animals have not been performed.

Pregnancy: Animal reproduction studies have not been conducted with Peglyte, and it is not known whether Peglyte can affect reproductive capacity or harm the fetus when administered to a pregnant patient. Peglyte should be given to a pregnant patient only if clearly needed.

Children: PEG lavage solution has been used for bowel cleansing and the treatment of constipation and fecal impaction in children. Treatment and dosage should be monitored by a physician.

Information for the Patient: Peglyte produces a watery stool which cleanses the bowel prior to examination.

For best results, no solid food should be consumed during the 3- to 4-hour period before Peglyte consumption. In no case should solid foods be ingested 3 hours before Peglyte administration.

The rate of administration is 240 mL every 10 minutes. Rapid drinking of each portion is preferred rather than drinking small amounts continuously.

The first bowel movement should occur approximately 1 hour after the start of Peglyte administration. Administration of Peglyte should be continued until the watery stool is clear and free of solid matter. This normally requires the consumption of approximately 3 to 4 L, although more or less may be required in some patients. The unused portion should be discarded.

Adverse Effects: Nausea, abdominal fullness, and bloating are the most frequent adverse effects, occurring in up to 50% of patients. Abdominal cramps, vomiting and anal irritation occur less frequently. These adverse effects are transient.

Isolated cases of urticaria, rhinorrhea and dermatitis have been reported which may represent allergic reactions.

Dosage: Prior to gastrointestinal examination or procedure: Peglyte can be administered orally or by nasogastric tube. Patients should fast at least 3 hours prior to administration. A 1-hour waiting period after the appearance of clear liquid stools should be allowed prior to examination to complete bowel evacuation. No foods except clear liquids should be permitted prior to examination after Peglyte administration.

Oral: The recommended adult oral dose is 240 mL every 10 minutes (see Precautions, Information for the Patient). Lavage is complete when fecal discharge is clear. Lavage is usually complete after the ingestion of 3 to 4 L.

Nasogastric Tube: Peglyte is administered at a rate of 20 to 30 mL/minute (1.2 to 1.8 L/hour).

Preparation of Solution: Add tap water to fill line. Replace cap tightly and mix or shake well until all ingredients have dissolved. (No additional flavorings or ingredients may be added to the solution.)

Chronic Constipation: 240 to 480 mL/day orally or as recommended by a physician.

Fecal Impaction: Fecal impaction should only be treated by a physician. Recommended adult dose is 2 to 3 L orally, over a 3- to 4-hour period.

Children: Dosage should be adjusted bearing in mind the weight of the child.

Supplied: Powder: Each 280 g container of powder contains: polyethylene glycol 3350 238.18 g, sodium sulfate 22.96 g, sodium bicarbonate 6.76 g, sodium chloride 5.85 g, potassium chloride 3.05 g, flavors 2.55 g and sodium saccharin 0.55 g.

When reconstituted to 4 L with water, each 1 L of solution contains: polyethylene glycol 3350 17.8 mmol, sodium 126 mmol, potassium 10.2 mmol, chloride 35.3 mmol, sulfate 40.4 mmol, bicarbonate 20.1 mmol. The reconstituted solution has a mild fruit flavor.

Containers of 4 L. Reconstituted solution should be used within 48 hours after mixing if stored at room temperature. If kept refrigerated (2 to 8°C), use within 30 days. Discard unused portion.

Solution: Each 1 L of solution contains: polyethylene glycol 17.8 mmol, sodium 126 mmol, potassium 10.2 mmol, chloride 35.3 mmol, sulfate 40.4 mmol, bicarbonate 20.1 mmol supplied as polyethylene glycol 59.55 g, sodium sulfate 5.74 g, sodium bicarbonate 1.69 g, sodium chloride 1.46 g, potassium chloride 0.76 g. The solution has a mild fruit flavor.

Peglyte (cont'd)

Containers of 1 L, cartons of 8, wrapped in groups of 4. Once opened the solution should be used within 48 hours if stored at room temperature. If kept refrigerated (2 to 8ºC) use within 30 days. Discard unused portion.

Note: Flavoring for Peglyte is premixed with powder inside jug.

Reviewed 1999

PENGLOBE® Ⓟ
Astra

Bacampicillin HCl

Antibiotic

Pharmacology: Bacampicillin is a prodrug of ampicillin and is microbiologically inactive. During absorption from the gastrointestinal tract, bacampicillin is hydrolyzed by esterases present in the intestinal wall. It is microbiologically active as ampicillin, and exerts a bactericidal action through the inhibition of the biosynthesis of cell wall mucopeptides.

Indications: For infections at the following sites: upper and lower respiratory tract; skin and soft tissue; urinary tract and acute uncomplicated gonococcal urethritis, when due to sensitive strains of the following organisms:

Gram-positive: streptococci (including S. faecalis and S. pneumoniae) and nonpenicillinase-producing staphylococci.

Gram-negative: H. influenzae, N. gonorrhoeae, E. coli, P. mirabilis, Salmonellae and Shigellae.

As follow-up oral therapy for infections initially treated with parenteral ampicillin.

Bacampicillin is not indicated in the treatment of infections caused by β-lactamase-producing organisms.

In vitro studies should be performed to identify causative organisms and determine their susceptibility to ampicillin.

Disc Susceptibility Tests: Ampicillin, 10 μg discs, should be used to estimate the in vivo susceptibility of organisms to bacampicillin.

Contraindications: In patients with a history of hypersensitivity to any of the penicillins or cephalosporins.

Bacampicillin should not be used to treat infections associated with infectious mononucleosis because of the high frequency of exanthema associated with the use of aminopenicillins in these patients.

Warnings: Serious and occasionally fatal hypersensitivity (anaphylactoid) reactions have been reported in patients on penicillin therapy. Although anaphylaxis is more frequent following parenteral therapy, it has occurred in patients administered oral penicillins. These reactions are more apt to occur in individuals with a history of sensitivity to multiple allergens.

Before initiating therapy with bacampicillin, careful inquiry should be made concerning previous hypersensitivity reactions to penicillins, cephalosporins and other allergens. If an allergic reaction occurs, the administration of bacampicillin should be discontinued and appropriate therapy instituted. Serious anaphylactoid reactions require immediate emergency treatment with epinephrine, oxygen and i.v. steroids. Airway management, including intubation, should also be used as indicated.

Precautions: General: The possibility of superinfections with mycotic organisms or bacterial pathogens should be kept in mind during therapy with bacampicillin. Oxygen, epinephrine, i.v. fluids and i.v. steroids should be used to treat anaphylactic reactions. Emergency intubation may be necessary in some cases.

Special Disease Conditions: In patients with severely impaired renal function (CL_{cr}<20 mL/min), reduced dosage should be considered. Patients with depressed immunologic function are more likely to develop superinfections and should be closely observed.

The passage of any penicillin from blood into the brain is facilitated by inflamed meninges and during cardiopulmonary bypass. In these circumstances and particularly in the presence of renal failure, when high serum concentrations can be attained, CNS adverse effects including myoclonia, convulsive seizures and depressed consciousness may occur. This has never been reported with oral ampicillin.

Laboratory Tests: Periodic assessment of organ system function, including renal, hepatic and hematopoietic evaluations should be made during prolonged therapy.

Patients with gonorrhea, who have a suspected lesion of syphilis, should have darkfield examinations before receiving bacampicillin and monthly serological tests for a minimum of 4 months.

Drug Interactions: Metabolism of bacampicillin produces low plasma concentrations of alcohol and acetaldehyde; although the risk of a disulfiram-alcohol interaction appears minimal, caution is recommended if concurrent use is unavoidable.

The concurrent administration of allopurinol and ampicillin increases substantially the incidence of rashes in patients receiving both drugs as compared to patients receiving ampicillin alone. There are no data available on the incidence of rash in patients treated concurrently with bacampicillin and allopurinol.

Several reports have indicated that breakthrough bleeding and loss of contraceptive protection has occurred in women taking oral contraceptives and concurrently taking ampicillin. Although no reports have been received with regard to bacampicillin, it is recommended that an alternative contraceptive method be used during concurrent use of bacampicillin and oral contraceptive agents.

Probenecid decreases the renal tubular secretion of ampicillin. Concurrent use with bacampicillin may result in increased and prolonged blood levels of ampicillin.

Pregnancy: Ampicillin diffuses across the placental barrier into the fetal circulation. No harmful effects on the reproductive process have been reported in humans.

Lactation: The ampicillin from bacampicillin passes into the breast milk but any risk to the nursing infant seems unlikely when therapeutic doses are used. The potential for allergic sensitization should, however, be considered.

Adverse Effects: The pattern of adverse reactions observed in patients treated with bacampicillin b.i.d. closely follows that of other aminopenicillins i.e. gastrointestinal symptoms and dermatological reactions dominate, although at a lower level. The lowest total incidence of adverse reactions was seen with bacampicillin 400 mg b.i.d.

More Common Reactions: Dermatological (400 mg b.i.d., 4.8%; 800 mg b.i.d., 4.3%): rash, urticaria, pruritus, increased sweating.

Note: Patients with mononucleosis infectiosa and with leukemia are at a higher risk of experiencing exanthema.

Upper Gastrointestinal (400 mg b.i.d., 3%; 800 mg b.i.d., 2%): nausea, vomiting, heartburn, dyspepsia, epigastric discomfort, glossitis, dry mouth, stomatitis.

Lower Gastrointestinal (400 mg b.i.d., 2.4%; 800 mg b.i.d., 4.3%): diarrhea, loose stool, abdominal pain, flatulence, constipation.

CNS (400 mg b.i.d., 0.6%; 800 mg b.i.d., 1.2%): dizziness, vertigo, headache, insomnia, somnolence.

Miscellaneous (400 mg b.i.d., 0.6%; 800 mg b.i.d., 1.6%): fatigue, myalgia, edema, vaginitis, dysuria, leukorrhea.

Less Common Reactions: Biochemical Abnormalities: Moderate rises in AST, ALT and alkaline phosphatase have been noted.

General: Serious hypersensitivity reactions such as anaphylaxis, angioedema, serum sickness, drug fever, vasculitis and Stevens-Johnson syndrome have been reported following use of penicillin class antibiotics. In addition, there have been 4 reports of Lyell's syndrome/toxic epidermal necrolysis in patients treated with bacampicillin.

In rare cases, esophageal ulcerations have been reported in association with tablet intake without adequate liquid.

In rare cases, colitis, enterocolitis or pseudomembranous colitis in association with bacterial pathogens have been reported.

Other rare reactions which have been reported, regardless of causal relationship to bacampicillin, include stomatitis ulcerative, hepatitis, jaundice, circulatory failure, hypotension, oliguria, coma, chest pain and superinfection.

Hematological and Lymphatic: eosinophilia, hemolytic anemia, thrombocytopenia and leukopenia. These reactions are usually reversible upon discontinuation of therapy.

Overdose: Symptoms: The treatment of overdosage would likely be needed only in patients with severely impaired renal function since patients with normal kidneys excrete penicillins at a very fast rate. Following oral ingestion, symptoms that may occur include diarrhea, nausea, vomiting and abdominal pain.

Treatment: The drug should be withdrawn, the stomach emptied and charcoal administered. Seizures caused by penicillins may be treated with anticonvulsive drugs. Hemodialysis lowers the serum level of penicillins.

Dosage: Chemically, 400 mg of bacampicillin HCl is equivalent to 278 mg of ampicillin on a molar basis. The absorption of bacampicillin is not significantly affected by food and therefore may be administered in association with meals.

To facilitate swallowing, bacampicillin should preferably be taken with a full glass of water (see Table I).

Table I—Penglobe

Adult Dosage

Site of Infection	Mild-Moderate	Severe
upper respiratory tract urinary tract skin and soft tissue	400 mg b.i.d.	800 mg b.i.d.
lower respiratory tract	800 mg b.i.d.	1 200–1 600 mg b.i.d.

Treatment should be continued for a minimum of 48 to 72 hours beyond the time the patient becomes asymptomatic or evidence of bacterial eradication has been obtained. At least 10 days' treatment is recommended for an infection caused by Group A β-hemolytic streptococci to prevent acute rheumatic fever or glomerulonephritis.

Urethritis due to N. gonorrhoeae: 1.6 g as a single dose with 1 g of probenecid. Bacampicillin is not recommended for the treatment of pharyngeal gonorrhea or secondary gonococcal infections (i.e. arthritis). There are inadequate clinical data to recommend an appropriate dosage regimen for the treatment of rectal gonorrhea.

Children: There are inadequate clinical data to recommend an appropriate dosage regimen.

Supplied: 400 mg: Each white to yellowish-white, scored tablet, engraved PEN/GLOBE on one side contains: bacampicillin HCl 400 mg. Nonmedicinal ingredients: Tablet Core: lactose, magnesium stearate and microcrystalline cellulose. Coating Layer: hydroxypropyl methylcellulose, polyethylene glycol and titanium dioxide. Energy: 0.42 kJ (0.1 kcal). Sodium- and tartrazine-free. Bottles of 100.

800 mg: Each white to yellowish-white, scored tablet, engraved PEN/GLOBE contains: bacampicillin HCl 800 mg. Nonmedicinal ingredients: Tablet Core: lactose, magnesium stearate and microcrystalline cellulose. Coating Layer: hydroxypropyl methylcellulose, polyethylene glycol and titanium dioxide. Energy: 0.84 kJ (0.2 kcal). Sodium- and tartrazine-free. Bottles of 100.

Store at room temperature. Protect from moisture.

(Shown in Product Recognition Section)

PENICILLIN G Ⓟ
PENICILLIN V Ⓟ
General Monograph, CPhA

Benzylpenicillin

Phenoxymethylpenicillin

Antibiotic

This monograph has been compiled by CPhA. It may contain information different from that approved by Therapeutic Products Programme, Health Canada, and the pharmaceutical manufacturers' approval has not been requested.

Pharmacology: Penicillins G and V, known as the natural penicillins, are bactericidal against susceptible organisms. Penicillins interfere with the synthesis of cell wall mucopeptides, resulting in the formation of defective cell walls that will lyse and eventually result in death of the organism.

The spectra of activity of penicillins G and V are similar. Penicillin G is more active against gram-negative organisms (i.e., Neisseria) and some anaerobes than is penicillin V. Penicillin G can also be given parenterally, enabling the attainment of high serum concentrations, and is used for the treatment of serious infections involving penicillin-susceptible bacteria. Penicillin V is more resistant to hydrolysis by acidic gastric secretions and is absorbed orally to a much greater extent than penicillin G; therefore, it is the preparation of choice for the treatment of penicillin-susceptible infections of mild to moderate severity, in which the oral route of administration is desirable.

The in-vitro spectrum of activity of the natural penicillins is as follows: Gram-positive Aerobic Bacteria: non-ß-lactamase-producing staphylococci, streptococci Groups A, B, C, G, H, K, L and M, S. pneumoniae (increasingly not susceptible), nonenterococcal group D streptococci, viridans streptococci and some strains of enterococci, C. diphtheriae, L. monocytogenes, B. anthracis and E. rhusiopathiae.

Gram-negative Aerobic Bacteria: non-ß-lactamase producing N. gonorrhoeae, N. meningitidis, non-beta-lactamase producing H. influenzae, H. parainfluenzae, B. pertussis, E. corrodens, P. multocida.
Gram-positive Anaerobic Bacteria: A. israelii, Bifidobacterium, C. tetani, C. perfringens, C. botulinum, Eubacterium, Lactobacillus, Peptococcus, Peptostreptococcus, Propionibacterium.
Gram-negative Anaerobic Bacteria: Fusobacterium, Veillonella; most Bacteroides species are resistant.
Spirochetes: T. pallidum, B. recurrentis, B. burgdorferi, Leptospira.
Pharmacokinetics: After oral administration, penicillin is absorbed mainly from the duodenum and upper jejunum. The extent of absorption depends on the presence of food in the gastrointestinal tract, gastric and intestinal pH and the relative acid-stability of the penicillin derivative. Both natural penicillins are hydrolyzed in the presence of acidic gastric secretions. Penicillin G is more acid-labile and should be taken on an empty stomach. Penicillin V is more stable in the presence of gastric acid and although it may be taken with meals, higher serum levels are achieved if it is taken on an empty stomach.

Peak serum levels are reached within 30 to 60 minutes and are 2 to 5 times higher with penicillin V than penicillin G. The oral form of penicillin G or V benzathine reaches a lower peak level when compared with other forms of oral penicillin but levels are sustained for a longer period of time.

Aqueous penicillin G (as the potassium or sodium salt) may be administered i.m. or i.v. Following i.m. injection of either salt, peak levels are attained within 15 to 30 minutes.

Repository preparations of penicillin G benzathine or penicillin G procaine are intended for deep i.m. injection and provide a tissue depot from which absorption takes place over several hours to several days. Penicillin G benzathine reaches its peak more slowly and is generally longer acting than penicillin G procaine.

The natural penicillins are readily distributed into ascitic, synovial, pleural and pericardial fluids. Distribution into tissues varies widely, with highest amounts in the kidney and lower concentrations in the liver, lungs, skin, intestines and muscle. Small amounts are found in all other body tissues and in the CSF. When the meninges are inflamed, the CSF concentration is about 5% of the serum concentration and can be therapeutic against sensitive organisms. Penicillins readily cross the placenta and are distributed into breast milk.

Penicillin V is more highly protein bound (75 to 89%) than penicillin G (45 to 68%).

In patients with normal kidney function, penicillin is excreted rapidly by filtration and active tubular secretion. The elimination half-life is about 30 minutes. In neonates and young infants and in individuals with impaired kidney function, excretion is considerably delayed, occasionally necessitating longer dosing intervals and smaller doses.

Penicillin G is removed by hemodialysis but only minimally removed by peritoneal dialysis. It is not known whether penicillin V is dialyzable.

Indications: Penicillin G is indicated for treatment of infections due to susceptible organisms (parenteral preparations for severe infections, oral preparations for less serious infections). Penicillin V is indicated for treatment of mild to moderately severe infections.

Both penicillin G and penicillin V are indicated in the treatment of: actinomycosis caused by Actinomyces species; anthrax caused by B. anthracis; bronchitis, acute otitis media, pharyngitis, sinusitis, skin and soft tissue infections caused by susceptible organisms; erysipelas caused by susceptible strains of group A streptococci; erysipeloid (including endocarditis and septicemia) caused by E. rhusiopathiae; acute, necrotizing, ulcerative gingivitis (Vincent's angina or "trench mouth") caused by anaerobes and spirochetes; P. multocida infections; rat-bite fever caused by S. moniliformis or S. minor; scarlet fever caused by group A streptococci; Lyme disease caused by B. burgdorferi. In addition, parenteral penicillin G is indicated for treatment of gonococcal arthritis caused by susceptible strains of N. gonorrhoeae; bone and joint infections, bacterial endocarditis, intra-abdominal infections, meningitis, pericarditis, pneumonia and septicemia caused by susceptible organisms; uncomplicated gonorrhea caused by susceptible strains (not a first-line agent); listeriosis caused by L. monocytogenes; tetanus; yaws caused by T. pallidum pertenue; tertiary and neurosyphilis; gas gangrene caused by Clostridium species; leptospirosis caused by Leptospira species.

Both penicillin G benzathine and penicillin G procaine are indicated for treatment of: bejel caused by T. pallidum endemicum; erysipeloid; pinta caused by T. carateum; yaws.

In addition, penicillin G procaine is indicated for treatment of the following infections involving sysceptible organisms: anthrax; bacterial endocarditis; erysipelas; acute necrotizing, ulcerative gingivitis; acute otitis media; pericarditis; pneumonia; rat-bite fever, scarlet fever; septicemia; skin and soft tissue infections; tertiary syphilis.

Penicillin G benzathine is also indicated for treatment of pharyngitis and for early or late benign syphilis (not neurosyphilis).

Penicillin G, penicillin V, penicillin G procaine and penicillin G benzathine are indicated in the prophylaxis of: diphtheria caused by C. diphtheriae, as an adjunct to antitoxin. Penicillins G and V are indicated in the prophylaxis of bacterial endocarditis but have been replaced by amoxicillin in the 1997 Recommendations by the American Heart Association for Prevention of Bacterial Endocarditis (see Endocarditis Prophylaxis in the Clin-Info section). Penicillin V and penicillin G benzathine are indicated in the prohylaxis of rheumatic fever caused by group A streptococci. Patients with a history of rheumatic fever who are receiving continuous prophylaxis may harbor penicillin-resistant organisms; use of another agent may be considered.

Contraindications: A clear history of penicillin allergy; infections caused by beta-lactamase producing organisms.

Oral penicillin should not be used as adjunctive prophylaxis for genitourinary instrumentation or surgery, lower intestinal tract surgery, sigmoidoscopy or childbirth, or for the active treatment of syphilis, gonorrhea, meningitis, bacterial endocarditis, diphtheria, gas gangrene or other severe infections due to penicillin-susceptible microorganisms.

Severe pneumonia, empyema, bacteremia, pericarditis, meningitis and septic arthritis should not be treated with oral penicillin during the acute stage.

Topical application of penicillin is contraindicated since hypersensitization is a frequent complication.

Penicillin G procaine is contraindicated in patients who are allergic to procaine. Hypersensitivity may be confirmed by injecting 0.1 mL of a 1 to 2% procaine HCl solution intradermally. Development of erythema, wheal, flare or eruption indicates procaine sensitivity.

Warnings: Serious and occasionally fatal hypersensitivity reactions have been reported in patients receiving penicillin therapy. Although anaphylaxis is more frequent following parenteral therapy, it has occurred in patients receiving oral penicillin (see Overdose: Treatment).

Cross-sensitivity among ß-lactam antibiotics such as penicillins, cephalosporins and carbapenems is known to occur. The precise incidence is unknown. The possibility of cross-sensitivity must be considered in all patients reporting an allergy to any ß-lactam antibiotic.

Extreme care must be taken **not** to inject penicillin G procaine or penicillin G benzathine intravenously, intra-arterially or near a peripheral nerve or vessel as severe and/or permanent neurovascular damage may occur. Injections should be discontinued if sudden severe pain occurs at the injection site.

Precautions: Oral administration should not be relied upon in patients with severe illness, or with nausea, vomiting, gastric dilatation, cardiospasm or intestinal hypermotility.

Occasionally, certain patients will not absorb therapeutic amounts of orally administered penicillin.

In streptococcal infections, therapy should be given for a minimum of 10 days. Cultures should be taken following treatment to ensure eradication of streptococci.

Prolonged use of antibiotics may promote the overgrowth of nonsusceptible organisms, including fungi.

Patients with impaired renal function (ClCr <0.17 mL/sec) require modification of dose and interval.

High doses of intravenous penicillin G (>10 million units) should be administered slowly because of potential electrolyte imbalances resulting from the sodium or potassium load. This is particularly important in patients with impaired renal function.

The passage of any penicillin from blood into brain is facilitated by inflamed meninges and during cardiopulmonary bypass. In the presence of such factors, particularly in renal failure when high serum concentrations can be attained, CNS adverse effects including myoclonia, seizures and depressed consciousness can be expected.

Drug Interactions: Aminoglycosides: A synergistic bactericidal effect occurs in vitro against some strains of enterococci and against viridans streptococci when penicillin G is used in conjunction with aminoglycosides. This effect is used therapeutically to treat bacterial endocarditis.
Bacteriostatic Antibiotics (e.g., chloramphenicol, erythromycin, tetracycline): may decrease the effectiveness of penicillin.
Oral Contraceptives: Whether penicillins decrease the effectiveness of oral contraceptives is controversial. Some clinicians recommend adding an alternative method of contraception for the duration of the cycle when a penicillin is taken.
Probenecid: Decreases renal tubular secretion of penicillin leading to higher and more prolonged serum concentrations, higher CSF concentrations and an increased risk of toxicity.
Pregnancy: Usual doses appear to be safe in pregnant women.
Lactation: Penicillin does not appear in breast milk in sufficient quantities to treat infections in the infant but does appear in trace quantities which could lead to allergic sensitization or disruption of the gastrointestinal flora.

Adverse Effects: Hypersensitivity: Hypersensitivity reactions are usually more severe following parenteral administration, however all degrees of hypersensitivity including fatal anaphylaxis have followed even oral administration of the drug. The most common manifestations of hypersensitivity are: skin eruptions (from mild rash to exfoliative dermatitis) with an overall incidence of approximately 2%, urticaria, chills, fever, edema, eosinophilia and anaphylaxis (overall incidence about 0.05%). A serum sickness-like reaction has been reported, characterized by fever, malaise, urticaria, arthralgia, myalgia, lymphadenopathy and splenomegaly.
Hematologic: eosinophilia (hypersensitivity), hemolytic anemia, transient neutropenia, leukopenia, thrombocytopenia and thrombocytopenic purpura. These reactions are more common with larger parenteral doses of penicillin.
Gastrointestinal: nausea, vomiting, epigastric distress, diarrhea, black hairy tongue, antibiotic associated pseudomembranous colitis.
Renal: Rarely, acute interstitial nephritis (fever, proteinuria and hematuria); high doses of parenterally administered penicillin sodium or potassium may result in electrolyte disturbances, especially in patients with poor renal function.
Hepatic: Hepatotoxicity may be associated with hypersensitivity.
CNS: Usually associated with administration of large parenteral dosages to patients with impaired renal function; manifested as hallucinations, confusion, lethargy, dysphasia, twitching, hyperreflexia, asterixis, localized or generalized seizures, coma or fatal encephalopathy.
Miscellaneous: Jarisch-Herxheimer Reaction: Frequently occurs 2 to 12 hours after penicillin is started to treat syphilis or other spirochetal infections and is thought to result from the phagocytized organism's release of endotoxins and/or other pyrogens. The reaction is characterized by headache, fever, chills, sweating, sore throat, myalgia, arthralgia, malaise, tachycardia, hypertension followed by hypotension. The reaction usually subsides within 24 hours.

Overdose: Symptoms: Hypersensitivity reactions including anaphylaxis may occur with any dosage. Oral ingestion of excessive amounts may cause nausea, vomiting, diarrhea, abdominal pain. Parenteral administration of high doses may lead to cardiovascular or electrolyte abnormalities or neurological effects such as drowsiness, seizures or coma.

Treatment: Following oral ingestion, gastric decontamination, induction of emesis (if patient is not obtunded, comatose or experiencing seizures) and administration of activated charcoal with a cathartic may be of benefit. Patients must be observed for signs of a hypersensitivity reaction (see below). If seizures, cardiac arrhythmias or fluid or electrolyte disturbances occur following parenteral administration appropriate measures must be taken. Dialysis may be helpful in removing Penicillin G.
Anaphylaxis: Mild cases involving only urticaria may be managed with antihistamine therapy. Severe anaphylaxis may require oxygen supplementation, airway management, epinephrine administration, ECG monitoring and i.v. fluids.

Dosage: Oral therapy is generally used for the treatment of mild to moderately severe infections. Maximal absorption of both natural penicillins occurs on an empty stomach (1 hour before or 2 hours after meals). Parenteral administration is required for the treatment of severe infections including meningitis, endocarditis, syphilis, gonorrhea and clostridial infections.

Dosage must be individualized according to the causative organism, severity of the infection and host factors such as age and renal function.
Penicillin V 500 000 units is equivalent to 300 mg.
Penicillin G 500 000 units is equivalent to 312 mg.

Usual therapeutic dosages are as follows:

Penicillin G or V Oral: Adults and children >12 years: 500 000 units every 6 to 8 hours. Children <12 years: 25 000 to 90 000 units/kg/day in 3 to 6 divided doses.

Aqueous Penicillin G (Sodium or Potassium) I.M./I.V.: Adults and children >12 years: Dosage may range from 1 million units daily i.m. to 20 million units daily i.v. in 4 to 6 divided doses. Higher doses may be required for more

Penicillin (cont'd)

serious infections. Intermittent i.v. infusions should be given over 1 to 2 hours.
Children 1 month to 12 years: 25 000 to 50 000 units/kg/day in 4 divided doses. Higher doses (100 000 to 400 000 units/kg/day, in divided doses every 4 to 6 hours) may be required to treat more severe infections. I.V. infusion should be given over 15 to 30 minutes.
Neonates 1 week to 1 month: 75 000 to 200 000 units/kg/day, in divided doses every 6 hours (if >2 kg) or every 8 hours (if <2 kg).
Neonates <1 week: 50 000 to 100 000 units/kg/day, in divided doses every 8 hours (if >2 kg) or every 12 hours (if ≤2 kg).

Dosage for meningitis caused by group B streptococci in neonates is 250 000 to 400 000 units/kg/day, in divided doses every 6 to 8 hours.
Dosage in renal failure: Patients with ClCr <0.17 mL/sec should receive approximately one half the usual dose at less frequent intervals (recommendations range from every 8 to every 18 hours).

Penicillin G Benzathine I.M.: Adults: single dose of 1 200 000 units by deep i.m. injection.
Children <27 kg: single dose of 300 000 to 600 000 units by deep i.m. injection; >27 kg: 900 000 units by deep i.m. injection. Extreme care must be taken to avoid injection into peripheral nerves or vessels. See Warnings.

Penicillin G Procaine I.M.: Adults and children >12 years: 600 000 to 1 200 000 units daily by deep i.m. injection.
Children <12 years: 25 000 to 50 000 units/kg once daily (not to exceed adult dose). Extreme care must be taken to avoid injection into or near peripheral nerves or vessels. See Warnings.

Rheumatic Fever Prophylaxis: Prevention of recurrent Group A beta-hemolytic streptococcal infections in patients who have had rheumatic fever and/or chorea: penicillin V 250 000 units orally twice daily on a continual basis.

Reviewed 1999

PENTACARINAT®

Rhône-Poulenc Rorer

Pentamidine Isethionate

Antiparasitic Agent

Pharmacology: Pentamidine isethionate is a member of a class of compounds known as an aromatic diamidines. The precise mechanism of antiprotozoal action of pentamidine isethionate has not been fully elucidated. Several mechanisms of action have been suggested including inhibition of DNA, RNA, phospholipid and protein synthesis, but the relative role of each mechanism to the overall antiprotozoal activity may vary for different types of protozoa. In vitro, pentamidine appears to have a direct cidal effect on P. carinii although the drug only moderately inhibits glucose metabolism, protein synthesis, RNA synthesis and intracellular amino acid transport.

Following administration of a single 4 mg/kg i.m. or i.v. dose of pentamidine isethionate in humans, peak plasma concentrations averaged 209 ng/mL approximately 40 minutes after the i.m. dose and 612 ng/mL after completion of a 2-hour infusion. Following daily i.m. or i.v. doses of 4 mg/kg, there appeared to be little variation in plasma concentrations from day to day and little increase with successive doses, although one study found increased trough concentrations and drug accumulation with multiple dosing.

Following oral inhalation of pentamidine isethionate via nebulization, broncho-alveolar concentrations of the drug were substantially higher than those attained following a comparable i.v. dose, while plasma concentrations were substantially lower; pentamidine appears to undergo limited absorption from the respiratory tract into the systemic circulation. Pentamidine appears to be extensively distributed and/or bound to body tissues. Following i.m. and i.v. administration of a single 4 mg/kg dose in patients with a normal kidney function, plasma concentrations declined in a biphasic manner with terminal elimination half-lives of 9.4 and 6.4 hours, respectively.

After repeated i.m. administration for 10 to 12 days, approximately 15% to 20% of the daily dose was recovered in the urine, apparently as unchanged drug. Pentamidine appears to be eliminated very slowly from tissues in which it accumulates (i.e. liver, lungs) and decreasing amounts of the drug could be detected in the urine for 6 to 8 weeks after cessation of therapy.

The extent of pentamidine distribution and accumulation following chronic inhalation therapy is not known.

In a series of patients treated for P. carinii pneumonia, the highest plasma pentamidine concentrations were found in those with elevated BUN levels. Since the major route of elimination is renal, the activity of pentamidine should be anticipated to be prolonged in the presence of severe renal function impairment. No pharmacokinetic data are available following oral inhalation of pentamidine in patients with impaired hepatic or renal function.

Indications: The therapeutic role of pentamidine and its prophylactic efficacy and long-term safety, relative to alternative therapies, in the treatment and prevention of pneumonia due to P. carinii has not been established. Comparative data are required.
Inhalation: For the prevention of P. carinii pneumonia (PCP) in high-risk, HIV-infected patients defined by one or both of the following criteria: i) a history of one or more episodes of PCP; ii) a peripheral CD_4+ (T_4 helper/inducer) lymphocyte count less than or equal to 200/mm³ or CD_4 less than 20% of lymphocyte count.

These indications are based on the results of an 18-month randomized, dose-response trial in high-risk HIV-infected patients and on existing epidemiological data from natural history studies.
Injection: For the treatment of pneumonia due to P. carinii (PCP).

Contraindications: Patients with a history of hypersensitivity to the drug or to any of its salts.

Warnings: Inhalation: Cases of acute pancreatitis have been reported in patients receiving aerosolized pentamidine. Pentamidine isethionate for inhalation should be discontinued if signs or symptoms of acute pancreatitis develop.

Rare cases of renal insufficiency and acute renal failure have also been reported in association with aerosolized pentamidine.
Injection: **Fatalities due to severe hypotension, hypoglycemia, acute pancreatitis and cardiac arrhythmias have been reported in patients treated with pentamidine by both the i.m. and i.v. routes. Profound severe hypotension may result after a single dose (see Precautions).** Severe life-threatening hypoglycemia can occur even after completion of therapy with pentamidine. Severe renal impairment resulting in death may also occur in the presence of various clinical complications (e.g. bacterial sepsis), concurrent administration of other nephrotoxic antibiotic agents or previous evidence of renal disease. The parenteral administration of pentamidine, therefore, should be limited to patients in whom a diagnosis of P. carinii pneumonia has been made.

Pentamidine injection should be used only in a hospital setting with facilities to monitor blood glucose, blood count and renal and hepatic functions (see Precautions).

Pentamidine should only be administered by injection under close supervision and the patient should be very carefully monitored for the development of serious adverse reactions (see Precautions and Adverse Effects).

Precautions: *Pregnancy:* Pentamidine should be used during pregnancy only if clearly indicated. It is not known whether pentamidine can cause fetal harm when administered to pregnant women; however, in a teratogenicity study in rabbits, the drug was embryotoxic as evidenced by the number of post-implantation losses and by delayed ossification.
Lactation: It is not known whether pentamidine is excreted in breast milk. Because many drugs are excreted in human milk, the drug should be used with caution in nursing mothers and cessation of nursing should be considered.
Children: Efficacy and safety of aerosolized pentamidine in children have not been clearly established.
Inhalation: Prior to initiating pentamidine prophylaxis, symptomatic patients should be investigated to exclude the presence of PCP. The recommended prophylactic dosage of pentamidine is insufficient to treat acute PCP.

The potential for development of acute PCP still exists in patients receiving aerosolized pentamidine prophylactically. Therefore, any patient with symptoms suggestive of PCP, including but not limited to dyspnea, fever or cough, should be evaluated for possible acute infection and treated appropriately. The use of aerosolized pentamidine may alter the clinical and radiographic features of PCP and could result in an atypical presentation, including but not limited to mild disease or focal infection.

Prophylactic therapy with aerosolized pentamidine does not prevent dissemination of P. carinii to extrapulmonary sites. Physicians should be aware of the possibility of such dissemination. Patients with signs of disseminated disease should be investigated aggressively even if they have no signs of lung infection.
Pulmonary: Inhalation of pentamidine may induce bronchospasm or cough. This has been noted particularly in some patients who have a history of smoking or asthma. In clinical trials, cough and bronchospasm were the most frequently reported adverse experiences associated with pentamidine aerosol administration (38% and 15%, respectively, of patients receiving the 300 mg dose); however less than 1% of the doses were interrupted or terminated due to these effects. For the majority of patients, cough and bronchospasm were controlled by administration of an aerosolized bronchodilator. In patients who experience bronchospasm or cough, administration of an inhaled bronchodilator prior to giving each pentamidine dose may minimize recurrence of the symptoms.

During treatment some patients experience a burning sensation in the back of their throat. This can usually be alleviated if the patient interrupts treatment to drink some liquid.
General: Although the administration of pentamidine is reported to result in minimal systemic absorption, the extent and consequence of pentamidine accumulation following chronic inhalation therapy are not known. As a result, patients receiving pentamidine should be closely monitored for the development of serious adverse reactions that have occurred in patients receiving parenteral pentamidine, including hypotension, hypoglycemia, pancreatitis, hyperglycemia, hypocalcemia, anemia, thrombocytopenia, leukopenia, hepatic or renal dysfunction, ventricular tachycardia and Stevens-Johnson's syndrome.
Drug Interactions: While specific studies of drug interactions with pentamidine have not been conducted, the majority of patients in clinical trials received concomitant medications, including zidovudine, with no reported interactions.
Environmental and occupational exposure: The administration of aerosolized pentamidine has raised questions regarding the safety of health care providers. These questions have addressed two basic concerns. 1) Direct toxicity: There have been reports of mucous membrane irritation (including chemical conjunctivitis) in care givers with close aerosol exposure and one case report noting a transient decrease in diffusing capacity in a therapist administering aerosolized pentamidine. Studies of ambient pentamidine concentrations when using a closed nebulizer system such as Respirgard II have reported very low levels in treatment areas, especially when nebulizer exhalation filters are used and attention is paid to turning off nebulizers when not in use. 2) Infectious exposure: Aerosolized pentamidine can be irritating to the tracheo-bronchial tree and, thereby, induces coughing in patients. Since HIV-infected patients can have potentially communicable respiratory infections (notably tuberculosis) concurrently, there exists the possibility that care givers may become exposed to potential respiratory infectious agents during the prophylactic administration of inhaled pentamidine. Consequently, careful screening of patients for infectious diseases (especially tuberculosis) and the use of expiratory filters in well-ventilated rooms are recommended. To reduce the risk of exposing health care providers to aerosolized pentamidine or potential respiratory infectious pathogens, the guidelines for administration of aerosolized pentamidine must be adhered to closely (see Dosage).
Injection: General: Pentamidine should be used with caution in patients with hypertension, hypotension, hypoglycemia, hyperglycemia, hypocalcemia, leukopenia, thrombocytopenia, anemia, and hepatic or renal dysfunction.

Patients may develop sudden, severe hypotension after receiving a single dose of pentamidine injection. Therefore, patients receiving the drug should be in a supine position and the blood pressure monitored closely during administration of the drug and several times thereafter until the blood pressure is stable. Equipment for emergency resuscitation should be readily available. Pentamidine should be infused over a period of at least 60 minutes and preferably over 2 to 3 hours to minimize the risk of hypotension. Severe hypotension with accompanying bradycardia has been observed in a patient after the sixth dose of pentamidine isethionate; this hypotension did not respond to i.v. colloids, graded compression stockings or corticosteroids but resolved within 4 days of stopping treatment.

Ventricular tachycardia and ECG abnormalities have also been reported in patients receiving pentamidine. ECGs may be required at regular intervals if signs of cardiotoxicity develop.

Pentamidine can produce hypoglycemia which may be severe and/or prolonged. It generally occurs after 5 to 7 days of therapy but can even occur up to several days after the drug is discontinued. The duration appears quite variable, persisting for 1 day up to several weeks. Pentamidine-induced hypoglycemia has been associated with pancreatic islet cell necrosis and inappropriately high plasma insulin concentrations. Hyperglycemia and diabetes mellitus, with or without preceding hypoglycemia, have also occurred, sometimes several months after termination of therapy with pentamidine isethionate. Hypoglycemia induced by pentamidine isethionate may be controlled by administration of i.v. dextrose or (oral) diazoxide but it is not known if such therapy can prevent the subsequent development of diabetes mellitus.

Leukopenia and thrombocytopenia, which can be severe (e.g. leukocyte count less than 1 000/mm³, platelet count less than 20 000/mm³), occur occasionally in patients receiving pentamidine. Anemia occurs rarely. In a few cases, pentamidine therapy has been associated with neutropenia.

Some patients may become nauseated or febrile after each injection of pentamidine. In such cases, the prophylactic use of an antiemetic and/or antipyretic (e.g. acetaminophen) may be considered.

Phlebitis can occur after i.v. injection.

Patient Monitoring: In order to monitor for possible toxicity, the following tests should be carried out before, during and after therapy: routine determinations of blood urea nitrogen (BUN), serum creatinine and serum electrolytes; daily blood glucose determinations during therapy and continuing several times after completion of therapy as required by clinical condition; twice weekly complete blood count and platelet count; liver function tests including bilirubin, alkaline phosphatase, ALT and AST, weekly or more frequently if indicated; weekly serum calcium determinations; ECGs as indicated.

Drug Interactions: There are no documented interactions of pentamidine with other medications. However, since nephrotoxic effects may be additive, the concurrent or sequential use of pentamidine with drugs having a nephrotoxic potential (e.g. aminoglycosides, amphotericin B, cisplatin or vancomycin) should be undertaken with caution. Pentamidine should be administered with caution to patients who are receiving drugs with hepatotoxic potential, drugs with potential pancreatic toxicity (e.g. 2', 3-dideoxyinosine [DDI]) or medication that can impair the hematopoietic system.

I.M. Administration: I.M. injections are often associated with pain, tenderness, erythema, and induration at the site of injection. Sterile abscesses have been noted. Therefore, **i.m. administration should be reserved for patients with adequate muscle mass and limited to the rare situations where i.v. infusion is not feasible.**

Adverse Effects: Inhalation: The most frequent adverse effects attibutable to the inhalation of pentamidine are cough and bronchospasm (reported by 38% and 15%, respectively, of patients receiving 300 mg every 4 weeks.

The most frequently reported adverse experiences in controlled clinical trials using the Respirgard II nebulizer were as follows: 53 to 72%: fatigue, bad (metallic) taste, shortness of breath and decreased appetite; 31 to 47%: dizziness and rash; 10 to 23%: nausea, pharyngitis, chest pain or congestion, night sweats, chills and vomiting.

In nearly all cases, no conclusions were drawn as to the relationship of adverse experiences (or their severity) to treatment or underlying disease.

Other less frequently occurring adverse experiences (reported by greater than 1% and up to 5% of patients in 2 clinical trials) were pneumothorax, diarrhea, headache, anemia (generally associated with the use of zidovudine), myalgia, abdominal pain and edema.

From a total experience with 1 130 patients, adverse events reported with a frequency of 1% or less were as follows. No causal relationship to treatment was established.

General: allergic reactions and extrapulmonary pneumocystosis.

Cardiovascular: tachycardia, hypotension, hypertension, palpitations, syncope, cerebrovascular accident, vasodilation and vasculitis.

Metabolic: hypoglycemia, hyperglycemia and hypocalcemia.

Gastrointestinal: gingivitis, dyspepsia, oral ulcer/abscess, gastritis, gastric ulcer, hypersalivation, dry mouth, splenomegaly, melena, hematochezia, esophagitis, colitis and acute pancreatitis.

Hematological: pancytopenia, neutropenia, eosinophilia, and thrombocytopenia.

Hepatorenal: hepatitis, hepatomegaly, hepatic dysfunction, renal failure, flank pain and nephritis.

Musculoskeletal: arthralgia.

Neurological: tremors, confusion, anxiety, memory loss, seizure, neuropathy, paresthesia, hypesthesia, drowsiness, emotional lability, vertigo, paranoia, neuralgia, hallucination, depression and unsteady gait.

Respiratory: rhinitis, laryngitis, laryngospasm, hyperventilation, hemoptysis, gagging, eosinophilic or interstitial pneumonitis, pleuritis, cyanosis, tachypnea and rales.

Skin: pruritus, erythema, dry skin, desquamation and urticaria.

Special senses: eye discomfort, conjunctivitis, blurred vision, blepharitis and loss of taste and smell.

Urogenital: incontinence.

Reproductive: miscarriage.

Injection: **Fatalities due to severe hypotension, hypoglycemia, acute pancreatitis and cardiac arrhythmias have been reported in patients treated with pentamidine isethionate injection. The parenteral administration of pentamidine should therefore, be limited to patients in whom the presence of P. carinii has been demonstrated by laboratory means or by clinical diagnosis where the patient cannot tolerate an invasive procedure.**

The most commonly reported and often the most serious adverse reaction is nephrotoxicity. It usually occurs as mild azotemia and/or increased serum creatinine level, reversible upon discontinuation of the drug; however, acute renal failure or severe renal insufficiency has only been occasionally observed.

Other severe and potentially lethal reactions include: hypotension, hypoglycemia and cardiac arrhythmias (see Warnings).

The following list of adverse effects is based on the largest series reported in the medical literature and on the review of the medical records of 341 patients who received pentamidine in Canada for P. carinii pneumonia, mainly by the i.v. route.

The number of patients with adverse reactions in the literature was 46.8% and in Canada was 58.1%. Adverse reactions requiring discontinuation of therapy: not available in the literature; 5.9% in the Canadian Series.

In the following information, a ( ) will be used to denote the incidence of adverse reactions in the literature and a (( )) will be used to denote the incidence of adverse reactions in the Canadian series (Data on file Rhône-Poulenc Rorer Canada Inc.).

Renal: azotemia, elevated creatinine level, renal insufficiency (23% of treated patients) ((21.7% of treated patients)).

Hepatic: increased AST, ALT, alkaline phosphatase or bilirubin (9.6%) ((10.6%)).

Hypoglycemia or diabetogenic effect (6.2%), ((7.6%)).

Cardiovascular: hypotension or syncope, ventricular tachycardia, ECG abnormalities (9.6%) ((8.8%)).

Hematologic: leukopenia, neutropenia, thrombocytopenia, rarely anemia (4.2%) ((21.4%)).

Allergic: drug fever, erythematous rash, maculopapular rash, unspecified rash, urticaria (1.5%) ((3.8%)).

Local Reactions: pain, erythema, rash, induration at i.m. injection site, sterile abscess, myonecrosis or phlebitis after i.v. injection (18%) ((2.3%)).

CNS: dizziness, headache, altered mental state, loss of consciousness, spasticity of lower extremities, convulsions, paresthesia (N/A) ((2.3%)).

Special Senses: buzzing in ears, metallic taste (N/A) ((less than 1%)).

Gastrointestinal: nausea, vomiting, anorexia, diarrhea ((8.2%)). Increased amylase level ((less than 1%)), hyponatremia ((less than 1%)), hypocalcemia (1.2%) ((less than 1%)), bleeding ((less than 1%)), other not specified (11.1%).

Note: Some patients had more than 1 adverse reaction.

Overdose: Symptoms and Treatment: There are no reports to date of acute toxicity associated with overdosage of pentamidine; consequently there is no specific information available on symptoms.

In general, overdosage of pentamidine would be expected to produce effects that are extensions of the common adverse reactions or of the serious metabolic sequelae observed (see Warnings and Precautions).

Available clinical pharmacology data suggest that a dose up to 40 times the recommended dose of inhaled pentamidine would be required to produce systemic levels similar to a single 4 mg/kg i.v. dose.

In case of suspected overdosage, treatment should be symptomatic and supportive.

Dosage: Inhalation: For prophylaxis of P. carinii pneumonia, pentamidine is administered as an aerosol via the Respirgard II nebulizer system, a continuous flow device that stores the drug during exhalations.

Adults: 300 mg once every 4 weeks.

Administration: The contents of one 300 mg vial should be dissolved in 6 mL of sterile water for injection. Place the entire reconstituted contents into the Respirgard II nebulizer reservoir.

The dose should be delivered until the nebulizer chamber is empty (approximately 30 to 45 minutes). The flow rate should be 5 to 7 L/minute from a 40 to 50 pounds per square inch (PSI) air or oxygen source. Alternatively, a 40 to 50 PSI air compressor can be used with flow limited by setting the flowmeter at 5 to 7 L/minute or by setting the pressure at 22 to 25 PSI. Low pressure (less than 20 PSI) compressors should not be used.

When the nebulizer mouthpiece is firmly in the patient's mouth, turn on the gas source. Instruct the patient to breathe only through the mouth, so that any exhaled drug or microorganisms will be trapped by the exhalation filter of the nebulizer.

The patient should be instructed to breathe at a normal rate, but also to take a deep breath at least once every minute by exhaling all of the air from the lungs and then inspiring deeply to refill them. If possible, the patient should hold his breath for a few seconds before exhaling.

Alternatives to this breathing pattern are: have the patient either lie in the supine position or take half of the therapy lying on either side.

If the patient feels a need to take a break, turn off the gas supply to the nebulizer for a few minutes until the patient feels able to resume therapy.

The Respirgard II nebulizer **should not be reused**. Discard appropriately.

Environmental and occupational exposure: The following guidelines are recommended for administration of aerosolized pentamidine in order to reduce the risk of exposing health care providers to aerosolized pentamidine or potential respiratory infectious agents:

1. Use an approved aerosol generator that facilitates the delivery of a particle size of 1 to 2 microns. This not only ensures optimal aerosol deposition but also minimizes coughing caused by larger, more irritating particles.
2. Use a filter on the expiratory side of the aerosol generator to minimize the release of pentamidine into the treatment area.
3. Pretreatment of susceptible patients with a bronchodilator may help to minimize coughing.
4. Adequate ventilation (at least 6 airflow changes per hour) in the treatment area is desirable to minimize the possible presence of tuberculosis organisms and to dispel any particles of aerosolized pentamidine that may have been accidentally released into the room.
5. Optional use by care-givers of surgical face masks and close fitting protective eyewear may reduce the likelihood of side effects in the upper respiratory tract and the irritating conjunctivitis that may occur.
6. Patients should be evaluated for the presence of tuberculosis prior to initiating prophylaxis for PCP. Health care workers administering aerosolized pentamidine should be screened periodically for tuberculosis.
7. Care must be taken to ensure that the aerosol generator is activated only during actual treatments and is turned off when not in use.
8. Care must be taken during aerosol perparation to minimize contact with mucous membranes.
9. Pregnant and nursing health care workers may wish to avoid exposure to pentamidine.
10. It is recommended that all health care workers should practice so-called universal precautions with all patients all of the time.

Injection: For treatment of P. carinii pneumonia, pentamidine may be administered i.v. or i.m. When administered i.v., pentamidine must be given only by slow infusion (i.e. over a period of at least 60 minutes and preferably over a period of 2 to 3 hours). I.M. administration should be reserved for patients with adequate muscle mass and for whom a slow i.v. infusion is not practical. The i.m. administration of pentamidine is normally not recommended because of poor local tolerance (see Precautions).

Since severe hypotension reactions may occur, patients receiving pentamidine should be in a supine position and blood pressure should be closely monitored during administration of the drug and several times thereafter until blood pressure is stable.

Adults: The recommended regimen is 4 mg/kg once a day for 14 to 21 days. The benefits and risks of therapy for longer than 14 doses are not well defined.

Patients with Renal Failure (creatinine clearance less than 35 mL/min): Life-threatening infections: 4 mg/kg once daily for 7 to 10 days then 4 mg/kg on alternate days to complete the course of 14 doses. Less severe infections: 4 mg/kg on alternate days for 14 doses.

Children: Clinical and pharmacokinetic data are extremely limited and further investigation is necessary to fully characterize

Pentacarinat (cont'd)

the pharmacokinetics of pentamidine in this age group. However, a dosage of 4 mg/kg has been used in children. Pentamidine should be considered only if there is no other alternate treatment available.

Administration: I.V. infusion: The further diluted solution should be administered over a period of at least 60 minutes and preferably over a period of 2 to 3 hours.
I.M. injection: The appropriate volume of reconstituted solution should be administered well within the body of a relatively large muscle mass.
Reconstitution: For Inhalation: The contents of 1 vial (300 mg) must be dissolved with 6 mL of sterile water for injection.
Incompatibilities: Do not use saline solution for reconstitution because the drug may precipitate. Do not mix the solution with any other drugs.
Stability and Storage: Store unreconstituted powder at room temperature and protect from light. Reconstituted powder should be used immediately and not stored for later use.
For I.V. Infusion: Reconstitute only with Sterile Water for Injection (see Table I).

Table I—Pentacarinat

Reconstitution Table

Vial Size	Volume to be Added to Vial	Approximate Available Volume	Approximate Average Concentration
200 mg	2 mL	2.10 mL	100 mg/mL
300 mg	3 mL	3.15 mL	100 mg/mL

Further dilute the appropriate volume of reconstituted solution with 50 to 500 mL of a 5% dextrose or 0.9% sodium chloride solution. Reconstituted pentamidine should not be mixed with any other injection solution. These are single dose vials; discard the unused portions.
Stability and Storage: Reconstituted solutions that have been further diluted in 5% dextrose solution to a concentration of approximately 2 mg/mL are stable for up to 24 hours at room temperature. Store unreconstituted powder at room temperature and protect from light.
For I.M. Injection: Reconstitute only with Sterile Water for Injection as for i.v. injection **but do not further dilute.**
Incompatibilities: After reconstitution but prior to parenteral administration, pentamidine should not be mixed with any injection solution other than 5% dextrose and 0.9% sodium chloride injections.

Information for the Patient: See Blue Section—Information for the Patient ''Pentacarinat''.

Supplied: 200 mg: Each vial of sterile powder for injection after reconstitution contains: pentamidine isethionate 200 mg. Nonmedicinal ingredients: none. Boxes of 5.

300 mg: Each vial of sterile powder for injection after reconstitution contains: pentamidine isethionate 300 mg. Nonmedicinal ingredients: none. Boxes of 5.

Store at room temperature. Protect from light.

PENTACEL™
Connaught

Haemophilus b Conjugate Vaccine (Tetanus Protein-Conjugate)—Component Pertussis Vaccine—Diphtheria and Tetanus Toxoids Adsorbed Combined with Inactivated Poliomyelitis Vaccine

Active Immunizing Agent

Supplied: Pentacel is a comarketing of 2 licensed vaccines: the lyophilized Haemophilus b Conjugate Vaccine (Tetanus Protein-Conjugate)-Act-HIB to be reconstituted with Component Pertussis Vaccine and Diphtheria and Tetanus Toxoids Adsorbed Combined with Inactivated Poliomyelitis Vaccine-Quadracel. Each 0.5 mL i.m. Act-HIB dose contains: 10 μg purified capsular polysaccharide covalently bound to 20 μg tetanus protein. Each 0.5 mL dose contains: pertussis toxoid 20 μg, filamentous hemagglutinin 20 μg, fimbriae 5 μg, pertactin 3 μg, diphtheria toxoid 15 Lf, tetanus toxoid 5 Lf, inactivated poliomyelitis vaccine, aluminum and 2-phenoxyethanol as a preservative. Trace amounts of polymyxin B and neomycin may be present from the cell growth medium.

Each package contains: 5×single dose vials Act-HIB, 5×0.5 mL ampuls (single dose) Quadracel and direction leaflets for each product. For instructions for reconstitution with Quadracel, see the Act-HIB direction leaflet. Store between 2 and 8°C. Do not freeze.

PENTAMIDINE ISETHIONATE FOR INJECTION BP Ⓟ
Faulding

Antiparasitic

Supplied: Each vial of sterile lyophilized powder contains: pentamidine isethionate for injection BP 300 mg. No preservative. Packs of 5. Store unopened vials below 25°C. Protect from light.

PENTAMYCETIN® Ⓟ
Sabex

Chloramphenicol

Antibiotic

Supplied: Ophthalmic Ointment 1%: Each g contains: chloramphenicol 10 mg. Nonmedicinal ingredients: mineral oil and petrolatum. Tubes of 3.5 g. Preservative-free. Store at room temperature.

Ophthalmic Solution: 0.25%: Each mL contains: chloramphenicol 2.5 mg. Nonmedicinal ingredients: boric acid/sodium borate (to adjust pH), sodium chloride and water for injection. Preservative-free. Plastic dropper bottles of 10 mL. Refrigerate.

0.5%: Each mL contains: chloramphenicol 5 mg. Nonmedicinal ingredients: boric acid/sodium borate (to adjust pH), sodium chloride and water for injection. Preservative-free. Plastic dropper bottles of 10 mL. Refrigerate.

PENTAMYCETIN®/HC Ⓟ
Sabex

Chloramphenicol—Hydrocortisone

Antibiotic—Corticosteroid

Supplied: Eye and Ear Ointment: Each g contains: chloramphenicol 10 mg and hydrocortisone acetate 10 mg. Nonmedicinal ingredients: mineral oil and petrolatum. Tubes of 3.5 g. Preservative-free. Store at room temperature.

Eye and Ear Suspension: Each mL contains: chloramphenicol 2 mg and hydrocortisone acetate 10 mg. Nonmedicinal ingredients: polysorbate 80, povidone, purified water, sodium carboxymethylcellulose, sodium hydroxide and/or hydrochloric acid (to adjust pH) and sodium chloride. Plastic dropper bottles of 5 mL. Preservative-free. Refrigerate.

PENTASA® Ⓟ
Hoechst Marion Roussel

5-Aminosalicylic Acid

Gastrointestinal Anti-inflammatory

Pharmacology: Pentasa is a unique, ethylcellulose-coated, delayed-release formulation of 5-ASA, an aminosalicylate, gastrointestinal anti-inflammatory agent for oral administration. Aminosalicylates are considered to be first line therapy for inflammatory bowel diseases. 5-ASA is known to be therapeutically active in Crohn's disease and ulcerative colitis.

Although the mechanism of action of 5-ASA is unknown, its therapeutic effect appears to be nonsystemic. 5-ASA has in vitro and in vivo pharmacologic effects that decrease leukotriene production, scavenge for free radicals, and inhibit leukocyte chemotaxis. It is currently unknown which, if any, of these mechanisms play a predominant role in the clinical effectiveness of 5-ASA.

Pentasa is designed to release therapeutic quantities of 5-ASA throughout the small (jejunum and ileum) and large (colon) bowel. Based on urinary excretion data, 20 to 30% of 5-ASA in Pentasa is absorbed. It is rapidly acetylated to N-acetyl-5-ASA. Plasma 5-ASA concentration peaks at approximately 1 μg/mL 3 hours following a 1 g Pentasa dose, and declines rapidly in a biphasic manner. N-acetyl-5-ASA peaks at approximately 1.8 μg/mL and its concentration also follows a biphasic decline. Pharmacological activities of N-acetyl-5-ASA are unknown and other metabolites have not been identified.

About 130 mg free 5-ASA is recovered in the feces following a single 1 g Pentasa dose, which is comparable to the amount of 5-ASA recovered from a molar equivalent sulfasalazine dose of 2.5 g. Elimination of free 5-ASA and salicylates in feces increases proportionately with Pentasa dose. N-acetyl-5-ASA is the primary compound excreted in the urine (19 to 30% of dose).

Indications: For the treatment of acute ulcerative colitis and for long-term maintenance therapy in order to maintain remission and prevent relapse of active disease.

For the management of mild to moderate Crohn's disease, and as a maintenance therapy for patients with Crohn's disease in remission induced by surgery or medication.

Contraindications: Patients with existing gastric or duodenal ulcer, patients with urinary tract obstruction and patients who have demonstrated hypersensitivity to 5-ASA or salicylates.

Warnings: Impaired Renal or Hepatic Function: Caution should be exercised if 5-ASA is administered to patients with impaired renal or hepatic function.

Single reports of nephrotic syndrome and interstitial nephritis associated with 5-ASA therapy have been described in the literature. Animal studies have demonstrated a dose-dependent nephrotoxicity. Patients with pre-existing renal disease, increased BUN or serum creatinine, or proteinuria should be carefully monitored.
Pregnancy: 5-ASA should be used during pregnancy only if clearly needed.

5-ASA is known to cross the placental barrier.
Lactation: Caution should be exercised when 5-ASA is administered to a nursing woman.
Children: Safety and efficacy have not been established in children. The potential benefits of its use should be weighed against the possible risks.

Precautions: General: 5-ASA has been associated with the production of an acute intolerance syndrome which may be difficult to distinguish from flare of inflammatory bowel disease. Symptoms include cramping, acute abdominal pain and bloody diarrhea, sometimes fever, headache and rash. If acute intolerance syndrome is suspected, prompt withdrawal is required. If a rechallenge is performed later in order to validate the hypersensitivity, it should be carried out under close medical supervision at reduced dose and only if clearly needed.

In Crohn's disease and ulcerative colitis studies, most patients who were intolerant or hypersensitive to sulfasalazine were able to take 5-ASA without evidence of allergic reaction (e.g., rash, fever, pruritus) or intolerance. Nevertheless, caution should be exercised when 5-ASA is used in patients known to be allergic to sulfasalazine. These patients should be instructed to discontinue therapy if signs of rash or fever become apparent.

Semen abnormalities and infertility in men, which are associated with sulfasalazine, have not been reported with 5-ASA during controlled clinical trials. Semen quality significantly improved when patients were transferred from sulfasalazine to 5-ASA.
Drug Interactions: There are no known interactions between 5-ASA and other drugs.

Adverse Effects: Ulcerative Colitis: In 2 placebo-controlled clinical trials involving over 600 patients, adverse event rates for 5-ASA were similar to, or less than, those seen in the placebo group (5-ASA 14% vs placebo 18%) and were not dose-related. No single event was reported at a rate greater than 4% in the patients who received 5-ASA. Of the most common events, only nausea, rash, and vomiting had a higher incidence in the 5-ASA group relative to placebo.
Crohn's Disease: In 2 placebo-controlled clinical trials involving over 540 patients with acute Crohn's disease, 21% of the 5-ASA patients and 12% of the placebo patients, reported treatment-related adverse events. The adverse event rate for the 5-ASA group was not dose-related. No single event was reported at a rate greater than 5% in patients who received 5-ASA.

The most commonly reported 5-ASA related events were nausea 4.9%, headache 4.4%, abdominal pain 3.9%, diarrhea 3.4%, rash 2.8%, vomiting 2.6%, stool abnormalities 1.6%, back pain 1.0%, asthenia 1.0%, dyspepsia 1.0%, and pruritus 1.0%.

In a 48-week, placebo-controlled, maintenance therapy trial conducted in 293 patients with Crohn's disease in remission, treatment-related events were reported by 31% of patients in both the 5-ASA and the placebo groups. The most commonly reported treatment-related events in the 5-ASA group were abdominal pain (5%), diarrhea (5%), nausea (3.5%), headache (3.5%), abdominal cramps (2.1%), loose stools (2.1%), dyspepsia (1.4%), heartburn (1.4%), exacerbation of headache (1.4%) and edema of the hands (1.4%).

When considering all clinical trials together (ulcerative colitis and Crohn's disease), more than 2 600 patients have received 5-ASA therapy. Generally, 5-ASA was well tolerated. The most common events (i.e., greater than 1%) were: diarrhea (3.4%), headache (2.4%), nausea (2.3%), abdominal pain (2.4%), vomiting (1.7%), dyspepsia (1.6%), and rash (1.5%).

The following events were reported infrequently (i.e., less than 1%) during trials. In many cases the relationship to 5-ASA has not been established.

Gastrointestinal: abdominal distention, anorexia, duodenal ulcer, dysphagia, eructation, esophageal ulcer, fecal incontinence, gastrointestinal bleeding, gastrointestinal disturbances, increase in bowel movements, melena, mouth irritation, mouth ulcer, oral moniliasis, pancreatitis, rectal bleeding, rectal urgency, thirst.

Dermatological: acne, alopecia, dry skin, eczema, erythema nodosum, erythematous rash, hirsutism, nail disorder, photosensitivity, pruritus, skin discoloration, sweating.

Nervous System: anxiety, abnormal dreams, dizziness, insomnia, somnolence, paresthesia.

Cardiovascular: postural hypotension, tachycardia, vasodilation.

Respiratory: dyspnea, increased coughing, pharyngitis.

Metabolic: alkaline phosphatase increase, amylase increase, C reactive protein increase, creatinine increase, GGTP increase, LDH increase, proteinuria, AST increase, ALT increase, weight decrease, weight increase.

Other: albuminuria, anemia, appetite decreased, arthralgia, breast pain, chest pain/pressure, chills, conjunctivitis, dry eyes, eye pain, ecchymosis, edema, eosinophilia, ESR increase, fatigue, fever, flu syndrome, leg cramps, malaise, menorrhagia, myalgia, scotoma, sore throat, urinary frequency, urinary infection, urination disorder, vaginitis, weakness.

Isolated case reports have described pericarditis, pancreatitis, nephrotic syndrome and interstitial nephritis associated with 5-ASA.

Overdose: Symptoms and Treatment: There is no clinical experience with 5-ASA overdosage. 5-ASA is an aminosalicylate and symptoms of salicylate toxicity may be possible, such as: tinnitus, vertigo, headache, confusion, drowsiness, sweating, hyperventilation, vomiting and diarrhea. Severe intoxication with salicylates can lead to disruption of electrolyte balance and blood pH, hyperthermia and dehydration. Since 5-ASA is an aminosalicylate, conventional therapy for salicylate toxicity may be beneficial in the event of acute overdosage. This includes prevention of further gastrointestinal tract absorption by emesis and, if necessary, by gastric lavage. Fluid and electrolyte imbalance should be corrected by the administration of appropriate i.v. therapy. Adequate renal function should be maintained.

Dosage: 5-ASA is effective as a single oral agent for the treatment of acute ulcerative colitis and for long-term maintenance therapy in order to maintain remission and prevent relapse of active disease.

5-ASA is also effective for the management of mild to moderate Crohn's disease and as a maintenance therapy for patients with Crohn's disease in remission induced by surgery or medication. Dosage should be adjusted for each patient's needs consistent with achieving a satisfactory therapeutic response.

Ulcerative Colitis: Therapy should be initiated at 0.5 g 4 times daily (2 g daily dose). If additional therapeutic benefit is needed, the dose may be increased to 1 g 4 times daily (4 g daily dose).

Crohn's Disease: The optimal dose for mild to moderate disease is 1 g 4 times daily (4 g daily dose). For patients with Crohn's disease in remission, a dose of 0.75 g 4 times daily (3 g daily dose) is recommended. The management of Crohn's disease in remission should start as soon as remission is achieved.

5-ASA should be taken before meals and at bedtime with fluids. Pentasa should not be chewed, broken or crushed before being swallowed.

Supplied: 250 mg: Each white to grey or light brown, speckled, scored, delayed-release tablet, with PENTASA on one side and 250 on the other, contains: 5-ASA 250 mg. Nonmedicinal ingredients: cellulose, ethylcellulose, magnesium stearate, povidone and talc. Gluten-free. Bottles or blister packs of 240 and 480.

500 mg: Each white to grey or light brown, speckled, scored, delayed-release tablet, with PENTASA on one side and 500 on the other, contains: 5-ASA 500 mg. Nonmedicinal ingredients: cellulose, ethylcellulose, magnesium stearate, povidone and talc. Gluten-free. Bottles or blister packs of 240 and 480.

Store at room temperature (15 to 30°C).

(Shown in Product Recognition Section)

Reviewed 1998

PENTASPAN®

DuPont Pharma

Pentastarch

Plasma Volume Expander

Pharmacology: The colloidal properties of pentastarch render it useful as a plasma volume expander. I.V. infusion of pentastarch results in expansion of the plasma volume in excess of the volume infused. This expansion persists for approximately 18 to 24 hours and is expected to improve the hemodynamic status for 12 to 18 hours.

Pentastarch molecules below 50 000 molecular weight are rapidly eliminated by renal excretion. A single dose of approximately 500 mL of pentastarch results in elimination in the urine of approximately 70% of the dose within 24 hours, and approximately 80% of the dose within 1 week. The remaining percentage of the administered dose is presumed to be eliminated at a slower rate. Although this process is variable, it generally results in an intravascular pentastarch concentration below the level of detection by 1 week. The hydroxyethyl group is not cleaved, but remains intact and attached to glucose units when excreted.

Indications: When plasma volume expansion is desired as an adjunct in the management of shock due to hemorrhage, surgery, sepsis, burns or other trauma. It is not a substitute for red blood cells or coagulation factors in plasma.

Contraindications: In patients with known hypersensitivity to hydroxyethyl starch, or with bleeding disorders, or with congestive heart failure where volume overload is a potential problem. Pentastarch should not be used in renal disease with oliguria or anuria not related to hypovolemia.

Warnings: General: Administration of large volumes of pentastarch will decrease hemoglobin concentration and dilute plasma proteins excessively. Administration should be kept below the recommended ceiling of 2 000 mL in 24 hours (see Dosage).

As with other plasma volume expanders, large volumes of pentastarch will alter the coagulation mechanisms, inasmuch as a prolongation of prothrombin, partial thromboplastin and clotting times will occur. The physician should also be alert to the possibility of transient prolongation of bleeding time.

Hypersensitivity has been seen (wheezing and urticaria and hypotension). Anaphylactic/anaphylactoid reactions have been reported with pentastarch; a causal relationship has not been established. If hypersensitivity effects occur, discontinue the drug and, if necessary, administer appropriate therapy.

Pregnancy: Pentastarch has been shown to be embryocidal in New Zealand rabbits and in Swiss mice when given in doses 5 times the human dose. There are no adequate and well-controlled clinical studies using pentastarch in pregnant women. Pentastarch should not be used during pregnancy unless potential benefits justify the potential risk to the fetus.

Lactation: It is not known whether pentastarch is excreted in human milk. Because many drugs are excreted in human milk, caution should be exercised when pentastarch is administered to a nursing woman.

Children: The safety and effectiveness of pentastarch in children have not been established.

Precautions: Pentastarch, like all plasma volume expanders, is not a substitute for red blood cells or coagulation factors in plasma.

The possibility of circulatory overload should be kept in mind.

Caution should be used when the risk of pulmonary edema and/or congestive heart failure is increased. Special care should be exercised in patients who have impaired renal clearance since this is the principal route by which pentastarch is eliminated.

The serum chemistries of 16 normal volunteers who were given pentastarch in doses of 500 to 2 000 mL (2×1 000 mL infusions on separate days) were essentially unchanged from pre- to 7 days post infusion, except for dilutional effects. There were no clinically significant abnormal values except for one creatinine phosphokinase level following an episode of venospasm. However, indirect bilirubin levels of 8.3 mg/L (normal 0 to 7 mg/L) have been reported in 2 out of 20 normal subjects who received multiple infusions of a 6% hetastarch product. Total bilirubin was within normal limits at all times; indirect bilirubin returned to normal by 96 hours following the final infusion. The significance, if any, of these elevations is not known; however, caution should be observed before administering pentastarch to patients with a history of liver disease.

Caution should be exercised when administering pentastarch to patients allergic to corn because such patients can also be allergic to pentastarch.

Elevated serum amylase levels may be observed temporarily following administration of pentastarch although no association with pancreatitis has been demonstrated. A 6% hetastarch injection product has not been shown to increase serum lipase. Similar effects may be expected with pentastarch.

Adverse Effects: Coagulation disorders or hemorrhage have been reported in association with the use of pentastarch as a plasma volume expander. Headache, diarrhea, nausea, weakness, temporary weight gain, insomnia, fatigue, fever, edema, paresthesia, acne, malaise, shakiness, dizziness, chest pain, chills, nasal congestion, anxiety and increased heart rate have also been reported in clinical studies involving pentastarch.

It is uncertain whether any of these adverse experiences are attributable to the drug, medical procedures, concurrent adjunctive medication, or a combination of these factors.

Hypersensitivity has been seen (wheezing, urticaria and hypotension). Anaphylactic/anaphylactoid reactions have been reported with pentastarch (see Warnings).

Overdose: Symptoms and Treatment: The treatment of overdosage would be essentially symptomatic and supportive.

Dosage: Pentastarch is administered by i.v. infusion only. Total dosage and rate of infusion depend upon the amount of blood or plasma lost. In adults, the amount usually administered is 500 to 2 000 mL. Total dosage does not usually exceed 2 000 mL/day or approximately 28 mL/kg of body weight for the typical 70 kg patient. In acute hemorrhagic shock, an administration rate approaching 20 mL/kg/hour may be used. Use beyond 72 hours has not been studied.

Parenteral drug products should be inspected for particulate matter and discoloration prior to administration whenever solution and container permit.

The solution is intended for i.v. administration using sterile equipment. It is recommended that i.v. administration apparatus be replaced at least once every 24 hours.

Special Instructions: Caution: Before administering to patient, review these directions: Visual Checking: 1. Do not remove the plastic infusion container from its overwrap until immediately before use. 2. While the overwrap is intact, identify the solution (Pentaspan), lot number and expiration date. 3. Check that the solution is clear. 4. Inspect the intact unit for signs of obvious damage. If present, the unit should not be used.

Removal of Overwrap: To open overwrap, tear at any notch located at either end of unit. After removing overwrap, check for minute leaks by squeezing container firmly. If leaks are found, discard unit as sterility may be impaired.

Preparation for Administration (Use aseptic technique): 1. Close flow control clamp of administration set. 2. Twist off plug from port designated "Infusion Set Port". 3. Insert spike of infusion set into port with a twisting motion until the set is firmly sealed. 4. Suspend container from hanger. 5. Follow manufacturer's recommended procedures for the administration set. 6. Discontinue administration and notify physician immediately if patient exhibits signs of adverse reactions.

Supplied: Each 100 mL of sterile, clear, pale yellow to amber-colored, nonpyrogenic solution contains: pentastarch 10 g, sodium chloride USP 0.9 g and water for injection USP qs. pH adjusted with sodium hydroxide to approximately 5.0. Approximate concentration of electrolytes (mEq/L): sodium 154, chloride 154. Calculated Osmolarity: approximately 326 mOsM. Plastic i.v. infusion bags of 250 and 500 mL. Exposure of pharmaceutical products to heat should be minimized. Avoid excessive heat. Protect from freezing. Store at room temperature (15 to 25°C).

Reviewed 1999

...Canada's Poison Control Centres are listed in the CLIN-INFO SECTION.

PENTA-THION®
Sabex

Vitamin C—Vitamin B₁

Vitamin Supplement

Supplied: Each pouch contains: vitamin C (ascorbic acid) 500 mg and vitamin B_1 (thiamine) 2 mg. Nonmedicinal ingredients: adenosine triphosphoric acid (ATP) and reduced glutathione, in soluble effervescent granules. Boxes of 20.

PENTA/3B®
PENTA/3B® Plus
PENTA/3B® + C
Sabex

Vitamin Supplement

Supplied: Penta/3b: Each film-coated tablet contains: vitamin B_1 250 mg, vitamin B_6 125 mg and vitamin B_{12} 250 µg. Nonmedicinal ingredients: cornstarch, hydroxypropyl methylcellulose, isopropyl alcohol, lactose, magnesium stearate, methanol, methylene chloride, Opaspray (FD&C Red #40), povidone, propylene glycol, stearic acid and vanillin. Bottles of 50 and 300.

Penta/3b plus: Each capsule contains: vitamin B_1 250 mg, vitamin B_2 2 mg, vitamin B_6 125 mg, niacinamide 20 mg, folic acid 0.1 mg, vitamin B_{12} 250 µg, vitamin C 75 mg, vitamin D 400 IU, vitamin E (as dl-alpha-tocopheryl acetate) 15 mg, vitamin A (as palmitate) 4 000 IU, and pantothenic acid (as calcium pantothenate) 9 mg. Nonmedicinal ingredients: gelatin capsule (FD&C Yellow No. 6, amaranth, FD&C Red No. 3, titanium dioxide and sodium lauryl sulfate), magnesium stearate and colloidal silicon dioxide. Bottles of 50 and 300.

Penta/3b + C: Each film-coated tablet contains: vitamin B_1 250 mg, vitamin B_6 125 mg, vitamin B_{12} 250 µg and vitamin C 250 mg. Nonmedicinal ingredients: colloidal silicon dioxide, deionized water, ethyl alcohol, hydroxypropyl methylcellulose, icing sugar, lactose, methanol, methylene chloride, opaspray (FD&C Yellow No. 5), polysorbate 80, povidone, propylene glycol, stearic acid and vanillin. Bottles of 50 and 300.

PENTAZOCINE Ⓝ
General Monograph, CPhA

see OPIOID ANALGESICS

PENTOBARBITAL ◈
General Monograph, CPhA

see BARBITURATES

PENTOTHAL® ◈
Abbott

Thiopental Sodium

I.V. Anesthetic

Indications: As the sole anesthetic agent for brief (15-minute) procedures; for induction of anesthesia prior to administration of other anesthetic agents; to supplement regional anesthesia; to provide hypnosis during balanced anesthesia with other agents for analgesia or muscle relaxation; for the control of convulsive states during or following inhalation anesthesia, local anesthesia, or other causes; in neurosurgical patients with increased intracranial pressure, if adequate ventilation is provided; and for narcoanalysis and narcosynthesis in psychiatric disorders.

Contraindications: Absolute Contraindications: Absence of suitable veins for i.v. administration; hypersensitivity (allergy) to barbiturates; variegate porphyria (South African) or acute intermittent porphyria; patients with severe respiratory embarrassment; status asthmaticus and; inflammatory conditions of the mouth, jaw, and neck.

Relative Contraindications: Severe cardiovascular disease; hypotension or shock; and conditions in which the hypnotic effect may be prolonged or potentiated-excessive premedication, Addison's disease, hepatic or renal dysfunction, myxedema, increased blood urea, severe anemia, asthma and myasthenia gravis.

Diluents in Pentothal Ready-to-Mix syringes should not be used for fluid replacement. Do not use unless diluent is clear and the syringe package is undamaged.

Warnings: Keep resuscitative and endotracheal intubation equipment and oxygen readily available. Maintain patency of the airway at all times.

This drug should be administered only by persons qualified in the use of i.v. anesthetics.

Avoid extravasation or intra-arterial injection.

May be habit forming.

I.V. administration of Sterile Water for Injection USP, without a solute, may result in hemolysis.

Use aseptic technique for preparing thiopental solutions.

Administer only clear, reconstituted solutions.

Use within 24 hours after reconstitution. Discard unused portions.

Precautions: General: A person competent in anesthesia management should be in constant attendance and adequate facilities for support of respiration and circulation should be available when thiopental for injection is being used.

Observe aseptic precautions at all times in preparation and handling of thiopental solutions.

If used in conditions involving relative contraindications, reduce dosage and administer slowly.

Thiopental should be administered with caution to patients with pre-existing hypotension or in conditions where the hypnotic effect may be prolonged or intensified, such as in the presence of liver disease and renal disease.

Care should be taken in administering the drug to patients with advanced cardiac disease, increased intracranial pressure, ophtalmoplegia plus, asthma, myasthenia gravis and endocrine insufficiency (pituitary, thyroid, adrenal, pancreas).

<u>*Drug Interactions:*</u> The following drug interactions have been reported with thiopental (see Table I).

Table I—Pentothal

Drug Interactions

Drug	Effect
Probenecid	Prolonged action of thiopental
Diazoxide	Hypotension
Opioid analgesics	Decreased antinociceptive action
Aminophylline	Thiopental antagonism
Midazolam	Synergism
Sulfisoxazole (i.v.)	Reduced thiopental dosage requirements

Pregnancy: It is not known whether thiopental can cause fetal harm when administered to a pregnant woman or can affect reproductive capacity. Thiopental should be given to a pregnant woman only if clearly needed.

Lactation: Thiopental readily crosses the placenta barrier and small amounts may appear in the milk of nursing mothers following administration of large doses.

Adverse Effects: Adverse reactions include respiratory depression, myocardial depression, cardiac arrhythmias, prolonged somnolence and recovery, hypotension, tachycardia, sneezing, coughing, bronchospasm, laryngospam and shivering. Anaphylactic and anaphylactoid reactions to thiopental have been reported. Symptoms, e.g., urticaria, bronchospasm, vasodilation and edema should be managed by conventional means.

Hypersensitivity reactions to barbiturates, including thiopental have been reported.

Rarely, immune hemolytic anemia with renal failure and radial nerve palsy have been reported.

Reactions which may occur because of the diluents, technique of preparation or mixing, or administration of reconstituted solutions of thiopental include febrile response or infection at site of injection, venous thrombosis or phlebitis extending from the site of injection and extravasation.

If an adverse reaction does occur, discontinue the injection, evaluate the patient, institute appropriate therapeutic counter measures and save the remainder of unused solution (or the used container or syringe) for examination if deemed necessary.

Overdose: Symptoms: Overdosage may occur from too rapid or repeated injections. Too rapid injection may be followed by an alarming fall in blood pressure even to shock levels. Apnea, occasional laryngospasm, coughing and other respiratory difficulties with excessive or too rapid injections may occur. In the event of suspected or apparent overdosage, the drug should be discontinued, a patent airway established (intubate if necessary) or maintained, and oxygen should be administered, with assisted ventilation if necessary. The lethal dose of barbiturates varies and cannot be stated with certainty. Lethal blood level may be as low as 1 mg/100 mL for short-acting barbiturates; less if other depressant drugs or alcohol are also present.

Cardiovascular collapse may also follow too rapid injection or overdosage. Treatment should be directed toward supporting the blood pressure and using volume expansion and/or vasopressor agents as appropriate.

Treatment: It is generally agreed that respiratory depression or arrest, due to unusual sensitivity to thiopental or overdosage, is easily managed if there is no concomitant respiratory obstruction. If the airway is patent, any method of ventilating the lungs (that prevents hypoxia) should be successful in maintaining other vital functions. Since depression of respiratory activity is one of the characteristic actions of the drug, it is important to observe respiration closely.

Should laryngospasm occur, it may be relieved by one of the usual methods, such as the use of a relaxant drug or positive pressure oxygen. Endotracheal intubation may be indicated in difficult cases.

Dosage: Thiopental is administered by i.v. route only. Individual response to the drug is so varied that there can be no fixed dosage. The drug should be titrated against patient requirements as governed by age, sex and body weight. Younger patients require relatively larger doses than middle-aged and elderly persons: the latter metabolize the drug more slowly. Prepuberty requirements are the same for both sexes, but adult females require less than adult males. Dose is usually proportional to body weight and obese patients require a larger dose than relatively lean persons of the same weight.

Reconstituted solutions of thiopental should be inspected visually for particular matter and discoloration, whenever solution and container permit.

Premedication: Premedication usually consists of atropine or scopolamine to suppress vagal reflexes and inhibit secretions. In addition, a barbiturate or an opiate is often given. Sodium pentobarbital injection is suggested because it provides a preliminary indication of how the patient will react to barbiturate anesthesia. Ideally, the peak effect of these medications should be reached shortly before the time of induction.

Test Dose: It is advisable to inject a small "test" dose of 25 to 75 mg: (1 to 3 mL of a 2.5% solution) of thiopental to assess tolerance or unusual sensitivity to thiopental, and pausing to observe patient reaction for at least 60 seconds. If unexpectedly deep anesthesia develops or if respiratory depression occurs, consider these possibilities: the patient may be unusually sensitive to thiopental, the solution may be more concentrated than had been assumed, or the patient may have received too much premedication.

Anesthesia: Moderately slow induction can usually be accomplished in the "average" adult by injection of 50 to 75 mg (2 to 3 mL of a 2.5% solution) at intervals of 20 to 40 seconds, depending on the reaction of the patient. Once anesthesia is established, additional injections of 25 to 50 mg can be given whenever the patient moves.

Slow injection is recommended to minimize respiratory depression and the possibility of overdosage. The smallest dose consistent with attaining the surgical objective is the desired goal. Momentary apnea following each injection is typical, and progressive decrease in the amplitude of respiration appears with increasing dosage. Pulse remains normal or increases slightly and returns to normal. Blood pressure usually falls slightly and returns toward normal. Muscles usually relax about 30 seconds after unconsciousness is attained, but this may be masked if a skeletal muscle relaxant is used. The tone of jaw muscles is a fairly reliable index. The pupils may dilate but later contract: sensitivity to light is not usually lost until a level of anesthesia deep enough to permit surgery is attained. Nystagmus and divergent strabismus are characteristic during early stages, but at the level of surgical anesthesia, the eyes are central and fixed. Corneal and conjunctival reflexes disappear during surgical anesthesia.

When thiopental is used for induction in balanced anesthesia with a skeletal muscle relaxant and an inhalation agent, the total dose of thiopental can be estimated and then injected in 2 to 4 fractional doses. With this technique, brief periods of apnea may occur which may require assisted or controlled pulmonary ventilation. As an initial dose, 210 to 280 mg (3 to 4 mg/kg) is usually required for rapid induction in the average adult (70 kg).

When thiopental is used as the sole anesthetic agent, the desired level of anesthesia can be maintained by injection of small, repeated doses as needed or by using a continuous i.v. drip in a 0.2 or 0.4% concentration. (Sterile Water should not be used as the diluent in these concentrations, since hemolysis will occur. Solutions may be prepared with Dextrose 5%

in water, Sodium Chloride Injection or Normosol-R.) With continuous drip, the depth of anesthesia is controlled by adjusting the rate of infusion.

Convulsive States: For the control of convulsive states following anesthesia (inhalation or local) or other causes, 75 to 125 mg (3 to 5 mL of a 2.5% solution) should be given as soon as possible after the convulsion begins. Convulsions following the use of a local anesthetic may require 125 to 250 mg of thiopental, given over a 10-minute period. If the convulsion is caused by a local anesthetic, the required dose of thiopental will depend upon the amount of local anesthetic given and its convulsant properties.

Neurosurgical Patients with Increased Intracranial Pressure: In neurosurgical patients, intermittent bolus injections of 1.5 to 3.5 mg/kg of body weight may be given to reduce intraoperative elevations of intracranial pressure, if adequate ventilation is provided.

Psychiatric Disorders: For narcoanalysis and narcosynthesis in psychiatric disorders, premedication with an anticholinergic agent may precede administration of thiopental. After a test dose, thiopental is injected at a slow rate of 100 mg/min (4 mL/min of a 2.5% solution) with the patient counting backwards from 100. Shortly after counting, the patient becomes confused but before actual sleep is produced, the injection is discontinued. Allow the patient to return to a semidrowsy state where conversation is coherent. Alternatively, thiopental may be administered by rapid i.v. drip using a 0.2% concentration in 5 % dextrose and water. At this concentration, the rate of administration should not exceed 50 mL/min.

Management of Some Complications: Respiratory depression (hypoventilation, apnea), which may result from either unusual responsiveness to thiopental or overdosage, is managed as stated above. Thiopental should be considered to have the same potential for producing respiratory depression as an inhalation agent, and patency of the airway must be protected at all times.

Laryngospasm may occur with light thiopental narcosis at intubation, or in the absence of intubation if foreign matter or secretions in the respiratory tract create irritation. Laryngeal and bronchial vagal reflexes can be suppressed, and secretions minimized by giving atropine or scopolamine premedication and a barbiturate or opiate. Use of a skeletal muscle relaxant or positive pressure oxygen will usually relieve laryngospasm. Tracheotomy may be indicated in difficult cases.

Myocardial depression, proportional to the amount of drug in direct contact with the heart, can occur and may cause hypotension, particularly in patients with an unhealthy myocardium. Arrhythmias may appear if Pco_2 is elevated, but they are uncommon with adequate ventilation. Management of myocardial depression is the same as for overdosage. Thiopental does not sensitize the heart to epinephrine or other sympathomimetic amines.

Extravascular infiltration should be a avoided. Care should be taken to insure that the needle is within the lumen of the vein before injection of thiopental. Extravascular injection may cause chemical irritation of the tissues varying from slight tenderness to venospasm, extensive necrosis and sloughing. This is due primarily to the high alkalinity (pH 10 to 11) of clinical concentrations of the drug. If extravasation occurs, the local irritant effects can be reduced by injection of 1 % procaine locally to relieve pain and enhance vasodilatation. Local application of heat also may help to increase local circulation and removal of the infiltrate.

Intra-arterial injection can occur inadvertently, especially if an aberrant superficial artery is present at the medial aspect of the antecubital fossa. The area selected for i.v. injection of the drug should be palpated for detection of an underlying pulsating vessel. Accidental intra-arterial injection can cause arteriospasm and severe pain along the course of the artery with blanching of the arm and fingers. Appropriate corrective measures should be instituted promptly to avoid possible development of gangrene. Any patient complaint of pain warrants stopping the injection. Methods suggested for dealing with this complication vary with the severity of symptoms. The following have been suggested: Dilute the injected thiopental by removing the tourniquet and any restrictive garments; leave the needle in place, if possible; inject the artery with a dilute solution of papaverine, 40 to 80 mg, or 10 mL of 1% procaine, to inhibit smooth muscle spasm; if necessary, perform sympathetic block of the brachial plexus and/or stellate ganglion to relieve pain and assist in opening collateral circulation (papaverine can be injected into subclavian artery, if desired); unless otherwise contraindicated, institute immediate heparinization to prevent thrombus formation; consider local infiltration of an alpha-adrenergic blocking agent such as phentolamine into the vasospastic area; and provide additional symptomatic treatment as required.

Shivering after thiopental anesthesia, manifested by twitching face muscles and occasional progression to tremors of the arms, head, shoulders and body, is a thermal reaction due to increased sensitivity to cold. Shivering appears if the room environment is cold and if a large ventilatory heat loss has been sustained with balanced inhalation anesthesia employing nitrous oxide. Treatment consists of warming the patient with blankets, maintaining room temperature near 22°C, and administration of chlorpromazine or methylphenidate.

Reconstitution of Solutions: Thiopental is supplied as a sterile, yellowish, hygroscopic powder stabilized with anhydrous sodium carbonate as a buffer.

The diluent (Sterile Water for Injection USP) in Pentothal Ready-to-Mix Syringes is supplied in a separate container to allow for mixing with the thiopental in the powder vial to permit immediate i.v. injection of reconstituted solution into a vein or attachment to a standard stopcock assembly.

Since thiopental contains no added bacteriostatic agent, extreme care in preparation and handling should be exercised at all times to prevent the introduction of microbial contaminants. Solutions should be **freshly prepared** and used promptly. Reconstituted solutions of thiopental may be kept, tightly stoppered, under refrigeration up to 24 hours, unused portions should be discarded after 24 hours. Sterilization by heating should not be attempted.

Directions for Preparing the Pentothal Solutions, Excluding Ready-to-Mix Syringes: See Table II. Solutions should be prepared **aseptically** with 1 of the 3 following diluents: Sterile Water for Injection, USP, sodium chloride injection, USP, or 5% dextrose injection, USP. Clinical concentrations used for intermittent i.v. administration vary between 2 and 5%. A 2 or 2.5% solution is most commonly used. A 3.4% concentration in sterile water for injection is isotonic; concentrations less than 2% in this diluent are not used because they cause hemolysis. For continuous i.v. drip administration, concentrations of 0.2 or 0.4% are used. Solutions may be prepared by adding Pentothal to 5% dextrose injection, USP, sodium chloride injection, USP, or Normosol-R pH 7.4.

Table II—Penthotal

Calculations For Various Concentrations

Concentration %	Desired mg/mL	Amounts to Use: Pentothal g	Amounts to Use: Diluent mL
0.2	2	1	500
0.4	4	1	250
		2	500
2.0	20	1	50
		5	250
		10	500
2.5	25	1	40
		5	200
5	50	1	20
		5	100

Directions for Preparing the Pentothal Ready-to-Mix Syringe: Use aseptic technique: Do not assemble until ready to use.

1. Remove caps from powder vial and injector.
2. Insert powder vial into injector and rotate clockwise approximately 3 turns.
3. Remove fliptop from diluent vial. Swab stopper. Remove needle cover. Insert needle into target area of diluent vial stopper.
4. Position syringe upright, depress powder vial to transfer air into diluent vial. Release pressure on powder vial and allow diluent to fill powder vial. Repeat until air in powder vial has been displaced.
5. Transfer remaining diluent by slowly pulling back on powder vial.
6. Remove and discard empty diluent vial. Replace needle cover. Shake until powder is completely dissolved.
7. **Use reconstituted solution only if it is clear, free from precipitate and not discolored.**

Medication, fluid path and needle are sterile if caps and protective covers are undisturbed and package is intact. Component exteriors are not sterile. Single dose unit. Discard unused portion. For i.v. use.

Compatibility: **Any solution of thiopental with a visible precipitate should be discarded.** The stability of thiopental solutions depends upon several factors, including the diluent, temperature of storage and the amount of carbon dioxide from room air that gains access to the solution. Any factor or condition which tends to lower pH (increased acidity) of thiopental solutions will increase the likelihood of precipitation of thiopental acid. Such factors include the use of diluents which are too acidic and the absorption of carbon dioxide, which can combine with water to form carbonic acid.

Solutions of succinylcholine, tubocurarine or other drugs which have an acid pH should not be mixed with thiopental solutions. The most stable solutions are those reconstituted in water or isotonic saline, kept under refrigeration and tightly stoppered.

Supplied: Combination Kits: 2.5 g/vial: Each kit contains: one 2.5 g thiopental sodium vial and one 100 mL bottle of water for injection to provide a 2.5% solution after reconstitution. Packages of 25 kits. Protect from freezing and high temperatures, above 38°C.

1 g/vial: Each kit contains: one 1 g thiopental sodium vial and one 50 mL vial of water for injection to provide a 2% solution after reconstitution. To obtain a 2.5% solution after reconstitution, use only 40 mL of water for injection. Packages of 25 kits. Protect from freezing and high temperatures, above 38°C.

5 g/vial: Each kit contains: one 5 g thiopental sodium vial and one 200 mL bottle of water for injection to provide a 2.5% solution after reconstitution. Packages of 25 kits. Protect from freezing and high temperatures, above 38°C.

Vials: 500 mg: Each vial of sterile, yellowish, hydroscopic powder for injection, stabilized with anydrous sodium carbonate as a buffer, contains: thiopental sodium 500 mg. Packages of 25 vials. Protect from freezing and high temperatures, above 38°C.

1 g: Each vial of sterile, yellowish, hydroscopic powder for injection, stabilized with anydrous sodium carbonate as buffer, contains: thiopental sodium 1 g. Packages of 25 vials. Protect from freezing and high temperatures, above 38°C.

Ready to Mix Syringes: 250 mg: Each single dose unit contains: thiopental sodium powder 250 mg accompanied with 10 mL of diluent, providing a reconstituted concentration of 2.5%. Store at controlled room temperature (15 to 30°C).

500 mg: Each single dose unit contains: thiopental sodium powder 500 mg accompanied with 20 mL of diluent, providing a reconstituted concentration of 2.5%. Store at controlled room temperature (15 to 30°C).

Reviewed 1998

PENTRAX®

Medicis

Fractar

Antipsoriatic—Antiseborrheic

Supplied: Each bottle of shampoo contains: Fractar, a patented extract of coal tar, equivalent to coal tar 5%. Plastic bottles of 120 and 240 mL.

PEPCID AC®

Johnson & Johnson • Merck

Famotidine

Histamine H_2 Receptor Antagonist

Pharmacology: Famotidine is a competitive inhibitor of histamine H_2-receptors. The primary clinically important pharmacologic activity of famotidine is inhibition of gastric juice secretion. Famotidine reduces the acid and pepsin content, as well as the volume, of basal, nocturnal, and stimulated gastric secretion.

Pharmacokinetics: Famotidine is incompletely absorbed. The bioavailability of oral doses is 40 to 45%. The bioavailability of the 10 mg chewable tablet was found to be equivalent to the 10 mg film-coated tablet. Bioavailability may be slightly increased by food; however, this effect is of no clinical significance. Bioavailability of Pepcid AC at recommended doses is not affected by customary doses of antacids. Famotidine undergoes minimal first-pass metabolism. After oral doses, peak plasma levels occur in 1 to 3 hours.

A C_{max} value of 41 ng/mL and of 40 ng/mL for the 10 mg film-coated and chewable tablet, respectively, was found in 1 bioequivalence study. Plasma levels after multiple doses are similar to those after single doses. Fifteen to 20% of famotidine in plasma is protein bound. Famotidine has an elimination half-life of 2.5 to 3.5 hours. Famotidine is eliminated by renal (65 to 70%) and metabolic (30 to 35%) routes. Renal clearance is 250 to 450 mL/min, indicating some tubular excretion.

Twenty-five to 30% of an oral dose and 65 to 70% of an i.v. dose are recovered in the urine as unchanged compound.

Pepcid AC (cont'd)

The only metabolite identified in man is the S-oxide. There is a close relationship between creatinine clearance values and the elimination half-life of famotidine. In patients with severe renal insufficiency, i.e., creatinine clearance less than 10 mL/min, elimination half-life of famotidine may exceed 20 hours (see Dosage). In elderly patients, there are no clinically significant age-related changes in the pharmacokinetics of famotidine.

Indications: The treatment of the following conditions where a controlled reduction of gastric secretion is required, such as acid indigestion, heartburn, sour or upset stomach. It is also indicated for the prevention of these symptoms when associated with the consumption of food and/or beverage.

Contraindications: Hypersensitivity to any component of this medication.

Precautions: General: In clinical trials, patients with other underlying acid gastrointestinal diseases (e.g., duodenal ulcer, gastric ulcer) did not experience complications; in general, they did not exhibit a clinically significant deterioration in their condition. However, if patients have difficulty swallowing or if abdominal discomfort persists, the underlying cause should be determined. Symptomatic response to therapy with famotidine does not preclude the presence of gastric malignancy.

Patients with severe kidney disease, previous history of ulcer disease complications, severe coexisting illness, those who are experiencing unintended weight loss in association with dyspeptic symptoms, and those who are middle-aged or older with new or recently changed dyspeptic symptoms should consult a physician before commencing therapy with famotidine.

Patients consuming NSAIDs may have dyspepsia as a side effect of these medicines and should consult a physician or a pharmacist before taking famotidine.

Therapy should not exceed 2 weeks of continuous treatment without medical consultation.

Drug Interactions: Studies with famotidine in man, in animal models, and in vitro have shown no significant interference with the disposition of compounds metabolized by the hepatic microsomal enzymes, e.g., cytochrome P450 system. Compounds tested in man have included warfarin, theophylline, phenytoin, diazepam, aminopyrine and antipyrine. Indocyanine green as an index of hepatic blood flow and/or hepatic drug extraction has been tested and no significant effects have been found.

Concomitant use of aluminum hydroxide/magnesium hydroxide at commonly used doses, does not influence the pharmacodynamics or bioavailability of Pepcid AC. Famotidine does not affect gastric alcohol dehydrogenase and, consequently, blood ethanol levels.

Pregnancy: Reproductive studies have been performed in rats and rabbits at oral doses of up to 2 000 and 500 mg/kg/day, respectively (approximately 2 500 and 625 times the maximum recommended prescription human dose [80 mg], respectively), and have revealed no evidence of impaired fertility or harm to the fetus due to famotidine. There are, however, no adequate or well-controlled studies in pregnant women.

Since the safe use of famotidine in pregnant women has not been established, pregnant women should not use famotidine unless directed otherwise by a physician.

Lactation: Famotidine is detectable in human milk. Nursing mothers should either stop this drug or should stop nursing.

Children: Safety and effectiveness in children have not been established. Pepcid AC should not be administered to children under 12 years of age.

Geriatrics: No dosage adjustment is required based on age (see Pharmacology, Pharmacokinetics).

Adverse Effects: Famotidine has been demonstrated to be generally well tolerated. Adverse reactions reported in $\geq 1\%$ of patients were headache and dizziness. These occurred with comparable frequency in patients treated with placebo.

Laboratory parameters may be affected during treatment with famotidine, but the changes are usually not considered serious. Among the laboratory changes that were reported during clinical trials were increases in AST, ALT, and WBC count, and decreases in hemoglobin and hematocrit. These changes were rarely of clinical significance.

No famotidine-treated patients/subjects had to be discontinued from therapy because of laboratory adverse experiences.

During marketed use of prescription doses, which are higher than those recommended for nonprescription use, the following adverse reactions have been reported; urticaria, liver enzyme abnormalities, cholestatic jaundice, anaphylaxis, angioedema. Toxic epidermal necrolysis has been reported very rarely with H_2-receptor antagonists.

The following adverse reactions have been reported; however, a causal relationship to therapy with famotidine has not been established: agitation, confusion, hallucinations, grand mal seizures, rare cases of impotence, thrombocytopenia, pancytopenia, leukopenia and agranulocytosis.

Gynecomastia has been reported rarely. In most cases that were followed up, it was reversible after discontinuing treatment.

Overdose: Symptoms and Treatment: There is no experience to date with deliberate overdosage. Doses of up to 800 mg/day have been employed in patients with pathological hypersecretory conditions with no serious adverse effects. In the event of overdosage, treatment should be symptomatic and supportive. Unabsorbed material should be removed from the gastrointestinal tract, the patient should be monitored, and supportive therapy should be employed.

The oral LD_{50} of famotidine in male and female rats and mice was >5 000 mg/kg.

Dosage: Adults and children 12 years of age or older: 10 mg, as required to relieve symptoms.

For prevention of acid-related symptoms associated with the consumption of food and/or beverage: 10 mg 1 hour before eating. Repeat if symptoms return, up to a maximum of 20 mg in a 24-hour period.

Therapy should not exceed 2 weeks of continuous treatment without medical consultation.

Concomitant Use with Antacids: Antacids may be given concomitantly if needed.

Information for the Patient: See Blue Section—Information for the Patient "Pepcid AC".

Supplied: Chewable Tablets: Each round, biconvex, pale rose (pink) colored, chewable tablet, with Pepcid AC embossed on one side, contains: famotidine 10 mg. Nonmedicinal ingredients: aspartame, cellulose acetate, citric acid (flavors), hydroxypropyl cellulose, hydroxypropyl methylcellulose, lactose, magnesium stearate, maltodextrin, mannitol, microcrystalline cellulose, modified food starch, red ferric oxide and starch. Boxes of 12 and 30 individually packaged in foil pouches.

Film-coated Tablets: Each rounded-square, pale rose (pink) colored, film-coated tablet, with Pepcid AC embossed on one side, contains: famotidine 10 mg. Nonmedicinal ingredients: hydroxypropyl cellulose, hydroxypropyl methylcellulose, magnesium stearate, microcrystalline cellulose, red ferric oxide, starch, talc and titanium dioxide. Boxes of 6, 12, 18 and 30 individually packaged in PVC/Aluminum blisters.

Store at room temperature (15 to 30°C). Protect from moisture.

(Shown in Product Recognition Section)

Reviewed 1997

PEPCID® Ⓟ
PEPCID® I.V. Ⓟ
MSD

Famotidine

Histamine H_2 Receptor Antagonist

Pharmacology: Famotidine is a competitive inhibitor of histamine H_2-receptors. The primary clinically important pharmacologic activity is inhibition of gastric juice secretion. Famotidine reduces the acid and pepsin content, as well as the volume, of basal, nocturnal, and stimulated gastric secretion.

In both normal volunteers and hypersecretors, famotidine inhibited basal nocturnal and daytime gastric secretion, as well as secretion stimulated by a variety of stimuli, such as pentagastrin and food.

After oral administration, the onset of the antisecretory effect occurred within 1 hour; the maximum effect was dose-dependent, occurring within 1 to 3 hours. Duration of inhibition of secretion was 10 to 12 hours. After i.v. administration, the maximum effect was achieved within 30 minutes. Single i.v. doses of 10 and 20 mg inhibited basal nocturnal secretion for a period of 10 to 12 hours. The 20 mg dose was associated with the longest duration of action in most subjects.

Single oral doses of 20 and 40 mg inhibited basal nocturnal acid secretion in all subjects; mean gastric acid secretion was inhibited by 86% and 94%, respectively, for a period of at least 10 hours. Similar doses given in the morning suppressed food-stimulated acid secretion in all subjects, with mean suppression of 76% and 84%, respectively, 3 to 5 hours after drug, and of 25% and 30%, respectively, 8 to 10 hours after drug; however, in some subjects who received the 20 mg dose, the antisecretory effect was dissipated earlier, within 6 to 8 hours. There was no cumulative effect with repeated doses. The basal nocturnal intragastric pH was raised by evening doses of 20 and 40 mg of famotidine to mean values of 5.0 and 6.4, respectively. When famotidine was given in the morning, the basal daytime interdigestive pH at 3 and 8 hours after 20 or 40 mg was raised to about 5.0.

Fasting and postprandial serum gastrin levels may be slightly elevated during periods of drug antisecretory effect and with chronic therapy an increase in gastric bacterial flora may occur. Gastric emptying and exocrine pancreatic function are not affected by famotidine.

The presence of gastroesophageal reflux disease appears to correlate best with the percentage of time over 24 hours during which the esophagus is exposed to acid. In gastroesophageal reflux disease patients, 20 mg twice a day and 40 mg twice a day of famotidine reduced intraesophageal acid exposure into the normal range as measured by 24 hour intraesophageal pH monitoring. In clinical studies of gastroesophageal reflux disease patients with endoscopically verified erosive or ulcerative esophagitis, 40 mg twice a day was more effective than 20 mg twice a day in healing esophageal lesions. Both dosage regimens were superior to placebo.

Systemic pharmacologic effects of famotidine in the CNS, cardiovascular, respiratory or endocrine systems have not been found to date. Serum prolactin levels do not rise after i.v. bolus doses of 20 mg famotidine and no antiandrogenic effects have been detected.

Pharmacokinetics: Famotidine is incompletely absorbed. The bioavailability of oral doses is 40 to 45% . Bioavailability may be slightly increased by food, or slightly decreased by antacids; however, these effects are of no clinical consequence. Famotidine undergoes minimal first-pass metabolism. After oral doses, peak plasma levels occur in 1 to 3 hours. Plasma levels after multiple doses are similar to those after single doses. Fifteen to 20% of famotidine in plasma is protein bound. Famotidine has an elimination half-life of 2.5 to 3.5 hours. It is eliminated by renal (65 to 70%) and metabolic (30 to 35%) routes. Renal clearance is 250 to 450 mL/min, indicating some tubular excretion.

Twenty-five to 30% of an oral dose and 65 to 70% of an i.v. dose are recovered in the urine as unchanged compound. The only metabolite identified in man is the S-oxide. There is a close relationship between creatinine clearance values and the elimination half-life of famotidine. In patients with severe renal insufficiency, i.e., creatinine clearance less than 10 mL/min, elimination half-life may exceed 20 hours and adjustment of dosing intervals may be necessary (see Precautions and Dosage). In elderly patients, there are no clinically significant age-related changes in the pharmacokinetics of famotidine.

Indications: Tablets: The treatment of the following conditions where a controlled reduction of gastric secretion is required: treatment of acute duodenal ulcer; prophylactic use in duodenal ulcer; treatment of acute benign gastric ulcer; treatment of pathological hypersecretory conditions (e.g., Zollinger-Ellison syndrome); treatment of gastroesophageal reflux disease (GERD); maintenance of remission of patients with GERD.

Injection: In some hospitalized patients with pathological hypersecretory conditions or intractable ulcers, or as an alternative to the oral dosage form for short-term use in patients who are unable to take oral medication.

Contraindications: Hypersensitivity to any component of this medication.

Precautions: Patients with Severe Renal Insufficiency: Dosing intervals may need to be prolonged in patients with advanced renal insufficiency (creatinine clearance<10 mL/min) to adjust for the longer elimination half-life of famotidine (see Pharmacology and Dosage).

Drug Interactions: Studies with famotidine in man, in animal models, and in vitro have shown no significant interference with the disposition of compounds metabolized by the hepatic microsomal enzymes, e.g., cytochrome P450 system. Compounds tested in man have included warfarin, theophylline, phenytoin, diazepam, aminopyrine and antipyrine. Indocyanine green as an index of hepatic blood flow and/or hepatic drug extraction has been tested and no significant effects have been found. In addition, studies with famotidine have shown no augmentation of expected blood alcohol levels resulting from alcohol ingestion.

Gastric Ulcer: Gastric malignancy should be excluded prior to initiation of therapy of gastric ulcer with famotidine. Symptomatic response of gastric ulcer to therapy does not preclude the presence of gastric malignancy.

Pregnancy: Reproductive studies have been performed in rats and rabbits at oral doses of up to 2 000 and 500 mg/kg/day, respectively (approximately 2 500 and 625 times the maximum recommended human dose, respectively), and have revealed no evidence of impaired fertility or harm to the fetus due to famotidine. There are, however, no adequate or well-controlled studies in pregnant women.

Since the safe use of famotidine in pregnant women has not been established, the benefits of treatment should be weighed against potential risks.

Lactation: Famotidine is detectable in human milk. Nursing mothers should either stop this drug or should stop nursing.

Children: Safety and effectiveness in children have not been established.

Geriatrics: No dosage adjustment is required based on age.

Adverse Effects: Famotidine is usually well tolerated; most adverse effects have been mild and transient. The adverse effects listed below have been reported during clinical trials in 2 333 patients. In those controlled clinical trials in which famotidine was compared to placebo, the overall incidence of adverse experiences in the group which received famotidine 40 mg at bedtime, was similar to the placebo group. No anti-androgenic or other adverse hormonal effects have been observed.

The following adverse effects have been reported at a rate of greater than 1% in patients on therapy with famotidine in controlled clinical trials, and may be causally related to the drug: headache (4.6%), dizziness (1.2%), constipation (1.2%) and diarrhea (1.6%).

Other reactions have been reported in clinical trials but occurred under circumstances where a causal relationship could not be established. However, in these rarely reported events, that possibility cannot be excluded. Therefore, these observations are listed to serve as alerting information to physicians.

Gastrointestinal (8.0%): nausea 1.6%, vomiting 0.9%, anorexia 0.5%, abdominal discomfort 0.3%, dry mouth 0.2%.

CNS/Psychiatric (7.3%): insomnia 0.6%, somnolence 0.4%, anxiety 0.3%, paresthesia 0.3%, depression 0.2%, libido decreased 0.1%.

Respiratory (4.4%): bronchospasm <0.1%.

Body as a Whole (3.0%): fatigue 0.6%, asthenia 0.3%, fever 0.2%.

Musculoskeletal (1.7%): musculoskeletal pain 0.1%, arthralgia 0.1%.

Skin (1.7%): pruritus 0.4%, rash 0.3%, alopecia 0.2%, flushing 0.2%, acne 0.1%, dry skin 0.1%.

Cardiovascular (1.0%): palpitations 0.2%.

Special Senses (0.9%): taste disorder 0.1%, tinnitus 0.1%, orbital edema <0.1%.

Urogenital (0.9%).

The adverse reactions reported for the tablets may also occur with the i.v. In addition, transient irritation at the injection site has been observed with the i.v.

The following additional adverse reactions have been reported since the drug was marketed: urticaria, liver enzymes abnormalities, cholestatic jaundice, anaphylaxis and angioedema. Toxic epidermal necrolysis has been reported very rarely with H_2-receptor antagonists.

The following adverse reactions have been reported; however, a causal relationship to therapy with famotidine has not been established: agitation, confusion, hallucinations, grand mal seizures, rare cases of impotence, thrombocytopenia, pancytopenia, leukopenia and agranulocytosis.

Gynecomastia has been reported rarely. In most cases that were followed up, it was reversible after discontinuing treatment.

Laboratory Abnormalities: Laboratory parameters may be affected during treatment with famotidine, but the changes are usually not considered serious. Among the laboratory changes that were reported during clinical trials were increases in AST, ALT, BUN, and serum creatinine. These changes were rarely of clinical significance.

Only 3 patients had to be discontinued from therapy because of laboratory adverse experiences, however laboratory abnormalities were present at baseline.

Overdose: Symptoms and Treatment: There is no experience to date with deliberate overdosage. Doses of up to 800 mg/day have been employed in patients with pathological hypersecretory conditions with no serious adverse effects. In the event of overdosage, treatment should be symptomatic and supportive. Unabsorbed material should be removed from the gastrointestinal tract, the patient should be monitored, and supportive therapy should be employed.

The oral LD_{50} of famotidine in male and female rats and mice was >5 000 mg/kg.

Dosage: Duodenal Ulcer: Acute Therapy: The recommended adult oral dosage of famotidine for acute duodenal ulcer is 40 mg once a day at bedtime. Treatment should be given for 4 to 8 weeks, but the duration of treatment may be shortened if healing can be documented. Healing occurs within 4 weeks in most cases of duodenal ulcer.

Maintenance Therapy: For the prevention of recurrence of duodenal ulcer, it is recommended that therapy be continued with a dose of 20 mg once a day at bedtime, for a duration of up to 6 to 12 months depending on the severity of the condition.

Benign Gastric Ulcer: Acute Therapy: The recommended adult oral dosage for acute benign gastric ulcer is 40 mg once a day at bedtime. Treatment should be given for 4 to 8 weeks, but the duration of treatment may be shortened if healing can be documented.

Pathological Hypersecretory Conditions (such as Zollinger-Ellison Syndrome): The dosage of famotidine in patients with pathological hypersecretory conditions varies with the individual patient. The recommended adult oral starting dose for pathological hypersecretory conditions is 20 mg every 6 hours. In some patients, a higher starting dose may be required. Doses should be adjusted to individual patient needs and should continue as long as clinically indicated. Doses up to 800 mg/day have been administered to some patients with severe Zollinger-Ellison syndrome.

Gastroesophageal Reflux Disease: The recommended dosage for the symptomatic relief of gastroesophageal reflux disease is 20 mg of famotidine twice a day.

For the treatment of esophageal erosion or ulceration associated with gastroesophageal reflux disease, the recommended dosage is 40 mg of famotidine twice a day.

For the maintenance of remission of patients with GERD, the recommended dosage is 20 mg of famotidine twice a day.

I.V. Administration: In some hospitalized patients with pathological hypersecretory conditions or intractable ulcers, or in patients who are unable to take oral medication, famotidine injection may be administered. The recommended dosage is 20 mg every 12 hours.

I.V. injection therapy should be changed to oral treatment as soon as the acute situation is under control.

Concomitant Use with Antacids: Antacids may be given concomitantly if needed.

Severe Renal Insufficiency: In patients with advanced renal insufficiency, i.e., with a creatinine clearance less than 10 mL/min, the elimination half-life of famotidine may exceed 20 hours reaching approximately 24 hours in anuric patients.

To avoid excess accumulation of the drug, the dosing interval of famotidine may be prolonged to 36 to 48 hours as indicated by the patient's clinical response.

Reconstitution: See Table I.

Table I—Pepcid I.V.

Dilution of Pepcid I.V. for Infusion

Pepcid I.V. Solution	Volume of Compatible I.V. Solution	Final Volume	Final Concentration	Rate of Infusion
2 mL	3 mL	5 mL	4 mg/mL	Not less than 2 minutes
2 mL	8 mL	10 mL	2 mg/mL	Not less than 2 minutes
2 mL	100 mL	102 mL	0.196 mg/mL	15–30 minutes

Famotidine i.v. solutions are compatible with: water for injection, 0.9% sodium chloride injection, 5% dextrose injection, 10% dextrose injection, lactated Ringer's injection and sodium bicarbonate injection 5%.

Diluted i.v. solutions should be used within 24 hours due to the possibility of microbial contamination during preparation. Note. Parenteral drug products should be inspected visually for particulate matter and discoloration prior to administration whenever solution and container permit.

Information for the Patient: See Blue Section—Information for the Patient "Pepcid Tablets".

Supplied: Tablets: 20 mg: Each beige, D-shaped, film-coated tablet, coded 963, contains: famotidine 20 mg. Nonmedicinal ingredients: hydroxypropyl cellulose, hydroxypropyl methylcellulose, magnesium stearate, microcrystalline cellulose, red ferric oxide, starch pregelatinized, talc, titanium dioxide and yellow ferric oxide. Blisters of 30. Store between 15 and 30°C in a tightly closed container. Protect from light.

40 mg: Each light brownish orange, D-shaped, film-coated tablet, coded 964, contains: famotidine 40 mg. Nonmedicinal ingredients: hydroxypropyl cellulose, hydroxypropyl methylcellulose, magnesium stearate, microcrystalline cellulose, red ferric oxide, starch pregelatinized, talc, titanium dioxide and yellow ferric oxide. Gluten- and tartrazine-free. Blisters of 30. Store between 15 and 30°C in a tightly closed container. Protect from light.

I.V.: Each mL of clear, colorless solution for i.v. injection contains: famotidine 10 mg. Also contains L-aspartic acid 4 mg, mannitol 20 mg and water for injection q.s. 1 mL. The multidose injection also contains benzyl alcohol 0.9% added as preservative. Nonpreserved unit dose vials of 2 mL. Packages of 10. Preserved multiple dose vials of 4 mL. Store between 2 and 8°C. Protect from light. If the solution freezes, bring the solution to room temperature; allow sufficient time to solubilize all the components. Should be used within 24 hours due to the possibility of microbial contamination during preparation.

(Shown in Product Recognition Section)

PEPTOL® Ⓟ

Carter Horner

Cimetidine

Histamine H_2 Receptor Antagonist

Pharmacology: Cimetidine inhibits competitively the action of histamine at the histamine H_2 receptor and it is not an anticholinergic agent. It inhibits both daytime and nocturnal basal gastric acid secretion. Similarly, gastric acid secretion stimulated by food, histamine, pentagastrin, insulin and caffeine is inhibited by cimetidine.

After oral administration, cimetidine is absorbed rapidly. The plasma half-life is about 2 hours. The drug is excreted primarily in the urine.

The level and duration of inhibition of both basal and stimulated gastric acid secretion has been shown to be dose-related. An 80% or higher inhibition for 24 hours can be obtained with a dosage regimen of 300 mg 4 times daily given with meals and before retiring. A reduction of total pepsin output determined by a decrease in the volume of gastric juice takes place following the administration of 300 mg cimetidine. No effect was detected on the rate of gastric emptying or lower esophageal sphincter pressure.

Indications: For conditions where the inhibition of gastric acid secretion is expected to be beneficial, such as: duodenal ulcer, nonmalignant gastric ulcer, gastroesophageal reflux disease, pathological hypersecretion associated with Zollinger-Ellison Syndrome, systemic mastocytosis and multiple endocrine adenomas.

Contraindications: None known.

Precautions: *Pregnancy* and *Lactation:* There has been no experience with cimetidine use in pregnant women. Reproduction studies in rats, mice and rabbits have revealed no impairment of fertility or fetal damage connected with cimetidine. The drug crosses the placental barrier and is secreted in the milk of animals. Cimetidine should be used in pregnant or lactating patients or women of childbearing potential only when the anticipated benefits outweigh the potential risks.

Children: Clinical experience is limited. Therefore, cimetidine cannot be recommended for children unless anticipated benefits outweigh potential risks. In a few cases, oral divided doses of 20 to 40 mg/kg daily have been administered.

Use in impaired renal function: Because cimetidine is excreted by the kidney, a reduced dosage should be administered to patients with an impaired renal function (see Dosage).

Drug Interactions: Cimetidine may interact with other drugs by several mechanisms: inhibition of the hepatic microsomal oxidative system (the most important in this connection), reduction of the hepatic blood flow, reduction of the gastric pH.

Potentially clinically significant interactions have been reported with: benzodiazepines (diazepam, chlordiazepoxide), warfarin, theophylline, phenytoin, beta adrenergic blocking agents (propranolol), lidocaine, carbamazepine, digitoxin. The most important clinical consequences of these interactions involve the inhibition of usual drug metabolism with subsequent higher steady-state blood concentrations and an increased incidence of side effects. Drugs with a narrow therapeutic index (phenytoin, warfarin, theophylline) are more likely to produce such problems.

Proper dose adjustment, especially when changes are made in dosage regimens should be implemented whenever the

Peptol (cont'd)

administration of cimetidine is necessary in conjunction with these drugs.

Adverse Effects: CNS: The most common symptoms reported have been confusion or delirium with dizziness, drowsiness, slurred speech, flushing and sweating. The occurrence of cimetidine-induced confusional states seems to be rare. The reported cimetidine CNS effects occurred either after high dosage, in elderly patients, in the presence of renal impairment, or in the presence of a previous psychiatric history.
Gastrointestinal: Mild and transient diarrhea, some increases in serum transaminase not requiring cimetidine discontinuance may occur.

Perforation of duodenal, esophageal and gastric ulcers has been reported following abrupt discontinuance of the drug. There is no firm evidence, however, that recurrences of ulcer disease occur sooner or more severely in patients withdrawn from cimetidine than in patients withdrawn from other forms of treatment.

Gastritis and duodenitis during cimetidine therapy have been described.

Rare cases of hepatitis and pancreatitis reacting favorably to cimetidine withdrawal have been reported.
Endocrine: Gynecomastia with and without elevated prolactin levels has been reported. Galactorrhea with elevated prolactin levels has also been reported in females only.

Decreased libido and impotence during cimetidine treatment has been described.
Hematology: Decreased white blood cell counts including agranulocytosis have been reported, including a few cases of recurrence on rechallenge. These patients generally presented other concomitant pathology and received other drugs known to produce neutropenia. Thrombocytopenia and a few cases of aplastic anemia have also been reported.
Renal: Small increases in plasma creatinine, which did not progress when treatment was continued and disappeared on its withdrawal, have been reported. Rare cases of interstitial nephritis have been reported.
Skin: Rash, giant urticaria, Stevens-Johnson syndrome and psoriasis secondary to cimetidine have been reported.
Miscellaneous: Fever and muscular pain have been reported.

Overdose: Symptoms and Treatment: A 25-year-old man after taking 12 g of cimetidine presented disorientation and nonsensical speech. He recovered fully after 24 hours.

A 35-year-old man after taking one hundred and twenty 200 mg cimetidine together with 400 mg oxazepam was unconscious for 6 hours and responded favorably to forced diuresis.

Dosage: Experience with cimetidine in children is limited and it has not been evaluated in clinical studies (see Precautions).

In clinical studies, cimetidine has been used in doses up to 2 400 mg/day in divided doses.
Acute Duodenal Ulcer: The daily oral dosage for adults is 800 mg before retiring, or 400 mg twice a day at breakfast and before retiring or 300 mg 4 times daily with meals and before retiring. While symptoms may disappear frequently during the first or second week of treatment, cimetidine administration should be continued for at least 4 weeks or until endoscopic healing is obtained. Concomitant antacids might be needed in some patients until symptoms disappear.

For patients known to be at risk of frequent recurrences of duodenal ulcer and for those patients who, in the judgment of the attending physician, might benefit from a longer-term reduction of gastric acid secretion, consideration should be given to a maintenance treatment.

It has been shown that in duodenal ulcer patients, following cimetidine-induced ulcer healing, a daily maintenance regimen of 400 mg at bedtime for 6 to 12 months reduces the incidence of recurrences. These patients should be reassessed periodically.
Nonmalignant Gastric Ulcer and Gastroesophageal Reflux Disease: The recommended adult oral dosage for these conditions is 300 mg, 4 times daily, with meals and at bedtime. Frequently patients may become asymptomatic during the first week or two, but treatment should be continued for at least 4 weeks or until endoscopic healing is documented.
Impaired Renal Function: Use of cimetidine in patients with severely impaired renal function has been very limited. Based on this experience, the recommended dosage in such patients is 300 mg every 12 hours. If the patient's condition requires it, the frequency of dosing may be increased to every 8 hours or, with caution, even further. Accumulation may occur in severe renal failure and the lowest frequency of dosing compatible with an adequate therapeutic response should be used. Hemodialysis removes circulating cimetidine and therefore the timing of dosage should be adjusted to the dialysis schedule.
Pathological Hypersecretory Conditions (e.g. Zollinger-Ellison Syndrome): Recommended adult oral dosage: 300 mg, 4 times a day, with meals and at bedtime. Some patients may require more frequent 300 mg doses to control symptoms. Dosage should be individually adjusted, without exceeding 2 400 mg daily. When necessary, 600 mg 4 times daily or 800 mg 3 times daily with meals and at bedtime.
Special Cases: In patients in whom control of gastric acid secretion is desirable, the recommended oral dosage is 300 mg, 4 times daily, with meals and at bedtime.

Supplied: 300 mg: Each round, blue, biconvex, film-coated tablet, one side engraved "300" and "FWH" on the other side, contains: cimetidine 300 mg. Nonmedicinal ingredients: alumina, cellulose, cornstarch, FD&C Blue No. 2, FD&C Red No. 3, glycerin, magnesium stearate, povidone, propylene glycol, sodium starch glycolate and titanium dioxide. Energy: 0.4 kJ (0.1 kcal). Sodium: <1 mmol (<1 mg). Alcohol-, gluten- and tartrazine-free. Bottles of 100 and 1 000.

400 mg: Each round, peach-colored, biconvex, film-coated tablet, one side engraved "400" and "FWH" on the other side, contains: cimetidine 400 mg. Nonmedicinal ingredients: alumina, cellulose, FD&C Yellow No. 6, magnesium stearate, polyethylene glycol, povidone, sodium starch glycolate, cornstarch and titanium dioxide. Energy: 0.8 kJ (0.2 kcal). Sodium: <1 mmol (<1 mg). Alcohol-, gluten- and tartrazine-free. Bottles of 100 and 500.

600 mg: Each ellipsoid, blue, biconvex tablet, bisected on one side, the other side engraved FWH 600, contains: cimetidine 600 mg. Nonmedicinal ingredients: alumina, cellulose, cornstarch, FD&C Blue No. 2, FD&C Red No. 3, glycerin, magnesium stearate, povidone, sodium starch glycolate and titanium dioxide. Energy: 1.2 kJ (0.3 kcal). Sodium: <1 mmol (<1 mg). Alcohol-, gluten- and tartrazine-free. Bottles of 100 and 500.

800 mg: Each ellipsoid, peach-colored, biconvex tablet, bisected on one side, the other side engraved FWH 800, contains: cimetidine 800 mg. Nonmedicinal ingredients: alumina, cellulose, cornstarch, FD&C Yellow No. 6, magnesium stearate, polyethylene glycol, povidone, sodium starch glycolate and titanium dioxide. Energy: 2.9 kJ (0.7 kcal). Sodium: <1 mmol (<1 mg). Alcohol-, gluten- and tartrazine-free. Bottles of 100 and 500.

(Shown in Product Recognition Section)

PERCOCET® Ⓝ
PERCOCET®-DEMI Ⓝ
DuPont Pharma

Oxycodone HCl—Acetaminophen
Opioid Analgesic

Pharmacology: The principal ingredient, oxycodone, is a semisynthetic opioid analgesic with multiple actions qualitatively similar to those of morphine; the most prominent of these involve the CNS and organs composed of smooth muscle. The principal actions of therapeutic value of the oxycodone in Percocet are analgesia and sedation.

Oxycodone is similar to codeine and methadone in that it retains at least one half of its analgesic activity when administered orally. It has been suggested that less rapid biotransformation in the liver may be due to the protective effect of a methoxy group in the 3-position, the site of glucuronide conjugation in morphine.

Percocet also contains the nonopioid, antipyretic analgesic, acetaminophen; the latter exerts its effects by a mechanism similar to that of the salicylates but, unlike the salicylates, does not have anti-inflammatory or uricosuric properties. Acetaminophen is rapidly and almost completely absorbed from the gastrointestinal tract, peak plasma levels being obtained within 10 minutes to 1 hour.

Indications: The relief of moderate to moderately severe pain, including conditions accompanied by fever.

Contraindications: Status asthmaticus, pre-existing respiratory depression or convulsive states, hypersensitivity to oxycodone or acetaminophen.

Warnings: Drug dependence: Oxycodone can produce drug dependence of the morphine type and, therefore, has the potential of being abused. Psychic dependence, physical dependence and tolerance may develop upon repeated administration of Percocet, and it should be prescribed and administered with the same degree of caution appropriate to the use of other oral medication containing opioids.
Occupational Hazards: Oxycodone may impair the mental and/or physical abilities required for the performance of potentially hazardous tasks such as driving a car or operating machinery. The patient using Percocet should be cautioned accordingly.
Interaction with other CNS depressants: Patients receiving other opioid analgesics, general anesthetics, monoamine oxidase inhibitors, tricyclic antidepressants, phenothiazines, other tranquilizers, sedative-hypnotics or other CNS depressants (including alcohol), concomitantly with Percocet may exhibit an additive CNS depression. When such combined therapy is contemplated, the dose of one or both agents should be reduced.
Pregnancy: Safe use in pregnancy has not been established relative to possible adverse effects on fetal development. Therefore, Percocet should not be given to pregnant women unless, in the judgment of the physician, the potential benefits outweigh the possible hazards. The administration of Percocet to obstetrical patients in labor may be associated with respiratory depression of the newborn.
Children: The more potent formula, Percocet, should not be administered to infants or children. However, Percocet-Demi, containing half the amount of oxycodone, can be considered for children of 6 years of age or older.

Precautions: Head injury and increased intracranial pressure: The respiratory depressant effects of opioids and their capacity to elevate cerebrospinal fluid pressure may be markedly exaggerated in the presence of head injury, other intracranial lesions or a pre-existing elevated intracranial pressure. Furthermore, opioids may produce adverse reactions which can obscure the clinical course of patients with head injuries.
Acute abdominal conditions: The administration of Percocet or other opioids may obscure the diagnosis or clinical course in patients with acute abdominal conditions.
Special risk patients: Percocet should be given with caution to certain patients such as the elderly or debilitated, because of the danger of cardiac or respiratory depression, as well as to those patients with hemorrhage, severe impairment of hepatic, respiratory or renal function, hypothyroidism, Addison's disease, prostatic hypertrophy or urethral stricture.
Headache: Because headache often involves a significant psychological component, an opioid analgesic should only be employed for the treatment of headache when no other treatment is effective, in order to minimize the risk of psychological and physical dependence.
Drug Interactions: The CNS depressant effects of Percocet may be additive with those of other CNS depressants (see Warnings).
Other: Patients should be instructed to store Percocet as for any medication, safely out of the reach of children.

Adverse Effects: The most frequently observed adverse reactions include: light-headedness, dizziness, sedation, nausea, and vomiting. These effects seem to be more prominent in ambulatory than in nonambulatory patients, and some of these adverse reactions may be alleviated if the patient lies down.

Other adverse reactions include: euphoria, dysphoria, constipation and pruritus.

Overdose: Symptoms: Serious overdose is characterized by respiratory depression (a decrease in respiratory rate and/or tidal volume, Cheyne-Stokes respiration, cyanosis), extreme somnolence progressing to stupor or coma, skeletal muscle flaccidity, cold and clammy skin and sometimes bradycardia and hypotension. In severe overdose, apnea, circulatory collapse, cardiac arrest, and death may occur. The ingestion of very large amounts of Percocet may, in addition, result in acute acetaminophen intoxication, characterized by anorexia, nausea, vomiting and sweating within 2 or 3 hours of ingestion, and possibly cyanosis with methemoglobinemia. Within 48 hours, liver function tests rise abnormally, and the liver becomes enlarged and tender. Within 3 to 5 days, jaundice, coagulation defects, myocardiopathy, encephalopathy and renal failure occur, followed by death due to hepatic necrosis. The ingestion of 10 g of acetaminophen is considered to result in intoxication, with the possibility of a fatal outcome if the amount exceeds 15 g. Hepatotoxicity occurs when plasma levels of 300 μg/mL are observed within 4 hours of ingestion.

Treatment: Primary attention should be given to the re-establishment of adequate respiratory exchange through provision of a patent airway and the institution of assisted or controlled ventilation. The opioid antagonist naloxone is a specific antidote against respiratory depression which may result from overdosage or unusual sensitivity to opioids, including oxycodone. Therefore, an appropriate dose of this antagonist should be administered, preferably by the i.v. route, simultaneously with efforts at respiratory resuscitation. Since the duration of action of oxycodone may exceed that of the antagonist, the patient should be kept under continued surveillance and repeat doses of the antagonist should be administered as needed to maintain adequate respiration. The instructions contained in the package insert provided by the manufacturer should be carefully observed.

An antagonist should not be administered in the absence of clinically significant respiratory or cardiovascular depression.

Oxygen, i.v. fluids, vasopressors and other supportive measures should be employed as indicated.

Gastric emptying by emesis or lavage may be useful in removing unabsorbed drug and should be carried out at an early stage of treatment. Plasma levels of acetaminophen should be determined. If hemodialysis is carried out within 10 hours of ingestion, it may be of some value.

The drug N-acetylcysteine is a specific antidote for acetaminophen intoxication. For directions for use, refer to the manufacturer's Product Monograph or the CPS.

Dosage: Dosage should be adjusted according to the severity of the pain and the patient's response. It may occasionally be necessary to exceed the usual dosage recommended below in cases of more severe pain or in those patients who have become tolerant to the analgesic effect of opioids.
Percocet: Adults: 1 tablet every 6 hours as needed for pain.
Percocet-Demi: Adults: 1 or 2 tablets every 6 hours. Children 12 years and older: one half tablet every 6 hours. Children 6 to 12 years: quarter of a tablet every 6 hours. Not indicated for children under 6 years of age.

Supplied: Percocet: Each white, scored tablet, embossed on one side with PERCOCET and on the other side with DuPont contains: oxycodone HCl 5 mg and acetaminophen 325 mg. Nonmedicinal ingredients: cornstarch, microcrystalline cellulose, povidone, pregelatinized starch, silicon dioxide and stearic acid. Lactose-, sodium- and tartrazine-free. Bottles of 100 and 500 and blister packs of 25.

Percocet-Demi: Each blue, quadrisected tablet, embossed on one side with PERCOCET-DEMI and on the other side with DuPont contains: 2.5 mg oxycodone HCl and acetaminophen 325 mg. Nonmedicinal ingredients: cornstarch, microcrystalline cellulose, FD&C Blue No. 2, povidone, pregelatinized starch, silicon dioxide and stearic acid. Lactose-, sodium- and tartrazine-free. Bottles of 100.

Store at room temperature (15 to 30°C).

(Shown in Product Recognition Section)

PERCODAN® Ⓝ
PERCODAN®-DEMI Ⓝ
DuPont Pharma

Oxycodone HCl—ASA

Opioid Analgesic

Pharmacology: The principal ingredient, oxycodone, is a semisynthetic opioid analgesic with multiple actions qualitatively similar to those of morphine; the most prominent of these involve the CNS and organs composed of smooth muscle. The principal actions of therapeutic value of the oxycodone in Percodan are analgesia and sedation.

Oxycodone is similar to codeine and methadone in that it retains at least one-half of its analgesic activity when administered orally. It has been suggested that less rapid biotransformation in the liver may be due to the protective effect of a methoxy group in the 3-position, the site of glucuronide conjugation in morphine.

Percodan also contains the nonopioid, anti-inflammatory and antipyretic analgesic, ASA.

Indications: The relief of mild to moderately severe pain, including conditions accompanied by fever and/or inflammation.

Contraindications: Status asthmaticus, pre-existing respiratory depression or convulsive states, gastrointestinal ulceration, hypersensitivity to oxycodone or ASA.

Warnings: Oxycodone can produce drug dependence of the morphine type and, therefore, has the potential of being abused. Psychic dependence, physical dependence and tolerance may develop upon repeated administration of Percodan, and it should be prescribed and administered with the same degree of caution appropriate to the use of other oral medication containing opioids.

Reye's Syndrome: Reye's syndrome is a rare but serious disease which can follow flu or chickenpox in children and teenagers. While the cause of Reye's syndrome is unknown, some reports claim ASA (or salicylates) may increase the risk of developing this disease.
Occupational Hazards: Oxycodone may impair the mental and/or physical abilities required for the performance of potentially hazardous tasks such as driving a car or operating machinery. The patient using Percodan should be cautioned accordingly.
Interaction with other CNS Depressants: Patients receiving other opioid analgesics, general anesthetics, monoamine oxidase inhibitors, tricyclic antidepressants, phenothiazines, other tranquilizers, sedative-hypnotics or other CNS depressants (including alcohol), concomitantly with Percodan may exhibit an additive CNS depression. When such combined therapy is contemplated, the dose of one or both agents should be reduced.
Pregnancy: Safe use in pregnancy has not been established relative to possible adverse effects on fetal development. Therefore, Percodan should not be given to a pregnant woman unless, in the judgment of the physician, the potential benefits outweigh the possible hazards. The administration of Percodan to obstetrical patients in labor may be associated with respiratory depression of the newborn.
Children: The more potent formula, Percodan, should not be administered to infants or children. However, Percodan-Demi, containing half the amount of oxycodone, can be considered for children of 6 years of age or older.

Precautions: Head injury and increased intracranial pressure: The respiratory depressant effects of opioids and their capacity to elevate cerebrospinal fluid pressure may be markedly exaggerated in the presence of head injury, other intracranial lesions or a pre-existing elevated intracranial pressure. Futhermore, opioids may produce adverse reactions which can obscure the clinical course of patients with head injuries.
Acute Abdominal Conditions: The administration of Percodan or other opioids may obscure the diagnosis or clinical course in patients with acute abdominal conditions.
Special Risk Patients: Percodan should be given with caution to certain patients such as the elderly or debilitated, because of the danger of cardiac or respiratory depression, as well as to those patients with hemorrhage, severe impairment of hepatic, respiratory or renal function, hypothyroidism, Addison's disease, prostatic hypertrophy or urethral stricture.
Headache: Because headache often involves a significant psychological component, an opioid analgesic should only be employed for the treatment of headache when no other treatment is effective, in order to minimize the risk of psychological and physical dependence.
Coagulation Abnormalities: Salicylates should be used with caution in patients with coagulation abnormalities.
<u>*Drug Interactions:*</u> The CNS depressant effects of oxycodone may be additive with those of other CNS depressants (see Warnings).

Salicylates may enhance the effect of anticoagulants and inhibit the effect of uricosuric agents.
Other: Patients should be instructed to store Percodan, as for any medication, safely out of the reach of children.

Adverse Effects: The most frequently observed adverse reactions include light-headedness, dizziness, sedation, nausea, and vomiting. These effects seem to be more prominent in ambulatory than in nonambulatory patients, and some of these adverse reactions may be alleviated if the patient lies down.

Other adverse reactions include euphoria, dysphoria, constipation and pruritus.

Overdose: Symptoms: Serious overdose with Percodan is characterized by respiratory depression (a decrease in respiratory rate and/or tidal volume, Cheyne-Stokes respiration, cyanosis), extreme somnolence progressing to stupor or coma, skeletal muscle flaccidity, cold and clammy skin, and sometimes bradycardia and hypotension. In severe overdosage, apnea, circulatory collapse, cardiac arrest and death may occur. The ingestion of very large amounts of Percodan may, in addition, result in acute salicylate intoxication.

Treatment: Primary attention should be given to the reestablishment of adequate respiratory exchange through provision of a patent airway and the institution of assisted or controlled ventilation. The opioid antagonist naloxone is a specific antidote against respiratory depression which may result from overdosage or unusual sensitivity to opioids, including oxycodone. Therefore an appropriate dose of this antagonist should be administered, preferably by the i.v. route, simultaneously with efforts at respiratory resuscitation. Since the duration of action of oxycodone may exceed that of the antagonist, the patient should be kept under continued surveillance and repeated doses of the antagonist should be administered as needed to maintain adequate respiration. The instructions contained in package insert provided by the manufacturer should be carefully observed.

An antagonist should not be administered in the absence of clinically significant respiratory or cardiovascular depression.

Oxygen, i.v. fluids, vasopressors and other supportive measures should be employed as indicated.

Gastric aspiration and lavage may be useful in removing unabsorbed drug.

Dosage: Adjust dosage according to the severity of the pain and the patient's response. It may occasionally be necessary to exceed the usual dosage recommended below in cases of more severe pain or in those patients who have become tolerant to the analgesic effect of opioids. The usual adult dose is 1 tablet every 6 hours as needed for pain.
Percodan: Adults: 1 tablet every 6 hours as needed for pain.
Percodan-Demi: Adults: 1 or 2 tablets every 6 hours. Children 12 years and older: one half tablet every 6 hours. Children 6 to 12 years: one quarter tablet every 6 hours. Not indicated for children under 6 years of age.

Supplied: Percodan: Each yellow, scored tablet, embossed on one side with PERCODAN and on the other side with DuPont, contains: oxycodone HCl 5 mg and ASA 325 mg. Nonmedicinal ingredients: cornstarch, FD&C Yellow No. 6, D&C Yellow No. 10 and microcrystalline cellulose. Lactose-, sodium- and tartrazine-free. Bottles of 100 and 500 and blister packs of 25. Store at room temperature (15 to 30°C).

Percodan-Demi: Each pink, scored tablet, embossed on one side with PERCODAN-DEMI and on the other side with DuPont, contains: oxycodone HCl 2.5 mg and ASA 325 mg. Nonmedicinal ingredients: cornstarch, FD&C Red No. 3, FD&C Blue No. 2 and microcrystalline cellulose. Lactose-, sodium- and tartrazine-free. Bottles of 100. Store at room temperature (15 to 30°C).

(Shown in Product Recognition Section)

PERGONAL® Ⓟ
Serono

Menotropins

Gonadotropins

Pharmacology: Menotropins is a purified preparation of gonadotropins extracted from the urine of postmenopausal women.

Indications: Women: Menotropins and human chorionic gonadotropin (hCG) given in a sequential manner are indicated for the induction of ovulation and to enable pregnancy in the anovulatory infertile patient, in whom the cause of anovulation is functional and is not due to primary ovarian failure.
Men: Menotropins with concomitant hCG is indicated for the stimulation of spermatogenesis in men who have primary or secondary hypogonadotropic hypogonadism.

Menotropins with concomitant hCG has proven effective in inducing spermatogenesis in men with primary hypogonadotropic hypogonadism due to a congenital factor or prepubertal hypophysectomy and in men with secondary hypogonadotropic hypogonadism due to hypophysectomy, craniopharyngioma, cerebral aneurysm or chromophobe adenoma.

Contraindications: Women: High levels of FSH indicating primary ovarian failure. The presence of uncontrolled thyroid and adrenal dysfunction. An organic intracranial lesion such as a pituitary tumor. The presence of any cause of infertility other than anovulation as stated in the Indications. Abnormal vaginal bleeding of undetermined origin. Ovarian cysts or enlargement not due to polycystic ovarian syndrome. A prior hypersensitivity to menotropins.
Pregnancy: Pergonal may cause fetal harm when administered to a pregnant woman. There are limited human data on the effects of menotropins when administered during pregnancy.
Men: Normal gonadotropin levels indicating normal pituitary function. Elevated gonadotropin levels indicating primary testicular failure. Infertility disorders other than hypogonadotropic hypogonadism.

Warnings: Caution: Menotropins is a drug that should only be used by physicians who are thoroughly familiar with infertility problems. It is a potent gonadotropic substance capable of causing mild to severe adverse reactions in women. Because of the potential hazards involved with the use of menotropins, physicians must become thoroughly familiar with the Indications, Contraindications, Warnings, and Precautions before instituting treatment. Gonadotropin therapy requires a certain

Pergonal (cont'd)

time commitment by physicians and supportive health professionals, and its use requires the availability of appropriate monitoring facilities (see Precautions, Laboratory Tests). In female patients it must be used with a great deal of care.

Overstimulation of the Ovary During Therapy: Ovarian Enlargement: Mild to moderate uncomplicated ovarian enlargement which may be accompanied by abdominal distension and/or abdominal pain occurs in approximately 20% of those treated with menotropins and hCG, and generally regresses without treatment within two or three weeks.

The Ovarian Hyperstimulation Syndrome (OHSS): OHSS is a medical event distinct from uncomplicated ovarian enlargement. OHSS may progress rapidly (within 24 hours to several days) to become a serious medical event. It is characterized by an apparent dramatic increase in vascular permeability which can result in a rapid accumulation of fluid in the peritoneal cavity, thorax, and potentially, the pericardium. The early warning signs of development of OHSS are severe pelvic pain, nausea, vomiting, and weight gain. The following symptomatology has been seen with cases of OHSS: abdominal pain, abdominal distension, gastrointestinal symptoms including nausea, vomiting and diarrhea, severe ovarian enlargement, weight gain, dyspnea, and oliguria. Clinical evaluation may reveal hypovolemia, hemoconcentration, electrolyte imbalances, ascites, hemoperitoneum, pleural effusions, hydrothorax, acute pulmonary distress, and thromboembolic events. (see Warnings, Pulmonary and Vascular Complications).

OHSS occurred in approximately 0.4% of patients when the recommended dose is administered and in 1.3% of patients when higher than recommended doses are administered. OHSS develops rapidly and most often after treatment with menotropins or hCG has been discontinued, reaching its maximum at about seven to ten days following treatment. Patients, therefore, should be followed for at least 2 weeks after menotropins or hCG administration. Cases of OHSS are more common, more severe, and more protracted if pregnancy occurs. Usually, OHSS resolves spontaneously with the onset of menses. If there is evidence that OHSS may be developing prior to hCG administration (see Precautions, Laboratory Tests), the hCG should be withheld.

If OHSS occurs, treatment should be stopped and the patient hospitalized. Treatment is primarily symptomatic, consisting of bed rest, fluid and electrolyte management, and analgesics if needed. The phenomenon of hemoconcentration associated with fluid loss into the peritoneal cavity, pleural cavity, and pericardial cavity has been seen to occur and should be thoroughly assessed in the following manner: fluid intake and output; weight; hematocrit; serum and urinary electrolytes; urine specific gravity; BUN and creatinine, and abdominal girth. These determinations are to be performed daily or more often if the need arises.

With OHSS there is an increased risk of injury to the ovary. The ascitic, pleural, and pericardial fluids should not be removed unless absolutely necessary to relieve symptoms such as pulmonary distress or cardiac tamponade. Pelvic examination may cause rupture of an ovarian cyst, which may result in hemoperitoneum, and should therefore be avoided. If this does occur, and if bleeding becomes such that surgery is required, the surgical treatment should be designed to control bleeding and to retain as much ovarian tissue as possible. Intercourse should be prohibited in those patients in whom significant ovarian enlargement occurs after ovulation because of the danger of hemoperitoneum resulting from ruptured ovarian cysts.

The management of OHSS may be divided into 3 phases: the acute, the chronic, and the resolution phases. Because the use of diuretics can accentuate the diminished intravascular volume, diuretics should be avoided except in the late phase of resolution as described below.

Acute Phase: Management during the acute phase should be designed to prevent hemoconcentration due to loss of intravascular volume to the third space and to minimize the risk of thromboembolic phenomena and kidney damage. Treatment is designed to normalize electrolytes while maintaining an acceptable but somewhat reduced intravascular volume. Full correction of the intravascular volume deficit may lead to an unacceptable increase in the amount of third space fluid accumulation. Management includes administration of limited i.v. fluids, electrolytes, and human serum albumin. Monitoring for the development of hyperkalemia is recommended.

Chronic Phase: After stabilizing the patient during the acute phase, excessive fluid accumulation in the third space should be limited by instituting severe potassium, sodium, and fluid restriction.

Resolution Phase: A fall in hematocrit and an increasing urinary output without an increased intake are observed due to the return of third space fluid to the intravascular compartment. Peripheral and/or pulmonary edema may result if the kidneys are unable to excrete third space fluid as rapidly as it is mobilized. Diuretics may be indicated during the resolution phase if necessary to combat pulmonary edema.

Pulmonary and Vascular Complications: Serious pulmonary conditions (e.g. atelectasis, acute respiratory distress syndrome) have been reported following gonadotropin therapy. In addition, thromboembolic events both in association with, and separate from, OHSS have been reported following therapy. Intravascular thrombosis and embolism, which may originate in venous or arterial vessels, can result in reduced blood flow to critical organs or the extremities. Sequelae of such events have included venous thrombophlebitis, pulmonary embolism, pulmonary infarction, cerebral vascular occlusion (stroke), and arterial occlusion resulting in loss of limb. In rare cases, pulmonary complications and/or thromboembolic events have resulted in death.

Multiple Births: Data from a clinical trial revealed the following results regarding multiple births: Of the pregnancies following therapy with menotropins and hCG, 80% resulted in single births, 15% in twins, and 5% of the total pregnancies resulted in 3 or more concepti. The patient and her husband should be advised of the frequency and potential hazards of multiple gestation before starting treatment.

Precautions: Careful attention should be given to diagnosis in the selection of candidates for menotropins therapy.

Women: Before treatment with menotropins is instituted, a thorough gynecologic and endocrinologic evaluation must be performed. This should include a hysterosalpingogram (to rule out uterine and tubal pathology) and documentation of anovulation by means of basal body temperature, serial vaginal smears, examination of cervical mucus, determination of serum (or urinary) progesterone, and endometrial biopsy. Primary ovarian failure should be excluded by the determination of serum gonadotropin levels. Careful examination should be made to rule out the presence of early pregnancy. Patients in late reproductive life have a greater predisposition to endometrial carcinoma as well as a higher incidence of anovulatory disorders. Cervical dilation and curettage should always be done for diagnosis before starting therapy in such patients who demonstrate abnormal uterine bleeding or other signs of endometrial abnormalities. Evaluation of the husband's fertility potential must also be performed before starting therapy.

In order to minimize the hazard associated with the occasional abnormal ovarian enlargement which may occur with menotropins-hCG therapy, the lowest dose consistent with expectation of good results should be used. Careful monitoring of ovarian response can further minimize the risk of overstimulation.

If the ovaries are abnormally enlarged on the last day of menotropins therapy, hCG should not be administered in this course of therapy; this will reduce the chances of development of the Ovarian Hyperstimulation Syndrome.

Men: Patient selection should be made based on a documented lack of pituitary function. Prior to hormonal therapy, these patients will have low or absent urinary gonadotropin levels. Patients with primary hypogonadotropic hypogonadism will have a subnormal development of masculinization, and those with secondary hypogonadotropic hypogonadism will have decreased masculinization.

Information for the Patient: Prior to therapy with Pergonal, patients should be informed of the duration of treatment and the monitoring of their condition that will be required. Possible adverse reactions (see Adverse Effects) and the risk of multiple births should also be discussed.

Laboratory Tests—Women (Treatment for Induction of Ovulation): In most instances, treatment with menotropins results only in follicular growth and maturation. In order to effect ovulation, hCG must be given following the administration of menotropins when clinical assessment of the patient indicates that sufficient follicular maturation has occurred. This may be estimated by measuring serum (or urinary) estrogen levels and sonographic visualization of the ovaries. The combination of both estradiol levels and ultrasonography is useful for monitoring the growth and development of follicles, timing hCG administration, as well as detecting ovarian enlargement and minimizing the risk of OHSS and multiple gestation.

Urinary and/or plasma estrogen determinations provide an indirect index of follicular maturity since as the follicles grow and develop, they secrete estrogens in increasing amounts. However, plasma and/or urinary estrogen levels represent the sum of ovarian activity. It is recommended that the number of growing follicles be confirmed using ultrasonography because plasma and/or urinary estrogens do not give an indication of the number of follicles.

Other clinical parameters which may have potential use for monitoring menotropins therapy include: changes in the vaginal cytology, appearance and volume of the cervical mucus, spinnbarkeit, and ferning of the cervical mucus.

The above clinical indices provide an indirect estimate of the estrogenic effect upon the target organs and, therefore, should only be used adjunctively with more direct estimates of follicular development, i.e., serum estradiol and ultrasonography.

The clinical confirmation of ovulation, with the exception of pregnancy, is obtained by direct and indirect indices of progesterone production. The indices most generally used are as follows: a rise in basal body temperature, increase in serum progesterone, and menstruation following the shift in basal body temperature.

When used in conjunction with indices of progesterone production, sonographic visualization of the ovaries will assist in determining if ovulation has occurred. Sonographic evidence of ovulation may include the following: fluid in the cul-de-sac, ovarian stigmata, and collapsed follicle.

Because of the subjectivity of the various tests for the determination of follicular maturation and ovulation, it cannot be overemphasized that the physician should choose tests with which he/she is thoroughly familiar.

Drug Interactions: No clinically significant drug/drug or drug/food interactions have been reported.

Carcinogenesis and Mutagenesis: Carcinogenicity and mutagenicity studies have not been performed.

Pregnancy: Contraindicated in pregnancy.

Lactation: It is not known whether this drug is excreted in human milk. Because many drugs are excreted in human milk, caution should be exercised if menotropins are administered to a nursing mother.

Adverse Effects: Women: The following adverse reactions reported are listed in decreasing order of potential severity: pulmonary and vascular complications (see Warnings); Ovarian Hyperstimulation Syndrome (see Warnings); hemoperitoneum; mild to moderate ovarian enlargement; abdominal pain; sensitivity to menotropins (febrile reactions after the administration of the drug have occurred. It is not clear whether or not these were pyrogenic responses or possible allergic reactions. In addition, reports of flu-like symptoms including fever, chills, musculoskeletal aches, joint pains, nausea, headache, and malaise have been received); ovarian cysts; gastrointestinal symptoms (nausea, vomiting, diarrhea, abdominal cramps, bloating); pain, rash, swelling, and/or irritation at site of injection; body rashes; dizziness, tachycardia, dyspnea, tachypnea, and breast tenderness.

The following medical events have been reported subsequent to pregnancies resulting from menotropins therapy: ectopic pregnancy; congenital abnormalities. [From a study of 287 completed pregnancies following menotropins-hCG therapy, 5 incidents of birth defects were reported (1.7%). One infant had multiple congenital anomalies consisting of imperforate anus, aplasia of the sigmoid colon, third degree hypospadias, cecovesicle fistula, bifid scrotum, meningocele, bilateral internal tibial torsion, and right metatarsus adductus. Another infant was born with an imperforate anus and possible congenital heart lesions; another had a supernumerary digit; another was born with hypospadias and exstrophy of the bladder; and the fifth child had Down's syndrome. None of the investigators felt that these defects were drug-related. Subsequently, one report of an infant death due to hydrocephalus and cardiac anomalies has been received.]

Menotropins do not appear to influence the incidence of abortion in the subfertile individual. The abortion rate for the subfertile individual is reported to be 20% in primary infertility and 30% in secondary infertility. The abortion rate following menotropins and hCG therapy has been 25%.

Ovarian cancer has been reported in a very small number of infertile women who have been treated with fertility drugs. A causal relationship between treatment with fertility drugs and ovarian cancer has not been established.

Men: Gynecomastia may occur occasionally during menotropins-hCG therapy. This is a known effect of hCG treatment. Erythrocytosis (hct 50% hgb 17.8 g%) was recorded in 1 patient.

Drug Abuse and Dependence: There have been no reports of abuse or dependence with menotropins.

Overdose: Symptoms and Treatment: Aside from possible Ovarian Hyperstimulation Syndrome (see Warnings), little is known concerning the consequences of acute overdosage with menotropins.

Dosage: Women: The doses of menotropins and hCG for the induction of ovulation must be individualized. For instance, patients with normal intrinsic gonadotropins require a short course of therapy. Patients with low or absent gonadotropins require a longer period. The most generally effective doses are:

Menotropins: 150 IU (2 ampuls)/day for 8 to 12 days.

Human chorionic gonadotropin (hCG): 5 000 to 10 000 U one day after the last dose of menotropins. Administer menotropins in daily i.m. doses until the indices of estrogenic activity, as indicated under Precautions, Laboratory Tests, are equivalent to or greater than those of the normal individual. This generally occurs by the eighth to twelfth day. Administer 5 000 to 10 000 U of hCG i.m. If the patient does not respond to 12 days of menotropins administration, generally no response can be expected and therapy should be discontinued.

During treatment with both menotropins and hCG and during a 2-week post-treatment period, patients should be examined at least every other day for signs of excessive ovarian stimulation. It is recommended that menotropins administration be stopped if the ovaries become significantly enlarged or abdominal pain occurs. Most often OHSS occurs after treatment has been discontinued and reaches its maximum at about 7 to 10 days postovulation. Patients should be followed for at least 2 weeks after hCG administration.

The couple should be encouraged to have intercourse daily, beginning on the day prior to the administration of HCG until ovulation becomes apparent from the indices employed for the determination of progestational activity. Care should be taken to ensure insemination.

Men: Menotropins with concomitant hCG should be administered to men with pituitary hypofunction who have been adequately masculinized by prior treatment with hCG. Testosterone levels should be in the normal range, and there should be adequate development of the secondary sexual characteristics.

The recommended dose of menotropins is 1 ampul 3 times a week. The recommended dose of hCG is 2 000 U twice a week. Therapy should be carried on for a minimum of 4 months to ensure detecting spermatozoa in the ejaculate, as it takes approximately 74±4 days in the human male for germ cells to reach the spermatozoa stage.

Dissolve the contents of 1 ampul of menotropins in 1 to 2 mL of sterile saline and administer i.m. immediately. The reconstituted menotropins may lose potency with time.

Supplied: Each ampul contains: FSH 75 IU and LH 75 IU plus lactose 10 mg in a sterile, lyophilized form. By biological assay, one IU of LH for the Second International Reference Preparation (2nd-IRP) for HMG (human menopausal gonadotropin) is biologically equivalent to approximately ½ U of human chorionic gonadotropin (hCG). Cartons of 1 ampul with diluent.

PERIACTIN®

Johnson & Johnson • Merck

Cyproheptadine HCl

Antihistaminic

Pharmacology: Cyproheptadine is a serotonin and histamine antagonist with anticholinergic and sedative effects recommended for the symptomatic treatment of allergic disorders and pruritic dermatoses, as well as certain types of vascular headaches.

Indications: Cyproheptadine has a wide range of antiallergic and antipruritic activity and can be used successfully in the treatment of acute and chronic allergies and pruritus, such as: dermatitis, including neurodermatitis and neurodermatitis circumscripta, eczema, eczematoid dermatitis, dermatographism, mild local allergic reactions to insect bites, hay fever and other seasonal rhinitis, perennial allergic and vasomotor rhinitis, allergic conjunctivitis due to inhalant allergens and foods, urticaria, including ''cold urticaria'', angioneurotic edema, drug and serum reactions, anogenital pruritus and pruritus of chickenpox, as well as certain types of vascular headaches.

Cyproheptadine may be used as therapy for anaphylactic reactions, adjunctive to epinephrine and other standard measures after the acute manifestations have been controlled.

Cyproheptadine has been reported to have a beneficial effect in many patients diagnosed as having **vascular** types of **headaches,** such as migraine and histamine cephalalgia. Patients who have not been able to obtain adequate relief from any other agent have reported amelioration of symptoms with cyproheptadine. The characteristic headache and feeling of malaise may disappear within an hour or two after the first dose.

Contraindications: Although peripheral anticholinergic effects are minimal with recommended doses, as with all anticholinergic agents, cyproheptadine is contraindicated in patients with angle-closure glaucoma, in patients predisposed to urinary retention, and in patients with stenosing peptic ulcer or pyloroduodenal obstruction, symptomatic prostatic hypertrophy or bladder neck obstruction.

It is also contraindicated with concurrent MAO inhibitor therapy and in patients allergic to cyproheptadine.

Geriatrics: This drug should not be prescribed for elderly debilitated patients.

Lactation and Children: Antihistamines should not be used in nursing mothers, or in newborn or premature infants.

In an acute asthmatic attack, cyproheptadine should not be used.

Precautions: Antihistamines should not be used to treat lower respiratory tract symptoms including those of acute asthma.

Children: Safety and effectiveness in children below the age of 2 years have not been established.

Overdosage of antihistamines, particularly in infants and children, may produce hallucinations, CNS depression, convulsions and death.

Antihistamines may diminish mental alertness; conversely, particularly in the young child, they may occasionally produce excitation.

Occupational Hazards: This drug may impair alertness in some patients. Patients should be warned about engaging in activities requiring mental alertness and motor coordination, such as driving a car or operating machinery. Antihistamines are more likely to cause dizziness, sedation and hypotension in elderly patients.

Although not reported with cyproheptadine, rarely, prolonged therapy with antihistamines may cause blood dyscrasias.

Cyproheptadine has an atropine-like action and, therefore, should be used with caution in patients with: history of bronchial asthma, increased intraocular pressure, hyperthyroidism, cardiovascular disease, hypertension.

Pregnancy: The use of any drug in pregnancy, lactation, or in women of childbearing age requires that the potential benefits be weighed against its possible hazards to mother and child. Lactation may be inhibited.

The safe use of this drug in pregnancy has not been established.

Lactation: It is not known whether this drug is excreted in human milk. Because many drugs are excreted in human milk, and because of the potential for serious adverse reactions in nursing infants from cyproheptadine, a decision should be made whether to discontinue nursing or to discontinue the drug, taking into account the importance of the drug to the mother (see Contraindications).

Drug Interactions: MAO inhibitors prolong and intensify the anticholinergic effects of antihistamines.

Patients using this drug should be cautioned against the ingestion of alcohol and other CNS depressants, such as: hypnotics, sedatives, tranquilizers, antianxiety agents. Additive effects may occur.

Adverse Effects: The adverse reactions that appear frequently are drowsiness and somnolence. Many patients who initially complain of drowsiness may no longer do so after the first 3 or 4 days of continuous administration. Drowsiness is often a desirable effect in patients with dermatitis and pruritus, since it tends to decrease the level of perception and may also decrease emotional tension caused by the disease.

Adverse reactions which have been reported with the use of antihistamines are as follows: CNS: sedation, sleepiness (often transient), dizziness, disturbed coordination, confusion, restlessness, excitation, nervousness, tremor, irritability, insomnia, paresthesias, neuritis, convulsions, euphoria, hallucinations, hysteria and faintness.

Integumentary: allergic manifestation of rash and edema, excessive perspiration, urticaria and photosensitivity.

Special Senses: acute labyrinthitis, blurred vision, diplopia, vertigo and tinnitus.

Cardiovascular: hypotension, palpitation, tachycardia, extrasystoles and anaphylactic shock.

Hematologic: hemolytic anemia, leukopenia, agranulocytosis and thrombocytopenia.

Digestive System: dryness of mouth, epigastric distress, anorexia, nausea, vomiting, diarrhea, constipation and jaundice.

Genitourinary: frequency of micturition, difficult micturition, urinary retention and early menses.

Respiratory: dryness of nose and throat, thickening of bronchial secretions, tightness of chest and wheezing and nasal stuffiness.

Miscellaneous: fatigue, chills and headache.

Overdose: Symptoms: Antihistamine overdosage reactions may vary from CNS depression or stimulation to convulsions and death, especially in infants and children. Also, atropine-like signs and symptoms (dry mouth; fixed, dilated pupils; flushing, etc.); gastrointestinal symptoms may occur as well.

Treatment: If vomiting has not occurred spontaneously the patient should be induced to vomit if conscious with syrup of ipecac.

If the patient is unable to vomit, perform gastric lavage followed by activated charcoal. Isotonic or ½ isotonic saline is the lavage of choice. Precautions against aspiration must be taken, especially in infants and children.

When life-threatening CNS signs and symptoms are present, i.v. physostigmine salicylate may be considered. Dosage and frequency of administration are dependent on age, clinical response, and recurrence after response. (See package circulars for physostigmine products.)

Saline cathartics, such as milk of magnesia, draw water into the bowel by osmosis and therefore are valuable for their action in rapid dilution of bowel content.

Stimulants should not be used.

Vasopressors may be used to treat hypotension.

Dosage: Allergies and Pruritus: Dosage must be individualized. Since the antiallergic effect of a single dose usually lasts 4 to 6 hours, the daily requirement should be given in divided doses 3 times a day or as often as necessary to provide continuous relief.

There is no recommended dosage schedule for children under 2 years of age.

Although intended primarily for administration to children, the syrup is also useful for administration to adults who cannot swallow tablets.

Adults: The therapeutic range is 4 to 20 mg a day, with the majority of patients requiring 12 to 16 mg a day. An occasional patient may require as much as 32 mg a day for adequate relief. It is suggested that the dosage be initiated with 4 mg 3 times a day and adjusted according to the size and response of the patient. **The dosage is not to exceed 32 mg a day.**

Children (7 to 14 years): It is suggested that dosage be initiated with 2 mg 3 or 4 times a day depending on the age of the patient. The usual maintenance dosage is 4 mg 2 or 3 times a day. This dosage may be adjusted as necessary according to the size and response of the patient. If an additional daily dose is required, it should be taken preferably at bedtime. **The dosage is not to exceed 16 mg a day.**

Children (2 to 6 years): It is suggested that dosage be initiated with 2 mg 2 or 3 times a day, every 8 to 12 hours, and adjusted as necessary according to the size and response of the patient. If an additional daily dose is required, it should be taken preferably at bedtime. **The dosage is not to exceed 12 mg a day.**

Caution: One teaspoonful is assumed to be equivalent to 5 mL. Attention is called to the potential error in the use of household units. A teaspoon may hold from 4 to 7 mL. It is recommended therefore, that a medicinal spoon (5 mL) or calibrated medicine glass be used.

Migraine and Vascular Types of Headache: Adults: For prophylaxis or therapy, recommended dosage is 4 mg immediately, to be repeated in ½ hour if necessary, not to exceed 8 mg in a 4- to 6-hour period. Relief usually is obtained in responsive patients with 8 mg and maintained by 4 mg every 4 to 6 hours.

Supplied: Syrup: Each 5 mL of clear, yellow, syrupy liquid contains: cyproheptadine HCl 2 mg. Nonmedicinal ingredients: alcohol 5%, flavors, glycerin, purified water, quinoline yellow, sodium hydroxide, sorbic acid as preservative and sucrose. Gluten-, lactose- and tartrazine-free. Bottles of 250 and 500 mL. Store syrup between 15 and 30°C. Do not expose to temperatures below −20°C. Keep container tightly closed, protected from sunlight.

Tablets: Each round, white, flat, compressed tablet, with bevelled edge, scored on one side with MSD 62 on the other, contains: cyproheptadine HCl 4 mg. Nonmedicinal ingredients: calcium phosphate dibasic, cornstarch, lactose and magnesium stearate. Gluten- and tartrazine-free. Bottles of 45, 100 and 500. Store between 15 and 30°C. Keep container tightly closed, protected from sunlight.

(Shown in Product Recognition Section)

For comparative information on Benzodiazepines, see the CPhA General Monograph in the WHITE SECTION.

PERI-COLACE®

Roberts

Docusate Sodium—Casanthranol

Laxative—Stool Softener

Indications: Occasional or temporary constipation.

Contraindications: When symptoms of appendicitis or intestinal obstruction are present.

Precautions: Do not use in presence of abdominal pain, nausea, fever or vomiting. Use with caution in lactating women as the compound may cause increased stooling in the infant. Frequent or prolonged use may result in dependence on laxatives. Do not administer Peri-Colace within 2 hours of another medicine, to avoid reductions of its effect.

Dosage: Adults: 1 or 2 capsules at bedtime, or as indicated. In severe cases, the dosage may be increased to 2 capsules twice daily or 3 capsules at bedtime.

Supplied: Each maroon gelatin capsule contains: docusate sodium, USP 100 mg and casanthranol (standardized preparation of anthraquinone derivatives from cascara sagrada) 30 mg. Sodium: <1 mmol (5.17 mg). Bottles of 60.

PERIDEX® Ⓟ

Zila Pharmaceuticals

Chlorhexidine Gluconate

Antigingivitis

Pharmacology: Chlorhexidine provides antimicrobial activity during oral rinsing which is maintained between rinsings. Microbiologic sampling of plaque has shown a general reduction of both aerobic and anaerobic bacterial counts ranging from 54 to 97% through 6 months' clinical use. Rinsing with chlorhexidine inhibits the buildup and maturation of plaque by reducing certain microbes regarded as gingival pathogens, thereby reducing gingivitis. Chlorhexidine provided antimicrobial activity during rinsing and for several hours thereafter.

No significant changes in bacterial sensitivity, overgrowth of potentially opportunistic organisms or other adverse changes in the oral microbial flora were observed following the use of chlorhexidine for 6 months. Three months after chlorhexidine use was discontinued, the number of bacteria in plaque had returned to pretreatment levels and sensitivity of plaque bacteria to chlorhexidine remained unchanged.

Pharmacokinetics: Studies conducted with human subjects and animals demonstrate that any ingested chlorhexidine is poorly absorbed from the gastrointestinal tract. Excretion of chlorhexidine occurred primarily through the feces (approximately 90%). Less than 1% of the chlorhexidine ingested by these subjects was excreted in the urine.

Indications: For use as part of a professional program for the treatment of moderate to severe gingivitis, and for management of associated gingival bleeding and inflammation between dental visits. For patients having coexisting gingivitis and periodontitis, see Precautions.

Contraindications: Should not be used by persons who are known to be hypersensitive to chlorhexidine or other formula ingredients.

Warnings: *Pregnancy:* Reproduction and fertility studies with chlorhexidine have been conducted. No evidence of impaired fertility was observed in male and female rates at doses up to 100 mg/kg/day, and no evidence of harm to the fetus was observed in rats and rabbits at doses up to 300 mg/kg/day and 40 mg/kg/day, respectively. These doses are approximately 100, 300, and 40 times that which would result from a person ingesting 30 mL of 0.12% chlorhexidine/day. Since controlled studies in pregnant women have not been conducted, the benefits of use of the drug in pregnant women should be weighed against possible risk to the fetus.

Lactation: It is not known whether this drug is excreted in human milk. In parturition and lactation studies with rats, no evidence of impaired parturition or of toxic effects to suckling pups was observed when chlorhexidine was administered to dams at doses that were over 100 times greater than the dose which would result if a person ingested the entire recommended dose of chlorhexidine on a daily basis.

Children: Since the safety and efficacy of chlorhexidine in children has not yet been fully established, the benefits of its use should be weighed against the possible risks.

Precautions: For patients having coexisting gingivitis and periodontitis, the absence of gingival inflammation following treatment with chlorhexidine may not be indicative of the absence of underlying periodontitis. Appropriate treatment of periodontitis is therefore indicated.

Chlorhexidine may cause staining of oral surfaces such as the film on tooth surfaces, restorations, and the dorsum of the tongue. Stain will be more pronounced in patients who have heavier accumulations of unremoved plaque.

Stain resulting from use of chlorhexidine does not adversely affect the health of gingivae or other oral tissue. Stain can be removed from most tooth surfaces by conventional professional prophylactic techniques. Additional time may be required to complete the prophylaxis.

Discretion should be used when treating patients with exposed root surfaces or anterior facial restorations with rough surfaces or margins. If natural stains cannot be removed from these surfaces by a dental prophylaxis, patients should be excluded from chlorhexidine treatment if the risk of permanent discoloration is unacceptable. Stains in these areas may be difficult to remove by dental prophylaxis and on rare occasions may necessitate replacement of these restorations.

A few patients may experience an alteration in taste perception while undergoing treatment with chlorhexidine. Most of these patients accommodate to this effect with continued use of chlorhexidine.

Rare instances of permanent taste alteration following chlorhexidine use have been reported via postmarketing product surveillance.

For maximum effectiveness the patient should avoid rinsing their mouth (with water or other mouthwashes), brushing their teeth, eating or drinking for about 30 minutes after using chlorhexidine.

Adverse Effects: No serious systemic reactions associated with the use of chlorhexidine were observed in clinical testing. However, some adverse reactions have been reported in studies with Peridex or other chlorhexidine-containing mouth rinses. The most common side effects associated with chlorhexidine oral rinses are an increase in staining of oral surfaces; an increase in supra gingival calculus; and an alteration in taste perception to which most patients accommodate (see Precautions). Epithelial irritation and superficial desquamation of the oral mucosa have been noted in studies of children using chlorhexidine which were reversible upon discontinuation.

There have been rare cases of parotid gland swelling and inflammation of the salivary glands, in patients using chlorhexidine.

Oral irritation and local allergy-type symptoms have been spontaneously reported as side effects associated with use of chlorhexidine rinse.

The following oral mucosal side effects were reported during placebo-controlled adult clinical trials: apthous ulcer, grossly obvious gingivitis, trauma, ulcerations, erythema, desquamation, coated tongue, keratinization, geographic tongue, mucocele, and short frenum. Each occurred at a frequency of less than 1%.

Among postmarketing reports, the most frequently reported oral mucosal symptoms associated with chlorhexidine are stomatitis, gingivitis, glossitis, ulcer, dry mouth, hypesthesia, glossal edema and paresthesia.

Overdose: Symptoms and Treatment: Ingestion of 30 or 60 mL of chlorhexidine by a small child (10 kg or less body weight) might result in gastric distress, including nausea, or signs of alcohol intoxication. Medical attention should be sought if more than 120 mL chlorhexidine is ingested by a small child or if signs of alcohol intoxication develop.

Dosage: Chlorhexidine therapy should be initiated directly following a dental prophylaxis. Patients using chlorhexidine should be re-evaluated and given a thorough prophylaxis at intervals no longer than 6 months; they should be referred for periodontal consultation as necessary.

Recommended use is twice daily oral rinsing for 30 seconds, morning and evening after tooth brushing. Usual dosage is 15 mL (marked in cap) of undiluted chlorhexidine. Chlorhexidine is not intended for ingestion and should be expectorated after rinsing. Rinsing the mouth (with water or other mouthwashes), brushing the teeth, or eating or drinking should be avoided for about 30 minutes after using chlorhexidine.

The suggested initial course of therapy is 3 months, at which time patients should be recalled for evaluation. At the time of the recall visit, the dental professional should: evaluate progress, remove any stain, and reinforce proper home care techniques; if gingival inflammation and bleeding is controlled, discontinue therapy and recall the patient in 3 months to assess gingival health; if gingival inflammation and bleeding persists, continue chlorhexidine therapy for an additional 3 months and schedule a 3-month recall for evaluation; evaluate for evidence of epithelial irritation, desquamation and parotitis.

The following generally accepted grading scheme may be of use in evaluating the severity of gingivitis: see Table I.

Table I—Peridex

Loe and Silness Gingival Index (GI)

Grade	Description
1	**Normal** gingiva, no inflammation, no discoloration, no bleeding.
2	**Mild** inflammation, slight color change, mild alteration of gingival surface. No bleeding.
3	**Moderate** inflammation, erythema, swelling, bleeding on probing or when pressure applied.
4	**Severe** inflammation, severe erythema and swelling, tendency toward spontaneous hemorrhage, some ulceration.

An occasional missed dose can be ignored if the patient is generally compliant with the prescribed regimen.

Information for the Patient: See Blue Section—Information for the Patient "Peridex".

Supplied: Each mL of blue oral rinse contains: chlorhexidine gluconate 0.12%. Nonmedicinal ingredients: alcohol, FD&C Blue No. 1, flavor, glycerin, PEG-40 sorbitan di-isostearate, saccharin sodium and water. Amber plastic bottles of 475 mL with child-resistant dispensing closures. Store above freezing (0°C).

Reviewed 1998

PERIDOL® Ⓟ

Technilab

Haloperidol

Antipsychotic

Supplied: Oral Solution: Each mL of colorless, odorless and tasteless solution contains: haloperidol 2 mg. Nonmedicinal ingredients: lactic acid, methylparaben and purified water. Bottles of 100 and 500 mL.

Tablets: 0.5 mg: Each uncoated, scored, white tablet contains: haloperidol 0.5 mg. Nonmedicinal ingredients: magnesium stearate, microcrystalline cellulose and starch. Bottles of 100 and 1 000.

1 mg: Each uncoated, scored, yellow tablet contains: haloperidol 1 mg. Nonmedicinal ingredients: D&C yellow #10 aluminum lake, FD&C yellow #6 aluminum lake, magnesium stearate, microcrystalline cellulose and starch. Bottles of 100 and 1 000.

2 mg: Each uncoated, scored, pink tablet contains: haloperidol 2 mg. Nonmedicinal ingredients: FD&C blue #1 aluminum lake, FD&C red #3 aluminum lake, magnesium stearate, microcrystalline cellulose and starch. Bottles of 100 and 1 000.

5 mg: Each uncoated, scored, green tablet contains: haloperidol 5 mg. Nonmedicinal ingredients: D&C yellow #10 aluminum lake, FD&C blue #1 aluminum lake, magnesium stearate, microcrystalline cellulose and starch. Bottles of 100 and 1 000.

10 mg: Each uncoated, scored, aqua tablet contains: haloperidol 10 mg. Nonmedicinal ingredients: D&C yellow #10 aluminum lake, FD&C blue #1 aluminum lake, magnesium stearate, microcrystalline cellulose and starch. Bottles of 100, 500 and 1 000.

PERINDOPRIL Ⓟ

General Monograph, CPhA

see ACE INHIBITORS

PERMAX® Ⓟ

Draxis Health

Pergolide Mesylate

Dopamine Agonist

Pharmacology: Pergolide mesylate, a synthetic ergot derivative, is a dopamine receptor agonist at both D_1 and D_2 receptor sites.

In Parkinson's disease, pergolide is believed to exert its therapeutic effect by directly stimulating postsynaptic dopamine receptors in the corpus striatum. In addition, pergolide suppresses the secretion of prolactin, causes a transient increase in serum concentration of growth hormone and a decrease in serum concentration of luteinizing hormone.

To-date only very limited pharmacokinetic data are available. Following oral administration of ^{14}C-pergolide, radioactivity in plasma appeared after 15 to 30 minutes, peaked at 1 to 2 hours, and was barely detectable after 96 hours. Radioactivity was eliminated as pergolide metabolites in urine (55%), in feces (40%) and in breath (5%). No unchanged pergolide was detected in excreta. At least 10 radioactive metabolites have been isolated including N-despropylpergolide, pergolide sulfoxide and pergolide sulfone. The latter 2 metabolites are dopamine agonists in animals. The other detected metabolites have not been identified and it is not known whether they are pharmacologically active.

Pergolide is approximately 90% bound to plasma proteins. This extent of protein binding may be important to consider when pergolide is coadministered with other drugs known to affect protein binding.

Indications: As an adjunct to levodopa (usually with a peripheral decarboxylase inhibitor) in the symptomatic management of Parkinson's disease.

Evidence to support the efficacy of pergolide was obtained in a double-blind, placebo-controlled multicenter study which enrolled patients with mild to moderate Parkinson's disease who were intolerant to l-dopa/carbidopa treatment as manifested by moderate to severe dyskinesia and/or on-off phenomena.

Pergolide has not been assessed in the treatment of newly diagnosed patients or as the sole medication in Parkinson's disease.

Contraindications: Patients who are hypersensitive to this drug or other ergot derivatives.

Warnings: Hypotension: Pergolide may cause syncope or hypotension (i.e., a fall in systolic blood pressure to less than 100 mmHg). It is therefore important to warn patients of the risk, to begin therapy with low doses, and to increase the dosage in carefully adjusted increments over a period of several weeks (see Dosage).

Syncope or excessive hypotension were observed in patients on pergolide therapy, especially during initiation of treatment. Episodes of moderate hypotension also occurred. With gradual dosage titration, tolerance to hypotension usually develops.

Care should be exercised when administering pergolide concomitantly with antihypertensive agents or other medications known to lower blood pressure.

Occupational Hazards: Patients receiving pergolide should be cautioned with regard to engaging in activities requiring rapid and precise responses, such as driving an automobile or operating machinery.

Hallucinosis: In controlled trials, pergolide with levodopa caused hallucinosis in about 14% of patients as opposed to 3% taking placebo with levodopa. This was of sufficient severity to cause discontinuation of treatment in about 3% of those enrolled; tolerance to this untoward effect was not observed.

Fatalities: In the placebo-controlled trial, 2 of 187 patients treated with placebo died as compared with 1 of 189 patients treated with pergolide. In the latter group, 3 additional patients died who continued on pergolide beyond the controlled phase of the study. Of the 2 299 patients treated with pergolide in premarketing studies 143 died while on the drug or shortly after discontinuing the drug. The patient population under evaluation was elderly, ill, and at high risk for death. It seems unlikely that pergolide played any role in these deaths, but the possibility that pergolide shortens survival of patients cannot be excluded with absolute certainty.

Precautions: General: The abrupt discontinuation of pergolide in patients receiving it chronically as an adjunct to levodopa may precipitate the onset of hallucinations and confusion; these may occur within a span of several days. Discontinuation of pergolide should be undertaken gradually whenever possible, even if the patient is to remain on levodopa.

A symptom complex resembling the neuroleptic malignant syndrome (NMS), characterized by elevated body temperature, muscular rigidity, altered consciousness, and autonomic instability, has been reported in antiparkinsonian therapy. Therefore, patients should be observed carefully when the dosage of pergolide is reduced abruptly or discontinued.

The administration of pergolide to patients receiving levodopa may cause and/or exacerbate pre-existing dyskinesia.

Cardiovascular Effects: Pergolide has not been systematically evaluated in patients with heart disease. In the multicenter clinical trial, patients with heart disease, i.e., recent angina pectoris, decompensated heart failure (New York Scale III or IV), myocardial infarction within the last 12 months, or any arrhythmia requiring antiarrhythmic therapy at the time of the study or within 12 months prior to the study were excluded. Since there is only limited experience with pergolide in these patients, pergolide should be administered only if in the judgement of the physician the potential benefits clearly outweigh the potential risks.

In a study comparing pergolide and placebo, patients taking pergolide were found to have significantly more episodes of atrial premature contractions (APCs) and sinus tachycardia.

Drug Interactions: Dopamine antagonists such as the neuroleptics (phenothiazines, butyrophenones, thioxanthenes) or metoclopramide ordinarily should not be administered concurrently with pergolide (a dopamine agonist) because these agents may diminish the effectiveness of pergolide.

Because pergolide is approximately 90% bound by plasma proteins, caution should be exercised if pergolide is coadministered with other drugs known to affect protein binding.

Pregnancy: In teratology studies performed in mice and rabbits, there was no evidence of harm to the fetus due to pergolide. There are however, no adequate and well-controlled studies in pregnant women. In a small number of women who received pergolide for endocrine disorders, there were 33 pregnancies that resulted in healthy babies and 6 pregnancies that resulted in congenital abnormalities (3 major, 3 minor); a causal relationship has not been established. Because human data are limited and because animal reproduction studies are not always predictive of human response, this drug should be used during pregnancy only, if in the opinion of the treating physician, the possible benefit to the patient outweighs the potential risks to the fetus.

Lactation: It is not known whether pergolide is excreted in human milk. The pharmacologic action of pergolide suggests that it may interfere with lactation. Because many drugs are excreted in human milk and because of the potential for serious adverse reactions to pergolide in nursing infants, a decision should be made whether to discontinue nursing or to discontinue the drug, taking into account the importance of the drug to the mother.

Children: Safety and effectiveness in children have not been established.

Adverse Effects: Commonly Observed: The most commonly observed adverse events associated with the use of pergolide are: nervous system complaints, including dyskinesia, dizziness, hallucinations, somnolence, and insomnia; gastrointestinal complaints, including nausea, constipation, diarrhea and dyspepsia; cardiovascular complaints, including postural hypotension, and respiratory system complaints, including rhinitis.

Adverse Reactions Resulting in Discontinuation of Treatment: Twenty-seven percent of approximately 1 200 patients, receiving pergolide for treatment of Parkinson's disease in premarketing clinical trials in the U.S. and Canada, discontinued treatment due to adverse reactions. Events most often causing discontinuation were related to the nervous system (15.5%), primarily hallucinations (7.8%) and confusion (1.8%).

Incidence of Adverse Reactions in Controlled Clinical Trials: Table I enumerates adverse events that occurred at a frequency of 1% or more among pergolide treated patients who participated in the double-blind controlled clinical trial comparing pergolide with placebo. The prescriber should be aware that these figures cannot be used to predict the incidence of side effects in the course of usual medical practice where patient characteristics and other factors differ from those which prevail in clinical trials. The cited figures, however, do provide the prescribing physician with some basis for estimating the relative contribution of drug and non-drug factors to the side effect incidence rate in the population studied.

Table I—Permax

Incidence of Treatment-Emergent Adverse Experiences in the Placebo-Controlled Clinical Trial

Adverse Reaction	Percentage of Patients Permax N=189	Reporting Events Placebo N=187
Body as a Whole System		
Pain	7.0	2.1
Abdominal Pain	5.8	2.1
Injury, accident	5.8	7.0
Headache	5.3	6.4
Asthenia	4.2	4.8
Chest Pain	3.7	2.1
Flu syndrome	3.2	2.1
Neck Pain	2.7	1.6
Back Pain	1.6	2.1
Surgical Procedure	1.6	<1
Chills	1.1	0
Face edema	1.1	0
Infection	1.1	0
Nervous System		
Dyskinesia	62.4	24.6
Dizziness	19.1	13.9
Hallucinations	13.8	3.2
Dystonia	11.6	8.0
Confusion	11.1	9.6
Somnolence	10.1	3.7
Insomnia	7.9	3.2
Anxiety	6.4	4.3
Tremor	4.2	7.5
Depression	3.2	5.4
Abnormal dreams	2.7	4.3
Personality disorder	2.1	<1
Psychosis	2.1	0
Abnormal gait	1.6	1.6
Akathisia	1.6	0
Extrapyramidal syndrome	1.6	1.1
Incoordination	1.6	<1
Paresthesia	1.6	3.2
Akinesia	1.1	1.1
Hypertonia	1.1	0
Neuralgia	1.1	<1
Speech disorder	1.1	1.6
Gastrointestinal		
Nausea	24.3	12.8
Constipation	10.6	5.9
Diarrhea	6.4	2.7
Dyspepsia	6.4	2.1
Anorexia	4.8	2.7
Dry mouth	3.7	<1
Vomiting	2.7	1.6
Cardiovascular System		
Postural hypotension	9.0	7.0
Sinus tachycardia	4.8	1.6
Vasodilation	3.2	<1
Palpitation	2.1	<1
Hypotension	2.1	<1
Syncope	2.1	1.1
Hypertension	1.6	1.1
Arrhythmia	1.1	<1
Myocardial infarction	1.1	<1
Respiratory System		
Rhinitis	12.2	5.4
Dyspnea	4.8	1.1
Epistaxis	1.6	<1
Hiccup	1.1	0
Metabolic and Nutritional System		
Peripheral edema	7.4	4.3
Edema	1.6	0
Weight gain	1.6	0
Special Senses		
Abnormal vision	5.8	5.4
Diplopia	2.1	0
Taste perversion	1.6	0
Eye disorder	1.1	0
Musculoskeletal System		
Arthralgia	1.6	2.1
Bursitis	1.6	<1
Myalgia	1.1	<1
Twitching	1.1	0
Skin and Appendages		
Rash	3.2	2.1
Sweating	2.1	2.7
Urogenital System		
Urinary frequency	2.7	6.4
Urinary tract infection	2.7	3.7
Hematuria	1.1	<1
Hemic and Lymphatic System		
Anemia	1.1	<1

Certain adverse experiences (e.g., dyskinesias, hallucinations) are frequently observed in patients receiving levodopa pergolide and/or other dopamine agonists. These are dose related and tend to improve with reduction of the dosage of levodopa or of pergolide. Hallucinations may infrequently persist after discontinuation of pergolide.

Postural hypotension and nausea are most frequently reported during the initial titration phase.

Abnormalities in laboratory tests may include elevations of AST, ALT, alkaline phosphatase and urea nitrogen.

Permax (cont'd)

Other Events Observed During the Premarketing Evaluation of Pergolide: This section reports event frequencies of adverse reactions that occurred in approximately 1 700 patients who took multiple doses of pergolide in premarketing studies worldwide. The conditions and duration of exposure to pergolide varied greatly, involving well-controlled studies as well as experience in open and uncontrolled clinical settings. In the absence of appropriate controls in some of the studies, a causal relationship to pergolide treatment cannot be determined.

The following definitions of frequency are used: **Frequent** adverse events are defined as those occurring in at least 1/100 patients; **infrequent** adverse events are those occurring in 1/100 to 1/1 000 patients; **rare** events are those occurring in less than 1/1 000 patients.

Body as a Whole System: Frequent: headache, asthenia, injury accident, abdominal pain, chest pain, back pain, fever, flu syndrome, neck pain. Infrequent: enlarged abdomen, malaise, neoplasm, hernia, pelvic pain, facial edema, chills, sepsis, cellulitis, moniliasis, abscess, jaw pain, hypothermia. Rare: acute abdominal syndrome, LE syndrome, erythromelalgia.

Nervous System: Frequent: hallucinations, psychosis, paranoid reaction, personality disorder, akinesia, dyskinesia, choreoathetosis, dystonia, tremor, abnormal gait, incoordination, speech disorders, dizziness, confusion, depression, anxiety, somnolence, insomnia, abnormal dreams, amnesia. Infrequent: neuropathy, hypertonia, delusions, convulsion, libido increase, euphoria, emotional lability, libido decrease, akathisia, vertigo, neuralgia, myoclonus, coma, apathy, paralysis, neurosis, hyperkinesia, ataxia, acute brain syndrome, torticollis, meningitis, manic reaction, hypokinesia, hostility, agitation. Rare: stupor, neuritis, intracranial hypertension, hemiplegia, facial paralysis.

Gastrointestinal: Frequent: nausea, vomiting, constipation, dyspepsia, anorexia, diarrhea, dry mouth, dysphagia. Infrequent: flatulence, abnormal liver function tests, increased appetite, salivary gland enlargement, thirst, gastroenteritis, gastritis, rectal disorder, peridontal abscess, intestinal obstruction, nausea and vomiting, gingivitis, esophagitis, cholelithiasis, tooth caries, hepatitis, stomach ulcer, melena, hepatomegaly, hematemesis, eructation. Rare: sialadenitis, peptic ulcer, pancreatitis, colitis, cholecystitis, aphthous stomatitis.

Cardiovascular: Frequent: postural hypotension, hypotension, syncope, hypertension, palpitations, arrhythmia, vasodilatation, congestive heart failure. Infrequent: myocardial infarct, tachycardia, cardiac arrest, abnormal ECG, angina pectoris, thrombophlebitis, bradycardia, ventricular extrasystoles, cerebrovascular accident, ventricular tachycardia, cerebral ischemia, atrial fibrillation, varicose vein, pulmonary embolus, AV block, shock. Rare: vasculitis, pulmonary hypertension, pericarditis, migraine, heart block, cerebral hemorrhage.

Respiratory: Frequent: rhinitis, dyspnea, pneumonia, pharyngitis, cough increased. Infrequent: sinusitis, bronchitis, epistaxis, voice alteration, hemoptysis, asthma, lung edema, hiccup, pleural effusion, laryngitis, emphysema, apnea. Rare: pneumothorax, lung fibrosis, larynx edema, hypoxia, hypoventilation, hyperventilation, hemothorax, carcinoma of lung.

Metabolic and Nutritional Findings: Frequent: peripheral edema, weight loss, weight gain. Infrequent: dehydration, hypokalemia, hypoglycemia, gout, hyperglycemia, iron deficiency anemia, hypercholesteremia. Rare: electrolyte imbalance, cachexia, acidosis, hyperuricemia.

Special Senses: Frequent: diplopia. Infrequent: otitis media, conjunctivitis, tinnitus, deafness, taste perversion, ear pain, eye pain, glaucoma, eye hemorrhage.

Rare: blindness, cataract, retinal detachment, retinal vascular disorder.

Musculoskeletal: Frequent: twitching, myalgia, arthralgia. Infrequent: bursitis, bone pain, tenosynovitis, myositis, bone sarcoma. Rare: osteoporosis, muscle atrophy.

Skin and Appendages: Frequent: sweating, rash. Infrequent: skin discoloration, pruritus, acne, skin ulcer, alopecia, dry skin, skin carcinoma, seborrhea, hirsutism, herpes simplex, eczema, fungal dermatitis. Rare: vesiculobullous rash, subcutaneous nodule, skin nodule, skin benign neoplasm, lichenoid dermatitis, herpes zoster.

Urogenital: Frequent: urinary tract infection, urinary frequency, urinary incontinence, prostatic disorder, dysmenorrhea, hematuria. Infrequent: dysuria, breast pain, menorrhagia, impotence, cystitis, urinary retention, menstrual disorder, abortion, vaginal hemorrhage, vaginitis, abnormal ejaculation, priapism, kidney calculus, fibrocystic breast, lactation, uterine hemorrhage, urolithiasis, salpingitis, pyuria, metrorrhagia, menopause, kidney failure, breast neoplasm. Rare: amenorrhea, bladder carcinoma, breast engorgement, epididymitis, hypogonadism, leukorrhea, nephrosis, pyelonephritis, urethral pain, uricaciduria, withdrawal bleeding.

Hemic and Lymphatic: Frequent: anemia. Infrequent: leukopenia, lymphadenopathy, leukocytosis, thrombocytopenia, petechia, megaloblastic anemia, cyanosis. Rare: purpura, lymphocytosis, eosinophilia, acute lymphoblastic leukemia.

Postmarketing Reports: Voluntary reports of adverse events temporally associated with pergolide that have been received since market introduction and which may have no causal relationship with the drug, include the following: neuroleptic malignant syndrome.

Overdose: Symptoms and Treatment: There is no clinical experience with massive overdosage. The largest overdose involved a young hospitalized adult patient who was not being treated with pergolide but who intentionally took 60 mg of pergolide. He experienced vomiting, hypotension and agitation. Another patient receiving a daily dosage of 7 mg of pergolide, unintentionally took 19 mg/day for 3 days, after which his vital signs were normal but he experienced severe hallucinations. Within 36 hours of resumption of the prescribed dosage level, the hallucinations stopped. One patient unintentionally took 14 mg/day for 23 days instead of her prescribed 1.4 mg/day dosage. She experienced severe involuntary movements and tingling in her arms and legs. Another patient who inadvertently received 7 mg instead of the prescribed 0.7 mg experienced palpitations, hypotension and ventricular extrasystoles. The highest total daily dose (prescribed for several patients with refractory Parkinson's disease) has exceeded 30 mg.

Animal studies indicate that the manifestations of overdosage in man might include nausea, vomiting, convulsions, decreased blood pressure, and CNS stimulation.

Management of overdosage may require supportive measures to maintain arterial blood pressure. Cardiac function should be monitored; an antiarrhythmic agent may be necessary. If signs of CNS stimulation are present, a phenothiazine or butyrophenone neuroleptic agent may be indicated; the efficacy of such drugs has not been assessed in reversing the effects of overdose. There is no experience with dialysis or hemoperfusion; these procedures are unlikely to be of benefit.

Dosage: Administration of pergolide should be initiated with a single daily dose of 0.05 mg for the first 2 days. The dose should then be gradually increased by 0.1 to 0.15 mg/day every third day over the next 12 days of therapy. The dosage may then be increased by 0.25 mg/day every third day until an optimal dosage is achieved.

Pergolide is usually administered in divided doses 3 times/day. During dosage titration, the dosage of levodopa/carbidopa may be cautiously decreased.

Since rapid escalation of the drug causes severe adverse reactions, it is recommended that a slow increase of pergolide be combined with a concomitant, gradual and limited reduction of levodopa dosage.

In clinical studies, the mean therapeutic dose of pergolide was 3 mg/day. The average concurrent levodopa/carbidopa daily dosage (expressed as levodopa) was approximately 650 mg/day. The safety of pergolide at doses above 5 mg/day has not been systematically evaluated.

Supplied: 0.05 mg: Each ivory-colored, modified rectangle-shaped tablet, scored and engraved with the company logo and Identi-code 4131, contains: pergolide mesylate 0.05 mg. Nonmedicinal ingredients: croscarmellose sodium, iron oxide yellow, lactose, l-methionine, magnesium stearate and povidone. Gluten- and tartrazine-free. Amber HDPE bottles of 30.

0.25 mg: Each green, modified rectangle-shaped tablet, scored and engraved with the company logo and Identi-code 4133, contains: pergolide mesylate 0.25 mg. Nonmedicinal ingredients: croscarmellose sodium, FD&C blue No. 2, iron oxide yellow, lactose, magnesium stearate and povidone. Gluten- and tartrazine-free. Amber HDPE bottles of 100.

1 mg: Each pink-colored, modified rectangle-shaped tablet, scored and engraved with the company logo and Identi-code 4135, contains: pergolide mesylate 1 mg. Nonmedicinal ingredients: croscarmellose sodium, iron oxide red pure, lactose, magnesium stearate and povidone. Gluten- and tartrazine-free. Amber HDPE bottles of 100.

Store at room temperature.

...Grateful acknowledgement is accorded to the "participating companies" whose support has facilitated the widespread distribution of *CPS*.

PERNOX®
Westwood-Squibb

Sulfur—Salicylic Acid Compound
Acne Therapy

Supplied: Each g of Pernox Regular or Lemon Scent contains: microfine polyethylene granules, sulfur 2%, salicylic acid 1.5%, in a surface-active combination of soapless cleansers and wetting agents. Pernox Regular: Nonmedicinal ingredients: D&C Yellow No. 10, EDTA, FD&C Blue No. 1, methylcellulose, modified food starch, perfume, poloxamer 184, polyethylene, sodium dioctyl sulfosuccinate, sodium dodecylbenzenesulfonate, sodium octoxynol-2 ethane sulfonate and water. Lemon Scent: Nonmedicinal ingredients: D&C Yellow No. 10, EDTA, methylcellulose, modified food starch, perfume, poloxamer 184, polyethylene, sodium dioctyl sulfosuccinate, sodium dodecylbenzenesulfonate, sodium octoxynol-2 ethane sulfonate and water. Plastic tubes of 110 g.

PERSANTINE® Ⓟ
Boehringer Ingelheim

Dipyridamole
Coronary Vasodilator—Inhibitor of Platelet Adhesion and Aggregation

Pharmacology: Dipyridamole normalizes increased platelet adhesiveness and tendency to aggregate (Hellem's method). Dipyridamole has been found to lengthen abnormally shortened platelet survival time in a dose-dependent manner; 400 mg/day or 100 mg/day plus 1 g ASA.

It is believed that platelet reactivity and interaction with prosthetic cardiac valve surfaces, resulting in abnormal shortened platelet survival time is a significant factor in connection with prosthetic heart valve replacement.

In a controlled clinical trial involving patients who had undergone surgical placement of prosthetic heart valves (mitral and/or aortic valve replacement), Persantine, in combination with anticoagulants, significantly decreased the incidence of postoperative thromboembolic events, without increasing hemorrhagic complications. The incidence of thromboembolic events in patients receiving dipyridamole in a dose of 400 mg/day in combination with anticoagulants was 1.3% compared to 14.3% to the control group treated with anticoagulant alone.

In vitro dipyridamole potentiates the aggregation-inhibiting effects of adenosine and prostaglandin E_1, inhibits platelet uptake of adenosine, serotonin and glucose and increases platelet cyclic AMP levels. At higher concentrations dipyridamole inhibits platelet aggregation induced by ADP or collagen.

Myocardial blood flow increases in a dose-dependent fashion after i.v. or oral dipyridamole, with flows 170% or more above normal. Maximal increases are achieved at about 2 μg/mL with 0.8 μg/mL being the threshold serum level. Single oral doses of 150 mg dipyridamole produce the maximal response. At normal therapeutic doses, no significant alterations of peripheral blood flow, systemic blood pressure, or heart rate have been observed.

Dipyridamole is a coronary vasodilator in man. The mechanism of vasodilation has not been fully elucidated, but may result from inhibition of uptake of adenosine, an important mediator of coronary vasodilation. The vasodilatory effects of dipyridamole are abolished by administration of the adenosine receptor antagonist theophylline.

How dipyridamole-induced vasodilation leads to abnormalities in thallium distribution (when administered i.v. for myocardial perfusion imaging) and ventricular function is also uncertain, but presumably represents a "steal" phenomenon. In this situation, relatively intact vessels dilate, and sustain enhanced flow, leaving reduced pressure and flow across areas of hemodynamically important coronary vascular constriction.

Pharmacokinetics: Dipyridamole is readily absorbed from the gastrointestinal tract, reaching peak plasma levels in man 1 to 3 hours following oral administration. Peak plasma levels are dose dependent and range from about 0.5 μg/mL after a 25 mg dose to 1.6 μg/mL after a 75 mg dose. Blood levels are quite variable, possibly depending on food intake and gastrointestinal peristalsis. Ingestion on an empty stomach may result in higher blood levels. Following i.v. administration, the distribution half-life in man is about 25 minutes and after oral administration about 3 hours. When plasma levels of drug are followed for up to 60 hours after i.v. or oral administration of 20 to 50 mg, plasma levels decline tri-exponentially with half-lives of 5 minutes (i.v. only), 53 minutes and about 10 to 12 hours. The volume of distribution is about 140 L with about 92 to 99% binding to plasma proteins, primarily alpha$_1$-acid glycoprotein.

Indications: Oral: Thromboembolic Disease: The prevention of post-operative thromboembolic complications associated with prosthetic heart valves.

Parenteral: Myocardial Perfusion Imaging: I.V. dipyridamole can be used to induce pharmacologic vasodilation for myocardial perfusion imaging.

Contraindications: Hypersensitivity to dipyridamole. I.V. administration of dipyridamole is not recommended in states of shock or collapse.

Warnings: Rare serious adverse reactions associated with the administration of i.v. dipyridamole for myocardial imaging have been reported. These have included fatal and non-fatal myocardial infarction, ventricular fibrillation, symptomatic ventricular tachycardia, stroke and transient cerebral ischemia.

Since excessive doses of dipyridamole (i.v. or oral) or i.v. doses given too rapidly can produce peripheral vasodilation, dipyridamole should be used with caution in patients with hypotension, rapidly worsening angina, subvalvular aortic stenosis or hemodynamic instability. In rare cases, such patients may be at risk for developing myocardial ischemia and infarction.

An i.v. bolus of dipyridamole (40 to 50 mg over 4 minutes) can result in chest pain in patients with coronary artery disease. Rarely, hypotension or ventricular arrhythmias occur with a rapid, i.v. bolus. The infusion rate should be monitored to minimize this risk. The symptoms can generally be reversed with an i.v. injection of 50 to 250 mg of aminophylline over several minutes.

Patients with a history or presence of bronchial hyperreactivity may be at risk of developing bronchospasm during the use of i.v. dipyridamole as an adjunct to myocardial perfusion imaging. Although the actual overall incidence of this occurrence is small (~0.2%), the clinical information to be gained through the use of i.v. dipyridamole should be weighed against the potential risk to the patient.

Precautions: I.V. dipyridamole as an adjunct to myocardial perfusion imaging should be used with caution in patients with unstable angina, as such patients may be at risk for severe myocardial infarction.

As with exercise induced stress, the use of i.v. dipyridamole as an adjunct to myocardial perfusion imaging may occasionally precipitate cardiac arrhythmias in patients with severe heart disease. Scanning should therefore be performed with constant monitoring of the patient's ECG. Parenteral aminophylline should be readily available and should be administered as a slow i.v. injection of 50 to 250 mg in the event of occurrences such as chest pain, bronchospasm, severe nausea/vomiting, hypotension, severe headache.

In the case of severe hypotension, the patient should be placed in a supine position with the head tilted down if necessary, before administration of parenteral aminophylline. If 250 mg of aminophylline does not relieve chest pain symptoms within a few minutes, sublingual nitroglycerin may be administered. If chest pain continues despite use of aminophylline and nitroglycerin, the possibility of myocardial infarction should be considered. If the clinical condition of a patient with an adverse event permits a 1-minute delay in the administration of parenteral aminophylline, thallium-201 may be injected and allowed to circulate for 1 minute before the injection of aminophylline. This will allow initial thallium perfusion imaging to be performed before reversal of the pharmacologic effects of dipyridamole on the coronary circulation.

Pregnancy: Reproductive studies have been performed in mice, rats, and rabbits at doses of up to 125 mg/kg and have not revealed evidence of impaired embryonic development attributable to dipyridamole. However, there have not been adequate, well-controlled studies in pregnant women and the drug should be used during pregnancy only if the expected benefits outweigh the potential risks.

Lactation: Dipyridamole is excreted in human milk. Caution should therefore be used when this drug is administered to nursing mothers.

Children: The safety and effectiveness of dipyridamole have not been established in the pediatric population.

Drug Interactions: The use of oral maintenance xanthines (e.g., theophylline, aminophylline) may abolish the coronary vasodilation produced by i.v. dipyridamole administration. This could lead to false-negative imaging results. Xanthine derivatives (e.g., found in coffee, tea) may weaken the effect of dipyridamole.

Caution is necessary when dipyridamole is used concurrently with anticoagulants or thrombolytics as the combined use of such agents may result in an increased risk of hemorrhage.

Dipyridamole may increase the hypotensive effect of blood pressure lowering drugs.

Dipyridamole may counteract the anticholinesterase effect of cholinesterase inhibitors. In patients with myasthenia gravis, readjustment of therapy may be necessary during treatment with dipyridamole.

Adverse Effects: Serious adverse events (fatal and non-fatal myocardial infarction, severe ventricular arrhythmias, and serious CNS abnormalities) associated with the i.v. administration of dipyridamole for myocardial imaging are described in Warnings.

Adverse reactions at therapeutic doses are usually minimal and transient. Occasionally, headache, dizziness, nausea, flushing, syncope or weakness and skin rash have occurred during initiation of therapy. Mild occasional gastric distress can be avoided by administration of tablets with a glass of milk. Gastric irritation, emesis and abdominal cramping may occur at high dosage levels. Rare cases of what appears to be an aggravation of angina pectoris have been reported, usually at the initiation of therapy.

On those uncommon occasions when adverse reactions have been persistent or intolerable to the patient, withdrawal of the medication has been followed promptly by cessation of the undesirable symptoms.

When dipyridamole is used in combination with ASA, the only side effect clearly attributable to dipyridamole is headache. This symptom shows an increase of 5.5% in the combination treated group over that occurring in a group of patients treated with ASA alone. Other adverse reactions which occur during combination therapy are similar to those mentioned above, together with the well documented side effects of ASA therapy, notably gastric distress and gastrointestinal bleeding.

At the higher doses of dipyridamole there may be an increase in the incidence of adverse reactions.

In very rare cases, increased bleeding during or after surgery has been reported.

When **i.v.** dipyridamole was used as an adjunct to myocardial perfusion imaging in a study of 3 911 patients, the following events occurred in greater than 1% of the patients (see Table I).

Table I—Persantine

Adverse Effects—I.V. Use

Event Description	Incidence (%) of Occurrence in 3 911 Patients
Chest Pain/Angina Pectoris	19.7
Headache	12.2
Dizziness	11.8
Electrocardiographic Abnormalities/ST-T changes	7.5
Electrocardiographic Abnormalities/Extrasystoles	5.2
Hypotension	4.6
Nausea	4.6
Flushing	3.4
Electrocardiographic Abnormalities/Tachycardia	3.2
Dyspnea	2.6
Pain Unspecified	2.6
Blood Pressure Lability	1.6
Hypertension	1.5
Paresthesia	1.3
Fatigue	1.2

Less common events (i.e., occurred in 1% or less of the patients in the study) included, in decreasing order of frequency:

Cardiovascular: electrocardiographic abnormalities unspecified, arrhythmia unspecified, palpitation, ventricular tachycardia, bradycardia, myocardial infarction, AV block, syncope, orthostatic hypotension, atrial fibrillation, supraventricular tachycardia, ventricular arrhythmia unspecified, heart block unspecified, cardiomyopathy, edema.

Central and Peripheral Nervous System: hypoesthesia, hypertonia, nervousness/anxiety, tremor, abnormal coordination, somnolence, dysphonia, migraine, vertigo.

Gastrointestinal: dyspepsia, dry mouth, abdominal pain, flatulence, vomiting, eructation, dysphagia, tenesmus, increased appetite.

Respiratory: pharyngitis, bronchospasm, hyperventilation, rhinitis, coughing, pleural pain.

Other: myalgia, back pain, injection site reaction unspecified, diaphoresis, asthenia, malaise, arthralgia, injection site pain, rigor, earache, tinnitus, vision abnormalities unspecified, dysgeusia, thirst, depersonalization, eye pain, renal pain, perineal pain, breast pain, intermittent claudication, leg cramping.

Overdose: Symptoms and Treatment: Hypotension, if it occurs, is likely to be of short duration but vasopressor substances may be used if necessary. Symptoms such as feeling warm, flushes, sweating, accelerated pulse, restlessness, feeling of weakness and dizziness, and anginal complaints may occur.

Dosage: Oral: Thromboembolic Disease: The recommended oral dose is 100 mg q.i.d., 1 hour before meals. A lower dose of 100 mg of dipyridamole daily together with 1 g ASA daily, prolongs platelet survival to the same extent.

Parenteral: Myocardial Perfusion Imaging: The dose of i.v. dipyridamole used as an adjunct to myocardial perfusion imaging should be adjusted according to the weight of the patient. Prior to use, dipyridamole i.v. should be diluted 1:1 with Dextrose Injection, USP 5%. The recommended dose is 0.142 mg/kg/minute, infused over 4 minutes. A total dose of greater than 60 mg is not recommended for use in any patient. The imaging agent should be injected within 5 minutes following the 4 minute infusion of dipyridamole. Do not mix i.v. dipyridamole with other drugs in the same syringe or infusion container.

Supplied: Tablets: 25 mg: Each orange, round, sugar-coated tablet, imprinted with the Ingelheim tower on one side contains: dipyridamole 25 mg. Nonmedicinal ingredients: acacia, carnauba wax, colloidal silica, FD&C Yellow No. 6, lactose, magnesium stearate, maize starch, polyethylene glycol, sucrose, talc, titanium dioxide and white wax. Energy: 1.01 kJ (0.24 kcal). Bottles of 100 and 500. Store at room temperature (15 to 30°C).

50 mg: Each coral-red, round, sugar-coated tablet, imprinted with the Ingelheim tower on one side contains: dipyridamole 50 mg. Nonmedicinal ingredients: acacia, calcium hydrogen phosphate, carnauba wax, colloidal silica, FD&C Yellow No. 6, magnesium stearate, maize starch, polyethylene glycol, red iron oxide, sucrose, talc, titanium dioxide and white wax. Energy: 1.01 kJ (0.24 kcal). Bottles of 100 and 500. Store at room temperature (15 to 30°C).

75 mg: Each reddish-orange, round, sugar-coated tablet, imprinted with the Ingelheim tower on one side contains: dipyridamole 75 mg. Nonmedicinal ingredients: acacia, calcium hydrogen phosphate, carnauba wax, colloidal silica, FD&C Yellow No. 6, magnesium stearate, maize starch, polyethylene glycol, sucrose, talc, titanium dioxide and white wax. Energy: 1.01 kJ (0.24 kcal). Bottles of 100 and 500. Store at room temperature (15 to 30°C).

100 mg: Each white, round, sugar-coated tablet, imprinted with the Ingelheim tower on one side contains: dipyridamole 100 mg. Nonmedicinal ingredients: acacia, calcium hydrogen phosphate, carnauba wax, colloidal silica, FD&C Yellow No. 6, magnesium stearate, maize starch, polyethylene glycol, sucrose, talc, titanium dioxide and white wax. Energy: 1.01 kJ (0.24 kcal). Bottles of 100. Store at room temperature (15 to 30°C).

Parenteral: Each mL contains: dipyridamole 5 mg. Nonmedicinal ingredients: hydrochloric acid, polyethylene glycol, tartaric acid and water for injection. Ampuls of 10 mL, packages of 5. Protect from direct light, and avoid freezing. Store at room temperature (less than 30°C).

PETHIDINE Ⓝ

General Monograph, CPhA

see OPIOID ANALGESICS

PETHIDINE INJECTION BP Ⓝ

Faulding

Meperidine HCl

Opioid Analgesic

Pharmacology: Meperidine is a narcotic analgesic with multiple actions qualitatively similar to those of morphine. The most prominent of these actions involve the CNS and organs which are composed of smooth muscle. Analgesia and sedation are the principal actions of therapeutic value.

Some evidence suggests that meperidine may produce less smooth muscle spasm, constipation, and depression of the cough reflex than equivalent analgesic doses of morphine. Meperidine parenteral doses of 80 to 100 mg is approximately

Pethidine Injection BP (cont'd)

equivalent in analgesic effect to 10 mg of morphine. Its onset of action is slightly more rapid than with morphine, and there is a slightly shorter duration of action. Meperidine is significantly less effective by the oral rather than parenteral route. However, the exact ratio of oral to parenteral effectiveness is unknown.

Indications: The relief of moderate to severe pain involved in many medical, surgical, obstetrical and dental situations.

Contraindications: Hypersensitivity to meperidine. Contraindicated in patients who are currently receiving or who have been receiving MAO inhibitors within 14 days. The mechanism of these reactions is unclear, but may be related to a pre-existing hyperphenylalaninemia. Some have resembled the syndrome of acute narcotic overdose characterized by coma, severe respiratory depression, cyanosis and hypotension. In other reactions, hyperexcitability, convulsions, tachycardia, hyperpyrexia and hypertension have been the predominant manifestations. Although it is unknown if other narcotics are exempt from the risk of such reactions, virtually all the reported reactions have occurred with meperidine. A sensitivity test should be performed if a narcotic is needed in such patients. The sensitivity test should involve repeated, small, incremental doses of morphine administered over the course of several hours. The patient's condition and vital signs should be under careful observation throughout the test. Severe reactions have been treated with i.v. hydrocortisone or prednisolone with the addition of i.v. chlorpromazine in those cases exhibiting hypertension and hyperpyrexia. The usefulness and safety of narcotic antagonists in the treatment of these reactions is unknown. There is a chemical incompatibility between solutions of meperidine and barbiturates.

Warnings: Drug Dependence: Meperidine can produce drug dependence similar to that of morphine and therefore has the potential for being abused. Psychic and physical dependence, as well as tolerance may develop upon repeated administration of meperidine. Meperidine should therefore be prescribed and administered with the same degree of caution appropriate to the use of morphine. As with other narcotics, meperidine is subject to the provisions of the Narcotic Control Act.

Drug Interactions: Interaction With Other CNS Depressants: In the case of patients who are concurrently receiving other narcotic analgesics, general anesthetics, phenothiazines, other tranquilizers (see Dosage), sedative-hypnotics (including barbiturates), tricyclic antidepressants, and other CNS depressants (including alcohol), meperidine should be used with great caution and in reduced dosage. The following conditions may result: respiratory depression, hypotension, and profound sedation or coma.

Head Injury and Increased Intracranial Pressure: Head injury, other intracranial lesions, or a pre-existing increase of intracranial pressure may markedly exaggerate the respiratory depressant effects of meperidine and its capacity to elevate cerebrospinal fluid pressure. Furthermore, adverse reactions produced by narcotics may obscure the clinical course of patients with head injuries. Meperidine must be used with extreme caution and only if its use is deemed essential in such patients.

I.V.: If necessary, meperidine may be given i.v., but the injection should be given very slowly, preferably in the form of diluted solution. Increased incidence of adverse reaction such as severe respiratory depression, apnea, hypotension, peripheral circulatory collapse, and cardiac arrest have occurred with rapid i.v. injection of narcotic analgesics, including meperidine. Meperidine should not be administered i.v. without the immediate availability of a narcotic antagonist and the facilities for assisted or controlled respiration. The patients should be lying down when meperidine is given parenterally, especially i.v.

Asthma and Other Respiratory Conditions: Meperidine should be used with extreme caution in the following patients who are: having an acute asthmatic attack, have chronic obstructive pulmonary disease or cor pulmonale, have a substantially decreased respiratory reserve, and have pre-existing respiratory depression, hypoxia, or hypercapnia. Even usual therapeutic doses of narcotics may decrease respiratory drive while simultaneously increasing airway resistance to the point of apnea in such patients.

Hypotensive Effect: Severe hypotension in the postoperative patient or any individual whose ability to maintain blood pressure has already been compromised by a depleted blood volume or the administration of drugs such as the phenothiazines or certain anesthetics may result from the administration of meperidine.

Occupational Hazards: Ambulatory Patients: The mental and/or physical abilities required for the performance of potentially hazardous tasks such as driving a car or operating machinery may be impaired by meperidine. The patient should be cautioned accordingly. Like other narcotics, meperidine may produce orthostatic hypotension in ambulatory patients.

Pregnancy: Meperidine should not be used in pregnant women prior to the labor period, unless the potential benefits outweigh the possible hazards. Safe use in pregnancy prior to labor has not been established relative to possible adverse effects on fetal development. Therefore when meperidine is used as an obstetrical analgesic, it crosses the placental barrier and respiratory depression or psychophysiologic functions can be produced in the newborn; resuscitation may be required (see Overdose: Symptoms and Treatment).

Lactation: Meperidine appears in the milk of nursing mothers given the drug.

Precautions: Supraventricular Tachycardias: Meperidine should be used with caution in patients with atrial flutter and other supraventricular tachycardias due to possible vagolytic action. This action may produce a significant increase in the ventricular response rate.

Convulsions: Meperidine may aggravate pre-existing convulsions in patients with convulsive disorders. Convulsions may occur in individuals without a history of convulsive disorders if dosage is escalated substantially above recommended levels because of tolerance development.

Acute Abdominal Conditions: In the case of patients with acute abdominal conditions, the administration of meperidine or other narcotics may obscure the diagnosis or clinical course.

Special Risk Patients: Elderly or debilitated patients, and those with severe impairment of hepatic or renal function, hypothyroidism, Addison's disease and prostatic hypertrophy or urethral stricture should be given meperidine with caution and the initial dose should be reduced.

Incompatibilities: Solutions of meperidine are chemically incompatible with aminophylline, barbiturates, heparin, iodines, methiallin, phenytoin, sodium bicarbonate, sulfadiazine and sulfisoxazole.

Adverse Effects: As with other narcotic analgesics, the major hazards of meperidine are respiratory depression and, to a lesser degree, circulatory depression; respiratory arrest, shock, and cardiac arrest have occurred. Lightheadedness, dizziness, sedation, nausea, vomiting, and sweating are among the most frequently observed adverse reactions. These effects seem to be more prominent in ambulatory patients and in those who are not experiencing severe pain. Lower doses are advisable in such individuals. Some adverse reactions in ambulatory patients may be alleviated if the patient lies down.

Other adverse reactions include: CNS: euphoria, dysphoria, weakness, headache, agitation, tremor, severe convulsions, uncoordinated muscle movements, transient hallucinations and disorientation and visual disturbances. Inadvertent injection about a nerve trunk may result in sensory-motor paralysis which is usually, though not always, transitory.

Gastrointestinal: dry mouth, constipation, biliary tract spasm.

Cardiovascular: flushing of the face, tachycardia, bradycardia, palpitation, hypotension (see Warnings), syncope and phlebitis following i.v. injection.

Genitourinary: urinary retention.

Allergic: pruritus, urticaria, other skin rashes, wheal and flare over the vein with i.v. injection.

Others: pain at injection site; local tissue irritation and induration following s.c. injection, particularly when repeated; antidiuretic effect.

Overdose: Symptoms: Serious overdosage with meperidine is characterized by respiratory depression (a decrease in respiratory rate and/or tidal volume, Cheyne-Stokes respiration, cyanosis), extreme somnolence progressing to stupor or coma, skeletal muscle flaccidity, cold and clammy skin, and sometimes bradycardia and hypotension. In severe overdosage, particularly by the i.v. route, apnea, circulatory collapse, cardiac arrest, and death may occur.

Treatment: In parenteral overdosage, circulation should be maintained with infusions of plasma or suitable electrolyte solution and assisted respiration may be necessary. If consciousness is impaired and respiratory depressed, an opioid antagonist should be administered. Naloxone, a pure antagonist, is now the treatment of choice. Administer i.v. naloxone (e.g., 0.4 mg) which may be repeated at 2- to 3-minute intervals. For children, the initial dose recommended is 0.01 mg/kg of naloxone. In neonates, a more rapid and improved antagonism was noted after 0.02 mg/kg was administered. A response should be seen after 2 or 3 doses. Note the duration of action of naloxone is usually shorter than that of meperidine and thus the patient should be carefully observed for signs of CNS depression returning.

Note: In a individual physically dependent on opioids, the administration of the usual dose of an opioid antagonist will precipitate an acute withdrawal syndrome. The severity of this syndrome will depend on the degree of physical dependence and the dose of antagonist administered. The use of opioid antagonists in such individuals should be avoided if possible. If an opioid antagonist must be used to treat serious respiratory

Table I—Pethidine Injection BP

Opioid Analgesics: Approximate Analgesic Equivalences[a]

Drug	Equivalent Dose mg[b] (compared to morphine 10 mg i.m.) Parenteral	Oral	Duration of Action (hours)
Strong Opioid Agonists			
Morphine (single dose)	10	60	3-4
(chronic dose)	10	20-30[c]	3-4
Hydromorphone	1.5-2	6-7.5	2-4
Anileridine	25	75	2-3
Levorphanol	2	4	4-8
Meperidine[d]	75	300	1-3
Oxymorphone	1.5	5 (rectal)	3-4
Methadone[e]			
Heroin	5-8	10-15	3-4
Weak Opioid Agonists			
Codeine	120	200	3-4
Oxycodone	5-10	10-15	2-4
Propoxyphene	50	100	2-4
Mixed Agonist-Antagonists[f]			
Pentazocine	60	180	3-4
Nalbuphine	10		3-6
Butorphanol	2		3-4

[a]References: Cancer Pain: A Monograph on the Management of Cancer Pain, Health and Welfare Canada, 1984.
Foley, K.M., New Engl. J. Med. 313: 84-95, 1985.
Aronoff, G.M. and Evans, W.O., In: Evaluation and Treatment of Chronic Pain, 2nd Ed., G.M. Aronoff (Ed.), Williams and Wilkins, Baltimore, pp. 359-368, 1992.
Cherny, N.I. and Portenoy, R.K., In: Textbook of Pain, 3rd Ed., P.D. Wall and R. Melzack (Eds.), Churchill Livingstone, London, pp. 1437-1467, 1994.

[b]Most of these data were derived from single-dose, acute pain studies and should be considered an approximation for selection of doses when treating chronic pain.

[c]For acute pain, the oral dose of morphine is 6 times the injectable dose. However, for chronic dosing, this ratio becomes 2 or 3:1, possibly due to the accumulation of active metabolites.

[d]These drugs are not recommended for the management of chronic pain.

[e]Extremely variable equianalgesic dose. Patients should undergo personalized titration starting at an equivalent to 1/10 of the morphine dose.

[f]Mixed agonist-antagonists can precipitate withdrawal in patients on pure opioid agonists.

depression in the physically dependent patient, the antagonist should be administered with extreme care and only 10 to 20% of the usual initial dose administered.

Dosage: Pain Relief: If i.v. administration is required, dosage should be adjusted for the patient and made with repeated slow i.v. injections of fractional doses (e.g., 10 mg/mL) with the use of an infusion pump. When administered concomitantly with phenothiazines and tranquilizers, meperidine dose should be reduced.
Preoperative Medication: Repeated slow i.v. injections of fractional doses (e.g., 10 mg/mL) via an infusion pump.
Support of Anesthesia: Repeated slow i.v. injections of fractional doses (e.g., 10 mg/mL) with the use of an infusion pump or continuous i.v. infusion of a more dilute solution (e.g., 1 mg/mL) should be used and titrated to patient needs and operative procedure.
Opioid Analgesics: Approximate Analgesic Equivalences: See Table I (on previous page).

Information for the Patient: See Blue Section—Information for the Patient "Pethidine Injection BP".

Supplied: Each mL of sterile solution contains: meperidine HCl 10 mg. Nonmedicinal ingredients: sodium chloride and water for injection. Preservative-free. Rapiject prefilled, single-dose syringes of 50 mL. Store between 15 and 25°C, protected from light.

New Product 1998

PHARMORUBICIN® Ⓡ

Pharmacia & Upjohn

Epirubicin HCl

Antineoplastic

Pharmacology: The mechanism of action of epirubicin, although not completely elucidated, is mainly related to its ability to bind to nucleic acids by intercalation of the planar anthracycline nucleus with the DNA double helix.

Binding to cell membranes as well as to plasma proteins may also be involved. Cell culture studies have demonstrated rapid cell penetration and perinucleolar chromatin binding, rapid inhibition of mitotic activity, mutagenesis and chromosomal aberrations.

Animal studies have shown activity in a wide spectrum of experimental tumors, immunosuppression, mutagenic and carcinogenic properties in rodents, and a variety of toxic effects, including myelosuppression in all species and atrophy of the seminiferous tubules of testes in rats and dogs.

Data from different animal species and in vitro models have shown that epirubicin is less toxic, and in particular less cardiotoxic than doxorubicin.

At equally effective doses, epirubicin produces less severe nonhematologic side effects such as vomiting and mucositis, than doxorubicin.

Pharmacokinetics: Pharmacokinetic studies show an initial rapid elimination of the parent compound from plasma. The terminal half-life of elimination of the parent drug from plasma approximates 30 to 40 hours in man. Urinary excretion accounts for approximately 9 to 10% of the administered dose in 48 hours. Biliary excretion represents the major route of elimination, about 40% of the administered dose being recovered in the bile in 72 hours. The major metabolites that have been identified are epirubicinol (13-OH epirubicin) and glucuronides of epirubicin and epirubicinol.

The 4'-0-glucuronidation distinguishes epirubicin from doxorubicin and may account for the faster elimination of epirubicin and its reduced toxicity. Plasma levels of the main metabolite, the 13-OH derivative (epirubicinol) are consistently lower and virtually parallel to those of the unchanged drug.

Impairment of hepatic function results in higher plasma levels.

Distribution studies in the rat have shown that epirubicin does not appear to cross the blood-brain barrier.

Indications: Epirubicin has been used successfully as a single agent and also in combination with other chemotherapeutic agents to produce regression in a variety of tumor types such as lymphoma, lung, cancer of the breast, ovary and stomach.

It is recommended for the treatment of metastatic breast cancer, small cell lung cancer (both limited and extensive disease), advanced non-small cell lung cancer, non-Hodgkin's lymphoma, Hodgkin's disease, Stage III and IV (FIGO) ovarian carcinoma and metastatic and locally unresectable gastric carcinoma.

In clinical studies epirubicin has been safely used in combination with fluorouracil and cyclophosphamide, when considered appropriate by the physician, in the adjuvant treatment of early stage breast cancer (Stage II to III A).

Several other solid tumors have shown responsiveness to epirubicin but data are not yet sufficient to justify specific recommendations.

Contraindications: Therapy should not be started in patients who have marked myelosuppression induced by prior treatment with other antitumor agents or by radiotherapy. Therapy should not be initiated in patients with a history of severe cardiac disease. Preliminary data suggest that in such cases cardiac toxicity may occur at doses lower than the recommended cumulative limit.

Epirubicin treatment is generally contraindicated in patients who have received prior treatment with maximum recommended cumulative doses of doxorubicin, daunorubicin, mitoxantrone or mitomycin C.

Warnings: Caution: Epirubicin is a potent drug and should be used only by physicians experienced with cancer chemotherapeutic drugs (see Precautions). Blood counts and hepatic function tests should be performed regularly. Irreversible cardiac toxicity may occur as the cumulative dose approaches 1 000 mg/m². Cardiac monitoring is advised in those patients who have received mediastinal radiotherapy, other anthracycline or anthracene therapy, with pre-existing cardiac disease, or received prior epirubicin cumulative doses exceeding 650 mg/m².

Serious irreversible myocardial toxicity with resultant congestive heart failure and/or cardiomyopathy may be encountered as the cumulative dose approaches 1 000 mg/m². This toxicity may occur at lower cumulative doses in patients who have received prior anthracycline, mitomycin C or anthracene therapy and/or mediastinal radiotherapy and in those with a history or presence of cardiac disease.

Although uncommon, left ventricular failure may occur, particularly in patients who have received a cumulative dose that exceeds 1 000 mg/m², or a lower cumulative dose in patients who have received radiotherapy to the mediastinal area. The total dose administered to a patient should also take into account prior or concomitant therapy with related anthracyclines and anthracenes. Congestive heart failure and/or cardiomyopathy may be encountered several weeks after discontinuation of therapy.

Available evidence appears to indicate that cardiotoxicity is cumulative across members of the anthracycline and anthracene class of drugs. Patients who have previously received other anthracyclines or anthracenes are at particular risk for possible cardiotoxic effects of epirubicin at a lower total dose than previously untreated patients and, therefore, should be carefully monitored.

Anthracycline-induced cardiac failure is often resistant to currently available therapeutic and physical measures used for the treatment of cardiac failure. Early clinical diagnosis of drug-induced heart failure is essential. Treatment measures include digitalis, diuretics, peripheral vasodilators, low salt diet and bed rest. Severe cardiac toxicity may occur precipitously without antecedent ECG changes. An ECG, echocardiogram or radionuclide angiography (MUGA) performed at baseline and prior to each dose or course after a cumulative dose of 650 mg/m² of epirubicin is suggested. Transient ECG changes consisting of T-wave flattening, S-T depression and arrhythmias occurring up to 2 weeks after a dose or course of epirubicin are presently not considered indications for suspension of epirubicin therapy.

Epirubicin cardiomyopathy has been reported to be associated with a reduction of the ejection fraction as determined by radionuclide scan or echocardiography. None of these tests have yet consistently identified those individual patients that are approaching their maximally tolerated cumulative dose of epirubicin. If test results indicate a change in cardiac status associated with epirubicin therapy, the benefit of continued therapy must be carefully weighed against the risk of producing irreversible cardiac damage.

Careful hematologic monitoring is required since bone marrow depression, primarily of leukocytes may occur.

With the recommended dosage schedule (see Dosage) leukopenia is transient, reaching its nadir 10 to 14 days after treatment, with recovery usually occurring by the 21st day. White blood cell counts as low as 1 000/mm³ are to be expected during treatment. Red blood cell and platelet levels should be monitored since they may also be suppressed. Hematologic toxicity may require dose reduction or delay or suspension of therapy. Persistent myelosuppression may result in infection or hemorrhage.

Epirubicin may potentiate the toxicity of other anticancer therapies as well as radiation-induced toxicity to the myocardium, mucosa and skin.

Toxicity to recommended doses of epirubicin is enhanced by hepatic impairment. Therefore, prior to dosing, an evaluation of hepatic function, using conventional clinical laboratory tests such as AST, ALT, alkaline phosphatase and bilirubin determinations is recommended (see Dosage).

Epirubicin must not be administered by i.m. or s.c. injection.

Severe local tissue necrosis can occur if epirubicin is extravasated during i.v. administration. Extravasation may occur with or without an accompanying stinging or burning sensation even if blood returns well on aspiration of the infusion needle (see Dosage). If signs or symptoms of extravasation occur, the injection or infusion should be terminated immediately and restarted in another vein.

Epirubicin and related compounds have also been shown to have mutagenic and carcinogenic properties when tested in experimental models.

Epirubicin imparts a red coloration to the urine for 1 to 2 days after administration. Patients should be advised to expect this during active therapy.

Pregnancy: There is no conclusive information about epirubicin adversely affecting human fertility, or causing teratogenesis; however, at high doses epirubicin is embryotoxic and teratogenic in rats and embryotoxic and abortifacient in rabbits. Therefore women of childbearing potential should be advised to avoid pregnancy. If epirubicin is to be used during pregnancy, or if the patient becomes pregnant during therapy, the patient should be informed of the potential hazard to the fetus.

Lactation: Mothers should be advised not to breast-feed while undergoing chemotherapy with epirubicin.

Precautions: Initial treatment requires close observation of the patient and extensive laboratory monitoring.

As with other cytotoxic drugs, epirubicin may induce hyperuricemia secondary to rapid lysis of neoplastic cells. The physician should monitor the patient's serum chemistry, blood uric acid levels and be prepared to institute appropriate measures that might be necessary to control this problem.

Epirubicin is not an antimicrobial agent.

Adverse Effects: Dose limiting toxicities are myelosuppression and cardiotoxicity (see Warnings). Other reactions reported are: Cutaneous: Reversible partial or complete alopecia occurs in most patients. Alopecia and lack of beard growth in males are usually reversible. Recall of skin reaction associated with prior radiotherapy may occur.

Gastrointestinal: Acute nausea and vomiting occur frequently in most patients. This may be alleviated by antiemetic therapy. Mucositis (stomatitis and esophagitis) has been reported to occur 5 to 10 days after administration. This may lead to ulceration and represents a site of origin for severe infections. Diarrhea has been reported.

Local: Severe cellulitis, vesication, local pain and tissue necrosis can occur if epirubicin is extravasated during administration (see Dosage). Erythematous streaking and/or transient urticaria along the vein proximal to the site of administration may occur. Venous sclerosis may result from injection into small veins or repeated injection into the same vein.

Hematological: The occurrence of secondary acute myeloid leukemia with or without a preleukemic phase has been reported rarely in patients concurrently treated with doxorubicin in association with DNA-damaging antineoplastic agents. Such cases could have a short (1 to 3 years) latency period.

Other: Phlebitis, fever, and malaise have been reported following administration.

Overdose: Symptoms and Treatment: Acute overdosage may cause an acute myocardial dysfunction within 24 hours. Pronounced mucositis, leukopenia and thrombocytopenia could be observed within 7 to 14 days. Treatment of acute overdosage consists of hospitalization of the severely myelosuppressed patient, platelet and granulocyte transfusions, antibiotics and symptomatic treatment of mucositis.

Dosage: See Guidelines for Safe Preparation and Handling. A variety of dose schedules have been used. The following recommendations are for use as a single agent or in combination with other chemotherapeutic agents. Dosage is usually calculated on the basis of body surface area. The lower dose should be given to patients with inadequate marrow reserves due to old age, or prior therapy, or neoplastic marrow infiltration.

Carcinoma of the Breast: Single Agent: The most commonly used dosage schedule in metastatic breast cancer when employed as a single agent for adults is 75 to 90 mg/m² administered at 21-day intervals. The recommended single dose may be divided over 2 successive days. An alternative schedule of weekly doses of 12.5 to 25 mg/m² has been used and has been reported to produce less clinical toxicity than higher doses given every 3 weeks.

Pharmorubicin (cont'd)

Combination Therapy: In metastatic breast cancer epirubicin can be used in combination with cyclophosphamide and 5-fluorouracil (Fec), at a dose of 50 mg/m².

Clinical studies have shown that epirubicin 50 to 60 mg/m² given on Days 1 and 8 every 4 weeks in combination with fluorouracil and cyclophosphamide, when considered appropriate by the physician, can be used safely in the adjuvant treatment of early stage breast cancer (Stage II to IIIA).

Small Cell Lung Cancer: Single Agent: Epirubicin, as a single agent, can be used at 90 to 120 mg/m² administered every 3 weeks.

Combination Therapy: Epirubicin has been used in several different combinations with other antineoplastic agents at doses ranging from 50 to 90 mg/m². The following combinations have proven effective: epirubicin in combination with either cisplatin or ifosfamide; epirubicin with cyclophosphamide and vincristine (CEV); epirubicin with cyclophosphamide and etoposide (CEVP-16) and epirubicin with cisplatin and etoposide.

Nonsmall Cell Lung Cancer: Single Agent: Epirubicin, as a single agent, can be used at doses of 120 to 150 mg/m² administered day 1, every 3 to 4 weeks.

Combination Therapy: Epirubicin, in combination with etoposide, cisplatinum, mitomycin, vindesine and vinblastine, can be used at doses of 90 to 120 mg/m² administered day 1, every 3 to 4 weeks.

NonHodgkin's Lymphoma: Single Agent: Epirubicin, as a single agent, can be used at doses of 75 to 90 mg/m² at 21-day intervals.

Combination Therapy: Epirubicin at doses of 60 to 75 mg/m² can be used in combination with cyclophosphamide, vincristine and prednisone with or without bleomycin (replacing doxorubicin in the CHOP, CHOP-Bleo or BACOP regimens) for the treatment of newly diagnosed non-Hodgkin's lymphoma.

Hodgkin's Disease: Combination Therapy: Epirubicin, in combination with bleomycin, vinblastine and dacarbazine, can be used at 35 mg/m² every 2 weeks or 70 mg/m² every 3 to 4 weeks (replacing doxorubicin in the ABVD regimen).

Ovarian Cancer: Single Agent: In patients with prior therapy, epirubicin can be used as a single agent at doses of 50 to 90 mg/m² at 3- to 4-week intervals.

Combination Therapy: In patients with prior therapy, epirubicin can be used in combination at doses of 50 to 90 mg/m² at 3 to 4 week intervals. Epirubicin at doses of 50 to 90 mg/m² in combination with cisplatin and cyclophosphamide can be used for initial therapy of ovarian cancer repeated at 3 to 4 week intervals.

Gastric Cancer: Single Agent: Epirubicin, as a single agent can be used for the treatment of locally unresectable or metastatic gastric carcinoma, at doses of 75 to 100 mg/m².

Combination Therapy: Epirubicin at a dose of 80 mg/m² can be used in combination with fluorouracil for the treatment of locally unresectable or metastatic gastric carcinoma.

As epirubicin is excreted primarily by the biliary system, its dosage must be reduced in patients with impaired liver function indicated by elevated bilirubin values as follows: Serum bilirubin 1.2 to 3 mg/dL give ½ normal dose; >3 mg/dL give ¼ normal dose.

Renal impairment does not appear to call for dose reduction in view of the limited amount of epirubicin excreted by this route.

Care in the administration of epirubicin will reduce the chance of perivenous infiltration. It may also decrease the chance of local reactions such as urticaria and erythematous streaking. On i.v. administration extravasation may occur with or without an accompanying stinging or burning sensation even if blood returns well on aspiration of the infusion needle. If any signs or symptoms of extravasation have occurred, the injection or infusion should be immediately terminated and restarted in another vein.

If it is known or suspected that s.c. extravasation has occurred, the following steps are recommended: attempt aspiration of the infiltrated epirubicin solution; local intermittent application of ice for up to 3 days; elevation of the affected limb; close observation of the lesion; consultation with a plastic surgeon familiar with drug extravasation if local pain persists or skin changes progress after 3 to 4 days. If ulceration begins, early wide excision of the involved area should be considered.

Preparation of Solution: Skin reactions may occur. Caution in handling of the powder and preparation of the solution must be exercised. The use of gloves, eye protection, masks and protective clothing is recommended. If epirubicin powder or solution contacts the skin or mucosa, immediately wash thoroughly with soap and water. If it is spilled into the conjunctiva immediately flush with saline or water.

Pharmorubicin RDF 10 and 50 mg vials should be reconstituted with 5 and 25 mL respectively of sodium chloride injection USP (0.9%) to give a final concentration of 2 mg/mL epirubicin HCl. Bacteriostatic diluents are not recommended.

After adding the diluent, the vial should be shaken until the contents are dissolved. A slight suspension may form which will completely dissolve on further shaking. The vials are under negative pressure and care should be taken to avoid a pressure build-up. The reconstituted solution is stable for 24 hours at room temperature and 48 hours under refrigeration at 2 to 8°C. The solution should be protected from exposure to direct light and any unused solution should be discarded.

It is recommended that epirubicin be slowly administered into the tubing of a freely running i.v. infusion of sodium chloride injection USP (0.9%) or 5% dextrose injection USP. The tubing should be attached to a Butterfly needle or other suitable device and inserted preferably into a large vein. If possible, avoid veins over joints or in extremities with compromised venous or lymphatic drainage. The rate of administration is dependent on the size of the vein and the dosage. However, the dosage should be administered in not less than 3 to 5 minutes. Local erythematous streaking along the vein as well as facial flushing may be indicative of too rapid administration. A burning or stinging sensation may be indicative of perivenous infiltration and the infusion should be immediately terminated and restarted in another vein. Perivenous infiltration may occur painlessly.

Unless specific compatibility data are available, mixing epirubicin with other drugs is not recommended.

Epirubicin has been used concurrently with other approved chemotherapeutic agents. Evidence is available that combination chemotherapy is superior to single agents. The benefits and risks of such therapy continue to be elucidated.

Guidelines for Safe Preparation and Handling: 1. Preparation of antineoplastic solutions should be done in a vertical laminar flow hood (Biological Safety Cabinet—Class II).

2. Personnel preparing epirubicin solutions should wear PVC gloves, safety glasses and protective clothing such as disposable gowns and masks. If epirubicin solutions contact the skin or mucosa, the area should be washed with soap and water immediately.

3. Personnel regularly involved in the preparation and handling of antineoplastics should have blood examinations on a regular basis.

4. Directions for dispensing from Pharmorubicin PFS Pharmacy Bulk Vial: **The use of Pharmacy Bulk Vials is restricted to hospitals with a recognized i.v. admixture program. The Pharmacy Bulk Vial is intended for single puncture, multiple dispensing and for i.v. use only.**

Entry into the vial must be made with a suitable, sterile transfer or dispensing device such as the Econ-o-set Sterile Transfer System. Multiple use of a syringe with needle is not recommended since it may cause leakage as well as it may increase the potential for microbial and particulate matter contamination.

In a suitable work area such as a laminar flow hood, swab the vial stopper with an antiseptic solution. Following carefully the manufacturer's instructions, insert the device into the vial. Withdraw contents of the vial into sterile syringes using strict aseptic techniques. Dispensing from the Pharmacy Bulk Vial should be completed within 8 hours of **the initial entry** because of the potential for microbial contamination. Discard any unused portion. The contents of the syringes filled from the Pharmacy Bulk Vial should be used within 24 hours at room temperature or 48 hours when refrigerated **from the time of the initial entry into the Pharmacy Bulk Vial.**

Disposal: 1. Avoid contact with skin and inhalation of airborne particles by use of PVC gloves and disposable gowns and masks.

2. All needles, syringes, vials and other materials which have come in contact with epirubicin should be segregated in plastic bags, sealed and marked as hazardous waste. Incinerate at 1 000°C or higher. Sealed containers may explode if a tight seal exists.

3. If incineration is not available, epirubicin may be detoxified by adding sodium hypochlorite solution (household bleach) to the vial, in sufficient quantity to decolorize the epirubicin, care being taken to vent the vial to avoid a pressure build-up of the chlorine gas which is generated. Dispose of detoxified vials in a safe manner.

Needles, Syringes, Disposable and Nondisposable Equipment: Rinse equipment with an appropriate quantity of sodium hypochlorite solution. Discard the solution in the sewer system with running water and discard disposable equipment in a safe manner. Thoroughly wash nondisposable equipment with soap and water.

Spillage/Contamination: Wear gloves, mask, protective clothing. Treat spilled powder or liquid with sodium hypochlorite solution. Carefully absorb solution with gauze pads or towels, wash area with water and absorb with gauze or towels again and place in polyethylene bag; seal, double bag and mark as hazardous waste. Dispose of waste by incineration or by other methods approved for hazardous materials. Personnel involved in cleanup should wash with soap and water.

Supplied: Pharmorubicin PFS: Each mL of isotonic solution **without preservatives** contains: epirubicin HCl 2 mg, sodium chloride USP 9 mg and water for injection q.s. Also contains hydrochloric acid NF for pH adjustment. Single glass and polypropylene vials of 5, 25 and 100 mL. Store under refrigeration (2 to 8°C), protect from light and retain in carton until time of use. Discard unused solution.

Pharmorubicin RDF: 10 mg: Each vial of sterile, red-orange lyophilized powder contains: epirubicin HCl 10 mg. Also contains lactose NF 50 mg and methylparaben NF 2 mg (added to enhance dissolution). Single vials. Protect from light. Store at 15 to 30°C.

50 mg: Each vial of sterile, red-orange lyophilized powder contains: epirubicin HCl 50 mg. Also contains lactose NF 250 mg and methylparaben NF 10 mg (added to enhance dissolution). Single vials. Protect from light. Store at 15 to 30°C.

Reviewed 1999

PHAZYME™ Preparations
R & C

Simethicone

Antiflatulent

Indications: For relief of discomfort due to gastrointestinal gas, resulting from aerophagia, dyspepsia. Also, for relief of gas distress associated with other functional or organic conditions such as: diverticulosis, spastic colon, hyperacidity, postcholecystectomy syndrome, chronic cholecystitis, chronic pancreatitis, chronic alcoholism, elevated diaphragm in late pregnancy, aerophagia and aerophagic pseudoangina.

Dosage: Phazyme-95: 1 softgel before meals and at bedtime. Or as directed by a physician.

Phazyme-125: 1 softgel before meals and at bedtime. Or as directed by a physician.

Phazyme Liquid Adult Formula: 2 teaspoonfuls up to 4 times daily with meals and at bedtime. Do not exceed 8 teaspoonfuls/day unless directed by a physician.

Supplied: Phazyme-95: Each softgel contains: simethicone USP 95 mg. Nonmedicinal ingredients: FD&C yellow No. 6, gelatin, glycerin, hydrogenated vegetable oil, lecithin, methyl paraben, polysorbate 80, propylparaben, purified water, soybean oil, titanium dioxide, vegetable shortening and yellow wax. Gluten-, lactose- and sucrose-free. Bottles of 12 and 50.

Phazyme-125: Each softgel contains: simethicone USP 125 mg. Nonmedicinal ingredients: FD&C Red No. 40, gelatin, glycerin, hydrogenated vegetable oil, lecithin, methylparaben, polysorbate 80, propylparaben, purified water, soybean oil, titanium dioxide, vegetable shortening and yellow wax. Gluten-, lactose- and sucrose-free. Blister packs of 36.

Phazyme Liquid Adult Formula: Each 10 mL of cherry- or mint-flavored liquid contains: simethicone USP 125 mg. Nonmedicinal ingredients: diluted hydrochloric acid, flavor (cherry, mint), glycerin, hydroxyethyl cellulose, polyoxyl 40 stearate, purified bentonite, purified water, sodium benzoate, sodium saccharin and titanium dioxide. Gluten-, lactose- and sucrose-free. Bottles of 300 mL.

PHENAPHEN® with Codeine Ⓝ
Wyeth-Ayerst

ASA—Codeine Phosphate—Phenobarbital

Analgesic—Sedative

Supplied: Phenaphen No. 2 : Each black and yellow capsule, monogrammed "AHR" in white contains: ASA 325 mg, phenobarbital 16.2 mg and codeine phosphate 16.2 mg. Nonmedicinal ingredients: cornstarch and lactose. Empty capsule: D&C Yellow No. 10, EEC amaranth E123, FD&C Blue No. 1, FD&C Yellow No. 6, gelatin, silicon dioxide and sodium lauryl sulfate. Energy: <1 kJ (<1 kcal). Tartrazine-free. Bottles of 100.

Phenaphen No. 3 : Each black and green capsule, monogrammed "AYERST" in white contains: ASA 325 mg, phenobarbital 16.2 mg and codeine phosphate 32.4 mg. Nonmedicinal ingredients: cornstarch and lactose. Empty capsule: D&C Yellow No. 10, EEC amaranth E123, FD&C Blue No. 1, FD&C Green No. 3, FD&C Yellow No. 6, gelatin, silicon dioxide and sodium lauryl sulfate. Energy: <1 kJ (<1 kcal). Tartrazine-free. Bottles of 100 and 500.

Phenaphen No. 4 : Each green and white capsule, monogrammed "AYERST" in white contains: ASA 325 mg, phenobarbital 16.2 mg and codeine phosphate 64.8 mg. Nonmedicinal ingredients: cornstarch and lactose. Empty capsule: D&C Yellow No. 10, FD&C Green No. 3, FD&C Yellow No. 6, gelatin, silicon dioxide, sodium lauryl sulfate and titanium dioxide. Energy: <1 kJ (<1 kcal). Tartrazine-free. Bottles of 50.

PHENAZO™ ℞

ICN

Phenazopyridine HCl

Urinary Analgesic

Supplied: 100 mg: Each maroon, sugar-coated tablet, printed ICN P17 contains: phenazopyridine HCl 100 mg. Nonmedicinal ingredients: croscarmellose sodium, gelatin, lactose, methylcellulose, starch and stearic acid. Bottles of 100 and 500.

200 mg: Each maroon, sugar-coated tablet, printed ICN P18 contains: phenazopyridine HCl 200 mg. Nonmedicinal ingredients: croscarmellose sodium, gelatin, lactose, methylcellulose, starch and stearic acid. Bottles of 100 and 500.

PHENERGAN® EXPECTORANT with Codeine Ⓝ

Novartis Consumer Health

Promethazine HCl—Potassium Guaiacolsulfonate—Codeine Phosphate

Cough Therapy

Indications: For symptomatic relief of coughs due to colds and minor upper respiratory tract infections. To facilitate expectoration and control cough associated with inflamed mucosa and tenacious sputum which does not respond to products of lesser potency.

Contraindications: Sensitivity to any of the components, patients receiving MAO inhibitors. Not recommended for children below 2 years of age.

Precautions: Before prescribing medication to suppress or modify cough, it is important to ascertain that the underlying cause of the cough is identified, that modification of the cough does not increase the risk of clinical or physiologic complications, and that appropriate therapy for the primary disease is provided.

Children: In young children the respiratory centre is especially susceptible to the depressant action of narcotic cough suppressants. Benefit to risk ratio should be carefully considered, especially in children with respiratory embarrassment, e.g., croup. Estimation of dosage relative to the child's age and weight is of great importance.

Not to be administered to children under 2 years of age.

Pregnancy: Since codeine crosses the placental barrier, the use of Phenergan Expectorant with Codeine in pregnancy is not recommended.

As codeine may inhibit peristalsis, patients with chronic constipation should be given Phenergan Expectorant with Codeine only after weighing the potential therapeutic benefit against the hazards involved.

Preparations containing codeine may be habit forming.

Use products with caution in patients with hypertension, glaucoma, hyperthyroidism, cardiac or peripheral vascular disease or diabetes mellitus.

Occupational Hazards: Patients should be cautioned not to operate vehicles or hazardous machinery until their response to the drug has been determined. Since the depressant effects of antihistamines are additive to those of other drugs affecting the CNS, patients should be cautioned against drinking alcoholic beverages or taking hypnotics, sedatives, psychotherapeutic agents or other drugs with CNS depressant effects during antihistaminic therapy.

See also guaifenesin monograph.

Adverse Effects: Dryness of the mouth, blurring of vision, dizziness or mild stimulation and insomnia may occur. Very rare cases of leukopenia and only one case of agranulocytosis following prolonged therapy with promethazine at high dosages have been reported.

Dosage: Adults: 5 to 10 mL every 4 to 6 hours, or as prescribed. Children (over 2 years of age): 2.5 to 5 mL every 4 to 6 hours, or as prescribed.

Supplied: Each 5 mL of brown syrup contains: promethazine HCl 5.65 mg, potassium guaiacolsulfonate 40 mg and codeine phosphate 10 mg. Energy: 67.1 kJ (16.0 kcal)/5 mL. Alcohol: 7.5% v/v. Sucrose: 3.6 g/5 mL. Tartrazine-free. Bottles of 500 mL.

PHENERGAN® Injectable

Rhône-Poulenc Rorer

Promethazine HCl

Antihistamine

Pharmacology: Promethazine is an antihistamine with sedative, antiemetic and antispasmodic properties. In addition, it exerts local anesthetic effects and potentiates analgesics, anesthetics and other CNS depressants.

Indications: Allergic reactions: hay fever, urticaria, vasomotor rhinitis, skin allergies, poison ivy, insect bites; for the relief of pruritus due to various dermatologic conditions. Nausea and vomiting of various etiologies: motion sickness, radiation sickness, surgery, anesthesia and gastroenteritis, centrally acting emetics, metabolic or endocrine disorders.

It is also employed as a sedative, hypnotic and tranquilizer in insomnia, nervousness, anxiety, tension; as a local anesthetic for the relief of pruritus and mild burns; as a pre- and postoperative medication in obstetrical analgesia and as a potentiator of anesthetics.

Contraindications: Hypersensitivity to phenothiazines, in patients with glaucoma or those in a coma due to CNS depressants.

Promethazine is not recommended for infants below 2 years of age.

Precautions: Promethazine can potentiate CNS depressants such as barbiturates, narcotics, analgesics, and general anesthetics; therefore, dosages of these agents should be reduced when administered concomitantly with promethazine.

Because of its antiemetic properties, promethazine can mask symptoms of intestinal obstruction or intracranial pressure; thus it is necessary to establish the etiology of nausea and vomiting before using high doses of the drug.

Occupational Hazards: Patients should be warned that promethazine may cause drowsiness or dizziness; in such cases, abstain from driving an automobile or operating machinery until this effect has worn off.

The i.m. parenteral route is used most frequently; promethazine should be injected deeply into a large muscle mass.

The i.v. route is well tolerated; however, perivascular extravasation which could be painful should be avoided and speed of injection should not exceed 25 mg/minute; it is preferrable to inject through the tubing of a running infusion set that is known to be functioning satisfactorily.

Children: Use is not recommended in infants up to 2 years of age because of the possible absence or deficiency of detoxifying enzymes and inefficient renal function usually noted in this age group, and also because of its possible effect on sleep pattern.

Adverse Effects: Promethazine is a phenothiazine derivative. Although the likelihood of those side effects associated with antipsychotic phenothiazines occurring with promethazine seem to be minimal, the possibility exists, especially at higher doses or with prolonged administration.

Adverse reactions with promethazine are those usually seen during antihistamine therapy; they are generally mild and rarely necessitate discontinuation of treatment.

Most frequent side effects are drowsiness and certain anticholinergic effects: dryness of the mouth and more rarely, blurring of vision, dizziness and asthenia.

More rarely, the following effects on the cardiovascular system may be seen, at the beginning of promethazine parenteral therapy mainly: hypotension and tachycardia; occasionally it will be accompanied by nausea and vomiting.

The following have been reported with a rare incidence: paradoxical reactions characterized by hyperexcitability and/or nightmares, especially in children; allergic reactions, including contact dermatitis; photosensitivity; leukopenia.

Overdose: Symptoms: Sedation, respiratory depression, possible convulsions, coma.

Treatment: No specific antidote. After gastric lavage, treatment is symptomatic. If a pressor agent is necessary, norepinephrine may be used, **not** epinephrine as it may further depress blood pressure. Centrally acting emetics are ineffective because of the strong antiemetic action of promethazine.

Dosage (dosage expressed in terms of promethazine base—administered as promethazine HCl): The preferred route of administration is by deep i.m. injection.

When administered i.v., the injection rate should not exceed 1 mL (25 mg)/minute. Avoid perivascular extravasation. When possible, injection should be made into the tubing of a running infusion.

Do not administer intra-arterially because of the possibility of severe arteriospasm and resultant gangrene.

Adults: Antihistaminic (H_1 receptor): 25 mg; may be repeated within 2 hours if necessary.

Antiemetic: 12.5 to 25 mg every 4 to 6 hours as needed.

Sedative-hypnotic: 25 to 50 mg as needed.

Do not exceed 100 mg daily.

Children (over 2 years of age): Antiemetic: 0.25 to 0.5 mg/kg of body weight i.m. every 4 to 6 hours as needed.

Sedative-hypnotic and premedication: 0.5 to 1 mg/kg of body weight i.m. as needed.

Supplied: Each mL of solution contains: promethazine base 25 mg (as the hydrochloride). Nonmedicinal ingredients: ascorbic acid, potassium metabisulfite, sodium sulfite and water for injection. Ampuls of 2 mL, boxes of 10.

PHENERGAN® Preparations

Novartis Consumer Health

Promethazine HCl

Antihistamine

Pharmacology: Promethazine is an antihistamine with sedative, antiemetic and antispasmodic properties. In addition, it exerts local anesthetic effects and potentiates analgesics, anesthetics and other CNS depressants.

Indications: Allergic reactions: hay fever, urticaria, vasomotor rhinitis, skin allergies, poison ivy, insect bites; for the relief of pruritus due to various dermatologic conditions. Nausea and vomiting of various etiologies: motion sickness, radiation sickness, surgery, anesthesia and gastroenteritis, centrally acting emetics, metabolic or endocrine disorders.

It is also employed as a sedative, hypnotic and tranquilizer in insomnia, nervousness, anxiety, tension; as a local anesthetic for the relief of pruritus and mild burns; as a pre- and postoperative medication in obstetrical analgesia and as a potentiator of anesthetics.

Contraindications: Hypersensitivity to phenothiazines, in patients with glaucoma or those in a coma due to CNS depressants.

Promethazine is not recommended for infants below 2 years of age.

Precautions: Promethazine can potentiate CNS depressants such as barbiturates, narcotics, analgesics, and general anesthetics; therefore, dosages of these agents should be reduced when administered concomitantly with promethazine.

Because of its antiemetic properties, promethazine can mask symptoms of intestinal obstruction or intracranial pressure; thus it is necessary to establish the etiology of nausea and vomiting before using high doses of the drug.

Occupational Hazards: Patients should be warned that promethazine may cause drowsiness or dizziness; in such cases, abstain from driving an automobile or operating machinery until this effect has worn off.

Children: Use is not recommended in infants up to 2 years of age because of the possible absence or deficiency of detoxifying enzymes and inefficient renal function usually noted in this age group, and also because of its possible effect on sleep pattern.

Adverse Effects: Promethazine is a phenothiazine derivative. Although the likelihood of those side effects associated with antipsychotic phenothiazines occurring with promethazine seem to be minimal, the possibility exists, especially at higher doses or with prolonged administration.

Adverse reactions with promethazine are those usually seen during antihistamine therapy; they are generally mild and rarely necessitate discontinuation of treatment.

Most frequent side effects are drowsiness and certain anticholinergic effects: dryness of the mouth and more rarely, blurring of vision, dizziness and asthenia.

Phenergan Preparations (cont'd)

More rarely, the following effects on the cardiovascular system may be seen, at the beginning of promethazine parenteral therapy mainly: hypotension and tachycardia; occasionally it will be accompanied by nausea and vomiting.

The following have been reported with a rare incidence: paradoxical reactions characterized by hyperexcitability and/or nightmares, especially in children; allergic reactions, including contact dermatitis; photosensitivity; leukopenia.

Overdose: Symptoms: Sedation, respiratory depression, possible convulsions, coma.

Treatment: No specific antidote. After gastric lavage, treatment is symptomatic. If a pressor agent is necessary, norepinephrine may be used, **not** epinephrine as it may further depress blood pressure. Centrally acting emetics are ineffective because of the strong antiemetic action of promethazine.

It must be borne in mind that overdosage has been reported after use of the cream over extensive skin areas.

Dosage: Oral (dosage expressed in terms of promethazine HCl): Adults: Antihistaminic (H_1 receptor): 25 mg at bedtime as needed.
Antiemetic: 25 mg initially, then 25 mg every 4 to 6 hours as needed.
Sedative-hypnotic: 25 to 50 mg as needed.

Do not exceed 100 mg daily.

Geriatric patients may be more sensitive to the effects of the usual adult dose.

Children (over 2 years of age): Antihistaminic (H_1 receptor): 0.125 mg/kg of body weight every 4 to 6 hours or 0.5 mg/kg of body weight at bedtime as needed; or 5 to 10 mg 3 times a day or 25 mg at bedtime as needed.
Antiemetic: 0.25 to 0.5 mg/kg of body weight every 4 to 6 hours as needed; or 25 mg every 4 to 6 hours as needed.
Sedative-hypnotic: 0.5 to 1 mg/kg of body weight as needed or 25 mg as needed.

Not recommended for use in infants before 2 years of age.

Topical: Apply 2 or 3 times a day to affected area. Avoid application to extensive skin areas. Do not exceed 10% of body surface.

Supplied: Cream: Each tube contains: promethazine base 2% in a scented, nongreasy water miscible base. Nonmedicinal ingredients: Fragrance, glyceryl monostearate, lanolin, methylparaben, propylparaben, stearyl alcohol, stearic acid, triethanolamine and water. Tubes of 30 g.

Tablets: Each tablet contains: promethazine HCl 25 mg (brown, coated) or 50 mg (blue, coated). Nonmedicinal ingredients: burnt umber, dibasic calcium phosphate, magnesium stearate, microcrystalline cellulose, polacrillin potassium and sodium oleate. Tartrazine-free. Bottles of 100.

PHENOBARBITAL ⊕

General Monograph, CPhA

see BARBITURATES

PHENOBARBITAL ⊕

Abbott

Anticonvulsant—Hypnotic—Sedative

Supplied: Each mL contains: phenobarbital 30 or 120 mg. Nonmedicinal ingredients: benzyl alcohol, hydrochloric acid, propylene glycol and water for injection. **Use cautiously in newborns.** Ampuls of 1 mL. Boxes of 50.

PHENYTOIN Ⓟ

General Monograph, CPhA

Diphenylhydantoin

Anticonvulsant

This monograph has been compiled by CPhA. It may contain information different from that approved by Therapeutic Products Programme, Health Canada, and the pharmaceutical manufacturers' approval has not been requested.

Pharmacology: Phenytoin is an anticonvulsant which elevates the seizure threshold in the motor cortex by limiting the posttetanic potentiation (PTP) of synaptic transmission. It exerts this effect by preventing the excessive accumulation of intracellular sodium during tetanic stimulation by either reducing the passive influx of sodium or increasing the efficiency of the sodium pump. By limiting PTP, phenytoin prevents the spread of seizure activity to adjacent cortical areas.

Phenytoin also possesses antiarrhythmic activity similar to that of quinidine and procainamide. It increases the conduction velocity of the AV node and Purkinje fibres especially when conduction has been depressed by digitalis glycosides. Phenytoin decreases the automaticity of cardiac tissue by prolonging the effective refractory period. It also decreases the force of cardiac contraction. It may produce hypotension following i.v. administration.

Phenytoin has little hypnotic activity.

Pharmacokinetics: Following oral administration, phenytoin is slowly absorbed from the gastrointestinal tract. Absorption may be variable and sometimes incomplete. The drug is slowly and erratically absorbed following i.m. administration due to precipitation of the drug at the injection site. Following absorption, the drug is rapidly distributed to all tissues. Peak serum drug concentrations are achieved between 3 and 12 hours after administration of an oral dose.

Phenytoin is greater than 90% protein bound. Free fraction may increase in patients with renal or hepatic failure and/or hypoalbuminemia. These patients are predisposed to toxicity.

The plasma half-life in man after oral phenytoin administration averages 22 hours, with a range of 7 to 42 hours. Time to steady state is highly variable, ranging from 1 to 5 weeks. Therapeutic drug concentrations can be obtained in 1 to 2 hours when the drug is administered intravenously. The clinically effective serum trough concentration is usually 40 to 80 μmol/L.

Phenytoin is metabolized in the liver to an inactive metabolite 5-(p-hydroxyphenyl)-5-phenylhydantoin (HPPH). This metabolite undergoes enterohepatic circulation. Approximately 60 to 75% of the daily dose of the drug is excreted in the urine as the glucuronide. Other minor metabolites also appear in the urine. In therapeutic doses, approximately 1% is excreted unchanged in the urine; in toxic doses, up to 10% of the ingested drug may be excreted unchanged by the kidneys.

Phenytoin kinetics are nonlinear and saturable, resulting in highly variable concentrations even with minor dosage changes. A small increase in dose may lead to a large increase in drug concentration as elimination becomes saturated.

Indications: Oral: Control of generalized tonic-clonic and complex partial seizures and in the treatment and prevention of seizures occurring during or following neurosurgery.
Parenteral: The treatment of status epilepticus and treatment and prevention of seizures occurring during or following neurosurgery.

Contraindications: Known hypersensitivity to hydantoin products. Because of its effect on ventricular automaticity, i.v. phenytoin is contraindicated in sinus bradycardia, sinoatrial block, second and third degree AV block, patients with Adams-Stokes syndrome.

Warnings: This drug must be administered slowly. I.V. administration should not exceed 50 mg/minute in adults. In neonates, the drug should be administered at a rate not exceeding 1 to 3 mg/kg/min. The response to phenytoin may be significantly altered by the concomitant use of other drugs (see Precautions, Drug Interactions).

Abrupt withdrawal of phenytoin in epileptic patients may precipitate seizures. When the need for dosage reduction, discontinuation, or substitution of other anticonvulsant medication arises, this should be done gradually. However, in the event of an allergic or hypersensitivity reaction, rapid initiation of alternative therapy may be necessary. In this case, alternative therapy should be an anticonvulsant drug not belonging to the hydantoin chemical class.

Severe cardiotoxic reactions and fatalities have been reported with atrial and ventricular conduction depression and ventricular fibrillation. Severe complications are most commonly encountered in elderly or gravely ill patients.

Phenytoin should be used with caution in patients with hypotension and severe myocardial insufficiency.

Hypotension is associated with rapid i.v. administration.

The i.m. route is not recommended for the treatment of status epilepticus since absorption of the drug may be erratic.

There have been a number of reports suggesting a relationship between phenytoin and the development of lymphadenopathy (local or generalized) including benign lymph node hyperplasia, pseudolymphoma, lymphoma, and Hodgkin's disease. Although a cause and effect relationship has not been established, the occurrence of lymphadenopathy indicates the need to differentiate such a condition from other types of lymph node pathology. Lymph node involvement may occur with or without symptoms and signs resembling serum sickness, e.g. fever, rash and liver involvement.

In all cases of lymphadenopathy, follow-up observation for an extended period is indicated and every effort should be made to achieve seizure control using alternative antiepileptic drugs.

Acute alcoholic intake may increase phenytoin serum levels while chronic use may decrease serum levels.

Pregnancy: The great majority of mothers on antiepileptic medication deliver normal infants. It is important to note that antiepileptic drugs should not be discontinued in patients in whom the drug is administered to prevent major seizures because of the strong possibility of precipitating status epilepticus with attendant hypoxia and threat to life. In individual cases where the severity and frequency of the seizure disorder are such that the removal of medication does not pose a serious threat to the patient, discontinuation of the drug may be considered prior to and during pregnancy, although it cannot be said with any confidence that even minor seizures do not pose some hazard to the developing embryo or fetus. The prescribing physician should weigh these considerations in treating or counseling epileptic women of childbearing potential.

In addition to reports of increased incidence of congenital malformations, such as cleft lip/palate and heart malformations in children of women receiving phenytoin and other antiepileptic drugs, there have been reports of fetal hydantoin syndrome. This consists of prenatal growth deficiency, microcephaly and mental deficiency in children born to mothers who have received phenytoin, barbiturates, alcohol, or trimethadione. However, these features are all interrelated and are frequently associated with intrauterine growth retardation from other causes.

There have been isolated reports of malignancies, including neuroblastoma, in children whose mothers received phenytoin during pregnancy.

An increase in seizure frequency during pregnancy occurs in a high proportion of patients, because of altered phenytoin absorption or metabolism. Periodic measurement of serum phenytoin levels is particularly valuable in the management of a pregnant epileptic patient as a guide to appropriate dosage adjustment; however, restoration of the original dosage will probably be indicated postpartum.

Neonatal coagulation defects have been reported within the first 24 hours in babies born to epileptic mothers receiving phenobarbital and/or phenytoin. Vitamin K has been shown to prevent or correct this defect and has been recommended to be given to the mother before delivery and to the neonate after birth.

Precautions: The liver is the chief site of biotransformation of phenytoin; patients with impaired liver function, elderly patients, or those who are gravely ill may be particularly susceptible to toxicity.

A small percentage of individuals who have been treated with phenytoin have been shown to metabolize the drug slowly. Slow metabolism may be due to limited enzyme availability and lack of induction; it appears to be genetically determined.

Phenytoin should be discontinued if a skin rash appears (see Warnings). If the rash is exfoliative, purpuric, or bullous or if lupus erythematosus, Stevens-Johnson syndrome or toxic epidermal necrolysis is suspected, use of this drug should not be resumed and alternative therapy should be considered (see Adverse Effects). If the rash is of a milder type (measles-like or scarlatiniform), therapy may be resumed after the rash has completely disappeared. If the rash recurs upon reinstitution of therapy, further phenytoin therapy is contraindicated. Patients should be instructed to call their physician if skin rash develops.

The importance of good dental hygiene should be stressed in order to minimize the development of gingival hyperplasia and its complications.

Hyperglycemia, resulting from the drug's inhibitory effects on insulin release, has been reported. Phenytoin may also raise the serum glucose level in diabetic patients.

Osteomalacia has been associated with phenytoin therapy and is considered to be due to phenytoin's interference with vitamin D metabolism.

Phenytoin is not indicated for seizures due to hypoglycemic or other metabolic causes.

Phenytoin is not effective for and may worsen absence (petit mal) seizures. If tonic-clonic (grand mal) and absence (petit mal) seizures are present, combined drug therapy is needed.

Each injection of i.v. phenytoin sodium should be followed by an injection of sterile saline through the same needle or i.v. catheter to avoid local venous irritation due to the alkalinity of the solution. Continuous infusion should be avoided.

Soft tissue irritation and inflammation has occurred at the site of injection with and without extravasation of i.v. phenytoin. Soft tissue irritation varying from slight tenderness to extensive necrosis and sloughing has been noted. s.c. or perivascular injection should be avoided.

Serum levels of phenytoin sustained above the optimal range may produce confusional states referred to as delirium, psychosis, or encephalopathy, or rarely, irreversible cerebellar dysfunction. Accordingly, at the first sign of acute toxicity, plasma level determinations are recommended. Dose reduction of phenytoin therapy is indicated if plasma levels are excessive; if symptoms persist, termination is recommended (see Warnings).

Patients should be cautioned about the use of other drugs or alcoholic beverages without first seeking the physician's advice.

Do not use capsules which are discolored.

Drug Interactions: There are many drugs which may increase or decrease phenytoin levels or which phenytoin may affect. The most commonly occurring drug interactions are listed below (see also Drug Interactions table in the Clin-Info section).

When adding or deleting phenytoin from a patient's therapeutic regimen, pharmacotherapy must be monitored closely as dosage adjustment may be necessary. Serum level determinations of each drug are especially helpful when possible drug interactions are suspected.

Drugs which may increase phenytoin serum levels include: amiodarone, chloramphenicol, cimetidine, disulfiram, erythromycin, fluconazole, fluoxetine, isoniazid, ketoconazole, methylphenidate, omeprazole, phenylbutazone, salicylates, sulfonamides, trazodone, warfarin and acute alcohol ingestion.

Drugs which may decrease phenytoin levels include: carbamazepine, chronic alcohol abuse, diazoxide, rifampin and theophylline.

Drugs which may either increase or decrease phenytoin serum levels include: phenobarbital, valproic acid, and sodium valproate. Similarly, the effect of phenytoin on phenobarbital, valproic acid and sodium valproate serum levels is unpredictable.

Drugs whose efficacy is impaired by phenytoin include: corticosteroids, diazoxide, digitalis glycosides, doxycycline, estrogens, furosemide, levodopa, methadone, oral contraceptives, quinidine, theophylline, vitamin D and warfarin.

Administration of phenytoin with sulcralfate, enteral feeds, antacids or calcium preparations should be separated by at least 3 hours to prevent a decrease in phenytoin absorption.

Concurrent use of i.v. phenytoin with lidocaine or propranolol may produce additive cardiac depressant effects.

Although not a true drug interaction, tricyclic antidepressants may precipitate seizures in susceptible patients and phenytoin dosage may need to be adjusted.

Drug-Laboratory Test Interactions: Phenytoin may produce lower than normal values for dexamethasone or metyrapone tests. Phenytoin may cause increased serum levels of glucose, alkaline phosphatase, and gamma glutamyl transpeptidase (GGT).

Pregnancy: See Warnings.

Lactation: If maternal levels are kept within therapeutic range, there is little risk of drug accumulation in the infant.

Adverse Effects: Cardiovascular: Severe cardiotoxic reactions and fatalities have been reported with atrial and ventricular conduction depression and ventricular fibrillation. Severe complications are most commonly encountered in elderly or gravely ill patients.

The most notable signs of toxicity associated with the i.v. use of this drug are cardiovascular collapse and/or CNS depression. Hypotension does occur when the drug is administered rapidly by the i.v. route. The rate of administration is very important; it should not exceed 50 mg/minute in adults, and 1 to 3 mg/kg/min in neonates. At this rate, toxicity should be minimized.

CNS: nystagmus, ataxia, slurred speech, decreased coordination and mental confusion. These are usually related to increased drug serum concentrations. Dizziness, insomnia, transient nervousness, motor twitching and headache have also been observed. There have also been rare reports of phenytoin induced dyskinesias, including chorea, dystonia and tremor, similar to those induced by phenothiazine and other neuroleptic drugs.

A predominantly sensory peripheral polyneuropathy has been observed in patients receiving long-term phenytoin therapy.

Connective Tissue: gingival hyperplasia, coarsening of the facial features, enlargement of the lips, systemic lupus erythematosus, hypertrichosis and Peyronie's disease.

Dermatological: scarlatiniform or morbilliform rashes sometimes accompanied by fever. Other more serious reactions which may be fatal have included bullous, exfoliative or purpuric dermatitis, lupus erythematosus, Stevens-Johnson syndrome and toxic epidermal necrolysis (see Precautions).

Gastrointestinal: nausea, vomiting, and constipation.

Hematological: thrombocytopenia, leukopenia, granulocytopenia, agranulocytosis, and pancytopenia with or without bone marrow suppression. Some reactions have been fatal. While macrocytosis and megaloblastic anemia have occurred, these conditions usually respond to folic acid therapy. Lymphadenopathy including benign lymph node hyperplasia, pseudolymphoma, lymphoma, and Hodgkin's disease have been reported (see Warnings).

Injection Site: Local irritation, inflammation, tenderness, necrosis, and sloughing have been reported with or without extravasation of i.v. phenytoin.

Other: Periarteritis nodosa, toxic hepatitis, liver damage, and immunoglobulin abnormalities may occur.

Overdose: Symptoms: The lethal dose in children is not known. The lethal dose in adults is estimated to be 2 to 5 g. The initial symptoms are nystagmus, ataxia and dysarthria. Other signs are tremor, hyperflexia, lethargy, slurred speech, nausea and vomiting. The patient may become comatose and hypotensive. Death is due to respiratory and circulatory depression.

There are marked variations among individuals with respect to phenytoin plasma levels where toxicity may occur. Nystagmus on lateral gaze usually appears at 80 μmol/L, ataxia at 119 μmol/L, dysarthria and lethargy appear when the plasma concentration is over 159 μmol/L, but as high a concentration as 198 μmol/L has been reported without evidence of toxicity. As much as 25 times the therapeutic dose has been taken resulting in a serum concentration of greater than 396 μmol/L with the achievement of complete recovery.

Treatment: The adequacy of the respiratory and circulatory systems should be carefully observed and appropriate supportive measures employed. Monitor ECG, serum levels and blood glucose. Empty stomach. Follow with activated charcoal and a cathartic. As phenytoin undergoes enterohepatic circulation and can form concretions which may remain in the gastrointestinal tract after initial stomach emptying, administration of activated charcoal should be repeated. Forced diuresis, hemodialysis, peritoneal dialysis, charcoal hemoperfusion, exchange transfusion and plasmapheresis are thought to be of no value.

In acute overdosage the possibility of other CNS depressants, including alcohol, should be borne in mind.

Dosage: Phenytoin and its sodium salt are administered orally, often in combination with phenobarbital or other anticonvulsant agents; however, monotherapy is preferred. In most adults, phenytoin may be administered as a once daily dose. Suspensions and chewable tablets are not generally recommended for once-a-day dosing. The sodium salt of phenytoin may be administered by direct i.v. injection for the initial treatment of status epilepticus and for prophylaxis of seizures in neurosurgery.

Serum concentrations should be monitored when switching a patient from the sodium salt to the free acid form.

Phenytoin sodium 100 mg is approximately equivalent to phenytoin acid 92 mg. This difference in phenytoin content should be considered when the dosage form is changed.

Oral: Individualize dosage to provide maximum benefit. In some cases, serum blood concentration determinations may be necessary for optimal dosage adjustments—the clinically effective serum concentration is usually in the range of 40 to 80 μmol/L. Serum blood level determinations are especially helpful when possible drug interactions or poor adherence to prescribed therapy are suspected. With recommended dosage, a period of 7 to 10 days may be required to achieve therapeutic blood concentrations and changes in dosage (increase or decrease) should generally not be carried out at intervals shorter than 7 to 10 days. A small increase in dose can result in a disproportionate increase in serum concentration and possible toxicity.

Adults: Patients who have received no previous treatment may be started on 100 mg of phenytoin 3 times daily. For most adults a satisfactory maintenance dose will be 300 to 400 mg daily; however, maintenance doses of up to 600 mg may be required. Clinical studies with phenytoin have indicated that both single and divided dosage schedules demonstrate similar rates of absorption and equilibrium concentrations in adults. This means that a patient stabilized with 100 mg doses 3 times daily by mouth may respond to the more convenient single daily dose of 300 mg. There has been no reported evidence of increased drug toxicity when single daily doses of 300 mg have been administered to patients previously receiving the same quantity in divided doses.

Children: Initially, 5 mg/kg/day in 2 or 3 equally divided doses with subsequent dosage individualized to a maximum of 300 mg daily. The usual maintenance dose varies between 4 and 8 mg/kg. Children over 6 years old may require the minimum adult dose (300 mg/day).

Parenteral: Do not exceed a rate of 50 mg/minute, i.v. in adults and 1 to 3 mg/kg/min in neonates. Because of the unpredictable differences in absorption of phenytoin when given i.m., the i.v. route is preferred.

Parenteral phenytoin should be injected slowly and directly into a large vein through a large-gauge needle or i.v. catheter or administered as an intermittent infusion (minibag or piggyback). Each injection should be followed by an injection of sterile saline through the same needle or catheter to avoid local venous irritation due to alkalinity of the solution.

Continuous monitoring of the ECG and blood pressure is essential when administered by direct injection. The patient should be observed for signs of respiratory depression. Determination of phenytoin plasma levels is advised when using phenytoin in the management of status epilepticus and in the subsequent establishment of maintenance dosage.

Status Epilepticus: In adults, a loading dose of 10 to 15 mg/kg should be administered slowly i.v. at a rate not exceeding 50 mg/minute (this will require approximately 20 minutes in a 70 kg patient). The loading dose should be followed by maintenance doses of 100 mg orally or i.v. every 6 to 8 hours.

Children: Recent work in neonates and children has shown that absorption of phenytoin is unreliable after oral administration, but a loading dose of 15 to 20 mg/kg i.v. will usually produce plasma concentrations of phenytoin within the generally accepted therapeutic range (40 to 80 μmol/L). The drug should be injected slowly i.v. at a rate not exceeding 1 to 3 mg/kg/min.

Other measures, including concomitant administration of an i.v. benzodiazepine such as diazepam, or an i.v. short-acting barbiturate, will usually be necessary for rapid control of seizures because of the required slow rate of administration of phenytoin.

If administration of parenteral phenytoin does not terminate seizures, the use of other anticonvulsants, i.v. barbiturates, general anesthesia, and other appropriate measures should be considered.

I.M. administration should not be used in the treatment of status epilepticus because the attainment of peak plasma levels may require up to 24 hours.

Neurosurgery: Prophylactic dosage: 100 to 200 mg i.m. at approximately 4 hour intervals during surgery and continued during the postoperative period.

When i.m. administration is required for a patient previously stabilized orally, compensating dosage adjustments are necessary to maintain therapeutic plasma levels. An i.m. dose 50% greater than the oral dose is necessary to maintain these levels. When returned to oral administration, the dose should be reduced by 50% of the original oral dose for 1 week to prevent excessive plasma levels due to sustained release from i.m. tissue sites.

If the patient requires more than a week of i.m. phenytoin, alternative routes should be explored, such as gastric intubation. For time periods less than 1 week, the patient shifted back from i.m. administration should receive one half the original oral dose for the same period of time the patient received i.m. phenytoin. Monitoring plasma levels will help prevent a fall into the subtherapeutic range.

Reviewed 1999

PHENYTOIN SODIUM INJECTION, USP ℞

Abbott

Anticonvulsant

Supplied: Each mL of sterile, non-pyrogenic solution contains: phenytoin sodium 50 mg in a vehicle containing propylene glycol 40% and alcohol 10% in water for injection; with sodium hydroxide for pH adjustment (10.0 to 12.3 approximately). The solution contains no bacteriostat, or any antimicrobial agent, and is intended as a single-dose only; any unused portion should be discarded. Ampuls of 2 and 5 mL. Boxes of 25 and 50.

pHisoHex® ℞
Sanofi

Hexachlorophene

Antibacterial—Skin Cleanser

Description: pHisoHex is an antibacterial sudsing emulsion. It contains entsufon (sodium octylphenoxyethoxyethyl ether sulfonate), lanolin cholesterols, petrolatum and 3% hexachlorophene on a total weight basis. It is a colloidal dispersion of the active ingredients in a stable emulsion. Entsufon is a synthetic detergent which is effective in many kinds of water—hard or soft, cold or hot—and under acid as well as alkaline conditions.

Indications: A general antibacterial cleansing agent with bacteriostatic activity against staphylococci and other gram-positive bacteria. It is indicated for use as a surgical scrub and for thorough washing and cleansing of the skin, to reduce bacterial colonization and to prevent the spread of infection.

Contraindications: Do not use on burned or denuded skin; as an occlusive dressing, wet pack or lotion; as vaginal pack or tampon, on mucous membranes or for routine prophylactic total body bathing.

Should not be used on persons hypersensitive to any of its components nor on persons who have demonstrated primary light sensitivity to halogenated phenol derivatives because of the possibility of cross-sensitivity to hexachlorophene.

Precautions: Rinse thoroughly after use especially from sensitive areas such as the scrotum and perineum. Patients should be closely monitored and use should be immediately discontinued at the first sign of any of the symptoms described below.

Rapid absorption of hexachlorophene may occur with resultant toxic blood levels when preparations containing hexachlorophene are applied to skin lesions such as ichthyosis congenita, the dermatitis of Letterer-Siwe's syndrome, or other generalized dermatological conditions. Application to burns has also produced neurotoxicity and death. Detectable blood levels of hexachlorophene following absorption through intact skin have been found in subjects who regularly scrubbed with hexachlorophene 3%.

Hexachlorophene should be discontinued promptly if signs or symptoms of cerebral irritability occur.

Children: Infants, especially premature infants or those with dermatoses, are particularly susceptible to hexachlorophene absorption. Systemic toxicity may be manifested by signs of CNS stimulation (irritation) sometimes with convulsions.

Infants have developed dermatitis, irritability, generalized clonic muscular contractions and decerebrate rigidity following application of 6% hexachlorophene powder. Examinations of brain stems of these cases revealed vacuolization like that which can be produced in newborn experimental animals following repeated topical application of 3% hexachlorophene. Moreover, a histological study has shown a positive correlation between hexachlorophene baths and brain tissue lesions in premature infants who died of unrelated causes.

Intended for external use only. If swallowed, it is especially harmful to infants and children. Do not pour into measuring cups, medicine bottles, or similar containers since it may be mistaken for baby formula or other medication.

Suds that get into the eyes accidentally during washing should be rinsed out promptly and thoroughly with water.

Periorbital skin and head application should be performed while the patient is conscious, so that eye irritation can be reported immediately.

Topical exposure of neonatal rats to 3% hexachlorophene solution caused reduced fertility in 7-month-old males, due to inability to ejaculate.

Pregnancy: Hexachlorophene is embryo toxic and produces some teratogenic effects in rats. There are no adequate studies in pregnant women. Hexachlorophene should be used during pregnancy only if the potential benefits justify potential risk to the fetus.

Hexachlorophene has been shown to be teratogenic and embryotoxic in rats when given by mouth or instilled into the vagina in large doses. Administration of 500 mg/kg diet or 20 to 30 mg/kg body weight/day by gavage to rats caused some malformations (angulated ribs, cleft palate, micro- and anophthalmia) and reduction in litter size. Placental transfer and excretion in milk of hexachlorophene has been demonstrated in rats. In another study, doses of up to 50 mg/kg diet failed to produce any effects in 3 generations of rats. Hexachlorophene did not interfere with reproduction in hamsters.

Lactation: Placental transfer and excretion in milk of hexachlorophene has been demonstrated in rats. It is not known whether this drug is excreted in human milk. Because of the potential risk to newborn infants, a decision is required to discontinue nursing or to discontinue the drug.

Children: pHisoHex should not be used routinely for bathing infants (see Precautions). For premature infants, see Precautions.

Adverse Effects: Adverse reactions may include dermatitis and photosensitivity. Hexachlorophene is not irritating to the skin in ordinary concentrations and hypersensitivity reactions are rare. Primary light sensitivity occurs rarely but patients who have developed photo-allergy to other halogenated phenol derivatives may sometimes exhibit cross-sensitivity to hexachlorophene. If a sensitivity reaction occurs, discontinue use of the product and consult a physician.

Sensitive skin may react with redness and/or mild scaling or dryness, especially when exposed to excessive rubbing, heat or cold.

Use of skin products containing alcohol may decrease the antibacterial action of pHisoHex.

Overdose: Symptoms: The accidental ingestion of pHisoHex in amounts from 30 to 120 mL has caused anorexia, vomiting, abdominal cramps, diarrhea, dehydration, convulsions, hypotension and shock, and in several reported instances has been fatal.

Treatment: If patients are seen early, the stomach should be evacuated by emesis or gastric lavage. Olive oil or vegetable oil (60 mL) may then be given to delay absorption of hexachlorophene, followed by a saline cathartic to hasten removal. Treatment is symptomatic and supportive; i.v. fluids (5% dextrose in physiologic saline solution) may be given for dehydration. Correct any other electrolyte derangement. If marked hypotension occurs, vasopressor therapy is indicated. Consider the use of opiates if gastrointestinal symptoms (cramping, diarrhea) are severe. Scheduled medical or surgical procedures should be postponed until the patient's condition has been evaluated and stablized.

Animal Toxicity: The oral LD_{50} of hexachlorophene in male rats is 66 mg/kg body weight, in females 56 mg/kg body weight, and in weanling rats 120 mg/kg body weight. In suckling rats (10-days old), it is 9 mg/kg body weight.

Dosage: To be used for scrubbing and washing following suggested procedure to effect thorough cleansing.

Surgical Hand Scrub: Wet hands and forearms with water. Apply approximately 5 mL of pHisoHex over the hands and rub into a copious lather by adding small amounts of water. Spread suds over hands and forearms and scrub well with a wet brush for 3 minutes, paying particular attention to the nails and interdigital spaces. A separate nail cleaner may be used. Rinse thoroughly under running water.

Apply 5 mL to hands again and scrub as above for another 3 minutes. Rinse thoroughly with running water and dry.

For repeat surgical scrubs during the day, scrub thoroughly with the same amount of pHisoHex for 3 minutes only. Rinse thoroughly with running water and dry.

Bacteriostatic Cleansing: Wet hands with water. Dispense approximately 5 mL of pHisoHex into the palm, work up a lather with water and apply to area to be cleansed.

Rinse thoroughly after each washing.

Infant care: pHisoHex should not be used routinely for bathing infants (see Precautions).

Premature Infants: (see Precautions).

Use of baby skin products containing alcohol may decrease the antibacterial action of pHisoHex.

pHisoHex should not be dispensed from, or stored in, containers with ordinary metal parts. Plastic or a special type of stainless steel must be used or undesirable discoloration of the product or oxidation of metal may occur.

Supplied: Each mL of white to slightly off-white emulsion contains: hexachlorophene 3%. Nonmedicinal ingredients: lanolin chlolesterols, lauryl myristyl diethanolamide, methylcellulose, petrolatum (white), polyethylene glycol 400, polyethylene glycol 400 monostearate, sodium benzoate and sodium octylphenoxyethoxyethyl ether sulfonate in purified water. Bottles of 150 mL, 450 mL and 3.75 L.

PHOSPHATE-NOVARTIS
Novartis Pharmaceuticals

Sodium Acid Phosphate

Hypercalciuria—Electrolyte Replenisher

Indications: Hypercalciuria, electrolyte replenisher.

Contraindications: Do not use this medication if hyperphosphatemia is present or in the presence of severe impairment of renal function (less than 30% of normal).

Warnings: Use carefully in patients with cardiac disease treated with digitalis and in conditions where high potassium concentration may be encountered such as: adrenal insufficiency, acute dehydration, severe renal insufficiency, in conditions such as in severe burns, where high tissue breakdown is expected.

Because of the sodium content of this product, use carefully in the presence of cardiac failure, liver cirrhosis or severe hepatic disease, edema, hypernatremia, hypertension and toxemia of pregnancy.

Precautions: High phosphate intake may result in high serum concentrations which may be associated with an increase in extraskeletal calcification. If long-term therapy is prescribed, the following patient monitoring may be warranted: evaluation of renal function, and serum determination of the following ions: calcium, phosphorus, potassium, sodium.

Pregnancy: No well-controlled studies have been conducted in humans or in animals to determine the effect of phosphate during pregnancy. Nevertheless, the benefit of treatment should be considered in relation to the risks before instituting treatment in a pregnant woman.

Lactation: It is not known if phosphates are excreted in breast milk. However, problems in nursing infants have not been documented.

Drug Interactions: Concurrent use of sodium phosphates with glucocorticoids and related compounds may result in hypernatremia.

Androgens and anabolic steroids may increase the risk of edema.

Oxalates and phytates in food, and aluminum and/or magnesium antacids may bind phosphates and prevent absorption.

Calcium containing drugs (e.g. dietary supplement and antacids) may increase the risk of calcium deposition in soft tissues.

Drugs containing potassium and ACE inhibitors may produce hyperkalemia.

Thiazide diuretics taken with phosphates may cause or worsen renal damage.

Iron supplements will form insoluble complex with phosphates resulting in a decreased absorption of iron.

Phosphates by producing marked acidification of urine may accelerate excretion of mexiletine and decrease salicylate excretion. Potassium content in this drug may enhance quinidine's effects.

Vitamin D enhances phosphate absorption and may increase potential for hyperphosphatemia if taken with high doses of phosphate.

Adverse Effects: The following reactions have been reported: nausea, vomiting, stomach pain, laxative effect or diarrhea, and less frequently: fluid retention associated with swelling of feet and/or weight gain, hyperkalemia associated with confusion; tiredness or weakness; irregular or slow heartbeat; numbness or tingling around lips, hands or feet; unexplained anxiety; breathing problems, hypernatremia associated with confusion; convulsions; decrease in urine volume or in frequency of urination; fast heartbeat; headache or dizziness; increased thirst; hyperphosphatemia or hypocalcemic tetany associated with muscle cramps; numbness, tingling, pain, or weakness in hands or feet; shortness of breath or troubled breathing.

Overdose: Symptoms and Treatment: Withhold further administration of phosphates. Correct deficient serum electrolyte concentrations (such as that of calcium). Implement general supportive measures.

Dosage: Adults: Usual dosage for hypercalciuria and as an electrolyte replenisher: 1 tablet 2 times a day with meals. Adjust dose according to patient response.

Children: Half of the adult dose.

Take tablets only when dissolved in water. Use preferably 250 mL of diluent. Use only on the advice of a physician.

Do not take if renal function is impaired or if sodium (table salt) restriction has been prescribed.

Supplied: Each white, round, flat tablet, approximately 25 mm in diameter with a coarse surface, contains: phosphorus 500 mg from anhydrous sodium acid phosphate 1 936 mg. Also contains potassium 123 mg (3.1 mmol), sodium 469 mg (20.4 mmol), sucrose and calcium cyclamate. Energy: 9.9 kJ (2.38 kcal). Lactose-, paraben-, starch-, sulfite- and tartrazine-free. Tubes of 20. Store at 15 to 30°C, protect from heat and humidity.

(Shown in Product Recognition Section)

PHOSPHATES SOLUTION

Pharmascience

Sodium Phosphates

Laxative

Pharmacology: Depending on dosage, sodium phosphates oral solution is useful as a laxative in the relief of constipation, or as a bowel evacuant for a variety of diagnostic, surgical and therapeutic indications. Dibasic sodium phosphate and monobasic sodium phosphate are poorly absorbed from the gastrointestinal tract and retain water in the lumen of the intestine. When administered orally, they produce a bowel movement in 0.5 to 6 hours, depending on dosage.

Indications: As a laxative, for the relief of occasional constipation. As a purgative, for use as part of a bowel cleansing regimen in preparing the patient for surgery or for preparing the colon for x-ray or endoscopic examination.

Contraindications: Do not use this product in patients who have kidney disease or are on a sodium-restricted diet, unless directed by a physician.

Warnings: Do not exceed recommended dose unless directed by a physician. Serious side effects may occur from excessive dosage.

Do not use in patients with congenital megacolon or congestive heart failure, as hypernatremic dehydration may occur. Use with caution in patients with impaired renal function as hypocalcemia, hyperphosphatemia, hypernatremia and acidosis may occur.

Since the solution contains dibasic sodium phosphate and monobasic sodium phosphate, there is a risk of acute elevation of sodium concentration in the serum and consequent dehydration, particularly in children with megacolon. Additional fluids by mouth are recommended where appropriate.

In addition, elevated levels of serum phosphates and decreased levels of serum calcium have been reported in patients with renal disease (and with prolonged use).

Do not use a laxative product when nausea, vomiting, or abdominal pain is present unless directed by a physician. Patients who have noticed a sudden change in bowel habits that persists over a period of 2 weeks should consult a physician before using a laxative. Rectal bleeding or failure to have a bowel movement may indicate a serious condition. Laxative products should not be used longer than 1 week unless directed by a physician.

Precautions: Not recommended for pregnant or nursing women, or children under 5 years old, except on the advice of a physician.

Overdose: Symptoms: Overdosage with Phosphates solution may cause hypocalcemia, hyperphosphatemia, hypernatremia, hypernatremic dehydration and acidosis.

Treatment: Hypocalcemia, Hyperphosphatemia, Hypernatremia and Acidosis: Calcium, phosphate, chloride and sodium levels should be taken to restore electrolyte balance with appropriate fluid replacements.

Hypernatremic Dehydration: Calcium, phosphate, chloride and sodium levels should be carefully monitored. Promptly administer parenteral fluids with lower concentrations of sodium and chloride then extracellular fluid (40 to 50 mEq/L) and moderate concentration of potassium (20 to 30 mEq/L) administered at a rate of 3 000 to 4 000 mL/m² of body surface during the first 12 to 24 hours dependent on the severity of dehydration and the clinical response.

Dosage: Do not exceed single daily dosage (see Table I).

Table I—Phosphates Solution

Dosage		
Laxative	Adults and children 12 years and over	20 mL
	Children 10 to under 12 years	10 mL
	Children 5 to under 10 years	5 mL
Purgative	Adults Only	45 mL

Directions for Use: Best taken on an empty stomach; upon rising, 30 minutes before a meal, or at bedtime for overnight action. Dilute recommended dosage with 120 mL (½ glass) cool water. Drink, then follow with 240 mL (1 glass) cool water.

Supplied: Each 5 mL of ginger-lemon flavored solution contains: monobasic sodium phosphate 2.4 g and dibasic sodium phosphate 0.9 g in a stable, buffered, aqueous solution. Plastic bottles of 45 mL.

Reviewed 1999

PHOSPHOLINE IODIDE® Ⓟ

Wyeth-Ayerst

Echothiophate Iodide

Glaucoma Therapy

Supplied: Each package contains all material needed for dispensing 5 mL of sterile eyedrops of the strength indicated on the label. Nonmedicinal ingredients: acetic acid glacial, potassium acetate and sodium hydroxide; sterile diluent: hydrochloric acid, mannitol, sodium phosphate dibasic and water for injection. Alcohol-, gluten-, paraben-, sulfite- and tartrazine-free. Vials of 3 mg (package for 0.06%), 6.25 mg (package for 0.125%), 12.5 mg (package for 0.25%).

Store in refrigerator until reconstituted. The eyedrops prepared from the materials in the package are stable for about a month at room temperature, or 3 months if kept in the refrigerator. Protect from freezing.

PHOTOFRIN®

Ligand

Porfimer Sodium

Antineoplastic Photosensitizing Agent

Pharmacology: Pharmacodynamics: The cytotoxic and antitumor actions of porfimer sodium are light and oxygen dependent. Photodynamic therapy (PDT) with porfimer sodium is a 2 stage process. The first stage is the i.v. injection of porfimer sodium. Clearance from a variety of tissues occurs over 40 to 72 hours; but tumor, skin, and organs of the reticuloendothelial system (including liver and spleen) retain porfimer sodium for a longer period. Illumination with 630 nm wavelength laser light constitutes the second and final stage of therapy. Tumor selectivity in treatment occurs through a combination of selective retention of porfimer sodium and selective delivery of light. PDT-induced cytotoxicity may be due to free radical (superoxide or hydroxyl) generation and the production of singlet oxygen via energy transfer from light to triplet oxygen. Tumor death also occurs through ischemic necrosis secondary to vascular occlusion that appears to be partly mediated by thromboxane A_2 release. The laser treatment induces a photochemical, not a thermal effect.

Pharmacokinetics: A pharmacokinetic study was performed on 12 lung cancer patients given 2 mg/kg of porfimer sodium via the i.v. route. Samples of plasma were obtained up to 56 days post injection. Porfimer sodium was slowly cleared from the body with a mean apparent elimination half-life of 21.5 days (range 11 to 28 days).

No special precautions in renally impaired patients are necessary because excretion is primarily via the fecal route. The influence of impaired hepatic function on porfimer sodium disposition has not been evaluated.

Porfimer sodium was approximately 90% protein bound in human serum, studied in vitro. The binding was independent of concentration over the concentration range of 20 to 100 μg/mL.

Clinical Studies: Papillary Bladder Cancer: A Phase III, multicentre, randomized, open-label study was performed in patients with superficial papillary transitional cell carcinoma of the urinary bladder, stage TaG1 with frequently recurring disease or stages TaG2, T1G1-3. Following transurethral resection, patients were randomized to either single doses of porfimer sodium plus light or an observation control arm and the time to tumor recurrence was compared between groups. Efficacy analysis was performed on 30 patients. The median follow-up time for all randomized patients was 456 days. In the porfimer sodium group, 9 of 17 patients (53%) recurred compared with 10 of 13 patients (77%) in the observation group. The median time to tumor recurrence for patients who received porfimer sodium was 379 days versus 93 days for the observed group.

Esophageal Cancer: A Phase III, multicentre, randomized, open-label clinical trial was conducted comparing PDT with porfimer sodium and controlled uniform laser light versus thermal ablation therapy using the Nd:YAG laser for the removal of tumor mass and subsequent local palliation of dysphagia in 236 patients with partially obstructing esophageal carcinoma. Each course of PDT with porfimer sodium consisted of 1 injection of the drug followed by up to 2 laser light applications. A maximum of 3 courses of PDT with porfimer sodium was allowed. Repeat Nd:YAG laser sessions were given until maximal anticipated tumor debulking and palliation of dysphagia were achieved. Thus, a course of Nd:YAG laser therapy consisted of multiple laser application sessions. An unlimited number of Nd:YAG courses was permitted. Efficacy results after 1 course of therapy, based on all 236 randomized patients, are provided in Table I. Based on all courses, 9 PDT-treated patients and 2 Nd:YAG-treated patients had no visible evidence of tumor and were considered to be in complete response (CR). In 6 PDT-treated patients and 2 Nd:YAG-treated patients, CR was verified by pathology.

In addition, PDT with porfimer sodium was utilized in a Phase III, multicentre, single-arm study in 19 patients with completely obstructing esophageal carcinoma using the same schedule as above. Based on Month 1 assessments for Course 1 for all 19 patients enrolled, 42% of patients showed improvement in dysphagia grade, 32% of patients achieved partial objective tumor responses (PR), and median time to palliation failure was 30 days. Based on all courses, three patients achieved a complete tumor response; one of these was verified by pathology.

Indications: Papillary Bladder Cancer: Photodynamic therapy (PDT) with porfimer sodium is indicated following transurethral resection in patients with recurring superficial papillary bladder cancer as second-line treatment for thsoe who have failed a standard intravesical therapy.

Esophageal Cancer: Photodynamic therapy with porfimer sodium is indicated for the reduction of obstruction and palliation of dysphagia in patients with completely or partially obstructing esophageal cancer.

Contraindications: Patients with porphyria or in patients with known allergies to porphyrins.

Papillary Bladder Cancer: Patients with prior total bladder irradiation, or with a functional bladder capacity less than 200 mL, must not be treated with PDT to the bladder; there is the possibility of irreversible bladder contracture from increased fibrosis.

Patients with coexisting bladder tumors of stage greater than T1, who have invasive cancer, must not receive PDT.

Esophageal Cancer: PDT is contraindicated in patients with an existing tracheoesophageal or bronchoesophageal fistula.

Warnings: Caution: Porfimer sodium is an injectable photosensitizing drug for use in photodynamic therapy (PDT) for treatment of cancer. PDT is a photochemical process requiring specific lasers and fiber optics. PDT with porfimer sodium should only be used by physicians trained in the treatment of cancer using PDT with porfimer sodium and only in those facilities properly equipped for the procedure. Porfimer sodium will only be distributed to institutions with proper facilities and physicians with proper training. Porfimer sodium may cause residual photosensitivity for

Table I—Photofrin

Course 1 Efficacy Results in the Randomized Trial

	Month 1 Improvement in Dysphagia (% of Pts)	Month 1 Objective Tumor Response Rate (% of Pts)	Median TPF[a] (Days)	Mean No. of Treatment Endoscopies Per Patient[b]
PDT w/ Photofrin (n=118)	35%	32%[c] (CR 2%, PR[d] 30%)	34	2.1
Nd:YAG (n=118)	29%	20% (CR 0%, PR 20%)	42	2.8

[a] Time to Palliation Failure.

[b] Treatments not compared statistically.

[c] Statistically significant difference between PDT and Nd:YAG ($p < 0.05$).

[d] Partial response, based on change in smallest esophageal luminal diameter.

Photofrin (cont'd)

30 days or more resulting in erythema and blistering of the skin where it is exposed to sunlight or brightly focused indoor light (e.g., from examination lamps, operating room lamps, floodlights, halogen lamps, etc.).

If the esophageal tumor is eroding into the trachea or bronchial tree, the likelihood of tracheoesophageal or bronchoesophageal fistula resulting from treatment is sufficiently high that PDT is not recommended.

Tumors eroding into a major blood vessel should not be treated with PDT.

Precautions: All patients who receive porfimer sodium will be photosensitive for 30 days or more and must observe precautions to avoid exposure of eyes and skin to direct sunlight or brightly focused indoor light (from examination lamps, operating room lamps, floodlights, halogen lamps, etc.) UV sunscreens are of no value because photoactivation is caused by visible light. When outdoors, patients should wear dark sunglasses. The patient should **not** be kept in a completely darkened room during this period of time, since photobleaching due to exposure to low light levels such as ambient room light may be important in decreasing the period of photosensitivity. After 30 days, patients may expose a small area of skin (finger, dorsum of hand) to the sun for 5 minutes to test for residual photosensitivity. If significant erythema or blistering results, the patient should continue precautions against sun and bright light exposure for another 2 weeks before retesting the effects of limited sun exposure.

As a result of PDT treatment in esophageal cancer, patients may complain of substernal chest pain because of inflammatory responses within the area of treatment. Such pain may be of sufficient intensity to warrant the short-term prescription of opiate analgesics.

Drug Interactions: There is no clinical information concerning drug-drug interactions involving porfimer sodium. However, it is possible that concomitant use of other agents known to produce photosensitivity reactions (e.g., tetracyclines, sulfonamides, phenothiazines, sulfonylurea hypoglycemic agents, thiazide diuretics, and griseofulvin) would have the potential to increase the photosensitivity reaction.

Since the basic effects of PDT are thought to involve vasoconstriction and platelet activation and aggregation at the site of treatment, as well as the generation of active oxygen species, treatments which alter blood flow or availability of oxygen would be expected to affect the effectiveness of PDT. Data from animal models and in vitro tissue culture studies suggest the following: thromboxane A_2 receptor antagonists, thromboxane synthetase inhibitors, drugs which quench active oxygen species, and compounds which react with hydroxyl radicals, including dimethyl sulfoxide (DMSO), ethanol, formate, and mannitol, have been shown to decrease the effectiveness of PDT. Steroids administered 24 to 48 hours following PDT enhanced antitumor effects, whereas steroids administered concomitantly inhibited the PDT effect. Animal or in vitro studies involving combination therapy with PDT and standard antineoplastic agents (including doxorubicin, mitomycin C, and BCG for bladder cancer, and mitomycin C in a colon cancer cell line) resulted in an increase in effectiveness compared with single therapies. Similarly, combinations of PDT with porfimer sodium and different photosensitizers with different biodistribution properties (including tetraphenylporphine sulfonate) resulted in enhanced tumor eradication in a murine mammary tumor model.

Pregnancy: There are no adequate and well controlled studies in pregnant humans. Porfimer sodium should be used during pregnancy only if the potential benefit justifies the potential risk to the fetus. Women of childbearing potential should practice an effective method of contraception during therapy, and have a pretreatment pregnancy test performed.

Lactation: Whether the drug is excreted in human milk is unknown, therefore, women receiving porfimer sodium must not breast-feed.

Children: Safety and effectiveness in children have not been established.

Adverse Effects: The skin of all patients who receive porfimer sodium, will be photosensitive for 30 days or more (see Precautions). Photosensitivity reactions are avoidable through proper patient education. Reactions that do occur are most often limited to mild or moderate severity. The incidence of photosensitivity across all indications in clinical studies was 20%; this incidence was highest (40%) in patients with papillary bladder cancer whose activity was less impeded by their malignancy or concurrent illness. Ocular discomfort (sensitivity to sun, bright lights or car headlights) has also been reported.

The toxicities associated with PDT across all indications are primarily local, in the immediate area that received laser light, and sometimes extending into adjacent tissues. The local/regional reactions are consistent with an inflammatory reaction induced by the photodynamic effect (see below for specific reactions by indication). The only other known systemic reaction (besides photosensitivity) is constipation.

Papillary Bladder Cancer: Patients with papillary bladder cancer may develop transient (up to several weeks) irritative bladder symptoms after photodynamic therapy with porfimer sodium. This post-PDT response, thought to be due to inflammation, includes increased micturition frequency (60% of patients), hematuria (56%), dysuria (36%), urgency (32%) and suprapubic pain (20%). Additional common urinary symptoms observed were strangury (32%), genital edema (24%), urinary incontinence (20%) and nocturia (12%) and urinary tract infection (12%). Transient reduction in bladder capacity may occur; irreversible bladder contracture occurred in 20% of patients, a median of 99 days post PDT.

Additional adverse reactions which occurred in ≥10% of patients with papillary bladder cancer were anxiety (12%), insomnia (20%), peripheral edema (16%), nonspecific pain (12%), nausea (12%) and constipation (12%).

Esophageal Cancer: In a clinical trial involving patients with partially-obstructing esophageal cancer PDT with porfimer sodium was compared to surgical ablation with the Nd:YAG laser. Adverse events that occurred significantly more often in PDT-treated than in Nd:YAG-treated patients (besides photosensitivity) were fever (33% versus 10%, respectively), pleural effusion (28% versus 6%), respiratory insufficiency (10% versus 1%), anemia (26% versus 12%), and constipation (23% versus 9%). With the exception of anemia and respiratory insufficiency, these reactions were generally mild or moderate in severity and easily managed. Anemia was manageable by transfusion and was more common in patients with large tumors (>10 cm) and in tumors in the lower more vascular area of the esophagus. The etiology of respiratory insufficiency is unclear. Fever and pleural effusion, as well as pain (22% versus 20%), esophageal edema (6% versus 2%) and atrial fibrillation (8% versus 4%) are thought to be manifestations of a local/regional inflammatory reaction. Esophageal edema occurred more frequently when the tumor was located in the upper third of the esophagus; atrial fibrillation was more likely to occur when the tumor was in the middle of the esophagus.

Other adverse reactions which occurred commonly (>10% of either group of patients) in both the PDT group and the ND:YAG laser group were insomnia (14% versus 9%), abdominal pain (19% versus 11%), hematemesis (11% versus 7%), nausea (21% versus 15%), vomiting (16% versus 8%), dyspnea (18% versus 15%), pneumonia (16% versus 13%) and chest pain (23% versus 19%). Some of these adverse events reflect symptoms of esophageal cancer or concurrent conditions such as respiratory disease, although they may have been exacerbated by either treatment.

Overdose: Symptoms and Treatment: There is no information on overdosage situations involving porfimer sodium. Effects of overdosage on the duration of photosensitivity are unknown. Laser treatment should not be given if an overdose of porfimer sodium is administered. In the event of an overdose, patients should protect their eyes and skin from direct sunlight or bright indoor lights for 30 days. At this time, patients should test for residual photosensitivity (see Precautions). Porfimer sodium is not dialyzable.

Overdose of Laser Light Following Porfimer Sodium Injection: Papillary Bladder Cancer: Whole bladder photoradiation at light levels exceeding the recommended dose may significantly increase adverse urinary symptoms seen after PDT treatment, and may create irreversible bladder contracture in some patients.

Esophageal Cancer: There is no information on overdose of laser light following porfimer sodium injection in patients with esophageal carcinoma.

Dosage: Photodynamic therapy (PDT) with porfimer sodium is a 2 stage process requiring administration of both drug and light. Physicians should be trained in the safe and efficacious treatment of papillary bladder or esophageal cancer using photodynamic therapy with porfimer sodium and associated light delivery devices. The first stage of PDT is the i.v. injection of porfimer sodium at 2 mg/kg. The second stage of therapy is illumination with laser light 40 to 50 hours following injection with porfimer sodium. In patients with bladder cancer, no further doses of drug or light should be administered due to increased risk of bladder contracture; for esophageal cancer, patients may receive a second laser light application 96 to 120 hours after drug administration, and, if needed, up to 2 more courses of drug and light may be given, with each injection separated by a minimum of 30 days.

Porfimer Sodium Administration: Porfimer sodium should be reconstituted according to the directions given under Reconstitution, and administered as a single slow i.v. injection over 3 to 5 minutes at 2 mg/kg body weight. As with all i.v. injections, care should be taken to prevent extravasation at the injection site. If extravasation occurs, the area should be protected from light for a minimum of 30 days. There is no known benefit from injecting the extravasation site with another substance.

Photoactivation of Porfimer Sodium: Uniform and complete light delivery to the tumor mass is essential for activation of porfimer sodium. Light from a laser is delivered to the tumor via Optiguide Fiber Optic Diffusers, designed specifically for use in photodynamic therapy. While there are numerous lasers available for medical applications, the use of the Optiguide Fiber Optics for photoactivation of porfimer sodium requires an accepted laser operating at a wavelength of 630±3 nm, and producing a stable power output. The choice of the type and size of the fiber optic diffuser tip will depend on the tumor location and size.

Photoactivation of porfimer sodium is controlled by the total energy delivered to the tumor site. This is determined by the power delivered from the Optiguide Fiber Optic to the tumor site and the total treatment time.

The Optiguide Package insert provides details relating to the assembly, function and operation of the fiber optic light delivery system, including accepted laser light sources, and should be used in conjunction with the information presented for each indication below.

Superficial Papillary Bladder Cancer: Whole bladder treatment will require a total light delivery of 15 joules/cm², using the spherical diffuser. Approximately 40 to 50 hours after injection with porfimer sodium, the patient should be anesthetized and the bladder distended with a volume of saline or water sufficient to smooth mucosal folds, without compromising circulation. This "treatment volume" should be within 50 to 75% of the bladder's functional capacity, as measured by cystometrography.

Referring to the Optiguide Package Insert, attach the Optiguide Model DSPH spherical diffuser to an aceptable laser light source. To minimize the treatment time and thus the period of bladder distention, the total power output at the fiber optic tip should be at least 1.25 watts but less than the maximum power specification for the fiber optic.

The cystocope should be positioned securely at the bladder neck using clamps and metal rods, a gooseneck or similar stationary apparatus, and should not be moved once it is secured. The patient is placed in Trendelenberg position which relaxes the abdominal wall to facilitate centering the treatment tip. By adjusting the position of the patient, the cystoscope is aimed at the point where the posterior wall meets the dome, which is the maximum distance from the bladder neck. The trigone should not be visible. Correct placement of the fiber tip in the center of the bladder is essential to ensure uniform irradiation of the bladder, as areas which receive excessive amounts of light may result in pain or sensitivity post-treatment. Correct placement can be achieved by one of two methods:

a. Ultrasound Imaging: Ultrasound imaging is recommended to verify the mid-bladder placement of the fiber tip, as well as to monitor the bladder volume during treatment: (1) after the bladder is filled, an initial examination of the bladder is made in cross-sectional and longitudinal planes using an ultrasound apparatus. (2) The probe is then placed in the longitudinal position in the midline of the abdomen just above the symphysis pubis. Once the bladder filling has begun, the fluid can be easily detected as a black or clear space in the ultrasound image. The probe may have to be moved side to side (right to left or left to right) to locate the optimum long axis of the bladder once the bladder is filled. (3) Once the bladder has been filled, the cystocope can easily be imaged by ultrasound. (4) Centering of the cystoscope and laser fiber should be done using the linear distance calipers on the ultrasound equipment.

b. Sounding: To determine the midpoint of the bladder by sounding, a urethral catheter with one end plugged to prevent leakage is directed to the dome. The maximum distance is measured from the bladder neck to the point where the posterior bladder wall meets the dome. The spherical diffuser tip is passed through the port of the cystocope to the midpoint of the neck-dome measurement. Once the spherical diffuser tip is situated at the midpoint of the bladder, the catheter should be withdrawn.

Calculation of Treatment Time: The surface area of the bladder wall and the subsequent treatment time required to deliver a total light dose of 15 joules/cm² should be calculated knowing the bladder treatment volume (i.e., the volume instilled to distend the bladder) and the laser power output from the fiber optic tip, as follows:

$$\text{Treatment time (seconds)} = \frac{\text{Dose (joules/cm}^2\text{)}}{\text{Power Density}}$$

where:

$$\text{Light dose} = 15 \text{ joules/cm}^2$$

$$\text{Power Density} = \frac{\text{Power output (watts)}}{\text{Bladder surface area}}$$

$$\text{Bladder surface area} = 4.83 \times (\text{bladder treatment volume})^{2/3}$$

Urine production or irrigant leakage during treatment can change the bladder surface area and therefore the power density and the delivered light dose. The bladder volume, power output at the fiber tip and positioning of the fiber tip should be checked at the beginning, middle (particularly if the total treatment time is to exceed 45 minutes) and end, and at any time that bleeding is observed or significant changes in bladder volume, fiber power output or fiber tip position are suspected. Whenever treatment is interrupted, "pause" the laser output, ensuring that the original laser settings and elapsed treatment time are retained. If the bladder appears to be filling during the procedure, sufficient urine should be evacuated to restore the original volume. By the end of the preocedure, the cumulative laser light dose should total 15 ± 1 joules/cm².

The patient should remain under observation for 24 hours postcystoscopy or until the physician determines that he or she may be safely discharged.

No further courses of treatment with porfimer sodium or light should be used to treat superficial papillary bladder cancer, due to increased risk of bladder contracture.

Esophageal Cancer: Approximately 40 to 50 hours after porfimer sodium administration, light is delivered to the tumor by cylindrical Optiguide Fiber Optic Diffusers passed through the operating channel of an endoscope. The diffusers may be used either interstitially or intraluminally. Complete photoactivation of porfimer sodium for reduction of obstruction and palliation of dysphagia in patients with complete or partially obstructing esophageal cancer requires 300 joules of energy for each cm of tumor length. This is achieved by using appropriate power levels for a treatment time of 12 minutes, 30 seconds. Optiguide cylindrical diffusers are available in several lengths (refer to Optiguide Package Insert) and the choice of diffuser tip length depends on the length of the tumor. Diffuser length should be sized to avoid exposure of nonmalignant tissue to light and to prevent overlapping of previously treated malignant tissue. The power (mW) should be set to 400×length (cm) of diffuser to deliver 300 joules of energy per cm of tumor length in 12 minutes, 30 seconds.

Tumors with lengths that differ from available diffuser lengths may require multiple use of a single Optiguide Fiber Optic Diffuser or the use of 2 or more Optiguide Fiber Optic Diffusers of differing lengths. An exposure time of 12.5 minutes is used for each segment treated. Diffusers or combinations of diffusers should be selected to minimize patient treatment time. Examples of diffuser lengths/tumor sizes follow: See Table II.

Debridement of residua should be performed via endoscopy 2 days after light treatment. Patients with residual tumor may be retreated with laser light at the time of debridement at the same dose as used in the initial treatment, provided the second light dose is administered 96 to 120 hours after porfimer sodium injection.

Patients may receive a second course of PDT a minimum of 30 days after initial therapy; up to 3 courses of PDT (each injection separated by a minimum of 30 days) can be given. Before each course of treatment, patients should be evaluated for the presence of a tracheoesophageal or bronchoesophageal fistula (see Contraindications).

Reconstitution: Photofrin in the 75 or 15 mg vial should be reconstituted as follows with 5% Dextrose for injection, USP resulting in a final concentration of 2.5 mg porfimer sodium/mL. See Table III.

Table III—Photofrin

Reconstitution

Vial Size*	Volume of Diluent to be Added to Vial	Approximate Available Volume	Concentration
75 mg	31.8 mL	30.0 mL	2.5 mg/mL
15 mg	6.6 mL	6.0 mL	2.5 mg/mL

* Some excess added to allow complete recovery of quantity specified below.

Store reconstituted solutions at 2 to 8°C protected from light. Discard unused portion after 24 hours.

Incompatibilites: Photofrin should only be reconstituted with Dextrose 5% in water. Photofrin should not be mixed with other drugs in the same solution.

Special Instructions: Spills and Disposal: Spills of porfimer sodium should be wiped up with a damp cloth, at which time the wearing of rubber gloves and eye protection are recommended. Skin and eye contact should be avoided. All contaminated materials should be disposed of in a polyethylene bag in a manner consistent with local regulations.

Accidental Exposure: Porfimer sodium is neither a primary ocular irritant nor a primary dermal irritant. Because of its potential to induce photosensitivity, porfimer sodium might be an eye and/or skin irritant in the presence of bright light. It is important to avoid contact with the eyes and skin during preparation and/or administration. As with therapeutic overdosage, any accidentally exposed persons must be protected from bright light.

Information for the Patient: See Blue Section—Information for the Patient "Photofrin".

Supplied: Each vial contains: porfimer sodium 15 or 75 mg as a sterile freeze-dried cake or powder. Sodium hydroxide and/or hydrochloric acid are used in the manufacturing process to adjust pH. There are no antimicrobial preservatives or formulation excipients. Vials of 15 and 75 mg. Store unreconstituted porfimer sodium for injection at 15 to 25°C.

Reviewed 1997

Table II—Photofrin

Diffuser Lengths/Tumor Sizes

Tumor Length	Diffuser Model	Diffuser Length	Number of Segments	Power (mW)	Minutes per Segment	Total Time (Minutes)
1.0 cm	DCYL 10	1.0 cm	1	400	12.5	12.5
1.5 cm	DCYL 15	1.5 cm	1	600	12.5	12.5
2.0 cm	DCYL 10	1.0 cm	2	400	12.5	25.0
2.5 cm	DCYL 25	2.5 cm	1	1 000	12.5	12.5
3.0 cm	DCYL 15	1.5 cm	2	600	12.5	25.0
3.5 cm	DCYL 10	1.0 cm	2	400	12.5	25.0
	DCYL 25	2.5 cm		1 000		
4.0 cm	DCYL 15	1.5 cm	2	600	12.5	25.0
	DCYL 25	2.5 cm		1 000		

PHYLLOCONTIN® ℞
PHYLLOCONTIN®-350 ℞

Purdue Frederick

Aminophylline

Bronchodilator

Pharmacology: Aminophylline is the ethylenediamine salt of theophylline. The pharmacodynamics of Phyllocontin and Phyllocontin-350 tablets are a function of theophylline blood levels.

Theophylline is a xanthine structurally related to theobromine and caffeine. As with other xanthine derivatives, the precise mechanism of action of theophylline has not been determined. Theophylline stimulates the CNS and skeletal muscles, stimulates cardiac muscle, relaxes certain smooth muscles including those of the bronchi, produces diuresis, and causes an increase in gastric secretion.

Phyllocontin and Phyllocontin-350 tablets are sustained release tablets which produce peak blood levels of theophylline between 3 and 5 hours. Once the steady state level has been reached, the therapeutic blood levels persist for 12 hours.

Theophylline is usually readily absorbed following oral administration. The extent of absorption is negligibly influenced by food. Following absorption 55 to 65% of theophylline is reversibly bound to plasma protein. Theophylline is distributed in the extracellular fluids and uniformly to all tissues. The drug has a mean biological half-life of 5 hours in adults and 3.5 hours in children with great individual variability. Theophylline is metabolized in the liver. The major metabolites are 1,3-dimethyluric acid, 1-methyluric acid and 3-methylxanthine with only 7 to 13% excreted unchanged.

The enzymes involved in theophylline metabolism are unknown, but do not include xanthine oxidase. Serum uric acid concentrations are not increased during theophylline administration and the drug is not contraindicated in the presence of gout or allopurinol administration. Theophylline clearance is markedly increased in smokers, likely due to stimulation of the metabolizing enzymes.

Indications: Symptomatic treatment of reversible bronchoconstriction associated with bronchial asthma, chronic obstructive pulmonary emphysema, chronic bronchitis and related bronchospastic disorders.

Contraindications: Should not be administered to patients with hypersensitivity to xanthines or ethylenediamine; to patients with coronary artery disease where cardiac stimulation might prove harmful or to patients with peptic ulcer.

Warnings: These sustained release tablets are not appropriate for use in an emergency where rapid relief of bronchospasm is required.

Children: Children are very sensitive to xanthines; the margin of safety above therapeutic doses is small. **Not** presently recommended for children under 12 years of age, as a dosage schedule in this age group has not been established.

Precautions: There is a marked variation in blood levels achieved in different patients given the same dose of theophylline. High serum levels may occur in some patients receiving doses considered to be conventional. Overdosage may lead to serious side effects such as tachycardia, arrhythmias, seizures, vascular collapse and even death, and may occur without warning signs such as nausea and vomiting. The variability in blood levels is primarily due to differences in the rate of metabolism. Therefore, it is important to individualize the dosage regimen.

Ideally, all individuals should have serum theophylline levels measured and a theophylline half-life calculated which would enable doses and dosing regimens to be tailored to each patient to maintain a therapeutic level, to ensure optimal clinical response and to avoid toxicity. The incidence of toxicity increases at serum theophylline levels greater than 82.5 µmol/L (15 µg/mL) and levels above 110 µmol/L (20 µg/mL) are usually quite toxic in most patients (adults). Concurrent tea, coffee or cocoa administration may interfere with analytical results.

The equivalent content of theophylline anhydrous is the active ingredient which determines clinical response. If there is a change in the theophylline product and if it involves a change in the theophylline anhydrous equivalence the physician should adjust the dosage to avoid overdosage or underdosage.

Patients with Special Diseases and Conditions: Theophylline clearance is decreased, which may result in increased serum levels and resultant toxicity in patients: with impaired liver or kidney function; over 55 years of age, particularly males and those with chronic lung disease; with cardiac failure from any cause; with active influenza or other viral disease or after influenza immunization; with high carbohydrate, low protein diet; taking certain drugs (see Drug Interactions).

Laboratory monitoring of serum theophylline levels is especially appropriate in the above individuals in order to maintain the appropriate theophylline dosage.

Theophylline is known to stimulate gastric acid secretion and may also act as a local gastrointestinal irritant. Therefore, the drug should only be used with caution in patients with a history of peptic ulcer disease.

Theophylline may cause arrhythmia and/or worsen preexisting arrhythmia. Any significant change in rate and/or rhythm warrants monitoring and further investigation.

Many patients who require theophylline may exhibit tachycardia due to their underlying disease process so that the cause/effect relationship to elevated serum theophylline concentrations may not be appreciated.

Use with caution in patients with severe cardiac disease, severe hypoxemia, hypertension, hyperthyroidism, acute myocardial injury, cor pulmonale, congestive heart failure, liver disease, and in the elderly (especially males).

Phyllocontin (cont'd)

Drug Interactions: Theophylline pharmacokinetics are altered by the concurrent use of various drugs as listed in Table I.

Table I—Phyllocontin

Effect of Various Drugs on Theophylline Pharmacokinetics

Drug	Effect on Theophylline Clearance and Elimination Half-life
Cimetidine, propranolol, allopurinol, macrolide antibiotics (erythromycin, troleandomycin), quinolone antibacterials (ciprofloxacin, norfloxacin), oral contraceptives.	↑ t½, ↓ clearance
Alkalinizing agents	↑ t½, ↓ clearance
Influenza vaccine	↑ t½, clearance reported to be decreased or no change
Phenytoin, barbiturates, carbamazepine, isoproterenol, rifampin	↓ t½, ↑ clearance
Tobacco	↓ t½, ↑ clearance
Acidifying agents	↓ t½, ↑ clearance

Concurrent use of theophylline influences the actions of certain drugs (see Table II).

Table II—Phyllocontin

Influence of Theophylline on Various Drugs

Drug	Influence of Theophylline
Digitalis glycosides	↑ cardiac effect
Thiazides	↑ diuresis
Nephrotoxic drugs	↑ nephrotoxicity
Lithium	↑ ratio of lithium/creatinine clearance, thus a decrease in serum lithium levels
Sympathomimetic amines	↑ toxicity, ↑ CNS stimulation
Coumarin anticoagulants	↓ anticoagulant activity ↑ prothrombin and fibrinogen blood concentrations ↓ prothrombin time
Allopurinol	↓ antihyperuricemic action
Probenecid and pyrazolon derivatives	↓ uricosuric action

Pregnancy: Theophylline crosses the placental barrier and also passes freely into breast milk, where concentrations are similar to plasma levels. Safe use in pregnancy has not been established relative to possible adverse effects on fetal development, but neither have adverse effects on fetal development been established. Therefore, use of theophylline in pregnant women should be balanced against the risk of uncontrolled disease.

Adverse Effects: The most common adverse reactions are gastric irritation, nausea, vomiting, epigastric pain and tremor. These are usually early signs of toxicity; however, with high doses, ventricular arrhythmias or seizures may be the first signs to appear.

Adverse reactions include: Gastrointestinal: nausea, vomiting, epigastric pain, hematemesis, diarrhea, anorexia, intestinal bleeding and reactivation of peptic ulcer.

CNS: headache, irritability, restlessness, insomnia, twitching, convulsions and reflex hyperexcitability.

Cardiovascular: palpitation, tachycardia, hypotension, circulatory failure, ventricular arrhythmias, extrasystoles and flushing.

Renal: albuminuria, diuresis and hematuria.

Others: hyperglycemia, tachypnea and inappropriate ADH syndrome.

Overdose: Symptoms: Insomnia, restlessness, mild excitement or irritability, and rapid pulse are the early symptoms, which may progress to mild delirium.

Sensory disturbances such as tinnitus or flashes of light are common. Anorexia, nausea and vomiting are frequently early observations of theophylline overdosage.

Fever, diuresis, dehydration and extreme thirst may be seen. Severe poisoning results in bloody, syrup-like "coffee ground" vomitus, tremors, tonic extensor spasm interrupted by clonic convulsions, extrasystoles, quickened respiration, stupor and finally coma. Cardiovascular disorders and respiratory collapse leading to shock, cyanosis and death follow gross overdosages.

Treatment: If potential oral overdosage is established, and seizure has not occurred, induce vomiting. Administer a cathartic (this is particularly important when a sustained release preparation has been taken). Administer activated charcoal.

If the patient is having a seizure, establish an airway. Administer oxygen. Treat the seizure with i.v. diazepam, 100 to 300 µg/kg up to 10 mg. Monitor vital signs, maintain blood pressure and provide adequate hydration.

Post Seizure Coma: Maintain airway and oxygenation. If a result of oral medication, follow the above recommendations to prevent absorption of the drug. Intubation and lavage will have to be performed instead of inducing emesis, and the cathartic and charcoal will need to be introduced via a large bore gastric lavage tube. Continue to provide full supportive care and adequate hydration while waiting for the drug to be metabolized. In general, the drug is metabolized sufficiently rapidly so as not to warrant consideration of dialysis. However, if serum levels exceed 275 µmol/L (50 µg/mL) charcoal hemoperfusion may be indicated.

Dosage: Adults: The recommended initial dose is 225 to 350 mg every 12 hours (equivalent to 182.25 to 283.5 mg anhydrous theophylline).

Dosage adjustments should be based on the patient's clinical response and/or serum theophylline levels, with increases of ½ tablet per dose at 3 to 4 day intervals. Individual requirements vary considerably; therefore, the physician should be prepared to adjust each patient's dose. Doses greater than 1 125 mg/day should not be given unless serum theophylline levels are monitored. Monitoring serum theophylline levels is important, especially during dosage adjustment.

At steady state, Phyllocontin and Phyllocontin-350 tablets produce peak theophylline levels 3 to 5 hours after dosing. For serum levels to be most useful, it is important that the patient not have missed any doses during the previous 3 days. The optimum serum theophylline concentration is in the 44 to 110 µmol/L (8.0 to 20.0 µg/mL) range, depending on the severity of the condition. The incidence of adverse effects increases at levels greater than 82.5 µmol/L (15 µg/mL). In cases where it is not possible to monitor theophylline levels, patients should be closely observed for signs of toxicity.

Phyllocontin and Phyllocontin-350 tablets should not be chewed or crushed; they may be halved.

Information for the Patient: See Blue Section—Information for the Patient "Phyllocontin/Phyllocontin-350".

Supplied: Phyllocontin: Each sustained release, round, flat-faced, off-white, scored tablet, engraved P on one side and PF on the reverse, contains: aminophylline USP 225 mg (equivalent to anhydrous theophylline 182.25 mg). Nonmedicinal ingredients: cetostearyl alcohol, hydroxyethyl cellulose, magnesium stearate, natural color, povidone and talc. Sodium- and tartrazine-free. Bottles of 100 and 500.

Phyllocontin-350: Each sustained release, square, off-white, scored tablet, engraved PF on one side and P 350 on the reverse, contains: aminophylline USP 350 mg (equivalent to anhydrous theophylline 283.5 mg). Nonmedicinal ingredients: cetostearyl alcohol, hydroxyethyl cellulose, magnesium stearate, natural color, povidone and talc. Sodium- and tartrazine-free. Bottles of 100 and 500.

(Shown in Product Recognition Section)

PHYTONADIONE

General Monograph, CPhA

see VITAMIN K

PILOCARPINE HYDROCHLORIDE

Rivex Ophthalmics

Miotic—Cholinergic

Supplied: Each mL of sterile ophthalmic solution contains: pilocarpine HCl 1%, 2% or 4%. Nonmedicinal ingredients: benzalkonium chloride, edetate disodium, hydrochloric acid, hydroxypropyl methylcellulose, purified water, sodium hydroxide, sodium phosphate dibasic and sodium phosphate monobasic. Plastic squeeze bottles of 15 mL with controlled tip applicators.

PILOCARPINE HYDROCHLORIDE

Technilab

Miotic—Cholinergic

Supplied: Each mL of sterile ophthalmic solution contains: pilocarpine HCl 1%, 2% or 4% (weight/volume). Nonmedicinal ingredients: benzalkonium chloride, boric acid, hydroxypropyl methylcellulose, purified water, sodium chloride (for the 1% solution only) and sodium citrate. Plastic squeeze bottles of 15 mL with dropper tip. Store between 15 and 30°C. Protect from light. Keep this bottle tightly closed when not in use.

PILOPINE HS®

Alcon

Pilocarpine HCl

Topical Miotic

Supplied: Each tube of gel contains: pilocarpine HCl 4%. Preserved with benzalkonium Cl 0.008%. Nonmedicinal ingredients: carbomer 940, edetate disodium, hydrochloric acid, purified water and sodium hydroxide. Tubes of 5 g.

PIPORTIL L4®

Rhône-Poulenc Rorer

Pipotiazine Palmitate

Antipsychotic

Pharmacology: Pipotiazine palmitate is the palmitic ester of pipotiazine, a piperidine phenothiazine with antipsychotic properties and weak sedative activity with prolonged duration of action. The onset of action appears usually within the first 2 to 3 days after injection and the effects of the drug on psychotic symptoms are significant within 1 week. Improvement in symptomatology lasts from 3 to 6 weeks, but adequate control may frequently be maintained with one injection every 4 weeks. However, in view of the variations in individual response, careful supervision is required throughout treatment.

Pipotiazine has actions similar to those of other phenothiazines. Among the different phenothiazine derivatives, it appears to be less sedating and to have a weak propensity for causing hypotension or potentiating the effects of CNS depressants and anesthetics. However, it produces a high incidence of extra pyramidal reactions.

Indications: The maintenance treatment of chronic non-agitated schizophrenic patients.

Contraindications: Should not be administered in the presence of circulatory collapse, altered states of consciousness or comatose states, particularly when these are due to intoxication with central depressant drugs e.g., alcohol, hypnotics, narcotics. In severely depressed patients, in the presence of blood dyscrasias, liver disease, renal insufficiency, pheochromocytoma, or in patients with severe cardiovascular disorders or a history of hypersensitivity to phenothiazine derivatives.

It is not indicated for the management of psychoneurotic patients or geriatric patients with confusion and/or agitation.

As with other phenothiazines, pipotiazine is contraindicated in patients with suspected or established subcortical brain damage, with or without hypothalamic damage, since a hyperthermic reaction with temperatures above 40°C may occur, sometimes not until 14 to 16 hours after drug administration.

Phenothiazine compounds should not be used in patients receiving large doses of hypnotics, due to the possibility of potentiation.

Children: The safety and efficacy of pipotiazine in children have not been established. Therefore, it is not indicated for use in children.

Warnings: Severe adverse reactions requiring immediate medical attention may occur and are difficult to predict. Therefore, pipotiazine should be administered under the supervision of physicians experienced in the use of psychotropic drugs and facilities should be readily available to cope with any emergency situation.

Occupational Hazards: The use of this drug may impair the mental and physical abilities required for the performance of potentially hazardous tasks, such as driving a car or operating machinery.

Potentiation of the effects of alcohol may also occur.

Pregnancy: Safety during pregnancy has not been established, and the drug should not be used in women of childbearing potential unless, in the opinion of the physician, the expected benefit to the patient outweighs the possible risk to the fetus.

Precautions: Phenothiazines, particularly those which are long acting, should be used with caution in patients with a history of convulsive disorders; treatment should not be initiated unless such patients are receiving appropriate anticonvulsive medication.

The increased incidence of seizures, which occasionally occur in epileptics started on antipsychotic medication, may be controlled by increasing the dosage of their anticonvulsant. Patients with a familial history of seizures or febrile convulsions are more likely to develop seizures than those who have no such history.

Hypotensive phenomena may develop in phenothiazine treated patients who are undergoing surgery. Careful observation is necessary and dosages of anesthetics or CNS depressants may have to be reduced. Antipsychotic agents should be temporarily discontinued in patients receiving spinal or epidural anesthesia, if possible, to allow time for the residual drug to be metabolized.

Particularly during the first 2 or 3 months of therapy, it is advisable to perform periodic liver function tests and blood counts as cholestatic jaundice and blood dyscrasias may occur, necessitating discontinuation of treatment. During long-term therapy renal function should be monitored and, if BUN becomes abnormal, treatment should be discontinued.

The effects of anticholinergic drugs may be potentiated by pipotiazine. Paralytic ileus, even resulting in death, may occur, especially in the elderly. Caution should be observed if constipation develops.

Retinal changes, lenticular and corneal deposits and abnormal skin pigmentation have been observed with other phenothiazines and may occur after prolonged therapy. The possibility of persistent tardive dyskinesia should be considered with long-term treatment.

Patients receiving pipotiazine should be cautioned against exposure to extreme heat or organophosporus insecticides.

Hypotension and ECG changes, particularly nonspecific and usually reversible Q and T wave distortions, have been associated with the administration of phenothiazines. Use with caution in patients with compensated cardiovascular and cerebrovascular disorders.

The antiemetic effects of most phenothiazines can obscure toxic signs due to overdosage of other drugs or they may mask the symptoms of diseases such as brain tumors or intestinal obstruction.

Unexpected, sudden deaths have occurred in hospitalized patients treated with phenothiazines. Previous brain damage or seizures may predispose. High doses should be avoided in known seizure patients. Sudden exacerbations of psychotic behavior patterns occurred in several patients shortly before death. Acute fulminating pneumonia or pneumonitis and aspiration of gastric contents also were observed. Therefore, the physician also should keep in mind the possible development of "silent pneumonias".

Neuroleptic drugs elevate prolactin levels; the elevation persists during chronic administration. Tissue culture experiments indicate that approximately 33% of human breast cancers are prolactin-dependent in vitro, a factor of potential importance if the prescription of these drugs is contemplated in a patient with a previously detected breast cancer. Although disturbances such as galactorrhea, amenorrhea, gynecomastia and impotence have been reported, the clinical significance of elevated serum prolactin levels is unknown for most patients. An increase in mammary neoplasms has been found in rodents after chronic administration of neuroleptic drugs. Neither clinical studies, nor epidemiologic studies conducted to date, however, have shown an association between chronic administration of these drugs and mammary tumorogenesis; the available evidence is considered too limited to be conclusive at this time.

Withdrawal Emergent Neurological Signs: Abrupt withdrawal after short-term administration of antipsychotic drugs does not generally pose problems. However, transient dyskinetic signs are experienced by some patients on maintenance therapy after abrupt withdrawal. The signs are very similar to those described under Tardive Dyskinesia, except for duration. Although it is not known whether gradual withdrawal of antipsychotic drugs will decrease the incidence of withdrawal emergent neurological signs, gradual withdrawal would appear to be advisable.

Geriatrics: The incidence of adverse reactions may be greater in patients over 55 years of age, since the half-lives of antipsychotic drugs are often prolonged. To minimize this possibility, the maintenance dosage should be reduced to the lowest effective level as soon as possible after initial titration and periodically reviewed.

Since psychiatric syndromes in the elderly can be caused by drugs or organic disease, withdrawal of the precipitating drug or treatment of the medical condition should supersede initiation of antipsychotic medication. These agents should not be used for non-psychiatric conditions for which other drugs are available, since the elderly are especially prone to develop adverse effects from antipsychotic drugs.

Adverse Effects: Neurological: The side effects most frequently reported are extrapyramidal reactions including tremor, rigidity, akathisia, dystonia, dyskinesia, oculogyric crises, opisthotonos, hyperreflexia and sialorrhea which tend to occur in the first few days after an injection. Pipotiazine tends to produce a higher incidence of extrapyramidal reactions than some other phenothiazine derivatives. Extrapyramidal reactions may be alarming, and the patient should be forewarned and reassured. These reactions may tend to subside as treatment is continued but are often dose related and may respond to a reduction of the dose. Antiparkinsonian medication may be required to control serious reactions or, if intractable, the drug may have to be withdrawn. The information available tends to indicate that persistent tardive dyskinesia results from heavy drug overloading of the extrapyramidal system. Therefore, caution should be exercised to avoid overdosing and the optimum dosage should not be exceeded since this will tend to elicit marked extrapyramidal reactions.

Persistent Tardive Dyskinesia: May occur in patients on long-term therapy or may be observed after drug therapy has been discontinued. The risk seems to be greater in elderly patients on high doses, especially females. The symptoms are persistent and in some patients appear to be irreversible. The syndrome is characterized by rhythmical involuntary movements of the tongue, face, mouth or jaw, e.g., protrusion of tongue, puffing of cheeks, puckering of mouth, chewing movements. These may be accompanied by involuntary movements of the extremities.

There is no known effective treatment for tardive dyskinesia; antiparkinsonian agents usually do not alleviate the symptoms. It is suggested that all antipsychotic agents be discontinued if these symptoms appear. Should it be necessary to reinstitute treatment, or increase the dosage of the agent, or switch to a different antipsychotic agent, the syndrome may be masked. It has been reported that fine vermicular movements of the tongue may be an early sign of the syndrome and if the medication is stopped at that time, the syndrome may not develop. The physician may be able to reduce the risk of this syndrome by minimizing the unnecessary use of neuroleptic drugs and reducing the dose or discontinuing the drug, if possible, when manifestations of this syndrome are recognized, particularly in patients over the age of 50.

Behavioral: Sleep disturbances, drowsiness, fatigue, insomnia, and depression have been reported and may, in severe cases, necessitate reduction in dosage. As with other phenothiazine derivatives, reactivation or aggravation of psychotic processes may be encountered.

Paradoxical effects such as agitation, anxiety, restlessness, excitement and bizarre dreams, have been observed in some patients.

Autonomic Nervous System: Dry mouth, nausea and constipation were most frequently seen during pipotiazine therapy. Tachycardia, hypotension, syncope, dizziness, blurred vision, vomiting, sweating, nasal congestion, and urinary incontinence have also been observed.

Patients with pheochromocytoma, cerebral vascular or renal insufficiency, or a severe cardiac reserve deficiency such as mitral insufficiency appear to be particularly prone to hypotensive reactions with phenothiazine compounds, and should therefore be observed closely when the drug is administered. Should hypotension occur in patients receiving pipotiazine and a vasopressor agent be required, i.v. levarterenol or phenylephrine should be used, and **not** epinephrine, since phenothiazine derivatives can reverse the pressor effect of the latter drug.

Other autonomic reactions which have occurred with phenothiazines are salivation, polyuria, glaucoma, bladder paralysis, adynamic ileus, and fecal compaction.

Metabolic and Endocrine: Anorexia, menstrual irregularities, impotence, and increased thirst have been reported with pipotiazine.

Weight changes, increased appetite, peripheral edema, galactorrhea, gynecomastia, false positive pregnancy tests, and changes in libido have also occurred in patients receiving phenothiazine therapy.

Allergic or Toxic: Pruritus, dermatitis and rash have been observed with pipotiazine. Other allergic reactions reported with phenothiazine derivatives are erythema, urticaria, seborrhea, eczema, exfoliative dermatitis, and photosensitivity. The possibility of an anaphylactoid reaction should be borne in mind.

Blood dyscrasias including leukopenia, agranulocytosis, pancytopenia, thrombocytopenic or nonthrombocytopenic purpura, eosinophilia, and anemia, have been associated with phenothiazine therapy. Routine blood counts are therefore advisable during prolonged therapy. If any soreness of the mouth, gums or throat or any symptoms of upper respiratory infection occur and confirmatory leukocyte count indicates cellular depression, therapy should be discontinued and other appropriate measures instituted immediately.

Cholestatic jaundice and biliary stasis may be encountered, particularly during the first months of therapy, and require immediate discontinuation of treatment.

Miscellaneous: The following adverse reactions have been reported in patients receiving phenothiazine derivatives: headache, asthma, laryngeal, cerebral and angioneurotic edema, altered cerebrospinal fluid proteins, systemic lupus erythematosus like syndrome, hyperpyrexia, ECG and EEG changes and hypotension severe enough to cause fatal cardiac arrest. Skin pigmentation, epithelial keratopathy, lenticular and corneal deposits have been associated with long-term administration.

Sudden, unexpected and unexplained deaths have been reported in hospitalized psychotic patients receiving phenothiazines. Previous brain damage or seizures may be predisposing factors; high doses should be avoided in known seizure patients. Several patients have shown flare-ups of psychotic behaviour patterns shortly before death. Autopsy findings have usually revealed acute fulminating pneumonia or pneumonitis, aspiration of gastric contents or intramyocardial lesions.

Potentiation of CNS depressants (barbiturates, narcotics, analgesics, alcohol, antihistamines), may occur.

Local tolerance to pipotiazine is good and reactions at the site of injection are seldom seen.

Overdose: Symptoms: Severe extrapyramidal manifestations, hypotension, lethargy and sedation are most likely to be observed. Initial hospitalization may be required and close medical supervision should be maintained until symptoms are well under control.

Treatment: Symptomatic and supportive. Severe extrapyramidal reactions may be treated with an appropriate antiparkinsonian agent. Maintain an adequate airway and, in cases of severe hypotension, administer i.v. levarterenol or phenylephrine (**not** epinephrine as it may further depress the blood pressure).

When a sufficient amount of time has elapsed or when the patient shows signs of relapse, treatment may be resumed at a lower dosage.

Dosage: Pipotiazine palmitate is to be administered as an i.m. injection only. As a long acting depot phenothiazine, it has been found useful in the maintenance therapy of non-agitated, chronic schizophrenic patients stabilized with shorter acting neuroleptics who might benefit from a transfer to a long acting injectable drug.

The changeover to pipotiazine palmitate should aim at maintaining a clinical outcome similar to or better than that obtained with the previously used antipsychotic agent in patients who cannot be relied upon to take oral medication regularly. In those patients who might benefit from a long acting neuroleptic, it is suggested to discontinue the previous antipsychotic medication prior to the changeover of drugs. The initial dose and the interval between injections should be selected on an individual basis, considering such factors as age, physical condition, symptoms and severity of illness, and previous drug history. Depending on the previous drug history or other individual factors, an initial dose of 50 to 100 mg may be administered. If necessary, further symptom control can usually be obtained by increasing the dose by increments of 25 mg every 2 or 3 weeks. The optimal dose and the interval between injections must be determined in accordance with the patient's response. A single injection of pipotiazine palmitate may effectively control the schizophrenic symptoms for 3 to 6 weeks. However, it is frequently possible to achieve adequate control with a dosage between 75 and 150 mg administered every 4 weeks. Some patients may not require more than 25 to 50 mg every 4 weeks, while in others, doses of up to 250 mg may be needed.

Lower doses should be used in patients over the age of 50 when initiating therapy.

The dosage should not be increased in order to prolong the interval between injections. Some patients may benefit from the use of lower doses administered every 3 weeks. Regular

Piportil L4 (cont'd)

and continuous supervision is considered essential in order to maintain the patient on the lowest effective individual dose and to make any additional adjustments in the dosage which may be required to avoid overdosage and troublesome adverse effects.

Although the incidence of extrapyramidal reactions is high, antiparkinsonian medication should be prescribed only to treat emergent symptoms that may occur. They should not be used prophylactically against such reactions.

A dry syringe and a needle of at least 21 gauge should be used. Use of a wet needle or syringe may cause the solution to become cloudy.

Supplied: 25 mg/mL: Each mL contains: pipotiazine palmitate 25 mg. Nonmedicinal ingredients: sesame oil. Ampuls of 1 mL, boxes of 3.

50 mg/mL: Each mL contains: pipotiazine palmitate 50 mg. Nonmedicinal ingredients: sesame oil. Ampuls of 1 mL, boxes of 3. Ampuls of 2 mL, boxes of 1.

Store at room temperature and protect from light.

PIPRACIL®

Wyeth-Ayerst

Piperacillin Sodium

Antibiotic

Pharmacology: Piperacillin is a third-generation, broad-spectrum, semisynthetic penicillin. Piperacillin is bactericidal and exerts its antibacterial action by inhibiting both septum and cell wall synthesis in the bacterial cell.

The bactericidal action of β-lactam antibiotics is related to their ability to reach and bind target proteins, the penicillin sensitive enzymes within the cytoplasmic membranes of the bacteria. These enzymes are involved in reactions essential to cell division and to maintenance of the integrity of the cell structure.

Piperacillin has been shown to have ready accessibility to target enzymes within the bacteria that mediate septum and cell wall synthesis and high inhibitory activity for cell wall enzymes. Piperacillin induces the formation of elongated forms with defective cell walls.

Pharmacokinetics: Piperacillin can be administered either i.m. or i.v. It is not absorbed when given orally. Piperacillin is rapidly absorbed after i.m. injection. In healthy volunteers, the mean peak serum concentration occurs approximately 30 minutes after a single dose of 2 g and is about 36 μg/mL. Peak serum concentrations are attained immediately after completion of i.v. injection or infusion. Serum levels after i.v. administration and renal clearance do not show dose proportionality because of saturation of the renal secretory mechanism. The serum half-life in healthy volunteers ranges from 36 minutes to 1 hour and 12 minutes.

The mean elimination half-life of piperacillin in healthy adult volunteers is 54 minutes following administration of 2 g and 68 minutes following 6 g. With concurrent administration of probenecid higher and more prolonged serum levels are reached. The oral administration of 1 g probenecid before injection produces an increase in piperacillin peak serum level of about 30%. The area under the curve (AUC) is increased by approximately 60%. Piperacillin binding to human serum proteins is low (16%). The substitution of 0.5% lidocaine for Sterile Water as a diluent in an i.m. pharmacokinetic study showed no significant difference in the area under the serum concentration curve, peak serum concentration or cumulative urine excretion of piperacillin. The serum half-lives were prolonged from 67 to 70 minutes at 3 g/day, 56 to 68 minutes at 4 g/day and 52 to 59 minutes at 6 g/day, however.

As with other penicillins, piperacillin is eliminated primarily by glomerular filtration and tubular secretion. It is rapidly excreted as unchanged drug in urine, reaching high concentrations after a single 2 g i.m. dose. In man, urinary excretion accounted for 42 to 62% of 1 to 6 g i.v. doses within 2 hours and 54 to 79% within 4 hours. Mean urinary recovery in 24 hours was 74 to 89% for i.v. doses and 57 to 59% for i.m. doses. Piperacillin urine concentrations, determined by microbioassay, were as high as 14 100 μg/mL following a 6 g i.v. dose and 8 500 μg/mL following a 4 g i.v. dose. These urine drug concentrations remained well above 1 000 μg/mL throughout the dosing interval. The elimination half-life is increased 2-fold in mild to moderate renal impairment and 5-to-6-fold in severe impairment.

Because piperacillin is excreted by the biliary route (10 to 20%) as well as the renal route, it can be used safely in appropriate dosage (see Dosage) in patients with mild to severe renal impairment and can be used in treatment of hepatobiliary infections.

Pharmacokinetic characteristics were similar for normal subjects compared to patients with cystic fibrosis, whether or not the latter received concomitant treatment with pancreatic enzymes and vitamins.

While piperacillin reduces platelet aggregation, these effects are less than those caused by ticarcillin or carbenicillin at equivalent therapeutic dosage.

There was no significant inactivation of amikacin, gentamicin or tobramycin in serum when the aminoglycoside was administered concomitantly with carbenicillin or piperacillin to subjects with normal renal function. In the urine, lowering of the concentration of tobramycin, and gentamicin to a lesser degree, by the presence of carbenicillin or piperacillin was observed. This possible inactivation effect was greater with carbenicillin than with piperacillin. No urinary inactivation of amikacin by either of these penicillins was observed. The clinical significance of these observations is unknown.

A follow-up study was conducted in patients with end-stage renal failure stabilized on chronic intermittent hemodialysis. No inactivation of piperacillin or carbenicillin in these patients was observed when gentamicin was administered concomitantly with either of these penicillins. Carbenicillin and piperacillin, however, inactivated gentamicin in these patients. Gentamicin was inactivated 4 times faster by carbenicillin than by piperacillin.

Indications: The treatment of systemic and local infections due to susceptible strains of gram-negative and gram-positive aerobic and anaerobic bacteria listed below. Because of its broad spectrum of activity, piperacillin is also suitable for the therapy of mixed infections, and the presumptive therapy of serious infections, when piperacillin-sensitive pathogens are suspected as the cause of disease.

Intra-abdominal infections including hepato-biliary and surgical infections caused by E. coli, P. aeruginosa, enterococci, Clostridium spp., anaerobic cocci, and Bacteroides spp., including B. fragilis.

Urinary tract infections (complicated and uncomplicated) caused by E. coli, Klebsiella spp., P. aeruginosa, P. mirabilis and enterococci.

Gynecological infections including endometritis and pelvic inflammatory disease caused by Bacteroides spp., including B. fragilis, anaerobic cocci, N. gonorrhoeae, and enterococci (S. faecalis).

Septicemia including bacteremia caused by E. coli, Klebsiella spp., Serratia spp., P. mirabilis, S. pneumoniae, enterococci, P. aeruginosa, Bacteroides spp., and anaerobic cocci.

Lower respiratory tract infections caused by E. coli, Klebsiella spp., Enterobacter spp., P. aeruginosa, Serratia spp., H. influenzae, Bacteroides species and anaerobic cocci. Although improvement has been noted in patients with cystic fibrosis, lasting bacterial eradication may not be achieved.

Skin and skin structure infections caused by E. coli, Klebsiella spp., Serratia spp., Acinetobacter spp., Enterobacter spp., P. aeruginosa, indole-positive Proteus spp., P. mirabilis, Bacteroides spp., including B. fragilis, anaerobic cocci and enterococci.

Bone and joint infections caused by P. aeruginosa, enterococci, Bacteroides spp., and anaerobic cocci.

Uncomplicated urethritis caused by N. gonorrhoeae.

Appropriate cultures should be made before initiating treatment. Presumptive therapy may be started while awaiting results of susceptibility tests. Treatment should be adjusted, if necessary, when results of these tests become available.

Mixed Infections: Piperacillin has also been shown to be clinically effective for the treatment of infections at various sites caused by streptococcus species, including Group A betahemolytic Streptococcus and S. pneumoniae. While infections caused solely by these organisms are ordinarily treated with narrower spectrum penicillins, mixed infections involving the above, and other organisms susceptible to piperacillin, may be effectively treated by the latter.

Piperacillin may be administered as single drug therapy in some situations where normally 2 antibiotics might be employed.

General: The efficacy of piperacillin has been demonstrated in infections produced by organisms resistant to other penicillins, some aminoglycosides and cephalosporins.

Combined Therapy with Other Antibiotics: In vitro synergism has been shown between piperacillin and some aminoglycosides in some bacterial strains. Piperacillin has been used clinically with aminoglycosides, especially in patients with impaired host defenses. Both drugs were used in full therapeutic doses.

Piperacillin can be used safely in combination with penicillinase-resistant penicillins, e.g. oxacillin, in mixed infections when beta-lactamase-positive S. aureus is isolated along with piperacillin-susceptible organisms.

Piperacillin may be administered concomitantly with a cephalosporin, provided that an additive or synergistic antibacterial action of the 2 antibiotics is ascertained through in vitro tests. Based on in vitro data, cefoxitin should **not** be given with piperacillin when infections caused by organisms producing inducible β-lactamases are suspected or confirmed.

Contraindications: A history of allergic reactions to any of the penicillins and/or cephalosporins.

Piperacillin when reconstituted with lidocaine for i.m. use is contraindicated in patients with a known history of hypersensitivity to local anesthetics of the amide type.

Warnings: Serious and occasionally fatal hypersensitivity (anaphylactic) reactions have been reported in patients receiving therapy with penicillins. These reactions are more apt to occur in persons with a history of sensitivity to multiple allergens.

Cross-sensitivity of patients to penicillins and cephalosporins has been reported. Before initiating therapy with piperacillin, careful inquiry should be made concerning previous hypersensitivity reactions to penicillins, cephalosporins and other allergens.

If an allergic reaction occurs, the antibiotic should be discontinued. The usual agents (antihistamines, pressor amines and corticosteroids) should be readily available.

Serious anaphylactoid reactions require immediate emergency treatment with epinephrine. Oxygen, i.v. steroids, airway management, including intubation, should also be administered as necessary.

Antibiotic-associated pseudomembranous colitis has been reported with nearly all antibacterial agents, including piperacillin, and may range in severity from mild to life-threatening. It is important to consider this diagnosis if significant diarrhea or colitis occurs during therapy. Mild cases usually respond to drug discontinuation alone. However, in moderate to severe cases, management with fluids and electrolytes, protein supplementation and treatment with an oral antibacterial drug effective against C. difficile (e.g., oral vancomycin) should be considered.

Precautions: While piperacillin possesses the characteristic low toxicity of the penicillin group of antibiotics, it is advisable to check periodically for organ dysfunction (including renal, hepatic and hematopoietic) during prolonged therapy.

Bleeding manifestations have occurred in some patients receiving beta-lactam antibiotics including piperacillin. These reactions have sometimes been associated with abnormalities of coagulation tests such as clotting time, platelet aggregation and prothrombin time and are more likely to occur in patients with renal failure.

If bleeding manifestations or significant leukopenia occur, piperacillin should be discontinued and appropriate therapy instituted.

The possibility of the emergence of resistant organisms and the development of superinfections should be kept in mind, particularly during prolonged treatment. If this occurs, appropriate measures should be taken.

As with other penicillins, patients may experience neuromuscular excitability or convulsions if higher than recommended doses are given i.v.

Since piperacillin is excreted not only renally but also by the biliary route, it can be used at reduced dosage (see Dosage) in patients with severely restricted kidney function and in those who have had nephrotoxic reactions to other drugs.

Piperacillin is a monosodium compound containing 1.85 mEq (42.5 mg) of Na^+/g based on molecular weight. This should be considered when treating patients requiring restricted salt intake. Periodic electrolyte determinations should be made in patients with low potassium reserves, and the possibility of hypokalemia should be kept in mind with patients who have potentially low potassium reserves, receiving cytotoxic therapy or diuretics. Electrolyte and cardiac status should also be monitored during prolonged treatment in patients with impaired cardiac function.

Antimicrobials used in high doses for short periods to treat gonorrhea may mask or delay the symptoms of incubating syphilis. Therefore, prior to treatment, patients with gonorrhea should also be evaluated for syphilis. Specimens for darkfield examination should be obtained from patients with any suspected primary lesion, and serologic tests should be performed. In all cases where concomitant syphilis is suspected, monthly serological tests should be made for a minimum of 4 months. The use of some penicillins (ampicillin, amoxicillin) has been associated with morbilliform rashes in some cases of infectious mononucleosis. Piperacillin should be used with caution, therefore, in the treatment of infections caused by susceptible organisms in patients with infectious mononucleosis.

As with other semisynthetic penicillins, piperacillin therapy has been associated with an increased incidence of fever and rash in cystic fibrosis patients.

Because of chemical instability, piperacillin should not be used for i.v. administration with solutions containing **only** sodium bicarbonate (see Dosage, Incompatability).

Piperacillin should not be added to blood products.

Drug Interactions: The mixing of piperacillin with an aminoglycoside in vitro can result in substantial inactivation of the aminoglycosides.

Concurrent administration of probenecid results in higher and more prolonged serum levels of piperacillin.

Whenever piperacillin is administered concurrently with another antibiotic the drugs should **not** be mixed in the same solution but must be administered separately.

Piperacillin, when used clinically in the early postoperative period, has been implicated in the prolongation of the neuromuscular blockage of vecuronium. In a controlled clinical study, the ureidopenicillins, including piperacillin, have been reported to prolong the action of vecuronium. Caution is indicated when piperacillin is used perioperatively with vecuronium and similar neuromuscular blocking agents.

Pregnancy and *Lactation:* Although reproduction studies in mice and rats performed at doses up to 4 times the human dose have shown no evidence of impaired fertility or harm to the fetus, safety of piperacillin use in pregnant women has not been determined. Because animal reproduction studies are not always predictive of human response, this drug should be used during pregnancy only if clearly needed. It has been found to cross the placenta in rats.

Caution should be exercised when piperacillin is administered to nursing mothers. It is excreted in low concentrations in milk.

Children: Dosages for children under the age of 12 have not been established.

Adverse Effects: Piperacillin is generally well tolerated. The most common adverse reactions have been local in nature, following i.v. or i.m. injection. The following adverse reactions may occur:

Local: In adult clinical trials thrombophlebitis was noted in 2.5% of patients. It is more likely to occur when an insufficiently diluted solution is injected into the vein. Pain, erythema, and/or induration at the injection site occurred in 1.0% of patients. Less frequent reactions, including ecchymosis, deep vein thrombosis and hematomas, have also occurred.

Hypersensitivity: Rash and/or pruritus was noted in 2.3% of patients. Drug fever was 2% (Note: The incidence of rash and fever is higher in patients with cystic fibrosis). Other less frequent findings included vesicular eruptions, positive Coombs' tests. Anaphylactoid reactions have been reported rarely (see Warnings). Other dermatologic manifestations such as erythema multiforme and Stevens-Johnson syndrome have been reported rarely.

Gastrointestinal: Diarrhea and loose stools were noted in 3% of patients. Other less frequent reactions included vomiting, nausea, bloody diarrhea. Pseudomembranous colitis has been reported rarely.

Hepatic: increases in liver enzymes (LDH, AST, ALT), hyperbilirubinemia. Rarely, cholestatic hepatitis.

Renal: elevations of creatinine or BUN. Rarely, interstitial nephritis.

CNS: headache, dizziness, fatigue. Convulsions with high doses.

Hemic and Lymphatic: reversible leukopenia, neutropenia, thrombocytopenia and/or eosinophilia, bleeding and decreases in prothrombin time have been reported. As with other betalactam antibiotics, reversible leukopenia (neutropenia) is more apt to occur in patients receiving prolonged therapy at high dosages or in association with drugs known to cause this reaction.

Serum Electrolytes: individuals with liver disease or individuals receiving cytotoxic therapy or diuretics, were reported rarely to demonstrate a decrease in serum potassium concentrations with high doses of piperacillin.

Musculoskeletal: rarely, prolonged muscle relaxation.

Other: superinfection, including candidiasis and hemorrhagic manifestations.

Overdose: Symptoms and Treatment: Other than general supportive treatment, no specific antidote is known. Excessive serum levels of piperacillin may be reduced by hemodialysis.

Table I—Pipracil

Dosage

Type of Infection	Usual Total Daily Dosage	Frequency of Administration
Serious infections such as septicemia, nosocomial pneumonia, intra-abdominal infections, aerobic and anaerobic gynecologic infections, and skin and soft-tissue infections	12 to 18 g i.v. (200 to 300 mg/kg)	Every 4 to 6 hours
Complicated urinary tract infections	8 to 16 g i.v. (125 to 200 mg/kg)	Every 6 to 8 hours
Uncomplicated urinary tract infections and most community-acquired pneumonia	6 to 8 g i.m. or i.v. (100 to 125 mg/kg)	Every 6 to 12 hours
Uncomplicated gonococcal urethritis	2 g i.m.[a]	Single dose

[a] 1 g of probenecid given orally ½ hour prior to injection.

Dosage in Renal Impairment (Adults)

Degree of Renal Impairment	Creatinine Clearance (mL/min)	Creatinine Serum Level (mg%)	Urinary Tract Infection (uncomplicated)	Urinary Tract Infection (complicated)	Serious Systemic Infection
Mild	>40	1.5 to 3.0	N/A[b]	N/A[b]	N/A[b]
Moderate	20 to 40	3.1 to 5.0	N/A[b]	9 g/day (3 g/every 8 hrs)	12 g/day (4 g every 8 hrs)
Severe	<20	>5	6 g/day (3 g every 12 hrs)	6 g/day (3 g every 12 hrs)	8 g/day (4 g every 12 hrs)
Patients on Hemodialysis[c]					6 g/day (2 g every 8 hrs)

[b] No adjustment necessary.

[c] Hemodialysis removes 30 to 50% of the drug in 4 hours; an additional dose of 1 g of piperacillin should be administered following each dialysis period. For patients with renal failure, hepatic insufficiency or biliary tract obstruction measurement of serum levels of piperacillin will provide additional guidance for adjusting dosage.

As with other penicillins, neuromuscular excitability or convulsions have occurred following large i.v. doses. General supportive measures, including administration of phenytoin and barbiturates or other anticonvulsant drugs may be considered. Daily doses of piperacillin of at least 24 g have been administered in man without observation of adverse effects.

For treatment of hypersensitivity reactions, see Warnings.

Dosage: Piperacillin may be administered i.m. or i.v. (either in a 3 to 5 minute injection or by infusion). Dosage and route of administration should be determined by the severity of the infection and condition of the patient. The usual dosage of piperacillin for serious infections is 3 to 4 g given every 4 to 6 hours as a 20- to 30-minute infusion. For serious infections the i.v. route should be used. See Table I.

The maximum daily dose usually administered to adults is 24 g/day, although higher doses have been used.

Infants and Children: Dosages in infants and children under 12 years of age have not been established.

Duration of therapy: The average duration of piperacillin treatment is from 7 to 10 days, except in the treatment of gynecologic infections, in which it is from 3 to 10 days; the duration should be guided by the patient's clinical and bacteriological progress. Some infections such as osteomyelitis may require significantly longer periods of therapy. For most acute infections, treatment should be continued for at least 48 to 72 hours after the patient becomes asymptomatic. Antibiotic therapy for Group A beta-hemolytic streptococcal infections should be maintained for at least 10 days to reduce the risk of rheumatic fever or glomerulonephritis.

Reconstitution and Administration: I.M. injection: I.M. injections should be limited to 2 g per injection site. This route of administration has been used primarily in the treatment of patients with uncomplicated gonorrhea and urinary tract infections. Injection should be given into the upper outer quadrant of the buttock (i.e., gluteus maximus).

When indicated by clinical and bacteriological findings, i.m. administration of 6 to 8 g daily of piperacillin, in divided doses, may be utilized for initiation of therapy. In addition, i.m. administration of the drug may be considered for maintenance therapy after clinical and bacteriological improvement has been obtained with i.v. piperacillin treatment.

The deltoid area should be used only if well-developed, and then only with caution to avoid radial nerve injury. I.M. injections should not be made into the lower or mid-third of the upper arm.

Solutions for Reconstitution (see Table II): Sterile water for injection or 0.5 to 1.0% lidocaine HCl (without epinephrine) in sterile water for injection. (Lidocaine is contraindicated in patients with a known history of hypersensitivity to local anesthetics of the amide type).

Table II—Pipracil

Reconstitution Table—I.M. Injection

Vial Size	Volume to Be Added	Approximate Available Volume	Approximate Available Concentration
2 g	4.0 mL	5.0 mL	0.4 g/mL
3 g	6.0 mL	7.5 mL	0.4 g/mL
4 g	8.0 mL	10.0 mL	0.4 g/mL

Shake well until dissolved.

Note: I.M. injections should be limited to 2 g per injection site. Injection should be given into the upper outer quadrant of the buttock (i.e., gluteus maximus).

For I.V. injection or infusion: I.V. Injection (Bolus): Reconstituted solution should be injected slowly over a 3- to 5-minute period to help avoid vein irritation.

I.V. Infusion: Infusion should be carried out over a period of about 20 to 40 minutes or intermittent infusion over a 30-minute to 2-hour period. During infusion it is desirable to discontinue the primary i.v. solution.

For i.v. injection or infusion, reconstitute piperacillin with sterile water for injection (see Table III).

Table III—Pipracil

Reconstitution Table—I.V. Injection or Infusion

Product Size	Volume of Diluent to Be Added	Approximate Available Volume	Approximate Average Concentration
2 g	10 mL	11 mL	0.18 g/mL
3 g	15 mL	17 mL	0.18 g/mL
4 g	20 mL	22 mL	0.18 g/mL

Shake well until dissolved.

The prepared solution may be further diluted to the desired volume (at least 15 mL/g for infusion) with any i.v. solutions or i.v. admixtures listed below.

Table IV—Pipracil

Reconstitution Table for Bulk Pharmacy Vial

Product Size	Volume of Diluent to Be Added	Approximate Available Volume	Approximate Average Concentration
40 g	172 mL	200 mL	0.20 g/mL

Shake well until dissolved.

The Pharmacy Bulk Vial is intended for multiple dispensing for **i.v. use only,** employing a single puncture. Following reconstitution (see Table IV), the solution should be further diluted to the desired volume in any appropriate i.v. solution or i.v. admixture listed below.

Pipracil (cont'd)

Any unused reconstituted solution should be discarded after 8 hours.

I.V. Solutions: Dextrose 5% in Water (D_5W), 0.9% sodium chloride (Normal Saline) [NS], dextrose 5% and 0.9% sodium chloride (D_5NS), Lactated Ringer's Injection, USP, dextran 6% in 0.9% sodium chloride.

I.V. Admixtures: Normal saline [+KCl 40 mEq/500 mL], 5% dextrose in water (D_5W) [+KCl 40 mEq/500 mL], Ringer's Injection, USP [+KCl 40 mEq/500 mL], 5% Dextrose/Normal Saline (D_5Ns) [+KCl 40 mEq/500 mL], Lactated Ringer's Injection, USP [+KCl 40 mEq/500 mL].
Note: Because of chemical instability, piperacillin should not be used for i.v. administered with solutions containing **only** sodium bicarbonate (see Incompatibility).

Stability of Solutions: Stability studies have demonstrated chemical stability (pH, potency and clarity) through 24 hours at room temperature and up to 72 hours refrigerated. Appropriate consideration of aseptic technique recommends discarding unused portions after storage for 24 hours at room temperature or 48 hours refrigerated.

Piperacillin is stable in both glass and plastic containers when reconstituted with recommended diluents and further diluted with the indicated i.v. solutions and i.v. admixtures.

Incompatibility: Piperacillin should not be added to blood products.

Because of chemical instability, piperacillin should not be used for i.v. administration with solutions containing sodium bicarbonate alone. It may be used with i.v. admixtures containing other ingredients as well as sodium bicarbonate for up to 24 hours at room temperature and 48 hours refrigerated.

Solutions containing piperacillin and protein hydrolysates or amino acids should be used within 12 hours if stored at room temperature and 24 hours if refrigerated.

Supplied: 2 g: Each vial contains: sterile piperacillin sodium lyophilized powder equivalent to 2 g of piperacillin. Tartrazine-free. Boxes of 10.

3 g: Each vial contains: sterile piperacillin sodium lyophilized powder equivalent to 3 g of piperacillin. Tartrazine-free. Boxes of 10.

4 g: Each vial contains: sterile piperacillin sodium lyophilized powder equivalent to 4 g of piperacillin. Tartrazine-free. Boxes of 10.

40 g: Each vial contains: sterile piperacillin sodium lyophilized powder equivalent to 40 g of piperacillin. Tartrazine-free. Single vials of 40 g.

Store at controlled room temperatures 15 to 30°C.

PITREX
Taro

Tolnaftate

Topical Antifungal

Supplied: Each g of cream contains: tolnaftate 1% in a water washable non-aqueous base of polyethylene glycol-400, polyethylene glycol-3350, white petrolatum, titanium dioxide and butylated hydroxytoluene. Paraben-free. Tubes of 15 g.

PLACEBO
Odan

Supplied: Each white scored tablet contains: lactose 100 mg. Nonmedicinal ingredients: cellulose, magnesium stearate, methylparaben, propylparaben and silicon dioxide. Gluten- and tartrazine-free. Bottles of 100 and 1 000.

PLAQUENIL® Ⓟ
Sanofi

Hydroxychloroquine Sulfate

Anti-inflammatory—Antimalarial

Pharmacology: Hydroxychloroquine has been beneficial for a high percentage of patients with rheumatoid arthritis and lupus erythematosus, especially chronic discoid lupus. The exact mode of action in controlling these diseases is unknown. The action of this compound against malarial parasites is similar to that of chloroquine phosphate.

Indications: For the treatment of rheumatoid arthritis, and discoid and systemic lupus erythematosus, in patients who have not responded satisfactorily to drugs with less potential for serious side effects. It is also indicated for the suppressive treatment and treatment of acute attacks of malaria due to P. vivax, P. malariae, P. ovale, and susceptible strains of P. falciparum. It is not active against the exo-erythrocytic forms of P. vivax, P. malariae and P. ovale and therefore will neither prevent infection due to these organisms when given prophylactically, nor prevent relapse of infection due to these organisms. It is highly effective as a suppressive agent in patients with vivax or malariae malaria in terminating acute attacks and significantly lengthening the interval between treatment and relapse. In patients with falciparum malaria, it abolishes the acute attack and effects complete cure of the infection, unless due to a resistant strain of P. falciparum.

Contraindications: Preexisting retinopathy of the eye, patients with known hypersensitivity to 4-aminoquinoline compounds and long-term therapy in children.

Warnings: Ophthalmic: Irreversible retinal damage has been observed in some patients who had received long-term or high-dosage 4-aminoquinoline therapy for discoid and systemic lupus erythematosus, or rheumatoid arthritis. Retinopathy is reported to be dose-related and is likely to be increased if recommended dosages are exceeded. When prolonged therapy with any antimalarial compound is contemplated, initial (baseline) and periodic (every 3 months) ophthalmologic examinations (including visual acuity, expert slit lamp, funduscopic, and visual field tests) should be done.

If there is any indication of abnormality in the visual acuity, visual field, or retinal macular areas (such as pigmentary changes, loss of foveal reflex), or any visual symptoms (such as light flashes and streaks) that are not fully explainable by difficulties of accommodation or coroneal opacities, the drug should be stopped immediately. The patient should be closely observed for possible progression. Retinal changes (and visual disturbances) may progress even after cessation of therapy.
Anti-inflammatory: Dermatological reactions to hydroxychloroquine may occur. It is not recommended for the treatment of psoriasis or porphyria as these conditions may be exacerbated by its use. The preparation should only be used in these conditions, when in the judgment of the physician, the benefit outweighs the risk.

All patients on long term therapy with this preparation should be questioned and examined periodically, including the testing of knee and ankle reflexes, to detect any evidence of muscular weakness. If weakness occurs, discontinue the drug.
Malaria: Plaquenil is not effective against chloroquine-resistant strains of P. falciparum, and is not active against the exo-erythrocytic forms of P. vivax, P. ovale and P. malariae and therefore will neither prevent infection due to these organisms when given prophylactically, nor prevent relapse of infection due to these organisms.
Pregnancy: Plaquenil should be avoided in pregnancy except for the suppression or treatment of malaria when, in the judgment of the physician, the potential benefits outweigh the potential hazards. It should be noted that the 4-aminoquinolines in therapeutic doses have been associated with central nervous system damage, including ototoxicity (auditory and vestibular toxicity, congenital deafness), retinal hemorrhages and abnormal retinal pigmentation.
Lactation: Careful consideration should be given to using hydroxychloroquine during lactation, since it has been known to be excreted in small amounts in human breast milk and it is known that infants are extremely sensitive to the toxic effects of 4-aminoquinolines.
Children: Safety and efficacy has not been established in rheumatoid arthritis or systemic lupus erythematosus in children. Children are especially sensitive to the 4-aminoquinoline compounds. The most reported fatalities follow the accidental ingestion of chloroquine, sometimes in small doses. Patients should be strongly warned to keep these drugs out of the reach of children.

Precautions: Observe caution in patients with hepatic or renal disease, in whom a reduction in dosage may be necessary, as well as in those taking medicines known to affect these organs.

Observe caution also in patients with gastrointestinal, neurological, or blood disorders, in those with a sensitivity to quinine, and in glucose-6-phosphate dehydrogenase deficiency, porphyria and psoriasis.

Methods recommended for early diagnosis of retinopathy consist of (1) funduscopic examination of the macula for fine pigmentary disturbances or loss of the foveal reflex and (2) examination of the central visual field with a small red test object for pericentral or paracentral scotoma or determination of retinal thresholds to red. Any unexplained visual symptoms, such as light flashes or streaks also should be regarded with suspicion as possible manifestations of retinopathy.

If serious toxic symptoms occur from overdosage or sensitivity, it has been suggested that ammonium chloride (8 g daily in divided doses for adults) 3 or 4 days a week be administered for several months after therapy has been stopped, as acidification of the urine increases renal excretion of the 4-aminoquinoline compounds by 20 to 90%. However, caution must be exercised in patients with impaired renal function and/or metabolic acidosis.

Although the risk of bone-marrow depression is low, periodic blood counts should be obtained in patients requiring prolonged therapy. If any severe blood disorder appears that is not attributable to the disease under treatment, discontinuation of the drug should be considered.
Drug Interactions: Concomitant hydroxychloroquine and digoxin therapy may result in increased serum digoxin levels; serum digoxin levels should be closely monitored in patients receiving combined therapy.
Occupational Hazards: Patients should be warned about driving and operating machinery since hydroxychloroquine can impair accommodation and cause blurring of vision. If the condition is not self-limiting, dosage may need to be temporarily reduced.

Adverse Effects: Retinopathy with changes in pigmentation and visual field defects, can occur following hydroxychloroquine administration, but is rare. In its early form, it appears reversible upon discontinuation of the drug. If allowed to develop however, there may be a risk of progression even after treatment withdrawal.

Corneal changes including edema and opacities have been reported. They are either symptomless or may cause disturbances such as halos, blurring of vision or photophobia. They are reversible upon discontinuation of therapy. Blurring of vision due to a disturbance of accommodation which is dose dependent and reversible may also occur.

Skin rashes sometimes occur; pigmentary changes in skin and mucous membranes, bleaching of hair, and alopecia have also been reported. These usually resolve readily upon cessation of therapy. Isolated cases of exfoliative dermatitis have been reported.

Other adverse reactions include gastrointestinal disturbances such as nausea, diarrhea, anorexia, abdominal pain and, rarely, vomiting. These symptoms usually resolve immediately upon reducing the dose or upon stopping the treatment.

Less frequently, muscle weakness, vertigo, tinnitus, nerve deafness, headache, nervousness, and emotional lability have been reported with this class of drugs.

Rarely, there have been reports of bone marrow depression, cardiomyopathy, neuromyopathy, psychosis and convulsions.

Isolated cases of abnormal liver function tests have been reported and two cases of fulminant hepatic failure have been published.

Hydroxychloroquine may exacerbate porphyria and precipitate attacks of psoriasis.

Overdose: Overdosage with the 4-aminoquinolines is dangerous particularly in infants, as little as 1 to 2 g having proved fatal.

Symptoms: The 4-aminoquinoline compounds are very rapidly and completely absorbed following ingestion and in accidental overdosage toxic symptoms may occur within 30 minutes. These consist of headache, drowsiness, visual disturbances, cardiovascular collapse, and convulsions, followed by sudden and early respiratory and cardiac arrest. The ECG may reveal atrial standstill, nodal rhythm, prolonged intraventricular conduction time, and progressive bradycardia leading to ventricular fibrillation and/or arrest.

Treatment: Treatment is symptomatic and must be prompt with immediate evacuation of the stomach by emesis (at home, before transportation to the hospital), or gastric lavage until the stomach is completely emptied. If finely powdered activated charcoal is introduced by the stomach tube, after lavage and within 30 minutes after ingestion of the tablets, it may inhibit further intestinal absorption of the drug. To be effective, the dose of activated charcoal should be at least five times the estimated dose of ingested hydroxychloroquine. Convulsions, if present should be controlled before attempting gastric lavage. If due to cerebral stimulation, cautious administration of an ultrashort-acting barbiturate may be tried but, if due to anoxia, convulsions should be corrected by oxygen administration, artificial respiration or, in shock with hypotension, by vasopressor therapy. Because of the importance of supporting respiration, tracheal intubation or tracheostomy, followed by gastric lavage, has also been advised. Exchange transfusions have been used to reduce the level of 4-aminoquiolines in the blood.

Consideration should be given to administering diazepam parenterally, since studies have reported it beneficial in reversing chloroquine cardiotoxicity.

A patient who survives the acute phase and is asymptomatic should be closely observed for at least 6 hours. Fluids may be forced, and sufficient ammonium chloride may be administered for a few days to acidify the urine to help promote urinary excretion.

Dosage: The dosages cited below are stated in terms of hydroxychloroquine sulfate. One 200 mg tablet is equivalent to 155 mg base. Each dose should be taken with a meal or a glass of milk.

Rheumatoid Arthritis: The compound is cumulative in action and will require several weeks to exert its beneficial therapeutic effects, whereas minor side effects may occur somewhat early. Several months of therapy may be required before maximum effects can be obtained. If objective improvement (such as reduced joint swelling, increased mobility) does not occur within 6 months, the drug should be stopped. Safe use of the drug in the treatment of juvenile rheumatoid arthritis has not been established.

Initial Dosage: Adults: 400 to 600 mg daily. In a few patients, the side effects may require temporary reduction of the initial dosage. Generally, after 5 to 10 days the dose may be gradually increased to the optimum response level, frequently, without return of side effects.

Maintenance Dosage: When a good response is obtained (usually in 4 to 12 weeks), the dosage is reduced by 50% and continued at an acceptable maintenance level of 200 to 400 mg daily. The incidence of retinopathy has been reported to be higher when the maintenance dose is exceeded.

If a relapse occurs after medication is withdrawn, therapy may be resumed or continued on an intermittent schedule if there are no ocular contraindications.

Combination Therapy: Hydroxychloroquine may be used safely and effectively in combination with corticosteroids, salicylates, NSAIDS, and methotrexate and other second line therapeutic agents. Corticosteroids and salicylates can generally be decreased gradually in dosage or eliminated after the drug has been used for several weeks. When gradual reduction of steroid dosage is suggested, it may be done by reducing every 4 to 5 days, the dose of cortisone by no more than 5 to 15 mg; of hydrocortisone from 5 to 10 mg; of prednisolone and prednisone from 1 to 2.5 mg; of methylprednisolone and triamcinolone from 1 to 2 mg and dexamethasone from 0.25 to 0.5 mg. Regimens of treatment using other agents than steroids and NSAIDS are under development. No definitive dose combinations have been established.

Lupus Erythematosus: Adults: Initially, the average dose is 400 mg once or twice daily. This may be continued for several weeks or months, depending upon the response of the patient. For prolonged maintenance therapy, a smaller dose, from 200 to 400 mg daily will suffice. The incidence of retinopathy has been reported to be higher when this maintenance dose is exceeded.

Malaria: Suppression: Adults: 400 mg on exactly the same day of each week.

Infants and Children: The weekly suppressive dose is 5 mg base/kg, but should not exceed the adult dose regardless of body weight.

Suppressive therapy should begin 2 weeks before exposure. When not administered before exposure, give an initial loading dose of 800 mg to adults, or 10 mg base/kg to children in 2 divided doses, 6 hours apart. The suppressive therapy should be continued for eight weeks after leaving the endemic area.

Treatment of the Acute Attack: Adults: An initial loading dose of 800 mg followed by 400 mg in 6 to 8 hours. This is followed by 400 mg on each of the next 2 days for a total of 2 g of hydroxychloroquine sulfate or 1.55 g base. Alternatively, the administration of a single dose of 800 mg has also proved effective. The dosage for adults may also be calculated by body weight.

Infants and Children: Dosage calculated by body weight is preferred. A total dose representing 25 mg of base/kg is administered over 3 days as follows:

First dose: 10 mg base/kg (not to exceed 620 mg base).

Second dose: 5 mg base/kg 6 hours after the first dose (not to exceed 310 mg base).

Third dose: 5 mg base/kg 18 hours after the second dose.

Fourth dose: 5 mg base/kg 24 hours after the third dose.

For radical cure of vivax and malariae malaria, concomitant therapy with an 8-aminoquinoline compound is necessary.

Supplied: Each white, film-coated, peanut-shaped tablet, with PLAQUENIL in black on one side, contains: hydroxychloroquine sulfate 200 mg (equivalent to 155 mg of base). Nonmedicinal ingredients: calcium phosphate (dibasic), carnauba wax, hydroxypropyl methylcellulose, magnesium stearate, polyethylene glycol, polysorbate 80, starch and titanium dioxide. Energy: 0.97 kJ (0.23 kcal). Gluten-, lactose-, sucrose- and tartrazine-free. Bottles of 100.

(Shown in Product Recognition Section)

Reviewed 1997

PLASBUMIN®-5

Bayer

Albumin (Human)

Plasma Substitute/Blood Derivative

Pharmacology: Albumin (human) 5% is oncotically equivalent volume for volume to normal human plasma.

When administered i.v. to an adequately hydrated subject, the oncotic (colloid osmotic) effect of Albumin (Human) 5% is to expand the circulating blood volume by an amount approximately equal to the volume infused. It is primarily used in the treatment of shock associated with hemorrhage, surgery, trauma, burns, bacteremia, renal failure, and cardiovascular collapse.

Albumin is a transport protein and it may be useful in severe jaundice in hemolytic disease of the newborn. This could also be of importance in acute liver failure where albumin might serve the dual role of supporting plasma oncotic pressure, as well as binding excessive plasma bilirubin.

Indications: Emergency Treatment of Hypovolemic Shock: Albumin (human) 5% is iso-oncotic with normal plasma and on i.v. infusion will expand the circulating blood volume by an amount approximately equal to the volume infused. In conditions associated mainly with a volume deficit, albumin is best administered as a 5% solution; but where there is an oncotic deficit, the 25% solution may be preferred. This is also an important consideration where the treatment of the shock state has been delayed. If the 25% solution is used, appropriate additional crystalloid should be administered.

Crystalloid solutions in volumes several times greater than that of Albumin (Human) 5% may be effective in treating shock in younger individuals who have no pre-existing illness at the time of the incident. Older patients, especially those with pre-existing debilitating conditions, or those in whom the shock is caused by a medical disorder, or where the state of shock has existed for some time before active therapy could be instituted, may not tolerate hypoalbuminemia as well.

Removal of ascitic fluid from a patient with cirrhosis may cause changes in cardiovascular function and even result in hypovolemic shock. In such circumstances, the use of albumin infusion may be required to support the blood volume.

Burn Therapy: An optimal therapeutic regimen with respect to the administration of colloids, crystalloids, and water following extensive burns has not been established. During the first 24 hours after sustaining thermal injury, large volumes of crystalloids are infused to restore the depleted extracellular fluid volume. Beyond 24 hours, albumin can be used to maintain plasma colloid osmotic pressure. Albumin (human) 25% may be preferred for this purpose.

Cardiopulmonary Bypass: With the relatively small priming volume required with modern pumps, preoperative dilution of the blood using albumin and crystalloid has been shown to be safe and well-tolerated. Although the limit to which the hematocrit and plasma protein concentration can be safely lowered has not been defined, it is common practice to adjust the albumin and crystalloid pump prime to achieve a hematocrit of 20% and a plasma albumin concentration of 2.5 g/100 mL in the patient.

Acute Liver Failure: In the uncommon situation of rapid loss of liver function, with or without coma, administration of albumin may serve the double purpose of supporting the colloid osmotic pressure of the plasma as well as binding excess plasma bilirubin.

Sequestration of Protein Rich Fluids: This occurs in such conditions as acute peritonitis, pancreatitis, mediastinitis, and extensive cellulitis. The magnitude of loss into the third space may require treatment of reduced volume or oncotic activity with an infusion of albumin.

Situations in which albumin administration is **not** warranted: In chronic nephrosis, infused albumin is promptly excreted by the kidneys with no relief of the chronic edema or effect on the underlying renal lesion. It is of occasional use in the rapid "priming" diuresis of nephrosis. Similarly, in hypoproteinemic states associated with chronic cirrhosis, malabsorption, protein losing enteropathies, pancreatic insufficiency, and undernutrition, the infusion of albumin as a source of protein nutrition is not justified.

Contraindications: Certain patients, e.g., those with a history of congestive cardiac failure, renal insufficiency or stabilized chronic anemia, are at special risk of developing circulatory overload. A history of allergic reaction to albumin is a specific contraindication for usage.

Warnings: Solutions which are turbid or which have been frozen should not be used. Do not begin administration more than 4 hours after the container has been entered. Partially used vials must be discarded. Vials which are cracked or which have been previously entered or damaged should not be used, as this may have allowed the entry of microorganisms. The 5% solution contains no preservative.

Precautions: General: Patients should always be monitored carefully in order to guard against the possibility of circulatory overload. The 5% solution is iso-oncotic with normal plasma and will not tend to aggravate tissue dehydration. Appropriate additional crystalloids should be administered, if required by the patient, to maintain normal fluid balance.

In hemorrhage, the administration of albumin should be supplemented by the transfusion of whole blood to treat the relative anemia associated with hemodilution. When circulating blood volume has been reduced, hemodilution following the administration of albumin persists for many hours. In patients with a normal blood volume, hemodilution lasts for a much shorter period. The rapid rise in blood pressure, which may follow the administration of a colloid with positive oncotic activity, necessitates careful observation to detect and treat severed blood vessels which may not have bled at the lower blood pressure.

Drug Interactions: Albumin (human) 5% is compatible with whole blood and packed red cells, as well as the standard carbohydrate and electrolyte solutions intended for i.v. use. It should not be mixed with protein hydrolysates, amino acid solutions nor those containing alcohol.

Pregnancy: Animal reproduction studies have not been conducted with albumin (human) 5%. It is also not known whether it can cause fetal harm when administered to a pregnant woman or can affect reproduction capacity. It should be given to a pregnant woman only if clearly needed.

Children: Safety and effectiveness in the pediatric population have not been established.

Adverse Effects: Adverse reactions to albumin are rare. Such reactions may be allergic in nature or be due to high plasma protein levels from excessive albumin administration. Allergic manifestations include urticaria, chills, fever, and changes in respiration, pulse and blood pressure.

Dosage: Albumin (human) 5% should always be administered by i.v. infusion. The choice between the use of 5% and 25% solutions depends upon whether the patient requires primarily volume (5% solution) or primarily colloid osmotic activity (25% solution). Below a serum oncotic level of 20 mmHg (equal to a total serum protein concentration of 5.2 g/100 mL) there is evidence which suggests that the risk of complications increases. When the oncotic pressure drops below this level, the patient should be treated with the 25% solution together with diuretics. This is especially important in high risk patients who have undergone abdominal, cardiovascular, thoracic or urologic surgery or who have acute bacteremia.

The volume administered and the speed of administration should be adapted to the response of the individual patient.

Hypovolemic Shock: The volume infused should be related to the estimated volume deficit and the speed of administration adapted to the response of the patient.

In neonates or infants, albumin (human) 5% may be given in large amounts. The recommended dose is 10 to 20 mL/kg equivalent to 0.5 to 1.0 g albumin/kg body weight.

Burns: After a burn injury (usually beyond 24 hours) there is a close correlation between the amount of albumin infused and the resultant increase in plasma colloid osmotic pressure. The aim should be to maintain the plasma albumin concentration in the region of 2.5 ± 0.5 g/100 mL with a plasma oncotic pressure of 20 mmHg (equivalent to a total plasma protein concentration of 5.2 g/100 mL). This is best achieved by the i.v. administration of albumin (human), usually as the 25% solution. The duration of therapy is decided by the loss of protein from burned areas and in the urine. In addition, oral or parenteral feeding with amino acids should be initiated. Long-term administration of albumin should not be considered as a source of nutrition.

Other dosage recommendations are given under Indications.

Preparation for Administration: Remove seal to expose stopper. Always swab stopper top immediately with suitable

Plasbumin-5 (cont'd)

antiseptic prior to entering vial. Parenteral drug products should be inspected visually for particulate matter and discoloration prior to administration, whenever solution and container permit.

Supplied: Each vial of sterile, aqueous solution for i.v. administration contains albumin (human) 5%, USP: 2.5 g (in 50 mL), 12.5 g (in 250 mL), 25 g (in 500 mL). Also contains sodium caprylate 0.004 M, and acetyltryptophan 0.004 M and is buffered with sodium carbonate. Preservative-free. Vials of 50 (pediatric size), 250 and 500 mL.

Each vial is heat-treated at 60°C for 10 hours against the possibility of transmitting the hepatitis viruses.

Store at room temperature not exceeding 30°C. Do not use after expiration date. Do not freeze.

PLASBUMIN®-25

Bayer

Albumin (Human)

Plasma Substitute/Blood Derivative

Pharmacology: Each 20 mL vial of albumin (human) 25% supplies the oncotic equivalent of approximately 100 mL citrated plasma; 50 mL supplies the oncotic equivalent of approximately 250 mL citrated plasma.

When administered i.v. to an adequately hydrated subject, the oncotic (colloid osmotic) effect of 20 mL albumin (human) 25% is such that it will draw approximately a further 70 mL of fluid from the extravascular tissues into the circulation within 15 minutes, thus increasing the total blood volume and reducing both hemoconcentration and whole blood viscosity. Accordingly, the main clinical indications are for hypoproteinemic states involving reduced oncotic pressure, with or without accompanying edema. Albumin (human) 25% can also be used as a plasma volume expander.

Albumin is a transport protein and it may be useful in severe hemolytic disease in the neonate who is awaiting exchange transfusion. The infused albumin may reduce the level of free bilirubin in the blood.

This could also be of importance in acute liver failure where albumin might serve the dual role of supporting plasma oncotic pressure, as well as binding excessive plasma bilirubin.

Indications: Emergency Treatment of Hypovolemic Shock: Albumin (human) 25% is hyperoncotic and on i.v. infusion will expand the plasma volume by an additional amount, 3 to 4 times the volume actually administered, by withdrawing fluid from the interstitial spaces, provided the patient is normally hydrated interstitially or there is interstitial edema. If the patient is dehydrated, additional crystalloids must be given, or alternatively, albumin (human) 5% should be used. The patient's hemodynamic response should be monitored and the usual precautions against circulatory overload observed. The total dose should not exceed the level of albumin found in the normal individual, i.e., about 2 g/kg body weight in the absence of active bleeding. Although albumin (human) 5% is to be preferred for the usual volume deficits, albumin (human) 25% with appropriate crystalloids may offer therapeutic advantages in oncotic deficits or in long-standing shock where treatment has been delayed.

Removal of ascitic fluid from a patient with cirrhosis may cause changes in cardiovascular function and even result in hypovolemic shock. In such circumstances, the use of an albumin infusion may be required to support the blood volume.

Burn Therapy: An optimal therapeutic regimen with respect to the administration of colloids, crystalloids, and water following extensive burns has not been established. During the first 24 hours after sustaining thermal injury, large volumes of crystalloids are infused to restore the depleted extracellular fluid volume. Beyond 24 hours albumin (human) 25% can be used to maintain plasma colloid osmotic pressure.

Hypoproteinemia With or Without Edema: During major surgery, patients can lose over half of their circulating albumin with the attendant complications of oncotic deficit. A similar situation can occur in sepsis or intensive care patients. Treatment with albumin (human) 25% may be of value in such cases.

Adult Respiratory Distress Syndrome (ARDS): This is characterized by deficient oxygenation caused by pulmonary interstitial edema complicating shock and postsurgical conditions. When clinical signs are those of hypoproteinemia with a fluid volume overload, albumin (human) 25% together with a diuretic may play a role in therapy.

Cardiopulmonary Bypass: With the relatively small priming volume required with modern pumps, preoperative dilution of the blood using albumin and crystalloid has been shown to be safe and well-tolerated. Although the limit to which the hematocrit and plasma protein concentration can be safely lowered has not been defined, it is common practice to adjust the albumin and crystalloid pump prime to achieve a hematocrit of 20% and a plasma albumin concentration of 2.5 g/100 mL in the patient.

Acute Liver Failure: In the uncommon situation of rapid loss of liver function with or without coma, administration of albumin may serve the double purpose of supporting the colloid osmotic pressure of the plasma as well as binding excess plasma bilirubin.

Neonatal Hemolytic Disease: The administration of albumin (human) 25% may be indicated prior to exchange transfusion, in order to bind free bilirubin, thus lessening the risk of kernicterus. A dosage of 1 g/kg body weight is given about 1 hour prior to exchange transfusion. Caution must be observed in hypervolemic infants.

Sequestration of Protein Rich Fluids: This occurs in such conditions as acute peritonitis, pancreatitis, mediastinitis, and extensive cellulitis. The magnitude of loss into the third space may require treatment of reduced volume or oncotic activity with an infusion of albumin.

Erythrocyte Resuspension: Albumin may be required to avoid excessive hypoproteinemia, during certain types of exchange transfusion, or with the use of very large volumes of previously frozen or washed red cells. About 25 g of albumin per litre of erythrocytes is commonly used, although the requirements in pre-existent hypoproteinemia or hepatic impairment can be greater. Albumin (human) 25% is added to the isotonic suspension of washed red cells immediately prior to transfusion.

Acute Nephrosis: Certain patients may not respond to cyclophosphamide or steroid therapy. The steroids may even aggravate the underlying edema. In this situation a loop diuretic and 100 mL albumin (human) 25% repeated daily for 7 to 10 days may be helpful in controlling the edema and the patient may then respond to steroid treatment.

Renal Dialysis: Although not part of the regular regimen of renal dialysis albumin (human) 25% may be of value in the treatment of shock or hypotension in these patients. The usual volume administered is about 100 mL, taking particular care to avoid fluid overload as these patients are often fluid overloaded and cannot tolerate substantial volumes of salt solution.

Situations in which albumin administration is **not** warranted: In chronic nephrosis, infused albumin is promptly excreted by the kidneys with no relief of the chronic edema or effect on the underlying renal lesion. It is of occasional use in the rapid "priming" diuresis of nephrosis. Similarly, in hypoproteinemic states associated with chronic cirrhosis, malabsorption, protein losing enteropathies, pancreatic insufficiency, and undernutrition, the infusion of albumin as a source of protein nutrition is not justified.

Contraindications: Certain patients, e.g., those with a history of congestive cardiac failure, renal insufficiency or stabilized chronic anemia, are at special risk of developing circulatory overload. A history of an allergic reaction to albumin is a specific contraindication to usage.

Warnings: Solutions which have been frozen should not be used. Do not use if turbid. Do not begin administration more than 4 hours after the container has been entered. Partially used vials must be discarded. Vials which are cracked or which have been previously entered or damaged should not be used, as this may have allowed the entry of microorganisms. Albumin (human) 25% contains no preservative.

Precautions: General: Patients should always be monitored carefully in order to guard against the possibility of circulatory overload. Albumin (human) 25% is hyperoncotic, therefore, in the presence of dehydration, albumin must be given with or followed by addition of fluids.

In hemorrhage the administration of albumin should be supplemented by the transfusion of whole blood to treat the relative anemia associated with hemodilution. When circulating blood volume has been reduced, hemodilution following the administration of albumin persists for many hours. In patients with a normal blood volume, hemodilution lasts for a much shorter period.

The rapid rise in blood pressure which may follow the administration of a colloid with positive oncotic activity necessitates careful observation to detect and treat severed blood vessels which may not have bled at the lower blood pressure.

Drug Interactions: Albumin (human) 25%, USP is compatible with whole blood, packed red cells, as well as the standard carbohydrate and electrolyte solutions intended for i.v. use. It should, however, not be mixed with protein hydrolysates, amino acid solutions nor those containing alcohol.

Pregnancy: Animal reproduction studies have not been conducted with albumin (human) 25%. It is also not known whether it can cause fetal harm when administered to a pregnant woman or can affect reproduction capacity. It should be given to a pregnant woman only if clearly needed.

Children: Safety and effectiveness in the pediatric population have not been established.

Adverse Effects: Adverse reactions to albumin are rare. Such reactions may be allergic in nature or due to high plasma protein levels from excessive albumin administration. Allergic manifestations include urticaria, chills, fever, and changes in respiration, pulse and blood pressure.

Dosage: Albumin (human) 25% should always be administered by i.v. infusion. If sodium restriction is required, it may be administered either undiluted or diluted in a sodium-free carbohydrate solution such as 5% dextrose in water.

Hypovolemic Shock: For treatment of hypovolemic shock, the volume administered and the speed of infusion should be adapted to the response of the individual patient.

Burns: After a burn injury (usually beyond 24 hours) there is a close correlation between the amount of albumin infused and the resultant increase in plasma colloid osmotic pressure. The aim should be to maintain the plasma albumin concentration in the region of 2.5 ± 0.5 g/100 mL with a plasma oncotic pressure of 20 mm Hg (equivalent to a total plasma protein concentration of 5.2 g/100 mL). This is best achieved by the i.v. administration of albumin (human) 25%. The duration of therapy is decided by the loss of protein from the burned areas and in the urine. In addition, oral or parenteral feeding with amino acids should be initiated, as the long-term administration of albumin should not be considered as a source of nutrition.

Hypoproteinemia With or Without Edema: Unless the underlying pathology responsible for the hypoproteinemia can be corrected, the i.v. administration of albumin (human) 25% must be considered purely symptomatic or supportive (see Situations in which albumin administration is **not** warranted). The usual daily dose of albumin for adults is 50 to 75 g and for children 25 g. Patients with severe hypoproteinemia who continue to lose albumin may require larger quantities. Since hypoproteinemic patients usually have approximately normal blood volumes, the rate of administration of albumin (human) 25% should not exceed 2 mL/min, as more rapid injection may precipitate circulatory embarrassment and pulmonary edema.

Other dosage recommendations are given under Indications.

Preparation for Administration: Remove seal to expose stopper. Always swab stopper top immediately with a suitable antiseptic prior to entering vial. Parenteral drug products should be inspected visually for particulate matter and discoloration prior to administration, whenever solution and container permit.

Supplied: Each vial of sterile, aqueous solution for i.v. administration contains albumin (human) 25%, USP: 5 g (in 20 mL), 12.5 g (in 50 mL), 25 g (in 100 mL). The solution also contains sodium caprylate 0.02 M and acetyltryptophan 0.02 M and is buffered with sodium carbonate. Preservative-free. Vials of 20, 50 and 100 mL.

Each vial is heat-treated at 60°C for 10 hours against the possibility of transmitting the hepatitis viruses.

Store at room temperature not exceeding 30°C. Do not use after expiration date. Do not freeze.

PLATINOL®-AQ Ⓟ

Bristol

Cisplatin

Antineoplastic

> Caution: Cisplatin is a potent drug and should be used only by physicians experienced with cancer chemotherapeutic drugs (see Warnings and Precautions). Blood counts as well as renal and hepatic function tests should be taken regularly. Discontinue the drug if abnormal depression of bone marrow or abnormal renal or hepatic function is seen.

Pharmacology: Cisplatin has biochemical properties similar to those of bifunctional alkylating agents producing interstrand and intrastrand crosslinks in DNA. It is apparently not cell-cycle specific.

Pharmacokinetics: Following bolus injection, or i.v. infusion over 2 to 7 hours, of doses ranging from 50 to 100 mg/m², plasma cisplatin half-life is approximately 30 minutes. The ratios of cisplatin to total, free (ultrafilterable) platinum in the plasma range from 0.4 to 1.1 after a dose of 100 mg/m².

Cisplatin does not undergo instantaneous and reversible binding to plasma proteins characteristic of normal drug-protein binding; however, the platinum from cisplatin becomes bound to plasma proteins. These complexes are slowly eliminated with a half-life of 5 days or more.

Following cisplatin doses of 20 to 120 mg/m², the concentrations of platinum are highest in liver, prostate and kidney, somewhat lower in bladder, muscle, testicle, pancreas and spleen and lowest in bowel, adrenal, heart, lung, cerebrum, and cerebellum. Platinum is present in tissues for as long as 180 days after the last administration. With the exception of intracerebral tumors, platinum concentrations in tumors are generally somewhat lower than the concentrations in the organ where the tumor is located. Different metastatic sites in the same patient may have different platinum concentrations. Hepatic metastases have the highest platinum concentrations, but these are similar to the platinum concentrations in normal liver.

Over a range of doses administered as bolus injections or infusions of up to 24 hours, approximately 10 to 40% of the platinum administered is excreted in the urine in 24 hours. Similar mean urinary recoveries of platinum are found following daily administration on 5 consecutive days. Intact cisplatin accounts for the majority of platinum excreted in the urine within 1 hour of administration. Renal clearance of cisplatin exceeds creatinine clearance. The renal clearance of free (ultrafilterable) platinum also exceeds creatinine clearance, is nonlinear and depends on dose, urine flow rate and individual variability in tubular secretion and reabsorption. No close correlation exists between the renal clearance of either free (ultrafilterable) platinum or cisplatin and creatinine clearance. There is a potential for accumulation of free (ultrafilterable) platinum in plasma when cisplatin is administered on a daily basis, but not when it is administered on an intermittent basis.

Although small amounts of platinum are present in the bile and large intestine after administration of cisplatin, fecal excretion of platinum appears to be insignificant.

Indications: As palliative therapy, to be employed in addition to other modalities, or in established combination therapy with other chemotherapeutic agents in the following: Metastatic testicular tumors: in patients who have already received appropriate surgical and/or radiotherapeutic and/or chemotherapeutic procedures. Metastatic ovarian tumors: as secondary therapy in patients refractory to standard chemotherapy. Advanced bladder cancer: as a single agent for patients with transitional cell bladder cancer.

Contraindications: In patients with pre-existing renal impairment, and hearing impairment, unless in the judgement of the physician and patient the possible benefits of treatment outweigh the risks.

Cisplatin should not be employed in myelosuppressed patients and is contraindicated in individuals who have demonstrated a previous hypersensitivity to it or other platinum-containing compounds.

When used as indicated, the physician must carefully weigh the therapeutic benefit versus risk of toxicity which may occur.

Warnings: Cisplatin produces cumulative nephrotoxicity which can be potentiated by aminoglycoside antibiotics (see Precautions).

Anaphylactic-like reactions to cisplatin have been reported and include facial edema, bronchoconstriction, tachycardia and hypotension. These reactions have occurred within minutes of administration to patients with prior exposure to cisplatin and have been alleviated by administration of epinephrine, corticosteroids and antihistamines.

There are reports of severe neuropathies in patients in whom regimens are employed using higher doses of cisplatin, or greater dose frequencies, than those recommended. These neuropathies may be irreversible and are seen as paresthesia in a stocking-glove distribution, areflexia, and loss of proprioception and vibratory sensation. Loss of motor function has also been reported.

Ototoxicity, which may be more pronounced in children, and is manifested by tinnitus, and/or loss of high frequency hearing and occasionally deafness, is significant. Since ototoxicity is cumulative, audiometric testing should be performed prior to initiating therapy and prior to each subsequent dose of drug (see Adverse Effects).

Pregnancy: Cisplatin can cause fetal harm when administered to a pregnant woman. Cisplatin is mutagenic in bacteria, produces chromosome aberrations in animal cells in tissue culture and is teratogenic and embryotoxic in mice. Patients should be advised to avoid becoming pregnant. If this drug is used during pregnancy or if the patient becomes pregnant while taking this drug, the patient should be apprised of the potential hazard to the fetus.

Cisplatin has been found to have carcinogenic potential in laboratory animals. The development of acute leukemia coincident with the use of cisplatin has been reported rarely in humans. In these reports cisplatin was generally given in combination with other leukemogenic agents.

As with any potent antineoplastic drug, the benefit to patient versus risk of toxicity must be carefully weighed.

Precautions: Cisplatin should be administered under the supervision of a qualified physician experienced with the use of antineoplastic therapy. Appropriate management of therapy and complications is possible only when adequate diagnostic and treatment facilities are readily available.

Cisplatin produces cumulative nephrotoxicity which can be potentiated by aminoglycoside antibiotics. Serum creatinine, BUN, creatinine clearance, magnesium, sodium, potassium and calcium levels should be measured prior to initiating therapy, and prior to each subsequent course. At the recommended dosage, cisplatin should not be given more frequently than once every 3 to 4 weeks (see Adverse Effects). Pretreatment hydration with 1 or 2 L of fluid infused for 8 to 12 hours prior to a cisplatin dose is recommended to minimize nephrotoxicity.

Since ototoxicity of cisplatin is cumulative, audiometric testing should be performed prior to initiating therapy and prior to each subsequent dose of drug (see Adverse Effects).

Peripheral blood counts should be monitored weekly. Liver function should be monitored periodically. Neurologic examinations should also be performed regularly (see Adverse Effects).

Drug Interactions: Plasma levels of anticonvulsants may become subtherapeutic during cisplatin therapy. In a randomized trial in advanced ovarian cancer, response duration was adversely affected when pyridoxine was used with altretamine (hexamethylmelamine) and cisplatin.

Pregnancy: See Warnings.

Lactation: Cisplatin has been reported to be excreted in human milk; patients receiving cisplatin should not breast-feed.

After reconstitution, cisplatin is physically incompatible with any i.v. set, needle and syringe containing aluminum. An interaction will occur between aluminum and platinum from cisplatin causing a black precipitate which is visible in the solution (see Dosage, Preparation of i.v Solutions).

As with other potentially toxic compounds, caution should be exercised in handling the solution of cisplatin. Skin reactions associated with accidental exposure to cisplatin may occur. The use of gloves is recommended. If cisplatin solution contacts the skin, immediately wash thoroughly with soap and water. If cisplatin solution contacts mucous membranes, flush thoroughly with water.

Adverse Effects: Nephrotoxicity: Dose-related and cumulative renal insufficiency is the major dose-limiting toxicity of cisplatin. Renal toxicity has been noted in 28 to 36% of patients treated with a single dose of 50 mg/m². It is first noted during the second week after a dose and is manifested by elevations in BUN and creatinine, serum uric acid and/or a decrease in creatinine clearance. Renal toxicity becomes more prolonged and severe with repeated courses of the drug. Renal function must return to normal before another dose of cisplatin can be given.

Renal function impairment has been associated with renal tubular damage. The administration of cisplatin using a 6- to 8-hour infusion with i.v. hydration, and mannitol diuresis has been used to reduce nephrotoxicity. However, renal toxicity still can occur after utilization of these procedures.

Ototoxicity: Ototoxicity has been observed in up to 31% of patients treated with a single dose of cisplatin, 50 mg/m², and is manifested by tinnitus and/or hearing loss in the high frequency range (4 000 to 8 000 Hz). Decreased ability to hear normal conversational tones may occur occasionally. Ototoxic effects may be more severe in children receiving cisplatin. Hearing loss can be unilateral or bilateral and tends to become more frequent and severe with repeated doses; however, deafness after the initial dose of cisplatin has been reported rarely. Ototoxicity may be enhanced with prior or simultaneous cranial irradiation and may be related to peak plasma concentration of cisplatin. It is unclear whether cisplatin-induced ototoxicity is reversible. Careful monitoring of audiometry should be performed prior to initiation of therapy and prior to subsequent doses of cisplatin. Vestibular toxicity has also been reported.

Hematologic: Myelosuppression occurs in 25 to 30% of patients treated with cisplatin. The nadirs in circulating platelets and leukocytes occur between days 18 and 23 (range 7.5 to 45) with most patients recovering by day 39 (range 13 to 62). Leukopenia and thrombocytopenia are more pronounced at higher doses (>50 mg/m²). Anemia (decrease of 2 g hemoglobin/100 mL) occurs at approximately the same frequency and with the same timing as leukopenia and thrombocytopenia. Cisplatin has been shown to sensitize red blood cells, sometimes resulting in a direct coombs' positive hemolytic anemia. The incidence, severity and relative importance of this effect in relation to other hematologic toxicity has not been established, but the possibility of an hemolytic process should be considered in any person who is receiving cisplatin and has unexplained fall in hemoglobin. The hemolytic process reverses on cessation of therapy.

The development of acute leukemia coincident with the use of cisplatin has been reported rarely in humans. In these reports, cisplatin was generally given in combination with other leukemogenic agents.

Gastrointestinal: Marked nausea and vomiting occur in almost all patients treated with cisplatin, and are occasionally so severe that the drug must be discontinued. Nausea and vomiting usually begin within 1 to 4 hours after treatment and last up to 24 hours. Various degrees of vomiting, nausea and/or anorexia may persist for up to 1 week after treatment.

Delayed nausea and vomiting (beginning or persisting 24 hours or more after chemotherapy) has occurred in patients attaining complete emetic control on the day of cisplatin therapy.

Diarrhea has also been reported.

Hyperuricemia: Hyperuricemia has been reported to occur at approximately the same frequency as increases in BUN and serum creatinine. It is more pronounced after doses greater than 50 mg/m², and peak levels of uric acid generally occur between 3 to 5 days after the dose. Allopurinol therapy for hyperuricemia effectively reduces uric acid levels.

Serum Electrolyte Disturbances: Hypomagnesemia, hypocalcemia, hyponatremia, hypokalemia and hypophosphatemia have been reported to occur in patients treated with cisplatin and are probably related to renal tubular damage. Tetany has occasionally been reported in those patients with hypocalcemia and hypomagnesemia. Generally, normal serum electrolyte levels are restored by administering supplemental electrolytes and discontinuing cisplatin. Inappropriate antidiuretic hormone syndrome has also been reported.

Neurotoxicity: Neurotoxicity, usually characterized by peripheral neuropathies, has occurred in some patients. Neuropathies resulting from cisplatin treatment may occur after prolonged therapy (4 to 7 months); however, neurologic symptoms have been reported to occur after a single dose. Although symptoms and signs usually develop during treatment, rarely they may begin after the last dose of cisplatin. The neuropathy may progress after stopping the treatment. Lhermitte's sign, dorsal column myelopathy, and autonomic neuropathy have also been reported.

Cisplatin therapy should be discontinued when symptoms are first observed. Preliminary evidence suggests peripheral neuropathy may be irreversible in some patients.

Muscle cramps of sudden onset and short duration have been reported. These were usually observed in patients who had received a relatively high cumulative dose of cisplatin, and who had a relatively advanced stage of peripheral neuropathy.

Loss of taste and seizures have also been reported.

Ocular Toxicity: Optic neuritis, papilledema and cerebral blindness have been reported infrequently in patients receiving standard recommended doses of cisplatin. Improvement and/or total recovery usually occurs after discontinuing cisplatin. Steroids with or without mannitol have been used, however, efficacy has not been established.

Blurred vision and altered color perception have been reported after the use of regimens with higher doses of cisplatin or greater dose frequencies than those recommended. The altered color perception manifests as a loss of color discrimination, particularly in the blue-yellow axis. The only

Platinol-AQ (cont'd)

finding on funduscopic exam is irregular retinal pigmentation of the macular area.

Anaphylactic-like Reactions: Anaphylactic-like reactions have been occasionally reported in patients previously exposed to cisplatin. The reactions consist of facial edema, wheezing, tachycardia and hypotension within a few minutes of drug administration. Reactions may be controlled by i.v. epinephrine, corticosteroids or antihistamines. Patients receiving cisplatin should be observed carefully for possible anaphylactic-like reactions and supportive equipment and medication should be available to treat such a complication.

Hepatic: Transient elevation of hepatic enzymes, and bilirubin can occur when cisplatin is administered in recommended doses.

Other Toxicities: Vascular toxicities coincident with the use of cisplatin in combination with other antineoplastic agents have been reported rarely. The events are clinically heterogeneous and may include myocardial infarction, cerebrovascular accident, thrombotic microangiopathy (hemolytic uremic syndrome) or cerebral arteritis. Various mechanisms have been proposed for these vascular complications. There are also reports of Raynaud's phenomenon occurring in patients treated with the combination of bleomycin, vinblastine with or without cisplatin. It has been suggested that hypomagnesemia developing coincident with the use of cisplatin may be an added, although not essential, factor associated with this event. However, it is currently unknown if the cause of Raynaud's phenomenon in these cases is the disease, underlying vascular compromise, bleomycin, vinblastine, hypomagnesemia, or a combination of any of these factors.

Other toxicities reported to occur infrequently are cardiac abnormalities, hiccups, elevated serum amylase and rash. Alopecia has also been reported.

Local soft tissue toxicity has rarely been reported following extravasation of cisplatin. Infiltration of solutions of cisplatin may result in tissue cellulitis, fibrosis and necrosis.

Overdose: Symptoms: Caution should be used to prevent inadvertent overdosage with cisplatin.

Acute overdosage with this drug may result in kidney failure, liver failure, deafness, ocular toxicity (including detachment of the retina), significant myelosuppression, intractable nausea and vomiting and/or neuritis. In addition, death can occur following overdosage.

Treatment: No proven antidote have been established for cisplatin overdosage. Hemodialysis even when initiated for hours after overdosage, appears to have little effect on removing platinum from the body because of rapid and high degree of protein binding of cisplatin. Management of overdosage should include general supportive measures to sustain the patient through the period of toxicity that may occur. Patients should be monitored for 3 to 4 weeks in case of delayed toxicity.

Dosage: The recommended dose in adults and children as single-agent therapy is 50 to 75 mg/m² as a single i.v. dose every 3 to 4 weeks, or 15 to 20 mg/m² i.v. daily for 5 days every 3 to 4 weeks.

A repeat course of cisplatin should not be given until the serum creatinine is below 1.5 mg/100 mL and/or the BUN is below 25 mg/100 mL. A repeat course should not be given until circulating blood elements are at an acceptable level (platelets ≥100 000 cells/mm³, WBC≥4 000 cells/mm³). Subsequent dose of cisplatin should not be given until an audiometric analysis indicates that auditory acuity is within normal limits.

When employed in combination with other antitumor drugs, the dose of cisplatin should be adjusted appropriately.

Pretreatment hydration with 1 to 2 L of fluid infused for 8 to 12 hours prior to a cisplatin dose is recommended. The drug is then diluted in 2 L of 5% Dextrose in 1/2 or 1/3N Saline containing 37.5 g of mannitol, and infused over a 6 to 8-hour period. Adequate hydration and urinary output must be maintained during the following 24 hours.

Caution should be exercised in preparing the solution of cisplatin (see Handling and Disposal). If cisplatin solution contacts the skin, immediately wash thoroughly with soap and water. If cisplatin solution contacts mucous membranes, flush thoroughly with water.

Preparation of I.V. Solutions: **I.V. needles, syringes or sets having aluminum components should not be employed in preparation or administration of cisplatin solutions.** An interaction will occur between aluminum and platinum from cisplatin causing formation of a black precipitate, which is visible in the reconstituted solution, and a loss of potency.

The diluted solution should not be refrigerated and should be used up within a 20 hour period from the time of dilution.

Cisplatin solution further diluted in the following infusion fluids, is stable for 6 to 8 hours at room temperature: 0.9% sodium chloride; 5% dextrose and 0.9% sodium chloride; 5% dextrose and 0.45% sodium chloride; 5% dextrose and 0.9% sodium chloride with mannitol; 5% dextrose and 0.45% sodium chloride with mannitol; 5% dextrose and 0.3% sodium chloride with mannitol.

The diluted infusion should be protected from light if it is not to be used within 6 hours.

Handling and Disposal: Preparation of cisplatin should be done in a vertical laminar flow hood (Biological Safety Cabinet—Class II).

Personnel preparing cisplatin should wear PVC gloves, safety glasses, disposable gowns and masks.

All needles, syringes, vials and other materials which have come in contact with cisplatin should be segregated and incinerated at 1 000°C or more. Sealed containers may explode. Intact vials should be returned to the manufacturer for destruction. Proper precautions should be taken in packaging these materials for transport.

Personnel regularly involved in the preparation and handling of cisplatin should have bi-annual blood examinations.

Supplied: Each mL contains: cisplatin 1 mg and sodium chloride 9 mg in water for injection. Nonmedicinal ingredients: sodium chloride and water for injection. Hydrochloric acid and/or sodium hydroxide is added to adjust pH. Amber glass vials of 50 and 100 mL. Store at room temperature between 15 and 25°C. Protect from light.

Reviewed 1999

PLAVIX™ Ⓟ

Sanofi/Bristol-Myers Squibb

Clopidogrel Bisulfate

Platelet Aggregation Inhibitor

Pharmacology: Mechanism of Action: The role of platelets in the pathophysiology of atherosclerotic disease and thrombotic events has been established. Long-term prophylactic use of antiplatelet drugs has shown consistent benefit in the prevention of ischemic stroke, myocardial infarction and vascular death in patients at increased risk of such outcomes, including those with established atherosclerosis or a history of atherothrombosis. Clopidogrel is a specific inhibitor of ADP-induced platelet aggregation.

Pharmacodynamics: Clopidogrel inhibits selectively the binding of adenosine-diphosphate (ADP) to its platelet receptor and the subsequent ADP-mediated activation of the GPIIb-IIIa complex, thereby inhibiting platelet aggregation. Biotransformation of clopidogrel is necessary to produce inhibition of platelet aggregation. An active metabolite responsible for the activity of the drug has not been identified. Clopidogrel also inhibits platelet aggregation induced by other agonists by blocking the amplification of platelet activation by released ADP. Clopidogrel does not inhibit phosphodiesterase activity.

Clopidogrel acts by modifying irreversibly the platelet ADP receptor. Consequently, platelets exposed to a single dose of clopidogrel are affected for the remainder of their lifespan and recovery of normal platelet function occurs at a rate consistent with platelet turnover (approximately 7 days). Single administration is not sufficient to reach a desired therapeutic effect.

Statistically significant and dose-dependent inhibition of platelet aggregation was noted 2 hours after single oral doses of clopidogrel. Repeated doses of 75 mg/day produced inhibition of ADP-induced platelet aggregation from the first day. Steady state was reached between Day 3 and Day 7. At steady state, with a dose of 75 mg/day, the average inhibition level observed was between 40 and 60%. The aggregation level and bleeding time gradually returned to baseline values within 5 to 7 days after treatment was discontinued. The precise correlation between inhibition of platelet aggregation, prolongation of bleeding time and prevention of atherothrombotic events has not been established.

Pharmacokinetics and Metabolism: Following repeated 75 mg oral doses of clopidogrel (base), plasma concentrations of the parent compound are very low and generally below the quantification limit (0.00025 mg/mL) beyond 2 hours after dosing. Clopidogrel is extensively metabolised by the liver to an unknown pharmacodynamically active chemical moiety. The main circulating metabolite (the carboxylic acid derivative), is inactive and represents about 85% of the circulating metabolites in plasma. The relationship between platelet aggregation and the concentration of the main circulating metabolite has not been established.

Clopidogrel is rapidly absorbed after oral administration of repeated 75 mg clopidogrel (base), with peak plasma levels (approx. 3 mg/L) of the main circulating metabolite occurring at approximately 1 hour after dosing. The pharmacokinetics of the carboxylic acid metabolite are linear (plasma concentrations increase in proportion to dose) in the dose range of 50 to 150 mg of clopidogrel. Absorption is at least 50%, based on urinary excretion of clopidogrel-related metabolites.

Clopidogrel and the main circulating metabolite bind reversibly in vitro to human plasma proteins (98% and 94%, respectively). The binding is non saturable in vitro up to a concentration of 100 μg/mL.

Following an oral dose of ^{14}C-labeled clopidogrel in humans, approximately 50% was excreted in the urine and approximately 46% in the feces in the 5 days after dosing. The elimination half-life of the main circulating metabolite was 8 hours after single and repeated administration. Covalent binding to platelets accounted for 2% of the radiolabel with a half-life of 11 days.

Administration of clopidogrel with meals did not significantly modify the bioavailability of clopidogrel as assessed by the pharmacokinetics of the main circulating metabolite.

Special Populations: Geriatric Patients: Although plasma concentrations of the main circulating metabolite are significantly higher in elderly (≥75 years) as compared to young healthy subjects, there were no differences in platelet aggregation and bleeding time (see Dosage).

Patients with Renal Impairment: After repeated doses of 75 mg/day, plasma levels of the main circulating metabolite were significantly lower in subjects with severe renal impairment (creatinine clearance from 5 to 15 mL/min) compared to subjects with moderate renal impairment (creatinine clearance 30 to 60 mL/min). Since no differences in Cmax, for both clopidogrel and the main circulating metabolite were observed, a compensatory phenomenon, i.e., biliary excretion, which has been observed in animals, may explain the lower values of AUC observed in subjects with severe chronic renal failure. The inhibition of ADP-induced platelet aggregation was lower (25%) than what was observed in healthy subjects in other clinical studies (see Dosage).

Sex Differences: No significant difference was observed in the plasma levels of the main circulating metabolite between males and females. In a small study comparing men and women (n=10 males and 10 females), less inhibition of ADP-induced platelet aggregation was observed in women. In the CAPRIE study (for details see below), the incidence of clinical outcome events was similar in men and women.

Clinical Studies: The safety and efficacy of clopidogrel in preventing atherothrombotic events has been evaluated in a blinded comparison with ASA (Clopidogrel vs Aspirin in Patients at Risk of Ischemic Events; CAPRIE). This was a 19 185-patient, 304-center, international, randomized, double-blind, parallel-group study comparing clopidogrel (75 mg daily) ASA (325 mg daily). Patients ranged in age from 21 to 94 years (mean 62 years). The study was composed of 72.4% men and 27.6% women and included patients with established atherosclerosis or history of atherothrombosis as manifested by myocardial infarction, ischemic stroke or peripheral arterial disease. Patients received randomized treatment for up to 3 years (mean treatment period 1.6 years) and were followed to 3 years or study termination, irrespective of whether study drug had been discontinued (mean follow-up 1.9 years).

The primary outcome of the trial was an intent to treat analysis of the time to first occurrence of new ischemic stroke (fatal or not), new myocardial infarction (fatal or not), or other vascular death. Deaths not easily attributable to nonvascular causes were all classified as vascular. See Table I.

Table I—Plavix

Outcome Events of the Primary Analysis

Patients	Clopidogrel 9 599	ASA 9 586
IS (fatal or not)	438 (4.56%)	461 (4.81%)
MI (fatal or not)	275 (2.86%)	333 (3.47%)
Other vascular death	226 (2.35%)	226 (2.36%)
Total	939 (9.78%)	1 020 (10.64%)

As shown in Table I, clopidogrel was associated with a lower incidence of outcome events of every kind. The overall risk reduction (9.78% vs. 10.64%) was 8.7%, P=0.045. Similar results were obtained when all-cause mortality and all-cause strokes were counted instead of vascular mortality and ischemic strokes (risk reduction 6.9%). In patients who survived an on-study stroke or myocardial infarction, the incidence of subsequent events was again lower in the clopidogrel group.

The CAPRIE trial was not designed to evaluate the relative benefit of clopidogrel in the individual patient subgroups. The benefit appeared to be strongest in patients who were enrolled because of peripheral arterial disease (PAD), followed by patients with stroke and then those with recent myocardial infarction.

Relative Risk Reduction
(95% CI)

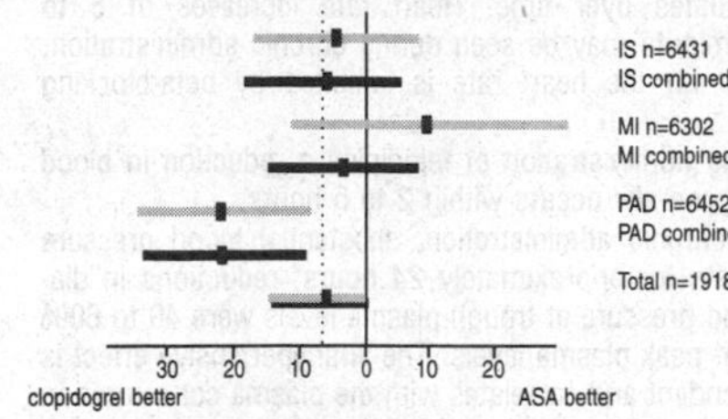

Relative Risk Reduction for the primary endpoint by enrollment criterion: recent MI (0–35 days), recent stroke (0–6 months) or established PAD.

Relative Risk Reduction for the primary endpoint by enrollment criterion (as described above) combined with history of that condition.

* The greater difference in values for MI and MI combined reflects the proportionally larger group of patients (2144) who had a past history of MI in the PAD and stroke groups.

An on-treatment efficacy analysis was also performed in which clopidogrel demonstrated a significant relative risk reduction in the overall event rate compared to ASA of 9.4% ($p=0.046$). The event curves separated early and continued to diverge over the 3-year, follow-up period.

Indications: For the secondary prevention of vascular ischemic events (myocardial infarction, stroke, vascular death) in patients with a history of symptomatic atherosclerotic disease.

Contraindications: Hypersensitivity to the drug substance or any component of the product. Active bleeding such as peptic ulcer and intracranial hemorrhage. Significant liver impairment or cholestatic jaundice.

Warnings: Active Gastrointestinal Lesions: Clopidogrel prolongs bleeding time. Although clopidogrel has shown a lower incidence of gastrointestinal bleeding compared to ASA in a large controlled clinical trial (CAPRIE), clopidogrel should not be used in patients who have lesions with a propensity to bleed (such as ulcers). In patients taking clopidogrel, drugs that might induce such lesions (such as ASA and NSAIDs) should only be used under medical supervision, after carefully assessing the risks.

Anticoagulant Drugs: In view of the possible increased risk of bleeding, anticoagulant drugs should be used with caution as tolerance and safety of simultaneous administration with clopidogrel has not been established (See Precautions, Drug interactions). Risk factors should be assessed for individual patients before using clopidogrel.

The safety of the coadministration of clopidogrel with warfarin has not been established. Consequently, concomitant administration of these two agents should be undertaken with caution.

Pregnancy: There are no adequate and well-controlled studies in pregnant women.

Reproduction studies have been performed in rats at doses up to 500 mg/kg/day and in rabbits at doses up to 300 mg/kg/day and have revealed no evidence of impaired fertility or harm to the fetus due to clopidogrel. Because animal reproduction studies are not always predictive of a human response, clopidogrel should be used during pregnancy only if the potential benefits outweigh the potential risks to the fetus.

Lactation: Studies in rats have shown that clopidogrel and/or its metabolites are excreted in milk. Therefore, clopidogrel should not be used by lactating women.

Children: Safety and effectiveness in subjects below the age of 18 have not been established.

Precautions: General: As with other antiplatelet agents, when considering prescribing clopidogrel, physicians should inquire whether the patient has a history of bleeding. Clopidogrel should be used with caution in patients who may be at risk of increased bleeding from recent trauma, surgery or other pathological condition(s). If a patient is to undergo elective surgery, consideration should be given to discontinue clopidogrel 7 days prior to surgery to allow for the reversal of the effect.

Platelet transfusion may be used to reverse the pharmacological effects of clopidogrel when quick reversal is required.

Patients with Renal Impairment: Therapeutic experience with clopidogrel is limited in patients with severe and moderate renal impairment. Therefore clopidogrel should be used with caution in these patients.

Patients with Hepatic Impairment: Experience is limited in patients with moderate hepatic impairment who may have bleeding diatheses. As with any patient exhibiting hepatic impairment, liver function should be carefully monitored and clopidogrel should be used with caution.

In the CAPRIE study, there were 344 hepatically impaired patients (Alkaline phosphatase >300 U/l, or ALT>120 U/l, or AST>75 U/l) and 168 received clopidogrel for a mean duration of 18 months. The adverse events were more common in this population, compared to the rest of the CAPRIE population, and more common in the clopidogrel (n=168) than in the ASA (n=176) group (any bleeding disorders, n=17 vs n=14; any rash, n=11 vs n=6; diarrhea, n=8 vs n=3, respectively).

Drug Interactions: Study of specific drug interactions yielded the following results.

ASA: ASA (2×500 mg once) did not modify the clopidogrel-mediated inhibition of ADP-induced platelet aggregation, but clopidogrel potentiated the effect of ASA on collagen-induced platelet aggregation. The safety of chronic concomitant administration of ASA and clopidogrel has not been established.

NSAIDs: The short-term concomitant administration of clopidogrel and naproxen increased occult gastrointestinal blood loss in a clinical study conducted in healthy volunteers. Consequently, there is a potential increased risk of gastrointestinal bleeding (See Warnings).

Heparin: Clopidogrel did not modify the effect of heparin on coagulation in a clinical study conducted in healthy volunteers. Coadministration of heparin had no effect on platelet aggregation inhibition induced by clopidogrel. However, the safety of this combination has not been established (See Warnings).

Warfarin: The safety of the coadministration of clopidogrel with warfarin has not been established. Consequently, concomitant administration of these two agents should be undertaken with caution (See Warnings).

Digoxin, Theophylline, Antacids: There was no modification of the pharmacokinetics of digoxin or theophylline with the coadministration of clopidogrel. Antacids did not modify the extent of clopidogrel absorption.

Other: No clinically significant pharmacodynamic interactions were observed when clopidogrel was coadministered in clinical studies to investigate drug interaction with atenolol, nifedipine, or both atenolol and nifedipine. The pharmacodynamic activity of clopidogrel was slightly enhanced by the coadministration of phenobarbital, however this was not considered to be clinically significant. Pharmacodynamic activity of clopidogrel was not changed with the coadministration of cimetidine. Pharmacodynamic activity of clopidogrel was not significantly influenced by the coadministration of estrogen.

Clinically significant adverse interactions were not detected in the CAPRIE study where patients received a variety of concomitant medications including diuretics, beta-blocking agents, angiotensin converting enzyme inhibitors, calcium antagonists, coronary vasodilators, antidiabetic agents, antiepileptic agents and hormone replacement therapy. Patients on HMG CoA reductase inhibitors and clopidogrel experienced a higher incidence of bleeding events (primarily epistaxis). There is no known physiological or pharmacological explanation for this observation. Patients on HMG CoA reductase inhibitors and ASA experienced a higher incidence of intracranial hemorrhage.

At high concentrations in vitro, clopidogrel inhibits cytochrome P450 (2C9). Accordingly, clopidogrel may interfere with the metabolism of phenytoin, tamoxifen, tolbutamide, warfarin, torsemide, fluvastatin, and many nonsteroidal anti-inflammatory agents. There are no data with which to predict the magnitude of these interactions. Caution should be used when any of these drugs is coadministered with clopidogrel.

Laboratory Test Interactions: None known.

Table II—Plavix

Summary of Selected Adverse Events

Adverse Event	Clopidogrel % Incidence (N=9 599)	ASA % Incidence (N=9 586)
Hemorrhages or Bleeding		
Intracranial hemorrhage	0.4	0.5
Gastrointestinal bleeding	2.0	2.7[a]
—requiring hospitalization	0.7	1.1
Purpura (primarily bruising and ecchymosis)	5.3[a]	3.7
Epistaxis	2.9	2.5
Eye bleeding	0.8	0.5
—conjunctival[b]	0.3	0.2
—with sequelae[b]	0.1	0.1
Platelet		
Severe thrombocytopenia ($0 \leq \times < 80$ G/L)	0.2	0.1
Thrombocytopenia ($80 \leq \times < 100$ G/L)	0.1	0.2
Skin		
Rash	4.2[a]	3.5
—severe[b]	0.1	0.1
—leading to discontinuation[b]	0.5	0.2
Pruritus	3.3[a]	1.6
Gastrointestinal		
Peptic, gastric, duodenal ulcer	0.7	1.2
Diarrhea	4.5[a]	3.4
—severe[b]	0.2	0.1
—leading to discontinuation[b]	0.4	0.3
Dyspepsia	5.2	6.1[a]
Constipation	2.4	3.3[a]
Stomatitis	0.2	0.1
Nausea	3.4	3.8
Abdominal pain	5.6	7.1[a]
Gastritis	0.8	1.3[a]
Cardiovascular and Rhythm		
Heart and rhythm disorder	4.3	5.0[a]
Pulmonary embolism	0.4	0.2
Other		
Allergic reaction	0.9	1.0
Influenza-like symptoms	7.5	7.0
Fatigue	3.3	3.4
Pain	6.4	6.3
Headache	7.6	7.2
Coughing	3.1	2.7

[a]Statistically significant difference between treatments ($p \leq 0.05$).
[b]Patients may be included in more than 1 category.

Plavix (cont'd)

Information to be Provided to the Patient: Patients should be informed that it may take longer than usual to stop bleeding when they take clopidogrel, and that they should report any unusual and prolonged bleeding to their physician before starting and during clopidogrel therapy. Patients should be told to inform physicians and dentists that they are taking clopidogrel before any surgery is scheduled and before any new drug is prescribed.

Adverse Effects: Clopidogrel has been evaluated for safety in more than 11 300 patients, including over 7 000 patients treated for 1 year or more. Clopidogrel was well tolerated compared to ASA in a large controlled clinical trial (CAPRIE). The overall tolerability of clopidogrel was similar regardless of age, gender and race. However, in women there was a slightly higher incidence of bleeding disorders, primarily epistaxis, in the clopidogrel group (11.36% vs 9.88%).

A summary of selected adverse effects, regardless of incidence observed in CAPRIE are presented in Table II (on previous page). In CAPRIE, patients with a known intolerance to ASA were excluded from the study.

The following rare events were reported in CAPRIE although there was no difference in the incidence between clopidogrel and ASA. Clopidogrel was not associated with an increase in the incidence of thrombocytopenia and neutropenia.

White Cell Disorders: Granulocytopenia (<1.2 G/L) occurred in 8 patients taking clopidogrel and 14 patients taking ASA. Among those, severe granulocytopenia (<0.45 G/L) was observed in 4 patients (0.04%) that received clopidogrel and 2 patients (0.02%) that received ASA. Two of the 9 599 patients who received clopidogrel had neutrophil counts of zero. None of the 9 586 patients who received ASA had neutrophil counts of zero.

Platelet, Bleeding and Clotting Disorders: One case of Henoch-Schonlein purpura (acute visceral symptoms: vomiting, diarrhea, abdominal distension, hematuria, renal colic) was reported in a patient taking clopidogrel. The patient recovered without sequelae within 1 month.

Skin Disorders: There was no notable difference between treatment groups in the incidence of bullous eruptions (0.23% clopidogrel versus 0.16% ASA). One case of a severe bullous eruption was reported in a patient taking clopidogrel.

Allergic Disorders: Three anaphylactic reactions were reported, 2 in the clopidogrel group and 1 in the ASA group. The patients recovered without sequelae. No anaphylactic shock was reported in either treatment group.

Overdose: Symptoms: One case of deliberate overdosage with clopidogrel was reported: a 34 year old woman took a single 1 050 mg dose of clopidogrel (equivalent to 14 standard 75 mg tablets). There were no associated adverse events. No special therapy was instituted, and she recovered without sequelae.

No adverse reactions were reported after single oral administration of 600 mg (equivalent to 8 standard 75 mg tablets) of clopidogrel in healthy volunteers. The bleeding time was prolonged by a factor of 1.7, which is similar to that typically observed with the therapeutic dose of 75 mg/day.

A single oral dose of clopidogrel at 1 500 or 2 000 mg/kg was lethal to mice and rats, and at 3 000 mg/kg to baboons.

Treatment: Platelet transfusion may be used to reverse the pharmacological effects of clopidogrel when quick reversal is required.

Dosage: The recommended dose of clopidogrel is 75 mg once daily with or without food.

No dosage adjustment is necessary for elderly patients or patients with renal impairment (see Pharmacology).

Information for the Patient: See Blue Section—Information for the Patient "Plavix".

Supplied: Each round, pink, film-coated tablet, engraved on one side with the number 75, contains: clopidogrel 75 mg. Nonmedicinal ingredients: anhydrous lactose, hydrogenated castor oil, microcrystalline cellulose, pregelatinized starch and polyethylene glycol 6000; coating: carnauba wax, ferric oxide (red), hydroxypropyl methylcellulose 2910, polyethylene glycol 6000 and titanium dioxide. Blister cards of 28, cartons of 1. Store away from heat and humidity. Store between 15 and 30°C.

(Shown in Product Recognition Section)

New Product 1998

...Consult a pharmacist for additional drug information.

PLENDIL® Ⓟ

Astra

Felodipine

Antihypertensive Agent

Pharmacology: Felodipine is a calcium ion influx inhibitor (calcium channel blocker). Felodipine is a member of the dihydropyridine class of calcium channel blockers.

Mechanism of Action: The therapeutic effect of this group of drugs is believed to be related to their specific cellular action of selectively inhibiting transmembrane influx of calcium ions into cardiac muscle and vascular smooth muscle. The contractile processes of these tissues are dependent upon the movement of extracellular calcium into the cells through specific ion channels. Felodipine blocks transmembrane influx of calcium through the slow channel without affecting to any significant degree the transmembrane influx of sodium through the fast channel. This results in a reduction of free calcium ions available within cells of the above tissues.

Felodipine does not alter total serum calcium. In vitro studies show that the effects of felodipine on contractile mechanisms are selective, with greater effects on vascular smooth muscle than on cardiac muscle. Negative inotropic effects can be detected in vitro, but such effects have not been seen in intact animals.

The effect of felodipine on blood pressure in man is principally a consequence of a dose-related decrease in peripheral vascular resistance, with a modest reflex increase in heart rate (see Pharmacodynamics).

Pharmacokinetics: Felodipine is completely absorbed from the gastrointestinal tract after oral administration. Due to rapid biotransformation of felodipine during its first pass through the portal circulation, the systemic availability is approximately 15% and is independent of the dose in the range of 5 to 20 mg/day. The plasma protein binding of felodipine is approximately 99%. It is bound predominately to the albumin fraction.

Felodipine is extensively metabolized by the liver, predominantly by cytochrome P450 CYP 3A4. After 72 hours, approximately 70% of a given dose is excreted as metabolites in the urine and 10% is secreted in the feces. Less than 0.5% of a dose is recovered unchanged in the urine. Six metabolites, which account for 23% of the oral dose, have been identified: none has significant vasodilating activity.

Felodipine has been observed to have a mean blood clearance of 914±355 mL/min in hypertensive patients, 606±245 mL/min in elderly hypertensive patients and 1 337±413 mL/min in young healthy volunteers. Its mean terminal half-life was 24.5±7.0 hours in hypertensive patients, 27.5±8.4 hours in elderly hypertensive patients and 14.1±5.6 hours in young healthy volunteers.

The extended release formulation prolongs the absorption phase of felodipine resulting in an increased time to reach peak plasma concentrations (t_{max}), and a reduced maximum plasma concentration (C_{max}). The mean t_{max} ranges from 2.5 to 5 hours. The area under the plasma concentration versus time curve and C_{max} are linearly related to the dose in the 10 to 40 mg range. Following administration of felodipine to hypertensive patients, mean C_{max} at steady state is approximately 20% higher after multiple doses than after a single dose. No increase in the AUC is found during multiple dosing. The inter-individual variation in C_{max} and AUC after repeated dosing is approximately 3-fold and indicates a need for individualized dosing.

The bioavailability of felodipine is not influenced by the presence of food in the gastrointestinal tract.

Studies in healthy male volunteers showed significant alterations in the pharmacokinetics of felodipine when felodipine was administered concomitantly with grapefruit juice. Following the administration of a single dose of plain felodipine 5 mg tablets with 200 mL grapefruit juice or 200 mL water AUC and C_{max} of felodipine increased about 3-fold as compared to administration with water. When felodipine extended release tablets were administered as Plendil 10 mg with 250 mL grapefruit juice felodipine AUC and C_{max} values doubled as compared to those observed with water. When grapefruit juice was taken for up to 24 hours prior to Plendil administration, a significant pharmacokinetic interaction was observed (see Precautions, Interaction with Grapefruit Juice).

Plasma concentrations of felodipine, after a single dose and at steady state, increase with age. Mean clearance of felodipine in elderly hypertensives (mean age 74 years) was only 45% of that in young volunteers (mean age 26 years). At steady state mean AUC for young patients was 39% of that for the elderly patients.

In patients with hepatic disease, the clearance of felodipine was reduced to about 60% of that seen in normal young volunteers.

Renal impairment does not alter the plasma concentration profile of felodipine. Although higher concentrations of the metabolites are present in the plasma due to decreased urinary excretion, these are hemodynamically inactive.

Animal studies have demonstrated that felodipine crosses the blood-brain barrier and the placenta.

Pharmacodynamics: The acute hemodynamic effect of felodipine is a reduction in total peripheral resistance which leads to a decrease in blood pressure associated with a modest reflex increase in heart rate. This reflex increase in heart rate frequently occurs during the first week of therapy and generally attenuates over time. Heart rate increases of 5 to 10 beats/minute may be seen during chronic administration. The effect on the heart rate is inhibited by beta-blocking agents.

Following administration of felodipine a reduction in blood pressure generally occurs within 2 to 5 hours.

During chronic administration, substantial blood pressure control lasts for approximately 24 hours; reductions in diastolic blood pressure at trough plasma levels were 40 to 60% of those at peak plasma levels. The antihypertensive effect is dose-dependent and correlates with the plasma concentration of felodipine.

Felodipine in therapeutic doses has no effect on conduction in the conducting system of the heart and no effect on the AV nodal refractoriness. No direct additional effects to those registered after beta-blockade are observed when felodipine is given concomitantly.

Renal vascular resistance is decreased by felodipine while glomerular filtration rate remains unchanged. Mild diuresis, natriuresis and kaliuresis have been observed during the first week of therapy. No significant effects on serum electrolytes were observed during short- and long-term therapy. No general salt and water retention occurs during long-term therapy. In clinical trials increases in norepinephrine plasma levels have been observed.

Indications: In the treatment of mild to moderate essential hypertension. Felodipine should normally be used in those patients in whom treatment with a diuretic or a beta-blocker was found ineffective or has been associated with unacceptable adverse effects.

Felodipine can be tried as an initial agent in those patients in whom the use of diuretics and/or beta-blockers is contraindicated or in patients with medical conditions in which these drugs frequently cause serious adverse effects.

Combination of felodipine with a thiazide diuretic or a beta-blocker has been found to be compatible and showed an additive antihypertensive effect. Safety and efficacy of concurrent use of felodipine with other antihypertensive agents has not been established.

Contraindications: In patients with a known hypersensitivity to felodipine or other dihydropyridines.

Pregnancy and *Lactation:* In women of childbearing potential, in pregnancy, and during lactation. Fetal malformations and adverse effects on pregnancy have been reported in animals.

Teratogenic Effects: Studies in pregnant rabbits administered doses of 0.46, 1.2, 2.3 and 4.6 mg/kg/day (from 0.4 to 4 times the maximum recommended human dose on a mg/m² basis) showed digital anomalies consisting of reduction in size and degree of ossification of the terminal phalanges in the fetuses. The frequency and severity of the changes appeared dose-related and were noted even at the lowest dose. These changes have been shown to occur with other members of the dihydropyridine class. Similar fetal anomalies were not observed in rats given felodipine.

In a teratology study in cynomolgus monkeys, no reduction in the size of the terminal phalanges was observed but an abnormal position of the distal phalanges was noted in about 40% of the fetuses.

Nonteratogenic Effects: In a study on fertility and general reproductive performance in rats, prolongation of parturition with difficult labor and an increased frequency of fetal and early postnatal deaths were observed in the groups treated with doses of 9.6 mg/kg/day and above.

Significant enlargement of the mammary glands in excess of the normal enlargement for pregnant rabbits was found with doses greater than or equal to 1.2 mg/kg/day. This effect occurred only in pregnant rabbits and regressed during lactation. Similar changes in the mammary glands were not observed in rats or monkeys.

Warnings: Congestive Heart Failure: The safety and efficacy of felodipine in patients with heart failure have not been established. Caution should, therefore, be exercised when using felodipine in hypertensive patients with compromised ventricular function, particularly in combination with a beta-blocker. Acute hemodynamic studies in a small number of patients with New York Heart Association Class II or III heart failure treated with felodipine have not demonstrated negative inotropic effects.

Hypotension, Myocardial Ischemia: Felodipine may, occasionally, precipitate symptomatic hypotension and rarely syncope. It may lead to reflex tachycardia which, particularly in patients with severe obstructive coronary artery disease, may result in myocardial ischemia. Careful monitoring of blood pressure during the initial administration and titration of felodipine is recommended.

Care should be taken to avoid hypotension especially in patients with a history of cerebrovascular insufficiency, and in those taking medications known to lower blood pressure.

Beta-blocker Withdrawal: Felodipine gives no protection against the dangers of abrupt beta-blocker withdrawal; any such withdrawal should be a gradual reduction of the dose of beta-blockers.

Outflow Obstruction: Felodipine should be used with caution in the presence of fixed left ventricular outflow obstruction.

Precautions: Peripheral Edema: Mild to moderate peripheral edema was the most common adverse event in the clinical trials. The incidence of peripheral edema was dose-dependent. Frequency of peripheral edema ranged from about 10% in patients under 50 years of age taking 5 mg daily to about 30% in those over 60 years of age taking 20 mg daily. This adverse effect generally occurs within 2 to 3 weeks of the initiation of treatment. Care should be taken to differentiate this peripheral edema from the effects of increasing left ventricular dysfunction.

Geriatrics: Patients over 65 years of age may have elevated plasma concentrations of felodipine and, therefore, may require lower doses of felodipine (see Pharmacology, Pharmacokinetics). These patients should have their blood pressure monitored closely during initial administration and after dosage adjustment of felodipine. A dosage of 10 mg daily should not be exceeded (see Dosage, Geriatrics).

Patients with Impaired Liver Function: Patients with impaired liver function may have elevated concentrations of felodipine and, therefore, may require lower doses of felodipine (see Pharmacology, Pharmacokinetics). These patients should have their blood pressure monitored closely during initial administration and after dosage adjustment of felodipine. A dosage of 10 mg daily should not be exceeded (see Dosage, Patients with Impaired Liver Function).

Gingival Hyperplasia: Felodipine can induce gingival enlargement in patients with pronounced gingivitis and parodontitis. However, such changes may be reversed by measures of good oral hygiene and mechanical debridement of the teeth.

Pregnancy and *Lactation:* See Contraindications.

Children: Felodipine is not recommended in children since the safety and efficacy in children have not been established.

Interaction with Grapefruit Juice: Published data show that through inhibition of cytochrome P450, grapefruit juice can increase plasma levels and augment pharmacodynamic effects of dihydropyridine calcium channel blockers. In view of the absolute bioavailability of felodipine, the potential for a significant increase in pharmacodynamic effects exists (see Pharmacology, Pharmacokinetics). Therefore, the consumption of grapefruit juice, prior to or during treatment with felodipine should be avoided.

Drug Interactions: As with all drugs, care should be exercised when treating patients with multiple medications. Dihydropyridine calcium channel blockers undergo biotransformation by the cytochrome P450 system, mainly via the CYP 3A4 isoenzyme. Coadministration of felodipine with other drugs which follow the same route of biotransformation may result in altered bioavailability of felodipine or these drugs. Dosages of similarly metabolized drugs, particularly those of low therapeutic ratio, and especially in patients with renal and/or hepatic impairment, may require adjustment when starting or stopping concomitantly administered felodipine to maintain optimum therapeutic blood levels.

Drugs known to be inhibitors of the cytochrome P450 system include: azole antifungals, cimetidine, cyclosporine, erythromycin, quinidine, warfarin.

Drugs known to be inducers of the cytochrome P450 system include: phenobarbital, phenytoin, rifampin.

Drugs known to be biotransformed via P450 include: benzodiazepines, flecainide, imipramine, propafenone, terfenadine, theophylline.

Cytochrome P450 Enzyme Inhibitors: Cimetidine: In healthy volunteers pharmacokinetic studies showed an approximately 50% increase in the area under the plasma concentration time curve (AUC) as well as the C_{max} of felodipine when given concomitantly with cimetidine. It is anticipated that a clinically significant interaction may occur in some hypertensive patients. Therefore, it is recommended that low doses of felodipine be used when given concomitantly with cimetidine.

Erythromycin: Concomitant treatment with erythromycin has been shown to cause an increase in felodipine plasma levels.

Cytochrome P450 Enzyme Inducers: Phenytoin, Carbamazepine and Phenobarbital: In a pharmacokinetic study maximum plasma concentrations of felodipine were considerably lower in epileptic patients on long-term anticonvulsant therapy (phenytoin, carbamazepine, phenobarbital) than in healthy volunteers. The mean area under the felodipine plasma concentration-time curve was also reduced in epileptic patients to approximately 6% of that observed in healthy volunteers. Since a clinically significant interaction may be anticipated, alternative antihypertensive therapy should be considered in these patients.

Alcohol: Alcohol can enhance the hemodynamic effects of felodipine.

Beta-adrenoceptor Blocking Agents: A pharmacokinetic study of felodipine in conjunction with metoprolol demonstrated no significant effects on the pharmacokinetics of felodipine. The AUC and C_{max} of metoprolol, however, were increased approximately 31 and 36%, respectively. In controlled clinical trials, however, beta-blockers including metoprolol were concurrently administered with felodipine and were well tolerated.

Digoxin: When given concomitantly with felodipine as conventional tablets the peak plasma concentration of digoxin was significantly increased. With the extended release formulation of felodipine there was no significant change in peak plasma levels or AUC of digoxin.

Other Concomitant Therapy: In healthy subjects there were no clinically significant interactions when felodipine was given concomitantly with indomethacin or spironolactone.

Adverse Effects: In 861 essential hypertensive patients treated once daily with 2.5 to 10 mg felodipine as monotherapy in controlled clinical trials, the most common clinical adverse events were peripheral edema and headache.

Adverse events that occurred with an incidence of 1.5% or greater at any of the recommended doses of 2.5 to 10 mg once a day, without regard to causality, are listed by dose in Table I. These events are reported from controlled clinical trials with patients who were randomized to either a fixed dose of felodipine or titrated from an initial dose of 2.5 or 5 mg once a day. **A dose of 20 mg once a day has been evaluated in some clinical studies. Although the antihypertensive effect of felodipine is increased at 20 mg once per day, there is a disproportionate increase in adverse events, especially those associated with vasodilatory effects (see Dosage).**

Adverse events that occurred in 0.5 up to 1.5% of patients who received felodipine in all controlled clinical trials at the recommended dosage range of 2.5 to 10 mg once a day are listed below. These events are listed in order of decreasing severity within each category regardless of relationship to felodipine therapy: Body as a Whole: chest pain, facial edema, flu-like illness.

Cardiovascular: tachycardia, premature beats, postural hypotension, bradycardia.

Gastrointestinal: abdominal pain, diarrhea, vomiting, dry mouth, flatulence, acid regurgitation, cholestatic hepatitis, gingival hyperplasia, salivary gland enlargement.

Metabolic: ALT increased.

Musculoskeletal: arthralgia, muscle cramps, myalgia.

Nervous/Psychiatric: insomnia, depression, anxiety disorders, irritability, nervousness, somnolence, decrease in libido, tremor, confusion.

Respiratory: dyspnea, epistaxis.

Dermatologic: pruritus, erythema multiforme, erythema nodosum, urticaria, photosensitivity reactions.

Special Senses: visual disturbances.

Urogenital: impotence, urinary frequency, urinary urgency, dysuria, polyuria.

Serious adverse events reported from controlled clinical trials and during marketing experience (incidence $<0.5\%$) were myocardial infarction, hypotension, syncope, angina pectoris, arrhythmia and anemia.

Isolated cases of angioedema have been reported. Angioedema may be accompanied by breathing difficulty.

Laboratory Tests: For the following laboratory values statistically significant decreases were observed; bilirubin, red blood count, hemoglobin, and urate. Statistically significant increases were found in erythrocyte sedimentation rate and thrombocyte count. In isolated cases, there were increased liver enzymes. None of the changes were considered to be of clinical significance.

Overdose: Symptoms: Overdosage can cause excessive peripheral vasodilation with marked hypotension and possibly bradycardia.

Treatment: If severe hypotension occurs, symptomatic treatment should be instituted. The patient should be placed supine with the legs elevated. The i.v. administration of fluids may be used to treat hypotension. Plasma volume may be increased by infusion of a plasma volume expander. When accompanied by bradycardia, atropine 0.5 to 1 mg should be administered i.v. Sympathomimetic drugs predominantly affecting the α_1-adrenoceptor may be given if the above-mentioned measures are considered insufficient. Removal of felodipine from the circulation by hemodialysis has not been established.

Dosage: Felodipine should be swallowed whole and not crushed or chewed.

The usual recommended initial dose is 5 mg once daily (see Geriatrics, and Patients with Impaired Liver Function).

Depending on the patient's response, the dosage should be adjusted accordingly. Dose adjustment, if necessary, should be done at intervals of not less than 2 weeks.

The maintenance dosage range is 2.5 to 10 mg once daily.

In clinical trials, doses above 10 mg daily showed an increased blood pressure response but a disproportionately higher incidence of peripheral edema and other vasodilatory adverse events.

Modification of the recommended dosage is usually not required in patients with renal impairment.

Table I—Plendil

Percent of patients with adverse events in controlled trials of Plendil (N=861)* as monotherapy without regard to causality (incidence of discontinuations shown in parentheses)

Body System / Adverse Events	Placebo N=334	2.5 mg N=255	5 mg N=581	10 mg N=408
Body as a Whole				
Peripheral Edema	3.3 (0.0)	2.0 (0.0)	8.8 (2.2)	17.4 (2.5)
Asthenia	3.3 (0.0)	3.9 (0.0)	3.3 (0.0)	2.2 (0.0)
Cardiovascular				
Palpitation	2.4 (0.0)	0.4 (0.0)	1.4 (0.3)	2.5 (0.5)
Warm Sensation/Flushing	0.9 (0.3)	3.9 (0.0)	6.2 (0.9)	8.4 (1.2)
Digestive				
Nausea	1.5 (0.9)	1.2 (0.0)	1.7 (0.3)	1.0 (0.7)
Dyspepsia	1.2 (0.0)	3.9 (0.0)	0.7 (0.0)	0.5 (0.0)
Constipation	0.9 (0.0)	1.2 (0.0)	0.3 (0.0)	1.5 (0.2)
Nervous				
Headache	10.2 (0.9)	10.6 (0.4)	11.0 (1.7)	14.7 (2.0)
Dizziness	2.7 (0.3)	2.7 (0.0)	3.6 (0.5)	3.7 (0.5)
Paresthesia	1.5 (0.3)	1.6 (0.0)	1.2 (0.0)	1.2 (0.2)
Respiratory				
Upper Respiratory Infection	1.8 (0.0)	3.9 (0.0)	1.9 (0.0)	0.7 (0.0)
Cough	0.3 (0.0)	0.8 (0.0)	1.2 (0.0)	1.7 (0.0)
Skin				
Rash	0.9 (0.0)	2.0 (0.0)	0.2 (0.0)	0.2 (0.0)

*Some patients have been exposed to more than one dose level of Plendil.

Plendil (cont'd)

Geriatrics: Patients over 65 years of age may develop elevated plasma concentrations of felodipine. A starting dose no higher than 2.5 mg once daily is recommended. A dosage of 10 mg daily should not be exceeded (see Precautions, Geriatrics).

Patients with Impaired Liver Function: Patients with impaired liver function may develop elevated plasma concentrations of felodipine. A starting dose no higher than 2.5 mg once daily is recommended. A dosage of 10 mg daily should not be exceeded (see Precautions, Patients with Impaired Liver Function).

Information for the Patient: See Blue Section—Information for the Patient "Plendil".

Supplied: 2.5 mg: Each yellow, circular, biconvex, film-coated, extended release tablet, engraved A/FL on one side and 2.5 on the other, contains: felodipine 2.5 mg. Nonmedicinal ingredients: Tablet Core: aluminum silicate, hydroxypropyl cellulose, hydroxypropyl methylcellulose, lactose anhydrous, microcrystalline cellulose, polyoxy 40 hydrogenated castor oil, propyl gallate and sodium stearyl fumarate; Coating Layer: carnauba wax, color iron oxide yellow, color titanium dioxide, hydrogen peroxide, hydroxypropyl methylcellulose and polyethylene glycol. Gluten- and tartrazine-free. Blister packages of 30; unit dose blister packages of 10×10.

5 mg: Each pink, circular, biconvex, film-coated, extended release tablet, engraved A/M on one side and 5 on the other, contains: felodipine 5 mg. Nonmedicinal ingredients: Tablet Core: aluminum silicate, hydroxypropyl cellulose, hydroxypropyl methylcellulose, lactose anhydrous, microcrystalline cellulose, polyoxy 40 hydrogenated castor oil, propyl gallate and sodium stearyl fumarate; Coating Layer: carnauba wax, color iron oxide red-brown, color iron oxide yellow, color titanium dioxide, hydrogen peroxide, hydroxypropyl methylcellulose and polyethylene glycol. Gluten- and tartrazine-free. Blister packages of 30; unit dose blister packages of 10×10.

10 mg: Each red-brown, circular, biconvex, film-coated, extended release tablet, engraved A/FE on one side and 10 on the other, contains: felodipine 10 mg. Nonmedicinal ingredients: Tablet Core: aluminum silicate, hydroxypropyl cellulose, hydroxypropyl methylcellulose, lactose anhydrous, microcrystalline cellulose, polyoxy 40 hydrogenated castor oil, propyl gallate and sodium stearyl fumarate; Coating Layer: carnauba wax, color iron oxide red-brown, color iron oxide yellow, color titanium dioxide, hydrogen peroxide, hydroxypropyl methylcellulose and polyethylene glycol. Gluten- and tartrazine-free. Blister packages of 30; unit dose blister packages of 10×10.

Note: These extended release tablets must not be divided, crushed or chewed.

Store between 15 and 30°C.

(Shown in Product Recognition Section)

Reviewed 1999

PMS-ATENOLOL

Pharmascience

Atenolol

β-adrenergic Receptor Blocking Agent

Supplied: 50 mg: Each white to off-white, biconvex, scored, film-coated tablet, embossed with pms-ATENOLOL 50 on one face, contains: atenolol 50 mg. Compliance packs of 30. Bottles of 100 and 500.

100 mg: Each white to off-white, biconvex, scored, film-coated tablet, embossed with pms-ATENOLOL 100 on one face, contains: atenolol 100 mg. Compliance packs of 30. Bottles of 100 and 500.

New Product 1998

PMS-BACLOFEN

Pharmascience

Baclofen

Muscle Relaxant—Antispastic

Supplied: 10 mg: Each white, oval, flat, beveled-edge, bisected tablet, inscribed "pms" on one side of line and "10" on the other, inscribed "Baclofen" on reverse side, contains: baclofen 10 mg. Bottles of 100 and 500.

20 mg: Each white, scored, capsule-shaped tablet, inscribed "pms" on one side of the score line and "20" on the other, inscribed "Baclofen" on reverse side, contains: baclofen 20 mg. Bottles of 100.

Store between 15 and 30°C. Protect from heat and humidity.

PMS-BENZYDAMINE

Pharmascience

Benzydamine HCl

Local Analgesic

Supplied: Each mL of clear green liquid contains: benzydamine HCl 0.15%. Nonmedicinal ingredients: alcohol, glycerin, methylparaben, propylparaben, sorbitol and water. HDPE bottles of 100 and 250 mL.

PMS-BUSPIRONE

Pharmascience

Buspirone HCl

Anxiolytic

Supplied: 5 mg: Each white, round tablet, inscribed "pms" on one side and "B" scored "5" on the other, contains: buspirone HCl 5 mg. Bottles of 100.

10 mg: Each white, caplet-shaped tablet, inscribed "BUSPIRONE" on one side and "pms" scored "10 mg" on the other, contains: buspirone HCl 10 mg. Bottles of 100.

PMS-CEFACLOR

Pharmascience

Cefaclor

Antibiotic

Supplied: Capsules: 250 mg: Each opaque purple and white capsule contains: cefaclor 250 mg. Bottles of 100 and 250.

500 mg: Each opaque purple and gray capsule contains: cefaclor 500 mg. Bottles of 100.

Oral Suspension: 125 mg: Each 5 mL dose of strawberry-flavored suspension contains: cefaclor 125 mg (25 mg/mL). Bottles of 100 and 150 mL.

250 mg: Each 5 mL dose of strawberry-flavored suspension contains: cefaclor 250 mg (50 mg/mL). Bottles of 100 and 150 mL.

375 mg: Each 5 mL dose of strawberry-flavored suspension contains: cefaclor 375 mg (75 mg/mL). Bottles of 70 and 100 mL.

PMS-CEPHALEXIN

Pharmascience

Cephalexin

Antibiotic

Supplied: Suspension: 125 mg/5mL: Each 5 mL of flavored suspension, contains: the equivalent of cephalexin 125 mg (mauve granules). Energy: 52.0 kJ (12.4 kcal)/5 mL. Sodium: <1 mmol (0.032 mg)/5 mL. Tartrazine-free. Identi-Code: W21. Bottles of 100 and 200 mL.

250 mg/5 mL: Each 5 mL of flavored suspension contains: the equivalent of cephalexin 250 mg (peach granules). Energy: 50.5 kJ (12.1 kcal)/5 mL. Sodium: <1 mmol (0.032 mg)/5 mL. Tartrazine-free. Identi-Code: W68. Bottles of 100 and 200 mL.

Tablets: 250 mg: Each round, peach-colored tablet contains: cephalexin 250 mg. Sodium- and tartrazine- free. Identi-Code: GP3. Bottles of 100.

500 mg: Each capsule-shaped, peach-colored tablet contains: cephalexin 500 mg. Sodium- and tartrazine-free. Identi-Code: GP4. Bottles of 100.

PMS-CHLORAL HYDRATE

Pharmascience

Chloral Hydrate

Hypnotic—Sedative

Supplied: Capsules: Each mint green, oval, soft gelatin capsule contains: chloral hydrate 500 mg USP. Tartrazine-free. Bottles of 100 and 500.

Syrup: Each mL of orange-flavored syrup contains: chloral hydrate USP 100 mg. White polyethylene bottles of 500 mL. Store at room temperature; avoid excessive heat.

PMS-CHOLESTYRAMINE

Pharmascience

Cholestyramine Resin

Antihypercholesterolemic—Antidiarrheal

Supplied: Light/Orange and Lemon-Lime Flavors: Each 5 g dose of powder contains: cholestyramine resin 4 g (dried basis). Sugar-free. Cans of 210 g (42 doses) and 400 g (80 doses). Cartons of 30 pouches (30 doses).

Regular: Each sachet (1 dose) of powder contains: cholestyramine resin 4 g (dried basis). Energy: 53.5 kJ (12.8 kcal)/9 g. Sodium- and tartrazine-free. Cartons of 30 sachets. Cans of 378 g (42 doses).

Store at room temperature (15 to 30°C).

PMS-CIMETIDINE

Pharmascience

Cimetidine

Histamine H_2 Receptor Antagonist

Supplied: 200 mg: Each film-coated, light green, round, biconvex tablet contains: cimetidine 200 mg. HDPE bottles of 100 and 500.

300 mg: Each film-coated, light green, round, biconvex tablet contains: cimetidine 300 mg. HDPE bottles of 100, 500 and 1 000.

400 mg: Each film-coated, light green, round, biconvex tablet contains: cimetidine 400 mg. HDPE bottles of 100, 500 and 1 000.

600 mg: Each film-coated, light green, round, biconvex tablet contains: cimetidine 600 mg. HDPE bottles of 100, 500 and 1 000.

800 mg: Each film-coated, light green, round, biconvex tablet contains: cimetidine 800 mg. HDPE bottles of 100 and 500.

PMS-CLOBETASOL

Pharmascience

Clobetasol 17-Propionate

Topical Corticosteroid

Supplied: Cream: Each g of cream contains: clobetasol 17-propionate 0.05% w/w. Tubes of 15 and 50 g.

Ointment: Each g of ointment contains: clobetasol 17-propionate 0.05% w/w. Tubes of 15 and 50 g.

Store between 15 and 30°C.

New Product 1998

PMS-CLONAZEPAM

Pharmascience

Clonazepam

Anticonvulsant

Supplied: PMS-Clonazepam: 0.25 mg: Each cylindrical, biconvex, blue tablet, imprinted CLONAZEPAM on one side and plain on the other side, contains: clonazepam 250 µg. Also contains lactose. Sodium- and tartrazine-free. Bottles of 100.

0.5 mg: Each cylindrical, biplane, beveled-edge, orange, scored tablet, imprinted CLONAZEPAM on one side and pms over 0.5 on the other side, contains: clonazepam 500 µg. Also contains lactose. Sodium- and tartrazine-free. Bottles of 100, 500 and 1 000.

1 mg: Each round, standard concave, pink tablet, imprinted CLONAZEPAM on one side and pms over 1.0 on the other side, contains: clonazepam 1 mg. Also contains lactose. Sodium- and tartrazine-free. Bottles of 100, 500 and 1 000.

2 mg: Each cylindrical, biplane, beveled-edge, white tablet, imprinted CLONAZEPAM on one side and pms over 2.0 on the other, contains: clonazepam 2 mg. Also contains lactose. Sodium- and tartrazine-free. Bottles of 100, 500 and 1 000.

PMS-Clonazepam-R: 0.5 mg: Each cylindrical, biplane, beveled-edge, orange, scored tablet, imprinted CLONAZEPAM on one side and pms over 0.5 on the other side, contains: clonazepam 500 µg. Also contains lactose. Sodium- and tartrazine-free. Bottles of 100 and 500.

Store between 15 and 30°C. Keep in tightly closed, light-resistant container.

PMS-DESIPRAMINE Ⓟ

Pharmascience

Desipramine HCl

Antidepressant

Supplied: 10 mg: Each round, biconvex, film-coated, blue tablet, inscribed "pms-10" on one side, contains: desipramine HCl 10 mg. Bottles of 100.

25 mg: Each round, biconvex, film-coated, yellow tablet, inscribed "pms-25" on one side, contains: desipramine HCl 25 mg. Bottles of 100 and 500.

50 mg: Each round, biconvex, film-coated, green tablet, inscribed "pms-50" on one side, contains: desipramine HCl 50 mg. Bottles of 100 and 500.

75 mg: Each round, biconvex, film-coated, orange tablet, inscribed "pms-75" on one side, contains: desipramine HCl 75 mg. Bottles of 50.

100 mg: Each round, biconvex, film-coated, orange tablet, contains: desipramine HCl 100 mg. Bottles of 100.

Store between 15 and 30°C.

PMS-DICITRATE™

Pharmascience

Sodium Citrate—Citric Acid

Systemic Alkalizer—Neutralizing Buffer

Supplied: Each 5 mL of clear solution contains: sodium citrate dihydrate 500 mg and citric acid monohydrate 334 mg. Each mL contains: Sodium 1 mmol (mEq) and is equivalent to bicarbonate 1 mmol (mEq). Sugar-free. Bottles of 500 mL. Unit dose packages of 30 mL.

Shake well before using. Keep tightly closed. Store at room temperature 15 to 30°C. Protect from freezing.

PMS-DICLOFENAC Ⓟ
PMS-DICLOFENAC SR Ⓟ

Pharmascience

Diclofenac Sodium

Anti-inflammatory—Analgesic

Supplied: PMS-Diclofenac: 25 mg: Each yellow, round, enteric-coated tablet, imprinted with P on one side and 25 on the other, contains: diclofenac sodium 25 mg. Bottles of 100 and 500.

50 mg: Each light brown, round, enteric-coated tablet, imprinted with P on one side and 50 on the other, contains: diclofenac sodium 50 mg. Bottles of 100 and 500.

PMS-Diclofenac SR: 75 mg: Each light pink, triangular, slow-release tablet, printed SR 75 on one side, contains: diclofenac sodium 75 mg. Bottles of 100 and 500.

100 mg: Each pink, round, slow-release tablet, imprinted with P on one side and SR 100 on the other, contains: diclofenac sodium 100 mg. Bottles of 100 and 250.

Protect from heat (store below 30°C) and humidity.

New Product 1998

PMS-DIPHENHYDRAMINE

Pharmascience

Diphenhydramine

Antihistamine

Supplied: Capsules: 25 mg: Each hard gelatin capsule with clear body and pink head, identified R one side and 191 on the other contains: diphenhydramine HCl USP 25 mg. Bottles of 100 and 1 000.

50 mg: Each hard gelatin capsule with pink head and body, identified R one side and 192 on the other contains: diphenhydramine HCl USP 50 mg. Bottles of 100 and 1 000.

Elixir: Each mL of solution contains: diphenhydramine HCl USP 2.5 mg. Bottles of 100 and 500 mL.

Injection: Each mL of the injection contains: diphenhydramine HCl 50 mg. Vials of 10 mL.

PMS-DOCUSATE CALCIUM

Pharmascience

Docusate Calcium

Stool Softener

Supplied: Each red, oblongated, soft gelatin capsule, identified PMS 240 contains: docusate calcium USP 240 mg. Unit doses of 30 and 100. Bottles of 30, 300 and 1 000. Blister sheets of 30.

PMS-DOCUSATE SODIUM

Pharmascience

Docusate Sodium

Stool Softener

Supplied: Capsules: Each orange, oval, soft gelatin capsule, identified PMS 100, contains: docusate sodium USP 100 mg. Sodium: <1 mmol (5.17 mg). Bottles of 30, 100 and 1 000.

Drops: Each mL of clear, red solution with vanillin odor, contains: docusate sodium USP 10 mg. Sodium: <1 mmol (2.5 mg). Plastic bottles of 500 mL.

Syrup: 4 mg: Each mL of clear, red solution with peppermint odor, contains: docusate sodium USP 4 mg. Also contains ethyl alcohol 0.03 mL/5 mL. Sodium: <1 mmol (3.7 mg). Unit dose packages of 25 mL. Graduated Pet-G plastic bottles of 500 mL.

50 mg: Each mL of clear, yellow, lemon-flavored syrup contains: docusate sodium USP 50 mg. Also contains alcohol 5% by volume. Sodium: <1 mmol (5.3 mg). Graduated Pet-G plastic bottles of 250 and 500 mL.

Syrup may be given in milk, fruit juice or infant formula to mask bitter taste.

Store between 15 and 30°C in a tight, light resistant container in a dry area. Protect from freezing. Keep out of reach of children.

PMS-DOMPERIDONE Ⓟ

Pharmascience

Domperidone Maleate

Upper Gastrointestinal Motility Modifier

Supplied: Each white to faintly cream, film-coated tablet contains: domperidone maleate 12.72 mg (equivalent to domperidone 10 mg). HDPE bottles of 100 and 500.

New Product 1998

PMS-EGOZINC

Pharmascience

Zinc Sulfate

Zinc Supplement

Supplied: Ointment: A smooth, colorless, translucent ointment contains: zinc sulfate monohydrate 0.5% in a petrolatum ointment base. Tubes of 30 g with applicator. Store at room temperature (15 to 30°C).

Suppositories: Each white opaque suppository contains: zinc sulfate monohydrate 10 mg. Boxes of 12 and 24. Store at room temperature (15 to 30°C).

Tablets: Each round, white, biconvex tablet, identified PMS-contains: zinc sulfate USP 220 mg equivalent to 50 mg of elemental zinc. Bottles of 100.

PMS-EGOZINC-HC Ⓟ

Pharmascience

Zinc Sulfate Monohydrate—Hydrocortisone Acetate

Anorectal Therapy

Supplied: Ointment: Each tube contains: zinc sulfate monohydrate 0.5% and hydrocortisone acetate 0.5% in a petroleum ointment base. Tubes of 30 g with applicator.

Suppositories: Each suppository contains: zinc sulfate monohydrate 10 mg, hydrocortisone acetate 10 mg in a triglyceride base. Boxes of 12 and 24. Store at room temperature (15 to 30°C).

New Product 1998

PMS-ERYTHROMYCIN Ⓟ

Pharmascience

Erythromycin

Antibiotic

Supplied: Each g of sterile ophthalmic ointment contains: erythromycin (base) 5 mg in a mineral oil and white petrolatum base. Tubes of 3.5 g. Unit dose tubes of 1 g, boxes of 50. Store at room temperature 15 to 30°C.

PMS-FLUOXETINE Ⓟ

Pharmascience

Fluoxetine HCl

Antidepressant—Antiobsessional—Antibulimic

Supplied: Capsules: 10 mg: Each green and grey capsule contains: fluoxetine HCl equivalent to fluoxetine 10 mg (32.3 µmol). Nonmedicinal ingredients: silicone and starch; capsule shell: benzyl alcohol, carboxymethylcellulose sodium, edetate calcium disodium, FD&C Blue No. 1, gelatin, iron oxide black, iron oxide yellow, methylparaben, sodium lauryl sulfate, sodium propionate and titanium dioxide. White HDPE bottles of 100.

20 mg: Each green and yellow capsule contains: fluoxetine HCl equivalent to fluoxetine 20 mg (64.7 µmol). Nonmedicinal ingredients: silicone and starch; capsule shell: benzyl alcohol, carboxymethylcellulose sodium, edetate calcium disodium, FD&C Blue No. 1, gelatin, iron oxide yellow, methylparaben, sodium lauryl sulfate, sodium propionate and titanium dioxide. White HDPE bottles of 100 and 500.

Liquid: Each 5 mL of clear, colorless, syrup solution, with an odor of mint, contains: fluoxetine HCl equivalent to fluoxetine 20 mg/5 mL. Nonmedicinal ingredients: benzoic acid, glycerin, mint flavor, purified water and sucrose. Energy: 50.3 kJ (12.0 kcal)/5 mL. Amber glass bottles of 120 mL.

Store at 15 to 25°C.

PMS-FLUPHENAZINE DECANOATE Ⓟ

Pharmascience

Fluphenazine Decanoate

Antipsychotic

Supplied: Each mL of injectable solution contains: fluphenazine decanoate BP 25 mg in sesame oil. Nonmedicinal ingredients: benzyl alcohol 1.2% as preservative. Glass vials of 5 mL.

PMS-FLUTAMIDE Ⓟ

Pharmascience

Flutamide

Nonsteroidal Antiandrogen

Supplied: Each round, pale yellow-colored, compressed tablet, scored on one side and inscribed "p" on the other, contains: flutamide 250 mg. Bottles of 100.

PMS-GEMFIBROZIL Ⓟ

Pharmascience

Gemfibrozil

Antihyperlipidemic

Supplied: Each white, film-coated, oval-shaped tablet, scored on one side with engraving "93" and "670" on each side of the score and plain on the other, contains: gemfibrozil 500 mg. HDPE bottles of 100, 250 and 500.

PMS-GLYBURIDE Ⓟ

Pharmascience

Glyburide

Oral Hypoglycemic

Supplied: 2.5 mg: Each white, cylindrical, biplane tablet with a "T" superimposed on a smaller "O" printed on one face, and single scored on the other with "A1" printed above and below the score line, contains: glyburide 2.5 mg. Nonmedicinal ingredients: lactose, magnesium stearate, maize starch, silicon dioxide and talc. Tartrazine-free. Bottles of 100 and 500.

5 mg: Each white, oblong, scored tablet, coded BM/EU on both faces, contains: glyburide 5 mg. Nonmedicinal ingredients: lactose, magnesium stearate, maize starch, silicon dioxide and talc. Tartrazine-free. Bottles of 100 and 500.

New Product 1998

PMS-HALOPERIDOL LA Ⓟ

Pharmascience

Haloperidol Decanoate

Antipsychotic

Supplied: 50 mg/mL: Each mL contains: haloperidol decanoate 70.52 mg, equivalent to haloperidol 50 mg. Nonmedicinal ingredients: benzyl alcohol and sesame oil. Multidose vials of 5 mL. Store between 15 and 30°C in airtight containers. Do not refrigerate or freeze. Protect from light.

100 mg/mL: Each mL contains: haloperidol decanoate 141.04 mg, equivalent to haloperidol 100 mg. Nonmedicinal ingredients: benzyl alcohol and sesame oil. Vials of 1 mL (boxes of 10 × 1 mL) and multidose vials of 5 mL. Store between 15 and 30°C in airtight containers. Do not refrigerate or freeze. Protect from light.

PMS-HYDROMORPHONE Ⓝ

Pharmascience

Hydromorphone HCl

Analgesic—Narcotic

Supplied: Suppositories: Each suppository contains: hydromorphone HCl 3 mg. Boxes of 10. Store between 15 to 30°C. Protect from light.

Syrup: Each mL of syrup contains: hydromorphone HCl 1 mg. Pet-G bottles of 500 mL. Store between 15 to 30°C. Protect from light.

Tablets: Each scored tablet contains: hydromorphone HCl 1 mg (light green), 2 mg (light orange), 4 mg (yellow) or 8 mg (white). Bottles of 100. Control packs of 25 (4×25). Protect from light.

PMS-HYDROXYZINE Ⓟ

Pharmascience

Hydroxyzine HCl

Anxiolytic—Antihistamine

Supplied: Capsules: 10 mg: Each soft orange gelatin capsule contains: hydroxyzine HCl 10 mg. Bottles of 100 and 500.

25 mg: Each soft green gelatin capsule contains: hydroxyzine HCl 25 mg. Bottles of 100 and 500.

50 mg: Each soft red gelatin capsule contains: hydroxyzine HCl 50 mg. Bottles of 100 and 500.

Syrup: Each mL of pale yellow, viscous, vanilla-flavored syrup contains: hydroxyzine HCl 2 mg. Glass bottles of 500 mL.

PMS-IPRATROPIUM Ⓟ

Pharmascience

Ipratropium Bromide

Bronchodilator

Supplied: Bottles: Each mL of clear, colorless or almost colorless, isotonic solution contains: ipratropium bromide 250 µg (0.025%). Amber glass bottles of 20 mL with screwcap.

Unit Dose Vials: 125 µg/mL: Each mL of clear, colorless, isotonic solution contains: ipratropium bromide 125 µg (0.0125%). Plastic single use polynebs of 2 mL, packages of 20.

250 µg/mL: Each mL of clear, colorless, isotonic solution contains: ipratropium bromide 250 µg (0.025%). Plastic single use polynebs of 1 mL, packages of 20. Plastic single use polynebs of 2 mL, packages of 10.

PMS-ISONIAZID Ⓟ

Pharmascience

Isoniazid

Tuberculosis Therapy

Supplied: Tablets: Each white, round, biconvex tablet scored on one side and PMS-identified on the other side contains: isoniazid USP 50 mg, 100 mg and 300 mg. Bottles of 100 and 1 000 (100 and 300 mg). Bottles of 100 (50 mg).

Syrup: Each 5 mL of clear liquid contains: isoniazid USP 50 mg. Bottles of 500 mL.

PMS-LACTULOSE

Pharmascience

Lactulose

Colonic Content Acidifier—Laxative

Supplied: Each mL of pale yellow, orange-flavored syrup contains: lactulose USP 667 mg. Also contains less than 147 mg galactose, less than 80 mg lactose and less than 80 mg of other sugars. Unit dose packages of 15 and 30 mL. Graduated Pet-G plastic bottles of 200, 250 and 500 mL. White plastic bottles of 1 L. Store between 15 to 30°C.

Protect from freezing. Prolonged exposure to high temperature or direct light may cause some darkening of solution or a cloudy appearance but no loss of therapeutic effect. Freezing will change solution to semisolid state, which returns to normal when warmed to room temperature. Dilution and subsequent storage not recommended.

PMS-LINDANE

Pharmascience

Lindane

Scabicide—Pediculicide

Supplied: Shampoo: Each mL contains: lindane USP (gamma benzene hexachloride) 1%, acetone, polyoxyethylene sorbitan monostearate, triethanolamine lauryl sulfate and deionized water. Bottles of 50 and 500 mL.

Lotion: Each mL of nongreasy lotion contains: lindane USP (gamma benzene hexachloride) 1% and a mixture of esters of p-hydroxybenzoic acid 0.4% as preservatives. Bottles of 50 and 500 mL.

PMS-LITHIUM CARBONATE Ⓟ
PMS-LITHIUM CITRATE Ⓟ

Pharmascience

Lithium Carbonate

Lithium Citrate

Antimanic Agent

Pharmacology: Although lithium is useful for its antimanic effect and in preventing relapses in patients with a clearcut diagnosis of bipolar affective disorder, it has very little, if any, direct effect on moods, normal or abnormal.

Lithium alters sodium transport in nerve and muscle cells, effects a shift toward intraneuronal metabolism of catecholamines and has an inhibitory action on the intracellular formation of cyclic AMP. However, the specific biochemical mechanism of action of lithium in mania is still largely unknown.

Lithium is inactive in most screening psychopharmacological tests but it produces marked potentiation of amphetamine hyperactivity in animals. It does not appear to protect against the action of stimulant and convulsive drugs and produces only slight potentiation of CNS depressants.

ECG changes with lithium have been reported in both animals and man.

Pharmacokinetics: The results of the comparative pharmacokinetics study for lithium citrate syrup (8 mmol/5 mL) vs lithium carbonate tablets (300 mg) are presented in Table I.

Table I—PMS-Lithium

Results of Comparative Pharmacokinetics Study

Parameter	Solid Mean±SD	Liquid Mean±SD
T_{max} (hours)	2.1±0.74	0.9±0.42*
C_{max} (mmol/L)	1.19±0.47	1.34±0.37
AUC (mmol/L·hour)	7.24±2.56	7.40±1.85
$T_{1/2}$ (hours)	15.18±3.57	13.57±6.43
V_D(L) (volume of distribution)	44.76±21.51	35.30±13.36
Cl (L/hour) (total body clearance)	2.02±0.68	1.87±0.35

*p<0.05.
SD=standard deviation.

The results of the study demonstrated that therapeutic serum lithium levels can be achieved with the liquid lithium citrate dosage equivalent (8 mmol in 5 mL) of 300 mg solid lithium carbonate.

Lithium ions are rapidly absorbed from the gastrointestinal tract following oral administration of lithium citrate. Peak plasma lithium concentrations are reached 0.5 to 1 hour after administration. The distribution of lithium in the body approximates that of total body water, but its passage across the blood-brain barrier is slow and at equilibration, the CSF lithium level reaches only approximately half the plasma concentration.

Lithium is excreted primarily in urine with less than 1% being eliminated with the feces. Lithium is filtered by the glomeruli and 4/5 (80%) of the filtered lithium is reabsorbed in the tubules, probably by the same mechanism responsible for sodium reabsorption. The renal clearance of lithium is proportional to its plasma concentration. The half-life of elimination of lithium is approximately 24 hours. A low salt intake resulting in low tubular concentration of sodium will increase lithium reabsorption and might result in retention or intoxication.

Renal lithium clearance is, under ordinary circumstances, remarkably constant in the same individual but decreases with age and falls when sodium intake is lowered. The dose necessary to maintain a given concentration of serum lithium depends on the ability of the kidney to excrete lithium. However, renal lithium excretion may vary greatly between individuals and lithium dosage must, therefore, be adjusted individually. In clinical reports, it has been noted that serum lithium may rise an average of 0.2 to 0.4 mmol/L after intake of 300 mg (8 mmol) and 0.3 to 0.6 mmol/L after intake of 600 mg (16 mmol) of lithium carbonate. It has been suggested that manic patients retain larger amounts of lithium during the active manic phase, but studies have been unable to confirm a clear difference in excretion patterns. However, patients in a manic state seem to have an increased tolerance to lithium.

Balance studies indicate that lithium may produce a transitory diuresis with increase in sodium and potassium excretion. A period of equilibrium or slight retention may follow, but persistent polyuria may occur in some patients. There is evidence that therapeutic doses of lithium decrease the 24-hour exchangeable sodium. Longitudinal metabolic studies have demonstrated cumulative lithium retention in some patients without undue rise in plasma lithium values, indicating a possible intracellular retention of lithium. There is some evidence that lithium may affect the metabolism of potassium, magnesium and calcium.

Indications: In the treatment of acute manic episodes in patients with manic-depressive disorders. Maintenance therapy has been found useful in preventing or diminishing the frequency of subsequent relapses in bipolar manic-depressive patients (with a strong history of mania).

In patients who find solid dosage forms difficult to swallow or where there are problems with compliance.

Contraindications: In patients with significant cardiovascular or renal disease. In patients with evidence of severe debilitation or dehydration, sodium depletion, brain damage, and in conditions requiring low sodium intake.

Warnings: Therapy with lithium citrate requires reaching plasma levels of lithium which are relatively close to the toxic level. Since lithium is excreted primarily by the kidney, adequate renal function and adequate salt and fluid intake (2 500 to 3 000 mL) are essential in order to avoid lithium accumulation and intoxication. Thus, a decision to initiate lithium therapy should be preceded by a thorough clinical examination and evaluation of each patient, including laboratory determinations, ECG, and a very careful assessment of renal function.

Means of obtaining accurate determinations of serum lithium levels should be available, since frequent serum determinations are required specially during the initial period of treatment. Lithium toxicity is closely related to serum lithium levels and during treatment, they should usually not exceed 1.5 mmol/L, if serious adverse reactions and lithium intoxication are to be avoided. This lithium level refers to a blood sample drawn before the patient has had his/her first lithium dose of the day, therefore, 9 to 12 hours after his/her last dose of drug. Serum lithium levels should usually be monitored 3 times weekly during the initial period of administration and periodically as required thereafter. If lithium levels exceed 1.5 to 2 mmol/L, the drug should be discontinued and, if appropriate, the administration resumed at a lower level after 24 hours. Prodromal toxic signs such as fatigue, muscular weakness, incoordination, drowsiness, coarse tremors, diarrhea and vomiting, provide a sensitive warning of lithium intoxication.

In view of the limited dosage range of lithium compared to other psychotropic agents, particular care is required for the patient to receive exactly the prescribed amount of lithium citrate.

Good kidney function and adequate salt and fluid intake are essential to maintain lithium excretion. When sodium intake is lowered, lithium excretion is reduced. Diminished intake or excessive loss of salt and fluids, as a result of vomiting, diarrhea, perspiration or use of diuretics will also increase lithium retention. Thus, lithium should not be given to patients on a salt-free diet and sodium depletion must be carefully avoided. Therefore, it is essential for the patients to maintain a normal diet including adequate salt and fluid intake during lithium therapy. Salt supplements and additional fluids may be required if excessive losses occur. Lithium citrate should generally not be given to patients receiving diuretics, since the risk of lithium toxicity is very high in such patients. If diuretics are used during lithium therapy, the serum lithium concentration must be closely monitored.

Chronic lithium therapy may be associated with diminution of renal concentrating ability, occasionally presenting as nephrogenic diabetes insipidus, with polyuria and polydipsia. Such patients should be carefully managed to avoid dehydration with resulting lithium retention and toxicity. This condition is usually reversible when lithium is discontinued. Morphologic changes with glomerular and interstitial fibrosis and nephron atrophy have been reported in patients on chronic lithium therapy. Morphological changes have also been seen in manic depressive patients never exposed to lithium. The relationship between renal functional and morphologic changes and their association with lithium therapy have not been established.

When kidney function is assessed for baseline data prior to starting lithium therapy or thereafter, routine urinalysis and other tests may be used to evaluate tubular function (e.g., urine specific gravity or osmolality following a period of water deprivation, or 24-hour urine volume) and glomerular function (e.g., serum creatinine or creatinine clearance). During lithium therapy, progressive or sudden changes in renal function, even within the normal range, indicate the need for re-evaluation of treatment.

An encephalopathic syndrome (characterized by weakness, lethargy, fever, tremulousness and confusion, extrapyramidal symptoms, leukocytosis, elevated serum enzymes, BUN and fasting blood sugar followed by irreversible brain damage has occurred in a few patients treated with lithium plus haloperidol. A causal relationship between these events and the concomitant administration of lithium and haloperidol has not been established; however, patients receiving such combined therapy should be monitored closely for early evidence of neurologic toxicity and treatment discontinued promptly if such signs appear (see Precautions, Drug Interactions). The possibility of similar adverse interactions with other antipsychotic medications exists (see Precautions, Drug Interactions).

Outpatients and their families should be warned that patients must discontinue lithium citrate therapy and contact their physician immediately if such clinical signs of lithium toxicity as diarrhea, vomiting, tremor, mild ataxia, drowsiness, fatigue or muscular weakness occur.

There is evidence of decreased tolerance to lithium once the acute manic episode breaks. Therefore, when the acute attack subsides, the dosage should be reduced rapidly in order to produce serum lithium levels no higher than between 0.6 and 1.2 mmol/L.

Precautions: General: Periodic review and monitoring of kidney and cardiovascular function is advisable during therapy with lithium. Other laboratory tests should be performed as indicated by the patient's clinical condition. The appearance of signs of toxicity or a rise in the blood level of lithium after the dosage is stabilized should alert the physician to determine the reasons for lithium accumulation.

Patients with Special Disease and Conditions: Patients with Cardiovascular Disease: Patients with underlying cardiovascular disease should be observed carefully for signs of arrhythmias.

Thyroid Disorder: Since the formation of nontoxic goiters has been reported during lithium therapy, the thyroid gland should be examined before treatment and appropriate thyroid function tests performed. Nontoxic goiters reported during prolonged lithium therapy have disappeared following discontinuation of the medication. Treatment with small doses of thyroxin or desiccated thyroid in patients who develop a diffuse nontoxic goiter may stop further growth or lead to shrinkage of the gland.

Concomitant Infection: In addition to sweating and diarrhea, concomitant infection with elevated temperatures may also necessitate a temporary reduction or cessation of medication.

Pregnancy or in Women of Childbearing Potential: Lithium should not be used during pregnancy or in women of childbearing potential unless it cannot be substituted by other appropriate therapy and in the opinion of the physician the expected benefits outweigh the possible hazards to the fetus.

In various animal species, lithium affects reproduction and has been noted to have teratogenic effects. A group of spontaneous reports concerning 37 mothers who received lithium during pregnancy included 2 who gave birth to infants with congenital malformations. Data from lithium birth registries suggests that the drug may increase the incidence of cardiac and other anomalies, especially Ebstein's anomaly.

When possible, lithium should be withdrawn for at least the first trimester unless it is determined that this would seriously endanger the mother.

If this drug is used during pregnancy, or if the patient becomes pregnant while taking the drug, the patient should be appraised for the potential hazards to the fetus.

When lithium is used during pregnancy, serum lithium concentrations should be carefully monitored and dosage adjusted if necessary since renal clearance of the drug and distribution of the drug into erythrocytes may be increased during pregnancy. Pregnant women receiving lithium may have subtherapeutic serum lithium concentrations if dosage of the drug is not increased during pregnancy. Immediately postpartum, renal clearance of lithium may decrease to prepregnancy levels; therefore, to decrease the risk of postpartum lithium intoxication, dosage of the drug should be reduced from 1 week before parturition.

Lactation: Lithium is excreted in human milk (concentrations of 33 to 50% of those in the mother's serum). Nursing should not be undertaken during lithium therapy except in rare and unusual circumstances where, in the opinion of the physician, the potential benefits to the mother outweighs possible hazards to the child.

Geriatrics: Geriatric patients appear to be more susceptible to adverse effects even when lithium levels are therapeutic.

Children: Since information regarding the safety and effectiveness of lithium in children under 12 years of age is not available, its use in such patients is not recommended. There has been a report of a transient syndrome of acute dystonia and hyperreflexia occurring in a 15 kg child who ingested 300 mg of lithium carbonate.

Discontinuation of Therapy: The majority of patients do not experience withdrawal symptoms or rebound phenomenon upon cessation of long-term lithium therapy. In view of the occasional reports of sudden relapses occurring with abrupt discontinuation, gradual discontinuation is recommended unless abrupt withdrawal is necessary because of toxicity.

Drug Interactions: Diuretics or Angiotensin Converting Enzyme (ACE) Inhibitors: Caution should be exercised when lithium and diuretics or ACE inhibitors are used concomitantly because sodium loss may reduce the renal clearance of lithium and increase serum lithium levels with risk of lithium toxicity. When such combinations are used, the lithium dosage may need to be decreased and more frequent monitoring of lithium plasma levels is recommended (see Warnings).

Haloperidol: It has been proposed that haloperidol and lithium could have a combined inhibitory effect on striatal adenylate cyclase. If haloperidol and lithium are used concomitantly, careful attention should be given to the dose of both agents as well as to early detection of neurotoxicity, particularly in the presence of 1 or more predisposing factors which include large doses of one or both drugs, the presence of acute mania, failure to discontinue drugs when adverse effects occur, preexisting brain damage, a history of extrapyramidal symptoms with neuroleptic therapy alone, the concurrent use of anticholinergic antiparkinsonian drugs, and the presence of other physiologic disturbances such as infection, fever, or dehydration (see Warnings).

Phenothiazines: Both pharmacokinetic interactions and clinical toxicity with the combined use of phenothiazines and lithium have been described. Lithium-induced reductions in plasma chlorpromazine levels, phenothiazine-induced increases in red cell uptake of lithium and chlorpromazine-induced increases in renal lithium excretion have been reported. Clinically, occasional cases of neurotoxicity have been reported and may be more likely to occur with thioridazine than other phenothiazines, when combined with lithium. Therefore, the clinician should be alert for altered response to either drug when used in combination and when either drug is withdrawn.

Nonsteroidal Anti-inflammatory Drugs (NSAIDs): NSAIDs have been reported to increase significantly steady-state plasma lithium levels. In some cases lithium toxicity has resulted from such interactions. In a patient stabilized on lithium and NSAIDs, discontinuation of the NSAIDs may result in inadequate serum lithium concentrations. When such combinations are used, increased plasma lithium level monitoring is recommended.

Selective Serotonin Reuptake Inhibitors (SSRI) Drugs: Lithium may enhance the serotonergic effects of SSRI drugs. Coadministration of lithium with SSRI drugs may lead to a higher incidence of serotonin associated side effects and lithium toxicity. Fluvoxamine: Several cases of adverse reactions including convulsions have been reported in patients receiving concomitant lithium and fluvoxamine. Fluoxetine: There have been reports of both increased and decreased lithium levels when lithium was used concomitantly with fluoxetine. Cases of lithium toxicity have been reported. Sertraline: In a placebo-controlled study in normal volunteers sertraline did not alter steady-state concentrations or renal clearance of lithium. However, there was a high incidence of apparently treatment-related side effects with the combination in this study, tremors being the most frequently observed. There is no clinical experience with lithium in sertraline treated patients.

Therefore, combined use of lithium and SSRI drugs should be carried out with caution. Lithium levels should be monitored when these drugs are administered concomitantly, so that appropriate adjustments to the lithium dose may be made if necessary.

Carbamazepine: Several cases of neurotoxicity (in the absence of toxic serum lithium concentrations) have been reported in patients receiving lithium and carbamazepine, but the combination has also been used to advantage in some manic patients. Patients should be monitored for evidence of lithium toxicity when carbamazepine is given concurrently. It is not yet established whether plasma lithium concentrations are useful in monitoring this interaction since the carbamazepine might increase the effect of lithium without increasing plasma lithium concentrations.

Neuromuscular Blocking Agents: In patients receiving chronic lithium therapy, the action of neuromuscular blocking agents (e.g., succinylcholine, pancuronium) may be prolonged.

Theophylline: Theophylline enhances the renal clearance of lithium in most patients, thus tending to reduce serum lithium concentrations. When initiating lithium therapy in a patient on chronic theophylline, lithium dosage requirements may be higher than anticipated. When initiating theophylline therapy in a patient on chronic lithium, there may be reduced lithium response. Discontinuation of theophylline in a patient on

PMS-Lithium (cont'd)

chronic lithium may result in excessive lithium response. Monitoring of serum lithium concentration is recommended.

Calcium Channel Blockers (CCBs): The addition of verapamil or diltiazem to patients stabilized on lithium therapy may result in neurotoxicity. The CCB effects may be additive to that of lithium on transmitter secretion in the nervous system. The use of CCBs in the treatment of patients with bipolar disorders receiving lithium should be commenced carefully with observation for neurotoxic effects. The therapeutic range of lithium may need to be toward the lower end when a CCB is coadministered.

Propranolol: Limited clinical data suggests that propranolol may increase lithium serum concentrations, and its coadministration with lithium may produce bradycardia. Pending further data, patients maintained on lithium should be monitored for changed lithium serum concentrations or exaggerated beta-blocker effects.

Tricyclic Antidepressants: Both lithium and tricyclic antidepressants lower the seizure threshold. An additive effect is possible.

Potassium Iodide: The hypothyroidic and goitrogenic effects of lithium and potassium iodide (and possibly other iodides) may be additive if the two drugs are used concurrently.

Diazepam: An isolated case has been reported of serious hypothermia during concurrent treatment with lithium and diazepam. Since hypothermia is potentially fatal if it occurs and its general incidence is not known, it would be prudent to watch for this interaction during concurrent treatment.

Sodium Bicarbonate: Patients on combined sodium bicarbonate and lithium therapy should be monitored for decreased lithium effects. Lithium blood levels may be helpful in assessing this interaction.

Sodium Chloride: Patients on salt-restricted diets who receive lithium are prone to developing symptoms of lithium toxicity. In contrast, increased sodium intake has been associated with reduced therapeutic response to lithium. Extremely large or small intakes of sodium chloride should be avoided in patients receiving lithium (see Warnings).

Urea: Limited clinical experience indicates that urea may enhance the renal excretion of lithium resulting in reduced lithium serum concentrations.

Other: Isolated cases of lithium toxicity have been reported to be induced by concomitant administration of mazindol, methyldopa and phenytoin.

Adverse Effects: Mild side effects may be encountered with lithium citrate even when serum lithium values remain below 1 mmol/L. The most frequent side effects are the initial post-absorptive symptoms, believed to be associated with a rapid rise in serum lithium levels. They include, gastrointestinal discomfort, nausea, vertigo, muscle weakness and a dazed feeling, and frequently disappear after stabilization of therapy. The more common and persistent adverse reactions are: fine tremor of the hands, and at times, fatigue, thirst and polyuria. These do not necessarily require reduction of dosage.

Mild to moderate toxic reactions may occur at lithium levels from 1.5 to 2 mmol/L, and moderate to severe reactions at levels above 2 mmol/L.

A number of patients may experience lithium accumulation during initial therapy, increasing to toxic levels and requiring immediate discontinuation of the drug. Some elderly patients with lower renal clearances for lithium may also experience different degrees of lithium toxicity, requiring reduction or temporary withdrawal of medication. However, in patients with normal renal clearance the toxic manifestations appear to occur in a fairly regular sequence related to serum lithium levels. The usually transient GI symptoms are the earliest side effects to occur. A mild degree of fine tremor of the hands may persist throughout therapy. Thirst and polyuria may be followed by increased drowsiness, ataxia, tinnitus and blurred vision, indicating early intoxication. As intoxication progresses the following manifestations may be encountered: confusion, increasing disorientation, muscle twitching, hyperreflexia, nystagmus, seizures, diarrhea, vomiting, and eventually coma and death.

The following adverse reactions have been reported and are usually related to serum lithium levels: Gastrointestinal: anorexia, nausea, vomiting, diarrhea, abdominal pain and weight loss.

Neuromuscular: general muscle weakness, ataxia, tremor, muscle hyperirritability, (fasciculation, twitching, especially of facial muscles and clonic movements of the limbs), choreoathetotic movement and hyperactive deep tendon reflexes.

Neurological: Cases of pseudotumor cerebri (increased intracranial pressure and papilledema) have been reported with lithium use. If undetected, this condition may result in enlargement of the blind spot, constriction of visual fields and eventual blindness due to optic atrophy. Lithium should be discontinued, if clinically possible, if this syndrome occurs.

Central and Peripheral Nervous System: urinary and fecal incontinence, slurred speech, blackout spells, seizures, cranial nerve involvement, psychomotor retardation, somnolence, toxic confusional states, restlessness, stupor and coma.

Cardiovascular: arrhythmia, hypotension, peripheral circulatory failure, cardiac collapse and peripheral edema.

ECG Changes: reversible flattening, isoelectricity or inversion of T-waves.

EEG Changes: diffuse slowing, widening of frequency spectrum, potentiation and disorganization of background rhythm. Sensitivity to hyperventilation and paroxysmal bilateral synchronous delta activity have also been described.

Autonomic Nervous System: blurred vision, dry mouth.

Thyroid Abnormalities: Euthyroid goiter and/or hypothyroidism (including myxedema) accompanied by lower T_3 and T_4. I^{131} iodine uptake may be elevated (see Precautions). Paradoxically, rare cases of hyperthyroidism have been reported.

Genitourinary: albuminuria, oliguria, polyuria, and glycosuria.

Dermatologic: drying and thinning of hair, anesthesia of skin, chronic folliculitis, xerosis cutis, alopecia, exacerbation of psoriasis, rash and pruritus.

Allergy: allergic vasculitis.

Metabolic and Nutritional Disorders: thirst, hyperglycemia and dehydration.

Hematopoietic and Lymphatic: anemia, leukopenia, leukocytosis.

General: general fatigue, leg ulcers, metallic taste, and slight elevation of plasma magnesium.

Miscellaneous Reactions Unrelated to Dosage: transient electroencephalographic and electrographic changes, hyperthyroidism, worsening of organic brain syndromes, excessive weight gain, edematous swelling of ankles or wrists. A single report has been received of the development of painful discoloration of fingers and toes and coldness of the extremities within one day of the starting of treatment of lithium. The mechanism through which these symptoms (resembling Raynaud's Syndrome) developed is not known. Recovery followed discontinuance.

Serious Reactions to Long-Term Therapy: In addition to other possible adverse reactions, the main concern during chronic lithium therapy centres on kidney functions, the thyroid, parathyroid, the bone and skin.

Overdose: Symptoms: Lithium toxicity is closely related to the concentration of lithium in the blood and is usually associated with serum levels in excess of 2 mmol/L. Early signs of toxicity which may occur at lower serum levels were described under Adverse Effects and usually respond to reduction of dosage. Lithium intoxication has been preceded by the appearance or aggravation of the following symptoms: sluggishness, drowsiness, lethargy, coarse tremors or muscle twitching, loss of appetite, vomiting and diarrhea. Occurrence of these symptoms requires immediate cessation of medication and careful clinical reassessment and management. Signs and symptoms of lithium intoxication have already been described under Adverse Effects.

In 8 cases of lithium poisoning described by Schou, the patients frequently developed muscle rigidity with hyperactive deep reflexes, generalized muscle tremors or fasciculations, attacks of hyperextension of the limbs with gasping and wide opening of the eyes, and sometimes epileptic seizures and various neurological dysfunction. There was progressive impairment of consciousness and, in some patients, the coma. EEG changes in some patients consisted of decrease of alpha activity and increase of theta and delta activity, the latter at times paroxysmal with maximal activity frontally. Periods of beta activity with sharp waves were also observed. The kidney function was probably impaired in several patients. Three of these patients died, all of pulmonary complications.

Treatment: No specific antidote for lithium poisoning is known. The treatment of lithium poisoning is symptomatic. Early symptoms of lithium toxicity can usually be treated by reduction or cessation of dosage of the drug and resumption of treatment at a lower dose after 24 to 48 hours. In severe cases of lithium poisoning, the first and foremost goal of treatment consists of elimination of this ion from the organism. Treatment of lithium poisoning is 1) lavage, 2) correction of fluid and electrolyte imbalance, and 3) regulation of kidney function. Sodium depletion in particular must be corrected. However, administration of large amounts of sodium in the absence of depletion of this electrolyte has not been very successful, in many as a means of speeding lithium excretion. Lithium excretion may be facilitated by the judicious use of intravenous urea, sodium bicarbonate, acetazolamide or aminophylline. Hemodialysis is an effective and rapid means of removing the ion from the severely toxic patient or in the presence of impaired renal function. Infection prophylaxis, regular chest x-rays and preservation of adequate respiration are essential.

Dosage: Since lithium acts without the production of sedation, some prefer lithium to neuroleptics or use these to supplement lithium therapy to obtain rapid control of overt manic behavior. Lithium also has a useful indication in those cases that fail to respond to neuroleptics.

Selection of patients and approach to lithium therapy: The results of lithium therapy depend largely on the nature and course of the illness itself, rather than on the symptoms. The selection of patients for long-term treatment requires a clearcut diagnosis of primary affective disorder, the condition for which the stabilizing effects of lithium have been found useful. The variables that have been more consistently associated with response to lithium therapy in patients with a primary affective disorder are: the good quality of remissions with good function and no significant symptomatology during the free intervals between previous episodes of illness; low frequency of episodes, typically 1 or 2 (and not more than 3 or 4) per year; and symptomatology during the acute episodes that meet strict criteria for a primary affective disorder (DSM-III: Research Diagnostic Criteria).

Screening for lithium candidates should include at least, a medical history and physical examination with emphasis on the CNS, urinary, cardiovascular, gastrointestinal and endocrine systems and the skin. It should also include: routine 24-hour urine volume, serum creatinine, record of weight, an ECG, possibly electrolytes and TSH, and for long-term treatment, creatinine clearance and a urine concentration test. Other examinations and tests should be used when indicated. Monitoring lithium treatment should include, for each visit, mental status, physical examination, weight, 12-hour serum lithium and a check for lithium side effects and compliance. It should also include serum creatinine every 2 months, plasma thyroid hormone and TSH every 6 to 12 months, particularly in female patients, and attention to renal and thyroid function should be maintained throughout, with tests used for baseline screening repeated as required.

The first objective of treatment is to establish an effective and safe daily dosage of lithium, with the aid of standardized 12-hour serum lithium levels maintained within the therapeutic range, as high as necessary for efficacy, and with the patient as much as possible free of significant side effects. Three daily doses should be used initially, at least until the daily dosage is established. The next aim is to move to an optimal dose, which should be as low as possible, consistent with protection against relapse. During follow-up, an adjustment to lower dosages may be required to minimize adverse effects, and a change in the lithium preparation used and/or the frequency of dosing, either towards multiple doses or towards a single dose, may be necessary to handle absorption-related adverse effects or concern over possible renal toxicity. Intermittent lithium treatment in carefully selected patients has been recommended by some lithium experts, but should not be undertaken without careful planning and great caution. The cooperation of patients and relatives is required throughout.

Before deciding on the institution of long-term treatment, it is essential to establish that the patient has clearly responded to a course of stabilizing lithium therapy and that the risk of such therapy is acceptable. Maintaining a patient with a lithium nonresponsive condition on long-term therapy poses an unacceptable risk. A decision with regards to long-term therapy can be made during a time-limited trial of lithium therapy with frequent reassessment of outcome. The following are among the factors to be reassessed before a decision is made: careful reconfirmation of the diagnosis of primary affective disorder; the health status of the patient; the side effects of lithium therapy experienced by the patient; and the response to treatment. Assessment of response to treatment is based strictly on firm evidence of relapse prevention during a reasonable trial period, but can be assisted by consideration of the predictors of response outlined above. Great pains should be taken to exclude false responders and false nonresponders. It should also be borne in mind that nonresponders are more susceptible to the adverse effects of lithium.

Acute Mania: The therapeutic dose of lithium citrate for the treatment of acute mania should be based primarily on the patient's clinical condition. It must be individualized for each patient according to blood levels and clinical response. Manic patients usually require serum lithium levels in excess of 1 mmol/L and the dosage should be adjusted to obtain serum levels between 1 and 1.5 mmol/L (in blood samples drawn before the patient has had his/her first lithium dose of the day).

In properly screened adult patients, the suggested initial daily dosage for acute mania is approximately 50 mmol, divided into 3 doses. In view of the large variability of renal lithium excretion between individuals, it is suggested that lithium treatment be started at a dose between 16 mmol/day (10 mL) and 24 mmol/day (15 mL), reaching a level of 32 mmol/day (20 mL) to 48 mmol/day (30 mL) in 3 divided doses on the second day. Depending on the patient's clinical condition, the initial dosage should be adjusted to produce the desired serum lithium level. The weight of the patient should also influence the choice of the initial dose. Lithium should be used cautiously and in reduced doses in the elderly patient, usually in the range of 16 mmol/day (10 mL) to 32 mmol/day (20 mL). Serum lithium levels should be monitored frequently and kept below 1.5 mmol/L.

Long-Term Control: After the acute manic episode subsides, usually within a week, the dosage of lithium citrate should be rapidly reduced to achieve serum levels between 0.6 and 1.2 mmol/L (with the level kept below 1.5 mmol/L), since there is evidence at this time of a decreased tolerance to lithium. The average suggested dosage at this stage is 24 mmol/day (15 mL) divided into 3 doses, with a range usually between 16 mmol/day (10 mL) and 32 mmol/day (20 mL). If a satisfactory response is not obtained in 14 days, lithium therapy should be discontinued. When the manic attack is controlled, lithium administration should be maintained during the expected duration of the manic phase, since early withdrawal might lead to relapse. It is essential to maintain clinical supervision of the patient and monitor lithium levels as required during treatment (see Warnings and Precautions).

Lithium may be used concomitantly with neuroleptic drugs (see Warnings and Precautions, Drug Interactions).

Serum lithium levels in uncomplicated cases receiving maintenance therapy during remission should be monitored at least every 2 months.

Patients abnormally sensitive to lithium may exhibit toxic signs at serum levels of 1 to 1.4 mmol/L. Elderly patients often respond to reduced dosage and may exhibit signs of toxicity at serum levels ordinarily tolerated by other patients.

Note: Blood samples for serum lithium determinations should be drawn immediately prior to the next dose when lithium concentrations are relatively stable (i.e., 8 to 12 hours after previous dose). Total reliance must not be placed on serum levels alone. Accurate patient evaluation require both clinical and laboratory analysis.

Supplied: PMS-Lithium Carbonate: 150 mg: Each hard gelatin capsule, orange cap inscribed pms over 150, white body inscribed LITH, contains: lithium carbonate USP 150 mg. Bottles of 100 and 500.

300 mg: Each hard gelatin, flesh-colored capsule, inscribed pms over 300 on the cap and LITH on the body, contains: lithium carbonate USP 300 mg. Bottles of 100 and 500.

600 mg: Each hard gelatin, blue capsule, inscribed pms over 600 on the cap and LITH on the body, contains: lithium carbonate USP 600 mg. Bottles of 100 and 500.

PMS-Lithium Citrate: Each 5 mL of cherry-flavored syrup contains: lithium ion 8 mmol (equivalent to approximately lithium carbonate 300 mg). Nonmedicinal ingredients: alcohol parabens, artificial cherry flavor, citric acid, glycerin, methylparaben, propylene glycol, propylparaben, sodium hydroxide and hydrochloric acid to adjust pH and sorbitol. Bottles of 500 mL. Store between 15 and 30°C. Store in a tight container. Avoid freezing.

PMS-LOXAPINE ℞
Pharmascience
Loxapine
Antipsychotic

Supplied: 5 mg: Each round, scored, biconvex, yellow, film-coated tablet, engraved "Loxapine 5" on one side and "pms" over score on the other side, contains: loxapine 5 mg as the succinate salt. HDPE bottles of 100 and 500.

10 mg: Each round, scored, biconvex, light green, film-coated tablet, engraved "Loxapine 10" on one side and "pms" over score on the other side, contains: loxapine 10 mg as the succinate salt. HDPE bottles of 100 and 500.

25 mg: Each round, scored, biconvex, pink, film-coated tablet, engraved "Loxapine 25" on one side and "pms" over score on the other side, contains: loxapine 25 mg as the succinate salt. HDPE bottles of 100 and 500.

50 mg: Each round, scored, biconvex, yellow, film-coated tablet, engraved "Loxapine 50" on one side and "pms" over score on the other side, contains: loxapine 50 mg as the succinate salt. HDPE bottles of 100 and 500.

PMS-MEFENAMIC ACID ℞
Pharmascience
Mefenamic Acid
Analgesic

Supplied: Each hard gelatin capsule with yellow opaque body and blue opaque cap, imprinted "p" logo on cap and "250" on body in black ink, contains: mefenamic acid 250 mg. Bottles of 100 and 500.

PMS-METHOTRIMEPRAZINE ℞
Pharmascience
Methotrimeprazine Maleate
Neuroleptic

Supplied: 5 mg: Each yellow tablet contains: methotrimeprazine 5 mg (as the maleate salt). Bottles of 100 and 500.

25 mg: Each yellow tablet contains: methotrimeprazine 25 mg (as the maleate salt). Bottles of 100 and 500.

50 mg: Each yellow tablet contains: methotrimeprazine 50 mg (as the maleate salt). Bottles of 100 and 500.

Store in tight containers, protected from light, at room temperature between 15 and 30°C.

New Product 1998

PMS-METHYLPHENIDATE ◈
Pharmascience
Methylphenidate HCl
CNS Stimulant

Supplied: 5 mg: Each orange, round, biconvex, scored tablet, embossed "PMS" and "5" and "130" on opposite sides, contains: methylphenidate HCl USP 5 mg. Bottles of 100 and 500.

10 mg: Each blue, round, biconvex, scored tablet, embossed "PMS" and "10" and "110" on opposite sides, contains: methylphenidate HCl USP 10 mg. Bottles of 100 and 500.

20 mg: Each yellow, round, biconvex, scored tablet, embossed "PMS" and "20" and "123" on opposite sides, contains: methylphenidate HCl USP 20 mg. Bottles of 100 and 500.

Store at controlled room temperature 15 to 30°C. Protect from moisture.

PMS-METOCLOPRAMIDE ℞
Pharmascience
Metoclopramide HCl
Upper Gastrointestinal Tract Motility Modifier—Antiemetic

Supplied: Oral Solution: Each mL contains: metoclopramide HCl 1 mg. Bottles of 500 mL.

Tablets: 5 mg: Each square shaped tablet, inscribed "PMS" on one side and plain on the other side, contains: metoclopramide HCl 5 mg. Bottles of 100 and 500.

10 mg: Each white, round, biconvex tablet, inscribed "PMS" on one side and scored on the other, contains: metoclopramide HCl 10 mg. Bottles of 100 and 500.

PMS-METOPROLOL-B ℞
Pharmascience
Metoprolol Tartrate
β-Adrenoceptor Blocking Agent

Supplied: 50 mg: Each compressed, white, biconvex, circular tablet, scored and engraved on one side Metop-B and on the other PMS/60, contains: metoprolol tartrate 50 mg. Bottles of 100 and 500.

100 mg: Each compressed, white, biconvex, circular tablet, scored and engraved on one side Metop-B and on the other PMS/100, contains: metoprolol tartrate 100 mg. Bottles of 100 and 500.

Protect from light and humidity.

PMS-METOPROLOL-L ℞
Pharmascience
Metoprolol Tartrate
β-blocking agent

Supplied: 50 mg: Each pink, oblong, biconvex, coated, scored tablet, engraved PMS 50 on one side and METOP-L on the other, contains: metoprolol tartrate 50 mg. Bottles of 100, 500 and 1 000.

100 mg: Each light blue, oblong, biconvex, coated, scored tablet, engraved PMS 100 on one side and METOP-L on the other, contains: metoprolol tartrate 50 mg. Bottles of 100, 500 and 1 000.

New Product 1998

PMS-NIFEDIPINE ℞
Pharmascience
Nifedipine
Antianginal Agent

Supplied: 5 mg: Each 3 minim oval, opaque, yellow, soft gelatin capsule, imprinted P5 in white on one side and NIFED in white on the other side, contains: nifedipine 5 mg in a clear yellow, oily liquid. Bottles of 100 and 500.

10 mg: Each 7 minim oval, opaque, yellow, soft gelatin capsule, imprinted P10 in white on one side and NIFEDIPINE in white on the other side, contains: nifedipine 10 mg in a clear yellow, oily liquid. Bottles of 100 and 500.

New Product 1998

PMS-NORTRIPTYLINE ℞
Pharmascience
Nortriptyline HCl
Antidepressant

Supplied: 10 mg: Each No. 3, yellow and white capsule contains: nortriptyline HCl equivalent to nortriptyline base 10 mg. HDPE bottles of 100.

25 mg: Each No. 1, yellow and white capsule contains: nortriptyline HCl equivalent to nortriptyline base 25 mg. HDPE bottles of 100.

PMS-NYSTATIN ℞
Pharmascience
Nystatin
Antifungal

Supplied: Each mL of yellow, cherry-flavored suspension contains: nystatin USP 100 000 units. White plastic unit dose bottles of 5 mL with screw caps. White plastic bottles of 24 or 48 mL (with graduated droppers). Graduated amber Pet-G bottles of 100 and 500 mL. Store at room temperature.

PMS-SALBUTAMOL RESPIRATOR SOLUTION ℞
Pharmascience
Salbutamol Sulfate
Bronchodilator

Supplied: Respirator Solutions: Each mL of sterile solution contains: salbutamol sulfate equivalent to salbutamol base 5 mg. Nonmedicinal ingredients: benzalkonium chloride (preservative). Containers of 10 mL. Store between 15 and 30°C. Protect from light. Discard if not used within 1 month after opening.

Respirator Solutions Unit Dose (Polyneb): Each unit dose (Polyneb) of sterile, isotonic solution contains: salbutamol sulfate equivalent to 1.25 mg, 2.5 mg or 5 mg of salbutamol

PMS-Salbutamol Respirator Solution (cont'd)

base in 2.5 mL. pH 3.5 to 4.5. Boxes of 20. Store below 25°C. Protect from light. Use within 3 months when removed from overwrap.

PMS-SENNOSIDES
Pharmascience

Sennosides

Laxative

Supplied: 8.6 mg: Each grey, film-coated tablet, identified PMS on one side and 411 on the other, contains: sennosides 8.6 mg. Bottles of 100, 500 and 1 000.

12 mg: Each pink, film-coated tablet, identified PMS on one side and 403 on the other, contains: sennosides 12 mg. Bottles of 100, 500 and 1 000.

PMS-SODIUM CROMOGLYCATE NEBULIZER SOLUTION ℞
Pharmascience

Cromolyn Sodium

Asthma Prophylaxis

Supplied: Each mL of inhalation solution contains: sodium cromoglycate 1% (w/v). Plastic nebules (Polynebs) of 2 mL, cartons of 50.

PMS-SODIUM POLYSTYRENE SULFONATE ℞
Pharmascience

Sodium Polystyrene Sulfonate

Cation Exchange Resin

Supplied: Oral Suspension: Each 60 mL of brown, cherry-flavored suspension contains: sodium polystyrene sulfonate USP 15 g and sorbitol 14.1 g. Also contains methylparaben and propylparaben as preservatives. Sodium: 65 mmol (1.5 g)/60 mL. Exchange capacity: approximately 3 mmol of potassium/4 mL (/g of resin) of suspension in vitro and approximately 1 mmol in vivo. Amber Pet G graduated bottles of 500 mL, unit dose plastic bottles of 60 mL.

Powder: Each g contains: a light brown, finely ground powder of sodium polystyrene sulfonate, a cation exchange resin prepared in the sodium phase with an in vitro exchange capacity of approximately 3 mmol (in vivo approximately 1 mmol) of potassium/g. Sodium: 4.1 mmol (94.3 mg)/g. Jars of 454 g.

Retention Enema: Each 120 mL of brown suspension contains: sodium polystyrene sulfonate USP 30 g and sorbitol 28.2 g. Also contains methylparaben and propylparaben as preservatives. Sodium: 65 mmol (1.5 g)/60 mL. Exchange capacity: approximately 3 mmol of potassium/4 mL (/g of resin) of suspension in vitro and approximately 1 mmol in vivo. Thin walled plastic bottles of 120 mL with special enema tip.

PMS-TEMAZEPAM ℞
Pharmascience

Temazepam

Hypnotic

Supplied: 15 mg: Each maroon and flesh, size 3 hard shell gelatin capsule, printed pms/15 in white, contains: temazepam 15 mg. Nonmedicinal ingredients: colloidal silicon dioxide, D&C Red #28, D&C Yellow #10, FD&C Blue #1, gelatin, lactose, magnesium stearate, sodium lauryl sulfate and titanium dioxide. The agents used to polish the capsules are alcohol, canner special salt and Tween 60. Bottles of 100.

30 mg: Each maroon and blue, size 3 hard shell gelatin capsule, printed pms/30 in white, contains: temazepam 30 mg. Nonmedicinal ingredients: colloidal silicon dioxide, D&C Red #28, FD&C Blue #1, gelatin, lactose, magnesium stearate, sodium lauryl sulfate and titanium dioxide. The agents used to polish the capsules are alcohol, canner special salt and Tween 60. Bottles of 100.

Store at controlled room temperature (15 to 30°C). Protect from moisture and light.

New Product 1998

PMS-TIAPROFENIC ℞
Pharmascience

Tiaprofenic Acid

Anti-inflammatory—Analgesic

Supplied: Each white, round, biconvex tablet, inscribed "pms" on one side and scored on the other, contains: tiaprofenic acid 200 or 300 mg. HDPE bottles of 100 and 500.

PMS-TIMOLOL ℞
Pharmascience

Timolol Maleate

Glaucoma Therapy

Supplied: 2.5 mg/mL: Each mL of clear, colorless to light yellow, sterile, isotonic, buffered, aqueous ophthalmic solution contains: timolol maleate equivalent to timolol 2.5 mg (0.25%). Nonmedicinal ingredients: benzalkonium chloride (as a preservative), dibasic sodium phosphate, monobasic sodium phosphate, sodium chloride (to adjust pH) and water for injection. Clear, colorless, plastic ophthalmic dispensers of 5 and 10 mL with controlled drop tips.

5 mg/mL: Each mL of clear, colorless to light yellow, sterile, isotonic, buffered, aqueous ophthalmic solution contains: timolol maleate equivalent to timolol 5 mg (0.5%). Nonmedicinal ingredients: benzalkonium chloride (as a preservative), dibasic sodium phosphate, monobasic sodium phosphate, sodium chloride (to adjust pH) and water for injection. Clear, colorless, plastic ophthalmic dispensers of 5 and 10 mL with controlled drop tips.

New Product 1998

PMS-TRAZODONE ℞
Pharmascience

Trazodone HCl

Antidepressant

Supplied: 25 mg: Each blue, round, biconvex, scored tablet, identified "Trazodone" on one side, and "pms" above the score and 25 below the score on the other side, contains: trazodone HCl 25 mg equivalent to 22.75 mg of trazodone base. High density polyethylene bottles of 100.

50 mg: Each orange, biconvex tablet, scored on one side, and "Trazodone" on the other side, contains: trazodone HCl 50 mg equivalent to 45.5 mg of trazodone base. High density polyethylene bottles of 100, 250 and 500.

100 mg: Each white, biconvex tablet, scored on one side, and "Trazodone" on the other side, contains: trazodone HCl 100 mg equivalent to 91 mg of trazodone base. High density polyethylene bottles of 100 and 500.

PMS-TRYPTOPHAN ℞
Pharmascience

L-Tryptophan

Adjunct in the Management of Affective Disorders

Supplied: Each white, capsule-shaped, clear film-coated tablet, imprinted with "P" logo on one side and "Tryptophan 1" on the other side, contains: L-tryptophan USP 1 g. Bottles of 100 and 500.

PMS-VALPROIC ACID ℞
PMS-VALPROIC ACID E.C. ℞
Pharmascience

Valproic Acid

Anticonvulsant

Supplied: PMS-Valproic Acid: Capsules: 250 mg: Each oblong, orange, soft gelatin capsule, identified "pms 250" in black, contains: valproic acid 250 mg. Bottles of 100 and 500.

500 mg: Each oblong, yellow, soft gelatin, enteric-coated capsule contains: valproic acid 500 mg. Bottles of 100 and 500.

Syrup: Each 5 mL of red-pink syrup contains: the equivalent of valproic acid 250 mg, as the sodium salt. Bottles of 450 mL.

PMS-Valproic Acid E.C.: Each oblong, yellow, soft gelatin, enteric-coated capsule contains: valproic acid 500 mg. Bottles of 100 and 500.

PMS-YOHIMBINE ℞
Pharmascience

Yohimbine HCl

Sympatholytic

Supplied: 2 mg: Each pink, uncoated, round tablet, engraved with Y on one side, contains: yohimbine HCl 2 mg. White polyethylene bottles of 100 and 500.

5.4 mg: Each white, uncoated, round tablet, inscribed P over 5.4 and YOHIMBINE on opposite sides, contains: yohimbine HCl 5.4 mg. White polyethylene bottles of 100 and 500.

6 mg: Each pink, uncoated, round tablet, engraved PMS-YOHIMBINE on one side and scored on the other, contains: yohimbine HCl 6 mg. White polyethylene bottles of 100 and 500.

Store between 15 and 30°C.

PNEUMOCOCCAL POLYSACCHARIDE VACCINE PNEUMO 23™
Connaught

Active Immunizing Agent

Pharmacology: Pneumococcal polysaccharide vaccine, Pneumo 23 is a capsular polysaccharide vaccine against disease caused by 23 of the most common types of S. pneumoniae (pneumococcus). Approximately 90% of cases of pneumococcal bacteremia and meningitis are caused by these 23 types. Although the overall incidence of pneumococcal infections in Canada is not known, invasive disease is most common in the very young, the elderly, and in certain specific groups at high risk.

In clinical studies involving more than 1 000 volunteers, serum capsular polysaccharide antibodies start to increase 10 to 15 days following immunization with the pneumococcal polysaccharide vaccine. Although the duration of protection has not yet been determined it may last approximately 5 to 10 years. Encouraging and concordant studies from a randomized controlled trial in France, from 3 of 4 case-control studies, and from the epidemiological analysis by the CDC, all support the consensus that pneumococcal polyvalent vaccines are effective in immunocompetent older persons with high-risk conditions. Almost 90% of elderly people achieve antibody levels 300 ng antibody nitrogen/mL. Clinical trials with the pneumococcal polysaccharide vaccine have also shown that healthy adults develop excellent antibody responses following pneumococcal vaccination: 80% or more of subjects develop at least a 2-fold rise in antibody levels. In humans, the capsular polysaccharide vaccine, after i.m. injection, induce IgG and IgM antibody type.

Indications: For the prevention of invasive infection, such as pneumonia or meningitis, caused by those types of pneumococci contained in the vaccine.

A single dose of pneumococcal vaccine should be given to persons in the following groups at increased risk of pneumococcal disease or its complications:

Adults: All persons ≥65 years of age. Adults with asplenia, splenic dysfunction or sickle-cell disease. Adults with the following conditions: chronic cardiorespiratory disease, cirrhosis, alcoholism, chronic renal disease, nephrotic syndrome, diabetes mellitus, chronic cerebrospinal fluid leak, HIV infection and other conditions associated with immunosuppression (Hodgkin's disease, lymphoma, multiple myeloma, immunosuppression for organ transplantation).

Children: Children ≥2 years of age with asplenia, splenic dysfunction or sickle-cell disease. All children ≥2 years of age with nephrotic syndrome, chronic cerebrospinal fluid leak, HIV infection and other conditions associated with immunosuppression.

The pneumococcal polysaccharide vaccine may be given simultaneously with influenza, meningococcal and Hib conjugate vaccines at separate sites with separate syringes.

Where possible, the vaccine should be given at least 10 to 14 days before splenectomy or initiation of immunosuppressive therapy.

Children: The pneumococcal polysaccharide vaccine is not recommended for children < 2 years of age.

History of a confirmed or suspected pneumococcal infection is not a contraindication and should be considered according to underlying risk status. The pneumococcal polysaccharide vaccine is not recommended for prevention of recurrent upper respiratory tract infections, particularly otitis media and sinusitis.

Revaccination: Adults should not be routinely given more than 1 dose of pneumococcal vaccine. Revaccination after 3 to 5 years should be considered for children with sickle-cell anemia, asplenia or nephrotic syndrome, who will be ≤10 years old at revaccination. Revaccination of older children and adults at highest risk of fatal infection (asplenic patients) should be considered for those who received pneumococcal vaccine 6 or more years previously, as well as for those shown to have rapid decline in pneumococcal antibody levels (patients with nephrotic syndrome, renal failure or transplant recipients).

Contraindications: General: Immunization with the pneumococcal polysaccharide vaccine, should be deferred in the presence of any acute illness, including febrile illness. A minor afebrile illness such as mild upper respiratory infection is not usually reason to defer immunization.

Absolute Contraindications: Allergy to any component of the pneumococcal polysaccharide vaccine (see Supplied) or an allergic or anaphylactic reaction to a previous dose of pneumococcal vaccine are contraindications to vaccination.

Immunization is contraindicated in persons who were given a pneumococcal vaccine within the previous 3 years.

Warnings: Pneumococcal polysaccharide vaccine will not immunize against types of pneumococci other than those contained in the vaccine.

If the pneumococcal polysaccharide vaccine is used in persons with malignancies receiving immunosuppressive therapies, including irradiation, antimetabolites, alkylating agents, cytotoxic drugs, or who are otherwise immunocompromised (including HIV infected individuals), the expected immune response may not be obtained.

In patients receiving antibiotic prophylaxis against pneumococcal infection, such prophylaxis should not be discontinued after immunization with the pneumococcal polysaccharide vaccine.

Corticosteroid therapy can result in immunosuppression although the exact dose and duration of therapy required to suppress the immune system is not well defined. Persons treated with high doses of systemic steroids, e.g., ≥2 mg/kg/day of prednisone orally for more than 2 weeks, should be considered to have a compromised immune system.

If the pneumococcal polysaccharide vaccine is given less than 14 days prior to splenectomy or initiation of chemotherapy, it may not elicit the expected immune response.

As with any vaccine, immunization with the pneumococcal polysaccharide vaccine may not protect 100% of susceptible individuals.

Very rare Arthus-like phenomenae have been reported. They are reversible without after-effects and mainly occur in persons with high initial pneumococcal antibody levels.

Precautions: General: The possibility of allergic reactions in individuals sensitive to components of the vaccine should be evaluated. Epinephrine HCl Solution (1:1 000) should be available for immediate use in case an anaphylactic or acute hypersensitivity reaction occurs. Health care providers should be familiar with current recommendations for the initial management of anaphylaxis in nonhospital settings.

Before an injection of any vaccine, all appropriate precautions should be taken to prevent adverse reactions. This includes a review of the patient's history with respect to possible hypersensitivity to the vaccine or similar vaccine, determination of previous immunization history, and the presence of any contraindications to immunization, current health status, and a current knowledge of the literature concerning the use of the vaccine under consideration.

Special care should be taken to ensure that the injection does not enter a blood vessel.

Caution: A separate, sterile syringe and needle, or a sterile disposable unit, must be used for each individual patient to prevent the transmission of infectious agents. There have been case reports of transmission of HIV and hepatitis by failure to scrupulously observe sterile technique.

Needles should not be recapped and should be disposed of properly.

Administer the vaccine s.c. or i.m., do **not** administer i.v.

It is recommended that the pneumococcal polysaccharide vaccine be given at least 2 weeks before splenectomy, the initiation of a chemotherapy or an immunosuppressive treatment.

Pregnancy: The safety of the pneumococcal polysaccharide vaccine in pregnant women has not been specifically evaluated.

Reproduction studies have not been conducted with the pneumococcal polysaccharide vaccine. The vaccine should be given to a pregnant woman only if clearly needed.

Lactation: The pneumococcal polysaccharide vaccine may be given to lactating women.

Adverse Effects: Local reactions at the injection site including pain, erythema, and induration occur in approximately 60% of vaccinees. These reactions are generally mild and transient.

Rarely, Arthus-like reactions have been reported. These occur mainly in persons with high pneumococcal antibody levels.

Systemic Reactions: Fever ≥38.5°C occurs in approximately 2% of vaccinees. Febrile episodes occur early after vaccination and generally resolve within 24 hours. Headache and/or general malaise occur in <8%.

Allergic-type reactions including urticaria, angioedema and anaphylaxis have been reported.

Rarely, more severe systemic reactions have been reported in the literature following administration of pneumococcal polysaccharide vaccines. These include thrombocytopenia, vasculitis, generalized rash, and relapse of known underlying immune conditions. The relationship, if any, between these reactions and pneumococcal vaccine is unknown.

Physicians, nurses, and pharmacists should report any adverse occurrences temporally related to the administration of the product in accordance with local requirements and to the Medical Director, Connaught Laboratories Limited, 1755 Steeles Avenue West, Toronto, Ontario, Canada, M2R 3T4.

Dosage: The immunizing dose is a single injection of 0.5 mL given i.m. or s.c.

Revaccination: One injection of 0.5 mL (see Indications).

Administration: Parenteral biological products should be inspected visually for extraneous particulate matter and/or discoloration before administration. If these conditions exist, the product should not be administered.

Before injection, the skin over the site to be injected should be cleansed with a suitable germicide.

Shake the prefilled syringe well before administering dose.

Administer the vaccine i.m. or s.c. The preferred site is the deltoid area.

After insertion of the needle, aspirate to ensure that the needle has not entered a blood vessel.

Do not inject i.v.

Each person who is immunized should be given a permanent personal immunization record. In addition, it is essential that the physician or nurse record the immunization history in the permanent medical record of each patient. This permanent office record should contain the name of the vaccine, date given, dose, manufacturer and lot number.

Supplied: Pneumococcal polysaccharide vaccine, is a clear, colorless liquid prepared from purified pneumococcal capsular antigens. Each dose of 0.5 mL contains: purified S. pneumoniae polysaccharides, 25 μg of each of the following serotypes: 1, 2, 3, 4, 5, 6B, 7F, 8, 9N, 9V, 10A, 11A, 12F, 14, 15B, 17F, 18C, 19A, 19F, 20, 22F, 23F, 33F; phenol as a preservative; isotonic buffered solution (composition: sodium chloride, disodium phosphate, monosodium phosphate, water for injection).

Prefilled syringes of 0.5 mL (single dose), packages of 10. Store between 2 and 8°C. **Do not freeze.** Product that has been exposed to freezing should not be used. Do not use vaccine after expiration date.

New Product 1998

PNEUMOVAX® 23

MSD

Pneumococcal Vaccine, Polyvalent

Pneumococcal Infection Immunization

Pharmacology: Pneumococcal infection is a leading cause of death throughout the world and a major cause of pneumonia, meningitis and otitis media. The emergence of strains of pneumococci with increased resistance to one or more of the common antibiotics and recent isolations of pneumococci with multiple antibiotic resistance emphasize the importance of vaccine prophylaxis against pneumococcal disease. Based on projection from limited observations in the United States, it has been estimated that 400 000 to 500 000 cases of pneumococcal pneumonia may occur annually. The overall case fatality rate ranges from 5 to 10%. About 25% of all persons with pneumococcal pneumonia develop bacteremia. Death occurs in about 28% of these bacteremic patients more than 50 years of age.

The annual incidence of pneumococcal meningitis is 1.1 per 100 000 population with an overall fatality rate of 19% (children, 6%; adults, 30%). Children with sickle cell disease have been estimated to have a risk of pneumococcal meningitis nearly 600 times greater than normal children.

Invasive pneumococcal disease causes high morbidity and mortality in spite of effective antimicrobial control by antibiotics. These effects of pneumococcal disease appear due to irreversible physiologic damage caused by the bacteria during the first 5 days following onset of illness, and occur irrespective of antimicrobial therapy. Older persons, individuals with chronic debilitating diseases, and persons with absent or impaired splenic function, including those with homozygous sickle cell anemia and sickle thalassemia, are especially susceptible to severe pneumococcal disease.

Presently, there are 83 known pneumococcal capsular types. However, the preponderance of pneumococcal disease is caused by only some capsular types. For example, a 10-year (1952 to 1962) surveillance at a New York medical center showed that 56% of all deaths due to pneumococcal pneumonia were caused by 6 capsular types and that approximately 78% of all pneumococcal pneumonias were caused by 12 capsular types. Such unequal distribution of pneumococcal capsular types causing disease has been shown throughout the world. It is on the basis of this information that the pneumococcal vaccine is composed of 23 capsular types, designed to provide coverage of approximately 90% of the most frequently reported types.

It has been established that the purified pneumococcal capsular polysaccharides induce antibody production and that such antibody is effective in preventing pneumococcal disease. Studies in humans have demonstrated the immunogenicity (antibody-stimulating capability) of each of the 23 capsular types when tested in polyvalent vaccines. Adults of all ages responded immunologically to the vaccines. Earlier studies with 12- and 14-valent pneumococcal vaccines in children 2 years of age and older and in adults showed immunogenic responses.

The protective efficacy of pneumococcal vaccines containing 6 and 12 capsular polysaccharides was investigated in controlled studies of gold miners in South Africa, in whom there is a high attack rate for pneumococcal pneumonia. Capsular type-specific attack rates for pneumococcal pneumonia were observed for the period from 2 weeks through about 1 year after vaccination. The rates for pneumonia caused by the same capsular types represented in the vaccines are given below. See Table I. Protective efficacy was 76% and 92%, respectively, in the 2 studies for the capsular types represented.

Table I—Pneumovax 23

Rates for Pneumonia

Number of Capsular Types in Pneumococcal Vaccine	Rate/1 000 for Pneumonia Caused by Homologous Capsular Types		
	Vaccinated Groups	Control Groups	Protective Efficacy
6	9.2	38.3	76%
12	1.8	22.0	92%

In similar studies carried out by Dr. R. Austrian and associates using similar pneumococcal vaccines, prepared for the National Institutes of Allergy and Infectious Disease by a different source, the reduction in pneumonias caused by the vaccine capsular types was 79%. Type-specific reduction in pneumococcal bacteremia was 82%. A preliminary report suggests efficacy of the vaccine in persons over 2 years of age in preventing severe pneumococcal disease and bacteremia in patients with sickle cell anemia and in individuals without spleens or those who have impaired splenic function.

The duration of protective effect of pneumococcal vaccine is presently unknown, but it has been shown in previous studies with other pneumococcal vaccines that antibody induced by the vaccine may persist for as long as 5 years. Type-specific antibody levels induced by pneumococcal vaccine (14-valent) have been observed to decline over a 42-month period of observation, but remain significantly above prevaccination levels in almost all recipients who manifest an initial response.

Pneumovax 23 (cont'd)

Indications: For immunization against pneumonia and bacteremia, caused by those types of pneumococci included in the vaccine, in all persons 2 years of age or older in whom there is an increased risk of morbidity and mortality from pneumococcal pneumonia. These include: (1) persons having chronic physical conditions such as chronic heart disease of any etiology, chronic bronchopulmonary diseases, chronic renal failure, and chronic metabolic disorders; (2) persons convalescing from severe disease; (3) persons 50 years of age or older who in the opinion of their physician are at increased risk of pneumococcal pneumonia.

Earlier studies suggest the 12- and 14-valent pneumococcal vaccines are efficacious for preventing severe pneumonic disease and bacteremia in persons over 2 years of age with sickle cell anemia and in individuals who have had a splenectomy or who have impaired splenic function, and in pediatric patients over 2 years of age with nephrotic syndrome. It is expected also that the vaccine will be found effective in preventing pneumococcal meningitis of bacteremic origin. However, pneumococcal vaccine may not be effective in preventing infection resulting from basilar skull fracture or from external communication with cerebrospinal fluid.

Use with other Vaccines: Simultaneous administration of pneumococcal polysaccharide vaccine and whole-virus influenza vaccine gives satisfactory antibody response without increasing the occurrence of adverse reactions. Simultaneous administration of the pneumococcal vaccine and split-virus influenza vaccine may also be expected to yield satisfactory results.

Revaccination: Adults: Routine revaccination of adults is not recommended; however, revaccination is recommended for adults with chronic conditions which increase the risk of fatal pneumococcal infection and for those shown to have a rapid decline in pneumococcal antibody levels (e.g., patients with nephrotic syndrome, renal failure, or transplant recipients).

One hundred ninety-eight subjects, participated in a randomized, double-blind, placebo-controlled study to compare the safety and tolerance of pneumococcal vaccine revaccination to placebo, in a group of subjects who had been immunized 4 or more years previously. Twenty-five subjects with no prior history of pneumococcal vaccination were in an open study group which served as a positive control for the lot of pneumococcal vaccine used. The demographic characteristics of the subjects enrolled in this study are shown in Table II.

Table II—Pneumovax 23

Pneumovax 23 Revaccination Study: Demographic Characteristics[a]

	Revaccinees (n=98)	Placebo (n=100)	Primary Vaccinees (n=25)
Age (years)			
Mean	75.8	76.6	76.4
Range	47.0-94.6	57.7-97.6	65.7-94.7
Sex (%)			
Male	45	44	36
Female	55	56	64
Time[b] (Mean±S.D.)			
Years since initial vaccination	6.1±1.41	6.09±1.51	0

[a]All subjects were Caucasian.
[b]Time elapsed between initial receipt of 14-valent pneumococcal vaccine and randomization.

The rate of local injection site reactions was higher for the Pneumovax 23 revaccination group than the placebo group, and the local reactions in the Pneumovax 23 revaccination group tended to have slightly longer duration than did those in the placebo group. However, the rate and duration of local injection site reactions in the Pneumovax 23 revaccination group were not significantly different from those in the primary vaccinee group, and almost all of the local reactions in the Pneumovax 23 revaccination group were of mild intensity. All 3 groups had similar rates of systemic adverse events.

Based on the above-mentioned clinical study, revaccination with pneumococcal vaccine is recommended for adults at highest risk of fatal pneumococcal infection who were initially vaccinated with pneumococcal vaccine 4 or more years previously without a serious or severe reaction.

In addition, the National Advisory Committee on Immunization (NACI) and the U.S. Immunization Practices Advisory Committee (ACIP) recommend that revaccination should be considered for adults at highest risk who received the 23-valent vaccine 6 or more years previously.

Because of an increased incidence and severity of adverse reactions among healthy adults revaccinated with pneumococcal vaccines at intervals under 3 years, routine revaccination with pneumococcal vaccine is not recommended. This was probably due to sustained high antibody levels. Also, persons who received the 14-valent vaccine should not be routinely revaccinated with the 23-valent vaccine, as increased coverage is modest and duration of protection is not well defined.

Children: The National Advisory Committee on Immunization (NACI) and the U.S. Immunization Practices Advisory Committee (ACIP) recommend that revaccination after 3 to 5 years should be considered for children at highest risk for pneumococcal infection (e.g., children with asplenia, sickle cell disease or nephrotic syndrome) who would be 10 years old or younger at revaccination.

Children at highest risk for pneumococcal infection may have lower peak antibody levels and/or more rapid antibody decline than do healthy adults. There is evidence that some of these high-risk children (e.g., asplenic children) benefit from revaccination with vaccine containing antigen 7F, 8, 19F.

Contraindications: Hypersensitivity to any component of the vaccine. Epinephrine injection (1:1 000) must be immediately available should an acute anaphylactoid reaction occur due to any component of the vaccine.

Revaccination with pneumococcal vaccine is contraindicated except as described under Indications.

Patients with Hodgkin's disease immunized less than 7 to 10 days prior to immunosuppressive therapy have in some instances been found to have postimmunization antibody levels below their preimmunization levels. Because of these results immunization less than 10 days prior to or during treatment is contraindicated. Patients with Hodgkin's disease who have received extensive chemotherapy and/or nodal irradiation have been shown to have an impaired antibody response to a 12-valent pneumococcal vaccine. Because, in some intensively treated patients, administration of that vaccine depressed pre-existing levels of antibody to some pneumococcal types, pneumococcal vaccine is not recommended at this time for patients who have received these forms of therapy for Hodgkin's disease.

Warnings: The pneumococcal vaccine will not immunize against capsular types of pneumococcus other than those contained in the vaccine.

If the vaccine is used in persons receiving immunosuppressive therapy, the expected serum antibody response may not be obtained.

Intradermal administration may cause severe local reactions.

In patients who require penicillin (or other antibiotics) prophylaxis against pneumococcal infection, such prophylaxis should not be discontinued after immunization with pneumococcal vaccine.

Precautions: General: Any febrile respiratory illness or other active infection is reason for delaying use of pneumococcal vaccine, except when, in the opinion of the physician, withholding the agent entails even greater risk.

Caution and appropriate care should be exercised in administering pneumococcal vaccine to individuals with severely compromised cardiac and/or pulmonary function in whom a systemic reaction would pose a significant risk.

Pregnancy: It is not known whether pneumococcal vaccine can cause fetal harm when administered to a pregnant woman or can affect reproduction capacity. The pneumococcal vaccine should be given to a pregnant woman only if clearly needed.

Lactation: It is not known whether this vaccine is excreted in human milk. Caution should be exercised when pneumococcal vaccine is administered to a nursing woman.

Children: Children under 2 years of age may not obtain a satisfactory antibody response to pneumococcal capsular types. Safety and effectiveness in children below the age of 2 years have not been established. Therefore, the vaccine should not be used in this age group.

Adverse Effects: Common: local injection site soreness, erythema and induration.

Occasional: Body as a whole: low grade fever (<38.3°C).

Rare: Body as a whole: headache, fever (>39°C), malaise, asthenia.

Hematologic/Lymphatic: Adenitis.

Hypersensitivity: anaphylactoid reactions, serum sickness.

Musculoskeletal: arthralgia, myalgia, arthritis.

Skin: rash, urticaria.

Patients with otherwise stabilized idiopathic thrombocytopenic purpura have, on rare occasions, experienced a relapse in their thrombocytopenia, occurring 2 to 14 days after vaccination, and lasting up to 2 weeks.

Reactions of greater severity, duration, or extent are unusual. Neurological disorders such as paresthesias and acute radiculoneuropathy including Guillain-Barré syndrome have been rarely reported in temporal association with administration of pneumococcal vaccine. No cause and effect relationship has been established.

Dosage: Do not inject i.v.

Parenteral drug products should be inspected visually for particulate matter and discoloration prior to administration, whenever solution and container permit. The pneumococcal vaccine is a clear, colorless solution.

Administer a single 0.5 mL dose of the pneumococcal vaccine s.c. or i.m. (preferably in the deltoid muscle or lateral midthigh), with appropriate precautions to avoid intravascular administration (see Indications). **Intradermal** administration should be avoided.

The vaccine is used directly as supplied. No dilution or reconstitution is necessary. Phenol in 0.25% concentration is present in the vaccine as a preservative.

Use a separate sterile syringe and needle free of preservatives, antiseptics and detergents for each individual patient.

It is important to use a separate sterile syringe and needle for each individual patient to prevent transmission of hepatitis B and other infectious agents from one person to another.

Supplied: Each 0.5 mL dose contains: 25 µg of each polysaccharide type dissolved in isotonic saline solution containing phenol 0.25% as preservative. See Table III.

Table III—Pneumovax 23

23 Pneumococcal Capsular Types Included in Pneumovax 23

Nomenclature	Pneumococcal Types																					
Danish	1	2	3	4	5	6B	7F	8	9N	9V	10A	11A	12F	14	15B	17F	18C	19F	19A	20	22F	23F	33F
U.S.	1	2	3	4	5	26	51	8	9	68	34	43	12	14	54	17	56	19	57	20	22	23	70

Single dose vials. Cartons of 1, boxes of 5. Store vials at 2 to 8°C. All vaccines must be discarded by the expiration date.

Reviewed 1998

PNU-IMUNE® 23

Wyeth-Ayerst

Pneumococcal Vaccine Polyvalent

Active Immunizing Agent

Pharmacology: Disease caused by S. pneumonia remains an important cause of morbidity and mortality particularly in the very young, the elderly and persons with certain high-risk conditions. The overall incidence of pneumococcal infections in Canada is not known. In 1992, 132 cases of pneumococcal meningitis were reported in Canada. In England, 34% of pneumonias in adults have been attributed to the pneumococcus.

Studies in the United States have detected rates of pneumococcal bacteremia of 15 to 19/100 000 for all persons, 50/100 000 for persons ≥65 years of age and 160/100 000 for children ≤2 years old. Certain population groups, e.g., Native Americans, may have considerably higher disease rates.

Mortality from pneumococcal disease is highest in patients with bacteremia or meningitis, patients with underlying medical conditions, and older persons. In some high-risk patients, mortality has been reported to be over 40% for bacteremic disease and 55% for meningitis, despite appropriate antimicrobial therapy.

In addition to the young and persons 65 years of age and older, patients with certain chronic conditions are at increased risk of developing pneumococcal infection and severe pneumococcal illness. Patients with chronic cardiovascular or pulmonary disease, diabetes mellitus, alcoholism and cirrhosis are generally immunocompetent but have increased risk. Other patients at greater risk because of decreased responsiveness to polysaccharide antigens or more rapid decline in serum antibody include those with functional or anatomic asplenia (e.g., sickle cell disease or splenectomy), Hodgkin's disease, lymphoma, multiple myeloma, chronic renal failure, nephrotic syndrome and organ transplantation. Studies indicate that patients with acquired immunodeficiency syndrome (AIDS) are also at increased risk of pneumococcal disease. Recurrent pneumococcal meningitis may occur in patients with cerebrospinal fluid leakage that complicates skull fractures or neurologic procedures.

The polysaccharide capsules of pneumococci give these organisms resistance to the phagocytic action of polymorphonuclear leukocytes and monocytes. However, type-specific antibody facilitates their destruction in the body by the mechanism of complement-medicated lysis.

Most healthy adults, including the elderly, demonstrate at least a 2-fold rise in type-specific antibodies within 2 or 3 weeks of immunization. Similar antibody responses have been reported in patients with alcoholic cirrhosis and diabetes mellitus. In contrast, elderly individuals with chronic pulmonary disease failed to mount a comparable immune response. In immunocompromised patients, the response to immunization may also be lower. Children under 2 years of age respond poorly to most capsular polysaccharide types. Further, response to some pneumococcal types (e.g., 6A and 14) important in pediatric infection is decreased in children less than 5 years of age.

In clinical studies with pneumococcal vaccine polyvalent, more than 90% of all adults showed 2-fold or greater increase in geometric mean antibody titre for each capsular type contained in the vaccine.

Patients over the age of 2 years with anatomical or functional asplenia and otherwise intact lymphoid function generally respond to pneumococcal vaccines with a serological conversion comparable to that observed in healthy individuals of the same age.

Patients with acquired immunodeficiency syndrome (AIDS) may have an impaired antibody response to pneumococcal vaccine. However, asymptomatic human immunodeficiency virus (HIV)-infected patients, or those with generalized lymphadenopathy, respond to the 23-valent pneumococcal vaccine.

Following immunization of healthy adults, antibody levels remain elevated for at least 5 years, but in some individuals these may fall to preimmunization levels within 10 years. A more rapid decline in antibodies may occur in children, particulary those who have undergone a splenectomy and those with sickle cell disease, in whom antibodies for some types can fall to preimmunization levels 3 to 5 years after immunization. Similar rates of decline can occur in children with nephrotic syndrome.

Controlled clinical trials in South Africa involving 12 000 gold miners have shown a 6-valent and a 13-valent pneumococcal vaccine to be 78.5% effective in preventing type-specific pneumococcal pneumonia and 82.3% effective in preventing pneumococcal bacteremia with the types contained in the vaccine. In a preliminary study of an 8-valent polysaccharide vaccine in a group consisting of 77 patients with sickle-cell disease and 19 asplenic persons, there were no pneumococcal infections in the immunized patients within 2 years of immunization. There were 8 cases of pneumococcal infection in 106 unimmunized, age-matched patients with sickle-cell disease. Antibody response to the asplenic patients was comparable to that of normal controls.

In a study carried out by Austrian and colleagues with 13-valent pneumococcal vaccines prepared for the National Institute of Allergy and Infectious Disease, the reduction in pneumonias caused by the capsular types present in the vaccines was 79%. Reduction in type-specific pneumococcal bacteremia was 82%.

In a double-blind study of a 14-valent pneumococcal vaccine carried out in Papua, New Guinea, pneumococcal infection was 84% lower in the immunized group and mortality from pneumonia 44% lower.

Five case-control studies in the U.S. have evaluated the efficacy of pneumococcal vaccine in the prevention of serious pneumococcal disease. Four of these studies showed the vaccine to be efficacious, with point estimates of efficacy ranging from 61 to 70%. One study failed to show efficacy in preventing pneumococcal bacteremia. This study was judged inadequate in determination of vaccination status and the selection of controls was considered potentially biased.

A prospective study failed to demonstrate efficacy against pneumococcal pneumonia and bronchitis. This study has been criticized for methodological flaws. In contrast, a prospective French study found pneumococcal vaccine to be 77% effective in reducing the incidence of pneumonia among nursing home residents.

Despite conflicting findings, the data continue to support the use of pneumococcal vaccine for certain well-defined groups at risk.

Indications: For immunization against pneumococcal disease caused by those pneumococcal types included in the vaccine.
Children: Children 2 years of age or older with chronic illnesses specifically associated with increased risk of pneumococcal disease or its complications (e.g., anatomic or functional asplenia [including sickle-cell disease], nephrotic syndrome, cerebrospinal fluid leaks, and conditions associated with immunosuppression).
Adults: All adults 65 or older with emphasis on immunization of the older adult while in good health.

Immunocompetent adults who are at increased risk of pneumococcal disease or its complications because of chronic illness (e.g., cardiovascular or pulmonary disease, diabetes mellitus, alcoholism, cirrhosis, or cerebrospinal fluid leaks).

Immunocompromised adults at increased risk of pneumococcal disease or its complications (e.g., splenic dysfunction or anatomic asplenia, Hodgkin's disease, lymphoma, multiple myeloma, chronic renal failure, nephrotic syndrome, or conditions such as organ transplantation associated with immunosuppression).
Special Groups: Persons living in special environments or social settings with an identified increased risk of pneumococcal disease or its complications.

Patients with acquired immunodeficiency syndrome (AIDS) have been shown to have an impaired antibody response to pneumococcal vaccine. However, asymptomatic or symptomatic human immunodeficiency virus (HIV)-infected patients or those with persistent generalized lymphadenopathy respond to the 23-valent vaccine.
Timing of Immunization: When elective splenectomy is being considered, pneumococcal vaccine should be given at least 2 weeks before surgery, if possible.

For planning cancer chemotherapy or other immunosuppressive therapy, the interval between immunization and initiation of chemotherapy or immunosuppression should be at least 2 weeks.

Contraindications: Hypersensitivity to any component of the vaccine, including thimerosal, a mercury derivative, is a contraindication to the use of the product.

Revaccination of adults is contraindicated. Adults previously immunized with any polyvalent pneumococcal vaccine should not receive pneumococcal vaccine polyvalent since an increased incidence and severity of adverse reactions among healthy adults receiving such reinjections have been noted most likely due to sustained high antibody levels.

The occurrence of any type of neurological symptoms or signs following administration of this product is a contraindication to further use.

Immunization should be deferred during the course of any febrile illness or acute infection. A minor illness such as mild upper respiratory infection is usually not a reason to defer immunization.

The clinical judgment of the attending physician should prevail at all times.

Warnings: Pneumococcal vaccine polyvalent is not recommended for children under two years of age, since antibody response to most capsular polysaccharide types is poor in this age group.

Pneumococcal Vaccine Polyvalent is not an effective agent for prophylaxis against capsular types of pneumococcus other than those contained in the vaccine.

Patients with impaired immune responsiveness whether due to the use of immunosuppressive therapy, a genetic defect, human immunodeficiency virus (HIV) infection, or other causes may have a reduced antibody response to active immunization procedures (see Precautions).

Patients who have received extensive chemotherapy and/or splenectomy for the treatment of Hodgkin's disease have been shown to have an impaired serum antibody response to pneumococcal vaccine.

In 1 study, administration of the vaccine to patients on immunosuppressive drugs and/or irradiation for Hodgkin's disease resulted in reduction of pre-existing antibody levels in several patients. It is unclear whether this effect was due to the vaccine or to the effects of irradiation and/or chemotherapy.

At least 2 weeks should elapse between immunization and the initiation of chemotherapy or immunosuppressive therapy.

Routine reimmunization with this vaccine is not recommended. For reimmunization (including recommendations regarding reimmunization of individuals at highest risk of fatal pneumococcal infection), see Dosage.

In 1 study, local reactions after reimmunization were more severe than after initial immunization when the interval between immunizations was 13 months.

Patients who have had episodes of pneumococcal pneumonia or other pneumococcal infection may have high levels of pre-existing pneumococcal antibodies that may result in increased reactions to pneumococcal vaccine polyvalent, mostly local, but occasionally systemic. Caution should be exercised if such patients are considered for immunization with pneumococcal vaccine polyvalent.

Do not administer the vaccine intradermally since severe reactions may occur.

As with other i.m. injections, pneumococcal vaccine polyvalent should be given with caution to individuals with thrombocytopenia or any coagulation disorder that would contraindicate i.m. injection (see Precautions, Drug Interactions).

As with any vaccine, pneumococcal vaccine polyvalent may not protect 100% of individuals receiving the vaccine.

In patients who require penicillin (or other antibiotics) prophylaxis against pneumococcal infection, such prophylaxis should not be discontinued after immunization with the pneumococcal vaccine.

Precautions: Pneumococcal vaccine polyvalent is for i.m. or s.c. use only.

Pneumococcal vaccine polyvalent should not be used in children under 2 years of age.

Caution and appropriate care should be exercised in administering pneumococcal vaccine to individuals with severely compromised cardiac and/or pulmonary function in whom a systemic reaction would pose a significant risk.

Prior to administration of any dose of pneumococcal vaccine polyvalent, the parent, guardian, or adult patient should be asked about the personal history, family history, recent health status and immunization history of the patient to be immunized to determine the existence of any contraindication to immunization with pneumococcal vaccine (see Contraindications and Warnings).

Before administration of any biological, the physician should take all known precautions for prevention of allergic or any other reactions. This includes: a review of the patient's history regarding possible sensitivity, the ready availability of epinephrine 1:1 000 and other appropriate agents used for control of immediate allergic reactions, and a knowledge of the recent literature pertaining to use of the biological concerned, including the nature of side effects and adverse reactions that may follow its use.

A separate sterile syringe and needle or a sterile disposable unit should be used for each individual patient to prevent transmission of infectious agents from one person to another. Needles should be disposed of properly and should not be recapped.

Patients with impaired immune responsiveness, whether due to use of immunosuppressive therapy (including irradiation, corticosteroids, antimetabolites, alkylating agents, any cytotoxic agents), a genetic defect, human immunodeficiency virus (HIV) infection or other causes, may have reduced antibody response to active immunization procedures. Deferral of administration of vaccine may be considered in individuals receiving immunosuppressive therapy.

This product is not contraindicated for use in individuals with HIV.

Special care should be taken to prevent injection into a blood vessel.
Children: **Pneumococcal vaccine polyvalent should not be used in children under 2 years of age.**
Pregnancy: Animal reproduction studies have not been conducted with pneumococcal vaccine polyvalent. It is also not known whether pneumococcal vaccine polyvalent can cause fetal harm when administered to a pregnant woman or effect reproduction capacity. Pneumococcal vaccine polyvalent is not recommended for use in pregnant women.
Lactation: It is not known whether the drug is excreted in human milk. Because many drugs are excreted in human milk, caution should be exercised when pneumococcal vaccine polyvalent is administered to a nursing woman.
Carcinogenesis, Mutagenesis, Impairment of Fertility: Pneumococcal vaccine polyvalent has not been evaluated for its carcinogenic or mutagenic potential, or impairment of fertility.
Drug Interactions: Simultaneous immunization is possible with attenuated live vaccines, inactivated vaccines and immunoglobulins, if the application is given at separate sites.

Children receiving immunosuppressive therapy may have a reduced response to active immunization procedures.

As with other i.m. injections, pneumococcal vaccine polyvalent should be given with caution to children on anticoagulant therapy.
Information to be Provided to the Patient: Prior to administration of this vaccine, health care personnel should inform the parent, guardian, or adult patient of the benefits and risks of immunization with pneumococcal vaccine. Guidance should be provided on measures to be taken should adverse events

Pnu-Imune 23 (cont'd)

occur, such as, antipyretic measures for elevated temperatures and the need to report adverse events to the health care provider.

Adverse Effects: Pneumococcal vaccine polyvalent is associated with a relatively low incidence of adverse reactions. The adverse reactivity observed in clinical studies was of short duration and not serious.

In a study of 32 individuals who received pneumococcal vaccine polyvalent, 23 (72%) experienced local reaction characterized by soreness at the injection site within 3 days after immunization.

Low grade fever (less than 37.8°C) and mild myalgia occur occasionally and are usually confined to the 24-hour period following immunization. Rash and arthralgia have been reported infrequently.

Although rare, fever over 38.9°C and marked local swelling have been reported with pneumococcal polysaccharide vaccine. Rash, urticaria, arthritis, arthralgia and adenitis have been reported rarely.

Patients with otherwise stabilized idiopathic thrombocytopenic purpura have, on rare occasions, experienced a relapse in their thrombocytopenia, occurring 2 to 14 days after immunization and lasting up to 2 weeks.

Reactions of greater severity or extent are unusual. Rarely, anaphylactoid reactions have been reported.

Temporal association of neurological disorders such as paresthesias and acute radiculoneuropathy, including Guillain-Barré syndrome, have been reported following parenteral injections of biological products including pneumococcal vaccine.

Overdose: Symptoms and Treatment: In case of anaphylactic reactions, the usual procedures for shock therapy apply.

Dosage: The immunization schedule consists of a single 0.5 mL dose given i.m. or s.c.

Administration: **Shake vigorously before withdrawing each dose to resuspend the contents of vial or syringe.**

The preferred sites are the anterolateral aspect of the thigh or the deltoid muscle of the upper arm. The vaccine should not be injected in the gluteal area or areas where there may be a major nerve trunk. Before injection, the skin at the injection site should be cleansed with a suitable germicide. After insertion of the needle, aspirate to help avoid inadvertent injection into a blood vessel.

The vaccine should be injected i.m. or s.c. **Intradermal administration should be avoided. Do not inject i.v.** (Vaccines applied mistakenly i.v. can result in anaphylactic reactions, including shock.)

Parenteral drug products should be inspected visually for particulate matter and discoloration prior to administration.

Directions for Use of the Lederject Disposable Syringe (see package insert for illustrations): Twist the plunger rod clockwise to be sure the rod is secure to rubber plunger base. **Shake syringe to resuspend contents.**

Hold needle shield in place with index finger and thumb of one hand while, with the other thumb, exert light pressure on plunger rod until the plunger base has been freed and demonstrates slight movement when pressure is applied.

Grasp the rubber needle shield at its base; twist and pull to remove.

To prevent needle-stick injuries, needles should not be recapped, purposely bent, or broken by hand.

Do not use this vaccine past the expiration date.

Simultaneous Administration with Other Vaccines: Many patients who receive pneumococcal vaccine should also be immunized with influenza vaccine which may be given simultaneously at a different site. In contrast to pneumococcal vaccine, influenza vaccine is recommended annually.

Reimmunization: The incidence of local reactions after reimmunization were found to be more severe than after initial immunization when the interval between immunizations was 13 months. Reports of reimmunization after longer intervals in children and adults, including a large group of elderly persons reimmunized at least 4 years after primary immunization, suggest a similar incidence of such reactions.

The USA Immunization Practices Advisory Committee (ACIP) recommendations regarding reimmunization are as follows: Persons who receive the 14-valent vaccine should not **routinely** be reimmunized with the 23-valent vaccine. However, reimmunization with 23-valent vaccine should be strongly considered for persons who received the 14-valent vaccine **if they are at highest risk** of fatal pneumococcal infection (e.g., asplenic patients). Reimmunization should also be carefully considered for adults at highest risk who received the 23-valent vaccine more than 6 years before and for those shown to have a rapid decline in antibody levels (e.g., patients with nephrotic syndrome, renal failure, or transplant patients). Reimmunization should be carefully considered after 3 to 5 years for children with nephrotic syndrome, asplenia, or sickle-cell anemia who would be 10 years old or younger at the time of reimmunization.

Supplied: Each dose (0.5 mL) of clear, colorless liquid contains: 25 µg of each of the 23 purified capsular polysaccharide types of S. pneumoniae. See Table I. Nonmedicinal ingredients: 2-(ethylmeralrithio) benzoic acid, phosphate buffer, sodium salt and thimerosal. Thimerosal (mercury derivative) is added to the vaccine to a final concentration of 1:10 000.

Table I—Pnu-Imune 23

23 Pneumococcal Capsular Types Included in Pnu-Imune 23

Nomenclature	
Danish	1 2 3 4 5 6B 7F 8 9N 9V 10A 11A 12F 14 15B 17F 18C 19F 19A 20 22F 23F 33F
U.S.	1 2 3 4 5 26 51 8 9 68 34 43 12 14 54 17 56 19 57 20 22 23 70

Vials of 2.5 mL (5 doses), for use with syringe only, packages of 1. Lederject disposable syringes of 0.5 mL (single dose), packages of 5. Store refrigerated away from the freezer compartment at 2 to 8°C. **Do not freeze.** Do not use vaccine past expiration date.

New Product 1998

PODOFILM® Ⓟ

Pharmascience

Podophyllum Resin

Wart Remover

Indications: For the removal of benign epithelial growths such as venereal warts (condylomata acuminata), common warts (verruca vulgaris), and benign papillomas such as granuloma inguinale and plantar warts.

Contraindications: Hypersensitivity to podophyllin. The consumption of alcoholic beverages for several hours after treatment, is to be avoided.

Precautions: Podophyllin is an extremely potent vesicant and is to be applied only by the doctor. It is recommended that care be used in the selection of patients to be treated with the product and method used, the doctor developing his own experience and technique. To avoid toxicity, it is recommended that applications be limited to small areas of intact skin. Do not use on tongue or any mucosal tissue. Do not use if growth or surrounding tissue is inflamed or irritated. Do not use on diabetics or people with poor blood circulation, nor on moles, birth-marks, or unusual warts with hair growing from them. Do not use in circumstances where the genital warts are either florid with a large surface area or so hemorrhagic that absorption of the toxin is probable. If vaginal condylomata are very extensive it is probably best to treat them on just one half of the vagina at a time to prevent severe inflammation and interference with micturition. Large areas should not be treated all at once since discomfort may be excessive and systemic absorption may result.

Pregnancy and *Lactation:* Use during pregnancy and or in nursing mothers is not recommended since there have been no adequate and well-controlled studies in the use of podophyllin in pregnant women or nursing mothers. It is recommended that the patient be advised of the effect and the possible results of treatment.

Adverse Effects: Systemic effects from topical use of podophyllum resin includes urticaria, transient fever, paresthesia, polyneuritis, paralytic ileus, pyrexia leukopenia, thrombocytopenia, coma, and death. Local effects include severe necrosis and scarring of the anogenital area, paraphimosis requiring circumcision and pseudoepitheliomatous hyperplasia.

Note: Podophyllin is a strong vesicant and may produce blisters if it comes in contact with normal skin or mucous membrane. If spilled on skin, wipe off at once, using acetone, alcohol or tape remover. Then wash vigorously with warm soapy water and rinse well. If spilled on mucous membrane or eyes, flush with water, remove the precipitated film, and flush with water for an additional 15 minutes. Patients vary in their sensitivity to podophyllin and in rare cases tingling, burning or extreme tenderness may develop. In these cases, patient should remove tape and soak the area in cool water for 10 to 15 minutes, repeating as required for relief. If soreness persists, puncture blister using sterile technique, apply antiseptic and cover with a Band-Aid. It is advisable to treat only 1 or 2 lesions on the first visit, until the sensitivity of the patient is known. For external use only.

Dosage: Care must be exercised when applying the drug so that the adjacent area is not affected. Normal skin adjacent to the lesion should be protected with petrolatum. Apply no more than 1 to 2 mL of podophyllin during 1 treatment.

Moist anogenital warts (condylomata acuminata): Treatment should be an office procedure and should be carried out by the physician. Using a cotton applicator or toothpick, apply the drug carefully to the lesion. Allow to dry before adding the next application. It should be allowed to dry before the patient leaves the office.

The initial application should be allowed to remain in place for 1 hour then washed off. If the initial application is not unusually inflammatory or painful, the product may be subsequently left on for 4 to 6 hours before being washed off. The medication should then be carefully removed with soap and water. Reapplication can be carried out at weekly intervals, if necessary.

It has been reported that use of podophyllum for cervical warts can lead to a false-positive PAP smear for as long as 6 months after the application of the podophyllum resin.

Common warts: Method A (no curettage): No cutting or prior treatment is required. Occasionally nails must be trimmed to expose subungual warts to medication. Using a Q-Tip or applicator stick, apply podophyllin (1 layer only) to the wart and a 1 to 3 mm margin around the wart. Allow to dry for a few minutes. Cover with a piece of nonporous plastic adhesive tape. Instruct patient to keep the tape on for at least 4 hours (up to 24 hours). Within 24 hours a blister forms which is often painful and inflamed. Have the patient return for observation in 1 to 2 weeks. Remove necrotic tissue and treat as before if any viable wart tissue remains. Allow tissue to re-epithelialize before retreatment.

Method B (with curettage) Proceed as in Method A except have patient return in 1 day for curettage. (Local anesthesia may be necessary). There are several advantages to this method: Treatment with podophyllin prior to curettage enhances identification of tissue planes, increases separability of wart tissue and retreatment is rarely necessary. Have the patient return for observation in 4 weeks. (The lesion normally heals completely within 1 to 3 weeks.) The use of a mild antibacterial agent until area heals is recommended.

Plantar warts: Pare away keratin covering the wart, avoid bleeding, avoid cutting viable tissue. Using a Q-Tip or applicator stick, apply podophyllin to both the wart and a 1 to 3 mm margin around the wart. Allow a few minutes to dry. Secure with nonporous plastic adhesive tape. Leave in place for 48 hours, then debride. If any viable wart tissue remains after debridement, reapply a small amount of podophyllin and bandage as above. Repeat treatments over several weeks are often necessary. When destruction of wart is complete, the healed site will appear smooth, with normal skin lines.

Pain Management: Warn the patient that the blister may be painful. Prescribe a mild analgesic, e.g. ASA with codeine, or acetaminophen with codeine. The tape may be removed and the area soaked in cool water for 10 to 15 minute periods, as needed, provided sufficient time has been allowed for the medication to penetrate. Local anesthesia may be needed during curettage (Method B).

Molluscum contagiosum: Coat each lesion with a thin film of podophyllin. After 1 week, treat any new lesions the same way and retreat any resistant lesions with podophyllum, this time covering with a small piece of occlusive tape. The tape should be removed in 6 to 8 hours.

Supplied: Each bottle contains: podophyllum resin 25% in an adherent film forming vehicle (tincture of benzoin compound). Bottles of 25 mL. Keep away from heat, fire and flame. Close tightly immediately after use. Store at room temperature.

POLARAMINE®

Schering

Dexchlorpheniramine Maleate

Antihistamine

Indications: For symptomatic relief of allergic conditions such as hay fever, urticaria, angioedema, vasomotor rhinitis, allergic eczema, contact dermatitis, pruritus ani and vulvae, and pruritus of nonspecific origin, as well as in certain cases of migraine headache.

Precautions: Occupational Hazards: Patients should be cautioned not to operate vehicles or hazardous machinery until their response to the drug has been determined.

Since the depressant effects of antihistamines are additive to those of other drugs affecting the CNS, patients should be cautioned against drinking alcoholic beverages or taking hypnotics, sedatives, psychotherapeutic agents or other drugs with CNS depressant effects during antihistaminic therapy.

Should not be used by persons who are allergic or sensitive to any of the components of the product. May cause excitability in children; children should be observed by parents.

Pregnancy and *Lactation:* The safe use of this product during pregnancy and lactation has not been established and therefore the compound should be used only if the potential benefit justifies the potential risk to the fetus or infant.

Antihistamines should be discontinued approximately 48 hours prior to skin testing procedures since these may prevent or diminish otherwise positive reactions to dermal reactivity indicators.

Adverse Effects: Occasionally nausea, mild drowsiness may be produced.

Overdose: Symptoms and Treatment: If accidental overdose occurs, seek medical assistance immediately.

Dosage: Adults and children over 12 years, 2 mg 3 or 4 times daily. Children 6 to 12 years, 1 mg 3 or 4 times daily.

Supplied: Each red, oval, scored tablet contains: dexchlorpheniramine maleate USP 2 mg. Nonmedicinal ingredients: cornstarch, FD & C Yellow No. 6, FD & C Red No. 40, lactose, magnesium stearate and povidone. Tartrazine-free. Bottles of 100.

(Shown in Product Recognition Section)

POLIOVIRUS VACCINE LIVE ORAL TRIVALENT

Connaught

Poliovirus Types 1, 2 and 3

Active Immunizing Agent

Pharmacology: The purpose of administering any attenuated, live virus vaccine is to stimulate the immune system to produce an active immunity by stimulating natural infection without producing clinical symptoms of the disease. To accomplish this with live poliovirus vaccine, it is necessary for the virus to multiply in the intestinal tract. A primary series of this vaccine is designed to produce an antibody response to poliovirus types 1, 2 and 3. This immune response is comparable to that induced by natural disease. The antibodies thus formed help protect the individual against clinical poliomyelitis infection by any one of the 3 types of poliovirus.

The immune response to Poliovirus Vaccine Live Oral Trivalent (OPV) is similar to that induced by natural infection with poliovirus and includes the development of secretory antibody within the intestinal tract. This is believed to prevent subsequent infection with "wild" polioviruses and their dissemination by the fecal-oral route to susceptible individuals in the community. OPV also interferes with simultaneous infection with "wild" poliovirus and is thus of particular value in the control of epidemics.

The virus persists in the throat for 1 to 2 weeks; it is excreted in the feces for several weeks, and, rarely, for more than 2 months. This may lead to infection of close contacts which is regarded as largely beneficial since it results in protection of more individuals than the number actually vaccinated. In a very small number of infected contacts, especially adults, paralytic disease may occur.

Indications: Primary immunization of infants, children and adolescents against poliomyelitis caused by poliovirus types 1, 2 and 3. Booster immunization of vaccinated adults. Immunization of unvaccinated adults travelling in less than 4 weeks to endemic areas when time does not permit administration of at least 2 doses of inactivated poliovirus vaccine (IPV).

Outbreak Control: If a case of paralytic poliomyelitis caused by "wild" virus appears in a community, OPV should be administered to all individuals (including infants) who have not been completely immunized or whose immunization status is uncertain.

IPV is not recommended for the control of outbreaks of poliomyelitis.

Contraindications: Do not administer Poliovirus Vaccine Live Oral Trivalent (OPV) parenterally.

Individuals with a known allergy to polymyxin B, neomycin or streptomycin should not receive the vaccine.

It is recommended that OPV **not** be administered to those acutely ill.

Administration of OPV is contraindicated in all cases of leukemia, lymphoma, generalized malignancy or advanced debilitated states. OPV must **never** be given to patients who are immunodeficient including persons known to be HIV infected, those on immunosuppressive therapy, and to persons who will have household, or similar close contact with such patients in the following 4 weeks. These patients and their contacts may be given IPV without risk, but the protection afforded to immunocompromised persons may be limited.

Warnings: The virus persists in the throat for 1 to 2 weeks; it is excreted in the feces for several weeks, and, rarely, for more than 2 months. This may lead to infection of close contacts which is regarded as largely beneficial since it results in protection of more individuals than the number actually vaccinated. In a very small number of infected contacts, especially adults, paralytic disease may occur.

Any vaccine showing particulate matter or turbidity should be discarded.

As with any vaccine, administration of Poliovirus Vaccine Live Oral Trivalent may not result in seroconversion in 100% of susceptible subjects given the vaccine.

Precautions: For unvaccinated adults not at special risk, primary immunization with IPV is recommended.

The possibility of allergic reactions in individuals sensitive to the components of the vaccine should be evaluated.

Epinephrine HCl Solution (1:1 000) should be available for immediate use in case an anaphylactic or acute hypersensitivity reaction occurs.

Pregnancy: There is no evidence to suggest that a pregnant women or her fetus is at greater risk from OPV than other persons and therefore OPV should be used for pregnant women during control of an outbreak. When polio vaccination is indicated in other circumstances during pregnancy, IPV should be used.

Drug Interactions: One live vaccine may interfere with the effectiveness of another, and to minimize this possibility, 2 or more live vaccines should preferably be administered either on the same day or be separated by an interval of at least 1 month.

Poliovirus vaccine live oral trivalent should not be mixed with chlorinated water. No other interactions with food are known.

Adverse Effects: In rare instances, OPV has been associated temporally with paralytic disease in vaccine recipients or their close contacts.

Between 1965 and 1988, vaccine-associated paralysis in Canadian recipients of OPV occurred at the rate of 1 case per 9.5 million doses of vaccine distributed, and in contacts of vaccinees, 1 case per 3.2 million doses distributed.

The effectiveness of OPV in preventing and controlling paralytic poliomyelitis is so great that the extremely small risk of vaccine-associated paralysis is not a contraindication to its widespread use in routine immunization programs for infants and children.

Dosage: Single Dose Dispenser: One dose is the entire expellable contents (0.5 mL) of the single dose dispenser.

Table II—Poliovirus Vaccine Live Oral Trivalent

Availability of Dosage Forms

	Single Dose Dispenser	10 Dose Dispenser
Poliovirus Type I	1 000 000 infectious particles	1 000 000 infectious particles
Poliovirus Type 2	100 000 infectious particles	100 000 infectious particles
Poliovirus Type 3	300 000 infectious particles	300 000 infectious particles
Streptomycin	not more than 1.6 ng by calculation	not more than 320 pg by calculation
Neomycin	not more than 2.0 μg	not more 0.4 μg
Polymyxin B	not more than 10 units	not more than 2 units

suspended in 53.5% w/w sucrose in phosphate buffer

10 Dose Dispenser: One dose is 2 drops from the 10 dose dispenser.

In infancy, the primary series is usually integrated with Diptheria, Tetanus and Pertussis (DPT) vaccination. Poliovirus Vaccine Live Oral Trivalent can be administered simultaneously with DPT, MMR (Measles, Mumps and Rubella) or H. influenzae type b (Hib) conjugate vaccines without increased side effects; the immune response to each antigen is adequate and comparable to that found in patients receiving these vaccines according to the routine schedule. It is recommended that individual live virus vaccines be administered either simultaneously or be separated by an interval of at least 30 days of one another because of theoretical concerns that the immune response to one live-virus vaccine might be impaired if given within 30 days of another. See Table I.

Table I—Poliovirus Vaccine Live Oral Trivalent

Recommended Immunization Schedule

Dose	Timing
1st	First Visit (commonly at 2 months of age)
2nd	2 months after First Visit
3rd	4 months after First Visit[a]
4th	16 months after First Visit
5th	Pre-school[b]
6th	At 14 to 16 years of age[a]

[a] This dose may be omitted if OPV has been used exclusively for the individual.

[b] This dose may be omitted if the previous dose was administered after the 4th birthday.

Methods of Administration: The vaccine must be administered orally. It must **not** be administered parenterally.

The vaccine must be completely thawed prior to use. For **single dose dispensers**, a single dose can be obtained by inverting the plastic dispenser and squeezing to dispense the **entire contents.**

For the **10 dose dispenser**, hold the tube upright and tap lightly to remove any product from the neck of the tube. Carefully remove the cap by twisting it slowly. Invert the plastic dispenser, hold vertically (tip down) and apply even pressure to express **2 drops.** Before replacing the cap, hold the tube upright and tap lightly to remove any product from the neck of the tube. Replace the cap with a careful slow twist to assure a good seal and to avoid damage to the tip of the dispenser. Damage to the tip could alter the drop size and so change the dose.

The vaccine should be administered by dispensing the dose into a plastic disposable spoon. **The 10 dose plastic dispenser must not be used for feeding the vaccine nor allowed to come into contact with any contaminated dispensing spoons.**

Each person who is immunized should be given a permanent personal immunization record. In addition, it is essential that the health care provider also maintain a permanent record of the immunization history of each individual. This office record should contain the name of the vaccine, date given, dose, manufacturer and lot number.

Information for the Patient: See Blue Section—Information for the Patient "Poliovirus Vaccine Live Oral Trivalent".

Supplied: Single and 10 dose plastic dispensers.

Store at −20°C or lower for a period not exceeding the expiry date on the label. Alternatively, the thawed vaccine may be stored between 2 and 8°C for up to 4 months. The vaccine must **not** be administered beyond the expiry date on the label.

Once **opened**, the 10 dose dispenser may be used for up to 3 days provided it is kept constantly between 2 and 8°C during this period. The contents of opened dispensers must be examined for turbidity prior to use. Vaccine showing turbidity must be discarded.

Each dose of Poliovirus Vaccine Live Oral Trivalent (OPV) is prepared in human diploid strain WI-38 cell cultures from attenuated poliovirus (Sabin) types 1, 2 and 3. See Table II for availability of dosage forms.

The vaccine is clear with color ranging from orange to pale yellow due to the presence of trace amounts of phenol red indicator.

A quick and easy reference for immunization schedules for infants and children can be found in the CLIN-INFO SECTION.

POLLINEX®-R
Bencard

Modified Ragweed Tyrosine Adsorbate
Vaccine

Pharmacology: Pollinex-R is an aqueous extract of short ragweed pollen (Ambrosia elatior) chemically modified with gluteraldehyde adsorbed onto tyrosine and then suspended in saline.

The exact mode of therapeutic action of Pollinex-R, as with other allergy vaccines, is unknown. It has been proposed the elevation of IgG blocking antibodies may interfere with the immediate hypersensitivity reaction of patients exposed to ragweed pollen. In addition, patients receiving Pollinex-R have lesser postseasonal increase in ragweed specific IgE antibody compared to placebo treated patients. It is possible that suppression of IgE antibody by Pollinex-R during the ragweed season could influence the response of ragweed allergic patients to the pollen in their environment.

Indications: For the preseasonal immunotherapy of adults and children, over 8 years of age, who have demonstrated ragweed allergic rhinitis by careful patient history and physical examination, supplemented by skin testing and/or immunological assay.

Pollinex-R is generally not expected to completely eliminate the various allergic symptoms but should reduce their severity. Pollinex-R should also be expected in many patients to reduce their dependence on other medication, such as antihistamines and other cough/cold over the counter medications that are taken during the season to alleviate rhinitis symptoms. There is evidence the use of more potent therapy, such as nasal and oral steroids, is reduced in patients who have received a course of Pollinex-R.

Contraindications: Pollinex-R should not be administered to a patient who has experienced a previous severe anaphylactic reaction to ragweed vaccine immunotherapy.

Warnings: Patients suffering from febrile conditions or an acute asthmatic attack should not be given Pollinex-R until 24 hours after their condition has returned to normal. Acute immediate anaphylactic reactions characterized by difficulty in breathing, cyanosis and shock have rarely occurred with Pollinex-R treatment, but if such should occur, standard emergency measures must be adopted with the use of a tourniquet above the injection site, epinephrine, oxygen, i.v. steroids and airway management including intubation if required. Similarly, delayed anaphylactic reactions have rarely been reported with Pollinex-R, however, the patient should be advised to report to their physician immediately if symptoms of such a reaction should be manifested.

Recent evidence suggests that patients on beta-blockers may be more prone to anaphylaxis during immunotherapy and in such patients, anaphylaxis may be less responsive to conventional treatment.

Hence, in such patients, the need for continued immunotherapy and/or continued beta-blocker use should be carefully reviewed.

Do not administer Pollinex-R during the ragweed season, which usually starts in mid-August through to the end of September, or until the first killing frost.

Precautions: All Pollinex-R administrations must be given by the s.c. route, by or under a physician's supervision. Never inject Pollinex-R directly into a blood vessel.

All patients should remain under observation in the doctor's office or clinic for 20 to 30 minutes after each vaccine injection and then should avoid strenuous physical exercise for at least 24 hours.

Advise patients not to eat a heavy meal immediately before receiving their Pollinex-R injection. It is advisable to administer an antihistamine about 1 hour prior to a Pollinex-R injection. Epinephrine HCl 1:1 000 solution should always be kept on hand for use in the very unlikely event of a severe immediate reaction.

It is extremely important to shake the syringe containing the vaccine prior to injection thus greatly reducing the possibility of needle blockage.

Pregnancy: Pollinex-R's safety for use in pregnancy has not been established.

Safety for use in combination with other allergens has not been established. Pollinex-R administration should not be instituted unless other ragweed pollen extract therapy has been discontinued.

Adverse Effects: Hypersensitivity: erythema, swelling, pruritus, wheal, papule, mild hives, anaphylactoid reaction.

Other: local reactions, such as pain accompanied by induration at the injection site; wheezing, stuffy and/or runny nose, tight chest.

Overdose: Symptoms and Treatment: It is not possible to administer to a patient an overdosage of Pollinex-R, as long as no more than 0.5 mL of the vaccine is administered starting with either syringe or vial number 1, followed in sequence by syringe or vial 2, 3 and lastly 4.

In patients with severe allergic reactions, general supportive measures (if the patient is in shock) or symptomatic therapy similar to that applied in all cases of hypersensitivity are recommended. Pressor amines, antihistamines and corticosteroids should be readily available. Pollinex-R is not suitable for such patients with severe allergic reactions.

Dosage: Pollinex-R must be given prior to the ragweed season which usually starts in mid August. The course of vaccine therapy should start toward the end of June and be given so that the last injection is received about the first week in August.

Syringes: The dosage regimen is outlined in Table I. Each course of Pollinex-R consists of a patient treatment pack of 4 sterile prefilled syringes clearly labeled 1, 2, 3 and 4 containing the following Pollinex-R strengths each in a 0.5 mL volume.

Table I—Pollinex-R

Syringes

Syringe Number	Strength in Protein Nitrogen Units (PNU)/0.5 mL	Strength in Noon Units/0.5 mL
1	110	300
2	250	700
3	710	2 000
4	2 100	6 000

The vaccine treatment regimen consists of the administration of Pollinex-R by s.c. injection. On the first occasion, the contents of No. 1 syringe are given, followed in order by syringe numbers 2, 3 and 4 at a recommended interval of approximately 7 days between injections. The operation of the syringe is as follows:

1. Withdraw the syringe from the cold storage condition well before time of administration and allow to attain room temperature. Do not heat.
2. **Do not remove the needle guard until ready for use.**
3. Withdraw syringe plunger slightly and shake the syringe thoroughly to ensure a homogeneous suspension.
4. Apply quick firm pressure on the plunger to burst internal seal (the rupture will be felt).
5. Release the pressure in the syringe by withdrawing the plunger slightly.
6. Shake the syringe thoroughly again, remove needle guard, then carefully express the air from the syringe with the needle held upwards, to minimize loss of contents.
7. **Slowly** inject the suspension **deep subcutaneously.**
8. **Do not inject into a blood vessel.**

Vials: Each patient treatment pack consists of 4 sterile vials clearly labeled 1, 2, 3 and 4 containing Pollinex-R strengths each in a volume of 1 mL as seen in Table II.

Table II—Pollinex-R

Vials

Vial Number	Strength in Protein Nitrogen Units/1.0 mL	Strength in Noon Units/1.0 mL
1	210	600
2	500	1 400
3	1 400	4 000
4	4 300	12 000

The vaccine treatment regimen consists of the administration of Pollinex-R by s.c. injection. On the first occasion, 0.5 mL of the contents of No. 1 vial are given, followed in order by 0.5 mL of vial numbers 2, 3 and 4 at a recommended interval of approximately 7 days between injections.

Procedure for vials:

1. Withdraw the vial from the cold storage condition well before time of administration and allow to attain room temperature. Do not heat.
2. Shake vial thoroughly to ensure a homogeneous suspension.
3. Using a sterile disposable syringe, withdraw 0.5 mL of suspension.
4. Carefully express the air from the syringe with the needle held upwards to minimize loss of contents.
5. **Slowly** inject the suspension **deep subcutaneously.**
6. **Do not inject into a blood vessel.**

Supplied: Prefilled Syringes: Each patient treatment package consists of 4 prefilled sterile syringes each containing 0.5 mL of suspension. Each syringe is labeled as to syringe number and strength in total Protein Nitrogen Units (see Table III).

Table III—Pollinex-R

Syringe Number	Dosage in Protein Nitrogen Units
1	110
2	250
3	710
4	2 100

Vials: Each patient treatment package consists of 4 sterile vials each containing 1 mL of suspension. Each vial is clearly labeled as to vial number and strength in total Protein Nitrogen Units (see Table IV).

Table IV—Pollinex-R

Vial Number	Total Protein Nitrogen Units/Vial
1	210
2	500
3	1 400
4	4 300

Store at 5°C.

Reviewed 1999

POLOCAINE® 3%
POLOCAINE® 2% with LEVONORDEFRIN 1:20 000
Astra

Mepivacaine HCl
Mepivacaine HCl—Levonordefrin
Local Anesthetic

Pharmacology: Mechanism of Action: Mepivacaine stabilizes the neuronal membrane by inhibiting the ionic fluxes required for the initiation and conduction of impulses, thereby effecting local anesthetic action. Local anesthetics of the amide type are thought to act within sodium channels of the nerve membrane.

Onset of Action: Mepivacaine has a rapid onset of action after infiltration, on average 2 to 3 minutes. Mandibular block requires 5 minutes or more to take full effect. The average duration of useful anesthesia after infiltration is about 20 minutes. After successful regional anesthesia, e.g., mandibular block, anesthesia lasts for 2 hours or longer.

Mepivacaine with levonordefrin provides anesthesia of longer duration for more prolonged procedures.

Hemodynamics: Mepivacaine, like other local anesthetics, may also have effects on excitable membranes in the brain and myocardium. If excessive amounts of drug reach systemic circulation rapidly, symptoms and signs of toxicity will appear, emanating from the central nervous and cardiovascular systems.

CNS toxicity (see Overdose: Symptoms and Treatment) usually precedes the cardiovascular effects since it occurs at lower plasma concentrations. Direct effects of local anesthetics on the heart include slow conduction, negative inotropism and eventually cardiac arrest.

Pharmacokinetics: The clearance of mepivacaine is almost entirely due to liver metabolism and depends upon the liver blood flow and the activity of the metabolizing enzymes. The total plasma clearance of mepivacaine is 0.8 L/min, the elimination half-life is 1.9 hours, and the hepatic extraction ratio is 0.5. The elimination half-life in neonates is 3 to 5 times longer than in adults.

Mepivacaine crosses the placenta and equilibrium in regard to free drug will be reached. Because the degree of protein binding in the fetus is less than in the mother, the total plasma concentration will be greater in the mother, although the free concentration will be the same.

Only 4% of mepivacaine is excreted unchanged. The drug is degraded by hydroxylation and conjugation but only 30% of the injected drug has been accounted for in the form of metabolites.

Levonordefrin is a sympathomimetic amine used as a vasoconstrictor in local anesthetic solutions. It has pharmacologic activity similar to that of epinephrine but is more stable. In equal concentrations, levonordefrin is less potent than epinephrine in raising blood pressure, and as a vasoconstrictor.

Indications: In dentistry for the production of local anesthesia by infiltration or nerve block.

Contraindications: In patients with a known history of hypersensitivity to local anesthetics of the amide type or to other components of the solution.

Warnings: Local anesthetics should only be employed by clinicians who are well versed in diagnosis and management of dose-related toxicity and other acute emergencies that might arise from the block to be employed and then only after ensuring the immediate availability of oxygen, other resuscitative drugs, cardiopulmonary equipment and the personnel needed for proper management of toxic reactions and related emergencies (see also Adverse Effects and Precautions). Delay in proper management of dose-related toxicity, underventilation from any cause, and/or altered sensitivity may lead to the development of acidosis, cardiac arrest and possibly, death.

To minimize the likelihood of intravascular injection, aspiration should be performed before the local anesthetic solution is injected. If blood is aspirated, the needle must be repositioned until no return of blood can be elicited by aspiration. Note, however, that the absence of blood in the syringe does not assure that intravascular injection will be avoided.

Polocaine 2% with levonordefrin contains sodium metabisulfite, a sulfite that may cause allergic-type reactions including anaphylactic symptoms and life-threatening or less severe asthmatic episodes in certain susceptible people. Sulfite sensitivity is seen more frequently in asthmatic than in nonasthmatic people.

Precautions: The safety and effectiveness of mepivacaine depends on proper dosage, correct technique, adequate precautions and readiness for emergencies. Standard textbooks should be consulted for specific techniques and precautions for various dental anesthetic procedures.

Resuscitative equipment, oxygen, and other resuscitative drugs should be available for immediate use (see Warnings and Overdose: Symptoms and Treatment). **The lowest dosage that results in effective anesthesia should be used to avoid high plasma levels and serious adverse effects. Injections should be made slowly, with frequent aspirations before and during the injection to avoid intravascular injection.**

Repeated doses of mepivacaine may cause significant increases in blood levels with each repeated dose because of slow accumulation of the drug or its metabolites. Tolerance to elevated blood levels varies with the status of the patient. Debilitated, elderly patients, acutely ill patients and children should be given reduced doses commensurate with their age and physical condition. Mepivacaine should also be used with caution in patients with epilepsy, impaired cardiac conduction, bradycardia, impaired hepatic function and in severe shock.

Because amide-type local anesthetics such as mepivacaine are metabolized by the liver, these drugs, especially repeat doses, should be used cautiously in patients with hepatic disease.

Patients with severe hepatic disease, because of their inability to metabolize local anesthetics normally, are at greater risk of developing toxic plasma concentrations. Mepivacaine should also be used with caution in patients with impaired cardiovascular function since they may be less able to compensate for functional changes associated with the prolongation of AV conduction produced by these drugs.

Local anesthetic procedures should not be used when there is inflammation and/or sepsis in the region of the proposed injection.

Mepivacaine 2% with levonordefrin should be used with caution in patients whose medical history and physical evaluation suggest the existence of untreated hypertension, poorly controlled thyrotoxicosis, diabetes, ischemic heart disease, heart block, cerebral vascular insufficiency and peripheral vascular disorder. This solution should also be used cautiously in areas of the body supplied by end arteries, such as digits, or otherwise having a compromised blood supply (see also Drug Interactions).

Careful and constant monitoring of cardiovascular and respiratory (adequacy of ventilation) vital signs and the patient's state of consciousness should be performed after each local anesthetic injection. It should be kept in mind at such times that restlessness, anxiety, incoherent speech, lightheadedness, numbness and tingling of the mouth and lips, metallic taste, tinnitus, dizziness, blurred vision, tremors, twitching, depression or drowsiness may be early warning signs of CNS toxicity.

Many drugs used during the conduct of anesthesia are considered potential triggering agents for familial malignant hyperthermia. It has been shown that the use of amide local anesthetics in malignant hyperthermia patients is safe. However, there is no guarantee that neural blockade will prevent the development of malignant hyperthermia during surgery. It is also difficult to predict the need for supplemental general anesthesia. Therefore, a standard protocol for the management of malignant hyperthermia should be available.

Mepivacaine should be used with caution in persons with known drug sensitivities. Patients allergic to para-aminobenzoic acid derivatives (procaine, tetracaine, benzocaine, etc.) have not shown cross-sensitivity to mepivacaine.

Head and Neck Area: Small doses of local anesthetics injected into the head and neck area, including retrobulbar, dental and stellate ganglion blocks, may produce adverse reactions caused by inadvertent injection to an artery. These reactions may be similar to systemic toxicity seen with unintentional intravascular injections of larger doses. Inadvertent injections into an artery can cause cerebral symptoms even at low doses. Confusion, convulsions, respiratory depression and/or respiratory arrest, and cardiovascular stimulation or depression leading to cardiac arrest have been reported. Patients receiving these blocks should have their circulation and respiration monitored and be constantly observed.

Drug Interactions: Mepivacaine should be used with caution in patients receiving other agents structurally related to amide-type local anesthetics, since the toxic effects are additive.

Mepivacaine 2% with levonordefrin or other vasopressors should not be used concomitantly with ergot-type oxytocic drugs, because a severe persistent hypertension may occur and cerebrovascular and cardiac accidents are possible. Likewise, Polocaine 2% with levonordefrin or solutions containing mepivacaine and another vasoconstrictor should be used with extreme caution in patients receiving MAO inhibitors or antidepressants of the triptyline or imipramine types, because severe prolonged hypertension may result. In situations when concurrent therapy is necessary, careful patient monitoring is essential. Phenothiazines and butyrophenones may reduce or reverse the pressor effect of levonordefrin.

If sedatives are employed to reduce patient apprehension, they should be used in reduced doses, since local anesthetic agents, like sedatives, are CNS depressants which in combination may have an additive effect.

Solutions containing levonordefrin or another vasoconstrictor, e.g., epinephrine, should be used with caution in patients undergoing general anesthesia with inhalation agents such as halothane, due to the risk of serious cardiac arrhythmias.

Information for the Patient: The patients should be informed that they may experience temporary loss of sensation and motor activity after infiltration or nerve block injections. The patients should be advised to exert caution to avoid inadvertent trauma to the lips, tongue, cheek mucosa or soft palate when these structures are anesthetized. The ingestion of food should therefore be postponed until normal function returns. The patient should be advised to consult the dentist if anesthesia persists or if a rash develops.

Pregnancy: It is reasonable to assume that a large number of pregnant women and women of childbearing age have been given mepivacaine. No specific disturbances to the reproductive process have so far been reported, e.g., no increased incidence of malformations. However, care should be given during early pregnancy when maximum organogenesis takes place.

Lactation: Mepivacaine is excreted in the breast milk, but in such small quantities that there is generally no risk of affecting the infant at therapeutic dose levels. It is not known whether levonordefrin enters breast milk, but it is unlikely to affect the breast-fed infant.

Adverse Effects: Adverse experiences following the administration of mepivacaine are similar in nature to those observed with other amide local anesthetic agents. These adverse experiences are, in general, dose-related and may result from high plasma levels caused by overdosage, rapid absorption, or inadvertent intravascular injection, or may result from a hypersensitivity, idiosyncrasy or diminished tolerance on the part of the patient.

Reactions to mepivacaine are very rare in the doses used in dental procedures. Psychogenic reactions to anticipation of or during the dental procedures, are however, common and may mimic the symptoms of a generalized systemic reaction to local anesthetics.

Serious adverse experiences are generally systemic in nature. The following types are those most commonly reported: CNS: CNS manifestations are excitatory and/or depressant and may be characterized by circumoral paresthesia, lightheadedness, nervousness, apprehension, euphoria, confusion, dizziness, drowsiness, hyperacusis, tinnitus, blurred vision, vomiting, sensations of heat, cold or numbness, twitching, tremors, convulsions, unconsciousness, respiratory depression and arrest. The excitatory manifestations may be very brief or may not occur at all, in which case the first manifestation of toxicity may be drowsiness merging into unconsciousness and respiratory arrest.

Cardiovascular: Cardiovascular manifestations are usually depressant and are characterized by bradycardia, hypotension, arrhythmia, and cardiovascular collapse, which may lead to cardiac arrest.

Allergic: Allergic reactions are characterized by cutaneous lesions, urticaria, edema, or in the most severe instances, anaphylactic shock. Allergic reactions of the amide type are extremely rare and may occur as a result of sensitivity either to the local anesthetic agent or to other components in the formulation.

Neurologic: The incidence of adverse neurological reactions, e.g., persistent neurological deficit, associated with the use of local anesthetics is very low. Neurological reactions may be dependent upon the particular drug used, the route of administration and the physical status of the patient. Many of these effects may be linked to the injection technique, with or without a contribution by the drug. Neurological reactions following regional nerve blocks have included persistent paresthesia and sensory disturbances.

Overdose: Acute emergencies are, in general, dose-related and may result from high plasma levels caused by excessive dosage, rapid absorption (i.e., rate of increase of plasma concentration) or unintentional intravascular injection, or may result from hypersensitivity or diminished tolerance on the part of the patient.

Symptoms: Acute Systemic Toxicity: CNS reactions are excitatory or depressant and may be characterized by nervousness, tinnitus, twitching, euphoria, drowsiness, blurred or double vision, dizziness, convulsions, unconsciousness and possibly respiratory arrest. The excitatory reactions may be very brief or may not occur at all, in which case the first manifestation of toxicity is drowsiness merging into unconsciousness and even respiratory arrest.

Cardiovascular reactions are depressant and may be characterized by hypotension, myocardial depression, bradycardia and possibly cardiac arrest. Signs and symptoms of depressed cardiovascular function may commonly result from a vasovagal reaction, particularly if the patient is in an upright position. Less commonly, they may occur as a direct effect of the drug. Failure to recognize premonitory signs such as sweating, a feeling of faintness, changes in pulse or sensorium, may result in progressive cerebral hypoxia and seizure or serious cardiovascular collapse.

Cardiovascular effects are usually only seen in the most severe cases and are generally preceded by signs of toxicity in the CNS.

Acidosis or hypoxia in the patient may increase the risk and severity of toxic reactions. Such reactions involve the CNS and the cardiovascular system.

Treatment: Treatment of Acute Toxicity: The immediate treatment of acute systemic toxicity is as follows:

Put the patient in a supine position. Raise the legs 30 to 45° above the horizontal level.

Ensure a patent airway. If ventilation is inadequate, ventilate the patient, with oxygen if available. This is important since toxicity increases with acidosis.

The treatment of convulsions consists of ensuring a patent airway and arresting convulsions. Should convulsions persist despite adequate ventilation, 5 to 15 mg diazepam or 50 to 200 mg thiopental should be administered i.v. to arrest the convulsions. Since this treatment may also depress respiration, the means of mechanically supporting or controlling ventilation should be available.

Supportive treatment of circulatory depression may require the administration of i.v. fluids and, when appropriate, a vasopressor (e.g., ephedrine 5 to 10 mg i.v. and repeated, if necessary, after 2 to 3 minutes), as governed by the clinical situation.

If the patient is unresponsive and the carotid pulse rate is totally absent, start external cardiac massage and mouth to mouth resuscitation.

Polocaine (cont'd)

Dosage: When used for local anesthesia in dental procedures the dosage depends on the area of the oral cavity to be anesthetized, the vascularity of the oral tissues, and the technique of anesthesia. The total dose must be adjusted to the age, size and physical status of the patient. The lowest dosage that results in effective local anesthesia should be administered. Injections should be made slowly with careful aspiration before and intermittently during injection to avoid inadvertent intravascular injection, which may have toxic effects. For specific techniques and procedures of a local anesthesia in the oral cavity, refer to standard textbooks.

Adults: Dosage requirements should be determined on an individual basis. In oral infiltration a dose of 1 to 2 mL, corresponding to 30 to 60 mg mepivacaine for Polocaine 3%, and 20 to 40 mg for Polocaine 2% with levonordefrin, is usually effective. For regional block, a dose of 1.5 to 5 mL (45 to 150 mg Polocaine 3% and 30 to 100 mg Polocaine 2% with Levonordefrin) is recommended. No more than 300 mg mepivacaine should be administered per procedure.

Children: In children under 10 years of age, the dose should not exceed 1 to 2 mL (30 to 60 mg mepivacaine for Polocaine 3%, and 20 to 40 mg for Polocaine 2% with levonordefrin) per procedure.

Due to the specific need for bone penetration, dental local anesthetics contain high concentrations of active drug, e.g., 20 or 30 mg/mL mepivacaine for Polocaine solutions. A combination of high pressure induced by the use of a dental cartridge system and a rapid rate of injection may lead to complications (see Overdose: Symptoms and Treatment) even after the injection of small amounts of local anesthetic. This is due to the high concentration, especially following accidental intravascular injection, when the injected drug could travel in a retrograde manner along the vessel and, in cases of intra-arterial injection in the head and neck area, reach the brain without the same degree of dilution that occurs with an i.v. injection.

Aspiration is recommended since it reduces the possibility of intravascular injection, thereby keeping the incidence of side effects and anesthetic failures to a minimum.

For best results, it is important that cartridges be used with a syringe of appropriate size. The Astra Self-Aspirating Syringe has been designed especially for Astra cartridges.

Sterilization, Storage and Technical Procedures: Cartridges should not be autoclaved, because the rubber plunger will typically be extruded thus compromising container integrity.

If disinfection of the cartridge is desired, its immersion should be avoided due to the risk of undesirable effects on the rubber membrane and aluminum cap, and the risk of contamination of the solution. Disinfection of the rubber membrane or the entire dental cartridge should be accomplished by wiping it with a cotton pledget that has been moistened with a disinfectant. Isopropyl alcohol (91%) or ethyl alcohol (70%) is recommended. Many commercially available brands of rubbing alcohol, as well as solutions of ethyl alcohol not of USP grade, contain denaturants which are injurious to rubber and therefore are not to be used.

Quaternary ammonium salts, such as benzalkonium chloride, are electrolytically incompatible with aluminum. Cartridges which are sealed with aluminum caps should not be immersed in any solution containing these salts.

Anti-rust tablets usually contain sodium nitrate or other similar agents which may be capable of releasing metal ions from syringes, needles and aluminum sealed cartridges. Accordingly, cartridges should not be kept in such solutions.

Adequate precautions should be taken to avoid prolonged contact between local anesthetic solutions containing a vasoconstrictor (low pH) and metal surfaces (e.g., needles or metal parts of syringes), since dissolved metal ions, particularly copper ions, may cause severe local irritation (swelling, edema) at the site of injection and accelerate the degradation of the vasoconstrictor.

To avoid leakage of solutions during injection, be sure to penetrate the centre of the rubber diaphragm perpendicularly with the needle when loading the syringe. An off-centre penetration produces an oval-shaped puncture that allows leakage around the needle.

In order to avoid traumatic nerve injuries leading to paresthesia in conjunction with dental nerve block, an atraumatic technique should be used. Dental cartridge systems may generate high pressures during injection, however, injected local anesthetics may travel in a retrograde manner along a nerve in cases of intraneural injection. If an accidental traumatic nerve injury has occurred, a vasoconstrictor, if present in the anesthetic solution, may aggravate the local neurotoxicity by decreasing the intraneural blood circulation. In order to minimize the risk of intraneural injection as well as fascicular injuries, the needle should always be withdrawn a little if paresthesia is elicited during injection. Furthermore, a short-bevelled needle should be considered for regional blocks (in which case a topical anesthetic may be used to reduce the pain of needle insertion), while a sharper (i.e., long-bevelled) needle can still be recommended for infiltration.

Store mepivacaine at controlled room temperature (15 to 30°C). Mepivacaine 2% with levonordefrin should be protected from light. Do not use if solution is pinkish or darker than slightly yellow, or if it contains a precipitate.

Polocaine is preservative-free and are for single use only. Discard unused portion.

Supplied: Polocaine 3%: Each mL of solution contains: mepivacaine HCl 30 mg. Nonmedicinal ingredients: sodium chloride, water for injection and sodium hydroxide and/or hydrochloric acid to adjust to pH 4.5 to 6.8. Preservative-free. Plastic dental cartridges of 1.8 mL. Boxes of 50.

Polocaine 2% with Levonordefrin: Each mL of solution contains: mepivacaine HCl 20 mg and levonordefrin (as the HCl) 0.05 mg. Nonmedicinal ingredients: sodium chloride, sodium metabisulfite, water for injection and sodium hydroxide and/or hydrochloric acid to adjust to pH 3.3 to 5.5. Preservative-free. Plastic dental cartridges of 1.8 mL. Boxes of 50.

Reviewed 1997

POLYCIDIN™ Eye/Ear Drops
POLYCIDIN™ Ophthalmic Ointment
CIBA Vision

Polymyxin B—Gramicidin
Polymyxin B—Bacitracin

Ophthalmic Antibiotic

Supplied: Eye/Ear Drops: Each mL contains: polymyxin B (as sulfate) 10 000 units, gramicidin 0.025 mg and benzalkonium chloride (preservative) 0.005%. Bottles of 10 mL.

Ointment: Each g contains: polymyxin B (as sulfate) 10 000 units and bacitracin (as zinc) 500 units. Tubes of 3.5 g.

Store between 15 and 30°C.

POLYCITRA-K®
Alza

Potassium Citrate

Potassium Supplement

Indications: Pleasant tasting, sugar-free, oral potassium citrate supplement. In the treatment or prevention of hypokalemia, treatment of digitalis intoxication, and for the treatment of potassium replacement and electrolyte recharge.

Contraindications: Ventricular fibrillation, hyperkalemia of various etiologies, in association with Addison's disease, suprarenal hyperplasia associated with a loss of salt, extensive tissue deterioration such as severe burns, acute dehydration and heat cramps. Severe renal impairment with oliguria or azotemia. Increased hypersensitivity to potassium, e.g., paramyotonia congenita or adynamia episodica hereditaria.

Warnings: The administration of potassium salts to patients with disturbed potassium elimination, e.g., patients with chronic nephropathy, may cause hyperkalemia and cardiac arrest. This phenomenon is more frequent with i.v. potassium administration while it may occur with oral treatment. Severe or even fatal hyperkalemia may appear rapidly, without any particular prodrome. Therefore, use of potassium salts requires a particular monitoring of kalemia with frequent evaluations and dosage adjustments.

Concurrent administration with potassium-sparing diuretics (spironolactone, triamterene, amiloride) might induce hyperkalemia. In the presence of renal impairment, the administration of potassium supplements must be closely monitored.

Precautions: The therapeutic use of potassium in potassium depletion cases requires a particular monitoring of the acid-base equilibrium, especially in presence of cardiac disease, renal disease or acidosis. Regular verifications of the serum electrolytes rate, of ECG and of the clinical state of the patient should take place. Potassium must be used cautiously in case of disease associated with heart block as the increase in potassium serum concentration may increase the blockage degree.

Adverse Effects: Nausea, vomiting, diarrhea and abdominal discomfort can result from potassium salt administration. In order to decrease the incidence of gastrointestinal irritation associated with the oral ingestion of concentrated potassium-salt preparations, patients must be instructed to dissolve completely each dose in the indicated quantity of water, to increase, if possible, the fluid intake and to take the product after a meal.

Overdose: Symptoms: Potassium concentrations above 4 mEq/L and above 2 g/day in the blood and urine respectively may cause hyperkalemia in the normal effort conditions.

Paresthesia of the extremities, apragmatism, mental confusion, tiredness, paralysis, hypotension, cardiac arrhythmias, cardiac block and arrest may occur. ECG alterations are characterized by the increase in the amplitude and frequency of T waves, the lowering of the ST segment, the decrease in R wave amplitude, the widening of the QRS complex, the extension of the PR interval and the disappearance of the P wave. Widening of the QRS complex is one of the major symptoms and must alert to the importance of rigorous measures. Hyperkalemia is often asymptomatic and only manifested by elevated serum concentration and the above-mentioned ECG alterations.

Treatment: Deletion of the potassium-containing food and drugs, and of the potassium-sparing diuretics. I.V. administration of 300 to 500 mL/hour of a 10% dextrose solution containing 10 to 20 units of crystalline insulin/1 000 mL. Use of the ion-exchange resins, hemodialysis or peritoneal dialysis. In presence of threatening cardiac arrythmias, administration of 10 to 50 mL of a 10% solution of calcium gluconate i.v. during 1 to 5 minutes to interfere with the cardiac toxicity. It is essential to keep the patient under ECG telecontrol. The fast decrease in serum concentrations, during the treatment of hyperkalemia in digitalis-stabilized patients may cause digitalis intoxication.

Dosage: Adults: Crystals: 3 packets (90 mEq)/day after meals. For prevention of hypokalemia: 1 packet (30 mEq)/day after meal. Contents of each packet should be mixed with 250 mL (a full glass) of cold water. Stir well before drinking. Drink only after complete effervescence.

Oral Solution: 15 to 30 mL (providing 30 to 60 mEq)/day, diluted in 250 mL of water or juice after meals. For prevention of hypokalemia: 10 to 20 mL (providing 20 to 40 mEq)/day.

To be taken immediately after meals or with food to reduce the possibility of upset stomach or laxative effect.

Supplied: Crystals: Each packet contains: 4.5 g of fruit-flavored, sugar-free crystals containing potassium 1 193 mg (from potassium citrate monohydrate), providing potassium 30 mEq equivalent to bicarbonate (HCO_3) 30 mEq. Boxes of 100.

Solution: Each 5 mL contains: potassium 398 mg (from potassium citrate monohydrate), providing potassium 10 mEq, equivalent to bicarbonate (HCO_3) 10 mEq. Self-measuring bottles of 475 mL.

Reviewed 1997

POLYSPORIN® ANTIBIOTIC BURN CREAM
Warner-Lambert Consumer Healthcare

Polymyxin B Sulfate—Gramicidin—Lidocaine HCl

Antibiotic—Anesthetic—Antipruritic

Indications: For treatment and prevention of infection of minor burns and scalds and relief of skin pain.

Contraindications: Hypersensitivity to any of the components.

Precautions: As with other antibiotic preparations, prolonged use may result in overgrowth of nonsusceptible organisms. Appropriate measures should be taken if this occurs.

If adverse reaction or irritation occurs, discontinue use and consult a physician. In the case of a serious burn, consult a physician.

Overdose: Symptoms and Treatment: Treatment is symptomatic.

Dosage: A small quantity may be applied 2 to 5 times daily as required.

Supplied: Each g of cream contains: polymyxin B sulfate 10 000 units, gramicidin 0.25 mg and lidocaine HCl 50 mg.

Nonmedicinal ingredients: mineral oil, paraben, petrolatum, polysorbate, propylene glycol, sodium hydroxide, water and wax. Tubes of 15 and 30 g. Store at 15 to 25°C.

POLYSPORIN® Preparations

Warner-Lambert Consumer Healthcare

Polymyxin B Sulfate—Gramicidin or Bacitracin

Antibiotic

Indications: Cream: Infection in dermatologic disorders particularly where the lesions are moist or weeping. Prophylactically, against bacterial contamination in burns, skin grafts, incisions and other clean lesions. For abrasions, minor cuts and wounds, the cream may prevent infection and permit normal healing.

Eye/Ear Drops: For external infections of the eye and ear when due to susceptible organisms. Used in situations in which drops may be preferred to an ointment, as in preoperative and postoperative use in surgery.

Ointment/Triple Antibiotic Ointment: For treating local infections due to susceptible organisms and amenable to local treatment; these include infected wounds, burns and skin grafts; pyodermas; folliculitis; infections of external ear.

Ophthalmic Ointment: For treatment of superficial ocular infections involving the conjunctiva and/or cornea caused by organisms susceptible to polymyxin B sulfate and bacitracin zinc.

Contraindications: Hypersensitivity to any of the components.

Eye/Ear Drops: Should not be given subconjunctivally or intraocularly, nor should it be used for the irrigation of fistulous tracts in or about the eye or its socket.

Precautions: As with any antibiotic containing medication, prolonged use may result in the overgrowth of nonsusceptible organisms, including fungi. Should superinfection occur, the preparation should be discontinued and/or appropriate therapy instituted.

Ophthalmic ointments may retard corneal healing.

Geriatrics: No specific information is available regarding the use of Polysporin in the elderly; however, the maximum dosage should be reduced in cases where a decrease in renal function may exist.

Pregnancy: Polysporin has been used for several years without any evidence of untoward effects in pregnancy. The clinical benefit of treatment to the patient must be balanced against any possible, but unknown hazards to the fetus.

Following application to extensive areas of raw skin, the possibility of systemic absorption of the active ingredients exists.

Allergic hypersensitivity following topical application of polymyxin B sulfate and bacitracin zinc is rare but has been reported. Rarely anaphylactic reactions following topical administration of bacitracin zinc have been reported. Following significant systemic absorption, polymyxin B can intensify and prolong the respiratory depressant effects of neuromuscular blocking agents.

Overdose: Symptoms and Treatment: If toxic symptoms develop following significant systemic absorption, treatment with Polysporin should be stopped and the patient's general status, renal function and neuromuscular function should be monitored and blood levels of polymyxin B sulfate and bacitracin zinc determined.

Dosage: Cream: Apply a small quantity 2 to 5 times daily, as required, rub in gently if condition permits.

Eye/Ear Drops: 1 or 2 drops in the affected eye or ear, 2 to 4 times daily, or more frequently as required.

Ointment: To be applied over the infected area 2 to 5 times a day. May be covered with a dressing or left exposed.

Ophthalmic Ointment: Apply every 3 or 4 hours, depending on the severity of the disease.

Triple Antibiotic Ointment: To be applied to the affected area 1 to 3 times daily. May be covered with a bandage or gauze or left uncovered.

Supplied: Cream: Each g contains: polymyxin B sulfate 10 000 units, gramicidin 250 μg (0.25 mg) in a white vanishing cream base, pH of 5. Nonmedicinal ingredients: mineral oil, paraben, petrolatum, poloxamer, propylene glycol, sodium hydroxide, water and wax. Tubes of 15 and 30 g.

Eye/Ear Drops: Each mL contains: polymyxin B sulfate 10 000 units, gramicidin 25 μg (0.025 mg). Nonmedicinal ingredients: alcohol, benzalkonium chloride, poloxamer, propylene glycol and water. Plastic dropper bottles of 10 mL.

Ointment: Each g contains: polymyxin B sulfate 10 000 units (equivalent to 1 mg polymyxin standard) and bacitracin 500 units. Nonmedicinal ingredients: BHT and petrolatum. Tubes of 15 and 30 g. Sterile ophthalmic in tubes of 3.5 g.

Triple Antibiotic Ointment: Each g contains: polymyxin B sulfate 10 000 units (equivalent to 1 mg polymyxin standard), bacitracin 500 units and gramicidin 0.25 mg. Nonmedicinal ingredients: BHT and petrolatum. Tubes of 15 and 30 g.

Store at 15 to 25°C.

POLYTAR® AF

Stiefel

Coal Tar—Salicylic Acid Compound

Antidandruff and Psoriasis Therapy

Supplied: Each mL of shampoo contains: decolorized coal tar 0.5%, pyrithione disulfide 1% w/v, salicylic acid 2% w/v and 0.5% menthol in a soapless shampoo base with conditioners. Buffered to natural pH balance of hair. Nonmedicinal ingredients: fragrance IDC 10316, hexylene glycol, menthol crystals, modified lauric diethanolam, oleyl alcohol, polymer JR-30 M, polysorbate 80, purified water USP, triethanolamine and triethanolamine lauryl sulfate. Plastic bottles of 150 mL.

POLYTAR® Preparations

Stiefel

Wood-Mineral Tar Compound

Antidandruff Therapy

Supplied: Shampoo: Mild: Each mL contains: Polytar 0.5%, a blend of wood and mineral tars in a soapless lather. Nonmedicinal ingredients: citric acid monohydrate, coconut diethanolamide, collagen protein derived, fragrance, hexylene glycol, imidurea NF, oleth 10, oleyl alcohol, polysorbate 80, polytar B, purified water USP, sodium chloride and triethanolamine lauryl sulfate. Buffered to a natural pH balance of hair. Plastic bottles of 150 and 350 mL.

Regular: Each mL contains: Polytar 1%, a blend of wood and mineral tars in a soapless lather. Nonmedicinal ingredients: citric acid monohydrate, coconut diethanolamide, fragrance, hexylene glycol, imidurea NF, oleyl alcohol, polysorbate 80, polytar B, purified water USP, sodium chloride and triethanolamine lauryl sulfate. Buffered to a natural pH balance of hair. Plastic bottles of 150 and 350 mL.

Soap: Each g bar contains: Polytar 1%, a blend of wood and mineral tars. Nonmedicinal ingredients: butylated hydroxytoluene, fragrance, polyvinyl pyrrolidone, purified water USP, soap chips and trisodium HEDTA. Bars of 75 g.

POLYTOPIC Cream
POLYTOPIC Ointment

Technilab

Polymyxin B Sulfate—Gramicidin
Polymyxin B Sulfate—Bacitracin

Antibiotic

Supplied: Cream: Each g of cream contains: polymyxin B sulfate USP 10 000 units and gramicidin USP 0.25 mg. Nonmedicinal ingredients: emulsifying wax, methylparaben, mineral oil, petrolatum, poloxamer, propylene glycol and purified water. Tubes of 15 and 30 g.

Ointment: Each g of ointment contains: polymyxin B sulfate USP 10 000 units and bacitracin USP 500 units. Nonmedicinal ingredients: light mineral oil and petrolatum. Tubes of 5, 15 and 30 g.

Store between 15 to 30°C.

POLYTRIM™ Ⓟ

Allergan

Trimethoprim Sulfate—Polymyxin B Sulfate

Antibacterial Agent

Pharmacology: When used topically, trimethoprim and polymyxin B are rarely sensitizing and absorption through intact skin and mucous membrane is insignificant.

Blood samples were obtained from 11 human volunteers at 20 minutes, 1 hour and 3 hours following instillation of 2 drops of a solution containing 1 mg trimethoprim and 10 000 units of polymyxin B/mL. On the 9 previous days, each patient received 2 drops of solution 4 times/day.

No detectable levels of drugs were noted with assay limits of 0.03 mg trimethoprim/mL of serum and 1 unit polymyxin B/mL of serum.

Indications: Polytrim is active against the following gram-positive and gram-negative organisms which may be associated with surface ocular bacterial infections:

Gram-positive: S. aureus, S. epidermidis, Streptococcus spp. (Group A beta-hemolytic and non-hemolytic), S. pneumoniae.

Gram-negative: P. aeruginosa, H. influenzae, H. aegyptius, E. coli, K. pneumoniae, P. mirabilis (indole-positive), Proteus spp. (indole-negative), E. aerogenes, C. freundii, C. diversus, A. calcoaceticus, M. lacunata (some strains), S. marcescens.

Sensitivity tests should be performed whenever possible to determine the optimum therapy for any given infection.

Polytrim is indicated for the following surface ocular bacterial infections when caused by susceptible strains of the above organisms: acute bacterial conjunctivitis, blepharitis, blepharoconjunctivitis.

Contraindications: In patients with known hypersensitivity to any of its components.

Warnings: Not for injection into the eye. If a sensitivity reaction to Polytrim occurs, discontinue use. Polytrim is not indicated for the prophylaxis or treatment of ophthalmia neonatorum.

Precautions: General: As with other antimicrobial preparations, prolonged use may result in overgrowth of nonsusceptible organisms, including fungi. If superinfection occurs, appropriate therapy should be initiated.

Information for the Patient: Avoid contamination of the dropper with material from the eye, fingers, or other source. This precaution is necessary to maintain sterility of the drops.

If redness, irritation, swelling or pain persists or increases, discontinue use immediately and contact your physician.

Children: The safety and effectiveness in children below the age of 2 months has not been established (see Warnings).

Adverse Effects: The most frequent adverse reaction to Polytrim is local irritation consisting of transient burning or stinging, itching or increased redness upon instillation. These reactions occur in less than 4 of 100 patients treated. Polytrim has a low incidence of hypersensitivity reactions (less than 2 of 100 patients treated) consisting of lid edema, itching, increased redness, tearing and/or circumocular rash.

Dosage: Adults: In mild to moderate infections, instill 1 or 2 drops in the affected eye every 3 hours (maximum of 6 doses/day) for a period of 7 to 10 days.

More severe infections may require instillation of 1 or 2 drops every hour until improvement is observed and then reduced to 1 or 2 drops every 3 hours.

Children: Children over 2 months of age are treated in the same manner as adults.

Supplied: Each mL of sterile ophthalmic solution contains: trimethoprim (as sulfate) 1 mg, polymyxin B (as sulfate) 10 000 units. Nonmedicinal ingredients: benzalkonium chloride 0.004% (as preservative), sodium chloride, sodium hydroxide or sulfuric acid and water for injection. Plastic drop-dose dispensers of 10 mL. Store at 15 to 25°C. Protect from light.

PONDOCILLIN® Ⓟ

Leo

Pivampicillin

Antibiotic

Pharmacology: Pivampicillin is the pivaloyloxymethyl ester of (the semi-synthetic penicillin) ampicillin. It is an inactive prodrug, which is converted during its absorption from the gastrointestinal tract to the microbiologically active ampicillin, together with formaldehyde and pivalic acid, by non-specific esterases present in most body tissues. Amounts in excess of 99% of the pivampicillin absorbed are converted to ampicillin within 15 minutes of absorption. Ampicillin has a bactericidal action resulting from inhibition of cell wall mucopeptide biosynthesis.

The absorption of pivampicillin was virtually unaffected by taking the dose with food. Although the peak serum level may be reduced and delayed when compared to doses given in the fasting state, the total bioavailability was not affected .

Pondocillin (cont'd)

Oral administration of 500 mg produced a mean peak serum level of 13 μg/mL ampicillin within 1 hour.

In healthy volunteers the plasma half-life of ampicillin is approximately one hour and there is no significant accumulation on repeated dosing.

The urinary excretion of ampicillin in healthy volunteers in the first 6 hours, expressed as a percentage of the dose administered, was around 70% for pivampicillin and 25 to 30% for ampicillin. Similar results have been obtained in patients.

The pivalic acid, released during the conversion of pivampicillin to ampicillin is excreted mainly in the urine in the form of labile conjugates with glycine.

Indications: For the treatment of respiratory tract infections (including acute bronchitis, acute exacerbations of chronic bronchitis and pneumonia); ear, nose and throat infections; gynecological infections; urinary tract infections (including acute uncomplicated gonococcal urethritis) when caused by non penicillinase-producing susceptible strains of the following organisms: gram-positive organisms, e.g., streptococci, pneumococci and staphylococci; gram-negative organisms, e.g., H. influenzae, N. gonorrhoeae, E. coli, P. mirabilis.

Contraindications: In patients with a history of hypersensitivity to any of the penicillins or cephalosporins; in secondary infections associated with infectious mononucleosis or lymphatic leukemia, because of the high frequency or exanthemata associated with ampicillin therapy in these conditions; in infections caused by β-lactamase (penicillinase)-producing bacteria.

Warnings: Pivampicillin suspension is not recommended for the treatment of severe infections in children.

Precautions: Before therapy, inquiry as to past penicillin, cephalosporin or other allergies is essential as reactions occur more frequently in hypersensitive persons. If allergic or anaphylactic reactions occur during therapy, discontinue treatment and initiate usual measures, i.e., antihistamines, pressor amines or corticosteroids.

During long-term therapy, renal, hepatic and hematopoietic functions should be checked periodically. Candidiasis and other super-infections may occur especially in debilitated and malnourished patients or in those with low resistance to infection due to corticosteroids, immunosuppressors or irradiation.

Long-term treatment or frequently repeated treatment courses should be used with caution as pivampicillin has been associated with an increased excretion of carnitine in urine and a reduction of serum carnitine. During absorption pivampicillin is hydrolyzed to pivalic acid and ampicillin. Pivalic acid is excreted partly as a conjugate with carnitine. Treatment with pivalic acid liberating antibiotics for a duration of 22 and 30 months in children resulted in total muscle carnitine depletion to 10% of reference values, however, no adverse clinical effects were reported which could be associated with primary or secondary carnitine deficiency. Following 7 to 10 days treatment at the highest recommended doses of pivampicillin there was a significant reduction in serum carnitine which returned to the normal range within 2 weeks of stopping therapy. Despite these reductions in serum carnitine, total body stores of carnitine were reduced by approximately 10%. The increased excretion of carnitine associated with the use of pivampicillin is considered to be without clinical significance in short-term treatment. Adverse effects which could be related to carnitine deficiency occur with similar frequency as with other antibiotics not liberating pivalic acid. Carnitine is synthesized in the liver and kidney of man. Carnitine is also available from the diet in meat and dairy products; however, endogenous biosynthesis can meet normal metabolic needs in vegetarians. Carnitine functions in the transport of fatty acids across the mitochondrial membrane as an essential cofactor in fatty acid oxidation. Almost all the body stores of carnitine (100 to 200 mmol, 16 to 32 g) are found in muscle (98%), liver and kidney (1.6%) and serum (0.4%). In patients with the extremely rare condition of carnitine deficiency, treatment with pivampicillin should be avoided. Concurrent treatment with valproic acid or other medications liberating pivalic acid should be avoided.

Neither measurement of serum carnitine nor concomitant administration of prophylactic doses of carnitine is recommended as a general measure for patients receiving pivalic acid liberating antibiotics.

Children: Endogenous carnitine production begins at birth and in normal children is fully developed during the first months of life. Although no adverse events which can be explained by a pivalic acid induced reduction in carnitine have been documented, use of pivampicillin in children less than 3 months of age should be avoided.

Pregnancy and *Lactation:* Safety for use during pregnancy has not been established. Ampicillin crosses the placenta and small amounts have been detected in breast milk. It is not known whether the pivalic acid component of pivampicillin is excreted in human milk. The administration of pivampicillin to a mother who is breast-feeding a child less than 3 months of age should take into account the importance of the drug to the mother and the possible risk to the infant (see precaution on carnitine above).

The passage of any penicillin from blood into brain is facilitated by inflamed meninges and during cardiopulmonary bypass. In the presence of such factors and particularly in the presence of renal failure when high serum concentrations can be attained, CNS adverse effects including myoclonia, convulsive seizures and depressed consciousness can be expected. Although this complication has not been reported with pivampicillin it should be anticipated.

Cases of gonorrhea with a suspected primary lesion of syphilis should have dark field examination before receiving treatment. In all other cases where concomitant syphilis is suspected, monthly serological tests should be made for a minimum of 4 months.

Adverse Effects: Hypersensitivity: Like ampicillin, erythematous maculopapular rashes have been reported fairly frequently. Urticarial reactions have also been reported. Anaphylactic reactions have occurred as with other penicillins. Rare cases of erythema multiforme and exfoliative dermatitis, though not observed with pivampicillin have been reported with ampicillin and, therefore, may be anticipated.

Note: Urticaria, other skin rashes and serum sickness-like reactions may be controlled with antihistamines and if necessary, systemic corticosteroids. Serious anaphylactic reactions require the immediate use of epinephrine, oxygen and i.v. corticosteroids. In some cases of infectious mononucleosis, where ampicillin has been administered, an extremely high incidence of generalized rash has been reported.

Gastrointestinal: nausea, vomiting, retrosternal pain and flatulence. Diarrhea has been reported but less frequently than with ampicillin. The incidence of these effects can be reduced by taking the medication with food. Glossitis, stomatitis, black 'hairy' tongue and enterocolitis have been associated with ampicillin therapy and therefore, may be anticipated with pivampicillin.

Hematologic: Eosinophilia, anemia, thrombocytopenia, thrombocytopenic purpura, leukopenia and agranulocytosis have been reported with ampicillin and, therefore, may be anticipated with pivampicillin.

Others: dizziness and pruritus. Transient changes in AST.

Overdose: Symptoms and Treatment: There is no experience of overdosage with pivampicillin. However, excessive doses are likely to induce nausea, vomiting and gastritis.

Treatment should be restricted to symptomatic and supportive measures.

Dosage: Suspension: Adults and children over 10 years: 15 mL (525 mg) twice daily; double in severe infections.

Children 7 to 10 years: 10 mL (350 mg) twice daily; 4 to 6 years: 7.5 mL (262.5 mg) twice daily; 1 to 3 years: 5 mL (175 mg) twice daily. In children 10 years of age or less the dosage range is 25 to 35 mg/kg/day and should not exceed the recommended adult dose of 500 mg twice daily.

Infants 3 to 12 months: 40 to 60 mg/kg body weight daily divided into 2 equal doses.

In short-term therapy (treatment less than 14 days), continue treatment for 72 hours beyond the time that evidence of bacterial eradication has been obtained (patient is asymptomatic). In group A beta hemolytic streptococci, continuation of therapy for at least 10 days is recommended.

In the treatment of urinary tract infection, frequent bacteriological and clinical appraisal is necessary. Smaller doses than those recommended should not be used.

In the management of acute exacerbations of chronic bronchitis 10 to 14 days of pivampicillin is usually recommended.

Tablets: Adults and children over 10 years: 500 mg twice daily; double in severe infections.

Gonococcal Urethritis: 1.5 g as a single dose with 1 g probenecid concurrently.

Supplied: Suspension: Each mL of reconstituted suspension contains: pivampicillin 35 mg. Nonmedicinal ingredients: aspartame, banana dry flavor, magnesium stearate, polyvidone, propylparahydroxybenzoate, sodium carraghenate, sodium chloride, sodium citrate, sorbitol and vanilla dry flavor. Bottles containing powder for suspension to prepare 100, 150 and 200 mL of reconstituted solution. Store powder for suspension below 25°C. The reconstituted suspension may be stored for 7 days at room temperature and 14 days under refrigeration.

Tablets: Each white film-coated, ovoid tablet, embossed with 128 on one side and an Assyrian Lion on the other, contains: pivampicillin 500 mg (equivalent to 377 mg ampicillin). Nonmedicinal ingredients: starch carboxy-methylsodium glycolate, magnesium stearate, methylcellulose (methocel A15), STA-RX 1500 and hydroxypropylmethylcellulose. Bottles of 100 and 500.

(Shown in Product Recognition Section)

PONSTAN® Ⓟ

Parke-Davis

Mefenamic Acid

Analgesic

Pharmacology: Mefenamic acid, an anthranilic acid derivative, is a nonsteroidal anti-inflammatory drug (NSAID) with demonstrated anti-inflammatory, analgesic and antipyretic activity in laboratory animals. Its mode of action is not completely understood, but may be related to prostaglandin synthetase inhibition. In animal studies the drug was found to inhibit prostaglandin synthesis and to compete for binding at the prostaglandin receptor site.

Pharmacokinetics: Mefenamic acid appears to be rapidly absorbed from the gastrointestinal tract following oral administration to humans. Peak plasma levels were reached 1 to 2 hours after the administration of two 250 mg capsules; the C_{max} of free mefenamic acid was 3.5 μg/mL and the half-life in plasma about 3 to 4 hours.

Following a single 1 000 mg oral dose, peak plasma levels of 10 μg/mL occurred in 2 to 4 hours, with a half-life of 2 hours. Following multiple doses, plasma levels are proportional to dose with no evidence of drug accumulation. Repeated administration of mefenamic acid (250 mg capsules q.i.d.) yielded peak plasma levels of 3.7 to 6.7 μg/mL within 1 to 2.5 hours after administration of each dose.

Mefenamic acid has 2 distinct metabolic products, namely a hydroxymethyl and a carboxy derivative, both have been identified in both plasma and urine. The parent drug and the metabolites are conjugated with glucuronic acid and excreted primarily in the urine but to a lesser extent also in the feces.

Following a single dose, 67% of the total dose is excreted in the urine as unchanged drug or as 1 of 2 metabolites. Twenty to twenty-five per cent of the dose is excreted in the feces during the first 3 days.

In controlled, double-blind, clinical trials, mefenamic acid was evaluated for the treatment of primary spasmodic dysmenorrhea. The parameters used in determining efficacy included pain assessment by both patient and investigator; the need for concurrent analgesic medication; and evaluation of change in frequency and severity of symptoms characteristic of spasmodic dysmenorrhea. Patients received either mefenamic acid 500 mg (2 capsules) as an initial dose and 250 mg every 6 hours, or placebo at onset of bleeding or of pain, whichever began first. After 3 menstrual cycles, patients were crossed over to the alternate treatment for an additional 3 cycles. Mefenamic acid was significantly superior to placebo in all parameters, and both treatments (drug and placebo) were equally tolerated.

Indications: For the relief of pain of moderate severity in conditions such as muscular aches and pains, primary dysmenorrhea, headaches and dental pain.

Contraindications: In patients who have previously exhibited hypersensitivity to it.

Because the potential exists for cross-sensitivity to ASA or other nonsteroidal anti-inflammatory drugs, mefenamic acid should not be given to patients in whom these drugs induce symptoms of bronchospasm, allergic rhinitis, or urticaria.

Mefenamic acid is contraindicated in patients with active ulceration or chronic inflammation of the upper or lower gastrointestinal tract.

Mefenamic acid should be avoided in patients with preexisting renal disease.

Warnings: If diarrhea occurs, the dsoage should be reduced or temporarily suspended (see Adverse Effects and Dosage). Certain patients who develop diarrhea may be unable to tolerate the drug because of recurrence of the symptoms on subsequent exposure.

Risk of Gastrointestinal Ulceration, Bleeding and Perforation with NSAID Therapy: Serious gastrointestinal toxicity such as bleeding, ulceration, and perforation, can occur at any time, with or without warning symptoms, in patients treated chronically with NSAID therapy. Although minor upper gastrointestinal problems, such as dyspepsia, are common, usually developing early in therapy, physicians should remain alert for ulceration and bleeding in patients treated chronically with NSAIDs even in the absence of previous gastrointestinal tract symptoms. In patients observed in clinical trials of several months to 2 years duration, symptomatic upper gastrointestinal ulcers, gross bleeding or perforation appear to occur in approximately 1% of patients treated for 3 to 6 months, and in about 2 to 4% of patients treated for 1 year. Physicians should inform patients about the signs and/or symptoms of serious gastrointestinal toxicity and what steps to take if they occur. Studies to date have not identified any subset of patients not at risk of developing peptic ulceration and bleeding. Except for a prior history of serious gastrointestinal events and other risk factors known to be associated with peptic ulcer disease, such as alcoholism, smoking, etc., no risk factors (e.g., age, sex) have been associated with increased risk. Elderly or debilitated patients seem to tolerate ulceration or bleeding less well than other individuals and most spontaneous reports of fatal gastrointestinal events are in this population. Studies to date are inconclusive concerning the relative risk of various NSAIDs in causing such reactions. High doses of any NSAID probably carry a greater risk of these reactions, although controlled clinical trials showing this do not exist in most cases. In considering the use of relatively large doses (within the recommended dosage range), sufficient benefit should be anticipated to offset the potential increased risk of gastrointestinal toxicity.

Precautions: If rash occurs, the drug should be promptly discontinued.

A false-positive reaction for urinary bile, using the diazo tablet test, may result after mefenamic acid administration. If biliuria is suspected, other diagnostic procedures, such as the Harrison spot test, should be performed.

In chronic animal toxicity studies mefenamic acid at 7 to 28 times the recommended human dose, caused minor microscopic renal papillary necrosis in rats, edema and blunting of the renal papilla in dogs, and renal papillary edema in monkeys. In humans, there have been reports of acute interstitial nephritis with hematuria, proteinuria and occasionally nephrotic syndrome. A second form of renal toxicity has been seen in patients with prerenal conditions leading to a reduction in renal blood flow or blood volume, where the renal prostaglandins have a supportive role in the maintenance of renal perfusion. In these patients administration of an NSAID may cause a dose-dependent reduction in prostaglandin formation and may precipitate overt renal decompensation. Patients at greatest risk of this reaction are those with impaired renal function, heart failure, liver dysfunction, those taking diuretics and the elderly. Discontinuation of NSAID therapy is typically followed by recovery to the pretreatment state. In normal human volunteers, BUN levels were slightly elevated following the prolonged administration of mefenamic acid at greater than therapeutic doses. Since mefenamic acid is eliminated primarily through the kidneys, it should not be administered to patients with significantly impaired renal function.

As with other nonsteroidal anti-inflammatory drugs, borderline elevations of liver function tests may occur. These abnormalities may remain essentially unchanged, or may be transient with continued therapy. Meaningful (3 times the upper limit of normal) elevations of ALT or AST occurred in controlled clinical trials in less than 1% of patients. A patient with symptoms and/or signs suggesting liver dysfunction, or in whom an abnormal liver test has occurred, should be evaluated for evidence of development of more severe hepatic reaction while on therapy with mefenamic acid. Severe hepatic reactions, including jaundice and cases of fatal hepatitis, have been reported with other nonsteroidal anti-inflammatory drugs. Although such reactions are rare, if abnormal liver tests persist or worsen, if clinical signs and symptoms consistent with liver disease develop, or if systemic manifestations occur (e.g., eosinophilia, rash, etc.), mefenamic acid should be discontinued.

Mefenamic acid may prolong ASA induced gastrointestinal bleeding. However, mefenamic acid itself appears to be less liable than ASA to cause gastrointestinal bleeding.

Mefenamic acid 500 mg and ASA 650 mg 4 times a day both caused significant further lowering of the prothrombin concentration (mefenamic acid 3.48% and ASA 2.75%) in patients in whom the concentration had been initially lowered by anticoagulant therapy. Caution, therefore, should be exercised in administering mefenamic acid to patients on anticoagulant therapy and should not be given when prothrombin concentration is in the range of 10 to 20% normal. Careful monitoring of blood coagulation factors is recommended.

It is recommended that estimations of hemoglobin and blood counts be carried out at regular intervals.

Mefenamic acid should be used with caution in known asthmatics.

Information for the Patient: Patients should be informed about the signs and/or symptoms of serious gastrointestinal toxicity and what steps to take if they occur. Patients should be advised that if diarrhea, other digestive problems or a skin rash arise, they should stop taking the drug promptly and consult their physician. Patients in whom ASA or other nonsteroidal anti-inflammatory drugs induce symptoms of bronchospasm, allergic rhinitis, or urticaria should be aware of potential cross-sensitivity to mefenamic acid. Women on mefenamic acid therapy should consult their physician if they decide to become pregnant.

Pregnancy: There are no adequate and well-controlled studies in pregnant women. Because animal reproduction studies are not always predictive of human response, this drug should be used only if clearly needed. The use of mefenamic acid in late pregnancy is not recommended because of the effects on the fetal cardiovascular system of drugs of this class.

Lactation: Trace amounts of mefenamic acid may be present in breast milk and transmitted to the nursing infant; thus mefenamic acid should not be taken by the nursing mother because of the effects of this class of drugs on the infant cardiovascular system.

Children: Safety and effectiveness in children below the age of 14 have not been established.

Geriatrics: Impairment of renal function, sometimes leading to acute renal failure, has been reported. Elderly or debilitated patients seem unable to tolerate ulceration or bleeding as well as some other individuals; most spontaneous reports of fatal gastrointestinal events are in this population (see Warnings).

Drug Interactions: Protein-bound Drugs: Because mefenamic acid is highly protein bound, it could be displaced from binding sites by, or it could displace from binding sites, other protein-bound drugs such as oral anticoagulants, hydantoins, salicylates, sulfonamides and sulfonylureas. Patients receiving mefenamic acid with any of these drugs should be observed for adverse effects.

Anticoagulants and Thrombolytic Agents: Mefenamic acid may prolong prothrombin time. Therefore when the drug is administered to patients receiving oral anticoagulant therapy, frequent monitoring of prothrombin time is necessary. In addition, the ulcerogenic potential of mefenamic acid and the effect of the drug on platelet function may further contribute to the hazard of concomitant therapy with any anticoagulant or thrombolytic agent (e.g., streptokinase).

Adverse Effects: The most frequently reported adverse reactions associated with the use of mefenamic acid involve the gastrointestinal tract. In controlled studies for up to 8 months, the following disturbances were reported in decreasing order of frequency: diarrhea (approximately 5% of patients), nausea with or without vomiting, other gastrointestinal symptoms and abdominal pain. In certain patients, the diarrhea was of sufficient severity to require discontinuation of medication. The occurrence of the diarrhea is usually dose related, generally subsides on reduction of dosage and rapidly disappears on termination of therapy. Other gastrointestinal reactions less frequently reported were anorexia, pyrosis, flatulence, constipation, enterocolitis, colitis, steatorrhea, cholestatic jaundice, hepatitis, pancreatitis, hepatorenal syndrome and mild hepatic toxicity.

Gastrointestinal ulceration with or without hemorrhage has been reported.

Hematopoietic: Cases of autoimmune hemolytic anemia have been associated with continuous administration of NSAIDs, including mefenamic acid, for 12 months or longer. In such cases the Coombs test results are positive, with evidence of both accelerated RBC production and RBC destruction. The process is reversible upon termination of mefenamic administration.

Decreases in hematocrit have been noted in 2 to 5% of patients and primarily in those who have received prolonged therapy.

Leukopenia, eosinophilia, thrombocytopenic purpura, agranulocytosis, pancytopenia, bone marrow hypoplasia and aplastic anemia have also been reported on occasion with NSAID treatment.

CNS: Dizziness, drowsiness, blurred vision, convulsions, insomnia, nervousness and headache have occurred.

Integumentary: Urticaria, rash, facial edema, angioedema, edema of the larynx, Stevens-Johnson syndrome, Lyell's syndrome (toxic epidermal necrolysis), erythema multiforme and perspiration have been reported.

Renal: As with other nonsteroidal anti-inflammatory agents, renal failure, including papillary necrosis, has been reported. In elderly patients renal failure has occurred after taking mefenamic acid for 2 to 6 weeks. The renal damage may not be completely reversible. Hematuria, dysuria and hyponatremia have also been reported with mefenamic acid.

Body as a Whole: anaphylaxis.

Special Senses: eye irritation, ear pain, reversible loss of color vision.

Other: glucose intolerance in diabetic patients, hypotension, asthma, palpitation, dyspnea.

Overdose: Symptoms and Treatment: Should accidental overdosage occur, the stomach should be emptied by inducing emesis or by careful gastric lavage followed by the administration of activated charcoal. Laboratory studies indicate that mefenamic acid should be adsorbed from the gastrointestinal tract by activated charcoal. Vital functions should be monitored and supported. Because mefenamic acid and its metabolites are firmly bound to plasma proteins, hemodialysis and peritoneal dialysis may be of little value.

Seizures, acute renal failure, and coma have been reported with mefenamic acid overdoses. Overdose has led to fatalities.

Dosage: Administration is by the oral route, preferably with food.

The recommended regimen in acute pain for adults and children over 14 years of age is 500 mg as an initial dose followed by 250 mg every 6 hours as needed, usually not to exceed 1 week.

For the treatment of primary dysmenorrhea, the recommended dosage is 500 mg as an initial dose followed by 250 mg every 6 hours, starting with the onset of bleeding and associated symptoms. Clinical studies indicate that effective treatment can be initiated with the start of menses and should not be necessary for more than 2 to 3 days.

Supplied: Each Coni-snap capsule with an ivory opaque body and an aqua blue opaque cap contains: mefenamic acid 250 mg. Nonmedicinal ingredients: gelatin, lactose and sodium lauryl sulfate. Capsule shell: D&C Yellow No. 10, FD&C Blue No. 1, FD&C Yellow No. 6, gelatin, silicon dioxide, sodium lauryl sulfate and titanium dioxide. Energy: 2.5 kJ (0.6 kcal). Sodium: <1 mmol (0.1 mg). Gluten-, paraben-, sulfite- and tartrazine-free. Bottles of 100 and 500.

(Shown in Product Recognition Section)

Reviewed 1999

PONTOCAINE®

Sanofi

Tetracaine HCl

Anesthetic

Pharmacology: Tetracaine is 2-(dimethylamino) ethyl p-(butylamino) benzoate monohydrochloride. It is a white crystalline odorless powder that is readily soluble in water, physiologic saline solution or dextrose solution. Tetracaine is a local anesthetic of the ester-linkage type, related to procaine. Tetracaine is detoxified by plasma esterases to para-aminobenzoic acid and diethylaminoethanol.

Indications: Where spinal anesthesia is indicated for operations requiring 2 to 3 hours of anesthesia; for surface anesthesia of the eye, nose and throat.

Tetracaine should be used only on the advice of a physician. Use of ophthalmic tetracaine preparations for self-administration is not recommended.

When applied to the eye tetracaine is less likely than cocaine to affect the corneal epithelium. Usually there is no dilatation of the pupil, except in isolated cases, no disturbance of accommodation, and no increase in intraocular pressure. As with any anesthetic agent, prolonged use in the eye, even in dilute solution is not advisable.

Contraindications: In patients with known hypersensitivity to tetracaine or to drugs of a similar chemical configuration (ester-type local anesthetics), or para-aminobenzoic acid or its derivatives; and in patients for whom spinal anesthesia as a technique is contraindicated.

Warnings: Resuscitative equipment and drugs should be immediately available whenever any local anesthetic drug is used.

Large doses of local anesthetics should not be used in patients with heart block.

As is the case with any anesthetic agent, prolonged use in the eye, even in dilute solution, is not advisable.

For anesthetizing the larynx, trachea, or esophagus, the total absorbed dose of tetracaine should not usually exceed 20 mg using a 0.5% solution by direct application or a 0.5% solution nebulized for oral inhalation. Absorption may be

Pontocaine (cont'd)

retarded by the addition of 0.06 mL epinephrine 1:1 000 to each mL of anesthetic solution. In order to avoid rapid absorption and high blood levels of the anesthetic, the solution should not be administered in a coarse stream or by forceful injection, and care should be taken in dose measurement. In every instance, the dose should be measured accurately.

Constitutional reactions following the use of tetracaine have frequently been attributable to an existing allergic hypersensitivity. However, serious untoward effects, some of which proved fatal, have also been due to the injudicious use of excessive doses.

Precautions: The safety and effectiveness of any spinal anesthetic depend upon proper dosage, correct technique, adequate precautions, and readiness for emergencies. The lowest dosage that results in effective anesthesia should be used to avoid high plasma levels and serious systemic side effects. Tolerance varies with the status of the patient; debilitated, elderly patients or acutely ill patients should be given reduced doses commensurate with their weight, age, and physical status. Reduced doses are also indicated for obstetric patients and those with increased intraabdominal pressure.

Protection of the anesthetized eye from irritating chemicals, foreign bodies, and rubbing is very important. Patients should be warned not to rub an eye to which tetracaine has been applied, because inadvertent damage may be done to the anesthetized cornea and conjunctiva.

Tetracaine should be applied more sparingly on open lesions, in cases of allergy, cardiac or hepatic disease, emaciation, hyperthyroidism and other endocrine disorders in which tolerance may be diminished.

Caution should be used in administering tetracaine to patients with abnormal or reduced levels of plasma esterases. Also see package circular.

As is the case with all spinal anesthetics, the patient's blood pressure should be monitored during anesthesia.

Spinal anesthetics should be used with caution in patients with severe disturbances of cardiac rhythm, shock or heart block.

Tetracaine should not be used if the patient is being treated with a sulfonamide because para-aminobenzoic acid inhibits the action of sulfonamides.

Hypotension should be corrected early if it develops during saddle block for normal vaginal delivery, since hypoxic fetal bradycardia may occur. If a vasoconstrictor is given to correct hypotension, the obstetrician should be cautioned that if an oxytocic drug is employed, severe persistent hypertension and even rupture of a cerebral blood vessel may occur during the postpartum period.

Children: Safety and effectiveness of tetracaine in children have not been established.

There is no evidence from human data that tetracaine may be carcinogenic or mutagenic or that it impairs fertility.

Pregnancy: Tetracaine should be given to a pregnant woman only if clearly needed and the benefits outweigh the risks.

Lactation: It is not known whether or not tetracaine is excreted in human milk. However, it is rapidly metabolized following absorption into the plasma.

Adverse Effects: Ophthalmology: Prolonged ophthalmic use of topical anesthetics has been associated with corneal epithelial erosions, retardation or prevention of healing of corneal erosions and reports of severe keratitis and permanent corneal opacification and scarring. Inadvertent damage may be done to the anesthetized cornea and conjunctiva by rubbing an eye to which topical anesthetics have been applied. Tetracaine occasionally causes transient smarting in the eye when concentrations higher than 0.5% are used. On rare occasions, local idiosyncratic reactions including lacrimation, photophobia, and chemosis, have been observed. Although exceedingly rare with ophthalmic application of local anesthetics, systemic toxicity, usually manifested as CNS stimulation followed by CNS and cardiovascular depression, may occur.

Rhinolaryngology: Excessive doses of rapid absorption producing high blood levels can result in systemic toxic reactions which can lead to cardiac arrest and death if not promptly and correctly treated. Systemic reactions to tetracaine are characteristic of those associated with other local anesthetics and can involve the central nervous system and cardiovascular system. A small number of reactions may result from hypersensitivity, idiosyncrasy or diminished tolerance to normal dosage.

CNS: Effects are characterized by excitation or depression. The first manifestation may be nervousness, dizziness, blurred vision, or tremors, followed by drowsiness, convulsions, unconsciousness, and possibly respiratory and cardiac arrest. Because excitement may be transient or absent, the first manifestation may be drowsiness, sometimes merging into unconsciousness and respiratory and cardiac arrest. Other CNS effects may be nausea, vomiting, chills, constriction of the pupils, or tinnitus.

Cardiovascular system reactions include depression of the myocardium, blood pressure changes (usually hypotension), and cardiac arrest.

Allergic reactions which may be due to hypersensitivity, idiosyncrasy or diminished tolerance, are characterized by cutaneous lesions (e.g., urticaria), edema, and other manifestations of allergy. Detection of sensitivity by skin testing is of limited value. Severe allergic reactions including anaphylaxis have occurred rarely and are not usually dose related.

Reactions associated with spinal anesthesia techniques: CNS: post-spinal headache, meningismus, arachnoiditis, palsies, or spinal nerve paralysis. Cardiovascular: hypotension due to vasomotor paralysis and pooling of the blood in the venous bed. Respiratory: respiratory impairment or paralysis due to the level of anesthesia extending to the upper thoracic and cervical segments. Gastrointestinal: nausea and vomiting.

Treatment of Systemic Toxic Reactions: Toxic effects of local anesthetics require symptomatic treatment; there is no specific cure. The most important measure is oxygenation of the patient by maintaining an airway and supporting ventilation. Supportive treatment of the cardiovascular system includes i.v. fluids and, when appropriate, vasopressors (preferably those that stimulate the myocardium). Convulsions are usually controlled with adequate oxygenation alone but i.v. administration in small increments of a barbiturate (preferably an ultrashort-acting barbiturate such as thiopental and thiamylal) or diazepam can be utilized. I.V. barbiturates or anticonvulsant agents should only be administered by those familiar with their use and only if ventilation and oxygenation have first been assured. Muscle relaxants such as succinylcholine may also be required.

In spinal anesthesia, sympathetic blockade also occurs as a pharmacological action, resulting in peripheral vasodilation and often hypotension. The extent of the hypotension will usually depend on the number of dermatomes blocked. The blood pressure should therefore be monitored in the early phases of anesthesia. If hypotension occurs, it is readily controlled by vasoconstrictors administered either by i.m. or the i.v. route, the dosage of which would depend on the severity of the hypotension and the response to treatment.

Dosage: Ophthalmology: 0.5% solution: usual dose, 1 or 2 drops. Prolonged use, especially for at-home self-medication by the patient, is not recommended. Epinephrine 1:1 000 may be added to produce vascular constriction when necessary.

Rhinolaryngology: For anesthetizing the larynx, trachea, or esophagus, the total absorbed dose of tetracaine 0.5% solution should not usually exceed 20 mg. Profound anesthesia lasting 30 minutes is obtainable either by direct application of 0.5% solution or by oral inhalation of nebulized 0.5% solution. The addition of 0.06 mL (1 minim) of epinephrine 1:1 000 to each mL of anesthetic solution is advisable to retard absorption and reduce maximum blood levels.

In every instance, special care should be taken to measure the dose accurately.

Spinal anesthesia: See Table I.

Table I—Pontocaine

Suggested Dosage for Spinal Anesthesia Using Niphanoid

Extent of anesthesia	Dose of Niphanoid (mg)	Volume of spinal fluid (mL)	Site of injection (lumbar interspace)
Perineum	5[a]	1	4th
Perineum and lower extremities	10	2	3rd or 4th
Up to costal margin	15 to 20[b]	3	2nd, 3rd, or 4th

[a]For vaginal delivery (saddle block), from 2 to 5 mg in dextrose.

[b]Doses exceeding 15 mg are rarely required and should be used only in exceptional cases. Inject solution at rate of about 1 mL per 5 seconds.

For a hyperbaric solution Pontocaine Niphanoid is first dissolved in dextrose solution 10% in a ratio of 1 mL dextrose to 10 mg of the anesthetic. Further dilution is made with an equal volume of spinal fluid. The resulting solution now contains 5% dextrose with 5 mg of anesthetic agent per mL.

A hypobaric solution may be prepared by dissolving the Niphanoid in sterile water for injection, USP (1 mg/mL).

Examine ampuls carefully before use. Do no use if discoloration is observed in the ampuls, or if crystals or cloudiness is observed in the reconstituted product. This formulation of sterile tetracaine hydrochloride does not contain preservatives; therefore, unused portions should be discarded and the reconstituted Niphanoid should be used immediately.

Sterilization: The drug in intact ampuls is sterile. The preferred method to destroy bacteria on the exterior of ampuls before opening is heat sterilization (autoclaving). The ampuls should be set in an upright position for autoclaving. Immersion in antiseptic solution is not recommended.

Autoclave at 15 pounds pressure, at 121°C, for 15 to 20 minutes. The crystals may lose their snow-like appearance and tend to adhere to the sides of the ampul. This effect may slightly decrease the rate at which the drug dissolves but does not interfere with its anesthetic potency.

Autoclaving increases the likelihood of crystal formation. Unused autoclaved ampuls should be discarded. In no case should unused autoclaved ampuls be placed back in stock for later use.

Supplied: Ampuls: Each ampul of dry powder contains: tetracaine HCl 20 mg. Gluten-, lactose-, preservative-, starch and sulfite-free. Ampuls of 20 mg, boxes of 10. Protect ampuls from light.

Ophthalmic Solution: Each mL of ophthalmic solution contains: tetracaine HCl 0.5% in purified water. Nonmedicinal ingredients: chlorobutanol (hydrous) and sodium chloride. Mono-Drop bottles of 15 mL.

Reviewed 1998

PORTAGEN®

Mead Johnson

Therapeutic Nutrient

Description: A nutritionally complete formulated liquid diet which contains medium chain triglycerides.

Indications: For use in the nutritional management of individuals who do not efficiently digest and absorb conventional long chain food fats. For use in pancreatic insufficiency, bile acid deficiency, intestinal resection, lymphatic anomalies, steatorrhea.

Precautions: The usual intake of water should be maintained when Portagen beverage is used as the sole source or major part of the diet. In persons with advanced cirrhosis of the liver, large amounts of medium chain triglycerides in the diet may result in elevated blood and spinal fluid levels of medium chain fatty acids (MCFA), due to impaired hepatic clearance of these fatty acids, which are rapidly absorbed via the portal vein. These elevated levels have been reported to be associated with reversible coma and pre coma in certain subjects with advanced cirrhosis, particularly with portacaval shunts. Therefore, diets containing high levels of medium chain triglyceride fat should be used with caution in persons with hepatic cirrhosis and complications thereof, such as portacaval shunts or tendency to encephalopathy.

Dosage: Children and adults: The recommended daily intake is 946 mL, prepared as follows: Normal dilution 125.6 kJ (30 kcal)/30 mL: Add 1½ packed level 8 fl. oz. measuring cups (204 g) of powder to 710 mL of water and mix. Then add additional water to make 946 mL of beverage. For infants: Normal dilution 84 kJ (20 kcal)/30 mL: Add 1 packed level 8 fl. oz. measuring cup (136 g) of powder to 710 mL of water and mix. Then add additional water to make 946 mL of formula. The usual intake of water should be maintained when Portagen is used as the whole or major part of the diet.

Prepared Portagen must be kept under refrigeration. Unused portion should be discarded after 24 hours.

Supplied: Each can of powder contains: corn syrup solids, medium chain triglycerides (fractionated coconut oil), sodium caseinate, sucrose, corn oil, calcium citrate, lecithin and essential vitamins and minerals. Energy: 2 067 kJ (490 kcal)/ 100 g. Osmolality: 320 mOsm/kg water. Cases of 12 (454 g).

POSTACNE®

Dermik Laboratories Canada

Sulfur

Acne Therapy

Indications: For use in early mild adolescent acne or excessively oily skin and as maintenance therapy for acne that has been controlled.

Precautions: Keep away from eyes. Discontinue use temporarily if excessive irritation or scaling occurs. For external use only.

Dosage: Shake lotion well. Apply a thin film over area, allow to dry, blend in with skin by gently brushing off excess.

Supplied: Each flesh tinted lotion contains: colloidal sulfur 2% w/v. Nonmedicinal ingredients: alkyl-aryl sulfonic acid, attapulgite clay, butylparaben, diethanolamine, edetic acid, ethyl alcohol, hydroxyethyl cellulose, iron oxides, lauric myristic acid, methylparaben, perfume, polyethylene glycol, polyethylene glycol monolaurate, polyoxyethylene laurate, precipitated sulfur, propylene glycol, purified water, silicon emulsion, sodium chloride, sodium metabisulfite, talc, titanium dioxide, xanthan gum and zinc oxide. Alcohol: 20% w/v. Bottles of 28.4 g with color blender.

POTABA® Ⓟ

Glenwood

Aminobenzoate Potassium

Antifibrotic

Indications: Peyronie's disease. Scleroderma. Dermatomyositis. Morphea and linear scleroderma.

Contraindications: Patients taking sulfonamides.

Warnings: *Pregnancy* and *Lactation:* Safety for use in pregnancy or during lactation has not been established.

Precautions: Should anorexia or nausea occur, therapy is interrupted until the patient is eating normally again. This permits prompt subsidence of symptoms and also avoids the possible development of hypoglycemia. Give cautiously to patients with renal disease. If a hypersensitivity reaction should occur, aminobenzoate should be stopped.

Adverse Effects: Anorexia, nausea, fever and rash have occurred infrequently and subside with omission of the drug. Desensitization can be accomplished and treatment resumed.

Dosage: Adults: 12 g given in 4 divided doses.

Tablets and capsules are given at the rate of 6 tablets or capsules 4 times daily, usually with meals, and at bedtime with a snack. Tablets must be crushed and taken with an adequate amount of liquid to prevent gastrointestinal upset.

Envules each contain 2 g of pure drug, and constitute the individual average dose. Six envules are given for a total of 12 g daily.

Information for the Patient: See Blue Section—Information for the Patient "Potaba".

Supplied: Capsules: Each capsule contains: aminobenzoate potassium USP 500 mg. Nonmedicinal ingredients: magnesium stearate NF, microcrystalline cellulose NF, povidone USP, silica gel NF, sodium starch glycolate NF, stearic acid NF. Bottles of 250 and 1 000.

Powder: Each envule contains: aminobenzoate potassium USP 2 g. Nonmedicinal ingredients: magnesium stearate NF, microcrystalline cellulose NF, povidone USP, silica gel NF, sodium starch glycolate NF, stearic acid NF. Boxes of 50.

Tablets: Each tablet contains: aminobenzoate potassium USP 500 mg. Nonmedicinal ingredients: magnesium stearate NF, microcrystalline cellulose NF, povidone USP, silica gel NF, sodium starch glycolate NF, stearic acid NF. Bottles of 100 and 1 000.

Store in a cool place and in well-closed containers.

POTASSIUM CHLORIDE

Abbott

Electrolyte Replenisher

Supplied: Each mL contains: potassium 2 mEq (potassium chloride 149 mg). Nonmedicinal ingredients: hydrochloric acid and water for injection. Single-dose vials of 10 mL (20 mEq K^+) or 20 mL (40 mEq K^+). Must be diluted for i.v. use. Trays of 25 vials.

POTASSIUM CHLORIDE FOR INJECTION CONCENTRATE USP

Astra

Electrolyte Replenisher

Indications: The treatment of potassium depletion in patients with hypokalemia; treatment of digitalis intoxication.

The i.v. route is indicated when the patient is unable to take potassium orally or if hypokalemia is severe.

Contraindications: Renal impairment with oliguria or azotemia, untreated Addison's disease, hyperadrenalism associated with adrenogenital syndrome, extensive tissue breakdown as in severe burns, acute dehydration, heat cramps, adynamia episodica hereditaria and hyperkalemia of any etiology.

Warnings: In patients with impaired mechanisms for excreting potassium, administration of potassium salts can produce hyperkalemia and cardiac arrest. This is of particular concern in patients given i.v. potassium. Potentially fatal hyperkalemia can develop rapidly and be asymptomatic.

Precautions: The use of potassium salts in patients with chronic renal disease, adrenal insufficiency or any other condition which impairs potassium excretion, requires particularly careful monitoring of the serum potassium concentration and appropriate dosage adjustment.

Hypokalemia should not be treated by the concomitant administration of potassium salts and a potassium-sparing diuretic (e.g. spironolactone or triamterene), since the simultaneous administration of these agents can produce severe hyperkalemia.

In patients on a low salt diet, hypokalemic hypochloremic alkalosis is a possibility that may require chloride as well as potassium supplementation.

The treatment of potassium depletion, particularly in the presence of cardiac disease, renal disease or acidosis, requires careful attention to acid-base balance and appropriate monitoring of serum electrolytes, the ECG and the patient's clinical status.

Potassium should be used with caution in diseases associated with heart block since increased serum potassium may increase the degree of block.

Parenteral potassium chloride solutions may cause pain if given in a small vein.

Adverse Effects: The symptoms and signs of potassium intoxication include paresthesias of the extremities, flaccid paralysis, listlessness, mental confusion, weakness and heaviness of the legs, fall in blood pressure, cardiac arrhythmias and heart block. Hyperkalemia may exhibit the following ECG abnormalities: disappearance of the P-wave, widening and slurring of QRS complex, changes of the S-T segment, tall peaked T-waves. Nausea, vomiting, diarrhea and abdominal discomfort have been reported.

Overdose: Symptoms: If excretory mechanisms are impaired or if i.v. potassium is administered too rapidly, potentially fatal hyperkalemia can result (see Contraindications and Precautions). However, hyperkalemia is usually asymptomatic and may be manifested only by an increased serum potassium concentration and characteristic ECG changes (peaking of T-waves, loss of P-waves, depression of S-T segment, and prolongation of the QT interval). Late manifestations include muscle paralysis and cardiovascular collapse from cardiac arrest. Should any of these manifestations occur, discontinue administration immediately.

Treatment: If hyperkalemia develops, the following measures should be considered: 1. Elimination of foods and medications containing potassium and of potassium-sparing diuretics. 2. I.V. administration of 300 to 500 mL/hour of 10% dextrose solution containing 10 to 20 units of insulin/1 000 mL. 3. Correction of acidosis, if present, with i.v. sodium bicarbonate. 4. Use of exchange resins, hemodialysis, or peritoneal dialysis. 5. Calcium gluconate.

In treating hyperkalemia in digitalized patients, too rapid a lowering of the serum potassium concentration can produce digitalis toxicity.

Dosage: For i.v. administration only; dilute before infusing. The dose and rate of injection are dependent upon the individual patient's condition. In patients whose serum potassium concentration is above 2.5 mEq/L, the rate of infusion should not exceed 10 mEq/hour, in a concentration less than 30 mEq/L. The total dose should not exceed 200 mEq/24 hours.

If urgent treatment is required (serum potassium concentration less than 2 mEq/L with ECG changes or paralysis), infuse potassium in a suitable concentration at a rate of 40 mEq/hour, up to a maximum of 400 mEq/24 hour period. In critical states, potassium may be infused in saline (unless saline is contraindicated) rather than in dextrose solutions, as the latter may decrease serum potassium concentrations.

Supplied: Each mL of sterile concentrated solution contains: potassium 2 mEq in water for injection. Single use glass vials and Polyamp Duofit units of 10 mL (20 mEq potassium) and 20 mL (40 mEq potassium). The osmolarity of the solutions is approximately 4.0 mOsm/mL (calc.). Store at room temperature (15 to 30°C). Discard unused portion.

POTASSIUM PHOSPHATES INJECTION

Abbott

Electrolyte Replenisher

Supplied: Each mL contains: phosphates 3 mmol and potassium 4.4 mEq in water for injection. Vials of 5 and 15 mL. Trays of 25.

POTASSIUM SALTS

General Monograph, CPhA

Potassium Replacement Therapy

This monograph has been compiled by CPhA. It may contain information different from that approved by Therapeutic Products Programme, Health Canada, and the pharmaceutical manufacturers' approval has not been requested.

Pharmacology: Potassium is the principal intracellular ion of body tissues. Potassium ions are involved in a number of essential physiological processes, such as the maintenance of intracellular acid-base balance and tonicity. Other functions include the transmission of nerve impulses, contraction of cardiac, skeletal and smooth muscle, gastric secretion, normal renal function, tissue synthesis and carbohydrate metabolism.
Hypokalemia: Potassium depletion may occur whenever the rate of loss exceeds the rate of intake. Causes of hypokalemia include: inadequate intake, diuretic therapy, diabetic ketoacidosis, metabolic alkalosis, potassium-losing nephropathy, severe diarrhea, prolonged vomiting, drainage of gastrointestinal fluids, hyperaldosteronism, hepatic cirrhosis with ascites, Bartter's syndrome and long-term corticosteroid therapy. The need for potassium supplementation in patients taking potassium-depleting medications may sometimes be avoided by increasing dietary intake of potassium. For information on food sources of potassium, see Mineral Food Sources in the Clin-Info section.

Potassium deficiency may cause vomiting, abdominal distention, paralytic ileus, acute muscular weakness, paralysis, paresthesia, polydipsia and an inability to concentrate urine, hypotension, cardiac arrhythmias, and coma. Hypokalemia may also potentiate digoxin toxicity.
Hyperkalemia: Manifestations of hyperkalemia include ECG changes which ultimately may progress to complete heart block, ventricular arrhythmias or cardiac arrest. Symptoms of hyperkalemia may or may not be present and include weakness, parasthesias, confusion and muscular or respiratory paralysis (see Overdose).
Pharmacokinetics: Potassium is readily absorbed from the gastrointestinal tract. Potassium is actively transported into cells from the extracellular fluid. Dextrose, insulin and bicarbonate facilitate movement of potassium into cells. Normal adult values for serum potassium range from 3.5 to 5.0 mmol/L. Serum potassium concentrations may not be an accurate indicator of total body stores, as intracellular potassium accounts for 98% of total body amount. Excretion is mainly in the urine (85 to 90%) and closely follows potassium intake. Potassium is readily removed by peritoneal dialysis or hemodialysis.
Slow-Release Preparations: Expanded wax matrix may be seen in stools; it is not an indication of poor bioavailability.

Indications: The prevention of potassium depletion when dietary intake of potassium is inadequate for this purpose; the treatment of potassium depletion in patients with hypokalemia; treatment of digitalis intoxication. The i.v. route is indicated when the patient is unable to take potassium orally or if hypokalemia is severe.

Contraindications: In hyperkalemia; renal impairment with oliguria, anuria or azotemia; ventricular fibrillation; untreated Addison's disease; salt-losing adrenal hyperplasia; in extensive tissue breakdown as in severe burns, acute dehydration and heat cramps; increased sensitivity to potassium administration (e.g., in congenital paramyotonia or adynamia episodica hereditaria) and hyperadrenalism associated with adrenogenital syndrome.

All solid dosage forms of potassium supplements are contraindicated in any patient in whom there is cause for arrest or delay in tablet passage through the gastrointestinal tract.

Potassium Salts (cont'd)

In these instances, potassium supplementation should be with a liquid preparation.

Slow-release potassium chloride preparations have produced esophageal ulceration in certain cardiac patients with esophageal compression due to an enlarged left atrium. The administration of these preparations is contraindicated in such patients as well as in patients with dysphagia.

Warnings: In patients with impaired mechanisms for excreting potassium, (e.g., renal function impairment), administration of potassium salts can produce hyperkalemia and cardiac arrest. This is of particular concern in patients receiving i.v. potassium but may also occur in patients taking oral potassium. Potentially fatal hyperkalemia can develop rapidly and may be asymptomatic. Careful monitoring of the serum potassium concentration and appropriate dosage adjustment is required.

The concomitant use of potassium supplements and drugs which increase serum potassium may result in severe hyperkalemia (see Precautions, Drug Interactions).

Slow-release preparations should be avoided in patients at high risk for potassium chloride-induced gastrointestinal lesions, i.e., patients with cardiomegaly, esophageal stricture or compression, dysphagia, recent gastric surgery, delayed intestinal transit, ulcerative bowel disease or diverticulitis. Enteric coated tablets have an unacceptably high rate of gastrointestinal symptoms (40 to 50 incidents per 100 000 patient years) and should not be used.

Administration of concentrated potassium injection can be fatal. Parenteral potassium chloride solutions must be well diluted, thoroughly mixed and administered by slow i.v. infusion. Pain at the injection site and phlebitis may occur. Extravasation is to be avoided.

Precautions: The treatment of potassium depletion, particularly in the presence of cardiac disease, renal disease or acidosis, requires careful attention to acid base balance and appropriate monitoring of serum electrolytes, the ECG and the patient's clinical status.

Use potassium with caution in diseases associated with heart block since increased serum potassium may increase the degree of block.

Potassium balance is markedly altered in patients with diabetic ketoacidosis. Generally, total potassium is depleted and patients present with potassium deficits of 3 to 5 mmol/kg or greater; however the serum potassium concentration may be high, normal or low depending on the degree of acidosis and volume depletion. Following insulin administration, monitor serum potassium concentrations closely as hyperkalemia can be rapidly converted to hypokalemia.

In patients on a low salt diet, hypokalemic hypochloremic alkalosis is a possibility that may require chloride as well as potassium supplementation. Salt substitutes which primarily contain potassium chloride may result in hyperkalemia especially in renal patients. Hypokalemia in patients with metabolic acidosis should be treated with an alkalinizing potassium salt such as the acetate, bicarbonate, gluconate or citrate.

Drug Interactions: Extreme caution is advised with concomitant administration of potassium and potassium-sparing diuretics (e.g., spironolactone, triamterene, amiloride) or angiotensin converting enzyme (ACE) inhibitors (e.g., benazepril HCl, captopril, cilazapril, enalapril maleate, enalaprilat, fosinopril sodium, lisinopril, quinapril HCl and ramipril) since the simultaneous administration of these agents can produce severe hyperkalemia.

Adverse Effects: Nausea, vomiting, diarrhea, unpleasant taste (liquids) and abdominal cramps have been reported. Severe adverse effects reported with potassium preparations have been hyperkalemia and arrhythmias (see Overdose); intestinal, esophageal and gastric ulceration (see Warnings).

Overdose: Symptoms: If excretory mechanisms are impaired or if potassium is administered too rapidly i.v., potentially fatal hyperkalemia can result. Paresthesia of the extremities, listlessness, mental confusion, gastrointestinal symptoms, weakness, heaviness of legs, paralysis, hypotension, cardiac arrhythmias, heart block and cardiac arrest may occur. Frequently hyperkalemia is asymptomatic and may be manifested only by increased serum potassium concentration and characteristic electrocardiographic changes.

Progressive ECG changes occur with increasing serum potassium levels and indicate the need for immediate treatment. ECG changes include increased amplitude and peaking of the T waves, depression of the ST segment, reduction in the amplitude of the R wave, widening of the QRS complex, prolongation of the PR interval, and a decrease in the amplitude and ultimately disappearance of the P wave. Widening of the QRS complex is one of the most ominous signs and indicates the need for aggressive treatment.

Treatment: Discontinue administration of potassium-rich foods, medications and i.v. solutions containing potassium, or medications which can induce hyperkalemia.

In patients with severe hyperkalemia (e.g., serum potassium exceeds 7 mmol/L) or if any ECG manifestations of hyperkalemia exist, immediate treatment is required. The plasma potassium concentration and ECG must be monitored, as well as serum electrolytes, creatinine, glucose and arterial blood gases. I.V. calcium may be administered to antagonize the cardiotoxic effects of potassium, e.g., 1.125 to 7 mmol elemental calcium (1.7 to 10.3 mL calcium chloride 10% or 4.8 to 30 mL calcium gluconate 10%) i.v. over 1 to 5 minutes; this may be repeated after 5 to 10 minutes. The use of i.v. calcium is not recommended in patients receiving digoxin. To promote a shift of potassium from the extracellular to the intracellular compartment, agents such as dextrose and insulin or sodium bicarbonate may be used. 300 to 500 mL of dextrose 10% containing 10 to 20 units of regular insulin per litre may be infused over a 1-hour period. Alternately, give 25 g of dextrose i.v. (e.g., 50 mL of a dextrose 50% prefilled syringe) accompanied by 5 to 10 units of regular insulin i.v. over 5 minutes. To correct acidosis and to promote intracellular potassium shift, sodium bicarbonate 50 mmol (e.g. 50 mL of a sodium bicarbonate 8.4% prefilled syringe) may be given i.v. over 5 minutes and repeated every 5 to 10 minutes as necessary. Bicarbonate must be used with caution in patients at risk for fluid overload.

When ECG approaches normal, measures to reduce body stores of potassium such as cation exchange resins (e.g., sodium or calcium polystyrene sulfonate) may be employed. Hemodialysis or peritoneal dialysis should be considered if the above measures fail or the patient is in renal failure.

In treating hyperkalemia in patients receiving digoxin, too rapid a lowering of the serum potassium concentration can produce digoxin toxicity.

Dosage: The usual dietary intake of potassium by the average adult is 40 to 80 mmol/day. For information on food sources of potassium, see Mineral Food Sources in the Clin-Info section.

Potassium depletion sufficient to cause hypokalemia usually requires the loss of ≥200 mmol of potassium from the total body store.

Dosage must be individualized according to the patient's needs. Whenever possible, potassium supplementation should be given orally (or via nasogastric tube). Dosage must be reduced in patients with renal failure and administered with great caution, if at all.

Table I lists the elemental potassium content of the various salts.

Table I—Potassium Salts

Elemental Potassium Content

Salt	Elemental k^+/g (mmol)
Potassium acetate	10.2
Potassium bicarbonate	10
Potassium chloride	13.4
Potassium citrate	9.3
Potassium gluconate	4.3

Potassium chloride is generally the salt of choice in treating hypokalemia, as hypochloremia is usually an accompanying factor. However, metabolic acidosis may rarely coincide with hypokalemia, in which case an alkalinizing salt may be preferable, e.g., bicarbonate, citrate or gluconate.

Oral: Adults: Tablets should be administered whole with a full glass of water, and should not be broken or chewed. Oral liquids, soluble powders and effervescent tablets should be mixed or dissolved completely in 100 to 200 mL of cold water, juice or other liquid and drunk slowly. Administer with or after meals in 2 or 3 divided doses/day to minimize gastric irritation and too rapid absorption.

Prevention of Hypokalemia: supplementary, approximately 20 to 40 mmol/day.

Treatment of Depletion: approximately 40 to a maximum of 100 mmol/day. In general a daily dose exceeding 60 mmol should not be required.

Parenteral: For i.v. administration only; dilute concentrated solutions before infusing. The dose and rate of infusion are dependent on the individual patient's condition.

Adults: Generally, potassium concentrations in peripheral i.v. solutions should not exceed 40 mmol/L. Higher concentrations (e.g., 60 mmol/L) may be needed in cases of severe hypokalemia and should be administered via a central line. Care must be taken to avoid extravasation.

In patients whose serum potassium concentration is above 2.5 mmol/L, the rate of infusion should not exceed 10 mmol/hour. The total dose should not exceed 200 mmol/24 hours.

For urgent treatment (serum potassium concentration <2 mmol/L with ECG changes or paralysis), infuse potassium at a rate of 40 mmol/hour, up to a maximum of 400 mmol/24 hour period. If doses greater than 20 mmol/hour are used, an infusion pump, ECG and frequent serum potassium monitoring are essential. In critical states, potassium may be infused in saline (unless saline is contraindicated) rather than in dextrose solutions, as the latter may decrease serum potassium concentrations by producing an intracellular shift.

Children: 2 to 3 mmol/kg/day or 40 mmol/m²/day with serum level monitoring.

Reviewed 1997

PRAMEGEL™

Medicis

Pramoxine—Menthol

Antipruritic

Supplied: Each bottle contains: pramoxine HCl 1% and menthol 0.5% in a specially formulated gel base containing D.S. alcohol, carbopol 940 and purified water. Plastic bottles of 120 mL.

PRAMOX® HC Ⓟ

Dermtek

Hydrocortisone Acetate—Pramoxine HCl

Topical Corticosteroid—Anesthetic—Antipruritic

Supplied: Cream: Each tube contains: hydrocortisone (as acetate) 1% and pramoxine HCl 1% in a white unscented vanishing cream. Tubes of 45 g.

Lotion: Each bottle contains: Hydrocortisone (as acetate) 1% and pramoxine HCL 1% in a water-miscible lotion base containing menthol. Bottles of 120 mL.

PRANDASE® Ⓟ

Bayer

Acarbose

Oral Antidiabetic Agent—Alpha-glucosidase Inhibitor

Pharmacology: Acarbose is a complex oligosaccharide that inhibits α-glucosidase activity in the brush border membrane of the small intestine. This delays the digestion of ingested carbohydrates, thereby resulting in a smoothing and lowering of blood glucose concentration following meals (postprandial). As a consequence of decreases in plasma glucose postprandial increases, acarbose reduces levels of glycosylated hemoglobin in patients with Type II (non-insulin dependent) diabetes mellitus. Systemic nonenzymatic protein glycosylation, as reflected by levels of glycosylated hemoglobin, is a function of average blood glucose concentration over time.

Mechanism of Action: Acarbose does not enhance insulin secretion. The antihyperglycemic action of acarbose results from a competitive, reversible inhibition of pancreatic α-amylase and membrane bound intestinal α-glucoside hydrolase enzymes. Pancreatic α-amylase hydrolyzes complex starches to oligosaccharides in the lumen of the small intestine, while the membrane-bound intestinal α-glucosidases hydrolyze oligosaccharides, trisaccharides and disaccharides to glucose and other monosaccharides in the brush border of the small intestine. In diabetic patients, this enzyme inhibition results in a delayed glucose absorption and a smoothing and lowering of postprandial hyperglycemia, resulting in improved glycemic control.

Because its mechanism of action is different, the effect of acarbose in enhancing glycemic control is additive to that of sulfonylureas when used in combination. In addition, acarbose diminishes the insulinotropic and weight-increasing effects of sulfonylureas.

Acarbose has no inhibitory activity against lactase and consequently does not induce lactose intolerance.

Pharmacokinetics: Absorption: One to 2% of an oral dose of acarbose is absorbed from the gastrointestinal tract as unchanged drug. When ^{14}C-labelled acarbose was administered orally, approximately 35% of the total radioactivity (changed and unchanged drug) was absorbed. An average of 51% of an oral dose was excreted in the feces as unabsorbed drug-related radioactivity within 96 hours of ingestion. Because acarbose acts locally within the gastrointestinal tract, this low systemic bioavailability of parent compound is therapeutically desired. Following oral dosing of healthy volunteers with ^{14}C-labelled acarbose, peak plasma concentrations of radioactivity were attained 14 to 24 hours after dosing, while peak plasma concentrations of active drug were attained at approximately 1 hour. The delayed absorption of acarbose-related radioactivity reflects the absorption of metabolites that may be formed by either intestinal bacteria or intestinal enzymatic hydrolysis.

Metabolism: Acarbose is metabolized exclusively within the gastrointestinal tract, principally by intestinal bacteria, but also by digestive enzymes. A fraction of these metabolites (approximately 34% of the dose) was absorbed and subsequently excreted in the urine. At least 13 metabolites have been separated chromatographically from urine specimens. The major metabolites have been identified as 4-methylpyrogallol derivatives (i.e., sulfate, methyl, and glucuronide conjugates). One metabolite (formed by cleavage of a glucose molecule from acarbose) also has α-glucosidase inhibitory activity. This metabolite, together with the parent compound, recovered from the urine, accounts for less than 2% of the total administered dose.

Excretion: The fraction of acarbose that is absorbed as intact drug is almost completely excreted by the kidneys. When acarbose was given i.v., 89% of the dose was recovered in the urine as active drug within 48 hours. In contrast, less than 2% of an oral dose was recovered in the urine as active (i.e., parent compound and active metabolite) drug. This is consistent with the low bioavailability of the parent drug. The plasma elimination half-life of acarbose activity is approximately 2 hours in healthy volunteers. Consequently, drug accumulation does not occur with 3 times a day (t.i.d.) oral dosing.

Patients with severe renal impairment (creatinine clearance <25 mL/min/1.73m²) attained about 5 times higher peak plasma concentrations of acarbose and 6 times larger AUCs than volunteers with normal renal function.

Indications: As monotherapy, acarbose is indicated as adjunct to prescribed diet for the management of blood glucose levels in non-insulin dependent diabetic patients who are inadequately controlled by diet alone.

Acarbose may also be used in combination with a sulfonylurea when diet plus either acarbose or a sulfonylurea do not result in adequate glycemic control. The effect of acarbose in enhancing glycemic control is additive to that of sulfonylureas when used in combination because of its different mechanism of action.

In initiating treatment for NIDDM, diet should be emphasized as the primary form of treatment. Caloric restriction and weight loss are essential in the obese diabetic patient. Proper dietary management alone may be effective in controlling blood glucose and symptoms of hyperglycemia. The importance of regular physical activity when appropriate should also be stressed. If this treatment program fails to result in adequate glycemic control, the use of acarbose should be considered. The use of acarbose must be viewed by both the physician and patient as a treatment in addition to diet, and not as a substitute for diet or as a convenient mechanism for avoiding dietary restraint. Acarbose should be considered as complementary to dietary therapy and physical exercise before resorting to other forms of treatment, such as oral hypoglycemics.

Contraindications: Patients with hypersensitivity to acarbose and patients with diabetic ketoacidosis. It is also contraindicated in patients with inflammatory bowel disease, colonic ulceration, partial intestinal obstruction or in patients predisposed to intestinal obstruction. In addition, acarbose should not be used in patients who have chronic intestinal diseases associated with marked disorders of digestion or absorption and in patients who suffer from states which may deteriorate as a result of increased gas formation in the intestine, e.g. larger hernias.

Warnings: Transaminases: Acarbose may give rise to elevations of serum transaminases and, in rare instances, hyperbilirubinemia. If elevated transaminase levels are observed, a reduction in dosage or withdrawal of therapy may be indicated, particularly if the elevations persist.

Precautions: General: Increased use of sucrose (cane sugar) and food that contains sucrose can lead to gastrointestinal symptoms (e.g., flatulence and bloating) and also loose stools and occasionally diarrhea as a result of increased carbohydrate fermentation in the colon during acarbose treatment.

Acarbose delays glucose absorption and lowers hyperglycemia following meals. Regular intake of acarbose should not be interrupted without the physician's knowledge, since such interruption can cause a rise in blood glucose.

Hypoglycemia: Because of its mechanism of action, acarbose when administered alone will not cause hypoglycemia in the fasted or postprandial state. Sulfonylurea agents may cause hypoglycemia. Because acarbose given with a sulfonylurea will cause a further lowering of blood glucose, it may increase the hypoglycemic potential of the sulfonylurea. Oral glucose (dextrose), whose absorption is not inhibited by acarbose, should be used instead of sucrose (cane sugar) in the treatment of mild to moderate hypoglycemia. Sucrose, whose hydrolysis to glucose and fructose is inhibited by acarbose, is unsuitable for the rapid correction of hypoglycemia. Severe hypoglycemia may require the use of either i.v. glucose infusion or glucagon injection.

Loss of Control of Blood Glucose: When diabetic patients are exposed to stress such as fever, trauma, infection or surgery, a temporary loss of control of blood glucose may occur. At such times, temporary insulin therapy may be necessary.

Geriatrics: No special precautions are necessary with acarbose treatment in the elderly. Elderly patients receiving acarbose may require more intensive supervision and follow-up.

Children: Safety and effectiveness of acarbose in patients <18 years of age have not been established.

Pregnancy: There are no adequate and well-controlled studies of acarbose in pregnant women and its use in these patients is not recommended.

Lactation: A small amount of radioactivity has been found in the milk of lactating rats after administration of radiolabelled acarbose. It is not known whether this drug is excreted in human milk. Because many drugs are excreted in human milk, acarbose should not be administered to a nursing woman.

Patients with Special Diseases and Conditions: See Warnings regarding elevated serum transaminases.

Renal: Plasma concentrations of acarbose in renally impaired volunteers were proportionally increased relative to the degree of renal dysfunction. Long-term clinical trials in diabetic patients with significant renal dysfunction (creatinine clearance <25 mL/min) have not been conducted. Therefore, treatment of these patients with acarbose is not recommended.

In one species of rats studied an increased incidence of renal tumors was observed. This was not seen in any other species of rats or other animals studied. When malnutrition was prevented in these rats, acarbose did not increase the incidence of renal tumors.

Drug Interactions: General: Certain drugs tend to produce hyperglycemia and may lead to loss of blood glucose control. These drugs include diuretics (thiazides, furosemide), corticosteroids, phenothiazines, thyroid products, estrogens, oral contraceptives, phenytoin, nicotinic acid, sympathomimetics and isoniazid. When such drugs are administered to a patient receiving acarbose, the patient should be closely observed for loss of blood glucose control. When such drugs are withdrawn from patients receiving acarbose in combination with sulfonylureas, patients should be observed closely for evidence of hypoglycemia.

Intestinal Absorbents: Intestinal absorbents (e.g., charcoal) and digestive enzyme preparations containing carbohydrate-splitting enzymes (amylase, pancreatin) may reduce the effect of acarbose and should not be taken concomitantly.

Antacids: The concomitant administration of acarbose and an antacid does not alter the effect of acarbose. The administration of antacid preparations is unlikely to ameliorate the gastrointestinal symptoms of acarbose and therefore should not be recommended to patients for this purpose.

Cholestyramine: The concomitant administration of cholestyramine may enhance the effects of acarbose, particularly with respect to reducing postprandial insulin levels. In healthy volunteers, a rebound phenomenon with respect to the postprandial insulin response was observed when both acarbose and cholestyramine therapy were withdrawn simultaneously.

Other Drugs: Studies in healthy volunteers have shown that acarbose has no effect on either the pharmacokinetics or pharmacodynamics of digoxin, nifedipine, propranolol or ranitidine.

Acarbose did not interfere with the absorption or disposition of the sulfonylurea glyburide in diabetic patients.

Acarbose delays the intestinal absorption of metformin but does not reduce its overall bioavailability.

Laboratory Tests: Therapeutic response to acarbose should be monitored by periodic postprandial blood glucose tests. Measurement of glycosylated hemoglobin levels is recommended for the monitoring of long-term glycemic control.

Adverse Effects: In placebo controlled pivotal studies of ≥6 months duration, adverse experiences were reported in 53% of patients receiving placebo and in 77% of patients treated with acarbose. The majority of adverse experiences were gastrointestinal symptoms which result from the pharmacodynamic action of the drug. The majority of symptoms were of mild or moderate intensity and were dose-dependent. The symptoms occurred early (within 1 to 2 months of treatment) and improved tolerability with longer duration of treatment was observed. Rarely, these gastrointestinal events may be severe and might be confused with ileus/ileus-like symptoms. Therapy was discontinued prematurely due to adverse events in 14% of acarbose-treated patients and 5% of placebo-treated patients.

The following adverse events (>3%) were reported at acarbose doses of 50 to 300 mg given 3 times daily (see Table I). The maximum recommended daily dose is 100 mg 3 times daily.

The only significant difference in the incidence of adverse events between acarbose and placebo were gastrointestinal symptoms (e.g., flatulence, diarrhea and abdominal pain) which can be minimized by starting on a low dose and titrating slowly (see Dosage).

Rarely, hypersensitive skin reactions, such as erythema, exanthema and urticaria and cases of hepatitis and jaundice have been reported.

Laboratory Tests: In clinical trials, at doses of 50 mg t.i.d. and 100 mg t.i.d., the incidence of serum transaminase elevations with acarbose was the same as with placebo. In approximately 3 million patient-years of international postmarketing experience with acarbose, 62 cases of serum transaminase elevations ≥500 IU/L have been reported, 29 of which were associated with jaundice. In most cases where followup was reported, hepatic dysfunction improved or resolved upon discontinuation of acarbose. Therefore, when appropriate, liver enzyme monitoring should be considered during the first 6 to 12 months.

Table I—Prandase

Adverse Effects

	Incidence of Adverse Events (%)			
	Diet		Combination with Sulfonylurea	
Adverse Event	Acarbose n=192	Placebo n=196	Acarbose n=205	Placebo n=203
Flatulence	127 (66)	58 (30)	141 (69)	56 (28)
Diarrhea	49 (26)	17 (8.7)	68 (33)	15 (7.4)
Abdominal Pain	22 (11)	11 (5.7)	31 (15)	15 (7.4)
Abdominal Cramps	10 (5.2)	5 (2.6)	15 (7.3)	4 (2.0)
Abdominal Distention	6 (3.1)	3 (1.5)	6 (2.9)	4 (2.0)
Nausea	7 (3.6)	5 (2.6)	15 (7.3)	12 (5.9)
Vomiting	3 (1.6)	2 (1.0)	7 (3.4)	6 (3.0)
Dyspepsia	9 (4.7)	9 (4.6)	8 (3.9)	6 (3.0)
Constipation	15 (7.7)	5 (2.6)	4 (2.0)	8 (3.9)
Flu Syndrome	12 (6.3)	14 (7.1)	16 (7.8)	15 (7.4)
Headache	10 (5.2)	5 (2.6)	9 (4.4)	13 (6.4)
Asthenia	0 (0)	5 (2.6)	8 (3.9)	8 (3.9)
Chest Pain	1 (0.5)	2 (1.0)	7 (3.4)	8 (3.9)

Prandase (cont'd)

Overdose: Symptoms and Treatment: Unlike sulfonylureas, an overdose of acarbose will not result in hypoglycemia. When acarbose is taken with drinks and/or meals containing carbohydrates (polysaccharides, oligosaccharides or disaccharides), overdosage can lead to abdominal distention, flatulence and diarrhea. In the event of acarbose being taken in an overdose independent of food, excessive intestinal symptoms need not be anticipated.

In cases of overdosage, the patient should not be given drinks or meals containing carbohydrates (polysaccharides, oligosaccharides and disaccharides) for the next 4 to 6 hours.

Dosage: There is no fixed dosage regimen for the management of diabetes mellitus with acarbose or any other pharmacologic agent. Dosage of acarbose must be individualized on the basis of both effectiveness and tolerance while not exceeding 100 mg t.i.d. Acarbose should be started at a low dose, with gradual dose escalation as described below, both to reduce gastrointestinal side effects and to permit identification of the minimum dose required for adequate glycemic control of the patient.

During treatment initiation and dose titration (see below), 2-hour postprandial plasma glucose should be used to determine the therapeutic response to acarbose and identify the minimum effective dose for the patient. Thereafter, glycosylated hemoglobin should be measured at intervals of approximately 3 months. The therapeutic goal should be to decrease both postprandial plasma glucose and glycosylated hemoglobin levels to optimal or near optimal by using the lowest effective dose of acarbose.

Initial Dosage: The usual starting dosage is 50 mg given orally once daily. After 1 to 2 weeks, the dosage should be increased to 50 mg b.i.d. with a subsequent increase to 50 mg t.i.d. after a further 1 to 2 weeks. Each dose should be taken with the first bite of a main meal.

Maintenance Dosage: Once a maintenance dose of 50 mg t.i.d. has been reached, some patients may benefit from further increasing the dosage to 100 mg t.i.d. The maintenance dose ranges from 50 mg t.i.d. to 100 mg t.i.d. The dosage should be adjusted at 4 to 8 week intervals based on 2-hour postprandial glucose levels and on tolerance. Consideration should be given to lowering the dose if no further reduction in postprandial glucose or glycosylated hemoglobin levels is observed after titration to 100 mg t.i.d. Once an effective and tolerated dosage is established, it should be maintained.

Maximum Dosage: Dosages above 100 mg t.i.d. are not recommended.

Patients Receiving Sulfonylureas: Sulfonylurea agents may cause hypoglycemia. Therefore, acarbose given in combination with a sulfonylurea may also cause hypoglycemia. If hypoglycemia occurs, appropriate adjustment in the sulfonylurea dosage should be made.

Information for the Patient: See Blue Section—Information for the Patient "Prandase".

Supplied: 50 mg: Each round, off-white, scored tablet, marked with "G50" on one side and the Bayer cross on the other, contains: acarbose 50 mg. Nonmedicinal ingredients: cornstarch, magnesium stearate, microcrystalline cellulose and silicon dioxide. Preservative- and dye-free. Blister packs in cartons of 120.

100 mg: Each round, off-white, scored tablet, marked with "G100" on one side and the Bayer cross on the other, contains: acarbose 100 mg. Nonmedicinal ingredients: cornstarch, magnesium stearate, microcrystalline cellulose and silicon dioxide. Preservative- and dye-free. Blister packs in cartons of 120.

Store between 15 and 25°C. At temperatures >25°C and at a relative humidity of >75%, discoloration may occur in tablets that have been removed from the pack. The tablets should therefore not be removed from the foil until immediately before use.

(Shown in Product Recognition Section)

Reviewed 1998

PRAVACHOL® Ⓟ

Squibb

Pravastatin Sodium

Lipid Metabolism Regulator

Pharmacology: Pravastatin is one of a new class of lipid-lowering compounds known as HMG-CoA reductase inhibitors (statins) that reduce cholesterol biosynthesis. These agents are competitive inhibitors of 3-hydroxy- 3-methylglutaryl-coenzyme A (HMG-CoA) reductase, the enzyme catalyzing the early rate-limiting step in cholesterol biosynthesis, conversion of HMG-CoA to mevalonate. Pravastatin is isolated from a strain of Penicillium citrinum. The active drug substance is the hydroxyacid form.

Pravastatin produces its lipid-lowering effect in 2 ways. First, as a consequence of its reversible inhibition of HMG-CoA reductase activity, it effects modest reductions in intracellular pools of cholesterol. This results in an increase in the number of low density lipoproteins (LDL)—receptors on cell surfaces and enhanced receptor-mediated catabolism and clearance of circulating LDL. Second, pravastatin inhibits LDL production by inhibiting hepatic synthesis of very low density lipoproteins (VLDL), the LDL precursor.

Epidemiologic and clinical studies have associated the risk of coronary artery disease (CAD) with elevated levels of Total-C, LDL-C and decreased levels of HDL-C. These abnormalities of lipoprotein metabolism are considered as major contributors to the development of the disease. Other factors, e.g., interactions between lipids/lipoproteins and endothelium, platelets and macrophages, have also been incriminated in the development of human atherosclerosis and of its complications.

In long-term, prospective clinical trials effective treatment of hypercholesterolemia/dyslipidemia has consistently been associated with a reduction in the risk of CAD.

Treatment with pravastatin has been shown to reduce circulating Total-C, LDL-C, and apolipoprotein B, modestly reduce VLDL-C and triglycerides (TG) while producing increases of variable magnitude in HDL-C and apolipoprotein A. Clinical trials suggest that pravastatin's effect on reducing clinical events appears to incorporate both cholesterol modification and some ancillary mechanism.

Pravastatin has complex pharmacokinetic characteristics.

Pharmacokinetics: Pravastatin is administered orally in the active form. Following oral ingestion, pravastatin is rapidly absorbed with peak plasma levels attained at about 1 to 1.5 hours. Average oral absorption of pravastatin, based on urinary recovery of radiolabeled drug after oral and i.v. dosing, is 34%; average absolute bioavailability of the parent drug is 17%. The therapeutic response to pravastatin is similar, whether taken with meals or 1 hour prior to meals, even though the presence of food in the gastrointestinal tract causes a reduction in systemic bioavailability (see Table I).

Table I—Pravachol

Percent Decrease in LDL-C

Pravastatin	10 mg b.i.d.	20 mg b.i.d.
With meals	-25%	-37%
Before meals*	-26%	-36%

* administered 1 hour or more prior to eating.

Pravastatin undergoes extensive first pass extraction in the liver (estimated hepatic extraction ratio, 66%), its primary site of action, and is excreted in the bile. Therefore, plasma levels of the drug are probably of limited value in predicting therapeutic effectiveness. Nevertheless, measurement of plasma pravastatin concentrations by gas chromatography and mass-spectrometry showed dose proportionality for area under the concentration-time curve (AUC) and maximum and steady-state plasma levels. Steady-state areas under the plasma concentration-time curves and maximum (C_{max}) or minimum (C_{min}) plasma concentrations showed no accumulation following once or twice-daily administration of pravastatin tablets.

Protein binding of pravastatin is approximately 50%. The plasma elimination half-life of pravastatin is between 1.5 and 2 hours (2.5 to 3 hours in hypercholesterolemic subjects). Approximately 20% of a radiolabeled oral dose is excreted in the urine and 70% in the feces. Pravastatin is extensively metabolized. The major metabolite is the 3 α-hydroxy isomer, which has one-tenth to one-fortieth of the inhibitory activity of the parent compound on HMG-CoA reductase.

After i.v. administration to healthy subjects, approximately 47% of the total drug clearance occurs via renal excretion of intact pravastatin, and about 53% is cleared by nonrenal routes, i.e., biliary excretion and biotransformation.

Studies of pravastatin administered as a single dose to healthy elderly male and female subjects (age 65 to 78 years) indicated a 30 to 50% increase in plasma levels.

No studies have been carried out in patients with renal insufficiency.

Indications: Therapy with lipid-altering agents should be considered a component of multiple risk factor intervention in those individuals at increased risk for atherosclerotic vascular disease due to hypercholesterolemia. Pravastatin should be used in addition to a diet restricted in saturated fat and cholesterol when the response to diet and other nonpharmacological measures alone has been inadequate (see Table II).

Hypercholesterolemia: As an adjunct to diet [at least an equivalent of the American Heart Association (AHA) Step 1 diet] for the reduction of elevated total and low density lipoprotein cholesterol (LDL-C) levels in patients with primary hypercholesterolemia (Types IIa and IIb), when the response to diet and other nonpharmacologic measures alone has been inadequate.

Prior to initiating therapy with pravastatin, secondary causes for hypercholesterolemia, such as obesity, poorly controlled diabetes mellitus, hypothyroidism, nephrotic syndrome, dysproteinemias, obstructive liver disease, other drug therapy or alcoholism, should be excluded and it should be determined that patients for whom treatment with pravastatin is being considered have an elevated LDL-C level as the cause for an elevated total serum cholesterol. A lipid profile should be performed to measure total cholesterol, high density lipoprotein cholesterol (HDL-C) and triglycerides (TG).

For patients with total triglycerides less than 4.52 mmol/L (400 mg/dL), LDL-C can be estimated using the following equation:

LDL-C (mmol/L) =
Total Cholesterol − [(0.37 × triglycerides) + HDL-C]
LDL-C (mg/dL) =
Total Cholesterol − [(0.16 × triglycerides) + HDL-C]

When total triglyceride levels exceed 4.52 mmol/L (400 mg/dL), this equation is less accurate and LDL-C concentrations should be determined by ultracentrifugation.

The US National Cholesterol Education Program's (NCEP) Treatment Guidelines are summarized in Table II.

Since the goal of treatment is to lower LDL-C, the NCEP recommends that LDL-C levels be used to initiate and assess treatment response. Only if LDL-C levels are not available, should the Total-C be used to monitor therapy.

As with other lipid-lowering therapy, pravastatin is not indicated when hypercholesterolemia is due to hyperalphalipoproteinemia (elevated HDL-C). The efficacy of pravastatin has not been evaluated in conditions where the major abnormality is elevation of chylomicrons, VLDL or LDL (i.e., hyperlipoproteinemia or dyslipoproteinemia types I, III, IV or V).

Coronary Heart Disease: Pravastatin was also found to reduce the rate of progression of atherosclerosis in patients with coronary heart disease as part of a treatment strategy to lower Total and LDL-cholesterol to target levels. In 2 trials including this type of patients* (i.e., in a secondary prevention intervention), pravastatin monotherapy was shown to reduce the rate of progression of atherosclerosis as evaluated by quantitative angiography and B-mode ultrasound. This effect may be associated with an improvement in the coronary endpoints (fatal or nonfatal myocardial infarction) (see Precautions).

* Pravastatin Limitation of Atherosclerosis in the Coronary/Carotid Arteries (PLAC I and II).

In hypercholesterolemic patients without clinically evident coronary heart disease, pravastatin is indicated to: reduce the risk of myocardial infarction; reduce the risk for undergoing

Table II—Pravachol

US National Cholesterol Education Program's (NCEP) Treatment Guidelines

Definite Atherosclerotic Disease[a]	Two or More Other Risk Factors[b]	LDL Cholesterol mmol/L (mg/dL) Drug Treatment Initiation Level	LDL Cholesterol mmol/L (mg/dL) Goal
No	No	≥4.9 (≥190)	<4.1 (<160)
No	Yes	≥4.1 (≥160)	<3.4 (<130)
Yes	Yes or No	≥3.4 (≥130)	≤2.6 (≤100)

[a]Coronary heart disease or peripheral vascular disease (including symptomatic carotid artery disease).

[b]Other risk factors (or coronary heart disease (CHD) include: age (males: ≥45 years; females: ≥55 years or premature menopause without estrogen replacement therapy); family history of premature CHD; current cigarette smoking; hypertension; confirmed HDL-C <0.91 mmol/L (<35 mg/dL); and diabetes mellitus. Subtract one risk factor if HDL-C is ≥1.6 mmol/L (≥60 mg/dL).

myocardial revascularization procedures; reduce the risk of cardiovascular mortality with no increase in death from noncardiovascular causes.

In the West of Scotland Study (WOS), the effect of pravastatin treatment on fatal and nonfatal coronary heart disease (CHD) was assessed in 6 595 patients (aged 45 to 66 years) without a previous myocardial infarction, but with elevated LDL-C levels between 4 to 6.7 mmol/L (156 to 254 mg/dL). The patients were followed for a median of 4.8 years.

Pravastatin significantly reduced the rate of first coronary events (either CHD death or nonfatal myocardial infarction) by 31% (248 events in the placebo group [CHD death = 44, nonfatal myocardial infarction = 204] vs 174 events in the pravastatin group [CHD death = 31, nonfatal myocardial infarction = 143], p = 0.0001). The effect of these cumulative cardiovascular event rates was evident after 6 months of treatment. The risk reduction with pravastatin was similar and significant throughout the entire range of baseline LDL cholesterol levels. This reduction was also similar and significant across the age range studied with a 40% risk reduction for patients younger than 55 years and a 27% risk reduction for patients 55 years and older.

Pravastatin also significantly decreased the risk for undergoing myocardial revascularization procedures (coronary artery bypass graft surgery by 37% [80 vs 51 patients, p = 0.009] and coronary angiography by 31% [128 vs 90, p = 0.007]). Cardiovascular deaths were decreased by 32% (73 vs 50, p = 0.03), and there was no increase in deaths from noncardiovascular causes.

The West of Scotland Study excluded female patients, elderly subjects and most patients with familial hypercholesterolemia (FH). Consequently it has not been established to what extent the findings of the WOS study can be extrapolated to these subpopulations of hypercholesterolemic patients.

In patients with heterozygous FH, optimal reduction in total and LDL cholesterol necessitates a combination drug therapy in the majority of patients. (For homozygous FH see Precautions, Use in Homozygous Familial Hypercholesterolemia.)

Because information on familial combined hyperlipidemic (FCH) patients is not available from the WOS study, the effect of pravastatin in this subgroup of high risk dyslipidemic patients could not be assessed.

Contraindications: Hypersensitivity to any component of this medication. Active liver disease or unexplained persistent elevations in liver function tests (see Warnings).

Pregnancy: Atherosclerosis is a chronic process and discontinuation of lipid-lowering drugs during pregnancy should have little impact on the outcome of long-term therapy of primary hypercholesterolemia. Cholesterol and other products of cholesterol biosynthesis are essential components for fetal development (including synthesis of steroids and cell membranes). Since HMG-CoA reductase inhibitors such as pravastatin decrease cholesterol synthesis and possibly the synthesis of other biologically active substances derived from cholesterol, they may cause fetal harm when administered to pregnant women. Therefore, pravastatin is contraindicated during pregnancy.

Lactation: See Precautions.

Warnings: Liver Dysfunction: HMG-CoA reductase inhibitors have been associated with biochemical abnormalities of liver function. As with other lipid-lowering agents, including nonabsorbable bile acid-binding resins, increases in liver enzymes to **less than** 3 times the upper limit of normal have occurred during therapy with pravastatin. The significance of these changes, which usually appear during the first few months of treatment initiation, is not known. In the majority of patients treated with pravastatin, in clinical trials, these increased values declined to pretreatment levels despite continuation of therapy at the same dose.

Marked persistent increases (greater than 3 times the upper limit of normal) in serum transaminases were seen in 6 out of 1 142 (0.5%) patients treated with pravastatin in clinical trials (see Adverse Effects). The increases usually appeared 3 to 12 months after the start of therapy with pravastatin. These elevations were not associated with clinical signs and symptoms of liver disease and usually declined to pretreatment levels upon discontinuation of therapy. Patients rarely had persistent marked abnormalities possibly attributable to therapy.

Liver function tests should be performed at baseline and periodically thereafter in all patients. Special attention should be given to patients who develop increased transaminase levels. Liver function tests should be repeated to confirm an elevation and subsequently monitored at more frequent intervals. **If increases in ALT and AST equal or exceed 3 times the upper limit of normal and persist, therapy should be discontinued.**

Caution should be exercised when pravastatin is administered to patients with a history of liver disease or heavy alcohol ingestion. Active liver disease or unexplained serum transaminase elevations are contraindications to the use of pravastatin; if such condition develops during therapy, the drug should be discontinued.

Muscle Effects: Elevations of creatinine phosphokinase levels (CPK [MM fraction]), myalgia, myopathy and rhabdomyolysis have been reported with the use of HMG-CoA reductase inhibitors, including pravastatin.

Muscle weakness and rhabdomyolysis have been reported in patients receiving other HMG-CoA reductase inhibitors concomitantly with itraconazole and cyclosporine.

The benefits and risks of using HMG-CoA reductase inhibitors concomitantly with immunosuppressive drugs, fibrates, erythromycin, systemic azole derivative antifungal agents or lipid-lowering doses of niacin should be carefully considered.

Myalgia has been associated with pravastatin therapy. Rare cases of rhabdomyolysis associated with pravastatin (and macrocreatine kinase in 1 case) have been reported.

Myopathy (markedly elevated CPK of greater than 10 times the upper limit of normal with myalgia) was very rarely reported in pravastatin treated patients in clinical trials. Rhabdomyolysis with renal dysfunction secondary to myoglobinuria has also very rarely been reported with pravastatin. However, myopathy should be considered in any patients with diffuse myalgia, muscle tenderness or weakness, and/or marked elevation of CPK.

As with other statins, the risk of myopathy including rhabdomyolysis may be substantially increased by concomitant immunosuppressive therapy including cyclosporine, and by concomitant therapy with gemfibrozil, erythromycin or niacin (see Precautions).

Myopathy has not been observed in clinical trials involving small numbers of patients who were treated with pravastatin together with immunosuppressants, fibric acid derivatives or niacin.

The use of fibrates alone is occasionally associated with myopathy. In a limited size clinical trial of combined therapy with pravastatin (40 mg/day) and gemfibrozil (1 200 mg/day), myopathy was not reported, although a trend towards CPK elevations and musculoskeletal symptoms was seen. **The combined use of pravastatin and fibrates should generally be avoided.**

No information is available on the combined therapy of pravastatin with erythromycin.

Pravastatin therapy should be discontinued if marked elevation of CPK levels occurs or if myopathy is diagnosed or suspected.

Interruption of therapy with pravastatin should be considered in any patient with an acute, serious condition, suggestive of a myopathy or having a risk factor predisposing to the development of renal failure or rhabdomyolysis, such as severe acute infection, hypotension, major surgery, trauma, severe metabolic, endocrine or electrolyte disorders and uncontrolled seizures.

Precautions: General: **In secondary prevention intervention, the effects of pravastatin-induced changes in lipoprotein levels, including reduction of total and LDL cholesterol, on total mortality have not been established.**

Before instituting therapy with pravastatin an attempt should be made to control hypercholesterolemia with appropriate diet, exercise, weight reduction in overweight and obese patients, and to treat other underlying medical problems (see Indications). The patient should be advised to inform subsequent physicians of the prior use of pravastatin.

Pravastatin may elevate creatine phosphokinase and transaminase levels. This should be considered in the differential diagnosis of chest pain in a patient on therapy with pravastatin.

Effect on the Lens: Current data from clinical trials do not indicate an adverse effect of pravastatin on the human lens.

Homozygous Familial Hypercholesterolemia: Pravastatin has not been evaluated in patients with rare homozygous familial hypercholesterolemia. Most HMG-CoA reductase inhibitors are less or not effective in this subgroup of hypercholesterolemic patients.

Effect on Lipoprotein(a): In some patients, the beneficial effect of lowered total cholesterol and LDL-C levels may be partly blunted by a concomitant increase in the lipoprotein (a)[Lp(a)] level. Further research is ongoing to elucidate the significance of Lp(a) variations. Therefore, until further experience is obtained, where feasible, it is suggested that measurements of serum Lp(a) be followed up in patients placed on pravastatin therapy.

Effect on CoQ10 Levels (Ubiquinone): A significant short-term decrease in plasma CoQ10 levels in patients treated with pravastatin has been observed. Longer clinical trials have also shown reduced serum ubiquinone levels during treatment with pravastatin and other HMG CoA reductase inhibitors. The clinical significance of a potential long-term statin-induced deficiency of CoQ10 has not yet been established. It has been reported that a decrease in myocardial ubiquinone levels could lead to impaired cardiac function in patients with borderline congestive heart failure.

Carcinogenesis: A 21-month oral study in mice, with doses of 10 to 100 mg/kg daily of pravastatin did not demonstrate any carcinogenic potential. In a 2-year oral study in rats, a statistically significant increase in the incidence of hepatocellular carcinoma was observed in male rats given 100 mg/kg daily (125 times the maximum human dose) of pravastatin. This change was not seen in male rats given 40 mg/kg daily (50 times the recommended human dose) or less, or in female rats at any dose level.

Pregnancy: **Pravastatin is contraindicated during pregnancy (see Contraindications).**

Safety in pregnant women has not been established. Although pravastatin was not teratogenic in rats at doses as high as 1 000 mg/kg daily nor in rabbits at doses of up to 50 mg/kg daily, pravastatin should be administered to women of childbearing age only when such patients are highly unlikely to conceive and have been informed of potential hazards. If a woman becomes pregnant while taking pravastatin, pravastatin should be discontinued and the patient advised again as to the potential hazards to the fetus.

Lactation: A negligible amount of pravastatin is excreted in human breast milk. Because of the potential for adverse reactions in nursing infants, if the mother is being treated with pravastatin, nursing should be discontinued or treatment with pravastatin stopped.

Children: Only limited experience with the use of statins in children is available. There is no experience to date with the use of pravastatin in such patients.

Geriatrics: Pharmacokinetic evaluation of pravastatin in patients over the age of 65 years indicates an increased AUC. There were no reported increases in the incidence of adverse effects in these or other studies involving patients in that age group. As a precautionary measure, the lowest dose should be administered initially.

Patients with Impaired Renal Function: There have been no studies on the use of pravastatin in patients with renal failure. As a precautionary measure, the lowest dose should be used in these patients (see Warnings, Muscle Effects).

Hypersensitivity: With lovastatin an apparent hypersensitivity syndrome has been reported rarely which has included one or more of the following features: anaphylaxis, angioedema, lupus-like syndrome, polymyalgia rheumatica, thrombocytopenia, leukopenia, hemolytic anemia, positive antinuclear antibody (ANA), erythrocytes sedimentation rate (ESR) increase, arthritis, arthralgia, urticaria, asthenia, photosensitivity, fever and malaise.

Although to date hypersensitivity syndrome has not been described as such, in few instances eosinophilia and skin eruptions appear to be associated with pravastatin treatment. If hypersensitivity is suspected pravastatin should be discontinued. Patients should be advised to report promptly any signs of hypersensitivity such as angioedema, urticaria, photosensitivity, polyarthralgia, fever, malaise.

Endocrine Function: HMG-CoA reductase inhibitors interfere with cholesterol synthesis and as such could theoretically blunt adrenal and/or gonadal steroid production.

In one long-term study investigating the endocrine function in hypercholesterolemic patients, pravastatin exhibited no effect upon basal and stimulated cortisol levels, as well as on aldosterone secretion. Although no change was reported in the testicular function, conflicting results were observed in the analysis of sperm motility after administration of pravastatin. A case of reversible impotence has been reported in a 57-year old man administered pravastatin 20 mg/day and metoprolol. A causal relationship to therapy with pravastatin has not been established. Further studies are needed to clarify the effects of HMG CoA reductase inhibitors on male fertility. Furthermore, the effects, if any, on the pituitary-gonadal axis in premenopausal women are unknown.

Patients treated with pravastatin who develop clinical evidence of endocrine dysfunction should be evaluated appropriately. Caution should be exercised if an HMG-CoA reductase inhibitor or other agent used to lower cholesterol levels is administered to patients receiving other drugs (e.g., ketoconazole, spironolactone, or cimetidine) that may decrease the levels of endogenous steroid hormones.

Pravachol (cont'd)

Drug Interactions: Concomitant Therapy with Other Lipid Metabolism Regulators: Combined drug therapy should be approached with caution as information from controlled studies is limited.

Bile Acid Sequestrants: Preliminary evidence suggests that the cholesterol-lowering effects of pravastatin and the bile acid sequestrants, cholestyramine/colestipol are additive.

When pravastatin was administered 1 hour before or 4 hours after cholestyramine or 1 hour before colestipol and a standard meal, there was no clinically significant decrease in bioavailability or therapeutic effect. Concomitant administration resulted in an approximately 40 to 50% decrease in the mean AUC of pravastatin (see Dosage, Concomitant Therapy).

Gemfibrozil, Nicotinic Acid and Probucol: Gemfibrozil, nicotinic acid and probucol do not statistically significantly affect the bioavailability of pravastatin. However, in a limited size clinical trial, a trend toward CPK elevations and musculoskeletal symptoms was seen in patients treated concurrently with pravastatin and gemfibrozil. No results are available from clinical studies involving combination of pravastatin with probucol.

Myopathy, including rhabdomyolysis, has occurred in patients who were receving coadministration of HMG-CoA reductase inhibitors with fibric acid derivatives and niacin, particularly in subjects with pre-existing renal insufficiency (see Warnings, Muscle Effects).

Other Concomitant Therapy: Digoxin: Coadministration of digoxin and other HMG CoA reductase inhibitors has been shown to increase the steady state digoxin concentrations. The potential effects of coadministration of digoxin and pravastatin are not known. As a precautionary measure, patients taking digoxin should be closely monitored.

Antipyrine: Antipyrine was used as a model for drugs metabolized by the microsomal hepatic enzyme system (cytochrome P450 system). Pravastatin had no effect on the pharmacokinetics of antipyrine.

Coumarin Anticoagulants: Bioavailability parameters at steady state for pravastatin were not altered following concomitant administration with warfarin. Dosing of the 2 drugs did not produce any changes in the anticoagulant action of warfarin (i.e., no increase was seen in mean prothrombin time after 6 days of concomitant therapy). However, until further clinical experience is gained careful monitoring of prothrombin time is recommended in patients taking coumarin anticoagulants concomitantly with pravastatin.

Antacids and Cimetidine: On the average, antacids (1 hour prior to pravastatin) reduce and cimetidine increases the bioavailability of pravastatin. These changes were not statistically significant. The clinical significance of these interactions is not known but is probably minimal as judged from the interaction with food (see Pharmacology).

No information is available regarding interactions with erythromycin (see Warnings, Muscle Effects).

Although specific interaction studies were not performed during clinical trials, no noticeable drug interactions were reported when pravastatin was added to diuretics, antihypertensives, digitalis, angiotensin converting-enzyme (ACE) inhibitors, calcium channel blockers, or nitroglycerin.

Propranolol: Coadministration of propranolol and pravastatin reduced the AUC values by 23% and 16% respectively.

Cyclosporine: In a multicentre study, the AUC values of pravastatin were shown to be 5-fold higher in the presence of cyclosporine. There was no accumulation of pravastatin after multiple doses.

Adverse Effects: Based on experience in a total of over 4 300 patients, of whom 3 537 were treated for 1 year or more and over 2 800 were treated for 2 years or more, pravastatin is generally well tolerated. Adverse events, both clinical and laboratory, are usually mild and transient. In all clinical studies (controlled and uncontrolled), approximately 2% of patients were discontinued from treatment due to adverse experiences attributable to pravastatin.

All adverse drug events (possibly, probably or definitively related to the drug) reported in ≥0.5% of patients in placebo-controlled studies of up to 6 years duration are presented in Table III.

The following additional events have occurred during long-term studies with pravastatin: pruritus, scalp hair abnormalities, skin dryness, abnormal stool, appetite change, chest pain (noncardiovascular), weakness, excess sweating, hot flashes, paresthesia, equilibrium disturbance, mood change, eye symptoms (including soreness, dryness or itching), tinnitus and impotence (see Precautions, Endocrine Function).

Table III—Pravachol

Adverse Drug Events Reported in Placebo-Controlled Studies

	Pravachol (N=4 123) %	Placebo (N=3 612) %
Gastrointestinal		
Nausea/Vomiting	1.4	0.7
Diarrhea	1.0	0.4
Constipation	1.4	0.7
Abdominal pain	0.8	0.5
Flatulence	1.0	0.2
Distention Abdomen	0.5	0.3
Dyspepsia/Heartburn	1.6	1.7
Musculoskeletal/Connective Tissue*		
Musculoskeletal Pain	0.9	0.5
Muscle Cramp	0.5	0.1
Nervous System		
Headache	0.7	0.2
Dizziness	0.5	0.1
Anxiety/Nervousness	0.8	0.8
General		
Fatigue	0.8	0.4
Special Senses		
Vision Disturbance	0.6	0.2
Lens Opacity	0.9	0.2
Dermatologic		
Rash	0.9	0.5
Renal/Genitourinary		
Urinary Abnormality	0.9	0.4

* Myalgia occurred as an adverse drug event in 0.2% of patients treated with pravastatin and 0.2% of patients treated with placebo.

In the West of Scotland Study (see Indications) involving 6 595 patients treated with pravastatin (n=3 216) or placebo (n=3 203), the adverse event profile in the pravastatin group was comparable to that of the placebo group over the median 4.8 years of the study.

The following have also been reported with other statins: hepatitis, cholestatic jaundice, anorexia, psychic disturbances including anxiety, hypospermia and hypersensitivity (see Precautions).

Lens: See Precautions.

Laboratory Test Abnormalities: Increases in serum transaminases and in creatine phosphokinase (CPK) in patients treated with pravastatin have been discussed (see Warnings).

Overdose: Symptoms: There have been 2 reports of overdosage with pravastatin, both of which were asymptomatic and not associated with clinical laboratory abnormalities.

Treatment: In the event of overdosage, treatment should be symptomatic and supportive, and appropriate therapy instituted. Until further experience is obtained, no specific therapy of overdosage can be recommended. The dialyzability of pravastatin and its metabolites is not known.

Dosage: Prior to initiating pravastatin, the patient should be placed on at least an equivalent of the AHA Step I diet, which should be continued during treatment. If appropriate, a program of weight control and physical exercise should be implemented.

Hypercholesterolemia and Coronary Heart Disease: The recommended starting dose is 10 to 20 mg once daily at bedtime. If serum cholesterol is markedly elevated [e.g., Total Cholesterol greater than 7.75 mmol/L (300 mg/dL)] dosage may be initiated at 40 mg/day. Pravastatin may be taken without regard to meals.

Since the maximal effect of a given dose is seen within 4 weeks, periodic lipid determinations should be performed and dosage adjusted according to the patient's response to therapy. **Consideration should be given to reducing the dosage of pravastatin if cholesterol levels fall below the targeted range, such as that recommended by the Second Report of the U.S. National Cholesterol Education Program (NCEP).** The recommended dosage range is 10 to 40 mg administered once a day at bedtime.

Concomitant Therapy: Some patients may require combination therapy with one or more lipid-lowering agents. Pharmacokinetic interaction with pravastatin administered concurrently with nicotinic acid, probucol, or gemfibrozil did not statistically significantly affect the bioavailability of pravastatin. The combined use of pravastatin and fibrates should however generally be avoided (see Warnings, Muscle Effects). No results are available from clinical studies involving the concomitant administration of pravastatin with probucol.

The lipid-lowering effects of pravastatin on Total and Low Density Lipoprotein Cholesterol are additive when combined with a bile acid-binding resin. However, when administering a bile acid-binding resin (e.g., cholestyramine, colestipol) and pravastatin, pravastatin should not be administered concomitantly, but should be given either 1 hour or more before or at least 4 hours following the resin (see Precautions, Drug Interactions, Concomitant Therapy with Other Lipid Metabolism Regulators).

Information for the Patient: See Blue Section—Information for the Patient "Pravachol".

Supplied: 10 mg: Each pink to peach, rounded, rectangular-shaped, biconvex tablet, with a P embossed on one side and PRAVACHOL 10 engraved on the other, contains: pravastatin sodium 10 mg. Nonmedicinal ingredients: croscarmellose sodium, lactose, magnesium oxide, magnesium stearate, microcrystalline cellulose, povidone and red ferric oxide. Bottles of 100. Packages of 30 and 100 individually foil wrapped tablets.

20 mg: Each yellow, rounded, rectangular-shaped, biconvex tablet, with a P embossed on one side and PRAVACHOL 20 engraved on the other, contains: pravastatin sodium 20 mg. Nonmedicinal ingredients: croscarmellose sodium, lactose, magnesium oxide, magnesium stearate, microcrystalline cellulose, povidone and yellow ferric oxide. Bottles of 100. Packages of 30 and 100 individually foil wrapped tablets.

40 mg: Each green, rounded, rectangular-shaped, biconvex tablet, with a P embossed on one side and PRAVACHOL 40 engraved on the other, contains: pravastatin sodium 40 mg. Nonmedicinal ingredients: croscarmellose sodium, D&C yellow no. 10, FD&C blue no. 1, lactose, magnesium oxide, magnesium stearate, microcrystalline cellulose and povidone. Bottles of 100. Packages of 30 and 100 individually foil wrapped tablets.

Store at room temperature (15 to 30°C). Protect from moisture and light.

(Shown in Product Recognition Section)

Reviewed 1999

PRED FORTE®
PRED MILD®
Allergan

Prednisolone Acetate

Ophthalmic Corticosteroid

Supplied: Each 5 mL (Pred Forte only) and 10 mL plastic dropper bottle contains: prednisolone acetate (microfine suspension) 1% (Pred Forte) or 0.12% (Pred Mild). Nonmedicinal ingredients: benzalkonium chloride, boric acid, disodium edetate, hydroxypropyl methylcellulose, polysorbate 80, purified water, sodium bisulfite, sodium chloride and sodium citrate.

PREDNISOLONE
General Monograph, CPhA

see CORTICOSTEROIDS: EYE EAR NOSE
see CORTICOSTEROIDS: SYSTEMIC

PREDNISOLONE SODIUM PHOSPHATE FORTE
Rivex Ophthalmics

Anti-inflammatory

Supplied: Each mL of sterile ophthalmic solution contains: prednisolone sodium phosphate 1%. Nonmedicinal ingredients: benzalkonium chloride, edetate disodium, hydrochloric acid, hydroxypropyl methylcellulose, purified water, sodium chloride, sodium hydroxide, sodium phosphate dibasic and sodium phosphate monobasic. Plastic squeeze bottles of 5 mL with controlled tip applicators.

PREDNISONE
General Monograph, CPhA

see CORTICOSTEROIDS: SYSTEMIC

PREEMIE SMA®
Wyeth-Ayerst

see SMA, PREEMIE

PREGNYL®
Organon

Chorionic Gonadotropin
Gonadotropin

Pharmacology: Chorionic gonadotropin is a glycoprotein substance, with a molecular weight of approximately 38 600, secreted by the placenta and obtained from the urine of pregnant women. It is composed of nonidentical and noncovalently linked α and β subunits. The α subunit of CG is essentially identical to the α subunits of the human pituitary gonadotropins, luteinizing hormone and follicle-stimulating hormone, as well as to the α subunit of human TSH; however, the β subunit of CG differs in amino acid sequence from these other hormones.

Chorionic gonadotropin occurs as a white or practically white, amorphous powder and is freely soluble in water.

The action of HCG is virtually identical to that of pituitary LH, although HCG appears to have a small degree of FSH activity as well. It stimulates production of gonadal steroid hormones by stimulating the interstitial cells (Leydig cells) of the testis to produce androgens and the corpus luteum of the ovary to produce progesterone.

Androgen stimulation in the male leads to the development of secondary sex characteristics and may stimulate testicular descent when no anatomical impediment to descent is present. This descent may be reversible, on extremely rare occasions, when HCG is discontinued.

HCG has no known effect on fat mobilization, appetite or sense of hunger, or body fat distribution.

Following i.m. administration, an increase in serum chorionic gonadotropin concentrations may be observed within 2 hours. Peak concentrations occur within 6 hours and persist for approximately 36 hours. Serum chorionic gonadotropin levels begin to decline at 48 hours reaching undetectable levels after 72 hours. Chorionic gonadotropin is distributed primarily in the testes and ovaries of the male and female respectively, with small amounts possibly distributing into the proximal tubules of the renal cortex.

Blood levels of chorionic gonadotropin decline in a biphasic manner. The initial phase half-life has been reported between 5.6 and 11 hours, whereas the terminal phase half-life has been reported between 23 and 37.2 hours. Following i.m. administration of therapeutic doses, approximately 10 to 12% of the dose is excreted in the urine within 24 hours.

Indications: Prepubertal cryptorchidism not due to anatomical obstruction. In general, HCG is thought to induce testicular descent in situations when descent would have occurred at puberty. HCG thus may help predict whether or not orchiopexy will be needed in the future. Descent following HCG administration is usually permanent.

Selected cases of hypogonadotropic hypogonadism (hypogonadism secondary to a pituitary deficiency) in males.

Induction of ovulation and pregnancy in the anovulatory, infertile woman in whom the cause of anovulation is secondary and not due to primary ovarian failure, and who has been appropriately pretreated with human menotropins.

Note: HCG has not been demonstrated to be effective adjunctive therapy in the treatment of obesity. There is no substantial evidence that it increases weight loss beyond that resulting from caloric restriction, that it causes a more attractive or "normal" distribution of fat, or that it decreases the hunger and discomfort associated with calorie-restricted diets.

Contraindications: Precocious puberty, prostatic carcinoma or other androgen-dependent neoplasm, prior allergic reaction to HCG.

Warnings: HCG should be used in conjunction with human menopausal gonadotropins only by physicians experienced with infertility problems who are familiar with the criteria for patient selection, contraindications, warnings, precautions, and adverse reactions described in the package insert for menotropins.

The principal serious adverse reactions during this use are: ovarian hyperstimulation, a syndrome of sudden ovarian enlargement, ascites with or without pain, and/or pleural effusion; rupture of ovarian cysts with resultant hemoperitoneum; multiple births; and arterial thromboembolism.

Precautions: Induction of androgen secretion by HCG may induce precocious puberty in patients treated for cryptorchidism. Therapy should be discontinued if signs of precocious puberty occur.

Since androgens may cause fluid retention, HCG should be used with caution in patients with cardiac or renal disease, epilepsy, migraine, or asthma.

Adverse Effects: Headache, irritability, restlessness, depression, fatigue, edema, precocious puberty, gynecomastia, pain at the injection site.

Ovarian cancer has been reported in a very small number of infertile women who have been treated with fertility drugs. A causal relationship between treatment with fertility drugs and ovarian cancer has not been established.

Dosage: For i.m. use only after reconstitution of the dry powder with the sterile diluent. Although the dosage regimen will depend upon the indication, the patient's age and weight, and the prescriber's preference, the following regimens have been advocated by various authorities.

Males: Prepubertal Cryptorchidism Not Due To Anatomical Obstruction: 4 000 USP units, 3 times weekly, for 2 to 3 weeks, or 1 000 USP units, 3 times weekly for 6 to 8 weeks. The dosage schedule may vary to some extent, depending upon the age when treatment is given. If the dosage is adequate, there will usually be some indication, following one such course of therapy, whether descent will occur or surgery be required.

A therapeutic trial with chorionic gonadotropin may constitute a valuable diagnostic aid to determine the need for surgery. Lack of response is usually an indication of anatomic obstruction. Furthermore, when surgery is required, the preliminary treatment may facilitate the procedure by increasing the size of the testes and the length of the cords. Postoperative gonadotropic therapy has also been suggested to prevent retraction of testes.

Age of Initiation of Treatment: Various ages ranging from early childhood to immediately before expected puberty have been suggested. The average appropriate age, however, appears to be 12 years.

Selected Cases of Hypogonadotropic Hypogonadism in Males: 4 000 to 5 000 USP units 3 times weekly for 6 to 8 weeks with a rest period of 2 to 3 weeks between courses of therapy.

Females: Induction of ovulation and pregnancy in the anovulatory infertile woman in whom the cause of anovulation is secondary and not due to primary ovarian failure and who has been appropriately pretreated with human menotropins (see prescribing information for menotropins for dosage and administration for that drug product).

5 000 to 10 000 USP units 1 day following the last dose of menotropins. (A dosage of 10 000 USP units is recommended in the labeling of menotropins.)

Directions for Reconstitution: Reconstitute chorionic gonadotropin for injection to the desired concentration by addition of the required amount of the solvent supplied. Remove 1 to 10 mL of the solvent and add to the vial with the lyophilized powder; agitate gently until the powder is completely dissolved.

When reconstituted with 10 mL of the solvent, the concentration of chorionic gonadotropin is 1 000 USP units/mL. The solvent contains benzyl alcohol 0.9%.

Supplied: Each package contains 2 vials: one multidose vial of Pregnyl 10 000 USP units plus 1 vial of 10 mL sterile Pregnyl solvent. Each vial of Pregnyl contains: sterile lyophilized human chorionic gonadotropin 10 000 USP units. Nonmedicinal ingredients: dibasic sodium phosphate anhydrous (pH may have been adjusted with sodium hydroxide and/or phosphoric acid) and monobasic sodium phosphate monohydrate. Each vial of Pregnyl solvent contains: Bacteriostatic Water for Injection 10 mL, benzyl alcohol 0.9%, sodium chloride 0.56% and trace amounts of sodium hydroxide and/or hydrochloric acid.

Store at 15 to 30°C. Reconstituted solution is stable for 30 days when refrigerated (2 to 8°C).

New Product 1998

PREMARIN® INTRAVENOUS
Wyeth-Ayerst

Conjugated Estrogens
Estrogen

Supplied: Each vial contains: conjugated estrogens, CSD 25 mg, in a sterile lyophilized cake. Nonmedicinal ingredients: hydrochloric acid, lactose, simethicone, sodium citrate and sodium hydroxide. The pH is adjusted to 7.3 with sodium hydroxide or hydrochloric acid. The reconstituted solution is suitable for i.v. or i.m. injection.

PREMARIN® TABLETS
Wyeth-Ayerst

Conjugated Estrogens
Estrogenic Hormones

Pharmacology: Estrogen drug products act by regulating the transcription of a limited number of genes. They may act directly at the cell's surface via non "estrogen receptor" mechanism or directly with the estrogen receptor inside the cell. Estrogens diffuse through cell membranes, distribute themselves throughout the cell, and bind to and activate the nuclear estrogen receptor, a DNA-binding protein which is found in estrogen-responsive tissues. The activated estrogen receptor binds to specific DNA sequences, or hormone-response elements, which enhance the transcription of adjacent genes and in turn lead to the observed effects. Estrogen receptors have been identified in the wall of blood vessels, in tissues of the reproductive tract, breast, pituitary, hypothalamus, liver, and bone of women.

Estrogens are important in the development and maintenance of the female reproductive system and secondary sex characteristics. By a direct action, they cause growth and development of the uterus, fallopian tubes, and vagina. With other hormones, such as pituitary hormones and progesterone, they cause enlargement of the breasts through promotion of ductal growth, stromal development, and the accretion of fat. Estrogens are intricately involved with other hormones, especially progesterone, in the processes of the ovulatory menstrual cycle and pregnancy, and affect the release of pituitary gonadotropins. They also contribute to the shaping of the skeleton, maintenance of tone and elasticity of urogenital structures, changes in the epiphyses of the long bones that allow for the pubertal growth spurt and its termination, and pigmentation of the nipples and genitals.

Estrogens occur naturally in several forms. The primary source of estrogen in normally cycling adult women is the ovarian follicle, which secretes 70 to 500 μg of estradiol daily, depending on the phase of the menstrual cycle. This is converted primarily to estrone, which circulates in roughly equal proportion to estradiol, and to small amounts of estriol. After menopause, most endogenous estrogen is produced by conversion of androstenedione, secreted by the adrenal cortex, to estrone by peripheral tissues. Thus, estrone—especially in its sulfate ester form—is the most abundant circulating estrogen in postmenopausal women. Although circulating estrogens exist in a dynamic equilibrium of metabolic interconversions, estradiol is the principal intracellular human estrogen and is substantially more potent than estrone or estriol at the receptor.

Conjugated estrogens used in therapy are soluble in water and are well absorbed from the gastrointestinal tract after release from the drug formulation. However, Premarin contains a modified-release formulation of conjugated estrogens that slowly releases estrogens over several hours.

Estrogens used in therapy are also well absorbed through the skin and mucous membranes. When applied for a local action, absorption is usually sufficient to cause systemic effects. When conjugated with aryl and alkyl groups for parenteral administration, the rate of absorption of oily preparations is slowed with a prolonged duration of action, such that a single i.m. injection of estradiol valerate or estradiol cypionate is absorbed over several weeks.

Administered estrogens and their esters are handled within the body essentially the same way as the endogenous hormones. Metabolic conversion of estrogens occurs primarily in the liver (first pass effect), but also at local target tissue sites. Complex metabolic processes result in a dynamic equilibrium of circulating conjugated and unconjugated estrogenic forms which are continually interconverted, especially between estrone and estradiol and between esterified and nonesterified forms. Although naturally occurring estrogens circulate in the

Premarin Tablets (cont'd)

blood largely bound to sex hormone-binding globulin (SHBG) and albumin, only unbound estrogens enter target tissue cells. A significant proportion of the circulating estrogen exists as sulfate conjugates, especially estrone sulfate, which serves as a circulating reservoir for the formation of more active estrogenic species. A certain proportion of the estrogen is excreted into the bile, then reabsorbed from the intestine and returned to the liver through the portal venous system. During this enterohepatic recirculation, estrogens are desulfated and resulfated and undergo degradation through conversion to less active estrogens (estriol and other estrogens), oxidation to nonestrogenic substances (catecholestrogens, which interact with catecholamine metabolism, especially in the CNS), and conjugation with glucuronic acids (which are then rapidly excreted in the urine).

When given orally, naturally occurring estrogens and their esters are extensively metabolized (first pass effect) and circulate primarily as estrone sulfate, with smaller amounts of other conjugated and unconjugated estrogenic species. This results in limited oral potency. By contrast, synthetic estrogens, such as ethinyl estradiol and the nonsteroidal estrogens, are degraded very slowly in the liver and other tissues, which results in their high intrinsic potency. Estrogen drug products administered by nonoral routes while not subject to true "first-pass" metabolism, do undergo significant hepatic uptake, metabolism, and enterohepatic recycling.

Indications: The relief of menopausal and postmenopausal symptoms occurring in naturally or surgically induced estrogen deficiency states including vulvar and vaginal atrophy.

The prevention and treatment of osteoporosis in naturally occurring or surgically induced estrogen-deficiency states. This is in addition to other important therapeutic measures such as adequate diet and regular exercise. In postmenopausal women already diagnosed as having osteoporosis and vertebral fractures, treatment with conjugated estrogens may prevent further loss of bone mass. Even when started as late as 6 years after menopause, estrogen prevents further loss of bone mass for as long as the treatment is continued. When estrogen therapy is discontinued, bone mass declines at a rate comparable to that of the immediate postmenopausal period.

Hypoestrogenism due to hypogonadism, castration, or primary ovarian failure.

Atrophic vaginitis.

Vulvar atrophy (with or without pruritus).

In patients with an intact uterus, conjugated estrogens should always be supplemented by administration of a progestin whose role is to prevent endometrial hyperplasia.

Contraindications: In patients with any of the following conditions: personal history of known or suspected estrogen-dependent neoplasia such as breast or endometrial cancer; undiagnosed abnormal vaginal bleeding; known or suspected pregnancy; active hepatic dysfunction or disease, especially of the obstructive type; active thrombophlebitis, thrombosis, or thromboembolic disorders; endometrial hyperplasia.

Premarin tablets should not be used in patients hypersensitive to their ingredients.

Warnings: There is evidence from several studies that estrogens, unopposed by progestins increase the risk of carcinoma of the endometrium in humans. The incidence of endometrial hyperplasia is reported to be lowered with coadministration of a progestin (see Dosage).

In some studies, women on estrogen replacement therapy, given alone or in combination with a progestin, have been reported to have an increased risk of thrombophlebitis, and/or thromboembolic disease. The physician should be aware of the possibility of thrombotic disorders (including thrombophlebitis, retinal thrombosis, cerebral embolism, and pulmonary embolism) during estrogen replacement therapy and alert to their earliest manifestations. Should any of these occur or be suspected, estrogen replacement therapy should be discontinued immediately. Patients who have risk factors for thrombotic disorders should be kept under careful observation.

Breast cancer is a multifactorial disease, which increases in frequency with age. Much of the etiology of breast cancer is unknown. Some published epidemiological studies have documented an association between a modest increase in the risk of developing breast cancer and the use of hormone replacement therapy in menopause when given for periods exceeding 10 years. Information is still lacking to show whether the risks of combination estrogen-progestin therapy differ from those of estrogen used alone. There is a need for caution in prescribing estrogens for women with a strong family history of breast cancer or who present breast nodules, fibrocystic disease of the breast, or abnormal mammograms. Other known risk factors for the development of breast cancer such as nulliparity, obesity, early menarche, late age at first full-term pregnancy and at menopause should also be evaluated. It is recommended that a mammography be performed before starting treatment and repeated at regular intervals in patients at high risk for breast cancer.

Precautions: Before conjugated estrogens are administered, the patient should have a complete physical examination including blood pressure determination. (There is no evidence that elevation of blood pressure may occur with use of estrogens in the menopause). Breasts and pelvic organs should be examined and a Papanicolaou smear should be taken.

The first follow-up examination should be done within 6 months of initiation of treatment. Thereafter, examinations should be made once a year and should include those procedures outlined above. Patients should be encouraged to practice frequent self-examination of the breasts.

If unexpected or abnormal vaginal bleeding occurs during therapy, diagnostic aspiration biopsy or curettage should be performed to rule out the possibility of uterine malignancy.

Diabetic patients or those with a predisposition to diabetes should be observed closely to detect any alterations in carbohydrate metabolism.

When liver or endocrine function tests are indicated, or surgical procedures are performed, the laboratory should be advised of the patient's therapy before specimens are forwarded.

Estrogen may cause sodium and water retention. Therefore, particular caution is indicated in cardiac or renal dysfunction, epilepsy, or asthma.

Pre-existing uterine leiomyomata may increase in size during estrogen use.

In patients with familial defects of lipoprotein metabolism, estrogen therapy may be associated with massive elevations of plasma triglycerides leading to pancreatitis and other complications.

A 2- to 4-fold increase in the risk of surgically confirmed gallbladder disease has been reported in postmenopausal women receiving oral estrogens.

Because the prolonged use of estrogens influences the metabolism of calcium and phosphorus, estrogens should be used with caution in patients with metabolic and malignant bone diseases associated with hypercalcemia and in patients with renal insufficiency.

Pregnancy: Estrogen therapy during pregnancy is associated with an increased risk of fetal congenital reproductive-tract disorders. In females there is an increased risk of vaginal adenosis, squamous cell dysplasia of the cervix, and cancer later in life; in the male, of urogenital abnormalities. Although some of these changes are benign, it is not known whether they are precursors of malignancy.

If feasible, estrogens should be discontinued at least 4 weeks before surgery or during periods of prolonged immobilization since they may be associated with an increased risk of thromboembolism.

Drug Interactions: Estrogens may diminish the effectiveness of anticoagulants, antidiabetic and antihypertensive agents. Preparations affecting liver enzymes (e.g., barbiturates, hydantoins, carbamazepine, meprobamate, phenylbutazone or rifampin) may interfere with the activity of orally administered estrogens.

Laboratory Tests: Certain endocrine and liver function tests may be affected by estrogen-containing products: Increased sulfobromophthalein retention. Increased prothrombin time and partial thromboplastin time; increased levels of fibrinogen and fibrinogen activity; increased coagulation factors VII, VIII, IX, X; increased norepinephrine-induced platelet aggregability; decreased antithrombin III. Increased thyroxin-binding globulin (TBG), leading to increased circulating total thyroid hormone (T_1) as measured by T_4 levels determined either by column or radioimmunoassay; free T_3 resin uptake is decreased, reflecting the elevated TBG; free T_4 concentration is unaltered. Other binding proteins may be elevated in serum, i.e., corticosteroid binding globulin (CBG), sex-hormone binding globulin (SHBG), leading to increased circulating corticosteroids and sex steroids respectively; free or biologically active hormone concentrations are unchanged. Reduced response to the metyrapone test. Reduced serum folate concentration. Increased serum triglyceride and phospholipid concentration, increased plasma HDL and HDL-2 subfraction concentrations, reduced LDL cholesterol concentration, increased triglyceride levels. Impaired glucose tolerance.

The interpretation of the above laboratory tests should take into consideration whether or not the woman has taken estrogen therapy. The pathologist should be informed that the patient is receiving estrogen therapy when relevant specimens are submitted.

Adverse Effects: The most serious adverse reactions associated with the use of estrogens and progestogens are indicated under Warnings and Precautions.

The following additional adverse reactions have been reported with estrogen therapy: Cardiovascular: venous thromboembolism; pulmonary thromboembolism.
Genitourinary: changes in vaginal bleeding pattern and abnormal withdrawal bleeding or flow; breakthrough bleeding, spotting; increase in size of uterine leiomyomata; vaginal candidiasis; change in amount of cervical secretion.
Breasts: tenderness, enlargement.
Gastrointestinal: nausea, vomiting; abdominal cramps, bloating; cholestatic jaundice; increased incidence of gallbladder disease; pancreatitis.
Skin: chloasma or melasma that may persist when drug is discontinued; erythema multiforme; erythema nodosum; hemorrhagic eruption; loss of scalp hair; hirsutism.
Eyes: steepening of corneal curvature; intolerance to contact lenses.
CNS: headache, migraine, dizziness; mental depression; chorea.
Miscellaneous: increase or decrease in weight; reduced carbohydrate tolerance; aggravation of porphyria; edema; changes in libido.

Overdose: Symptoms and Treatment: Serious ill effects have not been reported following acute ingestion of large doses of estrogen-containing oral contraceptives by young children.

Overdosage of estrogen may cause nausea and vomiting, and withdrawal bleeding may occur in females. All of the ingested drug should be removed by gastric lavage and symptomatic treatment given.

Dosage: Administration: Conjugated estrogens therapy may be given continuously with no interruption in therapy, or in cyclical regimens (regimens such as 25 days on drug followed by 5 days off drug) as is medically appropriate on an individualized basis.

Continuous, noncyclic therapy may be indicated in hysterectomized women or in cases where the signs and symptoms of estrogen deficiency become problematic during the treatment-free interval. In women with an intact uterus, a progestin should be coadministered for a **minimum** of 10, but preferably at least 12 to 14 days per cycle to avoid overstimulation of the endometrium. In addition, progestin should be administered to minimize the occurrence of endometrial hyperplasia. Unexpected or abnormal vaginal bleeding in such patients requires institution of prompt diagnostic measures, such as endometrial biopsy or curettage to rule out the possibility of uterine malignancy. Since progestins are administered to reduce the risk of hyperplastic changes of the endometrium, patients without a uterus do not require a progestin for this purpose.
Usual Dosage Range: Menopausal Symptoms: 0.625 to 1.25 mg daily, cyclically or continuously as is medically required. Adjust dosage upward or downward according to severity of symptoms and response of the patient. For maintenance, adjust dosage to lowest level providing effective control.
Osteoporosis (loss of bone mass): 0.625 mg daily.
Hypoestrogenism Due To: A. Female Hypogonadism: 0.3 mg to 0.625 mg daily, administered cyclically (e.g., 3 weeks on and 1 week off) or continuously as required. Doses are adjusted depending on the severity of symptoms and responsiveness of the endometrium.
B. Female Castration or Primary Ovarian Failure: 1.25 mg daily, cyclically or continuously as required. Adjust dosage upward or downward according to severity of symptoms and response of the patient. For maintenance, adjust dosage to lowest level that will provide effective control.
Atrophic Vaginitis: 0.3 mg to 1.25 mg daily depending upon the tissue response of the individual patient. Administer cyclically or continuously as required.
Vulvar Atrophy: 0.3 mg to 1.25 mg daily depending upon the tissue response of the individual patient. Administer cyclically or continuously as required.

Information for the Patient: See Blue Section—Information for the Patient "Premarin Tablets".

Supplied: 0.3 mg: Each green, oval, sugar-coated tablet imprinted with "Premarin" contains: conjugated estrogens CDS 0.3 mg. Nonmedicinal ingredients: calcium phosphate tribasic, calcium sulfate anhydrous, carnauba wax, D&C Yellow No. 10, edible ink, FD&C Blue No. 1, FD&C Yellow No. 6, glyceryl monooleate, lactose, magnesium stearate, methylcellulose, methylparaben, microcrystalline cellulose, polyethylene glycol, polysorbate 60, polyvinylpyrrolidone, propylparaben, shellac, sodium benzoate, sucrose, sucrose syrup and titanium dioxide. Energy: 4.19 kJ (1.0 kcal)/0.3 mg. Sodium: <1 mmol (0.024 mg)/ 0.3 mg. Alcohol-, gluten-, sulfite- and tartrazine-free. Bottles of 100 and 500. Blister cards of 25 and 30.

0.625 mg: Each maroon, oval, sugar-coated tablet imprinted with "Premarin" contains: conjugated estrogens CDS 0.625 mg. Nonmedicinal ingredients: calcium phosphate tribasic, calcium sulfate anhydrous, carnauba wax, edible ink, FD&C Blue No. 2, FD&C Red No. 3, FD&C Yellow No. 6, glyceryl monooleate, gum acacia, lactose, magnesium stearate, methylcellulose, microcrystalline cellulose, polyethylene glycol, polysorbate 60, propylparaben, shellac, sodium benzoate, sucrose, sucrose syrup and titanium dioxide. Energy: 4.19 kJ (1.0 kcal)/0.625 mg. Sodium: <1 mmol (0.0001 mg)/ 0.625 mg. Alcohol-, gluten-, sulfite- and tartrazine-free. Bottles of 100 and 1 000. Blister cards of 25 and 30.

0.9 mg: Each pink, oval, sugar-coated tablet imprinted with "Premarin" contains: conjugated estrogens CDS 0.9 mg. Nonmedicinal ingredients: calcium phosphate tribasic, calcium sulfate anhydrous, carnauba wax, edible ink, FD&C Blue No. 2, FD&C Red No. 3, glyceryl monooleate, lactose, magnesium stearate, methylcellulose, microcrystalline cellulose, polyethylene glycol, polysorbate 60, propylparaben, shellac, sucrose and titanium dioxide. Energy: 4.19 kJ (1.0 kcal)/0.9 mg. Sodium: <1 mmol (0.661 mg)/ 0.9 mg. Alcohol-, gluten-, sulfite- and tartrazine-free. Bottles of 100. Blister cards of 25 and 30.

1.25 mg: Each yellow, oval, sugar-coated tablet imprinted with "Premarin" contains: conjugated estrogens CDS 1.25 mg. Nonmedicinal ingredients: calcium phosphate tribasic, calcium sulfate anhydrous, carnauba wax, D&C Yellow No. 10, edible ink, FD&C Yellow No. 6, glyceryl monooleate, lactose, magnesium stearate, methylcellulose, microcrystalline cellulose, polyethylene glycol, polysorbate 60, propylparaben, shellac, sucrose and titanium dioxide. Energy: 4.19 kJ (1.0 kcal)/1.25 mg. Sodium: <1 mmol (0.016 mg)/1.25 mg. Alcohol-, gluten-, sulfite- and tartrazine-free. Bottles of 100 and 1 000. Blister cards of 25 and 30.

(Shown in Product Recognition Section)

Reviewed 1999

PREMARIN® VAGINAL CREAM Ⓟ

Wyeth-Ayerst

Conjugated Estrogens

Vaginitis Therapy

Pharmacology: Conjugated estrogens are a mixture of estrogens obtained exclusively from natural sources occurring as the sodium salts of water-soluble estrogen sulfates blended to represent the average composition of material derived from pregnant mares' urine. It contains estrone, equilin, and 17α-dihydroequilin, together with smaller amounts of 17α-estradiol, equilenin, and 17α-dihydroequilenin as salts of their sulfate esters.

Metabolic and Somatic Effects: Estrogens are responsible for the development and maintenance of the female reproductive system and secondary sex characteristics. Estrogens cause growth and development of the vagina, uterus and fallopian tubes, and the enlargement of the breasts. Indirectly, estrogens contribute to the shaping of the skeleton, maintenance of tone and elasticity of urogenital structures, cause changes in the epiphyses of the long bones producing pubertal growth spurt and termination, axillary and pubic hair growth, and pigmentation of the nipples and genitals.

Estrogens affect calcium and phosphorus metabolism and are involved in maintaining normal bone structure. In prolonged estrogen deficiency states, the administration of estrogens may alter associated degenerative bone changes.

Effect on Menstruation: An ebb and rise of the female gonadal hormone produces the normal menstrual cycle. In the pre- and anovulatory cycle, estrogens are the primary determinants for the onset of menstruation. Estrogens do not induce ovulation. Estrogen levels rise during the first half of the menstrual cycle. At midpoint in the second half of the cycle, the corpus luteum produces high levels of both estrogens and progesterone. Decline of estrogenic activity at the end of the menstrual cycle commonly brings on menstruation, although the cessation of progesterone secretion is the most important factor in this phase of the mature ovulatory cycle.

Effects on Nervous System: Estrogens also affect the psychologic and emotional aspects of feminine behavior. As estrogen levels increase during the menstrual cycle, women experience a sense of well-being and vigor. In the postmenopausal period, after the decline of endogenous estrogen production, estrogen administration aids in relieving nervous symptoms, such as anxiety, depression and irritability.

Indications: The treatment of atrophic vaginitis, dyspareunia and kraurosis vulvae.

For many years it has been known that topical or vaginal estrogen therapy would stimulate cell growth and development, improving the epithelial thickness of the vaginal mucosa and increasing secretions. Recent reports have shown that the intravaginal use of topical estrogen creams produces even higher blood estrogen levels than comparable oral doses. Therefore, precautions recommended with oral estrogen administration should also be observed with this route.

Contraindications: Estrogens should not be administered to patients with active hepatic dysfunction or disease, especially of the obstructive type; or a personal history of breast or endometrial cancer, except in special circumstances, or in patients with endometrial hyperplasia unless a progestogen is administered concomitantly.

Premarin is also contraindicated in the following situations: undiagnosed vaginal bleeding; a history of cerebrovascular accident, coronary thrombosis, or in the presence of classical migraine; a history of thrombophlebitis or thromboembolic disease; partial or complete loss of vision or diplopia due to ophthalmic vascular disease; when *pregnancy* is suspected.

Warnings: Before administration the patient should have a complete physical examination including blood pressure determination. Breasts, and pelvic organs should be examined and a Papanicolaou smear taken.

The first followup examination should be done preferably within 6 months after initiation of treatment. Thereafter, examinations should be made once a year and should include those procedures outlined above.

If any surgical procedures are performed, the pathologist should be advised of the patient's therapy when specimens are sent for examination. Liver function tests should be made periodically in subjects who have, or are suspected of having, hepatic disease.

If abnormal vaginal bleeding occurs during therapy, diagnostic aspiration biopsy or curettage should be performed to rule out the possibility of uterine malignancy.

Although the estrogen content or oral contraceptive therapy has been associated with an increased risk of various thromboembolic, thrombotic and vascular diseases, to date no such increased risk in postmenopausal users of estrogens has been detected. Nevertheless, the physician should be alert to the earliest manifestations of thrombotic disorders (thrombophlebitis, retinal thrombosis, cerebral embolism, and pulmonary embolism). If these occur or are suspected, estrogen therapy should be discontinued immediately.

In patients with metastatic carcinoma and hypercalcemia, estrogen medication should be used with caution.

Three independent retrospective studies have reported an association between postmenopausal oral estrogen therapy and an increased risk of endometrial carcinoma. These studies, however, lacked information regarding certain important intrinsic risk factors of the patients (especially pretreatment endogenous hormonal status) and the mode of administration of estrogen. The potential relationship of estrogen to endometrial carcinoma under clinical conditions has to be considered. However, a cause and effect relationship between estrogen administration and endometrial carcinoma cannot be established by these data at this time.

Precautions: Estrogen may cause sodium and water retention. Where this may be undesirable such as in cardiac or renal dysfunction, epilepsy, or asthma, particular caution is indicated.

Development or sudden enlargement, pain, or tenderness of uterine fibroids requires discontinuation of medication.

Elevation of blood pressure in previously normotensive or hypertensive patients generally necessitates cessation of therapy.

Diabetic patients or those with a predisposition to diabetes should be observed closely to detect any alterations in carbohydrate metabolism.

When liver or endocrine function tests are indicated, the results should not be considered reliable unless therapy has been discontinued for 2 to 4 months.

Note: Preliminary studies conducted by the Health Protection Branch have demonstrated that Premarin cream may react with the latex rubber of certain mechanical barrier devices used for prevention of sexually transmitted diseases and pregnancy (diaphragms and condoms).

Adverse Effects: The following adverse reactions have been reported with the use of estrogens in general. Some of these (indicated in brackets) have been documented with oral contraceptives specifically, and have not, to date been associated with cyclic menopausal or postmenopausal conjugated estrogen therapy.

Gastrointestinal: nausea, (anorexia, vomiting, abdominal cramps, bloating), cholestatic jaundice and increase in body weight.

Genitourinary: sodium and water retention, breakthrough bleeding, spotting and withdrawal bleeding, increased cervical mucus, endometrial hyperplasia, reactivation of endometriosis, (cystitis-like syndrome).

Endocrine and Metabolic: breast swelling and tenderness, increased blood sugar levels, and decreased glucose tolerance; in males—gynecomastia, reduced potency, and feminization.

CNS: headaches, increase or decrease of libido, (mental depression, nervousness, dizziness, fatigue, irritability).

Dermatologic hypersensitivity: allergic reactions and rashes, chloasma, (loss of scalp hair, hemorrhagic eruption, itching, erythema nodosum and erythema multiforme, pigmentation of the skin).

Cardiovascular: an increase in blood pressure in susceptible individuals and aggravation of migraine headaches.

Hematologic: A statistically significant association has been demonstrated between the use of oral contraceptive preparations containing estrogens and the following serious reactions: thrombophlebitis, pulmonary embolism and cerebral thrombosis. Although available evidence is suggestive of an association, such a relationship has been neither confirmed nor refuted for the following serious reactions: coronary thrombosis and neuro-ocular lesions (e.g. retinal thrombosis and optic neuritis); altered coagulation tests (increase in prothrombin and Factors VII, VIII, IX, X).

Overdose: Symptoms and Treatment: Excessive doses may result in nausea, vomiting and abdominal cramps, headache, dizziness and general malaise. Treatment should be discontinued and symptomatic treatment given.

Dosage: Administered cyclically for short-term use only: For the treatment of atrophic vaginitis, dyspareunia or kraurosis vulvae.

In patients with severe cases of atrophic vaginitis, the mucosa should first be conditioned with a short course of oral therapy, 1.25 mg daily for approximately 10 days. Vaginal treatment should be instituted at the lowest effective dosage, and the requirement for estrogen therapy reassessed regularly. In patients already receiving oral therapy, the oral dosage may be reduced taking into account the potential absorption from the vaginal medication. The degree of atrophy is directly responsible for the level of absorption and should be the guiding factor in dose adjustment.

Two to 4 g daily, intravaginally or topically, depending on the severity of the condition. Administration should be cyclic (e.g. 3 weeks on and 1 week off).

Appropriate diagnostic measures should be taken to rule out malignancy in the event of persistent or recurring abnormal vaginal bleeding.

Supplied: Each g of white, vaginal cream contains: 625 μg (0.625 mg) of conjugated estrogens CSD in a nonliquefying cream base. Nonmedicinal ingredients: cetyl alcohol, cetyl esters wax, glycerin, glyceryl monostearate, methyl stearate, mineral oil light, phenylethyl alcohol, propylene glycol monostearate, sodium lauryl sulfate, water purified and white wax. Gluten-, paraben-, sugar-, sulfite- and tartrazine-free. Tubes of 42.5 g with calibrated plastic applicator.

PRENAVITE®

Roberts

Iron—Calcium—Vitamins

Prenatal Supplement With Folic Acid

Indications: As a dietary supplement to meet increased needs in pregnancy and lactation.

Contraindications: Hemosiderosis, hemochromatosis, hemolytic anemias.

Precautions: Neurologic involvement may develop or progress, despite temporary remission of anemia, in patients with pernicious anemia who receive more than 100 μg of folic acid per day and who are inadequately treated with vitamin B_{12}. Periodic examinations and laboratory studies of pernicious anemia patients are essential.

Oral iron containing preparations may aggravate existing peptic ulcer, regional enteritis and ulcerative colitis.

Prenavite (cont'd)

Iron compounds taken orally can impair the absorption of tetracycline antibiotics. Antacids given concomitantly with iron compounds decrease iron absorption.

Adverse Effects: Rarely, in iron sensitive patients, mild gastrointestinal upsets may occur.

Dosage: One tablet daily during pregnancy and lactation or as recommended by physician.

Supplied: Each small, pink, film-coated tablet contains: vitamin A (acetate) 4 000 IU, vitamin D 400 IU, vitamin C 100 mg, folic acid 1.0 mg, iron (ferrous fumarate) 50 mg and calcium (calcium carbonate) 125 mg. Energy: 0.4 kJ (0.1 kcal). Sodium: <1 mmol (15 mg). Lactose- and tartrazine-free. Bottles of 60.

PREPARATION H® CLEANSING PADS
PREPARATION H® COOLING GEL
PREPARATION H® CREAM
PREPARATION H® OINTMENT
PREPARATION H® SUPPOSITORIES

Whitehall-Robins

Hamamelis Water—Glycerin
Phenylephrine HCl—Hamamelis Water
Live Yeast Derivative (Bio-Dyne)—Shark Liver Oil
Live Yeast Derivative (Bio-Dyne)—Shark Liver Oil
Live Yeast Derivative (Bio-Dyne)—Shark Liver Oil

Hemorrhoid Therapy—Anal Hygiene
Hemorrhoidal Treatment

Indications: Cleansing Pads: hemorrhoidal, toilet tissue irritation, anal cleansing wipe, everyday hygiene of the outer vaginal area, final cleansing step at diaper changing time.
Ointment/Cream/Suppositories/Cooling Gel: To help shrink swelling of hemorrhoidal tissues caused by inflammation and to give prompt temporary relief from pain and itching. Preparation H is of considerable value as a lubricant in easing painful bowel movements by protecting and soothing the painful area.

Precautions: In case of bleeding or if irritation/condition persists, patient should be instructed to discontinue use and contact physician.

Dosage: Cleansing Pads: As a personal wipe—use as a final cleansing step after regular toilet tissue, or instead of. As a compress, hemorrhoid sufferers will get additional relief by using cleansing pads as a compress. Fold pad and hold in contact with inflamed anal tissue for 15 to 30 minutes. Repeat several times daily while inflammation lasts.
Ointment/Cream/Cooling Gel: Apply freely night, morning, after each bowel movement and whenever symptoms occur. Lubricate applicator before each application and thoroughly cleanse after use.
Suppositories: Remove wrapper and insert one suppository night, morning, after each bowel movement and whenever symptoms occur. Store at controlled room temperature in a cool place, but not over 26°C.

Supplied: Cleansing Pads: Each pad contains: hamamelis water 50% and glycerin 10%. Nonmedicinal ingredients: DMDM hydantoin, paraben, octoxynol-9 and water. Jars of 40.

Cooling Gel: Each tube contains: phenylephrine HCl 0.25% w/w and hamamelis water 50% w/w in a nonstaining clear gel base. Nonmedicinal ingredients: edetate disodium, hydroxyethyl cellulose, parabens, propylene glycol, sodium citrate, sodium metabisulfite and water. Tubes of 25 and 50 g.

Cream: Each tube contains: yeast as a live cell derivative (Bio-Dyne: Skin Respiratory Factor) 1% and shark liver oil 3% in a nonstaining cream base. Nonmedicinal ingredients: butylated hydroxyanisole, cellulose, cetyl alcohol, citric acid, disodium edetate, glycerin, glyceryl monostearate, glycerol oleate, lanolin, parabens, propyl gallate, petrolatum, propylene glycol, simethicone emulsion, sodium benzoate, sodium lauryl sulfate, stearyl alcohol, water and xanthan gum. Tubes of 25 and 50 g.

Ointment: Each tube contains: yeast as a live cell derivative (Bio-Dyne: Skin Respiratory Factor) 1% and shark liver oil 3%. Nonmedicinal ingredients: chlorhexidine gluconate, falba, flavor, lanolin, mineral oil and petrolatum. Tubes of 25, 50 and 75 g.

Suppositories: Each 2.2 g individually wrapped suppository contains: yeast as a live cell derivative (Bio-Dyne: Skin Respiratory Factor) 22 mg (1%) and shark liver oil 66 mg (3%). Nonmedicinal ingredients: chlorhexidine gluconate, cocoa butter, D&C Red No. 33, D&C Yellow No. 10, FD&C Blue No. 1, FD&C Yellow No. 6, glycerin, polyethylene glycol, wax and witepsol. Packages of 12, 24, 36 and 48.

PRE-PEN® ℞

Rivex Pharma

Benzylpenicilloyl-Polylysine

Diagnostic—Penicillin Allergy

Pharmacology: The major antigenic determinant of penicillin hypersensitivity is the penicilloyl group, a degradation product of penicillin. Pre-Pen reacts specifically with penicilloyl skin sensitizing antibodies (reagins) to produce immediate wheal and flare reactions which may reflect increased risk of allergic reactions to subsequent penicillin therapy.

Indications: As a skin test reagent for the detection of penicilloyl reagins. Use is indicated whenever there is a need to determine the presence or absence of these reagins. Prospective skin testing in patients with known or possible histories of penicillin intolerance may be useful for assessing the allergic status. Retrospective skin testing may also be useful in determining if a prior drug reaction may have been due to penicillin exposure. Pre-Pen skin testing may be useful in patients undergoing allergy evaluations where exposure to penicillin in the environment may be a factor.

Contraindications: Skin testing for detection of reagin with specific haptenes is never without risk. Skin testing patients known to be extremely hypersensitive to penicillin should not be done unless there is a very strong medical reason for administering penicillin.

Warnings: There are insufficient data to assess the potential danger of sensitization to repeated skin testing with Pre-Pen. Rarely, a systemic allergic reaction may follow a skin test with Pre-Pen. This can be avoided by making the first application by scratch test and very carefully following the instructions in administering the intradermal test, using the intradermal route only if the scratch test has been entirely negative. Skin testing with penicillin and/or other penicillin-derived reagents should not be performed simultaneously.

Precautions: There are insufficient data derived from well-controlled studies to determine the value of the Pre-Pen skin test as a means of assessing the risk of administering therapeutic penicillin in the following situations: adult patients who give no history of clinical penicillin hypersensitivity; pediatric patients.

In addition, there are no data at present to assess the clinical value of Pre-Pen where exposure to penicillin is suspected as a cause of a drug reaction and in patients who are undergoing routine allergy evaluation.

Furthermore, there are no data relating the clinical value of Pre-Pen skin tests to the risk of administering semi-synthetic penicillins and cephalosporin-derived antibiotics.

Recognition that the following clinical outcomes are possible makes it imperative for the physician to weigh risk to benefit in every instance where the decision to administer or not to administer penicillin is based in part on a Pre-Pen skin test: an allergic reaction to therapeutic penicillin may occur in a patient with a negative skin test to Pre-Pen; it is possible for a patient to have an anaphylactic reaction to therapeutic penicillin in the presence of a negative Pre-Pen skin test and a negative history of clinical penicillin hypersensitivity; if penicillin is the absolute drug of choice in a life-threatening situation, successful desensitization with therapeutic penicillin may be possible irrespective of a positive skin test and/or a positive history of clinical penicillin hypersensitivity.

Pregnancy: Animal reproduction studies have not been conducted with Pre-Pen. It is not known whether it can cause fetal harm when administered to a pregnant woman or can affect reproduction capacity. The hazards of skin testing in such patients should be weighed against the hazards of penicillin therapy without skin testing.

Adverse Effects: Urticaria, generalized pruritus, local swelling, generalized flushing, anaphylaxis, bronchospasm, fainting and maculopapular eruption. The overall incidence of such reactions appears to be less than 1 in 1 000. There is indication, however, that the incidence is higher in patients with a history of penicillin intolerance.

Dosage: Skin testing is usually performed on the inner volar surface of the forearm. The skin test material may be applied by the scratch technique or by intradermal injection. (It is particularly desirable to start with a scratch test.) If the scratch test produces a positive reaction, it is not necessary or desirable to do the intradermal test. If no reaction occurs to the scratch test within 5 minutes, the intradermal test should be performed. There is sufficient material in the ampul to perform both tests.

Using a tuberculin syringe with a 26 gauge needle, withdraw the contents of the ampul. A drop is sufficient for the scratch test. At the appearance of a wheal and/or flare, the excess material should be wiped off to avoid a possible severe systemic reaction.

The intradermal test is performed by injecting not more than 0.03 mL of the material intradermally. It is important not to increase the volume of the injection, since tissue reaction to larger volumes can be confused and misinterpreted as weakly positive tests. Many allergists recommend injecting only enough material to make the smallest discernible bleb. Detection of skin response is facilitated if the size of the initial bleb is outlined on the skin with a fine-line ballpoint pen. Most skin reactions develop within 5 minutes, but patients who do not respond to the test should be observed for up to 20 minutes. Responses to Pre-Pen are graded as follows: (−) negative response: no increase in size of original bleb; (±) ambiguous response: wheal being only slightly larger than initial injection bleb, with or without accompanying erythematous flare; (+) positive response: marked increase in size of original bleb. Wheal may exceed 20 mm in diameter and exhibit pseudopodia.

It is desirable also to include a saline control to rule out skin reactions due to dermographia.

Supplied: Each single dose ampul contains: a sterile solution of benzylpenicilloyl-polylysine 0.20 mL in a concentration of 6.0×10^{-5} M (penicilloyl) in phosphate buffer 0.01 M and sodium chloride 0.15 M. Packages of 5.

Store in the refrigerator. Test materials subjected to ambient temperatures for over a day should be discarded.

PREPIDIL® GEL ℞

Pharmacia & Upjohn

Dinoprostone

Prostaglandin

Pharmacology: Dinoprostone gel, which contains a prostaglandin E_2 analogue as the active ingredient, causes cervical ripening preparatory to the onset of labor when it is administered endocervically. Although the local effects of prostaglandin E_2 on cervical maturation is not specifically known, experimental data indicates the drug enhances cervical hemodynamics which in turn promotes ripening of the cervix.

Indications: Administered to the cervical canal, for inducing cervical softening and dilatation of the cervix in pregnant women at or near term, where cervical features are not conducive to induction.

The use of the gel in this manner, in patients with unfavorable induction features prior to labor induction by conventional methods, has been shown to improve the overall outcome of labor induction attempt.

Contraindications: Endocervically administered dinoprostone gel is not recommended for use in the following: patients in whom oxytocic drugs are generally contraindicated or where prolonged contractions of the uterus are considered inappropriate. These include the following situations: patients with a history of cesarean section or major uterine surgery; patients with a major degree of cephalopelvic disproportion; patients with a history of difficult labor and/or traumatic delivery; grand multiparae with 6 or more previous term pregnancies; patients with suspected or clinically evident pre-existing fetal distress; patients with overdistention of the uterus (multiple pregnancy, polyhydramnios). Patients with ruptured membranes. Patients with known hypersensitivity to the prostaglandins. Patients with unexplained vaginal bleeding during this pregnancy. Patients with fetal malpresentation. Patients with gynecological, obstetrical or medical conditions that preclude vaginal delivery.

Dinoprostone gel should not be used simultaneously with other oxytocics (see Warnings).

Dinoprostone gel should not be used in patients with a history of epilepsy.

Warnings: Dinoprostone, like other effective oxytocic agents, should be used with strict adherence to recommended dosages, by medically trained personnel in hospital surroundings with appropriate obstetrical care facilities.

The use of oxytocin following pre-induction cervical ripening with dinoprostone gel has been studied. Prostaglandins may potentiate the effect of oxytocin on the uterus. Therefore, to preclude inappropriate augmentation of one oxytocic agent with another, it is recommended that induction with an oxytocic agent not be implemented until 6 to 12 hours after application of the gel for cervical ripening. Patients requiring oxytocin induction after administration should be carefully monitored.

Precautions: Prior to and during the use of dinoprostone uterine activity, fetal status and the character of the cervix (dilatation and effacement) should be carefully monitored to detect possible evidence of undesired responses. These include hypertonus, sustained uterine contractility or fetal distress. In cases where there is a known history of hypertonic uterine contractility or tetanic uterine contractions, it is recommended that uterine activity and the state of the fetus should be continuously monitored. The possibility of uterine rupture and/or cervical laceration should be born in mind where high-tone myometrial contractions are sustained.

Cephalopelvic relationships should be carefully evaluated before the use of dinoprostone.

Caution should be exercised in the administration of the gel in patients with the following medical conditions: asthma or a history of asthma; glaucoma or raised intraocular pressure.

Prolonged treatment of newborn infants with prostaglandin E_1 can induce proliferation of bone. There is no evidence that short term administration of prostaglandin E_2 can cause similar bone effects.

Caution should be taken not to administer dinoprostone gel above the level of the internal os. Placement of the gel into the extra-amniotic space has been associated with uterine hyperstimulation.

Patients with severe renal disease and/or severe hepatic disease accompanied by metabolic aberrations should be dosed with caution.

Drug Interactions: Dinoprostone, like all prostaglandins, may potentiate the uterine response to oxytocin. Patients requiring oxytocin induction, after pre-induction cervical ripening with dinoprostone, should be carefully monitored (see Warnings).

Adverse Effects: In clinical trials of dinoprostone gel the most commonly seen reactions were intrapartum fetal heart rate changes and unclassified fetal distress during or subsequent to gel administration. The adverse reaction incidences reported below are from the clinical trials (0.5 mg administered endocervically) in which oxytocin was used as the control. The control group had comparable incidences of adverse events. Fetal Effects (16%): intrapartum fetal heart rate changes and unclassified fetal distress during or subsequent to dinoprostone treatment (13%); uterine contractile abnormalities with fetal heart rate changes (3%); depressed neonates at birth (Apgar Scores below 7): 1 minute (13%) and 5 minutes (1%). Maternal Effects (10%): uterine contractile abnormalities without fetal heart rate changes (5%); vomiting and/or diarrhea (5%).

Overdose: Symptoms and Treatment: No cases of overdose have been reported. Should an overdose occur, any of the listed adverse reactions would be anticipated. Treatment of overdosage must be symptomatic at this time, since clinical studies with prostaglandin antagonists have not progressed to the point where recommendations may be made.

Dosage: The recommended dose is 0.5 mg. Each prefilled syringe contains 3 g (2.5 mL) of gel which, in turn contains 0.5 mg dinoprostone.

This product is intended for **single dose** administration.

Utilizing the catheter provided, administer the entire contents of the syringe by gentle expulsion into the cervical canal just below the level of the internal cervical os. Care should be taken not to administer the gel above the level of the internal os. Placement of the gel into the amniotic space has been associated with uterine hyperstimulation (see Precautions).

After placement of the gel, the patient should be instructed to remain in the dorsal position for 10 to 15 minutes to minimize gel leakage.

Supplied: Each prefilled syringe of translucent sterile gel with an accompanying catheter contains: dinoprostone 0.5 mg. Syringes of 3 g (2.5 mL). Nonmedicinal ingredients: colloidal silicon dioxide and triacetin. Available to hospitals only. This product has a shelf life of 24 months when stored at 4°C, under continuous refrigeration.

(Shown in Product Recognition Section)

PREPULSID® Ⓟ

Janssen-Ortho

Cisapride Monohydrate

Gastrointestinal Prokinetic Agent

Pharmacology: Cisapride is a gastrokinetic drug whose activity is considered to be due to enhancement of the physiological release of acetylcholine at the myenteric plexus.

Cisapride increases esophageal peristaltic activity and lower esophageal sphincter tone, thereby decreasing reflux of gastric contents into the esophagus and improving esophageal clearance. Gastric and duodenal emptying are also enhanced by cisapride as a consequence of increased gastric and duodenal contractility and antroduodenal coordination. Cisapride decreases duodenogastric reflux. It also enhances intestinal propulsive activity and improves both small and large bowel transit.

Cisapride lacks cholinomimetic effects and, therefore, does not increase basal or pentagastrin-induced gastric acid secretion. In vitro studies with animal tissues have shown that cisapride is a serotonin (5-HT_4) receptor agonist.

Pharmacokinetics: Following oral administration in man, cisapride is rapidly and completely absorbed. Peak plasma levels are attained within 1 or 2 hours. Plasma levels proportionally increase with oral doses from 5 to 20 mg. At steady-state, morning predose plasma levels and evening peak levels fluctuate between 10 to 20 ng/mL and 30 to 60 ng/mL respectively for 5 mg cisapride t.i.d., and between 20 to 40 ng/mL and 50 to 100 ng/mL for 10 mg t.i.d. The elimination half-life is 10 hours. Pharmacokinetics and steady-state levels are unrelated to the duration of treatment.

Cisapride is metabolized mainly by the cytochrome P450 3A4 enzyme. Cisapride undergoes extensive first-pass metabolism in the liver and in the gut wall. The main metabolic pathways are oxidative N-dealkylation and aromatic hydroxylation. The excretion of cisapride occurs mainly as metabolites in approximately the same amounts in urine and in feces. The excretion in maternal milk is limited.

Cisapride is extensively bound to plasma proteins (97.5%), mainly to albumin.

Indications: The symptomatic management of gastrointestinal motility disorders including: gastroesophageal reflux disease; gastroparesis, idiopathic or associated with diabetic neuropathy; and intestinal pseudo-obstruction.

Also for the prophylaxis of gastroesophageal reflux disease.

Contraindications: The concomitant oral or parenteral use of the following potent cytochrome P450 3A4 inhibiting drugs may lead to elevated cisapride blood levels and is contraindicated.

Antifungals: oral or i.v. fluconazole, itraconazole, ketoconazole.

Antibiotics: oral or i.v. erythromycin, clarithromycin.

Protease Inhibitors: ritonavir, indinavir (in vitro studies suggest that saquinavir is only a weak inhibitor).

Antidepressants: nefazodone.

Cisapride is also contraindicated for patients with: history of prolonged electrocardiographic QT intervals; renal failure; history of ventricular arrhythmias, ischemic heart disease, and congestive heart failure; uncorrected electrolyte disorders (hypokalemia, hypomagnesemia or in patients who might experience rapid reduction of plasma potassium such as those administered potassium-wasting diuretics and/or insulin in acute settings); respiratory failure; and concomitant medications known to prolong the QT interval and increase the risk of arrhythmia, such as certain antiarrhythmics, certain antipsychotics, certain antidepressants, astemizole and terfenadine.

The preceding lists of drugs are not comprehensive.

Cisapride is contraindicated in prematurely born infants (born at gestational age of less than 36 weeks), from 0 through 3 months after the delivery date.

Cisapride is contraindicated in patients with known sensitivity or intolerance to the drug.

Cisapride is contraindicated whenever gastrointestinal stimulation might be dangerous, i.e., gastrointestinal hemorrhage, mechanical obstruction or perforation. **(See also Warnings and Precautions, Drug Interactions.)**

Warnings: Serious cardiac arrhythmias including ventricular tachycardia, ventricular fibrillation, torsades de pointes, and QT prolongation have been reported in patients taking cisapride with other drugs that inhibit cytochrome P450 3A4. **Cisapride is contraindicated in patients taking any of these drugs.** Some of these contraindicated drugs are listed in the Contraindications section. Some of these patients did not have cardiac disease. However, most had been receiving multiple other medications and had pre-existing cardiac disease or risk factors for arrhythmias. QT prolongation, torsades de pointes (sometimes with syncope), cardiac arrest and sudden death have been reported in patients taking cisapride without the above-mentioned contraindicated drugs. Most patients had disorders that may have predisposed them to arrhythmias with cisapride. Some of these events have been fatal.

Cisapride is contraindicated in patients with the following risk factors for cardiac arrhythmia: uncorrected electrolyte disturbances (hypokalemia, hypomagnesemia such as seen in patients taking potassium-wasting diuretics, severe dehydration, vomiting, malnutrition, or in patients who might experience a rapid reduction of plasma potassium, such as insulin administered in acute settings), renal failure (particularly when on chronic dialysis), chronic obstructive pulmonary disease, respiratory failure, conditions associated with QT prolongation (such as congenital long QT syndrome, idiopathic QT prolongation, QT prolongation associated with diabetes mellitus, combination with medications known to prolong the QT interval), prolonged QT interval at baseline and history of significant cardiac disease (including serious ventricular arrhythmia, torsades de pointes, second or third degree AV block, congestive heart failure, ischemic heart disease and sinus node dysfunction).

Additionally, concomitant medications known to prolong the QT interval and increase the risk of arrhythmia, such as certain antiarrhythmics, including those of Class 1A (such as but not limited to quinidine and procainamide) and Class III (such as but not limited to amiodarone and sotalol); tricyclic antidepressants (such as but not limited to amitriptyline); certain tetracyclic antidepressants (such as but not limited to maprotiline); certain antipsychotic medications (such as but not limited to certain phenothiazines); astemizole and terfenadine should also be avoided.

The preceding lists of drugs are not comprehensive.

Potential benefits should be weighed against risks prior to the administration of cisapride to patients who have, or may develop prolongation of cardiac conduction intervals, particularly QT_c. In addition, patients with or suspected of having the above risk factors should be evaluated prior to the administration of cisapride. An ECG should be considered as part of this evaluation to exclude a prolonged QT interval.

(See also Contraindications and Precautions, Drug Interactions.)

Precautions: General: Before initiating therapy with cisapride, organic disease such as gastrointestinal hemorrhage, mechanical obstruction or perforation should be excluded by the physician.

Drug Interactions: The main metabolic pathway of cisapride is through cytochrome P450 3A4. In some cases where serious cardiac arrhythmias have occurred when cisapride was taken in conjunction with one of the cytochrome P450 3A4 inhibitors, elevated blood cisapride levels were noted at the time of QT prolongation. Therefore, the use of such drugs is contraindicated. Examples of these drugs include the following:

Antifungals: oral or i.v. fluconazole, itraconazole, ketoconazole.

Antibiotics: oral or i.v. erythromycin, clarithromycin.

Protease Inhibitors: ritonavir, indinavir (in vitro studies suggest that saquinavir is only a weak inhibitor).

Antidepressants: nefazodone.

Additionally, concomitant medications known to prolong the QT interval and increase the risk of arrhythmia, such as certain antiarrhythmics, including those of Class 1A (such as but not limited to quinidine and procainamide) and Class III (such as but not limited to amiodarone and sotalol); tricyclic antidepressants (such as but not limited to amitriptyline); certain tetracyclic antidepressants (such as but not limited to maprotiline); certain antipsychotic medications (such as but not limited to certain phenothiazines); astemizole and terfenadine should also be avoided.

The preceding lists of drugs are not comprehensive.

(See also Contraindications, Warnings and Adverse Effects.)

Since cisapride accelerates gastric emptying, the absorption from the stomach of other concomitantly administered drugs may be diminished whereas absorption of drugs from the small bowel may be accelerated.

In the case of drugs that require careful individual titration, such as anticonvulsants, it may be useful to monitor the

Prepulsid (cont'd)

plasma levels of such drugs when cisapride is given concomitantly.

In patients receiving anticoagulants, the coagulation times may increase. It is advisable to check the coagulation time within the first few days after the initiation and termination of cisapride therapy, with appropriate adaptation of the anticoagulant dose, if necessary.

Although cisapride does not affect psychomotor function, nor does it induce sedation or drowsiness when used alone, the sedative effects of benzodiazepines and of alcohol may be enhanced by cisapride.

The beneficial effects of cisapride on gastrointestinal motility are largely antagonized by anticholinergic drugs.

The oral bioavailability of cisapride increases slightly when used concomitantly with cimetidine or ranitidine; this is not considered to be clinically significant.

Patients With Hepatic or Renal Insufficiency: Because of the importance of the liver and kidneys in the metabolism and excretion of cisapride, the daily dose should be halved in patients with hepatic or renal insufficiency (see Dosage).

Geriatrics: Steady-state plasma levels of cisapride are generally higher than those of younger patients, due to a moderate prolongation of the elimination half-life. Initial therapeutic doses are similar to those used in younger patients but afterwards this dose can be adjusted depending on the therapeutic effects or possible side effects.

The rate of common adverse experiences in patients greater than 65 years of age in clinical trials was similar to that in younger adults.

Pregnancy: In a large population study in humans, cisapride has shown no increase in fetal anomalies. However, the anticipated therapeutic benefits should be weighed against potential hazards before giving cisapride during pregnancy, especially during the first trimester.

Lactation: Although the excretion of cisapride in human breast milk is minimal, it is advisable to discontinue breast-feeding while taking cisapride.

Adverse Effects: The most frequent side effects encountered are gastrointestinal in nature: diarrhea and abdominal discomfort. Most side effects are transient and rarely necessitate discontinuation of therapy.

Gastrointestinal (9.9%): diarrhea (5.1%), abdominal pain/cramps (2.1%), nausea, abdominal distention, constipation, borborygmi, flatulence, increased appetite (all <1%). There may be an increased incidence of abdominal cramps with 20 mg per intake. Should severe abdominal cramps occur, it is recommended to halve the dose per intake.

CNS (3.3%): headache (1.6%), mental disorders, sedation, fatigue, sleep disorders (all <0.5%).

Dermatological (0.9%): rash, pruritus (each <0.5%).

Cardiovascular (0.6%): orthostatic hypotension, palpitations, tachycardia, hot flushes (all <0.2%).

Genitourinary (0.5%): mastalgia, menstrual disorder, dose-related pollakiuria, urinary incontinence (all <0.1%).

Musculoskeletal (0.3%): back pain, heaviness in limbs (<0.2%).

Miscellaneous: vertigo/dizziness (1.2%), blurred vision (0.2%).

Postmarketing Reports: In addition, other side effects, such as edema (unspecified) and hemorrhoids have been observed during cisapride therapy. The relationship to the drug is unclear. Cases of hypersensitivity including rash, pruritus and urticaria, bronchospasm, and mild and transient headache or lightheadedness have been reported occasionally

Rare cases of cardiac arrhythmia, including ventricular tachycardia, ventricular fibrillation, torsades de pointes, and QT prolongation have been reported. Most of these patients had been receiving multiple other medications and had pre-existing cardiac disease or risk factors for arrhythmias.

Exceptional cases of reversible liver function abnormalities, with or without cholestasis, have been reported. Hyperprolactinemia which may cause gynecomastia and galactorrhea have also been reported; however, in large-scale surveillance studies the incidence (<0.1%) has not exceeded that commonly reported in the general population. All of these events were reversible. A causal relationship to cisapride has not been unequivocally established.

There are isolated reports of CNS effects, i.e., convulsive seizures and extrapyramidal effects. **(See also Contraindications—Warnings and Precautions, Drug Interactions.)**

Overdose: Symptoms: The symptoms that occur most frequently after overdosing are abdominal cramping and increased stool frequency. Rare cases of QT prolongation and ventricular arrhythmia have been reported. In infants (<1 year of age), mild sedation, apathy and atony were also observed.

Treatment: In case of overdosage, the administration of activated charcoal and close observation of the patient are recommended. It is recommended that patients be evaluated for possible QT prolongation and for factors that can predispose to the occurrence of torsades de pointes, such as electrolyte disturbances (especially hypokalemia or hypomagnesemia) and bradycardia.

Dosage: The tablets and oral suspension **should** be taken with a beverage. The suspension should be shaken before use. **The recommended doses should not be exceeded.**

Adults: Gastroesophageal Reflux Disease: Symptomatic Management: 5 to 10 mg 3 to 4 times daily, 15 minutes before meals and at bedtime or 20 mg twice daily, before breakfast and at bedtime.

Prophylaxis: 10 mg twice daily, before breakfast and at bedtime or 20 mg once daily, at bedtime. In patients with severe disease, it may be necessary to increase the dose to a maximum of 20 mg twice daily.

Gastroparesis and Pseudo-obstruction: The usual dose is 10 mg, 3 to 4 times daily, 15 minutes before meals and at bedtime. Although improvement will usually be obtained within the first weeks of treatment, maximal effect may not be seen until the patient has completed 8 to 12 weeks of continuous therapy.

Patients with Hepatic or Renal Insufficiency: Because of the importance of the liver and kidneys in the metabolism and excretion of cisapride, the daily dose should be halved in patients with hepatic or renal insufficiency.

Geriatrics: Therapeutic doses in the elderly are similar to those used in younger adults; however, because of a moderate prolongation of the elimination half-life, the steady-state plasma levels tend to be higher. More careful titration to the lowest effective dose may be necessary.

Supplied: Tablets: 5 mg: Each white, circular, biconvex, half-scored tablet, inscribed CIS/5 on the scored side and JANSSEN on the other side, contains: cisapride 5 mg as cisapride monohydrate. Nonmedicinal ingredients: colloidal anhydrous silica, lactose, magnesium stearate, maize starch, microcrystalline cellulose, polysorbate 20 and polyvidone K90. Bisulfites-, gluten- and tartrazine-free. HDPE bottles of 100 and 500.

10 mg: Each white, circular, biconvex, half-scored tablet, inscribed P/10 on the scored side and JANSSEN on the other side, contains: cisapride 10 mg as cisapride monohydrate. Nonmedicinal ingredients: colloidal anhydrous silica, lactose, magnesium stearate, maize starch, microcrystalline cellulose, polysorbate 20 and polyvidone K90. Bisulfites-, gluten- and tartrazine-free. HDPE bottles of 500.

20 mg: Each light blue, oval, biconvex, unscored tablet, inscribed with P/20 on one side and JANSSEN on the other, contains: cisapride 20 mg as cisapride monohydrate. Nonmedicinal ingredients: colloidal anhydrous silica, FD&C Blue No. 2 Aluminum Lake, lactose, magnesium stearate, maize starch, microcrystalline cellulose, polysorbate 20 and polyvidone K90. Bisulfites-, gluten- and tartrazine-free. HDPE bottles of 250.

Suspension: Each mL of white, cherry-cream-flavored suspension contains: cisapride 1 mg as cisapride monohydrate. Nonmedicinal ingredients: cherry-cream flavor, hypromellose 2910, methyl parahydroxybenzoate, microcrystalline cellulose and sodium carmellose, polysorbate 20, propyl parahydroxybenzoate, purified water, sodium chloride and sucrose. Sodium: <1 mmol (0.4 mg). Alcohol-, bisulfites-, gluten- and tartrazine-free. Amber glass bottles of 200 mL.

Store at room temperature (15 to 30°C). Protect from moisture and light.

(Shown in Product Recognition Section)

Reviewed 1999

PRESSYN® ℞

Ferring

Vasopressin

Antidiuretic Agent

Pharmacology: Vasopressin is a synthetic water-soluble pressor principle identical in sequence to lysine vasopressin.

Vasopressin exerts its antidiuretic action by increasing the reabsorption of water by the renal tubules. The drug can also cause contraction of smooth muscle of the gastrointestinal tract and all parts of the vascular beds, especially the capillaries, small arterioles, and venules, with less effect on the smooth musculature of the large veins.

The direct effect on the contractile elements is neither antagonized by adrenergic blocking agents nor prevented by vascular denervation.

Vasopressin injection USP is intended for i.m. or s.c. injection.

Indications: For the prevention or treatment of postoperative abdominal distention, dispelling of gas shadows in abdominal roentgenography and symptomatic control of diabetes insipidus.

Contraindications: Should not be used in patients having cardiorenal disease with hypertension, advanced arteriosclerosis, coronary thrombosis, angina pectoris, epilepsy or toxemia of pregnancy. Anaphylaxis or hypersensitivity to the drug or its components are also contraindications.

Chronic nephritis with nitrogen retention may be a contraindication (see Precautions).

Warnings: The drug should not be used except with extreme caution in patients with vascular disease, especially disease of the coronary arteries. In such patients even small doses of the drug may precipitate anginal pain and with larger doses, the possibility of myocardial infarction should be considered.

Vasopressin may produce water intoxication. The early signs of drowsiness, listlessness and headaches should be recognized to prevent convulsions and terminal coma.

Precautions: Vasopressin should be used cautiously in the presence of epilepsy, migraine, asthma, heart failure, or any state in which a rapid addition to extracellular water may produce hazard for an already overburdened system.

Chronic nephritis with nitrogen retention contraindicates the use of vasopressin until reasonable nitrogen blood levels have been attained.

Adverse Effects: Local or systemic allergic reactions may occur in hypersensitive individuals. The following side effects have been reported following the administration of vasopressin: tremor, sweating, vertigo, circumoral pallor, "pounding" in the head, abdominal cramps, passage of gas, nausea, vomiting, urticaria, bronchial constriction.

Anaphylaxis (cardiac arrest and/or shock) has been observed shortly after injection of vasopressin.

Dosage: Dosage should be individualized: 0.25 to 0.5 mL i.m. or s.c. at intervals of 3 to 4 hours, as required. Children's dosages in proportion.

Abdominal Distension: Adults, 0.25 to 0.5 mL.

Abdominal Roentgenography: Adults, 0.5 mL given 2 hours and 0.5 hours before exposure of films.

Diabetes Insipidus: The dose by i.m. or s.c. injection is 0.25 to 0.5 mL repeated 2 or 3 times daily as required.

Supplied: Each mL of aqueous solution contains: vasopressin 20 USP pressor units, chlorobutanol 0.5% as a preservative, and sodium chloride 9 mg/mL. The acidity of the solution is adjusted, if necessary to 2.5 to 4.5 with acetic acid. Ampuls of 5 mL, boxes of 1. Keep away from heat.

PRESUN® SUNBLOCK 28

Westwood-Squibb

Titanium Dioxide

Sunscreen

Indications: A waterproof, titanium dioxide sunscreen which physically blocks UVA and UVB rays and does not contain PABA or other chemical-sensitizing sunscreens. This broad spectrum, fragrance-free product is ideally suited for sensitive skin. This product is appropriate for daily sunscreen use for the whole family.

Precautions: For external use only. If irritation or rash develops, discontinue use. Use on children under 6 months of age with the advice of a physician. Avoid contact with eyes. Keep out of the reach of children. Protect from freezing.

Dosage: Apply evenly onto dry skin at least 15 minutes before sun exposure. Rub in until completely absorbed. Reapply to dry skin after prolonged swimming or excessive perspiration.

Supplied: Each g contains: titanium dioxide 16% w/w. Fragrance-, parabens- and potentially sensitizing chemicals-free. Nonmedicinal ingredients: aluminum hydroxide, BHT, C12-15 alcohols benzoate, benzyl alcohol, cetyl dimethicone copolyol, diazolidinyl urea, hexyl laurate, lauric acid, magnesium stearate, magnesium sulfate, octyldodecyl neopentanoate, phenyl trimethicone, polyglyceryl-4 isostearate, sodium chloride and water. Tubes of 100 g.

Reviewed 1997

PRESUN® ULTRA 30 Preparations

Westwood-Squibb

Octyl Methoxycinnamate—Octyl Salicylate—Oxybenzone—Butyl Methoxydibenzoylmethane (Parsol® 1789)

Sunscreen

Indications: A waterproof, non-PABA sunscreen for extremely sun-sensitive patients, or those patients who exhibit a sensitivity to PABA or its esters. Offers maximum UVA and UVB sun protection. Regular usage may help prevent premature aging and wrinkling of the skin due to sun overexposure.

Precautions: For external use only. If skin irritation develops, discontinue use. Avoid contact with eyes. Keep gel away from open flame.

Dosage: Gently smooth a liberal amount onto dry skin before sun exposure. Reapply to dry skin after prolonged swimming or excessive perspiration.

Supplied: Cream: Each g of non-PABA, fragrance-free, non-comedogenic, waterproof cream sunscreen contains: octyl methoxycinnamate 7.5%, octyl salicylate 5%, oxybenzone 3% and butyl methoxydibenzoylmethane (Parsol® 1789) 3%. Nonmedicinal ingredients: benzyl alcohol, carbomer 940, cetyl alcohol, DEA cetyl phosphate, dimethicone-225, disodium EDTA, isodecyl neopentanoate, isopropyl myristate, Kathon CG, PG dioctanoate, PVP/eicosene copolymer, stearic acid, triethanolamine and water. Bottles of 110 mL.

Clear Gel: Each g of non-PABA, fragrance free, non comedogenic waterproof gel sunscreen contains: octyl methoxycinnamate 7.5%, octyl salicylate 5%, oxybenzone 6% and butyl methoxydibenzoylmethane (Parsol® 1789) 3%. Nonmedicinal ingredients: acrylates/t-octylpropenamide, hydroxypropylcellulose, PPG-15 stearyl ether and SD alcohol G 1-B (64% w/w). Bottles of 110 mL.

Kids Cream: Each g of non-PABA, fragrance-free, non-comedogenic water-proof cream sunscreen contains: octyl methoxycinnamate 7.5%, octyl salicylate 5%, oxybenzone 3% and butyl methoxydibenzoylmethane (Parsol® 1789) 3%. Nonmedicinal ingredients: benzyl alcohol, carbomer 940, cetyl alcohol, DEA cetyl phosphate, dimethicone-225, disodium EDTA, isodecyl neopentanoate, isopropyl myristate, Kathon CG, PG dioctanoate, PVP/eicosene copolymer, stearic acid, triethanolamine and water. Bottles of 110 mL.

PREVACID® ℞

Abbott

Lansoprazole

H^+, K^+-ATPase Inhibitor

Note: When used in combination with antimicrobials for the eradication of H. pylori, the product monograph for those agents should be consulted.

Pharmacology: Lansoprazole inhibits the gastric H^+, K^+-ATPase (the proton pump) which catalyzes the exchange of H^+ and K^+. It is effective in the inhibition of both basal acid secretion and stimulated acid secretion.

In healthy subjects, single and multiple doses of lansoprazole (15 to 60 mg) have been shown in healthy subjects to decrease significantly basal gastric acid output and to increase significantly mean gastric pH and percent of time at pH >3 and 4. These doses have also been shown to reduce significantly meal-stimulated gastric acid output and gastric secretion volume. Single or multiple doses of lansoprazole (10 to 60 mg) reduced pentagastrin-stimulated acid output. In addition, lansoprazole has been demonstrated to reduce significantly basal and pentagastrin-stimulated gastric acid secretion among DU and hypersecretory patients, and basal gastric acid secretion among patients with GU disease.

A dose-response effect was analyzed by considering the results from clinical pharmacology studies that evaluated more than one dose of lansoprazole. The results indicated that, in general, as the dose was increased from 7.5 mg to 30 mg, there was a decrease in mean gastric acid secretion and an increase in the average time spent at higher pH values (pH >4).

The results of pharmacodynamic studies with lansoprazole in normal subjects suggest that doses of 7.5 to 10 mg are substantially less effective in inhibiting gastric acid secretion than doses of 15 mg or greater. In view of these results, the doses of lansoprazole evaluated in the principal clinical trials ranged from 15 to 60 mg daily.

Eradication of H. pylori: H. pylori is considered to be a major factor in the etiology of duodenal ulcer disease. The presence of H. pylori may damage the mucosal integrity due to the production of enzymes (catalase, lipases, phospholipases, proteases, and urease), adhesins and toxins; the inflammatory response generated in this manner contributes to mucosal damage.

The concomitant administration of an antimicrobial(s) and an antisecretory agent such as lansoprazole, improves the eradication of H. pylori as compared to individual drug administration. The higher pH resulting from antisecretory treatment, optimizes the environment for the pharmacologic action of the antimicrobial agent(s) against H. pylori.

Pharmacokinetics: Prevacid contains an enteric-coated granule formulation of lansoprazole to ensure that absorption of lansoprazole begins only after the granules leave the stomach (lansoprazole is acid-labile). Peak plasma concentrations of lansoprazole (C_{max} and the area under the plasma concentration curve (AUC) of lansoprazole are approximately proportional in doses of 15 to 60 mg after single oral administration. Lansoprazole pharmacokinetics are unaltered by multiple dosing and the drug does not accumulate.

Lansoprazole is highly bioavailable when administered orally. In a definitive absolute bioavailability study, the absolute bioavailability was shown to be 86% for a 15 mg capsule and 80% for a 30 mg capsule. First pass effect is apparently minimal.

Table I summarizes the pharmacokinetic parameters (T_{max}, T½, AUC and C_{max}) of lansoprazole in healthy subjects.

Elimination: Following single dose oral administration of lansoprazole, virtually no unchanged lansoprazole was excreted in the urine. After a single dose of ^{14}C-lansoprazole, approximately one-third of the dose was excreted in the urine and approximately two-thirds were recovered in the feces. This implies a significant biliary excretion of the metabolites of lansoprazole.

Metabolism: Lansoprazole is extensively metabolized in the liver. Two metabolites have been identified in measurable quantities in plasma, the hydroxylated sulfinyl and sulfone derivatives of lansoprazole. These metabolites have very little or no antisecretory activity. Within the parietal cell canaliculus, lansoprazole is thought to be transformed into 2 active metabolites which inhibit acid secretion by (H^+, K^+)–ATPase, but these metabolites are not present in the systemic circulation. The plasma elimination half-life of lansoprazole does not reflect its duration of suppression of gastric acid secretion. Thus, the plasma elimination hlaf-life is less than 2 hours while the acid inhibitory effect lasts mcre than 24 hours.

Special Populations: Patients With Hepatic Impairment: As would be expected with a drug that is primarily metabolized by the liver, in patients with mild (Child-Pugh Class A) or moderate (Child-Pugh Class B) chronic hepatic disease, the plasma 1.5 hours half-life of the drug increased to 5.2 hours compared to the 1.5 hours half-life in healthy subjects. An increase in AUC of 3.4 fold was observed in patients with hepatic impairment versus healthy subjects (7 096 versus 2 645 ng•h/mL) which was due to slower elimination of lansoprazole; however, C_{max} was not significantly affected.

Patients With Renal Impairment: In patients with mild (Cl_{cr} 40 to 80 mL/min), moderate Cl_{cr} 20 to 40 mL/min) and severe (Cl_{cr} <20 mL/min) chronic renal impairment, the disposition of lansoprazole was very similar to that of healthy volunteers.

Table I—Prevacid

Pharmacokinetic Parameters of Lansoprazole Pooled Across Phase I Studies

Parameter	T_{max} (h)	t½ (h)	AUC[a] (ng•h/mL)	C_{max}[a] (ng/mL)
Mean	1.68	1.53	2 133	824
Median	1.50	1.24	1 644	770
SD	0.80	1.01	1 797	419
% CV	47.71	65.92	84.28	50.81
Min	0.50	0.39	213	27
Max	6.00	8.50	14 203	2 440
N[b]	345	285	513	515

[a]Normalized to a 30 mg dose.

[b]Number of dosages associated with a parameter.

Absorption: Absorption is rapid, with mean peak plasma levels of lansoprazole occurring at approximately 1.7 hours. Peak plasma concentrations of lansoprazole (C_{max}) and the area under the plasma concentration curve (AUC) are approximately proportional to dose throughout the range that has been studied (up to 60 mg).

Absorption With Food: Food reduces the peak concentration and the extent of absorption by about 50%. Moreover, the results of a pharmacokinetic study that compared the bioavailability of lansoprazole following a.m. dosing (fasting) versus p.m. dosing (3 hours after a meal) indicated that both C_{max} and AUC values were increased by approximately 2-fold or more with a.m. dosing. Therefore, it is recommended that lansoprazole be administered in the morning prior to breakfast.

Absorption With Antacids: Simultaneous administration of lansoprazole with Maalox (aluminum and magnesium hydroxide) or Riopan (magaldrate) resulted in lower peak serum levels, but did not significantly reduce bioavailability of lansoprazole.

In a single-dose crossover study when 30 mg of lansoprazole was administered concomitantly with 1 g of sucralfate in healthy volunteers, absorption of lansoprazole was delayed and its bioavailability was reduced. The value of lansoprazole AUC was reduced by 17% and that for C_{max} was reduced by 21%.

In a similar study when 30 mg of lansoprazole was administered concomitantly with 2 g of sucralfate, lansoprazole AUC and C_{max} were reduced by 32% and 55%, respectively. When lansoprazole dosing occurred 30 minutes prior to sucralfate administration, C_{max} was reduced by only 28% and there was no statistically significant difference in lansoprazole AUC. Therefore, lansoprazole may be given concomitantly with antacids but should be administered at least 30 minutes prior to sucralfate.

Distribution: Lansoprazole is 97% bound to plasma proteins. The mean total body clearance (Cl) of lansoprazole was calculated to be 31±8 L/hour, and the volume of distribution (V_{ss}) was calculated to be 29±4 L.

The impact of dialysis on lansoprazole was evaluated from a pharmacokinetic standpoint, and there were no significant differences in AUC, C_{max} or t½ between dialysis day and dialysis-free day. Dialysate contained no measurable lansoprazole or metabolite. Lansoprazole is not significantly dialyzed.

Geriatrics: The results from the studies that evaluated the pharmacokinetics of lansoprazole in an older population revealed that in comparison with younger subjects, older subjects exhibited significantly larger AUCs and longer t½s. Lansoprazole did not accumulate in the older subjects upon multiple dosing since the longest mean t½ in the studies was 2.9 hours, and lansoprazole is dosed once daily. C_{max} in the elderly was comparable to that found in adult subjects.

Children: The pharmacokinetics of lansoprazole have not been investigated in patients <18 years of age.

Gender: In a study comparing 12 male and 6 female subjects, no gender differences were found in pharmacokinetics and intragastric pH results (see Precautions, Women).

Race: The pooled pharmacokinetic parameters of lansoprazole from 12 U.S. Phase I studies (N=513) were compared to the mean pharmacokinetic parameters from 2 Asian studies (N=20). The mean AUCs of lansoprazole in Asian subjects are approximately twice that seen in pooled US data, however, the inter-individual variability is high. The C_{max} values are comparable.

Indications: In the treatment of conditions where a reduction of gastric acid secretion is required, such as: duodenal ulcer; gastric ulcer; reflux esophagitis including patients with Barrett's esophagus, and patients poorly responsive to an adequate course of therapy with histamine H_2-receptor antagonists; pathological hypersecretory conditions including Zollinger-Ellison syndrome (see Dosage); eradication of H. pylori.

Triple Therapy: Lansoprazole, in combination with clarithromycin plus amoxicillin as triple therapy, is indicated for

Prevacid (cont'd)

the treatment of patients with H. pylori infection and active duodenal ulcer disease. Eradication of H. pylori has been shown to reduce the risk of duodenal ulcer recurrence (see Dosage).

(For additional information on triple therapy for the treatment of H. pylori infection and active duodenal ulcer recurrence, refer to the Hp-PAC product monograph).

Dual Therapy: Lansoprazole, in combination with amoxicillin as dual therapy, are indicated for the treatment of patients with H. pylori infection and active duodenal ulcer disease who are either allergic or intolerant to clarithromycin or in whom resistance is known or suspected. Eradication of H. pylori has been shown to reduce the risk of duodenal ulcer recurrence (see Dosage).

In patients with a recent history of duodenal ulcers who are H. pylori positive, eradication therapy may reduce the rate of recurrence of duodenal ulcers. The optimal timing for eradication therapy for such patients remains to be determined.

In patients who fail a therapy combination containing clarithromycin, susceptibility testing should be done. If resistance to clarithromycin is demonstrated or susceptibility testing is not possible, an alternative therapy combination is recommended.

Resistance to amoxicillin has not been demonstrated in clinical studies with lansoprazole and amoxicillin.

Table II summarizes the eradication rates for the H. pylori Triple- and Dual- Therapy treatment regimens.

Table II—Prevacid

Eradication Rates for the H. pylori Triple- and Dual- Therapy Treatment Regimens

Study	**Eradication Rates % (n/N)**
†Triple Therapy	
Evaluable Patients	
Trial #1 (M93-131)	92 (44/48)
Trial #2 (M95-392)	**86 (57/66)**
Combined	89 (101/114)
ITT (All Available Data)	
Trial #1 (M93-131)	94 (47/50)
Trial #2 (M95-392)	**87 (58/67)**
Combined	90 (105/117)
‡Dual Therapy	
Evaluable Patients	
Trial #1 (M93-131)	76 (39/51)
Trial #4 (M95-125)	**66 (38/58)**
Combined	71 (77/109)
ITT (All Available Data)	
Trial #1 (M93-131)	78 (42/54)
Trial #4 (M95-125)	**67 (41/61)**
Combined	72 (83/115)
#Dual Therapy	
Evaluable Patients	
Trial #1 (M93-131)	55 (28/51)
Trial #3 (M95-130)	**65 (55/85)**
Combined	61 (83/136)
ITT (All Available Data)	
Trial #1 (M93-131)	56 (28/50)
Trial #3 (M95-130)	**68 (56/83)**
Combined	63 (84/133)

ITT = intent-to-treat patients.
† Triple Therapy: Prevacid 30 mg b.i.d./clarithromycin 500 mg b.i.d./amoxicillin 1 g b.i.d.
‡ Dual Therapy: Prevacid 30 mg t.i.d./amoxicillin 1 g t.i.d.
# Dual Therapy: Prevacid 30 mg b.i.d./clarithromycin 500 mg b.i.d.

Patients were included in the analysis if they had documented duodenal ulcer (active) and H. pylori infection at baseline defined as at least 2 of 3 positive endoscopic tests from CLOtest, histology and/or culture.

Contraindications: In patients with known hypersensitivity to any component of the formulation.

Amoxicillin is contraindicated in patients with a known hypersensitivity to any penicillin. (Please refer to the Amoxicillin Product Monograph before prescribing).

Clarithromycin is contraindicated in patients with known hypersensitivity to clarithromycin, erythromycin or other macrolide antibacterial agents. Clarithromycin is also contraindicated in patients receiving concurrent therapy with astemizole, terfenadine, cisapride or pimozide. (Please refer to the Clarithromycin tablets Product Monograph before prescribing).

Warnings: Clarithromycin should not be used in pregnancy except where no alternative therapy is appropriate, particularly during the first 3 months of pregnancy. If pregnancy occurs while taking the drug, the patient should be apprised of the potential hazard to the fetus. Clarithromycin has demonstrated adverse effects on pregnancy outcome and/or embryo-fetal development in monkeys, mice, rats and rabbits at doses that produced plasma levels 2 to 17 times the serum levels obtained in humans treated at the maximum recommended doses (see Warnings section in the clarithromycin product monograph).

Pseudomembranous colitis has been reported with nearly all antibacterial agents, including clarithromycin and amoxicillin, and may range in severity from mild to life threatening. Therefore, it is important to consider this diagnosis in patients who present with diarrhea subsequent to the administration of antibacterial agents.

Treatment with antibacterial agents alters the normal flora of the colon and may permit overgrowth of clostridia. Studies indicate that a toxin produced by C. difficile is a primary cause of "antibiotic-associated colitis".

After the diagnosis of pseudomembranous colitis has been established, therapeutic measures should be initiated. Mild cases of pseudomembranous colitis usually respond to discontinuation of the drug alone. In moderate to severe cases, consideration should be given to management with fluids and electrolytes, protein supplementation, and treatment with an antibacterial drug effective against C. difficile.

Allergic reactions (including anaphylaxis) have been reported in patients receiving clarithromycin orally.

Serious and occasionally fatal hypersensitivity (anaphylactic) reactions have been reported in patients on penicillin therapy. These reactions are more apt to occur in individuals with a history of penicillin hypersensitivity and/or a history of sensitivity to multiple allergens.

There have been well documented reports of individuals with a history of penicillin hypersensitivity reactions who have experienced severe hypersensitivity reactions when treated with a cephalosporin. Before initiating therapy with any penicillin, careful inquiry should be made concerning previous hypersensitivity reactions to penicillins, cephalosporins, and other allergens. If an allergic reaction occurs, amoxicillin should be discontinued and the appropriate therapy instituted.

Serious anaphylactic reactions require immediate emergency treatment with epinephrine, oxygen, corticosteroids, and airway management, including intubation, as indicated.

When gastric ulcer is suspected the possibility of malignancy should be excluded before therapy with lansoprazole is instituted as treatment with this drug may alleviate symptoms and delay diagnosis.

Pregnancy: There are no adequate or well-controlled studies in pregnant women. Therefore, lansoprazole should be used during pregnancy only if the potential benefit justifies the potential risk to the fetus.

Reproductive studies conducted in pregnant rats at oral doses up to 150 mg/kg/day (40 times the recommended human dose based on body surface area), and in rabbits at oral doses up to 30 mg/kg/day (16 times the recommended human dose based on body surface area), did not disclose any evidence of a teratogenic effect. Maternal toxicity and a significant increase in fetal mortality were observed in the rabbit study at doses above 10 mg/kg/day. In rats, maternal toxicity and a slight reduction in litter survival and weights were noted at doses above 100 mg/kg/day.

Lactation: It is not known whether lansoprazole is excreted in human milk. Because drugs are excreted in human milk, it should not be given to nursing mothers unless its use is considered essential.

Children: Safety and effectiveness in children have not been established.

Patients With Hepatic Impairment: It is recommended that the initial dosing regimen need not be altered for patients with mild or moderate liver disease, but for patients with moderate impairment, doses higher than 30 mg/day should not be administered unless there are compelling clinical indications.

Precautions: General: Symptomatic response to therapy with lansoprazole does not preclude the presence of gastric malignancy.

H. pylori Eradication and Compliance: To avoid failure of the eradication treatment with a potential for developing antimicrobial resistance and a risk of failure with subsequent therapy, patients should be instructed to follow closely the prescribed regimen.

For the eradication of H. pylori, amoxicillin and clarithromycin should not be administered to patients with renal impairment since the appropriate dosage in this patient population has not yet been established.

Carcinogenicity: Safety concerns of long-term treatment relate to hypergastrinemia, possible ECL effect and carcinoid formation. ECL cell hyperplasia and gastric carcinoid tumors were observed in 4 animal studies.

In two 24-month carcinogenicity studies, Sprague-Dawley rats were treated orally with doses of 5 to 150 mg/kg/day about 1 to 40 times the exposure on a body surface (mg/m²) basis, of a 50 kg person of average height (1.46 m² body surface area) given the recommended human dose of 30 mg/day (22.2 mg/m²). Lansoprazole produced dose-related gastric enterochromaffin-like (ECL) cell hyperplasia and ECL cell carcinoids in both male and female rats. It also increased the incidence of intestinal metaplasia of the gastric epithelium in both sexes. In male rats lansoprazole produced a dose related increase of testicular interstitial cell adenomas. The incidence of these adenomas in rats receiving doses of 15 to 150 mg/kg/day (4 to 40 times the recommended human dose based on body surface area) exceeded the low background incidence (range=1.4 to 10%) for this strain of rats. Testicular interstitial cell adenoma also occurred in 1 of 30 rats treated with 50 mg/kg/day (13 times the recommended human dose based on body surface area) in a 1-year toxicity study.

In a 24-month carcinogenicity study, CD-1 mice were treated orally with doses of 15 to 600 mg/kg/day, 2 to 80 times the recommended human dose based on body surface area. Lansoprazole produced a dose-related increased incidence of gastric ECL cell hyperplasia. Lansoprazole also induced a low, non-dose-related incidence of carcinoid tumors in the gastric mucosa in several dose groups (one female mouse in the 15 mg/kg/day group, one male mouse in the 150 mg/kg/day group, and 2 males and 1 female in the 300 mg/kg/day group). It also produced an increased incidence of liver tumors (hepatocellular adenoma plus carcinoma). The tumor incidences in male mice treated with 300 and 600 mg/kg/day (40 to 80 times the recommended human dose based on body surface area) and female mice treated with 150 to 600 mg/kg/day (20 to 80 times the recommended human dose based on body surface area) exceeded the ranges of background incidences in historical controls for this strain of mice. Lansoprazole treatment produced adenoma of rete testis in male mice receiving 75 to 600 mg/kg/day (10 to 80 times the recommended human dose based on body surface area).

Analysis of gastric biopsy specimens from patients after short-term treatment of proton pump inhibitors have not detected ECL cell effects similar to those seen in animal studies. Longer term studies in humans revealed a slight increase in the mean ECL-cell density, although there was no microscopic evidence of cell hyperplasia. Similar results were seen in the maintenance treatment studies, where patients received up to 15 months of lansoprazole therapy. Serum gastrin values increased significantly from their baseline values but reached a plateau after 2 months of therapy. By 1 month post-treatment, fasting serum gastrin values returned to lansoprazole therapy baseline. Moreover, results from gastric biopsies from short-term, long-term and maintenance treatment studies indicate that there are no clinically meaningful effects on gastric mucosa morphology among lansoprazole-treated patients.

Retinal Atrophy: In animal studies, retinal atrophy was observed in rats dosed orally for 2 years with lansoprazole at doses of 15 mg/kg/day and above. These changes in rats are believed to be associated with the effects of taurine imbalance and phototoxicity in a susceptible animal model. Clinical data available from long-term lansoprazole studies are not suggestive of any drug-induced eye toxicity in humans. In humans, there are presently no concerns for ocular safety with short-term lansoprazole treatment and the risks associated with long-term use for nearly 5 years appear to be negligible. The finding of drug-induced retinol atrophy in the albino rat is considered to be species-specific with little relevance for humans.

Leydig Cell Hyperplasia/Leydig Cell Tumors: In the 24-month toxicology study in rats, after 18 months of treatment, Leydig cell hyperplasia increased above the concurrent and historical control level at dosages of 15 mg/kg/day or higher.

Testicular interstitial cell adenoma also occurred in 1 of 30 rats treated with 50 mg/kg/day (13 times the recommended human dose based on body surface area) in a 1-year toxicity study.

These changes are associated with endocrine alterations which have not been, to date, observed in humans.

Drug Interactions: Lansoprazole is metabolized through the cytochrome P450 system, specifically through CYP3A and CYP2C19. Studies have shown that lansoprazole does not have clinically significant interactions with warfarin, antipyrine, indomethacin, ASA, ibuprofen, phenytoin, prednisone, antacids (Maalox and Riopan), diazepam clarithromycin, propranolol, amoxicillin or terfenadine in healthy subjects. These compounds are metabolized through various cytochrome P450 Isozymes including CYP1A2, CYP2C19, CYP2D6 and CYP3A. When lansoprazole was administered concomitantly with theophylline CYP1A2, CYP3A, a minor increase (10%) in the clearance of theophylline was seen, which is unlikely to be of clinical concern. Nonetheless, individual patients may require adjustment of their theophylline dosage when lansoprazole is started or stopped to ensure clinically effective blood levels.

In a single-dose crossover study when 30 mg of lansoprazole was administered concomitantly with 1 g of sucralfate in healthy volunteers, absorption of lansoprazole was delayed and its bioavailability was reduced. The value of lansoprazole AUC was reduced by 17% and that for C_{max} was reduced by 21%.

In a similar study when 30 mg of lansoprazole was administered concomitantly with 2 g of sucralfate, lansoprazole AUC and C_{max} were reduced by 32% and 55%, respectively. When lansoprazole dosing occurred 30 minutes prior to sucralfate administration, C_{max} was reduced by only 28% and there was no statistically significant difference in lansoprazole AUC. Therefore, lansoprazole may be given concomitantly with antacids but should be administered at least 30 minutes prior to sucralfate.

Lansoprazole causes a profound and long lasting inhibition of gastric acid secretion; therefore, it is theoretically possible that lansoprazole may interfere with the absorption of drugs where gastric pH is an important determinant of bioavailability (e.g., ketoconazole, ampicillin esters, iron salts, digoxin).

Combination Therapy With Clarithromycin and/or Amoxicillin: For more information on drug interactions for clarithromycin and amoxicillin, refer to their respective Product Monographs, under Precautions, Drug Interactions.

Antibiotic Resistance in Relation to H. pylori Eradication: Three patients 3/82 (3.7%) who had isolates susceptible to clarithromycin pretreatment and were treated with the triple therapy regimen remained H. pylori positive posttreatment. None of the isolates from these 3 patients had susceptibility results available after treatment with triple therapy; therefore, it is unknown whether or not these patients developed resistance to clarithromycin. Sixteen percent of the patients treated with the dual therapy regimen developed clarithromycin resistance post-treatment. Therefore, development of clarithromycin resistance should be considered as a possible risk.

Patients With Renal Impairment: No dosage modification of lansoprazole is required in patients with renal insufficiency.

Geriatrics: Ulcer healing rates in elderly patients are similar to those in younger age groups. The incidence rates of adverse events and laboratory test abnormalities are also similar to those seen in other age groups. The initial dosing regimen need not be altered for elderly patients, but subsequent doses higher than 30 mg/day should not be administered unless additional gastric acid suppression is necessary.

Women: Over 800 women were treated with lansoprazole. Ulcer healing rates in females are similar to those in males. The incidence rates of adverse events are also similar to those seen in males.

Adverse Effects: Worldwide, over 7 000 patients have been treated with lansoprazole during Phase II and III short-term and long-term clinical trials involving various dosages and duration of treatment. In general, lansoprazole treatment has been well tolerated.

Short-term Studies: The following adverse events were reported to have a possible or probable relationship to drug as described by the treating physician in 1% or more of lansoprazole-treated patients who participated in placebo- and positive-controlled trials (see Tables III and IV). Numbers in parentheses indicate the percentage of the adverse events reported.

Can't find information on a particular drug? Check the CPhA General Monograph index at the beginning of the WHITE SECTION.

Table III—Prevacid

Incidence of Possibly or Probably Treatment-related Adverse Events in Short-term, Placebo-controlled Studies in TAP Safety Database

Body System/ Adverse Event*	Prevacid* (n=817), n (%)	Placebo (n=254), n (%)
Body as a Whole		
Abdominal Pain	19 (2.3)	3 (1.2)
Headache	63 (7.7)	31 (12.2)
Digestive System		
Diarrhea	29 (3.5)	6 (2.4)
Nausea	9 (1.1)	5 (2.0)
Liver Function Tests Abnormal	2 (0.2)	3 (1.2)
Vomiting	7 (0.9)	3 (1.2)
Nervous System		
Dizziness	8 (1.0)	2 (0.8)

* Events reported by at least 1% of patients on either treatment are included.

Table IV—Prevacid

Incidence of Possibly or Probably Treatment-related Adverse Events in Short-term, Positive-controlled Studies in TAP Safety Database

Body System/ Adverse Event*	Prevacid* (n=647), n (%)	Ranitidine (n=393), n (%)
Body as a Whole		
Abdominal Pain	8 (1.2)	3 (0.8)
Headache	26 (4.0)	14 (3.6)
Digestive System		
Diarrhea	27 (4.2)	8 (2.0)
Nausea	7 (1.1)	4 (1.0)
Nervous System		
Dizziness	8 (1.2)	3 (0.8)
Skin and Appendages		
Rash	7 (1.1)	1 (0.3)

* Events reported by at least 1% of patients on either treatment are included.

In the TAP Safety Database, all short-term, Phase II/III studies, one or more treatment-emergent Adverse Events (AEs) were reported by 715/1 359 (52.6%) Prevacid-treated patients; of those considered to be possibly or probably treatment-related AEs, one or more were reported by 276/1 359 (20.3%) Prevacid-treated patients. In all short-term, Phase II/III studies, one or more treatment-emergent AEs were reported by 150/254 (59.1%) placebo-treated patients; of those considered to be possibly or probably treatment-related AEs, one or more were reported by 56/254 (22%).

The most frequent AEs reported in the European short-term studies were diarrhea (3.3%), laboratory test abnormal (2.3%), headache (1.5%), constipation (1.2%), asthenia (1.1%), dizziness (1.1%), and abdominal pain (1.0%). The most frequent AEs reported in the Asian short-term studies were unspecified laboratory test abnormalities (7.3%), eosinophilia (1.0%) and increased ALT (1.0%).

Maintenance Studies: US Studies: Treatment-emergent adverse effects with an incidence of at least 2% in any treatment group of the maintenance treatment studies occurring from the start of maintenance treatment to the first recurrence of disease are displayed by body system and COSTART term, and by treatment group in Table V.

There were no frequently reported (≥2%, incidence) severe adverse effects in the treatment-emergent or the possibly/probably treatment-related event categories with onset at any point from the start of maintenance treatment to the time of first recurrence of disease.

European Studies: The adverse effects reported by at least 2% of patients in any treatment group are displayed by COSTART body system and term and by treatment group for controlled long-term European Studies in Table VI.

The adverse effects reported by at least 1% of patients receiving lead-in open-label lansoprazole treatment in long-term European Studies are diarrhea (5.7%), esophagitis (2.0%), abdominal pain (2.1%), gastritis (2.1%), flatulence (1.3%), headache (1.1%), constipation (1.0%), and nausea (1.0%). The incidence of adverse effects reported in the lead-in open-label period of the European Studies was similar to that seen in controlled studies; however, the overall incidence was lower for the lead-in open-label studies than for the H_2-receptor antagonist controlled studies (27.5% versus 49.8%, respectively).

Table V—Prevacid

Treatment-Emergent Adverse Effects Reported by ≥2% of the Placebo and Lansoprazole Patients to the Time of First Recurrence of Disease* in the Maintenance Treatment Studies

Treatment Group	Placebo	Lansoprazole
	Cumulative Effect N=236	**Cumulative Effect N=386**
Mean Exposure (Days)	**105.4**	**267.5**
Body System/COSTART Term	**% (n)**	**% (n)**
Total Patients		
Any event	39.4 (93)	70.5 (272)
Body as a Whole		
Abdominal pain	3.0 (7)	5.2 (20)
Accidental injury	2.1 (5)	5.4 (21)
Back pain	4.2 (10)	3.1 (12)
Chest pain	0.8 (2)	2.3 (9)
Flu syndrome	3.8 (9)	7.3 (28)
Headache	6.4 (15)	11.4 (44)
Infection	1.3 (3)	2.1 (8)
Pain	0.8 (2)	2.6 (10)
Digestive		
Diarrhea	5.5 (13)	9.8 (38)
Gastrointestinal anomaly (polyp)	0.8 (2)	4.4 (17)
Nausea	1.3 (3)	2.8 (11)
Tooth disorder	0.4 (1)	2.1 (8)
Vomiting	0.4 (1)	3.4 (13)
Musculoskeletal		
Arthralgia	1.3 (3)	4.4 (17)
Myalgia	1.3 (3)	2.1 (8)
Nervous System		
Dizziness	0.4 (1)	2.8 (11)
Respiratory		
Bronchitis	1.3 (3)	3.1 (12)
Cough Increased	0	2.3 (9)
Pharyngitis	9.3 (22)	17.1 (66)
Rhinitis	1.3 (3)	5.7 (22)
Sinusitis	2.5 (6)	6.5 (25)
Skin and Appendages		
Rash	3.0 (7)	4.7 (18)
Urogenital		
Urinary Tract Infection	2.5 (6)	4.1 (16)

*Until time of first recurrence, withdrawal or end of maintenance treatment.

Table VI—Prevacid

Treatment-Emergent Adverse Effects Reported by ≥2% of Patients Treated with H_2-Receptor Antagonists or Lansoprazole in Long-term, Phase II/III H_2-Receptor Antagonist Controlled European Studies

Treatment Group	Lansoprazole (N=263)	H_2-Receptor Antagonists (N=161)
Body System/COSTART Term	**% (n)**	**% (n)**
Total Patients		
Any event	49.8 (131)	46.6 (75)
Body as a Whole		
Abdominal pain	3.0 (8)	3.7 (6)
Back pain	2.3 (6)	0.6 (1)
Accidental injury	1.5 (4)	2.5 (4)
Infection	1.1 (3)	3.1 (5)
Cardiovascular		
Hypertension	1.9 (5)	2.5 (4)
Digestive		
Diarrhea	9.1 (24)	4.3 (7)
Gastritis	5.3 (14)	1.2 (2)
Constipation	2.7 (7)	2.5 (4)
Vomiting	1.9 (5)	3.1 (5)
Dyspepsia	1.1 (3)	3.1 (5)
Musculoskeletal		
Arthralgia	1.9 (5)	2.5 (4)
Nervous System		
Dizziness	1.9 (5)	2.5 (4)
Respiratory		
Respiratory disorder	2.3 (6)	3.1 (5)
Cough increased	1.1 (3)	2.5 (4)

Additional adverse experiences occurring in <1% of patients or subjects in domestic and/or international trials, or occurring since the drug was marketed, are shown below within each body system.

Prevacid (cont'd)

Body as a Whole: asthenia, candidiasis, chest pain (not otherwise specified), edema, fever, flu syndrome, halitosis, infection (not otherwise specified), malaise, carcinoma, general pain.
Cardiovascular: angina, cerebrovascular accident, hypertension/hypotension, myocardial infarction, palpitations, shock (circulatory failure), vasodilation.
Digestive: melena, cholelithiasis, abnormal stools/melena, bezoar, constipation, dry mouth/thirst, flatulence, gastroenteritis, gastrointestinal hemorrhage, hematemesis, anorexia, increased appetite, increased salivation, rectal hemorrhage, cardiospasm, dyspepsia, dysphagia, eructation, esophageal stenosis, esophageal ulcer, esophagitis, stomatitis, fecal discoloration, tenesmus, ulcerative colitis, gastric nodules/fundic gland polyps, carcinoid.
Endocrine: diabetes mellitus, goiter, hyperglycemia/hypoglycemia.
Hematologic and Lymphatic*: agranulocytosis, anemia, aplastic anemia, hemolysis, hemolytic anemia, leukopenia, neutropenia, pancytopenia, thrombocytopenia and thrombotic thrombocytopenic purpura.
Metabolic and Nutritional Disorders: gout, weight gain/loss, edema.
Musculoskeletal: arthritis/arthralgia, musculoskeletal pain, myalgia.
Nervous System: agitation, amnesia, apathy, confusion, dizziness, syncope, hallucinations, hostility aggravated, libido decreased, depression, hemiplegia, insomnia, somnolence, thinking abnormality, anxiety, nervousness, paresthesia.
Respiratory: asthma, bronchitis, cough increased, dyspnea, hemoptysis, hiccup, upper respiratory inflammation/infection, pneumonia, epistaxis.
Skin and Appendages: acne, pruritus, rash, urticaria, alopecia.
Special Senses: amblyopia, eye pain, visual field defect, tinnitus, ophthalmologic disorders, ear disorder, deafness, otitis media, taste perversion.
Urogenital: abnormal menses, albuminuria, breast enlargement/gynecomastia, breast tenderness, glycosuria, impotence, kidney calculus, hematuria, urinary urgency.
*The majority of hematologic cases received were foreign-sourced and their relationship to lansoprazole was unclear.
Combination Therapy With Clarithromycin and Amoxicillin: In clinical trials using combination therapy with lansoprazole plus clarithromycin and amoxicillin, and lansoprazole plus amoxicillin, no adverse reactions related to these drug combinations were observed. Adverse reactions that have occurred have been limited to those that have been previously reported with lansoprazole, clarithromycin, or amoxicillin.

For more information on adverse reactions with clarithromycin or amoxicillin, refer to their respective Product Monographs, under the Adverse Effects section.
Triple Therapy: Lansoprazole/clarithromycin/amoxicillin: The most frequently reported adverse events for patients who received triple therapy were diarrhea (7%), headache (6%), and taste perversion (5%). No treatment-emergent adverse events were observed at significantly higher rates with triple therapy than with any dual therapy regimen.
Dual Therapy: Lansoprazole/amoxicillin: The most frequently reported adverse events for patients who received lansoprazole t.i.d. plus amoxicillin t.i.d. dual therapy were diarrhea (8%) and headache (7%). No treatment-emergent adverse events were observed at significantly higher rates with lansoprazole t.i.d. plus amoxicillin t.i.d. dual therapy than with lansoprazole alone.
Laboratory Values: In addition, the following changes in laboratory parameters were reported as adverse events. Abnormal liver function tests, increased AST, increased ALT, increased creatinine, increased alkaline phosphatase, increased gamma globulins, increased GGTP, increase/decreased/abnormal WBC, abnormal AG ratio, abnormal RBC, bilirubinemia, eosinophilia, hyperlipemia, increased/decreased electrolytes, increased/decreased cholesterol, increased glucocorticoids, increased LDH, increased/decreased/abnormal platelets, and increased gastrin levels. Additional isolated laboratory abnormalities were reported.

In the placebo controlled studies, when AST and ALT were evaluated, 0.4% (1/250) placebo patients and 0.3% (2/795) lansoprazole patients had enzyme elevations greater than 3 times the upper limit of normal range at the final treatment visit. None of these patients reported jaundice at any time during the study.

For more information on laboratory value changes with clarithromycin or amoxicillin, refer to their respective Product Monographs, under the Adverse Effects section.

Postmarketing Experience: Hypersensitivity reactions have been reported, including anaphylaxis.

Overdose: Symptoms and Treatment: As in all cases where overdosing is suspected, treatment should be supportive and symptomatic. Any unabsorbed material should be removed from the gastrointestinal tract, and the patient should be carefully monitored. Lansoprazole is not removed from the circulation by hemodialysis. In one reported case of overdose, the patient consumed 600 mg of lansoprazole with no adverse reaction.

Oral doses up to 5 000 mg/kg in rats (approximately 1 300 times the recommended human dose based on body surface area) and mice (about 675.7 times the recommended human dose based on body surface area) did not produce deaths or any clinical signs.

Dosage: Duodenal Ulcer: The recommended adult oral dose is 15 mg daily before breakfast for 2 to 4 weeks (see Indications).

A small percentage of patients that are H. pylori negative will experience a disease recurrence and will require maintenance treatment with an antisecretory agent. Lansoprazole 15 mg daily before breakfast may be used up to 1 year for the maintenance treatment of recurrent duodenal ulcers.
H. pylori Eradication to Reduce the Risk of Duodenal Ulcer Recurrence: Triple Therapy: lansoprazole/clarithromycin/amoxicillin. The recommended adult oral dose is 30 mg lansoprazole, 500 mg clarithromycin, and 1 g amoxicillin, all given twice daily for 14 days (see Indications). Daily doses should be taken before meals.

(For additional information on triple therapy for the treatment of H. pylori infection and active duodenal ulcer recurrence, refer to the Hp-PAC product monograph).
Dual Therapy: Lansoprazole/amoxicillin: The recommended adult oral dose is 30 mg lansoprazole and 1 g amoxicillin, each given 3 times daily for 14 days (see Indications). Daily doses should be taken before meals.

Optimal therapeutic regimens consisting of a shorter treatment duration for the eradication of H. pylori are currently under investigation.

For the eradication of H. pylori, amoxicillin and clarithromycin should not be administered to patients with renal impairment since the appropriate dosage in this patient population has not yet been established.
Gastric Ulcer: The recommended adult oral dose is 15 mg daily before breakfast for 4 to 8 weeks.

No dosage adjustment is necessary in patients with renal insufficiency. No dosage adjustment is necessary in the initial lansoprazole dosing regimen in older patients and in patients with mild to moderate hepatic impairment. Dosing recommendations described in the labelling should be adhered to for older patients and hepatically impaired patients.

Lansoprazole is not indicated for maintenance therapy in the treatment of patients with gastric ulcer.
Reflux Esophagitis or Poorly Responsive Reflux Esophagitis including Patients with Barrett's Esophagus: The recommended adult oral dose is 30 mg daily before breakfast for 4 to 8 weeks (see Indications).
Maintenance Treatment of Healed Reflux Esophagitis: For the long-term management of patients with healed reflux esophagitis, 15 mg lansoprazole given once daily before breakfast has been found to be effective in controlled clinical trials of 12 month's duration.

The recommended adult oral dose of lansoprazole for maintenance treatment of patients with healed reflux esophagitis is 15 mg daily before breakfast (see Indications).
Treatment and Maintenance of Pathological Hypersecretory Conditions Including Zollinger-Ellison Syndrome: The dosage of lansoprazole in patients with pathologic hypersecretory conditions varies with the individual patient. The recommended adult oral starting dose is 60 mg once a day. Doses should be adjusted to individual patient needs and should continue for as long as clinically indicated. Dosages up to 90 mg b.i.d. have been administered. Daily dosage of greater than 120 mg should be administered in divided doses. Some patients with Zollinger-Ellison syndrome have been treated continuously with lansoprazole for more than 4 years.
Patients With Hepatic Impairment: The daily dose of lansoprazole should not exceed 30 mg (see Warnings).
Patients With Renal Impairment: No dosage modification of lansoprazole is necessary (see Precautions).
Geriatrics: The daily dose should not exceed 30 mg (see Precautions).
Concomitant Antacid Use: Simultaneous administration of lansoprazole with Maalox (aluminum and magnesium hydroxide) or Riopan (magaldrate) results in lower peak plasma levels, but does not significantly reduce bioavailability. Antacids may be used concomitantly if required. If sucralfate is to be given concomitantly, lansoprazole should be administered at least 30 minutes prior to sucralfate (see Pharmacology, Absorption With Antacids). In clinical trials, antacids were administered concomitantly with lansoprazole delayed-release capsules; this did not interfere with its effects.

Information for the Patient: See Blue Section—Information for the Patient "Prevacid".

Supplied: 15 mg: Each pink and green-colored, opaque, hard gelatin, delayed-release capsule of enteric-coated granules contains: lansoprazole 15 mg. Nonmedicinal ingredients: cellulosic polymers, colloidal silicon dioxide, D&C Red No. 28, FD&C Blue No. 1, FD&C Green No. 3, FD&C Red No. 40, gelatin, magnesium carbonate, methacrylic acid copolymer, polyethylene glycol, polysorbate 80, starch, sucrose, sugar spheres, talc and titanium dioxide. Bottles of 30 and 100.

30 mg: Each pink and black-colored, opaque, hard gelatin, delayed-release capsule of enteric-coated granules contains: lansoprazole 30 mg. Nonmedicinal ingredients: cellulosic polymers, colloidal silicon dioxide, D&C Red No. 28, FD&C Blue No. 1, FD&C Red No. 40, gelatin, magnesium carbonate, methacrylic acid copolymer, polyethylene glycol, polysorbate 80, starch, sucrose, sugar spheres, talc and titanium dioxide. Bottles of 30 and 100.

Store in a tight container protected from light and moisture. Store between 15 and 25°C.

Reviewed 1999

PREVEX®
TCD
Refined Petrolatum
Emollient

Supplied: Cream: Each tube contains: petrolatum USP 67%, specially refined, in a nonmedicinal anhydrous base. Nonmedicinal ingredients: cyclomethicone, microcrystalline wax and purified petrolatum. Perfume- and preservative-free. Tubes of 15 and 60 g.

Lotion: Each bottle contains: petrolatum USP 6% in a nonmedicinal base. Nonmedicinal ingredients: benzyl alcohol, calcium chloride, cetyl dimethicone copolyol, dimethicone, purified petrolatum, purified water and white petrolatum. Perfume-free. Bottles of 200 mL.

Oil: Each bottle contains: Jojoba and mineral oils. Perfume- and preservative-free. Bottles of 100 mL.

PREVEX® B Ⓟ
TCD
Betamethasone Valerate
Topical Corticosteroid

Supplied: Each g of cream contains: betamethasone valerate 0.1% in an anhydrous base. Nonmedicinal ingredients: cyclomethicone, microcrystalline wax and purified petrolatum. Tubes of 30 g. Store below 25°C.

PREVEX® Baby Diaper Rash Cream
TCD
Zinc Oxide
Protectant

Supplied: Each tube contains: zinc oxide USP 15% in a cream base. Nonmedicinal ingredients: cyclomethicone, microcrystalline wax and purified petrolatum. Perfume- and preservative-free. Tubes of 50 g.

PREVEX® HC Ⓟ
TCD
Hydrocortisone
Topical Corticosteroid

Supplied: Each tube of cream contains: hydrocortisone USP 1% in an anhydrous base. Nonmedicinal ingredients: cyclomethicone, microcrystalline wax and purified petrolatum. Tubes of 30 g. Store below 25°C.

PRIMACOR® Ⓟ
Sanofi

Milrinone Lactate

Inotrope—Vasodilator

Pharmacology: Milrinone is a positive inotrope and vasodilator, with little chronotropic activity, different in structure and mode of action from either the digitalis glycosides or catecholamines.

Milrinone, at relevant inotropic and vasorelaxant concentrations, is a selective inhibitor of peak III cAMP phosphodiesterase isozyme in cardiac and vascular muscle. This inhibitory action is consistent with cAMP mediated increases in intracellular ionized calcium and contractile force in cardiac muscle, as well as with cAMP dependent contractile protein phosphorylation and relaxation in vascular muscle. Additional experimental evidence also indicates that it is not a beta-adrenergic agonist, nor does it inhibit sodium-potassium adenosine triphosphatase activity as do the digitalis glycosides.

Clinical studies in patients with congestive heart failure have shown that milrinone produces dose and plasma level-related increase in left ventricular dP/dt, increase in forearm blood flow indicating a direct arterial vasodilator activity of the drug, and improves diastolic function as evidenced by improvement in left ventricular diastolic relaxation.

Studies in normal subjects have shown that milrinone produces increases in the slope of the left ventricular pressure-dimension relationship, indicating a direct inotropic effect of the drug. Both the inotropic and vasodilatory effects have been observed over the therapeutic range of milrinone plasma concentrations of 100 to 300 ng/mL.

Pharmacokinetics: Following i.v. loading injections of 12.5 to 125 µg/kg to congestive heart failure patients, i.v. milrinone had a volume of distribution of 0.38 L/kg, a mean terminal elimination half-life of 2.3 hours, and a clearance of 0.13 L/kg/h. Following i.v. infusions of 0.2 to 0.7 µg/kg/min to congestive heart failure patients, the drug had a volume of distribution of about 0.45 L/kg, a mean terminal elimination half-life of 2.4 hours, and a clearance of 0.14 L/kg/h. These pharmacokinetic parameters were not dose-dependent, while the area under the plasma concentration versus time curve following loading injections was significantly dose-dependent.

The steady-state milrinone plasma levels after approximately 6 to 12 hours of unchanging maintenance infusion of 0.5 µg/kg/min are approximately 200 ng/mL.

Milrinone has been shown (by ultracentrifugation) to be in excess of 70% bound to human plasma proteins at plasma concentrations of 70 to 400 ng/mL.

The primary route of excretion of milrinone in man is via the urine, with much smaller amounts recovered in the feces. The major urinary excretion products in man are milrinone (83%) and its 0-glucuronide metabolite (12%). Elimination in normal subjects via the urine is rapid, with approximately 60% recovered within the first 2 hours following dosing, and approximately 90% recovered within the first 8 hours following dosing. The mean renal clearance of milrinone is approximately 0.3 L/min while that of the metabolites is even greater, indicative of active secretion.

In patients with moderate to severe renal impairment, both C_{max} (210 ng/mL) and t_{max} (1.19 h) were increased compared to subjects with normal renal function (162 ng/mL and 0.64 h, respectively). The half-life of milrinone increased from 0.94 h in subjects with normal renal function to 1.71 h in patients with moderate renal impairment and to 3.09 h in patients with severe renal impairment.

Pharmacodynamics: In patients with congestive heart failure, i.v. milrinone produces prompt, significant improvements in cardiac output, pulmonary capillary wedge pressure, and vascular resistance without clinically significant increases in heart rate or myocardial oxygen consumption. Onset of action generally occurs within 5 to 15 minutes.

Improvement in left ventricular function and relief of congestive heart failure symptoms in patients with ischemic heart disease have been observed. The improvement has occurred without inducing symptoms or electrocardiographic signs of myocardial ischemia.

In studies in congestive heart failure patients, milrinone administered as a loading injection followed by a maintenance infusion produced the following pharmacodynamic changes (see Table I).

Patients evaluated for 48 hours maintained improvements in hemodynamic function, with no evidence of diminished response (tachyphylaxis), and in a small number of patients no evidence of tachyphylaxis was seen for as long as 72 hours of infusion.

Table I—Primacor

Pharmacodynamic Changes

Dosage Regimen: Loading Dose (µg/kg)	Dosage Regimen: Maintenance Infusion (µg/kg/min)	% change: CI	PCWP	SVR	HR	MAP
37.5	0.375	+25	−20	−17	+3	−5
50.0	0.50	+38	−23	−21	+3	−5
75.0	0.75	+42	−36	−37	+10	−17

The duration of therapy should depend upon patient responsiveness. Patients have been maintained on infusion of milrinone up to 5 days.

I.V milrinone is effective in fully digitalized patients without affecting glycoside plasma levels.

Milrinone has been shown to enhance atrio-ventricular nodal conduction rate (see Precautions).

Indications: For the short-term management of severe congestive heart failure including low output states following cardiac surgery. The majority of experience with the drug has been in patients receiving digoxin and diuretics. In some patients, milrinone has been shown to increase ventricular ectopy (see Warnings).

Contraindications: In patients who are hypersensitive to it or to any of its ingredients.

Warnings: Supraventricular and ventricular arrhythmias have been observed in the high risk population of congestive heart failure patients treated with milrinone. In using the drug, consideration should be given to the fact that in some patients, milrinone has been associated with an increase in ventricular ectopy including ventricular tachycardia or fibrillation (see Adverse Effects). The incidence of arrhythmias has not been shown to be related to the dose or plasma level of milrinone. Patients receiving milrinone should be closely monitored during infusion.

No clinical studies have been conducted in patients in the acute phase of post myocardial infarction. Until further clinical experience is gained, milrinone is not recommended in these patients.

Precautions: Milrinone should not be used in lieu of surgical relief of the obstruction in patients with severe obstructive aortic or pulmonic valvular disease. Like other inotropic agents, it may aggravate outflow tract obstruction in hypertrophic subaortic stenosis.

Milrinone has been shown to enhance AV nodal conduction rate, indicating a potential for an increased ventricular response rate in patients with atrial flutter/fibrillation which is not being controlled with digitalis therapy. Digitalization of these patients should be considered prior to the administration of milrinone.

During therapy with milrinone, blood pressure and heart rate should be monitored and the rate of infusion slowed or stopped in patients showing excessive decrease in blood pressure.

Patients who have received vigorous diuretic therapy may have insufficient cardiac filling pressure to respond adequately to milrinone, in which case cautious liberalization of fluid and electrolyte intake may be indicated.

Fluid and electrolyte changes and renal function should be carefully monitored during therapy with milrinone.

Improvement in cardiac output with resultant diuresis may necessitate a reduction in the dose of diuretic. Potassium loss due to excessive diuresis may predispose digitalized patients to arrhythmias. Therefore, hypokalemia should be corrected by potassium supplementation in advance of or during milrinone administration.

Renally Impaired Patients: Data obtained from patients with severe renal impairment (creatinine clearance = 0 to 30 mL/min) but without congestive heart failure have demonstrated that the presence of renal impairment significantly increases the terminal elimination half-life of milrinone. Reductions in the infusion rate may be necessary in patients with renal impairment (see Dosage).

Geriatrics: Experience so far suggests that no special dosage recommendations for the elderly patient are necessary.

Pregnancy: Milrinone did not appear to be teratogenic when administered i.v. to pregnant rats at doses up to 3 mg/kg/day or pregnant rabbits at doses up to 12 mg/kg/day, although an increase in resorption rate was apparent at both 8 and 12 mg/kg/day (i.v.) in the latter species.

There are no studies in pregnant women. Milrinone should be used during pregnancy only if the potential benefit justifies the potential risk to the fetus.

Lactation: Caution should be exercised when milrinone is administered to nursing women, since it is not known whether it is excreted in human milk.

Children: Safety and effectiveness in children have not been established.

Drug Interactions: No untoward clinical manifestations have been observed in patients in whom milrinone was used concurrently with the following drugs: digitalis glycosides; lidocaine, quinidine; hydralazine, prazosin; isosorbide dinitrate, nitroglycerin; chlorthalidone, furosemide, hydrochlorothiazide, spironolactone; captopril; heparin, warfarin; diazepam; insulin; and potassium supplements.

Chemical Interactions: Precipitation occurs immediately when furosemide is mixed with milrinone solution. Therefore, furosemide should not be administered in i.v. lines containing milrinone.

Other drugs should not be mixed with milrinone until further compatibility data are available.

Animal Toxicity: Oral and i.v. administration of toxic dosages of milrinone to rats and dogs resulted in myocardial degeneration/fibrosis and endocardial hemorrhage, principally affecting the left ventricular papillary muscles. Coronary vascular lesions characterized by periarterial edema and inflammation have been observed in dogs only. The myocardial/endocardial changes are similar to those produced by beta-adrenergic receptor agonists such as isoproterenol, while the vascular changes are similar to those produced by minoxidil and hydralazine. Doses within the recommended clinical dose range (up to 1.13 mg/kg/day) for congestive heart failure patients have not produced significant adverse effects in animals.

Adverse Effects: In clinical trials involving 413 patients who received milrinone, the most frequent adverse effects observed were ventricular arrhythmias (12.6%) and the most severe adverse effect observed was ventricular fibrillation (0.2%).

Adverse reactions occurring in patients treated with milrinone are shown below in order of decreasing frequency (percentages indicated in parentheses): ventricular arrhythmias (12.6), ventricular ectopic activity (9.0), ventricular tachycardia (3.6), ventricular fibrillation (0.2), supraventricular arrhythmias (3.6), hypotension (3.1), headache (2.4), angina pectoris/chest pain (1.4), hypokalemia (0.7), thrombocytopenia (0.5), tremor (0.5).

Overdose: Symptoms and Treatment: No specific antidote to milrinone is known, but general measures for circulatory support should be taken. Milrinone may produce hypotension because of its vasodilator effect. In case of overdose, administration of milrinone should be reduced or temporarily discontinued until the patient's condition stabilizes.

Dosage: Prior correction or adjustment of fluid/electrolytes may be necessary to obtain a satisfactory response with milrinone (see Precautions).

Milrinone injection is a clear colorless to pale yellow solution. Vials should be inspected visually and should not be used if particulate matter or discoloration is present.

Suitable diluents include normal or half normal saline or sterile 5% dextrose solution.

Diluted solution should be used within 24 hours.

Furosemide should not be added to milrinone injection due to a chemical interaction.

Drug Administration: Milrinone should be administered with a loading dose followed by a continuous infusion (maintenance dose) according to the following guidelines (see Table II).

Table II—Primacor

Drug Administration

Loading Dose

50 µg/kg: administered slowly over 10 minutes
(For ease of administration Primacor Injection may be diluted with suitable diluents or used undiluted if suitable equipment is available).

Maintenance Dose

	Infusion Rate	Total Daily Dose (24 hours)	
Minimum	0.375 µg/kg/min	0.60 mg/kg	Administer as a
Standard	0.50 µg/kg/min	0.77 mg/kg	continuous i.v.
Maximum	0.75 µg/kg/min	1.13 mg/kg	infusion

The infusion rate should be adjusted according to hemodynamic and clinical response. Patients should be closely monitored. In controlled clinical studies most patients showed an improvement in hemodynamic status as evidenced by increases in cardiac output and reduction in pulmonary capillary wedge pressure. Dosage may be titrated to the maximum

Primacor (cont'd)

hemodynamic effect but should not exceed 1.13 mg/kg/day. Duration of therapy should depend upon patient responsiveness.

I.V. infusions of milrinone should be administered as described in Table III.

Table III—Primacor

Infusion Delivery Rate

Primacor Dosage (µg/kg/min)	Concentration of Milrinone in Infusion 100 µg/mL[a] Delivery Rate (mL/kg/h)	150 µg/mL[b] (mL/kg/h)	200 µg/mL[c] (mL/kg/h)
0.375	0.22	0.15	0.11
0.400	0.24	0.16	0.12
0.500	0.30	0.20	0.15
0.600	0.36	0.24	0.18
0.700	0.42	0.28	0.21
0.750	0.45	0.30	0.22

In order to calculate flow rate (mL/h), multiply infusion delivery rate by patient weight in kg.

[a]Prepare by adding 180 mL diluent per 20 mg vial (20 mL) Primacor Injection.

[b]Prepare by adding 113 mL diluent per 20 mg vial (20 mL) Primacor Injection.

[c]Prepare by adding 80 mL diluent per 20 mg vial (20 mL) Primacor Injection.

Dosage Adjustment in Renally Impaired Patients: The loading dosage is not affected, but reductions in the maintenance infusion rate may be necessary according to Table IV (see Precautions, Renally Impaired Patients).

Table IV—Primacor

Dosage Adjustment in Renally Impaired Patients

Creatinine Clearance (mL/min/ 1.73m²)	Primacor Dosage (µg/kg/min)	Concentration of Milrinone in Infusion 100 µg/mL[a] Delivery Rate (mL/kg/h)	150 µg/mL[b] (mL/kg/h)	200 µg/mL[c] (mL/kg/h)
5	0.20	0.12	0.08	0.06
10	0.23	0.14	0.09	0.07
20	0.28	0.17	0.11	0.08
30	0.33	0.20	0.13	0.10
40	0.38	0.23	0.15	0.11
50	0.43	0.26	0.17	0.13

In order to calculate flow rate mL/h, multiply infusion delivery rate by patient weight in kg.

[a]Prepare by adding 180 mL diluent per 20 mg vial (20 mL) Primacor Injection.

[b]Prepare by adding 113 mL diluent per 20 mg vial (20 mL) Primacor Injection.

[c]Prepare by adding 80 mL diluent per 20 mg vial (20 mL) Primacor Injection.

Reconstituted Solutions: For ease of administration milrinone may be diluted with suitable diluents such as normal or half normal saline or sterile 5% dextrose solution, or may be used undiluted if suitable equipment is available.

Diluted solutions should be used within 24 hours.

For detailed information regarding dilution, see above.

Since precipitation occurs immediately when furosemide is mixed with milrinone solution, furosemide should not be administered in i.v. lines containing milrinone.

Supplied: Each mL of sterile, clear, colorless to pale yellow solution contains: milrinone lactate equivalent to 1 mg milrinone and anhydrous dextrose USP 47 mg, in water for injection. The pH is adjusted to between 3.2 and 4.0 with lactic acid or sodium hydroxide. The total concentration of lactic acid can vary between 0.95 and 1.29 mg/mL. Single dose vials of 10 and 20 mL. Store vials at room temperature (15 to 30°C). Avoid freezing.

PRIMAQUINE ℞

Sanofi

Primaquine Phosphate

Antimalarial

Pharmacology: Primaquine is an 8-aminoquinoline compound which eliminates tissue (exo-erythrocytic) infection. Thereby, it prevents the development of the erythrocytic forms of the parasite which are responsible for relapses in vivax and ovale malaria. Primaquine phosphate is also active against gametocytes of P. falciparum.

Indications: For the radical cure (prevention of relapse) of vivax and ovale malaria.

Contraindications: In acutely ill patients suffering from systemic disease manifested by tendency to granulocytopenia, such as rheumatoid arthritis and lupus erythematosus. In patients receiving concurrently other potentially hemolytic drugs or depressants of myeloid elements of the bone marrow.

Quinacrine appears to potentiate the toxicity of antimalarial compounds which are structurally related to primaquine; therefore, the use of quinacrine in patients receiving primaquine is contraindicated. Similarly, primaquine should not be administered to patients who have received quinacrine recently, as toxicity is increased.

Warnings: Discontinue the use of primaquine promptly if signs suggestive of hemolytic anemia occur such as darkening of urine, marked fall of hemoglobin or erythrocyte count.

Hemolytic reactions (moderate to severe) may occur in glucose-6-phosphate dehydrogenase (G-6-PD) deficient Caucasians, particularly in Sardinians and in individuals with a family or personal history of favism. Dark skinned persons have a great tendency to develop hemolytic anemia (due to congenital deficiency of erythrocytic G-6-PD) while receiving primaquine and related drugs.

Pregnancy: Safe usage of this preparation in pregnancy has not been established. Therefore, use of it during pregnancy should be avoided except when in the judgment of the physician the benefit outweighs the possible hazard.

Precautions: Anemia, methemoglobinemia, and leukopenia have been observed following administration of large doses of primaquine; therefore, the adult dosage of 1 tablet daily for 14 days should not be exceeded. It is also advisable to make routine blood examinations, particularly blood cell counts and hemoglobin determinations, during therapy.

If primaquine is prescribed for a patient who has shown a previous idiosyncrasy to primaquine (as manifested by hemolytic anemia, methemoglobinemia, or leukopenia) or who has a family or personal history of favism, or G-6-PD deficiency or nicotinamide adenine dinucleotide (NADH) methemoglobin reductase deficiency, the patient should be observed closely for tolerance.

Discontinue drug immediately if marked darkening of urine, or sudden decrease in hemoglobin concentration or leukocyte count occurs.

Adverse Effects: Gastrointestinal: Nausea, vomiting, epigastric distress, and abdominal cramps.

Hematologic: Leukopenia, hemolytic anemia in G-6-PD deficient individuals, and methemoglobinemia in NADH methemoglobin reductase deficient individuals.

Overdose: Symptoms: Abdominal cramps, vomiting, burning epigastric distress, CNS and cardiovascular disturbances, cyanosis, methemoglobinemia, moderate leukocytosis or leukopenia, and anemia. The most striking symptoms are granulocytopenia and acute hemolytic anemia in sensitive persons. Acute hemolysis occurs, but patients recover completely if the dosage is discontinued.

Treatment: Empty the stomach by emesis or aspiration and lavage. Assist respiration and administer i.v. fluids and vasopressors for hypotension. Ammonium chloride in doses up to 12 g daily orally may be given to enhance urinary excretion. Sodium lactate i.v. may be used to counter the depressant effects of primaquine on the heart. Electrical pacing of the heart may be needed.

Dosage: Primaquine phosphate is recommended only for the radical cure of vivax and ovale malaria, the prevention of relapse in vivax and ovale malaria, or following the termination of chloroquine phosphate suppressive therapy in an area where vivax or ovale malaria is endemic. Patients suffering from an attack of vivax or ovale malaria or having parasitized red blood cells should receive a course of chloroquine phosphate, which quickly destroys the erythrocytic parasites and terminates the paroxysm. Primaquine should be administered concurrently in order to eradicate the exo-erythrocytic parasites in an adult dosage of 1 tablet (equivalent to 15 mg base) daily for 14 days.

When primaquine is indicated for the prevention of delayed primary attacks and relapse of P. ovale or P. vivax malaria in individuals who have returned home from areas where these plasmodial species are endemic, primaquine is generally initiated during the last 2 weeks of, or immediately following, therapy with chloroquine or another suitable antimalarial agent.

Supplied: Each pink, film-coated tablet, imprinted W on one side and P97 on the other, contains: primaquine phosphate USP 26.3 mg (equivalent to primaquine base 15 mg). Nonmedicinal ingredients: cellulose (microcrystalline), hydroxypropylmethylcellulose, lactose, magnesium stearate, polyethylene glycol 400, polysorbate 80, red iron oxide, starch, talc and titanium dioxide. Gluten- and tartrazine-free. Bottles of 100.

(Shown in Product Recognition Section)

PRIMAXIN® ℞

MSD

Imipenem—Cilastatin Sodium

Antibiotic

Pharmacology: Imipenem exerts a bactericidal action by inhibiting cell wall synthesis in aerobic and anaerobic gram-positive and gram-negative bacteria.

Primaxin consists of 2 components: imipenem, a derivative of thienamycin, a carbapenem antibiotic; and cilastatin sodium, a specific inhibitor of dehydropeptidase-I a renal enzyme which metabolizes and inactivates imipenem. Cilastatin blocks the metabolism of imipenem in the kidney, so that concomitant administration of imipenem and cilastatin allows antibacterial levels of imipenem to be attained in the urine.

Inhibition of cell-wall synthesis is achieved in gram-negative bacteria by the binding of imipenem to penicillin binding proteins (PBPs). In the case of E. coli and selected strains of P. aeruginosa, imipenem has been shown to have highest affinity for PBP-2, PBP-1a and PBP-1b, with lower activity against PBP-3. The preferential binding of imipenem on PBP-2 and PBP-1b leads to direct conversion of the individual cell to a spheroplast resulting in rapid lysis and cell death without filament formation. When imipenem is removed prior to complete killing of gram-negative species, the remaining viable cells show a measurable lag, termed a "post-antibiotic effect" (PAE), prior to resumption of new growth.

Pharmacokinetics: Primaxin was administered via i.v. infusion over 20 minutes at a single dose of 250/250 mg to 4 male subjects (mean age: 31.5±0.6 years), at a single dose of 500/500 mg to 20 male subjects (mean age: 26.8±4.1 years), and at a single dose of 1000/1000 mg to 8 male subjects (mean age: 24.8±3.7 years). Peak plasma levels of imipenem and of cilastatin were measured at the end of a 20-minute infusion, and are presented in Table I. Plasma levels of imipenem antimicrobial activity are proportional to the dose and decline to below 1 µg/mL or less in 4 to 6 hours.

Table I—Primaxin

Range of Peak Plasma Levels of Imipenem and Cilastatin Following a 20-minute I.V. Infusion of Primaxin

	250/ 250 mg	500/ 500 mg	1 000/ 1 000 mg
Imipenem (µg/mL)	12–20	21–58	41–83
Cilastatin (µg/mL)	21–26	21–55	56–88

Primaxin was administered via the i.v. route over a 30-minute period, every 6 hours, for a period of 10 days, at a dose of 1 000/1 000 mg, to a group of 6 male volunteers (mean age 28.2±5).

The pharmacokinetic parameters for imipenem and cilastatin, when Primaxin was administered at a dose of 1 000/1 000 mg, are summarized in Table II (on following page).

Excretion and Metabolism: Imipenem, when administered alone, is metabolized in the kidneys by dehydropeptidase-I and therefore achieves relatively low levels in urine.

Cilastatin is a specific inhibitor of this enzyme and it prevents renal metabolism of imipenem. When imipenem and cilastatin are given concomitantly, approximately 70% of the administered imipenem and cilastatin are recovered unchanged in the urine within 10 hours of administration, after which no further urinary excretion is detectable. Urine concentrations of imipenem in excess of 10 µg/mL can be maintained for up to 8 hours with Primaxin, at the 500 mg dose.

The remainder of the administered dose of imipenem is recovered in the urine as antibacterially inactive metabolites, and fecal elimination of imipenem is essentially nil.

Approximately 10% of the cilastatin administered is found as the N-acetyl metabolite, which has inhibitory activity against dehydropeptidase comparable to that of the parent drug. Activity of dehydropeptidase-I in the kidney returns to normal levels within approximately 8 to 12 hours after the elimination of cilastatin from the bloodstream.

Table II—Primaxin

Pharmacokinetic Parameters: Imipenem and Cilastatin 1 000/1 000 mg (I.V. Infusion over 30 min)

Time (days)	Volume of Distribution (L)	Area under the Plasma Concentration Time Curve between 0 and 6 h (μg• h/mL)	Plasma Half-Lives (min)*	Dose Recovered in Urine through 6 h (mg)	Cumulative Renal Clearance (mL/min)	Plasma Clearance (mL/min)
			Imipenem			
Day 1	13.6	73.3	59.6	540.2	126.5	227.7
Day 5	11.4	74.5	61.3	651.8	139.9	227.8
Day 10	10.9	79.7	59.4	626.5	131.3	210.4
			Cilastatin			
Day 1	10.3	82.1	57.5	698.6	142.7	208.9
Day 5	9.5	73.0	50.7	ND	ND	236.5
Day 10	9.7	77.4	50.8	ND	ND	221.6

*Harmonic means.

No accumulation of imipenem and cilastatin in plasma is observed with regimens of Primaxin administered at therapeutic doses, in patients with normal renal function.

Serum Protein Binding: At serum concentration of 25 mg/L the human serum protein binding of imipenem is 20%. Cilastatin binding to protein was found to be approximately 35% in the human serum.

Impaired Renal Function: Primaxin was administered to 6 healthy male volunteers and 25 patients with different degrees of renal impairment at a dose of 250/250 mg, in single i.v. infusions over 5 minutes. The pharmacokinetic parameters for imipenem and cilastatin are summarized in Table III.

Indications: In the treatment of serious infections when caused by sensitive strains of bacteria. Where considered necessary, therapy may be initiated on the basis of clinical judgment before results of sensitivity testings are available. Continuation of therapy should be reevaluated on the basis of bacteriological findings and of the patient's clinical condition.

Imipenem is active in vitro against a wide range of gram-positive and gram-negative aerobic and anaerobic bacteria, including most strains which are beta-lactamase producing. Patients have responded while under treatment with Primaxin for single or mixed infections of the following body systems, when they were associated with a number of pathogenic species and strains of the genera listed: lower respiratory tract infections, urinary tract infections, intra-abdominal infections, gynecological infections, septicemia, endocarditis caused by S. aureus, bone and joint infections, skin structure infections.

Primaxin is **not** indicated for the treatment of meningitis.

Gram-positive Aerobes: L. monocytogenes, N. asteroides, Staphylococcus (excluding many strains which are methicillin resistant), Streptococcus (excluding S. faecium).

Gram-negative Aerobes: Acinetobacter, Citrobacter, Enterobacter, E. coli, H. influenzae, H. parainfluenzae, Klebsiella, M. morganii, Neisseria, Proteus (indole positive and indole negative strains), Providencia, P. aeruginosa, S. marcescens.

Gram-positive Anaerobes: Clostridium (excluding C. difficile), Peptococcus, Peptostreptococcus.

Gram-negative Anaerobes: B. fragilis, Bacteroides (non-fragilis).

Contraindications: In patients who have shown hypersensitivity to either component of this product.

Warnings: Primaxin should be administered with caution to any patient who has demonstrated some form of allergy, particularly to structurally-related drugs. If an allergic reaction to Primaxin occurs, discontinue the drug. Serious hypersensitivity reactions may require epinephrine and other emergency measures.

Pseudomembranous Colitis: Pseudomembranous colitis has been reported with the use of Primaxin. Therefore it is important to consider this diagnosis in patients who develop diarrhea during or after therapy. This colitis may range from mild to life-threatening in severity.

Mild cases of pseudomembranous colitis may respond to drug discontinuance alone. In more severe cases, management may include sigmoidoscopy, appropriate bacteriological studies, fluid, electrolyte and protein supplementation, and the use of a drug such as oral vancomycin, as indicated. Other causes of colitis should also be considered.

Precautions: General: Prolonged use may result in overgrowth of resistant organisms. Repeated evaluation of the patient's condition is essential. If superinfection occurs during therapy, appropriate measures should be taken.

CNS adverse experiences such as myoclonic activity, confusional states, or seizures have been reported especially when recommended dosages based on renal function and body weight were exceeded. These experiences have occurred most commonly in patients with CNS disorders (e.g., brain lesions or history of seizures) and/or who have compromised renal function. However, there were rare reports in which there was no recognized or documented underlying CNS disorder. Close adherence to recommended dosage schedules is urged especially in patients with known factors that predispose to seizures (see Dosage).

Anticonvulsant therapy should be continued in patients with a known seizure disorder. If focal tremors, myoclonus, or seizures occur, patients should be evaluated neurologically and placed on anticonvulsant therapy if not already instituted. If CNS symptoms continue, the dosage should be decreased or discontinued.

Impaired Renal Function: Dosage in patients with impaired renal function is based on the severity of infection but the maximum daily dose varies with the degree of renal functional impairment (see Dosage, Renal Insufficiency).

Pregnancy: Use in pregnant women has not been studied, therefore, Primaxin should be used during pregnancy only if clearly needed. Use of this drug in women of childbearing potential requires that the anticipated benefits be weighed against possible hazards.

Reproduction studies with bolus i.v. doses suggest an apparent intolerance to Primaxin (including emesis, inappetence, body weight loss, diarrhea and death) at doses equivalent to the average human dose in pregnant rabbits and cynomolgus monkeys that is not seen in non-pregnant animals in these or other species. In other studies, Primaxin was well tolerated in equivalent or higher doses (up to 11 times the average human dose) in pregnant rats and mice.

Lactation: It is not known whether Primaxin is excreted in milk. If its use is deemed essential, the patient should stop nursing.

Children: Efficacy and tolerability in infants under the age of 3 months have not yet been established; therefore, Primaxin is not recommended in the pediatric age group below the age of 3 months.

Drug Interactions: Concomitant administration of Primaxin and probenecid results in only minimal increases in plasma levels of imipenem and plasma half-life. It is not recommended that probenecid be given with Primaxin.

Primaxin should not be mixed with or physically added to other antibiotics. Primaxin has been administered concomitantly with some antibiotics, such as aminoglycosides.

There is no evidence to suggest that association of Primaxin with any other beta-lactam antibiotics has any therapeutic advantage.

Adverse Effects: Primaxin is generally well tolerated. The following adverse reactions were reported on 1 723 patients treated in clinical trials. Many of these patients were severely ill and had multiple background diseases and physiological impairments, making it difficult to determine causal relationship of adverse experiences to therapy with Primaxin.

Local: Adverse local clinical reactions that were reported as possibly, probably or definitely related to therapy with Primaxin were: phlebitis/thrombophlebitis 1.7%, infused vein pain 0.6%, vein induration 0.2%, infused vein infection 0.1%.

Systemic: Adverse clinical reactions that were reported as possibly, probably or definitely related to Primaxin were:

Gastrointestinal: nausea 2.0%, diarrhea 1.7%, vomiting 1.6%, tongue papillar hypertrophy 0.2%, pseudomembranous colitis (see Warnings) 0.1%, hemorrhagic colitis <0.1%, gastroenteritis <0.1%, abdominal pain <0.1%, glossitis <0.1%, heartburn <0.1%, pharyngeal pain <0.1%, increased salivation <0.1%.

CNS: fever 0.4%, dizziness 0.3%, seizures (see Precautions) 0.2%, somnolence 0.2%, confusion 0.2%, myoclonus 0.1%, vertigo 0.1%, headache 0.1%, encephalopathy <0.1%, paresthesia <0.1%.

Special Senses: transient hearing loss in patients with impaired hearing <0.1%, tinnitus <0.1%.

Respiratory: dyspnea 0.1%, hyperventilation <0.1%, thoracic spine pain <0.1%.

Cardiovascular: hypotension 0.4%, palpitations 0.1%, tachycardia <0.1%.

Renal: oliguria/anuria <0.1%, polyuria <0.1%.

Skin: rash 0.9%, pruritus 0.3%, urticaria 0.2%, skin texture changes 0.1%, candidiasis 0.1%, erythema multiforme <0.1%, facial edema <0.1%, flushing <0.1%, cyanosis <0.1%, hyperhidrosis <0.1%, pruritus vulvae <0.1%.

Body as a whole: polyarthralgia <0.1%, asthenia/weakness <0.1%.

Laboratory Changes: Adverse laboratory changes, without regard to drug relationship, that were reported during clinical trials were:

Hepatic: Increased ALT, AST, alkaline phosphatase, bilirubin and LDH.

Hemic: Increased eosinophils, positive Coombs test, decreased WBC and neutrophils, increased WBC, increased platelets, decreased platelets, decreased hemoglobin and hematocrit, increased monocytes, abnormal prothrombin time, increased lymphocytes, increased basophils.

Table III—Primaxin

Pharmacokinetic Parameters: Imipenem and Cilastatin in Patients with Renal Failure (Single Dose 250/250 mg, I.V. Infusion over 5 min)

Group No.	No. Pts	Mean Age (yrs)	Creatinine Clearance mL/min/1.73 m² (mL/s/1.73 m²)	% Dose Urinary Recovery	Renal Clearance (mL/min)	Plasma Clearance (mL/min)	[AUC][c] (μg• h/mL)	T½[d] (min)
				Imipenem				
I	6	22.8	>100 (>1.7)	46.2	101.9	219.5	19.8	56
II	6	41.8	31–99 (0.52–1.65)	51.0[e]	77.7[e]	157.2	30.3	92
III	9	50.8	10–30 (0.17–0.50)	26.1[g]	24.2[g]	86.2	51.6	139
IV	2	32 & 67	<10 (<0.17)	11.3	8.5	69.3	60.6	160
V_a	4	42.3	Hemodialysis[a]			184.0	23.1	74
V_b	4	61.5	Hemodialysis[b]	3.4	1.8	59.1	73.1	181
				Cilastatin				
I	6	22.8	>100 (>1.7)	59.4	100.7	168.5	25.4	54
II	6	41.8	31–99 (0.52–1.65)	71.2[e]	71.3[e]	99.9	45.7	84
III	9	50.8	10–30 (0.17–0.50)	61.9[f]	23.9[g]	38.4	135.3	198
IV	2	32 & 67	<10 (<0.17)	39.4	6.5	16.2	261.4	462
V_a	4	42.3	Hemodialysis[a]			74.9	56.7	132
V_b	4	61.5	Hemodialysis[b]	17.9	2.0	11.4	416.8	696

[a]Received dose during hemodialysis.
[b]Measurements done between dialysis sessions.
[c]AUC normalized to a 250 mg dose.
[d]Harmonic means.
[e]n=5
[f]n=6
[g]n=8

Primaxin (cont'd)

Electrolytes: Decreased serum sodium, increased potassium, increased chloride.

Renal: Increased BUN, creatinine.

Urinalysis: Presence of urine protein, urine red blood cells, urine white blood cells, urine casts, urine bilirubin, and urine urobilinogen.

Marketing Experience: The following reactions have been reported since the drug was marketed, but occurred under circumstances where a causal relationship could not be established. However, in these rarely reported events, that possibility cannot be excluded. Therefore, these observations are listed to serve as alerting information to physicians and pharmacists: toxic epidermal necrolysis; hepatitis; acute renal failure. The role of Primaxin in changes in renal function is difficult to assess, since factors predisposing to pre-renal azotemia or to impaired renal function usually have been present; psychic disturbances; anaphylactic reactions; taste perversion.

Overdose: Symptoms and Treatment: There are no data available on overdosage. Primaxin is cleared by hemodialysis.

Dosage: The dosage recommendations represent the quantity of imipenem to be administered by i.v. infusion only. An equivalent amount of cilastatin is also present in the solution.

The dosage should be determined by the severity of the infection, renal function, body weight, the antibiotic susceptibility of the causative organism(s) and the condition of the patient. Doses cited are based on body weight of 70 kg.

The median duration of treatment in clinical trials for infections of the various body systems ranged from 6 to 10 days except for endocarditis and bone and joint infections for which the median duration of treatment was 4 weeks.

Adults: 1 to 2 g daily administered in equally divided doses every 6 to 8 hours (see Table IV).

Table IV—Primaxin

Adult Dosage

Severity of infection	I.V. Administration: Dose (mg of Imipenem)	Dosage Interval	Daily Dose
Mild	250 mg	6 h	1 g
Moderate	500 mg	8 h	1.5 g
Severe (fully susceptible)	500 mg	6 h	2 g
Severe* infections due to less susceptible	1 000 mg	8 h	3 g
organisms or life-threatening conditions	1 000 mg	6 h	4 g

*Primarily some strains of P. aeruginosa.

The maximum daily dose should not exceed 4 g or 50 mg/kg, whichever is less.

Geriatrics: In patients with normal renal function the dosage is the same as given for adults above. Renal status of elderly patients may not be accurately portrayed by measurement of BUN or creatinine alone. Determination of creatinine clearance is suggested to provide guidance for dosing in such patients.

Renal Insufficiency: Patients with creatinine clearances of ≤5 mL/min/1.73 m² (≤0.08 mL/s/1.73 m²) should not receive Primaxin unless hemodialysis is instituted within 48 hours. Both imipenem and cilastatin are cleared from the circulation during hemodialysis. The patient should receive Primaxin after hemodialysis and at 12 hour intervals timed from the end of that hemodialysis session (see Table V). Dialysis patients, especially those with background CNS disease, should be carefully monitored; for patients on hemodialysis, Primaxin is recommended only when the benefit outweighs the potential risk of seizures (see Precautions). Currently, there are inadequate data to recommend the use of Primaxin in patients undergoing peritoneal dialysis.

When only the serum creatinine level is available, the following formula (based on sex, weight, and age of the patient) may be used to convert this value into creatinine clearance (mL/min). The serum creatinine should represent a steady state of renal function.

$$\text{Males: } \frac{\text{Weight (kg)} \times (140 - \text{age})}{72 \times \text{serum creatinine (mg/100 mL)}}$$

Females: 0.85×above value.

Table V—Primaxin

Maximum Dosage in Relation to Renal Function

Renal Function	Creatinine Clearance mL/min/1.73 m² (mL/s/1.73 m²)	Dose (g)	Dosage Interval (h)	Maximum Total Daily Dosage (g)
Mild impairment	31–70 (0.52–1.17)	0.5	6–8	1.5–2
Moderate impairment	21–30 (0.35–0.50)	0.5	8–12	1.0–1.5
Severe[a] impairment	0–20 (0–0.33)	0.25–0.5	12	0.5–1.0[b]

[a]Patients with creatinine clearance of 6 to 20 mL/min/1.73 m² (0.1 to 0.3 mL/s/1.73 m²) should be treated with 250 mg (or 3.5 mg/kg whichever is lower) every 12 hours for most pathogens. When the 500 mg dose is used in these patients, there may be an increased risk of seizures.

[b]The highest dose is only recommended for infections due to less susceptible organisms primarily some strains of P. aeruginosa.

When using the International System of units (SI), the estimated creatinine clearance (mL/s) in males can be calculated as follows:

$$\frac{(\text{lean body weight, kg}) \times (140 - \text{age, years}) \times 1.4736}{(72) \times (\text{serum creatinine concentration, } \mu\text{mol/L})}$$

and in females the estimated creatinine clearance (mL/s) is:

$$\frac{(\text{lean body weight, kg}) \times (140 - \text{age, years}) \times 1.2526}{(72) \times (\text{serum creatinine concentration, } \mu\text{mol/L})}$$

Primaxin is cleared by hemodialysis. After each dialysis session the dosage schedule should be restarted.

Infants and Children: In children and infants 3 months of age and older, the dosage is 60 to 100 mg/kg body weight divided into 4 equal doses given at 6-hour intervals. The higher dosages should be used for infants and young children. The total daily dosage should not exceed 2 g. Clinical data are insufficient to recommend an optimum dose for infants and children with impaired renal function.

Primaxin is not recommended for the therapy of meningitis. If meningitis is suspected, an appropriate antibiotic should be used.

Primaxin may be used in children with sepsis as long as they are not suspected of having meningitis.

Caution: Contents of vials not for direct infusion.

Each reconstituted 250 mg or 500 mg dose should be given by i.v. infusion over 20 to 30 minutes. Each 1 000 mg dose should be infused over 40 to 60 minutes. In patients who develop nausea during the infusion, the rate of infusion may be slowed.

Reconstitution: Vials: Contents of the vials must be suspended and transferred to 100 mL of an appropriate infusion solution.

A suggested procedure is to transfer approximately 10 mL from the 100 mL of the appropriate infusion solution to the vial (see Compatibility and Stability, List of Diluents). Shake well. Return the resulting 10 mL of suspension to the remaining 90 mL of the infusion solution.

Repeat, using 10 mL of the diluted suspension, to ensure complete transfer of the contents of the vial to the infusion solution.

Caution: Contents of vials not for direct infusion.

ADD-Vantage Vials: When administering Primaxin using the ADD-Vantage drug delivery system, the sterile powder is added directly to a single-dose flexible plastic ADD-Vantage diluent container.

Solutions for Reconstitution: Use Abbott Laboratories' ADD-Vantage diluent containers containing 100 mL or 250 mL of either: 5% Dextrose Injection or 0.9% Sodium Chloride Injection. Reconstitute as follows (Table VI).

Table VI—Primaxin

Reconstitution Table

Strength	Amount of Diluent to be Added (mL)*	Approximate Withdrawable Volume (mL)	Approximate Average Concentration (mg/mL)
250/250	100 or 250	100 or 250	2.5 or 1.0
500/500	100 or 250	100 or 250	5.0 or 2.0

* Shake to dissolve and let stand until clear.

Special Instructions (ADD-Vantage): To Open Diluent Container: Peel overwrap from the corner and remove container. Some opacity of the plastic due to moisture absorption during the sterilization process may be observed. This is normal and does not affect the solution quality or safety. The opacity will diminish gradually.

To Assemble Vial and Flexible Diluent Container (use aseptic technique): See package insert for figures.

1. Remove the protective covers from the top of the vial and the vial port on the diluent container as follows: a) To remove the breakaway vial cap, swing the pull ring over the top of the vial and pull down far enough to start the opening. Pull the ring approximately half way around the cap and then pull straight up to remove the cap. b) To remove the vial port cover, grasp the tab on the pull ring, pull up to break the 3 tie strings, then pull back to remove the cover.
2. Screw the vial into the vial port until it will go no further. **The vial must be screwed in tightly to assure a seal.** This occurs approximately ½ turn (180°) after the first audible click. The clicking sound does not assure a seal; the vial must be turned as far as it will go. Note: Once vial is seated, do not attempt to remove.
3. Recheck the vial to assure that it is tight by trying to turn it further in the direction of assembly.
4. Label appropriately.

To Prepare Admixture:

1. Squeeze the bottom of the diluent container gently to inflate the portion of the container surrounding the end of the drug vial.
2. With the other hand, push the drug vial down into the container telescoping the walls of the container. Grasp the inner cap of the vial through the walls of the container.
3. Pull the inner cap from the drug vial. Verify that the rubber stopper has been pulled out, allowing the drug and diluent to mix.
4. Mix container contents thoroughly and use within the specified time.

Preparation for Administration (use aseptic technique):

1. Confirm the activation and admixture of vial contents.
2. Check for leaks by squeezing container firmly. If leaks are found, discard unit as sterility may be impaired.
3. Close flow control clamp of administration set.
4. Remove cover from outlet port at bottom of container.
5. Insert piercing pin of administration set into port with a twisting motion until the pin is firmly seated. Note: See full directions on administration set carton.
6. Lift the free end of the hanger loop on the bottom of the vial, breaking the 2 tie strings. Bend the loop outward to lock it in the upright position, then suspend container from hanger.
7. Squeeze and release drip chamber to establish proper fluid level in chamber.
8. Open flow control clamp and clear air from set. Close clamp.
9. Attach set to venipuncture device. If device is not indwelling, prime and make venipuncture.
10. Regulate rate of administration with flow control clamp.

Warning: Do not use flexible containers in series connections.

Compatibility and Stability: List of Diluents: Sodium Chloride 0.9% Injection, Dextrose 5% or 10% Injection, Dextrose 5% Injection with 0.02% sodium bicarbonate solution, Dextrose 5% and Sodium Chloride 0.9% Injection, Dextrose 5% Injection with 0.225% or 0.45% saline solution, Normosol-M in D5-W, Dextrose 5% Injection with potassium chloride 0.15% solution, mannitol 2.5%, 5% and 10%.

Reconstituted Solutions: Solutions range from colorless to yellow. Variations of color within this range do not affect the potency of the product.

Primaxin, as supplied in vials or in ADD-Vantage vials and reconstituted as above maintains satisfactory potency for

4 hours at room temperature and for 24 hours under refrigeration (4°C). Primaxin has been found to be stable in Sodium Chloride 0.9% Injection for 10 hours at room temperature and 48 hours under refrigeration.

Supplied: 250 mg: Each vial of sterile powder mixture contains: imipenem anhydrous equivalent to imipenem 250 mg and cilastatin sodium equivalent to cilastatin 250 mg. Also contains sodium bicarbonate buffer. ADD-Vantage vials also available.

500 mg: Each vial of sterile powder mixture contains: imipenem anhydrous equivalent to imipenem 500 mg and cilastatin sodium equivalent to cilastatin 500 mg. Also contains sodium bicarbonate buffer. ADD-Vantage vials also available.

Store the dry powder between 15 and 30°C.

PRIMENE®
Clintec

Amino Acids

I.V. Nutritive Supplement

Pharmacology: Primene is a sterile, nonpyrogenic, hypertonic solution of essential and nonessential amino acids in a Pharmacy Bulk Package. A Pharmacy Bulk Package is a container of a sterile preparation for parenteral use in a pharmacy admixture program and is restricted to the preparation of admixtures for i.v. infusion.

Primene provides a mixture of essential and nonessential amino acids as well as taurine and cysteine. This amino acid injection has been specifically formulated to provide a well tolerated nitrogen source for nutritional support for neonates, infants and young children. The amino acid profile corresponds qualitatively and quantitatively to the protein needs in this patient population. Of the total amino acids, essential amino acids comprise 47.5% and branched chain amino acids comprise 24%.

Clinical studies in infants and young children who required TPN therapy showed that infusion of Primene resulted in a normalization of the plasma amino acid concentrations. In addition, weight gains, nitrogen balance, and serum protein concentrations were consistent with an improving nutritional status.

When infused with hypertonic dextrose as a calorie source, electrolytes, vitamins, and minerals, Primene provides total parenteral nutrition in infants and young children, with the exception of essential fatty acids.

The amounts of chloride present in Primene are not of clinical significance.

The electrolyte content of any additives that are introduced should be carefully considered and included in total input computations.

Indications: The nutritional support of infants (including those of low birth weight) and young children requiring TPN via either central or peripheral infusion routes. The purpose of the solution is to prevent nitrogen and weight loss or treat negative nitrogen balance in infants and young children where: the alimentary tract cannot or should not be used, gastrointestinal absorption of protein is impaired, or metabolic requirements for protein are substantially increased, as with extensive burns.

Contraindications: In patients with untreated anuria, hepatic coma, inborn errors of amino acid metabolism, including those involving branched chain amino acid metabolism such as maple syrup urine disease and isovaleric acidemia, or hypersensitivity to one or more amino acids present in the solution.

Warnings: This solution is for compounding only, not for direct infusion.

Proper administration of this injection requires knowledge of fluid and electrolyte balance and nutrition as well as clinical expertise in recognition and treatment of the complications which may occur.

Frequent clinical evaluation and laboratory determinations are necessary to monitor changes in fluid balance, electrolyte concentration, osmolarity, and acid base balance during prolonged parenteral therapy or whenever the condition of the patient warrants such evaluation. Studies should include blood sugar, serum proteins, blood ammonia levels, kidney and liver function tests, electrolytes, hemogram, arterial blood gases, serum osmolarities and blood cultures.

Administration of amino acid solutions to a patient with hepatic insufficiency may result in serum amino acid imbalances, hyperammonemia, prerenal azotemia, stupor and coma.

The i.v. administration of these solutions can lead to fluid or solute overload resulting in hyper or hypoosmolal states. The risk of hypoosmolal states is especially present in conditions associated with ADH secretion and is proportional to the infusion rate. Hyperammonemia is of special significance in infants. This reaction appears to be related to a deficiency of the urea cycle enzymes of genetic or product origin. It is essential that blood ammonia be measured frequently in infants.

Conservative doses of this injection should be given to patients with known or suspected hepatic dysfunction. Should symptoms of hyperammonemia develop, administration should be discontinued and the patient's clinical status re-evaluated.

Administration of amino acids in the presence of impaired renal function or gastrointestinal bleeding may augment an already elevated blood urea nitrogen. Patients with azotemia from any cause should not be infused with amino acids without regard to total nitrogen intake.

This injection should not be administered simultaneously with blood through the same infusion set because of the possibility of pseudoagglutination.

Precautions: It is essential to provide adequate calories concurrently if parenterally administered amino acids are to be retained by the body and utilized for protein synthesis. Concentrated dextrose solutions are an effective source of such calories. With the administration of Primene in combination with highly concentrated dextrose solutions, hyperglycemia, glycosuria and hyperosmolar syndrome may result. Blood and urine glucose should be monitored on a routine basis in patients receiving this therapy.

Sudden cessation in administration of a concentrated dextrose solution may result in insulin reaction due to continued endogenous production. Parenteral nutrition mixtures should be withdrawn slowly.

Special care must be taken when giving hypertonic dextrose to a diabetic or prediabetic patient. To prevent severe hyperglycemia in such patients, insulin may be required.

Electrolytes may be added with this injection as dictated by the patient's electrolyte profile.

Strongly hypertonic nutrient solutions should be administered through an indwelling i.v. catheter with the tip located in the superior vena cava.

Peripheral administration of Primene requires appropriate dilution and provision of adequate calories. Care should be taken to assure proper placement of the needle within the lumen of the vein. The venipuncture site should be inspected frequently for signs of infiltration. If venous thrombosis or phlebitis occurs, discontinue infusions or change infusion site and initiate appropriate treatment.

Because of its antianabolic activity, concurrent administration of tetracycline may reduce the protein-sparing effects of infused amino acids.

During administration of amino acids in the absence of supporting carbohydrate metabolism, an accumulation of ketone bodies in the blood often occurs. Correction of ketonemia usually can be accomplished by administering some carbohydrates.

Primene contains no added electrolytes. Patients, especially those with hypophosphatemia, may require the addition of phosphate. To prevent hypocalcemia, calcium supplementation should always accompany phosphate administration. To assure adequate intake, serum levels should be monitored frequently.

To minimize the risk of possible incompatibilities arising from mixing this injection with other additives that may be prescribed, the final infusate should be inspected for cloudiness or precipitation immediately after mixing, prior to administration, and periodically during administration.

Unit must be used with a vented set or a nonvented set with a vented spike adapter.

Special Precautions: Administration of amino acid solutions and other nutrients via central or peripheral venous catheter may be associated with complications which can be prevented or minimized by careful attention to all aspects of the procedure. This includes attention to solution preparation, administration and patient monitoring. It is essential that a carefully prepared protocol, based on current medical practices, be followed, preferably by an experienced team.

Although a detailed discussion of the complications is beyond the scope of this insert, the following summary lists those based on current literature:

Technical: The placement of a central venous catheter should be regarded as a surgical procedure. The physician should be fully acquainted with various techniques of catheter insertion as well as recognition and treatment of complications. For details of techniques and placement sites, consult the medical literature. X-ray is the best means of verifying catheter placement. Complications known to occur from the placement of central venous catheters are pneumothorax, hemothorax, hydrothorax, artery puncture and transection, injury to the brachial plexus, malposition of the catheter, formation of arteriovenous fistula, phlebitis, thrombosis, cardiac arrhythmia and catheter embolus.

Septic: The constant risk of sepsis is present during administration of parenteral nutrition solutions. Since contaminated solutions and infusion catheters are potential sources of infection, it is imperative that the preparation of the solution and the placement and care of catheters be accomplished under controlled aseptic conditions. If fever develops, the solution, its delivery system and the site of the indwelling catheter should be changed. Blood cultures should be taken and the remainder of fluid should be saved for examination when deemed necessary.

Solutions ideally should be prepared in the hospital pharmacy under a laminar flow hood. The key factor in their preparation is careful aseptic technique to avoid inadvertent touch contamination during mixing of solutions and addition of other nutrients.

These solutions should be used promptly after admixing. Any storage should be under refrigeration and limited to a brief period of time, preferably less than 24 hours.

Metabolic: The following metabolic complications have been reported: metabolic acidosis, hypophosphatemia, alkalosis, hyperglycemia and glycosuria, osmotic diuresis and dehydration, rebound hypoglycemia, elevated liver enzymes, hypo and hyper vitaminosis, electrolyte imbalances and hyperammonemia. Frequent clinical evaluation and laboratory determinations are necessary, especially during the first few days of therapy, to prevent or minimize these complications.

Adverse Effects: See Warnings and Precautions, Special Precautions.

In cases of excessive administration, there is a possibility of metabolic acidosis and of elevated blood urea nitrogen in children with renal insufficiency.

Overdose: Symptoms and Treatment: In the event of overhydration or solute overload, re-evaluate the patient and institute appropriate corrective measures. See Warnings and Precautions.

Dosage: The total daily dose of Primene depends on daily protein requirements and on the patient's metabolic and clinical response. The determination of nitrogen balance and accurate daily body weights, corrected for fluid balance, are probably the best means of assessing individual protein requirements. Dosage should also be guided by the patient's fluid intake limits and glucose and nitrogen tolerances, as well as by metabolic and clinical response.

The recommended dosage of Primene is 1.5 to 3.5 g of amino acids/kg body weight/day.

Typically, Primene is admixed with 50% dextrose and supplemented with electrolytes and administered continuously over a 24 hour period.

The healthy newborn child requires 2.2 g/kg of protein and 120 kcal/kg/day. For premature infants, especially those in catabolic state, these requirements could be even higher.

Total daily fluid intake should be appropriate for the patient's age and size. A fluid dose of 125 mL/kg body weight/day is appropriate for most infants on TPN. Provision of additional nitrogen may not be possible due to fluid intake limits, nitrogen, or glucose intolerance. In addition, the provision of sufficient intracellular electrolytes, principally potassium, magnesium, and phosphate, is required for optimum utilization of amino acids, and sufficient quantities of the major extracellular electrolytes sodium, calcium, and chloride, must be given. Therefore if oral feeding is not possible or advisable and TPN is necessary, the volume restrictions dictate how to administer Primene, dextrose and most electrolytes in the same hypertonic solution through i.v. lines. Even such hypertonic solutions will not provide the required daily calories. If prolonged TPN is required (5 days or more), i.v. lipid emulsions will also have to be administered. The following scenario can serve as an example. See Table I (on following page).

Premature baby, weight 1 kg, requiring 2.5 g/kg of amino acid/day and 125 mL/kg/day fluid volume.

When prolonged parenteral nutrition (more than 5 days) is required fat emulsion should also be considered in order to prevent essential fatty acid deficiency (EFAD). Serum lipids should be monitored for evidence of EFAD in patients maintained on fat free total parenteral nutrition.

In patients with hyperchloremic or other metabolic acidoses, sodium and potassium may be added as the acetate salts to provide bicarbonate precursor. Serum electrolytes, including magnesium and phosphorus, should be monitored frequently.

Primene (cont'd)

Table I—Primene

Example

Product	mL	g of nutrient/ 100 mL	Calories	Approx. mOsmols
Primene 10%	25 mL	2.5 g	10	20
Dextrose 50%	42 mL	21 g	71	110
Water for Injection and electrolytes	33 mL			e.g. 15
Total	100 mL		81	145
Lipid 20%	25 mL		50	
Total	125 mL		131	

Additional electrolytes and trace elements should be administered as required.

Central Vein Administration: When enteral feeding is inadvisable, Primene given by central venous infusion in combination with energy sources, vitamins, trace elements and electrolytes, will meet the requirements for weight maintenance or weight gain, depending on the dose selected. The energy component in parenteral nutrition by central infusion may be derived solely from dextrose or may be provided by a combination of dextrose and i.v. fat emulsion. The addition of i.v. fat emulsion provides essential fatty acids and permits a dietary balance of fat and carbohydrate, at the same time offering the option of reducing the dextrose load and/or increasing the total caloric input. An adequate energy supply is essential for optimal utilization of amino acids.

Hypertonic mixtures of amino acids and dextrose may be administered safely by continuous infusion through a central vein catheter with the tip located in the vena cava. Initial infusion rates should be slow, and gradually increased to the recommended 60 to 120 mL/kg body weight/day. In addition to meeting nitrogen needs, the administration rate is governed, especially during the first few days of therapy, by the patient's tolerance to dextrose. Daily intake of amino acids and dextrose should be increased gradually to the maximum required dose as indicated by frequent determinations of urine and blood sugar levels.

Peripheral Vein Administration: For patients requiring parenteral nutrition in whom the central vein route is not indicated, this injection can be mixed with low concentration dextrose solutions and administered by peripheral vein in conjunction with or without fat emulsions. Reduction of protein loss can be achieved by use of diluted Primene in combination with dextrose or with dextrose and i.v. fat emulsion by peripheral infusion. Complete peripheral i.v. nutrition can be achieved in patients with low caloric requirements by a Primene-dextrose-fat regimen.

In many patients, provision of adequate calories in the form of hypertonic dextrose may require the administration of exogenous insulin to prevent hyperglycemia and glycosuria.

Parenteral nutrition may be started with infusates containing lower concentrations of dextrose; dextrose content may be gradually increased to estimated caloric needs as the patient's glucose tolerance increases.

Sudden cessation in administration of concentrated dextrose solution may result in insulin reaction due to continued endogenous insulin production. Such solutions should be withdrawn slowly.

I.V. fat emulsions provide approximately 1.2 kcal/mL (10%) or 2 kcal/mL (20%) and may be administered along with amino acid-dextrose solutions by means of a short Y-connector near the infusion site to supplement caloric intake. Fat, however, should not be the sole caloric intake since studies have indicated that glucose is more nitrogen sparing in the stressed patient.

Parenteral drug products should be inspected visually for particulate matter and discoloration prior to administration whenever solution and container permit. Use of a final filter is recommended during administration of all parenteral solutions where possible.

A slight yellow color does not alter the quality and efficacy of the product.

Primene in the Pharmacy Bulk Package is intended for use in the preparation of sterile, i.v. admixtures. Additives may be incompatible with the fluid withdrawn from this container. Complete information is not available. Those additives known to be incompatible should not be used. Consult with pharmacist, if available. When compounding admixtures, use aseptic technique. Mix thoroughly. Do not store any unused portion of Primene.

Solutions should be used promptly after mixing. Any storage should be under refrigeration and limited to a brief period of time, preferably less than 24 hours.

Directions for Use of the Pharmacy Bulk Package Container: For compounding only, not for direct infusion: 1. The Pharmacy Bulk Package is to be used only in a suitable work area such as a laminar flow hood (or an equivalent clean air compounding area). 2. Remove outer seal and metal disc. Swab surface of stopper using approved technique. 3. Insert vented connector of solution transfer set and suspend unit. Refer to directions accompanying set. 4. Once container closure has been penetrated, withdrawal of contents should be completed without delay. After initial entry, maintain contents at room temperature (25°C) and dispense within 4 hours.

Stability and Storage Recommendations: Exposure of pharmaceutical products to heat should be minimized. Solutions should be used promptly after admixing. Any storage should be under refrigeration and limited to a brief period of time, preferably less than 24 hours. Protect from freezing. It is recommended the product be stored at temperatures between 15 and 25°C, protected from light.

Parenteral drug products should be inspected visually for particulate matter and discoloration prior to administration whenever solution and container permit. Use of a final filter is recommended during administration of all parenteral solutions where possible. A slight yellow color does not alter the quality and efficacy of the product.

Parenteral Products: To minimize the risk of possible incompatibilities arising from mixing this injection with other additives that may be prescribed, the final infusate should be inspected for cloudiness or precipitation immediately after mixing, prior to administration, and periodically during administration. When compounding admixtures, use aseptic technique. Mix thoroughly. Do not store any unused portion of Primene.

Supplied: Each 100 mL contains: See Table II.

Table II—Primene

Composition	
Amino Acids	10.0 g
Total Nitrogen	1.5 g
pH	5.5
(pH adjusted with malic acid)	
Essential Amino Acids	
L-Leucine-$C_6H_{13}NO_2$	1.00 g
L-Lysine-$C_6H_{14}N_2O_2$	1.10 g
L-Valine-$C_5H_{11}NO_2$	760 mg
L-Isoleucine-$C_6H_{13}NO_2$	670 mg
L-Phenylalanine-$C_9H_{11}NO_2$	420 mg
L-Histidine-$C_6H_9N_3O_2$	380 mg
L-Threonine-$C_4H_9NO_3$	370 mg
L-Cysteine HCl	246 mg
L-Methionine-$C_5H_{11}NO_2S$	240 mg
L-Tryptophan-$C_{11}H_{12}N_2O_2$	200 mg
Taurine-$C_2H_7NSO_3$	60 mg
L-Tyrosine-$C_9H_{11}NO_3$	45 mg
Nonessential Amino Acids	
L-Glutamic Acid-$C_5H_9NO_4$	1.00 g
L-Arginine-$C_6H_7NO_2$	840 mg
L-Alanine-$C_3H_7NO_2$	800 mg
L-Aspartic Acid-$C_6H_7NO_4$	600 mg
L-Serine-$C_3H_7NO_3$	400 mg
Glycine-$C_2H_5NO_2$	400 mg
L-Proline-$C_5H_9NO_2$	300 mg
L-Ornithine-$C_5H_{12}N_2O_2$	249 mg
Water for Injection USP	qs
Anion Profiles/L	
Chloride (from cysteine HCl)	15.6 mmol/L
Malic acid	qs to pH 5.5
Osmolarity (calc.)	780 mOsmol/L

Glass pharmacy bulk package of 250 mL.

Reviewed 1997

PRINIVIL® Ⓟ

MSD

Lisinopril

Angiotensin Converting Enzyme Inhibitor

Pharmacology: Lisinopril is an ACE inhibitor which is used in the treatment of hypertension, congestive heart failure and following myocardial infarction in hemodynamically stable patients.

Angiotensin converting enzyme (ACE) is a peptidyl dipeptidase which catalyzes the conversion of angiotensin I to the pressor substance, angiotensin II. Inhibition of ACE results in decreased plasma angiotensin II, which leads to increased plasma renin activity (due to removal of negative feedback of renin release) and decreased aldosterone secretion. Although the latter decrease is small, it results in a small increase in serum K+. In patients treated with lisinopril and a thiazide diuretic there was essentially no change in serum potassium (see Precautions).

ACE is identical to kininase II. Thus, lisinopril may also block the degradation of bradykinin, a potent vasodilator peptide. However, the role that this plays in the therapeutic effects of lisinopril is unknown.

While the mechanism through which lisinopril lowers blood pressure is believed to be primarily the suppression of the renin-angiotensin-aldosterone system, lisinopril also lowers blood pressure in patients with low-renin hypertension.

Pharmacodynamics: Administration of lisinopril to patients with hypertension results in a reduction of both supine and standing blood pressure. Abrupt withdrawal of lisinopril has not been associated with a rapid increase in blood pressure. In most patients studied, after oral administration of an individual dose of lisinopril, the onset of antihypertensive activity is seen at 1 hour with peak reduction of blood pressure achieved by 6 hours. Although an antihypertensive effect was observed 24 hours after dosing with recommended single daily doses, the effect was more consistent and the mean effect was considerably larger in some studies with doses of 20 mg or more than with lower doses. However, at all doses studied, the mean antihypertensive effect was substantially smaller 24 hours after dosing than it was 6 hours after dosing. On occasion, achievement of optimal blood pressure reduction may require 2 to 4 weeks of therapy.

In hemodynamic studies in patients with essential hypertension, blood pressure reduction was accompanied by a reduction in peripheral arterial resistance with little or no change in cardiac output and in heart rate. In a study in 9 hypertensive patients, following administration of lisinopril, there was an increase in mean renal blood flow that was not significant. Data from several small studies are inconsistent with respect to the effect of lisinopril on glomerular filtration rate in hypertensive patients with normal renal function, but suggest that changes, if any, are not large.

When lisinopril is given together with thiazide-type diuretics, its blood pressure lowering effect is approximately additive.

The antihypertensive effect of angiotensin converting enzyme inhibitors is generally lower in black than in non-black patients.

Administration of lisinopril to patients with congestive heart failure reduces afterload and preload of the heart, resulting in an increase in cardiac output, without reflex tachycardia. Exercise tolerance is improved.

Pharmacokinetics: Following oral administration of lisinopril, peak serum concentrations of lisinopril occur within about 7 hours. Declining serum concentrations exhibit a prolonged terminal phase which does not contribute to drug accumulation. This terminal phase probably represents saturable binding to ACE and is not proportional to dose. Lisinopril does not bind serum proteins other than ACE.

Lisinopril does not undergo metabolism and is excreted unchanged entirely in the urine. Based on urinary recovery, the extent of absorption of lisinopril is approximately 25%, with large intersubject variability (6 to 60%) at all doses tested (5 to 80 mg). Lisinopril absorption is not influenced by the presence of food in the gastrointestinal tract.

Following multiple doses of lisinopril, the effective half-life of accumulation is 12 hours.

In a study in elderly healthy subjects (65 years and above), a single dose of lisinopril 20 mg produced higher serum concentrations than those seen in young healthy adults given a similar dose. In another study, single daily doses of lisinopril 5 mg were given for 7 consecutive days to young and elderly healthy volunteers and to elderly patients with congestive heart failure. Maximum serum concentrations of lisinopril on Day 7 were higher in the elderly volunteers than in the young, and still higher in the elderly patients with congestive heart failure. Renal clearance of lisinopril was decreased in the elderly, particularly in the presence of congestive heart failure.

The elimination of lisinopril in patients with renal insufficiency is similar to that in patients with normal renal function until the glomerular filtration rate is 30 mL/min or less. With renal function ≤30 mL/min, peak and trough lisinopril levels increase, time to peak concentration increases and time to steady state is prolonged (see Dosage).

Studies in rats indicate that lisinopril crosses the blood-brain barrier poorly.

Indications: Hypertension: In the treatment of essential hypertension and in renovascular hypertension. It may be used alone or concomitantly with thiazide diuretics. A great majority of patients (>80%) with severe hypertension required combination therapy. Lisinopril has been used concomitantly with beta-blockers and calcium antagonists, but the data on such use are limited.

Lisinopril should normally be used in those patients in whom treatment with diuretic or beta-blocker was found ineffective or has been associated with unacceptable adverse effects. Lisinopril can also be tried as an initial agent in those patients in whom use of diuretics and/or beta-blockers is contraindicated or in patients with medical conditions in which these drugs frequently cause serious adverse effects.

Congestive Heart Failure: Lisinopril is indicated in the management of symptomatic congestive heart failure as adjunctive treatment with diuretics and, where appropriate, digitalis. Treatment with lisinopril should be initiated under close medical supervision, usually in a hospital.

Acute Myocardial Infarction: Lisinopril is indicated in the treatment of hemodynamically stable patients within 24 hours of an acute myocardial infarction, to improve survival. Patients should receive, as appropriate, the standard recommended treatments such as thrombolytics, ASA and beta-blocker(s).

Therapy with lisinopril should be reassessed after 6 weeks. If there is no evidence of symptomatic or asymptomatic left ventricular dysfunction, treatment with lisinopril can be stopped.

Lisinopril should not be used if systolic blood pressure is less than 100 mmHg, if clinically relevant renal failure is present, if there is a history of bilateral stenosis of the renal arteries, or if there is a known allergy to ACE inhibitors (see Precautions, Hypotension in Acute Myocardial Infarction, Renal Impairment.

When used in pregnancy during the second and third trimesters, ACE inhibitors can cause injury or even death to the developing fetus. When pregnancy is detected, lisinopril should be discontinued as soon as possible (see Warnings, Pregnancy and Information for the Patient).

In using lisinopril, attention should be given to the risk of angioedema (see Warnings).

Contraindications: In patients who are hypersensitive to this product and in patients with a history of angioneurotic edema relating to previous treatment with an angiotensin converting enzyme inhibitor.

Warnings: Angioedema: Angioedema has been reported in patients treated with lisinopril. This may occur at any time during treatment. Angioedema associated with laryngeal edema and/or shock may be fatal. If angioedema occurs, lisinopril should be promptly discontinued and the patient should be observed until the swelling subsides. Where swelling is confined to the face, lips and mouth the condition will usually resolve without further treatment, although antihistamines may be useful in relieving symptoms. These patients should be followed carefully until the swelling has resolved. However, where there is involvement of the tongue, glottis or larynx, likely to cause airway obstruction, s.c. epinephrine (0.5 mL 1:1 000) should be administered promptly when indicated.

The incidence of angioedema during ACE inhibitor therapy has been reported to be higher in black than in non-black patients.

Patients with a history of angioedema unrelated to ACE inhibitor therapy may be at increased risk of angioedema while receiving an ACE inhibitor (see Contraindications).

Hypotension: Symptomatic hypotension has occurred after administration of lisinopril, usually after the first or second dose or when the dose was increased. It is more likely to occur in patients who are volume depleted by diuretic therapy, dietary salt restriction, dialysis, diarrhea or vomiting or possibly in patients with renin-dependent renovascular hypertension (see Dosage). In patients with severe congestive heart failure, with or without associated renal insufficiency, excessive hypotension has been observed and may be associated with oliguria and/or progressive azotemia, and rarely with acute renal failure and/or death. Because of the potential fall in blood pressure in these patients, therapy should be started under very close medical supervision, usually in a hospital. Such patients should be followed closely for the first 2 weeks of treatment and whenever the dose of lisinopril and/or diuretic is increased. Similar considerations apply to patients with ischemic heart or cerebrovascular disease in whom an excessive fall in blood pressure could result in a myocardial infarction or cerebrovascular accident (see Adverse Effects).

If hypotension occurs, the patient should be placed in supine position and, if necessary, receive an i.v. infusion of normal saline. A transient hypotensive response is not a contraindication to further doses which usually can be given without difficulty once the blood pressure has increased after volume expansion.

In some patients with congestive heart failure who have normal or low blood pressure, additional lowering of systemic blood pressure may occur with lisinopril. If hypotension occurs, a reduction of dose or discontinuation of therapy should be considered.

Neutropenia/Agranulocytosis: Agranulocytosis and bone marrow depression have been caused by angiotensin converting enzyme inhibitors. Several cases of agranulocytosis and neutropenia have been reported in which a causal relationship to lisinopril cannot be excluded. Current experience with the drug shows the incidence to be rare. Periodic monitoring of white blood cell counts should be considered, especially in patients with collagen vascular disease and renal disease.

Pregnancy: ACE inhibitors can cause fetal and neonatal morbidity and mortality when administered to pregnant women. Several dozen cases have been reported in the world literature. When pregnancy is detected, lisinopril should be discontinued as soon as possible.

In rare cases (probably less than once in every thousand pregnancies) in which no alternative to ACE inhibitor therapy will be found, the mothers should be apprised of the potential hazards to their fetuses. Serial ultrasound examinations should be performed to assess fetal development and well-being and the volume of amniotic fluid.

If oligohydramnios is observed, lisinopril should be discontinued unless it is considered lifesaving for the mother. A nonstress test (NST) and/or a biophysical profiling (BPP) may be appropriate, depending upon the week of pregnancy. If concerns regarding fetal well-being still persist, a contraction stress testing (CST) should be considered. Patients and physicians should be aware, however, that oligohydramnios may not appear until after the fetus has sustained irreversible injury.

Infants with a history of in utero exposure to ACE inhibitors should be closely observed for hypotension, oliguria and hyperkalemia. If oliguria occurs, attention should be directed toward support of blood pressure and renal perfusion. Exchange transfusion or dialysis may be required as a means of reversing hypotension and/or substituting for impaired renal function, however, experience with those procedures has been limited.

Lisinopril has been removed from the neonatal circulation by peritoneal dialysis with some clinical benefit and may, theoretically be removed by exchange transfusion, although there is no experience with the latter procedure.

Human Data: It is not known whether exposure limited to the first trimester of pregnancy can adversely affect fetal outcome. The use of ACE inhibitors during the second and third trimesters of pregnancy has been associated with fetal and neonatal injury including hypotension, neonatal skull hypoplasia, anuria, reversible or irreversible renal failure, and death. Oligohydramnios has also been reported, presumably resulting from decreased fetal renal function; oligohydramnios in this setting has been associated with fetal limb contractures, craniofacial deformation, and hypoplastic lung development. Prematurity and patent ductus arteriosus have also been reported, although it is not clear whether these occurrences were due to the ACE inhibitor exposure.

Animal Data: Lisinopril was not teratogenic in mice treated on days 6 to 15 of gestation with up to 1 000 mg/kg/day (625 times the maximum recommended human dose). There was an increase in fetal resorptions at doses down to 100 mg/kg; at doses of 1 000 mg/kg this was prevented by saline supplementation. There was no fetotoxicity or teratogenicity in rats treated with up to 300 mg/kg/day (188 times the maximum recommended dose) of lisinopril at days 6 to 17 of gestation. In rats receiving lisinopril from day 15 of gestation through day 21 postpartum, there was an increased incidence in pup deaths on days 2 to 7 postpartum and a lower average body weight of pups on day 21 postpartum. The increase in pup deaths and decrease in pup weight did not occur with maternal saline supplementation.

Lisinopril, at doses up to 1 mg/kg/day, was not teratogenic when given throughout the organogenic period in saline supplemented rabbits. Saline supplementation (physiologic saline in place of tap water) was used to eliminate maternotoxic effects and enable evaluation of the teratogenic potential at the highest possible dosage level. The rabbit has been shown to be extremely sensitive to angiotensin converting enzyme inhibitors (captopril and enalapril) with maternal and fetotoxic effects apparent at or below the recommended therapeutic dosage levels in man.

Fetotoxicity was demonstrated in rabbits by an increased incidence of fetal resorptions at an oral dose of lisinopril of 1 mg/kg/day and by an increased incidence of incomplete ossification at the lowest dose tested (0.1 mg/kg/day). A single i.v. dose of 15 mg/kg of lisinopril administered to pregnant rabbits on gestation days 16, 21 or 26 resulted in 88 to 100% fetal death.

By whole body autoradiography, radioactivity was found in the placenta following administration of labelled lisinopril to pregnant rats, but none was found in the fetuses.

Precautions: Renal Impairment: As a consequence of inhibiting the renin-angiotensin-aldosterone system, changes in renal function have been seen in susceptible individuals. In patients whose renal function may depend on the activity of the renin-angiotensin-aldosterone system, such as patients with bilateral renal artery stenosis, unilateral renal artery stenosis to a solitary kidney, or severe congestive heart failure, treatment with agents that inhibit this system has been associated with oliguria, progressive azotemia, and rarely, acute renal failure and/or death. In susceptible patients, concomitant diuretic use may further increase risk.

In acute myocardial infarction, treatment with lisinopril should not be initiated in patients with evidence of renal dysfunction, defined as serum creatinine concentration exceeding 177 μmol/L and/or proteinuria exceeding 500 mg/24 hours. If renal dysfunction develops during treatment with lisinopril (serum creatinine concentration exceeding 265 μmol/L or a doubling from the pretreatment value), then the physician should consider withdrawal of lisinopril.

Use of lisinopril should include appropriate assessment of renal function.

Hypotension in Acute Myocardial Infarction: Treatment with lisinopril must not be initiated in patients with acute myocardial infarction who are at risk of further serious hemodynamic deterioration after treatment with a vasodilator. These include patients with systolic blood pressure of 100 mmHg or lower or those in cardiogenic shock.

During the first 3 days following the infarction, dosage reduction should occur if systolic blood pressure is between 100 and 120 mmHg (see Dosage, Acute Myocardial Infarction).

Patients with myocardial infarction in the GISSI-3 study treated with lisinopril had a higher (9.0% vs 3.7%) incidence of persistent hypotension (systolic blood pressure less than 90 mmHg for more than 1 hour) than patients treated with placebo.

Hyperkalemia: In clinical trials hyperkalemia (serum potassium >5.7 mEq/L) occurred in approximately 2.2% of hypertensive patients and 4% of patients with congestive heart failure. In most cases these were isolated values which resolved despite continued therapy. Hyperkalemia was a cause of discontinuation of therapy in approximately 0.1% of hypertensive patients. Risk factors for the development of hyperkalemia may include renal insufficiency, diabetes mellitus and the concomitant use of potassium-sparing diuretics, potassium supplements and/or potassium-containing salt substitutes (see Drug Interactions).

Valvular Stenosis: There is concern on theoretical grounds that patients with aortic stenosis might be at particular risk of decreased coronary perfusion when treated with vasodilators because they do not develop as much afterload reduction.

Surgery/Anesthesia: In patients undergoing major surgery or during anesthesia with agents that produce hypotension, lisinopril blocks angiotensin II formation, secondary to compensatory renin release. If hypotension occurs and is considered to be due to this mechanism, it can be corrected by volume expansion.

Patients with Impaired Liver Function: Hepatitis, jaundice (hepatocellular and/or cholestatic), elevations of liver enzymes and/or serum bilirubin have occurred during therapy with lisinopril in patients with or without pre-existing liver abnormalities (see Adverse Effects). In most cases the changes were reversed on discontinuation of the drug.

Should the patient receiving lisinopril experience any unexplained symptoms (see Information for the Patient), particularly during the first weeks or months of treatment, it is recommended that a full set of liver function tests and any

Prinivil (cont'd)

other necessary investigation be carried out. Discontinuation of lisinopril should be considered when appropriate.

There are no adequate studies in patients with cirrhosis and/or liver dysfunction. Lisinopril should be used with particular caution in patients with pre-existing liver abnormalities. In such patients baseline liver function tests should be obtained before administration of the drug and close monitoring of response and metabolic effects should apply.

Cough: A dry, persistent cough, which usually disappears only after withdrawal or lowering of the dose of lisinopril, has been reported.

Such possibility should be considered as part of the differential diagnosis of the cough.

Lactation: Milk of lactating rats contains radioactivity following administration of ^{14}C lisinopril.

It is not known whether this drug is secreted in human milk. Because many drugs are secreted in human milk, caution should be exercised when lisinopril is given to a nursing mother.

Geriatrics: In general, blood pressure response and adverse experiences were similar in younger and older patients given similar doses of lisinopril. Pharmacokinetic studies, however, indicate that maximum blood levels and area under the plasma concentration time curve (AUC) are doubled in older patients so that dosage adjustments should be made with particular caution (see Dosage).

Children: Safety and effectiveness in children have not been established.

Anaphylactoid Reactions during Membrane Exposure: Anaphylactoid reactions have been reported in patients dialysed with high-flux membranes (e.g. polyacrylonitrile [PAN]) and treated concomitantly with an ACE inhibitor. Dialysis should be stopped immediately if symptoms such as nausea, abdominal cramps, burning, angioedema, shortness of breath and severe hypotension occur. Symptoms are not relieved by antihistamines. In these patients consideration should be given to using a different type of dialysis membrane or a different class of antihypertensive agent.

Anaphylactoid Reactions during LDL Apheresis: Rarely, patients receiving ACE inhibitors during low density lipoprotein (LDL)-apheresis with dextran sulfate have experienced life-threatening anaphylactoid reactions. These reactions were avoided by temporarily withholding ACE inhibitor therapy prior to each apheresis.

Anaphylactoid Reactions during Hymenoptera Desensitization: There have been isolated reports of patients experiencing sustained life-threatening anaphylactoid reactions while receiving ACE inhibitors during desensitizing treatment with hymenoptera (bees, wasps) venom. In the same patients, these reactions have been avoided when ACE inhibitors were temporarily withheld for at least 24 hours, but they have reappeared upon inadvertent rechallenge.

Drug Interactions: Hypotension: Patients on Diuretic Therapy: Patients on diuretics and especially those in whom diuretic therapy was recently instituted may occasionally experience an excessive reduction of blood pressure after initiation of therapy with lisinopril. The possibility of symptomatic hypotension with lisinopril can be minimized by discontinuing the diuretic prior to initiation of treatment with lisinopril and/or lowering the initial dose of lisinopril (see Warnings, Hypotension and Dosage).

Agents Increasing Serum Potassium: Since lisinopril decreases aldosterone production, elevation of serum potassium may occur. Potassium sparing diuretics, such as spironolactone, triamterene or amiloride, or potassium supplements should be given only for documented hypokalemia and with caution and with frequent monitoring of serum potassium since they may lead to a significant increase in serum potassium. Potassium-containing salt substitutes should also be used with caution.

Agents Causing Renin Release: The antihypertensive effect of lisinopril is augmented by antihypertensive agents that cause renin release (e.g., diuretics).

Agents Affecting Sympathetic Activity: Agents affecting sympathetic activity (e.g. ganglionic blocking agents or adrenergic neuron blocking agents) may be used with caution. Beta-adrenergic blocking drugs add some further antihypertensive effect to lisinopril.

Indomethacin: Indomethacin may diminish the antihypertensive efficacy of concomitantly administered lisinopril.

Lithium Salts: As with other drugs which eliminate sodium, the lithium elimination may be reduced. Therefore, the serum lithium levels should be monitored carefully if lithium salts are to be administered.

Information for the Patient: Angioedema: Angioedema, including laryngeal edema, may occur especially following the first dose of lisinopril. Patients should be so advised and told to report immediately any signs or symptoms suggesting angioedema (swelling of face, extremities, eyes, lips, tongue, difficulty in breathing) and to take no more drug until they have consulted with the prescribing physician.

Hypotension: Patients should be cautioned to report lightheadedness especially during the first few days of therapy. If actual syncope occurs, the patients should be told to discontinue the drug until they have consulted with the prescribing physician.

All patients should be cautioned that excessive perspiration and dehydration may lead to an excessive fall in blood pressure because of reduction in fluid volume. Other causes of volume depletion such as vomiting or diarrhea may also lead to a fall in blood pressure; patients should be advised to consult with their physician.

Neutropenia: Patients should be told to report promptly any indication of infection (e.g., sore throat, fever) which may be a sign of neutropenia.

Impaired Liver Function: Patients should be advised to return to the physician if he/she experiences any symptoms possibly related to liver dysfunction. This would include "viral-like symptoms" in the first weeks to months of therapy (such as fever, malaise, muscle pain, rash or adenopathy which are possible indicators of hypersensitivity reactions), or if abdominal pain, nausea or vomiting, loss of appetite, jaundice, itching or any other unexplained symptoms occur during therapy.

Hyperkalemia: Patients should be told not to use salt substitutes containing potassium without consulting their physician.

Pregnancy: Patients should be advised to report promptly to their physician if they become pregnant, since the use of lisinopril during pregnancy can cause injury and even death of the developing fetus.

Note: As with many other drugs, certain advice to patients being treated with lisinopril is warranted. This information is intended to aid in the safe and effective use of this medication. It is not a disclosure of all possible adverse or intended effects.

Adverse Effects: In controlled clinical trials involving 3 269 patients (2 633 patients with hypertension and 636 patients with congestive heart failure), the most frequent clinical adverse reactions were: dizziness (4.4%), headache (5.6%), asthenia/fatigue (2.7%), diarrhea (1.8%) and cough (3%), all of which were more frequent than in placebo-treated patients. Discontinuation of therapy was required in 5.9% of patients.

For adverse reactions which occurred in hypertensive patients and patients with congestive heart failure treated with lisinopril in controlled clinical trials, comparative incidence data are listed in Table I.

Angioedema: Angioedema has been reported in patients receiving lisinopril (0.1%). Angioedema associated with laryngeal edema may be fatal. If angioedema of the face, extremities, lips, tongue, glottis and/or larynx occurs, treatment with lisinopril should be discontinued and appropriate therapy instituted immediately (see Warnings, Angioedema).

Hypotension: In hypertensive patients, hypotension occurred in 0.8% and syncope occurred in 0.2% of patients. Hypotension or syncope was a cause for discontinuation of therapy in 0.3% of hypertensive patients (see Warnings).

In patients with congestive heart failure, hypotension occurred in 5.2% and syncope occurred in 1.7% of patients. Hypotension and dizziness were causes for discontinuation of therapy in 1.7% of these patients.

Additional adverse reactions which were reported rarely, either during controlled clinical trials or after the drug was marketed, include:

Cardiovascular: myocardial infarction or cerebrovascular accident possibly secondary to excessive hypotension in high risk patients (see Warnings), tachycardia.

Dermatologic: alopecia, diaphoresis, pemphigus, pruritus, Stevens-Johnson syndrome, urticaria.

Gastrointestinal: abdominal pain, dry mouth, pancreatitis.

Hematologic: hemolytic anemia.

Hepatic: hepatitis, jaundice (hepatocellular and/or cholestatic), liver function abnormalities.

Nervous System: mental confusion, mood alterations, paresthesia.

Respiratory: bronchospasm.

Special Senses: taste disorders.

Table I—Prinivil

Incidence of Adverse Reactions Occurring in Patients Treated with Prinivil in Controlled Clinical Trials

	Hypertension (2 633 Patients) %	Congestive Heart Failure (636 Patients) %
Cardiovascular		
Hypotension	0.8	5.2
Orthostatic effects	0.9	1.3
Chest pain	1.1	7.4
Angina	0.3	3.8
Edema	0.6	2.5
Palpitation	0.8	1.9
Rhythm disturbances	0.5	0.6
Gastrointestinal		
Diarrhea	1.8	6.1
Nausea	1.9	4.9
Vomiting	1.1	2.4
Dyspepsia	0.5	1.9
Anorexia	0.4	1.4
Constipation	0.2	0.8
Flatulence	0.3	0.5
Nervous System		
Dizziness	4.4	14.2
Headache	5.6	4.6
Paresthesia	0.5	2.8
Depression	0.7	1.1
Somnolence	0.8	0.6
Insomnia	0.3	2.4
Vertigo	0.2	0.2
Respiratory		
Cough	3.0	6.4
Dyspnea	0.4	7.4
Orthopnea	0.1	0.9
Dermatologic		
Rash	1.0	5.0
Pruritus	0.5	1.4
Musculoskeletal		
Muscle cramps	0.5	2.2
Back pain	0.5	1.7
Leg pain	0.1	1.3
Shoulder pain	0.2	0.8
Other		
Asthenia/fatigue	2.7	7.1
Blurred vision	0.3	1.1
Fever	0.3	1.1
Flushing	0.3	0.3
Gout	0.2	1.7
Decreased libido	0.2	0.2
Malaise	0.3	1.1

Urogenital: acute renal failure, impotence, oliguria/anuria, renal dysfunction, uremia.

A symptom complex has been reported which may include fever, vasculitis, myalgia, arthralgia/arthritis, a positive ANA, elevated ESR, eosinophilia and leukocytosis. Rash, photosensitivity or other dermatologic manifestations may also occur.

Laboratory Test Findings: Serum Electrolytes: Hyperkalemia and hyponatremia have occurred (see Precautions).

Creatinine, Blood Urea Nitrogen: Increases in blood urea nitrogen and serum creatinine, usually reversible upon discontinuation of therapy, were observed in 1.1 and 1.6% of patients respectively with essential hypertension treated with lisinopril alone. Increases were more common in patients receiving concomitant diuretics and in patients with renal artery stenosis (see Precautions). Reversible increases in blood urea nitrogen (14.5%) and serum creatinine (11.2%) were observed in approximately 12.0% of patients with congestive heart failure on concomitant diuretic therapy. Frequently, these abnormalities resolved when the dosage of the diuretic was decreased.

Hematology: Decreases in hemoglobin and hematocrit (mean decreases of approximately 0.9 g % and 0.6 vol % respectively) occurred frequently in patients treated with lisinopril but were rarely of clinical importance in patients without some other cause of anemia.

An occasional case of neutropenia and bone marrow depression has been reported in the world literature.

Thrombocytopenia and leukopenia have been reported; a causal relationship to therapy with lisinopril cannot be excluded.

Hepatic: Elevations of liver enzymes and/or serum bilirubin have occurred (see Precautions).

Discontinuations: Overall, 1% of patients discontinued therapy due to laboratory adverse experiences, principally elevations in blood urea nitrogen (0.8%), serum creatinine (0.1%) and serum potassium (0.1%).

Overdose: Symptoms and Treatment: There are no data on overdosage in humans. The most likely manifestation of overdosage would be hypotension, for which the usual treatment would be i.v. infusion of normal saline solution.

Lisinopril may be removed from the general circulation by hemodialysis.

Dosage: Since absorption of lisinopril is not affected by food, the tablets may be administered before, during or after meals. Lisinopril should be administered in a single daily dose.

Dosage must be individualized.

Essential Hypertension: In patients with essential hypertension, not on diuretic therapy, the usual recommended starting dose is 10 mg once a day. Dosage should be adjusted according to blood pressure response: the usual dosage range is 10 to 40 mg/day, administered in a single daily dose. The antihypertensive effect may diminish toward the end of the dosing interval regardless of the administered dose, but most commonly with a dose of 10 mg daily. This can be evaluated by measuring blood pressure just prior to dosing to determine whether satisfactory control is being maintained for 24 hours. If it is not, an increase in dose should be considered. The maximum dose used in long-term controlled clinical trials was 80 mg/day. If blood pressure is not controlled with lisinopril alone, a low dose of a diuretic may be added. Hydrochlorothiazide 12.5 mg has been shown to provide an additive effect. After the addition of a diuretic, it may be possible to reduce the dose of lisinopril.

Diuretic Treated Patients: In hypertensive patients who are currently being treated with a diuretic, symptomatic hypotension may occur occasionally following the initial dose of lisinopril. The diuretic should be discontinued, if possible, for 2 to 3 days before beginning therapy with lisinopril to reduce the likelihood of hypotension (see Warnings). The dosage of lisinopril should be adjusted according to blood pressure response. If the patient's blood pressure is not controlled with lisinopril alone, diuretic therapy may be resumed as described above.

If the diuretic cannot be discontinued, an initial dose of 5 mg should be used under medical supervision for at least 2 hours and until blood pressure has stabilized for at least an additional hour (see Warnings, Hypotension and Precautions, Drug Interactions).

A lower starting dose is required in the presence of renal impairment, in patients in whom diuretic therapy cannot be discontinued, in patients who are volume and/or salt-depleted for any reason, and in patients with renovascular hypertension.

Dosage Adjustment in Renal Impairment: Dosage in patients with renal impairment should be based on creatinine clearance as outlined in Table II.

Table II—Prinivil

Dosage Adjustment in Renal Impairment

Creatinine Clearance mL/s (mL/min)	**Starting Dose mg/day**
≤1.17≥0.5 mL/s(≤70≥30 mL/min)	5.0-10.0 mg
≤0.5≥0.17 mL/s(≤30≥10 mL/min)	2.5-5.0 mg
<0.17 mL/s(<10 mL/min) (including patients on dialysis)	2.5 mg*

* Dosage and/or frequency of administration should be adjusted depending on the blood pressure response.

The dosage may be titrated upward until blood pressure is controlled or to a maximum of 40 mg daily. Anaphylactoid reactions have been reported in patients dialysed with high-flux membranes (e.g. polyacrylonitrile [PAN]) and treated concomitantly with an ACE inhibitor (see Precautions, Anaphylactoid Reactions during Membrane Exposure).

Geriatrics: In general, blood pressure response and adverse experiences were similar in younger and older patients given similar doses of lisinopril. Pharmacokinetic studies, however, indicate that maximum blood levels and area under the plasma concentration time curve (AUC) are doubled in older patients so that dosage adjustments should be made with particular caution.

Renovascular Hypertension: Some patients with renovascular hypertension, especially those with bilateral renal artery stenosis or stenosis of the artery to a solitary kidney, may develop an exaggerated response to the first dose of lisinopril. Therefore, a lower starting dose of 2.5 or 5 mg is recommended. Thereafter, the dosage may be adjusted according to the blood pressure response.

Congestive Heart Failure: Lisinopril is to be used in conjunction with a diuretic and where appropriate digitalis. Therapy must be initiated under close medical supervision, usually in a hospital. Blood pressure and renal function should be monitored, both before and during treatment with lisinopril, because severe hypotension and, more rarely, consequent renal failure have been reported (see Warnings, Hypotension and Precautions, Renal Impairment).

Initiation of therapy requires consideration of recent diuretic therapy and the possibility of severe salt/volume depletion. If possible, the dose of diuretic should be reduced before beginning treatment.

The recommended initial dose is 2.5 mg/day. If required, the dose should be increased gradually, depending on the patient response. The usual effective dosage range is 5 to 20 mg/day administered in a single daily dose. Dose titration may be performed over a 2 to 4 week period, or more rapidly if indicated by the presence of residual signs and symptoms of heart failure.

Acute Myocardial Infarction: Treatment with lisinopril may be started within 24 hours of the onset of symptoms in hemodynamically stable patients. Patients should receive, as appropriate, the standard recommended treatments such as thrombolytics, ASA and beta blocker(s) (see Indications, Acute Myocardial Infarction).

The first dose of lisinopril is 5 mg given orally, followed by 5 mg after 24 hours, 10 mg after 48 hours and then 10 mg once daily thereafter.

Patients with a low systolic blood pressure (between 100 and 120 mmHg) when treatment is started or during the first 3 days after the infarct should be given a lower dose, 2.5 mg orally (see Precautions, Hypotension and Acute Myocardial Infarction). After 3 days if hypotension occurs (systolic blood pressure less than or equal to 100 mmHg), a daily maintenance dose of 5 mg may be given with temporary reductions to 2.5 mg if needed. If prolonged hypotension occurs (systolic blood pressure less than 90 mmHg for more than 1 hour), lisinopril should be withdrawn.

Renal function should be assessed before and during therapy with lisinopril (see Precautions, Renal Impairment).

Dosing should normally continue for 6 weeks. At that time, patients with signs or symptoms of heart failure should continue with lisinopril (see Congestive Heart Failure).

Lisinopril is compatible with i.v. or transdermal glyceryl trinitrate.

Information for the Patient: See Blue Section—Information for the Patient "Prinivil".

Supplied: 5 mg: Each white, shield shaped, scored, compressed tablet, with code 19/19 on one side and PRINIVIL on the other, contains: lisinopril 5 mg. Nonmedicinal ingredients: calcium phosphate, cornstarch, magnesium stearate, mannitol. Bottles of 100. Blister packages of 30.

10 mg: Each yellow, shield shaped, compressed tablet, with code 106 on one side and PRINIVIL on the other, contains: lisinopril 10 mg. Nonmedicinal ingredients: calcium phosphate, cornstarch, iron oxide, magnesium stearate, mannitol. Bottles of 100. Blister packages of 30.

20 mg: Each peach, shield shaped, compressed tablet, with code 207 on one side and PRINIVIL on the other, contains: lisinopril 20 mg. Nonmedicinal ingredients: calcium phosphate, cornstarch, iron oxide, magnesium stearate, mannitol. Bottles of 100. Blister packages of 30.

Store at room temperature (15 to 30°C).

(Shown in Product Recognition Section)

Reviewed 1999

PRINZIDE®

MSD

Lisinopril—Hydrochlorothiazide

Angiotensin Converting Enzyme Inhibitor—Diuretic

Pharmacology: Prinzide combines the action of an angiotensin converting enzyme inhibitor, lisinopril, and a diuretic, hydrochlorothiazide.

Lisinopril: Angiotensin converting enzyme (ACE) is a peptidyl dipeptidase which catalyzes the conversion of angiotensin I to the pressor substance, angiotensin II. Inhibition of ACE results in decreased plasma angiotensin II, which leads to increased plasma renin activity (due to removal of negative feedback of renin release) and decreased aldosterone secretion. Although the latter decrease is small, it results in a small increase in serum potassium. In patients treated with lisinopril plus a thiazide diuretic, there was essentially no change in serum potassium (see Precautions).

ACE is identical to kininase II. Thus, lisinopril may also block the degradation of bradykinin, a potent vasodilator peptide. However, the role that this plays in the therapeutic effects of lisinopril is unknown.

While the mechanism through which lisinopril lowers blood pressure is believed to be primarily the suppression of the renin-angiotensin-aldosterone system, lisinopril also lowers blood pressure in patients with low-renin hypertension.

When lisinopril is given together with thiazide-type diuretics, its blood pressure lowering effect is approximately additive.

The antihypertensive effect of angiotensin converting enzyme inhibitors is generally lower in black than in non-black patients.

Pharmacodynamics: Administration of lisinopril to patients with hypertension results in a reduction of both supine and standing blood pressure. Abrupt withdrawal of lisinopril has not been associated with a rapid increase in blood pressure. In most patients studied, after oral administration of an individual dose of lisinopril, the onset of antihypertensive activity is seen 1 hour with peak reduction of blood pressure achieved by 6 hours. Although an antihypertensive effect was observed 24 hours after dosing with recommended single daily doses, the effect was more consistent and the mean effect was considerably larger in some studies with doses of 20 mg or more than with lower doses. However, at all doses studied, the mean antihypertensive effect was substantially smaller 24 hours after dosing than it was 6 hours after dosing. On occasion, achievement of optimal blood pressure reduction may require 2 to 4 weeks of therapy.

In hemodynamic studies in patients with essential hypertension, blood pressure reduction was accompanied by a reduction in peripheral arterial resistance with little or no change in cardiac output and in heart rate. In a study in 9 hypertensive patients, following administration of lisinopril, there was an increase in mean renal blood flow that was not significant. Data from several small studies are inconsistent with respect to the effect of lisinopril on glomerular filtration rate in hypertensive patients with normal renal function, but suggest that changes, if any, are not large.

Hydrochlorothiazide: Hydrochlorothiazide is a diuretic and antihypertensive which interferes with the renal tubular mechanism of electrolyte reabsorption. It increases excretion of sodium and chloride in approximately equivalent amounts. Natriuresis may be accompanied by some loss of potassium and bicarbonate. While this compound is predominantly a saluretic agent, in vitro studies have shown that it has a carbonic anhydrase inhibitory action which seems to be relatively specific for the renal tubular mechanism. It does not appear to be concentrated in erythrocytes or the brain in sufficient amounts to influence the activity of carbonic anhydrase in those tissues.

Hydrochlorothiazide is useful in the treatment of hypertension. It may be used alone or as an adjunct to other antihypertensive drugs. Hydrochlorothiazide does not affect normal blood pressure. The mechanism of its antihypertensive action is not known. Lowering of the sodium content of arteriolar smooth muscle cells and diminished response to norepinephrine have been postulated.

Onset of the diuretic action following oral administration occurs in 2 hours and the peak action in about 4 hours. Diuretic activity lasts about 6 to 12 hours.

Pharmacokinetics: Lisinopril: Following oral administration of lisinopril, peak serum concentrations occur within about 7 hours. Declining serum concentrations exhibit a prolonged terminal phase which does not contribute to drug accumulation. This terminal phase probably represents saturable binding to ACE and is not proportional to dose. Lisinopril does not bind to plasma proteins other than ACE.

Lisinopril does not undergo metabolism and is excreted unchanged entirely in the urine. Based on urinary recovery, the extent of absorption of lisinopril is approximately 25%, with large inter-subject variability (6 to 60%) at all doses tested (5 to 80 mg).

Lisinopril absorption is not influenced by the presence of food in the gastrointestinal tract.

Upon multiple dosing, lisinopril exhibits an effective half-life of accumulation of 12 hours.

In a study in elderly healthy subjects (65 years and above), a single dose of lisinopril 20 mg produced higher serum concentrations than those seen in young healthy adults given a similar dose. In another study, single daily doses of lisinopril 5 mg were given for 7 consecutive days to young and elderly healthy volunteers. Maximum serum concentrations of lisinopril on Day 7 were higher in the elderly volunteers than in the young.

Prinzide (cont'd)

The elimination of lisinopril in patients with renal insufficiency is similar to that in patients with normal renal function until the glomerular filtration rate is 30 mL/min or less. With renal function ≤30 mL/min, peak and trough lisinopril levels increase, time to peak concentration increases and time to steady state may be prolonged (see Dosage).

Studies in rats indicate that lisinopril crosses the blood-brain barrier poorly.

Hydrochlorothiazide: Hydrochlorothiazide is not metabolized but is eliminated rapidly by the kidney. The plasma half-life is 5.6 to 14.8 hours when the plasma levels can be followed for at least 24 hours. At least 61% of the oral dose is eliminated unchanged within 24 hours. Hydrochlorothiazide crosses the placental but not the blood-brain barrier and is excreted in breast milk.

Lisinopril–Hydrochlorothiazide: Concomitant administration of lisinopril and hydrochlorothiazide has little or no effect on the bioavailability of either drug. The combination tablet is bioequivalent to concomitant administration of the separate entities.

Indications: For the treatment of essential hypertension in patients for whom combination therapy is appropriate.

In using Prinzide, consideration should be given to the risk of angioedema (see Warnings).

Lisinopril should normally be used in those patients in whom treatment with diuretic or beta-blocker was found ineffective or has been associated with unacceptable adverse effects.

Prinzide is not indicated for initial therapy. Patients in whom lisinopril and diuretic are initiated simultaneously can develop symptomatic hypotension (see Precautions, Drug Interactions).

Patients should be titrated on the individual drugs. If the fixed combination represents the dosage determined by this titration, the use of Prinzide may be more convenient in the management of patients. If during maintenance therapy dosage adjustment is necessary, it is advisable to use individual drugs.

Pregnancy: **When used in pregnancy during the second and third trimesters, ACE inhibitors can cause injury or even death of the developing fetus. When pregnancy is detected Prinzide should be discontinued as soon as possible (see Warnings, Pregnancy, and Information for the Patient).**

Contraindications: Patients who are hypersensitive to any component of this product and patients with a history of angioneurotic edema relating to previous treatment with an angiotensin converting enzyme inhibitor. Because of the hydrochlorothiazide component, this product is contraindicated in patients with anuria or hypersensitivity to other sulfonamide-derived drugs.

Warnings: Angioedema: Angioedema has been reported in patients treated with Prinzide. This may occur at any time during treatment. Angioedema associated with laryngeal edema and/or shock may be fatal. If angioedema occurs, Prinzide should be promptly discontinued and appropriate monitoring should be instituted to ensure complete resolution of symptoms prior to dismissing the patient. Where swelling is confined to the face, lips and mouth the condition will usually resolve without further treatment, although antihistamines may be useful in relieving symptoms. These patients should be followed carefully until the swelling has resolved. However, where there is involvement of the tongue, glottis or larynx, likely to cause airway obstruction, s.c. epinephrine (0.5 mL 1:1 000) should be administered promptly when indicated.

The incidence of angioedema during ACE inhibitor therapy has been reported to be higher in black than in nonblack patients.

Patients with a history of angioedema unrelated to ACE inhibitor therapy may be at increased risk of angioedema while receiving an ACE inhibitor (see Contraindications).

Hypotension: Symptomatic hypotension has occurred after administration of lisinopril, usually after the first or second dose or when the dose was increased. It is more likely to occur in patients who are volume depleted by diuretic therapy, dietary salt restriction, dialysis, diarrhea or vomiting. Therefore, Prinzide should not be used to start therapy or when a dose change is needed. In patients with ischemic heart or cerebrovascular disease, an excessive fall in blood pressure could result in a myocardial infarction or cerebrovascular accident (see Adverse Effects). Because of the potential fall in blood pressure in these patients, therapy with lisinopril should be started under very close medical supervision, usually in a hospital. Such patients should be followed closely for the first 2 weeks of treatment and whenever the dose of lisinopril and/or hydrochlorothiazide is increased. In patients with severe congestive heart failure, with or without associated renal insufficiency, excessive hypotension has been observed and may be associated with oliguria and/or progressive azotemia, and rarely with acute renal failure and/or death.

If hypotension occurs, the patient should be placed in supine position and, if necessary, receive an i.v. infusion of normal saline. A transient hypotensive response is not a contraindication to further doses which usually can be given without difficulty once the blood pressure has increased after volume expansion.

Neutropenia/Agranulocytosis: Agranulocytosis and bone marrow depression have been caused by angiotensin converting enzyme inhibitors. Several cases of agranulocytosis and neutropenia have been reported in which a causal relationship to lisinopril cannot be excluded. Current experience with the drug shows the incidence to be rare. Periodic monitoring of white blood cell counts should be considered, especially in patients with collagen vascular disease and renal disease.

Azotemia: Azotemia may be precipitated or increased by hydrochlorothiazide. Cumulative effects of the drug may develop in patients with impaired renal function. If increasing azotemia and oliguria occur during treatment of severe progressive renal disease the diuretic should be discontinued.

Patients with Impaired Liver Function: Hepatitis, jaundice (hepatocellular and/or cholestatic), elevations of liver enzymes and/or serum bilirubin have occurred during therapy with lisinopril in patients with or without pre-existing liver abnormalities (see Adverse Effects). In most cases the changes were reversed on discontinuation of the drug.

Should the patient receiving Prinzide experience any unexplained symptoms (see Information for the Patient), particularly during the first weeks or months of treatment, it is recommended that a full set of liver function tests and any other necessary investigation be carried out. Discontinuation of Prinzide should be considered when appropriate.

There are no adequate studies in patients with cirrhosis and/or liver dysfunction. Prinzide should be used with particular caution in patients with pre-existing liver abnormalities. In such patients baseline liver function tests should be obtained before administration of the drug and close monitoring of response and metabolic effects should apply.

Thiazides should be used with caution in patients with impaired hepatic function or progressive liver disease, since minor alterations of fluid and electrolyte balance may precipitate hepatic coma.

Hypersensitivity Reactions: Sensitivity reactions to hydrochlorothiazide may occur in patients with or without a history of allergy or bronchial asthma.

The possibility of exacerbation or activation of systemic lupus erythematosus has been reported in patients treated with hydrochlorothiazide.

Pregnancy: ACE inhibitors can cause fetal and neonatal morbidity and mortality when administered to pregnant women. Several dozen cases have been reported in the world literature. When pregnancy is detected, Prinzide should be discontinued as soon as possible.

In rare cases (probably less than once in every thousand pregnancies) in which no alternative to ACE inhibitor therapy will be found, the mothers should be apprised of the potential hazards to their fetuses. Serial ultrasound examinations should be performed to assess fetal development and well-being and the volume of amniotic fluid.

If oligohydramnios is observed, then Prinzide should be discontinued unless it is considered lifesaving for the mother. A non-stress test (NST), and/or a biophysical profiling (BPP) may be appropriate, depending on the week of pregnancy. If concerns regarding fetal well-being still persist, a contraction stress testing (CST) should be considered. Patients and physicians should be aware, however, that oligohydramnios may not appear until after the fetus has sustained irreversible injury.

Infants with a history of in utero exposure to ACE inhibitors should be closely observed for hypotension, oliguria and hyperkalemia. If oliguria occurs, attention should be directed toward support of blood pressure and renal perfusion. Exchange transfusion or dialysis may be required as a means of reversing hypotension and/or substituting for impaired renal function, however, experience with those procedures has been limited.

Lisinopril has been removed from the neonatal circulation by peritoneal dialysis with some clinical benefit and may, theoretically, be removed by exchange transfusion, although there is no experience with the latter procedure.

Human Data: It is not known whether exposure limited to the first trimester of pregnancy can adversely affect fetal outcome. The use of ACE inhibitors during the second and third trimesters of pregnancy has been associated with fetal and neonatal injury including hypotension, neonatal skull hypoplasia, anuria, reversible or irreversible renal failure, and death. Oligohydramnios has also been reported, presumably resulting from decreased fetal renal function; oligohydramnios in this setting has been associated with fetal limb contractures, craniofacial deformation and hypoplastic lung development. Prematurity and patent ductus arteriosus have also been reported, although it is not clear whether these occurrences were due to the ACE-inhibitor exposure.

Animal Data: Lisinopril was not teratogenic in mice treated on days 6 to 15 of gestation with up to 1 000 mg/kg/day (625 times the maximum recommended human dose). There was an increase in fetal resorptions at doses down to 100 mg/kg; at doses of 1 000 mg/kg, this was prevented by saline supplementation. There was no fetotoxicity or teratogenicity in rats treated with up to 300 mg/kg/day (188 times the maximum recommended dose) of lisinopril at days 6 to 17 of gestation. In rats receiving lisinopril from day 15 of gestation through day 21 postpartum, there was an increased incidence in pup deaths on days 2 to 7 postpartum and a lower average body weight of pups on day 21 postpartum. The increase in pup deaths and decrease in pup weight did not occur with maternal saline supplementation.

Lisinopril, at doses up to 1 mg/kg/day, was not teratogenic when given throughout the organogenic period in saline supplemented rabbits. Saline supplementation (physiologic saline in place of tap water) was used to eliminate maternotoxic effects and enable evaluation of the teratogenic potential at the highest possible dosage level. The rabbit has been shown to be extremely sensitive to angiotensin converting enzyme inhibitors (captopril and enalapril) with maternal and fetotoxic effects apparent at or below the recommended therapeutic dosage levels in man.

Fetotoxicity was demonstrated in rabbits by an increase incidence of fetal resorptions at an oral dose of lisinopril of 1 mg/kg/day and by an increased incidence of incomplete ossification at the lowest dose tested (0.1 mg/kg/day). A single i.v. dose of 15 mg/kg of lisinopril administered to pregnant rabbits on gestation days 16, 21 or 26 resulted in 88% to 100% fetal death.

By whole body autoradiography, radioactivity was found in the placenta following administration of labeled lisinopril to pregnant rats, but none was found in the fetuses.

Precautions: Renal Impairment: As a consequence of inhibiting the renin-angiotensin-aldosterone system, changes in renal function have been seen in susceptible individuals. In patients whose renal function may depend on the activity of the renin-angiotensin-aldosterone system, such as patients with bilateral renal artery stenosis, unilateral renal artery stenosis to a solitary kidney, or severe congestive heart failure, treatment with agents that inhibit this system has been associated with oliguria, progressive azotemia, and rarely, acute renal failure and/or death. In susceptible patients, concomitant diuretic use may further increase risk.

Use of Prinzide should include appropriate assessment of renal function.

Thiazides may not be appropriate diuretics for use in patients with renal impairment and are ineffective at creatinine clearance values of 30 mL/min or below (i.e., moderate to severe renal insufficiency).

Hyperkalemia: In clinical trials hyperkalemia (serum potassium >5.7 mEq/L) occurred in approximately 1.4% of hypertensive patients. In most cases these were isolated values which resolved despite continued therapy. Hyperkalemia was not a cause of discontinuation of therapy. Risk factors for the development of hyperkalemia may include renal insufficiency, diabetes mellitus and the concomitant use of potassium-sparing diuretics, potassium supplements and/or potassium-containing salt substitutes (see Drug Interactions).

Valvular Stenosis: There is concern on theoretical grounds that patients with aortic stenosis might be at particular risk of decreased coronary perfusion when treated with vasodilators because they do not develop as much afterload reduction.

Metabolism: Hyperuricemia may occur, or acute gout may be precipitated in certain patients receiving thiazide therapy.

Thiazides may decrease serum PBI levels without signs of thyroid disturbance.

Thiazides have been shown to increase excretion of magnesium; this may result in hypomagnesemia.

Thiazides may decrease urinary calcium excretion. Thiazides may cause intermittent and slight elevation of serum calcium in the absence of known disorders of calcium metabolism. Marked hypercalcemia may be evidence of hidden hyperparathyroidism. Thiazides should be discontinued before carrying out tests for parathyroid function.

Increases in cholesterol, triglyceride and glucose levels may be associated with thiazide diuretic therapy.

Surgery/Anesthesia: In patients undergoing major surgery or during anesthesia with agents that produce hypotension, lisinopril blocks angiotensin II formation, secondary to compensatory renin release. If hypotension occurs and is considered to be due to this mechanism, it can be corrected by volume expansion.

Thiazides may increase the responsivenes to tubocurarine.

Cough: A dry, persistent cough, which usually disappears only after withdrawal or lowering of the dose of Prinzide, has been reported.

Such possibility should be considered as part of the differential diagnosis of the cough.

Lactation: Milk of lactating rats contains radioactivity following administration of ^{14}C lisinopril.

It is not known whether lisinopril is secreted in human milk; however, thiazides do appear in human milk. If the use of Prinzide is deemed essential, the patient should stop nursing.

Geriatrics: In general, blood pressure response and adverse experiences were similar in younger and older patients given similar doses of lisinopril. Pharmacokinetic studies, however, indicate that maximum blood levels and area under the plasma concentration time curve (AUC) are doubled in older patients so that dosage adjustments should be made with particular caution.

Children: Prinzide has not been studied in children and, therefore, use in this age group is not recommended.

Anaphylactoid Reactions during Membrane Exposure: Anaphylactoid reactions have been reported in patients dialysed with high-flux membranes (e.g., polyacrylonitrile [PAN]) and treated concomitantly with an ACE inhibitor. Dialysis should be stopped immediately if symptoms such as nausea, abdominal cramps, burning, angioedema, shortness of breath and severe hypotension occur. Symptoms are not relieved by antihistamines. In these patients consideration should be given to using a different type of dialysis membrane or a different class of antihypertensive agent.

Anaphylactoid Reactions during LDL Apheresis: Rarely, patients receiving ACE inhibitors during low density lipoprotein (LDL)-apheresis with dextran sulfate have experienced life-threatening anaphylactoid reactions. These reactions were avoided by temporarily withholding ACE inhibitor therapy prior to each apheresis.

Anaphylactoid Reactions during Hymenoptera Desensitization: There have been isolated reports of patients experiencing sustained life-threatening anaphylactoid reactions while receiving ACE inhibitors during desensitizing treatment with hymenoptera (bees, wasp) venom. In the same patients, these reactions have been avoided when ACE inhibitors were temporarily withheld for at least 24 hours, but they have reappeared upon inadvertent rechallenge.

<u>*Drug Interactions:*</u> Hypotension—Patients on Diuretic Therapy: Patients on diuretics, and especially those in whom diuretic therapy was recently instituted, may occasionally experience an excessive reduction of blood pressure after initiation of therapy with lisinopril. The possibility of hypotensive effects with lisinopril can be minimized by either discontinuing the diuretic or increasing the salt intake prior to initiation of treatment with lisinopril (see Warnings and Dosage).

Agents Increasing Serum Potassium: Since lisinopril decreases aldosterone production, elevation of serum potassium may occur. Potassium sparing diuretics, such as spironolactone, triamterene or amiloride, or potassium supplements should be given only for documented hypokalemia and with caution and with frequent monitoring of serum potassium since they may lead to a significant increase in serum potassium. Salt substitutes which contain potassium should also be used with caution.

Agents Causing Renin Release: The antihypertensive effect of Prinzide is augmented by antihypertensive agents that cause renin release (e.g., diuretics).

Agents Affecting Sympathetic Activity: Agents affecting sympathetic activity (e.g., ganglionic blocking agents or adrenergic neuron blocking agents) may be used with caution. Beta-adrenergic blocking drugs add some further antihypertensive effect to lisinopril.

Indomethacin: Indomethacin may diminish the antihypertensive efficacy of concomitantly administered lisinopril.

Lithium: Lithium generally should not be given with diuretics or ACE inhibitors. Diuretic agents and ACE inhibitors reduce the renal clearance of lithium and add a high risk of lithium toxicity.

d-tubocurarine: Thiazide drugs may increase the responsiveness to tubocurarine.

Insulin: Insulin requirements in diabetic patients treated with thiazide diuretics may be increased. Diabetes mellitus which has been latent may become manifest during thiazide administration.

Alcohol, Barbiturates or Narcotics: In the presence of thiazide diuretics, potentiation of orthostatic hypotension may occur.

Corticosteroids, ACTH: Intensified electrolyte depletion, particularly hypokalemia may occur when given concomitantly with thiazide diuretics.

Pressor Amines (e.g., norepinephrine): In the presence of thiazide diuretics, possible decreased response to pressor amines but not sufficient to preclude their use.

Nonsteroidal Anti-inflammatory Drugs: In some patients, the administration of a nonsteroidal anti-inflammatory agent can reduce the diuretic, natriuretic and antihypertensive effects of loop, potassium-sparing and thiazide diuretics. Therefore, when Prinzide and nonsteroidal anti-inflammatory agents are used concomitantly, the patient should be observed closely to determine if the desired effect of the diuretic is obtained.

Information for the Patient: Angioedema: Angioedema, including laryngeal edema, may occur during treatment with Prinzide. Patients should be so advised and told to report immediately any signs or symptoms suggesting angioedema (swelling of face, extremities, eyes, lips, tongue, difficulty in breathing) and to take no more drug until they have consulted with the prescribing physician.

Hypotension: Patients should be cautioned to report lightheadedness especially during the first few days of therapy. If actual syncope occurs, the patients should be told to discontinue the drug until they have consulted with the prescribing physician.

All patients should be cautioned that excessive perspiration and dehydration may lead to an excessive fall in blood pressure because of reduction in fluid volume. Other causes of volume depletion such as vomiting or diarrhea may also lead to a fall in blood pressure; patients should be advised to consult with their physician.

Neutropenia: Patients should be told to report promptly any indication of infection (e.g., sore throat, fever) which may be a sign of neutropenia.

Impaired Liver Function: Patients should be advised to return to the physician if he/she experiences any symptoms possibly related to liver dysfunction. This would include "viral-like symptoms" in the first weeks to months of therapy (such as fever, malaise, muscle pain, rash or adenopathy which are possible indicators of hypersensitivity reactions), or if abdominal pain, nausea or vomiting, loss of appetite, jaundice, itching or any other unexplained symptoms occur during therapy.

Hyperkalemia: Patients should be told not to use salt substitutes containing potassium without consulting their physician.

Pregnancy: Patients should be advised to report promptly to their physician if they become pregnant, since the use of Prinzide during pregnancy can cause injury and even death of the developing fetus.

Note: As with many other drugs, certain advice to patients being treated with Prinzide is warranted. This information is intended to aid in the safe and effective use of this medication. It is not a disclosure of all possible adverse or intended effects.

Adverse Effects: In clinical trials involving 930 patients, including 100 patients treated for 50 weeks or more, the most severe clinical adverse reactions were syncope (0.8%) and hypotension (1.9%). The most frequent clinical adverse reactions were: dizziness (7.5%), headache (5.2%), cough (3.9%), fatigue (3.7%) and orthostatic effects (3.2%).

Discontinuation of treatment due to adverse reactions occurred in 4.4% of patients, mainly because of dizziness, cough, fatigue or muscle cramps.

Adverse reactions that have occurred in clinical trials or in marketing experience are those which have been previously reported with lisinopril and hydrochlorothiazide when used separately for the treatment of hypertension.

Adverse reactions occurring in hypertensive patients treated with lisinopril and hydrochlorothiazide in controlled trials are shown in Table I.

Laboratory Test Findings: Hypokalemia, Hyperkalemia: See Precautions.

Creatinine, Blood Urea Nitrogen: Minor increases in blood urea nitrogen (3.8%) and serum creatinine (4.2%) were observed in patients with essential hypertension treated with Prinzide. More marked increases have also been reported and were more likely to occur in patients with bilateral renal artery stenosis (see Precautions).

Increases in blood urea nitrogen and serum creatinine, usually reversible upon discontinuation of therapy, were observed in 1.1 and 1.6% of patients respectively with essential hypertension treated with lisinopril alone.

Serum Uric Acid, Glucose, Magnesium, Cholesterol, Triglycerides and Calcium: See Precautions.

Table I—Prinzide

Incidence of Adverse Reactions Occurring in Patients Treated with Lisinopril and Hydrochlorothiazide in Controlled Trials

	Lisinopril 2 633 Patients (%)	Lisinopril Plus Hydrochlorothiazide 930 Patients (%)
Cardiovascular		
Hypotension	1.4	1.9
Orthostatic effects	0.9	3.2
Chest pain	1.1	1.0
Syncope	0.2	0.8
Angina	0.3	0.1
Edema	0.6	0.1
Palpitation	0.8	0.9
Rhythm disturbances	0.5	0.1
Chest discomfort	—	0.6
Gastrointestinal		
Diarrhea	1.8	2.5
Nausea	1.9	2.2
Vomiting	1.1	1.4
Dyspepsia	0.5	1.3
Anorexia	0.4	0.2
Constipation	0.2	0.3
Flatulence	0.3	0.2
Abdominal pain	1.4	0.9
Dry mouth	0.5	0.2
Nervous System		
Dizziness	4.4	7.5
Headache	5.6	5.2
Paresthesia	0.5	1.5
Depression	0.7	0.5
Somnolence	0.8	0.4
Insomnia	0.3	0.2
Vertigo	0.2	0.9
Respiratory		
Cough	3.0	3.9
Dyspnea	0.4	0.4
Upper respiratory infection	2.1	2.2
Dermatologic		
Rash	1.0	1.2
Pruritus	0.5	0.4
Flushing	0.3	0.8
Angioedema	0.1	—*
Musculoskeletal		
Muscle cramps	0.5	2.0
Back pain	0.5	0.8
Shoulder pain	0.2	0.5
Other		
Fatigue	—	3.7
Asthenia	2.7	1.8
Decreased libido	0.2	1.0
Fever	0.3	0.5
Impotence	0.7	1.2
Gout	0.2	0.2

*See Prinzide (Marketing Experience Only).

Hemoglobin and Hematocrit: Small decreases in hemoglobin and hematocrit (mean decreases of approximately 0.5 g % and 1.5 vol %, respectively) occurred frequently in hypertensive patients treated with Prinzide but were rarely of clinical importance unless another cause of anemia coexisted. In clinical trials, 0.4% of patients discontinued therapy due to anemia.

Other (Causal Relationship Unknown): Rarely, elevations of liver enzymes and/or serum bilirubin have occurred.

Adverse Reactions Reported in Uncontrolled Trials and/or Marketing Experience: Prinivil: Cardiovascular: Myocardial infarction or cerebrovascular accident possibly secondary to excessive hypotension in high risk patients (see Warnings), tachycardia.

Dermatologic: allopecia, urticaria, diaphoresis, pemphigus, Stevens-Johnson syndrome.

Gastrointestinal: abdominal pain, dry mouth, pancreatitis.

Hematologic: hemolytic anemia.

Hepatic: liver function abnormalities, hepatitis, jaundice (hepatocellular and/or cholestatic).

Nervous System: mood alterations, mental confusion.

Respiratory: bronchospasm.

Special Senses: taste disorder.

Urogenital: uremia, oliguria/anuria, renal dysfunction, acute renal failure, impotence.

Prinzide (cont'd)

A symptom complex has been reported which may include fever, vasculitis, myalgia, arthralgia/arthritis, a positive ANA, elevated ESR, eosinophilia and leukocytosis. Rash, photosensitivity or other dermatologic manifestations may also occur.

Prinzide (Marketing Experience Only): Angioedema of the face, extremities, lips, tongue, glottis and/or larynx has been reported (see Warnings).

Cases of pancreatitis have been reported.

No other adverse events have been reported with Prinzide which have not been reported with lisinopril or hydrochlorothiazide individually.

Overdose: Symptoms and Treatment: No specific information is available on the treatment of overdosage with Prinzide. Treatment is symptomatic and supportive. Therapy with Prinzide should be discontinued and the patient observed closely. Suggested measures include induction of emesis and/or gastric lavage, if ingestion is recent, and correction of dehydration, electrolyte imbalance and hypotension by established procedures.

Lisinopril: The most likely feature of overdosage would be hypotension, for which the usual treatment would be i.v. infusion of normal saline solution. Lisinopril may be removed from general circulation by hemodialysis.

Hydrochlorothiazide: The most common signs and symptoms observed are those caused by electrolyte depletion (hypokalemia, hypochloremia, hyponatremia) and dehydration resulting from excessive diuresis. If digitalis has also been administered, hypokalemia may accentuate cardiac arrhythmias.

Dosage: Dosage must be individualized. The fixed combination is not for initial therapy. The dose of Prinzide should be determined by the titration of the individual components.

Once the patient has been successfully titrated with the individual components as described below, either 1 Prinzide 10/12.5 mg or, 1 or 2 20/12.5 mg or 20/25 mg tablets once daily may be substituted if the titrated doses are the same as those in the fixed combination (see Indications and Warnings).

Patients usually do not require doses in excess of 50 mg of hydrochlorothiazide daily, particularly when combined with antihypertensive agents.

For lisinopril monotherapy the recommended initial dose in patients not on diuretics is 10 mg of lisinopril once a day. Dosage should be adjusted according to blood pressure response. The usual dosage range of lisinopril is 10 to 40 mg administered in a single daily dose. The antihypertensive effect may diminish toward the end of the dosing interval regardless of the administered dose, but most commonly with a dose of 10 mg daily. This can be evaluated by measuring blood pressure just prior to dosing to determine whether satisfactory control is being maintained for 24 hours. If it is not, an increase in dose should be considered. The maximum dose used in long-term controlled clinical trials was 80 mg/day. If blood pressure is not controlled with lisinopril alone, a low dose of a diuretic may be added. Hydrochlorothiazide 12.5 mg has been shown to provide an additive effect. After the addition of a diuretic, it may be possible to reduce the dose of lisinopril.

Diuretic Treated Patients: In patients who are currently being treated with a diuretic, symptomatic hypotension occasionally may occur following the initial dose of lisinopril. The diuretic should, if possible, be discontinued for 2 to 3 days before beginning therapy with lisinopril to reduce the likelihood of hypotension (see Warnings). The dosage of lisinopril should be adjusted according to blood pressure response. If the patient's blood pressure is not controlled with lisinopril alone, diuretic therapy may be resumed as described above.

If the diuretic cannot be discontinued, an initial dose of 5 mg of lisinopril alone should be administered and the patient remain under medical supervision for at least 2 hours, and until blood pressure has stabilized for at least an additional hour (see Warnings and Precautions, Drug Interactions).

Dosage Adjustment in Renal Impairment: In patients with creatinine clearance greater than 30 mL/min. the usual dose titration of the individual components is required.

For patients with creatinine clearance between 10 and 30 mL/min, the starting dose of lisinopril is 2.5 to 5 mg/day. The dosage may then be titrated upward until blood pressure is controlled or to a maximum of 40 mg daily.

When concomitant diuretic therapy is required in patients with moderate to severe renal impairment (creatinine clearance <30 mL/min), a loop diuretic, rather than a thiazide diuretic, is preferred for use with lisinopril. Therefore, for patients with moderate or severe renal dysfunction the lisinopril-hydrochlorothiazide combination tablet is not recommended (see Precautions, Renal Impairment—Anaphylactoid Reactions during Membrane Exposure).

Information for the Patient: See Blue Section—Information for the Patient "Prinzide".

Supplied: 10 mg/12.5 mg: Each blue, hexagon-shaped, biconvex tablet, coded MSD 145 on one side and PRINZIDE on the other, contains: lisinopril 10 mg and hydrochlorothiazide 12.5 mg. Nonmedicinal ingredients: calcium phosphate, cornstarch, indigotine on aluminum substrate, magnesium stearate and mannitol. Bottles of 100 and blister packages of 30.

20 mg/12.5 mg: Each yellow, round, fluted-edge tablet, coded MSD 140 on one side and PRINZIDE on the other, contains: lisinopril 20 mg and hydrochlorothiazide 12.5 mg. Nonmedicinal ingredients: calcium phosphate, cornstarch, iron oxide, magnesium stearate and mannitol. Bottles of 100.

20 mg/25 mg: Each orange, round, fluted-edge tablet, coded MSD 142 on one side and PRINZIDE on the other, contains: lisinopril 20 mg and hydrochlorothiazide 25 mg. Nonmedicinal ingredients: calcium phosphate, cornstarch, iron oxide, magnesium stearate and mannitol. Bottles of 100.

Store at controlled room temperature (15 to 30°C). Protect from moisture.

(Shown in Product Recognition Section)

Reviewed 1998

PRO-BANTHINE®

Roberts

Propantheline Bromide

Anticholinergic

Pharmacology: Propantheline bromide is a synthetic quaternary ammonium anticholinergic agent which inhibits gastrointestinal motility and spasm and diminishes gastric acid secretion. The drug also inhibits the action of acetylcholine at the postganglionic nerve endings of the parasympathetic nervous system. Its effects are similar to those of atropine although they last longer (6 hours). The antispasmodic effects on the gastrointestinal tract may occur at doses causing other less marked antimuscarinic effects. Propantheline is extensively metabolized in man primarily by hydrolysis to the inactive materials xanthene-9-carboxylic acid and (2-hydroxyethyl) diisopropylmethylammonium bromide. Approximately half of the hydrolysis of the drug occurs in the gastrointestinal tract prior to its absorption. After a single 15 mg oral dose of carbon-14 labeled drug given to a healthy man, 390 ng/mL peak plasma concentration of total ^{14}C material is attained at 6 hours. Unmetabolized drug represents only a small proportion of the total ^{14}C material. The plasma half-life of the total ^{14}C material is about 9 hours and approximately 70% of the dose is excreted in the urine, mostly as metabolites. The urinary excretion of the intact propantheline is about 5%.

Indications: Adjunctive therapy of peptic ulcer, symptomatic treatment of the irritable bowel syndrome (irritable colon, spastic colon, mucous colitis); renal colic and hyperhidrosis; adjunctive therapy of ulcerative colitis, diverticulitis, cholecystitis and pancreatitis.

Contraindications: Propantheline is contraindicated in patients with: glaucoma since mydriasis is to be avoided; obstructive disease of the gastrointestinal tract (pyloroduodenal stenosis, achalasia, paralytic ileus); obstructive uropathy due to prostatism; intestinal atony of elderly or debilitated patients; severe ulcerative colitis or toxic megacolon complicating ulcerative colitis; unstable cardiovascular adjustment in acute hemorrhage; myasthenia gravis.

Warnings: Heat Prostration: In the presence of a high environmental temperature, heat prostration (fever and heat stroke due to decreased sweating) can occur with the use of propantheline.

Intestinal Obstruction: Diarrhea may be an early symptom of incomplete intestinal obstruction especially in patients with ileostomy or colostomy. In this instance, treatment with propantheline bromide would be inappropriate and possibly harmful.

Occupational Hazards: Propantheline may produce drowsiness or blurred vision. Caution the patient regarding activities requiring mental alertness, such as operating a motor vehicle or other machinery or performing hazardous work, while taking the drug.

Severe Cardiac Disease: Give this medication with caution to patients with severe cardiac disease if even a slight increase in heart rate is undesirable.

Pregnancy: Reproduction studies have not been performed in animals. Information on possible adverse effects to the fetus is limited to uncontrolled data derived from marketing experience. Such experience has revealed no evidence of toxicity to mother or fetus. There are no controlled studies in animals or humans to determine whether this drug affects fertility in human males or females, has teratogenic potential, or has other adverse effects on the fetus. It should be used during pregnancy only when, in the opinion of the physician, the benefits outweigh any possible risk.

Lactation: Documentation is lacking or conflicting regarding the excretion of anticholinergics (especially atropine) in milk and the reduction in breast milk production by these drugs. Problems in humans have not been documented. Propantheline is considered to be compatible with breast-feeding; however, it is recommended to monitor closely the possible anticholinergic side effects to the infant.

Children: Since there is inadequate experience with the use of propantheline in children, safety and efficacy have not been established. Keep out of reach of children.

Precautions: Varying degrees of urinary hesitancy may occur in patients with prostatic hypertrophy. Urinary retention may be minimized if patients are advised to micturate just before taking the medication.

Propantheline should be used with caution in hiatal hernia associated with reflux esophagitis since it may lower esophageal sphincter pressure and aggravate this condition.

Elderly and Disease States: Propantheline should be used with caution in the elderly and in all patients with autonomic neuropathy, hepatic or renal disease, hyperthyroidism, coronary heart disease, congestive heart failure, cardiac tachyarrhythmias or hypertension, as these conditions may be aggravated.

Ulcerative Colitis: In patients with ulcerative colitis, large doses of propantheline may suppress intestinal motility to the point of producing paralytic ileus and, for this reason, may precipitate or aggravate toxic megacolon, a serious complication of the disease.

Bronchial Secretion: A decrease in bronchial secretion may lead to inspissation of these secretions and formation of bronchial mucous plugs especially in the elderly or debilitated with chronic pulmonary disease.

Drug Interactions: Anticholinergics may delay absorption of other medication given concomitantly.

Excessive cholinergic blockage may occur if propantheline is given concomitantly with belladonna alkaloids, synthetic or semisynthetic anticholinergic agents, narcotic analgesics such as meperidine, Type 1 antiarrhythmic drugs (e.g. disopyramide, procainamide or quinidine), antihistamines, phenothiazines, tricyclic antidepressants, or other psychoactive drugs. Propantheline may also potentiate the sedative effect of phenothiazines. Increased intraocular pressure may result from concurrent administration of anticholinergics and corticosteroids.

Concurrent use of propantheline with slow-dissolving tablets of digoxin may cause increased serum digoxin levels.

Adverse Effects: Varying degrees of drying of salivary secretions, decreased sweating. Ophthalmic side effects include blurred vision, mydriasis, cycloplegia, and increased ocular tension. In addition the following adverse reactions have been reported: urinary hesitancy and retention, tachycardia, palpitations, loss of the sense of taste, headache, nervousness, mental confusion, drowsiness, weakness, dizziness, insomnia, nausea, vomiting, constipation, bloated feeling, impotence, suppression of lactation and allergic reactions or drug idiosyncrasies including anaphylaxis, urticaria and other dermatoses.

Overdose: Symptoms and Treatment: The symptoms of overdosage with propantheline progress from an intensification of the usual side effects to CNS disturbances (from restlessness and excitement to psychotic behavior), circulatory changes (flushing, fall in blood pressure, circulatory failure), respiratory failure, paralysis and coma.

Measures to be taken are: (1) immediate lavage of the stomach, and (2) injection of physostigmine 0.5 to 2 mg i.v., and repeated as necessary up to a total of 5 mg. Fever may be treated symptomatically.

Excitement of a degree which demands attention may be managed with sodium thiopental 2% solution given slowly i.v. or chloral hydrate (100 to 200 mL of a 2% solution) by rectal infusion. In the event of progression of the curare-like effect to paralysis of the respiratory muscles, artificial respiration should be instituted and maintained until effective respiratory action returns.

Dosage: Dosage should be individualized.

The usual initial adult dosage is 15 mg 30 minutes before each meal and 30 mg at bedtime (i.e., 75 mg daily).

Subsequent dosage adjustments should be made according to the patient's individual response and tolerance. The administration of one 7.5 mg tablet 3 times a day may be sufficient for patients with mild manifestations, for geriatric patients, and for those of small stature.

When used in contrast radiology, 30 mg should be given 45 minutes before the procedure.

For other indications, the dose is 15 to 30 mg 4 times daily.

Supplied: 7.5 mg: Each white, convex, sugar-coated tablet, printed in red ink, 073 on one side and RPC on the other side, contains: propantheline bromide 7.5 mg. Nonmedicinal ingredients: beeswax white, calcium carbonate, carnauba wax, castor oil, cornstarch, lactose, light mineral oil, magnesium carbonate, magnesium stearate, sodium saccharin, sucrose, talc and titanium dioxide. Energy: 1.4 kJ (0.33 kcal). Bottles of 100.

15 mg: Each peach-colored, convex, sugar-coated tablet, printed in red ink, 074 on one side and RPC on the other side, contains: propantheline bromide 15 mg. Nonmedicinal ingredients: beeswax white, calcium carbonate, carnauba wax, castor oil, cornstarch, iron oxides, lactose, light mineral oil, magnesium carbonate, magnesium stearate, sodium saccharin, sucrose, talc and titanium dioxide. Energy: 1 kJ (0.24 kcal). Bottles of 100.

(Shown in Product Recognition Section)

PROBETA® ℞

Allergan

Levobunolol HCl—Dipivefrin HCl

Glaucoma Therapy

Pharmacology: Probeta is a combination of levobunolol (a noncardioselective beta-adrenoceptor blocking agent) and dipivefrin (an adrenergic agonist) which acts to lower elevated intraocular pressure (IOP). Elevated IOP presents a major risk factor in glaucomatous field loss. The higher the level of IOP, the greater the likelihood of optic nerve damage and visual field loss. Poor ocular perfusion may also contribute to nerve head damage and visual field loss.

Although the mechanism of action of Probeta has not been studied, it is believed to be a combination of the action of the 2 individual components. Thus, it is expected that Probeta reduces IOP by decreasing aqueous humor production and enhancing the outflow facility.

The onset of action of Probeta has not been directly evaluated, but is expected to reflect that of the 2 individual components. For dipivefrin, onset of action occurs within 30 minutes of instillation while for levobunolol the onset of action occurs approximately 1 hour after instillation, indicating that the onset of effect of Probeta would likely occur between 30 minutes and 1 hour after instillation. A significant effect on IOP occurs within 2 hours of instillation of Probeta, while peak effect, as measured by reduction in IOP, occurs between 4 and 6 hours after instillation.

Probeta, was evaluated in 2 controlled studies of 6 and 3 months duration. Analyses of the proportion of subjects with overall mean decreases in IOP of ≥ 3 mm Hg were performed. The results of the 6 month study showed that approximately 7 hours after the previous dose, 44% of the Probeta group experienced an overall mean IOP decrease of ≥ 3 mm Hg from a levobunolol-only baseline level. Twenty-two percent of the dipivefrin treated group and 24% of the levobunolol treated group experienced this degree of decrease in IOP.

The results of the 3 month study indicated that approximately 7 hours after the previous dose, 31% of the Probeta treated group experienced an overall mean IOP decrease of ≥ 3 mm Hg. Twenty-one percent of the subjects in the dipivefrin treated group and 24% in the levobunolol treated group experienced an overall mean IOP decrease of ≥ 3 mm Hg.

In both of these studies, the overall decrease (average mean decrease over time) in IOP was statistically significantly greater in the Probeta treated group than in the dipivefrin treated group or levobunolol treated group.

In a third clinical study of 6 weeks duration, Probeta provided a significantly better sustained mean diurnal decrease in IOP than that provided by either component alone. Probeta was more effective in lowering IOP than dipivefrin at hours 2, 4 and 6 and than levobunolol at hours 4 and 6.

When a decision to administer both a beta-adrenoceptor blocking and an adrenergic agonist is made, the administration of such drugs in combination has the advantage of greater patient compliance and convenience, with the added assurance that the appropriate dosage of both drugs is administered. When both types of drugs are in the same formulation, compatibility of ingredients is assured and the correct volume of drug is delivered and retained. Combination formulations also allow less preservative to be delivered to the ocular surface as compared to using 2 separate drugs.

Beta-adrenergic receptor blockade reduces cardiac output in both healthy subjects and patients with heart disease. In patients with severe impairment of myocardial function, beta-adrenergic receptor blockade may inhibit the stimulatory effect of the sympathetic nervous system necessary to maintain adequate cardiac function.

Beta-adrenergic receptor blockade in the bronchi and bronchioles results in increased airway resistance from unopposed para-sympathetic activity. Such an effect in patients with asthma or other bronchospastic conditions is potentially dangerous.

Indications: For the control of intraocular pressure in chronic open-angle glaucoma or ocular hypertension.

Contraindications: Bronchial asthma, or a history of bronchial asthma or severe chronic obstructive pulmonary disease; sinus bradycardia; second or third degree atrioventricular heart block; overt cardiac failure; or cardiogenic shock. Probeta should not be used in patients with narrow angles since any dilation of the pupil may predispose the patient to an attack of angle-closure glaucoma.

Probeta is contraindicated in individuals who are hypersensitive to any components of the medication.

Warnings: Because the diagnosis of narrow angle glaucoma is frequently missed during normotensive intervals (between attacks), it is very important that careful slit lamp and gonioscopic study be done before initiating therapy with this drug. Should an elevation of intraocular tension follow the instillation of Probeta, appropriate hypotensive therapy by the treating physician is recommended.

As with other topically applied ophthalmic drugs, Probeta may be absorbed systemically. The same adverse events found with systemic administration of beta-adrenergic blocking agents may occur with topical administration. For example, severe respiratory reactions and cardiac reactions including death due to bronchospasm in patients with asthma, and, rarely, death in association with cardiac failure, have been reported with topical application of beta-adrenergic blocking agents (see Contraindications and Precautions).

Precautions: General: Probeta should be used with caution in patients with known hypersensitivity to other beta-adrenoceptor blocking agents.

Probeta should be used with caution in patients who are receiving a beta-adrenergic blocking agent orally, because of the potential for additive effects on systemic beta-blockade. Generally, patients should not use more than one topical ophthalmic beta-adrenergic blocking agent simultaneously.

Because of the potential effects of beta-adrenergic blocking agents on blood pressure and pulse rates, this medication must be used cautiously in patients with cerebrovascular insufficiency. Should signs or symptoms develop that suggest reduced cerebral blood flow while using Probeta, alternative therapy should be considered.

Dipivefrin is a prodrug of epinephrine. Macular edema has been known to occur in aphakic patients treated with epinephrine. Discontinuation of epinephrine generally results in reversal of the maculopathy.

Cardiac Failure: Sympathetic stimulation may be essential for support of the circulation in individuals with diminished myocardial contractility, and its inhibition by beta-adrenergic receptor blockade may precipitate more severe failure.

Patients without a History of Cardiac Failure: Continued depression of the myocardium with beta-blocking agents over a period of time can, in some cases, lead to cardiac failure. At the first sign or symptom of cardiac failure, Probeta should be discontinued.

Obstructive Pulmonary Disease: Patients with chronic obstructive pulmonary disease (e.g., chronic bronchitis, emphysema) of mild or moderate severity, bronchospastic disease or a history of bronchospastic disease (other than bronchial asthma or a history of bronchial asthma, in which Probeta is contraindicated, see Contraindications), should in general not receive beta–blockers, including Probeta . However, if Probeta is deemed necessary in such patients, then it should be administered cautiously since it may block bronchodilation produced by endogenous and exogenous catecholamine stimulation of $beta_2$–receptors.

Major Surgery: The necessity or desirability of withdrawal of beta-adrenergic blocking agents prior to major surgery is controversial. Beta-adrenergic receptor blockade impairs the ability of the heart to respond to beta-adrenergically mediated reflex stimuli. This may augment the risk of general anesthesia in surgical procedures. Some patients receiving beta-adrenergic receptor blocking agents have been subject to protracted severe hypotension during anesthesia. Difficulty in restarting and maintaining the heartbeat has also been reported. For these reasons, in patients undergoing elective surgery, gradual withdrawal of beta-adrenergic blocking agents may be appropriate. If necessary during surgery, the effects of beta-adrenergic blocking agents may be reversed by sufficient doses of such agonists as isoproterenol, dopamine, dobutamine or levarterenol (see Overdose: Symptoms and Treatment).

Diabetes Mellitus: Beta-adrenergic blocking agents should be administered with caution in patients subject to spontaneous hypoglycemia or to diabetic patients (especially those with labile diabetes) who are receiving insulin or oral hypoglycemic agents. Beta-adrenergic blocking agents may mask the signs and symptoms of acute hypoglycemia.

Thyrotoxicosis: Beta-adrenergic blocking agents may mask certain clinical signs (e.g., tachycardia) of hyperthyroidism. Patients suspected of developing thyrotoxicosis should be managed carefully to avoid abrupt withdrawal of beta-adrenergic blocking agents which might precipitate a thyroid storm.

Muscle Weakness: Beta-adrenergic blockade has been reported to potentiate muscle weakness consistent with certain myasthenic symptoms (e.g., diplopia, ptosis and generalized weakness).

Pregnancy: No reproduction studies using Probeta were performed. Rat and rabbit reproduction and fertility studies using levobunolol or dipivefrin alone were conducted. Fetotoxicity (as evidenced by a greater number of resorption sites) has been observed in rabbits when doses of levobunolol equivalent to 200 to 700 times the recommended dose for the treatment of glaucoma were given.

No adverse effect on male or female rat fertility was seen at doses up to 1 800 times the human dose for levobunolol. Teratogenic studies with levobunolol in rats at doses up to 25 mg/kg/day (1 800 times the recommended human dose for glaucoma) showed no evidence of fetal malformation, fetotoxicity, and no adverse effects on postnatal development of offspring.

Reproduction studies using dipivefrin have been performed in rats and rabbits at daily oral doses of up to 10 mg/kg body weight and 5 mg/kg in teratogenicity studies. No evidence of impaired fertility or harm to the fetus due to dipivefrin were observed. There are, however, no adequate and well-controlled studies in pregnant women. Probeta should be used during pregnancy only if the potential benefit justifies the potential risk to the fetus.

Carcinogenesis, Mutagenesis: In a lifetime oral study of levobunolol in mice, there were statistically significant ($p \leq 0.05$) increases in the incidence of benign leiomyomas in female mice at 200 mg/kg/day (14 000 times the recommended human dose for glaucoma), but not at 12 or 50 mg/kg/day (850 and 3 500 times the human dose). In a two year oral study of levobunolol in rats, there was a statistically significant ($p \leq 0.05$) increase in the incidence of benign hepatomas in male rats administered 12 800 times the recommended human dose for glaucoma. Similar differences were not observed in rats administered oral doses equivalent to 350 times to 2 000 times the recommended human dose for glaucoma.

Levobunolol did not show evidence of mutagenic activity in a battery of microbiological and mammalian in vitro and in vivo assays.

Carcinogenicity and mutagenicity studies have not been performed with either dipivefrin or Probeta.

Lactation: It is not known whether or not Probeta is excreted in human milk. Systemic beta-blockers and topical timolol maleate are known to be excreted in human milk. Because of the potential for adverse reactions from Probeta in nursing infants, a decision should be made whether to discontinue this drug, taking into account the importance of the drug to the mother.

Children: The safety and effectiveness of Probeta have not been established in children.

<u>*Drug Interactions*</u>: Probeta may have additive effects in patients taking systemic antihypertensive drugs. These possible additive effects may include hypotension, including orthostatic hypotension, bradycardia, dizziness, and/or syncope. Conversely, systemic beta-adrenergic receptor blocking agents may potentiate the ocular hypotensive effect of Probeta.

Probeta (cont'd)

Close observation is recommended when a beta-blocker is administered to patients receiving catecholamine-depleting drugs such as reserpine because of possible additive effects and the production of hypotension and/or marked bradycardia, which may produce vertigo, syncope or postural hypotension.

Patients receiving beta-adrenergic blocking agents along with either oral or i.v. calcium antagonists should be monitored for possible atrioventricular conduction disturbances, left ventricular failure and hypotension. In patients with impaired cardiac function, simultaneous use should be avoided altogether.

The concomitant use of beta-adrenergic blocking agents with digitalis and calcium antagonists may have additive effects on prolonging atrioventricular conduction time.

Phenothiazine-related compounds and beta-adrenergic blocking agents may have additive hypotensive effects due to the inhibition of each other's metabolism.

While taking beta-blockers, patients with a history of severe anaphylactic reaction to a variety of allergens may be more reactive to repeated challenge, either accidental, diagnostic or therapeutic. Such patients may be unresponsive to the usual doses of epinephrine used to treat allergic reaction.

Adverse Effects: The ocular events experienced by patients evaluated (n=221) in controlled clinical trials are listed below in decreasing order of frequency: mild, transient burning and stinging (52%); vision problems/blurring (16%); conjunctival erythema (16%); foreign body sensation (10.4%); photophobia (6%); corneal staining (4.5%); itching (4.5%); follicular response (4.0%); eyelid erythema (3.6%); mydriasis (3.1%); eyelid edema (2.2%); tearing (2.2%); corneal endothelial changes (1.8%); conjunctival edema (1.3%); conjunctivitis (0.9%).

Systemic adverse events during clinical trials included headache, dizziness and nervousness. Insignificant increases in heart rate and systolic blood pressure were noted with Probeta.

Although levobunolol has minimal membrane stabilizing activity, there remains a possibility of decreased corneal sensitivity after prolonged use.

The following additional adverse reactions have been reported with levobunolol, dipivefrin, or the ophthalmic use of other beta-adrenergic receptor blocker agents:

Body As A Whole: asthenia, chest pain.

Cardiovascular: bradycardia, arrhythmia, hypotension, syncope, heart block, cerebral vascular accident, cerebral ischemia, congestive heart failure, palpitation, cardiac arrest.

CNS: somnolence, transient ataxia, lethargy.

Digestive: nausea, diarrhea.

Endocrine: masked symptoms of hypoglycemia in insulin-dependent diabetics (see Warnings).

Psychiatric: depression, increase in signs and symptoms of myasthenia gravis, paresthesia.

Respiratory: bronchospasm (predominantly in patients with pre-existing bronchospastic disease), respiratory failure, dyspnea and nasal congestion.

Skin: alopecia, Stevens-Johnson syndrome, hypersensitivity, including localized and generalized rash, urticaria and pruritus.

Special Senses: signs and symptoms of keratitis, discharge, and iridocyclitis.

Urogenital: Impotence.

Epinephrine therapy can lead to adrenochrome deposits in the conjunctiva and cornea.

Other reactions associated with the systemic use of nonselective adrenergic receptor blocking agents or epinephrine compounds should be considered potential effects with ophthalmic use of these agents.

Overdose: Symptoms and Treatment: No data are available regarding overdosage in humans. Should accidental **ocular** overdosage occur, flush eye(s) with clean water or normal saline. If an **ingested** overdose of Probeta occurs, evacuation of the stomach should be considered during the first few hours after the overdose.

The most common signs and symptoms to be expected with overdosage of systemic beta-adrenergic blocking agents are symptomatic bradycardia, hypotension, bronchospasm and acute cardiac failure. Should these symptoms occur, discontinue Probeta therapy and initiate appropriate supportive therapy.

Dosage: The recommended dose is 1 drop in the affected eye(s) given every 12 hours. As with any medication, upon initiation of therapy, careful monitoring of patients is advised. Keep out of reach of children. For external use only. Do not touch the dropper tip to the eye, skin or any surface since this may contaminate the solution. Protect from light and excessive heat. Discard any unused solution at the end of the prescribed treatment period.

Information for the Patient: See Blue Section—Information for the Patient "Probeta".

Supplied: Each mL of sterile ophthalmic solution contains: levobunolol HCl 5 mg and dipivefrin HCl 1 mg. Nonmedicinal ingredients: benzalkonium chloride 0.005% as preservative, edetate disodium, polyvinyl alcohol, purified water, sodium chloride and hydrochloric acid and/or sodium hydroxide to adjust pH. White opaque plastic dropper bottles with the C Cap Compliance Cap of 5 and 10 mL. Protect from light. Store at 15 to 25°C.

Reviewed 1997

PROCAN™ SR

Parke-Davis

Procainamide HCl

Antiarrhythmic Agent

Pharmacology: Procainamide depresses the excitability of cardiac muscle to electrical stimulation, and slows conduction in the atrium, the bundle of His, and the ventricle. The refractory period of the atrium is considerably more prolonged than that of the ventricle. With therapeutic plasma levels of the drug, contractility of the heart is usually not affected nor is cardiac output decreased to any extent unless myocardial damage exists. In the absence of any arrhythmia, the heart rate may occasionally be accelerated by conventional doses, suggesting that the drug possesses anticholinergic properties. Larger doses can induce atrioventricular block and ventricular extrasystoles which may proceed to ventricular fibrillation. These effects on the myocardium are reflected in the ECG; a widening of the QRS complex occurs most consistently; less regularly, the PR and QT intervals are prolonged, and the QRS and T waves show some decrease in voltage.

According to the Vaughn Williams antiarrhythmic drug classification, procainamide is a Class IA drug. Thus, procainamide reduces the maximal rate of phase-O depolarization, prolongs repolarization and refractory periods, and in general, decreases automaticity of cardiac cells.

Pharmacokinetics: Oral administration of conventional immediate-release procainamide capsules produces a therapeutic effect approximately 1 hour after a 1 g loading dose or 4 hours after initiating treatment every 3 hours with the maintenance dose. Peak plasma concentrations occur about 1 hour after oral administration, indicating an overall half-time for absorption of approximately 20 minutes. For ventricular arrhythmias, therapeutic plasma levels have been reported to be 3 to 10 μg/mL, with those for the majority of patients in the range of 4 to 8 μg/mL.

Procainamide's apparent volume of distribution (Vd) is usually between 1.75 and 2.5 L/kg body weight. About 75% of the procainamide is concentrated in highly perfused tissues. Approximately 20% is bound to plasma albumin.

Following oral administration of the conventional immediate-release procainamide capsules, over 90% is recovered in the urine as unchanged drug or metabolites indicating almost complete absorption of the drug. On the average, about 60% (range 30 to 80%) of the drug is excreted unchanged. The half-time for elimination from the body may vary from 2.5 to 6 hours or longer. The plasma clearance of procainamide is 400 to 600 mL/minute; renal clearance is 200 to 400 mL/minute.

In humans, procainamide is acetylated, and N-acetylprocainamide (NAPA), an active metabolite, can be detected in both plasma and urine. The dose fraction of procainamide excreted as NAPA is extremely variable, ranging from 6 to 52%.

Following oral administration of Procan SR tablets every 6 hours, the mean steady-state serum concentrations of procainamide and NAPA achieved are approximately equivalent to those of a comparable dose of the conventional immediate-release capsule administered every 3 hours.

When 500 mg sustained-release tablets were administered for 3 days, approximately 48% and 15% were recovered in the urine as procainamide and NAPA, respectively. Other metabolites e.g. free and conjugated p-aminobenzoic acid which usually account for about 10% of the dose, were not analyzed in this study.

Indications:

> No antiarrhythmic drug has been shown to reduce the incidence of sudden death in patients with asymptomatic ventricular arrhythmias. Most antiarrhythmic drugs have the potential to cause dangerous arrhythmias; some have been shown to be associated with an increased incidence of sudden death. In light of the above, physicians should carefully consider the risks and benefits of antiarrhythmic therapy for all patients with ventricular arrhythmias.

Ventricular Arrhythmias: For the treatment of documented life-threatening ventricular arrhythmias, such as sustained ventricular tachycardia. Procainamide may also be used for the treatment of patients with documented symptomatic ventricular arrhythmias when the symptoms are of sufficient severity to require treatment. Because of the proarrhythmic effects of procainamide its use should be reserved for patients in whom, in the opinion of the physician, the benefit of treatment clearly outweighs the risks.

For patients with sustained ventricular tachycardia, procainamide therapy should be initiated in the hospital. Hospitalization may also be required for certain other patients depending on their cardiac status and underlying cardiac disease.

The effects of procainamide in patients with recent myocardial infarction have not been adequately studied and, therefore, its use in this condition cannot be recommended.

Supraventricular Arrhythmias: In the treatment of atrial fibrillation, particularly if the condition is of recent development and the treatments of choice cannot be used or are ineffective. The drug may also be used in paroxysmal atrial tachycardia which cannot be controlled by reflex stimulation or by other measures.

Contraindications: Hypersensitivity to procainamide is an absolute contraindication; in this connection, cross-sensitivity to procaine and related drugs must be borne in mind. Procainamide should not be administered to patients with complete atrioventricular heart block; it is also contraindicated in cases of second-degree and third-degree AV block unless an electrical pacemaker is operative. Procainamide is also contraindicated in patients with systemic lupus erythematosus, and should not be used in patients having "les torsades de pointes" ventricular arrhythmias. It has been suggested that procainamide be contraindicated in patients with myasthenia gravis.

Warnings: Mortality: The results of the Cardiac Arrhythmia Suppression Trial (CAST) in post-myocardial infarction patients with asymptomatic ventricular arrhythmias showed a significant increase in mortality and in non-fatal cardiac arrest rate in patients treated with encainide or flecainide compared with a matched placebo-treated group. CAST was continued using a revised protocol with the moricizine and placebo arms only. The trial was prematurely terminated because of a trend towards an increase in mortality in the moricizine-treated group.

The applicability of these results to other populations or other antiarrhythmic agents is uncertain, but at present it is prudent to consider these results when using any antiarrhythmic agent.

Blood Dyscrasias: Agranulocytosis, bone marrow depression, neutropenia, hypoplastic anemia and thrombocytopenia have been reported at a rate of approximately 0.5% in patients receiving procainamide . Most of these patients received procainamide within the recommended dosage range. Fatalities have occurred (with approximately 20 to 25% mortality in reported cases of agranulocytosis). Since most of these events have been noted during the first 12 weeks of therapy, it is recommended that complete blood counts including white cell, differential and platelet counts be performed at weekly intervals for the first 3 months of therapy; and periodically thereafter. Complete blood counts should be performed promptly if the patient develops any signs of infection (such as fever, chills, sore throat or stomatitis), bruising or bleeding. If any of these hematologic disorders are identified, procainamide should be discontinued. Blood counts usually return to normal within 1 month of discontinuation. Caution should be used in patients with pre-existing marrow failure or cytopenia of any type (see Adverse Effects).

Patients should be instructed to report promptly any flu-type symptoms such as malaise and aches, as well as any soreness of the mouth, throat or gums, unexplained fever, skin rash, unusual bleeding or bruising, symptoms that resemble arthritis or symptoms of an upper respiratory tract infection.

Positive Antinuclear Antibody: The prolonged administration of procainamide often leads to the development of a positive antinuclear antibody (ANA) test with or without symptoms of lupus erythematosus-like syndrome. If a positive ANA titer develops, the benefit/risk ratio related to continued procainamide therapy should be assessed. This may necessitate a discontinuation of procainamide and substitution of alternative antiarrhythmic therapy.

Precautions: General: During administration of procainamide, evidence of untoward myocardial responses should be carefully watched for in all patients. In the presence of an abnormal myocardium, procainamide may at times produce untoward responses. In atrial fibrillation or flutter, the ventricular rate may increase suddenly as the atrial rate is slowed. Adequate digitalization reduces, but does not abolish, this danger. If myocardial damage exists, ventricular tachycardia is particularly hazardous.

Correction of atrial fibrillation, with resultant forceful contractions of the atrium, may cause a dislodgment of mural thrombi and produce an embolic episode. However, it has been suggested that, in a patient who is already discharging emboli, procainamide is more likely to stop than to aggravate the process.

Attempts to adjust the heart rate in a patient who has developed ventricular tachycardia during an occlusive coronary episode should be carried out with extreme caution. Caution is also required in marked disturbances of atrioventricular conduction such as AV block, bundle branch block, or severe digitalis intoxication, where the use of procainamide may result in additional depression of conduction and ventricular asystole or fibrillation. Widening of QRS complex on ECG calls for extréme caution. The effects of procainamide in digitalis intoxication, particularly where the arrhythmia is accompanied by marked conduction disturbances, are unpredictable and fatalities have occurred.

Because patients with severe organic heart disease and ventricular tachycardia may also have complete heart block, which is difficult to diagnose under these circumstances, this complication should always be kept in mind when treating ventricular arrhythmias with procainamide. If the ventricular rate is significantly slowed by procainamide without attainment of regular atrioventricular conduction, the drug should be stopped and the patient re-evaluated because asystole may result under these circumstances.

Serious hypotension can result from peripheral vasodilation, and by depressing myocardial contractility and cardiac output. At high plasma levels, procainamide may produce sinus tachycardia due to reflex sympathetic response to its hypotensive effect. Large doses may increase cardiac automaticity and can induce complete atrioventricular block, cardiac standstill or ventricular extrasystoles that may proceed to ventricular fibrillation. These effects on the myocardium are reflected in the ECG; a widening of the QRS complex occurs most consistently; less regularly, the PR and QT intervals are prolonged; the QRS and T waves show some decrease in voltage. These actions of procainamide may be intensified in patients with congestive heart failure.

Plasma procainamide and NAPA concentrations rise markedly with increases in blood urea nitrogen and correlate well with creatinine clearance. Should patients with impaired kidney function and/or liver disease receive unadjusted dosage, symptoms of overdosage (principally ventricular tachycardia and severe hypotension) may occur due to drug accumulation. Similarly, plasma concentrations have been found to be increased in elderly patients possibly due to declining renal function in this age group. The frequency of administration should be reduced in patients with renal or hepatic insufficiency or in elderly patients.

Plasma concentrations of procainamide and NAPA should be monitored in patients with renal disease, hepatic disease, cardiac failure, or low cardiac output states.

In patients with cardiac failure or shock or in patients with low cardiac output and extrarenal azotemia, the apparent volume of distribution and/or the elimination rate of procainamide can decrease considerably for a given dose, thereby resulting in increased plasma concentrations. Such patients should therefore be carefully monitored and the dose or frequency of administration reduced if warranted.

Antinuclear antibodies (ANA) are often found in patients receiving long-term procainamide therapy. The induction of ANA appears to be independent of dosage. Patients with procainamide-induced increases in ANA titers may develop a syndrome resembling systemic lupus erythematosus (SLE). The mechanism of this syndrome is uncertain. Polyarthralgia, arthritic symptoms, fever, skin lesions and pleuritic pain are common symptoms; to a lesser extent, myalgia, pleural effusion, pericarditis, headache, fatigue, weakness, nausea, and abdominal pain may occur. Rare cases of thrombocytopenia, Coombs' positive hemolytic anemia, increased AST, ALT, and serum amylase have been reported which may be related to this SLE-like syndrome.

It is recommended that tests for SLE be carried out at regular intervals in patients receiving maintenance procainamide therapy. The drug should be discontinued if there is rising ANA titer or clinical symptoms of SLE appear. The SLE-like syndrome may be reversible upon discontinuation of the drug. If discontinuation does not cause remission of the symptoms, corticosteroid therapy may be effective. If the SLE-like syndrome develops in a patient with recurrent life-threatening arrhythmias not controllable by other antiarrhythmic agents, corticosteroid suppressive therapy may be used concomitantly with procainamide.

Pregnancy: Animal reproduction studies have not been conducted with procainamide. It is also not known whether procainamide can cause fetal harm when administered to a pregnant woman or can affect reproduction capacity.

There has been some evidence of the diffusion of procainamide across the placental membrane. Therefore, due to the potential accumulation and slow rate of elimination of procainamide and N-acetylprocainamide in the fetus, the potential benefit of the use of procainamide during pregnancy should be weighed against the possible hazard to the fetus.

Lactation: Both procainamide and N-acetylprocainamide are secreted in human milk, and absorbed by the nursing infant. Because of the potential for serious adverse reactions in nursing infants, a decision to discontinue nursing or the drug should be made, taking into account the importance of the drug to the mother.

Children: Safety and effectiveness in children have not been established.

Drug Interactions: Antiarrhythmics: Concurrent use with procainamide may result in additive cardiac effects and/or additive toxic effects. In acute myocardial infarctions procainamide may potentiate the cardiac depressant action of beta blocking agents such as propranolol.

Anticholinergics: Procainamide enhances the anticholinergic effects. Extreme caution must be exercised with such a combination.

Anticholinesterases: Procainamide antagonizes the effect of anticholinesterases in myasthenia gravis, and paralysis returns.

Antihypertensives: Procainamide may potentiate the hypotensive effects of thiazide diuretics and other antihypertensive agents. Adjustment of dosage may be required.

Cimetidine: It has been reported that the histamine H_2-antagonist cimetidine reduces renal clearance of procainamide and NAPA resulting in higher plasma concentrations for longer durations. Caution should be exercised when administering these drugs concurrently especially in the elderly who have a reduced ability to clear all three. Dosage modification may be required.

Neuromuscular Blocking Agents: Procainamide potentiates the effects of skeletal muscle relaxants such as succinylcholine. It also may enhance or prolong the neuromuscular blocking activity of bacitracin, colistimethate, dihydrostreptomycin, gentamicin, gramicidin, kanamycin, neomycin, polymyxin B, streptomycin and viomycin, producing respiratory depression.

Antibiotics: Procainamide has also been reported to interact with kanamycin, neomycin and streptomycin to cause apnea and muscle weakness, due to an additive neuromuscular blocking effect.

Adverse Effects: The overall incidence of adverse effects with procainamide is about 9.2%. The most commonly occurring are gastrointestinal upset 3.9%, cardiovascular effects (ventricular dysrhythmias, bradycardia, hypotension and shock) 3.3% and drug fever 1.6%.

The most serious adverse reactions reported are granulocytopenia and the development of antinuclear antibodies (ANA). Granulocytopenia is most likely to occur within the first 3 months of therapy. Prolonged administration of procainamide often leads to the development of a positive ANA test with or without symptoms of lupus erythematosus-like syndrome (see Warnings).

Incidence greater than 1%: elevated ANA, sometimes associated with drug-induced lupus syndrome. Gastrointestinal symptoms, especially with large oral doses: anorexia, nausea, vomiting, diarrhea.

In patients on long-term procainamide therapy with sustained release preparations, the above reactions have been reported with an incidence greater than 5%.

Cardiovascular Effects: bradycardia, arrhythmias, cardiac failure, shock.

Hypersensitivity reactions, which may be manifested by one or more of the following: pruritus, urticaria, angioneurotic edema, maculopapular rash, fever, eosinophilia, hypergammaglobulinemia.

Incidence less than 1%: granulocytopenia (incidence about 0.5%), sometimes resulting in death, thrombocytopenia, immune hemolytic anemia, convulsions, psychosis with hallucinations, confusion, mental depression, giddiness, lightheadedness, weakness, bitter taste.

Rare: hypotension. A case was reported with fever and chills, plus nausea, vomiting, abdominal pain, acute hepatomegaly and a rise in serum glutamic oxaloacetic transaminase following a single dose of the drug. Vasculitis (hypersensitivity-type).

Overdose: Symptoms and Treatment: Signs and symptoms of overdosage of procainamide include severe hypotension, ventricular fibrillation, widening of the QRS complex, junctional tachycardia, intraventricular conduction delay, oliguria, lethargy, confusion, nausea and vomiting.

If ingestion is recent, gastric lavage or emesis may reduce absorption. Dopamine, phenylephrine or norepinephrine may be helpful in reversing severe hypotensive responses. Management of overdosage includes symptomatic treatment with ECG and blood pressure monitoring. Procainamide toxicity can usually be treated, if necessary, by administering vasopressors after adequate fluid volume replacement. I.V. infusion of 1/6 molar sodium lactate injection reportedly reduces the cardiotoxic effects of procainamide.

The urinary elimination of procainamide is proportional to the glomerular filtration rate but is also affected by changes in urinary pH. Procainamide is relatively lipid-soluble as a free base but the ionized form is not. Acid urine, therefore, leads to ion trapping of procainamide which enters the urine by passive diffusion from the plasma. Accordingly, renal clearance of procainamide can be considerably increased by maintaining a low urinary pH and high flow rates.

If procainamide toxicity causes severe hypotension and renal insufficiency, urinary elimination of procainamide and NAPA is decreased and hemodialysis may be required. Hemodialysis significantly reduces the serum half-life of procainamide and effectively removes procainamide and NAPA. Peritoneal dialysis is not effective.

Overdosage symptoms may result following a single 2 g dose of conventional immediate-release procainamide; 3 g may be dangerous, especially if patient is a slow acetylator, has decreased renal function or underlying organic heart disease.

It has been reported that 1 patient who ingested approximately 7 g of procainamide recovered after treatment consisting of i.v. norepinephrine, i.v. furosemide, attempted volume expansion with albumin, and hemodialysis. Also reported, is the case of an elderly patient who recovered after ingestion of approximately 19 g of procainamide. The patient was treated with i.v. isoproterenol and i.v. epinephrine. The latter report suggested that insertion of a ventricular pacing electrode is a reasonable precautionary measure in case high grade SV block develops.

Dosage: Procan SR is a sustained release dosage form not intended for initial therapy. For initial therapy by oral administration, conventional oral formulations of procainamide are recommended. Patients stabilized to an appropriate dosage level can be transferred to an equivalent daily dosage regimen of Procan SR tablets.

Procan SR tablets should not be crushed or chewed as this would interfere with the designed dissolution characteristics.

The tablet matrix of Procan SR may be seen in the stool since it does not disintegrate following release of procainamide.

The duration of action of procainamide supplied in this sustained-release dosage form allows dosing at intervals of every 6 hours, which may encourage patient compliance.

In elderly patients and in patients with impaired renal function (decreased creatinine clearance) excretion is delayed and reduced frequency of administration is required (see Precautions).

Atrial Fibrillation and Paroxysmal Atrial Tachycardia: Suggested Titration Dosage: (Standard tablets should be used.) Initial dose of 1.25 g of standard oral procainamide preparation, followed in 1 hour by 0.75 g if there have been no ECG changes, and then given at a dose of 0.5 to 1 g every 2 hours until arrhythmia is interrupted or the limit of tolerance is reached.

Ventricular Tachycardia: Suggested Titration Dosage: (Standard tablets should be used.) Initial dose of 1 g of standard oral procainamide preparation, followed by total daily dose of 50 mg/kg of body weight, given in divided doses at 3-hour intervals, to be increased until arrhythmia is interrupted or the limit of tolerance is reached.

Procan SR (cont'd)

Suggested Maintenance Dosage of Procan SR: 50 mg/kg of body weight daily given in divided doses at 6-hour intervals starting 2 to 3 hours after the last dose of standard oral procainamide. Although the dosage for each patient must be determined on an individual basis, Table I may be used as a guide for providing the total daily dosage using Procan SR.

Table I—Procan SR

Suggested Maintenance Dosage

Patient's Weight	Approximate Total Daily Dosage	Dosage with Procan SR
<55 kg	2 000 mg	Two 250 mg tablets or One 500 mg tablet q6h
55 to 91 kg	3 000 mg	One 750 mg tablet q6h
>91 kg	4 000 mg	Two 500 mg tablets q6h

Information for the Patient: See Blue Section—Information for the Patient "Procan SR".

Supplied: 250 mg: Each elliptical, green, film-coated, sustained-release tablet, imprinted PROCAN SR 250 mg, contains: procainamide HCl 250 mg. Nonmedicinal ingredients: carnauba wax, hydrogenated soybean oil, lactose, magnesium stearate and silicon dioxide colloidal; coating: candelilla wax, hydroxypropyl methylcellulose, methylparaben, opaspray green, polyethylene glycol, propylparaben and vanillin. Energy: 2.67 kJ (0.64 kcal). Sodium: <1 mmol (0.04 mg). Gluten-, sulfite- and tartrazine-free. Bottles of 100.

500 mg: Each elliptical, yellow, scored, film-coated, sustained-release tablet, imprinted PROCAN SR 500 mg, contains: procainamide HCl 500 mg. Nonmedicinal ingredients: carnauba wax, magnesium stearate, polyethylene glycol, silicon dioxide colloidal and sugar; coating: candelilla wax, hydroxypropyl methylcellulose, methylparaben, opaspray yellow, polyethylene glycol, propylparaben and vanillin. Energy: 2.31 kJ (0.55 kcal). Sodium: <1 mmol (0.06 mg). Gluten-, lactose-, sulfite- and tartrazine-free. Bottles of 100.

750 mg: Each elliptical, orange, scored, film-coated, sustained-release tablet, imprinted PROCAN SR 750 mg, contains: procainamide HCl 750 mg. Nonmedicinal ingredients: carnauba wax, magnesium stearate, polyethylene glycol and silicon dioxide colloidal; coating: alcohol, candelilla wax, hydroxypropyl methylcellulose, opaspray medium orange, polyethylene glycol, propylene glycol and vanillin. Energy: 0 kcal. Sodium: <1 mmol (0.07 mg). Gluten-, lactose-, paraben, sulfite- and tartrazine-free. Bottles of 100.

Protect from moisture. Store at controlled room temperature, 15 to 30°C.

(Shown in Product Recognition Section)

PROCTODAN™-HC

Odan

Pramoxine HCl—Hydrocortisone Acetate—Zinc Sulfate Monohydrate

Anorectal Therapy

Supplied: Each g of ointment contains: pramoxine HCl 1%, hydrocortisone acetate 0.5% and zinc sulfate monohydrate 0.5%. Nonmedicinal ingredients: methylparaben, propylparaben and petrolatum. Tubes of 15 and 30 g with rectal applicator.

New Product 1998

PROCTOFOAM™-HC

R & C

Hydrocortisone Acetate—Pramoxine HCl

Anorectal Therapy

Pharmacology: Proctofoam-HC combines the anti-inflammatory action of hydrocortisone with the surface anesthetic effect of pramoxine HCl.

Indications: The temporary relief of anorectal inflammation, pruritus, pain and swelling associated with hemorrhoids, proctitis, cryptitis, fissures, postoperative pain and pruritus ani.

Contraindications: The presence of active infection, abscess, extensive fistulas or sinus tracts, tuberculosis, varicella, vaccinia, acute herpes simplex, fungal infections, patients with a known sensitivity to any of the product's components.

Warnings: Contents are flammable and the aerosol container may explode if heated.

Do not insert any part of the aerosol container into the anus. Do not use in presence of open flame or spark. Contents under pressure. Do not place in hot water or near radiators, stoves or other sources of heat. Do not puncture or incinerate container or store at temperatures over 50°C.

Precautions: Do not use on infected lesions unless accompanied by appropriate anti-infective agents. Discontinue use if sensitivity develops.

A complete rectal examination to rule out any contraindicated pathology should be completed before instituting therapy.

Pregnancy and *Lactation:* The safety of topical corticosteroids during pregnancy and lactation has not been established. The potential benefit should be weighed in these conditions against possible hazard to the fetus or the nursing infant. When indicated, they should not be used extensively, in large amounts or for prolonged periods of time on pregnant patients or nursing mothers.

Prolonged or excessive use of this product could produce systemic corticosteroid effects. To minimize this possibility, when long-term therapy is anticipated, interrupt treatment periodically.

Advise patients to inform subsequent physicians of the prior use of corticosteroids.

Adverse Effects: Occasionally, patients may experience itching, burning and/or pain upon application of the foam.

The following local adverse reactions have been reported with the use of topical corticosteroids: dryness, itching, burning, local irritation, striae, skin atrophy, hypertrichosis, hypopigmentation and secondary infection. When occlusive dressings are used, pustules, miliaria, folliculitis and pyoderma may occur.

Adrenal suppression has occurred with prolonged use of large doses of topical corticosteroids, particularly under occlusion due to increased percutaneous absorption.

Posterior subcapsular cataracts have been reported following systemic use of corticosteroids.

Overdose: Symptoms and Treatment: No specific symptoms or therapy known. However, overdosage is improbable at the concentrations of pramoxine and hydrocortisone per 18 g unit of Proctofoam-HC. In case of accidental ingestion, institute symptomatic treatment.

Dosage: Shake the aerosol container well before using. Insert 1 applicatorful into anus 2 or 3 times daily and after each bowel evacuation. To relieve discomfort following hemorrhoidectomy, remove wing-tip cap and replace with topical cap. Transfer foam to a perianal pad and apply directly to the operative site as often as required.

Supplied: Each aerosol container with anal and topical applicator contains: 18 g of a mixture of hydrocortisone acetate USP 1%, pramoxine HCl USP 1% in a water-miscible mucoadhesive foam base formulated with cetyl alcohol, emulsifying wax, methylparaben, propylene glycol, propylparaben, steareth-10, triethanolamine, water and inert propellants, isobutane and propane. Each application provides 375 mg of mucoadhesive base containing 1% hydrocortisone acetate USP (3.75 mg/dose) and 1% pramoxine HCl USP (3.75 mg/dose). The aerosol container contains approximately 36 applications.

Contents are flammable and are under pressure. Do not use in presence of open flame or spark. Do not place in hot water or near radiators, stoves or other sources of heat. Do not puncture or incinerate container or store at temperatures over 50°C.

Reviewed 1998

PROCTOSEDYL®

Hoechst Marion Roussel

Hydrocortisone—Framycetin Sulfate—Cinchocaine HCl—Esculin

Anorectal Therapy

Indications: The reduction of swelling, pain and inflammation of hemorrhoids and other rectal lesions. The management of acute and chronic nonspecific proctitis, acute internal hemorrhoids, cryptitis, fissures and incomplete fistulas, internal and external pruritus ani. May be used in pre- and postoperative hemorrhoidectomy and repair of fissures.

Contraindications: Hydrocortisone must not be used in the presence of tuberculosis, fungal and viral infections. Sensitivity to any of the components.

Precautions: Discontinue use if sensitization occurs. Hydrocortisone should not be used until an adequate proctologic examination is completed and a diagnosis made. Other specific measures against infections, allergy, and other causal factors must not be neglected. The possibility, however rare, that prolonged use of this preparation might produce systemic corticosteroid effects, should be borne in mind. Patients should be advised to inform subsequent physicians of the previous use of hydrocortisone.

Pregnancy: The safe use of topical corticosteroids during pregnancy has not been fully established. Therefore, during pregnancy, they should not be used unnecessarily on extended areas, in large amounts or for prolonged periods of time.

Adverse Effects: Certain patients may experience burning upon application, especially if the mucous membrane is not intact.

Dosage: Ointment: For external treatment: Apply a small quantity morning and evening and after each bowel movement, to the affected area. For internal application: attach rectal cannula to tube, insert to full extent and squeeze tube gently from lower end while withdrawing.

Suppositories: 1 suppository morning and evening and after each bowel movement.

Supplied: Ointment: Each g contains: hydrocortisone BP 5 mg (0.5%), framycetin sulfate BP 10 mg (equivalent to 7 mg of framycetin base—1%), cinchocaine HCl BP 5 mg (0.5%), aesculin 10 mg (1%). Also contains 10% w/w anhydrous lanolin. Tubes of 15 and 30 g with rectal cannula. Store at cool temperature.

Suppositories: Each rectal suppository contains: hydrocortisone BP 5 mg (0.5 %), framycetin sulfate BP 10 mg (equivalent to 7 mg of framycetin base—1%), cinchocaine HCl BP 5 mg (0.5%), aesculin 10 mg (1%). Boxes of 12 and 24. Store at cool temperature.

PROCTOSONE®

Technilab

Hydrocortisone Acetate—Framycetin Sulfate—Cinchocaine HCl—Esculin

Anorectal Therapy

Supplied: Ointment: Each g of ointment contains: hydrocortisone (as acetate) 5 mg, framycetin sulfate 10 mg (equivalent to 7 mg of framycetin base), cinchocaine HCl 5 mg and esculin 10 mg. Nonmedicinal ingredients: lanolin, light mineral oil and petrolatum. Tubes of 15 and 30 g with rectal canula.

Suppositories: Each rectal suppository contains: hydrocortisone (as acetate) 5 mg, framycetin sulfate 10 mg (equivalent to 7 mg of framycetin base), cinchocaine HCl 5 mg and esculin 10 mg. Nonmedicinal ingredients: semisynthetic glycerides. Boxes of 12.

Store between 15 to 30°C.

PROCYCLID™

ICN

Procyclidine HCl

Antiparkinsonian Agent

Supplied: Elixir: Each mL of elixir contains: procyclidine HCl USP 0.5 mg. Nonmedicinal ingredients: cherry-mint flavor, citric acid, ethyl alcohol, propylene glycol, sodium benzoate and sodium cyclamate. Bottles of 500 mL.

Tablets: Each white, scored tablet imprinted ICN P6 contains: procyclidine HCl USP 5 mg. Nonmedicinal ingredients: colloidal silicone dioxide, lactose, magnesium stearate and starch. Bottles of 100 and 1 000.

PROCYTOX®

Carter Horner

Cyclophosphamide

Antineoplastic

Pharmacology: Although it is classified generally as an alkylating agent, cyclophosphamide itself is not an alkylating agent.

It appears to be inactive in vitro when tested on cultures of human leukocytes or carcinomatous cells of human origin. It appears active metabolites of the drug exhibit the alkylating action.

Cyclophosphamide's metabolism is initiated by the mixed function oxidase enzymes of the liver microsomes, which produce several metabolites the principal active one being 4-hydroxycyclophosphamide. Because of their highly polar nature and lability during isolation procedures, their identification has been difficult and the knowledge of cyclophosphamide's metabolic pathway is still incomplete. It appears that the metabolite 4-hydroxycyclophosphamide, is in equilibrium with its acyclic tautomeric form, aldophosphamide which when further oxidized, results in the known metabolite: carboxyphosphamide. Aldophosphamide to a lesser extent is metabolized to phosphoramide mustard and acrolein, both highly cytotoxic, and which might be the active metabolites of cyclophosphamide.

The rate of cyclophosphamide's metabolism is much more variable among humans, than in other species. The plasma half-life of the unchanged drug does not appear to be influenced by: age, race, degree of sensitivity to the drug, condition treated or dosage.

Plasma cyclophosphamide half-life in patients without prior drug exposure has been found to be 6.5 hr., after i.v. administration. A maximum of 20% of injected cyclophosphamide was excreted intact in the urine, irrespective of the dose used. 68% of the injected drug was excreted in the urine when administered for 5 successive days; its half-life was shorter and peak alkylating concentrations were constantly higher on the fifth day than on the first day.

Peak plasma concentrations of metabolites have been found to be almost proportional to the administered dose, but relatively wide individual variations have been reported. Peak plasma alkylating metabolite levels generally are reached at 2 to 3 hours after administration of the drug.

The average plasma alkylating metabolite concentration at 8 hours after i.v. administration of the drug was about 77% of the peak level when studied in 12 patients without prior drug exposure.

Cyclophosphamide does not bind to human plasma proteins in appreciable amounts, but with single i.v. doses about 12 to 14% of the total dose was bound to plasma proteins at plasma cyclophosphamide concentrations of 10 and 200 millimicron moles/mL. Repeated doses increased the amount bound to plasma proteins. Following 5 doses of 40 mg/kg, about 56% of the dose was bound.

The tissue distribution of cyclophosphamide has been examined in cancer patients following i.v. administration. It was found that both unchanged drug and metabolites pass the blood-brain barrier. Cerebral tissue contained drug levels in a concentration range similar to that found in blood.

Biopsies performed 2 hours after administration of the drug revealed that about 30% more drug was present in lymph nodes than in muscle, adipose tissue, or skin, but the relative proportions of unchanged drug metabolites were not established.

In experimental animals cyclophosphamide inhibits immune phenomena, inflammatory processes, delayed hypersensitivity reactions, experimental allergic inflammatory disease, and body defenses to infectious microorganisms. Although immunosuppressive and anti-inflammatory actions for cyclophosphamide have not been demonstrated conclusively in humans, they may be associated with the therapeutic use of the drug.

In humans, cyclophosphamide is absorbed from the gastrointestinal tract and from parenteral sites. It appears to be absorbed also when it is applied topically to neoplastic tissues situated on the body surface.

In humans, a generally higher proportion of the administered dose is excreted in the urine as metabolites. Recovery after i.v. administered cyclophosphamide ranged from 37 to 82%, with 20 to 45% of that recovered attributable to the unchanged drug. The total urinary excretion of unchanged cyclophosphamide ranged from 3% to 30% of the administered dose.

Indications: A. Frequently responsive myeloproliferative and lymphoproliferative disorders: malignant lymphomas (Stages III and IV, Peter's Staging System)—Hodgkin's disease, follicular lymphoma, lymphocytic lymphosarcoma, reticulum cell sarcoma, lymphoblastic lymphosarcoma, Burkitt's lymphoma; multiple myeloma; leukemias—chronic lymphocytic leukemia, chronic granulocytic leukemia (it is ineffective in acute blastic crises), acute myelogenous and monocytic leukemia, acute lymphoblastic (stem-cell) leukemia in children (cyclophosphamide given during remission is effective in prolonging its duration); mycosis fungoides (advanced disease).

B. Frequently responsive solid malignancies: neuroblastoma (in patients with disseminated disease), adenocarcinoma of the ovary, retinoblastoma.

C. Infrequently responsive malignancies: carcinoma of the breast, malignant neoplasms of the lung.

Contraindications: Sensitivity to cyclophosphamide or to any components of its dosage forms, severe leukopenia, thrombocytopenia, hepatic or renal dysfunction.

Warnings: Cyclophosphamide is a potent drug and should be used only by physicians experienced with cancer-chemotherapeutic drugs (see Precautions). Periodic monitoring of peripheral blood should be done. Renal function must be conducted prior to and during therapy.

The rate of metabolism of cyclophosphamide reportedly is increased by chronic administration of high doses of phenobarbital. The physician should be alert for possible combined drug actions, desirable or undesirable, involving cyclophosphamide even though cyclophosphamide has been used successfully concurrently with other drugs, including other cytotoxic drugs.

Since cyclophosphamide is an inhibitor of serum cholinesterase, patients receiving the drug may exhibit an increased sensitivity to neuromuscular blocking agents such as succinylcholine. If a patient receiving cyclophosphamide is to undergo surgery, advise the anesthesiologist. To avoid the risk of prolonged apnea, the dose of succinylcholine should be reduced when administered concomitantly with cyclophosphamide.

Cyclophosphamide has been reported to have oncogenic activity in rats and mice. The possibility that it may have oncogenic potential in humans should be considered. Cyclophosphamide may interfere with normal wound healing.

Pregnancy and *Lactation:* Cyclophosphamide can be teratogenic or cause fetal resorption in experimental animals. It should not be used in pregnancy, particularly in early pregnancy, unless the potential benefits outweigh the possible risks. Cyclophosphamide is excreted in breast milk and breast feeding should be terminated prior to institution of cyclophosphamide therapy.

Patients, male or female, capable of conception, ordinarily should be advised of the mutagenic potential of cyclophosphamide. Adequate methods of contraception appear desirable for such patients receiving cyclophosphamide.

Precautions: Administer cautiously to patients with any of the following conditions: leukopenia, thrombocytopenia, tumor cell infiltration of bone marrow, previous x-ray therapy, previous therapy with other cytotoxic agents, impaired hepatic or renal function.

Because cyclophosphamide may exert a suppressive action on immune mechanisms, consider the interruption or modification of dosage for patients who develop bacterial, fungal or viral infections. This is especially true for patients receiving concomitant steroid therapy and perhaps those with a recent history of steroid therapy, since infections in some of these patients have been fatal. Varicella-zoster infections appear to be particularly dangerous under these circumstances. Since cyclophosphamide has been reported to be more toxic in adrenalectomized dogs, adjustment of the doses of both replacement steroids and cyclophosphamide may be necessary for the adrenalectomized patient.

Adverse Effects: Hematopoietic: Leukopenia is an expected effect and ordinarily is used as a guide to therapy. Thrombocytopenia or anemia may occur in a few patients. These effects are almost always reversible when therapy is interrupted.

Gastrointestinal: Anorexia, nausea, or vomiting are common and related to dose as well as individual susceptibility. There are isolated reports of hemorrhagic colitis, oral mucosal ulceration and jaundice occurring during therapy.

Genitourinary: Sterile hemorrhagic cystitis can result from cyclophosphamide administration. This can be severe, even fatal, and is probably due to metabolites in the urine. Nonhemorrhagic cystitis and/or bladder fibrosis also have been reported to result from cyclophosphamide administration. Atypical epithelial cells may be found in the urinary sediment. Ample fluid intake and frequent voiding help to prevent the development of cystitis, but when it occurs it is ordinarily necessary to interrupt cyclophosphamide therapy. Hematuria usually resolves spontaneously within a few days after cyclophosphamide therapy is discontinued, but may persist for several months. In severe cases, replacement of blood loss may be required. Electrocautery to telangiectatic areas of the bladder and diversion of urine flow has been successfully used in treatment of protracted cases. Cryosurgery has also been used. Nephrotoxicity, including hemorrhage and clot formation in the renal pelvis, has been reported.

Gonadal suppression, resulting in amenorrhea or azoospermia, has been reported and appears to be related to dosage and duration of therapy. This side effect, possibly irreversible, should be anticipated in patients treated with cyclophosphamide. It is not known to what extent cyclophosphamide may affect prepuberal gonads. Ovarian fibrosis following cyclophosphamide therapy has been reported also.

Integument: It is ordinarily advisable to inform patients in advance of possible alopecia, a frequent complication of cyclophosphamide therapy. Regrowth of hair can be expected although occasionally the new hair may be of a different color or texture. The skin and fingernails may become darker during therapy. Nonspecific dermatitis has been reported to occur with cyclophosphamide.

Pulmonary: Interstitial pulmonary fibrosis has been reported in patients receiving high doses of cyclophosphamide over a prolonged period.

Miscellaneous: headache, dizziness, hypoprothrombinemia, diabetes mellitus, hyponatremia.

Overdose: Symptoms and Treatment: No specific antidote. Institute general supportive measures to sustain the patient through any period of toxicity that might occur.

Dosage: Chemotherapy with cyclophosphamide, as with other drugs used in cancer chemotherapy, is potentially hazardous and fatal complications can occur.

Cyclophosphamide should be administered only by physicians aware of the associated risks. Therapy may be aimed at either induction or maintenance of remission.

Induction therapy: The usual initial loading dose for patients with no hematologic deficiency is 40 to 50 mg/kg, usually administered i.v. This dose can be given at the rate of 10 to 20 mg/kg/day for 2 to 5 days according to the patient's tolerance. In patients having received other treatments (radiation therapy, other cytotoxic drugs) which might affect the functional capacity of the bone marrow or in patients with bone marrow neoplastic infiltration, the initial loading dose should be reduced by 30 to 50%.

The above mentioned doses are usually followed by a marked leukopenia. Recovery begins usually after 7 to 10 days. The white blood cell count should be monitored carefully during induction therapy.

If the treatment is started orally, a dose of 1 to 5 mg/kg/day should be administered, according to the patient's tolerance.

Maintenance therapy: The initial chemotherapeutic effect must be maintained in order to obtain suppression, reduction or retardation of neoplastic growths.

Various maintenance therapy schedules have been used: orally: 1 to 5 mg/kg daily; i.v.: 10 to 15 mg/kg, repeated every 7 to 10 days; i.v.: 3 to 5 mg/kg, twice a week.

It is advisable to give the largest maintenance dose that can be tolerated by the patient. The total WBC count should be used as an objective indication to determine the maintenance dose. Usually, a leukopenia of 3 000 to 4 000 cells/mm^3 is relatively safe to avoid serious infections or other complications.

Cyclophosphamide should be administered in the morning and followed by a fluid intake of 2 000 to 3 000 mL to ensure the prompt excretion of the active metabolites. The bladder must be emptied frequently to avoid the development of a cyclophosphamide cystitis.

Preparation and Handling of Solutions: As with most antineoplastic agents, care should be exercised in the preparation of solutions. Protective wear—i.e., gloves (unpowdered surgical latex gloves), safety glasses, disposable gown and mask—is recommended, as is the use of a vertical laminar flow hood (Biological Safety Cabinet—Class II), when possible. Personnel regularly handling these agents should have biannual blood examinations.

After use, all disposable materials which have come into contact with the agent should be segregated and incinerated at above 1 000°C.

Prepare Procytox solutions for parenteral use by adding Sterile Water for Injection, USP, or Bacteriostatic Water for Injection, USP (paraben or benzyl alcohol preserved) to the vial and shaking until dissolution. pH: 5.1 to 5.9. Extreme caution should be exercised with solutions containing benzyl alcohol in very young children. Use of sterile water for injection is recommended. See Table I (on following page).

Heating should not be used to facilitate dissolution.

Procytox solutions may be injected i.v., i.m., intraperitoneally or intrapleurally or they may be infused i.v. in Dextrose Injection USP (5% dextrose and 0.9% sodium chloride).

Solutions prepared with Bacteriostatic Water for Injection may be stored under refrigeration (4°C) if used within 6 days. Use solutions prepared with Sterile Water for Injection for single dose administration and discard any unused solution.

Extemporaneous liquid preparations of Procytox for oral administration may be prepared by dissolving Procytox for

Procytox (cont'd)

Table I—Procytox

Reconstitution Table

Vial Size			
Cyclophosphamide BP (mg)	**NaCl BP (mg)**	**Volume of Diluent to be Added to Vial (mL)**	**Nominal Concentration (mg/mL)**
200	90	10	20
500	225	25	20
1 000	450	50	20
2 000	900	100	20

Injection in Aromatic Elixir USP. These solutions when kept under refrigeration (4°C) should be used within 14 days.

Supplied: Injection: Each vial contains: cyclophosphamide 200, 500,1 000 or 2 000 mg. Nonmedicinal ingredients: sodium chloride. Gluten-, lactose- and tartrazine-free. Single vials and boxes of 10.

Tablets: 25 mg: Each white, coated, deeply convex and round tablet contains: cyclophosphamide 25 mg. Nonmedicinal ingredients: calcium carbonate, calcium phosphate, cellulose, gelatin, glycerin, lactose, magnesium stearate, polyethylene glycol, polysorbate, povidone, silicon dioxide, starch (corn), sucrose, talc, titanium dioxide and wax. Energy: 2.1 kJ (0.5 kcal). Gluten-, sodium- and tartrazine-free. Bottles of 100.

50 mg: Each white, coated, deeply convex and round tablet contains: cyclophosphamide 50 mg. Nonmedicinal ingredients: calcium carbonate, calcium phosphate, cellulose, gelatin, glycerin, lactose, magnesium stearate, polyethylene glycol, polysorbate, povidone, silicon dioxide, starch (corn), sucrose, talc, titanium dioxide and wax. Energy: 2.1 kJ (0.5 kcal). Gluten-, sodium- and tartrazine-free. Bottles of 30, 100 and 1 000.

Store injectables (before reconstitution) and tablets at room temperature; injectables after reconstitution must be refrigerated.

(Shown in Product Recognition Section)

PRODIEM® PLAIN

Novartis Consumer Health

Psyllium

Bulk Forming Laxative

Pharmacology: Psyllium is a high fiber bulk forming laxative. It absorbs water and expands to provide increased bulk and moisture content to the stool. The increased bulk encourages normal peristalsis and bowel motility.

Indications: The relief of simple, chronic, atonic, and spastic constipation and for constipation associated with pregnancy, convalescence and advanced age. For use in special diets lacking in residue fiber, mucous and ulcerative colitis and in the management of constipation associated with irritable bowel syndrome, diverticulitis, hemorrhoids and anal fissures.

Contraindications: The presence of nausea, fever or vomiting, abdominal pain or symptoms of an acute abdomen or fecal impaction.

Warnings: Do not use in patients with a history of psyllium allergy. Psyllium allergy is rare but can be severe. If an allergic reaction occurs, discontinue use.

Bulk forming agents have the potential to obstruct the esophagus, particularly in the presence of esophageal narrowing or when consumed with insufficient fluid. **Taking this product without adequate fluid may cause it to swell and block the throat or esophagus and may cause choking.** Patients should be made aware of the symptoms of esophageal obstruction, including chest pain/pressure, vomiting, and difficulty swallowing. Patients experiencing these symptoms should seek immediate medical attention. Patients with esophageal narrowing or dysphagia should not use this product.

Precautions: Taking this product without enough liquid may cause choking (see Warnings).

As with all laxatives, this product should not be taken for more than 1 week, unless a special schedule has been ordered by the physician.

Drug Interactions: As with all laxatives, this product should not be taken within 2 hours of another medication, because the desired effect of the other medication may be reduced.

Dosage: Adults: 5 to 10 g (1 or 2 teaspoonfuls) once or twice/day. This dose may be taken before breakfast and/or in the evening, depending on the condition being treated, its severity and individual responsiveness. Moisten the mouth with a sip of beverage. Place the measured dose on the tongue and swallow unchewed with at least 240 mL of any cool or warm beverage including juice, milk or water. The dosage may be taken a little at a time or all at once. **Do not chew.** Because of its mode of action, optimal effectiveness may take 2 to 3 days. Do not interrupt therapy.
Children 6 to 12 years: half the adult dose.

Supplied: Each 5 g (1 level teaspoonful) of light brown minty tasting granules contains: psyllium 3.25 g. Nonmedicinal ingredients: acacia, flavors, iron oxide, paraffin, sucrose, talc and titanium dioxide. Energy: 16 kJ (3.85 kcal). Potassium: 30 mg. Sodium: <1 mmol (1.2 mg). Sucrose: 0.96 g. Tartrazine-free. Brown plastic bottles of 100 and 250 g.

Reviewed 1999

PRODIEM® PLUS

Novartis Consumer Health

Psyllium—Senna

Bulk Forming Laxative—Mild Stimulant

Pharmacology: Prodiem Plus is a unique combination of a bulk forming fibre and a mild stimulant. It is a gentle method for the relief of acute and obstinate constipation without harsh chemical laxatives and is often effective in 12 to 24 hours

Psyllium is a high fibre bulk forming laxative. It absorbs water and expands to provide increased bulk and moisture content to the stool. The increased bulk encourages normal peristalsis and bowel motility.

Senna is a mild stimulant laxative in the family of the anthraquinones. The primary active principles of senna are sennosides. Precise mechanism of action is unknown. Recent studies suggest that stimulant laxatives alter fluid and electrolyte absorption, producing net intestinal fluid accumulation and laxation.

Indications: The relief of acute and obstinate constipation, the early stages of more severe simple constipation and constipation of the elderly caused by loss of muscle tone and neuromuscular reflex. For use in patients being weaned off harsh laxatives or where a straight bulk forming preparation has failed to provide regular bowel evacuation.

Contraindications: In the presence of nausea, fever or vomiting, abdominal pain or symptoms of an acute abdomen or fecal impaction, Prodiem Plus should not be used without consulting a physician.

Warnings: Should not be used in the presence of undiagnosed abdominal pain. Frequent or prolonged use without the direction of a physician is not recommended as it may lead to laxative dependence.

Do not use in patients with a history of psyllium allergy. Psyllium allergy is rare but can be severe. If an allergic reaction occurs, discontinue use.

Bulk forming agents have the potential to obstruct the esophagus, particularly in the presence of esophageal narrowing or when consumed with insufficient fluid. **Taking this product without adequate fluid may cause it to swell and block the throat or esophagus and may cause choking.** Patients should be made aware of the symptoms of esophageal obstruction, including chest pain/pressure, vomiting and difficulty swallowing. Patients experiencing these symptoms should seek immediate medical attention. Patients with esophageal narrowing or dysphagia should not use this product.

Precautions: For patients with a history of esophageal disorders. **Taking this product without enough liquid may cause choking (see Warnings).**

As with all laxatives, this product should not be taken for more than 1 week, unless a special schedule has been ordered by the physician.

Drug Interactions: As with all laxatives, this product should not be taken within 2 hours of another medication because the desired effect of the other medication may be reduced.

Adverse Effects: In therapeutic oral doses, all stimulant laxatives may produce some degree of abdominal discomfort, nausea, mild cramps, griping, and/or faintness. If mild cramping occurs, dosage should be reduced.

Dosage: Adults: 5 to 10 g (1 or 2 teaspoonfuls) once or twice/day. This dose may be taken before breakfast and/or in the evening, depending on the condition being treated, its severity and individual responsiveness. Moisten the mouth with a sip of beverage. Place the measured dose on the tongue and swallow unchewed with at least 240 mL of any cool or warm beverage including juice, milk or water. The dosage may be taken a little at a time or all at once. **Do not chew.**
Children 6 to 12 years: half the adult dose.

Supplied: Each 5 g (1 level teaspoonful) of dark brown, minty tasting granules contains: psyllium 2.71 g and senna pod 0.62 g (equivalent to 15 mg of sennosides). Nonmedicinal ingredients: acacia, flavors, iron oxide, paraffin, sucrose and talc. Energy: 16 kJ (3.85 kcal). Potassium: 30 mg. Sodium: <1 mmol (1.2 mg). Sucrose: 0.96 g. Tartrazine-free. Yellow plastic bottles of 100 and 250 g.

Reviewed 1999

PROFASI® HP

Serono

Chorionic Gonadotropin

Gonadotropin

Pharmacology: Chorionic gonadotropin, extracted from the urine of pregnant women, is a water-soluble polypeptide hormone produced by the human placenta composed of an alpha and a beta sub-unit. The alpha sub-unit is essentially identical to the alpha sub-units of the human pituitary gonadotropins, luteinizing hormone (LH) and follicle-stimulating hormone (FSH), as well as to the alpha sub-unit of human thyroid-stimulating hormone (TSH). The beta sub-units of these hormones differ in amino acid sequence.

Chorionic gonadotropin is biologically standardized and the potency is declared in terms of the USP Reference Standard.

The action of hCG is virtually identical to that of pituitary LH, although hCG appears to have a small degree of FSH activity as well.

Male: Chorionic gonadotropin is given in an attempt to stimulate the interstitial cells of the testes (cells of Leydig) to produce androgen. The response to chorionic gonadotropin may be considered similar to the effect produced by the interstitial cell stimulating hormone (ICSH) from the anterior lobe of the pituitary. Androgen stimulation in the male leads to the development of secondary sex characteristics and may stimulate testicular descent when no anatomical impediment to descent is present. This descent is usually reversible when hCG is discontinued. Chorionic gonadotropin is likely to be of benefit in all conditions directly related to insufficient secretion of androgen, provided the interstitial cells of the testes are capable of stimulation.

Female: Chorionic gonadotropin is administered in the second phase of the cycle in an attempt to maintain the functional integrity of the corpus luteum and to stimulate its secretion of progesterone. Response to chorionic gonadotropin may be considered similar to the effect produced by the luteotrophic hormone from the pituitary gland. During the normal menstrual cycle, LH participates with FSH in the development and maturation of the normal ovarian follicle, and the mid-cycle LH surge triggers ovulation. hCG can substitute for LH in this function.

During a normal pregnancy, hCG secreted by the placenta maintains the corpus luteum after LH secretion decreases, supporting continued secretion of estrogen and progesterone and preventing menstruation.

hCG has no known effect on fat mobilization, appetite or sense of hunger, or body fat distribution.

Indications: Note: hCG has not been demonstrated to be effective adjunctive therapy in the treatment of obesity. There is no substantial evidence that it increases weight loss beyond that resulting from caloric restriction, that it causes a more attractive or "normal" distribution of fat, or that it decreases the hunger and discomfort associated with calorie-restricted diets.

Male: Chorionic gonadotropin is indicated for the treatment of: Prepubertal Cryptorchidism (not due to anatomical obstruction). In general, hCG is thought to induce testicular descent in situations when descent would have occurred at puberty. hCG thus may help predict whether or not orchiopexy will be needed in the future. Although, in some cases, descent following hCG administration is permanent, in most cases, the response is temporary. Age of initiation of treatment: Various ages ranging from early childhood to immediately before expected puberty have been suggested. On the average, however, 12 years appears to be the appropriate age.
Delayed Adolescence: Chorionic gonadotropin will almost invariably set in motion the normal mechanism of puberty by stimulating the interstitial cells to secrete androgen, and normal development is likely to continue after therapy ceases.
Dwarfism (Pituitary): Before epiphyseal closure, the stimulative effects of chorionic gonadotropin on the interstitial cells of the testes may prove beneficial. Therapy has produced in some cases acceleration of longitudinal bone growth as well as sexual and somatic maturation.
Hypogonadotropic Eunuchoidism: Therapy is directed to the development of primary and secondary sex characteristics through the ability of chorionic gonadotropin to stimulate the interstitial cells of the testes to secrete androgen. In the patient of pubertal age, the response is usually dramatic. The adult patient does not respond as readily, but in view of the permanent effects frequently observed following therapy, it is recommended that in either group, treatment be initiated with this substance, and that androgen be administered only if chorionic gonadotropin proves ineffective.
Selected cases of hypogonadotropic hypogonadism (hypogonadism secondary to a pituitary deficiency) in males: On clinical grounds alone, it is often impossible to determine whether the hypogonadism is the result of primary testicular failure. When testicular biopsies and urinary gonadotropin assays are not available, a therapeutic trial with chorionic gonadotropin will serve to establish diagnosis and indicate type of treatment required.

Lack of response to therapy may be taken as an indication that the hypogonadism is not of pituitary origin, or that the testes are unresponsive to stimulation; if this is the case, substitution therapy with androgen is indicated.

Female: Chorionic gonadotropin is indicated for: Ovulation Induction: Induction of ovulation and pregnancy in the anovulatory, infertile woman in whom the cause of anovulation is secondary and not due to primary ovarian failure, and who has been appropriately pre-treated with human gonadotropins.
Abortion (Habitual): Recurrent abortion at the end of the first 3 to 6 weeks of pregnancy may be due to inadequate production of chorionic gonadotropin, and the administration of large daily doses of chorionic gonadotropin may provide a beneficial luteotropic effect in the habitual aborter. Preconceptional treatment may also encourage nidation and promote a more favorable environment for implantation and early development of the ovum.
Infrequent Scanty Bleeding (Functional): oligomenorrhea, amenorrhea (primary and secondary) and Frohlich's syndrome.
Functional Sterility: Functional sterility may not be due to ovulatory failure but to corpus luteum development and function inadequate for proper implantation and early development of the fertilized ovum. In such cases, chorionic gonadotropin may be used in an attempt to stimulate progesterone secretion and to encourage a return to normal ovarian function.

Contraindications: In the treatment of pituitary tumor, ovarian tumor, prostatic carcinoma and androgen dependent neoplasms, uncontrolled endocrine disorders (e.g., hyperprolactinemia, thyroid and adrenal dysfunction); in female, primary ovarian failure (ovarian dysgenesis and premature menopause), tubal occlusion unless the patient is undergoing superovulation for in vitro fertilization; in men, u-hCG will not be effective in cases where the FSH level is raised since this is indicative of primary testicular failure; urinary-hCG is not effective and is not indicated for weight reduction; precocious puberty; active thrombophlebitis or thromboembolic event; allergy to u-hCG.

Warnings: Female: Ovarian Hyperstimulation Syndrome (OHSS): In women undergoing ovulation induction, an excessive ovarian response to follicular stimulating agents may lead to the development of ovarian hyperstimulation syndrome if u-hCG is given to induce ovulation or to support the corpus luteum. It is of primary importance that u-hCG should be withheld in such cycles.

OHSS is generally categorized as mild, moderate or severe.
Mild OHSS Symptoms: some abdominal distention; nausea; vomiting; occasional diarrhea; ovaries enlarged to about 5 cm diameter appear 3 to 6 days after u-hCG administration. Therapy: rest; careful observation and symptomatic relief. Ovarian enlargement declines rapidly.
Moderate OHSS Symptoms: more pronounced abdominal distention; nausea, vomiting; occasional diarrhea; ovaries enlarge to about 12 cm. Therapy: bed rest; close observation in the case of conception occurring, to detect any progression to severe hyperstimulation. Pelvic examination of enlarged ovaries should be gentle, in order to avoid rupture of ovarian cysts. Symptoms subside spontaneously over 2 to 3 weeks.

Severe OHSS is a rare (less than 2% of cases when patients are normally monitored) but serious complication. Symptoms: ovaries enlarge to in excess of 12 cm diameter; pronounced abdominal distention; ascites; pleural effusion; decreased blood volume; reduced urine output; electrolyte imbalance and sometimes shock. Use of diuretics should be avoided in the primary phase of the syndrome, since they may precipitate cardiovascular shock in a patient who already has plasma hypovolemia. They may however be used during the resolution phase of OHSS, to help mobilize and eliminate fluid sequestered during the first phase. Therapy: hospitalization, treatment should be conservative and concentrate on restoring fluid depletion and preventing shock. Acute symptoms subside over several days if conception has not occurred. Symptoms may be prolonged if conception has occurred.
The risk of OHSS developing in women undergoing superovulation for an assisted conception technique may be lessened if all the follicles are aspirated prior to ovulation.

Rupture of ovarian cysts with resultant hemoperitoneum.
Thromboembolic Complications: Thromboembolic events have been reported following gonadotropin/u-hCG therapy both in association with and separated from OHSS. These included thrombophlebitis, pulmonary embolism, stroke, and arterial occlusion resulting in loss of a limb. In rare cases, thromboembolic events have resulted in death.
Pregnancy: Multiple Pregnancy: The incidence of multiple pregnancies and births is increased following gonadotropins/u-hCG therapy stimulation and ovulation induction in patients attempting in vivo conception. The risk of multiple pregnancy following ART is related to the number of oocytes/embryos replaced. However, the majority of multiple pregnancies are twins. Multiple pregnancies might result in premature deliveries.
Pregnancy Testing: A false positive result might be obtained if the test is carried out in a patient who has recently undergone (over the last 7 days) or is still having u-hCG administration.
Males: Androgens may cause fluid retention in the male if high doses of u-hCG are administered. In such cases dosage should be considerably reduced particularly in patients with cardiac or renal disease, epilepsy, migraine or asthma.
Sexual Precocity: u-hCG may cause sexual precocity when administered in young patients for cryptorchidism. If signs are observed, treatment should be stopped. If continued therapy is considered necessary, a reduced dosage regimen should be instituted.

Finally, u-hCG may induce gynecomastia.

Precautions: *Drug Interactions:* No clinically significant drug interactions have been reported during u-hCG therapy.

Adverse Effects: The following adverse reactions have been associated with the administration of chorionic gonadotropin: headache, irritability, restlessness, depression, fatigue, edema, precocious puberty, gynecomastia, pain at the site of injection.

Ovarian cancer has been reported in a very small number of infertile women who have been treated with fertility drugs. A causal relationship between treatment with fertility drugs and ovarian cancer has not been established.

Dosage: The dosage regimen employed in any particular case will depend upon the indication for use, the age and weight of the patient, and the physician's preference.

Male: Prepubertal Cryptorchidism (not due to anatomical obstruction): (1) 4 000 USP units, 3 times weekly, for 2 to 3 weeks, or (2) 1 000 USP units, 3 times weekly, for 6 to 8 weeks. The dosage schedule may vary to some extent depending upon the age when treatment is given.

If the dosage is adequate, there will usually be some indication, following 1 such course of therapy, whether descent will occur or surgery be required. A therapeutic trial with chorionic gonadotropin may constitute a valuable diagnostic aid to determine the need for surgery. Lack of response is usually an indication of anatomic obstruction. Furthermore, when surgery is required, this preliminary treatment may facilitate the procedure by increasing the size of the testes and the length of the cords. Postoperative gonadotropic therapy has also been suggested to prevent retraction of the testes.
Delayed Adolescence: 4 000 to 5 000 USP units 3 times weekly for 6 to 8 weeks with a rest period of 2 to 3 weeks between courses of therapy.
Dwarfism (Pituitary): 1 000 to 5 000 USP units 3 times weekly.
Hypogonadotropic Eunuchoidism: 4 000 to 5 000 USP units 3 times weekly for 6 to 8 weeks with a rest period of 2 to 3 weeks between courses of therapy.
Hypogonadism (after Sexual Maturity): 4 000 to 5 000 USP units 3 times weekly for 6 to 8 weeks with a rest period of 2 to 3 weeks between courses of therapy.

Female: Ovulation Induction: (For the gonadotropins dosage, see the prescribing information for that drug product.) 5 000 to 10 000 USP Units 1 day following the last dose of gonadotropins.
Abortion (Habitual): 1 000 to 2 000 USP units, or more, 1 or more times daily combined with other recognized therapeutic measures until the danger of abortion has passed.
Infrequent Scanty Bleeding (Functional): Oligomenorrhea, amenorrhea (primary and secondary), and Frohlich's Syndrome: See dosage for Functional Sterility.
Functional Sterility: 500 to 1 000 USP units may be given daily from the 15th to the 24th day. An alternative schedule is 1 500 USP units every other day, 3 times in all, on the 16th, 18th and 20th day of the cycle.

Chorionic gonadotropin is for **s.c. or i.m. use only.**
Preparation of Solution: Withdraw sterile air from the vial containing the lyophilized chorionic gonadotropin and inject it into the diluent vial. Remove up to 10 mL from the diluent vial and add to the chorionic gonadotropin vial; agitate gently until dissolution is complete.

Parenteral drug products should be inspected visually prior to administration. Do not inject if the reconstituted product contains particulate matter or is discolored.

Chorionic gonadotropin may be reconstituted by adding the required amount of diluent to obtain the desired dosage. See Table I.

Table I—Profasi

Reconstitution and Administration Alternatives

Desired Dosage (units)	Diluent Volume Options (mL)	Injection Volume (mL)
10 000	10	10
	5	5
	2.5	2.5
	1	1
5 000	10	5
	5	2.5
	2.5	1.25
4 000	10	4
	5	2
	2.5	1
2 000	10	2
	5	1
	2.5	0.5
1 000	10	1
	5	0.5

Supplied: Each vial of Profasi HP contains: chorionic gonadotropin, 10 000 USP Units. Nonmedicinal ingredients: mannitol, sodium dihydrogen phosphate and disodium phosphate for adjustment of pH. In addition, when reconstituted with the diluent provided (bacteriostatic water for injection, USP containing 0.9% benzyl alcohol), each vial contains benzyl alcohol 0.9%. Packages of 1 vial of Profasi HP (10 000 USP Units) and one 10 mL multiple-dose vial of Sterile Diluent (bacteriostatic water for injection, USP containing 0.9% benzyl alcohol).

Store the sterile lyophilized powder at room temperature (15 to 30°C) until the expiry date indicated on the label. When reconstituted the solution should be refrigerated (2 to 8°C) and should be used within 30 days.

Reviewed 1998

For comparative information on Corticosteroids: Inhaled, Topical, Systemic or Eye Ear Nose, see the CPhA General Monograph in the WHITE SECTION.

PROGLYCEM® Ⓟ
Schering

Diazoxide
Hyperglycemic Agent

Pharmacology: Diazoxide, a benzothiadiazine derivative, when administered orally produces a prompt dose-related increase in blood glucose level, due primarily to an inhibition of insulin release from the pancreas and also to an extrapancreatic effect.

The hyperglycemic effect begins within an hour and generally lasts no more than 8 hours in the presence of normal renal function.

Diazoxide decreases the excretion of sodium and water, resulting in fluid retention which may be clinically significant.

The effects on blood pressure are usually not marked with the oral preparation. This contrasts with the i.v. preparation (see Adverse Effects). Other pharmacologic actions include increased pulse rate; increased serum uric acid levels due to decreased excretion; increased serum levels of free fatty acids; decreased chloride excretion; decreased para-aminohippuric acid (PAH) clearance with no appreciable effect on glomerular filtration rate. The concomitant administration of a benzothiazide diuretic may intensify the hyperglycemic and hyperuricemic effects of diazoxide. In the presence of hypokalemia, hyperglycemic effects are also potentiated. Diazoxide-induced hyperglycemia is reversed by the administration of insulin or tolbutamide.

The inhibition of insulin release by diazoxide is antagonized by alpha-adrenergic blocking agents. Diazoxide is extensively bound (more than 90%) to serum proteins and is excreted by the kidneys. The plasma half-life following i.v. administration is about 28 hours. Limited data on oral administration revealed a half-life of 24 and 36 hours in 2 adults. In 4 children aged 4 months to 6 years, the plasma half-life varied from 9.5 to 24 hours on long-term oral administration. The half-life may be prolonged following overdosage and in patients with impaired renal function.

Indications: Oral diazoxide is useful in the management of hypoglycemia due to hyperinsulinism associated with the following conditions: Adults: inoperable islet cell adenoma or carcinoma or extrapancreatic malignancy.
Infants and Children: leucine sensitivity, islet cell hyperplasia, nesidioblastosis, extrapancreatic malignancy, islet cell adenoma, or adenomatosis. It may be used preoperatively as a temporary measure and post-operatively if hypoglycemia persists.

Diazoxide should be used only after a diagnosis of hypoglycemia due to one of the above conditions has been definitely established. When other specific medical therapy or surgical management either has been unsuccessful or is not feasible, treatment with diazoxide should be considered.

Contraindications: The use of diazoxide for functional hypoglycemia is contraindicated. The drug should not be used in patients hypersensitive to diazoxide or to other thiazides unless the potential benefits outweigh the possible risks.

Warnings: *Pregnancy* and *Lactation:* Diazoxide should not be used in women of child-bearing age except in life-threatening situations. Diazoxide may pass into the breast milk of nursing mothers. Reproduction studies using the oral preparation in rats have revealed increased fetal resorptions and delayed parturition, as well as fetal skeletal anomalies. Evidence of skeletal and cardiac teratogenic effects in rabbits has been noted with the i.v. administration. The drug has also been demonstrated to cross the placental barrier in animals and cause degeneration of the fetal pancreatic beta cells. Since there are no adequate data on fetal effects of this drug when given to pregnant women, safety in pregnancy has not been established.

When its use in pregnant women is considered, the indications should be limited to those specified above for adults (see Indications) and the potential benefits to the mother must be weighed against possible harmful effects to the fetus.

The antidiuretic property of diazoxide may lead to significant fluid retention, which in patients with compromised cardiac reserve may precipitate congestive heart failure. The fluid retention will respond to conventional therapy with diuretics.

It should be noted that concomitantly administered thiazides may potentiate the hyperglycemic and hyperuricemic actions of diazoxide (see Precautions, Drug Interactions).

Ketoacidosis and non-ketotic hyperosmolar coma have been reported in patients treated with recommended doses, usually during intercurrent illness. Prompt recognition and treatment are essential (see Overdose) and prolonged surveillance following the acute episode is necessary because of the long drug half-life of approximately 30 hours. The occurrence of these serious events may be reduced by careful education of patients regarding the need for monitoring the urine for sugar and ketones and for prompt reporting of abnormal findings and unusual symptoms to the physician.

In the presence of hypokalemia, the hyperglycemia effects of diazoxide are potentiated.

Transient cataracts occurred in association with hyperosmolar coma in an infant and subsided on correction of the hyperosmolarity. Cataracts have been observed in several animals receiving daily doses of i.v. or oral diazoxide.

Precautions: Treatment should be initiated under close clinical supervision, with careful monitoring of blood glucose and clinical response until the patient's condition has stabilized. This usually requires several days. If not effective in 2 or 3 weeks, the drug should be discontinued.

Prolonged treatment requires regular monitoring of the urine for sugar and ketones, especially under stress conditions, with prompt reporting of any abnormalities to the physician. Additionally, blood sugar levels should be monitored periodically by the physician to determine the need for dose adjustment.

The effects of diazoxide on the hematopoietic system and the level of serum uric acid should be kept in mind; the latter should be considered particularly in patients with hyperuricemia or a history of gout.

In some patients, higher blood levels have been observed with the liquid than with the capsule formulation. Dosage should be adjusted as necessary in individual patients if changed from 1 formulation to the other.

Since the plasma half-life of diazoxide is prolonged in patients with impaired renal function, a reduced dosage should be considered. Serum electrolyte levels should also be evaluated for such patients.

The antihypertensive effect of other drugs may be enhanced by diazoxide and this should be kept in mind when administering it concomitantly with antihypertensive agents.

Because of protein binding, administration of diazoxide with coumarin or its derivatives may require reduction in the dosage of the anticoagulant, although there has been no reported evidence of excessive anticoagulant effect. In addition, it may possibly displace bilirubin from albumin; this should be kept in mind particularly when treating newborns with increased bilirubinemia.

Drug Interactions: Diuretics: The hyperglycemic and hyperuricemic actions of diazoxide may be potentiated by the concomitant administration of thiazides or other commonly used diuretics.
Coumarin Anticoagulants: The administration of diazoxide to patients treated with coumarin and its derivatives may result in potentiation of hypoprothrombic action and may necessitate a decrease of anticoagulant dosage.
Phenytoin: The concomitant administration of diazoxide to phenytoin treated patients can cause loss of seizure control.
Chlorpromazine: The hyperglycemic action of diazoxide may be enhanced by concomitant administration of chlorpromazine.

Adverse Effects: Frequent and serious: Sodium and fluid retention is most common in young infants and in adults and may precipitate congestive heart failure in patients with compromised cardiac reserve. It usually responds to diuretic therapy (see Precautions, Drug Interactions).
Infrequent but serious: Diabetic ketoacidosis and hyperosmolar non-ketotic coma may develop very rapidly. Conventional therapy with insulin and restoration of fluid and electrolyte balance are usually effective if instituted promptly. Prolonged surveillance is essential in view of the long half-life of diazoxide (see Overdose).

Other frequent adverse reactions: Hirsutism of the lanugo type mainly on the forehead, back and limbs which occurs most commonly in children and women may be cosmetically unacceptable. It subsides on discontinuation of the drug.

Hyperglycemia or glycosuria may require reduction in dosage in order to avoid progression to ketoacidosis or hyperosmolar coma.

Gastrointestinal intolerance may include anorexia, nausea, vomiting, abdominal pain, ileus, diarrhea, transient loss of taste. Tachycardia, palpitations, increased levels of serum uric acid are common.

Thrombocytopenia with or without purpura may require discontinuation of the drug. Neutropenia is transient, is not associated with increased susceptibility to infection and ordinarily does not require discontinuation of the drug. Skin rash, headache, weakness and malaise may also occur.

Other adverse reactions which have been observed:
Cardiovascular: hypotension occurs occasionally which may be augmented by thiazide diuretics given concurrently. A few cases of transient hypertension, for which no explanation is apparent have been noted. Chest pain has been reported rarely.
Hematologic: eosinophilia; decreased hemoglobin/hematocrit; excessive bleeding; decreased IgG.
Hepato-Renal: increased AST, alkaline phosphatase, azotemia, decreased creatinine clearance, reversible nephrotic syndrome, decreased urinary output, hematuria, albuminuria.
Neurologic: anxiety, dizziness, insomnia, polyneuritis, paresthesia, pruritus, extrapyramidal signs.
Ophthalmologic: transient cataracts, subconjunctival hemorrhage, ring scotoma, blurred vision, diplopia, lacrimation.
Skeletal/Integumentary: monilial dermatitis, herpes, advance in bone age; loss of scalp hair.
Systemic: fever, lymphadenopathy.
Other: gout, acute pancreatitis/pancreatic necrosis, galactorrhea, enlargement of lump in breast.

Overdose: Symptoms and Treatment: An overdose of diazoxide causes marked hyperglycemia which may be associated with ketoacidosis. It will respond to prompt insulin administration and restoration of fluid and electrolyte balance. Because of the drug's long half-life (approximately 30 hours), the symptoms of overdosage require prolonged surveillance for periods up to 7 days, until the blood sugar level stabilizes within the normal range. One investigator reported successful lowering of diazoxide blood levels by peritoneal dialysis in 1 patient and by hemodialysis in another.

Dosage: Patients should be under close clinical observation when treatment is initiated. The clinical response and blood glucose level should be carefully monitored until the patient's condition has stabilized satisfactorily; in most instances, this may be accomplished in several days. If administration of diazoxide is not effective after 2 or 3 weeks, the drug should be discontinued.

The dosage must be individualized based on the severity of the hypoglycemic condition and the blood glucose level and the clinical response of the patient. The dosage should be adjusted until the desired clinical and laboratory effects are produced with the least amount of the drug. Special care should be taken to assure accuracy of dosage in infants and young children.
Adults and Children: The usual daily dosage is 3 to 8 mg/kg, divided into 2 or 3 equal doses every 8 or 12 hours. In certain instances, patients with refractory hypoglycemia may require higher dosages. Ordinarily, an appropriate starting dosage is 3 mg/kg/day, divided into 3 equal doses every 8 hours. Thus, an average adult would receive a starting dosage of approximately 200 mg daily.
Infants and Newborns: The usual daily dosage is 8 to 15 mg/kg, divided into 2 or 3 equal doses every 8 to 12 hours. An appropriate starting dosage is 10 mg/kg/day, divided into 3 equal doses every 8 hours.

Supplied: Capsules: Each opaque orange capsule, contains: diazoxide USP 100 mg. Nonmedicinal ingredients: lactose and magnesium stearate. Tartrazine-free. Bottles of 100.

Suspension: Each mL of chocolate-mint flavored suspension contains: diazoxide USP 50 mg. Nonmedicinal ingredients: alcohol (<5%), carboxymethylcellulose, chocolate cream flavor, hydrochloric acid, methylparaben, mint imitation flavor, pluronic F68, propylparaben, propylene glycol, sodium benzoate, sorbitol, veegum HV and water. Tartrazine-free. Bottles of 30 mL with dropper calibrated to deliver 10, 20, 30, 40 and 50 mg diazoxide. Protect from light.

PROGRAF® Ⓟ
Fujisawa

Tacrolimus
Immunosuppressant

Pharmacology: Tacrolimus is a macrolide immunosuppressant produced by Streptomyces tsukubaensis.
Mechanism of Action: Tacrolimus prolongs the survival of the host and transplanted graft in animal transplant models of liver, kidney, heart, bone marrow, small bowel and pancreas, lung and trachea, skin, cornea and limb.

Tacrolimus has been demonstrated to suppress some humoral immunity and, to a greater extent, cell-mediated reactions such as allograft rejection, delayed type hypersensitivity, Freund's adjuvant arthritis, experimental allergic encephalomyelitis and graft versus host disease in several animal species.

Tacrolimus inhibits T-lymphocyte activation, although the exact mechanism of action is not known. The minimum inhibitory tissue culture level of tacrolimus that prevents antigen stimulation of T-lymphocytes is 0.1 to 0.3 nM. Experimental evidence suggests that tacrolimus binds to an intracellular protein, FKBP-12. A complex of tacrolimus-FKBP-12, calcium, calmodulin and calcineurin is then formed and the phosphatase activity of calcineurin inhibited. This effect may prevent the generation of nuclear factor of activated T-cells (NF-AT), a nuclear component thought to initiate the gene transcription for the formation of lymphokines (interleukin-2, gamma interferon). The net result is the inhibition of T-lymphocyte activation (i.e., immunosuppression).

Pharmacokinetics: Tacrolimus activity is primarily due to the parent drug. After oral administration, absorption of tacrolimus into the systemic circulation from the gastrointestinal tract is incomplete and can be variable. Elimination of tacrolimus is via hepatic metabolism with a mean terminal elimination half-life of 18.8 hours in kidney transplant patients, 11.7 hours in liver transplant patients and 34.2 hours in healthy volunteers following i.v. administration. Due to intersubject variability in tacrolimus pharmacokinetics, individualization of dosing regimen is necessary for optimal therapy. Dosing individualization can be achieved by therapeutic drug monitoring of tacrolimus blood concentrations and evaluation of clinical status (see Dosage). Pharmacokinetic data indicate that whole blood concentrations rather than plasma concentrations serve as the more appropriate sampling compartment to describe tacrolimus pharmacokinetics.

Absorption: Absorption of tacrolimus from the gastrointestinal tract after oral administration is incomplete and can be variable. Mean (±S.D.) pharmacokinetic parameters of tacrolimus in whole blood after oral administration to volunteers in 2 studies are presented in Table I.

The two different dose strengths of tacrolimus capsules (1 and 5 mg) are bioequivalent (see Table I).

In 26 kidney transplant patients, peak concentrations (C_{max}) were achieved at approximately 1 to 3 hours. The absorption half-life of tacrolimus in 17 liver transplant patients averaged 0.6 hour (S.D. 1.0 hour) with peak concentrations (C_{max}) in blood and plasma being achieved at approximately 1.5 to 3.5 hours. Mean (±S.D.) pharmacokinetic parameters of tacrolimus in whole blood after initial dose in adult kidney and liver transplant patients are presented in Table II.

The absolute bioavailability of tacrolimus is approximately 17% in kidney transplant patients, 22% in adult liver transplant patients, 34% in pediatric liver transplant patients, and 18% in healthy volunteers.

Food Effects: The rate and extent of tacrolimus absorption is greatest under fasted conditions. The presence and composition of food decreased both the rate and extent of tacrolimus absorption when administered to healthy volunteers: See Table III.

Table III—Prograf

Food Effects

Parameter	Fasted (n=15)	High Carbohydrate[a] (n=15)	High Fat[b] (n=15)
C_{max} (ng/mL)	25.6±11.4	9.0±3.8	5.9±2.3
T_{max} (h)	1.4±0.6	3.2±1.1	6.5±3.0
AUC $_{0-t}$ (ng·h/mL)	233±121[c]	168±59[c]	147±56[c]

[a]668 kcal (4% fat; 85% carbohydrate).
[b]848 kcal (46% fat, 39% carbohydrate).
[c]AUC (0-96).

The effect was most pronounced with the high-fat meal: mean area under the curve (AUC_{0-96}) and C_{max} were decreased 37% and 77%, respectively; T_{max} was lengthened 5-fold. The high-carbohydrate meal decreased AUC_{0-96} and C_{max} by 28% and 65%, respectively.

The effect of food was also studied in 11 liver transplant patients. Tacrolimus was administered in the fasted state or 15 minutes after a breakfast of known fat content (34% of 400 total calories). The results indicate that the presence of food reduces the absorption of tacrolimus in these patients (decrease in AUC and C_{max} and increase in T_{max}). The relative oral bioavailability (whole blood) was reduced by 27.0 (±18.2%) compared to administration in the fasting state.

In healthy volunteers, the time of the meal also affected tacrolimus bioavailability. Relative to the fasted state, there was little effect on tacrolimus bioavailability when administered 1 hour prior to a high-fat breakfast, whereas bioavailability (both extent and rate of absorption) was greatly reduced when the drug was administered immediately or 1.5 hours after the meal. When given immediately following the meal, C_{max} was reduced 71%, AUC_{0-96} was reduced by 39%, and T_{max} was delayed 1.6 hours relative to the fasting condition. When administered 1.5 hours following the meal, C_{max} was reduced 63%, AUC_{0-96} was reduced 39%, and T_{max} was delayed 1.4 hours relative to the fasted condition.

Table I—Prograf

Pharmacokinetic Parameters After Oral Administration

Parameter	Bioequivalence Study		Pharmacokinetic Study
Age	19-53 yrs		19-50 yrs
Number	62	59	16
Dose	5×1 mg single dose	1×5 mg single dose	5×1 mg single dose
Absolute Bioavailability (%)		—	17.8±5.0
C_{max} (ng/mL)	25.2±9.7	26.5±10.8	29.7±7.2
T_{max} (h)	1.2±0.4	1.4±0.6	1.6±0.7
AUC $_{0-t}$ (ng·h/mL)	196±93[a]	209±97[a]	243±73[b]

[a]AUC (0-72).
[b]AUC (0-120).

Table II—Prograf

Pharmacokinetic Parameters After Initial Dose—Kidney and Liver Transplant

Parameter	Adult Kidney Transplant Patients	Adult Liver Transplant Patients
Age	19-66 yrs	33-65 yrs
Number	26	17
Oral Dose (in divided doses q12h)	0.2-0.3 mg/kg/day range	0.3 mg/kg/day mean dose
Absolute Bioavailability (%)	17.4±10.4	21.8±6.3
C_{max} (ng/mL)	19.2±10.3[a] 24.2±15.8[b]	68.5±30.0
T_{max} (h)	3.0[a] 1.5[b]	2.3±1.5
AUC $_{0-t}$ (ng·h/mL)	203±42[a,c] 288±93[b,c]	519±179[c]

[a]0.2 mg/kg/day.
[b]0.3 mg/kg/day.
[c]AUC (0-inf).

In fasted healthy volunteers given a single dose, the absorption of tacrolimus was proportional to dose; see Table IV.

Table IV—Prograf

Absorption

Parameter	Dose n=18 3 mg	n=18 7 mg	n=18 10 mg
C_{max} (ng/mL)	14.5±5.8 14.5±5.8*	31.2±10.1 13.4±4.3*	45.1±15.0 13.5±4.5*
T_{max} (h)	1.4±0.4	1.4±0.5	1.3±0.4
AUC_{0-96} (ng·h/mL)	131±77 131±77*	303±138 130±59*	420±166 126±50*

*Adjusted to 3 mg dose.

Distribution: The apparent volume of distribution (based on whole blood concentrations) of tacrolimus is approximately 1.41, 1.91 and 0.85 L/kg in kidney transplant patients, healthy volunteers and adult liver transplant patients, respectively; see Table V (on following page).

The plasma protein binding of tacrolimus is approximately 99% and is independent of concentration over a range of 5 to 50 ng/mL. Tacrolimus is bound to proteins, mainly albumin and α-1-acid glycoprotein, and has a high level of association with erythrocytes. The distribution of tacrolimus between whole blood and plasma depends on several factors, such as hematocrit, temperature at the time of plasma separation, drug concentration, and plasma protein concentration. In a U.S. study, the ratio of whole blood concentration to plasma concentration ranged from 12 to 67 (mean 35).

In 18 kidney transplant patients, tacrolimus trough concentrations from 3 to 30 ng/mL measured at 10 to 12 hours post dose (C_{min}) correlated well with the AUC $_{0-12}$ (correlation coefficient 0.93). In 24 liver transplant patients over a concentration range of 10 to 60 ng/mL, the correlation coefficient was 0.94.

Metabolism: Tacrolimus is extensively metabolized by the mixed-function oxidase system, primarily the cytochrome P450 enzyme system (CYPIIIA). A metabolic pathway leading to the formation of 8 possible metabolites has been proposed. Demethylation and hydroxylation were identified as the primary mechanisms of biotransformation in vitro. The major metabolite identified in incubations with human liver microsomes is 13-demethyl tacrolimus. In in vitro studies, a 31-demethyl metabolite has been reported to have the same activity as tacrolimus; the 13-demethyl, 15-demethyl and 15- and 31-double-demethylated metabolites were shown to retain an activity of less than 10%.

Excretion: The clearance of tacrolimus is 0.040, 0.083 and 0.042 L/h/kg in healthy volunteers, adult kidney transplant patients and adult liver transplant patients, respectively. In man, less than 1% of the dose administered is excreted unchanged in urine.

Special Populations: Pediatric Patients: A study in liver transplantation has been conducted in 16 pediatric patients (age range: 0.7 to 13.2 years). A mean terminal elimination half-life of 11.5 hours was determined following an i.v. dose of 0.037 mg/kg/day in 12 patients; the volume of distribution was 2.6 L/kg, whereas clearance was 0.135 L/h/kg. In 9 patients receiving capsule formulation, a mean C_{max} of 48.4 ng/mL was attained at a mean T_{max} of 2.7 hours following an oral dose of 0.152 mg/kg as tacrolimus capsules. The AUC (0-72h) was 337 ng·h/mL. The absolute bioavailability was 31%.

Whole blood trough concentrations from 31 pediatric patients (less than 12 years old) showed that pediatric patients need higher doses than adults to achieve similar tacrolimus trough concentrations, suggesting that the pharmacokinetic characteristics of tacrolimus are different in pediatric patients compared to adults (see Dosage).

Renal Insufficiency: Tacrolimus pharmacokinetics following a single i.v. administration have been determined in 12 patients (7 not on dialysis and 5 on dialysis) prior to their kidney transplant. The pharmacokinetic parameters obtained are presented in Table VI (on following page).

The disposition of tacrolimus in patients with renal dysfunction was not different from that in normal volunteers (see previous tables). The clearance was similar whereas volume of distribution was smaller and the mean terminal elimination half-life shorter than that of normal volunteers.

Hepatic Insufficiency: Tacrolimus pharmacokinetics have been determined in 6 patients with mild hepatic dysfunction (mean Pugh score: 6.2) following single i.v. and oral administrations. The pharmacokinetic parameters obtained are presented in Table VII (on following page).

Prograf (cont'd)

Table V—Prograf

Volume of Distribution

Parameter	Volunteers (n=8)	Kidney Transplant Patients (n=26)	Liver Transplant Patients (Adult) (n=17)
Mean I.V. Dose	0.025 mg/kg/4 h	0.02 mg/kg/4 h	0.05 mg/kg/12 h
V (L/kg)	1.91±0.31	1.41±0.66	0.85±0.3
Cl (L/h/kg)	0.040±0.009	0.083±0.050	0.053±0.017

Table VI—Prograf

Pharmacokinetic Parameters Following a Single I.V. Administration—Renal Insufficiency

Serum Creatinine (mg/dL)	3.9±1.6 (not on dialysis) 12.0±2.4 (on dialysis)
Age range (yrs)	25-65
Route	i.v.
Dose (mg)	1.17±0.28
AUC 0-60 (ng·h/mL)	393±123
AUC 0-inf (ng·h/mL)	499±155
V (L/kg)	1.07±0.20
Cl (L/h/kg)	0.038±0.014
$t_{1/2}$ (h)	26.3±9.2

Table VII—Prograf

Pharmacokinetic Parameters Following Single I.V. and Oral Administration—Hepatic Insufficiency

Number of Patients	6	
Age Range (yrs)	52-63	
Dose (mg)	7.7	1.3
Route	oral	i.v.
Absolute Bioavailability (%)	22.3±11.4	
C_{max} (ng/mL)	48.2±17.9	
T_{max} (h)	1.5±0.6	
AUC 0-72 (ng·h/mL)	488±320	367±107
V (L/kg)	3.7±4.7	3.1±1.6
Cl (L/h/kg)	0.034±0.019	0.042±0.020
$t_{1/2}$ (h)	66.1±44.8	60.6±43.8

The disposition of tacrolimus in patients with mild hepatic dysfunction was not substantially different from that in normal volunteers (see previous tables). In general, tacrolimus elimination half-life was longer and volume of distribution larger in patients with mild hepatic dysfunction compared to normal volunteers. The clearance in both populations was similar and since tacrolimus is extensively metabolized at multiple sites, patients with mild hepatic dysfunction may not require lower maintenance doses of tacrolimus than patients with normal hepatic function.

Clinical Studies: Kidney Transplantation: The safety and efficacy of tacrolimus-based immunosuppression following kidney transplantation were assessed in 2 randomized, multicentre, nonblinded, prospective studies. The active control groups were treated with cyclosporine-based immunosuppression. These studies were designed to evaluate whether the 2 regimens were therapeutically equivalent for 1-year patient and graft survival. Based on the results from these 2 studies, the tacrolimus-based regimen was found to be therapeutically equivalent to the cyclosporine-based regimen.

In 1 trial, 412 kidney transplant patients were enrolled at 19 clinical sites in the U.S.; 205 patients were randomized to tacrolimus-based immunosuppression and 207 patients were randomized to cyclosporine-based immunosuppression. All patients received prophylactic induction therapy consisting of an antilymphocyte antibody preparation, corticosteroids and azathioprine. Tacrolimus was initiated when renal function was stable as indicated by a serum creatinine ≤4 mg/dL (353.6 μmol/L). Tacrolimus was initiated a median of 4 days after transplantation. Patients less than 6 years of age were excluded.

In the second trial, 448 kidney transplant patients were enrolled at 15 clinical sites in Europe; 303 patients were randomized to tacrolimus-based immunosuppression and 145 patients were randomized to cyclosporine-based immunosuppression. Tacrolimus was initiated within 24 hours of transplantation and was administered with corticosteroids and azathioprine. Patients less than 18 years of age were excluded.

One-year patient and graft survival in the tacrolimus-based treatment groups were equivalent to those in the cyclosporine-based treatment groups. The overall 1-year patient survival (tacrolimus and cyclosporine combined) was 96.1% in the U.S. study and 94.2% in the European study. The overall 1-year graft survival was 89.6% in the U.S. study and 83.7% in the European study.

The 2 large, randomized clinical trials demonstrated that significantly fewer tacrolimus-treated patients (approximately 16% fewer) experienced an episode of acute rejection during the one-year treatment period compared with cyclosporine-treated patients ($p<.001$).

Significantly fewer tacrolimus-treated patients crossed over to cyclosporine therapy due to adverse events and acute rejection episodes compared to cyclosporine-treated patients transferring to tacrolimus therapy ($p=.007$). The majority of patients who crossed over from the cyclosporine therapy to tacrolimus therapy were due to rejection (n=27). The majority of patients who crossed over from tacrolimus therapy to cyclosporine therapy were due to adverse reactions (n=13) and rarely for rejection (n=2). Of 27 cyclosporine-treated patients demonstrating acute rejection episodes and transferred to tacrolimus, 21 of these patient rejection episodes resolved (77.8%). Of the 2 tacrolimus patients transferred to cyclosporine due to acute rejection, 1 of the rejection episodes resolved.

An open-label, rescue study assessed the effect of tacrolimus on 73 kidney transplant patients with biopsy-proven, corticosteroid-resistant acute rejection. Responses to tacrolimus therapy included improvement in 78% of patients, stabilization in 11% and progressive deterioration in 11%. Patient and graft survival 1 year postconversion to tacrolimus was 93% and 75% respectively.

Liver Transplantation: The safety and efficacy of tacrolimus administered in combination with adrenal corticosteroids was compared with cyclosporine-based immunosuppressive regimens in 2 randomized, prospective, open-labeled, multicentre studies after orthotopic liver transplantation. In addition, the efficacy of tacrolimus as rescue therapy in patients with liver allograft rejection refractory to standard therapy was examined in an open-labeled, nonrandomized, multicentre, historically controlled trial.

In 1 controlled trial, 529 patients were randomized to receive immunosuppression with tacrolimus (N=263) or cyclosporine-based regimens (N=266). Patient survival was equivalent with Kaplan-Meier actuarial 1-year estimates of 88% for both tacrolimus and cyclosporine-based regimens. Actuarial 1-year graft survival estimates were 82% for the tacrolimus group and 79% for the cyclosporine-based group. The incidences of acute rejection (68% vs 76%), steroid-resistant rejection requiring treatment with OKT3 (19% vs 36%), and refractory rejection (3% vs 15%) were lower in recipients of the tacrolimus regimen compared with cyclosporine-based regimens (see Table VIII). Cumulative adrenal corticosteroid use was lower in the tacrolimus group; however, equivalent doses of corticosteroids were not mandated for induction or maintenance in the 2 arms of the study. Other measures of efficacy, such as liver function tests and Karnofsky scores, showed similar improvement over time in both groups.

In the second controlled study, 545 patients were randomized to receive tacrolimus combined with adrenal corticosteroids (N=270) as a treatment for prevention of rejection of primary liver allograft patients, compared with cyclosporine-based therapy (N=275).

The estimated 1-year Kaplan-Meier patient survival rates were 81% for the tacrolimus treatment group and 75% for the cyclosporine-based treatment group. One-year estimated Kaplan-Meier graft survival rates were 76% for the tacrolimus group and 70% for the cyclosporine-based group. The acute rejection rate was 42% for the tacrolimus group compared with 55% for the cyclosporine-based group. The incidence of refractory rejection was also less in the tacrolimus group (3%) compared with the cyclosporine-based group (10%) (see Table IX). The cumulative amount of adrenal corticosteroids administered to patients in the tacrolimus group was less than in the cyclosporine-based group.

Table VIII—Prograf

Results of Clinical Studies

	Prograf (%)	CBIR[a] (%)	95% Confidence Intervals (%)[b]
Actuarial 1 Year Patient Survival Estimates	88	88	−5, 7
Actuarial 1 Year Graft Survival Estimates	82	79	−5, 10
Incidence of Acute Rejection	68	76	−17, 1
Incidence of Steroid-Resistant Rejection Requiring Orthoclone OKT3 Treatment	19	36	−25, −8
Incidence of Refractory Rejection	3	15	−18, −6

[a]Cyclosporine-based Immunosuppressive Regimens.
[b]Prograf minus CBIR.

Table IX—Prograf

Results of Clinical Studies

	Prograf (%)	CBIR[a] (%)	95% Confidence Intervals (%)[b]
Actuarial 1 Year Patient Survival Estimates	81	75	−1, 13
Actuarial 1 Year Graft Survival Estimates	76	70	−1, 14
Incidence of Acute Rejection	42	54.7	−23, −4
Incidence of Refractory Rejection	2.6	9.2	−12, −3

[a]Cyclosporine-based Immunosuppressive Regimens.
[b]Prograf minus CBIR.

In a nonrandomized historically controlled trial, 125 patients previously treated with cyclosporine-based regimens with refractory acute or chronic liver allograft rejection were treated with tacrolimus plus adrenal corticosteroids as rescue therapy. Actuarial Kaplan-Meier estimates of survival at 1 year post-conversion to tacrolimus were 71% for patient survival and 56% for graft survival. Other measures of efficacy such as clinical response scores, liver function tests, and Karnofsky performance status showed improvement over time after conversion to tacrolimus.

Indications: For the prophylaxis of organ rejection in patients receiving allogeneic liver or kidney transplants. Tacrolimus is also indicated for the treatment of refractory rejection in patients receiving allogeneic liver or kidney transplants. Tacrolimus is to be used concomitantly with adrenal corticosteroids. Because of the risk of anaphylaxis, tacrolimus injection should be reserved for patients unable to take tacrolimus capsules orally.

Contraindications: In patients with a hypersensitivity to tacrolimus. The injection is contraindicated in patients with a hypersensitivity to HCO-60 (polyoxyl 60 hydrogenated castor oil).

Warnings: Increased susceptibility to infection and the possible development of lymphoma may result from immunosuppression. Only physicians experienced in immunosuppressive therapy and management of organ transplant patients should prescribe tacrolimus. Patients receiving the drug should be managed in facilities equipped and staffed with adequate laboratory and supportive medical resources. The physician responsible for maintenance therapy should have complete information requisite for the follow-up of the patient.

Tacrolimus may cause neurotoxicity and nephrotoxicity, and the likelihood increases with higher blood levels. Nephrotoxicity has been noted in approximately 52% and 57% of kidney transplantation patients and in 40% and 36% of liver transplantation patients receiving tacrolimus in the U.S. and European randomized trials, respectively (see Adverse Effects). More overt nephrotoxicity is seen early after transplantation, characterized by increasing serum creatinine and a decrease in urine output. Impaired renal function requires close monitoring and may necessitate tacrolimus dosage reduction. In patients with persistent elevations of serum creatinine who are unresponsive to dosage adjustments, consideration should be given to changing to other immunosuppressive therapy.

Care should be taken in using tacrolimus with other nephrotoxic drugs. **In particular, to avoid excess nephrotoxicity, when switching patients from a cyclosporine-based regimen to a tacrolimus-based regimen, cyclosporine should be discontinued at least 24 hours prior to initiating tacrolimus. Tacrolimus dosing may be further delayed in the presence of elevated cyclosporine levels (see Precautions). When switching from tacrolimus to cyclosporine, tacrolimus should be discontinued for at least 24 hours.**

Mild to severe hyperkalemia was reported in 31% and 21% of kidney transplant patients and in 45% and 13% of liver transplant recipients treated with tacrolimus in the U.S. and European randomized trials, respectively (see Adverse Effects). Serum potassium levels should be monitored and potassium sparing diuretics should not be used during tacrolimus therapy (see Precautions).

Neurotoxicity, including tremor, headache, and other changes in motor function, mental status and sensory function were reported in approximately 55% of liver transplant recipients in the 2 randomized studies (see Adverse Effects). Tremor occurred more often in tacrolimus-treated kidney transplant patients in the U.S. and European studies (54 and 35%, respectively), compared to cyclosporine-treated patients. The incidence of other neurological events was similar in the 2 treatment groups in both kidney studies (see Adverse Effects). Tremor and headache have been associated with high whole blood concentrations of tacrolimus and may respond to dosage adjustment. Seizures have occurred in adult and pediatric patients receiving tacrolimus (see Adverse Effects). Coma and delirium also have been associated with high plasma concentrations of tacrolimus.

As in patients receiving other immunosuppressants, patients receiving tacrolimus are at increased risk of developing lymphomas and other malignancies, particularly of the skin. The risk appears to be related to the intensity and duration of immunosuppression rather than to the use of any specific agent. Lymphoproliferative disorder (LPD) related to Epstein-Barr Virus (EBV) infection has been reported in immunosuppressed organ transplant recipients.

The risk of LPD appears greatest in young children who are at risk for primary EBV infection while immunosuppressed, or who are switched to tacrolimus following long-term immunosuppression therapy. Experience on combining tacrolimus with immunosuppressive drugs other than adrenal corticosteroids is limited because of the potency of tacrolimus and the risk of over immunosuppression and such combinations are not recommended.

Tacrolimus has been studied in combination with azathioprine and steroids (triple therapy) in recipients of kidney transplants. In a Phase II European trial, tacrolimus triple therapy was administered to 31 adults receiving cadaveric kidney transplants. Within 6 weeks post-transplant there were no deaths or graft losses. Six patients (19.4%) experienced acute rejection, with 1 patient experiencing corticosteroid resistant rejection. Three patients (9.7%) developed transient hyperglycemia, but no patient required long-term therapy for diabetes. Other adverse events reported frequently included infections (51.6%), minor neurological disorders (54.8%), and hypertension (48.8%). The University of Pittsburgh has studied double therapy (tacrolimus and steroids) compared to triple therapy in 204 adult recipients of kidney transplants between August 1991 and October 1992. The 1 year actuarial patient and graft survival of double therapy were 95 and 90% versus 91 and 82% for triple therapy (p=NS). The incidence of rejection was significantly lower with triple therapy in cadaveric recipients (39% versus 58%) but not significantly different in recipients from living related donors. New onset diabetes was seen in 20.2% of double therapy patients versus 7.7% of triple therapy patients. A U.S. Phase II trial studied 92 adult recipients of cadaveric kidney transplants randomized to 3 target whole blood concentration ranges of tacrolimus. All patients received antilymphoblast globulin induction with azathioprine and steroids followed by tacrolimus triple therapy initiated within 2 weeks post-transplant. With follow-up to 6 weeks post-transplant there were no patient deaths, and 1 graft loss. The incidence of rejection was 14% combining all tacrolimus treatment groups. Adverse events requiring dose reduction were significantly associated with target tacrolimus blood concentrations (36 to 62%).

Data on the safety and efficacy of tacrolimus in combination with immunosuppressants other than steroids in liver transplant patients are more limited. In the European multicentre liver transplant study, many patients received azathioprine or ATG/ALG when tacrolimus therapy was withheld. Seven patients received azathioprine in combination with tacrolimus and steroids. Of these 7 patients, 1 died and 1 lost their graft in the first year post-transplant.

A few patients receiving tacrolimus injection have experienced anaphylactic reactions. Although the exact cause of these reactions is not known, other drugs with castor oil derivatives in the formulation have been associated with anaphylaxis in a small percentage of patients. Because of this potential risk of anaphylaxis, tacrolimus injection should be reserved for patients who are unable to take tacrolimus capsules.

Patients receiving tacrolimus injection should be under continuous observation for at least the first 30 minutes following the start of the infusion and at frequent intervals thereafter. If signs or symptoms of anaphylaxis occur, the infusion should be stopped. An aqueous solution of epinephrine 1:1 000 should be available at the bedside as well as a source of oxygen.

Precautions: General: Hypertension is a common side effect of tacrolimus therapy (see Adverse Effects). Mild or moderate hypertension is more frequently reported than severe hypertension. The incidence of hypertension decreases over time. Antihypertensive therapy may be required; the control of blood pressure can be accomplished with any of the common antihypertensive agents. Since tacrolimus may cause hyperkalemia, potassium-sparing diuretics should be avoided. While calcium channel blocking agents can be effective in treating tacrolimus-associated hypertension, care should be taken since interference with tacrolimus metabolism may require a dosage reduction (see Drug Interactions).

Insulin-dependent post-transplant diabetes mellitus (PTDM) was reported in 20% and 6% of tacrolimus-treated kidney transplant patients in the U.S. and European studies respectively. Since the development of PTDM is related to increased whole blood trough concentrations of tacrolimus and higher doses of corticosteroids, trough concentrations of tacrolimus and/or steroid doses may be decreased if the risk/benefit assessment permits. In the U.S. multicentre trial, Black and Hispanic kidney transplant patients were at an increased risk of development of PTDM, regardless of randomized treatment. Insulin-dependence was reversible in some patients without discontinuation of tacrolimus or steroids, and therefore, the need for insulin therapy should be reassessed periodically.

Hyperglycemia was associated with the use of tacrolimus in 47% and 33% of liver transplant recipients in the U.S. and European randomized studies, respectively, and may require treatment (see Adverse Effects). Insulin-dependent diabetes was associated with the use of tacrolimus. This may reverse with dose decrease; however, it may be irreversible after prolonged tacrolimus administration.

Myocardial Hypertrophy: Myocardial hypertrophy has been reported in association with the administration of tacrolimus, and is generally manifested by echocardiographically demonstrated concentric increases in left ventricular posterior wall and interventricular septum thickness. Hypertrophy has been observed in infants, children and adults. This condition appears reversible in most cases following dose reduction or discontinuance of therapy. In a group of 20 patients with pre- and post-treatment echocardiograms who showed evidence of myocardial hypertrophy, mean tacrolimus whole blood concentrations during the period prior to diagnosis of myocardial hypertrophy ranged from 11 to 53 ng/mL in infants (N=10) age 0.4 to 2 years, 4 to 46 ng/mL in children (n=7) age 2 to 15 years and 11 to 24 ng/mL in adults (N=3) age 37 to 53 years.

Pregnancy: Tacrolimus at oral doses of 0.32 and 1 mg/kg during organogenesis in rabbits, was associated with maternal toxicity as well as an increase in incidence of abortions; these doses are equivalent to 0.33X and 1.0X (based on body surface area corrections) the recommended clinical dose (0.3 mg/kg). At the higher dose only, an increased incidence of malformations and developmental variations was also seen. Tacrolimus, at oral doses of 3.2 mg/kg during organogenesis in rats, was associated with maternal toxicity and caused an increase in late resorptions, decreased numbers of live births, and decreased pup weight and viability.

Tacrolimus, given orally at 1 and 3.2 mg/kg (equivalent to 0.5X and 1.5X), the recommended clinical dose based on body surface area corrections to pregnant rats after organogenesis and during lactation, was associated with reduced pup weights.

Tacrolimus, given orally at 1 mg/kg (0.5 × the recommended clinical dose based on body surface area corrections) to male and female rats, prior to and during mating, as well as to dams during gestation and lactation, was associated with adverse effects on female reproduction and embryo lethality. Effects on female reproductive function (parturition) and embryo lethal effects were indicated by a higher rate of pre-implantation loss and increased numbers of undelivered and nonviable pups. When given at 3.2 mg/kg (1.5 × the recommended clinical dose based on body surface area correction), tacrolimus was associated with maternal and paternal toxicity as well as reproductive toxicity including marked adverse effects on estrus cycles, parturition, pup viability and pup malformations. Toxicities to parental rats were indicated by tremors and circling, as well as reduced weight gains and food consumption in males; and reduced food consumption during gestation and lactation in females. Adverse effects on reproductive parameters included: 1) increased copulatory intervals, 2) increased pre- and postimplantation loss of fetuses (resulting in smaller litter sizes), and 3) decreased numbers of dams delivering. No reduction in male or female fertility was evident. Adverse effects seen in pups were markedly reduced viability and a slight increase in the incidence of malformation (3 pups from 3 dams).

There are no adequate and well-controlled studies in pregnant women. Tacrolimus is transferred across the placenta. The use of tacrolimus during pregnancy has been associated with neonatal hyperkalemia and renal dysfunction. Tacrolimus should be used during pregnancy only if the potential benefit to the mother justifies potential risk to the fetus.

In experience reported by the University of Pittsburgh, 11 female transplant patients maintained on tacrolimus therapy throughout pregnancy delivered 12 babies, with 1 patient conceiving twice. These patients received tacrolimus from week 1 to 20 months prior to conception. Ten of the pregnancies were successful, 4 with C-sections. The neonates showed no growth retardation or congenital anomalies. Hyperkalemia was observed in the majority of babies, but resolved within 24 to 48 hours without adverse effects. Two babies (both premature 22 and 24 weeks) died shortly after birth. One pregnancy was complicated by diabetes, hypertension and proteinuria, the other by CMV infection requiring ganciclovir therapy. Additional information includes a report of 1 newborn who had temporary anuria associated with high cord blood tacrolimus concentration; however, renal function was normal within 1 week. Another reference reports on the successful pregnancy (normal healthy male) in a 28-year-old female with bolus steroids and increased doses of tacrolimus for liver graft rejection. In this case, the cord blood plasma concentration was approximately one half that noted in maternal plasma.

Lactation: Since tacrolimus is excreted in human milk, nursing should be avoided.

Children: Experience with tacrolimus in pediatric kidney transplant patients is limited. Successful liver transplants have been performed in pediatric patients (ages 4 months up to 16 years) using tacrolimus. The majority of these patients were under 5 years of age. The 2 randomized active-controlled trials of tacrolimus in primary liver transplantation included 56 pediatric patients. Thirty-one patients were randomized to tacrolimus and 25 to cyclosporine-based therapies. Additionally, a minimum of 120 pediatric patients (median age 22.5 months) who underwent 122 liver transplants were studied in an uncontrolled published trial of tacrolimus in living related donor liver transplantation. Pediatric patients generally required higher doses of tacrolimus to maintain blood trough concentrations of tacrolimus similar to adult patients (see Dosage). This is thought to be a result of age related differences in the oxidative capacity of the cytochrome P450 enzyme system (CYP3A) used to metabolize tacrolimus.

Heart failure, cardiomegaly and increased thickness of the myocardium have been reported in patients taking tacrolimus. Patients at risk for these effects are primarily children younger than 5 years undergoing liver "rescue", small bowel or multivisceral transplantation with trough whole blood tacrolimus levels exceeding 25 ng/mL. Also, these patients at risk often have experienced fluid overload, renal and/or hepatic dysfunction, hypertension and are receiving large doses of corticosteroids and other concomitant medications. Cardiovascular function for such patients should be carefully monitored. In addition, tacrolimus trough whole blood levels should be maintained below 25 ng/mL. If cardiac abnormalities develop, dose reduction or discontinuation of tacrolimus should be considered in cases where the perceived risk to the patient outweighs the benefit.

Patients with Renal or Hepatic Impairment: For patients with renal insufficiency some evidence suggests that the use of lower doses may be warranted (see Dosage).

Prograf (cont'd)

The use of tacrolimus in liver transplant recipients experiencing post-transplant hepatic impairment may be associated with increased risk of developing renal insufficiency related to high whole blood levels of tacrolimus. These patients should be monitored closely and dose adjustments should be considered. Some evidence suggests that the use of lower doses may be warranted in these patients (see Dosage).

Drug Interactions: Drug interaction studies with tacrolimus have not been conducted. Due to the potential for additive or synergistic impairment of renal function, care should be taken when administering tacrolimus with drugs that may be associated with renal dysfunction. These include, and are not limited to, aminoglycosides, amphotericin B, and cisplatin. Initial clinical experience with tacrolimus and cyclosporine resulted in additive/synergistic nephrotoxicity when both agents were co-administered. Patients switched from cyclosporine to tacrolimus should receive the first tacrolimus dose no sooner than 24 hours after the last cyclosporine dose. Dosing may be further delayed in the presence of elevated cyclosporine levels.

Since tacrolimus is metabolized mainly by the cytochrome P450 IIIA enzyme systems, substances known to inhibit these enzymes may decrease the metabolism of tacrolimus with resultant increases in whole blood or plasma levels. Drugs known to induce these enzyme systems may result in an increased metabolism of tacrolimus and decreased whole blood or plasma levels. Monitoring of blood levels and appropriate dosage adjustments are essential when such drugs are used concomitantly.

Drugs That May Increase Tacrolimus Blood Levels: calcium channel blockers: diltiazem, nicardipine, verapamil, nifedipine; antifungal agents: clotrimazole, fluconazole, itraconazole, ketoconazole; macrolide antibiotics: erythromycin, clarithromycin, troleandomycin; gastrointestinal prokinetic agents: metoclopramide, cisapride; other drugs: cyclosporine, methylprednisolone, cimetidine, danazole, bromocriptine.

Drugs That May Decrease Tacrolimus Blood Levels: anticonvulsants: carbamazepine, phenobarbital, phenytoin; antibiotics: rifampin, rifabutin.

Other Drug Interactions: Immunosuppressants may affect vaccination. Therefore, during treatment with tacrolimus, vaccination may be less effective. The use of live vaccines should be avoided; live vaccines may include, but are not limited to: measles, mumps, rubella, oral polio, BCG, yellow fever and TY 21a typhoid.

Grapefruit juice affects P450 IIIA-mediated metabolism and should be avoided.

There is no data available regarding the effect of antacids on tacrolimus absorption.

Laboratory Tests: Serum creatinine and potassium should be assessed regularly. Routine monitoring of metabolic and hematologic systems should be performed as clinically warranted.

Carcinogenesis, Mutagenesis and Impairment of Fertility: An increased incidence of malignancy is a recognized complication of immunosuppression in recipients of organ transplants. The most common forms of neoplasms are non-Hodgkin's lymphomas and carcinomas of the skin. As with other immunosuppressive therapies, the risk of malignancies in tacrolimus recipients may be higher than in the normal, healthy population. Lymphoproliferative disorders associated with Epstein-Barr virus infection have been seen. It has been reported that reduction or discontinuation of immunosuppression may cause the lesions to regress.

No evidence of genotoxicity was seen in bacterial (Salmonella and E. coli) or mammalian (Chinese hamster lung-derived cells) in vitro assays of mutagenicity. For the in vitro CHO/HGRPT assay of mutagenicity, or in vivo clastogenicity assays performed in mice, tacrolimus did not cause unscheduled DNA synthesis in rodent hepatocytes.

An 80-week study in mice administered tacrolimus at oral doses of 0.3, 1 and 3 mg/kg/day showed no evidence of tumorigenicity. The 104 week studies in rats administered tacrolimus at oral doses of 0.2, 0.5, 1.25, 2.5 and 5 mg/kg/day demonstrated no evidence of tumorigenicity.

No impairment of fertility was demonstrated in studies of male and female rats. In reproduction studies in rats and rabbits, adverse effects on the fetus were observed mainly at dose levels that were toxic to dams. However, in female rats dosed during organogenesis, embryo toxicity (expressed as reduced pup weights) was seen at a dose which was one-third of the maternally toxic dose. At this same dose, when administered prior to mating and during gestation, tacrolimus was associated with adverse effects on female reproductive parameters and embryolethality. This dose was equivalent to 0.5X the clinical dose (see Pregnancy).

Adverse Effects: Kidney Transplantation: The most common adverse reactions reported were infection, tremor, hypertension, decreased renal function, constipation, diarrhea, headache, abdominal pain and insomnia. Many of these adverse reactions were mild and responded to a reduction in dosage.

Insulin-dependent post-transplant diabetes mellitus (PTDM) was related to increased whole blood trough concentrations of tacrolimus and higher doses of corticosteroids. The median time to onset of PTDM was 68 days.

The incidence of adverse events was determined in 2 randomized Phase 3 comparative kidney transplant studies involving 508 patients receiving tacrolimus and 352 patients receiving cyclosporine. Adverse events that occurred in >15% of tacrolimus-treated patients (combined study results) are presented in Table X for the two controlled trials in kidney transplantation.

Table X—Prograf

Kidney Transplantation: Adverse Events Occurring in >15% of Prograf-treated Patients

	U.S. Study (%)		European Study (%)	
	Prograf (N=205)	CBIR* (N=207)	Prograf (N=303)	CBIR* (N=145)
Nervous System				
Tremor (See Warnings)	54	34	35	12
Headache (See Warnings)	44	38	21	14
Insomnia	32	30	24	26
Gastrointestinal				
Diarrhea	44	41	22	10
Nausea	38	36	17	16
Constipation	35	43	31	35
Vomiting	29	23	13	8
Dyspepsia	28	20	16	13
Cardiovascular				
Hypertension (See Precautions)	50	52	37	39
Urogenital				
Creatinine increased (See Warnings)	45	42	35	21
Metabolic and Nutritional				
Hypophosphatemia	49	53	3	5
Hypomagnesemia	34	17	4	1
Hyperkalemia (See Warnings)	31	32	21	16
Diabetes mellitus (See Precautions)	24	9	12	2
Hyperglycemia (See Precautions)	22	16	16	7
Hemic and Lymphatic				
Anemia	30	24	18	17
Leukopenia	15	17	17	15
Miscellaneous				
Infection	45	49	76	75
Peripheral edema	36	48	16	16
Asthenia	34	30	7	4
Abdominal pain	33	31	27	23
Pain	32	30	21	23
Fever	29	29	8	9
Respiratory System				
Dyspnea	22	18	12	11
Musculoskeletal				
Arthralgia	25	24	9	10

*Cyclosporine-based immunosuppressive regimen.

Less frequently observed adverse reactions in both kidney transplantation patients and liver transplantation patients are described under the Liver Transplantation subsection.

Liver Transplantation: The principal adverse reactions of tacrolimus are tremor, headache, diarrhea, hypertension, nausea and renal dysfunction. These occur with oral and i.v. administration of tacrolimus and may respond to a reduction in dosing. Diarrhea was sometimes associated with other gastrointestinal complaints such as nausea and vomiting.

Hyperkalemia and hypomagnesemia have occurred in patients receiving tacrolimus therapy. Hyperglycemia has been noted in many patients; some may require insulin therapy.

The incidence of adverse events reported in 2 randomized comparative liver transplant trials was determined in 514 patients receiving tacrolimus and steroids and 515 patients receiving a cyclosporine-based regimen (CBIR). The proportion of patients reporting more than 1 adverse event was 99.8% in the tacrolimus group and 99.6% in the CBIR group. Precautions must be taken when comparing the incidence of adverse events in the U.S. study to that in the European study. The 12 month post-transplant information from the U.S. study and from the European study is presented in Table XI (on following page). The 2 studies included different patient populations and patients were treated with immunosuppressive regimens of differing intensities. Adverse events reported in >15% in tacrolimus patients (combined study results) are presented in Table XI (on following page) for the 2 controlled trials in liver transplantation.

The following adverse events, not mentioned in Table XI (on following page), were reported with greater than 3% incidence in tacrolimus-treated patients. Nervous System (see Precautions): abnormal dreams, agitation, amnesia, anxiety, confusion, convulsion, depression, dizziness, emotional lability, encephalopathy, hallucinations, hypertonia, incoordination, myoclonus, nervousness, neuropathy, paresthesia, psychosis, somnolence, thinking abnormal.

Special Senses: abnormal vision, amblyopia, otitis media, tinnitus.

Digestive System: anorexia, cholangitis, cholestatic jaundice, dyspepsia, dysphagia, esophagitis, flatulence, gastritis, gastrointestinal hemorrhage, GGT increase, gastrointestinal perforation, hepatitis, ileus, increased appetite, jaundice, liver function test abnormal, liver damage, oral moniliasis, stomatitis, rectal disorder.

Cardiovascular: angina pectoris, chest pain, abnormal ECG, hemorrhage, hypotension, postural hypotension, tachycardia, thrombosis, vasodilatation.

Urogenital System (see Precautions): albuminuria, dysuria, hematuria, hydronephrosis, kidney failure, kidney tubular necrosis, toxic nephropathy, oliguria, urinary tract infection, urinary frequency.

Metabolic/Nutritional: acidosis, alkaline phosphatase increased, alkalosis, AST increased, ALT increased, bilirubinemia, dehydration, edema, healing abnormal, hypercalcemia, hypercholesterolemia, hyperlipemia, hyperphosphatemia, hyperuricemia, hypocalcemia, hypervolemia, hypoglycemia, hypokalemia, hypophosphatemia, hyponatremia, hypoproteinemia, lactic dehydrogenase increase, weight gain.

Endocrine System (see Precautions): diabetes mellitus.

Hemic/Lymphatic: coagulation disorder, ecchymosis, hypochromic anemia, leukopenia, prothrombin decreased.

Table XI—Prograf

Adverse Events

	U.S. Study (%)		European Study (%)	
	Prograf (N=250)	CBIR* (N=250)	Prograf (N=264)	CBIR* (N=265)
Nervous System				
Headache	64	60	37	26
Tremor	56	46	48	32
Insomnia	64	68	32	23
Paresthesia	40	30	17	17
Digestive System				
Diarrhea	72	47	37	27
Nausea	46	37	32	27
Constipation	24	27	23	21
LFT Abnormal	36	30	6	5
Anorexia	34	24	7	5
Vomiting	27	15	14	11
Cardiovascular				
Hypertension	47	56	38	43
Urogenital				
Kidney Function Abnormal	40	27	36	23
Creatinine Increased	39	25	24	19
Hyperkalemia	45	26	13	9
Hypokalemia	29	34	13	16
BUN Increased	30	22	12	9
Urinary Tract Infection	16	18	21	19
Oliguria	18	15	19	12
Metabolic and Nutritional				
Hyperglycemia	47	38	33	22
Hypomagnesemia	48	45	16	9
Peripheral Edema	26	26	12	14
Hemic and Lymphatic				
Anemia	47	38	5	1
Leukocytosis	32	26	8	8
Thrombocytopenia	24	20	14	19
Body as a Whole				
Abdominal Pain	59	54	29	22
Pain	63	57	24	22
Fever	48	56	19	22
Asthenia	52	48	11	7
Back Pain	30	29	17	17
Ascites	27	22	7	8
Respiratory				
Pleural Effusion	30	32	36	35
Atelectasis	28	30	5	4
Dyspnea	29	23	5	4
Skin and Appendages				
Pruritus	36	20	15	7
Rash	24	19	10	4

*Cyclosporine-based immunosuppressive regimen.

Body as a Whole: abdomen enlarged, abscess, back pain, chills, flu syndrome, generalized edema, hernia, peritonitis, photosensitivity reaction, sepsis.

Musculoskeletal: arthralgia, cramps, generalized spasm, leg cramps, myalgia, myasthenia, osteoporosis.

Respiratory: asthma, bronchitis, cough increased, lung disorder, pharyngitis, pneumothorax, pneumonia, pulmonary edema, respiratory disorder, rhinitis, sinusitis, voice alteration.

Skin and Appendages: acne, alopecia, fungal dermatitis, herpes simplex, hirsutism, pruritus, rash, skin disorder, sweating.

The following nervous system adverse events were also reported: acute brain syndrome (0.2%), coma (2.1%), delirium (1.2%), dysarthria (0.4%), dystonia (0.4%), encephalopathy (2.5%), flaccid paralysis (0.4%), hemiplegia (0.8%), nystagmus (0.8%), paralysis (0.4%) and stupor (0.2%).

There have been rare spontaneous reports of myocardial hypertrophy associated with clinically manifested ventricular dysfunction in patients receiving tacrolimus therapy (see Precautions, Myocardial Hypertrophy).

There has been a report of pure red cell aplasia in a renal transplant recipient who was receiving tacrolimus. This condition was reversed upon termination of the administration of tacrolimus.

Overdose: Symptoms and Treatment: Limited overdosage experience is available. Acute overdosages of up to 30 times the intended dose have been reported. All patients recovered with no sequelae. Acute overdosage has been followed by adverse reactions consistent with those listed in the Adverse Effects section, including mild elevations of renal function markers (creatinine), nausea, headache, hyperreflexia, oliguria, hypotension, tremor and elevations in liver enzymes. In one case transient urticaria and lethargy were observed and in another case acute anuric renal insufficiency developed. Based on the poor aqueous solubility and extensive erythrocyte and plasma protein binding, it is anticipated that tacrolimus is not dialyzable to any significant extent; there is no experience with charcoal hemoperfusion. The oral use of activated charcoal has been reported in treating acute overdoses, but experience has not been sufficient to warrant recommending its use. General supportive measures and treatment of specific symptoms should be followed in all cases of overdosage.

In acute oral and i.v. toxicity studies, mortalities were seen at or above the following doses: in adult rats, 52 × the recommended human oral dose: in immature rats, 16 × the recommended oral dose and in adult rats, 16 × the recommended human i.v. dose (all based on body surface area corrections).

Dosage: Injection: **For i.v. infusion only.**

Note: Anaphylactic reactions have occurred with injectables containing castor oil derivatives (see Warnings).

In patients unable to take oral capsules, therapy may be initiated with the injection. The initial dose of tacrolimus should be administered no sooner than 6 hours after transplantation. The recommended starting dose of injection is 0.05 to 0.10 mg/kg/day as a continuous i.v. infusion. Adult patients should receive doses at the lower end of the dosing range. Concomitant adrenal corticosteroid therapy is recommended early post transplantation. Continuous i.v. infusion of tacrolimus injection should be continued until the patient can tolerate oral administration of tacrolimus capsules.

Preparation for Administration and Stability: The injection must be diluted with 0.9% Sodium Chloride Injection or 5% Dextrose Injection to a concentration between 0.004 mg/mL and 0.02 mg/mL prior to use. Diluted infusion solution should be stored in glass or polyethylene containers and should be discarded after 24 hours. The diluted infusion solution should not be stored in a PVC container due to poor stability and the potential for extraction of phthalates. Parenteral drug products should be inspected visually for particulate matter and discoloration prior to administration, whenever solution and container permit.

Capsules: Kidney Transplantation: The recommended starting oral dose is 0.2 to 0.3 mg/kg/day administered every 12 hours in 2 divided doses. The initial dose may be administered within 24 hours of transplantation. Black patients may require higher doses to achieve comparable blood levels. Dosage and typical tacrolimus whole blood trough concentrations are shown in Table XII; blood concentration details are described in Blood Level Monitoring: Kidney Transplantation below.

Table XII—Prograf

Dosage and Whole Blood Trough Concentrations

Initial Oral Dose	0.2-0.3 mg/kg/day
Dosing Regimen	2 divided doses, q12h
Tacrolimus whole blood trough concentration	
Month 1-3	7-20 ng/mL
Month 4-12	5-15 ng/mL

Liver Transplantation: It is recommended that patients be converted from i.v. to oral tacrolimus capsules as soon as oral therapy can be tolerated. This usually occurs within 2 to 3 days. The first dose of oral therapy should be given 8 to 12 hours after discontinuing the i.v. infusion. The recommended starting oral dose is 0.15 to 0.30 mg/kg/day administered in 2 divided daily doses every 12 hours. The initial dose should be administered no sooner than 6 hours after transplantation. Adult patients should receive doses at the lower end of the dosing range.

Some centres use lower tacrolimus doses during maintenance therapy post transplantation. Dosing should be titrated based on clinical assessment of rejection and tolerability. Adjunct therapy with adrenal corticosteroids is recommended early post transplant.

Children: Pediatric liver transplantation patients without preexisting renal or hepatic dysfunction have required and tolerated higher doses than adults to achieve similar blood concentrations. Therefore, it is recommended that therapy be initiated in pediatric patients at the high end of the recommended i.v. and oral dosing ranges (0.1 mg/kg/day i.v. and 0.3 mg/kg/day oral). Dose adjustments may be required. Although experience in pediatric transplantation patients is limited, the dosing guidelines listed above should be followed.

Patients with Hepatic or Renal Dysfunction: Due to the potential for nephrotoxicity, patients with renal or hepatic impairment should receive doses at the lowest value of the recommended i.v. and oral dosing ranges. Further reductions in dose below these ranges may be required. Patients with postoperative oliguria may have the initiation of tacrolimus therapy delayed up to 48 hours or longer as circumstances warrant.

Conversion to Tacrolimus from Cyclosporine: Patients converted from cyclosporine to tacrolimus should receive the first tacrolimus dose no sooner than 24 hours after the last cyclosporine dose. Dosing may be further delayed in the presence of elevated cyclosporine levels. Patients converted from tacrolimus to cyclosporine should receive the first cyclosporine dose no sooner than 24 hours after the last tacrolimus dose. Dosing may be further delayed in the presence of elevated tacrolimus levels.

Blood Level Monitoring: Monitoring of tacrolimus blood levels in conjunction with other laboratory and clinical parameters is considered an essential aid to patient management. During the immediate postoperative period trough blood concentrations should be measured every 1 to 3 days. More intensive monitoring may be required in patients with hepatic or renal dysfunction. Following discharge from the hospital, the frequency of patient monitoring will decrease with time post-transplant.

Although there is a lack of direct correlation between tacrolimus levels and drug efficacy, data from Phase II and III studies of kidney and liver transplant patients has shown an increasing incidence of adverse events with increasing trough blood concentrations. Most stable patients are maintained with 12 hours trough whole blood levels of 5 to 20 ng/mL. Long-term post-transplant patients often are maintained at the low end of this target range.

Two methods are available for the assay of tacrolimus: microparticle enzyme immuno assay (MEIA) and enzyme linked immuno sorbent assay (ELISA). Both methods use the same monoclonal antibody for the tacrolimus parent compound. Whole blood is the matrix of choice and specimens should be collected into tubes containing ethylene diamine tetraacetic acid (EDTA) anticoagulant. Heparin anticoagulation is not recommended because of the tendency to form clots on storage. Samples which are not analyzed immediately should be stored in a refrigerator and assayed within 3 days; if samples are to be kept longer they should be deep frozen −20°C for up to 12 months.

Kidney Transplantation: Data from the U.S. and European studies indicate that trough concentrations of tacrolimus in whole blood, as measured by IMx, were most variable during the first week of dosing. During the first 3 months, 80% of the patients maintained trough concentrations between 7 to 20 ng/mL, and then between 5 to 15 ng/mL, through 1 year.

The relative risk of toxicity is increased with higher trough concentrations. Therefore, monitoring of whole blood trough concentrations is recommended to assist in the clinical evaluation of toxicity.

Liver Transplantation: Data from the U.S. clinical trial show that tacrolimus whole blood concentrations, as measured by ELISA, were most variable during the first week post-transplantation. After this early period, the median trough blood concentrations, measured at intervals from the second week to 1 year post-transplantation, ranged from 9.8 to 19.4 ng/mL.

Information for the Patient: See Blue Section—Information for the Patient "Prograf".

Supplied: Capsules: 1 mg: Each oblong, white capsule, branded with red "1 mg" on cap and Fujisawa logo "[f] 617" on capsule body contains: anhydrous tacrolimus 1 mg. Nonmedicinal ingredients: croscarmellose sodium, hydroxypropylmethylcellulose 2910, lactose and magnesium stearate; capsule shell: gelatin and titanium dioxide. Bottles of 100 and blister cards of 10×10.

5 mg: Each oblong, greyish/red capsule, branded with white "5 mg" on cap and Fujisawa logo "[f] 657" on capsule body, contains: anhydrous tacrolimus 5 mg. Nonmedicinal ingredients: croscarmellose sodium, hydroxypropylmethylcellulose 2910, lactose and magnesium stearate; capsule shell: gelatin, ferric oxide and titanium dioxide. Bottles of 100 and blister cards of 10×10.

Store and dispense at controlled room temperature, 15 to 30°C.

Injection: Each mL of sterile solution contains: the equivalent of anhydrous tacrolimus 5 mg. Nonmedicinal ingredients: dehydrated alcohol, USP, 83% v/v and polyoxyl 60 hydrogenated castor oil (HCO-60). Ampuls of 1 mL, boxes of 10. Store in carton and protect from light and dispense ampuls between 15 and 25°C.

(Shown in Product Recognition Section)

Reviewed 1999

PROLASTIN®

Bayer

Alpha$_1$-Proteinase Inhibitor (Human)

Alpha$_1$-Antitrypsin Replenisher

Pharmacology: Alpha$_1$-antitrypsin deficiency is a chronic, hereditary, usually fatal, autosomal recessive disorder in which a low concentration of alpha$_1$-PI (alpha$_1$-antitrypsin) is associated with slowly progressive, severe panacinar emphysema that most often manifests itself in the third to fourth decades of life. (Although the terms alpha$_1$-proteinase inhibitor and alpha$_1$-antitrypsin are used interchangeably in the scientific literature, the hereditary disorder associated with a reduction in the serum level of alpha$_1$-PI is conventionally referred to as alpha$_1$-antitrypsin deficiency while the deficient protein is referred to as alpha$_1$-proteinase inhibitor). The emphysema is typically worse in the lower lung zones. The pathogenesis of development of emphysema in alpha$_1$-antitrypsin deficiency is not well understood at this time. It is believed, however, to be due to a chronic biochemical imbalance between elastase (an enzyme capable of degrading elastin tissues, released by inflammatory cells, primarily neutrophils, in the lower respiratory tract) and alpha$_1$-PI (the principal inhibitor of neutrophil elastase), which is deficient in alpha$_1$-antitrypsin disease. As a result, it is believed that alveolar structures are unprotected from chronic exposure to elastase released from a chronic, low-level burden of neutrophils in the lower respiratory tract, resulting in progressive degradation of elastin tissues. The eventual outcome is the development of emphysema. Neonatal hepatitis with cholestatic jaundice appears in approximately 10% of newborns with alpha$_1$-antitrypsin deficiency. In some adults, alpha$_1$-antitrypsin deficiency is complicated by cirrhosis.

A large number of phenotypic variants of alpha$_1$-antitrypsin deficiency exists. The most severely affected individuals are those with the PiZZ variant, typically characterized by alpha$_1$-PI serum levels <35% normal. Epidemiologic studies of individuals with various phenotypes of alpha$_1$-antitrypsin deficiency have demonstrated that individuals with endogenous serum levels of alpha$_1$-PI ≤50 mg/dL (based on commercial standards) have a risk of >80% of developing emphysema over a lifetime. However, individuals with endogenous alpha$_1$-PI levels >80 mg/dL, in general, do not manifest an increased risk for development of emphysema above the general population background risk. From these observations, it is believed that the threshold level of alpha$_1$-PI in the serum required to provide adequate anti-elastase activity in the lung of individuals with alpha$_1$-antitrypsin deficiency is about 80 mg/dL (based on commercial standards for immunologic assay of alpha$_1$-PI).

In clinical studies of alpha$_1$-proteinase inhibitor (human), 23 subjects with the PiZZ variant of congenital deficiency of alpha$_1$-antitrypsin deficiency and documented destructive lung disease participated in a study of acute and/or chronic replacement therapy with alpha$_1$-proteinase inhibitor (human). The mean in vivo recovery of alpha$_1$-PI was 4.2 mg (immunologic)/dL/mg (functional)/kg body weight administered. The half-life of alpha$_1$-PI in vivo was approximately 4.5 days. Based on these observations, a program of chronic replacement therapy was developed. Nineteen of the subjects in these studies received alpha$_1$-proteinase inhibitor (human) replacement therapy, 60 mg/kg body weight, once weekly for up to 26 weeks (average 24 weeks of therapy). With this schedule of replacement therapy, blood levels of alpha$_1$-PI were maintained above 80 mg/dL (based on the commercial standards for alpha$_1$-PI immunologic assay). Within a few weeks of commencing this program, bronchoalveolar lavage studies demonstrated significantly increased levels of alpha$_1$-PI and functional antineutrophil elastase capacity in the epithelial lining fluid of the lower respiratory tract of the lung, as compared to levels prior to commencing the program of chronic replacement therapy with alpha$_1$-proteinase inhibitor (human).

All 23 individuals who participated in the investigations were immunized with hepatitis B vaccine and received a single dose of hepatitis B immune globulin (human) on entry into the investigation. Although no other steps were taken to prevent hepatitis, neither hepatitis B nor non-A, non-B hepatitis occurred in any of the subjects. All subjects remained seronegative for HIV antibody. None of the subjects developed any detectable antibody to alpha$_1$-PI or other serum protein.

Long-term controlled clinical trials to evaluate the effect of chronic replacement therapy with alpha$_1$-proteinase inhibitor (human) on the development of or progression of emphysema in patients with congenital alpha$_1$-antitrypsin deficiency have not been performed. Estimates of the sample size required of this rare disorder and the slow, progressive nature of the clinical course have been considered impediments in the ability to conduct such a trial. Studies to monitor the long-term effects will continue as part of the post-approval process.

Indications: For chronic replacement therapy of individuals having congenital deficiency of alpha$_1$-PI (alpha$_1$-antitrypsin deficiency) with clinically demonstrable panacinar emphysema. Clinical and biochemical studies have demonstrated that with such therapy, it is possible to increase plasma levels of alpha$_1$-PI, and that levels of functionally active alpha$_1$-PI in the lung epithelial lining fluid are increased proportionately. As some individuals with alpha$_1$-antitrypsin deficiency will not go on to develop panacinar emphysema, only those with evidence of such disease should be considered for chronic replacement therapy with alpha$_1$-proteinase inhibitor (human). Subjects with the PiMZ or PiMS phenotypes of alpha$_1$-antitrypsin deficiency should not be considered for such treatment as they appear to be at small risk for panacinar emphysema. Clinical data are not available as to the long-term effects derived from chronic replacement therapy of individuals with alpha$_1$-antitrypsin deficiency with alpha$_1$-proteinase inhibitor (human). Only adult subjects have received alpha$_1$-proteinase inhibitor (human) to date.

Alpha$_1$-proteinase inhibitor (human) is not indicated for use in patients other than those with PiZZ, PiZ(null) or Pi(null)(null) phenotypes.

Contraindications: Individuals with selective IgA deficiencies who have known antibody against IgA (anti-IgA antibody) should not receive alpha$_1$-proteinase inhibitor (human), since these patients may experience severe reactions, including anaphylaxis, to IgA which may be present.

Warnings: This product is prepared from pooled human plasma which may contain the causative agents of hepatitis and other viral diseases. Prescribed manufacturing procedures utilized at the plasma collection centres, plasma testing laboratories, and the fractionation facilities are designed to reduce the risk of transmitting viral infection. However, the risk of viral infectivity from this product cannot be totally eliminated.

Individuals who receive infusions of blood or plasma products may develop signs and/or symptoms of some viral infections, particularly non-A, non-B hepatitis. Alpha$_1$-proteinase inhibitor (human), has been heat-treated in solution at 60°C for 10 hours in order to reduce the potential for transmission of infectious agents. No cases of hepatitis, either hepatitis B or non-A, non-B hepatitis have been recorded to date in individuals receiving alpha$_1$-proteinase inhibitor (human). However, as all individuals received prophylaxis against hepatitis B, no conclusions can be drawn at this time regarding potential transmission of hepatitis B virus.

Precautions: General: 1. Administer within 3 hours after reconstitution. Do not refrigerate after reconstitution.

2. Administer only by the i.v. route.

3. As with any colloid solution, there will be an increase in plasma volume following i.v. administration of alpha$_1$-proteinase inhibitor (human). Caution should therefore be used in patients at risk for circulatory overload.

4. It is recommended that in preparation for receiving alpha$_1$-proteinase inhibitor (human), recipients be immunized against hepatitis B using a licensed Hepatitis B Vaccine, according to the manufacturer's recommendations. Should it become necessary to treat an individual with alpha$_1$-proteinase inhibitor (human), and time is insufficient for adequate antibody response to vaccination, individuals should receive a single dose of hepatitis B immune globulin (human), 0.06 mL/kg body weight, i.m., at the time of administration of the initial dose of Hepatitis B Vaccine.

5. Alpha$_1$-proteinase inhibitor (human) should be given alone, without mixing with other agents or diluting solutions.

6. Product administration and handling of the needles must be done with caution. Percutaneous puncture with a needle contaminated with blood can transmit infectious virus including HIV (AIDS) and hepatitis. Obtain immediate medical attention if injury occurs.

Place needles in sharps container after single use. Discard all equipment including any reconstituted Prolastin product in accordance with biohazard procedures.

Carcinogenesis, Mutagenesis, Impairment of Fertility: Long-term studies in animals to evaluate carcinogenesis, mutagenesis or impairment of fertility have not been conducted.

Pregnancy: Animal reproduction studies have not been conducted with alpha$_1$-proteinase inhibitor (human). It is also not known whether Prolastin can cause fetal harm when administered to a pregnant woman or can affect reproduction capacity. Prolastin should be given to a pregnant woman only if clearly needed.

Lactation: It is not known whether alpha$_1$-proteinase inhibitor (human) is excreted in human milk. Because many drugs are excreted in human milk, caution should be exercised when alpha$_1$-proteinase inhibitor (human) is administered to a nursing woman.

Children: Safety and effectiveness in children have not been established.

Adverse Effects: Therapeutic administration of alpha$_1$-proteinase inhibitor (human), 60 mg/kg weekly, has been demonstrated to be well tolerated. In clinical studies, 6 reactions were observed with 517 infusions of alpha$_1$-proteinase inhibitor (human), or 1.16%. None of the reactions was severe. The adverse reactions reported included delayed fever (maximum temperature rise was 38.9°C, resolving spontaneously over 24 hours) occurring up to 12 hours following treatment (0.77%), lightheadedness (0.19%), and dizziness (0.19%). Mild transient leukocytosis and dilutional anemia several hours after infusion have also been noted.

Since market entry, occasional reports of other flu-like symptoms, allergic-like reactions, dyspnea, rash, tachycardia, and, rarely, hypotension have also been received.

Dosage: Each bottle of alpha$_1$-proteinase inhibitor (human) has the functional activity, as determined by inhibition of porcine pancreatic elastase, stated on the label of the bottle.

The threshold level of alpha$_1$-PI in the serum believed to provide adequate anti-elastase activity in the lung of individuals with alpha$_1$-antitrypsin deficiency is 80 mg/dL (based on commercial standards for alpha$_1$-PI immunologic assay). However, assays of alpha$_1$-PI based on commercial standards measure antigenic activity of alpha$_1$-PI, whereas the labeled potency value of alpha$_1$-PI is expressed as actual functional activity, i.e., actual capacity to neutralize porcine pancreatic elastase. As functional activity may be less than antigenic activity, serum levels of alpha$_1$-PI determined using commercial immunologic assays may not accurately reflect actual functional alpha$_1$-PI levels. Therefore, although it may be helpful to monitor serum levels of alpha$_1$-PI in individuals receiving alpha$_1$-proteinase inhibitor (human), using currently available commercial assays of antigenic activity, results of these assays should not be used to determine the required therapeutic dosage.

The recommended dosage of alpha$_1$-proteinase inhibitor (human) is 60 mg/kg body weight administered i.v. once weekly. This dose is intended to increase and maintain a level of functional alpha$_1$-PI in the epithelial lining of the lower respiratory tract, providing adequate anti-elastase activity in the lung of individuals with alpha$_1$-antitrypsin deficiency.

Alpha$_1$-proteinase inhibitor (human) may be given at a rate of 0.08 mL/kg/min or greater and must be administered i.v. The recommended dosage of 60 mg/kg takes approximately 30 minutes to infuse.

Parenteral drug products should be inspected visually for particulate matter and discoloration prior to administration, whenever solution and container permit.

Reconstitution: 1. Warm the unopened diluent and concentrate to room temperature (not more than 37°C).

2. After removing the plastic flip-top caps, aseptically cleanse rubber stoppers of both bottles.

3. Remove the protective cover from the plastic transfer needle cartridge with tamper-proof seal and penetrate the stopper of the diluent bottle.

4. Remove the remaining portion of the plastic cartridge. Invert the diluent bottle and penetrate the rubber seal on the concentrate bottle with the needle at an angle.

5. The vacuum will draw the diluent into the concentrate bottle. For best results, and to avoid foaming, hold the diluent bottle at an angle to the concentrate bottle in order to direct the jet of diluent against the wall of the concentrate bottle.

6. After removing the diluent bottle and transfer needle, gently swirl the concentrate bottle until the powder is completely dissolved.

7. Swab top of reconstituted bottle of alpha$_1$-proteinase inhibitor (human), again.

8. Attach the sterile filter needle provided to syringe. With filter needle in place, insert syringe into reconstituted bottle and withdraw solution into syringe.

9. To administer alpha$_1$-proteinase inhibitor (human), replace filter needle with appropriate injection needle and follow procedure for i.v. administration.

10. The contents of more than 1 bottle may be drawn into the the same syringe before administration. If more than 1 bottle is used, withdraw contents from bottles using aseptic technique. Place contents into an administration container (plastic

minibag or glass bottle) using a syringe*. Avoid pushing an i.v. administration set spike into the product container stopper as this has been known to force the stopper into the vial, with a resulting loss of sterility.

*For a patient of average weight (about 70 kg), the volume needed will exceed the limit of 1 syringe.

Supplied: Each single use vial of sterile, stable, lyophilized preparation contains: purified human alpha$_1$-proteinase inhibitor with a functional activity of 500 or 1 000 mg. A suitable volume of Sterile Water for Injection USP (20 or 40 mL, respectively), a sterile double-ended transfer needle and a sterile filter needle are provided. Preservative-free. Must be administered by the i.v. route.

Alpha$_1$-proteinase inhibitor (human) is prepared from pooled human plasma of normal donors by modification and refinements of the cold ethanol method of Cohn. In order to reduce the potential risk of transmission of infectious agents, alpha$_1$-proteinase inhibitor (human) has been heat-treated in solution at 60±0.5°C for not less than 10 hours. However, no procedure has been found to be totally effective in removing viral infectivity from plasma fractionation products.

The specific activity of alpha$_1$-proteinase inhibitor (human) is ≥0.35 mg functional alpha$_1$-PI/mg protein and when reconstituted as directed, the concentration of alpha$_1$-PI is ≥20 mg/mL. When reconstituted, alpha$_1$-proteinase inhibitor (human) has a pH of 6.6 to 7.4, a sodium content of 100 to 210 mEq/L a chloride content of 60 to 180 mEq/L, a sodium phosphate content of 0.015 to 0.025 M, a polyethylene glycol content of not more than 5 ppm, and not more than 0.1% sucrose. Alpha$_1$-proteinase inhibitor (human) contains small amounts of other plasma proteins including alpha$_2$-plasmin inhibitor, alpha$_1$-antichymotrypsin, C_1-esterase inhibitor, haptoglobin, antithrombin III, alpha$_1$-lipoprotein, albumin, and IgA.

Each vial contains the labeled amount of functionally active alpha$_1$-PI in mg/vial, as determined by capacity to neutralize porcine pancreatic elastase.

Store under refrigeration (2 to 8°C). Freezing should be avoided as breakage of the diluent bottle might occur.

Reviewed 1997

PRO-LAX®
Rivex Pharma

Polyethylene Glycol 3350—Electrolytes
Laxative

Pharmacology: Pro-Lax contains PEG 3350, which is an inert, non-toxic, water-soluble polymer that acts as an osmotic agent. When administered as a solution, the PEG 3350 component of Pro-Lax prevents absorption by the intestinal tract of the portion of water ingested, thereby serving to hydrate and soften stools, and promote peristalsis. Pro-Lax does not affect electrolyte absorption in the intestine; sodium, potassium, chloride and bicarbonate ions are present in the same concentration as in the plasma, to counteract passive absorption or secretion of these ions. Active absorption of sodium is counteracted by the addition of sulfate.

Pro-Lax provides relief of constipation without irritating the digestive tract or stimulating nerve centres.

Indications: For the gentle relief and prevention of constipation.

Precautions: Do not use in the presence of abdominal pain, nausea, fever or vomiting (as these may be signs of appendicitis or an inflamed bowel). Overuse or extended use of any laxative may cause dependence for bowel function. Do not take any type of laxative for more than 1 week, unless directed by a physician. Laxatives should not be taken within 2 hours of another medicine because the desired effect of the other medicine may be reduced.

Keep out of the reach of children. Store in a cool, dry place.

Dosage: Take the entire contents of 1 sachet dissolved in a large (250 mL) glass of water. Stir rapidly to dissolve. This dose may be repeated once daily, depending on the severity of the condition being treated and the individual response, or as directed by a physician.

Supplied: Each flavored sachet contains: polyethylene glycol 3350 14.75 g, sodium sulfate 1.42 g, sodium bicarbonate 0.42 g, sodium chloride 0.37 g and potassium chloride 0.19 g. Nonmedicinal ingredients: aspartame and passion fruit flavor. Boxes of 10.

Reviewed 1999

PROLEUKIN® Ⓟ
Ligand

Aldesleukin
Antineoplastic Agent

Pharmacology: The exact mechanism by which aldesleukin mediates its anitiumor activity is unknown. Aldesleukin has been shown to possess the biological activity of human native interleukin-2.

In vitro studies performed on human cell lines demonstrate the immunoregulatory properties of aldesleukin, including: 1) enhancement of lymphocyte mitogenesis and stimulation of long-term growth of human interleukin-2 dependent cell lines; 2) enhancement of lymphocyte cytotoxicity; 3) induction of killer cell [lymphokine-activated (LAK) and natural (NK)] activity; and 4) induction of interferon-gamma production.

The in vivo administration aldesleukin in murine tumor models and in the clinic produces multiple immunological effects in a dose dependent manner. These effects include activation of cellular immunity with profound lymphocytosis, eosinophilia, and thrombocytopenia, and the production of cytokines including tumor necrosis factor, IL-1 and gamma interferon. In vivo experiments in murine tumor models have shown inhibition of tumor growth.

Pharmacokinetics: Aldesleukin exists as biologically active, noncovalently bound microaggregates with an average size of 27 recombinant interleukin-2 molecules. The solubilizing agent, sodium dodecyl sulfate, may have an effect on the kinetic properties of this product. The pharmacokinetic profile of aldesleukin is characterized by high plasma concentrations following a short i.v. infusion, rapid distribution to extravascular, extracellular space and elimination from the body by metabolism in the kidneys with little or no bioactive protein excreted in the urine.

Studies of i.v. aldesleukin in sheep and humans indicated that approximately 30% of the administered dose initially distributes to the plasma. This is consistent with studies in rats that demonstrate a rapid (<1 minute) and preferential uptake of approximately 70% of an administered dose into the liver, kidney, and lung.

The serum half-life (t ½) curves of aldesleukin remaining in the plasma are derived from studies done in 52 cancer patients following a 5-minute i.v. infusion. These patients were shown to have a distribution and elimination t ½ of 13 and 85 minutes, respectively.

The relatively rapid clearance rate of aldesleukin has led to dosage schedules characterized by frequent, short infusions. Observed serum levels are proportional to the dose of aldesleukin.

Following the initial rapid organ distribution described above, the primary route of clearance of circulating aldesleukin is the kidney. In humans and animals, aldesleukin is cleared from the circulation by both glomerular filtration and peritubular extraction in the kidney. This dual mechanism for delivery of aldesleukin to the proximal tubule may account for the preservation of clearance in patients with rising serum creatinine values. Greater than 80% of the amount of aldesleukin distributed to plasma, cleared from the circulation and presented to the kidney is metabolized to amino acids in the cells lining the proximal convoluted tubules. In humans, the mean clearance rate in cancer patients is 268 mL/min.

Immunogenicity: Fifty-seven of 77 renal cancer patients (74%) treated with the every 8-hour aldesleukin regimen developed low titres of non-neutralizing anti-interleukin-2 antibodies. Neutralizing antibodies were not detected in this group of patients, but have been detected in 1/106 (<1%) patients with i.v. aldesleukin using a wide variety of schedules and doses. The clinical significance of anti-interleukin-2 antibodies is unknown.

Clinical Experience: Two hundred and fifty-five patients with metastatic renal cell cancer were treated with single agent aldesleukin. Treatment was given by the every 8-hour regimen in 7 clinical studies conducted at 21 institutions. To be eligible for study, patients were required to have bidimensionally measurable disease; Eastern Cooperative Oncology Group (ECOG) Performance Status (PS) of 0 or 1 (see Table I); and normal organ function, including normal cardiac stress test and pulmonary function tests. Patients with brain metastases, active infections, organ allografts, and diseases requiring steroid treatment were excluded. In addition, it was noted that 218 of the 255 (85%) patients had undergone nephrectomy prior to treatment with aldesleukin.

Aldesleukin was given as either 600 000 or 720 000 IU/kg (0.037 mg/kg or 0.044 mg/kg respectively) by 15-minute i.v. infusion every 8 hours for up to 5 days (maximum of 14 doses). No treatment was given on days 6 to 14 and then dosing was repeated for up to 5 days on days 15 to 19 (maximum of 14 doses). These 2 cycles constituted 1 course of therapy. All patients were to be treated with 28 doses or until dose-limiting toxicity occurred requiring Intensive Care Unit (ICU)-level support. Patients received a median of 15 or 20 scheduled doses of aldesleukin for the higher and lower dosage regimens, respectively. Doses were held for specific toxicities (see Dosage, Dose Modification). A variety of serious adverse events were encountered including: hypotension; oliguria/anuria; mental status changes including coma; pulmonary congestion and dyspnea; gastrointestinal bleeding; respiratory failure leading to intubation; ventricular arrhythmias; myocardial ischemia and/or infarction; ileus or intestinal perforation; renal failure requiring dialysis; gangrene; seizures; sepsis and death (see Adverse Effects).

Due to the toxicities encountered during the clinical trials, investigators used the following concomitant medications. Acetaminophen and indomethacin were started immediately prior to aldesleukin to reduce fever. Renal function was particularly monitored because aldesleukin and indomethacin may both cause nephrotoxicity. Meperidine was added to control the rigors associated with fever. Ranitidine or cimetidine were given for prophylaxis of gastrointestinal irritation and bleeding. Antiemetics and antidiarrheals were used as needed to treat other gastrointestinal side effects. These medications were discontinued 12 hours after the last dose of aldesleukin. Hydroxyzine or diphenhydramine were used to control symptoms from pruritic rashes and continued until resolution of pruritus. Note: Prior to the use of any product mentioned in this paragraph, the physician should refer to the product monograph for the respective product.

For the 255 patients in the aldesleukin database, objective response was seen in 15% or 37 patients with 9 (4%) complete and 28 (11%) partial responders. The 95% confidence interval for response was 11 to 20%. Onset of tumor regression has been observed as early as 4 weeks after completion of the first course of treatment and tumor regression may continue for up to 12 months after the start of treatment. Durable responses were achieved with a median duration of objective (partial or complete) response by Kaplan-Meier projection of 23.2 months (1 to 50 months). The median duration of objective partial response was 18.8 months. The proportion of responding patients who will have response durations of 12 months or greater is projected to be 85% for all responders and 79% for patients with partial responses (Kaplan-Meier).

Complete Responders: 9 (4%); partial responders: 28 (11%); response rate: 15%; onset of response: 1 to 12 months; median duration of response: 23.2 months (range 1 to 50).

Response was observed in both lung and nonlung sites (e.g., liver, lymph node, renal bed recurrences, soft tissue). Patients with individual bulky lesions (>5×5 cm) as well as large cumulative tumor burden (>25 cm² tumor area) achieved durable responses.

An analysis of prognostic factors showed that performance status as defined by the ECOG (see Table I on following page) was a significant predictor of response. PS 0 patients had an 18% overall rate of objective response, which included all 9 complete response patients and 21 of 28 partial response patients. PS 1 patients had a lower rate of response (9%), all of which were partial responses. In this group it was notable that 6 of the 7 responders had resolution of tumor related symptoms and improved performance status to PS 0. All 7 patients were fully functional and 4 of the 7 returned to work, suggesting that responses among the PS 1 patients were clinically meaningful as well (see Table II on following page).

In addition, the frequency of toxicity was related to the performance status. As a group, PS 0 patients, when compared with PS 1 patients, had lower rates of adverse events with fewer on-study deaths (4% vs 6%), less frequent intubations (8% vs 25%), gangrene (0% vs 6%), coma (1% vs 6%), gastrointestinal bleeding (4% vs 8%), and sepsis (6% vs 18%). These differences in toxicity are reflected in the shorter mean time to hospital discharge for PS 0 patients (2 vs 3 days) as well as the smaller percentage of PS 0 patients experiencing a delayed (>7 days) discharge from the hospital (8% vs 19%).

Indications: The treatment of adults (≥18 years of age) with metastatic renal cell carcinoma.

Proleukin (cont'd)

Table I—Proleukin

Performance Status Scale

Performance Status Equivalent ECOG*	Karnofsky	Performance Status Definitions
0	100	Asymptomatic
1	80-90	Symptomatic: fully ambulatory
2	60-70	Symptomatic; in bed less than 50% of day
3	40-50	Symptomatic: in bed more than 50% of day
4	20-30	Bedridden

Zubrod, CG, et al. J Chron Dis 11:7-33, 1960.
*Eastern Cooperative Oncology Group.

Table II—Proleukin

Proleukin Response Analyzed By ECOG* Performance Status (PS)

Pre-Treatment ECOG PS	No. of Patients Treated (n=255)	Response CR PR	% of Patients Responding	On-Study Death Rate
0	166	9 21	18%	4%
1	80	0 7	9%	6%
≥2	9	0 0	0%	0%

*Eastern Cooperative Oncology Group.

Careful patient selection is mandatory prior to the administration of aldesleukin. See Contraindications, Warnings and Precautions regarding patient screening, including recommended cardiac and pulmonary function tests and laboratory tests.

Evaluation of clinical studies to date reveals that patients with more favorable ECOG performance status (ECOG PS 0) at treatment initiation respond better to aldesleukin, with a higher response rate and lower toxicity (see Pharmacology, Clinical Experience). Therefore, selection of patients for treatment should include assessment of performance status, as described in Table I.

Experience in patients with PS>1 is extremely limited.

Contraindications: In patients with a known history of hypersensitivity to interleukin-2 or any component of the aldesleukin formulation.

Patients with an abnormal thallium stress test or pulmonary function tests are excluded from treatment with aldesleukin. Patients with organ allografts should be excluded as well. In addition, retreatment with aldesleukin is contraindicated in patients who experienced the following toxicities while receiving an earlier course of therapy: sustained ventricular tachycardia (≥5 beats); cardiac rhythm disturbances not controlled or unresponsive to management; recurrent chest pain with ECG changes, consistent with angina or myocardial infarction; intubation required >72 hours; pericardial tamponade; renal dysfunction requiring dialysis >72 hours; coma or toxic psychosis lasting >48 hours; repetitive or difficult to control seizures; bowel ischemia/perforation; gastrointestinal bleeding requiring surgery.

Warnings: Intensive therapy with aldesleukin for injection should be administered only to well informed patients in a hospital setting under the supervision of a qualified physician experienced in the use of anticancer agents. An intensive care facility and specialists skilled in cardiopulmonary or intensive care medicine must be available.

Aldesleukin administration has been associated with capillary leak syndrome (CLS) which results from extravasation of plasma proteins and fluid into the extravascular space and loss of vascular tone. CLS results in hypotension and reduced organ perfusion which may be severe and can result in death. The CLS may be associated with cardiac arrhythmias (supraventicular and ventricular), angina, myocardial infarction, respiratory insufficiency requiring intubation, gastrointestinal bleeding or infarction, renal insufficiency, and mental status changes.

Because of the severe adverse events which generally accompany aldesleukin therapy at the recommended dosages, thorough clinical evaluation should be performed to exclude from treatment patients with significant cardiac, pulmonary, renal, hepatic, or CNS impairment.

Therapy with aldesleukin should be restricted to patients with normal cardiac and pulmonary functions as defined by thallium stress testing and formal pulmonary function testing. Extreme caution should be used in patients with normal thallium stress tests and pulmonary function tests who have a history of prior cardiac or pulmonary disease.

Aldesleukin may exacerbate pre-existing autoimmune disease. Because not all patients who develop interleukin-2-associated autoimmune phenomena have a pre-existing history of autoimmune disease, awareness and close monitoring for thyroid abnormalities or other potentially autoimmune phenomena is warranted. Two patients with quiescent Crohn's disease had activation of their disease following treatment with aldesleukin, and both required surgical intervention.

Aldesleukin may exacerbate disease symptoms in patients with clinically unrecognized or untreated CNS metastases. All patients should have thorough evaluation and treatment of CNS metastases prior to receiving aldesleukin therapy. They should be neurologically stable with a negative computed tomography (CT) scan. In addition, extreme caution should be exercised in treating patients with a history of seizure disorder because aldesleukin may cause seizures.

Aldesleukin administration should be held in patients developing moderate to severe lethargy or somnolence; continued administration may result in coma.

Aldesleukin treatment is associated with impaired neutrophil function (reduced chemotaxis) and with an increased risk of disseminated infection, including sepsis and bacterial endocarditis, in treated patients. Consequently, pre-existing bacterial infection should be adequately treated prior to initiation of aldesleukin therapy. Additionally, all patients with indwelling central lines should receive antibiotic prophylaxis effective against S. aureus. Antibiotic prophylaxis which has been associated with a reduced incidence of staphylococcal infections in aldesleukin studies includes the use of oxacillin, nafcillin, ciprofloxacin, or vancomycin. Disseminated infections acquired in the course of aldesleukin treatment are a major contributor to treatment morbidity and use of antibiotic prophylaxis and aggressive treatment of suspected and documented infections may reduce the morbidity of aldesleukin treatment.

Note: Prior to the use of any product mentioned in this paragraph, the physician should refer to the product monograph for the respective product.

Precautions: General: Patients should have normal cardiac, pulmonary, hepatic, and CNS function at the start of therapy. Patients who have had a nephrectomy are still eligible for treatment if they have serum creatinine levels ≤1.5 mg/dL.

Adverse events are predictable and frequent, often serious, and sometimes life-threatening.

Capillary leak syndrome (CLS) begins immediately after aldesleukin treatment starts and is marked by increased capillary permeability to protein and fluids and reduced vascular tone. In most patients, this results in a concomitant drop in mean arterial blood pressure within 2 to 12 hours after the start of treatment. With continued therapy, clinically significant hypotension (defined as systolic blood pressure below 90 mm Hg or a 20 mm Hg drop from baseline systolic pressure) and hypoperfusion will occur. In addition, extravasation of protein and fluids into the extravascular space will lead to edema and effusions.

Medical management of CLS begins with careful monitoring of the patient's fluid and organ perfusion status. This is achieved by frequent determination of blood pressure and pulse, and by monitoring organ function, which includes assessment of mental status and urine output. Hypovolemia is assessed by catheterization and central pressure monitoring.

Flexibility in fluid and pressor management is essential for maintaining organ perfusion and blood pressure. Consequently, extreme caution should be used in treating patients with fixed requirements for large volumes of fluid (e.g., patients with hypercalcemia).

Patients with hypovolemia are managed by administering i.v. fluids, either colloids or crystalloids. I.V. fluids are usually given when the central venous pressure (CVP) is below 3 to 4 mm H_2O. Correction of hypovolemia may require large volumes of i.v. fluids but caution is required because unrestrained fluid administration may exacerbate problems associated with edema formation or effusions.

With extravascular fluid accumulation, edema is common and some patients may develop ascites or pleural effusions. Management of these events depends on a careful balancing of the effects of fluid shifts so that neither the consequences of hypovolemia (e.g., impaired organ perfusion) nor the consequences of fluid accumulations (e.g., pulmonary edema) exceeds the patient's tolerance.

Clinical experience has shown that early administration of dopamine (1 to 5 µg/kg/min) to patients manifesting capillary leak syndrome, before the onset of hypotension, can help to maintain organ perfusion particularly to the kidney and thus preserve urine output. Weight and urine output should be carefully monitored. If organ perfusion and blood pressure are not sustained by dopamine therapy, clinical investigators have increased the dose of dopamine to 6 to 10 µg/kg/min or have added phenylephrine HCl (1 to 5 µg/kg/min) to low dose dopamine (see Pharmacology, Clinical Experience). Prolonged use of pressors, either in combination or as individual agents, at relatively high doses, may be associated with cardiac rhythm disturbances. Note: Prior to the use of any product mentioned in this paragraph, the physician should refer to the product monograph for the respective product.

Failure to maintain organ perfusion, demonstrated by altered mental status, reduced urine output, a fall in the systolic blood pressure below 90 mm Hg or onset of cardiac arrhythmias, should lead to holding the subsequent doses until recovery of organ perfusion and a return of systolic blood pressure above 90 mm Hg are observed (see Dosage, Dose Modification).

Recovery from CLS begins soon after cessation of aldesleukin therapy. Usually, within a few hours, the blood pressure rises, organ perfusion is restored and resorption of extravasated fluid and protein begins. If there has been excessive weight gain or edema formation, particularly if associated with shortness of breath from pulmonary congestion, use of diuretics, once blood pressure has normalized, has been shown to hasten recovery.

Oxygen is given to the patient if pulmonary function monitoring confirms that PaO_2 is decreased.

Aldesleukin administration may cause anemia and/or thrombocytopenia. Packed red blood cell transfusions have been given both for relief of anemia and to insure maximal oxygen carrying capacity. Platelet transfusions have been given to resolve absolute thrombocytopenia and to reduce the risk of gastrointestinal bleeding. In addition, leukopenia and neutropenia are observed.

Aldesleukin administration results in fever, chills, rigors, pruritus, and gastrointestinal side effects in most patients treated at recommended doses. These side effects have been aggressively managed as described in Pharmacology, Clinical Experience.

Renal and hepatic function are impaired during aldesleukin treatment. Use of concomitant medications known to be nephrotoxic or hepatotoxic may further increase toxicity to the kidney or liver. In addition, reduced kidney and liver function secondary to aldesleukin treatment may delay elimination of concomitant medications and increase the risk of adverse events from those drugs.

Patients may experience mental status changes including irritability, confusion, or depression while receiving aldesleukin. These mental status changes may be indicators of bacteremia or early bacterial sepsis. Mental status changes due solely to aldesleukin are generally reversible when drug administration is discontinued. However, alterations in mental status may progress for several days before recovery begins.

Impairment of thyroid function has been reported following aldesleukin treatment. A small number of these patients required thyroid replacement therapy. This impairment of thyroid function may be a manifestation of autoimmunity.

Aldesleukin enhancement of cellular immune function may increase the risk of allograft rejection in transplant patients.

Laboratory Tests: The following clinical evaluations are recommended for all patients, prior to beginning treatment and then daily during drug administration: standard hematologic tests—including complete blood count (CBC), differential and platelet counts; blood chemistries—including electrolytes, renal and hepatic function tests; and chest x-rays.

All patients should have baseline pulmonary function tests with arterial blood gases. Adequate pulmonary function should be documented (FEV1>2L or ≥75% of value predicted for height and age) prior to initiating therapy. All patients should be screened with a stress thallium study. Normal ejection fraction and unimpaired wall motion should be documented. If a thallium stress test suggests minor wall motion abnormalities of questionable significance, a stress echocardiogram to document normal wall motion may be useful to exclude significant coronary artery disease.

Daily monitoring during therapy with aldesleukin should include vital signs (temperature, pulse, blood pressure, and respiration rate) and weight. In a patient with a decreased blood pressure, especially less than 90 mm Hg, constant cardiac monitoring for rhythm should be conducted. If an abnormal complex or rhythm is seen, an ECG should be performed. Vital signs in these hypotensive patients should be taken hourly and central venous pressure (CVP) checked.

During treatment, pulmonary function should be monitored on a regular basis by clinical examination, assessment of vital signs and pulse oximetry. Patients with dyspnea or clinical signs of respiratory impairment (tachypnea or rales) should be further assessed with arterial blood gas determination. These tests are to be repeated as often as clinically indicated.

Cardiac function is assessed daily by clinical examination and assessment of vital signs. Patients with signs or symptoms of chest pain, murmurs, gallops, irregular rhythm or palpitations should be further assessed with an ECG examination and creatinine phosphokinase (CPK) evaluation. If there is evidence of cardiac ischemia or congestive heart failure, a repeat thallium study should be done.

Drug Interactions: Aldesleukin may affect central nervous function. Therefore, interactions could occur following concomitant administration of psychotropic drugs (e.g., narcotics, analgesics, antiemetics, sedatives, tranquilizers).

Concurrent administration of drugs possessing nephrotoxic (e.g., aminoglycosides, indomethacin), myelotoxic (e.g., cytotoxic chemotherapy), cardiotoxic (e.g., doxorubicin) or hepatotoxic (e.g., methotrexate, asparaginase) effects with aldesleukin may increase toxicity in these organ systems. The safety and efficacy of aldesleukin in combination with chemotherapies have not been established.

Although glucocorticoids have been shown to reduce aldesleukin-induced side effects including fever, renal insufficiency, hyperbilirubinemia, confusion, and dyspnea, concomitant administration of these agents with aldesleukin may reduce the antitumor effectiveness of aldesleukin and thus should be avoided.

Beta-blockers and other antihypertensives may potentiate the hypotension seen with aldesleukin.

Delayed Adverse Reactions to Iodinated Contrast Media: A review of the literature revealed that 12.6% (range 11 to 28%) of 501 patients treated with various interleukin-2 containing regimens who were then subsequently administered radiographic iodinated contrast media experienced acute, atypical adverse reactions. The onset of symptoms usually occurred within hours (most commonly 1 to 4 hours) following the administration of contrast media. These reactions include fever, chills, nausea, vomiting, pruritus, rash, diarrhea, hypotension, edema, and oliguria. Some clinicians have noted that these reactions resemble the immediate side effects caused by interleukin-2 administration, however the cause of contrast reactions after interleukin-2 therapy is unknown. Most events were reported to occur when contrast media was given within 4 weeks after the last dose of interleukin-2. These events were also reported to occur when contrast media was given several months after interleukin-2 treatment.

Carcinogenesis, Mutagenesis, Impairment of Fertility: There have been no studies conducted assessing the carcinogenic or mutagenic potential of aldesleukin.

There have been no studies conducted assessing the effect of aldesleukin on fertility. It is recommended that this drug not be administered to fertile persons of either sex not practising effective contraception.

Pregnancy: Animal reproduction studies have not been conducted with aldesleukin. It is also not known whether aldesleukin can cause fetal harm when administered to a pregnant woman or can affect reproduction capacity. Aldesleukin should be given to a pregnant women only if clearly needed.

Lactation: It is not known whether this drug is excreted in human milk. Because many drugs are excreted in human milk and because of the potential for serious adverse reactions in nursing infants from aldesleukin, a decision should be made whether to discontinue nursing or to discontinue the drug, taking into account the importance of the drug to the mother.

Children: Safety and effectiveness in children under 18 years of age have not been established.

Adverse Effects: The rate of drug-related deaths in the 255 metastatic renal cell carcinoma patients on study who received single-agent aldesleukin was 4% (11/255).

Frequency and severity of adverse reactions to aldesleukin have generally been shown to be dose-related and schedule-dependent. Most adverse reactions are self-limiting and are usually, but not invariably, reversible within 2 or 3 days of discontinuation of therapy.

Examples of adverse reactions with permanent sequelae include: myocardial infarction, bowel perforation/infarction, and gangrene.

The most frequently reported serious adverse reactions include hypotension, renal dysfunction with oliguria/anuria, dyspnea or pulmonary congestion, and mental status changes (i.e., lethargy, somnolence, confusion, and agitation). Other serious toxicities have included myocardial ischemia, myocarditis, gangrene, respiratory failure leading to intubation, gastrointestinal bleeding requiring surgery, intestinal perforation/ileus, coma, seizure, sepsis, and renal impairment requiring dialysis. The incidence of these events has been higher in PS 1 patients than in PS 0 patients (see Pharmacology, Clinical Experience).

The following data on adverse reactions are based on 373 patients (255 with renal cell cancer and 118 with other tumors) treated with the recommended every 8-hour, 15-minute-infusion dosing regimen. These patients had metastatic or recurrent carcinoma and were enrolled in investigational trials in the United States and Canada.

Organ systems in which reactions occurred in a significant number of the patients treated are found in Table III.

Table III—Proleukin

Incidence of Adverse Events

Events by Body System	**% of Patients**
Cardiovascular	
Hypotension	85
(requiring pressors)	71
Sinus Tachycardia	70
Arrhythmias	22
Atrial	8
Supraventricular	5
Ventricular	3
Junctional	1
Bradycardia	7
Premature Ventricular Contractions	5
Premature Atrial Contractions	4
Myocardial Ischemia	3
Myocardial Infarction	2
Cardiac Arrest	2
Congestive Heart Failure	1
Myocarditis	1
Stroke	1
Gangrene	1
Pericardial Effusion	1
Endocarditis	1
Thrombosis	1
Pulmonary	
Pulmonary Congestion	54
Dyspnea	52
Pulmonary Edema	10
Respiratory Failure (leading to intubation)	9
Tachypnea	8
Pleural Effusion	7
Wheezing	6
Apnea	1
Pneumothorax	1
Hemoptysis	1
Hepatic	
Elevated Bilirubin	64
Elevated Transaminase	56
Elevated Alkaline Phosphatase	56
Jaundice	11
Ascites	4
Hepatomegaly	1
Hematologic	
Anemia	77
Thrombocytopenia	64
Leukopenia	34
Coagulation Disorders	10
Leukocytosis	9
Eosinophilia	6
Abnormal Laboratory Findings	
Hypomagnesemia	16
Acidosis	16
Hypocalcemia	15
Hypophosphatemia	11
Hypokalemia	9
Hyperuricemia	9
Hypoalbuminemia	8
Hypoproteinemia	7
Hyponatremia	4
Hyperkalemia	4
Alkalosis	4
Hypoglycemia	2
Hyperglycemia	2
Hypocholesterolemia	1
Hypercalcemia	1
Hypernatremia	1
Hyperphosphatemia	1
Gastrointestinal	
Nausea and Vomiting	87
Diarrhea	76
Stomatitis	32
Anorexia	27
Gastrointestinal Bleeding	13
(requiring surgery)	2
Dyspepsia	7
Constipation	5
Intestinal Perforation/Ileus	2
Pancreatitis	<1
Neurologic	
Mental Status Changes	73
Dizziness	17
Sensory Dysfunction	10
Special Sensory Disorders (vision, speech, taste)	7
Syncope	3
Motor Dysfunction	2
Coma	1
Seizure (grand mal)	1
Renal	
Oliguria/Anuria	76
BUN Elevation	63
Serum Creatinine Elevation	61
Proteinuria	12
Hematuria	9
Dysuria	3
Renal Impairment Requiring Dialysis	2
Urinary Retention	1
Urinary Frequency	1
Dermatologic	
Pruritus	48
Erythema	41
Rash	26
Dry Skin	15
Exfoliative Dermatitis	14
Purpura/Petechiae	4
Urticaria	2
Alopecia	1
Musculoskeletal	
Arthralgia	6
Myalgia	6
Arthritis	1
Muscle Spasm	1
Endocrine	
Hypothyroidism	<1
General	
Fever and/or Chills	89
Pain (all sites)	54
Abdominal	15
Chest	12
Back	9
Fatigue/Weakness/Malaise	53
Edema	47
Infection (including urinary tract, injection site, catheter tip, phlebitis, sepsis)	23
Weight Gain (≥10%)	23
Headache	12
Weight Loss (≥10%)	5
Conjunctivitis	4
Injection Site Reactions	3
Allergic Reactions (nonanaphylactic)	1

Other serious adverse events were derived from trials involving more than 1 800 patients treated with aldesleukin-based regimens using a variety of doses and schedules. These events each occurred with a frequency of <1% and included: liver or renal failure resulting in death, duodenal ulceration, fatal intestinal perforation, bowel necrosis, fatal cardiac arrest, myocarditis and supraventricular tachycardia, permanent or transient blindness secondary to optic neuritis, fatal malignant hyperthermia, pulmonary edema resulting in death, respiratory arrest, fatal respiratory failure, fatal stroke, transient ischemic attack, meningitis, cerebral edema, pericarditis, allergic interstitial nephritis, tracheo-esophageal fistula, fatal pulmonary emboli, and severe depression leading to suicide.

Exacerbation of pre-existing autoimmune disease (Crohn's Disease and Thyroid Disease, see Warnings) and delayed adverse reactions to iodinated contrast media (see Precautions) have also been reported. In clinical investigations, persistent but nonprogressive vitiligo has been observed in malignant melanoma patients treated with interleukin-2.

Overdose: Symptoms and Treatment: Side effects following the use of aldesleukin are dose-related. Administration of more than the recommended dose has been associated with a more rapid onset of expected dose-limiting toxicities. Adverse reactions generally will reverse when the drug is stopped, particularly because its serum half-life is short (see Pharmacology, Pharmacokinetics). Any continuing symptoms should be treated supportively. Life-threatening toxicities have been ameliorated by the i.v. administration of dexamethasone,

Proleukin (cont'd)

which may result in loss of therapeutic effect from aldesleukin. Note: Prior to the use of dexamethasone, the physician should refer to the product monograph for this product.

Dosage: 18 millions IU=1.1 mg of proteins. Aldesleukin for injection should be administered by a 15-minute i.v. infusion every 8 hours. Before initiating treatment, carefully review the Indications, Contraindications, Warnings, Precautions, and Adverse Effects sections, particularly regarding patient selection, possible serious adverse events, patient monitoring and withholding dosage.

The following schedules have been used to treat adult patients with metastatic renal cell carcinoma. Each course of treatment consists of two 5-day treatment cycles separated by a rest period.

1. 600 000 IU/kg (0.037 mg/kg) administered every 8 hours by a 15-minute i.v. infusion for a total of 14 doses. Following 9 days of rest, the schedule is repeated for another 14 doses, for a maximum of 28 doses per course.
2. 720 000 IU/kg (0.044 mg/kg) administered every 8 hours by a 15-minute i.v. infusion for a total of 14 doses. Following 9 days of rest, the schedule is repeated for another 14 doses, for a maximum of 28 doses per course.
3. During clinical trials, doses were frequently held for toxicity (see Dose Modifications). Patients treated with 600 000 IU/kg (0.037 mg/kg) received a median of 20 of the 28 doses during the first course of therapy, and patients treated with 720 000 IU/kg (0.044 mg/kg) received a median of 15 of the 28 doses during the first course of therapy.

Retreatment: Patients should be evaluated for response approximately 4 weeks after completion of a course of therapy and again immediately prior to the scheduled start of the next treatment course. Additional courses of treatment may be given to patients only if there is some tumor shrinkage following the last course and retreatment is not contraindicated (see Contraindications). Each treatment course should be separated by a rest period of at least 7 weeks from the date of hospital discharge. Tumors have continued to regress up to 12 months following the initiation of aldesleukin therapy.

Dose Modifications: Dose modification for toxicity should be accomplished by holding or interrupting a dose rather than reducing the dose to be given. Decisions to stop, hold, or restart aldesleukin therapy must be made after a global assessment of the patient. With this in mind, the following guidelines should be used.

Treatment with Aldesleukin should be permanently discontinued for: See Table IV.

Doses should be held and restarted according to the following: see Table V.

Stability and Storage Recommendations: Store vials of lyophilized aldesleukin in a refrigerator at 2 to 8°C.

Reconstituted or diluted aldesleukin is stable for up to 48 hours at refrigerated and room temperatures, 2 to 25°C. However, since this product contains no preservatives, the reconstituted and diluted solutions should be stored in the refrigerator.

Do not use beyond the expiration date printed on the vial. Note: This product contains no preservative.

Reconstitution: Reconstitution and dilution procedures other than those recommended may alter the delivery and/or pharmacology of aldesleukin and thus should be avoided.

1. Proleukin is a sterile, white to off-white, preservative-free, lyophilized powder suitable for i.v. infusion upon reconstitution and dilution. **Each vial contains 22 million IU (1.3 mg) of aldesleukin and should be reconstituted aseptically with 1.2 mL of Sterile Water for Injection, USP. When reconstituted as directed, each mL contains 18 million IU (1.1 mg) of aldesleukin.** The resulting solution should be a clear, colorless to slightly yellow liquid. The vial is for single-use only and any unused portion should be discarded.
2. During reconstitution the Sterile Water for Injection, USP should be directed at the side of the vial and the contents gently swirled to avoid excess foaming. **Do not shake.**
3. The dose of aldesleukin, reconstituted in Sterile Water for Injection, USP (without preservative) should be diluted aseptically in 50 mL of 5% Dextrose Injection, USP and infused over a 15-minute period. Although glass bottles and plastic (polyvinyl chloride) bags have been used in clinical trials with comparable results, it is recommended that plastic bags be used as the dilution container since experimental studies suggest that use of plastic containers results in more consistent drug delivery. **In-line filters should not be used when administering aldesleukin.**
4. Before and after reconstitution and dilution, store in a refrigerator at 2 to 8°C. Do not freeze. Administer aldesleukin within 48 hours of reconstitution. The solution should be brought to room temperature prior to infusion in the patient.
5. Reconstitution or dilution with Bacteriostatic Water for Injection, USP, or 0.9% Sodium Chloride Injection, USP should be avoided because of increased aggregation. Animal studies have shown that dilution with albumin can alter the pharmacology of aldesleukin. Aldesleukin should not be mixed with other drugs.
6. Parenteral drug products should be inspected visually for particulate matter and discoloration prior to administration, whenever solution and container permit.

Table IV—Proleukin

Toxicities for which Treatment should be Permanently Discontinued

Organ System	**Permanently discontinue treatment for the following toxicities**
Cardiovascular	Sustained ventricular tachycardia (≥5 beats)
	Cardiac rhythm disturbances not controlled or unresponsive to management
	Recurrent chest pain with ECG changes, documented angina or myocardial infarction
	Pericardial tamponade
Pulmonary	Intubation required >72 hours
Renal	Renal dysfunction requiring dialysis >72 hours
CNS	Coma or toxic psychosis lasting >48 hours
	Repetitive or difficult to control seizures
Gastrointestinal	Bowel ischemia/perforation/gastrointestinal bleeding requiring surgery

Table V—Proleukin

Toxicities for which Doses should be Held and Restarted

Organ System	**Hold dose for**	**Subsequent doses may be given if**
Cardiovascular	Atrial fibrillation, Supraventricular tachycardia, or bradycardia that requires treatment or is recurrent or persistent	Patient is asymptomatic with full recovery to normal sinus rhythm
	Systolic BP <90 mm Hg with increasing requirements for pressors	Systolic BP ≥90 mm Hg and stable or decreasing requirements for pressors
	Any ECG change consistent with myocardial infarction or ischemia with or without chest pain; suspicion of cardiac ischemia	Patient is asymptomatic, myocardial infarction has been ruled out, clinical suspicion of angina is low
Pulmonary	O_2 saturation <94% on room air or <90% with 2 L O_2 by nasal prongs	O_2 saturation ≥94% on room air or ≥90% with 2 L O_2 by nasal prongs
CNS	Mental status changes, including moderate confusion or agitation	Mental status changes completely resolved
Systemic	Sepsis syndrome, patient is clinically unstable	Sepsis syndrome has resolved, patient is clinically stable, infection is under treatment
Renal	Serum creatinine ≥4.5 mg/dL or a serum creatinine of 4 mg/dL in the presence of severe volume overload, acidosis, or hyperkalemia	Serum creatinine <4 mg/dL and fluid and electrolyte status is stable
	Persistent oliguria, urine output of ≤10 mL/h for 16 to 24 hours with rising serum creatinine	Urine output >10mL/h with a decrease of serum creatinine ≥1.5 mg/dL or normalization of serum creatinine
Hepatic	Signs of hepatic failure including encephalopathy, increasing ascites, liver pain, hypoglycemia	All signs of hepatic failure have resolved*
Gastrointestinal	Stool guaiac repeatedly >3-4+	Stool guaiac negative
Skin	Bullous dermatitis or marked worsening of pre-existing skin condition (avoid topical steroid therapy)	Resolution of all signs of bullous dermatitis

*Discontinue all further treatment for that course. Consider starting a new course of treatment at least 7 weeks after cessation of adverse event and hospital discharge.

Supplied: When reconstituted with 1.2 mL Sterile Water for Injection, USP, each mL contains: aldesleukin 18 million IU (1.1 mg), mannitol 50 mg and sodium dodecyl sulfate 0.18 mg, buffered with approximately 0.17 mg monobasic sodium phosphate and 0.89 mg dibasic sodium phosphate to a pH of 7.5 (range 7.2 to 7.8). Preservative-free. Single use vials of 22 million IU (1.3 mg).

Before and after reconstitution and dilution, store in a refrigerator at 2 to 8°C.

Reviewed 1997

PROLOPA® Pr

Roche

Levodopa—Benserazide

Antiparkinsonian Agent

Pharmacology: The symptoms of Parkinson's disease are to a high degree associated with striatal dopamine deficiency and degeneration of the dopamine containing neurons in the nigrostriatal bundle. However, administration of dopamine is ineffective in the treatment of Parkinson's syndrome, because it does not cross the blood-brain barrier.

Levodopa, which does permeate the blood-brain barrier, appears to correct the akinesia of Parkinson's disease by the formation of dopamine at nigro striatal dopaminergic sites that remain functional. While rigidity and tremor also improve with levodopa therapy, these symptoms seem to be related to a disturbed balance of neurotransmitters.

When levodopa is given alone, a large proportion of it does not reach the brain, because it is rapidly converted to dopamine by aromatic acid decarboxylase at extracerebral sites. Large doses must therefore be given in order to allow for sufficient levodopa to reach the brain and provide the dopamine needed to correct the deficiency observed in patients with Parkinson's disease. These large doses of levodopa result in a sharp increase in the levels of circulating dopamine and other dopa metabolites, and the excessive quantities of these substances in extracerebral tissues may explain in part some of the side effects of levodopa, such as nausea and vomiting and cardiac arrhythmias. The high incidence of these adverse effects requires a very slow titration of levodopa and may interfere with the administration of an effective drug dosage.

The decarboxylase inhibitor, benserazide, at the recommended therapeutic doses, does not cross the blood-brain barrier. Thus, administration of this agent makes it possible to inhibit the peripheral decarboxylation of levodopa without significantly affecting its metabolism in the brain. In this way, the formation of circulating dopamine is minimized and the incidence of extracerebral side effects may thereby be reduced while at the same time permitting more levodopa to reach the brain. Combined therapy with levodopa and benserazide reduces the amount of levodopa required for optimum therapeutic benefit and permits an earlier response to therapy.

Nevertheless, combined therapy does not decrease the adverse reactions due to central effects of levodopa. In fact, dyskinesias and oscillations in performance occur at lower dosages of levodopa and earlier in treatment during combined therapy.

Plasma levels of levodopa are markedly increased when the drug is given in combination with benserazide compared to those obtained after levodopa alone. There is also a reduction in the level of dopa metabolites when levodopa is combined with benserazide. Clinical trials have suggested that the combination of levodopa and benserazide in a 4 to 1 ratio is effective in reducing peripheral adverse effects and the amount of levodopa required for therapeutic improvement.

The pharmacokinetics of ^{14}C-benserazide administered alone and in combination with levodopa has been studied in 6 patients with Parkinson's disease. Three of these patients were administered 50 mg of the inhibitor by both i.v. and oral routes. Three additional patients received oral does of 50 mg ^{14}C-benserazide alone and also in combination with 200 mg of levodopa.

Comparison of the time-plasma concentration curves of total radioactivity in the patients receiving oral and i.v. ^{14}C-benserazide indicated that between 66 and 74% of the administered dose was absorbed from the gastrointestinal tract. Peak plasma concentrations of radioactivity were detected 1 hour after oral administration in 5 of the 6 patients.

Elimination of the ^{14}C-label was primarily by urinary excretion with 86 to 90% of an i.v. dose recovered in the urine while 53 to 64% of the oral dose was detected in the urine. The majority of the ^{14}C radioisotope was accounted for in the urine within 48 hours after administration. Fecal recovery studies conducted over 5 to 8 days accounted for the majority (approximately 30%) of the remainder of administered ^{14}C-benserazide.

In still another experiment in man, where ^{14}C-dopa had been administered either i.v. (0.1 mg/kg) or orally (3 mg/kg), the administration of benserazide (16 to 24 mg orally) enhanced the ^{14}C-dopa and ^{14}C-methyldopa plasma concentrations 6- to 10-fold over those observed with the administration of ^{14}C-dopa alone. Also, the ^{14}C-phenolcarboxylic acid concentration was 1/5 to 1/10th that which was observed when ^{14}C-dopa was administered alone.

Pyridoxine HCl (vitamin B_6) accelerates the decarboxylation of levodopa and is therefore contraindicated in patients on levodopa alone. However, the efficacy of combination therapy is generally unaffected by pyridoxine.

Indications: Treatment of Parkinson's syndrome with exception of drug-induced parkinsonism.

The administration of Prolopa is associated with amelioration of the symptoms of Parkinson's syndrome with the advantage that combined therapy significantly diminishes the incidence of the levodopa-induced peripheral side effects of nausea, vomiting and possibly cardiac arrhythmias.

This results in an advantage for those patients who previously were unable to tolerate an optimal daily dosage of levodopa. Improved gastrointestinal tolerance also provides for a more rapid induction of therapy, e.g., optimum dosage can in most cases be achieved within 2 to 3 weeks.

However, combined therapy with levodopa and benserazide increases the incidence of centrally mediated abnormal movements earlier in therapy and can lead to an earlier appearance of oscillations in performance. Thus, when combined therapy with levodopa and benserazide is instituted it is important to strive at using and maintaining a dosage regimen which balances efficacy with freedom from dyskinesias.

Despite the dramatic symptomatic improvement it produces in many patients with Parkinson's disease, levodopa does not arrest the progression of the disease and there is evidence to indicate that drug adverse effects increase with continuing use. Combined therapy, because of the advantages already described, is therefore indicated only when its use is capable of improving the quality of life of the patient. However, there is little to be gained by substituting combined therapy for levodopa in patients already on stable, effective and well tolerated levodopa therapy.

Contraindications: As with levodopa, patients in whom sympathomimetic amines are contraindicated should not receive Prolopa.

MAO inhibitors cannot be given concomitantly and should be withdrawn at least 2 weeks prior to initiating therapy with Prolopa.

Prolopa should not be administered to patients with clinical or laboratory evidence of uncompensated cardiovascular, endocrine, renal, hepatic, hematologic or pulmonary disease. Prolopa is also contraindicated in patients with narrow angle glaucoma.

Prolopa is contraindicated in patients with a known sensitivity to levodopa or benserazide.

Warnings: Before initiating therapy in patients already receiving levodopa, the levodopa should be discontinued at least 12 hours before Prolopa is started. Prolopa therapy should be instituted at a level that will provide approximately 15% of the previous amount of levodopa (see Dosage).

Prolopa is not indicated in the management of intention tremor, Huntington's chorea, or drug-induced extrapyramidal effects.

Since Prolopa may induce CNS side effects effects shortly after beginning its use, and at lower doses of levodopa, it is important to administer the dosage in careful increments and to observe patients carefully for the development of abnormal involuntary movements. These movements and oscillations in performance may appear earlier with combination therapy. Should they occur, a dosage reduction is indicated.

All patients should be carefully observed for signs of depression with suicidal tendencies or other serious behavioral changes. Extreme caution should be used in treating patients with a history of psychotic disorders or who are receiving psychotherapeutic agents such as reserpine, phenothiazines or tricyclic antidepressants.

Care should be exercised in administering Prolopa to patients with a history of myocardial infarction or who have atrial, nodal or ventricular arrhythmias. Patients with cardiac abnormalities should have their treatment with Prolopa initiated in a facility with adequate monitoring equipment and provision for intensive care.

Care should be exercised in administering this drug to patients with a history of melanoma or with suspicious undiagnosed skin lesions.

Children and Young Adults: The safety of Prolopa in patients under the age of 18 has not been established. Animal studies have suggested the possibility of skeletal abnormalities when benserazide is administered before ossification is complete.

It should also be borne in mind that Prolopa stimulates human growth hormone secretion.

Pregnancy and *Lactation:* Although Prolopa's effects on human pregnancy are unknown, levodopa has caused visceral and skeletal malformations in rabbits. Before prescribing the combination of levodopa and benserazide, physicians should consider the possibility that a woman of childbearing potential may be pregnant and should weigh the anticipated benefits of the drug against its possible hazards to the mother and to the fetus. In the event women of childbearing age become pregnant or wish to become pregnant while taking Prolopa the physician should consider the desirability of discontinuing this drug. Prolopa should not be given to nursing mothers.

Precautions: General: Regular assessments of cardiovascular, hepatic, hematopoietic and renal function should be performed in all patients during extended therapy. Patients with a history of convulsive disorders should be treated cautiously if Prolopa is incorporated into their regimen. The possibility of upper gastrointestinal hemorrhage occurring in patients with a history of peptic ulcer must be borne in mind when treating them with Prolopa.

Physical Activity: Patients with severe parkinsonism who improve on Prolopa therapy should be advised to resume normal activities gradually and with caution as rapid mobilization may increase the risk of injury, especially in those patients with osteoporosis or phlebothrombosis. Physiotherapy and appropriate safeguards may be useful during this phase.

Patients with Wide-Angle Glaucoma: Patients with chronic wide-angle glaucoma can be treated cautiously with Prolopa, provided the intraocular pressure is well controlled. The intraocular pressure should be monitored carefully during therapy. Rarely pupillary dilatation and activation of later Horner's syndrome have been reported during levodopa treatment.

Drug Interactions: (a) Cardiovascular Drugs: Postural hypotensive episodes have been reported; therefore, Prolopa should be administered cautiously and blood pressure monitored in patients on antihypertensive medication. It may be necessary to adjust the dosage of the latter particularly during the initial stages of therapy with Prolopa. (b) Psychoactive Drugs: If concomitant administration of psychoactive drugs is necessary, they should be administered with great caution. Patients should be carefully observed for unusual untoward drug effect (see Contraindications and Warnings). (c) Anesthetics: If general anesthesia is required, Prolopa can be discontinued the night before surgery and therapy recommended as soon as the patient is able to receive oral medication.

Adverse Effects: The most common serious adverse reactions occurring with Prolopa are the abnormal involuntary movements. Dosage reduction can diminish those reactions though often at the expense of increasing parkinsonism. Other serious adverse reactions are oscillations in performance, psychiatric disorders and, less frequently, cardiovascular effects.

Involuntary movements: choreiform, dystonic and other involuntary movements. Muscle twitching and blepharospasm occur less often and may be taken as early signs of overdosage. The appearance of these reactions should prompt a reduction in the dose administered. The incidence of involuntary movements reported by several investigators was 30 to 40% in the first month and 50 to 60% or more by 6 to 9 months.

Oscillations in Performance: Periodic oscillations in performance constitute the most serious problem encountered after prolonged levodopa therapy and appear earlier with combined therapy than when levodopa is used alone. Three types have been described:

End of Dose Akinesia: episodic re-emergence of Parkinsonian symptoms 3 or more hours after each dose of levodopa, often following a period of dyskinesia. This type of akinesia tends to occur progressively earlier after each dose during prolonged therapy and is regarded as resulting from a temporary insufficiency of dopamine at the appropriate receptor sites.

On-off Phenomenon: a rapid alternation between a state of satisfactory motility, usually with oral-facial dyskinesias, and a rigid akinetic state without dyskinesias. This oscillation of performance is also regarded as being associated with a temporary insufficiency of dopamine.

Akinesia Paradoxica (Hypotonic Freezing): irregular episodes of sudden freezing, usually of short duration, with the patient unable to move, accompanied by hypotonia and postural instability. These episodes are at times accompanied by autonomic symptoms. Hypotonic freezing is regarded as possibly associated with a severe temporary deficiency in norepinephrine in progressively depleted and damaged norepinephrine pathways.

Psychiatric Disorders: paranoid ideation, psychotic episodes, depression (with or without development of suicidal tendencies) and dementia. In depressed patients, levodopa may give rise to an improvement in mood in a small number of individuals. However, when administered to patients with bipolar depression, it tends regularly to produce hypomania. Various psychiatric disturbances have been reported in about 20% of patients.

Other adverse reactions that occur less frequently during treatment with Prolopa are:

Cardiovascular: arrhythmias and orthostatic hypotensive episodes, hypertension, nonspecific ECG changes, flushing, phlebitis and angina pectoris have also been reported.

Neurologic: ataxia, faintness, impairment of gait, headache, increased hand tremor, akinetic episodes, torticollis, trismus, tightness of the mouth, lips or tongue, oculogyric crisis, weakness, numbness, bruxism and convulsions.

Intellectual function: progressive impairment of intellectual and autonomic functions has been described, particularly in akinetic patients, after prolonged levodopa therapy.

Psychiatric: increased libido with serious antisocial behavior, euphoria, lethargy, sedation, stimulation, fatigue and malaise, confusion, insomnia, nightmares, hallucinations and delusions, agitation and anxiety.

Gastrointestinal: nausea and vomiting, constipation, diarrhea, epigastric and abdominal distress or pain, flatulence, eructation, hiccups, sialorrhea, difficulty in swallowing, bitter taste, dry mouth, duodenal ulcer, gastrointestinal bleeding, burning sensation of the tongue.

Dermatologic: dark sweat, sweating, edema, hair loss, pallor and rash.

Hematological: hemolytic anemia, leukopenia, agranulocytosis.

Musculoskeletal: low back pain, muscle spasm and twitching, musculoskeletal pain.

Respiratory: cough, hoarseness, bizarre breathing pattern, postnasal drip.

Genitourinary: dark urine, hematuria, nocturia and urinary frequency, retention or incontinence and changes in libido.

Ophthalmologic: blurred vision, diplopia, dilated pupils, activation of latent Horner's syndrome.

Miscellaneous: fever, weight variation.

Laboratory abnormalities: Elevations of BUN, serum uric acid, AST, ALT, LDH, bilirubin, alkaline phosphatase or PBI have been observed. Positive Coombs' tests have been observed during extended therapy, both with Prolopa and with levodopa alone but hemolytic anemia is extremely rare.

Overdose: Symptoms: Symptoms of acute overdosage may be qualitatively similar to those listed under Adverse Effects and to those observed in patients overdosed with levodopa alone, but will possibly be of greater magnitude.

Treatment: General supportive measures should be employed, along with immediate gastric lavage. I.V. fluids should be administered judiciously and an adequate airway maintained. ECG monitoring should be instituted and the patient carefully observed for the development of arrhythmias and if required appropriate antiarrhythmic therapy should be provided. To date, the value of dialysis in the treatment of Prolopa overdosage is not known. Consideration should be

Prolopa (cont'd)

given to the possibility of multiple drug ingestion by the patient. Pyridoxine is ineffective in reversing the effects of Prolopa overdosage.

Dosage: In order to achieve maximal benefit and reduce the incidence of adverse reactions, therapy with Prolopa must be individualized and drug administration must be continuously matched to the needs and tolerance of the patient. Because of the increased availability of levodopa to the CNS when administered in combined therapy, titration and adjustments of dosage should be made in small steps and the dosage ranges recommended should usually not be exceeded. The appearance of involuntary movements should be regarded as a sign of levodopa toxicity and as an indication of overdosage, usually requiring a reduction in dosage. Treatment should aim at maximal benefit without dyskinesias.

Levodopa should be discontinued for at least 12 hours before initiating therapy with Prolopa.

Capsules should be swallowed whole and not opened or dissolved in liquid.

Initiation of treatment in patients not on levodopa therapy: The initial recommended dose is 1 capsule of Prolopa 100-25 once or twice a day. This dose may be carefully increased by 1 capsule every third or fourth day until an optimal therapeutic effect is obtained without dyskinesias. Near the upper limits of dosage, the increments should be made slowly, say at 2- to 4-week intervals. The dosage should be divided, aiming at a frequency of dosing of at least 4 times daily taken with or immediately after meals.

The optimal dosage for most patients is usually 4 to 8 capsules of Prolopa 100-25 daily (400 to 800 mg of levodopa) divided into 4 to 6 doses. Most patients require no more than 6 capsules of Prolopa 100-25 (600 mg of levodopa)/day.

Individual patient response varies. Some patients, e.g., post encephalitic Parkinson patients, may only tolerate a slower rate of increase in dosage, e.g., 1 capsule of Prolopa 100-25 at weekly intervals, since these patients are more sensitive to levodopa and usually only tolerate lower dosages.

Prolopa 200-50 capsules are intended only for maintenance therapy once the optimal dosage has been determined using Prolopa 100-25 capsules. No patient should receive more than 5 to 6 capsules of Prolopa 200-50 daily (1 000 to 1 200 mg of levodopa in combined therapy) during the first year of therapy.

Treatment should be continued for at least 3 to 6 weeks before it is concluded that Prolopa therapy has not benefited the patient.

Initiation of treatment in patients on levodopa therapy: Allow at least 12 hours or more to elapse between the last dose of levodopa and the first dose of Prolopa. A dosage of Prolopa should be used that will provide approximately 15% of the previous levodopa daily dosage. For example, if a patient is receiving 4 000 mg of levodopa/day, the dosage of Prolopa 100-25 should not exceed 6 capsules/day (600 mg of levodopa) divided into 4 to 6 doses.

Adjustment and maintenance of therapy in all patients: Prolopa 200-50 capsules may be used for maintenance therapy once the optimal dosage has been determined using Prolopa 100-25 capsules. Prolopa 50-12.5 capsules should be used when frequent dosing is required to minimize adverse effects. During the first year of treatment the total daily dosage should not exceed 1 000 to 1 200 mg of levodopa in combined therapy.

The variability in dosage response of patients is considerable. Some individuals may experience oscillations in performance with a diurnal rhythm of periods of symptomatic control alternating with periods of akinesia (end of dose), with return of Parkinson's symptoms, which can frequently be corrected by rescheduling individual doses. A low protein diet tends to potentiate and stabilize the effects of levodopa, whereas a high protein diet may decrease the effect of levodopa, although with combined therapy this effect may be less prominent. The predominant limiting factor in treatment with Prolopa is the occurrence of involuntary movements. These frequently can be controlled by reducing the dosage of levodopa and varying the frequency of individual doses. A progressive decrease in the threshold for dyskinetic manifestations and an increase in the incidence of oscillations in performance have been reported after a certain time on levodopa therapy. These appear earlier in the course of combined treatment with Prolopa than with levodopa alone.

In an attempt to avoid the emergence, or decrease the incidence of these manifestations, it is recommended that, after the initial period, the daily maintenance dosage of levodopa as combined therapy should be reduced slowly (at a rate of about 50 mg a month) over a period of a few months, to a maintenance level without dyskinesias. After 1 year of therapy, the patient should usually receive not more than 6 capsules of Prolopa 100-25 daily (600 mg of levodopa) divided into at least 4 to 6 doses.

Other antiparkinson agents, e.g., anticholinergics, may be continued during Prolopa therapy, and should not be abruptly withdrawn. However, as treatment proceeds, their dosage may need to be altered.

Interruption of therapy: If Prolopa therapy is interrupted for a brief period, the previous dosage may be administered as soon as the patient is again able to take oral medication. If, however, therapy is interrupted for a longer period, a lower dosage should be given and the dosage should be adjusted gradually. In many cases, patients can be returned rapidly to their previous therapeutic dosage.

Supplied: Prolopa 50-12.5: Each light grey and blue capsule, imprinted ROCHE C and PROLOPA 50-12.5 (black ink) alternating between cap and body, contains: levodopa 50 mg and benserazide base 12.5 mg in the form of benserazide HCl. Nonmedicinal ingredients: gelatin, indigotine, iron oxide, magnesium stearate, mannitol, microcrystalline cellulose, povidone, talc and titanium dioxide. Energy: 0.7 kJ (0.2 kcal). Gluten-, lactose-, paraben-, sodium-, sulfite- and tartrazine-free. Bottles of 100.

Prolopa 100-25: Each blue and flesh colored capsule, imprinted ROCHE C and PROLOPA 100-25 (black ink) alternating between cap and body, contains: levodopa 100 mg and benserazide base 25 mg in the form of benserazide HCl. Nonmedicinal ingredients: gelatin, indigotine, iron oxide, magnesium stearate, microcrystalline cellulose, povidone, talc and titanium dioxide. Energy-, gluten-, lactose-, paraben-, sodium-, sulfite- and tartrazine-free. Bottles of 100.

Prolopa 200-50: Each blue and caramel colored capsule, imprinted ROCHE C and PROLOPA 200-50 (black ink) alternating between cap and body, contains: levodopa 200 mg and benserazide base 50 mg in the form of benserazide HCl. Nonmedicinal ingredients: gelatin, indigotine, iron oxide, magnesium stearate, microcrystalline cellulose, povidone, talc and titanium dioxide. Energy-, gluten-, lactose-, paraben-, sodium-, sulfite- and tartrazine-free. Bottles of 100.

Keep in a tightly closed, light-resistant container. Store at 15 to 30°C.

(Shown in Product Recognition Section)

PROLOPRIM® Ⓟ

Glaxo Wellcome

Trimethoprim

Antibacterial

Pharmacology: Trimethoprim blocks the production of tetrahydrofolic acid from dihydrofolic acid by binding to and reversibly inhibiting the enzyme dihydrofolate reductase. This binding is very much stronger for the bacterial enzyme than for the corresponding mammalian enzyme; thus, trimethoprim selectively interferes with bacterial biosynthesis of nucleic acids and proteins by causing a deficiency of endogenously produced thymine. The effect is usually bactericidal in the absence of an adequate external supply of thymine or thymidine.

Trimethoprim is rapidly absorbed following oral administration. Peak blood levels occur 1 to 4 hours after oral administration. The half-life is 8 to 10 hours. Trimethoprim blood levels are dose and time dependent.

A single oral dose of 100 mg produced serum trimethoprim levels ranging from 0.42 to 1.68 µg/mL at 2 hours and 0.32 to 1.55 µg/mL at 4 hours after dosing. Single 200 mg doses of trimethoprim produced serum levels approximately twice as high: ranging from 1.87 to 3.11 µg/mL at 2 hours and 1.57 to 2.58 µg/mL at 4 hours after dosing. Table I gives the mean serum concentrations as a function of time for both of these doses.

Trimethoprim exists in the blood as free, protein bound and metabolized forms. The free form is considered to be the therapeutically active form. Approximately 44% of trimethoprim is protein bound in the blood.

Excretion is chiefly by the kidneys through glomerular filtration and tubular secretion. Urine concentrations are considerably higher than are concentrations in the blood. Approximately 85% of the excreted drug is in its unmetabolized form.

Urine levels are time and dose related. After a single 100 mg oral dose, urinary trimethoprim levels ranged from 30 to 160 µg/mL during the 0 to 4 hour collection period and declined to 18 to 91 µg/mL during the 8 to 24 hour collection period. 50% to 60% of trimethoprim was excreted in the urine within 24 hours. Single doses of 200 mg produced urinary trimethoprim levels approximately twice as high. In one study, urinary concentrations ranged from 74 to 394 µg/mL for the 0 to 4 hour collection period and in a second study from 71 to 91 µg/mL for a 0 to 12 hour collection period. These levels are well above the MIC's required to be effective against the majority of urinary pathogens.

Concentrations of trimethoprim in prostatic and vaginal secretions are consistently greater than those found in the serum. Oral administration of 5 to 8.1 mg/kg for 1 to 2 days produced trimethoprim levels of 1.9 to 5.6 µg/mg in prostatic tissue, and levels of 2.5 to 5.6 µg/mL in prostatic secretions. Administration of 320 mg/day of trimethoprim in combination with sulfamethoxazole for 10 days produced levels of 2.5 to 10 µg/mL in vaginal secretions.

Sufficient trimethoprim is excreted in the feces to eliminate susceptible organisms from the fecal flora. The dominant fecal organisms, Bacteroides and Lactobacillus are not susceptible to trimethoprim; trimethoprim does not cause intestinal upset due to imbalance in the normal colonic flora.

Emergence of resistant strains of fecal bacteria has not been a problem, thus preventing urogenital superinfection by such organisms from the gut.

Trimethoprim should be given with caution to patients with possible folate deficiency. Trimethoprim in vivo and in vitro, in concentrations achieved in plasma by standard dosages, caused no disturbances of folate metabolism in human bone marrow. Folates may be administered concomitantly without interfering with the antibacterial action of trimethoprim except in Enterococci infections.

Indications: For treatment of acute, uncomplicated urinary tract infections due to susceptible strains of E. coli and K. pneumoniae. Limited clinical experience suggests the probability of therapeutic response in infections due to susceptible strains of P. mirabilis and Enterobacter.

Cultures and susceptibility tests should be performed to determine the susceptibility of the bacteria to trimethoprim. Therapy may be initiated prior to obtaining the results of these tests.

For infections associated with urinary tract complications such as obstruction, or where tissue involvement is suspected, the combination of trimethoprim/sulfamethoxazole has been shown to be superior to trimethoprim alone.

Contraindications: Hypersensitivity to trimethoprim. Individuals with documented megaloblastic anemia due to folate deficiency.

Pregnancy and *Lactation:* During pregnancy and during the nursing period.

Warnings: Rare incidents of serious hypersensitivity reactions has been reported on trimethoprim therapy. In elderly patients concurrently receiving certain diuretics, primarily thiazides, an increased incidence of thrombocytopenia with purpura has been reported.

Rare incidents of trimethoprim interfering with hematopoiesis have been reported, especially when administered in large doses and/or for prolonged periods.

The presence of clinical signs such as sore throat, fever, pallor, purpura or jaundice may be early indications of serious blood disorders. Complete blood counts should be obtained if any of these signs are noted in a patient receiving trimethoprim and the drug discontinued if a significant reduction in the count of any formed blood element is found.

Table I—Proloprim

Mean Serum Concentrations as a Function of Time

Dose (mg)	No. of Volunteers	Mean Serum Concentration of Trimethoprim (µg/mL at indicated times (h) after dosing) 0.5	1	2	4	8	24
100	18	0.68	1.06	1.11	0.96	0.68	0.20
200	6	1.50	2.29	2.12	2.03	1.58	0.43

Precautions: Trimethoprim should be given with caution to patients with possible folate deficiency. Folates may be administered concomitantly without interfering with the antibacterial action of trimethoprim, except in Enterococci infections.

An increased incidence of skin rashes has been observed when double the recommended dosage was administered.

General: Children: The safety of trimethoprim in infants under 2 months of age has not been demonstrated. The effectiveness of trimethoprim as a single agent has not been established in children under 12 years of age.

Fertility: No adverse effects on fertility or general reproductive performance were observed in rats given trimethoprim in oral dosages as high as 70 mg/kg/day for males and 14 mg/kg/day for females.

Impaired Renal or Hepatic Function: Trimethoprim should also be given with caution to patients with impaired renal or hepatic function (see Pharmacology and Dosage).

Drug Interactions: Trimethoprim may inhibit the hepatic metabolism of phenytoin. Trimethoprim, given at a common clinical dosage increased the phenytoin half-life and decreased the phenytoin metabolic clearance rate. When administering these drugs concurrently, one should be alert for possible excessive phenytoin effect.

Occasional reports suggest that patients receiving pyrimethamine as malarial prophylaxis at doses in excess of 25 mg weekly may develop megaloblastic anemia should cotrimoxazole be prescribed concurrently. The same interaction is likely if trimethoprim be prescribed concurrently.

Trimethoprim may potentiate the anticoagulant activity of warfarin via stereo-selective inhibition of its metabolism.

Laboratory Test Interactions: Trimethoprim can interfere with a serum methotrexate assay as determined by the competitive binding protein technique (CBPA) when a bacterial dihydrofolate reductase is used as the binding protein. No interference occurs, however, if methotrexate is measured by a radioimmunoassay (RIA).

The presence of trimethoprim may also interfere with the Jaffé alkaline picrate reaction assay for creatinine resulting in overestimations of about 10% in the range of normal values.

Adverse Effects: Hematologic: neutropenia, anemia (megaloblastic, hemolytic, aplastic), leukopenia, thrombocytopenia, methemoglobinemia.

Dermatologic: rash, pruritus and phototoxic skin eruptions. At the recommended dosage regimens of 100 mg b.i.d. or 200 mg once daily each for 10 days, the incidence of rash is 2.9 to 6.7%. In clinical studies which employed high doses of trimethoprim, an elevated incidence of rash was noted. These rashes were maculopapular, morbilliform, pruritic and generally mild to moderate appearing 7 to 14 days after the initiation of therapy.

Hypersensitivity: Rare reports of exfoliative dermatitis, erythema multiforme, Stevens-Johnson syndrome, Lyell syndrome and anaphylaxis have been reported.

Gastrointestinal: nausea, vomiting, abdominal cramps, glossitis, stomatitis. There have been rare reports of cholestatic jaundice. Elevations of serum transaminase and bilirubin have been noted, but the significance of this finding is unknown.

Metabolic: hyperkalemia, hyponatremia.

Neurologic: Aseptic meningitis has rarely been reported.

Others: headache, joint pain, apathy, fatigue, muscle weakness, nervousness, fever and increases in BUN and serum creatinine levels.

The following adverse reactions have not been reported in patients receiving trimethoprim; however, based upon clinical experience with chemically related drugs, the possibility of these reactions occurring should be recognized.

CNS: convulsions, ataxia, tinnitus and vertigo.

Overdose: Symptoms: Acute: Signs of acute overdosage with trimethoprim may appear following ingestion of 1 g or more of the drug and include nausea, vomiting, dizziness, headaches, mental depression, confusion, and bone marrow depression (see Chronic).

Treatment: Treatment consists of gastric lavage and general supportive measures. Acidification of the urine will increase renal elimination of trimethoprim. Peritoneal dialysis is not effective and hemodialysis only moderately effective in eliminating the drug.

Chronic: Use of trimethoprim in high doses and/or for extended periods of time may cause bone marrow depression manifested as thrombocytopenia, leukopenia and/or megaloblastic anemia. If signs of bone marrow depression occur, trimethoprim should be discontinued and the patient should be given leucovorin; 5 to 15 mg leucovorin daily has been recommended by some investigators.

Dosage: Adults: 100 mg every 12 hours or 200 mg every 24 hours, each for 10 days.

The use of trimethoprim in patients with a creatinine clearance of less than 15 mL/min is not recommended. For patients with creatinine clearance of 15 to 30 mL/min, the dose should be 50 mg every 12 hours.

Supplied: 100 mg: Each white, biconvex tablet imprinted with PROLOPRIM 09A on the same side as score mark, contains: trimethoprim 100 mg. Nonmedicinal ingredients: lactose, sodium starch glycolate (potato), cornstarch and magnesium stearate. Bottles of 100 and 500.

200 mg: Each yellow, round, biconvex tablet imprinted with PROLOPRIM R2C on the same side as score mark, contains: trimethoprim 200 mg. Nonmedicinal ingredients: sodium starch glycolate (potato), cornstarch, magnesium stearate and quinoline yellow WS. Bottles of 100.

Store at 15 to 30°C. Protect from light and keep dry.

(Shown in Product Recognition Section)

Reviewed 1997

PROMAZINE HYDROCHLORIDE ℞

Abbott

Antipsychotic—Antiemetic

Supplied: Each mL contains: promazine HCl 50 mg. Nonmedicinal ingredients: ascorbic acid, sodium chloride, sodium hydroxide, sodium metabisulfite and water for injection. Ampuls of 1 mL. Boxes of 10.

PROMETHAZINE HYDROCHLORIDE INJECTION ℞

Bioniche

Antihistamine

Supplied: Each mL of sterile solution contains: promethazine base 25 mg (as the HCl). Also contains potassium metabisulfite 0.75 mg, sodium sulfite 1 mg and trisodium citrate and citric acid to adjust pH. Ampuls of 1 and 2 mL, boxes of 10. Store at room temperature (15 to 30°C). Protect from light.

PROMETRIUM™ ℞

Schering

Progesterone

Progestin

Pharmacology: Micronized progesterone is an oral dosage form of the naturally occurring steroid; it is chemically identical to progesterone of ovarian origin. Micronization of progesterone improves its absorption by the digestive tract by increasing the surface area in contact between the steroid and the mucous membrane. Pharmacokinetic studies indicate that plasma progesterone levels within the luteal range are achieved with peak levels at 2 to 4 hours following administration of progesterone (see Table I).

Table I—Prometrium

Mean (n = 15) Day 5 Progesterone C_{max} and AUC Values after Administration of Prometrium 200 and 300 mg once Daily

	Prometrium Dose (mg/day)	
	200	300
C_{max} (nmol/L)	121.2	192.7
AUC_{0-10} (nmol•hr/L)	321.8	558.7

Progesterone is metabolized primarily by the liver and is excreted mainly in the urine. Patients with illness related to the liver and/or kidneys should be monitored closely.

Progesterone exerts significant antiproliferative effects on the endometrium and suppresses endometrial mitotic activity through suppression of nuclear estradiol receptors, reduction of epithelial and stromal DNA synthesis and induction of 17β-estradiol dehydrogenase and isocitric dehydrogenase.

Indications: In women with intact uteruses as an adjunct to postmenopausal estrogen replacement therapy to significantly reduce the risk of endometrial hyperplasia and carcinoma.

Contraindications: Severe liver disease such as cholestatic jaundice or hepatitis or a history of severe liver disease, hepatic cell tumors, Rotor syndrome or Dubin-Johnson syndrome.

Unexplained abnormal vaginal bleeding.

Known or suspected breast malignancy or pathology.

Known or suspected progesterone-dependent neoplasia.

Conditions or a history of conditions of rare occurrence which have occurred or have worsened with pregnancy or the use of sex steroids i.e. herpes gestationis, jaundice of pregnancy, otosclerosis, severe pruritus, or porphyria.

Cerebral apoplexy or thrombophlebitis.

Known sensitivity to progesterone capsules or any of its individual components. **Prometrium contains peanut oil and should never be used by patients allergic to peanuts.**

Warnings: Treatment should be discontinued if the results of liver function tests become abnormal or if cholestatic jaundice appears.

Several published epidemiological studies have documented an association between a modest increase in the risk of developing breast cancer and the use of hormone replacement therapy in menopause when given for periods exceeding 10 years. Information is still lacking to show whether the risks of combination estrogen-progestin therapy differ from those of estrogen used alone.

Instruction for breast self-examination should be given to all women.

Precautions: Occupational Hazards: Transient and occasional somnolence or dizziness may occur in some patients 1 to 4 hours after ingestion of progesterone, particularly if administered with food. Activities requiring concentration, good attention, good coordination or reflex action should be avoided when the above-mentioned neurological symptoms occur. In most cases, these problems can be avoided by taking the capsules at the recommended times. The 200 mg dosage should be taken at bedtime. The 300 mg dosage should be divided into 2 doses, 100 mg 2 hours after breakfast and 200 mg at bedtime.

Chloasma is occasionally seen during the use of estrogen and/or progestin-containing preparations, especially in women with a history of chloasma gravidarum. In women with a tendency to chloasma, exposure of the skin to natural or artificial sunlight may induce or aggravate the condition.

There are no indications of an increased cardiovascular risk associated with natural progesterone use. However, a slightly increased risk of these disorders has been reported with estrogen/progestin-containing oral contraceptive preparations, therefore patients with cardiovascular disorders (or a history of this condition) should be kept under close medical supervision.

Pregnancy: If the patient is exposed to progesterone during the first 4 months of pregnancy or if she becomes pregnant while taking this drug she should be appraised of the potential risks to the fetus.

Lactation: Detectable amounts of progesterone have been identified in the milk of mothers receiving progesterone. The possible effects of progesterone on the nursing infant have not been determined.

Abnormal uterine bleeding due to its prolongation, irregularity or heaviness, occurring during therapy, should prompt diagnostic measures such as endometrial biopsy, hysteroscopy or uterine curettage to rule out the possibility of uterine pathology.

The pretreatment physical examination, prior to initiation of hormone replacement therapy, should include blood pressure determination, breast, abdomen and pelvic organ examination as well as Papanicolaou smear. This examination should exclude the presence of genital or breast neoplasia before considering hormone replacement therapy.

Pathologists should be advised of progestin therapy when relevant specimens are submitted.

Adverse Effects: Adverse events which could be considered to be possibly associated with progesterone therapy are: breakthrough bleeding, spotting, and menstrual irregularity.

Under the recommended conditions of use (200 mg h.s.), dizziness, somnolence, cramps or nausea have been reported occasionally.

Fatigue, headache, vertigo, lightheadedness or migraine have been reported rarely.

Breast: Breast tenderness may occur with the use of progesterone.

Other adverse events which are generally attributed to synthetic progestins and which may possibly occur during progesterone treatment include: chloasma, pruritus, jaundice, rash, fluid retention, mental depression and thrombotic disorders.

The following laboratory results may be altered by the use of progesterone: levels of gonadotropin, plasma progesterone and urinary pregnanediol.

Overdose: Symptoms and Treatment: The toxicity of progesterone is very low. Symptoms that may possibly occur are:

Prometrium (cont'd)

nausea, vomiting, somnolence and dizziness. No specific antidote is available. If necessary, symptomatic treatment can be given.

Dosage: Hormone Replacement Therapy: In general, the dosage is 200 mg daily for the last 14 days of estrogen treatment per cycle (i.e., from day 8 to day 21 for a 28 day cycle, and from day 12 to day 25 for a 30 day cycle). Estrogens should be administered daily at the lowest effective dose. Patients being treated with high dosages of estrogen (equivalent to 1.25 mg conjugated estrogens or higher) should be administered 300 mg daily for the last 12 to 14 days of estrogen treatment.

The 200 mg daily dosage should be taken at bedtime. Patients receiving 300 mg daily should take 1 capsule (100 mg) in the morning and 2 capsules (200 mg) at bedtime. The morning dose should be taken 2 hours after breakfast.

If a patient is treated with 200 mg daily (total dose at bedtime) and she forgets to take this dose, she should take an extra dose of 1 capsule (100 mg) the following morning and continue taking the rest of the capsules as prescribed. If a patient is treated with 300 mg daily, and she forgets to take a morning or evening dose, she should not take the missed dose.

The dosage of progesterone should be proportional to the dosage of estrogen. With adequate adjustment of the dosage of progesterone, patients should experience either regular withdrawal uterine bleeding or cessation of bleeding (amenorrhea).

Abnormal uterine bleeding due to its prolongation, irregularity or heaviness, in any patient receiving hormone replacement therapy, requires institution of prompt diagnostic measures such as endometrial biopsy, hysteroscopy or uterine curettage to rule out uterine pathology.

Information for the Patient: See Blue Section—Information for the Patient "Prometrium".

Supplied: Each capsule contains: micronized progesterone 100 mg. Nonmedicinal ingredients: arachis (peanut) oil, gelatin, glycerin, lecithin; coloring agent: titanium dioxide. Unit dose blister packages of 28, bottles of 100. Store at controlled room temperature 15 to 30°C. Protect from light.

(Shown in Product Recognition Section)

PRONESTYL® Ⓟ
PRONESTYL®-SR Ⓟ

Squibb

Procainamide HCl

Antiarrhythmic Agent

Pharmacology: Procainamide increases the effective refractory period of the atria, and to a lesser extent the bundle of His-Purkinje system and ventricles of the heart. It reduces impulse conduction velocity in the atria, His-Purkinje fibers, and ventricular muscle, but has variable effects on the atrioventricular node, a direct slowing action and a weaker vagolytic effect which may speed atrioventricular conduction slightly. Myocardial excitability is reduced in the atria, Purkinje fibers, papillary muscles, and ventricles by an increase in the threshold for excitation, combined with inhibition of ectopic pacemaker activity by retardation of the slow phase of diastolic depolarization, thus decreasing automaticity especially in ectopic sites. Contractility of the undamaged heart is usually not affected by therapeutic concentrations, although slight reduction of cardiac output may occur, and may be significant in the presence of myocardial damage. Therapeutic levels of procainamide may exert vagolytic effects and produce slight acceleration of heart rate, while high or toxic concentrations may prolong atrioventricular conduction time or induce atrioventricular block, or even cause abnormal automaticity and spontaneous firing, by unknown mechanisms.

The ECG may reflect these effects by showing slight sinus tachycardia (due to the anticholinergic action) and widened QRS complexes and, less regularly, prolonged QT and PR intervals (due to longer systole and slower conduction), as well as some decrease in QRS and T wave amplitude. These direct effects of procainamide on electrical activity, conduction, responsiveness, excitability and automaticity are characteristic of a Group 1A antiarrhythmic agent, the prototype for which is quinidine; procainamide effects are very similar. However, procainamide has weaker vagal blocking action than does quinidine, does not induce alpha-adrenergic blockade, and is less depressing to cardiac contractility.

Pharmacokinetics: The action of procainamide begins almost immediately after i.v. administration. Following i.m. injection, the therapeutic effect appears in 15 to 60 minutes. Oral administration of procainamide capsules produces a therapeutic effect approximately 1 hour after a 1 g loading dose or 4 hours after initiating treatment every 3 hours with the maintenance dose. Peak plasma concentrations occur about 1 hour after oral administration, indicating an overall half-time for absorption of approximately 20 minutes. For ventricular arrhythmias, therapeutic plasma levels have been reported to be 3 to 10 μg/mL, with those for the majority of patients in the range of 4 to 8 μg/mL.

Procainamide's apparent volume of distribution (Vd) is usually between 1.75 and 2.5 L/kg body weight. About 75% of the procainamide is concentrated in highly perfused tissues. Approximately 20% is bound to plasma albumin.

Following oral administration of the conventional procainamide capsule, over 90% is recovered in the urine as unchanged drug or metabolites indicating almost complete absorption of the drug.

On the average, about 60% (range 30 to 80%) of the drug is excreted unchanged. The half-time for elimination from the body may vary from 2.5 to 6 hours or longer. The plasma clearance of procainamide is 400 to 600 mL/minute; renal clearance is 200 to 400 mL/minute.

In humans, procainamide is acetylated, and N-acetylprocainamide (NAPA), an active metabolite, can be detected in both plasma and urine. The dose fraction of procainamide excreted as NAPA is extremely variable, ranging from 6% to 52%.

Following oral administration of sustained release tablets every 6 hours, the mean steady-state serum concentrations of procainamide and NAPA achieved are approximately equivalent to those of a comparable dose of the conventional capsule administered every 3 hours.

When 500 mg sustained release tablets were administered for 3 days, approximately 48% and 15% were recovered in the urine as procainamine and NAPA, respectively. Other metabolites e.g., free and conjugated p-aminobenzoic acid which usually account for about 10% of the dose, were not analyzed in this study.

Indications:

> No antiarrhythmic drug has been shown to reduce the incidence of sudden death in patients with asymptomatic ventricular arrhythmias. Most antiarrhythmic drugs have the potential to cause dangerous arrhythmias; some have been shown to be associated with an increased incidence of sudden death. In light of the above, physicians should carefully consider the risks and benefits of antiarrhythmic therapy for all patients with ventricular arrhythmias.

Ventricular Arrhythmias: For the treatment of documented life-threatening ventricular arrhythmias, such as sustained ventricular tachycardia. Procainamide may also be used for the treatment of patients with documented symptomatic ventricular arrhythmias when the symptoms are of sufficient severity to require treatment. Because of the proarrhythmic effects of procainamide, its use should be reserved for patients in whom, in the opinion of the physician, the benefit of treatment clearly outweighs the risks.

For patients with sustained ventricular tachycardia, procainamide therapy should be initiated in the hospital. Hospitalization may also be required for certain other patients depending on their cardiac status and underlying cardiac disease.

The effects of procainamide in patients with recent myocardial infarction have not been adequately studied and, therefore, its use in this condition cannot be recommended.

Supraventricular Arrhythmias: In the treatment of atrial fibrillation, particularly if the condition is of recent development and the treatments of choice cannot be used or are ineffective. The drug may also be used in paroxysmal atrial tachycardia which cannot be controlled by reflex stimulation or by other measures.

Pronestyl-SR is a sustained release formulation indicated as maintenance therapy for patients stabilized on regular Pronestyl.

Contraindications: Hypersensitivity to the drug is an absolute contraindication; in this connection, cross sensitivity to procaine and related drugs must be borne in mind. Procainamide should not be administered to patients with complete atrioventricular heart block. Procainamide is also contraindicated in cases of high degree AV block unless an electrical pacemaker is operative. Procainamide should not be used in patients with myasthenia gravis.

Because of the possibility of precipitous lowering of blood pressure with i.v. procainamide, it should not be used in patients with severe congestive heart failure, renal failure or shock.

An established diagnosis of systemic lupus erythematosus is a contraindication to procainamide therapy, since aggravation of symptoms is highly likely.

In the particular ventricular arrhythmia called torsades de pointes, Group 1A antiarrhythmic drugs are contraindicated. Administration of procainamide in such cases may aggravate this type of ventricular tachycardia instead of suppressing it.

Warnings: Mortality: The results of the Cardiac Arrhythmia Suppression Trial (CAST) in post-myocardial infarction patients with asymptomatic ventricular arrhythmias showed a significant increase in mortality and in non-fatal cardiac arrest rate in patients treated with encainide or flecainide compared with a matched placebo-treated group. CAST was continued using a revised protocol with the moricizine and placebo arms only. The trial was prematurely terminated because of a trend towards an increase in mortality in the moricizine treated group.

The applicability of these results to other populations or other antiarrhythmic agents is uncertain, but at present it is prudent to consider these results when using any antiarrhythmic agent.

Blood Dyscrasias: Agranulocytosis, bone marrow depression, neutropenia, hypoplastic anemia and thrombocytopenia in patients receiving procainamide have been reported at a rate of approximately 0.5%. Most of these patients received procainamide within the recommended dosage range. Fatalities have occurred (with approximately 20 to 25% mortality in reported cases of agranulocytosis). Since most of these events have been noted during the first 12 weeks of therapy, it is recommended that complete blood counts including white cell, differential and platelet counts be performed at weekly intervals for the first 3 months of therapy, and periodically thereafter. Complete blood counts should be performed promptly if the patient develops any signs of infection (such as fever, chills, sore throat or stomatitis), bruising or bleeding. If any of these hematologic disorders are identified, procainamide therapy should be discontinued. Blood counts usually return to normal within 1 month of discontinuation. Caution should be used in patients with pre-existing marrow failure or cytopenia of any type (see Adverse Effects).

Patients should be instructed to report promptly any flu type symptoms such as malaise and aches, as well as any soreness of the mouth, throat or gums, unexplained fever, skin rash, unusual bleeding or bruising, or symptoms that resemble arthritis or symptoms of an upper respiratory tract infection.

Positive ANA: The prolonged administration of procainamide often leads to the development of a positive anti-nuclear antibody (ANA) test with or without symptoms of lupus erythematosus-like syndrome. If a positive ANA titer develops, the benefit/risk ratio related to continued procainamide therapy should be assessed. This may necessitate discontinuation of procainamide and substitution of alternative antiarrhythmic therapy.

Sulfite Sensitivity: Pronestyl injection contains sodium bisulfite, that may cause allergic-type reactions including anaphylactic symptoms and life-threatening or less severe asthmatic episodes in susceptible individuals.

The overall prevalence of sulfite sensitivity in the general population is unknown and probably low. Sulfite sensitivity is seen more frequently in asthmatic than in nonasthmatic individuals.

Precautions: The solution intended for i.v. use should be diluted prior to administration (see Dosage).

Patients should be closely observed for possible hypersensitivity reactions, especially if procaine or local anesthetic sensitivity is suspected, and for muscular weakness if myasthenia gravis is a possibility.

During administration of the drug, evidence of untoward myocardial responses should be carefully watched for in all patients. In the presence of an abnormal myocardium, procainamide may at times produce untoward responses. In atrial fibrillation or flutter, the ventricular rate may increase suddenly as the atrial rate is slowed. Adequate digitalization reduces, but does not abolish this danger. If myocardial damage exists, ventricular tachycardia is particularly hazardous. Correction of atrial fibrillation, with resultant forceful contractions of the atrium, may cause a dislodgement of mural thrombi and produce an embolic episode. However, it has been suggested that in a patient who is already discharging emboli, procainamide is more likely to stop than to aggravate the process.

Adjustment of the heart rate in a patient who has developed ventricular tachycardia during an occlusive coronary episode should be carried out with extreme caution. Caution is also required in marked disturbances of atrioventricular conduction such as AV block, bundle branch block, or severe digitalis intoxication, where the use of procainamide may result in additional depression of conduction and ventricular asystole or fibrillation. Widening of the QRS complex on the ECG calls for extreme caution. The effects of procainamide in digitalis intoxication, particularly where the arrhythmia is accompanied by marked conduction disturbances, are unpredictable and fatalities have occurred.

ECG monitoring should be carried out during i.v. therapy and, whenever practical, during i.m. therapy. If ECGs give evidence of impending heart block, parenteral administration should be discontinued at once. Since patients with severe organic heart disease and ventricular tachycardia may also have complete heart block which is difficult to diagnose under these circumstances, this complication should always be kept in mind when treating ventricular arrhythmias with procainamide. If the ventricular rate is significantly slowed by procainamide without attainment of regular atrioventricular conduction, the drug should be discontinued and the patient re-evaluated as asystole may result under these circumstances.

Serious hypotension can result from peripheral vasodilation and by depressing myocardial contractility and cardiac output. At high plasma levels, procainamide may produce sinus tachycardia due to reflex sympathetic response to its hypotensive effect. Large doses may increase cardiac automaticity and can induce complete atrioventricular block, cardiac standstill or ventricular extrasystoles that may proceed to ventricular fibrillation. These effects on the myocardium are reflected in the ECG; a widening of the QRS complex occurs most consistently; less regularly, the PR and QT intervals are prolonged; and the QRS and T waves show some decrease in voltage. These actions of procainamide may be intensified in patients with congestive heart failure.

During the first day following acute myocardial infarction, absorption of oral procainamide can be very poor. Therefore, when warranted, it is suggested that the drug be administered i.m. or i.v.

Plasma procainamide and NAPA concentrations rise markedly with increases in BUN and correlate well with creatinine clearance. Should patients with impaired kidney function and/or liver disease receive unadjusted dosage, symptoms of overdosage (principally ventricular tachycardia and severe hypotension) may occur due to drug accumulation. Similarly, plasma concentrations have been found to be increased in elderly patients possibly due to declining renal function in this age group. The frequency of administration should be reduced in patients with renal or hepatic insufficiency or in elderly patients.

Plasma concentrations of procainamide and NAPA should be monitored in patients with renal disease, hepatic disease, cardiac failure or low cardiac output states.

In patients with cardiac failure or shock or in patients with low cardiac output and extrarenal azotemia, the apparent volume of distribution and/or the elimination rate of procainamide can decrease considerably for a given dose, thereby resulting in increased plasma concentrations. Such patients should therefore be carefully monitored and the dose or frequency of administration reduced if warranted.

Instances of a syndrome resembling systemic lupus erythematosus have been reported in connection with oral maintenance procainamide therapy. The mechanism of this lupus erythematosus-like syndrome is uncertain. Polyarthralgia, arthritis, fever, pleuritic pain and skin lesions are common symptoms; to a lesser extent myalgia, pleural effusion and pericarditis may occur. Rare cases of thrombocytopenia or Coombs' positive hemolytic anemia have been reported, and may be related to this syndrome. Patients receiving procainamide for extended periods of time or in whom symptoms suggestive of lupus erythematosus-like syndrome appear, should have antinuclear antibody titers measured at regular intervals. The drug should be discontinued if there is a rising titer (ANA) or clinical symptoms of lupus erythematosus-like syndrome appear. Lupus erythematosus-like syndrome is usually reversible upon discontinuation of the drug. If discontinuation of the drug does not cause remission of the symptoms, steroid therapy may be effective. If lupus erythematosus-like syndrome develops in a patient with recurrent life-threatening arrhythmias not controllable by other antiarrhythmic agents, steroid suppressive therapy may be used concomitantly with procainamide.

Laboratory Tests: Laboratory tests including complete blood count, ECG, and serum creatinine or urea nitrogen may be indicated, depending on the clinical situation, and periodic checking of the complete blood count and antinuclear antibody is helpful in early detection of untoward reactions (see Warnings, Blood Dyscrasias).

Pregnancy: Animal reproduction studies have not been conducted with procainamide. It is also not known whether procainamide can cause fetal harm when administered to a pregnant woman or can affect reproduction capacity.

There has been some evidence of the diffusion of procainamide across the placental membrane. Therefore, due to the potential accumulation and slow rate of elimination of procainamide and N-acetylprocainamide in the fetus, the potential benefit of the use of procainamide during pregnancy should be weighed against the possible hazard to the fetus.

Lactation: Both procainamide and N-acetylprocainamide are excreted in human milk, and absorbed by the nursing infant. Because of the potential for serious adverse reactions in nursing infants, a decision should be made to discontinue nursing or discontinue the drug, taking into account the importance of the drug to the mother.

Children: Safety and effectiveness in children have not been established.

Drug Interactions: Antiarrhythmics: Concurrent use with procainamide may result in additive or antagonistic cardiac effects and/or additive toxic effects. Dosage reduction may be necessary.

Concurrent use with Class I antiarrhythmic agents (e.g., quinidine or disopyramide) may produce enhanced prolongation of conduction or depression of contractility and hypotension, especially in patients with cardiac decompensation. Such use should be reserved for patients with serious arrhythmias unresponsive to a single drug, and should be employed only if close observation is possible.

Concurrent use with amiodarone may result in increased plasma procainamide and N-acetylprocainamide concentrations and subsequent toxicity. The dosage of i.v. procainamide should be reduced by 20 to 30% during concomitant administration. In addition, additive electrophysiologic effects may occur during concomitant use with agents that prolong the QT interval.

Beta Blockers: Procainamide may potentiate the cardiac depressant action of beta blocking agents such as propranolol.

Anticholinergics: Procainamide enhances the anticholinergic effects. Extreme caution must be exercised with such a combination.

Anticholinesterases: Procainamide antagonizes the effect of anticholinesterases in myasthenia gravis and paralysis returns.

Antihypertensives: Procainamide may potentiate the hypotensive effects of thiazide diuretics and other antihypertensive agents. Adjustment of dosage may be required.

Cimetidine: It has been reported that the histamine H_2-antagonist cimetidine reduces renal clearance of procainamide and NAPA resulting in higher plasma concentrations for longer durations. Caution should be exercised when administering these drugs concurrently especially in the elderly who have a reduced ability to clear all three. Dosage modification may be required.

Neuromuscular Blocking Agents: Procainamide potentiates the effects of skeletal muscle relaxants such as succinylcholine. It also may enhance or prolong the neuromuscular blocking activity of bacitracin, colistimethate, dihydrostreptomycin, gentamicin, gramicidin, kanamycin, neomycin, polymyxin B, streptomycin, and viomycin, producing respiratory depression.

Antibiotics: Procainamide has also been reported to interact with kanamycin, neomycin and streptomycin to cause apnea and muscle weakness, due to an additive neuromuscular blocking effect.

Trimethoprim: The renal clearance of procainamide and NAPA is reduced by trimethoprim, resulting in increased pharmacodynamic response.

Adverse Effects: The overall incidence of adverse effects with procainamide is about 9.2%. The most commonly occurring are gastrointestinal upset 3.9%, cardiovascular effects (ventricular dysrhythmias, bradycardia, hypotension and shock) 3.3% and drug fever 1.6%.

The most serious adverse reactions reported are granulocytopenia and the development of ANA. Granulocytopenia is most likely to occur within the first 3 months of therapy. Prolonged administration of procainamide often leads to the development of a positive ANA test with or without symptoms of lupus erythematosus-like syndrome perhaps more often in patients who are slow acetylators.

Because procainamide is a peripheral vasodilator, rapid i.v. administration may produce transient but at times severe lowering of blood pressure, particularly in conscious patients. I.M. injection is less likely to be accompanied by serious falls in blood pressure, and hypotension following oral administration is rare. Serious disturbances of cardiac rhythm such as ventricular asystole or fibrillation are also more common with i.v. administration. Precautionary measures to be followed during i.v. injection are given in the section on Dosage.

Incidence greater than 1%: Elevated ANA, sometimes associated with drug-induced lupus syndrome. Gastrointestinal symptoms, especially with large oral doses: anorexia, nausea, vomiting, diarrhea. (In patients on long-term procainamide therapy with sustained release preparations, the above reactions have been reported with an incidence greater than 5%.) Cardiovascular Effects: bradycardia, arrhythmias, cardiac failure, shock. Hypersensitivity reactions, which may be manifested by one or more of the following: pruritus, urticaria, angioneurotic edema, maculopapular rash, fever, eosinophilia, hypergammaglobulinemia, flushing.

Incidence less than 1%: granulocytopenia (incidence about 0.5%), sometimes resulting in death; thrombocytopenia; immune hemolytic anemia; convulsions; psychosis with hallucinations; confusion; mental depression; giddiness; lightheadedness; weakness; bitter taste.

Rare: hypotension, second degree heart block (oral route); a case was reported with fever and chills plus nausea, vomiting, abdominal pain, acute hepatomegaly, and a rise in serum glutamic oxaloacetic transaminase following a single dose of the drug; vasculitis (hypersensitivity-type).

Overdose: Symptoms: Signs and symptoms of overdosage of procainamide include severe hypotension, ventricular fibrillation, widening of the QRS complex, prolonged P-R- and Q-T intervals, lowering of the R and T waves, increasing A-V block, junctional tachycardia, intraventricular conduction delay, oliguria, lethargy, confusion, nausea and vomiting.

Plasma levels above 10 µg/mL are increasingly associated with toxic findings, which are seen occasionally in the 10 to 12 µg/mL range, more often in the 12 to 15 µg/mL range, and commonly in patients with plasma levels greater than 16 µg/mL. If available, procainamide and N-acetylprocainamide plasma levels may be helpful in assessing the potential degree of toxicity and response to therapy. Transient high plasma levels of procainamide may induce hypotension after i.v. administration, and occasionally after oral therapy. This hypotension affects systolic more than diastolic pressures, especially in hypertensive patients. Such high levels may also produce CNS depression, tremor, and even respiratory depression.

Treatment: If ingestion is recent, gastric lavage or emesis may reduce absorption. Dopamine, phenylephrine or norepinephrine may be helpful in reversing severe hypotensive responses.

Management of overdosage includes symptomatic treatment with ECG and blood pressure monitoring. Procainamide toxicity can usually be treated, if necessary, by administering vasopressors after adequate fluid volume replacement. I.V. infusion of 1/6 molar sodium lactate injection reportedly reduces the cardiotoxic effects of procainamide.

The urinary elimination of procainamide is proportional to the glomerular filtration rate but is also affected by changes in urinary pH. Procainamide is relatively lipid-soluble as a free base but the ionized form is not. Acid urine, therefore, leads to ion trapping of procainamide which enters the urine by passive diffusion from the plasma. Accordingly, renal clearance of procainamide can be considerably increased by maintaining a low urinary pH and high flow rates.

If procainamide toxicity causes severe hypotension and renal insufficiency, urinary elimination of procainamide and NAPA is decreased and hemodialysis may be required. Hemodialysis significantly reduces the serum half-life of procainamide and effectively removes procainamide and NAPA. Peritoneal dialysis is not effective.

It has been reported that one patient who ingested approximately 7 g of procainamide HCl recovered after treatment consisting of i.v. norepinephrine, i.v. furosemide, attempted volume expansion with albumin, and hemodialysis. Also reported is the case of an elderly patient who recovered after ingestion of approximately 19 g of procainamide HCl. The patient was treated with i.v. isoproterenol and i.v. epinephrine. The latter report suggested that insertion of a ventricular pacing electrode is a reasonable precautionary measure in case high grade AV block develops.

Dosage: Selection of the dose and route of administration should be made with the following in mind: The optimum plasma level is 4 to 8 µg/mL.

Therapeutic Urgency: Oral administration is preferred. When parenteral therapy is necessary, i.m. administration is the method of choice. I.V. use should be limited to emergencies and continuous ECG monitoring is mandatory when this route is used.

Pronestyl (cont'd)

In elderly patients and in patients with impaired renal function (decreased creatinine clearance) excretion is delayed and reduced frequency of administration is required (see Precautions).

An alkaline urine indicates a reduction in excretion rate, and the necessity for reduced frequency of administration.

Patients with cardiac failure, shock, low cardiac output and extrarenal azotemia should be carefully monitored and the dose or frequency of administration reduced if necessary.

Excretion rates appear to be unchanged by furosemide and other diuretics but are decreased by the use of acetazolamide, due to the production of alkaline urine.

Following stabilization on i.v. therapy, conversion to oral procainamide should be carried out as soon as practical.

Should toxic or sub-therapeutic levels be suspected, the patient's plasma procainamide should be determined and adjusted accordingly.

Patients vary in response to a dose of procainamide. Nevertheless, the following **guidelines** should be considered when deciding upon the patient's actual requirements: Parenteral dose: I.M: If the oral route is not feasible because of vomiting or unreliable absorption, 0.5 to 1 g may be given i.m., repeated every 3 hours until oral therapy is possible.

I.V.: The 10% (100 mg/mL) solution can be used for i.v. administration. This solution should be further diluted to facilitate accurate control of dosage. The dose should be administered at a rate not greater than 25 to 50 mg/minute by either direct i.v. administration or infusion. Slow administration allows some initial tissue distribution. Solutions prepared with 5% dextrose should be discarded after 8 hours.

Caution: I.V. use of procainamide may be accompanied by a hypotensive response, sometimes precipitous. For this reason, the dose schedules described below should be monitored electrocardiographically, so that the drug may be stopped when the arrhythmia is interrupted or when excessive widening of the QRS complex or prolongation of the PR interval suggests the occurrence of myocardial toxicity. Patients should be kept in a supine position and blood pressure should be measured almost continuously during the i.v. administration. If the fall in blood pressure exceeds 15 mmHg, the i.v. administration should be temporarily discontinued. Solutions of phenylephrine HCl injection, or norepinephrine injection, should be available to counteract severe hypotensive responses.

Direct I.V. Administration: Each mL of the 10% (100 mg/mL) solution should be further diluted to 10 to 20 mL with 5% Dextrose Injection USP prior to direct i.v. administration to facilitate control of dosage rate.

To reduce the possibility of a hypotensive response, 100 mg doses may be administered every 5 minutes by direct i.v. injection, at a rate not exceeding 50 mg/minute, until the arrhythmia is suppressed or a dose of 1 g has been administered. Blood pressure must be monitored and the ECG read before each dose. An effect is usually seen after the first or second injection. It is unusual to require more than 5 or 6 injections to achieve satisfactory antiarrhythmic effects.

To maintain therapeutic levels, procainamide infusion may then be started at a rate of 2 to 6 mg of procainamide per minute (see Table I) depending on the patient's body weight, circulatory condition and renal function.

I.V. Infusion: An alternative method of achieving and then maintaining a therapeutic plasma concentration is to infuse 500 to 600 mg of procainamide at a constant rate over a period of 25 to 30 minutes and then to change to another infusion for maintenance at a rate of 2 to 6 mg/minute (see Table I).

Table I—Pronestyl/Pronestyl-SR

Dilutions and Rates for I.V. Infusions*

Approximate Final Concentration	Infusion Bottle Size (mL)	mL of Pronestyl (100 mg/mL) to be added	Infusion Rate
0.2% (2 mg/mL)	500	10	1–3 mL/min
	250	5	
0.4% (4 mg/mL)	500	20	0.5–1.5 mL/min
	250	10	

* Caution: The flow rate of all i.v. infusion solutions must be closely monitored. These dilutions are calculated to deliver 2 to 6 mg/minute at the infusion rates listed.

I.V. therapy should be terminated as soon as the patient's basic cardiac rhythm appears to be stabilized and, if indicated, the patient should be placed on oral procainamide maintenance therapy. A period of about 3 to 4 hours (1 half-life) should elapse after the last i.v. dose of procainamide before administering the first oral dose of procainamide.

Surgical Use: For arrhythmias occurring during surgery, the suggested parenteral dose is 0.5 to 1.0 g preferably given i.m.

Oral Dose: Capsules: For ventricular tachycardia: An initial loading dose of 1 g followed thereafter by a total daily dose of 50 mg/kg of body weight in divided doses at 3 hour intervals is recommended (see Table II).

Table II—Pronestyl/Pronestyl-SR

Oral Dose for Ventricular Tachycardia

To provide 50 mg/kg/day:*	
give patients weighing less than 55 kg,	250 mg every 3 hours;
give patients weighing between 55 and 91 kg,	375 mg every 3 hours;
give patients over 91 kg,	500 mg every 3 hours.

* This dosage schedule is for use as a guide for treating the average patient but all patients must be considered on an individual basis.

In atrial arrhythmias, an initial dose of 1.25 g may be followed in 1 hour by 0.75 g if there have been no ECG changes. A dose of 0.5 to 1 g may then be given every 2 hours until the arrhythmia is interrupted or the limit of tolerance is reached. Suggested maintenance dosage is 0.5 to 1 g every 4 to 6 hours.

Pronestyl-SR Tablets are a sustained release dosage form not intended for initial therapy. For initial therapy by oral administration, conventional oral formulations of procainamide are recommended (see Supplied). Patients stabilized to an appropriate dosage level can be transferred to an equivalent daily dosage regimen of sustained release tablets.

The duration of action of procainamide supplied in this sustained release form allows dosing at intervals of every 6 hours, which may encourage patient compliance.

For Ventricular Tachycardia: The suggested maintenance dosage of sustained release tablets is 50 mg/kg of body weight daily given in divided doses at 6 hour intervals (see Table III).

Table III—Pronestyl/Pronestyl-SR

Maintenance Dosage of Pronestyl-SR for Ventricular Tachycardia

To provide approximately 50 mg/kg/day:*	
give patients weighing less than 55 kg,	500 mg every 6 hours;
give patients weighing between 55 and 91 kg,	500 mg or 1 g every 6 hours;
give patients over 91 kg,	1 g every 6 hours.

* This dosage schedule is for use as a guide for treating the average patient; however, each patient must be considered on an individual basis.

For Atrial Fibrillation and Paroxysmal Atrial Tachycardia: The suggested maintenance dosage of sustained release tablets is 0.5 to 1 g every 6 hours.

Patients should be advised not to break or chew the sustained release tablet, as this would interfere with designed dissolution characteristics.

Supplied: Pronestyl: Capsules: 250 mg: Each yellow capsule contains: procainamide HCl 250 mg. Nonmedicinal ingredients: lactose, magnesium stearate and talc. Capsule shell: D&C yellow No. 10, FD&C yellow No. 6, gelatin, printing ink and titanium dioxide. Tartrazine-free. Bottles of 100.

375 mg: Each white and orange capsule contains: procainamide HCl 375 mg. Nonmedicinal ingredients: magnesium stearate and talc. Capsule shell: FD&C yellow No. 6, gelatin, printing ink and titanium dioxide. May or may not contain lactose. Tartrazine-free. Bottles of 100.

500 mg: Each yellow and orange capsule contains: procainamide HCl 500 mg. Nonmedicinal ingredients: magnesium stearate and talc. Capsule shell: D&C yellow No. 10 and FD&C yellow No. 6. May or may not contain lactose. Tartrazine-free. Bottles of 100.

Keep containers tightly closed. Store at room temperature.

Injection: Each mL of parenteral solution for i.m. or i.v. use contains: procainamide HCl 100 mg (10%). Nonmedicinal ingredients: benzyl alcohol 0.9% (w/v) and sodium bisulfite 0.09% as preservatives and water for injection. Hydrochloric acid or sodium hydroxide for pH adjustments (pH 4.0 to 6.0). Vials of 10 mL.

Store vials at room temperature (15 to 30°C) and protect from light, freezing and exposure to excessive heat. The 10% solution, which is colorless initially, may in time develop a slightly yellow color. This change does not prevent its use, but a solution which becomes discolored in any other way should not be used.

Pronestyl-SR: Each greenish-yellow, biconvex, oval, veneer-coated, sustained release tablet contains: procainamide HCl 500 mg. Nonmedicinal ingredients: carbomer 934P, carnauba wax, microcrystalline cellulose, povidone, silica gel and stearic acid. Coating: alcohol, D&C yellow No. 10, ethylcellulose, FD&C blue No. 2, hydroxypropyl cellulose, hydroxypropyl methylcellulose, printing ink, titanium dioxide and triethyl citrate. Bottles of 100. Store at room temperature; avoid excessive heat.

(Shown in Product Recognition Section)

Reviewed 1997

PROPADERM® Ⓟ
Roberts

Beclomethasone Dipropionate
Topical Corticosteroid

Supplied: Cream: Each g contains: beclomethasone dipropionate 0.025%. Cartoned tubes of 15 and 45 g.

Lotion: Each mL contains: beclomethasone dipropionate 0.025%. Plastic squeeze bottles of 60 mL.

PROPANTHEL™
ICN

Propantheline Bromide
Anticholinergic

Supplied: Each round, peach-colored, sugar-coated tablet, imprinted ICN P8, contains: propantheline bromide, USP 15 mg. Nonmedicinal ingredients: calcium stearate, croscarmellose sodium, dibasic calcium phosphate, microcrystalline cellulose, opalux light peach color and wax solution. Bottles of 100 and 1 000.

PROPECIA® Ⓟ
MSD

Finasteride
Type II 5 Alpha-reductase Inhibitor

Pharmacology: Finasteride is a competitive and specific inhibitor of Type II 5 alpha-reductase, an intracellular enzyme that converts the androgen testosterone into dihydrotestosterone (DHT). Two distinct isozymes of 5 alpha-reductase are found in mice, rats, monkeys, and humans: Type I and II. Each of these isozymes is differentially expressed in tissues and developmental stages. In humans, Type I 5 alpha-reductase is predominant in the sebaceous glands of most regions of skin, including scalp and liver. Type I 5 alpha-reductase is responsible for approximately one-third of circulating DHT. The Type II 5 alpha-reductase isozyme is primarily found in prostate, seminal vesicles, epididymides and hair follicles as well as liver, and is responsible for two-thirds of circulating DHT.

In humans, the mechanism of action of finasteride is based on its preferential inhibition of the Type II isozyme. Using native tissues (scalp and prostate), in vitro binding studies examining the potential of finasteride to inhibit either isozyme revealed a 100-fold selectivity for the human Type II 5 alpha-reductase over Type I isozyme (IC_{50}=500 and 4.2 nM for Type I and II, respectively). For both isozymes, the inhibition by finasteride is accompanied by reduction of the inhibitor to dihydrofinasteride and adduct formation with NADP+. The turnover for the enzyme complex is slow ($t_{1/2}$ approximately 30 days for the Type II enzyme complex and 14 days for the Type I complex).

Finasteride has no affinity for the androgen receptor and has no androgenic, antiandrogenic, estrogenic, antiestrogenic, or progestational effects. Inhibition of Type II 5 alpha-reductase blocks the peripheral conversion of testosterone to DHT, resulting in significant decreases in serum and tissue DHT concentrations. Finasteride produces a rapid reduction in serum DHT concentration, reaching 65% suppression within 24 hours of oral dosing with a 1 mg tablet.

In men with male pattern hair loss (androgenetic alopecia), the balding scalp contains miniaturized hair follicles and increased amounts of DHT compared with hairy scalp. Administration of finasteride decreases scalp and serum DHT concentrations in these men. By this mechanism, finasteride interrupts a key factor in the development of androgenetic alopecia in those patients genetically predisposed.

In a study in 15 healthy male subjects, the mean bioavailability of finasteride 1 mg tablets was 65% (range, 26 to 170%), based on the ratio of AUC relative to a 5 mg i.v. dose infused over 60 minutes. Following the i.v. infusion, mean plasma clearance was 165 mL/min (range, 70 to 279 mL/min) and mean steady-state volume of distribution was 76 L (range, 44 to 96 L). In a separate study, the bioavailability of finasteride was not affected by food.

Approximately 90% of circulating finasteride is bound to plasma proteins. Finasteride has been found to cross the blood-brain barrier.

Indications: For the treatment of male pattern hair loss (androgenetic alopecia) in **men** who have mild to moderate scalp hair loss of the vertex and anterior mid-scalp. Clinical studies were conducted in men between 18 to 41 years of age.

Not indicated for use in women or children.

Contraindications: *Pregnancy:* Use in women when they are or may potentially be pregnant (see Warnings and Precautions, Exposure to Finasteride—Risk to Male Fetus).

Hypersensitivity to any component of this product.

Not indicated for use in women or children.

Warnings: *Pregnancy* and *Lactation:* Finasteride is not indicated for use in women. Women should not handle crushed or broken finasteride tablets when they are or may potentially be pregnant (see Contraindications). Because of the ability of Type II 5 alpha-reductase inhibitors such as finasteride to inhibit conversion of testosterone to dihydrotestosterone, finasteride may cause abnormalities of the external genitalia of a male fetus when administered to a pregnant woman. It is not known whether finasteride is excreted in human milk.

Precautions: General: Caution should be used in the administration of finasteride in patients with liver function abnormalities, as finasteride is metabolized in the liver.

Other causes of alopecia should be ruled out prior to prescribing finasteride. Efficacy and duration of treatment should be assessed periodically by the treating physician.

Exposure to Finasteride—Risk to Male Fetus: Women should not handle crushed or broken tablets of finasteride when they are or may potentially be pregnant because of the possibility of absorption of finasteride and the subsequent potential risk to a male fetus (see Warnings, Pregnancy and Lactation). Finasteride tablets are coated and will prevent contact with the active ingredient during normal handling, provided that the tablets have not been broken or crushed.

Geriatrics: Clinical studies with finasteride have not been conducted in elderly men with male pattern hair loss.

Children: Finasteride is not indicated for use in children.

Drug Interactions: No drug interactions of clinical importance have been identified. Finasteride does not appear to affect significantly the cytochrome P450-linked drug metabolizing enzyme system. Compounds which have been tested in man have included antipyrine, digoxin, glyburide, propranolol, theophylline and warfarin, and no interactions were found. However, patients on medication with narrow therapeutic indices, such as phenytoin, should be carefully monitored when treatment with finasteride is initiated.

Other Concomitant Therapy: Although specific interaction studies were not performed, in clinical studies finasteride doses of 1 mg or more were used concomitantly with ACE inhibitors, acetaminophen, alpha blockers, benzodiazepines, beta blockers, calcium-channel blockers, cardiac nitrates, diuretics, H_2 antagonists, HMG-CoA reductase inhibitors, prostaglandin synthetase inhibitors (NSAIDs), and quinolones, without evidence of clinically significant adverse interactions.

Drug/Laboratory Test Interactions: In clinical studies with finasteride in men 18 to 41 years of age, the mean value of serum prostate-specific antigen (PSA) decreased from 0.7 ng/mL at baseline to 0.5 ng/mL at month 12. When finasteride is used in older men who have benign prostatic hyperplasia (BPH), PSA levels are decreased by approximately 50%. Until further information is gathered in men >41 years of age without BPH, consideration should be given to doubling the PSA level in men undergoing this test while taking finasteride.

Information to be Provided to the Patient: Patients should be advised that: finasteride is to be used by men only and should be taken daily as prescribed.

In general, daily use for 3 months or more is necessary before hair growth is increased and/or further hair loss is prevented.

The clinical benefits of finasteride can only be maintained with continuous use of finasteride.

A small number of men may experience less desire to have sex and/or difficulty in achieving an erection. In clinical studies, these side effects disappeared in men who stopped taking finasteride and in most men who continued treatment.

If the patient experiences sustained impairment in sexual function or any other unintended effect, the patient should be advised to consult with the prescribing physician regarding continuation of the medication.

As with all other medications, it is important that any other treating physician(s) be aware of the patient's use of finasteride.

Women who are or may potentially be pregnant must not use finasteride. They should not handle crushed or broken tablets of finasteride.

Adverse Effects: Finasteride for male pattern hair loss has been evaluated for safety in clinical studies involving more than 3 200 men and is generally well tolerated. In 3 12-month, placebo-controlled, double-blind, multicenter studies of comparable design, the overall safety profiles of finasteride and placebo were similar. Discontinuation of therapy due to any clinical adverse experience occurred in 1.7% of 945 men treated with finasteride and 2.1% of 934 men treated with placebo.

In these studies, the following drug-related adverse experiences were reported in $\geq$1% of men treated with finasteride or placebo, respectively: decreased libido (1.8%, 1.3%), erectile dysfunction (1.3%, 0.7%) and ejaculation disorder (1.2%, 0.7%; primarily decreased volume of ejaculate:[0.8%, 0.4%]). Integrated analysis of clinical adverse experiences showed that during treatment with finasteride, 36 (3.8%) of 945 men had reported one or more of these adverse experiences as compared to 20 (2.1%) of 934 men treated with placebo ($p=0.04$).

Resolution of these adverse reactions occurred in men who discontinued therapy with finasteride and in 58% who continued therapy. In a separate study, the effect of finasteride on ejaculate volume was measured and was not different from that seen with placebo.

A sexual function questionnaire was self-administered by patients participating in the 2 vertex baldness trials to detect more subtle changes in sexual function. At month 12, statistically significant differences were found in 3 of 4 domains (sexual interest, erections, and perception of sexual problems) when compared to placebo. However, no significant difference was seen in the question on overall satisfaction with sex life.

The adverse reactions profile for 547 patients who continued on finasteride for up to 24 months was similar to that observed in the 12-month controlled studies.

Finasteride is also in use for the treatment of older men with BPH at 5 times the dosage recommended for male pattern hair loss. Additional adverse reactions that have been reported at the 5 mg dosage in men with BPH are: breast tenderness and enlargement, and hypersensitivity reactions, including lip swelling and rash. In the clinical studies with finasteride, the incidence of these events was not different from placebo.

Laboratory Tests: No difference in standard laboratory parameters was observed between patients treated with placebo or finasteride.

Overdose: Symptoms and Treatment: Patients have received single doses of finasteride up to 400 mg and multiple doses of finasteride up to 80 mg/day for 3 months without adverse reactions.

No specific treatment for overdosage with finasteride is recommended.

Dosage: The recommended dosage is one 1 mg tablet daily. Finasteride may be taken with or without food.

In general, daily use for 3 months or more is necessary before hair growth is increased and/or further hair loss is prevented. Continued use is recommended to obtain maximum benefit. Withdrawal of treatment leads to reversibility of effect within 12 months.

Dosage in Renal Insufficiency: Adjustments in dosage are not necessary in patients with varying degrees of renal insufficiency (creatinine clearances as low as 0.15 mL/s [9 mL/min]) as pharmacokinetic studies did not indicate any change in the disposition of finasteride.

Information for the Patient: See Blue Section—Information for the Patient "Propecia".

Supplied: Each tan-colored, 8-sided, film-coated convex tablet, with the code MSD 71 on one side and PROPECIA 1 on the other, contains: finasteride 1 mg. Nonmedicinal ingredients: docusate sodium, hydroxypropylcellulose, lactose monohydrate, magnesium stearate, methylhydroxypropylcellulose, microcrystalline cellulose, pregelatinized starch, red ferric oxide, sodium starch glycolate, talc, titanium dioxide and yellow ferric oxide. Blister packages of 28. Store at room temperature 15 to 30°C and protect from moisture.

(Shown in Product Recognition Section)

New Product 1998

PROPINE® Ⓟ

Allergan

Dipivefrin HCl

Glaucoma Therapy

Pharmacology: Dipivefrin is a member of a class of drugs known as prodrugs. Prodrugs are chemical modifications of valuable therapeutic agents which make the parent compound a more useful drug. These modifications are undertaken to enhance absorption, decrease side effects and enhance stability and comfort. Enhanced absorption makes the prodrug a more efficient delivery system for the parent drug because less drug will be needed to produce the desired therapeutic response.

Dipivefrin is a prodrug of epinephrine formed by the diesterification of epinephrine and pivalic acid. The addition of pivaloyl groups to the epinephrine molecule enhances its lipophilic character and as a consequence, its penetration into the anterior chamber.

Indications: As initial or adjunctive therapy for the control of elevated intraocular pressure in chronic open angle glaucoma and in ocular hypertensive patients.

Contraindications: Should not be used in patients with narrow angles since any dilation of the pupil may predispose the patient to an attack of angle-closure glaucoma. This product is contraindicated in patients who are hypersensitive to any of its components. Not recommended for use in children.

Warnings: Because the diagnosis of narrow-angle glaucoma is missed during normotensive intervals (between attacks), it is very important that careful slit lamp and gonioscopic study be done before initiating therapy with this drug. Should an elevation of intraocular tension follow the instillation of dipivefrin solution, appropriate hypotensive therapy by the treating physician is recommended.

Precautions: Avoid contamination of the dropper tip which may result from contact with the eye or skin or any other surface.

Pregnancy: Pregnancy Category B: Reproduction studies have been performed in rats and rabbits at daily oral doses up to 10 mg/kg body weight (5 mg/kg in teratogenicity studies), and have revealed no evidence of impaired fertility or harm to the fetus due to dipivefrin. There are, however, no adequate and well-controlled studies in pregnant women. Because animal reproduction studies are not always predictive of human response, this drug should be used during pregnancy only if clearly needed.

Lactation: It is not known whether this drug is excreted in human milk. Because many drugs are excreted in human milk, caution should be exercised when dipivefrin is administered to a nursing woman.

Children: Clinical studies for safety and efficacy in children have not been done.

Adverse Effects: Dipivefrin is well tolerated and possesses few side effects. The most common side effects reported during clinical trials were burning/stinging/irritation upon instillation. Other side effects occasionally reported include conjunctivitis, blurred vision, browache and photophobia.

Adverse effects of epinephrine although not usually seen with dipivefrin therapy include reactive hyperemia, hypersensitivity or orbital pain, mydriasis and follicular conjunctivitis.

On rare occasions, systematic adverse effects such as occipital headache, palpitation, paleness, acceleration of the heart beat, trembling and perspiration have been observed following epinephrine therapy; the slight possibility of their occurrence following dipivefrin therapy should be borne in mind.

Propine (cont'd)

Aphakic Patients: Macular edema in aphakic patients have been known to occur with epinephrine therapy. Discontinuation of epinephrine generally results in prompt reversal. Very rarely have cases of macular edema in aphakic patients been reported with dipivefrin. Reversal occurred upon discontinuation of therapy.
Adrenochrome Deposits: Although epinephrine therapy has led to adrenochrome deposits in the conjunctiva and cornea, these have been reported rarely following the use of dipivefrin.

Overdose: Symptoms and Treatment: Overdosage has not been reported to date. In the event of such an occurrence, symptomatic treatment, as for epinephrine, should be initiated.

Dosage: Adults: 1 drop in each affected eye every 12 hours. Keep out of reach of children.

Supplied: Each mL contains: dipivefrin hydrochloride 1 mg in a sterile, isotonic aqueous ophthalmic solution. Also contains benzalkonium chloride 0.005% as preservative, and edetate disodium, sodium chloride, and hydrochloric acid to adjust the pH. Plastic dropper bottles of 10 and 15 mL.

Store at room temperature; keep tightly closed. Protect from light and excessive heat. Do not use if solution is discolored. Not for injection.

PROPOFOL INJECTION Ⓟ
Abbott

I.V. Emulsion—Anesthetic—Sedative

Supplied: Each mL of white, oil in water emulsion contains: propofol 10 mg for i.v. administration. Nonmedicinal ingredients: egg phosphatide, glycerin, sodium hydroxide to adjust pH, soybean oil and water for injection. It is isotonic with a pH of 6.5 to 8.5. Ready-to-use 20 mL ampuls, trays of 5. Glass infusion vials of 20, 50 and 100 mL, cartons of 5 and 1 respectively. Store between 15 and 25°C; do not freeze. The emulsion should be visually inspected for particulate matter, emulsion separation and discoloration prior to use. Any unused portions or solutions containing propofol should be discarded at the end of the surgical procedure.

New Product 1998

PROPOXYPHENE Ⓝ
General Monograph, CPhA

see OPIOID ANALGESICS

PROPYL-THYRACIL® Ⓟ
Frosst

Propylthiouracil

Hyperthyroidism Therapy

Indications: The medical management of hyperthyroidism. The treatment of thyrotoxicosis prior to surgery. In conjunction with radioiodine to hasten recovery while awaiting the effects of radiation. The management of thyroid storm in addition to other therapeutic measures.

Contraindications: Lactation. Hypersensitivity or idiosyncratic reaction to propylthiouracil.

Warnings: *Pregnancy:* Propylthiouracil readily crosses the placenta and can cause goiter or cretinism in the developing fetus. Thyroid does not cross the placenta to a degree significant enough to protect the fetus against the effects of propylthiouracil. If used for the management of thyrotoxicosis during pregnancy, propylthiouracil should be used in the smallest possible dose.

Precautions: The dose of propylthiouracil should be reduced or temporarily discontinued if signs of hypothyroidism occur during treatment.

Blood formula should be determined prior to institution of treatment. Patients receiving propylthiouracil should be advised to notify their physician if fever, sore throat, unusual bleeding or bruising, or skin rash occurs. In such cases, white blood cell and differential counts should be made to determine whether severe leukopenia or agranulocytosis has developed.

Propylthiouracil has occasionally been reported to cause hypoprothrombinemia which would increase the effect of anticoagulants. Doses of oral anticoagulants, administered concurrently, should be adjusted accordingly.

The vascularity and size of the thyroid gland may increase during treatment with propylthiouracil. This suggests overtreatment and indicates the need for reduced dosage.

When propylthiouracil is administered pre-operatively, iodine, in the form of a strong iodine solution (Lugol's solution or potassium iodide solution) should be given concomitantly for 7 to 10 days prior to surgery. The rationale for this is to reduce the vascularity and fragility of the thyroid gland.

Adverse Effects: Blood: Agranulocytosis is the most serious potential side effect. The incidence is less than 0.5%. It usually develops in the first few months of therapy, is dose related and is reversible on rapid withdrawal of the drug.

Leukopenia with granulocytopenia, hemolytic anemia, thrombocytopenia, hypoprothrombinemia with hemorrhagic manifestations, aplastic anemia, myeloblastic leukemia and hyperglobulinemia have been reported.
Skin: Urticaria, pruritus and a mild papular rash which may be accompanied by purpura are the most common skin reactions (about 3%).

Loss or depigmentation of the hair are less frequent.

Two cases of vesicular eruption in the newborn have been reported, secondary to maternal propylthiouracil therapy.
Miscellaneous: Nausea, vomiting, abdominal discomfort, drowsiness, headache, dizziness, arthralgia and paresthesia occur occasionally.
Very Rare Reactions: Drug fever, lymphadenopathy, splenomegaly, hepatitis, cholestatic jaundice, neuritis, nephritis, sialadenopathy, recurrent keratitis, conjunctival disorders, connective tissue disorders resembling polyarteritis, arthritis, lupus erythematosus and an ototoxic reaction presenting as unilateral sensorineural hearing impairment.

Overdose: Symptoms and Treatment: Acute poisoning with propylthiouracil has not been reported.

Overdosage can result in enlargement of the thyroid gland, with signs and symptoms of hypothyroidism. This can be readily reversed by reducing or even temporarily withdrawing medication. Thyroxine replacement therapy, until the patient becomes euthyroid, may be indicated.

Overdosage in pregnant women may result in congenital goiter and hypothyroidism in the fetus. The newborn child should be examined carefully for signs of hypothyroidism and immediate thyroid therapy should be instituted if hypothyroidism is confirmed.

Hemorrhage may be controlled by the administration of vitamin K_1 and the dosage of propylthiouracil should be reduced.

Dosage: Treatment should be individualized, according to the severity of symptoms and signs of hyperthyroidism and response to therapy.

Adults: The recommended initial dose is 50 to 100 mg every 8 hours, with increases as necessary up to a maximum of 500 mg/day. In some cases, initial doses as high as 900 mg/day may be required.

When doses larger than 300 mg/day are needed, the drug should be administered every 4 to 6 hours.

Usually after one or 2 weeks, but certainly after 3 weeks of therapy, objective signs of clinical improvement should be seen.

Delayed responses are sometimes noted when the thyroid is unusually large and when iodine in any form has previously been given.

The patient should be examined regularly by the physician and the dose adjusted until the patient is euthyroid (usually after 6 to 8 weeks). At this stage, the dose should be reduced by 33% every 4 to 6 weeks to a maintenance dose of 50 mg 2 or 3 times daily, administered at regular intervals.

The course of therapy may last from 6 months to 3 years. Usually within 1 to 2 years, a prolonged remission in 50% of the cases can be expected.

When remission is observed, propylthiouracil should be withdrawn over a period of 1 to 2 months under close supervision.

Children: Initial Dose Guideline: 150 mg/m²/24 hours.
For Children 10 Years of Age and Older: 150 to 300 mg/day in divided doses, at regular intervals.
For Children 6 to 10 Years of Age: 50 to 150 mg/day in divided doses, at regular intervals.
General Maintenance Dose: 50 mg twice daily when euthyroid.

Renal Failure: The following schedule is recommended (see Table I).

Table I—Propyl-Thyracil

Dosage Schedule in Renal Failure

Glomerular Filtration Rate (creatinine clearance)	10-50 mL/min	<10 mL/min
Reduce dose by	25% of the usual maintenance dose	50% of the usual maintenance dose

Supplied: Each white, phi-marked, scored tablet contains: propylthiouracil 50 or 100 mg. Gluten-, lactose- and tartrazine-free. Bottles of 100.

(Shown in Product Recognition Section)

PROSCAR® Ⓟ
MSD

Finasteride

5 Alpha-reductase Inhibitor

Pharmacology: Finasteride is a synthetic 4-azasteroid compound which is a competitive and specific inhibitor of 5 alpha-reductase, an intracellular enzyme which metabolizes testosterone into the more potent androgen dihydrotestosterone (DHT). Finasteride has very low affinity for the androgen receptor.

Benign prostatic hyperplasia (BPH) is a common finding in men over the age of 50 and its prevalence increases with age. The development of the prostate gland and subsequent BPH are partially dependent upon the conversion of testosterone to DHT within the prostate. As with other androgen mediated processes, BPH is a slowly progressing disorder and therefore, reversal of the clinical manifestations of BPH may require several months of treatment.

Within 24 hours after oral administration of a single 5 mg dose of finasteride, circulating DHT levels are reduced by approximately 60%. In patients with BPH, finasteride, given for 12 months at a dose of 5 mg/day, was shown to reduce circulating DHT concentrations by approximately 70%.

In one year clinical trials, patients treated with 5 mg daily dose of finasteride demonstrated a suppression of DHT associated with an approximate 20% mean decrease in prostate volume, an increase of ≥ 3 mL/s in maximum urinary flow rate in about 35% of patients, and an improvement in total, as well as obstructive symptoms. This control of BPH was maintained throughout the long-term open extensions of these trials for up to 36 months. However, the effects of finasteride are reversible if treatment is stopped.

Compared to baseline values, patients showed an improvement in all three primary efficacy parameters at first evaluation—month 3 for prostate volume and week 2 for urinary flow and symptoms. Compared to placebo, a statistically significant difference in the decrease in prostate volume and prostate specific antigen (PSA) occurred after 3 months. Statistically significant differences in favor of finasteride compared to placebo were also seen in maximum urinary flow rates by 4 months and in both total and obstructive symptoms scores by 7 months. However, not all patients responded.

In a study in 15 healthy male subjects, the mean bioavailability of a 5 mg finasteride tablet was 63% (range, 34 to 108%), based on the ratio of the area under the curve (AUC) relative to a 5 mg i.v. dose infused over 60 minutes. Maximum finasteride plasma concentration averaged 37 ng/mL (range, 27 to 49 ng/mL) and was reached 1 to 2 hours postdose. The mean plasma half-life of elimination was 6 hours (range, 3 to 16 hours). Following the i.v. infusion, mean plasma clearance was 165 mL/min (range, 70 to 279 mL/min) and mean steady-state volume of distribution was 76 L (range, 44 to 96 L). In a separate study, the bioavailability of finasteride was not affected by food.

Approximately 90% of circulating finasteride is bound to plasma proteins. Finasteride has been found to cross the blood-brain barrier.

No dosage adjustment is necessary for the elderly or patients with renal insufficiency.

Indications: For the treatment of symptomatic benign prostatic hyperplasia (BPH), to cause regression of the enlarged prostate, improve urinary flow and improve the symptoms associated with BPH.

There is a regression of the enlarged prostate gland in most patients treated with finasteride. Approximately 50 to 60% of patients experienced a significant increase in urinary flow (greater than 10%) and improvement in symptoms of benign prostate enlargement when treated with finasteride. Although some patients may respond sooner, a minimum of 6 months of treatment may be necessary to determine whether an individual will respond to finasteride. Eighty-five to 90% of those patients who do respond to finasteride, do so during the first 12 months of treatment. It is not possible to identify prospectively those patients who will respond (see Dosage).

Prior to initiating therapy with finasteride, thorough evaluation should be performed to identify other conditions, such as infection, prostate cancer, stricture disease, hypotonic bladder or other neurogenic disorders, that might mimic BPH.

Contraindications: Finasteride is not indicated for use in women or children.

Finasteride is contraindicated in the following: Hypersensitivity to any component of this product.

Pregnancy: Use in women when they are or may potentially become pregnant (see Precautions, Exposure to Finasteride—Risk to Male Fetus).

Warnings: *Pregnancy* and *Lactation:* Finasteride is contraindicated for use in women when they are or may potentially become pregnant (see Contraindications). Because of the ability of 5 alpha-reductase inhibitors such as finasteride to inhibit conversion of testosterone to dihydrotestosterone, finasteride may cause abnormalities of the external male genitalia when administered to a woman carrying a male fetus. It is not known whether finasteride is excreted in human milk.

Precautions: General: Since the beneficial response to finasteride may not be manifested immediately, patients with large residual urine volume and/or severely diminished urinary flow should be carefully monitored for obstructive uropathy. These patients may not be candidates for this therapy.

Finasteride is not indicated for those patients who are candidates for immediate surgery.

No studies have been conducted to determine if finasteride can be used for the control of prostatic hyperplasia in asymptomatic patients.

The long-term (>10 years) beneficial and adverse effects of finasteride have not yet been established.

Prior to treatment with finasteride, the patient should undergo a thorough urological evaluation to determine the severity of the condition, and to exclude the need for immediate surgery or the possibility of carcinoma of the prostate. Periodic follow-up evaluations should be performed to determine whether a clinical response has occurred.

Prostate Cancer: Digital rectal examinations, as well as other evaluations for prostate cancer are recommended prior to initiating therapy with finasteride and periodically thereafter. Serum PSA is being increasingly used as one of the components of the screening process to detect prostate cancer. Generally, a baseline PSA>10 ng/mL (Hybritech) prompts further evaluation and consideration of biopsy; for PSA levels between 4 and 10 ng/mL, further evaluation is generally considered advisable. The physician should be aware that a baseline PSA<4 ng/mL does not exclude the diagnosis of prostate cancer.

Finasteride causes a decrease in serum PSA levels in patients with BPH even in the presence of prostate cancer. This reduction of PSA levels should be considered when evaluating PSA laboratory data and does not suggest a beneficial effect of finasteride on prostate cancer. In controlled clinical trials finasteride did not appear to alter the rate of prostate cancer detection.

Any sustained increases in PSA levels while on finasteride should be carefully evaluated, including consideration of non-compliance to therapy with finasteride.

Clinical experience with finasteride in men with prostate cancer (n=72) suggests that the reduction in PSA from malignant prostate disease appears to be no greater than the percentage reduction of PSA from benign prostate disease.

Exposure to Finasteride—Risk to Male Fetus: Crushed or broken Proscar tablets should not be handled by women when they are or may become pregnant because of the possibility of absorption of finasteride and the subsequent potential risk to a male fetus (see Warnings).

Children: Finasteride is not indicated for use in children.

Safety and effectiveness in children have not been established.

Drug Interactions: No drug interactions of clinical importance have been identified. Finasteride, at prescribed doses, does not appear to affect significantly the cytochrome P_{450}-linked drug metabolizing enzyme system. Compounds which have been tested in man have included propranolol, digoxin, glyburide, warfarin, theophylline and antipyrine. However, patients on medications with narrow therapeutic indices, such as phenytoin, should be carefully monitored when treatment with finasteride is initiated.

Other Concomitant Therapy: Although specific interaction studies were not performed, in clinical studies finasteride was used concomitantly with ACE-inhibitors, alpha-blockers, beta-blockers, calcium channel blockers, cardiac nitrates, diuretics, H_2 antagonists, HMG-CoA reductase inhibitors, nonsteroidal anti-inflammatory drugs (NSAIDs), quinolones and benzodiazepines without evidence of clinically significant adverse interactions.

Adverse Effects: Based on experience in a total of over 1 950 patients, of whom 1 645 patients were treated for 1 year and over 360 for more than 1 year, finasteride is well tolerated. In these clinical studies, 1.4% of patients were withdrawn due to adverse reactions attributable to finasteride.

In controlled clinical studies of 12 months duration involving 543 patients treated with finasteride 5 mg, adverse reactions considered by the investigators as possibly, probably or definitely drug-related, occurring with a frequency greater than 1% and greater than with placebo were: impotence (3.7% on finasteride, 1.1% on placebo), decreased libido (3.3%, 1.6%) and decreased volume of ejaculate (2.8%, 0.9%).

The adverse experience profile for approximately 1 100 patients treated with 5 mg/day finasteride for 24 months, 400 patients treated for 36 months and 50 patients treated for 48 months was similar to that observed in the 12-month studies. There is no evidence of increased adverse experiences with increased duration of treatment with finasteride. The incidence of new drug related sexual adverse experiences decreases with duration of treatment and, in over 60% of patients who develop sexual adverse experiences, they resolve with continued treatment.

The following additional adverse reactions have been reported in postmarketing experience: breast tenderness and enlargement; hypersensitivity reactions, including lip swelling and skin rash.

Laboratory Tests: When PSA laboratory determinations are evaluated, consideration should be given to the fact that PSA levels are decreased in patients treated with finasteride (see Precautions, Prostate Cancer).

In most patients, a rapid decrease in PSA is seen within the first months of therapy, after which time PSA levels stabilize to a new baseline. The post-treatment baseline approximates half of the pretreatment value. This decrease is predictable over the entire range of PSA values, although it may vary in individual patients. Therefore, in typical patients treated with finasteride for 6 months or more, PSA values should be doubled for comparison to normal ranges in untreated men. There is considerable overlap in PSA levels among men with and without prostate cancer. Therefore, in men with BPH, PSA values within the normal reference range do not rule out prostate cancer, regardless of finasteride treatment.

No other difference in standard laboratory parameters was observed between patients treated with placebo or finasteride.

Overdose: Symptoms and Treatment: Patients have received single doses of finasteride up to 400 mg and multiple doses of finasteride up to 80 mg/day for 3 months without adverse effects.

No specific treatment of overdosage with finasteride is known.

Dosage: The recommended dosage is one 5 mg tablet daily with or without food.

Although early improvement may be seen, a therapeutic trial of at least 6 months **but not exceeding 1 year** may be necessary, in some patients, to assess whether a beneficial response has been achieved. If no clinical benefit is evident within this period, patients should be re-evaluated and the decision for continuation or discontinuation of finasteride therapy should be based upon assessment of their disease status.

Renal Insufficiency: Adjustments in dosage are not necessary in patients with varying degrees of renal insufficiency [creatinine clearances as low as 0.15 mL/s (9 mL/min)] as pharmacokinetic studies did not indicate any change in the disposition of finasteride.

Geriatrics: No adjustment in dosage is required although pharmacokinetic studies indicated the elimination of finasteride is decreased in patients more than 70 years of age.

Information for the Patient: See Blue Section—Information for the Patient "Proscar".

Supplied: Each blue, apple-shaped, film-coated tablet, with the code MSD 72 on one side and PROSCAR on the other, contains: finasteride 5 mg. Nonmedicinal ingredients: cellulose and cellulose derivatives, docusate sodium, FD&C Blue 2/aluminum lake, lactose, magnesium stearate, sodium starch glycolate, starch, talc, titanium dioxide and yellow ferric oxide. Blister packages of 30. Store at room temperature (15 to 30°C) and protect from light to prevent discoloration.

Crushed or broken tablets should not be handled by women when they are or may potentially become pregnant (see Contraindications and Warnings).

(Shown in Product Recognition Section)

Reviewed 1998

PROSTIGMIN® Preparations 🄿

ICN

Neostigmine

Parasympathomimetic

Pharmacology: Neostigmine inhibits the destruction of acetylcholine by cholinesterase, thus permitting freer transmission of nerve impulses across the neuromuscular junction. It also has a direct effect on voluntary muscle fibres and possibly on autonomic ganglion cells and neurons of the CNS.

After absorption or i.v. administration, 80% of a dose is excreted by the kidney in the unchanged (50%) and metabolized (30%) forms in 24 hours. The elimination half-life is approximately 51 to 91 minutes.

Indications: Ampuls: Prophylaxis and treatment of postoperative intestinal atony, urinary retention; in serious cases of myasthenia gravis; to neutralize effect of curare in surgical anesthesia and shock therapy.

Tablets: Myasthenia gravis.

Contraindications: Bronchial asthma or mechanical obstruction of intestinal or urinary tract. Known hypersensitivity to neostigmine.

Precautions: When large doses are given, simultaneous administration of atropine sulfate may be advisable. Because of the possibility of hypersensitivity in an occasional patient, atropine should always be at hand, together with antishock medications. Hypotension and bradycardia may occur if the effect of gallamine or curare is antagonized by neostigmine.

Adverse Effects: The untoward effects of neostigmine are most commonly related to overdosage and generally are of two varieties: muscarinic and nicotinic. Among the former group are nausea, vomiting, diarrhea, abdominal cramps, increased salivation, increased bronchial secretions, miosis, and diaphoresis. Muscarinic untoward effects can usually be counteracted by atropine. Nicotinic untoward effects are chiefly muscle cramps, fasciculation and weakness, which can be difficult to distinguish from exacerbation of underlying myasthenia gravis.

Overdose: Symptoms: Muscarinic and nicotinic effects (see Adverse Effects). Distinguish from myasthenic crisis with edrophonium chloride, if necessary.

Treatment: Control muscarinic effects with i.v. atropine, followed by i.m. atropine every 2 to 4 hours. Assist ventilation and treat convulsions or shock if necessary.

Dosage: Intestinal Atony, Postoperative: Prophylaxis: 250 µg s.c. or i.m. before or immediately after operation, repeated every 4 to 6 hours s.c. Treatment: 500 µg (1 mL 1:2 000) s.c., i.m. (or possibly i.v.) repeated at intervals of 4 to 5 hours.

Urinary Retention: Prophylaxis: 250 µg (1 mL 1:4 000) as for intestinal atony. Treatment: 500 µg (1 mL 1:2 000) s.c. or i.m. and apply heat to the lower abdomen. If urination does not occur within one hour, the patient should be catheterized. After the patient has voided, continue the 500 µg injections at 3-hour intervals for at least 5 additional injections.

Myasthenia Gravis: 75 to 300 mg orally, spaced over 24 hours as required. Occasionally parenteral therapy is needed in seriously ill patients and up to 1 mg i.m. every hour may be necessary in myasthenic crises.

Curare Antagonist (to neutralize the effect of curare in surgical anesthesia and shock therapy): 0.5 to 2 mg i.v. Atropine sulfate 0.6 to 1.2 mg i.v. should also be given.

Supplied: Injections: Prostigmin 1:2 000: Each mL contains: neostigmine methylsulfate 0.5 mg (500 µg) and sodium hydroxide to adjust pH to 5.9. Each mL of ampul solution also contains 1.8 mg methylparaben and 0.2 mg propylparaben as preservatives. Alcohol- and sulfite-free. Each mL of vial solution contains 4.5 mg phenol as preservative and sodium acetate and acetic acid as buffer. Paraben-, and sulfite-free. Vials of 10 mL. Packs of 10.

Prostigmin 1:1 000: Each mL contains: neostigmine methylsulfate 1 mg, with 4.5 mg phenol as preservative, sodium acetate and acetic acid as buffer and sodium hydroxide to adjust pH to 5.9. Paraben- and sulfite-free. Vials of 10 mL, packs of 10.

Prostigmin 1:400: Each mL contains: neostigmine methylsulfate 2.5 mg, with 4 mg phenol as preservative, sodium

Prostigmin Preparations (cont'd)

chloride for isotonicity and sodium hydroxide to adjust pH to 6.0. Paraben- and sulfite-free. Vials of 5 mL, packs of 5 and 10.

All injections contain sodium <0.01 mmol/mL. Parenteral vials contain phenol; parenteral ampuls contain parabens.

Tablets: Each white, cylindrical, biplane tablet with bevelled edges, single-scored on one side, contain: neostigmine bromide 15 mg. Also contains lactose 150 mg. Energy: 3.5 kJ (0.8 kcal). Gluten-, paraben-, sodium-, sulfite- and tartrazine-free. Bottles of 100.

Store injections at 15 to 30°C and protect from light. Protect tablets from excessive heat (40°C), and keep in a tightly closed container.

PROSTIN® E_2 Ⓟ

Pharmacia & Upjohn

Dinoprostone

Prostaglandin

Pharmacology: Orally administered dinoprostone stimulates the myometrium of the gravid uterus to contract in a manner that is similar to the contractions observed in the term uterus during spontaneous labor. Whether or not this action results from a direct or indirect effect of dinoprostone on the myometrium has not been determined with certainty.

Dinoprostone's ability to stimulate gastrointestinal tract smooth muscle may be responsible for the nausea, vomiting and/or diarrhea that is sometimes associated with the use of dinoprostone.

I.V. administered dinoprostone is extremely rapidly distributed and metabolized in man. Within 1.5 minutes only about 3% of the administered dose remains in the blood as unchanged drug, whereas over 40% of the dose is present as the metabolite, 11α-hydroxy-9, 15-dioxoprost-5-enoic acid. At least 9 metabolites of dinoprostone have been identified in human blood and urine. Studies with these metabolites in the rat blood pressure assay and smooth muscle assays indicate a much lower level of activity than the parent compound. In the amount present from a therapeutic dose of dinoprostone in man, there is felt to be essentially no activity. Dinoprostone is cleared from the blood with a half-life of less than 1 minute and the metabolites with a half-life of less than 10 minutes.

Indications: As a uterine stimulant for induction of labor at or near term in:

1. Elective induction.
2. Indicated induction such as: postmaturity, hypertension, toxemia of pregnancy, premature rupture of amniotic membranes, Rh incompatibility, diabetes mellitus, intrauterine death, or fetal growth retardation.

Contraindications: Gynecological, obstetrical or medical conditions that preclude vaginal delivery. Hypersensitivity to dinoprostone. Do not use dinoprostone simultaneously with other oxytocics.

Dinoprostone is considered inappropriate in such conditions as: a) Patients with a history of cesarean section or prior major uterine surgery. b) Patients with cephalopelvic disproportion. c) Patients with fetal malpresentation. d) Patients with suspected or clinically evident pre-existing fetal distress. e) Patients with a prior history of difficult labor and/or traumatic delivery. f) Patients with overdistension of the uterus (multiple pregnancy, polyhydramnios). g) Patients with pre-existing uterine hypertonus. h) Circumstances that make it impossible for a responsible physician to be present. i) Grand multiparae with 6 or more previous term pregnancies.

Warnings: Dinoprostone, like other effective oxytocics, should be used with strict adherence to recommended dosages, by medically trained personnel in hospital surroundings that can provide immediate intensive care and facilities for immediate surgical intervention.

The sequential use of oxytocin immediately following dinoprostone has been carried out. It has been found that prostaglandins might potentiate the effect of oxytocin. **Therefore, infusion of oxytocin should not be started until at least 1 hour has elapsed following the last oral dose of dinoprostone.**

Reports of epileptic seizures with other forms of prostaglandin by routes other than oral have been published. The association of prostaglandin with seizures has not been conclusively proven. One epileptic patient under poor control, when treated with dinoprostone tablets, did experience a grand mal seizure. Therefore, dinoprostone tablets should be used in known epileptics only when their epilepsy is under good control and then only with maximum care and observation on the part of the physician in charge. Elective induction of labor should not be employed in these patients.

Precautions: In patients with a history of asthma, increased intraocular pressure, or glaucoma, dinoprostone should be used with caution.

During oral administration, uterine activity, fetal status and the progression of cervical dilatation should be carefully evaluated to detect possible evidence of unphysiological responses, e.g. hypertonus, sustained uterine contraction, or fetal distress. Uterine activity and the state of the fetus should be monitored throughout labor.

As with the use of any effective oxytocic agent, uterine rupture and/or cervical laceration should be borne in mind.

Animal studies lasting several weeks at high doses have shown that prostaglandins of the E and F series can induce proliferation of bone. Such effects have also been noted in newborn infants who have received prostaglandin E_1 during prolonged treatment. There is no evidence that short-term administration of dinoprostone can cause similar bone effects.

Cephalopelvic relationships should be carefully evaluated before the use of dinoprostone.

Adverse Effects: The most frequent adverse reactions observed with the use of dinoprostone for the induction of labor are vomiting, with or without nausea and diarrhea. These adverse effects occur in about 21% of patients induced with a total dose of 0.5 to 3.0 mg (1 to 6 tablets) of dinoprostone in about 39% of patients induced with a total dose of 3.5 to 6.0 mg (7 to 12 tablets) of dinoprostone and in about 50% of patients induced with a total dose of more than 6.0 mg (more than 12 tablets) of dinoprostone.

Fetal heart rate changes were observed in 6.5% of patients induced with dinoprostone.

Uterine hypertonus occurred in 3.1% of patients. It is usually manageable by the temporary discontinuation of dinoprostone, a reduction in the dose of dinoprostone and the administration of oxygen. In the rare instance where these measures are not effective, prompt delivery is indicated.

Other adverse effects reported in less than 1% of patients include the following: headache, hypertension, hypotension, postpartum hemorrhage, fever, dizziness, chills, hiccough, flushing, tachycardia, dyspnea, bronchospasm, rash. The relationship of these adverse effects to dinoprostone therapy has not been established.

Overdose: Symptoms: No cases of accidental or intentional overdosage with dinoprostone tablets have been reported. Should such overdosage occur in nonpregnant patients it would be expected that nausea and vomiting and possibly diarrhea would occur.

Hyperpyrexia may occur. Pregnant patients should be carefully observed for severe uterine hypercontractility.

Treatment: Because of dinoprostone's extremely short duration of action once it is absorbed, no specific treatment to counteract drug effect need be taken. However, vomiting should be induced (if not already occurring) to remove any unabsorbed drug from the stomach.

In one published report, the i.v. infusion of 500 mL of 10% ethanol/hour for 1 hour inhibited uterine activity initiated and maintained by an infusion of either prostaglandin F_2-α or E_2 when given simultaneously with the prostaglandin.

Dosage: An initial 0.5 mg (1 tablet) dose should be given followed in one hour by a second dose of 0.5 mg (1 tablet). All subsequent doses should be given hourly. The lowest dosage that will produce satisfactory uterine response should be used. All doses should be taken with a small amount of water.

For patients with a parity of 2 or greater, and those with a Bishop Score of 6 or greater (see Table I), 0.5 mg should be administered hourly and maintained throughout the induction (unless excessive uterine activity dictates elimination of the hourly dose). In nulliparous or multiparous patients who are historically resistant to induction (Bishop Score of 0 to 5), an increment in individual doses may be justified. If satisfactory labor has not been initiated in these patients after 2 hours of dinoprostone administration, subsequent doses may be increased by 0.5 mg increments at each hourly interval. **A single dose should never exceed 1.5 mg (3 tablets).**

Once labor has been initiated (regardless of the dose), 0.5 mg (1 tablet) should be given hourly for maintenance of the progress of labor. It may, however, prove reasonable to occasionally eliminate this maintenance dose to determine if labor will progress without additional medication.

If vomiting occurs at any time during the treatment period, examine the vomitus for the presence of an intact dinoprostone tablet. If one is found, the dose should be repeated at once. If only a part or parts of the tablet is (are) seen (this is considered as evidence of tablet disintegration) or, if no tablet is seen in the vomitus, the dose **should not** be repeated and the next dose should be given only at the scheduled time. If 2 successive doses are vomited and an intact tablet is seen each time the patient should be allowed to rest until the next scheduled dose. The effectiveness of medication to treat the nausea and/or vomiting which may occur with the use of dinoprostone has not been determined.

Uterine activity is considered excessive if the frequency of contractions is greater than 5 per 10 minutes and/or the internal tonus consistently exceeds 15 mm Hg. In this event, dinoprostone administration should be stopped to allow stabilization and evaluation. **Note:** The i.v. administration of 10% ethyl alcohol may reverse the effect of dinoprostone.

If dinoprostone fails to elicit regular uterine contraction **by the end of 8 hours,** the case should be classified as a failed induction. Subsequent management is left to the physician's discretion.

The total treatment period with dinoprostone should not, in any instance, exceed 18 hours.

Table I—Prostin E_2

Bishop Method of Pelvic Scoring

Pelvic Score				
cm	0	1-2	3-4	5-6
Dilatation	0	1	2	3
%	0-30	40-50	60-70	80
Effacement	0	1	2	3
	-3	-2	-1 0	+1 +2
Station	0	1	2	3
	Firm	Med.	Soft	
Consistency	0	1	2	
	Post.	Mid.	Ant.	
Position	0	1	2	

Supplied: Available to hospitals only. Each white rectangular compressed tablet imprinted "U" on one side and "76" on the other side contains: dinoprostone 0.5 mg. Nonmedicinal ingredients: cornstarch, lactose, magnesium stearate, microcrystalline cellulose and silicon dioxide. Gluten-free. Glass bottles of 10. Tablets are stable for at least 2 years if stored under normal refrigeration (4°C). Once bottle is opened, use tablets within 90 days.

(Shown in Product Recognition Section)

PROSTIN® E_2 Vaginal Gel Ⓟ

Pharmacia & Upjohn

Dinoprostone

Prostaglandin

Pharmacology: Dinoprostone is a synthetic analogue of Prostaglandin E_2 (PGE_2). The major clinical application of PGE_2 relates to its effect on uterine smooth muscle. This property has led to its obstetrical use for term labor induction and preterm evacuation of uterine contents (for fetal death in utero, hydatidiform mole and abortion). Similarly, this effect on other smooth muscle beds results in prominent dose-related side effects of nausea, vomiting and abdominal cramping. It also acts as a vasodilator and may be associated with modest hypotension. Changes that occur in the cervix during pharmacologically induced softening, effacement and dilatation (collectively referred to as cervical ripening) appear to involve more than smooth muscle contraction. While a small amount of smooth muscle is found in this structure, the body of the cervix is composed mainly of fibrous connective tissue and surrounding collagenous matrix.

Although the exact mechanisms are not fully understood, it is theorized that the pharmacologic action of PGE_2 is related to its ability to regulate intracellular cyclic 3′, 5′-adenosine monophosphate (cAMP) levels and cellular membrane calcium ion transport. In many tissues, PGE_2 appears to stimulate the syntheses of cAMP by activating the enzyme, adenylate cyclase. It has been proposed that the prostaglandins are released by hormonal stimulation and, in turn, stimulate the enzyme. It should be noted, however, that some effects of prostaglandins are independent of cAMP and are mediated through that of cGMP.

In controlled clinical trials of 964 patients (484 on dinoprostone vaginal gel; 480 on oxytocin), 67% of PGE_2 treated patients and 67% of oxytocin treated patients had achieved satisfactory labor at 12 hours while 69% of PGE_2 treated patients and 68% of oxytocin treated patients were successfully induced. There was a trend toward fewer cesarean sections in the PGE_2 treated group.

Indications: For the induction of labor in term or near term pregnant women who have favorable induction features, a singleton pregnancy and a vertex presentation.

Contraindications: Dinoprostone should not be used in patients with known hypersensitivity to dinoprostone or any other constituents of the gel (colloidal silicon dioxide and triacetin).

Labor should not be induced in patients who have any of the following: Patients in whom oxytocic drugs are generally contraindicated or where prolonged contractions of the uterus are considered inappropriate. These include the following situations: patients with a history of cesarean section or major uterine surgery; patients with cephalopelvic disproportion; patients with a history of difficult labor and/or traumatic delivery; grand multiparae with 6 or more previous term pregnancies; patients with suspected or clinically evident pre-existing fetal distress; patients with overdistention of the uterus (multiple pregnancy, polyhydraminos); patients with pre-existing uterine hypertonus; circumstances that make it impossible for a responsible physician to be present.

Patients with ruptured membranes; engagement of the head has not taken place; patients with unexplained vaginal bleeding during this pregnancy; patients with fetal malpresentation; patients with gynecological, obstetrical or medical conditions that preclude vaginal delivery.

Dinoprostone vaginal gel should not be used simultaneously with other oxytocics (see Precautions).

Warnings: Dinoprostone like other effective oxytocic agents, should be used with strict adherence to recommended dosages, by medically trained personnel in hospital surroundings with appropriate obstetrical care facilities.

The sequential use of oxytocin less than 12 hours following dinoprostone vaginal gel has not been carried out. Therefore, infusion of oxytocin should not be started until 12 to 24 hours has elapsed following the use of dinoprostone vaginal gel.

Reports of epileptic seizures with other forms of prostaglandins have been published. The association of prostaglandin with seizures has not been conclusively proven. One epileptic patient under poor control, when treated with dinoprostone tablets, did experience a grand mal seizure. Therefore, it is recommended that dinoprostone vaginal gel be used in known epileptics only when their epilepsy is under good control and then only with maximum care and observation on the part of the physician in charge. Elective induction of labor should not be employed in these patients.

Precautions: Prior to and during the use of labor inducing agents including dinoprostone vaginal gel, uterine activity, fetal status and the character of the cervix (dilation and effacement) should be carefully monitored to detect possible evidence of undesired responses. These include hypertonus, sustained uterine contractility or fetal distress.

As with other effective oxytocic agents, it is recommended, during labor induction with dinoprostone vaginal gel, that continuous electronic monitoring of uterine activity and fetal heart rate be employed; particularly in cases where there is a known history of hypertonic uterine contractility or tetanic uterine contractions.

Cephalopelvic relationships should be carefully evaluated before the use of labor inducing agents, including dinoprostone vaginal gel.

Dinoprostone vaginal gel for labor induction should be used with caution in patients with compromised cardiovascular, hepatic or renal function and in patients with asthma or glaucoma.

Dinoprostone vaginal gel is an intravaginal product. Not to be used intracervically.

Consistent with treatment with any labor inducing agent, patients who develop uterine hypertonus or hypercontractility or in whom nonreassuring fetal heart patterns develop should be managed in a manner that addresses the welfare of the fetus and mother.

As with any oxytocic agent, the possibility of uterine rupture and/or cervical laceration should be considered in the presence of excessive uterine activity or unusual uterine pain, or where high-tone myometrial contractions are sustained.

In approximately 54% of 484 patients treated in controlled clinical trials with dinoprostone vaginal gel for labor induction, the membranes were artificially ruptured after administration of the gel.

Animal studies lasting several weeks at high doses have shown that prostaglandins of the E and F series can induce proliferation of bone. Such effects have also been noted in newborn infants who have received prostaglandin E_1 during prolonged treatment. There is no evidence that short-term administration of dinoprostone can cause similar bone effect.

Drug Interactions: Dinoprostone vaginal gel, like all prostaglandins, may potentiate the uterine response to oxytocin. The response to oxytocin may be accentuated in the presence of exogenous prostaglandin therapy.

Adverse Effects: In clinical trials of 965 patients treated with dinoprostone compared to placebo (26 patients) and oxytocin (739 patients), Table I shows the profile of events observed.

Table I—Prostin E_2

Pooled events n (%)

	Placebo n=26	PGE_2 n=965	Oxytocin n=739
fetal distress	1 (3.9)	42 (4.4)	37 (5.0)
failure to progress	2 (7.7)	12 (1.2)	14 (1.9)
failed induction		15 (1.6)	14 (1.9)
hypercontractility		30 (3.1)	29 (3.9)
fetal heart rate abnormalities		82 (8.5)	77 (10.4)

Overdose: Symptoms and Treatment: No cases of overdose have been reported. Should an overdose occur, any of the listed adverse reactions would be anticipated. Treatment of overdosage must be symptomatic at this time, since clinical studies with prostaglandin antagonists have not progressed to the point where recommendations may be made.

Dosage: For intravaginal use only. Not to be used intracervically.

For the induction of labor in term or near term pregnant women who have favorable induction features, a singleton pregnancy and a vertex presentation: an initial dose of 1 mg of dinoprostone vaginal gel placed into the posterior fornix of the vaginal canal is recommended. A dose of 1 or 2 mg of the gel may be repeated, once, 6 hours later depending upon the patient's response to the initial dose.

Patients should remain in a lateral or supine position for 30 minutes after administration to prevent leakage of the gel.

Dinoprostone vaginal gel prefilled syringes contain overfill and are designed to deliver a dose of 1 or 2 mg of dinoprostone.

The syringe should be assembled by following the sequence in the diagram (see package insert).

Method of Assembly: Remove syringe from sterile package. Remove peel-off seal from end of syringe. Remove protective end cap (to serve as plunger extension). Insert protective end cap into plunger stopper assembly in barrel of syringe. Administer syringe contents.

Supplied: Each syringe of semi-translucent viscous vaginal gel contains: dinoprostone 1 or 2 mg/3 g (2.5 mL). Nonmedicinal ingredients: colloidal silicon dioxide and triacetin gel. The contents of one syringe (a single dose container/closure system) to be used for one patient. Discard after use. The gel has a shelf life of 36 months when stored at 2 to 8°C, under continuous refrigeration.

(Shown in Product Recognition Section)

PROSTIN® VR Ⓟ

Pharmacia & Upjohn

Alprostadil

Prostaglandin

Pharmacology: Alprostadil (also known as prostaglandin E_1) relaxes the ductus arteriosus in early postnatal life and supports its patency when continuously infused i.v. or intra-arterially in neonates with congenital heart defects who depend on a patent ductus for survival. The desired pharmacological effects are obtained with an initial dosage of 0.1 μg/kg/minute. Higher doses do not offer added benefit. Postnatally the ductus arteriosus rapidly loses its responsiveness to alprostadil and consequently alprostadil appears to be most effective within 96 hours after birth, particularly when the pre-infusion arterial pO_2 is less than 40 mm Hg.

The estimated half-life of alprostadil is 5 to 10 minutes. I.V. administered alprostadil is rapidly distributed and metabolized and the pulmonary vascular bed removes about 68% of the drug in a single pass. Alprostadil is weakly bound to serum albumin. The major route of elimination of alprostadil and its metabolites is via the kidneys. In laboratory animals and humans, alprostadil can lower blood pressure, probably by relaxing the smooth muscle of the cardiovascular system. Alprostadil can elevate body temperature and this effect has been observed in some neonates receiving the drug.

Indications: To temporarily maintain the patency of the ductus arteriosus until corrective or palliative surgery can be performed in neonates who have congenital heart defects and who depend upon a patent ductus arteriosus for survival.

Alprostadil should be administered only by medically trained personnel in facilities in which pediatric patients can receive or have access to pediatric intensive care.

Contraindications: In the following patients: Cyanotic neonates with persistent fetal circulation. Neonates with total anomalous pulmonary venous return below the diaphragm, neonates with polysplenia or asplenia in whom pulmonary atresia is combined with anomalous pulmonary venous return which may be obstructed.

In such patients alprostadil may precipitate pulmonary edema because of increased pulmonary blood flow.

Warnings: Approximately 10 to 12% of neonates treated with alprostadil experienced apnea. Apnea is seen most often in neonates weighing less than 2 kg at birth and usually appears during the first hour of drug infusion. Therefore alprostadil should be used in facilities with immediately available intensive care for intubation and assisted ventilation.

Pathologic studies of the ductus arteriosus and pulmonary arteries of infants with prostaglandin E_1 have disclosed histologic changes compatible with a weakening effect upon these structures. The specificity or clinical relevance of these findings is not known.

Cortical proliferation of the long bones has followed long-term infusions of alprostadil in infants. The proliferation appeared to regress after withdrawal of the drug.

The administration of alprostadil to neonates may result in gastric outlet obstruction secondary to antral hyperplasia. This effect appears to be related to duration of therapy and cumulative dose of the drug. Neonates receiving alprostadil at recommended doses for more than 120 hours should be closely monitored for evidence of antral hyperplasia and gastric outlet obstruction.

Alprostadil should be infused for the shortest period of time at the lowest dose which will produce the desired effects. Risk of long-term treatment infusion of alprostadil should be weighed against the possible benefits that critically ill infants may derive from its administration.

Precautions: Alprostadil should be used with caution in infants with suspected bleeding tendencies.

Care should be taken to avoid the use of alprostadil in neonates with respiratory distress syndrome (hyaline membrane disease), which sometimes can be confused with cyanotic heart disease. If full diagnostic facilities are not immediately available, cyanosis (pO_2 less than 40 mm Hg) and restricted pulmonary blood flow apparent on an x-ray are good indicators of congenital heart defects.

In all neonates, blood pressure should be monitored by appropriate methods such as an umbilical artery catheter, or by a Doppler transducer. **Should arterial pressure fall significantly, reduce the rate of infusion immediately.**

Since alprostadil appears most effective within 96 hours after birth due to a decreasing responsiveness of the ductus arteriosus with time after birth, every effort should be made to start infusion of the drug during this period.

Long-term carcinogenicity and fertility studies have not been done.

The Ames and Alkaline Elution assays reveal no potential for mutagenesis.

In infants with restricted pulmonary blood flow, the increase in blood oxygenation is inversely proportional to pre-treatment pO_2 values; that is, patients with low pO_2 values (less than 40 torr) respond best, and patients with high pO_2 values (greater than 40 torr) usually have little response.

In infants with restricted pulmonary blood flow, measure efficacy of alprostadil by monitoring an improvement in blood oxygenation. In infants with restricted systemic blood flow, measure efficacy by monitoring improvement of systemic blood pressure and blood pH.

Drug Interactions: No drug interactions have been reported to occur between alprostadil and the standard therapy employed in neonates with congenital heart defects. Standard therapy includes antibiotics, such as penicillin or gentamicin; vasopressors, such as dopamine or isoproterenol; cardiac glycosides; and diuretics, such as furosemide.

Adverse Effects: In infants whose ductus arterious must be kept patent, the most frequent adverse reactions observed with alprostadil infusion are related to its known pharmacological effects. The following incidences are based on experience in 436 patients.

Cardiovascular System: The most common adverse reactions reported in these patients were flushing 10.1%, bradycardia 6.7%, hypotension 3.9%, tachycardia 2.8%, cardiac arrest

Prostin VR (cont'd)

1.1% and edema 1.1%. The following reactions were reported in less than 1% of patients: congestive heart failure, hyperemia, pneumo-pericardium, second degree heart block, shock, spasm of the right infundibulum (conus arteriosus), supraventricular tachycardia, ventricular fibrillation, ventricular hypertrophy, tachyphylaxis.

CNS: The most common adverse reactions reported were fever in 13.8% and seizures in 4.1% of patients. The following reactions were reported in less than 1% of patients: intracranial bleeding, hyper-extension of neck, hyperirritability, hypothermia, jitteriness, lethargy, stiffness.

Respiratory System: The most common adverse reaction reported was apnea in 11.5% of patients. The following reactions were reported in less than 1% of patients: bradypnea, bronchial wheezing, hypercapnia, pneumothorax, respiratory depression, respiratory distress, tachypnea.

Gastrointestinal System: The most common adverse reaction reported was diarrhea in 2.6% of patients. The following reactions were reported in less than 1% of patients: gastric regurgitation, hyperbilirubinemia, peritonitis.

Hematologic: The most common adverse reaction reported was disseminated intravascular coagulation in 1.1% of patients. The following reactions were reported in less than 1% of patients: anemia, bleeding, thrombocytopenia, hypochromic anemia.

Urinary tract: The following reactions were reported in less than 1% of patients: anuria, hematuria, renal failure.

Metabolic: The most common adverse reaction reported was hypokalemia in 1.1% of patients. The following reactions were reported in less than 1% of patients: hypoglycemia, hyperkalemia.

Infection: Sepsis was reported in 1.6% and peritonsillitis in less than 1% of patients.

Ductus arteriosus histological changes: One group of investigators reported edema of the media, separation of the medial components by clear spaces, pathological interruption of the internal elastic lamina, and intimal lacerations some of which extended into the media in the ductus arteriosus of 4 patients.

Cortical proliferation of long bones: Following long term infusion of alprostadil, cortical proliferation of long bones has been reported.

This hypertrophic osteoarthropathy appeared to be reversible on discontinuation of the drug.

Overdose: Symptoms and Treatment: Apnea, bradycardia, pyrexia, hypotension and flushing may be signs of drug overdose. If apnea or bradycardia occur, the infusion should be discontinued and the appropriate medical treatment initiated. Caution should be used if the infusion is restarted. If pyrexia or hypotension occur, the infusion rate should be reduced until these symptoms subside. Flushing is usually attributed to incorrect intra-arterial catheter placement and is usually alleviated by repositioning the tip of the catheter.

Dosage: The initial infusion rate of alprostadil should be 0.1 μg/kg of body weight/minute. When the desired effect on the ductus arteriosus is achieved, decrease infusion to the lowest possible dose while maintaining the desired effect. This may be accomplished by reducing the dosage from 0.1 to 0.05 to 0.025 to 0.01 μg/kilogram of body weight/minute. Although doses up to 0.4 μg/kilogram of body weight/minute have been used, doses above 0.1μg/kilogram of body weight/minute generally do not offer additional benefits.

The preferred route of administration of alprostadil is by continuous i.v. infusion into a large vein. Alternatively, alprostadil may be administered through an umbilical artery catheter placed at the ductal opening. Adverse effects have occurred with both routes of administration, but higher incidence of flushing has been associated with intra-arterial than with i.v. administration.

If undiluted alprostadil comes in direct contact with a plastic container, plasticizers are leached from the sidewalls. The solution may turn hazy and the appearance of the container may change. Should this occur, the solution should be discarded and the plastic container replaced. This appears to be a concentration-dependent phenomenon. To minimize the possibility of haze formation, alprostadil should be added directly to the i.v. infusion solution avoiding contact with the walls of plastic containers.

Dilution Instructions: To prepare infusion solutions, dilute 1 mL of Prostin VR with sterile Sodium Chloride Injection or sterile Dextrose Injection. Dilute to volumes appropriate for the pump delivery system available. Prepare fresh infusion solution every 24 hours. **Discard any solution more than 24 hours old.**

For administration using a pump capable of delivering small volume constant infusions (i.e., not limited to discrete infusion rates) dissolve 1 mL Prostin VR (500 μg alprostadil) in 25 to 100 mL sterile 0.9% Sodium Chloride injection USP or sterile 5% Dextrose Injection USP to provide a solution containing 500 μg alprostadil. The infusion rate to deliver 0.1 μg/kg of body weight/minute can be calculated as follows:

$$\text{Infusion rate (mL/hr)} = \frac{\dfrac{\text{Volume containing } 500\ \mu g}{\text{alprostadil} \times \text{body weight (kg)}}}{83.3}$$

For administration using an infusion pump limited to discrete infusion rates, infuse 2 to 4 mL/hour. The volume of saline or glucose to be added to the 1 mL Prostin VR is to be calculated as follows:

$$\text{Volume of saline or glucose needed (mL)} = \frac{\text{Pump rate (mL/hr)} \times 83.3}{\text{body weight (kg)}} - 1$$

The infusion solution may be mixed conveniently in a graduated mixing chamber inserted between the i.v. bottle and the pump.

Change the dosage from 0.1 μg/kg of body weight/minute to 0.05 μg/kg of body weight/minute by reducing the pump rate to one-half the original rate.

Supplied: Each 1 mL ampul contains: alprostadil 500 μg in anhydrous ethanol. Ampuls of 1 mL. Store in a refrigerator at 2 to 8°C. Prepare fresh dilutions every 24 hours. Discard any dilution more than 24 hours old.

PROTAMINE SULFATE INJECTION

Pharmaceutical Partners

Heparin Antagonist

Pharmacology: When administered alone, protamine has an anticoagulant effect. However, when it is given in the presence of heparin (which is strongly acidic), a stable salt is formed which results in the loss of anticoagulant activity of both drugs.

Protamine has a rapid onset of action. Neutralization of heparin occurs within 5 minutes after i.v. administration. Although the metabolic fate of the heparin-protamine complex has not been elucidated, it has been postulated that protamine in the heparin-protamine complex may be partially metabolized or may be attacked by fibrinolysin, thus freeing heparin.

Indications: Treatment of heparin overdosage.

Contraindications: Patients who have shown previous intolerance to the drug.

Warnings: Hyperheparinemia or bleeding has been reported in experimental animals and in some patients 30 minutes to 18 hours after cardiac surgery (under cardiopulmonary bypass) in spite of complete neutralization of heparin by adequate doses of protamine at the end of the operation.

Therefore, it is important to keep the patient under close observation after cardiac surgery. Additional doses of protamine should be administered if indicated by coagulation studies; such as the heparin titration test with protamine and the determination of plasma thrombin time.

Too rapid administration of protamine can cause severe hypotensive and anaphylactoid-like reactions (see Dosage). Facilities to treat shock should be available.

Precautions: General: **Because of the anticoagulant effect of protamine, it is unwise to give more than 100 mg over a short period unless there is certain knowledge of a larger requirement.**

Previous exposure to protamine through use of protamine-containing insulins or during heparin neutralization may predispose susceptible individuals to the development of untoward reactions from the subsequent use of this drug. Reports of the presence of antiprotamine antibodies in the serums of infertile or vasectomized men suggest that some of these individuals may react to the use of protamine.

Patients with a history of allergy to fish may develop hypersensitivity reactions to protamine, although to date no relationship has been established between allergic reactions to protamine and fish allergy.

Drug Interactions: Protamine has been shown to be incompatible with certain antibiotics, including several of the cephalosporins and penicillins (see Dosage).

Carcinogenesis, Mutagenesis, Impairment of Fertility: Studies have not been performed to determine potential for carcinogenicity, mutagenicity or impairment of fertility.

Pregnancy: Animal reproduction studies have not been conducted with protamine. It is also not known whether protamine can cause fetal harm when administered to a pregnant woman or can affect reproduction capacity. Protamine should be given to a pregnant woman only if clearly needed.

Lactation: It is not known whether this drug is excreted in human milk. Because many drugs are excreted in human milk, caution should be exercised when protamine is administered to a nursing woman.

Children: Safety and effectiveness in children have not been established.

Adverse Effects: I.V. injections of protamine may cause a sudden fall in blood pressure, bradycardia, pulmonary hypertension, dyspnea, or transitory flushing and a feeling of warmth. There have been reports of anaphylaxis that resulted in respiratory embarrassment (see Precautions). Other reported adverse reactions include systemic hypertension, nausea, vomiting and lassitude. Back pain has been reported rarely in conscious patients undergoing such procedures as cardiac catheterization.

Because fatal reactions often resembling anaphylaxis have been reported after administration of protamine, the drug should be given only when resuscitation techniques and treatment of anaphylactoid shock are readily available.

Overdose: Symptoms and Treatment: Because of the anticoagulant effect of protamine, overdosage of this drug may theoretically result in hemorrhage. However, in one study, overdosage of 600 to 800 mg of i.v. protamine had only minimal, transient effects on blood coagulation tests. The patient should be followed with coagulation studies and treated symptomatically.

The LD_{50} of protamine is 100 mg/kg in mice.

Dosage: Each mg of protamine will neutralize approximately 90 USP units of heparin activity derived from beef lung tissue or about 115 USP units of heparin activity derived from porcine intestinal mucosa.

Protamine sulfate injection should be given by very slow i.v. injection in doses not to exceed 50 mg of protamine in any 10 minute period (see Warnings).

Protamine is intended for injection without further dilution; however, if further dilution is desired, 5% Dextrose Injection or 0.9% Sodium Chloride Injection may be used. Diluted solutions should not be stored since they contain no preservative.

Protamine should not be mixed with other drugs without knowledge of their compatibility, because protamine has been shown to be incompatible with certain antibiotics, including several of the cephalosporins and penicillins.

Because heparin disappears rapidly from the circulation, the dose of protamine required also decreases rapidly with the time elapsed following i.v. injection of heparin. For example, if the protamine is administered 30 minutes after the heparin, one-half the usual dose may be sufficient.

The dosage of protamine should be guided by blood coagulation studies (see Warnings).

Parenteral drug products should be visually inspected for particulate matter and discoloration prior to administration, whenever solution and container permit.

Supplied: Each mL of sterile, nonpyrogenic, isotonic solution contains: protamine sulfate 10 mg, sodium chloride 9 mg and water for injection q.s. Sulfuric acid and/or dibasic sodium phosphate (heptahydrate) may have been added for pH adjustment. Preservative-free. Flip-top vials of 5 mL, packages of 25. Individually packaged flip-top vials of 30 mL with 25 mL fill. Store at controlled room temperature 15 to 30°C. Do not freeze. Discard unused portion.

Note: The 25 mL vials are designed for antiheparin treatment in certain cases in which large doses of heparin have been given during surgery and are to be neutralized by large doses of protamine after surgical procedures.

PROTAMINE SULFATE INJECTION

Sabex

Heparin Antagonist

Supplied: Each mL of preservative-free, sterile, isotonic solution contains: protamine sulfate 10 mg. Nonmedicinal ingredients: sodium chloride, sulfuric acid/or dibasic sodium phosphate to adjust pH and water for injection. Single use vials of 5 and 25 mL, boxes of 10 and 1, respectively. Discard unused portion. Store between 15 and 30°C. Do not freeze

New Product 1998

PRO•TEC SPORT™
Allergan

Octyl Methoxycinnamate—Octyl Salicylate—Oxybenzone

UVA/UVB Protection

Supplied: Each bottle of waterproof, sweatproof, oil-free base, SPF 20 sunscreen formula, contains: octyl methoxycinnamate 7.5%, octyl salicylate 5% and oxybenzone 5%. Nonmedicinal ingredients: acrylates/C10-30 alkyl acrylate crosspolymer, C12-15 alkyl benzoate, carbomer 940, disodium EDTA, glycerin, imidazolidinyl urea, methylparaben, propylparaben, purified water, sorbitan stearate, steareth-2, steareth-100, tocopheryl acetate, tricontanyl PVP and triethanolamine. Tubes of 15 and 118 mL.

PROTOPAM® CHLORIDE ℞
Wyeth-Ayerst

Pralidoxime Chloride

Cholinesterase Reactivator

Supplied: Cartons of six 20 mL single dose vials: 1 g each: of sterile pralidoxime chloride powder for i.v. injection. Solutions may be prepared by adding 20 mL Sterile Water for Injection USP. Nonmedicinal ingredients: sodium hydroxide. I.M. or s.c. injections may be given when i.v. injection is not feasible. pH range: 3.5 to 4.5.

PROTROPIN® ℞
Roche

Somatrem

Growth Hormone

Pharmacology: Somatrem is a polypeptide (methionyl human growth hormone) produced by recombinant DNA technology using the gene for human growth hormone.

Somatrem has the same amino acid sequence as pituitary-derived human growth hormone plus an additional amino acid, methionine, on the N-terminus of the molecule. The two molecules also have the same disulfide bond arrangement and the same secondary and tertiary structure.

In vitro and in vivo preclinical testing and clinical testing have demonstrated that somatrem is therapeutically equivalent to pituitary-derived human growth hormone in pharmacokinetics and in stimulation of linear growth as well as other actions.

Somatrem treatment of children who lack adequate secretion of endogenous growth hormone resulted in an increase in growth rate and an increase in levels of insulin-like growth factor-I, similar to that seen with pituitary-derived human growth hormone.

Actions that have been demonstrated for somatrem, somatropin and/or pituitary-derived human growth hormone include:

Tissue Growth: Skeletal Growth: Somatrem stimulates skeletal growth in children with growth failure due to a lack of adequate secretion of endogenous growth hormone. Skeletal growth is accomplished at the epiphyseal plates at the end of a growing long bone. Growth and metabolism of epiphyseal plate cells are directly stimulated by growth hormone and one of its mediators, insulin-like growth factor-I. Serum levels of insulin-like growth factor-I are low in children and adolescents who are growth hormone deficient, but increase during treatment with Protropin. New bone is formed at the epiphyses in response to growth hormone. This results in linear growth until these growth plates fuse at the end of puberty.

Cell Growth: Treatment with pituitary-derived human growth hormone results in an increase in both the number and the size of skeletal muscle cells.

Organ Growth: Pituitary-derived human growth hormone influences the size of internal organs, including kidneys, and also increases red cell mass. Treatment of hypophysectomized or genetic dwarf rats with growth hormone results in organ growth that is proportional to the overall body growth.

Protein Metabolism: Linear growth is facilitated in part by growth hormone-stimulated protein synthesis. This is reflected by nitrogen retention as demonstrated by a decline in urinary nitrogen excretion and blood urea nitrogen during growth hormone therapy.

Carbohydrate Metabolism: Growth hormone is a modulator of carbohydrate metabolism. Children with inadequate secretion of growth hormone sometimes experience fasting hypoglycemia which is improved by treatment with growth hormone. Growth hormone therapy may decrease glucose tolerance. Administration of growth hormone to normal adults and patients who lack adequate secretion of endogenous growth hormone results in increases in mean serum fasting and postprandial insulin levels. However, mean fasting and postprandial glucose levels and mean hemoglobin A_{1C} levels remain within the normal range.

Lipid Metabolism: Acute administration of pituitary-derived human growth hormone to humans results in lipid mobilization. Nonesterified fatty acids increase in plasma within 2 hours of pituitary-derived human growth hormone administration. In growth hormone-deficient patients, long-term administration of growth hormone often decreases body fat. Mean cholesterol levels decrease in patients treated with growth hormone.

Mineral Metabolism: The retention of total body potassium in response to growth hormone administration is thought to result from cellular growth. Sodium retention also occurs. Serum levels of inorganic phosphorus may increase slightly in patients with inadequate secretion of endogenous growth hormone after growth hormone therapy due to metabolic activity associated with bone growth as well as increased tubular reabsorption of phosphate by the kidney. Serum calcium is not significantly altered in these patients (see Precautions, Laboratory Tests).

Connective Tissue Metabolism: Growth hormone stimulates the synthesis of chondroitin sulfate and collagen as well as the urinary excretion of hydroxyproline.

Indications: For the long-term treatment of children who have growth failure due to growth hormone inadequacy.

Contraindications: Should not be used in patients with closed epiphyses.

Somatrem should not be used in patients with active neoplasia. Growth hormone therapy should be discontinued if evidence of neoplasia develops.

Somatrem, when reconstituted with Bacteriostatic Water for Injection, USP (benzyl alcohol preserved) should not be used in newborns or in patients with a known sensitivity to benzyl alcohol (see Warnings).

Warnings: Benzyl alcohol as a preservative in Bacteriostatic Water for Injection, USP has been associated with toxicity in newborns. When administering somatrem in newborns or in patients sensitive to benzyl alcohol, reconstitute with Sterile Water for Injection, USP. When Sterile Water for Injection, USP is used, **use only one somatrem dose per vial and discard the unused portion.**

Precautions: General: Somatrem should be prescribed by physicians experienced in the diagnosis and management of patients with growth failure.

Because somatrem may induce a state of insulin resistance, patients should be observed for evidence of glucose intolerance.

Patients with a history of an intracranial lesion should be examined frequently for progression or recurrence of the lesion.

Intracranial hypertension (IH) with papilledema, visual changes, headache, nausea and/or vomiting has been reported in a small number of patients treated with growth hormone products. Symptoms usually occurred within the first 8 weeks of the initiation of the growth hormone therapy. In all reported cases, IH-associated signs and symptoms resolved after termination of therapy or a reduction of the growth hormone dose. Funduscopic examination of patients is recommended at the initiation and periodically during the course of growth hormone therapy.

Slipped capital femoral epiphysis may occur more frequently in patients with endocrine disorders or in patients undergoing rapid growth. Physicians and parents should be alert to the development of a limp or complaints of hip or knee pain in somatrem-treated patients.

Progression of scoliosis can occur in children who experience rapid growth. Because growth hormone increases growth rate, patients with a history of scoliosis who are treated with growth hormone should be monitored for progression of scoliosis. Growth hormone has not been shown to increase the incidence of scoliosis.

Local or systemic allergic reactions may occur. Parents/patient should be informed that such reactions are possible and that prompt medical attention should be sought if allergic reactions occur.

Laboratory Tests: Serum levels of inorganic phosphorus, alkaline phosphatase, and parathyroid hormone may increase with somatrem therapy. Changes in thyroid hormone laboratory measurements may develop during human growth hormone treatment of children who lack adequate endogenous growth hormone secretion. As untreated hypothyroidism prevents optimal response to somatrem, patients should have periodic thyroid function tests and should be treated with thyroid hormone when indicated.

Drug Interactions: Concomitant glucocorticoid therapy may inhibit the growth promoting effect of somatrem. If glucocorticoid replacement is required, the glucocorticoid dose should be carefully adjusted.

Children: Prudence is indicated for children aged 6 months to 3 years, when administering somatrem reconstituted in Bacteriostatic Water for Injection, USP (benzyl alcohol preserved); although there is no information on the toxicity of benzyl alcohol for this age group, the toxic dose for premature neonates is in the range of 100 to 250 mg/kg/day.

Pregnancy: Reproduction studies have not been conducted with somatrem. It is not known whether somatrem can cause fetal harm when administered to a pregnant woman or can affect reproduction capacity. Somatrem should be given to a pregnant woman only if clearly needed.

Lactation: It is not known whether somatrem is excreted in human milk. Because many drugs are excreted in human milk, caution should be exercised when somatrem is administered to a nursing mother.

Carcinogenicity and Mutagenicity: Carcinogenicity and mutagenicity studies have not been conducted with somatrem. Patients developing neoplasia should be reported to HPB by the treating physician.

Information for the Patient: Patients being treated with growth hormone and/or their parents should be informed of the potential benefits and risks associated with treatment. If home use is determined by the physician to be desirable, instructions on appropriate use should be given, including a review of the contents of the Patient Information Insert. This information is intended to aid in the safe and effective administration of the medication. It is not a disclosure of all possible adverse or intended effects.

If home use is prescribed, a puncture-resistant container for the disposal of used syringes and needles should be recommended to the patient. Patients and/or parents should be thoroughly instructed in the importance of proper disposal and cautioned against any reuse of needles and syringes (see Blue Section—Information for the Patient "Protropin").

Adverse Effects: A small percentage of patients may develop antibodies to the protein. Growth hormone antibody binding capacities below 2 mg/L have not been associated with growth attenuation. In some cases when binding capacity exceeds 2 mg/L, growth attenuation has been observed. In clinical studies and postmarketing experience of patients treated with somatrem, approximately 0.4 % of patients screened for antibody production developed antibodies with binding capacities >2 mg/L at 6 months. Reports of growth deceleration associated with binding capacities >2 mg/L in these patients are rare (<0.1 %). If growth deceleration is observed which is not attributable to another cause, the patient should be tested for antibodies to growth hormone. Although no evidence exists to indicate that the methionine on the N-terminus of somatrem causes antibodies to growth hormone, the physician should consider transferring the patient to somatropin if the patient has an antibody binding capacity >2 mg/L and has exhibited growth attenuation.

In addition to an evaluation of compliance with the prescribed treatment program and thyroid status, testing for antibodies to human growth hormone should be carried out in any patient who fails to respond to therapy.

No other adverse effects of anti-growth hormone antibody formation were observed in additional short-term immunologic and renal function studies carried out in a group of patients after approximately 2 years of treatment. The antibodies to growth hormone were determined to be of the IgG class; no antibodies to growth hormone of the IgE class were detected.

Leukemia has been reported in a small number of growth hormone deficient patients who were treated with growth hormone. It is uncertain whether this increased risk is related to the pathology of growth hormone deficiency, growth hormone therapy, or other associated treatments such as radiation therapy for intracranial tumors. The risk to an individual patient, if any, remains to be established.

In studies of children treated with somatrem, injection site pain was reported infrequently.

Adverse drug reactions which have been reported infrequently (<1 %) in growth hormone-treated patients include mild and transient peripheral edema.

Other rare (<0.1 %) adverse drug reactions reported in growth hormone-treated patients include the following:

Protropin (cont'd)

1) Musculoskeletal: carpal tunnel syndrome, 2) Skin: increased growth of pre-existing nevi (malignant nevi transformation has not been reported), 3) Endocrine: gynecomastia and pancreatitis.

Overdose: Symptoms and Treatment: Theoretical risks of long-term human growth hormone treatment with doses exceeding the recommended dose levels could be signs and symptoms of gigantism and/or acromegaly.

Dosage: Dosage and administration schedule should be individualized for each patient. A dose of up to 0.3 mg/kg/**week** (approximately 0.9 IU/kg/week) administered daily in divided doses by s.c. or i.m. injection is recommended.

The total number of mg **per daily dose** is calculated as follows:

dose (mg)/injection=
patient weight (kg)×up to 0.043 (mg/kg).

Therapy should not be continued if final height is achieved or epiphyseal fusion occurs. Patients who fail to respond adequately while on somatrem therapy should be evaluated to determine the cause of unresponsiveness.

Reconstitution: Protropin is dispensed in vials of 5 mg (15 IU) and 10 mg (30 IU). Each 5 mg vial of Protropin should be reconstituted with 1 to 5 mL of Bacteriostatic Water for Injection, USP (benzyl alcohol preserved). (Vials are reconstituted to a concentration of 1 mg somatrem/mL with 5 mL of the water.)

Each 10 mg vial of Protropin should be reconstituted with 1 to 10 mL of Bacteriostatic Water for Injection, USP (benzyl alcohol preserved). (Vials are reconstituted to a concentration of 1 mg somatrem/mL with 10 mL of the water.)

When Protropin is reconstituted to 1 mg somatrem/mL, the recommended daily somatrem dose of 0.043 mg/kg contains 0.387 mg/kg benzyl alcohol.

See Warnings for reconstitution of Protropin for use in newborns and persons sensitive to benzyl alcohol and see Precautions for use in children age 6 months to 3 years.

To prepare the solution, slowly inject the Bacteriostatic Water for Injection, USP (benzyl alcohol preserved) into the Protropin vial, aiming the stream of liquid against the glass wall of the vial. Then swirl the somatrem vial with a **gentle** rotary motion until the contents are completely dissolved. **Do not shake.** Because somatrem is a protein, shaking can result in a cloudy solution. The somatrem solution should be **clear**, i.e., it should not have any solid particles floating on the surface. If you notice lumps or solid particles of powder, continue to gently swirl the solution until all of the powder has dissolved. If the solution does not become clear, **do not** inject it. Note also that occasionally, after refrigeration, small colorless particles of protein may be present in the Protropin solution. This is not unusual for solutions containing proteins. Allow the vial to come to room temperature and gently swirl until solution is clear. If the solution remains cloudy or hazy, **do not** inject it.

Injection: Before needle insertion, the septum of both the Protropin and diluent vials should be wiped with alcohol or an antiseptic solution to prevent contamination of the contents by microorganisms that may be introduced by repeated needle insertions. Protropin must be administered using sterile, disposable syringes and needles. The syringes should be of small enough volume that the prescribed dose can be drawn from the vial with reasonable accuracy. If the route of injection selected is i.m., the needle should be of sufficient length (usually 1 inch or more [2.5 cm]) to ensure that the injection reaches the muscular layer. The site of injection should be rotated each time Protropin is administered.

Stability and Storage: Before Reconstitution: Protropin and Bacteriostatic Water for Injection, USP (benzyl alcohol preserved), must be refrigerated at 2 to 8°C. **Avoid freezing the vials of Protropin and Bacteriostatic Water for Injection, USP (benzyl alcohol preserved).** Expiration dates are stated on the labels.

After Reconstitution: Vial contents are stable for 14 days when reconstituted with Bacteriostatic Water for Injection, USP (benzyl alcohol preserved) and refrigerated at 2 to 8°C. **Avoid freezing the reconstituted vials of Protropin.** See Warnings for storage information regarding reconstituted somatrem for **use in newborns** and persons sensitive to benzyl alcohol.

Unusual Handling Conditions: Vials of **unreconstituted** somatrem may be held at ambient temperature (not to exceed 37°C) for a total time not to exceed 7 days. Vials of **reconstituted** somatrem should not be exposed to temperatures greater than 25°C (controlled room temperature) for more than 24 hours in total.

Information for the Patient: See Blue Section—Information for the Patient "Protropin".

Supplied: 5 mg: Each vial of sterile, lyophilized powder contains: somatrem 5 mg (approx. 15 IU). Nonmedicinal ingredients: mannitol, sodium phosphate dibasic and sodium phosphate monobasic. May also contain phosphoric acid (used for pH adjustment). Cartons of two 5 mg vials and one multiple use vial with diluent [10 mL Bacteriostatic Water for Injection, USP (benzyl alcohol preserved)].

10 mg: Each vial of sterile, lyophilized powder contains: somatrem 10 mg (approx. 30 IU). Nonmedicinal ingredients: mannitol, sodium phosphate dibasic and sodium phosphate monobasic. May also contain phosphoric acid (use for pH adjustment). Cartons of two 10 mg vials and two multiple use vials with diluent [10 mL Bacteriostatic Water for Injection, USP (benzyl alcohol preserved)].

Reviewed 1998

PROVERA® Ⓟ

Pharmacia & Upjohn

Medroxyprogesterone Acetate

Progestin

Pharmacology: Medroxyprogesterone, an orally active progestational steroid (progestin) derived from a natural source (soy beans), when administered to women with adequate levels of estrogen (endogenous or exogenous), transforms a proliferative endometrium into a secretory endometrium. Furthermore, the anticancer activity of medroxyprogesterone at pharmacologic doses, may be dependent on its effect on the hypothalamic/pituitary/gonadal axis, estrogen receptors and metabolism of steroids at the tissue level.

Bioavailability: In a randomized cross-over study using 22 healthy male volunteers, the bioavailability of Provera 2.5 mg and Provera 10 mg tablets was studied following 10 mg single oral doses in the following regimens: (a) four 2.5 mg tablets or; (b) one 10 mg tablet as a single dose during a fasting period which began 9 hours before and lasted until 4 hours after the dose. Treatment phases were separated by a 14 day washout period. Blood samples were collected prior to and at the following times after drug administration: 0.5, 1, 2, 3, 4, 6, 8, 10, 12, 16, 24, 36, 72, 96 and 120 hours. The resulting serum samples were analyzed for medroxyprogesterone using a radioimmunoassay procedure.

Relevant bioavailability parameters are included in Table I.

Table I—Provera

Bioavailability Parameters of Medroxyprogesterone Acetate Following Oral Administration

Provera Dose (mg)	Tmax (hr)	Cmax (ng/mL)	AUC (ng/hr/mL)
2.5 mg (4 tablets)	1.68	22.10	390.66–466.62
10 mg (1 tablet)	1.91	19.26	399.95–471.96

Dose=single oral dose.
Tmax=time to reach peak serum concentration.
Cmax=peak serum concentration.
AUC=area under the curve.

The bioavailability of Provera 100 mg tablets was assessed in a clinical study using 16 healthy, male volunteers. A single dose of medroxyprogesterone 100 mg was administered orally to subjects who fasted overnight and for 2 hours after the dose was administered. Blood samples were collected prior to, and at the following times, after drug administration: 0.5, 1, 2, 3, 4, 6, 8, 10, 12, 26, 32, 50, 74, 98, and 170 hours. Serum samples were analyzed for medroxyprogesterone using a radioimmunoassay procedure.

Relevant bioavailability parameters are included in Table II.

Table II—Provera

Bioavailability Parameters of Medroxyprogesterone Acetate Following Oral Administration

Provera Dose (mg)	Tmax (hr)	Cmax (ng/mL)	AUC (ng/hr/mL)
100 mg	4.1	35.2	974.2

Dose=single oral dose.
Tmax=time to reach peak serum concentration.
Cmax=peak serum concentration.
AUC=area under the curve.

Medroxyprogesterone has an apparent half-life of about 30 hours.

Medroxyprogesterone is rapidly absorbed from the gastrointestinal tract and metabolized in the liver to several progestin metabolites. The major drug-related material found in circulation following oral administration has been characterized as both free and glucuronide-conjugated metabolites of medroxyprogesterone.

Medroxyprogesterone is primarily eliminated via fecal excretion, to which biliary secretion may contribute. Approximately 44% of an oral dose is eliminated through urinary excretion in the form of metabolites.

The only metabolite of medroxyprogesterone that has been isolated and unequivocally identified is 6α-methyl-6β,17α,21-trihydroxy-4-pregnene-3,20-dione-17-acetate, and appears to be the primary urinary metabolite. This metabolite accounts for approximately 8% of an oral dose, and is found to be excreted as an glucuronide conjugate.

Indications: For hormonal replacement therapy, to oppose the effects of estrogen on the endometrium and significantly reduce the risk of hyperplasia and carcinoma.

For functional menstrual disorders due to hormonal imbalance in non-pregnant women, in the absence of organic pathology.

As adjunctive and/or palliative treatment of recurrent and/or metastatic endometrial carcinoma.

As adjunctive and/or palliative treatment of hormonally-dependent, recurrent metastatic breast cancer in post-menopausal women.

Contraindications: Thrombophlebitis, thromboembolic disorders, cerebral apoplexy or patients with a past history of these conditions. Known sensitivity to medroxyprogesterone, or to any of the tablet's excipients (see Supplied). Undiagnosed vaginal bleeding. Undiagnosed urinary tract bleeding. Undiagnosed breast pathology.

Pregnancy: Pregnancy (either for diagnosis or therapy) (see Warnings).

Warnings: Liver function tests should be performed periodically in patients who have or are suspected of having hepatic disease. The physician should be alert to the earliest manifestations of impaired liver function. Should these occur or be suspected, the drug should be discontinued and the patient's status re-evaluated.

Although medroxyprogesterone has not been causally associated with the induction of thromboembolic disorders, the physician should be alert to the earliest manifestations of these disorders. Should any occur, or be suspected, while the patient is undergoing therapy with medroxyprogesterone, the drug should be discontinued immediately. The patient's status and need for treatment should be carefully assessed before continuing therapy.

Pregnancy: Usage in pregnancy is not recommended. Progestational agents are also not recommended as a diagnostic test for pregnancy. If the patient is exposed to medroxyprogesterone during pregnancy or if she becomes pregnant while taking the drug, she should be apprised of the potential risk to the fetus.

Discontinue medication pending examination, if there is sudden partial or complete loss of vision, or if there is a sudden onset of proptosis, diplopia or migraine. If examination reveals papilledema or retinal vascular lesions, the drug should **not** be continued.

Clinical suppression of adrenocortical function has not been observed at low dose levels. However, the high doses of medroxyprogesterone used in the treatment of certain cancers may, in some cases, produce Cushingoid symptoms (e.g., "moon" facies, fluid retention, glucose intolerance, and blood pressure elevation).

Lactation: Detectable amounts of progestin have been identified in the milk of mothers receiving the drug. Infants exposed to medroxyprogesterone via breast milk have been studied for developmental and behavioral effects through puberty. No adverse effects have been noted.

Anaphylactic and anaphylactoid reactions have occasionally been reported in patients treated with medroxyprogesterone.

Precautions: Prior to administering medroxyprogesterone, a thorough examination should be conducted with special reference to breast and pelvic organs, and include a Papanicolaou smear. This evaluation should exclude the presence of genital or breast neoplasia before considering the use of this drug. For those patients who will be receiving this drug for the treatment of endometrial or breast cancer, the caution expressed by the preceding sentence does not apply.

Because this drug may cause some degree of fluid retention, conditions which might be influenced by this factor, such as epilepsy, migraine, asthma, cardiac or renal dysfunction require careful observation.

In cases of breakthrough bleeding, as in all cases of irregular bleeding per vagina, organic causes should be considered. In cases of undiagnosed vaginal bleeding, adequate diagnostic measures are indicated.

Patients should be advised of the menstrual bleeding patterns expected with the sequential regimen (see Dosage).

Upon sequential administration of medroxyprogesterone to women with adequate levels of estrogen (endogenous or exogenous), withdrawal bleeding usually occurs within 7 days after stopping this drug. Bleeding that occurs during medroxyprogesterone administration period indicates a need for a longer duration, or a higher dose.

Patients who have a history of mental depression should be carefully monitored while receiving therapy with medroxyprogesterone. Some patients may complain of premenstrual like depression while taking this medication.

A decrease in glucose tolerance has been observed in some patients on progestins. The mechanism of this decrease is obscure. For this reason, diabetic patients should be carefully observed while receiving medroxyprogesterone therapy.

The age of the patient constitutes no absolute limiting factor although treatment with progestins may mask the onset of the climacteric.

The pathologist should be advised of progestin therapy when relevant specimens are submitted.

Aminoglutethimide administered concomitantly with medroxyprogesterone may significantly depress the bioavailability of this drug.

Rifampin can increase the metabolism of exogenously administered progestational agents. The extent to which rifampin may alter the metabolism of medroxyprogesterone remains to be determined; the possibility of an interaction should be considered.

Adverse Effects: The following adverse reactions have been associated with the use of medroxyprogesterone: Breast: tenderness, galactorrhea.

Reproductive System: breakthrough bleeding, spotting, change in menstrual flow, amenorrhea, changes in cervical erosion and cervical secretions.

CNS: headache, nervousness, dizziness, depression, insomnia, somnolence, fatigue, premenstrual syndrome-like symptoms.

Thromboembolic Phenomena: including thrombophlebitis and pulmonary embolism.

Skin and Mucous Membranes: sensitivity reactions ranging from pruritus, urticaria, angioneurotic edema to generalized rash and anaphylaxis; acne, alopecia, hirsutism.

Gastrointestinal: abdominal discomfort, nausea, bloating.

Miscellaneous: pyrexia, increase in weight, peripheral edema, ''moon'' facies.

The following laboratoy tests may be affected by the use of medroxyprogesterone: gonadotropin levels, plasma progesterone levels, urinary pregnanediol levels, plasma testosterone levels (in the male), plasma estrogen levels (in the female), plasma cortisol levels, glucose tolerance test, metyrapone test.

Overdose: Symptoms: In female patients, overdosage may result in a period of amenorrhea of a variable length and may be followed by irregular menses for several cycles.

No cases of overdosage in male patients have been reported. However, such overdosage, if it were to occur, would not likely result in any particular symptomatology.

Treatment: There is no known therapy for overdosage of medroxyprogesterone. Doses as high as 1 000 mg for the therapy of endometrial carcinoma have been used without adverse effect.

Dosage: Hormone Replacement Therapy: Progestin Challenge Test: Subsequent to the diagnosis of menopause, the progestin challenge test is recommended for amenorrheic women with an intact uterus. Medroxyprogesterone 10 mg daily should be administered for 10 days.

A negative test is identified by the absence of withdrawal bleeding, and implies the absence of endometrial stimulation due to insufficient estrogen secretion. In these women, hormone replacement therapy consisting of estrogen therapy, and concurrent medroxyprogesterone, should be considered.

A positive test is indicated by the presence of withdrawal bleeding which occurs within 7 days after stopping medroxyprogesterone treatment. Withdrawal bleeding implies the presence of sufficient endogenous estrogen to stimulate the endometrium. Medroxyprogesterone therapy should be administered, as above, until withdrawal bleeding no longer occurs. This cessation of withdrawal bleeding indicates the absence of endometrial stimulation due to a decline in estrogen secretion. In these women, hormone replacement therapy consisting of estrogen therapy, and concurrent medroxyprogesterone should be considered.

Sequential Therapy: see Table III.

Table III—Provera

Sequential Therapy

Days of the Month: 1 2 3 4 5 6 7 8 9 10 11	12 13 14	15 16 17 18 19 20 21 22 23 24	25 26 27 28 29 30 31
Sequential Estrogen–25 days			
	Start	Provera 5–10 mg/day	
Continuous Estrogen–everyday			
Provera 5–10 mg/day	Stop		

In women with an intact uterus receiving estrogen replacement therapy, medroxyprogesterone may be given in a dosage of 5 to 10 mg daily for 12 to 14 days. The recommended starting dose should be 10 mg/day, administered for 12 to 14 days. A dose of 5 mg/day for 12 to 14 days may be appropriate for some women.

Note: The lowest dose required to protect the endometrium from estrogenic-hyperstimulation should be used. A good indicator is the lowest dose that will consistently result in withdrawal bleeding within 7 days after stopping medroxyprogesterone treatment. Bleeding that occurs during treatment indicates a need for a longer duration, or higher dose.

Functional Menstrual Disorders: Secondary Amenorrhea: After ruling out pregnancy, medroxyprogesterone may be administered in doses ranging from 5 to 10 mg daily depending upon the degree of progestational effect desired. The dose should be given daily for 12 to 14 days every month.

Note: In patients with poorly developed endometria, conventional estrogen therapy should be given in conjunction with medroxyprogesterone.

Dysfunctional Uterine Bleeding: In dysfunctional uterine bleeding, medroxyprogesterone may be given in doses ranging from 5 to 10 mg/day, for 10 to 14 days, beginning on the assumed or calculated 12th to 16th day of the cycle. This regimen should be repeated for 2 subsequent cycles or longer if necessary.

When bleeding is due to a deficiency of both ovarian hormones, as indicated by a poorly developed proliferative endometrium, conventional estrogen therapy should be given in conjunction with medroxyprogesterone. If bleeding is controlled satisfactorily, at least 2 subsequent cycles of treatment should be given.

If dysfunctional uterine bleeding is not controlled by hormone therapy, appropriate diagnostic measures should be undertaken to rule out uterine pathology.

Endometrial Cancer: 200 to 400 mg/day is the usual dose. It is suggested that if neither subjective nor objective improvement is noted within 2 to 3 months, therapy should be discontinued. Where improvement is noted and the disease process appears to be stabilized, it may be possible to maintain this improvement with a 200 mg/day dose.

Breast Cancer: The recommended dose is 400 mg daily, given in divided doses. The patient should be continued on therapy as long as she is responding to treatment. Although doses of up to 2 400 mg daily have been reported, controlled studies using 800 mg daily did not demonstrate any appreciable increase in response rates compared to the 400 mg daily dose.

Medroxyprogesterone is not recommended as primary therapy, but as adjunctive and palliative treatment in advanced, inoperable cases including those with recurrent metastatic disease.

Note: Response to hormonal therapy for endometrial or breast cancer may not be evident until 8 to 10 weeks of therapy. Rapid progression of disease at any time during therapy should result in termination of treatment with medroxyprogesterone.

Supplied: Provera Pak: 5 mg: Each blue tablet embossed ''U 286'' contains: medroxyprogesterone acetate 5 mg. Nonmedicinal ingredients: cornstarch, FD&C, lactose, starch and sucrose. Blisters of 14, cartons of 10.

10 mg: Each white tablet embossed ''Upjohn 50'' contains: medroxyprogesterone acetate 10 mg. Nonmedicinal ingredients: cornstarch, FD&C, lactose, starch and sucrose. Blisters of 10, cartons of 10.

Tablets: 2.5 mg: Each orange, round compressed tablet embossed ''U 64'', contains: medroxyprogesterone acetate 2.5 mg. Nonmedicinal ingredients: calcium stearate, cornstarch, FD&C Yellow #6, lactose, mineral oil, sucrose and talc. Gluten-free. Bottles of 100 and 500. Blisters of 30, cartons of 3.

5 mg: Each blue, round, scored, compressed tablet embossed ''U 286'', contains: medroxyprogesterone acetate 5 mg. Nonmedicinal ingredients: calcium stearate, cornstarch, FD&C Blue #2, lactose, mineral oil, sucrose and talc. Gluten-free. Bottles of 100 and 500.

10 mg: Each white, round, scored, compressed tablet, embossed ''Upjohn 50'', contains: medroxyprogesterone acetate 10 mg. Nonmedicinal ingredients: calcium stearate, cornstarch, lactose, mineral oil, sucrose and talc. Gluten-free. Bottles of 100 and 500.

100 mg: Each white, round, scored, compressed tablet embossed ''U 467'', contains: medroxyprogesterone acetate 100 mg. Nonmedicinal ingredients: calcium stearate, cornstarch, lactose, mineral oil, sodium laurylsulfate, sucrose and talc. Gluten-free. Bottles of 100.

Store at controlled room temperature (15 to 30°C).

(Shown in Product Recognition Section)

PROVIODINE®

Rougier

Povidone-Iodine

Antiseptic

Pharmacology: Proviodine is iodine complexed with povidone (polyvinyl-pyrrolidone). The compound is soluble in water forming a golden brown solution. Like iodine, the solution of the iodine complex is bactericidal and fungicidal. However, unlike solutions of iodine, it is non-staining. The antiseptic action of povidone-iodine solutions is due to the available iodine present in the complex.

Indications: Derma: Useful as a topical antimicrobial in preventing infections in lacerations, minor cuts, abrasions and burns caused by iodine susceptible pathogenic organisms. Helps prevent acute and chronic inflammatory infections such as in acne vulgaris. In pyodermas, as a topical adjunct to systemic antimicrobial therapy.

Detergent: Pre and postoperative scrubbing or washing. General antiseptic use.

Douche: For nonspecific vaginitis, vaginitis and vulvovaginitis associated with Trichomonas vaginalis and monilial infection. Routine cleansing douche and deodorant. Adjunctive use in preoperative vaginal prepping.

Hydro: Not intended for topical application but may be used as an additional antiseptic measure for hydrotherapy baths.

Ointment: First aid antisepsis in abrasions, cuts, minor burns, bacterial or mycotic dermatoses. The treatment of infected wounds and lacerations.

Ovules: For nonspecific vaginitis, vaginitis and vulvovaginitis associated with Trichomonas vaginalis and monilial infection.

Solution: Pre and postoperative skin and mucous membrane antisepsis. For disinfection and prevention of infection in abrasions, cuts, burns and wounds. For oral infections (stomatitis, etc.) and dental procedures.

Vaginal Gel: For nonspecific vaginitis, vaginitis and vulvovaginitis associated with Trichomonas vaginalis and monilial infection.

Precautions: Use with caution in patients known to be allergic to iodine. If irritation, redness or swelling develops, discontinue use of the product and institute appropriate measures. Blue stains on starched linen will wash off with soap and water.

Lactation: Povidone-iodine as vaginal douche may produce elevated breast milk iodine levels.

Proviodine (cont'd)

Adverse Effects: Although rare, local hypersensitivity reactions have occurred. Serum PBI may increase temporarily in some patients after topical application of povidone-iodine.

Dosage: Derma: Wet affected skin areas. Apply a sufficient amount of Proviodine Derma and work up rich lather. Allow lather 2 to 3 minutes contact with the affected areas. Rinse thoroughly. Does not stain skin or natural fabrics.

Detergent: Use about 5 mL on wet hands. Carefully follow steps and techniques of thorough antiseptic cleansing, scrubbing, brushing and rinsing, as usually followed prior to surgery.

Preoperative preparation of the patient: Apply approximately 1 mL/50 cm^2 of surface on previously shaved, wet skin. Rub thoroughly. Clean with sterile gauze soaked with water. For additional antiseptic protection, paint operating site with undiluted Proviodine Solution. Allow to dry for a few minutes.

Douche: Therapeutic douche: 2 capfuls (30 mL) diluted in 1.14 L of lukewarm water once daily for 6 to 12 days. Hygienic douche: 1 capful diluted in 1.14 L of lukewarm water, 1 to 2 times per week. Also for sitz baths. Dilutions: Generally between 5 to 10% in vol. (60 to 115 mL/1.14 L water).

Hydro: Dilute according to additional disinfection required or to individual patient need. Hydrotherapy: In general, effective concentration is 4 p.p.m. (30 mL/68.1 L water) or more. In certain cases, a higher concentration may be required.

Ointment: Apply locally 1 to 3 times per day. Cover with gauze or bandage if required.

Ovules: Insert 1 ovule high into the vagina preferably at bedtime. The use of the applicator is optional. Treatment is usually for 20 consecutive days and must be continued even during menstruation. Repeat treatment if necessary.

Solution: Preoperative preparations: swab or wet soak on operating site for 15 minutes following usual technique. Avoid pooling of the product beneath the patient. General use: swab with the nondiluted solution. Mouthwash: dilute in 1 or 2 parts of water.

Vaginal Gel: (Treatment for 12 days or more.) Insert syringe well into vagina and empty contents with plunger. Use once daily at bedtime. A vaginal douche with Proviodine Douche (dilute 30 mL/1.14 L of lukewarm water) is advisable every morning during treatment with Gel. Treatment may be continued through the menstrual cycle and during menstruation if required. If severe or prolonged irritation occurs, cease treatment.

Supplied: Derma: Each mL of sudsing, antiseptic liquid cleanser contains: povidone-iodine 7.5% (0.75% available iodine). Plastic bottles of 200 mL.

Detergent: Each mL of liquid contains: povidone-iodine 7.5% (0.75% available iodine). Bottles of 115 mL, 500 mL and 5 L.

Douche: Each mL of liquid contains: povidone-iodine 10% (1% available iodine). Bottles of 200 mL with 15 mL measuring cap.

Hydro: Each mL of liquid contains: povidone-iodine 10% (1% available iodine) with no foaming agent. Plastic jugs of 5 L.

Ointment: Each g contains: povidone-iodine 100 mg (10 mg of available iodine/g). Tubes of 30 g and jars of 500 g.

Ovules: Each ovule contains: povidone-iodine 250 mg (equivalent to 25 mg available iodine), in a readily soluble and water diffusible vehicle. Boxes of 20 with applicator.

Solution: Each mL of liquid contains: povidone-iodine 10% (1% available iodine). Bottles of 115 mL, 500 mL and 5 L.

Vaginal Gel: Each 5 g applicatorful of gel contains: povidone-iodine 500 mg (equivalent to 50 mg available iodine). Tubes of 90 g with applicators.

PROZAC® Ⓟ

Lilly

Fluoxetine HCl

Antidepressant—Antiobsessional—Antibulimic

Pharmacology: The antidepressant, antiobsessional, and antibulimic actions of fluoxetine are presumed to be linked to its ability to selectively inhibit the neuronal reuptake of serotonin. At clinically relevant doses fluoxetine blocks the uptake of serotonin into human platelets. Antagonism of muscarinic, histaminergic and α_1-adrenergic receptors has been hypothesized to be associated with various anticholinergic, sedative and cardiovascular effects of classical tricyclic antidepressant drugs. In vitro receptor binding studies have demonstrated that fluoxetine binds to these and other membrane receptors [opiate, serotonergic (5-HT$_1$, 5-HT$_2$), adrenergic (α_1, α_2, β) and dopaminergic] much less potently than do the tricyclic drugs.

Pharmacokinetics: Fluoxetine is well absorbed after oral administration. In man, following a single oral 40 mg dose, peak plasma concentrations of fluoxetine from 15 to 55 ng/mL are observed after 6 to 8 hours. The capsule and oral solution dosage forms of fluoxetine are bioequivalent. Food does not appear to affect the systemic bioavailability of fluoxetine, although it may delay its absorption inconsequentially. Thus fluoxetine may be administered with or without food.

Fluoxetine is extensively metabolized in the liver to norfluoxetine, and other, unidentified metabolites. The pharmacological activity of norfluoxetine, which is formed by demethylation of fluoxetine appears to be similar to that of the parent drug. Norfluoxetine contributes to the long duration of action of Prozac. The primary route of elimination appears to be hepatic metabolism to inactive metabolites excreted by the kidney.

Clinical Issues Related to Metabolism/Elimination: Variability in Metabolism: The metabolism of fluoxetine, like that of a number of other compounds, including tricyclic antidepressants and some selective serotonin reuptake inhibitors, involves the P450IID6 system. Concomitant therapy with fluoxetine and the aforementioned drugs may lead to clinically significant drug interactions (see Precautions, Drug Interactions).

Accumulation and Slow Elimination: The relatively slow elimination of fluoxetine and its active metabolite, norfluoxetine, results in significant accumulation of these active moieties in chronic use. Therefore, it may take up to 1 to 2 months for the active drug substance(s) to disappear from the body. This persistence of active moieties is important to keep in mind when fluoxetine is discontinued, or when drugs that are predicted to interact with fluoxetine are to be administered soon after its discontinuation (see Warnings, Implications of the long elimination half-life of fluoxetine and Precautions, Drug Interactions).

Kinetic Data: After 30 days of dosing at 20 mg/day, mean plasma concentrations of fluoxetine 79.1$\pm$33.4 ng/mL and of norfluoxetine 129$\pm$42.0 ng/mL have been observed. Plasma concentrations of fluoxetine (elimination half-life of 1 to 3 days after acute administration and 4 to 6 days after chronic administration) were higher than those predicted by single dose studies. Norfluoxetine appears to have linear pharmacokinetics. Its mean terminal half-lives after a single dose and multiple dose were 8.6 days and 9.3 days respectively.

Steady-state plasma levels are attained after 4 to 5 weeks of continuous drug administration. Patients receiving fluoxetine at doses of 40 to 80 mg/day over periods as long as 3 years exhibited, on average, plasma concentrations similar to those seen among patients treated for 4 to 5 weeks at the same dose.

Age: The effects of age upon the metabolism of fluoxetine have been investigated in a subset of 260 elderly, but otherwise healthy, depressed patients (mean age: 67.4 yr, range 60 to 85 yr) who received 20 mg fluoxetine for 6 weeks. Mean plasma concentrations were found to be 89.5$\pm$53.6 ng/mL for fluoxetine and 119$\pm$51.3 ng/mL for norfluoxetine. However, the effects of concomitant illness and/or concomitant drugs have not been evaluated.

Protein Binding: Approximately 94% of fluoxetine is protein bound. The interaction between fluoxetine and other highly protein bound drugs has not been evaluated, but may be important (see Precautions).

Liver Disease: In patients with cirrhosis, the elimination half-life of fluoxetine was prolonged, with a mean of 7.6 days compared to a range of 2 to 3 days seen in healthy subjects; norfluoxetine half-life was also prolonged, with a mean of 12 days compared to a range of 7 to 9 days in healthy subjects. Fluoxetine should therefore be used with caution in patients with liver disease (see Precautions and Dosage).

Renal Disease: In single dose studies, the pharmacokinetics of fluoxetine and norfluoxetine were similar among subjects with all levels of impaired renal function including anephric patients on chronic hemodialysis. However, with chronic administration, additional accumulation of fluoxetine or its metabolites (possibly including some not yet identified) may occur in patients with severely impaired renal function and the use of a lower or less frequent dose is advised (see Precautions).

Clinical Trials: The efficacy of fluoxetine was established in 5- and 6-week placebo-controlled clinical trials in depressed outpatients ($\geq$18 years of age), who met the DSM-III-R criteria for major depressive disorder.

Two, 6-week placebo-controlled clinical trials in depressed elderly patients, who met the DSM-III-R criteria for major depressive disorder (mean age 67.4 years, range 60 to 85 years) have shown Prozac, 20 mg/day, to be effective.

Indications: Depression: For the symptomatic relief of depressive illness.

Bulimia Nervosa: Fluoxetine has been shown to significantly decrease binge-eating and purging activity when compared with placebo treatment.

Obsessive-Compulsive Disorder: Fluoxetine has been shown to significantly reduce the symptoms of obsessive-compulsive disorder in double-blind, placebo-controlled clinical trials.

The obsessions or compulsions must be experienced as intrusive, markedly distressing, time-consuming, or interfering significantly with the person's social or occupational functioning.

The efficacy of fluoxetine in hospitalized patients has not been adequately studied.

The effectiveness of fluoxetine in long-term use (i.e., for more than 5 to 6 weeks in depression, for more than 16 weeks in bulimia nervosa, or for more than 13 weeks in obsessive compulsive disorder), has not been systematically evaluated in controlled trials. Therefore, the physician who elects to use fluoxetine for extended periods should periodically re-evaluate the long-term usefulness of the drug for the individual patient.

Contraindications: In patients with known hypersensitivity to the drug.

MAO Inhibitors: There have been reports of serious, sometimes fatal, reactions (including hyperthermia, rigidity, myoclonus, autonomic instability with possible rapid fluctuations of vital signs, and mental status changes that include extreme agitation progressing to delirium and coma) in patients receiving fluoxetine in combination with a MAO inhibitor and in patients who have recently discontinued fluoxetine and then started on a MAO inhibitor. Some cases presented with features resembling neuroleptic malignant syndrome. Therefore, **fluoxetine should not be used in combination with a MAO inhibitor or within a minimum of 14 days of discontinuing therapy with a MAO inhibitor.** Since fluoxetine and its major metabolite have very long elimination half-lives, at least 5 weeks should be allowed after stopping fluoxetine before starting a MAO inhibitor. Limited reports suggest that i.v. administered dantrolene or orally administered cyproheptadine may benefit patients experiencing such reactions.

Warnings: Allergic Reactions (Rash and Accompanying Events): During premarketing testing of more than 5 600 patients given fluoxetine, approximately 4% developed a rash and/or urticaria. Among these cases, almost a third were withdrawn from treatment because of the rash and/or systemic signs or symptoms associated with the rash. Clinical findings reported in association with these allergic reactions include rash, fever, leukocytosis, arthralgias, edema, carpal tunnel syndrome, respiratory distress, lymphadenopathy, proteinuria, and mild transaminase elevation. Most patients improved promptly with discontinuation of fluoxetine and/or adjunctive treatment with antihistamines or steroids, and all patients experiencing these events were reported to recover completely.

In premarketing clinical trials 2 patients are known to have developed a serious cutaneous systemic illness. In neither patient was there an unequivocal diagnosis, but one was considered to have a leukocytoclastic vasculitis, and the other severe desquamation that was considered variously to be a vasculitis or erythema multiforme. Other patients have had systemic manifestations suggestive of serum sickness.

Since the introduction of fluoxetine, systemic events, possibly related to vasculitis, have developed in patients with rash. Although these events are rare, they may be serious, involving the lung, kidney, or liver. Death has been reported to occur in association with these systemic events.

Anaphylactoid events, including bronchospasm, angioedema, and urticaria alone and in combination, have been reported.

Pulmonary events, including inflammatory processes of varying histopathology and/or fibrosis, have been reported rarely. These events have occurred with dyspnea as the only preceding symptom.

Whether these systemic events and rash have a common underlying cause or are due to different etiologies or pathogenic processes is not known. Furthermore, a specific underlying immunologic basis for these events has not been identified. Upon the appearance of rash or of other allergic phenomena for which an alternative etiology cannot be identified, fluoxetine should be discontinued. Particular caution should be exercised in patients with a history of allergic reactions.

Implications of the Long Elimination Half-Life of Fluoxetine: Because of the long elimination half-lives of fluoxetine and its major active metabolite norfluoxetine, changes in dose will not be fully reflected in plasma for several weeks, affecting both strategies for titration to final dose and withdrawal from treatment (see Pharmacology and Dosage). Even when dosing is stopped, active drug substance will persist in the body for weeks due to the long elimination half-lives of fluoxetine and norfluoxetine. This is of potential consequence when drug discontinuation is required or when drugs are prescribed that might interact with fluoxetine and norfluoxetine following discontinuation of fluoxetine.

Precautions: Anxiety and Insomnia: During premarketing clinical trials, anxiety, nervousness and insomnia were reported by 10 to 15% of patients treated with fluoxetine. These symptoms led to discontinuation of the drug in 5% of the patients.
Weight Change: Significant weight loss, especially in underweight depressed patients and the elderly, may be an undesirable result of treatment with fluoxetine.
Mania/Hypomania: During premarketing clinical trials in a patient population comprised primarily of unipolar depressives, hypomania or mania occurred in approximately 1% of fluoxetine treated patients. The incidence in a general patient population which might also include bipolar depressives is unknown. The likelihood of hypomanic or manic episodes may be increased at the higher dosage levels. Such reactions require a reduction in dosage or discontinuation of the drug.
Seizures: Fluoxetine should be used with caution in patients with a history of convulsive disorders. The incidence of seizures associated with fluoxetine during clinical trials did not appear to differ from that reported with other marketed antidepressants; however, patients with a history of convulsive disorders were excluded from these trials.

Concurrent administration with electroshock therapy should be avoided because of the absence of experience in this area. There have been rare reports of a prolonged seizure in patients on fluoxetine receiving ECT treatment.
Hypokalemia: Self-induced vomiting often leads to hypokalemia which may lower seizure threshold and/or may lead to cardiac conduction abnormalities. Electrolyte levels of bulimic patients should be assessed prior to initiation of treatment.
Suicide: The possibility of a suicide attempt is inherent in depression and may persist until significant remission occurs. Therefore, high risk patients should be closely supervised throughout therapy and consideration should be given to the possible need for hospitalization. In order to minimize the opportunity for overdosage, prescriptions for fluoxetine should be written for the smallest quantity of drug consistent with good patient management.
Concomitant Illness: Clinical experience with fluoxetine in patients with concomitant systemic illness is limited and it should be used cautiously in such patients, especially those with diseases or conditions that could affect metabolism or hemodynamic responses.

Fluoxetine has not been evaluated or used to any appreciable extent in patients with a recent history of myocardial infarction or unstable heart disease. Patients with these diagnoses were systematically excluded from premarketing clinical studies. Retrospective evaluation of ECGs in some of these studies showed no conduction abnormalities that resulted in heart block. The mean heart rate was reduced by approximately 3 beats/minute.

Fluoxetine should be given with caution to patients suffering from anorexia nervosa and only if the expected benefits (e.g., co-morbid depression) markedly outweigh the potential weight reducing effect of the drug.

In patients with diabetes, fluoxetine may alter glycemic control. Hypoglycemia has occurred during therapy with fluoxetine and hyperglycemia has developed following discontinuation of the drug. As is true with many other types of medication when taken concurrently by patients with diabetes, insulin and/or oral hypoglycemic dosage may need to be adjusted when therapy with fluoxetine is instituted or discontinued.

Since fluoxetine is extensively metabolized, excretion of unchanged drug in urine is a minor route of elimination. However, until adequate number of patients with severe renal impairment have been evaluated in the course of chronic treatment, fluoxetine should be used with caution in such patients.

Since clearances of fluoxetine and norfluoxetine may be decreased in patients with impaired liver function including cirrhosis, a lower or less frequent dose should be used in such patients.
Hyponatremia: Several cases of hyponatremia (some with serum sodium lower than 110 mmol/L) have been reported. The hyponatremia appeared to be reversible when fluoxetine was discontinued. Although these cases were complex with varying possible etiologies, some were possibly due to the syndrome of inappropriate antidiuretic hormone secretion (SIADH). The majority of these occurrences have been in older patients and in patients taking diuretics or who were otherwise volume depleted.

In a placebo-controlled, double-blind trial in elderly patients, 10 of 313 fluoxetine-treated patients and 6 of 320 placebo-treated patients had a lowering of serum sodium below the reference range. The lowest observed concentration of sodium in a fluoxetine treated patient was 129 mmol/L.
Platelet Function: There have been rare reports of altered platelet function and/or abnormal results from laboratory studies in patients taking fluoxetine. While there have been reports of abnormal bleeding in several patients taking fluoxetine, it is unclear whether fluoxetine had a causative role.
Occupational Hazards: Patients should be cautioned against driving an automobile or performing hazardous tasks until they are reasonably certain that treatment with fluoxetine does not affect them adversely.
Pregnancy: Safe use of fluoxetine during pregnancy has not been established. Therefore, it should not be administered to women of childbearing potential unless, in the opinion of the treating physician, the expected benefits to the patient markedly outweigh the possible hazards to the child or fetus.
Lactation: Fluoxetine and its metabolites are excreted in breast milk, and have been observed to reach high plasma levels in nursing infants. Women who are taking fluoxetine should not breast-feed unless, in the opinion of the treating physician, breast-feeding is necessary, in which case the infant should be closely monitored.

In one breast milk sample, the concentration of fluoxetine plus norfluoxetine was 70.4 ng/mL. The concentration in the mother's plasma was 295 ng/mL. No adverse effects on the infant were reported. In another case, a 6-week infant, nursed by a mother on fluoxetine, developed crying, decreased sleep, vomiting and watery stools. The breast milk showed concentrations of 69 ng/mL for fluoxetine and 90 ng/mL for norfluoxetine. In the infant's plasma, the concentrations of fluoxetine and norfluoxetine on the second day of feeding were 340 and 208 ng/mL, respectively.
Children: Safety and effectiveness in patients below the age of 18 have not been established.
Geriatrics: Evaluation of patients over the age of 60 who received fluoxetine 20 mg daily revealed no unusual pattern of adverse events relative to the clinical experience in younger patients. These data are however insufficient to rule out possible age-related differences during chronic use, particularly in elderly patients who have concomitant systemic illnesses or who are receiving concomitant drugs.
Drug Interactions: MAO Inhibitors: Combined use of fluoxetine and MAO inhibitors is contraindicated (see Contraindications).
Tricyclic Antidepressants: In two studies, previously stable plasma levels of imipramine and desipramine have increased greater than 2- to 10-fold when fluoxetine has been administered in combination. This influence may persist for 3 weeks or longer after fluoxetine is discontinued. Thus, the dose of tricyclic antidepressant (TCA) may need to be reduced and plasma TCA concentrations may need to be monitored temporarily when fluoxetine is coadministered or has been recently discontinued. See Pharmacology, Accumulation and Slow Elimination and Precautions, P450 and Isoenzyme (IID6).
Lithium: There have been reports of both increased and decreased **lithium** levels when lithium was used concomitantly with fluoxetine. Cases of lithium toxicity have been reported. Lithium levels should be monitored when these drugs are administered concomitantly.
Tryptophan: Five patients receiving fluoxetine in combination with **tryptophan** experienced adverse reactions, including agitation, restlessness and gastrointestinal distress.
Diazepam: The half-life of concurrently administered **diazepam** may be prolonged in some patients. Experience with the use of fluoxetine in combination with other CNS-active drugs is limited and caution is advised if such concomitant medication is required (see Warnings).
Phenytoin: In patients on stable, maintenance doses of phenytoin, plasma phenytoin concentrations increased substantially and symptoms of phenytoin toxicity appeared (nystagmus, diplopia, ataxia and CNS depression) following initiation of concomitant fluoxetine treatment.
Drugs Tightly Bound to Plasma Protein: Because fluoxetine is highly bound to plasma protein, the administration of fluoxetine to a patient taking another drug which is tightly bound to protein (e.g., warfarin, digitoxin) may cause a shift in plasma concentrations potentially resulting in an adverse effect. Conversely, adverse effects may result from displacement of protein bound fluoxetine by other tightly bound drugs.
Drugs Metabolized by P450 Isoenzyme (IID6): Approximately 3 to 10% of the normal population has a genetic defect that leads to reduced levels of activity of the cytochrome P450 isoenzyme P450IID6. Such individuals have been referred to as "poor metabolizers" of drugs such as debrisoquine, dextromethorphan, sparteine, tricyclic antidepressants (e.g., nortryptiline, amitriptyline, imipramine and desipramine), phenothiazine neuroleptics (e.g., perphenazine and thioridazine) and Type 1C antiarrhythmics (e.g., propafenone and flecainide).

Conversely, approximately 90 to 97% of the normal population do not have this genetic defect, and are known as "extensive metabolizers". Fluoxetine, like other agents that are metabolized by the P450IID6 system, inhibits the activity of this isoenzyme, and thus may make normal "extensive" metabolizers resemble "poor metabolizers". Therapy with medications that are predominantly metabolized by the P450IID6 system and that have a relatively narrow therapeutic index (e.g., flecainide, encainide, vinblastine, carbamazepine and tricyclic antidepressants) should be initiated at the low end of the dose range if a patient is receiving fluoxetine concurrently, or has taken it in the previous 5 weeks.

If fluoxetine is added to the treatment regimen of a patient already receiving a drug metabolized by P450IID6 the need for decreased dose of the original medication should be considered. The aforementioned drugs with a narrow therapeutic index represent the greatest concern.
Dependence Liability: Fluoxetine has not been systematically studied, in animals or humans, for its potential for abuse, tolerance, or physical dependence. Physicians should carefully evaluate patients for history of drug abuse and follow such patients closely, observing them for signs of misuse or abuse of fluoxetine.

Adverse Effects: Commonly Observed: In clinical trials, the most commonly observed adverse events associated with the use of fluoxetine and not seen at an equivalent incidence among placebo treated patients were: CNS complaints, including headache, nervousness, insomnia, drowsiness, fatigue or asthenia, anxiety, tremor, and dizziness or lightheadedness; gastrointestinal complaints, including nausea, diarrhea, dry mouth and anorexia; and excessive sweating.
Adverse Events Leading to Discontinuation of Treatment: Fifteen percent of approximately 4 000 patients who received fluoxetine in North American clinical trials discontinued treatment due to an adverse event. The more common events causing discontinuation from depression trials in adults and elderly, included: psychiatric, primarily nervousness, anxiety, and insomnia; digestive, primarily nausea; nervous system, primarily dizziness, asthenia and headaches; skin, primarily rash and pruritus.

In obsessive compulsive disorder studies, 12.1% of fluoxetine treated patients discontinued treatment early because of adverse events. Anxiety, and rash, at incidences of less than 2%, were the most frequently reported events. In bulimia nervosa studies, 10.2% of fluoxetine treated patients discontinued treatment early because of adverse events. Insomnia, anxiety and rash, at incidences of less than 2%, were the most frequently reported events.
Serious Adverse Reactions: Suicidal thoughts and acts are far more common among depressed patients than in the general population. It is estimated that suicide is 22 to 36 times more prevalent in depressed persons than in the general population. A comprehensive meta-analysis of pooled data from 17 double blind clinical trials in patients with major depressive disorder compared fluoxetine (n=1 765) with a tricyclic antidepressant (n=731) or placebo (n=569), or both. The pooled incidence of emergence of substantial suicidal ideation was 1.2% for fluoxetine, 2.6% for placebo, and 3.6% for tricyclic antidepressants.

In countries where the drug has already been marketed, the following potentially serious adverse reactions have been reported: interactions with MAO inhibitors and possibly other drugs, allergic reactions, cardiovascular reactions, syndrome of inappropriate ADH secretion, and grand mal seizure. Death and life-threatening events have been associated with some of these reactions, although causal relationship to fluoxetine has not been established.

Postmarketing experience also confirms the profile of adverse reactions commonly reported during clinical trials with fluoxetine, including allergic skin reactions.
Adverse Experience Reports: The pattern of treatment-emergent adverse experience incidence (≥5%) for both fluoxetine and placebo was somewhat different in bulimia and obsessive compulsive disorder trials than in the adult and elderly depression studies, and is summarized in Table I (on following page).

The following adverse reactions, were reported on at least one occasion by patients during treatment with fluoxetine either during clinical trials or after marketing. All reported events are included except those where a drug cause was

Prozac (cont'd)

Table I—Prozac

Adverse Experience Reports

Body System/ Adverse Event	Depression (Adults) Fluoxetine (N=1730)	Depression (Adults) Placebo (N=799)	Depression (Elderly) Fluoxetine (N=335)	Depression (Elderly) Placebo (N=336)	OCD Fluoxetine (N=264)	OCD Placebo (N=89)	Bulimia Fluoxetine (N=418)	Bulimia Placebo (N=210)
Nervous								
headache	20.3	15.5	27.5	23.8	32.6	23.6	30.1	26.9
nervousness	14.9	8.5	12.2	7.4	14.4	14.6	10.8	5.2
insomnia	13.8	7.1	18.2	12.5	29.6	22.5	33.1	15.0
somnolence	11.6	6.3	9.3	5.7	17.1	6.7	12.7	7.1
anxiety	9.4	5.5	13.1	8.0	13.6	6.7	16.3	11.1
tremor	7.9	2.4	7.8	3.9	9.1	1.1	13.7	2.0
dizziness	5.7	3.3	11.0	10.1	13.3	11.2	11.4	5.4
libido, decreased	1.6	—	—	—	11.4	2.3	5.9	0.9
depression	—	—	—	—	8.0	14.6	10.1	16.4
emotional lability	—	—	—	—	—	—	2.7	7.8
Digestive								
nausea	21.1	10.1	16.7	7.4	26.5	13.5	29.7	13.5
diarrhea	12.3	7.0	14.3	8.9	18.2	13.5	7.5	6.7
dry mouth	9.5	6.0	6.6	4.8	12.1	3.4	9.9	8.6
anorexia	8.7	1.5	10.7	1.8	16.7	10.1	8.8	4.4
dyspepsia	6.4	4.3	11.0	5.1	9.9	4.5	10.7	6.7
gastrointestinal disorder	—	—	—	—	5.7	1.1	5.7	5.9
constipation	—	—	6.9	6.3	4.2	6.7	4.8	4.6
flatulence	—	—	7.2	2.4	3.4	5.6	—	—
Skin and Appendages								
sweating, excessive	8.4	3.8	7.2	3.3	7.2	—	8.9	1.6
rash	—	—	—	—	6.4	3.4	5.1	4.9
Body as a Whole								
asthenia	4.4	1.9	12.8	10.1	15.2	10.1	21.7	9.6
flu syndrome	—	—	—	—	9.9	6.7	10.1	5.9
back pain	—	—	6.9	8.6	2.7	5.6	3.9	7.0
infection	—	—	—	—	—	—	6.2	6.2
abdominal pain	—	—	6.0	5.7	4.9	11.2	9.6	6.5
myalgia	—	—	3.3	5.4	—	—	4.7	9.4
Respiratory								
upper respiratory infection	7.6	6.0	—	—	—	—	—	—
rhinitis	—	—	9.0	14.3	22.7	23.6	23.0	29.1
pharyngitis	—	—	—	—	10.6	9.0	11.1	5.5
sinusitis	—	—	3.3	6.8	—	—	5.7	6.9
yawn	—	—	—	—	7.2	—	11.1	0.8
Cardiovascular								
vasodilatation	—	—	—	—	5.3	—	—	—
Urogenital								
menstrual disorder	—	—	—	—	3.4	5.6	8.3	4.8
dysmenorrhea	—	—	—	—	3.4	5.6	6.1	7.8
urinary frequency	—	—	—	—	—	—	6.2	1.6
urinary tract infection	—	—	—	—	—	—	5.1	2.0

remote or the event term so general as to be unhelpful. Multiple events may have been reported by a single patient and related to a single condition, which may have preexisted. Therefore, while the following events occurred during treatment with fluoxetine, they were not necessarily caused by it.

Events are further classified within body system categories and enumerated in order of decreasing frequency using the following definitions: frequent adverse events are defined as those occurring on 1 or more occasions in at least 1% of patients; infrequent adverse events are those occurring in less than 1% but at least 1/1 000 patients; rare events are those occurring in less than 1/1 000 patients.

Allergic or Toxic: Frequent: rash, pruritus.

Infrequent: chills and fever, urticaria, maculopapular rash.

Rare: allergic reaction, erythema multiforme, vesiculobullous rash, serum sickness, contact dermatitis, erythema nodosum, purpuric rash, leukocytoclastic vasculitis, leukopenia, thrombocythemia, arthralgia, angioedema, bronchospasm, lung fibrosis, allergic alveolitis, larynx edema, respiratory distress.

Neurologic: Frequent: headache, tremor, dizziness or lightheadedness, asthenia.

Infrequent: abnormal gait, ataxia, akathisia, buccoglossal syndrome, hyperkinesia, hypertonia, incoordination, neck rigidity, extrapyramidal syndrome, convulsions, photophobia, myoclonus, vertigo, migraine, tinnitus, hypoesthesia, neuralgia, neuropathy, acute brain syndrome.

Rare: dysarthria, dystonia, torticollis, decreased reflexes, nystagmus, paralysis, paresthesia, carpal tunnel syndrome, stupor, coma, abnormal EEG, chronic brain syndrome, dyskinesia and other movement disorders (including worsening of preexisting conditions or appearance in patients with risk factors [e.g., Parkinson's disease, treatment with neuroleptics or other drugs known to be associated with movement disorders]) neuroleptic malignant syndrome-like events.

Behavioral: Frequent: insomnia, anxiety, nervousness, agitation, abnormal dreams, drowsiness and fatigue.

Infrequent: confusion, delusions, hallucinations, manic reaction, paranoid reaction, psychosis, depersonalization, apathy, emotional lability, euphoria, hostility, amnesia, increased libido.

Rare: antisocial reaction, hysteria, suicidal ideation, violent behaviors.

Autonomic: Frequent: excessive sweating.

Infrequent: dry mouth, constipation, urinary retention, vision disturbance, diplopia, mydriasis, hot flushes.

Cardiovascular: Infrequent: chest pain, hypertension, syncope, hypotension (including postural hypotension), angina pectoris, arrhythmia, tachycardia.

Rare: bradycardia, ventricular arrhythmia, first degree AV block, bundle branch block, myocardial infarct, cerebral ischemia, cerebral vascular accident, thrombophlebitis.

Gastrointestinal: Frequent: nausea, disturbances of appetite, diarrhea.

Infrequent: vomiting, stomatitis, dysphagia, eructation, esophagitis, gastritis, gingivitis, glossitis, melena, thirst, abnormal liver function tests.

Rare: bloody diarrhea, hematemesis, gastrointestinal hemorrhage, duodenal ulcer, stomach ulcer, mouth ulceration, hyperchlorhydria, colitis, enteritis, cholecystitis, cholelithiasis, hepatitis, hepatomegaly, liver tenderness, jaundice, increased salivation, salivary gland enlargement, tongue discoloration, fecal incontinence, pancreatitis.

Respiratory: Frequent: bronchitis, rhinitis, yawn.

Infrequent: asthma, dyspnea, hyperventilation, pneumonia, hiccups, epistaxis.

Rare: apnea, lung edema, hypoxia, pleural effusion, hemoptysis.

Endocrine: Frequent: weight loss.

Infrequent: generalized edema, peripheral edema, face edema, tongue edema, hypoglycemia, hypothyroidism, weight gain.

Rare: dehydration, gout, goitre, hyperthyroidism, hypercholesteremia, hyperglycemia, hyperlipemia, hyperprolactinemia, hypokalemia, hyponatremia, iron deficiency anemia, syndrome of inappropriate ADH secretion.

Hematologic: Infrequent: anemia, lymphadenopathy, hemorrhage.

Rare: bleeding time increased, leukocytosis, lymphocytosis, thrombocytopenia, thrombocytopenic purpura, thrombocythemia, retinal hemorrhage, petechia, purpura, sedimentation rate increased, aplastic anemia, pancytopenia, immune-related hemolytic anemia.

Dermatologic: Infrequent: acne, alopecia, dry skin, herpes simplex.

Rare: eczema, psoriasis, seborrhea, skin hypertrophy, skin discoloration, herpes zoster, fungal dermatitis, hirsutism, ecchymoses.

Musculoskeletal: Frequent: muscle pain, back pain, joint pain.

Infrequent: arthritis, bone pain, bursitis, tenosynovitis, twitching.

Rare: bone necrosis, osteoporosis, pathological fracture, chondrodystrophy, myositis, rheumatoid arthritis, muscle hemorrhage.

Urogenital: Frequent: painful menstruation, impotence, sexual dysfunction, urinary tract infection, frequent micturition.

Infrequent: abnormal ejaculation, menopause, amenorrhea, menorrhagia, ovarian disorder, vaginitis, leukorrhea, fibrocystic breast, breast pain, cystitis, dysuria, urinary urgency, urinary incontinence.

Rare: breast enlargement, galactorrhea, abortion, dyspareunia, uterine spasm, vaginal hemorrhage, metrorrhagia, hematuria, albuminuria, polyuria, pyuria, epididymitis, orchitis, pyelonephritis, salpingitis, urethritis, kidney calculus, urethral pain, urolithiasis.

Miscellaneous: Frequent: chills, abnormal vision.

Infrequent: amblyopia, conjunctivitis, cyst, ear pain, eye pain, jaw pain, neck pain, pelvic pain, hangover effect, malaise.

Rare: abdomen enlarged, blepharitis, cataract, corneal lesion, glaucoma, iritis, ptosis, strabismus, deafness, taste loss, moniliasis, hydrocephalus, LE syndrome.

Overdose: During clinical trials, there were 2 deaths among approximately 38 reports of acute overdose with fluoxetine, either alone or in combination with other drugs and/or alcohol. One death involved a combined overdose with approximately 1 800 mg of fluoxetine and an undetermined amount of maprotiline. Plasma concentrations of fluoxetine and maprotiline were 4.57 mg/L and 4.18 mg/L, respectively.

A second death involved 3 drugs yielding plasma concentrations as follows: fluoxetine, 1.93 mg/L; norfluoxetine, 1.10 mg/L; codeine, 1.80 mg/L; temazepam 3.80 mg/L.

One other patient who reportedly took up to 3 000 mg of fluoxetine experienced 2 grand mal seizures that remitted spontaneously without specific treatment. Since vomiting occurred, the amount of drug absorbed may have been less than that ingested.

In the postmarketing phase, there have been 16 confirmed reports of overdose of fluoxetine taken alone. The amount of drug ingested has varied from 80 mg to 2 000 mg and the patients have ranged in age from 13 to 51 years. There have been no deaths in this group of patients, some of whom were treated vigorously with activated charcoal in the acute phase. Furthermore, patient recoveries were remarkable in the absence of serious adverse events with the exception of a 13 year old male who ingested 1 880 mg and experienced 2 brief seizures but thereafter had an uneventful recovery.

Since introduction, reports of death attributed to overdosage of fluoxetine alone have been rare.

Symptoms: Nausea and vomiting were prominent in overdoses involving higher fluoxetine doses. Other prominent symptoms of overdose included agitation, restlessness, hypomania, and other signs of CNS excitation, including seizures.

Treatment: Establish and maintain an airway; ensure adequate oxygenation and ventilation. Activated charcoal, which may be used with sorbitol, may be as or more effective than emesis or lavage, and should be considered in treating overdose.

Cardiac and vital signs monitoring is recommended, along with general symptomatic and supportive measures. Based on experience in animals, which may not be relevant to humans, fluoxetine-induced seizures which fail to remit spontaneously may respond to diazepam.

There are no specific antidotes for fluoxetine.

Due to the large volume of distribution of fluoxetine, forced diuresis, dialysis, hemoperfusion, and exchange transfusion are unlikely to be of benefit.

In managing overdosage, consider the possibility of multiple drug involvement. The physician should consider contacting a poison control centre on the treatment of any overdosage.

Dosage: Since it may take up to 4 or 5 weeks to reach steady state plasma levels of fluoxetine, sufficient time should be allowed to elapse before dosage is gradually increased. Higher dosages are usually associated with an increased incidence of adverse reactions.

Depression: Adults: The recommended initial dosage is 20 mg administered once daily in the morning. A gradual dose increase should be considered only after a trial period of several weeks if the expected clinical improvement does not occur. Dosage should not exceed a maximum of 80 mg/day since clinical experience with doses above 80 mg/day is very limited.

Geriatrics: Fluoxetine was evaluated in depressed elderly patients only at a dosage of 20 mg/day. A lower or less frequent dosage may be effective and should be considered in elderly patients with concurrent disease or on multiple medications.

Children: The safety and effectiveness of fluoxetine in patients below the age of 18 years have not been established.

Bulimia Nervosa: Adults: The recommended dosage is 60 mg/day, although studies show that lower doses may also be efficacious. Electrolyte levels should be assessed prior to initiation of treatment.

Obsessive-Compulsive Disorder: A dose range of 20 mg/day to 60 mg/day is recommended for the treatment of obsessive-compulsive disorder.

For any indication, the total fluoxetine dosage should not exceed a maximum of 80 mg/day since clinical experience with doses above 80 mg/day is very limited.

During maintenance therapy, the dosage should be kept at the lowest effective level.

A lower or less frequent dosage should be used in patients with renal and/or hepatic impairment and in those on multiple medications.

Switching Patients to a Tricyclic Antidepressant (TCA): Dosage of a TCA may need to be reduced, and plasma TCA concentrations may need to be monitored temporarily when fluoxetine is coadministered or has been recently discontinued (see Drug Interactions, Tricyclic Antidepressants).

Switching Patients to or from a MAO Inhibitor: At least 14 days should elapse between discontinuation of an MAO inhibitor and initiation of therapy with fluoxetine. In addition, at least 5 weeks, perhaps longer, should be allowed after stopping fluoxetine before starting an MAO inhibitor (see Contraindications).

Supplied: Capsules: 10 mg: Each green and grey capsule, printed with Lilly 3104 and Prozac 10 mg, contains: fluoxetine HCl equivalent to fluoxetine 10 mg. Nonmedicinal ingredients: silicone and starch. The capsule shell contains: benzyl alcohol, carboxymethylcellulose, edetate calcium disodium, FD&C Blue No. 1, gelatin, iron oxide black, iron oxide yellow, methylparaben, sodium, sodium lauryl sulfate, sodium propionate and titanium dioxide. Amber bottles of 100.

20 mg: Each green and white capsule, printed with Lilly 3105 and Prozac 20 mg, contains: fluoxetine HCl equivalent to fluoxetine 20 mg. Nonmedicinal ingredients: silicone and starch. The capsule shell contains: benzyl alcohol, carboxymethylcellulose, edetate calcium disodium, FD&C Blue No. 1, gelatin, iron oxide yellow, methylparaben, sodium, sodium lauryl sulfate, sodium propionate and titanium dioxide. Amber bottles of 100.

Liquid: Each 5 mL clear, colorless, syrup solution, with an odor of mint, contains: fluoxetine HCl equivalent to fluoxetine 20 mg/5 mL. Nonmedicinal ingredients: benzoic acid, glycerin, mint flavor, purified water and sucrose. Energy: 50.3 kJ (12.0 kcal)/5 mL. Amber glass bottles of 120 mL (M-5120).

Store at 15 to 25°C.

Reviewed 1997

PSORIGEL®

Galderma

Coal Tar

Antipsoriatic

Supplied: Each tube contains: Owentar, equivalent to 7.5% coal tar solution USP (crude coal tar 1.5%) in a hydro alcoholic (ethyl alcohol 33.3%) gel vehicle. Nonmedicinal ingredients: alcohol SD-40, citric acid and/or sodium hydroxide (to adjust pH), hydroxyethyl cellulose, fragrance, laureth-4, propylene glycol and purified water. Plastic tubes of 110 g.

PULMICORT® NEBUAMP® Pr

Astra

Budesonide

Glucocorticosteroid—Asthma Therapy

Pharmacology: Budesonide is a potent nonhalogenated synthetic glucocorticosteroid with strong topical and weak systemic effects.

Budesonide has a high topical anti-inflammatory potency and it is rapidly biotransformed in the liver. This favorable separation between topical anti-inflammatory activity and systemic effect is due to strong glucocorticosteroid receptor affinity and an effective first pass metabolism with a short half-life.

The late reaction can be significantly inhibited if Pulmicort Nebuamp is given at least 2 hours before a bronchial challenge. Pretreatment for 1 to 4 weeks with inhaled budesonide may inhibit the immediate bronchial reaction.

After therapeutic use of orally inhaled budesonide, several weeks may pass before the full effect is obtained.

Indications: Patients with bronchial asthma, who require maintenance treatment with inhaled glucocorticosteroids for control of the underlying airways inflammation and who are unable to efficiently use other inhaled formulations.

Contraindications: Status asthmaticus; not to be used in primary treatment of acute episodes of asthma or in patients with moderate to severe bronchiectasis, known hypersensitivity to any components, active or quiescent pulmonary tuberculosis, untreated fungal, bacterial or viral infections of the respiratory system.

Warnings: Deaths due to adrenal insufficiency have occurred in asthmatic patients during and after transfer from systemic corticosteroids to inhaled corticosteroids; therefore, particular care is needed in patients who are transferred from systemically active corticosteroids to budesonide. After withdrawal from systemic corticosteroids, a number of months are required for recovery of hypothalamic-pituitary-adrenal (HPA) function. During this period of HPA suppression, patients may exhibit signs and symptoms of adrenal insufficiency when exposed to trauma, surgery or infections, particularly gastroenteritis. Although budesonide may provide control of asthmatic symptoms during these episodes, it does **not** provide the systemic steroid which is necessary for coping with these emergencies.

During periods of stress or a severe asthmatic attack, patients who have been withdrawn from systemic corticosteroids should be instructed to resume systemic steroids (in large dosages) immediately and to contact their physicians for further instruction. These patients should also be instructed to carry a warning card indicating that they may need supplementary systemic steroids during periods of stress or a severe asthma attack. To assess the risk of adrenal insufficiency in emergency situations, routine tests of adrenal cortical function, including measurement of early morning and evening cortisol levels, should be performed periodically in all patients. An early morning resting cortisol level may be accepted as normal only if it falls at or near the normal mean level.

Patients previously on high doses of systemic steroids may regain earlier symptoms not related to asthma such as rhinitis and eczema when transferred from oral therapy to budesonide. These symptoms are a result of the generally lower systemic steroid action which will be experienced. Patients may also suffer from tiredness, headache, pain in muscles and joints and, occasionally, nausea and vomiting. Temporary resumption of systemic steroids may be necessary to treat these conditions.

The development of pharyngeal and laryngeal candidiasis is cause for concern because the extent of its penetration of the respiratory tract is unknown. If oral pharyngeal candidiasis develops, appropriate antifungal therapy should be implemented to eradicate the infection. The incidence of candidiasis can generally be held to a minimum by having patients rinse their mouths out with water after each nebulization treatment (see Dosage).

Glucocorticosteroids may mask some signs of infections and new infections may appear during its use.

Budesonide is not to be regarded as a bronchodilator and is not indicated for rapid relief of bronchospasm.

The nebulizer chamber should be cleaned after every administration. Wash the nebulizer chamber and mouthpiece or face mask in hot tap water using a mild detergent. Rinse well and dry by connecting the nebulizer chamber to the compressor or air inlet.

Due to a low output of budesonide, ultrasonic nebulizers should not be used for administration of budesonide.

Precautions: Two cases of mortality due to cerebral edema and encephalopathy were reported during clinical trials. There was no apparent cause and effect relationship.

There is still insufficient data for the long-term systemic effect of budesonide. The long-term effects of budesonide in developmental or immunologic processes in the mouth, pharynx, trachea, eyes and lungs are unknown. With the recommended therapeutic doses, the risk/benefit ratio seems to be very low. However, as with any other glucocorticosteroid, patients should be carefully followed up for systemic adverse effects, particularly during long-term therapy.

In transferring patients from a systemic steroid to budesonide, the reduction of the systemic steroid must be very gradual and carefully supervised by the physician since systemic withdrawal symptoms (e.g. joint and/or muscular pain, lassitude, depression) may occur in spite of maintenance or improvement of respiratory functions (see Dosage).

It is essential that the patient be instructed that budesonide is a preventative agent which must be taken at regular intervals and is not to be used to relieve an acute asthmatic attack.

Treatment should not be stopped abruptly, but tapered off gradually (see Dosage, Clinical Management).

Pulmonary infiltrates with eosinophilia may occur in patients on budesonide therapy. The causative role of inhalational steroids cannot be ruled out.

Pregnancy: Administration of budesonide during pregnancy should be avoided unless there are compelling reasons. In experimental animal studies, budesonide was found to cross the placental barrier. Like other glucocorticosteroids, budesonide is teratogenic to rodent species. High doses of budesonide administered s.c. produced fetal malformations, primarily skeletal defects, in rabbits, rats and mice. The relevance of these findings to humans has not yet been established. In the absence of further studies in humans, budesonide should be used during pregnancy only if the potential benefits clearly outweigh the risk to the fetus. Infants born of mothers who have received substantial doses of corticosteroids, especially oral steroids, during pregnancy should be carefully observed for hypoadrenalism.

Lactation: Glucocorticoids are secreted in human milk. It is not known whether budesonide would be secreted in human milk, but it is suspected to be likely. The use of budesonide in nursing mothers requires that the possible benefits of the drug be weighed against the potential hazards to the mother or infant.

Corticosteroids may mask some signs of infections and new infections may appear. A decreased resistance to localized infection has been observed during corticosteroid therapy. During long-term therapy, pituitary-adrenal function and height (in children) should be periodically assessed.

Patients should be advised to inform subsequent physicians of the prior use of corticosteroids.

There may be enhanced systemic effects of budesonide in patients with an advanced liver cirrhosis, and in those with hypothyroidism.

ASA should be used cautiously in conjunction with corticosteroids in hypoprothrombinemia.

Special care is needed in patients with lung tuberculosis and fungal and viral infections. Children who are on immunosuppressant drugs are more susceptible to infections than healthy children. Chickenpox and measles, for example, can have a more serious or fatal course in children on immunosuppressant corticosteroids. In such children, or in adults who have not had these diseases, particular care should be taken to avoid exposure. If exposed, therapy with varicella zoster immune globulin (VZIG) or pooled i.v. immunoglobulin (IVIG), as appropriate, may be indicated. If chickenpox develops, treatment with antiviral agents may be considered.

If, however, a viral upper respiratory infection is present, the patient should adhere to the regular asthma medication. In patients who are known to deteriorate rapidly when they

Pulmicort Nebuamp (cont'd)

have a viral respiratory infection, a short course of oral corticosteroid therapy should be considered.

Clinical studies have shown that viral upper respiratory infections cause significantly fewer problems in patients who are on regular treatment with topical glucocorticosteroids.

To ensure the proper dosage and administration of the drug, the patient should be instructed by a physician or other health professional in the use of Pulmicort Nebuamp and the nebulizing equipment.

Adequate oral hygiene is of primary importance in minimizing overgrowth of microorganisms such as C. albicans (see Dosage).

Drug Interactions: The kinetics of budesonide were investigated in a study of healthy subjects without and with cimetidine, 1 000 mg daily. After a 4 mg oral dose the values for C_{max} (nmol/L) and systemic availability (%) of budesonide without and with cimetidine (3.3 vs 5.1 nmol/L and 10 vs 12% respectively) indicated a slight inhibitory effect on hepatic metabolism of budesonide, caused by cimetidine. This should be of little clinical importance.

Adverse Effects: During clinical trials, the most common side effects were cough, throat irritation and hoarseness (2 to 4%). Bad taste, headache, nausea and dryness of the throat were reported less frequently. Other side effects reported on occasion during budesonide treatment were tiredness, thirst and diarrhea. Facial skin irritation has occurred in a few cases when a nebulizer with a face mask has been used. To prevent irritation, the facial skin should be washed after use of the face mask. Skin reactions (urticaria, rash, dermatitis, etc.) may, in rare cases, occur in association with local corticosteroid therapy.

Psychiatric symptoms such as nervousness, restlessness and depression as well as behavioral disturbances in children have been observed.

As with other inhalation therapy, the potential for paradoxical bronchospasm should be kept in mind. If it occurs, the preparation should be discontinued immediately and alternative therapy instituted.

Systemic effects and oropharyngeal complications caused by budesonide were found to be dose-dependent. Candidiasis has been reported by some patients and may occur at therapeutic doses. In rare cases, budesonide may provoke bronchoconstriction in hyperreactive patients.

In patients in whom systemic steroids are reduced or stopped, withdrawal symptoms due to decreased systemic activity occur frequently (see Dosage, Clinical Management).

Overdose: Symptoms and Treatment: Occasional overdosing will not give any obvious symptoms in most cases but it will decrease the plasma cortisol level. Other pharmacological effects are an increase in the number and percentage of circulating neutrophils, while the number and percentage of eosinophils will decrease concurrently. Stopping the treatment or decreasing the dose will abolish the induced effects.

Habitual overdosing may cause hypercorticism and hypothalamic-pituitary-adrenal (HPA) suppression. Decreasing the dose or stopping the therapy will abolish these effects, although the restitution of the HPA-axis may be a slow process, and during periods with pronounced physical stress (severe infections, trauma, surgical operations, etc.) it may be advisable to supplement with systemic steroids.

Dosage: Pulmicort Nebuamp should be administered from suitable nebulizers. Due to a low output of budesonide, ultrasonic nebulizers should not be used.

The amount of budesonide suspension delivered to the patient in a nebulizer is variable and dependent upon several factors, including the following: nebulization time, volume fill, the characteristics of the nebulizing equipment, the inspiratory/expiratory ratio and tidal volume of the patient, the use of either a face-mask or a mouth piece.

Data from ex vivo studies have estimated that the dose of nebulized budesonide delivered to the patient varies between 9 to 19% of the nominal dose.

The nebulization time and the dose delivered are dependent on flow rate, volume of nebulizer chamber and volume fill.

Nebulization should take place using a gas flow (oxygen or compressed air) of 6 to 10 L/minute and the suspension nebulized over a 10 to 15 minute period. A suitable volume fill for most nebulizers is 2 to 4 mL. The manufacturer's instructions concerning cleaning and maintenance of the nebulizer should be strictly followed.

Initial Dose: The dosage is individual. The intitial dose should be: Children (3 months to 12 years) 0.25 to 0.5 mg twice daily. In some cases, the dosage may be further increased up to 1 mg twice daily.

Adults: usually 1 to 2 mg twice daily. In some cases, the dosage may be further increased.

Maintenance Dose: The maintenance dose is individual. After the desired clinical effect has been obtained, the maintenance dose should be gradually reduced to the smallest amount necessary for control of symptoms.

See Table I.

Table I—Pulmicort Nebuamp

Dosage

	Volume of Pulmicort Nebuamp		
Dose (mg)	**0.125 mg/mL**	**0.25 mg/mL**	**0.5 mg/mL**
0.125 mg	1 mL*	—	—
0.25 mg	2 mL	1 mL*	—
0.5 mg	4 mL	2 mL	—
0.75 mg	—	3 mL	—
1 mg	—	—	2 mL
1.5 mg	—	—	3 mL
2 mg	—	—	4 mL

* This should be mixed with 0.9% saline to a volume of 2 mL.

In patients where an increased therapeutic effect is desired, an increased dose of budesonide is recommended because of the lower risk of systemic effects as compared with a combined treatment with oral glucocorticosteroids.

If only half the contents of an ampul are used, add sterile normal saline to make up the required volume fill.

Clinical Management: Patients—Nonsteroid Dependent: Treatment with the recommended doses usually gives a therapeutic effect within 10 days. However, certain patients might have an excessive collection of mucous secretion in the bronchi which reduces the penetration of budesonide into the bronchial mucosa. In these cases, it is desirable to initially give a short (about 2 weeks) oral corticosteroid regimen in addition to budesonide. The oral treatment is started on a rather large dose which is then gradually reduced. Thereafter, treatment with budesonide only is sufficient. Exacerbations of the asthma caused by bacterial infections are controlled by adequate antibiotic regimens and also by increasing the budesonide dosage.

Patients—Steroid Dependent: Transferral of patients dependent upon oral steroids to treatment with budesonide demands special care mainly because of the slow restitution of the disturbed hypothalamic-pituitary-adrenal function caused by extended treatment with oral corticosteroids. When budesonide treatment is initiated, the patient should be in a relatively stable phase. Budesonide is then given in combination with the previously used oral steroid dose for about 10 days. After this period of time, reduction of the oral corticoid dose may be started gradually. The oral dose is thus reduced to the lowest level which, in combination with budesonide, gives a stable respiratory capacity. In adults, the usual rate of withdrawal of the systemic corticosteroid is the equivalent of 2.5 mg of prednisone every 4 days if the patient is under close observation. **If continuous supervision is not feasible, the withdrawal of the systemic steroid should be slower,** approximately 2.5 mg of prednisone (or equivalent) every 10 days. A slow rate of withdrawal cannot be overemphasized. If withdrawal symptoms appear, the previous dosage of the systemic drug should be resumed for a week before further decrease is attempted. During withdrawal, some patients may experience symptoms of systemically active steroid withdrawal, e.g., joint and/or muscular pain, lassitude and depression, despite maintenance or even improvement of respiratory function. Such patients should be encouraged to continue with budesonide, but should be watched carefully for objective signs of adrenal insufficiency such as hypotension and weight loss. If evidence of adrenal insufficiency occurs, the systemic steroid dosage should be boosted temporarily and thereafter further withdrawal should continue more slowly.

In many cases it may be possible to completely replace the oral steroid with budesonide treatment. In other patients, a low oral steroid maintenance dosage may be required. The length of time needed for the body to regain its natural production of corticosteroid in sufficient quantity is often extended. **Thus, during severe asthma attacks or physically stressing situations such as severe infections, trauma and surgical operations, it is necessary to resume systemic steroids (in large dosages) in order to avoid adrenocorticoid insufficiency.** Acute exacerbations, especially in connection with increased viscosity and mucous plugging, may require complementary treatment with a short course of oral corticosteroids which are gradually tapered as symptoms subside.

During transfer from oral therapy to budesonide, a lower general steroid action is experienced. The patients might regain earlier symptoms (rhinitis, eczema) or suffer from tiredness, headache, pain in muscles and joints and, occasionally, nausea and vomiting. In these cases, further medical support may be required.

Note: Patients should be instructed to rinse their mouths out with water after each nebulization treatment. This will help prevent the occurrence of candidiasis and potential systemic effects. Cleansing dentures has the same effect.

Storage: Store at 5 to 30°C in an upright position. Keep protected from light. Once envelope is opened, use ampuls within 3 months. Opened ampuls must be used within 12 hours.

Information for the Patient: See Blue Section—Information for the Patient "Pulmicort Nebuamp".

Supplied: Each ampul contains: budesonide 0.125 mg/mL, 0.25 mg/mL or 0.5 mg/mL. Nonmedicinal ingredients: citric acid, disodium edetate, polysorbate 80, sodium chloride, sodium citrate and water, purified. LD-polyethylene ampuls of 2 mL. Sheets of 5 ampuls packed in foil-laminate envelopes. Cartons of 6 envelopes.

(Shown in Product Recognition Section)

Reviewed 1998

PULMICORT® TURBUHALER® Ⓟ

Astra

Budesonide

Glucocorticosteroid for the Treatment of Bronchial Asthma

Pharmacology: Budesonide is a potent nonhalogenated synthetic glucocorticosteroid with strong topical and weak systemic effects.

Budesonide has a high topical anti-inflammatory potency and it is rapidly biotransformed in the liver. This favorable separation between topical anti-inflammatory activity and systemic effect is due to strong glucocorticosteroid receptor affinity and an effective first pass metabolism with a short half-life.

The late reaction can be significantly inhibited if budesonide is given at least 2 hours before a bronchial challenge. Pretreatment for 1 to 4 weeks with inhaled budesonide may inhibit the immediate bronchial reaction.

After initiation of therapeutic use of orally inhaled budesonide, several weeks may pass before the full effect is obtained.

Indications: Patients with bronchial asthma: in patients who require inhaled steroids and in patients for whom a reduction of systemic glucocorticoids is desirable.

Contraindications: Status asthmaticus; not to be used in primary treatment of acute episodes of asthma or in patients with moderate to severe bronchiectasis. Hypersensitivity to budesonide. Active or quiescent pulmonary tuberculosis. Untreated fungal, bacterial or viral infections of the respiratory system.

Warnings: Budesonide is not intended for rapid relief of acute episodes of asthma where an inhaled short-acting bronchodilator is required. If patients find short-acting bronchodilator treatment ineffective, or they need more inhalations than usual, medical attention must be sought. In this situation consideration should be given to the need for increased anti-inflammatory therapy, e.g., higher doses of inhaled budesonide or a course of oral corticosteroid.

Deaths due to adrenal insufficiency have occurred in asthmatic patients during and after transfer from systemic corticosteroids to inhaled corticosteroids; therefore particular care is needed in patients who are transferred from systemically active corticosteroids to budesonide. After withdrawal from systemic corticosteroids, a number of months are required for recovery of hypothalamic-pituitary-adrenal (HPA) function. During this period of HPA suppression, patients may exhibit signs and symptoms of adrenal insufficiency when exposed to trauma, surgery or infections, particularly gastroenteritis, or other conditions associated with severe electrolyte loss.

Although budesonide may provide control of asthmatic symptoms during these episodes, it does **not** provide the systemic steroid which is necessary for coping with these emergencies.

During periods of stress or a severe asthmatic attack, patients who have been withdrawn from systemic corticosteroids should be instructed to resume systemic steroids (in large dosages) immediately and to contact their physicians for further instruction. These patients should also be instructed to carry a warning card indicating that they may need supplementary systemic steroids during periods of stress or a severe asthma attack. To assess the risk of adrenal insufficiency in emergency situations, routine tests of adrenal cortical function, including measurement of early morning and evening cortisol levels, should be performed periodically in all patients. An early morning resting cortisol level may be accepted as normal only if it falls at or near the normal mean level.

Patients previously on high doses of systemic steroids may regain earlier symptoms not related to asthma such as rhinitis and eczema when transferred from oral therapy to budesonide. These symptoms are a result of the generally lower systemic steroid action which will be experienced. Patients may also suffer from tiredness, headache, pain in muscles and joints and, occasionally, nausea and vomiting. Temporary resumption of systemic steroids may be necessary to treat these conditions.

The development of pharyngeal and laryngeal candidiasis is cause for concern because the extent of its penetration of the respiratory tract is unknown. If oral pharyngeal candidiasis develops, appropriate antifungal therapy should be implemented to eradicate the infection. The incidence of candidiasis can generally be held to a minimum by having patients rinse their mouths out with water after each inhalation (see Dosage).

Glucocorticosteroids may mask some signs of infection and new infections may appear during their use.

There is no evidence that control of asthma can be achieved by administration of budesonide in doses higher than those recommended. During such episodes, patients may require therapy with systemic corticosteroids.

Precautions: In transferring patients from a systemic steroid to budesonide, the reduction of the systemic steroid must be very gradual and carefully supervised by the physician since systemic withdrawal symptoms (e.g., joint and/or muscular pain, lassitude, depression), may occur in spite of maintenance or improvement of respiratory functions (see Dosage).

It is essential that the patient be instructed that budesonide is a preventative agent which must be taken at regular intervals and is not to be used to relieve an acute asthmatic attack.

The long-term effects of budesonide on developmental or immunologic processes in the mouth, pharynx, trachea, eyes and lungs are unknown. With the recommended therapeutic doses of budesonide, there is little risk of adverse systemic effects.

In children, treated for 2 to 6 years, with budesonide via Turbuhaler at daily doses up to 400 µg, no effect was demonstrated on statural growth compared with nonsteroidal therapy. However, to allow for individuals that are excessively sensitive, it is recommended that height is monitored in growing children.

Treatment with budesonide should not be stopped abruptly, but tapered off gradually.

Pulmonary infiltrates with eosinophilia may occur in patients on budesonide therapy. Although this is possible in some patients who are administered inhalational steroids, their causative role cannot be ruled out.

Pregnancy: Administration during pregnancy should be avoided unless there are compelling reasons. In experimental animal studies, budesonide was found to cross the placental barrier. Like other glucocorticosteroids, budesonide is teratogenic to rodent species. High doses of budesonide administered s.c. produced fetal malformations, primarily skeletal defects, in rabbits, rats, and in mice. The relevance of these findings to humans has not yet been established. In the absence of further studies in humans, budesonide should be used during pregnancy only if the potential benefits clearly outweigh the risk to the fetus. Infants born of mothers who have received substantial doses of corticosteroids, especially oral steroids, during pregnancy should be carefully observed for hypoadrenalism.

Lactation: Glucocorticoids are secreted in human milk. It is not known whether budesonide would be secreted in human milk, but it is suspected to be likely. The use of budesonide in nursing mothers, requires that the possible benefits of the drug be weighed against the potential hazards to the mother, or infant.

Children under 6 years of age: Budesonide via Turbuhaler is not presently recommended for children younger than 6 years of age due to limited clinical data in this age group.

Corticosteroids may mask some signs of infections and new infections may appear. A decreased resistance to localized infection has been observed during corticosteroid therapy. During long-term therapy, pituitary-adrenal function and height (in children) should be periodically assessed.

Patients should be advised to inform subsequent physicians of the prior use of corticosteroids.

There may be enhanced systemic effects of budesonide in patients with an advanced liver cirrhosis, and in those with hypothyroidism. Reduced liver function may affect the elimination of corticosteroids. The i.v. pharmacokinetics of budesonide however, are similar in cirrhotic patients and in healthy subjects. The pharmacokinetics after oral ingestion of budesonide were affected by compromised liver function as evidenced by increased systemic availability. This is however, of little importance for budesonide, as after inhalation the oral contribution to the systemic availability is very small.

ASA should be used cautiously in conjunction with corticosteroids in hypoprothrombinemia.

Special care is needed in patients with lung tuberculosis and fungal and viral infections. Children who are on immunosuppressant drugs are more susceptible to infections than healthy children. Chickenpox and measles, for example, can have a more serious or fatal course in children on immunosuppressant corticosteroids. In such children, or in adults who have not had these diseases, particular care should be taken to avoid exposure. If exposed, therapy with varicella zoster immune globulin (VZIG) or pooled i.v. immunoglobulin (IVIG), as appropriate, may be indicated. If chickenpox develops treatment with antiviral agents may be considered.

If, however, a viral upper respiratory infection is present, the patient should adhere to the regular asthma medication. In patients who are known to deteriorate rapidly when they have a viral respiratory infection, a short course of oral corticosteroid therapy should be considered.

Clinical studies have shown that viral upper respiratory infections cause significantly fewer problems in patients who are on regular treatment with topical glucocorticosteroids.

To ensure the proper dosage and administration of the drug, the patient should be instructed by a physician or other health professional in the use of Pulmicort Turbuhaler.

Adequate oral hygiene is of primary importance in minimizing overgrowth of microorganisms such as C. albicans (see Dosage).

Drug Interactions: Budesonide has not been observed to interact with any drug used for the treatment of asthma.

Cimetidine: The kinetics of budesonide were investigated in a study of healthy subjects without and with cimetidine, 1 000 mg daily. After a 4 mg oral dose the values for C_{max} (nmol/L) and systemic availability (%) of budesonide without and with cimetidine (3.3 vs 5.1 nmol/L and 10 vs 12%, respectively) indicated a slight inhibitory effect on hepatic metabolism of budesonide, caused by cimetidine. This should be of little clinical importance.

Ketoconazole: Ketoconazole, a potent inhibitor of cytochrome P450 3A, the main metabolic enzyme for corticosteroids, increases plasma levels of orally ingested budesonide.

Omeprazole: At recommended doses, omeprazole has no effect on the pharmacokinetics of oral budesonide.

Adverse Effects: No major side effects attributable to the use of budesonide, in all dosage forms, have been reported. During clinical trials, the frequency of subjectively reported side effects was low.

The most common side effects were cough, throat irritation, and hoarseness (2 to 4%). Bad taste, headache, nausea and dryness of the throat were reported less frequently. Other side effects reported on occasion during budesonide treatment were tiredness, thirst and diarrhea. Skin reactions (urticaria, rash, dermatitis, angioedema, etc.) may, in rare cases, occur in association with local corticosteroid therapy. In rare cases, skin bruising has been reported following treatment with inhaled glucocorticosteroids.

Psychiatric symptoms such as nervousness, restlessness and depression, as well as behavioral disturbances in children, have been observed.

As with other inhalation therapy, the potential for paradoxical bronchospasm should be kept in mind. If it occurs, the preparation should be discontinued immediately and alternative therapy instituted.

In rare cases, signs or symptoms of systemic glucocorticosteroid effect including hypofunction of the adrenal gland and oropharyngeal complications may occur, depending on dose, exposure time, concomitant and previous steroid exposure, and individual sensitivity. Candidiasis has been reported by some patients and may occur at therapeutic doses.

In patients in whom systemic steroids are reduced or stopped, withdrawal symptoms due to decreased systemic activity occur frequently (see Dosage, Clinical Management).

Overdose: Symptoms and Treatment: Occasional overdosing will not give any obvious symptoms in most cases but it will decrease the plasma cortisol level. Other pharmacological effects are an increase in the number and percentage of circulating neutrophils, where the number and percentage of eosinophils will decrease concurrently. Stopping the treatment or decreasing the dose will abolish the induced effects.

Habitual overdosing may cause hypercorticism and hypothalamic-pituitary-adrenal suppression. Decreasing the dose or stopping the therapy will abolish these effects, although the restitution of the HPA-axis may be a slow process and during periods with pronounced physical stress (severe infections, trauma, surgical operations, etc.) it may be advisable to supplement with systemic steroids.

Dosage: Adults and Children over 12 years of age: When treatment with inhaled glucocorticosteroids is started, during periods of severe asthma, and while reducing or discontinuing oral glucocorticosteroids the dosage should be 400 to 2 400 µg daily divided into 2 to 4 administrations.

The maintenance dose is usually 200 to 400 µg twice daily but higher doses may be necessary for longer or shorter periods of time in some patients. The dose should be individualized to the patient's need and should be the lowest possible dose that fills the therapeutic objective.

Once daily dosing may be considered in patients who require a dosage of 400 µg budesonide per day. The dose may then be given in the morning or in the evening. If deterioration of asthma occurs, the frequency of dosing and the daily dose should be increased.

Treatment with budesonide should not be stopped abruptly, but tapered off gradually.

Children 6 to 12 years: When starting therapy with budesonide in children, during periods of severe asthma and while reducing or discontinuing oral corticosteroids, the dosage should be 200 to 400 µg daily, given in divided doses twice daily at 100 to 200 µg per inhalation.

The maintenance dose is individual and should be the lowest dose which keeps the patient symptom-free. Administration twice daily is usually adequate in stable asthmatics.

Children under 6 years of age: Budesonide via Turbuhaler is not recommended for children in this age group.

Clinical studies in man have shown an improved efficacy for the same amount of budesonide delivered via Turbuhaler inhaler as compared with the pressurized aerosol with Nebuhaler spacer device. It may be possible to reduce the dose of Pulmicort Turbuhaler when the patient is in a stable phase.

In patients where an increased therapeutic effect is desired, an increased dose of Turbuhaler is recommended because of the lower risk of systemic effects as compared with a combined treatment with oral glucocorticosteroids.

Since the effect of budesonide depends on its regular use and on the proper technique of inhalation, patients must be instructed to use their Turbuhaler daily, as prescribed by their physician and not as they feel necessary. They must also be instructed in the correct method which is described in Information for the Patient.

Turbuhaler: Turbuhaler is a breath-activated dry powder inhaler which does not require a coordinated inhalation technique. It contains only the active ingredient budesonide—no propellants or preservatives, and as such, offers those patients sensitive to excipients, an alternate dosage form. Note: The patient may not taste or feel any medication when inhaling from Turbuhaler. This lack of feeling does not mean that the patient is not receiving benefit from Pulmicort Turbuhaler.

Clinical Management: Patients—Nonsteroid Dependent: Treatment with the recommended doses of budesonide usually gives a therapeutic effect within 10 days. However, certain patients might have an excessive collection of mucous secretion in the bronchi which reduces the penetration of budesonide into the bronchial mucosa. In these cases, it is desirable to initially give a short (about 2 weeks) oral corticosteroid regimen in addition to budesonide. The oral treatment is started on a rather large dose which is then gradually reduced. Thereafter, treatment with budesonide only is sufficient. Exacerbations of the asthma caused by bacterial infections are controlled by adequate antibiotic regimens and also by increasing the budesonide dosage.

Patients—Steroid Dependent: Transferral of patients dependent upon oral steroids to treatment with budesonide demands special care mainly because of the slow restitution of the disturbed hypothalamic-pituitary-adrenal function caused by extended treatment with oral corticosteroids. When treatment is initiated, the patient should be in a relatively stable phase. Budesonide is then given in combination with the previously used oral steroid dose for about 10 days. After this period of time, reduction of the oral corticoid dose may be started gradually. The oral dose is thus reduced to the lowest level which, in combination with budesonide, gives a stable respiratory capacity.

Pulmicort Turbuhaler (cont'd)

In adults, the usual rate of withdrawal of the systemic corticosteroid is the equivalent of 2.5 mg of prednisone every 4 days if the patient is under close observation. **If continuous supervision is not feasible, the withdrawal of the systemic steroid should be slower,** approximately 2.5 mg of prednisone (or equivalent) every 10 days. A slow rate of withdrawal cannot be overemphasized. If withdrawal symptoms appear, the previous dosage of the systemic drug should be resumed for a week before further decrease is attempted. During withdrawal, some patients may experience symptoms of systemically active steroid withdrawal, e.g., joint and/or muscular pain, lassitude, and depression, despite maintenance or even improvement of respiratory function. Such patients should be encouraged to continue with budesonide but should be watched carefully for objective signs of adrenal insufficiency such as hypotension and weight loss. If evidence of adrenal insufficiency occurs, the systemic steroid dosage should be boosted temporarily and thereafter further withdrawal should continue more slowly.

In many cases it may be possible to completely replace the oral steroid with budesonide treatment. In other patients, a low oral steroid maintenance dosage may be required. The length of time needed for the body to regain its natural production of corticosteroid in sufficient quantity is often extended. **Thus, during severe asthma attacks or physically stressing situations such as severe infections, trauma, and surgical operations, it is necessary to resume systemic steroids (in large dosages) in order to avoid adrenocorticoid insufficiency.** Acute exacerbations, especially in connection with increased viscosity and mucous plugging, may require complementary treatment with a short course of oral corticosteroids which are gradually tapered as symptoms subside.

During transfer from oral therapy to budesonide, a lower general steroid action is experienced. The patients might regain earlier symptoms (rhinitis, eczema) or suffer from tiredness, headache, pain in muscles and joints and, occasionally, nausea and vomiting. In these cases, further medical support may be required.

Note: The medication from Turbuhaler is delivered to the lungs as the patient inhales and, therefore, it is important to instruct the patient to breathe in forcefully and deeply through the mouthpiece. When prescribing Turbuhaler to young children it is necessary to ascertain that they can follow the instructions for use. The patient may not taste or feel any medication when using Turbuhaler due to the small amount of drug dispensed.

Patients should be instructed to rinse their mouths out with water after each inhalation. This will help prevent the occurrence of candidiasis. Cleansing dentures has the same effect.

Information for the Patient: See Blue Section—Information for the Patient "Pulmicort Turbuhaler".

Supplied: Each dry powder inhaler contains: 200 doses of 100, 200 and 400 µg or 100 doses of 200 µg of micronized budesonide. Each inhalation from Pulmicort Turbuhaler will provide either 100, 200 or 400 µg of budesonide active substance; no additives or carrier substances are included. Pulmicort Turbuhaler cannot be refilled and should be discarded when empty.

(Shown in Product Recognition Section)

Reviewed 1999

PULMOZYME™ Pr

Roche

Dornase Alfa Recombinant

Enzyme that Cleaves DNA

Pharmacology: Dornase alfa for inhalation is a sterile, clear, colorless, highly purified solution of recombinant human deoxyribonuclease 1 (rhDNase), an enzyme which selectively cleaves DNA. The protein is produced by genetically engineered Chinese Hamster Ovary (CHO) cells containing DNA encoding for the native human protein, deoxyribonuclease 1 (Dnase). The product is purified by tangential flow filtration and column chromatography. The purified glycoprotein contains 260 amino acids with an approximate molecular weight of 37 000 daltons. The primary amino acid sequence is identical to that of the native human enzyme.

Pulmozyme is administered by inhalation of an aerosol mist produced by a compressed air driven nebulizer system (see Dosage).

General: In cystic fibrosis (CF) patients, retention of viscous purulent secretions in the airways contributes both to reduced pulmonary function and to exacerbations of infection.

Purulent pulmonary secretions contain very high concentrations of extracellular DNA released by degenerating leukocytes that accumulate in response to infection. In vitro, dornase alfa hydrolyzes the DNA in sputum of CF patients and reduces sputum viscoelasticity.

Pharmacokinetics: When 2.5 mg dornase alfa was administered by inhalation to 18 CF patients, mean sputum concentrations of 3 µg/mL DNase were measurable within 15 minutes. Mean sputum concentrations declined to an average of 0.6 µg/mL 2 hours following inhalation. Inhalation of up to 10 mg t.i.d. of dornase alfa by 4 CF patients for 6 consecutive days, did not result in a significant elevation of serum concentrations of DNase above normal endogenous levels. After administration of up to 2.5 mg of dornase alfa twice daily for 6 months to 321 CF patients, no accumulation of serum DNase was noted.

Clinical Experience: Phase III Studies: Dornase alfa has been evaluated in a large, randomized, placebo-controlled trial of clinically stable cystic fibrosis patients, 5 years of age and older, with baseline forced vital capacity (FVC) greater than or equal to 40% of predicted and receiving standard therapies for cystic fibrosis. Patients were treated with placebo (325 patients), 2.5 mg of dornase alfa once a day (322 patients), or 2.5 mg of dornase alfa twice a day (321 patients) for 6 months administered via a Hudson T Updraft II nebulizer with a Pulmo-Aide compressor.

Both doses of dornase alfa resulted in significant reductions compared with the placebo group in the number of patients experiencing respiratory tract infections requiring use of parenteral antibiotics. Administration of dornase reduced the relative risk of developing a respiratory tract infection by 27% and 29% for the 2.5 mg daily dose and the 2.5 mg twice daily dose, respectively (see Table I). The data suggest that the effects of dornase alfa on respiratory tract infections in older patients (>21 years) may be smaller than in young patients, and that twice daily dosing may be required in the older patients. Patients with baseline FVC>85% may also benefit from twice a day dosing (see Table I). The reduced risk of respiratory infection observed in dornase alfa treated patients did not directly correlate with improvement in FEV_1, during the initial 2 weeks of therapy.

Within 8 days of the start of treatment with dornase alfa mean FEV_1 increased 7.9% in those treated once a day and 9% in those treated twice a day compared to the baseline values. The overall mean FEV_1 observed during long-term therapy increased 5.8% from baseline at the 2.5 mg daily dose level and 5.6% from baseline at the 2.5 mg twice daily dose level. Placebo recipients did not show significant mean changes in pulmonary function testing.

For patients 5 years of age or older, with baseline FVC greater than or equal to 40%, administration of dornase alfa decreased the incidence of occurrence of first respiratory tract infection requiring parenteral antibiotics, and improved mean FEV_1 regardless of age or baseline FVC.

Table I—Pulmozyme

Incidence of Occurrence of First Respiratory Tract Infection Requiring Parenteral Antibiotics in a Controlled Trial

	Placebo n=325	2.5 mg qd n=322	2.5 mg b.i.d. n=321
Percent of Patients Infected	43%	34%	33%
Relative Risk (vs placebo)		0.73	0.71
p-value (vs placebo)		0.015	0.007
Subgroup by Age and Baseline FVC	**Placebo (n)**	**2.5 mg qd (n)**	**2.5 mg b.i.d. (n)**
Age			
5-20 years	42% (201)	25% (199)	28% (184)
21 years and older	44% (124)	48% (123)	39% (137)
Baseline FVC			
40-85%, Predicted	54% (194)	41% (201)	44% (203)
>85%, Predicted	27% (131)	21% (121)	14% (118)

Other Studies: Dornase alfa did not produce a pulmonary function benefit in short-term usage in patients with FVC less than 40% of predicted. Studies are in progress to assess the impact of chronic use on pulmonary function and infection risk in this population.

Clinical trials have indicated that dornase alfa therapy can be continued or initiated during an acute respiratory exacerbation.

Short-term dose ranging studies demonstrated that doses in excess of 2.5 mg b.i.d. did not provide further improvement in FEV_1. Patients who have received drug on a cyclical regimen (i.e., administration of dornase alfa 10 mg b.i.d. for 14 days followed by a 14-day wash out period) showed rapid improvement in FEV_1 with the initiation of each cycle and a return to baseline with each dornase alfa withdrawal.

Indications: Daily administration of dornase alfa for inhalation in conjunction with standard therapies is indicated in the management of cystic fibrosis patients to reduce the frequency of respiratory infections requiring parenteral antibiotics and to improve pulmonary function. Safety and efficacy of daily administration have not been demonstrated in patients under the age of 5 years, or with FVC<40% of predicted, or for longer than 12 months.

Contraindications: Patients with known hypersensitivity to dornase alfa, Chinese Hamster Ovary cell products or any component of the product.

Warnings: None.

Precautions: General: Dornase alfa should be used in conjunction with standard therapies for CF.

Information for the Patient: Pulmozyme must be stored in the refrigerator at 2 to 8°C and protected from light. It should be kept refrigerated during transport and should not be exposed to room temperatures for a total time of 24 hours. The solution should be discarded if it is cloudy or discolored. Pulmozyme contains no preservative and, once opened, the entire ampul must be used or discarded. Patients should be instructed in the proper use and maintenance of the nebulizer and compressor system used in its delivery.

Pulmozyme should not be diluted or mixed with other drugs in the nebulizer. Mixing of Pulmozyme with other drugs could lead to adverse physicochemical and/or functional changes in Pulmozyme or the admixed compound.

Drug Interactions: Clinical trials have indicated that dornase alfa can be effectively and safely used in conjunction with standard cystic fibrosis therapies including oral, inhaled and parenteral antibiotics, bronchodilators, enzyme supplements, vitamins, oral and inhaled corticosteroids and analgesics. No formal drug interaction studies have been performed.

Carcinogenesis, Mutagenesis, Impairment of Fertility: Carcinogenesis: A 2-year inhalation (head-only) toxicity study of dornase alfa in rats to assess oncogenic potential is in progress. Mutagenesis: Ames tests using 6 different tester strains of bacteria (4 of S. typhimurium and 2 of E. coli), at concentrations up to 5 000 µg/plate, a cytogenetic assay using human peripheral blood lymphocytes at concentrations up to 2 000 µg/plate, and a mouse lymphoma assay at concentrations up to 1 000 µg/plate, with and without metabolic activation, revealed no evidence of mutagenesis potential. Dornase alfa was tested in a micronucleus (in vivo) assay for its potential to produce chromosome damage in bone marrow cells of mice following a bolus i.v. dose of up to 10 mg/kg on 2 consecutive days. No evidence of chromosomal damage was noted.

Impairment of Fertility: In studies with rats receiving up to 10 mg/kg/day, a dose representing systemic exposures greater than 600 times that expected following the recommended human dose, fertility and reproductive performance on both males and females was not affected.

Pregnancy: Reproduction studies have been performed in rats and rabbits with i.v. doses up to 10 mg/kg/day, representing systemic exposures greater than 600 times that expected following the recommended human dose. These studies have revealed no evidence of impaired fertility, harm to the fetus, or effects on development due to dornase alfa. There are, however, no adequate and well-controlled studies in pregnant women. Because animal reproductive studies are not always predictive of the human response, this drug should be used during pregnancy only if clearly needed.

Lactation: It is not known whether the drug is excreted in human milk. Because many drugs are excreted in human milk, caution should be exercised when dornase alfa is administered to a nursing woman.

Children: Safety and effectiveness in children under the age of 5 years has not been studied.

Adverse Effects: Patients have been exposed to dornase alfa for up to 12 months in clinical trials. In a large, randomized, placebo-controlled clinical trial, over 600 patients received dornase alfa once or twice daily for 6 months; most adverse events were not more common on dornase alfa than on placebo and probably reflected the sequelae of the underlying lung disease. In most cases events that were increased were mild, transient in nature, and did not require alterations in dosing. Few patients experienced adverse events resulting in permanent discontinuation from dornase alfa and the discontinuation rate was similar between placebo (2%) and dornase alfa (3%).

Events that were more frequent in dornase alfa treated patients than in placebo treated patients are listed in Table II.

Table II—Pulmozyme

Adverse Events Reported in a Controlled Trial

Adverse Event	Placebo n=325	Pulmozyme qd n=322	Pulmozyme b.i.d. n=321
Voice alteration	7%	12%	16%
Pharyngitis	33%	36%	40%
Laryngitis	1%	3%	4%
Rash	7%	10%	12%
Chest pain	16%	18%	21%
Conjunctivitis	2%	4%	5%

Events Observed at Similar Rates in Pulmozyme and Placebo Treated Patients: Body as a Whole: abdominal pain, asthenia, fever, flu syndrome, malaise, sepsis.

Digestive: intestinal obstruction, gallbladder disease, liver disease, pancreatic disease.

Metabolic Nutritional: diabetes mellitus, hypoxia, weight loss.

Respiratory: apnea, bronchiectasis, bronchitis, change in sputum, cough increase, dyspnea, hemoptysis, lung function decrease, nasal polyps, pneumonia, pneumothorax, rhinitis, sinusitis, sputum increase, wheeze.

Mortality rates observed in a controlled trial were similar for the placebo (1%) and dornase alfa (1%). Causes of death were consistent with progression of cystic fibrosis and included apnea, cardiac arrest, cardiopulmonary arrest, cor pulmonale, heart failure, massive hemoptysis, pneumonia, pneumothorax and respiratory failure.

Allergic Reactions: There have been no reports of anaphylaxis attributed to the administration of dornase alfa to date. Skin rash and urticaria have been observed and were mild and transient in nature. Within all of the studies, a small percentage (average of 2 to 4%) of patients treated with dornase alfa developed serum antibodies to dornase alfa. None of these patients developed anaphylaxis, and the clinical significance of serum antibodies to dornase alfa is unknown.

Overdose: Symptoms and Treatment: Single-dose inhalation studies in rats and monkeys at doses up to 180-times higher than doses routinely used in clinical studies are well tolerated. Single dose oral administration of dornase alfa in doses up to 200 mg/kg are also well tolerated by rats.

Cystic fibrosis patients have received up to 20 mg b.i.d. for up to 6 days and 10 mg b.i.d. intermittently (2 weeks on/ 2 weeks off drug) for 168 days. These doses were well tolerated.

Dosage: The recommended dose for use in most cystic fibrosis patients is one 2.5 mg single-use ampul inhaled once daily using a recommended nebulizer. Some patients may benefit from twice daily administration (see Table I). Clinical trials have been performed with the following nebulizers and compressors: the disposable jet nebulizer Hudson T Up-draft II and disposable jet nebulizer Marquest Acorn II in conjunction with a Pulmo-Aide compressor, and with the reusable PARI LC Jet+ nebulizer, in conjunction with the PARI PRONEB compressor. Safety and efficacy have been demonstrated only with these recommended nebulizer systems. No clinical data are currently available that support the safety and efficacy of administration of dornase alfa with other nebulizer systems. The patient should follow the manufacturer's instructions on the use and maintenance of the equipment.

Pulmozyme should not be diluted or mixed with other drugs in the nebulizer. Mixing of Pulmozyme with other drugs could lead to adverse physicochemical and/or functional changes in Pulmozyme or the admixed compound.

Supplied: Each mL of sterile, clear, colorless, aqueous solution contains: dornase alfa 1 mg. Nonmedicinal ingredients: calcium chloride dihydrate and sodium chloride. Nominal pH is 6.3. Preservative-free. Single-use ampuls of 2.5 mL. Cartons of 14 (each in a foil pouch) and 30 (5 foil pouches of 6 ampuls). Keep refrigerated during transport and do not expose to room temperatures for a total time of 24 hours. Store under refrigeration (2 to 8°C). Ampuls should be protected from light. Do not use beyond the expiration date stamped on the ampul. Unused ampuls should be stored in their protective foil pouch under refrigeration.

PUREGON™ Ⓟ
Organon

Follitropin Beta

Gonadotropin

Pharmacology: Puregon is a freeze-dried preparation containing highly purified human follicle stimulating hormone (hFSH) prepared by recombinant DNA technology. The active substance, follitropin beta, is a heterodimeric glycoprotein with a molecular mass of approximately 35-45kD. It is produced by a Chinese hamster ovary (CHO) cell line transfected with a plasmid containing two subunit genes encoding human FSH. Structural analysis has shown that the amino acid sequence of follitropin beta is identical to that of natural hFSH. The oligosaccharide side chains are very similar to those reported for natural hFSH but not completely identical. These small differences do not affect the degree of charge heterogeneity, receptor binding affinity and bioactivity of follitropin relative to natural hFSH. Follitropin beta, as purified from the CHO cell culture supernatant, is of high biochemical purity (≥99%), high specific biological activity (approximately 10 000 IU/mg protein), and devoid of luteinizing hormone (LH) activity.

Follicle stimulating hormone (FSH) is essential for normal female and male gamete growth and maturation, and gonadal steroid production. Deficiencies in the endogenous production of FSH may lead to infertility.

FSH is critical for the onset and duration of follicular development and consequently for the timing and number of follicles reaching maturity in females. The primary action of follitropin beta in women with gonadal dysfunction is the stimulation of follicular development and steroid production. Follitropin may also be used to promote multiple follicular development in medically assisted reproduction programs (i.e., IVF/ET/ISCI) and gamete or zygote intra-fallopian transfer (GIFT/ZIFT). In order to induce ovulation, in the absence of an endogenous LH surge, human chorionic gonadotropin (hCG) must be given after follitropin administration once follicular maturation has occurred.

After i.m. or s.c. administration of follitropin beta, high concentrations of FSH are reached within about 12 hours. FSH levels remain high for 24 to 48 hours due to follitropin beta's relatively long elimination half-life of about 40 hours (ranging from 12 to 70 hours). Plasma FSH concentrations, after repeated administration of follitropin beta, are approximately 1.5 to 2.5 times higher than after single dose administration.

There are no significant pharmacokinetic differences between i.m. and s.c. administration of follitropin beta.

Indications: For development of multiple follicles in ovulatory patients participating in an Assisted Reproduction Technology (ART) program and for induction of ovulation and pregnancy in anovulatory infertile females in whom the cause of infertility is functional and not due to primary ovarian failure.

Contraindications: Women who exhibit a high circulating FSH level indicating primary ovarian failure; uncontrolled thyroid or adrenal dysfunction; tumor of the ovary, breast, uterus, hypothalamus or pituitary gland; pregnancy and lactation; heavy or irregular vaginal bleeding of undetermined origin; ovarian cysts or enlargement not due to polycystic ovary syndrome (PCOD); prior hypersensitivity to follitropin beta or other components of Puregon; and conditions incompatible with pregnancy (e.g., malformation of sexual organs or fibroid tumors of the uterus).

Warnings: Follitropin beta is a potent gonadotropic agent that is capable of causing severe adverse effects in women. It should be used only by physicians who are experienced in the management of fertility disorders and only when facilities for appropriate clinical and endocrinologic evaluations are available.

Overstimulation of the Ovary During Therapy: To minimize the risk associated with abnormal ovarian enlargement in women receiving follitropin beta and hCG for the induction of ovulation and pregnancy, the drugs should be administered at the lowest possible effective dosage. Since follitropin beta may cause ovarian enlargement and/or hyperstimulation, patients should be assessed for signs of excessive ovarian stimulation during therapy and for a 2-week post-treatment period. Careful monitoring of ovarian response (i.e., ultrasonography and/or estradiol level determination) can minimize the risk of overstimulation.

Mild to moderate uncomplicated ovarian enlargement, which may be accompanied by abdominal distention and/or abdominal pain, occurs in approximately 20% of patients treated with gonadotropins and hCG, and generally regresses without treatment within 2 to 3 weeks. If unwanted hyperstimulation occurs, the administration of follitropin beta should be discontinued immediately. In this case, hCG must not be given because the administration of an LH-active gonadotropin at this stage may induce ovarian hyperstimulation syndrome, in addition to multiple ovulations. This warning is particularly important with respect to patients with anovulation or oligoovulation (polycystic ovarian disease and hypothalamic hypogonadism).

Clinical symptoms of mild ovarian hyperstimulation syndrome are gastrointestinal problems (abdominal distention, nausea, diarrhea), painful breasts, and mild to moderate enlargement of ovaries because of ovarian cysts.

Severe ovarian hyperstimulation syndrome (OHSS) is characterized by ovarian enlargement (large cysts prone to rupture) accompanied by hemoconcentration, decreased urinary output, ascites with or without pain and/or pleural effusion.

If severe OHSS occurs, treatment should be stopped and the patient hospitalized. Ovarian hyperstimulation syndrome develops rapidly within 3 to 4 days and generally during the 2-week period following the hCG injection.

Hemoconcentration associated with fluid loss into the abdominal cavity has been observed to occur and should be thoroughly assessed as follows: 1) fluid intake and output; 2) weight and abdominal girth; 3) hematocrit; 4) serum and urinary electrolytes; 5) urine specific gravity. Other monitoring should include serum albumin and total proteins. These determinations should be performed daily or more often if needed. Treatment consists primarily of bed rest, fluid, electrolyte and albumin replacement, and analgesics as needed. Generally, removal of ascitic fluid (paracentesis) should be reserved for the more severe cases of third space fluid shift or abdominal discomfort.

Hemoperitoneum may occur from ruptured ovarian cysts. This is usually the result of sexual intercourse or a vigorous pelvic examination. Should this occur and be accompanied by bleeding to the extent that surgery is necessary, partial resection of the enlarged ovary or ovaries may be required. Intercourse should be prohibited in those patients in whom significant ovarian enlargement occurs after ovulation due to the risk of hemoperitoneum resulting from ruptured ovarian cysts.

Arterial Thromboembolism: Arterial thromboembolism has been reported in patients who have received gonadotropin and hCG, both in association with and separate from ovarian hyperstimulation syndrome. Complications resulting from thromboembolism have included venous thrombophlebitis, pulmonary embolism, pulmonary infarction, stroke, arterial occlusion necessitating limb amputation, and (rarely) death.

Other Reproductive Complications: Multiple ovulations with resulting multiple births occur (mostly twins) frequently (~20% of pregnancies) following treatment with gonadotropins and hCG. Prior to gonadotropin and hCG therapy, the patient and her male sexual partner should be informed of the possibility and potential risks associated with multiple births.

Spontaneous abortion rates have been reported from 10 to 25% of all patients following gonadotropin treatment. Increased abortion rates are more common in women over 35 years of age, in women with polycystic ovarian disease, and are more common in the infertile couple. The increased frequency of multiple pregnancy is also associated with an increased rate of abortion.

Precautions: A thorough gynecologic and endocrinologic evaluation must be performed prior to treatment with follitropin beta. The evaluation may include hysterosalpinography to detect uterine and tubal pathology. Anovulation should be confirmed by menstrual history, observation of the basal body temperature pattern, determination of serum progesterone concentration in the luteal phase, or an endometrial biopsy. Tumors of the thyroid, adrenals, pituitary and ovary may cause anovulation and patients with such tumors should be excluded from follitropin beta therapy.

Determination of serum gonadotropin concentrations should be obtained to rule out primary ovarian failure.

The presence of early pregnancy should be ruled out by a biochemical pregnancy test. Evaluation of the fertility potential of the male sexual partner should also be performed (a semen analysis) before starting follitropin beta therapy.

Lactation: Follitropin beta is not intended for use during lactation.

Carcinogenesis and Mutagenesis: Follitropin beta displays no mutagenic potential. Carcinogenicity studies have not been performed.

Drug Interactions: Concurrent use of follitropin beta and clomiphene may enhance the follicular response. After pituitary

Puregon (cont'd)

desensitization effected by a GnRH agonist, a higher dose of follitropin beta may be necessary to elicit an adequate follicular response.

Adverse Effects: The most frequently reported adverse events in clinical trials were related to the reproductive (total 8.8%; ovarian hyperstimulation syndrome 5%, ectopic pregnancy 2.1%, vaginal hemorrhage 1%) and gastrointestinal system (total 3.6%, abdominal pain 2%). Miscarriages were reported in 3.1% of the study population. The incidence of adverse reactions was similar to that observed with urinary gonadotropin. Table I shows adverse events, listed by body system, which have been reported in clinical studies evaluating the efficacy and safety of follitropin beta.

In addition, each of the following adverse events were reported by 1 to 3 patients receiving follitropin beta: eczema, itching, rash, hyperemesis, bloating, constipation, gastroesophageal reflux, vomiting, tooth disorder, increased bilirubin, dyspnea, hematoma, cystitis, dysuria, face edema, frequent micturition, premature labor, metrorrhagia, ovarian disorder, vaginal discharge, vulvovaginitis, hydatidiform mole, back pain, feeling unwell, hot flushes, influenza-like symptoms, lumbar pain, pain, swollen abdomen, syncope, abscess, Herpes zoster, otitis media, sepsis and genital infection.

Post-treatment sera were analyzed following 3 treatment cycles and no evidence of induction of anti-FSH or anti-CHO cell-derived protein antibodies were found.

The following adverse reactions have been reported with gonadotropin therapy in general: mild to moderate ovarian enlargement; febrile reactions which may be associated with chills, musculoskeletal aches, joint pains, malaise, headache and fatigue; breast tenderness; dry skin; hair loss; hives; and hemoperitoneum.

The following adverse events have been reported subsequent to pregnancies resulting from gonadotropin therapy: ectopic pregnancy; congenital abnormalities including chromosomal abnormalities and birth defects (imperforate anus, aplasia of the sigmoid colon, hypospadias, cecovesical fistula, bifid scrotum, bilateral internal tibial torsion, right metatarsus adductus, cardiac lesions, supernumerary digit, exstrophy of the bladder, Down's syndrome, Trisomy 13, Trisomy 18, hydrocephaly, omphalocele, meningocele, external ear defect, dislocated ankle and hip, dilated cardiomyopathy). None of these events were considered drug-related and the incidence does not exceed that found in the general population. Spontaneous abortion was also observed in patients receiving urinary gonadotropin therapy.

Overdose: Symptoms and Treatment: The acute toxicity of gonadotropin preparations has been shown to be very low. However, too high a dosage for more than 1 day may lead to hyperstimulation of the ovaries (see Warnings).

Dosage: Ovulation Induction: The dosage of follitropin beta required to produce follicular maturation must be individualized according to ovarian response. The growth and development of follicles, timing of hCG administration, detection of ovarian enlargement and minimization of the risk of OHSS and multiple gestation requires careful clinical assessment. This may be achieved through pelvic ultrasonography, monitoring of estrogen levels, and/or clinical evaluation of estrogen activity.

Generally, an initial dose of 75 IU/day, administered i.m. or s.c., for 5 to 7 days is recommended. If there is no apparent ovarian response, the daily dose is gradually increased until estrogen levels start to rise. A daily ascent rate of 40 to 100% is considered to be optimal. The maximum individualized daily dose of follitropin beta safely used in clinical trials was 300 IU. The daily effective dose is maintained until preovulatory conditions are reached. If estrogen levels rise too rapidly (i.e., more than a daily doubling for 2 consecutive days), the daily dose should be decreased. Preovulatory conditions are reached when plasma estradiol levels of 1 000 to 3 000 pmol/L are attained, and/or when there is ultrasonographic evidence of a dominant follicle of at least 18 mm in mean diameter. Usually, 7 to 14 days of treatment is sufficient to reach this state. Once preovulatory conditions are reached, the administration of follitropin beta should be discontinued and ovulation induced by administration of 5 000 to 10 000 IU human chorionic gonadotropin (hCG).

Beginning the day prior to administration of human chorionic gonadotropin the couple should be encouraged to have intercourse at least 3 times per week until ovulation occurs.

Clinical confirmation of ovulation is obtained through the indices of progesterone production. Increasing progesterone secretion by the corpus luteum and a concomitant increase in basal body temperature are indirect signs of ovulation. A serum progesterone level over 30 nmol/L also provides adequate proof of a functional corpus luteum. Lower concentrations of serum progesterone may be supplemented by luteal phase injections of hCG. Within the following 9 days after the initial hCG administration, 2 to 3 injections of 1 000 to 3 000 IU hCG each may be given to prevent insufficiency of the corpus luteum.

Patients should be closely monitored for 2 weeks following follitropin beta and hCG treatment to ensure that hyperstimulation does not occur. If the ovaries become abnormally enlarged, there is more than a 1 kg/day gain in weight, or abdominal pain occurs, administration of hCG should be stopped. Most ovarian hyperstimulation occurs after follitropin beta treatment has been completed and reaches its maximum at about 7 to 10 days after hCG administration (see Warnings).
Controlled Ovarian Hyperstimulation in Medically Assisted Reproduction Programs: The dosage regimen may vary according to the physician's preference or the patient's response. In general, stimulation of follicular growth is achieved by starting with daily i.m. or s.c. administration of 150 to 225 IU follitropin beta for a period of 4 days. Thereafter, the dose may be adjusted according to the individual's ovarian response.

Maturation of follicles is monitored by pelvic ultrasonography and measurement of plasma estrogen levels. In responding patients, daily maintenance doses of 75 to 300 IU for 6 to 12 days are usually sufficient, although longer treatment may be necessary. The maximum individualized daily dose safely used in clinical studies was 450 IU. There is limited experience with higher doses. When ultrasonic evaluation indicates the presence of at least 3 follicles of sufficient size and there is evidence of a good estradiol response, the final phase of maturation of the follicles is induced by administration of hCG. HCG is given 30 to 40 hours after the last administration of follitropin beta in a dose of 5000 to 10 000 IU.

After embryo transfer, up to 3 repeat injections of 1 000 to 3000 IU hCG each may be given within the following 9 days to provide luteal phase support.

Follitropin beta may be given alone, or in combination with clomiphene citrate to stimulate the endogenous production of gonadotropins, (see Precautions, Drug Interactions) or in combination with a GnRH agonist to prevent premature luteinization.

Administration: To prepare the solution, inject 1 mL of the solvent (sodium chloride injection, 4.5 mg/mL) into the ampul of follitropin beta. Swirl gently until the solution is clear. **Do not shake. Do not use** if the liquid is not clear.

Immediately administer the reconstituted follitropin beta either s.c. or i.m. Any unused reconstituted material should be discarded.

S.C. Administration: The best site for s.c. injection is in the abdomen around the navel. Pinch up a large area of skin between the finger and thumb. Vary the injection site with each injection. The needle should be inserted at the base of the pinched-up skin at a 45° angle. S.C. injection of follitropin beta may be carried out by patients or their partners, provided proper instructions are given by the physician. Self-administration of follitropin beta should only be performed by patients who are well motivated, adequately trained and with access to expert advice.

I.M. Administration: The best site for i.m. administration is the upper outer quadrant of the buttock muscle. Stretching the skin helps the needle to go in more easily and pushes the tissue beneath the skin out of the way. This helps the solution to disperse correctly. The needle should be inserted right up to the hilt at an angle of 90° to the skin surface. Pushing in with a quick thrust causes the least discomfort.

Information for the Patient: See Blue Section—Information for the Patient "Puregon".

Supplied: Each ampul of lyospheres contains: follitropin beta (recombinant FSH) 50 or 100 IU. Nonmedicinal ingredients: hydrochloric acid, polysorbate 20, sodium citrate anhydrous, sodium hydroxide and sucrose. Ampuls of 2 mL. Each ampul

Table I—Puregon

Percent Incidence of Most Frequently (>0.1%) Reported Adverse Events (AEs) in Clinical Trials

Body System	Follitropin Beta* (n=1 074)	Urinary Gonadotropin (n=498)
	Percent	
Patients with at least one AE	17.3	19.7
Patients with known severe AE	5.0	6.2
Patients with drug-related AEs*	8.7	8.2
Reproductive System	**8.8**	**9.4**
Ovarian hyperstimulation syndrome	5.0	4.0
Ectopic pregnancy	2.1	3.4
Vaginal hemorrhage	1.0	1.0
Vaginitis	0.4	0.2
Gastrointestinal	**3.6**	**4.2**
Abdominal pain	2.0	2.4
Abdominal pain-upper/lower	0.7	0.6
Nausea	0.5	0.8
Abdominal discomfort	0.4	0.2
Fetal Disorders	**3.1**	**4.2**
Miscarriage	3.1	4.2
Body as a Whole	**1.2**	**1.0**
Application site disorders	**1**	**0.6**
Injection site pain	1	0.6
Urinary	**0.8**	**0.4**
Urinary tract infection	0.5	0.2
Neoplasms	**0.8**	**0.8**
Ovarian cyst	0.7	0.8
Central and Peripheral Nervous System	**0.7**	**0.6**
Headache	0.7	0.4
Resistance Mechanism Disorders	**0.5**	**0.2**
Skin and Appendages	**0.4**	**0.6**
Autonomous Nervous System (hyperemesis, loose stools, vasovagal syncope	**0.4**	**0**
Respiratory (dyspnea, rhinitis, sore throat, upper respiratory tract infection)	**0.4**	**0.6**
Platelet/ Bleeding, Clotting Disorders	**0.2**	**0**
Psychiatric (Nervousness)	**0.1**	**0**
Vision/Eye Abnormalities	**0.1**	**0.2**
Hearing/Vestibular Disorders	**0**	**0.2**

*Related: Definitely, probably, or possibly related to the study drug.

of sovlent contains: sodium chloride 4.5 mg/mL. Ampuls of 1 mL. Boxes of 3×3.

Store at 2 to 30°C Protect from light. For single use only. Discard unused portion.

New Product 1998

PURIFIED PROTEIN DERIVATIVE

Connaught

PPD-B (Mantoux)

Diagnostic Antigen

Indications: If there is reason to believe that an individual is infected with a mycobacterium other than M. tuberculosis var. hominis, as an added diagnostic procedure, PPD-B (Mantoux), 0.05 µg per test dose may be injected using Tuberculin PPD (Mantoux), 5 TU (bioequivalent) per test dose, as a control. Injections are usually made in the same forearm not less than 5 to 7.5 cm apart, but if necessary may be made on opposite forearms. Since it is well known that cross-reactivity between Tuberculin PPD and PPD-B takes place, it is generally accepted that an individual who shows a larger positive reaction to PPD-B than to Tuberculin PPD is possibly infected with a mycobacterium other than M. tuberculosis var. hominis. Skin testing with PPD-B (Mantoux) can therefore be used as a differential diagnostic test.

Contraindications: There are no contraindications.

Warnings: Caution: Reactivity to the test may be depressed or suppressed for as long as 4 to 6 weeks in individuals who have received concurrent or recent immunization with certain virus vaccines (measles, influenza), have had viral infections (rubeola, influenza, mumps and probably others) or who are receiving corticosteroids or immunosuppressive agents.

Dosage: The test dose for Tuberculin PPD (Mantoux) is 0.1 mL containing 5 TU (0.05 µg of PPD), and for PPD-B (Mantoux), the test dose is 0.1 mL containing 0.05 µg of Purified Protein Derivative.

Administration: The site of the test is the flexor surface of the forearm about 10 cm below the bend of the elbow.

The skin of the forearm is first cleansed with alcohol and allowed to dry.

The test material is administered intracutaneously with a 1 mL syringe calibrated in tenths and fitted with a short, 3/8'' or 1/2'', 26-or 27-gauge needle.

Disposable sterile syringes and needles may be used. Glass syringes and needles should be sterilized by autoclaving (121°C for 30 minutes), by boiling or by the use of dry heat. Do not sterilize by means of alcohol.

The rubber cap of the vial should be wiped with cotton moistened with alcohol or other suitable antiseptic. The needle is then inserted gently through the cap and a small amount (0.1 mL) of the Tuberculin PPD or PPD-B (Mantoux) is drawn into the syringe, used for rinsing and then completely expelled.

The required amount of antigen is then drawn into the syringe.

The point of the needle is inserted into the most superficial layers of the skin with the needle bevel pointing upward. If the intracutaneous injection is performed properly, a definite white bleb will rise at the needle point, about 1 cm in diameter. This will disappear within minutes. No dressing is required.

If several persons are being tested at one time, it is advisable to use a separate sterilized needle for each individual injection.

Interpretation of the Test: The test is read 48 to 72 hours after administration of the test antigens. The widest diameter of distinctly palpable induration, measured at right angles to the long axis of the arm, should be recorded. Presence of redness, edema or necrosis should also be recorded. Any distinct induration measuring 10 mm or over is considered a positive reaction. Indurations between 5 to 9 mm are considered doubtful.

An individual who does not show a positive reaction to the test dose of PPD-B (Mantoux) may be considered as negative for ''atypical'' mycobacterial infections.

A positive reaction to PPD-B (Mantoux) larger than to Tuberculin PPD (Mantoux) indicates a sensitivity, which may be the result of a previous infection with atypical mycobacteria. Thus a control test with Tuberculin PPD (Mantoux) should always be performed as indicated above under the heading Indications.

Those individuals giving a positive reaction 10 mm or greater to PPD-B (Mantoux) may or may not show evidence of infection by M. tuberculosis. Chest X-ray examination in these cases is recommended as a means of determining the presence or absence, of pulmonary tuberculosis.

As a result of 2 studies using Tuberculin PPD (Mantoux) and PPD-B (Mantoux), it has been found that in cases of high sensitivity to Tuberculin PPD (indurations greater than 10 mm), the probability of misclassification is of the order of 10%, while in cases of low sensitivity (5 to 9 mm) this probability would increase to about 50%. Therefore, even for those individuals highly sensitized to Tuberculin PPD, a greater response to PPD-B (Mantoux) than to Tuberculin PPD may be due to cross-reactivity and does not necessarily indicate that an individual is infected with ''atypical'' mycobacteria.

Thus, although testing with PPD-B (Mantoux) can be a valuable aid in detecting those who have been infected with mycobacteria other than M. tuberculosis, additional tests such as bacteriological identification, animal tests, etc. should be carried out before an accurate diagnosis can be reached as to the nature of the mycobacterial strain involved.

Supplied: PPD-B (Mantoux): Purified Protein Derivative (PPD-B), for intracutaneous (Mantoux) testing for ''atypical'' mycobacterial infections in humans, is prepared from M. avium-intracellulare (Battey bacillus) grown on a protein-free synthetic medium. It is available in the form of a stabilized solution in sterile isotonic phosphate-buffered saline containing Tween 80 0.0005%. Phenol 0.28% has been added as a preservative. The solution is standardized by intracutaneous testing in Battey-sensitized guinea pigs against the Connaught House Standard. Each mL contains: PPD-B (Mantoux) 0.5 µg. Vials of 1 mL containing 10 test doses. When stored in the cold, 2 to 8°C, the stabilized PPD-B (Mantoux) solution keeps its potency for at least 1 year after the date of release for distribution. The preparation is ready for immediate use without further dilution.

Tuberculin PPD (Mantoux): Vials of tuberculin PPD (Mantoux) 5 TU (bioequivalent) to be used as the control containing 10 and 50 test doses.

Store in a refrigerator at 2 to 8°C.

Reviewed 1998

PURINETHOL® Ⓟ

Glaxo Wellcome

Mercaptopurine

Antileukemic

Pharmacology: Clinical studies have shown the absorption of an oral dose of mercaptopurine in man is incomplete and variable, averaging approximately 50% of the administered dose. The factors influencing absorption are unknown. I.V. administration of an investigational preparation of mercaptopurine revealed a plasma half-disappearance time of 21 minutes in children and 47 minutes in adults. The volume of distribution usually exceeded that of the total body water.

Mercaptopurine is extensively metabolized and excreted via the kidneys and the active metabolites have a longer half-life than the parent drug. Following the oral administration of ^{35}S-6-mercaptopurine in one subject, a total of 46% of the dose could be accounted for in the urine (as parent drug and metabolites) in the first 24 hours. Metabolites of mercaptopurine were found in urine within the first 2 hours after administration. Radioactivity (in the form of sulfate) could be found in the urine for weeks afterwards. The half-life of orally administered 6-mercaptopurine in the circulation is approximately 90 minutes.

There is a negligible entry of mercaptopurine into cerebrospinal fluid.

Plasma protein binding averages 19% over the concentration range 10 to 50 µg/mL (a concentration only achieved by i.v. administration of mercaptopurine at doses exceeding 5 to 10 mg/kg).

Monitoring plasma levels of mercaptopurine during therapy is of questionable value. It is technically difficult to determine plasma concentrations which are seldom greater than 1 to 2 µg/mL after a therapeutic oral dose. More significantly mercaptopurine enters rapidly into the anabolic and catabolic pathways for purines and the active intracellular metabolites have appreciably longer half-lives than the parent drug. The biochemical effects of a single dose of mercaptopurine are evident long after the parent drug has disappeared from plasma. Because of this rapid metabolism of mercaptopurine to active intracellular derivatives, hemodialysis would not be expected to appreciably reduce toxicity of the drug. There is no known pharmacologic antagonist to the biochemical actions of mercaptopurine in vivo.

Azathioprine is cleaved in vivo to mercaptopurine. Mercaptopurine competes with hypoxanthine and guanine for the enzyme hypoxanthine-guanine phosphoribosyltransferase (HGPRTase) and is itself converted to thioinosinic acid (TIMP). This intracellular nucleotide inhibits several reactions involving inosinic acid (IMP) including the conversion of IMP to xanthylic acid (XMP) and the conversion of IMP to adenylic acid (AMP) via adenylosuccinate (SAMP). In addition, 6-methylthioinosinate (MTIMP) is formed by the methylation of TIMP. Both TIMP and MTIMP have been reported to inhibit glutamine-5-phosphoribosylpyrophosphate amidotransferase, the first enzyme unique to the de novo pathway for purine ribonucleotide synthesis.

Experiments indicate that radiolabeled mercaptopurine may be recovered from the DNA in the form of deoxythioguanosine. Some mercaptopurine is converted to nucleotide derivatives of 6-thioguanine (6-TG) by the sequential actions of inosinate (IMP) dehydrogenase and xanthylate (XMP) aminase, converting TIMP to thioguanylic acid (TGMP).

Animal tumors that are resistant to mercaptopurine have lost the ability to convert mercaptopurine to TIMP. However, it is clear that resistance to mercaptopurine may be acquired by other means as well, particularly in human leukemias.

It is not known exactly which of any one or more of the biochemical effects of mercaptopurine and its metabolites are directly or predominantly responsible for cell death.

The catabolism of mercaptopurine and its metabolites is complex. In man, after oral administration of ^{35}S-6-mercaptopurine, urine contains intact mercaptopurine, thiouric acid (formed by direct oxidation by xanthine oxidase, probably via 6-mercapto-8-hydroxypurine) and a number of 6-methylated thiopurines. The methylthiopurines yield appreciable amounts of inorganic sulfate. The importance of the metabolism by xanthine oxidase relates to the fact that allopurinol inhibits this enzyme and retards the catabolism of mercaptopurine and its active metabolites. A significant reduction in mercaptopurine dosage is mandatory if a potent xanthine oxidase inhibitor and mercaptopurine are used simultaneously in a patient (see Warnings).

Indications: For remission induction, remission consolidation, and maintenance therapy of the acute leukemias. The response to this agent depends upon the particular sub-classification of the acute leukemia (lymphatic, myelogenous, undifferentiated) and the age of the patient (child or adult). Mercaptopurine is also indicated for the palliative treatment of chronic myelogenous (granulocytic) leukemia.

Acute Lymphatic (Lymphocytic, Lymphoblastic) Leukemia: Acute lymphatic leukemia occurring in children responds, in general, more favorably to mercaptopurine than the same disorder occurring in adults. Given as a single agent for remission induction, mercaptopurine induces complete remission in approximately 25% of children and 10% of adults. These results can be improved upon considerably by using multiple, carefully selected agents in combination. Reliance upon mercaptopurine alone is seldom justified. The duration of complete remission induced in children with acute lymphatic leukemia is so brief without the use of maintenance therapy that some form of drug therapy is considered essential following remission induction. Mercaptopurine, as a single agent, is capable of significantly prolonging complete remission duration in children; however, combination therapy with multiple agents has produced results superior to that achieved with mercaptopurine alone. The effectiveness of mercaptopurine in maintenance programs in adult acute lymphatic leukemia has not been established.

Acute Myelogenous (and Acute Myelomonocytic) Leukemia: As a single agent, mercaptopurine will induce complete remission in approximately 10% of children and adults with acute myelogenous leukemia or its sub-classifications. These results are inferior to those achieved with combination chemotherapy employing optimum treatment schedules.

Chronic Myelogenous (Granulocytic) Leukemia: Mercaptopurine is 1 of several agents with demonstrated efficacy in the treatment of chronic myelogenous leukemia. Approximately 30 to 50% of patients with chronic myelogenous leukemia obtain an objective response to mercaptopurine. This is less than the 90% objective responses with busulfan, and, of these two agents, busulfan is usually regarded as the preferred drug for initial therapy.

CNS Leukemia: Mercaptopurine is not effective for prophylaxis or treatment of CNS leukemia.

Other Neoplasms: Mercaptopurine is not effective in chronic lymphatic leukemia, the lymphomas (including Hodgkin's Disease), or solid tumors.

Contraindications: Mercaptopurine should not be used unless a diagnosis of acute leukemia or chronic myelogenous leukemia has been adequately established and the responsible physician is knowledgeable in assessing response to chemotherapy. Mercaptopurine should not be used in patients whose disease has demonstrated prior resistance to this drug. In

Purinethol (cont'd)

animals and man there is usually complete cross-resistance between mercaptopurine and thioguanine.

Warnings: Caution: Purinethol is a potent drug and should be used only by physicians experienced with cancer chemotherapy drugs. Blood counts should be taken once or twice weekly. Discontinue or reduce the dosage upon evidence of abnormal depression of the bone marrow. Liver function must be evaluated prior to and at weekly intervals at the beginning of therapy and monthly thereafter.

Bone Marrow Toxicity: The most consistent dose-related toxicity is bone marrow suppression. This may be manifest by anemia, leukopenia, thrombocytopenia, or any combination of these. Any of these findings may also indicate progression of the underlying disease. It is imperative that patients be instructed to report promptly the development of fever, sore throat, signs of local infection, bleeding from any site, or symptoms suggestive of anemia. Since mercaptopurine may have a delayed effect, it is important to withdraw the medication temporarily at the first sign of an abnormally large fall in any of the formed elements of the blood.

There are rare individuals with an inherited deficiency of the enzyme thiopurine methyltransferase (TPMT) who may be unusually sensitive to the myelosuppressive effects of mercaptopurine and prone to developing rapid bone marrow suppression following the initiation of treatment. Substantial dosage reductions may be required to avoid the development of life-threatening bone marrow suppression in these patients. This toxicity may be more profound in patients treated with concomitant allopurinol (see Warnings, Drug Interactions).

Hepatotoxicity: Mercaptopurine is hepatotoxic in animals and man; deaths have been reported from hepatic necrosis. Hepatic injury can occur with any dosage, but seems to occur with greatest frequency when doses of 2.5 mg/kg/day are exceeded. The histologic pattern of mercaptopurine hepatotoxicity includes features of both intrahepatic cholestasis and parenchymal cell necrosis, either of which may predominate. It is not clear how much of the hepatic damage is due to direct toxicity from the drug and how much may be due to a hypersensitivity reaction. In some patients jaundice has cleared following withdrawal of mercaptopurine and reappeared with its reintroduction.

Published reports have cited widely varying incidences of overt hepatotoxicity; several reports have indicated that as many as 10 to 40% of patients with acute leukemia develop jaundice while receiving treatment with mercaptopurine.

Usually, clinically detectable jaundice appears early in the course of treatment (1 or 2 months). However, jaundice has been reported as early as 1 week and as late as 8 years after the start of treatment with mercaptopurine.

Monitoring of serum transaminase levels, alkaline phosphatase, and bilirubin levels may allow early detection of hepatotoxicity. It is advisable to monitor these liver function tests at weekly intervals when first beginning therapy and at monthly intervals thereafter. Liver function tests may be advisable more frequently in patients who are receiving mercaptopurine with other hepatotoxic drugs or with known preexisting liver disease.

The concomitant administration of mercaptopurine with other hepatotoxic agents requires especially careful clinical and biochemical monitoring of hepatic function. Combination therapy involving mercaptopurine with other drugs not felt to be hepatotoxic should nevertheless be approached with caution. The combination of mercaptopurine with doxorubicin was reported to be hepatotoxic in 19 of 20 patients undergoing remission-induction therapy for leukemia resistant to previous therapy.

The hepatotoxicity has been associated in some cases with anorexia, diarrhea, jaundice, and ascites. Hepatic encephalopathy has occurred. The onset of clinical jaundice, hepatomegaly, or anorexia with tenderness in the right hypochondrium are immediate indications for withholding mercaptopurine until the exact etiology can be identified. Likewise, any evidence of deterioration in liver function studies, toxic hepatitis, or biliary stasis should prompt discontinuation of the drug and lead to a search for an etiology of the hepatotoxicity.

Drug Interactions: Allopurinol: When allopurinol and mercaptopurine are administered concomitantly, it is imperative that the dose of mercaptopurine be reduced one-third to one-quarter of the usual dose. Failure to observe this dosage reduction will result in a delayed catabolism of mercaptopurine and the strong likelihood of inducing severe toxicity.

Warfarin: Inhibition of the anticoagulant effect of warfarin when given with mercaptopurine has been reported.

Thioguanine: see Precautions.

Trimethoprim-Sulfamethoxazole: see Precautions.

Immunosuppression: Mercaptopurine recipients may manifest decreased cellular hypersensitivities and impaired allograft rejection. Induction of immunity to infectious agents or vaccines will be subnormal in these patients; the degree of immunosuppression will depend on antigen dose and temporal relationship to drug. This drug effect is similar to that of azathioprine and should be carefully considered with regard to intercurrent infections and risk of subsequent neoplasia.

Mutagenesis and Carcinogenesis: Mercaptopurine causes chromosomal aberrations in animals and man and induces dominant-lethal mutations in male mice. Carcinogenic potential exists in man. Cases have been documented of the occurrence of acute nonlymphatic leukemia in patients who received mercaptopurine for non-neoplastic disorders.

Teratogenesis: Mercaptopurine has embryopathic effects in rats. Women receiving mercaptopurine in the first trimester of pregnancy have an increased incidence of abortion; the risk of malformation in offspring surviving first trimester exposure is not accurately known. In a series of 28 women receiving mercaptopurine after the first trimester of pregnancy, 3 mothers died undelivered, 1 delivered a stillborn child, and 1 aborted; there were no cases of macroscopically abnormal fetuses.

Since such experience cannot exclude the possibility of fetal damage, mercaptopurine should be used during pregnancy only if the benefit clearly justifies the possible risk to the fetus, and particular caution should be given to the use of mercaptopurine in the first trimester of pregnancy.

Effects on Fertility: The effect of mercaptopurine on human fertility is unknown for either males or females.

Lactation: Mothers receiving mercaptopurine should not breast-feed.

Precautions: General: The safe and effective use demands a thorough knowledge of the natural history of the condition being treated. For example, remission induction of adult acute leukemia virtually always necessitates the production of moderate to severe bone marrow hypoplasia. The degree of myelosuppression acceptable in this disease would not be desirable in the management of chronic granulocytic leukemia. After selection of an initial dosage schedule, therapy will frequently need to be modified depending upon the patient's response and manifestations of toxicity.

The most frequent, serious, toxic effect of mercaptopurine is myelosuppression resulting in leukopenia, thrombocytopenia and anemia. These toxic effects are often unavoidable during the induction phase of adult acute leukemia if remission induction is to be successful. Whether or not these manifestations demand modification or cessation of dosage depends both upon the response of the underlying disease and a careful consideration of supportive facilities (granulocyte and platelet transfusions) which may be available. Life-threatening infections and bleeding have been observed as a consequence of mercaptopurine induced granulocytopenia and thrombocytopenia. Severe hematologic toxicity may require supportive therapy with platelet transfusions for bleeding, and antibiotics and granulocyte transfusions if sepsis is documented.

If it is not the intent to induce bone marrow hypoplasia, it is important to discontinue the drug temporarily at the first evidence of an abnormally large fall in white blood cell count, platelet count or hemoglobin concentration as leukocyte and platelet counts continue to fall after treatment is stopped. In many patients with severe depression of the formed elements of the blood due to mercaptopurine, the bone marrow appears hypoplastic on aspiration or biopsy, whereas in other cases it may appear normocellular. The qualitative changes in the erythroid elements towards the megaloblastic series, characteristically seen with the folic acid antagonists and some other antimetabolites, are not seen with this drug.

It is recommended that evaluation of the hemoglobin or hematocrit, total white blood cell count and differential count, and quantitative platelet count be obtained weekly while the patient is on mercaptopurine therapy. In cases where the cause of fluctuations in the formed elements in the peripheral blood is obscure, bone marrow examination may be useful for the evaluation of marrow status. The decision to increase, decrease, continue or discontinue a given dosage of mercaptopurine must be based not only on the absolute hematologic values, but also upon the rapidity with which changes are occurring. In many instances, particularly during the induction phase of acute leukemia, complete blood counts will need to be done more frequently than once weekly (often daily) in order to evaluate the effect of the therapy. The dosage of mercaptopurine may need to be reduced when this agent is combined with other drugs whose primary toxicity is myelosuppression.

Impaired Renal Function: It is probably advisable to start with smaller dosages in patients with impaired renal function, since the latter might result in slower elimination of the drug and a greater cumulative effect.

Drug Interactions: Allopurinol: see Warnings.

Warfarin: see Warnings.

Thioguanine: There is usually complete cross-resistance between mercaptopurine and thioguanine.

Trimethoprim-Sulfamethoxazole: The dosage of mercaptopurine may need to be reduced when mercaptopurine is combined with other drugs whose primary or secondary toxicity is myelosuppression. Enhanced marrow suppression has been noted in some patients also receiving trimethoprim-sulfamethoxazole.

Pregnancy: As with all cytotoxic chemotherapy, adequate contraceptive precautions should be advised if either partner is receiving mercaptopurine (see Warnings).

Adverse Effects: Hematologic: The most frequent adverse reaction to mercaptopurine is myelosuppression. The induction of complete remission of acute lymphatic leukemia frequently is associated with marrow hypoplasia. Maintenance of remission generally involves multiple drug regimens whose component agents cause myelosuppression. Anemia, leukopenia, and thrombocytopenia are frequently observed. Dosages and schedules are adjusted to prevent life-threatening cytopenias (see Warnings and Precautions).

Gastrointestinal: Intestinal ulceration has been reported. Nausea, vomiting and anorexia are uncommon during initial administration, but they may occur during toxicity. Mild diarrhea and sprue-like symptoms have been noted occasionally, but it is difficult at present to attribute these to the medication. Oral lesions are rarely seen, and when they occur they resemble thrush rather than antifolic ulcerations.

An increased risk of pancreatitis may be associated with the investigational use of mercaptopurine in inflammatory bowel disease.

Renal: Hyperuricemia frequently occurs in patients receiving mercaptopurine as a consequence of rapid cell lysis accompanying the antineoplastic effect. Adverse effects can be minimized by increased hydration, urine alkalinization, and the prophylactic administration of a xanthine oxidase inhibitor such as allopurinol. The dosage of mercaptopurine should be reduced to one-third to one-quarter of the usual dose if allopurinol is given concurrently.

Miscellaneous: While dermatologic reactions can occur as a consequence of disease, the administration of mercaptopurine has been associated with skin rashes and hyperpigmentation.

Drug fever has been very rarely reported with mercaptopurine. Before attributing fever to mercaptopurine, every attempt should be made to exclude more common causes of pyrexia, such as sepsis, in patients with acute leukemia.

Overdose: Symptoms and Treatment: Signs and symptoms of overdosage may be immediate such as anorexia, nausea, vomiting and diarrhea; or delayed such as myelosuppression, liver dysfunction, and gastroenteritis. There is no known pharmacologic antagonist of mercaptopurine. The drug should be discontinued immediately if unintended toxicity occurs during treatment. If a patient is seen immediately following an accidental overdosage of the drug, induced emesis may be useful. Dialysis cannot be expected to clear mercaptopurine. Hemodialysis is thought to be of marginal use due to the rapid intracellular incorporation of mercaptopurine into active metabolites with long persistence.

Dosage: Induction and Consolidation Therapy: Administered orally. The dosage which will be tolerated or will be effective varies from patient to patient, and therefore careful titration is necessary to obtain the optimum therapeutic effect without incurring excessive, unintended toxicity. The usual initial dosage for children and adults is 2.5 mg/kg of body weight per day (100 to 200 mg in the average adult and 50 mg in an average 5-year-old child). Children with acute leukemia have tolerated this dose without difficulty in most cases; it may be continued daily for several weeks or more in some patients. If after 4 weeks at this dosage, there is no clinical improvement and no definite evidence of leukocyte or platelet depression, the dosage may be increased by up to 5 mg/kg daily.

A dosage of 2.5 mg/kg per day may result in a rapid fall in leukocyte count within 1 to 2 weeks in some adults with acute leukemia and high total leukocyte counts, as well as in certain adults with chronic myelocytic leukemia.

The total daily dosage may be given at one time. It is calculated to the nearest multiple of 25 mg. The dosage of mercaptopurine should be reduced to one-third to one-quarter of the usual dose if allopurinol is given concurrently. Since the drug may have a delayed action, it should be discontinued at the first sign of an abnormally large or rapid fall in the leukocyte or platelet count. If subsequently the leukocyte count or platelet count remains constant for 2 or 3 days, or rises, treatment may be resumed.

Maintenance Therapy: If a complete hematologic remission is obtained with mercaptopurine either alone or in combination with other agents, maintenance therapy should be considered. This is indicated in children with acute lymphatic leukemia. The use of mercaptopurine in maintenance schedules for adults with acute leukemia has not been established to be effective. If remission is achieved, maintenance doses will vary from patient to patient. A usual daily maintenance dose of mercaptopurine is 1.5 to 2.5 mg/kg/day as a single dose. It is to be emphasized that in children with acute lymphatic leukemia in remission, superior results have been obtained when mercaptopurine has been combined with other agents (most frequently with methotrexate) for remission maintenance. Mercaptopurine should rarely be relied upon as a single agent for the maintenance of remissions induced in acute leukemia.

Special Instructions: Tablets should be returned to the manufacturer for destruction. Proper precautions should be taken in packaging these materials for transport.

All materials which have come in contact with cytotoxic drugs should be segregated and incinerated at 1 000°C or more. Sealed containers may explode.

Personnel regularly involved in the preparation and handling of cytotoxic agents should have bi-annual blood examinations.

Care should be taken when handling or halving the tablets so as not to contaminate hands or to inhale the drug.

Supplied: Each pale yellow to buff, scored tablet, imprinted with "PURINETHOL" and "O4A", contains: mercaptopurine 50 mg. Nonmedicinal ingredients: cornstarch, lactose, magnesium stearate, potato starch and stearic acid. Bottles of 25. Store in a dry place between 15 and 25°C, protected from light.

(Shown in Product Recognition Section)

Reviewed 1998

PYLORID® ℞

Glaxo Wellcome

Ranitidine Bismuth Citrate

Histamine H_2-receptor Antagonist with H. pylori Suppressive Activity

Note: For additional safety information on clarithromycin and ranitidine, consult the individual product monographs.

Pharmacology: Ranitidine bismuth citrate is a complex of ranitidine, a histamine H_2-receptor antagonist, and bismuth citrate, which together produce H. pylori suppressive activity. Following ingestion, ranitidine bismuth citrate dissociates in intragastric fluid, giving rise to ranitidine, and soluble and insoluble forms of bismuth. Histamine H_2-receptor antagonists are effective in the treatment of peptic ulcer disease and this therapeutic effect results from their ability to suppress gastric acid secretion. In vitro, bismuth-containing compounds have bactericidal activity against the microorganism H. pylori, in vivo, growth is inhibited and the bactericidal effects of antibiotics (e.g., clarithromycin) greatly enhanced.

Ranitidine bismuth citrate, when used in conjunction with clarithromycin, is effective in the eradication of H. pylori infection. Ranitidine bismuth citrate and clarithromycin have been shown to act synergistically.

Ranitidine bismuth citrate inhibits both daytime and nocturnal basal gastric acid secretions as well as gastric acid secretion stimulated by food. A 400 mg dose of ranitidine bismuth citrate is as effective as a 150 mg dose of ranitidine at inhibiting daytime and nocturnal gastric acidity. Ranitidine bismuth citrate does not alter plasma pepsinogen I and II concentrations or pepsin activity. Ranitidine bismuth citrate has no clinically relevant effects on fasting or postprandial plasma gastrin.

Mucosal penetration and absorption of bismuth from ranitidine bismuth citrate is not affected by the degree of gastritis or the presence of H. pylori.

Ranitidine bismuth citrate has no observed effects on the CNS, cardiovascular system, or respiratory system in rats dosed 50 times, and in dogs and monkeys dosed 6.25 times the human dose. In addition, it has no effects on duodenal bicarbonate secretion, PGE_2 output, or transmucosal potential difference.

Pharmacokinetics: Following ingestion, ranitidine bismuth citrate dissociates in intragastric fluid, giving rise to ranitidine and soluble and insoluble forms of bismuth. Approximately 50% of the ranitidine is absorbed with a typical mean peak ranitidine concentration of 433 ng/mL (95%, CI 391, 479 ng/mL) occurring 0.5 to 5 hours after a 400 mg dose. Absorption of ranitidine derived from ranitidine bismuth citrate tablets is not significantly impaired by administration of food. The elimination half life of ranitidine is 3 hours.

The principal route of elimination for ranitidine is in the urine, accounting for 30 to 40% of the dose. Renal clearance (580 to 680 mL/min) is primarily by active tubular secretion. In renally impaired patients, decreases in ranitidine renal clearance are highly correlated with declining renal function, while nonrenal elimination is unaltered by renal impairment, averaging 140 mL/min. Elimination half life may exceed 6 hours in severely impaired patients, e.g., creatinine clearance less than 25 mL/min. The volume of distribution for ranitidine is 0.8 to 1.8 L/kg. Serum protein binding averages 15%.

Although oral absorption of bismuth is variable, less than 1% of bismuth derived from ranitidine bismuth citrate is absorbed after oral administration, with a typical mean peak bismuth concentration of 4.2 ng/mL (95%, CI 3.1, 5.6 ng/mL) occurring 15 to 60 minutes after a 400 mg dose.

Absorption of bismuth derived from ranitidine bismuth citrate is not clinically significantly affected by administration of food or antacids. The absorption of bismuth from ranitidine bismuth citrate is increased when gastric pH exceeds 6 at the time of dosing (AUC increased from a mean of 16 to 48.3 ng·h/mL).

Bismuth accumulates in the plasma/serum in rats and rabbits during once daily dosing, reaching steady-state concentrations in the rat between 1 and 6 months. In the dog, there is no evidence for accumulation of bismuth in the plasma during repeat dosing.

Bismuth accumulates relatively slowly in tissues in animals during once daily dosing, reaching steady-state concentrations between 1 and 6 months. There is slow elimination from tissues and bismuth can still be detected 6 months after cessation of treatment in long-term toxicity studies.

In man, bismuth accumulates in plasma during twice daily dosing with ranitidine bismuth citrate, reaching at least 70% of steady-state concentrations (less than 20 ng/mL) after 4 weeks of dosing at twice the recommended dose. Elimination of bismuth is polyexponential, with a terminal elimination half life of 11 to 28 days.

The principal route of excretion for bismuth is in the urine, with an average renal clearance of 30 to 60 mL/min, indicating net tubular reabsorption. Bismuth concentrations may be elevated in renally impaired and elderly patients as a result of decreased renal elimination. Bismuth also undergoes minor excretion in the bile. Unabsorbed bismuth is excreted in the feces. Bismuth is 98% bound to human plasma proteins, primarily albumin.

Indications: Ranitidine bismuth citrate in combination with clarithromycin is indicated for the treatment of patients with an active duodenal ulcer associated with H. pylori infection. The eradication of H. pylori has been demonstrated to reduce the risk of duodenal ulcer recurrence.

It is recommended that all patients not eradicated of H. pylori following ranitidine bismuth citrate plus clarithromycin treatment be considered to have H. pylori resistant to clarithromycin. Patients who fail therapy should not be retreated with a regimen containing clarithromycin. See Tables I and II.

Contraindications: The ranitidine bismuth citrate is contraindicated for patients known to have hypersensitivity to the drug or its ingredients.

Ranitidine bismuth citrate should not be used in patients with a history of porphyria.

Renal Impairment: Administration of ranitidine bismuth citrate is not recommended in patients with creatinine clearance less than 25 mL/min.

Warnings: Treatment with a H_2-antagonist may mask symptoms associated with carcinoma of the stomach and, therefore, may delay diagnosis of that condition. Accordingly,

Table I—Pylorid

Result of USA Studies in Patients with Active Ulcer who are H. pylori Positive

Study Number	Treatment[a]	Eradication[b] Rate (C.I.)	(n)	Ulcer Healing (4 weeks)[c] Rate (C.I.)	(n)	Overall Success[d] (24 weeks) Rate (C.I.)	(n)
Study 1	Pylorid 400 mg b.i.d. + Clarithromycin 500 mg t.i.d. for 2 weeks	84% (60-97)	(19)	75% (53-90)	(24)	59% (45-73)	—
Study 2	Pylorid 400 mg b.i.d. + Clarithromycin 500 mg t.i.d. for 2 weeks	73% (50-89)	(22)	71% (51-87)	(28)	51% (37-65)	—

[a] Based on an initial 2 weeks of coprescription with clarithromycin followed by a further 2 weeks of Pylorid 400 mg b.i.d. to facilitate ulcer healing.

[b] Patients had at least 2 negative and no positive eradication test results 28 days after the completion of treatment. The following patients were excluded: patients not infected with H. pylori prestudy, dropouts, patients with major protocol violations, patients with missing H. pylori tests, and patients that were not assessed for H. pylori eradication 4 weeks after the end of treatment because they were found to have an unhealed ulcer and were H. pylori negative at the end of treatment.

[c] Dropouts and patients with major protocol violations were excluded.

[d] Based on a life table analysis of overall success rate in the intent-to-treat Population. Overall success is defined as ulcer healing and absence of ulcer recurrence during the 24-week followup period.

Table II—Pylorid

Result of International Studies in Patients with Active Ulcer who are H. pylori Positive

Study Number	Treatment[a]	Eradication[b] Rate (C.I.)	(n)	Ulcer Healing (4 weeks)[c] Rate (C.I.)	(n)	Overall Success[d] (24 weeks) Rate (C.I.)	(n)
Study 1	Pylorid 400 mg b.i.d. + Clarithromycin 250 mg q.i.d. for 2 weeks	82% (60-95)	(22)	88% (71-96)	(32)	—	—
Study 2	Pylorid 400 mg b.i.d. + Clarithromycin 250 mg q.i.d. for 2 weeks	94% (84-99)	(52)	89% (80-95)	(75)	89% (81-97)	—

[a] Based on an initial 2 weeks of coprescription with clarithromycin followed by a further 2 weeks of Pylorid 400 mg b.i.d. to facilitate ulcer healing.

[b] Patients had at least 2 negative and no positive eradication test results 28 days after the completion of treatment. The following patients were excluded: patients not infected with H. pylori or unevaluable for H. pylori prestudy, prematurely withdrawn patients, patients with unhealed ulcer at the completion of the 4-week randomized treatment period, patients with missing H. pylori tests.

[c] Patients without a duodenal ulcer prestudy were excluded.

[d] Based on a life table analysis of overall success rate in the Intent-to-Treat Population. Overall success is defined as ulcer healing and absence of ulcer recurrence during the 24-week followup period.

Pylorid (cont'd)

where gastric ulcer is suspected the possibility of malignancy should be excluded before therapy with ranitidine bismuth citrate.

Pregnancy: There are no adequate and well-controlled studies in pregnant women, and therefore, the safety of ranitidine bismuth citrate in human pregnancy has not been established. In animal reproductive studies there was no evidence of teratogenicity. Because animal reproduction studies are not always predictive of human response, administration of ranitidine bismuth citrate is not recommended during pregnancy.

Lactation: It has been demonstrated during repeat dosing of ranitidine bismuth citrate in the lactating rat that low levels of ranitidine and bismuth are excreted in the milk with consequent exposure to the pups. The passage of ranitidine bismuth citrate into human breast milk has not been evaluated, therefore, ranitidine bismuth citrate should not be used by women who are breast-feeding.

Children: Safety and effectiveness of ranitidine bismuth citrate in children (under 18 years) has not been established.

Precautions: Selection of Patients: Whenever possible appropriate tests should be conducted prior to administration of the eradication regimen to determine the presence of H. pylori.

Darkening of the stool was reported in up to 19% of patients treated with ranitidine bismuth citrate in USA placebo-controlled trials. Stool darkening should not be confused with melena (blood in the stool). Adequate followup tests should be conducted if the physician suspects melena.

The doses of ranitidine bismuth citrate should not be taken in close succession repeatedly on consecutive days, since this could result in increased gastric pH to about 6, increased bismuth plasma levels and AUC. It is recommended that ranitidine bismuth citrate be taken in the morning and evening (see Dosage).

Although not seen in clinical trials with ranitidine bismuth citrate, bismuth intoxication from prolonged overdosage or deliberate self poisoning with soluble bismuth compounds can result in neurotoxicity and nephrotoxicity (see Overdose: Symptoms and Treatment).

A plasma bismuth concentration over 77.5 ng/mL (equivalent to 50 ng/mL whole blood) has been reported in the literature as a level of possible clinical concern, however, this value has subsequently been questioned as being too conservative due to a failure to take account of the time elapsed between last ingestion of bismuth and when blood samples were taken for analyses.

Drug Interactions: Although ranitidine has been reported to bind weakly to cytochrome P450 in vitro, the amount contained in 400 mg of ranitidine bismuth citrate does not inhibit the action of the cytochrome P450-linked oxygenase enzymes in the liver. However, there have been isolated reports of drug interactions that suggest ranitidine may affect the bioavailability of certain drugs by some mechanism as yet unidentified (e.g., a pH dependent effect on absorption).

Coadministration with clarithromycin results in a 50% increase in plasma concentrations of ranitidine from ranitidine bismuth citrate, and in 31% increased concentration of 14-hydroxy-clarithromycin.

Coadministration with ASA results in a slight decrease in the rate of salicylate absorption that is clinically unimportant.

Coadministration with a high dose of antacid (170 mEq) results in a 28% decrease in plasma concentrations of ranitidine, and may decrease plasma concentrations of bismuth from ranitidine bismuth citrate. These effects are not clinically significant.

Geriatrics: Ulcer healing and relapse rates in elderly patients (≥65 years of age) were no different from those in younger age groups. The incidence of adverse events and laboratory abnormalities were also not different from those seen in other age groups. Serum levels of ranitidine may be increased in elderly patients, however serum bismuth levels were similar to those seen in younger patients.

Renal Impairment: No dosage adjustment is required in patients with mild to moderate renal impairment (see Dosage).

Adverse Effects: Worldwide clinical trials of ranitidine bismuth citrate tablets included over 4 000 patients given ranitidine bismuth citrate alone or in combination with amoxicillin or clarithromycin.

Incidence of Drug-related Adverse Events in Placebo-controlled Clinical Trials: Table III lists drug-related adverse events that occurred at a frequency of ≥1% among patients treated with ranitidine bismuth citrate who participated in worldwide placebo-controlled trials.

Table III—Pylorid

Drug-related Adverse Events During Treatment

	Placebo n=818 (%)	Pylorid 400 mg b.i.d n=4 195 (%)	Pylorid plus clarithromycin 1-1.5 g daily n=348 (%)
Gastrointestinal			
Diarrhea	1	1	6
Constipation	<1	1	<1
Nausea/Vomiting	1	1	1
Neurological			
Headache	1	2	4
Miscellaneous			
Taste Disturbance	<1	<1	6

As with other medicines containing bismuth, ranitidine bismuth citrate may cause blackening of the stools and tongue, these are reversible, usually within 1 month after cessation of treatment.

Although not seen at a frequency of ≥1%, the following events may also be associated with the use of ranitidine bismuth citrate:

Gastrointestinal: abdominal discomfort, gastric pain.

Hepatic: transient changes in the liver enzymes ALT and AST.

Hypersensitivity: There have been rare reports of hypersensitivity reactions, including pruritus, skin rash and anaphylaxis.

Hematological: There have been rare reports of mild anemia.

Overdose: Symptoms and Treatment: There has been limited experience with overdosage. Adverse events related to overdosage with ranitidine are usually reversible, nonspecific, and nonlife threatening and result in no adverse sequelae. Although not seen in clinical trials with ranitidine bismuth citrate, bismuth intoxication from prolonged overdosage or deliberate self poisoning with soluble bismuth compounds can result in neurotoxicity and nephrotoxicity.

Treatment: In the event of an overdose or suspected bismuth toxicity, gastric lavage should be employed to remove unabsorbed material from the gastrointestinal tract, and symptom monitoring and other supportive therapy should be employed, if indicated. The ranitidine and bismuth components may be removed from the plasma by hemodialysis.

Dosage: The recommended dose should be taken twice daily, in the morning and evening, with or without food.

Eradication of H. pylori Infection: The recommended adult oral dosage is 400 mg twice daily plus clarithromycin (500 mg 3 times daily or 250 mg 4 times daily) for the first 2 weeks followed by ranitidine bismuth citrate 400 mg twice daily for a further 2 weeks to facilitate ulcer healing.

Geriatrics: No dosage adjustment is necessary in elderly patients (see Precautions, Geriatrics).

Renal Impairment: Because the principal route of excretion is renal, care should be exercised when administering ranitidine bismuth citrate to patients with renal impairment. However, for patients with mild to moderate renal impairment (creatinine clearance 25 to 50 mL/min), no dosage adjustment is necessary. Administration of ranitidine bismuth citrate is not recommended in patients with severe renal impairment (creatinine clearance less than 25 mL/min) (see Contraindications).

Information for the Patient: See Blue Section—Information for the Patient "Pylorid".

Supplied: Each light blue, film-coated, elongated octagonal-shaped tablet, identified by a logo on one side, contains: ranitidine bismuth citrate 400 mg, equivalent to ranitidine base 162 mg, trivalent bismuth 128 mg and citrate 110 mg. Nonmedicinal ingredients: indigo carmine aluminum lake, magnesium stearate, methylhydroxypropylcellulose, microcrystalline cellulose, polyvidone K30, sodium carbonate (anhydrous), titanium dioxide and triacetin. Double foil blister packs, cartons of 14 and 28. Store between 2 and 30°C in a dry place.

(Shown in Product Recognition Section)

New Product 1998

Nonmedicinal ingredients are listed alphabetically within the supplied information of product monographs. Refer to the WHITE SECTION.

PYRIBENZAMINE®

Novartis Consumer Health

Tripelennamine HCl

Antihistamine

Indications: Seasonal or nonseasonal allergic reactions.

Precautions: Occupational Hazards: Patients should be cautioned not to operate vehicles or hazardous machinery until their response to the drug has been determined.

Since the depressant effects of antihistamines are additive to those of other drugs affecting the CNS, patients should be cautioned against drinking alcoholic beverages or taking hypnotics, sedatives, psychotherapeutic agents or other drugs with CNS depressant effects during antihistaminic therapy. In longterm therapy, rare instances of acute hypersensitivity reactions as well as leukopenia and agranulocytosis have been reported.

Pregnancy and *Lactation:* Safety during lactation and in pregnancy, particularly during the first trimester, has not been established; therefore, this drug should be used only when its use is deemed essential to the patient's welfare.

Adverse Effects: Drowsiness, gastric discomfort, nausea, dry mouth, vertigo, rash, irritability, dizziness, bladder discomfort, symptoms of excitation (especially in young children), may occur.

Overdose: Symptoms: Usually, profound sedation. In children under 2 years, and rarely in adults, central stimulation, perhaps with convulsions, may occur; followed by central depression.

Treatment: Gastric lavage, or in the absence of coma, emetics. In excitation, short acting barbiturates i.v. In profound sedation with respiratory depression, stimulants and oxygen as required. Children may show hyperthermia, as in atropine poisoning.

Dosage: Adults: 50 mg 4 times daily (not more than 600 mg per day).

Supplied: Each pale blue, round, biconvex, scored tablet, imprinted CIBA on one side and LJ on the other, contains: tripelennamine HCl 50 mg. Nonmedicinal ingredients: acacia, cornstarch, FD&C Green No. 3, gelatin, lactose, magnesium stearate, talc and water. Energy: 2.26 kJ (0.54 kcal). Alcohol-, bisulfite-, gluten-, sodium-, parabens- and tartrazine-free. Boxes of 18 and 48.

PYRIDIUM® Ⓟ

Parke-Davis

Phenazopyridine HCl

Urinary Analgesic

Pharmacology: Phenazopyridine is excreted in the urine where it exerts a topical analgesic effect on the mucosa of the urinary tract. This action helps to relieve pain, burning, urgency and frequency. The precise mechanism of action is unknown.

Pharmacokinetics: The pharmacokinetic properties of phenazopyridine have not been determined. Phenazopyridine and its metabolites are rapidly excreted by the kidneys. In a small number of healthy subjects, 90% of a 600 mg/day oral dose of phenazopyridine was eliminated in the urine in 24 hours, 41% as unchanged drug and 49% as metabolites.

Indications: For the symptomatic relief of pain, burning, urgency, frequency, and other discomforts resulting from irritation of the mucosa of the lower urinary tract caused by infection, trauma, surgery, endoscopic procedures, or the passage of sounds or catheters.

The use of phenazopyridine for relief of symptoms should not delay definitive diagnosis and treatment of causative conditions. The drug should be used for symptomatic relief of pain and not as a substitute for specific surgery or antimicrobial therapy.

Phenazopyridine is compatible with antimicrobial therapy and can help relieve pain and discomfort during the interval before antimicrobial therapy controls the infection.

Treatment of a urinary tract infection with phenazopyridine should not exceed 2 days. There is no evidence that the combined administration of phenazopyridine and an antimicrobial provides greater benefit than administration of the antimicrobial alone after 2 days.

Contraindications: In patients who are hypersensitive to the drug or its ingredients. Phenazopyridine is contraindicated in patients with renal insufficiency or severe liver disease.

Precautions: General: The patient should be advised that phenazopyridine produces an orange to red color in the urine and feces, and may cause staining. Phenazopyridine may cause discoloration of body fluids and staining of contact lenses has been reported. A yellowish color of the skin or sclera may indicate accumulation of phenazopyridine resulting from impaired renal function and necessitates discontinuance of the drug. It should be noted that a decline in renal function is common in elderly patients. Phenazopyridine may mask pathological conditions and interfere with laboratory test values using colorimetric, spectrophotometric or fluorometric analysis methods.

Cautious use in patients with G-6-PD deficiency is advised since these patients are susceptible to oxidative hemolysis and may have greater potential to develop hemolytic anemia.

Information for the Patient: The patient should be advised to take phenazopyridine with or following food or after eating a snack to reduce stomach upset.

The patients should be aware that phenazopyridine causes a reddish orange discoloration of the urine and feces, and may stain clothing. Phenazopyridine may cause discoloration of body fluids and staining of contact lenses has been reported. There have been reports of teeth discoloration when the product has been broken or held in the mouth prior to swallowing.

Patients should be instructed to take phenazopyridine for only 2 days if an antibacterial agent is administered concurrently for the treatment of a urinary tract infection. If symptoms persist beyond those 2 days, the patient should be instructed to contact his or her physician.

Laboratory Tests: Phenazopyridine may interfere with laboratory test values using colorimetric, photometric or fluorometric analysis methods. Altered urine laboratory test values may include ketone (sodium nitroprusside), bilirubin (foam test, talc-disk-Fouchet-spot test, Franklin's tablet-Fouchet test, p-nitrobenzene diazonium p-toluene sulfonate reagent), diacetic acid (Gerhardt ferric chloride test), free hydrochloric acid, glucose (glucose oxidase tests), 17-hydroxycorticosteroids (modified Glenn-Nelson), 17-ketosteroids (Holtorff Koch modification of Zimmerman), porphyrins, albumin (discolors bromophenol blue test areas of commercial reagent strips, nitric acid ring test), phenolsulfophthalein, urobilinogen (color interference with Ehrlich's reagent), and urinalysis (spectrophotometric or color-based tests). Phenazopyridine also imparts an orange-red color to stools which may interfere with color tests.

Drug Interactions: The interaction of phenazopyridine with other drugs has not been studied in a systematic manner. However, the medical literature to date suggests that no significant interactions have been reported.

Carcinogenesis, Mutagenesis, Impairment of Fertility: Long-term administration of phenazopyridine has been associated with tumors of the large intestine in rats and of the liver in mice. Available epidemiological data are insufficient to evaluate the carcinogenicity of phenazopyridine in humans. In vitro studies indicate that phenazopyridine in the presence of metabolic activation is mutagenic in bacteria and mutagenic and clastogenic in mammalian cells.

Pregnancy: Reproductive studies with phenazopyridine (in combination with sulfacytine) in rats given up to 110 mg/kg/day and in rabbits given up to 39 mg/kg/day during organogenesis revealed no evidence of harm to offspring.

One prospective study in humans demonstrated that phenazopyridine traverses the placenta into the fetal compartment. There are no adequate and well-controlled studies in pregnant women. Therefore, phenazopyridine should be used in pregnant women only if the benefit clearly outweighs the risk.

Lactation: It is not known whether phenazopyridine or its metabolites are excreted in human milk. Because many drugs are excreted in human milk, a decision should be made to discontinue nursing or to discontinue the drug, taking into account the importance of drug therapy to the mother.

Children: Adequate and well-controlled studies have not been performed in the pediatric population. No pediatric-specific problems have been documented.

Adverse Effects: The following adverse events have been reported:

CNS: headache.

Gastrointestinal: nausea, vomiting and diarrhea.

Dermatologic and Hypersensitivity: rash, pruritus, discoloration, anaphylactoid-like reaction and hypersensitivity hepatitis.

Hematologic: methemoglobinemia, hemolytic anemia, potential hemolytic agent in G-6-PD deficiency, sulfhemoglobinemia.

Other: visual disturbances, renal and hepatic toxicity usually associated with overdose, renal calculi, jaundice, discoloration of body fluids and aseptic meningitis.

Overdose: Symptoms: Exceeding the recommended dose in patients with normal renal function or administering the recommended dose to patients with impaired renal function (common in elderly patients) may lead to increased serum levels and toxic reactions.

Methemoglobinemia generally follows a massive, acute overdose. Methylene blue, 1 to 2 mg/kg/dose given i.v. as a 1% solution as needed, should cause prompt reduction of the methemoglobinemia and disappearance of the cyanosis which is an aid in diagnosis. Oxidative Heinz body hemolytic anemia also may occur, and "bite cells" (degmacytes) may be present in a chronic overdosage situation. Red blood cell G-6-PD deficiency may predispose to hemolysis; however, hemolysis may occur at normal doses in patients with G-6-PD Mediterranean. Renal toxicity and occasional failure and hepatic impairment may also occur.

Treatment: Treatment is symptomatic and supportive.

Dosage: Adults: 200 mg 3 times daily after meals.

When used concomitantly with an antibacterial agent for the treatment of a urinary tract infection, the administration of phenazopyridine should not exceed 2 days. If symptoms persist, the patient should be re-evaluated.

Supplied: 100 mg: Each reddish brown, coated tablet, imprinted with a white PD 180 monogram on one side, contains: phenazopyridine HCl 100 mg. Nonmedicinal ingredients: carnauba wax, cornstarch, D&C red No. 7, FD&C blue No. 2, FD&C yellow No. 6, gelatin, lactose, magnesium stearate, methylcellulose, sodium starch glycolate, sucrose, titanium dioxide and white wax. Energy: 1.76 kJ (0.42 kcal)/100 mg. Sodium: 0.32 mg. gluten-, paraben-, sulfite- and tartrazine-free. Bottles of 100.

200 mg: Each reddish brown, coated tablet, imprinted with a white PD 181 monogram on one side, contains: phenazopyridine HCl 200 mg. Nonmedicinal ingredients: carnauba wax, cornstarch, D&C red No. 7, FD&C blue No. 2, FD&C yellow No. 6 gelatin, lactose, magnesium stearate, methylcellulose, sodium starch glycolate, sucrose, titanium dioxide and white wax. Energy: 3.2 kJ (0.76 kcal)/200 mg. Sodium: 0.32 mg. Gluten-, paraben-, sulfite- and tartrazine-free. Bottles of 100.

Store at controlled room temperature (15 to 30°C).

(Shown in Product Recognition Section)

Reviewed 1996

PYRIDOXINE

General Monograph, CPhA

see VITAMIN B_6

PYRIDOXINE HCl

Abbott

Vitamin

Supplied: Each mL contains: pyridoxine HCl 100 mg. Nonmedicinal ingredients: sodium hydroxide and water for injection. Ampuls of 1 mL, boxes of 10.

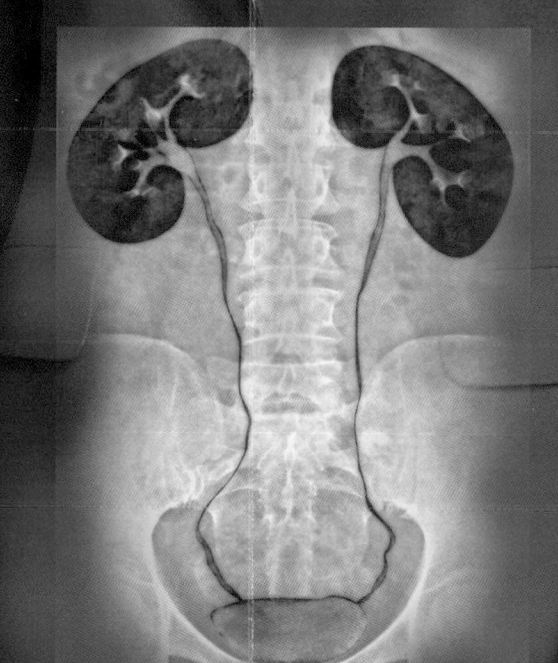

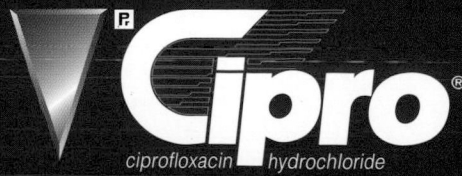

What is the difference between these two hypertensives?

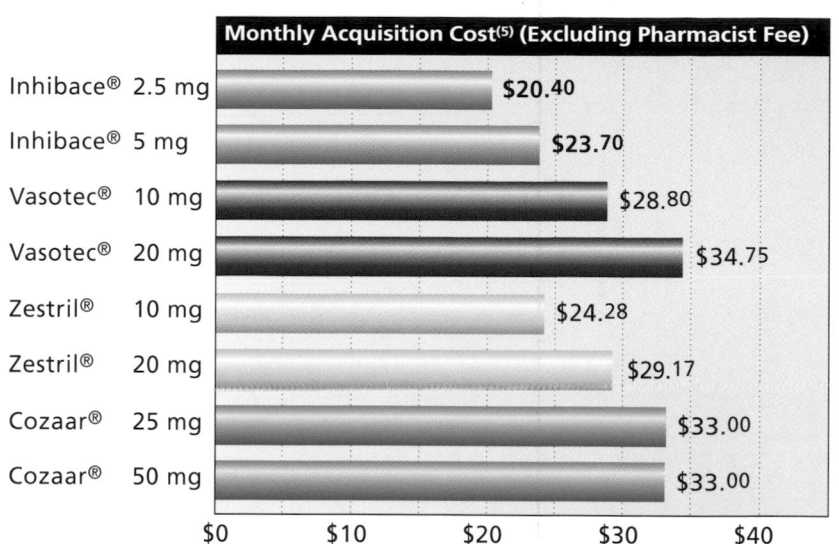

Q

QUADRACEL™

Connaught

Component Pertussis Vaccine—Diphtheria and Tetanus Toxoids Adsorbed Combined with Inactivated Poliomyelitis Vaccine

Active Immunizing Agent

Pharmacology: Immunization against diphtheria, tetanus, pertussis and polio has been associated with a striking decrease in the incidence of morbidity and mortality from these diseases. Simultaneous vaccination with a combination vaccine containing pertussis, diphtheria and tetanus toxoids and poliomyelitis vaccines have been used in Canada since 1958.

Diphtheria is a serious communicable disease caused by toxigenic strains of C. diphtheriae. The organism may be harbored in the nasopharynx, skin or other sites of asymptomatic carriers, making eradication of the disease difficult. Routine immunization against diphtheria in infancy and childhood has been widely practised in Canada since 1930, resulting in a decline in morbidity and mortality. Fewer than 5 cases are now reported annually in Canada. The case-fatality rate remains 5 to 10%, with the highest death rates in the very young and elderly. The disease occurs most frequently in unimmunized or partially immunized individuals. Diphtheria toxoid is a cell-free preparation of diphtheria toxin detoxified with formaldehyde. The immunity conferred is antitoxic, not antibacterial, and thus protects against the potentially lethal systemic effects of diphtheria toxin but not directly against local infection.

Tetanus is an acute and often fatal disease caused by an extremely potent neurotoxin produced by C. tetani. The organism is ubiquitous and its occurrence in nature cannot be controlled. Immunization is highly effective, provides long-lasting protection, and is recommended for the whole population. Only 2 to 3 cases of tetanus are now reported annually in Canada. Tetanus toxoid is prepared by detoxification of tetanus toxin with formaldehyde.

Injection of bacterial proteins such as diphtheria and tetanus toxoids results in the production of protective antibodies. A primary series consisting of 2 or more injections is required to prime the immune system and produce a satisfactory protective antibody level. Tetanus antitoxin levels of >0.01 IU/mL are generally accepted as good evidence of immunity from tetanus. Diphtheria antitoxin levels of ≥0.01 IU/mL are thought to be the minimal level required for protection. Levels >0.05 IU/mL are considered optimal for protection. After completion of a primary series, circulating antibodies to tetanus and diphtheria toxoids gradually decline but are thought to persist at protective levels for up to 10 years. Tetanus and diphtheria toxoid boosters are recommended every 10 years.

Pertussis (whooping cough) is a highly communicable bacterial disease caused by B. pertussis. Severity and mortality are greatest in infancy, and even infants born to apparently immune mothers are highly susceptible to infection, particularly if maternal immunity was induced by whole cell pertussis vaccine. During the last 30 years, vaccination with whole cell pertussis vaccine has been widely practised in Canada and the incidence and mortality from pertussis have declined remarkably. However, outbreaks of pertussis continue to occur across Canada, with an annual reported rate of 1 000 to 8 000 cases over the past 5 years. Deaths and brain damage from pertussis infections still occur, particularly in young infants who have not been vaccinated. Controversy regarding the safety of whole cell pertussis vaccine during the 1970s led to several studies of the benefits and risks of this vaccination during the 1980s. These epidemiologic analyses clearly indicate that the benefits of the pertussis immunization program outweigh the risks. Acellular pertussis vaccines consisting of purified fractions of the B. pertussis bacterium have been used effectively to control pertussis in children 2 years of age or older in Japan since 1981.

A randomized controlled efficacy study was conducted in Sweden using the formulation of Tripacel which contained lower concentrations of PT, FHA than the current formulation. In this study, 2 500 infants received Tripacel and 2 500 infants received a control vaccine containing diphtheria and tetanus toxoids. Tripacel demonstrated a clinical efficacy of 85% against pertussis disease (defined as 21 days of paroxysmal cough with culture, serologic, or epidemiologic confirmation). The current formulation of Tripacel produced comparable or higher serologic responses to the defined pertussis antigens (PT, FHA, fimbriae and pertactin) when compared to the lower antigen formulation in clinical trials, either as a primary immunizing agent or as a booster vaccine. Tripacel has been shown to have lower rates of local and systemic reactions compared directly against whole cell DPT vaccines when administered to infants and older children.

Poliomyelitis is caused by infection with 1 of the 3 antigenic types of poliovirus. Following introduction of poliovirus vaccine in Canada in 1955, the indigenous disease has been virtually eliminated. The last significant outbreak of poliomyelitis occurred in 1978 to 1979, when there were 11 cases of paralytic disease among unimmunized contacts of imported cases. The last case of poliomyelitis attributed to imported, wild virus occurred in 1988. However, circulation of wild viruses does occur in rare circumstances, and it remains crucial that the highest possible level of vaccine-induced immunity be maintained in the population. Inactivated Poliomyelitis Vaccine (Diploid Cell Origin)— IPV, (sometimes referred to as e-IPV), is an enhanced formalin-inactivated product which has a higher potency than the original IPV. The 3 poliovirus types are propagated in human diploid cells. A primary series induces protective antibody levels in more than 99% of recipients.

In clinical trials conducted in Canada, more than 1 000 children have received Quadracel alone or used to reconstitute Act-HIB, Haemophilus b Conjugate Vaccine (Tetanus Protein-Conjugate). Whether given at 2, 4, 6 months, at 18 to 19 months (fourth dose) or at the 4- to 6-year booster, Quadracel produced comparable antitetanus, diphtheria and polio responses to the DPT Polio Adsorbed control. Anti-PRP responses were comparable as well. Although Quadracel contains 15 Lf of diphtheria toxoid versus the 25 Lf of diphtheria toxoid in DPT Polio Adsorbed, no significant differences in diphtheria antitoxin responses were seen in any of the age groups. Responses to pertussis antigens PT, FHA and pertactin were significantly higher in Quadracel recipients than in recipients of DPT Polio Adsorbed. See Table I.

Table I—Quadracel

Comparison of Quadracel with Whole Cell Pertussis Combinations Serologic Results

	Geometric Mean Titre (GMT)					
	7 Months		19-20 Months		4-6 Years	
Antigen	DPT Polio/ PRP-T* (n=105)	Quadracel (n=108)	DPT Polio/ PRP-T* (n=94)	Quadracel (n=92)	DPT Polio (n=30)	Quadracel (n=126)
Diphtheria	0.29	0.36	6.82	7.07	17.0	15.1
Tetanus	0.63	1.61	5.40	6.78	5.54	5.10
Agglutinins	438	444	642	848	1 315	1 939
PT	15.2	103	44.6	116	47.9	123.2
FHA	31.4	165	72.6	156	119.3	176.2
Pertactin	8.9	40.5	26.4	77	41.2	64.2
FIM	355	332	719	877	479	738
Polio 1	889	702	11 873	9 311	15 462	10 903
Polio 2	2 597	2 595	21 038	18 331	23 661	27 337
Polio 3	2 726	1 837	10 675	12 492	10 540	9 165

*Act-HIB reconstituted with Connaught's DPT Polio Adsorbed.

With the exception of tetanus, no differences were found in immunogenicity when Quadracel was used to reconstitute Act-HIB or the 2 vaccines were given at separate sites. Anti-PRP responses were comparable. All children were protected against polio. Pertussis responses were not affected by method of administration. Tetanus antitoxin levels were lower in the combined vaccine groups, but all children had protective levels (≥0.01 EU*/mL). Following the 18-month dose, all children had tetanus antitoxin levels ≥0.10 EU*/mL.

Quadracel was significantly less reactogenic than DPT Polio Adsorbed.

*EU=Elisa Units.

Indications: For the primary immunization of infants, at or above the age of 2 months and as a booster in children up to their 7th birthday against diphtheria, tetanus, whooping cough and poliomyelitis.

When both vaccines are indicated, Quadracel may be used to reconstitute Act-HIB (Haemophilus b Conjugate Vaccine Tetanus Protein-Conjugate) for simultaneous administration of all 5 antigens in a single injection. Quadracel must not be mixed in the same syringe with any other vaccines.

Because simultaneous administration of common childhood vaccines is not known to affect the efficacy or safety of any of the routine recommended childhood vaccines, if return of a vaccine recipient for further immunization is doubtful, simultaneous administration of all vaccines appropriate for age and previous vaccination status (including MMR, other H. influenzae type b conjugate vaccines, hepatitis B vaccine) at separate sites with separate syringes is indicated.

Infants born prematurely whose clinical condition is satisfactory should be vaccinated according to their chronological age from birth.

Contraindications: General: Immunization with Quadracel should be deferred in the presence of any acute illness, including febrile illness. A minor afebrile illness such as mild upper respiratory infection is not usually reason to defer immunization.

Quadracel should not be administered to children after their 7th birthday or to adults because of the quantity of diphtheria toxoid and because pertussis is less severe in these age groups than in infants and young children.

Absolute Contraindications: Allergy to any component of Quadracel (see Supplied), or an allergic or anaphylactic reaction to a previous dose of DPT Polio Adsorbed are contraindications to vaccination.

Relative Contraindications (based on experience with whole cell pertussis vaccine): Hypotonic-hyporesponsive episodes: No long-term sequelae have been associated with hypotonic-hyporesponsive episodes; however, it may be prudent in areas of low pertussis incidence to withhold the pertussis component and continue immunization with DT Polio Adsorbed in children who have experienced a hypotonic-hyporesponsive episode following a previous dose of pertussis-containing vaccine. Children can continue immunization with Quadracel if the incidence of disease is high in their area.

Deferral: Deferral of the pertussis component of Quadracel should be considered in children with a progressive, evolving, or unstable neurologic condition (including seizures) because administration of the pertussis component may coincide with the onset of overt manifestations of such disorders and result in confusion about causation. It is prudent to delay initiation of immunization with pertussis vaccine until further observation and study have clarified the child's neurologic status. In addition, the effect of treatment, if any, can be assessed.

Immunization with Quadracel should be reinstituted when the condition has resolved, been corrected or controlled.

When immunization with pertussis vaccine is contraindicated or deferred, immunization with diphtheria and tetanus toxoids and poliomyelitis vaccine, when necessary, may be continued using DT Polio Adsorbed.

The use of fractional doses in an attempt to reduce the severity of adverse reactions cannot be recommended because there is insufficient evidence on the safety or efficacy of such smaller doses.

Elective immunization of individuals over 6 months of age should be deferred during an outbreak of poliomyelitis.

Human Immunodeficiency Virus (HIV) Infected Persons: HIV-infected individuals, both asymptomatic and symptomatic, should be immunized against diphtheria, pertussis, tetanus and poliomyelitis according to standard schedules.

Warnings: I.M. injections should be given with care in patients suffering from coagulation disorders because of the risk of hemorrhage.

Quadracel (cont'd)

If Quadracel is used in persons with malignancies, receiving immunosuppressive therapies, including irradiation, antimetabolites, alkylating agents, cytotoxic drugs, or who are otherwise immunocompromised (including HIV infected individuals), the expected immune response may not be obtained.

Corticosteroid therapy can result in immunosuppression although the exact dose and duration of therapy required to suppress the immune system is not well defined. Persons treated with high doses of systemic steroids, e.g., ≥2 mg/kg/day of prednisone orally for more than 2 weeks, should be considered to have a compromised immune system.

As with any vaccine, immunization with Quadracel may not protect 100% of susceptible individuals.

Precautions: General: Care is to be taken by the health care provider for the safe and effective use of Quadracel.

The possibility of allergic reactions in individuals sensitive to components of the vaccine should be evaluated. Epinephrine HCl solution (1:1 000) and other appropriate agents should be available for immediate use in case an anaphylactic or acute hypersensitivity reaction occurs. Health care providers should be familiar with current recommendations for the initial management of anaphylaxis in nonhospital settings.

Before an injection of any vaccine, all appropriate precautions should be taken to prevent adverse reactions. This includes a review of the patient's history with respect to possible hypersensitivity to the vaccine or similar vaccine, determination of previous immunization history, and the presence of any contraindications to immunization, current health status, and a current knowledge of the literature concerning the use of the vaccine under consideration.

Antipyretic Prophylaxis: Administration of acetaminophen (15 mg/kg/dose) or other appropriate antipyretic at the time of immunization and at 4 and 8 hours after immunization decreases the incidence of febrile and local reactions. Since convulsions after whole cell pertussis vaccine are almost always associated with fever, antipyretic prophylaxis may benefit children at increased risk of seizures. For such children, administration of an antipyretic every 4 to 6 hours for as long as 24 hours after vaccination should be considered. Caregivers should be aware that antipyretic therapy could also obscure fever caused by concomitant, unrelated infection.

Special care should be taken to ensure that the product is not injected into a blood vessel.

A separate, sterile needle and syringe or a sterile disposable unit must be used for each individual patient to prevent the transmission of infectious agents. There have been case reports of transmission of HIV and hepatitis by failure to scrupulously observe sterile technique. In particular, the same needle and/or syringe must never be used to re-enter a multidose vial to withdraw vaccine even when it is to be used for inoculation of the same patient. This may lead to contamination of the vial contents and infection of patients who subsequently receive vaccine from the vial.

Needles should not be recapped and should be disposed of properly.

A family history of convulsions in parents and siblings is not a contraindication to pertussis vaccination and children with such family histories should receive pertussis-containing vaccine according to the recommended schedule. Parents of infants and children with family histories of convulsions should be informed of their children's increased risk of seizures following administration of any vaccine causing a febrile reaction. Acetaminophen prophylaxis is particularly recommended for children with a personal or family history of convulsions.

Frequent booster doses of tetanus or diphtheria toxoids in the presence of adequate or excessive serum levels of tetanus or diphtheria antitoxins have been associated with increased incidence and severity of reactions and should be avoided.

Before administration of Quadracel, health care personnel should inform the parent or guardian of the patient of the benefits and risks of immunization, and also inquire about the recent health status of the patient to be injected.

Adverse Effects: In clinical trials done in Canada, Quadracel had consistently lower rates of local and systemic reactions than DPT Polio Adsorbed, whether combined with Act-HIB or given at separate sites. See Tables II and III.

Local Reactions: As with whole cell DPT and DPT Polio, there is a trend for increasing local reaction rates at the fourth and fifth doses, but with Quadracel these are still lower than those observed following whole cell DPT and DPT Polio.

In a clinical trial comparing 3 acellular pertussis and 1 whole cell DPT Vaccine in Sweden 20 745 infants received Tripacel, Component Pertussis Vaccine Combined with Diphtheria and Tetanus Toxoids Adsorbed at 2, 4 and 6 months of age. The following serious adverse events were reported: fever >40°C (within 3 days of immunization) 7; hypotonic-hyporesponsive episode 29; convulsions (within 3 days of immunization) 4; acute severe neurologic event lasting more than 30 minutes 1; infantile spasms 2; invasive bacterial infections 9; deaths 4*.

*Not attributed to the vaccine.

Table II—Quadracel

Local Adverse Reactions (%) Within 24 Hours of Vaccination with Quadracel

Reaction	2 Months (n=111)	4 Months[a] (n=109)	6 Months[a] (n=109)	18-19 Months[b] (n=92)	4-6 Years[c] (n=163)
Redness	1	7	12	15	19
Swelling	5	4	7	8	19
Tenderness	19	17	10	22	75

[a] Received Quadracel for previous dose(s).
[b] Received whole cell pertussis combination vaccine for first 3 doses.
[c] Received whole cell pertussis combination vaccine for first 4 doses.

Table III—Quadracel

Systemic Adverse Reactions (%) Within 24 Hours of Vaccination with Quadracel

Reaction	2 Months (n=111)	4 Months[a] (n=109)	6 Months[a] (n=109)	18-19 Months[b] (n=92)	4-6 Years[c] (n=163)
Fever	21	20	17	19	17
Fussiness	45	42	35	33	20
Crying	30	28	24	4	—
Decreased Activity	51	29	22	14	23
Decreased Eating	34	21	17	15	23
Vomiting	8	3	6	3	5
Diarrhea	8	8	10	8	2

[a] Received Quadracel for previous dose(s).
[b] Received whole cell pertussis combination vaccine for first 3 doses.
[c] Received whole cell pertussis combination vaccine for first 4 doses.

Rates of events were less than or comparable to the rates in the other acellular pertussis vaccine and whole cell DPT groups in this study.

Rarely, an anaphylactic reaction (i.e., hives, swelling of the mouth, difficulty breathing, hypotension, or shock) has been reported after receiving preparations containing diphtheria, tetanus, and/or pertussis antigens.

Arthus-type hypersensitivity reactions, characterized by severe local reactions (generally starting 2 to 8 hours after an injection), may follow receipt of tetanus and diphtheria toxoids. A few cases of peripheral neuropathy have been reported following tetanus toxoid administration, although a causal relationship has not been established.

Persistent nodules at the site of injection have occurred following the use of adsorbed vaccine, but this complication is unusual. Sterile abscess at the site of injection have been reported following use of adsorbed vaccines (6 to 10 per million doses).

Persistent, inconsolable crying lasting 3 or more hours (1%) and high-pitched, unusual screaming (0.1%) have also been reported after whole cell DPT vaccination. The incidence of both of these events is significantly lower with Quadracel. Convulsions and a hypotonic-hyporesponsive state have each been reported to occur at a frequency of about 1:1 750 injections of whole cell DPT. Most convulsions are brief, generalized and self-limited, and are usually associated with fever. Neither febrile nor afebrile convulsions have been shown to be associated with subsequent seizure disorder. Complete recovery, with no persistent sequelae, has been observed on follow-up of children with hypotonic-hyporesponsive episodes or convulsions (see Contraindications and Precautions).

Although there has been a concern about the possible association of severe neurologic illness (including encephalopathy) occurring within 72 hours of the administration of whole cell pertussis-containing vaccines to previously healthy infants, the risk of an association is so small compared to the background rate for these types of events that the question of causation probably cannot be answered.

Reanalysis of the National Childhood Encephalopathy study (NECS) in the United Kingdom has failed to confirm that there was an increased risk of permanent brain damage following acute neurological illness occurring within 7 days of whole cell pertussis vaccination. Additional studies have also failed to demonstrate an association between pertussis vaccine and permanent neurologic sequelae.

Sudden infant death syndrome (SIDS) has been reported in temporal relationship to the administration of vaccines containing diphtheria and tetanus toxoids and pertussis vaccine (DPT). Review of the evidence does not indicate a causal relationship between whole cell DPT vaccine and SIDS. Studies showing a temporal relation between these events are consistent with the expected occurrence of SIDS over the age range in which DPT immunization usually occurs.

Physicians, nurses and pharmacists should report any adverse occurrences temporally related to the administration of the product in accordance with local requirements and report to the Medical Director at Connaught Laboratories Limited, 1755 Steeles Avenue West, Toronto, Ontario, Canada, M2R 3T4.

Dosage: For primary immunization of infants the following routine immunization schedule is recommended: one 0.5 mL dose administered at 2, 4, 6 and 18 months of age.

If, for any reason this schedule is delayed, it is recommended that 3 doses of 0.5 mL be administered with an interval 4 to 8 weeks between doses, followed by a fourth dose of 0.5 mL administered approximately 1 year following the third dose.

A booster dose of 0.5 mL should be administered between 4 and 6 years of age (i.e., at the time of school entry). This booster dose is unnecessary if the fourth primary immunizing dose has been administered after the fourth birthday.

Thereafter, routine booster immunizations should be with Td, at intervals of 10 years. **Persons 7 years of age and older should not be immunized with Quadracel.**

Parenteral biological products should be inspected visually for extraneous particulate matter and/or discoloration prior to administration. If these conditions exist, the product should not be administered.

Shake the vial or ampul well to distribute uniformly the suspension before withdrawing each dose. Before withdrawing a dose from an ampul, tap the container first to ensure that any vaccine in the ampul neck falls to the lower portion of the ampul. Once the ampul has been opened, any of its contents not used immediately should be discarded. When administering a dose from a rubber-stoppered vial, do not remove either the rubber stopper or the metal seal holding it in place. Aseptic technique must be used for withdrawal of each dose (see Precautions).

Before injection, the skin over the site to be injected should be cleansed with a suitable germicide.

Administer the vaccine **i.m.** The preferred site is into the deltoid muscle or into the anterolateral aspect of the mid-thigh (vastus lateralis muscle). In children >1 year of age, the deltoid is the preferred site since use of the anterolateral thigh results in frequent complaints of limping due to muscle pain.

After insertion of the needle, aspirate to ensure that the needle has not entered a blood vessel.

Do not inject i.v.

Each person who is immunized should be given a permanent personal immunization record. In addition, it is essential that the physician or nurse record the immunization history in the permanent medical record of each patient. This permanent office record history should contain the name of the vaccine, date given, dose, manufacturer and lot number.

Supplied: Each 0.5 mL of sterile, cloudy, uniform suspension contains: pertussis toxoid (PT) 20 μg, filamentous hemagglutinin (FHA) 20 μg, fimbriae (agglutinogens 2+3) 5 μg, pertactin (69kDa membrane protein) 3 μg, diphtheria toxoid 15 Lf, tetanus toxoid 5 Lf, aluminum 0.33 mg, purified inactivated poliomyelitis vaccine: Type 1(Mahoney); Type 2 (M.E.F.1); Type 3 (Saukett); and 2-phenoxyethanol 0.6%±0.1% added as preservative. By calculation, the vaccine contains 20 ppm Tween 80 less than 0.05% albumin (human) and less than 1 ppm of bovine serum. Trace amounts of polymyxin B and neomycin may be present from the cell growth medium. Single dose ampuls of 0.5 mL, boxes of 5.

Store between 2 and 8°C. **Do not freeze.** Product which has been exposed to freezing should not be used. Do not use vaccine after expiration date.

Reviewed 1998

QUELICIN® CHLORIDE INJECTION ℞

Abbott

Succinylcholine Chloride

Neuromuscular Blocking Agent

Supplied: 20 mg/mL: Each mL contains: succinylcholine chloride 20 mg. May also contain sodium hydroxide and/or hydrochloric acid to adjust the pH at approximately 3.7, and sodium chloride for tonicity. Single-dose unit; any unused portion should be discarded. Ampuls of 2 or 5 mL. Boxes of 25 or 50.

20 mg/mL: Each mL contains: succinylcholine chloride 20 mg with methylparaben and propylparaben as preservatives in an isotonic solution. Also contains hydrochloric acid, sodium chloride and sodium hydroxide. pH adjusted to about 4. Multidose vials of 10 mL, boxes of 25. Multidose vials of 20 mL, boxes of 50.

100 mg/mL: Each mL contains: succinylcholine chloride 100 mg and sodium hydroxide and/or hydrochloric acid to adjust pH to about 4. This solution **must be diluted** for i.v. use. Any unused reconstituted portion should be discarded. Vials of 10 mL containing 5 mL solution, boxes of 25. For dilution only.

All units must be kept refrigerated (2 to 8°C) to prevent loss of potency. These products are stable for up to 7 days at room temperature without significant loss of potency.

QUESTRAN® ℞
QUESTRAN® LIGHT ℞

Bristol

Cholestyramine Resin

Antidiarrheal—Antihypercholesterolemic

Pharmacology: Cholestyramine is a quarternary ammonium anion exchange resin with a polystyrene polymer skeleton. As the chloride salt, it binds bile acids both in vitro and in vivo, exchanging chloride for bile acid.

Cholesterol is probably the sole precursor of bile acids. During normal digestion, bile acids are secreted into the intestines. A major portion of the bile acids is absorbed from the intestinal tract and returned to the liver via the enterohepatic circulation. Only very small amounts of bile acids are found in normal serum.

Cholestyramine resin absorbs and combines with the bile acids in the intestine to form an insoluble complex which is excreted in the feces. This results in a partial removal of bile acids from the enterohepatic circulation by preventing their absorption.

The increased fecal loss of bile acids due to cholestyramine resin administration leads to an increased oxidation of cholesterol to bile acids, a decrease in beta lipoprotein or low density lipoprotein plasma levels and a decrease in serum cholesterol levels. Although in man cholestyramine resin produces an increase in hepatic synthesis of cholesterol, plasma cholesterol levels fall.

Indications: As adjunctive therapy to diet and exercise for the reduction of elevated serum cholesterol in patients with primary hypercholesterolemia (elevated low density lipoproteins); such reduction of serum cholesterol may reduce the risks of atherosclerotic coronary artery disease and myocardial infarction. Cholestyramine resin may be useful to lower elevated cholesterol in patients with combined hypercholesterolemia and hypertriglyceridemia but it is not indicated where hypertriglyceridemia is the abnormality of most concern.

Cholestyramine resin is indicated as a symptomatic control of bile acid induced diarrhea due to short bowel syndrome.

Cholestyramine resin is indicated for the relief of pruritus associated with partial biliary obstruction.

Contraindications: In patients with complete biliary obstruction where bile is not excreted into the intestine and in those individuals who have shown hypersensitivity to any of its components.

Warnings: Cholestyramine resin should not be taken in its dry form. Always admix the drug with water or other fluids before ingesting.

Since cholestyramine resin may bind other drugs given concurrently, patients should take other drugs at least 1 hour before or 4 to 6 hours after cholestyramine resin (or at as great an interval as possible) to avoid impeding their absorption.

Pregnancy: Since cholestyramine resin is not absorbed systemically, it is not expected to cause fetal harm when administered during pregnancy in recommended dosages. There are, however, no adequate and well-controlled studies in pregnant women and, the known interference with absorption of fat soluble vitamins may be detrimental even in the presence of supplementation.

Lactation: Caution should be exercised when cholestyramine resin is administered to a nursing mother. The possible lack of proper vitamin absorption described in the Pregnancy section may have an effect on nursing infants.

Use in pregnancy or lactation requires that the potential benefits of drug therapy be weighed against the possible hazards to the mother and the child.

Children: The effects of long-term drug administration, as well as its effect in maintaining lowered cholesterol levels in pediatric patients, are unknown. A pediatric dosage schedule has not been established.

The National Cholesterol Education Program (NCEP) Expert Panel recommends, however, that drug therapy be considered in children 10 years or older, who have previously undergone an adequate trial of diet therapy but still have unacceptable high serum cholesterol levels. In certain situations where a young child has extremely high serum cholesterol levels, drug treatment may even be initiated before 10 years of age. If the child is started on drug therapy, a carefully assessed diet therapy should also be continued in order to obtain optimal results.

Because bile acid sequestrants may interfere with absorption of fat-soluble vitamins, appropriate monitoring of growth and development is essential if cholestyramine is used in children.

Geriatrics: Appropriate studies on the relationship of age to the effects of cholestyramine have not been performed in the geriatric population. However, patients over 60 years of age may be more likely to experience gastrointestinal side effects.

Carcinogenesis and Mutagenesis: Studies were conducted in rats in which cholestyramine resin was used as a tool to investigate the role of various intestinal factors (e.g., fat, bile salts and microbial flora). The incidence of intestinal tumors, induced by potent carcinogens, was observed to be greater in cholestyramine resin treated rats, than in control rats. This observation was not evident in all studies conducted in rats, as results from one study indicated a statistically insignificant increase in tumor incidence whereas a more recent study did not demonstrate any presence of tumors following ingestion of cholestyramine. The relevance of this laboratory observation from studies in rats to the clinical use of cholestyramine resin is not known.

Precautions: Before instituting therapy with cholestyramine resin an attempt should be made to control serum cholesterol by appropriate dietary regimen, weight reduction, and the treatment of any underlying disorder such as hypothyroidism, diabetes mellitus, nephrotic syndrome, dysproteinemias and obstructive liver disease which might be the cause of hypercholesterolemia. In addition, the current medications of the patient should be reviewed for their potential to increase serum LDL-C or total cholesterol. A favorable trend in cholesterol reduction should occur during the first month of cholestyramine resin therapy. The therapy should be continued to sustain cholesterol reduction.

There is a possibility that prolonged use of cholestyramine resin, since it is a chloride form of anion exchange resin, may produce hyperchloremic acidosis. This would especially be true in younger and smaller patients where the relative dosage may be higher.

Cholestyramine resin may produce or worsen pre-existing constipation. Dosage should be reduced or discontinued in such cases. Fecal impaction and aggravation of hemorrhoids may occur. Every effort should be made to avert severe constipation and its inherent problems in those patients with clinically symptomatic coronary artery disease.

Cholestyramine potentially may cause steatorrhea or accentuate pre-existing steatorrhea and this may require reduction and adjustment of dosage.

Effect on Vitamin Absorption: Because cholestyramine binds bile acids, it may interfere with normal fat digestion and absorption and thus may prevent absorption of fat soluble vitamins such as A, D and K. When cholestyramine resin is given for long periods of time, concomitant supplementation of water-miscible parenteral forms of vitamins A and D should be considered.

Chronic use of cholestyramine may be associated with increased bleeding tendency due to hypoprothrombinemia associated with vitamin K deficiency. This will usually respond promptly to parenteral vitamin K_1 and recurrences can be prevented by oral administration of vitamin K_1.

Reduction of serum or red cell folate has been reported over long-term administration of cholestyramine resin. Supplementation with folic acid should be considered in these cases.

Laboratory Tests: Serum cholesterol levels should be determined frequently during the first few months of therapy and periodically thereafter. Serum triglyceride levels should be measured periodically to detect whether significant changes have occurred.

Drug Interactions: Since cholestyramine is an anion-exchange resin, it may have strong affinity for anions other than the bile acids. Drugs that are affected by coadministration of bile acid sequestrants vary widely in pharmacologic effect and mechanisms, magnitude of doses, and chemical characteristics. Therefore, it is not possible to predict a priori whether or not co-administration with cholestyramine will interfere with absorption. It should be assumed that concomitantly administered drugs have the potential for interacting with cholestyramine unless clinical studies have shown otherwise.

Cholestyramine resin may delay or reduce the absorption of concomitant oral medication such as phenylbutazone, warfarin, chlorothiazide (acidic), as well as tetracycline, penicillin G, phenobarbital, thyroid and thyroxine preparations, and digitalis. The discontinuance of cholestyramine resin could pose a hazard to health if a potentially toxic drug such as digitalis has been titrated to a maintenance level while the patient was taking cholestyramine resin. The concomitant drug should be re-titrated to avoid overdosage when cholestyramine is discontinued. Also, cholestyramine resin may interfere with the pharmacokinetics of drugs (e.g., estrogens) that undergo enterohepatic recirculation.

Drug interaction studies have been conducted with cholestyramine and various HMG-CoA reductase inhibitors. Although cholestyramine has been shown to reduce the bioavailability of HMG-CoA reductase inhibitors, the clinical cholesterol-lowering effects of an HMG-CoA reductase inhibitor and cholestyramine have been shown to be additive.

Since cholestyramine resin may bind other drugs given concurrently, patients should take other drugs at least 1 hour before or 4 to 6 hours after cholestyramine resin (or at as great an interval as possible) to avoid impeding their absorption.

Adverse Effects: The most common adverse reaction is constipation. When used as a cholesterol lowering agent predisposing factors for most complaints of constipation are high dose and increased age (more than 60 years old). Most instances of constipation are mild, transient, and controlled with conventional therapy. Some patients require a temporary decrease in dosage or discontinuation of therapy.

Less frequent adverse reactions: abdominal discomfort, flatulence, nausea, vomiting, diarrhea, heartburn, anorexia, dyspepsia and steatorrhea, bleeding tendencies due to hypoprothrombinemia (vitamin K deficiency) as well as vitamin A (night blindness has been reported rarely) and D deficiencies, hyperchloremic acidosis in children, osteoporosis, rash and irritation of the skin, tongue and perianal area.

Occasional calcified material has been observed in the biliary tree, including calcification of the gallbladder, in patients to whom cholestyramine resin has been given. This may be a manifestation of the liver disease and not drug related.

One patient experienced biliary colic on each of 3 occasions on which he took cholestyramine. One patient diagnosed with acute abdominal symptom complex was found to have a "pasty mass" in the transverse colon x-ray.

Other adverse reactions (not necessarily drug related) reported in patients taking cholestyramine resin include: Gastrointestinal: gastrointestinal-rectal bleeding, black stools, hemorrhoidal bleeding, bleeding from known duodenal ulcer, dysphagia, hiccups, ulcer attack, sour taste, pancreatitis, rectal pain, diverticulitis, eructation.

Laboratory Test Changes: liver function abnormalities.

Hematologic: decreased or increased prothrombin time, ecchymosis, anemia, dental bleeding.

Questran (cont'd)

Hypersensitivity: urticaria, asthma, wheezing, shortness of breath.
Musculoskeletal: backache, muscle and joint pains, arthritis.
Neurologic: headache, anxiety, vertigo, dizziness, fatigue, tinnitus, syncope, drowsiness, femoral nerve pain, paresthesia.
Eye: uveitis.
Renal: hematuria, dysuria, burnt odor of urine, diuresis.
Miscellaneous: weight loss, weight gain, increased libido, swollen glands, edema, dental caries.

Overdose: Symptoms and Treatment: One case of overdosage with cholestyramine resin has been reported in a patient taking 150% of the maximum recommended daily dosage for several weeks. No ill effects were observed.
Should overdosage occur, the chief potential harm would be obstruction of the gastrointestinal tract. The location of such potential obstruction, the degree of obstruction, and the presence or absence of normal gut motility would determine treatment.

Dosage: To familiarize the patient with cholestyramine resin and to minimize gastrointestinal side effects, it is desirable to begin all therapy with one dose daily. Dosage is then increased within a day or two to the desired level for effective control.

Motivation of the patient to continue the prescribed regimen in spite of gastrointestinal problems is important. Physician's encouragement and supervision are essential for successful management.

The recommended adult dose is 4 g of cholestyramine resin, 1 to 6 times daily. Dosage may be adjusted as required to meet the patient's needs. A pediatric dosage schedule has not been established.

Cholestyramine resin should not be taken in its dry form. Always mix the powder with water or other fluids before ingesting (see Preparation Instructions).
Preparation Instructions: The color of cholestyramine resin may vary somewhat from batch to batch but this variation does not affect the performance of the product. Mix contents of 1 packet or 1 level scoop of Questran with 120 to 180 mL to 180 mL of a preferred beverage (water, milk, fruit juice or other noncarbonated beverage).

Mix contents of 1 packet of Questran Light with 60 to 90 mL of a preferred beverage (water, milk, fruit juice or other noncarbonated beverage).

Cholestyramine resin may also be mixed with highly fluid soups or pulpy fruits with high moisture content such as applesauce or crushed pineapple.

Supplied: Questran: Each packet (1 dose) of powder contains: anhydrous cholestyramine resin 4 g. Nonmedicinal ingredients: acacia, citric acid, D&C yellow No. 10, FD&C yellow No. 6, flavor, polysorbate 80, propylene glycol alginate and sucrose. Energy: 53.5 kJ (12.8 kcal)/9 g. Sodium- and tartrazine-free. Cartons of 30 packets. Cans of 378 g (42 doses).

Questran Light: Each packet (1 dose) of powder contains: anhydrous cholestyramine resin 4 g. Nonmedicinal ingredients: aspartame, citric acid, D&C yellow No. 10, FD&C red No. 40, flavor, propylene glycol alginate, silicon dioxide, sucrose and xanthan gum. Energy: 6.7 kJ (1.6 kcal). Sodium- and tartrazine-free. Cartons of 30 packets.

Store at room temperature (15 to 30°C). Protect from temperatures above 30°C. Protect from moisture.

(Shown in Product Recognition Section)

QUIBRON®-T Ⓟ
QUIBRON®-T/SR Ⓟ

Bristol

Theophylline

Bronchodilator

Pharmacology: Theophylline is a xanthine derivative structurally related to theobromine and caffeine. It has 2 distinct actions in the airways of patients with reversible obstruction: smooth muscle relaxation (i.e., bronchodilation) and suppression of the response of the airways to stimuli (i.e., nonbronchodilator prophylactic effects).

While its mechanisms of action are not known with certainty, studies in animals suggest that theophylline bronchodilation is mediated by phosphodiesterase inhibition; theophylline also increases the force of diaphragm muscle contraction.
Pharmacokinetics: Immediate Release Formulation: The pharmacokinetics of theophylline varies widely among patients and cannot be predicted by age, sex, body weight or other demographic characteristics. Therefore, careful consideration should be given to dosing and monitoring (see Warnings, Precautions and Dosage).

Theophylline is rapidly and completely absorbed after oral administration in an immediate-release solid oral dosage form (Quibron-T). After a single dose of 5 mg/kg in adults, a mean peak serum concentration of about 10 µg/mL (range 5 to 15 µg/mL) can be expected 1 to 2 hours after the dose. Coadministration of theophylline with food or antacids does not cause clinically significant changes in absorption.
Sustained Release Formulation: Administration of a sustained release formulation of theophylline (Quibron-T/SR) produces peak blood levels between 5 and 7 hours. Once steady state levels have been reached, the therapeutic plasma levels (between 8 and 15 µg/mL) persist for 12 hours in most adults.

Indications: For the symptomatic treatment of reversible bronchospasm associated with bronchial asthma, chronic bronchitis, emphysema and related bronchospastic disorders.

Contraindications: In those patients who have shown hypersensitivity to theophylline or to other xanthine derivatives or to any other component in the formulations; in coronary artery disease when, in the physician's judgement, myocardial stimulation might prove harmful; in patients with active peptic ulcer disease; and in patients with seizure disorders.

Warnings: Children exhibit a higher degree of sensitivity to xanthines than adults; the margin of safety above the therapeutic dose is small. The use of theophylline tablets and theophylline sustained-release tablets in children less than 9 years of age is not recommended at present as dose schedules for this age group have not been established.

Theophylline should be used with extreme caution in patients with cardiac arrhythmias (not including bradyarrhythmias).

Generalized seizures, life-threatening cardiac arrhythmias, and death may occur at serum theophylline concentrations >30 µg/mL with chronic dosing. Seizures associated with serum theophylline concentrations >30 µg/mL are often resistant to anticonvulsant therapy and may result in irreversible brain injury if not rapidly controlled. Death from theophylline toxicity is most often secondary to cardiorespiratory arrest and/or hypoxic encephalopathy after prolonged generalized seizures or intractable cardiac arrhythmias.

Whenever a patient receiving theophylline develops nausea or vomiting, particularly repetitive vomiting, or other signs or symptoms consistent with theophylline toxicity (even if another cause may be suspected), additional doses of theophylline should be withheld and a serum theophylline concentration measured immediately. In patients with suspected decreased serum protein binding (e.g., patients with cirrhosis or women during the third trimester of pregnancy), the concentration of unbound theophylline should be measured and the dosage adjusted to achieve a concentration of 6 to 12 µg/mL.
Conditions that Reduce Theophylline Clearance: There are several readily identifiable causes of reduced theophylline clearance. If the total daily dose is not appropriately reduced in the presence of the risk factors listed below, severe and potentially fatal theophylline toxicity can occur.
Age: elderly (>60 years old).
Pregnancy: (3rd trimester).
Concurrent Diseases: acute pulmonary edema; congestive heart failure; cor-pulmonale; fever (≥39°C for 24 hours or more, or lesser temperature elevations for longer periods); hypothyroidism; liver disease (cirrhosis, acute hepatitis); sepsis with multiorgan failure; shock.
Cessation of smoking.
Drug Interactions (see Precautions).

Theophylline dose should not be increased to treat acute exacerbations of chronic lung disease, since increasing the dose elevates the risk of adverse effects and offers little benefit in comparison with other acute treatment options such as the use of β_2-selective agonists and systemically administered corticosteroids.

Precautions: There is a marked variation in blood levels achieved in different patients given the same dose of theophylline. This may lead to serious side effects in some patients. This variability in blood levels is probably due to differences in the rate of metabolism. Therefore, it is advisable to individualize the dose regimens. Ideally, all individuals should have serum theophylline levels measured and a theophylline half-life calculated which would enable doses and dosing regimens to be tailored to each patient to maintain a therapeutic level, to insure optimal clinical response and to avoid toxicity. The possibility of overdose must be considered in all patients and especially when large doses are used, because fatalities have been reported. Overdosage of theophylline may cause peripheral vascular collapse.

Special caution is necessary in patients with severe pulmonary or cardiovascular disease and in patients with hepatic dysfunction as metabolism of theophylline may be impaired in these patients leading to the possibility of toxic blood levels on fixed dosage regimens.

Caution should be exercised when theophylline is used concurrently with sympathomimetic amines or other xanthines, as such use may increase the incidence and severity of adverse reactions. Theophylline tablets and theophylline sustained-release tablets should not be given within 12 hours of the ingestion of other xanthines.

Theophylline may cause an elevation of urine catecholamines and plasma free fatty acids.
Carcinogenesis, Mutagenesis, and Impairment of Fertility: Studies in Ames salmonella, in vivo and in vitro cytogenetics, micronucleus and Chinese hamster ovary test systems did not show evidence of genotoxicity with theophylline.

In a study in mice at oral doses approximately 1 to 3 times the human dose (on a mg/m² basis) fertility was impaired, as evidenced by decreases in the number of live pups per litter, decreases in the mean number of litters per fertile pair, and increases in the gestation period at the high dose and proportion of live pups in a litter at the mid and high dose. Systemic toxicity was observed in rats and mice in 13-week toxicity studies, at approximately twice the human dose on a mg/m² basis, including decreases in testicular weight.
Pregnancy: Theophylline passes freely across the placenta. There are no adequate and well controlled studies in pregnant women. Theophylline was not shown to be teratogenic in mice at oral doses up to approximately twice the human dose (on a mg/m² basis) or in rats at oral doses up to approximately 3 times the recommended human dose (on a mg/m² basis). At a dose of 220 mg/kg, embryotoxicity was observed in rats in the absence of maternal toxicity. Safe use in pregnancy has not been established relative to possible adverse effects on fetal development, but neither has adverse effects on fetal development been established. Therefore, use of theophylline in pregnant women should be balanced against the risk of uncontrolled asthma.
Lactation: Theophylline is excreted into breast milk and may cause irritability or other signs of mild toxicity in nursing human infants. An infant ingesting a L of breast milk containing 10 to 20 µg/mL of theophylline a day is likely to receive 10 to 20 mg of theophylline a day. The concentration of theophylline in breast milk is approximately equivalent to the maternal serum concentration.
Children: The maintenance dose of theophylline must be selected with caution in pediatric patients since the rate of theophylline clearance is highly variable (see Pharmacology).
Geriatrics: Elderly patients are at significantly greater risk of serious acute or chronic adverse events from theophylline than younger patients. Theophylline clearance is reduced in patients older than 60 years old, resulting in increased serum theophylline concentrations at a given dose. Protein binding may be decreased in the elderly, resulting in a proportionately larger fraction of the total serum theophylline concentration in the pharmacologically active, unbound form. For these reasons, the maximum daily dose of theophylline in patients older than 60 ordinarily should not exceed 400 mg.

Drug Interactions: The drugs listed below can produce clinically significant interactions with theophylline, resulting in altered theophylline levels. Adding a drug that increases theophylline levels or stopping a drug that decreases theophylline levels can lead to serious toxicity.

Drugs that **increase** serum theophylline concentrations: alcohol, allopurinol (≥600 mg/day), clarithromycin, disulfiram, erythromycin, estrogen, interferon (human recombinant α-A) methotrexate, mexiletine, pentoxifylline, propafenone, thiabendazole, ticlopidine, troleandomycin, verapamil.

Inhibitors of cytochrome P450 1A2: cimetidine, ciprofloxacin, enoxacin, fluvoxamine, propranolol, tacrine.

Drugs that **decrease** serum theophylline concentrations: isoproterenol i.v., moricizine, rifampin, sulfinpyrazone.
Inducers of microsomal enzyme activity: aminoglutethimide, carbamazepine, phenobarbital, phenytoin.
Other Interactions: Adenosine: Higher doses of adenosine may be required to achieve the desired effects because theophylline blocks adenosine receptors.
Benzodiazepines (e.g., diazepam, flurazepam, midazolam, lorazepam): Larger doses of benzodiazepines may be required to produce the desired level of sedation.

Ephedrine may cause increased frequency of nausea, nervousness, and insomnia because of synergistic CNS effects.

Halothane may cause increased risk of ventricular arrhythmias via sensitization of the myocardium to catecholamines by halothane combined with theophylline-induced increases in endogenous catecholamines.

Ketamine may lower the theophylline seizure threshold. Induction of anesthesia with ketamine in patients receiving theophylline has been reported to produce seizures.

Lithium: Theophylline increases renal clearance of lithium, so the dose of lithium may have to be increased.

Pancuronium: Larger doses of pancuronium may be required due the antagonism of the drug's effects by theophylline.

Effect of Other Drugs on Theophylline Serum Concentration Measurements: Cefazolin and cephalothin may interfere with certain HPLC theophylline assays. In patients with renal dysfunction, caffeine and xanthine metabolites may cause falsely high theophylline readings on assays using a dry reagent office method. The immunoassays that are specific for theophylline may be used, since other xanthines are not detected by these assays.

Xanthine derivatives, such as theophylline, potentiate the diuretic action of thiazide diuretics. They also potentiate the cardiac effect of digitalis glycosides.

Xanthines have been shown to be nephrotoxic with prolonged use at high dosage. Coincident toxicity should therefore be borne in mind when other potentially nephrotoxic drugs are administered concurrently.

The methylxanthines increase blood levels of prothrombin and fibrinogen, shorten the prothrombin time and thus antagonize the effects of coumarin anticoagulants.

Combined use of several xanthines, or concomitant use of xanthines with sympathomimetics, may cause excessive CNS stimulation.

Xanthines may antagonize the antihyperuricemia action of allopurinol.

Xanthines antagonize the uricosuric action of probenecid and of sulfinpyrazone and uricosuric activity of pyrazolon derivatives.

Adverse Effects: When peak serum concentrations exceed 20 μg/mL, theophylline produces a wide range of adverse events, such as persistent vomiting, cardiac arrhythmias, and potentially intractable and life-threatening seizures (see Warnings and Overdose). Seizures have also been reported rarely in elderly patients or patients with an underlying neurological disease when serum theophylline concentrations were not in the toxic range (<20 μg/mL). Seizures occurring at this plasma level are generally transient and without neurologic sequelae.

Common adverse events include transient caffeine-like effects such as nausea, vomiting, headache, and insomnia, which occur in about 50% of patients in whom theophylline therapy is initiated at doses higher than the recommended initial doses. In a small percentage of patients (3% of children and 10% of adults) caffeine-like effects persist during maintenance therapy.

The following adverse events have also been reported: Gastrointestinal: abdominal pain, epigastric pain, hematemesis, diarrhea, anorexia, reactivation of peptic ulcer, intestinal bleeding.

Metabolic: hypokalemia, hyperglycemia, acid/base disturbance, and rhabdomyolysis, inappropriate secretion of antidiuretic hormone syndrome.

CNS: nervousness, irritability, restlessness, tremors, reflex hyperexcitability, muscle twitching, disorientation, seizures and death.

Cardiovascular: sinus tachycardia and other supraventricular tachycardias, ventricular premature beats, atrial fibrillation, multifocal atrial tachycardia or flutter (especially in patients with hypoxia secondary to COPD), ventricular arrhythmias with hemodynamic instability and hypotension/shock, flushing, palpitation, circulatory failure.

Respiratory: tachypnea.

Renal: albuminuria, transient diuresis and hematuria.

Other: rash.

The likelihood of adverse effects may be reduced by initiation of theophylline therapy at a low dose and slow titration to a predetermined age-related maximum dose (see Dosage).

Overdose: Death from theophylline toxicity is most often secondary to cardiorespiratory arrest and/or hypoxic encephalopathy after prolonged generalized seizures or intractable cardiac arrhythmias causing hemodynamic compromise. Seizures associated with serum theophylline concentrations >30 μg/mL are often resistant to anticonvulsant therapy and may result in irreversible brain injury if not rapidly controlled.

In general, patients with an acute overdose are less likely to experience seizures than patients with chronic overdosage, unless the peak serum theophylline concentration is >100 μg/mL. Patients >60 years old are at the greatest risk for severe toxicity and mortality after chronic overdosage. Preexisting or concurrent disease may also significantly increase the susceptibility of a patient to a particular toxic manifestation, e.g., neurologic disorders predispose to seizures or cardiac disease predispose to cardiac arrhythmias.

Other manifestations of theophylline toxicity include acute myocardial infarction, and urinary retention in men with obstructive uropathy as well as the following laboratory findings: increases in serum calcium, creatine kinase, myoglobin and leukocyte count, and decreases in serum phosphate and magnesium.

Symptoms: Insomnia, restlessness, mild excitement or irritability and rapid pulse are the early symptoms, which may progress to mild delirium.

Sensory disturbances such as tinnitus or flashes of light are common. Anorexia, nausea and vomiting are frequently early observations of theophylline overdosage.

Fever, diuresis, dehydration and extreme thirst may be seen. Severe poisoning results in bloody, syrup-like coffee-ground vomitus, tremors, tonic extensor spasm interrupted by clonic convulsions, extra systoles, quickened respiration, stupor and finally coma. Cardiovascular disorders and respiratory collapse, leading to shock, cyanosis and death follow gross overdosages.

Treatment: Charcoal hemoperfusion is the most effective method of extracorporeal removal, increasing theophylline clearance up to 6-fold, but serious complications may occur. Hemodialysis bears a lower risk of serious complications than multiple-dose oral activated charcoal, and is equally effective. Peritoneal dialysis is ineffective for theophylline removal.

Serum theophylline concentrations may rebound 5 to 10 μg/mL after discontinuation of charcoal hemoperfusion or hemodialysis, due to redistribution of theophylline from the tissue compartment.

If potential oral overdose is established and seizure has not occurred: Induce vomiting. Administer a cathartic. Administer activated charcoal.

If the patient is having a seizure: Establish an airway. Administer oxygen. Treat the seizure with i.v. diazepam, 0.1 to 0.3 mg/kg up to 10 mg. Monitor vital signs, maintain blood pressure and provide adequate hydration.

Postseizure Coma: Maintain airway and oxygenation. If as a result of oral medications, follow above recommendations to prevent absorption of drug, but intubation and lavage will have to be performed instead of inducing emesis and the cathartic and charcoal will need to be introduced via a large bore gastric lavage tube. Continue to provide full supportive care and adequate hydration while waiting for drug to be metabolized. In general, the drug is metabolized sufficiently rapidly so as not to warrant consideration of dialysis.

Dosage: Quibron-T: Table I outlines the usual recommended starting dose for children (9 to 12) and adults (over 12 years).

Table I—Quibron-T

Recommended Starting Dose

Body Weight kg	Recommended Starting Dose Adults	Recommended Starting Dose Children (9-12)
20-30	—	100
30-40	—	150
40-60	150	—
60-75	200	—
75-100	300	—

Dosage should be calculated on the basis of ideal body weight. Doses shown in mg of theophylline should be repeated every 8 hours, when Quibron-T tablets are prescribed.

Quibron-T/SR: The average initial dose for children (age 9 to 12) is ½ (150 mg) of a Quibron-T/SR tablet every 12 hours.

The average initial dose for adults is 1 (300 mg) Quibron-T/SR tablet every 12 hours.

Dose Adjustment: Quibron-T and Quibron-T/SR tablets can be divided as follows: ⅓ tablet=100 mg; ½ tablet=150 mg; ⅔ tablet=200 mg; 1 tablet=300 mg.

If the desired response is not achieved with the above initial dosage recommendation, and there are no adverse reactions, the dose may be increased by 2 to 3 mg/kg body weight/day at 3-day intervals. Within any 24 hours, a maximum dose of 900 mg or 13 mg/kg (whichever is less) should not be exceeded for adults. For children (9 to 12) maximum daily dose should not exceed 15 mg/kg. Children are extremely sensitive to xanthines and the margin of safety above therapeutic doses is small.

Individual requirements may vary considerably and the physician should be prepared to adjust the patient's dose accordingly.

Because of the large intersubject variability, monitoring of plasma theophylline concentrations is extremely important, especially in the initial stages of therapy (see Precautions). Concurrent tea, coffee or cocoa administration may affect assay results.

Optimal therapeutic serum levels are considered to be between 8 to 15 μg/mL.

Supplied: Quibron-T: Each rectangular shaped tablet with trisects and bisects contains: theophyllineanhydrous 300 mg. Bottles of 100.

Quibron-T/SR: Each sustained release, rectangular shaped tablet with trisects and bisects contains: theophylline anhydrous 300 mg. Nonmedicinal ingredients: magnesium stearate. Bottles of 100.

(Shown in Product Recognition Section)

Reviewed 1999

QUINAPRIL ℞
General Monograph, CPhA

see ACE INHIBITORS

QUINATE
Rougier

Quinidine Gluconate

Antiarrhythmic Agent

Pharmacology: Quinidine depresses excitability, conduction velocity and contractility of most cardiac tissues by a direct action on cardiac cells. Indirectly, cardiac tissues will also be affected by the anticholinergic and α-adrenoceptor blocking properties of quinidine.

According to Vaughan Williams-Harrison antiarrhythmic drug classification, quinidine is a Class IA agent. Thus, quinidine reduces the maximal rate of phase 0 depolarization, prolongs repolarization and refractory periods and, in general, decreases automaticity of cardiac cells.

Pharmacokinetics: Absorption of oral quinidine is assumed to be essentially complete, though bioavailability is approximately 70% due to a first-pass removal by the liver. Peak plasma levels are variable among individuals. After a single dose given orally, quinidine can be detected in blood within 15 minutes and peak concentrations are achieved within 1 to 3 hours. Peak plasma levels during a multiple daily dose regimen may not be reached before the seventh day of administration. Quinidine concentrations are generally higher and appear earlier when the drug is administered on an empty stomach but the amount of drug absorbed is not diminished by the presence of food in the digestive tract.

Although quinidine is 80% bound to plasma constituents (mainly α-1 acid glycoprotein), its distribution in the body is predominantly extravascular. The terminal elimination half-life is approximately 7 hours and is primarily associated with its metabolism by the liver (50 to 90% of the dose administered). Quinidine half-life vary considerably between individuals even among healthy subjects. Total body clearance is approximately 4 mL/kg/min and is also variable. The metabolites may be therapeutically active. Ten to 20% of an administered dose is excreted unchanged in urine. Renal excretion is due to glomerular filtration and secretion by proximal renal tubules and is dependant upon urinary pH, renal clearance diminishes as urinary pH, renal clearance diminishes as urinary pH increases. Fecal excretion accounts for less than 5% of the oral dose.

The average therapeutic range is between 6 to 15 μmol/L (2 and 5 μg/mL) of plasma. Toxic reactions are almost certain to appear at concentrations above 24.7 μmol/L (8 μg/mL). Levels may differ based on the assay method used.

Indications:

> No antiarrhythmic drug has been shown to reduce the incidence of sudden death in patients with asymptomatic ventricular arrhythmias. Most antiarrhythmic drugs have the potential to cause dangerous arrhythmias; some have been shown to be associated with an increased incidence of sudden death. In light of the above, physicians should carefully consider the risks and benefits of antiarrhythmic therapy for all patients with ventricular arrhythmias.

Quinate (cont'd)

Ventricular Arrhythmias: For the treatment of documented life-threatening ventricular arrhythmias, such as sustained ventricular tachycardia. Quinidine may also be used for the treatment of patients with documented symptomatic ventricular arrhythmias when the symptoms are of sufficient severity to require treatment. Because of the proarrhythmic effects of quinidine, its use should be reserved for patients in whom, in the opinion of the physician, the benefit of treatment clearly outweighs the risks.

For patients with sustained ventricular tachycardia, quinidine therapy should be initiated in the hospital. Hospitalization may be required for certain other patients depending on their cardiac status and underlying cardiac disease.

The effects of quinidine in patients with recent myocardial infarction have not been adequately studied and, therefore, their use in this condition cannot be recommended.

Supraventricular Arrhythmias: For premature atrial or AV junctional contractions, paroxysmal atrial or AV junctional tachycardia, atrial flutter, atrial fibrillation when this therapy is appropriate and maintenance therapy after electrical conversion of atrial flutter and/or fibrillation to sinus rhythm.

Contraindications: Hypersensitivity or idiosyncrasy to quinidine or other cinchona derivatives, history of thrombocytopenic purpura associated with previous quinidine administration, myasthenia gravis, digitalis intoxication manifested by AV conduction disorders, complete AV block with an AV nodal or idioventricular pacemaker, and ectopic impulses and rhythms due to escape mechanisms and intraventricular conduction defects (especially with marked widening of the QRS complex).

Warnings: Mortality: The results of the Cardiac Arrhythmia Suppression Trial (CAST) is post-myocardial infarction patients with asymptomatic ventricular arrhythmias showed a significant increase in mortality and in non-fatal cardiac arrest rate in patients treated with encainide or flecainide compared with a matched placebo-treated group. CAST was continued using a revised protocol with the moricizine and placebo arms only. The trial was prematurely terminated because of a trend towards increase in mortality in the moricizine treated group.

The applicability of these results to other populations or other antiarrhythmic agents is uncertain, but at present it is prudent to consider these results when using any antiarrhythmic agent.

Quinidine Cardiotoxicity: Manifestation of quinidine cardiotoxicity, such as excessive prolongation of the QT interval, widening of the QRS complex, and ventricular arrhythmias, mandates immediate discontinuation of the drug and/or close clinical and electrocardiographic monitoring.

Treatment should be discontinued if the duration of the QRS complex increases more than 50% or the P-waves disappear. A significant fall in blood pressure, the onset of ventricular premature contractions or ventricular tachycardia due to quinidine requires the immediate discontinuation of treatment.

Atrial Flutter Treatment: In the treatment of atrial flutter, reversion to sinus rhythm may be preceded by a progressive reduction in the degree of AV block to a 1:1 ratio, resulting in an extremely rapid ventricular rate. This possible hazard may be reduced by digitalization prior to administration of quinidine.

Cardiac Depression: In predisposed individuals, such as those with marginally compensated cardiovascular disease, quinidine may produce clinically important depression of the cardiovascular system such as hypotension, bradycardia or heartblock. The depressant action of quinidine on cardiac contractility and arterial blood pressure limits its use in congestive heart failure and in hypotensive states unless these conditions are due to or aggravated by the arrhythmia. The potential disadvantage and benefits must be weighed.

Syncopal Episodes: Occasionally, patients taking quinidine have syncopal episodes which usually results from tachycardia or fibrillation. The syndrome has not been shown to be related to dose or plasma levels. Syncopal episodes frequently terminate spontaneously, but sometimes are fatal.

Incomplete AV block: Quinidine should be used with extreme caution in patients with incomplete AV block. This can lead to complete AV block and asystole.

Digitalis Intoxication: Quinidine may cause abnormalities of cardiac rhythm in digitalized patients and, therefore, should be closely monitored. Reports indicate that plasma concentrations of digoxin increase and may even double when quinidine is administered concurrently. Patients on concomitant therapy should be carefully monitored. Reduction of digoxin dosage may have to be considered.

Hepatotoxicity: A few cases of hepatoxicity, including granulomatous hepatitis, due to quinidine hypersensitivity have been reported in patients taking quinidine. Unexplained fever and/or elevation of hepatic enzymes, particularly in the early stages of therapy, warrant consideration of possible hepatotoxicity. Monitoring liver function during the first 4 to 8 weeks should be considered. Cessation of quinidine in these cases usually results in the disappearance of toxicity.

Precautions: Test for Hypersensitivity: A test dose of a single tablet of quinidine by mouth should be given initially in order to ascertain any possible hypersensitivity to quinidine. Hypersensitivity to quinidine, although rare, should be constantly considered, especially during the first week of therapy.

Large doses: Continuous ECG monitoring and determination of plasma quinidine concentration are indicated when large doses (>3.25 g quinidine gluconate/day) are used.

Serum Potassium: Quinidine's activity is enhanced by potassium and reduced if hypokalemia is present.

Established Atrial Fibrillation: The use of quinidine in established atrial fibrillation is controversial. Weigh the benefits of such use in each patient against the possible hazards.

Pregnancy: It is not known whether quinidine can cause fetal harm when administered to pregnant women. Quinidine, the levostereoisomer of quinidine, has caused fetal blindness and has been implicated in congenital deafness. Quinidine should be used during pregnancy only when clearly indicated.

Lactation: Very small quantities pass into breast milk; no effects have been described in infants.

Children: Safety and efficacy of quinidine in children have not been determined.

Drug Interactions: See Table I.

Table I—Quinate

Drug Interactions

Quinidine with	Effect
anticholinergic drugs	additive, e.g., vagal block
urine alkalinization	increased quinidine blood level
acidifying agents	decreased quinidine blood level
coumarin	decreased coagulation
neuromuscular blockers (including neomycin)	potentiation of blockade
phenothiazines, reserpine	additive cardiac depression
antihypertensives	potentiation of blood pressure fall
hepatic enzyme inducers nifedipine	reduction in plasma quinidine
amiodarone, cimetidine	increase in plasma quinidine
digoxin	increase in plasma digoxin
quinine	additive (all quinine/quinidine properties)
verapamil	hypotension
potassium	increased cardiotoxicity
aluminum hydroxide	decreased absorption
drugs increasing QT	additive or potentiation

Adverse Effects: Quinidine has a low therapeutic index. Adverse effects occur in as many as a third of cases.

The most frequent adverse reactions are gastrointestinal in nature: nausea, vomiting, diarrhea and abdominal pain.

Cinchonism: Symptoms of mild cases includes tinnitus, dysphonia and occasionally loss of hearing, some blurring of vision and gastrointestinal upset; more severe cases show headache, photophobia, altered color perception and possibly confusion, delirium and psychosis. Other symptoms observed include palpitations, convulsions, faintness and flushing, localized edema, vertigo, tremor, light-headedness, excitement, apprehension, coma and even death.

Idiosyncratic and Hypersensitivity Reactions: angioedema, febrile reactions, skin eruptions, acute asthmatic episodes, confusion, headache, anorexia, nausea, vomiting, diarrhea, precordial pain, abdominal pain, hepatic toxicity including granulomatous hepatitis, vascular collapse and respiratory arrest.

Cardiovascular: QRS widening, increase QT (and JT) interval, vasculitis, arterial embolism (following conversion of long standing atrial fibrillation to sinus rhythm), decreased cardiac contractility, hypotension (cardiac depression and vasodilatation), syncope (due to paroxysmal ventricular tachycardia or fibrillation), proarrhythmias (due to an increased frequency of existing arrhythmia or development of new arrhythmias including ventricular tachycardia, fibrillation or torsades de pointes) and asystole.

Nervous System: apprehension, excitement, psychomotor agitation, hallucinations, delusions or paranoia, delirium; confusion, memory loss, depression; vertigo, disturbed hearing and/or vision.

Hematologic: thrombocytopenia including thrombotic purpura, hemolytic anemia, agranulocytosis, pancytopenia, hypoprothrombinemia and leukocytosis or shift in leukocyte count.

Liver: moderate increase in enzyme levels, granulomatous hepatitis (see Warnings), hepatocellular necrosis and centrilobular cholestasis.

Kidney: nephrotic syndrome.

Skin: rash, flushing with pruritus, urticaria, photosensitivity and discoloration (bluish-gray).

Musculoskeletal: very rare cases of lupus erythematosus, carpal tunnel syndrome and arthritis.

Overdose: Symptoms: Large doses may cause cinchonism, ventricular tachycardia, severe hypotension, cardiac standstill and ventricular fibrillation. Serious hypersensitivity reactions are manifested by respiratory embarrassment or cardiovascular collapse.

Treatment: If ingestion is recent, perform gastric lavage, or induce emesis. (The use of an emetic may interfere with some of the following procedures.) Administration of 25 to 50 g of activated charcoal is indicated to reduce absorption of any remaining quinidine. Administration of hypertonic cathartic (30 g sodium sulfate in 250 mL water) will hasten passage of unabsorbed quinidine through the gastrointestinal tract. If the charcoal preparation contains 70% sorbitol, the use of an additional hypertonic saline is not necessary. Maintain body temperature. Monitor electrolytes; especially potassium, calcium and magnesium. Support blood pressure and maintain renal function. Phenytoin or lidocaine may be used to control arrhythmias. Ventricular tachycardia may require DC cardioversion or pacing. Standard bradycardia or heart block that compromises blood pressure may require a temporary pacemaker. Angioneurotic or asthmatic phenomena may require the use of epinephrine and antihistamines. Hemoglobinuria may necessitate blood transfusion and attention to renal function. The use of alkali to prevent precipitation in the tubules may prove helpful.

Dosage: Administer a preliminary test dose of a single tablet of quinidine gluconate to determine whether the patient has a quinidine idiosyncrasy. Continuous ECG monitoring is recommended in all cases in which quinidine is used in large doses. Gastrointestinal symptoms such as nausea, vomiting, diarrhea and colic may be minimized by giving the drug with food.

Premature Supraventricular Contractions: 325 to 488 mg 3 to 4 times daily.

Paroxysmal Supraventricular Tachycardia: 650 to 975 mg every 2 or 3 hours until the paroxysm is terminated.

Atrial Flutter: Quinidine should be administered after digitalization for this indication. Dosage is to be individualized.

Conversion of Atrial Fibrillation: Various schedules of quinidine administration have been utilized. One widely used technique is to give 325 mg orally every 2 or 3 hours for 5 to 8 doses, with subsequent daily increase of the individual dose until sinus rhythm is restored or toxic effects occur. The total daily dose should not exceed 4.9 to 6.5 g in any regimen. The patient may require anticoagulation for up to 2 to 3 months before conversion. Prior to quinidine administration, the ventricular rate and congestive failure (if present) should be brought under control by digitalis therapy.

Maintenance Therapy: 325 to 488 mg 3 or 4 times daily.

Supplied: Each round, green, biconvex, film-coated tablet, engraved with Rougier logo, contains: quinidine gluconate 325 mg (equivalent to approximately 202 mg of anhydrous quinidine). Amber glass bottles of 50 and 500. Keep in a light-resistant package at room temperature.

QUINIDEX EXTENTABS®

Wyeth-Ayerst

Quinidine Sulfate

Antiarrhythmic Agent

Supplied: Each round, white, biconvex, coated tablet, monogrammed "Quinidex AHR" contains: quinidine sulfate USP 300 mg in a sustained release form. Nonmedicinal ingredients: guar gum, magnesium oxide light, magnesium stearate, myverol type 18-40, water purified (retained) and zein. Printing:

ink black edible. Coating materials: acacia spray dried, calcium sulfate hydrated, carnauba wax, distilled acetylated monoglycerides, gelatin, pharmaceutical glaze (refined wax free 4 Lb cut), polysorbate 60, sucrose, titanium dioxide and white wax. Energy: 4.6 kJ (1.1 kcal). Alcohol-, gluten-, lactose-, paraben-, sulfite- and tartrazine-free. Bottles of 50.

(Shown in Product Recognition Section)

QUINIDINE

General Monograph, CPhA

Quinidine

Antiarrhythmic—Antimalarial

This monograph has been compiled by CPhA. It may contain information different from that approved by Therapeutic Products Programme, Health Canada, and the pharmaceutical manufacturers' approval has not been requested.

Pharmacology: Quinidine is a class IA antiarrhythmic agent according to the Vaughan-Williams classification. It depresses most cardiac tissues by a direct action on cardiac cells.

Quinidine depresses the rapid inward depolarizing sodium current, thereby reducing the amplitude of the action potential without affecting the resting potential. The slope of the slow depolarization phase of Purkinje fibres is reduced, and the threshold voltage for reactivation is increased by an effect on the sodium current. The result is a reduction in excitability, conduction velocity and contractility in most parts of the heart, with an increase in the refractory periods and duration of action potential in the atria, ventricles and Purkinje tissues. Quinidine also raises the ventricular defibrillation threshold.

Quinidine also has anticholinergic activity, and acts peripherally as an α-adrenergic antagonist (i.e., a vasodilator).

By slowing conduction and prolonging the effective refractory period, quinidine can interrupt or prevent re-entrant arrhythmias, including atrial flutter, atrial fibrillation and paroxysmal supraventricular tachycardia.

In patients with sick sinus syndrome, quinidine may cause marked sinus node depression and bradycardia. In most patients, however, quinidine is associated with an increase in sinus rate and AV conduction, presumably through the combination of its anticholinergic effects and reflex increases in sympathetic activity.

Quinidine prolongs the QT interval in a dose-related fashion. At high serum levels, and especially in the presence of hypokalemia, this may lead to increased ventricular automaticity and polymorphic ventricular tachycardias, including torsades de pointes.

In patients with normal conduction time, a 50% increase in QRS duration is dangerous, and therefore, the increase in the QRS interval should not exceed 25% of the control value.

Quinidine has antimalarial activity and is used i.v. to treat severe and complicated P. falciparum malaria. It has been associated with clearing of parasitemia and high rates of survival. Although quinidine and its optical isomer, quinine, are both effective, i.v. quinine is an emergency release drug and may not be readily available.

Quinidine is available in Canada as the bisulfate, gluconate, polygalacturonate and sulfate salts (see Table I).

Table I—Quinidine

Comparison of Available Salts

Quinidine Salt	Equivalent Dose (mg)	% Quinidine Base
Quinidine bisulfate	250	66
Quinidine gluconate	267	62
Quinidine polygalacturonate	275	60
Quinidine sulfate	200	83

Pharmacokinetics: Each salt dissociates in the gastrointestinal tract to release quinidine base, which is rapidly and almost completely absorbed from the small intestine. Extended-release formulations and the different salts of the drug are absorbed at different rates. Quinidine concentrations are generally higher and appear earlier when the drug is administered on an empty stomach, but the amount of drug absorbed is not diminished by the presence of food in the digestive tract. Extended-release preparations are generally preferred as the plasma concentration profile is smoother, and doses can be given at 8- to 12-hour intervals compared to the usual 6-hour dosing schedule for regular-release formulations.

All salts and formulations have approximately the same bioavailability of 70%. Peak plasma levels will vary among individuals primarily as a result of individual variations in first pass metabolism. Quinidine is widely distributed to all tissues except the brain. Quinidine crosses the placenta and is distributed into breast milk. At therapeutic plasma concentrations, the plasma protein binding of quinidine is 70 to 90% in adults and older children, but in infants and neonates it may be as low as 50 to 70%.

The elimination half-life is approximately 6 to 8 hours in adults and 3 to 4 hours in children but varies considerably among individuals. Quinidine is metabolized in the liver via the action of cytochrome-P450. Some of its metabolites may be therapeutically active. Decreased liver function does not seem to significantly affect the plasma clearance of the drug. Approximately 10 to 50% is excreted unchanged in the urine within 24 hours. Renal excretion is by glomerular filtration and secretion by proximal renal tubules. Renal clearance diminishes as urinary pH increases. Fecal excretion accounts for less than 5% of the oral dose.

The average therapeutic range is 6 to 15 μmol/L (2 to 5 μg/mL) of plasma. However, levels differ based on the assay method used. Currently available methods which are more specific than older methods report lower plasma quinidine concentrations. Toxicity is almost certain at concentrations above 25 μmol/L (8 μg/mL). The concentration necessary to produce a therapeutic effect will depend on the individual as well as the type, severity and duration of the arrhythmia. When efficacy is established, a serum drug concentration should be determined against which future levels should be compared if arrhythmia recurs or modifications made to the formulation or salt. Sampling is usually done just prior to the next dose.

Small amounts of quinidine are removed by hemodialysis; the drug is not removed by peritoneal dialysis.

Indications:

No antiarrhythmic drug has been shown to reduce the incidence of sudden death in patients with asymptomatic ventricular arrhythmias. Most antiarrhythmic drugs have the potential to cause dangerous arrhythmias; some have been shown to be associated with an increased incidence of sudden death. In light of the above, physicians should carefully consider the risks and benefits of antiarrhythmic therapy for all patients with ventricular arrhythmias.

Supraventricular Arrhythmias: Quinidine is the drug of choice for new onset (less than 1 year) atrial fibrillation or flutter when direct current cardioversion is undesirable. Ventricular rate should be controlled first with an agent that inhibits AV node conduction such as digoxin, beta-blockers or verapamil. Conversion of atrial fibrillation may be associated with embolism; therefore, anticoagulant treatment may be necessary before administration of quinidine. Quinidine is also the drug of choice for maintenance of sinus rhythm after cardioversion in patients with atrial fibrillation or flutter and for prevention of recurrent atrial fibrillation or flutter although this latter role is being re-evaluated.

Quinidine may also be used for prevention of paroxysmal atrial tachycardia due to AV nodal re-entry in patients with structural heart disease when digoxin or beta-blockers have failed or cannot be used.

Quinidine is not recommended to be used for atrial fibrillation or flutter of longer than 1 year's duration or in patients with an enlarged left atrium as successful conversion is very unlikely.

Ventricular Arrhythmias: For the treatment of documented life-threatening ventricular arrhythmias, such as sustained ventricular tachycardia. Quinidine may also be used for the treatment of patients with documented symptomatic ventricular arrhythmias when the symptoms are of sufficient severity to require treatment. Because of the proarrhythmic effects of quinidine, its use should be reserved for patients in whom the benefit of treatment clearly outweighs the risks.

For patients with sustained ventricular tachycardia, quinidine therapy should be initiated in the hospital. Hospitalization may also be required for certain other patients depending on their cardiac status and underlying cardiac disease.

The effects of quinidine in patients with recent myocardial infarction have not been adequately studied and, therefore, their use in this condition cannot be recommended.

Parenterally, quinidine may be used in the treatment of the above conditions when oral therapy is not feasible or when rapid therapeutic effect is required.

P. falciparum Malaria: I.V. quinidine is indicated for the treatment of life-threatening P. falciparum malaria.

Contraindications: Second-degree or complete atrioventricular block, junctional or idioventricular conduction disturbance that might be aggravated by quinidine, uncompensated heart failure, digitalis intoxication, prolonged QT interval (see also Warnings); patients manifesting clinical signs or having a past history of idiosyncrasy or hypersensitivity to quinidine or other cinchona derivatives (e.g., febrile reactions, skin eruptions, thrombocytopenic purpura, SLE syndrome); history of drug-induced torsades de pointes; myasthenia gravis.

Warnings: Mortality: The results of the Cardiac Arrhythmia Suppression Trial (CAST) in postmyocardial infarction patients with asymptomatic ventricular arrhythmias showed a significant increase in mortality and in nonfatal cardiac arrest rate in patients treated with encainide or flecainide compared with a matched placebo-treated group. CAST was continued using a revised protocol with the moricizine and placebo arms only. The trial was prematurely terminated because of a trend towards an increase in mortality in the moricizine treated group.

The applicability of these results to other populations or other antiarrhythmic agents is uncertain, but at present it is prudent to consider these results when using any antiarrhythmic agent.

Patients with non-life-threatening arrhythmias received quinidine or a class IB or IC antiarrhythmic in a series of unrelated clinical trials. In a meta-analysis of these trials, mortality was greatest among the patients who had received quinidine.

Quinidine should be used with extreme caution in the presence of: incomplete AV block (since a complete block and asystole may result); digitalized patients (quinidine may cause unpredictable abnormalities of rhythm); partial bundle branch block; severe congestive heart failure, cardiogenic shock, severe bradycardia and hypotensive states (quinidine may have a depressant effect on myocardial contractility and arterial pressure); hepatic and renal insufficiency (especially renal tubular acidosis, because of the potential for quinidine accumulation).

In the treatment of atrial fibrillation or flutter, conversion to sinus rhythm may be preceded by an extremely rapid ventricular rate as the degree of AV block is progressively reduced. Agents which inhibit AV node conduction such as digoxin, beta-blockers or verapamil, should be used prior to the initiation of quinidine therapy for atrial fibrillation or flutter.

Cardiotoxicity: Quinidine cardiotoxicity may be manifested by increased PR and QT intervals, 50% widening of QRS, ventricular ectopic beats or tachycardia. Appearance of these toxic signs during quinidine administration mandates immediate discontinuation of the drug and close clinical and ECG monitoring.

Syncopal Episodes: Quinidine syncope may occur as a complication of long-term therapy. It is manifested by sudden loss of consciousness and ventricular arrhythmias with bizarre QRS complexes of the torsades de pointes type. This syndrome does not appear to be related to dose or plasma levels, but occurs more often with prolonged QT intervals. Syncopal episodes frequently terminate spontaneously, but sometimes are fatal. If quinidine-induced syncope occurs, the drug should be discontinued immediately.

Vagal Stimulation: Because quinidine antagonizes the effect of vagal excitation upon the atrium and the AV node, the administration of parasympathomimetic drugs or the use of any other procedure to enhance vagal activity may fail to terminate paroxysmal supraventricular tachycardia in patients receiving quinidine.

Digitalis Intoxication: Quinidine slows the elimination of digoxin and simultaneously reduces digoxin's apparent volume of distribution. As a result, serum digoxin levels may double or even triple. When used concurrently, digoxin dosage should be reduced by approximately 50%, plasma concentrations should be monitored and patients observed closely for digoxin toxicity.

Hepatotoxicity: A few cases of hepatotoxicity, including granulomatous hepatitis, due to quinidine hypersensitivity have been reported. Unexplained fever and/or elevation of hepatic enzymes, particularly in the early stages of therapy, warrant consideration of possible hepatotoxicity. Cessation of quinidine in these cases usually results in the disappearance of toxicity.

Precautions: Proarrhythmic effects, or worsening of arrhythmias, can occur and are more likely in patients with sustained ventricular arrhythmias and left ventricular dysfunction.

A test dose of quinidine (orally or i.m.) should be given initially in order to identify possible hypersensitivity to quinidine. Although rare, the possibility of hypersensitivity should be constantly considered, especially during the first week of therapy.

Quinidine (cont'd)

When initiating therapy, hospitalization for close clinical observation, ECG monitoring and plasma level monitoring is indicated when large doses (i.e., >2 g/day) are used, or in patients at increased risk such as those with a history of syncope or presyncope due to ventricular arrhythmias.

Serum Potassium: Quinidine's activity is enhanced by potassium and reduced if hypokalemia is present.

Established Atrial Fibrillation: The use of quinidine in established atrial fibrillation is controversial. Weigh the benefits of such use in each patient against possible hazards.

Parenteral Administration: Overly rapid infusion of quinidine may cause peripheral vascular collapse and severe hypotension. Blood pressure and ECG should be monitored continuously during i.v. administration; quinidine administration should be discontinued if there is a significant fall in blood pressure. Because the kinetics of absorption may vary with the patient's peripheral perfusion, i.m. injection of quinidine is not recommended. I.M. injections are typically followed by moderate to severe local pain. Some patients will develop tender nodules at the site of injection that persist for several weeks.

P. falciparum Malaria: Complicated P. falciparum infection represents a medical emergency, and prompt administration of a schizonticidal drug is essential. All patients with severe P. falciparum malaria requiring i.v. administration of quinidine should be treated in an intensive care facility where hemodynamic and ECG monitoring is available. Even in patients without pre-existing cardiac disease, antimalarial use of quinidine has occasionally been associated with hypotension, QT prolongation, and cinchonism.

Pregnancy: It is not known whether quinidine can cause fetal harm when administered to pregnant women. There have been no teratogenic effects reported since the introduction of the drug, although quinine, the levostereoisomer of quinidine, has caused fetal blindness and has been implicated in congenital deafness. No clinical or epidemiologic studies have, however, been done. Quinidine should be used during pregnancy only when clearly indicated.

Lactation: Quinidine is present in breast milk at levels slightly lower than those in maternal serum. If possible, administration of quinidine should be avoided in nursing women.

Children: Safety and efficacy of antiarrhythmic use of quinidine in children has not been established. In antimalarial trials, quinidine was as safe and effective in pediatric patients as in adults. Children in these trials received the same doses (on a mg/kg basis) as adults.

Drug Interactions: See Table II.

Adverse Effects: Gastrointestinal: The most frequent adverse reactions occurring in approximately 30% of patients are gastrointestinal disorders (diarrhea, nausea, vomiting and anorexia). These can occur as isolated reactions to therapeutic levels of quinidine, but they may also be the first signs of cinchonism. Gastrointestinal side effects may be less severe with extended-release formulations or the polygalacturonate salt.

Cinchonism is most often a sign of chronic toxicity but may appear in sensitive patients after a single dose. Symptoms include tinnitus and other hearing disturbances, nausea, diarrhea, vertigo, blurred vision, headache, dizziness, confusion and tremor.

Cardiac: Ventricular tachycardia (most frequently torsades de pointes or ventricular fibrillation), decreased contractility, reduction in blood pressure, syncope and ECG abnormalities (marked increase in PR, QRS and QT intervals) can occur.

Hypersensitivity: fever, urticaria, flushing, exfoliative rash, bronchospasm, psoriasiform rash, photosensitivity, pruritus, lymphadenopathy, vasculitis, thrombocytopenic purpura, uveitis, angioedema, the sicca syndrome and SLE-like syndrome. Serious reactions are manifested by respiratory arrest or cardiovascular collapse.

Hematologic: hemolytic anemia, aplastic anemia, thrombocytopenia, neutropenia, leukocytosis, leukopenia, agranulocytosis, hemolysis in patients with G6PD deficiency.

CNS: headache, vertigo, apprehension, excitement, confusion, delirium, ataxia, mental depression.

Ophthalmic: mydriasis, blurred vision, disturbed color perception, photophobia, diplopia, night blindness, scotomata, reduced visual fields, optic neuritis.

Musculoskeletal: arthralgia, myalgia, increased serum skeletal muscle creatine phosphokinase.

Hearing: tinnitus, decreased auditory capacity, transitory deafness.

Liver: increased hepatic enzyme levels, hepatitis (see Warnings).

Overdose: Symptoms: Large doses may cause ataxia, respiratory distress, apnea, vomiting, diarrhea, severe hypotension, syncope, anuria, tachyarrhythmias, depressed automaticity and conduction, heart block, heart failure, irritability, lethargy, seizures, paresthesia, coma and death. Symptoms of cinchonism have also occurred.

Treatment: If ingestion is recent, gastric lavage and/or administration of activated charcoal with sorbitol may reduce absorption and hasten the passage of any remaining unabsorbed quinidine through the gastrointestinal tract. Avoid the use of charcoal if ileus is present. Maintain body temperature. Monitor electrolytes, especially potassium, calcium and magnesium. Support blood pressure and maintain renal function. Phenytoin or lidocaine may be used to control arrhythmias. Ventricular tachycardia may require DC cardioversion or pacing. Standard therapy for asystole should be employed. Refractory bradycardia or heart block that compromises blood pressure may require a temporary pacemaker. Torsades de pointes may require electrical conversion, treatment with magnesium or isoproterenol, or atrial or ventricular overdrive pacing. Angioneurotic or asthmatic phenomena may require the use of epinephrine and antihistamines.

Table II—Quinidine

Drug Interactions

Quinidine With	**Potential Effect**
Amiloride	Increased prolongation of QRS interval
Amiodarone	Increased quinidine levels and prolonged cardiac conduction
Antiarrhythmics (e.g., disopyramide, flecainide, mexiletine)	Increased serum concentrations of several antiarrhythmics; enhanced cardiac depressant effects and potential toxicity
Anticholinergics	Additive anticholinergic effect
Antihypertensives	Enhancement of hypotensive effect
β-blockers	Decreased metabolism of some β-blockers; additive cardiac depressant effects
Cholinergic drugs (e.g., neostigmine, edrophonium, pyridostigmine)	Quinidine may antagonize cholinergic effects. May result in failure of quinidine to terminate PSVT.
Cimetidine	Increased half-life and plasma levels of quinidine
Digoxin	Markedly increased digoxin levels (see Warnings)
Hepatic enzyme inducers (e.g., barbiturates, phenytoin, rifampin)	Enhanced hepatic metabolism and decreased levels of quinidine
Neuromuscular blockers (e.g., tubocurarine, succinylcholine, pancuronium)	Potentiation of neuromuscular blockade
Nifedipine	Decreased quinidine levels
Potassium	Quinidine effects enhanced by potassium and reduced by hypokalemia
Quinine	Additive effects of both drugs
Tricyclic antidepressants	Decreased clearance of some tricyclic antidepressants; additive QT prolongation
Urinary alkalinizers (e.g., acetazolamide, sodium bicarbonate, some antacids)	Decreased renal excretion of quinidine and increased blood levels
Verapamil	Increased quinidine levels, hypotension
Warfarin	Enhanced hypoprothrombinemic effect and bleeding

Dosage: Equivalent doses for each of the available quinidine salts can be found in Table I (on previous page).

Oral: Dosage based on quinidine sulfate equivalent. Administer a preliminary test dose of a single tablet of quinidine sulfate to determine whether the patient has a quinidine idiosyncrasy. Continuous or frequent ECG monitoring is desirable when quinidine therapy is initiated, especially if using large doses, i.e., >2 g quinidine sulfate daily. Gastrointestinal symptoms such as nausea, vomiting, diarrhea and colic may be minimized by giving the drug with food.

Premature Atrial and Ventricular Contractions: 200 to 300 mg of quinidine sulfate 3 or 4 times daily. Alternatively, a loading dose of 12 mg/kg, followed by a maintenance dose of 6 mg/kg every 4 to 6 hours has been recommended.

Paroxysmal Supraventricular Tachycardia: 400 to 600 mg of quinidine sulfate every 2 or 3 hours until the paroxysm is terminated.

Atrial Fibrillation or Flutter: Various schedules of quinidine administration have been utilized. One widely used technique is to give 200 mg of quinidine sulfate orally every 2 or 3 hours for up to 8 doses, with subsequent daily increase of the individual dose until sinus rhythm is restored or toxic effects occur. The total daily dose should not exceed 3 to 4 g of quinidine sulfate in any regimen.

The patient should be anticoagulated before conversion of atrial fibrillation. Ventricular rate should be brought under control with digoxin, verapamil or β-blockers. Congestive heart failure should be controlled if present. Patients should be digitalized before quinidine administration for atrial flutter.

Maintenance Therapy: 200 to 300 mg of quinidine sulfate 3 or 4 times daily.

Extended-release tablets may be given every 8 to 12 hours.

Parenteral: Dosage based on quinidine gluconate equivalent. If the patient has not received quinidine before and time permits, an initial dose of 200 mg of quinidine gluconate may be give i.m. as a test for idiosyncrasy. The test dose is given i.m. regardless of whether subsequent administration is to be i.m. or i.v.

The patient must be under close clinical observation. Frequent or continuous ECG and frequent measurement of blood pressure are recommended, especially during i.v. injection, to detect any change in rate or rhythm. I.V. administration of the drug must be stopped when any one of the following occurs: severe adverse effects, restoration of sinus rhythm, prolongation of QRS complex in excess of 25% beyond that observed prior to the injection, disappearance of P waves, or if the patient develops significant tachycardia, symptomatic bradycardia or hypotension.

I.M.: Because the kinetics of absorption may vary with the patient's peripheral perfusion, intramuscular injection of quinidine is not recommended, except as a test dose.

I.V.: In about 50% of patients who respond successfully to quinidine, arrhythmias can be terminated by a total dose of less than 5 mg/kg of quinidine gluconate but some patients may require up to 10 mg/kg. If conversion to sinus rhythm has not been achieved after infusion of 10 mg/kg, the infusion should be discontinued and other means of conversion considered.

For i.v. administration, dilute 10 mL of quinidine gluconate 80 mg/mL injection to 50 mL with 5% dextrose for injection. Infusions of quinidine must be delivered slowly, preferably under control of a volumetric pump, no faster than 0.25 mg/kg/min (or 1 mL/kg/hour of the diluted solution).

Treatment of P. falciparum Malaria: 2 regimens have been empirically shown to be effective, with or without concomitant exchange transfusions. As soon as practical, standard oral antiplasmodial therapy should be instituted.

a) Continuous I.V. Infusion: loading dose of 10 mg/kg of quinidine gluconate (6.2 mg/kg base) in a volume of 250 mL normal saline infused over 1 to 2 hours, followed immediately by maintenance infusion of 0.02 mg/kg/min of quinidine gluconate (0.0125 mg/kg/min base) for up to 72 hours, or until oral therapy can be instituted to complete 7 days of treatment.

b) Intermittent I.V. Infusion: loading dose of 24 mg/kg of quinidine gluconate (15 mg/kg base) in a volume of 250 mL normal saline infused over 4 hours followed by maintenance infusion, beginning 8 hours after the beginning of the loading dose, of 12 mg/kg of quinidine gluconate (7.5 mg/kg base) infused over 4 hours, every 8 hours until the patient can swallow. Oral therapy can then be substituted to complete 7 days of treatment.

Reviewed 1997

QUINIDINE SULFATE
Abbott

Antiarrhythmic

Supplied: Each mL contains: quinidine sulfate 190 mg in propylene glycol as a vehicle. Ampuls of 1 mL, boxes of 10.

QUINIDINE SULFATE
Glaxo Wellcome

Antiarrhythmic

Pharmacology: Quinidine depresses excitability, conduction velocity and contractility of most cardiac tissues by a direct action on cardiac cells. Indirectly, cardiac tissues will also be affected by the anticholinergic and α-adrenoceptor blocking properties of quinidine.

According to Vaughan Williams' antiarrhythmic drug classification, quinidine is a Class 1A agent. Thus, quinidine reduces the maximal rate of phase 0 depolarization, prolongs repolarization and refractory periods and, in general, decreases automaticity of cardiac cells.

Pharmacokinetics: Absorption of oral quinidine sulfate assumed to be essentially complete, though bioavailability is approximately 70% due to a first-pass removal by the liver. Peak plasma levels are variable among individuals. After a single dose given orally, quinidine can be detected in blood within 15 minutes and peak concentrations are achieved within 1 to 3 hours. Peak plasma levels during a multiple daily dose regimen may not be reached before the seventh day of administration. Quinidine concentrations are generally higher and appear earlier when the drug is administered on an empty stomach but the amount of drug absorbed is not diminished by the presence of food in the digestive tract.

Although quinidine is 80% bound to plasma constituents (mainly α-1 acid glycoprotein), its distribution in the body is predominantly extravascular. The terminal elimination half-life is approximately 7 hours and is primarily associated with its metabolism by the liver (50 to 90% of the dose administered). Quinidine half-life varies considerably between individuals, even among healthy subjects. Total body clearance is approximately 4 mL/kg/min and is also variable. The metabolites may be therapeutically active. Ten to 20% of an administered dose is excreted unchanged in urine. Renal excretion is due to glomerular filtration and secretion by proximal renal tubules and is dependent upon urinary pH, renal clearance diminishes as urinary pH increases. Fecal excretion accounts for less than 5% of the oral dose.

The average therapeutic range is between 6 to 15 μmol/L (2 and 5 μg/mL) of plasma. Toxic reactions are almost certain to appear at concentrations above 24.7 μmol/L (8 μg/mL). Levels may differ based on the assay method used.

Indications:

> No antiarrhythmic drug has been shown to reduce the incidence of sudden death in patients with asymptomatic ventricular arrhythmias. Most antiarrhythmic drugs have the potential to cause dangerous arrhythmias; some have been shown to be associated with an increased incidence of sudden death. In light of the above, physicians should carefully consider the risks and benefits of antiarrhythmic therapy for all patients with ventricular arrhythmias.

Ventricular Arrhythmias: For the treatment of documented life-threatening ventricular arrhythmias, such as sustained ventricular tachycardia. Quinidine may also be used for the treatment of patients with documented symptomatic ventricular arrhythmias when the symptoms are of sufficient severity to require treatment. Because of the proarrhythmic effects of quinidine, its use should be reserved for patients in whom, in the opinion of the physician, the benefit of treatment clearly outweighs the risks.

For patients with sustained ventricular tachycardia, quinidine therapy should be initiated in the hospital. Hospitalization may be required for certain other patients depending on their cardiac status and underlying cardiac disease.

The effects of quinidine in patients with recent myocardial infarction have not been adequately studied and, therefore, their use in this condition cannot be recommended.

Supraventricular Arrhythmias: For premature atrial or AV junctional contractions, paroxysmal atrial or AV junctional tachycardia, atrial flutter, atrial fibrillation when this therapy is appropriate and maintenance therapy after electrical conversion of atrial flutter and/or fibrillation to sinus rhythm.

Contraindications: Hypersensitivity or idiosyncrasy to quinidine or other cinchona derivatives, history of thrombocytopenic purpura associated with previous quinidine administration, myasthenia gravis, digitalis intoxication manifested by AV conduction disorders, complete AV block with an AV nodal or idioventricular pacemaker, ectopic impulses and rhythms due to escape mechanisms, and intraventricular conduction defects (especially with marked widening of the QRS complex).

Warnings: Mortality: The results of the Cardiac Arrhythmia Suppression Trial (CAST) in post-myocardial infarction patients with asymptomatic ventricular arrhythmias showed a significant increase in mortality and in non-fatal cardiac arrest rate in patients treated with encainide or flecainide compared with a matched placebo-treated group. CAST was continued using a revised protocol with the moricizine and placebo arms only. The trial was prematurely terminated because of a trend towards increase in mortality in the moricizine-treated group.

The applicability of these results to other populations or other antiarrhythmic agents is uncertain, but at present it is prudent to consider these results when using any antiarrhythmic agent.

Quinidine Cardiotoxicity: Manifestation of quinidine cardiotoxicity, such as excessive prolongation of the QT interval, widening of the QRS complex, and ventricular arrhythmias, mandates immediate discontinuation of the drug and/or close clinical and ECG monitoring.

Treatment should be discontinued if the duration of the QRS complex increases more than 50% or the P-waves disappear. A significant fall in blood pressure, the onset of ventricular premature contractions or ventricular tachycardia due to quinidine requires the immediate discontinuation of treatment.

Atrial Flutter Treatment: In the treatment of atrial flutter, reversion to sinus rhythm may be preceded by a progressive reduction in the degree of AV block to a 1:1 ratio, resulting in an extremely rapid ventricular rate. This possible hazard may be reduced by digitalization prior to administration of quinidine.

Cardiac Depression: In predisposed individuals, such as those with marginally compensated cardiovascular disease, quinidine may produce clinically important depression of the cardiovascular system such as hypotension, bradycardia or heartblock. The depressant action of quinidine on cardiac contractility and arterial blood pressure limits its use in congestive heart failure and in hypotensive states unless these conditions are due to or aggravated by the arrhythmia. The potential disadvantage and benefits must be weighed.

Syncopal Episodes: Occasionally, patients taking quinidine have syncopal episodes which usually result from tachycardia or fibrillation. The syndrome has not been shown to be related to dose or plasma levels. Syncopal episodes frequently terminate spontaneously, but sometimes are fatal.

Incomplete AV block: Quinidine should be used with extreme caution in patients with incomplete AV block. This can lead to complete AV block and asystole.

Digitalis Intoxication: Quinidine may cause abnormalities of cardiac rhythm in digitalized patients and, therefore, should be closely monitored. Reports indicate that plasma concentrations of digoxin increase and may even double when quinidine is administered concurrently. Patients on concomitant therapy should be carefully monitored. Reduction of digoxin dosage may have to be considered.

Hepatotoxicity: A few cases of hepatotoxicity, including granulomatous hepatitis, due to quinidine hypersensitivity have been reported in patients taking quinidine. Unexplained fever and/or elevation of hepatic enzymes, particularly in the early stages of therapy, warrant consideration of possible hepatotoxicity. Monitoring liver function during the first 4 to 8 weeks should be considered. Cessation of quinidine in these cases usually results in the disappearance of toxicity.

Precautions: Test for Hypersensitivity. A test dose of a single tablet of quinidine sulfate (200 mg) by mouth should be given initially in order to ascertain any possible hypersensitivity to quinidine. Hypersensitivity to quinidine, although rare, should be constantly considered, especially during the first week of therapy.

Large doses: Continuous ECG monitoring and determination of plasma quinidine concentration are indicated when large doses (>2 g/day) are used.

Serum Potassium: Quinidine's activity is enhanced by potassium and reduced if hypokalemia is present.

Established Atrial Fibrillation: The use of quinidine in established atrial fibrillation is controversial. Weigh the benefits of such use in each patient against the possible hazards.

Pregnancy: It is not known whether quinidine can cause fetal harm when administered to pregnant women. Quinine, the levostereoisomer of quinidine, has caused fetal blindness and has been implicated in congenital deafness. Quinidine should be used during pregnancy only when clearly indicated.

Lactation: Very small quantities pass into breast milk; no effects have been described in infants.

Children: Safety and efficacy of quinidine in children have not been determined.

Drug Interactions: See Table I.

Table I—Quinidine Sulfate

Drug Interactions

Quinidine with	Effect
anticholinergic drugs	additive, e.g., vagal block
urine alkalinization	increased quinidine blood level
acidifying agents	decreased quinidine blood level
coumarin	decreased coagulation
neuromuscular blockers (including neomycin)	potentiation of blockade
phenothiazines, reserpine	additive cardiac depression
antihypertensives	potentiation of blood pressure fall
hepatic enzyme inducers, nifedipine	reduction in plasma quinidine
amiodarone, cimetidine	increase in plasma quinidine
digoxin	increase in plasma digoxin
quinine	additive (all quinine/quinidine) properties
verapamil	hypotension
potassium	increased cardiotoxicity
aluminum hydroxide	decreased absorption
drugs increasing QT	additive or potentiation

Adverse Effects: Quinidine has a low therapeutic index. Adverse effects occur in as many as ⅓ of cases.

The most frequent adverse reactions are gastrointestinal in nature: nausea, vomiting, diarrhea and abdominal pain.

Cinchonism: Symptoms of mild cases include tinnitus, dysphonia and occasionally loss of hearing; some blurring of vision and gastrointestinal upset. More severe cases show headache, photophobia, altered color perception and possibly confusion, delirium and psychosis. Other symptoms observed include palpitations, convulsions, faintness and flushing, localized edema, vertigo, tremor, light-headedness, excitement, apprehension, coma and even death.

Idiosyncratic and Hypersensitivity Reactions: angioedema, febrile reactions, skin eruptions, acute asthmatic episodes, confusion, headache, anorexia, nausea, vomiting, diarrhea, precordial pain, abdominal pain, hepatic toxicity including granulomatous hepatitis, vascular collapse and respiratory arrest.

Cardiovascular: QRS widening, increase QT (and JT) interval, vasculitis, arterial embolism (following conversion of long-standing atrial fibrillation to sinus rhythm), decreased cardiac contractility, hypotension (cardiac depression and vasodilatation), syncope (due to paroxysmal ventricular tachycardia or fibrillation), proarrhythmic effects (increased frequency of existing arrhythmia or development of new arrhythmias including ventricular tachycardia, fibrillation or torsades de pointes), and asystole.

Nervous System: apprehension, excitement, psychomotor agitation, hallucinations, delusion or paranoia, delirium; confusion, memory loss, depression; vertigo, disturbed hearing and/or vision.

Hematologic: thrombocytopenia including thrombotic purpura, hemolytic anemia, agranulocytosis, pancytopenia, hypoprothrombinemia and leukopenia.

Liver: moderate increase in enzyme levels, granulomatous hepatitis (see Warnings), hepatocellular necrosis and centrilobular cholestasis.

Kidney: nephrotic syndrome.

Skin: rash, flushing with pruritus, urticaria, photosensitivity and discoloration (bluish-gray).

Musculoskeletal: very rare cases of lupus erythematosus, carpal tunnel syndrome and arthritis.

Overdose: Symptoms: Large doses may cause cinchonism, ventricular tachycardia, severe hypotension, cardiac standstill and ventricular fibrillation. Serious hypersensitivity reactions are manifested by respiratory embarrassment or cardiovascular collapse.

Quinidine Sulfate (cont'd)

Treatment: If ingestion is recent, perform gastric lavage, or induce emesis. (The use of an emetic may interfere with some of the following procedures.) Administration of 25 to 50 g of activated charcoal is indicated to reduce absorption of any remaining quinidine. Administration of hypertonic cathartic (30 g sodium sulfate in 250 mL water) will hasten passage of unabsorbed quinidine through the gastrointestinal tract. If the charcoal preparation contains 70% sorbitol, the use of an additional hypertonic saline is not necessary. Maintain body temperature. Monitor electrolytes; especially potassium, calcium and magnesium. Support blood pressure and maintain renal function. Phenytoin or lidocaine may be used to control arrhythmias. Ventricular tachycardia may require DC cardioversion or pacing. Standard therapy for cardiac standstill should be employed. Refractory bradycardia or heart block that compromises blood pressure may require a temporary pacemaker. Angioneurotic or asthmatic phenomena may require the use of epinephrine and antihistamines. Hemoglobinuria may necessitate blood transfusion and attention to renal function. The use of alkali to prevent precipitation in the tubules may prove helpful.

Dosage: Administer a preliminary test dose of a single tablet of quinidine to determine whether the patient has a quinidine idiosyncrasy. Continuous ECG monitoring is recommended in all cases in which quinidine is used in large doses. Gastrointestinal symptoms such as nausea, vomiting, diarrhea and colic may be minimized by giving the drug with food.

Premature Supraventricular Contractions: 200 to 300 mg 3 to 4 times daily. Alternatively a loading dose of 12 mg/kg, followed by a maintenance dose of 6 mg/kg every 4 to 6 hours has been recommended.

Paroxysmal Supraventricular Tachycardia: 400 to 600 mg every 2 or 3 hours until the paroxysm is terminated.

Atrial Flutter: Quinidine should be administered after digitalization for this indication. Dosage is to be individualized.

Conversion of Atrial Fibrillation: Various schedules of quinidine administration have been utilized. One widely used technique is to give 200 mg of quinidine orally every 2 or 3 hours for 5 to 8 doses, with subsequent daily increase of the individual dose until sinus rhythm is restored or toxic effects occur. The total daily dose should not exceed 3 to 4 g in any regimen. The patient may require anticoagulation for up to 2 to 3 months before conversion. Prior to quinidine administration, the ventricular rate and congestive failure (if present) should be brought under control by digitalis therapy.

Maintenance Therapy: 200 to 300 mg 3 or 4 times daily.

Supplied: Each white, biconvex tablet, scored on one side and imprinted with "Wellcome" on the upper half and "P4A" on the lower half of the score, contains: quinidine sulfate 200 mg. Nonmedicinal ingredients: cornstarch, magnesium stearate and stearic acid. Bottles of 100 and 500. Store between 15 and 30°C and protect from light.

(Shown in Product Recognition Section)

QUININE

General Monograph, CPhA

Antimalarial

This monograph has been compiled by CPhA. It may contain information different from that approved by Therapeutic Products Programme, Health Canada, and the pharmaceutical manufacturers' approval has not been requested.

Pharmacology: Quinine decreases the response of skeletal muscle to tetanic stimulation by increasing the refractory period of the muscle and affecting calcium distribution in individual muscle fibres. The excitability of the motor end-plate is also decreased causing a reduction in the response of the muscle to acetylcholine and repetitive nerve stimulation.

Quinine has antimalarial activity and is used orally in combination with a second drug to treat nonsevere P. falciparum infections acquired in zones where chloroquinine resistance has been reported. Patients with nonsevere infections unable to tolerate oral therapy or those patients with severe and complicated P. falciparum infections should receive i.v. drug therapy. Although quinine and its optical isomer, quinidine, are both effective, i.v. quinine is an emergency release drug and may not be readily available.

Pharmacokinetics: Following oral administration, quinine is rapidly and almost completely absorbed from the gastrointestinal tract. It is widely distributed to body tissues and approximately 70% protein bound. Quinine readily crosses the placenta and is excreted into breast milk. Concentrations in CSF are 2 to 7% of plasma levels. Quinine is metabolized by the liver and excreted mainly in the urine. Anywhere from <5 to 20% of the drug is excreted unchanged in the urine. Renal excretion of the drug is enhanced at low urinary pH. The elimination half-life of quinine in healthy individuals ranges from 7 to 12 hours. Plasma concentrations of the drug may be higher and the half-life longer in patients with malaria due to impaired hepatic metabolism of the drug.

Indications: Quinine is indicated orally in combination with a second drug in the treatment of uncomplicated chloroquine-resistant P. falciparum malaria. For those patients unable to tolerate oral therapy or those with severe P. falciparum infections, i.v. quinine or i.v. quinidine, in combination with a second drug, is indicated.

Quinine may also be used to treat chloroquine-resistant P. vivax malaria but higher doses may be required. Expert advice from an infectious or tropical disease specialist should be sought for the management of these cases.

Quinine is also used to treat and prevent nocturnal recumbency leg muscle cramps.

Contraindications: Quinine is contraindicated in patients who have a known hypersensitivity to the drug. Cross-sensitivity between quinine and quinidine may occur.

Quinine should not be used in patients with G-6-PD deficiency; tinnitus; optic neuritis; myasthenia gravis; hypoglycemia; pregnancy unless required to treat a severe, life-threatening malaria infection in the mother; history of blackwater fever and thrombocytopenic purpura (associated with previous quinine ingestion).

Precautions: Quinine has quinidine-like activity; the same precautions should be taken with quinine as with quinidine in patients with atrial fibrillation. Advise patients to notify physician if cutaneous, angioedematous, visual or auditory symptoms occur. If evidence of hemolysis appears, stop the drug immediately.

Drug Interactions: Antacids: Concomitant administration of antacids and quinine may decrease or delay the absorption of oral quinine.

Anticoagulants, warfarin: Quinine may enhance the anticoagulant effects of warfarin.

Astemizole: Concomitant use of quinine and astemizole may lead to elevated plasma levels of astemizole and desmethylastemizole, accompanied by prolongation of the QT interval.

Cimetidine: Cimetidine may inhibit the metabolism of quinine and increase the risk of quinine toxicity.

Digitalis Glycosides: Quinine increases plasma concentrations of digoxin. Monitor digoxin and digitoxin serum concentrations in patients receiving quinine.

Mefloquine: Concomitant use of quinine and mefloquine may cause ECG abnormalities or cardiac arrest. The risk of seizures may also be increased. Quinine therapy for malaria should be initiated with caution in patients who have received mefloquine for prophylaxis.

Neuromuscular blockers: Quinine may potentiate the effects of neuromuscular blockers such as pancuronium, succinylcholine and tubocurarine resulting in respiratory difficulties.

Urinary alkalinizers: Agents such as sodium bicarbonate and acetazolamide which increase urinary pH may inhibit the renal excretion of quinine and increase the risk of quinine toxicity.

Pregnancy: Quinine causes congenital malformations. Its use during pregnancy should be avoided (see Contraindications).

Lactation: Quinine is distributed into breast milk. Administration of quinine, when possible, should be avoided in nursing women.

Children: Quinine is safe for use in children at recommended doses for the treatment of malaria.

Adverse Effects: The usual therapeutic doses of quinine frequently induce symptoms of mild to moderate cinchonism (tinnitus, headache, impaired hearing, nausea, blurred vision) but these symptoms are seldom severe enough to necessitate cessation of treatment. Serious adverse effects are relatively rare; however, more marked symptoms of cinchonism as well as vomiting, abdominal pain, diarrhea and vertigo may develop, particularly when plasma concentrations exceed 3.2 μmol/L.

Reactions to continued or large doses include: visual disturbances such as disturbed color perception, photophobia, blurred vision, night blindness, amblyopia, scotomata, diplopia, mydriasis, spasm of the retinal vessels and in severe cases, optic atrophy, hot and flushed skin, fever, profuse sweating, asthma and angioedema.

Cardiovascular: Conduction disturbances, ventricular tachycardia and anginal symptoms have occurred with prolonged quinine therapy in highly sensitive patients.

Gastrointestinal: nausea, vomiting, diarrhea and abdominal pain. Nausea and vomiting may be related to CNS effects of quinine.

Hematologic: Thrombocytopenic purpura, leukopenia, pancytopenia, coagulopathy, hypoprothrombinemia and agranulocytosis have been reported. Massive hemolysis is a rare complication of quinine therapy.

Hypersensitivity Reactions: Cutaneous flushing, pruritus, scarlatiniform, maculopapular or urticarial skin eruptions, fever, facial edema, gastrointestinal distress, dyspnea, tinnitus and impairment of vision have been reported. Extreme flushing of the skin with intense, generalized pruritus is most common. Hemoglobinuria and asthma have been reported rarely.

Hypoglycemia, which may be severe and recurrent, has been reported in some patients with severe malaria caused by P. falciparum who received quinine therapy, and there was some evidence that quinine-induced insulin secretion may have been one of several possible precipitating factors.

Overdose: Symptoms: Symptoms of cinchonism such as tinnitus, headache, vertigo, nausea, vomiting, abdominal pain, diarrhea. Visual disturbances may be severe, ranging from blurring and diplopia to acute complete blindness. Blindness is usually transitory, but may rarely be permanent. Cardiovascular toxicity may include conduction disturbances, cardiac arrhythmias, and hypotension leading to cardiac arrest and circulatory collapse. CNS reactions can include restlessness, confusion, seizures, respiratory arrest, delirium and coma.

Treatment: Empty stomach using gastric lavage. Administer activated charcoal and repeat every 4 hours. Administer one dose of a cathartic with the charcoal or separately. Treatment is mostly symptomatic with attention to maintaining blood pressure, renal function and respiration, and treating arrhythmias. The value of using vasodilators and stellate ganglion block to prevent or reverse visual impairment is controversial. Hemodialysis and peritoneal dialysis are of little or no value in the management of quinine overdose.

Dosage: Quinine sulfate 300 mg is approximately equivalent to quinine base 250 mg. Quinine dihydrochloride 300 mg is approximately equivalent to quinine base 250 mg.

Malaria: Oral: Uncomplicated chloroquine-resistant P. falciparum malaria: quinine sulfate should be administered in conjunction with doxycycline, clindamycin or the combination product pyrimethamine/sulfadoxine.

Adults: Quinine sulfate 600 mg 3 times daily, after meals, for 3 to 7 days.

Children: Quinine sulfate 9 mg/kg to a maximum of 600 mg, 3 times daily, after meals, for 3 to 7 days.

Parenteral: Parenteral quinine is available in Canada only through the Special Access Program, Health Canada. For information about this program see Special Access Program in the Clin-Info section. Parenteral quinidine gluconate may also be used to treat severe, life-threatening P. falciparum malaria (see Quinidine, General Monograph).

Severe P. falciparum malaria: The 2 dosage regimens listed below are equally effective. Either regimen should be administered in conjunction with doxycycline, clindamycin or the combination product pyrimethamine/sulfadoxine. Therapy should be switched to oral quinine sulfate when the patient can swallow, to complete a 7-day treatment course. If parenteral therapy is required for more than 48 hours, the maintenance dose of quinine should be reduced by one-third to one-half.

a) If an infusion pump is available: Quinine dihydrochloride 7 mg/kg i.v. over 30 minutes followed immediately by quinine dihydrochloride 10 mg/kg diluted in 10 mL/kg isotonic fluid, i.v. over 4 hours; repeat every 8 hours until oral therapy can be instituted.

b) Without an infusion pump: Quinine dihydrochloride 20 mg/kg i.v. over 4 hours, then quinine dihydrochloride 10 mg/kg diluted in 10 mL/kg isotonic fluid, i.v. over 4 hours; repeat every 8 hours until oral therapy can be instituted.

Nocturnal Recumbency Leg Cramps: Oral: Quinine sulfate 200 to 300 mg at bedtime. If leg cramps persist, an additional dose may be taken following the evening meal. If leg cramps do not occur for several consecutive nights during therapy, quinine may be discontinued to assess the need for continued therapy.

Reviewed 1999

QUINOBARB® ♦

Rougier

Quinidine Phenylethylbarbiturate

Antiarrhythmic—Sedative

Supplied: Each scored, uncoated, pink tablet stamped on one side with W.L. logo, contains: quinidine phenylethylbarbiturate 100 mg. Energy: 2.76 kJ (0.65 kcal). Bottles of 100 and 500.

QUINTASA® Ⓟ

Ferring

5-Aminosalicylic Acid

Lower Gastrointestinal Anti-inflammatory

Pharmacology: 5-aminosalicylic acid (5-ASA) has been recognized as the therapeutically active moiety of sulfasalazine, a drug used to treat inflammatory bowel disease. 5-ASA has in vitro and in vivo pharmacologic effects that decrease leukotriene production, scavenge for free radicals and inhibit leukocyte chemotaxis. While its exact mode of action is currently unknown, any of these biochemical mechanisms may play a role in the clinical effectiveness of 5-ASA.

Regardless of its mode of action, 5-ASA appears to exert its therapeutic effect by topical action on the affected areas of inflammation. Dosage forms designed for rectal administration, such as enemas and suppositories are, therefore, especially suited to deliver the active ingredient, 5-ASA, directly to the affected areas along the mucosal lumen of the rectum, sigmoid and distal large bowel.

The local and systemic bioavailability of 5-ASA enema and suppositories were assessed in 12 healthy volunteers during steady-state conditions. Systemic absorption of 5-ASA was low; 15% of the 2 g daily dose was recovered in the urine (mostly as the acetylated metabolite) after administration of the enema, with 10% urinary recovery observed after administration of the suppositories. This compares to 20 to 30% of the 5-ASA dose being absorbed systemically following oral administration.

Maximum plasma concentrations of 5-ASA and of N-acetyl-5-ASA (approximately) 0.7 μg/mL and 1.2 μg/mL respectively for the enema; 0.3 μg/mL and 0.8 μg/mL respectively for the suppositories) were reached 2 hours following administration of the enema and 5 to 6 hours following administration of the suppositories.

More importantly, local availability, as shown by recovery of free 5-ASA in the feces, is higher for both the enema (mean 30%) and the suppositories (mean 45%) than for the oral dosage forms of 5-ASA.

Indications: Rectal Suspension: For the treatment of acute distal ulcerative colitis extending to the splenic flexure and for long-term maintenance therapy in order to maintain remission and prevent relapse of active disease.
Suppositories: For the treatment of acute ulcerative proctitis and for long-term maintenance therapy in order to maintain remission and prevent relapse of active disease.

Contraindications: Hypersensitivity to salicylic acid derivatives. Severely impaired hepatic and/or renal function. Contraindicated in patients with peptic ulcer.

Warnings: Impaired Renal or Hepatic Function: Caution should be exercised if 5-ASA is administered to patients with impaired renal or hepatic function.

Single reports of nephrotic syndrome and interstitial nephritis associated with 5-ASA therapy have been described in the literature. Animal studies have demonstrated a dose-dependent nephrotoxicity. Patients with pre-existing renal disease, increased BUN or serum creatinine, or proteinuria should be carefully monitored.
Pregnancy: 5-ASA should be used during pregnancy only if clearly needed. 5-ASA is known to cross the placental barrier.
Lactation: Caution should be exercised when 5-ASA is administered to a nursing woman.
Children: The safety and efficacy of 5-ASA have not been established in children. The potential benefits of its use should be weighed against the possible risks.

Precautions: General: 5-ASA has been associated with the production of an acute intolerance syndrome which may be difficult to distinguish from flare of inflammatory bowel disease. Symptoms include cramping, acute abdominal pain and bloody diarrhea, sometimes fever, headache and rash. If acute intolerance syndrome is suspected, prompt withdrawal is required. If a rechallenge is performed later in order to validate the hypersensitivity, it should be carried out under close medical supervision at reduced dose and only if clearly needed.

In ulcerative colitis studies, most patients who were intolerant or hypersensitive to sulfasalazine were able to take 5-ASA without evidence of allergic reaction (e.g., rash, fever, pruritus) or intolerance. Nevertheless, caution should be exercised when 5-ASA is used in patients known to be allergic to sulfasalazine. These patients should be instructed to discontinue therapy if signs of rash or fever become apparent.

Semen abnormalities and infertility in men, which are associated with sulfasalazine, have not been reported with 5-ASA during controlled clinical trials. Semen quality significantly improved when patients were transferred from sulfasalazine to 5-ASA.

<u>Drug Interactions:</u> There are no known interactions between 5-ASA and other drugs.

Adverse Effects: The nature and frequency of adverse events reported during clinical trials involving over 200 patients treated with 5-ASA were similar to those observed with the oral dosage forms, were not dose-related and were not significantly different from those seen with placebo.

The most common events, as shown in Table I, were: abdominal pain, diarrhea, nausea and headache.

Table I—Quintasa

Adverse Events Occurrence Rates (by Daily Dose)*

Symptom	Placebo N=70	Quintasa 1 g/100 mL N=73	Quintasa 2 g/100 mL N=73	Quintasa 4 g/100 mL N=73
Pain (Abdominal)	2 (2.9%)	2 (2.7%)	2 (2.8%)	3 (4.1%)
Diarrhea	3 (4.3%)	1 (1.4%)	1 (1.4%)	3 (4.1%)
Nausea	2 (2.9%)	3 (4.1%)	—	1 (1.4%)
Headache	2 (2.9%)	—	—	3 (4.1%)
Flatulence	1 (1.4%)	1 (1.4%)	2 (2.8%)	—
Alopecia	—	2 (2.7%)	1 (1.4%)	—
Pain (Back)	1 (1.4%)	1 (1.4%)	1 (1.4%)	—
Rash (Maculopapular) (Vesicobullous)	—	1 (1.4%)	1 (1.4%)	1 (1.4%)
Rectal Disease	—	—	1 (1.4%)	2 (2.7%)
Colitis Ulcer (Proctitis Ulcer)	1 (1.4%)	1 (1.4%)	—	—
Conjunctivitis	1 (1.4%)	—	—	1 (1.4%)
Constipation	—	2 (2.7%)	—	—
Fever	—	1 (1.4%)	1 (1.4%)	—
Asthenia	—	1 (1.4%)	—	—
Dizziness	—	1 (1.4%)	—	—
Edema (Face)	—	—	—	1 (1.4%)
Glossitis	—	—	1 (1.4%)	—
Insomnia	—	—	1 (1.4%)	—
Joint Disease	—	1 (1.4%)	—	—
Malaise	—	—	1 (1.4%)	—
Melena	1 (1.4%)	—	—	—
Nausea/Vomiting	1 (1.4%)	—	—	—
Skin (Dry)	—	1 (1.4%)	—	—
Somnolence	—	1 (1.4%)	—	—
Sputum Increase	—	1 (1.4%)	—	—
Stool (Abnormal)	1 (1.4%)	—	—	—
Weight Decrease	—	1 (1.4%)	—	—
Total	7 (10.0%)	11 (15.1%)	10 (14.1%)	9 (12.3%)

* Patient counts should not be totaled vertically as some patients experienced more than one event and are presented more than once in this table.

When considering all clinical trials together, more than 1 750 patients have received Quintasa therapy, with either oral or rectal dosage forms. Generally, 5-ASA was well tolerated. The following events were reported infrequently (i.e., less than 1%) during trials. In many cases the relationship to 5-ASA has not been established.
Gastrointestinal: abdominal distention, anorexia, duodenal ulcer, eructation, esophageal ulcer, fecal incontinence, gastrointestinal bleeding, increased alkaline phosphatase, melena, dysphagia, mouth ulcer, oral moniliasis, rectal bleeding, rectal urgency, AST increase, stool abnormalities (color or texture change), thirst.
Dermatological: acne, alopecia, dry skin, eczema, erythema nodosum, nail disorder, photosensitivity, pruritus, sweating.
CNS: dizziness, insomnia, somnolence, paresthesia.
Cardiovascular: vasodilation.
Other: albuminuria, asthenia, breast pain, ecchymosis, edema, fever, leg cramps, malaise, menorrhagia, myalgia, urinary frequency.

Isolated case reports have described pericarditis, pancreatitis, nephrotic syndrome and interstitial nephritis associated with 5-ASA.

Overdose: Symptoms and Treatment: There is no clinical experience with 5-ASA overdosage. 5-ASA is an aminosalicylate and symptoms of salicylate toxicity may be possible, such as: tinnitus, vertigo, headache, confusion, drowsiness, sweating, hyperventilation, vomiting and diarrhea. Severe intoxication with salicylates can lead to disruption of electrolyte balance and blood pH, hyperthermia, and dehydration. Since 5-ASA is an aminosalicylate, conventional therapy for salicylate toxicity may be beneficial in the event of acute overdosage. This includes prevention of further gastrointestinal tract absorption by emesis and, if necessary by gastric lavage. Fluid and electrolyte imbalance should be corrected by the administration of appropriate i.v. therapy. Adequate renal function should be maintained.

Dosage: Rectal Suspension: The recommended dose ranges from 1 to 4 g of 5-ASA, depending on disease activity, self-administered once daily at bedtime, in unit dose packages containing 1 g, 2 g or 4 g of 5-ASA. Dosage may be adjusted according to the individual patient's needs consistent with therapeutic goals. Prolonged retention is expected to achieve the best therapeutic response.
Suppositories: The usual dose is 1 suppository containing 1 g of 5-ASA, self-administered once daily at bedtime. Prolonged retention is expected to achieve the best therapeutic response. The frequency of dosage may be adjusted according to the individual patient's needs consistent with therapeutic goals.

Information for the Patient: See Blue Section—Information for the Patient "Quintasa".

Supplied: Enema: Each unit dose (100 mL) of rectal suspension enema contains: 5-ASA 1 g, 2 g or 4 g. Nonmedicinal ingredients: hydrochloric acid, purified water, sodium acetate, sodium edetate, sodium metabisulfite. Cartons of 7 enemas. Plastic bags are included in the carton to aid in hygenic disposal of enema bottles.

Suppositories: Each suppository contains: 5-ASA 1 g. Nonmedicinal ingredients: magnesium stearate, polyethyleneglycol, povidone, talc. Cartons of 30 suppositories in individual foil pouches with finger protectors. Store at controlled room temperature below 25°C. Dispense in the respective unit-dose containers.

R

R & C®

R & C

see "R and C"

RABIES VACCINE INACTIVATED (DIPLOID CELL ORIGIN), DRIED

Connaught

Vaccine

Pharmacology: The administration of Rabies Vaccine Inactivated (Diploid Cell Origin), Dried stimulates the rapid development of specific antibodies.

Pre-exposure Immunization: Pre-exposure clinical trials have been carried out since 1979 with the present vaccine or its less purified predecessors in over 600 volunteers. Following 3 injections of 1 mL each of vaccine, all developed antibodies at a level of 1 IU/mL or greater.

In a clinical trial done in Canada in 1989 and 1990, 119 individuals who had rabies vaccine antibody titers of less than 0.16 IU received pre-exposure immunization by either the i.m. or s.c. route. Following administration of 3 doses of vaccine on days 0, 7 and 21, 100% of recipients had protective rabies antibody titers with postimmunization levels ranging from 2.8 IU/mL to 82.2 IU/mL. The i.m. route produced significantly higher levels of rabies antibodies.

In clinical trials in 1983 and 1984 in which 187 individuals received 3 injections of vaccine at 0, 7 and 21 days, and were tested 4 weeks following the third injection, all had antibody levels equal to or greater than 3 IU/mL by the Rapid Fluorescent Focus Inhibition Test (RFFIT).

The National Advisory Committee on Immunization considers a protective antibody level to be 1:32 by the RFFIT test. The WHO currently considers a minimal acceptable antibody titer to be 0.5 IU/mL. The CDC currently considers a minimal acceptable antibody titer to be 1:5 by the RFFIT test.

Persistence of antibody following three 1 mL injections of the primary immunization series with Rabies Vaccine Inactivated (Diploid Cell Origin), Dried in 197 adults showed a 10-fold drop in geometric mean levels in one year from 30 IU/mL to 3 IU/mL. However, the mean antibody response of 3 IU/mL is still considerably above the minimal acceptable antibody level of 0.5 IU/mL.

Reinforcement Immunization: Since 1979 single dose reinforcement immunization has been administered to more than 400 individuals. A single reinforcement dose of 1 mL of vaccine administered between 1983 and 1984 to 84 individuals immunized at different times previously with various rabies vaccines induced an antibody response in all and at least a 4-fold increase in all but 7 of those tested.

Post-Exposure Immunization: Rabies Vaccine Inactivated (Diploid Cell Origin), Dried administered as 1 mL injections **i.m.** on day 0, 3, 7, 14 and 28 evoked detectable antibody in vaccinees by day 7. Antibody levels continued to rise reaching peak values at day 28.

Testing of vaccinees at day 90 showed some decline from peak antibody levels but all were many times above the accepted protective level.

When Rabies Immune Globulin (Human) in a dosage of 20 IU per kg of bodyweight was administered at the same time as the initial vaccine injection, serum rabies antibody was demonstrable 2 days following the injection. Significantly higher antibody levels were present on days 2, 3, and 7 than when rabies vaccine only was administered indicating the importance of rabies immune globulin in providing antibody in the early period following exposure. There was no significant difference in antibody levels following rabies vaccine with and without rabies immune globulin at 14, 28, 49 and 90 days indicating that rabies immune globulin did not suppress the response to vaccine.

Indications: Pre-exposure immunization, both primary series and periodic reinforcement, and for postexposure immunization against rabies.

Pre-exposure Immunization: Pre-exposure rabies vaccination is an elective procedure and should be offered to persons at potentially high risk of contact with rabid animals, e.g., certain laboratory workers, veterinarians, animal control and wildlife workers, spelunkers, forest rangers, conservation officers, and certain travellers including those: working (even for a short time) in a rabies-infected country, if their activities may involve exposure to some special risk; spending time (e.g., 1 month or more) in a foreign country where rabies is a constant threat; or travelling in such a country, for any length of time, far away from a major medical centre. Three doses of Human Diploid Cell Vaccine (HDCV) are required, one on days 0, 7 and 21.

Reinforcement Immunization: Persons with continuing high risk of exposure such as certain veterinarians should have their serum tested every 2 years; others working with live rabies virus in laboratories or vaccine-production facilities and who are at risk of inapparent exposure should be tested every 6 months. Those with inadequate titers should be given a booster dose of HDCV. Persons previously immunized with other vaccines should be given sufficient doses of HDCV to produce an adequate antibody response. An acceptable antibody titer is considered to be 1:32 by the rapid fluorescent-focus inhibition test.

Postexposure Immunization: A decision on the management of a person who has been exposed to the risk of rabies infection must be made rapidly and judiciously since delay in starting a course of vaccine reduces its effectiveness, and the disease once established is almost always fatal.

Rabies prophylaxis must be considered in every incident where potential exposure to rabies virus has occurred. The following factors should be taken into consideration.

Species of Animal: The animals in Canada most often proven rabid are foxes, skunks, cattle, dogs, cats and bats. The distribution of animal rabies and the species involved vary considerably across Canada so it is important to consult the local medical officer of health or government veterinarian. Human exposures to livestock are usually confined to salivary contamination, with the exception of horses and swine in which biting incidents have been reported. Risk of infection following exposure to rabid cattle is low, and only about 30 cases have ever been recorded. Squirrels, hamsters, guinea-pigs, gerbils, chipmunks, rats, mice, other rodents or rabbits and hares are rarely found to be infected with rabies and are not known to cause human rabies in Canada and the U.S.; their bites seldom, if ever, call for rabies prophylaxis.

Incident: Each incident requires full investigation including an assessment of the risk of rabies in the animal species involved and the behavior of the particular animal. An unprovoked attack is more apt to indicate that the animal is rabid. Nevertheless, rabid cats and dogs may become uncharacteristically quiet. Bites inflicted on a person attempting to feed or handle an apparently healthy animal should generally be regarded as provoked.

Type of Exposure: Exposure to rabies virus is considered to have occurred when the animal's teeth break the skin in a bite or if the animal's saliva or other potentially infectious material (such as brain tissue) comes into contact with an open wound or mucous membrane. If the virus-containing material is dry, the virus can be considered to be non-infectious. Contact with blood, urine or feces or petting a rabid animal does not constitute an exposure and is not an indication for prophylaxis. The occurrence of rabies following exposure to virus-laden aerosols in a laboratory and in a bat-infested cave has been reported. The only known cases of human-to-human transmission of rabies occurred in patients who received corneal transplants from persons who had died of unrecognized rabies. Tissues from persons who die of encephalitis of unknown etiology should not be used as donor transplants.

Vaccination Status of Biting Animal: A small number of vaccinated animals have developed rabies. Therefore, symptoms suggesting rabies, even in a vaccinated animal, must be carefully evaluated. The vaccination history in itself should not influence the need for post-exposure treatment nor the need to sacrifice the animal for assessment.

The following recommendations are intended as a guide for the management of persons following possible exposure to rabies and may need to be modified in accordance with the specific circumstances of the exposure to rabies.

Local Treatment of Wounds: Immediate washing and flushing with soap and water, detergent, or water alone is imperative and is probably the most effective procedure in the prevention of rabies. Suturing the wound should be avoided if possible. Tetanus prophylaxis and antibacterial drugs should be given as required.

Immunizing Agents: There are 2 types of immunizing products: Vaccines, which contain inactivated virus and induce an active immune response beginning in 7 to 10 days and persisting for at least a year; and Rabies Immune Globulin (RIG), which provides rapid protection that persists for only short period of time (half-life about 21 days).

Vaccine and immune globulin should be used concurrently for optimum post-exposure prophylaxis against rabies, except in certain previously immunized persons, as indicated below.

Vaccine: Postexposure prophylaxis should be started as soon as possible after exposure and should be offered to exposed persons regardless of the elapsed interval. Prophylaxis may be started as late as 6 or more months after exposure.

Five doses of HDCV should be given: The first dose (on day 0) as soon as possible after exposure, and additional doses on each of days 3, 7, 14 and 28 days after the first dose. A single dose of RIG should also be given on day 0 as described below. Routine follow-up antibody determination is unnecessary, except in the case of persons with immunodeficiency or those receiving immunosuppressive therapy.

Indication for Discontinuation of Postexposure Prophylaxis: A course of vaccine may be discontinued if fluorescent antibody tests on the brain of an animal killed at the time of attack prove to be negative.

Postexposure Therapy of Previously Immunized Persons: Persons previously vaccinated with HDCV should receive 2 vaccine doses, 1 immediately and another 3 days later. RIG should not be given in these cases. Antibody determination is not helpful because two booster doses are recommended whatever the result.

If vaccine other than HDCV had been used for previous immunization and seroconversion has not been demonstrated, full post-exposure rabies prophylaxis with HDCV including rabies immune globulin should be started. A serum sample may be collected before vaccine is given and if adequate antibody is demonstrated, the course can be discontinued provided that the 2 doses of vaccine indicated above have been given.

Contraindications: There are no specific contraindications to the use of Rabies Vaccine Inactivated (Diploid Cell Origin), Dried in the postexposure situation; however, care should be taken if the vaccine is to be administered to persons known to be sensitive to bovine serum, polymyxin, neomycin or thimerosal, as even trace amounts may cause an allergic reaction in such individuals.

General: Pre-exposure immunization with Rabies Vaccine Inactivated (Diploid Cell Origin), Dried should be deferred in the presence of any acute illness, including febrile illness.

Absolute Contraindications: Allergy to any component of Rabies Vaccine Inactivated (Diploid Cell Origin), Dried, or an allergic or anaphylactic reaction to a previous dose of Rabies Vaccine Inactivated (Diploid Cell Origin), Dried are contraindications to pre-exposure vaccination.

Warnings: Local and/or mild systemic reactions may occur after vaccine injection but these are usually transient and do not contraindicate continuing immunization.

This vaccine must not be used s.c. or intradermally.

Corticosteroids, other immunosuppressive agents, antimalarials, and immunosuppressive illnesses can interfere with the development of active immunity after vaccination and may predispose the patient to rabies. Pre-exposure prophylaxis should be administered to such persons with the awareness that the immune response may be inadequate. Immunosuppressive agents should not be administered during post-exposure therapy unless essential for the treatment of other conditions. When rabies post-exposure prophylaxis is administered to persons receiving steroids or other immunosuppressive therapy, or who are immunosuppressed, it is important that a serum sample be tested for rabies antibody to ensure that an acceptable antibody response has developed.

Corticosteroid therapy can result in immunosuppression although the exact dose and duration of therapy required to suppress the immune system is not well defined. Persons treated with high doses of systemic steroids, e.g., ≥ 2 mg/kg/day of prednisone orally for more than 2 weeks, should be considered to have a compromised immune system.

As with any vaccine, immunization with Rabies Vaccine Inactivated (Diploid Cell Origin), Dried may not protect 100% of susceptible individuals.

Since the vaccine contains traces of bovine serum, polymyxin, neomycin and thimerosal, the possibility of allergic reactions in individuals sensitive to these substances should be borne in mind when considering the use of this vaccine.

Precautions: General: The possibility of allergic reactions in individuals sensitive to components of the vaccine should be

Rabies Vaccine Inactivated (Diploid Cell Origin), Dried (cont'd)

evaluated. Epinephrine HCl solution (1:1 000) and other appropriate agents should be available for immediate use in case an anaphylactic or acute hypersensitivity reaction occurs. Before an injection of any vaccine, all appropriate precautions should be taken to prevent adverse reactions. This includes a review of the patient's history with respect to possible hypersensitivity to the vaccine or similar vaccine, determination of previous immunization history, and the presence of any contraindications to immunization.

Special care should be taken to ensure that the product is not injected into a blood vessel.

A separate, **sterile** syringe and needle, or a **sterile** disposable unit, must be used for each individual patient to prevent the transmission of infectious agents. There have been case reports of transmission of HIV and hepatitis by failure to scrupulously observe sterile technique.

Do not recap needles.

If the vaccine is administered to persons with immunodeficiency or receiving immunosuppressive therapy the expected antibody response may not be obtained.

Pregnancy: The safety of Rabies Vaccine in pregnancy has not been established. Because of the potential consequences of inadequately treated rabies exposure and limited data that indicate that fetal abnormalities have not been associated with rabies vaccination, pregnancy is not considered a contraindication to postexposure prophylaxis. If there is a substantial risk of exposure to rabies, pre-exposure prophylaxis may also be indicated during pregnancy.

Adverse Effects: Local reactions which may occur include redness, soreness, hardness, swelling, pain and itching at the site of injection. Generalized reactions such as fever, chills, malaise, headache, abdominal pain and joint pain may also occur. These reactions are usually of short duration lasting a few hours to 1 to 2 days and have onset within a few hours of vaccine injection.

In a simulated post-exposure clinical trial done in Texas in 1984, 31 persons each received 5 doses of rabies vaccine on days 0, 3, 7, 14 and 28. These persons were not given rabies immune globulin. Local reactivity was mild and subsided within 24 to 48 hours. Systemic reactivity was infrequent, mild and usually consisted of headache, dizziness and malaise. There were no severe reactions reported. The incidence of adverse events following any dose are shown in Tables I and II.

Table I—Rabies Vaccine Inactivated (Diploid Cell Origin), Dried

Local Reactions (% of 31 Patients)

Reaction	%
Muscle Ache	68
Tenderness	45.1
Pain	26
Enlarged Nodes	23
Redness	9.7
Swelling	9.7
Induration	6.5
Pain in axilla	6.5
Itchiness	3.2

Table II—Rabies Vaccine Inactivated (Diploid Cell Origin), Dried

Systemic Reactions (% of 31 Patients)

Reaction	%
Malaise	26
Headache	26
Nausea	13
Joint Pain	13
Pharyngitis	13
Dizziness	9.7
Abdominal Pain	9.7
Fever	6.5
Upper Respiratory Tract Infection	6.5
Ear Ache	3.2
Cough	3.2

Neurological events have been reported following administration of rabies vaccine of human diploid cell origin. These have included 3 cases of neurologic illness resembling Guillain Barré syndrome and a few other subacute central and peripheral nervous system disorders.

Systemic allergic reactions characterized by generalized urticaria and accompanied in some cases by arthralgia, angioedema, fever, nausea and vomiting have been reported following administration of Human Diploid Cell Rabies Vaccines (HDCV). These reactions are uncommon in persons receiving primary immunization but have occurred in up to 7% of persons receiving a booster dose, with onset after 2 to 21 days. These reactions have been shown to follow the development of IgE antibodies to beta propiolactone-altered human serum albumin in the vaccine. Vaccines purified by zonal centrifugation appear to be less likely to be associated with such reactions. Immediate anaphylactic reactions have occurred in 1 in 10 000 persons given HDCV. In clinical trials with this vaccine, no immune-complex-like reactions have been reported.

Physicians, nurses, and pharmacists should report any adverse occurrences temporally related to the administration of the product in accordance with local requirements and to the Medical Director, Connaught Laboratories Limited, 1755 Steeles Avenue West, Toronto, Ontario, Canada, M2R 3T4.

Dosage: Do not inoculate in the gluteal area.

Pre-exposure Immunization: Three injections each of 1 mL each of Rabies Vaccine Inactivated (Diploid Cell Origin), Dried should be administered **i.m.** into the deltoid muscle on days 0, 7 and 21.

Reinforcement Immunization: The booster dose of 1 mL of vaccine should be administered **i.m.** into the deltoid muscle.

Postexposure Immunization: Five dose of 1 mL of HDCV should be given by **i.m.** injection into the deltoid muscle in adults or into the anterolateral zone of the thigh in small children; the first dose (on day 0) as soon as possible after exposure, and additional doses on each of days 3, 7, 14 and 28 after the first dose. A single dose of RIG should also be given on day 0 as described below.

Rabies Immune Globulin: A dose of 20 IU/kg of RIG should be administered on one occasion, as soon as possible after exposure. Up to one half the dose should be infiltrated around the wound if practical; the remainder should be given i.m. using a separate syringe and needle. Because of interference with active antibody production, **the recommended dose should not be exceeded.**

Since vaccine-induced antibody begins to appear within 1 week, there is no value in administering RIG more than 8 days after initiating a vaccine course.

Under no circumstances should vaccine be administered in the same syringe or at the same site as RIG.

Parenteral biological products should be inspected visually for extraneous particulate matter and/or discoloration before administration. If these conditions exist, the product should not be administered.

Shake the vial to distribute uniformly the suspension before withdrawing each dose. When administering a dose from a rubber-stoppered vial, do not remove either the rubber stopper or the metal seal holding it in place. Aseptic technique must be used for withdrawal of each dose.

Before injection, the skin over the site to be injected should be cleansed with a suitable germicide.

Administer the vaccine **i.m.** The preferred site is into the anterolateral aspect of the mid-thigh (vastus lateralis muscle) or into the deltoid muscle. After insertion of the needle, aspirate to ensure that the needle has not entered a blood vessel.

Do not inject i.v.

Each person who is immunized should be given a permanent personal immunization record. In addition, it is essential that the physician or nurse record the immunization history in the permanent medical record of each patient. This permanent office record should contain the name of the vaccine, date given, dose, manufacturer and lot number.

Supplied: Rabies Vaccine Inactivated (Diploid Cell Origin), Dried is a sterile diploid cell culture rabies virus vaccine for human use. It is a purified and concentrated suspension of "fixed" rabies virus (CL-77) adapted to and prepared in monolayers of MRC-5 human diploid cells grown in a defined medium. The viral harvest is inactivated with β-propiolactone. The inactivated material is clarified by membrane filtration and further processed by continuous gradient zonal centrifugation and dialysis. In addition to the presence of viral protein, human albumin is added to a concentration of 2% as a stabilizer. Traces of bovine serum, polymyxin, neomycin and proteins originating from the cell substrate may also be present.

The potency of the vaccine is equal to or greater than 2.5 IU of rabies antigen per dose as established by testing in parallel with the Standard Rabies Vaccine in the NIH mouse potency test (FDA).

The vaccine is freeze-dried in single dose vials for reconstitution to 1 mL with the sterile diluent provided. The sterile diluent contains thimerosal 0.01% as a preservative. The reconstituted vaccine is orange to red in color due to phenol red indicator.

Packages of 1 single dose vial of vaccine and 1 vial of sterile diluent for reconstitution of a single dose.

The freeze-dried vaccine and sterile diluent should be stored and transported between 2 and 8°C. **Do not freeze. The vaccine should be used immediately after reconstitution.** Product which has been exposed to freezing should not be used. Do not use vaccine beyond the expiry date.

Reviewed 1998

RAFTON® Liquid
RAFTON® Tablets

Ferring

Alginic Acid Compound

Gastroesophageal Reflux Therapy

Pharmacology: Rafton forms a protective neutralizing foam barrier in the stomach that effectively stops the upward flow of stomach acids into the esophagus providing fast relief of heartburn.

Indications: For the effective relief of day or night-time heartburn or for discomfort of the esophagus due to upward flow of stomach acids.

Precautions: Each 5 mL of liquid contains approximately 30 mg of sodium and each tablet contains approximately 22 mg of sodium which should be noted for patients on severely restricted diets.

The cations of magnesium and aluminum interfere with the absorption of tetracycline, iron and phosphate. In addition, oral magnesium may accumulate in the plasma of patients with impaired renal function. Patients suffering from renal failure or those taking any form of tetracycline should not use Rafton.

Adverse Effects: Nausea, vomiting, eructation, flatulence.

Overdose: Symptoms and Treatment: Should overdose occur, gastric distention may result and it is best treated conservatively.

Dosage: Adults: 10 to 20 mL of liquid or 2 to 4 tablets 1 to 4 times daily chewed thoroughly, after meals and upon retiring. Administration may be followed by a half glass of water. Recommended dose, not more than 16 tablets or 80 mL/day. Do not swallow tablets whole.

Supplied: Liquid: Each 5 mL of tan-colored, fruit-flavored suspension contains: sodium alginate 250 mg and aluminum hydroxide 100 mg. Nonmedicinal ingredients: calcium carbonate precipitated, cetylpyridinium chloride, guarana flavor, purified water, silicon dioxide, sodium (30 mg), sodium bicarbonate, sodium cyclamate (sweetener), methylparaben, propylparaben, and xanthan gum. Alcohol-, gluten-, lactose, sucrose- and tartrazine-free. Bottles of 340 mL.

Tablets: Each round, fruit-flavored tablet, imprinted with "Rafton" on both sides, contains: alginic acid 200 mg and aluminum hydroxide 80 mg. Nonmedicinal ingredients: calcium stearate, magnesium trisilicate, guarana flavor, sodium (22 mg), sodium bicarbonate, sucrose (1.2 g), and sucrose pregranulated. Gluten-, lactose-, starch- and tartrazine-free. Bottles of 40 and 100.

RAGWEED TYROSINE ADSORBATE, MODIFIED

Bencard

see POLLINEX-R

RAMIPRIL 🄿

General Monograph, CPhA

see ACE INHIBITORS

R & C™ Shampoo/Conditioner

R & C

Pyrethrins—Piperonyl Butoxide

Pediculicide—Ovicide

Indications: For the treatment of infestations with head lice (P. capitis), body lice (P. corporis), crab lice (P. pubis) and their nits.

Contraindications: Should not be used by persons allergic to chrysanthemum, pyrethrin or synthetic pyrethroids.

Precautions: For external use only. Harmful if swallowed. It should not be inhaled. During shampooing, contact should be avoided with eyelashes, eyes, nose and mouth and other mucous areas. If contact does take place, flush with water.

A physician should be consulted if accidental ingestion should occur. If physician not available drink 1 or 2 glasses of water and induce vomiting. No attempt should be made to induce vomiting with an unconscious person. The patient should be exposed to air.

In case of infection or skin irritation, discontinue use and consult a physician. Consult a physician if an infestation of lice to eyebrows or eyelashes occurs. Destroy container when empty.

Dosage: To the dry hair, apply sufficient shampoo to thoroughly soak the hair and the skin of the infested and adjacent hairy areas. Allow the shampoo/conditioner to remain on the area for 10 minutes. Add small quantities of water, working the shampoo/conditioner into the hair and skin until a lather forms. Rinse thoroughly. The dead lice and their nits should be removed with the inpacked nit comb. Repeat in 7 to 10 days if necessary. Do not exceed 2 consecutive applications within 24 hours.

Lice infestations are spread by contact. Each family member should be examined carefully. If infested, they should be treated immediately to prevent the spread of the infestation or cause a reinfestation with previously treated family members. All contaminated clothing and other articles such as combs, brushes, hats, etc. should be dry cleaned or washed in very hot water. Upholstery, carpets and other areas where lice may linger and cause a reinfestation should be sprayed with R & C II Spray Insecticide.

Supplied: Each plastic bottle contains: pyrethrins 0.33%; piperonyl butoxide technical 3.0% (equivalent to 2.4% active piperonyl butoxide and 0.6% related compounds). Nonmedicinal ingredients: fragrance, isocetyl alcohol, isopropanol, lavramine oxide, laureth-4, laureth-23, petroleum hydrocarbon, triethanolamine lauryl sulfate, water. Plastic bottles of 50 and 200 mL, each with a nit comb.

R & C™ II Spray

R & C

Pyrethrins—Piperonyl Butoxide

Spray Insecticide

Indications: For use on lice and lice eggs on garments, bedding, mattresses and furniture.

Warnings: Not for use on humans or animals.

Precautions: Contents under pressure. Do not puncture or incinerate can. Do not use near heat or store at temperatures above 50°C. Avoid spraying in eyes. May be absorbed through skin. Avoid breathing spray mist. May cause skin irritation. Avoid contact with skin. Do not contaminate feed and foodstuffs. Do not wear treated garments or use bedding until thoroughly cleaned and infestation is eliminated. Intentional misuse by deliberately concentrating and inhaling the contents can be harmful or fatal. Keep out of reach of children.

Call a physician in case of accident. If in eyes, flush with plenty of clear water. If on skin, wash thoroughly with soap and water.

Dosage: Shake well before and occasionally during use. Spray on an inconspicuous area to test for possible staining or discoloration. Inspect after drying, then proceed to spray entire area to be treated. Hold container upright with nozzle away from you. Depress valve and spray from a distance of 20 to 25 cm. Spray each 900 cm² for about 3 seconds. For garments and bedding: spray those that cannot be either laundered or dry cleaned immediately. For mattresses and furniture: spray, then air until completely dry at least 4 hours before re-use. Vacate room after treatment and ventilate before reoccupying. Repeat treatment if re-infestation occurs.

Supplied: Each 142 g pressurized spray can contains: pyrethrins 0.3% and piperonyl butoxide 1.5% with ozone friendly propellant.

Let your network of health care professionals know that there is information on chronic medication management before surgery in the CLIN-INFO SECTION.

RAXAR™ ℞

Glaxo Wellcome

Grepafloxacin HCl

Antibacterial

Pharmacology: Grepafloxacin is a broad-spectrum fluoroquinolone antibiotic. It has in vitro activity against a wide range of gram-positive and gram-negative aerobic microorganisms, as well as some atypical microorganisms. Grepafloxacin exerts its antibacterial activity by inhibiting bacterial topoisomerase II (DNA gyrase) and topoisomerase IV, essential enzymes for duplication, transcription, and repair of bacterial DNA. Grepafloxacin is bactericidal at concentrations equal to or slightly greater than minimum inhibitory concentrations (MICs). Fluoroquinolones differ in chemical structure and mode of action from other classes of antimicrobial agents such as beta-lactam antibiotics, aminoglycosides, and macrolides. Beta-lactamase production and alterations in penicillin binding proteins have no effect on grepafloxacin activity. Therefore, microorganisms resistant to the latter classes of antimicrobial agents may be susceptible to fluoroquinolones including grepafloxacin. Conversely, microorganisms resistant to quinolones, including grepafloxacin may be susceptible to these other classes of antimicrobial agents.

Although cross-resistance has been observed between grepafloxacin and some other fluoroquinolones, some microorganisms resistant to other fluoroquinolones may be susceptible to grepafloxacin. Conversely some microorganisms resistant to grepafloxacin may be susceptible to some other fluoroquinolones.

Grepafloxacin has been shown to be active against most strains of H. influenzae (including beta-lactamase-producing strains), M. catarrhalis (including beta-lactamase-producing strains), and N. gonorrhoeae (including strains resistant to penicillin or tetracycline), both in vitro and in specific clinical infections as described in the Indications section.

Pharmacokinetics: Absorption: Grepafloxacin is rapidly and extensively absorbed following oral administration of grepafloxacin tablets. The absolute bioavailability is approximately 70%.

Multiple oral doses of 400 and 600 mg once a day, provided steady-state concentrations of grepafloxacin within 7 days.

There was no difference between the fasting and postprandial state and milk had no effect on the pharmacokinetic properties of grepafloxacin tablets. Neutralization of gastric acidity by histamine type-2 receptor antagonists did not affect the absorption or other pharmacokinetic properties of grepafloxacin tablets.

Distribution: Grepafloxacin distributes widely into extravascular spaces. Binding of grepafloxacin to human plasma proteins is low (approximately 50%). Following oral administration, grepafloxacin is rapidly and extensively distributed into tissues and body fluids, including the respiratory tract and sputum as well as male and female genital tract tissues. High intracellular concentrations are achieved significantly above the plasma concentrations.

Metabolism and Excretion: The plasma elimination half-life of grepafloxacin at steady-state was approximately 12 hours. Grepafloxacin is eliminated predominantly through hepatic metabolism and biliary excretion. Renal excretion of unchanged drug is a lesser route of elimination (less than 10% of an oral dose is excreted as unchanged grepafloxacin in urine).

The nonconjugated metabolites have little antimicrobial activity compared with the parent drug. The conjugated metabolites have no antimicrobial activity.

The metabolism and excretion of grepafloxacin is significantly reduced in patients with hepatic disease (see Contraindications, Precautions and Dosage).

Renal clearance of grepafloxacin was 0.458±0.04 mL/min/kg in adults with normal renal function. Varying degrees of renal function did not substantially affect the pharmacokinetic properties of grepafloxacin.

Table I shows the typical pharmacokinetic parameters of grepafloxacin in healthy male subjects.

Indications: For treatment of adults 18 years of age and older with infections caused by susceptible strains of the designated microorganisms in the infections listed as follows: acute bacterial exacerbations of chronic bronchitis caused by H. influenzae, S. pneumoniae, or M. catarrhalis (see Dosage); community-acquired pneumonia caused by H. influenzae, S. pneumoniae, M. catarrhalis, M. pneumoniae, or L. pneumophila; uncomplicated gonorrhea (urethral in males and endocervical and rectal in females) caused by N. gonorrhoeae (see Warnings); nongonococcal cervicitis and urethritis caused by C. trachomatis.

Appropriate culture and susceptibility testing should be performed to determine susceptibility of the causative microorganism(s) to grepafloxacin. Therapy may be started while awaiting the results of this testing. Antimicrobial therapy should be appropriately adjusted according to the results of such testing.

Contraindications: Patients with known or suspected hypersensitivity to grepafloxacin, other quinolone antibiotics or any other components of grepafloxacin tablets. Also contraindicated in patients with hepatic disease (see Pharmacology, Precautions and Dosage). Because prolongation of the QT interval has been observed in healthy volunteers receiving grepafloxacin, it is contraindicated in patients with existing QT prolongation. Grepafloxacin is also contraindicated in patients being treated concomitantly with medications known to produce an increase in the QT interval and/or torsades de pointes (e.g., class I antiarrhythmic agents, [e.g., disopyramide, flecainide, quinidine, procainamide], class III antiarrhythmic agents [e.g., amiodarone, sotalol], as well as erythromycin, terfenadine, astemizole, cisapride, pentamidine, tricyclic antidepressants, some antipsychotics including phenothiazines) unless appropriate cardiac monitoring can be assured (e.g., in hospitalized patients).

Warnings: The safety and efficacy of grepafloxacin in patients under 18 years of age, pregnant women, or lactating women have not been established (see Precautions, Children, Pregnancy and Lactation). Histopathological examination of the weight-bearing joints of juvenile dogs revealed permanent lesions of the cartilage. Related quinolone-class drugs also produce lesions of cartilage of weight-bearing joints and other signs of arthropathy in immature animals of various species.

Achilles and other tendon ruptures that required surgical repair or resulted in prolonged disability have been reported in patients receiving quinolone antibiotics. Grepafloxacin should be discontinued if the patient experiences pain, inflammation, or rupture of a tendon.

Table I—Raxar

Typical Pharmacokinetic Parameters of Grepafloxacin in Healthy Male Subjects*

Oral Bioavailability	F	72%
Time to maximum concentration	t_{max}	2 h
Volume of distribution	Vd/F	5L/kg
Plasma protein binding		48-52%
Oral clearance	Cl/F	5.2 mL/min/kg
Renal clearance	Clr	0.5 mL/min/kg
% Dose excreted in urine	fe%	10%
Elimination half-life (mean)	$t_{1/2}$	12h (10.14-15.7)
Peak concentration after single dose 400 mg	C_{max}	0.93 µg/mL
Peak concentration after single dose 600 mg	C_{max}	1.41 µg/mL
Area under time concentration curve after single dose 400 mg	AUC_∞	11.35 µg·h/mL
Area under time concentration curve after single dose 600 mg	AUC_∞	19.73 µg·h/mL
Peak concentration at steady-state after multiple dose 400 mg	C_{max}	1.35 µg/mL
Peak concentration at steady-state after multiple dose 600 mg	C_{max}	2.30 µg/mL
Area under time concentration curve over a dosing interval at steady-state after multiple dose 400 mg	AUC_{0-24}	14.4 µg·h/mL
Area under time concentration curve over a dosing interval at steady-state after multiple dose 600 mg	AUC_{0-24}	28.5 µg·h/mL

*Plasma levels in females were higher than in male subjects, with C_{max} and AUC values in female subjects about 39 to 42% and 33 to 50% higher than in male subjects, respectively.

Raxar (cont'd)

The efficacy of grepafloxacin for treatment of syphilis is not known. Antimicrobial agents used in high doses for short periods of time to treat gonorrhea may mask or delay the symptoms of incubating syphilis. All patients with gonorrhea should have a serologic test for syphilis at the time of diagnosis. Patients treated with grepafloxacin should have a follow-up serologic test for syphilis 3 months after treatment for gonorrhea.

In healthy male and female volunteers who received grepafloxacin, prolongation of the QTc interval was observed. Because of a potential risk of cardiac arrhythmias, including torsades de pointes, patients should not receive grepafloxacin concomitantly with medications known to prolong the QT interval, e.g., class I antiarrhythmic agents, (e.g., disopyramide, flecainide, quinidine, procainamide), class III antiarrhythmic agents (e.g., amiodarone, sotalol), as well as erythromycin, terfenadine, astemizole, cisapride, pentamidine, tricyclic antidepressants, some antipsychotics including phenothiazines when appropriate cardiac monitoring cannot be assured, e.g., during outpatient therapy (see Contraindications). Grepafloxacin is not recommended for use in patients with ongoing proarrhythmic conditions (e.g., electrolyte imbalances, such as hypokalemia and hypomagnesemia, significant bradycardia, congestive heart failure, myocardial ischemia, and atrial enlargement).

Serious and occasionally fatal hypersensitivity (anaphylactoid or anaphylactic) reactions have been reported in patients receiving therapy with quinolones, often following the first dose. Some reactions have been accompanied by cardiovascular collapse, hypotension, shock, seizure, loss of consciousness, tingling, angioedema, (including tongue, laryngeal, throat or facial edema/swelling, etc.), airway obstruction (including bronchospasm, shortness of breath, and acute respiratory distress), dyspnea, urticaria/hives, itching, and other serious skin reactions. Only a few of these patients had a history of prior hypersensitivity reactions. Grepafloxacin should be discontinued if an allergic reaction or any other sign of hypersensitivity appears. Serious acute hypersensitivity reactions require immediate treatment.

Serious and sometimes fatal events of uncertain etiology have been reported in patients receiving therapy with quinolones. Serious events are extremely rare and generally occur following administration of multiple doses. Clinical manifestations of serious adverse events may include one or more of the following: fever, rash or severe dermatologic reactions (e.g., toxic epidermal necrolysis, Stevens-Johnson syndrome, etc.); vasculitis, arthralgia, myalgia, serum sickness; allergic pneumonitis; interstitial nephritis, acute renal insufficiency/failure; hepatitis, jaundice, acute hepatic necrosis/failure; tendon pain, inflammation, or rupture; anemia (including hemolytic and aplastic anemia), thrombocytopenia, including thrombotic thrombocytopenic purpura, leukopenia, agranulocytosis, pancytopenia, and/or other hematologic abnormalities. Grepafloxacin should be discontinued immediately at the first appearance of any such reaction and appropriate intervention should be instituted (see Adverse Effects).

Convulsions, increased intracranial pressure, and toxic psychosis have been reported in patients receiving quinolones. Quinolones may also cause CNS stimulation which may lead to tremors, restlessness, lightheadedness, confusion, or hallucinations. If these reactions occur in patients receiving grepafloxacin, the drug should be discontinued and appropriate treatment measures instituted. As with other quinolones, grepafloxacin should be used with caution in patients with known or suspected CNS disorders, such as severe cerebral arteriosclerosis, epilepsy, and other factors that predispose to seizures (see Adverse Effects).

Pseudomembranous colitis has been reported with nearly all antibacterial agents, including quinolones, and may range in severity from mild to life-threatening. Therefore, it is important to consider this diagnosis in patients who present with diarrhea subsequent to the administration of antibacterial agents. Treatment with broad-spectrum antibiotics alters the normal flora of the colon and may permit overgrowth of clostridia. Studies indicate that a toxin produced by C. difficile is a primary cause of "antibiotic-associated colitis". After the diagnosis of pseudomembranous colitis has been established, appropriate therapeutic measures should be initiated.

Precautions: General: Phototoxicity reactions have been observed in patients who were exposed to direct sunlight while receiving some quinolones, including grepafloxacin. Excessive sunlight should be avoided. Therapy should be discontinued if phototoxicity occurs.

Geriatrics: Grepafloxacin tablets were administered to 343 elderly adults (age >65 years old) in clinical trials. There was no apparent difference in the frequency, type, or severity of adverse reactions in elderly adults compared with other adults.

The pharmacokinetic properties of grepafloxacin in younger adults and elderly adults did not differ significantly.

Children: The safety and effectiveness of grepafloxacin in children and adolescents below the age of 18 years has not been established.

Pregnancy: Grepafloxacin should be used during pregnancy only if the potential benefit justifies the potential risk to the fetus (see Warnings). Adequate and well-controlled studies have not been conducted in pregnant women. Reproductive studies performed in rats and rabbits indicate that placental transfer of grepafloxacin occurs. Studies in these species did not show any evidence of teratogenicity, impairment of fertility or impairment of peri- or postnatal development of their offspring following administration of grepafloxacin.

Lactation: Limited evidence indicates that grepafloxacin is excreted in human milk. Grepafloxacin was detected in breast milk of one patient who was studied on the ninth day of treatment at 4 to 5 hours after oral administration of 400 mg of grepafloxacin.

It is known that other quinolones are secreted in human milk. Because of the potential for serious adverse experiences from grepafloxacin in nursing infants, a decision should be made to discontinue nursing or discontinue administration of the drug, taking into account the importance of the drug to the mother (see Warnings).

Patients with Hepatic Disease: Grepafloxacin is contraindicated in patients with hepatic disease (see Dosage).

Two studies were performed to assess the effect of hepatic failure on grepafloxacin pharmacokinetics. In both studies, subjects were given a single 400 mg dose of grepafloxacin. Subjects with normal hepatic function, with mild (Child-Pugh class A) hepatic failure, or moderate hepatic failure (Child-Pugh class B) were evaluated. In one study, oral clearance was reduced by approximately 50% in patients with mild hepatic failure (n=5) relative to subjects with normal hepatic function (n=6). In the second study, oral clearance as reduced by approximately 15% in subjects with mild hepatic failure (n=5) relative to subjects with normal hepatic function (n=8). Due to the different results for the 2 studies, it is not possible to determine an appropriate dose adjustment for subjects with mild hepatic failure. In both studies, oral clearance was decreased by >50% in subjects with moderate hepatic failure (n=9, n=3) compared to subjects with normal hepatic function (n=6, n=8).

Drug Interactions: Antacids, Sucralfate, Metal Cations, Multivitamins: Quinolones form chelates with alkaline earth and transition metal cations. Administration of quinolones with antacids containing aluminum, magnesium, or calcium, with sucralfate, with metal cations such as iron, or with multivitamins containing zinc may substantially interfere with the absorption of quinolones, resulting in systemic concentrations considerably lower than desired. These agents should not be taken within 4 hours before or after grepafloxacin administration.

Theophylline: Grepafloxacin is a competitive inhibitor of the metabolism of theophylline. Serum theophylline concentrations increase when grepafloxacin is initiated in a patient maintained on theophylline. In a pharmacokinetic study in 12 adults receiving concomitant theophylline during a 10-day course of grepafloxacin, oral clearance of theophylline decreased from 0.78±0.25 (without grepafloxacin: mean±S.D.) to 0.40±0.08 mL/min/kg (with grepafloxacin), steady-state peak theophylline concentration increased from 8.30±1.54 μg/mL to 15.12±3.69 μg/mL, and AUC over a 12-hour interval increased from 85.9±16.6 to 165.9±36.9 μg·h/mL. In these normal volunteers, concomitant administration of grepafloxacin and theophylline increased the frequency of theophylline-related adverse events.

When initiating a multi-day course of grepafloxacin in a patient maintained on theophylline, the theophylline maintenance dose should be halved for the period of concurrent use of grepafloxacin and monitoring of serum theophylline concentrations should be initiated as a guide to further dosage adjustments.

Caffeine: Grepafloxacin, like other quinolones, may inhibit the metabolism of caffeine. In some patients, this may lead to reduced clearance of caffeine, prolongation of its plasma half-life, and enhanced effects of caffeine.

Drugs Metabolized by Cytochrome P450 Enzymes: Grepafloxacin is metabolized primarily by the cytochrome P450 enzymes, particularly the isoenzyme CYP1A2 and to a lesser extent the isoenzyme CYP3A4. Like most quinolone drugs, grepafloxacin may competitively inhibit cytochrome P450 enzyme activity. This may result in impaired metabolism of certain other drugs that are also metabolized by this system such as cimetidine, cyclosporine, terfenadine, astemizole, cisapride, midazolam and triazolam.

Probenecid: In clinical studies, probenecid did not significantly alter the pharmacokinetic properties of a single 200 mg oral dose of grepafloxacin.

Warfarin: Grepafloxacin did not alter the anticoagulant effect of warfarin in a study of 16 adults receiving grepafloxacin 600 mg daily. In this same study, warfarin did not alter the pharmacokinetic properties of grepafloxacin. However, because some quinolones have been reported to enhance the effects of warfarin or its derivatives, prothrombin time or other suitable anticoagulation test should be monitored closely if a quinolone antimicrobial is administered with warfarin or its derivatives.

Nonsteroidal Anti-inflammatory Drugs (NSAIDs): Drug interactions resulting in seizures have been reported between some quinolones and NSAIDs. In animal studies grepafloxacin did not induce seizures when administered with a variety of NSAIDs.

Antidiabetic Agents: Disturbances of blood glucose, including hyperglycemia and hypoglycemia, have been reported in patients treated concomitantly with quinolones and an antidiabetic agent. Therefore, careful monitoring of blood glucose is recommended when these agents are coadministered.

Adverse Effects: Adverse reactions were assessed in clinical trials involving approximately 2 500 patients receiving single-dose or multiple-dose regimens of grepafloxacin.

Multiple-dose Regimens: Most of the adverse reactions reported in clinical trials were transient in nature, mild to moderate in severity, and required no treatment. Twenty of 1 069 patients (1.9%) receiving grepafloxacin 400 mg daily and 94 of 1 406 patients (6.7%) receiving grepafloxacin 600 mg daily discontinued grepafloxacin due to an adverse reaction.

Table II lists drug-related adverse reactions that occurred with frequencies of 1% or greater in patients treated with grepafloxacin in multiple-dose clinical trials.

Table II—Raxar

Drug-related Adverse Reactions in Grepafloxacin-treated Patients on Multiple-dose Regimens in Clinical Trials

Adverse Reaction	400 mg daily (n=1 069) (%)	600 mg daily (n=1 406) (%)
Nausea	11.1	14.4
Unpleasant taste	9.0	16.2
Headache	4.6	4.2
Dizziness	4.3	4.9
Diarrhea	3.5	4.3
Vaginitis	3.3	1.1
Abdominal pain	2.2	1.9
Vomiting	1.7	6.1
Pruritus	1.5	1.2
Dyspepsia	1.5	2.3
Leukorrhea	1.4	0.0
Asthenia	1.4	1.9
Infection	1.3	0.3
Insomnia	1.3	2.4
Rash	1.1	1.8
Anorexia	0.8	1.6
Somnolence	0.9	1.5
Photosensitivity reaction	0.7	1.9
Constipation	0.7	1.6
Nervousness	0.6	1.7

Additional drug-related events, occurring in multiple-dose clinical trials at a rate of less than 1%, were: Body as a Whole: allergic reaction, back pain, body odor, chest pain, chills, facial edema, pain, fever, malaise, neck rigidity, pelvic pain.

Cardiovascular: arrhythmia, hypotension, palpitations, peripheral vascular disorder, postural hypotension, syncope, tachycardia, vasodilation.

Digestive: abnormal liver function tests, abnormal stools, cheilitis, dysphagia, eructation, flatulence, gastritis, gastrointestinal disorder, dry mouth, gingivitis, glossitis, increased appetite, melena, mouth ulceration, oral moniliasis, rectal disorder, rectal hemorrhage, stomatitis, tenesmus, thirst, tongue discoloration, tongue disorder, tongue edema.

Hemic and Lymphatic: anemia, eosinophilia, hypochromic anemia, leukocytosis, leukopenia, lymphadenopathy, lymphocytosis, lymphoma-like reaction, prothrombin decreased, prothrombin increased, reticuloendothelial hyperplasia, thrombocytopenia, thromboplastin increased.

Metabolic and Nutritional: dehydration, edema, electrolyte abnormality, gout, hyperglycemia, hyperkalemia, hyperlipidemia, hypernatremia, hyperuricemia, hypoglycemia, increased alkaline phosphatase, increased BUN, increased creatinine, increased gamma glutamyl transpeptidase, increased serum phosphorus, increased AST, increased ALT, peripheral edema, weight loss.
Musculoskeletal: arthralgia, myalgia.
CNS: abnormal dreams, abnormal gait, agitation, anxiety, confusion, depression, emotional lability, hallucinations, hyperkinesia, hypesthesia, hypokinesia, paresthesia, speech disorder, stupor, thinking abnormal, tremor, vertigo.
Respiratory: asthma, atelectasis, bronchitis, dyspnea, epistaxis, hemoptysis, increased cough, laryngismus, pharyngitis, pleural effusion, rhinitis, sputum increased.
Skin and Appendages: acne, alopecia, dry skin, epidermal necrolysis, exfoliative dermatitis, fungal dermatitis, herpes simplex, maculopapular rash, skin disorder, sweating, urticaria, vesiculobullous rash.
Special Senses: amblyopia, conjunctivitis, deafness, dry eyes, ear disorder, eye pain, lacrimation disorder, parosmia, photophobia, taste loss, tinnitus.
Urogenital: albuminuria, balanitis, dysuria, hematuria, impotence, polyuria, urethral pain, uricaciduria, urinary frequency, urinary tract disorder, urination impaired, urine abnormality, vulvovaginal disorder.
Single-dose Regimens: In clinical trials, patients were treated for uncomplicated gonorrhea using a single dose of grepafloxacin 400 mg. Table III lists the drug-related adverse reactions which occurred with frequencies of 1% or greater in patients treated with grepafloxacin in single dose clinical trials.

Table III—Raxar

Drug-related Adverse Reactions in Grepafloxacin-treated Patients on a Single-dose Regimen in Clinical Trials

Adverse Reaction	400 mg daily (n=487) (%)
Vaginitis	5.0
Nausea	3.3
Dizziness	2.1
Vomiting	2.1
Headache	1.8
Leukorrhea	1.7
Abdominal pain	1.2
Diarrhea	1.2
Pruritus	1.2
Unpleasant taste	1.2

Additional drug-related events, occurring in single-dose clinical trials at a rate of less than 1%, were: Body as a Whole: asthenia, chest pain, chills, flu-like syndrome, infection, malaise.
Cardiovascular: syncope, vasodilation.
Digestive: anorexia, constipation, increased appetite, tenesmus.
Hemic and Lymphatic: lymphadenopathy.
CNS: hyperkinesia, insomnia, nervousness, somnolence.
Respiratory: rhinitis.
Skin and Appendages: acne, rash, sweating.
Urogenital: balanitis.

Overdose: Symptoms and Treatment: Information on overdosage with grepafloxacin is limited. In the event of acute overdosage, the stomach should be emptied by inducing vomiting or by gastric lavage. The patient should be carefully observed and given supportive treatment. As with other quinolones, adequate hydration and electrolyte balance must be maintained. Due to the possibility of prolongation of the QT interval and complications including arrhythmias, ECG monitoring for at least 24 hours after overdosage with grepafloxacin is recommended. It is not known if grepafloxacin can be efficiently removed by hemodialysis or peritoneal dialysis.

Dosage: Grepafloxacin may be taken with or without meals. Table IV summarizes the recommended daily dosages.

Clinical trials of grepafloxacin in the treatment of acute exacerbations of chronic bronchitis suggest that grepafloxacin 600 mg once daily may be more effective against S. pneumoniae than grepafloxacin 400 mg once daily.

As with other broad-spectrum antimicrobial agents, prolonged use of grepafloxacin may result in overgrowth of nonsusceptible organisms. Repeated evaluation of the patient's condition and microbial susceptibility testing is essential. If superinfection occurs during therapy, appropriate measures should be taken.
Patients with Renal Failure: Grepafloxacin was well tolerated in a study of a limited number of patients with impaired renal function. Since renal excretion is a lesser route of elimination of grepafloxacin, dosage adjustment is not required in patients with impaired renal function.
Patients with Hepatic Disease: Metabolism and excretion of grepafloxacin are reduced in patients with hepatic disease.

Grepafloxacin is contraindicated in patients with hepatic disease (see Contraindications and Pharmacology).

Information for the Patient: See Blue Section—Information for the Patient "Raxar".

Supplied: Each white to pale yellow, film-coated, round, biconvex, beveled edged tablet, imprinted with "GX CK3" on one side, contains: grepafloxacin HCl 200 mg. Nonmedicinal ingredients: grey printing ink, hydroxypropyl cellulose, hydroxypropyl methylcellulose, low-substituted hydroxypropyl cellulose, magnesium stearate, microcrystalline cellulose, talc and titanium dioxide. Plastic bottles of 60. Store at controlled room temperature between 15 to 30°C protected from light. Replace cap securely after each opening.

(Shown in Product Recognition Section)

New Product 1998

Table IV—Raxar

Recommended Daily Dosages

Infection	Dose	Frequency	Duration (days)
Acute bacterial exacerbations of chronic bronchitis	400 or 600 mg	once daily	7-10
Community-acquired pneumonia	600 mg	once daily	10
Nongonococcal urethritis or cervicitis	400 mg	once daily	7
Uncomplicated gonorrhea	400 mg	single dose	1

REACTINE™

Pfizer Consumer

Cetirizine HCl

Histamine H_1-Receptor Antagonist

Pharmacology: Cetirizine, a human metabolite of hydroxyzine, is a histamine H_1 receptor antagonist anti-allergic compound; its principal effects are mediated via selective inhibition of peripheral H_1 receptors. Cetirizine is distinguished from other histamine H_1 receptor antagonists by the presence of a carboxylic acid function. This difference may be partly responsible for the selectivity of cetirizine seen in pharmacologic models and its distinctive pharmacokinetic properties in humans.

The antihistaminic activity of cetirizine has been well documented in a variety of animal and human models. In vivo animal models have shown negligible anticholinergic or antiserotonergic activity. In vitro receptor binding studies have detected no measurable affinity for other than H_1 receptors. Autoradiographic studies have shown negligible penetration into the brain. Systemically administered cetirizine does not significantly occupy cerebral H_1 receptors.

Cetirizine does not exacerbate asthma and is effective in a variety of histamine mediated disorders. Oral doses of 5 to 20 mg in humans strongly inhibit the skin wheal and flare response caused by the intradermal injection of histamine. The onset of activity occurs within 20 (50% of subjects) to 60 (95% of subjects) minutes and persists for at least 24 hours following a single dose. The effects of intradermal injection of various other mediators or histamine releasers as well as components of the allergic inflammatory response to cutaneous antigen challenge are also inhibited.

Randomized, multi-centre, double-blind, placebo-controlled clinical trials have demonstrated the effectiveness of cetirizine in relieving the symptoms associated with seasonal allergic rhinitis, perennial allergic rhinitis and chronic idiopathic urticaria. The clinical trials have shown only weak anticholinergic effects. There is no evidence that tolerance to the antihistaminic effects of cetirizine occurs or that cetirizine has any abuse potential or dependency liability.

Objective measurements to evaluate the effects of cetirizine on the CNS at doses up to 20 mg showed no significant effects on daytime drowsiness, reaction times, mental alertness, objective CNS depression and various other tests of cognitive function as compared to placebo.

Specific ECG studies in healthy volunteers at doses up to 60 mg/day (3 times the maximum clinically studied dose) for 1 week did not prolong QT_c intervals nor was there any evidence of QT_c prolongation in clinical trials which included ECG evaluations.

Cetirizine given at the maximum clinically studied dose of 20 mg daily did not prolong the QT_c when given in combination with either ketoconazole 400 mg daily or erythromycin 50 mg q8h for 10 days. Moreover, cetirizine did not significantly alter the pharmacokinetics of either ketoconazole or erythromycin nor were the pharmacokinetics of cetirizine altered by either ketoconazole or erythromycin.

Pharmacokinetics: Cetirizine is rapidly absorbed after oral administration. Peak plasma levels after a 10 mg dose are approximately 300 ng/mL and occur at about 1 hour. Co-administration of cetirizine with food does not affect bioavailability as measured by AUC but absorption is delayed by about 1 hour, with 23% lower C_{max}. Plasma protein binding is 93% in the concentration range observed in clinical studies. The plasma elimination half-life is approximately 8 to 9 hours and does not change with multiple dosing. Pharmacokinetics are dose independent and plasma levels are proportional to the dose administered over the clinically studied range of 5 to 20 mg.

Cetirizine is less extensively metabolized than other antihistamines and approximately 60% of an administered dose is excreted unchanged in 24 hours. The high bioavailability associated with generally low inter-subject variation in blood levels is attributable primarily to low first-pass metabolism. Only 1 metabolite has been identified in humans—the product of oxidative dealkylation of the terminal carboxymethyl group. The antihistaminic activity of this metabolite is negligible.

Consequently, based on (1) its relatively low level of metabolic elimination, (2) no effect on corrected QT intervals at plasma concentrations 3 times the maximal therapeutic levels and (3) no apparent interactions with ketoconazole or erythromycin, cetirizine is unlikely to have clinically significant interactions with other macrolides such as clarithromycin or other imidazole antifungals such as itraconazole in patients with normal renal and hepatic function. Although no data with these other drugs are available at the present time, there is no epidemiological evidence (the safety database comprised 6 490 patients evaluated in U.S. and Canadian studies) of interactions between macrolide antibiotics and/or imidazole antifungals taken orally, and cetirizine/hydroxyzine. The epidemiologic data do not suggest an increase of adverse events, cardiac or non-cardiac, in patients treated with cetirizine and concomitant macrolide or imidazole antifungal medication.

In patients with mild to moderate hepatic and renal impairment, total body clearance of cetirizine is reduced and AUC and half-life increased by about 2 to 3 fold. Clearance is reduced in proportion to the decline in creatinine clearance. Plasma levels are unaffected by hemodialysis. The plasma elimination half-life in dialysis patients is approximately 20 hours and the plasma AUC is increased by about 3-fold.

The AUC and C_{max} in pediatric subjects are higher in proportion to their lower body weight, and half-life is reduced to 5.6 hours.

Indications: The relief of symptoms associated with seasonal allergic rhinitis, perennial allergic rhinitis and chronic idiopathic urticaria; i.e., sneezing, rhinorrhea, post nasal discharge, tearing and redness of the eyes, pruritus and hives.

Contraindications: Those patients with a known hypersensitivity to it or to its parent compound, hydroxyzine.

Warnings: *Pregnancy:* No teratogenic effects were caused by oral doses as high as 60, 188 and 133 times the maximum clinically studied human dose in mice, rats and rabbits, respectively. No effects on reproduction and fertility were observed at doses as high as 40 and 10 times the maximum recommended human dose in male and female mice, respectively. An oral dose 60 times the maximum clinically studied human dose in female mice did not affect parturition or lactation. Although the animal studies are not indicative of any adverse effects during pregnancy at clinically relevant doses, such studies are not always predictive of a human response. There are no adequate and well-controlled studies in pregnant women. Until such data become available, cetirizine should not be used during pregnancy, unless advised otherwise by a physician.

Lactation: Studies in beagle dogs indicate that approximately 3% of the dose is excreted in milk. The extent of excretion in human milk is unknown. Use of cetirizine in nursing mothers is not recommended, unless directed otherwise by a physician.
Children: Unless directed otherwise by a physician, cetirizine should not be administered to children below 12 years of age

Reactine (cont'd)

since its safety and effectiveness in this age group has not yet been established.

Occupational Hazards: Activities Requiring Mental Alertness: Studies using objective measurements have shown no effect of cetirizine hydrochloride on cognitive function, motor performance or sleep latency. However, in clinical trials the appearance of some CNS effects, particularly somnolence, have been observed. If drowsiness occurs, do not drive or operate machinery.

Geriatrics: Cetirizine was well tolerated by patients aged 65 and over. Clearance of cetirizine is reduced in proportion to creatinine clearance. In patients whose creatinine clearance is reduced (i.e., those with moderate renal impairment), a starting dose of 5 mg/day is recommended (see Pharmacology, Pharmacokinetics).

Occasional instances of liver function test (transaminase) elevations have occurred during cetirizine therapy. This incidence was 1.6% in the short-term trials and 4.4% in the 6 month trials. These liver enzyme elevations, mainly ALT, were generally reversible. There was no evidence of jaundice or hepatitis, and the clinical significance is presently unknown. Consequently, cetirizine should be used with caution in patients with pre-existing liver disease. In patients with moderate hepatic impairment, a starting dose of 5 mg is recommended.

Asthmatics: Cetirizine has been safely administered to patients with mild to moderate asthma. Cetirizine did not cause exacerbation of asthma symptoms.

Drug Interactions: No clinically significant drug interactions have been found with theophylline, pseudoephedrine, cimetidine, erythromycin and ketoconazole. Epidemiologic data suggests that there also would not be interaction with other macrolide antibiotics or imidazole antifungals. In clinical trials cetirizine has been safely administered with beta-agonists, NSAIDS, oral contraceptives, narcotic analgesics, corticosteroids, H_2 antagonists, cephalosporins, penicillins, thyroid hormones and thiazide diuretics. Interaction studies with cetirizine and alcohol or diazepam indicate that cetirizine does not increase alcohol-induced or diazepam-induced impairment of motor and mental performance.

Adverse Effects: In clinical development programs (domestic and international), cetirizine has been evaluated in more than 6 000 treated patients at daily doses ranging from 5 to 20 mg. The most common adverse reactions were headache and somnolence. The incidence of headache associated with cetirizine was not different from placebo. The incidence of somnolence associated with cetirizine was dose related and predominantly mild to moderate. The incidence of somnolence in fixed dose studies was 6% for placebo, 11% at 5 mg and 13.7% at 10 mg. Dry mouth was reported by 5% of patients (vs 2.3% for placebo). Fatigue was reported by 5.9% of patients (vs 2.6% for placebo).

Most adverse reactions reported during cetirizine therapy were mild to moderate. The incidence of discontinuation due to adverse reactions in patients receiving cetirizine was not significantly different from placebo (1.0% vs 0.6%, respectively, in placebo-controlled trials). There was no difference by gender or by body weight with regard to the incidence of adverse reactions.

Occasional instances of transient, reversible hepatic transaminase elevations have occurred during cetirizine therapy, without evidence of jaundice, hepatitis or other clinical findings.

Adverse events which were reported at an incidence of greater than 1/100 in clinical trials are listed in Table I.

The following events were observed infrequently (equal to or less than 1%), in 3 982 patients who received cetirizine in U.S. trials, including an open study of 6 months' duration; a causal relationship with cetirizine administration has not been established.

Application Site: application site reaction, injection site inflammation.

Autonomic Nervous System: anorexia, urinary retention, flushing, saliva increased.

Cardiovascular: palpitation, tachycardia, hypertension, arrhythmia, cardiac failure.

CNS and Peripheral Nervous System: parasthesia, confusion, hyperkinesia, hypertonia, migraine, tremor, vertigo, cramps legs, ataxia, dysphonia, coordination abnormal, hyperesthesia, hypoesthesia, myelitis, paralysis, ptosis, speech disorder, twitching, visual field defect.

Endocrine: thyroid disorder.

Table I—Reactine

Adverse Reactions Reported in Placebo-controlled U.S. Reactine Trials (Maximum Dose of 10 mg) at Rates of 1% or Greater

Adverse Experience	Reactine % (N=2 034)	Placebo % (N=1 612)	Difference of Percentage
Headache	17.6	17.9	(0.3)*
Somnolence	13.7	6.3	7.4
Fatigue	5.9	2.6	3.3
Dry Mouth	5.0	2.3	2.7
Nausea	2.5	2.9	(0.4)*
Pharyngitis	2.0	1.9	0.1
Dizziness	2.0	1.2	0.8
Insomnia	1.4	1.2	0.2
Epistaxis	1.2	0.6	0.6
Coughing	1.0	0.6	0.4
Abdominal Pain	1.0	0.9	0.1
Dyspesia	0.8	1.6	(0.8)*
Pruritus	0.3	1.2	(0.9)*

( )* = Higher frequency in placebo group.

Gastrointestinal: appetite increased, dyspepsia, abdominal pain, diarrhea, flatulence, constipation, vomiting, stomatitis ulcerative, tongue disorder, tooth caries, aggravated stomatitis, tongue discoloration, tongue edema, gastritis, hemorrhage rectum, hemorrhoids, melena, hepatic function abnormal.

Genitourinary: polyuria, urinary tract infection, cystitis, dysuria, hematuria, urine abnormal.

Hearing and vestibular: earache, tinnitus, deafness, ototoxicity.

Metabolic/Nutritional: thirst, edema, dehydration, diabetes mellitus.

Musculoskeletal: myalgia, arthralgia, bone disorder, arthrosis, tendon disorder, arthritis, muscle weakness.

Psychiatric: insomnia, nervousness, depression, emotional lability, concentration impaired, anxiety, depersonalization, paroniria, thinking abnormal, agitation, amnesia, libido decreased, euphoria.

Resistance Mechanism: healing impaired, herpes simplex, infection, infection fungal, infection viral.

Respiratory: epistaxis, rhinitis, coughing, respiratory disorder, bronchospasm, dyspnea, upper respiratory tract infection, hyperventilation, sinusitis, sputum increased, bronchitis, pneumonia.

Reproductive: dysmenorrhea, menstrual disorder, breast pain female, intermenstrual bleeding, leukorrhea, menorrhagia, pregnancy unintended, vaginitis, testes disorder.

Recticuloendothelial: lymphadenopathy.

Skin: pruritus, rash, skin disorder, skin dry, urticaria, acne, dermatitis, rash erythematous, sweating increased, alopecia, angioedema, furunculosis, bullous eruption, eczema, hyperkeratosis, hypertrichosis, photosensitivity reaction, photosensitivity toxic reaction, rash maculopapular, seborrhea, purpura.

Special Senses: taste perversion, taste loss, parosmia.

Vision: eye abnormality, vision abnormal, eye pain, conjunctivitis, xerophthalmia, glaucoma, ocular hemorrhage.

Body as a Whole: weight increase, back pain, malaise, pain, chest pain, fever, asthenia, edema generalized, edema periorbital, edema peripheral, rigors, edema legs, face edema, hot flushes, abdomen enlarged, allergic reaction, nasal polyp.

Weight gain was reported as an adverse event in 0.4% of cetirizine patients in placebo-controlled trials. In an open study of 6 months' duration, the mean weight gain was 2.8% after 20 weeks, with no further increase at 26 weeks.

Occasional instances of transient, reversible hepatic transaminase elevations have occurred during cetirizine therapy.

In foreign marketing experience the following additional rare, but potential severe adverse events have been reported: hemolytic anemia, thrombocytopenia, orofacial dyskinesia, severe hypotension, anaphylaxis, hepatitis, glomerulonephritis, stillbirth, and cholestasis.

In a 6-week, placebo-controlled study of 186 patients with allergic rhinitis and mild to moderate asthma, cetirizine 10 mg daily improved rhinitis symptoms and did not alter pulmonary function. This study supports the safety of administering cetirizine to allergic rhinitis patients with mild to moderate asthma.

Overdose: Symptoms and Treatment: Overdose has not been reported with cetirizine in North America. In foreign marketing experience, somnolence has been reported in cases of overdose up to 150 mg. If an acute overdose occurs, evacuation of the stomach should be considered during the first few hours after this overdose. Treatment should be symptomatic and supportive taking into account any concomitantly ingested medications. There is no known specific antidote to cetirizine. Cetirizine is not effectively removed by dialysis, and dialysis will be ineffective unless a dialyzable agent has been concomitantly ingested. The minimal lethal oral dose in rodents is at least 590 times the maximum clinically studied dose.

Dosage: Adults and Children over 12 Years: The recommended initial dose is 5 to 10 mg, depending on symptom severity. The time of administration with or without food may be varied to suit individual patient needs.

Clinical studies to date support treatment for up to 6 months thus medical recommendation is advised for long-term use.

Geriatrics: In patients with moderate hepatic and/or renal impairment, a starting dose of 5 mg/day is recommended.

Information for the Patient: See Blue Section—Information for the Patient "Reactine".

Supplied: 5 mg: Each white (dye-free), film-coated, scored, ovoid tablet contains: cetirizine HCl 5 mg. Nonmedicinal ingredients: cornstarch, hydroxypropyl methylcellulose, lactose, magnesium stearate, polyethylene glycol, povidone and titanium dioxide. Blister packages (for OTC use) of 14 and 21.

10 mg: Each white (dye-free), film-coated, scored, ovoid tablet contains: cetirizine HCl 10 mg. Nonmedicinal ingredients: cornstarch, hydroxypropyl methylcellulose, lactose, magnesium stearate, polyethylene glycol, povidone and titanium dioxide. Bottles of 100 and 500. Blister packages (for OTC use) of 6, 12, 18 and 30.

Store at room temperature between 15 and 30°C.

(Shown in Product Recognition Section)

Reviewed 1998

REBIF™ ℗

Serono

Interferon beta-1a

Immunomodulator

Pharmacology: General: Interferons are a family of naturally occurring proteins, which have molecular weights ranging from 15 000 to 21 000 daltons. Three major classes of interferons have been identified: alpha, beta and gamma. Interferon beta, interferon alpha and interferon gamma have overlapping yet distinct biologic activities.

Interferon beta-1a acts through various mechanisms: Immunomodulation through the induction of cell membrane components of the major histocompatibility complex i.e., MHC Class I antigens, an increase in natural killer (NK) cell activity, and an inhibition of IFN-γ induced MHC Class II antigen expression, as well as a sustained reduction in TNF level. Antiviral effect through the induction of proteins like 2′-5′ oligoadenylate synthetase and p78. Antiproliferative effect through direct cytostatic activity and indirect through antitumoral immune response enhancement.

The mechanism of action of interferon beta-1a in relapsing-remitting multiple sclerosis is still under investigation.

Relapsing-remitting Multiple Sclerosis: Two pivotal studies, including a total of 628 patients, evaluated the long-term safety and efficacy of interferon beta-1a when administered s.c. 3 times weekly to relapsing-remitting multiple sclerosis patients. The results indicate that interferon beta-1a alters the natural course of relapsing-remitting multiple sclerosis. Efficacy was demonstrated with respect to the 3 major aspects of this disease: disability (patients EDSS 0-5), exacerbations, and burden of disease and activity as measured by MRI scans.

Prisms Study: In the larger trial, a total of 560 patients diagnosed with clinically definite or laboratory-supported relapsing-remitting multiple sclerosis EDSS 0-5 with at least a 1-year history before study entry, were enrolled and randomized to the 3 treatments (placebo, 22 μg (6MIU) interferon beta-1a, or 44 μg (12MIU) interferon beta-1a) in a ratio of 1:1:1. About 90% of patients completed the 2 years of treatment, and very few patients withdrew from the study due to adverse events.

The main criteria for inclusion were: history of 2 or more acute exacerbations in the 2 years prior to study entry, no previous systemic treatment with interferons, no treatment with corticosteroids or ACTH in the 2 months preceding study entry and no exacerbation in the 8 weeks prior to study entry.

Patients were evaluated at 3-month periods, during exacerbations and coinciding with MRI scanning. Each patient underwent cranial proton density/T_2-weighted (PD/T_2) MRI scans at baseline and every 6 months during the study. A subset of patients underwent PD/T_2 and T_1-weighted (T_1) Gd-MRI scans 1 month before the start of treatment, at baseline and then monthly until the end of the first 9 months of treatment. Of

Table I—Rebif

Effect on Exacerbation

Efficacy Parameters	Placebo	Rebif 66 μg/ week	Rebif 132 μg/ week	p-value Rebif 66 μg/week vs Placebo	p-value Rebif 132 μg/week vs Placebo
Mean # exacerbations over the 2-year study	2.56	1.82	1.73	0.0002	<0.0001
Percentage of exacerbation-free patients at 2 years	14.6%	25.6%	32%	0.0140	<0.0001
Median time to first exacerbation (months)	4.5	7.6	9.6	0.0008	<0.0001
Median time to second exacerbation (months)	15.0	23.4	>24*	0.0020	<0.0001
Mean # of moderate and severe exacerbations during the 2-year period	0.99	0.71	0.62	0.0025	0.0003

*Median time to second exacerbation not reached in 132 μg/week dose group.

Table II—Rebif

Effect on Time to First Progression in Disability

Efficacy Parameters	Placebo	Rebif 66 μg/ week	Rebif 132 μg/ week	p-value Rebif 66 μg/week vs Placebo	p-value Rebif 132 μg/week vs Placebo
Time to confirmed progression in disability, first quartile (months)	11.8	18.2	21.0	0.0398	0.0136
Median change in EDSS score at 2 years	0.5	0	0	0.0263	0.0519

Table III—Rebif

Effect on Multiple Sclerosis Pathology as Detected by MRI Scans

Efficacy Parameters	Placebo	Rebif 66 μg/ week	Rebif 132 μg/ week	p-value Rebif 66 μg/week vs Placebo	p-value Rebif 132 μg/week vs Placebo
Burden of disease (BOD) Median % change	+10.9	−1.2	−3.8	<0.0001	<0.0001
MRI activity					
All patients					
Number of active lesions (per 6 months)	2.25	0.75	0.5	<0.0001	<0.0001
% active scans	75%	50%	25%	<0.0001	<0.0001
Patients with monthly MRIs (9 months)					
Number active lesions (per month)	0.88	0.17	0.11	<0.0001	<0.0001
% active scans	44	12.5	11	<0.0001	<0.0001
Patients with monthly MRIs throughout the study (2 years)					
Number active lesions	0.9	0.1	0.02	0.0905	0.0105
% active scans	52	10	2	0.0920	0.0117

those, another subset of 39 continued with the monthly scans throughout the 24-month treatment period.

This study demonstrated that interferon beta-1a at a total dose of 66 or 132 μg weekly, significantly improved all 3 major outcomes, including exacerbation rate, disease activity and burden of disease as measured by MRI scanning and progression of disability (see Table I). In addition, the study showed that interferon beta-1a is effective in delaying the progression in disability in patients with an EDSS of 4.0 or higher who are known to progress more rapidly. Also, the drug reduced the requirements for steroids to treat multiple sclerosis and, at 132 μg weekly interferon beta-1a reduced the number of hospitalizations for multiple sclerosis.

The results after 1 year of treatment were also significant (see Tables II and III).

Requirement for Steroids: The proportion of patients requiring steroids for MS (excluding non-MS indications) was higher in the placebo group (more than 50%) than in either of the 2 interferon beta-1a groups (around 40% in each group).

Hospitalization for Multiple Sclerosis: The observed mean numbers of hospitalizations for MS in the interferon beta-1a 66 and 132 μg weekly groups represented reductions of 21% and 48%, respectively, from that in the placebo group.

Immunogenicity: Antibodies to IFN-beta were tested in all patients pre-entry, and at Months 6, 12, 18 and 24. The results of testing for the presence of neutralizing antibodies (NAb) are shown in Table IV.

Table IV—Rebif

Percentage of Patients Positive for Neutralizing Antibodies

Placebo	Rebif 66 μg weekly	Rebif 132 μg weekly
0%	24%	12.5%

Due to concern about the potential impact of neutralizing antibody formation on efficacy, exacerbation counts (primary endpoint) were analyzed according to patients' neutralizing antibody status. Over the 2 years of the study, there was no trend to a higher exacerbation rate in the neutralizing antibody-positive groups compared to the neutralizing antibody-negative groups. There is no clear indication that the development of serum neutralizing antibodies affected either safety or efficacy in either of the interferon beta-1a groups.

Cohort of Patients with High Baseline EDSS (baseline EDSS >3.5): Additional analyses were conducted in order to study the efficacy of interferon beta-1a in populations of patients with adverse predictive outcome factors, who were likely to be at higher risk for progression in disability. The primary predictive factor examined was baseline EDSS >3.5. Patients in this cohort have a more severe degree of disability and are at higher risk for progression than those with lower EDSS: natural history studies have shown that patients at EDSS levels of 4.0 to 5.0 spend less time at these EDSS levels than at lower levels of disability.

Treatment with interferon beta-1a at both doses significantly reduced the mean exacerbation count per patient compared to placebo treatment. Progression in this group of patients is of particular concern, as it involves development of difficulty in ambulation. The 132 μg weekly dose significantly prolonged time to confirmed progression whereas the 66 μg weekly dose did not. Both doses of interferon beta-1a significantly affected percent change from baseline in MRI burden of disease in the high-EDSS cohort, and the 132 μg weekly dose significantly reduced the number of T2 active lesions in this population. The efficacy results in this cohort of patients with established disability confirms that the 132 μg weekly dose has a marked effect on progression in disability and the underlying pathology of the disease. See Tables V, VI, VII and Tables VIII and IX (on following page).

Cross-over Study: The other study was an open cross-over design, with MRI evaluations conducted in a blinded fashion. Enrolled in this study were 68 patients between the ages of 15 and 45 years, with clinically definite and/or laboratory supported relapsing-remitting MS for up to 10 years in duration. The main inclusion criteria included: at least 2 relapses in the previous 2 years, EDSS score between 1 and 5, no corticosteroid or plasmapheresis treatments or administration of gamma globulins within the 3 months prior to study, no immunomodulating or immunosuppressive therapy for the 6 months prior to the study and absence of HBsAg and HIV antibodies. Once enrolled, patients remained under clinical observation for 6 months with assessments of their neurological status and other parameters, and extensive monitoring of exacerbations. Patients were then randomized to treatment with either 11 μg (3MIU) (n=35) or 33 μg (9MIU) (n=33) of interferon beta-1a, self-administered s.c. 3 times per week. The total dose was therefore 33 or 99 μg weekly.

Six-months Observation vs 6-months Treatment: Treatment with interferon beta-1a at both doses used in this study, achieved a statistically significant reduction in both the MRI evidence of MS activity in the brain and the clinical relapse rate versus the corresponding observation periods. This pattern of improvement was also reflected in additional MRI measures. In the biannual T_2-weighted scans, a reduction in the mean number of new lesions and in the mean number of enlarging lesions was demonstrated (see Table X on following page).

Two-year Results: At the end of this study, 62 patients continued treatment for a further 18 months. Each of these patients continued to receive the dose to which they were randomized. Validation of the results of the 2-year treatment period is ongoing; however, the results from the continuation of treatment at both doses demonstrate that interferon beta-1a maintained its dose-dependent effect in reducing the relapse rate and the brain lesion volume detected by T_2 weight MRI

Table V—Rebif

Effect on Exacerbation (High-EDSS cohort)

Efficacy Parameters	Placebo	Rebif 66 μg/week	Rebif 132 μg/week
Mean # exacerbations	3.07	1.83	1.22
# and % of exacerbations-free patients	2 (7%)	7 (20%)	10 (32%)
p-value* (Rebif vs placebo)		p=0.0121	p=0.0002

*Log-linear model.

Table VI—Rebif

Progression in Disability by One Point on the EDSS (High-EDSS cohort)

Treatment Group	% of progressors*	# Patients	Time to Progression Median (days)	Time to Progression Q1 (days)
Placebo	56%	28	638	218
Rebif 66 μg weekly	41%	35	not reached	226
Rebif 132 μg weekly	27%	31	not reached	638

*Excludes patients lost to follow-up without progression.

Table VII—Rebif

Progression in Disability: Statistical Comparisons

Test	Group Comparison	p-value
Log-rank test	66 μg weekly vs Placebo	p=0.4465
	132 μg weekly vs Placebo	p=0.0481

Rebif (cont'd)

Table VIII—Rebif

MRI Burden of Disease: % Change (High-EDSS Cohort)

	Placebo	Rebif 66 μg/week	Rebif 132 μg/week
Burden of disease—Median % change	5.3	−2.3	−6.9
Burden of disease—Mean % change	12.2	13.6	0.7
p-value* (Rebif vs placebo)		p=0.0146	p=0.0287

*ANOVA on the ranks.

Table IX—Rebif

Number of T2 Active Lesions (High-EDSS Cohort)

Treatment Group	Number of T_2 Active Lesions: Median	Mean	p-value*
Placebo	1.9	2.6	
Rebif 66 μg weekly	0.9	1.7	Rebif 66 μg vs Placebo: p=0.0612
Rebif 12 μg weekly	0.5	0.9	Rebif 132 μg vs Placebo: p=0.0042

*ANOVA on the ranks.

Table X—Rebif

Biannual T_2-Weighted Scans

	Dosage	Observation Period	Treatment Period	Reduction %	p-value
Exacerbation Rate/Patient	33 μg weekly	0.914	0.429	53%	p=0.007
	99 μg weekly	0.788	0.242	69%	p=0.003
# Exacerbation-free Patients	33 μg weekly	15/35	23/35		p=0.059
	99 μg weekly	17/33	26/33		p=0.02
# of Monthly Lesions/Patient	33 μg weekly	3.47	1.77	49%	<0.001
	99 μg weekly	2.42	0.86	64%	<0.001
Volume of Lesions/Patient	33 μg weekly	557 mm³	220 mm³	61%	<0.001
	99 μg weekly	379 mm³	100 mm³	73%	<0.001
Total Mean # of New T_2 Lesions	33 μg weekly	5.67	1.97	65%	<0.001
	99 μg weekly	3.93	1.18	70%	<0.001
Total Mean # of T_2 Enlarged Lesions	33 μg weekly	2.26	0.97	57%	p=0.001
	99 μg weekly	1.81	0.45	75%	p=0.004

Table XI—Rebif

Summary of Double-blind, Placebo-controlled Studies

Study	# patients/ % Previously Treated	# Lesions Treated	Treatment	Results
1	25/80%	3	0.12 or 3.67 μg of Rebif/lesion, or placebo, 3 times per week for 3 weeks	Rebif at a dose of 3.67 μg/lesion is efficacious, as evidenced by the induction of complete disappearance of lesions and the reduction in the area of lesions. The 0.12 μg dose of Rebif did not show advantages over placebo treatment.
2	100/72%	6	3.67 μg of Rebif/lesion, or placebo, 3 times per week for 3 weeks	There was a significant increase in Major Response rate at Month 3 in patients who received Rebif vs placebo (p<0.0001). The Complete Response rate at Month 3 was significantly in favor of patients who received Rebif (p≤0.0162).
3	100/52%	8	3.67 μg of Rebif/lesion, or placebo, 3 times per week for 3 weeks	For the Israeli centre, the results from Week 6, supported by those from study Day 19 demonstrate the efficacy of Rebif. Because of the study design and the noncompliance with the study protocol at the German centre, indications of efficacy were not supported by the results from the analyses where patients from both centres were pooled.
4	124/72%	6	3.67 μg of Rebif/lesion, or placebo, 3 times per week for 3 weeks	This study showed that Rebif was effective with the proportion of patients achieving a complete or Partial Response at Day 19 and Week 6, and a significant reduction in the total area of lesions on Day 19 and Week 6. Because of the study design, the effect of Rebif at Month 3 was not demonstrated.

scans compared to the observation period, which corroborates the findings of the longer, placebo-controlled study.

Condyloma Acuminatum: The results from 4 double-blind, placebo-controlled studies, including 349 patients (aged 17 to 62), each reveal that interferon beta-1a, when injected intralesionally at a dose of 3.67 μg (1 MIU)/lesion 3 times per week for 3 weeks, is efficacious in the treatment of condyloma acuminatum in men and women. This efficacy is evidenced by both the induction of complete disappearance of lesions as well as the reduction in the area of lesions. The majority of treated patients in these studies had recurrent warts that had failed previous treatments. The number of lesions treated per patient was between 3 and 8, as stated in Table XI.

Immunogenicity: The determination of the presence of antibodies to human IFN-β was performed in all 4 studies. A total of four patients had anti beta-interferon antibodies at pre-entry, and 6 other patients had at least a positive result for total binding antibodies at some point during the study. Antibodies were of low titer, and none of the antibodies were neutralizing to human IFN-β biological activity.

Indications: Multiple Sclerosis: For the treatment of relapsing-remitting multiple sclerosis in patients with an EDSS between 0 and 5.0, to reduce the number and severity of clinical exacerbations, slow the progression of physical disability, reduce the requirement for steroids, and reduce the number of hospitalizations for treatment of multiple sclerosis. The efficacy has been confirmed by T_1-Gd enhanced and T_2 (burden of disease) MRI evaluations. Evidence of efficacy beyond 2 years is not known since the primary evidence of efficacy derives from 2-year trials.

Condyloma Acuminatum: For the patient who has less than 9 lesions, and who has failed several prior treatments. In the case of patients with 9 or more lesions, if the first treatment is successful, the remaining lesions could be treated with a second course of therapy. Interferon beta-1a should also be considered for the treatment of condyloma acuminatum in patients for whom the side effects from other treatments, e.g., scarring, are of concern. While not all patients who were treated with interferon beta-1a attained a complete response, patients whose lesions decreased in size and had at least a partial response may have also benefitted from treatment because lesion shrinkage may facilitate subsequent management with other therapies, as has been reported with IFN-α.

Contraindications: Patients with a known hypersensitivity to natural or recombinant interferon beta, albumin (human), or any other component of the formulation.

Warnings: Interferon beta-1a should be used under the supervision of a physician.

Relapsing-remitting Multiple Sclerosis: Depression and suicidal ideation are known to occur at an increased frequency in the multiple sclerosis population. The use of interferon beta-1a has not been associated with an increase in the incidence and/or severity of depression, or with an increased incidence of suicide attempts or suicide. In the relapsing-remitting multiple sclerosis study, a similar incidence of depression was seen in the placebo-treated group and in the 2 interferon beta-1a patient groups. Nevertheless, patients with depression should be closely monitored for signs of significant worsening of depression or suicidal ideation.

The first injection should be performed under the supervision of an appropriately qualified health care professional.

Condyloma: All injections should be administered by a qualified health care professional.

Precautions: General: Patients should be informed of the most common adverse events associated with interferon beta administration, including symptoms of the flu-like syndrome (see Adverse Effects). These symptoms tend to be most prominent at the initiation of therapy and decrease in frequency and severity with continued treatment.

Serum neutralizing antibodies against interferon beta-1a may develop. The precise incidence and clinical significance of antibodies is as yet uncertain.

Intralesional injections can be painful to some patients treated for condyloma acuminata. In such cases an anesthetic cream such as lidocaine-prilocaine can be used.

Pregnancy and *Lactation*: Interferon beta-1a should not be administered in case of pregnancy and lactation. There are no studies of interferon beta-1a in pregnant women. At high doses in monkeys, abortifacient effects were observed with other interferons. Fertile women receiving interferon beta-1a should take appropriate contraceptive measures. Patients planning for pregnancy and those becoming pregnant should be informed of the potential hazards of interferons to the fetus and interferon beta-1a should be discontinued. It is not known whether interferon beta-1a is excreted in human milk. Because of the potential for serious adverse reactions in nursing infants, a decision should be made either to discontinue nursing or to discontinue interferon beta-1a therapy.

Children: There is no experience with interferon beta-1a in children under 16 years of age with multiple sclerosis or condyloma, and therefore, interferon beta-1a should not be used in this population.

Patients with Special Diseases and Conditions: Caution should be used and close monitoring considered when administering interferon beta-1a to patients with severe renal and hepatic failure, patients with severe myelosuppression, and depressive patients.

Drug Interactions: No formal drug interaction studies have been conducted with interferon beta-1a in humans. Interferons have been reported to reduce the activity of hepatic cytochrome P450-dependent enzymes in humans and animals. Caution should be exercised when administering interferon beta-1a in combination with medicinal products that have a narrow therapeutic index and are largely dependent on the hepatic cytochrome P450 system for clearance, e.g., antiepileptics and some classes of antidepressants. The interaction of interferon beta-1a with corticosteroids or ACTH has not been studied systematically. Clinical studies indicate that multiple sclerosis patients can receive interferon beta-1a and corticosteroids or ACTH during relapses. Interferon beta-1a should not be mixed with other drugs in the same syringe.

Laboratory Tests: Relapsing-remitting Multiple Sclerosis: Laboratory abnormalities are associated with the use of interferons. Therefore, in addition to those laboratory tests normally required for monitoring patients with multiple sclerosis, complete and differential white blood cell counts, platelet counts and blood chemistries, including liver function tests are recommended during interferon beta-1a therapy.

Condyloma Acuminatum: Same as relapsing-remitting multiple sclerosis but tend not to be as severe because of dose and length of treatment.

Information to Be Provided to the Patient: Flu-like symptoms (fever, headache, chills, muscle aches) are not uncommon following initiation of therapy with interferon beta-1a. Acetaminophen may be used for relief of flu-like symptoms. Patients should contact their physician or pharmacist if they experience any undesirable effects.

Depression may occur in patients with relapsing-remitting multiple sclerosis and may occur while patients are taking interferon beta-1a. Patients should be asked to contact their physician should they feel depressed.

Patients should be advised not to stop or modify their treatment unless instructed by their physician.

Instruction on Self-Injection Technique and Procedures: Patients treated for relapsing-remitting multiple sclerosis should be instructed in the use of aseptic technique when administering interferon beta-1a. Appropriate instruction for reconstitution of interferon beta-1a and self-injection should be given including careful review of the interferon beta-1a patient leaflet. The first injection should be performed under the supervision of an appropriately qualified health care professional. Injection sites should be rotated at each injection. Injections may be given prior to bedtime as this may lessen the perception of side effects. Patients should be cautioned against the re-use of needles or syringes and instructed in safe disposal procedures. A puncture resistant container for disposal of used needles and syringes should be supplied to the patient along with instructions for safe disposal of full containers.

In the controlled MS trial reported injection site reactions were commonly reported by patients at one or more times during therapy. In general, they did not require discontinuation of therapy, but the nature and severity of all reported reactions should be carefully assessed. Patient understanding and use of aseptic self-injection technique and procedures should be periodically re-evaluated.

Adverse Effects: Multiple Sclerosis: As with other interferon preparations, flu-like symptoms are not uncommon. The use of interferon beta may cause flu-like syndrome, asthenia, pyrexia, chills, arthralgia, myalgia, headache, and injection site reactions.

Less frequent adverse reactions include cold sores, stuffy nose, light headedness, mucosal irritation, hematological disorders (leukopenia, lymphopenia, granulocytopenia), and alterations in liver function tests such as elevated AST and ALT. These effects are usually mild and reversible. Tachyphylaxis with respect to most side effects is well recognized. Fever and flu-like symptoms can be treated with acetaminophen. Depending on the severity and persistence of the side effects, the dose may be lowered or temporarily interrupted, at the discretion of the physician.

Most injection site reactions are mild to moderate. Rare cases of skin ulceration/necrosis at the site of injection have been reported with long-term treatment.

The most frequently reported adverse events and the most common laboratory abnormalities observed during the placebo-controlled study in relapsing-remitting multiple sclerosis (560 patients, 2 years' treatment) are presented in Table XII for patients on placebo and interferon beta-1a. The frequencies are patients who reported this event at least once during the study, as a percentage of the total number of patients, by study-arm.

The adverse events experienced during the study are listed below, by WHOART System Organ Class. The most common amongst the injection site reactions was in the form of mild erythema. The majority of the other injection site reactions were also mild in the 2 interferon beta-1a groups. Necrosis

Table XII—Rebif

Adverse Events and Laboratory Test Abnormalities—Remitting Multiple Sclerosis

	Placebo	Rebif 66 μg weekly	Rebif 132 μg weekly
Adverse Events			
Injection site disorders (all)	**38.5**	**89.9**	**92.4**
Upper respiratory tract infections	**85.6**	**75.1**	**74.5**
Headache	62.6	64.6	70.1
Flu-like symptoms	51.3	56.1	58.7
Fatigue	35.8	32.8	41.3
Depression	27.8	20.6	23.9
Fever	**15.5**	**24.9**	**27.7**
Back pain	21.4	19.6	23.4
Myalgia	19.8	24.9	25.0
Nausea	23.0	24.9	24.5
Insomnia	21.4	19.6	23.4
Diarrhea	18.7	17.5	19.0
Laboratory Test Abnormalities			
Lymphopenia	11.2	20.1	28.8
Leukopenia	3.7	12.7	22.3
Granulocytopenia	3.7	11.6	15.2
AST increase	3.7	10.1	17.4
ALT increase	4.3	19.6	27.2

For the events in bold, observed differences reached statistical significance as compared to placebo.

was reported in 8 patients treated with interferon beta-1a. Two of these patients were in the 66 μg weekly and 6 in the 132 μg weekly groups. All patients completed the planned treatment period, with only 1 requiring temporary dose reductions and another patient stopping treatment for 2 weeks. Those that required treatment, received antibiotics.

Adverse events experienced by patients enrolled in the double-blind, placebo-controlled, multiple sclerosis study are presented in Table XIII.

In addition to the above listed adverse events, the following events have been experienced less frequently, in one or both of the relapsing-remitting multiple sclerosis studies: asthenia, fluid retention, anorexia, gastroenteritis, heartburn, paradentium affections, dental abscess or extraction, stomatitis, glossitis, sleepiness, anxiety, irritability, confusion, lymphadenopathy, weight gain, bone fracture, dyspnea, cold sores, fissure at the angle of the mouth, menstrual disorders, cystitis and vaginitis.

Condyloma Acuminatum: Most common adverse events for patients treated for Condyloma acuminatum are shown in Table XIV (on following page).

Other adverse events were experienced by less than 5% of the patients, and included eye pain, skin disorder, rhinitis, bronchitis, coughing, diarrhea, abdominal pain, postural hypotension, palpitation, vasodilatation, rectal disorder, lymphocytosis, thrombocytopenia, delirium, somnolence, joint pain, joint stiffness, lightheadedness, paresthesia distal, disorientation, irritability, sleeplessness, lethargy, bruise, purpura, sweating increased, shortness of breath, upper respiratory tract infection, tachycardia, flushing, urethral pain, infection, chest pain, lymphadenopathy, PBI increased, arthralgia, dizziness, nervousness, tremor, abnormal vision, vulvovaginal disease, balanitis, penis disease, testis disease, urethritis, infection urinary tract, vaginitis, leukopenia, herpes simplex, pruritus, rash mac pap, skin neoplasia and rash.

Overdose: Symptoms and Treatment: No case of overdose has thus far been described. However, in case of overdosage, patients should be hospitalized for observation and appropriate supportive treatment should be given.

Dosage: Relapsing-remitting Multiple Sclerosis: The recommended dosage of interferon beta-1a is 22 μg (6 MIU) given 3 times per week by s.c. injection. This dose is effective in the majority of patients to delay progression of the disease. Patients with a higher degree of disability (an EDSS of 4 or higher) may require a dose of 44 μg (12 MIU) 3 times per week.

Treatment should be initiated under supervision of a physician experienced in the treatment of the disease. When first starting treatment with interferon beta-1a, in order to allow tachyphylaxis to develop thus reducing adverse events, it is recommended that 20% of the total dose be administered during the initial 2 weeks of therapy, 50% of total dose be administered in week 3 and 4, and the full dose from the fifth week onwards.

Table XIII—Rebif

Adverse Events—Remitting Multiple Sclerosis

Body System Preferred Term	Placebo (n=187)	Rebif 66 μg weekly (n=189)	Rebif 132 μg weekly (n=184)
Application Site			
Injection site inflammation[a,b]	15.0%	65.6%	65.8%
Injection site reaction[a,b]	13.4%	31.2%	34.8%
Injection site pain[b]	14.4%	20.1%	22.8%
Body as a Whole—General			
Influenza-like symptoms	51.3%	56.1%	58.7%
Fatigue	35.8%	32.8%	41.3%
Fever[a,b]	15.5%	24.9%	27.7%
Leg pain	14.4%	10.1%	13.0%
Rigors[b,c]	5.3%	6.3%	13.0%
CNS/Peripheral Nervous System			
Headache	62.6%	64.6%	70.1%
Dizziness	17.6%	14.3%	16.3%
Paresthesia	18.7%	19.6%	16.3%
Hypoesthesia	12.8%	12.2%	7.6%
Respiratory			
Rhinitis	59.9%	52.4%	50.5%
Upper Respiratory Tract Infection	32.6%	36.0%	29.3%
Pharyngitis[b]	38.5%	34.9%	28.3%
Coughing	21.4%	14.8%	19.0%
Bronchitis	9.6%	10.6%	9.2%
Gastrointestinal			
Nausea	23.0%	24.9%	24.5%
Abdominal pain	17.1%	22.2%	19.6%
Diarrhea	18.7%	17.5%	19.0%
Vomiting	12.3%	12.7%	12.0%
Musculoskeletal			
Back pain	19.8%	23.3%	24.5%
Myalgia	19.8%	24.9%	25.0%
Arthralgia	17.1%	15.3%	19.0%
Skeletal pain	10.2%	14.8%	9.8%
Psychiatric			
Depression	27.8%	20.6%	23.9%
Insomnia	21.4%	19.6%	23.4%
White Cell and Reticulo-endothelium			
Lymphopenia[a,b]	11.2%	20.1%	28.8%
Leukopenia[a,b,c]	3.7%	12.7%	22.3%
Granulocytopenia[a,b]	3.7%	11.6%	15.2%
Lymphadenopathy	8.0%	11.1%	12.0%
Skin and Appendages			
Pruritus	11.8%	9.0%	12.5%
Liver and Biliary			
ALT increased[a,b]	4.3%	19.6%	27.2%
AST increased[a,b,c]	3.7%	10.1%	17.4%
Urinary			
Urinary tract infection	18.7%	18.0%	16.8%
Vision			
Vision abnormal	7.0%	7.4%	13.0%
Secondary Terms			
Fall	16.0%	16.9%	15.8%

n=Number of patients.

[a] Significant difference between placebo and Rebif 66 μg weekly groups ($p \le 0.05$).

[b] Significant difference between placebo and Rebif 132 μg weekly groups ($p \le 0.05$).

[c] Significant difference between Rebif 66 μg and Rebif 132 μg weekly groups ($p \le 0.05$).

At the present time, it is not known for how long patients should be treated. Safety and efficacy with interferon beta-1a have been demonstrated following 2 years of treatment. Therefore, it is recommended that patients should be evaluated after 2 years of treatment with interferon beta-1a and a decision for longer-term treatment be made on an individual basis by the treating physician.

Preparation of Solution: Lyophilized Formulation (Relapsing-remitting Multiple Sclerosis): Reconstitute the contents of a vial of interferon beta-1a with 0.5 mL of the accompanying sterile diluent (see Table XV on following page). The reconstituted solution should be used immediately.

Rebif (cont'd)

Table XIV—Rebif

Adverse Events—Condyloma Acuminatum

Body System/ Preferred Term	Trial 1 n=25	Trial 2 n=52	Trial 3 n=50	Trial 4 n=65
Body as a Whole, General				
Asthenia	24%	3.8%	36.0%	15.4%
Fever	8%	21.2%	4%	0%
Flu-syndrome	4%	7.7%	24%	26.1%
Injection site reaction	8%	11.5%	—	—
Injection site inflammation	—	5.8%	—	—
Headache	28%	42.3%	20%	36.9%
Bodily discomfort	—	15.4%	—	—
Back pain	—	9.6%	—	10.8%
Pain	—	—	—	9.2%
Pelvic pain	4%	—	6%	—
Chills	—	28.8%	—	6.2%
Malaise	—	1.9%	16%	1.5%
Injection site pain	4%	36.5%	66%	13.8%
Noninflammatory swelling	—	7.7%	—	—
Fatigue	—	28.8%	—	—
Digestive				
Nausea	8%	17.3%	—	1.5%
Vomiting	8%	1.9%	—	3%
Musculoskeletal				
Myalgia	12%	3.8%	2%	9.2%
Muscle ache	—	26.9%	—	—
Muscle pain	—	1.9%	—	—
Respiratory				
Pharyngitis	16%	0%	—	3%

Table XV—Rebif

Reconstitution Table—Relapsing-remitting Multiple Sclerosis

Strength	Volume of Diluent to be Added to Vial	Approximate Available Volume	Nominal Concentration/mL
11 µg (3 MIU)	0.5 mL	0.5 mL	22 µg (6 MIU)
44 µg (12 MIU)	0.5 mL	0.5 mL	88 µg (24 MIU)

Liquid Formulation: The liquid formulation in a prefilled syringe is ready for use. These syringes are graduated to facilitate therapy initiation. The prefilled syringes contain 22 µg and 44 µg of interferon beta-1a respectively. The prefilled syringes are ready for s.c. use only.

Condyloma Acuminatum: The recommended dosage is 3.67 µg (1 MIU) per lesion 3 times per week for 3 weeks. The recommended route of administration is intra- or peri-lesional. The prefilled syringes are not to be used for this indication.

Preparation of Solution: Lyophilized Formulation (Condyloma Acuminatum): Reconstitute the contents of a vial of interferon beta-1a in sterile diluent in order to obtain a final concentration of 1 MIU per 0.1 mL solution (see Table XVI). The reconstituted solution should be used immediately.

Table XVI—Rebif

Reconstitution Table—Condyloma Acuminatum

Strength	Volume of Diluent to be Added to Vial	Approximate Available Volume	Nominal Concentration/mL
11 µg (3 MIU)	0.3 mL	0.3 mL	37 µg (10 MIU)
44 µg (12 MIU)	1.2 mL	1.2 mL	37 µg (10 MIU)

Information for the Patient: See Blue Section—Information for the Patient "Rebif".

Supplied: Rebif is a purified, sterile glycoprotein product produced by recombinant DNA techniques and formulated for use by injection. The active ingredient is produced by genetically engineered Chinese Hamster Ovary (CHO) cells. Interferon beta-1a is a highly purified glycoprotein that has 166 amino acids and an approximate molecular weight of 22 500 daltons. It contains a single N-linked carbohydrate moiety attached to Asn-80 similar to that of natural human interferon beta.

The specific activity of Rebif is approximately 0.27 million international units (MIU)/µg interferon beta-1a. The unit measurement is derived by comparing the antiviral activity of the product to an in-house natural hIFN-β NIH standard that is obtained from human fibroblasts (BILS 11), which has been calibrated against the NIH natural hIFN-β standard (GB 23-902-531).

Liquid: Each prefilled syringe with 0.5 mL of solution contains: interferon beta-1a 22 µg (6 MIU) or 44 µg (12 MIU). Nonmedicinal ingredients: albumin (human), mannitol and sodium acetate buffer. Preservative-free. Packs of 1, 3 and 12. Refer to the date indicated on the labels for the expiry date. Liquid in a prefilled syringe should be stored at 2 to 8°C. Do not freeze.

Lyophilized Powder: Each 3 mL of sterile, lyophilized powder contains: interferon beta-1a, 11 µg (3 MIU) or 44 µg (12 MIU). Nonmedicinal ingredients: albumin (human), mannitol and sodium acetate and sodium hydroxide. Each ampul of diluent contains: 2 mL of NaCl 0.9% in water for injection. Preservative-free. Cartons of 1, 3 and 12 with ampuls of diluent. Refer to the date indicated on the labels for the expiry date. Store at 2 to 8°C. The reconstituted solution should be administered immediately. Although not recommended, it may be used later during the day of reconstitution if stored in a refrigerator (2 to 8°C). Do not freeze. The reconstituted solution may have a yellow coloration which is a normal product characteristic.

New Product 1998

RECOMBIVAX HB®

MSD

Hepatitis B Vaccine (Recombinant)

Vaccine

Pharmacology: Hepatitis B virus is one of at least 3 hepatitis viruses that cause a systemic infection, with major pathology in the liver. The others are hepatitis A virus, and non-A, non-B hepatitis viruses.

Hepatitis B virus is an important cause of viral hepatitis. There is no specific treatment for this disease. The incubation period for type B hepatitis is relatively long; 6 weeks to 6 months may elapse between exposure and the onset of clinical symptoms. The prognosis following infection with hepatitis B virus is variable and dependent on at least 3 factors: (1) Age—Infants and younger children usually experience milder initial disease than older persons; (2) Dose of Virus—The higher the dose, the more likely acute icteric hepatitis B will result; and, (3) Severity of Associated Underlying Disease—Underlying malignancy or pre-existing hepatic disease predisposes to increased mortality and morbidity.

Persistence of viral infection (the chronic hepatitis B virus carrier state) occurs in 5 to 10% of persons following acute hepatitis B, and occurs more frequently after initial anicteric hepatitis B than after initial icteric disease. Consequently, carriers of hepatitis B surface antigen (HBsAg) frequently give no history of recognized acute hepatitis. It has been estimated that more than 170 million people in the world today are persistently infected with hepatitis B virus. The Centers for Disease Control (CDC) estimate that there are approximately 0.5 to 1.0 million chronic carriers of hepatitis B virus in the USA and that this pool of carriers grows by 2 to 3% (8 000 to 16 000 individuals) annually. Chronic carriers represent the largest human reservoir of hepatitis B virus.

The serious complications and sequelae of hepatitis B virus infection include massive hepatic necrosis, cirrhosis of the liver, chronic active hepatitis, and hepatocellular carcinoma. Chronic carriers of HBsAg appear to be at increased risk of developing hepatocellular carcinoma, which accounts for 80 to 90% of primary liver carcinomas. Although a number of etiologic factors are associated with development of hepatocellular carcinoma, the single most important etiologic factor appears to be active infection with the hepatitis B virus.

There is also evidence that several diseases other than hepatitis have been associated with hepatitis B virus infection through an immunologic mechanism involving antigen-antibody complexes. Such diseases include a syndrome with rash, urticaria and arthralgia resembling serum sickness; polyarteritis nodosa; membranous glomerulonephritis; and infantile papular acrodermatitis.

Although the vehicles for transmission of the virus are predominantly blood and blood products, viral antigen has also been found in tears, saliva, breast milk, urine, semen and vaginal secretions. Hepatitis B virus is capable of surviving for days on environmental surfaces. Infection may occur when hepatitis B virus, transmitted by infected body fluids, is implanted via mucous surfaces or percutaneously introduced through accidental or deliberate breaks in the skin.

Transmission of hepatitis B virus infection is often associated with close interpersonal contact with an infected individual and with crowded living conditions. In such circumstances, transmission by inoculation via routes other than overt parenteral ones may be quite common. Perinatal transmission of hepatitis B infection from infected mother to child, at, or shortly after birth, can occur if the mother is a HBsAg carrier or if the mother has an acute hepatitis B infection in the third trimester. Infection in infancy by the hepatitis B virus usually leads to the chronic carrier state. Among infants born to women whose sera are positive for both the hepatitis B surface antigen and the e antigen, 85 to 90% are infected and become chronic carriers.

Hepatitis B is endemic throughout the world, and is a serious medical problem in population groups at increased risk (see Indications). The prevalence of HBsAg in the general population varies between less than 0.5% in the U.S. and Western Europe, 1 to 2% in South America and Southern Europe, 3 to 5% in North Africa and in many parts of the Federation of Russia (formerly known as USSR) and 9 to 10% and higher in sub-Saharan Africa and Southeast Asia. The overall prevalence of serologic markers of infection varies between 7 and 10% in the U.S. and 60 and 80% in Southeast Asia or Africa. Even in countries like those in Northern and Western Europe and other highly developed countries with a relatively low prevalence of hepatitis B, certain populations are at high risk of acquiring the disease and have cumulative infection rates of up to 70% (see Indications). In countries or areas with a high prevalence rate, the entire population is at risk and infection tends to occur during childhood.

Numerous epidemiological studies have shown that persons who develop anti-HBs following active infection with the hepatitis B virus are protected against the disease on re-exposure to the virus.

Clinical studies have established that hepatitis B vaccine (recombinant), when injected into the deltoid muscle, induced protective levels of antibody in greater than 90% of healthy individuals who received the recommended 3 dose regimen. Studies with hepatitis B vaccine derived from plasma have shown that a lower response rate (81%) to vaccine may be obtained if the vaccine is administered as a buttock injection. A protective antibody (anti-HBs) level has been defined as 10 or more sample ratio units (SRU) as determined by radioimmunoassay or a positive by enzyme immunoassay.

Responsiveness to the vaccine was age dependent. The seroconversion rate for children 1 to 10 years of age was 100%. In contrast, the conversion rate for adults ranged from 95 to 98% for those from 20 to 39 years of age and 91% for those of 40 years of age or older.

Immunocompromised persons respond less well to Recombivax HB than do healthy individuals. Vaccine-induced levels of anti-HBs are lower in predialysis and hemodialysis patients than are the levels in healthy individuals. Eighty-six percent of predialysis and hemodialysis patients who received three 40 µg doses of Recombivax HB developed protective levels of anti-HBs.

The protective efficacy of 5 µg doses of Recombivax HB has been demonstrated in neonates born of mothers positive for both HBsAg and HBeAg. In a clinical study of infants who received 1 dose of Hepatitis B Immune Globulin (HBIg) at birth followed by the recommended 3-dose regimen of Recombivax HB, efficacy in prevention of chronic hepatitis B infection was 96% in 47 infants at 6 months and 100% in 19 infants at 9 months.

The duration of protective effect of Recombivax HB is unknown at present, and the need for booster doses not defined. However, a booster dose or revaccination with the dialysis formulation may be considered in predialysis/dialysis patients if the anti-HBs level is less than 10 mIU/mL 1 to 2 months after the third dose.

Recent studies have established the relative efficacies of immune globulin and/or hepatitis B vaccine in accidental percutaneous or permucosal exposure to HBsAg-positive blood; or sexual exposure to HBsAg-positive persons (see Dosage).

It has been demonstrated that doses of up to 5 mL of Hepatitis B Immune Globulin, when administered simultaneously with the first dose of Recombivax HB at separate body sites, did not interfere with the induction of protective antibodies against hepatitis B virus elicited by the 3-dose vaccine regimen.

Reports in the literature describe a more virulent form of hepatitis B associated with superinfections or coinfections by delta virus, an incomplete RNA virus. Delta virus can only infect and cause illness in persons infected with hepatitis B virus since the delta agent requires a coat of HBsAg in order to become infectious. Therefore, persons immune to hepatitis B virus infection should also be immune to delta virus infection.

Indications: For immunization against infection caused by all known subtypes of hepatitis B virus.

Hepatitis B vaccine (recombinant) will not prevent hepatitis caused by other agents, such as hepatitis A virus, non-A, non-B hepatitis viruses, or other viruses known to infect the liver.

Vaccination with hepatitis B vaccine (recombinant) is recommended in persons of all ages, especially those who are or will be at increased risk of infection with hepatitis B virus.

The incidence of infection is known to vary greatly in different geographic areas and in different populations throughout the world. Vaccination strategy should vary accordingly.

Areas with High Prevalence: In these areas, most of the population are at risk of acquiring hepatitis B, often at a young age. Therefore, vaccination should be targeted to infants born to HBsAg-positive mothers, infants and children and susceptible adults.

Areas with Low Prevalence: In these areas vaccination may be limited to those who are in groups identified as being at increased risk of infection. The following categories might be identified in low-prevalence areas:

A. Infants born to HBsAg-positive mothers.

B. Health Care Personnel: dentists and oral surgeons; physicians and surgeons; nurses; paramedical personnel and custodial staff who may be exposed to the virus via blood or other patient specimens (i.e., body fluids and tissues); dental hygienists and dental nurses; laboratory personnel handling blood, blood products and other patient specimens (i.e., body fluids and tissues); and dental, medical and nursing students, preferably soon after acceptance in the university.

C. Selected Patients and Patient Contacts: patients and staff in hemodialysis units and hematology/oncology units; patients requiring frequent and/or large-volume blood transfusions or clotting factor concentrates (e.g., persons with hemophilia, thalassemia); patients (residents) and staff of institutions for the mentally handicapped; classroom contacts of deinstitutionalized mentally handicapped persons who have persistent hepatitis B antigenemia and who show aggressive behavior; and household and other intimate contacts of persons with persistent hepatitis B antigenemia.

D. Military Personnel Identified as Being at Increased Risk.

E. Morticians and Embalmers.

F. Blood Bank and Plasma Fractionation Workers.

G. Persons at Increased Risk of the Disease Due to Their Sexual Practices such as: persons who have heterosexual activity with multiple partners; persons who repeatedly contract sexually transmitted diseases; homosexually active males and female prostitutes.

H. Prisoners.

I. Users of Illicit Injectable Drugs.

Contraindications: Hypersensitivity to any component of the vaccine.

Warnings: Because of the long incubation period for hepatitis B, it is possible for unrecognized infection to be present at the time hepatitis B vaccine (recombinant) is given. Hepatitis B vaccine (recombinant) may not prevent hepatitis B in such patients.

Patients who develop symptoms suggestive of hypersensitivity after an injection should not receive further injections of hepatitis B vaccine (recombinant) (see Contraindications).

Precautions: General: Persons with immuno-deficiency or those receiving immunosuppressive therapy require larger vaccine doses and respond less well than healthy individuals.

As with any parenteral vaccine, epinephrine should be available for immediate use should an anaphylactoid reaction occur.

Any serious active infection is reason for delaying use of hepatitis B vaccine (recombinant), except when, in the opinion of the physician, withholding the vaccine entails a greater risk.

Caution and appropriate care should be exercised in administering hepatitis B vaccine (recombinant) to individuals with severely compromised cardiopulmonary status or to others in whom a febrile or systemic reaction could pose a significant risk.

Pregnancy: Animal reproduction studies have not been conducted with hepatitis B vaccine (recombinant). It is also not known whether hepatitis B vaccine (recombinant) can cause fetal harm when administered to a pregnant woman or can affect reproductive capacity. Hepatitis B vaccine (recombinant) should be given to a pregnant woman only if clearly needed.

Lactation: It is not known whether hepatitis B vaccine (recombinant) is excreted in human milk. However, studies with hepatitis B vaccine (recombinant) in 12 lactating women have failed to reveal evidence of this vaccine being secreted.

Children: Hepatitis B vaccine (recombinant) has been shown to be generally well-tolerated and highly immunogenic in infants and children of all ages. Newborns have responded well; maternally transferred antibodies did not interfere with the active immune response to the vaccine. See Dosage for recommended pediatric dosage and recommended dosage for infants born to HBsAg-positive mothers. The safety profile and effectiveness of the dialysis formulation in children have not been established.

Adverse Effects: Hepatitis B vaccine (recombinant) is generally well tolerated. No serious adverse reactions attributable to vaccination were reported during the course of clinical trials involving administration of hepatitis B vaccine (recombinant) to over 1 000 individuals. The frequency of complaints was somewhat lower following the second and third vaccine doses compared with the first dose. As with any vaccine, there is the possibility that broad use of the vaccine could reveal rare adverse reactions not observed in clinical trials.

No adverse reactions were reported during clinical trials which could be related to yeast.

In a group of studies 3 258 doses of hepatitis B vaccine (recombinant) were administered to 1 252 healthy adults. Vaccine recipients were monitored for 5 days after each dose, and the following adverse reactions were reported in Table I.

Table I—Recombivax HB

Adverse Effects	% of Doses
Local Reactions in Injection Site	
Injection site reactions, consisting principally of local pain, soreness and tenderness and including pruritus, erythema, ecchymoses, swelling, warmth and nodule formation.	16.7
Body as a Whole	
Fatigue/Asthenia	4.2
Malaise	1.2
Fever ≥37.8°C	3.2
Sweating	0.5
Chills	0.2
Flushing	0.2
Aching	0.4
Sensation of warmth	0.4
Digestive	
Nausea	1.8
Diarrhea	1.1
Vomiting	0.3
Abdominal Pains/Cramps	0.3
Dyspepsia	0.2
Diminished Appetite	0.1
Integumentary	
Pruritus	0.3
Rash	0.2
Urticaria	0.1
Musculoskeletal	
Myalgia	0.4
Arthralgia	0.5
Back Pain	0.2
Neck Pain	0.2
Shoulder Pain	0.2
Neck stiffness	0.2
Nervous System	
Headache	4.1
Light headedness	0.3
Vertigo/dizziness	0.5
Paresthesia	0.1
Respiratory	
Pharyngitis	1.2
Rhinitis	0.8
Cough	0.2
Upper respiratory infection (NOS)	1.0
Influenza	0.3
Special Senses	
Earache	0.2

Other incidences reported in less than 1% of injections:
Cardiovascular: hypotension.
Hemic/lymphatic: lymphadenopathy.
Integumentary; angioedema.
Psychiatric/behavioral: insomnia/disturbed sleep.
Urogenital: dysuria.

Additional Adverse Effects: The following additional adverse reactions have been reported with use of the marketed vaccine; however, in many instances a causal relationship to the vaccine has not been established.

Hematologic: Increased erythrocyte sedimentation rate.

Hypersensitivity: Anaphylaxis and symptoms of immediate hypersensitivity reactions including edema, dyspnea, chest discomfort, bronchial spasm, or palpitation have been reported within the first few hours after vaccination. An apparent hypersensitivity syndrome (serum-sickness-like) of delayed onset has been reported days to weeks after vaccination, including: arthritis (usually transient), and dermatologic reactions such as erythema multiforme, ecchymoses and erythema nodosum (see Precautions).

Nervous system: Peripheral neuropathy including Bell's Palsy; Guillain-Barré syndrome, and optic neuritis.

Special Senses: tinnitus.

Dosage: The deltoid muscle is the preferred site for i.m. injection in adults. The anterolateral thigh is the recommended site for i.m. injection in infants and children. Data suggest that injections given in the buttocks are given frequently into fatty tissue instead of into muscle. Such injections may result in lower seroconversion rate than is expected.

The vaccine should be used as supplied. No dilution or reconstitution is necessary. The full recommended dose of the vaccine should be used.

It is recommended to record lot numbers when the vaccine is administered to a recipient.

I.M.: Do not inject i.v. or intradermally. Hepatitis B vaccine (recombinant)] is for i.m. injection. It may, however, be administered s.c. to persons at risk of hemorrhage following i.m. injections. However, when other aluminum-adsorbed vaccines have been administered s.c., an increased incidence of local reactions including subcutaneous nodules has been observed. Therefore, s.c. administration should be used only in persons (e.g., hemophiliacs) at risk of hemorrhage following i.m. injections.

Shake well before withdrawal and use.

Thorough agitation at the time of administration is necessary to maintain suspension of the vaccine. Parenteral drug products should be inspected visually for particulate matter and discoloration prior to administration. After thorough agitation, Recombivax HB is a slightly opaque, white suspension.

It is important to use a separate sterile syringe and needle for each individual patient to prevent transmission of hepatitis and other infectious agents from one person to another.

The immunization regimen consists of 3 doses of vaccine given according to the following schedule: 1st dose: at elected date; 2nd dose: 1 month later; 3rd dose: 6 months after the first dose.

The volume of vaccine to be given on each occasion is as shown in Table II.

Table II—Recombivax HB

Dosage Volumes

Group	Initial (mL)	1 Month (mL)	6 Months (mL)
Infants*/children (birth to 10 years of age) Pediatric formulation 5 μg/0.5 mL	0.25	0.25	0.25
Adolescents (11 -19 years of age) Pediatric formulation 5 μg/0.5 mL	0.5	0.5	0.5
Adults Adult formulation 10 μg/1 mL	1.0	1.0	1.0

*Infants born of HBsAg-negative mothers.

Recombivax HB Dialysis Formulation: Recombivax HB dialysis formulation (40 μg/mL) is intended only for adult predialysis/dialysis patients.

The recommended vaccination regimen for predialysis/dialysis patients is as shown in Table III.

Table III—Recombivax HB

Recommended Vaccination Regimen for Predialysis/Dialysis Patients

Group	Initial (mL)	1 Month (mL)	6 Months (mL)
Predialysis/dialysis Dialysis formulation 40 μg/1 mL	1.0	1.0	1.0

Recombivax HB (cont'd)

Dosage for Infants Born to HBsAg-positive Mothers: Infants born to HBsAg-positive mothers are at high risk of becoming chronic carriers of hepatitis B virus and of developing the chronic sequelae of hepatitis B virus infection. Well-controlled studies have shown that administration of three 0.5 mL doses of hepatitis B immune globulin starting at birth is 75% effective in preventing establishment of the chronic carrier state in these infants during the first year of life. Protection is transient under these circumstances and the effectiveness of the passively administered hepatitis B immune globulin declines thereafter. Results from clinical studies indicate that administration of one 0.5 mL dose of hepatitis B immune globulin at birth and three 5 µg (0.5 mL) doses, the first dose given within 1 week after birth, was 96% effective in preventing establishment of the chronic carrier state in infants born to HBsAg- and HBeAg-positive mothers. Testing for HBsAg and anti-HBs is recommended at 12 to 15 months to monitor the final success or failure of therapy. If HBsAg is not detectable, and anti-HBs is present, the child has been protected.

The recommended dosage for infants born to HBsAg-positive mothers is as shown in Table IV.

Table IV—Recombivax HB

Recommended Dosage for Infants Born to HBsAg Positive Mothers

Treatment	Birth (mL)	Within 7 days (mL)	1 Month (mL)	6 Months (mL)
Recombivax HB (Pediatric dose) 5 µg/0.5 mL		0.5[a]	0.5	0.5
Hepatitis B immune globulin	0.5			

[a] The first dose of Recombivax HB (Pediatric formulation) may be given at birth at the same time as hepatitis B immune globulin, but should be administered in the opposite anterolateral thigh. This procedure may be preferable to ensure absorption of the vaccine.

Acute Exposure to Blood Containing HBsAg: There are no prospective studies directly testing the efficacy of a combination of hepatitis B immune globulin and hepatitis B vaccine (recombinant) in preventing clinical hepatitis B following percutaneous, ocular or mucous membrane exposure to hepatitis B virus. However, recent studies have established the relative efficacies of immune globulins and/or hepatitis B vaccine in various exposure situations. Since most persons with such exposures (e.g., health care workers) are candidates for the hepatitis B vaccine and since combined hepatitis B immune globulin plus vaccine is more efficacious than hepatitis B immune globulin alone in perinatal exposures, the following guidelines are recommended for persons who have been exposed to hepatitis B virus such as through (1) percutaneous (needlestick), ocular, mucous membrane exposure to blood known or presumed to contain HBsAg , (2) human bites by known or presumed HBsAg carriers, that penetrate the skin, or (3) following intimate sexual contact with known or presumed HBsAg carriers:

Hepatitis B immune globulin (0.06 mL/kg) should be given as soon as possible after exposure and within 24 hours if possible. Hepatitis B vaccine 1 mL (10 µg/1 mL) should be given i.m. within 7 days of exposure and second and third doses given 1 and 6 months, respectively, after the first dose.

For Syringe Use Only: Withdraw the recommended dose from the vial using a sterile needle and syringe free of preservatives, antiseptics, and detergents.

Supplied: Adults: Each 1 mL dose of sterile suspension contains: hepatitis B surface antigen 10 µg adsorbed onto approximately 0.5 mg of aluminum hydroxide. Formaldehyde-treated. Thimerosal (mercury derivative) 1:20 000 added as a preservative. Single dose vials of 1 mL; 3-dose vials of 3 mL.

Children: Each 0.5 mL dose of pediatric, sterile suspension, contains: hepatitis B surface antigen 5 µg adsorbed onto approximately 0.25 mg of aluminum hydroxide. Formaldehyde-treated. Thimerosal (mercury derivative) 1:20 000 added as a preservative. Single dose vials of 0.5 mL.

Adult Dialysis Formulation: Each 1 mL dose of sterile suspension contains: hepatitis B surface antigen 40 µg adsorbed onto approximately 0.5 mg of aluminum hydroxide. Formaldehyde-treated. Single dose vials of 1 mL.

Store unopened and opened vials at 2 to 8°C. Storage above or below the recommended temperature may reduce potency. **Do not freeze because freezing destroys potency.** The vaccine is used directly as supplied. No dilution or reconstitution is necessary. Do not use vaccine after the expiration date.

Reviewed 1998

RECTOCORT ℞

Welcker-Lyster

Hydrocortisone Acetate

Topical Corticosteroid

Supplied: Ointment: Each 100 g of ointment contains: hydrocortisone acetate 840 mg equivalent to hydrocortisone 750 mg. Tubes of 15 and 30 g.

Suppositories: Each suppository contains: hydrocortisone acetate 11.2 mg equivalent to hydrocortisone 10 mg. Boxes of 12 and 24.

RECTOGEL
RECTOGEL HC ℞

Riva

Zinc Sulfate Monohydrate—Benzocaine

Zinc Sulfate Monohydrate—Benzocaine—Hydrocortisone Acetate

Anorectal Therapy

Supplied: Rectogel: Each tube contains: zinc sulfate monohydrate 0.5% and benzocaine 10% in a petroleum base. Nonmedicinal ingredients: methyl- and propylparaben. Tubes of 15 and 30 g with applicator.

Rectogel HC: Each tube contains: zinc sulfate monohydrate 0.5%, benzocaine 10% and hydrocortisone acetate 1% in a petroleum base. Nonmedicinal ingredients: methyl- and propylparaben. Tubes of 15 and 30 g with applicator.

Store in a cool place under 22°C.

New Product 1998

RED AWAY®

Rivex Ophthalmics

Naphazoline HCl

Vasoconstrictor

Supplied: Each mL of sterile ophthalmic solution contains: naphazoline HCl 0.1%. Nonmedicinal ingredients: benzalkonium chloride, boric acid, edetate disodium, hydrochloric acid, purified water, sodium carbonate and sodium chloride. Plastic squeeze bottles of 15 mL with controlled tip applicators.

REDOXON®

Roche

Ascorbic Acid

Vitamin

Indications: Prevention and treatment of deficiency of ascorbic acid. Ascorbic acid is essential for the formation of collagen and intercellular material, and hence for the development of cartilage, bone and teeth, and for wound healing. It influences the formation of hemoglobin, erythrocyte maturation, and certain immunological reactions in the body. The reducing properties of ascorbic acid are useful in the treatment of idiopathic methemoglobinuria. Useful in large doses to acidify urine.

Precautions: Ascorbic acid may affect the activity of other drugs. In acid urine the excretion of weak acids, such as some sulfonamides, is decreased and that of weak bases, such as quinidine, is increased; the clinical significance of these effects is not known. Other possible hazards are interference by large doses with the effects of warfarin and precipitation of crisis in patients with sickle cell anemia.

Large doses of ascorbic acid may give false negative tests in enzyme dip tests for glycosuria and false positive tests when Benedict's Solution is used as a test for glycosuria.

Adverse Effects: The most frequently noted adverse effect of large doses of ascorbic acid is diarrhea. Also, acidification of the urine by large amounts of ascorbic acid may cause the precipitation of urate, oxalate, or cystine stones in the urinary tract.

Dosage: Dissolve tablets in a glass of water immediately before use. The minimum human daily requirement of ascorbic acid for an adult is about 30 mg and for infants 5 mg/kg. The minimum protective dose against clinical scurvy is 10 mg daily. These quantities are normally supplied in the diet, but individuals vary greatly in their requirements, and the higher the metabolic rate (as in pregnancy and lactation) the greater the need; more is required in adolescence, pregnancy and lactation, infections, thyrotoxicosis, and postoperative states. For prophylactic purposes, doses of at least double the minimum requirements are advised, while in cases of known deficiency, or where there is excessive excretion, doses of 100 to 500 mg are employed. A daily allowance of 75 mg for a man and 70 mg for a woman, the latter dose being increased to 100 mg in pregnancy and 150 mg during lactation, has been recommended. For the prevention of infantile scurvy, 5 mg of ascorbic acid may be added to the feeds of bottle fed infants. Oral doses of 150 mg twice daily are used in idiopathic methemoglobinuria. Doses of 1 g every 6 hours are used to acidify urine.

Supplied: Each cylindrical, biplane, rough surfaced, effervescent tablet contains: ascorbic acid 1 g. Tablet forms available: Orange [orange color, orange odor and taste; energy: 26.0 kJ (6.2 kcal); sodium: 12.4 mmol (284 mg)]. Nonmedicinal ingredients: acacia, apocarotenal, carrageenan, dextrin, dl-α-tocopherol, flavor, hydogenated vegetable oil, riboflavin, sodium bicarbonate, sodium chloride, sodium saccharin, sucrose and tartaric acid. Lemon: [yellow color, lemon odor and taste; energy: 24.9 kJ (5.9 kcal); sodium: 12.8 mmol (292 mg)]. Nonmedicinal ingredients: citric acid, cornstarch, flavor, riboflavin, sodium bicarbonate, sodium chloride, sodium saccharin, sucrose and tartaric acid.

Gluten-, lactose-, paraben-, sulfite- and tartrazine-free. Tubes of 10, packs of 12. Keep tube tightly closed in a dry place, between 15 to 30°C. Desiccant in the cap harmless if swallowed.

(Shown in Product Recognition Section)

REDOXON-B®

Roche

Vitamin B Complex—Ascorbic Acid

Vitamin-Mineral Supplement

Indications: For supportive nutritional supplementation in conditions in which water soluble vitamins are required prophylactically or therapeutically.

Dosage: Adults: 1 effervescent tablet daily, or as directed by the physician, dissolved in ½ glass of cold water immediately before use.

Supplied: Each cylindrical, biplane, rough surfaced, orange-flavored, effervescent tablet contains: ascorbic acid 1 000 mg, vitamin B_1 (as thiamine monophosphate ester chloride) 15 mg, vitamin B_2 (as riboflavin 5-phosphate sodium) 15 mg, niacinamide 50 mg, vitamin B_6 (as pyridoxine HCl) 10 mg, pantothenic acid (as calcium pantothenate) 23 mg, biotin 150 µg, vitamin B_{12} 10 µg and magnesium (as carbonate and sulfate) 100 mg. Nonmedicinal ingredients: acacia, aspartame, apocarotenal, calcium carbonate, carrageenan, citric acid, dextrin, dl-α-tocopherol, flavor, hydrogenated vegetable oil, mannitol, sodium bicarbonate, sodium chloride, sodium lauryl sulfate and sucrose. Energy: 8 kcal (33 kJ). Sodium: (11.5 mmol) 265 mg. Gluten-, lactose-, paraben-, sulfite- and tartrazine-free. Tubes of 10, packs of 12.

Keep tube tightly closed in a dry place, between 15 to 30°C. Desiccant in the cap harmless if swallowed.

(Shown in Product Recognition Section)

REDOXON-CAL®

Roche

Vitamins D_3—Pyridoxine HCl—Ascorbic Acid—Calcium

Vitamin—Mineral Supplement

Indications: Increased requirements of nutritional substances during the years of general growth and development; pregnancy and lactation; disease and convalescence; geriatrics. Also indicated in the delayed healing of wounds and fractures, for the prevention of vitamin and calcium deficiency, osteoporosis, osteomalacia, faulty development of bones and teeth and for improvement of metabolism and general growth and development.

Dosage: Adults: 1 effervescent tablet daily dissolved in 240 mL of water immediately before use. School children: ½ to 1 effervescent tablet daily or as recommended. Pediatric dosage is correspondingly smaller.

Supplied: Each orange effervescent tablet contains: ascorbic acid 1 000 mg, vitamin D_3 300 IU, pyridoxine HCl 15 mg and calcium (as calcium carbonate) 250 mg. Nonmedicinal ingredients: acacia, aspartame, beta-apo-8′-carotenal, carrageenan, citric acid, cornstarch, dextrin, dl-α-tocopherol, flavor, gelatin, hydrogenated vegetable oil, povidone, sodium bicarbonate, sodium chloride, sucrose and sucrose esters of fatty acids. Energy: 14.7 kJ (3.5 kcal). Sodium: 7.6 mmol (175 mg). Gluten-, lactose-, paraben-, sulfite- and tartrazine-free. Tubes of 10, packs of 12.

(Shown in Product Recognition Section)

REFRESH™
Allergan

Polyvinyl Alcohol

Ocular Lubricant

Supplied: Each unit dose container of 0.4 mL contains: polyvinyl alcohol 1.4%. Also contains povidone, purified water and sodium chloride. May also contain hydrochloric acid or sodium hydroxide to adjust pH. Preservative-free. Use immediately after opening. Do not store opened container.

REGLAN® Ⓟ
Wyeth-Ayerst

Metoclopramide HCl

Upper Gastrointestinal Tract Motility Modifier—Antiemetic

Supplied: Injectable: Each 2 mL vial contains: metoclopramide HCl 10 mg (5 mg/mL). Nonmedicinal ingredients: hydrochloric acid, sodium hydroxide and water for injection. Preservative-free. Cartons of 10.

Each 10 mL vial for i.v. infusion (with dilution) contains: metoclopramide HCl 50 mg (5 mg/mL). Nonmedicinal ingredients: hydrochloric acid, sodium hydroxide and water for injection. Preservative-free. Cartons of 10. (For the prophylaxis of nausea and vomiting associated with cancer chemotherapeutic regimens that include cisplatin as a component.)

Each 30 mL single use vial for i.v. infusion (with dilution) contains: metoclopramide HCl 150 mg (5 mg/mL). Nonmedicinal ingredients: hydrochloric acid, sodium hydroxide and water for injection. Preservative-free. Cartons of 10. (For the prophylaxis of nausea and vomiting associated with cancer chemotherapeutic regimens that include cisplatin as a component.)

Liquid: Each mL of orange-colored, chocolate-flavored liquid contains: metoclopramide HCl 1 mg. Nonmedicinal ingredients: citric acid anhydrous, FD&C Yellow 6 Sunset, flavors (Cheri-Beri artificial, chocolate imitation, custard imitation) glycerin, methylparaben, propylparaben, sorbitol and water purified. Energy: 51.9 kJ (12.4 kcal)/5 mL. Bottles of 100 mL.

Tablets: Each blue, scored, compressed tablet, engraved AYERST, contains: metoclopramide HCl 10 mg. Nonmedicinal ingredients: FD&C Blue 1 Aluminum Lake, magnesium stearate, mannitol, microcrystalline cellulose and stearic acid. Energy: <1 kJ (<1 kcal). Bottles of 100 and 500.

All dosage forms are gluten-, lactose-, sulfite- and tartrazine-free.

(Shown in Product Recognition Section)

The safety of immunization programs is in part maximized through monitoring vaccine-associated adverse events. To report a vaccine-associated adverse event, complete the form "Report of Vaccine-associated Adverse Event" found in the CLIN-INFO SECTION.

REGULAR STRENGTH ACETAMINOPHEN
REGULAR STRENGTH ACETAMINOPHEN with Codeine Ⓝ
WestCan

Acetaminophen

Acetaminophen—Caffeine—Codeine Phosphate

Analgesic—Antipyretic

Supplied: Regular Strength Acetaminophen: Each tablet contains: acetaminophen 325 mg. Bottles of 24, 100, 125 and 500 (child resistant caps supplied for 24, 100 and 125).

Regular Strength Acetaminophen with Codeine: Each tablet contains: acetaminophen 325 mg, caffeine 15 mg and codeine phosphate 8 mg. Bottles of 30, 50, 100 and 200 (child resistant caps supplied for 30, 50 and 100).

REJUVA-A® Ⓟ
Stiefel

Tretinoin

Agent for the Treatment of Photodamaged Skin

Pharmacology: Tretinoin, a member of the retinoid class of compounds, is both pharmacologically and structurally related to vitamin A which regulates epithelial cell growth and differentiation. Retinoic acid may exert its effects at the molecular level by binding to specific steroid-like nuclear receptors known as retinoic acid receptors. Binding of retinoic acid to a retinoic acid receptor will promote events at the cellular level by regulating gene transcription and affecting activities such as cellular differentiation and proliferation but the exact mechanism underlying these processes remain to be elucidated.

Topical tretinoin has been reported to correct many of the structural abnormalities of photoaged skin. Tretinoin has been shown to produce epidermal and dermal changes. At the epidermal level, tretinoin increased the epidermal thickness (acanthosis) and the mean granular layer, decreased tonofilament and desmosome strength and increased secretion of a glycosaminoglycan-like substance into the intercellular space. In addition, the cohesion of the epidermal cells and activity of the melanocytes are reduced.

Functional changes in the epidermis include an increase in trans-epidermal water loss and permeability. At the level of the dermis, vasodilatation and angiogenesis of the superficial vasculature, along with increased papillary dermal collagen, have been reported.

The long-term (1 year) safety and efficacy of tretinoin cream in the treatment of photoaging was evaluated during a double-blind, randomized, parallel group, multicentre, placebo controlled study. A total of 147 patients (110 active, 37 placebo) were entered; all were caucasian with chronic, moderate to severe actinically damaged facial skin. The patients applied the medication over their entire face once a day before retiring and were evaluated by the investigators after 1, 3, 6, 9 and 12 months of therapy.

Among the various expressions of the entity of the disease, significant clinical benefits were demonstrated for tretinoin cream versus placebo for the following: reduction in fine wrinkles from Month 3; reduction in moderate, moderately severe and severe coarse wrinkles from Month 6; reduction in the severity of dermatosis at Month 9.

In addition, histological findings demonstrated that skin treated with tretinoin cream showed significant decrease in the thickness of the stratum corneum and increases in the thickness of the stratum granulosum and spinulosum. Skin receiving the placebo cream showed no significant difference in the thickness of the different epidermal strata.

Indications: For the treatment of photodamaged skin (heliodermatitis).

The safety and efficacy of tretinoin cream (0.025%) for the prevention and treatment of actinic keratosis has not been established.

Contraindications: Patients with known hypersensitivity to retinoids or to any ingredient contained in the preparation.

Warnings: Tretinoin cream should be used as part of a comprehensive skin protection program, including use of sunscreen products and protective clothing.

Tretinoin cream is intended for external use only and should be kept away from the nostrils and other mucous membranes because of its irritant effect. Avoid the angles of the nose and nasolabial fold (if treatment in these areas is necessary, apply very sparingly). Topical use may induce severe local erythema and peeling at the site of application. If the degree of local irritation warrants, patients should be directed to use the medication less frequently, discontinue use temporarily or discontinue use altogether. Tretinoin has been reported to cause severe irritation of eczematous skin, and tretinoin cream should only be used with utmost caution in patients with this condition.

Pregnancy: **Topical tretinoin should be used by women of childbearing years only after contraceptive counseling. It is recommended that topical tretinoin should not be used by pregnant women.**

There have been rare reports of birth defects among babies born to women exposed to **topical** tretinoin during pregnancy. However, there are no well-controlled prospective studies of the use of topical tretinoin in pregnant women. A retrospective study of mothers exposed to topical tretinoin during the first trimester of pregnancy found no increase in the incidence of birth defects.

Topical retinoid teratology studies in rats and rabbits have been inconclusive. As with all retinoids, tretinoin administered **orally** at high doses is teratogenic.

Lactation: **It is not known whether tretinoin is excreted in human milk. Nevertheless, a decision should be made whether to discontinue nursing or to discontinue the drug, taking into account the importance of the drug to the mother.**

Children: **Safety and effectiveness in children have not been established.**

Precautions: General: Care should be used when tretinoin cream is applied to treat wrinkles around the eyes (Crow's feet) and mouth.

If a sunburn occurs, it is advisable to interrupt therapy until the severe erythema and peeling subside. **Patients whose occupations require considerable exposure to the sun and those inherently sensitive to the sun should exercise particular caution and are advised to use a sunscreen of at least SPF 15. Protective clothing over treated areas is recommended when sun exposure cannot be avoided.**

Carcinogenesis: Carcinogenic studies have not been conducted with tretinoin cream. Studies in hairless albino mice suggest that tretinoin may accelerate the tumorigenic potential of ultraviolet radiation. Although the significance of these studies to man is not clear, patients should avoid or minimize exposure to sun.

Information Provided to the Patient: A patient information leaflet has been prepared and is included with each package of Rejuva-A (see Blue Section—Information for the Patient "Rejuva-A").

Drug Interactions: Concomitant topical medication should be used with caution during therapy with tretinoin cream because of possible intensified reactions. Particular caution should be exercised when using cosmetics with a strong drying effect and products with high concentration of alcohol, as well as those containing a peeling agent concomitantly (such as sulfur, resorcinol, benzoyl peroxide or salicylic acid) with tretinoin cream. It may be advisable to "rest" a patient's skin until the effects of previously used peeling agents subside before initiating tretinoin cream therapy.

Tretinoin is compatible with almost all oral drugs except for photosensitizers. In treating thin-skinned, sensitive regions such as the neck area with tretinoin, it is recommended to apply tretinoin cream thinly every third night, in the beginning, and then every other night as tolerance develops.

Excessive exposure to sunlight or ultraviolet rays (sunlamps) should be avoided during tretinoin cream treatment because the additional irradiation may lead to a more intense action.

If a sunburn occurs, it is advisable to interrupt therapy until the severe erythema and peeling subside. Patients whose occupations require considerable exposure to the sun should exercise particular caution and advised to use a sunscreen of at least SPF 15.

Adverse Effects: In the long-term clinical trial with tretinoin cream, erythema and peeling/dryness were the most reported side effects in the tretinoin cream group with only 5 of 110 patients from this group withdrawing because of adverse events (erythema and peeling).

The skin of certain sensitive individuals, particularly those with fair complexions, may become excessively red, edematous, blistered or crusted when exposed to tretinoin cream. Pain, burning sensation, tenderness, irritation or pruritus have also been occasionally reported. If any of these effects occur, the medication should be discontinued until the integrity of

Rejuva-A (cont'd)

the skin has been restored or the treatment schedule adjusted to the level the patient can tolerate. Temporary hyper- or hypopigmentation has been reported with repeated application of tretinoin. To date, all adverse clinical effects of tretinoin encountered have been reversible upon discontinuance of therapy. In many instances, reinstitution of therapy with tretinoin failed to produce the adverse effect previously experienced.

Overdose: Symptoms and Treatment: Topical: If medication is applied excessively, marked redness, peeling or discomfort may occur.

Inadvertent oral ingestion of tretinoin cream may lead to the same adverse effects as those associated with excessive oral intake of vitamin A including teratogenesis in women of childbearing years. Therefore, in such cases, pregnancy testing should be carried out in women of childbearing years.

Dosage: Tretinoin cream is especially suitable for the treatment of sun sensitive Type I and II skin types e.g., fair skinned people with red or blond hair and blue or hazel eyes, who always burn easily, severely with no or minimal tanning.

Tretinoin cream should be applied to the affected area once a day just before retiring. The area under treatment should be thoroughly cleansed with a mild soap and water and patted dry with a soft towel followed by application of tretinoin cream with a gentle rubbing motion using the fingertips.

It is recommended to start the therapy by applying one pea-size amount to the forehead and spread it evenly over the entire face. After tolerance to the medication is established, the dose may be doubled by applying a pea-size amount to each temple. For those patients who experience excessive irritation or discomfort, the frequency of application should be decreased to every other night or even every third night.

Treatment should be discontinued if a severe local inflammatory response is experienced. In cases where it has been necessary to discontinue therapy or to reduce the frequency of application, therapy may be reinstituted when the adverse effects have ceased.

Therapeutic results will occur gradually. Nine to twelve months of therapy may be required before beneficial effects are seen. At that time, frequency of application may be reduced to 2 or 3 times/week.

Information for the Patient: See Blue Section—Information for the Patient "Rejuva-A".

Supplied: Rejuva-A Cream is available in Rejuva-A Skin Revitalizing System which also contains Rejuva Moisturizing Day Cream SPF 15.

Rejuva-A: Each g of cream contains: tretinoin 0.025% in a moisturizing cream base. Nonmedicinal ingredients: butylated hydroxytoluene, carbomer 934, cyclomethicone, diisopropyl adipate, germaben II, glycerin, light mineral oil, phenyl trimethicone, polysorbate 60, purified water, sodium hydroxide, sorbitan monostearate and stearyl alcohol. Tubes of 20 g.

Rejuva Moisturizing Day Cream SPF 15: Each g of cream contains: parsol 1989, parsol MCX. Nonmedicinal ingredients: butylated hydroxytoluene, carbomer 934, cyclomethicone, diisopropyl adipate, germaben II, glycerin, isoarachidyl neopentanoate, light mineral oil, phenyl trimethicone, polysorbate 60, purified water, sodium hydroxide and stearyl alcohol. Tubes of 20 g.

New Product 1998

RELAFEN™ Ⓟ

SmithKline Beecham

Nabumetone

Nonsteroidal Anti-inflammatory Agent

Pharmacology: Nabumetone is a nonacidic, nonsteroidal anti-inflammatory drug (NSAID) with a naphthylalkanone structure which is virtually insoluble in water. It exhibits anti-inflammatory, analgesic and antipyretic properties in pharmacologic studies. As with the acidic NSAIDs, its mode of action is not known. However, the ability to inhibit prostaglandin synthesis may be involved in the anti-inflammatory effect.

Nabumetone, as the parent compound, is a pro-drug which undergoes rapid hepatic biotransformation to its principal active metabolite, 6-methoxy-2-naphthylacetic acid (6-MNA), a potent inhibitor of prostaglandin biosynthesis.

Nabumetone was compared to ASA in inducing gastrointestinal blood loss. Food intake was not monitored. Studies utilizing ^{51}Cr-tagged red blood cells in healthy males showed no difference in fecal blood loss after 3 or 4 weeks' therapy of nabumetone 1 000 or 2 000 mg daily when compared to either placebo-treated or nontreated subjects. In contrast, ASA 3 600 mg daily produced an increase in fecal blood loss when compared to the nabumetone, placebo- or nontreated subjects.

In 1 week repeat dose studies in healthy volunteers, nabumetone 1 000 mg daily had little effect on collagen-induced platelet aggregation and no effect on bleeding time.

Pharmacokinetics: After oral administration, approximately 80% of a radio-labeled dose of nabumetone is found in the urine, indicating that nabumetone is well absorbed from the gastrointestinal tract. Nabumetone itself is not quantifiable in the plasma because, after absorption, it undergoes rapid biotransformation to the principal active metabolite, 6-MNA. Approximately 35% of a 1 000 mg dose of nabumetone is converted to 6-MNA and 50% is converted into unidentified metabolites which are subsequently excreted in the urine. Following oral administration, peak plasma levels of 6-MNA occur between 2.5 and 4 hours (range 1 to 12 hours). Preliminary in vivo and in vitro studies suggest that unlike other NSAIDs, there is no evidence of enterohepatic recirculation of the active metabolite. Steady state is generally achieved between 3 and 6 days and the elimination half-life is variable from 23 (±3.7) hours in young healthy patients to 30 (±8.1) hours in the elderly.

The active metabolite penetrates into the synovial fluids at measurable sustained levels in osteoarthritis and rheumatoid arthritis patients. There is wide inter-individual variation in plasma concentrations of 6-MNA. A correlation between plasma 6-MNA levels and efficacy has not been established.

6-MNA is more than 99% bound to plasma proteins. The free fraction is dependent on total concentration of 6-MNA and is proportional to dose over the range of 1 000 to 2 000 mg. It is 0.2% to 0.3% at concentrations typically achieved following administration of nabumetone 1 000 mg and is approximately 0.6% to 0.8% of the total concentrations at steady-state following daily administration of 2 000 mg.

Table I—Relafen

Mean Pharmacokinetic Parameters of Nabumetone Active Metabolite (6-MNA) at Steady-state Following Oral Administration of 1 000 or 2 000 mg Doses of Nabumetone

Abbreviations (units)	Young Adults Mean±SD 1 000 mg n=31	Young Adults Mean±SD 2 000 mg n=12	Elderly Mean±SD 1 000 mg n=27
T_{max} (hours)*	3.0 (1.0 to 12.0)	2.5 (1.0 to 8.0)	4.0 (1.0 to 10.0)
t½ (hours)	22.5±3.7	26.2±3.7	29.8±8.1
Cl_{ss}/F (mL/min)	26.1±17.3	21.0±4.0	18.6±13.4
VD_{ss}/F(L)	55.4±26.4	53.4±11.3	50.2±25.3

*T_{max} is reported as median (range) values.

Concomitant administration of an aluminum-containing antacid had no significant effect on the bioavailability of the active metabolite of nabumetone. When administered with food or milk, there is more rapid absorption; however, the total amount of 6-MNA in the plasma is unchanged.

Geriatrics: Steady-state plasma concentrations in elderly patients were generally higher than in young healthy subjects (see Table I for summary of pharmacokinetic parameters of 6-MNA).

Renal Insufficiency: In studies of patients with renal insufficiency, the mean terminal half-life of 6-MNA was increased in patients with severe renal dysfunction (creatinine clearance <30 mL/min/1.73 m^2). In patients undergoing hemodialysis, steady-state plasma concentrations of the active metabolite were similar to those observed in healthy subjects. Due to extensive protein binding, 6-MNA is not dialyzable.

Hepatic Impairment: Data in patients with severe hepatic impairment are limited. Biotransformation of nabumetone to 6-MNA and the further metabolism of 6-MNA to inactive metabolites is dependent on hepatic function and could be reduced in patients with severe hepatic impairment (history of or biopsy-proven cirrhosis).

Indications: For acute and chronic relief of the signs and symptoms of rheumatoid arthritis and osteoarthritis.

Contraindications: In patients who have previously exhibited hypersensitivity to nabumetone.

Nabumetone should not be given to patients in whom ASA or other NSAIDs induce asthma, urticaria or other allergic type reactions. Fatal anaphylactoid reactions have occurred in such individuals.

Warnings: Risk of Gastrointestinal Ulceration, Bleeding and Perforation with NSAID Therapy: Peptic ulceration, perforation and gastrointestinal bleeding, sometimes severe and occasionally fatal have been reported during therapy with NSAIDs including nabumetone.

Nabumetone should be given under close medical supervision to patients prone to gastrointestinal irritation particularly those with a history of peptic ulcer, diverticulosis or other inflammatory disease of the gastrointestinal tract. In these cases the physician must weigh the benefits of treatment against the possible hazards.

Patients taking any NSAID including this drug should be instructed to contact a physician immediately if they experience symptoms or signs suggestive of peptic ulceration or gastrointestinal bleeding. These reactions can occur without warning symptoms or signs and at any time during the treatment.

Elderly, frail and debilitated patients appear to be at higher risk from a variety of adverse reactions from NSAIDs. However, data from clinical studies with nabumetone have indicated that there were no overall differences in efficacy or safety between older patients and younger ones. As with other NSAIDs, the lowest dose should be sought for each patient. Therefore, after observing the response to initial therapy, the dose should be adjusted to meet individual patients' requirements. See Precautions for further advice.

Pregnancy and *Lactation:* As the safety and efficacy of nabumetone in human pregnancy and lactation have not been established, its use is therefore not recommended.

Teratogenic effects were not observed in rats or rabbits. Postnatal development was not affected even though the active metabolite of nabumetone (6-MNA) is found in the milk of lactating rats. Nabumetone and/or its active metabolites have been shown to cross the placental barrier of rats.

Children: Nabumetone is not recommended for use in children because the safety and efficacy in children have not been established.

Precautions: Gastrointestinal: If peptic ulceration is suspected or confirmed, or if gastrointestinal bleeding or perforation occurs, nabumetone should be discontinued, and appropriate treatment instituted and the patient closely monitored.

There is no definitive evidence that the concomitant administration of histamine H_2-receptor antagonists and/or antacids will either prevent the occurrence of gastrointestinal side effects or allow continuation of nabumetone therapy when and if these adverse reactions occur.

Hepatic Impairment: As with other NSAIDs, borderline elevations of one or more liver tests may occur. These abnormalities may progress, may remain essentially unchanged, or may be transient with continued therapy. A patient with symptoms and/or signs suggesting liver dysfunction, or in whom an abnormal liver test has occurred, should be evaluated for evidence of the development of more severe hepatic reaction while on therapy with this drug.

Severe hepatic reactions, including jaundice and cases of fatal hepatitis have been reported with other NSAIDs. Although such reactions are rare, if abnormal liver tests persist or worsen, if clinical signs and symptoms consistent with liver disease develop, or if systemic manifestations occur (e.g. eosinophilia, rash, etc.), this drug should be discontinued.

During long-term therapy, liver function tests should be monitored periodically. If this drug is to be used in the presence of impaired liver function, it must be done under strict observation.

Renal Impairment: As with other NSAIDs, long-term administration of nabumetone to animals has resulted in renal papillary necrosis and other abnormal renal pathology. In humans, there have been reports of acute interstitial nephritis with hematuria, proteinuria, and occasionally nephrotic syndrome.

A second form of renal toxicity has been seen in patients with prerenal conditions leading to the reduction in renal blood flow or blood volume, where the renal prostaglandins have a supportive role in the maintenance of renal perfusion. In these patients, administration of a NSAID may cause a dose-dependent reduction in prostaglandin formation and may precipitate overt renal decompensation. Patients at greatest risk of this reaction are those with impaired renal function, heart failure, liver dysfunction, those taking diuretics, and the elderly. Discontinuation of nonsteroidal anti-inflammatory therapy is usually followed by recovery to the pre-treatment state.

Nabumetone and its metabolites are eliminated primarily by the kidneys; therefore, the drug should be used with great caution in patients with impaired renal function. Although studies have shown that no adjustment of dosage is generally necessary in patients with renal insufficiency, as with other NSAIDs, patients with severely impaired renal function should be monitored more closely than patients with normal renal function.

During long-term therapy, kidney function should be monitored periodically.

Geriatrics: Use in the elderly and debilitated patient should be monitored more closely as NSAID use in this population is known to be associated with a higher risk of adverse events. Data from controlled clinical studies (where 24% of 1 677 patients were ≥65 years of age) and UK postmarketing studies with nabumetone (where 43% of 10 800 patients were ≥65 years of age) indicate that there were no differences in efficacy or safety between older and younger patients.

Fluid and Electrolyte Balance: Fluid retention and edema have been observed in patients treated with nabumetone. Therefore, as with many other NSAIDs, the possibility of precipitating congestive heart failure in elderly patients or those with compromised cardiac function should be borne in mind. Nabumetone should be used with caution in patients with heart failure, hypertension or other conditions predisposing to fluid retention.

With NSAID treatment, there is a potential risk of hyperkalemia particularly in patients with conditions such as diabetes mellitus or renal failure; elderly patients; or in patients receiving concomitant therapy with β-adrenergic blockers, angiotensin converting enzyme inhibitors or some diuretics. Serum electrolytes should be monitored periodically during long-term therapy, especially in those patients at risk.

Hematology: Drugs inhibiting prostaglandin biosynthesis do interfere with platelet function to some degree; therefore, patients who may be adversely affected by such an action should be carefully observed when nabumetone is administered. Blood dyscrasias associated with the use of NSAIDs are rare, but could have severe consequences.

Hypersensitivity: As with other NSAIDs, allergic reactions may occur. Manifestations of allergic reactions include urticaria, dyspnea, and in rare instances anaphylaxis, or severe skin reactions such as Stevens-Johnson syndrome.

Infection: In common with other anti-inflammatory drugs, nabumetone may mask the usual signs of infection.

Ophthalmology: Blurred and/or diminished vision has been reported with the use of nabumetone and other NSAIDs. If such symptoms develop this drug should be discontinued and an ophthalmologic examination performed; ophthalmic examination should be carried out at periodic intervals in any patients receiving this drug for an extended period of time.

Occupational Hazards: Dizziness or other disturbances of the CNS may occur following therapy with nabumetone. Patients experiencing these symptoms should be cautioned against driving or operating machinery.

Drug Interactions: In vitro studies have shown that, because of its affinity for protein, the active metabolite of nabumetone may displace other protein-bound drugs such as sulfonylureas, tolbutamide, chlorpropamide and warfarin, from their binding site. Although clinical pharmacology studies demonstrated no significant drug interaction between warfarin and nabumetone, concomitant administration of nabumetone and warfarin or other highly protein-bound drugs should be undertaken with caution.

Digoxin levels should be monitored, and if necessary, a dosage adjustment made when administered concomitantly with nabumetone. NSAIDs have also been reported to increase steady-state plasma lithium concentrations. It is recommended that these concentrations be monitored when initiating, adjusting or discontinuing nabumetone treatment. Rare cases of fatal renal toxicity have occurred when methotrexate and NSAIDs are given concomitantly.

Concomitant administration of an aluminum-containing antacid had no significant effect on the bioavailability of 6-MNA. When administered with food or milk, there is more rapid absorption; however, the total amount of 6-MNA in the plasma is unchanged.

Concomitant administration of acetaminophen, ASA or cimetidine did not affect the bioavailability of the principal circulating metabolite in volunteer subjects.

In controlled rheumatoid arthritis trials, nabumetone has been used in combination with gold, d-penicillamine, and corticosteroids. There was no evidence of untoward effects associated with their concurrent administration.

Adverse Effects: The most common adverse reactions encountered with NSAIDs are gastrointestinal, of which peptic ulcer, with or without bleeding, is the most severe. Fatalities have occurred on occasion particularly in the elderly.

Adverse reaction information was derived from blinded-controlled and open-labeled clinical trials and from worldwide marketing experience. Over 6 000 patients have been treated with nabumetone in clinical trials, and over 49 000 patients included in postmarketing surveillance studies and nabumetone has been prescribed extensively in those countries where the drug has received registration clearance.

In large scale postmarketing studies the adverse event profile was highly consistent with the profile seen in clinical trials of nabumetone. The pattern of adverse events remained similar in patients treated with nabumetone for several years, similar in patients taking 1 to 2 g doses, and was similar in patients aged <65 or ≥65 years.

In the description below, information on adverse experiences observed in U.S. clinical studies is presented. Of the 1 677 patients who received nabumetone during U.S. clinical trials, 1 524 were treated for at least 1 month 1 327 for at least 3 months, 929 for at least a year and 750 for at least 2 years. Over 300 patients have been treated for 5 years or longer.

The most frequently reported adverse reactions were related to the gastrointestinal tract. They were diarrhea, dyspepsia and abdominal pain. Of 1 677 patients treated with nabumetone in controlled clinical trials (1 140 followed for 1 year and 927 for 2 years), the cumulative incidence of peptic ulcers was 0.3% at 3 to 6 months, 0.5% at 1 year and 0.8% at 2 years.

The following is a listing of adverse events reported in long-term clinical trial follow-up involving treatment for up to 8 years. Adverse events listed at an estimated incidence of ≤0.01% are based on spontaneous reports from worldwide marketing experience. Where available, percentages are based upon the total number of observations, thus patients reporting multiple incidents of an adverse event have been recorded for each occurrence. Causal relationship to nabumetone has not necessarily been established for all of the events listed below.

Adverse Events: Gastrointestinal: diarrhea (14%), dyspepsia (13%), abdominal pain (12%), nausea (9%), flatulence (6%), constipation (4%), positive stool guaiac (2%), dry mouth (2%), gastritis (1%), vomiting (1%), melena 1%), eructation 0.7%), gastoenteritis (0.7%), anorexia (0.7%), rectal bleeding (0.5%), gastric ulcer (0.4%), duodenal ulcer (0.4%), stomatitis (0.4%), dysphagia (0.3%), increased appetite (0.2%), glossitis (0.2%), pancreatitis (0.1%), gingivitis (0.1%), duodenitis (0.1%), bilirubinuria (0.1%), gastrointestinal bleeding (0.1%), cholestatic jaundice (≤0.01%), gallstones (≤0.01%).

CNS: headache (8%), dizziness (6%), insomnia (3%), fatigue (2%), somnolence (2%), increased sweating (1%), nervousness (1%), depression (0.9%), vertigo (0.9%), malaise (0.8%), paresthesia (0.8%), asthenia (0.7%), anxiety (0.4%), confusion (0.3%), agitation (0.1%), tremor (0.1%), nightmares (<0.01%).

Dermatologic: rash (7%), pruritus (4%), alopecia (0.9%), urticaria (0.7%), acne (0.4%), bullous eruptions (0.2%), photosensitivity (0.2%), pseudoporphyria cutanea tarda (≤0.01%), erythema multiforme (≤0.01%), Stevens-Johnson syndrome (≤0.01%), toxic epidermal necrolysis (≤0.01%).

Special Senses: tinnitus (4%), abnormal vision (2%), taste disorder (0.2%).

Cardiovascular: hypertension (1.7%), palpitations (1%), syncope (0.3%), thrombophlebitis (0.2%), vasculitis (0.1%), angina (0.1%), arrhythmia (0.1%), myocardial infarction (0.1%).

Respiratory: dyspnea (1%), cough (0.6%), asthma (0.4%), eosinophilic pneumonia (≤0.01%), hypersensitivity pneumonitis (≤0.01%).

Renal/Genitourinary: dysuria (0.7%), albuminuria (0.5%), hematuria (0.4%), impotence (0.2%), renal stones (0.2%), hyperuricemia (0.1%), azotemia (0.1%), interstitial nephritis (≤0.01%), vaginal bleeding (≤0.01%).

Other: edema (0.7%), weight gain (0.7%), weight loss (0.4%), fever (0.4%), chills (0.2%), hyperglycemia (0.2%), hypokalemia (0.1%).

Hematologic/Lymphatic: anemia (0.5%), leukopenia (0.4%), thrombocytopenia (0.2%), granulocytopenia (0.1%), aplastic anemia (<0.01%).

Hepatic: liver function abnormalities (0.5%).

Allergic/Hypersensitivity: angioneurotic edema (<0.01%), anaphylactoid reaction (<0.01%), anaphylaxis (<0.01%).

Overdose: Symptoms and Treatment: Nabumetone overdose has been rarely reported. If acute overdosage occurs, it is recommended that the stomach be emptied by vomiting or lavage and institution of general supportive measures as necessary. In addition, the use of activated charcoal, up to 60 g, may effectively reduce nabumetone absorption. Coadministration of nabumetone with activated charcoal orally in man has resulted in an 80% decrease in maximum plasma concentrations of the active metabolite.

Dosage: Osteoarthritis and Rheumatoid Arthritis: The starting and usual adult dose is 1 000 mg daily taken as a single dose with or without food. The dosage may be increased to 1 500 mg or 2 000 mg/day given either as a single dose or in 2 divided doses.

Since nabumetone has an average plasma half-life of 23 hours in healthy young subjects and 30 hours in elderly patients, plasma levels of 6-MNA will approximate steady-state within 1 week of dosing. For this reason, dosage adjustments during therapy should not be made more frequently than at 1 week intervals, except in the case of side effects. In patients with severe renal or hepatic impairment, dosage level adjustments should be made on an individual basis.

Information for the Patient: See Blue Section—Information for the Patient "Relafen".

Supplied: 500 mg: Each white, pillow-shaped, film-coated tablet, with RELAFEN embossed on one side and 500 embossed on the other side, contains: nabumetone 500 mg. Nonmedicinal ingredients: hydroxypropyl methylcellulose, microcrystalline cellulose, sodium starch glycolate and sodium lauryl sulfate. Film coating: coloring and titanium dioxide. Polyethylene bottles of 60.

750 mg: Each beige, pillow-shaped, film-coated tablet, with RELAFEN embossed on one side and 750 embossed on the other side, contains: nabumetone 750 mg. Nonmedicinal ingredients: hydroxypropyl methylcellulose, microcrystalline cellulose, sodium starch glycolate and sodium lauryl sulfate. Film coating: coloring and titanium dioxide. Polyethylene bottles of 100.

Store between 15 and 30°C in a dry place and dispense in a light-resistant container.

(Shown in Product Recognition Section)

Reviewed 1999

RELEFACT® TRH

Hoechst Marion Roussel

Protirelin

Synthetic Thyrotropin Releasing Hormone

Pharmacology: Protirelin stimulates the secretion of pituitary thyroid stimulating hormone (TSH). This effect may be used clinically to assess the functional integrity of the hypothalamic-pituitary-thyroid axis by estimating TSH concentrations in the peripheral plasma.

In addition to its stimulatory effect on secretion of pituitary TSH, it has been shown that protirelin increases secretion of prolactin.

Approximately 65% of acromegalic patients, tested with TRH, respond with a rise in circulating Human Growth Hormone (HGH) levels; the clinical significance of this is as yet not clear. It is possible that synthetic TRH testing may result in increases of circulating HGH levels in other pathophysiologic states, including renal failure, hepatic disease, hypothyroidism, anorexia nervosa, or mental depression.

TSH response, following i.v. administration of synthetic TRH, may be blunted in some patients with mental depression; an association between hypothyroidism and clinical depression is claimed by several sources.

A proportion of patients with Cushing's syndrome, tested with synthetic TRH, respond with a blunted, or absent, rise in TSH and a concomitant rise in Adrenocorticotropic Hormone (ACTH).

The possibility that protirelin testing may affect other hormonal systems in certain pathophysiologic states cannot be excluded.

Studies in human euthyroid subjects have shown that i.v. injections of synthetic TRH, in doses ranging from 25 to 800 μg,

Relefact TRH (cont'd)

produce an elevation of plasma TSH. Peak levels were observed between 10 and 30 minutes following injection.

Upon synthetic TRH administration, patients with hyperthyroidism, primary hypothyroidism, or hypopituitarism show various TSH secretion patterns differing from that obtained with euthyroid subjects.

Interpretation of the response of patients to protirelin injection is based on the increase of plasma levels of TSH. The changes observed in various conditions following protirelin administration are briefly outlined below. (Thyroxine (T4), liothyronine (T3), and plasma protein bound-iodine (PBI) levels may also show increases from baseline values). Hyperthyroidism: no rise in serum TSH; euthyroid Graves Disease: blunted or no TSH response; primary hypothyroidism: exaggerated and prolonged elevation in TSH levels; hypopituitarism: a deficiency in TSH secretion may be observed after stimulation with protirelin, in which case the TSH response is blunted or absent.

When 5 different doses of synthetic TRH, ranging from 10 to 800 μg, were administered i.v. to healthy male and female adult subjects, TSH and prolactin levels were significantly affected. The male subgroup showed a dose-related response at doses ranging from 10 to 400 μg with no further increase in levels of serum TSH at a dose of 800 μg. The female subgroup showed a significant increase in serum level of TSH at the 25 μg dose when compared to the 10 μg dose; however, no significant difference took place in serum TSH levels at the four highest doses (25 to 800 μg) of synthetic TRH injection.

From the data outlined above, and using the T3-TRH bioassay, the plasma half-life was calculated to be approximately 5 minutes. In the same tests, clearance was calculated to be 140 mL/min.

Indications: May be used as a diagnostic test for the evaluation of the hypothalamic-pituitary-thyroid axis.

Contraindications: Known hypersensitivity to protirelin.

Pregnancy: Until further evidence of a lack of drug-induced fetal abnormalities becomes available, protirelin should not be used in pregnant patients.

Protirelin should not be administered to patients in whom marked, rapid changes in blood pressure would be dangerous.

Warnings: *Pregnancy:* Since the teratogenic properties of synthetic TRH have not been established in women of childbearing potential, perform the test during the first 10 days following the onset of menstruation or when pregnancy is ruled out.

No studies have been conducted in human pregnancy which would relate to fetal safety of protirelin. Animal reproduction studies, performed in rats and rabbits with doses 1½ and 6 times the human dose, have shown an increase in the number of resorption sites in the pregnant rabbit.

Due to an effect on smooth muscle contraction, protirelin should be administered with caution to patients with cardiac disease, hypertension, labile blood pressure, renal insufficiency or bronchial asthma.

Upon i.v. protirelin administration, transient changes (increases, decreases) in blood pressure have been observed. Therefore, blood pressure should be measured before protirelin is administered and at frequent intervals during the first 15 minutes after its administration. Increases in systolic blood pressure (usually less than 30 mm Hg) and/or increases in diastolic blood pressure (usually less than 20 mm Hg) have been observed more frequently than decreases in blood pressure. These changes have not ordinarily persisted for more than 15 minutes, nor have they routinely necessitated corrective therapy.

More severe degrees of hypertension or hypotension (with or without syncope) have been reported in a few patients. Hypotensive episodes have involved administration of synthetic TRH alone, and combinations of (synthetic) TRH and insulin with/without luteinizing hormone releasing hormone (LHRH/GnRH). Symptoms also included decreased cardiac output, absent pulses, and apnea. Patients recovered, some experiencing transient bradycardia during recovery.

To minimize the incidence and/or severity of hypotension the patient should be supine before, during and for at least 15 minutes after administration of Relefact TRH. This is particularly important for persons with labile blood pressure, documented hypertension and older persons with compromised cardiovascular function.

If a clinically important change in blood pressure occurs, monitoring of blood pressure should be continued until it returns to baseline levels.

Pituitary apoplexy requiring acute neurosurgical intervention has been reported in patients with pituitary adenomas following the administration of protirelin injection in combination with LHRH/GnRH and insulin.

Severe headaches, with and without temporary amaurosis, have been reported in patients with pituitary tumors given TRH in combination with LHRH/GnRH. Patients rechallenged with LHRH/GnRH did not experience event recurrence; rechallenge with TRH resulted in recurrence of symptoms.

Convulsions or seizures, with and without unconsciousness, have been reported in patients with predisposing conditions of epilepsy, brain lesion, pituitary tumor, or head injury, following administration of TRH or the combination TRH with LHRH/GnRH.

Precautions: Failure of response to synthetic TRH in some euthyroid patients has been reported. Consequently, protirelin testing is most valuable when used in conjunction with other diagnostic aids.

Protirelin is a peptide, and must therefore be regarded as potentially allergenic.

The protirelin diagnostic test should not be repeated in the same individual within 7 days because frequent administration may lead to erroneous test results.

Thyroid hormones reduce the TSH response to protirelin. Accordingly, patients to whom protirelin is to be administered (for diagnostic testing) should be taken off liothyronine (T3) approximately 7 days prior to testing, and should be taken off thyroid medications containing levothyroxine (T4) at least 14 days prior to testing. Thyroid hormone therapy is **not** to be discontinued when the protirelin test is employed to evaluate the effectiveness of thyroid suppression with a particular dose of T4 in patients with nodular or diffuse goitre, or when the TRH test is administered to adjust dosage of thyroid hormone given to patients with primary hypothyroidism.

Drug Interactions: Generally, the withdrawal of adrenocorticoids, administered in the therapy of known hypopituitarism, is not recommended. Pharmacologic doses of glucocorticoids reduce the TSH response to protirelin, but physiologic doses do not appear to have a significant effect on this response.

The diagnostic use of dexamethasone has been shown to reduce TSH response to TRH testing; ethynylestradiol has been shown to cause a rise in serum levels of TSH.

Caffeine and theophylline may enhance the activity of TRH; hence, patients should avoid beverages containing these substances 12 to 14 hours before administration of protirelin.

Administration of levodopa (L-Dopa) has been reported to reduce the TSH response to synthetic TRH.

The ingestion of ASA caused the peak level of TSH to decrease approximately 30% as compared to values obtained without ASA administration. In both cases, the TSH peak occurred 30 minutes postadministration of protirelin.

Other pharmacologic/hormonal agents which may depress the TSH response to TRH include dopamine, bromocriptine, chlorpromazine, thioridazine, phentolamine, cyproheptadine, methysergide, or somatostatin.

Adverse Effects: Generally, side effects have been of a minor nature, with prompt onset and persistence for a few minutes following injection of protirelin. One third, or more, of patients tested with protirelin may expect to experience an adverse effect. The most common side effects are nausea, an urge to micturate, and a sensation of bad taste. Other monitored adverse effects include flushed sensations, light-headedness, abdominal discomfort, headaches, dry mouth, anxiety, sweating, tightness in the throat, pressure in the chest, tingling sensations and drowsiness.

CNS: Severe headaches, with and without temporary amaurosis, have been reported in patients with pituitary tumors given TRH in combination with LHRH/GnRH. Pituitary apoplexy has developed in patients with pituitary adenomas given protirelin in combination with LHRH/GnRH and insulin. Convulsions or seizures, with and without unconsciousness, have been reported in patients with predisposing conditions of epilepsy, brain lesion, pituitary tumor, or head injury after administration of TRH or the combination TRH with LHRH/GnRH (see Warnings).

Cardiovascular: Marked changes in blood pressure, leading to clinically significant hypertension and hypotension, with or without syncope, have been reported in a small number of patients (see Warnings).

Endocrine: In postpartum patients, an increase in breast engorgement and lactation has been observed following administration of synthetic TRH.

Overdose: Symptoms: Although no specific symptoms of overdosage have been characterized in patients receiving up to 1 mg i.v. of synthetic TRH, tremors have been observed in all species of animals and at all doses tested during acute toxicity studies.

Treatment: Should any serious reaction develop, it should be treated using routine hospital procedures.

Dosage: Adults: 200 to 400 μg (0.2 to 0.4 mg). Children: 7 μg/kg (0.007 mg/kg) body weight, up to adult dose. Doses greater than 400 μg are not expected to elicit a greater TSH response.

Tests employing i.v. protirelin administration are based on the serum TSH response to a standard dose of synthetic TRH. It is essential for each laboratory to establish its own range of normal values for serum TSH before attempting quantitative assessment of TSH response to synthetic TRH administration.

When a patient is prepared for a protirelin test, the following measures should be taken: Since elevated serum lipids tend to interfere wth TSH radio-immunoassay, patients should be fasted overnight (caution is advised in patients with known hypopituitarism). Patients should be instructed to abstain from beverages containing caffeine or theophylline for 12 to 14 hours before administration of protirelins (see Drug Interactions).

Test Procedure: Blood pressure should be measured before protirelin is administered and at frequent intervals during the first 15 minutes after its administration. It is advisable to monitor blood pressure throughout the test procedure (see Warnings). The patient should be supine before, during, and for at least 15 minutes after administration of protirelin (see Warnings). Attention should be given throughout the procedure to avoid aspiration of stomach contents should nausea and possible vomiting occur. One blood sample, for baseline TSH assay, should be drawn immediately prior to the injection of protirelin. Protirelin is injected i.v. as a bolus. A second blood sample, for peak TSH assay, should be drawn at 20 to 30 minutes following protirelin injection. To detect possible delayed TSH responses, it may be necessary to draw further blood samples at 45 to 60 minutes post injection.

Supplied: Each mL of solution contains: protirelin 200 μg (0.2 mg). Nonmedicinal ingredients: mannitol and sodium chloride for isotonicity and sodium phosphate monobasic as buffer. Clear glass prescored ampuls of 1 mL, boxes of 5. Store at room temperature (below 25°C), do not freeze.

RENEDIL® Ⓟ

Hoechst Marion Roussel

Felodipine

Antihypertensive Agent

Pharmacology: Felodipine is a calcium ion influx inhibitor (calcium channel blocker). Felodipine is a member of the dihydropyridine class of calcium channel blockers.

Mechanism of Action: The therapeutic effect of this group of drugs is believed to be related to their specific cellular action of selectively inhibiting transmembrane influx of calcium ions into cardiac muscle and vascular smooth muscle. The contractile processes of these tissues are dependent upon the movement of extracellular calcium into the cells through specific ion channels. Felodipine blocks transmembrane influx of calcium through the slow channel without affecting to any significant degree the transmembrane influx of sodium through the fast channel. This results in a reduction of free calcium ions available within cells of the above tissues.

Felodipine does not alter total serum calcium. In vitro studies show that the effects of felodipine on contractile mechanisms are selective, with greater effects on vascular smooth muscle than on cardiac muscle. Negative inotropic effects can be detected in vitro, but such effects have not been seen in intact animals.

The effect of felodipine on blood pressure in man is principally a consequence of a dose-related decrease in peripheral vascular resistance, with a modest reflex increase in heart rate (see Pharmacodynamics).

Pharmacokinetics: Felodipine is completely absorbed from the gastrointestinal tract after oral administration. Due to rapid biotransformation of felodipine during its first pass through the portal circulation the systemic availability is approximately 20% and is independent of the dose in the range of 5 to 20 mg/day. The plasma protein binding of felodipine is approximately 99%. It is bound predominately to the albumin fraction.

Felodipine is extensively metabolized in the liver, predominantly by cytochrome P450 CYP 3A4. After 72 hours, approximately 70% of a given dose is excreted as metabolites in the urine and 10% is secreted in the feces. Less than 0.5% of a dose is recovered unchanged in the urine. Six metabolites, which account for 23% of the oral dose, have been identified: none has significant vasodilating activity.

Felodipine has been observed to have a mean blood clearance of 914 ± 355 mL/minute in hypertensive patients, 606 ± 245 mL/minute in elderly hypertensive patients and 1 337 ± 413 mL/minute in young healthy volunteers. Its mean terminal half-life was 24.5 ± 7.0 hours in hypertensive patients, 27.5 ± 8.4 hours in elderly hypertensive patients and 14.1 ± 5.6 hours in young healthy volunteers.

The extended release formulation prolongs the absorption phase of felodipine resulting in an increased time to reach peak plasma concentrations (t_{max}), and a reduced maximum plasma concentration (C_{max}). The mean t_{max} ranges from 2.5 to 5 hours. The area under the plasma concentration versus time curve and C_{max} are linearly related to the dose in the 10 to 40 mg range. Following administration of felodipine to hypertensive patients, mean C_{max} at steady state is approximately 20% higher after multiple doses than after a single dose. No increase in the AUC is found during multiple dosing. The inter-individual variation in C_{max} and AUC after repeated dosing is approximately 3-fold and indicates a need for individualized dosing.

The bioavailability of felodipine is not influenced by the presence of food in the gastrointestinal tract.

Studies in healthy male volunteers showed significant alterations in the pharmacokinetics of felodipine when felodipine was administered concomitantly with grapefruit juice. Following the administration of a single dose of plain felodipine 5 mg tablets with 200 mL grapefruit juice or 200 mL water AUC and C_{max} of felodipine increased about 3-fold as compared to administration with water. When felodipine extended release tablets were administered as felodipine 10 mg with 250 mL grapefruit juice, felodipine AUC and C_{max} values doubled as compared to those observed with water. When grapefruit juice was taken for up to 24 hours prior to felodipine administration, a significant pharmacokinetic interaction was observed (see Precautions, Interaction with Grapefruit Juice).

Plasma concentrations of felodipine, after a single dose and at steady state, increase with age. Mean clearance of felodipine in elderly hypertensives (mean age 74 years) was only 45% of that in young volunteers (mean age 26 years). At steady state mean AUC for young patients was 39% of that for the elderly patients.

In patients with hepatic disease, the clearance of felodipine was reduced to about 60% of that seen in normal young volunteers.

Renal impairment does not alter the plasma concentration profile of felodipine. Although higher concentrations of the metabolites are present in the plasma due to decreased urinary excretion, these are hemodynamically inactive.

Animal studies have demonstrated that felodipine crosses the blood-brain barrier and the placenta.

Pharmacodynamics: The acute hemodynamic effect of felodipine is a reduction in total peripheral resistance which leads to a decrease in blood pressure associated with a modest reflex increase in heart rate. This reflex increase in heart rate frequently occurs during the first week of therapy and generally attenuates over time. Heart rate increases of 5 to 10 beats/minute may be seen during chronic administration. The effect on the heart rate is inhibited by β-blocking agents.

Following administration of felodipine a reduction in blood pressure generally occurs within 2 to 5 hours.

During chronic administration, substantial blood pressure control lasts for approximately 24 hours; reductions in diastolic blood pressure at trough plasma levels were 40 to 50% of those at peak plasma levels. The antihypertensive effect is dose-dependent and correlates with the plasma concentration of felodipine.

Felodipine in therapeutic doses has no effect on conduction in the conducting system of the heart and no effect on the AV nodal refractoriness. No direct additional effects to those registered after β-blockade are observed when felodipine is given concomitantly.

Renal vascular resistance is decreased by felodipine while glomerular filtration rate remains unchanged. Mild diuresis, natriuresis and kaliuresis have been observed during the first week of therapy. No significant effects on serum electrolytes have been observed during short- and long-term therapy. No general salt and water retention occurs during long-term therapy. In clinical trials increases in norepinephrine plasma levels have been observed.

Indications: In the treatment of mild to moderate essential hypertension. Felodipine should normally be used in those patients in whom treatment with a diuretic or a β-blocker was found ineffective or has been associated with unacceptable adverse effects.

Felodipine can be tried as an initial agent in those patients in whom the use of diuretic and/or β-blockers is contraindicated or in patients with medical conditions in which these drugs frequently cause serious adverse effects.

Combination of felodipine with a thiazide diuretic or a β-blocker has been found to be compatible and showed an additive antihypertensive effect. Safety and efficacy of concurrent use of felodipine with other antihypertensive agents has not been established.

Contraindications: Patients with a known hypersensitivity to felodipine or other dihydropyridines. In women of childbearing potential, in pregnancy, and during lactation. Fetal malformations and adverse effects on pregnancy have been reported in animals.

Teratogenic Effects: Studies in pregnant rabbits administered doses of 0.46, 1.2, 2.3 and 4.6 mg/kg/day (from 0.4 to 4 times the maximum recommended human dose on a mg/m² basis) showed digital anomalies consisting of reduction in size and degree of ossification of the terminal phalanges in the fetuses. The frequency and severity of the changes appeared dose-related and were noted even at the lowest dose. These changes have been shown to occur with other members of the dihydropyridine class. Similar fetal anomalies were not observed in rats given felodipine.

In a teratology study in cynomolgus monkeys, no reduction in the size of the terminal phalanges was observed but an abnormal position of the distal phalanges was noted in about 40% of the fetuses.

Nonteratogenic Effects: In a study on fertility and general reproductive performance in rats, prolongation of parturition with difficult labor and an increased frequency of fetal and early postnatal deaths were observed in the groups treated with doses of 9.6 mg/kg/day and above.

Significant enlargement of the mammary glands in excess of the normal enlargement for pregnant rabbits was found with doses greater than or equal to 1.2 mg/kg/day. This effect occurred only in pregnant rabbits and regressed during lactation. Similar changes in the mammary glands were not observed in rats or monkeys.

Warnings: Congestive Heart Failure: The safety and efficacy of felodipine in patients with heart failure has not been established. Caution should, therefore, be exercised when using felodipine in hypertensive patients with compromised ventricular function, particularly in combination with a β-blocker. Acute hemodynamic studies in a small number of patients with New York Heart Association Class II or III heart failure treated with felodipine have not demonstrated negative inotropic effects.

Hypotension, Myocardial Ischemia: Felodipine may, occasionally, precipitate symptomatic hypotension and rarely syncope. It may lead to reflex tachycardia which, particularly in patients with severe obstructive coronary artery disease, may result in myocardial ischemia. Careful monitoring of blood pressure during the initial administration and titration of felodipine is recommended.

Care should be taken to avoid hypotension especially in patients with a history of cerebrovascular insufficiency, and in those taking medications known to lower blood pressure.

β-Blocker Withdrawal: Felodipine gives no protection against the dangers of abrupt β-blocker withdrawal; any such withdrawal should be a gradual reduction of the dose of β-blockers.

Outflow Obstruction: Felodipine should be used with caution in the presence of fixed left ventricular outflow obstruction.

Precautions: Peripheral Edema: Mild to moderate peripheral edema was the most common adverse event in the clinical trials. The incidence of peripheral edema was dose-dependent. Frequency of peripheral edema ranged from about 10% in patients under 50 years of age taking 5 mg daily to about 30% in those over 60 years of age taking 20 mg daily. This adverse effect generally occurs within 2 to 3 weeks of the initiation of treatment. Care should be taken to differentiate this peripheral edema from the effects of increasing left ventricular dysfunction.

Geriatrics: Patients over 65 years of age may have elevated plasma concentrations of felodipine and, therefore, may require lower doses of felodipine (Pharmacology, Pharmacokinetics). These patients should have their blood pressure monitored closely during initial administration and after dosage adjustment of felodipine. A dosage of 10 mg daily should not be exceeded (see Dosage, Geriatrics).

Impaired Liver Function: Patients with impaired liver function may have elevated plasma concentrations of felodipine and, therefore, may require lower doses of felodipine (Pharmacology, Pharmacokinetics). These patients should have their blood pressure monitored closely during initial administration and after dosage adjustment of felodipine. A dosage of 10 mg daily should not be exceeded (see Dosage, Impaired Liver Function).

Gingival Hyperplasia: Felodipine can induce gingival enlargement in patients with pronounced gingivitis and parodontitis. However, such changes may be reversed by measures of good oral hygiene and mechanical debridement of the teeth.

Pregnancy and *Lactation*: See Contraindications.

Children: Felodipine is not recommended in children since the safety and efficacy in children have not been established.

Interaction with Grapefruit Juice: Published data indicate that through inhibition of cytochrome P450, grapefruit juice can increase plasma levels and augment pharmacodynamic effects of dihydropyridine calcium channel blockers. In view of the absolute bioavailability of felodipine, the potential for a significant increase in pharmacodynamic effects exists (see Pharmacology, Pharmacokinetics). Therefore, consumption of grapefruit juice prior to or during treatment with felodipine should be avoided.

Drug Interactions: As with all drugs, care should be exercised when treating patients with multiple medications. Dihydropyridine calcium channel blockers undergo biotransformation by the cytochrome P450 system, mainly via the CYP 3A4 isoenzyme. Coadministration of felodipine with other drugs which follow the same route of biotransformation may result in altered bioavailability of felodipine or these drugs. Dosages of similarly metabolized drugs, particularly those of low therapeutic ratio, and especially in patients with renal and/or hepatic impairment, may require adjustment when starting or stopping concomitantly administered felodipine to maintain optimum therapeutic blood levels.

Drugs known to be inhibitors of the cytochrome P450 system include: azole antifungals, cimetidine, cyclosporine, erythromycin, quinidine and warfarin.

Drugs known to be inducers of the cytochrome P450 system include: phenobarbital, phenytoin and rifampin.

Drugs known to be biotransformed via P450 include: benzodiazepines, flecainide, imipramine, propafenone, terfenadine and theophylline.

Cytochrome P450 Enzyme Inhibitors: Cimetidine: In healthy volunteers pharmacokinetic studies showed an approximately 50% increase in the area under the plasma concentration time curve (AUC) as well as the C_{max} of felodipine when given concomitantly with cimetidine. It is anticipated that clinically significant interaction may occur in some hypertensive patients. Therefore, it is recommended that low doses of felodipine be used when given concomitantly with cimetidine.

Erythromycin: Concomitant treatment with erythromycin has been shown to cause an increase in felodipine plasma levels.

Cytochrome P450 Enzyme Inducers: Phenytoin, Carbamazepine and Phenobarbital: In a pharmacokinetic study maximum plasma concentrations of felodipine were considerably lower in epileptic patients on long-term anticonvulsant therapy (phenytoin, carbamazepine, phenobarbital) than in healthy volunteers. The mean area under the felodipine plasma concentration-time curve was also reduced in epileptic patients to approximately 6% of that observed in healthy volunteers. Since a clinically significant interaction may be anticipated, alternative antihypertensive therapy should be considered in these patients.

Alcohol: Alcohol may enhance the hemodynamic effects of felodipine.

β-adrenoceptor Blocking Agents: A pharmacokinetic study of felodipine in conjunction with metoprolol demonstrated no significant effects on the pharmacokinetics of felodipine. The AUC and C_{max} of metoprolol, however, were increased approximately 31 and 36%, respectively. In controlled clinical trials, however, β-blockers including metoprolol were concurrently administered with felodipine and were well tolerated.

Digoxin: When given concomitantly with felodipine as conventional tablets the peak plasma concentration of digoxin was significantly increased. With the extended release formulation of felodipine there was no significant change in peak plasma levels or AUC of digoxin.

Other Concomitant Therapy: In healthy subjects there were no clinically significant interactions when felodipine was given concomitantly with indomethacin or spironolactone.

Adverse Effects: In 861 essential hypertensive patients treated once daily with 2.5 to 10 mg of felodipine as monotherapy in controlled clinical trials, the most common clinical adverse events were peripheral edema and headache.

Adverse events that occurred with an incidence of 1.5% or greater at any of the recommended doses of 2.5 to 10 mg once a day, without regard to causality, are listed by dose in Table I (on following page). These events are reported from controlled clinical trials with patients who were randomized to either a fixed dose of felodipine or titrated from an initial dose of 2.5 or 5 mg once a day. **A dose of 20 mg once a day**

Renedil (cont'd)

has been evaluated in some clinical studies. Although the antihypertensive effect of felodipine is increased at 20 mg once a day, there is a disproportionate increase in adverse events, especially those associated with vasodilatory effects (see Dosage).

Table I—Renedil

Percent of patients with adverse events in controlled trials of Renedil (N=861)* as monotherapy without regard to causality (incidence of discontinuations shown in parentheses)

Body System Adverse Events	Placebo N=334	2.5 mg N=255	5 mg N=581	10 mg N=408
Body as a Whole				
Peripheral edema	3.3 (0.0)	2.0 (0.0)	8.8 (2.2)	17.4 (2.5)
Asthenia	3.3 (0.0)	3.9 (0.0)	3.3 (0.0)	2.2 (0.0)
Cardiovascular				
Palpitation	2.4 (0.0)	0.4 (0.0)	1.4 (0.3)	2.5 (0.5)
Warm sensation/ flushing	0.9 (0.3)	3.9 (0.0)	6.2 (0.9)	8.4 (1.2)
Digestive				
Nausea	1.5 (0.9)	1.2 (0.0)	1.7 (0.3)	1.0 (0.7)
Dyspepsia	1.2 (0.0)	3.9 (0.0)	0.7 (0.0)	0.5 (0.0)
Constipation	0.9 (0.0)	1.2 (0.0)	0.3 (0.0)	1.5 (0.2)
Nervous				
Headache	10.2 (0.9)	10.6 (0.4)	11.0 (1.7)	14.7 (2.0)
Dizziness	2.7 (0.3)	2.7 (0.0)	3.6 (0.5)	3.7 (0.5)
Paresthesia	1.5 (0.3)	1.6 (0.0)	1.2 (0.0)	1.2 (0.2)
Respiratory				
Upper respiratory infection	1.8 (0.0)	3.9 (0.0)	1.9 (0.0)	0.7 (0.0)
Cough	0.3 (0.0)	0.8 (0.0)	1.2 (0.0)	1.7 (0.0)
Skin				
Rash	0.9 (0.0)	2.0 (0.0)	0.2 (0.0)	0.2 (0.0)

* Some patients have been exposed to more than one dose level of Renedil.

Adverse events that occurred in 0.5 up to 1.5% of patients who received felodipine in all controlled clinical trials at the recommended dosage range of 2.5 to 10 mg once a day are listed below. These events are listed in order to decreasing severity within each category regardless of relationship to felodipine therapy.

Body as a Whole: chest pain, facial edema, flu-like illness.

Cardiovascular: tachycardia, premature beats, postural hypotension, bradycardia.

Gastrointestinal: abdominal pain, diarrhea, vomiting, dry mouth, flatulence, acid regurgitation, cholestatic hepatitis, gingival hyperplasia, salivary gland enlargement.

Metabolic: ALT increased.

Musculoskeletal: arthralgia, muscle cramps, myalgia.

Nervous/Psychiatric: insomnia, depression, anxiety disorders, irritability, nervousness, somnolence, decrease in libido, tremor, confusion.

Respiratory: dyspnea, epistaxis.

Dermatologic: pruritus, erythema multiforme, erythema nodosum, urticaria, photosensitivity reactions.

Special Senses: visual disturbances.

Urogenital: impotence, urinary frequency, urinary urgency, dysuria, polyuria.

Serious adverse events reported from controlled clinical trials and during marketing experience (incidence $<0.5\%$) were myocardial infarction, hypotension, syncope, angina pectoris, arrhythmia and anemia.

Isolated cases of angioedema have been reported. Angioedema may be accompanied by breathing difficulty.

Laboratory Tests: For the following laboratory values statistically significant decreases were observed: bilirubin, red blood count, hemoglobin, and urate. Statistically significant increases were found in erythrocyte sedimentation rate and thrombocyte count. In isolated cases, there were increased liver enzymes. None of the changes were considered to be of clinical significance.

Overdose: Symptoms: Overdosage can cause excessive peripheral vasodilation with marked hypotension and possibly bradycardia.

Treatment: If severe hypotension occurs, symptomatic treatment should be instituted. The patient should be placed supine with the legs elevated. The i.v. administration of fluids may be used to treat hypotension. Plasma volume may be increased by infusion of a plasma volume expander. When accompanied by bradycardia, atropine 0.5 to 1 mg should be administered i.v. Sympathomimetic drugs predominantly affecting the α_1-adrenoceptor may be given if the above-mentioned measures are considered insufficient. Removal of felodipine from the circulation by hemodialysis has not been established.

Dosage: Felodipine should be swallowed whole and not crushed or chewed.

The usual recommended initial dose is 5 mg once daily (see Geriatrics and Impaired Liver Function).

Depending on the patient's response, the dosage should be adjusted accordingly. Dose adjustment, if necessary, should be done at intervals of not less than 2 weeks.

The maintenance dosage range is 2.5 to 10 mg once daily.

In clinical trials, doses above 10 mg daily showed an increased blood pressure response but a disproportionately higher incidence of peripheral edema and other vasodilatory adverse events.

Modification of the recommended dosage is usually not required in patients with renal impairment.

Geriatrics: Patients over 65 years of age may develop elevated plasma concentrations of felodipine. A starting dose no higher than 2.5 mg once daily is recommended. A dosage of 10 mg daily should not be exceeded (see Precautions, Geriatrics).

Impaired Liver Function: Patients with impaired liver function may develop elevated plasma concentrations of felodipine. A starting dose no higher than 2.5 mg once daily is recommended. A dosage of 10 mg daily should not be exceeded (see Precautions, Impaired Liver Function).

Information for the Patient: See Blue Section—Information for the Patient "Renedil".

Supplied: 2.5 mg: Each yellow, circular, biconvex, film-coated, extended release tablet, engraved ⍑ on one side and 2.5 on the other; contains: felodipine 2.5 mg. Nonmedicinal ingredients: aluminum silicate, hydroxypropyl cellulose, hydroxypropyl methylcellulose, lactose anhydrous, microcrystalline cellulose, polyoxy 40 hydrogenated castor oil, propyl gallate and sodium stearyl fumarate; coating layer: hydroxypropyl methylcellulose, polyethylene glycol, color titanium dioxide, color iron oxide yellow, carnauba wax and hydrogen peroxide. Gluten- and tartrazine-free. Compliance packages of 2 × 15.

5 mg: Each pink, circular, film-coated, extended release tablet, engraved ⍑ on one side and 5 on the other, contains: felodipine 5 mg. Nonmedicinal ingredients: aluminum silicate, hydroxypropyl cellulose hydroxypropyl methylcellulose, lactose anhydrous, microcrystalline cellulose, polyoxy 40 hydrogenated castor oil, propyl gallate and sodium stearyl fumarate; coating layer: hydroxypropyl methylcellulose, polyethylene glycol, color titanium dioxide, color iron oxide yellow, color iron oxide red-brown, carnauba wax and hydrogen peroxide. Gluten- and tartrazine-free. Compliance packages of 2 × 15.

10 mg: Each red-brown, circular, film-coated, extended release tablet, engraved ⍑ on one side and 10 on the other, contains: felodipine 10 mg. Nonmedicinal ingredients: aluminum silicate, hydroxypropyl cellulose, hydroxypropyl methylcellulose, lactose anhydrous, microcrystalline cellulose, polyoxy 40 hydrogenated castor oil, propyl gallate and sodium stearyl fumarate; coating layer: hydroxypropyl methylcellulose, polyethylene glycol, color titanium dioxide, color iron oxide yellow, color iron oxide red-brown, carnauba wax and hydrogen peroxide. Gluten- and tartrazine-free. Compliance packages of 2 × 15.

Note: These extended release tablets must not be divided, crushed or chewed.

Store at 15 to 30°C.

(Shown in Product Recognition Section)

Reviewed 1999

RENOVA® ℞

Janssen-Ortho

Tretinoin

Agent for the Treatment of Photodamaged Skin

Pharmacology: Tretinoin significantly reduces clinical signs of photodamaged skin such as fine wrinkles, mottled hyperpigmentation and roughness.

While the exact mechanism of action of tretinoin is unknown, the clinical improvements are accompanied by the following histologic changes: increased epidermal and granular layer thickness, reduced melanin content and stratum corneum alterations.

Indications: For the treatment of fine wrinkling, mottled hyperpigmentation and roughness of the skin. These signs are usually associated with photodamaged (sun-damaged) skin and intrinsic aging but may be associated with other conditions.

The safety and efficacy of tretinoin for the prevention or treatment of actinic or solar keratoses have not been established.

Contraindications: Individuals with a history of sensitivity reactions to any of its components. It should be discontinued if hypersensitivity to any of its ingredients is noted.

Warnings: Tretinoin should be used under medical supervision as part of a comprehensive skin protection program, including use of sunscreen products and protective clothing.

Excessive use of tretinoin should be avoided. Tretinoin should be kept away from the eyes, mouth, angles of the nose or mucous membranes. Topical use may induce severe local erythema, pruritus, burning or stinging and peeling at the site of application. If the degree of local irritation warrants, patients should be directed to use the medication less frequently, discontinue use temporarily, or discontinue use altogether.

Tretinoin has been reported to cause severe irritation on eczematous skin and should be used with utmost caution in patients with this condition.

Pregnancy: **Topical tretinoin should be used by women of childbearing years only after contraceptive counselling. It is recommended that topical tretinoin should not be used by pregnant women.**

There have been a few reports of birth defects among babies born to women exposed to **topical** tretinoin during pregnancy. To date, there have been no adequate and well-controlled prospective studies performed in pregnant women, and the teratogenic blood level of tretinoin is unclear. However, a retrospective cohort study of babies born to women exposed to topical tretinoin during the first trimester of pregnancy found no excess birth defects among these babies when compared with babies born to women in the same cohort who were not similarly exposed.

Oral tretinoin has been shown to be teratogenic and fetotoxic in rats when given in doses 1 000 and 500 times the topical human dose, respectively.

In 9 out of 10 **topical** teratology studies of tretinoin conducted in rats and rabbits using several formulations, there has been no evidence of teratogenicity. In 1 out of 10 studies, there was an increase in fetal malformations; however, a clear causal relationship of topical tretinoin and these findings could not be established. In a repeat of this study, there were no fetal malformations. Topical tretinoin can produce treatment-related fetal effects (delayed ossification of bones and an increase in supernumerary ribs). The fetal no effect dose is 1 mg/kg/day (200 times the recommended clinical dose).

Lactation: It is not known whether tretinoin is excreted in human milk. Nevertheless, a decision should be made whether to discontinue nursing or to discontinue the drug, taking into account the importance of the drug to the mother.

Children: Safety and effectiveness in children have not been established.

Precautions: General: If a reaction suggesting sensitivity, chemical irritation, or a systemic adverse effect should occur, use of tretinoin should be discontinued.

Exposure to sunlight, including sunlamps, should be avoided or minimized during the use of tretinoin, and patients with sunburn should be advised not to use the product until fully recovered because of heightened susceptibility to sunlight as a result of the use of tretinoin. **Patients who may be required to have considerable sun exposure due to occupation and those inherently sensitive to the sun should exercise particular caution. Use of sunscreen products and protective clothing over treated areas is recommended when exposure cannot be avoided.** Weather extremes, such as wind or cold, also may be irritating to patients under treatment with tretinoin.

Carcinogenesis: The mutagenic potential of tretinoin was evaluated in the Ames assay and the in vivo mouse micronucleus assay, both of which were negative. In a lifetime study of topical tretinoin in CD-1 mice, there was no evidence of carcinogenic potential. Studies in hairless albino mice suggest that tretinoin may accelerate the tumorigenic potential of weakly carcinogenic light from a solar simulator. Although the significance of these studies to man is not clear, patients should avoid or minimize exposure to sun.

Information for the Patient: A patient information leaflet has been prepared and is included with each package of Renova emollient cream (see Blue Section—Information for the Patient "Renova"). The skin of certain sensitive individuals may become excessively red, swollen, blistered, or crusted. Tretinoin should be discontinued if patients experience severe or persistent irritation, and they should be advised to consult their physician.

Drug Interactions: Concomitant topical medication, medicated or abrasive soaps, shampoos and cleansers, cosmetics that have a strong drying effect, and products with high concentrations of alcohol, as well as astringents and products that may irritate the skin, should be used with caution because they may increase irritation with tretinoin.

Adverse Effects: In double-blind, vehicle-controlled studies involving 199 patients who received tretinoin for facial photodamage, adverse reactions associated with the use of tretinoin emollient cream were limited primarily to the skin. Local reactions such as peeling or dry skin, burning or stinging, erythema, and pruritus were reported by most subjects during therapy with tretinoin emollient cream. These signs and symptoms were usually of mild to moderate severity and were generally well tolerated. These skin reactions occurred early in therapy and, except for dryness and peeling which tended to persist during therapy, generally decreased over the course of therapy.

Overdose: Symptoms and Treatment: Tretinoin emollient cream is indicated for topical use only. If medication is applied excessively, no more rapid or better results will be obtained and marked redness, peeling, or discomfort may occur. Oral ingestion of this drug may lead to the same side effects as those associated with excessive oral intake of Vitamin A.

Dosage: The emollient cream should be applied once daily at bedtime, to lightly cover the entire face. In some cases it has been necessary to temporarily discontinue therapy or to reduce the frequency of application. When the patient is able to tolerate the treatment, therapy can be resumed or the frequency of application can be increased.

Improvement in facial photodamage with tretinoin treatment occurs gradually over the course of therapy. Six months of therapy may be required before definite beneficial effects are seen.

Patients treated with tretinoin should use an effective sunscreen with a minimum SPF of 15 as well as protective clothing when exposure to the sun cannot be avoided.

Information for the Patient: See Blue Section—Information for the Patient "Renova".

Supplied: Each g of yellow cream with a characteristic floral odor contains: tretinoin 0.5 mg w/w. Nonmedicinal ingredients: citric acid (monohydrate), butylated hydroxytoluene, dimethicone 50cs, edetate disodium, fragrance, hydroxyoctacosanyl hydroxystearate, light mineral oil, methoxy PEG-22/dodecyl glycol copolymer, methylparaben, PEG-45/dodecyl glycol copolymer, purified water, quaternium-15, sorbitol solution, stearoxytrimethyl-silane and stearyl alcohol. Tubes of 20 g. Store between 15 and 25°C. **Do not freeze.**

Reviewed 1999

REOPRO™ Ⓟ

Lilly

Abciximab

Chimeric Monoclonal Antiplatelet Antibody

Pharmacology: General: Abciximab is the Fab fragment of the chimeric monoclonal antibody 7E3. It selectively binds to the glycoprotein IIb/IIIa (GPIIb/IIIa) receptor located on the surface of human platelets. Abciximab inhibits platelet aggregation by preventing the binding of fibrinogen, von Willebrand factor and other adhesive molecules to GPIIb/IIIa receptor sites on activated platelets.

Pharmacokinetics: Following i.v. administration of abciximab, free plasma concentrations decreased very rapidly with an initial half-life of several minutes and a second phase half-life of about 30 minutes. This disappearance from the plasma is probably related to rapid binding to the platelet GPIIb/IIIa receptors (approximately 80 000 to 100 000 GPIIb/IIIa receptors on the surface of each platelet). After a single bolus injection of abciximab, the inhibitory effects on platelet function, as measured by inhibition of platelet aggregation, were evident within 10 minutes. The antibody remains in the circulation for several days in a platelet-bound state. Its disappearance follows a monoexponential time course.

I.V. administration of a 0.25 mg/kg bolus dose of abciximab followed by continuous infusion of 5 or 10 μg/min for periods of 12 to 96 hours produced relatively constant total plasma concentrations from the first time point measured (usually 2 hours) for all infusion rates and durations. However, although the total plasma concentrations resulting from the 5 μg/min infusion were only slightly lower than those from the 10 μg/min infusion, the 5 μg/min infusion was ineffective in inhibiting platelet function over the whole infusion period. At the termination of the infusion period, plasma concentrations fell rapidly for approximately 6 hours, then declined at a much slower rate.

Pharmacodynamics: I.V. administration in humans of single bolus doses of abciximab from 0.15 to 0.30 mg/kg resulted in a dose-dependent blockade of platelet GPIIb/IIIa receptors and produced dose-dependent inhibition of platelet function as measured by ex vivo platelet aggregation in response to ADP or by prolongation of bleeding time. At the 2 highest doses (0.25 and 0.30 mg/kg) at 2 hours postinjection, over 80% of the GPIIb/IIIa receptors were blocked and platelet aggregation in response to 20 μM ADP was almost abolished. The median bleeding time increased to over 30 minutes at both doses compared with a baseline value of approximately 5 minutes.

I.V. administration in humans of a single bolus dose of 0.25 mg/kg followed by a continuous infusion of 10 μg/min for periods of 12 to 96 hours produced sustained high-grade platelet inhibition (ex vivo platelet aggregation in response to 5 or 20 μM ADP less than 20% of baseline and bleeding time greater than 30 minutes) for the duration of the infusion in most patients. Results in patients who received the 0.25 mg/kg bolus followed by a 5 μg/min infusion for 24 hours showed a similar initial inhibition of platelet aggregation, but the response was not maintained throughout the infusion period. Following cessation of the infusion, platelet function typically returned to baseline values over a period of 24 to 48 hours.

Indications: As an adjunct to percutaneous transluminal coronary angioplasty or atherectomy (PTCA) for the prevention of acute cardiac ischemic complications in patients at high risk for abrupt closure of the treated coronary vessel. Patients at high risk for abrupt closure include those undergoing PTCA with at least 1 of the following conditions: unstable angina or a non-Q-wave myocardial infarction; an acute Q-wave myocardial infarction within 12 hours of the onset of symptoms; other high-risk clinical and/or morphologic characteristics (as adapted from the classification of the ACC/AHA; see Table I): 2 type B lesion characteristics in the artery to be dilated, 1 type B lesion characteristic in the artery to be dilated in a woman of at least 65 years of age, 1 type B lesion characteristic in the artery to be dilated in a patient with diabetes mellitus, 1 type C lesion characteristic in the artery to be dilated, or angioplasty of an infarct-related lesion within 7 days of myocardial infarction.

The principal data supporting the safety and efficacy of abciximab for this indication are from a full evaluation of the EPIC trial. Data included from the EPILOG and CAPTURE trials are based on interim analyses and are included because of their relevance to bleeding events. Any appropriate references to efficacy in these trials will be made in a revised Product Monograph following a full evaluation of trial data by Centocor and the Canadian Health Protection Branch.

Abciximab is intended for use with ASA and heparin and has been studied only in that setting as described in Pharmacology.

The EPIC Trial: The Evaluation of c7E3 to Prevent Ischemic Complications (EPIC) trial was a multicenter, double-blind, placebo-controlled trial of abciximab in patients undergoing percutaneous transluminal coronary angioplasty or atherectomy (PTCA). In the EPIC trial, 2 099 patients between 26 and 83 years of age who were at high risk for abrupt closure of the treated coronary vessel were randomly allocated to 1 of 3 treatments: 1) an abciximab bolus (0.25 mg/kg) followed by an abciximab infusion (10 μg/min) for 12 hours (bolus plus infusion group); 2) an abciximab bolus (0.25 mg/kg) followed by a placebo infusion (bolus group); or 3) a placebo bolus followed by a placebo infusion (placebo group). Patients at high risk during or following PTCA were defined as those with unstable angina or a non-Q-wave myocardial infarction (n=489), those with an acute Q-wave myocardial infarction within 12 hours of symptom onset (n=66), and those who were at high risk because of coronary morphology and/or clinical characteristics as defined in Table I (n=1 544). Treatment with study agent in each of the 3 arms was initiated 10 to 60 minutes before the onset of PTCA. All patients initially received an i.v. heparin bolus (10 000 to 12 000 units) and boluses of up to 3 000 units thereafter to a maximum of 20 000 units during PTCA. Heparin infusion was continued for 12 hours to maintain a therapeutic elevation of activated partial thromboplastin time (APTT, 1.5 to 2.5 times normal). Unless contraindicated, ASA (325 mg) was administered orally 2 hours prior to the planned procedure and then once daily.

The primary endpoint was the occurrence of any of the following events within 30 days of PTCA: death, myocardial infarction (MI), or the need for urgent intervention for recurrent ischemia (i.e., urgent PTCA, urgent coronary artery bypass graft (CABG) surgery, a coronary stent, or an intra-aortic balloon pump). The 30-day (Kaplan-Meier) primary endpoint event rates for each treatment group by intention-to-treat analysis of all randomized patients are shown in Table II (on following page). The 4.5% lower incidence of the primary endpoint in the bolus plus infusion treatment group, compared with the placebo group, was statistically significant, whereas the 1.3% lower incidence in the bolus treatment group was not. A lower incidence of the primary endpoint was observed in the bolus plus infusion treatment arm for all 3 high-risk subgroups: patients with unstable angina, patients presenting within 12 hours of the onset of symptoms of an acute myocardial infarction, and patients with other high-risk clinical and/or morphologic characteristics as defined in Table I. The treatment effect was largest in the first 2 subgroups and smallest in the third subgroup.

Mortality was uncommon and similar rates were observed in all arms. The rate of acute myocardial infarctions was significantly lower in the groups treated with abciximab. While 80% of myocardial infarctions in the study were non-Q-wave infarctions, patients in the bolus plus infusion arm experienced a lower incidence of both Q-wave and non-Q-wave infarctions. Urgent intervention rates were lower in the groups treated with abciximab, mostly because of lower rates of emergency PTCA and, to a lesser extent, emergency CABG surgery. The primary endpoint events in the bolus plus infusion treatment group were reduced mostly in the first 48 hours and this benefit was sustained through 30 days and 6 months. At 6 months, this event rate remained lower in the bolus plus infusion arm (12.3%) than in the placebo arm (17.6%).

The primary endpoint component with the most marked reduction in event rates with bolus plus infusion treatment was urgent PTCA (81% reduction from 4.5% in the placebo group to 0.9% in the bolus plus infusion group, $p<0.001$). The ischemic events that led to urgent PTCA were characterized by prolonged periods of chest pain with ECG changes suggesting that these events were of a serious nature. Placebo treated patients began experiencing ischemic events requiring urgent repeat PTCA within the first hour after randomization, and continued to have events over the first 48 hours. Patients treated with the bolus only regimen did not experience events in the first 4 hours following randomization, but subsequently followed a pattern similar to that seen in

Table I—ReoPro

Classification of Coronary Lesions According to ACC/AHA Criteria	
Type A Lesions (high success, >85%; low risk)	
Discrete (<10 mm length)	Little or no calcification
Concentric	Less than totally occlusive
Readily accessible	Not ostial in location
Nonangulated segment, <45°	No major branch involvement
Smooth contour	Absence of thrombus
Type B Lesions (moderate success, 60 to 85%; moderate risk)	
Tubular (10 to 20 mm length)	Moderate to heavy calcification
Eccentric	Total occlusions <3 months old
Moderate tortuosity of proximal segment	Ostial in location
Moderately angulated segment >45°, <90°	Bifurcation lesions requiring double guide wires
Irregular contour	Some thrombus present
Type C Lesions (low success, <60%; high risk)	
Diffuse (>2 cm length)	Total occlusion >3 months old
Excessive tortuosity of proximal segment	Inability to protect major side branches
Extremely angulated segments >90°	Degenerated vein grafts with friable lesions

ReoPro (cont'd)

placebo-treated patients. The patients receiving the bolus plus infusion regimen had fewer events; these events did not begin until approximately 11 hours after randomization and the event rate quickly achieved a plateau. Bolus plus infusion patients exhibited stability over the 30-day period of follow-up compared with the other 2 treatment groups. These results suggest that the 12-hour infusion of abciximab inhibited platelet function long enough for the PTCA site to undergo transition to a lower thrombogenic state.

The marked reduction in myocardial infarction and urgent intervention is consistent with the biological activity of abciximab as a potent antithrombotic agent. The clinical data suggest that both potent and sustained inhibition of platelet aggregation, as provided by the bolus plus infusion regimen, is required to suppress the major complications of angioplasty. Furthermore, the myocardial infarctions prevented by the bolus plus infusion regimen included those that would be expected to be associated with a poorer long-term prognosis—Q-wave and large non-Q-wave infarctions—as well as smaller non-Q-wave infarctions (see Table III).

Abciximab should not be administered to patients with known sensitivity to the product, to any component of the product or to murine monoclonal antibodies.

The most common complication encountered in the EPIC clinical trial was bleeding, with statistically significant increases in both major and minor bleeding events and in bleeding requiring transfusions (see Adverse Effects). However, the trial results suggested that heparin administered in high, non-weight-adjusted doses might be the principal cause of the bleeding when used with abciximab. In addition, a comparison of bleeding frequencies at the various EPIC trial sites suggested that certain patient and access site management techniques, including early sheath removal, could reduce the bleeding rate.

The EPILOG Trial: A large trial (Evaluation of PTCA to Improve Long-term Outcome by c7E3 GPIIb/IIIa Receptor Blockade or EPILOG) was initiated to formally test the hypothesis that use of a low-dose, weight-adjusted heparin regimen and early sheath removal could significantly lower the bleeding rate and while maintaining abciximab efficacy.

EPILOG was a 3-treatment arm trial of abciximab+standard dose, weight-adjusted heparin (bolus of 100 U/kg heparin to achieve an ACT of ≥300 seconds; maximum initial bolus 10 000 units), Abciximab+low dose, weight-adjusted heparin (bolus of 70 U/kg heparin to achieve an ACT of ≥200 seconds; maximum initial bolus 7,000 units) and placebo+standard dose, weight-adjusted heparin in a broad population of PTCA patients (but excluding patients with myocardial infarction, unstable angina and obvious contraindications). The abciximab dose regimen was the same as that used in the EPIC trial, except that the continuous infusion dose was weight-adjusted (0.125 μg/kg/min). Improved patient and access site management as well as a strong recommendation for early sheath removal were also incorporated into the trial which was designed to enroll 4 800 patients with an interim safety analysis at 1 500.

At the 1 500 patient interim analysis, 2 major and positive findings led to the termination of the trial. These findings were: 1) the bleeding rate of abciximab+low dose, weight-adjusted heparin was reduced to the same order as placebo. Bleeding rates in both arms were lower than that seen in the EPIC trial with a standard, non-weight-adjusted heparin dose regimen (see Table IV). 2) In spite of the modification of the heparin regimen, efficacy in the abciximab+low dose and the abciximab+standard dose, weight-adjusted heparin arms was maintained. There was no significant difference between the 2 abciximab treatment arms.

The CAPTURE Trial: The Chimeric Anti-Platelet Therapy in Unstable Angina Refractory to Standard Medical Therapy (CAPTURE) trial was designed to determine if potent antiplatelet therapy would reduce ischemic complications in patients with refractory unstable angina scheduled for PTCA. Enrollment was planned for 1 400 patients who were randomly allocated to abciximab or placebo treatment for approximately 24 hours preceding PTCA and continued until 1 hour afterwards. This dose regimen differs from that used in the EPIC trial and included in the current prescribing information. The CAPTURE trial incorporated weight adjustment of the heparin dose, but did not investigate the effect of a low heparin dose on bleeding and efficacy, and arterial sheaths were left in place for approximately 30 hours.

An important and positive finding that was apparent at an interim analysis at 1 050 patients, leading to termination of the trial, dealt with safety. The rate of major bleeding not associated with CABG was 1.7% in the placebo group and 2.9% in the abciximab group (p=0.21, 2-tailed) and transfusions were 3.6% and 7.8%, respectively (p=0.006, 2-tailed).

The bleeding rates in the CAPTURE trial are moderately higher than in the EPILOG trial, probably due to higher heparin dosing in CAPTURE and the extended time until sheath removal. Major bleeding not related to CABG was markedly lower in the ReoPro treated patients in the EPILOG low dose, weight adjusted heparin arm (1.4%), the EPILOG standard dose, weight adjusted heparin arm (1.8%) and the CAPTURE trial (2.9%) than in the original EPIC trial (10.6%). In contrast to the EPIC trial, no statistically significant differences in the major non-CABG bleeding rates were observed in the EPILOG and CAPTURE trials between abciximab and placebo treatment arms.

Table II—ReoPro

Primary Outcome Events

Event	Placebo (n=696)	Bolus (n=695)	Bolus + Infusion (n=708)
	Number of Patients (%)		
Primary Endpoint[a]	89 (12.8)	79 (11.5)	59 (8.3)
p-value vs placebo		0.428	0.008
Components of Primary Endpoint[b]			
Death	12 (1.7)	9 (1.3)	12 (1.7)
Acute myocardial infarctions in surviving patients	55 (7.9)	40 (5.8)	31 (4.4)
Urgent interventions in surviving patients without an acute myocardial infarction	22 (3.2)	30 (4.4)	16 (2.2)

[a]Patients who experienced more than one event in the first 30 days are counted only once.
[b]Patients are counted only once under the most serious component (death>acute MI>urgent intervention).

Table III—ReoPro

Number of Patients with MI by Type of MI

	Total (n=2 099)	Placebo (n=696)	Bolus (n=695)	Bolus+ Infusion (n=708)	Dose Response p-Value
Q-wave	29 (1.4%)	16 (2.3%)	7 (1.0%)	6 (0.8%)	0.020
% reduction vs placebo			56.2%	63.1%	
p-value vs placebo			0.090	0.032	
Large non-Q-wave[a]	68 (3.2%)	28 (4.0%)	19 (2.7%)	21 (3.0%)	0.265
% reduction vs placebo			32.0%	26.3%	
p-value vs placebo			0.235	0.310	
Small non-Q-wave	43 (2.0%)	16 (2.3%)	17 (2.4%)	10 (1.4%)	0.239
% reduction vs placebo			−6.4%	38.6%	
p-value vs placebo			0.862	0.240	
All MI[b]	140 (6.7%)	60 (8.6%)	43 (6.2%)	37 (5.2%)	0.011
% reduction vs placebo			28.2%	39.4%	
p-value vs placebo			0.101	0.015	

[a]Enzymes 5 times the upper range of normal values.
[b]p-values do not match Table II because logrank statistics were used in Table II, while Chi-square statistics were used in this table.

Table IV—ReoPro

EPILOG Interim Analysis—Bleeding Rates

	Bleeding Rates (%)				
	EPILOG Trial			EPIC Trial	
	Placebo+ Std Dose Wt Adj Heparin (n=492)	ReoPro+Low Dose Wt Adj Heparin (n=510)	ReoPro+Std Dose Wt Adj Heparin (n=498)	Placebo+Std Non-Wt Adjusted Heparin (n=696)	ReoPro+Std Non-Wt Adj Heparin (n=708)
Major bleeding, all	3.1	1.8	3.5	6.6	14.0
Major bleeding, non-CABG related	1.0	1.4	1.8	3.3	10.6
Hemorrhagic stroke	0.0	0.2	0.2	0.3	0.4

Contraindications: Abciximab should not be administered to patients with known sensitivity to abciximab, to any component of the product or to murine monoclonal antibodies.

Because inhibition of platelet aggregation increases the risk of bleeding, abciximab is contraindicated in the following clinical situations: active internal bleeding; recent (within 6 weeks) gastrointestinal or genitourinary bleeding of clinical significance; history of cerebrovascular accident (CVA) within 2 years or a CVA with a significant residual neurological deficit; recent (within 6 weeks) major surgery or trauma; intracranial neoplasm, arteriovenous malformation or aneurysm; known bleeding diathesis or severe uncontrolled hypertension; preexisting thrombocytopenia; vasculitis; use of i.v. dextran before PTCA, or intent to use it during PTCA; administration of oral anticoagulants within 7 days unless prothrombin time is ≤1.2 times control.

Warnings: Abciximab has been shown to be of benefit in patients who have high risk of ischemic complications in relation to PTCA. However, due to the increased risk of bleeding, careful assessment of risk:benefit should be made in individual patients before commencing therapy with abciximab.

Increased Risk of Bleeding (see Adverse Effects): The most common complication encountered during abciximab therapy is bleeding. The types of bleeding associated with abciximab therapy fall into two broad categories: bleeding observed at the arterial access site for cardiac catheterization and internal bleeding involving the gastrointestinal tract, genitourinary tract, or retroperitoneal sites.

In the following conditions, clinical data suggest that the risks of major bleeds due to abciximab therapy may be increased and should be weighed against the anticipated benefits: patients who weigh less than 75 kg, patients >65 years old, patients with a history of prior gastrointestinal disease and patients receiving thrombolytics.

The following conditions are also associated with an increased risk of bleeding in the angioplasty setting which may be additive to that of abciximab: PTCA within 12 hours of the onset of symptoms for acute myocardial infarction, prolonged PTCA (lasting more than 70 minutes) and failed PTCA

Heparin anticoagulation may contribute to the risk of bleeding. See Bleeding, Precautions: Patient Monitoring.

Should serious bleeding occur that is not controllable with pressure, the infusion of abciximab and any concomitant heparin should be stopped (see Restoration of Platelet Function).

Bleeding Precautions: Requirement for Specialist Facilities: Abciximab should only be administered in conjunction with extensive specialist medical and nursing care. In addition, there must be availability of laboratory tests of hematology function and facilities for administration of blood products.

Concomitant ASA and Heparin Therapy: Abciximab should be used as an adjunct to ASA and heparin therapy.

ASA: ASA should be administered orally at a daily dose of approximately but not less than 300 mg.

Heparin: Heparin Bolus Pre-PTCA: If a patient's activated clotting time (ACT) is less than 200 seconds prior to the start of the PTCA procedure, an initial bolus of heparin should be given upon gaining arterial access according to the following algorithm: ACT <150 seconds: administer 70 U/kg; ACT 150-199 seconds: administer 50 U/kg.

The initial heparin bolus dose should not exceed 7 000 U.

ACT should be checked a minimum of 2 minutes after the heparin bolus. If the ACT is <200 seconds, additional heparin boluses of 20 U/kg may be administered. Should the ACT remain <200 seconds, additional 20 U/kg boluses are to be given until an ACT ≥200 seconds is achieved.

Should a situation arise where higher doses of heparin are considered clinically necessary in spite of the possibility of a greater bleeding risk, it is recommended that heparin be carefully titrated using weight-adjusted boluses and that the target ACT not exceed 300 seconds.

Heparin Bolus during PTCA: During the PTCA procedure, ACT should be checked every 30 minutes. If ACT is <200 seconds, additional heparin boluses of 20 U/kg may be administered. Should the ACT remain <200 seconds, additional 20 U/kg boluses may to be given until an ACT ≥200 seconds is achieved. ACT should be checked prior to and a minimum of 2 minutes after each heparin bolus.

Heparin Infusion after PTCA: Discontinuation of heparin immediately following completion of the procedure, with removal of the arterial sheath within 6 hours, is **strongly recommended**. In individual patients, if prolonged heparin therapy after PTCA or later sheath removal is used, then an initial infusion rate of 7 U/kg/h is recommended (see Bleeding Precautions: Femoral Artery Sheath Removal).

Femoral Artery Access Site: Abciximab is associated with an increase in bleeding rate particularly at the site of arterial access for femoral artery sheath placement. The following are specific recommendations for access site care: Femoral Artery Sheath Insertion: when appropriate, place only an arterial sheath for vascular access (avoid venous sheath placement); puncture only the anterior wall of the artery or vein when establishing vascular access; the use of a through and through technique to identify the vascular structure is **strongly discouraged.**

While Femoral Artery Sheath Is In Place: Check sheath insertion site and distal pulses of affected leg(s) every 15 minutes for 1 hour, then hourly for 6 hours; maintain complete bed rest with head of bed ≤30°; maintain affected leg(s) straight via sheet tuck method or soft restraint; medicate for back/groin pain as necessary; educate patient on post-PTCA care via verbal instructions.

Femoral Artery Sheath Removal: heparin should be discontinued at least 4 hours prior to arterial sheath removal; check APTT or ACT prior to arterial sheath removal: do not remove sheath unless APTT ≤50 seconds or ACT ≤175 seconds; apply pressure to access site for at least 30 minutes following sheath removal, using either manual compression or a mechanical device; apply pressure dressing after hemostasis has been achieved.

After Femoral Artery Sheath Removal: check groin for bleeding/hematoma and distal pulses every 15 minutes for the first hour or until stable, then hourly; continue complete bed rest with head of bed ≤30° and affected leg(s) straight for 6 to 8 hours following femoral artery sheath removal, 6 to 8 hours following discontinuation of abciximab or 4 hours following discontinuation of heparin, whichever is later; remove pressure dressing prior to ambulation; continue to medicate for discomfort.

Management of Femoral Access Site Bleeding/Hematoma Formation: In the event of groin bleeding with or without hematoma formation, the following procedures are recommended: Lower head of bed to 0°; apply manual pressure/compression device until hemostasis has been achieved; any hematoma should be measured and monitored for enlargement; change pressure dressing as needed; if heparin is being given, obtain APTT and adjust heparin as needed; maintain i.v. access if sheath has been removed.

If groin bleed continues or the hematoma expands during abciximab infusion despite the above measures, the abciximab infusion should be immediately discontinued and the arterial sheath removed according to the guidelines listed above. After sheath removal i.v. access should be maintained until bleeding is controlled.

Potential Bleeding Sites: Careful attention should be paid to all potential bleeding sites, including arterial and venous puncture sites, catheter insertion sites, cutdown sites, and needle puncture sites.

Retroperitoneal Bleeding: Abciximab is associated with an increased risk of retroperitoneal bleeding in association with femoral vascular puncture. The use of venous sheaths should be minimized and only the anterior wall of the artery or vein should be punctured when establishing vascular access.

Gastrointestinal Bleeding Prophylaxis: In order to prevent spontaneous gastrointestinal bleeding it is recommended that patients are pretreated with H_2-histamine receptor antagonists or liquid antacids. Antiemetics should be given as needed to prevent vomiting.

General Nursing Care: Unnecessary arterial and venous punctures, i.m. injections, routine use of urinary catheters, nasotracheal intubation, nasogastric tubes and automatic blood pressure cuffs should be avoided. When obtaining i.v. access, noncompressible sites (e.g., subclavian or jugular veins) should be avoided. Saline or heparin locks should be considered for blood drawing. Vascular puncture sites should be documented and monitored. Gentle care should be provided when removing dressings.

Patient Monitoring: Before administration of abciximab, platelet count, ACT, prothrombin time (PT) and APTT should be measured to identify pre-existing coagulation abnormalities. Hemoglobin and hematocrit measurements should be obtained prior to the abciximab administration, at 12 hours following the abciximab bolus injection, and again at 24 hours following the bolus injection. Twelve lead electrocardiograms (ECG) should be obtained prior to the bolus injection of abciximab, and repeated once the patient has returned to the hospital ward from the catheterization laboratory, and at 24 hours after the bolus injection of abciximab. Vital signs (including blood pressure and pulse) should be obtained hourly for the first 4 hours following the abciximab bolus injection, and then at 6, 12, 18 and 24 hours following the abciximab bolus injection.

Thrombolytics, Anticoagulants and Other Antiplatelet Agents: Because abciximab inhibits platelet aggregation, caution should be employed when used with other drugs affecting hemostasis such as heparin, oral anticoagulants such as warfarin, thrombolytics and antiplatelet agents other than ASA, such as dipyridamole, ticlopidine or low molecular weight dextrans.

There are limited data on the use of abciximab in patients receiving thrombolytic agents. However these data suggest an increase in the risk of bleeding when abciximab is administered to patients treated with thrombolytics at doses sufficient to produce a systemic fibrinolytic state. If urgent intervention is required for refractory symptoms in a patient receiving abciximab (or who has received the drug in the previous 48 hours), it is recommended that PTCA be attempted first to salvage the situation. Prior to further surgical interventions, the bleeding time should be determined by the Ivy method and should be 12 minutes or less. Should PTCA and any other appropriate procedures fail, and should the angiographic appearance suggest that the etiology is due to thrombosis, consideration may be given to the administration of adjunctive thrombolytic therapy via the intracoronary route. A systemic fibrinolytic state should be avoided.

Thrombocytopenia: To reduce the possibility of thrombocytopenia, platelet counts should be monitored prior to treatment, 2 to 4 hours following the bolus dose of abciximab and at 24 hours. If a patient experiences an acute platelet decrease, additional platelet counts should be determined. These platelet counts should be drawn in separate tubes containing ethylenediaminetetraacetic acid (EDTA), citrate and heparin to exclude pseudothrombocytopenia due to in vitro anticoagulant interaction. If true thrombocytopenia is verified, abciximab should be immediately discontinued and the condition appropriately monitored and treated. A daily platelet count should be obtained until it returns to normal. If a patient's platelet count drops to 60 000 cells/µL, heparin and ASA should be discontinued. If a patient's platelet count drops below 50 000 cells/µL, platelets should be transfused.

Restoration of Platelet Function: Transfusion of donor platelets has been shown to restore platelet function following abciximab administration in animal studies and transfusions of fresh random donor platelets have been given empirically to restore platelet function in humans. In the event of serious uncontrolled bleeding or the need for surgery, a bleeding time should be determined. If the bleeding time is greater than 12 minutes, 10 units of platelets may be given. Abciximab may be displaced from endogenous platelet receptors and subsequently bind to platelets which have been transfused. Nevertheless, a single transfusion may be sufficient to reduce receptor blockade to 60 to 70% at which level platelet function is restored. Repeat platelet transfusions may be required to maintain the bleeding time at or below 12 minutes.

Precautions: Children: Safety and effectiveness of abciximab in children below the age of 18 have not been established.

Obstetrics: In vitro and in vivo mutagenicity studies have not demonstrated any mutagenic effect. Long-term studies in animals have not been performed to evaluate the carcinogenic potential or effects on fertility in male or female animals.

Animal reproduction studies have not been conducted with abciximab. It is also not known whether abciximab can cause fetal harm when administered to a pregnant woman or can affect reproduction capacity. Abciximab should be given to a pregnant woman only if clearly needed.

Lactation: It is not known if this drug is excreted in human milk. Because many drugs are excreted in human milk, caution should be exercised when abciximab is administered to a nursing woman.

Readministration: There are no data concerning readministration of abciximab. Administration of abciximab may result in human antichimeric antibody (HACA) formation (see Adverse Effects) that can cause allergic or hypersensitivity reactions (including anaphylaxis), thrombocytopenia or diminished benefit upon readministration of abciximab.

Allergic Reactions: Anaphylaxis may occur at any time during administration. If it does, administration of abciximab should be immediately stopped and standard appropriate resuscitative measures should be initiated.

Drug Interactions: Although drug interactions with abciximab have not been studied systematically, abciximab has been administered to patients with ischemic heart disease treated concomitantly with a broad range of medications used in the treatment of angina, myocardial infarction and hypertension. These medications have included heparin, warfarin, beta-adrenergic receptor blockers, calcium channel antagonists, angiotensin converting enzyme inhibitors, i.v. and oral nitrates, and ASA. Heparin, other anticoagulants, thrombolytics, and antiplatelet agents may be associated with an increase in bleeding. Patients with HACA titers may have allergic or hypersensitivity reactions when treated with other diagnostic or therapeutic monoclonal antibodies.

Adverse Effects: Clinical toxicity has been infrequent with the administration of abciximab. Adverse events reasonably related to study agent that were reported by investigators for more than 0.5% of the 2 038 treated patients in the pivotal trial are shown in Table V (on following page). Although extremely unlikely, anaphylaxis may potentially occur at any time during administration. If it does, immediate cessation of infusion, s.c. administration of 0.3 to 0.5 mL of aqueous epinephrine (1:1 000 dilution), corticosteroids, respiratory assistance and other resuscitative measures are essential.

Bleeding: In the pivotal trial, bleeding was classified as major or minor by the criteria of the Thrombolysis in Myocardial Infarction (TIMI) study group. Major bleeding events (intracranial hemorrhage or decrease in hemoglobin greater than 5 g/dL) and minor bleeding events (spontaneous gross hematuria or hematemesis or observed blood loss with a hemoglobin decreasing more than 3 g/dL or with a decrease in hemoglobin of at least 4 g/dL with no observed blood loss) are summarized in Table VI (on following page).

Major bleeding events occurred in 14% (99/708) of patients treated with the bolus plus infusion regimen, 11.1% (77/695) of patients treated with the bolus regimen and 6.6% (46/696) of the patients treated with placebo. If bleeding associated with CABG is excluded, these major bleeding rates become 10.6% (75/708), 8.6% (60/695) and 3.3% (23/696), respectively. The rates for major and minor bleeding observed in the EPILOG and CAPTURE trials are described in Indications.

The principal site of bleeding in the majority of the abciximab-treated patients was the femoral artery access site. The incidence of intracranial hemorrhage was the same in all 3 groups (3 in the bolus plus infusion group, 1 of which was in a patient who did not receive abciximab but is included in the intent to treat analysis; 1 in the bolus group; and 2 in the placebo group). The incidence of CABG-related blood loss was also the same in all 3 groups (24 or 3.4% in the bolus plus infusion group, 21 or 3% in the bolus group, and 26 or 3.7% in the placebo group). There was no increase in the need for surgical intervention as a consequence of bleeding in either of the abciximab-treated groups. The incidence and site of major bleeding events not associated with CABG and the frequencies of transfusions and surgical interventions for bleeding in patients with these bleeding events are listed in Table VII (on following page).

If patients undergoing CABG and other patients are also included, transfusions of blood products were given to 16.8% of the bolus plus infusion patients, 14% of the bolus patients and 7.5% of the placebo patients. Similarly, including all patients in the analysis, surgical intervention for bleeding remained infrequent in all 3 treatment groups, being 1.7%

ReoPro (cont'd)

Table V—RePro

Patients Who Experienced Adverse Events Reasonably Related to Study Agent

	Total (n=2 038)	Placebo (n=681)	Bolus (n=679)	Bolus+ Infusion (n=678)
Hypotension	119 (5.8%)	21 (3.1%)	46 (6.8%)	52 (7.7%)
Nausea	84 (4.1%)	23 (3.4%)	21 (3.1%)	40 (5.9%)
Vomiting	63 (3.1%)	18 (2.6%)	18 (2.7%)	27 (4.0%)
Thrombocytopenia	27 (1.3%)	3 (0.4%)	8 (1.2%)	16 (2.4%)
Hematoma	27 (1.3%)	7 (1.0%)	11 (1.6%)	9 (1.3%)
Bradycardia	25 (1.2%)	3 (0.4%)	12 (1.8%)	10 (1.5%)
Fever	23 (1.1%)	6 (0.9%)	7 (1.0%)	10 (1.5%)
Vascular disorder	21 (1.0%)	5 (0.6%)	12 (1.8%)	5 (0.7%)

Table VI—ReoPro

Number of Patients with Bleeding Events[a]

	Total (n=2 099)	Placebo (n=696)	Bolus (n=695)	Bolus+ Infusion (n=708)	Dose Response p-Value
Patients with major bleeding[b]	222 (10.6%)	46 (6.6%)	77 (11.1%)	99 (14.0%)	<0.001
% change vs placebo			+67.6%	+111.6%	
p-value vs placebo			0.003	<0.001	
Patients with minor bleeding[b]	295 (14.1%)	68 (9.8%)	107 (15.4%)	120 (16.9%)	<0.001
% change vs placebo			+57.6%	+73.5%	
p-value vs placebo			0.002	<0.001	
Patients with insignificant or no bleeding	1 559 (74.3%)	572 (82.2%)	505 (72.7%)	482 (68.1%)	<0.001
% change vs placebo			−11.6%	−17.2%	
p-value vs placebo			<0.001	<0.001	
Patients not evaluated	23 (1.1%)	10 (1.4%)	6 (0.9%)	7 (1.0%)	0.422
% change			−39.9%	−31.2%	
p-value			0.452	0.475	

[a]Patients with blood loss associated with CABG are included in this table.
[b]Patients who had blood loss in more than one classification are counted only once according to the most severe classification. Patients with blood loss of the same classification are also counted once.

Table VII—ReoPro

Characteristics of Major Bleeding Events

	Placebo	Bolus	Bolus+Infusion
Major bleeding[a]	23/696 (3.3%)	60/695 (8.6%)	75/708 (10.6%)
Site of major bleed[b]			
Intracranial	2 (8.7%)	1 (1.7%)	3[c] (4%)
Gross hematuria	1 (4.3%)	4 (6.7%)	4 (5.3%)
Other genitourinary	2 (8.7%)	5 (8.3%)	8 (10.7%)
Hematemesis	0 (0%)	5 (8.3%)	11 (14.7%)
Other gastrointestinal	1 (4.3%)	11 (18.3%)	11 (14.7%)
Access sites	17 (73.9%)	42 (71.7%)	54 (72%)
Groin	16	43	50
Retroperitoneal	2	2	12
Brachial	0	1	0
Other	1	1	4
Oral	1 (4.3%)	4 (6.7%)	4 (5.3%)
Otic	0 (0%)	1 (1.7%)	0 (0%)
Other	1 (4.3%)	8 (13.3%)	11 (14.7%)
Decrease in Hct/Hgb only	3 (13.0%)	7 (11.7%)	11 (14.7%)
Transfusions[b]			
RBC/Whole blood	14 (60.9%)	42 (70%)	55 (73.3%)
Platelets	2 (8.7%)	10 (16.7%)	10 (13.3%)
Hypotension[b,d]	8 (34.8%)	18 (30%)	23 (0.3%)
Surgical intervention for bleeding[b]	6 (26.1%)	12 (20%)	5 (6.7%)

[a]Patients may be included for more than one bleeding site or transfusion type. Blood loss associated with CABG is not included in this table.
[b]Percentages are based on the number of patients with major bleeding.
[c]Includes one patient randomized but not treated.
[d]Hypotension that was serious, life-threatening, or fatal.

(12/708) in the bolus plus infusion group, 2.6% (18/695) in the bolus group and 1.4% (10/696) in the placebo group.

In this study 37/708 (5.2%) of bolus plus infusion patients, 25/695 (3.6%) of bolus patients and 24/696 (3.4%) of placebo patients exhibited an in-hospital thrombocytopenia defined as any platelet count <100 000 cells/μL. The median change in platelet count was similar in both treatment groups and showed little change over the course of hospitalization, or at the 2 and 4-week follow-up periods. There was, however, a higher rate of platelet transfusions in patients who received the bolus plus infusion regimen (5.5% in the bolus plus infusion group, 4.2% in the bolus group and 2.6% in the placebo group).

Taken together, these data show that administration of abciximab in combination with ASA and heparin may cause bleeding complications, usually at the arterial puncture site. Women over 65 years of age and low weight patients had the highest risk of bleeding events. The relationship of bleeding to lower weight suggests that heparin may play a role. While the abciximab bolus was weight adjusted, heparin administration was not. The most frequent actions taken in response to major bleeding events following abciximab bolus plus infusion were application of pressure or a change of dressing (72%), discontinuation or reduction of heparin administration (46.7%) and discontinuation or reduction of abciximab administration (28%).

Human antichimeric antibody (HACA) may appear in response to the administration of abciximab. Positive responses occurred in 5.2% (32/616) of the bolus patients and 6.5% (40/616) of the bolus plus infusion patients who could be evaluated. None of the 605 placebo patients who could be evaluated had a positive HACA response. Most of the patients with a positive HACA result had a low-titer response. All of the 32 patients who had a positive HACA result in the bolus group and 34 of the 40 patients who had a positive HACA result in the bolus plus infusion group had a titer 1:1 600. There were 6 patients in the bolus group who had HACA titers ranging between 1:6 400 and 1:51 200. However, there was no excess of hypersensitivity or allergic reactions related to abciximab treatment compared with placebo treatment.

Overdose: Symptoms and Treatment: There has been no experience of overdosage with abciximab in human clinical trials. However, refer to Reversal of Antiplatelet Effects in the Warnings section. It is recommended that infusion be discontinued after 12 hours to avoid effects of prolonged platelet receptor blockade.

Dosage: Abciximab is intended for use in patients undergoing PTCA. The safety and efficacy of ReoPro have only been investigated with concomitant administration of heparin and ASA as described in Pharmacology.

In patients with failed PTCAs, the continuous infusion of abciximab should be stopped because there is no evidence for abciximab efficacy in that setting.

In the event of serious bleeding that cannot be controlled by compression, abciximab and heparin should be discontinued immediately (see Warnings, Restoration of Platelet Function).

Adults: The recommended dose is a 0.25 mg/kg i.v. bolus administered over 1 minute, 10 to 60 minutes prior to PTCA, followed by a 10 μg/min continuous i.v. infusion for 12 hours.

Children: There is no experience on the use of abciximab in children.

Administration Instructions: Parenteral drug products should be inspected visually for particulate matter prior to administration. Preparations of abciximab containing visibly opaque particles should **not** be used.

Hypersensitivity reactions should be anticipated whenever protein solutions such as abciximab are administered. Epinephrine, dopamine, theophylline, antihistamines and corticosteroids should be available for immediate use. If symptoms of an allergic reaction or anaphylaxis appear, the infusion should be stopped and appropriate treatment given.

As with all parenteral drug products, aseptic procedures should be used during the administration of abciximab.

Withdraw the necessary amount of abciximab for bolus injection through a sterile, nonpyrogenic, low protein-binding 0.2 or 0.22 μm filter (Millipore SLGV025LS or equivalent) into a syringe. Ten to 60 minutes prior to PTCA, the bolus injection should be administered over 1 minute.

Withdraw the necessary amount of abciximab for the continuous infusion through a sterile, nonpyrogenic, low protein-binding 0.2 or 0.22 μm filter (Millipore SLGV025LS or equivalent) into a syringe. Inject into sterile 0.9% saline or 5% dextrose and infuse at a rate of 10 μg/min for 12 hours via a continuous infusion pump equipped with an in-line sterile, nonpyrogenic, low protein-binding 0.2 or 0.22 μm filter (Abbott #4524 or equivalent). For example, withdraw 4.5 mL abciximab and inject into 250 mL of 0.9% saline or 5% dextrose and infuse at 17 mL/hr for 12 hours.

Once mixed, the solution can be stored up to 12 hours at 2 to 8°C. Discard the unused portion at the end of the 12-hour infusion.

Although incompatibilities have not been observed with i.v. infusion fluids or commonly used cardiovascular drugs, it is recommended that abciximab be administered in a separate i.v. line whenever possible and not mixed with other medications.

No incompatibilities have been observed with glass bottles or polyvinyl chloride bags and administration sets.

Supplied: Each mL of clear, colorless, sterile, nonpyrogenic solution for i.v. use contains: abciximab 2 mg. Nonmedicinal ingredients: polysorbate 80, sodium chloride and sodium phosphate. Preservative-free. Vials of 5 mL, packages of 1. Store at 2 to 8°C. Do not freeze. Do not shake. Do not use beyond the expiration date. Discard any unused portion left in the vial.

New Product 1998

REPLENS®

Roberts

Polycarbophil

Vaginal Moisturizer—Lubricant

Pharmacology: Polycarbophil, the key ingredient, is a bioadhesive polymer which can carry up to 60 times its weight in water. It adheres to the epithelial cells lining the vaginal walls and delivers electrolytes and water. The polymer is detached only upon the shedding of the outer layer of cells or mucin, a normal healthy process which occurs every 2 or 3 days. The polycarbophil is negatively charged and this causes the water and electrolytes to be driven into the underlying cells. Electrolytes are also driven into the vasculature causing vasodilation, which results in (i) an increase in blood supply to the tissue and (ii) a greater transudation of fluids which pass into and through the tissues. The electrolytes and water moisturize and lubricate the vaginal tissue and thus relieve the discomfort caused by vaginal dryness. The increased blood flow can lead to enhanced secretion as vaginal fluids diffuse from blood.

In addition, the polymer, polycarbophil, has a low pH of 2.8 and has the ability to keep the pH of the vagina stable. It maintains vaginal pH in the physiologically normal range (4.5 to 5.5, or fairly acid) thereby making it less susceptible to bacterial infection.

Indications: Relieves vaginal dryness, itching and painful intercourse for up to 3 days with a single application.

Warnings: Keep out of the reach of children. Replens is not a contraceptive. Does not contain spermicide or hormones.

Dosage: Use as needed. One application every 2 to 3 days is recommended.

Supplied: Each single-use disposable applicator delivers 2.5 g. Nonstaining, fragrance-free, paraben-free, unflavored and nongreasy. Nonmedicinal ingredients: carbomer 934P, glycerin, hydrogenated palm oil glyceride, mineral oil, polycarbophil, purified water and sorbic acid. Individually-wrapped prefilled applicators, boxes of 3 and 8.

(Shown in Product Recognition Section)

REQUIP™ Ⓟ

SmithKline Beecham

Ropinirole HCl

Antiparkinsonian Agent—Dopamine Agonist

Pharmacology: Ropinirole is a non-ergoline dopamine agonist, which activates postsynaptic dopamine receptors.

In vitro studies have shown that ropinirole binds with high affinity to cloned human D_2, D_3, and D_4 receptors. The antiparkinson activity of ropinirole is believed to be due to its stimulatory effects on central postsynaptic dopamine D_2 receptors within the caudate-putamen.

Ropinirole is a potent agonist both in vitro and in vivo and restores motor function in animal models of Parkinson's disease. Ropinirole has been shown to reverse the motor deficits induced by the neurotoxin 1-methyl-4-phenyl-1,2,3,6-tetrahydropyridine (MPTP) in primates.

Neither ropinirole nor its metabolites bind with high affinity to dopamine D_1 receptors. Ropinirole also has very low affinity for 5-HT_1, 5-HT_2, benzodiazepine, $GABA_A$, muscarinic, α-or β-adrenoreceptors. Ropinirole binds to opiate receptors with low affinity, however, studies show that this weak opiate activity has no consequences at pharmacological doses in vivo.

In rats, ropinirole binds to melanin-containing tissues (e.g., the eye) to a greater degree than nonpigmented tissues, and tissue levels decline with a half-life of 16 to 20 days. It is unknown whether or not ropinirole accumulates in these tissues over time.

In healthy normotensive subjects, single oral doses of ropinirole, in the range of 0.01 to 2.5 mg, had little or no effect on supine blood pressure and pulse rate. Upon standing, ropinirole caused decreases in systolic and mainly diastolic blood pressure at doses above 0.25 mg. In some subjects, these changes were associated with the emergence of orthostatic symptoms, bradycardia, and, in 1 case, transient sinus arrest in the context of a severe vasovagal syncope. The effect of repeat dosing and slow titration of ropinirole was not studied in healthy volunteers. The mechanism of ropinirole-induced orthostatic symptoms probably relates to its dopamine D_2-mediated blunting of the noradrenergic response to standing and subsequent decrease in peripheral vascular resistance. Orthostatic signs and symptoms were often accompanied by nausea.

Ropinirole had no dose-related effect on ECG wave form and rhythm in young healthy male volunteers.

At doses ≥ 0.8 mg ropinirole suppressed serum prolactin concentrations in healthy male volunteers.

Pharmacokinetics: Absorption, Bioavailability and Distribution: Ropinirole is rapidly absorbed with median peak concentrations occurring within 1.5 hours after oral dosing. Despite complete absorption, absolute bioavailability of ropinirole is reduced to approximately 50% as a result of first-pass metabolism. Relative bioavailability from a tablet compared to an oral solution is 85%. Over the therapeutic dose range, C_{max} and AUC values increase in proportion to the increase in dose (see Table I).

The average oral clearance is approximately 47 L/h (range 17 to 113 L/h) and is constant over the entire dosage range. The terminal elimination half-life is approximately 6 h (range 2 to 27 h) and the volume of distribution at steady-state is approximately 480 L (range 216 to 891 L) or 7 L/kg (range 3.1 to 12.9 L/kg).

Table I—Requip

Steady-state Pharmacokinetic Parameters (Mean and Range) of Ropinirole in Patients with Parkinson's Disease Administered Ropinirole in a t.i.d. Regimen

Unit Dose (mg)	C_{max} (ng/mL)	C_{min} (ng/mL)	T_{max}* (h)	AUC_{0-8} (ng·h/mL)
1	5.3 (3.1-9.0)	2.6 (0.9-4.2)	2.0 (0.5-7.0)	27.5 (14.9-46.5)
2	9.8 (5.0-18.0)	4.8 (2.3-10.0)	1.0 (0.6-4.0)	53.8 (23.9-108)
4	23.7 (14.2-40.9)	13.1 (4.8-23.9)	1.0 (1.0-3.0)	136 (66.1-241)

*Median.

Steady-state concentrations are expected to be achieved within 2 days of dosing. There is, on average, a 2-fold higher steady-state plasma concentration of ropinirole following the recommended t.i.d. regimen compared to those observed following a single oral dose.

Food delayed the rate of absorption of ropinirole (median T_{max} was increased by 2.6 hours and C_{max} was decreased by 25%) in Parkinsonian patients. However, there was no marked change in the overall systemic availability of the drug. Ropinirole may be given with or without food. While administration of the drug with food may improve gastrointestinal tolerance, in severely fluctuating patients, the morning dose may be given without food in order to avoid a delay in time to switch "ON".

Population pharmacokinetic analyses have shown that frequently coadministered medications, such as levodopa, selegiline, amantadine, anticholinergic drugs, ibuprofen, benzodiazepines and antidepressants did not alter the pharmacokinetics of ropinirole.

Plasma protein binding is low (10 to 40%).

Ropinirole has a blood to plasma ratio of 1.2.

Metabolism: Ropinirole is extensively metabolized by the liver. The N-despropyl metabolite is the major metabolite circulating in the plasma. Based on AUC data, the plasma levels of the metabolite were consistently higher than those of the parent drug suggesting a nonsaturable conversion of ropinirole to the N-despropyl metabolite. The affinity of the N-despropyl metabolite for human cloned D_2 receptors is lower than the affinity of ropinirole. In addition the metabolite does not cross the blood-brain barrier; thus, it is unlikely to contribute to the therapeutic effects of ropinirole. The plasma concentrations of the hydroxylated metabolite are low and account for about 1 to 5% of the ropinirole concentrations. Although the hydroxylated metabolite was more active than ropinirole in in vitro D_2 receptor binding studies, at therapeutic doses it is not expected to contribute to the activity of ropinirole.

In vitro studies indicate that the major cytochrome P450 isozyme involved in the metabolism of ropinirole is CYP1A2. In patients with Parkinson's disease, ciprofloxacin, an inhibitor of CYP1A2, significantly increased the systemic availability of ropinirole, while theophylline, a substrate of CYP1A2, was devoid of such activity (see Precautions, Drug Interactions).

Elimination: Recovery of radioactivity after oral and i.v. administration of ^{14}C-ropinirole was approximately 88% and 90% of the dose, respectively. Urinary excretion of unchanged ropinirole is low and represents approximately 5 to 10% of the dose. N-despropyl ropinirole is the predominant metabolite found in the urine (40%), followed by the glucuronide of the hydroxy metabolite (10%), and the carboxylic acid metabolite (10%) formed from N-despropyl ropinirole.

Population Subgroups: Renal and Hepatic Impairment: Based on population pharmacokinetics, no clinically significant differences were observed in the pharmacokinetics of ropinirole in Parkinsonian patients with moderate renal impairment (creatinine clearance between 30 to 50 mL/min; n=18, mean age 74 years) compared to age-matched patients with creatinine clearance above 50 mL/min (n=44, mean age 70 years). Therefore, no dosage adjustment is necessary in Parkinsonian patients with mild to moderate renal impairment (see Precautions and Dosage).

The use of ropinirole in patients with severe renal impairment or hepatic impairment has not been studied. Administration of ropinirole to such patients is not recommended (see Precautions and Dosage).

Gender: Population pharmacokinetic analysis indicated that the oral clearance and volume of distribution of ropinirole at steady-state were similar in male patients (n=99, mean age 60 years) and female patients who were not taking concomitant estrogens (n=56, mean age 65 years).

Estrogen Replacement Therapy: In women, on long-term treatment with conjugated estrogens (n=16, mean age 63 years), the oral clearance of ropinirole was decreased by an average of 36% compared to the oral clearance in women not receiving supplemental estrogens (n=56, mean age 65 years). The average terminal elimination half-life was 9 hours in the estrogen group and 6.5 hours in patients not taking estrogens (see Precautions and Dosage).

Age: Population pharmacokinetic analysis revealed that the oral clearance of ropinirole, seen in patients under the age of 65 years (n=97), was reduced from 62.1 L/h to 45.5 L/h in patients between the ages of 65 and 75 years (n=63). In patients older than 75 years (n=11), oral clearance was similar to that seen in the 65 to 75 year age group (41.7 L/h). However, since the dose of ropinirole is to be individually titrated to clinical response, dosage adjustment is not necessary in the elderly (above 65 years).

Clinical Trials: Up to May 31, 1996, 1 599 patients have been exposed to ropinirole, with 481 patients being exposed for over 1 year and 241 patients being exposed for over 2 years.

Evidence to support the efficacy of ropinirole in treating the signs and symptoms of Parkinson's disease was obtained in multicentre, double-blind studies. These studies included either patients who had minimal or no prior dopaminergic therapy, or patients who were not optimally controlled with current levodopa-decarboxylase inhibitor therapy. In patients with early disease, ropinirole improved motor function (assessed by the motor component of the UPDRS [Unified Parkinson's Disease Rating Scale]) and delayed the need to initiate treatment with levodopa. In patients with more advanced disease, ropinirole reduced "off" time (based upon patient diaries recording time "on" and "off") and permitted a reduction in levodopa dose. The subsequent section describes some of the studies in which ropinirole was titrated (see Dosage) to the maximal dose of 8 mg t.i.d.

In clinical trials where dosing was titrated to optimal clinical effect, the mean daily dose of ropinirole at 24 weeks was 9.5 mg in early therapy (n=282) and was 13.5 mg in adjunct therapy (n=303).

In the pivotal clinical trials, including studies where the dose was titrated to the target maximum of 24 mg/day, the mean daily dose of ropinirole at endpoint was 10.7 mg in early therapy (n=458) and 12.5 mg in adjunct therapy (n=456).

In the total patient database (n=1 599) over 50% of patients were dosed between 6 and 15 mg of ropinirole per day in both early and adjunct therapy. Less than 22% of patients exceeded a total daily dose of 15 mg.

Requip (cont'd)

During the clinical trials, the dose of ropinirole was titrated to optimal clinical response and tolerance. Retrospective analysis showed that female patients required lower doses than male patients but were exposed to ropinirole for similar periods of time.

Early Therapy: In a double-blind, randomized, placebo-controlled, 6-month study, ropinirole-treated patients (n=116) demonstrated a 24% improvement in UPDRS motor scores from baseline, compared to placebo-treated patients (n=125), who demonstrated a 3% worsening in motor scores. On the Clinical Global Impression (CGI) scale, 33% of ropinirole-treated patients and 12% of placebo-treated patients were rated as "very much improved" and "much improved". "Rescue levodopa" was needed by 11% of ropinirole-treated and 29% of placebo-treated patients. All differences were statistically significant.

In a double-blind, randomized 5-year study, at the 6-month interim analysis, ropinirole (n=179) was compared to levodopa-benserazide (n=89). The decrease in UPDRS motor scores versus baseline was greater with levodopa than with ropinirole. However, the proportion of "responders" (UPDRS improvement of at least 30%) did not differ between levodopa and ropinirole. Results on the CGI indicated that there was no difference between ropinirole and levodopa in less severely afflicted patients (Hoehn and Yahr stage I to II) but levodopa was more efficacious in patients with more severe disease.

Adjunct Therapy: In a double-blind, randomized, clinical trial of 6-month duration, ropinirole (n=94) was compared to placebo (n=54) as adjunct therapy to levodopa. The primary efficacy parameter, defined as both a 20% or greater reduction in levodopa dose and a 20% or greater reduction in "off" time, was achieved by 28% of ropinirole-treated patients and 11% of placebo-treated patients. This difference was statistically significant. The daily dose of levodopa was reduced by 19% and 2.8% in the ropinirole and placebo-treated patients, respectively.

Therapeutic Effect—Plasma Concentrations: The relationship between efficacy and plasma concentrations of ropinirole was assessed from population pharmacokinetic data obtained in 141 male and female patients who participated in 2 prospective studies.

In general, the average plasma concentrations of ropinirole at steady-state (C_{ss}) were higher in patients classified as responders versus non-responders, although considerable overlap in the range of C_{ss} between the 2 groups was noted. Mean (±SD) ropinirole C_{ss} for responders and non-responders were 22.8±10.8 ng/mL and 15.1±9.7 ng/mL, respectively.

Indications: In the treatment of the signs and symptoms of idiopathic Parkinson's disease.

Ropinirole can be used both as early therapy, without concomitant levodopa and as an adjunct to levodopa.

Contraindications: Patients with a known hypersensitivity to ropinirole or the excipients of the drug product.

Warnings: Orthostatic Symptoms: Dopamine agonists appear to impair the systemic regulation of blood pressure with resulting orthostatic symptoms of dizziness or lightheadedness, with or without documented hypotension. These symptoms appear to occur especially during dose escalation. Therefore, patients treated with dopamine agonists should be carefully monitored for signs and symptoms of orthostatic hypotension, especially during dose escalation (see Dosage) and should be informed of this risk (see Blue Section, Information for the Patient).

Hallucinations: In controlled trials, ropinirole caused hallucination in 5.1% of patients during early therapy (1.4% in the placebo group) and in 10.1% of patients receiving ropinirole and levodopa (4.2% receiving placebo and levodopa). Hallucination was of sufficient severity that it led to discontinuation in 1.3% and 1.9% of patients during early and adjunct therapy, respectively. The incidence of hallucination was dose-dependent both in early and adjunct therapy studies.

Precautions: Cardiovascular: Since ropinirole has not been studied in patients with a history or evidence of significant cardiovascular disease including myocardial infarction, unstable angina, cardiac decompensation, cardiac arrhythmias, vaso-occlusive disease (including cerebral) or cardiomyopathy, it should be used with caution in such patients.

There is limited experience with ropinirole in patients treated with antihypertensive and antiarrhythmic agents. Consequently, in such patients, the dose of ropinirole should be titrated with caution.

Table II—Requip

Adverse Events With Incidence ≥1% From All Placebo-Controlled Early and Adjunct Therapy Studies

	Early Therapy		Adjunct Therapy	
	Requip N=157 % occurrence	Placebo N=147 % occurrence	Requip N=208 % occurrence	Placebo N=120 % occurrence
Autonomic Nervous System				
Sweating Increased	6.4	4.1	7.2	1.7
Mouth Dry	5.1	3.4	5.3	0.8
Flushing	3.2	0.7	1.4	0.8
Body as a Whole				
Peripheral Edema	13.4	4.1	3.9	2.5
Fatigue	10.8	4.1	*	–
Injury	–	–	10.6	9.2
Pain	7.6	4.1	5.3	3.3
Asthenia	6.4	1.4	–	–
Drug Level Increased	4.5	2.7	6.7	3.3
Chest Pain	3.8	2.0	–	–
Malaise	3.2	0.7	1.4	0.8
Therapeutic Response Decreased	1.9	0.7	–	–
Cellulitis	1.3	0.0	–	–
Influenza-Like Symptoms	–	–	1.0	0.0
Fever	–	–	1.4	0.0
Cardiovascular				
Syncope	11.5	1.4	2.9	1.7
Hypotension Postural	6.4	4.8	–	–
Hypertension	4.5	3.4	3.4	3.3
Hypotension	1.9	0.0	2.4	0.8
Cardiac Failure	–	–	1.0	0.0
Central and Peripheral Nervous System				
Dizziness	40.1	21.8	26.0	15.8
Dyskinesia	–	–	33.7	12.5
Headache	17.2	17.0	16.8	11.7
Ataxia (Falls)	–	–	9.6	6.7
Tremor	–	–	6.3	2.5
Paresthesia	–	–	5.3	2.5
Hyperesthesia	3.8	2.0	–	–
Dystonia	–	–	4.3	4.2
Hypokinesia	–	–	5.3	4.2
Paresis	–	–	2.9	0.0
Speech disorder	–	–	1.0	0.0
Vertigo	1.9	0.0	–	–
Carpal Tunnel Syndrome	1.3	0.7	–	–
Gastrointestinal				
Nausea	59.9	21.8	29.8	18.3
Vomiting	12.1	6.8	7.2	4.2
Dyspepsia	9.6	4.8	–	–
Constipation	8.3	7.5	5.8	3.3
Abdominal Pain	6.4	2.7	8.7	7.5
Diarrhea	–	–	4.8	2.5
Anorexia	3.8	1.4	–	–
Flatulence	2.5	1.4	1.9	0.8
Tooth Disorder	1.9	0.7	1.0	0.8
Saliva Increased	–	–	2.4	0.8
Colitis	1.3	0.0	–	–
Dysphagia	1.3	0.0	2.4	0.8
Periodontitis	1.3	0.0	1.4	0.8
Eructation	–	–	1.4	0.0
Fecal Incontinence	–	–	1.0	0.0
Hemorrhoids	–	–	1.0	0.0
Gastroesophageal Reflux	–	–	1.0	0.0
Gastrointestinal Disorder (NOS)	–	–	1.0	0.0
Tooth Ache	–	–	1.0	0.0
Hearing and Vestibular				
Tinnitus	1.3	0.0	–	–
Heart Rate and Rhythm				
Palpitation	3.2	2.0	2.9	2.5
Extrasystoles	1.9	0.7	–	–
Tachycardia	1.9	0.0	1.0	0.0
Fibrillation Atrial	1.9	0.0	–	–
Tachycardia Supraventricular	1.3	0.0	–	–
Bradycardia	–	–	1.0	0.0
Liver and Biliary				
Gamma-GT Increased	1.3	0.7	1.0	0.0
Hepatic Enzymes Increased	1.3	0.0	–	–
Metabolic and Nutritional				
Alkaline Phosphate Increased	2.5	1.4	1.0	0.0
Weight Decrease	–	–	2.4	0.8
Hypoglycemia	1.3	0.0	–	–

Table II—Requip (Continued)

Adverse Events With Incidence ≥1% From All Placebo-Controlled Early and Adjunct Therapy Studies

	Early Therapy		Adjunct Therapy	
	Requip N=157 % occurrence	Placebo N=147 % occurrence	Requip N=208 % occurrence	Placebo N=120 % occurrence
Musculoskeletal				
Arthralgia	–	–	6.7	5.0
Arthritis	–	–	2.9	0.8
Arthritis Aggravated	1.3	0.0	1.4	0.0
Myocardial, Endocardial, Pericardial Valve				
Myocardial Ischemia	1.3	0.7	–	–
Psychiatric				
Somnolence	40.1	6.1	20.2	8.3
Anxiety	–	–	6.3	3.3
Confusion	5.1	1.4	8.7	1.7
Hallucination	5.1	1.4	10.1	4.2
Nervousness	–	–	4.8	2.5
Yawning	3.2	0.0	–	–
Amnesia	2.5	1.4	4.8	0.8
Dreaming Abnormal	–	–	2.9	1.7
Depersonalization	–	–	1.4	0.0
Paranoid Reaction	–	–	1.4	0.0
Agitation	1.3	0.7	1.0	0.0
Concentration Impaired	1.9	0.0	1.0	0.0
Illusion	1.3	0.0	–	–
Thinking Abnormal	–	–	1.4	0.8
Apathy	–	–	1.0	0.0
Increased Libido	–	–	1.0	0.0
Personality Disorder	–	–	1.0	0.0
Red Blood Cell				
Anemia	–	–	2.4	0.0
Reproductive Male				
Impotence	2.5	1.4	–	–
Prostatic Disorder	–	–	1.0	0.0
Penis Disorder	–	–	1.3	0.0
Resistance Mechanism				
Upper Respiratory Tract Infection	–	–	8.7	8.3
Infection Viral	10.8	3.4	7.2	6.7
Respiratory				
Pharyngitis	6.4	4.1	–	–
Rhinitis	3.8	2.7	–	–
Sinusitis	3.8	2.7	–	–
Dyspnea	3.2	0.0	2.9	1.7
Bronchitis	2.5	1.4	–	–
Respiratory Disorder	1.9	1.4	1.9	0.0
Pneumonia	1.3	0.7	1.0	0.8
Coughing	–	–	1.4	0.8
Skin/Appendages				
Pruritus	–	–	1.0	0.0
Urinary				
Urinary Tract Infection	5.1	4.1	6.3	2.5
Cystitis	1.3	0.7	–	–
Micturition Frequency	–	–	1.4	0.0
Pyuria	–	–	1.9	0.8
Urinary Incontinence	–	–	1.9	0.8
Urinary Retention	1.3	0.7	–	–
Dysuria	–	–	1.0	0.0
Vascular Extracardiac				
Peripheral Ischemia	2.5	0.0	–	–
Vision				
Vision Abnormal	5.7	3.4	–	–
Eye Abnormality	3.2	1.4	–	–
Diplopia	–	–	1.9	0.8
Xerophthalmia	1.9	0.0	1.4	0.8
Cataract	–	–	1.4	0.8
Lacrimation Abnormal	–	–	1.4	0.0
White Cell and Reticuloendothelial				
Eosinophilia	–	–	1.4	0.0

*Incidence of adverse event <1%.

Neuroleptic Malignant Syndrome: A symptom complex resembling the neuroleptic malignant syndrome (characterized by elevated temperature, muscular rigidity, altered consciousness, and autonomic instability), with no other obvious etiology, has been reported in association with rapid dose reduction, withdrawal of, or changes in antiparkinsonian therapy.

A single spontaneous report of a symptom complex resembling the neuroleptic malignant syndrome has been observed in a 66-year-old diabetic male patient with Parkinson's disease, who developed fever, muscle stiffness, and drowsiness 8 days after beginning ropinirole treatment. The patient also experienced acute bronchitis, which did not respond to antibiotic treatment. Ropinirole was discontinued 3 days before the patient died. The reporting physician considered these events to be possibly related to ropinirole treatment (see Dosage).

A single spontaneous report of severe muscle pain has been reported in a 66-year-old male patient around his thigh. The reporting physician considered the event to be probably related to ropinirole treatment.

Retinal Pathology in Rats: In a 2-year carcinogenicity study in albino Sprague-Dawley rats, retinal atrophy was observed at incidences of 0, 4.4, 1.4 and 10% of male rats and 0, 4.4, 2.9 and 12.9% of female rats dosed at 0, 1.5, 15 and 50 mg/kg/day respectively. The incidence was significantly higher in both male and female animals dosed at 50 mg/kg/day. The 50 mg/kg/day dose represents a 2.8-fold greater exposure (AUC) and a 13.1-fold greater exposure (C_{max}) to ropinirole in rats than the exposure would be in humans at the maximum recommended dose of 24 mg/day. The relevance of this finding to humans is not known.

Pregnancy: The use of ropinirole during pregnancy is not recommended.

Ropinirole given to pregnant rats during organogenesis (gestation days 8 through 15) resulted in decreased fetal body weight at 60 mg/kg/day (approximately 3 to 4 times the AUC at the maximal human dose of 8 mg t.i.d.), increased fetal death at 90 mg/kg/day (approximately 5 times the AUC at the maximal human dose of 8 mg t.i.d.) and digital malformations at 150 mg/kg/day (approximately 8 to 9 times the AUC at the maximal human dose of 8 mg t.i.d.). These effects occurred at maternally toxic doses. There was no indication of an effect on development of the conceptus at a maternally toxic dose of 20 mg/kg/day in the rabbit. In a perinatal-postnatal study in rats, 10 mg/kg/day of ropinirole (approximately 0.5 to 0.6 times the AUC at the maximal human dose of 8 mg t.i.d.) impaired growth and development of nursing offspring and altered neurological development of female offspring.

Lactation: Since ropinirole suppresses lactation, it should not be administered to mothers who wish to breast-feed infants.

Studies in rats have shown that ropinirole and/or its metabolites cross the placenta and are excreted in breast milk. Consequently, the human fetus and/or neonate may be exposed to dopamine agonist activity.

Use in Women receiving Estrogen Replacement Therapy: In female patients on long-term treatment with conjugated estrogens, oral clearance was reduced and elimination half-life prolonged compared to patients not receiving estrogens (see Pharmacology, Pharmacokinetics). In patients already receiving estrogen replacement therapy, ropinirole may be titrated in the recommended manner according to clinical response. However, if estrogen replacement therapy is stopped or introduced during treatment with ropinirole, adjustment of the ropinirole dosage may be required.

Children: Safety and effectiveness in the pediatric population have not been established.

Renal and Hepatic Impairment: No dosage adjustment is needed in patients with mild to moderate renal impairment (creatinine clearance of 30 to 50 mL/min; see Pharmacology, Pharmacokinetics).

Because the use of ropinirole in patients with severe renal impairment or hepatic impairment has not been studied, administration of ropinirole to such patients is not recommended.

Drug Interactions: Psychotropic Drugs: Neuroleptics and other centrally active dopamine antagonists may diminish the effectiveness of ropinirole. Therefore, concomitant use of these products is not recommended.

Based on population pharmacokinetic assessment, no interaction was seen between ropinirole and tricyclic antidepressants or benzodiazepines.

Antiparkinson Drugs: Based on population pharmacokinetic assessment, there were no interactions between ropinirole and drugs commonly used to treat Parkinson's disease, i.e., selegiline, amantadine, and anticholinergics.

Levodopa: The potential pharmacokinetic interaction of levodopa/carbidopa (100 mg/10 mg b.i.d.) and ropinirole (2 mg t.i.d.) was assessed in levodopa naive (de novo) male and female patients with Parkinson's disease (n=30, mean age 64 years). The rate and extent of availability of ropinirole at steady-state were essentially the same with or without levodopa. Similarly, the rate and extent of availability of levodopa, as well as its elimination half-life, were essentially the same in the presence and absence of ropinirole.

Inhibitors of CYP1A2: Ciprofloxacin: The effect of ciprofloxacin (500 mg b.i.d.) on the pharmacokinetics of ropinirole (2 mg t.i.d.) was studied in male and female patients with Parkinson's disease (n=12, mean age 55 years). The extent of systemic availability of ropinirole was significantly increased when coadministered with ciprofloxacin (AUC increased by 1.84 fold). Thus, in patients already receiving CYP1A2 inhibitors such as ciprofloxacin, ropinirole therapy may be instituted in the recommended manner and the dose titrated according to clinical response. However, if therapy with a drug known

Requip (cont'd)

to be an inhibitor of CYP1A2 is stopped or introduced during treatment with ropinirole, adjustment of the ropinirole dosage will be required.

Substrates of CYP1A2: Theophylline: The effect of oral theophylline (300 mg b.i.d.) on the pharmacokinetics of ropinirole (2 mg t.i.d.) was studied in male and female patients with Parkinson's disease (n=12, mean age 59 years). There was no marked change in the rate or extent of availability of ropinirole when coadministered with theophylline. Similarly, coadministration of ropinirole with i.v. theophylline (5 mg/kg) did not result in any marked change in the pharmacokinetics of theophylline. It is therefore unlikely that substrates of CYP1A2 would significantly alter the pharmacokinetics of ropinirole, and vice-versa.

Digoxin: The effect of ropinirole (2 mg t.i.d.) on the pharmacokinetics of digoxin (0.125 to 0.25 mg once a day) was studied in male and female patients with Parkinson's disease (n=10, mean age 72 years). Coadministration at steady-state with ropinirole resulted in a 10% decrease in digoxin AUC although mean trough digoxin plasma concentrations were unaltered. However, the effect of higher recommended doses of ropinirole on the pharmacokinetics of digoxin is not known.

Alcohol: No information is available on the potential for interaction between ropinirole and alcohol. As with other centrally active medications, patients should be cautioned against taking ropinirole with alcohol.

Occupational Hazards: Psychomotor Performance: As orthostatic symptoms of dizziness or lightheadedness as well as somnolence may occur during ropinirole therapy patients should be cautioned not to drive a motor vehicle or operate potentially hazardous machinery until they are reasonably certain that ropinirole therapy does not affect their ability to engage in such activities.

Adverse Effects: Adverse Reactions Associated with Discontinuation of Treatment: Of 1 599 patients who received ropinirole during the premarketing clinical trials, 17.1% in early-therapy studies and 17.3% in adjunct-therapy studies discontinued treatment due to adverse reactions. The events resulting in discontinuation of ropinirole in 1% or more of patients were as follows: Early therapy: nausea (6.4%), dizziness (3.8%), aggravated Parkinson's disease (1.3%), hallucination (1.3%), headache (1.3%), somnolence (1.3%) and vomiting (1.3%). Adjunct therapy: dizziness (2.9%), dyskinesia (2.4%), confusion (2.4%), vomiting (2.4%), hallucination (1.9%), nausea (1.9%), anxiety (1.9%), and increased sweating (1.4%). Patients over 75 years of age (n=130) showed slightly higher incidences of withdrawal due to hallucination, confusion and dizziness than patients less than 75 years of age.

Most Frequent Adverse Events: Adverse events occurring with an incidence of greater than, or equal to, 10% were as follows: Early therapy: nausea, dizziness, somnolence, headache, peripheral edema, vomiting, syncope, fatigue and viral infection. Adjunct therapy: dyskinesia, nausea, dizziness, somnolence and headache.

Dopamine agonists with an ergoline chemical structure have been associated with adverse experiences such as retroperitoneal fibrosis, erythromelalgia and pulmonary reactions. Ropinirole has a novel, non-ergoline chemical structure and no reports of such events have been observed in clinical trials.

Incidence of Adverse Events in Placebo-Controlled Trials: The incidence of postural hypotension, an event commonly associated with initiation of dopamine agonist therapy, was not notably different from placebo in clinical trials. However, decreases in systolic blood pressure to <90 mmHg have been observed in 13% (<65 years), 16% (65 to 75 years) and 7.6% (>75 years) of patients treated with ropinirole.

Table II (on previous page) lists adverse events that occurred at an incidence of 1% or more among ropinirole-treated patients who participated in placebo-controlled trials for up to 1 year. Patients were dosed in a range of 0.75 mg to 24 mg/day. Reported adverse events were classified using a standard World Health Organization (WHO)-based dictionary terminology.

The prescriber should be aware that these figures cannot be used to predict the incidence of adverse events in the course of usual medical practice where patient characteristics and other factors differ from those which prevailed in the clinical trials. Similarly, the cited frequencies cannot be compared with figures obtained from other clinical investigations involving different treatments, uses and investigators. The cited figures, however, do provide the prescribing physician with some basis for estimating the relative contribution of drug and nondrug factors to the adverse events incidence rate in the population studied.

In addition to the events listed in Table II (on previous page), the following adverse events were recorded with rates equal to, or more common in, placebo-treated patients:

Early Therapy: fever, hot flushes, injury, rigors, ataxia, dyskinesia, dystonia, hyperkinesia, involuntary muscle contractions, paresthesia, aggravated Parkinsonism, tremor, diarrhea, gingivitis, increased saliva, bradycardia, gout, hyperglycemia, decreased weight, arthralgia, arthritis, back pain, myalgia, basal cell carcinoma, anxiety, depression, abnormal dreaming, insomnia, nervousness, prostatic disorder, upper respiratory tract infection, coughing, rash, hematuria and leg cramps.

Adjunct Therapy: asthenia, chest pain, fatigue, hot flushes, postural hypotension, abnormal gait, hyperkinesia, aggravated Parkinsonism, vertigo, abdominal pain, constipation, back pain, myalgia, depression, insomnia, paroniria (WHO dictionary term for nightmares), viral infection, upper respiratory tract infection, pharyngitis, rhinitis, rash, rash erythematous, taste perversion, hematuria, leg cramps and diplopia, myocardial infarction, extrasystoles supraventricular.

Events Observed During the Premarketing Evaluation of Ropinirole: Of the 1 599 patients who received ropinirole in therapeutic studies, the following adverse events, which are not included in Table II (on previous page) or in the listing above, have been noted up to May 1996. In the absence of appropriate controls in some of the studies, a causal relationship between these events and treatment with ropinirole cannot be determined.

Events are categorized by body system and listed in order of decreasing frequency according to the following definitions: *frequent* adverse events are those occurring on one or more occasions in at least 1/100 patients; *infrequent* adverse events are those occurring in 1/100 to 1/1 000 patients; *rare* events are those occurring in fewer than 1/1 000 patients.

Autonomic Nervous System: *rare,* cold clammy skin.

Body as a Whole: *infrequent,* pallor, allergy, enlarged abdomen, substernal chest pain, edema, allergic reaction, ascites, precordial chest pain, therapeutic response increased, ischemic necrosis, edema generalised; *rare,* periorbital edema, face edema, halitosis.

Cardiovascular: *infrequent,* cardiac failure, heart disorder, specific abnormal ECG, aneurysm, cardiomegaly, abnormal ECG, aggravated hypertension; *rare,* cyanosis, fluid overload, heart valve disorder.

Central and Peripheral Nervous System: *frequent,* neuralgia; *infrequent,* hypertonia, speech disorder, choreoathetosis, abnormal coordination, dysphonia, extrapyramidal disorder, migraine, aphasia, coma, convulsions, hypotonia, nerve root lesion, peripheral neuropathy, paralysis, stupor; *rare,* cerebral atrophy, grand mal convulsions, hemiparesis, hemiplegia, hyperreflexia, neuropathy, ptosis, sensory disturbance, hydrocephaly.

Collagen: *rare,* rheumatoid arthritis.

Endocrine: *infrequent,* gynecomastia, hypothyroidism; *rare,* SIADH (syndrome of inappropriate antidiuretic hormone secretion), increased thyroxine, goitre, hyperthyroid.

Gastrointestinal: *frequent,* gastrointestinal disorder (NOS); *infrequent,* gastritis, gastroenteritis, gastroesophageal reflux, increased appetite, esophagitis, peptic ulcer, diverticulitis, hemorrhoids, hiccup, tooth caries, increased amylase, duodenal ulcer, duodenitis, fecal incontinence, gastrointestinal hemorrhage, glossitis, rectal hemorrhage, melena, pancreatitis, rectal disorder, altered saliva, stomatitis, ulcerative stomatitis, tongue edema, gastric ulcer, tooth disorder; *rare,* esophageal stricture, esophageal ulceration, hemorrhagic gastritis, gingival bleeding, hematemesis, lactose intolerance, salivary duct obstruction, tenesmus, tongue disorder, hemorrhagic duodenal ulcer, aggravated tooth caries.

Hearing: *infrequent,* earache, decreased hearing, vestibular disorder, ear disorder (NOS); *rare,* hyperacusis, deafness.

Heart Rate and Rhythm: *infrequent,* arrhythmia, bundle branch block, cardiac arrest, supraventricular extrasystoles, ventricular tachycardia; *rare,* atrioventricular block.

Liver and Biliary: *Infrequent,* abnormal hepatic function, increased ALT, bilirubinemia, cholecystitis, cholelithiasis, hepatocellular damage, increased AST; *rare,* biliary pain, aggravated bilirubinemia, gallbladder disorder.

Metabolic and Nutritional: *frequent,* increased blood urea nitrogen; *infrequent,* increased LDH, increased NPN, hyperuricemia, increased weight, hyperphosphatemia, diabetes mellitus, glycosuria, hypercholesterolemia, acidosis, hypokalemia, hyponatremia, thirst, increased creatine phosphokinase, dehydration, aggravated diabetes mellitus, hyperkalemia; *rare,* electrolyte abnormality, enzyme abnormality, hypochloremia, obesity, increased phosphatase acid, decreased serum iron.

Musculoskeletal: *frequent,* arthrosis; *infrequent,* arthropathy, osteoporosis, tendinitis, bone disorder, bursitis, muscle weakness, polymyalgia rheumatica, skeletal pain, torticollis, *rare,* muscle atrophy, myositis, Dupuytren's contracture, spine malformation.

Myocardial, Endocardial, Pericardial Valve: *frequent,* angina pectoris; *infrequent,* myocardial infarction, aggravated angina pectoris; *rare,* mitral insufficiency.

Neoplasm: *infrequent,* carcinoma, malignant female breast neoplasm, dermoid cyst, malignant skin neoplasm, prostate adenocarcinoma, adenocarcinoma, neoplasm (NOS); *rare,* bladder carcinoma, benign brain neoplasm, breast fibroadenosis, malignant endometrial neoplasm, esophageal carcinoma, malignant larynx neoplasm, malignant lymphoma, malignant neoplasm, neuroma, lipoma, rectal carcinoma, uterine neoplasm.

Platelet Bleeding and Clotting: *infrequent,* purpura, thrombocytopenia, hematoma.

Psychiatric: *frequent,* aggravated depression, agitation; *infrequent,* increased libido, sleep disorder, apathy, dementia, delirium, emotional lability, psychosis, aggressive reaction, delusion, psychotic depression, euphoria, decreased libido, manic reaction, neurosis, personality disorder, somnambulism; *rare,* suicide attempt.

Red Blood Cell: *infrequent,* hypochromic anemia, anemia B_{12} deficiency; *rare,* polycythemia.

Female Reproductive: *infrequent,* amenorrhea, menstrual disorder, vaginal hemorrhage, uterine disorders (NOS); *rare,* female breast enlargement, intermenstrual bleeding, mastitis, uterine hemorrhage, dysmenorrhea.

Male Reproductive: *Infrequent,* epididymitis, balanoposthitis, ejaculation failure, penis disorder, perineal pain; *rare,* Peyronie's disease, ejaculation disorder, testis disorder.

Resistance Mechanism: *frequent,* infection; *infrequent,* herpes zoster, moniliasis, otitis media, sepsis, herpes simplex, fungal infection, abscess, bacterial infection, genital moniliasis; *rare,* poliomyelitis.

Respiratory: *frequent,* pneumonia; *infrequent,* asthma, epistaxis, laryngitis, pleurisy, increased sputum, pulmonary edema; *rare,* hypoxia, respiratory insufficiency, vocal cord paralysis.

Skin and Appendages: *infrequent,* dermatitis, alopecia, skin discoloration, dry skin, skin hypertrophy, skin ulceration, fungal dermatitis, eczema, hyperkeratosis, photosensitivity reaction, psoriasis, maculopapular rash, psoriaform rash, seborrhea, skin disorder, urticaria, furunculosis; *rare,* bullous eruption, nail disorder, nevus, photosensitivity allergic reaction, aggravated psoriasis, skin exfoliation, abnormal skin odor.

Other Special Senses: *rare,* parosmia.

Urinary: *infrequent,* albuminuria, dysuria, nocturia, polyuria, renal calculus, abnormal urine, micturition disorder; *rare,* oliguria, pyelonephritis, renal cyst, acute renal failure, renal pain, uremia, urethral disorder, urinary casts, bladder calculus, nephritis.

Vascular Extracardiac: *infrequent,* cerebrovascular disorder, vein disorder, varicose vein, peripheral gangrene, phlebitis, vascular disorder; *rare,* atherosclerosis, limb embolism, pulmonary embolism, gangrene, superficial phlebitis, subarachnoid hemorrhage, deep thrombophlebitis, leg thrombophlebitis, thrombosis, arteritis.

Vision: *infrequent,* conjunctivitis, blepharitis, abnormal accommodation, blepharospasm, eye pain, glaucoma, photophobia, scotoma; *rare,* blindness, blindness temporary, hemianopia, keratitis, photopsia, macula lutea degeneration, vitreous detachment, retinal disorder.

White Cell and Reticuloendothelial System: *infrequent,* leukocytosis, leukopenia, lymphopenia, lymphedema, lymphocytosis; *rare,* lymphadenopathy, granulocytopenia.

Overdose: Symptoms and Treatment: There were no reports of intentional overdose of ropinirole in the premarketing clinical trials. A total of 27 patients accidentally took more than their prescribed dose of ropinirole, with 10 patients ingesting more than 24 mg/day. The largest overdose reported in premarketing clinical trials was 435 mg taken over a 7-day period (62.1 mg/day). Of patients who received a dose greater than 24 mg/day, one experienced mild oro-facial dyskinesia, another patient experienced intermittent nausea. Other symptoms reported with accidental overdoses were: agitation, increased dyskinesia, grogginess, sedation, orthostatic hypotension, chest pain, confusion, vomiting and nausea.

It is anticipated that the symptoms of ropinirole overdose will be related to its dopaminergic activity. General supportive measures are recommended. Vital signs should be maintained, if necessary. Removal of any unabsorbed material (e.g., by gastric lavage) should be considered.

Dosage: Ropinirole should be taken 3 times daily. While administration of ropinirole with meals may improve gastrointestinal tolerance, ropinirole may be taken with or without food (see Pharmacology, Pharmacokinetics).

The recommended starting dosage is 0.25 mg 3 times daily. Based on individual patient response, dosage should then be titrated by weekly increments of 0.25 mg/dose as described in Table III. After week 4, daily dosage may be increased by 0.5 to 1 mg/dose on a weekly basis up to 24 mg/day. Doses greater than 24 mg/day have not been tested in clinical trials. Smaller dose increments are recommended for patients who may be at risk for orthostatic symptoms. In clinical trials, initial benefits were observed with 3 mg/day and higher doses.

Table III—Requip

Dosage Titration

	Week			
	1	**2**	**3**	**4**
Unit Dose (mg)	0.25	0.5	0.75	1.0
Total Daily Dose (mg)	0.75	1.5	2.25	3.0

When ropinirole is administered as adjunct therapy to levodopa, the dose of levodopa may be decreased gradually as tolerated once a therapeutic effect with ropinirole has been observed (see Pharmacology, Clinical Trials).

Ropinirole should be discontinued gradually over a 7-day period. The frequency of administration should be reduced from 3 times daily to twice daily for 4 days. For the remaining 3 days, the frequency should be reduced to once daily prior to complete withdrawal of ropinirole.

Renal and Hepatic Impairment: In patients with mild to moderate renal impairment, ropinirole may be titrated in the recommended manner according to clinical response. Patients with severe renal impairment or on hemodialysis have not been studied and administration of ropinirole to such patients is not recommended.

Patients with hepatic impairment have not been studied and administration of ropinirole to such patients is not recommended.

Estrogen Replacement Therapy: In patients already receiving estrogen replacement therapy, ropinirole may be titrated in the recommended manner according to clinical response. However, if estrogen replacement therapy is stopped or started during treatment with ropinirole, adjustment of the ropinirole dosage may be required.

Information for the Patient: See Blue Section—Information for the Patient "Requip".

Supplied: 0.25 mg: Each white, pentagonal, film-coated, beveled-edged Tiltab tablet, imprinted with SB and 4890, contains: ropinirole HCl 0.25 mg. Nonmedicinal ingredients: croscarmellose sodium, hydrous lactose, hydroxypropyl methylcellulose, magnesium stearate, microcrystalline cellulose, polyethylene glycol, polysorbate 80 and titanium dioxide. Sucrose-, tartrazine- or any other azo dyes-free. Bottles of 100.

1 mg: Each pale green, pentagonal, film-coated, beveled-edged Tiltab tablet, imprinted with SB and 4892, contains: ropinirole HCl 1 mg. Nonmedicinal ingredients: croscarmellose sodium, FD&C Blue No. 2 aluminum lake, hydrous lactose, hydroxypropyl methylcellulose, iron oxide yellow, magnesium stearate, microcrystalline cellulose, polyethylene glycol and titanium dioxide. Sucrose-, tartrazine- or any other azo dyes-free. Bottles of 100.

2 mg: Each pale pink, pentagonal, film-coated, beveled-edged Tiltab tablet, imprinted with SB and 4893, contains: ropinirole HCl 2 mg. Nonmedicinal ingredients: croscarmellose sodium, hydrous lactose, hydroxypropyl methylcellulose, iron oxide red, iron oxide yellow, magnesium stearate, microcrystalline cellulose, polyethylene glycol and titanium dioxide. Sucrose-, tartrazine- or any other azo dyes-free. Bottles of 100.

5 mg: Each pale blue, pentagonal, film-coated, beveled-edged Tiltab tablet, imprinted with SB and 4894, contains: ropinirole HCl 5 mg. Nonmedicinal ingredients: croscarmellose sodium, FD&C Blue No. 2 aluminum lake, hydrous lactose, hydroxypropyl methylcellulose, magnesium stearate, microcrystalline cellulose, polyethylene glycol, talc and titanium dioxide. Sucrose-, tartrazine- or any other azo dyes-free. Bottles of 100.

Store between 15 and 30°C, in tightly closed containers. Protect from light.

(Shown in Product Recognition Section)

New Product 1998

RESONIUM CALCIUM

Sanofi

Calcium Polystyrene Sulfonate

Ion Exchange Resin

Pharmacology: Calcium polystyrene sulfonate is a cation exchange resin prepared in the calcium phase. Each gram of resin has a theoretical in vitro exchange capacity of about 1.3 to 2 mmol of potassium. In vivo, the actual amount of potassium bound will be less than this. The sodium content of the resin is less than 1 mg/g. The calcium content is 1.6 to 2.4 mmol/g. The resin is insoluble in water. Calcium polystyrene sulfonate is not absorbed from the gastrointestinal tract.

Calcium polystyrene sulfonate acts by a cumulative process throughout the gastrointestinal tract, removing potassium ions which are carried away in the feces.

As the resin passes through the colon, it comes into contact with fluids containing increasing amounts of potassium. Whereas in the cecum the concentration of Na^+ and K^+ are similar to those in the small intestine, in the stool water of the sigmoid colon there may be 6 to 38 mmol/L sodium and 14 to 44 mmol/L potassium. The result is that potassium is taken up in increasing amounts in exchange for calcium ions. The length of time the resin remains in the body is a decisive factor in its effectiveness. For this reason oral administration is more effective than the use of enemas which should, if possible, be retained for 9 hours. The efficiency of potassium exchange is unpredictably variable. The resin is not selective for potassium.

Indications: In patients with hyperkalemia associated with anuria or severe oliguria to reduce serum levels of potassium and to remove excess potassium from the body. Calcium polystyrene sulfonate is indicated in all states of hyperkalemia due to acute and chronic renal failure; for example following abortion, complicated labor, incompatible blood transfusion, crush injury, prostatectomy, severe burns, surgical shock, and in cases of severe glomerulonephritis and pyelonephritis.

Calcium polystyrene sulfonate can also be useful in patients requiring dialysis. Serum potassium levels in acute renal failure often reach dangerous heights before a rise in blood urea indicates the need for hemodialysis. Calcium polystyrene sulfonate can be used to reduce these potassium levels and thereby postpone the need for the use of the artificial kidney machine until other causes make it necessary.

Patients on regular hemodialysis therapy may develop shunt difficulties and underdialysis occurs, resulting in serious hyperkalemia. In these circumstances it is advisable to give the resin to control hyperkalemia during the period of underdialysis, monitoring serum potassium and calcium levels at regular intervals.

When patients on routine hemodialysis present a dietary management problem and tend towards hyperkalemia, calcium polystyrene sulfonate can be used to control blood potassium levels. Similarly, patients on prolonged peritoneal dialysis may develop intermittent hyperkalemia after a few weeks, possibly due to dietary problems. These patients also can be satisfactorily controlled with calcium polystyrene sulfonate.

Contraindications: Should not be administered to patients with: serum potassium <5 mmol/L; conditions associated with hypercalcemia (e.g., hyperparathyroidism, multiple myeloma, sarcoidosis or metastic carcinoma); a history of hypersensitivity to polystyrene sulfonate resins; obstructive bowel disease.

Oral administration of calcium polystyrene sulfonate is contraindicated in neonates. Administration of the resin in neonates with reduced gut motility (postoperatively or drug induced) is contraindicated.

Warnings: In neonates, calcium polystyrene sulfonate should not be given by the oral route.

Rare instances of colonic necrosis and intestinal obstruction have been reported with sodium polystyrene sulfonate due to concretion formation. This appears to be related to the use of a sorbitol enema with either inadequate or no lavage after use of the resin.

Precautions: The possibility of severe potassium depletion should be considered and adequate biochemical control, by daily estimation of serum electrolytes and blood urea levels, is essential during treatment. To prevent serious hypokalemia, administration of the resin should be discontinued as soon as the serum potassium level falls to 5 mmol/L to prevent serious hypokalemia. Hypercalcemia has been reported in well dialyzed patients receiving calcium resin, and in the occasional patient with chronic renal failure. Serum calcium levels should be estimated at weekly intervals to detect the early development of hypercalcemia, and the dose of administered calcium resin reduced to levels at which hypercalcemia and hypokalemia are prevented.

Like all cation-exchange resins, calcium polystyrene sulfonate is not totally selective for potassium. Hypomagnesemia and/or hypercalcemia may occur. Accordingly, patients should be monitored for all applicable electrolyte disturbances.

In the event of clinically significant constipation, treatment with the resin should be discontinued until normal bowel motions are resumed. Magnesium-containing laxatives should not be used (see Drug Interactions).

The patient should be positioned carefully when ingesting the resin, to avoid aspiration, which may lead to bronchopulmonary complications.

Children: In both children and neonates, particular care should be observed with rectal administration, as excessive dosage or inadequate dilution could result in impaction of the resin.

Drug Interactions: Digitalis: The toxic effects of digitalis on the heart, especially various ventricular arrhythmia and A-V nodal dissociation, are likely to be exaggerated by hypokalemia, even in the face of serum digoxin concentrations in the 'normal range'.

Cation Donating Agents: These may reduce the effectiveness of the resin in binding potassium.

Nonabsorbable Cation-donating Antacids and Laxatives: Systemic alkalosis has been reported after cation-exchange resins were administered orally in combination with nonabsorbable cation-donating antacids and laxatives such as magnesium hydroxide and aluminum.

Aluminum Hydroxide: Intestinal obstruction due to concretions of aluminum hydroxide has been reported when aluminum hydroxide was combined with the resin (sodium form).

Sorbitol in enemas: (see Warnings).

Pregnancy and *Lactation:* Calcium polystyrene sulfonate is not absorbed from the gastrointestinal tract. No data are available about the use of polystyrene sulfonate resins in human pregnancy and lactation.

Adverse Effects: In accordance with its pharmacological actions, calcium polystyrene sulfonate may give rise to hypokalemia and hypercalcemia and their related clinical manifestations (see Overdose: Symptoms and Treatment).

Intestinal intolerance due to the gritty consistency and bulk of the resin may be manifested by the appearance of general adverse effects including nausea, vomiting, gastric irritation, anorexia, constipation and occasionally, diarrhea. These adverse effects may be relieved by intermittent therapy and the use of mild laxatives where constipation is a factor.

Fecal impaction following rectal administration in children, and gastrointestinal concretions following oral administration to neonates, have been reported. Rarely intestinal obstruction has been reported. This could possibly be a reflection of coexisting pathology or inadequate dilution of the resin.

Some cases of acute bronchitis and/or bronchopneumonia associated with inhalation of particles of calcium polystyrene sulfonate have been described.

Overdose: Symptoms: Biochemical disturbances resulting from overdosage may give rise to clinical signs and symptoms of hypokalemia, including irritability, confusion, delayed thought processes, muscle weakness, hyperreflexia, and eventually frank paralysis. Apnea may be a serious consequence of this progression. ECG changes may be consistent with hypokalemia or hypercalcemia; cardiac arrhythmia may occur.

Treatment: Appropriate measures should be taken to correct serum electrolytes (potassium, calcium). The resin should be removed from the alimentary tract by appropriate use of laxatives or enemas.

Dosage: Treatment with the resin should be given as soon as the serum potassium level rises above 6 mmol/L (23.5 mg/100 mL). The action may be delayed for 1 or 2 days since maximal exchange probably takes place in the colon. Exchange will continue until all the resin has been voided (this may be 1 or 2 days after administration has been discontinued). For this reason, resin therapy should be stopped when

Resonium Calcium (cont'd)

the serum potassium level has fallen to 5 mmol/L, or the continued action may lead to potassium depletion. The following doses are suggested only as a general guide. The precise daily dose should be decided on the basis of regular serum electrolyte determination.

The amount of potassium taken up by the resin will be largely determined by the length of time it is exposed to the high potassium concentration in the fecal water in the colon. For this reason, a tendency towards constipation should be encouraged and purgative drugs should be avoided.

Adults: For adults the usual dose is 15 g, 3 or 4 times a day. The resin is given by mouth in a little water, or it may be made into a paste with some sweetened vehicle, but not orange juice or other fruit juices that are known to contain potassium. The amount of fluid usually ranges from 3 to 4 mL/g of resin. If there is difficulty with swallowing, it may be given through a gastric tube, 2 to 3 mm in diameter.

In cases where vomiting may make oral administration difficult, or in patients who have upper gastrointestinal problems, including paralytic ileus, the resin may be given rectally as a suspension of 30 g resin in 100 mL of 2% methylcellulose and 100 mL of water, as a daily retention enema. In the initial stages, administration by this route as well as orally may help to achieve a more rapid lowering of the serum potassium level.

The rectal route is less effective than the oral, and since the longer the resin is retained the greater is the amount of potassium removed, the enema should, if possible, be retained for at least 9 hours. If both routes are used initially, it is probably unnecessary to continue rectal administration once the oral resin has reached the rectum.

Children: Acute hyperkalemia: Children should be given 1 g/kg body weight of calcium polystyrene sulfonate daily in divided doses. In maintenance therapy the dose may be reduced to 0.5 g/kg body weight daily in divided doses.

Calcium polystyrene sulfonate should be given orally, preferably with a drink or a little jam or honey. It should not be given in fruit drinks and some carbonated beverages, since these have a high potassium content. When the resin is refused by mouth, it may be given rectally suspended in a proportional amount of 10% dextrose in water, using a dose at least as great as that which whould have been given orally. It should not be given in fruit drinks and some carbonated beverages, since these have a high potassium content. Following retention of the enema, the colon should be irrigated to ensure adequate removal of the resin.

Neonates: Oral administration of calcium polystyrene sulfonate is contraindicated in neonates. Administration of the resin in neonates with reduced gut motility (postoperatively or drug induced) is contraindicated. Only rectal administration should be considered. With rectal administration, the minimum effective dosage within the range of 0.5 to 1 g/kg should be employed, diluted as for adults and with adequate irrigation to ensure recovery of the resin. It should not be given in fruit drinks and some carbonated beverages, since these have a high potassium content.

Supplied: Each polystyrene pack contains: 300 g of the flavored calcium polystyrene sulfonate powdered resin. Also contains saccharin and vanillin. Sodium: <1 mmol (1 mg)/g. Alcohol-, gluten-, lactose-, parabens-, starch-, sucrose-, sulfite- and tartrazine-free. A plastic measure is included which holds 15 g of resin.

Reviewed 1999

RESOURCE®
Novartis Nutrition

Therapeutic Nutrient

Indications: A complete balanced low-residue liquid nutrition supplement for use in feeding situations where the patient's diet requires support or where conditions preclude normal food intake.

Precautions: Not for parenteral use. Shake Tetra Pak of liquid well before opening.

Dosage: Oral: As a supplement with or between meals: 1 to 3 Tetra Paks daily, 1 050 to 3 150 kJ (250 to 750 kcal). Does not require dilution with water. When used as the sole daily feeding, should be administered to meet individual requirements. Eight Tetra Paks meet or surpass 100% of the Canadian RNI (adult males, 25 to 49) for protein and essential vitamins and minerals.

Tube Feeding: Follow a physician's or dietitian's directions. When initiating feeding, the flow rate, volume and dilution are dependent on patient condition and tolerance. Care should be taken to avoid contamination of this product during preparation and administration. Additional fluid requirements should be met by giving water orally with or after feedings, or when flushing the feeding tube.

Supplied: Each 235 mL ready-to-use brik contains: Ⓤ-D water, corn syrup solids, sugar, sodium and calcium caseinates, corn oil, soy protein isolate, potassium citrate, natural and artificial flavor, calcium phosphate tribasic, sodium citrate, soy lecithin, potassium chloride, magnesium chloride, choline chloride, ascorbic acid, potassium hydroxide, carrageenan, zinc sulfate, ferrous sulfate, alpha tocopheryl acetate, niacinamide, D-calcium pantothenate, manganese sulfate, copper gluconate, thiamine hydrochloride, pyridoxine hydrochloride, riboflavin, vitamin A palmitate, folic acid, maltol, biotin, potassium iodide, vitamin K_1, cyanocobalamin and vitamin D_3. See Table I.

Note: Ingredient content may differ slightly between vanilla, chocolate and strawberry. Consult the product labeling for exact composition.

Energy Distribution: protein 14%, fat 32%, carbohydrates 54%; 447 kJ (106 kcal)/100 mL.

Table I—Resource

Analysis	100 mL	
Energy	447 (106)	kJ (kcal)
Protein	3.7	g
Carbohydrates	14.6	g
Fat	3.7	g
Linoleic Acid	2.2	g
Sodium	89.4	mg
Potassium	162	mg
Vitamin A	266	IU
Vitamin C	16.0	mg
Thiamine	0.16	mg
Riboflavin	0.18	mg
Niacin	2.1	mg
Calcium	55.3	mg
Iron	0.95	mg
Vitamin D	21.3	IU
Vitamin E	2.4	IU
Vitamin B_6	0.21	mg
Folic Acid	0.0213	mg
Vitamin B_{12}	0.00064	mg
Phosphorus	55.3	mg
Iodine	0.0085	mg
Magnesium	21.3	mg
Zinc	1.6	mg
Copper	0.11	mg
Biotin	0.016	mg
Pantothenic Acid	0.53	mg
Vitamin K	0.0038	mg
Choline	55.3	mg
Chloride	102	mg
Manganese	0.21	mg
Osmolality	430	mOsm/kg water

Resource has a calorie to nitrogen ratio of 179:1 which is suggested as reasonable for effective protein utilization. Gluten- and lactose-free.

Aseptic Tetra Brik Paks of 235 mL (vanilla, chocolate, strawberry), cases of 27.

Store unopened at room temperature; protect from heat. Once opened, store covered in refrigerator and use within 24 hours. Chilling enhances flavor.

RESOURCE® DIABETIC
Novartis Nutrition

Therapeutic Nutrient

Indications: A high nitrogen, fibre containing complete liquid formula. Designed for persons with Type 1 or Type 2 diabetes or stress hyperglycemia and normal gastrointestinal function. For oral or tube feeding use.

Not recommended when a low residue tube feeding is required.

Precautions: Not for parenteral administration.

Dosage: 1 250 mL or 5 550 kJ (5 cans or 1 330 kcal) provides at least 100% of the Canadian RNI (adult males, 25 to 49) for protein and essential vitamins and minerals. Ready-to-use and does not require dilution with water. For oral use it may be fed at room temperature or chilled.

Tube Feeding: Feed at room temperature. Follow a physician's or dietitian's directions. When initiating feedings, the flow rate, volume and dilution are dependent on the patient's condition and tolerance. Care should be taken to avoid contamination of the product during preparation and administration. Additional fluid requirements should be met by giving water orally with or after feedings or when flushing the feeding tube.

Feeding should be initiated at a slow rate. Rate and volume of feeding can be increased gradually over 48 hours if well tolerated. If intolerance develops, return to previously tolerated rate, or dilute formula to half strength until desired rate is achieved, then switch to full strength. Do not alter strength and volume at the same time. Rinse the tube with 20 to 30 mL water after each intermittent feeding or every 3 to 4 hours during continuous feeding to avoid clogging and provide additional water.

Supplied: Each 250 mL ready-to-use can contains: Ⓤ-D water, sodium and calcium caseinates, corn syrup solids, high oleic sunflower oil, fructose, soy polysaccharides, soybean oil, soy protein isolate, artificial flavor, calcium phosphate tribasic, potassium citrate, potassium hydroxide, magnesium chloride, monoglycerides, sodium ascorbate, soy lecithin, sodium citrate, choline chloride, L-carnitine, potassium chloride, taurine, chromium yeast, selenium yeast, molybdenum yeast, zinc sulfate, alpha tocopheryl acetate, ferrous sulfate, niacinamide, D-calcium pantothenate, manganese sulfate, copper gluconate, pyridoxine HCl, thiamine HCl, riboflavin, beta carotene, vitamin A palmitate, folic acid, biotin, potassium iodide, vitamin K, cyanocobalamin, vitamin D_3. See Table I.

Energy Distribution: protein 24%, fat 40%, carbohydrate 36%; 444 kJ (106 kcal)/100 mL. Contains 3 g/250 mL of dietary fibre (from soy polysaccharide).

Table I—Resource Diabetic

Analysis	100 mL	
Energy	444 (106)	kJ (kcal)
Protein	6.4	g
Carbohydrate	9.5	g
Fat	4.7	g
Linoleic Acid	0.96	g
Dietary Fibre	1.2	g
Sodium	96	mg
Potassium	140	mg
Vitamin A	360	IU
Vitamin C	20	mg
Thiamine	0.16	mg
Riboflavin	0.18	mg
Niacin	2.1	mg
Calcium	93	mg
Iron	0.95	mg
Vitamin D	21	IU
Vitamin E	2.4	IU
Vitamin B_6	0.21	mg
Folic Acid	0.042	mg
Vitamin B_{12}	0.0006	mg
Phosphorus	93	mg
Iodine	0.013	mg
Magnesium	21	mg
Zinc	1.2	mg
Copper	0.11	mg
Biotin	0.032	mg
Pantothenic Acid	1.1	mg
Vitamin K	0.0051	mg
Choline	16	mg
Chloride	80	mg
Manganese	0.27	mg
Selenium	0.0051	mg
Chromium	0.011	mg
Molybdenum	0.0079	mg
L-carnitine	11	mg
Taurine	7.9	mg
Osmolality	450	mOsm/kg

Resource Diabetic is high in protein and low in carbohydrate. It contains fructose with no added sucrose. Lactose- and gluten-free.

Cans of 250 mL, cases of 24. Store unopened at room temperature. Once opened, store covered in refrigerator and use within 24 hours.

Reviewed 1998

...Remind your patients—"Keep all medication out of the reach of children."

RESOURCE® FRUIT BEVERAGE
Novartis Nutrition

Therapeutic Nutrient

Indications: For patients requiring oral supplementation. For the dietary management of increased protein and calorie needs in the following patient groups: oncology, anorexia, pre-and post-operative, bowel preparation and fat malabsorption. Follow physician's instructions for use.

Precautions: Not for parenteral administration.

Dosage: 8 Tetra Paks [1 880 mL or 6 020 kJ (1 440 kcal)] provides 1 440 kcal and at least 100% of the Canadian RNI (adult males, 25 to 49) for protein and essential vitamins and minerals.

Supplied: Each 235 mL container contains: water, sugar, whey protein concentrate, magnesium gluconate, phosphoric acid, artificial flavor, corn syrup solids, citric acid, calcium chloride, soybean oil, choline bitartrate, L-cysteine, ascorbic acid, zinc sulfate, color, polyglycerol esters of fatty acids, alpha tocopheryl acetate, ferrous sulfate, niacinamide, acetic acid, d-calcium pantothenate, copper gluconate, manganese sulfate, thiamine hydrochloride, pyridoxine hydrochloride, vitamin A palmitate, ethyl maltol, riboflavin, folic acid, biotin, potassium iodide, vitamin K_1, vitamin D_3, cyanocobalamin. See Table I.

Energy Distribution: protein 19%, fat 2%, carbohydrate 79%; 320 kJ (77 kcal)/100 mL.

Table I—Resource Fruit Beverage

Analysis	100 mL	
Energy	320 (77)	kJ (kcal)
Protein	3.7	g
Carbohydrate	15.3	g
Fat	0.2	g
Linoleic Acid	0.09	g
Sodium	29.8	mg
Potassium	4.3	mg
Vitamin A	266	IU
Vitamin C	16	mg
Thiamine	0.16	mg
Riboflavin	0.18	mg
Niacin	2.1	mg
Calcium	57.4	mg
Iron	0.95	mg
Vitamin D	21.3	IU
Vitamin E	2.4	IU
Vitamin B_6	0.21	mg
Folic Acid	0.021	mg
Vitamin B_{12}	0.00064	mg
Phosphorus	68.1	mg
Iodine	0.0085	mg
Magnesium	21.3	mg
Zinc	1.6	mg
Copper	0.11	mg
Biotin	0.016	mg
Pantothenic Acid	0.53	mg
Vitamin K	0.0038	mg
Choline	55.3	mg
Chloride	93.6	mg
Manganese	0.21	mg
Osmolality	700	mOsm/kg water

Tetra Paks of 235 mL (wild berry, peach, orange flavors), cases of 27.

RESOURCE® JUST FOR KIDS
Novartis Nutrition

Therapeutic Nutrient

Indications: A standard lactose-, gluten- and fiber-free liquid formula designed to meet the nutritional needs of children 1 to 12 years of age with normal gastrointestinal function. Appropriate for both oral or tube feeding use.

Precautions: Not for parenteral administration. Not for patients with galactosemia.

Dosage: 1 200 mL or 5 020 kJ (5.1 aseptic Tetra Brik Paks or 1 200 kcal) provides at least 100% of the Canadian RNI (adult males, 25 to 49) for protein and essential vitamins and minerals for children 1 to 12 years of age. Ready-to-use and does not require dilution with water. For oral use it may be fed at room temperature or chilled.

Tube Feeding: Feed at room temperature. Follow a physician's or dietitian's directions. When initiating feedings, the flow rate, volume and dilution are dependent on the patient's condition and tolerance. Care should be taken to avoid contamination of the product during preparation and administration. Additional fluid requirements should be met by giving water orally with or after feedings or when flushing the feeding tube.

Feeding should be initiated at a slow rate. Rate and volume of feeding can be increased gradually over 48 hours if well tolerated. If intolerance develops, return to previously tolerated rate, or dilute formula to half strength until desired rate is achieved, then switch to full strength. Do not alter strength and volume at the same time. Rinse the tube with 20 to 30 mL water after each intermittent feeding or every 3 to 4 hours during continuous feeding to avoid clogging and provide additional water.

Supplied: Each Tetra Brik Pak contains: Ⓤ-D water, maltodextrin, sugar, sodium and calcium caseinates, high oleic sunflower oil, soybean oil, medium chain triglycerides, whey protein concentrate, calcium phosphate tribasic, natural & artificial flavor, soy lecithin, potassium phosphate dibasic, potassium citrate, calcium citrate, choline bitartrate, magnesium chloride, carrageenan, ascorbic acid, potassium chloride, microcrystalline cellulose, potassium hydroxide, taurine, cellulose gum, L-carnitine, ferrous sulfate, zinc sulfate, niacinamide, calcium pantothenate, alpha tocopheryl acetate, copper gluconate, pyridoxine HCl, thiamine HCl, manganese sulfate, BHA/BHT (to preserve freshness), riboflavin, vitamin A palmitate, maltol, beta carotene, biotin, chromic acetate, folic acid, potassium iodide, sodium molybdate, sodium selenite, vitamin K_1, vitamin D_3, cyanocobalamin. See Table I.

Table I—Resource Just For Kids

Analysis	100 mL	
Energy	418 (100)	kJ (kcal)
Protein	3.3	g
Carbohydrate	11	g
Fat	5.0	g
Linoleic Acid	1.1	g
Sodium	41	mg
Potassium	130	mg
Vitamin A	260	IU
Vitamin C	8.3	mg
Thiamine	0.21	mg
Riboflavin	0.21	mg
Niacin	1.7	mg
Calcium	120	mg
Iron	1.4	mg
Vitamin D	33	IU
Vitamin E	1.3	IU
Vitamin B_6	0.26	mg
Folic Acid	0.027	mg
Vitamin B_{12}	0.00013	mg
Phosphorus	80	mg
Iodine	0.01	mg
Magnesium	17	mg
Zinc	1.2	mg
Copper	0.1	mg
Biotin	0.032	mg
Pantothenic Acid	1.0	mg
Vitamin K	0.0034	mg
Choline	30	mg
Chloride	70	mg
Manganese	0.25	mg
Selenium	0.0039	mg
Chromium	0.0067	mg
Molybdenum	0.0042	mg
L-carnitine	4.0	mg
Taurine	17	mg
Osmolality	370	mOsm/kg

Aseptic Tetra Brik Paks of 235 mL (vanilla), cases of 27. Store unopened at room temperature. Once opened, store covered in refrigerator and use within 24 hours.

Reviewed 1998

RESOURCE® PLUS
Novartis Nutrition

Therapeutic Nutrient

Indications: A high-calorie liquid preparation providing complete, balanced nutrition. Energy density is 1 490 kJ (355 kcal)/Tetra Pak and provides a concentrated source of calories in a limited volume for patients with high protein requirements. When utilized to provide total nutrition, Resource Plus can deliver high energy intakes required by hypermetabolic patients who are nutritionally depleted, and are unable to tolerate large fluid volume intake. As a dietary supplement, Resource Plus can supply extra energy and protein for those patients unable or unwilling to consume adequate nutrition (i.e. geriatric and cancer patients).

Precautions: Not for parenteral use. Shake Tetra Pak of liquid well before opening.

Dosage: Oral: As a supplement with or between meals: 1 to 3 Tetra Paks daily, 1 490 to 4 470 kJ (355 to 1 065 kcal). Does not require dilution with water. When used as the sole daily feeding, should be administered to meet individual requirements. 1 410 mL, 6 Tetra Paks meet or surpass 100% of the Canadian RNI (adult males, 25 to 49) for protein and essential vitamins and minerals.

Tube Feeding: Follow a physician's or dietitian's directions. When initiating feeding, the flow rate, volume and dilution are dependent on patient condition and tolerance. Care should be taken to avoid contamination of this product during preparation and administration. Additional fluid requirements should be met by giving water orally with or after feedings, or when flushing the tube.

Supplied: Each 235 mL ready-to-use brik contains: Ⓤ-D water, corn syrup solids, sodium and calcium caseinates, corn oil, sugar, maltodextrin, soy protein isolate, potassium citrate, soy lecithin, sodium citrate, calcium phosphate tribasic, natural and artificial flavor, magnesium chloride, potassium chloride, choline chloride, ascorbic acid, potassium hydroxide, carrageenan, zinc sulfate, alpha tocopheryl acetate, ferrous sulfate, niacinamide, D-calcium pantothenate, copper gluconate, manganese sulfate, thiamine hydrochloride, pyridoxine hydrochloride, riboflavin, vitamin A palmitate, maltol, folic acid, biotin, potassium iodide, vitamin K_1, cyanocobalamin and vitamin D_3. See Table I.

Note: Ingredient content may differ slightly between chocolate, strawberry and vanilla flavors. Consult the product labeling for exact composition.

Energy Distribution: protein 15%, fat 32%, carbohydrates 53%; 634 kJ (150 kcal)/100 mL.

Table I—Resource Plus

Analysis	100 mL	
Energy	634 (150)	kJ (kcal)
Protein	5.5	g
Carbohydrates	20.1	g
Fat	5.3	g
Linoleic Acid	3.1	g
Sodium	127	mg
Potassium	208	mg
Vitamin A	378	IU
Vitamin C	16.2	mg
Thiamine	0.26	mg
Riboflavin	0.27	mg
Niacin	3.2	mg
Calcium	71.1	mg
Iron	1.45	mg
Vitamin D	29.7	IU
Vitamin E	3.3	IU
Vitamin B_6	0.32	mg
Folic Acid	0.0319	mg
Vitamin B_{12}	0.00095	mg
Phosphorus	71.1	mg
Iodine	0.0113	mg
Magnesium	31.9	mg
Zinc	2.39	mg
Copper	0.16	mg
Biotin	0.0238	mg
Pantothenic Acid	0.85	mg
Vitamin K	0.0055	mg
Choline	53.2	mg
Chloride	160	mg
Manganese	0.21	mg
Osmolality	600	mOsm/kg water

Resource Plus has a calorie to nitrogen ratio of 170:1, which is suggested as reasonable for effective protein utilization. Gluten- and lactose-free.

Aseptic Tetra Brik Paks of 235 mL (vanilla, strawberry, chocolate), cases of 27.

Store unopened at room temperature; avoid freezing; protect from heat. Once opened, store covered in refrigerator and use within 24 hours. Chilling enhances flavor.

...Consult a pharmacist for additional drug information.

RESTORIL®

Novartis Pharmaceuticals

Temazepam

Hypnotic

Pharmacology: General: Temazepam is a benzodiazepine with hypnotic properties.

Benzodiazepines act as depressants of the CNS. It is believed that benzodiazepines enhance or facilitate the effects of the inhibitory neurotransmitter gamma-aminobutyric acid (GABA).

Benzodiazepines act as agonists at the benzodiazepine receptor sites. The benzodiazepine-GABA receptor-chloride ionophore complex functions mainly in the gating of the chloride channel. Benzodiazepines are thought to produce their pharmacological effects by facilitating GABA-mediated transmission in the CNS, which reportedly increase the frequency of the chloride channel opening.

In sleep laboratory studies, the effect of temazepam 15 and 30 mg, was compared to placebo over a 2-week period. There was a linear dose-response improvement in total sleep time and sleep latency with significant drug-placebo differences occurring for total sleep time at both doses, and for sleep latency at the higher dose. REM sleep was essentially unchanged and slow wave sleep was decreased.

Rebound Insomnia: A transient syndrome, known as "rebound insomnia", whereby the symptoms that led to treatment with a benzodiazepine recur in an enhanced form, may occur on withdrawal of hypnotic treatment. In the sleep laboratory studies, no measurable effects on daytime alertness or performance occurred following temazepam treatment or during the withdrawal period, even though a transient sleep disturbance in some sleep parameters was observed following the withdrawal of the higher doses.

The duration of hypnotic effect and the profile of unwanted effects may be influenced by the alpha (distribution) and beta (elimination) half-lives of the administered drug and any active metabolites formed. When half-lives are long, the drug or metabolite may accumulate during periods of nightly administration and be associated with impairments of cognitive and motor performance during waking hours. If half-lives are short, the drug and metabolites will be cleared before the next dose is ingested, and carry-over effects related to sedation or CNS depression should be minimal or absent. However, during nightly use and for an extended period, pharmacodynamic tolerance or adaptation to some effects of benzodiazepine hypnotics may develop.

If the drug has a very short elimination half-life, it is possible that a relative deficiency (i.e., in relation to the receptor site) may occur at some point in the interval between each night's use. This sequence of events may account for two clinical findings reported to occur after several weeks of nightly use of rapidly eliminated benzodiazepine hypnotics: 1) increased wakefulness during the last third of the night and 2) the appearance of increased daytime anxiety (see Warnings).

Pharmacokinetics: Orally administered temazepam is well absorbed in man. In a single and multiple dose absorption, distribution, metabolism and excretion (ADME) study, using ^{3}H labelled drug, temazepam was found to have minimal (8%) first-pass metabolism. There were no active metabolites formed and the only significant metabolite present in blood was the O-conjugate. Oral administration of 15 to 45 mg temazepam in man resulted in rapid absorption with significant blood levels achieved in 30 minutes and peak levels at 2 to 3 hours. Drug levels in blood declined in a biphasic manner with a short half-life ranging from 0.4 to 0.6 hours and a terminal half-life from 3.5 to 18 hours (mean 9 hours). The inactive O-conjugate metabolite was formed with a half-life of 10 hours and excreted with a half-life of approximately 2 hours. Thus, O-conjugation is the rate limiting step in the biodisposition. In a multiple dose study, steady-state was approximated after the second daily dose with no evidence of accumulation after 5 consecutive daily doses of 30 mg temazepam. Steady-state plasma levels at 2.5 hours were 382±192 ng/mL.

Approximately 96% of unchanged drug is bound to plasma protein.

Twenty-four hours after a single oral dose of temazepam approximately 80 to 90% of the drug was recovered in urine, primarily as the O-conjugate. Total recovery from feces and urine in single- and multiple-dose studies was approximately 95%, with only 3 to 13% of the radioactivity detectable in feces. Less than 1% of the dose was excreted as unchanged drug or N-desmethyltemazepam. A dose-proportional relationship has been established for the area under the plasma concentration/time curve over the 15 to 30 mg dose range.

At the dose of 30 mg once a day for 8 weeks, no evidence of enzyme induction was found in man.

Indications: Sleep disturbance may be the presenting manifestation of a physical and/or psychiatric disorder. Consequently, a decision to initiate symptomatic treatment of insomnia should only be made after the patient has been carefully evaluated.

Temazepam is indicated for the symptomatic relief of transient and short-term insomnia characterized by difficulty in falling asleep, frequent nocturnal awakenings and/or early morning awakenings.

Treatment with temazepam should usually not exceed 7 to 10 consecutive days. Use for more than 2 to 3 consecutive weeks requires complete re-evaluation of the patient. Prescriptions for temazepam should be written for short-term use (7 to 10 days) and it should not be prescribed in quantities exceeding a 1-month supply.

The use of hypnotics should be restricted for insomnia where disturbed sleep results in impaired daytime functioning.

Contraindications: In patients with a known hypersensitivity to the drug, any component of its formulation, or to other benzodiazepines; myasthenia gravis; sleep apnea syndrome.

Temazepam is contraindicated in patients who in the past manifested paradoxical reactions to alcohol and/or sedative medications.

Warnings: General: Benzodiazepines should be used with extreme caution in patients with a history of substance or alcohol abuse.

Geriatrics: The lowest possible effective dose should be prescribed for elderly patients. Inappropriate, heavy sedation in the elderly, may result in accidental events or falls.

The failure of insomnia to remit after 7 to 10 days of treatment may indicate the presence of a primary psychiatric and/or medical illness or the presence of sleep state misperception.

Worsening of insomnia or the emergence of new abnormalities of thinking or behavior may be the consequence of an unrecognized psychiatric or physical disorder. These have also been reported to occur in association with the use of drugs that act at the benzodiazepine receptors.

Pregnancy: The use of temazepam during pregnancy is not recommended.

Benzodiazepines may cause fetal damage when administered during pregnancy. During the first trimester of pregnancy, several studies have suggested an increased risk of congenital malformations associated with the use of benzodiazepines. During the last weeks of pregnancy, ingestion of therapeutic doses of a benzodiazepine hypnotic has resulted in neonatal CNS depression due to transplacental distribution.

If the drug is prescribed to a woman of childbearing potential, the patient should be warned of the potential risk to a fetus and advised to consult her physician regarding the discontinuation of the drug if she intends to become pregnant or suspects that she is pregnant.

Memory Disturbance: Anterograde amnesia of varying severity has been reported following therapeutic doses of benzodiazepines. The event is rare with temazepam. Anterograde amnesia is a dose-related phenomenon and elderly subjects may be at particular risk. Cases of transient global amnesia and "traveller's amnesia" have also been reported in association with benzodiazepines, the latter in individuals who have taken the drug, often in the middle of the night, to induce sleep while travelling.

Transient global amnesia and traveller's amnesia are unpredictable and not necessarily dose-related phenomena. Patients should be warned not to take temazepam under circumstances in which a full night's sleep and clearance of the drug from the body are not possible before they need again to resume full activity.

Abnormal thinking and psychotic behavioral changes have been reported to occur in association with the use of benzodiazepines including temazepam, although rarely.

Some of the changes may be characterized by decreased inhibition, e.g., aggressiveness or extroversion that seem excessive, similar to that seen with alcohol and other CNS depressants (e.g., sedative/hypnotics). Particular caution is warranted in patients with a history of violent behavior and a history of unusual reactions to sedatives including alcohol and the benzodiazepines. Psychotic behavioral changes that have been reported with benzodiazepines include bizarre behavior, hallucinations, and depersonalization. Abnormal behaviors associated with the use of benzodiazepines have been reported more with chronic use and/or high doses but they may occur during the acute, maintenance or withdrawal phases of treatment.

It can rarely be determined with certainty whether a particular instance of abnormal behaviors listed above is drug induced, spontaneous in origin, or a result of an underlying psychiatric disorder. Nevertheless, the emergence of any new behavioral sign or symptom of concern requires careful and immediate evaluation.

Confusion: The benzodiazepines affect mental efficiency, e.g., concentration, attention and vigilance. The risk of confusion is greater in the elderly and in patients with cerebral impairment.

Anxiety, Restlessness: An increase in daytime anxiety and/or restlessness have been observed during treatment with temazepam.

This may be a manifestation of interdose withdrawal due to the short elimination half-life of the drug.

Depression: Caution should be exercised if temazepam is prescribed to patients with signs or symptoms of depression that could be intensified by hypnotic drugs. The potential for self-harm (e.g., intentional overdose) is high in patients with depression and thus, the least amount of drug that is feasible should be available to them at any one time.

Potentiation of Drug Effects: Temazepam may potentiate the effects of other CNS depressant drugs such as alcohol, barbiturates, nonbarbiturate hypnotics, antihistamines, narcotics, antipsychotic and antidepressant drugs, and anticonvulsants. Therefore, different benzodiazepines should usually not be used simultaneously and careful consideration should be given if other CNS depressants are administered in combination with temazepam. Patients should be advised against the simultaneous use of other CNS depressant drugs and should be cautioned not to take alcohol because of the potentiation of effects that might occur.

Precautions: Drug Interactions: Temazepam may produce additive CNS depressant effects when coadministered with alcohol, sedative antihistamines, anticonvulsants, or psychotropic medications which themselves can produce CNS depression.

Compounds which inhibit certain hepatic enzymes (particularly cytochrome P450) may enhance the activity of benzodiazepines.

Drug Abuse, Dependence and Withdrawal: Withdrawal symptoms, similar in characteristic to those noted with barbiturates and alcohol (convulsions, tremor, abdominal and muscle cramps, vomiting, sweating dysphoria, perceptual disturbances and insomnia) have occurred following abrupt discontinuation of benzodiazepines, including temazepam.

The more severe symptoms are usually associated with higher dosages and longer usage, although patients given therapeutic dosages for as few as 1 to 2 weeks can also have withdrawal symptoms including daytime anxiety between nightly doses. Consequently, abrupt discontinuation should be avoided and a gradual dosage tapering schedule is recommended in any patient taking more than the lowest dose for more than a few weeks. The recommendation for tapering is particularly important in patients with a history of seizures.

The risk of dependence is increased in patients with a history of alcoholism, drug abuse, or in patients with marked personality disorders. Interdose daytime anxiety and rebound anxiety may increase the risk of dependency in temazepam treated patients. As with all hypnotics, repeat prescriptions should be limited to those who are under medical supervision.

Patients with Specific Conditions: Temazepam is O-conjugated in the liver and is primarily excreted by the kidney. Hence, temazepam should be given with caution to patients with impaired hepatic or renal function. Temazepam should also be given with caution to patients with severe pulmonary insufficiency: respiratory depression has been reported in patients with compromised respiratory function.

Temazepam should be used with caution in severely depressed patients or those in whom there is any evidence of latent depression; it should be recognized that suicidal tendencies may be present and protective measures may be necessary.

Patients Requiring Mental Alertness: Because of temazepam's CNS depressant effect, patients receiving the drug should be cautioned against engaging in hazardous occupations requiring complete mental alertness such as operating machinery or driving a motor vehicle. For the same reason, patients should be warned against the concomitant ingestion of temazepam and alcohol or CNS depressant drugs.

Pregnancy: For teratogenic effects see Warnings. Nonteratogenic effects: a child born to a mother who is on benzodiazepines may be at risk for withdrawal symptoms from the drug during the postnatal period. Also, neonatal flaccidity has been reported in an infant born to a mother who had been receiving benzodiazepines.

Lactation: It is not known whether or not temazepam is excreted in human milk. Therefore, it should not be given to nursing mothers.

Children: The safety and effectiveness of temazepam in children below the age of 18 have not been established.

Geriatrics and Debilitated Patients: Elderly patients are especially susceptible to dose-related adverse effects, such as drowsiness, dizziness, or impaired coordination. Inappropriate, heavy sedation may result in accidental events/falls. Therefore, the lowest possible dose should be used in these subjects.

Debilitated patients, or those with organic brain syndrome, are prone to CNS depression after even low doses of benzodiazepines and may experience paradoxical reactions to these drugs. Therefore, temazepam should be used only at the lowest possible dose and adjusted when necessary under careful observation, depending on the response of the patient.

Because temazepam is eliminated by O-conjugation, minimal accumulation occurs.

Adverse Effects: During controlled clinical trials in which 1 076 patients received temazepam at bedtime, the adverse events occurring in 1% or more of patients are listed in Table I.

Table I—Restoril

Adverse Effects

	Restoril % incidence (n=1 076)	Placebo % incidence (n=783)
Drowsiness	9.1	5.6
Headache	8.5	9.1
Fatigue	4.8	4.7
Nervousness	4.6	8.2
Lethargy	4.5	3.4
Dizziness	4.5	3.3
Nausea	3.1	3.8
Hangover	2.5	1.1
Anxiety	2.0	1.5
Depression	1.7	1.8
Dry mouth	1.7	2.2
Diarrhea	1.7	1.1
Abdominal Discomfort	1.5	1.9
Euphoria	1.5	0.4
Weakness	1.4	0.9
Confusion	1.3	0.5
Blurred Vision	1.3	1.3
Nightmares	1.2	1.7
Vertigo	1.2	0.8

The following adverse events have been reported with an incidence of 0.5 to 0.9%:

CNS: anorexia, ataxia, equilibrium loss, tremor, increased dreaming.

Cardiovascular: dyspnea, palpitations.

Gastrointestinal: vomiting.

Muskuloskeletal: backache.

Special Senses: hyperhidrosis, burning eyes.

The following adverse events have been reported with an incidence of less than 0.5%: amnesia, hallucinations, horizontal nystagmus and paradoxical reactions including restlessness, overstimulation, and agitation.

Overdose: Symptoms and Treatment: Manifestations of acute overdosage of temazepam, as with other benzodiazepines, can be expected to reflect the increasing CNS effects of the drug and include somnolence, confusion and coma, with reduced or absent reflexes. With large overdoses, respiratory depression, hypotension and finally coma will result. If the patient is conscious, vomiting should be induced mechanically or with emetics (e.g., syrup of ipecac 20 to 30 mL). Gastric lavage should be employed as soon as possible, utilizing concurrently a cuffed endotracheal tube if the patient is unconscious, in order to prevent aspiration and pulmonary complications. Maintenance of adequate pulmonary ventilation is essential and fluids should be administered i.v. to encourage diuresis. The use of pressor agents, such as norepinephrine bitartrate or metaraminol, i.v. may be necessary to combat hypotension but only if considered essential. The value of dialysis in emergency therapy for benzodiazepine overdosage has not been determined. If excitation occurs, barbiturates should not be used. It should be borne in mind that multiple agents may have been ingested.

The benzodiazepine antagonist, flumazenil, is a specific antidote in known or suspected benzodiazepine overdose. For conditions of use see flumazenil product monograph.

Dosage: The lowest effective dose should be used. Treatment should usually not exceed 7 to 10 consecutive days.

Use of temazepam for more than 2 to 3 consecutive weeks requires complete re-evaluation of the patient.

An appropriate hypnotic dose should produce the desired hypnotic effect while avoiding oversedation and impairment of performance the next day.

Adults: The recommended adult dose is 30 mg before retiring, **15 mg may be sufficient for some patients.**

Geriatrics and debilitated patients: The initial dose should not exceed 15 mg before retiring (see Precautions).

Temazepam is intended only for short-term use and therefore, should not be prescribed in quantities exceeding those required for that cycle of administration. Prescription should not be renewed without further assessment of the patient's needs.

Children: Not indicated in children under 18 years of age.

Information for the Patient: See Blue Section—Information for the Patient "Restoril".

Supplied: 15 mg: Each maroon and flesh, size 3 hard shell gelatin capsule, printed SANDOZ and RESTORIL 15 in white, contains: temazepam 15 mg. Nonmedicinal ingredients: colloidal silicon dioxide, D&C Red #28, D&C Yellow #10, FD&C Blue #1, gelatin, lactose, magnesium stearate, sodium lauryl sulfate and titanium dioxide. The agents used to polish the capsules are alcohol, canner special salt and Tween 60. Bottles of 100.

30 mg: Each maroon and blue, size 3 hard shell gelatin capsule, printed SANDOZ and RESTORIL 30 in white, contains: temazepam 30 mg. Nonmedicinal ingredients: colloidal silicon dioxide, D&C Red #28, FD&C Blue #1, gelatin, lactose, magnesium stearate, sodium lauryl sulfate and titanium dioxide. The agents used to polish the capsules are alcohol, canner special salt and Tween 60. Bottles of 100.

Store at controlled room temperature (15 to 30°C). Protect from moisture and light.

(Shown in Product Recognition Section)

RETIN-A® ℞

Janssen-Ortho

Tretinoin

Comedolytic Agent

Pharmacology: Studies in animals have shown that tretinoin supplies all the physiologic requirements of vitamin A except those needed for vision and reproduction. When animals were fed a diet in which vitamin A was replaced by vitamin A acid, there was no storage in the liver. This suggests that the acid may be the tissue-active form which is important for epithelial growth and general health, while the alcohol or ester form is necessary for vision and reproduction.

Repeated skin applications of vitamin A acid over a period of days have produced detectable changes in the skin. Initially, the change is mild erythema, followed by flaking or peeling of the stratum corneum, which in itself is associated with a marked thinning of the stratum corneum and increased cellular turnover in the skin.

Local application of vitamin A has been reported to have reduced abnormal cornification in follicular orifices, and vitamin A acid was reported to be more potent than vitamin A alcohol or its esters when applied locally in ointments to human skin.

Although the exact mode of action of tretinoin is unknown, current evidence suggests that topical tretinoin decreases cohesiveness of follicular cells with decreased microcomedo formation. Additionally, tretinoin stimulates mitotic activity and increased turnover of follicular epithelial cells, causing extrusion of the comedones.

Indications: For topical application in the treatment of acne vulgaris.

Contraindications: Patients who have demonstrated a hypersensitivity to the drug.

Warnings: General: Excessive use of tretinoin should be avoided. In order to minimize the potential for additional skin irritation, care should be taken to avoid contact with the eyes, eyelids, angles of the nose, mouth, mucous membranes or other areas where treatment is not intended. Tretinoin may cause irritation of circumoral and other sensitive skin areas. Tretinoin should not be applied to severely inflamed skin or to open lesions.

Simultaneous use of harsh abrasives and other skin treatments, including sun lamp, should be avoided if possible.

In some patients temporary skin irritation may occur, especially in early weeks of treatment. Should these reactions occur to an excessive degree, and the skin becomes extremely red, swollen and crusted, use of tretinoin should be discontinued immediately.

An apparent exacerbation may develop due to the drug effect on previously seen deep lesions. This is an anticipated part of the therapeutic effect. Therapy should be continued.

Pregnancy: **Topical tretinoin should be used by women of childbearing years only after contraceptive counselling. It is recommended that topical tretinoin should not be used by pregnant women.**

There have been a few reports of birth defects among babies born to women exposed to **topical** tretinoin during pregnancy. To date, there have been no adequate and well-controlled prospective studies performed in pregnant women and the teratogenic blood level of tretinoin is not clear. However, a well-conducted retrospective cohort study of babies born to women exposed to topical tretinoin during the first trimester of pregnancy found no excess birth defects among these babies when compared with babies born to women in the same cohort who were not similarly exposed.

Oral tretinoin has been shown to be teratogenic and fetotoxic in rats when given in doses 1 000 and 500 times the topical human dose, respectively.

In 9 out of 10 topical teratology studies of tretinoin conducted in rats and rabbits using several formulations, there has been no evidence of teratogenicity. In 1 out of 10 studies there was an increase in fetal malformations; however, a clear causal relationship of topical tretinoin in these findings could not be established. In a repeat of this study, there were no fetal malformations. Topical tretinoin can produce treatment-related fetal effects (delayed ossification of bones and an increase in supernumerary ribs). The fetal no effect dose is 1 mg/kg/day (200 times the recommended clinical dose).

Lactation: It is not known whether tretinoin is excreted in human milk. Nevertheless, a decision should be made whether to discontinue nursing or to discontinue the drug taking into account the importance of the drug to the mother. Since many drugs are excreted in human milk, caution should be exercised when tretinoin is administered to a nursing mother.

Precautions: General: For external use only.

Cosmetics may be used, but the areas to be treated should be cleansed thoroughly before the medication is applied. Astringent toiletries should be avoided.

Patients will be able to remove hair as usual (e.g., plucking, electrolysis, depilatories) but should avoid these procedures at night before applying tretinoin as they might result in skin irritation.

Permanent wave solutions, waxing preparations, medicated soaps and shampoos can sometimes irritate even normal skin. Caution should be used so that these products do not come into contact with skin treated with tretinoin.

Exposure to sunlight, including ultraviolet sunlamps, may provoke additional irritation. Therefore, exposure should be avoided or minimized during the use of tretinoin. A patient experiencing considerable sun exposure due to occupational duties, and/or any patient inherently sensitive to the sun, should exercise particular caution. When exposure to sunlight cannot be avoided, use of sunscreen products and protective clothing over treated areas is recommended.

Hyper- or hypopigmentation has occasionally been reported when the product is used to the point of producing severe irritation. This is reversible when the medication is stopped.

Children: Safety and effectiveness have not been established in children.

Gels are flammable. Note: Keep away from heat and flame. Keep tube tightly closed.

Local Irritation: It is not recommended to initiate treatment with tretinoin or continue its use in the presence of skin irritation (e.g., erythema, peeling, pruritus, sunburn, etc.) until these symptoms subside.

In certain sensitive individuals, tretinoin may induce severe local erythema, swelling, pruritus, warmth, burning or stinging, blistering, crusting and/or peeling at the site of application. If the degree of local irritation warrants, the patient should be instructed to either apply the medication less frequently or discontinue its use temporarily.

Tretinoin has been reported to cause severe irritation on eczematous skin and should be used with utmost caution in patients with this condition. If a patient experiences severe or persistent irritation, the patient should be advised to discontinue application of tretinoin completely, and if necessary, consult a physician.

Weather extremes, such as wind, cold and low humidity may be irritating to skin treated with tretinoin and may increase its dryness.

Drug Interactions: Concomitant topical medication, medicated or abrasive soaps and cleansers, soaps and cosmetics that

Retin-A (cont'd)

have a strong drying effect, and products with high concentrations of alcohol, astringents, spices or lime should be used with caution because of possible interaction with tretinoin. Particular caution should be exercised in using preparations containing sulfur, resorcinol, or salicylic acid with tretinoin. It is also advisable to "rest" a patient's skin until the effects of such preparations subside before use of tretinoin is begun.

Adverse Effects: Some degree of local irritation is expected. The most commonly reported undesirable effects are dry skin, burning, stinging, warmth, erythema, pruritus, rash, peeling and temporary hypo- and hyperpigmentation. Rarely reported undesirable effects are blistering and crusting of the skin, eye irritation and edema. These reactions were usually mild to moderate in severity, generally well-tolerated and self-limiting, occurred early during the course of therapy and generally decreased over time with the exception of dry skin, which tended to persist.

True contact allergy to topical tretinoin is rarely encountered.

Changes in the skin may be anticipated, indicating an active effect of the medication. Expected changes include mild erythema and flaking or peeling of the stratum corneum. In certain very sensitive patients, the skin may become very erythematous, edematous, blistered or crusted. In such cases, application of tretinoin should be discontinued until the skin has fully recovered. Further applications should be at a level that the individual can tolerate. All adverse reactions observed are reversible when treatment is discontinued.

Overdose: Symptoms and Treatment: If medication is applied excessively, no more rapid or better results will be obtained and marked redness, peeling, or discomfort may occur. Tretinoin is intended for topical use only. In the event of accidental ingestion, if the ingestion is recent, the stomach should be emptied immediately by gastric lavage or by induction of emesis. All other treatment should be appropriately supportive. Oral ingestion of the drug may lead to the same side effects as those associated with excessive oral intake of vitamin A including teratogenesis in women of childbearing years. Therefore, in such cases pregnancy testing should be carried out in women of childbearing years. Reduce amount or frequency of application if undesirable reactions occur.

Dosage: Excessive use should be avoided.

Adults: Apply daily to the affected areas, preferably at bedtime, after cleansing with a mild, nonmedicated soap and water. The treated area should be washed no more than twice per day. After washing, the skin should be dried gently and completely without rubbing it. Allow at least 20 to 30 minutes to dry before applying medication. Only a sufficient quantity of medication should be applied to cover the affected areas lightly, using a gauze swab, cotton wool or the tips of clean fingers. Over-saturation should be avoided since excess medication could run into the eyes, angles of the nose or other areas where treatment is not intended.

Discontinue treatment if a severe local inflammatory response is experienced. Reinstitute therapy when the reaction has subsided and apply preparation every other day or less frequently. Should discomfort still be experienced, stop treatment completely.

Maintenance dose should be the least number of applications that will prevent recurrence of the condition. Maintenance therapy should be administered daily for best results.

Application of tretinoin may cause a transitory feeling of warmth or slight stinging. When administered according to recommended guidelines, tretinoin may produce a slight erythema similar to that of mild sunburn. In cases where it is necessary to temporarily discontinue therapy or reduce the frequency of application, therapy should be resumed or the frequency of application increased when the patient becomes able to tolerate the treatment.

Excess application of tretinoin does not provide more rapid or better results. In fact, marked redness, peeling or discomfort can occur. If excess application occurs accidentally or through over-enthusiastic use, tretinoin should be discontinued for several days before resuming therapy.

Therapeutic effects may be noticed after 2 to 3 weeks of use but more than 6 weeks of therapy may be required before definite beneficial effects are seen. During the early weeks of treatment, an apparent exacerbation of inflammatory lesions may occur. This is due to the action of the medication on deep, previously unseen lesions and should not be considered a reason to discontinue therapy. Once a satisfactory response has been obtained, it may be possible to maintain this improvement with less frequent applications.

Children: Safety and effectiveness have not been established in children.

Information for the Patient: See Blue Section—Information for the Patient "Retin-A".

Supplied: Cream: Each g of smooth, yellow, oil-in-water cream, contains: tretinoin 0.01%, 0.025%, 0.05% or 0.1% in a bland, hydrophilic base. Nonmedicinal ingredients: butylated hydroxytoluene, isopropyl myristate, polyoxyl (40) stearate, purified water, sorbic acid, stearic acid, stearyl alcohol and xanthan gum (Keltrol). Tubes of 30 g.

Gel: Each g of smooth, clear, viscous yellow gel, contains: tretinoin 0.01% or 0.025%. Nonmedicinal ingredients: butylated hydroxytoluene, ethanol undenatured and hydroxypropyl cellulose. Tubes of 30 g.

Keep container closed when not in use. Store between 15 and 25°C.

Reviewed 1999

RETISOL-A® Ⓟ

Stiefel

Tretinoin

Acne Therapy

Pharmacology: The precise mechanism of action of tretinoin on the skin is not fully understood. It is known that tretinoin is both pharmacologically and structurally related to vitamin A which regulates epithelial cell growth and differentiation. Tretinoin itself is known to have an irritant and keratolytic effect on the skin. These 2 actions which occur simultaneously have been shown histologically in both animal and man to be associated with an increased growth rate and with a decrease in the cohesiveness of the epidermal cells. The result is a slightly thickened epidermis with an accelerated turnover rate and shedding of keratinized cells as very fine barely perceptible scales.

In acne vulgaris the induced fine scaling of the skin surface is accompanied by an increased production of less cohesive epidermal sebaceous cells which consequently flow out of the follicle at a more rapid rate. The thickened mass of sebaceous cellular debris, the comedones, appear to be initially extruded and then prevented from recurring by these actions. Histopathologically, acne is the impaction plus distention of the sebaceous follicles by tightly packed horny cells and disruption of the follicular epithelium. It has been postulated that tretinoin inhibits the synthesis or quality of the substance which binds the horny cells within the sebaceous follicle.

Indications: The treatment of acne vulgaris, primarily where comedones, papules and pustules predominate. Tretinoin is not effective in most cases of severe pustular and deep cystic nodular varieties (acne conglobata).

Contraindications: Patients with known hypersensitivity to retinoids or to any ingredient contained in the preparation.

Warnings: Tretinoin is intended for external use only and should be kept away from eyes, nose, mouth, and other mucous membranes because of its irritant effect.

Do not apply to eyelids or to the skin at the corners of the eyes and mouth. Avoid the angles of the nose and nasolabial fold (if treatment in these areas is necessary, apply very sparingly). Topical use may induce severe local erythema and peeling at the site of application. If the degree of local irritation warrants, patients should be directed to use the medication less frequently, discontinue use temporarily or discontinue use altogether. Tretinoin has been reported to cause severe irritation of eczematous skin and tretinoin should only be used with utmost caution in patients with this condition.

Pregnancy: **Topical tretinoin should be used by women of childbearing years only after contraceptive counselling. It is recommended that topical tretinoin should not by used by pregnant women.**

There have been rare reports of birth defects among babies born to women exposed to **topical** tretinoin during pregnancy. However, there are no well controlled prospective studies of the use of topical tretinoin in pregnant women. A retrospective study of mothers exposed to topical tretinoin during the first trimester of pregnancy found no increase in the incidence of birth defects.

Topical retinoid teratology studies in rats and rabbits have been inconclusive. As with all retinoids, tretinoin administered **orally** at high doses is teratogenic.

Lactation: **It is known whether tretinoin is excreted in human milk. Nevertheless, a decision should be made whether to discontinue nursing or to discontinue the drug taking into account the importance of the drug to the mother.**

Precautions: Concomitant topical medications should be used with caution during therapy with tretinoin because of possible intensified reactions. Particular caution should be exercised when using preparations containing a peeling agent concomitantly (such as sulfur, resorcinol, benzoyl peroxide or salicylic acid) with tretinoin. It may be advisable to "rest" a patient's skin until the effects of previously used peeling agents subside before initiating tretinoin therapy.

Excessive exposure to sunlight or ultraviolet rays (sunlamps) should be avoided during tretinoin treatment, because the additional irradiation may lead to a more intense action.

If a sunburn occurs, it is advisable to interrupt therapy until the severe erythema and peeling subside. Patients whose occupations require considerable exposure to the sun should exercise particular caution.

Adverse Effects: The skin of certain sensitive individuals, particularly those with fair complexion, may become excessively red, edematous, blistered or crusted when exposed to tretinoin. Pain, burning sensation, tenderness, irritation or pruritus have also been occasionally reported. If any of these effects occur, the medication should be discontinued until the integrity of the skin has been restored or the treatment schedule adjusted to the level the patient can tolerate. Temporary hyper- or hypopigmentation has been reported with repeated application of tretinoin. To date, all adverse clinical effects of tretinoin encountered have been reversible upon discontinuance of therapy. In many instances, reinstitution of therapy with tretinoin failed to produce the adverse effect previously experienced.

Overdose: Symptoms and Treatment: Topical: If medication is applied excessively, marked redness, peeling or discomfort may occur.

Dosage: Tretinoin should be applied to the affected area once a day. The area under treatment (not just clinical lesions) should be thoroughly cleansed with a mild soap, such as Acne-Aid Soap, and dried, followed by application of tretinoin with a gentle rubbing motion. Application may be accompanied by a transitory feeling of warmth or a stinging sensation. Treatment should be discontinued if a severe local inflammatory response is experienced.

In cases where it has been necessary to discontinue therapy or to reduce the frequency of applications, therapy may be resumed, when the adverse effects have ceased. In some patients, during the early weeks of therapy, an apparent exacerbation of the acne lesions may occur.

Therapeutic results may be noticed after 2 to 3 weeks of therapy; however, results may not be optimal until after 8 to 10 weeks of treatment. Once the acne lesions have responded satisfactorily, it may be possible to maintain the improved state with less frequent applications.

Patients being treated with tretinoin may continue to use water-based cosmetics; however, the area of skin to be treated should be thoroughly cleansed and dried before tretinoin application.

Information for the Patient: See Blue Section—Information for the Patient "Retisol-A".

Supplied: Each g of cream contains: tretinoin 0.01%, 0.025%, 0.05% or 0.1% in a moisturizing cream base with 7.5% Parsol MCX and 2% Parsol 1789 (SPF 15). Nonmedicinal ingredients: 2-ethyl-hexyl-p-methoxycinnamate, butyl methoxyl dibenzoyl M, butylated hydroxytoluene, carbomer 934 NF, cyclomethicone NF, diisopropyl adipate NF, glycerin USP, imidurea/parabens, isoarachidyl neopentanoate, light mineral oil USP, phenyl timethicone, polysorbate 60 NF, purified water USP, sodium hydroxide 10%, sorbitan monostearate NF and stearyl alcohol NF. Tubes of 25 g. Store between 15 and 30°C.

RETROVIR® (AZT™) Ⓟ

Glaxo Wellcome

Zidovudine

Antiretroviral Agent

Pharmacology: Zidovudine is a potent inhibitor of the in vitro replication of some retroviruses including human immunodeficiency virus, HIV. Zidovudine is a thymidine analogue in which the 3-hydroxy (-OH) group is replaced by an azido(-N_3) group. Cellular thymidine kinase converts zidovudine into zidovudine monophosphate. The monophosphate is further converted into the diphosphate by cellular thymidylate kinase and to the triphosphate derivative by other cellular enzymes. Zidovudine triphosphate interferes with the HIV viral RNA dependent DNA polymerase (reverse transcriptase) and thus inhibits viral replication. Zidovudine triphosphate also inhibits cellular α-DNA polymerase, but at concentrations 100-fold higher than those required to inhibit reverse transcriptase. In vitro, zidovudine triphosphate has been shown to be incorporated into growing chains of DNA by viral reverse transcriptase. When incorporation by the viral enzyme occurs, the DNA chain is terminated. Studies in cell culture suggest that zidovudine incorporation by cellular α-DNA polymerase may occur, but only to a very small extent and not in all test systems. Cellular γ-DNA polymerase shows some sensitivity to inhibition by the zidovudine triphosphate with 50% inhibitory concentration (IC_{50}) values 400 to 900 times greater than that for HIV reverse transcriptase.

Pharmacokinetics: Pharmacokinetic studies of zidovudine following i.v. dosing in adults indicate dose-independent kinetics over the range of 1 to 5 mg/kg with a mean zidovudine half-life of 1.1 hours. Zidovudine is rapidly metabolized in the liver to 3′-azido-3′-deoxy-5′-0-β-D-glucopyranuronosylthymidine (GZDV, formerly called GAZT), and both are rapidly eliminated by the kidney. A second metabolite, 3′-amino-3′-deoxythymidine (AMT) has been identified in the plasma following single dose i.v. administration of zidovudine. After oral dosing in adults, zidovudine is rapidly absorbed from the gastrointestinal tract with peak serum concentrations occurring within 0.5 to 1.5 hours, with an average oral bioavailability of 65%. Retrovir capsules and syrup are bioequivalent. In pediatric patients older than 3 months, the pharmacokinetics of zidovudine are similar to those in adult patients.

Indications: Monotherapy: Adults: Zidovudine is indicated for the initial treatment of HIV-infected adults with CD4 cell counts of approximately 500 cells/mm³ or less. Therapy with zidovudine has been shown to prolong survival and decrease the incidence of opportunistic infections in patients with advanced HIV disease at the time of initiation of therapy and to delay disease progression in asymptomatic HIV-infected patients.

Zidovudine should be considered as initial therapy for adult HIV-infected patients who have not received previous antiretroviral treatment. However, randomized studies have shown that for some patients with advanced disease on prolonged therapy with zidovudine, modifying the antiviral regimen may be more effective in delaying disease progression than remaining on monotherapy with zidovudine.

Children: Zidovudine is also indicated for HIV-infected children over 3 months of age who have HIV-related symptoms or who are asymptomatic with abnormal laboratory values indicating significant HIV-related immunosuppression.

Maternal-Fetal HIV Transmission: Zidovudine is also indicated for the prevention of maternal-fetal HIV transmission as part of a regimen that includes oral zidovudine beginning between 14 and 34 weeks of gestation, i.v. zidovudine during labor, and administration of zidovudine syrup to the newborn after birth. However, transmission to infants may still occur in some cases despite the use of this regimen. The efficacy of this regimen for preventing HIV transmission in women who have received zidovudine for a prolonged period before pregnancy has not been evaluated. The safety of zidovudine for the mother or fetus during the first trimester of pregnancy has not been assessed.

The utility of zidovudine for the prevention of maternal-fetal HIV transmission was demonstrated in a randomized, double-blind, placebo-controlled trial (ACTG 076) conducted in HIV-infected pregnant women who had little or no previous exposure to zidovudine and CD4 cell counts of 200 to 1 818 cells/mm³ (median in the treated group: 560 cells/mm³). Oral zidovudine was initiated between 14 and 34 weeks of gestation (median 11 weeks of therapy) followed by i.v. administration of zidovudine during labor and delivery. After birth, infants received oral zidovudine syrup for 6 weeks. The study showed a statistically significant difference in the incidence of HIV infection in the infants (based on viral culture from peripheral blood) between the group receiving zidovudine and the group receiving placebo. Of 363 infants evaluated in the study, the estimated risk of HIV infection was 8.3% in the group receiving zidovudine and 25.5% in the placebo group, a relative reduction in transmission risk of 67.5%.

Zidovudine was well tolerated by mothers and infants. There was no difference in pregnancy-related adverse events between the treatment groups. The mean difference in hemoglobin values was less than 1.0 g/dL for infants receiving zidovudine compared to infants receiving placebo. Infants did not require transfusion and hemoglobin values spontaneously returned to normal within 6 weeks after completion of therapy with zidovudine. The long-term consequences of in utero and infant exposure to zidovudine are unknown.

Combination Therapy with zidovudine and zalcitabine: Zidovudine in combination with zalcitabine is indicated for the treatment of selected patients with advanced HIV disease (CD4 cell count ≤300 cells/mm³). In patients without prior exposure to zidovudine, this indication is based on greater increases in CD4 cell counts that were maintained longer for patients treated with combination therapy as compared to monotherapy with zidovudine. In patients with no prior exposure to zidovudine, there have been no studies showing clinical benefit from combination therapy compared to zidovudine alone.

Contraindications: Patients who have potentially life-threatening allergic reactions to any of the components of the formulations.

Warnings: Bone Marrow Suppression: Zidovudine should be used with extreme caution in patients who have bone marrow compromise evidenced by granulocyte count <1 000 cells/mm³ or hemoglobin <9.5 g/dL. In all of the placebo-controlled studies, but most frequently in patients with advanced symptomatic disease, anemia and granulocytopenia were the most significant adverse events observed (see Adverse Effects). There have been reports of pancytopenia associated with the use of zidovudine, which was reversible in most instances after discontinuation of the drug.

Myopathy: Myopathy and myositis with pathological changes similar to that produced by HIV disease have been associated with prolonged use of zidovudine.

Lactic Acidosis/Severe Hepatomegaly with Steatosis: Rare occurrences of lactic acidosis in the absence of hypoxemia, and severe hepatomegaly with steatosis have been reported with the use of antiretroviral nucleoside analogues, including zidovudine and zalcitabine, and are potentially fatal; it is not known whether these events are causally related to the use of these drugs. Lactic acidosis should be considered whenever a patient receiving therapy with zidovudine develops unexplained tachypnea, dyspnea, or fall in serum bicarbonate level. Under these circumstances, therapy with zidovudine should be suspended until the diagnosis of lactic acidosis has been excluded. Caution should be exercised when administering zidovudine to any patient, particularly obese women, with hepatomegaly, hepatitis, or other known risk factors for liver disease. These patients should be followed closely while on therapy with zidovudine. The significance of elevated aminotransferase levels (suggesting hepatic injury) in HIV-infected patients prior to starting zidovudine or while on zidovudine is unclear. Treatment with zidovudine should be suspended in the setting of rapidly elevating aminotransferase levels, progressive hepatomegaly, or metabolic/lactic acidosis of unknown etiology.

Other Serious Adverse Reactions: Several serious adverse events have been reported with use of zidovudine in clinical practice. Reports of pancreatitis, sensitization reactions (including anaphylaxis in one patient), vasculitis, and seizures have been rare. These adverse events, except for sensitization, have also been associated with HIV disease. Changes in skin and nail pigmentation have been associated with the use of zidovudine.

Coadministration of zidovudine with other drugs metabolized by glucuronidation should be avoided because the toxicity of either drug may be potentiated (see Precautions, Drug Interactions).

The full safety and efficacy profile of zidovudine has not been defined, particularly in regard to prolonged use and especially in HIV-infected individuals who have less advanced disease. The incidence of adverse reactions appears to increase with disease progression, and patients should be monitored carefully, especially as disease progression occurs.

Combination Therapy with zidovudine and zalcitabine: At present, there are no results from controlled studies evaluating the effect of combined use of zidovudine and zalcitabine on the clinical progression of HIV infections such as survival or the incidence of opportunistic infections.

In patients who have shown clinical or immunologic deterioration, consideration should be given to the use of alternative antiretroviral therapy.

The major clinical toxicities of zalcitabine are peripheral neuropathy and much less frequently pancreatitis. Toxicities associated with zidovudine monotherapy are likely to occur in patients treated with combined zidovudine and zalcitabine therapy. It is recommended that physicians refer to the product monograph for zalcitabine before prescribing combination therapy with zidovudine and zalcitabine.

Precautions: General: Zidovudine is eliminated from the body primarily by renal excretion following metabolism in the liver (glucuronidation). In patients with severely impaired renal function, dosage reduction is recommended (see Pharmacology and Dosage). Although very little data are available, patients with severely impaired hepatic function may be at greater risk of toxicity.

Infancy: A positive test for HIV-antibody in children under 15 months of age may represent passively acquired maternal antibodies, rather than an active antibody response to infection in the infant. Thus, the presence of HIV-antibody in a child less than 15 months of age must be interpreted with caution, especially in the asymptomatic infant. Auxiliary diagnostic tests may be required to confirm infection in such children.

Children: See Indications, Adverse Effects and Dosage. The pharmacokinetics of zidovudine in pediatric patients greater than 3 months of age is similar to that of zidovudine in adult patients.

Pregnancy: A randomized, double-blind, placebo-controlled trial was conducted in HIV-infected pregnant women to determine the utility of zidovudine for the prevention of maternal-fetal HIV-transmission. Congenital abnormalities occurred with similar frequency between infants born to mothers who received zidovudine and infants born to mothers who received placebo. Abnormalities were either problems in embryogenesis (prior to 14 weeks) or were recognized on ultrasound before or immediately after initiation of study drug.

Pregnant women considering the use of zidovudine during pregnancy for prevention of HIV-transmission to their infants should be advised that transmission may still occur in some cases despite therapy. The long-term consequences of in utero and infant exposure to zidovudine are unknown. The long-term effects of early or short-term use of zidovudine in pregnant women are also unknown.

Antiretroviral Pregnancy Registry: To monitor maternal-fetal outcomes of pregnant women exposed to zidovudine, an Antiretroviral Pregnancy Registry has been established. Physicans are encouraged to register patients by calling 1-800-668-6051.

Lactation: It is not known whether zidovudine is excreted in human milk or whether zidovudine reduces the potential for transmission of HIV in breast milk. Lactating mice administered zidovudine (200 mg/kg intraperitoneally) were found to have milk concentrations of zidovudine 5 times the corresponding serum zidovudine concentration. Milk concentrations of zidovudine declined at a slower rate than serum zidovudine concentrations.

It is advisable to caution mothers against breast-feeding to avoid postnatal transmission of HIV to a child who may not yet be infected.

Drug Interactions: Ganciclovir: Use of zidovudine in combination with ganciclovir increases the risk of hematologic toxicities in some patients with advanced HIV disease. Should the use of this combination become necessary in the treatment of patients with HIV disease, dose reduction or interruption of one or both agents may be necessary to minimize hematologic toxicity. Hematologic parameters, including hemoglobin, hematocrit, and white blood cell count with differential, should be monitored frequently in all patients receiving this combination.

Interferon-alpha: Hematologic toxicities have also been seen when zidovudine is used concomitantly with interferon-alpha. As with the concomitant use of zidovudine and ganciclovir, dose reduction or interruption of one or both agents may be necessary, and hematologic parameters should be monitored frequently.

Bone Marrow Suppressive Agents/Cytotoxic Agents: Coadministration of zidovudine with drugs that are cytotoxic or which interfere with RBC/WBC number or function (e.g., dapsone, flucytosine, vincristine, vinblastine, or adriamycin) may increase the risk of hematologic toxicity.

Probenecid: Limited data suggest that probenecid may increase zidovudine levels by inhibiting glucuronidation and/or reducing renal excretion of zidovudine. Some patients who have used zidovudine concomitantly with probenecid have developed flu-like symptoms consisting of myalgia, malaise, and/or fever and maculopapular rash.

Phenytoin: Phenytoin plasma levels have been reported to be low in some patients receiving zidovudine, while in one case a high level was documented. However, in a pharmacokinetic interaction study in which 12 HIV-positive volunteers received a single 300 mg phenytoin dose alone and during steady-state zidovudine conditions (200 mg every 4 hours), no change in phenytoin kinetics was observed. Although not designed to optimally assess the effect of phenytoin on zidovudine kinetics, a 30% decrease in oral zidovudine clearance was observed with phenytoin.

Methadone: In a pharmacokinetic study of 9 HIV-positive patients receiving methadone-maintenance (30 to 90 mg daily) concurrent with 200 mg of zidovudine every 4 hours, no changes were observed in the pharmacokinetics of methadone upon initiation of therapy with zidovudine and after 14 days of treatment with zidovudine. No adjustments in methadone-maintenance requirements were reported. However, plasma levels of zidovudine were elevated in some patients while

Retrovir (AZT) (cont'd)

remaining unchanged in others. The exact mechanism and clinical significance of these data are unknown.

Fluconazole: Preliminary data suggest that fluconazole interferes with the oral clearance and metabolism of zidovudine. In a pharmacokinetic interaction study in which 12 HIV-positive men received zidovudine alone and in combination with fluconazole, increases in the mean peak serum concentration (79%), AUC (70%) and half-life (38%) were observed at steady state. The clinical significance of this interaction is unknown.

Other Nucleoside Analogues: Some experimental nucleoside analogues which are being evaluated in HIV-infected patients may affect RBC/WBC number or function and may increase the potential for hematologic toxicity of zidovudine. Some experimental nucleoside analogues affecting DNA replication, such as ribavirin, antagonize the in vitro antiviral activity of zidovudine against HIV and thus, concomitant use of such drugs should be avoided.

Other Agents: Some drugs such as trimethoprim-sulfamethoxazole, pyrimethamine, and acyclovir may be necessary for the management or prevention of opportunistic infections. In the placebo-controlled trial in patients with advanced HIV disease, increased toxicity was not detected with limited exposure to these drugs. However, there is one published report of neurotoxicity (profound lethargy) associated with concomitant use of zidovudine and acyclovir. Preliminary data from a drug interaction study (n=10) suggest that coadministration of 200 mg zidovudine and 600 mg rifampin decreases the area under the plasma concentration curve by an average of 48%±34%. However, the effect of once daily dosing of rifampin on multiple daily doses of zidovudine is unknown.

Adverse Effects: Adults: The frequency and severity of adverse events associated with the use of zidovudine in adults are greater in patients with more advanced infection at the time of initiation of therapy.

Anemia and Granulocytopenia: In all of the placebo-controlled studies, but most frequently in patients with advanced symptomatic HIV disease, anemia and granulocytopenia were the most significant adverse events observed.

Significant anemia most commonly occurred after 4 to 6 weeks of therapy and in many cases required dose adjustment, discontinuation of zidovudine and/or blood transfusions. Frequent blood counts are strongly recommended in patients with advanced HIV disease taking zidovudine. For asymptomatic HIV-infected individuals and patients with early HIV disease, most of whom have better marrow reserve, blood counts may be obtained less frequently, depending upon the patient's overall status. If anemia or granulocytopenia develops, dosage adjustments may be necessary (see Dosage).

Table I summarizes the relative incidence of hematologic adverse events observed in clinical studies by severity of HIV disease present at the start of treatment.

Other Adverse Events (Advanced HIV Disease): The anemia reported in patients with advanced HIV disease receiving zidovudine appeared to be the result of impaired erythrocyte maturation as evidenced by macrocytosis while on drug. Although mean platelet counts in patients receiving zidovudine were significantly increased compared to mean baseline values, thrombocytopenia did occur in some of these patients with advanced disease. Twelve percent of patients receiving zidovudine compared to 5% of patients receiving placebo had >50% decreases from baseline platelet count. Mild drug-associated elevations in total bilirubin levels have been reported as an uncommon occurrence in patients treated for asymptomatic HIV infection. The HIV-infected adults participating in these clinical trials often had baseline symptoms and signs of HIV disease and/or experienced adverse events at some time during the study. It was often difficult to distinguish adverse events possibly associated with administration of zidovudine from underlying signs of HIV disease or intercurrent illnesses.

Table II summarizes clinical adverse events or symptoms which occurred in at least 5% of all patients with advanced HIV disease treated with 1 500 mg/day of zidovudine in the original placebo-controlled study. Of the items listed in the table, only severe headache, nausea, insomnia and myalgia were reported at a significantly greater rate in patients receiving zidovudine.

Table II—Retrovir (AZT)

Percentage (%) of Patients with Clinical Events in the Advanced HIV Disease Study

Adverse Event	**Retrovir (AZT) 1 500 mg/day* %(n=144)**	**Placebo %(n=137)**
Body as a Whole		
Asthenia	19	18
Diaphoresis	5	4
Fever	16	12
Headache	42	37
Malaise	8	7
Gastrointestinal		
Anorexia	11	8
Diarrhea	12	18
Dyspepsia	5	4
Gastrointestinal pain	20	19
Nausea	46	18
Vomiting	6	3
Musculoskeletal		
Myalgia	8	2
Nervous		
Dizziness	6	4
Insomnia	5	1
Paresthesia	6	3
Somnolence	8	9
Respiratory		
Dyspnea	5	3
Skin		
Rash	17	15
Special Senses		
Taste Perversion	5	8

*The currently recommended dose is 500 to 600 mg daily.

Table I—Retrovir (AZT)

Relative Incidence of Hematologic Adverse Events

Asymptomatic HIV Infection Study (n=1 338)	**Granulocytopenia (<750 cells/mm³)** Retrovir (AZT) 1 500 mg/day[a]	Retrovir (AZT) 500 mg/day	Placebo	**Anemia (Hgb<8g/dL)** Retrovir (AZT) 1 500 mg/day[a]	Retrovir (AZT) 500 mg/day	Placebo
CD4≤500	6.4% (n=457)	1.8%[b] (n=453)	1.6% (n=428)	6.4% (n=457)	1.1%[b] (n=453)	0.2% (n=428)
Early Symptomatic HIV Disease Study (n=713)	**Granulocytopenia (<750 cells/mm³)** Retrovir (AZT) 1 200 mg/day[a]	Placebo		**Anemia (Hgb<8g/dL)** Retrovir (AZT) 1 200 mg/day[a]	Placebo	
CD4>200	4%(n=361)	1%(n=352)		4%(n=361)	0%(n=352)	
Advanced Symptomatic HIV Disease Study (n=281)	**Granulocytopenia (<750 cells/mm³)** Retrovir (AZT) 1 500 mg/day[a]	Placebo		**Anemia (Hgb<7.5g/dL)** Retrovir (AZT) 1 500 mg/day[a]	Placebo	
CD4>200	10%(n=30)[b]	3%(n=30)		3%(n=30)[b]	0%(n=30)	
CD4≤200	47%(n=114)	10%(n=107)		29%(n=114)	5%(n=107)	
Advanced Symptomatic HIV Disease Dose Comparison Study (n=524)	**Granulocytopenia (<750 cells/mm³)** Retrovir (AZT) 1 200 mg/day[a]	600 mg/day		**Anemia (Hgb<8.0g/dL)** Retrovir (AZT) 1 200 mg/day[a]	600 mg/day	
CD4≤200	51%(n=262)	37%(n=262)		39%(n=262)	29%(n=262)	

[a]The currently recommended dose is 500 to 600 mg/day.
[b]Not statistically significant compared to placebo.

Clinical adverse events which occurred in less than 5% of all adult patients treated with 1 500 mg/day of zidovudine in the advanced HIV study are listed below. Since many of these adverse events were seen in placebo-treated patients as well as patients treated with zidovudine, their possible relationship to the drug is unknown.

Body as a Whole: body odor, chills, edema of the lip, flu syndrome, hyperalgesia, back pain, chest pain, lymphadenopathy.

Cardiovascular: vasodilation.

Gastrointestinal: constipation, dysphagia, edema of the tongue, eructation, flatulence, bleeding gums, rectal hemorrhage, mouth ulcer.

Musculoskeletal: arthralgia, muscle spasm, tremor, twitch.

Nervous: anxiety, confusion, depression, emotional lability, nervousness, syncope, loss of mental acuity, vertigo.

Respiratory: cough, epistaxis, pharyngitis, rhinitis, sinusitis, hoarseness.

Skin: acne, pruritus, urticaria.

Special Senses: amblyopia, hearing loss, photophobia.

Urogenital: dysuria, polyuria, urinary frequency, urinary hesitancy.

Other Adverse Events (Early Symptomatic/Asymptomatic HIV Disease): All events of a severe or life-threatening nature were monitored for adults in the placebo controlled studies in early HIV disease and asymptomatic HIV infection. Data concerning the occurrence of additional signs or symptoms were also collected. No distinction was made between events possibly associated with the administration of the study medication and those due to the underlying disease. Tables III and IV summarize all those events reported significantly more frequently by patients receiving zidovudine in these studies.

Table III—Retrovir (AZT)

Percentage (%) of Patients with Clinical Events in the Early HIV Disease Study

Adverse Event	**Retrovir (AZT) 1 200 mg/day* (n=361) %**	**Placebo (n=352) %**
Body as a Whole		
Asthenia	69	62
Gastrointestinal		
Dyspepsia	6	1
Nausea	61	41
Vomiting	25	13

* The currently recommended dose is 500 to 600 mg daily.

Table IV—Retrovir (AZT)

Percentage (%) of Patients with Clinical Events[a] in an Asymptomatic HIV Infection Study

Adverse Event	**Retrovir (AZT) 1 500 mg/day[b] (n=457) %**	**Retrovir (AZT) 500 mg/day (n=453) %**	**Placebo (n=428) %**
Body as a Whole			
Asthenia	10.1	8.6[c]	5.8
Headache	58.0[c]	62.5	52.6
Malaise	55.6	53.2	44.9
Gastrointestinal			
Anorexia	19.3	20.1	10.5
Constipation	8.1	6.4[c]	3.5
Nausea	57.3	51.4	29.9
Vomiting	16.4	17.2	9.8
Nervous			
Dizziness	20.8	17.9[c]	15.2

[a]Reported in ≥5% of study population.
[b]The currently recommended dose is 500 to 600 mg/day.
[c]Not statistically significant versus placebo.

Several serious adverse events have been reported with the use of zidovudine in clinical practice. Myopathy and myositis with pathological changes similar to that produced by HIV disease have been associated with prolonged use of zidovudine. Reports of hepatomegaly with steatosis, hepatitis, pancreatitis, lactic acidosis, sensitization reactions (including anaphylaxis in one patient), hyperbilirubinemia, vasculitis, and seizures have been rare. These adverse events, except for sensitization, have also been associated with HIV disease. A single case of macular edema has been reported with the use of zidovudine. Changes in skin and nail pigmentation have been associated with the use of zidovudine (see Warnings).

Combination Therapy with Zidovudine and Zalcitabine: Only limited safety data are available on the combined use of zidovudine with zalcitabine. The major toxicities of zalcitabine are peripheral neuropathy and, less frequently, pancreatitis.

Table V includes clinical adverse events in the combination zalcitabine and zidovudine Protocol N3447/ACTG 106. Only 8 patients were treated with the recommended combination regimen.

Table V—Retrovir (AZT)

Number and Percentage (%) of Patients with Clinical Adverse Experiences Occurring in >3% of Patients Considered Possibly or Probably Related to Study Drug

'HIVID' + Zidovudine Combination Trial Pooled Concomitant Regimens	**N3447/ACTG 106* No Prior Zidovudine n=47 (%)**	
Body System Adverse Event	**Mild/ Moderate/ Severe**	**Moderate/ Severe**
Peripheral Neuropathy	12 (25.5)	2 (4.3)
Gastrointestinal		
Nausea	17 (36.2)	4 (8.5)
Oral Ulcers	13 (27.7)	2 (4.3)
Abdominal pain	10 (21.3)	4 (8.5)
Diarrhea	7 (14.9)	5 (10.6)
Vomiting	7 (14.9)	1 (2.1)
Anorexia	6 (12.8)	3 (6.4)
Constipation	3 (6.4)	1 (2.1)
Skin and Appendages		
Pruritus	7 (14.9)	2 (4.3)
Rash	7 (14.9)	1 (2.1)
Erythematous rash	3 (6.4)	1 (2.1)
Night sweats	3 (6.4)	1 (2.1)
Maculopapular rash	2 (4.3)	1 (2.1)
Follicular rash	2 (4.3)	0 (0.0)
Central and Peripheral NS		
Headache	18 (38.3)	4 (8.5)
Musculoskelatal		
Myalgia	7 (14.9)	1 (2.1)
Arthralgia	4 (8.5)	1 (2.1)
Body as a Whole		
Fatigue	16 (34.0)	4 (8.5)
Fever	7 (14.9)	1 (2.1)
Rigors	4 (8.5)	1 (2.1)
Chest pain	3 (6.4)	1 (2.1)
Weight decrease	3 (6.4)	2 (4.3)
Respiratory		
Pharyngitis	4 (8.5)	1 (2.1)

* Median duration of treatment ranged from 22 to 92 weeks among the arms.

Children: Anemia and Granulocytopenia: The incidences of anemia and granulocytopenia among children with advanced HIV disease receiving zidovudine occurred with similar incidence to that reported for adults with AIDS or advanced ARC (see above). Table VI summarizes the occurrence of anemia (Hgb<7.5 g/dL) and granulocytopenia (<750/mm³) among 124 children receiving zidovudine for a mean of 267 days (range 3 to 855 days).

Table VI—Retrovir (AZT)

Anemia and Granulocytopenia in Children

Advanced Pediatric HIV Disease	**Granulocytopenia (<750 cells/mm³)**		**Anemia (Hgb<7.5 g/dL)**	
	n	%	n	%
(n=124)	48	39	28*	23

* Twenty-two children received one or more transfusions due to a decline in hemoglobin to <7.5 g/dL; an additional 15 children were transfused for hemoglobin levels>7.5 g/dL. Fifty-nine percent of the patients transfused had a pre-study history of anemia or transfusion requirement.

Management of neutropenia and anemia included, in some cases, dose modification and/or blood product transfusions. In the open-label studies, 17% had their dose modified (generally a reduction in dose by 30%) due to anemia, and 25% had their dose modified (temporary discontinuation or reduction by 30%) for neutropenia. Four children had zidovudine permanently discontinued because of neutropenia.

Macrocytosis was observed among the majority of children enrolled in the studies.

Other Adverse Events (Children): The clinical adverse events reported among adult recipients of zidovudine may also occur in children.

In the open-label studies involving 124 children, 16 different clinical adverse events were reported by 24 children. No event was reported by more than 5.6% of the study populations. Due to the open-label design of the studies, it was difficult to determine possible events related to the use of zidovudine versus disease-related events. Therefore, all clinical events reported as associated with therapy with zidovudine or of unknown relationship to therapy with zidovudine are presented in Table VII.

Table VII—Retrovir (AZT)

Percentage (%) of Pediatric Patients with Clinical Events in Open Label Studies

Adverse Event	**n**	**%**
Body as a Whole		
Fever	4	3.2
Phlebitis*/Bacteremia	2	1.6
Headache	2	1.6
Gastrointestinal		
Nausea	1	0.8
Vomiting	6	4.8
Abdominal Pain	4	3.2
Diarrhea	1	0.8
Weight Loss	1	0.8
Nervous		
Insomnia	3	2.4
Nervousness/Irritability	2	1.6
Decreased Reflexes	7	5.6
Seizure	1	0.8
Cardiovascular		
Left Ventricular Dilation	1	0.8
Cardiomyopathy	1	0.8
S_3 Gallop	1	0.8
Congestive Heart Failure	1	0.8
Generalized Edema	1	0.8
ECG Abnormality	3	2.4
Urogenital		
Hematuria/Viral Cystitis	1	0.8

* Peripheral vein i.v. catheter site.

Prevention of Maternal-Fetal Transmission of HIV: In a randomized, double-blind, placebo-controlled trial in HIV-infected women and their infants conducted to determine the utility of zidovudine for the prevention of maternal-fetal HIV transmission, zidovudine syrup at 2 mg/kg was administered every 6 hours for 6 weeks to infants beginning within 12 hours after birth. The most commonly reported adverse experiences were anemia (hemoglobin <9.0 g/dL) and neutropenia (<1 000 cells/mm³). Anemia occurred in 22% of the infants who received zidovudine and in 12% of the infants who received placebo. The mean difference in hemoglobin values was less than 1.0 g/dL for infants receiving zidovudine compared to infants receiving placebo. No infants with anemia required transfusion and all hemoglobin values spontaneously returned to normal within 6 weeks after completion of therapy with zidovudine. Neutropenia was reported with similar frequency in the group that received zidovudine (21%) and in the group that received placebo (27%). The long-term consequences of in utero and infant exposure to zidovudine are unknown.

Overdose: Symptoms and Treatment: Cases of acute overdose in both children and adults have been reported with doses up to 50 g. None were fatal.

The only consistent finding in these cases of overdose was spontaneous or induced nausea and vomiting. Hematological changes were transient and not severe. Some patients experienced nonspecific CNS symptoms such as headache, dizziness, drowsiness, lethargy, and confusion. One report of a grand mal seizure possibly attributable to zidovudine occurred in a 35-year-old male 3 hours after ingesting 36 g of zidovudine. No other cause could be identified. All patients recovered without permanent sequelae. Hemodialysis and peritoneal dialysis appear to have a negligible effect on the removal of zidovudine while elimination of its primary metabolite, GZDV is enhanced.

Dosage: Capsules and Syrup: Adults: Asymptomatic HIV Infection: The recommended dose for adults is 100 mg (one 100 mg capsule or 10 mL of syrup) administered orally every 4 hours while awake for a total daily dose of 500 mg.

Symptomatic HIV Disease: The recommended dose for adults is 100 mg (one 100 mg capsule or 10 mL of syrup) administered orally every 4 hours around the clock for a total daily dose of 600 mg.

The effectiveness of the oral dose compared to higher dosing regimens in improving the neurologic dysfunction associated with HIV disease is unknown. A small randomized study has found a greater effect of higher doses of zidovudine on improvement of neurological symptoms in patients with preexisting neurological disease.

Children: The recommended oral dose in children 3 months to 12 years of age is 180 mg/m² every 6 hours (720 mg/m²/day). This dose is equivalent to 1 200 mg/day in adults. Do not exceed 200 mg for any individual dose.

I.V. Infusion: Adults: The recommended dose is 1 to 2 mg/kg administered as a 1 hour infusion every 4 hours around the clock (6 times daily). Patients should receive i.v. zidovudine only until oral therapy can be administered.

The i.v. dosing regimen equivalent to the oral administration of 100 mg every 4 hours is approximately 1 mg/kg i.v. every 4 hours.

Zidovudine injection is administered i.v. at a constant rate over 1 hour. Rapid infusion or bolus injection should be avoided. Zidovudine injection should not be given i.m.

The effectiveness of the i.v. dose compared to higher dosing regimens in improving the neurologic dysfunction associated with HIV disease is unknown. A small randomized study has found a greater effect of higher doses of zidovudine on improvement of neurological symptoms in patients with preexisting neurological disease.

Children: The recommended dose of zidovudine i.v. injection in children 3 months to 12 years of age is 120 mg/m² every 6 hours, infused over 1 hour (480 mg/m²/day). Do not exceed 160 mg for any individual dose.

Prevention of Maternal-Fetal HIV Transmission: The recommended dosing regimen for administration to pregnant women (>14 weeks of pregnancy) and their newborn infants is:

Maternal Dosing: 100 mg orally 5 times/day until the start of labor. During labor and delivery, i.v. zidovudine should be administered at 2 mg/kg (total body weight) over 1 hour followed by a continuous i.v. infusion at 1 mg/kg/hour (total body weight) until clamping of the umbilical cord.

Infant Dosing: 2 mg/kg orally every 6 hours starting within 12 hours after birth and continuing through 6 weeks of age. Infants unable to receive oral dosing may be administered zidovudine i.v. at 1.5 mg/kg, infused over 30 minutes, every 6 hours. See Precautions if hepatic disease or renal insufficiency is present.

Combination Therapy With Zidovudine and Zalcitabine: For the treatment of adult patients with advanced HIV infection (CD4 cell count ≤300 cells/mm³), the daily recommended combination regimen is 200 mg of zidovudine administered concomitantly with one 0.75 mg tablet of zalcitabine every 8 hours (600 mg zidovudine total daily dose and 2.25 mg zalcitabine total daily dose).

Monitoring of Patients: Hematologic toxicities appear to be related to pretreatment bone marrow reserve and to dose and duration of therapy. In patients with poor bone marrow reserve, particularly in patients with advanced symptomatic HIV disease, frequent monitoring of hematologic indices is recommended to detect serious anemia or granulocytopenia (see Adverse Effects). In patients who experience hematologic toxicity, reduction in hemoglobin may occur as early as 2 to 4 weeks, and granulocytopenia usually occurs after 6 to 8 weeks.

Patients treated with zidovudine should be under close clinical observation to manage potential opportunistic infections associated with HIV disease. Prompt recognition of infection or toxicities and appropriate management is required.

Dose Adjustment: Significant anemia (hemoglobin of <7.5 g/dL or reduction of >25% of baseline) and/or significant granulocytopenia (granulocyte count of <750 cells/mm³ or reduction of >50% from baseline) may require a dose interruption until evidence of marrow recovery is observed (see Adverse Effects). In patients who develop significant anemia, dose modification does not necessarily eliminate the need for transfusion.

For less severe anemia or granulocytopenia, a reduction in daily dose may be adequate. If marrow recovery occurs following dose modification, gradual increases in dose may be appropriate depending on hematologic indices and patient tolerance.

In end stage disease patients maintained on hemodialysis or peritoneal dialysis, recommended dosing is 100 mg every 6 to 8 hours for oral administration and 1 mg/kg every 6 to 8 hours for i.v. infusion (see Pharmacology, Pharmacokinetics).

There are insufficient data to recommend dose adjustment of zidovudine in patients with impaired hepatic function.

Combination Therapy with Zidovudine and Zalcitabine: For recipients of combination therapy with zidovudine and zalcitabine, dose adjustments for either drug should be based on the known toxicity profile of the individual drugs. For toxicities more likely to be associated with zalcitabine (i.e., peripheral neuropathy, severe oral ulcers), zalcitabine should be interrupted or the dose reduced.

Retrovir (AZT) (cont'd)

For patients experiencing toxicities more likely to be associated with zidovudine (i.e., anemia, granulocytopenia), zidovudine should be interrupted or the dose reduced first.

For any interruption of zalcitabine and especially if zalcitabine is permanently discontinued, the zidovudine dosage should be adjusted from 200 mg every 8 hours to 100 mg every 4 hours.

For severe toxicities or toxicities in which the causative drug is unclear, or those persisting after dose interruption or reduction of one drug, the other drug should also be interrupted or the dose reduced.

Method of Preparation of Retrovir (AZT) Injection: **Retrovir (AZT) injection must be diluted prior to administration.** The calculated dose should be removed from the 20 mL vial and added to a recommended diluent to achieve a concentration no greater than 4 mg/mL. Retrovir (AZT) injection does not contain preservatives. Unused portion of the vial should be discarded.

Recommended Diluents: 5% Dextrose Injection, 0.9% Sodium Chloride Injection, 5% Dextrose Injection and 0.45% Sodium Chloride Injection, Lactated Ringer's Injection, 5% Dextrose and Lactated Ringer's Injection.

The diluted solution should be administered within 8 hours if stored at 25°C or 24 hours if refrigerated at 2 to 8°C to minimize potential administration of a microbially contaminated solution.

Parenteral drug products should be inspected visually for particulate matter and discoloration prior to administration whenever solution and container permit. Should either be observed, the solution should be discarded and fresh solution prepared.

Incompatibility: Admixture in biologic or colloidal fluids (e.g., blood products, protein solutions) is not recommended.

Information for the Patient: See Blue Section—Information for the Patient "Retrovir (AZT)".

Supplied: Capsules: Each gelatin capsule, with a white opaque cap and body with dark blue band, printed with 'Wellcome' and Unicorn logo on cap and 'Y9C' and '100' on body, contains: zidovudine 100 mg. Nonmedicinal ingredients: cornstarch, magnesium stearate, microcrystalline cellulose, and sodium starch glycolate. Capsule shell: gelatin and imprinted with edible black ink. The blue band around the capsule contains gelatin and indigotine. Bottles of 100. Store at room temperature between 15 and 25°C. Protect from light and moisture.

I.V. Injection: Each mL of solution contains: zidovudine 10 mg in water for injection. Hydrochloric acid or sodium hydroxide may have been added to adjust pH to approximately 5.5. Preservative-free. Single use amber vials of 20 mL, boxes of 10. Store at room temperature between 15 and 25°C. Protect from light. Do not freeze.

Syrup: Each 5 mL of colorless to pale yellow, strawberry-flavored syrup contains: zidovudine 50 mg. Nonmedicinal ingredients: candied sugar flavor, citric acid, glycerin, strawberry flavor and sucrose. Sodium benzoate (0.2%) is added as a preservative and sodium hydroxide may have been added to adjust pH. Bottles of 240 mL. Store at 15 to 25°C. Protect from light.

(Shown in Product Recognition Section)

REVERSA® AHA Preparations

Dermtek

Glycolic Acid

Exfoliant

Supplied: Cream: Each g of water washable cream contains: glycolic acid 5 and 8%. Jars of 60 g.

Eye/Lip Contour: Each g of cream contains: glycolic acid 2%. The vehicle is perfume-free, contains vitamin E and panthenol. Tubes of 15 g.

Gel Cleanser: Each mL of water-soluble and perfume-free gel contains: nonirritating cleansing and moisturizing ingredients: glycerin, propylene glycol, sodium hyaluronate and hydrolyzed glycosaminoglycans, nonoxynol 9. Oil- and alcohol-free. Bottles of 130 mL with pump.

HQ: Each g of hydroalcoholic gel contains: hydroquinone USP 3% w/w. The vehicle contains 10% glycolic acid. Bottles of 30 mL with pump.

Lotion: Each mL of water washable lotion contains: glycolic acid 10%. Bottles of 175 mL.

Solution: Each mL of clear, hydroalcoholic solution contains: glycolic acid 8%. Bottles of 120 mL.

REVIA® Ⓟ

DuPont Pharma

Naltrexone HCl

Opioid Antagonist

Pharmacology: Pharmacodynamic Actions: Naltrexone is a pure opioid antagonist. It markedly attenuates or completely blocks, reversibly, the subjective effects of i.v. administered opioids. [In this context, the term opioid is used to describe 1) classic morphine-like agonists and 2) analgesics possessing agonist and antagonist activity (e.g., butorphanol, nalbuphine and pentazocine).]

When coadministered with morphine, on a chronic basis, naltrexone blocks the physical dependence to morphine and presumably other opioids. Naltrexone has few, if any, intrinsic actions besides its opioid blocking properties. However, it does produce some pupillary constriction, by an unknown mechanism.

While the mechanism of action is not fully understood, the preponderance of evidence suggests that naltrexone blocks the effects of opioids by competitive binding (i.e., analogous to competitive inhibition of enzymes) at opioid receptors. This makes the blockade produced potentially surmountable, but overcoming full naltrexone blockade by administration of very high doses of opiates has resulted in excessive symptoms of histamine release in experimental subjects.

The mechanism of action of naltrexone in the treatment of alcoholism is not understood; however, involvement of the endogenous opioid system is suggested by preclinical data. Naltrexone, an opioid receptor antagonist, competitively binds to such receptors and may block the effects of endogenous opioids. Opioid antagonists have been shown to reduce alcohol consumption by animals, and naltrexone has been shown to reduce alcohol consumption in clinical studies.

Naltrexone is not aversive therapy and does not cause a disulfiram-like reaction either as a result of opiate use or ethanol ingestion.

The administration of naltrexone is not associated with the development of tolerance or dependence.

In subjects physically dependent on opioids, naltrexone will precipitate withdrawal symptomatology.

Clinical studies indicate that 50 mg of naltrexone will block the pharmacologic effects of 25 mg of i.v. administered heroin for periods as long as 24 hours. Other data suggest that doubling the dose of naltrexone provides blockade for 48 hours, and tripling the dose of naltrexone provides blockade for about 72 hours.

Pharmacokinetics/Bioavailability: Following oral administration, naltrexone undergoes rapid and nearly complete absorption with approximately 96% of the dose absorbed from the gastrointestinal tract. Although well absorbed orally, naltrexone is subject to extensive "first-pass" hepatic metabolism with an oral bioavailability estimate ranging from 5 to 40%. The activity of naltrexone is believed to be due to both parent and the 6-β-naltrexol metabolite.

Following the administration of 50 mg naltrexone tablets to 24 healthy adult male volunteers, the C_{max} for naltrexone and its major metabolite, 6-β-naltrexol were 8.6 ng/mL and 99.3 ng/mL, respectively. The maximum concentration (C_{max}) and area under the curve (AUC), for both naltrexone and 6-β-naltrexol are dose proportional over the range of 50 to 200 mg. The time to maximum concentration (T_{max}) is 1 hour for both naltrexone and 6-β-naltrexol. The mean elimination half-life ($T_{1/2}$) values for naltrexone and 6-β-naltrexol are 4 hours and 12.9 hours, respectively. The mean elimination half-life ($T_{1/2}$) and time to maximum concentration (T_{max}) for naltrexone and 6-β-naltrexol are independent of dose.

The volume of distribution for naltrexone following i.v. administration is estimated to be 1 350 L. In vitro tests with human plasma show naltrexone to be 21% bound to plasma protein over the therapeutic dose range.

The systemic clearance (after i.v. administration) of naltrexone approximates 3.5 L/min, which exceeds liver blood flow (~1.35 L/min), and suggests that naltrexone is a highly extracted drug (>98% metabolized) and that extrahepatic sites of drug metabolism exist. The major metabolite of naltrexone is 6-β-naltrexol. Two other minor metabolites are 2-hydroxy-3-methoxy-6-β-naltrexol and 2-hydroxy-3-methyl-naltrexone. Naltrexone and its metabolites are also conjugated to form additional metabolic products. A renal clearance ranging from 30 to 127 mL/min for naltrexone suggests it is primarily cleared by glomerular filtration. A renal clearance of 230 to 369 mL/min for 6-β-naltrexol suggests an additional renal tubular secretory mechanism. Naltrexone and its metabolites are excreted primarily by the kidney (56 to 79% of the dose), with fecal excretion being a minor elimination pathway. The urinary excretion of unchanged naltrexone accounts for less than 2% of an oral dose; urinary excretion of unchanged and conjugated 6-β-naltrexol accounts for approximately 43% of an oral dose. The pharmacokinetic profile of naltrexone suggests that naltrexone and its metabolites undergo enterohepatic recycling.

Adequate studies of naltrexone in patients with severe hepatic or renal impairment have not been conducted; however, a recent preliminary communication stated that naltrexone bioavailability is increased in patients with liver cirrhosis as compared to healthy subjects.

Clinical Trials: Treatment of Narcotic Addiction: Naltrexone has been shown to produce complete blockade of the euphoric effects of opioids in both volunteer and addict populations. When administered by means that enforce compliance, it will produce an effective opioid blockade, but has not been shown to affect the use of cocaine or other nonopioid drugs of abuse.

The drug is reported to be of greatest use in good prognosis narcotic addicts who take the drug as part of a comprehensive occupational rehabilitative program, behavioral contract, or other compliance enhancing protocols.

Alcoholism: The efficacy of naltrexone as an aid to the treatment of alcoholism was tested in placebo-controlled, outpatient, double-blind trials. These studies used a dose of naltrexone 50 mg once daily for 12 weeks as an adjunct to social and psychotherapeutic methods. Patients with psychosis, dementia, and secondary psychiatric diagnosis were excluded from these studies.

In one of these studies, 104 alcohol-dependent patients were randomized to receive either naltrexone 50 mg once daily or placebo. In this study, naltrexone proved superior to placebo in measures of drinking including abstention rates (51 vs 23%), number of drinking days, and relapse rates (31 vs 60%). In a second study with 82 alcohol-dependent patients, the group of patients receiving naltrexone were shown to have lower relapse rates (21 vs 41%), less alcohol craving, and fewer drinking days compared with patients who received placebo.

The clinical use of naltrexone as adjunctive pharmacotherapy for the treatment of alcoholism was also evaluated in a multicentre safety study. This study of 865 individuals with alcoholism included patients with comorbid psychiatric conditions, concomitant medications, polysubstance abuse and HIV disease. Results of this study demonstrated that the side-effect profile of naltrexone appears to be similar in both alcoholic and opioid dependent populations.

Naltrexone was not uniformly helpful to all patients, and the expected effect of the drug is a modest improvement in the outcome of conventional treatment.

Indications: To provide blockade of the pharmacologic effects of exogenously administered opioids as an adjunct to the maintenance of the opioid-free state in detoxified, formerly opioid-dependent individuals. There are no data that demonstrate an unequivocally beneficial effect of naltrexone on the rates of recidivism among detoxified formerly opioid-dependent individuals who self-administer the drug. Naltrexone is expected to have a therapeutic effect only when given under conditions that support continued use of the medication.

Naltrexone is indicated in the treatment of alcohol dependence, as a component of a comprehensive psychotherapeutic or psychological alcoholism counselling program to support abstinence, and reduce the risk of relapse. The efficacy of naltrexone beyond 12 weeks of treatment has not been established.

Contraindications: Patients receiving opioid analgesics. Opioid dependent patients. Patients in acute opioid withdrawal (see Warnings). Any individual who has failed to pass the Narcan challenge (see Dosage). Any individual who has a positive urine screen for opioids. Any individual with a history of sensitivity to naltrexone. It is not known if there is any cross-sensitivity with naloxone or other phenanthrene containing opioids.

Any individual with acute hepatitis or liver failure.

Warnings: Unintended Precipitation of Withdrawal: To prevent occurrence of an acute withdrawal syndrome, or exacerbation of a pre-existing subclinical withdrawal syndrome, patients should remain opioid-free for a minimum of 7 to 10 days before starting naltrexone. Since the absence of an opioid drug in the urine often is not sufficient proof that the patient is opioid-free, a Narcan challenge may be required to minimize the possibility of precipitating a withdrawal reaction following administration of naltrexone. The Narcan challenge test is described in the Dosage Section.

Hepatotoxicity: Naltrexone has the capacity to cause dose related hepatocellular injury. Prior to making a decision to initiate treatment with naltrexone, the physician should establish whether the patient has subclinical liver injury or disease (see Precautions, Laboratory Tests). Naltrexone is contraindicated in acute hepatitis or liver failure, and its use even in patients with evidence of less severe liver disease or a history of recent liver disease must be carefully considered in light of its hepatotoxic potential.

The evidence that identified naltrexone as a hepatotoxin was not obtained in studies involving its use at the doses recommended for opiate blockade, or for treatment of alcohol dependence (50 mg/day). However, the margin of separation between the apparently safe and the hepatotoxic doses appears to be only 5-fold or less.

Patients should be warned of the risk of hepatic injury and advised to stop the use of naltrexone and seek medical attention if they experience symptoms of acute hepatitis.

Evidence of naltrexone's hepatotoxic potential is derived primarily from a placebo controlled study in which naltrexone was administered to obese subjects at a dose approximately 5-fold that recommended for the blockade of opiate receptors (300 mg/day). In the study, 5 of 26 naltrexone recipients developed elevations of serum transaminases (i.e., peak ALT values ranging from a low of 121 to a high of 532, or 3 to 19 times their baseline values) after 3 to 8 weeks of treatment. Although the patients involved were generally clinically asymptomatic and the transaminase levels of all patients on whom follow-up was obtained returned to (or toward) baseline values in a matter of weeks, the lack of any transaminase elevations of similar magnitude in any of the 24 placebo patients in the same study is persuasive evidence that naltrexone is a direct (i.e., not an idiosyncratic) hepatotoxin. This conclusion is also supported by evidence from other placebo controlled studies in which exposure to naltrexone at doses from 1-to 2-fold the amount recommended for the treatment of alcoholism or opiate blockade (50 mg/day) consistently produced more numerous and more significant elevations of serum transaminase than did placebo, and reports of transaminase elevations in 3 of 9 patients with Alzheimer's Disease who received naltrexone (up to 300 mg/day) for 5 to 8 weeks in an open clinical trial have been reported.

Although no cases of hepatic failure due to naltrexone administration have ever been reported, physicians are advised to consider this as a possible risk of treatment and to use the same care in prescribing naltrexone as they would other drugs with the potential for causing hepatic injury.

Self-Administration of Exogenous Opiates: While naltrexone is a potent antagonist with a prolonged pharmacologic effect (24 to 72 hours), the blockade produced by naltrexone is surmountable. This is useful in patients who may require analgesia, but poses a potential risk to individuals who attempt, on their own, to overcome the blockade by administering large amounts of exogenous opioids. Indeed, any attempt by a patient to overcome the antagonism by taking opioids is very dangerous and may lead to a fatal overdose. Injury may arise because the plasma concentration of exogenous opioids attained immediately following their acute administration may be sufficient to overcome the competitive receptor blockade. As a consequence, the patient may be in immediate danger of suffering life-endangering opioid intoxication (e.g., respiratory arrest, circulatory collapse). Also, lesser amounts of exogenous opioids may prove dangerous if they are taken in a manner (i.e., relatively long after the last dose of naltrexone) and in an amount so that they persist in the body longer than effective concentrations of naltrexone and its metabolites. **Patients should be told of the serious consequences of surmounting the opiate blockade (see Information for the Patient).**

Precautions General: Emergency Pain Management in Patients Receiving Fully Blocking Doses of Naltrexone: In an emergency situation in patients receiving fully blocking doses of naltrexone, a suggested plan of management is regional analgesia, conscious sedation with a benzodiazepine, use of nonopioid analgesics or general anesthesia. In a situation requiring analgesia which can only be achieved with opioids, the amount of opioid required may be greater than usual, and the resulting respiratory depression may be deeper and more prolonged. In such circumstances, a rapidly acting opioid analgesic which minimizes the duration of respiratory depression is preferred. The amount of analgesic administered should be titrated to the needs of the patient. No methods to reverse opioid overdose in patients receiving naltrexone have been established by clinical trials. However, the use of the opioid antagonist naloxone, should be considered when attempting reversal.

Additionally, nonreceptor mediated actions may occur (e.g., facial swelling, itching, generalized erythema, presumably due to histamine release). Irrespective of the drug chosen to reverse naltrexone blockade, the patient should be monitored closely by appropriately trained personnel in a hospital setting equipped and staffed for cardiopulmonary resuscitation.

Interference with the Action of Narcotic Containing Drug Product: Patients taking naltrexone may not benefit from opioid containing medicines, such as cough and cold preparations, antidiarrheal preparations, and opioid analgesics. Where a nonopioid containing alternative is available, it should be used.

Actions Suggested when Withdrawal is Accidently Precipitated with Naltrexone: Severe opioid withdrawal syndromes precipitated by the accidental ingestion of naltrexone have been reported in opioid-dependent individuals. Symptoms of withdrawal have usually appeared within 5 minutes of ingestion of naltrexone and have lasted for up to 48 hours. Mental status changes including confusion, somnolence and visual hallucinations have occurred. Significant fluid losses from vomiting and diarrhea have required i.v. fluid administration. In all cases patients were closely monitored and therapy tailored to meet individual requirements.

Hepatic-Renal Failure: Since naltrexone is extensively metabolized by the liver and excreted predominantly in the urine, caution should be observed in administering the drug to patients with impaired hepatic or renal function.

Drug Interactions: Studies to evaluate possible interactions between naltrexone and drugs other than opiates have not been performed. Consequently, caution is advised if the concomitant administration of naltrexone and other drugs is required.

The safety and efficacy of concomitant use of naltrexone and disulfiram is unknown, and the concomitant use of 2 potentially hepatotoxic medications is not ordinarily recommended unless the probable benefits outweigh the known risks.

Lethargy and somnolence have been reported following doses of naltrexone and thioridazine.

Suicide: The risk of suicide is known to be increased in patients with substance abuse with or without concomitant depression. The risk is not abated by treatment with naltrexone (see Adverse Effects).

Laboratory Tests: Tests designed to detect hepatic injury should be obtained prior to initiation of naltrexone therapy and periodically thereafter (see Warnings, Hepatotoxicity).

Periodic testing of all patients after initiation of treatment is critical if the occurrence of naltrexone induced liver damage is to be detected at the earliest possible time. Evaluations, using appropriate batteries of tests to detect liver injury are recommended on a monthly basis during the first 6 months of use; thereafter, clinical judgment about the frequency of monitoring must be relied upon.

Laboratory tests which may be used for the separation and detection of morphine, methadone, or quinine in the urine and with which naltrexone does not interfere include thin-layer, gas-liquid, and high pressure liquid chromatographic methods.

Impairment of Fertility: Naltrexone (100 mg/kg, approximately 140 times the human therapeutic dose) caused a significant increase in pseudopregnancy in the rat. A decrease in the pregnancy rate of mated female rats also occurred. The relevance of these observations to human fertility is not known.

Pregnancy: There are no adequate and well-controlled studies in pregnant women. Naltrexone should be used in pregnancy only when the potential benefits justify the potential risk to the fetus.

Labor and Delivery: It is not known whether naltrexone affects the duration of labor and delivery.

Lactation: It is not known whether naltrexone is excreted in human milk. Because many drugs are excreted in human milk, naltrexone should be administered to a nursing mother only when the potential benefits justify the potential risk to the infant.

Children: The safe use of naltrexone in subjects younger than 18 years of age has not been established.

Adverse Effects: While extensive clinical studies evaluating the use of naltrexone in detoxified, formerly opioid dependent individuals failed to identify any single, serious untoward risk of naltrexone use, placebo controlled studies employing up to 5-fold higher doses of naltrexone (up to 300 mg/day) than that recommended for use in opiate receptor blockade have shown that naltrexone causes hepatocellular injury in 5 of 26 patients exposed at this higher dose (see Warnings and Precautions, Laboratory Tests).

Aside from this finding, however, available evidence does not incriminate naltrexone, used at any dose, as a cause of any other serious untoward event for the patient who is "opioid free". It is critical to recognize that naltrexone can precipitate or exacerbate withdrawal signs and symptoms in any individual who is not completely free of exogenous opioids (see Contraindications, Warnings and Dosage).

Opioid Withdrawal-like Symptoms: Studies in alcoholic populations and in volunteers in clinical pharmacology studies have suggested that a small fraction of patients may experience an opioid withdrawal-like symptom complex consisting of tearfulness, mild nausea, abdominal cramps, restlessness, bone or joint pain, myalgia, and nasal symptoms. This may represent the unmasking of occult opioid use, or it may represent symptoms attributable to naltrexone. A number of alternative dosing patterns have been recommended to try to reduce the frequency of these complaints (see Individualization of Dosage).

Narcotic Addiction: Events Other than Hepatocellular Injury Reported During Clinical Testing: The following adverse reactions have been reported both at baseline and during the naltrexone clinical trials in narcotic addiction at an incidence rate of more than 10%: difficulty sleeping, anxiety, nervousness, abdominal pain/cramps, nausea and/or vomiting, low energy, joint and muscle pain and headache.

The incidence was less than 10% for: loss of appetite, constipation, increased thirst, increased energy, feeling down, irritability, dizziness, skin rash, delayed ejaculation, decreased potency and chills.

The following events occurred in less than 1% of subjects: Respiratory: nasal congestion, itching, rhinorrhea, sneezing, sore throat, excess mucus or phlegm, sinus trouble, heavy breathing, hoarseness, cough, shortness of breath.

Cardiovascular: nose bleeds, phlebitis, edema, increased blood pressure, nonspecific ECG changes, palpitations, tachycardia.

Gastrointestinal: excessive gas, hemorrhoids, diarrhea, ulcer.

Musculoskeletal: painful shoulders, legs or knees, tremors, twitching.

Genitourinary: increased frequency of, or discomfort during urination, increased or decreased sexual interest.

Dermatologic: oily skin, pruritus, acne, athlete's foot, cold sore, alopecia.

Psychiatric: depression, paranoia, fatigue, restlessness, confusion, disorientation, hallucinations, nightmares, bad dreams.

Special Senses: eyes—blurred, burning, light sensitive, swollen, aching, strained; ears—"clogged", aching, tinnitus.

General: increased appetite, weight loss, weight gain, yawning, somnolence, fever, dry mouth, head "pounding", inguinal pain, swollen glands, "side" pains, cold feet, "hot spells".

Other: Depression, suicide, attempted suicide and suicidal ideation have been reported in the postmarketing experience with naltrexone used in the treatment of narcotic dependence. No causal relationship has been demonstrated.

Laboratory Tests: With the exception of liver test abnormalities in investigator studies (see Warnings and Precautions), results of laboratory tests, like adverse reports, have not shown consistent patterns of abnormalities that can be attributed to treatment with naltrexone.

In the trials evaluating naltrexone for the blockade of opiate receptors, abnormal liver function tests and lymphocytosis were the two most common categories of abnormalities reported. These abnormalities are common among populations of parenteral opioid users and alcoholics. As is the case with the untoward events described above, a large proportion of patients had abnormal tests at baseline, further supporting the conclusion that the abnormalities observed are not attributable to naltrexone.

Idiopathic thrombocytopenic purpura was reported in one patient who may have been sensitized to naltrexone in a previous course of treatment with naltrexone. The condition cleared without sequelae after discontinuation of naltrexone and corticosteroid treatment.

Alcoholism: In two randomized, double-blind placebo controlled 12-week trials to evaluate the efficacy of naltrexone as adjunctive treatment of alcohol dependence, a total of 93 patients received naltrexone at a dose of 50 mg once daily. The most common (incidence greater than 10%) adverse events associated with the use of naltrexone in these trials (incidence at least 5% greater than in patients receiving placebo) were: somnolence, nervousness, vomiting, weight decrease, dry mouth and decreased libido. The incidences of adverse events leading to discontinuation of naltrexone in these trials were: vomiting (5%); agitation (2%); insomnia (2%); nervousness (1%); drowsiness (1%); and malaise (1%). Discontinuation rate for headache was 1% for patients on naltrexone and 2% for patients on placebo. No serious adverse events were reported during these 2 trials.

ReVia (cont'd)

In an open label safety study with approximately 570 individuals with alcoholism receiving naltrexone, the following new onset adverse reactions occurred in 2% or more of the patients: nausea (10%); headache (7%); dizziness (4%); nervousness (4%); fatigue (4%); insomnia (3%); vomiting (3%); anxiety (2%); somnolence (2%); dry mouth (2%); dyspepsia (2%).

In an open label safety study with approximately 570 individuals with alcoholism receiving naltrexone, the following adverse events were responsible for discontinuation in ≥ 1% of patients: nausea (6%); headache (3%); dizziness (3%); anxiety (2%); nervousness (2%); fatigue (1%); vomiting (1%); depression (1%); euphoria (1%); mouth dry (1%); insomnia (1%).

Depression (up to 6%), suicidal ideation/attempted suicide (up to 2%) have been reported in individuals on naltrexone, placebo and in concurrent control groups undergoing treatment for alcoholism. Although no causal relationship with naltrexone is suspected, physicians should be aware that treatment with naltrexone does not reduce the risk of suicide in these patients (see Precautions).

Drug Abuse and Dependence: Naltrexone is a pure opioid antagonist. It does not lead to physical or psychological dependence. Tolerance to the opioid antagonist effect is not known to occur.

Overdose: Symptoms: There is limited clinical experience with naltrexone overdosage in humans. In one study, subjects who received 800 mg daily of naltrexone for up to 1 week showed no evidence of toxicity.

Treatment: Consideration should be given to contacting a Poison Control Centre for the most up-to-date information. In view of the lack of actual experience in the treatment of naltrexone overdose, patients should be treated symptomatically in a closely supervised environment.

Dosage: Initiation of Naltrexone Therapy: **Do not attempt treatment with naltrexone unless, in the medical judgment of the prescribing physician, there is no reasonable possibility of opioid use within the past 7 to 10 days. If there is any question of occult opioid dependence, perform a Narcan challenge test and do not attempt to initiate naltrexone therapy until Narcan challenge is negative (see below).**

Treatment of Narcotic Dependence: Initiate treatment with naltrexone using the following guidelines:

1. Treatment should not be attempted until the patient has remained opioid-free for 7 to 10 days. Self-reporting of abstinence from opioids should be verified by analysis of the patient's urine for absence of opioids. The patient should not be manifesting withdrawal signs or reporting withdrawal symptoms.
2. If there is any question of occult opioid dependence perform a Narcan challenge test (see below). If signs of opioid withdrawal are still observed following Narcan challenge, treatment with naltrexone should not be attempted. The Narcan challenge can be repeated in 24 hours.
3. Treatment should be initiated carefully, slowly increasing the dose of naltrexone administered. This can be accomplished by administration of 25 mg of naltrexone initially. The patient should be observed for 1 hour. If no withdrawal signs occur, the patient may be given the rest of the daily dose.

Once the patient has been started on naltrexone, 50 mg every 24 hours will produce adequate clinical blockade of the actions of parenterally administered opioids (i.e., this dose will block the effects of a 25 mg i.v. heroin challenge). A flexible approach to a dosing regimen may be employed in cases of supervised administration. Thus, patients may receive 50 mg of naltrexone every weekday with a 100 mg dose on Saturday or patients may receive 100 mg every other day, or 150 mg every third day. While the degree of opioid blockade may be somewhat reduced by using higher doses at longer dosing intervals, improved patient compliance may result from dosing every 48 to 72 hours.

Several of the clinical studies reported in the literature have employed the following dosing regimen: 100 mg on Monday, 100 mg on Wednesday, and 150 mg on Friday. This dosing schedule appeared to be acceptable to many naltrexone patients successfully maintaining their opioid-free state.

Treatment of Alcoholism: A dose of 50 mg once daily is recommended.

Naltrexone should be used as part of a comprehensive treatment program for alcohol dependence. Factors associated with a good outcome include: appropriate management of comorbid conditions; use of community-based support groups; and good medication compliance. To achieve the best possible treatment outcome, appropriate compliance enhancing techniques should be implemented for all components of the treatment program, especially medication compliance.

The efficacy of naltrexone beyond 12 weeks of treatment has not been established.

Narcan Challenge Test: The Narcan challenge test should **not** be performed in a patient showing clinical signs or symptoms of opioid withdrawal, or in a patient whose urine contains opioids. The Narcan challenge test may be administered by either the i.v. or s.c. routes.

I.V. Challenge: Following appropriate screening of the patient, 2 mL (0.8 mg) of Narcan (0.4 mg/mL), should be drawn into a sterile syringe. If the i.v. route of administration is selected, 0.5 mL (0.2 mg) of Narcan should be injected, and while the needle is still in the patient's vein, the patient should be observed for 30 seconds for evidence of withdrawal signs or symptoms. If there is no evidence of withdrawal, the remaining 1.5 mL (0.6 mg) of Narcan should be injected, and the patient observed for an additional period of 20 minutes for signs and symptoms of withdrawal.

S.C. Challenge: If the s.c. route is selected, 2 mL (0.8 mg) should be administered s.c. and the patient observed for signs or symptoms of withdrawal for 45 minutes.

Conditions and Technique for Observation of Patients: During the appropriate period of observation, the patient's vital signs should be monitored and the patient should be observed for signs of withdrawal. It is also important to question the patient carefully. The signs and symptoms of opioid withdrawal include, but are not limited to, the following: withdrawal signs: stuffiness or running nose, tearing, yawning, sweating, tremor, vomiting or piloerection; withdrawal symptoms: feeling of temperature change, joint or bone and muscle pain, abdominal cramps, skin crawling, etc.

Interpretation of the Challenge: **Warning: The elicitation of the enumerated signs or symptoms indicates a potential risk for the subject, and naltrexone should not be administered.** If no signs or symptoms of withdrawal are observed, elicited, or reported, **naltrexone may be administered.** If there is any doubt in the observer's mind that the patient is not in an opioid-free state, or is in continuing withdrawal, naltrexone should be withheld for 24 hours and Narcan should be readministered as follows: Confirmatory rechallenge (if necessary): 4 mL (1.6 mg) of Narcan (0.4 mg/mL) should be injected i.v. and the patient again observed for signs and symptoms of withdrawal. If none are present, naltrexone may be administered. **If signs and symptoms of withdrawal are present, administration of naltrexone should be delayed until repeated Narcan challenge indicates the patient is no longer at risk.**

Information for the Patient: See Blue Section—Information for the Patient "ReVia".

Supplied: Each pale yellow, film-coated, capsule-shaped tablet, debossed on one side with "DuPont" and scored and debossed "11" on the other, contains: naltrexone HCl 50 mg. Nonmedicinal ingredients: colloidal silicon dioxide, crospovidone, lactose monohydrate, magnesium stearate, microcrystalline cellulose, and Pale Yellow Opadry YS-1-6378-G. Bottles of 50. Store at controlled room temperature (15 to 30°C). Dispense in a tight container as defined in the USP.

(Shown in Product Recognition Section)

Reviewed 1997

REVITALOSE-C-1000®

Rivex Pharma

Vitamin C

Vitamin Therapy

Indications: Vitamin C supplements for therapeutic use only.

Dosage: Contents of 1 yellow unidose daily or every other day before meals, or as directed by physician. May be mixed with water or fruit juice. For oral administration only.

Supplied: Each unidose vial contains: vitamin C 1 000 mg. Nonmedicinal ingredients: alcohol, glycerin, methylparaben, propylparaben and purified water. Alcohol: 0.3%. Drinkable unidose vials of 5 mL, packages of 24.

Many medications require special consideration when administered to geriatric patients. Refer to Drugs and Older Individuals found within the CLIN-INFO SECTION.

REVITONUS® C-1000

Sabex

Vitamin C—Gland Extracts

Vitamin Supplement

Supplied: Brown Ampul: Each 10 mL ampul contains: gland extracts (nonmedicinal ingredients) from: fresh adrenal cortex 1.33 g, fresh testicular gland 3 g and fresh grey matter 3 g. Other nonmedicinal ingredients: caramel, ethyl alcohol (1% v/v), methylparaben, orange terpenless oil, propylparaben, purified water and sucrose. Sodium: <1 mmol (15 mg).

Yellow Ampul: Each 10 mL ampul contains: vitamin C (ascorbic acid) 1 000 mg. Nonmedicinal ingredients: ethyl alcohol (0.1% v/v), glycerin, methylparaben, propyl gallate, propylparaben, purified water, sodium hydroxide (to adjust pH) and tartrazine (FD&C Yellow No. 5). Sodium: <1 mmol (15 mg).

Unit packs of 20 ampuls (10 yellow + 10 brown).

RHEOMACRODEX®

Medisan Pharmaceuticals

Dextran 40

Plasma Volume Expander

Pharmacology: The biological properties of dextrans are functions of molecular structure, average molecular weight and molecular weight distribution. For Rheomacrodex these have been selected so that the preparation exerts both a general and a microcirculatory flow improving effect, at the same time producing a rapid increase in plasma volume. Following the infusion of Rheomacrodex, approximately 60% of the dextran is excreted through normally functioning kidneys within 6 hours, and about 70% within 24 hours. The remainder is broken down in the body by endogenous dextranases.

Rheomacrodex possesses thromboprophylactic properties.

The usual blood-grouping, simple cross-matching and indirect Coombs' test are not affected by a preceding infusion of Rheomacrodex. The only techniques interfered with are those in which enzymes are used.

Indications: Reduced capillary circulation as in shock, burns, fat embolism, pancreatitis, peritonitis and paralytic ileus.

Disturbances of arterial and venous circulation as in imminent gangrene, leg ulcer, Raynaud's disease, nonhemorrhagical cerebral insults, etc.

Prophylaxis of postoperative and post-traumatic thromboembolism.

In vascular and plastic surgery, to improve local circulation and to reduce the tendency to thrombosis in transplants.

In open heart surgery, as an additive to the perfusion fluid in the heart lung machine.

Contraindications: Marked hemorrhagic tendency, as in thrombocytopenia. Oliguria or anuria in manifest renal disease. Pronounced heart failure. Known hypersensitivity to dextran.

Warnings: *Pregnancy:* Although anaphylactic reactions to Rheomacrodex are rare, the product should only be used during pregnancy when strictly indicated since anaphylactic reactions in the mother have been reported to cause anoxic brain damage with or without death of the fetus.

Precautions: Rheomacrodex is a hyper-colloid-osmotic solution and the risk of circulatory overload must therefore be constantly borne in mind, particularly in the presence of latent or manifest heart failure. Where infusion is rapid, the increase in plasma volume may temporarily be as much as twice the volume of liquid infused, since every gram of dextran circulating retains 20 to 25 mL water. The total dose and the rate of infusion are adjusted according to the clinical state of the patient, and are followed where necessary by observations of the arterial blood pressure and the central venous pressure. If Rheomacrodex is administered to dehydrated patients, the electrolyte and water balance should be corrected with crystalloid solutions. If, in the course of treatment with Rheomacrodex, there is the appearance of oliguria with viscous, syrupy urine, diuresis should be promoted by the administration of crystalloid solutions. If, in spite of this, the oliguria persists, a diuretic, such as furosemide or mannitol, should be given.

Adverse Effects: Hypersensitivity reactions may occur. Symptomatology varies from mild reactions with flushing, urticaria and chills to more serious reactions involving hypotension and circulatory collapse. Such reactions are generally reversible, though fatalities have been reported in elderly patients and others with depressed cardiovascular function. The incidence of reactions is lower after trauma and during surgery. The increased secretion of corticosteroids under such conditions may provide a degree of protection. Thus, in the prophylaxis of shock or thrombosis in connection with surgery, infusion should not be started until the induction of anesthesia or surgical intervention has commenced. Treatment in shock or after trauma, however, is instituted as soon as possible.

Reactions are generally limited to the first few minutes of the first infusion of dextran, when the patient should be closely observed with facilities at hand for emergency treatment. If complications occur, the infusion should be discontinued and symptomatic treatment as for allergic reactions instituted (adrenaline, corticosteroids, antihistamines, etc.). In circulatory collapse, rapid volume substitution with some other infusion solution should be instituted.

Capillary oozing, which may arise from wound surfaces, is principal evidence of an increase in perfusion pressure and improvement in capillary flow.

Dosage: The dosage is calculated individually, and is adjusted for each case depending on its clinical course. The rate of infusion should be slow where there is a risk of overloading the circulation (see Precautions).

Reduced capillary circulation in shock, etc.: Initially, 500 to 1 000 mL (10 to 20 mL/kg) is given i.v., depending on other treatment also being given. Thereafter, 500 mL (approximately 10 mL/kg) is infused during the same 24 hours. This second dose can be repeated daily for a maximum of 5 days.

Disturbances of arterial and venous circulation: Initially, 500 to 1 000 mL (10 to 20 mL/kg) is given in the first 24 hours. In addition, 500 mL is given on the following day and every alternate day thereafter up to a maximum of 2 weeks.

Prophylaxis of postoperative and post-traumatic thromboembolism: 500 to 1 000 mL (10 to 20 mL/kg) is infused i.v. To minimize the risk of complications, the infusion should begin during surgery or as soon as possible after trauma. Treatment may be supplemented with a further 500 mL on the following day.

In cases at high risk of thrombosis (fracture of the neck of the femur, malignant disease of abdomen or prostate, prolonged immobilization, a history of previous thromboses, etc.) treatment is begun as above with 500 to 1 000 mL. On the following day and on every alternate day thereafter for a maximum of 2 weeks, a further 500 mL is given.

In vascular and plastic surgery: 500 mL (approximately 10 mL/kg) is given i.v. during the operation. A further 500 mL is given postoperatively. 500 mL is given on the following day and every alternate day thereafter up to a maximum of 2 weeks.

In open heart vascular surgery: 10 to 20 mL/kg Rheomacrodex is added to the perfusion fluid. The dextran concentration in the perfusion fluid must not, however, exceed 3%. The postoperative dosage is the same as that recommended for reduced capillary circulation.

Rheomacrodex 10% in dextrose should be used in cases of reduced renal capacity for excretion of sodium chloride or when restricted administration of sodium chloride is indicated (to decrease the supply of electrolytes when large volumes of fluid are required).

Administration: Since globulin precipitation and spontaneous red cell aggregation may occur when mixing bottled blood with electrolyte-free sugar solution, Rheomacrodex 10% in dextrose should not be given through the same apparatus as blood. This does not apply to Rheomacrodex 10% in saline.

Supplied: Rheomacrodex 10% in dextrose: Each L contains: dextran 40 Pharmacia Standard 2.5 mmol, D-glucose USP 250 mmol and water for injection q.s. Energy: 720 kJ. Bottles of 500 mL.

Rheomacrodex 10% in normal saline: Each L contains: dextran 40 Pharmacia Standard 2.5 mmol, sodium 150 mmol, chloride 150 mmol and water for injection q.s. Bottles of 500 mL.

Both forms are isotonic with blood. Dextran 40 has a certain tendency to crystallize when subjected to variations in temperature or when stored for a long time at high room temperature. Therefore store at a constant temperature, not exceeding 30°C. Keep from cold during transport.

Did you know that the *CPS* provides information on certain drugs or drug classes in the shaded monographs in the WHITE SECTION? Check out the index at the beginning of the section.

RHEUMATREX™ Ⓟ

Wyeth-Ayerst

Methotrexate Sodium

Antirheumatic

> Caution: Methotrexate should be used only by physicians whose knowledge and experience includes the use of antimetabolite therapy.
>
> Because of the possibility of serious toxic reactions the patient should be informed by the physician of the risks involved and should be under a physician's constant supervision.
>
> Deaths have been reported with the use of methotrexate in the treatment of rheumatoid arthritis.
>
> In the treatment of rheumatoid arthritis, methotrexate use should be restricted to patients with severe, recalcitrant, disabling disease, which is not adequately responsive to other forms of therapy, and only when the diagnosis has been established and after appropriate consultation.

Pharmacology: Methotrexate has as its mechanism of action the competitive inhibition of the enzyme folic acid reductase. Folic acid must be reduced to tetrahydrofolic acid by this enzyme in the process of DNA synthesis and cellular replication. Methotrexate inhibits the reduction of folic acid and interferes with tissue-cell reproduction. In rheumatoid arthritis, the mechanism of action is unknown, it may affect immune function.

In patients with rheumatoid arthritis, effects of methotrexate on articular swelling and tenderness can be seen as early as 3 to 6 weeks. Although methotrexate clearly ameliorates symptoms of inflammation (pain, swelling, stiffness), there is no evidence that it induces remission of rheumatoid arthritis nor has a beneficial effect been demonstrated on bone erosions and other radiologic changes which result in impaired joint use, functional disability, and deformity.

Most studies of methotrexate in patients with rheumatoid arthritis are relatively short term (3 to 6 months). Data from long-term studies indicate that an initial clinical improvement is maintained for at least 2 years with continued therapy.

Absorption: In adults, oral absorption of methotrexate appears to be dose dependent. Peak serum levels are reached within 1 to 2 hours. At doses of 30 mg/m² or less, methotrexate is generally well absorbed with a mean bioavailability of about 60%.

Distribution: Methotrexate is rapidly distributed throughout the body. In a study in oncology patients, methotrexate was distributed to total body water within 1 hour following i.v. or small oral doses. Methotrexate competes with reduced folates for active transport across cell membranes by means of a single carrier-mediated active transport process. At serum concentrations greater than 100 micromolar, passive diffusion becomes a major pathway by which effective intracellular concentrations can be achieved. Methotrexate in serum is approximately 50% protein bound. Laboratory studies demonstrate that it may be displaced from plasma albumin by various compounds including sulfonamides, salicylates, tetracyclines, chloramphenicol and phenytoin.

Methotrexate does not penetrate the blood-cerebrospinal fluid barrier in therapeutic amounts when given orally.

In dogs, synovial fluid concentrations after oral dosing were higher in inflamed than uninflamed joints. Although salicylates did not interfere with this penetration, prior prednisone treatment reduced penetration into inflamed joint to the level of normal joints.

Metabolism: After absorption, methotrexate undergoes hepatic and intracellular metabolism to polyglutamated forms which can be converted back to methotrexate by hydrolase enzymes. These polyglutamates act as inhibitors of dihydrofolate reductase and thymidylate synthase. Small amounts of methotrexate polyglutamates may remain in tissues for extended periods. The retention and prolonged drug action of these active metabolite(s) vary among different cells and tissues. Methotrexate is partially metabolized by intestinal flora after oral administration.

Excretion: The terminal half-life reported for methotrexate is approximately 3 to 10 hours for patients receiving treatment for psoriasis or rheumatoid arthritis or low dose antineoplastic therapy (less than 30 mg/m²).

Renal excretion is the primary route of elimination and is dependent upon dosage and route of administration. With i.v. administration, 58 to 92% of a 0.1 mg/kg dose was excreted in the urine within 24 hours. Oral administration gave only slightly lower rates of excretion. Repeated doses daily result in more sustained serum levels and some retention of methotrexate over each 24-hour period, which may result in accumulation of the drug within tissues. There is limited biliary excretion amounting to 10% or less of the administered dose. Enterohepatic recirculation of methotrexate has been proposed.

Renal excretion occurs by glomerular filtration and active tubular secretion. Nonlinear elimination due to saturation of renal tubular reabsorption has been observed in psoriatic patients at doses between 7.5 and 30 mg. Impaired renal function as well as concurrent use of drugs such as weak organic acids that also undergo tubular secretion, can markedly increase methotrexate serum levels. Excellent correlation has been reported between methotrexate clearance and endogenous creatinine clearance.

Methotrexate clearance rates vary widely and are generally decreased at higher doses. Delayed drug clearance has been identified as one of the major factors responsible for methotrexate toxicity. It has been postulated that the toxicity of methotrexate for normal tissues is more dependent upon the duration of exposure to the drug rather than the peak level achieved. When a patient has delayed drug elimination due to compromised renal function, a third space effusion, or other causes, methotrexate serum concentrations may remain elevated for prolonged periods.

The potential for toxicity from delayed excretion is reduced by the administration of leucovorin during the final phase of methotrexate plasma elimination. Pharmacokinetic monitoring of methotrexate serum concentrations may help identify those patients at high risk for methotrexate toxicity and aid in proper adjustment of leucovorin dosing.

Methotrexate has been detected in human breast milk. The highest breast milk to plasma concentration ratio reached was 0.08:1.

Indications: In the management of selected adults with severe, active, classical or definite rheumatoid arthritis (American Rheumatism Association criteria) who have had an insufficient therapeutic response to, or are intolerant of, an adequate trial of first line therapy including full dose NSAIDs and usually a trial of at least one or more disease-modifying antirheumatic drugs.

ASA, NSAIDs, and/or low dose steroids may be continued, although the possibility of increased toxicity with concomitant use of NSAIDs including salicylates has not been fully explored.

Steroids may be reduced gradually in patients who respond to methotrexate.

Combined use of methotrexate with gold, penicillamine, hydroxychloroquine, sulfasalazine or cytotoxic agents, has not been studied and may increase the incidence of adverse effects. Rest and physiotherapy as indicated should be continued.

Methotrexate has a long history of clinical use as a folate antagonist and is the most widely used antimetabolite in chemotherapy, and severe psoriasis.

In 1951, the use of a folate antagonist to treat rheumatoid arthritis, a nonmalignant disease was reported. Moderate to marked improvement in patients with rheumatoid arthritis given methotrexate in intermittent dosage has been reported. As shown in many subsequent studies, methotrexate is effective in the treatment of rheumatoid arthritis at doses much lower than those used in chemotherapy. The use of methotrexate in severe active rheumatoid arthritis has been discussed in an increasing number of publications including several recent review articles.

Short-term, placebo-controlled trials have established the efficacy of methotrexate sodium in recalcitrant rheumatoid arthritis. In a placebo-controlled study, patients who crossed over to methotrexate showed significant improvement in all clinical variables. For those crossed over to placebo from methotrexate an increase in the mean number of tender/painful joints was evident as early as 3 weeks and deterioration in other clinical variables was observed within 6 weeks after crossover to placebo.

In several long-term studies patients have shown continued disease control with acceptable toxicity and few withdrawals from treatment.

The improvement in disease activity produced by methotrexate in clinical studies became maximal after 6 months of treatment and was maintained for a number of years. Several investigators observed a reduction in steroid dose during long-term therapy. However, in patients who discontinued methotrexate, a severe flare of rheumatoid arthritis occurred.

A short-term study showed an increased effect of methotrexate was evident at 10 mg/m² (15 to 22 mg) compared with half this amount and placebo.

Rheumatrex (cont'd)

In clinical trials versus auranofin, the response with methotrexate was consistently greater than that with auranofin for all measures of efficacy. About 44% of patients in the auranofin group discontinued treatment, 12 (8%) due to lack of efficacy, 37 (26%) due to toxicity and 14 (10%) for administrative or other reasons. This dropout rate was higher than for the methotrexate group as only 25% of patients discontinued treatment; 4 (3%) due to lack of efficacy, 17 (12%) due to toxicity, and 14 (10%) for administrative or other reasons.

In long-term prospective studies, data up to January 1989 show that out of 47 patients followed for more than 1 year, only 2 have withdrawn due to lack of efficacy (4%) and 2 due to adverse reactions (4%).

The results obtained by a variety of investigators suggest that a higher percentage of patients may be able to continue treatment with methotrexate than with other agents like gold and other antirheumatic drugs. In a life-table analysis, 78.7% of patients with rheumatoid arthritis remained on treatment with methotrexate after 12 months, a higher percentage than with other antirheumatic drugs. Other studies have shown similar favorable results for methotrexate.

The most common adverse effects seen in clinical trials were gastrointestinal disturbances and transient elevations of serum liver enzymes. Pulmonary toxicity is uncommon and may represent a hypersensitivity reaction. Incidence and severity of adverse experiences were similar for younger and older patients.

In summary, methotrexate represents an effective therapy in appropriately selected patients with severe refractory rheumatoid arthritis. It has been used for many years for thousands of patients in the clinical practice setting and in carefully controlled clinical trials. In short-term trials it has proven effective and well tolerated in most patients, in long-term trials continuingly effective and acceptable, and in comparative trials comparable to or better than available conventional therapy.

Contraindications: *Pregnancy:* Methotrexate has caused fetal deaths and congenital anomalies.

Blood dyscrasias, such as bone marrow hypoplasia, leukopenia, thrombocytopenia, significant anemia; liver disease including fibrosis, cirrhosis, recent or active hepatitis; active infectious disease and during immunization procedures; hypersensitivity to methotrexate; nursing mothers; overt or laboratory evidence of immunodeficiency syndrome(s).

Warnings: Malignant lymphomas, which may regress following withdrawal of methotrexate, may occur in patients receiving low-dose methotrexate and, thus, may not require cytotoxic treatment. Discontinue methotrexate first and, if the lymphoma does not regress, appropriate treatment should be instituted.

Methotrexate should be used only by physicians whose knowledge and experience includes the use of antimetabolite therapy.

Because of the possibility of serious toxic reactions the patient should be informed by the physician of the risks involved and should be under a physician's constant supervision.

In the treatment of rheumatoid arthritis, methotrexate use should be restricted to patients with severe, recalcitrant, disabling disease, which is not adequately responsive to other forms of therapy, and only when the diagnosis has been established and after appropriate consultation.

Periodic monitoring for toxicity, including CBC with differential and platelet counts, and liver and renal function tests is a mandatory part of methotrexate therapy. Periodic liver biopsies may be indicated in some situations. Patients at increased risk for impaired methotrexate elimination (e.g., renal dysfunction, pleural effusions or ascites) should be monitored more frequently (see Precautions, Laboratory Tests).

Methotrexate causes hepatotoxicity, fibrosis and cirrhosis, but generally only after prolonged use. Acutely, liver enzyme elevations are frequently seen, these are usually transient and asymptomatic, and also do not appear predictive of subsequent hepatic disease. Liver biopsy after sustained use often shows histologic changes, and fibrosis and cirrhosis have been reported; these latter lesions often are not preceded by symptoms or abnormal liver function tests.

Methotrexate-induced lung disease is a potentially dangerous lesion, which may occur acutely at any time during therapy and which has been reported at doses as low as 7.5 mg/week. It is not always fully reversible. Pulmonary symptoms (especially a dry, nonproductive cough) may require interruption of treatment and careful investigation.

Concomitant use of drugs with hepatotoxic potential should be avoided.

Methotrexate therapy should not be initiated in subjects who have an excessive alcohol intake.

Methotrexate is toxic to the hematopoietic system and may produce depression of bone marrow, anemia, leukopenia, thrombocytopenia and bleeding.

Unexpectedly severe (sometimes fatal) marrow suppression and gastrointestinal toxicity have been reported with concomitant administration of methotrexate (usually in high dosage) along with some nonsteroidal anti-inflammatory drugs.

For men and women in the fertile age, appropriate steps should be taken to avoid conception during methotrexate therapy. Methotrexate has been reported to cause fetal deaths and/or congenital anomalies. After discontinuation of methotrexate therapy, the risk of genetic abnormalities may persist. Thus, both men and women are advised to avoid intercourse leading to conception for an undefined period (at least 8 weeks) after taking the drug to ensure the re-establishment of the normal production of germinal cells.

Diarrhea and ulcerative stomatitis require interruption of therapy; otherwise, hemorrhagic enteritis and death from intestinal perforation may occur.

Like other cytotoxic drugs, methotrexate may induce "tumor lysis syndrome" in patients with rapidly growing tumors. Appropriate supportive and pharmacologic measures may prevent or alleviate this complication.

Severe, occasionally fatal, skin reactions have been reported following single or multiple doses of methotrexate. Reactions have occurred within days of oral, i.m., i.v., or intrathecal methotrexate administration. Recovery has been reported with discontinuation of therapy (see Precautions, Organ System Toxicity, Skin).

Potentially, fatal opportunistic infections, especially P. carinii pneumonia, may occur with methotrexate therapy.

Methotrexate therapy in patients with impaired renal function should be undertaken with extreme caution, and at reduced dosages, because renal dysfunction will prolong methotrexate elimination.

Interruption of methotrexate therapy should be considered as a result of toxicity in the following situations: pulmonary symptoms (especially a dry nonproductive cough) or a nonspecific pneumonitis, persistent evidence of impaired liver function, suppression of the hematopoietic system, ulcerative stomatitis, significant hepatic fibrosis or cirrhosis, impaired renal function, severe diarrhea, pregnancy.

Precautions: Methotrexate has a high potential toxicity, usually dose-related. The physician should be familiar with the various characteristics of the drug and its established clinical usage. Patients undergoing therapy should be subject to appropriate supervision so that signs or symptoms of possible toxic effects or adverse reactions may be detected and evaluated with minimal delay. Pretreatment and periodic tests and hematologic studies are essential to the use of methotrexate. Hematopoietic suppression may occur abruptly and while on an apparent safe dosage. Any profound drop in blood-cell count indicates immediate stopping of the drug and appropriate therapy.

In all instances where the use of methotrexate is considered for therapy, the physician must evaluate the need and usefulness of the drug against the risks of toxic effects or adverse reaction. Most adverse reactions are reversible if detected early. When such effects or reactions do occur, the drug should be reduced in dosage or discontinued and appropriate corrective measures should be taken, according to the clinical judgment of the physician. Reinstitution of methotrexate therapy should be carried out with caution, with adequate consideration of further need for the drug and alertness as to possible recurrence of toxicity.

The toxicity profile of methotrexate has been studied in older individuals. Due to the potential for diminished hepatic and renal function in this population, these patients should be closely monitored for early signs of toxicity.

When methotrexate is discontinued a 'flare' of arthritis usually occurs within 3 to 6 weeks.

Both the physician and the pharmacist should emphasize to the patient the importance of the **weekly** dosage regimens; mistaken daily use may cause serious and sometimes life-threatening or fatal toxicity.

Methotrexate is excreted principally by the kidneys. Its use in the presence of impaired renal function may result in accumulation of toxic amounts or even additional renal damage. The patient's renal status should be determined prior to and during methotrexate therapy and proper caution exercised should significant renal impairment be disclosed. Drug dosage should be reduced or discontinued until renal function is improved or restored.

If stomatitis, vomiting, diarrhea, or decreased fluid intake occur which may result in dehydration, methotrexate should be discontinued until recovery ensues.

Methotrexate should be used with extreme caution in the presence of infection, peptic ulcer, ulcerative colitis, debility, in extreme youth and old age, and in the presence of a significant third space (e.g., pleural effusion).

Methotrexate should be stopped if there is a significant drop in blood counts. Patients with profound granulocytopenia and fever should be evaluated immediately and usually require parenteral broad-spectrum antibiotic therapy. In severe bone marrow depression, blood or platelet transfusions may be necessary.

Pulmonary symptoms (especially a dry, nonproductive cough) or a nonspecific pneumonitis occurring during methotrexate therapy may be indicative of a potentially dangerous lesion and require interruption of treatment and careful investigation. Although clinically variable, the typical patient with methotrexate-induced lung disease presents with fever, cough, dyspnea, hypoxemia and an infiltrate on chest x-ray; infection needs to be excluded. This lesion can occur at all dosages.

Since it is reported that methotrexate may have an immunosuppressive action, this factor must be taken into consideration in evaluating the use of the drug where immune responses in a patient may be important or essential. Therefore, immunization may be ineffective and immunization with live virus is contraindicated.

Laboratory Tests: Patients undergoing methotrexate therapy should be closely monitored so that toxic effects are detected promptly. Baseline assessment should include a complete blood count with differential and platelet counts, hepatic enzymes, renal function tests, and a chest x-ray. During therapy of rheumatoid arthritis, monitoring of these parameters is recommended: hematology at least monthly, and liver and renal function every 1 to 3 months. More frequent monitoring is usually indicated during antineoplastic therapy. During initial or changing doses, or during periods of increased risk of elevated methotrexate blood levels (e.g., dehydration), more frequent monitoring may also be indicated.

A relationship between abnormal liver function tests and fibrosis or cirrhosis of the liver has not been established. Transient liver function test abnormalities are observed frequently after methotrexate administration and are usually not cause for modification of methotrexate therapy. Persistent liver function test abnormalities just prior to dosing and/or depression of serum albumin may be indicators of serious liver toxicity and require evaluation (see Organ System Toxicity, Hepatic).

Liver function tests, including serum albumin, should be performed periodically prior to dosing but are often normal in the face of developing fibrosis or cirrhosis. These lesions may be detectable only by biopsy.

When to perform a liver biopsy in rheumatoid arthritis patients has not been established, either in terms of cumulative methotrexate dose or duration of therapy.

Pulmonary function tests may be useful if methotrexate-induced lung disease is suspected, especially if baseline measurements are available.

Drug Interactions: Methotrexate may be displaced from its protein binding sites by phenylbutazone, salicylates, phenytoin and sulfonamides. Renal tubular transport is diminished by probenecid, salicylates, and weak organic acids such as some NSAIDs. Oral antibiotics such as tetracycline, chloramphenicol and nonabsorbable broad spectrum antibiotics, may decrease intestinal absorption of methotrexate or interfere with enterohepatic circulation by inhibiting bowel flora and suppressing metabolism of the drug by bacteria. Trimethoprim/sulfamethoxazole has been reported to increase bone marrow depression in a few patients receiving methotrexate. Therefore, caution should be used when NSAIDs, salicylates, and the aforementioned drugs are administered concomitantly with methotrexate.

In patients with rheumatoid arthritis, the controlled clinical trials have included concurrent use of constant dosage regimens of NSAIDs without observed problems. Therefore, until more is known about the NSAIDs/methotrexate interaction, it is recommended that methotrexate dosage be carefully controlled during treatment with NSAIDs.

Vitamin preparations containing folic acid or its derivatives may alter responses to methotrexate.

Organ System Toxicity: Potentially fatal opportunistic infections, especially P. carinii pneumonia, may occur with methotrexate therapy. When a patient presents with pulmonary symptoms, the possibility of P. carinii pneumonia should be considered.

Gastrointestinal: If vomiting, diarrhea, or stomatitis occur, which may result in dehydration, methotrexate should be discontinued until recovery occurs. Methotrexate should be used with extreme caution in the presence of peptic ulcer disease or ulcerative colitis.
Hematologic: Methotrexate can suppress hematopoiesis and cause anemia, leukopenia, and/or thrombocytopenia. In patients with malignancy and pre-existing hematopoietic impairment, the drug should be used with caution, if at all. In controlled clinical trials in rheumatoid arthritis (n=128), leukopenia (WBC <3 000/mm³) was seen in 2 patients, thrombocytopenia (platelets <100 000/mm³) in 6 patients, and pancytopenia in 2 patients.

In psoriasis and rheumatoid arthritis, methotrexate should be stopped immediately if there is a significant drop in blood counts. In the treatment of neoplastic diseases, methotrexate should be continued only if the potential benefit warrants the risk of severe myelosuppression. Patients with profound granulocytopenia and fever should be evaluated immediately and usually require parenteral broad-spectrum antibiotic therapy.
Hepatic: Methotrexate has the potential for acute (elevated transaminases) and chronic (fibrosis and cirrhosis) hepatotoxicity. Chronic toxicity is potentially fatal; it generally has occurred after prolonged use (generally 2 years or more) and after a total dose of at least 1.5 g. In studies in psoriatic patients, hepatotoxicity appeared to be a function of total cumulative dose and appeared to be enhanced by alcoholism, obesity, diabetes and advanced age. An accurate incidence rate has not been determined; the rate of progression and reversibility of lesions is not known. Special caution is indicated in the presence of pre-existing liver damage or impaired hepatic function.

In psoriasis, liver function tests, including serum albumin, should be performed periodically prior to dosing but are often normal in the face of developing fibrosis or cirrhosis. These lesions may be detectable only by biopsy. The usual recommendation is to obtain a liver biopsy at 1) pretherapy or shortly after initiation of therapy (2 to 4 months), 2) a total cumulative dose of 1.5 g, and 3) after each additional 1.5 g. Moderate fibrosis or any cirrhosis normally leads to discontinuation of the drug; mild fibrosis normally suggests a repeat biopsy in 6 months. Milder histologic findings such as fatty change and low grade portal inflammation are relatively common pretherapy. Although these mild changes are usually not a reason to avoid or discontinue methotrexate therapy, the drug should be used with caution.

In rheumatoid arthritis, age at first use of methotrexate and duration of therapy have been reported as risk factors for hepatotoxicity; other risk factors, similar to those observed in psoriasis, may be present in rheumatoid arthritis but have not been confirmed to date. Persistent abnormalities in liver function tests may precede appearance of fibrosis or cirrhosis in this population. There is a combined reported experience in 217 rheumatoid arthritis patients with liver biopsies both before and during treatment (after a cumulative dose of at least 1.5 g) and 714 patients with a biopsy only during treatment. There are 64 (7%) cases of fibrosis and 1 (0.1%) case of cirrhosis. Of the 64 cases of fibrosis, 60 were deemed mild. The reticulin stain is more sensitive for early fibrosis and its use may increase these figures. It is unknown whether even longer use will increase these risks.

Liver function tests should be performed at baseline and at 4 to 8 week intervals in patients receiving methotrexate for rheumatoid arthritis. Pretreatment liver biopsy should be performed for patients with a history of excessive alcohol consumption, persistently abnormal baseline liver function test values or chronic hepatitis B or C infection. During therapy, liver biopsy should be performed if there are persistent liver function test abnormalities or there is a decrease in serum albumin below the normal range (in the setting of well controlled rheumatoid arthritis).

If the results of a liver biopsy show mild changes (Roenigk grades I, II, IIIa), methotrexate may be continued and the patient monitored as per recommendations listed above. Methotrexate should be discontinued in any patient who displays persistently abnormal liver function tests and refuses liver biopsy or in any patient whose liver biopsy shows moderate to severe changes (Roenigk grade IIIb or IV).
Infection or Immunologic States: Methotrexate should be used with extreme caution in the presence of active infection, and is usually contraindicated in patients with overt or laboratory evidence of immunodeficiency syndromes. Immunization may be ineffective when given during methotrexate therapy. Immunization with live virus vaccines is generally not recommended. There have been reports of disseminated vaccinia infections after smallpox immunization in patients receiving methotrexate therapy. Hypogammaglobulinemia has been reported rarely.

Potentially fatal opportunistic infections, especially P. carinii pneumonia, may occur with methotrexate therapy. When a patient presents with pulmonary symptoms, the possibility of P. carinii pneumonia should be considered.
Neurologic: There have been reports of leukoencephalopathy following i.v. administration of methotrexate to patients who have had craniospinal irradiation. Serious neurotoxicity, frequently manifested as generalized or focal seizures, has been reported with unexpectedly increased frequency among pediatric patients with acute lymphoblastic leukemia who were treated with intermediate-dose i.v. methotrexate (1 g/m²). Symptomatic patients were commonly noted to have leukoencephalopathy and/or microangiopathic calcifications on diagnostic imaging studies. Chronic leukoencephalopathy has also been reported in patients with osteosarcoma who received repeated doses of high-dose methotrexate with leucovorin rescue even without cranial irradiation. Discontinuation of methotrexate does not always result in complete recovery.

A transient acute neurologic syndrome has been observed in patients treated with high dosage regimens. Manifestations of this neurologic disorder may include behavioral abnormalities, focal sensorimotor signs and abnormal reflexes. The exact cause is unknown.
Pulmonary: Pulmonary symptoms (especially a dry nonproductive cough) or a nonspecific pneumonitis occurring during methotrexate therapy may be indicative of a potentially dangerous lesion and require interruption of treatment and careful investigation. Although clinically variable, the typical patient with methotrexate induced lung disease presents with fever, cough, dyspnea, hypoxemia, and an infiltrate on chest X-ray; infection needs to be excluded. This lesion can occur at all dosages.
Renal: High doses of methotrexate used in the treatment of osteosarcoma may cause renal damage leading to acute renal failure. Nephrotoxicity is due primarily to the precipitation of methotrexate and 7-hydroxymethotrexate in the renal tubules. Close attention to renal function including adequate hydration, urine alkalinization and measurement of serum methotrexate and creatinine levels are essential for safe administration.
Skin: Severe, occasionally fatal, dermatologic reactions, including toxic epidermal necrolysis, Stevens-Johnson syndrome, exfoliative dermatitis, skin necrosis, and erythema multiforme, have been reported in children and adults, within days of oral, i.m., i.v., or intrathecal methotrexate administration. Reactions were noted after single or multiple, low, intermediate or high doses of methotrexate in patients with neoplastic and nonneoplastic diseases.
Other Precautions: Methotrexate should be used with extreme caution in the presence of debility.

Methotrexate exits slowly from third space compartments (e.g., pleural effusions or ascites). This results in a prolonged terminal plasma half-life and unexpected toxicity. In patients with significant third space accumulations, it is advisable to evacuate the fluid before treatment and to monitor plasma methotrexate levels.

Lesions of psoriasis may be aggravated by concomitant exposure to ultraviolet radiation. Radiation dermatitis and sunburn may be "recalled" by the use of methotrexate.

Adverse Effects: The most common adverse reactions reported in studies of rheumatoid arthritis patients involved the gastrointestinal system. Symptoms included nausea, stomatitis, gastrointestinal discomfort, diarrhea, vomiting and anorexia. Clinical laboratory findings included elevation of liver enzymes and, occasionally, decreased white-cell counts. In general, the incidence and severity of side effects are considered to be dose-related.

The incidence of adverse reactions in double-blind studies of patients with rheumatoid arthritis treated with low-dose oral (7.5 to 15 mg/week) pulse methotrexate are listed below. Virtually all of these patients were on concomitant NSAIDs and some were also taking low dosages of corticosteroids.
Incidence greater than 10%: liver enzymes 15%, nausea/vomiting.
Incidence between 3 and 10%: stomatitis, headache, and thrombocytopenia.
Incidence between 1 and 3%: alopecia, dizziness, leukopenia and pancytopenia.
Incidence less than 1%: chest pain, coughing, epistaxis, pruritus, tinnitus, decreased hematocrit, headache, upper respiratory infection, anorexia, arthralgias, chest pain, dysuria, eye discomfort, fever, infection, sweating and vaginal discharge.

Other reactions, usually reported at higher dosage in antineoplastic chemotherapy are as follows: Skin: urticaria, photosensitivity, depigmentation, ecchymosis, telangiectasia, acne, furunculosis, erythema multiforme, toxic epidermal necrolysis, Stevens-Johnson syndrome, skin necrosis, exfoliative dermatitis. Lesions of psoriasis may be aggravated by concomitant exposure to ultraviolet radiation.
Infections: There have been case reports of sometimes fatal opportunistic infections in patients receiving methotrexate therapy for neoplastic and nonneoplastic diseases. P. carinii pneumonia was the most common infection. Other reported infections included nocardiosis, histoplasmosis, cryptococcosis, Herpes zoster, H. simplex hepatitis, and disseminated H. simplex.
Blood: anemia, hypogammaglobulinemia, hemorrhage from various sites, septicemia.
Alimentary: pharyngitis, hematemesis, melena, gastrointestinal ulceration and bleeding, enteritis, hepatic toxicity resulting in acute liver atrophy, necrosis, fatty metamorphosis, periportal fibrosis, or hepatic cirrhosis, gingivitis.
Urogenital: renal failure, azotemia, cystitis, hematuria, defective oogenesis or spermatogenesis, transient oligospermia, menstrual dysfunction, infertility, abortion, fetal defects, severe nephropathy, gynecomastia.
Cardiovascular: pericarditis, pericardial effusion, hypotension, and thromboembolic events (including arterial thrombosis, cerebral thrombosis, deep vein thrombosis, retinal vein thrombosis, thrombophlebitis, and pulmonary embolus).
Pulmonary: interstitial pneumonitis deaths have been reported and chronic interstitial obstructive pulmonary disease has occasionally occurred.
CNS: drowsiness, blurred vision, leukoencephalopathy or encephalopathy. Aphasia, hemiparesis, paresis, and convulsions have also occurred. Following low doses, occasional patients have reported transient subtle cognitive dysfunction, mood alteration or unusual cranial sensations.

Other reactions attributed to the use of methotrexate such as metabolic changes, precipitation of diabetes, osteoporotic effects, loss of libido/impotence and even sudden death have been reported. Radiation dermatitis and sunburn may be 'recalled'. A few cases of anaphylactoid reactions have been reported.

Overdose: Symptoms and Treatment: Discontinue methotrexate at the first sign of ulceration or bleeding, diarrhea or marked depression of hematopoietic system.

As soon as possible after an inadvertent overdosage of methotrexate, leucovorin should be given at 10 mg/m² i.v. or i.m. every 6 hours until the serum methotrexate levels are below 10^{-8} M. If there is adequate gastrointestinal function, doses subsequent to the initial dose may be given orally. Concomitant hydration (3 L/day) and urinary alkalinization with sodium bicarbonate should be employed. The bicarbonate dose should be adjusted to maintain a urinary pH at 7 or greater. Serum samples should be assayed for creatinine levels and methotrexate levels at 24-hour intervals. If the 24-hour serum creatinine level has increased 50% over baseline or if the 24-hour methotrexate level is $>5\times10^{-6}$ M or the 48-hour methotrexate level is 9×10^{-7} M or higher, the doses of leucovorin should be increased to 100 mg/m² i.v. every 3 hours until the methotrexate level is $<10^{-8}$ M. The infusion rate for leucovorin should not exceed 16 mL (160 mg leucovorin)/minute.

Dosage: The patient should be fully informed of the risks involved and should be under constant supervision of the physician. Assessment of hematologic, hepatic, renal and pulmonary function should be made by history, physical examination, and laboratory tests before beginning, periodically during, and before reinstituting methotrexate therapy. Appropriate steps should be taken in men and women to avoid conception during methotrexate therapy.

Both the physician and the pharmacist should emphasize to the patient the importance of the weekly dosage regimens; mistaken daily use may cause serious and sometimes life-threatening or fatal toxicity.

All schedules should be continually tailored to the individual patient. An initial test dose may be given prior to the regular dosing schedule to detect any extreme sensitivity to adverse effects. Complete blood count with platelets should be evaluated 7 to 10 days later.

Recommended starting dosage schedules are: single oral doses of 7.5 mg once weekly or divided oral doses of 2.5 mg at 12-hour intervals for 3 doses given as a course once weekly.

Therapeutic response usually begins within 3 to 6 weeks and the patient may continue to improve for another 12 weeks or more.

The dosage in each schedule may be increased to 15 mg/week after 6 weeks in nonresponsive patients. If necessary dosage may be gradually increased further to achieve optimal response but not ordinarily to exceed a total weekly dosage of 20 mg.

Once response has been achieved, each schedule should be reduced, if possible, to the lowest possible amount of drug

Rheumatrex (cont'd)

and with the longest possible rest period. Although rare, some patients may be maintained on a dose of 2.5 mg/week.

The optimal duration of therapy is unknown. Limited data available from long-term studies indicate that the initial clinical improvement is maintained for at least 2 years with continued therapy. When methotrexate is discontinued, the arthritis usually worsens within 3 to 6 weeks.

Safe Handling and Disposal: Methotrexate is a potent antineoplastic drug. Good medical practice will minimize exposure of persons involved with frequent handling of this drug as outlined below.

Handling: Methotrexate or solutions of methotrexate have no vesicant properties and do not show acute toxicity on topical contact with the skin or mucous membranes. However, persons involved with handling cytotoxic drugs should avoid contact with skin and inhalation of airborne particles. Personnel regularly involved in the preparation and handling of antineoplastics should have biannual examinations.

Disposal: Avoid contact with skin and inhalation of airborne particles by use of PVC gloves and disposable gowns and masks. Tablets: Place container and tablets in a plastic bag, seal, and mark as hazardous waste. Incinerate at 1 000°C or higher. If incineration is not available, dissolve tablets in a suitable quantity of 1 normal sodium hydroxide solution, and autoclave the mixture for 1 hour. Discard in the sewer system with copious amounts of running water.

Cleaning: Nondisposable equipment that has come in contact with methotrexate solutions may be rinsed with water and washed thoroughly with soap and water.

Information for the Patient: See Blue Section—Information for the Patient "Rheumatrex".

Supplied: Each round, yellow, scored tablet, engraved "LL" and "M1", contains: methotrexate sodium equivalent to methotrexate 2.5 mg. Nonmedicinal ingredients: lactose, monohydrate, magnesium stearate, (food grade) and starch pregelatinized. Dye- and tartrazine-free. Bottles of 100. Store at 15 to 30°C.

Reviewed 1999

RHINALAR® ℞
Roche

Flunisolide Nasal Mist
Allergic Rhinitis Therapy

Pharmacology: Flunisolide has demonstrated marked anti-inflammatory and antiallergic efficacy in classical animal test systems. It is a corticosteroid which is several hundred times more potent in animal anti-inflammatory assays than the cortisol standard. Clinical studies with flunisolide have shown a topical activity on the nasal mucous membrane with minimal associated systemic activity at the low spray doses administered. The improvement of symptoms is based on its direct local effect rather than on indirect effect through systemic absorption.

Indications: Treatment of perennial and seasonal allergic rhinitis when tolerance to or effectiveness of conventional treatment is unsatisfactory.

Contraindications: Active or quiescent tuberculosis or untreated fungal, bacterial or viral infections. Hypersensitivity to the product. Children under 6 years of age.

Warnings: Glucocorticoids may mask some signs of infection, and new infections may appear during their use.

Pregnancy: Safety in pregnancy has not been established. Use of Rhinalar during the first 3 months of pregnancy is not recommended. If used during the second and third trimester, weigh the expected benefits against the potential hazards to the fetus.

In patients previously on high doses of systemic corticosteroids, withdrawal of steroids may cause symptoms such as tiredness, aches and pains and depression. In severe cases, adrenal insufficiency may occur necessitating a temporary resumption of systemic corticosteroids.

Flunisolide is not recommended for those patients with a history of recurrent nasal bleeding.

Precautions: Replacement of systemic corticosteroids with flunisolide should be gradual and carefully monitored by a physician.

Although absorption sufficient to produce systemic effects has not been shown in clinical studies with flunisolide nasal mist, the potential of adrenal suppression still exists and this must be considered as a possibility with prolonged excessive usage. Patients on long-term therapy should be reassessed periodically to avoid unnecessary continued use.

Since onset of action may be somewhat slower than that of topical or oral sympathomimetic amines or antihistamines, it should be used for several days before evaluating therapy.

If beneficial effect is not evident after approximately 7 days, reevaluate the patient.

If hypersensitivity reactions occur, discontinue therapy and institute appropriate treatment.

Corticosteroid therapy can decrease resistance to localized infection. If nasopharyngeal infections occur during therapy, institute appropriate treatment.

Despite the very low absorption of flunisolide when administered intranasally, the following must be kept in mind: a) corticosteroid effects may be enhanced in patients with hypothyroidism and in those with cirrhosis. b) in hypoprothrombinemia, acetylsalicylic acid should be used cautiously in conjunction with corticosteroids.

Advise patients to inform subsequent physicians of the prior use of corticosteroids.

During local corticosteroid therapy, the possibility of atrophic rhinitis and/or pharyngeal candidiasis should be kept in mind.

Flunisolide should not be used during an asthmatic attack.

Because of the inhibitory effect of corticosteroids on wound healing, in patients who have had recent nasal septal ulcers, recurrent epistaxis, nasal surgery or trauma, a nasal corticosteroid should be used with caution until healing has occurred.

Adverse Effects: Side effects noted have been consistent with what one would expect in applying a topical medication to an already inflamed membrane. The most frequent adverse effect observed were aftertaste and a mild transient nasal burning and stinging. Occasionally, this was severe enough to warrant discontinuation of therapy.

Other adverse effects seen in patients, in order of decreasing prevalence were: nasal irritation, epistaxis, runny and stuffy nose, sore throat, hoarseness, throat irritation, change or loss in the sense of smell or taste and nasal septal perforation. Exceptionally, these may require discontinuation of therapy. Rarely, a permanent loss in the sense of smell and/or taste has been reported.

Overdose: Symptoms and Treatment: Acute overdosage has not been reported. When used at excessive doses, the potential of steroid effects such as hypercorticism and adrenal suppression does exist. Decreasing the dose will abolish these manifestations.

Dosage: Flunisolide nasal mist is for administration by the intranasal route only. Starting dose: adults, 2 sprays into each nostril twice daily. Increase to 3 times daily if needed. Children 6 to 14 years of age, 1 spray into each nostril 3 times daily. Maintenance dose: After the desired clinical effect is obtained, the maintenance dose should be the smallest amount necessary to control the symptoms. Some patients may be maintained on as little as 1 spray (approximately 25 µg) in each nostril/day. Patients on long-term therapy should be reassessed periodically to avoid unnecessary continued use. There is no evidence that exceeding the maximum recommended dosage is more effective. Therefore, maximum daily dose should not exceed 6 sprays in each nostril for adults and 3 sprays in each nostril for children 6 to 14 years of age.

The effect of flunisolide, unlike that of vasoconstrictors, is not immediate. Full therapeutic benefit requires regular usage. Explain the absence of an immediate effect to the patient in order to ensure cooperation and continuation of treatment with the regular dosage schedule.

In the presence of excessive nasal mucus secretion or edema of the nasal mucosa, the drug may fail to reach the site of action. In such cases, use a nasal vasoconstrictor for 2 to 3 days prior to flunisolide.

Supplied: Each metered spray contains: approximately 25 µg of flunisolide dissolved in an aqueous solution (0.025%) containing propylene glycol, polyethylene glycol, citric acid, sodium citrate and benzalkonium chloride as a preservative. Solution is formulated without fluorocarbons. Plastic bottles of 25 mL fitted with a metered pump device which delivers approximately 25 µg of flunisolide/spray via a nozzle which is inserted into the nostril. Store at 15 to 30°C. Store bottle in an upright position.

Reviewed 1997

For comparative information on ACE Inhibitors, see the CPhA General Monograph in the WHITE SECTION.

RHINARIS®
Pharmascience

Polyethylene Glycol—Propylene Glycol
Dry Nose—Rhinitis Therapy

Indications: For the temporary relief of perennial rhinitis and relief of blockage and stuffiness in the nose and sneezing caused by hay fever or other allergies, common cold, chronic irritation, debility, inflammation of the nasal sinuses, unfavorable climate, nasal and/or post nasal discharge, pain and malaise.

Adverse Effects: Propylene glycol may produce some local irritation on application to mucous membranes. Patients who are hypersensitive to topical preparations containing propylene glycol should use Rhinaris with caution.

For full therapeutic benefit Rhinaris requires regular usage. Patients should be advised that they may expect relief 15 to 20 minutes after administration. Patients may expect a mild but transient stinging sensation upon administration.

Dosage: Lubricating Nasal Gel: Adults and children: Apply a small amount of gel into each nostril every 4 hours or as needed. Protect from freezing.

Lubricating Nasal Mist: Adults: 1 or 2 sprays into each nostril every 4 hours or as needed. Children: Over 2 years: 1 spray into each nostril every 4 hours or as needed. Protect from freezing.

Supplied: Lubricating Nasal Gel: Each g of gel contains: polyethylene glycol 15% and propylene glycol 20%. pH: 5.5. Tubes of 5 and 30 g.

Lubricating Nasal Mist: Each mL of solution contains: polyethylene glycol 15% and propylene glycol 5%. pH: 6. Plastic bottles of 30 mL fitted with a metered pump.

Reviewed 1998

RHINOCORT® AQUA ℞
Astra

Budesonide
Glucocorticosteroid

Pharmacology: Budesonide is a potent nonhalogenated synthetic glucocorticosteroid with strong topical and weak systemic effects.

Budesonide has a high topical anti-inflammatory potency and it is rapidly biotransformed in the liver. This favorable separation between topical anti-inflammatory activity and systemic effect is due to strong glucocorticosteroid receptor affinity and an effective first pass metabolism with a short half-life. The mechanism of action of intranasally administered budesonide has not yet been completely defined.

Pharmacokinetics: The systemic availability of oral budesonide in man is low (about 10%). With reference to the metered dose, the systemic availability of budesonide from Rhinocort Aqua is 33%. After application of budesonide in solution directly on the nasal mucosa, all the dose is systemically available, indicating that budesonide does not undergo local metabolism in the nose.

The maximal plasma concentration after administration of 400 µg budesonide from Rhinocort Aqua is 1 nmol/L and is reached within 0.7 hours.

Indications: The treatment of seasonal allergic and allergic/nonallergic perennial and vasomotor rhinitis unresponsive to conventional therapy. Also indicated for the treatment of nasal polyps and in the prevention of nasal polyps after polypectomy.

Contraindications: Hypersensitivity to any of the nasal spray's components. Active or quiescent tuberculosis. Untreated fungal, bacterial, or viral infections. Children under 6 years of age.

Warnings: In patients previously on prolonged periods or high doses of systemic steroids, withdrawal of steroids may cause symptoms such as tiredness, aches and pains, and depression. In severe cases, adrenal insufficiency may occur necessitating a temporary resumption of systemic steroids.

Careful attention must be given to patients with asthma or other clinical conditions in whom a rapid decrease in systemic steroids may cause a severe exacerbation of their symptoms.

Pregnancy: See Precautions.

Precautions: Glucocorticosteroids may mask some signs of infection and new infections may appear during their use.

In transferring patients from a systemic steroid to budesonide, the reduction of the systemic steroid must be very gradual and carefully supervised by the physician since systemic withdrawal symptoms (e.g., joint and/or muscular pain, lassitude, depression) may occur in spite of maintenance or improvement of respiratory functions (see Dosage).

Patients should be informed that the full effect of budesonide therapy is not achieved until 2 to 3 days of treatment have been completed. In rare cases the full effect of budesonide therapy is not achieved until 2 weeks of treatment have been completed. Treatment of seasonal rhinitis should, if possible, start before the exposure to allergens.

Treatment with budesonide should not be stopped abruptly but tapered off gradually.

Special care is needed in patients with fungal and viral nasal infections. Children who are on immunosuppressant drugs are more susceptible to infections than healthy children. Chickenpox and measles, for example, can have a more serious or fatal course in children on immunosuppressant corticosteroids. In such children, or in adults who have not had these diseases, particular care should be taken to avoid exposure. If exposed, therapy with varicella zoster immune globulin (VZIG) or pooled i.v. immunoglobulin (IVIG), as appropriate, may be indicated. If chickenpox develops, treatment with antiviral agents may be considered.

Concomitant treatment may sometimes be required to counteract eye symptoms caused by allergy.

The long-term effects of budesonide in human subjects are still unknown, in particular, its local effects, and on developmental or immunologic processes. The nasal mucosa of those patients receiving long-term, continuous therapy should be inspected at least twice a year. The possibility of atrophic rhinitis and/or pharyngeal candidiasis should be kept in mind. Children: Until greater clinical experience has been gained, the continuous, long-term treatment of children is not recommended.

When budesonide is administered intranasally, the following should be kept in mind: a) glucocorticosteroid effects may be enhanced in patients with hypothyroidism and in those with cirrhosis. Reduced liver function may affect the elimination of corticosteroids. The i.v. pharmacokinetics of budesonide however, are similar in cirrhotic patients and in healthy subjects. The pharmacokinetics after oral ingestion of budesonide were affected by compromised liver function as evidenced by increased systemic availability. This is however, of limited clinical importance for intranasally administered budesonide, as the oral contribution to the systemic availability is relatively small. b) in hypoprothrombinemia, salicylates should be used cautiously in conjunction with glucocorticosteroids.

Because of the inhibitory effect of corticosteroids on wound healing in patients who have had recent nasal surgery or trauma, a nasal corticosteroid should be used with caution until healing has occurred.

Pregnancy: The safety of budesonide in pregnancy has not been established. Therefore, its use during pregnancy should be avoided unless there are compelling reasons, particularly in the first trimester of pregnancy. In experimental animal studies, budesonide was found to cross the blood-placenta barrier. Like other glucocorticosteroids, budesonide is teratogenic to rodent species. High doses of budesonide administered s.c. produced fetal malformations, primarily skeletal defects, in rabbits, rats, and in mice. The relevance of these findings to humans has not yet been established. In the absence of further studies in humans, budesonide should be used during pregnancy only if the potential benefits clearly outweigh the risk to the fetus. Infants born of mothers who have received substantial doses of glucocorticosteroids during pregnancy should be carefully observed for hypoadrenalism.

Lactation: Glucocorticosteroids are secreted in human milk. It is not known whether budesonide would be secreted in human milk, but it is suspected to be likely. The use of budesonide in nursing mothers requires that the possible benefits of the drug be weighed against the potential hazards to the mother or infant.

Children under 6 Years of Age: Budesonide is not presently recommended for children younger than 6 years of age due to limited clinical data in this age group.

Glucocorticosteroids may mask some signs of infections and new infections may appear. A decreased resistance to localized infection has been observed during glucocorticosteroid therapy. During long-term therapy, pituitary-adrenal function, hematological status and height (in children) should be periodically assessed.

Patients should be advised to inform subsequent physicians of the prior use of glucocorticosteroids.

To ensure the proper dosage and administration of the drug, the patient should be instructed by a physician or other health professional in the use of Rhinocort Aqua (see Blue Section—Information for the Patient).

Dose-related suppression of plasma and urinary cortisol has been observed in healthy volunteers after short-term administration of budesonide. Although no important changes in basal plasma cortisol levels were manifested in patients with rhinitis using budesonide at recommended doses, caution is advised.

Drug Interactions: To date budesonide has not been observed to interact with other drugs used for the treatment of rhinitis. Cimetidine: The kinetics of budesonide were investigated in a study in healthy subjects without and with cimetidine, 1 000 mg daily. After a 4 mg oral dose the values for C_{max} (nmol/L) and systemic availability (%) of budesonide without and with cimetidine (3.3 vs 5.1 nmol/L and 10 vs 12%, respectively) indicated a slight inhibitory effect on hepatic metabolism of budesonide, caused by cimetidine. This should be of little clinical importance.

Ketoconazole: Ketoconazole, a potent inhibitor of cytochrome P450 3A, the main metabolic enzyme for corticosteroids, increases plasma levels of orally ingested budesonide.

Omeprazole: At recommended doses, omeprazole has no effect on the pharmacokinetics of oral budesonide.

Adverse Effects: The adverse reactions reported with budesonide are consistent with what one would expect when applying a topical treatment to an already inflamed membrane. All side effects were transient. The most commonly reported side effects include: nasal and throat irritation, nasal bleeding, crusting, dryness. Other adverse events reported are sneezing (at initiation of therapy), itching throat, sore throat, cough, fatigue, nausea/dizziness and headache. When patients are transferred to budesonide from a systemic steroid, allergic conditions such as asthma or eczema may be unmasked. In rare cases, skin reactions (urticaria, rash, dermatitis, angioedema, etc.) may occur in association with local corticosteroid therapy. Extremely rare cases of ulcerations of the mucous membranes and nasal septal perforation have been reported following the use of intranasal corticosteroids.

Overdose: Symptoms and Treatment: Like any other nasally administered corticosteroid, acute overdosing is unlikely in view of the total amount of active ingredient present. However, when used chronically in excessive doses or in conjunction with other corticosteroid formulations, systemic corticosteroid effects such as hypercorticism and adrenal suppression may appear. If such changes recur, the dosage of budesonide should be discontinued slowly consistent with accepted procedures for discontinuation of chronic steroid therapy (see Dosage).

The restoration of the hypothalamic-pituitary-axis may be a slow process and during periods with pronounced physical stress such as severe infections, trauma, and surgical operations, a supplement with systemic steroids may be advisable.

Dosage: See Warnings.

Careful attention must be given to patients previously treated for prolonged periods with systemic corticosteroids when transferred to budesonide. Initially, budesonide and the systemic corticosteroid must be given concomitantly, while the dose of the latter is gradually decreased. The usual rate of withdrawal of the systemic steroid is the equivalent of 2.5 mg of prednisone every 4 days if the patient is under close supervision. If continuous supervision is not feasible, the withdrawal of the systemic steroid should be slower, approximately 2.5 mg of prednisone (or equivalent) every 10 days. If withdrawal symptoms appear, the previous dose of the systemic steroid should be resumed for a week before further decrease is attempted.

Rhinitis: Adults and Children Over 6 Years: Initially: The recommended starting dose is 256 μg daily. The dose can be administered once daily in the morning or divided into 2 administrations morning and evening. For example: 128 μg (2 sprays) into each nostril in the morning or, 64 μg (1 spray) into each nostril morning and evening.

Maintenance: After the desired clinical effect is obtained, the maintenance dose should be reduced to the smallest amount necessary to control the symptoms.

Treatment or Prevention of Nasal Polyps: The recommended dose is 64 μg (1 spray) into each nostril morning and evening (total daily dose is 256 μg).

Children under 6 Years: Not recommended for children in this age group.

Patients should be informed that the full effect of budesonide therapy may not become evident until 2 to 3 days of treatment have been completed. Full therapeutic benefit requires regular usage. Explain the absence of an immediate effect to the patient in order to ensure cooperation and continuation of the treatment with a regular dosage regime. Treatment of seasonal rhinitis should, if possible, start before exposure to the allergens. Concomitant treatment may sometimes be necessary to counteract eye symptoms caused by the allergy. In continuous long-term treatment, the nasal mucosa should be inspected regularly, e.g., every 6 months.

If the nasal passages are severely blocked, the drug may fail to reach the site of action. In such cases, a course of oral steroids or decongestants may be required before initiating budesonide therapy.

Although systemic effects are negligible at recommended doses, budesonide treatment should not be continued beyond 3 weeks in the absence of significant symptomatic improvement. Budesonide should not be used in the presence of untreated localized infections involving the nasal mucosa.

Information for the Patient: See Blue Section—Information for the Patient "Rhinocort Aqua".

Supplied: Each metered dose contains: budesonide 64 μg in a white to off-white, thixotropic suspension in water. Nonmedicinal ingredients: carboxymethylcellulose sodium, disodium edetate, glucose anhydrous, hydrochloric acid, microcrystalline cellulose, polysorbate 80, potassium sorbate and purified water. Amber glass bottles of 120 doses, provided with a pump spray mechanism, nasal adapter and patient instruction leaflet. Store at room temperature (15 to 30°C).

Reviewed 1999

RHINOCORT® TURBUHALER® ℞

Astra

Budesonide

Glucocorticosteroid

Pharmacology: Budesonide is a potent nonhalogenated synthetic glucocorticosteroid with strong topical and weak systemic effects.

Budesonide has a high topical anti-inflammatory potency and it is rapidly biotransformed in the liver. This favorable separation between topical anti-inflammatory activity and systemic effect is due to strong glucocorticosteroid receptor affinity and an effective first pass metabolism with a short half-life. The mechanism of action of intranasally administered budesonide has not yet been completely defined.

Pharmacokinetics: The systemic availability of oral budesonide in man is low (about 10%). With reference to the metered dose, the systemic availability of budesonide from Rhinocort Turbuhaler is 22%. After application of budesonide in solution directly on the nasal mucosa, all the dose is systemically available, indicating that budesonide does not undergo local metabolism in the nose.

The maximal plasma concentration after administration of 800 μg budesonide from Rhinocort Turbuhaler is 1.1 nmol/L and is reached within 0.4 hours.

Indications: The treatment of seasonal allergic and allergic/non-allergic perennial and vasomotor rhinitis unresponsive to conventional therapy. Also indicated for the treatment of nasal polyps and the prevention of nasal polyps after polypectomy.

Contraindications: Hypersensitivity to budesonide. Active or quiescent tuberculosis. Untreated fungal, bacterial or viral infections. Children under 6 years of age.

Warnings: In patients previously on prolonged periods or high doses of systemic steroids, withdrawal of steroids may cause symptoms such as tiredness, aches and pains, and depression. In severe cases, adrenal insufficiency may occur necessitating a temporary resumption of systemic steroids.

Careful attention must be given to patients with asthma or other clinical conditions in whom a rapid decrease in systemic steroids may cause a severe exacerbation of their symptoms.

Pregnancy: See Precautions.

Precautions: In transferring patients from a systemic steroid to budesonide, the reduction of the systemic steroid must be very gradual and carefully supervised by the physician since systemic withdrawal symptoms (e.g., joint and/or muscular pain, lassitude, depression), may occur in spite of maintenance or improvement of respiratory functions (see Dosage).

Patients should be informed that the full effect of budesonide therapy is not achieved until 2 to 3 days of treatment have been completed. In rare cases the full effect of budesonide therapy is not achieved until 2 weeks of treatment have been completed. In rare cases the full effect of budesonide therapy is not achieved until 2 weeks of treatment have been completed. Treatment of seasonal rhinitis should, if possible, start before the exposure to allergens.

During long-term therapy, pituitary-adrenal function, hematological status and height (in children) should be periodically assessed.

Rhinocort Turbuhaler (cont'd)

Treatment with budesonide should not be stopped abruptly but tapered off gradually.

Glucocorticosteroids may mask some signs of infection and new infections may appear during their use. A decreased resistance to localized infections has been observed during glucocorticosteroid therapy; this may require treatment with appropriate therapy or stopping the administration of budesonide.

Special care is needed in patients with fungal and viral nasal infections. Children who are on immunosuppressant drugs are more susceptible to infections than healthy children. Chickenpox and measles for example, can have a more serious or fatal course in children on immunosuppressant corticosteroids. In such children, or in adults who have not had these diseases, particular care should be taken to avoid exposure. If exposed, therapy with varicella zoster immune globulin (VZIG) or pooled i.v. immunoglobulin (IVIG), as appropriate, may be indicated. If chickenpox develops, treatment with antiviral agents may be considered.

Concomitant treatment may sometimes be required to counteract eye symptoms caused by allergy.

The long-term effects of budesonide are still unknown, in particular, its local effects; the possibility of atrophic rhinitis and/or pharyngeal candidiasis should be kept in mind.

Children: Until greater clinical experience has been gained, the continuous, long-term treatment of children is not recommended.

When budesonide is administered intranasally, the following should be kept in mind: a) glucocorticosteroid effects may be enhanced in patients with hypothyroidism and in those with cirrhosis. Reduced liver function may affect the elimination of corticosteroids. The i.v. pharmacokinetics of budesonide however, are similar in cirrhotic patients and in healthy subjects. The pharmacokinetics after oral ingestion of budesonide were affected by compromised liver function as evidenced by increased systemic availability. This is however, of limited clinical importance for intranasally administered budesonide, as after inhalation, the oral contribution to the systemic availability is relatively small. b) in hypoprothrombinemia, salicylates should be used cautiously in conjunction with glucocorticosteroids.

Because of the inhibitory effect of corticosteroids on wound healing in patients who have had recent nasal surgery or trauma, a nasal corticosteroid should be used with caution until healing has occurred.

Pregnancy: The safety of budesonide in pregnancy has not been established. Therefore, its use during pregnancy should be avoided unless there are compelling reasons, particularly in the first trimester of pregnancy. In experimental animal studies, budesonide was found to cross the blood-placenta barrier. Like other glucocorticosteroids, budesonide is teratogenic to rodent species. High doses of budesonide administered s.c. produced fetal malformations, primarily skeletal defects, in rabbits, rats and mice. The relevance of these findings to humans has not yet been established. In the absence of further studies in humans, budesonide should be used during pregnancy only if the potential benefits clearly outweigh the risk to the fetus. Infants born of mothers who have received substantial doses of glucocorticosteroids during pregnancy should be carefully observed for hypoadrenalism.

Lactation: Glucocorticosteroids are secreted in human milk. It is not known whether budesonide would be secreted in human milk but it is suspected to be likely. The use of budesonide in nursing mothers requires that the possible benefits of the drug be weighed against the potential hazards to the mother or infant.

Children under 6 years of age: Budesonide is not presently recommended for children younger than 6 years of age due to limited clinical data in this age group.

Patients should be advised to inform subsequent physicians of the prior use of glucocorticosteroids.

Dose-related suppression of plasma and urinary cortisol has been observed in healthy volunteers after short-term administration of budesonide. Although no important changes in basal plasma cortisol levels were manifested in patients with rhinitis using budesonide at recommended doses, caution is advised.

To ensure the proper dosage and administration of the drug, the patient should be instructed by a physician or other health professional in the use of Rhinocort Turbuhaler (see Blue Section - Information for the Patient).

Drug Interactions: To date budesonide has not been observed to interact with other drugs used for the treatment of rhinitis. Cimetidine: The kinetics of budesonide were investigated in a study in healthy subjects without and with cimetidine, 1 000 mg daily. After a 4 mg oral dose the values for C_{max} (nmol/L) and systemic availability (%) of budesonide without and with cimetidine (3.3 vs 5.1 nmol/L and 10 vs 12%, respectively) indicated a slight inhibitory effect on hepatic metabolism of budesonide, caused by cimetidine. This should be of little clinical importance.

Ketoconazole: Ketoconazole, a potent inhibitor of cytochrome P450 3A, the main metabolic enzyme for corticosteroids, increases plasma levels of orally ingested budesonide.

Omeprazole: At recommended doses, omeprazole has no effect on the pharmacokinetics of oral budesonide.

Adverse Effects: The adverse reactions reported are consistent with what one would expect when applying a topical treatment to an already inflamed membrane. All side effects are transient. The most commonly reported side effects include: nasal and throat irritation, nasal bleeding, crusting, dryness. Other adverse events reported are sneezing (at initiation of therapy), itching throat, sore throat, cough, fatigue, nausea/dizziness and headache. When patients are transferred to budesonide from a systemic steroid, allergic conditions such as asthma or eczema may be unmasked. In rare cases, skin reactions (urticaria, rash, dermatitis, angioedema, etc.) may occur in association with local corticosteroid therapy. Extremely rare cases of ulcerations of the mucous membranes and nasal septal perforation have been reported following the use of intranasal corticosteroids.

Overdose: Symptoms and Treatment: Like any other nasally administered corticosteroid, acute overdosing is unlikely in view of the total amount of active ingredient present. However, when used chronically in excessive doses or in conjunction with other corticosteroid formulations, systemic corticosteroid effects such as hypercorticism and adrenal suppression may appear. If such changes recur, the dosage of budesonide should be discontinued slowly, consistent with accepted procedures for discontinuation of chronic steroid therapy (see Dosage).

The restoration of the hypothalamic-pituitary-axis may be a slow process, and during periods with pronounced physical stress such as severe infections, trauma and surgical operations, a supplement with systemic steroids may be advisable.

Dosage: See Warnings.

Careful attention must be given to patients previously treated for prolonged periods with systemic corticosteroids when transferred to budesonide. Initially, budesonide and the systemic corticosteroid must be given concomitantly, while the dose of the latter is gradually decreased. The usual rate of withdrawal of the systemic steroid is the equivalent of 2.5 mg of prednisone every 4 days if the patient is under close supervision. If continuous supervision is not feasible, the withdrawal of the systemic steroid should be slower, approximately 2.5 mg of prednisone (or equivalent) every 10 days. If withdrawal symptoms appear, the previous dose of the systemic steroid should be resumed for a week before further decrease is attempted.

Rhinitis: Initial Dose: Adults: 2 applications into each nostril in the morning (total daily dose: 400 μg).

Children (6 years and older): 2 applications into each nostril in the morning (total daily dose: 400 μg). This dose should not be exceeded in children.

Maintenance Dose: Adults and Children (6 years and older): Use the lowest effective dose necessary to control symptoms. Children under 6 years: Not recommended for children in this age group.

Treatment or Prevention of Nasal Polyps: One application (100 μg) into each nostril, morning and evening (total daily dose 400 μg).

Patients should be informed that the full effect of budesonide therapy may not become evident until 2 to 3 days of treatment have been completed. Full therapeutic benefit requires regular usage. Explain the absence of an immediate effect to the patient in order to ensure cooperation and continuation of the treatment with a regular dosage regime. Treatment of seasonal rhinitis should, if possible, start before exposure to the allergens. Concomitant treatment may sometimes be necessary to counteract eye symptoms caused by the allergy. In continuous long-term treatment, the nasal mucosa should be inspected regularly, e.g., every 6 months.

If the nasal passages are severely blocked, the drug may fail to reach the site of action. In such cases, a course of oral steroids or decongestants may be required before initiating budesonide therapy.

The patient may not taste or feel any medication when using Rhinocort Turbuhaler due to the small amount of drug dispensed.

Although systemic effects are negligible at recommended doses, budesonide treatment should not be continued beyond 3 weeks in the absence of significant symptomatic improvement. Budesonide should not be used in the presence of untreated localized infections involving the nasal mucosa.

Information for the Patient: See Blue Section—Information for the Patient "Rhinocort Turbuhaler".

Supplied: Each dry powder inhaler contains: 200 doses of micronized budesonide 100 μg/dose. Each inhalation from Turbuhaler will provide 100 μg of budesonide active substance; no additives or carrier substances are included. Turbuhaler cannot be refilled and should be discarded when empty. Store at 15 to 30°C.

Reviewed 1999

RHO®-ATENOLOL Ⓟ

Rhodiapharm

Atenolol

Beta-adrenergic Receptor Blocking Agent

Supplied: 50 mg: Each plain white scored tablet, 7 mm in diameter, embossed with "RHO" on one side and "50" on the other, contains: atenolol 50 mg. Nonmedicinal ingredients: colloidal silicon dioxide, magnesium stearate, microcrystalline cellulose, polyethylene glycol, sodium croscarmellose, sodium lauryl sulfate and talc. Blister packs of 15, boxes of 30.

100 mg: Each white biconvex tablet, 10 mm in diameter, with a grooved cross on one side and embossed with "RHO 100" on the other side, contains: atenolol 100 mg. Nonmedicinal ingredients: colloidal silicon dioxide, magnesium stearate, microcrystalline cellulose, polyethylene glycol, sodium croscarmellose, sodium lauryl sulfate and talc. Blister packs of 15, boxes of 30.

Store at room temperature (15 to 30°C). Protect from light and moisture.

New Product 1998

RHO®-CLONAZEPAM Ⓟ

RhoxalPharma

Clonazepam

Anticonvulsant

Supplied: 0.5 mg: Each orange, round, biconvex tablet, scored on one side and embossed RHO 0.5 on the other side, contains: clonazepam 0.5 mg, USP. Nonmedicinal ingredients: FD&C Yellow No. 6, lactose, magnesium stearate and pregelatinized starch. Bottes of 100 and 500.

1 mg: Each green, round, biconvex tablet, scored on one side and embossed RHO 1 on the other side, contains: clonazepam 1 mg, USP. Nonmedicinal ingredients: D&C Yellow No. 10 aluminium lake, FD&C Blue No. 2 aluminium lake, lactose, magnesium stearate and pregelatinized starch. Bottles of 100 and 500.

2 mg: Each white, round, biconvex tablet, scored on one side and embossed RHO 2 on the other side, contains: clonazepam 2 mg, USP. Nonmedicinal ingredients: lactose, magnesium stearate and pregelatinized starch. Bottles of 100 and 500.

Store in air-tight, light-resistant containers at controlled room temperature (15 to 30°C). Tablets have an expiration date of 2 years following the date of manufacture.

New Product 1998

RHODACINE® Ⓟ

Rhodiapharm

Indomethacin

Anti-inflammatory—Analgesic

Supplied: Capsules: 25 mg: Each cream-colored, hard gelatin #3 capsule, imprinted with IND. 25, contains: indomethacin USP 25 mg as white granules. Nonmedicinal ingredients: colloidal silicon dioxide, copolyvidone, cornstarch, croscarmellose sodium, gelatin, lactose monohydrate, magnesium stearate and talc; capsule shell: titanium dioxide. Amber glass bottles of 100. Store at room temperature (15 to 30°C) and protect from light.

50 mg: Each light brown, hard gelatin #3 capsule, imprinted with IND. 50, contains: indomethacin USP 50 mg as white granules. Nonmedicinal ingredients: colloidal silicon dioxide, copolyvidone, cornstarch, croscarmellose sodium, gelatin, lactose monohydrate, magnesium stearate and talc; capsule shell: ferric oxide black, ferric oxide red, ferric oxide yellow and titanium dioxide; imprint ink: iron oxide. Amber glass bottles of 100. Store at room temperature (15 to 30°C) and protect from light.

Suppositories: 50 mg: Each white, torpedo-shaped suppository contains: indomethacin USP 50 mg. Nonmedicinal ingredients: colloidal silicon dioxide and hydrogenated vegetable glycerides. Aluminum foil blister-strips of 5, boxes of 10. Store at room temperature and away from heat.

100 mg: Each white, torpedo-shaped suppository contains: indomethacin USP 100 mg. Nonmedicinal ingredients: colloidal silicon dioxide and hydrogenated vegetable glycerides. Aluminum foil blister-strips of 5, boxes of 10. Store at room temperature and away from heat.

RHODIAPROX® Ⓟ

Rhodiapharm

Naproxen

Anti-inflammatory—Analgesic—Antipyretic

Supplied: Each white opaque torpedo-shaped suppository contains: naproxen 500 mg. Nonmedicinal ingredients: anhydrous silicon dioxide and semi-synthetic solid glycerides. Individually wrapped in polyethylene lined white polyvinyl shells in perforated strips, boxes of 30. Store between 15 and 30°C. Protect from freezing.

New Product 1998

RHODIS™ Ⓟ
RHODIS-EC™ Ⓟ
RHODIS SR™ Ⓟ

Rhodiapharm

Ketoprofen

Anti-inflammatory—Analgesic

Supplied: Rhodis: Capsules: Each ivory and dark green capsule contains: ketoprofen 50 mg. Nonmedicinal ingredients: D&C yellow No 10, FD&C green No 3, FD&C yellow No 6, gelatin, lactose, magnesium stearate and titanium dioxide. Tartrazine-free. Bottles of 100 and 500.

Suppositories: Each white to off-white suppository contains: ketoprofen 100 mg. Nonmedicinal ingredients: colloidal silicon dioxide and hydrogenated vegetable glycerides. Tartrazine-free. Boxes of 30. Store below 30°C.

Rhodis EC: 50 mg: Each yellow, round, biconvex, enteric-coated tablet, plain on one side and identified 50 on the other, contains: ketoprofen 50 mg. Nonmedicinal ingredients: carnauba wax, cornstarch, D&C Yellow No 10 aluminum lake, dextrin, FD&C Yellow No 6 aluminum lake, lactose, magnesium stearate, polacrilin potassium, polyvinyl acetate phthalate, sucrose, talc, titanium dioxide and triethyl citrate. Tartrazine-free. Bottles of 100 and 500.

100 mg: Each yellow, round, biconvex, enteric-coated tablet, plain on one side and identified 100 on the other, contains: ketoprofen 100 mg. Nonmedicinal ingredients: carnauba wax, cornstarch, D&C Yellow No 10 aluminum lake, dextrin, FD&C Yellow No 6 aluminum lake, lactose, magnesium stearate, polyvinyl acetate phthalate, polacrilin potassium, stearic acid, sucrose, talc, titanium dioxide and triethyl citrate. Tartrazine-free. Bottles of 100 and 500.

Rhodis SR: Each white, round, biconvex, enteric-coated tablet, marked RH on one side and identified RHODIS SR 200 on the other, contains: ketoprofen 200 mg. Nonmedicinal ingredients: calcium phosphate dibasic, carnauba wax, cellulose acetate phthalate, diethyl phthalate, ethyl acetate, hydroxyethyl cellulose and magnesium stearate. Tartrazine-free. Bottles of 100 and 500.

RHO®-FLUPHENAZINE DECANOATE Ⓟ

Rhodiapharm

Fluphenazine Decanoate

Antipsychotic

Supplied: Injectable: Each mL of injectable solution contains: fluphenazine decanoate BP 25 mg. Nonmedicinal ingredients: benzyl alcohol and sesame oil. Multidose vials of 5 mL.

Concentrate: Each mL of injectable solution contains: fluphenazine decanoate B.P. 100 mg. Nonmedicinal ingredients: benzyl alcohol and sesame oil. Ampuls of 1 mL.

Store between 15 and 25°C. Protect from light.

RHO®-HALOPERIDOL DECANOATE Ⓟ

Rhodiapharm

Haloperidol Decanoate

Antipsychotic

Supplied: Ampuls: Each mL of slightly amber, viscous solution contains: haloperidol 100 mg (as haloperidol decanoate 141 mg). Nonmedicinal ingredients: benzyl alcohol and sesame seed oil. Ampuls of 1 mL.

Vials: 50 mg: Each mL of slightly amber, viscous solution contains: haloperidol 50 mg (as haloperidol decanoate 70.5 mg). Nonmedicinal ingredients: benzyl alcohol and sesame seed oil. Vials of 5 mL.

100 mg: Each mL of slightly amber, viscous solution contains: haloperidol 100 mg (as haloperidol decanoate 141 mg). Nonmedicinal ingredients: benzyl alcohol and sesame seed oil. Vials of 5 mL.

Store between 15 and 25°C, protected from light. As with other depot neuroleptics, precipitation may occur if the drug is stored for long periods in the cold. The precipitate should clear on storage at room temperature.

Warning: All parenteral drug products should be inspected visually for clarity, particulate matter, precipitate, discoloration and leakage prior to administration, whenever solution and container permit. The normal color of haloperidol decanoate injection is slightly amber. Solutions showing haziness, particulate matter, precipitate, discoloration or leakage should not be used.

RHO®-LOPERAMIDE

RhoxalPharma

Loperamide HCl

Antidiarrheal

Supplied: Each light green capsule-shaped tablet (caplet) contains: loperamide HCl 2 mg. Nonmedicinal ingredients: D&C Yellow #10 aluminium lake (quinoline lake), FD&C Blue #1 aluminium lake HT (brilliant blue lake), lactose monohydrate, magnesium stearate, microcrystalline cellulose, pregelatinized starch and sodium starch glycolate. Bottles of 100 and 500. Store in well-closed containers at controlled room temperature (15 to 30°C).

New Product 1998

RHO®-METFORMIN Ⓟ

RhoxalPharma

Metformin HCl

Antihyperglycemic Agent

Supplied: Each white, round, biconvex, film-coated tablet, embossed M21 on one side and RHO 500 on the other, contains: metformin HCl 500 mg. Nonmedicinal ingredients: acetylated monoglycerides, carnauba wax, hydroxypropyl cellulose, hydroxypropyl methylcellulose, isopropyl alcohol, microcrystalline cellulose, magnesium stearate, methylene chloride, povidone, sodium croscarmellose, titanium dioxide and white wax. Bottles of 100 and 500. The product has a shelf-life of 24 months when stored in airtight containers at controlled room temperature (15 to 30°C) and protected from light.

New Product 1998

RHO®-NITRAZEPAM Ⓟ

RhoxalPharma

Nitrazepam

Hypnotic—Anticonvulsant

Supplied: 5 mg: Each white, round, scored RHO 5 tablet, contains: nitrazepam 5 mg, BP. Nonmedicinal ingredients: lactose, magnesium stearate, microcrystalline cellulose and sodium croscarmellose. Bottles of 100 and 500.

10 mg: Each white, round, scored RHO 10 tablet, contains: nitrazepam 10 mg, BP. Nonmedicinal ingredients: lactose, magnesium stearate, microcrystalline cellulose and sodium croscarmellose. Bottles of 100 and 500.

Store at controlled room temperature (15 to 30°C). Protect from light.

New Product 1998

RHO®-SALBUTAMOL Ⓟ

Rhodiapharm

Salbutamol Sulfate

Bronchodilator

Supplied: Each mL of respirator solution contains: salbutamol sulfate equivalent to salbutamol 5 mg. Nonmedicinal ingredients: benzalkonium chloride, sulfuric acid and water for injection. Bottles of 10 mL. Store between 15 and 25°C. Protect from light. In hospitals, dilute respirator solution with sterile normal saline. Should be used within 24 hours from time of dilution when stored at room temperature or within 48 hours when stored under refrigeration.

RHO®-SOTALOL Ⓟ

RhoxalPharma

Sotalol HCl

Antiarrhythmic

Supplied: 80 mg: Each light blue, capsule-shaped tablet, embossed RHO 80, contains: sotalol HCl 80 mg, BP. Nonmedicinal ingredients: colloidal silicon dioxide, FD&C Blue No. 2 aluminum lake, lactose monohydrate, magnesium stearate and microcrystalline cellulose. Bottles of 100 and 500.

160 mg: Each light blue, capsule-shaped tablet, embossed RHO 160, contains: sotalol HCl 160 mg, BP. Nonmedicinal ingredients: colloidal silicon dioxide, FD&C Blue No. 2 aluminum lake, lactose monohydrate, magnesium stearate and microcrystalline cellulose. Bottles of 100 and 500.

240 mg: Each light blue, capsule-shaped tablet, embossed RHO 240, contains: sotalol HCl 240 mg, BP. Nonmedicinal ingredients: colloidal silicon dioxide, FD&C Blue No. 2 aluminum lake, lactose monohydrate, magnesium stearate and microcrystalline cellulose. Bottles of 100 and 500.

Store in tight, light-resistant containers at controlled room temperature (15 to 30°C).

New Product 1998

RHOTRAL Ⓟ

Rhodiapharm

Acebutolol HCl

Antihypertensive—Antianginal Agent

Supplied: 100 mg: Each white, scored, shield-shaped tablet, marked 100 and RH on one side and RHOTRAL on the other, contains: acebutolol base 100 mg (as the HCl). Nonmedicinal ingredients: acetic anhydride, calcium phosphate dibasic, carnauba wax, cellulose, colloidal silicon dioxide, magnesium stearate, polacrilin potassium, talc, titanium oxide and zein. Gluten-, lactose- and tartrazine-free. Bottles of 100 and 500.

200 mg: Each blue, scored, shield-shaped tablet, marked 200 and RH on one side and RHOTRAL on the other, contains: acebutolol base 200 mg (as the HCl). Nonmedicinal ingredients: acetic anhydride, calcium phosphate dibasic, carnauba wax, cellulose, colloidal silicon dioxide, FD&C Blue No. 1 aluminum lake, magnesium stearate, polacrilin potassium, talc, titanium oxide and zein. Gluten-, lactose- and tartrazine-free. Bottles of 100 and 500.

400 mg: Each white, scored, shield-shaped tablet, marked 400 and RH on one side and RHOTRAL on the other, contains: acebutolol base 400 mg (as the HCl). Nonmedicinal ingredients: acetic anhydride, carnauba wax, colloidal silicon dioxide, cornstarch, diethyl phthalate, lactose, magnesium stearate, methylcellulose, talc, titanium dioxide and zein. Gluten- and tartrazine-free. Bottles of 100 and 500.

RHOTRIMINE® ℞
Rhodiapharm

Trimipramine Maleate

Antidepressant

Supplied: Capsules: Each pink/peach capsule contains: trimipramine base 75 mg (as the maleate). Nonmedicinal ingredients: calcium phosphate dibasic, D&C Yellow No. 10, FD&C Blue No. 1, FD&C Red No. 3, gelatin, magnesium stearate, polacrilin potassium and titanium oxide. Tartrazine-free. Bottles of 100 and 500.

Tablets: 12.5 mg: Each pink tablet, plain on one side and identified RH on the other, contains: trimipramine base 12.5 mg (as the maleate). Nonmedicinal ingredients: acetic anhydride, cellulose, colloidal silicon dioxide, diethyl phthalate, erythrosine, FD&C Red No. 3, lactose, magnesium stearate, sodium croscarmellose, talc, titanium oxide and zein. Tartrazine-free. Bottles of 100 and 500.

25 mg: Each pink tablet, plain on one side and identified 25 on the other, contains: trimipramine base 25 mg (as the maleate). Nonmedicinal ingredients: acetic anhydride, cellulose, colloidal silicon dioxide, diethyl phthalate, erythrosine, FD&C Red No. 3, lactose, magnesium stearate, sodium croscarmellose, talc, titanium oxide and zein. Tartrazine-free. Bottles of 100 and 500.

50 mg: Each pink tablet, plain on one side and identified 50 on the other, contains: trimipramine base 50 mg (as the maleate). Nonmedicinal ingredients: acetic anhydride, cellulose, colloidal silicon dioxide, diethyl phthalate, erythrosine, FD&C Red No. 3, lactose, magnesium stearate, sodium croscarmellose, talc, titanium oxide and zein. Tartrazine-free. Bottles of 100 and 500.

100 mg: Each pink tablet, plain on one side and identified 100 on the other, contains: trimipramine base 100 mg (as the maleate). Nonmedicinal ingredients: acetic anhydride, cellulose, colloidal silicon dioxide, diethyl phthalate, erythrosine, FD&C Red No. 3, lactose, magnesium stearate, sodium croscarmellose, talc, titanium oxide and zein. Tartrazine-free. Bottles of 100 and 500.

RHOVAIL® ℞
RHO-Pharm

Ketoprofen

Anti-inflammatory—Analgesic

Supplied: 150 mg: Each transparent pink capsule with opaque white cap contains: ketoprofen 150 mg as white pellets. Nonmedicinal ingredients: colloidal silicon dioxide, ethyl cellulose, FD&C Red No 3, gelatin, shellac, starch, sucrose, talc and titanium dioxide. Bottles of 100 and 250.

200 mg: Each transparent pink capsule with opaque blue cap contains: ketoprofen 200 mg as white pellets. Nonmedicinal ingredients: colloidal silicon dioxide, ethyl cellulose, FD&C Blue No 1, FD&C Red No 3, gelatin, shellac, starch, sucrose, talc and titanium dioxide. Bottles of 100 and 250.

RHOVANE® ℞
Rhodiapharm

Zopiclone

Hypnotic

Supplied: Each oval, scored blue tablet, marked RHOVANE on one side and the logo LOGO on the other, contains: zopiclone 7.5 mg. Nonmedicinal ingredients: acetic anhydride, calcium phosphate, carnauba wax, cellulose, croscarmellose sodium, diethyl phthalate, FD&C Blue No. 1 aluminum lake, magnesium stearate, titane oxide and zein. Amber polystyrene bottles of 100 and 500. Store in a dry place, at room temperature (15 to 30°C). Protect from light.

RIBOFLAVIN
General Monograph, CPhA

see VITAMIN B_2

RIDAURA® ℞
Pharmascience

Auranofin

Antirheumatic Agent

Pharmacology: Auranofin is a gold preparation and therefore has the potential for serious gold toxicity. The mechanism by which auranofin exerts its therapeutic effect has not been established.

In patients with adult rheumatoid arthritis or psoriatic arthritis, auranofin may modify disease activity as manifested by synovitis and associated symptoms, and reflected by laboratory parameters such as elevated ESR. There is no substantial evidence, however, that gold-containing compounds induce remission of rheumatoid arthritis.

Clinically the usual time of onset of therapeutic response to auranofin is 3 to 4 months. Continuing therapy beyond this time depends upon patient responsiveness, which includes improvement in parameters such as joint swelling, tenderness, pain, morning stiffness and grip strength. Continuing therapy beyond 6 months is unwarranted in patients showing insufficient improvement in the above parameters, and auranofin should be discontinued because of potential serious adverse reactions.

Pharmacokinetics: In 5 rheumatoid arthritic patients, the oral administration of a single 6 mg (equivalent to 1.74 mg of gold) dose of a solution of radiolabeled auranofin demonstrated that approximately 25% of the oral dose was absorbed. Peak plasma radioactive gold concentrations of 0.039 to 0.11 μg ^{195}Au/mL were reached in 1.5 to 2.5 hours. The mean plasma terminal half-life was 17 days, while the mean total body terminal half-life was 58 days. By day 10 post-administration, 77% of the initially administered labeled gold had been excreted, 73% in the feces and 4% in the urine. Six months after this single dose, approximately 99.6% of the initially administered labeled gold had been excreted, with 0.4% retained in the body.

Following 6 months of therapy with unlabeled auranofin 3 mg twice daily, a single 6 mg dose of radiolabeled auranofin was administered. Peak plasma radioactive gold concentrations of 0.027 to 0.138 μg ^{195}Au/mL were reached in 1.0 to 1.5 hours. The mean plasma half-life was 25.5 days, while the mean total body terminal half-life was 80.8 days. By day 10 post-administration, 75% of the labeled gold had been excreted, 70% in the feces and 5% in the urine.

In clinical studies, steady state blood gold levels were achieved in about 3 months. With auranofin at 6 mg/day, mean blood gold levels of 0.62±0.195 μg/mL (91 patients) have been observed after 3 months of treatment and 0.68±0.452 μg/mL (63 patients) after 6 months. In blood, approximately 40% of auranofin gold is associated with red cells and 60% associated with serum proteins. In contrast, 99% of injectable gold is associated with serum proteins.

Mean blood gold concentrations are proportional to dose; however, no correlation between blood gold concentrations and safety or efficacy has been established.

Indications: In the management of adults with active (classical or definite) rheumatoid arthritis who have not responded to adequate trials of conventional anti-inflammatory therapy. Auranofin might also be of benefit in patients with psoriatic arthritis.

It should be considered only when salicylates or other nonsteroidal anti-inflammatory drugs, and, when appropriate, steroids, have proven to be inadequate for controlling the symptoms of rheumatoid arthritis.

Physicians planning to use auranofin should be experienced with chrysotherapy and should thoroughly familiarize themselves with the toxicity and benefits of auranofin.

In controlled clinical trials, comparing auranofin with injectable gold, auranofin was associated with fewer drop-outs due to adverse reactions, while injectable gold was associated with fewer drop-outs for inadequate or poor therapeutic effects. Physicians should consider these findings when deciding on the use of auranofin in patients who are candidates for chrysotherapy.

Auranofin should be added to an ongoing comprehensive treatment program which includes physical as well as other drug therapy. The usual time of onset of therapeutic response is 3 to 4 months; some patients require as long as 6 months to show a full clinical response.

Auranofin is not indicated in other arthropathies, such as osteoarthritis.

Contraindications: In patients with a history of serious gold-induced toxicity such as necrotizing enterocolitis, pulmonary fibrosis, exfoliative dermatitis or hypersensitivity. Auranofin should not be prescribed for patients with progressive renal disease, severe hepatocellular disease, bone marrow aplasia or other severe hematological disorders.

Pregnancy: Auranofin has been shown to be embryotoxic in rats at dose levels of 5 mg/kg/day or higher and both embryotoxic and teratogenic in rabbits at doses of 0.5 mg/kg/day or higher. Therefore, it should not be given to pregnant women. Furthermore, women of childbearing potential should be made aware of the necessity to avoid pregnancy during treatment and for at least 6 months after because of the slow excretion of gold and its persistence in the body tissues after discontinuation of treatment.

Lactation: Gold is excreted in rodent milk following the administration of auranofin. It is not known whether Ridaura is excreted in human milk; however, injectable gold appears in the milk of nursing mothers following administration. Therefore, it is recommended that Ridaura should not be given during nursing.

Warnings: Auranofin contains gold and, like other gold-containing drugs, can cause gold toxicity. Danger signs of possible gold toxicity include the following: fall in hemoglobin, leukopenia below 4 000 WBC/mm³, granulocytes below 1 500/mm³, decrease in platelets below 150 000/mm³, proteinuria, hematuria, pruritus, rash, stomatitis or persistent diarrhea. Therefore, it is recommended that white blood cells with differential platelet count, hemoglobin, urinary protein and renal and liver function be measured prior to therapy to establish a baseline and to identify pre-existing conditions (see Contraindications).

The possibility of adverse reactions should be explained to patients before starting therapy (see Information for the Patient).

Patients should be advised to report promptly any unusual signs and symptoms occurring during treatment such as sore throat or tongue, mouth ulceration, skin rash, easy bruising, purpura, epistaxis, bleeding gums or menorrhagia.

When the following adverse reactions occur, therapy may require modification or additional monitoring as outlined below:

Thrombocytopenia: Thrombocytopenia has occurred in approximately 1 to 3% of patients (see Adverse Effects) treated with auranofin, some of whom developed bleeding. The thrombocytopenia appears to be peripheral in origin in most cases and is usually reversible upon withdrawal of auranofin. Its onset bears no relationship to the duration of therapy and its course may be rapid. While patients' platelet counts require monitoring every 2 weeks for the first 3 months and at least monthly thereafter, the occurrence of a precipitous decline in platelets or a platelet count less than 100 000/mm³ or signs and symptoms (e.g., purpura, ecchymoses or petechiae) suggestive of thrombocytopenia indicates a need to immediately withdraw auranofin and all other therapies with the potential to cause thrombocytopenia, and to obtain additional platelet counts. No additional auranofin should be given unless the thrombocytopenia resolves and further studies show it was not due to gold therapy.

Proteinuria: Proteinuria has developed in approximately 3 to 9% of patients (see Adverse Effects) treated with auranofin. Urinalysis should be performed every 2 weeks for the first 3 months and at least monthly thereafter. If clinically significant proteinuria or microscopic hematuria is found, auranofin and all other therapies with the potential to cause proteinuria or microscopic hematuria should be stopped immediately.

There has been little experience with the concomitant use of auranofin and penicillamine, chloroquine/hydroxychloroquine, immunosuppressive agents (e.g., cyclophosphamide, azathioprine, or methotrexate) or high doses of corticosteroids and therefore, such use cannot be recommended.

Precautions: General: The potential benefits of using auranofin in patients with inflammatory bowel disease, skin rash or history of bone marrow depression, should be weighed against: 1) the potential risks of gold toxicity on organ systems previously compromised or with decreased reserve, and 2) the difficulty in quickly detecting and correctly attributing the toxic effect.

The following adverse effects have been reported with the use of gold preparations and require modification of auranofin treatment or additional monitoring. See Adverse Effects for the approximate incidence of those reactions specifically reported with auranofin.

Gastrointestinal: Gastrointestinal reactions reported with gold therapy include diarrhea/loose stools, nausea, vomiting, anorexia and abdominal cramps. The most common reaction is diarrhea/loose stools reported in approximately 47% of patients. This is generally manageable by reducing the dosage (e.g., from 6 mg daily to 3 mg). In 4% of the patients it has been necessary to discontinue auranofin permanently.

Ulcerative enterocolitis is a rare serious gold reaction. Therefore, patients with gastrointestinal symptoms should be monitored for the appearance of gastrointestinal bleeding.

Cutaneous: Dermatitis is the most common reaction to parenteral gold therapy and the second most common reaction to auranofin. **Any eruption, especially if pruritic, that develops during treatment should be considered a gold reaction until proven otherwise.** Pruritus often exists before dermatitis becomes apparent, and therefore should be considered to be a warning signal of a cutaneous reaction. Gold dermatitis may be aggravated by exposure to sunlight; an actinic rash may develop. The most serious form of cutaneous reaction reported with parenteral gold is generalized exfoliative dermatitis.

In patients with psoriatic arthritis who were involved in all clinical trials with Ridaura, 5/438 (1.1%) Ridaura-treated patients and 2/183 (1.1%) placebo-treated patients had an exacerbation of their psoriasis requiring withdrawal.

Mucous Membrane: Stomatitis, another common gold reaction, may be manifested by shallow ulcers on the buccal membranes, on the borders of the tongue, and on the palate or in the pharynx. Stomatitis may occur as the only adverse reaction or with a dermatitis. Sometimes diffuse glossitis or gingivitis develops. A metallic taste may precede these oral mucous membrane reactions and should be considered a warning signal.

Renal: Auranofin, like other gold preparations, can produce a nephrotic syndrome or glomerulitis with proteinuria and hematuria. These renal reactions are usually relatively mild and subside completely if recognized early and treatment is discontinued. They may become severe and chronic if treatment is continued after the onset of the reaction. Therefore, it is important to perform urinalysis regularly and to discontinue treatment promptly if proteinuria or hematuria develops.

Hematologic: Blood dyscrasias including leukopenia, granulocytopenia and thrombocytopenia have all been reported as reactions to injectable gold and auranofin. These reactions may occur separately or in combination at any time during treatment. In addition, a case of pure red cell aplasia has been reported as a reaction to auranofin. Because these reactions have potentially serious consequences, **blood dyscrasias should be constantly watched for, through monitoring of the formed elements of the blood, every 2 weeks for the first 3 months and at least monthly thereafter.**

Ocular: There have been some reports of gold deposits in the lens or corneas of patients treated with auranofin. These deposits have not led to any eye disorders or any degree of visual impairment, and have cleared within 3 to 6 months of cessation of therapy. Initial and periodic ophthalmic examinations are recommended in patients being treated with auranofin.

Miscellaneous: Rare reactions attributed to gold include cholestatic jaundice; gold bronchitis and interstitial pneumonitis and fibrosis; peripheral neuropathy; partial or complete hair loss; fever. The physician should be constantly on guard for any of the above changes, and as a precaution, suitable laboratory monitoring should be done at appropriate intervals.

Children: The safety and effectiveness of auranofin in children under age 16 have not yet been established. Consequently, use in this age group cannot be recommended.

Carcinogenesis: In a 24-month study in rats, animals treated with auranofin at 0.4, 1.0 or 2.5 mg/kg/day orally (3, 8 or 21 times the human dose) or gold sodium thiomalate at 2 or 6 mg/kg injected twice weekly (4 or 12 times the human dose) were compared to untreated control animals. There was a significant increase in instances of renal tubular cell karyomegaly and cytomegaly and renal adenoma in the animals treated with 1.0 or 2.5 mg/kg/day of auranofin and 2 or 6 mg/kg twice weekly of gold sodium thiomalate. Malignant renal epithelial tumors were seen in the 2.5 mg/kg/day auranofin and in the 6 mg/kg twice weekly gold sodium thiomalate-treated animals.

In a 12 month study, rats treated with auranofin at 23 mg/kg/day (192 times the human dose) developed adenomas of the renal tubular epithelium, whereas those treated with 3.6 mg/kg/day (30 times the human dose) did not.

Drug Interactions: One report suggests that, in a single patient, concurrent administration of auranofin and phenytoin was associated with increased phenytoin blood levels.

Adverse Effects: The adverse reactions listed below are based on observations on 4 784 rheumatoid arthritis patients treated with auranofin, of whom 2 729 were treated for more than 1 year and 573 for more than 3 years. The overall incidence of adverse reactions was 62%, of whom 18.6% discontinued therapy. The most common adverse reactions were diarrhea (47%), rash (24%), pruritus (17%), abdominal pain (14%) and stomatitis (13%). More serious adverse reactions were anemia (1.6%), leukopenia (1.9%), thrombocytopenia (0.9%) and proteinuria (5.0%). The highest incidence was during the first 6 months of treatment. However, reactions can occur at any time throughout the course of therapy.

Clinical trials were conducted assessing Ridaura in the treatment of 438 psoriatic arthritis patients. The nature and incidence of adverse reactions were similar to those observed in rheumatoid arthritis patients.

Reactions occurring in more than 1% of auranofin-treated patients: Gastrointestinal: loose stools or diarrhea (47%); abdominal pain (14%); nausea with or without vomiting (10%); anorexia*; flatulence*; constipation and dysgeusia.
Dermatological: rash (24%); pruritus (17%); hair loss; urticaria.
Mucous membrane: stomatitis (13%); conjunctivitis*; glossitis.
Hematological: anemia; leukopenia; thrombocytopenia; eosinophilia.
Renal: proteinuria*; hematuria.
Hepatic: elevated liver enzymes.
Miscellaneous: weight loss.
*Reactions marked with an asterisk occurred in 3 to 9% of the patients. The other reactions listed occurred in 1 to 3%.

Reactions occurring in less than 1% of auranofin-treated patients: Gastrointestinal: gastrointestinal bleeding; melena; stool positive for occult blood; dysphagia (<0.1%); ulcerative enterocolitis (<0.1%).
Dermatological: angioedema (<0.1%).
Mucous membrane: gingivitis.
Hematological: neutropenia; agranulocytosis (<0.1%); aplastic anemia (<0.1%).
Renal: membranous glomerulonephritis (<0.1%); nephrotic syndrome (<0.1%).
Hepatic: jaundice (<0.1%).
Respiratory: interstitial pneumonitis (<0.1%).
Neurological: peripheral neuropathy (<0.1%).

Overdose: Symptoms and Treatment: In case of acute overdosage, immediate induction of emesis or gastric lavage and appropriate supportive therapy are recommended.

Auranofin overdosage experience is limited. A 50-year-old female, previously on 6 mg daily, took 27 mg (9 capsules) daily for 10 days and developed an encephalopathy and peripheral neuropathy. Auranofin was discontinued and she eventually recovered.

There has been no experience with treating auranofin overdosage with modalities such as chelating agents; however, they have been used with injectable gold and may be considered when treating auranofin overdosage.

Dosage: Adults: Usual starting dosage is 6 mg/day. This dose may be given: twice a day—one 3 mg capsule with breakfast and one with the evening meal; or once a day—two 3 mg capsules with breakfast or two 3 mg capsules with the evening meal.

Auranofin should be discontinued in those patients in whom no response is observed after 4 months administration. In those patients in whom a partial response is observed after 4 months, it may be continued at 6 mg/day, or the dose may be increased to 9 mg/day (one 3 mg capsule 3 times a day), for an additional 2 months. Auranofin should be discontinued in patients in whom a satisfactory clinical response has not occurred after 6 months treatment. Daily dosages above 9 mg are not recommended.

Because of possible serious adverse reactions, some rheumatologists suggest reducing the dosage or discontinuing gold altogether when patients are in clinical remission (ARA criteria) lasting for at least 6 months, keeping in mind that cessation of therapy may allow the disease to progress further. Each patient must be evaluated individually.

Transferring from Injectable Gold: In a controlled clinical trial, patients on injectable gold were transferred to auranofin by discontinuing the injectable agent and starting oral therapy with 6 mg daily. At 6 months, control of disease activity of patients transferred to auranofin and those maintained on the injectable agent was not different. Data beyond 6 months are not available. When patients are transferred to auranofin, they should be informed of its adverse reaction profile, in particular the gastrointestinal reactions (see Precautions).

Information for the Patient: See Blue Section—Information for the Patient "Ridaura".

Supplied: Each tan and brown opaque capsule, monogrammed RIDAURA contains: auranofin 3 mg. Also contains lactose 115.8 mg. Energy: 2.80 kJ (0.67 kcal). Sodium: <1 mmol (0.271 mg). Gluten-, parabens-, sucrose-, sulfites- and tartrazine-free. Bottles of 60. Store at room temperature (15 to 30°C). Dispense in a tight, light-resistant container.

RIFADIN® Pr

Hoechst Marion Roussel

Rifampin

Antituberculous Antibiotic

Pharmacology: Rifampin inhibits DNA-dependent RNA polymerase activity in susceptible cells. Specifically, it interacts with bacterial RNA polymerase. This is the probable mechanism of action by which rifampin exerts its therapeutic effect.

Pharmacokinetics: Absorption is more rapid when rifampin is administered 1 hour before meals. Peak blood levels in normal adults vary widely from individual to individual. Peak levels occur between 2 and 4 hours following the oral administration of a 600 mg dose with average peak values of 7 to 10 µg/mL.

Rifampin is distributed throughout the body and is detectable in many organs and body fluids, including the cerebrospinal fluid. The highest concentrations are present in the liver and bile.

In normal subjects, the biological half-life of rifampin is approximately 3 hours with variations from 1 to 5 hours. Rifampin is eliminated from the blood equally in the urine and feces as unchanged drug and metabolites.

The principal metabolite in man is the biologically active desacetylrifampin. Desacetylation of rifampin in the body does not substantially modify its antimycobacterial activity. In Kirschner's medium, the MIC against M. tuberculosis varied from 0.1 to 2 µg/mL.

Indications: As a treatment of tuberculosis.

To achieve a complete kill of the bacillary population and to avoid selection of drug-resistant mutants, rifampin must be used concomitantly with at least one other active antituberculous drug. The selection of the specific drug for partner is determined by the in vitro sensitivity of the causative organisms, comparative safety and effectiveness, the patient's previous clinical history and the absorption/distribution pattern of the drug.

It is also indicated for the prophylaxis of bacterial meningitis or carriage of N. meningitidis or H. influenza b in persons exposed to a primary case.

Contraindications: Jaundice associated with reduced bilirubin excretion. History of previous sensitivity to any of the rifamycins. Premature and newborn infants in whom the liver is not yet capable of functioning with full efficiency. Rifampin passes into the breast milk and therefore should not be used during lactation.

Warnings: Rifampin has been shown to produce liver dysfunction. There have been fatalities associated with jaundice in patients with liver disease or receiving rifampin concomitantly with other hepatotoxic agents. Since an increased risk may exist for individuals with liver disease, benefits must be weighed carefully against the risk of further liver damage. Periodic liver function monitoring is mandatory.

Periodic blood counts should also be carried out in patients receiving long-term treatment.

Pregnancy: The effect of combinations of rifampin with other antituberculous drugs on the human fetus is not known. No obvious effect on the fetus was detected after the administration of rifampin to 15 pregnant patients. An increase in congenital malformations, primarily spina bifida and cleft palate, has been reported in the offspring of mice and rats given oral doses of rifampin 100 mg/kg/day during pregnancy.

Rifampin should not be used in pregnant women or women with childbearing potential. If rifampin therapy is judged to be essential, such treatment should be implemented only after carefully weighing the potential benefits of therapy against the risks which may be involved. In women with childbearing potential, treatment with rifampin should be undertaken only when the possibility of pregnancy during therapy is judged to be remote.

Precautions: Rifampin increases the requirements for anticoagulant drugs of the coumarin type. This effect is not observed until the fifth day following initiation of treatment. The decrease in prothrombin time usually lasts between 5 and 7 days, and is the result of rifampin's ability to cause induction of drug metabolizing enzyme systems of the liver. As a result, the rate of metabolism of those drugs which are substrates for these enzymes can be altered, resulting in reduced pharmacological effects of the drugs involved. In patients receiving anticoagulants, it is recommended that daily prothrombin times be performed until the dose of the anticoagulant required has been established.

The intermittent administration of high doses of rifampin >120 mg/dose has been reported to be associated with a hypersensitivity reaction, characterized by fever and myalgia.

Rifadin (cont'd)

The incidence of this reaction is greater when rifampin is given on a once-a-week basis than on a twice or thrice weekly basis. It is recommended that when resuming treatment with rifampin after short or prolonged interruptions, it be given in small, gradually increasing doses. During the transitional period, the renal and hemapoietic systems should be closely monitored. The drug should be stopped immediately if renal failure, thrombocytopenia purpura or hemolytic anemia develop and should not be reinstituted.

Safe conditions for the use of ethambutol alone or in combination with rifampin have not been established for children under the age of 13 years. Although renal insufficiency does not alter blood levels of rifampin, marked increases in ethambutol levels are observed under similar conditions; this, therefore, should be taken into consideration in such patients receiving rifampin/ethambutol combination therapy. Caution is recommended when instituting therapeutic regimens in which isoniazid is to be used concurrently with rifampin, in patients with impaired liver function, the elderly and malnourished.

From experimental studies, it would appear that BSP and rifampin compete with one another at the liver cell-bile canaliculus boundary. Clinically, this phenomena can be reflected by spurious BSP levels. It is recommended that the BSP test be carried out at least 5 hours after the last dose of rifampin.

Urine, feces, saliva, sputum, sweat and tears may be colored red-orange by rifampin and its metabolites. Individuals to be treated should be made aware of these possibilities in order to prevent undue anxiety.

Patients should be advised that soft contact lenses may be permanently stained.

It has been reported that oral contraceptives have failed to prevent conception in some patients receiving rifampin in association with other antituberculosis drugs. It is therefore necessary that alternative or additional contraceptive measures be recommended.

Current evidence indicates that administration of rifampin is associated with induction of some drug metabolizing enzyme systems of the liver. As a result, the rate of metabolism of those drugs which are substrates for these enzymes can be altered, resulting in reduced pharmacological effects of the drugs involved. Clinically significant changes have been reported for the oral anticoagulants, hypoglycemic agents, dapsone, digitalis preparations and corticosteroids (as well as for oral contraceptives and ethambutol). Readjustment in the dosage and monitoring of the effects of these drugs may therefore be necessary when they are used concomitantly with rifampin.

Microbiological techniques for assaying the serum concentrations of folic acid and vitamin B_{12} are not suitable for use during treatment with rifampin.

Upon completion of the treatment with rifampin, a renewed readjustment of the dosage should be made.

Adverse Effects: Rifampin is usually well tolerated at recommended dosage levels.

Gastrointestinal disturbances such as heartburn, epigastric distress, anorexia, nausea, vomiting, gas, cramps and diarrhea have been noted in some patients. Headache, drowsiness, fatigue, ataxia, dizziness, inability to concentrate, mental confusion, visual disturbances, muscular weakness, fever, pains in extremities and generalized numbness have also been noted. Pruritus, urticaria, skin rashes, eosinophilia, sore mouth, sore tongue, dyspnea and acute renal failure have occasionally been encountered. The following menstrual disturbances: breakthrough bleeding, spotting, amenorrhea, monthly prolongation of both menstrual interval and menses have been reported.

Thrombocytopenia, purpura, leukopenia, hemolytic anaemia and decreased hemoglobin have been observed. Thrombocytopenia has occurred when rifampin and ethambutol were administered concomitantly according to an intermittent dose schedule twice weekly and in high doses. Elevations in BUN and serum uric acid have been reported.

Transient abnormalities in liver function tests (elevations of serum bilirubin, BSP, alkaline phosphatase and serum transaminases) have been observed, particularly during the first few weeks of treatment.

A few cases of jaundice with evidence of hepatocellular damage have been reported in patients receiving rifampin. In some of them it was possible, under careful laboratory control, to resume treatment after an interval without recurrence of abnormalities.

Clinical trials have furnished no evidence to suggest that rifampin has any harmful effects on the cochleovestibular system.

Overdose: Symptoms and Treatment: For acute overdosage, general supportive measures should be employed, along with gastric lavage. No specific antidote is known.

Dosage: Treatment of tuberculosis: Adults: 600 mg in a single daily dose. Should intolerance occur, the daily dosage may be reduced to 450 mg. In patients with impaired liver function, a daily dose of 8 mg/kg should not be exceeded. A daily dosage of 10 mg/kg is recommended for frail and elderly persons.
Children: 10 to 20 mg/kg not to exceed 600 mg/day. Data is not available for the determination of dosage for children under 5 years of age.

In treatment of pulmonary tuberculosis, rifampin must be used in conjunction with at least one other antituberculous agent. In general, therapy should be continued until bacterial conversion has been established and maximum clinical improvement has occurred.

To ensure optimum absorption, rifampin should be taken on an empty stomach (1 hour before breakfast).
Prophylaxis versus H. influenzae type b: Adults: 600 mg every 24 hours for 4 days. Children (>1 month): 20 mg/kg (up to 600 mg) every 24 hours for 4 days. Neonates (<1 month): 10 mg/kg every 24 hours for 4 days.
Prophylaxis versus N. meningitidis: Adults: 600 mg every 12 hours for 2 days. Children (>1 month): 10 mg/kg (up to 600 mg) every 12 hours for 2 days. Neonates (<1 month): 5 mg/kg every 12 hours for 2 days.

Supplied: 150 mg: Each maroon, opaque capsule contains: rifampin 150 mg. Nonmedicinal ingredients: cornstarch, D&C Red No. 28, FD&C Blue No. 1, FD&C Red No. 40, gelatin, magnesium stearate, talc and titanium dioxide. Tartrazine-free. Bottles of 100.

300 mg: Each maroon and scarlet, opaque capsule contains: rifampin 300 mg. Nonmedicinal ingredients: cornstarch, D&C Red No. 28, FD&C Blue No. 1, FD&C Red No. 40, gelatin, magnesium stearate, talc and titanium dioxide. Tartrazine-free. Bottles of 100.

(Shown in Product Recognition Section)

Reviewed 1998

RIFAMPIN ℞

General Monograph, CPhA

Antibiotic

This monograph has been compiled by CPhA. It may contain information different from that approved by Therapeutic Products Programme, Health Canada, and the pharmaceutical manufacturers' approval has not been requested.

Pharmacology: Rifampin is a semisynthetic derivative of rifamycin B, an antibiotic produced by Streptomyces mediterranei. Rifampin is active against microorganisms of the genus Mycobacterium, including M. tuberculosis, M. kansasii, M. marinum, M. avium-intracellulare (M. avium complex) and M. leprae. Rifampin is also active against some gram-negative bacteria including N. meningitidis and H. influenzae type b, in addition to some gram-positive bacteria including S. aureus and S. epidermidis. Because of rapid emergence of resistant strains, it is generally recommended that rifampin be used in combination with other antibacterial agents.

Rifampin inhibits DNA-dependent RNA poymerase which leads to suppression of RNA synthesis in susceptible bacteria. The site of action appears to be the β subunit of the enzyme.

Rifampin may be bacteriostatic or bactericidal, depending on the concentration of the drug and the relative susceptibility of the organism. Rifampin is most effective when cell division is occurring.

Rifampin inhibits DNA dependent RNA polymerase activity in susceptible cells. Specifically, it interacts with bacterial RNA polymerase. This is the probable mechanism of action by which rifampin exerts its therapeutic effect.

Pharmacokinetics: Rifampin is readily absorbed and peak blood concentrations are reached between 2 and 4 hours following the oral administration of a 600 mg dose. Absorption of rifampin tends to be delayed if the drug is taken after food (see Dosage).

Rifampin is distributed throughout the body and is detectable in many organs and body fluids, including the cerebrospinal fluid, where concentrations are increased if the meninges are inflamed. High concentrations are found in the liver, bile and urine. Approximately 80% of rifampin in the serum is bound to protein. Rifampin crosses the placenta and is excreted in breast milk (see Warnings).

In normal subjects the serum half-life of rifampin is approximately 3 hours, with variations from 1 to 5 hours. Neither the peak concentration nor the half-life of rifampin is significantly altered in patients with impaired or absent renal function; these parameters are, however, increased in patients with impaired liver function or bile flow obstruction.

The principal metabolite of rifampin is desacetylated rifampin. To a large extent, desacetylated rifampin retains the antimycobacterial properties of rifampin, and is detectable in the blood, bile and urine following an oral dose of rifampin. Rifampin and its metabolite are excreted principally by the liver into the bile; however, the maximum excretory capacity of the liver is surpassed at doses larger than 5 mg/kg. In contrast, the amount of rifampin excreted by the kidney in the urine is proportional to the concentration of the drug in the blood and high urinary concentrations result with recommended dosages.

Indications: Active tuberculosis, whether it is in the primary or chronic phase. To prevent or delay the emergence of drug resistance, rifampin must be used in combination with at least one other effective antitubercular drug. Choice of appropriate drug combinations should be based on in vitro sensitivity studies, comparative safety as well as the patient's previous clinical history.

Rifampin is sometimes used in multiple-drug regimens for the treatment of infections caused by M. avium complex, M. kansasii, M. marinum, M. leprae (leprosy), L. pneumophila (Legionnaires' disease) and some gram-negative and gram-positive bacteria.

Rifampin is used for prophylaxis of selected individuals exposed to persons with invasive disease due to N. meningitidis and H. influenzae type b.

Contraindications: Jaundice. Hypersensitivity to rifamycins. Premature and newborn infants in whom liver function is not yet mature.

Warnings: Rifampin has been shown to produce hepatic dysfunction. There have been fatalities associated with jaundice in patients with pre-existing liver disease or in patients receiving rifampin in combination with other hepatotoxic agents. Predisposing factors include chronic liver disease and alcoholism. Therefore, the benefits must be weighed carefully against the risk in individuals with impaired liver function. It is essential that liver function be regularly assessed in patients with impaired liver function.

Pregnancy: Rifampin crosses the placenta. Reproductive and fetal toxicity studies in rats and mice with rifampin alone have indicated teratogenic effects, most commonly spina bifida and cleft palate, at doses of 100 mg/kg and above. Although the effect of rifampin alone or in combination with other antitubercular drugs on the human fetus is not known, the drug has been used (combined with isoniazid and/or ethambutol) to treat clinical tuberculosis in pregnant women.

Generally, rifampin should not be used in pregnant women. However, if rifampin therapy is judged to be essential, such treatment should be implemented only after carefully weighing the potential benefits of therapy against the risks which may be involved, particularly during the first 3 months of pregnancy. In women with childbearing potential, treatment with rifampin should be undertaken only when the possibility of pregnancy during therapy is judged to be remote. Oral contraceptive therapy has failed at times and alternative or additional contraceptive measures are essential in women who are receiving rifampin.

When administered during the last few weeks of pregnancy, rifampin has been shown to cause postnatal hemorrhage in the mother and infant; therefore, vitamin K should be given during labor to mothers receiving rifampin and to their offspring immediately after birth. In the newborn, careful surveillance for bleeding symptoms and decrease of coagulation factors is mandatory.

Lactation: Rifampin transfers into breast milk in limited amounts and is thought to represent a low risk to the nursing infant.

Precautions: Urine, feces, saliva, sputum, sweat and tears may be colored reddish orange by rifampin and its metabolites. To prevent undue anxiety, patients should be made aware of this possibility.

Soft contact lenses should not be worn during rifampin therapy as they may become permanently stained.

For prophylaxis of individuals exposed to persons with invasive disease due to N. meningitidis and H. influenzae type b, rifampin should be given only to selected individuals. Contact the local public health unit or refer to specific guidelines (i.e., Guidelines for control of meningococcal disease, Canada Communicable Disease Report 1994; 20:17-27) for further recommendations on which contacts should receive prophylaxis.

Daily treatment with rifampin is often better tolerated than intermittent therapy, since rare hypersensitivity reactions may occur. Resumption of treatment after termination of a course of long-term therapy with the drug involves risks and therefore, should if possible, be avoided. If intermittent administration is unavoidable, the risk of adverse reactions may be minimized if the drug-free interval or rest period is less than or closely resembles the interval of the previous drug treatment period. When resuming treatment with rifampin, the drug should be reintroduced gradually, beginning with a daily dose of 75 mg and increasing the dose by 75 mg daily until the required dosage is reached (see Dosage). During the transitional period, renal and hepatic function should be closely monitored. Corticosteroids may be useful in preventing adverse reactions since antigen-antibody complexes are suspected causes. If, as may happen in exceptional cases, the patient develops thrombocytopenia, purpura, hemolytic anemia or renal failure, treatment should be stopped at once and not reinstituted at a later date.

Rifampin should be used with caution in patients with porphyria as it could induce delta-aminolaevulinic acid synthetase activity.

Drug Interactions: Since the chemotherapy of tuberculosis involves the use of at least two drugs, the possible adverse reactions of each drug should be borne in mind, as well as the interactions that may occur. Caution is recommended when instituting therapeutic regimens in which isoniazid is to be used concurrently with rifampin, in patients with impaired liver function, the elderly and in malnourished patients.

Rifampin is a potent inducer of hepatic drug metabolism (cytochrome P-450). As a consequence, the rate of metabolism of numerous drugs can be accelerated, which can result in reduced pharmacological effects of the drugs involved or toxicity when rifampin is discontinued. Adjustments in the dosage and monitoring of the effects of these drugs is therefore necessary when used concomitantly with rifampin. This is particularly important when rifampin administration is either initiated or withdrawn. The effect on enzyme induction may develop gradually over several days after starting rifampin and may take even longer to dissipate after withdrawal of rifampin.

Interactions of significance involving enzyme induction include: Anticoagulants, Oral: Reduced hypothrombinemic effect may occur. Avoid rifampin in patients on warfarin if possible. If rifampin is used, monitor INR or PT closely and adjust warfarin dose accordingly.

Antihyperglycemics: Reduced antihyperglycemic response may occur.

Calcium Channel Blockers: Rifampin reduces the bioavailability and protein binding of verapamil and induces the metabolism of diltiazem, nifedipine and verapamil, possibly resulting in loss of efficacy.

Clarithromycin: Rifampin reduces the serum levels of clarithromycin.

Corticosteroids: There may be exacerbation of the disease for which steroids are being administered (e.g., Addison's disease, allograft failure, asthma).

Cyclosporine: Possible loss of therapeutic effect (e.g., graft-versus-host disease or graft rejection). Monitor cyclosporine concentration carefully and adjust dose accordingly.

Fluconazole: Concomitant administration of fluconazole and rifampin resulted in a 25% decrease in AUC and a 20% shorter half-life of fluconazole. The dosage of fluconazole should be increased by 25% when fluconazole is administered with rifampin.

Isoniazid: Hepatotoxicity has been reported to occur more frequently when rifampin and isoniazid are given concurrently. The incidence may be higher in slow isoniazid acetylators, those receiving high doses of isoniazid, prior general anesthesia and those with pre-existing liver disease.

Ketoconazole: In addition to enhanced metabolism of ketoconazole, rifampin concentrations may be reduced when concurrently administered with ketoconazole as a result of decreased rifampin absorption. Separate rifampin and ketoconazole doses by 12 hours.

Oral Contraceptives and Estrogens: Unplanned pregnancies and menstrual irregularities may occur. The effect of oral contraceptives can no longer be relied upon and it is necessary that alternative or additional contraceptive measures be used.

Other Agents: beta-blockers, chloramphenicol, cyclic antidepressants, diazepam, digoxin, disopyramide, itraconazole, methadone, mexiletine, phenytoin, propafenone, quinidine, theophyllines, tocainide and zidovudine.

Adverse Effects: CNS: headache, drowsiness, fatigue, ataxia, dizziness, inability to concentrate, mental confusion, visual disturbances.

Dermatological: Pruritus, urticaria, skin rashes, have occasionally been encountered.

Gastrointestinal: Sore mouth, sore tongue, dyspepsia, epigastric distress, anorexia, nausea, vomiting, gas, cramps and diarrhea have been noted. Isolated cases of pseudomembranous colitis have been reported.

Hematologic: Thrombocytopenia, eosinophilia, hemolytic anemia, purpura, transient leukopenia and decreased hemoglobin have been observed. Thrombocytopenia has occurred when rifampin and ethambutol were administered concomitantly according to an intermittent dose schedule twice weekly and in high doses.

Hepatic: Transient abnormalities in liver function tests (elevations of serum bilirubin, alkaline phosphatase and serum aminotransferases) have been observed. In isolated cases, induction of porphyria has been noted.

A few cases of jaundice with evidence of hepatocellular damage have been reported in patients receiving rifampin. In some of them it was possible to resume rifampin treatment without recurrence of abnormalities. However, hepatitis and fatalities associated with jaundice have also been reported (see Warnings).

Hypersensitivity: Hypersensitivity reactions, especially a flu-like syndrome (fever, chills, dizziness, pain in extremities, dyspnea), have been noted. Hematuria, renal insufficiency and acute renal failure have also occurred infrequently. These hypersensitivity reactions are usually associated with high-dose intermittent rifampin therapy (900 to 1 200 mg twice weekly) or resumption of treatment after termination of a course of long-term therapy (see Precautions).

Miscellaneous: Disturbances of menstruation including breakthrough bleeding, spotting, amenorrhea, and prolongation of both the menstrual interval and menses have been reported in women taking rifampin either alone or in conjunction with oral contraceptives. Elevations in serum urea and serum uric acid have been reported.

Overdose: Symptoms: Overdosage of rifampin produces symptoms that are principally extensions of common side effects. These include nausea, vomiting, lethargy. Brownish-red or orange discoloration of the skin, urine, sweat, saliva, tears, and feces is proportional to amount ingested.

Following massive overdosage of rifampin, liver involvement, manifested by enlargement (possibly with tenderness), jaundice and increased bilirubin levels and liver enzymes, can develop within a few hours. Hepatotoxicity may be more marked in patients with prior hepatic impairment.

Treatment: For acute overdosage, general supportive measures should be employed. Empty the stomach using ipecac syrup or gastric lavage. Activated charcoal may be administered to reduce further absorption.

Dosage: To ensure optimal absorption, rifampin should be taken on an empty stomach (1 hour before a meal). Should gastric intolerance occur, the daily dosage may be taken after meals and/or reduced.

M. tuberculosis (in combination with at least one other antituberculosis agent): Adults: 10 mg/kg once daily, to a maximum of 600 mg. Children: 10 to 20 mg/kg once daily, to a maximum of 600 mg. The duration of therapy for uncomplicated pulmonary or extrapulmonary tuberculosis should be a minimum of 6 months.

Prophylaxis of N. meningitidis: Adults: 600 mg every 12 hours for 2 days. Children: ≥1 month: 10 mg/kg (maximum 600 mg) every 12 hours for 2 days; <1 month: 5 mg/kg every 12 hours for 2 days.

Prophylaxis of H. influenzae Type b: Adults: 600 mg every 24 hours for 4 days. Children: >1 month: 20 mg/kg (max 600 mg) every 24 hours for 4 days; 1 month or less: 10 mg/kg every 24 hours for 4 days.

M. avium complex: In combination with other agents, the adult dose is 600 mg daily until culture-negative for 1 year.

M. kansasii: In combination with other agents, the adult dose is 600 mg daily until culture-negative for 1 year.

M. leprae (leprosy): In combination with dapsone, the adult dose is 600 mg once monthly for at least 6 months.

M. marinum: In combination with ethambutal, the adult dose is 600 mg daily for at least 3 months.

Prosthetic Valve Endocarditis caused by S. aureus or S. epidermidis: In combination with other agents, the adult dose is 300 mg every 8 hours for 14 days.

Reviewed 1999

Nonmedicinal ingredients are listed alphabetically within the supplied information of product monographs. Refer to the WHITE SECTION.

RIFATER™ Ⓟ

Hoechst Marion Roussel

Rifampin—Isoniazid—Pyrazinamide

Antituberculous Antibiotic

Pharmacology: Rifater is an antibacterial fixed combination product containing 120 mg rifampin, 50 mg isoniazid and 300 mg pyrazinamide used for the treatment of tuberculosis. Rifampin, isoniazid and pyrazinamide are bactericidal agents active against both intracellular and extracellular tuberculosis organisms.

Rifampin inhibits DNA-dependent RNA polymerase activity in susceptible cells. Specifically, it interacts with bacterial RNA polymerase, but does not inhibit the mammalian enzyme. Cross-resistance to rifampin has only been shown with other rifamycins. Isoniazid kills actively growing tubercle bacilli by inhibition of mycolic acid synthesis. The mechanism of action of pyrazinamide is unknown. In vitro and in vivo the drug is active only at a slightly acidic pH.

Pharmacokinetics: Pharmacokinetic studies in normal volunteers have shown that the 3 ingredients in Rifater have comparable bioavailability whether they are given together as individual dose forms or as Rifater.

Once daily doses of 4 to 7 tablets in tuberculosis patients resulted in the following steady-state pharmacokinetics: See Table I.

Table I—Rifater

Pharmacokinetics Parameters

	Half-Life (h)	C_{max} (mg/L)	T_{max} (h)	AUC (mg/L·h)
Isoniazid	2.5	7.6	1.5	34.2
Rifampin	2.0	9.5	2.2	47.9
Pyrazinamide	7.7	41.7	1.8	509.4

Indications: In the initial phase of the short-course treatment of pulmonary tuberculosis. During this phase, which should last 2 months, Rifater should be administered on a daily, continuous basis. When indicated, the addition of other antituberculosis drugs, such as streptomycin and/or ethambutol, should be considered.

Following the initial phase and treatment with Rifater, treatment should be continued with rifampin and isoniazid for at least 4 months. Treatment should be continued for longer if the patient is still sputum or culture positive, if resistant organisms are present, or if the patient is HIV positive. Susceptibility tests should be performed in the event of persistent positive cultures during the course of treatment.

In the treatment of tuberculosis, the small number of resistant cells present within large populations of susceptible cells can rapidly become the predominant type. Since resistance can emerge rapidly, susceptibility tests should be performed in the event of persistent positive cultures during the course of treatment. Bacteriologic smears or cultures should be obtained before the start of therapy to confirm the susceptibility of the organism to rifampin, isoniazid, and pyrazinamide and they should be repeated throughout therapy to monitor response to the treatment. If test results show resistance to any of the components of Rifater and the patient is not responding to therapy, the drug regimen should be modified.

Contraindications: In patients with a history of hypersensitivity to rifampin, isoniazid, pyrazinamide, or any of the components of the product. Other contraindications include patients with severe hepatic damage; severe adverse reactions to isoniazid, such as drug fever, chills, and arthritis; patients with acute liver disease of any etiology; and patients with acute gout.

Warnings: Rifater is a combination of 3 drugs, each of which has been associated with liver dysfunction.

Isoniazid: **Severe and sometimes fatal hepatitis associated with isoniazid therapy may occur and may develop even after many months of treatment. The risk of developing hepatitis is age related. Approximate case rates by age are: 0/1 000 for persons under 20 years of age, 3/1 000 for persons in the 20 to 34 year age group, 12/1 000 for persons in the 35 to 49 year age group, 23/1 000 for persons in the 50 to 64 year age group, and 8/1 000 for persons over 65 years of age. The risk of hepatitis is increased with daily consumption of alcohol. Precise data to provide a fatality rate for isoniazid-related hepatitis is not available; however, in a U.S. Public Health Service Surveillance Study of 13 838 persons taking isoniazid, there were 8 deaths among 174 cases of hepatitis.**

Rifater (cont'd)

Therefore, patients given isoniazid should be carefully monitored and interviewed at monthly intervals. Serum transaminase concentration becomes elevated in about 10 to 20% of patients, usually during the first few months of therapy, but it can occur at any time. Usually enzyme levels return to normal despite continuance of the drug, but in some cases progressive liver dysfunction occurs. Patients should be instructed to report immediately any of the prodromal symptoms of hepatitis, such as fatigue, weakness, malaise, anorexia, nausea, or vomiting. If these symptoms appear or if signs suggestive of hepatic damage are detected, isoniazid should be discontinued promptly since continued use of the drug in these cases has been reported to cause a more severe form of liver damage.

Patients with tuberculosis should be given appropriate treatment with alternative drugs. If isoniazid must be reinstituted, it should be reinstituted only after symptoms and laboratory abnormalities have cleared. The drug should be restarted in very small and gradually increasing doses and should be withdrawn immediately if there is any indication of recurrent liver involvement. Treatment should be deferred in persons with acute hepatic diseases.

Ophthalmologic examinations (including ophthalmoscopy) should be done before isoniazid is started and periodically thereafter, even without occurrence of visual symptoms.

Rifampin: Rifampin has been shown to produce liver dysfunction. Fatalities associated with jaundice have occurred in patients with liver disease and in patients taking rifampin with other hepatotoxic agents. Patients with impaired liver function should only be given rifampin in cases of necessity and then with caution and under strict medical supervision. In these patients, careful monitoring of liver function, especially serum ALT and serum AST should be carried out prior to therapy and then every 2 to 4 weeks during therapy. If signs of hepatocellular damage occur, Rifater, because it contains rifampin should be withdrawn.

In some cases, hyperbilirubinemia resulting from competition between rifampin and bilirubin for excretory pathways of the liver at the cell levels can occur in the early days of treatment. An isolated report showing a moderate rise in bilirubin and/or transaminase level is not in itself an indication for interrupting treatment; rather, the decision should be made after repeating the tests, noting trends in the levels, and considering them in conjunction with the patient's clinical condition.

Rifampin has enzyme-inducing properties, including induction of delta aminolevulinic acid synthetase. Isolated reports have associated porphyria exacerbation with rifampin administration.

Pyrazinamide: Patients started on pyrazinamide should have baseline serum uric acid and liver function determinations. Patients with pre-existing liver disease or those patients at increased risk for drug-related hepatitis (e.g., alcohol abusers) should be followed closely.

Because it contains pyrazinamide, Rifater should be discontinued and not be resumed if signs of hepatocellular damage or hyperuricemia accompanied by an acute gouty arthritis appear. If hyperuricemia accompanied by an acute gouty arthritis occurs without liver dysfunction, patients should be transferred to a regimen not containing pyrazinamide.

Precautions: General: Rifater should be used with caution in patients with a history of diabetes mellitus, as management may be more difficult.

A complete blood count (CBC), liver function tests, and blood uric acid determinations should be obtained prior to instituting therapy and periodically throughout the course of therapy. Because of a possible transient rise in transaminase and bilirubin values, blood for baseline clinical chemistries should be obtained before Rifater dosing.

Isoniazid: All drugs should be stopped and an evaluation of the patient should be made at the first sign of a hypersensitivity reaction.

Use of isoniazid should be carefully monitored in the following:

1. Patients who are receiving phenytoin concurrently. Isoniazid may decrease the excretion of phenytoin or may enhance its effects. To avoid phenytoin intoxication, appropriate adjustment of the anticonvulsant dose should be made.
2. Daily users of alcohol. Daily ingestion of alcohol may be associated with a higher incidence of isoniazid hepatitis.
3. Patients with current chronic liver disease or severe renal dysfunction.

Rifampin: For treatment of tuberculosis, rifampin is usually administered on a daily basis. High doses of rifampin (greater than 600 mg) given once or twice weekly have resulted in a high incidence of adverse reactions, including the "flu syndrome" (fever, chills and malaise); hematopoietic reactions (leukopenia, thrombocytopenia, or acute hemolytic anemia); cutaneous, gastrointestinal, and hepatic reactions; shortness of breath; shock and renal failure. Rifampin has been observed to increase the requirements for anticoagulant drugs of the coumarin type. In patients receiving anticoagulants and rifampin concurrently, it is recommended that the prothrombin time be performed daily or as frequently as necessary to establish and maintain the required dose of anticoagulant.

The patient should be advised that the reliability of oral contraceptives may be affected; consideration should be given to using alternative contraceptive measures.

Pyrazinamide: Pyrazinamide inhibits renal excretion of urates, frequently resulting in hyperuricemia which is usually asymptomatic. If hyperuricemia is accompanied by acute gouty arthritis, Rifater, because it contains pyrazinamide, should be discontinued.

Pregnancy: It is not known whether Rifater can affect reproduction capacity. When administered during the last few weeks of pregnancy, rifampin can cause postnatal hemorrhages in the mother and infant. In this case, treatment with vitamin K may be indicated for postnatal hemorrhage.

Teratogenic Effects: Animal reproduction studies have not been conducted with Rifater. It is also not known whether Rifater can cause fetal harm when administered to a pregnant woman. Rifater should be given to a pregnant woman only if clearly needed.

Isoniazid: It has been reported that in both rats and rabbits, isoniazid may exert an embryocidal effect when administered orally during pregnancy, although no isoniazid-related congenital anomalies have been found in reproduction studies in mammalian species (mice, rats, and rabbits). Rifater, because it contains isoniazid, should be prescribed during pregnancy only when therapeutically necessary. The benefit of preventive therapy should be weighed against a possible risk to the fetus. Preventive treatment generally should be started after delivery because of the increased risk of tuberculosis for new mothers.

Rifampin: Although rifampin has been reported to cross the placental barrier and appear in cord blood, the effect of rifampin, alone or in combination with other antituberculosis drugs, on the human fetus is not known. An increase in congenital malformations, primarily spina bifida and cleft palate, has been reported in the offspring of rodents given oral doses of 150 to 250 mg/kg/day of rifampin during pregnancy. The possible teratogenic potential in women capable of bearing children should be carefully weighed against the benefits of Rifater therapy.

Pyrazinamide: Animal reproductive studies have not been conducted with pyrazinamide. It is also not known whether pyrazinamide can cause fetal harm when administered to a pregnant woman. Rifater, because it contains pyrazinamide, should be given to a pregnant woman only if clearly needed.

Non-Teratogenic Effects: it is not known whether Rifater can affect reproduction capacity.

Rifampin: When administered during the last few weeks of pregnancy, rifampin can cause postnatal hemorrhages in the mother and infant. In this case, treatment with vitamin K may be indicated for postnatal hemorrhage.

Lactation: Since rifampin, isoniazid, and pyrazinamide are known to pass into maternal breast milk, a decision should be made whether to discontinue nursing or to discontinue Rifater, taking into account the importance of the drug to the mother.

Children: Safety and effectiveness in children have not been established.

Carcinogenesis, Mutagenesis, Impairment of Fertility: Increased frequency of chromosomal aberrations was observed in vitro in lymphocytes obtained from patients treated with combinations of rifampin, isoniazid, and pyrazinamide and combinations of streptomycin, rifampin, isoniazid, and pyrazinamide.

Isoniazid: Isoniazid has been reported to induce pulmonary tumors in a number of strains of mice.

Rifampin: There are no known human data on long-term potential for carcinogenicity, mutagenicity, or impairment of fertility. A few cases of accelerated growth of lung carcinoma have been reported in man, but a causal relationship with the drug has not been established. An increase in the incidence of hepatomas in female mice (of a strain known to be particularly susceptible to the spontaneous development of hepatomas) was observed when rifampicin was administered in doses 2 to 10 times the average daily human dose for 60 weeks followed by an observation period of 46 weeks. No evidence of carcinogenicity was found in male mice of the same strain, mice of a different strain, or rats under similar experimental conditions. Rifampin has been reported to possess immunosuppressive potential in rabbits, mice, rats, guinea pigs, human lymphocytes in vitro, and humans. Antitumor acitvity in vitro has been shown with rifampin.

There was no evidence of mutagenicity in bacteria, Drosophila melanogaster, or mice. An increase in chromatid breaks was noted when whole blood cell cultures were treated with rifampin.

Pyrazinamide: In lifetime bioassays in rats and mice, pyrazinamide was administered in the diet at concentrations of up to 10 000 ppm. This resulted in estimated daily doses of 2 g/kg for the mouse, or 40 times the maximum human dose, and 0.5 g/kg for the rat, or 10 times the maximum human dose. Pyrazinamide was not carcinogenic in rats or male mice and no conclusion was possible for female mice.

Pyrazinamide was not mutagenic in the Ames bacterial test, but induced chromosomal aberrations in human lymphocyte cell cultures.

Drug Interactions: Isoniazid: Enzyme Inhibition: Isoniazid is known to inhibit certain cytochrome P-450 enzymes. Coadministration of isoniazid with drugs that undergo biotransformation through these metabolic pathways may decrease elimination. Dosages of drugs metabolized by these enzymes may require adjustment when starting or stopping concomitantly administered isoniazid to maintain optimum therapeutic blood levels.

Isoniazid has been reported to inhibit the metabolism of the following drugs: anticonvulsants (e.g., carbamazepine, phenytoin, primidone, valproic acid), benzodiazepines (e.g., diazepam), haloperidol, ketoconazole, theophylline, and warfarin. It may be necessary to adjust the dosages of these drugs if they are given currently with Rifater because it contains isoniazid. The impact of the competing effects of rifampin and isoniazid on the metabolism of these drugs is unknown.

Other Interactions: Concomitant antacid administration may reduce the absorption of isoniazid. Ingestion with food may also reduce the absorption of isoniazid. Daily doses of isoniazid should be given on an empty stomach at least 1 hour before the ingestion of antacids or food.

Corticosteroids (e.g., prednisolone) may decrease the serum concentration of isoniazid by increasing acetylation rate and/or renal clearance. Para-aminosalicylic acid may increase the plasma concentration and elimination half-life of isoniazid by competition of acetylating enzymes.

Pharmacodynamic Interactions: Daily ingestion of alcohol may be associated with a higher incidence of isoniazid hepatitis. Isoniazid, when given concomitantly with rifampin, has been reported to increase the hepatotoxicity of both drugs. Patients receiving both rifampin and isoniazid as in Rifater should be monitored closely for hepatotoxicity.

In case reports, the CNS effects of meperidine (drowsiness), cycloserine (dizziness, drowsiness), and disulfiram (acute behavioral and coordination changes) may be exaggerated when concomitant isoniazid is given. Concurrent isoniazid and levodopa administration may produce symptoms of excess catecholamine stimulation (agitation, flushing, palpitations) or lack of levodopa effect.

Isoniazid may produce hyperglycemia and lead to loss of glucose control in patients on oral hypoglycemics.

Fast acetylation of isoniazid may produce high concentrations of hydrazine which facilitates deflorination of enflurane. Renal function should be monitored in patients receiving this drug combination.

Food Interactions: Because isoniazid has some monoamine oxidase inhibiting activity, an interaction with tyramine-containing foods (cheese, red wine) may occur. Diamine oxidase may also be inhibited, causing exaggerated response (e.g., headache, sweating, palpitations, flushing, hypotension) to foods containing histamine (e.g., skipjack, tuna, other tropical fish). Tyramine- and histamine-containing foods should be avoided.

Rifampin: Enzyme Induction: Rifampin is known to induce certain cytochrome P-450 enzymes. Coadministration of rifampin with drugs that undergo biotransformation through these metabolic pathways may accelerate elimination. To maintain optimum therapeutic blood levels, dosages of drugs metabolized by these enzymes may require adjustment when starting or stopping concomitantly administered rifampin.

Rifampin has been reported to accelerate the metabolism of the following drugs: anticonvulsants (e.g., phenytoin), antiarrhythmics (e.g., disopyramide, mexiletine, quinidine, tocainide), anticoagulants, antifungals (e.g., fluconazole, itraconazole, ketoconazole), barbiturates, beta-blockers, calcium channel blockers (e.g., diltiazem, nifedipine, verapamil), chloramphenicol, ciprofloxacin, corticosteroids, cyclosporine, cardiac glycoside preparations, clofibrate, oral contraceptives, dapsone, diazepam, haloperidol, oral hypoglycemic agents (sulfonylureas), narcotic analgesics, nortriptyline, progestins, and theophylline. It may be necessary to adjust the dosages of these drugs if they are given concurrently with Rifater since it contains rifampin.

Concurrent use of ketoconazole and rifampin has resulted in decreased serum concentration of both drugs. Concurrent use of rifampin and enalapril has resulted in decreased concentrations of enalaprilat, the active metabolite of enalapril. Dosage adjustments should be made if indicated by the patient's clinical condition.

Other Interactions: Concomitant antacid administration may reduce the absorption of rifampin. Daily doses of rifampin should be given at least 1 hour before the ingestion of antacids.

Probenecid and cotrimoxazole have been reported to increase the blood level of rifampin.

When rifampin is given concomitantly with either halothane or isoniazid the potential for hepatotoxicity is increased. The concomitant use of Rifater and halothane should be avoided. Patients receiving both rifampin and isoniazid as in Rifater should be monitored closely for hepatotoxicity (see Warnings).

Plasma concentrations of sulfapyridine may be reduced following the concomitant administration of sulfasalazine and rifampin. This finding may be the result of alteration in the colonic bacteria responsible for the reduction of sulfasalazine to sulfapyridine and mesalamine.

Drug/Laboratory Tests Interaction: Rifampin: Therapeutic levels of rifampin have been shown to inhibit standard microbiological assays for serum folate and vitamin B_{12}. Therefore, alternate assay methods should be considered. Transient abnormalities in liver function tests (e.g., elevation in serum bilirubin, abnormal bromsulphalein [BSP] excretion, alkaline phosphatase and serum transaminases), and reduced biliary excretion of contrast media used for visualization of the gallbladder have also been observed. Therefore, these tests should be performed before the morning dose of Rifater.

Rifampin and isoniazid have been reported to alter vitamin D metabolism. In some cases, reduced levels of circulating 25-hydroxy vitamin D and 1,25-dihydroxy vitamin D have been accompanied by reduced serum calcium and phosphate, and elevated parathyroid hormone.

Pyrazinamide: Pyrazinamide has been reported to interfere with Acetest and Ketostix urine tests to produce a pink-brown color.

Information for the Patient: Food Interactions: Because isoniazid has some monoamine oxidase inhibiting activity, an interaction with tyramine-containing foods (cheese, red wine) may occur. Diamine oxidase may also be inhibited, causing exaggerated response (e.g., headache, sweating, palpitations, flushing, hypotension) to foods containing histmaine (e.g., skipjack, tuna, other tropical fish). Tyramine- and histamine-containing foods should be avoided.

Rifater, because it contains rifampin may produce a reddish coloration of the urine, sweat, sputum, and tears, and the patient should be forewarned of this. Soft contact lenses may be permanently stained.

Patients should be instructed to take Rifater either 1 hour before or 2 hours after a meal.

Patients should be instructed to notify their physicians promptly if they experience any of the following: fever, loss of appetite, malaise, nausea and vomiting, darkened urine, yellowish discoloration of the skin and eyes, pain or swelling of the joints.

Compliance with the full course of therapy must be emphasized, and the importance of not missing any doses must be stressed.

Laboratory Tests: A complete blood count (CBC), liver function tests, and blood uric acid determinations should be obtained prior to instituting therapy and periodically throughout the course of therapy. Because of a possible transient rise in transaminase and bilirubin values, blood for baseline clinical chemistries should be obtained before Rifater dosing.

Adverse Effects: The adverse reactions reported during therapy with Rifater are consistent with reactions described or listed below for the individual components.

Isoniazid: The most frequent reactions are those affecting the nervous system and the liver (see Warnings).

Nervous System: Peripheral neuropathy is the most common toxic effect. It is dose-related, occurs most often in the malnourished and in those predisposed to neuritis (e.g., alcoholics and diabetics), and is usually preceded by paresthesias of the feet and hands. The incidence is higher in "slow inactivators".

Other neurotoxic effects, which are uncommon with conventional doses, are convulsions, toxic encephalopathy, optic neuritis and atrophy, memory impairment, and toxic psychosis.

Gastrointestinal: Nausea, vomiting, and epigastric distress.

Hepatic: elevated serum transaminases (ALT, AST), bilirubinemia, bilirubinuria, jaundice, and occasionally severe and sometimes fatal hepatitis. The common prodromal symptoms are anorexia, nausea, vomiting, fatigue, malaise, and weakness. Mild and transient elevation of serum transaminase levels occurs in 10 to 20% of persons taking isoniazid. The abnormality usually occurs in the first 4 to 6 months of treatment but can occur at any time during therapy. In most instances, enzyme levels return to normal with no necessity to discontinue medication. In occasional instances, progressive liver damage occurs, with accompanying symptoms. In these cases, the drug should be discontinued immediately. The frequency of progressive liver damage increases with age. It is rare in persons under 20, but occurs in up to 2.3% of those over 50 years of age.

Hematologic: agranulocytosis: hemolytic, sideroblastic, or aplastic anemia; thrombocytopenia; and eosinophilia.

Hypersensitivity Reactions: fever, skin eruptions (morbilliform, maculopapular, purpuric, or exfoliative), lymphadenopathy, and vasculitis.

Metabolic and Endocrine: pyridoxine deficiency, pellagra, hyperglycemia, metabolic acidosis, and gynecomastia.

Miscellaneous: rheumatic syndrome and systemic lupus erythematosus-like syndrome.

Rifampin: Gastrointestinal: heartburn, epigastric distress, anorexia, nausea, vomiting, jaundice, flatulence, cramps, and diarrhea have been noted in some patients. Although C. difficile has been shown in vitro to be sensitive to rifampin, pseudomembranous colitis has been reported with the use of rifampin (and other broad spectrum antibiotics). Therefore, it is important to consider this diagnosis in patients who develop diarrhea in association with antibiotic use. Rarely, hepatitis or a shock-like syndrome with hepatic involvement and abnormal liver function tests has been reported.

Hematologic: Thrombocytopenia has occurred primarily with high dose intermittent therapy, but has also been noted after resumption of interrupted treatment. It rarely occurs during well-supervised daily therapy. This effect is reversible if the drug is discontinued as soon as purpura occurs. Cerebral hemorrhage and fatalities have been reported when rifampin administration has been continued or resumed after the appearance of purpura.

Transient leukopenia, hemolytic anemia, and decreased hemoglobin have been observed.

CNS: Headache, fever, drowsiness, fatigue, ataxia, dizziness, inability to concentrate, mental confusion, behavioral changes, muscular weakness, pains in extremities, and generalized numbness have been observed.

Rare reports of myopathy have also been observed.

Ocular: Visual disturbances have been observed.

Endocrine: Menstrual disturbances have been observed.

Renal: Elevations in BUN and serum uric acid have been reported. Rarely, hemolysis, hemoglobinuria, hematuria, interstitial nephritis, renal insufficiency and acute renal failure have been noted. These are generally considered to be hypersensitivity reactions. They usually occur during intermittent therapy or when treatment is resumed following intentional or accidental interruption of a daily dosage regimen, and are reversible when rifampin is discontinued and appropriate therapy instituted.

Dermatologic: Cutaneous reactions are mild and self-limiting and do not appear to be hypersensitivity reactions. Typically, they consist of flushing and itching with or without a rash. More serious cutaneous reactions which may be due to hypersensitivity occur but are uncommon.

Hypersensitivity Reactions: Occasionally, pruritus, urticaria, rash, pemphigoid reaction, eosinophilia, sore mouth, sore tongue and conjunctivitis have been observed.

Miscellaneous: Edema of the face and extremities has been reported. Other reactions which have occurred with intermittent dosage regimens include "flu" syndrome (such as episodes of fever, chills, headache, dizziness and bone pain), shortness of breath, wheezing, decrease in blood pressure and shock. The "flu" syndrome may also appear if rifampin is taken irregularly by the patient or if daily administration is resumed after a drug-free interval.

Pyrazinamide: The principal adverse effect is a hepatic reaction (see Warnings). Hepatotoxicity appears to be dose related, and may appear at any time during therapy. Pyrazinamide can cause hyperuricemia and gout (see Precautions).

Gastrointestinal: Gastrointestinal disturbances including nausea, vomiting, and anorexia have also been reported.

Hematologic and Lymphatic: Thrombocytopenia and sideroblastic anemia with erythroid hyperplasia, vacuolation of erythrocytes and increased serum iron concentration have occurred rarely with this drug. Adverse effects on blood clotting mechanisms have also been rarely reported.

Other: Mild arthralgia and myalgia have been reported frequently. Hypersensitivity reactions including rashes, urticaria, and pruritus have been reported. Fever, acne, photosensitivity, porphyria, dysuria and interstitial nephritis have been reported rarely.

Overdose: There is no human experience with Rifater overdosage.

Isoniazid: Untreated or inadequately treated cases of gross isoniazid overdosage can be fatal, but good response has been reported in most patients treated within the first few hours after drug ingestion.

Ingested acutely, as little as 1.5 g isoniazid may cause toxicity in adults. Doses of 35 to 40 mg/kg have resulted in seizures.

Ingestion of 80 to 150 mg/kg isoniazid has been associated with severe toxicity and, if untreated, significant mortality.

Rifampin: Nonfatal overdoses with as high as 12 g of rifampin have been reported.

One case of fatal overdose is known: a 26-year-old man died after self-administering 60 g of rifampin.

Pyrazinamide: Overdosage experience with pyrazinamide is limited.

Symptoms: The following signs and symptoms have been seen with each individual component in an overdosage situation.

Isoniazid: Isoniazid overdosage produces signs and symptoms within 30 minutes to 3 hours. Nausea, vomiting, dizziness, slurring of speech, blurring of vision, visual hallucinations (including bright colors and strange designs) are among the early manifestations. With marked overdosage, respiratory distress and CNS depression, progressing rapidly from stupor to profound coma, are to be expected, along with severe, intractable seizures. Severe metabolic acidosis, acetonuria, and hyperglycemia are typical laboratory findings.

Rifampin: Nausea, vomiting, and increasing lethargy will probably occur within a short time after rifampin overdosage; unconsciousness may occur when there is severe hepatic disease. Brownish-red or orange discoloration of the skin, urine, sweat, saliva, tears and feces will occur, and its intensity is proportional to the amount ingested.

Liver enlargement, possibly with tenderness, can develop within a few hours after severe overdosage; bilirubin levels may increase and jaundice may develop rapidly. Hepatic involvement may be more marked in patients with prior impairment of hepatic function. Other physical findings remain essentially normal. A direct effect upon the hematopoietic system, electrolyte levels, or acid-base balance is unlikely.

Pyrazinamide: In 1 case of pyrazinamide overdosage, abnormal liver function tests developed. These spontaneously reverted to normal when the drug was stopped.

Treatment: The airway should be secured and adequate respiratory exchange should be established in cases of overdosage with Rifater.

Obtain blood samples for immediate determination of gases, electrolytes, BUN, glucose, etc.; type and cross-match blood in preparation for possible hemodialysis.

Gastric lavage within the first 2 to 3 hours after ingestion is advised, but it should not be attempted until convulsions are under control. To treat convulsions, administer i.v. diazepam or short-acting barbiturates, and i.v. pyridoxine (usually 1 mg/1 mg isoniazid ingested). Following evacuation of gastric contents, the instillation of activated charcoal slurry into the stomach may help absorb any remaining drug from the gastrointestinal tract. Antiemetic medication may be required to control severe nausea and vomiting.

Rapid control of metabolic acidosis is fundamental to management. Give i.v. sodium bicarbonate at once and repeat as needed, adjusting subsequent dosage on the basis of laboratory findings (e.g., serum sodium, pH, etc).

Forced osmotic diuresis must be started early and should be continued for some hours after clinical improvement to hasten renal clearance of drug and help prevent relapse; monitor fluid intake and output.

Hemodialysis is advised for severe cases; if this is not available, peritoneal dialysis can be used along with forced diuresis.

Along with measures based on initial and repeated determination of blood gases and other laboratory tests as needed, utilize meticulous respiratory and other intensive care to protect against hypoxia, hypotension, aspiration pneumonitis, etc.

Dosage: Adults: Patients should be given the following single daily dose either 1 hour before or 2 hours after a meal with a full glass of water: Patients weighing 44 kg or less: 4 tablets; patients weighing between 45 to 54 kg: 5 tablets; patients weighing 55 kg or greater: 6 tablets.

Rifater (cont'd)

Rifater is recommended in the initial phase of short-course therapy which is usually continued for 2 months. When indicated, the addition of other antituberculosis drugs, such as streptomycin and/or ethambutol, should be considered.

Following the initial phase, treatment should be continued with rifampin and isoniazid for at least 4 months. Treatment should be continued for longer if the patient is still sputum or culture positive, if resistant organisms are present, or if the patient is HIV positive.

Concomitant administration of pyridoxine (B_6) is recommended in the malnourished, in those predisposed to neuropathy (e.g., alcoholics and diabetics), and in adolescents.
Children: The ratio of the drugs in Rifater may not be appropriate in children (e.g., higher mg/kg doses of isoniazid are usually given in children than adults) (see Precautions).

Supplied: Each light beige, round, sugar-coated tablet contains: rifampin 120 mg, isoniazid 50 mg and pyrazinamide 300 mg. Nonmedicinal ingredients: acacia, aluminum hydroxide, calcium stearate, carnauba wax, colophony, kaolin, magnesium carbonate, paraffin, povidone, ferric oxide, silicon dioxide, sodium carboxymethylcellulose, sodium lauryl sulfate, sucrose, talc, titanium dioxide and white beeswax. Bottles of 60. Store at controlled room temperature (15 to 30°C). Protect from moisture.

(Shown in Product Recognition Section)

RIMACTANE® ℞

Novartis Pharmaceuticals

Rifampin

Antituberculous Antibiotic

Pharmacology: Rifampin inhibits DNA-dependent RNA polymerase activity in susceptible cells. Specifically, it interacts with bacterial RNA polymerase. This is the probable mechanism of action by which rifampin exerts its therapeutic effect.
Pharmacokinetics: Absorption: Peak blood levels in normal adults vary widely from individual to individual. Peak levels occur between 2 and 4 hours following the oral administration of a 600 mg dose. The average peak value is 7 μg/mL.

In one study, cumulation was noted upon multiple dosage of rifampin, 10 mg/kg/day, to newborns. Peak values appeared to be delayed in the newborns which were not seen in children up to 18 months of age. It is suggested that the drug is less readily eliminated from the newborn, probably because of the low flow of bile during the first days of life. In all of these children and infants the mean serum level of rifampin corresponded to one third to one tenth the levels in adults receiving proportionally the same dose.

Absorption is more rapid when rifampin is administered 1 hour before meals.
Distribution: Rifampin is distributed throughout the body and is detectable in many organs and body fluids, including the cerebrospinal fluid. The highest concentrations are present in the liver and bile.

The apparent volume of distribution is 1.6 L/kg in adults and 1.1 L/kg in children. Binding to serum proteins amounts to 84 to 91%.

Rifampin crosses the blood brain barrier in the case of inflamed meninges only, but concentrations in the cerebrospinal fluid may remain above the MIC for M. tuberculosis for up to 2 months with continuous therapy of 600 mg/day orally.

Rifampin crosses the human placenta and is secreted in human breast milk. However, a breast fed infant would not receive more than 1% of the usual therapeutic dose.
Biological Half-life: In normal subjects the biological half-life of rifampin is approximately 3 hours with variations from 1 to 5 hours. Biliary obstruction causes a longer half-life but kidney blockage does not appear to cause a change.
Excretion: Rifampin is eliminated from the blood equally in the urine and feces as unchanged drug and metabolites. Approximately half of the original dose eliminated by the bile is unchanged drug. The proportion of unchanged drug to metabolite is less in the urine than in the bile. In the presence of complete renal shutdown, the drug is excreted entirely in the bile.

The principal metabolite in man is the biologically active desacetyl-rifampin. Its excretion appears to be a dynamically changing picture at all times.

Desacetylation of rifampin in the body does not substantially modify its antimycobacterial activity.

Indications: Active pulmonary tuberculosis, whether it is in the primary or chronic phase.

Contraindications: Jaundice associated with reduced bilirubin excretion. Known or suspected sensitivity to any of the rifamycins or their excipients.

Premature and newborn infants in whom the liver is not yet capable of functioning with full efficiency.
Lactation: Rifampin passes into breast milk and, therefore, should not be used during lactation.

Warnings: Rifampin has been shown to produce liver dysfunction. There have been fatalities associated with jaundice in patients with liver disease or receiving the drug concomitantly with other hepatotoxic agents. Since an increased risk may exist for individuals with liver disease, benefits must be weighed carefully against the risk of further liver damage. If such treatment is necessary, the dosage must be reduced so that 6 to 8 mg/kg body weight is not exceeded. Periodic liver function monitoring is mandatory. Periodic blood counts should also be carried out in patients receiving long-term treatment.
Pregnancy: The effect of combinations of rifampin with other antituberculous drugs on the human fetus is not known. No obvious effect on the fetus was detected after the administration of rifampin to 15 pregnant patients. An increase in congenital malformations, primarily spina bifida and cleft palate, has been reported in the offspring of mice and rats given oral doses of 100 mg/kg/day during pregnancy.

Rifampin should not be used in pregnant women or women with childbearing potential. If therapy is judged to be essential, such treatment should be implemented only after carefully weighing the potential benefits of therapy against the risks, particularly if used during the first 3 months of pregnancy.

The possibility of pregnancy should be ruled out prior to treatment with rifampin; patients should be advised to avoid pregnancy.

When administered during the last few weeks of pregnancy, rifampin has been shown to cause postnatal hemorrhage in the mother and infant, therefore vitamin K should be given during labor to mothers receiving rifampin and to their offspring immediately after birth. In the newborn, careful surveillance for bleeding symptoms and decrease of coagulation factors is mandatory.

Precautions: To delay the emergence of drug resistance, which can be a serious problem, rifampin must be used concomitantly with at least one other antituberculous drug. The selection of the specific drug for concurrent therapy is determined by the in vitro sensitivity tests on the organisms and the patient's previous clinical history.

The possibility of a drug interaction, as well as the individual properties and special precautions relating to drugs used in concomitant therapy should be taken into consideration. For example, when rifampin is prescribed in addition to PAS preparations containing bentonite (aluminum hydrosilicate, closely related to kaolin), absorption of rifampin can be impaired; therefore, rifampin should be taken first, followed by the bentonite-containing preparation after an interval of 8 to 12 hours. Similarly, a reduction in the bioavailability of rifampin after oral dosing has been observed when given concomitantly with opiates and anticholinergic drugs. To avoid this interaction, rifampin should be taken a few hours before these preparations.

Daily treatment with rifampin is often better tolerated than intermittent therapy, since rare hypersensitivity reactions may occur. Resumption of treatment after termination of a course of long-term therapy with the drug involves risks and therefore should, if possible, be avoided. If unavoidable, possible adverse reactions may be minimized if the drug-free interval or rest period is less than or closely resembles the interval of the previous drug treatment period. When resuming treatment with rifampin, the drug should be re-introduced gradually, beginning with a daily dose of 75 mg and increasing the dose by 75 to 150 mg on the first day. The desired therapeutic dose should be reached within 3 to 4 days. During the transitional period, renal function should be closely monitored. Corticosteroids may be useful in attenuating possible immunological reactions. If as may happen in exceptional cases, the patient develops thrombocytopenia, purpura, hemolytic anemia, or renal failure, treatment should be stopped at once and not re-instituted at a later date.

Rifampin has been observed to increase the requirements for anticoagulant drugs of the coumarin type. This effect was not observed until the fifth day following the initiation of treatment. The decrease in prothrombin time lasts 5 to 7 days on the average. The cause of this phenomenon is unknown. In patients receiving anticoagulants it is recommended that daily prothrombin times be performed until the dose of the anticoagulant required has been established.

Safe conditions for the use of ethambutol alone or in combination with rifampin have not been established for children under the age of 13 years. Although renal insufficiency does not alter blood levels of rifampin, marked increases in ethambutol levels are observed under similar conditions; this, therefore, should be taken into consideration in such patients receiving rifampin/ethambutol combination therapy. Caution is recommended when instituting therapeutic regimens in which isoniazid is to be used concurrently with rifampin, in patients with impaired liver function, the elderly and malnourished.

From experimental studies it would appear that bromsulphalein (BSP) and rifampin compete with one another at the liver cell-bile canaliculus boundary. In clinical studies, BSP elevation was reported following rifampin administration. Therefore, the rationale of using the BSP as a test of liver function during therapy is nullified.

Urine, feces, saliva, sputum, sweat, and tears may be colored red-orange by rifampin and its metabolites. Individuals to be treated should be made aware of these possibilities in order to prevent undue anxiety. Patients should be advised that soft contact lenses may be permanently stained.

It has been reported that oral contraceptives have failed to prevent conception in some patients receiving rifampin in association with other antituberculosis drugs. It is therefore necessary that alternative or additional contraceptive measures be recommended.
Drug Interactions: Current evidence indicates that administration of rifampin may be associated with induction of drug metabolizing enzyme systems of the liver. As a result, the rate of metabolism of those drugs which are substrates for these enzymes can be altered, resulting in reduced pharmacological effects of the drugs involved. The activity of the following drugs may be impaired, and their dosage must therefore be re-assessed during and after treatment with rifampin: oral anticoagulants; oral antidiabetic agents; digitalis preparations; antiarrhythmic agents; tocainide; propafenone; quinidine; mexiletine; methadone (withdrawal signs may set in); hydantoins (phenytoin, ethotoin); hexobarbital; nortriptyline; benzodiazepines; corticosteroids (Addison patients may develop a crisis; exacerbation of pemphigus may occur; treatment for corticoid-dependent asthma may become more difficult or impossible); sex hormones (menstrual disorders may appear); oral contraceptives (their effect can no longer be relied upon); theophyllines (aminophylline, theophylline); dapsone; chloramphenicol; azole antifungal agents (ketoconazole, itraconazole); cyclosporin A; azathioprine (transplants may be rejected); β-blockers; nifedipine; verapamil; enalapril; cimetidine.

Rifampin should be used with caution in patients with porphyria as it could induce delta-aminolaevulinic acid synthetase activity.

Microbiological techniques for assaying the serum concentrations of folic acid and vitamin B_{12} are not suitable for use during treatment with rifampin.

Rifampin causes temporary competitive inhibition of bromosulphalein excretion. To guard against false positive results, the bromosulphalein test should be performed in the morning before administration of rifampin.

Adverse Effects: Rifampin is usually well tolerated at recommended dosage levels. The adverse reactions are stated in terms of occurrence rate: frequent (>10%), occasional (>1% and <10%), rare (>0.001% and <1%) and isolated cases (<0.001%).
Gastrointestinal: Occasionally anorexia, nausea, abdominal pains, gaseous distension; rarely vomiting or diarrhea; isolated cases of erosive gastritis and pseudomembranous colitis.
CNS: Occasionally tiredness, drowsiness, headache, lightheadedness, dizziness; rarely ataxia, mental confusion; isolated cases of muscular weakness and visual disturbances. Clinical trials have furnished no evidence to suggest that rifampin has any harmful effects on the cochleovestibular system.
Skin and Appendages: Occasionally flushing, itching with or without skin rash, urticaria and reddening of the eyes; isolated cases of severe signs and symptoms such as exudative conjunctivitis or generalized hypersensitivity reactions involving the skin (e.g. exfoliative dermatitis, Lyell's syndrome) and pemphigoid reactions.
Endocrine: In rare instances disturbances in the menstrual cycle; induction of a crisis in Addison patients (see Precautions, Drug Interactions).
Hematologic: Eosinophilia, thrombocytopenia, purpura, transient leukopenia, hemolytic anemia and decreased hemoglobin have been observed. Thrombocytopenia has occurred when rifampin and ethambutol were administered concomitantly according to an intermittent dose schedule twice weekly and

in high doses. Elevations in BUN and serum uric acid have been reported.

Thrombocytopenia and thrombocytopenic purpura are encountered more frequently under intermittent therapy than on continuous daily treatment, during which they occur only in isolated cases.

Hepatic: Frequently an asymptomatic increase in liver enzymes; rarely hepatitis or jaundice; here account must be noted of the liver toxicity of chemotherapeutic agents (e.g. isoniazid or pyrazinamide) employed in combination with rifampin. Induction of porphyria in isolated cases has been reported.

Unwanted effects chiefly occurring during intermittent therapy or upon resumption of treatment after temporary interruption: In patients taking rifampin other than on a daily basis or in those resuming treatment with the drug after a temporary interruption, an influenza-like syndrome ("flu syndrome") may occur, this being very probably of immunopathological origin. It is characterized by fever, shivering and possibly headache, dizziness and musculoskeletal pain. In rare cases the "flu-syndrome" may be followed by thrombocytopenia, purpura, dyspnea, asthma-like attacks, hemolytic anemia, shock and acute renal failure. These serious complications may, however, also set in suddenly with no preceding "flu syndrome", chiefly when treatment is resumed after a temporary interruption or when rifampin is given only once a week in high doses (25 mg/kg or more). When rifampin is administered in lower doses (600 mg) 2 to 3 times a week, the syndrome is only rarely encountered, its incidence then being comparable to that observed during daily medication.

Overdose: For acute overdosage, general supportive measures should be employed, along with gastric lavage. No specific antidote is known.

Symptoms: Reddish-brown or orange discoloration of the skin, sputum, lacrimal fluid, sweat, feces ("red man syndrome"); nausea, vomiting, abdominal pains; enlargement of the liver, jaundice, elevated liver enzyme levels; possibly acute pulmonary edema, lethargy, clouding consciousness, convulsions.

Treatment: Gastric lavage together with instillation of an activated charcoal suspension via the stomach tube; general supportive measures to maintain vital functions; forced diuresis; hemodialysis; in the presence of severe liver damage, cholecystostomy if necessary. Bear in mind that other drugs used in combination with rifampin may also have been taken in an over dosage and necessitate additional specific measures.

Dosage: Adults: 600 mg in a single daily dose. Should intolerance occur, the daily dosage may be reduced to 450 mg. In patients with impaired liver function, a daily dose of 8 mg/kg should not be exceeded. A daily dosage of 10 mg/kg is recommended for frail and elderly persons.

Children: 10 to 20 mg/kg not to exceed 600 mg/day. Data is not available for the determination of dosage for children under 5 years of age.

In treatment of pulmonary tuberculosis, rifampin must be used in conjunction with at least one other antituberculosis agent, each prescribed in its usual dosage. In general, therapy should be continued until bacterial conversion has been established and maximum clinical improvement has occurred.

To ensure optimum absorption, rifampin should be taken on an empty stomach (1 hour before breakfast).

When administering combined treatment with isoniazid, one should not exceed the dosage recommended for the latter.

Supplied: Each opaque, brownish-red, hard gelatin capsule containing an orange to reddish-brown powder, branded in black ink "CG" and the identification code letters "CS" (or "300") contains: rifampin 300 mg. Nonmedicinal ingredients: calcium stearate, gelatin, iron oxides and titanium dioxide. Energy: 0.8 kJ (0.2 kcal). Bottles of 100. Protect from heat (store at 2 to 30°C), light and humidity. Keep out of reach of children.

(Shown in Product Recognition Section)

Reviewed 1997

RIMSO®-50 Ⓟ

Roberts

Dimethyl Sulfoxide

Genitourinary Disorders

Pharmacology: Dimethyl sulfoxide has a wide spectrum of primary pharmacologic activity including: membrane penetrant, solute carrier across membranes, anti-inflammatory, analgesia, diuresis, cholinesterase inhibition, muscle relaxation, vasodilation, penetrant of blood-brain barrier. Although the mode of action of dimethyl sulfoxide as a treatment for various inflammatory genitourinary disorders is speculative at this time, hypotheses centre around the following: anti-inflammation, analgesic, improvement of blood supply, softening of collagen due to action on cross linking.

Dimethyl sulfoxide is metabolized by oxidation to dimethyl sulfone or by the reduction to dimethyl sulfide. Dimethyl sulfoxide and dimethyl sulfone are excreted in the urine and feces. Dimethyl sulfide is eliminated through the breath and skin and is responsible for the characteristic odor exuded from patients. The drug can persist in serum for more than 2 weeks after a single intravesical instillation. No residual accumulation of dimethyl sulfoxide has occurred in patients who have received treatment for protracted periods of time. Following topical application dimethyl sulfoxide is absorbed and generally distributed in the tissues and body fluids.

Indications: The symptomatic relief of chronic inflammatory genitourinary disorders (cystitis, interstitial cystitis, radiation cystitis, trigonitis and prostatitis).

Contraindications: None known.

Warnings: Dimethyl sulfoxide has not been approved as being safe and effective for indications other than those listed. There is no clinical evidence of effectiveness in the treatment of bacterial infections of the urinary tract.

Dimethyl sulfoxide can initiate the liberation of histamine and occasional hypersensitivity reactions have occurred with topical administration. Hypersensitivity has not occurred in patients receiving intravesical dimethyl sulfoxide; however, the physician should be cognizant of this possibility.

If anaphylactoid symptoms develop, appropriate therapy should be instituted. Some data indicate that dimethyl sulfoxide potentiates other concomitantly administered medications.

Precautions: Changes in the refractive index and lens opacities have been seen in animals with chronic administration. No ophthalmic changes attributable to intravesical instillation have been reported in patients carefully followed for up to 17 months; however, full eye evaluations, including slit lamp examinations are recommended prior to and at 6 month intervals during treatment.

Patients should be investigated with respect to biochemical parameters, particularly renal and hepatic function, at 6-month intervals.

Intravesical instillation may be harmful to patients with urinary tract malignancy due to dimethyl sulfoxide induced vasodilation.

Pregnancy: Intraperitoneally administered high doses have caused teratogenic responses in animal studies. Oral or topical doses did not cause fetal abnormalities. The safety of dimethyl sulfoxide in the human fetus has not been established and it should be given to pregnant women only when the potential benefits to the mother have been weighed against possible hazards to the child.

Lactation: Although data are lacking, it must be assumed that dimethyl sulfoxide is excreted in human milk. Mothers receiving dimethyl sulfoxide should not nurse their infants.

Adverse Effects: A garlic like taste may be noted by the patient within a few minutes after instillation. This taste may last several hours and because of the presence of metabolites, an odor on the breath and skin may remain for 72 hours. Transient chemical cystitis has been noted following instillation of 100% dimethyl sulfoxide. The patient may experience moderately severe discomfort on administration. Usually this becomes less prominent with repeated administration.

Dosage: Adults: For the treatment of chronic inflammatory genitourinary disorders, instill 50 mL of solution directly into the bladder by a catheter or asepto syringe and allow to remain for 15 minutes. For patients with prostatitis, a catheter should be passed gently to the level of the membranous urethra and the medication slowly instilled directly into the prostatic urethra and then into the bladder. Application of an analgesic lubricant gel such as lidocaine jelly to the urethra is suggested prior to insertion of the catheter to avoid spasm. The medication is expelled by spontaneous voiding. It is recommended that the treatment be repeated every 2 weeks until maximum symptomatic relief is obtained. Thereafter, time intervals between therapy may be increased appropriately.

In selected cases where symptomatic relief is not complete, the bladder may be gently distended by gravity instillation with up to 500 mL of a dimethyl sulfoxide solution (one part dimethyl sulfoxide to one part sterile water) prepared in a glass delivery container immediately prior to the procedure. After retention the solution is expelled. Discard any remaining solution. A standard dose of 50 mL of dimethyl sulfoxide should then be instilled for an additional 15 minutes, followed again by expulsion.

Administration of oral analgesic medication or suppositories containing belladonna and opium prior to the instillation of dimethyl sulfoxide can reduce bladder spasm.

In patients with severe bladder symptoms and sensitive bladders, the initial treatment, and possibly the second and third (depending on patient response) should be done under anesthesia (saddle block has been suggested).

Dimethyl sulfoxide is recommended for bladder instillation only.

Supplied: Each 50 mL cartoned bottle contains: 54 g of sterile and pyrogen free 500 mg/g (50% w/w) dimethyl sulfoxide in a clear, colorless and aqueous solution. Protect from light. Store at controlled room temperature (15 to 30°C). Do not autoclave.

RIOPAN®
RIOPAN® PLUS

Whitehall-Robins

Magaldrate
Magaldrate—Simethicone

Antacid
Antacid—Antiflatulent

Indications: Symptomatic relief of heartburn, indigestion and upset stomach due to excess acid, and relief of gas with Riopan Plus.

Precautions: Individuals with kidney disease should not take this product except with the advice and supervision of a physician. Do not take with tetracycline antibiotics. Antacids can interfere with the absorption of iron preparations. Do not take for longer than 2 weeks or if symptoms recur, unless otherwise directed by a physician.

Adverse Effects: Mild constipation may occur in a small percentage of patients.

Dosage: Riopan: Suspension: Adults: 5 to 20 mL, 20 minutes to 1 hour after meals and at bedtime, or as directed by a physician.

Chewable Tablets: Adults: 1 to 4 tablets, 20 minutes to 1 hour after meals and at bedtime, or as directed by a physician. Chew well before swallowing.

Riopan Plus: 10 to 20 mL, 20 minutes to 1 hour after meals and at bedtime, or as directed by a physician.

Supplied: Riopan: Chewable Tablets: Each white, round mint-flavored tablet contains: magaldrate USP 480 mg. Energy: 7.50 kJ (1.8 kcal). Sodium: <1 mmol (0.7 mg). Nonmedicinal ingredients: flavor, magnesium stearate, polyethylene glycol, sorbitol, sucrose and titanium dioxide. Gluten-, parabens-, sulfite- and tartrazine-free. Bottles of 60 and 100.

Suspension: Each 5 mL of mint-flavored suspension contains: magaldrate USP 480 mg. Energy: 0 kJ (0 kcal). Sodium: <1 mmol (0.7 mg)/tsp. Nonmedicinal ingredients: acacia, ammonia solution, calcium cyclamate, calcium hypochlorite, hydroxypropyl methylcellulose, menthol, peppermint oil and water. Alcohol-, gluten-, parabens-, sugar-, sulfite- and tartrazine-free. Bottles of 350 and 600 mL. Protect from freezing. Shake well.

Riopan Plus: Each 5 mL of mint-flavored suspension contains: magaldrate USP 480 mg and simethicone 20 mg. Energy: 0.0 kcal. Sodium: <1 mmol (0.7 mg). Nonmedicinal ingredients: acacia, calcium cyclamate, cellulose, flavors, monochloramine solution, sodium polyoxyl 8 stearate, sorbitan monostearate and water. Alcohol-, gluten-, parabens-, sugar-, sulfite- and tartrazine-free. Bottles of 350 mL. Protect from freezing. Shake well.

Store at room temperature (15 to 30°C).

RIPHENIDATE ⬥

Technilab

Methylphenidate HCl

CNS Stimulant

Supplied: 10 mg: Each round, biconvex white tablet with bluish tint, imprinted MD on one side and 530 on the other, contains: methylphenidate HCl 10 mg. Nonmedicinal ingredients: FD&C Green #3, lactose, magnesium stearate, micro crystalline cellulose and sodium starch glycolate. Bottles of 100 and 500.

Riphenidate (cont'd)

20 mg: Each round, biconvex, peach-colored tablet, imprinted MD on one side and 532 on the other, contains: methylphenidate HCl 20 mg. Nonmedicinal ingredients: FD&C Yellow #6, lactose, magnesium stearate, microcrystalline cellulose and sodium starch glycolate. Bottles of 100 and 500.

Store between 15 to 30°C. Protect from heat and humidity.

RISPERDAL® Oral Solution Ⓟ
RISPERDAL® Tablets Ⓟ

Janssen-Ortho

Risperidone Tartrate

Risperidone

Antipsychotic Agent

Pharmacology: Risperidone, a benzisoxazole derivative, is a novel antipsychotic drug which binds with high affinity to the serotonin type 2 (5-HT_2), dopamine D_2, and α_1-adrenergic receptors. Risperidone binds with a lower affinity to the α_2-adrenergic and histamine H_1 receptors. Risperidone does not bind to dopamine D_1 or muscarinic cholinergic receptors.

Receptor occupancy was also demonstrated in vivo in humans. Using positron emission tomography, risperidone was shown to block both 5-HT_2 and dopamine D_2 receptors in 3 healthy volunteers.

Pharmacokinetics: Risperidone was well absorbed after oral administration, had high bioavailability, and showed dose-proportionality in the therapeutic dose range, although inter-individual plasma concentrations varied considerably. Food did not affect the extent of absorption, thus, risperidone can be given with or without meals.

The bioequivalence of the oral formulations (oral solution and tablets) has been demonstrated. A summary table of comparative bioavailability data for unchanged risperidone is presented in Table I.

Peak plasma concentrations of parent drug are reached within 1 to 2 hours after drug intake. Risperidone is mainly metabolized via hydroxylation and oxidative N-dealkylation. The major metabolite is 9-hydroxy-risperidone which has similar activity to the parent drug. Consequently, the clinical effect is brought about by the active moiety, namely risperidone plus 9-hydroxy-risperidone.

The hydroxylation of risperidone is dependent upon debrisoquine 4-hydroxylase i.e., the metabolism of risperidone is sensitive to the debrisoquine hydroxylation type genetic polymorphism. Consequently, the concentrations of parent drug and active metabolite differ substantially in extensive and poor metabolizers. However, the concentration of the active moiety (risperidone plus 9-hydroxy-risperidone) did not differ substantially between extensive and poor metabolizers, and elimination half-lives were similar in all subjects (approximately 20 to 24 hours).

Risperidone is rapidly distributed. The volume of distribution is 1 to 2 L/kg. Steady-state concentrations of risperidone and the active moiety were reached within 1 to 2 days and 5 to 6 days, respectively. In plasma, risperidone is bound to albumin and alpha$_1$-acid glycoprotein (AGP). The plasma protein binding of risperidone is approximately 88%, that of the metabolite 77%. One week after administration, 70% of the dose is excreted in the urine and 14% in the feces. In urine, risperidone plus 9-hydroxy-risperidone represent 35 to 45% of the dose. The remainder is inactive metabolites.

Table II—Risperdal

Median Pharmacokinetic Parameters of the Active Moiety (risperidone plus 9-hydroxy-risperidone) Following a Single, 1 mg Oral Dose of Risperidone in Different Patient Populations

Parameters	Young	Elderly	Liver Disease	Renal Disease Moderate	Renal Disease Severe
N	8	12	6	7	7
age (yr)	30	69	51	56	52
range	25–35	65–78	35–73	34–68	29–66
T_{max}, h	2	1.5	1	1	2
C_{max}, ng/mL	9.1	10.2	7.4	13.0	13.3
$t_{1/2}$, h	17	23	15	25	29
$AUC_{0-\infty}$, ng•h/mL	132	189	108	272	417
Cl_{ren}, mL/min/1.73 m²	55	41	61	17	9.5
risperidone, % unbound	16	14	23	16	16

Legend: N: number of subjects.
T_{max}: time to peak plasma concentration.
C_{max}: peak plasma concentration.
$t_{1/2}$: elimination half-life.
$AUC_{0-\infty}$: area under plasma concentration time curve.
Cl_{ren}: renal clearance.

Table II summarizes the pharmacokinetic parameters observed in various subpopulations.

The results indicate that a 1 mg dose of risperidone produced modest pharmacokinetic changes in elderly subjects. In patients with impaired renal function, the changes were substantial; C_{max} and AUC were increased, half-life prolonged and clearance decreased.

In patients with impaired liver function, the unbound fraction of risperidone was somewhat increased due to diminished concentration of both α_1-AGP and albumin.

Clinical Studies: In controlled trials, risperidone was evaluated in a dose range of 1 to 16 mg/day and compared to both placebo and haloperidol. The studies indicated that risperidone is an effective antipsychotic agent improving both positive and negative symptoms. Optimal therapeutic response was seen in the 4 to 8 mg/day dose range, indicating a bell-shaped dose-response relationship. Parkinsonian side effects were mild but dose-related. Risperidone elevated serum prolactin levels. Due to the α_1-adrenergic blocking activity, orthostatic hypotension with compensatory tachycardia was also observed.

Indications: For the management of manifestations of schizophrenia and related psychotic disorders. In controlled clinical trials, risperidone was found to improve both positive and negative symptoms of schizophrenia.

Contraindications: In patients with a known hypersensitivity to the drug or the excipients of the product.

Warnings: Cardiovascular: During clinical trials, risperidone has been observed to cause orthostatic hypotension and tachycardia, especially during the initial dose titration period and the first few weeks of treatment. Rare cases of syncope, cardiac arrhythmias and first degree AV-block have been reported. The likelihood of excessive hypotension or syncope can be minimized by limiting the initial dose of the drug to 1 mg b.i.d. in adult patients and to 0.5 mg b.i.d. in special patient populations, and by increasing the dose slowly (see Dosage). A dose reduction should be considered if hypotension occurs.

Patients with a history of clinically significant cardiac disorders were excluded from clinical trials. Therefore, risperidone should be used with caution in patients with cardiovascular diseases (e.g., heart failure, myocardial infarction, cerebrovascular disease, conduction abnormalities) and other conditions such as dehydration and hypovolemia. Special care should be taken to avoid hypotension in patients with a history of cerebrovascular insufficiency or ischemic heart disease, and in patients taking medications to lower blood pressure.

Neuroleptic Malignant Syndrome (NMS): Neuroleptic malignant syndrome is a potentially fatal symptom complex that has been reported in association with neuroleptic drugs, including risperidone.

Clinical manifestations of NMS are hyperthermia, muscle rigidity, altered mental status (including catatonic signs) and evidence of autonomic instability (irregular blood pressure, tachycardia, cardiac arrhythmias and diaphoresis). Additional signs may include elevated creatine phosphokinase, myoglobinuria (rhabdomyolysis) and acute renal failure.

In arriving at a diagnosis, it is important to identify cases where the clinical presentation includes both serious medical illness (e.g., pneumonia, systemic infection, etc.) and untreated or inadequately treated extrapyramidal signs and symptoms. Other important considerations in the differential diagnosis include central anticholinergic toxicity, heat stroke, drug fever and primary CNS pathology.

The management of NMS should include: 1) immediate discontinuation of all antipsychotic drugs including risperidone, and other drugs not essential to concurrent therapy; 2) intensive symptomatic treatment and medical monitoring and 3) treatment of any concomitant serious medical problems for which specific treatments are available. There is no general agreement about specific pharmacological treatment regimens for uncomplicated NMS.

If a patient requires antipsychotic drug treatment after recovery from NMS, the potential reintroduction of drug therapy should be carefully considered. The patient should be carefully monitored, since recurrence of NMS has been reported.

Tardive Dyskinesia (TD): A syndrome consisting of potentially irreversible, involuntary, dyskinetic movements may develop in patients treated with conventional antipsychotic drugs. Although TD appears to be most prevalent in the elderly, especially elderly females, it is impossible to predict at the onset of treatment which patients are likely to develop TD.

It has been suggested that the occurrence of parkinsonian side effects is a predictor for the development of TD. In clinical studies, the observed incidence of drug-induced parkinsonism was lower with risperidone than with haloperidol. In the optimal clinical dose range, the difference between risperidone and haloperidol was significant. The risk of developing TD may be less with risperidone.

The risk of developing TD and the likelihood that it will become irreversible are believed to increase as the duration of treatment and the total cumulative dose of antipsychotic drugs administered to the patient increase. However, the syndrome can develop, although less commonly, after relatively brief periods of treatment at low doses. There is no known treatment for established cases of TD. The syndrome may remit, partially or completely, if antipsychotic drug treatment is withdrawn. Antipsychotic drug treatment itself, however, may suppress the signs and symptoms of TD, thereby masking the underlying process. The effect of symptom suppression upon the long-term course of TD is unknown.

Table I—Risperdal

Summary Table of the Comparative Bioavailability Data
Risperdal Oral Solution 1 mg/mL vs Risperdal 1 mg Tablet from Measured Data

Parameter	Unchanged Risperidone — Geometric Mean, Arithmetic Mean (CV%): Risperdal Oral Solution	Risperdal Tablet	% Ratio of Geometric Means (=solution/tablet)
AUC_t last (ng·h/mL)	34.1 46.5 (85.9%)	36.2 51.6 (95.0%)	94.2
AUC_I (ng·h/mL)	35.9 49.3 (87.7%)	38.1 53.8 (95.1%)	94.2
C_{max} (ng/mL)	6.36 6.77 (34.9%)	6.96 7.52 (36.2%)	91.4
T_{max}* (h)	1.3 (38.5%)	1.3 (30.8%)	—
$t_{1/2}$* (h)	8.7 (105%)	7.2 (72.8%)	—

*The T_{max} and $t_{1/2}$ parameters have been expressed as the arithmetic mean (CV%) only.

In view of these considerations, risperidone should be prescribed in a manner that is most likely to minimize the risk of TD. As with any antipsychotic drug, risperidone should be reserved for patients who appear to be obtaining substantial benefit from the drug. In such patients, the smallest dose and the shortest duration of treatment should be sought. The need for continued treatment should be reassessed periodically.

If signs and symptoms of TD develop during treatment with risperidone, withdrawal of the drug should be considered. However, some patients may require treatment with risperidone despite the presence of the syndrome.

Precautions: Occupational Hazards: Interference with Mental Alertness: Risperidone may interfere with activities requiring mental alertness. Therefore, patients should be cautioned not to drive or operate machinery until their individual susceptibility is known.

Seizures: Conventional neuroleptics are known to lower seizure threshold. In clinical trials, seizures have occurred in a few risperidone-treated patients. Therefore, caution should be used in administering risperidone to patients having a history of seizures or other predisposing factors.

Drug Interactions: The risk for potential interaction between risperidone and other drugs has not been evaluated systematically. Risperidone may enhance the effects of alcohol, centrally-acting drugs, as well as the effects of antihypertensive agents. Because of its potential for inducing hypotension, risperidone may enhance the hypotensive effects of other therapeutic agents with this potential.

Risperidone may antagonize the effects of levodopa and dopamine agonists.

Carbamazepine has been shown to decrease substantially the plasma levels of risperidone and its active metabolite, 9-hydroxy-risperidone. Similar effects may be observed with other hepatic enzyme inducers. Consequently, in the presence of carbamazepine or other hepatic enzyme inducers, the dose of risperidone may have to be adjusted. On discontinuation of these drugs, the dosage of risperidone should be re-evaluated and, if necessary, decreased.

The metabolism of risperidone, a substrate of the hepatic cytochrome P450 isozyme (P450IID6), is affected by the debrisoquine hydroxylation polymorphism (see Pharmacology, Pharmacokinetics). Potential interaction between risperidone and drugs that are also substrates of this enzyme, namely phenothiazines, tricyclic antidepressants, selective serotonin reuptake inhibitors, and some beta-blockers, should be considered.

In vitro studies, in which risperidone was given in the presence of various, highly protein-bound agents, indicated that clinically relevant changes in protein binding would not occur either for risperidone or for any of the drugs tested.

Endocrine Effects: Antipsychotic drugs elevate prolactin levels with the effect persisting during chronic administration. In controlled clinical trials, risperidone elevated substantially serum prolactin levels; in female patients, mean levels ranged between 48 and 57 ng/mL at doses ranging from 4 to 16 mg/day. The prolactin levels were considerably higher in risperidone-treated patients than in haloperidol-treated patients. Since tissue culture experiments indicate that approximately one-third of human breast cancers are prolactin dependent in vitro, risperidone should only be administered to patients with previously detected breast cancer if the benefits outweigh the potential risks. Caution should also be exercised when considering risperidone treatment in patients with pituitary tumors. Possible manifestations associated with elevated prolactin levels are amenorrhea, galactorrhea, and menorrhagia (see Adverse Effects).

In carcinogenicity studies, the administration of risperidone resulted in an increase in the incidence of mammary neoplasms in both rats and mice. In addition, adenomas of the endocrine pancreas in male rats and pituitary adenomas in female mice have been noted. These changes have been attributed to elevated prolactin levels and have also been observed with other dopamine receptor antagonists. To date, neither clinical studies nor epidemiological studies have shown an association between chronic administration of these drugs and mammary tumorigenesis.

With continued treatment, weight gain (mean: 2.3 kg in long-term studies) has been seen.

Pregnancy: The safety of risperidone for use during pregnancy has not been established. In animal studies, risperidone did not show direct reproductive toxicity. However, due to its prolactin elevating and CNS depressant activities, reproductive performance and pup survival were adversely affected in rats. Risperidone was not teratogenic in either rats or rabbits.

Risperidone should not be used during pregnancy unless the expected benefits outweigh the potential risks to the fetus.

Lactation: It is not known whether risperidone is excreted in human milk. Risperidone appeared in the milk of lactating dogs. The concentration of risperidone was similar in milk and plasma, while that of 9-hydroxy-risperidone was higher in the milk than in plasma.

Nursing should not be undertaken while a patient is receiving risperidone.

Geriatrics: Since the elimination of risperidone is somewhat slower in the elderly (see Pharmacology, Pharmacokinetics), doses exceeding 3 mg/day are not recommended in these patients (see Dosage).

Children: The safety and efficacy of risperidone in children under the age of 18 have not been established.

Patients with Hepatic Impairment: To date, clinical experience is lacking in this patient population. Although the pharmacokinetics in patients with liver insufficiency were comparable to those in young volunteers, the free fraction of risperidone was increased. Since this may lead to a more pronounced pharmacological effect, it is recommended to halve the starting dose and the subsequent dose increments (see Dosage).

Patients with Renal Impairment: The pharmacokinetics of risperidone were significantly altered in patients with renal disease (see Pharmacology, Pharmacokinetics). Since clinical experience is lacking in this patient population, dosage recommendations cannot be made at this time.

Patients with Parkinson's Disease: Risperidone, like other dopamine antagonists, may cause a deterioration in the condition of parkinsonian patients and should therefore be used with caution.

Adverse Effects: The most frequent adverse reactions observed during clinical trials with risperidone were insomnia, agitation, extrapyramidal disorder, anxiety, and headache (see Table III and Table IV [on following page]). In some instances it has been difficult to differentiate adverse events from symptoms of the underlying psychosis.

The most serious adverse reactions were rare cases of syncope, cardiac arrhythmias, first degree AV-block, and seizures.

An estimated 9% of approximately 1 800 patients who received risperidone in controlled clinical trials discontinued treatment due to adverse reactions. The more common events causing discontinuation included: **Psychiatric** (4.1%): primarily psychosis, agitation, suicide attempt, somnolence. **Neurological** (3.2%): primarily extrapyramidal disorder, dizziness. **Cardiovascular** (1.2%): primarily hypotension. Other events leading to discontinuation included: tachycardia/palpitations (0.6%), nervousness (0.4%), nausea (0.3%) and insomnia (0.3%).

Parkinsonian side effects were usually mild and were reversible upon dose reduction and/or administration of antiparkinsonian medication.

Occasionally, hypotension (including orthostatic), and tachycardia (including reflex tachycardia) have been observed following the administration of risperidone (see Warnings).

Table III—Risperdal

Treatment-Emergent Adverse Experience Incidence in 6- to 8-Week Controlled Clinical Trials[a]

	Percentage of Patients		
	Risperdal		
Body System/ Preferred Term	**≤10 mg/day (N=324)**	**16 mg/day (N=77)**	**Placebo (N=142)**
Psychiatric			
Insomnia	26	23	19
Agitation	22	26	20
Anxiety	12	20	9
Somnolence	3	8	1
Aggressive reaction	1	3	1
Neurological			
Extrapyramidal symptoms[b]	17	34	16
Headache	14	12	12
Dizziness	4	7	1
Gastrointestinal			
Constipation	7	13	3
Nausea	6	4	3
Dyspepsia	5	10	4
Vomiting	5	7	4
Abdominal pain	4	1	0
Saliva increased	2	0	1
Toothache	2	0	0
Respiratory			
Rhinitis	10	8	4
Coughing	3	3	1
Sinusitis	2	1	1
Pharyngitis	2	3	0
Dyspnea	1	0	0
Body as a Whole			
Back pain	2	0	1
Chest pain	2	3	1
Fever	2	3	0
Dermatological			
Rash	2	5	1
Dry skin	2	4	0
Seborrhea	1	0	0
Infections			
Upper respiratory	3	3	1
Visual			
Abnormal vision	2	1	1
Musculoskeletal			
Arthralgia	2	3	0
Cardiovascular			
Tachycardia	3	5	0

[a] Events reported by at least 1% of patients treated with Risperdal ≤10 mg/day are included, and are rounded to the nearest %. Comparative rates for Risperdal 16 mg/day and placebo are provided as well. Events for which the Risperdal incidence (in both dose groups) was equal to or less than placebo are not listed in the table, but included the following: nervousness, injury, and fungal infection.

[b] Includes tremor, dystonia, hypokinesia, hypertonia, hyperkinesia, oculogyric crisis, ataxia, abnormal gait, involuntary muscle contractions, hyporeflexia, akathisia and extrapyramidal disorders. Although the incidence of 'extrapyramidal symptoms' does not appear to differ for the '≤10 mg/day' group and placebo, the data for individual dose groups in fixed dose trials do suggest a dose/response relationship.

Risperdal (cont'd)

Risperidone elevated plasma prolactin levels. Associated manifestations, namely amenorrhea, galactorrhea, and menorrhagia, have occurred.

Weight gain, erectile dysfunction, ejaculatory dysfunction, orgastic dysfunction, and rash have also been observed during treatment with risperidone. In one study, in which testosterone levels were measured, testosterone decreased below the normal range in 6 out of 85 patients.

As with classical neuroleptics, cases of water intoxication, either due to polydipsia or to inappropriate secretion of antidiuretic hormone (ADH), have occasionally been reported during treatment with risperidone.

Adverse Events for North American Studies: Table III (on previous page) enumerates adverse events that occurred at an incidence of 1% or more, and were at least as frequent among risperidone-treated patients receiving doses of ≤10 mg/day than among placebo-treated patients in the pooled results of two 6- to 8-week controlled trials. Patients received risperidone doses of 2, 6, 10, or 16 mg/day in the dose comparison trial, or up to a maximum dose of 10 mg/day in the titration study. This table shows the percentage of patients in each dose group (≤10 mg/day or 16 mg/day) who spontaneously reported at least one episode of an event at some time during their treatment. Patients given doses of 2, 6, or 10 mg did not differ substantially in these rates. Reported adverse events were classified using the World Health Organization preferred terms.

Table IV lists the overall incidence of adverse reactions noted for all international controlled clinical trials including the North American trials. Some adverse events were reported at a higher incidence in the North American trials than appears in the table, due to differences in reporting practices and/or methodology.

Adverse Reactions During Long-term Treatment: Long-term treatment with risperidone was carried out in 386 chronic schizophrenic patients, with 213 patients receiving the drug for at least 1 year. The UKU side effect rating scale was used to elicit adverse events.

Listed (in decreasing order) are those events which showed deterioration during treatment compared to baseline in at least 10% of patients. **Psychic:** asthenia/lassitude/increased fatiguability, concentration difficulties, sleepiness/sedation, reduced duration of sleep, increased duration of sleep, failing memory, increased dream activity. **Autonomic:** orthostatic dizziness, constipation, nausea/vomiting, polyuria/polydipsia, palpitations/tachycardia, reduced salivation, accommodation disturbances, increased tendency to sweating, diarrhea. **Other:** weight gain, weight loss, amenorrhea, ejaculatory dysfunction, erectile dysfunction, diminished sexual desire, tension headache, increased sexual desire, orgastic dysfunction.

Postmarketing: International postmarketing reporting revealed the following adverse drug reactions during risperidone treatment: edema, increased hepatic enzyme levels, skin manifestations of allergy including a case of Stevens-Johnson syndrome, systemic manifestations of allergy including a case of anaphylactic shock, neuroleptic malignant syndrome and rare cases of tardive dyskinesia, hypertension, leukopenia and priapism. Rarely, mild to moderate neutropenia associated in a few cases with thrombopenia has been reported. To date, a causal relationship to risperidone has not been established. As with other neuroleptics, sudden deaths have been reported during risperidone treatment. Most of the patients had preexisting cardiovascular disease or were morbidly obese. A relationship to risperidone has not been established at this time.

Overdose: Symptoms: Cases of overdosing have been reported with risperidone; the estimated doses were between 20 and 360 mg. Symptoms observed were due to excessive pharmacological effects, namely drowsiness and sedation, tachycardia and hypotension, and extrapyramidal symptoms. In 1 case (240 mg) hyponatremia and hypokalemia were observed, with prolonged QT_c and widened QRS complex on the ECG. Additionally, hypokalemia and prolonged QT interval were observed in 1 patient who ingested 360 mg of risperidone.

Treatment: Since there is no specific antidote to risperidone, treatment is primarily supportive. Gastric lavage (after intubation, if the patient is unconscious) and administration of activated charcoal together with a laxative should be considered.

A patent airway must be established and maintained to ensure adequate oxygenation and ventilation. Cardiovascular monitoring should commence immediately and should include continuous electrocardiographic monitoring to detect possible arrhythmias. Hypotension and circulatory collapse may be counteracted by use of i.v. fluids. Epinephrine should not be used. In cases of severe extrapyramidal reactions, antiparkinsonian medication should be administered. Close medical supervision and monitoring should continue until the patient recovers.

In managing overdosage, the physician should consider the possibility of multiple drug involvement.

Dosage: In order to avoid orthostatic hypotension, the dose of risperidone should be titrated gradually.

Adults: Patients should be titrated gradually over 3 days on a b.i.d. schedule to a 6 mg daily dose, generally beginning with a 2 mg daily dose. The dosage should be increased to 4 mg on the second day and to 6 mg on the third day. Some patients may benefit from lower initial doses and/or a slower titration schedule.

Further dosage adjustments, if indicated, should generally occur at intervals of not less than 1 week since steady state for the active metabolite would not be achieved for approximately 1 week in the typical patient. When dosage adjustments are necessary, small dose increments/decrements are recommended.

Once a therapeutically effective maintenance dose has been established, risperidone may be administered once daily or twice daily.

In controlled clinical trials, optimal therapeutic effects were seen in the 4 to 8 mg/day dose range. Some patients may need higher doses, while in some patients further dosage increases may result in decreased therapeutic effect. Higher doses were associated with more extrapyramidal symptoms and other adverse effects. Since the safety of doses above 16 mg total daily dose has not been evaluated, doses above this level should not be used.

Geriatrics: In elderly patients, the doses of risperidone should be titrated slowly from a 0.5 mg b.i.d. starting dose to a maximum daily dose of 3 mg. Since the elimination of risperidone is somewhat slower in these patients, the potential for accumulation should be considered (see Pharmacology, Pharmacokinetics).

Postmarketing, treatment with risperidone in the elderly has been reported in publications for over 300 patients.

Patients Prone to Hypotension: Caution should be exercised in patients prone to hypotension and the use of a lower starting dose (0.5 mg b.i.d.) should be considered.

Impaired Liver Function: The pharmacokinetics of risperidone did not change in patients with impaired liver function in response to a 1 mg single dose. However, clinical experience is lacking in these patients. Until further experience is gained, the following dosage schedule is recommended. The starting dose should be 0.5 mg b.i.d. This dosage can be individually adjusted in 0.5 mg b.i.d. increments to 1 to 2 mg b.i.d.

Impaired Kidney Function: Since the pharmacokinetics of risperidone changed substantially in patients with renal disease, even in response to a 1 mg single dose (see Pharmacology, Pharmacokinetics and Precautions), and since to date no clinical experience is available, dosage recommendations cannot be made in this patient population.

Switching from Other Antipsychotics: When medically appropriate, gradual discontinuation of the previous treatment, while risperidone therapy is initiated is recommended. In all cases the period of overlapping antipsychotic administration should be minimized. When switching patients from depot antipsychotics, initiate risperidone therapy in place of the next scheduled injection. The need for continuing existing antiparkinsonian medications should be re-evaluated periodically.

Information for the Patient: See Blue Section—Information for the Patient "Risperdal Oral Solution".

Supplied: Oral Solution: Each mL of oral solution contains: risperidone 1 mg as risperidone tartrate. Nonmedicinal ingredients: benzoic acid, purified water, sodium hydroxide and tartaric acid. Bottles of 100 mL with a calibrated (in mg and in mL) pipette. The minimum calibrated volume is 0.25 mL, while the maximum calibrated volume is 3 mL. Store between 15 and 30°C. Protect from light and freezing. Keep out of reach of children. Patient Instructions (including illustrations)

Table IV—Risperdal

Adverse Reactions Reported at a Frequency of ≥1% in All International Trials*

Body System/ Adverse Reaction	Risperdal ≤10 mg/day (N=1 202)	Risperdal >10 mg/day (N=535)	Placebo (N=176)
Psychiatric			
Insomnia	13	10	16
Agitation	9	7	16
Anxiety	7	6	7
Somnolence	4	2	1
Nervousness	2	2	3
Impaired concentration	1	0	0
Aggressive reaction	1	1	3
Suicide attempt	1	2	1
Psychosis	1	1	0
Neurological			
Extrapyramidal disorder	7	13	7
Headache	6	3	10
Dizziness	3	2	1
Hyperkinesia (includes akathisia)	2	3	2
Tremor	1	2	2
Rigidity	1	2	2
Hypokinesia	1	1	1
Dystonia	1	2	1
Oculogyric crisis	1	1	1
Dyskinesia	1	1	1
Gastrointestinal			
Constipation	3	2	2
Nausea	3	1	2
Vomiting	2	2	3
Increased salivation	2	2	1
Dyspepsia	1	2	3
Anorexia	1	0	1
Abdominal pain	1	0	1
Respiratory			
Rhinitis	3	1	3
Coughing	1	1	1
Special Senses			
Abnormal vision	2	0	1
Cardiovascular			
Tachycardia	1	2	0
Other			
Fatigue	2	1	1

*Events reported by at least 1% of patients treated with Risperdal are rounded to the nearest %.

for using the Risperdal calibrated dispensing-pipette are provided (see Blue Section—Information for the Patient). Tests indicate that risperidone oral solution is compatible in the following beverages: water, coffee, orange juice and low-fat milk; however, it is **not** compatible with cola or tea.

Tablets: 1 mg: Each white, film-coated, half-scored, oblong tablet, marked JANSSEN and R 1, contains: risperidone 1 mg. Nonmedicinal ingredients: colloidal anhydrous silica, hypromellose, lactose, magnesium stearate, maize starch, microcrystalline cellulose, propylene glycol and sodium lauryl sulfate. Blister packages of 60 and HDPE bottles of 250.

2 mg: Each orange, film-coated, oblong tablet, marked JANSSEN and R 2, contains: risperidone 2 mg. Nonmedicinal ingredients: colloidal anhydrous silica, hypromellose, lactose, magnesium stearate, maize starch, microcrystalline cellulose, propylene glycol, sodium lauryl sulfate, sunset yellow (E110) aluminum lake, talc and titanium dioxide (E171). Blister packages of 60 and HDPE bottles of 250.

3 mg: Each yellow, film-coated, oblong tablet, marked JANSSEN and R 3, contains: risperidone 3 mg. Nonmedicinal ingredients: colloidal anhydrous silica, hypromellose, lactose, magnesium stearate, maize starch, microcrystalline cellulose, propylene glycol, quinoline yellow (E104), sodium lauryl sulfate, talc and titanium dioxide (E171). Blister packages of 60 and HDPE bottles of 250.

4 mg: Each green, film-coated, oblong tablet, marked JANSSEN and R 4, contains: risperidone 4 mg. Nonmedicinal ingredients: colloidal anhydrous silica, hypromellose, indigotindisulfonate (E132) aluminum lake, lactose, magnesium stearate, maize starch, microcrystalline cellulose, propylene glycol, quinoline yellow (E104), sodium lauryl sulfate, talc and titanium dioxide (E171). Blister packages of 60 and HDPE bottles of 250.

Store tablets between 15 and 30°C, protected from light and moisture. Keep out of the reach of children.

(Shown in Product Recognition Section)

Reviewed 1999

RITALIN® ◈
RITALIN® SR ◈
Novartis Pharmaceuticals
Methylphenidate HCl
CNS Stimulant

Pharmacology: Methylphenidate is a mild CNS stimulant.

The mode of action in man is not completely understood, but methylphenidate presumably activates the brain stem arousal system and cortex to produce its stimulant effect.

There is neither specific evidence which clearly establishes the mechanism whereby methylphenidate produces its mental and behavioral effects in children, nor conclusive evidence regarding how these effects relate to the condition of the CNS.

Pharmacokinetics: Methylphenidate is rapidly and extensively absorbed from the tablets following oral administration; however, owing to extensive first-pass metabolism, bioavailability is low (approx. 30%) and large individual differences exist (11 to 52%). In one study, the administration of methylphenidate with food accelerated absorption, but had no effect on the amount absorbed.

Peak plasma concentrations of 10.8 and 7.8 ng/mL were observed, on average, 2 hours after administration of 0.30 mg/kg in children and adults, respectively. However, peak plasma concentrations showed marked variability between subjects. Both the area under the plasma concentration curve (AUC), and the peak plasma concentrations (C_{max}) showed dose-proportionality.

Methylphenidate is eliminated from the plasma with a mean half-life of 2.4 hours in children and 2.1 hours in adults. The apparent mean systemic clearance is 10.2 and 10.5 L/h/kg in children and adults, respectively for a 0.3 mg/kg dose. These data indicate that the pharmacokinetic behavior of methylphenidate in hyperactive children is similar to that in normal adults. The apparent distribution volume of methylphenidate in children was approximately 20 L/kg, with substantial variability (11 to 33 L/kg).

Following oral administration of methylphenidate, 78 to 97% of the dose is excreted in the urine and 1 to 3% in the feces in the form of metabolites within 48 to 96 hours. The main urinary metabolite is ritalinic acid (α-phenyl-2-piperidine acetic acid, PPAA); unchanged methylphenidate is excreted in the urine in small quantities (<1%). Peak PPAA plasma concentrations occurred at approximately the same time as peak methylphenidate concentrations, however, levels were several-fold greater than those of the unchanged drug. The half-life of PPAA was approximately twice that of methylphenidate.

In blood, methylphenidate and its metabolites are distributed between plasma (57%) and erythrocytes (43%). Methylphenidate and its metabolites exhibit low plasma protein binding (approx. 15%).

Methylphenidate in the extended-release tablets is more slowly but as extensively absorbed as in the regular tablets. Relative bioavailability of the Ritalin SR tablet, compared to the Ritalin tablet, measured by the urinary excretion of the methylphenidate major metabolite (PPAA), was 105% (49 to 168%) in children and 101% (85% to 152%) in adults. The time to peak rate in children was 4.7 hours (1.3 to 8.2 hours) for the extended-release tablets and 1.9 hours (0.3 to 4.4 hours) for the regular tablets. The elimination half-life and the cumulative urinary excretion of PPAA are not significantly different between the two dosage forms. An average of 67% of the extended-release tablet dose was excreted in children as compared to 86% in adults.

Indications: Attention-Deficit Hyperactivity Disorder (ADHD), previously known as Attention-Deficit Disorder. Other terms being used to describe this behavioral syndrome include: Minimal Brain Dysfunction in Children, Hyperkinetic Child Syndrome, Minimal Brain Damage, Minimal Cerebral Dysfunction, Minor Cerebral Dysfunction.

Methylphenidate is indicated as an integral part of a total treatment program which typically includes other remedial measures (psychological, educational, social) for a stabilizing effect in children with a behavioral syndrome characterized by the following group of developmentally inappropriate symptoms: moderate-to-severe distractibility, short attention span, hyperactivity, emotional lability, and impulsivity. The diagnosis of this syndrome should not be made with finality when these symptoms are only of comparatively recent origin. Non-localizing (soft) neurological signs, learning disability, and abnormal EEG may or may not be present, and a diagnosis of CNS dysfunction may or may not be warranted.

Special Diagnostic Considerations: Specific etiology of this syndrome is unknown, and there is no single diagnostic test. Adequate diagnosis requires the use not only of medical but of special psychological, educational and social resources. Characteristics commonly reported include: chronic history of short attention span, distractibility, emotional lability, impulsivity, and moderate-to-severe hyperactivity; minor neurological signs and abnormal EEG. Learning may or may not be impaired. The diagnosis must be based upon a complete history and evaluation of the child and not solely on the presence of one or more of these characteristics.

Drug treatment is not indicated for all children with this syndrome. Stimulants are not intended for use in the child who exhibits symptoms secondary to environmental factors and/or primary psychiatric disorders, including psychosis. Appropriate educational placement is essential and psychosocial intervention is generally necessary. When remedial measures alone are insufficient, the decision to prescribe stimulant medication will depend upon the physician's assessment of the chronicity and severity of the child's symptoms.

Narcolepsy.

Contraindications: Anxiety, tension, agitation, thyrotoxicosis, tachyarrhythmias, severe angina pectoris and glaucoma. Known or suspected hypersensitivity to the drug or its excipients. Also contraindicated in patients with motor tics or with a family history or diagnosis of Tourette's syndrome.

Warnings: Methylphenidate should not be used in children under 6 years of age, since safety and efficacy in this age group have not been established.

Although a causal relationship has not been established, suppression of growth (i.e., weight gain and/or height) has been reported with the long-term use of stimulants in children. Therefore, patients requiring long-term therapy should be carefully monitored. In addition, the use of "Drug Holidays" is recommended, that is, withholding the drug on weekends and during school holidays in as much as the clinical situation permits.

Methylphenidate should not be used for severe depression of either exogenous or endogenous origin. Clinical experience suggests that in psychotic children, administration of methylphenidate may exacerbate symptoms of behavior disturbance and thought disorder.

Methylphenidate should not be used for the prevention or treatment of normal fatigue states.

There is some clinical evidence that methylphenidate may lower the convulsive threshold in patients with prior history of seizures, with prior EEG abnormalities in absence of seizures and, very rarely, in patients with no prior EEG evidence nor history of seizures. Clinical experience has shown that a small number of patients may experience an increase in seizure frequency when treated with methylphenidate. If seizure frequency rises, the drug should be discontinued.

Use cautiously in patients with hypertension. Blood pressure should be monitored at appropriate intervals in all patients taking methylphenidate, especially those with hypertension.

Pregnancy and *Lactation:* Experience to establish safe use of methylphenidate during pregnancy is limited. In rat studies, methylphenidate did not affect reproductive performance or fertility, and had no embryotoxic, fetotoxic or teratogenic effects at doses 2 to 5 times the human therapeutic dose, however the implications of these findings to human use is not clear. Therefore, methylphenidate should not be given to pregnant women unless the potential benefit outweighs the risk to fetus. It is not known whether the active substance methylphenidate and/or its metabolites pass into the breast milk. For safety reasons, the physician should assess the patient's medical condition and advise one of the following options: refrain from breast-feeding their infants while taking methylphenidate, or discontinue the drug while nursing.

Drug Dependence: Methylphenidate should be given cautiously to emotionally unstable patients, such as those with a history of drug dependence or alcoholism, because such patients may increase dosage on their own initiative.

Chronically abusive use can lead to marked tolerance and psychic dependence with varying degrees of abnormal behavior. Frank psychotic episodes can occur, especially with parenteral abuse. Careful supervision is required during drug withdrawal, since severe depression as well as the effects of chronic overactivity can be unmasked. Long-term follow-up may be required because of the patient's basic personality disturbances.

Available clinical data indicate that treatment with methylphenidate during childhood and/or adolescence does not seem to result in increased predisposition for addiction.

Precautions: Patients with an element of agitation may react adversely; discontinue therapy if necessary.

Periodic CBC, differential, and platelet counts are advised during prolonged therapy.

Drug treatment is not indicated in all cases of Attention Deficit Hyperactivity Disorders and should be considered only in light of the complete history and evaluation of the child. The decision to prescribe methylphenidate should depend on the physician's assessment of the chronicity and severity of the child's symptoms and their appropriateness for his/her age. Prescription should not depend solely on the presence of one or more of the behavioral characteristics. When these symptoms are associated with acute stress reactions, treatment with methylphenidate is usually not indicated.

Long-term effects of methylphenidate in children have not been well established.

Occupational Hazards: Because methylphenidate may affect performance, patients should be cautioned against engaging in hazardous activities (i.e., operation of automobiles or dangerous machinery).

Drug Interactions: Methylphenidate may decrease the hypotensive effect of guanethidine. Use cautiously with pressor agents and MAO inhibitors.

Human pharmacologic studies have shown that methylphenidate may inhibit the metabolism of coumarin anticoagulants, anticonvulsants (phenobarbital, phenytoin, primidone), phenylbutazone and tricyclic antidepressants (imipramine, desipramine). Downward dosage adjustments of these drugs may be required when given concomitantly with methylphenidate.

Alcohol may exacerbate the CNS adverse reactions of psychoactive drugs, including methylphenidate. Therefore, patients should be advised to abstain from alcohol during treatment.

Adverse Effects: Nervousness and insomnia are the most common adverse reactions reported with methylphenidate but are usually controlled by reducing dosage and omitting the drug in the afternoon or evening. Decreased appetite is also common but usually transient.

Central and Peripheral Nervous System: Occasional: dizziness, drowsiness, headache, and dyskinesia may occur. Isolated cases of the following have been reported: hyperactivity, convulsions, muscle cramps, choreo-athetoid movements, tics, or exacerbation of pre-existing tics, cerebral arteritis and/or occlusion, Tourette's syndrome, and psychotic episodes including hallucinations which subsided when methylphenidate was discontinued. Psychic dependence in emotionally unstable persons has occurred rarely with chronic treatment. Although a definite causal relationship has not been established, isolated cases of transient depressed mood have been reported.

Ritalin (cont'd)

Symptoms of visual disturbances have been encountered in rare cases. Difficulties with accommodation and blurring of vision have been reported.

Gastrointestinal: Occasional: nausea, vomiting and abdominal pain may occur at the start of treatment and may be alleviated if taken with food. Dry mouth.

Cardiovascular: Occasional: palpitations, blood pressure and pulse changes (both up and down), tachycardia, angina and cardiac arrhythmias.

Rare: angina pectoris.

Skin and/or Hypersensitivity: Occasional: rash, pruritus, urticaria, fever, arthralgia, and alopecia. Isolated cases of exfoliative dermatitis, erythema multiforme with histopathological findings of necrotizing vasculitis, and thrombocytopenic purpura.

Hematologic: Isolated: leukopenia, thrombocytopenia and anemia.

Other: Rare: weight loss during prolonged therapy.

In children, loss of appetite, abdominal pain, weight loss during prolonged therapy, insomnia, and tachycardia may occur more frequently; however, any of the other adverse reactions listed above may also occur. In rare instances, minor retardation of growth may also occur during prolonged therapy in children (see Warnings).

Overdose: Symptoms: Signs and symptoms of acute overdosage, resulting principally from overstimulation of the CNS and from excessive sympathomimetic effects, may include the following: vomiting, agitation, tremors, hyperreflexia, muscle twitching, convulsions (may be followed by coma), euphoria, confusion, hallucinations, delirium, sweating, flushing, headache, hyperpyrexia, tachycardia, palpitations, cardiac arrhythmias, hypertension, mydriasis and dryness of mucous membranes.

Treatment: Appropriate supportive measures. The patient must be protected against self-injury and against external stimuli that would aggravate overstimulation already present. If signs and symptoms are not too severe and the patient is conscious, gastric contents may be evacuated by induction of emesis or gastric lavage. In the presence of severe intoxication, use a carefully titrated dosage of short-acting barbiturate before performing gastric lavage.

Intensive care must be provided to maintain adequate circulation and respiratory exchange; external cooling procedures may be required for hyperpyrexia.

Efficacy of peritoneal dialysis or extracorporeal hemodialysis for methylphenidate overdosage has not been established.

Dosage: Dosage should be individualized according to the needs and responses of the patient.

Children (6 years and over): Ritalin: Ritalin should be initiated in small doses, (e.g., 5 to 10 mg t.i.d.) with weekly increments of 5 to 10 mg in the daily dosage. Dosage should be individualized on the basis of factors such as age, body weight and individual response. Timing of drug administration should be aimed to coincide with periods of greatest academic, behavioral and social difficulties for the patient.

Daily dosage above 60 mg is not recommended.

If improvement is not observed after appropriate dosage adjustments over a one month period, the drug should be discontinued.

Ritalin SR: Ritalin SR tablets have a duration of action of approximately 8 hours. Therefore, Ritalin SR tablets may be used in place of Ritalin tablets when the 8 hour dosage of Ritalin SR corresponds to the titrated 8-hour dosage of Ritalin. Ritalin SR tablets must be swallowed whole and never be crushed or chewed.

If paradoxical aggravation of symptoms or other adverse effects occur, reduce dosage, or if necessary, discontinue the drug.

Methylphenidate should be periodically discontinued to assess the child's condition. Improvement may be sustained when the drug is either temporarily or permanently discontinued.

Drug treatment should not and need not be indefinite and usually may be discontinued after puberty.

Adults: Ritalin: Administer in divided doses 2 or 3 times daily. Average daily dosage is 20 to 30 mg. Some patients may require 40 to 60 mg daily. In others, 10 to 15 mg daily will be adequate. Patients who are unable to sleep if medication is taken late in the day, should take the last dose before 6 p.m.

Ritalin SR: Ritalin SR tablets have a duration of action of approximately 8 hours. Therefore, Ritalin SR tablets may be used in place of Ritalin tablets when the 8-hour dosage of Ritalin SR corresponds to the titrated 8-hour dosage of Ritalin. Ritalin SR tablets must be swallowed whole and never be crushed or chewed.

Information for the Patient: See Blue Section—Information for the Patient "Ritalin/Ritalin SR".

Supplied: Ritalin: 10 mg: Each pale blue, round, flat-faced, beveled-edged tablet, scored and imprinted "AB" on one side with "CIBA" on the other, contains: methylphenidate HCl 10 mg. Nonmedicinal ingredients: cornstarch, FD&C Green No. 3, lactose, magnesium stearate, polyethylene glycol, sugar and talc. Energy: 1.88 kJ (0.45 kcal). Bottles of 100 and 500.

20 mg: Each pale yellow, round, flat-faced, beveled-edged tablet, scored and imprinted "PN" on one side with "CIBA" on the other, contains: methylphenidate HCl 20 mg. Nonmedicinal ingredients: D&C Yellow No. 10, lactose, magnesium stearate, polyethylene glycol, sugar, tragacanth and talc. Energy: 2.4 kJ (0.58 kcal). Bottles of 100 and 500.

Ritalin SR: Each white, round, biconvex, film-coated, extended release tablet, "16" printed on one side with "CIBA" printed on the other in black ink, contains: methylphenidate HCl 20 mg. Nonmedicinal ingredients: cellulose compounds, cetostearyl alcohol, castor oil compounds, lactose, magnesium stearate, talc and titanium dioxide. Energy: 1.55 kJ (0.37 kcal). Bottles of 100.

Protect from heat (store between 2 and 30°C) and humidity.

(Shown in Product Recognition Section)

Reviewed 1997

RIVANASE AQ. Ⓟ

Riva

Beclomethasone Dipropionate

Corticosteroid

Supplied: Each spray of suspension delivered by the nasal applicator contains: beclomethasone dipropionate 50 μg. Nonmedicinal ingredients: benzalkonium chloride, cellulose, dextrose, phenyl ethanol, polysorbate and sodium carboxymethyl cellulose. Glass bottles of 200 doses fitted with a metering atomizing pump and a nasal applicator. Store between 15 and 30°C and protect from light. Discard 3 months after first use.

RIVA-SENNA

Riva

Standardized Sennosides

Peristaltic Stimulant

Supplied: Each round, light brown tablet contains: standardized sennosides 8.6 mg. Nonmedicinal ingredients: colloidal silicone, magnesium stearate, polyvinylpyrrolidone, sodium croscarmellose, sodium lauryl sulfate and starch. Sugar- and tartrazine-free. Bottles of 100 and 1 000.

RIVASOL
RIVASOL HC Ⓟ

Riva

Zinc Sulfate Monohydrate
Zinc Sulfate Monohydrate—Hydrocortisone Acetate

Anorectal Therapy

Supplied: Rivasol: Each tube contains: zinc sulfate monohydrate 0.5% in a petroleum base. Nonmedicinal ingredients: methyl- and propylparaben. Tubes of 15 and 30 g with applicator.

Rivasol HC: Each tube contains: zinc sulfate monohydrate 0.5% and hydrocortisone acetate 0.5% in a petroleum base. Nonmedicinal ingredients: methyl- and propylparaben. Tubes of 15 and 30 g with applicator.

Store in a cool place under 22°C.

New Product 1998

RIVOTRIL® Ⓟ

Roche

Clonazepam

Anticonvulsant

Pharmacology: Clonazepam has pharmacological properties characteristic of the benzodiazepine class of drugs. Clonazepam has sedative, hypnotic and anticonvulsant properties. As an anticonvulsant it is useful in the management of minor motor seizures (myoclonic seizures) and may be of some value in selected patients with absence spells (petit mal) who have failed to respond satisfactorily to the succinimides. Clonazepam is capable of suppressing the spike and wave discharge in absence seizures (petit mal) and decreasing the frequency, amplitude, duration and spread of discharge in minor motor seizures.

Single oral dose administration of clonazepam to humans gives maximum blood levels of drug, in most cases, within 1 to 2 hours. The half-life of the parent compound varies from approximately 18 to 50 hours, and the major route of excretion is in the urine.

Indications: Alone or as an adjunct in the management of myoclonic and akinetic seizures and petit mal variant (Lennox-Gastaut syndrome). May also be of some value in patients with absence spells (petit mal) who have failed to respond to succinimides.

Up to nearly 33% of the patients in some studies have shown a loss of anticonvulsant activity, often within the first 3 months of clonazepam administration. In some cases, dosage adjustment may re-establish efficacy.

Contraindications: Significant liver disease, narrow angle glaucoma, sensitivity to benzodiazepines.

Warnings: *Pregnancy:* Recent reports indicate an association between the use of anticonvulsant drugs and an elevated incidence of birth defects in children born to epileptic women taking such medication during pregnancy. The incidence of congenital malformations in the general population is regarded to be approximately 2%; in children of treated epileptic women this incidence may be increased 2 to 3 fold. The increase is largely due to specific defects, e.g., congenital malformations of the heart, and cleft lip and/or palate. Nevertheless, the great majority of mothers receiving anticonvulsant medications deliver normal infants.

Data are more extensive with respect to phenytoin and phenobarbital, but these drugs are also the most commonly prescribed anticonvulsants. Some reports indicate a possible similar association with the use of other anticonvulsants, including trimethadione and paramethadione. However, the possibility also exists that other factors, e.g., genetic predisposition or the epileptic condition itself may contribute to or may be mainly responsible for the higher incidence of birth defects.

Anticonvulsants should not be discontinued in patients in whom the drug is administered to prevent major seizures, because of the strong possibility of precipitating status epilepticus with attendant hypoxia and risk to both the mother and the unborn child. With regard to drugs given for minor seizures, the risk of discontinuing medication prior to or during pregnancy should be weighed against the risk of congenital defects in the particular case and with the particular family history.

Epileptic women of childbearing age should be encouraged to seek professional counsel and should report the onset of pregnancy promptly to their physician. Where the necessity for continued use of antiepileptic medication is in doubt, appropriate consultation might be indicated.

In a reproductive study in rabbits, clonazepam administration was associated with an increased incidence of cleft palate and other anomalies at 2 dose concentrations. Accordingly, clonazepam should be used in women of childbearing potential only when the expected benefits to the patient warrant the possible risk to a fetus.

Lactation: Mothers receiving clonazepam should not breast-feed their infants.

Children: Because of the possibility that adverse effects on childhood physical or mental development could become apparent only after years, a risk-benefit consideration of the long-term use of clonazepam is important in pediatric patients.

Precautions: Although simultaneous administration of several anticonvulsants may be considered with clonazepam, such combined therapy may result in an increase of central depressant adverse effects. In addition, the dosage of each drug may be required to be adjusted to obtain the optimum effect.

Abrupt withdrawal of clonazepam particularly in those patients on long-term, high dose therapy, may precipitate status epilepticus. Therefore, as with any other anticonvulsants, gradual withdrawal is essential when discontinuing clonazepam. While clonazepam is being gradually withdrawn, the simultaneous substitution of incremental doses of another anticonvulsant may be indicated.

A paradoxical increase in seizure activity or the appearance of new seizure types has occurred in a very few patients during clonazepam treatment. When used in patients in whom several different types of seizures coexist, clonazepam may increase the incidence or precipitate the onset of generalized tonic-clonic seizures (grand mal). These phenomena may require the addition of appropriate anticonvulsants or an increase in their dosages. The concomitant use of valproic acid and clonazepam may produce absence status.

Occupational Hazards: Caution patients receiving clonazepam against engaging in hazardous occupations requiring complete mental alertness, such as operating machinery or driving a motor vehicle.

They also should be warned against the concomitant use of alcohol and other CNS depressant drugs.

The CNS depressant action of benzodiazepines may be potentiated by other drugs such as alcohol, narcotics, barbiturates, nonbarbiturate hypnotics, anxiolytics, phenothiazines, thioxanthene and butyrophenone antipsychotic agents, MAO inhibitors and tricyclic antidepressants.

Benzodiazepines have produced habituation, dependence and withdrawal symptoms similar to those noted with barbiturates and alcohol. Therefore, patients who may be prone to increasing the dose of drugs on their own initiative should be under careful monitoring when receiving clonazepam.

Periodic liver function tests and blood counts are recommended during long-term clonazepam therapy.

Clonazepam and its metabolites are excreted by the kidneys; to avoid excessive accumulation, exercise caution in administering the drug to patients with impaired renal function.

Hypersecretion in the upper respiratory passages has at times been a troublesome adverse reaction during clonazepam therapy, especially in small mentally retarded children who ordinarily have difficulty handling secretions. Treatment with clonazepam should be instituted with caution in patients with chronic respiratory diseases.

Adverse Effects: The most frequently occurring adverse reactions to clonazepam are referable to CNS depression. Drowsiness occurs in approximately 50% of patients and ataxia in approximately 30%. In some cases, these may diminish with time. Behaviour problems have been noted in approximately 25% of patients and increased salivation in 7%.

Others, listed by system, are: CNS: Alterations in behaviour, which have been variously reported as aggressiveness, argumentative behaviour, hyperactivity, agitation, depression, euphoria, irritability, forgetfulness and confusion. These behavioural reactions are particularly likely to occur in patients with a prior history of psychiatric disturbances and are known to occur in patients with chronic seizure disorders.

Other adverse reactions involving the CNS have included nystagmus, unsteady gait, slurred speech, dysarthria, vertigo, insomnia, and diplopia. Isolated reports of akinesia, hemiparesis, tremor, hypotonia, headache and choreiform movements have been received. Minor changes in EEG patterns specifically low-voltage fast activity.

Gastrointestinal: increased salivation, nausea, vomiting, anorexia, constipation, diarrhea, encopresis, dry mouth, increased appetite, abdominal pain, hepatomegaly.

Genitourinary: rare instances of dysuria, nocturia, incontinence, urinary retention, enuresis.

Integumentary: nonspecific erythematous, papular and maculopapular rashes, swelling of the face and eyelids, urticaria, pruritus. Hirsutism and hair loss have also been reported, but drug relationship has not been established.

Musculoskeletal: muscle weakness, low back pain.

Respiratory: hypersecretion in the upper respiratory passages, rhinorrhea, dyspnea, respiratory depression.

Hematopoietic: anemia, leukopenia (WBC below 4 000/mm³), thrombocytopenia, eosinophilia.

Liver function: slight, transient elevations of transaminase and alkaline phosphatase.

Miscellaneous: palpitations, coated tongue, dehydration, fever, lymphadenopathy, weight gain or loss, changes in libido, gynecomastia, hallucinations, dysdiadochokinesis, coma, aphonia.

Overdose: Symptoms: The cardinal manifestations of overdosage are drowsiness and confusion, reduced reflexes and coma. There are minimal effects on respiration, pulse and blood pressure, unless the overdosage is extreme. Patients have recovered from dosages of up to 60 mg without special treatment. When the effects of the drug overdosage begin to wear off, the patient exhibits some jitteriness and over stimulation.

Treatment: Gastric lavage may be beneficial if performed soon after ingestion of clonazepam. Supportive measures should be instituted as indicated: maintenance of an adequate airway, i.v. fluids and monitoring of pulse, blood pressure and respiration. CNS stimulants and vasopressors may be used if necessary. Dialysis appears to be of no value.

Dosage: Must be determined individually according to clinical response and tolerance and depends primarily on the patient's age.

Children: In order to minimize drowsiness, the initial dose for infants and children (up to 10 years of age or 30 kg) should be between 10 and 30 μg/kg/day and should not exceed 50 μg/kg/day given in 2 or 3 divided doses. Dosage should be increased by no more than 250 to 500 μg every third day until a maintenance dose of 100 to 200 μg/kg has been reached, unless seizures are controlled or adverse effects preclude further increase. Whenever possible, the daily dose should be divided into 3 equal doses. If doses are not equally divided, the larger dose should be given before retiring.

Adults: The initial adult dose should not exceed 1.5 mg/day divided into 3 doses. Dosage may be increased in increments of 0.5 to 1 mg every 3 days until seizures are adequately controlled or until adverse effects preclude any further increase. Maintenance dosage must be individualized for each patient depending upon response. A recommended adult maintenance dose is 8 to 10 mg/day in 3 divided doses. Dosages in excess of 20 mg/day should be administered with caution.

The use of multiple anticonvulsants may result in an increase of depressant adverse effects. This should be borne in mind whenever clonazepam is added to an already existing anticonvulsant regimen.

Supplied: 0.5 mg: Each pale yellow, cylindrical, biplane, scored tablet, edges bevelled, with ROCHE 0.5 on one side, cross-scored on the other, contains: clonazepam 0.5 mg. Nonmedicinal ingredients: cornstarch, iron oxide, lactose, magnesium stearate, potato starch and talc. Energy: 2.4 kJ (0.6 kcal). Gluten-, paraben-, sodium-, sulfite- and tartrazine-free. Bottles of 100 and 500.

2 mg: Each white, cylindrical, biplane, scored tablet, edges bevelled, with ROCHE •2• on one side, cross-scored on the other, contains: clonazepam 2 mg. Nonmedicinal ingredients: cornstarch, lactose, magnesium stearate and microcrystalline cellulose. Energy: 2.4 kJ (0.6 kcal). Gluten-, paraben-, sodium-, sulfite- and tartrazine-free. Bottles of 100 and 500.

Keep in a tightly closed, light-resistant container. Store at 15 to 30°C.

(Shown in Product Recognition Section)

ROBAXACET®
ROBAXACET® EXTRA STRENGTH

Whitehall-Robins

Methocarbamol—Acetaminophen

Skeletal Muscle Relaxant—Analgesic

Pharmacology: This product provides a dual approach to the management of discomforts associated with musculoskeletal disorders.

The mechanism of action of methocarbamol has not been established, but may be due to general CNS depression. It has no direct action on the contractile mechanism of striated muscle, the motor end plate or the nerve fiber. Acetaminophen is a non-opiate, non-salicylate analgesic and antipyretic.

Methocarbamol is metabolized to yield a dealkylated and a hydroxylated product. These two metabolites are found primarily as glucuronide and sulfate conjugates. The half-life of methocarbamol and its metabolites is about 2 hours. Animal studies reveal that methocarbamol crosses the placental barrier and the blood-brain barrier. Acetaminophen is conjugated in the liver to form glucuronide and sulfate conjugates. Its plasma half-life has been reported to be from 1 to 2 hours.

Indications: Pain due to or associated with skeletal muscle spasm such as acute and chronic back strains and sprains, whiplash and other traumatic injuries, myositis, pain and spasm associated with arthritis, torticollis, joint strains and sprains, bursitis, low back pain due to ill defined causes.

Contraindications: Hypersensitivity to methocarbamol or acetaminophen.

Warnings: Do not exceed recommended dosage as severe liver damage due to acetaminophen toxicity may occur. Avoid alcohol.

Precautions: Occupational Hazards: Until the potential for producing drowsiness and dizziness has been determined, the patient should be cautioned against the operation of motor vehicles or machinery.

Since methocarbamol may possess a general CNS depressant effect, patients receiving Robaxacet should be cautioned about combined effects with alcohol and other CNS depressants.

Drug Interactions: Methocarbamol may cause a color interference in certain screening tests for 5-hydroxyindoleacetic acid (5-HIAA) and vanillylmandelic acid (VMA).

Carcinogenesis, Mutagenesis: Long-term studies in animals have not been performed to evaluate carcinogenic or mutagenic potential.

Pregnancy: There are no adequate and well-controlled studies of Robaxacet in pregnant women. This product should be used during pregnancy only when, in the judgment of the physician, the potential benefits outweigh the potential hazards.

Lactation: It is not known whether methocarbamol or its metabolites are secreted in human milk; there is some indication that small quantities of acetaminophen are secreted.

Children: Safety and effectiveness in children 12 years of age and younger have not been established.

Adverse Effects: The most common complaints to methocarbamol are drowsiness, nausea and dizziness or lightheadedness (seen in approximately 4 to 5% of patients). The following reactions have been associated with the drug, some of them rarely; in some instances, causal relationships have not been established: headache, nasal congestion, blurred vision, rash, pruritus and urticaria.

Adverse reactions that have been associated with the use of acetaminophen include: nausea, vomiting or diarrhea. Rarely, hypersensitivity reactions have been reported, as manifested by thrombocytopenic purpura, hemolytic anemia and agranulocytosis.

Gastrointestinal discomfort may be minimized by taking the dose with food.

Overdose: Symptoms: Methocarbamol: No deaths or major toxicity have been reported from overdosage with methocarbamol, administered parenterally or orally. One adult survived the deliberate ingestion of 22 to 30 g of methocarbamol without serious toxicity. Another survived 30 to 50 g. The principal symptom was drowsiness in both cases. However, 3 deaths have been reported when methocarbamol was combined with alcohol and other drugs.

Acetaminophen: Acetaminophen in massive overdosage may cause hepatic toxicity in some patients.

In adults, hepatic toxicity has rarely been reported with acute overdoses of less than 5 g. Importantly, young children seem to be more resistant than adults to the hepatotoxic effect of an acetaminophen overdose. Despite this, the measures outlined below should be initiated in any adult or child suspected of having ingested an acetaminophen overdose.

Early symptoms following a potentially hepatotoxic overdose may include: nausea, vomiting, diaphoresis and general malaise. Clinical and laboratory evidence of hepatic toxicity may not be apparent until 48 to 72 hours postingestion.

Treatment: Methocarbamol: Supportive measures include maintenance of an adequate airway, monitoring urinary output and vital signs and the administration of i.v. fluids, if necessary. There is no experience with forced diuresis or with dialysis in the treatment of methocarbamol overdose. Likewise, the usefulness of hemodialysis in managing methocarbamol overdose is unknown.

Acetaminophen: The stomach should be emptied promptly by lavage or by induction of emesis with syrup of ipecac. Patients' estimates of the quantity of a drug ingested are notoriously unreliable. Therefore, if an acetaminophen overdose is suspected, a serum acetaminophen assay should be obtained as early as possible, but no sooner than 4 hours following ingestion. Liver function studies should be obtained initially and repeated at 24-hour intervals.

The antidote, N-acetylcysteine, should be administered as early as possible, and within 16 hours of the overdose ingestion for optimal results. Following recovery, there are no residual, structural or functional hepatic abnormalities.

Dosage: Robaxacet Tablets/Caplets: Adults and Children over 12 years: 2 caplets/tablets 4 times daily. Three caplets/tablets 4 times daily may be used in severe conditions for 1 to 3 days. These dosage recommendations provide 3.2 and 4.8 g, respectively, methocarbamol and 2.6 and 3.9 g, respectively, acetaminophen/day.

Robaxacet (cont'd)

Robaxacet Extra Strength: Adults and Children over 12 years: 2 caplets 4 times daily. This recommended dosage provides 3.2 g methocarbamol and 4 g acetaminophen/day.

Supplied: Robaxacet: Caplets: Each green and white caplet, green layer scored and white layer engraved "WR", contains: methocarbamol 400 mg and acetaminophen 325 mg. Nonmedicinal ingredients: cellulose, cornstarch, crospovidone, D&C Yellow No. 10, FD&C Blue No. 1, magnesium stearate, polyethylene glycol, povidone, pregelatinized starch, sodium lauryl sulfate, sodium starch glycolate and stearic acid. Energy: <1 kJ (<1 kcal). Sodium: <1 mmol (0.82 mg). Bottles of 40. Boxes of 18. Store at room temperature (15 to 30°C).

Tablets: Each green and white tablet, green layer scored and white layer engraved "WR", contains: methocarbamol 400 mg and acetaminophen 325 mg. Nonmedicinal ingredients: cornstarch, D&C Yellow No. 10, FD&C Blue No. 1, magnesium stearate, povidone, sodium lauryl sulfate, sodium starch glycolate and stearic acid. Energy: <1 kJ (<1 kcal). Sodium: <1 mmol (0.82 mg). Bottles of 40 and 500. Boxes of 18. Store at room temperature (15 to 30°C).

Robaxacet Extra Strength: Each green and white caplet, green layer scored and engraved "EX", and white layer engraved "W-R", contains: methocarbamol 400 mg and acetaminophen 500 mg. Nonmedicinal ingredients: cellulose, cornstarch, crospovidone, D&C Yellow No. 10, FD&C Blue No. 1, magnesium stearate, polyethylene glycol, povidone, pregelatinized starch, sodium lauryl sulfate, sodium starch glycolate and stearic acid. Energy: <1 kJ (<1 kcal). Sodium: <1 mmol (0.46 mg). Bottles of 40. Boxes of 18. Store at room temperature (15 to 30°C).

ROBAXACET®-8 Ⓝ

Whitehall-Robins

Methocarbamol—Acetaminophen—Codeine Phosphate

Muscle Relaxant—Analgesic

Pharmacology: The mechanism of action of methocarbamol has not been established, but may be due to general CNS depression. It has no direct action on the contractile mechanism of striated muscle, the motor end plate or the nerve fiber. Methocarbamol is metabolized to yield a dealkylated and a hydroxylated product. These 2 metabolites are found primarily as glucuronide and sulfate conjugates. Based on elimination of radioactivity, the half-life of methocarbamol and its metabolites is about 2 hours. Animal studies reveal that methocarbamol crosses the placental barrier and blood-brain barrier.

Acetaminophen is a nonopiate, nonsalicylate analgesic and antipyretic. Acetaminophen is conjugated in the liver to form glucuronide and sulfate conjugates. Its plasma half-life has been reported to be from 1 to 2 hours.

Codeine is readily absorbed from the gastrointestinal tract, and a therapeutic dose reaches peak analgesic effectiveness in about 2 hours and persists for 4 to 6 hours. Oral codeine (60 mg) given to healthy males has been shown to achieve peak blood levels of 0.016 mg/100 mL at approximately 1 hour post-dose. The codeine plasma half-life for a 60 mg oral dose is about 2.9 hours. Blood levels causing CNS depression begin at 0.05 to 0.19 mg/100 mL.

The single lethal dose of codeine in adults is estimated to be approximately 0.5 to 1.0 g. Codeine is rapidly distributed from blood to body tissues and taken up preferentially by parenchymatous organs such as liver, spleen and kidney. It passes the blood-brain barrier and is found in fetal tissue and breast milk. The drug is not bound by plasma protein nor is it accumulated in body tissues. Codeine is metabolized in the liver to morphine and norcodeine, each representing about 10% of the administered dose of codeine. About 90% of the dose is excreted within 24 hours, primarily through the kidneys. Urinary excretion products are free and glucuronide-conjugated codeine (about 70%), free and conjugated norcodeine (about 10%), free and conjugated morphine (about 10%), normorphine (under 4%) and hydrocodone (1%). The remainder of the dose appears in the feces.

Indications: Relief of acute episodes of severe pain associated with skeletal muscle spasm: acute torticollis, acute strains and sprains, acute low back pain, acute tenosynovitis, ankle sprain, fracture, trauma, acute bursitis, acute myositis, whiplash injury.

Contraindications: Hypersensitivity to methocarbamol, acetaminophen or codeine.

Warnings: Do not exceed recommended dosage as severe liver damage due to acetaminophen toxicity may occur. Avoid alcohol.

Precautions: General: The administration of Robaxacet-8 or other narcotics may obscure the diagnosis or clinical course in patients with acute abdominal conditions. In the presence of head injury, other intracranial lesions or a pre-existing increase in intracranial pressure, the respiratory depressant effects of narcotics and their capacity to elevate cerebrospinal fluid pressure may be markedly exaggerated. Furthermore, narcotics produce adverse reactions which may obscure the clinical course of patients with head injuries.

Robaxacet-8 should be given with caution to certain patients such as the elderly or debilitated, and those with severe impairment of hepatic or renal function, hypothyroidism, Addison's disease and prostatic hypertrophy or urethral stricture.

Occupational Hazards: Robaxacet-8 may impair the mental and/or physical abilities required for the performance of potentially hazardous tasks such as driving a car or operating machinery. The patient using this drug should be cautioned accordingly.

Drug Interactions: Patients receiving other narcotic analgesics, general anesthetics, phenothiazines, tranquilizers, sedative-hypnotics or other CNS depressants (including alcohol) concomitantly with Robaxacet-8 may exhibit an additive CNS depression. When such combined therapy is contemplated, the dose of one or both agents should be reduced.

The use of MAO inhibitors or tricyclic antidepressants with codeine preparations may increase the effect of either the antidepressant or codeine. The concurrent use of anticholinergics with codeine may produce paralytic ileus.

Methocarbamol may cause a color interference in certain screening tests for 5-hydroxyindoleacetic acid (5-HIAA) and vanillylmandelic acid (VMA).

Carcinogenesis, Mutagenesis: Long-term studies in animals have not been performed to evaluate carcinogenic or mutagenic potential.

Pregnancy: There are no adequate and well-controlled studies of Robaxacet-8 in pregnant women. This product should be used during pregnancy only when in the judgment of the physician the potential benefits outweigh the potential hazards.

Labor and Delivery: The effects of Robaxacet-8 on the mother and fetus, on the duration of labor and delivery, or on later growth, development and functional maturation of the child is unknown.

Lactation: It is not known whether methocarbamol or its metabolites are secreted in human milk; however, there are indications small quantities of acetaminophen and codeine have been found in breast milk.

Children: Safety and effectiveness of this product in children 12 years of age or younger have not been established.

Adverse Effects: The most common complaints to methocarbamol are drowsiness, nausea and dizziness or lightheadedness (seen in approximately 4 to 5% of patients). The following reactions have been associated with the drug, some of them rarely; in some instances, causal relationships have not been established: headache, nasal congestion, blurred vision, rash, pruritus and urticaria.

Adverse reactions that have been associated with the use of acetaminophen include: nausea, vomiting or diarrhea. Rarely, hypersensitivity reactions have been reported, as manifested by thrombocytopenic purpura, hemolytic anemia and agranulocytosis.

The most frequently observed adverse reactions to codeine include lightheadedness, dizziness, drowsiness, nausea, vomiting, constipation and depression of respiration. Less common reactions to codeine include euphoria, dysphoria, pruritus and skin rashes.

Gastrointestinal discomfort may be minimized by taking Robaxacet-8 with food.

Drug Abuse and Dependence: Codeine can produce drug dependence of the morphine type, and therefore has the potential for being abused. Psychic dependence, physical dependence and tolerance may develop upon repeated administration of this drug, and it should be prescribed and administered with the same degree of caution appropriate to the use of other oral narcotic-containing medications.

Overdose: Symptoms: Methocarbamol: No deaths or major toxicity have been reported from overdosage with methocarbamol, administered parenterally or orally. One adult survived the deliberate ingestion of 22 to 30 g of methocarbamol without serious toxicity. Another survived 30 to 50 g. The principal symptom was drowsiness in both cases.

Acetaminophen and Codeine: Serious overdose with acetaminophen and codeine is characterized by respiratory depression (a decrease in respiratory rate and/or tidal volume; Cheyne-Stokes respiration; cyanosis), extreme somnolence progressing to stupor or coma, skeletal muscle flaccidity, cold and clammy skin, and sometimes bradycardia and hypotension. In severe overdosage, apnea, circulatory collapse, cardiac arrest and death may occur. The ingestion of very large amounts of this drug may, in addition, result in acute hepatic toxicity from acetaminophen.

Treatment: Methocarbamol: Supportive measures include maintenance of an adequate airway, monitoring urinary output and vital signs, and the administration of i.v. fluids, if necessary. There is no experience with forced diuresis or with dialysis in the treatment of methocarbamol overdosage. Likewise, the usefulness of hemodialysis in managing methocarbamol overdose is unknown.

Acetaminophen and Codeine: Primary attention should be given to reestablishment of adequate respiratory exchange through provision of a patent airway and the institution of assisted or controlled ventilation. The narcotic antagonist naloxone is a specific antidote against respiratory depression which may result from overdosage or unusual sensitivity to narcotics, including codeine. Therefore, an appropriate dose of naloxone (usual initial adult dose: 0.4 mg) should be administered, preferably by the i.v. route, and simultaneously with efforts at respiratory resuscitation. Since the duration of action of codeine may exceed that of the antagonist, the patient should be kept under continued surveillance and repeated doses of the antagonist should be administered as needed to maintain adequate respiration. An antagonist should not be administered in the absence of clinically significant respiratory or cardiovascular depression. Oxygen, i.v. fluids, vasopressors and other supportive measures should be employed as indicated. Gastric emptying may be useful in removing unabsorbed drug.

Acetaminophen in massive overdosage may cause hepatotoxicity in some patients. Clinical and laboratory evidence of hepatotoxicity may be delayed for up to 1 week. Close clinical monitoring and serial hepatic enzyme determinations are therefore recommended.

The antidote, N-acetylcysteine, should be administered as early as possible, and within 16 hours of the overdose ingestion for optimal results. Following recovery, there are no residual, structural or functional hepatic abnormalities.

Dosage: Adults: 1 or 2 tablets 3 or 4 times a day.

Supplied: Each coated, blue and white caplet, blue layer engraved "WR", white layer scored, contains: methocarbamol 400 mg, acetaminophen 325 mg and codeine phosphate 8 mg. Nonmedicinal ingredients: calcium sulfate, cellulose, cornstarch, FD&C Blue No. 1, magnesium stearate, polyethylene glycol, povidone, sodium lauryl sulfate, sodium starch glycolate and stearic acid. Energy: <1 kJ (<1 kcal). Sodium: <1 mmol (0.9 mg). Bottles of 100. Boxes of 18.

ROBAXIN®
ROBAXIN®-750

Whitehall-Robins

Methocarbamol

Skeletal Muscle Relaxant

Pharmacology: The mechanism of action of methocarbamol has not been established, but may be due to general CNS depression. It has no direct action on the contractile mechanism of striated muscle, the motor end plate or the nerve fiber. Methocarbamol is metabolized to yield a dealkylated and a hydroxylated product. These 2 metabolites are found primarily as glucuronide and sulfate conjugates. Based on elimination of radioactivity, the half-life of methocarbamol and its metabolites is about 2 hours. Animal studies reveal that methocarbamol crosses the placental barrier and blood-brain barrier.

Indications: An adjunct to rest, physical therapy and other measures for the relief of discomforts associated with acute, painful musculoskeletal conditions.

Contraindications: Hypersensitivity to methocarbamol.

Precautions: Occupational Hazards: Methocarbamol may impair the ability of the patient to engage in potentially hazardous activities such as operating machinery or driving a motor vehicle; ambulatory patients should therefore be cautioned accordingly. Patients should be cautioned about combined effects of methocarbamol with alcohol and with other CNS depressants.

Methocarbamol may cause a color interference in screening tests for 5-hydroxyindoleacetic acid (5-HIAA) and vanillylmandelic acid (VMA).

Pregnancy: Safe use in pregnancy has not been established with regard to possible adverse effects in fetal development.

Lactation: It is not known whether methocarbamol is excreted in human milk.

Children: Safety and effectiveness in children 12 years of age and less have not been established.

Adverse Effects: Following oral administration, minor untoward effects such as lightheadedness, dizziness, drowsiness and mild nausea occasionally occur, and frequently disappear on reduction of dosage (seen in approximately 4 to 5% of patients). Allergic manifestations such as urticaria, pruritus, rash or conjunctivitis with nasal congestion have been reported in a few hypersensitive patients.

Overdose: Symptoms: No deaths or major toxicity have been reported from overdosage with methocarbamol, administered parenterally or orally. One adult survived the deliberate ingestion of 22 to 30 g of methocarbamol without serious toxicity. Another survived 30 to 50 g. The principal symptom was drowsiness in both cases.

Treatment: Reduction of dosage. Supportive therapy for 24 hours as methocarbamol is excreted within that period of time.

Dosage: Adults: 6 g daily for first 48 to 72 hours of acute skeletal muscle spasm. Severe conditions: 8 g daily. Thereafter reduce dosage to 4 g daily.

Supplied: Robaxin: Each white, scored, compressed tablet, engraved "WR", contains: methocarbamol 500 mg. Nonmedicinal ingredients: cornstarch, magnesium stearate, povidone, sodium lauryl sulfate, sodium starch glycolate and stearic acid. Energy: <1 kJ (<1 kcal). Sodium: <1 mmol (0.4 mg). Bottles of 50 and 500.

Robaxin-750: Each white, scored, capsule-shaped tablet, monogrammed "WR", contains: methocarbamol 750 mg. Nonmedicinal ingredients: cornstarch, magnesium stearate, povidone, sodium lauryl sulfate, sodium starch glycolate and stearic acid. Energy: <1 kJ (<1 kcal). Sodium: <1 mmol (0.59 mg). Bottles of 50.

ROBAXIN® INJECTABLE

Wyeth-Ayerst

Methocarbamol

Skeletal Muscle Relaxant

Supplied: Each 10 mL vial contains: methocarbamol 1 g, in sterile aqueous solution. Nonmedicinal ingredients: hydrochloric acid and/or sodium hydroxide to adjust pH, polyethylene glycol 300 and water for injection. pH: 3.5 to 6.0. Vials of 10 mL, boxes of 5.

ROBAXISAL®
ROBAXISAL® EXTRA STRENGTH

Whitehall-Robins

Methocarbamol—ASA

Skeletal Muscle Relaxant—Analgesic

Pharmacology: The mechanism of action of methocarbamol has not been established, but may be due to general CNS depression. It has no direct action on the contractile mechanism of striated muscle, the motor end plate or the nerve fibre. Methocarbamol is metabolized to yield a dealkylated and a hydroxylated product. These 2 metabolites are found primarily as glucuronide and sulfate conjugates. Based on elimination of radioactivity, the half-life of methocarbamol and its metabolites is bout 2 hours. Animal studies reveal that methocarbamol crosses the placental barrier and blood-brain barrier.

ASA interferes with the production of prostaglandins in various organs and tissues through acetylation and inactivation of the enzyme cyclooxygenase. The main action of the drug is thought to be peripheral; however, it may have similar activity in the CNS. The reduction in tissue levels of prostaglandins may be responsible for the analgesic and anti-inflammatory effects of the drug. ASA is most effective against pain of low to moderate intensity associated with inflammation.

Indications: Pain due to or associated with skeletal muscle spasm such as acute and chronic back strains and sprains, whiplash and other traumatic injuries, myositis, pain and spasm associated with arthritis, torticollis, joint strains and sprains, bursitis, low back pain due to ill defined causes.

Contraindications: Methocarbamol or salicylate sensitivity; patients who have had a bronchospastic reaction, generalized urticaria, angioedema, severe rhinitis, laryngeal edema or shock precipitated by ASA or nonsteroidal anti-inflammatory drugs. Some patients sensitive to ASA, may be cross-sensitive to other nonsteroidal anti inflammatory drugs. Patients with asthma associated nasal poylps have an increased risk of sensitivity to ASA.

Do not use in patients with active peptic ulcer.

This product should not be used in children, teenagers, and young adults with varicella or influenza, unless directed by a physician.

Precautions: Occupational Hazards: Methocarbamol may impair the ability of the patient to engage in potentially hazardous activities such as operating machinery or driving a motor vehicle; ambulatory patients should therefore be cautioned accordingly. Patients should be cautioned about combined effects of methocarbamol with alcohol and with other CNS depressants.

Methocarbamol may cause a color interference in screening tests for 5-hydroxyindoleacetic acid (5-HIAA) and vanillylmandelic acid (VMA).

Pregnancy: Safe use in pregnancy has not been established with regard to possible adverse effects in fetal development.

Lactation: It is not known whether methocarbamol is excreted in human milk.

Children: Safety and effectiveness in children 12 years of age and less have not been established.

Use with caution in patients with active or a history of gastrointestinal ulcerations. Concomitant ingestion of alcohol increases the risk of gastrointestinal bleeding.

Use cautiously in patients with decreased renal function, bleeding tendencies, significant anemia, hypoprothrombinemia, thrombocytopenia, vitamin K deficiency and severe hepatic damage.

Discontinue 5 to 7 days prior to elective surgery because of increased risk of bleeding.

Adverse Effects: The most frequent adverse reaction to methocarbamol is dizziness, lightheadedness and nausea. Less frequent reactions are drowsiness, blurred vision, headache, fever, allergic manifestations such as urticaria, pruritus and rash (seen in approximately 4 to 5% of patients). Adverse reactions associated with the use of ASA include nausea and other gastrointestinal discomforts, gastritis, gastric erosion, vomiting, constipation, diarrhea, angioedema, asthma, rash, pruritus, urticaria. Gastrointestinal discomfort may be minimized by administering with food.

Overdose: Symptoms: drowsiness, dizziness, rapid and deep breathing, nausea, vomiting, vertigo, tinnitus, flushing, sweating, thirst and tachycardia. In more severe cases, acid-base disturbances including respiratory alkalosis and metabolic acidosis can occur. Severe case may show fever, hemorrhage, excitement, confusion, convulsions or coma and respiratory failure.

Treatment: Reduction of dosage. Supportive therapy for 24 hours. In children with salicylate intoxication, sodium bicarbonate is recommended. Judicious use of 5% carbon dioxide with 95% oxygen may be of benefit. Abnormal electrolyte patterns should be corrected with appropriate fluid therapy.

Dosage: Robaxisal Tablets/Caplets: Adults: 2 caplets/tablets 4 times a day. 3 caplets/tablets 4 times a day may be given in severe conditions for 1 to 3 days in patients well able to tolerate salicylates.

Robaxisal Extra Strength: Adults: maximum 2 caplets, 4 times daily.

Supplied: Robaxisal: Caplets: Each pink and white, coated caplet, white layer monogrammed "WR", contains: methocarbamol 400 mg and ASA 325 mg. Nonmedicinal ingredients: cellulose, cornstarch, FD&C Red No. 3, magnesium stearate, polyethylene glycol, povidone, sodium lauryl sulfate, sodium starch glycolate, stearic acid and water. Energy: <1 kJ (<1 kcal). Sodium: <1 mmol (0.32 mg). Bottles of 40. Boxes of 18. Store at room temperature 15 to 30°C.

Tablets: Each pink and white tablet, white layer monogrammed "WR", contains: methocarbamol 400 mg and ASA 325 mg. Nonmedicinal ingredients: cornstarch, FD&C Red No. 3, magnesium stearate, povidone, sodium lauryl sulfate, sodium starch glycolate, stearic acid and water. Energy: <1 kJ (<1 kcal). Sodium: <1 mmol (0.32 mg). Bottles of 40 and 500. Boxes of 18. Store at room temperature 15 to 30°C.

Robaxisal Extra Strength: Each pink and white, coated caplet, white layer monogrammed "W-R", pink layer scored and engraved "EX", contains: methocarbamol 400 mg and ASA 500 mg. Nonmedicinal ingredients: cellulose, cornstarch, FD&C Red No. 3, magnesium stearate, polyethylene glycol, povidone, sodium lauryl sulfate, sodium starch glycolate and stearic acid. Energy: <1 kJ (<1 kcal). Sodium: <1 mmol (0.36 mg). Bottles of 40. Boxes of 18. Store at room temperature 15 to 30°C.

ROBAXISAL®-C Ⓝ

Whitehall-Robins

Methocarbamol—ASA—Codeine Phosphate

Skeletal Muscle Relaxant—Analgesic

Pharmacology: The mechanism of action of methocarbamol has not been established, but may be due to general CNS depression. It has no direct action on the contractile mechanism of striated muscle, the motor end plate or the nerve fibre. Methocarbamol is metabolized to yield a dealkylated and a hydroxylated product. These 2 metabolites are found primarily as glucuronide and sulfate conjugates. Based on elimination of radioactivity, the half-life of methocarbamol and its metabolites is about 2 hours. Animal studies reveal that methocarbamol crosses the placental barrier and blood-brain barrier.

ASA interferes with the production of prostaglandins in various organs and tissues through acetylation and inactivation of the enzyme cyclooxygenase. The main action of the drug is thought to be peripheral; however, it may have similar activity in the CNS. The reduction in tissue levels of prostaglandins may be responsible for the analgesic and anti-inflammatory effects of the drug. ASA is most effective against pain of low to moderate intensity associated with inflammation.

Codeine is readily absorbed from the gastrointestinal tract, and a therapeutic dose reaches peak analgesic effectiveness in about 2 hours and persists for 4 to 6 hours. Oral codeine (60 mg) given to healthy males has been shown to achieve peak blood levels of 0.016 mg/100 mL at approximately 1 hour post-dose. The codeine plasma half-life for a 60 mg oral dose is about 2.9 hours. Blood levels causing CNS depression begin at 0.05 to 0.19 mg/100 mL.

Indications: Relief of acute episodes of severe pain associated with skeletal muscle spasm: acute torticollis, acute strains and sprains, acute low back pain, acute tenosynovitis, ankle sprain, fracture, trauma, acute bursitis, acute myositis, whiplash injury.

Contraindications: Hypersensitivity to methocarbamol, ASA, or codeine.

Patients who have had a bronchospastic reaction, generalized urticaria, angioedema, severe rhinitis, laryngeal edema or shock precipitated by ASA or nonsteroidal anti-inflammatory drugs. Some patients sensitive to ASA, may be cross-sensitive to other nonsteroidal anti-inflammatory drugs as well as tartrazine dye. Patients with asthma associated nasal poylps have an increased risk of sensitivity to ASA.

Do not use in patients with active peptic ulcer.

Precautions: General: The administration of opioids may obscure the diagnosis or clinical course in patients with acute abdominal conditions. In the presence of head injury, other intracranial lesions or a pre-existing increase in intracranial pressure, the respiratory depressant effects of opioids and their capacity to elevate cerebrospinal fluid pressure may be markedly exaggerated. Furthermore, narcotics produce adverse reactions which may obscure the clinical course of patients with head injuries.

Occupational Hazards: Robaxisal-C may impair the mental and/or physical abilities required for the performance of potentially hazardous tasks such as driving a car or operating machinery. The patient using this drug should be cautioned accordingly.

Drug Interactions: Patients receiving other opioid analgesics, general anesthetics, phenothiazines, tranquilizers, sedative-hypnotics or other CNS depressants (including alcohol) concomitantly with Robaxisal-C may exhibit an additive CNS depression. When such combined therapy is contemplated, the dose of one or both agents should be reduced.

The use of MAO inhibitors or tricyclic antidepressants with codeine preparations may increase the effect of either the antidepressant or codeine. The concurrent use of anticholinergics with codeine may produce paralytic ileus.

Methocarbamol may cause a color interference in certain screening tests for 5-hydroxyindoleacetic acid (5-HIAA) and vanillylmandelic acid (VMA).

Robaxisal-C (cont'd)

Carcinogenesis, Mutagenesis: Long-term studies in animals have not been performed to evaluate carcinogenic or mutagenic potential.
Pregnancy: There are no adequate and well-controlled studies in pregnant women. This product should be used during pregnancy only when in the judgment of the physician the potential benefits outweigh the potential hazards.

Adverse Effects: Methocarbamol: The most common complaints to methocarbamol are drowsiness, nausea and dizziness or lightheadedness (seen in approximately 4 to 5 % of patients). The following reactions have been associated with the drug, some of them rarely; in some instances, causal relationships have not been established: headache, nasal congestion, blurred vision, rash, pruritus and urticaria.
ASA: Gastrointestinal: ulcer, hemorrhage, dyspepsia, heartburn, epigastric distress, nausea, vomiting, diarrhea, abdominal pain may occur with increasing incidence at higher dosages.
Hepatic: Reversible hepatotoxicity particularly in patients with juvenile rheumatoid arthritis and systemic lupus erythematosus has been reported rarely.
Otic: Tinnitus and hearing loss, usually completely reversible, may occur in patients receiving large doses of ASA or with long-term use and are dose related.
Skin: Skin eruptions and lesions have been reported. Stevens-Johnson's syndrome has rarely been associated with ASA.

Chronic salicylate intoxication may result from high doses or from prolonged therapy with high doses. Tinnitus and hearing loss are the most frequent signs of chronic intoxication. Other manifestations such as dimness of vision, headache, dizziness, mental confusion, drowsiness, sweating, thirst, hyperventilation, tachycardia, nausea, vomiting and sometimes diarrhea may occur.
Codeine: Drug Abuse and Dependence: Codeine can produce drug dependence of the morphine type, and therefore has the potential for being abused. Psychic dependence, physical dependence and tolerance may develop upon repeated administration of this drug, and it should be prescribed and administered with the same degree of caution appropriate to the use of other oral opioid-containing medications.

Overdose: Symptoms: Methocarbamol: No deaths or major toxicity have been reported from overdosage with methocarbamol, administered parenterally or orally. One adult survived the deliberate ingestion of 22 to 30 g of methocarbamol without serious toxicity. Another survived 30 to 50 g. The principal symptom was drowsiness in both cases.
Codeine: Respiratory depression (reduced respiratory rate and/or tidal volume; Cheyne-Stokes respiration; cyanosis), extreme somnolence progressing to stupor or coma, skeletal muscle flaccidity, cold or clammy skin, and sometimes hypotension and bradycardia. Severe overdosage may result in apnea, circulatory collapse, cardiac arrest and death. Miosis can be one characteristic of morphine derivative overdose. Mydriasis can take place in terminal narcosis, severe hypoxia or as a toxic effect of pethidine or its congeners.
ASA: Symptoms of acute toxicity with ASA may occur with doses greater than 150 mg/kg. Doses greater than 500 mg/kg are potentially fatal. Acid-base and electrolyte disturbances, dehydration, hyperpyrexia, hyperglycemia or hypoglycemia are the principal physiologic manifestations of acute ASA toxicity. Other symptoms of toxicity include burning pain in the mouth or throat, dizziness, tinnitus and sweating. In more severe cases, presence of CNS symptoms such as lethargy, disorientation, or confusion may be a predictor for the development of pulmonary edema. Coma and convulsions may be delayed for 24 to 48 hours. Cardiac arrhythmias have been reported. Bleeding disorders, cerebral edema, oliguria are also possible.

Treatment: Gastric lavage, administration of activated charcoal. If respiratory depression occurs, give attention to the re-establishment of respiratory exchange by ventilation and administration of a narcotic antagonist, e.g., naloxone.

Dosage: Adults: 1 or 2 tablets 3 or 4 times a day.

Supplied: Robaxisal-C ⅛: Each yellow and white tablet, yellow layer monogrammed "WR", contains: methocarbamol 400 mg, ASA 325 mg, codeine phosphate 8 mg. Nonmedicinal ingredients: cornstarch, D&C Yellow No. 10, FD&C Yellow No. 6, magnesium stearate, povidone, sodium starch glycolate and stearic acid. Energy: <1 kJ (<1 kcal). Bottles of 100. Boxes of 18.

Robaxisal-C ¼: Each orange and white tablet, orange layer monogrammed "WR", contains: methocarbamol 400 mg, ASA 325 mg and codeine phosphate 16.2 mg. Nonmedicinal ingredients: cornstarch, FD&C Yellow No. 6, magnesium stearate, povidone, sodium starch glycolate and stearic acid. Energy: <1 kJ (<1 kcal). Bottles of 24 and 250.

Robaxisal-C ½: Each coral and white caplet, coral layer monogrammed "WR", contains: methocarbamol 400 mg, ASA 325 mg, codeine phosphate 32.4 mg. Nonmedicinal ingredients: cellulose, cornstarch, FD&C Red No. 2, FD&C Yellow No. 6, magnesium stearate, povidone, sodium starch glycolate and stearic acid. Energy: <1 kJ (<1 kcal). Bottles of 24 and 250.

Store at room temperature (15 to 30°C).

ROBIDONE® Ⓝ
Wyeth-Ayerst
Hydrocodone Bitartrate
Antitussive

Supplied: Each mL of green, aromatic liquid contains: hydrocodone bitartrate 1 mg. Nonmedicinal ingredients: citric acid anhydrous, D&C Yellow No. 10, FD&C Blue No. 1 Brilliant FCF, FD&C Yellow No. 6 Sunset, flavor creme de menthe artificial, glycerin, invert sugar 73% solution, purified water, sodium benzoate, sodium chloride and sorbitol solution. Alcohol: 3.2 %. Energy: 44.8 kJ (10.7 kcal)/5 mL. Sodium: <1 mmol (11.75 mg)/5 mL. Bottles of 100 mL and 1 L.

ROBINUL®
ROBINUL® FORTE
Wyeth-Ayerst
Glycopyrrolate
Anticholinergic

Indications: The management of gastrointestinal disorders amenable to anticholinergic therapy, such as: duodenal ulcer, duodenitis, pylorospasm; gastric ulcer, gastritis, hiatal hernia, hyperchlorhydria, pyrosis, aerophagia, gastroenteritis; esophagitis; cholecystitis, chronic pancreatitis; spastic and irritable colon, ulcerative colitis, functional bowel distress, diverticulitis, acute enteritis, diarrhea; and splenic flexure syndrome, neurogenic gastrointestinal disturbances.

Contraindications: Glaucoma, urinary bladder neck obstruction, pyloric obstruction, stenosis with significant gastric retention, prostatic hypertrophy, duodenal obstruction, cardiospasm (megaesophagus), achalasia of the esophagus.

Warnings: *Pregnancy* and *Lactation:* Use of the drug in pregnancy, lactation or in the childbearing years requires that the potential benefits of the drug be weighed against the possible hazards to mother and child.

In the presence of a high environmental temperature, heat prostration can occur (fever, heat stroke due to decreased sweating) with all anticholinergic agents.

Diarrhea may be an early symptom of incomplete intestinal obstruction, especially in patients with ileostomy or colostomy. In this instance, treatment with this drug would be inappropriate and possibly harmful.
Occupational Hazards: Glycopyrrolate may produce drowsiness or blurred vision. In this event, the patients should be warned not to engage in activities requiring mental alertness such as operating a motor vehicle or other machinery, and not to perform hazardous work while taking this drug.

Precautions: Investigate any tachycardia before giving anticholinergic, (atropine-like) drugs since they may increase the heart rate.

The use of anticholinergic drugs in the treatment of gastric ulcer may produce a delay in gastric emptying and may complicate such therapy (antral stasis). The use of an indwelling nasogastric tube should be considered whenever more than 2 doses in succession are to be administered.

Do not rely on the use of the drug in the presence of complications of biliary tract disease.

Adverse Effects: Dry mouth, blurring of vision, constipation, urinary hesitancy, rash, urinary difficulties, nausea, bitter taste, nervousness, abdominal cramps; tachycardia, palpitation, dilatation of the pupil, increased ocular tension, weakness, vomiting, headache, dizziness, drowsiness, dysuria.

Overdose: Symptoms and Treatment: Symptomatic and supportive.

Empty the stomach as quickly as possible by emesis followed by gastric lavage. Following gastric lavage activated charcoal (30 g) may be administered every four to six hours during the first 24 hours after ingestion.

Monitor cardiac function for any signs of dysrhythmia.

Maintain an open airway and adequate fluid intake; regulate body temperature.

Use standard medical measures to manage circulatory shock and metabolic acidosis. Cardiac arrhythmias may be treated with neostigmine, pyridostigmine, or propranolol. If signs of cardiac failure occur, consider the use of a short acting digitalis preparation. Close monitoring of cardiac function for not less than 5 days is advisable.

Anticonvulsants may be given to control seizures.

Dialysis is of no value because of low plasma concentrations of the drug.

Physostigmine given i.v. can be used to reverse the symptoms of anticholinergic poisoning. Give physostigmine 1 to 3 mg slow i.v. (over 2 minutes). If no clinical changes or cholinergic signs occur within 15 to 30 minutes, an additional 1 to 2 mg may be administered. Repeat doses of 1 to 2 mg i.v. every 30 minutes up to two hours.

Physostigmine is not innocuous and carries the risk of inducing seizures and cholinergic crisis. It should not be used routinely. If excessive sweating, nausea or vomiting occur, reduce dosage of physostigmine. Atropine in a dose of 50% of the amount of injected physostigmine should be kept on hand and administered if excessive cholinergic symptoms develop.

Dosage: Average Recommended Adult Dose: 1 to 2 tablets 3 times daily (morning, mid-afternoon, and bedtime). To obtain optimum results, dosage should be adjusted to the individual patient's response. After the more severe symptoms associated with acute conditions have subsided, the dose may be reduced to the minimum required to maintain symptomatic relief. For maintenance, a dosage of 1 mg twice a day will frequently afford adequate control.

Supplied: Robinul: Each pink, scored, compressed tablet, engraved "AYERST", contains: glycopyrrolate 1 mg. Nonmedicinal ingredients: calcium phosphate dibasic dihydrate, FD&C Red No. 3 Aluminum Lake, lactose, magnesium stearate, povidone and sodium starch glycolate. Energy: <1 kJ (<1 kcal). Bottles of 100. Store at controlled room temperature (20 to 25°C). Protect from light.

Robinul Forte: Each pink, scored, compressed tablet, engraved "AYERST", contains: glycopyrrolate 2 mg. Nonmedicinal ingredients: calcium phosphate dibasic dihydrate, FD&C Red No. 3 Aluminum Lake, lactose, magnesium stearate, povidone and sodium starch glycolate. Energy: <1 kJ (<1 kcal). Bottles of 100. Store at controlled room temperature (20 to 25°C). Protect from light.

ROBINUL® INJECTABLE
Wyeth-Ayerst
Glycopyrrolate
Anticholinergic

Pharmacology: Glycopyrrolate, like other anticholinergic (antimuscarinic) agents, competitively antagonizes the action of acetylcholine on structures innervated by postganglionic cholinergic nerves and on smooth muscles that respond to acetylcholine but lack cholinergic innervation.

Glycopyrrolate antagonizes muscarinic symptoms (e.g., bronchorrhea, bronchospasm, bradycardia and intestinal hypermotility) induced by cholinergic drugs such as the anticholinesterases.

As a premedicant, glycopyrrolate injectable reduces excessive pharyngeal, tracheal and bronchial secretions and, during anesthesia, it appears to protect the heart against excessive vagal stimulation.

Glycopyrrolate's polar ammonium moiety limits its passage across lipid membranes, such as the blood-brain barrier in contrast to the belladonna alkaloids, which are nonpolar tertiary amines. Consequently, glycopyrrolate injectable does not cause CNS effects seen with the belladonna alkaloids.

The onset of action following i.m. glycopyrrolate injection is 20 to 40 minutes. Peak effects occur approximately 30 to 45 minutes after administration and the duration of action ranges from 4 to 6 hours. With i.v. injection, the onset of action is generally evident within 1 minute; the duration of action varies, as does that of all other anticholinergics. Following i.v. glycopyrrolate, the vagal blocking effects persist for 2 to 3 hours and the antisialagogue effects persist up to 7 hours.

Indications: The management of gastrointestinal disorders amenable to anticholinergic therapy when oral medication is not tolerated or a rapid anticholinergic effect is desired.

May also be used as a preanesthetic antimuscarinic agent. During reversal of neuromuscular blockade induced by nondepolarizing muscle relaxants, it protects against the peripheral muscarinic effects (e.g., bradycardia and excessive secretions) of cholinergic agents such as neostigmine and pyridostigmine.

Contraindications: Known hypersensitivity to glycopyrrolate and in treatment of gastrointestinal disorders in the presence of glaucoma, obstructive uropathy (e.g., bladder neck obstruction due to prostatic hypertrophy), obstructive disease of the gastrointestinal tract (e.g., pyloroduodenal stenosis), paralytic ileus, intestinal atony or chronic lung disease of the elderly or debilitated patient, unstable cardiovascular status in acute hemorrhage, severe ulcerative colitis, toxic megacolon complicating ulcerative colitis, myasthenia gravis.

Due to its benzyl alcohol content, Robinul Injectable should not be used in newborns.

Warnings: *Pregnancy* and *Lactation:* Use of glycopyrrolate in pregnancy, lactation or in the childbearing age requires that the drug's potential benefits be weighed against the possible hazards to mother and child.

In the presence of a high environmental temperature, heat prostration can occur (fever, heat stroke due to decreased sweating) with all anticholinergic agents.

Diarrhea may be an early symptom of incomplete intestinal obstruction, especially in patients with ileostomy or colostomy. In this instance, treatment with glycopyrrolate would be inappropriate and possibly harmful.

Occupational Hazards: Since glycopyrrolate may produce drowsiness or blurred vision, warn patients not to engage in activities requiring mental alertness such as operating a motor vehicle or other machinery, and not to perform hazardous work while taking the drug.

Precautions: The i.v. administration of any anticholinergic in the presence of cyclopropane anesthesia can result in ventricular arrhythmias; therefore, observe caution if glycopyrrolate injectable must be used during cyclopropane anesthesia. If the drug is given in small incremental doses of 100 μg or less, the likelihood of producing ventricular arrhythmias is reduced.

Investigate any tachycardia before giving anticholinergic (atropine like) drugs since they may increase the heart rate.

With overdosage, a curare like action may occur, i.e., neuromuscular blockade leading to muscular weakness and possible paralysis. However, it has not yet been reported.

Use glycopyrrolate injectable with caution in elderly and in all patients with autonomic neuropathy; hepatic or renal disease; ulcerative colitis (large doses may suppress intestinal motility to the point of producing a paralytic ileus and for this reason precipitate or aggravate the serious complication of toxic megacolon); hyperthyroidism; coronary heart disease; congestive heart failure; cardiac arrhythmias; hypertension; prostatic hypertrophy; hiatal hernia associated with reflux esophagitis, since anticholinergic drugs may aggravate this condition; incipient glaucoma (acute glaucoma can be precipitated in susceptible individuals).

Anticholinergic drugs used in the treatment of gastric ulcer may produce a delay in gastric emptying time and may complicate such therapy (antral stasis). Consider the use of an indwelling nasogastric tube whenever more than 2 doses in succession are to be administered.

Do not rely on the use of glycopyrrolate in the presence of complications of biliary tract disease.

Adverse Effects: Symptoms of CNS effects have not been observed with glycopyrrolate injectable. Adverse reactions to anticholinergics may include xerostomia; urinary hesitancy and retention; blurred vision due to mydriasis and cycloplegia; photophobia; increased ocular tension including acute glaucoma; tachycardia; palpitation; decreased sweating and heat prostration; loss of taste; headache; nervousness; drowsiness; weakness; dizziness, insomnia, nausea; vomiting; impotence; suppression of lactation; constipation; bloated feeling; severe allergic reaction or drug idiosyncrasies including anaphylaxis, urticaria and other dermal manifestations; some degree of mental confusion and/or excitement, especially in elderly persons.

Overdose: Symptoms: Widespread paralysis of organs innervated by parasympathetic nerves should create a suspicion of poisoning by antimuscarinic agents. Dry mucous membranes, widely dilated and unresponsive pupils, tachycardia, cutaneous flush and fever are significant. A curariform neuromuscular block may occur and lead to respiratory paralysis.

Treatment: To combat peripheral anticholinergic effects, a quaternary ammonium anticholinesterase such as neostigmine methylsulfate may be given in a dose of 1.0 mg for each 1.0 mg of glycopyrrolate injectable known to have been administered.

To combat hypotension, pressor amines may be tried. To combat respiratory depression, administer oxygen and respiratory stimulant or artificial respiration. Catheterization sometimes is necessary.

Dosage: May be administered by i.m. or i.v. routes without dilution. **Not for use in newborns. Children with disorders such as Down's syndrome should not have anticholinergics, or if they are necessary, the usual dose should be reduced by half.**

Gastroenterology: Usual adult dose is 0.1 mg administered at 4 hour intervals 3 or 4 times daily. Where more profound effect is required, 0.2 mg may be given. Frequency of administration depends upon individual patient response, but a 4 hour interval between injections is recommended. Some patients may need only a single dose, others may require administration 2, 3, or 4 times a day.

Data on the use of glycopyrrolate injectable in the management of gastrointestinal disorders in children are not available.

Preanesthetic medication: Adults and children: 0.005 mg/kg may be given by i.m. injection 30 to 60 minutes prior to the anticipated time of induction of anesthesia or at the time the preanesthetic narcotic and/or sedative are administered.

Note: Children (up to 12 years of age) may require up to 0.010 mg/kg of body weight.

The timing of administration of glycopyrrolate injectable with relation to the time of anesthetic induction is not as critical as with the belladonna alkaloids, since glycopyrrolate has a prolonged duration of action, providing protection 2 to 3 times as long as that provided by atropine or scopolamine.

Intraoperative Medication: Glycopyrrolate injectable may be used during surgery to counteract drug induced or vagal traction reflexes with the associated arrhythmias (e.g., bradycardia). The usual attempts should be made to determine the etiology of the arrhythmia and the surgical or anesthetic manipulations necessary to correct parasympathetic imbalance should be performed. It should be administered i.v. to adults as single doses of 0.1 mg and repeated, as needed, at intervals of 2 to 3 minutes. The pediatric dose is 0.005 mg/kg i.v., not to exceed 0.1 mg in a single dose which may be repeated, as needed, at intervals of 2 to 3 minutes.

Reversal of Neuromuscular Blockade: The recommended adult and pediatric dose is 0.2 mg of glycopyrrolate for each 1 mg of neostigmine or 5 mg of pyridostigmine. In order to minimize the appearance of cardiac side effects, the drugs may be administered simultaneously by i.v. injection and may be mixed in the same syringe. Mixtures containing more than 5 mg of neostigmine or 25 mg of pyridostigmine plus 1 mg of glycopyrrolate are not recommended.

Compatibility with Other Agents: Drug Interaction during anesthesia: Glycopyrrolate has been used clinically with at least the following medications: a barbiturate (sodium thiopental); narcotic analgesics (morphine, alphaprodine, fentanyl); sedative/tranquilizers (droperidol, diazepam); gaseous anesthetics (diethyl ether, halothane, methoxyflurane, enflurane); parenteral anesthetics (ketamine); peripherally-acting skeletal muscle relaxants (succinyl choline, gallamine, d-tubocurarine, pancuronium); cholinergic agents (neostigmine, pyridostigmine); and other anticholinergics (atropine).

There are no known unique or unanticipated drug-drug interactions with other agents except that glycopyrrolate injectable should be used with caution, if at all, during cyclopropane anesthesia (see Precautions).

Supplied: Each mL of solution contains: glycopyrrolate 0.2 mg. Nonmedicinal ingredients: benzyl alcohol, hydrochloric acid, sodium hydroxide and water for injection. Vials of 2 mL. Multiple dose vials of 20 mL.

Need a manufacturer's address? Use the YELLOW SECTION.

ROBITUSSIN®
ROBITUSSIN® DM
ROBITUSSIN® COUGH & COLD
ROBITUSSIN® EXTRA STRENGTH
ROBITUSSIN® EXTRA STRENGTH DM
ROBITUSSIN® EXTRA STRENGTH COUGH & COLD
ROBITUSSIN® PEDIATRIC
ROBITUSSIN® PEDIATRIC COUGH & COLD

Whitehall-Robins

Guaifenesin
Guaifenesin—Dextromethorphan HBr
Guaifenesin—Dextromethorphan HBr—Pseudoephedrine HCl
Guaifenesin
Guaifenesin—Dextromethorphan HBr
Guaifenesin—Dextromethorphan HBr—Pseudoephedrine HCl
Dextromethorphan HBr
Dextromethorphan HBr—Pseudoephedrine HCl

Expectorant
Expectorant—Antitussive
Expectorant—Antitussive—Decongestant
Expectorant
Expectorant—Antitussive
Expectorant—Antitussive—Decongestant
Antitussive
Antitussive—Decongestant

Pharmacology: Guaifenesin, as the expectorant, enhances the output of lower respiratory tract fluid. The enhanced flow of less viscid secretions promotes ciliary action, and facilitates the removal of inspissated mucus. As a result, dry, unproductive coughs become more productive and less frequent.

Dextromethorphan is a synthetic, non-narcotic, centrally-acting cough suppressant. The antitussive effectiveness of dextromethorphan has been demonstrated in both animal and human clinical studies, and the incidence of toxic effects has been remarkably low.

Pseudoephedrine produces vasoconstriction resulting in a nasal decongestant effect.

Indications: For the management of coughs associated with cold, bronchitis, laryngitis, tracheitis, pharyngitis and influenza.

Contraindications: Hypersensitivity to guaifenesin, dextromethorphan or sympathomimetic amines; marked hypertension; patients who are receiving MAO inhibitors should not take Robitussin DM, Cough & Cold, Extra Strength DM, Extra Strength Cough & Cold, Pediatric or Pediatric Cough & Cold.

Patients with diabetes, heart or thyroid disease, high blood pressure, glaucoma or difficulty in urination due to prostate enlargement should not take Robitussin Cough & Cold, Extra Strength Cough & Cold or Pediatric Cough & Cold.

Precautions: Before prescribing medication to suppress or modify cough, it is important to ascertain that the underlying cause of the cough is identified, that modification of the cough does not increase the risk of clinical or physiologic complications, and that appropriate therapy for the primary disease is provided.

If cough worsens, lasts for more than 1 week or is accompanied by high fever, or in patients with hypertension, consult a physician. Do not exceed recommended dosage. Keep safely out of reach of children.

Adverse Effects: The following may possibly occur: Robitussin, Robitussin Extra-Strength: nausea, gastrointestinal upset, drowsiness.

Robitussin Cough & Cold, Robitussin Extra-Strength Cough & Cold: nausea, vomiting, dry mouth, nervousness, insomnia.

Robitussin DM, Robitussin Extra Strength DM: drowsiness, dizziness, nausea, vomiting, confusion.

Robitussin (cont'd)

Robtiussin Pediatric: drowsiness, dizziness, nausea, vomiting, stomach ache.
Robitussin Pediatric Cough & Cold: drowsiness, dizziness, nausea, vomiting, stomach ache, insomnia, confusion, CNS stimulation, muscular weakness, dry mouth, palpitation, difficulty in micturition.

Dosage: Robitussin: Take every 6 hours as follows: Adults 12 years and over: 10 to 20 mL. Children 6 to under 12 years: 5 mL. Children 2 to under 6 years: 2.5 mL. Children under 2 years: consult a physician.

Robitussin DM and Cough & Cold: Take every 6 to 8 hours as follows: Adults 12 years and over: 10 mL. Children 6 to under 12 years: 5 mL. Children 2 to under 6 years: 2.5 mL. Children under 2 years: consult a physician.

Robitussin Extra Strength, Extra Strength DM and Extra Strength Cough & Cold: Take every 6 to 8 hours as follows: Adults 12 years and over: 10 mL. Children 6 to under 12 years: 5 mL.

Robitussin Pediatric and Pediatric Cough & Cold: Take every 6 to 8 hours as follows: Adults 12 years and over: 20 mL. Children 6 to 12 years: 10 mL. Children 2 to under 6 years: 5 mL. Children under 2 years: consult a physician.

Supplied: Robitussin: Each 5 mL of red, cherry-flavored syrup contains: guaifenesin 100 mg. Nonmedicinal ingredients: alcohol, caramel color, citric acid, flavor, glycerin, invert sugar, FD&C Red No. 40, sodium benzoate, sodium chloride and water. Energy: 15.3 kJ (3.7 kcal). Sodium: <1 mmol (2.8 mg). Bottles of 100 and 250 mL.

Robitussin DM: Each 5 mL of red, cherry-flavored syrup contains: guaifenesin 100 mg and dextromethorphan HBr 15 mg. Nonmedicinal ingredients: alcohol, citric acid, flavors, FD&C Red No. 40, FD&C Yellow No. 6, glycerin, invert sugar, sodium benzoate and water. Energy: 12.4 kJ (3.0 kcal). Sodium: <1 mmol (0.8 mg). Bottles of 100 and 250 mL.

Robitussin Cough & Cold: Each 5 mL of pink, cherry-flavored syrup contains: guaifenesin 100 mg, pseudoephedrine HCl 30 mg and dextromethorphan HBr 15 mg. Nonmedicinal ingredients: alcohol, citric acid, flavors, D&C Red No. 33, FD&C Red No. 40, glycerin, invert sugar, sodium benzoate, maltol and water. Energy: 17.6 kJ (4.2 kcal). Sodium: <1 mmol (0.8 mg). Bottles of 100 and 250 mL.

Robitussin Extra Strength: Each 5 mL of red, cherry-flavored syrup contains: guaifenesin 200 mg. Nonmedicinal ingredients: citric acid, corn syrup, FD&C Red No. 40, flavors, glycerin, polyethylene glycol, propylene glycol, sodium benzoate, sodium carboxymethylcellulose, sodium saccharin, sorbitol and water. Energy: 49 kJ (11.7 kcal). Sodium: <1 mmol (4.1 mg). Bottles of 100 and 250 mL.

Robitussin Extra Strength Cough & Cold: Each 5 mL of red, cherry-flavored syrup contains: guaifenesin 200 mg, dextromethorphan HBr 15 mg, pseudoephedrine HCl 30 mg. Nonmedicinal ingredients: citric acid, corn syrup, FD&C Red No. 40, flavors, glycerin, polyethylene glycol, propylene glycol, sodium benzoate, sodium carboxymethylcellulose, sodium saccharin, sorbitol and water. Energy: 49 kJ (11.7 kcal). Sodium: <1 mmol (4.1 mg). Bottles of 100 and 250 mL.

Robitussin Extra Strength DM: Each 5 mL of red, cherry-flavored syrup contains: guaifenesin 200 mg, dextromethorphan HBr 15 mg. Nonmedicinal ingredients: citric acid, corn syrup, FD&C Red No. 40, flavors, glycerin, maltol, polyethylene glycol, propylene glycol, sodium benzoate, sodium carboxymethylcellulose, sodium saccharin, sorbitol and water. Energy: 49 kJ (11.7 kcal). Sodium: <1 mmol (4.1 mg). Bottles of 100 and 250 mL.

Robitussin Pediatric: Each 5 mL of red, cherry-flavored syrup contains: dextromethorphan HBr 7.5 mg. Nonmedicinal ingredients: citric acid, flavors, FD&C Red No. 40, glycerin, propylene glycol, sodium benzoate, sodium cyclamate, sorbitol and water. Energy: 14.8 kJ (3.5 kcal). Sodium: <1 mmol (9.3 mg). Bottles of 100 mL.

Robitussin Pediatric Cough & Cold: Each 5 mL of red, cherry-flavored syrup contains: dextromethorphan HBr 7.5 mg and pseudoephedrine HCl 15 mg. Nonmedicinal ingredients: citric acid, FD&C Red No. 40, flavors, glycerin, propylene glycol, sodium benzoate, sodium saccharin, sorbitol and water. Energy: 23.6 kJ (5.6 kcal). Sodium: <1 mmol (1.7 mg). Bottles of 100 mL.

Store at room temperature (15 to 30°C).

Reviewed 1998

ROBITUSSIN® AC Ⓝ
ROBITUSSIN® with Codeine Ⓝ

Whitehall-Robins

Guaifenesin—Codeine Phosphate—Pheniramine Maleate

Expectorant—Antitussive—Antihistamine

Indications: To facilitate expectoration and control cough associated with inflamed mucosa.

Contraindications: Hypersensitivity to codeine, guaifenesin or pheniramine, or pre-existing respiratory depression.

Precautions: Before prescribing medication to suppress or modify cough, it is important to ascertain that the underlying cause of the cough is identified, that modification of the cough does not increase the risk of clinical or physiologic complications, and that appropriate therapy for the primary disease is provided.

In young children the respiratory centre is especially susceptible to the depressant action of narcotics. Benefit to risk ratio should be carefully considered especially in children with respiratory embarrassment, e.g., croup. Estimation of dosage relative to the child's age and weight is of great importance.

Tolerance, psychological dependence and physical dependence may develop in patients receiving codeine phosphate over a prolonged period.

Use with extreme caution in patients having an acute asthmatic attack, patients with chronic obstructive pulmonary disease or cor pulmonale, patients having a substantially decreased respiratory reserve and patients with pre-existing respiratory depression, hypoxia or hypercapnia. Usual therapeutic doses may decrease respiratory drive while simultaneously increasing airway resistance to the point of apnea. In patients with asthma or pulmonary emphysema, codeine may, due to its drying action on the respiratory mucosa, increase viscosity of bronchial secretions and suppress the cough reflex.

Use with caution in sedated or debilitated patients, in patients who have undergone thoracotomies or laparotomies, since suppression of the cough reflex may lead to retention of secretions postoperatively in these patients.

The respiratory depressant effects of codeine and its capacity to elevate cerebrospinal fluid pressure may be markedly exaggerated in the presence of head injury or intracranial lesions or pre-existing increase in intracranial pressure. Narcotics produce adverse reactions which may obscure the clinical course of a patient with head injuries. In such patients, codeine must be used with extreme caution and only if its use is deemed essential.

Use with caution in patients with seizures as the seizures may be exacerbated or induced by opioids.

Use with caution in patients with cardiac arrhythmias due to the cholinergic effects of the drug.

Codeine should be given with caution and the initial dose should be reduced in certain patients such as the debilitated and those with severe impairment of hepatic or renal function, hypothyroidism, Addison's disease, prostatic hypertrophy or urethral stricture.

Geriatrics: Elderly patients may be more susceptible to the adverse effects of codeine, especially respiratory depression. Use with caution; the initial dose should be reduced and the effects monitored.

The administration of codeine or other narcotics may obscure the diagnosis or clinical course in patients with acute abdominal conditions.

Codeine should not be used in patients with diarrhea associated with pseudomembranous colitis.

Use with caution in patients with acute ulcerative colitis or other severe inflammatory bowel disease due to the risk of toxic megacolon.

Caution should be exercised and dosage may need to be reduced when administered with other drugs that depress the CNS (including alcohol), with MAO inhibitors, phenothiazines or tricyclic antidepressants.

Do not administer to patients with glaucoma or prostate enlargement.

Occupational Hazards: Warn patients against driving or operating machinery if they become drowsy or show impaired mental and/or physical abilities while taking codeine.

Pregnancy: Since codeine phosphate crosses the placental barrier, its use in pregnancy is not recommended.

Lactation: Codeine is excreted in small amounts which are probably insignificant with usual analgesic or antitussive doses.

Adverse Effects: Adverse reactions due to codeine phosphate may include drowsiness, nausea, vomiting and constipation. Infrequent adverse effects include palpitation, dry mouth, skin rash, pruritus and, rarely, hyperhidrosis and agitation have been reported. Respiratory depression is seen in higher dosage, and there is a potential for tolerance, psychological dependence or physical dependence to occur.

Overdose: Symptoms: May result in euphoria, dysphoria, visual disturbances, hypotension and coma or death from respiratory depression.

Treatment: Symptomatic and supportive therapy. Maintain ventilation and administer oxygen as needed. The narcotic antagonist naloxone should be administered. If the patient is conscious and has not lost the gag reflex, empty the stomach by inducing emesis with ipecac syrup. If the patient is extremely drowsy, unconscious, convulsing or has no gag reflex, perform gastric lavage. Follow with activated charcoal (50 to 100 g in adults) and a cathartic.

Dosage: Robitussin AC: Take every 4 to 6 hours as follows: Adults 12 years and over: 5 to 10 mL. Children 6 to under 12 years: 2.5 to 5 mL. Children 2 to under 6 years: Consult physician. Children under 2 years: Not recommended.
Robitussin with Codeine: Take every 4 to 6 hours as follows: Adults 12 years and over: 15 mL. Children 6 to 12 years: 7.5 mL. Children 2 to 6 years: Consult a physician. Children under 2 years: Not recommended.

Supplied: Robitussin AC: Each 5 mL of orange, cherry-flavored syrup contains: guaifenesin 100 mg, codeine phosphate 10 mg and pheniramine maleate 7.5 mg. Nonmedicinal ingredients: alcohol, caramel, citric acid, FD&C Red No. 40, FD&C yellow No. 6, flavors, glycerin, invert sugar, sodium benzoate and water. Energy: 15 kJ (3.6 kcal). Sodium: <1 mmol (0.8 mg). Bottles of 100 and 500 mL and 1 L.

Robitussin with Codeine: Each 5 mL of red, cherry-flavored syrup contains: codeine phosphate 3.3 mg, guaifenesin 100 mg and pheniramine maleate 7.5 mg. Nonmedicinal ingredients: alcohol, citric acid, D&C Red No. 33, FD&C Blue No. 1, FD&C Yellow No. 6, flavors, glycerin, invert sugar, sodium benzoate and water. Energy: 15 kJ (3.6 kcal). Sodium: <1 mmol (0.8 mg). Bottles of 100 and 250 mL.

Store at room temperature (15 to 30°C).

ROBITUSSIN® COUGH & COLD LIQUI-GELS®
ROBITUSSIN® COUGH, COLD & FLU LIQUI-GELS®

Whitehall-Robins

Guaifenesin—Pseudoephedrine HCl—Dextromethorphan HBr

Guaifenesin—Pseudoephedrine HCl—Dextromethorphan HBr—Acetaminophen

Expectorant—Antitussive—Decongestant

Expectorant—Antitussive—Decongestant—Analgesic

Pharmacology: Guaifenesin, as the expectorant, enhances the output of lower respiratory tract fluid. The enhanced flow of less viscid secretions promotes ciliary action, and facilitates the removal of inspissated mucus. As a result, dry, unproductive coughs become more productive and less frequent.

Dextromethorphan is a synthetic, non-narcotic, centrally-acting cough suppressant. The antitussive effectiveness of dextromethorphan has been demonstrated in both animal and clinical studies, and the incidence of toxic effects has been remarkably low.

Pseudoephedrine produces vasoconstriction resulting in a nasal decongestant effect.

Indications: For the management of coughs associated with cold, bronchitis, laryngitis, tracheitis, pharyngitis and influenza.

Contraindications: Hypersensitivity to guaifenesin, dextromethorphan, pseudoephedrine or acetaminophen; marked hypertension, patients who receive MAO inhibitors or medication for high blood pressure should not take these products. Patients with diabetes, heart or thyroid disease, high blood pressure, glaucoma or prostate enlargement should not take these products. Patients with impaired liver or kidney or alcohol dependency should not take Robitussin Cough, Cold & Flu Liqui-Gels.

Precautions: Before prescribing medication to suppress or modify cough, it is important to ascertain that the underlying cause of the cough is identified, that modification of the cough does not increase the risk of clinical or physiologic complications, and that appropriate therapy for the primary disease is provided.

If cough worsens, lasts for more than 1 week or is accompanied by high fever, or in patients with hypertension, consult a physician. Do not exceed recommended dosage. Keep safely out of reach of children.

Adverse Effects: Robitussin Cough & Cold Liqui-Gels: As with other products containing sympathomimetic amines, headache, dizziness, insomnia, tremor, confusion, CNS stimulation, muscular weakness, dry mouth, nausea, vomiting, difficulty in micturition, palpitation, tightness in the chest and syncope may be encountered.
Robitussin Cough, Cold & Flu Liqui-Gels: In addition to the above, allergic reaction such as rash or itching may occur.

Dosage: Robitussin Cough & Cold Liqui-Gels: To be taken every 6 hours as follows: Children under 6 years: on the advice of a physician. Children 6 to 12 years: 1 capsule. Adults and children over 12 years: 2 capsules. Maximum 4 doses/day.
Robitussin Cough, Cold & Flu Liqui-Gels: To be taken every 4 hours as follows: Children under 6 years: on the advice of a physician. Children 6 to 12 years: 1 capsule. Adults and children over 12 years: 2 capsules. Maximum 4 doses/day.

Supplied: Robitussin Cough & Cold Liqui-Gels: Each red capsule contains: guaifenesin 200 mg, dextromethorphan HBr 10 mg and pseudoephedrine HCl 30 mg. Nonmedicinal ingredients: FD&C Blue No. 1, FD&C Red No. 40, gelatin, glycerin, pharmaceutical shellac, polyethylene glycol, povidone, propylene glycol, sorbitol and titanium dioxide. Energy: 5.2 kJ (1.24 kcal). Alcohol-, bisulfite-, gluten-, lactose-, parabens-, sodium- and tartrazine-free. Blister packs of 12.

Robitussin Cough, Cold & Flu Liqui-Gels: Each yellow capsule contains: guaifenesin 100 mg, dextromethorphan HBr 10 mg, pseudoephedrine HCl 30 mg and acetaminophen 250 mg. Nonmedicinal ingredients: D&C Yellow No. 10, FD&C Red No. 40, gelatin, glycerin, iron oxide, lecithin, polyethylene glycol, povidone, propylene glycol, simethicone and water. Energy: 5.7 kJ (1.36 kcal). Blister packs of 12.

Reviewed 1997

ROCALTROL® ℞
Roche

Calcitriol
Vitamin D₃ Metabolite

Pharmacology: The supply of vitamin D in man depends on dietary intake and/or exposure to the ultraviolet rays of the sun for conversion of 7-dehydrocholesterol to vitamin D_3 (cholecalciferol). Vitamin D_3 (cholecalciferol) must be metabolized in the liver and the kidneys before it is fully active on its target tissues. The initial transformation is catalyzed by a vitamin D_3-25-hydroxylase enzyme (25-OH-ase) present in the liver, and the product of this reaction is 25-hydroxy-vitamin D_3 (25-OH-D_3). The latter undergoes hydroxylation in the mitochondria of kidney tissue. This reaction is activated by the renal 25-hydroxy-vitamin D_3-1 alphahydroxylase (alpha-OH-ase) to produce 1,25-$(OH)_2D_3$ (calcitriol).

Calcitriol's two known sites of action are intestine and bone, but additional evidence suggests that it also acts on the kidney and the parathyroid gland.

In acutely uremic rats, calcitriol stimulates calcium absorption. It is the most active known form of vitamin D_3 in stimulating intestinal calcium transport. This agent also promotes the intestinal absorption of phosphorus through stimulation of an active transport system distinct from the calcium transport process.

Calcitriol stimulates bone resorption which serves to mobilize calcium for the circulation, when an intestinal source of calcium is absent. This effect is related to the role of vitamin D in maintaining the homeostasis of calcium and phosphorus in plasma. In addition, calcitriol may interact directly with osteoblasts.

Calcitriol's effects on the renal transport of calcium and phosphate appear to be influenced by the presence or absence of the parathyroid glands, vitamin D status, volume expansion and the dose of vitamin D metabolite used. With the available information it is not possible to determine which vitamin D metabolite, if any, influences divalent ion transport by the renal tubule under physiologic conditions or if so, whether an interaction with parathyroid hormone is required.

The presence of a direct negative feedback effect of calcitriol on the parathyroid gland has been suspected. Some investigators have postulated that calcitriol may exert a direct influence on the parathyroids. Although inhibition of PTH secretion by calcitriol has been demonstrated in vitro, the data obtained from in vivo studies are more equivocal.

Indications: The management of hypocalcemia and osteodystrophy in patients with chronic renal failure undergoing dialysis. Hypocalcemia and its clinical manifestations associated with: postsurgical hypoparathyroidism, idiopathic hypoparathyroidism, pseudohypoparathyroidism. Vitamin D resistant rickets (familial hypophosphatemia).

Contraindications: Hypersensitivity to calcitriol, vitamin D or its analogues and derivatives; hypercalcemia; evidence of vitamin D overdosage.

Warnings: Since calcitriol is a potent cholecalciferol derivative with profound effects on intestinal absorption of dietary calcium and inorganic phosphate, it should not be used concomitantly with other vitamin D products or their derivatives.

Calcitriol therapy should only be considered when adequate laboratory facilities for monitoring of blood and urine chemistries are available. During treatment, progressive hypercalcemia, either due to hyper-responsiveness or overdosage, may become so severe as to require emergency treatment.

Chronic hypercalcemia can lead to generalized vascular calcification, nephrocalcinosis, calcifications of the cornea or other soft tissues. During calcitriol treatment, **the serum total calcium (mg/dL) times serum inorganic phosphate product (CaxP) should not exceed 70.**

Dialysate calcium level of 7 mg % or above in addition to excessive dietary calcium supplements may lead to frequent episodes of hypercalcemia.

In patients on digitalis, hypercalcemia may precipitate cardiac arrhythmias; in such patients, use calcitriol with extreme caution.

To control serum inorganic phosphate levels and dietary phosphate absorption in patients undergoing dialysis, oral aluminum carbonate or aluminum hydroxide gel must be used. Magnesium containing antacids may contribute towards hypermagnesemia in patients on chronic renal dialysis and should be avoided during calcitriol therapy.

Pregnancy: Safety in women who are or may become pregnant has not been established; use of calcitriol in these cases may be considered only when the potential benefits have been weighed against possible hazards to mother and fetus.

Lactation: Since calcitriol may be excreted in human milk, avoid breast feeding during treatment.

Precautions: Patient selection and follow-up: Patients with renal osteodystrophy and hypocalcemia, poorly managed by conventional vitamin D therapy are likely to respond to calcitriol. The desired therapeutic margin of calcitriol is narrow; therefore, determine the optimal daily dose carefully for each patient by dose titration to obtain satisfactory response in the biochemical parameters and clinical manifestations (see Dosage).

Excessive dosage of calcitriol induces hypercalcemia and hypercalciuria; therefore, early in treatment during dosage adjustment determine serum calcium at least twice weekly. A fall in serum alkaline phosphatase values may indicate impending hypercalcemia. Should hypercalcemia develop, discontinue the drug immediately until the serum calcium has normalized. This may take several days to a week.

In patients with normal renal function, chronic hypercalcemia may be associated with an increase in serum creatinine. While the elevation of serum creatinine is usually reversible, it is important in such patients to pay careful attention to those factors which may lead to hypercalcemia. Therapy should always be started at the lowest possible dose and increased with careful monitoring of serum calcium concentrations. An estimate of daily dietary calcium intake should be made and the intake adjusted when indicated.

Patients with normal renal function should avoid dehydration. Adequate fluid intake should be maintained.

Patients with vitamin D resistant rickets (familial hypophosphatemia) should pursue their oral phosphate therapy. However, the possible stimulation of intestinal phosphate absorption should be taken into account since this effect may modify the requirement for phosphate supplements.

Essential laboratory tests: Serum calcium, inorganic phosphorus, magnesium, alkaline phosphatase as well as 24 hour urinary calcium and phosphorus should be determined periodically during calcitriol maintenance therapy. During the initial phase of the medication, determine serum calcium more frequently (at least twice weekly). Periodic ophthalmological examinations and radiological evaluation of suspected anatomical regions for early detection of ectopic calcifications are advisable.

Drug Interactions: Hypercalcemia in patients on digitalis may precipitate cardiac arrhythmias. Intestinal absorption of calcitriol may be impaired by resins such as cholestyramine and by use of mineral oil as a laxative. Although the precise mechanism involved is unknown, long-term anticonvulsant treatment, particularly with phenytoin and barbiturates, may interfere with the actions of vitamin D. Patients under concurrent treatment with such agents may require slightly higher doses of calcitriol.

Information for the Patient: Inform the patient and his or her immediate relatives about the need for compliance with dosage instructions, strict adherence to prescribed calcium intake, dietary and supplementary, and avoidance of unapproved nonprescription drugs or medications. Patients should also be made aware of the symptoms of hypercalcemia and should seek medical attention if such symptoms are noted (see Adverse Effects).

Adverse Effects: Most frequent: hypercalcemia (20 to 30%). Less frequent: headache, nausea, vomiting, constipation, abdominal cramps, pruritus, conjunctivitis, agitation, extremity pain, apprehension, polyuria, insomnia, elevated AST and/or ALT, elevated alkaline phosphatase, hypercalciuria, hypermagnesemia, hyperphosphatemia, elevated lymphocytes, elevated hematocrit, elevated neutrophils, elevated hemoglobin.

The adverse effects of calcitriol are, in general, similar to those encountered with excessive vitamin D intake. The early and late signs and symptoms associated with vitamin D intoxication and hypercalcemia are:

a. Early: weakness, headache, somnolence, nausea, cardiac arrhythmias, excessive thirst, vomiting, dry mouth, constipation, muscle pain, bone pain, metallic taste.

b. Late: polyuria, polydipsia, anorexia, weight loss, nocturia, conjunctivitis (calcific), pancreatitis, photophobia, rhinorrhea, pruritus, hyperthermia, decreased libido, elevated BUN, albuminuria, hypercholesterolemia, elevated AST and ALT, ectopic calcification, hypertension, cardiac arrhythmias, and rarely, overt psychosis.

Overdose: Symptoms: Calcitriol administration to patients in excess of their daily requirements can cause hypercalcemia, hypercalciuria and hyperphosphatemia. Conversely, high calcium and phosphate intake concomitantly with therapeutic doses of calcitriol may cause similar abnormalities. In dialysis patients, high levels of calcium in the dialysis bath may contribute to hypercalcemia.

Treatment: Accidental Overdosage: Employ general supportive measures. If drug ingestion is discovered within a relatively short time, induction of emesis or gastric lavage may be of benefit in preventing further absorption. If the drug has passed through the stomach, mineral oil administration may promote fecal elimination. Obtain serial serum electrolyte determinations (especially calcium ion), rate of urinary calcium excretion and assessment of ECG abnormalities due to hypercalcemia. Such monitoring is critical in patients receiving digitalis. Discontinuation of supplemental calcium and low calcium diet are also indicated in accidental overdosage. Due to the relatively short pharmacological action of calcitriol, further measures are probably unnecessary. Should, however, persistent and markedly elevated serum calcium concentrations occur, a variety of therapeutic alternatives may be considered, depending on the patient's underlying condition. These include the use of drugs such as phosphates and corticosteroids as well as measures to induce an appropriate forced diuresis. Peritoneal dialysis has been used against a calcium-free dialysate.

Treatment of Hypercalcemia in Patients undergoing Hemodialysis: General treatment of hypercalcemia (more than 1 mg/dL or 0.25 mmol/L above the upper limit of the normal range) consists of immediate discontinuation of calcitriol therapy, institution of a low calcium diet and withdrawal of calcium supplements. Determine serum calcium concentrations daily until normocalcemia ensues. Hypercalcemia frequently resolves in 2 to 7 days. When serum calcium concentrations have returned to within normal limits, calcitriol therapy may be reinstituted at a dose of 0.25 μg/day less than prior therapy. Monitor serum calcium concentrations carefully (at least twice weekly) during this period of dosage adjustment and subsequent dosage titration. Correct persistent or markedly elevated serum calcium concentrations by dialysis against a calcium-free dialysate.

Dosage: Determine the optimum daily dose carefully for each patient. The effectiveness of calcitriol therapy is predicated on the assumption that each patient is receiving an adequate daily calcium intake. The recommended daily intake for calcium is in the order of 800 mg for adults and 350 mg for infants during the first 6 months of life.

To ensure an adequate daily calcium intake, instruct patients regarding appropriate dietary measures or prescribe a calcium

Rocaltrol (cont'd)

supplement. However, because of improved calcium absorption from the gastrointestinal tract, some patients may be maintained on a lower calcium intake or no supplementation at all.

Dialysis Patients: Adults: Titration: Initial calcitriol dose is 0.25 μg/day. If a satisfactory response in the biochemical parameters and clinical manifestations of the disease state is not observed, dosage may be increased by 0.25 μg/day at 2 to 4 week intervals. During this titration period, obtain serum calcium levels at least twice weekly, and if hypercalcemia is noted, discontinue the drug immediately until normocalcemia ensues.

Maintenance: Patients with normal or only slightly reduced serum calcium levels may respond to calcitriol at doses of 0.25 μg every other day. Most patients undergoing hemodialysis respond to between 0.5 and 1 μg/day.

In order to decrease the risk of hypercalcemic episodes, a downward adjustment of the calcitriol dose may be advisable once a reduction in serum alkaline phosphatase has been achieved.

Hypoparathyroidism and Vitamin D Resistant Rickets:

Adults: Initial dose: 0.25 μg/day. If a satisfactory response in the biochemical parameters and clinical manifestations of the disease are not observed, the dose may be increased by 0.25 μg/day at 2 to 4 week intervals. During the dosage titration period, serum calcium levels should be measured at least twice weekly and, if hypercalcemia is present, calcitriol should be immediately discontinued until normocalcemia ensues. Consideration should also be given to lowering the calcium intake.

Malabsorption is occasionally noted in patients with hypoparathyroidism; hence, larger doses may be needed.

Children: Initiation of Treatment: x-linked hypophosphatemic rickets: 0.01 to 0.02 μg/kg/day (mean 0.018 μg/kg/day).

Vitamin D dependency rickets type 1: 0.010 to 0.025 μg/kg/day (mean 0.017 μg/kg/day).

Hypoparathyroidism: 0.03 to 0.05 μg/kg/day (mean 0.04 μg/kg/day).

Response is checked after 2 weeks to ascertain that the dose has not produced hypercalcemia. Biochemical evaluation should include serum calcium (total and ionized if available), phosphate, alkaline phosphatase, and creatinine. If satisfactory biochemical improvement has not occurred, the dose is increased by about 25% and the effect re-evaluated in 2 weeks. Until the desired response to treatment is achieved, the dose is gradually increased or decreased in this manner. Improvement in the radiographic lesions of rickets takes several weeks to become apparent.

For severely hypocalcemic or symptomatic patients, an initial dose as high as 0.05 μg/kg/day may be used to treat the hypocalcemia. In this situation, the serum calcium concentration should be monitored very closely (hospitalization recommended), and as soon as the patient is out of danger from hypocalcemia, the dose reduced.

Maintenance: x-linked hypophosphatemic rickets=0.01 to 0.05 μg/kg/day (mean 0.022 μg/kg/day).

Vitamin D dependency rickets type 1=0.0046 to 0.015 μg/kg/day.

Hypoparathyroidism=0.014 to 0.040 μg/kg/day (mean 0.025 μg/kg/day).

Assessment of serum calcium (total and ionized), phosphate, alkaline phosphatase and creatinine should be made at 3 to 4 month intervals once treatment has been established and for as long as the medication is administered.

Hypercalcemia can occur at any time while the patient is treated with Calcitriol (even if the dose has not been changed). Patients with rachitic or osteomalacic bone changes may become hypercalcemic as the bones become remineralized and therefore take up less calcium from the blood. To decrease the risk of hypercalcemia, a downward adjustment of the calcitriol dose may be advisable once a reduction in serum alkaline phosphatase has been achieved.

The single most important indicator of calcitriol overdose appears to be hypercalcemia as determined by accurate and frequent measurement of the serum calcium concentration. Signs of hypercalcemia such as polyuria, nocturia, polydipsia, nausea, vomiting, anorexia, weight loss, and constipation should be watched for but are less sensitive indicators of toxicity. Most hypercalcemic patients are asymptomatic.

If hypercalcemia occurs, calcitriol is discontinued for 1 to 2 weeks or until hypercalcemia disappears. Hypercalcemia frequently resolves in 2 to 7 days. Therapy is then resumed with a dose about 25% lower than that which caused intoxication.

If the dose has been increased or decreased for any reason, the calcium level should be re-evaluated at 2-week intervals.

Fasting urine samples for measurement of calcium/creatinine ratio may be used to monitor the development of hypercalciuria.

Kidney ultrasounds may be indicated yearly during calcitriol therapy. However, the clinical significance of the finding of nephrocalcinosis is not known.

Calcitriol solution must be measured accurately and can be administered directly into the mouth of the infant. The bottle should be closed tightly each time after use, and when stored between 15 and 30°C and protected from light, the solution is stable for 6 weeks after opening.

Supplied: Capsules: 0.25 μg: Each white/brownish-red oval soft gelatin capsule contains: calcitriol 0.25 μg. Energy: 6.5 kJ (1.5 kcal). Nonmedicinal ingredients: butylated hydroxyanisole, butylated hydroxytoluene, canthaxanthin, fractionated coconut oil, gelatin, glycerin hydrogenated partially hydrolyzed starch and titanium dioxide. Alcohol-, gluten-, lactose-, sulfite- and tartrazine-free. Bottles of 100.

0.50 μg: Each brownish-red oval soft gelatin capsule contains: calcitriol 0.50 μg. Energy: 6.5 kJ (1.5 kcal). Nonmedicinal ingredients: butylated hydroxyanisole, butylated hydroxytoluene, canthaxanthin, fractionated coconut oil, gelatin, glycerin hydrogenated partially hydrolyzed starch and titanium dioxide. Alcohol-, gluten-, lactose-, sulfite- and tartrazine-free. Bottles of 100.

Solution: Each mL of clear, colorless, oily solution contains: calcitriol 1.0 μg. Nonmedicinal ingredients: butylated hydroxyanisole, butylated hydroxytoluene and fractionated coconut oil. Bottles of 10 mL, boxes of 5.

Store capsules and solution at 15 to 30°C and protect from light. Discard solution 6 weeks after first opening the bottle.

(Shown in Product Recognition Section)

ROCEPHIN® Ⓟ
Roche

Ceftriaxone Sodium
Antibiotic

Pharmacology: In vitro studies indicate that the bactericidal action of ceftriaxone results from the inhibition of cell-wall synthesis. In E. coli, ceftriaxone showed a high affinity for penicillin binding proteins (PBP) 1a and 3 and a moderate affinity for 1b and 2. In H. influenzae, the highest affinity was shown for PBP 4 and PBP 5. The binding affinity to PBP 4 was 35 fold that of PBP 3, ten fold that of PBP 2 and approximately 100 fold that of PBP 1. The morphological changes resulting from the PBP binding include filament formation or cell wall and septal thickening, and then cell lysis.

Indications: The treatment of the following infections when caused by susceptible strains of the designated microorganisms:

Lower Respiratory Tract Infections: caused by E. coli, H. influenzae, K. pneumoniae and species, S. aureus, S. pneumoniae and species (excluding enterococci).

Urinary tract Infections (complicated and uncomplicated): caused by E. coli, Klebsiella species, P. mirabilis and P. vulgaris.

Bacterial Septicemia: caused by E. coli, H. influenzae, K. pneumoniae, S. aureus and S. pneumoniae, (excluding enterococci).

Skin and Skin Structure Infections: caused by K. pneumoniae and species, P. mirabilis, S. aureus, S. epidermidis and Streptococcus species (excluding enterococci).

Bone and Joint Infections: caused by S. aureus, S. pneumoniae and Streptococcus species (excluding enterococci).

Intra-Abdominal Infections: caused by E. coli and K. pneumoniae.

Meningitis: caused by H. influenzae, N. meningitidis, and S. pneumoniae. Ceftriaxone should not be used for the treatment of meningitis caused by L. monocytogenes.

Uncomplicated Gonorrhea (cervical/urethral, pharyngeal and rectal): caused by N. gonorrhoeae (penicillinase and nonpenicillinase producing strains).

Susceptibility Testing: Specimens for bacteriologic culture should be obtained prior to therapy in order to identify the causative organisms and to determine their susceptibilities to ceftriaxone. Therapy may be instituted before results of susceptibility testing are known. However, modification of the treatment may be required once these results become available.

Prophylaxis: The preoperative administration of a single 1 g dose of ceftriaxone may reduce the incidence of postoperative infections in patients undergoing vaginal or abdominal hysterectomy, coronary artery bypass surgery, or in patients at risk of infection undergoing biliary tract surgery. If signs of post surgical infection should appear, specimens for culture should be obtained for identification of the causitive organism(s) so that the appropriate therapy may be instituted.

Contraindications: Known allergy to ceftriaxone, other cephalosporins or penicillins.

Warnings: Before therapy is instituted, careful inquiry should be made concerning previous hypersensitivity reactions to ceftriaxone, other cephalosporins, penicillins or other allergens. Ceftriaxone should only be administered with caution to any patient who has demonstrated any form of allergy particularly to drugs. Serious, and occasionally fatal hypersensitivity (anaphylactoid) reactions have been reported in patients receiving cephalosporins. The reactions are more likely to occur in persons with a history of sensitivity to multiple allergens. Ceftriaxone should be administered with caution to patients with type I hypersensitivity reaction to penicillin. If an allergic reaction occurs, the administration of ceftriaxone should be discontinued and appropriate therapy instituted.

Pseudomembranous colitis has been reported with the use of ceftriaxone (and with broad-spectrum and other antibiotics). Therefore, it is important to consider its diagnosis in patients who develop diarrhea. Treatment with broad-spectrum antibiotics, including ceftriaxone, alters the normal flora of the colon and may permit overgrowth of Clostridia. Studies indicate that a toxin produced by C. difficile is one primary cause of antibiotic-associated colitis. Mild cases of colitis may respond to drug discontinuation alone. Moderate to severe cases should be managed with fluid, electrolyte, and protein supplementation as indicated. When the colitis is not relieved by discontinuation of ceftriaxone administration or when it is severe, consideration should be given to the administration of vancomycin or other suitable therapy. Other possible causes of the colitis should also be considered.

There have been reports of sonographic abnormalities in the gallbladder of patients treated with ceftriaxone; some of these patients also had symptoms of gallbladder disease. These abnormalities appear on sonography as an echo without acoustical shadowing or as an echo with acoustical shadowing suggesting sludge which may be misinterpreted as gallstones. The chemical nature of the sonographically-detected material has been determined to be predominantly a ceftriaxone-calcium salt. The condition appears to be transient and reversible upon discontinuation of ceftriaxone and institution of conservative management. Therefore, ceftriaxone should be discontinued in patients who develop signs and symptoms suggestive of gallbladder disease and/or sonographic findings described above. The effect of pre-existing gallbladder disease is not known.

Very rare cases of nephrolithiasis (renal precipitation) have been reported, mostly in children older than 3 years and who have been treated with either high daily doses (e.g., ≥80 mg/kg/day) or total doses exceeding 10 g and presenting other risk factors (e.g., fluid restrictions, confinement to bed, etc.). This event may be symptomatic, may lead to renal insufficiency, and appears to be reversible upon discontinuation of ceftriaxone.

Precautions: General: Hypoprothrombinemia and alterations in prothrombin time have occurred rarely (see Adverse Effects). Patients with impaired vitamin K synthesis or low vitamin K stores (e.g. chronic hepatic disease and malnutrition) may require monitoring of hematology and coagulation parameters during treatment.

Vitamin K administration (10 mg weekly) may be necessary if the prothrombin time is prolonged before or during treatment.

Prolonged treatment may result in overgrowth of non-susceptible organisms and organisms initially sensitive to the drug. Development of resistant organisms during the administration of ceftriaxone in clinical trials has been observed in 6% of the 94 patients infected with P. aeruginosa, in 33% of 3 patients infected with Citrobacter species and in 10% of the 10 patients infected with Enterobacter species. If superinfection occurs, appropriate measures should be taken.

Ceftriaxone should be administered with caution to individuals with a history of gastrointestinal disease, particularly colitis.

Renal and Hepatic Impairment: Although transient elevations of BUN and serum creatinine have been observed in clinical studies, there is no other evidence that ceftriaxone, when administered alone, is nephrotoxic.

In severe renal impairment (creatinine clearance of less than 10 mL/min), periodic monitoring of serum ceftriaxone concentrations is recommended. The maximum daily dose should not exceed 2 g. In severe renal impairment associated with clinically significant hepatic impairment, close monitoring of serum ceftriaxone concentrations, at regular intervals, is recommended. If there is evidence of accumulation, dosage should be decreased accordingly.

Drug Interactions: Interactions between ceftriaxone and other drugs have not been fully evaluated.

Pregnancy: Safety in the treatment of infections during pregnancy has not been established. Ceftriaxone should only be used during pregnancy if the likely benefit outweighs the potential risk to the fetus and/or the mother. Ceftriaxone has been detected in the umbilical cord blood, amniotic fluid and placenta. At parturition, 1 hour after a 2 g i.v. dose, average ceftriaxone concentrations in maternal serum, umbilical cord serum, amniotic fluid, and placenta were 106±40 μg/mL, 19.5±11.5 μg/mL, 3.8±3.2 μg/mL and 20.9±4.4 μg/g.

Lactation: Ceftriaxone is excreted in human milk at low concentrations, (e.g. the peak concentration of total drug in milk ranged between 0.45 to 0.65 μg/mL, approximately 5 hours after the administration of 1 g i.v. or i.m.). The clinical significance of this is unknown, therefore, caution should be exercised.

Neonates: Safety in neonates (birth to 1 month of age) has not been established. In vitro studies have shown that ceftriaxone can displace bilirubin from serum albumin. Caution should be exercised when considering ceftriaxone treatment for hyperbilirubinemic neonates especially if premature.

Geriatrics: The elimination of ceftriaxone may be reduced in elderly patients possibly due to impairment of both renal and hepatic function.

Drug-Laboratory Test Interactions: Ceftriaxone may interfere with urine glucose determinations utilizing the copper-reduction test (Clinitest), but not utilizing the glucose-oxidase test (Diastix or Tes-Tape). In patients treated with ceftriaxone the Coombs' test may rarely become false-positive; and ceftriaxone, like other antibiotics, may result in false-positive tests for galactosemia.

Adverse Effects: During clinical trials in postmarketing experience the following adverse reactions have been observed: Clinical Adverse Experiences: Dermatological: rash (1.3%); exanthema, allergic dermatitis and pruritus (0.1 to 1.0%); urticaria (postmarketing reports). Isolated cases of severe cutaneous adverse reactions (erythema multiforme, Stevens Johnson syndrome, or Lyell's syndrome/toxic epidermal necrolysis) have also been reported.

Hematological: anemia (0.1 to 1.0%); auto-immune hemolytic anemia and serum sickness (<0.1%); granulocytopenia (postmarketing reports). Isolated cases of agranulocytosis (<500/mm³) have been reported, most of them after 10 days of treatment and following total doses of 20 g or more.

Hepatic: jaundice, reports (in asymptomatic and symptomatic patients) of ultrasonographic shadows suggesting precipitations in the gallbladder and reports of gallbladder sludge (<0.1%).

Urogenital: moniliasis and vaginitis (0.1 to 1.0%); oliguria and nephrolithiasis (postmarketing reports).

Gastrointestinal: diarrhea (3.3%); nausea, vomiting, dysgeusia and gastric pain (0.1 to 1.0%); abdominal pain, colitis, flatulence, dyspepsia, pseudomembranous colitis and stomatitis (<0.1%); glossitis (postmarketing reports).

Neurological: dizziness and headache (0.1 to 1.0%); ataxia and paresthesia (<0.1%).

Miscellaneous: fever, chills, diaphoresis, malaise, burning tongue, flushing, edema and anaphylactic shock (0.1 to 1.0%); bronchospasm, palpitations and epistaxis (<0.1%); glottic/laryngeal edema (postmarketing reports).

Local Reactions at Injection Site: pain (9.4%)[a]; induration and tenderness (1 to 2%); phlebitic reactions (0.1 to 1.0%); thrombophlebitis (<0.1%).

[a]Pain on i.m. injection is usually mild and less frequent when the drug is administered in sterile 1% lidocaine solution.

Laboratory: Hematologic: eosinophilia (4.6%), thrombocytosis (5.1%), leukopenia (2.0%); neutropenia, lymphopenia, thrombocytopenia, increase or decrease in hematocrit, prolongation of prothrombin time and decrease in hemoglobin (0.1 to 1.0%); leukocytosis, lymphocytosis, monocytosis, basophilia and decrease in prothrombin time (<0.1%).

Hepatic: increase in AST (4.0%)[b], ALT (4.8%)[b], increase in alkaline phosphatase (1.0%); increase in bilirubin (0.1 to 1.0%).

Urinary: increase in BUN (1.1%)[c]; increase in creatinine, erythrocyturia, proteinuria and presence of casts in urine (0.1 to 1.0%); glycosuria (<0.1%).

[b]Incidence is more frequent in patients less than 1 year old.

[c]Incidence is more frequent in patients less than 1 year old and over 50 years old.

Overdose: Symptoms and Treatment: Ultrasonographic shadows suggesting precipitations in the kidneys accompanied by calcium ceftriaxone precipitate in the urine was observed in 1 patient dosed at 10 g/day (2.5 times the maximum recommended dose). No other case of overdosage has been reported to date. No specific information on symptoms or treatment is available. Excessive serum concentration of ceftriaxone cannot be reduced by hemodialysis or peritoneal dialysis. Treatment should be symptomatic.

Dosage: Ceftriaxone may be administered i.v. or i.m. after reconstitution.

Dosage and route of administration should be determined by the severity of infection, susceptibility of the causative organisms, and condition of the patient (see Tables I and II). The i.v. route is preferable for patients with septicemia or other severe or life-threatening infections.

Table I—Rocephin

Dosage in Adults

Type of Infection	Route	Dose	Frequency	Total Daily Dose
Moderate and Severe Infections	i.v./i.m.	1 or 2 g 0.5 or 1 g	q24h or q12h	1 or 2 g 1 or 2 g
There is limited experience with daily doses of 3 to 4 g administered as a single dose or 2 equally divided doses. The total daily dose should not exceed 4 g.				
Uncomplicated Gonorrhea	i.m.	250 mg	Single dose	—

Table II—Rocephin

Dosage in Infants and Children (1 Month to 12 Years of Age)

Type of Infection	Route	Dose	Frequency	Total Daily Dose
Serious Miscellaneous Infections	i.v./i.m.	25 or 37.5 mg/kg	q12h	50 or 75 mg/kg
The total daily dose should not exceed 2 g. If body weight is 50 kg or more the adult dose should be used.				
Meningitis	i.v./i.m.	50 mg/kg*	q12h	100 mg/kg

*With or without a loading dose of 75 mg/kg. The total daily dose should not exceed 4 g.

With the exception of gonorrhea, which is treated with a single dose, the administration of ceftriaxone should be continued for a minimum of 48 to 72 hours after the patient defervesces or after evidence of bacterial eradication has been obtained, usually 4 to 14 days. In bone and joint infections the average duration of treatment during clinical trials was 6 weeks, with a range of 1 to 13 weeks, depending on the severity of the infection.

When treating infections caused by beta hemolytic streptococcus, it is recommended that therapy be continued for at least 10 days. The average duration of therapy for infections associated with beta hemolytic streptococcus during clinical trials was 2 weeks, with a range of 1 to 5 weeks, depending on the site and severity of the infection.

Prophylaxis (Vaginal or Abdominal Hysterectomy, Coronary Artery Bypass Surgery, Biliary Tract Surgery): For preoperative use as prophylaxis before vaginal or abdominal hysterectomy, coronary artery bypass surgery, or biliary tract surgery in patients at risk of infection, a single dose of 1 g administered ½ to 2 hours before surgery is recommended.

Impairment of Renal and/or Hepatic Function: In patients with mild to moderate renal impairment, changes in the dosage regimen are not required, **provided liver function is intact.** In cases of preterminal renal failure (creatinine clearance less than 10 mL/min), periodic monitoring of serum ceftriaxone concentrations is recommended. The daily dosage should be limited to 2 g or less. In patients with liver damage, there is no need for the dosage to be reduced **provided renal function is intact.** In cases of coexistent renal and clinically significant hepatic insufficiency, close monitoring of serum ceftriaxone concentrations, at regular intervals, is recommended. If there is evidence of accumulation, dosage should be decreased accordingly.

I.M.: The reconstituted solution should be administered by deep intragluteal injection. It is recommended that not more than 1 g be injected at a single site. Pain on i.m. injection is usually mild and less frequent when ceftriaxone is administered in sterile 1% lidocaine solution.

I.V. (Bolus): The reconstituted solution should be administered over approximately 5 minutes. If the distal port of an i.v. administration set is used, stop the primary flow, inject the reconstituted solution and then restart the primary flow. This will prevent mixing with the primary fluid and possible incompatibilities.

Short I.V. Infusion: The further diluted i.v. solution should be given over a period of 10 to 15 minutes in infants and children and 20 to 30 minutes in adults.

Note: Ceftriaxone solution should not be physically mixed with aminoglycoside antibiotics nor administered at the same site because of possible chemical incompatibility. There have also been literature reports of physical incompatibilities between ceftriaxone and vancomycin, amsacrine, or fluconazole.

Reconstitution: I.M.: See Tables III and IV. Reconstitute the powder with the appropriate diluent: Sterile Water for Injection, 0.9% Sodium Chloride Injection, 5% Dextrose Injection, Bacteriostatic Water for Injection, 1% lidocaine solution.

Table III—Rocephin

Regular Volume Reconstitution Table (I.M.)

Vial Size	Volume to be Added to Vial mL	Approximate Available Volume mL	Approximate Average Concentration g/mL
0.25 g	0.9	1	0.25
1.0 g	3.3	4	0.25
2.0 g	6.6	8	0.25

Shake well until dissolved.

Table IV—Rocephin

Low Volume Reconstitution Table (I.M.)

Vial Size	Volume to be Added to Vial mL	Approximate Available Volume mL	Approximate Average Concentration g/mL
0.25 g	Not recommended for this vial size		
1.0 g	2.2	2.8	0.35
2.0 g	4.4	5.6	0.35

Shake well until dissolved.

Note: Solutions prepared for i.m. use or any solution containing lidocaine or bacteriostatic water for injection should never be administered i.v.

I.V.: Reconstitute only with Sterile Water for Injection. See Table V.

Table V—Rocephin

Reconstitution Table (I.V.)

Vial Size	Volume to be Added to Vial mL	Approximate Available Volume mL	Approximate Average Concentration g/mL
0.25 g	2.4	2.5	0.1
1.0 g	9.6	10.1	0.1
2.0 g	19.2	20.5	0.1

Shake well until dissolved. The prepared solution may be further diluted to the desired volume with any of the following: 0.9% Sodium Chloride Injection, 0.9% Sodium Chloride Injection in ADD-Vantage flexible diluent container, 50 mL and 100 mL, 5% Dextrose Injection, 5% Dextrose Injection in ADD-Vantage flexible diluent container, 50 mL and 100 mL, Dextrose and Sodium Chloride Injection.

ADD-Vantage System Reconstitution for Preparation of I.V. Infusion Solutions: To open diluent container: Peel overwrap from the corner and remove container. Some opacity of the plastic due to moisture absorption during the sterilization process may be observed. This is normal and does not affect the solution quality or safety. The opacity will diminish gradually. To assemble vial and flexible diluent container (use aseptic technique): Remove the protective covers from the top of the vial and the vial port on the diluent container as follows: a) To remove the breakaway vial cap, swing the pull ring over the top of the vial and pull down far enough to start the opening, then pull straight up to remove the cap. Do not access vial with syringe. b) To remove the vial port cover, grasp the tab on the pull ring, pull up to break the 3 tie strings, then pull back to remove the cover.

Screw the vial into the vial port until it will go no further. **The vial must be screwed in tightly to assure a seal.** This occurs approximately ½ turn (180°) after the first audible click. The clicking sound does not assure a seal; the vial must

Rocephin (cont'd)

be turned as far as it will go. Note: Once vial is sealed, do not attempt to remove.

Recheck the vial to assure that it is tight by trying to turn it further in the direction of assembly.

Label appropriately.

To reconstitute the drug: Squeeze the bottom of the diluent container gently to inflate the portion of the container surrounding the end of the drug vial.

With the other hand, push the drug vial down into the container telescoping the walls of the container. Grasp the inner cap of the vial through the walls of the container.

Pull the inner cap from the drug vial. Verify that the rubber stopper has been pulled out, allowing the drug and diluent to mix.

Mix container contents thoroughly and use within the specified time.

Preparation for administration (use aseptic technique): Confirm the activation and admixture of vial contents. Check for leaks by squeezing container firmly. If leaks are found, discard unit as sterility may be impaired. Close flow control clamp of administration set. Remove cover from outlet port at bottom of container. Insert piercing pin of administration set into port with a twisting motion until the pin is firmly seated. Note: See full directions on administration set carton. Lift the free end of the hanger loop on the bottom of the vial, breaking the 2 tie strings. Bend the loop outward to lock it in the upright position, then suspend container from hanger. Squeeze and release drip chamber to establish proper fluid level in chamber. Open flow control clamp and clear air from set. Close clamp. Attach set to venipuncture device. If device is not indwelling, prime and make venipuncture. Regulate rate of administration with flow control clamp.

Warning: Do not use flexible container in series connections.

Stability: The ADD-Vantage system is designed to minimize drug waste by allowing the drug and diluent to be mixed at bedside just prior to administration. However, in those rare instances where the admixed unit cannot be administered within the specified time, it may be stored as specified under Stability and Storage. Reconstituted ADD-Vantage units should **not** be stored in a frozen state (−20°C).

Pharmacy Bulk Vial: Reconstitution for Preparation of I.V. Infusion Solutions: The closure of the pharmacy bulk vial shall be penetrated only one time after reconstitution, using a suitable sterile transfer device or dispensing set which allows measured dispensing for the contents (see Table VI).

Table VI—Rocephin

Reconstitution Table for Pharmacy Bulk Vial

Vial Size	Volume to be Added to Vial mL	Approximate Available Volume mL	Approximate Average Concentration g/mL
10 g	95	101	0.1

Shake well until dissolved. Withdraw the required amount and dilute with one of the solutions for I.V. Infusion. Any unused solution remaining within a period of 8 hours should be discarded.

Stability and Storage: I.M.: Solutions should be reconstituted immediately before use. If storage is required, these solutions may be stored under refrigeration and should be used within 48 hours.

I.V. Bolus Injections (without further dilution): Reconstituted solutions should be administered within 24 hours when stored at room temperature and within 72 hours when refrigerated (2 to 8°C).

I.V. Infusion: Further diluted reconstituted solutions should be administered within 24 hours when stored at room temperature.

Solutions further diluted with 0.9% Sodium Chloride Injection, or with 5% Dextrose Injection should be administered within 72 hours when stored under refrigeration (2 to 8°C).

Solutions further diluted with Dextrose and Sodium Chloride Injection as diluent should not be refrigerated. These solutions are not physically compatible when refrigerated.

Extended Use of I.V. Admixtures: Although i.v. admixtures may often be physically and chemically stable for longer periods, **due to microbiological considerations, they are usually recommended for use within a maximum of 24 hours at room temperature or 72 hours when refrigerated (2 to 8°C).** Hospitals and institutions that have recognized admixture programs and use validated aseptic techniques for preparation of i.v. solutions may extend the storage times for Rocephin admixtures with 0.9% Sodium Chloride Injection or 5% Dextrose Injection in glass or polyvinyl chloride infusion containers, in concentrations of 3 to 40 mg/mL, to 7 days when stored under refrigeration (2 to 8°C).

Warning: As with all parenteral drug products, i.v. admixtures should be visually inspected prior to administration, whenever solution and container permit. Solutions showing any evidence of haziness or cloudiness, particulate matter, precipitation, discoloration or leakage should not be used.

Frozen I.V. Infusion Solutions: Hospitals and institutions that have recognized admixture programs and use validated aseptic techniques for preparation of i.v. solutions may freeze and store ceftriaxone i.v. infusion solutions when prepared in accordance with the following instructions.

I.V. infusion solutions prepared from reconstituted ceftriaxone further diluted with 5% Dextrose Injection or 0.9% Sodium Chloride Injection, in flexible polyvinylchloride infusion containers, in concentrations up to 40 mg ceftriaxone per mL, may be stored at −10 to −20°C for periods up to 3 months.

The frozen solutions should be thawed in a refrigerator (2 to 8°C) overnight and should subsequently be used within 24 hours when stored at room temperature or 7 days when stored under refrigeration (2 to 8°C).

After thawing, check for leaks by squeezing the bag firmly. If leaks are found, discard the container as sterility may be impaired. Do not use unless the solution is clear and seals/outlet ports are intact. Ceftriaxone solutions range from light yellow to amber in color. Parenteral drug products should be inspected visually for particulate matter and discoloration prior to administration whenever the solution and container permit.

Do not refreeze the previously frozen ceftriaxone i.v. infusion solutions. **Do not freeze** Rocephin in ADD-Vantage flexible diluent containers.

Incompatibility: Ceftriaxone should not be physically mixed with other antimicrobial agents, vancomycin, amsacrine, or fluconazole.

Ceftriaxone should not be added to blood products, protein hydrolysates or amino acids.

Ceftriaxone should not be added to solutions containing calcium.

Supplied: Each vial of sterile white to pale yellow crystalline powder contains: ceftriaxone sodium (expressed as anhydrous free acid), equivalent to ceftriaxone 0.25 g, 1 g or 2 g; and vials for use only with Abbott Laboratories Limited ADD-Vantage 0.9% Sodium Chloride Injection USP or 5% Dextrose Injection USP in 50 mL and 100 mL containers equivalent to 1 g of ceftriaxone; and as a pharmacy bulk vial containing the equivalent of ceftriaxone 10 g (not for direct administration). **The availability of the pharmacy bulk vial is restricted to hospitals with a recognized i.v. admixture program.** No added excipients. Sodium: 3.6 mmol (83 mg)/g of ceftriaxone activity. pH 6 to 8. Solutions are yellowish in color.

Sterile powder should be stored at a controlled room temperature (between 15 and 30°C) and protected from light.

Reviewed 1999

ROFACT™ Ⓟ

ICN

Rifampin

Antituberculous Antibiotic

Supplied: 150 mg: Each scarlet opaque cap and body capsule, printed ICN R11 contains: rifampin USP 150 mg. Nonmedicinal ingredients: croscarmellose sodium, magnesium stearate, microcrystalline cellulose, sodium lauryl sulfate and talc. Bottles of 100.

300 mg: Each brown opaque cap and scarlet opaque body capsule, printed ICN R12 contains: rifampin USP 300 mg. Nonmedicinal ingredients: croscarmellose sodium, magnesium stearate, sodium lauryl sulfate and talc. Bottles of 100.

ROFERON®-A Ⓟ

Roche

Interferon alfa-2a

Biological Response Modifier

Pharmacology: The mechanisms by which interferon alfa-2a, or any other interferon, exerts antitumor activity are not clearly understood. However, it is believed that the direct antiproliferative action against tumor cells and modulation of the host immune response play important roles in the antitumor activity.

Interferon alfa-2a has been shown to exert antiproliferative activity against a variety of human tumors in vitro and to inhibit the growth of some human tumor xenografts in immuno-compromised (nude) mice.

The serum concentrations of recombinant interferon alfa-2a exhibited a large intersubject variation in both healthy volunteers and patients with disseminated cancer.

In healthy people, recombinant interferon alfa-2a exhibited an elimination half-life of 3.7 to 8.5 hours (mean 5.1 hours), volume of distribution at steady-state of 0.223 to 0.748 L/kg (mean 0.4 L/kg) and a total body clearance of 2.14 to 3.62 mL/min/kg (mean 2.79 mL/min/kg) after a 36 million IU (2.2×10^8 pg) i.v. infusion. After i.m. and s.c. administrations of 36 million IU, peak serum concentrations ranged from 1 500 to 2 580 pg/mL (mean 2 020 pg/mL) at a mean time to peak of 3.8 hours and from 1 250 to 2 320 pg/mL (mean 1 730 pg/mL) at a mean time to peak of 7.3 hours, respectively. The apparent fraction of the dose absorbed after i.m. or s.c. injection was greater than 80%.

The pharmacokinetics of recombinant interferon alfa-2a after single i.m. doses to patients with disseminated cancer were similar to those found in healthy volunteers. Dose proportional increases in serum concentrations were observed after single doses up to 198 million IU. There were no changes in the distribution or elimination of recombinant interferon alfa-2a during twice daily (0.5 to 36 million IU), once daily (1 to 54 million IU), or 3 times weekly (1 to 136 million IU) dosing regimens up to 28 days of dosing. Multiple i.m. doses of recombinant interferon alfa-2a resulted in an accumulation of 2 to 4 times the single dose serum concentrations. Pharmacokinetic information in patients with hairy cell leukemia is presently unknown.

Indications: For use in the treatment of hairy cell leukemia, Kaposi's sarcoma in patients with AIDS (Acquired Immune Deficiency Syndrome), chronic active hepatitis B, chronic myelogenous leukemia (CML), and thrombocytosis associated with CML, renal cell carcinoma, cutaneous T-cell lymphoma (CTCL) and chronic hepatitis C.

Contraindications: In patients with known hypersensitivity to the drug, its components or other interferon preparations; in patients with chronic hepatitis associated with advanced, decompensated cirrhosis of the liver and in patients with chronic hepatitis who are being or have recently been treated with immunosuppressive agents, excluding short-term "steroid withdrawal".

Roferon-A Albumin (Human) Free which contains benzyl alcohol as a preservative, is contraindicated in patients with hypersensitivity to benzyl alcohol (also see Precautions, Children).

Warnings: Initial therapy with interferon alfa-2a should be conducted under the guidance of a qualified physician experienced in the use of cancer chemotherapeutic agents, in a unit having adequate facilities for monitoring of the relevant clinical and laboratory parameters. Treatment with interferon alfa-2a is not recommended in patients with severe pre-existing cardiac disease or severe renal or hepatic dysfunction as the benefit-risk ratio may not warrant therapy.

Precautions: General: If acute hypersensitivity reactions to interferon alfa-2a develop, the drug should be discontinued.

Moderate to severe adverse reactions may require modification of the patient's dosage regimen, or in some cases, termination of drug therapy.

CNS adverse reactions have been reported. These reactions included confusion, somnolence, dizziness and depression. Seizures and coma have been rarely observed. Most of these abnormalities were mild and were reversible within a few days to a few weeks upon dose reduction or discontinuation of therapy. Interferon alfa-2a should be used with caution in patients with seizure disorders and/or compromised CNS functions. Periodic examination of the neuropsychiatric status of all patients is recommended.

Interferon alfa-2a should be administered with caution to patients with cardiac disease or with any history of cardiac illness. No direct cardiotoxic effect has been demonstrated, but it is likely that acute self-limiting toxicities (i.e., fever, chills), frequently associated with interferon alfa-2a administration may exacerbate pre-existing cardiac conditions. Myocardial infarction occurred rarely in patients receiving interferon alfa-2a.

Those patients who have pre-existing cardiac abnormalities and/or are in advanced stages of cancer should have ECGs taken prior to and during the course of treatment.

When mild to moderate renal or hepatic impairment is present, close monitoring of these functions is required.

Hyperglycemia has been observed rarely in patients treated with interferon alfa-2a. Symptomatic patients should have their blood glucose measured and followed-up accordingly. Patients with diabetes mellitus should have their blood glucose measured and adjusted according to their antidiabetic regimen.

Careful periodic monitoring of all patients is recommended. Suicidal behavior has been observed rarely in patients receiving interferon alfa-2a. Therapy should be discontinued in patients exhibiting suicidal behavior.

The development of auto-antibodies may play a role in the development of autoimmune disorders. Autoimmune phenomena such as vasculitis, arthritis, hemolytic anemia, thyroid dysfunction and lupus erythematosus syndrome have been observed rarely in patients receiving interferon alfa-2a.

Pregnancy: Safe use in human pregnancy has not been established. As with other anticancer drugs, interferon alfa-2a should not be administered to fertile persons of either sex not practising effective contraception. In pregnancy, interferon alfa-2a should be administered only if the benefit to the woman justifies the potential risk to the fetus. The excipient benzyl alcohol can be transmitted via the placenta. The possibility of toxicity should be taken into account in premature infants after the administration of Roferon-A Albumin (Human) Free immediately prior to birth or Cesarean section.

Lactation: It is not known whether this drug is excreted in human milk. Because many drugs are excreted in human milk and because of the potential for serious adverse reactions in nursing infants, a decision should be made whether to discontinue nursing or to postpone treatment, taking into account the importance of the drug to the mother.

Children: Safety and effectiveness in patients under 18 years of age have not been established. Roferon-A Albumin (Human) Free is not recommended for use in the newborn or children under the age of 2 years since it contains benzyl alcohol as a preservative.

Patients with Special Diseases: Caution should be exercised when administering interferon alfa-2a to patients with severe myelosuppression.

Drug Interactions: Interactions between interferon alfa-2a and other drugs have not been fully evaluated.

As interferon alfa-2a may affect central nervous functions, interactions could occur following concurrent administration of centrally acting drugs.

Alfa-Interferons may affect the oxidative metabolic process by reducing the activity of microsomal cytochrome enzymes in the P450 group. Although the clinical relevance is still unclear, this should be taken into account when prescribing concomitant therapy with drugs metabolized by this route. Reduced clearance of theophylline following the concomitant administration of alfa-interferons has been reported.

It has been observed that the neurotoxic, hematotoxic or cardiotoxic effects of previously or concurrently administered drugs may be increased by interferons. Interactions could occur following concurrent administration of centrally acting drugs.

Caution should be exercised when interferon alfa-2a is used in combination with other agents that are known to cause myelosuppression. Synergistic toxicity has been observed when interferon alfa-2a is administered in combination with zidovudine (AZT). The effects of interferon alfa-2a when combined with other drugs used in the treatment of AIDS-related diseases are not known.

Laboratory Tests: Periodic complete blood counts and liver function tests should be performed during the course of interferon alfa-2a treatment. They should be performed prior to therapy and at appropriate periods during therapy. Interferon has suppressive effects on the bone marrow, leading to a fall in the white blood count, particularly the granulocytes, the platelet count and commonly the hemoglobin concentration.

Information for the Patient: Patients should be informed not only of the potential benefits and risks of therapy, but also that they will probably experience adverse reactions.

Patients should be well hydrated, especially during the initial stages of treatment.

Adverse Effects: The following data on adverse reactions are based on information derived from the treatment of patients with a wide variety of malignancies including patients with hairy cell leukemia, AIDS related Kaposi's sarcoma and chronic active hepatitis B and patients with chronic hepatitis C. Most patients suffered from advanced forms of the diseases. Also, most patients received doses that were significantly higher than the doses now recommended and this probably affected the frequency and severity of adverse reactions.

General Symptoms: The majority of the patients experienced flu-like symptoms such as fatigue, fever, chills, anorexia, myalgia, headache, arthralgias and diaphoresis. Dose attenuation usually decreased the severity of the adverse effects.

Gastrointestinal: Slightly more than half of the patients studied experienced anorexia and/or nausea. Emesis, diarrhea and mild to moderate abdominal pain were less frequently observed. Constipation, flatulence, hypermotility or heartburn occurred rarely. Reactivation of peptic ulcer and nonlife-threatening gastrointestinal bleeding have also been reported.

Alterations of hepatic function shown by an elevation of AST, alkaline phosphatase, LDH and bilirubin have been observed and generally did not require dose adjustment. Hepatitis was rarely reported.

CNS: Dizziness, vertigo, decreased mental status, depression, drowsiness, confusion, behavioral disturbances such as anxiety and nervousness and sleep disturbances were reported. Severe somnolence, convulsions, coma, seizures and encephalopathy and suicidal behavior are rare complications.

Peripheral Nervous System: Paresthesias, sleep disturbances, visual disturbances, numbness, neuropathy and tremor occurred occasionally, ischemic retinopathy rarely.

Cardiovascular: Reactions were seen in less than a fifth of the patients and consisted of transient hypotensive or hypertensive episodes, edema, chest pain, cyanosis, arrhythmias and palpitations. Rare cases of pulmonary edema, congestive heart failure, cardiorespiratory arrest and myocardial infarction have been reported.

Skin and Appendages: Rash, pruritus, mild to moderate hair loss, dryness of skin, rhinorrhea, urticaria, epistaxis and reactivation of herpes labialis were reported.

Renal and Urinary: Abnormalities consisted primarily of proteinuria and increased red and white cell counts in sediment. Elevations of BUN, serum creatinine and uric acid have been rarely observed. Rare cases of acute renal failure have been reported, mainly in cancer patients with renal disease and/or nephrotoxic comedications as concomitant risk factors.

Hematopoietic: Transient leukopenia occurred in about one third of the patients, but rarely required dosage reduction.

Thrombocytopenia was less frequently seen. Decreased hemoglobin and hematocrit occurred rarely. Recovery of severe hematological deviations to pretreatment levels usually occurred within 7 to 10 days after stopping interferon alfa-2a treatment.

Other: Weight loss, change in taste, and dryness or inflammation of the oropharynx have been reported, bleeding gums, ecchymosis and pneumonia rarely. Hyperglycemia has been observed rarely in patients treated with interferon alfa-2a.

Neutralizing antibodies to interferon alfa-2a were detected in 14.6 to 38% of patients in clinical trials with hairy cell leukemia, AIDS related Kaposi's sarcoma, chronic active hepatitis B, renal cell carcinoma, chronic myelogenous leukemia and chronic hepatitis C.

No data on neutralizing antibodies yet exist from clinical trials in which the presently marketed material, which is stored at 4°C, has been used. In a mouse model, however, the relative immunogenicity of interferon alfa-2a increases with time when the material is stored at 25°C - no such increase in immunogenicity is observed when interferon alfa-2a is stored at 4°C, the presently recommended storage conditions.

In general, the higher the cumulative dose of interferon alfa-2a received, the more likely a patient will produce antibodies to interferon alfa-2a. Antibodies to human leukocyte interferon may occur spontaneously in certain clinical conditions (cancer, systemic lupus erythematosus, herpes zoster) in patients who have never received exogenous interferon.

Overdose: Symptoms and Treatment: There are no reports of overdosage but repeated large doses of interferon are associated with profound lethargy, fatigue, prostration, and coma. Such patients should be hospitalized for observation and appropriate supportive treatment given.

Dosage: The following dosage schedules are recommended and should not be exceeded: Adults: **Hairy Cell Leukemia:** Induction dose of 3 million IU daily for 16 to 24 weeks administered as an i.m. injection. Maintenance 3 million IU 3 times/week. S.C. administration may be utilized in thrombocytopenic patients (platelet count $<$50 000) or in patients at risk for bleeding.

AIDS related Kaposi's Sarcoma: Induction dose of 36 million IU daily for 4 to 10 weeks as a s.c. or i.m. injection. Maintenance dose of 36 million IU 3 times/week.

Patients with Kaposi's sarcoma should be treated for 30 to 90 days before the physician determines the possible benefits of continued therapy in patients whose disease did not progress.

Chronic Active Hepatitis B: Recommended dose is 4.5 million IU administered s.c. 3 times/week for 6 months.

If markers for viral replication or HB_eAg do not decrease after 1 month of therapy, the dose can be escalated. The dosage may be further adjusted to the patient's tolerance to medication. If no improvement has been observed after 3 to 4 months of treatment, discontinuation of therapy should be considered.

Therapeutic trials in patients with chronic active hepatitis B show that interferon alfa-2a therapy at doses equivalent to $\geq$4.5 million IU 3 times weekly for 6 months is associated with inhibition of viral replication, development of a specific humoral immune response and a reduction or disappearance of necroinflammatory disease of the liver. Response to therapy is generally signalled by a transient asymptomatic acute hepatitis "flare" with a serum transaminase peak accompanied by a fall in the level of genomic and antigenic (especially HB_e) markers of viral replication. Loss or reduction of HB_s antigenemia usually occurs over a period of many months. The appearance of anti-HB_e and in some patients anti-HB_s antibody in the serum signals antiviral immunity. Maximal response to therapy often occurs weeks or months after the end of treatment. Patients with active disease respond better to therapy than those with hypoactive disease as defined by liver biopsy and/or serum ALT levels. Doses $\leq$1.5 million IU 3 times weekly for 16 weeks are suboptimally effective. Some patients may require doses up to the equivalent of 18 million IU for 6 months to benefit from therapy.

Chronic Myelogenous Leukemia: It is recommended that interferon alfa-2a should be given by s.c. or i.m. injection for 8 to 12 weeks to patients 18 years or more. The recommended schedule is: days 1 to 3: 3 million IU daily, days 4 to 6: 6 million IU daily; days 7 to 84: 9 million I.U. daily.

Duration of Treatment: Patients should be treated for a minimum of 8 weeks, preferably for at least 12 weeks before the physician decides whether or not to continue treatment in responding patients or to discontinue treatment in patients not showing any changes in hematological parameters. Responding patients should be treated until complete hematological response is achieved or for a maximum of 18 months. All patients with complete hematologic responses should continue treatment with 9 million IU daily (optimum) or 9 million IU 3 times/week (minimum) in order to achieve a cytogenic response in the shortest possible time. The optimal duration of interferon alfa-2a treatment for a chronic myelogenous leukemia has not been determined, although cytogenic responses have been observed 2 years after treatment started.

Thrombocytosis associated with CML: Thrombocytosis is a frequent concomitant phenomenon in CML. The morbid nature of severe thrombocytosis is reflected by the frequent manifestation of a serious thrombotic or hemorrhagic diathesis. In a large Phase 3 clinical trial, when 206 interferon alfa-2a treated CML patients were available for hematologic response assessment, 75 subjects had a baseline thrombocyte count of $>450\times10^9$/L. Platelet control was achieved in 73 patients (97%).

Therefore, therapy is recommended with interferon alfa-2a for the treatment of patients with excessive thrombocytosis in CML, even in the absence of cytogenetic response.

The recommended dosage for thrombocytosis in CML is the same as that recommended above for the treatment of CML.

Renal Cell Carcinoma: Induction dose of at least 18×10^6 IU daily as a s.c. or i.m. injection and if possible, 36×10^6 IU daily for 8 to 12 weeks using the recommended escalation schedules: 3×10^6 IU daily, days 1 to 3; 9×10^6 IU daily, days 4 to 6; 18×10^6 IU daily, days 7 to 9 and if tolerated, increase to: 36×10^6 IU daily, days 10 to 84.

Maintenance doses should be given to those patients responding to induction therapy. The maintenance dose should be identical to the maximum tolerated dose but should not exceed 36×10^6 IU 3 times/week.

Interferon alfa-2a has also shown to be effective in combination with vinblastine. 18×10^6 IU of interferon alfa-2a given i.m. 3 times/week for 8 to 12 weeks with concurrent vinblastine i.v. injected with doses of 0.1 mg/kg body weight, once every 3 weeks has shown increased effectiveness over interferon alfa-2a alone at these relatively lower doses. However, the objective response rate of the combination was similar to the response rate under optimal conditions for treatment of interferon alfa-2a alone.

Cutaneous T-Cell Lymphoma: Induction dose of at least 18×10^6 IU daily for 8 to 12 weeks administered by s.c. or i.m. injections. The recommended escalation schedule is as follows: 3×10^6 IU daily, days 1 to 3; 9×10^6 IU daily, days 4 to 6; 18×10^6 IU daily, days 7 to 84.

Roferon-A (cont'd)

Maintenance dose of 18×10⁶ IU 3 times/week. Patients should be treated for a minimum of 8 weeks and preferably for at least 12 weeks before the physician decides whether to continue treatment in responding patients or to discontinue treatment in nonresponding patients. Minimum treatment duration for patients who respond is suggested to be 12 months in order to maximize the chance of achieving a complete response and improve the chance of a prolonged response. Patients have been treated for up to 40 consecutive months.

In clinical trials, 55 of 85 evaluable patients with CTCL received the recommended dosage regimen and the following objective responses were observed: see Table I.

Table I—Roferon-A

Responses to Recommended Dosage Regimen in Patients with CTCL

	Stage I or II CTCL (n=37)	Stage III or IV CTCL (n=18)
Overall Response	73%	39%
95% C.I.*	56-86%	17-64%
Complete Response	35%	6%
95% C.I.*	20-53%	—
Partial Response	38%	33%
95% C.I.*	22-55%	13-59%

*C.I.=Confidence Index.

Chronic Hepatitis C: Interferon alfa-2a is indicated for the treatment of adult patients with chronic hepatitis C who are positive for HCV antibodies and have elevated ALT without liver decompensation (Child's Class A).

Initial Dosage: Interferon alfa-2a should be administered at a dose of 6 million IU by s.c. or i.m. injection 3 times/week for 3 months as induction therapy.

Maintenance Dosage: Patients whose serum ALT has normalized require maintenance therapy with 3 million IU interferon alfa-2a 3 times/week for an additional 3 months to consolidate the complete response.

Patients whose serum ALT has not normalized should stop treatment.

Note: The majority of patients who relapse after adequate treatment do so within 4 months of the end of treatment.

Special Dosage Instructions: Dosage should be modified to take into account the constitutional symptoms, the myelosuppressive effects, and the other clinical or laboratory test abnormalities caused by interferon alfa-2a therapy.

Dosage adjustments may be more important when administering interferon alfa-2a to patients receiving concomitant therapies or who may have compromised bone marrow reserve due to prior x-ray treatment or chemotherapy.

Geriatrics: Elderly patients may be more susceptible to the side effects and caution is recommended in the treatment of such patients.

Children: Safety and efficacy in patients under 18 years of age have not been established.

Administration: The s.c. or i.m. routes of administration should be used. S.C. administration is particularly suggested for, but not limited to, patients who are thrombocytopenic (platelet count <50 000) or who are at risk for bleeding. See also Information for the Patient for information on self-administration.

Stability and Storage: Solutions: See expiration date on the outer package. Store in a refrigerator at 2 to 8°C. Do not freeze or shake.

Information for the Patient: See Blue Section—Information for the Patient "Roferon-A".

Supplied: Alluman (Human) Free: 3 million IU: Each mL contains: interferon alfa-2a 3 million IU. Nonmedicinal ingredients: sodium chloride 7.21 mg, ammonium acetate 0.77 mg, polysorbate 80 0.2 mg with benzyl alcohol 10 mg as preservative and sodium hydroxyde or glacial acetic acid to adjust pH. Vials of 1 mL.

4.5 million IU: Each mL contains: interferon alfa-2a 4.5 million IU. Nonmedicinal ingredients: sodium chloride 7.21 mg, ammonium acetate 0.77 mg, polysorbate 80 0.2 mg with benzyl alcohol 10 mg as preservative and sodium hydroxide or glacial acetic acid to adjust pH. Vials of 1 mL.

6 million IU: Each mL contains: interferon alfa-2a 6 million IU. Nonmedicinal ingredients: sodium chloride 7.21 mg, ammonium acetate 0.77 mg, polysorbate 80 0.2 mg with benzyl alcohol 10 mg as preservative and sodium hydroxide or glacial acetic acid to adjust pH. Vials of 1 mL.

9 million IU: Each mL contains: interferon alfa-2a 9 million IU. Nonmedicinal ingredients: sodium chloride 7.21 mg, ammonium acetate 0.77 mg, polysorbate 80 0.2 mg with benzyl alcohol 10 mg as preservative and sodium hydroxide or glacial acetic acid to adjust pH. Vials of 1 mL.

18 million IU: Each mL contains: interferon alfa-2a 6 million IU. Nonmedicinal ingredients: sodium chloride 7.21 mg, ammonium acetate 0.77 mg, polysorbate 80 0.2 mg with benzyl alcohol 10 mg as preservative and sodium hydroxide or glacial acetic acid to adjust pH. Vials of 3 mL.

See expiration date on the outer package. Store in a refrigerator at 2 to 8°C. Do not freeze or shake.

Reviewed 1999

ROGAINE® Ⓟ

Pharmacia & Upjohn

Minoxidil

Hair Growth Stimulant

Pharmacology: When applied topically, minoxidil topical solution has been shown to stimulate hair growth in individuals with alopecia androgenetica (male pattern baldness). Although the exact mechanism of action of minoxidil in the treatment of alopecia androgenetica is not known, there may be more than one mechanism by which minoxidil stimulates hair growth; they include: vasodilation of the microcirculation around the hair follicles which may stimulate hair growth; direct stimulation of the hair follicle cells to enter into a proliferative phase: resting phase (telogen) follicles being stimulated to pass into active phase (anagen) follicles; alteration of the effect of androgens on genetically predetermined hair follicles: minoxidil may affect the androgen metabolism in the scalp by inhibiting the capacity of androgens to affect the hair follicles.

Following topical application of minoxidil topical solution, minoxidil is poorly absorbed from normal intact skin, with an average of 1.4% (range 0.3 to 4.5%) of the total applied dose reaching the systemic circulation. The effects of concomitant dermal diseases or occlusion on absorption are unknown. Serum minoxidil levels resulting from topical administration are governed by the drug's percutaneous absorption rate; increases in surface area of application do not result in proportionate increases in the serum minoxidil level. Steady state is achieved by the end of the third dosing interval (36 hours) when the drug is administered twice daily. Approximately 95% of the systemically absorbed minoxidil from topical dosing is eliminated within 4 days. The metabolic biotransformation of minoxidil absorbed following topical application has not been fully determined.

Absorption from the gastrointestinal tract following oral administration of minoxidil tablets is essentially complete (at least 95%). Approximately 90% of orally administered minoxidil is metabolized, predominantly by conjugation with glucuronic acid at the N-oxide position in the pyrimidine ring and by conversion to more polar products.

Known metabolites exert much less pharmacologic effect than minoxidil itself and all are excreted principally in the urine. Minoxidil does not bind to plasma proteins; its renal clearance corresponds to glomerular filtration rate and it does not cross the blood brain barrier. Minoxidil and its metabolites are hemodialyzable, although this does not rapidly reverse its pharmacological effect.

Increased hair growth has not been associated with increased systemic absorption of topical minoxidil. The onset of hair growth stimulation requires twice daily applications of minoxidil topical solution for 4 or more months, and is variable among patients. Upon discontinuation of topically applied minoxidil, new hair growth has been anecdotally reported to stop and restoration of pretreatment appearance to occur within 3 to 4 months.

Indications: The treatment of alopecia androgenetica (male pattern baldness).

Contraindications: Hypersensitivity to minoxidil, propylene glycol or ethanol.

Pregnancy and *Lactation:* Minoxidil topical solution should not be used by pregnant or nursing women.

Warnings: Although the following systemic effects have not been associated with the topical use of minoxidil topical solution, there is some absorption of minoxidil from the skin and the potential exists for systemic effects such as tachycardia, angina, edema or potentiation of the orthostatic hypotension produced by guanethidine. Patients should be observed periodically for any suggestion of systemic effects of minoxidil. In the event of systemic side effects discontinue administration of the drug. If necessary, fluid retention and edema can be managed with diuretic treatment. Tachycardia and angina can be controlled by administration of beta-adrenergic blocking drugs or other sympathetic nervous system suppressants. Patients should discontinue use of minoxidil topical solution and contact their physician in the event of systemic effects and/or severe dermatologic reactions.

Pregnancy and *Lactation:* The safety for use of minoxidil topical solution in pregnancy has not been established. Orally administered minoxidil has been shown to reduce the conception rate in rats and to show evidence of increased fetal resorption in rabbits when administered at 5 times the human oral dose. There was no evidence of teratogenic effects in rats and rabbits.

Systemically absorbed minoxidil is secreted in human milk.

Children: Safety and effectiveness of minoxidil topical solution in patients under 18 years of age has not been established.

Patients With Underlying Cardiovascular Disease: Patients should not use minoxidil topical solution if they have a history of underlying coronary artery disease, cardiac dysrhythmias, congestive heart failure, or valvular heart disease. Patients with hypertension, including those under treatment with antihypertensive agents, should be monitored closely and their medication adjusted if necessary. Minoxidil topical solution should be used with caution in patients with any other cardiovascular disease present.

Precautions: Before prescribing minoxidil topical solution, ensure that the patient reads and understands the contents of the patient-package insert including the application instructions.

Minoxidil topical solution will cause burning and irritation of the eye. In the event of accidental contact with sensitive surfaces (eye, abraded skin, mucous membranes), the area should be bathed with copious amounts of cool tap water.

Inhalation of the spray mist should be avoided.

Accidental ingestion of minoxidil topical solution could lead to serious adverse effects.

The effects of minoxidil topical solution in patients with concomitant dermal diseases, or in those using topical corticosteroids or other dermatologic preparations are unknown. It has not been clearly determined whether occlusion will increase the absorption of minoxidil after administration of the topical solution. As is the case with other topically applied drugs, decreased integrity of the epidermal barrier caused by inflammation or disease processes in the skin, may increase percutaneous absorption of minoxidil.

Geriatrics: Studies involving subjects over the age of 65 years have not been performed hence the safety and effectiveness of minoxidil topical solution in these patients has not been established.

Drug Interactions: There are currently no known drug interactions associated with the use of minoxidil topical solution. Although it has not been clinically demonstrated, there exists the possibility of potentiating orthostatic hypotension in patients concurrently taking guanethidine.

Adverse Effects: The most frequently encountered adverse effects in clinical trials with minoxidil topical solution were minor dermatologic reactions. In light of the findings that systemic levels of minoxidil from topical application are low in relation to systemic levels from oral dosing, this distribution of encountered adverse effects is to be expected. Local irritation was the most common adverse reaction reported, including scaling, erythema/flushing, dermatitis, dry skin, hypertrichosis (in areas other than where minoxidil topical solution was applied), burning sensation and rash.

Infrequent adverse reactions including allergic reactions (sensitivity, hives, generalized erythema and facial swelling); dizziness; tingling sensation; headache; weakness; neuritis; edema; eye irritation; altered taste; ear infection (otitis externa); and visual disturbances have been reported. Rarely reported adverse reactions included alopecia, hair abnormalities, chest pain, blood pressure changes, pulse changes, hepatitis, and kidney stones.

The occurrence rates for adverse reactions derived from the total adverse reactions of all patients (placebo [one-third of these patients received placebo treatment for 4 months] 2% minoxidil and 3% minoxidil treated) enrolled in 2 pivotal efficacy/safety studies (2 326 patients), are as follows: Dermatological: itching (3%); scaling, erythema, dermatitis, dry skin (1 to 2%); hypertrichosis, burning sensation, rash, folliculitis, desquamation, alopecia (hair loss), skin abscess,

acne, eczema, eruptions, excoriation, flaking scalp, hair abnormalities, nail disorders, seborrhea, other skin irritations (0.1 to 1.0%).
Cardiovascular: flushing (1 to 2%); chest pain, changes in blood pressure, changes in pulse rate, fainting (0.1 to 1.0%).
CNS: headache, dizziness (1 to 2%).
Allergic: fever (1 to 2%); allergic reaction, non-specific allergic reaction, hives, allergic rhinitis, facial swelling and sensitivity, chills (0.1 to 1.0%).
Renal: edema (1 to 2%); kidney stones (0.1 to 1.0%).
Respiratory: shortness of breath (0.1 to 1.0%).
Neurological: neuritis (1 to 2%); weakness (0.1 to 1.0%).
Hepatic: hepatitis (0.1 to 1.0%).
Special senses: eye irritations, bitter taste, ear infection (otitis externa), taste alteration, visual disturbance (0.1 to 1.0%).

Overdose: Symptoms and Treatment: Accidental ingestion of minoxidil topical solution may produce systemic effects related to the vasodilatory action of minoxidil (5 mL of the 2% topical solution contains 100 mg minoxidil, the maximum recommended adult oral dose for the treatment of hypertension). There have been only a few instances of deliberate or accidental overdosage with oral minoxidil (Loniten tablets).

In a reported case of accidental ingestion, a 3-year-old male swallowed 1 to 2 mL of a 3% concentration of topical minoxidil solution. After vomiting he was treated in an emergency room. The child was found to be alert and active with no obvious signs of distress. His temperature was 37°C, pulse 152, respiration 32, and systolic blood pressure 110 by palpation. Cardiovascular, chest, lungs, abdomen, head, skin and neurological examinations were normal. Blood levels taken indicated a total minoxidil level (glucuronide and unchanged) of 320.6 ng/mL. The child was discharged without sequelae.

Signs and symptoms of drug overdosage would most likely include cardiovascular effects associated with fluid retention, lowered blood pressure and tachycardia. Fluid retention can be managed with appropriate diuretic therapy. Tachycardia can be controlled by administration of a beta-adrenergic blocking agent.

If exaggerated hypotension is encountered, it is most likely to occur in association with residual sympathetic nervous system blockade from previous therapy (guanethidine-like effects or alpha-adrenergic blockade). The recommended treatment is i.v. administration of normal saline.

Sympathomimetic drugs, such as norepinephrine or epinephrine, should be avoided because of their excessive cardiac-stimulating action. Phenylephrine, angiotensin II, vasopressin and dopamine, which reverse the effects of orally administered minoxidil, should only be used if inadequate perfusion of a vital organ is evident.

Oral LD_{50} in rats has ranged from 1 321 to 3 492 mg/kg; in mice 2 457 to 2 648 mg/kg. Minoxidil and its metabolites are hemodialyzable, although this does not rapidly reverse its pharmacological effect.

Dosage: For external use only. Use only as directed.

A total dose of 1 mL minoxidil topical solution should be applied twice per day to the scalp, beginning at the centre of the affected area. This dose should be used regardless of the size of the affected area. The total daily dose should not exceed 2 mL. The method of application varies according to the disposable applicator used, as indicated below. After applying minoxidil topical solution, wash hands thoroughly. Do not apply the topical solution to any other area of the body.

Apply minoxidil topical solution when the hair and scalp are thoroughly dry. Do not use a hairdryer to speed the drying of the topical solution, because blowing air on the scalp may decrease the effectiveness of the drug.

A. **Pump-Spray Applicator:** (Works best for applying minoxidil topical solution to large areas): (1) Remove large outer cap and keep it. (2) Remove small inner cap and discard it. (3) Insert the pump spray applicator into bottle and screw on firmly. (4) After aiming the pump toward the centre of the bald area of the scalp, press the pump once and spread minoxidil topical solution with fingertips to cover all of the bald area. Repeat for a total of 6 times, to apply a dose of 1 mL. **Avoid breathing spray mist.** (5) Replace large outer cap over the pump spray applicator when not in use.

B. **Rub-On Applicator:** Works best for applying minoxidil topical solution to small areas of the scalp. (1) Remove large outer cap and keep it. (2) Remove small inner cap and discard it. (3) Insert the rub-on applicator into bottle and screw on firmly. (4) Hold the bottle upright and squeeze it **once** to fill the upper chamber to the black line. The chamber now contains 1 full dose (1 mL). (5) Hold the bottle upside down, then rub applicator on the scalp to apply minoxidil topical solution over the entire bald area—until the chamber is completely empty. (6) Replace large outer cap over the rub-on applicator when not in use.

C. **Extended Spray-Tip Applicator:** Works best for applying minoxidil topical solution to small areas of the scalp, or under hair. (1) Remove large outer cap and discard it. (2) Remove small inner cap and discard it. (3) Insert the pump spray applicator into the bottle and screw on firmly. (4) Remove small spray head from top of pump spray applicator. (5) Fit the extended spray tip applicator onto the spray shaft and push down firmly. (6) Remove the small cap on the end of the extended tip and keep it. (7) After aiming the applicator toward the centre of the bald area of the scalp, press the pump once and spread the minoxidil topical solution with fingertips to cover all of the bald area. Repeat for a total of 6 times, to apply a dose of 1 mL. **Avoid breathing spray mist.** (8) If desired, replace the small cap onto the end of extended tip when not in use.

Clinical experience with minoxidil topical solution indicates that twice daily application for 4 or more months may be required before evidence of hair growth stimulation can be expected. Onset and degree may be variable among patients. Relapse to pretreatment appearance following discontinuation of medication has been anecdotally reported to occur within 3 to 4 months.

Information for the Patient: See Blue Section—Information for the Patient "Rogaine".

Supplied: Each mL of clear, colorless to slightly yellow solution contains: minoxidil 20 mg (2%) in alcohol (63%), propylene glycol and water. Bottles containing 60 mL of solution with the following metered disposable applicators: pump spray, extended tip and rub-on assemblies.

ROGITINE® ℞

Novartis Pharmaceuticals

Phentolamine Mesylate

Alpha-adrenoreceptor Blocker

Pharmacology: Phentolamine produces an alpha-adrenergic block of relatively short duration. It also has direct but less marked positive inotropic and chronotropic effects on cardiac muscle and vasodilator effects on vascular smooth muscle.

Indications: Prevention and control of hypertensive episodes in patients with pheochromocytoma, preoperatively and during surgical excision.

Prevention of dermal necrosis and sloughing following i.v. administration or extravasation of norepinephrine.

Diagnosis of pheochromocytoma (phentolamine test).

Contraindications: Myocardial infarction, history of myocardial infarction, coronary insufficiency, angina or other evidence suggestive of coronary artery disease. Hypotension. Hypersensitivity to phentolamine or related compounds.

Warnings: Blood pressure must be monitored for appropriate selection of patients, dosage, and duration of therapy. Myocardial infarction, cerebrovascular spasm, and cerebrovascular occlusion have been reported to occur following the administration of phentolamine, usually in association with marked hypotensive episodes with shock-like states which occasionally occur.

For screening tests in patients with hypertension, the generally available urinary assay of catecholamines or other biochemical assays have largely supplanted the phentolamine and other pharmacological tests for reasons of accuracy and safety. None of the chemical or pharmacological tests are infallible in the diagnosis of pheochromocytoma. The phentolamine test is not the procedure of choice and should be reserved for cases in which additional confirmatory evidence is necessary, and the relative risks involved in conducting the test have been considered.

Precautions: Tachycardia and cardiac arrhythmias may occur with the use of phentolamine or other alpha-adrenergic blocking agents. When possible, defer administration of cardiac glycosides until cardiac rhythm returns to normal.

Due to its stimulatory effect on the gastrointestinal tract, including gastric secretion, phentolamine should be used with caution in patients with gastritis or peptic ulcer.

Use caution in administering phentolamine to patients with renal impairment; since the drug is primarily excreted by the kidney, a reduction in dosage may be necessary.

Pregnancy and *Lactation:* Animal studies indicate that high doses of phentolamine to pregnant rats and mice resulted in slightly decreased growth and slight skeletal immaturity in the fetuses. At very high doses a slightly lower rate of implantation was found in the rat. There are no studies in pregnant or nursing women. The use of phentolamine is therefore not recommended unless the potential benefits justify the potential risks.

Occupational Hazards: Phentolamine may cause central nervous symptoms, e.g. dizziness, which may impair the patient's reactions. Patients must therefore be warned against engaging in activities that require quick reactions, such as driving motor vehicles or operating machines.

Drug Interactions: See Dosage, Diagnosis of Pheochromocytoma, Preparation.

Adverse Effects: Orthostatic hypotension and tachycardia occur frequently. Acute and prolonged hypotensive episodes and cardiac arrhythmias have been reported (see Warnings). In addition, weakness, dizziness, flushing, nasal stuffiness, nausea, vomiting, diarrhea, anorexia, abdominal discomfort, conjunctival injections, sedation, anginal pain, and precordial pain may occur.

Priapism, penile hematoma and fibrosis have been reported following local injection. Neither the route of administration nor this use are approved or recommended.

Overdose: Death has occurred following use of phentolamine 5 mg for diagnostic purposes; fatal reactions do not appear to be related to the presence/absence of pheochromocytoma. A 47 year old man survived 440 mg infused in one day.

Symptoms: The main clinical manifestations of overdosage with phentolamine are arterial hypotension, tachycardia, cardiac stimulation, arrhythmias, increase in systemic venous capacity, and possibly shock. These effects may be accompanied by headache, hyperexcitability and visual disturbances, sweating, increased gastric motility, vomiting and diarrhea, hypoglycemia.

Treatment: Severe hypotension should be treated by discontinuing treatment with phentolamine and maintaining the patient in the supine position with the feet raised.

Norepinephrine, cautiously titrated in continuous i.v. infusion, can be considered the pharmacological antagonist. The effect of phentolamine may wear off in a short time and administration of norepinephrine may have to be adjusted accordingly. Do not use epinephrine since this may cause a further fall in blood pressure.

The ECG should be monitored when a pressor agent is used because major arrhythmias may occur. Should excessive cardiac stimulation and hypertensive crisis arise, administer a beta blocking agent by slow i.v. infusion. Treat hypoglycemia with i.v. glucose until compensated.

Dosage: Prevention or control of hypertensive episodes in the patient with pheochromocytoma, preoperatively and during surgical excision:

For use in preoperative reduction of elevated blood pressure, inject 2 to 5 mg of phentolamine i.v. or i.m. 1 or 2 hours before surgery (and repeat if necessary). For children, use the minimum effective dose e.g. 1 mg for a child over 8 years old.

During surgical removal of pheochromocytoma, repeat i.v. phentolamine as indicated to help prevent or control paroxysms of hypertension, respiratory depression, convulsions, or other effects of epinephrine intoxication. (Post-operatively, norepinephrine may be given to control the hypotension which commonly follows complete removal of a pheochromocytoma).

Prevention of dermal necrosis and sloughing following i.v. administration or extravasation of norepinephrine:

Infiltrate phentolamine mesylate (5 to 10 mg in 10 mL saline) into the area of extravasation within 12 hours.

Diagnosis of pheochromocytoma (phentolamine test): The test is most reliable in detecting pheochromocytoma in patients with sustained hypertension, and least reliable in those with paroxysmal hypertension. False positive tests may occur in patients with hypertension without pheochromocytoma.

I.V.: Preparation: Review the Contraindications, Warnings, and Precautions. Withhold all medication such as sedatives, analgesics, and all other medication unless deemed essential (e.g. digitalis and insulin) for at least 24 hours (preferably 48 to 72 hours) prior to the test. Special precautions should be taken with agents that have a long half-life and may interact with phentolamine (e.g. guanethidine, reserpine and antidepressants). Withhold antihypertensive drugs until blood pressure returns to the untreated, hypertensive level. Do not perform test on a patient who is normotensive.

Procedure: Keep patient at rest in the supine position throughout the test, preferably in a quiet, darkened room. Delay phentolamine injection until blood pressure is stabilized, as evidenced by blood pressure readings taken every 10 minutes for at least one-half hour. Dissolve 5 mg phentolamine mesylate in 1 mL Sterile Water for Injection. Dose for adults is 5 mg; for children, 1 mg. Insert the syringe needle into vein, delay injection until pressor response to venipuncture has subsided. Inject phentolamine rapidly. Record blood

Rogitine (cont'd)

pressure immediately after injection, at 30-second intervals for the first 3 minutes, and at 60-second intervals for the next 7 minutes.

Interpreting the Test: **Positive response,** suggestive of pheochromocytoma, is indicated by a drop in blood pressure of more than 35 mm Hg systolic and 25 mm Hg diastolic pressure. A typical positive response may be a drop of 60 mm Hg systolic and 25 mm Hg diastolic. Maximal depressor pressure effect usually is evident within 2 minutes after injection. Return to pre-injection pressure commonly occurs within 15 to 30 minutes, but may return more rapidly.

If blood pressure falls to a dangerous level, treat patient as outlined under Overdose.

A positive response should always be confirmed by other diagnostic procedures, preferably the measurement of urinary catecholamines or their metabolites.

Negative response is indicated when the blood pressure is unchanged, elevated, or is reduced less than 35 mm Hg systolic and 25 mm Hg diastolic after injection of phentolamine. A negative response to this test does not exclude the diagnosis of pheochromocytoma, especially in patients with paroxysmal hypertension in whom the incidence of false negative responses is high.

I.M.: If the i.m. test for pheochromocytoma is preferred, preparation is the same as for the i.v. test. Then dissolve 5 mg phentolamine mesylate in 1 mL Sterile Water for Injection. Dose for adults is 5 mg i.m., for children, 3 mg. Record blood pressure every 5 minutes for 40 to 45 minutes following i.m. injection. Positive response is indicated by a drop in blood pressure of 35 mm Hg systolic and 25 mm Hg diastolic or greater within 20 minutes following injection.

Supplied: Each vial contains: phentolamine mesylate 5 mg in lyophilized form. Nonmedicinal ingredients: mannitol. Alcohol-, bisulfite-, gluten-, lactose-, parabens-, sodium- and tartrazine-free. Boxes of 10 vials. Protect from heat (store between 2 and 30°C) and light. Use the reconstituted solution upon preparation; storage is not recommended.

ROVAMYCINE® Ⓟ

Rhône-Poulenc Rorer

Spiramycin

Antibiotic

Pharmacology: It is active against the following gram-positive organisms: S. aureus (including penicillin resistant strains), beta-hemolytic streptococci, S. viridans, S. faecalis and S. pneumoniae, C. diphtheriae, clostridia.

Except for B. pertussis, H. influenzae (approximately 50% of strains) and neisseria, gram-negative organisms are generally considered as resistant to spiramycin.

Bacterial resistance to spiramycin has been reported to develop, including cross resistance between spiramycin and erythromycin. However, most of the erythromycin resistant strains of S. aureus are still sensitive to spiramycin.

Indications: The treatment of infections of the respiratory tract, buccal cavity, skin and soft tissues due to susceptible organisms.

N. gonorrhoeae: as an alternate choice of treatment for gonorrhea in patients allergic to the penicillins. Before treatment of gonorrhea, the possibility of concomitant infection due to T. pallidum should be excluded.

Contraindications: Hypersensitivity to the drug.

The levels of spiramycin attained in the CSF are much lower than those in the blood and are too low to be clinically useful. Therefore spiramycin must not be used in patients with meningitis.

Precautions: Administer antibiotics, including spiramycin cautiously to any patient who has demonstrated some form of allergy, particularly to drugs.

The possibilty of superinfection caused by overgrowth of nonsusceptible organisms should be kept in mind during prolonged or repeated therapy. If superinfection occurs, discontinue the drug and take appropriate measures.

Pregnancy: Safety of this product for use during pregnancy has not been established.

Adverse Effects: Spiramycin has a low toxicity and rarely produces serious adverse effects; these include epigastric pain and abdominal discomfort, nausea, vomiting, diarrhea and skin sensitization.

Overdose: Symptoms: No case of accidental overdosage has been reported. In oral doses over 4 g/day, abdominal discomfort, nausea or diarrhea may occur.

Treatment: No specific treatment has been proposed. Management should be symptomatic.

Dosage: Adults: 6 000 000 to 9 000 000 U (4 to 6 capsules of Rovamycine '500') per 24 hours, in 2 divided doses. In severe infections, the daily dosage may be increased to 12 000 000 to 15 000 000 U (8 to 10 capsules of Rovamycine '500' per day).

Gonorrhea: 12 000 000 to 13 500 000 U (8 or 9 capsules) in a single dose.

Children: The usual daily dosage is based on 150 000 U/kg body weight in 2 or 3 divided doses; the following calculated dosages are given as a guide (see Table I).

Table I—Rovamycine

Dosage Guide for Children

Body Weight	Dosage in Capsules of Rovamycine '250' (750 000 U Spiramycin/capsule)
15 kg	3 capsules/day
20 kg	4 capsules/day
30 kg	6 capsules/day

Spiramycin is stable in gastric juices and absorption is not affected by food. In severe infections, the daily dosage may be increased by one half.

In the treatment of beta-hemolytic streptococcal infections, adequate spiramycin dosage should be administered for 10 days.

Supplied: Rovamycine '250': Each orange and red capsule contains: spiramycin 750 000 U. Nonmedicinal ingredients: FD&C Blue No. 1, FD&C Red No. 28, FD&C Red No. 40, FD&C Yellow No. 6, gelatin, lactose, magnesium stearate, sodium croscarmellose and titanium dioxide. Tartrazine-free. Bottles of 50.

Rovamycine '500': Each gray and red capsule contains: spiramycin 1 500 000 U. Nonmedicinal ingredients: FD&C Blue No. 1, FD&C Red No. 28, FD&C Red No. 40, gelatin, iron oxides, lactose, magnesium stearate, sodium croscarmellose and titanium dioxide. Tartrazine-free. Bottles of 50.

(Shown in Product Recognition Section)

ROYCHLOR®

Waymar

Potassium Chloride

Potassium Replacement Therapy

Indications: The treatment of potassium depletion found in patients with hypokalemia and metabolic alkalosis, digitalis intoxication, inadequate dietary potassium intake and those patients receiving digitalis and diuretics, e.g. congestive heart failure, and hepatic cirrhosis with ascites. For treatment of hypertensive patients undergoing longterm diuretic therapy, hyperaldosteronism states with normal renal function, potassium losing nephropathy and certain diarrheal states.

Contraindications: In ventricular fibrillation, hyperkalemia of any etiology, in association with Addison's disease, salt losing adrenal hyperplasia, in extensive tissue breakdown as in severe burns, acute dehydration and heat cramps. Renal impairment with oliguria or azotemia. Increased sensitivity to potassium administration, e.g., in congenital paramyotonia or adynamia episodica hereditaria.

Warnings: In patients with impaired mechanisms for excreting potassium, e.g. chronic renal disease, administration of potassium salts can produce hyperkalemia and cardiac arrest. This occurs most commonly in patients given i.v. potassium but may also occur in patients given oral potassium. Potentially fatal hyperkalemia can develop rapidly and be asymptomatic. Careful monitoring of the serum potassium concentration and appropriate dosage adjustment is recommended.

Caution is advised with concomitant administration of potassium and potassium sparing diuretics e.g., spironolactone or triamterene, since hyperkalemia may develop. Hypokalemia in patients with metabolic acidosis should be treated with an alkalinizing potassium salt such as the acetate, bicarbonate, gluconate or citrate.

Precautions: The treatment of potassium depletion, particularly in the presence of cardiac disease, renal disease or acidosis, requires careful attention to acid base balance and appropriate monitoring of serum electrolytes, the ECG and the patient's clinical status.

Use potassium with caution in diseases associated with heart block since increased serum potassium may increase the degree of block.

Adverse Effects: Nausea, vomiting, and diarrhea have been reported. These symptoms are due to irritation of the gastrointestinal tract and are best avoided by increasing fluid intake when possible, taking the dose with meals or reducing the dose. Severe adverse effects reported with potassium preparations have been hyperkalemia, intestinal esophageal and gastric ulceration.

Overdose: Symptoms and Treatment: In patients under normal conditions of exertion, concentrations of potassium in the blood of greater than 4 mEq/L, and in the urine of greater than 2 g/24 hours, may indicate hyperkalemia. Paresthesia of the extremities, listlessness, mental confusion, weakness, paralysis, hypotension, cardiac arrhythmias, heart block and cardiac arrest may occur. ECG changes include increased amplitude and peaking of the T waves, depression of the ST segment, reduction in the amplitude of the R wave, widening of the QRS complex, prolongation of the PR interval and a decrease in the amplitude and ultimately disappearance of the P wave. Widening of the QRS complex is one of the most ominous signs and indicates the need for aggressive treatment.

Frequently hyperkalemia is asymptomatic and may be manifested only by increased serum potassium concentration and characteristic electrocardiographic changes as above.

Treatment of Hyperkalemia: 1. Eliminate foods and medications containing potassium, and discontinue potassium sparing diuretics.

2. I.V. administration of 300 to 500 mL/hour of 10% dextrose solution containing 10 to 20 units of crystalline insulin/ 1 000 mL.

3. Correct acidosis, if present, with i.v. sodium bicarbonate.

4. Use exchange resins, hemodialysis or peritoneal dialysis.

5. In the presence of life threatening cardiac arrhythmias, to antagonize the cardiac toxicity, administer i.v. 10 to 50 mL calcium gluconate 10% over 1 to 5 minutes. Continuous ECG monitoring is mandatory.

In cases of digitalization, too rapid a lowering of plasma potassium concentration can cause digitalis toxicity.

Dosage: The usual adult dosage is 20 mEq in 90 mL or more of water twice daily after meals. Citrus fruit juices or citrated soft drinks may be used in place of water to dilute Roychlor-10%. Larger single doses, for example, 40 mEq, should be given with 240 mL of water after meals to minimize the possibility of a saline laxative effect. If given concomitantly in chronic diuretic therapy, administer on alternating days.

Prevention of hypokalemia: supplementary, approximately 20 to 40 mEq/day.

Treatment of depletion: 40 to a maximum of 100 mEq daily.

Supplied: Each 15 mL of clear, yellow colored liquid supplies: 20 mEq each of elemental potassium and chloride (as potassium chloride 1.5 g) with sugar and flavoring. Unit Dose package of 15 mL, bottles of 500 and 2 400 mL.

ROYFLEX®

Waymar

Triethanolamine Salicylate

Topical Analgesic

Indications: Analgesic rub for sore muscles, joint attachments, stiffness, sprains and minor arthritic and rheumatic conditions.

Contraindications: Salicylate hypersensitivity.

Precautions: Avoid contact with eyes, mucous membranes and broken skin. A 85 g tube contains the salicylate equivalent of about 5.4 g ASA. If applied to excessive skin areas may cause typical salicylate untoward effects such as tinnitus, nausea or vomiting.

Dosage: Apply to area of soreness with gentle massage, 2 or 3 times daily.

Supplied: Each 85 g tube contains: triethanolamine salicylate 10% w/w in a greaseless, nonstaining, odorless, vanishing cream base.

ROYVAC®
Waymar

Magnesium Citrate—Bisacodyl

Bowel Evacuant

Indications: Preparation of the colon for radiology (prior to barium enemas or i.v. pyelograms) surgery and many proctological procedures.

Precautions: Do not use any of these preparations when undiagnosed abdominal pain, nausea or vomiting are present. Frequent or prolonged use of these preparations may result in dependence on laxatives. Do not administer Royvac to persons who cannot swallow without chewing. Rectal bleeding or failure to respond may indicate a serious condition. Consult physician.

Adverse Effects: If full schedule of fluid intake is not followed, patient may become weak or dizzy due to dehydration.

Dosage: Your physician is preparing you for a medical procedure that requires thorough cleansing of the intestinal tract.

Be sure to follow each step and complete all instructions or the entire procedure may have to be repeated. **Important:** A high fluid intake is essential to the success of this regimen. You **must** drink a large glass (225 mL) of fluid at specified times. Drink only black coffee, plain tea, **strained** fruit juice, soft drinks or water at the times indicated. **No milk or cream.** Water is the preferred liquid to ensure success of this procedure.

Be sure to drink all the fluids specified.

On the Day Before the Examination: 12 Noon: Liquid lunch: Clear soup, plain gelatin, 225 mL of fluid. **(No milk products.)**
12:30 p.m. (or ½ hour after lunch): Drink entire contents of oral solution (#1 in your kit) over ice. A strong bowel cleansing action should be expected 3 to 6 hours after drinking this preparation.
1:00 p.m.: 225 mL of fluid.
3:00 p.m.: Take all 3 tablets (#2 in your kit) with a large glass of water **Do not crush or chew tablets. Swallow tablets whole,** one at a time.
4:00 p.m.: 225 mL of fluid.
5:00 p.m.: Liquid dinner: Clear soup, plain gelatin, 225 mL of fluid. **(No milk products.)**
6:00 p.m.: 225 mL of fluid.
9:00 p.m.: 225 mL of fluid.
10:00 p.m.: Remove foil wrapping from suppository (#3 in your kit). Insert suppository into rectum as far as possible. Wait at least 10 to 15 minutes before evacuating even if the urge is strong.
Bedtime: 225 mL of fluid. Drink additional quantities of the recommended fluids if up during the night.

On the Day of the Examination: No foods until after the examination is completed. One glass of fluid is permitted prior to the examination.

There are alternate time schedules for patients unable to start at noon the day before the examination. Available from manufacturer upon request.

Supplied: Each Royvac kit contains: **Solution:** Each bottle contains: magnesium citrate 17.46 g. Bottles of 296 mL. **Suppository (1):** Each suppository contains: bisacodyl 10 mg. **Tablets (3):** Each tablet contains: bisacodyl 5 mg. Store at 15 to 30°C.

RUBRAMIN®
Squibb

Vitamin B_{12}

Hematopoietic

Pharmacology: Vitamin B is essential for growth, cell reproduction, hematopoiesis, nucleoprotein and myelin synthesis.

Within 48 hours after injection of 100 to 1 000 μg of vitamin B_{12}, 50 to 98% of the injected dose may appear in the urine. The major portion is excreted within the first 8 hours.

Indications: For vitamin B_{12} deficiency occurring in: pernicious anemia with or without neurological complications. Other macrocytic, megaloblastic anemias where etiology suggests malabsorption of vitamin B_{12} such as following gastrectomy; gastric carcinoma; megaloblastic anemia associated with such gastrointestinal disorders as sprue syndrome, blind loops and anastomoses and fish tapeworm.
Note: In macrocytic megaloblastic anemia of pregnancy and sprue syndromes, cyanocobalamin may fail to produce satisfactory response, folic acid being indicated alone or in combination with cyanocobalamin.

The injection is also suitable for use as the flushing dose in the Schilling (vitamin B_{12} absorption) Test for pernicious anemia.

Contraindications: Sensitivity to cobalt or vitamin B_{12}.

Warnings: Patients who have early Leber's disease (hereditary optic nerve atrophy) have been found to suffer severe and swift optic atrophy when treated with vitamin B_{12}.

Hypokalemia and sudden death may occur when severe megaloblastic anemia is treated intensively. Lack of therapeutic response may be due to infection, uremia, concomitant treatment with chloramphenicol or misdiagnosis.

Precautions: Before administering vitamin B_{12}, an intradermal test dose is recommended for patients known to be sensitive to cobalamines.

Most antibiotics, methotrexate and pyrimethamine invalidate folic acid and vitamin B_{12} diagnostic microbiological blood assays.

Colchicine, para-aminosalicylic acid or excessive alcohol intake for longer than 2 weeks may produce malabsorption of vitamin B_{12}. Doses of vitamin B_{12} exceeding 10 μg daily may produce a hematologic response in patients who have a folate deficiency.

Indiscriminate administration of vitamin B_{12} may mask the true diagnosis of pernicious anemia. A dietary deficiency of only vitamin B_{12} is rare. Multiple vitamin deficiency is expected in any dietary deficiency.

Adverse Effects: Mild transient diarrhea, polycythemia vera, peripheral vascular thrombosis, itching, transitory exanthema, feeling of swelling of entire body, pulmonary edema and congestive heart failure early in treatment, anaphylactic shock and death have been reported following vitamin B_{12} administration.

Dosage: In patients with Addisonian (pernicious) anemia, parenteral therapy with vitamin B_{12} is the recommended method of treatment and will be required for the remainder of the patient's life. Oral therapy is not dependable. Serum potassium must be watched closely the first 48 hours; and potassium should be replaced if necessary. Reticulocyte plasma count, vitamin B_{12} and folic acid levels must be obtained prior to treatment and between the fifth and seventh day of therapy.

In patients with other types of vitamin B_{12} deficiency due to malabsorption, the malabsorption should be corrected. In all patients a well balanced dietary intake should be prescribed and poor dietary habits should be corrected.
Treatment of vitamin B_{12} deficiency: 30 μg daily for 5 to 10 days followed by 100 μg monthly injected i.m. or deep s.c. Folic acid should be administered concomitantly early in the treatment unless folic acid levels are adequate.
Note: Cyanocobalamin should not be administered i.v.
Schilling Test: The flushing dose is 1 000 μg.

Supplied: Each mL of clear, sterile, red aqueous solution for injection contains: vitamin B_{12} 1 000 μg. Nonmedicinal ingredients: benzyl alcohol 1.5% w/v, sodium chloride, sodium hydroxide or hydrochloric acid (for pH adjustment) and water for injection. Vials of 10 mL. Store at room temperature. Protect from freezing, sunlight and excessive heat.

RYLOSOL ℞
ICN

Sotalol HCl

Antiarrhythmic

Supplied: 80 mg: Each light blue, capsule-shaped tablet, embossed ICN S31, contains: sotalol HCl BP 80 mg. Nonmedicinal ingredients: colloidal silicon dioxide, FD&C blue #2, lactose monohydrate, magnesium stearate and microcrystalline cellulose. Bottles of 100 and 500.

160 mg: Each light blue, capsule-shaped tablet, embossed ICN S32, contains: sotalol HCl BP 160 mg. Nonmedicinal ingredients: colloidal silicon dioxide, FD&C blue #2, lactose monohydrate, magnesium stearate and microcrystalline cellulose. Bottles of 100 and 500.

240 mg: Each light blue, capsule-shaped tablet, embossed ICN S33, contains: sotalol HCl BP 240 mg. Nonmedicinal ingredients: colloidal silicon dioxide, FD&C blue #2, lactose monohydrate, magnesium stearate and microcrystalline cellulose. Bottles of 100 and 500.

Information on drug administration with respect to food can be found in the CLIN-INFO SECTION.

RYTHMODAN® ℞
RYTHMODAN®-LA ℞
Hoechst Marion Roussel

Disopyramide

Antiarrhythmic Agent

Pharmacology: In both animal and man the electrophysiological and hemodynamic effects of disopyramide are qualitatively similar to those of quinidine and procainamide.

Although the exact mechanism of action has not been completely elucidated, it would appear from animal studies that disopyramide exerts its antiarrhythmic activity in the following manner: 1. Reduces automaticity in cardiac Purkinje fibers by depressing the slope of Phase 4 diastolic depolarization. The action manifests itself both in normal Purkinje fibers and in fibers damaged by either ischemia or infarction. 2. Depresses conduction velocity in atria, AV node, Purkinje fibers and ventricular muscle by decreasing the rate of rise of phase 0 depolarization in these fibers. 3. Prolongs action potential duration and effective refractory period in atria, Purkinje fibers and ventricular muscle. 4. Depresses excitability of both atrial and ventricular muscles by its direct effect on the myocardium. 5. Although the anticholinergic action of disopyramide may cause an increase in the sinus rate of normal hearts, the usual effect on the rapid cardiac rate associated with an arrhythmia is a decrease with possibly a reduction in blood pressure. Disopyramide exerts a negative inotropic action on cardiac muscle.

Disopyramide is rapidly absorbed after oral administration and reaches peak levels in about 1 to 2 hours. Absorption is slower with the long acting form, peak levels being reached in 4.5 to 6.2 hours.

Serum levels of disopyramide are correlated with antiarrhythmic activity. Usual therapeutic plasma levels are 2 to 4 μg/mL. At these concentrations, disopyramide in the blood is about equally distributed between plasma and erythrocytes. Plasma protein binding of disopyramide in humans varies with drug concentration. At therapeutic concentrations, protein binding is about 50%. Toxic plasma levels have not been defined in man, but are thought to exceed 10.5 μg/mL.

Mean plasma half-life of disopyramide in healthy humans is 6.7 hours (range of 4 to 10 hours) while with the long acting form it is 14.5 hours, and even longer in ill, hospitalized patients. Patients with impaired renal function (creatinine clearance less than 40 mL/minute), have demonstrated disopyramide half-lives of 10 to 18 hours. Hepatic impairment may also prolong the half-life. Little or no tissue accumulation occurs.

In healthy humans, urinary and fecal excretion of disopyramide and its metabolites account for about 80% and 10% of the dose, respectively. Forty percent (40%) to 60% of a given dose is excreted in the urine as the unchanged drug and 15% to 25% as the mono-N-dealkylated metabolite. The remainder of a given dose is excreted via the bile into the feces. The plasma concentration of this metabolite is about 1/10th that of disopyramide.

Indications:

> No antiarrhythmic drug has been shown to reduce the incidence of sudden death in patients with asymptomatic ventricular arrhythmias. Most antiarrhythmic drugs have the potential to cause dangerous arrhythmias; some have been shown to be associated with an increased incidence of sudden death. In light of the above, physicians should carefully consider the risks and benefits of antiarrhythmic therapy for all patients with ventricular arrhythmias.

Disopyramide is indicated for the treatment of documented life-threatening ventricular arrhythmias, such as sustained ventricular tachycardia. Disopyramide may also be used for the treatment of patients with documented symptomatic ventricular arrhythmias when the symptoms are of sufficient severity to require treatment. Because of the proarrhythmic effects of disopyramide its use should be reserved for patients in whom, in the opinion of the physician, the benefit of treatment clearly outweighs the risks.

For patients with sustained ventricular tachycardia, disopyramide therapy should be initiated in the hospital. Hospitalization may also be required for certain other patients depending on their cardiac status and underlying cardiac disease.

The effects of disopyramide in patients with recent myocardial infarction have not been adequately studied and, therefore, its use in this condition cannot be recommended.

Rythmodan (cont'd)

Contraindications: In the presence of shock, renal failure, severe intraventricular conduction defects, pre-existing second and third degree AV block (if no pacemaker is present), known hypersensitivity to the drug.

Disopyramide should not be used in the presence of uncompensated or inadequately compensated congestive heart failure (see Warnings).

Disopyramide is contraindicated in most patients with extensive myocardial disease, but may on occasion be used in these patients under the close supervision of a cardiologist if in his opinion the patient's condition justifies it. When used in these patients continuous ECG monitoring in a CCU facility is mandatory.

Due to its anticholinergic activity, disopyramide is contraindicated in most patients with glaucoma or in patients in whom urinary retention is present (see Precautions).

Warnings: Mortality: The results of Cardiac Arrhythmia Suppression Trial (CAST) in post-myocardial infarction patients with asymptomatic ventricular arrhythmias showed a significant increase in mortality and in non-fatal cardiac arrest rate in patients treated with encainide or flecainide compared with a matched placebo-treated group. CAST was continued using a revised protocol with the moricizine and placebo arms only. The trial was prematurely terminated because of a trend towards an increase in mortality in the moricizine treated group.

The applicability of these results to other populations or other antiarrhythmic agents is uncertain, but at present it is prudent to consider these results when using any antiarrhythmic agent.

Negative Inotropic Properties: Heart Failure: Because of its negative inotropic effect disopyramide may cause or worsen congestive heart failure. Therefore, this drug should not be used in patients with heart failure, and should be especially avoided in patients with a previous history of heart failure except in the very special circumstances described below:

In patients in whom the failure is exacerbated or caused by an arrhythmia, disopyramide may be used to suppress the ectopy but it must be borne in mind that any such benefit on cardiac function may be overcome by the depressant effect on cardiac output, and thereby result in even worse failure even though routine methods of anti-failure therapy including optimal digitalization are attempted. Careful monitoring is essential under these circumstances.

Patients with compensated heart failure may be treated with disopyramide, but careful attention must be given to the maintenance of cardiac function including optimal digitalization. Close observation is mandatory, as any benefit of disopyramide either therapeutic or prophylactic could be accompanied by an unacceptable lowering of cardiac output.

For most patients the encroachment on their cardiac reserve may be of minimal clinical consequence, but in patients with a limited reserve as a result of pump dysfunction and/or imbalanced work load, even a minor encroachment on reserve can precipitate clinically evident failure or make its control more difficult, and even result in a gross low output congestive cardiac failure state (see Precautions, Drug Interactions).

Hypotension: On rare occasions disopyramide has caused syncope with sudden loss of consciousness. In the cases reported, this was believed to be due to an excessive hypotensive action of the drug or, in some cases, due to concomitant use with other hypotensive or negative inotropic agents.

Severe hypotension following disopyramide administration has been observed usually in patients with primary myocardial disease (cardiomyopathy), and also in inadequately compensated congestive heart failure or advanced myocardial disease with low output state, or in patients on other hypotensive medication e.g., beta-adrenergic blockers or verapamil. An oral loading dose of disopyramide should not be given to such patients; initial dosage and subsequent dosage adjustments should be made under close supervision.

If severe hypotension develops, disopyramide should be discontinued promptly (see Precautions, Drug Interactions).

Other Cardiac Effects: QRS Widening: Significant widening (greater than 25%) of the QRS complex may occur during disopyramide administration; in such cases disopyramide should be discontinued.

Q-T Prolongation: As with other quinidine-like antiarrhythmic drugs, prolongation of the Q-T interval (corrected) and worsening of the arrhythmia may occur with disopyramide, particularly in response to higher doses. Patients who have evidenced prolongation of the Q-T interval in response to quinidine may be at particular risk. If a Q-T prolongation greater than 25% is observed and if ectopy continues, the patient should be monitored closely, and consideration be given to discontinuing disopyramide.

Disopyramide, as with other quinidine-like antiarrhythmic drugs, has been associated with torsades de pointes.

Heart Block: If first degree heart block develops in a patient receiving disopyramide, the dosage should be reduced. If the block persists despite reduction of dosage, continuation of the drug must depend upon weighing the benefit being obtained against the risk of higher degree of heart block. Development of second or third degree AV block or unifascicular or trifascicular block requires discontinuation of disopyramide therapy, unless the ventricular rate is adequately controlled by a temporary or implanted ventricular pacemaker.

Precautions: Patients with Special Diseases or Conditions: Atrial Tachyarrhythmias: Disopyramide is usually ineffective in atrial flutter and its usefulness in atrial fibrillation is not proven. If atrial flutter or fibrillation is present, the patient should be fully digitalized prior to disopyramide use so that drug-induced changes in AV conduction do not result in an increase of ventricular rate beyond physiologically acceptable limits.

Conduction Abnormalities: Disopyramide therapy in patients with sick sinus syndrome (including bradycardia-tachycardia syndrome), Wolff-Parkinson White (WPW) syndrome or bundle branch block requires care, since the effect of disopyramide in these conditions is difficult to predict. Sinoatrial node function deterioration has been reported in 6 sick sinus syndrome patients treated with disopyramide.

Digitalis Intoxication: Since disopyramide has not been studied in patients with digitalis intoxication, it should be used with caution in these patients.

Anticholinergic Activity: Glaucoma: In patients with a family history of angle-closure glaucoma, intraocular pressure should be measured before initiating disopyramide therapy. Disopyramide should not be administered to patients with angle-closure glaucoma unless topical application of miotics (e.g. pilocarpine ophthalmic drops) is used to counteract the anticholinergic effects of the drug.

Urinary Retention: Urinary retention may occur in patients of either sex, but males with benign prostatic hypertrophy are at particular risk. If acute urinary retention develops, disopyramide therapy should be temporarily discontinued, except in occasional instances, in which continued control of the arrhythmia with disopyramide is considered mandatory. In such cases, overriding measures should be taken (e.g., catheter drainage or operative relief). If disopyramide is discontinued, and later reintroduced, a lower dose should be used.

Myasthenia Gravis: Disopyramide should be used with special care in myasthenia gravis since its anticholinergic properties could precipitate a myasthenic crisis.

Renal Impairment: More than 50% of disopyramide is excreted unchanged in urine. Therefore, in impaired renal function reduce the dose and increase the dosing interval (see Dosage); ECG should be carefully monitored for prolongation of PR interval, QRS widening, or other signs of overdosage (see Pharmacology and Overdose: Symptoms and Treatment).

Rythmodan-LA tablets should not be used in patients with severe renal impairment.

Hepatic Impairment: Hepatic impairment also increases disopyramide plasma half-life; reduce dosage for patients with such impairment. The ECG should be carefully monitored for signs of overdosage.

Rythmodan-LA tablets should not be used in severe hepatic impairment.

Hypokalemia: Although there is no experience with disopyramide in severe hypokalemia, other antiarrhythmic agents are frequently ineffective in such patients; a significant potassium deficit should be corrected before instituting disopyramide therapy.

Hypoglycemia: Significant lowering of blood glucose has occasionally been reported during disopyramide administration. The physician should be alert to this possibility, especially in patients with congestive heart failure, chronic malnutrition, hepatic, renal or other diseases, or who are taking drugs (e.g., β-adrenergic blockers, alcohol) which could compromise preservation of the normal gluco-regulatory mechanisms in the absence of food. In these patients blood glucose levels should be carefully monitored (see Drug Interactions).

Pregnancy: Animal studies have not demonstrated any teratogenic effect and only minimal evidence of impaired fertility.

Disopyramide has been reported to stimulate contraction of the pregnant uterus.

Disopyramide should be used in pregnant women only when it is clearly indicated and the benefit/risk ratio has been carefully evaluated.

Lactation: Disopyramide is excreted in human milk. Therefore, if use of the drug is deemed essential in lactating women, an alternative method of infant feeding should be instituted.

Children: The safety and effectiveness of disopyramide in children have not been established.

Drug Interactions: Concomitant Antiarrhythmic Therapy: The concomitant use of disopyramide with other Class I antiarrhythmic agent and/or β-adrenergic blockers should be reserved for patients with life-threatening arrhythmias who are demonstrably unresponsive to single agent antiarrhythmic therapy. Such use may produce serious negative inotropic effects, or may excessively prolong conduction. This should be considered particularly in patients with any degree of cardiac decompensation or those with a prior history, thereof. Patients receiving more than one antiarrhythmic drug must be carefully monitored.

Administer disopyramide cautiously to patients who have recently received other antiarrhythmic drugs. Disopyramide should not be started until at least one half-life after stopping the other antiarrhythmic agent. (Half-life of quinidine is about 6 hours. Half-life of procainamide is about 3 hours.) In these cases loading dose of disopyramide should not be used. Excessive widening of QRS or excessive negative inotropic effect may occur.

Quinidine: Concomitant administration of disopyramide and quinidine resulted in slight increases in plasma disopyramide levels and slight decreases in plasma quinidine levels.

Verapamil: Although the interaction is poorly documented, the concurrent use of verapamil and disopyramide may aggravate or precipitate congestive heart failure or result in excessive hypotension (see Warnings).

Digoxin: Concomitant digoxin and disopyramide therapy has not resulted in changes in serum digoxin levels.

Anticholinergic Agents: The anticholinergic effect of disopyramide may be additive with that of other agents having anticholinergic properties.

Drugs Affecting Hepatic Microsomal Enzymes: Drugs (e.g.: phenobarbital, rifampin, phenytoin) that induce hepatic microsomal enzymes may accelerate the metabolism of disopyramide, resulting in lower plasma concentrations. When microsomal enzymes inducers are used concomitantly with disopyramide, serum concentrations of disopyramide should be closely monitored to avoid subtherapeutic concentrations.

Erythromycin: There are 2 reported cases of patients with clinically stable cardiac condition under disopyramide therapy where the addition of erythromycin resulted in polymorphic ventricular tachycardia, QTc prolongation, and elevation of disopyramide serum levels. Erythromycin appears to inhibit disopyramide metabolism in the liver. Additional documentation is needed to substantiate this possible interaction. However closer monitoring is advised when the two drugs are combined.

Ethanol: In healthy subjects, ethanol did not affect the half-life or total body clearance of disopyramide. However, combination could result in hypoglycemia in patients at risk (see Precautions).

Insulin: There has been 1 report of potentiation of the hypoglycemic effect of insulin by disopyramide (see Hypoglycemia).

Warfarin: Potentiation of the hypoprothrombinemic effect of warfarin has been reported in several patients receiving disopyramide and warfarin. However, in a study in several patients receiving disopyramide and warfarin concomitantly, the hypoprothrombinemic effect of warfarin was not increased and, in 2 patients, actually was decreased slightly. Further study is needed to determine whether a potential interaction exists.

Adverse Effects: Rare occurrence of congestive heart failure, hypotension, widening QRS, sinus arrest, nodal rhythm dissociation, cardiac arrest and cardiovascular collapse have been reported. An occasional paradoxical ventricular tachycardia evolving sometimes to fibrillation has been observed. A definite relationship to the drug was not always established in the above cardiovascular effects.

The most common adverse reactions which are dose dependent are associated with the anticholinergic properties of the drug. These may be transitory, but may be persistent and can be severe. Urinary retention is the most serious anticholinergic effect.

The following reactions were reported in more than 10% of patients: Anticholinergic: dry mouth (16 to 30%), urinary retention (7 to 13%), constipation.

Gastrointestinal: nausea, indigestion, vomiting, diarrhea, flatulence, bad taste in the mouth, anorexia.

The following reactions were reported in 1 to 10% of patients: Anticholinergic: blurred vision, dry eyes/nose/throat.

Cardiovascular: hypotension with or without CHF, increased CHF, cardiac conduction disturbances, proarrhythmic effects (6%), edema, dyspnea, cyanosis, chest pain.

Dermatologic: skin reactions including pruritus, urticaria, morbilliform eruption, abdominal rash, photosensitization.

General: dizziness, vertigo, drowsiness, profuse sweating.

Genitourinary: urinary hesitancy and frequency.
Other: raised AST levels.

The following were reported in less than 1% of patients: dysuria, headache, feeling of warmth, pallor, peripheral paresthesia, fatigue, malaise, insomnia, confusion, transitory psychosis, elevated BUN, elevated creatinine, decreased hemoglobin/hematocrit, hypoglycemia, neutropenia, idiosyncratic reaction to drug. In a few instances cholestatic jaundice has been reported. A definite causal relationship has not been established.

A high plasma concentration has been associated with impotence.

Overdose: Symptoms: Five patients who took deliberate overdoses of oral disopyramide presented with an early loss of consciousness after an apneic period, cardiac arrhythmias and loss of spontaneous respiration, leading to death. Serum levels in these patients were as high as 114 mg/L taken at various times after ingestion, including post-mortem.

Toxic plasma levels of disopyramide produce excessive widening of QRS complex and QT interval, worsening of congestive heart failure, hypotension, varying kinds and degrees of conduction disturbance, bradycardia and finally asystole. Obvious anticholinergic effects are also observed.

Treatment: Discontinue drug and initiate gastric lavage; no specific antidote has been identified: treatment of overdosage should be symptomatic and may include the administration of isoproterenol, dopamine, intra-aortic balloon counterpulsation, mechanically assisted respiration and hemoperfusion with charcoal.

Hemodialysis may be employed to rapidly lower serum concentration of drug. In vitro studies with human blood have demonstrated good dialyzability. Its clearance was 33 mL/minute at a blood flow 250 mL/minute when an initial plasma concentration of 22 μg/mL was dialyzed using an artificial kidney (Cordis-DOW-4).

The ECG should be monitored and supportive therapy with vasopressors, sympathomimetics, cardiac glycosides and diuretics should be given, as required.

Should progressive heart block develop, endocardial pacing should be implemented. In case of any impaired renal function, measures to increase glomerular filtration rate may reduce the toxicity (disopyramide is excreted primarily by the kidney). Altering the urinary pH in man does not affect plasma half-life or the amount of disopyramide excreted in urine.

The anticholinergic effects could be reversed with neostigmine, at the discretion of the physician.

Dosage: The dosage should be individualized for each patient based upon response and tolerance and patient weight.

Capsules: Usual daily dose: 400 to 800 mg given in 4 divided doses. Rarely, control may be maintained on daily doses of less than 400 mg.

If rapid control of arrhythmia is essential, an initial dosage schedule for most adults is a single loading dose of 300 mg followed by 100 mg every 6 hours. If satisfactory control of the arrhythmia is not obtained with the maintenance dose of 100 mg every 6 hours, increase to 150 mg or subsequently to 200 mg every 6 hours if necessary.

For patients with cardiomyopathy or possible cardiac decompensation, loading doses should not be given, an initial dosage should be limited to 100 mg every 6 hours. Subsequent dosage adjustments should be made gradually with close monitoring for possible development of hypotension and/or congestive heart failure (see Warnings).

For patients of small stature (body weight less than 50 kg) and for patients with mild hepatic or renal insufficiency (creatinine clearance above 60 mL/minute) a loading dose of 200 mg is recommended followed by 100 mg every 6 hours. The recommended maintenance dose of these patients is 400 mg/day given in doses of 100 mg every 6 hours.

In patients with severe hepatic or renal insufficiency (creatinine clearance below 50 mL/minute) an initial loading dose of 100 mg is recommended. These patients are best managed with repeated plasma disopyramide determinations and subsequent dosage and frequency of administration (see Table I) should be based on the results of these determinations (see Precautions).

Table I—Rythmodan

Dosage Interval for Patients with Renal Insufficiency (Rythmodan Capsules)

Creatinine clearance (mL/min)	40–30	30–15	<15
Approximate maintenance-dosing interval	q8h	q12h	q24h

No loading dose should be given to patients who are being transferred from other oral antiarrhythmic agents such as quinidine or procainamide (see Precautions, Drug Interactions).

Long Acting Tablets: Rythmodan-LA should not be used to initiate therapy; the patient should be titrated to the appropriate disopyramide dosage level using disopyramide capsules. Patients stabilized on disopyramide to a dosage level of 500 to 600 mg/day can be transferred to Rythmodan-LA one 250 mg twice daily. Patients titrated to other dosage levels should remain on disopyramide capsules. The first Rythmodan-LA dose should be taken 6 hours after the last disopyramide capsule dose. Rythmodan-LA should not be used in patients with cardiomyopathies, or severe renal or hepatic insufficiency.

Supplied: Capsules: Each hard gelatin capsule contains: disopyramide 100 mg (green/yellow, marked RY RL) or 150 mg (opaque white, marked RY 150). Bottles of 100.

LA Tablets: Each circular, off-white, biconvex, film-coated tablet with a break line contains: disopyramide phosphate equivalent to 250 mg disopyramide base. Tablets are marked RY and R on one side and the Roussel logo on the other. Bottles of 100.

(Shown in Product Recognition Section)

RYTHMOL® Ⓟ

Knoll

Propafenone HCl

Antiarrhythmic Agent

Pharmacology: Propafenone is an antiarrhythmic agent which possesses class 1c properties in the modified electrophysiological classification of Vaughan-Williams. It has a direct stabilizing action on myocardial cell membranes. The electrophysiological effect of propafenone manifests itself as a reduction of the upstroke velocity (Phase 0) of the monophasic action potential, while phase 4 spontaneous automaticity is depressed. Diastolic excitability threshold is increased and effective refractory period prolonged. In Purkinje fibers, and to a lesser extent myocardial fibers, propafenone reduces the fast inward sodium current.

In addition to a local anesthetic effect, approximately equal to procaine, propafenone has weak beta-blocking activity. Clinical trials employing isoproterenol challenge and exercise testing suggest that the affinity of propafenone for beta-adrenergic receptors, as calculated from dose ratios and drug concentrations, is about 1/40 that of propranolol. Propafenone also inhibits the slow calcium influx at high concentrations, however, this action is weak (approximately 1/100 of verapamil) and does not contribute to its antiarrhythmic effect.

Electrophysiology studies have shown that propafenone prolongs atrioventricular conduction and in some instances significantly lengthens sinus nodal recovery times with a non-significant effect on sinus cycle length. AV nodal conduction time (AH interval) as well as His-Purkinje conduction time (HV interval) are prolonged. Propafenone increases atrial, AV nodal and ventricular effective refractory periods. Propafenone causes a dose-dependent increase in the PR interval and QRS complex duration. Non-significant increases in the QT_c interval and occasional slowing of the heart rate have also been observed.

Propafenone can exert a negative inotropic effect on the myocardium. Increases in pulmonary capillary wedge pressure and systemic and pulmonary vascular resistance, with a concurrent mild depression of cardiac output and cardiac index, have occurred following propafenone administration. Decreases in left ventricular function have been recorded in patients with depressed baseline function.

Pharmacokinetics: Following oral administration, propafenone is nearly completely absorbed but undergoes extensive first-pass hepatic metabolism resulting in a dose-dependent absolute bioavailability ranging from 3 to 40%. Bioavailability is enhanced by administration of the drug with food. Peak plasma concentrations occur within 3 hours. There is a non-linear increase in both plasma concentration and bioavailability with increase in dosage, presumably due to saturation of first pass hepatic metabolism as the liver is exposed to higher concentrations of propafenone. This departure from dose linearity occurs when single doses above 150 mg are given. A 300 mg dose gives plasma levels 6 times that of a 150 mg dose. Similarly, for a 3-fold increase in daily dose from 300 to 900 mg/day there is a 10-fold increase in steady state plasma concentration.

Patients may be categorized into fast (90%) or slow (10%) metabolizers of propafenone, resulting in low or high plasma concentrations respectively. This variability in metabolism is thought to be due to a genetically determined deficiency in one pathway. Propafenone undergoes extensive hepatic metabolism with <1% excreted as unchanged drug. In man, the major metabolites are: 5-hydroxypropafenone (5-OHP) and N-depropylpropafenone (NDPP); both occurring in concentrations less than 20% of the parent compound. In vitro preparations and animal studies have shown that the 5-OHP metabolite possesses antiarrhythmic and beta-adrenoreceptor blocking activity comparable to propafenone. For fast metabolizers of propafenone, the elimination half-life is 5.5±2.1 hours; for slow metabolizers, the elimination half-life is 17.2±8 hours. In slow metabolizers, as opposed to fast metabolizers, a linear relationship between propafenone dose and plasma concentration was observed. Slow metabolizers had higher propafenone plasma concentrations which they required for suppression of arrhythmia since they did not produce the active metabolite 5-OHP. These higher propafenone plasma concentrations may lead to clinically evident beta-blockade. Despite these differences in pharmacogenetics, steady-state conditions are achieved after 3 to 4 days in all patients.

Therapeutic plasma levels of propafenone appear to be in the range of 0.5 to 2.0 μg/mL. Propafenone is 97% bound to plasma proteins.

Indications:

> No antiarrhythmic drug has been shown to reduce the incidence of sudden death in patients with asymptomatic ventricular arrhythmias. Most antiarrhythmic drugs have the potential to cause dangerous arrhythmias; some have been shown to be associated with an increased incidence of sudden death. In light of the above, physicians should carefully consider the risks and benefits of antiarrhythmic therapy for all patients with ventricular arrhythmias.

For the treatment of documented life-threatening ventricular arrhythmias, such as sustained ventricular tachycardia. May also be used for the treatment of patients with documented symptomatic ventricular arrhythmias when the symptoms are of sufficient severity to require treatment. Because of the proarrhythmic effects of propafenone, its use should be reserved for patients in whom, in the opinion of the physician, the benefit of treatment clearly outweighs the risks.

For patients with sustained ventricular tachycardia, propafenone therapy should be initiated in the hospital. Initiation in hospital may also be required for certain other patients depending on their cardiac status and underlying cardiac disease.

The effects of propafenone in patients with recent myocardial infarction have not been adequately studied and, therefore, its use in this condition cannot be recommended.

There is no evidence from controlled clinical trials that the use of propafenone favorably affects survival or the incidence of sudden death.

Contraindications: In the presence of the following: severe or uncontrolled congestive heart failure (see Warnings); cardiogenic shock; sinoatrial, atrioventricular and intraventricular disorders of impulse conduction and sinus node dysfunction (e.g. sick sinus syndrome) in the absence of an artificial pacemaker; severe bradycardia (less than 50 beats/min); marked hypotension; bronchospastic disorders; severe disorders of electrolyte balance; severe hepatic failure (see Precautions); known hypersensitivity to the drug.

Warnings: Mortality: The results of the Cardiac Arrhythmia Suppression Trials (CAST) in post-myocardial infarction patients with asymptomatic ventricular arrhythmias showed a significant increase in mortality and in the non-fatal cardiac arrest rate in patients treated with flecainide or encainide compared with a matched placebo-treated group. CAST was continued using a revised protocol with the moricizine and placebo arms only. The trial was prematurely terminated because of a trend towards an increase in mortality in the moricizine treated group.

The applicability of these results to other populations or other antiarrhythmic agents is uncertain, but at present it is prudent to consider these results when using any antiarrhythmic agent.

Proarrhythmic Effects: Propafenone may cause new or worsen existing arrhythmias. Such proarrhythmic effects range from an increase in frequency of PVCs to the development of more severe ventricular tachycardia, ventricular fibrillation or torsades de pointes. It is therefore essential that each patient

Rythmol (cont'd)

administered propafenone be evaluated clinically and electrocardiographically prior to, and during therapy to determine whether the response to propafenone supports continued treatment.

Overall in clinical trials with propafenone, 4.7% of all patients had new or worsened ventricular arrhythmia possibly representing a proarrhythmic event (0.7% was an increase in PVCs, 4.0% a worsening, or new appearance, of VT or VF). Of the patients who had worsening of VT (4%), 92% had a history of VT and/or VT/VF, 71% had coronary artery disease, and 68% had a prior myocardial infarction. The incidence of proarrhythmia in patients with less serious or benign arrhythmias which include patients with an increase in frequency of PVCs, was 1.6%. Although most proarrhythmic events occurred during the first week of therapy, late events also were seen and the CAST study (see above) suggests that a risk is present throughout treatment.

Congestive Heart Failure: During treatment with oral propafenone in patients with depressed baseline function (mean EF=33.5%), no significant decreases in ejection fraction were seen. In clinical trial experience, new or worsened CHF has been reported in 3.7% of patients; of those 0.9% were considered probably or definitely related to propafenone. Of the patients with congestive heart failure probably related to propafenone, 80% had preexisting heart failure and 85% had coronary artery disease. CHF attributable to propafenone developed rarely (<0.2%) in patients who had no previous history of CHF.

Propafenone exerts both beta blockade and a dose related direct negative inotropic effect on myocardium. Therefore, patients with congestive heart failure should be compensated before receiving propafenone, and then closely monitored with careful attention being given to the maintenance of cardiac function. If congestive heart failure worsens, propafenone should be discontinued (unless congestive heart failure is due to the cardiac arrhythmia) and, if indicated, restarted at a lower dosage only after adequate cardiac compensation has been established.

Caution should be exercised when using propafenone in patients with minimal cardiac reserve or in those who are receiving other drugs with negative inotropic potential.

Effects on Cardiac Conduction: Propafenone slows cardiac conduction which may result in a dose-related prolongation of PR interval and QRS complex, development of first or higher degree AV block, bundle branch block and intraventricular conduction delay (see Adverse Effects). Therefore, development of signs of increasing depression of cardiac conductivity during drug therapy requires a reduction in dosage or a discontinuation of propafenone unless the ventricular rate is adequately controlled by a pacemaker.

Hematologic Disturbances: Agranulocytosis has been reported infrequently in patients taking propafenone. The onset is generally within 4 to 6 weeks and presenting symptoms have included fever, fatigue, and malaise. Agranulocytosis occurs in less than 0.1% of patients taking propafenone. Patients should be instructed to immediately report fever, fatigue, malaise or any signs of infection, especially in the first 3 months of therapy. Prompt discontinuation of propafenone therapy is recommended when a decreased white blood cell count or other signs and symptoms warrant consideration of agranulocytosis/granulocytopenia. Cessation of propafenone therapy is usually followed by recovery of blood counts within 2 weeks.

Nonallergic Bronchospasm (e.g. chronic bronchitis, emphysema): Patients with bronchospastic disease should, in general, not receive propafenone or other agents with beta-adrenergic blocking activity (see Contraindications).

Precautions: Effects on Pacemaker Threshold: Patients with permanent pacemakers should have their existing thresholds re-evaluated after initiation of or change in propafenone therapy because of a possible increase in endocardial stimulation threshold.

Patients with Impaired Hepatic Function: Since propafenone is highly metabolized by the liver it should be administered cautiously to patients with impaired hepatic function (see Contraindications). Administration of propafenone to these patients results in an increase in bioavailability to approximately 70% compared to 3 to 40% for patients with normal liver function, prolongation of the half-life, a decrease in the systemic clearance, and a reduction in the serum protein binding of the drug. As a result, the dose given to patients with impaired hepatic function should be reduced (see Dosage). It is important to monitor ECG intervals for signs of excessive pharmacological effects (see Overdose) and/or adverse effects, until an individualized dosage regimen has been determined.

Patients with Impaired Renal Function: To date there is no experience with use of oral propafenone in patients with impaired renal function. Since a considerable percentage of propafenone metabolites are excreted in the urine (18.5 to 38% of the dose/48 hours), propafenone should be used cautiously in patients with renal impairment and only after consideration of the benefit/risk ratio. These patients should be carefully monitored for signs of toxicity (see Overdose). The dose in these patients has not been determined.

Neuromuscular Dysfunction: Exacerbation of myasthenia gravis has been reported during propafenone therapy.

Elevated ANA Titres: In long-term studies positive antinuclear antibody (ANA) titres have been reported in 21% of patients receiving propafenone. However, it is impossible to determine what exact percentage of patients had a new positive ANA titre as a result of propafenone therapy. This laboratory finding has not been associated with clinical symptoms. One case of Lupus-like syndrome has been reported which resolved upon discontinuation of therapy. Laboratory evaluation for antinuclear antibodies should be performed initially and at regular intervals. It is recommended that patients in whom an abnormal ANA test has occurred be evaluated regularly. If worsening elevation of ANA titres or clinical symptoms are detected, the drug should be discontinued.

Impaired Spermatogenesis: Clinical evaluation of spermatogenesis was undertaken in 11 normal subjects, given oral propafenone 300 mg twice daily for 4 days which was then increased to 300 mg three times daily for an additional 4 days. Patients were followed for 128 days post-treatment and demonstrated a 28% reduction in semen sample volume following the last dose (day 8) and a 27% reduction in sperm count, on day 72. FSH and testosterone levels were also slightly decreased. Neither the decrease in sperm count nor the decrease in sample volume were sustained beyond the single visit in which they occurred, and both values remained within the laboratories normal reference range. Reduced spermatogenesis was also observed in animal experiments. The significance of these findings is uncertain.

Geriatrics: A slight increase in the incidence of dizziness was observed in elderly patients. Because of the possible increased risk of impaired hepatic or renal function in this age group, propafenone should be used with caution. The effective dose may be lower in these patients.

Children: The use of propafenone in children is not recommended, since safety and efficacy has not been established.

Pregnancy: Propafenone has been shown to be embryotoxic in the rat when given in doses of 600 mg/kg and in the rabbit when given in doses of 150 mg/kg. In a perinatal and postnatal study in rats, propafenone produced dose dependent increases in maternal and neonatal mortality, decreased maternal and pup body weight gain and reduced neonatal physiological development.

There are no studies in pregnant women. Propafenone should be used during pregnancy only when the potential benefit outweighs the risk to the fetus.

Labor and Delivery: It is not known whether the use of propafenone during labor or delivery has immediate or delayed adverse effects on the fetus, or whether it prolongs the duration of labor or increases the need for forceps delivery or other obstetrical intervention.

Lactation: Propafenone and 5-hydroxypropafenone are excreted in human milk. Because of possible serious adverse reactions in nursing infants, an alternative method of infant feeding should be considered when the use of propafenone is considered essential.

Drug Interactions: Quinidine: Small doses of quinidine completely inhibit the hydroxylation metabolic pathway, making all patients, in effect, slow metabolizers (see Pharmacology).

Table I—Rythmol

Adverse Events

	Incidence By Total Daily Dose			Overall Incidence At Any Dose	% of Patients who Discontinued
	450 mg	600 mg	900 mg	(N=2 127)	
Cardiovascular System					
Dyspnea	2.2%	2.3%	3.6%	5.3%	1.6%
Proarrhythmia	2.0	2.1	2.9	4.7	4.7
Angina	1.7	2.1	3.2	4.6	0.5
Congestive Heart Failure	0.8	2.2	2.6	3.7	1.4
Ventricular Tachycardia	1.4	1.6	2.9	3.4	1.2
Palpitations	0.6	1.6	2.6	3.4	0.5
First Degree AV Block	0.8	1.2	2.1	2.5	0.3
Syncope	0.8	1.3	1.4	2.2	0.7
QRS Duration, Increased	0.5	0.9	1.7	1.9	0.5
Bradycardia	0.5	0.8	1.1	1.5	0.5
PVC's	0.6	0.6	1.1	1.5	0.1
Edema	0.6	0.4	1.0	1.4	0.2
Bundle Branch Block	0.3	0.7	1.0	1.2	0.5
Atrial Fibrilation	0.7	0.7	0.5	1.2	0.4
Intraventricular Conduction Delay	0.2	0.7	0.9	1.1	0.1
Hypotension	0.1	0.5	1.0	1.1	0.4
CNS					
Dizziness	3.6%	6.6%	11.0%	12.5%	2.4%
Headaches	1.5	2.5	2.8	4.5	1.0
Blurred Vision	0.6	2.4	3.1	3.8	0.8
Ataxia	0.3	0.6	1.5	1.6	0.2
Insomnia	0.3	1.3	0.7	1.5	0.3
Tremor(s)	0.3	0.8	1.1	1.4	0.3
Drowsiness	0.6	0.5	0.7	1.2	0.2
Gastrointestinal					
Nausea and/or Vomiting	2.4%	6.1%	8.9%	10.7%	3.4%
Unusual Taste	2.5	4.9	6.3	8.8	0.7
Constipation	2.0	4.1	5.3	7.2	0.5
Dyspepsia	1.3	1.7	2.5	3.4	0.9
Diarrhea	0.5	1.6	1.7	2.5	0.6
Dry Mouth	0.9	1.0	1.4	2.4	0.2
Anorexia	0.5	0.7	1.6	1.7	0.4
Abdominal Pain/Cramping	0.8	0.9	1.1	1.7	0.4
Flatulence	0.3	0.7	0.9	1.2	0.1
Other					
Fatigue	1.8%	2.8%	4.1%	6.0%	1.0%
Rash	0.6	1.4	1.9	2.6	0.8
Weakness	0.6	1.6	1.7	2.4	0.7
Atypical Chest Pain	0.5	0.7	1.4	1.8	0.2
Anxiety	0.7	0.5	0.9	1.5	0.6
Diaphoresis	0.6	0.4	1.1	1.4	0.3
Pain, Joints	0.2	0.4	0.9	1.0	0.1

There is, as yet, too little information to recommend concomitant use of propafenone and quinidine.

Digitalis: Propafenone produces dose-related increases in serum digoxin levels ranging from approximately 35% at 450 mg/day to 85% at 900 mg/day of propafenone without affecting digoxin renal clearance. These elevations of digoxin levels were maintained for up to 16 months during concomitant administration. Plasma digoxin levels of patients on concomitant therapy should be measured, and digoxin dosage should ordinarily be reduced when propafenone is started, especially if a relatively large digoxin dose is used or if plasma concentrations are relatively high.

Beta-Antagonists: In a study involving healthy subjects, concomitant administration of propafenone and propranolol has resulted in substantial increases in propanolol plasma concentration and elimination half-life with no change in propafenone plasma levels from control values. Similar observations have been reported with metoprolol. Propafenone appears to inhibit the hydroxylation pathway for the two beta-antagonists (just as quinidine inhibits propafenone metabolism). Increased plasma concentrations of metoprolol could overcome its relative cardioselectivity. In propafenone clinical trials, patients who were receiving beta-blockers concurrently did not experience an increased incidence of side effects. While the therapeutic range for beta-blockers is wide, a reduction in dosage may be necessary during concomitant administration with propafenone.

Warfarin: Concurrent administration of propafenone and warfarin leads to a 39% increase in warfarin plasma levels with a corresponding prolongation in prothrombin times of approximately 25%. It is therefore recommended that in patients treated with propafenone and warfarin concomitantly, prothrombin time should be carefully monitored and the dose of warfarin adjusted as necessary.

Cimetidine: Concomitant administration of propafenone and cimetidine resulted in a 20% increase in plasma concentrations of propafenone. Therefore, patients should be carefully monitored and the dose adjusted when appropriate.

Local Anesthetics: Concomitant use of local anesthetics and propafenone may increase the risk of CNS side effects.

Desipramine: Concomitant administration of propafenone and desipramine may result in elevated serum desipramine levels. Both desipramine, a tricyclic antidepressant, and propafenone are cleared by oxidative pathways of demethylation and hydroxylation carried out by the hepatic P-450 cytochrome.

Cyclosporine: Propafenone therapy may increase levels of cyclosporine.

Theophylline: Propafenone may increase theophylline concentration during concomitant therapy with the development of theophylline toxicity.

Rifampin: Rifampin may accelerate the metabolism and decrease the plasma levels and antiarrhythmic efficacy of propafenone.

Adverse Effects: In 2 127 patients treated with propafenone in North American controlled and open clinical trials, the most common adverse reactions reported were dizziness (12.5%) nausea and/or vomiting (10.7%), unusual taste (8.8%) and constipation (7.2%). The adverse effects judged to be most severe were aggravation or induction of arrhythmia (4.7%), congestive heart failure (3.7%) and ventricular tachycardia (3.4%). The incidences for these 3 adverse reactions in patients with a previous history of MI were 6.9%, 5.3% and 5.5%, while in patients without a history of MI the incidences were 3.0%, 2.4% and 1.8%, respectively. Approximately 20% of patients had propafenone discontinued due to adverse reactions.

Adverse reactions were dose related and occurred most frequently during the first month of therapy.

The adverse events in Table I (on previous page) were observed in greater than 1% of patients.

In addition, the following adverse reactions were reported less frequently than 1% either in clinical trials or in marketing experience (*adverse events from marketing experience are given in italics*). Causality and relationship to propafenone therapy cannot necessarily be judged from these events.

Cardiovascular: artrial flutter, AV dissociation, cardiac arrest, flushing, hot flashes, sick sinus syndrome, sinus pause or arrest, supraventricular tachycardia, Torsades de Pointes.

Nervous System: abnormal dreams, abnormal speech, abnormal vision, *apnea, coma,* confusion, depression, memory loss, numbness, paresthesias, psychosis/mania, seizures (0.3%), tinnitus, unusual smell sensation, vertigo.

Gastrointestinal: A number of patients with liver abnormalities associated with propafenone therapy have been reported in foreign post-marketing experience. Some appeared due to hepatocellular injury, some were cholestatic and some showed a mixed picture. Some of these reports were simply discovered through clinical chemistries, others because of clinical symptoms. One case was rechallenged with a positive outcome.

Cholestasis (0.1%), elevated liver enzymes (alkaline phosphatase, serum transaminases) (0.2%), gastroenteritis, hepatitis (0.03%).

Hematologic: agranulocytosis (see Warnings), anemia, bruising, granulocytopenia, *increased bleeding time,* leukopenia, purpura, thrombocytopenia.

Other: alopecia, eye irritation, *hyponatremia/inappropriate ADH secretion,* impotence, increased glucose, kidney failure, positive ANA (0.7%), *lupus erythematosis,* muscle cramps, muscle weakness, nephrotic syndrome, pain, pruritus.

Overdose: Symptoms and Treatment: The symptoms of overdose include hypotension, somnolence, convulsions, bradycardia, conduction disturbances, ventricular tachycardia and/or ventricular fibrillation.

If ingestion is recent, perform gastric lavage or induce emesis. Supportive measures such as mechanical respiratory assistance and cardiac massage may be necessary.

Defibrillation and the use of a temporary pacemaker, as well as infusion of isoproterenol and dopamine have been effective in controlling cardiac rhythm and blood pressure. Convulsions have been alleviated with i.v. diazepam.

Detoxification measures such as forced diuresis, hemoperfusion and hemodialysis have not proven useful.

Dosage: The dose of propafenone must be individually determined on the basis of patient's response and tolerance. The usefulness of monitoring plasma levels for optimization of therapy has not been established. The recommended dose titration regimen can be used for both fast and slow metabolizers (see Pharmacology).

The initial dose is 150 mg given every 8 hours (450 mg/day). Dosage may be increased at 3 to 4 day intervals to 300 mg every 12 hours (600 mg/day). Should a further increase in dosage be necessary a maximum dose of 300 mg every 8 hours (900 mg/day) may be given.

In those patients in whom widening of the QRS complex (>0.12 s) or prolongation or PR interval (>0.24 s) occurs, the dosage should be reduced.

Administration of propafenone with food is recommended.

In patients with mild to moderate hepatic insufficiency (see Precautions), therapy should be initiated with 150 mg given once daily. The dosage may be increased at a minimum of 4 day intervals to 150 mg twice (300 mg/day) daily then to 150 mg every 8 hours (450 mg/day) and, if necessary, to 300 mg every 12 hours (600 mg/day).

There is no information on dosing with propafenone in patients with renal impairment. It should be used cautiously in these patients and only after consideration of the benefit/risk ratio. These patients should be carefully monitored for signs of toxicity. Lower doses may be required (see Precautions).

In elderly patients the effective dose of propafenone may be lower (see Precautions).

There is no information on the appropriate regimen for the transfer from lidocaine to propafenone.

Supplied: 150 mg: Each white, film-coated, round, unscored tablet contains: propafenone HCl 150 mg. Nonmedicinal ingredients: hydroxypropylmethylcellulose, magnesium stearate, maize starch, polyethylene glycol, sodium dodecyl sulfate, talc, titanium dioxide and vinyl pyrrolidone-vinyl acetate copolymer. Bottles of 100.

300 mg: Each white, film-coated, round, scored tablet contains: propafenone HCl 300 mg. Nonmedicinal ingredients: hydroxypropylmethylcellulose, magnesium stearate, maize starch, polyethylene glycol, sodium lauryl sulfate, talc, titanium dioxide and vinyl pyrrolidone-vinyl acetate copolymer. Bottles of 100.

Do not use beyond the expiry date indicated on the label.

(Shown in Product Recognition Section)

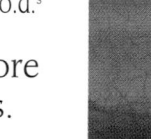

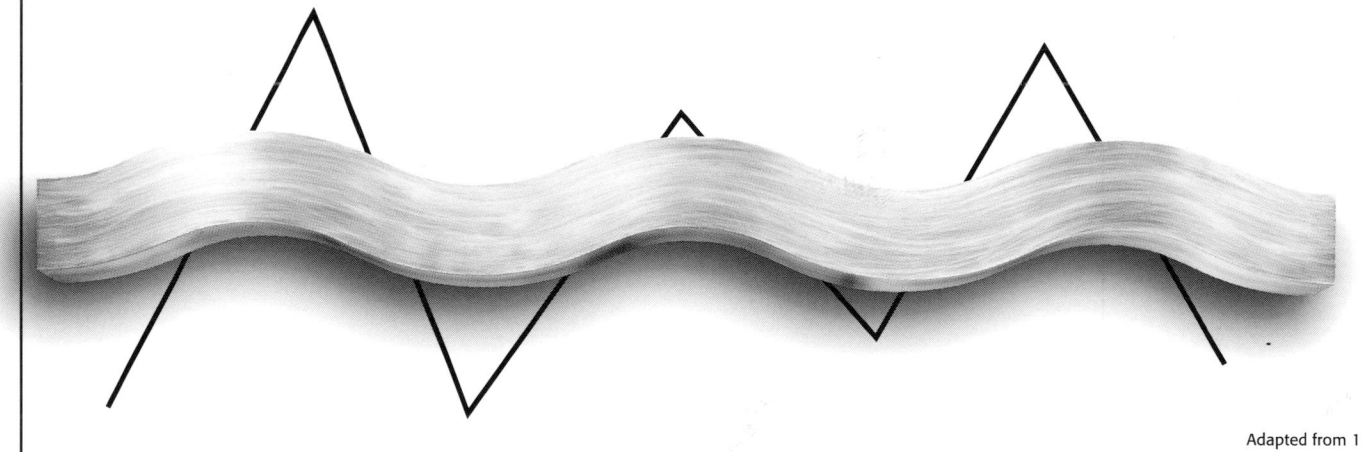

S

692® Tablets Ⓝ
Frosst
see "Six ..." in monographs

SABRIL® Ⓟ
Hoechst Marion Roussel

Vigabatrin

Antiepileptic

Pharmacology: Vigabatrin is an irreversible inhibitor of gamma-aminobutyric acid transaminase (GABA-T), the enzyme responsible for the catabolism of the inhibitory neurotransmitter gamma-aminobutyric acid (GABA) in the brain. The mechanism of action of vigabatrin is attributed to irreversible enzyme inhibition of GABA-T, and consequent increased levels of the inhibitory neurotransmitter, GABA.

Decreased serum levels of ALT and AST have been observed during treatment with vigabatrin and may be the result of inhibition of these transaminases by vigabatrin. The clinical significance of these findings is unknown.

The duration of effect of vigabatrin is thought to be dependent on the rate of GABA-T resynthesis rather than on the plasma concentration of vigabatrin.

Clinical Trials: In clinical trials, including double-blind, placebo-controlled studies involving 354 patients with drug-resistant complex partial seizures, vigabatrin reduced seizure frequency by 50% or more in approximately half of the patients studied. The efficacy of vigabatrin in children with refractory partial seizures was similar to that seen in adult patients.

A multicentre, double-blind, placebo-controlled, parallel group study was performed to evaluate the safety and efficacy of vigabatrin versus placebo as first line monotherapy in the treatment of newly diagnosed infantile spasms. The study involved a 2- to 3-day baseline period, a 5-day double-blind treatment phase, and a 6-month open-label follow-up. Complete cessation of spasms on the final day of double-blind treatment was achieved by 45% of vigabatrin patients (N=20) and by 15% of placebo patients (N=20). According to the Clinical Global Impression of Improvement, 80% of vigabatrin patients and 15% of placebo patients were considered to be moderately or markedly improved. These differences between the treatment groups were statistically significant. In the 6-month open-label extension of this study, 51% of patients (N=35) could be maintained on vigabatrin monotherapy, while 49% required the addition of other antiepileptic drugs.

In a retrospective analysis of 192 infants diagnosed with infantile spasms who had been treated with vigabatrin as first-line monotherapy (mean steady-state dose of 99 mg/kg/day), 162 patients (84%) experienced an initial decrease in spasm frequency of at least 50% with 131 patients (68%) experiencing a complete resolution of spasms. Demographic factors which seemed to be predictive of a positive response to vigabatrin included an etiology of tuberous sclerosis and an age of onset of illness of less than 3 months. According to long-term (mean 9.2 months) follow-up data for this retrospective study, 42% of the 192 patients could be successfully maintained on vigabatrin monotherapy, while the remainder required additional antiepileptic treatments. Of the 131 patients who were considered to be complete responders, 85 (65%) experienced neither relapse of infantile spasms nor onset of other seizure types during long-term follow-up.

Pharmacokinetics: Vigabatrin is rapidly absorbed following oral administration and peak plasma concentrations are reached within 2 hours. Vigabatrin is widely distributed with an apparent volume of distribution slightly greater than total body water. The primary route of elimination is via the kidney, with little metabolic transformation occurring. Following a single dose, approximately 70% is excreted in the urine as unchanged drug within the first 24 hours post-dose. The plasma elimination half-life is approximately 5 to 8 hours in young adults and 12 to 13 hours in the elderly. In renal impairment the elimination is prolonged and the rate of renal clearance is directly related to creatinine clearance (see Precautions and Dosage). Vigabatrin does not induce the hepatic cytochrome P450 system nor is it extensively metabolized or plasma-protein bound. Administration of vigabatrin with food slightly reduces the rate, but not the extent of absorption.

Indications: For the adjunctive management of epilepsy which is not satisfactorily controlled by conventional therapy.

Vigabatrin is indicated as initial monotherapy for the management of infantile spasms (West syndrome). Clinical experience indicates that at least 50% of patients may require the addition of other antiepileptic drugs owing to relapse or emergence of other seizure types following an initial response to the treatment of infantile spasms with vigabatrin.

Vigabatrin should be used under close monitoring by a neurologist.

Contraindications: In pregnancy and lactation (see Warnings) and in patients with a known hypersensitivity to vigabatrin or to any components of the product.

Warnings: Ophthalmological Abnormalities: In the course of international postmarketing surveillance, a number of ophthalmological abnormalities, including visual field constriction, bilateral optic disc pallor, subtle peripheral retinal atrophy, optic atrophy, and optic neuritis have been reported in patients receiving vigabatrin often in combination with other antiepileptic agents.

According to these reports, the time to onset of symptomatic visual field constriction, when specified, has ranged from less than one month to over 6 years. Preliminary data suggest that the onset of symptoms tends to be reported most frequently within the first year of treatment.

Initial and periodic (approximately every 3 months) ophthalmological examinations are recommended during vigabatrin treatment including expert mydriatic peripheral fundus examination and visual field perimetry.

Patients should be questioned at frequent intervals during treatment for narrowing of the field of vision or loss of visual acuity and should be advised to report any emerging visual problems promptly to their physicians.

The use of vigabatrin should be discontinued in patients exhibiting any of the above ophthalmological abnormalities, unless the benefits of continued treatment in terms of seizure control are considered to outweigh the risk of visual impairment.

In view of the difficulties of assessing visual field in infants and young pediatric patients, vigabatrin should be used in these patient groups only if clearly indicated. The need for continued use of vigabatrin should be reassessed periodically. Frequent examination by a pediatric ophthalmologist are recommended for all infants and young children receiving vigabatrin.

Neurotoxicity in Animals: Rat, Mouse and Dog: Safety studies carried out in the rat, mouse and dog at doses of 30 to 50 mg/kg/day and higher, caused dose- and time-dependent microvacuolation within certain white matter tracts of the brain (the cerebellum, reticular formation and thalamus in rodents and the columns of the fornix and optic tracts in dogs were most affected). The microvacuolation was caused by the separation of the outer lamellar sheath of myelinated fibres, a change characteristic of noninflammatory intramyelinic edema.

In both the rat and dog (mouse was not tested), the intramyelinic edema was reversible after stopping the administration of vigabatrin; however, in the mouse and rat, residual changes consisting of swollen axons and mineralized microbodies were observed.

Monkey: In monkeys, the oral administration of 300 mg/kg/day for 16 months produced minimal microvacuolation with equivocal differences between treated and control animals. Low oral absorption of vigabatrin in the monkey resulted in an actual absorbed dose of 75 mg/kg/day. In spite of the poor absorption, cerebrospinal fluid (CSF) levels of vigabatrin in the monkeys were comparable to those seen in rats treated with 300 mg/kg/day; however, GABA levels in the CSF and the brain cortex in treated monkeys were not significantly different from untreated monkeys. This finding may explain the reason for the equivocal effects, since the intramyelinic edema associated with vigabatrin treatment appears to be related to increased brain GABA levels.

Evoked Potentials: Evoked Potentials in Animals: In the dog, studies indicate that intramyelinic edema is associated with increased latencies in somatosensory and visually evoked potentials. Magnetic resonance imaging (MRI) changes also correlated with intramyelinic edema in the fornix, thalamus and hypothalamus.

Evoked Potentials in Man: No increased evoked potential latencies have been observed in man. Two hundred and twenty-one patients treated for 4 to 5 months showed no significant evoked potential latency changes at the end of treatment as compared to baseline. MRI results in man did not show the changes observed in dogs who had intramyelinic edema.

Postmortem neuropathological changes seen in 11 patients who were treated with vigabatrin (mean duration of treatment was 28 months, and the longest treatment was 6 years) showed no myelin vacuolation in the white matter that was considered to be outside of the control range.

Although clinical trials have not revealed the type of neurotoxicity seen in animal studies, increased CSF GABA levels have been observed in humans. It is recommended that patients treated with vigabatrin be closely observed for adverse effects on neurological function, with special attention to visual disturbance.

Pregnancy and *Lactation:* In a teratology study in the rabbit a dose-related incidence, 2% and 9%, of cleft palate was observed at doses of 150 and 200 mg/kg/day, respectively.

In animal reproductive studies neurohistopathology was not performed on the fetuses; therefore, it is not known whether microvacuolation occurred in utero. The possibility that microvacuolation or other neurotoxicity may occur in human fetuses cannot be disregarded.

Precautions: Patients with a History of Psychosis: Behavioral disturbances such as aggression and psychotic episodes have been reported following initiation of vigabatrin therapy. A history of abnormal behavior or psychosis appears to be a predisposing factor for such reactions, therefore treatment in such patients should be initiated cautiously at low doses and with frequent monitoring.

Geriatrics and Patients with Renal Impairment: Vigabatrin is eliminated via the kidney and caution should be exercised when administering the drug to elderly patients and to patients with renal impairment (see Dosage).

Patients with Myoclonic Seizures: As with other antiepileptic drugs, some patients may experience an increase in seizure frequency with vigabatrin. Patients with myoclonic seizures may be particularly liable to this effect.

Discontinuation of Therapy: As with other antiepileptic drugs, abrupt discontinuation may lead to rebound seizures. If a patient is to be withdrawn from vigabatrin treatment, it is recommended that this be done gradually by reducing the dose over a 2- to 4-week period if possible.

Drug Interactions: During concurrent vigabatrin administration, mean decreases of 16 to 33% in phenytoin levels have been reported. A 9 to 21% reduction in phenobarbital levels has also been seen in patients receiving concomitant vigabatrin treatment. The clinical relevance of these decreases is not known.

Occupational Hazards: Patients with uncontrolled epilepsy should not drive or handle potentially dangerous machinery. During clinical trials, the most common adverse reactions observed were drowsiness and fatigue. Patients should be advised to refrain from activities requiring mental alertness or physical coordination until they are sure that vigabatrin does not affect them adversely.

Adverse Effects: Vigabatrin is generally well tolerated in epileptic patients. Adverse events are mainly CNS-related and probably a secondary consequence of increased GABA levels caused by vigabatrin. The safety of vigabatrin was evaluated in 438 epileptic patients treated in double-blind, placebo-controlled clinical trials. The relationship of adverse events to vigabatrin therapy was not clearly established as patients were taking other antiepileptic drugs concomitantly.

Most Frequent Adverse Events (incidence higher than placebo): fatigue, headache, drowsiness, dizziness, depression, weight increase, agitation, tremor, abnormal vision, amnesia.

Postmarketing Ophthalmological Adverse Events: cases of peripheral visual field constriction, bilateral optic disc pallor, subtle peripheral retinal atrophy, and optic atrophy have been reported. There are also rare reports of optic neuritis (see Warnings).

Table I (on following page) provides a listing of all treatment emergent adverse events that were reported with an incidence of 2% or greater in double-blind, placebo-controlled clinical trials of vigabatrin as add-on therapy for the treatment of epilepsy.

The sedative effect of vigabatrin decreases with continuing treatment.

Other adverse events that have been reported less frequently include hypomania, mania, psychosis and suicide attempt.

Rare instances of marked sedation, stupor and confusion associated with nonspecific slow wave activity on EEG have been described soon after the introduction of vigabatrin

Sabril (cont'd)

Table I—Sabril

Treatment Emergent Adverse Event Incidence (≥ 2%) in Double-Blind, Placebo-Controlled Add-On Clinical Trials

Body System Adverse Event	Placebo* N=320 n	%	Sabril* N=438 n	%
Body as a Whole				
weight increase	12	3.8	54	12.3
pain	21	6.6	33	7.5
asthenia	15	4.7	19	4.3
appetite increase	6	1.9	15	3.4
fever	7	2.2	14	3.2
chest pain	8	2.5	12	2.7
accident injury	14	4.4	12	2.7
Cardiovascular				
edema, dependent	2	0.6	13	3.0
Dermatologic				
rash	15	4.7	20	4.6
skin disorder	11	3.4	18	4.1
Gastrointestinal				
nausea	25	7.8	39	8.9
diarrhea	17	5.3	31	7.1
dyspepsia	22	6.9	27	6.2
abdominal pain	12	3.8	25	5.7
constipation	10	3.1	24	5.5
vomiting	15	4.7	24	5.5
tooth disorder	4	1.2	12	2.7
Hematologic				
purpura	11	3.4	20	4.6
Musculoskeletal				
arthralgia	13	4.1	32	7.3
back pain	13	4.1	23	5.3
arthrosis	7	2.2	11	2.5
Nervous System				
fatigue	44	13.8	118	26.9
headache	79	24.7	113	25.8
drowsiness	46	14.4	97	22.1
dizziness	41	12.8	82	18.7
tremor	22	6.9	48	11.0
vision abnormal	18	5.6	47	10.7
amnesia	12	3.8	45	10.3
nystagmus	15	4.7	42	9.6
diplopia	17	5.3	39	8.9
ataxia	14	4.4	35	8.0
confusion	7	2.2	30	6.8
paresthesia	6	1.9	25	5.7
coordination abnormal	7	2.2	22	5.0
seizures (not specified)	7	2.2	22	5.0
gait abnormal	10	3.1	20	4.6
concentration impaired	3	0.9	16	3.7
speech disorder	3	0.9	15	3.4
hypoesthesia	7	2.2	13	3.0
vertigo	4	1.2	13	3.0
hyporeflexia	1	0.3	12	2.7
Psychiatric				
depression	10	3.1	57	13.0
agitation	24	7.5	48	11.0
insomnia	19	5.9	29	6.6
anxiety	11	3.4	24	5.5
emotional lability	9	2.8	21	4.8
thinking abnormal	1	0.3	15	3.4
aggressive reaction	6	1.9	12	2.7
nervousness	7	2.2	12	2.7
personality disorder	3	0.9	9	2.1
Respiratory				
throat irritation	19	5.9	29	6.6
congestion	21	6.6	22	5.0
upper respiratory tract infection	10	3.1	21	4.8
sinusitis	6	1.9	10	2.3
coughing	14	4.4	9	2.1
Special Senses				
eye pain	1	0.3	11	2.5
earache	4	1.2	10	2.3
Urogenital				
dysmenorrhea	4	1.2	15	3.4
urinary tract infection	0	0	13	3.0
menstrual disorder	5	1.6	10	2.3
Other				
infection viral	36	11.3	56	12.8

*Added on to patient's existing antiepilepsy drug therapy.

therapy. These events have been reversible following dose reduction or discontinuation of vigabatrin.

Rare reports of hypersensitivity reactions (including angioedema and urticaria) have been received.

As with other antiepileptic drugs, some patients may experience an increase in seizure frequency with vigabatrin treatment (see Precautions).

Laboratory data indicate that vigabatrin treatment does not lead to renal or hepatic toxicity. Chronic treatment with vigabatrin may be associated with a slight decrease in hemoglobin, which rarely attains clinical significance.

Pediatric Safety: Safety data are available in 299 children, aged 2 months to 16 years (1 patient was 18 years of age), participating in clinical trials with vigabatrin. Relationship of adverse events to vigabatrin therapy was not clearly established as children were taking other antiepileptic drugs concomitantly.

The most frequent adverse event observed in children was "hyperactivity" (reported as hyperkinesia 7.7%, agitation 2.3%, excitation 0.3% or restlessness 0.7%), which was observed in 11% of children, an incidence higher than that seen in adults. There have been postmarketing reports of visual field constriction, optic disc pallor, optic atrophy, and optic neuritis in pediatric patients receiving vigabatrin treatment (see Warnings). Other commonly reported adverse events were somnolence (8%) and weight gain (3%).

The following adverse events were reported in children with a frequency greater than 1% (see Table II).

Table II—Sabril

Adverse Events Reported By More Than 1% of Pediatric Patients

Body System Adverse Event	Number of Patients	Incidence
Nervous		
somnolence	24	8.0
hyperkinesia	23	7.7
aggression	8	2.7
insomnia	8	2.7
agitation	7	2.3
ataxia	7	2.3
emotional lability	3	1.0
headache	3	1.0
increased seizures	3	1.0
Digestive		
vomiting	6	2.0
nausea	3	1.0
increased saliva	3	1.0
Body as a Whole		
weight gain	9	3.0
fatigue	8	2.7
hypotonia	3	1.0

Overdose: Symptoms and Treatment: There is no specific antidote. The usual supportive measures should be employed. Measures to remove unabsorbed drug should be considered. Activated charcoal has been shown to not significantly adsorb vigabatrin in an in vitro study. The effectiveness of hemodialysis in the treatment of vigabatrin overdose is unknown. In isolated case reports in renal failure patients receiving therapeutic doses of vigabatrin, hemodialysis reduced vigabatrin plasma concentrations by 40 to 60%

Cases of vigabatrin overdose have been reported. The doses of vigabatrin taken were usually between 7.5 and 30 g; however, ingestions of up to 65 g have been reported. When reported, the most common symptoms included drowsiness, loss of consciousness and coma. Other less frequently reported symptoms included vertigo, headache, psychosis, respiratory depression or apnea, bradycardia, hypotension, agitation, irritability, confusion, abnormal behavior or speech disorder.

Dosage: Vigabatrin is intended for oral administration once or twice daily and may be taken with or without food. Vigabatrin should be added to the patient's current antiepileptic therapy.

The recommended doses may be taken as tablets or sachets. The entire contents of the sachet(s) should be dissolved in a glass of cold or room temperature water, juice or milk immediately before oral administration. Instructions to the patient on the use of vigabatrin are provided in the Information for the Patient section.

Adults: The recommended starting dose is 1 g/day, although patients with severe seizure manifestations may require a starting dose of up to 2 g/day. The daily dose may be increased or decreased in increments of 0.5 g depending on clinical response and tolerability. The optimal dose range is between 2 to 4 g/day. Increasing the dose beyond 4 g/day does not usually result in improved efficacy and may increase the occurrence of adverse reactions.

Children: The recommended starting dose in children is 40 mg/kg/day, increasing to 80 to 100 mg/kg/day depending on response. Therapy may be started at 0.5 g/day, and raised by increments of 0.5 g/day weekly depending on clinical response and tolerability. See Table III.

Table III—Sabril

Recommended Doses in Children

Body Weight	Daily Dose	No. Tablets/Day*
10-15 kg	0.5-1 g/day	1-2 tablets/day
16-30 kg	1-1.5 g/day	2-3 tablets/day
31-50 kg	1.5-3 g/day	3-6 tablets/day
>50 kg	2-4 g/day	4-8 tablets/day

*Sachets may be used at an equivalent daily dose.

Infants (Treatment of Infantile Spasms): The recommended dose for the management of infantile spasms (West Syndrome) is between 50 to 100 mg/kg/day, depending on the severity of the spasms. This dose may be titrated over a period of 1 week if necessary. Doses of up to 150 mg/kg/day have been used with good tolerability.

The total daily dose should be divided and administered on a b.i.d. basis. The entire contents of the vigabatrin sachet(s) should be dissolved in a 10 mL volume of water, fruit juice, milk or infant formula, and the appropriate aliquot of this volume administered using an oral syringe.

Geriatrics and Renally Impaired Patients: Vigabatrin is almost exclusively eliminated via the kidney and, therefore, caution should be exercised when administering the drug to the elderly, and more particularly to patients with creatinine clearance less than 60 mL/minute. It is recommended that such patients be started on a lower dose of vigabatrin and observed closely for adverse events such as sedation and confusion.

Information for the Patient: See Blue Section—Information for the Patient "Sabril".

Supplied: Sachets: Each sachet of white to off-white granular powder contains: vigabatrin 0.5 g. Lactose-free. Cartons of 50.

Tablets: Each white to off-white, film-coated, oval, biconvex tablet, imprinted "SABRIL" on one side, contains: vigabatrin 500 mg. Nonmedicinal ingredients: cellulose, hydroxypropyl methylcellulose, magnesium stearate, polyethylene glycol, povidone, sodium starch glycolate and titanium dioxide. Lactose-free. HDPE bottles of 100.

Store at controlled room temperature (15 to 30°C). Protect from moisture.

(Shown in Product Recognition Section)

Reviewed 1999

SAIZEN® Ⓟ

Serono

Somatropin

Human Growth Hormone

Pharmacology: Saizen is a polypeptide hormone consisting of 191 amino acid residues and its structure is identical to that of growth hormone extracted from human pituitary glands. It is produced by recombinant (rDNA) technology in a mammalian cell expression system.

Saizen is also therapeutically equivalent to human growth hormone of pituitary origin. Saizen provides an exogenous supply of human growth hormone for those patients lacking the ability to produce adequate endogenous supplies.

Linear Growth: Somatropin stimulates growth in patients with pituitary growth hormone deficiency. Treatment of human growth hormone deficient children with somatropin results in increased growth rates and somatomedin-C levels similar to those seen for children treated with growth hormone of pituitary origin.

Skeletal Growth: The measurable increase in growth (body length) after somatropin treatment results from its effect on cartilaginous growth areas of the long bones. It is known that somatropin's effect is mediated by a sulfation factor, somatomedin-C, which permits the incorporation of sulfate into cartilage. Somatomedin-C is present in low concentration in the serum of growth hormone deficient patients and increases during somatropin therapy.

Cell Growth: Somatropin brings about cellular growth as demonstrated by an increase in the muscular, visceral and red cell mass. In muscle tissue, the increase in mass is associated with a corresponding increase in both number and dimension of muscular fibre cells.

Carbohydrate Metabolism: Somatropin has an effect on carbohydrate metabolism. The diabetogenic effect of somatropin is well-known in clinical medicine. Acromegalic patients often suffer from diabetes mellitus while hypopituitary children experience hypoglycemia. In healthy patients, very large doses of somatropin may interfere with glucose tolerance. A simultaneous increase in the plasma insulin level is observed upon somatropin administration. The diabetogenic activity of somatropin is perhaps due to several concomitant factors: reduced transport of glucose into peripheral tissues; increased release of glucose from the liver; reduced concentration of insulin at the muscular level; reduced glycolysis from the block of the enzyme triose phosphate dehydrogenase, mediated by non-esterified fatty acids.

Protein Metabolism: Somatropin has an effect on protein metabolism. Somatropin is an anabolic agent that stimulates intracellular transport of amino acids, net retention of nitrogen and protein synthesis which can be quantified by observing the decline in urinary nitrogen excretion and BUN.

Lipid Metabolism: Lipid metabolism is also affected by somatropin. This occurs when intracellular lipolysis is stimulated, thus increasing the plasma concentration of free fatty acids and stimulating the oxidation of fatty acids. In the diabetic patient, somatropin has been shown to accentuate ketogenesis.

Connective Tissue Metabolism: Connective tissue metabolism is affected by somatropin's ability to stimulate the synthesis of chondroitin sulfate and collagen as well as the urinary excretion of hydroxyproline.

Mineral Metabolism: Somatropin affects mineral metabolism by inducing the net retention of phosphorus and potassium and to a lesser degree sodium. Somatropin induces the increased intestinal absorption of calcium and the increased renal tubular reabsorption of phosphorus with increased serum and inorganic phosphate. Increased serum alkaline phosphatase may also be observed during somatropin therapy.

Indications: For the long-term treatment of patients with growth failure due to inadequate secretion of normal endogenous growth hormone. Other causes for growth failure should be ruled out.

Contraindications: Somatropin is ineffective and should not be used in patients with closed epiphyses.

Somatropin is contraindicated in the presence of any progression of underlying intracranial tumor. Intracranial tumor should be inactive prior to instituting therapy and somatropin should be discontinued if there is evidence of recurrent activity. Patients should be examined frequently for progression or recurrence of the underlying disease process.

Pregnancy and *Lactation:* Somatropin is not recommended for use during pregnancy and lactation.

Treatment with somatropin should be discontinued when the patient has reached satisfactory adult height, or the epiphyses are fused.

Somatropin reconstituted with bacteriostatic diluent should not be administered to newborns or patients sensitive to benzyl alcohol.

Warnings: Benzyl alcohol as a preservative in bacteriostatic diluent has been associated with toxicity in newborns. For administration to newborns and patients sensitive to benzyl alcohol, Saizen 1.33 and 3.33 mg should be reconstituted with sodium chloride injection, USP and Saizen 5 mg should be reconstituted with Water for Injection, USP. When reconstituted with Sodium Chloride Injection, USP or with Water for Injection, USP, the reconstituted solution should be administered immediately and any unused solution should be discarded.

Precautions: Somatropin treatment should be carried out under regular guidance of a physician experienced in the diagnosis and management of growth hormone deficiency.

Because human growth hormone may induce a state of insulin-resistance, the patient should be observed for evidence of glucose intolerance. Human growth hormone should be used with caution in patients with diabetes mellitus or a family history of diabetes mellitus.

Hypothyroidism may develop during somatropin therapy. Serum thyroid function tests should be performed periodically during somatropin administration and thyroid hormone replacement initiated when indicated because untreated hypothyroidism will jeopardize the response to growth hormone.

Serum levels of organic phosphorus, alkaline phosphatase, and IGF-a may increase with somatropin therapy.

Leukemia has been reported in a small number of growth hormone deficient patients, treated with growth hormone. Based on the current evidence, experts cannot conclude that growth hormone therapy is responsible for these occurrences.

Scoliosis has also been reported in patients treated with growth hormone.

Slipped capital femoral epiphysis may occur more frequently in patients with endocrine disorders. Physicians and parents should be alert to the development of a limp or complaints of hip or knee pain in somatropin-treated patients.

Bone age should be monitored periodically during somatropin administration especially in patients who are pubertal and/or receiving concomitant thyroid replacement therapy. Under these circumstances, epiphyseal maturation may progress rapidly.

Concomitant glucocorticoid therapy may inhibit the response to somatropin and should not exceed 10 to 15 mg hydrocortisone equivalent/m² body surface area during somatropin treatment.

Patients with growth hormone deficiency secondary to an intracranial lesion should be examined frequently for progression or recurrence of the underlying disease process.

When growth hormone is administered s.c. at the same site over a long period, local tissue atrophy may result. This can be avoided by rotating the injection site daily.

In case of severe or recurrent headache, visual problems, nausea and/or vomiting, a fundoscopy for papilloedema is recommended. If papilloedema is confirmed, a diagnosis of benign intracranial hypertension should be considered and if appropriate the growth hormone treatment should be discontinued.

At present, there is insufficient evidence to guide clinical decision making in patients with resolved intracranial hypotension. If growth hormone treatment is restarted, careful monitoring for symptoms of intracranial hypotension is necessary.

Carcinogenicity studies have not been conducted. Mutagenicity studies showed no mutagenic activity with somatropin.

Patients developing neoplasia should be reported to HPB by the treating physician.

Pregnancy: Reproduction studies have not been conducted. It is not known whether somatropin can cause fetal harm when administered to a pregnant women or can affect reproduction capacity. Somatropin should only be given to a pregnant woman if the benefits outweigh the risks.

Lactation: It is not known whether this drug is excreted in human milk. Because many drugs are excreted in human milk, caution should be exercised when somatropin is administered to a nursing mother.

Information for the Patient: A package insert containing information for the patient is included in each package.

Patients and caregivers should receive appropriate training and instruction for administering Saizen.

Your physician or nurse will tell you what syringe and needle to use for mixing and how much diluent to add to the Saizen vial.

Adverse Effects: As with all protein pharmaceuticals, a small percentage of patients may develop antibodies to the protein. Anti-growth hormone (GH) antibody capacities below 2 mg/L have not been associated with growth attenuation. In some cases when binding capacity exceeds 2 mg/L, growth attenuation has been described. In clinical studies with somatropin involving 280 patients (204 naive and 76 transfer patients), 1 patient at 6 months of therapy developed anti-GH antibodies with binding capacities exceeding 2 mg/L. Despite the high binding capacity, these antibodies were not growth attenuating. The patient was subsequently shown to have a hGH-N gene defect. Thus, genetic analysis should be undertaken in any patient in whom anti-GH antibodies with high binding capacities occur. No antibodies against proteins of the host cells were detected in the sera of patients treated up to 5 years.

Any patient with well-documented growth hormone deficiency who fails to respond to therapy should be tested for antibodies to human growth hormone and for thyroid status.

In clinical studies in which somatropin was administered to growth hormone deficient children, the following events were infrequently seen: local reactions at the injection site (such as pain, numbness, redness and swelling), headache and hypothyroidism.

Toxicity in newborns has been associated with benzyl alcohol as a preservative (see Warnings).

Overdose: Symptoms and Treatment: Acute overdosage could produce transient hypoglycemia followed by hyperglycemia. Long-term overdosage could result in signs and symptoms of gigantism and/or acromegaly consistent with the known effects of excess human growth hormone.

Dosage: Should be individualized for each patient according to body weight. It is recommended that somatropin be administered s.c. or i.m. at a dose of 0.2 mg/kg/week. The dosage can be increased to 0.27 mg/kg/week if there is insufficient response to treatment.

After determining the appropriate dose for a patient, reconstitute each vial of Saizen with the diluent supplied. For use in newborns and patients sensitive to benzyl alcohol, see Warnings.

Administration: Should be administered using sterile, disposable syringes and needles. The syringe used should be of appropriately small volume to ensure the accurate dose withdrawal. The calculated dose should be withdrawn for either s.c. or i.m. injection. The remaining contents should be discarded.

S.C. Injection: The weekly dose can be divided into 3 single doses (corresponding to 0.067 mg/kg per injection) or into 6 or 7 single daily doses (corresponding to 0.033 to 0.028 mg/kg per injection). The injection site should be altered to prevent lipoatrophy. For s.c. injections, the use of a needle which is 1.25 cm long is recommended.

I.M. Injection: The weekly dose should be divided into 3 single injections (corresponding to 0.067 mg/kg). For i.m. injections, the use of a needle which is at least 2.5 cm long is recommended to ensure the injection reaches the i.m. layer.

Stability and Storage Recommendations: 1.33 & 3.33 mg Vials: Store lyophilized product under refrigeration at 2 to 8°C. 5 mg Vial: Store lyophilized product at room temperature. Do not use Saizen after the expiry date shown on label.

Reconstitution: The recommended diluents for reconstitution are: 1.33 mg Vial: Sodium Chloride Injection, USP; 3.33 mg Vial: Sodium Chloride Injection, USP and Bacteriostatic Sodium Chloride Injection, USP; 5 mg Vial: Water for Injection, USP and Bacteriostatic Water for Injection, USP.

Incompatibility: Saizen should not be mixed with other drugs.

Preparation of Solution: To prevent possible contamination of the vial, wipe the rubber stopper with an antiseptic solution before puncturing it with the needle. After determining appropriate patient dose, reconstitute each vial of Saizen as described below.

After determining appropriate patient dose, reconstitute each 1.33 mg vial of Saizen with up to 1 mL of Sodium Chloride Injection, USP, each 3.33 mg vial of Saizen with up to 5 mL of Bacteriostatic Sodium Chloride Injection, USP (benzyl alcohol preserved), and each 5 mg vial of Saizen with 1 to 3 mL of Bacteriostatic Water for Injection, USP (benzyl alcohol preserved).

To reconstitute, inject the diluent into the vial aiming the liquid against the glass vial wall. Swirl the vial with a **gentle** rotary motion until contents are dissolved completely. **Do not shake.** If shaken, the solution will appear opalescent; however, this opalescence does not indicate any decrease in potency. Parenteral drug products should be inspected visually prior to administration. Do not inject if the reconstituted product contains particulate matter or is discolored. For use in patients sensitive to the diluent see Warnings.

Stability of Solution and Storage: 1.33 mg Vial: When reconstituted with Sodium Chloride Injection, USP, the reconstituted solution should be administered immediately. Any unused solution should be discarded.

3.33 mg Vial: When reconstituted with Sodium Chloride Injection, USP, the reconstituted solution should be administered immediately. Any unused solution should be discarded.

When reconstituted with Bacteriostatic Sodium Chloride Injection, USP, the reconstituted solution may be stored at 2 to 8°C for up to 14 days.

5 mg Vial: When reconstituted with Water for Injection, USP, the reconstituted solution should be administered immediately. Any unused solution should be discarded.

When reconstituted with Bacteriostatic Water for Injection, USP, the reconstituted solution may be stored at 2 to 8°C for up to 14 days.

Supplied: 1.33 mg: Each vial of sterile, nonpyrogenic, lyophilized powder contains: somatropin 1.33 mg. Nonmedicinal ingredients: disodium phosphate dihydrate, mannitol, sodium chloride and sodium dihydrogen phosphate. Cartons of 1 and 10 vials with diluent (1 mL Sodium Chloride Injection, USP).

3.33 mg: Each vial of sterile, nonpyrogenic, lyophilized powder contains: somatropin 3.33 mg. Nonmedicinal ingredients: disodium phosphate dihydrate, mannitol and sodium dihydrogen phosphate monohydrate. Cartons of 1 and 10 vials with diluent (5 mL Bacteriostatic Sodium Chloride Injection, USP).

5 mg: Each vial of sterile, nonpyrogenic, lyophilized powder contains: somatropin 5 mg. Nonmedicinal ingredients: phosphoric acid and sucrose. Cartons of 1 and 2 vials with diluent (10 mL Bacteriostatic Water for Injection, USP).

Reviewed 1999

SALAC™
Medicis
Salicylic Acid
Acne Therapy

Supplied: Each plastic container contains: salicylic acid 2%. Plastic containers of 180 mL.

SALAGEN® Ⓟ
Pharmacia & Upjohn
Pilocarpine HCl
Cholinomimetic Agent

Pharmacology: Pilocarpine tablets are made from the naturally occurring alkaloid pilocarpine which is obtained from the leaflets of the South American shrub Pilocarpus jaborandi. Pilocarpine is a cholinomimetic (cholinergic parasympathomimetic) agent capable of exerting a broad spectrum of pharmacologic effects with predominant muscarinic action. Dependent upon the dosage and the individual, oral pilocarpine will increase secretion by the exocrine glands (e.g., sweat, salivary, lacrimal, gastric, pancreatic, intestinal and respiratory mucous cells) and stimulate smooth muscle (e.g., gastrointestinal tract, bronchi, ureters, urinary bladder, gallbladder and biliary tract). Pilocarpine may also produce arrhythmias and/or paradoxical effects on the cardiovascular system manifest by hypertension after a brief episode of hypotension.

The bioavailability of oral multiple-dose pilocarpine tablets has been determined in 19 healthy male volunteers. Pilocarpine 5 mg and 10 mg were administered orally for 2 days, at 8 a.m., noon, and 6 p.m. for a total of 6 doses. The results are presented in Table I.

Table I—Salagen

Bioavailability Parameters Following Multiple-Dose Oral Pilocarpine Tablets[a]

Dose	T_{max} (h)	C_{max} (ng/mL)	AUC[b] h(ng/mL)	$t_{1/2}$ (h)
5 mg (n=10)	1.25	14.61	33.04	0.76
10 mg (n=9)	0.85	41.35	107.96	1.35

[a]Pilocarpine tablets given orally, 3 times daily, for 2 days; the results determined after the final dose.
[b]Trapezoidal values.

Pharmacokinetics in elderly male volunteers (n=11) were comparable to those in younger men. In 5 healthy elderly female volunteers, the mean C_{max} and AUC were approximately twice that of elderly males and young normal male volunteers.

When taken with a high-fat meal by 12 healthy male volunteers, there was a decrease in the rate of absorption of pilocarpine from pilocarpine HCl tablets. Mean T_{max} were 1.47 and 0.87 hours, and mean C_{max} were 51.8 and 59.2 ng/mL for fed and fasted, respectively.

The results of an in vitro protein binding study indicate ^{3}H-pilocarpine is not bound to plasma proteins as determined in either rat or human plasma.

Limited information is available about the metabolism and elimination of pilocarpine in humans. Inactivation of pilocarpine is thought to occur at neuronal synapses and probably in plasma. Pilocarpine and its minimally active or inactive degradation products, which include pilocarpic acid, are excreted in the urine.

Indications: For the treatment of the symptoms of xerostomia (dry mouth) due to salivary gland hypofunction caused by radiotherapy for cancer of the head and neck.

For the treatment of the symptoms of xerostomia (dry mouth) and xerophthalmia (dry eyes) in patients with Sjögren's syndrome.

Contraindications: In patients with uncontrolled asthma; when miosis is undesirable (e.g., acute iritis and in narrow-angle (angle closure) glaucoma); in patients with known sensitivity to pilocarpine, or to any of the tablet's excipients.

Warnings: Cardiovascular Disease: Patients with significant cardiovascular disease may be unable to compensate for transient changes in hemodynamics or rhythm induced by pilocarpine. Pulmonary edema has been reported as a complication of pilocarpine toxicity. Pilocarpine should be administered with caution and under close medical supervision to patients with significant cardiovascular disease.

Pulmonary Disease: Pilocarpine has been reported to increase airway resistance, bronchial smooth muscle tone, and bronchial secretions. Pilocarpine should be administered with caution and under close medical supervision to patients with significant pulmonary disease (e.g., controlled asthma, chronic bronchitis, or chronic obstructive pulmonary disease).

Should any adverse changes in the patient's cardiopulmonary condition occur, or be suspected, therapy with pilocarpine should be discontinued immediately.

Precautions: General: Pilocarpine toxicity is characterized by an exaggeration of its parasympathomimetic effects.

The dose-related cardiovascular pharmacologic effects of pilocarpine include hypotension, hypertension, bradycardia, and tachycardia (see also Warnings).

Pilocarpine should be administered with caution to patients with known or suspected cholelithiasis or biliary tract disease. Contractions of the gallbladder and biliary smooth muscle could precipitate complications including cholecystitis, cholangitis, and biliary obstruction.

Pilocarpine may increase ureteral smooth muscle tone and could theoretically precipitate renal colic or "ureteral reflux" in patients with renal dysfunction (e.g., nephrolithiasis).

Hepatic Insufficiency: Based on decreased plasma clearance observed in patients with mild to moderate hepatic impairment, the starting dose in patients with moderate to severe hepatic impairment should be 5 mg twice daily, followed by titration based on tolerability.

Cholinergic agonists, like pilocarpine, may cause increased acid secretion. This possibility should be considered when treating patients with active peptic ulcer disease.

Cholinergic agonists, like pilocarpine, may have dose-related CNS effects. This should be considered when treating patients with underlying cognitive or psychiatric disturbances.

Occupational Hazards: Ocular administration of pilocarpine has been reported to cause visual blurring and impairment of depth perception which may result in decreased visual acuity, especially at night and in patients with central lens changes. Patients should be cautioned about driving at night or performing hazardous activities in reduced lighting while receiving therapy with pilocarpine.

Drug Interactions: Pilocarpine should be administered with caution to patients taking beta-adrenergic antagonists because of the possibility of conduction disturbances. Drugs with parasympathomimetic effects administered concurrently with pilocarpine would be expected to result in additive pharmacologic effects. Pilocarpine might antagonize the anticholinergic effects of drugs used concomitantly. These effects should be considered when anticholinerigc properties may be contributing to the therapeutic effect of concomitant medication (e.g., atropine, inhaled ipratropium).

While no formal drug interaction studies have been performed, the following concomitant drugs were used in at least 10% of patients in either or both Sjögren's pivotal studies: acetaminophen, ASA, artificial tears, calcium, conjugated estrogens, hydroxychloroquine sulfate, ibuprofen, levothyroxine sodium, medroxyprogesterone acetate, methotrexate, multivitamins, naproxen, omeprazole and prednisone. There were no reports of drug toxicities during either trial.

Children: Safety and effectiveness of pilocarpine have not been studied in children under 18 years of age.

Impairment of Fertility: The data obtained from a study in rats suggest that pilocarpine may impair the fertility of male and female humans. Therefore, pilocarpine tablets should be administered to individuals who are attempting to conceive a child only if the potential benefit justifies potential impairment of fertility.

Pregnancy: The safety of pilocarpine has not been established in human pregnancy. Therefore, pilocarpine should only be used during pregnancy if the potential benefit to the mother justifies the potential risk to the fetus.

Lactation: It is not presently known whether this drug is excreted in human milk. Because many drugs are excreted in human milk and because of the potential for serious adverse reactions in nursing infants from pilocarpine, a decision should be made whether to discontinue nursing or to discontinue the drug.

Dependence Liability: Pilocarpine does not have the potential for addiction; consequently, there have been no reports of addiction with the use of pilocarpine. There are no known withdrawal effects associated with pilocarpine either in animals or in humans. The pharmacologic effects, other than salivation, are not pleasurable, thus, there is no reason to suspect it will be abused.

Adverse Effects: Head and Neck Cancer Patients: In the controlled clinical studies, 217 patients of whom 147 (68%) were male and 70 (32%) were female were administered pilocarpine. The mean age of the patients was approximately 58 years; the majority of patients were between 50 and 64 years (51%), 33% were 65 years and older, and 16% were younger than 50 years.

No serious drug-related adverse events were reported with use of pilocarpine in these controlled clinical trials.

Table II presents the adverse events observed during treatment with pilocarpine which were considered to be a consequence of the expected pharmacologic effects of pilocarpine. These adverse events were dose-dependent and generally of mild or moderate intensity. Such adverse events usually subside within 6 hours of discontinuation of therapy.

Table II—Salagen

The Most Frequent Adverse Events, by Dose, Associated with Salagen Tablets (% of Patients Reporting)

Adverse Event	Placebo t.i.d. (n=152) %	5 mg t.i.d. (15 mg/day) (n=141) %	10 mg t.i.d. (30 mg/day) (n=121) %
Sweating	9	29	68
Nausea	4	6	15
Rhinitis	7	5	14
Chills	<1	3	14
Vasodilatation (Flushing)	3	8	13
Urinary Frequency	7	9	12
Dizziness	4	5	12
Asthenia	3	6	12

Table III presents adverse events (incidence ≥3%) reported at dosages of 15 to 30 mg/day in the controlled clinical trials.

Table III—Salagen

Adverse Events (Incidence ≥3%) Reported at Dosages of 15-30 mg/day Salagen Tablets (% of Patients Reporting)

Adverse Event	Placebo t.i.d. (n=152) %	5-10 mg t.i.d. (15-30 mg/day) (n=217) %
Headache	8	13
Dyspepsia	5	7
Lacrimation	8	6
Diarrhea	5	6
Edema	4	5
Abdominal Pain	4	4
Amblyopia	2	4
Vomiting	1	4
Pharyngitis	8	3
Hypertension	1	3

The following events were reported by head and neck cancer patients at incidences of 1 to 2% at dosages of 15 to 30 mg/day: Cardiovascular: tachycardia.

Digestive: dysphagia, taste perversion.

Musculoskeletal: myalgias.

Nervous: tremor.

Respiratory: epistaxis, sinusitis, voice alteration.

Skin: pruritus, rash.

Special Senses: abnormal vision, conjunctivitis.

In long-term treatment were 2 patients with underlying cardiovascular disease of whom 1 experienced a myocardial infarct and another an episode of syncope. The association with drug is uncertain.

Sjögren's Syndrome Patients: In the controlled clinical studies, 376 patients of whom 19 (5%) were male and 357 (95%) were female were administered pilocarpine. The mean age of the patients was approximately 55 years; the majority of patients were between 40 and 69 years (70%), 16% were 70 years and older, and 14% were younger than 40 years of age.

No serious drug-related adverse events were reported with use of pilocarpine tablets in these controlled clinical trials.

Table IV (on following page) presents the adverse events observed during treatment with pilocarpine tablets which were considered to be a consequence of the expected pharmacologic effects of pilocarpine. These adverse events were dose-dependent and generally of mild or moderate intensity.

Table IV—Salagen

Most Frequent Adverse Events, by Dose, Associated with Salagen Tablets (% of Patients Reporting)

Adverse Event	Placebo q.i.d. (n=253) %	2.5 mg q.i.d. (10 mg/day) (n=121) %	5 mg q.i.d. (20 mg/day) (n=255) %	5-7.5 mg q.i.d. (20-30 mg/day) (n=114) %
Sweating	7	11	40	47
Urinary Frequency	4	11	10	6
Chills	2	1	4	1
Vasodilatation (Flushing)	2	2	9	3
Increased Salivation	0	0	3	4

Table V presents additional adverse events (incidence ≥3%) reported at dosages of 10 to 30 mg/day in the controlled clinical trials.

Table V—Salagen

Adverse Events (Incidence ≥3%) Reported at Dosages of 10-30 mg/day Salagen Tablets (% of Patients Reporting)

Adverse Event	Placebo q.i.d. (n=253) %	2.5-7.5 mg q.i.d. (10-30 mg/day) (n=376) %
Headache	19	18
Flu Syndrome	9	12
Nausea	9	12
Dyspepsia	7	8
Rhinitis	8	8
Diarrhea	7	7
Dizziness	7	6
Pain	2	4
Abdominal Pain	4	5
Pharyngitis	5	4
Sinusitis	5	4
Asthenia	2	3
Rash	3	3
Infection	6	3

The following events were reported by Sjögren's patients at incidences of 1 to 2% at dosages of 10 to 30 mg/day: Body as a Whole: accidental injury, allergic reaction, fever, abnormal lab test.

Cardiovascular: palpitation, tachycardia.

Digestive: constipation, flatulence, glossitis, stomatitis, vomiting.

Metabolic and Nutritional: edema, face edema.

Musculoskeletal: back pain, myalgia.

Nervous: somnolence.

Respiratory: cough increased, epistaxis.

Skin: pruritus.

Special Senses: blurred vision, tinnitus.

Urogenital: urinary incontinence, urinary tract infection, vaginitis.

Overdose: Symptoms: Toxicity from pilocarpine is characterized chiefly by exaggeration of parasympathomimetic effects and resembles "muscarinic poisoning" (e.g., consumption of mushrooms of the genus Inocybe). Dose-dependent symptoms include salivation, sweating, vomiting, respiratory distress, hypotension, diarrhea, nausea and shock. Mental confusion and cardiac arrhythmias can also occur.

A fatal overdose with oral administration of ocular pilocarpine, resulting from poisoning, has been reported in the literature. The symptoms included: salivation, pinpoint pupils, sweating, dyspnea, tachypnea, tachycardia, and pulmonary edema.

There are several reports of pilocarpine overdosage reported with the treatment of angle-closure glaucoma. Cardiovascular decompensation has been noted in patients with acute closed-angle glaucoma who have received intraocular instillation of pilocarpine in excess of 60 to 100 mg over short periods prior to eye surgery. Other reported symptoms occurring in this situation include nausea, vomiting, profuse sweating, tremor, hypotension, sinus bradycardia, AV block, changes in mental state, and shock.

Treatment: Overdosage with pilocarpine should be treated with atropine titration (0.5 to 1 mg given s.c. or i.v.) and supportive measures to maintain respiration and circulation. Epinephrine (0.3 to 1 mg, s.c. or i.m.) may also be of value in the presence of severe cardiovascular depression or bronchoconstriction. It is not known if pilocarpine is dialyzable.

Dosage: The usual dose for initiation of treatment is 5 mg 3 or 4 times daily. Titration up to 10 mg (2 tablets)/dose, not to exceed a total of 30 mg (6 tablets)/day, may be considered for patients who have not responded adequately and who can tolerate the lower doses. The lowest dose that is tolerated and effective should be used for maintenance.

The starting dose in patients with moderate to severe hepatic impairment should be 5 mg twice daily, followed by titration based on tolerability.

Treatment should begin at the first signs of xerostomia. Clinical experience indicates that the relief of xerostomia improves over time with the administration of pilocarpine. Administration at the above recommended dosage, for 12 or more weeks may be required before relief of xerostomia can be expected. Onset and degree of relief may vary among patients.

Information for the Patient: See Blue Section—Information for the Patient "Salagen".

Supplied: Each white, round, biconvex, film-coated unscored tablet, printed with "SAL" on one side and "5" on the other side, contains: pilocarpine HCl 5 mg. Nonmedicinal ingredients: microcrystalline cellulose and stearic acid; coating: hydroxypropyl methylcellulose, polyethylene glycol, polysorbate 80 and titanium dioxide; ink: ethanol, ethylene glycol monoethyl ether, lecithin, methyl alcohol, N-butyl alcohol, propylene glycol, shellac and synthetic black iron oxide. Polish: carnauba wax. Bottles of 100. Store at room temperature (15 to 30°C).

Reviewed 1999

SALAZOPYRIN® ℞
SALAZOPYRIN EN-TABS® ℞

Pharmacia & Upjohn

Sulfasalazine

Anti-inflammatory

Pharmacology: About 20% of sulfasalazine is absorbed in the small intestine after oral administration. A small percentage of the absorbed sulfasalazine is excreted in the urine and the rest via the bile into the small intestine (enterohepatic circulation). This portion together with the unabsorbed sulfasalazine enters the colon where it is split by bacteria into 2 main metabolites, sulfapyridine and 5-aminosalicylic acid. The peak serum concentration is reached after 3 to 5 hours. The mean serum half-life after a single dose is about 6 hours; after repeated doses it is about 8 hours. After intake of sulfasalazine enteric coated tablets, sulfasalazine has been detected in serum somewhat later than after intake of plain tablets, as expected, the peak serum concentration being observed between 3 and 12 hours.

Sulfapyridine is absorbed, partially acetylated and/or hydroxylated in the liver and/or conjugated with glucuronic acid. In patients who are slow acetylators the serum concentration of free sulfapyridine is higher than in fast acetylators. The major part is excreted in the urine. Nonacetylated sulfapyridine is bound to serum proteins and reaches a maximum serum concentration after 12 hours. Sulfapyridine has a tendency towards accumulation. It does not disappear completely from the serum until 3 days after withdrawal of the drug.

The total urinary recovery of sulfasalazine and its sulfapyridine metabolites in healthy subjects during 3 days after the administration of a single 2 g dose of sulfasalazine averaged about 91%.

The absorbed 5-aminosalicylic acid is partly excreted in the urine, mainly as acetyl-5-aminosalicylic acid. A larger portion of 5-aminosalicylic acid is excreted in the feces.

The mode of action of sulfasalazine is unclear, suggested as being: anti-inflammatory, immunosuppressive and bacteriostatic.

In clinical inflammatory bowel disease cases, the anti-inflammatory effects seem to relieve the acute symptoms of diarrhea, gut inflammation, mucosal edema and bleeding. The long-term protection afforded by sulfasalazine therapy may be due to immunosuppressive properties of the drug.

Anti-inflammatory Effects: Sulfasalazine inhibits superoxide production by granulocytes stimulated with immune complexes or formyl peptides. In addition 5-ASA is a powerful scavenger of oxygen free radicals. Other granulocyte functions inhibited by sulfasalazine include degranulation, chemotaxis and random migration. These inhibitory effects on inflammatory cell functions may contribute to the beneficial clinical activity of sulfasalazine.

Sulfasalazine is a relatively weak inhibitor of the cyclo-oxygenase enzyme, but a potent inhibitor of 15-prostaglandin dehydrogenase (PGDH), the main metabolic pathway for the prostaglandins.

On the lipoxygenase side of the arachidonic acid cascade, sulfasalazine has been shown to exert an inhibitory activity on several enzymes including 5-LO and LTC_4 synthetase. In line with this effect sulfasalazine has been shown to inhibit the release of lipoxygenase product from inflammatory cells and tissue.

Taken together, these effects of sulfasalazine on arachidonic acid metabolizing enzymes would lead to a decrease in pro-inflammatory lipoxygenase products with a simultaneous increase in immunosuppressive, anti-inflammatory prostaglandins, which may have a bearing on the clinical activity.

Effects on Immunological Functions: Since the disorders in which sulfasalazine has clinical activity are considered to be of autoimmune nature, the effect of sulfasalazine on immune competent cells is of interest. Both natural killer cell activity and T-cell proliferation are inhibited by sulfasalazine in in vitro systems.

Antibacterial Effects: Studies in vitro have shown that both sulfasalazine and its main metabolites inhibit bacterial growth. A reduction in several bacterial species of the gut flora has also been observed after clinical treatment with sulfasalazine.

Pharmacokinetics: Patients with Rheumatoid Arthritis: The pharmacokinetics of sulfasalazine and its metabolites after a 2 g single oral dose were compared in patients with rheumatoid arthritis and patients with ulcerative colitis. The study showed a large individual variability, which is also found in studies in healthy volunteers, but no difference between the two patient groups except for a significantly higher peak concentration of sulfapyridine in rheumatoid arthritis patients. The area under the plasma concentration curve (AUC) for sulfapyridine was also increased but the difference was not significant.

Bioavailability in Elderly Patients with Rheumatoid Arthritis: The pharmacokinetics of sulfasalazine and its metabolites were compared in young (mean age 40.5 years) and elderly (mean age 74.4 years) rheumatoid arthritis patients after a single oral (2 g) dose taken fasting and at steady state. For sulfasalazine the only difference found between the two age groups was a prolonged half-life in the elderly, but no significant difference in either the plasma concentration at steady state and the renal clearance. For sulfapyridine both T_{max} and volume of distribution were significantly increased in the elderly after the single doses, but this difference with age disappeared at chronic dosing. The data indicates that there is no major age dependent difference in the pharmacokinetics of sulfasalazine but the acetylation phenotype is much more important.

Indications: Adjunctive therapy in the treatment of severe ulcerative colitis, proctitis or distal ulcerative colitis and Crohn's disease. It is especially useful for chronic administration.

The EN-tabs are indicated for the treatment of active rheumatoid arthritis, when treatment with an adequate conventional first line therapy has failed.

Contraindications: Hypersensitivity to sulfonamides or salicylates.

In infants under 2 years of age.

Intestinal and urinary obstructions.

Patients with porphyria should not receive sulfonamides, as these drugs have been reported to precipitate an acute attack.

Should not be used in patients in whom acute asthmatic attacks, urticaria, rhinitis or other allergic manifestations are precipitated by ASA or other nonsteroidal anti-inflammatory agents. Fatal anaphylactic reactions have occurred in such individuals.

Warnings: Sulfasalazine should be used only after critical appraisal of the risk to benefit in patients with hepatic or renal damage, blood dyscrasias, severe allergy or bronchial asthma. Pancreatitis has been observed in some susceptible individuals.

Deaths associated with the administration of sulfasalazine have been reported from hypersensitivity reactions, agranulocytosis, aplastic anemia, other blood dyscrasias, renal and liver damage, irreversible neuromuscular and CNS changes

Salazopyrin (cont'd)

and fibrosing alveolitis. The presence of clinical signs such as sore throat, fever, pallor, purpura or jaundice may be indications of serious blood disorders. Complete blood counts as well as urinalysis with careful microscopic examination should be done frequently in patients receiving this drug.

Oligospermia with infertility have been observed in men treated with sulfasalazine. Withdrawal of the drug appears to reverse these effects.

Patients, especially those with glucose-6-phosphate dehydrogenase deficiency, should be observed closely for signs of hemolytic anemia. This reaction is frequently dose related. If toxic or hypersensitivity reactions occur, the drug should be discontinued immediately.

Precautions: Patients hypersensitive to furosemide, thiazide diuretics, carbonic anhydrase inhibitors, may also be hypersensitive to this medication.

Sulfasalazine should be administered under medical supervision. Sulfasalazine shares the toxic potentialities of other sulfonamides, especially sulfapyridine and the usual precautions of sulfonamide therapy should be observed.

Bone marrow depression (most often expressed as leukopenia) has been reported, usually within the first 3 months of starting treatment. In the majority of patients this has been reversed on stopping the drug. A full blood count, including differential white blood cell count, should be carried out before starting treatment and monitored closely during the first 3 months of treatment. Thereafter patients should be screened if their condition changes or if they present any symptoms of infection. A falling trend in the blood count is a better indicator than a single value.

Red cell and platelet counts should be carried out before and periodically during therapy.

Sulfasalazine should be used with caution in patients with reduced kidney or liver function. Liver function tests and urinalysis should be carried out before and periodically during therapy.

When concurrent therapy with other drugs is administered, as in rheumatoid arthritis, the recommended frequency of monitoring is as follows: initially, every second week during first 3 months after onset of treatment, every 6 months thereafter.

Sulfasalazine may produce an orange-yellow color of the urine. Similar discoloration of the skin and yellow staining of soft contact lenses have occasionally been reported.

Isolated instances have been reported when the EN-tabs have passed undisintegrated. This may be due, in part, to a lack of intestinal esterase in these patients. If this is observed, the administration of EN-tabs should be discontinued.

Adequate fluid intake must be maintained in order to prevent crystalluria and stone formation.

Pregnancy and Reproduction: Teratogenic Effects: Reproduction studies have been performed in rats and rabbits at doses up to 6 times the human dose and have revealed no evidence of impaired female fertility or harm to the fetus due to sulfasalazine.

The outcome of pregnancy in a group of pregnant women with intestinal bowel disease (IBD) treated with sulfasalazine alone or sulfasalazine and concomitant steroid therapy was compared with untreated IBD pregnancies. The incidence of fetal morbidity and mortality was comparable between the groups and to the expected outcome in the general population.

Sulfasalazine should be used during pregnancy only if clearly needed.

Nonteratogenic Effects: Sulfasalazine and sulfapyridine pass the placental barrier. Although sulfapyridine has been shown to have a poor bilirubin displacing capacity, the potential for kernicterus in newborns should be kept in mind.

A case of agranulocytosis has been reported in an infant whose mother was taking both Salazopyrin and prednisone throughout pregnancy.

Lactation: Caution should be exercised when sulfasalazine is administered to a nursing woman, since it is excreted in the milk. The concentration of sulfapyridine in milk is about 30 to 60% of that in serum. However, since sulfapyridine has a poor bilirubin displacing capacity, the risk for kernicterus in healthy suckling children may be low with therapeutic doses.

Drug Interactions: The following drug interactions and/or related problems have been selected on the basis of their potential clinical significance (possible mechanism in parentheses where appropriate):

Note: Combinations containing any of the following medications, depending on the amount present, may also interact with this medication.

Antibiotics.

Anticoagulants, coumarin or indandione derivatives.

Anticonvulsants, hydantoin.

Antidiabetic agents, oral.

Digitalis glycosides or folic acid (sulfasalazine may inhibit absorption and lower the serum concentrations of these medications; folic acid requirements may be increased in patients receiving sulfasalazine); (patients taking digitalis glycosides should be monitored closely for evidence of altered digitalis effect).

Methenamine (in acid urine methenamine breaks down into formaldehyde which may form an insoluble precipitate with certain sulfonamides and may also increase the danger of crystalluria; concurrent use is not recommended).

Methotrexate (may be displaced from protein binding sites and/or metabolism may be inhibited by sulfonamides, resulting in increased or prolonged effects and/or toxicity; dosage adjustments may be necessary during and after sulfonamide therapy).

Oxyphenbutazone or phenylbutazone (effects may be potentiated when used concurrently with sulfonamides because of displacement from plasma protein binding sites).

Photosensitizing medications, other (caution in concurrent use of sulfasalazine with these medications is recommended because of possible additive photosensitizing effects).

Probenecid (decreases renal tubular secretion of sulfonamides when used concurrently, resulting in increased and more prolonged sulfonamide concentrations and/or toxicity; sulfonamide dosage adjustments may be necessary during and after probenecid therapy and sulfonamide serum determinations may be useful in prolonged probenecid therapy).

Sulfinpyrazone (concurrent use may displace sulfonamides from protein binding sites and may decrease renal excretion, resulting in increased sulfonamide concentrations and/or toxicity; sulfonamide dosage adjustments may be necessary during and after sulfinpyrazone therapy).

Medical Problems: Use of this medication should be carefully considered when the following medical problems exist: blood dyscrasias, glucose-6-phosphate dehydrogenase (G6PD) deficiency, hepatic function impairment, intestinal and urinary tract obstruction, porphyria or renal function impairment.

Laboratory Tests: The following may be especially important in patient monitoring (other tests may be warranted in some patients, depending on their condition): Complete blood count, including differential white blood cell count and platelets, should be carried out before starting treatment and monitored closely during the first 3 months of treatment. Thereafter, patients should be screened if their condition changes or if they present with any symptoms of infection. A falling trend in the blood count is a better indicator than a single value.

Liver function tests and urinalysis with careful microscopic examination should be carried out before and periodically during therapy.

Proctoscopy and sigmoidoscopy (may be required periodically during treatment to determine patient response and dosage adjustments).

Adverse Effects: Adverse reactions with sulfasalazine may be more frequent and more severe in patients who are slow acetylators.

Most side effects are dose dependent, and the symptoms can be alleviated by reducing the dosage. Increased incidences of adverse reactions are seen with the daily dosage of 4 g or more, or total serum sulfapyridine levels above 50 μg/mL. Hypersensitivity reactions have been noted, in which a dose reduction is irrelevant.

It has been shown that the frequency and severity of the rather common dyspeptic manifestations experienced by patients with gastric intolerance to uncoated tablets are markedly reduced when using enteric coated tablets.

The most commonly reported adverse reactions are: nausea, vomiting, gastric distress, methemoglobinemia, anorexia, headache and apparently reversible oligospermia. These occur in about one-third of patients. Less frequent adverse reactions are skin rash, erythema, pruritus, urticaria, fever, Heinz-body anemia, hemolytic anemia, leukopenia, megaloblastic (macrocytic) anemia, and cyanosis, which may occur in a frequency of 1 in every 30 patients or less.

Although the listing which follows includes a few adverse reactions which have not been reported with this specific drug, the pharmacological similarities among the sulfonamides require that each of these reactions be considered when sulfasalazine is administered.

Other adverse reactions which occur rarely, in approximately 1 in 1 000 patients or less are: Blood Dyscrasias: aplastic anemia, agranulocytosis, purpura, thrombocytopenia and hypoprothrombinemia.

Hypersensitivity: erythema multiforme (Stevens-Johnson syndrome), exfoliative dermatitis, epidermal necrolysis (Lyell's syndrome) with corneal damage, anaphylaxis, serum sickness syndrome, pneumonitis with or without eosinophilia, vasculitis, fibrosing alveolitis, pleuritis, pericarditis with or without tamponade, allergic myocarditis, polyarteritis nodosa, L.E. syndrome, hepatitis and hepatic necrosis with or without immune complexes, parapsoriasis varioliformis acuta (Mucha Habermann syndrome), photosensitization, arthralgia, periorbital edema, conjunctival and scleral injection and alopecia.

Gastrointestinal: hepatitis, pancreatitis, bloody diarrhea, impaired folic acid absorption, impaired digoxin absorption, stomatitis, diarrhea and abdominal pains.

CNS: transverse myelitis, convulsions, transient lesions of the posterior spinal column, peripheral neuropathy, mental depression, vertigo, hearing loss, insomnia, ataxia, hallucinations, tinnitus and drowsiness. Three cases of aseptic meningitis have been reported during the use of enteric coated sulfasalazine in the treatment of rheumatic disease.

Renal: toxic nephrosis with oliguria and anuria, nephrotic syndrome, hematuria, crystalluria and proteinuria.

Other: urine discoloration and skin discoloration. The sulfonamides bear certain chemical similarities to some goitrogens, diuretics, acetazolamide and the thiazides, and oral hypoglycemic agents. Goiter production, diuresis, and hypoglycemia have occurred rarely in patients receiving sulfonamides. Cross-sensitivity may exist with these agents. Rats appear to be especially susceptible to the goitrogenic effects of sulfonamides and long-term administration has produced thyroid malignancies in this species.

Overdose: Symptoms: Similar to those of any sulfonamide, the most likely symptoms would be gastrointestinal disturbances, drowsiness, convulsions, hematuria, crystalluria or anuria. Serum sulfapyridine concentrations may be used to monitor progress of recovery from overdosage.

Treatment: Gastric lavage or emesis plus catharsis as indicated. Alkalinize urine. If kidney function is normal, force fluids. If anuria is present, restrict fluids and salt, and treat appropriately. Catheterization of the ureters may be indicated for complete renal blockage by crystals. The low molecular weight of sulfasalazine and its metabolites may facilitate their removal by dialysis. For agranulocytosis, discontinue the drug immediately, hospitalize the patient and institute appropriate therapy.

For hypersensitivity reactions, discontinue treatment immediately. Such reactions may be controlled with antihistamines and, if necessary, systemic corticosteroids.

Dosage: The dosage should be adjusted according to the response to the treatment and the patient's tolerance to the drug. The tablets/enteric coated tablets should be taken at regular and even intervals over the 24-hour period. The uncoated tablets should preferably be taken with a meal. For intestinal inflammatory diseases the nighttime dose interval should not exceed 8 hours.

Patients not previously treated with sulfasalazine should increase the dose gradually during the first few weeks. The incidence of adverse reactions tends to increase with daily dosages of 4 g or more; patients receiving these doses should be advised of this possibility and should be carefully observed for the appearance of adverse reactions.

Geriatrics: Based on pharmacokinetic studies, no special dosage instructions are required for elderly patients.

Renal Deficiency: Sulfasalazine should be used with caution in patients with renal deficiency.

Inflammatory Bowel Disease, Ulcerative Colitis, Crohn's Disease: **Acute attacks:** Adults: Severe attacks: 2 to 4 tablets, 3 to 4 times daily. Moderate and mild attacks: 2 tablets 3 to 4 times daily.

Children: 25 to 35 kg: 1 tablet 3 times daily; 35 to 50 kg: 2 tablets 2 to 3 times daily.

Prophylaxis: Adults: In the state of remission in ulcerative colitis the maintenance dose recommended for keeping the patient free from symptoms is 2 tablets 2 to 3 times a day. Treatment with this dosage should continue indefinitely, unless adverse effects are observed. In case of deterioration, raise the dosage to 2 to 4 tablets, 3 to 4 times a day.

Children: 25 to 35 kg: 1 tablet twice daily; 35 to 50 kg: 1 tablet 2 to 3 times daily.

Patients experiencing gastrointestinal side effects with the uncoated tablet should use the enteric coated tablets or a lower dose.

Rheumatoid Arthritis: Adults: 2 enteric coated tablets, 2 times daily.

When starting therapy, it is suggested to increase the daily dose as follows: 1st week: 1 enteric coated tablet in the evening. 2nd week: 1 enteric coated tablet in the morning and 1 enteric coated tablet in the evening. 3rd week: 1 enteric coated tablet in the morning and 2 enteric coated tablets in the evening. 4th week and after: 2 enteric coated tablets in the morning and 2 enteric coated tablets in the evening.

If no response has been seen after 2 months' treatment, the dose may be increased to 3 g/day. Some patients may do well with 1.5 g/day.

A clinical effect generally appears 1 to 2 months after initiation of treatment. Concurrent therapy with analgesics and/or anti-inflammatory agents is recommended until the therapeutic effect of the EN-tabs is apparent. The EN-tabs are effective and well tolerated in long-term treatment.

Children: The use of sulfasalazine in Juvenile Rheumatoid Arthritis is not recommended since its efficacy/safety has not been established.

Information for the Patient: See Blue Section—Information for the Patient "Salazopyrin, Salazopyrin EN-tabs".

Supplied: EN-tabs: Each orange, elliptical, biconvex, enteric coated tablet, engraved with "KPh" on one side and "102" on the other side, contains: sulfasalazine USP 500 mg. Nonmedicinal ingredients: beeswax, carnauba wax, cellulose acetate phthalate, glyceryl monostearate, polyethylene glycol, propylene glycol and talc. Tartrazine-free. Bottles of 100 and 300.

Tablets: Each yellow-orange, round, biconvex tablet, engraved with "KPh" on one side and "101" and a score on the other side, contains: sulfasalazine USP 500 mg. Nonmedicinal ingredients: silicon dioxide, starch and magnesium stearate. Tartrazine-free. Bottles of 100, 300 and 500.

Reviewed 1999

SALBUTAMOL

BDH

Salbutamol Sulfate

Bronchodilator

Supplied: 1 mg/mL: Each mL of sterile aqueous solution contains: salbutamol sulfate equivalent to salbutamol base 1 mg. Sodium hydroxide and sulfuric acid may be included to adjust pH. Preservative-free. Plastic sterinebs of 2.5 mL. Cartons of 20 with information leaflets. Store between 2 and 25°C. Protect from light.

2 mg/mL: Each mL of sterile aqueous solution contains: salbutamol sulfate equivalent to salbutamol base 2 mg. Sodium hydroxide and sulfuric acid may be included to adjust pH. Preservative-free. Plastic sterinebs of 2.5 mL. Cartons of 20 with information leaflets. Store between 2 and 25°C. Protect from light.

SALBUTAMOL NEBUAMP®

Astra

Salbutamol Sulfate

Bronchodilator

Pharmacology: Salbutamol produces bronchodilation through stimulation of β_2-adrenergic receptors in bronchial smooth muscle, thereby causing relaxation of muscle fibers. This action is manifested by an increase in pulmonary function as demonstrated by spirometric measurements. A measurable decrease in airway resistance is typically observed 5 to 15 minutes after inhalation of salbutamol. The onset of maximum improvement in pulmonary function usually occurs after 60 to 90 minutes, and significant bronchodilator activity has been maintained from 3 to 6 hours.

Indications: In the treatment of severe bronchospasm associated with exacerbations of chronic bronchitis and bronchial asthma. It can be used by "wet" nebulization. When administered through a nebulizer, it should be used with compressed air or oxygen.

Contraindications: In those patients who have shown hypersensitivity to any of the ingredients, and in patients with cardiac tachyarrhythmias.

Children: Use of salbutamol in children under 5 years of age has not been established.

Warnings: In accordance with the present practice for asthma treatment, concomitant anti-inflammatory therapy should be part of the regimen if inhaled salbutamol needs to be used on a regular daily basis (see Dosage).

In common with other β-adrenergic agents, salbutamol can induce reversible metabolic changes. These are most pronounced during infusions of the drug and include hyperglycemia and hypokalemia. Potentially serious hypokalemia may result from β_2-agonist therapy, mainly from parenteral and nebulized administration. Particular caution is advised in acute severe asthma as this effect may be potentiated by concomitant treatment with xanthine derivatives, steroids, diuretics and hypoxia. Hypokalemia will increase the susceptibility of digitalis-treated patients to cardiac arrhythmias (see Precautions). It is recommended that serum potassium levels be monitored in such situations. Large doses of i.v. salbutamol have been reported to aggravate pre-existing diabetes mellitus and precipitate ketoacidosis. Concurrent administration of corticosteroids can exaggerate this effect. The relevance of these observations to the use of inhaled salbutamol is unknown.

Special care and supervision are required in patients with idiopathic hypertrophic subvalvular aortic stenosis, in whom an increase in the pressure gradient between the left ventricle and the aorta may occur, causing increased strain on the left ventricle.

β-adrenergic blocking drugs, especially the noncardioselective ones, may effectively antagonize the action of salbutamol and produce bronchospasm resistant to salbutamol injection. Therefore, salbutamol and nonselective β-blocking drugs, such as propranolol, should not usually be prescribed together.

Care should be taken in patients suffering from cardiovascular disorders, especially coronary insufficiency, cardiac arrhythmias and hypertension, in patients with convulsive disorders, diabetes mellitus or hyperthyroidism, and in patients who are usually responsive to sympathomimetic amines.

Some patients have been reported to have developed severe paradoxical bronchospasm with repeated excessive use of sympathomimetic inhalation preparations. The cause of this refractory state is unknown. It is advisable that in this event the use of the preparation be discontinued immediately and alternate therapy instituted, since in the reported cases the patients did not respond to other forms of therapy until the drug was withdrawn.

Fatalities have been reported following the excessive use of inhaled sympathomimetic drugs, the exact cause of which is unknown, however, cardiac arrest following the unexpected development of a severe acute asthmatic crisis and subsequent hypoxia is suspected. Therefore, it is essential that the physician instruct the patient of the need for further evaluation if the patient's asthma becomes worse. In individual patients, any β_2-adrenergic agonist, including salbutamol, may have a clinically significant cardiac effect.

It has been reported that the use of intermittent positive pressure ventilation (IPPV) in acute asthma attacks, in several cases was related to lethal episodes of hypoxia and pneumothorax. This method of drug administration may be ineffective in patients with severe obstruction and greatly increased airway resistance, and it may induce severe hypercapnia and hypoxia. During IPPV therapy, the monitoring of arterial blood gases is highly desirable.

Immediate hypersensitivity reactions including angioedema, urticaria, bronchospasm, anaphylaxis, hypotension, rash, oropharyngeal edema and collapse have been reported very rarely.

Precautions: If therapy does not produce a significant improvement or if the patient's condition worsens, medical advice must be sought in order to determine a new plan of treatment. In the case of acute or rapidly worsening dyspnea, a doctor should be consulted immediately.

Failure to respond for at least 3 hours to a previously effective dose of salbutamol indicates a deterioration of the condition and the physician should be contacted promptly. Patients should be warned not to exceed the recommended dose.

Increasing the use of β_2-agonists is usually a sign of worsening asthma. Under these conditions it is inadequate to simply increase their use, particularly over an extended period of time. Reassessment of the patient's therapy plan is required and concomitant anti-inflammatory therapy should be considered.

To ensure the proper dosage administration of the drug, the patient should be instructed by the physician or other health professional in the proper use of the nebulizer. During inhalation, children should be assisted or supervised by an adult who knows the proper use of the nebulizer.

Use of inhaled salbutamol by means other than nebulization or IPPV is not recommended until the safety and the dosage regimen for alternate methods of delivery have been established.

<u>*Drug Interactions:*</u> Salbutamol should be administered with extreme caution to patients being treated with MAO inhibitors or tricyclic antidepressants since the action of salbutamol on the cardiovascular system may be potentiated.

The concomitant use of salbutamol and other sympathomimetic agents is not recommended since such combined use may lead to deleterious cardiovascular effects. This recommendation does not preclude the judicious use of an aerosol bronchodilator of the adrenergic stimulant type in patients receiving salbutamol tablets. Such concomitant use should be individualized, and not given on a routine basis. If regular coadministration is required, this indicates that disease control is suboptimal and alternative therapy should be considered.

Salbutamol and β-receptor blocking agents inhibit the effect of each other.

A small number of cases of acute angle closure glaucoma has been reported in patients treated with a combination of nebulized salbutamol and ipratropium bromide. A combination of nebulized salbutamol with nebulized anticholinergics should therefore be used cautiously. Patients should receive adequate instruction in correct administration and be warned not to let the solution or mist enter the eye.

Pregnancy: The safety of salbutamol in pregnancy and in lactation has not been established.

Teratogenic Effects: Administration of drugs during pregnancy should only be considered if the expected benefit to the mother is greater than any possible risk to the fetus.

Salbutamol has been in widespread use for many years in human beings without apparent ill consequence, however, as with the majority of drugs, there is little published evidence of its safety in the early stages of human pregnancy. There are no adequate and well-controlled studies in pregnant women. Salbutamol has been shown to be teratogenic in mice when given in doses corresponding to 14 times the human aerosol dose, when given s.c. in doses corresponding to the human nebulization dose, when given s.c. in doses corresponding to 0.2 times the maximum human (child weighing 21 kg) oral dose, and when given s.c. in doses corresponding to 0.4 times the maximum human oral dose.

Labor and Delivery: Salbutamol should be used during pregnancy only if the potential benefit justifies the potential risk to the fetus. It has been reported that high doses of salbutamol administered i.v. inhibit uterine contractions. Although this effect is extremely unlikely as a consequence of the use of inhaled formulations, it should be kept in mind. Oral salbutamol has been shown to delay preterm labor in some reports. There are presently no well-controlled studies which demonstrate that it will stop preterm labor or prevent labor at term. Therefore, cautious use of salbutamol is required in pregnant patients when given for relief of bronchospasm so as to avoid interference with uterine contractility.

As maternal pulmonary edema has been reported during or following premature labor in patients receiving β_2-agonists, careful attention should be given to fluid balance, and cardiorespiratory function should be monitored.

Lactation: As salbutamol is probably secreted in breast milk and because of the potential for tumorigenicity shown in some animal studies, a decision should be made whether to discontinue nursing or to discontinue the drug, taking into account the importance of the drug to the mother. It is not known whether salbutamol in breast milk has a harmful effect on the neonate.

Adverse Effects: The most frequent adverse reactions are nervousness and tremor. Tension due to effects on skeletal muscle, headache, tachycardia, palpitations, transient muscle cramps, insomnia, nausea, weakness, dizziness and sweating have also been reported. Other rare adverse events have been drowsiness, flushing, restlessness, irritability, chest discomfort, difficulty in micturition, hypertension, angina, vomiting, vertigo, central nervous stimulation, unusual taste and drying or irritation of the oropharynx.

Children: As with other β_2-agonists, hyperactivity has been reported rarely in children.

Potentially serious hypokalemia may result from β_2-agonist therapy, mainly from parenteral and nebulized administration.

Hypersensitivity reactions including angioedema, urticaria, bronchospasm, hypotension, rash, oropharyngeal edema and collapse have been reported very rarely.

As with other inhalation therapies, the potential for paradoxical bronchospasm should be kept in mind. If it occurs, the preparation should be discontinued immediately and alternative therapy instituted.

Overdose: Symptoms and Treatment: Overdosage may cause tachycardia, cardiac arrhythmia, hypokalemia, hypertension and, in extreme cases, sudden death. In order to antagonize the effect of salbutamol, the judicious use of a cardioselective β-adrenergic blocking agent (e.g. metoprolol, atenolol), may be considered, bearing in mind the danger of inducing an asthmatic attack. Serum potassium levels should be monitored.

Dosage: Dosage should be individualized, and patient response should be monitored by the prescribing physician on an ongoing basis.

Salbutamol Nebuamp (cont'd)

If a previously effective dose fails to provide the usual relief, or if the effects of a dose last for less than 3 hours, patients should seek medical advice immediately since this is usually a sign of seriously worsening asthma.

In accordance with the present practice for asthma treatment, concomitant anti-inflammatory therapy should be part of the regimen if salbutamol needs to be used on a regular daily basis.

Adults: The average dose for a single treatment is 2.5 to 5 mg salbutamol up to 4 times daily. See Table I.

Children: For children 5 to 12 years of age, the average dose for a single treatment is 1.25 to 2.5 mg salbutamol. For more refractory cases, the single dose may be increased to 5 mg of salbutamol. Treatment may be repeated 4 times a day, if necessary. See Table I.

Table I—Salbutamol Nebuamp

Dosage

	Volume of Salbutamol Nebuamp		
Dose of Salbutamol Base in mg	**0.05% (0.5 mg/mL)**	**0.1% (1.0 mg/mL)**	**0.2% (2.0 mg/mL)**
1.25	2.5 mL (1 unit)	—	—
2.5	5.0 mL (2 units)	2.5 mL (1 unit)	—
5.0	—	5.0 mL (2 units)	2.5 mL (1 unit)

If a more severe attack has not been relieved by a treatment, further treatment may be required. In these cases, patients should immediately consult their doctor or the nearest hospital. Increasing demand for salbutamol in bronchial asthma is usually a sign of worsening asthma and indicates that the treatment plan should be reviewed.

Salbutamol is to be used with a respirator or nebulizer, and only under the direction of a physician.

Special Instructions: Salbutamol Nebuamp can be used by 2 methods: nebulization and intermittent positive pressure ventilation.

Nebulization: When used in a nebulizer, a mouthpiece or a face mask may be applied. The nebulizer should be connected to a compressed air or oxygen pump. Gas flow should be approximately 6 to 10 L/min. With an average volume of 3 mL, a single treatment lasts approximately 10 minutes. It is advisable to prepare one dose at a time.

Cleansing and maintenance of the nebulizer must be carefully followed according to the manufacturer's instructions.

Intermittent Positive Pressure Ventilation: When administered through intermittent positive pressure ventilation, the inspiratory pressure is usually 10 to 20 cm H_2O and the duration of administration varies from 5 to 20 minutes, depending upon the patient and the control of the apparatus. This length of administration provides a more gradual and more complete lysis of bronchospasm. It has been reported that the use of intermittent positive pressure ventilation in acute asthma attacks, in several cases was related to lethal episodes of hypoxia and pneumothorax. This method of drug administration may be ineffective in patients with severe obstruction and greatly increased airway resistance, and it may induce severe hypercapnia and hypoxia.

During intermittent positive pressure ventilation therapy, the monitoring of arterial blood gases is highly desirable.

Information for the Patient: See Blue Section—Information for the Patient "Salbutamol Nebuamp".

Supplied: Each 2.5 mL of sterile solution of 0.05%, 0.1% and 0.2% contains: salbutamol sulfate equivalent to salbutamol base 0.5, 1 and 2 mg/mL. The solutions are prediluted with sodium chloride 0.9%. The pH is adjusted to 3.0 to 4.5, with sulfuric acid and/or sodium hydroxide. Preservative-free. Single use polyethylene units of 2.5 mL. Cartons of 20 (2 strips of 10). Store between 15 and 25°C. Protect from light. Do not use if solution contains a precipitate.

Reviewed 1999

SALINE FROM OTRIVIN®

Novartis Consumer Health

Sodium Chloride

Nasal Moisturizer

Indications: Provides relief from dry and irritated nasal passages by moisturizing dry inflamed nasal membranes due to low humidity, allergies, overuse of nasal decongestants, use of antihistamines, minor nose bleeds and minor idiopathic nasal irritation.

Useful for maintenance of daily nasal hygiene. To help remove encrusted material from nasal passages and to thin out thick nasal mucus to aid in its easy removal.

Precautions: Do not use if hypersensitive to any of the ingredients.

Pregnancy: The product is safe for use during pregnancy.

Adverse Effects: No known associated side effects.

Dosage: Saline Spray: Adults: Hold head upright and spray once or twice in each nostril 1 to 3 times daily.

Infants and Children: Spray once in each nostril 1 to 3 times daily.

Saline Drops: Adults: Tilt head backwards and squeeze 2 to 3 drops into each nostril 1 to 3 times daily.

Infants and Children: Tilt child's head backwards and squeeze 1 drop into each nostril 1 to 3 times daily.

Supplied: Saline Spray: Each plastic squeeze bottle contains: sodium chloride 0.7%. Nonmedicinal ingredients: benzalkonium chloride, edetate disodium, hydroxypropyl methylcellulose, sodium phosphate, sorbitol and water. Plastic squeeze bottles of 30 mL. Protect from heat.

Saline Drops: Each plastic bottle contains: sodium chloride 0.7%. Nonmedicinal ingredients: benzalkonium chloride, edetate disodium, hydroxypropyl methylcellulose, sodium phosphate, sorbitol and water. Plastic bottles of 25 mL. Protect from heat.

SALINEX®

Technilab

Sodium Chloride

Nasal Solution

Supplied: Each mL of aqueous solution contains: sodium chloride 9 mg. Also contains benzalkonium chloride, glycerin and purified water. Bottles of 30 mL with dropper-tip. Vials of 30 mL.

SALINOL

Technilab

Polyethylene Glycol—Propylene Glycol

Nasal Lubricant

Supplied: Gel: Each g contains: polyethylene glycol 152 mg and propylene glycol 200 mg in a base containing sodium chloride 9 mg. Tubes of 30 g.

Solution: Each mL contains: polyethylene glycol 160 mg and propylene glycol 50 mg in a physiological solution of sodium chloride 9 mg. Polyethylene bottles of 30 mL.

SALOFALK® ℞

Axcan Pharma

5-Aminosalicylic Acid

Lower Gastrointestinal Anti-inflammatory

Pharmacology: 5-Aminosalicylic Acid (5-ASA) is the therapeutically active metabolite of sulfasalazine (SAS), a drug used to treat inflammatory bowel disease. Sulfasalazine is also an effective agent to both treat active disease and maintain remission in ulcerative colitis, however its use in Crohn's disease is minimal. Furthermore its use is limited by numerous adverse reactions. Over the past decade, human trials have shown that 5-ASA is the active principle of sulfasalazine and that it is effective in treating acute episodes of ulcerative colitis as well as maintaining remission.

When sulfasalazine is given orally, the majority of the dose migrates intact to the large bowel where bacterial enzymatic action cleaves the azo bond releasing sulfapyridine and 5-ASA. Sulfapyridine serves as a carrier for the active 5-ASA and has been cited by investigators as being responsible for the majority of adverse reactions and sensitivities of sulfasalazine. 5-ASA, administered rectally, induces few side effects.

The mode of action of 5-ASA is still under investigation with several biochemical mechanisms being proposed. At present, the action of 5-ASA in treating inflammatory bowel disease appears to be associated with the metabolism of arachidonic acid. Studies suggest that interference of 5-ASA with either leukotriene or prostaglandin metabolism may play a major role in suppressing the inflammatory response mechanism.

Regardless of the mode of action, 5-ASA appears to be only effective topically. Rectal administration, therefore, allows for direct targeting of free 5-ASA to the sites of inflammation along the mucosal lumen of the rectum, sigmoid and distal large bowel. Systemic absorption of rectally administered 5-ASA is low as shown by urinary recoveries which range from 5 to 35% of the amount given. Rectally administered 5-ASA thus acts locally on the recto-sigmoidal colon. In contrast, oral administration of free 5-ASA leads to high systemic absorption with little chance of topical effectiveness in the distal bowel. Salofalk tablets are therefore enteric-coated to allow passage through the stomach intact, delivering 5-ASA above pH 6 to the distal small bowel and proximal colon and ensuring availability throughout the terminal ileum and colon.

The only major metabolite of 5-ASA identified in man is N-acetyl-5-aminosalicylic acid. Following rectal administration, both free and acetylated forms can be found in plasma within 1 to 2 hours post administration. Usually plasma concentrations are low and do not exceed a maximum of about 10 μg/mL at rectal daily doses of up to 4 g. Urinary clearance of absorbed drug occurs rapidly, mainly as the acetylated metabolite. Plasma levels are therefore negligible approximately 24 hours after dosing. Unabsorbed drug is excreted as both the free and acetylated forms via feces.

5-ASA and its major metabolite N-acetyl-5-aminosalicylic acid are short lived in serum being excreted rapidly. N-acetyl-5-ASA exhibits a half-life reported to range from 5 to 10 hours and up to 24 hours. In patients with active ulcerative colitis or Crohn's disease receiving 500 mg of 5-ASA t.i.d. orally, mean steady-state plasma levels of 5-ASA and N-acetyl-5-ASA averaged 0.7 and 1.2 μg/mL respectively and were reached within 4 to 6 hours after administration. Treatment with a smaller dose (250 mg t.i.d.) achieved levels of 0.4 and 1 μg/mL respectively. The elimination half-life thus appears to be dose dependent (1.4 ± 0.6 hours at 500 mg t.i.d. vs 0.6 ± 0.2 hours at 250 mg t.i.d.).

Indications: Rectal Suspension: 4 g/60 g: In the management of distal ulcerative colitis (DUC) extending to the splenic flexure including refractory DUC defined to include patients who are difficult to manage with conventional therapies and patients who are allergic to sulfasalazine. Also as adjunctive therapy in more extensive disease as well as for the prevention of relapse in distal ulcerative colitis. 2 g/60 g: For the prevention of relapse in distal ulcerative colitis.

Suppositories: In the management of ulcerative proctitis and as adjunctive therapy in more extensive distal ulcerative colitis.

Tablets: In the treatment of acute ulcerative colitis and in the prevention of relapse of Crohn's disease in patients following bowel resection.

Contraindications: Active peptic ulcer. Hypersensitivity to salicylates. Infants under 2 years of age. Urinary tract obstructions.

Warnings: 5-ASA should be used only after critical appraisal of the risk to benefit ratio in the following situations: liver and kidney disease; bleeding and clotting disorders; pregnancy and lactation; children between 2 and 12 years of age. Caution should be exercised in patients with elevated BUN.

Patients with pyloric stenosis may have prolonged retention of 5-ASA enteric-coated tablets.

Precautions: Periodic urinalysis to assess kidney function is recommended since prolonged therapy may damage the kidneys. Caution should be exercised when 5-ASA is first used in patients known to be allergic to sulfasalazine. These patients should be instructed to discontinue therapy at first sign of rash or fever.

Epigastric pain, also commonly associated with inflammatory bowel disease and prednisone or sulfasalazine therapy should be investigated in order to exclude pericarditis and pancreatitis either as adverse drug reactions to 5-ASA or secondary manifestations of inflammatory bowel disease.

Drug Interactions: No known drug interactions exist. The hypoglycemic effect of sulfonylureas may be enhanced. Interactions with coumarins, methotrexate, probenecid, sulfinpyrazone, spironolactone, furosemide and rifampin cannot be excluded. Potentiation of undesirable glucocorticoid effects on the stomach is possible.

Children and *Pregnancy:* In children between the ages of 2 and 12, information on the safety and efficacy of 5-ASA is limited. Use of the drug should be limited to situations where a clear benefit is expected. The same precaution applies in the first 3 months of pregnancy.

Adverse Effects: Adverse reactions linked to the sulfapyridine moiety of sulfasalazine are avoided with 5-ASA. Hypersensitivity reactions have been reported in a sub-group of patients known to be allergic to sulfasalazine including rash, fever, and dizziness. The apparent frequency is estimated at 3 to 4%, with reactions occurring at the onset of therapy and resolving promptly following discontinuance.

In rare cases, following 5-ASA administration, exacerbation of ulcerative colitis characterized by cramping, acute abdominal pain and diarrhea has been reported. Acute pancreatitis, hepatitis and pleural effusion have also been reported in association both with 5-ASA and SAS, as have rare instances of pericarditis. Both pancreatitis and pericarditis have also been reported as manifestations of inflammatory bowel disease. Finally, acute or chronic interstitial nephritis has been reported in association with orally-administered 5-ASA.

Other reported side effects include headache, flatulence, nausea, and alopecia, but do not appear to be common. During placebo controlled clinical trials involving the administration of rectal 5-ASA, the following adverse reactions were reported in more than 0.1%: (see Table I).

Table I—Salofalk

Adverse Effects

Symptom	Salofalk n=841 %	Placebo n=176 %
Abdominal pain, cramps and discomfort	7.9	7.9
Headache	6.7	11.3
Gas or flatulence	6.0	4.5
Nausea	5.6	6.8
Flu	5.2	0.5
Weakness, malaise or fatigue	3.3	4.5
Fever	3.0	0.0
Rash	2.8	2.2
Spots	2.2	5.1
Cold, sore throat	2.0	2.8
Diarrhea	2.1	3.9
Leg, joint pain	2.0	1.1
Dizziness	1.7	2.8
Bloating	1.4	1.1
Back pain	1.3	0.5
Pain on insertion of tip (enema)	1.3	0.5
Hemorrhoids	1.3	0.0
Itching	1.1	0.5
Rectal pain	1.1	0.0
Constipation	0.9	2.2
Hair loss	0.8	1.1
Peripheral edema	0.5	6.2
Urinary tract infection, urinary burning	0.5	2.2
Rectal pain, soreness or burning	0.5	1.7
Asthenia	0.1	2.2
Insomnia	0.1	1.7
Upper respiratory tract infection	0.1	0.5
Pericarditis	0.1	0
Pancreatitis	0.1	0
Exacerbation of inflammatory bowel disease	0.1	0

Dosage: Rectal Suspension: Acute Episodes: Adults: The rectal suspension is self-administered on a daily basis during acute episodes of disease. Usually 1 unit-dose (4 g/60 g 5-ASA) is taken upon retiring and retained during the entire rest period. Best results are expected with prolonged retention.

The usual course of therapy is 1 unit of 4 g/60 g daily at bedtime. Response to treatment and adjustment in dosing frequency should be determined by periodic examination, including endoscopy and the assessment of symptomatology including rectal bleeding, stool frequency, and general well-being.

Daily dosing is continued until a significant response is achieved or the patient achieves remission.

Prevention of Relapse: Rectal suspension 2 g/60 g is self-administered in the same manner on a daily basis. If alternatively the 4 g/60 g preparation is used, the dose can usually be reduced to alternate days or every third day, depending upon disease activity. Abrupt discontinuance of 5-ASA is not recommended. Dose tapering is recommended and each patient should be titrated to meet individual needs. Maintenance therapy is recommended to assure continued remission. If symptoms, diarrhea and rectal bleeding recur, dosage should be increased to the previous effective level.

Suppositories: Two 250 mg or one 500 mg suppository is self-administered on a daily b.i.d. or t.i.d. basis. The usual adult dose is 1 to 1.5 g/day, and dosing is continued until a significant response is achieved or until the patient achieves remission. Dose tapering is recommended. Abrupt discontinuance is not recommended. Best results are expected with prolonged retention.

Tablets: In acute inflammatory stage, the tablets must be taken reliably and consistently by the patient in order to ensure therapeutic success. Tablets should be swallowed whole before meals with plenty of fluid. For the treatment of acute ulcerative colitis, four 250 mg or two 500 mg tablets, 3 or 4 times/day (total adult dose: 3 g/day to 4 g/day). Abrupt discontinuance is not recommended. Prolonged treatment may be required.

For the treatment or the prevention of recurrence of Crohn's disease in patients following bowel resection, the total adult dose is 3 g/day in divided doses. Prolonged treatment may be required.

Information for the Patient: See Blue Section—Information for the Patient "Salofalk".

Supplied: Rectal Suspension: 2 g/60 g: Each unit of use rectal retention enema contains: 5-ASA 2 g/60 g (58.25 mL). Also contains sodium benzoate and potassium metabisulfite. Boxes of 7. Store in a cool place, below 25°C.

4 g/60 g: Each unit of use rectal retention enema contains: 5-ASA 4 g/60 g (58.25 mL). Also contains sodium benzoate and potassium metabisulfite. Boxes of 7. Store in a cool place, below 25°C.

Suppositories: 250 mg: Each suppository contains: 5–ASA 250 mg. Boxes of 30. Store in a cool place, below 25°C.

500 mg: Each suppository contains: 5–ASA 500 mg. Boxes of 30. Store in a cool place, below 25°C.

Tablets: 250 mg: Each enteric-coated tablet contains: 5-ASA 250 mg. Gluten-, lactose-, sulfite- and tartrazine-free. Boxes of 150 (15 strips of 10 tablets). Store at controlled room temperature (15 to 30°C) and protect from light.

500 mg: Each enteric-coated tablet contains: 5-ASA 500 mg. Gluten-, lactose-, sulfite- and tartrazine-free. Boxes of 150 (15 strips of 10 tablets). Bottles of 500. Store at controlled room temperature (15 to 30°C) and protect from light.

(Shown in Product Recognition Section)

Reviewed 1999

SANDIMMUNE® I.V. ℞

Novartis Pharmaceuticals

see NEORAL/SANDIMMUNE I.V.

SANDOMIGRAN® ℞
SANDOMIGRAN DS® ℞

Novartis Pharmaceuticals

Pizotifen

Vascular Headache Prophylaxis

Pharmacology: The mode of action of pizotifen in the prophylactic management of vascular headaches has not yet been elucidated. Pizotifen is a serotonin and histamine antagonist, with sedative and weak anticholinergic effects.

In man, some radioactivity was noted in blood at 2 hours after a single oral dose of 1 mg of labeled pizotifen and peak concentrations occurred at 5 to 7 hours. Blood concentrations decreased slowly thereafter and small but significant amounts were still found after 96 hours. No data on metabolism and distribution is available. Excretion was relatively slow. In 3 subjects, the total excretion of the drug over a period of 120 hours accounted for 86% of the administered dose. The biological half-life averaged 26 hours.

Indications: The prophylactic management of vascular headaches. In various clinical trials, about ⅓ to ⅔ of patients with migraine experienced some benefit from pizotifen and in most trials it was more effective than placebo in reducing the frequency or severity of attacks. Therefore, a therapeutic trial of pizotifen may be indicated for prophylactic management of severe vascular headaches which are difficult to control. However, the drug is of no value in the treatment of the acute migrainous attack or in the treatment of tension headaches. As with other antiserotonin agents, the benefits of pizotifen decrease after a period of time in a certain number of patients.

Contraindications: Although peripheral anticholinergic effects are minimal in the recommended doses, anticholinergic agents, including pizotifen, are contraindicated in patients taking MAO inhibitors, in patients with pyloroduodenal obstruction and stenosing pyloric ulcer. Pizotifen is contraindicated for patients who have a known sensitivity to the drug.

Children: Until further studies are completed, pizotifen is not recommended for children under the age of 12.

Precautions: In view of the weak anticholinergic effect of pizotifen, caution is required in patients with narrow-angle glaucoma or with urinary retention (e.g., prostatic hypertrophy). In general, patients with narrow-angle glaucoma should not be given drugs with possible anticholinergic effects, unless they are required and the patient is under special care and medical supervision for this condition.

Pregnancy: Since it is desirable to keep drug administration to a minimum during pregnancy, pizotifen should be given only when the benefits derived from treatment exceed the possible risks to mother and fetus.

Some patients developed tolerance to pizotifen with prolonged use of the drug. Increase in dosage may overcome this tolerance.

After prolonged use hepatotoxic effects might occur and patients should be advised to report for adequate laboratory evaluation.

Patients with diabetes, cardiovascular disease and known or suspected impaired renal or hepatic function should be given pizotifen with caution, and appropriate laboratory tests should be done at regular intervals.

Lens opacities occurred in 2 cases but did not appear to be drug-related. However, it is recommended that any impairment in vision be reported to the attending physician for further investigation.

As with all drugs, pizotifen should be kept out of the reach of children.

Occupational Hazards: Since drowsiness may occur with pizotifen, sensitive patients should be cautioned against activities requiring rapid and precise responses such as driving an automobile or operating dangerous machinery until their response has been determined.

Drug Interactions: Since the effects of antihistamines can potentiate those of other drugs affecting the CNS, patients should be cautioned against drinking alcoholic beverages or taking hypnotics, sedatives, psychotherapeutic agents or other drugs with CNS depressant effects during pizotifen therapy.

Adverse Effects: Increased appetite, weight gain and drowsiness are the most frequent side effects. An appropriate diet should be recommended by the physician for patients benefiting from the drug but gaining excessive weight. A gradual increase in the dosage of pizotifen is recommended to minimize or reduce the incidence of drowsiness.

Relative to the occurrence of the above-mentioned reactions the following adverse effects have been less frequently observed: fatigue, nausea, dizziness, headache, confusion, edema, hypotension, depression, weakness, epigastric distress, dry mouth, nervousness, impotence and muscle pain.

Overdose: Symptoms: Sedation, drowsiness, tachycardia, ataxia, nausea and CNS depression.

Antihistamine poisoning in children exhibits excitation, hallucinations, ataxia, incoordination, convulsions, fixed dilated pupils, flushed facies, and fever, leading to coma and cardiorespiratory collapse.

In adults, drowsiness precedes excitement, convulsions and postictal depression.

Treatment: If vomiting has not occurred spontaneously, induce emesis or perform gastric lavage. Supportive measures should be instituted to maintain respiration and vital signs should be monitored; benzodiazepines for excitatory states or convulsions. Analeptics should be avoided.

Sandomigran (cont'd)

Dosage: Treatment should be initiated with a dose of 0.5 mg at bedtime. This is increased gradually to 0.5 mg 3 times daily. Average maintenance dose is 1.5 mg/day. The dosage range is 1 to 6 mg/day.

Since vascular headache is a paroxysmal but basically chronic disorder, treatment must extend over an adequate period of time in order to obtain maximal benefit. While some patients have responded rather quickly, most investigators agree that a 4-week trial period should be instituted to determine the true efficacy of pizotifen in specific cases. The periodic nature of the disorder will have to be considered in determining when and for how long therapy should be maintained.

Since some investigators have observed a change in headache pattern after several months of therapy, a drug-free interval is advisable to reassess the necessity of continuing treatment. The dosage should be reduced gradually during the last 2 weeks of each treatment course to avoid a "headache rebound".

Supplied: Sandomigran: Each biconvex, ivory-colored, sugar-coated tablet contains: pizotifen 0.5 mg as derived from 0.73 mg of pizotifen malate. Nonmedicinal ingredients: cornstarch, isopropyl alcohol, lactose, magnesium stearate, povidone, talc and tartrazine. Bottles of 100.

Sandomigran DS: Each circular, flat, white compressed, tablet bevelled edge, scored on one side and engraved "SANDOZ" on the other, contains: pizotifen 1 mg as derived from 1.46 mg of pizotifen malate. Nonmedicinal ingredients: lactose, magnesium stearate and microcrystalline cellulose. Bottles of 100.

(Shown in Product Recognition Section)

SANDOSOURCE™ PEPTIDE

Novartis Nutrition

High Nitrogen Semi-Elemental Diet

Indications: A high nitrogen, semi-elemental diet designed for patients with impaired gastrointestinal function. Sixty percent of the protein is available as free amino acids and low molecular weight peptides. Suggested indications include bowel resection, malabsorption syndrome, select trauma/surgery, Crohn's disease, pancreatic disorders, short bowel syndrome and gastrointestinal disorder related to HIV/AIDS.

Precautions: Not for parenteral administration.

Dosage: 1 750 mL or 7 320 kJ (7 cans or 1 750 kcal) provides at least 100% of the Canadian RNI (adult males, 25 to 49) for protein and essential vitamins and minerals.

Ready-to-use: Feed at room temperature. Follow a physician's or dietitian's directions. When initiating feedings, the flow rate, volume and dilution are dependent on the patient's condition and tolerance. Care should be taken to avoid contamination of the product during preparation and administration. Additional fluid requirements should be met by giving water orally with or after feedings or when flushing the feeding tube.

Feeding should be initiated at a slow rate. Rate and volume of feeding can be increased gradually over 48 hours if well tolerated. If intolerance develops, return to previously tolerated rate or dilute formula to half strength until desired rate is achieved, then switch to full strength. Do not alter strength and volume at the same time. Rinse the tube with 20 to 30 mL water after each intermittent feeding or every 3 to 4 hours during continuous feeding to avoid clogging and provide additional water.

Supplied: Each 250 mL of ready-to-use can contains: ®-D water, maltodextrin, casein hydrolysate, medium chain triglycerides, soybean oil, sodium caseinate, potassium citrate, L-arginine, L-leucine, calcium phosphate tribasic, L-isoleucine, cellulose gel, calcium carrageenan, L-valine, sodium ascorbate, citric acid, soy lecithin, magnesium chloride, L-methionine, sodium citrate, choline chloride, L-tryptophan, taurine, cellulose gum, potassium chloride, L-carnitine, alpha tocopheryl acetate, zinc sulfate, niacinamide, ferrous sulfate, calcium pantothenate, copper gluconate, manganese sulfate, pyridoxine HCl, thiamine HCl, riboflavin, beta carotene, vitamin A palmitate, BHA/BHT (to preserve freshness), folic acid, chromic acetate, biotin, sodium molybdate, potassium iodide, sodium selenite, phytonadione (vitamin K_1), cyanocobalamin (vitamin B_{12}), cholecalciferol (vitamin D_3). See Table I.

Table I—Sandosource Peptide

Analysis	100 mL	
Energy	418 (100)	kJ (kcal)
Protein	5.0	g
Carbohydrate	16.3	g
Fat	1.7	g
Linoleic Acid	0.39	g
Sodium	120	mg
Potassium	160	mg
Vitamin A*	286	IU
Vitamin C	17.1	mg
Thiamine	0.17	mg
Riboflavin	0.19	mg
Niacin	2.3	mg
Calcium	57.1	mg
Iron	1.0	mg
Vitamin D	23	IU
Vitamin E	2.6	IU
Vitamin B_6	0.23	mg
Folic Acid	0.046	mg
Vitamin B_{12}	0.0007	mg
Phosphorus	57.1	mg
Iodine	0.009	mg
Magnesium	23	mg
Zinc	1.3	mg
Copper	0.11	mg
Biotin	0.034	mg
Pantothenic Acid	1.14	mg
Vitamin K	0.0046	mg
Choline	23	mg
Chloride	97	mg
Manganese	0.17	mg
Selenium	0.0057	mg
Chromium	0.0086	mg
Molybdenum	0.014	mg
Carnitine	10	mg
Taurine	20	mg
Osmolality	490	mOsm/kg water

*Includes vitamin A activity from beta carotene.

Cans of 250 mL, cases of 24. Store unopened at room temperature. Once opened, store covered in refrigerator and use within 24 hours.

SANDOSTATIN® Ⓟ

Novartis Pharmaceuticals

Octreotide Acetate

Synthetic Octapeptide Analogue of Somatostatin

Pharmacology: Octreotide is a synthetic octapeptide analogue of naturally occurring somatostatin with similar pharmacological effects, but with a prolonged duration of action. It inhibits pathologically increased secretion of growth hormone (GH) and of peptides and serotonin produced within the gastroentero-pancreatic (GEP) endocrine system.

The precise mode of action of octreotide on portal hypertension is still unclear. Octreotide is thought to reduce splanchnic blood flow primarily by inhibiting vasoactive gastrointestinal hormone secretion and exerting a direct vasomotor effect on splanchnic vessels, thus reducing portal blood flow. Using human sephanous veins, it has been shown that vasoconstriction is mediated by type 2 somatostatin receptors.

After s.c. injection octreotide is rapidly and completely absorbed. Peak plasma concentrations are reached within 30 minutes. The half-life after s.c. administration is 100 minutes. After i.v. injection the elimination is biphasic with α and β half-lives of approximately 10 and 90 minutes, respectively. The volume of distribution is 0.4 L/kg body weight and the total body clearance is 160 mL/min. Plasma protein binding amounts to 65% with only negligible amounts bound to red blood cells.

In normal healthy subjects, octreotide has been shown to inhibit: release of growth hormone (GH) stimulated by arginine infusion, exercise and insulin-induced hypoglycemia; postprandial release of insulin, glucagon, gastrin, other peptides of the GEP endocrine system, and arginine-stimulated release of insulin and glucagon; thyrotropin releasing hormone (TRH) stimulated release of thyroid stimulating hormone (TSH).

Indications: General: For control of symptoms in patients with metastatic carcinoid and vasoactive intestinal peptide-secreting tumors (VIPomas) as well as in patients with acromegaly.

Data are insufficient to determine whether octreotide decreases the size, rate of growth, or development of metastases in patients with these tumors.

Octreotide is also indicated for the prevention of complications following pancreatic surgery in patients undergoing high risk procedures.

Octreotide is also indicated for the emergency management of bleeding gastroesophageal varices in patients with cirrhosis and as protection from rebleeding. Octreotide is used in association with specific intervention such as endoscopic sclerotherapy.

Carcinoid Tumors: For the symptomatic treatment of metastatic carcinoid tumors where it suppresses or inhibits the severe diarrhea and flushing episodes associated with the disease.

Vasoactive Intestinal Peptide Tumors (VIPomas): For the treatment of the profuse watery diarrhea associated with VIP-secreting tumors. Significant improvement has been noted in the overall condition of these otherwise therapeutically unresponsive patients. Therapy with octreotide results in improvement in electrolyte abnormalities, e.g., hypokalemia, often enabling reduction of fluid and electrolyte support.

Acromegaly: Octreotide is indicated to reduce blood levels of growth hormone and IGF-I (somatomedin C) including acromegalic patients who have had inadequate response to, or cannot be treated with surgical resection, pituitary irradiation and/or bromocriptine mesylate at maximally tolerated doses.

Since the effects of pituitary irradiation may not become maximal for several years, adjunctive therapy with octreotide to reduce blood levels of GH and IGF-I offers potential benefit before the effects of irradiation are manifested.

A clinically relevant growth hormone (GH) reduction (by 50% or more) occurs in almost all patients, and normalization (plasma GH$<$5 ng/mL) can be achieved in about half of the cases.

In most patients, octreotide markedly reduces the clinical symptoms of the disease such as headache, skin and soft tissue swelling, hyperhydrosis, arthralgia and paresthesia. In patients with a large pituitary adenoma, octreotide treatment may result in some skrinkage of the tumor mass.

Prevention of Complications Following Pancreatic Surgery: Octreotide inhibits basal and stimulated exocrine pancreatic secretion and when administered peri– and postoperatively in patients undergoing high risk pancreatic surgery, reduces the incidence and severity of typical postoperative complications (e.g., pancreatic fistula, abscess and subsequent sepsis and postoperative acute pancreatitis).

Bleeding Gastroesophageal Varices: In patients presenting with bleeding gastroesophageal varices due to underlying cirrhosis, octreotide administration in combination with specific intervention (e.g., sclerotherapy) provides better control of bleeding and early rebleeding, reduces transfusion requirements and improves 5-day survival.

Contraindications: Patients with a hypersensitivity to octreotide or to any component of the formulations.

Warnings: Octreotide therapy, like the natural hormone somatostatin, may be associated with cholelithiasis, presumably by altering fat absorption and possibly by decreasing the motility of the gallbladder. Because patients with somatostatinomas have been reported to be at risk for these dysfunctions, patients being treated with octreotide should be monitored periodically for gallbladder disease. Surgical intervention has been required in a few patients who developed severe abdominal pain associated with cholelithiasis while on octreotide therapy.

It is recommended that patients on extended therapy be evaluated periodically using ultrasound evaluations of the gallbladder and bile ducts.

Precautions: General: Sudden escape from symptomatic control by octreotide may occur infrequently, with rapid recurrence of severe symptoms. Dosage adjustment therefore may be required.

As GH-secreting pituitary tumors may sometimes expand, causing serious complications (e.g., visual field defects), it is essential that all patients be carefully monitored. If evidence of tumor expansion appears, alternative procedures may be advisable.

Octreotide therapy is occasionally associated with mild transient hypo- or hyperglycemia due to alterations in the balance between the counter-regulatory hormones, insulin, glucagon and growth hormone. Patients should be closely observed on introduction of octreotide therapy and at each change of dosage for symptomatic evidence of hyper- and hypoglycemia. In insulin-dependent diabetics, reduction of insulin requirements may result following initiation of octreotide therapy. Predicting the effect of octreotide on glucose tolerance in any given patient is not possible at this time. It is recommended that all acromegalic patients have their serum glucose carefully monitored during initiation and titration of octreotide therapy.

Since there is an increased risk, during bleeding episodes in cirrhotic patients, for the development of insulin-dependent diabetes or for changes in insulin requirement in patients with pre-existing diabetes, an appropriate monitoring of blood glucose is required.

Data on the effect of chronic therapy with octreotide on hypothalamic/pituitary function have not been obtained. A progressive drop in T_4 levels has been reported, culminating in clinical and biochemical hypothyroidism after 19 months of therapy in 1 clinical trial patient (carcinoid) receiving 1 500 µg of octreotide daily. Therefore, baseline and periodic thyroid function tests using total and free T_4 are advised.

There is evidence that octreotide therapy may alter absorption of dietary fats in some patients. It is suggested that periodic quantitative 72-hour fecal fat and serum carotene determinations be performed to aid in the assessment of possible drug-induced aggravation of fat malabsorption.

In patients with severe renal failure requiring dialysis, the half-life of the drug may be increased, necessitating adjustment of the maintenance dosage.

Decreased gallbladder contractility and bile stasis may result from prolonged treatment with octreotide. Development of gallstones has been reported in 10 to 20% of long-term recipients of this drug, therefore baseline and periodic ultrasonography is recommended to assess the presence of gallstones (see Warnings). If gallstones do occur, they are usually asymptomatic. Symptomatic gallstones should receive medical attention.

Information for the Patient: Careful instruction in sterile s.c. injection techniques should be given to the patients and to other persons who may administer octreotide injections (see Blue Section—Information for the Patient).

Laboratory Tests: Laboratory tests that may be helpful as biochemical markers in determining and following patient response depend on the specific tumor. Based on diagnosis, measurement of the following substances may be useful in monitoring the progress of therapy: Carcinoid: 5-HIAA (urinary 5-hydroxyindole acetic acid), plasma serotonin, plasma Substance P. VIPoma: VIP (plasma vasoactive intestinal peptide). Acromegaly: Growth hormone - IGF-I (somatomedin C). Responsiveness to octreotide may be evaluated by determining growth hormone levels at 1- to 4-hour intervals for 8 to 12 hours postdose. Alternatively, a single measurement of IGF-I (somatomedin C) level may be made 2 weeks after drug initiation or dosage change.

Baseline and periodic total and/or free T_4 measurements should be performed during chronic therapy (see Precautions).

Drug Interactions: Many patients with carcinoid syndrome or VIPomas being treated with octreotide have also been, or are being, treated with many other drugs to control the symptomatology or progression of the disease, generally without serious drug interaction. Included are chemotherapeutic agents, H_2 antagonists, antimotility agents, drugs affecting glycemic states, solutions for electrolyte and fluid support or hyperalimentation, antihypertensive diuretics and antidiarrheal agents.

Where symptoms are severe and octreotide therapy is added to other therapies used to control glycemic states, such as sulfonylureas, insulin and diazoxide, to beta-blockers or to agents for the control of fluid and electrolyte balance, patients must be monitored closely and adjustment made in the other therapies as the symptoms of the disease are controlled. Evidence currently available suggests these imbalances in fluid and electrolytes or glycemic states are secondary to correction of pre-existing abnormalities and not to a direct metabolic action of octreotide. Adjustment of the dosage of drugs, such as insulin, affecting glucose metabolism may be required following initiation of octreotide therapy in patients with diabetes.

Since octreotide has been associated with alterations in nutrient absorption, its effect on absorption of any orally administered drugs should be carefully considered. A single case of transplant rejection episode (renal/whole pancreas) in a patient immunosuppressed with cyclosporine has been reported. Octreotide treatment to reduce exocrine secretion and close a fistula in this patient resulted in decreases in blood levels of cyclosporine and may have contributed to the rejection episode. Octreotide has also been found to delay the intestinal absorption of cyclosporine or cimetidine.

Drug Laboratory Test Interactions: No known interference exists with clinical laboratory tests, including amine or peptide determinations.

Carcinogenesis/Mutagenesis/Impairment of Fertility: Studies in laboratory animals have demonstrated no mutagenic potential of octreotide. No long-term studies in animals to assess carcinogenicity have been completed. Octreotide did not impair fertility in rats at doses up to 1 000 µg/kg/day.

Pregnancy: Reproduction studies have been performed in rats and rabbits at doses up to 30 times the highest human dose and have revealed no evidence of impaired fertility or harm to the fetus due to octreotide. There are, however, no adequate and well-controlled studies in pregnant women. Because animal reproduction studies are not always predictive of human response, this drug should be used during pregnancy only if clearly needed.

Lactation: It is not known whether this drug is excreted in human milk. Because many drugs are excreted in milk, caution should be exercised when octreotide is administered to a nursing woman.

Children: Experience with octreotide in the pediatric population is limited. The youngest patient to receive the drug was 1 month old. Doses of 1 to 10 µg/kg body weight were well tolerated in the young patients. A single case of an infant (nesidioblastosis) was complicated by a seizure thought to be independent of octreotide.

Adverse Effects: The main side effects encountered with octreotide administration are local (at the site of injection) and gastrointestinal.

GEP and Acromegaly: See Table I.

Table I—Sandostatin

Composite Listing of Adverse Reactions in 196 GEP Endocrine Tumor Patients and 114 Acromegalic Patients Treated with Sandostatin

Adverse Reaction Profile According to Body System	GEP Endocrine Tumor Patients (n=196)%	Acromegalic Patients (n=114)%
Gastrointestinal		
Diarrhea	6.6	57.9
Abdominal discomfort	4.1	43.9
Stools (loose)	3.1	36.0
Nausea	8.7	29.8
Flatulence	0.5	13.2
Constipation	1.0	8.8
Abdominal distention	—	7.9
Stools (abnormal)	0.5	6.1
Cholelithiasis	<1.0	4.4
Rectal gas	—	4.4
Vomiting	2.6	4.4
Fatty stools	3.6	—
Gastrointestinal bleeding	0.5	—
Rectal disorders	0.5	—
Hemorrhoids	—	1.8
Cholecystitis	—	1.8
Eructations	—	1.8
Integumentary		
Pain at injection site	8.2	9.6
Acne	—	4.4
Bruise	0.5	4.4
Pruritus	—	4.4
Alopecia/baldness/hair loss	1.0	3.5
Musculoskeletal		
Back ache/pain	0.5	4.4
Joint pain	—	4.4
Arthritis	—	2.6
Arm/leg heavy-tired	—	2.6
Leg ache/pain	—	2.6
Osteoarthritis	—	1.8
Vertebral disk disorder	—	1.8
Twitching	—	1.8
Respiratory		
Throat pain	0.5	2.6
Flu symptoms	—	6.1
Cold symptoms	—	6.1
Sinusitis	—	3.5
Nasal congestion	—	1.8
Cardiovascular		
Leg cramps	—	3.5
Dyspnea	—	1.8
Epistaxis	—	1.8
Chest pain	0.5	—
Edema	1.0	2.6
Ischemic attack	0.5	—
Hypertension	0.5	—
Thrombophlebitis	0.5	—
Cramps	—	2.6
Autonomic		
Visual disturbances	0.5	2.6
Mouth dry/furry/xerostomia	0.5	1.8
Flushing	0.5	1.8
Numbness	—	1.8
Hot flash	—	1.8
CNS		
Headache	1.5	18.4
Dizziness	1.5	14.9
Fatigue	1.0	9.6
Anxiety/Nervousness	0.5	2.6
Asthenia	0.5	—
Bell's palsy	0.5	—
Seizure	0.5	—
Depression	0.5	2.6
Sleepiness/insomnia	0.5	1.8
Weakness	1.0	—
Moody	—	2.6
Appetite loss	—	1.8
Irritability	—	1.8
Tinnitus	—	1.8
Urogenital		
Urinary tract infection	—	6.1
Pollakiuria	—	3.5
Vaginal infection	—	2.6
Vaginal itch	—	1.8
Breast lump	—	1.8
Dysuria	—	1.8
Kidneys, pain in	—	1.8
Polyuria	—	1.8
Prostatitis	—	1.8
Tumor breast	—	1.8
Hematologic		
Hematoma, injection site	—	9.6
Endocrine		
Hypoadrenalism	—	2.6
Hypothyroidism	—	1.8
Hypogonadism	—	1.8
Hypoglycemia	—	1.8
Miscellaneous		
Foot pain	—	1.8
Fever	—	1.8
Otitis	—	1.8
Weight gain	—	1.8

Local reactions after s.c. administration include pain, and sensations of stinging, tingling or burning at the site of injection, with redness and swelling. These rarely last more than 15 minutes. Local discomfort may be reduced by allowing the solution to reach room temperature before injection and by slowly injecting octreotide.

Acromegalic patients had a higher incidence of diarrhea, abdominal discomfort, nausea and loose stools than patients (included in the original NDS) treated with octreotide for other indications. It is believed that the primary reason for this observation is that patients who received octreotide for carcinoid syndrome, VIPoma and other gastro-entero-pancreatic tumors had these gastrointestinal symptoms at baseline and would only report them as adverse events if they became more frequent or severe during octreotide treatment.

The adverse event rate for octreotide during study B301 is presented in comparison to placebo (see Table II on following page). This comparison more accurately reflects the difference in adverse event rates between Sandostatin and placebo.

Gastrointestinal side effects include anorexia, nausea, vomiting, crampy abdominal pain, abdominal bloating, flatulence, loose stools, diarrhea and steatorrhea. Although measured fecal fat excretion may increase, there is no evidence to date that long-term treatment with octreotide has led to nutritional deficiency due to malabsorption. In rare instances, gastrointestinal side effects may resemble acute intestinal obstruction with progressive abdominal distension, severe epigastric pain, abdominal tenderness and guarding. Occurrence of gastrointestinal side effects may be reduced by avoiding meals around the time of octreotide administration, that is, by timing injections between meals or at bedtime.

Prevention of Complications Following Pancreatic Surgery: Local reactions at the site of injection were the most frequently reported side effects in 247 patients undergoing pancreatic surgery treated with octreotide for 7 consecutive days starting on the day of the operation, at least 1 hour before laparotomy. Pruritus, exanthema, vomiting, biliary sludge and fever were

Sandostatin (cont'd)

Table II—Sandostatin

Number % Patients in U.S. Studies B301, B302, B303 with Adverse Events by Treatment and by Body System Events Occurring in ≥3%

Body System	Specific Adverse Event	Placebo B301 n=55 (%)	Sandostatin B301 n=60 (%)	Sandostatin B301, B302 & B303 n=114 (%)
Skin	Pain at injection site	2 (3.6)	5 (8.3)	11 (9.6)
	Acne		2 (3.3)	5 (4.4)
	Bruise	1 (1.1)	2 (3.3)	5 (4.4)
	Pruritus			5 (4.4)
	Alopecia/baldness/hair loss	—	—	4 (3.5)
Musculoskeletal	Back ache/pain			5 (4.4)
	Joint pain	2 (3.6)	1 (1.7)	5 (4.4)
Respiratory	Flu symptoms	—	2 (3.3)	7 (6.1)
	Cold symptoms	—	2 (3.3)	7 (6.1)
	Sinusitis	—	—	4 (3.5)
Cardiovascular	Leg cramps	—	—	4 (3.5)
Hematologic	Hematoma, injection site	6 (10.9)	1 (1.7)	11 (9.6)
Gastrointestinal	Diarrhea	6 (10.9)	32 (53.3)	66 (57.9)
	Abdominal discomfort	7 (12.7)	14 (23.3)	50 (43.9)
	Stools loose	8 (14.5)	16 (26.7)	41 (36.0)
	Nausea	6 (10.9)	17 (28.3)	34 (29.8)
	Flatulence	2 (3.6)	6 (10.0)	15 (13.2)
	Constipation	—	1 (1.7)	10 (8.8)
	Abdominal distention	—	2 (3.3)	9 (7.9)
	Stools abnormal	—	3 (5.0)	7 (6.1)
	Cholelithiasis	—	—	5 (4.4)
	Rectal gas	—	—	5 (4.4)
	Vomiting	1 (1.8)	3 (5.0)	5 (4.4)
Urogenital	Urinary tract infection	—	3 (5.0)	7 (6.1)
	Pollakiuria	2 (3.6)	1 (1.7)	4 (3.5)
Central Nervous	Headache	6 (10.9)	8 (13.3)	21 (18.4)
	Dizziness	6 (10.9)	5 (8.3)	17 (14.9)
	Fatigue	2 (3.6)	3 (5.0)	11 (9.6)

each reported in 0.4% of patients and flushes and rash occurred in 0.8% of patients.

Bleeding Gastroesophageal Varices: Raised blood glucose levels were reported in 23 of 98 cirrhotic patients treated with octreotide 25 μg/h administered by i.v. infusion over 5 days for the emergency management of bleeding esophageal varices. Diarrhea occurred in 5% of patients.

General: Prolonged use of octreotide may result in gallstone formation (see Precautions). Pancreatitis may develop in patients on long-term treatment with octreotide who develop cholelithiasis.

Because of its inhibitory action on growth hormone, glucagon and insulin, octreotide may impair glucose regulation. Postprandial glucose tolerance may be impaired and in some instances, with chronic administration, a state of persistent hyperglycemia may be induced. Hypoglycemia has also been observed.

Acute pancreatitis has been reported in rare instances. Generally, this effect is seen within the first hours or days of octreotide treatment and resolves on withdrawal of the drug.

Rarely, hair loss has been reported in patients receiving octreotide treatment.

There have been isolated reports of hepatic dysfunctions associated with octreotide administration. These consist of the following: acute hepatitis without cholestasis and normalization of transaminase values on withdrawal of octreotide has occurred; the slow development of hyperbilirubinemia in association with elevation of alkaline phosphatase, gamma glutamyl transferase and, to a lesser extent, transaminases.

Overdose: Symptoms: No life-threatening reactions have been reported after acute overdosage; the maximum single dose of octreotide given to an adult to date has been 1 000 μg by i.v. bolus injection. The observed signs and symptoms were a brief drop in heart rate, facial flushing, abdominal cramps, diarrhea, an empty feeling in the stomach and nausea, all of which resolved within 24 hours of drug administration.

One patient received an accidental overdosage of octreotide by continuous infusion (250 μg/h for 48 hours instead of 25 μg/h). He experienced no side effects.

Treatment: Symptomatic.

Dosage: Parenteral drug products should be inspected visually for particulate matter and discoloration prior to administration. **Do not use if particulates and/or discoloration are observed.**

S.C. injection is the recommended route of administration of octreotide for control of symptoms in most instances. I.V. bolus injections have been used under emergency conditions. Multiple injections at the same site within short periods of time should be avoided. The initial dosage is 50 μg, administered s.c., once or twice daily. Thereafter, the number of injections and dosage may be increased gradually based on patient tolerability, clinical response and effects on levels of tumor-produced hormones (in cases of carcinoid tumors on the urinary excretion of 5-hydroxyindole-acetic acid). Dosage information for patients with specific tumors is listed below. The drug is usually given in a b.i.d. or t.i.d. schedule.

Carcinoid Tumors: The suggested daily dosage of octreotide during the first 2 weeks of therapy ranges from 100 to 600 μg/day in 2 to 4 divided doses (mean daily dosage is 300 μg). In the clinical studies, the **median** daily maintenance dosage was approximately 450 μg, but clinical and biochemical benefits were obtained in some patients with as little as 50 μg, while others required doses up to 1 500 μg/day. However, experience with doses above 750 μg/day is limited.

VIPomas: Daily dosages of 200 to 300 μg in 2 to 4 divided doses are recommended during the initial 2 weeks of therapy (range 150 to 750 μg) to control symptoms of the disease. On an individual basis, dosage may be adjusted to achieve a therapeutic response, but usually doses above 450 μg/day are not required.

Acromegaly: Daily dosages of 100 μg to 300 μg b.i.d. or t.i.d. are recommended at the beginning of treatment. Dosage adjustment should be based on monthly assessment of GH levels and clinical symptoms, and on tolerability. In most patients, the optimal daily dose will be 200 to 300 μg/day. A maximum dose of 1 500 μg should not be exceeded.

If no relevant reduction of GH levels and no improvement of clinical symptoms have been achieved within 3 months of starting treatment with octreotide, therapy should be discontinued.

Prevention of Complications Following Pancreatic Surgery: Daily dosage of 100 μg t.i.d., administered s.c., for 7 consecutive days starting on the day of the operation at least 1 hour before laparotomy.

Bleeding Gastroesophageal Varices in Patients with Cirrhosis: The recommended dose of octreotide is 25 μg/h by continuous i.v. infusion for 48 hours. In patients with high risk of rebleeding, infusion should be maintained up to a maximum of 5 days.

Immediately prior to use, the contents of the ampul or multidose vial should be diluted in physiological saline. The volume of dilution will depend on the infusion system used and should be adjusted to ensure a continuous infusion of octreotide at the recommended rate. Once diluted, the solution should be used within 24 hours. Discard unused portion.

As with all parenteral drugs, i.v. admixtures should be inspected visually for clarity, particulate matter, precipitation, discoloration and leakage prior to administration, whenever solution and container permit.

Stability and Storage: For prolonged storage, ampuls should be kept at temperatures of 2 to 8°C and protected from light.

Octreotide multidose vials should be kept at temperatures of 2 to 8°C. The multidose vials must be protected from light and from freezing.

For day-to-day use, both the ampuls and the multidose vials may be stored at room temperature for up to 2 weeks; they must be protected from light. The ampuls should be opened just prior to administration and any unused portion discarded.

Solution for Continuous I.V. Infusion: Immediately prior to use, the contents of the ampul or multidose vial should be diluted in physiological saline. The volume of dilution will depend on the infusion system used and should be adjusted to ensure a continuous infusion of octreotide at a rate of 25 μg/h. Table III shows examples of dilutions which may be used:

As with all parenteral drugs, i.v. admixtures should be inspected visually for clarity, particulate matter, precipitation, discoloration and leakage prior to administration, whenever solution and container permit.

Sandostatin diluted in physiological saline is stable for 24 hours when stored at room temperature. Discard unused portion.

Table III—Sandostatin

Examples of Dilutions

Sandostatin Concentration μg/mL	Sandostatin Size mL	Sandostatin Volume mL	Volume of Physiological Saline	Approximate Available Volume mL	Nominal Concentration μg/mL	Infusion Rate mL/h (μg/h)
500	1	1	49	50	10	2.5 (25)
200	5	2.5	47.5	50	10	2.5 (25)
200	5	3	93	96	6.25	4 (25)

Information for the Patient: See Blue Section—Information for the Patient "Sandostatin".

Supplied: Ampuls: Each ampul contains: octreotide (as acetate) 50 μg, 100 μg or 500 μg. Nonmedicinal ingredients: lactic acid and mannitol. Sodium hydrogen carbonate is added to provide a buffered solution. Ampuls of 1 mL, boxes of 5.

Vials: Each multidose vial contains: octreotide (as acetate) 1 000 μg (200 μg/mL). Nonmedicinal ingredients: lactic acid, mannitol and phenol. Sodium hydrogen carbonate is added to provide a buffered solution. Vials of 5 mL.

(Shown in Product Recognition Section)

Reviewed 1999

SANOREX® Ⓟ

Novartis Pharmaceuticals

Mazindol

Anorexiant

Pharmacology: Mazindol is an imidazo-isoindole anorectic agent which shares many pharmacological properties with the amphetamines and their congeners. The effects of mazindol include CNS stimulation as well as an anorectic action.

It has not been established, however, that the action of such drugs in treating obesity is exclusively one of appetite suppression. Other CNS actions or metabolic effects may be involved as well. As with similar drugs, rebound weight gain may occur after discontinuation of mazindol.

Tolerance to the anorectic action has been demonstrated with all drugs of this class in which this phenomenon has been studied.

Absorption of mazindol occurs with a half-life of 1 hour. A single oral dose of 1 or 2 mg can be identified in the blood after 30 minutes. Maximum plasma concentrations are attained on average after 3.6 hours. Plasma protein binding is 77%. The elimination half-life in plasma is approximately 10 hours. Urinary excretion of unchanged substance and metabolites amounts to 40 to 50%, of which about 4% represents unchanged substance.

Indications: As a short-term (i.e., a few weeks) adjunct to continued dietary treatment in the medical management of obesity, in patients who have not responded to an appropriate weight reducing diet alone. Mazindol is recommended only for obese patients with an initial body mass index ≥30 kg/m², or ≥27 kg/m² in the presence of other risk factors (e.g., hypertension, diabetes, hyperlipidemia). See Table I.

Table I—Sanorex

Body Mass Index (BMI), kg/m²

Weight (pounds)	**Height (cm)**					
	5′0″	**5′3″**	**5′6″**	**5′9″**	**6′0″**	**6′3″**
140	**27**	25	23	21	19	18
150	**29**	**27**	24	22	20	19
160	31	**28**	26	24	22	20
170	33	30	**28**	25	23	21
180	35	32	**29**	**27**	25	23
190	37	34	31	**28**	26	24
200	39	36	32	30	**27**	25
210	41	37	34	31	**29**	26
220	43	39	36	33	30	**28**
230	45	41	37	34	31	**29**
240	47	43	39	36	33	30
250	49	44	40	37	34	31

Contraindications: In patients with glaucoma, severe hypertension, recent myocardial infarction, severe renal, hepatic or cardiac insufficiency, cardiac decompensation, elevated venous pressure, cerebral ischemia, uremia, for patients with a history of drug abuse, patients in agitated states, and in schizophrenia.

Mazindol should not be administered during therapy with MAO inhibitors or within 14 days following withdrawal of these agents (to avoid hypertensive crisis). Patients who display hypersensitivity or idiosyncratic reactions to mazindol should not be given further treatment with the drug.

Warnings: Primary Pulmonary Hypertension: **Anorexigens increase the risk of developing primary pulmonary hypertension, an often fatal disorder.**

Although mazindol was not identified, an epidemiological study has indicated that use of other anorexigens for longer than 3 months was associated with a 23-fold increase in the risk of developing Primary Pulmonary Hypertension (PPH). There was no significant increase in risk for persons who had used these agents for 3 months or less. Obesity itself (body mass index ≥30 kg/m²) was also independently associated with an increase of about two-fold in the risk of developing PPH. In the general population, the yearly occurrence of PPH is estimated to be about 1 to 2 cases per 1 000 000 persons. Therefore, the estimated risk associated with the long-term use of anorexigen drugs is about 23 to 46 cases per million persons exposed per year. The study further suggested that the risk of PPH rises with increasing duration of use of these drugs. The effect of intermittent compared to continuous use of anorexigens on the risk of PPH has not been determined.

The onset or aggravation of exertional dyspnea, or unexplained symptoms of angina pectoris, syncope, or lower extremity edema suggest the possibility of occurrence of pulmonary hypertension. Under these circumstances, treatment should be immediately discontinued, and the patient should be evaluated for the possible presence of PPH.

Drug Dependence: Experience with anorectic drugs with amphetamine-like properties has established that their use over prolonged periods can produce severe psychological dependence and has led to extensive abuse. Abstinence effects and self-administration of mazindol have been observed in animals. While the abuse potential of mazindol has not been further defined, the possibility of dependence should be kept in mind when evaluating the desirability of mazindol as part of a weight reduction program.

Tolerance: Tolerance to the anorectic effect of mazinol may occur within a few weeks. If this occurs, discontinuation of the medication is indicated. The dose should not be increased.

Pregnancy and *Lactation:* Mazindol should not be administered to women who are or who are likely to become pregnant unless, in the opinion of the prescribing physician, the potential benefits outweigh the possible risks to mother and fetus. Reproduction studies in rats and rabbits showed an increase in perinatal mortality in the offspring of animals treated with mazindol. Howovor, there was not a clear demonstration of a direct teratogenic effect of mazindol in these studies. Mazindol should not be administered to lactating women.

Children: Mazindol is not recommended for use in children 12 years of age and under and should be kept out of the reach of children.

Precautions: Mazindol should be used with caution in patients with hypertension, and frequent monitoring of blood pressure is indicated. There is insufficient evidence to indicate that mazindol would not have an adverse effect in some hypertensive patients. The drug is not recommended in individuals with symptomatic cardiovascular disease including arrhythmias.

Insulin requirements in diabetes mellitus may be altered by mazindol administration and the concomitant dietary regimen.

It is recommended that mazindol be administered continuously for a period no greater than 6 weeks. Mazindol should be prescribed at the lowest effective dose in the smallest possible quantities to avoid possible overdosage.

Occupational Hazards: Patients should be cautioned against engaging in activities requiring rapid and precise responses, such as driving an automobile or operating machinery until their response to mazindol has been determined.

Drug Interactions: Mazindol may markedly potentiate the pressor effect of exogenous catecholamines. If it should be necessary to administer a pressor amine to a patient in shock who has recently taken mazindol, extreme caution is advised in administering such agents (beginning with low initial doses and careful titration), as well as in monitoring blood pressure.

Mazindol may enhance CNS stimulation caused by CNS stimulants, thyroid hormones or amantadine.

Mazindol may decrease the hypotensive effect of some antihypertensive agents, especially clonidine, guanethidine, methyldopa and rauwolfia alkaloids.

Concomitant treatment with inhalation anesthesia (especially halothane) may result in cardiac arrhythmias.

Adverse Effects: Most frequently encountered have been nervousness, insomnia, dry mouth, constipation and nausea. Other side effects are: CNS: overstimulation, restlessness, dizziness, dysphoria, anxiety, tremor, headache, depression, drowsiness and weakness.

Cardiovascular: tachycardia, palpitations, flushing, changes in blood pressure (hypertension, hypotension). Very rarely (<0.01%) pulmonary hypertension has been reported following the use of mazindol. Although long-term treatment with other anorexigens has been associated with an increased risk of pulmonary hypertension, a causal relationship of this event to mazindol has not been established (see Warnings).

Gastrointestinal: vomiting, unpleasant taste, diarrhea and abdominal discomfort.

Integumental: rash, excessive sweating, pallor, clamminess, numbness and tingling of hands.

Endocrine: Impotence, changes in libido have rarely been observed with mazindol.

Ocular: mydriasis and blurred vision.

Other: dysuria and precordial pain.

Overdose: The highest acute overdosage with mazindol taken by adults was over 200 mg. One patient who had taken between 117 and 234 mg over 3 days presented with a clinical picture characteristic for such an acute overdosage, namely bradycardia and loss of memory as a sign of confusion. He made a full recovery. One poorly documented report describes a lethal outcome in a young drug abuser who had taken between 100 and 200 mg of mazindol and also had consumed ethanol.

Another lethal outcome was reported for a patient who had ingested an unknown dose of mazindol and who died as a consequence of the strong salt solution given orally to induce vomiting.

Symptoms: In cases in which overdosages have been reported, the following symptoms have been found: nausea, vomiting, headache, cardiac arrhythmia, dyspnea, micturition disturbances, excitation, convulsions, coma, hyperactivity and tachycardia.

Treatment: Symptomatic treatment may include the following: Emesis: If the patient is conscious, vomiting should be induced with ipecac syrup (15 to 30 mL).

Gastric Lavage Followed by Administration of Activated Charcoal: Patients should have pharyngeal and laryngeal reflexes. In unconscious patients gastric lavage should not be attempted unless cuffed endotracheal intubation has been performed to prevent aspiration and pulmonary complications.

Sedation: Give chlorpromazine (0.5 to 1 mg/kg, i.m.) every 30 minutes as needed to control symptoms of CNS overstimulation. A short acting barbiturate is generally considered the second best choice. Lidocaine may be administered to counteract cardiac arrhythmias.

There are no data on the treatment of acute mazindol overdosage with hemodialysis or peritoneal dialysis. However, mazindol is soluble only in acid solvents so dialysis with basic or neutral solvents would not remove the drug.

Dosage: 1 mg 3 times daily 1 hour before meals or 1 to 2 mg daily, as a single dose, 1 hour before the first main meal of the day. Should gastrointestinal discomfort occur, mazindol may be taken with meals.

The lowest effective dose should be chosen. To determine the lowest effective dose, therapy may be initiated at 1 mg once a day, and adjusted to the need and response of the patient.

Mazindol should be used for a duration of no more than a few weeks (see Warnings and Precautions).

Supplied: 1 mg: Each white, oval uncoated tablet contains: mazindol 1 mg. Nonmedicinal ingredients: alcohol, calcium sulfate, cornstarch, FD&C Yellow #5, FD&C Yellow #6, lactose, magnesium stearate, povidone and talc. Bottles of 100.

2 mg: Each scored, compressed peach tablet imprinted "Sanorex" on one side and "JC" on the other contains: mazindol 2 mg. Nonmedicinal ingredients: alcohol, calcium sulfate, cornstarch, FD&C Yellow #5, FD&C Yellow #6, lactose, magnesium stearate, povidone, talc and tartrazine. Bottles of 100.

(Shown in Product Recognition Section)

Reviewed 1998

SANS-ACNE® Ⓟ

Galderma

Erythromycin—Ethyl Alcohol

Acne Therapy

Pharmacology: The mechanism by which topically applied erythromycin acts in the treatment of inflammatory papular lesions of acne vulgaris is unknown. Ethyl alcohol is a drying and peeling agent.

Indications: The treatment of the inflammatory papular lesions of acne vulgaris.

Not indicated for the treatment of comedones, cysts or nodules. It is not indicated for use in Grade IV acne.

Contraindications: In persons who have shown hypersensitivity to erythromycin or any of the other ingredients.

Warnings: Sans-Acne is for external use only and should be kept away from the eyes, nose, mouth and other mucous membranes because of its irritant effects. Concomitant topical anti-acne therapy should be used with caution because a cumulative irritancy effect may occur, especially with preparations having peeling, desquamating or abrasive properties.

Precautions: The use of antibiotic-containing preparations such as Sans-Acne may result in the overgrowth of antibiotic-resistant organisms. If this occurs, administration should be

Sans-Acne (cont'd)

discontinued and appropriate measures taken. Cross-resistance between erythromycin and clindamycin has been reported to occur on rare occasions.

Pregnancy and *Lactation:* Safety during pregnancy or lactation has not been established.

Adverse Effects: Adverse reactions reported with topical erythromycin preparations such as Sans-Acne include mild to severe skin irritation symptoms including dryness, tenderness, pruritus, desquamation, scaling, coriaceousness, fissuring around the mouth, erythema, urticaria, oiliness and burning sensation.

Overdose: Symptoms and Treatment: Accidental ingestion could cause alcoholic intoxication and/or intestinal tract irritation (manifested by abdominal discomfort, cramping, diarrhea or vomiting). Treat with a demulcent.

If Sans-Acne comes into contact with the eye, irrigate with copious amounts of water or irrigation solutions such as Eyestream for at least 5 minutes. If discomfort persists, consult a physician.

Excessive frequency of application may result in excessive dryness and scaling, pruritus, tenderness, erythema, desquamation and burning sensation. Discontinue use until condition subsides. Appropriate anti-inflammatory measures may be employed.

Dosage: The topical solution should be applied twice a day to areas affected by acne. These areas should be washed first with a mild soap, rinsed well, and patted dry. Sans-Acne should be applied with the applicator top. If fingertips are used, wash hands thoroughly after application. Care should be taken to avoid eye, nose, mouth and other mucous membranes.

Ethyl alcohol contributes significantly to the efficacy of the product due to its drying and peeling properties. Because ethyl alcohol is potentially irritating, the frequency of application may require adjustment to once a day.

Instructions for installing applicator: Remove and discard temporary shipping cap. Push applicator firmly into bottle using white cap as holder. Screw cap down to seat applicator.

Supplied: Each mL of clear solution contains: erythromycin 2% and ethyl alcohol 44%. Also contains caprylic/capric triglyceride with citric acid and/or sodium hydroxide to adjust pH. Plastic (HDPE) bottles of 60 mL with optional applicators. Store in an upright position, tightly closed at room temperature. Keep away from open flame.

SANSERT®

Novartis Pharmaceuticals

Methysergide Maleate

Vascular Headache Prophylaxis

Pharmacology: Methysergide inhibits or blocks the effects of serotonin and potentiates the action of the catecholamines. The physiological function of serotonin in body processes has not been fully elucidated, but there is evidence that it may play a role in vascular headache. Suggestions have been made by investigators as to the mechanism whereby methysergide produces its clinical effects, but this has not been finally established.

Methysergide is rapidly absorbed after oral administration and is widely distributed to body tissues. It is metabolized to methylergonovine and glucuronide metabolites. Approximately 50% of an oral dose is excreted in the urine as unchanged drug and metabolites. The elimination half-life is about 10 hours.

Indications: The prophylactic treatment of: severe recurring vascular headaches occurring one or more times weekly; vascular headaches that are so severe or uncontrollable that preventive therapy is indicated regardless of frequency.

Methysergide has proven effective in reducing or eliminating the pain and frequency of attacks of classical migraine, common migraine and cluster headache (histaminic cephalalgia).

Contraindications: Pregnancy, peripheral vascular disease, severe arteriosclerosis, severe hypertension, coronary artery disease, valvular heart disease, phlebitis or cellulitis of the lower limbs, pulmonary or collagen disease, impaired liver or renal function, urinary tract diseases, cachectic or septic states.

Precautions: In a small number of patients receiving longterm methysergide therapy, retroperitoneal fibrosis has been noted and is usually manifested by signs and symptoms of urinary tract obstruction. A related condition (pleuropulmonary fibrosis) has been noted in a small number of patients and may be indicated by the presence of chest pain, dyspnea or pleural friction rub. Cardiac murmurs or vascular bruits have been noted occasionally. The development of any of these conditions should alert the physician to stop the medication. Spontaneous reversal of clinical and laboratory findings can be anticipated following discontinuation of the drug.

Continuous therapy should not exceed 6 months without institution of a reasonable drug free interval of 3 to 4 weeks. It is usually wise to decrease the dose of the drug gradually over 2 to 3 weeks before complete discontinuation in order to avoid "headache rebound". At the first signs of impaired peripheral circulation, prompt withdrawal of the drug is recommended.

Methysergide is specifically designed for the prophylaxis of vascular headache and has no place in the management of the acute attack. The drug is not recommended for use in children.

Adverse Effects: Within the recommended dose levels, the following adverse effects have been reported: Fibrotic complications: As mentioned (see Precautions) symptoms compatible with a diagnosis of retroperitoneal or pleuropulmonary fibrosis have been noted in a few patients receiving maintenance methysergide therapy. While a presumptive causal relationship appears to be present in some, in others such a relationship is uncertain.

Retroperitoneal fibrosis: This nonspecific fibrotic process is usually confined to the connective tissue above the pelvic brim and may present clinically with one or more symptoms such as general malaise, fatigue, weight loss, backache, low grade fever (elevated sedimentation rate), urinary obstruction (girdle or flank pain, dysuria, polyuria, oliguria, elevated BUN) vascular insufficiency of the lower limbs (leg pain, Leriche syndrome, edema of legs, thrombophlebitis). The single most useful diagnostic procedure in suspected cases of retroperitoneal fibrosis is i.v. pyelography. Typical deviation and obstruction of one or both ureters may be observed.

Pleuropulmonary complications: A similar nonspecific fibrotic process, limited to the pleural and immediately subjacent pulmonary tissues, usually presents clinically with dyspnea, tightness and pain in the chest, pleural friction rub, and pleural effusion. If a chest x-ray is confirmatory, medication should be stopped.

Cardiac complications: nonrheumatic fibrotic thickening of the aortic root and of the aortic and mitral valves usually present clinically with cardiac murmurs and dyspnea.

Other fibrotic complications: One case of fibrotic plaques simulating Peyronie's disease has been described.

Spontaneous reversal of clinical and laboratory findings can be anticipated, a fact which should be borne in mind to avoid unnecessary surgical intervention.

Cardiovascular complications: Encroachment of retroperitoneal fibrosis on the aorta, inferior vena cava and their common iliac branches may result in vascular insufficiency of the lower limbs, the presenting features of which are mentioned under retroperitoneal fibrosis.

Intrinsic vasoconstriction of large and small arteries, involving one or more vessels or merely a segment of a vessel, may occur at any stage of therapy and therefore, all patients should be warned of this possibility and cautioned to report immediately chest pain, abdominal pain, or cold, numb, painful extremities with or without paresthesias and diminished or absent pulses. Progression to ischemic tissue damage has rarely been reported. Prompt withdrawal of the drug at the first signs of impaired circulation is recommended to obviate such effects. Postural hypotension and tachycardia have also been observed.

Gastrointestinal symptoms: Nausea, vomiting, diarrhea, heartburn and abdominal pain tend to appear early and can frequently be obviated by gradual introduction of the medication and by administration of the drug with meals. Constipation and elevation of gastric acidity have also been reported.

CNS symptoms: insomnia, drowsiness, mild euphoria, dizziness, ataxia, lightheadedness, hyperesthesia, unworldly feelings (described variously as "dissociation", "hallucinatory experiences", etc.). Some of these symptoms may be associated with vascular headaches, per se, and may, therefore be unrelated to methysergide.

Dermatological manifestations: Facial flush, telangiectasia, and nonspecific rashes have rarely been reported. Increased hair loss may occur, but in many instances the tendency has abated despite continued therapy.

Edema: Peripheral edema, and more rarely, localized brawny edema may occur. Dependent edema has responded to lowered doses, salt restriction, or diuretics.

Weight gain: Weight gain may be a reason to caution patients regarding their caloric intake.

Hematological manifestations: neutropenia, eosinophilia.

Miscellaneous: weakness, arthralgia, myalgia, alopecia.

Overdose: Symptoms: 1) Euphoria, hyperactivity, dizziness, pallor, sweating, lethargy. 2) Peripheral vasospasm, with diminished or absent pulses, coldness, mottling and blueness of the extremities. 3) Dilated pupils; hypoactive deep tendon reflexes, areflexia. 4) Tachycardia. 5) Cramps, abdominal pain, nausea, vomiting, diarrhea.

Note: Ischemic tissue damage has not been reported in acute methysergide maleate overdosage.

Treatment: Elimination of the offending drug: 1) Emesis: If the patient is conscious, induce vomiting with syrup of ipecac (adults and children over 1 year of age: 15 mL; children under 1 year of age: 10 mL). 2) Perform gastric lavage followed by the administration of activated charcoal if the pharyngeal and laryngeal reflexes are present and if less than 4 hours have elapsed since ingestion. Do not attempt gastric lavage on an unconscious patient unless cuffed endotracheal intubation has been performed to prevent aspiration and pulmonary complications. 3) Catharsis: Following gastric lavage, a saline cathartic (sodium or magnesium sulfate 30 g in 250 mL of water) may be introduced and left in the stomach. 4) Diuresis: There is no evidence that forced diuresis accelerates methysergide elimination. As a general supportive measure, however, i.v. fluids may be given with advantage.

Treatment of peripheral vasospasm: Marked peripheral vasospasm with coldness and poor or absent pulses requires careful observation with regular palpation of the limb pulses. Warmth, but not heat, and protection must be afforded the ischemic limbs. In the cases of methysergide overdosage reported to date, the use of vasodilators has not been necessary. However,if vasospasm is persistent or there is evidence of impending ischemic tissue damage, sodium nitroprusside or tolazoline may be used with benefit.

General supportive measures: 1) Good nursing care is of prime importance and should include regular observation and accurate recording of the vital signs, and, in particular, the state of the peripheral circulation. 2) Careful supervision and recording of fluid intake and output is essential.

Dosage: Starting dose: 2 mg at night, increased gradually to 2 mg 3 times a day with meals. Since vascular headache is a paroxysmal but basically chronic disorder, treatment must extend over an adequate period of time in order to obtain maximum benefit. While some cases have responded rather quickly, most investigators agree that a three-week trial period should be instituted to determine the true efficacy of methysergide. Moreover, the periodic nature of the disorder will have to be taken into account in determining when and for how long therapy should be maintained. Average maintenance dosage is 4 to 8 mg daily with meals and the maximum daily dosage is 12 mg.

There must be a medication free interval of 3 to 4 weeks after every 6 month course of treatment (see Precautions) and the patient should be examined regularly (or followed up).

Methysergide is not recommended for use in children.

Supplied: Each circular, biconvex, greenish yellow, sugar-coated tablet, branded with "SAN DOZ" should be on one side in blue-green ink, contains: methysergide maleate USP 2 mg. Nonmedicinal ingredients: alcohol, cornstarch, gelatin, lactose, malic acid, stearic acid, talc and tartrazine. Bottles of 100.

(Shown in Product Recognition Section)

SANTYL®

Knoll

Collagenase

Enzymatic Debriding Agent

Pharmacology: Collagenase possesses the ability to digest insoluble collagen, undenatured and denatured, by peptide bond cleavage, under physiological conditions of pH and temperature. This ability makes it particularly effective in the removal of detritus from dermal lesions, contributing towards the more rapid formation of granulation tissue and subsequent epithelialization of dermal ulcers and severely burned areas. Collagen in healthy tissue or in newly formed granulation tissue is not digested.

Indications: For the debridement of dermal ulcers or severely burned areas.

Contraindications: Patients who have shown local or systemic hypersensitivity to collagenase.

Warnings: Debilitated patients should be closely monitored for systemic bacterial infections because of the theoretical possibility that debriding enzymes may increase the risk of bacteremia.

Precautions: The enzyme's optimal pH range is 6 to 8. Significantly lower pH conditions have a definitive adverse effect on the enzyme's activity and appropriate precautions should be taken.

The enzymatic activity is also adversely affected by detergents, hexachlorophene and heavy metal ions such as mercury and silver which are used in some antiseptics and by cobalt, magnesium and manganese. When it is suspected such materials have been used, the site should be carefully cleansed by repeated washings with normal saline before collagenase is applied. Soaks containing metal ions or acidic solutions (such as Burow's aluminum acetate solution) should be avoided because of the metal ion and low pH. Cleansing materials such as hydrogen peroxide or Dakin's (dilute sodium hypochlorite) solution do not interfere with the activity of the enzyme.

The ointment should be confined to the area of the lesion in order to avoid the risk of irritation or maceration of normal skin, however, the enzyme does not damage newly forming granulation tissue. A slight erythema has been noted occasionally in the surrounding tissue particularly when the enzyme ointment was not confined to the lesion. This can be readily controlled by more careful application or by protecting the healthy skin with a material such as zinc oxide paste. Since the enzyme is a protein, sensitization may develop with prolonged use.

Adverse Effects: Although no allergic sensitivity on toxic reactions have been noted in the recorded clinical investigations to date, one case of systemic manifestations of hypersensitivity has been reported in a patient treated for more than 1 year with a combination of collagenase and cortisone.

Irritation, maceration or erythema have been noted where prolonged contact of normal skin with collagenase ointment has been allowed, either by application of the ointment to areas of normal skin or by excessive application of ointment to the wound crater with subsequent spread to normal skin when dressings are applied. The reported incidence for this type of reaction was 1.8%.

Overdose: Symptoms: To date, the irritation, maceration or erythema reported on prolonged contact of normal skin with collagenase ointment constitute the only symptoms of overdosage reported.

Treatment: Collagenase ointment can be rendered inert by the application of Burow's solution (aluminum acetate topical solution, USP, pH 3.6 to 4.4) to the treatment site. If this should be necessary, reapplication should be made only with caution.

Dosage: For external use only.

Collagenase ointment should be applied once daily, or more frequently if the dressing becomes soiled (as from incontinence) in the following manner:

Prior to application the lesions should be gently cleansed with a gauze pad saturated with sterile normal saline, to remove any film and digested material. If a stronger cleansing solution is required, hydrogen peroxide, or Dakin's solution may be used, followed by sterile normal saline.

Whenever infection is present, as evidenced by positive cultures, pus, inflammation or odor, it is desirable to use an appropriate antibacterial agent. Should the infection not respond, therapy with collagenase ointment should be discontinued until remission of the infection.

Collagenase ointment should be applied (using a wooden tongue depressor or spatula) directly to deep wounds, or when dealing with shallow wounds, to a sterile gauze pad which is then applied to the wound. The wound is covered with an appropriate dressing such as a sterile gauze pad and properly secured.

Use of an occlusive dressing may promote softening of eschar, if present. Alternatively, crosshatching thick eschar with a #11 blade is helpful in speeding up debridements. It is also desirable to remove as much loosened detritus as can be done readily with forceps and scissors.

All excess ointment should be removed each time the dressing is changed.

Use of collagenase ointment should be terminated when debridement of necrotic tissue is complete and granulation is well underway.

Supplied: Each g of ointment contains: 250 units of collagenase activity/g of white petrolatum USP. Preservative-free. Collapsible metal tubes of 15 and 30 g. Do not store above 25°C. Do not use beyond the expiry date indicated on the label.

SARNA® HC ℞

Stiefel

Hydrocortisone

Topical Corticosteroid

Supplied: 1.0%: Each mL of lotion contains: hydrocortisone USP 1.0% in a soothing emollient base containing camphor and menthol. Plastic bottles of 150 mL with flip-top.

2.5%: Each mL of lotion contains: hydrocortisone USP 2.5% in a soothing emollient base containing camphor and menthol. Plastic tubes of 75 mL.

Nonmedicinal ingredients: camphor, cetyl alcohol, citric acid anhydrous, colloidal silicone dioxide, DMDM hydantoin, edetate disodium, fragrance, glyceryl stearate blend, isopropyl myristate, menthol crystals, PEG 400 monostearate, purified water USP, stearic acid, white petrolatum and xantham gum.

SARNA-P®

Stiefel

Camphor—Menthol—Pramoxine HCl

Antipruritic—Surface Anesthetic

Supplied: Each mL of lotion contains: pramoxine HCl 1%, camphor 0.5% and menthol 0.5% in a soothing, moisturizing emollient base. Nonmedicinal ingredients: carbomer 1342, cetyl alcohol, dimethylol dimethylhydantoin, fragrance, glyceryl stearate blend, isopropyl myristate, polyethylene glycol, purified water USP, sodium hydroxide, stearic acid triple pressed and white petrolatum. Plastic bottles of 150 mL with flip-top.

S.A.S.™ ℞

ICN

Sulfasalazine

Ulcerative Colitis Therapy

Supplied: S.A.S.-500: Each round, biconvex, yellowish-brown, compressed tablet, printed ICN S11 and scored one side, contains: sulfasalazine USP 500 mg. Nonmedicinal ingredients: microcrystalline cellulose, polyethylene glycol and povidone. Bottles of 100 and 500.

S.A.S. Enteric-500: Each oval shaped, biconvex, yellowish-brown enteric coated tablet, printed ICN S14 contains: sulfasalazine USP 500 mg. Nonmedicinal ingredients: microcrystalline cellulose, polyethylene glycol and povidone. Bottles of 100 and 500.

SASTID®

Stiefel

Sulfur—Salicylic Acid

Acne Therapy

Supplied: Each g of neutral soap contains: precipitated sulfur USP 10% and salicylic acid USP 3%. Nonmedicinal ingredients: brown RC 1654, butylated hydroxytoluene, D+C Green #5, fragrance A-3093, polyvinyl pyrrolidone, purified water USP, soap chips, stearic hydrazide, trisodium HEDTA and trolamine. Bars of 75 g.

SAVLODIL® 1:100

Zeneca

Chlorhexidine Gluconate—Cetrimide

Antiseptic

Indications: An antimicrobial agent with cleansing properties for the antiseptic treatment of wounds and burns and swabbing in obstetrics.

Contraindications: For persons who have previously shown a hypersensitivity reaction to either chlorhexidine or cetrimide. However, such reactions are extremely rare.

Warnings: For external use only. Keep out of the eyes and avoid contact with the brain, meninges or middle ear. Do not inject. Do not use in body cavities or as an enema. Do not use in or around the eyes. If Savlodil comes into contact with the eyes, wash out promptly and thoroughly with water.

Discard any surplus solutions immediately after use since sterility can no longer be assured.

Precautions: Hypochlorite bleaches may cause brown stains to develop in fabrics which have previously been in contact with chlorhexidine solutions. Use a perborate bleach instead. Savlodil is incompatible with soap and other anionic agents.

Adverse Effects: Irritative skin reactions can occasionally occur and rare hypersensitivity to cetrimide preparations, usually developing after repeated applications, has been reported. Generalized allergic reactions to chlorhexidine have also been reported but are extremely rare.

Overdose: Treatment: Accidental or Deliberate Poisoning: Accidental ingestion: Carry out gastric lavage with milk, raw egg, gelatin or mild soap. Do not induce vomiting. Employ supportive measures as appropriate. Central paralysis cannot be countered by curare antagonists or CNS stimulants but sympathomimetic drugs have been given. Mechanically assisted ventilation with oxygen may be necessary. Persistent convulsions may be controlled with cautious doses of diazepam or a short-acting barbiturate. Do not give alcohol in any form.

Accidental i.v. infusion: Blood transfusion may be necessary to counteract hemolysis.

Dosage: Apply undiluted.

Supplied: Each mL of sterile solution contains: chlorhexidine gluconate 0.015% w/v and cetrimide 0.15% w/v. Nonmedicinal ingredients: benzyl benzoate, deodorizer liq., glucono delta lactone, isopropyl alcohol, red & yellow dye, sodium hydroxide, Terpineol and water. Plastic containers of 450 mL. Savlodil sterile solution without surplus alcohol is available in unit-dose packages of 30 mL, boxes of 10.

Store at temperature not exceeding 25°C. Protect from light. Protect from freezing.

SAVLON® HOSPITAL CONCENTRATE

Zeneca

Chlorhexidine Gluconate—Cetrimide

Antiseptic—Disinfectant

Pharmacology: Chlorhexidine is effective against a wide range of gram-negative and gram-positive vegetative bacteria, yeasts, dermatophyte fungi and lipophilic viruses. It is inactive against bacterial spores except at elevated temperatures.

Studies with cetrimide have shown it to be active against a wide range of vegetative bacteria, both gram-positive and gram-negative, including S. aureus the commonest cause of infection in wounds and burns. Certain gram-negative bacteria, particularly strains of Pseudomonas and Proteus remain the least susceptible of the pathogenic bacteria to cetrimide, requiring a higher concentration than other species to produce an effective kill.

Because of its cationic nature, chlorhexidine binds strongly to skin, mucosa and other tissues and is thus very poorly absorbed. No detectable blood levels have been found in man following oral use. Percutaneous absorption, if it occurs at all, is insignificant. Cetrimide is also cationic in nature, binding strongly to skin and other tissues, and thus absorption is negligible.

Indications: An antimicrobial preparation with cleansing properties for general antiseptic purposes.

Contraindications: For persons who have previously shown a hypersensitivity reaction to either chlorhexidine or cetrimide. However, such reactions are extremely rare.

Warnings: For external use only. Dilute before use. Avoid contact with the middle ear, brain and meninges. Not for injection. Do not use in body cavities or as an enema. Keep away from the eyes and mucous membranes. If cetrimide/chlorhexidine solutions come into contact with the eyes, wash out promptly and thoroughly with water. If concentrated cetrimide solutions come into contact with the skin, rinse promptly and thoroughly with water. Prolonged skin contact with alcoholic solutions should be avoided. Allow to dry before proceeding. Solutions applied to wounds, burns or broken skin should be sterile.

Syringes, needles or instruments which have been immersed in Savlon solutions should be thoroughly rinsed in sterile water or saline before use. **Add diluent slowly to prevent excessive foaming.**

Savlon Hospital Concentrate (cont'd)

Dilute with water of acceptable chemical and bacteriologic purity or alcohol of acceptable purity (e.g. ethyl alcohol 95% USP or isopropyl alcohol 95% USP).

As a precaution against bacterial contamination, aqueous stock solutions should contain at least 4% v/v of isopropanol or 7% v/v of ethanol which may be denatured (e.g. Industrial Methylated Spirit).

Savlon solutions used for instrument storage should contain 0.4% w/v sodium nitrite to inhibit metal corrosion. Such solutions must be changed every 7 days. Prolonged immersion of rubber appliances in Savlon solutions is undesirable.

Savlon solutions may affect glass cement and therefore are not suitable for the disinfection of endoscopes. As cork may protect certain gram-negative organisms from the action of antiseptics, Savlon solutions must be stored in bottles with glass, plastic or rubber closures.

Precautions: Fabrics which have been in contact with chlorhexidine may develop a brown stain if bleached with a hypochlorite. A perborate bleach may be used instead. Chlorhexidine and cetrimide are incompatible with anionic agents.

Solutions should be prepared with purified water, freshly distilled or freshly boiled. Containers and closures should be thoroughly cleansed (preferably sterile). Diluted solutions should not be used later than 1 week after the container has been opened. Unused portions of sterilized solutions should be discarded after the original container has been opened since sterility can no longer be assured.

Only glass, high density polyethylene or polypropylene containers should be used to store Savlon solutions.

Avoid exposure of alcoholic solutions to sparks or open flame. Allow sufficient time for dissemination of flammable fumes which could constitute a burn or fire hazard. Remove excess alcohol from swabbed areas with sterile dry gauze.

Rubber articles are adversely affected by prolonged or repeated immersion in Savlon solutions.

Polyethylene tubing and catheters, and articles made of plastic should not remain immersed for more than 30 minutes.

Adverse Effects: Irritative skin reactions can occasionally occur and rare hypersensitivity to cetrimide preparations, usually developing after repeated application, has been reported. There have been rare reports of severe burn-like reactions to concentrated cetrimide solutions. Should such a reaction occur, treat as a chemical burn. Generalized allergic reactions to chlorhexidine have also been reported, but are extremely rare. In all these cases, stop application of the product.

Overdose: Treatment: Accidental or Deliberate Poisoning: Accidental oral or rectal administration: If the product is swallowed, give large quantities of milk, raw egg, gelatin or mild soap. Avoid vomiting or lavage if it is believed that a concentrated solution has been ingested.

Central paralysis cannot be countered by curare antagonists or CNS stimulants, but sympathomimetic drugs have been given.

Mechanically assisted ventilation with oxygen may be necessary. Persistent convulsions may be controlled with cautious doses of a short-acting barbiturate. Do not give alcohol in any form.

Accidental intravenous infusion: Massive hemolysis can occur which will require blood transfusion.

Accidental intrauterine administration: Introduction into the uterus can lead to systemic absorption causing hemolysis and pulmonary embolism.

Dosage: Dilute as indicated in Table I.

Supplied: Each mL of a deep orange aqueous preparation contains: chlorhexidine gluconate 1.5% w/v and cetrimide 15% w/v. Nonmedicinal ingredients: benzyl benzoate, deodoriser, dye red and yellow, glucono delta lactone, isopropyl alcohol, sodium hydroxide, terpineol and water. Plastic containers of 4.5 L. Store at a temperature not exceeding 25°C in airtight containers. Protect from light.

Table I—Savlon Hospital Concentrate

Dilution Use	Dilution Rate	Mode of Preparation
Patient Use Cleansing/disinfection of wounds and burns[a] Swabbing in obstetrics, gynecology and urology **Inanimates** Cleansing/disinfectant soak for used metal instruments Clean instrument disinfection (30 minutes' immersion)[c] Cleansing/disinfection of equipment, furniture and fittings in the vicinity of the patient Storage of clinical thermometers and sterile instruments	1 in 100 (1%) aqueous	10 mL made up to 1 L with Purified Water[b]
Patient Use Cleansing/disinfection[a] of wounds and burns where extra detergency/antimicrobial effects are indicated **Inanimates** Cleansing/disinfectant[c] soak for used items which are normally contaminated with adherent substances, e.g. catheters, rubber appliances, etc.	1 in 30 (approx.) aqueous	35 mL made up to 1 L with Purified Water[b]
Patient Use Rapid skin disinfection before operation and other invasive procedures **Inanimates** Disinfection of clean[c] instruments and equipment (2 minutes' immersion). Disinfection of clinical thermometers	1 in 30 (approx.) in 70% alcohol	35 mL with 200 mL Purified Water[b] made up to 1 L with 95% alcohol

Always add diluent slowly to prevent excessive foaming. Sodium nitrite tablets should be dissolved in the water first. The resulting solution should then be added slowly with agitation between each addition.

[a] Sterilize the dilution by autoclaving at 115–116°C for 30 minutes or 121–123°C for 15 minutes.

[b] Purified Water USP may be prepared by distillation, ion-exchange treatment, reverse osmosis. It contains no added substance.

[c] Endoscopes should not be introduced into solutions of Savlon.

SCABENE®

Medican

Esdepallethrin—Piperonyl Butoxide

Scabicide

Pharmacology: Esdepallethrin: Esdepallethrin is an insecticide of the synthetic pyrethroid group, and it acts on the nervous system of insects. The pyrethroids disrupt the ionic conductivity of neurones.

In vitro experiments on isolated nerves of invertebrates and vertebrates were performed to clarify this mode of activity at the cellular level.

Whenever an insect or an acarian comes in contact with an insecticide, it develops an excitation state, shaking and paralysis. The neuromuscular system is affected first, followed by paralysis and death.

Piperonyl Butoxide: Piperonyl butoxide inhibits the oxidative catabolism normally used by the insect to inactivate the pyrethroids. Thus the insecticidal activity of esdepallethrin is synergized by piperonyl butoxide.

Indications: For the treatment of scabies in the infant, child and adult.

Contraindications: Should not be used in patients with a known hypersensitivity, allergy or intolerance to any synthetic pyrethroid.

Warnings: Use of Scabene on eczematous lesions or on open and weeping wounds may provoke a transient worsening of these lesions. It is very important to follow closely the directions for use, particularly in children of less than 2 years of age.

Pregnancy: Scabene should not be used on pregnant women unless the expected benefits are judged greater than the risks that may be associated with the use of the product.

Precautions: General: Scabene should be sprayed in a well-ventilated area to avoid respiratory tract irritation in sensitive patients. Avoid all contact with the eyes.

Children: Protect nose and mouth of infants and small children with a clean handkerchief during the spraying.

Adverse Effects: No systemic adverse effects have been reported during clinical trials.

None of the side effects noted seemed attributable to the treatment. The only undesirable effects that may be due to the treatment are: transitory cutaneous tingling (7.6% of the cases); respiratory tract irritation (1.8%); cutaneous tingling and respiratory tract irritation (5.2%); slight ocular tingling (0.3%).

All the above were either mild or moderate, as far as the cutaneous reports are concerned.

Overdose: Symptoms: The accidental ingestion or inhalation of a large quantity of Scabene can cause nausea, vomiting and muscular paralysis.

Treatment: For ingestion: Gastric lavage must be performed. For inhalation: Move the patient to a well-ventilated area and apply symptomatic treatments.

Dosage: Adults: Apply preferably in the evening around 6 p.m. Spray the contents of the can all over the body surface including the genitals, and particularly interdigital spaces, folds and the areas most affected. Avoid spraying on the face and scalp.

Keep the product in contact with the skin for at least 12 hours, then soap and rinse abundantly to remove the product.

A second treatment should not be necessary, unless the post scabicidal pruritus persists after 10 to 15 days.

If the face is involved, rub the lesions with absorbent cotton soaked with Scabene.

To avoid recontamination, family members should also be treated, and clothing and bedding should be disinfected.

Children (under 2 years): Same procedure as for adults but with the following recommendations: The contact time should not exceed 12 hours. Protect the nose and mouth with a handkerchief while applying treatment.

Supplied: Each mL of aerosol contains: esdepallethrin 0.63% w/w and piperonyl butoxide 5.04% w/w. Nonmedicinal ingredients: butane/isobut/propane, dietylene glycol MEE, ethyl alcohol 95% and glycolized POE glycerin. Aerosol spray can of 160 g with a net volume content of 200 mL treats family of 4. Contents under pressure. Do not immerse in hot water or place near a radiator, oven or other source of heat. Do not puncture or incinerate or expose to a temperature exceeding 50°C.

SCHEINPHARM ARTIFICIAL TEARS

Schein Pharmaceutical

Polyvinyl Alcohol

Ocular Lubricant

Supplied: Each mL of sterile ophthalmic solution contains: polyvinyl alcohol 1.4%. Nonmedicinal ingredients: benzalkonium chloride (as preservative), edetate disodium, sodium chloride and water for injection. Bottles of 15 and 30 mL. Store at 15 to 30°C. Keep bottle tightly closed when not in use.

SCHEINPHARM ARTIFICIAL TEARS PLUS

Schein Pharmaceutical

Polyvinyl Alcohol

Ocular Lubricant

Supplied: Each mL of sterile ophthalmic solution contains: polyvinyl alcohol 1.4%. Nonmedicinal ingredients: chlorobutanol (as preservative), povidone, sodium chloride and water for injection. Bottles of 15 mL. Store at 15 to 30°C. Keep bottle tightly closed when not in use.

SCHEINPHARM ATENOLOL Ⓟ

Schein Pharmaceutical

Atenolol

Beta-adrenergic Receptor Blocking Agent

Supplied: 50 mg: Each scored, white to off-white biconvex, film-coated tablet, embossed with "50" on one face, contains: atenolol 50 mg. Nonmedicinal ingredients: gelatin, glycerol, heavy magnesium carbonate, hydroxypropyl methylcellulose, magnesium stearate, maize starch, sodium lauryl sulfate and titanium dioxide. Bottles of 100 and 500. Blister packs of 30.

100 mg: Each scored, white to off-white biconvex, film-coated tablet, embossed with "100" on one face, contains: atenolol 100 mg. Nonmedicinal ingredients: gelatin, glycerol, heavy magnesium carbonate, hydroxypropyl methylcellulose, magnesium stearate, maize starch, sodium lauryl sulfate and titanium dioxide. Bottles of 100 and 500. Blister packs of 30.

Store at room temperature protected from light and moisture.

SCHEINPHARM B12

Schein Pharmaceutical

Cyanocobalamin

Hematopoietic

Supplied: Each mL of injectable solution contains: cyanocobalamin 1 000 µg. Nonmedicinal ingredients: benzyl alcohol 1.5% w/v, glacial acetic acid, sodium acetate, sodium chloride, sodium hydroxide and/or hydrochloric acid (for pH adjustment) and water for injection. Multidose vials of 10 and 30 mL. Store at room temperature 15 to 30°C. Protect from light.

SCHEINPHARM CEFACLOR Ⓟ

Schein Pharmaceutical

Cefaclor

Antibiotic

Supplied: 250 mg: Each capsule contains: cefaclor 250 mg. Nonmedicinal ingredients: D&C Red #28, FD&C Blue #1, gelatin, magnesium stearate, sodium lauryl sulfate, sodium starch glycolate and titanium dioxide. Bottles of 100 and 500.

500 mg: Each capsule contains: cefaclor 500 mg. Nonmedicinal ingredients: D&C Red #28, D&C Yellow #10, FD&C Blue #1, gelatin, magnesium stearate, sodium lauryl sulfate, sodium starch glycolate and titanium dioxide. Bottles of 100 and 500.

New Product 1998

SCHEINPHARM™ CLOTRIMAZOLE

Schein Pharmaceutical

Clotrimazole

Antifungal

Supplied: Each g of topical cream contains: clotrimazole 10 mg (1%) in a vanishing cream base. Nonmedicinal ingredients: benzyl alcohol 1%, cetyl stearyl alcohol, 2-octyl dodecanol, polysorbate 60, purified water, sorbitan monostearate and synthetic spermaceti. Tubes of 30 g in cartons. Plastic tubs of 500 g. Store below 30°C. Avoid freezing.

SCHEINPHARM DESONIDE Ⓟ

Schein Pharmaceutical

Desonide

Glucocorticoid

Supplied: Cream: Each g contains: desonide 0.05%. Tubes of 15 and 60 g. Jars of 454 g.

Ointment: Each g contains: desonide 0.05%. Tubes of 60 g.

SCHEINPHARM DIPHENHYDRAMINE

Schein Pharmaceutical

Diphenhydramine HCl

Antihistamine

Supplied: Each mL of injectable solution contains: diphenhydramine HCl USP 50 mg. Nonmedicinal ingredients: benzethonium chloride 0.1 mg as preservative, sodium hydroxide and/or hydrochloric acid (for pH adjustment between 5.0 and 6.0) and water for injection. Multiple dose vials of 10 mL. Store at room temperature 15 to 30°C. **Do not permit to freeze. Protect from light.**

SCHEINPHARM™ DOBUTAMINE Ⓟ

Schein Pharmaceutical

Dobutamine HCl

Inotropic

Supplied: Each mL of sterile solution contains: dobutamine HCl 12.5 mg, sodium metabisulfite 0.24 mg and water for injection. Hydrochloric acid and/or sodium hydroxide may have been added to adjust pH. Single use vials of 250 mg/20 mL. I.V. use only. Cartons of 10. Store at 15 to 30°C.

SCHEINPHARM™ FERROUS FUMARATE

Schein Pharmaceutical

Ferrous Fumarate

Hematinic

Supplied: Each red capsule contains: ferrous fumarate USP 300 mg (elemental iron 100 mg). Bottles of 60. Security seal on the cap. Do not use if seal is broken. Keep out of the reach of children. This package contains enough drug to seriously harm a child.

SCHEINPHARM GENTAMICIN Ⓟ

Schein Pharmaceutical

Gentamicin Sulfate

Ocular Antibiotic

Supplied: Each mL of sterile, aqueous solution buffered to approximately pH 7 for ophthalmic use, contains: gentamicin (as gentamicin sulfate) 0.3%. Nonmedicinal ingredients: benzalkonium chloride 0.004% as preservative, dibasic sodium phosphate, edetate sodium, monobasic sodium phosphate, sodium chloride and water for injection. Store at 15 to 30°C. Keep container tightly closed and avoid exposure to excessive heat.

SCHEINPHARM PENICILLIN G SODIUM Ⓟ

Schein Pharmaceutical

Penicillin G Sodium

Antibiotic

Supplied: 1 000 000 IU: Each vial of dry, sterile powder contains: penicillin G sodium 1 million IU. Powder buffered with sodium citrate and citric acid. Sodium: 2 mmol/1 million IU of penicillin G sodium.

5 000 000 IU: Each vial of dry, sterile powder contains: penicillin G sodium 5 million IU. Powder buffered with sodium citrate and citric acid. Sodium: 2 mmol/1 million IU of penicillin G sodium.

10 000 000 IU: Each vial of dry, sterile powder contains: penicillin G sodium 10 million IU. Powder buffered with sodium citrate and citric acid. Sodium: 2 mmol/1 million IU of penicillin G sodium.

Store at controlled room temperature not exceeding 25°C.

SCHEINPHARM PILOCARPINE Ⓟ

Schein Pharmaceutical

Pilocarpine HCl

Miotic—Cholinergic

Supplied: Each mL of sterile ophthalmic solution contains: pilocarpine HCl 1%, 2%, 4% or 6% (w/v). Nonmedicinal ingredients: benzalkonium chloride (preservative), boric acid, hydroxypropyl methylcellulose, sodium chloride (in 1% only), sodium citrate, sodium hydroxide and/or hydrochloric acid to adjust pH in water for injection. Plastic squeeze bottles with dropper tip of 15 mL. Store at 8 to 27°C. Keep container tightly closed when not in use.

SCHEINPHARM TESTONE-CYP ◈

Schein Pharmaceutical

Testosterone Cypionate

Androgen

Supplied: Each mL of injectable solution contains: testosterone cypionate 100 mg. Nonmedicinal ingredients: benzyl alcohol 0.9% as preservative in cotton-seed oil. Multidose vials of 10 mL. Store at room temperature 15 to 30°C. Warming and shaking the vial should redissolve any crystals that may have formed during storage at temperatures lower than recommended. **Protect from light.**

SCHEINPHARM™ TOBRAMYCIN Ⓟ

Schein Pharmaceutical

Tobramycin Sulfate

Antibiotic

Supplied: 10 mg/mL: Each mL of solution contains: tobramycin sulfate equivalent to tobramycin 10 mg. Nonmedicinal ingredients: edetate disodium, phenol, sodium metabisulfite and water for injection. May contain sodium hydroxide and/or sulfuric acid for pH adjustment. Rubber stoppered vials of 2 mL for single use, cartons of 25.

40 mg/mL: Each mL of solution contains: tobramycin sulfate equivalent to tobramycin 40 mg. Nonmedicinal ingredients: edetate disodium, phenol, sodium metabisulfite and water for injection. May contain sodium hydroxide and/or sulfuric acid for pH adjustment. Rubber stoppered vials of 2 mL for single use, cartons of 25. Rubber stoppered vials of 30 mL for multiple dose use, cartons of 1.

Store at controlled room temperature (15 to 30°C).

SCHEINPHARM TRIAMCINE-A Ⓟ

Schein Pharmaceutical

Triamcinolone Acetonide

Corticosteroid

Supplied: Each mL of injectable suspension contains: triamcinolone acetonide 40 mg. Nonmedicinal ingredients: benzyl alcohol 0.9% as preservative, carboxymethylcellulose sodium, polysorbate, sodium chloride, hydrochloric acid and/or sodium hydroxide (for pH adjustment) and water. pH is between 5.0 and 7.5. At the time of manufacture, the air in the container is replaced by nitrogen. Multidose vials of 5 mL. Store at room temperature 15 to 30°C.

SCHERING® BASE
Schering

Indications: A water miscible nonmedicated emollient cream with moisturizing and protective properties suitable for extemporaneous preparation or dilution of dermatological creams. It is also indicated in the treatment of dry or chapped skin.

Supplied: Nonmedicinal ingredients: ceteth-20, cetostearyl alcohol, chlorocresol, mineral oil, monobasic sodium phosphate, phosphoric acid, sodium hydroxide, water and white petrolatum. Jars of 450 g.

SCOPOLAMINE
General Monograph, CPhA

Hyoscine

Anticholinergic

This monograph has been compiled by CPhA. It may contain information different from that approved by Therapeutic Products Programme, Health Canada, and the pharmaceutical manufacturers' approval has not been requested.

Pharmacology: Scopolamine (hyoscine) is a belladonna alkaloid. Scopolamine hydrobromide is the trihydrate hydrobromide salt of scopolamine.

Scopolamine, like atropine, is an antimuscarinic agent which produces competitive antagonism of the actions of acetylcholine, which can be overcome with increasing concentrations of acetylcholine. The anticholinergic properties of scopolamine and atropine differ in that scopolamine has a more potent activity on the iris, ciliary body and certain secretory (salivary, bronchial and sweat) glands. Atropine has more potent activity on the heart, intestine and bronchial muscle and a more prolonged duration of action.

Scopolamine, at usual dosages, produces CNS depression. However, excitement, restlessness, hallucinations, or delirium may paradoxically occur, especially in the presence of severe pain.

Scopolamine hydrobromide injection has been used as a preanesthetic medication in combination with narcotic analgesics to reduce excessive salivation and secretions of the respiratory tract and to produce tranquilization and amnesia.

In addition to its systemic anticholinergic effects, scopolamine is effective in motion sickness. The mechanism of action of scopolamine in the CNS is not well known but may include anticholinergic effects. The ability of scopolamine to prevent motion-induced nausea is believed to be associated with inhibition of vestibular input to the CNS, which results in inhibition of the vomiting reflex. In addition, scopolamine may have a direct action on the vomiting centre within the reticular formation of the brain stem.

Scopolamine is not effective as a single agent for the prophylaxis of chemotherapy-induced nausea and vomiting.

Pharmacokinetics: Scopolamine is rapidly absorbed following i.m. or s.c. injection. It is well absorbed from the gastrointestinal tract as well as percutaneously, following topical application of a transdermal system behind the ear. The drug is thought to be almost completely metabolized in the liver and excreted in the urine. The duration of action of the parenteral formulation is 4 hours while that of the transdermal system is up to 72 hours.

Indications: Scopolamine is used principally for the prevention of nausea and vomiting associated with motion sickness in adults (transdermal application). It is also used as an adjunct to anesthesia to produce sedation and amnesia.

Contraindications: Hypersensitivity to scopolamine or to any ingredient or component in the formulation or administration system; glaucoma or predisposition to angle-closure glaucoma; prostatic hypertrophy; pyloric obstruction; tachycardia secondary to cardiac insufficiency or thyrotoxicosis; paralytic ileus.

Warnings: Occupational Hazards: Since drowsiness, disorientation and confusion may occasionally occur with the use of scopolamine, patients should be cautioned about engaging in activities that require mental alertness, such as driving a motor vehicle or operating dangerous machinery.

In patients with a history of possible raised intraocular pressure, scopolamine should be employed only after an ophthalmic exam excludes glaucoma (see Contraindications).

Potentially alarming idiosyncratic reactions may occur with therapeutic doses.

Children: Safety and efficacy in children have not been established. Children are particularly susceptible to the side effects of belladonna alkaloids. The transdermal system should not be used in children because it is not known whether this system will release an amount of scopolamine that could produce serious adverse effects in children.

Precautions: Use with caution in patients taking drugs which act on the CNS, or patients with urinary bladder neck obstruction.

Caution should be exercised when administering an antiemetic or antimuscarinic drug to patients suspected of having intestinal obstruction, or to patients with gastroparesis, constipation or tachyarrhythmias.

The transdermal system should be used with special caution in the elderly or in individuals with impaired metabolic, liver or kidney function. Use with caution in patients with fever or exposed to high environmental temperatures.

In epileptics, isolated cases of increased seizure frequency have been reported.

In certain cases, especially in the elderly, confusional states and/or visual hallucinations may occur. Should this occur, the scopolamine transdermal system should be removed at once. If severe symptoms persist, appropriate countermeasures should be taken as required (see Overdose).

Drug Interactions: Scopolamine should be employed with caution in patients taking drugs which act on the CNS. This applies particularly to patients taking medications with anticholinergic properties, e.g., belladonna alkaloids, antihistamines, antidepressants (tricyclics and MAO inhibitors), phenothiazines, amantadine and quinidine. These combinations should be avoided whenever possible; if they are used concomitantly, the lowest effective dose of each agent should be used.

Any parasympatholytic or sympathomimetic agent or barbiturate should be administered with caution to persons wearing scopolamine transdermal patches.

Pregnancy: Scopolamine readily crosses the placenta. The use of scopolamine in women of childbearing potential requires that the potential benefit of the drug be weighed against the possible risk to the mother and fetus.

Lactation: Scopolamine appears in minute quantities in milk. Since neonates are particularly sensitive to anticholinergic agents, caution is indicated.

Adverse Effects: Cardiovascular: bradycardia (at low doses), tachycardia initially at high doses, then bradycardia; hypotension.

CNS: sedation, drowsiness; irritability, disorientation, hallucinations, impairment of memory and concentration, dizziness, confusion, tremor (more common in children); acute toxic psychosis (resolves 3 hours after i.m. dose, and 24 to 36 hours after removal of the transdermal patch).

Gastrointestinal: dry mouth (most common side effect; may be relieved by increasing fluid intake or using sugarless candy or gum); constipation.

Ocular: blurred vision, dilated pupils. Hand to eye contamination may result in anisocoria (unequal pupils) and confuse a neurologic examination.

Dermatological: occasional local irritation following transdermal application. Isolated cases of rashes and erythemas have been reported.

Other: difficulty in urinating, rashes, erythemas (rare).

Adverse Effects after Withdrawal of Transdermal Scopolamine: In certain instances, there have been complaints of transient dizziness, nausea, vomiting, headache and disturbances of balance following discontinuation of scopolamine, usually after several days of use.

Overdose: Symptoms: Scopolamine overdose may cause symptoms of CNS excitation: restlessness, giddiness, disorientation, memory disturbances, hallucinations and confusion. Other manifestations are: tachycardia, hyperthermia, dilated pupils, photophobia and blurring of vision, decreased gastrointestinal motility and urinary retention. Severe overdose may result in convulsions, cardiac arrhythmias, respiratory depression and coma.

Treatment: If the patient is wearing a transdermal patch, remove it. Treatment of acute antimuscarinic overdose consists mainly of symptomatic and supportive treatment. Patients should be hospitalized and closely monitored, including continuous ECG monitoring. Hemodialysis and peritoneal dialysis are not effective.

Physostigmine i.v. has been used in the treatment of anticholinergic toxicity. Its use is controversial and should be reserved for life-threatening situations. Physostigmine carries the risk of inducing seizures, bronchospasm, hypertension, severe arrhythmias and asystole. If used, a test dose of 0.5 mg i.v. of physostigmine is given initially, followed by 1 to 2 mg i.v. (maximum 1 mg/min). If no clinical changes or cholinergic signs occur within 15 to 30 minutes, cautiously repeat this dose. Repeat doses of 1 to 2 mg i.v. every 30 minutes up to 2 hours. As the CNS effects of physostigmine wear off rapidly, it is important to monitor the patient continuously. Adverse effects of physostigmine can be reversed with i.v. atropine.

Low doses of diazepam may prove useful in the presence of excitation states and convulsions. Higher doses should be avoided in view of the possibility of additional respiratory depression. In severe cases artificial respiration may be necessary.

In the event of hyperthermia, urgent action should be taken to dissipate heat (e.g., cold baths).

Dosage: Parenteral (Scopolamine Hydrobromide): Adults: 0.3 to 0.6 mg i.m., i.v. or s.c.; if necessary, these doses may be repeated 3 or 4 times daily.

Children: 0.006 mg/kg or 0.2 mg/m² i.m., i.v. or s.c.

Transdermal (Scopolamine): Adults: To obtain optimum effect, one transdermal scopolamine system should be applied to the dry, hairless skin behind the ear approximately 12 hours before the antiemetic effect is required.

The hands should be washed and dried thoroughly following application. Only 1 disc should be worn at a time. Once the disc has been affixed, it should not be touched again while it is being worn. Upon removal, the system should be discarded and the hands and application site washed thoroughly to prevent any traces of scopolamine from coming into direct contact with the eyes; if scopolamine were to contact the eyes, it could cause temporary dilation of the pupils (sometimes in 1 eye only) and blurring of vision.

Should a system become displaced, it should be removed and replaced with a second system on a different skin site in the postauricular area. If scopolamine administration is required for longer than 72 hours, the first system should be removed and a second system placed on a different skin site in the postauricular area.

Children: The transdermal system should not be used in children.

Reviewed 1997

SCOPOLAMINE HYDROBROMIDE
Abbott

Anticholinergic

Supplied: Each mL contains: scopolamine hydrobromide 0.4 mg or 0.6 mg. Nonmedicinal ingredients: hydrobromic acid and water for injection. Ampuls of 1 mL, boxes of 10.

SEBCUR®
Dermtek

Salicylic Acid

Antiseborrheic Agent

Supplied: Each bottle of shampoo contains: salicylic acid 4% in an anionic base with protein and conditioner. Plastic bottles of 120 mL.

SEBCUR/T®
Dermtek

Salicylic Acid—Coal Tar

Antipsoriatic Agent

Supplied: Each bottle of shampoo contains: salicylic acid 4%, coal tar solution 10% in an anionic base with protein and conditioner. Plastic bottles of 120 and 240 mL.

SEBULEX®
Westwood-Squibb

Sulfur—Salicylic Acid

Antiseborrheic Agent

Supplied: Each mL of shampoo contains: sulfur 2%, salicylic acid 2% in a surface-active combination of soapless cleansers and wetting agents. Nonmedicinal ingredients: D&C

Yellow #10, EDTA, FD&C Blue #1, fragrance, PEG-6 lauramide, PEG-14M, sodium dodecylbenzenesulfonate, sodium dioctyl sulfosuccinate, sodium octoxynol-2 ethane sulfonate and water. Plastic bottles of 100, 200 and 300 mL.

SEBULON®

Westwood-Squibb

Zinc Pyrithione

Antiseborrheic Agent

Supplied: Each mL contains: zinc pyrithione 2%. Nonmedicinal ingredients: acetamide MEA, benzyl alcohol, cocamide DEA, D&C Green #5, disodium oleamido PEG-2 sulfosuccinate, FD&C Green #3, fragrance, guar gum, magnesium aluminum silicate, quaternium-15, TEA lauryl sulfate and water. Plastic bottles of 100 mL.

SEBUTONE®

Westwood-Squibb

Salicylic Acid—Sulfur—Coal Tar

Antiseborrheic Agent

Supplied: Each mL contains: coal tar extract (equivalent to 0.5% coal tar USP), sulfur 1.5%, salicylic acid 1.5% in soapless cleansers. Nonmedicinal ingredients: D&C Yellow No. 10, EDTA, FD&C Blue No. 1, fragrance, lanolin oil, PEG-6 lauramide, PEG-90 M, sodium chloride, sodium dodecylbenzenesulfonate, sodium dioctyl sulfosuccinate, titanium dioxide, sodium octoxynol-2 ethane sulfonate and water. Plastic bottles of 200 mL.

SECARIS®

Pharmascience

Polyethylene Glycol—Propylene Glycol

Rhinitis Therapy

Indications: For the temporary relief of perennial rhinitis and relief of blockage and stuffiness in the nose and sneezing caused by hay fever or other allergies, common cold, chronic irritation, debility, inflammation of the nasal sinuses, unfavorable climate, nasal and/or post nasal discharge, pain and malaise, and administration of oxygen therapy.

Adverse Effects: Propylene glycol may produce some local irritation on application to mucous membranes. Patients who are hypersensitive to topical preparations containing propylene glycol should use Secaris with caution.

For full therapeutic benefit Secaris requires regular usage. Patients should be advised that they may expect relief 15 to 20 minutes after administration. Patients may expect a mild but transient stinging sensation upon administration.

Dosage: Intranasal: a small amount of gel applied into each nostril every 4 hours as needed.

Supplied: Each g of lubricant nasal gel contains: polyethylene glycol 15% and propylene glycol 20%, adjusted to pH 5.5. Tubes of 5 and 30 g.

SECOBARBITAL ♦

General Monograph, CPhA

see BARBITURATES

SECRETIN

Ferring

Diagnostic Stimulant of Pancreatic Secretion

Pharmacology: Secretin is a natural hormone occurring in the mucosa of the proximal part of the small intestine. The main action of secretin is to increase the volume and bicarbonate content of the pancreatic secretion.

Secretin also stimulates the production and increases the bicarbonate concentration of hepatic bile. It has an inhibitory effect on gastrointestinal motility and gastric acid secretion as well as a blood gastrin-reducing action.

Secretin stimulates gastrin release in patients with gastrinomas (Zollinger-Ellison syndrome) in contrast to the effect in normal subjects and patients with peptic ulcer disease.

Exogenous secretin disappears from the circulation with a half-life of around 4 minutes in normal subjects.

Indications: The diagnosis of pancreatic disorders. Signs of insufficiency of the pancreas are diminished excretory volume and reduced bicarbonate concentration. The latter indicates pancreatic inflammatory disease, while volume reduction is indicative of pancreatic duct obstruction, commonly associated with neoplasm.

The stimulating effect of secretin on gastrin-producing tumors (gastrinomas) can be used in the screening or differential diagnosis of patients suspected of gastrinomas (Zollinger-Ellison syndrome).

A secretin test may be helpful in the diagnosis of pancreatic cancer by cytological investigation of pancreatic juice.

Further information can be obtained by carrying out a cholecystokinin test at the same time as the secretin test.

Contraindications: Acute Pancreatitis: The secretin test is not recommended in cases of acute pancreatitis, as values for volume flow and bicarbonate concentration are usually within normal ranges in patients recovering from acute attacks. In other pancreatic diseases the excretory pattern is normally more clearly defined, chronic pancreatitis showing a reduction in bicarbonate concentration with normal flow, and pancreatic cancer showing a reduction in flow with a normal bicarbonate concentration, flow depending upon the location of the tumor in the pancreas.

Warnings: History of atopic asthma and/or allergy (see Precautions).

Precautions: Although no side effects have so far been reported, it is recommended that patients undergoing the secretin test are given a small i.v. test dose of 0.1 to 1 clinical units (CU) Secretin with constant monitoring before embarking on the test proper. Special care should be taken in patients with known hypersensitivity.

Employ slow i.v. injection of freshly prepared secretin.

Adverse Effects: No adverse reactions to secretin have so far been reported.

Overdose: Symptoms and Treatment: A preparation of secretin has been tested for acute toxicity in mice It can be concluded that albino mice tolerated i.v. administered secretin at a dose level of 3 750 CU/kg without showing toxicity signs.

Dosage: The solution should be prepared immediately before use. The contents of a vial of Secretin are dissolved in 7.5 mL of Sodium Chloride Injection USP, giving a concentration of 10 CU/mL. Other concentrations can be obtained using the desired amount of Sodium Chloride Injection USP. Discard any unused portion of the reconstituted solution.

For Standard Secretin Test: 1 CU/kg body weight, given by slow i.v. injection. A dose level of 1 CU/kg body weight of secretin has been established as near maximal for pancreatic response and further increase in dose does not enhance diagnostic discrimination.

After i.v. injection of 1 CU/kg body weight, the following normal values have been established: volume 3.6 to 3.8 mL/kg, peak bicarbonate concentration 101 to 103 mEq/L and bicarbonate output 0.32 to 0.34 mEq/kg. Individual variations are great.

These values provide an estimate of normal pancreatic function, but usually the wide range of the values makes an interpretation difficult. An abnormal value indicates the possibility of pancreatic damage, but does not prove the diagnosis. A volume response of less than 2 mL/kg body weight, peak bicarbonate concentration of less than 80 mEq/L and bicarbonate output of less than 0.15 mEq/kg body weight indicates impaired function.

A double-lumen tube is passed through the mouth after a 12 to 15 hours fast, under fluoroscopic guidance so that proper placement of the proximal tube in the gastric antrum and of the distal tube beyond the papilla of Vater is accomplished. The position of the tube must be verified prior to the test period. Constant suction with a negative pressure of 25 to 40 mm of mercury is applied to both outlets and maintained throughout the test. Uncontaminated duodenal contents are clear (not turbid) and bile-stained, having a pH of about 6.0. When these conditions are manifest, a control period of collection of fluid for 10 to 20 minutes is observed. The patient should be tested for sensitivity to secretin prior to its injection.

A standard dose of 1 CU/kg body weight of secretin is injected i.v. A 60-minute collection period has been found to be quite satisfactory but a collection period of 80 minutes may result in less variation in the volume, bicarbonate, and enzyme parameters. After the secretin injection, the aspirations are fractioned into 4 collection periods, the first 2 at 10-minute intervals and the last 2 at 20 minute intervals. The separation of specimens into 10 to 20 minute aliquots affords some assurance of a more complete collection. Wide variations in volume would suggest incomplete aspiration or contamination with juices other than pancreatic. The tube is cleared by injection of air after each aliquot is obtained. The duodenal aspirates are collected in containers surrounded by ice. Each aspirate is then analyzed for volume and bicarbonate concentrations. The duodenal aspirate may also be submitted for careful cystologic study.

For secretin stimulation test in the diagnosis of gastrinomas (Zollinger-Ellison syndrome): 1 to 2 CU/kg body weight given by slow i.v. injection.

After establishing the basal serum gastrin level, 1 to 2 CU/kg body weight are administered by i.v. injection and blood samples collected at 2, 5 and 10 minutes post injection for determination of serum gastrin levels. An increase greater than or equal to 110 pg/mL over basal level indicates presence of gastrinoma (Zollinger-Ellison syndrome).

The standard of activity used for Secretin Ferring is the clinical unit (CU) as defined by Jorpes and Mutt.

Supplied: Each 10 mL rubber-stoppered bottle of lyophilized sterile powder contains: secretin 75 clinical units (CU), L-cysteine HCl 1 mg and mannitol 20 mg. Cartons of 1. The lyophilized powder should be stored at −20°C.

SECTRAL® Ⓟ

Rhône-Poulenc Rorer

Acebutolol HCl

Antihypertensive—Antianginal Agent

Pharmacology: Acebutolol hydrochloride is a beta-adrenergic receptor blocking agent. In vitro and in vivo animal studies show it has a preferential effect on $beta_1$-adrenoreceptors, chiefly located in cardiac muscle. This preferential effect is not absolute, however, and at higher doses, acebutolol inhibits $beta_2$-adrenoreceptors, chiefly located in the bronchial and vascular musculature. It possesses some partial agonist activity (or intrinsic sympathomimetic activity—ISA). It is used in the treatment of hypertension and/or prophylaxis of angina pectoris.

The mechanism of the antihypertensive effect has not been established. Among the factors that may be involved are: competitive ability to antagonize catecholamine-induced tachycardia at the β-receptor sites in the heart, thus decreasing cardiac output; inhibition of renin release by the kidneys; inhibition of the vasomotor centres.

The mechanism of the anti-anginal effect is also uncertain. An important factor may be the reduction of myocardial oxygen requirements by blocking catecholamine-induced increases in heart rate, systolic blood pressure, and the velocity and extent of myocardial contraction.

Acebutolol is well absorbed from the gastrointestinal tract. It undergoes extensive first-pass hepatic biotransformation, with an absolute bioavailability of approximately 40% for the parent compound. The major metabolite, an N-acetyl derivative (diacetolol), is pharmacologically active. This metabolite is equipotent to acebutolol and, in cats, is more cardioselective; therefore, this first-pass phenomenon does not attenuate the therapeutic effect of acebutolol. Food intake does not have a significant effect on the area under the plasma concentration-time curve (AUC) of acebutolol although the rate of absorption and peak concentration decreases slightly.

The plasma elimination half-life of acebutolol is approximately 3 to 4 hours, while that of its metabolite, diacetolol, is 8 to 13 hours. The time to reach peak concentration for acebutolol is 2.5 hours and for diacetolol, after oral administration of acebutolol, 3.5 hours.

Within the single oral dose range of 200 to 400 mg, the kinetics are dose proportional. However, this linearity is not seen at higher doses, probably due to saturation of hepatic biotransformation sites. In addition, after multiple dosing the lack of linearity is also seen by AUC increases of approximately 100% as compared to single oral dosing. Elimination via renal excretion is approximately 30 to 40% and by non-renal mechanisms 50% to 60%, which includes excretion into the bile and direct passage through the intestinal wall.

Acebutolol has a low binding affinity for plasma proteins (about 26%). Acebutolol and its metabolite, diacetolol, are relatively hydrophilic and therefore only minimal quantities have been detected in the cerebrospinal fluid.

Indications: Hypertension: In patients with mild to moderate hypertension. It is usually used in combination with other

Sectral (cont'd)

drugs, particularly a thiazide diuretic. However, it may be tried alone as an initial agent in those patients in whom, in the judgment of the physician, treatment should be started with a β-blocker rather than a diuretic.

In patients with severe hypertension a β-adrenergic blocking agent may be used as part of a multiple drug regimen which would normally include a diuretic and a vasodilator.

The combination of acebutolol with a diuretic or peripheral vasodilator has been found to be compatible and generally more effective than acebutolol alone. Limited experience with other antihypertensive agents has not shown evidence of incompatibility.

Acebutolol is not indicated in the emergency treatment of hypertensive crises.

Angina Pectoris: In the long-term management of patients with angina pectoris due to ischemic heart disease.

Contraindications: Acebutolol should not be used in the presence of: sinus bradycardia, second and third degree AV block, right ventricular failure secondary to pulmonary hypertension, congestive heart failure, cardiogenic shock, anesthesia with agents that produce myocardial depression, e.g. ether.

Warnings: Increase in antinuclear antibody (ANA) titer was observed in approximately 12.5% of patients on chronic acebutolol therapy. Rare instances (<1%) of a syndrome resembling lupus erythematosus have been reported with maintenance therapy. Similar symptoms were occasionally observed with some other β-blockers. In addition to increased ANA titer, polyarthralgia, myalgia and pleuritic pain were the main presenting symptoms. Symptoms and ANA titers appear reversible upon discontinuation of acebutolol therapy. The drug should be withdrawn if symptoms appear or if the results of ANA testing are significantly positive. Patients should be followed up both clinically and serologically until resolution of symptoms.

Cardiac Failure: Special caution should be exercised when administering acebutolol to patients with a history of heart failure. Sympathetic stimulation is a vital component supporting circulatory function in congestive heart failure, and inhibition with β-blockade always carries the potential hazard of further depressing myocardial contractility and precipitating cardiac failure. Acebutolol acts selectively without abolishing the inotropic action of digitalis on the heart muscle. However, the positive inotropic action of digitalis may be reduced by the negative inotropic effect of acebutolol when the 2 drugs are used concomitantly.

The effects of β-blockers and digitalis are additive in depressing AV conduction.

In patients without a history of cardiac failure, continued depression of myocardium over a period of time can, in some cases, lead to cardiac failure. Therefore, at the first sign or symptom of impending cardiac failure, patients should be fully digitalized and/or given a diuretic and the response observed closely. If cardiac failure continues despite adequate digitalization and diuretic therapy, acebutolol therapy should be immediately withdrawn.

Abrupt Cessation of Therapy: Patients with angina should be warned against abrupt discontinuation of acebutolol. There have been reports of severe exacerbation of angina, and of myocardial infarction or ventricular arrhythmias occurring in patients with angina pectoris, following abrupt discontinuation of β-blocker therapy. The last 2 complications may occur with or without preceding exacerbation of angina pectoris. Therefore, when discontinuation is planned in patients with angina pectoris, the dosage should be gradually reduced over a period of about 2 weeks and the patient should be carefully observed. The same frequency of administration should be maintained. In situations of greater urgency, acebutolol therapy should be discontinued stepwise and under conditions of closer observation. If angina markedly worsens or acute coronary insufficiency develops, it is recommended that treatment with acebutolol be reinstituted promptly, at least temporarily.

Various skin rashes and conjunctival xerosis have been reported with β-blockers, including acebutolol. A severe syndrome (oculo-muco-cutaneous syndrome) whose signs include conjunctivitis sicca and psoriasiform rashes, otitis, and sclerosing serositis has occurred with the chronic use of one β-adrenergic-blocking agent (practolol). This syndrome has not been observed with acebutolol or any other such agent. However, physicians should be alert to the possibility of such reactions and should discontinue treatment in the event that they occur.

Severe sinus bradycardia may occur with the use of acebutolol from unopposed vagal activity remaining after blockade of $beta_1$-adrenergic receptors; in such cases, dosage should be reduced.

In patients with thyrotoxicosis, the possible deleterious effects from long-term use of acebutolol have not been adequately appraised. It may give a false impression of improvement by masking the clinical signs of continuing hyperthyroidism or its complications. Therefore, abrupt withdrawal of acebutolol may be followed by an exacerbation of the symptoms of hyperthyroidism, including thyroid storm.

Pregnancy: Reproduction studies have been performed with acebutolol in rats and rabbits at doses of up to 60 mg/kg/day by the oral route and 18 mg/kg/day by the i.v. route. In one rabbit study where acebutolol was administered by the i.v. route, the following malformations were observed: rib defects, gastroschisis, ventricular septal defect, dysplasia of urogenital system and umbilical hernia. These results could not be confirmed in a repeat i.v. study and were not seen in a study using the oral route.

Studies have also been performed with diacetolol (the major metabolite in man) at doses of up to 450 mg/kg/day orally in rabbits and 1 800 mg/kg/day orally in rats. There was a significant elevation of postimplantation loss in rabbit dams receiving 450 mg/kg/day, a level at which food consumption and body weight gain were reduced; a non-statistically significant increase in incidence of bilateral cataracts was also noticed in rat fetuses from dams treated with 1 800 mg/kg/day.

There has been no experience with the use of acebutolol in pregnant women; however, studies have shown that both acebutolol and diacetolol cross the placenta. Acebutolol should not be given to pregnant patients. Its use in women with child bearing potential requires that the anticipated benefit be cautiously weighed against possible hazards.

Lactation: Acebutolol and diacetolol appear in breast milk with a milk plasma ratio of 7.1 and 12.2 respectively. Use in nursing mothers is not recommended.

Precautions: Patients with bronchospastic disease should, in general, not receive a β-blocker. Because of its relative $beta_1$-selectivity, however, low doses of acebutolol may be used with caution in patients with bronchospastic disease who do not respond to, or who cannot tolerate, alternative treatment. Since $beta_1$-selectivity is not absolute and is dose-dependent, the lowest possible dose of acebutolol should be used initially, preferably in divided doses to avoid the higher plasma levels associated with the longer dose-interval. A bronchodilator such as theophylline or a $beta_2$-stimulant should be made available in advance with instructions concerning its use. There may be increased difficulty in treating an allergic type reaction in patients on β-blockers. In these patients, the reaction may be more severe due to pharmacological effects of β-blockers and problems with fluid changes. Epinephrine should be administered with caution since it may not have its usual effects in the treatment of anaphylaxis. On the one hand, larger doses of epinephrine may be needed to overcome the bronchospasm, while on the other, these doses can be associated with excessive α-adrenergic stimulation with consequent hypertension, reflex bradycardia and heart-block and possible potentiation of bronchospasm. Alternatives to the use of large doses of epinephrine include vigorous supportive care such as fluids and the use of β-agonists including parenteral salbutamol or isoproterenol to overcome bronchospasm, and norepinephrine to overcome hypotension.

Acebutolol should be administered with caution to patients subject to spontaneous hypoglycemia, or to diabetic patients (especially those with labile diabetes) who are receiving insulin or oral hypoglycemic agents. Beta-adrenergic blockers may mask the premonitory signs and symptoms of acute hypoglycemia.

Acebutolol should be administered with caution to patients with impaired renal function. Acebutolol is excreted through the gastrointestinal tract, but the active metabolite diacetolol, is eliminated predominantly by the kidney. There is a linear relationship between renal clearance of diacetolol and creatinine clearance. The daily dose of acebutolol should be reduced in patients with a creatinine clearance less than 50 mL/min.

Geriatrics: Acebutolol has been used in the elderly without specific adjustment of dosage. However, this patient population may require lower maintenance doses because the bioavailability of both acebutolol and its metabolite are approximately doubled in this age group. This increased bioavailability is probably due to decreases in first-pass metabolism and renal function in the elderly.

Acebutolol dosage should be individually adjusted when used concomitantly with other antihypertensive agents (see Dosage).

Liver function tests should be performed at regular intervals during long-term treatment.

Elective or Emergency Surgery: The management of patients being treated with β-blockers and undergoing elective or emergency surgery is controversial. Although β-adrenergic-receptor blockade impairs the ability of the heart to respond to β-adrenergically-mediated reflex stimuli, abrupt discontinuation of therapy with acebutolol may be followed by severe complications (see Warnings). Some patients receiving β-adrenergic-blocking agents have been subject to protracted severe hypotension during anesthesia. Difficulty in restarting and maintaining the heartbeat has also been reported. For these reasons, in patients with angina undergoing elective surgery, acebutolol should be withdrawn gradually following the recommendation given under Abrupt Cessation of Therapy (see Warnings). According to available evidence, all clinical and physiological effects of β-blockade are no longer present 72 hours after cessation of medication.

In emergency surgery, since acebutolol is a competitive inhibitor of β-adrenergic-receptor agonists, its effects may be reversed, if necessary, by sufficient doses of such agonists as isoproterenol.

Children: There is no experience with acebutolol in the treatment of pediatric age groups and therefore use in children is not recommended.

Drug Interactions: Catecholamine-depleting drugs, such as reserpine, may have an additive effect when given with β-blocking agents. Patients treated with acebutolol plus catecholamine depletors should, therefore be observed closely for evidence of marked bradycardia or hypotension which may present as vertigo, syncope/pre-syncope, or orthostatic changes in blood pressure without compensatory tachycardia.

Exaggerated hypertensive responses have been reported from the combined use of β-adrenergic antagonists and α-adrenergic stimulants, including those contained in proprietary cold remedies and vasoconstrictive nasal drops. Patients receiving β-blockers should be warned of this potential hazard.

No significant interactions with digoxin, hydrochlorothiazide, hydralazine, sulfinpyrazone, oral contraceptives, tolbutamide or warfarin have been observed.

Should it be decided to discontinue therapy in patients receiving β-blockers and clonidine concurrently, the β-blocker should be discontinued several days before the gradual withdrawal of clonidine. It has been suggested that withdrawal of clonidine in the presence of beta-blockade may exaggerate the clonidine withdrawal syndrome (see also prescribing information for clonidine).

Adverse Effects: The frequency of treatment-related side effects is derived from clinical trials in 3 090 patients with hypertension, angina pectoris or arrhythmia.

The most serious adverse reactions encountered with acebutolol are congestive heart failure, severe bradycardia and bronchospasm occurring in less than 1% of patients.

The most common adverse reactions reported are fatigue (4%), dyspnea (2.5%), nausea (2%), dizziness (2%), hypotension (1%) and rashes (1%).

Adverse reactions grouped by systems are as follows: Cardiovascular: congestive heart failure (see Warnings); secondary effects of decreased cardiac output which include: syncope, vertigo, lightheadedness and postural hypotension; severe bradycardia; lengthening of PR interval; second and third degree AV block; sinus arrest; palpitation; chest pain; cold extremities; Raynaud's phenomenon; hot flushes; pain in legs; edema.

CNS: headache, dizziness, mental depression, tiredness, drowsiness or somnolence, lightheadedness, anxiety, tinnitus, weakness, confusion, vivid dreams, paresthesia, insomnia.

Gastrointestinal: nausea and vomiting, heartburn, indigestion, flatulence, abdominal pain, diarrhea, constipation.

Respiratory: dyspnea, cough, shortness of breath, wheezing, bronchospasm.

Allergic-Dermatological: (see Warnings); urticaria; pruritus; sweating; exfoliative dermatitis; psoriasiform rash; lupus-like syndrome with arthralgia, myalgia, dyspnea and pleuritic pain, reversible upon cessation of the drug.

EENT: blurred vision and non-specific visual disturbances, itching eyes, conjunctivitis.

Miscellaneous: weight gain, loss of appetite, decrease in libido, shivering, micturition (frequency), nocturia.

Laboratory Tests: Occasional reports of increased transaminase, alkaline phosphatase and lactic dehydrogenase values. Positive antinuclear antibodies (see Warnings).

Overdose: Symptoms: The most common signs to be expected with a β-adrenergic blocking agent are bradycardia, congestive heart failure, hypotension, bronchospasm and hypoglycemia.

Treatment: If overdosage occurs, in all cases therapy with acebutolol should be discontinued and the patient observed closely.

In addition, if required, the following therapeutic measures are suggested: 1. Bradycardia: atropine or another anticholinergic drug.
2. Heart block (second or third degree): isoproterenol or transvenous cardiac pacemaker.
3. Congestive heart failure: conventional therapy.
4. Hypotension (depending on associated factors): epinephrine rather than isoproterenol or norepinephrine may be useful in addition to atropine and digitalis (see Precaution concerning the use of epinephrine in β-blocked patients).
5. Bronchospasm: aminophylline or isoproterenol.
6. Hypoglycemia: i.v. glucose.

Acebutolol and its major metabolite are dialyzable.

It should be remembered that acebutolol is a competitive antagonist of isoproterenol and hence large doses of isoproterenol can be expected to reverse many of the effects of excessive doses of acebutolol. However, the complications of excess isoproterenol should not be overlooked.

Dosage: The dose of acebutolol must always be adjusted to the individual requirements of the patient in accordance with the following guidelines:

Hypertension: Acebutolol is usually used in conjunction with other antihypertensive agents, particularly thiazide diuretics but may be used alone (see Indications).

Treatment should be initiated with doses of 100 mg twice daily. If an adequate response is not seen after 1 week, the dosage should be increased to 200 mg twice daily. In some cases, the daily dosage may need further increments of 100 mg twice daily at intervals of not less than 2 weeks, up to the maximum of 400 mg twice daily.

The maintenance dose is within the range of 400 to 800 mg daily. Patients who show a satisfactory response at a daily dose of 400 mg or less may be given the total dose once daily in the morning. Daily doses above this should be divided into 2 equal doses.

Angina Pectoris: The initial dose is 200 mg twice daily. If after 2 weeks a satisfactory response has not been obtained, the dosage should be increased to a maximum of 300 mg twice daily.

The usual maintenance dose in angina pectoris is in the range of 200 to 600 mg daily administered in 2 divided doses.

In patients adequately controlled on 400 mg daily, a lower maintenance dose of 100 mg twice a day may be tried.

Geriatrics: Older patients have an approximately 2-fold increase in bioavailability and are likely to require lower maintenance doses.

Impaired Renal Function: The daily dose of acebutolol should be reduced by 50% when creatinine clearance is less than 50 mL/min and by 75% when it is less than 25 mL/min (see Precautions).

Acebutolol and its metabolite are dialyzable.

Supplied: 100 mg: Each white, scored, shield-shaped tablet, marked with [logo] on one side and SECTRAL 100 on the other, contains: acebutolol base 100 mg (as the hydrochloride). Nonmedicinal ingredients: acetic anhydride, calcium phosphate dibasic, carnauba wax, cellulose, colloidal silicon dioxide, magnesium stearate, polacrilin potassium, talc, titanium oxide and zein. Gluten-, lactose- and tartrazine-free. Bottles of 100 and 500.

200 mg: Each blue, scored, shield-shaped tablet, marked with [logo] on one side and SECTRAL 200 on the other, contains: acebutolol base 200 mg (as the hydrochloride). Nonmedicinal ingredients: acetic anhydride, calcium phosphate dibasic, carnauba wax, cellulose, colloidal silicon dioxide, FD&C Blue No 1 aluminum lake, magnesium stearate, polacrilin potassium, talc, titanium oxide and zein. Gluten-, lactose- and tartrazine-free. Bottles of 100 and 500.

400 mg: Each white, scored, shield-shaped tablet, marked with [logo] on one side and SECTRAL 400 on the other, contains: acebutolol base 400 mg (as the hydrochloride). Nonmedicinal ingredients: acetic anhydride, carnauba wax, colloidal silicon dioxide, cornstarch, diethyl phthalate, lactose, magnesium stearate, methylcellulose, talc, titanium oxide and zein. Gluten- and tartrazine-free. Bottles of 100 and 500.

(Shown in Product Recognition Section)

SELAX®
Odan

Docusate Sodium

Stool Softener

Supplied: Capsules: Each light red soft gelatin capsule contains: docusate sodium USP 100 mg. Nonmedicinal ingredients: ethyl vanillin, FD&C Yellow #6, glycerin, methylparaben, PEG 400, propylene glycol and propylparaben. Gluten- and tartrazine-free. Bottles of 100 and 1 000 and unidose of 100.

Syrup: Each 5 mL of clear red syrup, with peppermint-cherry flavor contains: docusate sodium USP 20 mg. Nonmedicinal ingredients: amaranth, flavor (cherry, orange, peppermint), methylparaben, propylene glycol, propylparaben, purified water and sucrose. Alcohol-, gluten- and tartrazine-free. Bottles of 250 and 500 mL.

SELDANE® Ⓟ
Hoechst Marion Roussel

Terfenadine

Histamine H_1-Receptor Antagonist

Pharmacology: The antihistaminic effect of terfenadine in humans has been demonstrated by its effect against the histamine-induced skin wheal. In several studies with normal volunteers, terfenadine has produced a marked and dose-related reduction of histamine wheals at single oral doses of 20 to 200 mg, with the maximum effect being obtained at 60 mg. The effect of terfenadine was evident within 2 hours, reached its peak by the 4th hour, and persisted for at least 8 hours after dosing. Similarly, attenuation of histamine-induced skin wheals was observed in normal human volunteers after multiple oral doses of terfenadine at 20, 40, and 60 mg, t.i.d. or b.i.d. Reduction in wheal size was observed for at least 10 to 12 hours after the final dose of terfenadine. A single dose of 120 mg terfenadine produced significant reduction in wheal size beginning at 2 hours and lasting for 24 hours.

Clinical studies have shown that the incidence of drowsiness with terfenadine was not different from that of placebo. In normal male volunteers, the incidence of sedation occurring after terfenadine administration (single oral doses of 600 mg or daily oral doses of 30 mg q.i.d. for 6 weeks, 100 mg t.i.d. for 13 weeks, and 200 mg t.i.d. for 10 weeks) was similar to placebo.

Pharmacokinetics: Terfenadine has been shown to be well absorbed in humans following oral administration as a tablet, capsule, or suspension. On the basis of a mass balance study using ^{14}C labeled terfenadine the oral absorption of terfenadine was estimated to be at least 70%. Terfenadine itself undergoes extensive (99%) first pass metabolism to 2 primary metabolites, an active acid metabolite and an inactive dealkylated metabolite.

Pharmacokinetic studies following oral administration of ^{14}C labeled or unlabeled terfenadine in man have shown that the acid metabolite, but no parent compound, was detectable in plasma within 30 minutes, reached maximum concentration at about 3 hours and disappeared with a terminal elimination half-life of about 17 hours. Following single dose terfenadine administration, plasma kinetics of the acid metabolite were linear up to 180 mg; at 240 mg, the area under the plasma concentration-time curve was 14% lower and C_{max} was 19% lower than anticipated. Multiple dose studies confirmed dose proportionality. Systemic availability of terfenadine is low under normal conditions and plasma levels of intact terfenadine are below the limit of quantification (less than 10 ng/mL). From information gained in the ^{14}C study it appears that approximately 40% of the total dose is eliminated renally (40% as acid metabolite, 30% dealkyl metabolite, and 30% minor unidentified metabolites). Sixty percent of the dose is eliminated in the feces (50% as the acid metabolite, 2% unchanged terfenadine, and the remainder as minor unidentified metabolites).

Studies investigating the effect of hepatic and renal insufficiency on the metabolism and excretion of terfenadine are incomplete.

In cases of renal impairment, terfenadine acid metabolite plasma concentrations were noted to increase as renal function decreased, particularly when creatinine clearance fell below 40 mL/minute. Following a single dose of 120 mg of terfenadine, a 2 to 3 fold increase was observed in AUC for the acid metabolite in 6 patients with end-stage renal disease (creatinine clearance $<$10 mL/min) and 6 patients with severe renal disease (creatinine clearance 10 to 39 mL/min) compared to healthy subjects receiving the same dose; plasma terfenadine concentrations were below 10 ng/mL. It is not known if significant plasma terfenadine concentrations might accumulate in patients with significant degrees of renal impairment or end-stage renal disease, if dosed to steady state. Dosage adjustment to one tablet daily is recommended for patients with significant renal impairment but particularly with creatinine clearance below 40 mL/minute (see Dosage).

Preliminary information indicates that in cases of hepatic impairment, significant concentrations of unchanged terfenadine can be detected with the rate of acid metabolite formation being decreased. A single-dose study in patients with hepatic impairment revealed increased parent terfenadine and impaired metabolism suggesting that additional drug accumulation may occur after repetitive dosing in such patients. In subjects with normal hepatic function unchanged terfenadine plasma concentrations have not been detected. Although in rare cases there was measurable plasma terfenadine in apparently normal individuals without identifiable risk factors, the implications of this finding with respect to the variability of terfenadine metabolism in the normal population cannot be assessed without further study. Further studies of terfenadine metabolism in the general population are pending.

Elevated levels of parent terfenadine, whether due to significant hepatic dysfunction, concomitant medications, or overdose, have been associated with QT interval prolongation and serious cardiac adverse events (see Precautions). Terfenadine is contraindicated for use in patients with significant hepatic dysfunction, congenital QT syndrome and electrolyte abnormalities as well as in patients taking concomitant medications or foods that (a) prolong the QT interval, and/or (b) interfere with the metabolism of terfenadine at the cytochrome P_{450} 3A4 isoenzyme level or (c) have the potential for inducing electrolyte abnormalities (see Contraindications).

A study comparing the pharmacokinetics of a single 120 mg dose of terfenadine tablets in young (25 to 35 years old) and elderly (65 to 71 years old) male subjects revealed that the apparent clearance of the acid metabolite was reduced by about 25% and the half-life increased by 14% in elderly subjects. Mean C_{max} and T_{max} were very similar between the 2 groups, indicating that absorption was not impaired in the elderly.

In vitro studies demonstrate that terfenadine is extensively (97%) bound to human serum protein while the acid metabolite is approximately 70% bound to human serum protein. Based on data gathered from in vitro models of antihistaminic activity, the acid metabolite of terfenadine has approximately 30% of the H_1 blocking activity of terfenadine. The relative contribution of terfenadine and the acid metabolite to the pharmacodynamic effects have not been clearly defined. Since unchanged terfenadine is usually not detected in plasma and active acid metabolite concentrations are relatively high, the acid metabolite may be the entity responsible for the majority of efficacy after oral administration of terfenadine.

A relative bioavailability study comparing terfenadine tablets and suspension was conducted in 21 normal male volunteers. Plasma concentration measurements after a 60 or 180 mg (3×60 mg) tablet dose were compared to those obtained following the same doses of terfenadine suspension. Although the suspension produced higher peak plasma concentrations for the 60 and 180 mg doses and in a more rapid time for the 60 mg dose than did the tablet, the time to peak for the 180 mg dose and the AUC values obtained with the 2 formulations at either dose are not statistically significantly different from one another. The suspension and tablet dosage of terfenadine, therefore, are considered bioequivalent.

EEG studies, psychomotor function tests, and subjective ratings of mood or feelings in human volunteers have revealed virtually no differences between placebo and terfenadine at daily doses of 40 to 240 mg. In addition, 120 mg terfenadine did not potentiate the impairment of performance in psychomotor tests or subjective feelings caused by 10 mg diazepam or 0.75 g/kg alcohol.

Indications: For symptomatic relief of acute pollenosis (seasonal rhinitis, hay fever, rhinoconjunctivitis), and allergic dermatoses (including urticaria).

Contraindications: Concomitant administration of terfenadine with oral or topical forms of ketoconazole or other systemic antifungals with a similar structure such as fluconazole, itraconazole, or metronidazole is contraindicated.

Concomitant administration of terfenadine with oral or topical forms of erythromycin or other macrolide antibiotics prone to the formation of inactive cytochrome P_{450} - metabolite complexes is contraindicated.

Concomitant administration of terfenadine with drugs known to prolong the QT interval is contraindicated. These include certain class IA and III antiarrhythmic drugs (quinidine, procainamide, amiodarone, sotalol, bretylium), certain psychiatric drugs (thioridazine, pimozide, phenothiazines, haloperidol, tricyclic antidepressants, lithium, chloral hydrate), astemizole, certain antimalarial drugs (quinine, chloroquine, halofantrine,

Seldane (cont'd)

mefloquine) and others such as amantidine, pentamidine, cisapride and probucol.

Concomitant administration of terfenadine is contraindicated with drugs or foods that inhibit the metabolism of terfenadine. This includes serotonin reuptake inhibitors (fluoxetine, fluvoxamine, nefazodone, sertraline), HIV protease inhibitors (indinavir, ritonavir, saquinavir) and grapefruit juice. Certain calcium channel blocking agents that are primarily metabolized by the hepatic CYP 3A4 isoenzyme such as the dihydropyridines, also have the potential to elevate plasma terfenadine levels.

Terfenadine is contraindicated in patients with significant hepatic dysfunction such as hepatitis, jaundice, or chronic alcoholism, and in patients with electrolyte abnormalities (e.g., hypokalemia, hypomagnesemia) or in patients taking certain diuretics, systemic corticosteroids in supraphysiological doses or liquid protein diets all of which have the potential for inducing electrolyte abnormalities.

Terfenadine is contraindicated in patients with heart disease unless authorized by a physician (see Precautions).

Terfenadine is contraindicated in patients with a known hypersensitivity to the drug.

Precautions: General: Terfenadine undergoes extensive metabolism in the liver by a specific cytochrome P-450 isoenzyme. This metabolic pathway may be impaired in patients with significant hepatic dysfunction (alcoholic cirrhosis, hepatitis) or who are taking drugs such as ketoconazole or erythromycin (a macrolide antibiotic), or other potent inhibitors of this isoenzyme. Interference with this metabolism can lead to elevated terfenadine plasma levels associated with QT prolongation and increased risk of ventricular tachyarrhythmias (such as torsades de pointes, ventricular tachycardia, and ventricular fibrillation) at the recommended dose.

In some cases, severe arrhythmias have been preceded by episodes of syncope. Syncope in patients receiving terfenadine should lead to discontinuation of treatment and full evaluation of potential arrhythmias.

Other patients who may be at risk for these adverse cardiovascular events include patients who may experience new or increased QT prolongation while receiving certain drugs or having conditions leading to QT prolongation. These include patients taking antiarrhythmics, certain psychotropics, probucol or astemizole; patients with electrolyte abnormalities such as hypokalemia or hypomagnesemia; or patients taking diuretics with potential for inducing electrolyte abnormalities.

Patients with Heart Disease: The relationship of underlying heart disease to the development of ventricular tachyarrhythmias while taking terfenadine is unclear, nevertheless, terfenadine should not be used in patients with conditions that may lead to QT prolongation such as congenital QT syndrome (see Contraindications).

Drug Interactions: Ketoconazole: Spontaneous adverse reaction reports of patients taking concomitant oral ketoconazole with recommended doses of terfenadine demonstrate QT interval prolongation and rare serious cardiac events, e.g., death, cardiac arrest, and ventricular arrhythmia including torsades de pointes. Pharmacokinetic data indicate that ketoconazole markedly inhibits the metabolism of terfenadine, resulting in elevated plasma terfenadine levels. Presence of unchanged terfenadine is associated with statistically significant prolongation of the QT and QTc intervals. Concomitant administration of oral ketoconazole and terfenadine is contraindicated (see Contraindications).

Due to the chemical similarity of fluconazole, itraconazole, metronidazole, and miconazole to ketoconazole, concomitant use of these products with terfenadine is not recommended pending full investigation of potential interactions. Reports of torsades de pointes and elevated parent terfenadine have been received in patients taking terfenadine while participating in clinical trials of itraconazole.

Macrolide Antibiotics including Erythromycin: Preliminary data suggest that erythromycin may exert an effect on terfenadine metabolism similar to that of ketoconazole. Although erythromycin measurably decreases the clearance of the terfenadine acid metabolite, its influence on terfenadine levels is still under investigation. The presence of unchanged terfenadine is associated with statistically significant prolongation of the QT and QTc intervals. A few spontaneous accounts of QT interval prolongation with ventricular arrhythmia including torsades de pointes have been reported in patients receiving erythromycin and troleandomycin.

Concomitant administration of terfenadine with erythromycin is contraindicated (see Contraindications). Pending full characterization of potential interactions, concomitant administration of terfenadine with other macrolide antibiotics, including troleandomycin, azithromycin, and clarithromycin, is contraindicated. Studies to evaluate potential interactions of terfenadine with azithromycin and clarithromycin are in progress.

Other drugs that have shown significant cytochrome P_{450} 3A inhibition: Concomitant treatment with potent inhibitors of the hepatic cytochrome P_{450} 3A4 isoenzyme may be associated with decrease of terfenadine metabolism. Accumulation of unchanged terfenadine may cause prolongation of the QT interval with risk of life-threatening cardiac arrhythmias. These include **serotonin reuptake inhibitors** as well as **HIV protease inhibitors**. In absence of clinical studies demonstrating safety, coadministration of terfenadine with drugs that have shown significant CYP 3A inhibition is contraindicated (see Contraindications).

Drug/Food Interaction: Drug/food interaction studies raise the possibility that the simultaneous administration of grapefruit juice with terfenadine may lead to accumulation of unmetabolized parent terfenadine in some patients. Peak plasma levels of unmetabolized terfenadine were ≥ 5 ng/mL with some subjects exceeding 10 ng/mL. Mean QTc intervals increased by 4 to 14 msec compared to terfenadine alone, without adverse events. This increase is unlikely to be clinically significant in view of the large variation observed in the QTc interval with normal subjects (15 to 70 msec) (Morganroth 1991, 1993). When grapefruit juice was administered 2 hours after terfenadine dosing, there was less effect on the terfenadine pharmacokinetics and no increase in the mean QTc interval. Terfenadine should not be taken with grapefruit juice (see Contraindications).

Pregnancy: Although there has been no evidence of teratogenicity in animal reproduction studies, nor has fetal toxicity been observed in the absence of maternal toxicity, terfenadine, like most medications, should not be used in pregnancy unless, in the opinion of the physician, potential benefits outweigh any possible risks.

Lactation: The carboxylic acid metabolite is detectable in human breast milk after terfenadine administration. Therefore, infants should not be breast-fed milk by a patient receiving terfenadine unless in the physician's judgment the potential benefits to the patient outweigh the potential risk to the infant.

Children: Until appropriate data are available, the long-term use of terfenadine in children should be under the direction of a physician. At the present time, there are inadequate data respecting the use of terfenadine in children under the age of 3 years.

Adverse Effects: Cardiovascular: Rare reports of severe cardiovascular adverse effects have been received which include ventricular tachyarrhythmias (torsades de pointes, ventricular tachycardia, ventricular fibrillation, and cardiac arrest), hypotension, palpitations, syncope, and dizziness. Rare reports of deaths resulting from ventricular tachyarrhythmias have been received. Hypotension, palpitations, syncope, and dizziness could reflect undetected ventricular arrhythmia. In some patients, death, cardiac arrest, or torsades de pointes have been preceded by episodes of syncope (see Precautions). Rare reports of serious cardiovascular adverse events have been received, some involving QT prolongation and torsades de pointes, in apparently normal individuals without identifiable risk factors. There is no conclusive evidence of a causal relationship of these events with terfenadine. Although in rare cases there was measurable plasma terfenadine, the implications of this finding with respect to the variability of terfenadine metabolism in the normal population cannot be assessed without further study. In controlled clinical trials in otherwise normal patients with rhinitis, small increases in QTc interval were observed at doses of 60 mg b.i.d. In studies at 300 mg b.i.d. a mean increase in QTc of 10% (range −4 to 30%) (mean increase of 46 ms) was observed.

Two population based retrospective epidemiologic studies were undertaken to quantify the frequency of ventricular tachyarrhythmias in users of terfenadine. The results indicated that the risk of a serious cardiovascular event occurring with terfenadine is very small. However, rare patients are at increased risk for severe cardiac events in settings which result in elevated terfenadine and/or metabolite levels (e.g., concomitant use of ketoconazole or certain macrolide antibiotics, impaired hepatic function, overdose). Also, rare patients may be at increased risk in settings which lead to prolonged QT interval (e.g., hypokalemia or other electrolyte imbalances, underlying cardiac disorders which lead to QT prolongation). Terfenadine is contraindicated for use in patients with these conditions (see Contraindications).

General: Experience from clinical studies, including both controlled and uncontrolled studies involving more than 7 000 patients who received terfenadine, provides information on adverse experience incidence for periods of a few days up to 6 months. The usual dose in these studies was 60 mg twice daily, but in a small number of patients, the dose was as low as 20 mg twice a day, or as high as 600 mg daily.

In controlled clinical studies, using the recommended dose of 60 mg b.i.d., the incidence of reported adverse effects in patients receiving terfenadine was generally similar to that reported in patients receiving placebo as shown in Table I.

Table I—Seldane

	Percent of Patients Reporting				
	Controlled Studies[a]			All Clinical Studies[b]	
Adverse Event	**Seldane N=1 647**	**Placebo N=1 218**	**Control N=1 307[c]**	**Seldane N=7 266**	**Placebo N=3 284[d]**
CNS					
Appetite increase	0.4	0.2	0.0	0.3	0.1
Dizziness	0.9	1.1	0.7	0.7	1.0
Drowsiness	8.6	7.1	19.1	5.8	6.9
Fatigue	2.6	1.3	6.0	2.4	3.0
Headache	7.5	9.4	8.0	7.9	10.9
Insomnia	0.6	0.8	0.4	0.9	1.4
Nervousness	0.6	0.1	0.4	0.6	0.5
Weakness	0.4	0.4	0.1	0.2	0.4
Gastrointestinal					
(Abdominal distress, nausea, vomiting, change in bowel habits)	5.2	4.5	3.0	4.5	5.0
Eye, Ear, Nose, Throat					
Cough	1.6	1.1	0.8	1.2	1.5
Dry mouth/nose/throat	2.3	2.2	4.7	2.4	2.9
Epistaxis	0.2	0.7	0.4	0.3	0.4
Eye complaints, nonvisual	0.4	0.4	0.5	0.6	0.8
Nasal stuffiness	0.5	0.7	0.5	1.2	1.5
Sore throat	1.3	1.6	1.6	1.6	1.4
Skin					
Eruption (including rash and urticaria), itching	1.2	2.0	1.5	1.1	2.3
Other					
Infection, upper respiratory	1.1	1.8	1.1	1.1	1.4
Temperature rise	0.3	0.8	0.5	0.6	0.8

[a]Double-blind controlled studies of terfenadine 60 mg b.i.d. for 6 weeks or less.
[b]Duration of treatment was up to 6 months.
[c]Positive Controls: astemizole, clemastine, d-chlorpheniramine, chlorpheniramine, hydroxyzine, mequitazine.
[d]Includes both single and double-blind placebo.

Other side effects have been reported spontaneously during marketing of terfenadine; their relationship to terfenadine has neither been proved nor disproved. These include: alopecia (hair loss or thinning), anaphylaxis, angioedema, bronchospasm, confusion, depression, erythema multiforme, galactorrhea, insomnia, menstrual disorders (including dysmenorrhea), musculoskeletal symptoms, nightmares, paresthesia, photosensitivity, seizures, sweating, sinus tachycardia, thrombocytopenia, tremor, urinary frequency and visual disturbances.

In clinical trials, several instances of mild, or in 1 case, moderate transaminase elevations were seen in patients receiving terfenadine. Mild elevations were also seen in placebo treated patients. Postmarketing experiences include isolated reports of jaundice, cholestatic hepatitis and hepatitis. In most cases available information is incomplete.

Overdose: Symptoms and Treatment: Signs and symptoms of overdosage may be absent or mild (e.g., headache, nausea, confusion); but adverse cardiac events including cardiac arrest, ventricular arrhythmias including torsades de pointes and QT prolongation have been reported at overdoses as low as 360 mg and have occurred up to 15 hours after the dose. They occur more frequently at doses in excess of 600 mg, and QTc prolongation of up to 30% have been observed at a dose of 300 mg b.i.d. Seizures and syncope have also been reported. Use of doses in excess of 60 mg b.i.d. is not recommended. In overdose cases where ventricular arrhythmias are associated with significant QTc prolongation, treatment with antiarrhythmics known to prolong QTc intervals is not recommended. In the treatment of torsades de pointes, standard measures to control heart rate are recommended.

In cases of overdose, cardiac monitoring for at least 24 hours is recommended and for as long as QTc is prolonged, along with standard measures to remove any unabsorbed drug. Limited experience with the use of hemoperfusion (N=1) or hemodialysis (N=3) was not successful in completely removing the acid metabolite of terfenadine from the blood. There is no information about the dialysability of terfenadine.

Treatment of the signs and symptoms of overdose should be symptomatic and supportive after the acute stage.

Dosage: Tablets: Adults and children over 12 years: 1 tablet morning and evening or 2 tablets once a day, preferably in the morning, unless otherwise directed by a physician.
Caplets: Adults and children over 12 years: 1 caplet once a day, preferably in the morning, unless otherwise directed by a physician.
Suspension: Adults and children over 12 years: 2 teaspoonfuls (60 mg) morning and evening, unless otherwise directed by a physician. Children 7 to 12 years of age: 1 teaspoonful (30 mg) morning and evening. Children 3 to 6 years of age: ½ teaspoonful (15 mg) morning and evening. Children under 3 years: As directed by a physician. Use in children should be limited to periods of 1 week or less unless otherwise directed by a physician.

Patients with significant renal impairment, particularly in those with a creatinine clearance below 40 mL/min: 1 tablet or 2 teaspoonfuls (60 mg) once a day.

Terfenadine should not be taken with grapefruit juice.

Do not exceed recommended dosage.

Supplied: Caplets: Each white, capsule-shaped tablet (caplet) contains: terfenadine 120 mg. Nonmedicinal ingredients: cornstarch, gelatin, lactose, magnesium stearate and sodium bicarbonate. Blister packages of 6, 12 and 18.

Suspension: Each mL of white, cherry flavored suspension contains: terfenadine 6 mg. Nonmedicinal ingredients: artificial cherry flavor, benzyl alcohol, magnesium aluminum silicate, polysorbate, purified water, sodium carboxymethylcellulose and sodium cyclamate. Sweetened with lycasin. Amber polyethylene bottles of 100 mL.

Tablets: Each white, round, flat-faced, beveled-edge tablet contains: terfenadine 60 mg. Nonmedicinal ingredients: cellulose, colloidal silicon dioxide, hydrogenated vegetable oil, magnesium stearate, silica and starch. Gelatin- and lactose-free. Blister packages of 12, 24 and 36.

(Shown in Product Recognition Section)

Reviewed 1999

For comparative information on Heparins: Unfractionated or Low Molecular Weight, see the CPhA General Monograph in the WHITE SECTION.

SELECT™ 1/35 Ⓟ

Dispensapharm

Norethindrone—Ethinyl Estradiol

Oral Contraceptive

Pharmacology: Estrogen-progestogen combinations act primarily through the mechanism of gonadotropin suppression due to the estrogenic and progestational activity of their components. Although the primary mechanism of action is inhibition of ovulation, alterations in the cervical mucus and the endometrium may also contribute to effectiveness.

Indications: Prevention of pregnancy.

Contraindications: History of or actual thrombophlebitis or thromboembolic disorders; history of or actual cerebrovascular disorders; history of or actual myocardial infarction or coronary arterial disease; active liver disease or history of or actual benign or malignant liver tumors; history of or known or suspected carcinoma of the breast; history of or known or suspected estrogen-dependent neoplasia; undiagnosed abnormal vaginal bleeding; any ocular lesion arising from ophthalmic vascular disease, such as partial or complete loss of vision or defect in visual fields; when pregnancy is suspected or diagnosed.

Warnings: Predisposing Factors for Coronary Artery Disease: Cigarette smoking increases the risk of serious cardiovascular side effects and mortality. Birth control pills increase this risk, especially with increasing age. Convincing data are available to support an upper age limit of 35 years for oral contraceptive use by women who smoke.

Other women who are independently at high risk for cardiovascular disease include those with diabetes, hypertension, abnormal lipid profile, or a family history of these. Whether oral contraceptives accentuate this risk is unclear.

In low-risk, nonsmoking women of any age, the benefits of oral contraceptive use outweigh the possible cardiovascular risks associated with low dose formulations. Consequently, oral contraceptives may be prescribed for these women up to the age of menopause.

> Cigarette smoking increases the risk of serious adverse effects on the heart and blood vessels. This risk increases with age and becomes significant in oral contraceptive users over 35 years of age. Women should be counseled not to smoke.

Discontinue Medication at the Earliest Manifestation of the Following: A. Thromboembolic and cardiovascular disorders such as: thrombophlebitis, pulmonary embolism, cerebrovascular disorders, myocardial ischemia, mesenteric thrombosis, and retinal thrombosis.
B. Conditions that predispose to venous stasis and to vascular thrombosis, e.g., immobilization after accidents or confinement to bed during long-term illness. Other nonhormonal methods of contraception should be used until regular activities are resumed. For use of oral contraceptives when surgery is contemplated, see Precautions.
C. Visual defects, partial or complete.
D. Papilledema or ophthalmic vascular lesions.
E. Severe headache of unknown etiology or worsening of preexisting migraine headache.

Precautions: Physical Examination and Follow-up: Before oral contraceptives are used, a thorough history and physical examination should be performed, including a blood pressure determination. Breasts, liver, extremities and pelvic organs should be examined and a Papanicolaou smear should be taken if the patient has been sexually active.

The first follow-up visit should be done 3 months after oral contraceptives are prescribed. Thereafter, examinations should be performed at least once a year or more frequently if indicated. At each annual visit, examination should include those procedures that were done at the initial visit as outlined above or per recommendations of the Canadian Workshop on Screening for Cancer of the Cervix. Its suggestion was that, for women who had 2 consecutive negative Pap smears, screening could be continued every 3 years up to the age of 69.

Pregnancy: Fetal abnormalities have been reported to occur in the offspring of women who have taken estrogen-progestogen combinations in early pregnancy. Rule out pregnancy as soon as it is suspected.

Lactation: The use of oral contraceptives during the period a mother is breast-feeding her infant may not be advisable. The hormonal components are excreted in breast milk and may reduce its quantity and quality. The long-term effects on the developing child are not known.

Hepatic Function: Patients who have had jaundice including a history of cholestatic jaundice during pregnancy should be given oral contraceptives with great care and under close observation.

The development of severe generalized pruritus or icterus requires that the medication be withdrawn until the problem is resolved.

If a patient develops jaundice that proves to be cholestatic in type, the use of oral contraceptives should not be resumed. In patients taking oral contraceptives, changes in the composition of the bile may occur and an increased incidence of gallstones has been reported.

Hepatic nodules have been reported to be associated with use of oral contraceptives, particularly in long-term users of oral contraceptives. These nodules include benign hepatic adenomas, focal nodular hyperplasia and other hepatic lesions. In addition, hepatocellular carcinoma has been reported. Although these lesions are extremely rare, they have caused fatal intra-abdominal hemorrhage and should be considered in women presenting with an abdominal mass, acute abdominal pain, or evidence of intra-abdominal bleeding.

Hypertension: Patients with essential hypertension whose blood pressure is well-controlled may be given oral contraceptives but only under close supervision. If a significant elevation of blood pressure in previously normotensive or hypertensive subjects occurs at any time during the administration of the drug, cessation of medication is necessary.

Migraine and Headache: The onset or exacerbation of migraine or the development of headache of a new pattern which is recurrent, persistent or severe, requires discontinuation of oral contraceptives and evaluation of the cause.

Diabetes: Current low dose oral contraceptives exert minimal impact on glucose metabolism. Diabetic patients, or those with a family history of diabetes, should be observed closely to detect any worsening of carbohydrate metabolism. Patients predisposed to diabetes who can be kept under close supervision may be given oral contraceptives. Young diabetic patients whose disease is of recent origin, well-controlled, and not associated with hypertension or other signs of vascular disease such as ocular fundal changes, should be monitored more frequently while using oral contraceptives.

Ocular Disease: Patients who are pregnant or are taking oral contraceptives, may experience corneal edema that may cause visual disturbances and changes in tolerance to contact lenses, especially of the rigid type. Soft contact lenses usually do not cause disturbances. If visual changes or alterations in tolerance to contact lenses occur, temporary or permanent cessation of wear may be advised.

Breasts: Increasing age and a strong family history are the most significant risk factors for the development of breast cancer. Other established risk factors include obesity, nulliparity and late age at first full-term pregnancy. The identified groups of women that may be at increased risk of developing breast cancer before menopause are long-term users of oral contraceptives (more than 8 years) and starters at early age. In a few women, the use of oral contraceptives may accelerate the growth of an existing but undiagnosed breast cancer. Since any potential increased risk related to oral contraceptive use is small, there is no reason to change prescribing habits at present.

Women receiving oral contraceptives should be instructed in self-examination of their breasts. Their physicians should be notified whenever any masses are detected. A yearly clinical breast examination is also recommended because, if a breast cancer should develop, drugs that contain estrogen may cause a rapid progression.

Vaginal Bleeding: Persistent irregular vaginal bleeding requires assessment to exclude underlying pathology.

Fibroids: Patients with fibroids (leiomyomata) should be carefully observed. Sudden enlargement, pain, or tenderness require discontinuation of the use of oral contraceptives.

Emotional Disorders: Patients with a history of emotional disturbances, especially the depressive type, may be more prone to have a recurrence of depression while taking oral contraceptives. In cases of a serious recurrence, a trial of an alternate method of contraception should be made which may help to clarify the possible relationship. Women with premenstrual syndrome (PMS) may have a varied response to oral contraceptives, ranging from symptomatic improvement to worsening of the condition.

Select 1/35 (cont'd)

Metabolic and Endocrine Diseases: In metabolic or endocrine diseases and when metabolism of calcium and phosphorus is abnormal, careful clinical evaluation should precede medication and a regular follow-up is recommended.

Connective Tissue Disease: The use of oral contraceptives in some women has been associated with positive lupus erythematous cell tests and with clinical lupus erythematous. In some instances exacerbation of rheumatoid arthritis and synovitis has been observed.

Laboratory Tests: Results of laboratory tests should be interpreted in the light of the fact that the patient is on oral contraceptives. The laboratory tests listed below are modified.

A. Liver Function Tests: Aspartate serum transaminase (AST): variously reported elevations. Alkaline phosphatase and gamma glutamine transaminase (GGT): slightly elevated.

B. Coagulation Tests: Minimal elevation of test values reported for such parameters as Factors VII, VIII, IX and X. Increased platelet aggregation, decreased antithrombin III.

C. Thyroid Function Tests: Protein binding of thyroxine is increased as indicated by increased total serum thyroxine concentrations and decreased T_3 resin uptake.

D. Lipoproteins: Small changes of unproven clinical significance may occur in lipoprotein cholesterol fractions.

E. Gonadotropins: LH and FSH levels are suppressed by the use of oral contraceptives. Wait 2 weeks after discontinuing the use of oral contraceptives before measurements are made.

Tissue Specimens: Pathologists should be advised of oral contraceptive therapy when specimens obtained from surgical procedures and Pap smears are submitted for examination.

Return to Fertility: After discontinuing oral contraceptive therapy, the patient should delay pregnancy until at least 1 normal spontaneous cycle has occurred in order to date the pregnancy. An alternate contraceptive method should be used during this time.

Amenorrhea: Women having a history of oligomenorrhea, secondary amenorrhea, or irregular cycles may remain anovulatory or become amenorrheic following discontinuation of estrogen-progestin combination therapy.

Amenorrhea, especially if associated with breast secretion, that continues for 6 months or more after withdrawal, warrants a careful assessment of hypothalamic-pituitary function.

Thromboembolic Complications—Postsurgery: There is an increased risk of postsurgery thromboembolic complications in oral contraceptive users after major surgery. If feasible, oral contraceptives should be discontinued and an alternative method substituted at least 1 month prior to **major** elective surgery. Oral contraceptives should not be resumed until the first menstrual period after hospital discharge following surgery.

Drug Interactions: The concurrent administration of oral contraceptives with other drugs may result in an altered response to either agent. Reduced effectiveness of the oral contraceptive, should it occur, is more likely with the low dose formulations. It is important to ascertain all drugs that a patient is taking, both prescription and nonprescription, before oral contraceptives are prescribed.

Refer to the revised 1994 Report on Oral Contraceptives, Health Canada, for possible drug interactions with oral contraceptives.

Noncontraceptive Benefits of Oral Contraceptives: Several health advantages other than contraception have been reported.

Effects on Menses: increased menstrual cycle regularity; decreased menstrual blood loss; decreased incidence of iron deficiency anemia secondary to reduced menstrual blood loss; decreased incidence of dysmenorrhea.

Effects Related to Ovulation Inhibition: decreased incidence of functional ovarian cysts; decreased incidence of ectopic pregnancy.

Effects on Other Organs of the Reproductive Tract: decreased incidence of acute salpingitis; decreased incidence of endometrial cancer (50%); decreased incidence of ovarian cancer (40%); potential beneficial effects on endometriosis; improvement of acne vulgaris, hirsutism, and other androgen-mediated disorders.

Effects on Breasts: decreased incidence of benign breast disease (fibroadenomas and fibrocystic breast disease); decreased incidence of breast biopsies.

The noncontraceptive benefits of oral contraceptives should be considered in addition to the efficacy of these preparations when counselling patients regarding contraceptive method selection.

> Oral contraceptives **do not protect** against sexually transmitted diseases including HIV/AIDS. For protection against STDs, it is advisable to use latex condoms **in combination with** oral contraceptives.

Adverse Effects: An increased risk of the following serious adverse reactions has been associated with the use of oral contraceptives: thrombophlebitis; pulmonary embolism; mesenteric thrombosis; neuro-ocular lesions, (e.g., retinal thrombosis); myocardial infarction; cerebral thrombosis; cerebral hemorrhage; hypertension; benign hepatic tumors; gallbladder disease.

The following adverse reactions also have been reported in patients receiving oral contraceptives: nausea and vomiting, usually the most common adverse reaction, occurs in approximately 10% or less of patients during the first cycle. Other reactions, as a general rule, are seen less frequently or only occasionally.

Other adverse reactions: gastrointestinal symptoms (such as abdominal cramps and bloating); breakthrough bleeding; spotting; change in menstrual flow; dysmenorrhea; amenorrhea during and after treatment; infertility after discontinuance of treatment; edema; chloasma or melasma which may persist; breast changes: tenderness, enlargement, and secretion; change in weight (increase or decrease); endocervical hyperplasias; possible diminution in lactation when given immediately postpartum; cholestatic jaundice; migraine; increase in size of uterine leiomyomata; rash (allergic); mental depression; reduced tolerance to carbohydrates; vaginal candidiasis; premenstrual-like syndrome; intolerance to contact lenses; change in corneal curvature (steepening); cataracts; optic neuritis; retinal thrombosis; changes in libido; chorea; changes in appetite; cystitis-like syndrome; rhinitis; headache; nervousness; dizziness; hirsutism; loss of scalp hair; erythema multiforme; erythema nodosum; hemorrhagic eruption; vaginitis; porphyria; impaired renal function; Raynaud's phenomenon; auditory disturbances; hemolytic uremic syndrome; pancreatitis; arterial thromboembolism.

Overdose: Symptoms and Treatment: Numerous cases of the ingestion, by children, of estrogen-progestogen combinations have been reported. Although mild nausea may occur, there appears to be no other reaction. Treatment should be limited to a laxative such as citrate of magnesia with the aim of removing unabsorbed material as rapidly as possible.

Dosage: Information for the Patient on How to Take the Birth Control Pill:

1. **Read these directions:**
   - before you start taking your pills, and
   - any time you are not sure what to do.
2. **Look at your pill pack** to see if it has 21 or 28 pills:
   - 21-Pill Pack: 21 active pills (with hormones) taken daily for 3 weeks, and then no pills taken for 1 week

     or
   - 28-Pill Pack: 21 active pills (with hormones) taken daily for 3 weeks, and then 7 "reminder" pills (no hormones) taken daily for 1 week.
3. It is recommended that you use a second method of birth control (e.g., latex condoms and spermicidal foam or gel) for the first 7 days of the first cycle of pill use. This will provide a back-up in case pills are forgotten while you are getting used to taking them.
4. **When receiving any medical treatment, be sure to tell your doctor that you are using birth control pills.**
5. **Many women have spotting or light bleeding, or may feel sick to their stomach during the first 3 months on the pill.** If you do feel sick, do not stop taking the pill. The problem will usually go away. If it does not go away, check with your doctor or clinic.
6. **Missing pills also can cause some spotting or light bleeding,** even if you make up the missed pills. You also could feel a little sick to your stomach on the days you take 2 pills to make up for missed pills.
7. **If you miss pills at any time, you could get pregnant. The greatest risks for pregnancy are:**
   - when you start a pack late, or
   - when you miss pills at the beginning or at the very end of the pack.
8. **Always be sure you have ready:**
   - **another kind of birth control** (such as latex condoms and spermicidal foam or gel) to use as a back-up in case you miss pills, and
   - **an extra, full pack of pills.**
9. **If you experience vomiting or diarrhea, or if you take certain medicines,** such as antibiotics, your pills may not work as well. Use a back-up method, such as latex condoms and spermicidal foam or gel, until you can check with your doctor or clinic.
10. **If you forget more than 1 pill 2 months in a row,** talk to your doctor or clinic about how to make pill-taking easier or about using another method of birth control.
11. **If your questions are not answered here, call your doctor or clinic.**

When to start the first pack of pills: Be sure to read these instructions:

- before you start taking your pills, and
- any time you are not sure what to do.

Decide with your doctor or clinic what is the best day for you to start taking your first pack of pills. Your pills may be either a 21-day or a 28-day type.

A. 21-Day Combination: With this type of birth control pill, you are on pills for 21 days and off pills for 7 days. You must not be off the pills for more than 7 days in a row.

1. **The first day of your menstrual period (bleeding) is Day 1 of your cycle.** Your doctor may advise you to start taking the pills on Day 1, on Day 5, or on the first Sunday after your period begins. If your period starts on Sunday, start that same day.
2. Take 1 pill at approximately the same time every day for 21 days; **then take no pills for 7 days.** Start a new pack on the eighth day. You will probably have a period during the 7 days off the pill. (This bleeding may be lighter and shorter than your usual period.)

B. 28-Day Combination: With this type of birth control pill, you take 21 pills that contain hormones and seven pills that contain no hormones.

1. **The first day of your menstrual period (bleeding) is Day 1 of your cycle.** Your doctor may advise you to start taking the pills on Day 1, on Day 5, or on the first Sunday after your period begins. If your period starts on Sunday, start that same day.
2. Take 1 pill at approximately the same time every day for 28 days. Begin a new pack the next day, **not missing any days.** Your period should occur during the last 7 days of using that pill pack.

What to do during the month:

1. **Take a pill at approximately the same time every day until the pack is empty.**
   - Try to associate taking your pill with some regular activity such as eating a meal or going to bed.
   - Do not skip pills even if you have bleeding between monthly periods or feel sick to your stomach (nausea).
   - Do not skip pills even if you do not have sex very often.
2. **When you finish a pack:**
   - **21 pills: Wait 7 days** to start the next pack. You will have your period during that week.
   - **28 pills:** Start the next pack **on the next day.** Take one pill every day. Do not wait any days between packs.

What to do if you miss pills: Table I (on following page) outlines the actions you should take if you miss 1 or more of your birth control pills. Match the number of pills missed with the appropriate starting time for your type of pill pack.

Note: 28-Day Pack: If you forget any of the 7 "reminder" pills (without hormones) in Week 4, just safely dispose of the pills you missed. Then keep taking 1 pill each day until the pack is empty. You do not need to use a back-up method.

Always be sure you have on hand:

- a back-up method of birth control (such as latex condoms and spermicidal foam or gel) in case you miss pills, and
- an extra, full pack of pills.

If you forget more than 1 pill 2 months in a row, talk to your doctor or clinic, about ways to make pill-taking easier or about using another method of birth control.

Dosage: A. **21-Day Pack:** With this type of birth control pill, the patient is 21 days on pills with 7 days off pills. The patient must not be off the pills for more than 7 days in a row.

1. **The first day of the patient's menstrual period (bleeding) is Day 1 of a cycle.** The doctor may advise the patient to start taking the pills on Day 1, on Day 5, or on the first Sunday after a period begins. If a period starts on Sunday, the patient starts that same day.
2. The pack must be labeled correctly before starting. The pack is preprinted with a Sunday starting day. If the patient is starting on a day other than a Sunday, she should use the Flexi-start sticker labels provided. The patient peels off the label with the chosen starting day and applies it over the preprinted days on top of the card.
3. The patient takes 1 pill at approximately the same time every day for 21 days; **then she takes no pills for 7 days.** She starts a new pack on the eighth day. She will probably have a period during the 7 days off the pill. (This bleeding may be lighter and shorter than a usual period.)

Table I—Select 1/35

What to Do if You Miss Pills

Sunday Start	Other Than Sunday Start
Miss 1 pill	**Miss 1 pill**
Take it as soon as you remember, and take the next pill at the usual time. This means that you might take 2 pills in one day.	Take it as soon as you remember, and take the next pill at the usual time. This means that you might take 2 pills in one day.
Miss 2 pills in a row	**Miss 2 pills in a row**
First 2 Weeks: 1. Take 2 pills the day you remember and 2 pills the next day. 2. Then take 1 pill a day until you finish the pack. 3. Use a back-up method of birth control if you have sex in the 7 days after you miss the pills.	**First 2 Weeks:** 1. Take 2 pills the day you remember and 2 pills the next day. 2. Then take 1 pill a day until you finish the pack. 3. Use a back-up method of birth control if you have sex in the 7 days after you miss the pills.
Third Week: 1. Keep taking 1 pill a day until Sunday. 2. On Sunday, safely discard the rest of the pack and start a new pack that day. 3. Use a back-up method of birth control if you have sex in the 7 days after you miss the pills. 4. You may not have a period this month. **If you miss 2 periods in a row, call your doctor or clinic.**	**Third Week:** 1. Safely dispose of the rest of the pill pack and start a new pack that same day. 2. Use a back-up method of birth control if you have sex in the 7 days after you miss the pills. 3. You may not have a period this month. **If you miss 2 periods in a row, call your doctor or clinic.**
Miss 3 or more pills in a row	**Miss 3 or more pills in a row**
Anytime in the Cycle: 1. Keep taking 1 pill a day until Sunday. 2. On Sunday, safely discard the rest of the pack and start a new pack that day. 3. Use a back-up method of birth control if you have sex in the 7 days after you miss the pills. 4. You may not have a period this month. **If you miss 2 periods in a row, call your doctor or clinic.**	**Anytime in the Cycle:** 1. Safely dispose of the rest of the pill pack and start a new pack that same day. 2. Use a back-up method of birth control if you have sex in the 7 days after you miss the pills. 3. You may not have a period this month. **If you miss 2 periods in a row, call your doctor or clinic.**

B. **28-Day Pack:** With this type of birth control pill, the patient takes 21 pills which contain hormones and 7 pills which contain no hormones.

1. **The first day of the patient's menstrual period (bleeding) is Day 1 of a cycle.** The doctor may advise the patient to start taking the pills on Day 1, on Day 5, or on the first Sunday after a period begins. If a period starts on Sunday, the patient starts that same day.
2. The pack must be labeled correctly before starting. The pack is preprinted with a Sunday starting day. If the patient is starting on a day other than a Sunday, she should use the Flexi-start sticker labels provided. The patient peels off the label with the chosen starting day and applies it over the preprinted days on top of the card.
3. The patient takes 1 pill at approximately the same time every day for 28 days. She begins a new pack the next day, **not missing any days on the pills.** The patient's period should occur during the last 7 days of using that pill pack.

What to do during the month:

1. **The patient takes a pill at approximately the same time every day until the pack is empty.**

- The patient should try to associate taking the pill with some regular activity like eating a meal or going to bed.
- The patient must not skip pills even if she has bleeding between monthly periods or feels sick to her stomach (nausea).
- The patient must not skip pills even if she does not have sex very often.

2. **When a pack is finished:**
   - **21 pills: The patient must wait 7 days** to start the next pack. A period will begin during that week.
   - **28 pills:** The patient starts the next pack **on the next day.** She takes 1 pill every day. She does not wait any days between packs.

Information for the Patient: See Blue Section—Information for the Patient "Oral Contraceptives".

Supplied: Each white circular tablet, impressed "Syntex" on one side and "BX" on the other contains: norethindrone 1 mg and ethinyl estradiol 0.035 mg. Inert orange-colored tablets are impressed "Syntex" on one side. Nonmedicinal ingredients: Active tablets: cornstarch, lactose, magnesium stearate and povidone. Placebo tablets: cornstarch, lactose, magnesium stearate, povidone and sunset yellow FCF **or** FD&C Yellow No. 6 lake, lactose, lactose hydrous, magnesium stearate and microcrystalline cellulose. Dispensers of 21 days (21 active tablets) and 28 days (21 active and 7 inert tablets).

(Shown in Product Recognition Section)

Reviewed 1998

SELECTIVE SEROTONIN REUPTAKE INHIBITORS P

General Monograph, CPhA

Fluoxetine
Fluvoxamine
Paroxetine
Sertraline

Antidepressant—Antiobsessional—Antibulimic—Antipanic

This monograph has been compiled by CPhA. It may contain information different from that approved by Therapeutic Products Programme, Health Canada, and the pharmaceutical manufacturers' approval has not been requested.

Pharmacology: Selective Serotonin Reuptake Inhibitors (SSRIs) are potent and highly selective inhibitors of the reuptake of serotonin at the presynaptic neuronal membrane. This results in increased serotonin concentrations in the synapse, leading to improved serotonergic transmission. SSRIs have very little effect on the reuptake of norepinephrine or dopamine and do not possess clinically important binding affinity for adrenergic, histaminergic, muscarinergic, GABA or benzodiazepine receptors.

The SSRIs do not resemble each other structurally. Although 2 of these agents possess 3 rings, the structures of the SSRIs differ significantly from those of tricyclics and all other antidepressants currently available.

Many clinical applications have been found for this group of drugs, including use in depressive illness, bulimia nervosa, panic disorder, social phobia and obsessive-compulsive disorder. The role of serotonin in these disorders has been the subject of extensive investigation. Although the precise mechanism of action of SSRIs cannot be unequivocally stated, their known effects on serotonin transmission, combined with their clinical effectiveness, have contributed to many of the currently accepted theories of the pathophysiology of these disorders.

Pharmacokinetics: The SSRIs are well absorbed after oral administration. With the exception of sertraline, whose bioavailability appears to be moderately increased in the presence of food, the absorption of SSRIs is not significantly altered when they are taken with meals. As with other classes of antidepressants, clinical improvement may take anywhere from 1 to 4 weeks or more.

The SSRIs are metabolized in the liver and eliminated in the urine and feces to varying degrees. These agents should be used cautiously in patients with significant hepatic or renal impairment. Only fluoxetine and sertraline form active metabolites (see Table I).

The pharmacokinetics of these agents have been shown not to be significantly altered in healthy elderly patients; however, caution is advised with respect to initial dosage.

Table I lists various pharmacokinetic properties of the SSRIs.

Indications: Table II lists the current labeled indications for the available SSRIs. The SSRIs continue to be investigated for use in many other clinical conditions. Further experience with these agents may yield additional labeled indications for their use.

Table II—SSRIs

Labeled Indications

SSRI	Depressive Illness	Bulimia Nervosa	Obsessive-Compulsive Disorder	Panic Disorder
Fluoxetine	Yes	Yes	Yes	—
Fluvoxamine	Yes	—	Yes	—
Paroxetine	Yes	—	Yes	Yes
Sertraline	Yes	—	Yes	Yes

Contraindications: Patients with known hypersensitivity to the respective agents.

Because of reports of serious and sometimes fatal reactions such as serotonin syndrome in patients taking an MAO inhibitor either with or shortly after discontinuation of an SSRI, a 2-week washout period is recommended between therapy with these classes of drugs (see Warnings). In the case of fluoxetine with its very long elimination half-life, a 5-week period is recommended between discontinuation of fluoxetine and initiation of therapy with an MAO inhibitor (see Warnings, Precautions).

Warnings: SSRIs should not be used concurrently with MAO inhibitors. A potentially fatal reaction known as serotonin syndrome may result from the combination of serotonergic agents with different mechanisms of action (see Precautions, Drug Interactions). The signs and symptoms of serotonin syndrome include mental status changes, agitation, myoclonus, hyperreflexia, tremor and diarrhea. In some cases it has resembled neuroleptic malignant syndrome. The syndrome may be mild and may remit within 12 to 24 hours following discontinuation

Table I—SSRIs

Pharmacokinetic Properties (based on multiple-dosing[a])

SSRI (active metabolite)	Protein Binding (%)	Time to Steady-state (days)	Elimination Half-life	Comments
Fluoxetine (norfluoxetine[b])	94.5	14-28	4-6 days (9 days)	Will be present in the body for several weeks after discontinuation.
Fluvoxamine	80	10-14	17-22 hours	—
Paroxetine	95	7-14	24 hours	—
Sertraline (N-desmethyl-sertraline[c])	98	7	25-26 hours (62-104 hours)	Presence of food increases the peak serum concentration by 30% and the AUC by 39%.

[a] The pharmacokinetics of some agents become nonlinear with multiple-dosing, due to partial saturation of the specific cytochrome P450 system believed to be involved; therefore, the half-lives expressed in the table are those seen with multiple-dosing, which more closely reflects clinical use.
[b] Norfluoxetine is believed to be as potent and effective as the parent compound.
[c] N-desmethylsertraline is considered to be 5 to 10 times **less** potent than the parent compound.

Selective Serotonin Reuptake Inhibitors (cont'd)

of the serotonergic agents and with supportive therapy. However, it may be associated with severe hyperthermia and serious or fatal complications. A significant washout period is recommended between therapy with SSRIs and other serotonergic agents, especially MAO inhibitors (see Contraindications).

Because of the long elimination half-life of fluoxetine and its active metabolite, it is important to consider that these compounds will be present in the body for weeks after discontinuation.

Rash (e.g., maculopapular, purpuric, pustular, vesiculobullous, follicular, urticaria, erythema multiforme) has occurred in 2 to 4% of patients treated with SSRIs. Dermatologic reactions usually occur within the first few weeks of therapy. In a small number of patients, systemic signs and symptoms have accompanied dermatologic reactions. Anaphylactoid reactions (e.g., bronchospasm, urticaria, angioedema) and serious systemic illness have been reported rarely. It is generally recommended that SSRIs be discontinued if rash, urticaria or any signs of hypersensitivity occur during therapy.

Precautions: Concomitant Illness: Cardiovascular Disease: SSRIs are considered to be less cardiotoxic than tricyclic antidepressants. They do not tend to significantly affect ECG, blood pressure, or ejection fraction. However, their relative safety in patients with established heart disease remains to be more clearly defined.

Diabetes: Fluoxetine may affect glycemic control. Hypoglycemia has occurred during therapy, as has hyperglycemia upon its discontinuation. It may be necessary to make adjustments to the dosage of insulin or oral antihyperglycemic agents when fluoxetine is initiated or discontinued.

Renal Impairment: Although renal excretion is considered to be a minor route of elimination of SSRIs and their active metabolites, caution is prudent when SSRIs are used in patients with significant renal impairment, until further experience is gained.

Hepatic Disease: The clearance of SSRIs is significantly reduced in patients with liver disease because of their extensive hepatic metabolism. SSRIs should be used with caution in these patients, with lower and less frequent dosing.

Hyponatremia: Hyponatremia has occurred in patients receiving SSRIs. In most cases it occurred in older patients who were on diuretic therapy or who were otherwise volume depleted. There is a possible association between hyponatremia during SSRI therapy and the syndrome of inappropriate antidiuretic hormone secretion. The hyponatremia appears to be reversible on discontinuation of the SSRI.

Mania/Hypomania: Precipitation of a manic or hypomanic state has occurred in patients treated with SSRIs. This effect may be dose-related and may occur more frequently in patients with bipolar disorder. SSRIs should be used with caution in patients with a history of mania. If mania or hypomania occur during SSRI therapy, the dosage should be decreased or the drug discontinued.

Seizures: Seizures have occurred in patients receiving therapeutic doses of SSRIs. The overall incidence (0.1 to 0.2 %) appears to be similar to, or less than, the incidence of seizures in patients receiving other antidepressants; however, patients with a history of seizures were excluded from many of the clinical trials. SSRIs should be used with caution in patients with a history of seizures and discontinued if seizures occur.

Suicide: Although the SSRIs are considerably less toxic in overdose than many other antidepressants, they should be prescribed in the smallest quantity consistent with good patient therapy, given the potential for attempted suicide in depressed patients. Because of the known comorbidity between depression and obsessive-compulsive disorder or panic disorder, the same precaution is recommended when SSRIs are used to treat these conditions.

Withdrawal: A withdrawal syndrome consisting of abdominal cramps, flu-like symptoms and electric shock sensations has been described following abrupt discontinuation of SSRIs. It is usually mild and transient, but may indicate that SSRIs should be gradually tapered.

Pregnancy: Experience with the use of SSRIs in pregnancy is limited. Because their safety in pregnancy has not been clearly established, they should be used in pregnancy only in cases where the potential benefit of treatment is considered to outweigh the possible risk to the fetus.

Lactation: SSRIs are excreted in breast milk. Experience with their use in lactating women is limited and their effects on nursing infants are not well known. SSRIs should be used with caution during lactation.

Children: SSRIs have not been specifically approved in Canada for use in children; however they have been used and continue to be studied in this age group. Further experience with these agents in children is expected to result in specific guidelines for their use in this group.

Geriatric: SSRIs are generally well tolerated in the elderly. Lower initial dosages may be indicated in some elderly patients.

Drug Interactions: SSRIs have the potential to interact with other drugs by many different mechanisms, given that they are hepatically metabolized, inhibit several microsomal isoenzymes and because they are among the many classes of drugs that affect serotonin transmission. Because of their long elimination half-lives, they have the potential to interact with other drugs even after they have been discontinued. Table III illustrates many of the interactions that have occurred with SSRIs. Not every interaction has been reported with each of the SSRIs.

few reported cases of fatal overdose attributable to an SSRI alone. Some of the symptoms of SSRI overdose are thought to be extensions of their pharmacologic effects. The symptoms of overdose include somnolence, nausea and vomiting, ECG changes, nystagmus, dilated pupils, coma.

Treatment: Although SSRIs have exhibited a fairly wide margin of safety, it is recommended that SSRI overdose be managed aggressively since fatalities have occurred with both multiple and single ingestions.

There is no specific treatment or antidote for SSRI overdose. Management should involve symptomatic and supportive care. The possibility of multiple drug involvement should be considered.

The first priority should be to establish and maintain a patent airway, with adequate ventilation and oxygenation. Vital signs and ECG should be monitored. If the ingestion was recent (i.e., within 4 hours or less) and there are no signs or symptoms of cardiac toxicity, the stomach should be emptied, either by induced emesis or gastric lavage. If the patient is comatose, having seizures or does not exhibit a gag reflex, lavage should be performed only if an endotracheal tube with cuff inflated is in place to prevent aspiration.

Administration of activated charcoal, which may be used with sorbitol or a saline cathartic, may be as effective as gastric emptying and may be given either following or instead of induced emesis or lavage.

Hemodialysis, forced diuresis, peritoneal dialysis and exchange transfusion are not thought to be of benefit in the treatment of SSRI overdose.

Table III—SSRIs

Drug Interactions

Interacting Drug(s)	Outcome	(Proposed) Mechanism	Recommendations
Cyproheptadine	Decreased SSRI effects (e.g., worsening of depressive symptoms).	Serotonin antagonism by cyproheptadine.	Watch for reduced antidepressant response to SSRI if cyproheptadine started during therapy.
Drugs metabolized by cytochrome P450 systems, especially CYP2D6, CYP3A4 and CYP2C9 (e.g., astemizole, benzodiazepines, carbamazepine, clozapine, cyclosporine, phenothiazines, phenytoin, terfenadine, tricyclic antidepressants).	Increased serum levels and potentiated clinical and adverse effects of interacting drug.	Inhibition of cytochrome P450 enzyme system(s) involved in the metabolism of the interacting drug.	Clinicians should be aware of the possible interaction and appropriately monitor patients established on these agents when an SSRI is introduced or discontinued. Dosage adjustments may be indicated. In the case of astemizole and terfenadine, alternative antihistamine therapy such as cetirizine, loratadine or fexofenadine should be suggested.
Serotonergic agents (e.g., MAO inhibitors, amphetamine derivatives, dextromethorphan, dihydroergotamine, lithium, meperidine, pentazocine, selegiline, sumatriptan, TCAs, trazodone, tryptophan).	Serotonin Syndrome (see Warnings).	Additive serotonin effects.	Concurrent use of SSRIs and MAO Inhibitors is contraindicated. Sequential use could be hazardous as well (see Warnings). Clinicians should be aware of the possibility of serious reactions arising from concurrent use of SSRIs and other serotonergic drugs. If possible, the use of 2 or more agents with serotonergic activity should be avoided.
Warfarin	Increased hypoprothrombinemic response.	The mechanism of this effect is unclear. It has been observed that SSRIs may possess an intrinsic inhibitory effect on hemostasis.	Monitor patients on warfarin more closely when an SSRI is initiated or discontinued. Clinicians should bear in mind that there might be an increased risk of bleeding even when the hypoprothrombinemic response is in the desired range.

Adverse Effects: The SSRIs have been associated with numerous adverse effects, some of which occur quite frequently; however, these effects often subside with continued therapy and have rarely resulted in discontinuation. The incidences of some adverse effects have varied among the available SSRIs and indeed when the same drug is used for different indications. Please refer to individual product monographs for detailed accounts of the incidences of adverse effects when used for various indications.

The following is a listing of the adverse effects of SSRIs in general. Within each frequency category, the adverse effects are presented in alphabetical order.

Most common (overall incidence $>10\%$): diarrhea, headache, insomnia, nausea, nervousness, sexual dysfunction (males: mainly ejaculatory delay; females: decreased libido, anorgasmia), somnolence and weight loss.

Relatively common (overall incidence 1 to 10%): abnormal dreams, abdominal pain, anorexia, dizziness, dysmenorrhea, dyspnea, excessive sweating, excessive yawning, flatulence, flu-like symptoms, hot flushes, joint and muscle pain, lymphadenopathy, palpitations, rash, taste perception changes, tremor, visual disturbances, upper respiratory tract infection.

Relatively rare (overal incidence $<1\%$): abnormal bleeding, anemia, hypoglycemia, orthostatic hypotension, platelet function changes, weight gain.

Overdose: Symptoms: Most cases of overdose of SSRIs have involved multiple drug ingestions, including tricyclic antidepressants, benzodiazepines and/or alcohol. Most fatalities involved combined ingestions; however, there have been a

Dosage: As with other antidepressants, it may take several weeks to realize the full clinical benefit of SSRI therapy for any indication. The optimal duration of therapy has not been clearly determined; current practice supports a minimum continuation period of 6 months for first episodes of depression and 1 year or longer for recurrent depression.

To avoid a possible withdrawal reaction, SSRIs may be gradually tapered rather than abruptly discontinued. A 2-week washout period is recommended between therapy with SSRIs and other serotonergic drugs, especially MAO inhibitors. In the case of fluoxetine, a 5-week washout period is advised between discontinuation of fluoxetine and commencement of therapy with MAO inhibitors (see Contraindications, Warnings and Precautions, Drug Interactions).

The absorption of SSRIs is not significantly altered in the presence of food, with the exception of sertraline, whose peak serum level and AUC are significantly increased. It is recommended that sertraline be taken with meals and that the other SSRIs may be taken with food as desired, especially if this helps reduce stomach upset caused by the drug.

Since SSRIs can cause either somnolence or insomnia, the timing of daily doses can be tailored depending on the individual patient's response (i.e., patients who experience somnolence may take their SSRI at bedtime and vice versa).

SSRIs have not been specifically approved in Canada for use in children; however they have been used and continue to be studied in this age group. Further experience with these agents in children is expected to result in specific guidelines for their use in this group.

SSRIs are generally well tolerated in the elderly. Lower initial dosages may be indicated in some elderly patients, e.g., the very elderly or those with comorbid conditions or malnutrition.

SSRIs should be used with caution and at a lower and less frequent dosage in patients with hepatic disease. Caution is also advised when they are used in patients with severe renal impairment.

Patients should be informed that many of the side effects of SSRIs are transient in nature and can mimic the signs and symptoms of the condition being treated.

Table IV lists the adult dosages of the SSRIs for their labeled indications.

Table IV—SSRIs

Dosage

SSRI	Depression	Bulimia Nervosa	Obsessive-Compulsive Disorder	Panic Disorder
Fluoxetine	Initial: 10 to 20 mg daily in the morning.[a,b,c] Usual effective dose: 20 mg daily. Usual maximum: 80 mg daily.[d]	Usual Effective Dose: 60 mg daily.[e,f]	Initial: 20 mg daily in the morning.[a,b,c] Usual effective dose: 20 to 60 mg daily. Usual Maximum: 80 mg daily.[d]	
Fluvoxamine	Initial: 50 mg daily at bedtime.[g] Usual Effective Dose: 100 to 200 mg daily.[h] Usual Maximum: 300 mg daily.		Initial: 50 mg daily at bedtime.[g] Usual Effective Dose: 100 to 300 mg daily. Usual Maximum: 300 mg daily.[h]	
Paroxetine	Initial: 20 mg daily in the morning. Usual Effective Dose: 20 mg daily.[i] Usual Maximum: 50 mg daily.		Initial: 20 mg daily in the morning. Usual Effective Dose: 40 mg daily.[i] Usual Maximum: 60 mg daily	Initial: 10 mg daily in the morning. Usual Effective Dose: 40 mg daily. Usual Maximum: 60 mg daily.
Sertraline	Initial: 50 mg daily with evening meal, or with breakfast.[j] Usual Effective Dose: 50 to 100 mg daily. Usual Maximum: 200 mg daily.			Initial: 25 mg daily.[j] Usual Effective Dose: 50 to 200 mg daily. Usual Maximum: 200 mg daily.

[a] May be taken with food to lessen stomach irritation.
[b] If sedation occurs, dose may be taken at bedtime.
[c] After several weeks, dose may be increased by 20 mg daily at weekly (or longer) intervals.
[d] Higher doses have been used in some patients with refractory depression.
[e] Lower dosage might be effective.
[f] Because SSRIs can cause hyponatremia which may further complicate the electrolyte changes associated with purging behaviors, it may be advisable to assess electrolyte levels prior to initiation of SSRI therapy.
[g] Dosage may be increased every few days by 50 mg daily if necessary.
[h] Doses higher than 150 mg daily should be divided so that the maximum bedtime dose is 150 mg.
[i] If necessary, may be gradually increased by 10 mg daily at 1-to 2-week intervals, to 40 mg daily.
[j] If necessary, dosage may be increased at 1-week or longer intervals.

New Monograph 1998

SELEXID® Ⓟ

Leo

Pivmecillinam HCl

Antibiotic

Pharmacology: Pivmecillinam is an orally administered form of the β-lactam antibiotic mecillinam. This hydrochloride of the pivaloyloxymethyl ester of mecillinam is microbiologically inactive in the ester form. Pivmecillinam is an inactive prodrug which is converted during its absorption from the gastrointestinal tract to the microbiologically active mecillinam, together with formaldehyde and pivalic acid, by non-specific esterases present in most body tissues.

Mecillinam is bactericidal with a different spectrum of activity from other β-lactam antibiotics, in that it is primarily active against gram-negative organisms and relatively ineffective against gram-positive organisms.

The effects of mecillinam on E. coli, and presumably other gram-negative rods are different from those of other β-lactam antibiotics. These unique biochemical and morphological effects of mecillinam on E. coli have been attributed to its high affinity for penicillin binding protein 2, which affects cell shape. Mecillinam does not interact with other penicillin binding proteins which constitute the preferential targets of other β-lactam antibiotics.

Pivmecillinam's absorption is virtually unaffected by food. Although the peak serum level may be reduced and delayed when compared to doses given in the fasting state, the total bioavailability is not affected.

Significantly higher peak serum levels were observed in ambulant volunteers given 400 mg pivmecillinam when compared to those obtained when the subjects were supine.

Studies in a group of 10 fasting volunteers given single doses of 200, 400 and 800 mg have shown that pivmecillinam was well absorbed. Detectable serum levels were present after 15 minutes. The mean peak serum concentrations achieved were 3.3 μg/mL (200 mg), 5.2 μg/mL (400 mg) and 8.1 μg/mL (800 mg). Mean serum curves showed that serum levels and the area under the serum/time curve were increased proportionately with higher doses. The delay before the peak level was achieved and a reduced percentage urinary recovery with the 800 mg dose suggested that a threshold value for absorption had been reached.

A mean peak serum level of 3.9 μg/mL was recorded in 33 patients with urinary tract infections following a single oral dose of 400 mg pivmecillinam.

A mean peak serum level of 4.6 μg/mL was recorded 35 to 100 minutes after dosing in 9 children aged 6 months to 9½ years, given 10 mg pivmecillinam base/kg bodyweight as a suspension.

In healthy volunteers the plasma half-life of mecillinam is approximately 1 hour and there is no significant accumulation on repeated dosing. No accumulation of mecillinam was recorded in the serum of 11 patients receiving 600 mg pivmecillinam twice daily, between the 2nd and 5th day.

In one study of 6 elderly subjects given a 400 mg dose of pivmecillinam, the serum elimination half-life was markedly prolonged (3.97 hours), despite apparently normal renal function, compared to that in healthy volunteers (0.88 hours). The difference appeared to be due to a decreased ability in the elderly to eliminate mecillinam.

The concurrent administration of 1 g probenecid delayed renal excretion of mecillinam in volunteers given a 400 mg dose of pivmecillinam. The average maximum serum level was increased from 4.3 μg/mL to 5.7 μg/mL and the area under the serum/time curve raised from 8.3 to 14.3 μg/mL/hr by taking the dose with probenecid.

The urinary excretion of mecillinam in healthy volunteers in the first 6 hours was 60 to 80%. Mecillinam is excreted partly in the bile and lower levels were present in patients with nonfunctioning compared to functioning gall bladders, with only small amounts excreted in the bile of severely jaundiced subjects.

The conversion of pivmecillinam to mecillinam during absorption results in the release of pivalic acid and formaldehyde from the ester component. Pivalic acid is excreted mainly in the urine in the form of labile conjugates with glycine, and the formaldehyde is oxidized rapidly to formic acid and partly excreted into the respiratory air as carbon dioxide and partly incorporated into normal metabolic pathways as one carbon unit.

Around 50 to 70% of an administered dose (as mecillinam) was removed from the body by hemodialysis during a 4-hour period. Only 4% of a dose was removed by peritoneal dialysis during 14 to 18 hourly exchanges.

Pivmecillinam had only a transient effect on the aerobic fecal flora and in contrast to ampicillin did not increase populations of resistant Enterobacteriaceae, which would be a potential hazard to the patient and contaminate the environment.

Indications: In the treatment of urinary tract infections caused by sensitive strains of E. coli, Klebsiella species, Enterobacter species and Proteus species.

Contraindications: Hypersensitivity to penicillins or cephalosporins.

Warnings: Serious and occasionally fatal hypersensitivity (anaphylactoid) reactions have been reported in patients receiving penicillins. The reactions are more likely to occur in persons with a history of sensitivity to multiple allergens. Before therapy, careful inquiry should be made concerning previous hypersensitivity reactions to penicillins, cephalosporins or other allergens. If an allergic reaction occurs, the administration of pivmecillinam should be discontinued and appropriate therapy instituted.

Precautions: Even though pivmecillinam has exhibited characteristic low toxicity of the penicillins, periodic assessment of renal, hepatic and hematopoietic functions should be made during prolonged therapy.

Pivmecillinam is excreted mostly by the kidneys. In patients with renal impairment, the dosage administered should be reduced in proportion to the degree of loss of renal function. In severe renal function impairment, it is suggested that the plasma level of the drug be monitored to avoid excessive concentrations.

The passage of any penicillin from blood into brain is facilitated by inflamed meninges and during cardiopulmonary bypass. In the presence of these conditions and particularly when accompanied by renal failure, sufficiently high penicillin serum concentrations can be obtained to produce CNS adverse effects. These include myoclonia, convulsive seizure and depressed consciousness. Although these reactions have not yet been reported for pivmecillinam, physicians should be aware of the possibility of their occurrence.

The possibility of superinfections with mycotic or bacterial pathogens should be kept in mind during therapy. If superinfections, usually involving Pseudomonas or Candida, or hypersensitivity reactions occur, the drug should be discontinued and/or appropriate therapy instituted.

Long-term treatment or frequently repeated treatment courses should be used with caution as pivmecillinam has been associated with an increased excretion of carnitine in urine and a reduction of serum carnitine. During absorption pivmecillinam is hydrolyzed to pivalic acid and mecillinam. Pivalic acid is excreted partly as a conjugate with carnitine. Treatment with pivalic acid liberating antibiotics for a duration of 22 and 30 months in children resulted in total muscle carnitine depletion to 10% of reference values, however, no adverse clinical effects were reported which could be associated with primary or secondary carnitine deficiency. Following 7 to 10 days treatment at the highest recommended doses of

Selexid (cont'd)

pivmecillinam there was a significant reduction in serum carnitine which returned to the normal range within 2 weeks of stopping therapy. Despite these reductions in serum carnitine, total body stores of carnitine were reduced by approximately 10%. The increased excretion of carnitine associated with the use of pivmecillinam is considered to be without clinical significance in short-term treatment. Adverse effects which could be related to carnitine deficiency occur with similar frequency as with other antibiotics not liberating pivalic acid. Carnitine is synthesized in the liver and kidney of man. Carnitine is also available from the diet in meat and dairy products; however, endogenous biosynthesis can meet normal metabolic needs in vegetarians. Carnitine functions in the transport of fatty acids across the mitochondrial membrane as an essential cofactor in fatty acid oxidation. Almost all the body stores of carnitine (100 to 200 mmols, 16 to 32 g) are found in muscle (98%), liver and kidney (1.6%) and serum (0.4%). In patients with the extremely rare condition of carnitine deficiency, treatment with pivmecillinam should be avoided. Concurrent treatment with valproic acid or other medications liberating privalic acid should be avoided.

Neither measurement of serum carnitine nor concomitant administration of prophylactic doses of carnitine is recommended as a general measure for patients receiving pivalic acid liberating antibiotics.

Children: Endogenous carnitine production begins at birth and in normal children is fully developed during the first months of life. Although no adverse events which can be explained by a pivalic acid induced reduction in carnitine have been documented, use of pivmecillinam in children less than 3 months of age should be avoided.

Pregnancy and *Lactation:* The safety of pivmecillinam in the treatment of pregnant women or nursing mothers has not been established. Therefore, in nursing mothers an alternate feeding method should be considered.

Adverse Effects: As with other β-lactam antibiotics, it is expected that adverse reactions will be essentially limited to hypersensitivity phenomena. The following adverse reactions can occur during therapy:

Hypersensitivity: generalized: drug fever and anaphylactoid reactions; skin: skin rashes, urticaria, itching and exanthema.

Gastrointestinal: nausea, vomiting, anorexia, dyspepsia and diarrhea.

Hematological: anemia, thrombocytopenia, thrombocytopenic purpura, eosinophilia, leukopenia and agranulocytosis have been reported during therapy with β-lactam antibiotics. These reactions are usually reversible on discontinuation of therapy and are believed to be hypersensitivity phenomena.

Hepatic and Renal: Transient increases in alkaline phosphatase and transaminase levels have been observed in some patients. Clinical manifestations of hepatic and renal disorders, which could be ascribed solely to this product have not been observed.

Other Reactions: headache, giddiness and lethargy.

Overdose: Symptoms and Treatment: There is no experience of overdosage. However, excessive doses are likely to induce nausea, vomiting and gastritis. Treatment should be restricted to symptomatic and supportive measures.

Dosage: 200 mg pivmecillinam HCl is equivalent to 185 mg pivmecillinam (137 mg mecillinam). Adults and children weighing more than 40 kg:

For acute uncomplicated cystitis and urethritis: 2 to 4 tablets (equivalent to 370 mg to 740 mg pivmecillinam) daily in 2 or 3 equal divided doses.

In acute uncomplicated cystitis, therapy should be continued for at least 3 days or at least 48 hours after signs and symptoms of infection have disappeared.

For chronic urinary tract infections (see Precautions regarding long-term use): 2 tablets (370 mg pivmecillinam) 3 or 4 times daily. Continue therapy until urine is sterile.

Supplied: Each white film-coated tablet with convex surface, an Assyrian lion printed on 1 side and the number 137 on the other, contains: pivmecillinam HCl 200 mg equivalent to pivmecillinam 185 mg (mecillinam 137 mg). Nonmedicinal Ingredients: cellulose microcrystalline (Avicel pH 102), hpm cellulose 6 CPS, hydroxypropyl cellulose, magnesium stearate. Bottles of 100. Store at room temperature.

(Shown in Product Recognition Section)

SENOKOT® Preparations

Purdue Frederick

Standardized Sennosides

Peristaltic Stimulant

Description: The laxative agent in Senokot is a natural vegetable derivative (senna), standardized for predictable results. The principal constituents of Senokot are senna glycosides. These include sennosides A & B, and the glycoside derivatives of rhein and chrysophanic acid. These glycosides, when converted into aglycones in the colon, function as laxative agents.

Indications: Granules, Syrup and Tablets: For relief of functional constipation (chronic or occasional).

Suppositories: For use when more rapid evacuation is desired than with oral administration; when the oral route is impractical or contraindicated; when the use of an enema is inconvenient, disturbing to the patient, or potentially painful; in preparation for surgery (except in "acute abdomen") and for diagnostic procedures requiring removal of residual air and gas pockets in the colon; for treatment of postpartum constipation; and in all types of functional constipation where a suppository is preferred to, or more convenient than, oral laxatives.

Contraindications: The "acute abdomen".

Precautions: If griping occurs, reduce dosage. Administer with caution to nursing mothers. Frequent or prolonged use may result in dependence on laxatives.

Dosage: Administer preferably at bedtime.

Granules: Adults: 1 to 2 level teaspoons at bedtime as required. Maximum, 2 level teaspoons twice a day.

Pregnancy and Children (6 to 12 years): 1/2 to 1 level teaspoon at bedtime, not to exceed 1 teaspoon twice a day.

Children (2 to 5 years): 1/4 to 1/2 level teaspoon not to exceed 1/2 teaspoon twice a day.

Suppositories: Adults: unwrap 1 suppository, moisten with water, and insert in the rectum close to the posterior rectal wall; children over 25 kg, one-half suppository.

Syrup: Adults: 10 to 15 mL at bedtime, as required. Maximum, 15 mL twice a day.

Pregnancy and Children (6 to 12 years): 5 to 10 mL at bedtime, not to exceed 10 mL twice a day.

Children (2 to 5 years): 3 to 5 mL. Maximum 5 mL twice a day.

Infants (less than 2 years): Consult physician.

Adjust dosage as necessary.

Tablets: Adults: 2 to 4 tablets at bedtime, as required. Maximum, 4 tablets twice a day.

Pregnancy and children (6 to 12 years): 1 to 2 tablets at bedtime, not to exceed 2 tablets twice a day.

Supplied: Granules: Light brown, each level teaspoonful (3 g) contains: standardized sennosides 15 mg with cocoa malt flavoring 0.3 g and 2.2 g sugar equivalent to 36.2 kJ (8.8 kcal). Sodium: $<$1 mmol/3 g. Tartrazine-free. Bottles of 100 and 200 g.

Suppositories: Each brown suppository contains: standardized sennosides 30 mg in a dispersible vehicle containing guar gum, a surfactant, and hydrogenated cocoanut oil. Individually packed in white plastic, imprinted "Senokot". Boxes of 6. Store at room temperature.

Syrup: Each mL contains: standardized sennosides 1.7 mg. pH: 5.2 to 5.8. Also contains parabens 220 mg/100 mL and alcohol 6 g/100 mL. Sugar 66 g/100 mL equivalent to 1 246 kJ (304 kcal). Sodium and tartrazine-free. Bottles of 100, 250 and 500 mL. Expiration period: 2 years from date of manufacture.

Tablets: Each "S" stamped, light brown, sugar free tablet contains: standardized sennosides 8.6 mg. Also contains lactose and cornstarch. Sodium- and tartrazine-free. Packages of 10, bottles of 30, 100 and 1 000 tablets and unit dose in boxes of 1 000.

(Shown in Product Recognition Section)

SENOKOT®•S

Purdue Frederick

Standardized Sennosides—Docusate Sodium

Peristaltic Stimulant—Surfactant

Description: The laxative agent in Senokot•S is a natural vegetable derivative (senna), standardized for predictable results. The principal constituents of Senokot•S are senna glycosides. These include sennosides A & B, and the glycoside derivatives of rhein and chrysophanic acid. These glycosides, when converted into aglycones in the colon, function as laxative agents.

Docusate sodium is a surface active agent useful in the medical management of certain types of constipation and fecal impaction.

Indications: Relief of functional constipation through combined stool softening and peristaltic stimulation. Specifically indicated for postpartum patients, for use by patients with heart disease where straining at stool must be avoided, and in constipation in the presence of hemorrhoids, anal fissures or other conditions where hard, dry stools may cause discomfort.

Contraindications: The "acute abdomen".

Precautions: If griping occurs, subsequent dosage should be reduced. Administer with caution to nursing mothers. Frequent or prolonged use may result in dependence on laxatives. Do not administer concomitantly with mineral oil since the docusate sodium component of Senokot•S may increase absorption of oil.

Dosage: Adults: 1 to 2 tablets at bedtime, as required. Maximum, 4 tablets twice a day.

Pregnancy and Children (6 to 12 years): ½ to 1 tablet at bedtime, not to exceed 2 tablets twice a day.

Supplied: Each orange, film-coated tablet, stamped S/S on one side, contains: standardized sennosides 8.6 mg and docusate sodium 50 mg. Also contains cornstarch. Sodium: $<$1 mmol (2.6 mg). Tartrazine-free. Packages of 10, bottles of 20, 60 and 1 000.

(Shown in Product Recognition Section)

SENSORCAINE®
SENSORCAINE® with Epinephrine
SENSORCAINE® FORTE

Astra

Bupivacaine HCl
Bupivacaine HCl—Epinephrine
Bupivacaine HCl—Epinephrine

Local Anesthetic

Pharmacology: Mechanism of Action: As with other local anesthetics, bupivacaine blocks the generation and the conduction of nerve impulses.

Onset of Action: The onset of action with bupivacaine is rapid and anesthesia is long-lasting. As with other local anesthetics, the duration of action depends on the injection site, the route of administration, and the concentration and volume of anesthetic. It has also been noted that there is a period of analgesia that persists after the return of sensation, during which time the need for potent analgesics is reduced.

Systemic absorption of local anesthetics produces effects on the cardiovascular and central nervous systems. At blood concentrations achieved with therapeutic doses, changes in cardiac conduction, excitability, refractoriness, contractility, and peripheral vascular resistance are minimal. However, toxic blood concentrations depress cardiac conduction and excitability, which may lead to atrioventricular block, ventricular arrhythmias and to cardiac arrest. In addition, myocardial contractility is depressed and peripheral vasodilation occurs, leading to decreased cardiac output and arterial blood pressure. Clinical reports and animal research suggest that these cardiovascular changes are more likely to occur with bupivacaine than other local anesthetics.

Following systemic absorption, local anesthetics can produce CNS stimulation, depression or both. Apparent central stimulation is usually manifested as restlessness, tremors and shivering, progressing to convulsions, followed by depression and coma, progressing ultimately to respiratory arrest. However, the local anesthetics have a primary depressant effect on the medulla and on higher centres. The depressed stage may occur without a prior excited stage.

Pharmacokinetics: The rate of systemic absorption of local anesthetics is dependent upon the total dose and concentration of drug administered and the route of administration.

Peak levels of bupivacaine in the blood are reached in 20 to 45 minutes, depending on injection site and type of block. A decline to insignificant levels is achieved during the next 3 to 6 hours.

The half-life of bupivacaine in adults is 3.5±2 hours and in neonates 8.1 to 14 hours. The elderly may have a prolonged half-life. Bupivacaine is primarily metabolized in the liver via conjugation with glucuronic acid. The major metabolite of bupivacaine is 2,6-pipecoloxylidine.

Local anesthetics are bound to plasma proteins in varying degrees. Generally, the lower the plasma concentration of drug, the higher the percentage of drug bound to plasma proteins.

Local anesthetics appear to cross the placenta by passive diffusion. The rate and degree of diffusion is governed by: the degree of plasma protein binding, the degree of ionization, and the degree of lipid solubility. Fetal/maternal ratios of local anesthetics appear to be inversely related to the degree of plasma protein binding, because only the free, unbound drug is available for placental transfer. Bupivacaine, with a high protein binding capacity (95%), has a low fetal/maternal ratio (0.2 to 0.4). The extent of placental transfer is also determined by the degree of ionization and lipid solubility of the drug.

Lipid soluble, non-ionized drugs readily enter the fetal blood from the maternal circulation.

Depending upon the route of administration, local anesthetics are distributed to some extent to all body tissues, with high concentrations found in highly perfused organs such as the liver, lungs, heart and brain.

Various pharmacokinetic parameters of the local anesthetics can be significantly altered by the presence of hepatic or renal disease, factors affecting urinary pH, renal blood flow, the route of drug administration, the age of the patient and certain concomitant medication. Patients with hepatic disease, especially those with severe hepatic disease, may be more susceptible to the potential toxicities of the amide-type local anesthetics.

The acute toxicity of bupivacaine is higher than that of mepivacaine, lidocaine or prilocaine.

The kidney is the main excretory organ for most local anesthetics and their metabolites. Urinary excretion is affected by renal perfusion and factors affecting urinary pH. Only 6% of bupivacaine is excreted unchanged in the urine.

When administered in recommended doses and concentrations, bupivacaine solutions do not ordinarily produce irritation or tissue damage and do not cause methemoglobinemia.

Indications: Local or Regional Anesthesia: Sensorcaine or Sensorcaine with Epinephrine solutions are indicated for the production of local or regional anesthesia or analgesia for surgery and for obstetrical procedures. Standard procedures for infiltration, peripheral nerve block or epidural block should be observed.

Sensorcaine solutions are not recommended for i.v. regional anesthesia (Bier block) (see Contraindications).

Standard textbooks should be consulted to determine the accepted procedures and techniques for the administration of bupivacaine.

Dental Anesthesia: Sensorcaine Forte 0.5% is indicated for the production of local anesthesia for dental procedures by infiltration injection or nerve block in adults. Sensorcaine Forte is not recommended for use in children.

Contraindications: In obstetrical paracervical block anesthesia. Its use by this technique has resulted in fetal bradycardia and death.

Patients with a known hypersensitivity to bupivacaine or to any local anesthetic agent of the amide type or to other components of bupivacaine solutions. Local anesthetic procedures should not be used when there is inflammation and/or sepsis in the region of the proposed injection.

For i.v. regional anesthesia (Bier block) since unintentional leakage of bupivacaine over the tourniquet might cause systemic toxic reactions. Cardiac arrest and death have occurred (see Dosage).

Local anesthetics are contraindicated for epidural anesthesia in patients with pronounced hypotension, such as cardiogenic shock and hypovolemic shock.

Warnings: Local anesthetics should only be employed by clinicians who are well versed in diagnosis and management of dose-related toxicity and other acute emergencies which might arise from the block to be employed, and then only after ensuring the immediate availability of oxygen, other resuscitative drugs, cardiopulmonary resuscitative equipment, and the personnel resources needed for proper management of toxic reactions and related emergencies (see Adverse Effects and Precautions). Delay in proper management of dose-related toxicity, under ventilation from any cause and/or altered sensitivity may lead to the development of acidosis, cardiac arrest and, possibly, death.

It is essential that aspiration for blood or CSF (where applicable) be done prior to injecting any local anesthetic, both the original dose and all subsequent doses, to avoid intravascular or subarachnoid injection. However, a negative aspiration does not ensure against an intravascular or subarachnoid injection.

Sensorcaine with Epinephrine and Sensorcaine Forte solutions which contain a vasoconstrictor should be used with extreme caution for patients whose medical history and physical evaluation suggest the existence of hypertension, arteriosclerotic heart disease, cerebral vascular insufficiency, heart block, peripheral vascular disorder, thyrotoxicosis and diabetes, etc., as well as patients receiving drugs likely to produce alterations in blood pressure. These solutions should also be used cautiously in areas with limited blood supply such as the fingers, the toes, the ears, the nose and the penis.

Bupivacaine or other vasopressors should not be used concomitantly with ergot-type oxytocic drugs, because a severe persistent hypertension may occur. Likewise, Sensorcaine with Epinephrine and Sensorcaine Forte or solutions containing bupivacaine and another vasoconstrictor should be used with extreme caution in patients receiving MAO inhibitors or antidepressants of the triptyline or imipramine types, because severe prolonged hypertension may result.

Sensorcaine with Epinephrine and Sensorcaine Forte solutions contain sodium metabisulfite, a sulfite that may cause allergic-type reactions including anaphylactic symptoms and life-threatening or less severe asthmatic episodes in certain susceptible people. The overall prevalence of sulfite sensitivity in the general population is unknown and probably low. Sulfite sensitivity is seen more frequently in asthmatic than in nonasthmatic people.

Prior use of chloroprocaine, or any other local anesthetic, may interfere with subsequent use of bupivacaine. Because of this, and because safety of intercurrent use with bupivacaine and other local anesthetics has not been established, such use is not recommended.

Precautions: The safety and effectiveness of local anesthetics depend on proper dosage, correct technique, adequate precautions and readiness for emergencies. Resuscitative equipment, oxygen and other resuscitative drugs should be available for immediate use (see Warnings and Adverse Effects). During major regional nerve blocks, the patients should have i.v. fluids running via an indwelling catheter to assure a functioning i.v. pathway. **The lowest dosage of local anesthetic that results in effective anesthesia should be used to avoid high plasma levels and serious adverse effects. Injections should be made slowly, with frequent aspirations before and during the injection to avoid intravascular injection.**

Injection of repeated doses of local anesthetics may cause significant increases in plasma levels with each repeated dose due to slow accumulation of the drug or its metabolites or to slow metabolic degradation. Tolerance to elevated blood levels varies with the physical condition of the patient. Debilitated, elderly patients and acutely ill patients should be given reduced doses commensurate with their age and physical condition. Local anesthetics should also be used with caution in patients with hypotension or heart block.

Careful and constant monitoring of cardiovascular and respiratory vital signs (adequacy of ventilation) and the patient's state of consciousness should be performed after each local anesthetic injection. It should be kept in mind at such times that restlessness, anxiety, incoherent speech, lightheadedness, numbness and tingling of the mouth and lips, metallic taste, tinnitus, dizziness, blurred vision, tremors, twitching, depression, or drowsiness may be early warning signs of CNS toxicity.

Because amide-type local anesthetics such as bupivacaine are metabolized by the liver, these drugs, especially repeat doses, should be used cautiously in patients with hepatic disease. Patients with severe hepatic disease, because of their inability to metabolize local anesthetics normally, are at a greater risk of developing toxic plasma concentrations. Local anesthetics should also be used with caution in patients with impaired cardiovascular function because they may be less able to compensate for functional changes associated with the prolongation of AV conduction produced by these drugs.

Use in Epidural Anesthesia: During epidural administration, bupivacaine should be administered in incremental doses of 3 to 5 mL with sufficient time between doses to detect toxic manifestations of unintentional intravascular or intrathecal injection.

Frequent aspirations should be performed before and during each supplemental injection. An intravascular injection is still possible even if aspirations for blood are negative.

During the administration of epidural anesthesia, it is recommended that a test dose be administered initially and the effects monitored before the full dose is given. When using a "continuous" catheter technique, test doses should be given prior to both the original and all reinforcing doses, because plastic tubing in the epidural space can migrate into a blood vessel or through the dura. When clinical conditions permit, the test dose should contain epinephrine (10 to 15 μg have been suggested) to serve as a warning of unintentional intravascular injection. If injected into a blood vessel, this amount of epinephrine is likely to produce a transient "epinephrine response" within 45 seconds, consisting of an increase in heart rate and systolic blood pressure, circumoral pallor, palpitations and nervousness in the unsedated patient. The sedated patient may exhibit only a pulse rate increase of 20 or more beats per minute for 15 or more seconds. Therefore, following the test dose, the heart rate should be monitored for a heart rate increase. Patients on beta-blockers may not manifest changes in heart rate, but blood pressure monitoring can detect an evanescent rise in systolic blood pressure. The test dose should also contain 10 to 15 mg of bupivacaine solution or an equivalent dose of a short-acting amide anesthetic such as 30 to 40 mg of lidocaine, to detect an unintentional intrathecal administration. This will be manifested within a few minutes by signs of spinal block (e.g. decreased sensation of the buttocks, paresis of the legs, or in the sedated patient, absent knee jerk).

Dental Anesthesia: Because of the long duration of anesthesia, when Sensorcaine Forte 0.5% is used for dental injections, patients should be cautioned about the possibility of inadvertent trauma to tongue, lips, and buccal mucosa and advised not to chew solid foods or test the anesthetized area by biting or probing.

Changes in sensorium such as excitation, disorientation, drowsiness, may be early indications of a high blood level of the drug and may occur following inadvertent intravascular administration or rapid absorption of Sensorcaine Forte 0.5%. Solutions containing a vasoconstrictor should be used cautiously in areas with limited blood supply, in the presence of diseases that may adversely affect the patient's cardiovascular system, or in patients with peripheral vascular disease.

Use in Head and Neck Area: Small doses of local anesthetics injected into the head and neck area, including dental and stellate ganglion blocks, may produce adverse reactions similar to systemic toxicity seen with unintentional intravascular injections of larger doses. Confusion, convulsions, respiratory depression and/or respiratory arrest, and cardiovascular stimulation or depression leading to cardiac arrest, have been reported. These reactions may be due to intra-arterial injection of the local anesthetic with retrograde flow to the cerebral circulation. Patients receiving these blocks should have their circulation and respiration monitored and be constantly observed. Resuscitative equipment and personnel for treating adverse reactions should be immediately available. Dosage recommendations should not be exceeded (see Dosage).

Drug Interactions: See Warnings concerning solutions containing a vasoconstrictor. Bupivacaine should be used with caution in patients receiving antiarrhythmic drugs, since the toxic effects are additive.

If sedatives are employed to reduce patient apprehension, use reduced doses, since local anesthetic agents, like sedatives, are CNS depressants which in combination may have an additive effect.

Bupivacaine should be used cautiously in persons with known drug allergies or sensitivities, particularly to the amide-type local anesthetics.

Serious dose-related cardiac arrhythmias may occur if preparations containing a vasoconstrictor such as epinephrine are employed in patients during or following the administration of chloroform, halothane, cyclopropane, trichloroethylene or other related agents. In deciding whether to use these products concurrently in the same patient, the combined action of both agents upon the myocardium, the concentration and volume of vasoconstrictor used, and the time since injection, when applicable, should be taken into account.

Clinically Significant Drug Interactions: The administration of local anesthetic solutions containing epinephrine or norepinephrine to patients receiving MAO inhibitors or tricyclic antidepressants may produce severe, prolonged hypertension. Concurrent use of these agents should generally be avoided. In situations when concurrent therapy is necessary, careful patient monitoring is essential. Concurrent administration of vasopressor drugs and of ergot-type oxytocic drugs may cause severe, persistent hypertension or cerebrovascular accidents.

Phenothiazines and butyrophenones may reduce or reverse the pressor effect of epinephrine.

The H_2-antagonists cimetidine and ranitidine have been shown to reduce the clearance of bupivacaine; ranitidine to a lesser degree than cimetidine. Concomitant administration may increase likelihood of toxicity of bupivacaine.

Carcinogenesis, Mutagenesis and Impairment of Fertility: Long-term studies in animals of most local anesthetics, including bupivacaine, to evaluate the carcinogenic potential have not been conducted. Mutagenic potential or the effect

Sensorcaine (cont'd)

on fertility have not been determined. There is no evidence from human data that bupivacaine may be carcinogenic or mutagenic or that it impairs fertility.

Pregnancy: Decreased pup survival in rats and embryocidal effect in rabbits have been observed when bupivacaine was administered to these species in doses comparable to 9 and 5 times, respectively, the maximum recommended daily human dose (400 mg).

There are no adequate and well-controlled studies in pregnant women of the effect of bupivacaine on the developing fetus. Bupivacaine solutions should be used during pregnancy only if the potential benefit justifies the potential risk to the fetus. This does not exclude the use of bupivacaine solutions at term for obstetrical anesthesia or analgesia.

Labor and Delivery: Bupivacaine solutions are contraindicated in obstetrical paracervical block anesthesia.

Local anesthetics rapidly cross the placenta, and when used for epidural block anesthesia, can cause varying degrees of maternal, fetal and neonatal toxicity (see Pharmacology). The incidence and degree of toxicity depend upon the procedure performed, the type and amount of drug used, and the technique of drug administration. Adverse reactions in the parturient, fetus and neonate involve alterations of the CNS, peripheral vascular tone and cardiac function. Maternal hypotension has resulted from regional anesthesia. Local anesthetics produce vasodilation by blocking sympathetic nerves. Elevating the patient's legs and positioning her on her left side will help prevent decreases in blood pressure. The fetal heart rate also should be monitored continuously, and electronic fetal monitoring is highly advisable.

Epidural anesthesia may alter the forces of parturition through changes in uterine contractility or maternal expulsive efforts. Epidural anesthesia has been reported to prolong the second stage of labor by removing the parturient's urge to bear down or by interfering with motor function. The use of bupivacaine 0.25% has been shown to interfere less than the 0.5% solution. Obstetrical anesthesia may increase the need for forceps assistance.

The use of some local anesthetic drug products during labor and delivery may be followed by diminished muscle strength and tone for the first day or two of life. This has not been reported with bupivacaine solutions.

It is extremely important to avoid aortocaval compression by the gravid uterus during administration of regional block to parturients. To do this, the patient must be maintained in the left lateral decubitus position, or a blanket roll or sandbag may be placed beneath the right hip and the gravid uterus displaced to the left.

Lactation: Because bupivacaine enters breast milk in small quantities at therapeutic dose levels, caution should be exercised when this drug is administered to nursing women.

Children: Until further experience is gained in children younger than 2 years, administration of bupivacaine solution in this age group is not recommended.

Adverse Effects: Reactions to bupivacaine are characteristic of those associated with other amide-type local anesthetics. A major cause of adverse reactions to this group of drugs may be associated with its excessive plasma levels, which may be due to overdosage, unintentional intravascular injection or slow metabolic degradation.

Systemic: The most commonly encountered acute adverse experiences that demand immediate countermeasures are related to the CNS and the cardiovascular system. These adverse experiences are generally dose related and due to high plasma levels which may result from overdosage, rapid absorption from the injection site, diminished tolerance or from unintentional intravascular injection of the local anesthetic solution. In addition to systemic dose-related toxicity, unintentional subarachnoid injection of drug during the intended performance of lumbar epidural block or nerve blocks near the vertebral column (especially in the head and neck region) may result in under ventilation or apnea (''Total or High Spinal''). Also, hypotension due to loss of sympathetic tone and respiratory paralysis or under ventilation due to cephalad extension of the motor level of anesthesia may occur. This may lead to secondary cardiac arrest, if untreated. Factors influencing plasma protein binding, such as acidosis, systemic diseases that alter protein production or competition with other drugs for protein binding sites, may diminish individual tolerance.

CNS: These are characterized by excitation and/or depression. Restlessness, anxiety, dizziness, tinnitus, blurred vision or tremors may occur, possibly proceeding to convulsions. However, excitement may be transient or absent, with depression being the first manifestation of an adverse reaction. This may quickly be followed by drowsiness merging into unconsciousness and respiratory arrest. Other CNS effects may be nausea, vomiting, chills and constriction of the pupils. The incidence of convulsions associated with the use of local anesthetics varies with the procedure used and the total dose administered.

Cardiovascular: High doses or unintentional intravascular injection may lead to high plasma levels and related depression of the myocardium, decreased cardiac output, heart block, hypotension, bradycardia, ventricular arrhythmias, including ventricular tachycardia and ventricular fibrillation and cardiac arrest. Reactions due to systemic absorption may be either slow or rapid in onset. Cardiovascular collapse and cardiac arrest can occur rapidly (see Warnings, Precautions and Overdose). In some patients, bupivacaine may cause a marked peripheral vasoconstriction in unanesthetized areas which may last for several hours.

Allergic: Allergic type reactions are rare and may occur as a result of sensitivity to local anesthetics of the amide-type. These reactions are characterized by signs such as urticaria, pruritus, erythema, angioneurotic edema (including laryngeal edema), tachycardia, sneezing, nausea, vomiting, dizziness, syncope, excessive sweating, elevated temperature, and possibly, anaphylactoid symptomatology (including severe hypotension). Cross-sensitivity among members of the amide-type local anesthetic group has been reported. The usefulness of screening for sensitivity has not been definitely established.

Neurologic: The incidence of adverse neurologic reactions associated with the use of local anesthetics may be related to the total dose of local anesthetic administered and is also dependent upon the particular drug used, the route of administration and the physical status of the patient. Many of these effects may be related to local anesthetic techniques, with or without a contribution from the drug.

In the practice of lumbar epidural block, occasional unintentional penetration of the subarachnoid space by the catheter or needle may occur. Subsequent adverse effects may depend partially on the amount of drug administered intrathecally and the physiological and physical effects of a dural puncture. A high spinal is characterized by paralysis of the legs, loss of consciousness, respiratory paralysis and bradycardia.

Neurologic effects following unintentional subarachnoid administration during epidural anesthesia may include spinal block by varying magnitude (including high or total spinal block), hypotension secondary to spinal block, urinary retention, fecal and urinary incontinence, loss of perineal sensation and sexual function, persistent anesthesia, paresthesia, weakness, paralysis of the lower extremities and loss of sphincter control, all of which may have slow, incomplete or no recovery; headache, backache, septic meningitis, meningismus, slowing of labor, increased incidence of forceps delivery, or cranial nerve palsies due to traction or nerves from loss of cerebrospinal fluid.

Overdose: Symptoms and Treatment: Acute emergencies from local anesthetics are generally related to high plasma levels encountered during therapeutic use of local anesthetics or to unintended subarachnoid injection of local anesthetic solution (see Adverse Effects, Warnings and Precautions).

Management of Local Anesthetic Emergencies: The first consideration is prevention, best accomplished by careful and constant monitoring of cardiovascular and respiratory vital signs and the patient's state of consciousness after each local anesthetic injection. At the first sign of change, oxygen should be administered.

The first step in the management of systemic toxic reactions, as well as under ventilation or apnea due to unintentional subarachnoid injection of drug solution, consists of immediate attention to the establishment and maintenance of a patent airway and effective assisted or controlled ventilation with 100% oxygen with a delivery system capable of permitting immediate positive airway pressure by mask. This may prevent convulsions if they have not already occurred.

If necessary, use drugs to control the convulsions. Succinylcholine given i.v. will paralyze the patient without depressing the central nervous or cardiovascular systems and facilitate ventilation. A bolus i.v. dose of diazepam or thiopental will permit ventilation and counteract CNS stimulation, but these drugs also depress the CNS, respiratory and cardiac function, add to postictal depression, and may result in apnea.

I.V. barbiturates, anticonvulsant agents, or muscle relaxants should only be administered by those familiar with their use. Immediately after the institution of these ventilatory measures, the adequacy of the circulation should be evaluated. Supportive treatment of circulatory depression may require administration of i.v. fluids, and when appropriate, a vasopressor dictated by the clinical situation (such as ephedrine or epinephrine to enhance myocardial contractile force).

If difficulty is encountered in the maintenance of a patent airway or if prolonged ventilatory support (assisted or controlled) is indicated, endotracheal intubation, employing drugs and techniques familiar to the clinician, may be indicated after initial administration of oxygen by mask.

Recent clinical data from patients experiencing local anesthetic induced convulsions demonstrated rapid development of hypoxia, hypercarbia and acidosis with bupivacaine within a minute of the onset of convulsions. These observations suggest the oxygen consumption and carbon dioxide production are greatly increased during local anesthetic convulsions and emphasize the importance of immediate and effective ventilation with oxygen which may avoid cardiac arrest.

If not treated immediately, convulsions with simultaneous hypoxia, hypercarbia and acidosis, plus myocardial depression from the direct effects of the local anesthetic may result in cardiac arrhythmias, bradycardia, asystole, ventricular fibrillation or cardiac arrest. Respiratory abnormalities, including apnea, may occur. Under ventilation or apnea due to unintentional subarachnoid injection of local anesthetic solution may produce these same signs and also lead to cardiac arrest if ventilatory support is not instituted. If cardiac arrest should occur, a successful outcome may require prolonged resuscitative efforts.

The supine position is dangerous in pregnant women at term because of aortocaval compression by the gravid uterus. Therefore, during treatment of systemic toxicity, maternal hypotension or fetal bradycardia following regional block, the parturient should be maintained in the left lateral decubitus position if possible, or manual displacement of the uterus off the great vessels be accomplished.

The mean seizure dosage of bupivacaine in Rhesus monkeys was found to be 4.4 mg/kg with mean arterial plasma concentration of 4.5 μg/mL. The i.v. and s.c. LD_{50} in mice are 6 to 8 mg/kg and 38 to 54 mg/kg respectively.

Dosage: The dosage varies and depends upon the area to be anesthetized, the number of neuronal segments to be blocked, the depth of anesthesia and degree of muscle relaxation required, individual tolerance, tissue vascularity and the technique of anesthesia. The lowest concentration of anesthetic and the lowest dosage needed to provide effective anesthesia should be administered. The rapid injection of a large volume of local anesthetic solution should be avoided and fractional doses should be used when feasible. For specific techniques and procedures, refer to standard textbooks.

For most indications, the duration of anesthesia with bupivacaine solutions is such that a single dose is sufficient. Clinical experience is inadequate to permit precise recommendations about multiple dosage or intermittent dose techniques (see Maximum Dosage).

Bupivacaine is contraindicated in obstetrical paracervical block and for use in i.v. regional anesthesia (Bier block).

Adults: The dosages in Table I (on following page) are recommended as a guide for use in the average adult, defined as a healthy 70 kg young male. Higher dosages are not recommended for patients weighing more than 70 kg. For elderly or debilitated patients, these dosages should be reduced. The use of Sensorcaine solutions containing epinephrine will prolong the anesthetic action.

Children: Bupivacaine solutions can be used in children over 2 years of age. A guide of recommended dosages is provided in Table II (on following page).

Maximum Dosage: The maximum dosage limit must be determined by evaluating the size and physical status of the patient and considering the usual rate of systemic absorption from a specific injection site. Most experience to date is with single doses up to 175 mg of bupivacaine and 225 mg of bupivacaine with epinephrine. It is recommended that the dose of bupivacaine at any time should not exceed 2 mg/kg or 150 mg. Doses should not be repeated more frequently than every 3 to 6 hours and total daily dose should not exceed 400 mg.

Use in Epidural Anesthesia: For epidural anesthesia, a test dose of a local anesthetic should be administered (see Precautions). Sensorcaine with Epinephrine 0.5%, 2 to 3 mL, can be used if a vasoconstrictor is not contraindicated (see Table I). Verbal contact and repeated monitoring of heart rate and blood pressure should be maintained for 5 minutes after the test dose. In the absence of signs of subarachnoid or intravascular injection, the main dose may be given.

During epidural administration, bupivacaine solutions should be administered slowly in incremental doses of 3 to 5 mL, with sufficient time between doses to detect toxic manifestations of unintentional intravascular or intrathecal injection. No more than 50 to 150 mg at any dosing interval is recommended.

Table I—Sensorcaine

Dosage Recommendations in Adults (70 kg) for Sensorcaine Solutions

Type of Block	Conc. (%)	Each dose mL	mg	Motor Block[a]
Local infiltration	0.25	up to max.	up to max.	
Epidural (for vaginal delivery and vacuum extraction)	0.5 0.25	10–20 10–20	50–100 25–50	moderate to complete partial to moderate
Epidural (for Caesarean section)	0.5	15–30	75–150	complete
Epidural (for surgery)	0.5	15–30	75–150	
Epidural (test dose)	0.5[b]	2–3	10–15	
Brachial Plexus	0.5 0.25	10–30 10–40	50–150 25–100	moderate to complete moderate
Caudal	0.5 0.25	15–30 15–30	75–150 37.5–75	moderate to complete moderate
Peripheral nerves	0.5 0.25	5 to max. 5 to max.	25 to max. 12.5 to max.	moderate to complete moderate to complete
Sympathetic[c]	0.25	20–50	50–125	
Dental Anesthesia				
Infiltration	0.5[b]	1 to 1.8	5 to 9	
Nerve Block	0.5[b]	1.8 to 3.6	9 to 18	

[a] With continuous techniques, repeat doses increase the degree of motor block. The first repeat dose of 0.5% may produce complete motor block. Intercostal nerve block with 0.25% may also produce complete motor block for intra-abdominal surgery.
[b] With epinephrine 1:200 000 (5 μg/mL).
[c] See Precautions.

Table II—Sensorcaine

Dosage Recommendations in Children (over 2 years of age) for Sensorcaine Solutions

Type of Block	Conc. (%)	Each Dose mL/kg	mg/kg
Caudal	0.25 0.5	0.4–0.8 0.2–0.4	1–2 1–2
Lumbar Epidural	0.25 0.5	0.6–1.0 0.3–0.5	1.5–2.5 1.5–2.5
Dorsal (Penile)	0.25 (without epinephrine) 0.5 (without epinephrine)	0.1–0.2 0.06–0.1	0.3–0.5 0.3–0.5
Intercostal	0.25* 0.5*	0.8–1.2 0.4–0.6	2–3 2–3
Local infiltration for hernia repair	0.25 0.5	0.2–0.8 0.1–0.4	0.5–2 0.5–2

Note: The use of bupivacaine for anesthesia and/or analgesia may be supplementary to light general anesthesia.
* With epinephrine 1:200 000 (5 μg/mL).

Repeat doses should be preceded by a test dose containing epinephrine if the vasoconstrictor is not contraindicated.

Dental Anesthesia: Sensorcaine Forte 0.5% is recommended for infiltration and block injection in the maxillary and mandibular areas when a longer duration of local anesthetic action is desired, such as for oral surgical procedures generally associated with significant postoperative pain. The average dose of 1.8 mL (9 mg) per injection site will usually be sufficient; an occasional second dose of 1.8 mL (9 mg) may be used if necessary to produce adequate anesthesia after making allowances for 2 to 10 minutes' onset time. The lowest effective dose should be employed and time should be allowed between injections. It is recommended that the total dose for all injection sites, spread out over a single dental sitting should not ordinarily exceed 90 mg for a healthy adult patient (ten 1.8 mL injections of Sensorcaine Forte 0.5%). Injections should be made slowly and with frequent aspirations. Until further experience is gained, bupivacaine in dentistry is not recommended for children younger than 12 years.

Supplied: Sensorcaine: Each mL of sterile, isotonic solution contains: bupivacaine HCl 2.5 mg (0.25%) or 5 mg (0.5%). Nonmedicinal ingredients: sodium chloride, sodium hydroxide and/or hydrochloric acid and water for injection. pH is 4.0 to 6.5. Single use vials of 10 and 20 mL. Polyamp Duofit (plastic ampuls suitable for Luer fit and Luer lock syringes) of 10 and 20 mL. Store at 15 to 30°C.

Sensorcaine with Epinephrine (1:200 000): Each mL of sterile, isotonic solution contains: bupivacaine HCl 2.5 mg (0.25%) or 5 mg (0.5%) and epinephrine 5 μg (1:200 000). Nonmedicinal ingredients: citric acid, sodium chloride, sodium hydroxide and/or hydrochloric acid, sodium metabisulfite and water for injection. pH is 3.3. to 5.5. Single use vials of 10 and 20 mL. Store at 15 to 30°C. Protect from light.

Sensorcaine Forte (1:200 000): Each mL of sterile isotonic solution contains: bupivacaine HCl 5 mg (0.5%) and epinephrine 5 μg (1:200 000). Nonmedicinal ingredients: citric acid, sodium chloride, sodium hydroxide and/or hydrochloric acid, sodium metabisulfite and water for injection. pH is 3.3 to 5.5. Dental cartridges of 1.8 mL. Store at 15 to 30°C. Protect from light.

The dental cartridges of Sensorcaine Forte 0.5% may be disinfected with either isopropyl alcohol (91%) or ethyl alcohol (70%).

Do not use if solution is pinkish or darker than slightly yellow or if it contains precipitate.

Bupivacaine solutions are without preservative and for single use only. Discard unused portion.

Reviewed 1998

SEPTRA® Ⓟ
SEPTRA® DS Ⓟ
SEPTRA® INJECTION Ⓟ

Glaxo Wellcome

Trimethoprim—Sulfamethoxazole

Antibacterial

Pharmacology: Septra is an antibacterial agent with a wide spectrum of activity. It contains 2 active antibacterial components, trimethoprim and sulfamethoxazole, which act synergistically on many species of bacteria.

Sulfamethoxazole and trimethoprim act sequentially in two successive steps in the biosynthesis of nucleic acids. Trimethoprim is an inhibitor of dihydrofolate reductase, the enzyme which reduces dihydrofolic acid to its tetrahydro form. This biochemical step is essential in the production of the folate coenzymes which are involved in the biosynthesis of thymine, purine, serine and methionine. Sulfamethoxazole exerts its antibacterial activity by competing with PABA (para-aminobenzoic acid).

Most pathogenic bacteria meet their need for dihydrofolic acid by synthesizing it from PABA, pteridine and glutamic acid. Animals, in contrast, depend on exogenous sources for their folic acid needs and do not rely upon intracellular synthesis.

Under usual circumstances, sulfamethoxazole or trimethoprim acting alone do not produce a complete block in this biosynthesis of nucleic acids. Instead, they cause sufficient reduction in the synthesis of folate coenzymes to produce bacteriostasis. When the two agents act together, the superimposition of their effects produces a complete block in the synthesis, leading to the death of the organism. Thus the effect of the dual action is to reduce the minimum inhibitory concentrations (MIC) of each agent (synergism) and to convert a bacteriostatic action to a bactericidal action.

The activity of Septra therefore depends upon the ability of both sulfamethoxazole and trimethoprim to affect the folate metabolism of the bacterium; however, for Septra to be therapeutic it must not affect the folate metabolism of the host.

Since sulfamethoxazole affects only the de novo synthesis of dihydrofolic acid by bacteria, it does not affect folate metabolism of animals. Since in animals, as in bacteria, the folates have to be recycled to the active form by dihydrofolate reductase, trimethoprim could be expected to affect mammalian folate metabolism. Trimethoprim, however, was especially selected from similar folate inhibitors because of its low toxicity for animals and high toxicity for bacteria. This difference has since been shown to be due to the fact that the affinity of trimethoprim for the dihydrofolate reductase of bacteria is some 40 000 times greater than for the corresponding mammalian enzyme.

Pharmacokinetics: Both trimethoprim and sulfamethoxazole are rapidly absorbed following oral administration; detectable levels of both drugs appear in the blood in about 5 minutes with significant levels being reached within 1 hour. Peak blood levels for both compounds are attained usually in 2 to 4 hours, are maintained for about 7 hours, and detectable amounts are still present after 24 hours. When the two drugs are administered together, the individual blood levels are similar to those achieved when the drugs are administered separately, thus indicating no effect in absorption of one drug by the other.

The ratio of 1 part trimethoprim to 5 parts sulfamethoxazole achieves drug concentrations in the blood in the ratio of approximately 1:20, a ratio considered to be optimal against a wide range of bacteria. Unlike sulfamethoxazole, trimethoprim concentrates in tissues; biopsy material from a small number of patients taking trimethoprim preoperatively indicated that the concentration of trimethoprim in the tissues exceeded that of the plasma sampled at the same time—most significant in the lung (by 10 times). A similar pattern occurs in animals. Levels of trimethoprim in the sputum were also found to be higher than in the plasma following oral administration of trimethoprim-sulfamethoxazole. The concentrations of both drugs have also been found to be well-maintained in lymph and tissue fluids.

In serum, the degree of protein-binding by trimethoprim varies with the concentration, but it normally is about 44% bound to plasma protein. Sulfamethoxazole was found to be about 70% bound to plasma protein. Addition of sulfamethoxazole reduced the binding of trimethoprim by 3 to 4%, but there was no change in the protein-binding of sulfamethoxazole (about 66%) at therapeutically attainable concentrations of the two drugs.

Studies conducted on the individual components administered separately, indicate that in the presence of a high fluid intake, approximately 50%, and in the presence of a low fluid intake, approximately 40% of the orally ingested trimethoprim is excreted unchanged in the urine within 24 hours. Approximately 10% of the excreted drug is in the form of metabolites with little or no antibacterial activity. Some trimethoprim is excreted in the bile, where concentrations twice those of plasma are obtained, but as it is almost completely reabsorbed; very little appears in the feces. Studies with radiolabelled trimethoprim indicated that it is almost completely absorbed following oral administration in man; less than 4% of the radioactivity appeared in the feces over a period of 6 days. Radioactivity was eliminated from the plasma and urine at almost identical rates; almost all of an oral dose being excreted in the urine within 48 hours. The biological half-life of trimethoprim was calculated to be 10 hours (range of 6.2 to 12 hours in 4 patients), which corresponds well to the half-life of 9 to 11 hours determined in man for sulfamethoxazole.

About 60% of the orally ingested sulfamethoxazole is excreted in the urine within 48 hours. Of the excreted drug, approximately half is the N^4 acetylated derivative, a fifth is the N^4 conjugate, a sixth is the unchanged parent compound, and about a tenth is another N^4 free compound.

Although the amount of each drug excreted is similar when given separately or in combination, the method of excretion by the kidney is quite different. Sharpstone demonstrated that there is net tubular reabsorption of filtered sulfamethoxazole, at least in patients with normal renal function, whereas with trimethoprim there is a tubular secretory mechanism of excretion in patients with normal or impaired renal function.

Renal clearance of sulfamethoxazole increased with rising urine flow-rate, was independent of urine pH when this was less than 7, but increased with alkalinization of the urine above a pH of 7. The clearance of trimethoprim was unaffected by alteration in urine flow-rate but increased sharply with falling urine pH.

Septra (cont'd)

In patients with impaired renal function, sulfamethoxazole excretion was only slightly decreased, whereas trimethoprim excretion decreased markedly in severe renal impairment.

Indications: Septra has been effective in the treatment of infections associated with the following gram-positive and gram-negative organisms:

Gram-Negative Organisms: H. influenzae, N. gonorrhoeae, E. coli, Klebsiella species, E. aerogenes, P. mirabilis, P. vulgaris, Salmonella species, Shigella species, V. cholerae.

Gram-Positive Organisms: S. pyogenes, S. viridans, S. albus, S. aureus, D. pneumoniae.

Other Organisms: B. melitensis, N. asteroides, N. brasiliensis, P. brasiliensis, P. carinii, S. somaliensis.

Sensitivity tests should be performed whenever possible to determine choice of therapy. These tests should be repeated if there is a failure to respond, relapse or early recurrence.

Septra may be indicated for the following infections when caused by susceptible strains of the above organisms.

Urinary Tract Infections: acute, recurrent and chronic urinary tract infections.

Genital Tract Infections: uncomplicated gonococcal urethritis.

Upper and Lower Respiratory Tract Infections: upper and lower respiratory tract infections, and particularly chronic bronchitis.

Gastrointestinal Tract Infections: including cholera, bacillary dysentery, typhoid and paratyphoid.

Skin and Soft Tissue Infections.

Other Infections: Brucellosis, mycetoma, nocardiosis, South American blastomycosis and acute and chronic osteomyelitis.

Septra is also indicated in the treatment of infants and children with a diagnosis of P. carinii pneumonitis, especially if they are immunosuppressed.

Septra is not indicated in infections associated with Pseudomonas, Mycoplasma, nor when the infection is caused by a virus.

This drug has not yet been fully evaluated in streptococcal infections.

Contraindications: In patients with a known hypersensitivity to trimethoprim or sulfonamides and in patients with documented megaloblastic anemia due to folate deficiency, evidence of marked liver parenchymal damage, or blood dyscrasias.

In patients with marked renal impairment where repeated serum assays cannot be carried out (see also Precautions).

Pregnancy and *Lactation:* In pregnant patients and in nursing mothers, because sulfonamides pass the placenta and are excreted in the milk and may cause kernicterus.

Children: In infants less than 2 months of age.

Warnings: Fatalities associated with the administration of sulfonamides, although rare, have occurred due to severe reactions, including Stevens-Johnson syndrome, toxic epidermal necrolysis, fulminant hepatic necrosis, agranulocytosis, aplastic anemia, other blood dyscrasias, and hypersensitivity of the respiratory tract.

Septra should be discontinued at the first appearance of skin rash or any sign of adverse reaction. Clinical signs, such as rash, sore throat, fever, arthralgia, cough, shortness of breath, pallor, purpura, or jaundice may be early indications of serious reactions. Cough, shortness of breath, and/or pulmonary infiltrates may be indicators of pulmonary hypersensitivity to sulfonamides. In rare instances a skin rash may be followed by more severe reactions, such as Stevens-Johnson syndrome, toxic epidermal necrolysis, hepatic necrosis, or serious blood disorder. Complete blood counts should be done frequently in patients receiving sulfonamides.

Septra should not be used in the treatment of streptococcal pharyngitis. Clinical studies have documented that patients with group A β-hemolytic streptococcal tonsillopharyngitis have a greater incidence of bacteriologic failure when treated with Septra than to those patients treated with penicillin, as evidenced by failure to eradicate this organism from the tonsillopharyngeal area.

Septra Injection contains sodium metabisulfite, a sulfite that may cause allergic-type reactions including anaphylactic symptoms and life-threatening or less severe asthmatic episodes in certain susceptible people. The overall prevalence of sulfite sensitivity in the general population is unknown and probably low. Sulfite sensitivity is seen more frequently in asthmatic than in nonasthmatic people.

Precautions: General: Septra should be given with caution to patients with impaired renal or hepatic function, to those with possible folate deficiency (e.g., the elderly, chronic alcoholics, rheumatoid arthritics, patients receiving anticonvulsant therapy, patients with malabsorption syndrome, and patients in malnutrition states), and to those with severe allergy or bronchial asthma. Because of possible interference with folate metabolism, regular blood counts are advisable in these patients as well as patients who are on long-term therapy. Changes indicative of folic acid impairment have, in certain specific situations, been reversed by folinic acid therapy.

In glucose-6-phosphate dehydrogenase-deficient individuals, hemolysis may occur. This reaction is frequently dose-related.

The administration of Septra to patients known or suspected to be at risk of acute porphyria should be avoided. Both trimethoprim and sulfonamides (although not specifically sulfamethoxazole) have been associated with clinical exacerbation of porphyria.

The possibility of superinfection with a nonsensitive organism should be borne in mind.

Local irritation and inflammation due to extravascular infiltration of the infusion has been observed with Septra Injection. If these occur, the infusion should be discontinued and restarted at another site.

Renal Impairment: In patients with renal impairment, a reduced or less frequent dosage is recommended in order to avoid accumulation of trimethoprim in the blood (see Dosage). Nonionic diffusion is the main factor in the renal handling of trimethoprim, and as renal failure advances, trimethoprim excretion decreases. For such patients, serum assays are necessary. Septra should not be used when the serum creatinine level is above 2 mg/100 mL, in order to avoid possible permanent impairment of renal function.

Geriatrics: There may be an increased risk of severe adverse reactions in elderly patients, particularly when complicating conditions exist, e.g., impaired kidney and/or liver function, or concomitant use of other drugs. Severe skin reactions, or generalized bone marrow suppression (see Warnings and Adverse Effects), or a specific decrease in platelets (with or without purpura) are the most frequently reported severe adverse reactions in elderly patients. In those concurrently receiving certain diuretics, primarily thiazides, an increased incidence of thrombocytopenia with purpura has been reported. Appropriate dosage adjustments should be made for patients with impaired kidney function (see Dosage).

Use in the Treatment of and Prophylaxis for P. carinii Pneumonia in Patients with Acquired Immunodeficiency Syndrome (AIDS): The incidence of side effects, particularly rash, fever, leukopenia, and elevated aminotransferase (transaminase) values in AIDS patients who are being treated with Septra for P. carinii pneumonia has been reported to be greatly increased compared with the incidence normally associated with the use of Septra in non-AIDS patients. The incidence of hyperkalemia and hyponatremia appears to be increased in AIDS patients receiving Septra. Adverse effects are generally less severe in patients receiving Septra for prophylaxis. A history of mild intolerance to Septra in AIDS patients does not appear to predict intolerance of subsequent secondary prophylaxis. However, if a patient develops skin rash or any sign of adverse reaction, therapy with Septra should be re-evaluated (see Warnings).

The concomitant use of leucovorin with trimethoprim-sulfamethoxazole for the acute treatment of P. carinii pneumonia in patients with HIV infection was associated with increased rates of treatment failure and morbidity in a placebo-controlled study.

Information for the Patient: Patients should be instructed to maintain an adequate fluid intake in order to prevent crystalluria and stone formation.

Drug Interactions: In elderly patients concurrently receiving certain diuretics, primarily thiazides, an increased incidence of thrombocytopenia with purpura has been reported.

It has been reported that Septra may prolong the prothrombin time in patients who are receiving the anticoagulant warfarin. This interaction should be kept in mind when Septra is given to patients already on anticoagulant therapy, and the coagulation time should be reassessed.

Septra may inhibit the hepatic metabolism of phenytoin. Septra, given at a common clinical dosage, increased the phenytoin half-life by 39% and decreased the phenytoin metabolic clearance rate by 27%. When administering these drugs concurrently, one should be alert for possible excessive phenytoin effect.

Sulfonamides can also displace methotrexate from plasma protein binding sites, thus increasing free methotrexate concentrations. Folate supplementation should be considered.

Concomitant use of trimethoprim with digoxin has been shown to increase plasma digoxin levels in a proportion of elderly patients.

Reversible deterioration in renal function has been observed in patients treated with Septra and cyclosporine following renal transplantation.

When trimethoprim is administered simultaneously with drugs that form cations at physiological pH, and are also partly excreted by active renal secretion (e.g., procainamide, amantadine), there is the possibility of competitive inhibition of this process which may lead to an increase in plasma concentration of one or both of the drugs.

Drug/Laboratory Test Interactions: Septra, specifically the trimethoprim component, can interfere with a serum methotrexate assay as determined by the competitive binding protein technique (CBPA) when a bacterial dihydrofolate reductase is used as the binding protein. No interference occurs, however, if methotrexate is measured by a radioimmunoassay (RIA).

The presence of trimethoprim and sulfamethoxazole may also interfere with the Jaffé alkaline picrate reaction assay for creatinine, resulting in overestimations of about 10% in the range of normal values.

Adverse Effects: The most common adverse effects are gastrointestinal disturbances (nausea, vomiting, anorexia) and allergic skin reactions (such as rash and urticaria). **Fatalities associated with the administration of sulfonamides, although rare, have occurred due to severe reactions, including Stevens-Johnson syndrome, toxic epidermal necrolysis, fulminant hepatic necrosis, agranulocytosis, aplastic anemia, other blood dyscrasias, and hypersensitivity of the respiratory tract** (see Warnings).

Hematologic: leukopenia, neutropenia, thrombocytopenia, megaloblastic anemia, aplastic and hemolytic anemia, methemoglobinemia, purpura, agranulocytosis, hypoprothrombinemia, eosinophilia and bone marrow depression.

Allergic: Stevens-Johnson syndrome, toxic epidermal necrolysis, anaphylaxis, allergic myocarditis, erythema multiforme, toxicoderma, exfoliative dermatitis, angioedema, drug fever, chills, Henoch-Schönlein purpura, serum sickness-like syndrome, generalized allergic reactions, generalized skin eruptions, photosensitivity, conjunctival and scleral injection, pruritus, urticaria and rash. In addition, periarteritis nodosa and systemic lupus erythematosus have been reported.

Gastrointestinal: hepatitis, including cholestatic jaundice and hepatic necrosis, elevation of serum transaminase, alkaline phosphatase and bilirubin, pseudomembranous enterocolitis, jaundice, pancreatitis, stomatitis, glossitis, dry mouth, nausea, pyrosis, gastric intolerance, gastritis or gastroenteritis, dyspepsia emesis, abdominal pain, constipation, flatulence, diarrhea, anorexia.

Genitourinary: renal failure, interstitial nephritis, kidney changes (as indicated by abnormal elevations in blood urea nitrogen, blood nonprotein nitrogen, serum creatinine and urine protein levels), toxic nephrosis with oliguria and anuria, crystalluria, hematuria, urgency and dysuria.

Metabolic: hyperkalemia and hyponatremia.

Neurologic: aseptic meningitis, convulsions, peripheral neuritis, ataxia, tremor, vertigo, tinnitus, headache.

Psychiatric: hallucinations, depression, apathy, nervousness.

Endocrine: The sulfonamides bear certain chemical similarities to some goitrogens, diuretics (acetazolamide and the thiazides), and oral hypoglycemic agents. Cross-sensitivity may exist with these agents. Diuresis and hypoglycemia have occurred rarely in patients receiving sulfonamides.

Musculoskeletal: arthralgia and myalgia.

Respiratory: pulmonary infiltrates, cough, shortness of breath, dyspnea.

Miscellaneous: weakness, fatigue, insomnia, vision troubles, alopecia, epistaxis.

Overdose: Symptoms: Acute: The amount of a single dose of Septra that is either associated with symptoms of overdosage or is likely to be life-threatening has not been reported. Signs and symptoms of overdosage reported with sulfonamides include anorexia, colic, nausea, vomiting, dizziness, headache, drowsiness, and unconsciousness. Pyrexia, hematuria, and crystalluria may be noted. Blood dyscrasias and jaundice are potential late manifestations of overdosage. Signs of acute overdosage with trimethoprim include nausea, vomiting, dizziness, headache, mental depression, confusion, and bone marrow depression.

Chronic: Use of Septra at high doses and/or for extended periods of time may cause bone marrow depression manifested as thrombocytopenia, leukopenia, and/or megaloblastic anemia. If signs of bone marrow depression occur, the patient should be given leucovorin; 5 to 15 mg leucovorin daily has been recommended by some investigators.

Treatment: General principles of treatment include the institution of gastric lavage or emesis; forcing oral fluids; and the administration of i.v. fluids if urine output is low and renal function is normal. Acidification of the urine will increase renal elimination of trimethoprim. The patient should be monitored with blood counts and appropriate blood chemistries, including electrolytes. If a significant blood dyscrasia or jaundice occurs, specific therapy should be instituted for these complications. Peritoneal dialysis is not effective and hemodialysis is only moderately effective in eliminating trimethoprim and sulfamethoxazole.

There is no known antidote for sulfonamide poisoning; however, leucovorin is an effective antidote for adverse effects in the hemopoietic system caused by trimethoprim.

Dosage: Oral: Adults and children over 12 years of age: Standard dosage: 2 Septra tablets or 1 Septra DS tablet twice daily (morning and evening). Minimum dosage and dosage for long-term treatment: 1 Septra tablet or ½ Septra DS tablet twice daily. Maximum dosage (overwhelming infections): 3 Septra tablets or 1.5 Septra DS tablets twice daily. Gonorrhea (non-complicated): 2 Septra tablets or 1 Septra DS tablet 4 times daily for 2 days.

Children 6 to 12 years: 5 to 10 mL pediatric suspension twice daily. Ten mL of pediatric suspension is equivalent to 1 adult Septra tablet.

Children 2 to 5 years: 2.5 to 5 mL pediatric suspension twice daily. Five mL of pediatric suspension is equivalent to ½ of an adult Septra tablet.

Children under 2 years: 2.5 mL pediatric suspension twice daily.

In children this corresponds to an approximate dose of 6 mg trimethoprim/kg/day, plus 30 mg sulfamethoxazole/kg/day, divided into 2 equal doses.

Therapy should be continued for at least 5 days in acute infections or until the patient is asymptomatic for at least 48 hours. If the drug has to be given for protracted periods, consideration should be given to dosage reduction.

Children with P. carinii pneumonitis: 20 mg trimethoprim/kg/day and 100 mg sulfamethoxazole/kg/day in 4 divided doses. Children under 1 year (9 kg): 5 mL pediatric suspension or ½ of an adult tablet 4 times daily. Children 1 to 2 years (18 kg): 10 mL pediatric suspension or 1 adult tablet 4 times daily. Children 2 to 5 years (27 kg): 15 mL pediatric suspension or 1.5 adult tablet 4 times daily. Children 6 to 12 years (36 kg): 20 mL pediatric suspension or 2 adult tablets 4 times daily. Adults: 3 Septra tablets or 1.5 Septra DS tablets twice daily. In P. carinii pneumonitis the recommended dose should be continued for at least a 14-day period.

Acute Urinary Tract Infections: 2 tablets twice daily until urine is sterile. Patients with a history of chronic reinfection: 1 tablet twice daily as a prophylaxis.

Chest Infections: Adequate dosage is important in chest infections in order to maintain high sputum concentrations. Most trials of sulfamethoxazole-trimethoprim in acute exacerbations of chronic bronchitis report satisfactory results with the standard dosage (2 tablets twice daily); but in 1 trial involving patients with advanced disease, results were much better with the maximum dosage of 3 tablets twice daily. It has also been suggested to continue the drug for 2 days following eradication of purulent sputum and not to prescribe a predetermined course. In chronic chest infections, 1 tablet twice daily may be adequate for prophylaxis, but in some patients the standard dosage (2 tablets twice daily) may be necessary.

Acute Salmonellosis: 2 tablets twice daily, continue for at least 7 days after defervescence. Carriers: 1 tablet twice daily until repeated stool cultures are negative.

Other diseases, including certain tropical diseases rarely seen in Canada, have also been successfully treated with Septra. See Table I.

I.V.: Septra injection may be used only in patients who are unable to take oral medication or where there is a need for rapid attainment of high serum concentrations. Oral treatment should be substituted as soon as possible.

Method of dilution: Caution: Direct i.v. injection is not recommended.

Septra injection must be diluted in one of the following diluents: Ringer's solution; sodium chloride 0.18%+dextrose 4% solution; dextrose 5% solution; dextrose 10% solution; 10% Dextran 40 in sodium chloride 0.9% solution; 10% Dextran 40 in dextrose 5% solution; 6% Dextran 70 in sodium chloride 0.9% solution; 6% Dextran 70 in dextrose 5% solution.

Each 5 mL ampul should be diluted with 125 mL of one of the above solutions. The prepared solution must be kept at room temperature and administration started within 5 hours. Do not mix the prepared infusion solution with other drugs or solutions.

Note: If, upon visual inspection, there is cloudiness or evidence of precipitation after mixing, the solution should be discarded and a fresh solution prepared.

Table I—Septra

Dosage—Other Diseases

Disease	Usual Dosage Adults	Usual Dosage Children	Duration
Cholera	2 tabs b.i.d. or 1 DS b.i.d	2.5 to 10 mL pediatric suspension b.i.d	7 days
Nocardiosis	3 tabs b.i.d. or 1½ DS b.i.d	5 to 15 mL pediatric suspension or ½ to 1½ adult tablets b.i.d	12 weeks
South American Blastomycosis	2 tabs b.i.d. or 1 DS b.i.d	2.5 to 10 mL pediatric suspension b.i.d	4 to 12 weeks
Brucellosis	2 tabs b.i.d. or 1 DS b.i.d	2.5 to 10 mL pediatric suspension b.i.d	2 weeks to 3 months
Osteomyelitis Acute	2 tabs b.i.d. or 1 DS b.i.d.	10 mL pediatric suspension or 1 adult tablet b.i.d	10 to 45 days
Chronic	2 tabs b.i.d. or 1 DS b.i.d	10 mL pediatric suspension or 1 adult tablet b.i.d.	4 to 20 months

Pneumocystis carinii Pneumonitis: Children and adults: The recommended daily i.v. dose is 20 mg trimethoprim/kg and 100 mg sulfamethoxazole/kg. This daily dose is to be divided into 4 equal doses infused over a period of 0.5 to 1 hour, at 6 hour intervals, until oral therapy can be instituted (see Table II).

Table II—Septra

Pneumocystis carinii Pneumonitis—Dosage I.V. in Children and Adults

Volume of Undiluted Septra Injection per kg of Body Weight* (conversion factor 1.25 mL/kg)

Body Weight (kg)	Volume of Undiluted Septra Injection (mL) Total Daily Dose	Dose Every 6 hours (q.i.d.)
5	6.3	1.6
10	12.5	3.1
20	25.0	6.3
40	50.0	12.5
60	75.0	18.8
80	100.0	25.0

* Septra Injection must be properly diluted (see Method of dilution) and administered at 6-hour intervals.

Serious Systemic Infections: Adults: The i.v. dose depends on the severity of the infection. A dose of 160 to 240 mg trimethoprim and 800 to 1 200 mg sulfamethoxazole may be given every 6, 8 or 12 hours. This dose must be properly diluted (see Method of dilution) and infused over a period of 0.5 to 1 hour.

Children: The recommended daily dose for children is 5 to 10 mg trimethoprim/kg/day and 25 to 50 mg sulfamethoxazole/kg/day. This daily dose must be properly diluted and administered in equally divided doses by infusion over a period of 0.5 to 1 hour (see Table III).

Table III—Septra

Serious Systemic Infections—Dosage I.V. in Children and Adults

Volume of Undiluted Septra Injection per kg of Body Weight* (conversion factor 0.31 to 0.63 mL/kg)

Body Weight (kg)	Volume of Undiluted Septra for Infusion (mL) Total Daily Dose	Dose Every 12 hours (b.i.d.)	Dose Every 8 hours (t.i.d.)	Dose Every 6 hours (q.i.d.)
5	1.6 to 3.2	0.8 to 1.6	0.5 to 1.1	0.4 to 0.8
10	3.1 to 6.3	1.6 to 3.2	1.0 to 2.1	0.8 to 1.6
20	6.2 to 12.6	3.1 to 6.3	2.1 to 4.2	1.6 to 3.2
40	12.4 to 25.2	6.2 to 12.6	4.1 to 8.4	3.1 to 6.3
60	18.6 to 37.8	9.3 to 18.9	6.2 to 12.6	4.7 to 9.5

* Septra Injection must be properly diluted (see Method of dilution) and administered in equally divided doses.

Patients with Impaired Renal Function: When renal function is impaired, a reduced dosage should be employed using Table IV.

Table IV—Septra

Recommended Dose Regimen in Patients with Impaired Renal Function

Creatinine Clearance (mL/min)	Recommended Dose Regimen
Above 25	Usual standard regimen
15 to 25	One half the usual regimen
Below 15	Use not recommended

Supplied: Septra: Adult Tablets: Each white, round tablet, coded SEPTRA Y2B on the same side as score mark, contains: trimethoprim 80 mg and sulfamethoxazole 400 mg. Sodium: <1 mmol (0.29 to 0.42 mg). Nonmedicinal ingredients: docusate sodium, magnesium stearate, povidone and sodium starch glycolate. Bottles of 500. Store at 15 to 30°C. Protect from light and keep dry.

Pediatric Suspension: Each 5 mL contains: trimethoprim 40 mg and sulfamethoxazole 200 mg. Sodium: <1 mmol (0.56 to 0.83 mg). Nonmedicinal ingredients: alcohol, cellulose, citric acid, flavor cherry, glycerin, methylparaben, polysorbate, Ponceau 4R, purified water and sucrose. Bottles of 400 and 800 mL. Store at 15 to 25°C. Protect from light and freezing.

Septra DS: Each white, oval double strength tablet, coded SEPTRA DS O2C with score mark on reverse side, contains: trimethoprim 160 mg and sulfamethoxazole 800 mg. Sodium: <1 mmol (0.57 to 0.84 mg). Nonmedicinal ingredients: docusate sodium, magnesium stearate, povidone and sodium starch glycolate. Bottles of 250. Store at 15 to 30°C. Protect from light and keep dry.

Septra Injection: Each 5 mL ampul or vial contains: trimethoprim 80 mg and sulfamethoxazole 400 mg. Nonmedicinal ingredients: ethanol, propylene glycol, sodium hydroxide, sodium metabisulfite, tromethamine and water for injection. Store at 15 to 30°C. Protect from light.

(Shown in Product Recognition Section)

Reviewed 1998

SER-AP-ES® Ⓟ

Novartis Pharmaceuticals

Reserpine—Hydralazine HCl—Hydrochlorothiazide

Antihypertensive

Pharmacology: Ser-Ap-Es combines the antihypertensive activity of 3 agents: reserpine, the diuretic hydrochlorothiazide and the peripheral vasodilator hydralazine.

Reserpine probably produces its antihypertensive effect through depletion of tissue stores of catecholamines (epinephrine and norepinephrine) from peripheral sites which results in a decreased cardiac output. A decrease in peripheral resistance produced by reserpine may also contribute to its antihypertensive effect.

Ser-Ap-Es (cont'd)

Although the precise mechanism of action of hydralazine is not fully understood, the major effects are on the cardiovascular system. Hydralazine apparently lowers blood pressure by exerting a peripheral vasodilating effect through a direct relaxation of vascular smooth muscle. Hydralazine, by altering cellular calcium metabolism, interferes with the calcium movements within the vascular smooth muscle that are responsible for initiating or maintaining the contractile state.

The peripheral vasodilating effect of hydralazine results in decreased arterial blood pressure (diastolic more than systolic); decreased peripheral vascular resistance; and an increased heart rate, stroke volume, and cardiac output. The vasodilating effect is much greater on arterioles than on veins and vascular resistance decreases more in the coronary, cerebral, splanchnic and renal circulations than in skin and muscle.

Hydralazine usually increases renin activity in plasma, presumably as a result of increased secretion of renin by the renal juxtaglomerular cells in response to reflex sympathetic discharge. This increase in renin activity leads to the production of angiotensin II, which then causes stimulation of aldosterone and consequent sodium reabsorption and fluid retention.

Sodium retention and excessive sympathetic stimulation of the heart caused by hydralazine may be precluded by coadministration of a thiazide diuretic and a beta-blocker. Beta-adrenergic blocking drugs and hydralazine are complementary in their pharmacologic effects, a beta-adrenergic blocking agent minimizes hydralazine-induced increases in cardiac rate and output, and hydralazine prevents the reflex increase in peripheral resistance induced by beta-blockers.

Hydrochlorothiazide inhibits reabsorption of sodium and chloride in the distal renal tubule, thus promoting water loss. The higher urine volume increases potassium loss; therefore, restricting salt intake decreases potassium loss.

The blood pressure lowering effects of hydrochlorothiazide are initially due to volume reduction but the persisting effect includes other undetermined mechanisms that reduce peripheral resistance. A high salt intake reverses its antihypertensive effect.

Pharmacokinetics: When given orally, reserpine is readily absorbed from the gastrointestinal tract. Its action is slow in onset; the effects appear after 3 to 6 days and continue for many days after withdrawal of treatment. Reserpine is extensively metabolized by the liver and both metabolites and unchanged drug are slowly excreted in the urine and feces.

Hydralazine is rapidly and fairly completely absorbed after oral administration. In the plasma only small amounts of the free drug can be traced, the bulk circulating in conjugated form, i.e. pyruvic acid hydrazone. Peak serum concentrations are reached within 1 to 2 hours after a dose.

Plasma levels of hydralazine vary widely among individuals. Orally administered hydralazine undergoes extensive, saturable first-pass metabolism (systemic availability: 26 to 55%), this first-pass effect being dependent on the individual's acetylator status. In response to the same oral dose, slow-acetylators show higher "apparent" plasma hydralazine levels than rapid acetylators and require lower doses to maintain control of blood pressure.

Hydralazine is widely distributed in the body. The apparent volume of distribution of hydralazine is approximately 50% body weight. Binding to plasma proteins (chiefly albumin) is 88 to 90%.

Hydralazine crosses the placental barrier and is excreted in the breast milk.

The pattern of the metabolites depends on the subject's acetylator and presumably hydroxylator status. The main metabolite, NAc-HPZ (N-acetyl-hydrazine-phthalazinone), was found to be the relevant indicator for the drug-related phenotype. The plasma half-life generally ranges between 1.7 and 3.0 hours in most subjects, but in rapid acetylators it is shorter, averaging 45 minutes.

Hydralazine and its metabolites are rapidly excreted by the kidney and 80% of the oral dose appears in the urine within 48 hours. The bulk of the hydralazine excreted is in the form of acetylated and hydroxylated metabolites, some of which are conjugated with glucuronic acid; 2 to 14% is excreted as "apparent" hydralazine.

Oral doses of hydrochlorothiazide are well absorbed and reach peak effect in about 4 hours, with a 6 to 12 hour duration. About 40 to 70% of hydrochlorothiazide binds to plasma proteins. The distribution volume during the terminal elimination phase is estimated at 3 to 6 L/kg (equivalent to 210 to 240 L for 70 kg body weight). It is excreted unchanged in the urine with a half-life of 3 to 5 hours. On average, 50 to 75% of an oral dose is found in the urine in unchanged form.

Elderly patients, patients with renal failure, and patients with hepatic dysfunction: Clearance of hydrochlorothiazide is significantly reduced in the elderly and in patients with impaired renal function, resulting in substantially increased plasma concentrations. Decreased clearance in the elderly is thought to be due to deterioration of renal function. Cirrhosis of the liver does not alter the pharmacokinetics of hydrochlorothiazide. The effective doses of Ser-Ap-Es in elderly patients and patients with renal impairment may be lower than those in younger patients with normal renal function (see Dosage).

The plasma half-life of hydralazine is prolonged for up to 16 hours in patients with impaired renal function at a creatinine clearance of <20 mL/min (see Contraindications), and the active substance may accumulate in severe hepatic dysfunction. Reserpine is excreted more slowly in patients with renal insufficiency, but compensation occurs through fecal excretion. The dosage of Ser-Ap-Es, or the dosing intervals should therefore be adjusted in accordance with therapeutic requirements and tolerability, in order to avoid cumulative effects.

Indications: For the treatment of hypertension, especially when complicated by anxiety, impaired or degenerating renal function or edema.

Contraindications: Mental depression (especially with suicidal tendencies) or history of depressive illness. Parkinson's disease. Epilepsy. Electroconvulsive therapy. Active gastric or duodenal ulcer. Ulcerative colitis. Digitalis intoxication. Aortic insufficiency. Pheochromocytoma. MAO inhibitor therapy (MAO inhibitors should be withdrawn at least 14 days before treatment with reserpine). Anuria. Severe renal (creatinine clearance <30 mL/min) or hepatic failure. Hypertension during pregnancy. Refractory hypokalemia and hyponatremia. Hypercalcemia. Symptomatic hyperuricemia (history of gout or uric acid calculi). Conditions involving enhanced potassium loss, for example salt-losing nephropathies and prerenal impairment of kidney function. Known or suspected hypersensitivity to reserpine, hydrochlorothiazide, hydralazino-phthalazine derivatives and other related derivatives. Idiopathic systemic lupus erythematosus (SLE) and related diseases. Severe tachycardia and heart failure with a high cardiac output (e.g., in thyrotoxicosis). Myocardial insufficiency due to mechanical obstruction (e.g., in the presence of aortic or mitral stenosis or constrictive pericarditis). Isolated right-ventricular heart failure due to pulmonary hypertension (cor pulmonale). Acute dissecting aneurysm of the aorta. Coronary artery disease.

Warnings and Precautions: This fixed combination drug is not intended for initial therapy of hypertension. Hypertension requires therapy titrated to the individual patient. If the fixed combination represents the dosage determined, its use may be convenient in patient management. The treatment of hypertension is not static, but must be re-evaluated as conditions in each patient warrant.

Depression may be aggravated or unmasked by reserpine. Discontinue Ser-Ap-Es at first signs of depression; the possibility of suicide should be kept in mind, both during treatment and several months after withdrawal.

The possibility of exacerbation or activation of systemic lupus erythematosus has been reported with thiazide diuretics. In addition, hydralazine may provoke in a few patients a clinical picture simulating systemic lupus erythematosus (SLE) including glomerulonephritis. In its mild form this syndrome is reminiscent of rheumatoid arthritis (arthralgia, sometimes associated with fever and skin rash). When fully developed, a syndrome resembling disseminated lupus erythematosus occurs. Should this SLE-like syndrome develop, treatment should be discontinued immediately. Symptoms and signs usually regress when the drug is discontinued but residua have been detected many years later. Long-term treatment with adrenocorticosteroids may be necessary.

The frequency of these untoward effects increases with dosage and duration of exposure to the drug and is higher in slow than in fast acetylators. When treated with the same dosage, slow acetylators have higher serum concentrations than fast acetylators. The lowest effective dosage should therefore be used for maintenance therapy. If 100 mg daily fails to elicit an adequate clinical effect, the patient's acetylator status should be evaluated.

Slow acetylators and women run a greater risk of developing this SLE-like syndrome. In such cases dosage should be kept below 100 mg daily (hydralazine), and the patients carefully monitored for clinical signs and symptoms suggestive of this syndrome.

Complete blood counts, examination of lupus erythematosus cell preparations, antinuclear antibody titre determinations and urine analysis are indicated before and periodically (e.g. every 6 months) during prolonged therapy with hydralazine even if the patient is asymptomatic. These tests are also indicated if the patient develops arthralgia, fever, chest pain, continued malaise or other unexplained signs or symptoms. If the results of these tests are abnormal, treatment should be discontinued.

Antinuclear antibody may be found in the blood of as many as 50% of patients receiving hydralazine who remain asymptomatic. A positive antinuclear antibody titre requires that the physician carefully weigh the implications of the test results against the benefits to be derived from antihypertensive therapy with hydralazine.

Microhematuria and/or proteinuria, in particular together with positive titres of antinuclear antibodies, may be initial signs of immune-complex glomerulonephritis associated with the SLE-like syndrome.

The chronotropic and inotropic effects of hydralazine increase myocardial oxygen requirements. It can cause electrocardiographic changes of myocardial ischemia, and in patients with coronary artery disease may precipitate angina pectoris or congestive heart failure. Hydralazine has been implicated in the production of myocardial infarction.

Ser-Ap-Es must therefore be used with caution in patients with suspected coronary artery disease. It should be given only in combination with a beta-blocker or other suitable sympatholytic agents. The beta-blocker medication should be commenced a few days before the start of treatment with hydralazine.

Patients who have survived a myocardial infarction should not receive Ser-Ap-Es until postinfarction stabilization has been achieved.

The "hyperdynamic" circulation caused by hydralazine may accentuate specific cardiovascular inadequacies (e.g. hydralazine may increase pulmonary artery pressure in patients with mitral valvular disease).

Patients with impaired hepatic function or progressive liver disease, should be carefully monitored for rare but serious effects of hydralazine on the liver. Also, minor alterations in fluid and electrolyte balance or of serum ammonia may precipitate hepatic coma, especially in patients with liver cirrhosis.

Discontinue the drug at least 2 weeks before elective surgery or electroshock therapy. Preoperative withdrawal of reserpine does not insure that circulatory instability will not occur. It is important that the anesthesiologist be aware of the patient's drug intake and consider this in the overall management since hypotension has occurred in patients receiving rauwolfia preparations. Anticholinergic and/or adrenergic drugs (metaraminol, norepinephrine) have been employed to treat adverse vagocirculatory effects.

Postural hypotension may result from hydralazine, but is less common than with ganglionic blocking agents.

Since reserpine may increase gastrointestinal motility and secretion, it should be used cautiously in patients with a history of gastric or duodenal ulceration, acute erosive gastritis, ulcerative colitis or other gastrointestinal disorders. Reserpine may precipitate biliary colic in patients with gallstones.

Debilitated persons or patients with cardiac disease require special care in adjusting dosage in order to avoid hypotension and edema.

In patients suffering from coronary and/or cerebral arteriosclerosis Ser-Ap-Es should be employed with extreme caution. Any abrupt lowering of the blood pressure should be avoided. It is also advisable to exercise caution in patients with heart failure, recent myocardial infarction, sinus bradycardia, or disorders of cardiac conduction.

The possibility of sensitivity reactions should be considered in patients with, and without, a history of allergy or bronchial asthma. Due to the effect of catecholamine depletion, special care should be exercised when treating patients with a history of bronchial asthma. Asthmatics are more apt to be hypersensitive to catecholamine depletion, and their condition may be aggravated.

Disturbances in serum electrolyte balance, particularly hypokalemia, may occur during treatment with thiazides. Since the excretion of electrolytes is increased, an excessively strict low-salt diet should be avoided.

Patients receiving thiazides should be carefully observed for clinical signs of fluid or electrolyte imbalance. Serum and urine electrolyte determinations are particularly important in digitalized patients and in patients vomiting excessively or receiving parenteral fluids. Warning signs or symptoms of fluid and electrolyte imbalance include dryness of mouth, thirst, weakness, lethargy, drowsiness, restlessness, muscle pains or cramps, muscular fatigue, gastrointestinal disturbances, hypotension, oliguria, tachycardia, and cardiac arrhythmias or corresponding ECG changes. Should hypochloremic alkalosis or hyponatremia occur, consider appropriate therapy.

Hypokalemia may develop, especially with brisk diuresis, in patients presenting with vomiting, diarrhea, malnutrition, nephrosis, liver cirrhosis, hyperaldosteronism, or during concomitant use of corticosteroids or ACTH.

Hypokalemia may be avoided or treated with foods high in potassium content or, if necessary, with potassium supplements. Titrated coadministration of an oral potassium salt (e.g., KCl) may be considered in patients receiving digitalis; in patients exhibiting signs of coronary heart disease, unless they are also receiving an ACE inhibitor; in patients on high doses of β-adrenergic agonist; and in all cases where plasma potassium concentration are <3.0 mmol/L. If oral potassium preparations are not tolerated, Ser-Ap-Es may be combined with a potassium sparing diuretic.

Combined treatment consisting of hydrochlorothiazide and a potassium salt or a potassium-sparing diuretic must be avoided in patients also receiving ACE inhibitors.

In all cases of combined treatment, maintenance or normalization of the potassium balance should be checked closely. If hypokalemia is accompanied by clinical signs (e.g., muscular weakness, paresis or ECG alteration), Ser-Ap-Es should be discontinued.

For chronic treatment with hydrochlorothiazide, serum potassium concentrations should be checked initially and then after 3 to 4 weeks. Thereafter—if the potassium balance is not disturbed by additional factors (e.g., vomiting, diarrhea, change in renal function, etc.)—checks should be carried out every 4 to 6 months.

During treatment with thiazides, hyponatremia accompanied by neurological symptoms (nausea, debility, progressive disorientation, apathy) has been observed in isolated cases. In these patients, serum electrolytes should be monitored at more frequent intervals.

Water restriction rather than actual salt replacement may be considered appropriate treatment of any chloride deficit except in rare instances when hyponatremia is life threatening. Then appropriate salt replacement is the therapy of choice.

Patients receiving relatively high doses of thiazides may develop hypomagnesemia accompanied by such signs and symptoms as nervousness, muscle spasm, and cardiac arrhythmias.

Monitoring of serum electrolytes is particularly indicated in the elderly, in patients with ascites due to liver cirrhosis, and in patients with edema due to nephrotic syndrome. These patients are more susceptible to regulatory disorders affecting electrolyte and fluid balance. For the latter condition, hydrochlorothiazide should be used only under close control in normokalemic patients with no signs of volume depletion or severe hypoalbuminemia.

Thiazides may decrease serum protein bound iodine levels without signs of thyroid disturbance. Calcium excretion is decreased.

In hypertensive patients with normal kidneys who are treated with hydralazine, there is evidence of increased renal blood flow and a maintenance of glomerular filtration rate. In some instances improved renal function has been noted where control values were below normal prior to hydralazine administration. However, as with any antihypertensive agent, hydralazine should be used with caution in patients with advanced renal damage.

In patients with renal impairment, serum levels of hydralazine increased as compared to those in patients with normal renal function, there is also the risk of cumulative effects of hydrochlorothiazide in these patients. Therefore the dose or the dosing interval has to be adapted according to the clinical response, in order to avoid accumulation of the "apparent" active substance.

In patients with hepatic dysfunction, serum levels of hydralazine increased as compared to those in patients with normal hepatic function, therefore the dose or the dosing interval has to be adapted according to the clinical response, in order to avoid accumulation of the "apparent" active substance.

Pathological changes in the parathyroid glands, with hypercalcemia and hypophosphatemia, have been observed in a few patients on prolonged thiazide therapy. The common complications of hyperparathyroidism such as renal lithiasis, bone resorption, and peptic ulceration have not been seen. Discontinue thiazides before carrying out tests for parathyroid function.

Azotemia may be precipitated or increased by thiazides. Discontinue if increasing azotemia and oliguria occur during treatment of severe progressive renal disease.

Treatment with thiazide diuretics should be initiated cautiously in postsympathectomy patients since the antihypertensive effects may be enhanced.

Thiazides may raise the serum uric acid level and provoke attacks of gout in predisposed patients. In cases where prolonged and significant elevation of blood uric acid concentrations are considered potentially deleterious, concomitant use of a uricosuric agent is effective in reversing hyperuricemia without loss of diuretic and/or antihypertensive activity.

A decreased glucose tolerance evidenced by hyperglycemia and glycosuria may develop inconsistently with the administration of thiazides. This condition, usually reversible on discontinuation of therapy, responds to control with antidiabetic treatment. Diabetics and those predisposed should be checked regularly.

In patients with hyperlipidemia, serum lipids should be regularly monitored. In the event of a rise in all serum lipids, withdrawal of the thiazide should be considered.

Ser-Ap-Es should not be used as a first-line drug for long-term treatment in patients with overt diabetes mellitus or in subjects receiving therapy for hypercholesterolemia (diet or combined).

Peripheral neuritis, evidenced by paresthesias, numbness and tingling in the extremities has been observed with hydralazine. Published evidence suggests an antipyridoxine effect and the addition of pyridoxine to the regimen if symptoms develop.

Blood dyscrasias consisting of reduction in hemoglobin and red cell count, leukopenia, agranulocytosis and purpura have been reported with hydralazine. Periodic blood counts are advised during therapy. If such abnormalities develop, therapy should be discontinued.

Occupational Hazards: A pronounced lowering of the blood pressure may adversely affect the patient's reactions. Caution should therefore be exercised when driving or operating machinery while being treated with Ser-Ap-Es.

Pregnancy: No animal reproduction studies have been conducted with Ser-Ap-Es; it is contraindicated in pregnancy for the following reasons.

Animal studies indicate that high doses of hydralazine are teratogenic in mice, possibly in rabbits, but not in rats. Teratogenic effects observed were cleft palate and malformation of facial and cranial bones. There are no adequate and well-controlled studies in pregnant women. Although clinical experience does not include any positive evidence of adverse effects on the human fetus, hydralazine should be used during pregnancy only if the benefit clearly justifies the potential risk to the fetus.

Reserpine crosses the placental barrier. When administered shortly before term, it may lead to lethargy, nasal congestion, increased tracheobronchial secretions, and anorexia in the newborn infant. It should therefore not be given during the last 3 months prior to the calculated date of confinement.

The routine use of thiazide diuretics in an otherwise healthy woman with or without edema is inappropriate and exposes mother and fetus to unnecessary hazard. Thiazides cross the placental barrier and may carry the same risk to the fetus (jaundice, thrombocytopenia, etc.) as have occurred in adults.

Edema in pregnancy, resulting from restriction of venous return by the expanded uterus, is treated through elevation of the lower extremities and use of support hose. In a small percentage, more generalized edema may occur and also does not indicate use of diuretics. Rarely, gross edema giving extreme discomfort and due to no other apparent cause may be treated with a short course of diuretic if the above methods and salt restriction fail. Pathological edema such as cardiac, nephrotic or hepatic edema may indicate use of diuretics. Hydrochlorothiazide, like other diuretics, can cause placental hypoperfusion. Since they do not prevent or alter the course of EPH (Edema, Proteinuria, Hypertension)-gestosis (preeclampsia), these drugs must not be used to treat hypertension in pregnant women.

As thiazides increase blood uric acid concentration, levels should be taken before and during pregnancy but their value in assessing the onset of toxemia may still be lost.

Lactation: Reserpine, hydralazine, and hydrochlorothiazide each pass into the breast milk. Reserpine can cause effects in the infant as mentioned above. A choice must be made between withdrawing Ser-Ap-Es or weaning the infant. Hydrochlorothiazide may suppress lactation. Alternatives to Ser-Ap-Es should be considered in nursing mothers.

Geriatrics: The elderly may be more sensitive to the hypotensive effects. In addition, the risk of hydralazine-induced hypothermia may be increased in elderly patients.

Children: Although there is some experience with the use of hydralazine in children, controlled clinical trials to establish safety and effectiveness in this age group have not been conducted.

Keep out of reach of children.

Drug Interactions: Concomitant treatment with other vasodilators, calcium antagonists, ACE inhibitors, diuretics, centrally acting agents (e.g., methyldopa), antihypertensives, tricyclic antidepressants and major tranquilizers, as well as the consumption of alcohol, may potentiate the hypotensive effect of Ser-Ap-Es.

Administration of hydralazine shortly before or after diazoxide may lead to marked hypotension. When potent antihypertensive drugs, such as diazoxide, are used in combination with hydralazine, patients should be continuously observed for several hours for any excessive fall in blood pressure.

Thiazide diuretics may enhance the hyperglycemic effects of diazoxide.

Concurrent administration of hydralazine with beta-blockers subject to a strong first-pass effect (e.g., propranolol) may increase their bioavailability. Downward dosage adjustment of these drugs may be required when they are given concomitantly.

Hydralazine may reduce the pressor responses to epinephrine.

MAO inhibitors are contraindicated since large quantities of catecholamines may be released, causing a sharp transient rise in blood pressure. MAO inhibitors should be withdrawn at least 14 days before treatment with reserpine. Likewise, reserpine must be withdrawn for a similar period of time prior to MAO inhibition, since severe interactions (hyperactivity, hypertensive crises) could occur.

Ser-Ap-Es should be used cautiously with digitalis and antiarrhythmic drugs as arrhythmias have occurred with rauwolfia preparations.

Hypokalemia or hypomagnesemia, potential unwanted effects with thiazides, can sensitize or exaggerate the response of the heart to the toxic effects of digitalis (e.g., arrhythmias).

Concurrent use of guanethidine and rauwolfia derivatives may cause bradycardia, mental depression and postural hypotension.

The central depressant actions of alcohol, analgesics, antihistamines, and psychoactive drugs (tricyclic antidepressants) are potentiated by reserpine.

Reserpine diminishes the activity of levodopa.

Reserpine may potentiate the effects of epinephrine or other substances displaying sympathomimetic properties. (For example, caution is advised when using antitussives and cold preparations, nasal decongestants, and eye drops).

Concurrent use of tricyclic antidepressants may increase the antihypertensive effects of reserpine.

Reserpine interferes with colorimetric tests for urinary 17-ketosteroids and 17-hydroxycorticosteroids, producing spurious (low) values.

Concomitant administration of certain NSAIDs (e.g., indomethacin) may weaken the diuretic and antihypertensive activity of thiazides, and there have been isolated reports of a deterioration of renal function in predisposed patients.

The hypokalemic effect of diuretics may be increased by corticosteroids, ACTH, amphotericin and carbenoxolone.

Thiazides may increase the responsiveness to curare derivatives and ganglionic blocking agents.

Diuretics enhance the cardiotoxic (e.g., ECG changes) and neurotoxic (e.g., ataxia, confusion, and mental disorientation) effects of lithium and these drugs should not be administered concurrently. In those rare instances when these drugs must be given together, patients should be observed closely for signs and symptoms of lithium toxicity. Close monitoring of serum electrolytes and lithium concentrations and maintenance of adequate fluid, potassium and sodium intake are also necessary.

Postural hypotension may occur and may be potentiated by alcohol, barbiturates or narcotics.

Arterial responsiveness to norepinephrine may be decreased by hydrochlorothiazide, but not sufficiently to preclude effectiveness of the pressor agent in therapy.

It may prove necessary to readjust the dosage of insulin or oral hypoglycemic agents.

Allopurinol: Coadministration of thiazide diuretics may increase the incidence of hypersensitivity reactions to allopurinol.

Amantadine: Coadministration of thiazide diuretics may increase the risk of adverse effects caused by amantadine.

Antineoplastic agents (e.g., cyclophosphamide, methotrexate): Concomitant use of thiazide diuretics may reduce renal excretion of cytotoxic agents and enhance the myelosuppressive effects.

Anticholinergics (e.g., atropine, biperiden): The bioavailability of thiazide-type diuretics may be increased by anticholinergic agents apparently due to a decrease in gastrointestinal motility and the stomach-emptying rate.

Ser-Ap-Es (cont'd)

Cholestyramine: Absorption of thiazide diuretics is decreased by cholestyramine. A decrease in the pharmacological effect may be expected.
Vitamin D: Concomitant use of thiazide diuretics may decrease urinary excretion of calcium, and coadministration of vitamin D may potentiate the increase in serum calcium.
Cyclosporine: Concomitant treatment with diuretics may increase the risk of hyperuricemia and gout-type complications.
Calcium Salts: Concomitant use of thiazide-type diuretics may cause hypercalcemia by increasing tubular calcium reabsorption.
Methyldopa: There have been reports in the literature of hemolytic anemia occurring with concomitant use of hydrochlorothiazide and methyldopa.

Adverse Effects: The most common adverse reactions are tachycardia, palpitation, anginal symptoms, flushing, headache, and gastrointestinal disturbances. These are more frequent at the start of treatment, especially if the dosage is raised rapidly. However, such reactions generally subside in the further course of treatment or following a reduction of dosage.

The most severe reactions are neuropathy, blood dyscrasias, and an acute rheumatoid state resulting in a syndrome resembling disseminated lupus erythematosus (see Warnings and Precautions).

When adverse reactions occur, they are usually reversible and disappear when the drug is discontinued. The individual components of Ser-Ap-Es are present in lower doses than when given separately to treat hypertension. The frequency of the adverse reactions indicated, were reported from the use of the individual components.

Frequency estimates are as follows: Frequent: >10%. Occasional: 1 to 10%. Rare: 0.001 to 1%. Isolated cases: <0.001%.
Gastrointestinal: Occasional: increased salivation and gastric secretions, dry mouth (xerostomia), increased intestinal motility and diarrhea, nausea and vomiting. Rare: anorexia, increased appetite, aggravation of peptic ulcer or ulcerative colitis, constipation, gastric irritation, gastrospasm, gastrointestinal discomfort, abdominal distress, liver enlargement, abnormal liver function sometimes in association with hepatitis, paralytic ileus and intrahepatic cholestasis or jaundice. Isolated: higher dosages can cause gastrointestinal hemorrhage, pancreatitis.
Cardiovascular: Frequently: tachycardia, palpitation. Occasional: edema, in patients with hypertensive vascular disease (which generally ameliorates upon cessation of therapy, or with the administration of a diuretic agent), sinus bradycardia, anginal symptoms, flushing, hypotension and postural hypotension with higher doses (may be aggravated by alcohol, anesthetics or sedatives). Rare: angina-like syndrome, cardiac arrhythmias (particularly when used concurrently with digitalis or quinidine), heart failure. Isolated: loss of consciousness (syncope), cardiac insufficiency, cerebrovascular disturbances, paradoxical pressor responses.
Respiratory: asthma in susceptible or hypersensitive persons. Occasional: nasal congestion, dyspnea. Rare: pleural pain. Isolated: epistaxis, respiratory distress including pneumonitis and pulmonary edema.
Nervous System: Frequently: headache. Occasional: mental depression, nightmares (which may be an early sign of mental depression), drowsiness, lassitude, dizziness, nervousness, insomnia and sleep disturbances, respiratory depression. Rare: extrapyramidal symptoms (including parkinsonian syndrome), paradoxical anxiety, agitation, impaired concentration, fever, malaise, stupor, dull sensorium, and peripheral neuritis evidenced by paresthesia numbness and tingling. Isolated: cerebral edema, polyneuritis, tremor, hallucinations.
Musculoskeletal: Occasionally: arthralgia, joint swelling, myalgia.
Sense Organs: Isolated cases of hearing impairment, deafness, glaucoma, uveitis, conjunctival hyperemia, conjunctival injection, conjunctivitis, nasal congestion, increased lacrimation, blurred vision, exophthalmos, xanthopsia and optic atrophy. Visual disturbances particularly in the first few weeks of treatment.
Urogenital: Occasional: decreased libido, impotence. Rare: impaired ejaculation, proteinuria, increased plasma creatinine, hematuria sometimes in association with glomerulonephritis.
Dermatological: Occasional: urticaria and other forms of skin rash, systemic lupus erythematosus-like syndrome (see Warnings and Precautions). Rare: photosensitization, pruritus. Isolated: necrotizing vasculitis and toxic epidermal necrolysis, cutaneous lupus erythematosus-like reactions, reactivation of cutaneous lupus erythematosus.
Endocrine: Occasional: weight gain. Rare: galactorrhea, gynecomastia, weight decrease. Isolated: swelling of the breasts.
Hematological: Rare: anemia, leukopenia, neutropenia, eosinophilia, thrombocytopenia with or without purpura. Isolated: anemia (aplastic, hemolytic), agranulocytosis, bone marrow depression, lymphadenopathy, pancytopenia, splenomegaly and leukocytosis.
Electrolyte and Metabolic Disorders: Frequently: mainly at higher doses, hypokalemia, and rise in blood lipids. Occasionally: hyponatremia, hypomagnesemia, and hyperuricemia. Rare: hypercalcemia, hyperglycemia, glycosuria and worsening of diabetic metabolic state. Due to the possibility of hyperparathyroidism, hypercalcemia requires further diagnostic classification. Isolated: hyperchloremic alkalosis.

Overdose: Symptoms: Impairment of consciousness may occur and may range from drowsiness to coma, depending upon the severity of overdosage. Lethargy, tiredness, apathy, confusion, agitation, tachycardia, sweating or depression may also ensue. Flushing of the skin, conjunctival injection and miosis (lasting for several days) are to be expected. Convulsions (especially in children), hypotension, hypothermia, central respiratory depression, cardiac arrhythmias (particularly sinus bradycardia), muscle spasms (associated with electrolyte disturbances), myocardial ischemia with angina pectoris and myocardial infarction and shock may develop in cases of severe overdosage. Extrapyramidal disorders, headache, nausea, dizziness, paresthesia, vomiting, increased intestinal motility and diarrhea, increased salivary and gastric secretion, and swelling of the nasal mucosa may also occur.

Further possible symptoms include dry mouth, thirst, restlessness, muscular weakness, mental confusion, delirium, severe diarrhea, oliguria and hypovolemia. If digitalis had also been administered, hypokalemia may accentuate myocardial abnormalities (e.g., cardiac arrhythmias).

Hydrochlorothiazide may precipitate hepatic coma in cirrhotics, potentiate other antihypertensive agents, and decrease responsiveness to norepinephrine.

Treatment: There is no specific antidote.

Remove unabsorbed Ser-Ap-Es from the stomach by induction of emesis or gastric lavage, taking adequate precautions against aspiration and for protection of the airway. Administration of activated charcoal slurry and possibly an osmotic cathartic may help reduce absorption. Infusions may be helpful to promote urinary excretion. These procedures may have to be omitted or carried out after cardiovascular status has been stabilized, since they might precipitate cardiac arrhythmias or increase the depth of shock.

Treat the effects of Ser-Ap-Es overdosage symptomatically. Symptomatic management should pay particular attention to cardiac rate and output, blood volume, electrolyte balance, dehydration, paralytic ileus, urinary function, hepatic coma, and cerebral activity.

In the presence of postural hypotension, place the patient in an appropriate position (supine) and administer a plasma expander. I.V. electrolyte and fluid replacement may be indicated. The use of dopamine to elevate systolic blood pressure to 90 mmHg may be considered in an emergency. If hypotension is severe enough to require treatment with a vasopressor, use one having a direct action upon vascular smooth muscle (e.g., phenylephrine, norepinephrine, metaraminol). The ECG should be monitored while the vasopressor is being administered. Digitalization may be necessary. Renal function must be monitored and supported as required.

If bradycardia becomes marked, especially with cardiac arrhythmias, consider the use of vagal blocking agents along with other appropriate measures.

Administration of sympathomimetic drugs (e.g., dopamine) may be indicated. Diarrhea if severe or persistent, should be treated symptomatically with an anticholinergic agent to reduce intestinal hypermotility, with due attention to maintenance of hydration and electrolyte balance.

To combat convulsions administer anticonvulsants (e.g., diazepam) slowly i.v.

In the event of severe respiratory depression, administer oxygen or artificial respiration.

Since reserpine is long acting, observe the patient carefully for at least 72 hours, administering treatment as required.

Dosage: 1 or 2 tablets, twice daily, initially for 2 weeks; then adjust as needed. For maintenance, the lowest effective dosage should be used. The preparation should be taken with liquid at mealtimes.
Renal Impairment, Geriatric and Hepatic Dysfunction: The standard dosage is recommended for patients with normal renal function. In elderly patients, with hepatic dysfunction, and/or patients with mild renal insufficiency, the dosage or dosing interval should be adjusted carefully in accordance with therapeutic requirements and tolerability. In patients with impaired renal function (creatinine clearance ≤30 mL/min) who require treatment with a diuretic, it is preferable to give a loop diuretic rather than a thiazide diuretic (see Contraindications).
Note: With hydralazine, the incidence of toxic reactions, particularly the lupus erythematosus syndrome, is highest in the group of patients receiving large doses of hydralazine. The dose of hydralazine should not be increased above 100 mg/day without determining the acetylator phenotype.

The influence of food on the bioavailability of hydralazine is uncertain. Contradictory results have been obtained.

Geriatric patients may be more sensitive to the effects of the usual adult dose. Response should be monitored and the dosage adjusted accordingly to lowest effective levels. In patients with hepatic dysfunction or renal impairment the dose or the dosing interval should be adapted according to the clinical response, in order to avoid accumulation of the ''apparent'' active substance.

Information for the Patient: See Blue Section—Information for the Patient ''Ser-Ap-Es''.

Supplied: Each pink, round, flat-faced, bevel-edged tablet, engraved ''CIBA'' on one side and ''AC'' on the other, contains: reserpine 0.1 mg, hydralazine HCl 25 mg and hydrochlorothiazide 15 mg. Nonmedicinal ingredients: acacia, cornstarch, Erythrosine Lake, FD&C Green No. 3, lactose, polyethylene glycol, stearic acid, sugar and Sunset Yellow Lake. Energy: 4 kJ (0.97 kcal). Alcohol-, bisulfite-, gluten-, parabens-, sodium- and tartrazine-free. Bottles of 100. Protect from heat (store at 2 to 30°C), light and humidity.

(Shown in Product Recognition Section)

Reviewed 1997

SERAX® ℞

Wyeth-Ayerst

Oxazepam

Anxiolytic—Sedative

Supplied: 10 mg: Each light yellow, scored Titradose tablet, imprinted SERAX and 10, contains: oxazepam 10 mg. Nonmedicinal ingredients: D&C Yellow No. 10 Aluminum Lake, FD&C Yellow No. 6 Aluminum Lake, lactose, magnesium stearate, microcrystalline cellulose and polacrilin potassium. Energy: 2.97 kJ (0.71 kcal). Gluten- and tartrazine-free. Bottles of 100 and 500.

15 mg: Each yellow, scored Titradose tablet, imprinted SERAX and 15, contains: oxazepam 15 mg. Nonmedicinal ingredients: D&C Yellow No. 10 Aluminum Lake, FD&C Yellow No. 6 Aluminum Lake, lactose, magnesium stearate, microcrystalline cellulose and polacrilin potassium. Energy: 2.85 kJ (0.68 kcal). Gluten- and tartrazine-free. Bottles of 100 and 500.

30 mg: Each peach, scored Titradose tablet, imprinted SERAX and 30, contains: oxazepam 30 mg. Nonmedicinal ingredients: FD&C Yellow No. 6 Aluminum Lake, lactose, magnesium stearate, microcrystalline cellulose and polacrilin potassium. Energy: 2.64 kJ (0.63 kcal). Gluten- and tartrazine-free. Bottles of 100 and 500.

(Shown in Product Recognition Section)

SERC® ℞

Solvay Pharma

Betahistine HCl

Antivertigo

Pharmacology: Betahistine was found to have a histamine-like action in animals. Since parenteral histamine has been used in the treatment of Ménière's disease, studies were conducted to test the action of betahistine in this condition. Unlike some other antivertigo drugs, testing with nystagmus induced by caloric and rotational stimulation has demonstrated that betahistine does not decrease the vestibular response, as recorded by electronystagmography. In addition, the absorption, metabolism and action of betahistine when administered by the oral route are not known. However, clinical studies indicate that betahistine may be useful in reducing the vertigo of Ménière's disease.

Indications: May be of value in reducing the episodes of vertigo in Ménière's disease. No claim is made for the effectiveness of betahistine in the symptomatic treatment of any form of vertigo other than that associated with Ménière's disease.

Contraindications: Not to be administered to patients with active peptic ulcer or a history of this condition; pheochromocytoma.
Children: Not recommended for use in children.

Precautions: Caution should be exercised if betahistine is administered to patients with bronchial asthma. Betahistine should not be used concurrently with antihistaminic agents.
Pregnancy and *Lactation:* Safe use of betahistine during pregnancy or lactation, or in women of childbearing age has not yet been established.

Adverse Effects: Occasionally, patients have experienced gastric upset, nausea and headache.

Dosage: Usual adult dosage has been 4 to 8 mg orally 3 times a day. Therapy is adjusted as needed to maintain patient response. Dosage has ranged from 8 to 32 mg per day. Maximum recommended daily dosage is 32 mg.

Supplied: Each round, pink tablet, scored on one side and engraved with "unimed" on the other, contains: betahistine HCl 4 mg. Nonmedicinal ingredients: cornstarch, FD&C Red No. 3, lactose, magnesium stearate and purified silica. Gluten- and tartrazine-free. Bottles of 100.

(Shown in Product Recognition Section)

SERENTIL® ℞
Novartis Pharmaceuticals

Mesoridazine Besylate
Antipsychotic

Pharmacology: Pharmacological studies in laboratory animals have established that mesoridazine has a spectrum of pharmacological activity comparable to thioridazine, except that its effects, other than cataleptic which is weaker, are more pronounced.

Following oral administration, mesoridazine is well absorbed with peak blood levels occurring at 4 hours.

Approximately 30 to 40% of a dose is recovered in the urine and 25 to 30% is recovered in the feces, even after i.m. administration.

Indications: The treatment of both the acute and chronic states of schizophrenia; organic brain syndrome and mental retardation associated with psychotic symptoms or where psychomotor disturbances are predominant; treatment of some patients with symptoms of alcohol withdrawal.

Contraindications: Severe CNS depression, comatose states, blood dyscrasias, bone marrow depression, liver damage, hypersensitivity to mesoridazine; cross sensitivity to other phenothiazines may occur. Hypertension or hypotensive heart disease of extreme degree.

Precautions: Occupational Hazards: Where patients are participating in activities requiring complete mental alertness (e.g. driving) it is advisable to administer the phenothiazine cautiously and to increase the dosage gradually.

Attention should be paid to the fact that phenothiazines are capable of potentiating CNS depressants (e.g. anesthetics, analgesics, hypnotics, antihistamines, opiates, alcohol, etc.) as well as atropine and phosphorus insecticides. They may also potentiate quinidine's inhibitory effect on cardiac contractility.

Since ocular pigmentary changes have been reported with phenothiazines of the piperidine class the possibility of this side effect cannot be excluded.

Prolongation of the QT interval, flattening and inversion of the T wave and appearance of a wave tentatively identified as a bifid T or a U wave have been observed in some patients receiving phenothiazine tranquilizers, including mesoridazine. These changes appear to be reversible and related to a disturbance in repolarization. Mesoridazine should be given with caution to patients with heart disease.

Leukopenia, granulocytopenia and/or agranulocytosis have been reported following phenothiazine therapy. The possibility of the occurrence of blood dyscrasia cannot, therefore, be ruled out. Therefore, patients should be observed for any signs or symptoms of blood dyscrasia. It is also advisable to perform regular blood counts, particularly during the first 2 or 3 months of therapy and on the appearance of suspicious clinical signs.

Hypotension, which is typically orthostatic, may occur especially in the elderly and in alcoholic patients with either dosage form. Assumption of the head down supine position will ordinarily bring the blood pressure back to normal. On rare occasions, and more so after parenteral administration of the drug, prolonged and severe hypotension may occur, requiring the use of vasopressors. The administration of epinephrine should be avoided in the treatment of phenothiazine induced hypotension in view of the fact that phenothiazines may induce a reverse epinephrine effect and aggravate the hypotension.
Pregnancy and *Lactation:* Safe use of mesoridazine in human pregnancy has not been established. Therefore, it should not be administered to women of childbearing potential, particularly during the first trimester of pregnancy, unless the expected benefit to the patient outweighs the potential risk to the fetus. Mesoridazine may appear in human breast milk.

Adverse Effects: Drowsiness and hypotension are the most prevalent adverse effects encountered. Sedation, hypotension and other autonomic effects tend to occur more frequently early in the treatment or when initial high doses are used.

When these reactions occur they can usually be controlled by a reduction in dosage. In mild cases of hypotension, the head down position may be adequate. In severe cases of hypotension, a pressor agent such as levarterenol bitartrate may be used. Epinephrine should not be administered, since it may result in a further fall of blood pressure.

The following adverse reactions have been reported with phenothiazine derivatives and may occur with mesoridazine:
Behavioral reactions: oversedation; impaired psychomotor function; paradoxical effects, such as agitation, excitement, insomnia, bizarre dreams, aggravation of psychotic symptoms; and toxic confusional states.
CNS: extrapyramidal reactions, including Parkinsonism (with motor retardation, rigidity, masklike facies, tremor, salivation, etc.); dystonic reactions (including facial grimacing, tics, torticollis, oculogyric crises, etc.); and akathisia. Persistent dyskinesias resistant to treatment have also been reported. In addition, slowing of EEG, disturbed body temperature, and lowering of the convulsive threshold have occurred.

Tardive dyskinesia may appear in some patients on long-term antipsychotic therapy or may appear after drug therapy has been discontinued. The risk appears to be greater in elderly patients on high-dose therapy, especially females. The symptoms are persistent and in some patients appear to be irreversible. The syndrome is characterized by rhythmical involuntary movements of the tongue, face, mouth or jaw (e.g. protrusion of tongue, puffing of cheeks, puckering of mouth, chewing movements). Sometimes these may be accompanied by involuntary movements of extremities.

There is no known effective treatment for tardive dyskinesia; antiparkinsonian agents usually do not alleviate the symptoms of this syndrome. All antipsychotic agents should be discontinued if these symptoms appear. Should it be necessary to reinstitute treatment, or increase the dosage of the agent, or switch to a different antipsychotic agent, the syndrome may be masked. The physician may be able to reduce the risk of this syndrome by minimizing the unnecessary use of neuroleptics and reducing the dose or discontinuing the drug, if possible, when manifestations of this syndrome are recognized, particularly in patients over the age of 50. Fine vermicular movements of the tongue may be an early sign of the syndrome. If the medication is stopped at that time, the syndrome may not develop.
Autonomic nervous system: dry mouth, fainting, stuffy nose, photophobia, blurred vision, miosis.
Gastrointestinal: anorexia, increased appetite, gastric irritation, nausea, vomiting, constipation, paralytic ileus.
Endocrine system: altered libido, menstrual irregularities, lactation, false positive pregnancy tests, inhibition of ejaculation, gynecomastia, weight gain.
Skin: itching, rash, hypertrophic papillae of the tongue, angioneurotic edema, erythema, exfoliative dermatitis, contact dermatitis.
Cardiovascular effects: hypotension, tachycardia, ECG changes (see Precautions).
Blood dyscrasias: agranulocytosis, leukopenia, granulocytopenia, eosinophilia, thrombocytopenia, anemia, aplastic anemia, pancytopenia.
Allergic reactions: fever, laryngeal edema, angioneurotic edema, asthma.
Hepatotoxicity: jaundice, biliary stasis.
Urinary disturbances: retention, incontinence.
Abnormal pigmentation: more recently, a peculiar skin-eye syndrome has been recognized as an adverse effect following long-term treatment with phenothiazines. This reaction is marked by progressive pigmentation of areas of skin or conjunctiva and/or discoloration of the exposed sclera and cornea. Opacities of the anterior lens and cornea described as irregular or stellate in shape have also been reported. Although retinal pigmentation has not been observed with mesoridazine, patients receiving higher doses of mesoridazine for prolonged periods should have periodic complete eye examinations.
Miscellaneous: Unexpected and sudden deaths have been reported in hospitalized psychotic patients receiving phenothiazines. In some unexpected deaths, myocardial lesions have been observed. Previous brain damage or seizures may also be predisposing factors: high doses should be avoided in known seizure patients. Several patients have shown sudden exacerbations of psychotic behavior patterns shortly before death. Autopsy findings have also revealed acute fulminating pneumonia or pneumonitis and aspiration of gastric contents. The physician should therefore be alerted to the possible development of "silent pneumonias".

Overdose: Symptoms: Agitation, drowsiness, confusion, delirium in milder cases. Coma and areflexia in more severe cases. Respiratory depression is a late manifestation of severe phenothiazine intoxication. Motor restlessness, convulsions, acute extrapyramidal symptoms such as dystonia and oculogyric crisis have not been reported but are possible.

Treatment: There is no specific treatment for phenothiazine poisoning: 1. Elimination of the offending drug should be attempted by emesis or gastric lavage followed by the administration of activated charcoal, cathartic diuresis, exchange transfusion in children. Dialysis has been found ineffective.
2. Maintenance of adequate pulmonary ventilation.
3. Correction of hypotension. In severe cases administer dopamine or levarterenol i.v. Epinephrine is contraindicated.
4. General supportive measures and good nursing are required until the patient is well out of the CNS depression.

Dosage: Adjust to individual needs, using the lowest effective dose. When maximum response is achieved, dosage may be reduced gradually to a maintenance level. Dosage should be increased slowly in elderly patients.
Schizophrenia: 75 to 400 mg daily; usual dose: 150 mg per day in divided doses. Mental retardation and chronic brain syndrome: 75 to 300 mg daily; usual dose: 100 mg per day in divided doses. Alcohol withdrawal symptoms: 50 to 200 mg daily; usual dose: 100 mg per day in divided doses. Maximum symptom reduction can usually be achieved without exceeding 200 mg daily.

Supplied: Each red, sugar coated tablet imprinted SANDOZ on one side contains: mesoridazine besylate 10 mg (imprinted 10), 25 mg (imprinted 25) or 50 mg (imprinted 50). Also contains lactose (10, 25 and 50 mg) and cornstarch (10 and 50 mg). Bottles of 100 (10, 25 and 50 mg).

(Shown in Product Recognition Section)

SEREVENT® ℞
Glaxo Wellcome

Salmeterol Xinafoate
Bronchodilator—β_2-adrenergic Stimulant

Pharmacology: Salmeterol is a selective, long-acting (12 hours), slow onset (10 to 20 minutes) β_2-adrenoceptor agonist with a long side-chain which binds to the exo-site of the receptor.

Salmeterol offers more effective protection against histamine-induced bronchoconstriction and produces a longer duration of bronchodilation, lasting for at least 12 hours, than recommended doses of conventional short-acting β_2-agonists.

In contrast to conventional short-acting β_2-agonists, the onset of the bronchodilator effect of salmeterol usually occurs in 10 to 20 minutes. However, the full benefits only become apparent after the first or second dose of the drug. Regular dosing produces sustained improvement in lung function thereby reducing symptoms of airways obstruction.

In vitro tests on human lung, have shown salmeterol is a potent and long-lasting inhibitor of the release of mast cell mediators, such as histamine, leukotrienes and prostaglandin D_2.

In man, salmeterol inhibits the early and late phase response to inhaled allergen. The late phase response is inhibited for over 30 hours after a single dose, when the bronchodilator effect is no longer evident. The full clinical significance of these findings is not yet clear. The mechanism is different from the anti-inflammatory effect of corticosteroids and corticosteroids should not be stopped or reduced because salmeterol is prescribed.
Pharmacokinetics: Salmeterol acts locally in the lung; plasma levels therefore do not predict therapeutic effect. Because of the low therapeutic dose, systemic levels of salmeterol are

Serevent (cont'd)

low or undetectable after inhalation of recommended doses (50 μg twice daily).

Salmeterol is predominantly cleared by hepatic metabolism; liver function impairment may lead to accumulation of salmeterol in plasma. Therefore, patients with hepatic disease should be closely monitored.

Indications: For long-term, twice-daily (morning and evening) administration in the maintenance treatment of asthma in patients 12 years of age and older with reversible obstructive airway disease, including patients with nocturnal asthma, who are using optimal corticosteroid treatment and experiencing breakthrough symptoms requiring regular use of a short-acting bronchodilator. It should not be used in patients whose asthma can be managed by occasional use of short-acting, inhaled β_2-agonists.

Corticosteroids should not be stopped or reduced because salmeterol is prescribed.

Salmeterol is a slow onset, long-acting, β_2-agonist and should not be used as a rescue medication.

To relieve acute asthmatic symptoms a rapidly but short-acting inhaled bronchodilator (e.g., salbutamol) should be used.

Contraindications: Patients with cardiac tachyarrhythmias and those with a known hypersensitivity to any ingredient of the preparations.

Serevent dry powder for inhalation (Serevent Diskhaler Disk and Serevent Diskus) formulations contain lactose (see Supplied) and are contraindicated in patients with an allergy to lactose, milk or in those who have ever had any unusual or allergic reaction to salmeterol xinafoate.

Warnings: Important Information: Salmeterol should not be initiated in patients with significantly worsening or acutely deteriorating asthma, which may be a life-threatening condition (see Precautions). Serious acute respiratory events, including fatalities, have been reported worldwide, when salmeterol has been initiated in this situation.

Although it is not possible from these reports to determine whether salmeterol contributed to these events or simply failed to relieve the deteriorating asthma, the use of salmeterol in this setting is inappropriate.

Salmeterol should not be used to treat acute symptoms. It is crucial to inform patients of this and prescribe a short-acting, inhaled β_2-agonist for this purpose as well as warn them that increasing inhaled β_2-agonist use is a signal of deteriorating asthma (see Precautions).

Salmeterol is not a substitute for inhaled or oral corticosteriods. Corticosteroids should not be stopped or reduced when salmeterol is initiated (see Precautions).

Role of Long-acting β_2-Agonist in the Management of Asthma: The management of asthma should normally follow a stepwise programme, and **patient response should be monitored clinically and by lung function tests.** Sudden or progressive deterioration in asthma control is potentially life-threatening; treatment plan must be re-evaluated, and consideration be given to increasing corticosteroid therapy. **In patients at risk, daily peak flow monitoring with precise instructions for acceptable variation limits should be considered.**

Increased use of inhaled, short-acting β_2-agonists is a marker of destabilization of asthma and requires re-evaluation of the patient and consideration of alternative treatment regimens, especially inhaled or systemic corticosteroids.

Long-acting β_2-agonists are an alternative additional therapy for patients with moderate asthma with unsatisfactory symptom control despite an optimal dose of inhaled steroids in adults particularly when there are nocturnal symptoms.

Before introducing long-acting β_2-agonists, adequate education should be provided to the patient on how to use the drug and what to do if asthma flares up.

Use With Short-acting β_2-Agonists: When patients begin treatment with salmeterol, those who have been taking short-acting, inhaled β_2-agonists on a regular daily basis should be advised to discontinue their regular daily-dosing regimen and should be clearly instructed to use short-acting, inhaled β_2-agonists only for symptomatic relief if they develop asthma symptoms while taking salmeterol (see Precautions, Drug Interactions).

Cardiovascular Effects: Although clinically not significant, a small increase in QTc intervals have been reported at therapeutic doses. It is not known if this becomes clinically significant when concomitant medications causing similar effects are prescribed and/or in the presence of heart diseases, hypokalemia, or hypoxia.

In a very large scale postmarketing surveillance study in the U.K., involving over 24 000 patients comparing safety of salmeterol and salbutamol in the treatment of asthma, the overall cardiovascular deaths on salmeterol treatment were 0.17% vs 0.12% on salbutamol (P=0.308). The subdivision of these deaths into groups dependent on asthma severity are shown in Table I.

Table I—Serevent

Investigator Assessment of Severity of Asthma

	Mild (%)	Moderate (%)	Severe (%)
Salmeterol	0.04	0.11	0.55
Salbutamol	0.14	0.07	0.27

Test for interaction p=0.233.

Fatalities have been reported following excessive use of aerosol preparations containing sympathomimetic amines, the exact cause of which is unknown. Cardiac arrest was reported in several instances.

In individual patients any ß2-adrenergic agonist may have a clinically significant cardiac effect.

Paradoxical Bronchospasm: As with other inhaled asthma medications, paradoxical bronchospasm (which can be life-threatening) has been reported following the use of salmeterol inhalation aerosol. If it occurs, treatment with salmeterol inhalation aerosol should be discontinued immediately and alternative therapy instituted.

Immediate Hypersensitivity Reactions: Immediate hypersensitivity reactions may occur after administration of salmeterol, as demonstrated by rare cases of urticaria, angioedema, rash and bronchospasm.

Upper Airway Symptoms: Symptoms of laryngeal spasm, irritation, or swelling, such as stridor and choking, have been reported rarely in patients receiving salmeterol.

Others: In common with other β-adrenergic agents, salmeterol can induce reversible metabolic changes (e.g., hyperglycemia, hypokalemia).

β-adrenergic blocking drugs, especially the noncardioselective ones, may effectively antagonise the action of salmeterol.

Pregnancy and *Lactation:* The safety of salmeterol in pregnancy and lactation has not been established.

Precautions: General: Do Not Introduce Salmeterol as a Treatment for Acutely Deteriorating Asthma: Salmeterol is intended for the maintenance treatment of asthma (see Indications) and should not be introduced in acutely deteriorating asthma, which is a potentially life-threatening condition. There are no data demonstrating that salmeterol provides greater efficacy than or additional efficacy to short-acting, inhaled β_2-agonists in patients with worsening asthma. Serious acute respiratory events, including fatalities, have been reported worldwide in patients receiving salmeterol. In most cases these have occurred in patients with severe asthma (e.g., patients with a history of corticosteroid dependence, low pulmonary function, intubation, mechanical ventilation, frequent hospitalizations, or previous life-threatening acute asthma exacerbations) and/or in some patients in whom asthma has been acutely deteriorating (e.g., unresponsive to usual medications, increasing need for inhaled short-acting β_2-agonists, increasing need for systemic corticosteroids, significant increase in symptoms, recent emergency room visits, sudden or progressive deterioration in pulmonary function). However, they have occurred in a few patients with less severe asthma as well. It was not possible from these reports to determine whether salmeterol contributed to these events or simply failed to relieve the deteriorating asthma.

Do Not Use Salmeterol to Treat Acute Symptoms: A short-acting, inhaled β_2-agonist, not salmeterol, should be used to relieve acute asthma symptoms. When prescribing salmeterol, the physician must also provide the patient with a short-acting, inhaled β_2-agonist (e.g., salbutamol) for treatment of symptoms that occur acutely, despite regular twice daily (morning and evening) use of salmeterol.

When beginning treatment with salmeterol, patients who have been taking short-acting, inhaled β_2-agonists on a regular basis (e.g., q.i.d.) should be instructed to discontinue the regular use of these drugs and use them only for symptomatic relief if they develop acute asthma symptoms while taking salmeterol (see Precautions, Information to be Provided to the Patient).

Watch for Increasing Use of Short-acting, Inhaled β_2-Agonists, Which is a Marker of Deteriorating Asthma: Asthma may deteriorate acutely over a period of hours or chronically over several days or longer. If the patient's short-acting inhaled β_2-agonist becomes less effective or the patient needs more inhalation than usual, this may be a marker of destabilization of asthma. In this setting, the patient requires immediate re-evaluation with reassessment of the treatment regimen. Increasing the daily dosage of salmeterol in this situation is not appropriate. Salmeterol should not be used more frequently than twice daily (morning and evening) at the recommended dose of 2 inhalations.

Do Not Use Salmeterol as a Substitute for Oral or Inhaled Corticosteroids: There are no data demonstrating that salmeterol has a clinical anti-inflammatory effect and could be expected to take the place of, or reduce the dose of, corticosteroids. Patients must be warned not to stop or reduce corticosteroid therapy even if they feel better as a result of initiating salmeterol. Any change in corticosteroid dosage should be made **only** after clinical evaluation (see Precautions, Information to be Provided to the Patient).

Do Not Exceed Recommended Dosage: As with other inhaled β_2-adrenergic drugs, salmeterol should not be used more often or at higher doses than recommended. Fatalities have been reported in association with excessive use of inhaled sympathomimetic drugs. Large doses of inhaled or oral salmeterol (12 to 20 times the recommended dose) have been associated with clinically significant prolongation of the QTc interval, which has the potential for producing ventricular arrhythmias.

Adolescent Patients and Asthma Severity Reassessment: In adolescent patients the severity of asthma may be variable with age and periodic reassessment should be considered to determine if continued maintenance therapy with salmeterol is still indicated. Compliance, especially neglect of anti-inflammatory therapy and overuse of short-acting β_2-agonists, should be carefully followed in adolescents receiving long-acting β_2-agonists.

Cardiovascular and Other Effects: No clinically significant effect on the cardiovascular system is usually seen after the administration of inhaled salmeterol in recommended doses, but the cardiovascular and CNS effects seen with all sympathomimetic drugs (e.g., increased blood pressure, heart rate, excitement) can occur after use of salmeterol and may require discontinuation of the drug. Salmeterol, like all sympathomimetic amines, should be used with caution in patients with cardiovascular disorders, especially coronary insufficiency, cardiac arrhythmias, and hypertension; in patients with convulsive disorders or thyrotoxicosis; and in patients who are unusually responsive to sympathomimetic amines.

As has been described with other β-adrenergic agonist bronchodilators, clinically significant changes in systolic and/or diastolic blood pressure, pulse rate, and ECGs have been seen infrequently in individual patients in controlled clinical studies with salmeterol.

Metabolic Effects: Doses of the related β_2-adrenoceptor agonist salbutamol, when administered i.v., have been reported to aggravate pre-existing diabetes mellitus and ketoacidosis. No effects on glucose have been seen with salmeterol at recommended doses. Administration of β_2-adrenoceptor agonists may cause a decrease in serum potassium, possibly through intracellular shunting, which has the potential to increase the likelihood of arrhythmias. The decrease is usually transient, not requiring supplementation.

Clinically significant changes in blood glucose and/or serum potassium were seen rarely during clinical studies with long-term administration of salmeterol at recommended doses.

Drug Interactions: Short-acting β-Agonists: Aerosol bronchodilators of the short-acting adrenergic stimulant type may be used for relief of breakthrough symptoms while using salmeterol. But increasing use of such preparations to control symptoms indicates deterioration of asthma control and the patient's therapy plan should be reassessed.

The regular, concomitant use of salmeterol and other oral sympathomimetic agents is not recommended, since such combined use may lead to deleterious cardiovascular effects.

MAO Inhibitors and Tricyclic Antidepressants: Salmeterol should be administered with extreme caution to patients being treated with MAOIs or tricyclic antidepressants because the action of salmeterol on the vascular system may be potentiated by these agents.

Corticosteroids and Cromoglycate: In clinical trials, inhaled corticosteroids and/or inhaled cromolyn sodium did not alter the safety profile of salmeterol when administered concurrently.

Methylxanthines: The concurrent use of i.v. or orally administered methylxanthines (e.g., aminophylline, theophylline) by patients receiving salmeterol has not been completely evaluated.

β-blocking drugs: Nonselective β-blocking drugs, should never be prescribed in asthma since they may antagonize the bronchodilating action of salmeterol. Cardioselective β-blocking drugs should be used with caution in asthmatics.

Other Drugs: Use with caution in patients receiving other medications causing hypokalemia and/or increased QTc interval (diuretics, high dose steroids, antiarrhythmics, astemizole, terfenadine) and MAO inhibitors or tricyclic antidepressants, since cardiac and vascular effects may be potentiated.

Pregnancy: In animal studies, some effects on the fetus, typical for a β-agonist occurred at exposure levels substantially higher than those that occur with therapeutic use. Extensive use of other β-agonists has provided no evidence that effects in animals are relevant to human use. There are no adequate and well-controlled studies with salmeterol in pregnant women. Salmeterol should be used during pregnancy only if the potential benefit justifies the potential risk to the fetus.

Labor and Delivery: There are no well-controlled human studies that have investigated effects of salmeterol on preterm labor or labor at term. Because of the potential for β-agonist interference with uterine contractility, use of salmeterol during labor should be restricted to those patients in whom the benefits clearly outweigh the risks.

Lactation: Plasma levels of salmeterol after inhaled therapeutic doses are very low (85 to 200 pg/mL) in humans and therefore levels in milk should be correspondingly low. Studies in lactating animals indicate that salmeterol is likely to be secreted in only very small amounts in breast milk. However, since there is no experience with use of salmeterol by nursing mothers, a decision should be made whether to discontinue nursing or to discontinue the drug, taking into account the importance of the drug to the mother. Caution should be exercised when salmeterol is administered to a nursing woman.

Children: The safety and effectiveness of salmeterol in children younger than 12 years of age have not been established.

Geriatrics: No apparent differences in the efficacy and safety of salmeterol were observed when geriatric patients were compared with younger patients in clinical trials. As with other β_2-agonists, however, special caution should be observed when using salmeterol in elderly patients who have concomitant cardiovascular disease that could be adversely affected by this class of drug. Based on available data, no adjustment of salmeterol dosage in geriatric patients is warranted.

Proper Inhaler Technique: Patients' inhaler technique should be checked to make sure that aerosol actuation is synchronized with inspiration of breath for optimum delivery of the drug to the lungs.

Spacer or Other Devices: The safety and effectiveness of salmeterol when used with a spacer or other devices have not been adequately studied.

Information to be Provided to the Patient: See package insert for the type of inhaler that is being prescribed. It is important that patients be instructed on how to use the salmeterol inhalation device correctly and how it should be used in relation to other asthma medications they are taking. Patients should be given the following information: i) The recommended dosage (inhalations twice daily, morning and evening) should not be exceeded. ii) Salmeterol is not meant to relieve acute asthma symptoms and extra doses should not be used for that purpose. Acute symptoms should be treated with a short-acting, inhaled β_2-agonist such as salbutamol (the physician should provide the patient with such medication and instruct the patient in how it should be used). iii) The physician should be notified immediately if any of the following situations occur, which may be a sign of seriously worsening asthma: decreased effectiveness of short-acting, inhaled β_2-agonists; need for more inhalations than usual of short-acting, inhaled β_2-agonists. iv) Salmeterol should not be used as a substitute for oral or inhaled corticosteroids. The dosage of these medications should not be stopped or reduced without consulting the physician, even if the patient feels better after initiating treatment with salmeterol. v) Patients should be cautioned regarding potential adverse cardiovascular effects, such as palpitations or chest pain. vi) In patients receiving salmeterol, other inhaled medications should be used only as directed by the physician. vii) The parents/guardians of adolescent children who have been prescribed salmeterol should be alerted to the general concern regarding asthma therapy compliance, especially neglect of anti-inflammatory therapy and overuse of short-acting β_2-agonists.

Adverse Effects: Adverse reactions to salmeterol are similar in nature to reactions to other selective beta$_2$-adrenoceptor agonists, e.g., palpitation; immediate hypersensitivity reactions, including urticaria, rash, bronchospasm; edema and angioedema; headache; tremor; nervousness; paradoxical bronchospasm. There have also been reports of arthralgia and muscle cramps. Cardiac arrhythmias (including atrial fibrillation, supraventricular tachycardia and extrasystoles) have been reported, usually in susceptible patients.

In controlled, multidose clinical trials involving almost 2 000 patients, the most frequently occurring adverse events were headache, tremor and palpitations, which are pharmacologically predictable effects of β_2-adrenoceptor agonists. Tremor tended to be transient, dose-related and reduced with regular therapy. Headache and palpitations were reported but the incidence was not significantly different from placebo (see Table II).

Table II—Serevent

Incidence of Adverse Effects Compared to Placebo

	Salmeterol 50 μg b.i.d.	Placebo
No. of Patients Reporting	1 462	195
Headache	62 (4.2%)	5 (2.6%)
Tremor	20 (1.4%)	4 (2.1%)
Palpitations	22 (1.5%)	4 (2.1%)

In a subsequent controlled clinical trial patients received either salmeterol in combination with beclomethasone dipropionate (BDP) or BDP alone. A short-acting, inhaled β_2-adrenergic drug was also provided for prn use to all patients. The incidence of pharmacologically predictable adverse events was similar in all groups except for tremor which was significantly higher in the salmeterol 100 μg group compared with the other two groups (see Table III).

Table III—Serevent

Incidence of Adverse Effects with Salmeterol and BDP in Combination and BDP Alone

	Salmeterol 50 μg b.i.d. + BDP[a] 500 μg b.i.d.	Salmeterol 100 μg b.i.d.[b] + BDP[a] 500 μg b.i.d.	BDP[a] 1 000 μg
No. of Patients	243	244	251
Headache	26 (11%)	38 (16%)	43 (17%)
Tremors	6 (2%)	19 (8%)	2 (<1%)
Palpitations	4 (2%)	6 (2%)	4 (2%)
Tachycardia	4 (2 %)	5 (2%)	2 (<1%)

[a]BDP = Beclomethasone dipropionate.
[b]100 μg b.i.d. is not a recommended dose.

As with other inhalation therapy, the potential for paradoxical bronchospasm, should be kept in mind. If it occurs, the preparation should be discontinued immediately and alternative therapy instituted.

In US clinical trials, other events occurring in the salmeterol treatment group at a frequency of 1 to 3% were rhinitis, laryngitis, nausea, viral gastroenteritis, nausea and vomiting, diarrhea, abdominal pain, urticaria, dental pain, pain in joint, back pain, muscle cramp/contraction, myalgia/myositis, muscular soreness, nervousness, malaise/fatigue, tracheitis/bronchitis, rash/skin eruption, and dysmenorrhea.

In small dose-response studies, tremor, nervousness, and palpitations appeared to be dose related.

Postmarketing Experience: In extensive worldwide postmarketing experience, serious exacerbations of asthma, including some that have been fatal, have been reported. In most cases, these have occurred in patients with severe asthma and/or in some patients in whom asthma has been acutely deteriorating (see Warnings), but they have occurred in a few patients with less severe asthma as well. It was not possible from these reports to determine whether salmeterol contributed to these events or simply failed to relieve the deteriorating asthma.

Postmarketing experience includes rare reports of upper airway symptoms of laryngeal spasm, irritation, or swelling, such as stridor and chocking. Hypertension and arrhythmias have been reported.

Overdose: Symptoms and Treatment: Overdosage of β_2-agonists may cause tremor, headache and tachycardia, cardiac arrhythmias, hypokalemia, hypertension and, in extreme cases, sudden death. Treatment should be symptomatic; cardiac and respiratory function should be monitored and support provided if necessary. The preferred antidote for overdosage with salmeterol is the judicious use of a cardioselective β-blocking agent. Cardioselective β-blocking drugs should be used with caution, bearing in mind the danger of inducing an asthmatic attack. Serum potassium level should be monitored.

Dosage: Salmeterol should not be initiated in patients with significantly worsening or acutely deteriorating asthma, which may be a life-threatening condition (see Precautions).

Salmeterol is not a replacement for inhaled or oral corticosteroid therapy; its use is complementary to it. Patients must be warned not to stop or reduce anti-inflammatory therapy without medical advice, even if they feel better on salmeterol.

Salmeterol should not be used to treat acute symptoms. It is crucial to inform patients of this and prescribe a short-acting β_2-agonist for this purpose. The need for additional symptomatic bronchodilator therapy is usually reduced with salmeterol (see Precautions). Medical attention should be sought if patients find that short-acting relief bronchodilator treatment becomes less effective or if they need more inhalations than usual.

Bronchodilators should not be the only or the main treatment in patients with moderate to severe or unstable asthma. Patients with severe asthma require regular medical assessment since death may occur. These patients will require high dose inhaled or oral corticosteroid therapy. Sudden worsening of symptoms may require increased corticosteroids dosage which should be administered under medical supervision.

Since there may be serious adverse effects associated with excessive dosing, the dosage or frequency of administration should not be increased.

As twice-daily regular treatment, salmeterol provides 24-hour bronchodilation and can replace regular use of a fast-acting, short duration (4 hours) inhaled bronchodilator (e.g., salbutamol, terbutaline and ipratropium bromide), or an oral bronchodilator (e.g., salbutamol), when optimum corticosteroid therapy is being used. Salmeterol is administered by the inhaled route only.

Children: At present, there are insufficient clinical data to recommend the use of salmeterol in children younger than 12 years of age.

Geriatrics and Patients with Impaired Renal Function: There is no need to adjust the dose in the otherwise healthy elderly or in patients with impaired renal function (see Precautions, Drug Interactions and Warnings). Because salmeterol is predominantly cleared by hepatic metabolism, patients with hepatic disease should be closely monitored.

Maintenance Therapy: Patients 12 years of age and older: **Inhalation Aerosol:** inhalations [2 x 25 μg of salmeterol (as the xinafoate)] twice daily. **Diskhaler Disk:** Serevent Diskhaler Disks are for use with a Serevent Diskhaler device only. 1 blister [50 μg of salmeterol (as the xinafoate)] twice daily. **Diskus:** 1 blister [50 μg of salmeterol (as the xinafoate)] twice daily.

Adolescent Patients (12 to 16 years): In adolescent patients the severity of asthma may be variable with age and periodic reassessment should be considered to determine if continued maintenance therapy with salmeterol is still indicated (see Precautions).

Salmeterol should not be used more than twice daily.

For full therapeutic benefit, regular usage of salmeterol is recommended in the treatment of reversible airways obstruction.

Information for the Patient: See Blue Section—Information for the Patient "Serevent".

Supplied: Diskhaler Disks: Each circular, double-foil blister pack contains: 4 regularly distributed blisters, each containing a dry powder blend of microfine salmeterol (as the xinafoate salt). Each blister contains: salmeterol 50 μg. Nonmedicinal ingredients: lactose. Cartons of 15 disks (4 blisters/disk). Do not expose to extremes of temperature. Store below 25°C. Protect from humidity. A disk may be kept in the Diskhaler at all times but a blister should only be pierced immediately prior to use. Failure to observe this instruction will affect operation of the Diskhaler. Diskhalers are available individually.

Diskus: Each dose of dry powder of microfine salmeterol (as the xinafoate salt) for inhalation contains: the equivalent of salmeterol 50 μg. Nonmedicinal ingredients: lactose. Formats of 60 doses. Store below 30°C and in a dry place.

Inhalation Aerosol: Each pressurized metered-dose inhaler contains: a nonaqueous suspension of microfine salmeterol (as the xinafoate salt). Each actuation contains: salmeterol 25 μg. Nonmedicinal ingredients: dichlorodifluoromethane, lecithin and trichlorofluoromethane. Metered-dose formats of 60 and 120. Store between 15 and 30°C and protected from frost and direct sunlight. As with most inhaled medications in pressurized, metered-dose inhalers, the therapeutic effect of

Serevent (cont'd)

this medication may decrease when the canister is cold. **Important: Contents under pressure.** The canister should not be broken, punctured or burnt, even when apparently empty.

(Shown in Product Recognition Section)

Reviewed 1999

SEROPHENE®

Serono

Clomiphene Citrate

Ovulatory Agent

Pharmacology: The stimulation of an ovulatory response in cyclic clomiphene therapy is believed to be related to its antiestrogenic properties; by competing with estrogen for binding sites at the hypothalamic level, it may cause increased secretion of luteinizing hormone (LH) and follicle-stimulating hormone (FSH), with subsequent ovarian stimulation and preovulatory LH surge, resulting in maturation of the ovarian follicle and development of the corpus luteum.

The involvement of the pituitary is indicated by increased urinary excretion of gonadotropins and by the response of the ovary as manifested by increased urinary estrogen excretion.

Following therapy with clomiphene presumptive signs of ovulation resemble those associated with normal menstrual cycle. It should be noted, however, that during drug administration and for several days thereafter, the effects of endogenous estrogen on the vaginal mucosa and cervical mucus are inhibited.

Suggested criteria for ovulation following clomiphene may include the ovulatory peak of estrogen excretion, a biphasic basal body temperature curve, urinary excretion of pregnanediol at post-ovulatory or higher levels, and endometrial histologic findings characteristic of the luteal phase. In most patients, ovulation appears to occur from 6 to 12 days after completion of therapy at recommended dosage.

A review of 14 publications appearing between 1964 and 1983 showed that an ovulatory response occurred in 74% of 8 228 patients with ovulatory dysfunction who received clomiphene citrate. Successful therapy characterized by pregnancy occurred in 31% of the 8 228 patients.

Indications: In the treatment of ovulatory failure in patients desiring pregnancy, whose husbands have adequate sperm and who have potentially functional hypothalamic-hypophyseal ovarian systems and adequate endogenous estrogen. Impediments to this goal must be excluded or adequately treated before beginning therapy. The workup and treatment of candidates for clomiphene therapy should be supervised by physicians experienced in management of gynecologic or endocrine disorders. The workup of the patient must begin with a careful and detailed history of menstrual and reproductive function, and a complete physical examination. It should be followed by a selective and careful laboratory investigation, based on historical and physical findings.

The following considerations are appropriate for selection of patients: If any doubt exists as to the presence of early pregnancy, therapy should be withheld until a diagnosis of pregnancy has been excluded. The husband's potential fertility and potency should be ascertained by semen analysis and other indicated examinations. Mechanical impediments to conception, such as tubal obstruction, should be excluded or adequately treated before undertaking therapy. The diagnosis of ovulatory dysfunction should be established by such standard techniques as basal body temperature curves, serial vaginal smears, cervical mucus, endometrial biopsy, and pregnanediol determination. Appropriate diagnostic measures should be undertaken to exclude primary pituitary failure or primary ovarian failure. Intact pituitary and ovaries are required for successful therapy. Ovulatory dysfunction in the presence of abnormally high levels of pituitary gonadotropins is indicative of ovarian failure, and patients in this category cannot be expected to respond to clomiphene. Adequacy of endogenous estrogen, as estimated by vaginal smears, cervical mucus, endometrial biopsy, or urinary estrogen determination, furnishes a measure of ovarian function and indirectly of pituitary function. Bleeding after progesterone administration (progesterone alone, not combined with estrogen) furnishes evidence of an adequate level of endogenous estrogen. A good level of endogenous estrogen provides a favorable prognosis for treatment. A reduced estrogen level, although less favorable does not always preclude successful therapy. Patients with abnormal or excessive bleeding should have particularly careful evaluation prior to therapy. It is most important to ensure that neoplastic lesions are not overlooked. Clinical evaluation of liver function should always precede therapy. When disorders such as diabetes, adrenal disease, or thyroid disease are identified during the investigation, specific treatment should be undertaken and subfertility therapy reconsidered only after the underlying disorder has been adequately treated. Clomiphene cannot be expected to be a substitute for specific therapy of these conditions.

Contraindications: *Pregnancy:* Clomiphene should not be administered during pregnancy since studies in rats and rabbits have shown it to be teratogenic. Studies in humans have not been done. However, there have been reports of congenital malformations and fetal death associated with clomiphene administration in humans, although a direct causal relationship has not been established. To prevent inadvertent administration during early pregnancy, careful pelvic examination must be done prior to each course of therapy, the basal body temperature must be recorded throughout all treatment cycles, and the patient should be carefully observed to determine whether ovulation has occurred. If the basal body temperature following clomiphene is biphasic and is not followed by menses, the patient should be examined carefully for the presence of an ovarian cyst and should have a pregnancy test. The next course of therapy should be delayed until the possibility of pregnancy has been excluded.

Medical Problems: Clomiphene should not be used when the following medical problems exist (reasons given where appropriate):

Liver Disease: Clomiphene therapy is contraindicated in patients with active liver disease or history of hepatic function impairment.

Abnormal Bleeding: Clomiphene is contraindicated in patients with abnormal bleeding of undetermined origin. (Careful evaluation is recommended; neoplastic lesions should not be overlooked.) Clomiphene is not indicated for the management of menstrual disorders.

Fibroid tumors of the uterus.

Ovarian Cyst: Clomiphene should not be given in the presence of an ovarian cyst, since further enlargement of the ovary may occur.

Mental depression.

Thrombophlebitis.

Warnings: Occupational Hazards: Visual symptoms: Patients should be advised that blurring or other visual symptoms, dizziness or light-headedness may occasionally occur during therapy. Patients should be warned that visual symptoms may render such activities as driving a car or operating machinery more hazardous than usual, particularly under conditions of variable lighting. The significance of these visual symptoms is not yet understood (see Adverse Effects). If the patient has any visual symptoms, treatment should be discontinued and a complete ophthalmologic evaluation carried out.

Precautions: Diagnosis prior to therapy: Careful attention should be given to diagnosis in candidates for clomiphene therapy. Complete pelvic examination including cervical cytology is mandatory prior to treatment, and pelvic examination should be repeated before each subsequent course. Clomiphene should not be given in the presence of an ovarian cyst, since further enlargement of the ovary may occur.

Patients in later reproductive life have a greater tendency to endometrial carcinoma as well as a higher incidence of anovulatory disorders. Dilation and curettage should always be done for diagnosis before starting therapy in such patients. If abnormal bleeding is present, full diagnostic measures are mandatory.

Overstimulation of the Ovary During Therapy: In order to minimize the hazard associated with the occasional abnormal ovarian enlargement associated with therapy (see Adverse Effects), the lowest dose consistent with expectation of good results should be used. The patient should be advised of the possibility of ovarian cyst formation and should be instructed to return for repeat pelvic examination between 2 and 3 weeks after starting each course of treatment. Some patients with polycystic ovarian syndrome who are unusually sensitive to gonadotropin may have an exaggerated response to usual doses. It should be borne in mind that maximal enlargement of the ovary, whether physiologic or abnormal, does not occur until several days after discontinuation of the recommended dose. The patient who complains of pelvic pain after receiving clomiphene should be examined with care. If enlargement of the ovary occurs, additional clomiphene therapy should not be given until the ovaries have returned to pretreatment size, and the dosage or duration of the next course should be reduced. Experience has shown that the ovarian enlargement and cyst formation associated with therapy regress spontaneously within a few days or weeks after discontinuing treatment. Unless surgical indication for laparotomy exists, such cystic enlargement should always be managed conservatively.

Multiple Pregnancy: The incidence of multiple pregnancy (including triplets, quadruplets and quintuplets) has been increased up to ten-fold when conception takes place during a cycle in which clomiphene citrate therapy is given. During clinical studies, 353 infants were born of 163 multiple pregnancies. Of these infants, 293 survived, including 27 of 62 infants from triplet, quadruplet and quintuplet pregnancies. The patient and her husband should be advised of the frequency and potential hazards of multiple pregnancy before starting treatment.

Diagnostic Interference: Plasma desmosterol concentrations (only with long-term use, possibly indicating interference with cholesterol synthesis), plasma transcortin concentrations, serum thyroxine concentrations, sex hormone-binding globulin concentrations, sulfobromophthalein (BSP) retention (indicating hepatotoxicity), thyroxine-binding globulin (TBG) concentrations (may be increased).

Carcinogenicity: Two cases of bilateral breast carcinoma in women treated with clomiphene have been reported.

Patient Check-ups: The following procedures may be especially important in patient monitoring (other tests may be warranted in some patients, depending on condition):

Complete pelvic examination for evaluation of ovarian size (recommended prior to each course of treatment with clomiphene). Daily basal body temperature. Estrogen excretion determinations. Histological studies of luteal phase endometrium. Serum progesterone concentrations. Urinary excretion of pregnanediol (recommended during or after a cycle of clomiphene treatment to determine whether ovulation has occurred). Endometrial biopsy (recommended prior to initiation of clomiphene treatment in older patients to rule out the presence of endometrial carcinoma). Liver function tests (recommended prior to initiation of therapy with clomiphene). Ophthalmologic, including slit-lamp, examination (recommended if treatment with clomiphene is continued for more than 1 year).

Adverse Effects: Note: At recommended dosage, adverse effects usually are rare. Incidence and severity of adverse effects tend to be related to dose and duration of treatment and are usually reversible after clomiphene therapy is discontinued.

Use of clomiphene is associated with an increased incidence of multiple pregnancies and, therefore, possible premature deliveries.

Clomiphene may cause a decrease in cervical mucus which may interfere with response.

The following adverse effects have been selected on the basis of their potential clinical significance (possible cause in parenthesis where appropriate—not necessarily inclusive).

Those indicating need for medical attention: Incidence more frequent than 5%: Abdominal discomfort (bloating, stomach or pelvic pain) may be most often related to ovulatory or premenstrual phenomena, to ovarian enlargement or to enlargement of fibroids.

At recommended dosage, abnormal ovarian enlargement (see Precautions) is infrequent, although the usual cyclic variations in ovarian size may be exaggerated. Similarly, cyclic ovarian pain (mittelschmerz) may be accentuated. With higher or prolonged dosage, more frequent ovarian enlargement and cyst formation (usually luteal) may occur, and the luteal phase of the cycle may be prolonged. Rare instances of massive ovarian enlargement are on record. Southam and Janovski described such an instance in a patient with polycystic ovary syndrome whose clomiphene citrate therapy consisted of 100 mg daily for 14 days. Abnormal ovarian enlargement usually regresses spontaneously, and while laparotomy was performed on several such patients, investigators believe most of these patients should have been treated conservatively.

Note: Maximum ovarian enlargement occurs several days after clomiphene therapy is discontinued.

Blurred vision (ocular toxicity): Visual symptoms (see Warnings for further recommendations) described usually as blurring or spots or flashes, disappear within a few days or weeks after clomiphene is discontinued. These symptoms appear to be due to intensification and prolongation of after-images. Symptoms often first appear or are accentuated with exposure to a more brightly lit environment. While measured visual acuity has not generally been affected, one patient taking 200 mg daily developed visual blurring on the seventh day of treatment, which progressed to severe diminution of visual acuity by the tenth day. No other abnormality was found and the visual acuity returned to normal on the third day after treatment was stopped. Another patient treated during clinical studies developed scotomata during prolonged administration, which disappeared on placebo. Monolateral exophthalmos associated with laboratory evidence of hyperthyroidism was observed in one patient concomitant with completion of the third course of clomiphene citrate. In a 34-year-old patient who had taken 3 courses of clomiphene citrate, slit-lamp microscopic examination showed a mild amount of posterior cortical subcapsular opacity in each eye. Ophthalmoscopic examination revealed normal findings. The ocular diagnosis was posterior cortical senile cataracts.

Yellowing of eyes and skin (hepatotoxicity).

Those indicating need for medical attention only if they continue or are bothersome: Incidence more frequent than 10%: Hot flashes: The vasomotor symptoms resemble long menopausal hot flashes, are not usually severe and disappear promptly after treatment is discontinued.

Incidence less frequent or rare: 1 to 2%: Breast discomfort; dizziness or light-headedness; headache; heavy menstrual periods or bleeding between periods; mental depression, nervousness, restlessness, sleeplessness, or tiredness; nausea or vomiting.

Other less frequently reported symptoms during therapy have included: urticaria or allergic dermatitis, weight gain, increased urinary frequency or volume, constipation or diarrhea. Moderate, reversible hair loss has been reported in a few patients, primarily on continuous therapy.

Clomiphene has not been reported to cause significant abnormality in the hematologic or renal systems, in protein-bound iodine, or in serum cholesterol. Analysis by gas liquid chromatography (GLC) of serum sterols from patients on prolonged, continuous administration of clomiphene yields a peak compatible with an elevated level of desmosterol. This peak is indicative of an interference with cholesterol synthesis. However, the serum sterol GLC pattern from patients receiving recommended doses of clomiphene is not significantly altered.

Sulfobromophthalein (BSP) retention of greater than 5% has been reported in 32 of 141 patients in whom it was measured, including 5 of 43 patients who received approximately the dose of clomiphene citrate now recommended. Retention was usually minimal unless associated with prolonged continuous clomiphene citrate administration or with apparently unrelated liver disease. In some patients, pre-existing BSP retention decreased even though clomiphene citrate therapy was continued. Other liver function tests were usually normal. In a later study in which patients were given 6 consecutive monthly courses of clomiphene citrate (l00 mg daily for 3 days) or matching placebo, BSP tests were done on 94 patients. Values in excess of 5% retention were recorded in 11 patients, 6 of whom had received drug and 5 placebo. One patient developed jaundice on the nineteenth day of treatment (50 mg/day); liver biopsy revealed bile stasis without evidence of hepatitis. A male prison subject who received 200 mg daily for 77 days developed the clinical picture of infectious hepatitis; his cellmate was discovered to have had infectious hepatitis four months earlier.

Ovarian cancer has been reported in a very small number of infertile women who have been treated with fertility drugs. A causal relationship between treatment with fertility drugs and ovarian cancer has not been established.

Birth defects: From 2 339 completed pregnancies associated with clomiphene administration, 58 birth defects have been reported, for a cumulative rate of 2.5%. They have been reported in 4 conceptions in the abortion/stillbirth category, 14 of 353 infants from multiple pregnancies, and 39 of 1 676 infants from single pregnancies. Three live-born infants failed to survive.

Reported defects were congenital heart lesions (8 infants), Down's syndrome (5 infants), club foot (4 infants), congenital gut lesions (4 infants), hypospadias (3 infants), microcephaly (2 infants), harelip and cleft palate (2 infants), congenital hip (2 infants), polydactyly (both of twins), conjoined twins with teratomatous malformation, patent ductus arteriosus, amaurosis (blindness), arteriovenous fistula, inguinal hernia, umbilical hernia, syndactyly, pectus excavatum, myopathy, dermoid cyst of scalp, omphalocele, spina bifida occulta, ichthyosis, persistent lingual frenulum, and 7 infants with multiple somatic defects.

Eight of the entire group of 58 infants were born to 7 of 153 mothers who received a course of clomiphene citrate during the first 6 weeks after conception.

An interval of 4, 4 and 10 months respectively elapsed between the last clomiphene citrate therapy and conception in 3 mothers. In a fourth mother, conception occurred during a subsequent ovulation induced by gonadotropin therapy.

The cumulative rate of congential abnormalities does not exceed that reported in the general population.

Overdose: Symptoms and Treatment: There is no known antidote, but gastric lavage should be performed.

Dosage: Patients receiving clomiphene should be under supervision of a physician experienced in the treatment of gynecologic or endocrine disorders. Patients should be chosen for therapy only after careful diagnostic evaluation (see Indications).

The plan of therapy should be outlined in advance. Impediments to achieving the goal of therapy must be excluded or adequately treated before beginning clomiphene.

Patients who have been hypoestrogenic for prolonged periods may require pretreatment with estrogen to provide a more normal endometrium for ovum implantation. Estrogen therapy should be discontinued immediately before initiation of clomiphene citrate.

In some patients, a single injection of 5 000 to 10 000 USP units of human chorionic gonadotropin (hCG) is given 3 to 7 days after the last dose of clomiphene to stimulate the midcycle LH surge which results in ovulation.

Many patients will respond to 50 mg clomiphene daily for 5 days (see Recommended Dosage). In the determination of a recommended starting dose schedule, efficacy must be balanced against potential side effects. For example, the data available so far suggest that ovulation and pregnancy are slightly more attainable on 100 mg/day for 5 days than on 50 mg/day for 5 days. As the dosage is increased, however, ovarian overstimulation and other side effects may be expected to increase. Furthermore, although the data does not yet establish a relationship between dosage and multiple births, it would seem reasonable on pharmacologic grounds that such a relationship does exist. For these reasons, it would seem prudent to begin the treatment of the usual patient with a lower dose, 50 mg daily for 5 days, and to increase the dose only in those patients who do not respond to the first course (see Recommended Dosage).

Patients with unusual sensitivity to pituitary gonadotropins (for example, those with polycystic ovarian syndrome) may require a lower dosage or shorter duration of clomiphene therapy. Use of clomiphene is not recommended in patients with ovarian cysts because further enlargement may occur. A patient's report of abdominal pain during clomiphene therapy indicates immediate pelvic examination. If ovarian enlargement or cyst formation has occurred, it is recommended that clomiphene therapy be withdrawn until the ovaries have returned to pretreatment size, usually within a few days or weeks. Dosage and duration of next course of clomiphene should be reduced. If the patient receiving clomiphene experiences any visual disturbances, it is recommended that clomiphene therapy be withdrawn and a complete ophthalmologic examination performed. Ocular side effects usually disappear within a few days or weeks after the last dose of clomiphene.

The majority of patients who are going to respond will respond to the first course of therapy, and 3 courses should constitute an adequate therapeutic trial. Treatment beyond this is not recommended in the patient who does not exhibit evidence of ovulation. If ovulatory menses does not occur after 3 to 4 cycles of clomiphene therapy at the maximum dose, or pregnancy after a treatment-free interval of 3 to 6 months, the diagnosis should be reevaluated.

Pregnancy: In most patients, ovulation appears to occur from 6 to 12 days after completion of therapy. For regularity of cyclic ovulatory response, it is also important that each course of clomiphene be started on or about the fifth cycle day, once ovulation has been established. The importance of properly timed coitus cannot be over-emphasized. Conception should be attempted 2 days prior to ovulation, with intercourse every other day, starting within 48 hours after ovulation.

If a cycle of clomiphene is followed by a biphasic course of basal body temperature and menses do not ensue, the next cycle of clomiphene should be delayed until it is confirmed that the patient is not pregnant.

In common with other therapeutic modalities, therapy follows the rule of diminishing returns, such that likelihood of conception diminishes with each succeeding course of therapy. If pregnancy has not been achieved after 3 ovulatory responses, further treatment is not recommended. Patients should be advised of the possibility of multiple pregnancy and its potential hazards if conception occurs during a cycle in which clomiphene is given.

Recommended Dosage: Adults: Oral: 50 mg (1 tablet)/day for 5 days, starting on the fifth day of the menstrual cycle if bleeding occurs, or at any time in the patient who has had no recent uterine bleeding. If ovulation without conception occurs, this cycle is repeated until conception or for 3 or 4 cycles. When ovulation occurs at the regimen of 50 mg daily for 5 days, there is no advantage to increasing the dose in subsequent cycles of treatment. If ovulation does not occur, the dose is increased to 100 mg a day for 5 days (starting as early as 30 days after the previous course), repeated if ovulation without conception occurs. Some patients require up to 250 mg/day to induce ovulation.

Note: The majority of patients who are going to respond will respond to the first course of therapy, and 3 courses should constitute an adequate therapeutic trial. If ovulatory menses do not occur after 3 cycles of clomiphene therapy at the maximum dose, or pregnancy after a treatment-free interval of 3 to 6 months, the diagnosis should be re-evaluated. Treatment beyond this is not recommended in the patient who does not exhibit evidence of ovulation.

Usual adult prescribing limits: Doses over 100 mg/day for 5 days have been associated with a higher incidence of side effects, and patients receiving these doses should be carefully monitored.

Information for the Patient: See Blue Section—Information for the Patient "Serophene".

Supplied: Each round, white, flat, beveled-edge scored tablet, identified S on one side, contains: clomiphene citrate USP 50 mg . Bottles of 50. Blister packs of 10. Store in well-closed containers between 15 to 30°C. Protect from light.

SEROQUEL® Ⓟ

Zeneca

Quetiapine Fumarate

Antipsychotic

Pharmacology: Quetiapine, a dibenzothiazepine derivative, is an antipsychotic agent which interacts with a broad range of neurotransmitters. Quetiapine exhibits affinity for brain serotonin $5HT_2$ and $5HT_{1A}$ receptors (in vitro, Ki=288 and 557 nM, respectively), and dopamine D_1 and D_2 receptors (in vitro, Ki=558 and 531 nM, respectively). It is this combination of receptor antagonism with a higher selectivity for $5HT_2$ relative to D_2 receptors which is believed to contribute to the antipsychotic properties and low extrapyramidal symptoms (EPS) liability of quetiapine. Quetiapine also has very high affinity for histaminergic H_1 receptors (in vitro, Ki=10 nM) and adrenergic α_1 receptors (in vitro, Ki=13 nM), with a lower affinity for adrenergic α_2 receptors (in vitro, Ki=782 nM), little affinity for cholinergic muscarinic receptors, and no appreciable affinity for benzodiazepine receptors.

Pharmacokinetics: The pharmacokinetics of quetiapine are linear within the clinical dose range, and are similar in men and women, or smokers and nonsmokers.

Absorption: Quetiapine is well absorbed following oral administration. In studies with radiolabelled drug, approximately 73% of the total radioactivity is recovered in the urine and 21% in the feces over a period of 1 week. The bioavailability of quetiapine is marginally affected by administration with food, with C_{max} and AUC values increased by 25% and 15%, respectively.

Peak plasma concentrations of quetiapine generally occur within 2 hours after oral administration.

Distribution: Quetiapine has a mean apparent volume of distribution of 10 ± 4 L/kg, and is approximately 83% bound to plasma proteins.

Elimination and Metabolism: The elimination half-life of quetiapine is approximately 6 to 7 hours upon multiple dosing within the proposed clinical dosage range. Quetiapine is extensively metabolized by the liver, with parent compound accounting for less than 5% of the dose in the urine and feces, 1 week following the administration of radiolabeled quetiapine.

Major routes of metabolism of quetiapine involve oxidation of the alkyl side chain, hydroxylation of the dibenzothiazepine ring, sulphoxidation, and phase 2 conjugation. The principal human plasma metabolites are the sulfoxide, and the parent acid metabolite, neither of which are pharmacologically active.

In vitro investigations established that CYP 3A4 is the primary enzyme responsible for cytochrome P450-mediated metabolism of quetiapine.

In vitro studies suggest that quetiapine and its metabolites would have little inhibitory effect on in vivo metabolism of other drugs mediated by cytochromes P450 1A2, 2C9, 2C19, 2D6 and 3A4.

Special Populations: The mean clearance of quetiapine in the elderly is approximately 30 to 50% of that seen in adults aged 18 to 65 years (see Precautions and Dosage).

At single low (subclinical) doses, the mean plasma clearance of quetiapine was reduced by approximately 25% in subjects with severe renal impairment (creatinine clearance less than 30 mL/min/1.73 m²) and in subjects with hepatic impairment (stable alcoholic cirrhosis). However, the individual clearance

Seroquel (cont'd)

values remained within the range observed for healthy subjects (see Precautions and Dosage).

Drug Interactions: The prototype cytochrome P450 3A4 inducer, phenytoin, increased quetiapine oral clearance by over 5-fold (see Precautions, Drug Interactions). Coadministration of thioridazine also increased quetiapine oral clearance by 65% (see Precautions, Drug Interactions). Fluoxetine, imipramine, haloperidol, and risperidone did not significantly alter the pharmacokinetics of quetiapine (see Precautions, Drug Interactions).

No clinically important interaction was observed between quetiapine and cimetidine (a nonspecific enzyme inhibitor). Quetiapine did not affect the single dose pharmacokinetics of lithium, lorazepam, or antipyrine.

Clinical Trials: The efficacy of quetiapine in the short-term management of schizophrenia was demonstrated in 3 short-term (6-week) controlled trials of inpatients who met a DSM-III-R diagnosis of schizophrenia. The results of the trials follow.

In a 6-week, placebo-controlled trial (n=361) involving 5 fixed doses of quetiapine (75, 150, 300, 600 and 750 mg/day on a t.i.d. schedule), the 4 highest doses of quetiapine were generally superior to placebo on the BPRS total score, the BPRS psychosis cluster and the CGI severity score, with the maximal effect seen at 300 mg/day, and the effects of doses of 150 to 750 were generally indistinguishable. Quetiapine, at a dose of 300 mg/day, was superior to placebo on the SANS.

In a 6-week, placebo-controlled trial (n=286) involving titration of quetiapine in high (up to 750 mg/day on a t.i.d. schedule) and low (up to 250 mg/day on a t.i.d. schedule) doses, only the high dose quetiapine group (mean dose, 500 mg/day) was generally superior to placebo on the BPRS total score, the BPRS psychosis cluster, the CGI severity score and the SANS.

In a 6-week dose and dose regimen comparison trial (n=618) involving 2 fixed doses of quetiapine (450 mg/day on both b.i.d. and t.i.d. schedules and 50 mg/day on a b.i.d. schedule), only the 450 mg/day (225 mg b.i.d. schedule) dose group was generally superior to the 50 mg/day (25 mg b.i.d.) quetiapine dose group on the BPRS total score, the BPRS psychosis cluster, the CGI severity score, and on the SANS.

Clinical trials have demonstrated that quetiapine is effective when given twice a day, although quetiapine has a pharmacokinetic half-life of approximately 7 hours. This is further supported by the data from a positron emission tomography (PET) study which identified that for quetiapine, $5HT_2$ and D_2 receptor occupancy is maintained for up to 12 hours. The safety and efficacy of doses greater than 800 mg/day have not been evaluated.

In the placebo-controlled clinical trials, there were no differences between the quetiapine and placebo treatment groups in the incidence of EPS or concomitant use of anticholinergics. The placebo-controlled trial evaluating fixed doses of quetiapine across the range of 75 to 750 mg/day showed no evidence of dose-related increase in EPS or in the use of concomitant anticholinergics.

In clinical trials, quetiapine did not produce sustained elevations in prolactin. Raised prolactin levels can be associated with adverse effects such as galactorrhea, amenorrhea and impotence. In the multiple fixed-dose clinical trial there were no differences in prolactin levels at study completion for quetiapine, across the recommended dose range, and placebo.

Indications: For the management of the manifestations of schizophrenia. The antipsychotic efficacy of quetiapine was established in short-term (6-week) controlled inpatient trials (see Pharmacology). The efficacy of quetiapine in long-term use, that is, for more than 6 weeks, has not been systematically evaluated in controlled trials.

Contraindications: Patients with a known hypersensitivity to this medication or any of its ingredients.

Warnings: Neuroleptic Malignant Syndrome (NMS): Neuroleptic malignant syndrome is a potentially fatal symptom complex that has been reported in association with antipsychotic drugs, including quetiapine.

The clinical manifestations of NMS are hyperthermia, muscle rigidity, altered mental status, and evidence of autonomic instability (irregular pulse or blood pressure, tachycardia, diaphoresis, and cardiac dysrhythmia). Additional signs may include elevated creatine phosphokinase, myoglobinuria (rhabdomyolysis) and acute renal failure.

In arriving at a diagnosis, it is important to identify cases where the clinical presentation includes both serious medical illness (e.g., pneumonia, systemic infection, etc.) and untreated or inadequately treated extrapyramidal signs and symptoms. Other important considerations in the differential diagnosis include central anticholinergic toxicity, heat stroke, drug fever and primary CNS pathology.

The management of NMS should include immediate discontinuation of antipsychotic drugs, including quetiapine, and other drugs not essential to concurrent therapy; intensive symptomatic treatment and medical monitoring; and treatment of any concomitant serious medical problems for which specific treatments are available. There is no general agreement about specific pharmacological treatment regimens for uncomplicated NMS.

If a patient requires antipsychotic drug treatment after recovery from NMS, the potential reintroduction of drug therapy should be carefully considered. The patient should be carefully monitored since recurrences of NMS have been reported.

Tardive Dyskinesia (TD): A syndrome of potentially irreversible, involuntary, dyskinetic movements may develop in patients treated with antipsychotic drugs. Although the prevalence of the syndrome appears to be highest among the elderly, especially elderly women, it is impossible to rely upon estimates to predict which patients are likely to develop the syndrome.

It has been hypothesized that agents with a lower EPS liability may also have a lower liability to produce TD. In controlled clinical trials with quetiapine, the incidence of EPS was not statistically significantly different than placebo across the recommended therapeutic dose range. This may predict that quetiapine has less potential than standard antipsychotic agents to induce TD.

The risk of developing TD and the likelihood that it will become irreversible are believed to increase as the duration of treatment and the total cumulative dose of antipsychotic drugs administered to the patient increase. However, the syndrome can develop, although much less commonly, after relatively brief treatment periods at low doses.

There is no known treatment for established cases of TD, although the syndrome may remit, partially or completely, if antipsychotic treatment is withdrawn. Antipsychotic treatment, itself, however, may suppress (or partially suppress) the signs and symptoms of the syndrome and thereby may possibly mask the underlying process. The effect that symptomatic suppression has upon the long-term course of the syndrome is unknown.

Given these considerations, quetiapine should be prescribed in a manner that is most likely to minimize the occurrence of TD. Chronic antipsychotic treatment should generally be reserved for patients who appear to suffer from a chronic illness that is known to respond to antipsychotic drugs, and for whom alternative, equally effective, but potentially less harmful treatments are not available or appropriate. In patients who do require chronic treatment, the smallest dose and the shortest duration of treatment producing a satisfactory clinical response should be sought. The need for continued treatment should be reassessed periodically.

If signs and symptoms of TD appear in a patient on quetiapine, drug discontinuation should be considered. However, some patients may require treatment with quetiapine despite the presence of the syndrome.

Precautions: Hypotension and Syncope: As with other drugs that have high α_1 adrenergic receptor blocking activity, quetiapine may induce orthostatic hypotension, dizziness, and sometimes syncope, especially during the initial dose titration period. Syncope was reported in 1% (22/2 162) of patients treated with quetiapine, compared with 0% (0/206) on placebo, and 0.5% (2/420) on active control drugs. The risk of hypotension and syncope may be reduced by more gradual titration to the target dose (see Dosage). Quetiapine should be used with caution in patients with known cardiovascular disease (e.g., history of myocardial infarction or ischemic heart disease, heart failure or conduction abnormalities), cerebrovascular disease, or other conditions predisposing to hypotension (e.g., dehydration, hypovolemia and treatment with antihypertensive medications).

Cataracts: The development of cataracts was observed in association with quetiapine treatment in chronic dog studies at 4 times the recommended human dose. Lens changes have also been observed in patients during long-term quetiapine treatment, but a causal relationship to quetiapine use has not been established. The possibility of lenticular changes during long-term use of quetiapine in man, thus cannot be excluded at this time. Eye examinations (e.g., slit lamp exam) prior to or shortly after initiation of treatment with quetiapine and at 6-month intervals thereafter, are recommended. If clinically significant lens changes associated with quetiapine use are observed, discontinuation of quetiapine should be considered.

Seizures: In controlled clinical trials, there was no difference in the incidence of seizures in patients treated with quetiapine or placebo (incidence of 0.4% or 3 events per 100 patient years in patients given quetiapine, compared with 0.5% or 6.9 events for 100 patient years for placebo). Nevertheless, as with other antipsychotics, caution is recommended when treating patients with a history of seizures or with conditions associated with a lowered seizure threshold.

Hypothyroidism: Clinical trials demonstrated that quetiapine is associated with a dose-related decrease in total and free thyroxine (T_4). On average quetiapine was associated with about a 20% mean reduction in thyroxine levels (both total and free). Forty-two percent of quetiapine-treated patients showed at least a 30% reduction in total T_4 and 7% showed at least a 50% reduction. Maximum reduction of thyroxine levels generally occurred during the first 2 to 4 weeks of treatment with quetiapine. These reductions were maintained without adaption or progression during longer term treatment. Decreases in T_4 were not associated with systematic changes in TSH or clinical signs or symptoms of hypothyroidism. About 0.4% (10/2 386) of patients treated with quetiapine experienced persistent increases in TSH, and 0.25% of patients were treated with thyroid replacement.

Cholesterol and Triglyceride Elevations: In short-term placebo-controlled trials, quetiapine-treated patients showed mean increases from baseline in cholesterol and triglyceride of 11% and 17%, respectively, compared to mean decreases in the placebo-treated patients. There was little relation between these changes and weight changes observed during the trial.

Transaminase Elevations: During premarketing clinical trials, therapy with quetiapine was associated with elevation of hepatic transaminases, primarily ALT. Within a clinical trial database of 1 892 quetiapine-treated patients, with baseline ALT levels ≤60 IU/L, 5.3% (101/1 892) had treatment-emergent ALT elevations to >120 IU/L, 1.5% (29/1 892) had elevations to >200 IU/L, and 0.2% (3/1 892) had elevations to >400 IU/L. No patients had values in excess of 800 IU/L. None of the quetiapine-treated patients who had elevated transaminase values manifested clinical symptomatology associated with liver impairment. The majority of transaminase elevations were seen during the first 2 months of treatment. Most elevations were transient (80%) while patients continued on quetiapine therapy. Of the 101 quetiapine-treated patients whose enzyme levels increased to >120 IU/L, 40 discontinued treatment while their ALT values were still raised. In 114 quetiapine-treated patients whose baseline ALT was >90 IU/L, only 1 experienced an elevation to >400 IU/L.

Precautions should be exercised when using quetiapine in patients with pre-existing hepatic disorders, in patients who are being treated with potentially hepatotoxic drugs, or if treatment-emergent signs or symptoms of hepatic impairment appear.

For patients who have known or suspected abnormal hepatic function prior to starting quetiapine, standard clinical assessment, including measurement of transaminase levels is recommended. Periodic clinical reassessment with transaminase levels is recommended for such patients, as well as for patients who develop any signs and symptoms suggestive of a new onset liver disorder during quetiapine therapy.

Hyperprolactinemia: Elevation of prolactin levels was not seen in clinical trials with quetiapine, increased prolactin levels were observed in rat studies with this compound. As is common with compounds which stimulate prolactin release, the administration of quetiapine resulted in an increase in the incidence of mammary neoplasms in rats. The physiological differences between rats and humans with regard to prolactin make the clinical significance of these findings unclear. To date, neither clinical nor epidemiological studies have shown an association between chronic administration of drugs that stimulate prolactin release, and mammary tumorigenesis. Tissue culture experiments, however, indicate that approximately one third of human breast cancers are prolactin dependent in vitro; a factor of potential importance if prescription of these drugs is contemplated in a patient with previously detected breast cancer.

Possible manifestations associated with elevated prolactin levels are amenorrhea, galactorrhea, and menorrhagia.

Weight Gain: Quetiapine was associated with weight gain. In clinical trials mean weight gain after 4 to 8 weeks of treatment was approximately 2.1 kg, after 18 to 26 weeks, 3.5 kg, and at 1 year, 5.6 kg.

Occupational Hazards: Potential Effect on Cognitive and Motor Performance: Somnolence was a commonly reported adverse event in patients treated with quetiapine, especially during the initial dose titration period. Since quetiapine may cause sedation and impair motor skill, patients should be cautioned about performing activities requiring mental alertness, such as operating a motor vehicle or hazardous machinery, until they are reasonably certain that quetiapine therapy does not affect them adversely.

Antiemetic Effect: Consistent with its dopamine antagonist effects, quetiapine may have an antiemetic effect. Such an effect may mask signs of toxicity due to overdosage of other drugs, or may mask symptoms of disease such as brain tumor or intestinal obstruction.

Body Temperature Regulation: Although not reported with quetiapine, disruption of the body's ability to reduce core body temperature has been attributed to antipsychotic agents. Appropriate care is advised when prescribing quetiapine for patients who will be experiencing conditions which may contribute to an elevation of core temperature, e.g., exercising strenuously, exposure to extreme heat, receiving concomitant medication with anticholinergic activity, or being subject to dehydration.

Suicide: The possibility of suicide or attempted suicide is inherent in psychosis, and thus close supervision and appropriate clinical management of high-risk patients should accompany drug therapy.

Drug Interactions: Given the primary CNS effects of quetiapine, it should be used with caution in combination with other centrally acting drugs. Quetiapine potentiated the cognitive and motor effects of alcohol in a clinical trial in subjects with psychotic disorders. Alcoholic beverages should be avoided while taking quetiapine. Because of its potential for inducing hypotension, quetiapine may enhance the effects of certain antihypertensive agents. As it exhibits in vitro dopamine antagonism, quetiapine may antagonize the effects of levodopa and dopamine agonists.

CYP 3A4 is the primary enzyme responsible for cytochrome P450-mediated metabolism of quetiapine. Thus, coadministration of compounds (such as ketoconazole, erythromycin, clarithromycin, diltiazem, verapamil, or nefazodone) which inhibit CYP 3A4, may increase the concentration of quetiapine. In a clinical study examining the pharmacokinetics of quetiapine following coadministration with cimetidine, (a nonspecific P450 enzyme inhibitor), no clinically significant interaction was observed. Clinical study data on quetiapine coadministration with specific CYP 3A4 inhibitors, however are not available. Caution is thus advised when considering coadministration of quetiapine with potent CYP 3A4 inhibitors (such as systemic ketoconazole or erythromycin).

Coadministration of quetiapine and phenytoin (microsomal enzyme inducer) caused 5-fold increases in clearance of quetiapine. Increased doses of quetiapine may be required to maintain control of psychotic symptoms in patients coadministered quetiapine and phenytoin, or other hepatic enzyme inducers (e.g., carbamazepine, barbiturates, rifampin). The dose of quetiapine may need to be reduced if phenytoin is withdrawn and replaced with a noninducer (e.g., sodium valproate).

Coadministration of thioridazine (200 mg b.i.d.) with quetiapine (300 mg b.i.d.), increased the clearance of quetiapine by 65%. However, fluoxetine (60 mg daily), imipramine (75 mg b.i.d.), haloperidol (7.5 mg b.i.d.), and risperidone (3 mg b.i.d.) did not significantly alter the steady-state pharmacokinetics of quetiapine.

The pharmacokinetics of lithium were not altered when coadministered with quetiapine.

Quetiapine did not induce the hepatic enzyme systems involved in the metabolism of antipyrine.

Geriatrics: The number of patients 65 years of age or over, with schizophrenia or related disorders, exposed to quetiapine, during clinical trials was limited (n=38). When compared to younger patients the mean plasma clearance of quetiapine was reduced by 30 to 50% in elderly subjects. In addition, as this population has more frequent hepatic, renal, CNS, and cardiovascular dysfunctions, and more frequent use of concomitant medication, caution should be exercised with the use of quetiapine in the elderly patient (see Dosage).

Children and Adolescents: The safety and efficacy of quetiapine in children under the age of 18 years have not been established.

Patients with Hepatic or Renal Impairment: Quetiapine is extensively metabolized by the liver. There is little experience with quetiapine in patients with hepatic or renal impairment, except in a low (subclinical) single dose study (see Pharmacology). Quetiapine should thus be used with caution in patients with known hepatic or renal impairment, especially during the initial dosing period (see Dosage).

Pregnancy: Patients should be advised to notify their physician if they become pregnant or intend to become pregnant during treatment with quetiapine. The safety and efficacy of quetiapine during human pregnancy have not been established. Therefore, quetiapine should only be used during pregnancy if the expected benefits justify the potential risks.

Lactation: The degree to which quetiapine is excreted into human milk is unknown. Women who are breast-feeding should therefore be advised to avoid breast-feeding while taking quetiapine.

Adverse Effects: The stated frequencies of adverse events represent the proportion of individuals who experienced, at least once, a treatment-emergent adverse event of the type listed. An event was considered treatment-emergent if it occurred for the first time or worsened while receiving therapy following baseline evaluation.

The prescriber should be aware that the figures in the tables and tabulations cannot be used to predict the incidence of side effects in the course of usual medical practice where patient characteristics and other factors differ from those that prevailed in the clinical trials. Similarly, the cited frequencies cannot be compared with figures obtained from other clinical investigations involving different treatments, uses, and investigators. The figures cited, however, do provide the prescribing physician with some basis for estimating the relative contribution of drug and nondrug factors to the side effect incidence in the populations studied.

Commonly Observed Adverse Events in Short-term Placebo-controlled Clinical Trials: The following treatment-emergent adverse events, derived from Table I, commonly occurred during acute therapy with quetiapine (incidence of at least 5%, and an incidence at least 5% higher than that observed with placebo): somnolence, dizziness, dry mouth, postural hypotension, and elevated ALT levels.

Adverse Events Associated with Discontinuation: Short-term Placebo-controlled Clinical Trials: Overall, 3.9% of quetiapine-treated patients (n=510) discontinued treatment due to adverse events compared with 2.9% of placebo-treated patients (n=206). Somnolence, the single most common adverse event leading to withdrawal from quetiapine treatment, led to the withdrawal of 4 quetiapine-treated patients and no placebo-treated patients. Postural hypotension, hypotension, and/or tachycardia led to withdrawal of 1.8% of quetiapine-treated subjects, compared to 0.5% of placebo-treated subjects.

Combined Short- and Long-term Controlled Trial Database: In a premarketing controlled clinical trial database of 1 710 quetiapine-treated patients, 5% discontinued due to an adverse event. Somnolence was the single most common adverse event leading to withdrawal of 24 patients from quetiapine, and was the only adverse event leading to withdrawal that occurred in more than 1% of patients. Cardiovascular adverse events (e.g., postural hypotension, hypotension, tachycardia, dizziness) accounted for 20% of all subject withdrawals from quetiapine treatment. Sixteen (0.9%) quetiapine-treated subjects were withdrawn due to elevated liver enzymes. Four quetiapine-treated subjects were withdrawn because of leukopenia. Two of these subjects had at least one clinically significant, nonbaseline low neutrophil count. Two quetiapine-treated subjects were withdrawn from the trial because of suspected neuroleptic malignant syndrome (NMS).

Incidence of Adverse Events in Placebo-controlled Clinical Trials: Table I enumerates the incidence, rounded to the nearest percent, of treatment-emergent adverse events that occurred during acute therapy (up to 6 weeks) of schizophrenia in 1% or more of patients treated with quetiapine (doses of 150 mg/day or more) where the incidence in patients treated with quetiapine was greater than the incidence in placebo-treated patients.

Weight Gain: As with other antipsychotics, quetiapine may be associated with weight gain. During acute therapy (up to 6 weeks) in placebo-controlled clinical trials, mean weight gain in patients taking quetiapine was 2.3 kg compared to a mean weight gain of 0.1 kg in patients taking placebo. In long-term trials average weight gain was 5.6 kg after 1 year of treatment (see Precautions).

Seizures: There have been occasional reports of seizures in patients administered quetiapine, although the frequency was no greater than that observed in patients administered placebo in controlled clinical trials (see Precautions).

Table I—Seroquel

Adverse Events Reported for at Least 1% of Quetiapine-treated Subjects (doses ≥150 mg/day) and for a Higher Percentage of Quetiapine-treated Subjects Than Subjects Who Received Placebo in Short-term, Placebo-controlled Phase II-III trials*

Body System and COSTART Term	Percentage of Subjects With Adverse Events* Quetiapine (n=449)	Placebo (n=202)
Whole Body		
Headache	20	17
Abdominal pain	4	1
Back pain	2	1
Fever	2	1
Nervous System		
Somnolence	18	11
Dizziness	10	4
Digestive		
Constipation	9	5
Dry mouth	7	2
Dyspepsia	6	2
Gamma glutamyl transpeptidase increased	2	1
Cardiovascular		
Postural hypotension	8	2
Tachycardia	7	5
Palpitation	1	0
Metabolic and Nutritional		
ALT increased	7	2
AST increased	4	1
Weight gain	2	0
Endocrine		
Hypothyroidism	1	0
Skin and Appendages		
Rash	4	3
Respiratory		
Rhinitis	3	1
Hemic and Lymphatic		
Leukopenia	2	0
Special Senses		
Ear pain	1	0

*Subjects may have had more than one adverse event.

Neuroleptic Malignant Syndrome: As with other antipsychotics, rare cases of possible neuroleptic malignant syndrome have been reported in patients treated with quetiapine (see Warnings).

Vital Signs: As with other antipsychotics with α_1 adrenergic blocking activity, quetiapine may induce postural hypotension, associated with dizziness, tachycardia and, in some patients, syncope, especially during the initial dose titration period (see Precautions). In placebo-controlled clinical trials, postural hypotension was reported with an incidence of 8% in quetiapine-treated patients compared to 2% in placebo-treated patients. Quetiapine was associated with a mean baseline to endpoint increase in heart rate of 3.9 beats/min, compared to 1.6 beats/min among placebo-treated patients.

Laboratory Changes: Transient leukopenia and/or neutropenia have been observed in patients administered quetiapine. Occasionally, eosinophilia has been observed. There were no cases of persistent severe neutropenia or agranulocytosis reported in controlled clinical trials with quetiapine.

Asymptomatic elevations in serum transaminases (AST, ALT) or γ-GT levels have been observed in some patients administered quetiapine. These elevations were usually reversible on continued quetiapine treatment (see Precautions).

Small elevations in nonfasting serum triglyceride levels and total cholesterol have been observed during treatment with quetiapine (see Precautions).

Quetiapine treatment was associated with small dose-related decreases in thyroid hormone levels, particularly total T4 and free T4. The reduction in total and free T4 was maximal within the first 2 to 4 weeks of quetiapine treatment, with no further reduction during long-term treatment. There was no evidence of clinically significant changes in TSH concentration over time. In nearly all cases, cessation of quetiapine treatment was associated with a reversal of the effects on total and free T_4, irrespective of the duration of treatment (see Precautions).

ECG Changes: Between group comparisons for pooled placebo-controlled trials revealed no statistically significant quetiapine/placebo differences in the proportions of patients

Seroquel (cont'd)

experiencing potentially important changes in ECG parameters, including QT, QTc, and PR intervals. However, the proportions of patients meeting the criteria for tachycardia were compared in four 3- to 6-week, placebo-controlled clinical trials revealing a 1% (4/399) incidence for quetiapine compared to 0.6% (1/156) incidence for placebo. Quetiapine use was associated with a mean increase in heart rate, assessed by ECG, of 7 beats/minute compared to a mean increase of 1 beat/minute among placebo patients. This slight tendency to tachycardia may be related to quetiapine's potential for inducing orthostatic changes (see Precautions).

Extrapyramidal Symptoms (EPS): Table II enumerates the percentage of patients with treatment-emergent extrapyramidal symptoms in a short-term acute phase clinical trial comparing 5 fixed doses of quetiapine with placebo (n=50 patients/group), as assessed by: spontaneous complaints of parkinsonism (extrapyramidal syndrome, hypertonia, tremor and cogwheel rigidity), or akathisia; Simpson-Angus scores (mean change from baseline); and use of anticholinergic medication to treat emergent EPS.

Overdose: Symptoms: In clinical trials, experience with quetiapine in overdosage is limited. Doses in excess of 10 g have been taken; no fatalities were reported and patients recovered without sequelae.

In general, reported signs and symptoms were those resulting from an exaggeration of the drug's known pharmacological effects e.g., drowsiness and sedation, tachycardia and hypotension.

Treatment: There is no specific antidote to quetiapine. In cases of severe intoxication, the possibility of multiple drug involvement should be considered, and intensive care procedures are recommended, including establishing and maintaining a patent airway, ensuring adequate oxygenation and ventilation, and monitoring and support of the cardiovascular system.

Close medical supervision and monitoring should be continued until the patient recovers.

Dosage: The usual starting dose is 25 mg b.i.d., titrated with increments of 25 to 50 mg b.i.d./day, as tolerated, to a target dose of 300 mg/day given b.i.d. within 4 to 7 days.

Further dosage adjustments may be indicated depending on the clinical response and tolerability in the individual patient. Dosage adjustments should generally occur at intervals of not less than 2 days, as steady state for quetiapine would not be achieved for approximately 1 to 2 days in the typical patient. When adjustments are necessary, dose increments/decrements of 25 to 50 mg b.i.d. are recommended.

Quetiapine can be administered with or without food (see Pharmacology, Pharmacokinetics).

Clinical trials suggest that the usual effective treatment dose will be in the range of 300 to 600 mg/day (see Pharmacology, Clinical Trials). However, some patients may require as little as 150 mg/day. The safety of doses above 800 mg/day has not been evaluated.

The need for continuing existing extrapyramidal symptoms medications should be re-evaluated periodically as quetiapine has not been associated with treatment-emergent extrapyramidal symptoms across the clinical dose range.

Geriatrics: In clinical trials, 38 patients with schizophrenia or related disorders, 65 years of age or over, were treated with quetiapine (see Precautions). Given the limited experience with quetiapine in the elderly, and the higher incidence of concomitant illness and concomitant medication in this population, quetiapine should be used with caution. The mean plasma clearance of quetiapine was reduced by 30 to 50% in elderly subjects when compared to younger patients. The rate of dose titration may thus need to be slower, and the daily therapeutic target dose lower, than that used in younger patients.

Hepatic Impairment: Quetiapine is extensively metabolized by the liver (see Pharmacology). Therefore, quetiapine should be used with caution in patients with known hepatic impairment, especially during the initial dosing period. The rate of dose titration may need to be slower, and the daily therapeutic dose lower, than that used in nonhepatically impaired patients (see Precautions).

Renal Impairment: As clinical experience is lacking, caution is advised (see Precautions).

Information for the Patient: See Blue Section—Information for the Patient "Seroquel".

Supplied: 25 mg: Each peach colored, round, biconvex, intagliated, film-coated tablet, with "SEROQUEL" and "25" on one side and plain on the other, contains: quetiapine fumarate equivalent to quetiapine free base 25 mg. Nonmedicinal ingredients: tablet core: calcium hydrogen phosphate, lactose monohydrate, magnesium stearate, microcrystalline cellulose, povidone and sodium starch glycolate type A; coating: hydroxypropyl methylcellulose, polyethylene glycol, red ferric oxide, titanium dioxide and yellow ferric oxide. Blister packages of 60. High density polyethylene (HDPE) bottles of 100.

100 mg: Each yellow colored, round, biconvex, intagliated, film-coated tablet, with "SEROQUEL" and "100" on one side and plain on the other, contains: quetiapine fumarate equivalent to quetiapine free base 100 mg. Nonmedicinal ingredients: tablet core: calcium hydrogen phosphate, lactose monohydrate, magnesium stearate, microcrystalline cellulose, povidone and sodium starch glycolate type A; coating: hydroxypropyl methylcellulose, polyethylene glycol, titanium dioxide and yellow ferric oxide. Blister packages of 90. High density polyethylene (HDPE) bottles of 100.

200 mg: Each white, round, biconvex, intagliated, film-coated tablet, with "SEROQUEL" and "200" on one side and plain on the other, contains: quetiapine fumarate equivalent to quetiapine free base 200 mg. Nonmedicinal ingredients: tablet core: calcium hydrogen phosphate, lactose monohydrate, magnesium stearate, microcrystalline cellulose, povidone and sodium starch glycolate type A; coating: hydroxypropyl methylcellulose, polyethylene glycol and titanium dioxide. Blister packages of 90. High density polyethylene (HDPE) bottles of 100.

Store between 15 and 30°C.

(Shown in Product Recognition Section)

New Product 1998

Table II—Seroquel

Treatment-emergent Extrapyramidal Symptoms, Assessed by Spontaneous Reports, Simpson Scale, and Incidence of Anticholinergic Use

		Seroquel				
	Placebo	**75 mg**	**150 mg**	**300 mg**	**600 mg**	**750 mg**
Spontaneous reports of parkinsonian symptoms*	10%	6%	4%	4%	8%	4%
Spontaneous reports of akathisia	8%	2%	2%	0%	0%	2%
Simpson scale	−0.6	−1.0	−1.2	−1.6	−1.8	−1.8
Incidence of anticholinergic use	14%	11%	10%	8%	12%	11%

*Patients may have had more than one parkinsonism adverse event.

SERPASIL® Ⓟ

Novartis Pharmaceuticals

Reserpine

Antihypertensive—Antipsychotic

Pharmacology: Reserpine probably produces its antihypertensive effect through depletion of tissue stores of catecholamines (epinephrine and norepinephrine) from peripheral sites which results in a decreased cardiac output. A decrease in peripheral resistance produced by reserpine may also contribute to its antihypertensive effect. In contrast, its sedative and tranquilizing properties are thought to be related to depletion of 5-hydroxytryptamine from the brain.

When given orally, reserpine is readily absorbed from the gastrointestinal tract. Its action is slow in onset; the effects appear after 3 to 6 days and continue for many days after withdrawal of treatment. Reserpine is extensively metabolized by the liver and the metabolites and unchanged drug are slowly excreted in the urine and feces.

Indications: For the treatment of essential hypertension. In severe forms of hypertension, reserpine should be given in conjunction with other antihypertensive agents (hydralazine and/or thiazides). Reserpine is also indicated for the management of agitated psychotic states (schizophrenia) in those patients unable to tolerate phenothiazines, or requiring treatment of co-existing hypertension.

Contraindications: Mental depression (especially with suicidal tendencies or history of depressive illness), Parkinson's disease, epilepsy, electroconvulsive therapy, active gastric or duodenal ulcer, ulcerative colitis, digitalis intoxication, aortic insufficiency, pheochromocytoma, MAO inhibitor therapy (MAO inhibitors should be withdrawn at least 14 days before treatment with reserpine) and hypersensitivity to reserpine and related derivatives.

Warnings and Precautions: Depression may be unmasked by reserpine. Discontinue reserpine at first signs of depression; the possibility of suicide should be kept in mind.

Discontinue the drug at least 2 weeks before elective surgery or electroshock therapy. Preoperative withdrawal of reserpine does not insure that circulatory instability will not occur. It is important that the anesthesiologist be aware of the patient's drug intake and consider this in the overall management since hypotension has occurred in patients receiving rauwolfia preparations. Anticholinergic and/or adrenergic drugs (metaraminol, levarterenol) have been employed to treat adverse vagocirculatory effects.

Since reserpine may increase gastrointestinal motility and secretion, it should be used cautiously in patients with a history of gastric or duodenal ulceration, acute erosive gastritis, ulcerative colitis or other gastrointestinal disorders. Reserpine may precipitate biliary colic in patients with gallstones.

Debilitated persons or patients with cardiac disease require special care in adjusting dosage in order to avoid hypotension and edema.

In patients suffering from coronary and/or cerebral arteriosclerosis reserpine should be employed with extreme caution. Any abrupt lowering of the blood pressure should be avoided. It is also advisable to exercise caution in patients with heart failure, recent myocardial infarction, sinus bradycardia, or disorders of cardiac conduction.

Due to the effect of catecholamine depletion, special care should be exercised when treating patients with a history of bronchial asthma. Asthmatics are more apt to be hypersensitive, and their condition may be aggravated.

Occupational Hazards: The patient's reaction time can be impaired, even with low doses of reserpine. Caution should therefore be exercised when driving or operating machinery.

Pregnancy: The safety of reserpine for use during pregnancy, particularly the first trimester, has not been established, therefore, the drug should be used in pregnancy only when its use is deemed essential to the patient's welfare.

Reserpine crosses the placental barrier. When administered shortly before term, it may lead to lethargy, nasal congestion, increased tracheobronchial secretions, and anorexia in the newborn infant. It should therefore not be given during the last 3 months prior to the calculated date of confinement.

Lactation: Since reserpine passes into breast milk and can cause effects in the infant as mentioned above, a choice must be made between withdrawing the drug or weaning the infant.

Drug Interactions: MAO inhibitors are contraindicated since large quantities of catecholamines may be released, causing a sharp transient rise in blood pressure. MAO inhibitors should be withdrawn at least 14 days before treatment with reserpine. Likewise, reserpine must be withdrawn for a similar period of time prior to MAO inhibition.

Reserpine should be used cautiously with digitalis and antiarrhythmic drugs as arrhythmias have occurred with rauwolfia preparations.

Concurrent use of guanethidine and rauwolfia derivatives may cause bradycardia, mental depression and postural hypotension.

Concomitant treatment with other antihypertensives (e.g., guanethidine, methyldopa, beta-blockers, vasodilators, calcium antagonists, ACE inhibitors) intensifies the hypotensive effect of reserpine.

The central depressant action of alcohol, analgesics, antihistamines, and psycho-active drugs (tricyclic antidepressants) is potentiated by reserpine.

Reserpine diminishes the activity of levodopa.

Reserpine may potentiate the effect of adrenaline or other substances displaying sympathomimetic properties. (For example, caution is advised when using antitussives and cold preparations, nasal decongestants, and eye drops).

Concurrent use of tricyclic antidepressants may increase the antihypertensive effects of reserpine.

Reserpine interferes with colorimetric tests for urinary 17-ketosteroids and 17-hydroxycorticosteroids, producing spurious (low) values.

Adverse Effects: When adverse reactions occur, they are usually reversible and disappear when the drug is discontinued.

Gastrointestinal: Occasional: increased salivation and gastric secretions, dry mouth (xerostomia), increased intestinal motility and diarrhea. Rare: nausea, vomiting, anorexia,

increased appetite, aggravation of peptic ulcer or ulcerative colitis. Isolated: higher dosages can cause gastrointestinal hemorrhage.
Cardiovascular: Occasional: edema, in patients with hypertensive vascular disease (which generally ameliorates upon cessation of therapy, or with the administration of a diuretic agent), sinus bradycardia. Rare: angina-like syndrome, cardiac arrhythmias (particularly when used concurrently with digitalis or quinidine), hypotension, postural hypotension with higher doses, flushing. Isolated: loss of consciousness (syncope), cardiac insufficiency, cerebrovascular disturbances.
Respiratory Tract: asthma in susceptible or hypertensive persons. Occasional: nasal congestion, dyspnea. Isolated epistaxis.
CNS: Occasional: mental depression, nightmares (which may be an early sign of mental depression), drowsiness, lassitude, dizziness, nervousness, insomnia and sleep disturbances, respiratory depression. Rare: extrapyramidal symptoms (including parkinsonian syndrome), paradoxical anxiety, impaired concentration, headache, stupor, dull sensorium. Isolated: cerebral edema.
Sense Organs: Isolated cases of hearing impairment, deafnesss, glaucoma, uveitis, conjunctival hyperemia, conjunctival injection, lacrimation, blurred vision and optic atrophy.
Urogenital system: Occasional: decreased libido. Rare: impotence, impaired ejaculation. Isolated: dysuria.
Dermatological: pruritus, skin rash, purpura.
Endocrine system: Occasional: weight gain. Rare: galactorrhea, gynecomastia. Isolated: swelling of the breasts.
Hematological: Isolated: anemia, thrombocytopenia.

Overdose: Symptoms: Impairment of consciousness may occur and may range from drowsiness to coma, depending upon the severity of overdosage. Lethargy, tiredness, apathy, confusion, agitation or depression may also ensue. Flushing of the skin, conjunctival injection and miosis (lasting for several days) are to be expected. Convulsions (especially in children), hypotension, hypothermia, central respiratory depression, cardiac arrhythmias (particularly sinus bradycardia), myocardial infarction and shock may develop in cases of severe overdosage. Extrapyramidal disorders, headache, nausea, vomiting, increased intestinal motility and diarrhea, increased salivary and gastric secretion, and swelling of the nasal mucosa may also occur.

Treatment: Remove unabsorbed reserpine from the stomach by induction of emesis or gastric lavage, taking adequate precautions against aspiration and for protection of the airway. Administration of activated charcoal slurry may help reduce absorption.

Treat the effects of reserpine overdosage symptomatically.

In the presence of postural hypotension, place the patient in an appropriate position and administer a plasma expander. If hypotension is severe enough to require treatment with a vasopressor, use one having a direct action upon vascular smooth muscle (e.g., phenylephrine, levarterenol, metaraminol).

If bradycardia becomes marked, especially with cardiac arrhythmias, consider the use of vagal blocking agents along with other appropriate measures.

If diarrhea occurs, administer an anticholinergic agent.

To combat convulsions administer anticonvulsants (e.g., diazepam) slowly i.v.

In the event of severe respiratory depression, artifical respiration must be instituted.

Since reserpine is long acting, observe the patient carefully for at least 72 hours, administering treatment as required.

Dosage: The dosage should be as low as possible, to reduce the possibility of adverse effects at higher dosages.

The drug should be administered with food, meals or milk.
Hypertension: In patients not receiving other antihypertensive agents, the usual initial dose is 0.5 mg daily for 1 or 2 weeks. For maintenance, reduce to 0.125 to 0.25 mg daily. Higher doses should be used cautiously, because serious mental depression and other adverse effects may be increased considerably. Elderly and debilitated patients may require lower doses than other adults.
Psychiatric Disorder: Initial dose is usually 0.5 mg daily. The dosage is to be titrated (according to the patient's response) to the lowest effective dose, and therefore may range from 0.125 to1.0 mg.

Supplied: Each white, round, biconvex tablet, imprinted CIBA on one side and SP with bisect on the other, contains: reserpine 0.25 mg. Nonmedicinal ingredients: alcohol, lactose, magnesium stearate, polyethylene glycol, sugar, talc and tragacanth. Energy: 2 kJ (0.49 kcal). Also contains lactose. Alcohol-, bisulfite-, gluten-, parabens-, sodium- and tartrazine-free. Bottles of 100.

SERTRALINE ℞
General Monograph, CPhA

see SELECTIVE SEROTONIN REUPTAKE INHIBITORS

SERZONE® ℞
Bristol-Myers Squibb

Nefazodone HCl
Antidepressant

Pharmacology: Nefazodone is a synthetically derived analogue of the phenylpiperazine series with a chemical structure unrelated to selective serotonin reuptake inhibitors (SSRI), tricyclics, tetracyclics, or MAO inhibitors. It is metabolized in vivo to compounds which likewise exhibit pharmacological activity.

Nefazodone blocks the 5-HT_2 receptor (postsynaptic) and inhibits serotonin and norepinephrine reuptake (presynaptic).

Nefazodone has no significant affinity for alpha 2-adrenergic, beta-adrenergic, histaminergic, dopaminergic, cholinergic, benzodiazepine, and serotonergic receptors of the 5-HT_{1A} subtype. Nefazodone has alpha 1-adrenergic blocking activity.

Pharmacokinetics: The pharmacokinetics of nefazodone and its major metabolites are subject to considerable inter- and intrasubject variability. Orally administered nefazodone is rapidly and completely absorbed, with peak plasma concentrations occurring 1 to 3 hours after dosing. However, nefazodone is subject to extensive presystemic metabolism, and its systemic bioavailability is estimated to range between 15 and 23%. Single doses of 50, 100 and 200 mg of nefazodone, administered as the hydrochloride salt in capsule formulation, result in mean peak plasma concentrations of 84, 196 and 392 ng/mL, respectively. Steady-state plasma nefazodone concentrations are attained within 3 to 4 days of initiation or adjustment of b.i.d. dosing. At steady state, nefazodone exibits non-linear pharmacokinetics with peak serum levels and AUCs increasing more than proportionally with dose increases. The mean peak plasma concentrations for doses of 50, 100, and 200 mg b.i.d. were 270, 730 and 2 050 ng/mL, respectively, and the corresponding AUC values were 540, 2 270 and 9 250 ng·h/mL.
Effect of Food: Food delays the absorption of nefazodone and decreases its systemic exposure by approximately 20%. These effects are small and are unlikely to be clinically significant in light of the extensive inter- and intra-subject variability in pharmacokinetics.
Distribution: Nefazodone is widely distributed in body tissues, including the CNS. In humans, the volume of distribution ranges from 0.22 to 0.87 L/kg.
Metabolism: A clinical pharmacokinetic study using orally administered ^{14}C-radiolabelled nefazodone has demonstrated extensive presystemic metabolism. Nefazodone accounted for approximately 3% of the total radioactivity in the plasma. Nefazodone undergoes N-dealkylation as well as aliphatic and aromatic hydroxylation. Three major metabolites have been identified in the plasma: hydroxynefazodone (HO-NEF), metachlorophenyl-piperazine (mCPP), and a triazole-dione metabolite. The elimination half-lives for HO-NEF, mCPP and the triazole-dione metabolite are 1.5 to 4 hours, 4 to 9 hours, and 18 hours, respectively. Both hydroxynefazodone and metachlorophenyl-piperazine (mCPP) have inhibitory effects on serotonin reuptake, but mCPP also has agonist activity at some serotonergic receptor subtypes. The pharmacologic profile of the triazole-dione metabolite has not been well characterized. The pharmacokinetics of NEF, HO-NEF and mCPP exhibit extensive inter- and intra-subject variability in humans. In healthy male volunteers receiving multiple 100 mg b.i.d. and 200 mg b.i.d. doses of nefazodone, the AUC values of HO-NEF and mCPP were approximately 35% and 5%, respectively, of those for the parent compound. The pharmacokinetics of HO-NEF are nonlinear; however, mCPP exhibits linear pharmacokinetics. Triazole-dione, exhibits only weak 5-HT_2 antagonistic activity, but AUC values at steady state are approximately 2.7 fold higher than those for nefazodone.
Elimination: The mean elimination half-life of nefazodone ranges from 2 to 4 hours. The plasma elimination half-life of nefazodone is dose-dependent. In a 3-way crossover study in healthy male volunteers, steady-state $t_{1/2}$ values were 1.9 h for a 50 mg b.i.d. dose, 2.9 h for a 100 mg b.i.d. dose, and 3.7 h for a 200 mg b.i.d. dose. When ^{14}C-labelled nefazodone is administered orally, about 50 to 65% of the radioactivity was excreted in the urine as metabolites. Less than 1% of the administered nefazodone was detected unchanged in urine; identified metabolites of nefazodone accounted for 80% of the radioactivity detected in urine. The excretion of nefazodone and HO-NEF is negligible; approximately 1% of the administered dose is excreted as mCPP and about 7% as para-hydroxy-mCPP (p-OH-mCPP). Fecal excretion accounted for 20 to 40% of the administered radiolabel. In 24 healthy male volunteers, the oral clearance (CL/F) at steady state decreased from 115±32 L/h (mean±sd) at a dose of 50 mg to 29±13 L/h at a dose of 300 mg.
Geriatrics: After single doses of 300 mg nefazodone to men and women, the peak plasma concentration and AUC of nefazodone and hydroxynefazodone are up to twice as high in older patients (≥65 years). After multiple doses, however, these parameters are 10 to 20% higher in the older patients. These data suggest that treatment in the elderly patients should be initiated at one-half of the usual dose of nefazodone.
Hepatically Impaired Patients: In patients with hepatic cirrhosis, the steady-state AUC values for nefazodone and HO-NEF are approximately 25% greater than those observed in normal volunteers. The AUC values for mCPP are approximately 3-fold greater than those observed in normal volunteers. Therefore, if nefazodone is administered to patients with liver disease, treatment should be initiated at one-half the usual dose of nefazodone, with subsequent adjustments being performed on the basis of tolerance and therapeutic response.
Renally Impaired Patients: The pharmacokinetics of nefazodone, HO-NEF, and mCPP were investigated in a multiple dose study of nefazodone involving patients with varying degrees of renal impairment (creatinine clearance ranging from 7 to 60 mL/min/1.73m^2). No significant relationships were observed between the pharmacokinetic parameters and the degree of renal impairment. However, in patients with severely impaired renal function, nefazodone should be used with caution (see Precautions).
Protein Binding: At concentrations of 25 to 2 500 ng/mL, nefazodone is extensively (>99%) bound to plasma proteins in vitro.
Pharmacodynamics: Hemodynamic Effects: In a crossover study involving healthy volunteers at least 65 years old, nefazodone caused a modest decrease in mean supine blood pressure and pulse rate without producing orthostatic hypotension or alterations in cardiac conduction compared to placebo.
Psychomotor Effects: In one study, psychomotor impairment in nefazodone-treated patients was shown after 7 days of b.i.d. treatment, but not after acute dosing. In 12 elderly subjects (≥60 yrs), chronic administration of nefazodone resulted in statistically significant decreases in driving performance (200 mg b.i.d.) and increased reaction times (100 to 200 mg b.i.d.). In young adult subjects (N=12), increased reaction times were observed during chronic dosing with 200 mg b.i.d. nefazodone. In another 7-day study involving subjects of at least 65 years old, psychomotor and cognitive function tests generally sensitive to the effects of psychotropic medication were not markedly altered by nefazodone.
Nocturnal Penile Tumescence: In a sleep architecture study conducted in healthy volunteers, the percent total sleep time spent in the tumescent state was 28% for placebo and 37% for a 400 mg dose of nefazodone.
Endocrine Effects: In normal male volunteers (N=8), single 50, 100, and 200 mg doses of nefazodone were associated with dose-dependent increases in plasma prolactin and growth hormone levels. At 150 min postadministration of a 200 mg dose, mean plasma prolactin levels were double baseline values but remained within the normal range. This increase in prolactin was not evident following 7 days of dosing with 100 mg b.i.d. of nefazodone. Mean plasma levels of growth hormone were increased approximately 15 fold over baseline levels 150 minutes after single 100 to 200 mg doses of nefazodone. When nefazodone was administered for 7 days according to a 100 mg b.i.d. regimen, plasma growth hormone levels were increased approximately 10 fold over baseline. The peak levels of growth hormone were in excess of the normal values but declined to normal range within the dosing interval. Plasma levels of ACTH and cortisol also tended to be increased (not significant) after single doses of 100 and 200 mg. The effects of nefazodone on hormonal levels in female subjects have not been investigated.

Indications: For the symptomatic relief of depressive illness.

The effectiveness of nefazodone in long-term use (i.e., for more than 6 to 8 weeks) has not been systematically evaluated in controlled trials. Therefore, the physician who elects to use nefazodone for extended periods should periodically reevaluate the long-term usefulness of the drug for the individual patient.

Contraindications: Hypersensitivity: In patients with known hypersensitivity to nefazodone, any component of the formulation or other phenylpiperazine antidepressants.

Serzone (cont'd)

MAO Inhibitors: Nefazodone should not be used in combination with MAO inhibitors or within 2 weeks of terminating treatment with MAO inhibitors. MAO inhibitors should not be introduced until at least 7 days after the cessation of nefazodone therapy (see Precautions, Drug Interactions).
Terfenadine, Astemizole, Cisapride: Coadministration of terfenadine, astemizole or cisapride with nefazodone is contraindicated (see Precautions, Drug Interactions).

Warnings: Interaction with Triazolobenzodiazepines: Nefazodone has been reported to increase the plasma levels of certain triazolobenzodiazepines (e.g., triazolam and alprazolam) metabolized by cytochrome P450IIIA4 resulting in an enhancement of the psychomotor impairment caused by these agents (see Precautions, Drug Interactions).

If alprazolam is to be coadministered with nefazodone, a 50% reduction in the initial alprazolam dosage is recommended. The concomitant use of nefazodone and triazolam is not recommended.
Interactions with HMG-CoA Reductase Inhibitors: There have been rare reports of increased creatine phosphokinase and/or rhabdomyolysis in patients receiving nefazodone in combination with the 3-hydroxy-3-methylglutaryl-coenzyme A (HMG-CoA) reductase inhibitors, lovastatin or simvastatin, known substrates for cytochrome P450IIIA4. Severe myopathy and rhabdomyolysis have been observed in patients receiving HMG-CoA reductase inhibitors in combination with inhibitors of the P450IIIA4 isoenzyme. As nefazodone is known to inhibit this isoenzyme, extreme caution should be observed if the combined use of nefazodone with simvastatin, lovastatin, atorvastatin, or cerivastatin is to be undertaken.
Priapism: Nefazodone has been associated with the occurence of rare events of priapism. In some of the cases reported, surgical intervention was required. Male patients with prolonged or inappropriate erections should immediately discontinue nefazodone and consult their physicians. If the condition persists for more than 24 hours, a urologist should be consulted to determine appropriate management.

Precautions: General: Suicide: The possibility of a suicide attempt in seriously depressed patients is inherent to the illness and may persist even during apparent improvement in symptoms. Close supervision of high risk patients should continue throughout therapy and consideration should be given to the possible need for hospitalization. In order to reduce the risk of overdose, prescriptions for nefazodone (nefazodone HCl) should be written for the smallest quantity of tablets consistent with good patient management.
Seizures: As with other antidepressants, nefazodone should be used with caution in patients with a history of seizures. During clinical trials, the overall incidence of seizures was 0.04% in patients treated with nefazodone. Patients with a history of convulsive disorders were excluded from these studies. Rare occurences of convulsions (including grand mal seizures) following nefazodone administration have been reported postmarketing. A causal relationship to nefazodone has not been established. The drug should be discontinued in any patient who develops seizures.
Activation of Mania/Hypomania: Activation of mania/hypomania is a known risk in a small proportion of patients with Major Affective Disorder treated with antidepressants, and also occurred during clinical trials with nefazodone (0.3% of unipolar and 1.6% of bipolar patients). Nefazodone should be used cautiously in patients with a history of mania.
Renal and Hepatic Impairment: Caution is advisable when using nefazodone in patients with diseases or conditions such as hepatic or renal impairment, that could affect the metabolism and excretion of the drug. In patients with cirrhosis of the liver, the AUC values of nefazodone and HO-NEF are increased by approximately 25%. In patients with severely impaired renal function, chronic administration may result in additional accumulation of nefazodone or its metabolites. Therefore, the use of a lower or less frequent dose is advised. No specific relationship between pharmacokinetic parameters and degree of renal impairment has been observed (see Pharmacology).
Occupational Hazards: Interference with Cognitive and Motor Performance: Patients should be cautioned about operating hazardous machinery, including automobiles, until they are reasonably certain that the drug treatment does not adversely affect their ability to engage in such activities. Psychomotor impairment in nefazodone-treated subjects was evident after 7 days of b.i.d. treatment, but not after acute dosing (see Pharmacology).
Cardiovascular Effects: Nefazodone treatment was associated with modest blood pressure lowering effects in clinical trials. Orthostatic hypotension and syncope have been reported in some nefazodone-treated patients. The rates for adverse events characterized as postural hypotension in clinical trials with nefazodone were as follows: nefazodone (3%), tricyclic antidepressants (10.9%), SSRI (2.2%), and placebo (1%). Therefore, nefazodone should be used with caution in patients with known cardiovascular or cerebrovascular disease that could be exacerbated by hypotension (history of myocardial infarction, angina or ischemic stroke) and conditions that would predispose patients to hypotension (dehydration, hypovolemia, and treatment with antihypertensive medication).

Sinus bradycardia and first degree AV block were observed in 1.5% and 1.2% of patients who received recommended therapeutic doses of the drug in clinical trials. Corresponding rates of occurrence during placebo treatment were 0.4% and 0.6%.

Nefazodone has not been evaluated or used to any appreciable extent in patients with a recent history of myocardial infarction or unstable heart disease. Hence, the usual precautions should be observed in these patients.
Prolactin Levels: In male volunteers, prolactin levels were increased to twice the baseline values following the acute administration of nefazodone, although individual values remained within the normal range (2 to 15 ng/mL). Such an increase was not seen following 7-day dosing. Prolactin levels were not determined in women, however, no clinical evidence of hyperprolactinemia (e.g., amenorrhea, galactorrhea, abnormal menstrual cycle length) was observed in the 446 women who received nefazodone for more than 60 days in clinical studies.

In women with existing breast cancer, or a history of this disease, the possible risk of hyperprolactinemia should be weighed against the benefits of therapy. Tissue culture experiments indicate that approximately ⅓ of human breast cancers are prolactin-dependent in vitro. Neither clinical studies nor epidemiological studies conducted to date, however, have shown an association between administration of hyperprolactinemia-inducing drugs and mammary tumorigenesis: available evidence is considered too limited to be conclusive at this time.
Pregnancy: There have been no controlled studies with nefazodone in pregnant women. Reproduction studies, however, have been performed in rabbits and rats at doses equivalent to 16 and 25 times the maximum daily human dose of 600 mg and have revealed no evidence of teratogenicity due to nefazodone. Because animal reproductive studies are not always predictive of human response, this drug should be used during pregnancy only if the potential benefits outweigh the potential risk.
Lactation: It is not known whether and, if so, in what amount nefazodone or its metabolites are excreted in human milk. In lactating rats, nefazodone and 2 of its metabolites (HO-NEF and mCPP) are excreted in milk. Because many drugs are excreted in human milk, lactating women should not nurse their infants while receiving nefazodone.
Children: Safety and effectiveness in children below age 18 have not been established.
Geriatrics: Nefazodone has not been systematically studied in geriatric patients. Due to the increased systemic exposure to nefazodone seen in single dose trials in elderly patients (see Pharmacology), nefazodone treatment should be initiated at half the usual dose, with titration upward as needed to achieve a therapeutic response with optimal tolerability (see Dosage). In clinical trials, most elderly patients achieved optimal therapeutic response at daily doses of 200 to 400 mg. The usual precautions should be observed in elderly patients who have concomitant medical illnesses or who are receiving concomitant drugs.
Drug Abuse and Dependence: Nefazodone showed no potential for abuse in a controlled study of abuse liability in human subjects. Nefazodone has not been systematically studied in humans for its potential for tolerance, physical dependence or withdrawal emergent symptoms.

In animal studies, nefazodone did not act as a reinforcer for i.v. self-administration in monkeys trained to self-administer cocaine. However, physicians should carefully evaluate patients for a history of drug abuse and follow such patients closely, observing them for signs of misuse or abuse.
Electro-Convulsive Therapy (ECT): There have been no clinical studies establishing the benefit of the combined use of ECT and nefazodone.
Drug Interactions: Drugs for Which a Potentially Clinically Important Interaction is Observed or Anticipated: Terfenadine, Astemizole and Cisapride: The concurrent use of terfenadine, astemizole or cisapride with nefazodone is contraindicated. Nefazodone has been shown in vitro to be an inhibitor of cytochrome $P_{450}IIIA_4$. Terfenadine, astemizole and cisapride are all metabolized by the cytochrome $IIIA_4$, and it has been demonstrated that ketoconazole, erythromycin, and other inhibitors of $IIIA_4$ can block the metabolism of these drugs, resulting in increased plasma concentrations of parent drug. Increased plasma concentrations of terfenadine, astemizole and cisapride are associated with QT prolongation and with rare cases of serious cardiovascular adverse events, including death, due principally to ventricular tachycardia of the torsades de pointes type. Torsades de pointes has been reported in a patient receiving cisapride in combination with nefazodone (see Contraindications).
MAO Inhibitors: In patients receiving antidepressants with pharmacological properties similar but not identical to nefazodone (i.e., selective serotonin reuptake inhibitors) in combination with an MAO inhibitor, there have been reports of serious, sometimes fatal, reactions. These reactions have also been reported in patients who have recently discontinued these drugs and have been started on an MAO inhibitor. Symptoms have included hyperthermia, rigidity, myoclonus, autonomic instability with possible rapid fluctuations of vital signs, seizures, and mental status changes that include extreme agitation progressing to delirium and coma. Because nefazodone is an inhibitor of serotonin reuptake, it is recommended that nefazodone not be used in combination with an MAO inhibitor, or within 14 days of discontinuing treatment with an MAO inhibitor. At least 1 week should be allowed after stopping nefazodone before starting an MAO inhibitor (see Contraindications).
Drugs Metabolized by Cytochrome $P_{450}IIIA_4$ Isozyme: Nefazodone has been shown in vitro to be an inhibitor of cytochrome $P_{450}IIIA_4$. This is consistent with the interaction observed between nefazodone and the triazolobenzodiazepines (triazolam and alprazolam), drugs metabolized by this isozyme. Consequently, caution is indicated in the combined use of nefazodone with any drugs known to be metabolized by the $IIIA_4$ isozyme (e.g., calcium channel antagonists, cyclosporine, clarithromycin, erythromycin, ketoconazole, itraconazole, lovastatin, simvastatin, atorvastatin, midazolam, vinblastine) (see Warnings and Precautions). In the case of terfenadine, astemizole and cisapride, combined use with nefazodone is contraindicated.
Triazolobenzodiazepines: Triazolam: The concomitant use of nefazodone and triazolam should be avoided. When a single oral 0.25 mg dose of triazolam was coadministered with nefazodone (200 mg b.i.d.) at steady state, triazolam peak concentrations, half-life and AUC were increased 1.7, 3 and 4 fold respectively. The pharmacokinetics of nefazodone were not altered. The concomitant use of triazolam and nefazodone was also associated with an increase in psychomotor impairment presumably due to increased triazolam plasma concentrations. The interactive effects of higher doses of these agents have not been studied. The metabolism of triazolam has been attributed to the specific hepatic microsomal isozyme, $P_{450}IIIA_4$. Potential interactions between nefazodone and other drugs metabolized by this isozyme (e.g., cyclosporine, midazolam, nifedipine, quinidine, lidocaine and erythromycin) should be considered.
Alprazolam: When alprazolam (1 mg b.i.d.) and nefazodone (200 mg b.i.d.) were coadministered, peak concentrations, AUC, and half-life values for alprazolam increased by approximately 2 fold at steady state. Nefazodone plasma concentrations were unaffected by alprazolam, although levels of the mCPP metabolite were increased. The concomitant use of alprazolam and nefazodone was also associated with an increase in psychomotor impairment presumably due to increased alprazolam plasma concentrations. If alprazolam is coadministered with nefazodone, a 50% reduction in the alprazolam dosage is recommended; no dosage adjustment is required for nefazodone. The interactive effects of higher doses of these agents, such as the dosage levels of alprazolam used in panic disorder, have not been studied.
Interactions with HMG-CoA Reductase Inhibitors: There have been rare reports of increased creatine phosphokinase, and/or rhabdomyolysis in patients receiving nefazodone in combination with the 3-hydroxy-3-methylglutaryl-coenzyme A (HMG-CoA) reductase inhibitors, lovastatin or simvastatin, known substrates for cytochrome P450IIIA4 (see Warnings).
Fluoxetine: Pretreatment or coadministration of fluoxetine with nefazodone significantly increases the AUC values of the nefazodone metabolite mCPP by approximately 3 to 6 fold. Patients who are transferred immediately from fluoxetine to nefazodone may experience some transient adverse events (e.g., nausea, lightheadedness, headache). These adverse events may be minimized by allowing a washout period before initiating nefazodone therapy and reducing the initial dose of nefazodone. Because of the long half-life of fluoxetine and its metabolites, this washout period may range from 4 to

8 weeks, depending on the dose of fluoxetine and other individual patient variables. Nefazodone does not affect the pharmacokinetics of fluoxetine or norfluoxetine.

Digoxin: When nefazodone and digoxin were coadministered to healthy male volunteers who were phenotyped as $P_{450}IID_6$ extensive metabolizers, C_{max}, C_{min}, and AUC of digoxin were increased by 29%, 27%, and 15%, respectively. Digoxin had no effects on the pharmacokinetics of nefazodone and its active metabolites. Because of the narrow therapeutic index of digoxin, caution should be exercised when nefazodone and digoxin are coadministered; plasma level monitoring for digoxin is recommended.

Drugs for Which Either No Interaction or a Clinically Unimportant Interaction is Observed, or Known: Lorazepam: When lorazepam (2 mg b.i.d.) and nefazodone (200 mg b.i.d.) were coadministered to steady state, there was no change in any pharmacokinetic parameter for either drug compared to each drug administered alone. Therefore, dosage adjustment is not necessary for either drug when co-administered.

Alcohol: In a controlled trial with healthy volunteers, nefazodone did not potentiate the psychomotor or cognitive impairment of alcohol. It is prudent however to avoid concomitant use of alcohol and nefazodone.

Haloperidol: In healthy volunteers, the AUC of haloperidol (single 5 mg dose) was increased by 35%, with no significant increase in the C_{max} or T_{max} when coadministered with nefazodone (200 mg b.i.d.) at steady state. There were no changes in the pharmacokinetic parameters of nefazodone.

Lithium: Concurrent administration of nefazodone (100 mg b.i.d.) with lithium (800 mg/day) did not cause any adverse interactions.

Cimetidine: No significant clinical or pharmacokinetic interactions between nefazodone (200 mg b.i.d.) and cimetidine (300 mg q.i.d.) were observed in a multiple dose clinical trial involving healthy volunteers.

Propranolol: The coadministration of nefazodone and propranolol to healthy male volunteers, including poor and extensive $P_{450}IID_6$ metabolizers, resulted in 30% and 14% reductions in C_{max} and AUC of propranolol, respectively, and a 14% reduction in C_{max} for the metabolite, 4-hydroxypropranolol. The kinetics of nefazodone, hydroxynefazodone and triazole-dione were not affected by coadministration of propranolol. However, C_{max}, C_{min} and AUC of m-chlorophenylpiperazine were increased by 23%, 54% and 28%, respectively. Nefazodone may modestly enhance the heart rate lowering effect of propranolol in some situations. No change in initial dose of either drug is necessary and dose adjustments should be made on the basis of clinical response and tolerability.

Drugs Metabolized by Cytochrome $P_{450}IID_6$: A subset (3 to 10%) of the population has reduced activity of drug-metabolizing enzyme Cytochrome $P_{450}IID_6$. Such individuals are referred to commonly as "poor metabolizers" of drugs such as quinidine, dextromethorphan and the tricyclic antidepressants. The pharmacokinetics of nefazodone and its major metabolites are not altered in these "poor metabolizers." Although plasma concentrations of mCPP are increased in this population, the adjustment of nefazodone dosage is not required when administrated to "poor metabolizers." Nefazodone and its metabolites have been shown in vitro to be extremely weak inhibitors of $P_{450}IID_6$. Thus, it is not likely that nefazodone will decrease the metabolic clearance of drugs metabolized by this isozyme (e.g., alprenolol, metoprolol, timolol, flecainide, paroxetine, fluoxetine, thioridazine, haloperidol).

Drugs Metabolized by IA_2 Isozyme: Nefazodone and its metabolites have been shown in vitro not to inhibit cytochrome $P_{450}IA_2$. Thus, metabolic interactions between nefazodone and drugs metabolized by this isozyme are unlikely (e.g., clozapine, tacrine, theophylline).

Antihypertensives: There have been reports of postural hypotension and syncope in nefazodone-treated patients. Concomitant administration of antihypertensive therapy and nefazodone should be initiated cautiously and a reduction in the dose of the antihypertensive drug may be required (see Precautions, Cardiovascular Effects).

Protein Binding: Nefazodone is extensively (>99%) bound to plasma proteins in man. The effect of nefazodone on plasma protein binding of potentially coadministered drugs should be considered. Conversely, adverse effects could result from displacement of nefazodone by other highly bound drugs.

General Anesthetics: Little is known about the potential for interaction between nefazodone and general anesthetics; therefore, prior to elective surgery, nefazodone should be discontinued for as long as clinically feasible.

Other Drugs: During interaction studies, nefazodone was **not** found to have a significant effect on the pharmacokinetics or pharmacodynamics of theophylline or warfarin.

Adverse Effects: Commonly Observed Adverse Events: In clinical trials, the most commonly observed adverse experiences associated with the use of nefazodone which occurred at a higher rate than among placebo-treated patients were dry mouth, nausea, somnolence, dizziness, constipation, asthenia, lightheadedness and blurred vision. Over a 6-week period there was evidence of progressive adaptation with continued therapy to the following adverse experiences: nausea, somnolence, dry mouth, dizziness, asthenia, constipation, lightheadedness and blurred vision.

Adverse Events Associated with Discontinuation of Treatment: Approximately 11% of the 2 256 patients who received nefazodone in short-term worldwide premarketing clinical trials discontinued treatment due to adverse experiences. The most common events causing discontinuation included: nausea (2.4%), headache (2.0%), dizziness (1.2%), asthenia (1.0%) and insomnia (1.2%).

Serious Adverse Events: Serious adverse events occurring in all patients treated with nefazodone in clinical trials were: syncope (1 case), abdominal pain (1 case) and gastrointestinal bleeding (1 case).

Incidence in Controlled Clinical Trials: Table I shows adverse events that occurred in 1% or more of patients treated with nefazodone who participated in controlled clinical trials of 6 to 8 weeks duration. Only those adverse events which occurred at rates which were at least 1% higher during nefazodone treatment than during placebo treatment are included.

Table I—Serzone

Treatment-Emergent Adverse Experience Incidence in Placebo-Controlled Clinical Trials

	Number (%) of Patients	
Body System / Adverse Events	**Nefazodone 50 to 600 mg/day n=1 489**	**Placebo n=1 007**
Body as a Whole		
Asthenia	175 (11.8)	72 (7.2)
Flu Syndrome	67 (4.5)	30 (3.0)
Chills	42 (2.8)	7 (0.7)
Fever	27 (1.8)	8 (0.8)
Cardiovascular		
Postural Hypotension	44 (3.0)	10 (1.0)
Digestive		
Nausea	327 (22.0)	144 (14.3)
Dry Mouth	282 (18.9)	127 (12.6)
Constipation	168 (11.3)	72 (7.2)
Diarrhea	133 (8.9)	78 (7.8)
Vomiting	53 (3.6)	25 (2.5)
Anorexia	42 (2.8)	17 (1.7)
Musculoskeletal		
Myalgia	53 (3.5)	22 (2.2)
Arthralgia	33 (2.2)	8 (0.8)
Nervous System		
Somnolence	297 (20.0)	132 (13.1)
Dizziness	184 (12.4)	63 (6.3)
Insomnia	169 (11.4)	103 (10.2)
Lightheadedness	165 (11.1)	46 (4.6)
Paresthesia	73 (4.9)	16 (1.6)
Vasodilatation	65 (4.4)	25 (2.5)
Confusion	53 (3.6)	12 (1.2)
Abnormal Dreams	52 (3.5)	17 (1.7)
Memory Impairment	52 (3.5)	12 (1.2)
Incoordination	44 (3.0)	10 (1.0)
Hypesthesia	20 (1.3)	5 (0.5)
Ataxia	17 (1.2)	-(-.-)
Respiratory		
Rhinitis	81 (5.4)	44 (4.4)
Special Senses		
Blurred Vision	83 (5.6)	31 (3.1)
Visual Disturbances	46 (3.1)	6 (0.6)
Eye Disorder	25 (1.7)	3 (0.3)

Other Events Observed During the Premarketing Evaluation of Nefazodone: In placebo-controlled clinical trials, sinus bradycardia (≤50 bpm and a decrease of ≥15 bpm) was observed in 1.5% of nefazodone-treated patients compared to 0.4% of placebo-treated patients ($p<0.05$) (see Precautions).

In the tabulations that follow, a dictionary based on COSTART terminology has been used to classify reported adverse experiences. The adverse events, arranged by body system, were reported on at least one occasion by patients during clinical trials with nefazodone. The frequencies reported are based on 4 579 patients exposed to nefazodone. All reported events are included except those already listed in Table I or those for which a drug cause was remote or the event term was either overly general or excessively specific so as to be uninformative. It is important to emphasize that, although the experiences reported did occur during treatment with nefazodone, they were not necessarily caused by it. Experiences are further classified within body system categories and enumerated in order of decreasing frequency using the following definitions: frequent adverse experiences are defined as those occurring on 1 or more occasions in at least 1/100 patients; infrequent adverse experiences are those occurring in less than 1/100 but at least 1/1 000 patients; rare adverse experiences are those occurring in less than 1/1 000 patients.

Body as a Whole: **frequent:** headache, infection, abdominal pain, back pain, chest pain and neck pain; **infrequent:** neck rigidity, allergic reaction, photosensitivity reaction, hangover effect, malaise, enlarged abdomen, face edema, substernal chest pain, hernia, mucous membrane disorder, cyst, halitosis, overdose and pelvic pain; **rare:** cellulitis, unexpected benefit, aggravation reaction, intentional injury, neoplasm, abscess, carcinoma, altered hormone level, hypertrophy, abnormal lab test and moniliasis.

Cardiovascular: **frequent:** hypotension and palpitation; **infrequent:** presyncope, migraine, hypertension, tachycardia, ventricular extrasystoles, peripheral vascular disorder, bradycardia, syncope, angina pectoris, arrhythmia, abnormal ECG; **rare:** atrial fibrillation, pallor, phlebitis, congestive heart failure, coronary artery disease, extra systoles, AV block, hemorrhage, varicose vein, AV block first degree, AV block second degree, bigeminy, bundle branch block, cardiomyopathy, cardiovascular disorder, pancarditis, supraventricular extrasystoles, supraventricular tachycardia.

Digestive: **frequent:** gastroenteritis, dyspepsia, flatulence and increased appetite; **infrequent:** nausea and vomiting, liver function tests abnormality, gastritis, abnormal stools, eructation, periodontal abscess, colitis, mouth ulceration, stomatitis, gingivitis, peptic ulcer, rectal hemorrhage, esophagitis and dysphagia; **rare:** glossitis, bloody diarrhea, hepatitis, gastrointestinal hemorrhage, oral moniliasis, ulcerative colitis, salivary gland enlargement, cheilitis, cholecystitis, cholelithiasis, intestinal obstruction and melena.

Endocrine: **rare:** goiter and hypothyroidism.

Hemic and Lymphatic: **infrequent:** ecchymosis, leukopenia, lymphadenopathy and anemia; **rare:** eosinophilia, leukocytosis, hypochromic anemia, petechia, purpura, thrombocythemia and thrombocytopenia.

Metabolic and Nutritional: **frequent:** weight gain, peripheral edema and edema; **infrequent:** thirst, weight loss, increased ALT and AST, gout and increased lactate dehydrogenase; **rare:** hypercholesteremia, hypervolemia, hyponatremia, hypoglycemia, dehydration, alcohol intolerance, increased alkaline phosphatase, increased amylase, calcium disorder, diabetes mellitus, electrolyte abnormality, hyperglycemia and hypokalemia.

Musculoskeletal: **frequent:** cramp; **infrequent:** arthritis, muscle stiffness, tenosynovitis, bursitis and tendon disorder; **rare:** myasthenia, myositis, tendinous contracture and bone and joint disorder.

Nervous System: **frequent:** CNS stimulation, agitation, anxiety, decreased concentration, tremor, depression, psychomotor retardation and decreased libido; **infrequent:** increased libido, vertigo, emotional lability, dysphoria, hypertonia, depersonalization, euphoria, amnesia, twitching, hallucinations, hypomanic reaction, derealization, neuralgia, suicidal thoughts, hostility, suicide attempt, decreased attention, paranoid reaction, abnormal gait, apathy, myoclonus, sleep disorder, abnormal thinking, dysarthria, speech disorder, increased salivation; **rare:** affect abnormal, abnormal behavior, convulsion, delirium, delusions, drug dependency (other drug), hyperesthesia, neuropathy, neurosis, torticollis, hypotonia, ptosis, akathisia, hyperalgesia, personality disorder manic reaction, cerebrovascular accident, hyperkinesia, aphasia, mental retardation, neuritis, drug dependence, dystonia, meningitis, multiple sclerosis, decreased reflexes, stupor, vasospasm and neuroleptic malignant syndrome.

Respiratory: **frequent:** cough, pharyngitis, sinusitis, dyspnea and bronchitis; **infrequent:** hiccup, epistaxis, pneumonia, asthma, laryngitis, voice alteration, hyperventilation and yawn; **rare:** emphysema, pleural disorder and lung disorder.

Skin and Appendages: **frequent:** increased sweating, rash and pruritus; **infrequent:** dry skin, acne, urticaria, alopecia, herpes simplex, herpes zoster, maculopapular rash and eczema; **rare:** hirsutism, skin carcinoma, furunculosis, s.c. nodule, nail disorder, vesiculobullous rash, fungal dermatitis, skin melanoma, leukoderma, lichenoid dermatitis, psoriasis, seborrhea, skin discoloration, skin disorder and decreased sweating.

Serzone (cont'd)

Special Senses: **frequent:** tinnitus, taste perversion and eye pain; **infrequent:** ear pain, visual field defect, dry eye, abnormality of accommodation, conjunctivitis, diplopia, keratoconjunctivitis, mydriasis, photophobia, hyperacusis and deafness; **rare:** exophthalmos, glaucoma, night blindness, taste loss, otitis media, retinal degeneration, lacrimation disorder, vestibular disorder, cataract, blepharitis, blindness, chromatopsia, corneal ulcer and retinal disorder.

Urogenital: **frequent:** dysmenorrhea, vaginitis, urinary frequency, urinary tract infection and impotence; **infrequent:** cystitis, dysuria, breast pain, urinary urgency, metrorrhagia, polyuria, amenorrhea, urinary retention, prostatic disorder, breast enlargement, breast neoplasm, hematuria, kidney calculus, urinary incontinence, menstrual disorder, abnormal ejaculation, unintended pregnancy, vaginal hemorrhage, menorrhagia, anorgasmia, nocturia, urinary tract disorder, psychosexual dysfunction and urine abnormality; **rare:** breast carcinoma, cervix neoplasm, dyspareunia, mastitis, menopause, menorrhagia, oliguria, enlarged uterine fibroids and uterine hemorrhage.

Adverse Events Observed During the Postmarketing Evaluation of Nefazodone: Adverse events not listed above which have been reported in temporal association with nefazodone since market introduction include: seizures, hepatic events, serotonin syndrome, priapism, severe allergic reactions such as anaphylactoid reaction, exfoliative dermatitis and Stevens-Johnson syndrome; arrhythmias, rhabdomyolysis and pancytopenia.

The hepatic events included jaundice, liver failure, liver necrosis and liver damage. In rare cases, these events resulted in liver transplantation and/or death.

Rare reports of rhabdomyolysis involving patients receiving a combination of nefazodone and lovastatin or simvastatin have been received.

The causal realtionship between nefazodone treatment and the emergence of these adverse events has not been established.

Overdose: Symptoms: Overdoses of nefazodone alone of up to 30 g have been reported. Commonly reported symptoms from overdose of nefazodone alone included nausea, vomiting, somnolence, bradycardia and hypotension. Coma and death have occurred in patients ingesting overdoses of nefazodone in combination with other drugs.

Treatment: There is no specific antidote for nefazodone. Treatment should be symptomatic and supportive. Any patient suspected of having taken an overdose should have the stomach emptied by gastric lavage. In managing overdosage, consider the possibility of multiple drug involvement.

Dosage: Adults: Nefazodone should usually be initiated at 100 to 200 mg/day (50 to 100 mg b.i.d.). The dose may then be increased in increments of 100 to 200 mg/day, administered in 2 divided doses, at intervals of not less than 1 week, depending on clinical response and tolerability.

In controlled clinical trials designed to establish the efficacy of nefazodone, patients were given doses ranging from 100 to 600 mg/day, administered in divided doses. These studies indicate that most patients responded at daily doses ranging from 300 to 500 mg. Several weeks on treatment may be required to obtain the full therapeutic effect.

Geriatrics or Debilitated Patients: The recommended initial dose for these patients is 100 mg/day (50 mg b.i.d.). These patients often have reduced nefazodone clearance and/or increased sensitivity to the side effects of CNS-active drugs. It may be appropriate to modify the rate of subsequent dose titration and final target dose based on a careful assessment of the patient's clinical response.

Switching Patients to or from an MAO Inhibitor: At least 14 days should elapse between discontinuation of an MAO inhibitor and initiation of therapy with nefazodone. In addition, at least 7 days should be allowed after stopping nefazodone before starting an MAO inhibitor (see Warnings and Precautions).

Renal Impairment: No significant relationship between pharmacokinetics and degree of renal impairment has been observed. However, with chronic administration, additional accumulation of nefazodone or its metabolites may occur in patients with severely impaired renal function, and use of the lower end of the dose range is advised.

Information for the Patient: See Blue Section—Information for the Patient "Serzone".

Supplied: 50 mg: Each pink, hexagonal, flat-faced, beveled-edged tablet, engraved with "BMS 50" on one side and "31" on the other, contains: nefazodone 50 mg. Nonmedicinal ingredients: colloidal silicon dioxide, magnesium stearate, microcrystalline cellulose, povidone, red ferric oxide and sodium starch glycolate. Bottles of 60.

100 mg: Each white, hexagonal, flat-faced, beveled-edged tablet, engraved with "BMS 100" and a bisect score on one side and "32" and a bisect score on the other, contains: nefazodone HCl 100 mg. Nonmedicinal ingredients: colloidal silicon dioxide, magnesium stearate, microcrystalline cellulose, povidone and sodium starch glycolate. Bottles of 60.

150 mg: Each peach, hexagonal, flat-faced, beveled-edged tablet, engraved with "BMS 150" and a bisect score on one side and "39" and a bisect score on the other, contains: nefazodone HCl 150 mg. Nonmedicinal ingredients: colloidal silicon dioxide, magnesium stearate, microcrystalline cellulose, povidone, red ferric oxide, sodium starch glycolate and yellow ferric oxide. Bottles of 60.

200 mg: Each light yellow, hexagonal, flat-faced, beveled-edged tablet, engraved with "BMS 200" on one side and "33" on the other, contains: nefazodone HCl 200 mg. Nonmedicinal ingredients: colloidal silicon dioxide, magnesium stearate, microcrystalline cellulose, povidone, sodium starch glycolate and yellow ferric oxide. Bottles of 60.

Store at room temperature (between 15 and 30°C). Keep container tightly closed.

(Shown in Product Recognition Section)

Reviewed 1999

SEVORANE™ Ⓟ

Abbott

Sevoflurane

Inhalation Anesthetic

Pharmacology: Sevoflurane is an inhalational anesthetic agent for use in induction and maintenance of general anesthesia. Sevoflurane has a nonpungent odor and does not cause respiratory irritability. Sevoflurane is suitable for mask induction in adults and pediatric. Minimum alveolar concentration (MAC) of sevoflurane in oxygen for a 40-year-old adult is 2.1%. The MAC of sevoflurane decreases with age (see Dosage, Table V on following pages).

Pharmacokinetics: Uptake, Metabolism and Elimination: Solubility: Because of the low solubility of sevoflurane in blood (blood/gas partition coefficient at 37°C=0.63 to 0.69), a minimal amount of sevoflurane is required to be dissolved in the blood before the alveolar partial pressure is in equilibrium with the arterial partial pressure. Therefore there is a rapid rate of increase in the alveolar (end-tidal) concentration (F_A) toward the inspired concentration (F_I) during induction and rapid elimination via the lungs when it is discontinued.

Metabolism: Sevoflurane is metabolized by cytochrome P450 2E1, to hexafluoroisopropanol (HFIP) with the release of inorganic fluoride and CO_2. Once formed, HFIP is rapidly conjugated with glucuronic acid and eliminated as a urinary metabolite. No other metabolite pathways for sevoflurane have been identified. In vivo metabolism studies suggest that approximately 5% of the sevoflurane dose may be metabolized.

Cytochrome P450 2E1 is the principal isoform identified for sevoflurane metabolism and this may be induced by chronic exposure to isoniazide and ethanol. This is similar to the metabolism of isoflurane and enflurane and is distinct from that of methoxyflurane which is metabolized via a variety of cytochrome P450 isoforms. The metabolism of sevoflurane is not inducible by barbiturates. Inorganic fluoride concentrations peak within 2 hours of the end of sevoflurane anesthesia and return to baseline concentrations within 48 hours post-anesthesia in the majority of cases (67%). The rapid and extensive pulmonary elimination of sevoflurane minimizes the amount of ansthetic available for metabolism.

In 12 clinical trials with sevoflurane, approximately 7% (55 out of 886) of adults evaluated for inorganic fluoride had serum concentrations greater than 50 µmol; there were no reports of toxicity associated with elevated fluoride ion levels.

Renal and Hepatic Impaired Patients: Limited pharmacokinetic data in these patients appear to suggest that the half-life of sevoflurane may be increased. The clinical significance is unknown at this time.

Elimination: Up to 3.5% of the sevoflurane dose appears in the urine as inorganic fluoride. Studies on fluoride indicate that up to 50% of fluoride clearance is nonrenal (via fluoride being taken up into bone).

Compound A Production in Anesthesia Circuit: The only known degradation reaction in the clinical setting is through direct contact with CO_2 absorbents (soda lime and Baralyme) producing Compound A (pentafluoroisopropenyl fluoromethyl ether).

The concentrations of Compound A measured in the anesthesia circuit when sevoflurane is used as indicated are not known to be deleterious to humans. Fresh gas flow rates below 2 L/min in a circle absorber system are not recommended, as safety at lower rates has not yet been established.

Pharmacodynamics: Emergence times in pediatric patients are faster for sevoflurane (12 minutes) than for halothane (19 minutes). Time to first analgesia in pediatric patients is earlier in sevoflurane (approximately 52 minutes) than with halothane (approximately 68 minutes). The facts should be taken into account in cases where postanesthesia pain is anticipated.

Cardiovascular Effects: Sevoflurane was studied in 14 healthy volunteers (18 to 35 years old) comparing sevoflurane-O_2 (Sevo/O_2) to sevoflurane-N_2O/O_2 (Sevo/N_2O/O_2) during 7 hours of anesthesia. During controlled ventilation, hemodynamic parameters were measured.

A study investigating the epinephrine-induced arrhythmogenic effect of sevoflurane vs isoflurane in adult patients undergoing transsphenoidal hypophysectomy (n=40) demonstrated that the threshold dose of epinephrine (i.e., the dose at which the first sign of arrhythmia was observed) producing multiple ventricular arrhythmias was 5 µg/kg in both groups.

Cardiovascular Surgery/Coronary Artery Bypass Graft (CABG) Surgery: Sevoflurane was compared to isoflurane as an adjunct with opioids in a multicentre study of 273 patients undergoing CABG surgery. The average MAC dose was 0.49 for sevoflurane and 0.53 for isoflurane. No statistical differences were observed between the 2 treatment groups with respect to incidence (sevoflurane 7%, isoflurane 11%) and duration (sevoflurane approximately 18 minutes, isoflurane approximately 17 minutes) of ischemic events, number of patients with diagnosis of myocardial infarction (sevoflurane 8%, isoflurane 10%), time to hemodynamic stability (sevoflurane approximately 5 hours, isoflurane approximately 6 hours), or use of cardioactive drugs (sevoflurane 53%, isoflurane 47%).

Non-Cardiac Surgery Patients at Risk for Myocardial Ischemia: Sevoflurane-N_2O was compared to isoflurane-N_2O for maintenance of anesthesia in a multicentre study of 214 patients who were at mild-to-moderate risk for myocardial ischemia who underwent elective noncardiac surgery. The average MAC dose was 0.49 for both drugs. No statistical differences were observed between the treatment groups for the incidence of any hemodynamic variation (tachycardia, bradycardia, hypertension, hypotension, and ischemia without hemodynamic abnormality). No statistical differences were observed between the 2 regimens with respect to intraoperative incidence of myocardial ischemia (sevoflurane 6%, isoflurane 3%) or postoperative incidence of ischemic events (sevoflurane 10%, isoflurane 16%). No statistical differences were observed between the treatment groups for the incidences of study drug-related adverse experience by body system or by COSTART term (sevoflurane 60%, isoflurane 61%). There was 1 death in sevoflurane group while 4 deaths occurred in the isoflurane group. None of these deaths were considered by the investigator to be drug-related.

Pediatric Anesthesia: The concentration of sevoflurane required for maintenance of general anesthesia is age-dependent (see Dosage, Table V). Incidences of bradycardia (more than 20 beats/min less than normal) is lower for sevoflurane (3%) than for halothane (7%). Emergence times for sevoflurane are faster than with halothane (12 vs 19 minutes, respectively). A higher incidence of agitation occurs with sevoflurane (208/837 patients or 25%) when compared with halothane (114/661 patients or 17%).

Indications: For induction and maintenance of general anesthesia in adult and pediatric patients for inpatient and outpatient surgery.

Contraindications: Sevoflurane should not be used in patients with known history of sensitivity to sevoflurane or to other halogenated agents or with known or suspected genetic susceptibility to malignant hyperthermia. Sevoflurane should not be used when general anesthesia is contraindicated.

Warnings: Sevoflurane should be administered only by persons trained in the administration of general anesthesia. Facilities for maintenance of a patent airway, artificial ventilation, oxygen enrichment, and circulatory resuscitation must be immediately available. Since levels of anesthesia may be altered rapidly, only vaporizers producing predictable concentrations of sevoflurane should be used.

Because clinical experience in administering sevoflurane to patients with renal insufficiency (creatinine >1.5 mg/dL) is limited, its safety in these patients has not been established (see Pharmacology).

Fresh gas flow rates of less than 2 L/min in a circle absorber system are not recommended, as safety at lower rates has not yet been established.

Compound A is produced when sevoflurane interacts with soda lime and Baralyme (see Pharmacology). Its concentration in a circle absorber system increases with increasing absorber temperature and increasing sevoflurane concentrations and with decreasing fresh gas flow rates. Although Compound A is a dose-dependent nephrotoxin in rats, there have been no cases of renal toxicity reported in humans, when sevoflurane is used as recommended.

Malignant Hyperthermia: In susceptible individuals, potent inhalation anesthetic agents, including sevoflurane, may trigger a skeletal muscle hypermetabolic state leading to high oxygen demand and the clinical syndrome known as malignant hyperthermia.

In clinical trials, one case of malignant hyperthermia was reported. In genetically susceptible pigs, sevoflurane induced malignant hyperthermia. The clinical syndrome is signaled by hypercapnia, and may include muscle rigidity, tachycardia, tachypnea, cyanosis, arrhythmias, and/or unstable blood pressure. Some of these nonspecific signs may also appear during light anesthesia, acute hypoxia, hypercapnia and hypovolemia.

Treatment of malignant hyperthermia includes discontinuation of triggering agents, administration of i.v. dantrolene sodium, and application of supportive therapy. (Consult information for i.v. dantrolene sodium for additional information on patient management.) Renal failure may appear later, and urine flow should be monitored and sustained if possible.

Precautions: During the maintenance of anesthesia, increasing the concentration of sevoflurane produces dose-dependent decreases in blood pressure. Due to sevoflurane's insolubility in blood, these hemodynamic changes may occur more rapidly than with other volatile anesthetics. Excessive decreases in blood pressure or respiratory depression may be related to depth of anesthesia and may be corrected by decreasing the inspired concentration of sevoflurane.

The recovery from general anesthesia should be assessed carefully before patient is discharged from the postanesthesia care unit.

Drug Interactions: In clinical trials, no significant adverse reactions occurred with other drugs commonly used in the perioperative period, including: CNS depressants, autonomic drugs, skeletal muscle relaxants, anti-infective agents, hormones and synthetic substitutes, blood derivatives and cardiovascular drugs.

I.V. Anesthetics: Sevoflurane administration is compatible with barbiturates, nonbarbiturates (such as propofol) and benzodiazepines.

Benzodiazepines and Opioids: Benzodiazepines and opioids would be expected to decrease the MAC of sevoflurane in the same manner as with other inhalational anesthetics. Sevoflurane administration is compatible with benzodiazepines and opioids as commonly used in surgical practice.

Nitrous Oxide: As with other halogenated volatile anesthetics, the anesthetic requirement for sevoflurane is decreased when administered in combination with nitrous oxide. Using 50% N_2O, the MAC equivalent dose requirement is reduced approximately 50% in adults, and approximately 25% in pediatric patients (see Dosage).

Neuromuscular Blocking Agents: As is the case with other volatile anesthetics, sevoflurane increases both the intensity and duration of neuromuscular blockade induced by nondepolarizing muscle relaxants. The effect of sevoflurane on succinylcholine and the duration of depolarizing neuromuscular blockade has not been studied.

Geriatrics: MAC decreases with increasing age. The average concentration of sevoflurane to achieve MAC in an 80 year old is approximately 50% of that required in a 20 year old. In adults, the incidence of bradycardia is greater with sevoflurane than with isoflurane (see Adverse Effects).

Children: The concentration of sevoflurane required for maintenance of general anesthesia is age-dependent (see Dosage). Incidences of bradycardia (more than 20 beats/min less than normal) is lower for sevoflurane (3%) than for halothane (7%). Emergence times for sevoflurane are faster than with halothane (12 vs 19 minutes, respectively). A higher incidence of agitation occurs with sevoflurane (208/837 patients or 25%) when compared with halothane (114/661 patients or 17%).

Neurosurgery: Due to the limited number of patients who received sevoflurane during neurosurgical procedures (n=22), safety in neurosurgery has not been fully established at this time and sevoflurane should be used with caution. In a study of 20 patients, there was no difference between sevoflurane and isoflurane with regard to recovery from anesthesia. In 2 studies, a total of 22 patients with intracranial pressure (ICP) monitors received either sevoflurane or isoflurane. There was no difference between sevoflurane and isoflurane with regard to ICP response to inhalation of 0.5, 1.0, and 1.5 MAC inspired concentrations of volatile agent during N_2O-O_2-fentanyl anesthesia. During progressive hyperventilation from $PaCO_2=40$ to $PaCO_2=30$, ICP response to hypocarbia was preserved with sevoflurane at both 0.5 and 1.0 MAC concentrations. In patients at risk for elevations of ICP, sevoflurane should be administered cautiously in conjunction with ICP-reducing maneuvers such as hyperventilation.

Renal and Hepatic Impaired Patients: Because clinical experience in administering sevoflurane in patients with renal insufficiencies (creatinine >1.5 mg/dL) is limited (n=35), its safety in these patients has not been established. Therefore, sevoflurane should be used with caution in patients with renal insufficiency. Limited pharmacokinetic data in these patients appear to suggest that the half-life of sevoflurane may be increased. The clinical significance is unknown at this time (see Pharmacology).

In a limited number of patients with mild to moderate hepatic impairment (n=16), the hepatic function was not affected by sevoflurane. The safety of sevoflurane in patients with severe hepatic impairment has not yet been demonstrated; therefore, sevoflurane should be used with caution in these patients.

Pregnancy: There are no adequate and well-controlled studies in pregnant women. Sevoflurane should be used during pregnancy only if clearly needed.

Cesarean Section: Due to the limited number of patients studied, safety in cesarean section has not been fully established at this time and sevoflurane should be used with caution. Sevoflurane has been used as part of general anesthesia for elective cesarean section in 29 women. There were no untoward effects in mother or neonate.

Labor, Delivery and *Lactation:* The safety of sevoflurane in labor, delivery and lactation has not yet been demonstrated; therefore, sevoflurane should be used with caution in these patients.

Information for the Patient: Although recovery of consciousness following sevoflurane administration generally occurs within minutes, the impact on intellectual function for 2 or 3 days following anesthesia has not been studied. As with other anesthetics, small changes in moods may persist for several days following administration. Patients should be advised that performance of activities requiring mental alertness, such as operating a motor vehicle or hazardous machinery, may be impaired for some time after general anesthesia.

Adverse Effects: Adverse events are derived from controlled clinical trials conducted in the US, Canada and Europe. The reference drugs were isoflurane, enflurane, and propofol in adults and halothane in pediatric patients. The studies were conducted using a variety of premedications, other anesthetics, and surgical procedures of varying length. Most adverse events reported were mild and transient, and may reflect the surgical procedures, patient characteristics (including disease) and/or medications administered.

Of the 5 182 patients enrolled in the clinical trials, 2 906 were exposed to sevoflurane, including 118 adults and 507 pediatric patients who underwent mask induction. Each patient was counted once for each type of adverse event. Adverse events reported in patients in clinical trials are presented within each body system in order of decreasing frequency in Tables I, II, III and Table IV (on following page). One case of malignant hyperthermia was reported in preregistration clinical trials.

Table I—Sevorane

Adverse Events During the Induction Period (from onset of anesthesia by mask induction to surgical incision) Possibly or Probably Related Incidence >1%

Body System	Adverse Event	Incidence
Adult Patients (n=118)		
Cardiovascular	Bradycardia	5%
	Hypotension	4%
	Tachycardia	2%
Nervous System	Agitation	7%
Respiratory	Laryngospasm	8%
	Airway Obstruction	8%
	Breathholding	5%
	Cough Increased	5%
Pediatric Patients (n=507)		
Cardiovascular	Tachycardia	6%
	Hypotension	4%
Nervous System	Agitation	15%
	Increased Salivation	2%
Respiratory	Breathholding	5%
	Cough Increased	5%
	Laryngospasm	3%
	Apnea	2%

Note: Similar incidence of adverse events was noted when all adverse reactions were recorded, not only possibly or probably related.

Table II—Sevorane

Adverse Events for All Patients During All Anesthetic Periods Possibly or Probably Related Incidence >1% (n=2 906)

Body System	Adverse Event	Incidence
Body as a Whole	Fever	1%
	Shivering	6%
	Hypothermia	1%
	Movement	1%
	Headache	1%
Cardiovascular	Hypotension	11%
	Hypertension	2%
	Bradycardia	5%
	Tachycardia	2%
Nervous System	Somnolence	9%
	Agitation	9%
	Dizziness	4%
	Increased Salivation	4%
Digestive	Nausea	25%
	Vomiting	18%
Respiratory	Cough Increased	11%
	Breathholding	2%
	Laryngospasm	2%

Table III—Sevorane

All Adverse Events for All Patients During All Anesthetic Periods Incidence >1%

Body System	Adverse Event	Incidence Sevorane (n=2 906)	Incidence Ref. Agent (n=2 276)
Body as a Whole	Fever	11%	12%
	Shivering	7%	8%
	Hypothermia	2%	2%
	Movement	1%	1%
	Headache	2%	3%
Cardiovascular	Hypotension	15%	16%
	Hypertension	10%	9%
	Bradycardia	7%	8%
	Tachycardia	4%	4%
Nervous System	Somnolence	14%	17%
	Agitation	11%	9%
	Dizziness	8%	9%
	Increased Salivation	7%	11%
Digestive	Nausea	37%	36%
	Vomiting	25%	27%
Respiratory	Cough Increased	24%	29%
	Breathholding	3%	3%
	Laryngospasm	2%	3%

Sevorane (cont'd)

Table IV—Sevorane

All Adverse Events For All Patients During All Anesthetic Periods

Body System	Adverse Event Incidence < 1% (reported in 3 or more patients) (n = 2 906)
Body as a Whole	Asthenia, pain
Cardiovascular	Arrhythmia, ventricular extrasystoles, supraventricular extrasystoles, complete AV block, bigeminy, hemorrhage, inverted T wave, atrial fibrillation, atrial arrhythmia, second degree AV block, syncope, S-T depressed
Nervous System	Crying, nervousness, confusion, hypertonia, dry mouth, insomnia
Respiratory	Sputum increased, apnea, hypoxia, wheezing, bronchospasm, hyperventilation, pharyngitis, hiccup, hypoventilation, dyspnea, stridor
Metabolism and Nutrition	Increases in LDH, AST, ALT, BUN, alkaline phosphatase, creatinine, bilirubinemia, glycosuria, fluorosis, albuminuria, hypophosphatemia, acidosis, hyperglycemia
Hemic and Lymphatic	Leukocytosis, thrombocytopenia
Skin and Special Senses	Pruritus, taste perversion, rash, conjunctivitis
Urogenital	Urination impaired, urine abnormality, urinary retention, oliguria

See Warnings for information regarding malignant hyperthermia.

Postmarketing Experience: There have been postmarketing reports of rare events of malignant hyperthermia (see Warnings). Cases of dystonic movement with spontaneous resolution have been reported in children receiving sevoflurane for induction of anesthesia. There have also been reports of postoperative hepatitis. Due to the uncontrolled nature of these spontaneous reports, a causal relationship to sevoflurane has not been established.

Laboratory Findings: Transient elevations in glucose, liver function tests, and WBC count may occur as with use of other anesthetic agents.

Overdose: Symptoms and Treatment: In the event of overdosage, or what may appear to be overdosage, the following action should be taken: discontinue administration of sevoflurane, maintain a patent airway, initiate assisted or controlled ventilation with oxygen and maintain adequate cardiovascular function.

Dosage: Fresh gas flow rates of less than 2 L/min in a circle absorber system are not recommended, as safety at lower rates has not yet been established.

The concentration of sevoflurane being delivered from a vaporizer during anesthesia should be known. This may be accomplished by using a vaporizer calibrated specifically for sevoflurane. The administration of general anesthesia must be individualized based on the patient's response.

Preanesthetic Medication: No specific premedication is either indicated or contraindicated with sevoflurane. The decision as to whether or not to premedicate and the choice of premedication is left to the discretion of the anesthesiologist.

Induction: Sevoflurane has a nonpungent odor and does not cause respiratory irritability; therefore, it is suitable for mask induction in pediatrics and adults.

Maintenance: Surgical levels of anesthesia can usually be achieved with concentrations of 0.5 to 3% sevoflurane with or without the concomitant use of nitrous oxide. Sevoflurane can be administered with any type of anesthesia circuit.

Table V—Sevorane

MAC Values According to Age

Age of Patient	Number of Patients	MAC in Oxygen	MAC in 65% N_2O/35% O_2
Infants	26		
1–<6 months		3.0%	–
6–<12 months		2.8%	–
Children	39		
1–<3 years		2.6%	2.0%
3–12 years		2.5%	–
Adults	41		
25 years		2.5%	1.4%
40 years		2.1%	1.1%
60 years		1.6%	0.9%
80 years		1.4%	0.7%

Note 1: In 12 neonates of full-term gestational age, MAC was determined to be 3.3%.

Note 2: In 3- to <5-year-old pediatric patients, 60% N_2O/40% O_2 was used.

Supplied: Each bottle contains: sevoflurane. Additives- and chemical stabilizer-free. Amber colored bottles of 250 mL. Store at room temperature (15 to 30°C).

Reviewed 1998

SH-206

Pharmascience

Acetic Acid—Camphor—Lemon Extract Oil—Sodium Lauryl Ether Sulfate

Pediculicide

Pharmacology: A clinical study conducted in 81 patients suffering of pediculosis demonstrates the efficacy of SH-206 shampoo. The patients (school children and adults), were suffering of head pediculosis (80 cases).

A clinical study was carried out in which the scalp and hair were examined for the presence (or absence) of lice by means of a magnifier. The SH-206 shampoo was used as follows: after wetting the hair, approximately 15 mL of the shampoo was applied and left in contact with the scalp and hair for 10 minutes.

The results of a parasitological study demonstrated an efficacy of 100% (total destruction of lice and nits). The results of the clinical study show that the SH-206 shampoo was well tolerated; no discontinuation due to allergies or local irritations occurred.

A comparative clinical study of 70 children (4 to 14 years old) infested by Pediculus humanus capitis equally demonstrated the efficacy of the SH-206 shampoo in the treatment of head lice infestation. The patients were included in the study in their order of arrival and were assigned a treatment by the use of a table of random numbers. Fifty children (21 boys and 29 girls) were treated with SH-206 shampoo; twenty children (8 boys and 12 girls) served as a control group. After examining the hair in order to determine the number of lice and nits. The SH-206 shampoo was applied by lathering the previously wetted hair at a dosage of 9 to 15 mL and left in contact for 10 minutes.

The results observed after the first application demonstrated the undeniable efficacy of the SH-206 shampoo on lice (Pediculus humanus capitis) and their nits. A statistical study of the results obtained in comparison with a control group confirmed the efficacy of the SH-206 shampoo. A very good skin tolerance was also observed throughout the study.

Action: Even though the way in which this product acts is not yet fully understood, it is believed, as a result of gas chromatography studies, that the sodium lauryl ether sulfate molecules form, along with acetic acid and certain active ingredients present in the essential oils, a micellar system from which the acid part is liberated to act on the insect. It is believed that the micellar system helps dissolve the cement secreted by the female lice, their cuticle as well as the shells of the nits, therefore allowing the active ingredients to exert their toxic effects.

Observation with a magnifier showed that the administration of SH-206 shampoo first excited the lice which tried to release themselves, then caused ascending progressive paralysis followed by death due to circulatory arrested.

Indications: Recommended for the treatment of pediculosis caused by hair lice (Pediculus humanus capitis).

Contraindications: Should not be used on individuals with a history of sensitivity to the product or to one or more of its ingredients. Not recommended for use on children under 30 months of age.

Warnings: For external use only. As for all medication, keep out of the reach of children.

Precautions: SH-206 shampoo must not come into contact with eyes, nose, mouth, or other mucous membranes. In case of accidental contact, thoroughly rinse affected area with water. Should irritation persist or in case of sensibility, discontinue medication and consult a physician.

Adverse Effects: Application of SH-206 shampoo on damaged skin will lead to slight pruritus, but does not necessitate a cessation of the treatment.

Dosage: First Application: First, wet hair. Apply a sufficient amount of SH-206 shampoo to cover the hair (about 10 mL) and lather. Scrub vigorously for 2 minutes especially in the occipital and periauricular areas. Let set for 10 minutes. Rinse thoroughly with lukewarm water. Use a fine-toothed comb to remove dead lice and nits.

Second Application: 48 hours after the first application, it is necessary to repeat the above treatment.

Note: SH-206 shampoo treatment need not be followed by regular shampooing.

Information for the Patient: See Blue Section—Information for the Patient "SH-206".

Supplied: Each bottle of clear acid solution, slightly viscous and quick to lather, contains: acetic acid 3.65%, camphor 0.76%, lemon extract oil 0.76% and sodium lauryl ether sulfate 33.55%. Amber glass bottles of 60 mL with nit comb.

Reviewed 1998

SIALOR®

Solvay Pharma

Anetholtrithion

Sialogogue

Pharmacology: In addition to its choleretic activity, anetholtrithion has a positive effect on drug induced asialias which may be due to the drug's direct action on the secretory cells of the salivary glands.

Approximately 30% of an orally administered dose is absorbed from the gastrointestinal tract, with 80% being excreted in the urine and the remainder in the bile.

In man, the average amounts of anetholtrithion recovered as the free p-hydroxyphenyltrithione metabolite or its o-glucuronide are 1.5 to 3 and 12%, respectively. The yellow coloration of the urine resulting from anetholtrithion ingestion is due to the presence of the 2 metabolites.

Indications: The treatment of oral symptoms of xerostomia in order to reverse drug-induced hyposialosis related to the administration of certain drugs (neuroleptics, tranquilizers, antidepressants, synthetic antiparkinsonian agents) or following a course of radiotherapy of the head and neck area.

Contraindications: Jaundice, cirrhosis, biliary tract or common bile duct obstruction.

Precautions: Rarely, soft stools may be produced. If this persists, reduce the dosage to 25 mg in the morning and 25 mg in the evening.

Pregnancy and *Lactation:* Anetholtrithion's safety for use in human pregnancy has not been established. Therefore, the drug should not be used in pregnancy or lactation unless its use is deemed essential to the welfare of the mother and/or fetus.

Overdose: Symptoms and Treatment: Symptomatic: gastric lavage, induce diuresis.

Dosage: 25 mg, 3 times a day before meals. Treatment may be continuous or intermittent with 5 drug free days/month in association with the drugs responsible for the asialia. In hyposialosis related to radiotherapy, administration may be continued indefinitely. Usually, anetholtrithion's full therapeutic effect is gradually achieved after several days of treatment.

Supplied: Each orange-red, sugar coated tablet contains: anetholtrithion 25 mg. Nonmedicinal ingredients: anticaking sucrose, cochineal red A, E wax, gelatin, gum arabic, guar gum, hydrated colloidal silica, lactose, magnesium stearate, sucrose, sunset yellow S, talc, titanium dioxide and wheat starch. Boxes of 60.

SIMILAC® LF
Abbott
Milk Protein (Lactose-free)
Infant Formula

Indications: For infants with lactose intolerance.

Precautions: Product contains cow's milk protein and should not be given to infants with a cow's milk protein allergy.

Dosage: As determined by the individual infant's needs for the first year of life. Consult your physician for specific feeding recommendations.

Supplied: Ingredients: corn syrup solids, sucrose, total milk protein, high oleic sunflower or high oleic safflower oil, coconut oil, soya oil, minerals (potassium citrate, potassium chloride, calcium phosphate dibasic, sodium citrate, magnesium chloride, magnesium phosphate dibasic, ferrous sulfate, zinc sulfate, cupric sulfate, potassium iodide, manganese sulfate, sodium selenite), vitamins (ascorbic acid, alpha-tocopheryl acetate, niacinamide, calcium pantothenate, vitamin A palmitate, thiamine hydrochloride, riboflavin, pyridoxine hydrochloride, folic acid, vitamin K_1 [phylloquinone], biotin vitamin D_3, cyanocobalamin), choline chloride, taurine, inositol, ascorbyl palmitate, l-carnitine and beta-carotene (see Table I).

Note: Slight variation may exist in ingredients between the different Similac LF preparations. Consult the product label for exact composition.

Energy Distribution: protein 9%, fat 48%, carbohydrate 43%; 2 846 kJ (680 kcal)/L.

Table I—Similac LF

Analysis	1 000 mL (1 L)	
Energy	2 842 (680)	kJ (kcal)
Protein	15	g
Carbohydrate	72	g
Fat	37	g
Vitamin A	601	RE
Vitamin D	400	IU
Vitamin C	55	mg
Vitamin E	18.2	IU
Vitamin B_{12}	0.0015	mg
Vitamin K	0.055	mg
Thiamine	0.65	mg
Riboflavin	0.45	mg
Niacin	7	mg
Vitamin B_6	0.41	mg
Folic Acid	0.1	mg
Pantothenic Acid	3	mg
Biotin	0.03	mg
Choline	82	mg
Calcium	570	mg
Phosphorus	360	mg
Sodium	200	mg
Potassium	720	mg
Chloride	440	mg
Magnesium	41	mg
Iron	12	mg
Zinc	5	mg
Copper	0.6	mg
Carnitine	11	mg
Iodine	0.09	mg
Manganese	0.034	mg
Inositol	40	mg
Taurine	45	mg
Selenium	0.015	mg
Osmolality	223	mOsm/kg H_2O

Liquid Concentrate: Cans of 385 mL.

Liquid Ready-to-Feed: Cans of 235 and 945 mL.

Powder: Tins of 370 g.

Store unopened liquid and powder at room temperature. Prepared bottles and opened can (covered) should be refrigerated and used within 48 hours. Opened powder should be stored in a cool, dry place (but not in refrigerator) and used within 1 month. Formula remaining in bottle after feeding should be discarded.

General monographs are developed by CPhA editorial staff and reviewed by the *CPS* Editorial Advisory Panel to provide additional therapeutic information.

SINEMET® Ⓟ
DuPont Pharma
Levodopa—Carbidopa
Antiparkinson Agent

Pharmacology: The symptoms of Parkinson's disease are related to depletion of dopamine in the corpus striatum. Administration of dopamine is ineffective in the treatment of Parkinson's disease because it does not cross the blood-brain barrier. However, levodopa, the metabolic precursor of dopamine, does cross the blood-brain barrier, and is converted to dopamine in the basal ganglia. This is thought to be the mechanism whereby levodopa relieves the symptoms of Parkinson's disease.

When levodopa is administered orally it is rapidly converted to dopamine by decarboxylation in extracerebral tissues so that only a small portion of a given dose is transported unchanged to the CNS. For this reason, large doses of levodopa are required for adequate therapeutic effect and these may often be attended by nausea and other adverse reactions, some of which are attributable to dopamine formed in extracerebral tissues.

Since levodopa competes with certain aminoacids, the absorption of levodopa may be impaired in some patients on a high protein diet.

Carbidopa inhibits decarboxylation of peripheral levodopa. It does not cross the blood-brain barrier and does not affect the metabolism of levodopa within the CNS. Since its decarboxylase inhibiting activity is limited to extracerebral tissues, administration of carbidopa with levodopa makes more levodopa available for transport to the brain. Combined therapy with levodopa and carbidopa reduces the amount of levodopa required for optimum therapeutic benefit by about 75 to 80%, permits an earlier response to therapy, and also reduces the incidence of nausea, vomiting and cardiac arrhythmias. Combined therapy, however, does not decrease adverse reactions due to central effects of levodopa.

Following simultaneous administration of carbidopa and levodopa in man, both plasma levels and plasma half-life of levodopa are markedly increased over those found when the same dosage of levodopa is given alone, while plasma levels of dopamine and homovanillic acid are reduced or do not change. Nevertheless, the plasma levels vary greatly between patients.

Pyridoxine HCl (vitamin B_6), in oral doses of 10 to 25 mg, may reverse the effects of levodopa by increasing the rate of aromatic amino acid decarboxylation. Carbidopa inhibits this action of pyridoxine.

Indications: For the treatment of Parkinson's disease.

Sinemet is not recommended for the treatment of drug-induced extrapyramidal reactions.

Although the administration of carbidopa permits control of Parkinson's disease with much lower doses of levodopa, there is no conclusive evidence at present that this is beneficial other than reducing nausea and vomiting, permitting more rapid titration, and providing a somewhat smoother response to levodopa. Carbidopa does not decrease adverse reactions due to central effects of levodopa. By permitting more levodopa to reach the brain, particularly when nausea and vomiting is not a dose-limiting factor, certain adverse CNS effects, e.g., dyskinesias, may occur at lower dosages and sooner during therapy with Sinemet than with levodopa.

Contraindications: Monoamine oxidase inhibitors (except low doses of selective MAO-B inhibitors) and Sinemet should not be given concomitantly. These inhibitors must be discontinued at least 2 weeks prior to initiating therapy with Sinemet.

Sinemet should not be administered to patients with clinical or laboratory evidence of uncompensated cardiovascular, endocrine, hematologic, hepatic, pulmonary (including bronchial asthma), or renal disease; or to patients with narrow angle glaucoma.

As with levodopa, Sinemet should not be given when administration of a sympathomimetic amine is contraindicated.

Sinemet is contraindicated in patients with known hypersensitivity to any component of this medication.

Because levodopa may activate a malignant melanoma, Sinemet should not be used in patients with suspicious, undiagnosed skin lesions or a history of melanoma.

Warnings: When patients already receiving levodopa are switched to Sinemet, levodopa must be discontinued for at least 12 hours or more before Sinemet is started. Sinemet should be substituted at a dosage that will provide approximately 20% of the previous levodopa dosage (see Dosage).

Patients who are taking Sinemet should be instructed not to take additional levodopa unless it is prescribed by the physician.

The levodopa induced involuntary movements and "on-and-off" phenomenon may appear earlier with combination therapy.

As with levodopa, Sinemet may cause involuntary movements and mental disturbances. These reactions are thought to be due to increased brain dopamine following administration of levodopa. Because carbidopa permits more levodopa to reach the brain and thus, more dopamine to be formed, dyskinesias may occur at lower dosages and sooner with Sinemet than with levodopa. The occurrence of dyskinesias may require dosage reduction.

Patients should be monitored carefully for the development of depression with suicidal tendencies. Patients with past or current psychoses should be treated with caution.

Care should be exercised in administering Sinemet to patients with a history of myocardial infarction or who have atrial, nodal, or ventricular arrhythmias. In such patients, cardiac function should be monitored with particular care during the period of initial dosage adjustment in a facility with provisions for intensive cardiac care.

A symptom complex resembling the neuroleptic malignant syndrome including muscular rigidity, elevated body temperature, mental changes, and increased serum creatine phosphokinase has been reported when antiparkinsonian agents were withdrawn abruptly. Therefore, patients should be observed carefully when the dosage of Sinemet is reduced abruptly or discontinued, especially if the patient is receiving neuroleptics.

As with levodopa there is a possibility of upper gastrointestinal hemorrhage in patients with a history of peptic ulcer.

Precautions: General: Periodic evaluations of hepatic, hematopoietic, cardiovascular and renal function are recommended during extended therapy in all patients with Sinemet.

Since levodopa competes with certain amino acids, the absorption of levodopa may be impaired in some patients on a high protein diet.

Children: The safety of Sinemet in patients under 18 years of age has not been established.

Pregnancy and *Lactation:* Although the effects of Sinemet on human pregnancy and lactation are unknown, both levodopa and combinations of carbidopa and levodopa have caused visceral and skeletal malformations in rabbits. Therefore, use of Sinemet in women of childbearing potential requires that the anticipated benefits of the drug be weighed against possible hazards to the mother and to the fetus. Sinemet should not be given to nursing mothers.

Physical Activity: Patients who improve while on therapy with Sinemet should increase physical activities gradually, with caution, consistent with other medical considerations such as the presence of osteoporosis or phlebothrombosis.

Glaucoma: Pupillary dilatation and activation of latent Horner's syndrome have been reported during levodopa treatment. Patients with chronic wide angle glaucoma should therefore be treated cautiously with Sinemet. The intraocular pressure should be well controlled and the patient monitored carefully for changes in intraocular pressure during therapy.

Drug Interactions: Caution should be exercised when the following drugs are administered concomitantly with Sinemet.

Antihypertensive Drugs: Symptomatic postural hypotension can occur when Sinemet is added to the treatment of a patient receiving antihypertensive drugs. Therefore, when therapy with Sinemet is started, dosage adjustment of the antihypertensive drug may be required. For patients receiving monoamine oxidase inhibitors, see Contraindications.

Psychoactive Drugs: Phenothiazines and butyrophenones may reduce the therapeutic effects of levodopa. The beneficial effects of levodopa in Parkinson's disease have been reported to be reversed by phenytoin and papaverine. Patients taking these drugs with Sinemet should be carefully observed for loss of antiparkinsonian effect. There have been rare reports of adverse reactions, including hypertension and dyskinesia, resulting from the concomitant use of tricyclic antidepressants and Sinemet.

Anesthetics: When general anesthesia is required, Sinemet should be discontinued the night before. Therapy with Sinemet may be continued as soon as the patient is able to take medication by mouth.

Adverse Effects: The most common serious adverse reactions occurring with Sinemet (levodopa and carbidopa) are choreiform, dystonic and other involuntary movements. Other serious adverse reactions are mental changes including paranoid ideation and psychotic episodes, depression with or without development of suicidal tendencies, and dementia. Convulsions also have occurred; however, a causal relationship with Sinemet has not been established.

A common but less serious effect is nausea.

Sinemet (cont'd)

Less frequent adverse reactions are cardiac irregularities and/or palpitation, orthostatic hypotensive episodes, bradykinetic episodes (the on-off phenomenon), anorexia, vomiting and dizziness.

Rarely, gastrointestinal bleeding, development of duodenal ulcer, hypertension, phlebitis, hemolytic and non-hemolytic anemia, thrombocytopenia, leukopenia and agranulocytosis have occurred.

Other adverse reactions that have been reported with levodopa or Sinemet are listed below:

Nervous System: ataxia, paresthesia, numbness, increased hand tremor, muscle twitching, muscle cramps, blepharospasm (which may be taken as an early sign of excess dosage, consideration of dosage reduction may be made at this time), trismus and activation of latent Horner's syndrome.

Psychiatric: confusion, sleepiness, dementia, euphoria, insomnia, nightmares, hallucinations, delusions, paranoid ideation, agitation and anxiety.

Cardiovascular: arrhythmias, nonspecific ECG changes, flushing and phlebitis.

Gastrointestinal: bitter taste, sialorrhea, dry mouth, dysphagia, burning sensation of the tongue, hiccups, bruxism, abdominal pain and distress, development of duodenal ulcer, gastrointestinal bleeding, constipation, diarrhea and flatulence.

Integumentary: flushing, increased sweating, dark sweat, malignant melanoma (see Contraindications), skin rash and hair loss.

Genitourinary: urinary retention, urinary incontinence, urinary frequency, hematuria, dark urine, nocturia and priapism.

Special Senses: diplopia, blurred vision, dilated pupils and oculogyric crises.

Hematologic: leukopenia, hemolytic and non-hemolytic anemia, thrombocytopenia and agranulocytosis.

Miscellaneous: weakness, faintness, fatigue, chest pain, headache, hoarseness, malaise, hot flashes, sense of stimulation, dyspnea, bizarre breathing patterns and neuroleptic malignant syndrome.

Laboratory Tests: Laboratory tests which have been reported to be abnormal are alkaline phosphatase, AST, ALT, lactic dehydrogenase, bilirubin, and blood urea nitrogen.

Other abnormalities have occurred with Sinemet and are listed below:

False-positive reaction for urinary ketone bodies when using a test tape for ketonuria (reaction will not be altered by boiling the urine specimen).

False-negative tests may result with the use of glucose-oxidase methods of testing for glycosuria.

Overdose: Symptoms and Treatment: Management of acute overdosage with Sinemet is basically the same as management of acute overdosage with levodopa alone. However, pyridoxine is not effective in reversing the actions of Sinemet.

General supportive measures should be employed, along with immediate gastric lavage. I.V. fluids should be administered judiciously and an adequate airway maintained. ECG monitoring should be instituted and the patient carefully observed for the possible development of arrhythmias; if required, appropriate antiarrhythmic therapy should be given. The possibility that the patient may have taken other drugs as well as Sinemet should be taken into consideration. To date, no experience has been reported with dialysis; hence, its value in overdosage is not known.

Dosage: In order to reduce the incidence of adverse reactions and achieve maximal benefit, therapy with Sinemet must be individualized and drug administration must be continuously matched to the needs and tolerance of the patient. It should be borne in mind that the therapeutic range of Sinemet is narrower than that of levodopa alone because of its greater milligram potency. Therefore, titration and adjustment of dosage should be made in small steps and the dosage ranges recommended should usually not be exceeded. The appearance of involuntary movements should be regarded as a sign of levodopa toxicity and as an indication of overdosage, requiring dose reduction. Treatment should, therefore, aim at maximal benefit without dyskinesias.

If a patient being treated with levodopa is switched to therapy with Sinemet, levodopa must be discontinued at least 12 hours or more before therapy with Sinemet is initiated.

Sinemet tablets are available in a 4:1 ratio (Sinemet 100/25) and in a 10:1 ratio of levodopa to carbidopa (Sinemet 100/10 and Sinemet 250/25). Tablets of the 2 ratios may be given separately or combined as needed to provide the optimal dosage.

Studies have shown that peripheral dopa decarboxylase is saturated by carbidopa at doses between 70 to 150 mg/day. Patients receiving less than 70 mg per day of carbidopa are more likely to experience nausea and vomiting. Experience with total daily dosages of carbidopa greater than 200 mg is limited.

For patients who require only low doses of levodopa, e.g., less than 700 mg, Sinemet 100/25 may be helpful.

Induction of Therapy in Patients not Receiving Levodopa: Dosage is best initiated with 1 tablet of Sinemet 100/25 three times a day. This dosage schedule provides 75 mg of carbidopa/day. Dosage may be carefully increased by 1 tablet every 3 days until the optimal dosage has been reached which does not produce dyskinesias.

While increasing the dosage during the induction period, the doses should be divided, aiming at a frequency of dosing of at least 4 times a day. If further titration is necessary after a daily dosage level of 6 tablets of Sinemet 100/25 has been reached, tablets of Sinemet 100/10 or Sinemet 250/25 may be used as needed to provide the optimal dosage.

Usually no patient should receive more than 1 500 mg of levodopa a day. Some patients, including those with postencephalitic parkinsonism, are more sensitive to levodopa and require specially careful dosage adjustment.

Induction of Therapy in Patients Receiving Levodopa: **Levodopa must be discontinued at least 12 hours or more before Sinemet is started.** A dosage of Sinemet should be used that will provide approximately 20% of the previous levodopa daily dosage; this can be started in the morning after the day in which the treatment with levodopa has been stopped. For example, if a patient is receiving 4 000 mg of levodopa per day, the dosage of Sinemet should not provide more than 750 mg of levodopa per day divided into 4 to 6 doses.

Tablets of Sinemet 100/25 should be used to start medication for patients requiring lower dosages of levodopa.

Adjustment and Maintenance of Therapy: Therapy should be individualized and adjusted according to the desired therapeutic response. At least 70 to 100 mg of carbidopa per day should be provided. When a greater proportion of carbidopa is required, 1 tablet of Sinemet 100/25 may be substituted for each tablet of Sinemet 100/10. When more levodopa is required, Sinemet 250/25 should be substituted for Sinemet 100/25 or 100/10. If necessary, the dosage of Sinemet 250/25 may be increased by 1/2 or 1 tablet every day or every other day to a maximum of 8 tablets a day. Experience with total daily dosages of carbidopa greater than 200 mg is limited.

Because both therapeutic and adverse responses occur more rapidly with Sinemet than with levodopa alone, patients should be monitored closely during the dose adjustment period. Specifically, involuntary movements will occur more rapidly with Sinemet than with levodopa. The occurrence of involuntary movements may require dosage reduction. Blepharospasm may be a useful early sign of excess dosage in some patients.

Current evidence indicates that other standard antiparkinsonian drugs may be continued while Sinemet is being administered although their dosage may have to be adjusted.

If general anesthesia is required, therapy with Sinemet may be continued as long as the patient is permitted to take fluids and medication by mouth. If therapy is interrupted temporarily, the usual daily dosage may be administered as soon as the patient is able to take oral medication.

Supplied: Sinemet 100/10: Each dark dapple-blue, oval, uncoated tablet, engraved 100/10 on one side and SINEMET on the other, contains: levodopa 100 mg and carbidopa 10 mg expressed as anhydrous carbidopa. Nonmedicinal ingredients: cornstarch, indigotine, magnesium stearate, microcrystalline cellulose and pregelatinized starch. Bottles of 100.

Sinemet 100/25: Each yellow, oval, scored, uncoated tablet, coded Sinemet 650, contains: levodopa 100 mg and carbidopa 25 mg expressed as anhydrous carbidopa. Nonmedicinal ingredients: cornstarch, magnesium stearate, microcrystalline cellulose, pregelatinized starch and quinoline yellow. Bottles of 100 and 500.

Sinemet 250/25: Each light dapple-blue, oval, scored, uncoated tablet, coded Sinemet 654, contains: levodopa 250 mg and carbidopa 25 mg expressed as anhydrous carbidopa. Nonmedicinal ingredients: cornstarch, indigotine, magnesium stearate, microcrystalline cellulose and pregelatinized starch. Bottles of 100 and 500.

All strengths gluten-, lactose- and tartrazine-free. Store at 15 to 30°C in a tightly closed container. Protect from sunlight.

(Shown in Product Recognition Section)

SINEMET® CR Ⓟ

DuPont Pharma

Levodopa—Carbidopa

Antiparkinson Agent

Pharmacology: Sinemet CR, a combination of levodopa, the metabolic precursor of dopamine, and carbidopa, an aromatic amino acid decarboxylase inhibitor, is available in a polymer-based controlled-release tablet formulation. Sinemet CR can be useful in reducing "off" time in patients treated previously with a conventional levodopa/decarboxylase inhibitor combination who have had predictable peak dose dyskinesias and unpredictable motor fluctuations.

The symptoms of Parkinson's disease are related to depletion of dopamine in the corpus striatum. While the administration of dopamine is ineffective in the treatment of Parkinson's disease because it does not cross the blood-brain barrier, levodopa, the metabolic precursor of dopamine, does cross the blood-brain barrier and is converted to dopamine in the basal ganglia. This is thought to be the mechanism whereby levodopa relieves the symptoms of Parkinson's disease.

Levodopa is rapidly decarboxylated to dopamine in extracerebral tissues so that only a small portion of a given dose is transported unchanged to the CNS. For this reason, large doses of levodopa are required for adequate therapeutic effect and these may often be attended by nausea and other adverse reactions, some of which are attributable to dopamine formed in extracerebral tissues.

Carbidopa, a decarboxylase inhibitor, does not cross the blood-brain barrier and does not affect the metabolism of levodopa within the CNS. Since its decarboxylase inhibiting activity is limited to extracerebral tissues, administration of carbidopa with levodopa makes more levodopa available for transport to the brain. Combined therapy with levodopa and carbidopa reduces the amount of levodopa required for optimum therapeutic benefit by about 75 to 80%, permits an earlier response to therapy, and also reduces the incidence of nausea, vomiting and cardiac arrhythmias. Combined therapy, however, does not decrease adverse reactions due to central effects of levodopa.

Following years of treatment with preparations containing levodopa, an increasing number of parkinsonian patients develop fluctuations in motor performance and dyskinesias. The advanced form of motor fluctuations ("on-off" phenomenon) is characterized by unpredictable swings from mobility to immobility. Although the causes of the motor fluctuations are not completely understood, it has been demonstrated that they can be attenuated by treatment regimens that produce steady plasma levels of levodopa.

In clinical trials, patients with motor fluctuations experienced reduced "off" time with Sinemet CR when compared with Sinemet. Global ratings of improvement and activities of daily living in the "on" and "off" states, as assessed by both patient and physician, were slightly better in some patients during therapy with Sinemet CR than with Sinemet. In patients without motor fluctuations, Sinemet CR provided therapeutic benefit similar to Sinemet but with less frequent dosing.

Pyridoxine hydrochloride (vitamin B_6), in oral doses of 10 mg to 25 mg, may reverse the effects of levodopa by increasing the rate of aromatic amino acid decarboxylation. Carbidopa inhibits this action of pyridoxine.

Pharmacokinetics: Sinemet CR 200/50 contains levodopa, 200 mg and carbidopa, 50 mg, per tablet, in a controlled-release formulation designed to release the active ingredients over a 4- to 6-hour period.

The absorption of levodopa following Sinemet CR 200/50 is gradual and continuous for 4 to 5 hours although the majority of the dose is absorbed in 2 to 3 hours. With conventional Sinemet tablets, absorption is rapid and is virtually complete in 2 to 3 hours. The pharmacokinetic parameters of levodopa, following the administration of Sinemet CR 200/50 and conventional Sinemet tablets to healthy elderly volunteers, are presented in Table I (on following page).

Table I—Sinemet CR

Mean Pharmacokinetic Parameters of Levodopa Following the Administration of Two Sinemet 100/25 Tablets or One Sinemet CR 200/50 Tablet in Healthy Elderly Volunteers

	Single Dose		Steady-state	
	Sinemet	**Sinemet CR 200/50**	**Sinemet**	**Sinemet CR 200/50**
Bioavailability*%	—	—	99	71
C_{max}, μg/mL	3.26	1.15	3.20	1.14
Trough Cp at 8 h, μg/mL	0.048	0.090	0.074	0.163
Peak time, h	0.5	2.1	0.7	2.4
AUC, μg·h/mL	5.31	4.01	5.62	4.19

*Relative to an i.v. dose.

In general, peak levodopa plasma levels are lower, bioavailability is less and time to reach peak levels is delayed when using Sinemet CR. Levodopa plasma levels following a single dose are essentially identical to those following repeated administration. However, with Sinemet CR, levodopa plasma concentrations fluctuate less, namely peak plasma levels are lower and end of dose levels (trough concentrations) higher than after conventional therapy.

The bioavailability of 2 half tablets of Sinemet CR 200/50 is approximately 20% greater than that of 1 intact tablet. The bioavailability of Sinemet CR is somewhat increased in the presence of food. Dose-proportionality has been demonstrated over the dose range of 1 and 2 Sinemet CR 200/50 tablets.

The pharmacokinetics of levodopa following administration of Sinemet CR 100/25 were studied in patients with Parkinson's disease. Chronic 3 month, open-label, twice daily dosing with Sinemet CR 100/25 (range: 200 mg levodopa, 50 mg carbidopa up to 600 mg levodopa, 150 mg carbidopa/day) did not result in accumulation of plasma levodopa. The dose-adjusted bioavailability for 1 Sinemet CR 100/25 tablet was equivalent to that for 1 Sinemet CR 200/50 tablet. The mean peak concentration of levodopa following the administration of 1 Sinemet CR 100/25 tablet was greater than 50% of that following 1 Sinemet CR 200/50 tablet. Mean time-to-peak plasma levels may be slightly less for Sinemet CR 100/25 than for Sinemet CR 200/50.

Indications: For the treatment of Parkinson's disease.

At this time, experience in patients not previously treated with levodopa/decarboxylase inhibitors or levodopa alone is limited.

Sinemet CR is not recommended for the treatment of drug-induced extrapyramidal reactions.

Contraindications: MAO inhibitors (except low doses of selective MAO-B inhibitors) and Sinemet CR should not be given concomitantly. These inhibitors must be discontinued at least 2 weeks prior to initiating therapy with Sinemet CR.

Sinemet CR should not be administered to patients with clinical or laboratory evidence of uncompensated cardiovascular, endocrine, hematologic, hepatic, pulmonary (including bronchial asthma) or renal disease; or to patients with narrow angle glaucoma.

As with levodopa, Sinemet CR should not be given when administration of a sympathomimetic amine is contraindicated.

Sinemet CR is contraindicated in patients with known hypersensitivity to any component of this medication.

Because levodopa may activate a malignant melanoma, Sinemet CR should not be used in patients with suspicious undiagnosed skin lesions or a history of melanoma.

Warnings: When patients are receiving levodopa monotherapy or Sinemet, this medication must be discontinued at least 8 hours before therapy with Sinemet CR is started. (For appropriate dosage substitutions, see Dosage.)

As with levodopa or Sinemet, Sinemet CR may cause involuntary movements and mental disturbances. These reactions are thought to be due to increased brain dopamine following administration of levodopa. These adverse reactions may be more prolonged with Sinemet CR than with Sinemet. All patients should be observed carefully for the development of depression with concomitant suicidal tendencies. Patients with past or current psychoses should be treated with caution.

A symptom complex resembling the neuroleptic malignant syndrome including muscular rigidity, elevated body temperature, mental changes, and increased serum creatine phosphokinase has been reported when antiparkinsonian agents were withdrawn abruptly. Therefore, patients should be observed carefully when the dosage of Sinemet CR is reduced abruptly or discontinued, especially if the patient is receiving neuroleptics.

Care should be exercised in administering Sinemet CR to patients with a history of recent myocardial infarction who have residual atrial, nodal, or ventricular arrhythmias. In such patients, cardiac function should be monitored with particular care during the period of initial dosage administration and titration, in a facility with provisions for intensive cardiac care.

Sinemet CR should be administered cautiously to patients with a history of peptic ulcer disease or of convulsions.

Precautions: General: Periodic evaluations of hepatic, hematopoietic, cardiovascular and renal function are recommended during extended therapy (see Adverse Effects).

Patients with chronic wide angle glaucoma may be treated cautiously with Sinemet CR, provided the intraocular pressure is well controlled and the patient monitored carefully for changes in intraocular pressure during therapy.

Children: Safety of Sinemet CR in patients under 18 years of age has not been established.

Pregnancy and *Lactation:* Although the effects of Sinemet CR on human pregnancy and lactation are unknown, both levodopa and combinations of carbidopa and levodopa have caused visceral and skeletal malformations in rabbits. Therefore, use of Sinemet CR in women of childbearing potential requires that the anticipated benefits of the drug be weighed against possible hazards to the mother and to the fetus. Sinemet CR should not be given to nursing mothers.

Drug Interactions: Caution should be exercised when the following drugs are administered concomitantly with Sinemet CR.

Antihypertensive Drugs: Symptomatic postural hypotension has occurred when levodopa/decarboxylase inhibitor combinations were added to the treatment of patients receiving antihypertensive drugs. Therefore, when therapy with Sinemet CR is started, dosage adjustment of the antihypertensive drug may be required.

Psychoactive Drugs: Phenothiazines and butyrophenones may reduce the therapeutic effects of levodopa. The beneficial effects of levodopa in Parkinson's disease have been reported to be reversed by phenytoin and papaverine. Patients taking these drugs with Sinemet CR should be observed carefully for loss of therapeutic response.

There have been rare reports of adverse reactions, including hypertension and dyskinesia, resulting from the concomitant use of tricyclic antidepressants and carbidopa-levodopa preparations. (For patients receiving MAO inhibitors, see Contraindications.)

Other Drugs: Although specific interaction studies were not performed with other concomitant drugs, in clinical trials of Sinemet CR patients were allowed to receive tricyclic antidepressants, benzodiazepines, propranolol, thiazides, digoxin, H_2 antagonists, salicylates and other nonsteroidal anti-inflammatory drugs. Sinemet CR was also used with other antiparkinson agents (see Dosage).

Adverse Effects: In controlled clinical trials involving 748 patients with moderate to severe motor fluctuations, Sinemet CR did not produce side effects which were unique to the controlled release formulation.

The adverse reaction reported most frequently was dyskinesia (12.8%). Occasionally, prolonged, and at times, severe afternoon dyskinesias have occurred in some patients.

Other adverse reactions that were reported frequently were: nausea (5.5%), hallucinations (5.3%), confusion (4.9%), dizziness (3.5%), headache (2.5%), depression (2.5%), chorea (2.5%), dry mouth (2.3%), somnolence (2.1%), dream abnormalities (2.1%), dystonia (2%) and asthenia (2%).

Adverse reactions occurring less frequently (less than 2%) were: Body as a Whole: chest pain (1.7%), fatigue (0.9%), weight loss (0.8%).

Cardiovascular: orthostatic hypotension (0.8%), palpitation (0.8%), hypotension (0.5%).

Nervous System/Psychiatric: insomnia (1.7%), falling (1.6%), on-off phenomenon (1.2%), paresthesia (0.9%), disorientation (0.8%), anxiety disorders (0.8%), decreased mental acuity (0.7%), extrapyramidal disorder (0.7%), gait abnormalities (0.7%), agitation (0.5%), memory impairment (0.5%).

Gastrointestinal: anorexia (1.9%), constipation (1.5%), vomiting (1.3%), diarrhea (1.2%), gastrointestinal pain (0.9%), dyspepsia (0.8%).

Musculoskeletal: muscle cramps (0.9%).

Respiratory: dyspnea (1.6%).

Special Senses: blurred vision (1.1%).

Other adverse reactions that have been reported with levodopa or Sinemet and may be potential side effects with Sinemet CR are listed below.

Nervous System: ataxia, numbness, increased hand tremor, muscle twitching, blepharospasm, trismus, activation of latent Horner's syndrome.

Psychiatric: sleepiness, euphoria, paranoid ideation and psychotic episodes, and dementia.

Cardiovascular: arrhythmias, non-specific ECG changes, flushing, phlebitis.

Gastrointestinal: bitter taste, sialorrhea, dysphagia, bruxism, hiccups, gastrointestinal bleeding, flatulence, burning sensation of tongue, development of duodenal ulcer.

Integumentary: increased sweating, dark sweat, rash, hair loss.

Genitourinary: urinary frequency, retention, incontinence, hematuria, dark urine, nocturia and priapism.

Special Senses: diplopia, dilated pupils, oculogyric crises.

Hematologic: leukopenia, hemolytic and non-hemolytic anemia, thrombocytopenia, agranulocytosis.

Miscellaneous: weakness, faintness, hoarseness, malaise, hot flashes, sense of stimulation, bizarre breathing patterns, hypertension, neuroleptic malignant syndrome, malignant melanoma (see Contraindications).

Convulsions have occurred; however, a causal relationship with levodopa or levodopa/carbidopa combinations has not been established.

Laboratory Tests: Laboratory tests which have been reported to be abnormal are alkaline phosphatase, AST, ALT, lactic dehydogenase, bilirubin and blood urea nitrogen.

Abnormalities in various laboratory tests have occurred with Sinemet and may also occur with Sinemet CR.

Carbidopa-levodopa preparations may cause a false-positive reaction for urinary ketone bodies when a test tape is used for determination of ketonuria. This reaction will not be altered by boiling the urine specimen. False-negative tests may result with the use of glucose-oxidase methods of testing for glycosuria.

Overdose: Symptoms and Treatment: Management of acute overdosage with Sinemet CR is basically the same as management of acute overdosage with levodopa; however, pyridoxine is not effective in reversing the actions of Sinemet CR.

ECG monitoring should be instituted and the patient observed carefully for the development of arrhythmias; if required, appropriate antiarrhythmic therapy should be given. The possibility that the patient may have taken other drugs as well as Sinemet CR should be taken into consideration. To date, no experience has been reported with dialysis; hence, its value in overdosage is not known.

Dosage: Sinemet CR tablets contain a 4:1 ratio of levodopa to carbidopa. Sinemet CR 200/50 contains levodopa 200 mg/carbidopa 50 mg/tablet. Sinemet CR 100/25 contains levodopa 100 mg/carbidopa 25 mg/tablet. The daily dosage of Sinemet CR must be determined by careful titration. Patients should be monitored closely during the dose adjustment period, particularly with regard to appearance or worsening of nausea or abnormal involuntary movements, including dyskinesias, chorea and dystonia.

Sinemet CR 200/50 may be administered as whole or as half tablets. Sinemet CR 100/25 should only be administered as whole tablets. To maintain the controlled release properties of the product, tablets should not be chewed or crushed.

Standard antiparkinson drugs, other than levodopa alone, may be continued while Sinemet CR is being administered, although their dosage may have to be adjusted. The delayed onset of action with Sinemet CR may require the supplemental use of conventional Sinemet tablets for optimal control in the mornings.

Initial Dosage and Titration for Patients Currently Treated with Conventional Levodopa/Decarboxylase Inhibitor Combinations: Dosage with Sinemet CR 200/50 should be substituted at an amount that eventually provides approximately 10 to 30% more levodopa/day. The interval between doses should be prolonged by 30 to 50%. Initially, patients should receive Sinemet CR 200/50 at a dosage that provides the same

Sinemet CR (cont'd)

amount of levodopa, but with a longer dosing interval. Depending on clinical response, the dosage may be increased.

A guide for the initiation of treatment with Sinemet CR 200/50 is shown in Table II.

Table II—Sinemet CR

Guideline for Initial Conversion from Sinemet to Sinemet CR 200/50

Sinemet Total Daily Dose* Levodopa (mg)	Sinemet CR 200/50 (levodopa 200 mg/carbidopa 50 mg) Suggested Dosage Regimen
300–400	1 tablet b.i.d.
500–600	1½ tablets b.i.d. or 1 tablet t.i.d.
700–800	a total of 4 tablets in 3 or more divided doses (e.g., 1½ tablets a.m., 1½ tablets early p.m., and 1 tablet later p.m.)
900–1 000	a total of 5 tablets in 3 or more divided doses (e.g., 2 tablets a.m., 2 tablets early p.m., and 1 tablet later p.m.)

*For dosing ranges not shown in Table II, see Dosage.

Sinemet CR 100/25 is available to facilitate titration when 100 mg steps are required and as an alternative to the half tablet of Sinemet CR 200/50.

Initial Dosage for Patients Currently Treated with Levodopa Alone: Levodopa must be discontinued at least 8 hours before therapy with Sinemet CR 200/50 is started. Sinemet CR should be substituted at a dosage that will provide approximately 25% of the previous levodopa dosage. In patients with mild to moderate disease, the initial dose is usually 1 tablet of Sinemet CR 200/50 2 times daily.

Patients Without Prior Levodopa Therapy: Experience with Sinemet CR is limited in the de novo parkinsonian patients.

Sinemet CR 100/25 may be used in early stage patients who have not had prior levodopa therapy or to facilitate titration when necessary in patients receiving Sinemet CR 200/50. The initial recommended dose is 1 tablet of Sinemet CR 100/25 twice daily. For patients who require more levodopa, a daily dose of 1 to 4 tablets of Sinemet CR 100/25 twice a day is generally well-tolerated.

When appropriate, levodopa therapy may also be initiated with Sinemet CR 200/50. The initial recommended dose in patients with mild to moderate disease is 1 tablet of Sinemet CR 200/50 two times daily. Initial dosages should not exceed 600 mg/day of levodopa or be given at intervals of less than 6 hours.

Titration: Doses and dosing intervals must be adjusted on an individual basis, depending upon therapeutic response. An interval of at least 3 days between dosage adjustments is recommended. Most patients have been adequately treated with 2 to 8 tablets of Sinemet CR 200/50/day, administered as divided doses at intervals ranging from 4 to 12 hours during the waking day.

If the divided doses of Sinemet CR 200/50 are not equal, it is recommended that the smaller doses be given at the end of the day.

Maintenance: Because Parkinson's disease is progressive, periodic clinical evaluations are recommended and adjustment of the dosage regimen of Sinemet CR may be required.

Addition of Other Antiparkinson Medications: Anticholinergic agents, dopamine agonists, amantadine and lower doses of selective MAO-B inhibitors can be given with Sinemet CR. When combining therapies, dosage adjustments may be necessary.

Interruption of Therapy: Patients should be observed carefully if abrupt reduction or discontinuation of Sinemet CR is required, especially if the patient is receiving neuroleptics (see Precautions).

If general anesthesia is required, Sinemet CR may be continued as long as the patient is permitted to take oral medication. If therapy is interrupted temporarily, the usual dosage should be administered as soon as the patient is able to take oral medication.

Supplied: Sinemet CR 100/25: Each pink-colored, oval-shaped, biconvex, compressed tablet, engraved SINEMET CR on one side and 601 on the other, contains: levodopa 100 mg and carbidopa 25 mg. Nonmedicinal ingredients: hydroxypropyl cellulose, magnesium stearate, polyvinyl acetate-crotonic acid copolymer and red ferric oxide. Gluten- and tartrazine-free. Bottles of 100. Store between 15 and 30°C. Protect from sunlight.

Sinemet CR 200/50: Each peach-colored, oval-shaped, biconvex, scored compressed tablet, engraved Sinemet CR on one side and 521/521 on the other, contains: levodopa 200 mg and carbidopa 50 mg. Nonmedicinal ingredients: D&C yellow No. 10, hydroxypropyl cellulose, magnesium stearate, polyvinyl acetate-crotonic acid copolymer and red ferric oxide. Gluten- and tartrazine-free. Bottles of 100. Store between 15 and 30°C. Protect from sunlight.

(Shown in Product Recognition Section)

SINEQUAN™ Ⓟ
Pfizer

Doxepin HCl
Antidepressant

Pharmacology: Doxepin is a psychotropic agent with antidepressant and anxiolytic properties. It also has sedative and anticholinergic effects, and, in the higher dosage range, it produces peripheral adrenergic blocking effects. Studies of electroencephalograms in humans have shown decreases in amplitude, and amplitude variability, also, the delta, theta and 24-35 CPS activities increased.

Indications: The drug treatment of: 1. Psychoneurotic patients with anxiety and/or depressive reactions. Anxiety neurosis associated with somatic disorders; alcoholic patients with anxiety and/or depression. 2. Psychotic depression, including manic-depressive illness (depressed type) and involutional melancholia.

Contraindications: Doxepin is contraindicated in individuals who have shown hypersensitivity to the drug or to other dibenzoxepin compounds.

Children: It is not recommended for use in children since safety and efficacy in this age group have not been established.

Because of its anticholinergic activity doxepin should not be administered to patients with a history of glaucoma, increased intraocular pressure or urinary retention.

Tricyclic agents are generally contraindicated during the acute recovery phase following myocardial infarction and in the presence of acute congestive heart failure, as well as in patients with a history of blood dyscrasias and severe liver disease.

Doxepin should not be administered concomitantly with MAO inhibitors, since such a combination may cause a syndrome of intensive sympathetic stimulation. Drugs of this type should be discontinued at least 2 weeks before instituting therapy with doxepin.

Warnings: Tricyclic antidepressant drugs, particularly when given in high doses, can induce sinus tachycardia, changes in conduction time and arrhythmias. A few instances of unexpected death have been reported in patients with cardiovascular disorders. Myocardial infarction and stroke have also been reported with drugs of this class. Therefore, doxepin should be administered with extreme caution to patients with a history of cardiovascular disease, those with circulatory lability and elderly patients. In such cases, treatment should be initiated with low doses with progressive increases only if required and tolerated, and the patients should be under close surveillance at all dosage levels.

Since tricyclic agents are known to reduce the seizure threshold, doxepin should be used with caution in patients with a history of convulsive disorders. Concurrent administration of ECT and doxepin may be hazardous and, therefore, such treatment should be limited to patients for whom it is essential.

Close supervision is required when doxepin is given to hyperthyroid patients or those receiving thyroid medication because of the possibility of cardiovascular toxicity. At doses above 150 mg/day, it may block the antihypertensive effect of guanethidine and related compounds.

Pregnancy and *Lactation:* The safety of doxepin during pregnancy and lactation has not been established and therefore, it should not be used in women of childbearing potential or nursing mothers, unless, in the opinion of the physician, the potential benefits to the patient outweigh the possible hazards to the fetus.

Precautions: Occupational Hazards: Since drowsiness may occur with the use of this drug, patients should be advised against driving or engaging in activities requiring mental alertness and physical coordination until their response to the drug has been well established.

Patients should be warned that the effects of other drugs acting on the central nervous system, such as alcohol, barbiturates and other CNS depressants, may be potentiated by doxepin.

The possibility of suicide in seriously depressed patients may remain until significant remission occurs. Such patients should be closely supervised throughout therapy and consideration should be given to the possible need for hospitalization. This type of patient should not have easy access to large quantities of doxepin.

Tricyclic antidepressants may precipitate or aggravate psychotic manifestations in schizophrenic patients and hypomanic or manic episodes in manic-depressive patients. This may require a reduction of dosage, discontinuation of the drug, and/or administration of an antipsychotic agent.

Tricyclic antidepressants may also give rise to paralytic ileus, particularly in the elderly and in hospitalized patients. Therefore, appropriate measures should be taken if constipation occurs.

When doxepin is given concomitantly with anticholinergic or sympathomimetic drugs, close supervision and careful adjustment of dosages are required.

Doxepin should be discontinued prior to elective surgery for as long as the clinical situation will allow.

Doxepin should be used with caution in patients with impaired liver function or with a history of hepatic damage or blood dyscrasias. Periodic blood counts and liver function tests should be performed when patients receive doxepin in large doses or over prolonged periods.

Adverse Effects: Although some of the adverse reactions included in the following list have not been reported with doxepin pharmacological similarities among the tricyclic antidepressants require that each of the reactions be considered when prescribing doxepin.

Behavioral: drowsiness, fatigue, excitement, agitation, restlessness, insomnia, nightmares, hypomania, anxiety, confusion, disorientation, disturbed concentration, delusions, hallucinations, activation of latent psychosis.

Neurological: seizures, alteration in EEG patterns, dizziness, tremors, extrapyramidal symptoms, numbness, tingling, paresthesias of the extremities, peripheral neuropathy, tinnitus, syndrome of inappropriate ADH (antidiuretic hormone) secretion.

Cardiovascular: hypotension, hypertension, tachycardia, palpitations. A quinidine-like effect and other reversible ECG changes such as flattening or inversion of T-waves, bundle branch block, depressed S-T segments, prolonged conduction time and asystole, arrhythmias, heart block, fibrillation, myocardial infarction, stroke and unexpected death in patients with cardiovascular disorders have been reported with other tricyclic antidepressants.

Autonomic: dry mouth, blurred vision, disturbances of accommodation, mydriasis, constipation, nasal stuffiness, delayed micturition, sublingual adenitis, paralytic ileus, urinary retention, dilation of the urinary tract, precipitation of latent and aggravation of existing glaucoma, vertigo.

Endocrine: increased or decreased libido, impotence, menstrual irregularity, testicular swelling, breast enlargement and galactorrhea in the female, gynecomastia in the male, elevation and lowering of blood sugar levels.

Allergic or Toxic: pruritus, skin rash, photosensitization, edema, drug fever, leukopenia, urticaria, petechiae, obstructive jaundice and bone marrow depression, including agranulocytosis, eosinophilia, purpura and thrombocytopenia.

Gastrointestinal: nausea, epigastric distress, vomiting, flatulence, abdominal pain, diarrhea, peculiar taste, stomatitis.

Miscellaneous: weakness, headache, weight gain or loss, excessive appetite, anorexia, increased perspiration, urinary frequency, lacrimation, alopecia, parotid swelling, black tongue, hepatitis.

Withdrawal Symptoms: Abrupt cessation of treatment with tricyclic antidepressants after prolonged administration may produce nausea, headache and malaise. These symptoms are not indicative of addiction.

Overdose: Symptoms: Excessive drowsiness leading to minor alterations of consciousness and even unresponsiveness could be an early indication of excessive dosage. However, overdosage with doxepin is more likely to be manifested by increased psychomotor agitation and convulsions leading to apnea and coma. The ECG changes (broadening of QRS and T-wave abnormalities) tend to be a late finding and are not always accompanied by cardiovascular hemodynamic changes.

Treatment: In general, treatment of overdosage should be symptomatic and supportive. Cardiac arrhythmias and CNS involvement pose the greatest threat with tricyclic antidepressant overdosage and may occur suddenly even when initial symptoms appear to be mild. Therefore, patients who may have ingested an overdosage of doxepin, particularly children, should be hospitalized and kept under close surveillance.

If the patient is conscious, induced emesis followed by gastric lavage, with appropriate precautions to prevent pulmonary aspiration, should be accomplished as soon as possible. Following lavage, activated charcoal may be administered to reduce absorption. An adequate airway should be established in comatose patients and assisted ventilation instituted, if necessary. The possibility of occurrence of seizures should be kept in mind. External stimulation should be minimized to reduce the tendency to convulsions. Convulsions, should they occur, may respond to standard anticonvulsant therapy; however, barbiturates should be avoided since they may potentiate respiratory depression, particularly in children, and aggravate hypotension and coma.

ECG monitoring in an intensive care unit is recommended in all patients, particularly in the presence of ECG abnormalities, and should be maintained for several days after the cardiac rhythm has returned to normal. A patient who has ingested a toxic overdose of a tricyclic antidepressant may remain medically and psychiatrically unstable for several days due to sustained excessive drug levels. Unexpected cardiac deaths have occurred up to 6 days after overdosage with other antidepressants. The QRS interval of the electrocardiogram appears to be a reliable correlate of the severity of overdosage. If the QRS interval exceeds 100 milliseconds any time during the first 24 hours after overdosage, cardiac function should be continuously monitored for 5 or 6 days. Because of its effect on cardiac conduction, digitalis should be used only with caution. If rapid digitalization is required for the treatment of congestive heart failure, special care should be exercised in using the drug.

Shock should be treated with supportive measures such as i.v. fluids, oxygen and corticosteroids. Pressor agents, such as norepinephrine (but **not** epinephrine), are rarely indicated and should be given only after careful consideration and under continuous monitoring.

The slow i.v. administration of physostigmine salicylate has been reported to reverse most of the cardiovascular and CNS anticholinergic manifestations of tricyclic overdosage. The recommended dosage in adults has been 1 to 2 mg in **very slow** i.v. injection. In children, the initial dosage should not exceed 0.5 mg and should be adjusted to age and response. Since physostigmine has a short duration of action, administration may have to be repeated at 30- to 60-minute intervals.

Deaths by deliberate or accidental overdosage have occurred with this class of drugs. Since the propensity for suicide is high in depressed patients, a suicide attempt by other means may occur during the recovery phase. The possibility of simultaneous ingestion of other drugs should also be considered.

Dosage: The optimum daily dosage of doxepin depends on the condition which is being treated and the response of the individual. Some patients respond promptly: others may not respond for 2 weeks or longer. An initial dosage of 25 mg 3 times daily may be used in most patients. This dosage should be increased as required by 25 mg increments at appropriate intervals until a therapeutic response is obtained. The usual optimum dosage range is 100 to 150 mg per day. In some patients, up to 300 mg per day may be required, but there is rarely any benefit to be obtained by increasing this dosage. In elderly patients it is advisable to proceed more cautiously with dosage increments and to initiate treatment with a lower dosage.

Once a satisfactory therapeutic response has been obtained, it is generally possible to reduce the dosage and still maintain this effect.

For maintenance therapy in depressed patients, the total daily dosage, up to 150 mg, may be given on a once-a-day schedule. This dosage should be established as described above and should preferably be given at bedtime. The 150 mg capsule strength is intended for maintenance therapy only and is not recommended for initiation of treatment.

Supplied: 10 mg: Each pink/scarlet capsule contains: doxepin HCl equivalent to 10 mg of doxepin. Nonmedicinal ingredients: cornstarch, magnesium stearate and sodium lauryl sulfate; capsule shell: D&C Yellow No. 10, FD&C Blue No. 1 FD&C Red No. 2, FD&C Red No. 3, FD&C Yellow No. 6, gelatin, silicon dioxide, sodium lauryl sulfate and titanium dioxide. Tartrazine-free. Bottles of 100.

25 mg: Each pink/blue capsule contains: doxepin HCl equivalent to 25 mg of doxepin. Nonmedicinal ingredients: cornstarch, magnesium stearate and sodium lauryl sulfate; capsule shell contains FD&C Blue No. 1, FD&C Red No. 3, gelatin, silicon dioxide, sodium lauryl sulfate and titanium dioxide. Tartrazine-free. Bottles of 100.

50 mg: Each flesh/pink capsule contains: doxepin HCl equivalent to 50 mg of doxepin. Nonmedicinal ingredients: cornstarch, magnesium stearate and sodium lauryl sulfate; capsule shell contains D&C Yellow No. 10, FD&C Blue No. 1, FD&C Red No. 3, gelatin, silicon dioxide, sodium lauryl sulfate and titanium dioxide. Tartrazine-free. Bottles of 100.

75 mg: Each flesh/flesh capsule contains: doxepin HCl equivalent to 75 mg of doxepin. Nonmedicinal ingredients: cornstarch, magnesium stearate and sodium lauryl sulfate; capsule shell contains D&C Yellow No. 10, FD&C Red No. 3, gelatin, silicon dioxide, sodium lauryl sulfate and titanium dioxide. Tartrazine-free. Bottles of 100.

100 mg: Each flesh/blue capsule contains: doxepin HCl equivalent to 100 mg of doxepin. Nonmedicinal ingredients: cornstarch, magnesium stearate and sodium lauryl sulfate; capsule shell contains D&C Yellow No. 10, FD&C Blue No. 1, FD&C Red No. 3, gelatin, silicon dioxide, sodium lauryl sulfate and titanium dioxide. Tartrazine-free. Bottles of 100.

150 mg: Each pink capsule contains: doxepin HCl equivalent to 150 mg of doxepin. Nonmedicinal ingredients: cornstarch, magnesium stearate and sodium lauryl sulfate; capsule shell contains FD&C Blue No. 1, FD&C Red No. 3, gelatin, silicon dioxide, sodium lauryl sulfate and titanium dioxide. Tartrazine-free. Bottles of 100.

Store between 15 and 30°C.

(Shown in Product Recognition Section)

SINGULAIR® ℞
MSD

Montelukast Sodium

Leukotriene Receptor Antagonist

Pharmacology: Mechanism of Action: The cysteinyl leukotrienes (LTC_4, LTD_4, LTE_4), are potent inflammatory eicosanoids released from various cells including mast cells and eosinophils. These important proasthmatic mediators bind to cysteinyl leukotriene receptors (CysLT) found in the human airway and cause a number of airway actions, including bronchoconstriction, mucous secretion, vascular permeability, and eosinophil recruitment.

Montelukast is a potent, orally active compound that significantly improves parameters of asthmatic inflammation. Based on biochemical and pharmacological bioassays, it binds with high affinity and selectivity to the $CysLT_1$ receptor (in preference to other pharmacologically important airway receptors such as the prostanoid, cholinergic, or β-adrenergic receptor). Montelukast potently inhibits physiologic actions of LTC_4, LTD_4, and LTE_4 at the $CysLT_1$ receptor without any agonist activity.

A second cysteinyl leukotriene receptor ($CysLT_2$) is present in the lung but appears to be confined to blood vessels. To date, neither receptor has been cloned so the presence of CysLT receptors has been delineated principally through receptor binding and pharmacological assays. Montelukast is not believed to antagonize the $CysLT_2$ receptor.

Pharmacokinetics: Absorption: Montelukast is rapidly and nearly completely absorbed following oral administration. For the 10 mg film-coated tablet, the mean peak plasma concentration (C_{max}) is achieved 3 hours (T_{max}) after administration in adults in the fasted state. The mean oral bioavailability is 64%. The oral bioavailability and C_{max} are not influenced by a standard meal. Safety and efficacy were demonstrated in clinical trials where the 10 mg film-coated tablet was administered without regard to the timing of food ingestion.

For the 5 mg chewable tablet, the C_{max} is achieved 2 hours after administration in adults in the fasted state. The mean oral bioavailability is 73%. Food does not have a clinically important influence with chronic administration.

Distribution: Montelukast is more than 99% bound to plasma proteins. The steady-state volume of distribution of montelukast averages 8 to 11 L. Studies in rats with radiolabeled montelukast indicate minimal distribution across the blood-brain barrier. In addition, concentrations of radiolabeled material at 24 hours postdose were minimal in all other tissues.

Metabolism: Montelukast is extensively metabolized. In studies with therapeutic doses, plasma concentrations of metabolites of montelukast are undetectable at steady state in adults and pediatric patients.

In vitro studies using human liver microsomes indicate that cytochrome P450 3A4 and 2C9 are involved in the metabolism of montelukast. Based on further in vitro results in human liver microsomes, therapeutic plasma concentrations of montelukast do not inhibit cytochromes P450 3A4, 2C9, 1A2, 2A6, 2C19, or 2D6.

Elimination: The plasma clearance of montelukast averages 45 mL/min in healthy adults. Following an oral dose of radiolabeled montelukast, 86% of the radioactivity was recovered in 5-day fecal collections and $<0.2\%$ was recovered in urine. Coupled with estimates of montelukast oral bioavailability, this indicates montelukast and its metabolites are excreted almost exclusively via the bile.

In several studies, the mean plasma half-life of montelukast ranged from 2.7 to 5.5 hours in healthy young adults. The pharmacokinetics of montelukast are nearly linear for oral doses up to 50 mg. No difference in pharmacokinetics was noted between dosing in the morning or in the evening. During once-daily dosing with 10 mg montelukast, there is little accumulation of the parent drug in plasma ($\sim 14\%$).

Special Populations: Gender: The pharmacokinetics of montelukast are similar in males and females.

Geriatrics: The pharmacokinetic profile and the oral bioavailability of a single 10 mg oral dose of montelukast are similar in elderly and younger adults. The plasma half-life of montelukast is slightly longer in the elderly. No dosage adjustment in the elderly is required.

Race: Pharmacokinetic differences due to race have not been studied. In clinical studies, there do not appear to be any differences in clinically important effects.

Hepatic Insufficiency: Patients with mild to moderate hepatic insufficiency and clinical evidence of cirrhosis had evidence of decreased metabolism of montelukast resulting in approximately 41% higher mean montelukast area under the plasma concentration curve (AUC) following a single 10 mg dose. The elimination of montelukast is slightly prolonged compared with that in healthy subjects (mean half-life, 7.4 hours). No dosage adjustment is required in patients with mild to moderate hepatic insufficiency. There are no clinical data in patients with severe hepatic insufficiency (Child-Pugh score >9).

Renal Insufficiency: Since montelukast and its metabolites are not excreted in the urine, the pharmacokinetics of montelukast were not evaluated in patients with renal insufficiency. No dosage adjustment is recommended in these patients.

Adolescents and Children: The plasma concentration profile of montelukast following the 10 mg film-coated tablet is similar in adolescents ≥ 15 years old and young adults. The 10 mg film-coated tablet is recommended for use in patients ≥ 15 years old.

Pharmacokinetic studies using either the chewable tablet or film-coated tablet show that the plasma profile of the 5 mg chewable tablet in pediatric patients 6 to 14 years of age is similar to that of the 10 mg film-coated tablet in adults. The 5 mg chewable tablet should be used in pediatric patients 6 to 14 years of age.

<u>Drug Interactions</u> (also see Precautions, Drug Interactions): Montelukast 10 mg once daily to pharmacokinetic steady state: did not cause clinically significant changes in the kinetics of an i.v. dose of theophylline; did not change the pharmacokinetic profile of warfarin or influence the effect of a single 30 mg oral dose of warfarin on prothrombin time or INR (International Normalized Ratio); did not change the pharmacokinetic profile or urinary excretion of immunoreactive digoxin; did not change the plasma concentration profile of terfenadine or its carboxylated metabolite and does not prolong the QTc interval following coadministration with terfenadine 60 mg twice daily.

Montelukast at doses of ≥ 100 mg daily to pharmacokinetic steady state: did not significantly alter the plasma concentrations of either component of an oral contraceptive containing norethindrone 1 mg/ethinyl estradiol 35 μg; did not cause any clinically significant change in plasma profiles of either prednisone and prednisolone following administration of either oral prednisone or i.v. prednisolone.

Phenobarbital, which induces hepatic metabolism, decreased the AUC of montelukast approximately 40% following a single 10 mg dose of montelukast; no dosage adjustment for montelukast is recommended (see Precautions).

Pharmacodynamics: Montelukast causes potent inhibition of airway cysteinyl leukotriene receptors as demonstrated by the ability to inhibit bronchoconstriction due to inhaled LTD_4 in asthmatic patients. Doses as low as 5 mg cause substantial blockage of LTD_4-induced bronchoconstriction.

Singulair (cont'd)

Montelukast causes bronchodilation within 2 hours of oral administration; these effects were additive to the bronchodilation caused by a β-agonist.

Clinical studies in adults 15 years of age and older demonstrated there is no additional clinical benefit to montelukast doses above 10 mg once daily. This was shown in 2 chronic asthma studies using doses up to 200 mg once daily and in 1 exercise challenge study using doses up to 50 mg, evaluated at the end of the once daily dosing interval.

Indications: In adults and children 6 years of age and older for the prophylaxis and chronic treatment of asthma, including prevention of day- and night-time symptoms, the treatment of ASA-sensitive asthmatic patients, and the prevention of exercise-induced bronchoconstriction.

Montelukast is effective alone or in combination with other agents used in the maintenance treatment of chronic asthma. Montelukast and inhaled corticosteroids may be used concomitantly with additive effects to control asthma or to reduce the inhaled corticosteroid dose while maintaining clinical stability.

Contraindications: Hypersensitivity to any component of this product.

Precautions: The efficacy of oral montelukast for the treatment of acute asthma attacks has not been established. Therefore, oral tablets of montelukast should not be used to treat acute asthma attacks. Patients should be advised to have appropriate rescue medication available.

While the dose of concomitant inhaled corticosteroid may be reduced gradually under medical supervision, montelukast should not be abruptly substituted for inhaled or oral corticosteroids.

Geriatrics: In clinical studies, there were no age-related differences in the efficacy or safety profiles of montelukast.

Children: Montelukast has been studied in pediatric patients 6 to 14 years of age (see Dosage). Safety and effectiveness in pediatric patients younger than 6 years of age have not been studied.

Pregnancy: Montelukast has not been studied in pregnant women. Montelukast should be used during pregnancy only if clearly needed.

Lactation: It is not known if montelukast is excreted in human milk. Because many drugs are excreted in human milk, caution should be exercised when montelukast is given to a nursing mother.

Drug Interactions: Montelukast may be administered with other therapies routinely used in the prophylaxis and chronic treatment of asthma. In drug-interactions studies, the recommended clinical dose of montelukast did not have clinically important effects on the pharmacokinetics of the following drugs: theophylline, prednisone, prednisolone, oral contraceptives (ethinyl estradiol/norethindrone 35/1), terfenadine, digoxin and warfarin.

Although additional specific interaction studies were not performed, montelukast was used concomitantly with a wide range of commonly prescribed drugs in clinical studies without evidence of clinical adverse interactions. These medications included thyroid hormones, sedative-hypnotics, nonsteroidal anti-inflammatory agents, benzodiazepines and decongestants.

The area under the plasma concentration curve (AUC) for montelukast was decreased approximately 40% in subjects with coadministration of phenobarbital. No dosage adjustment for montelukast is recommended.

Occupational Hazards: Effects on Ability to Drive and Use Machines: There is no evidence that montelukast affects the ability to drive and use machines.

Information to be Provided to the Patient: Patients should be advised to take montelukast daily as prescribed, even when they are asymptomatic as well as during periods of asthma worsening, and to contact their physicians if their asthma is not well controlled. Patients should be advised that oral tablets of montelukast are not for the treatment of acute asthma attacks. They should have appropriate rescue medication available.

Chewable Tablets: Phenylketonurics: Phenylketonuric patients should be informed that the chewable tablet contains phenylalanine (a component of aspartame) 0.842 mg/5 mg chewable tablet.

Adverse Effects: Clinical Studies: Montelukast has been generally well tolerated. Side effects, which usually were mild, generally did not require discontinuation of therapy. The overall incidence of side effects reported with montelukast was comparable to placebo in both patient populations studied (pediatric patients 6 to 14 years of age, and adults 15 years of age and older).

Adults 15 Years of Age and Older: Montelukast has been evaluated for safety in approximately 2 600 adult patients 15 years of age and older in clinical studies. In 2 similarly designed, 12-week placebo-controlled clinical trials, only abdominal pain and headache were reported as drug-related in ≥1% of patients treated with montelukast and at a greater incidence than in patients treated with placebo. The incidences of these events were not significantly different in the 2 treatment groups.

In placebo-controlled clinical trials, the following adverse experiences reported with montelukast occurred in ≥1% of patients and at an incidence greater than or equal to that in patients treated with placebo, regardless of drug relationship (see Table I).

Table I—Singulair

Adverse Experiences Occurring in ≥1% of Patients with an Incidence ≥ to that in Patients Treated with Placebo, Regardless of Drug Relationship

	Singulair 10 mg/day (%) (n=1 955)	Placebo (%) (n=1 180)
Body as a Whole		
Asthenia/Fatigue	1.8	1.2
Fever	1.5	0.9
Pain, Abdominal	2.9	2.5
Trauma	1.0	0.8
Digestive		
Diarrhea	3.1	3.1
Dyspepsia	2.1	1.1
Gastroenteritis, Infectious	1.5	0.5
Pain, Dental	1.7	1.0
Nervous System/Psychiatric		
Dizziness	1.9	1.4
Headache	18.4	18.1
Insomnia	1.3	1.3
Respiratory		
Congestion, Nasal	1.6	1.3
Cough	2.7	2.4
Influenza	4.2	3.9
Skin/Skin Appendages		
Rash	1.6	1.2
Laboratory Adverse Experiences*		
ALT Increased	2.1	2.0
AST Increased	1.6	1.2
Pyuria	1.0	0.9

*Number of patients tested (Singulair and placebo, respectively): ALT and AST, 1 935, 1 170; pyuria, 1 924, 1 159.

Cumulatively, 544 patients were treated with montelukast for at least 6 months, 253 for 1 year and 21 for 2 years in clinical trials. With prolonged treatment, the adverse experience profile did not change.

Children 6 to 14 Years of Age: Montelukast has also been evaluated for safety in approximately 320 pediatric patients 6 to 14 years of age. Cumulatively, 143 pediatric patients were treated with montelukast for at least 3 months, 44 for 6 months or longer in clinical trials. The safety profile in pediatric patients is generally similar to the adult safety profile and to placebo. With prolonged treatment, the adverse experience profile did not change.

Overdose: Symptoms: No specific information is available on the treatment of overdosage with montelukast. In chronic asthma studies, montelukast has been administered at doses up to 200 mg/day to patients for 22 weeks and in short-term studies, up to 900 mg/day to patients for approximately 1 week without clinically important adverse experiences.

Treatment: It is not known whether montelukast is dialyzable by peritoneal dialysis or hemodialysis.

Dosage: Adults 15 Years of Age and Older: One 10 mg tablet daily to be taken at bedtime.

Children 6 to 14 Years of Age: One 5 mg chewable tablet daily to be taken at bedtime. No dosage adjustment within this age group is necessary. Safety and effectiveness in pediatric patients younger than 6 years of age have not been established.

General Recommendations: The therapeutic effect of montelukast on parameters of asthma occurs within 1 day. Montelukast may be taken with or without food. Patients should be advised to continue taking montelukast while their asthma is controlled, as well as during periods of worsening asthma.

No dosage adjustment is necessary for the elderly, for patients with renal insufficiency, or mild to moderate hepatic impairment, or for patients of either gender.

Therapy with Montelukast in Relation to Other Treatments for Asthma: Montelukast can also be added to a patient's existing treatment regimen.

Bronchodilator Treatments: Montelukast can be added to the treatment regimen of patients who are not adequately controlled on bronchodilator alone. When a clinical response is evident (usually after the first dose), the patient's bronchodilator therapy can be reduced as tolerated.

Inhaled Corticosteroids: Treatment with montelukast provides additional clinical benefit to patients treated with inhaled corticosteroids. A reduction in the corticosteroid dose can be made as tolerated. The dose should be reduced gradually with medical supervision. In some patients, the dose of inhaled corticosteroids can be tapered off completely. It remains to be determined whether the withdrawal from inhaled corticosteroids can be maintained for extended periods, or possibly indefinitely. Montelukast should not be abruptly substituted for inhaled corticosteroids.

Oral Corticosteroids: Limited data suggest that montelukast may provide additional clinical benefit in patients currently treated with oral corticosteroids.

Information for the Patient: See Blue Section—Information for the Patient "Singulair".

Supplied: Chewable Tablets: Each pink, round, biconvex-shaped, chewable tablet, with the code MSD 275 on one side and SINGULAIR on the other, contains: montelukast sodium 5.2 mg, which is the molar equivalent to free acid 5 mg. Nonmedicinal ingredients: aspartame, cherry flavor, croscarmellose sodium, hydroxypropyl cellulose, magnesium stearate, mannitol, microcrystalline cellulose and red ferric oxide. Blister packages of 30.

Tablets: Each beige, rounded square-shaped, film-coated tablet, with the code MSD 117 on one side and SINGULAIR on the other, contains: montelukast sodium 10.4 mg, which is the molar equivalent to free acid 10 mg. Nonmedicinal ingredients: croscarmellose sodium, hydroxypropyl cellulose, lactose monohydrate, magnesium stearate and microcrystalline cellulose; film-coating: carnauba wax, hydroxypropyl methylcellulose, hydroxypropyl cellulose, red iron oxide, titanium dioxide and yellow iron oxide. Blister packages of 30.

Store at room temperature 15 to 30°C, protected from moisture and light.

(Shown in Product Recognition Section)

New Product 1998

SINTROM® Ⓟ

Novartis Pharmaceuticals

Nicoumalone

Oral Anticoagulant

Pharmacology: Nicoumalone reduces the concentration of prothrombin in blood and increases the prothrombin time by inhibiting the formation of prothrombin in the liver. The drug also interferes with the production of factors VII, IX and X, as well as protein C, so their concentration in the blood is lowered during therapy.

Coumarin derivatives are vitamin K antagonists. They inhibit the γ-carboxylation of certain glutamic acid molecules which are located at several sites near the amino terminal end of vitamin K dependent coagulation factors. γ-carboxylation has a significant bearing on the interaction of the coagulation factors with calcium ions. Without this reaction, blood clotting cannot be initiated. Precisely how coumarin derivatives prevent vitamin K from bringing about γ-carboxylation of the glutamic acid molecules in the coagulation factors has not yet been determined.

Depending on the size of the initial dose, maximal effect on prothrombin time is usually achieved within 36 to 48 hours. Following a single therapeutic dose or cessation of therapy, the prothrombin time usually returns to normal within 48 hours.

Nicoumalone is rapidly absorbed by the oral route. At least 60% of the dose is systemically available. Peak plasma concentrations are generally attained within 1 to 3 hours of oral administration, with levels of 0.3±0.05 μg/mL observed following a single 10 mg dose. The peak plasma concentrations and the areas under the blood conentration-time curve (AUC) are proportional to the size of the dose over a range of 8 to 16 mg.

No correlation can be established between the plasma concentrations of nicoumalone and the apparent prothrombin level due to variation in plasma concentrations among patients. At any given prothrombin level, patients over 70 years of age generally have higher plasma concentrations than younger patients.

The bulk of the nicoumalone administered is found in the plasma fraction of the blood. 98.7% of the drug is bound to plasma proteins, notably to albumin.

The calculated apparent volume of distribution of nicoumalone is 0.16 to 0.18 L/kg for the R(+) enantiomer and 0.22 to 0.34 L/kg for the S (−) enantiomer.

Nicoumalone passes into the breast milk, but the quantities are too small to be detected by the usual analytical methods. The drug also crosses the placental barrier.

Nicoumalone is extensively metabolized. At least 2 primary pathways are involved. Oxidation of nicoumalone results in 2 hydroxy metabolites. Reduction of the keto group on nicoumalone forms 2 different alcohol metabolites. A major portion of the amino metabolite, produced by reduction of the nitro group, is further transformed to the corresponding acetamido metabolite. An additional unidentified strongly polar metabolite fraction was also noted. These metabolites appear to be pharmacologically inactive in man.

Nicoumalone is eliminated from the plasma with a half-life of 8 to 11 hours. Only 0.1% to 0.3% of the dose is excreted unchanged in the urine. Over a period of 1 week, the cumulative excretion of metabolites and unchanged active substance in the urine and feces is 60% and 29% of the dose respectively.

Indications: The prophylaxis and treatment of venous thrombosis and its extension, the treatment of atrial fibrillation with embolization, the prophylaxis and treatment of pulmonary embolism and as an adjunct in the treatment of coronary occlusion and transient cerebral ischemic attacks.

Contraindications: Nicoumalone is contraindicated in all pathological states in which the risk of hemorrhage is greater than the possible clinical benefits, e.g., hemorrhagic blood diathesis and/or blood dyscrasias. Recent or contemplated surgery of CNS or eye; traumatic surgery resulting in large open surfaces. Bleeding tendencies associated with active ulceration or overt bleeding of gastrointestinal, genitourinary or respiratory tracts; cerebrovascular hemorrhage; aneurysms: cerebral, dissecting aorta; pericarditis and pericardial effusions; subacute bacterial endocarditis. Threatened abortion, eclampsia and preeclampsia. Severe hypertension. Severe parenchymal lesions of the liver and kidneys. Increased fibrinolytic activity as encountered after operations on the lung, prostate, uterus, etc.

Pregnancy: Nicoumalone passes through the placental barrier, and the danger of hemorrhage to the fetus exists to the point of fatal hemorrhage in utero, even within the accepted therapeutic range of maternal prothrombin level. There have been reports of birth malformation in children born to mothers who have been treated with coumarin anticoagulants during the first trimester of pregnancy. Therefore, nicoumalone must not be employed during pregnancy. In women of childbearing age, contraceptive measures are necessary during treatment. If the patient becomes pregnant while taking this drug, she should be apprised of the potential risks to the fetus. The possibility of termination of the pregnancy should be discussed in light of those risks.

Known hypersensitivity to nicoumalone and related coumarin derivatives. I.M. injections (see Precautions). Inadequate laboratory facilities or lack of patient cooperation (e.g., unsupervised and senile patients, alcoholics and patients with psychiatric disorders).

Miscellaneous: polyarthritis, ascorbic acid deficiency, major regional block anesthesia.

Precautions: Nicoumalone is a potent drug and its effects tend to be cumulative and prolonged. At the earliest sign of bleeding the drug should be withdrawn.

Treatment of each patient is a highly individualized matter. Dosage can be controlled only by periodic determination of prothrombin time or other suitable coagulation test (see Dosage). Determinations of clotting and bleeding times are not effective measures for control of therapy. It is recommended that the blood samples for laboratory tests always be taken at the same time of the day.

Since heparin prolongs the one stage prothrombin time when it is given with nicoumalone, a period of from 4 to 5 hours after the last i.v. dose and 12 to 24 hours after the last s.c. dose of heparin should elapse before blood is drawn, if a valid prothrombin time is to be obtained.

Elderly patients on anticoagulant medication should be monitored with special care.

Factors which increase or decrease the absorption, storage or utilization of vitamin K may interfere with anticoagulant dosage. It is important that the diet not only be adequate but stable from day to day in order to regulate the dosage.

Caution should be used in patients with hepatic dysfunction since the production of coagulation factors and detoxification of oral anticoagulants can be affected by diseases of the liver.

Patients with impaired renal function do not appear to be subject to unusual risks. However, caution should be exercised in view of the possibility of a compromised state of platelet-mediated hemostasis.

Nicoumalone may show greater activity in certain conditions or diseases due to reduced protein binding (e.g., thyrotoxicosis, tumors, renal diseases, infections and inflammation). Strict medical supervision is necessary in these situations.

Diagnostic or therapeutic interventions (e.g., angiography, lumbar puncture, minor surgery, tooth extractions, etc.) may require the shortening of thromboplastin time. This should be done with meticulous care.

During treatment with anticoagulants, i.m. injections may cause hematomas and are therefore contraindicated. There is no evidence that s.c. or i.v. injections lead to such complications.

Out-patients should be advised to carry an oral anticoagulant card so that appropriate actions can be taken in the event of injuries or accidents.

Abrupt cessation of anticoagulant therapy is generally not recommended; taper dose gradually over 3 to 4 weeks.

Administration of anticoagulants in the following conditions will be based upon clinical judgment in which the risk of hemorrhage due to anticoagulants is weighed against the risk of thrombosis or embolization in untreated cases: prolonged dietary deficiency (cachexia, vitamin K); moderate to severe hepatic or renal insufficiency (see also Contraindications); infectious diseases or disturbances of intestinal flora (sprue, antibiotic therapy); severe trauma of head, bones or muscles associated with extreme raw surfaces; indwelling catheters; spinal punctures; moderate to severe hypertension (see also Contraindications); miscellaneous: polycythemia vera; vasculitis; severe diabetes; menometrorrhagia; severe allergic and anaphylactic disorders.

The following factors, alone or in combination, may be responsible for **increased** prothrombin time response:

Endogenous: hepatic disorders; vitamin K deficiency (hypoprothrombinemia) of obstructive jaundice, steatorrhea and infectious hepatitis; poor nutritional state; diarrhea; elevated temperature; congestive heart failure, carcinoma; collagen disease.

Exogenous: drug interactions (see above); carbon tetrachloride; alcohol; dietary deficiencies in protein, ascorbic acid, choline or cystine; narcotics with prolonged use; drugs affecting the blood elements; hepatotoxic drugs; anesthetics; prolonged hot weather, anticoagulant overdosage; unreliable prothrombin determinations.

The following factors, alone or in combination, may be responsible for **decreased** prothrombin time response:

Endogenous: edema; hyperlipemia; diabetes mellitus; hereditary resistance to coumarin therapy; hypothyroidism.

Exogenous: drug interactions (see above); vitamin K in polyvitamin preparations; diet high in vitamin K; anticoagulant underdosage; unreliable prothrombin determinations.

N.B.: A patient may be exposed to a combination of the above factors, some of which may increase and some decrease his sensitivity to nicoumalone. Because the net effect on his prothrombin time response may be unpredictable under these circumstances, more frequent laboratory monitoring is advisable.

Lactation: Nicoumalone passes into the breast milk, but in quantities so small that no undesirable effects on the infant are to be expected. As a precaution, however, it is recommended that the infant be given 1 mg of vitamin K_1 per week for prophylactic purposes. Clinical monitoring of the infant for signs of prothrombin abnormalities is also advised.

Drug Interactions: Coumarin anticoagulants have been involved in a number of serious adverse drug interactions. Important mechanisms associated with these interactions include disturbances of absorption, reduced availability of vitamin K necessary for γ-carboxylation of prothrombin-complex factors, inhibition or induction of metabolizing enzymes and interference with plasma protein binding. The anticoagulant effects may be increased or decreased by drug interactions. It is therefore essential to monitor the patient's response with additional prothrombin time determinations (e.g., twice weekly), and adjust dosage of nicoumalone appropriately, whenever other medications are initiated, discontinued or taken haphazardly.

The anticoagulant effect may be potentiated by concurrent treatment with the following drugs (increased prothrombin time): acetaminophen, allopurinol, anabolic steroids, androgens, antiarrhythmic agents (e.g., amiodarone, quinidine), antibiotics (e.g., erythromycin, tetracyclines, neomycin, chloramphenicol), chloral hydrate*, clofibric acid as well as its derivatives and structural analogues, diazoxide, disulfiram, ethacrynic acid, glucagon, histamine H_2-receptor antagonists (e.g., cimetidine), imidazole derivatives (e.g., metronidazole and, even when administered locally, miconazole), mefenamic acid, mercaptopurine, MAO inhibitors, nalidixic acid, oral hypoglycemics (e.g. tolbutamide), phenyramidol, quinine, sulfonamides (including co-trimoxazole), sulfinpyrazone, thyroid hormone (including dextrothyroxine).

*Increased and decreased prothrombin time responses have been reported.

During treatment with drugs which affect hemostasis, the anticoagulant effect may be potentiated, thereby increasing the risk of gastrointestinal hemorrhage. Chief among these drugs are heparin and platelet-aggregation inhibitors such as salicylic acid and its derivatives (e.g. ASA, paraaminosalicylic acid or PAS, diflunisal) and phenylbutazone or other pyrazolone derivatives (e.g. sulfinpyrazone). Use of nicoumalone together with these substances is therefore highly unadvisable.

Increased risk of hemorrhage has been reported with the combined use of oral anticoagulants and nonsteroidal anti-inflammatory agents. It is therefore recommended that more frequent coagulation tests be performed.

The anticoagulant effect may be diminished by concurrent treatment with the following drugs (decreased prothrombin time): aminoglutethimide, barbiturates, carbamazepine, cholestyramine (see below), corticosteroids, diuretics*, ethchlorvynol, griseofulvin, meprobamate, oral contraceptives, rifampin.

*Increased and decreased prothrombin time responses have been reported.

Cholestyramine reduces intestinal absorption, notably by interrupting the enterohepatic circulation; for this reason, it can be recommended as treatment for overdosage of a coumarin derivative.

A two way interaction between nicoumalone and phenytoin has been suggested. Phenytoin has been reported to decrease the serum concentrations of nicoumalone and to increase the plasma prothrombin-proconvertin concentrations. Presumably, phenytoin acts as a stimulator of nicoumalone metabolism. Conversely, nicoumalone has been reported to increase the serum concentrations and prolong the serum half-life of phenytoin by inhibiting its metabolism. Patients receiving nicoumalone and phenytoin concurrently should be closely observed for signs of phenytoin toxicity. Frequent monitoring of the prothrombin time is also essential. Other hydantoin anticonvulsants may interact with nicoumalone in a manner similar to that of phenytoin.

During concomitant treatment with sulfonylurea derivatives, their hypoglycemic effect may be potentiated.

Since neither the severity nor the early signs of interactions can be predicted, patients taking nicoumalone, especially if they suffer from hepatic dysfunction, should refrain from consuming alcohol.

Adverse Effects: Depending on the intensity of therapy, the patient's age and nature of the underlying disease, the complications most frequently reported with anticoagulants have been hemorrhages at various site. Prospective studies give no indication that the incidence of bleeding depends on duration of treatment. If hemorrhage occurs in a patient whose thromboplastin time is within the therapeutic range, the case must be clarified diagnostically (in view of such possibilities as ulceration, tumor and congenital coagulation disorders). Predilection sites of hemorrhage include the gastrointestinal tract (melena), the brain, the urogenital tract (macroscopic and microscopic hematuria), the uterus (metrorrhagia and menorrhagia), the liver and gallbladder (hematobilia), and the eye. Usually, hemorrhage is evident but the possibility of intestinal hemorrhage must be considered when a patient has abdominal symptoms.

Gastrointestinal disorders (loss of appetite, nausea, diarrhea, vomiting), allergic reactions (urticaria, dermatitis and fever) and reversible loss of hair (alopecia) have rarely been noted with similar coumarin derivatives.

Isolated cases of hemorrhagic skin necrosis have been reported, even when the prothrombin time was within apparently safe limits. The adverse reaction is usually associated with congenital protein C deficiency. Isolated cases of liver damage have also occurred.

Sintrom (cont'd)

Overdose: Symptoms: The patient's individual sensitivity to oral anticoagulants, the size of the overdosage and the duration of anticoagulant administration have a decisive bearing on the onset and severity of the effects.

Hemorrhages in the region of various organs are the most prominent clinical feature. Depending on the size of the dose and the patient's reaction to it, hemorrhages set in 1 to 5 days after ingestion. Effects of overdosage may take the form of nose-bleed, hematemesis, hemoptysis, gastrointestinal hemorrhage, vaginal bleeding, hematuria (with renal colic), cutaneous hemorrhage, bleeding into the joints and menorrhagia.

Tachycardia, hypotension, and peripheral circulatory disorders due to loss of blood, as well as nausea, vomiting, diarrhea, and colicky pains in the abdomen are further signs and symptoms of poisoning.

Laboratory tests reveal an extremely low Quick value (or high INR value), pronounced prolongation of the recalcification time or thromboplastin time and disturbed γ-carboxylation of factors II, VII, IX and X.

Treatment: Antidote: Phytomenadione (vitamin K_1) is capable of counteracting, within 3 to 5 hours, the inhibitory effect of nicoumalone on hepatic γ-carboxylation of the vitamin K-dependent coagulation factors.

If at the time of taking a single overdose the patient's thromboplastin time is normal, the drug can be partly eliminated by inducing vomiting or gastric lavage. Administration of activated charcoal or a rapid-acting laxative may also prevent or reduce absorption of the ingested anticoagulant. Cholestyramine may increase the drug's elimination.

In the event of clinically insignificant hemorrhages, such as brief nose-bleed or small isolated hematomas, a temporary reduction of the dose of nicoumalone is often sufficient.

In cases of mild to severe hemorrhage administer 1 to 10 mg vitamin K_1 by slow i.v. infusion (rate not to exceed 1 mg/minute). Vitamin K_1 should not be injected i.m. Additional doses (up to a maximum of 40 mg daily) should be administered at 4 hour intervals. It should be noted that doses in excess of 5 mg can cause resistance to oral anticoagulants lasting several days. Should an anticoagulant prove necessary, heparin may be employed as a temporary measure while resuming oral anticoagulant therapy. Heparin should be subsequently withdrawn when the therapeutic range has been reached.

Only rarely is whole blood needed. If life-threatening hemorrhage has occurred, the effect of treatment with nicoumalone can be abolished by i.v. infusion of deep-frozen plasma concentrates or fresh whole blood in order to substitute for the missing coagulation factors II, VII, IX and X.

Dosage: Sensitivity to anticoagulants varies from patient to patient and may also fluctuate in the course of treatment. It is therefore essential to carry out regular coagulation tests in adequate facilities for standardized laboratory control and to adapt the dosage accordingly. If this is not possible, nicoumalone should not be used.

The daily dose should be prescribed as a single dose and always taken at the same time of day.

Initial Dose: First Day: 8 to 12 mg. Second Day: 4 to 8 mg. If the thromboplastin time is initially abnormal, treatment must be commenced with great caution.

Maintenance Therapy and Coagulation Tests: In view of the marked individual differences encountered, the maintenance dose should be established and adjusted by reference to the results of periodically performed laboratory tests to determine the patient's blood coagulation time. The Quick value (or INR value, see below) should be carefully maintained within the therapeutic range. Such values should be determined daily from the beginning of treatment until the maintenance dose is established, then repeated at regular intervals (e.g. once a month), so that possible fluctuations outside the therapeutic range can be avoided. Depending on the Quick value (or INR value), as well as on the individual patient and nature of the disease, the maintenance dose is usually 1 to 10 mg daily.

As a routine test procedure, measurement of thromboplastin time yields good results. For the purpose of standardization, an "International Normalized Ratio" (INR) has been introduced. International comparability is made possible with the help of calibrated thromboplastins. An International Sensitivity Index value is determined for the reference thromboplastin using the WHO procedure. To obtain the INR value, the ratio between the test thromboplastin time and the normal thromboplastin time is raised to the power of the specified International Sensitivity Index value of the reference thromboplastin. As the Quick value decreases, the thromboplastin time for the patient's blood increases; thus the INR value increases.

Depending on the clinical picture, the therapeutic range to be aimed at generally lies between INR values of 2 to 4.5; within this range the majority of the patients treated develop neither a recurrence of thrombosis nor any severe hemorrhagic complications.

Supplied: 1 mg: Each peach colored, biconvex round tablet contains: nicoumalone 1 mg. Nonmedicinal ingredients: alcohol, colloidal silicon dioxide, cornstarch, FD&C Yellow No. 6, gelatin, glycerin, lactose, magnesium stearate and talc. Energy: 0.67 kJ (0.16 kcal). Bisulfite-, gluten-, parabens-, sodium- and tartrazine-free. Bottles of 100.

4 mg: Each white, flat-faced, beveledged, round tablet, imprinted GEIGY on one side and double scored on the other, contains: nicoumalone 4 mg. Nonmedicinal ingredients: colloidal silicon dioxide, cornstarch, lactose, magnesium stearate and talc. Energy: 1.76 kJ (0.42 kcal). Alcohol-, bisulfite-, gluten-, parabens-, sodium- and tartrazine-free. Bottles of 100.

(Shown in Product Recognition Section)

SINUTAB®
SINUTAB® with CODEINE Ⓝ
SINUTAB® NON DROWSY
SINUTAB® SA
SINUTAB® NIGHTIME

Warner-Lambert Consumer Healthcare

Acetaminophen—Pseudoephedrine HCl—Chlorpheniramine Maleate

Acetaminophen—Pseudoephedrine HCl—Chlorpheniramine Maleate—Codeine

Acetaminophen—Pseudoephedrine HCl

Acetaminophen—Phenylpropanolamine HCl—Phenyltoloxamine Citrate

Acetaminophen—Pseudoephedrine HCl—Diphenhydramine HCl

Analgesic—Antihistamine—Decongestant

Indications: Symptomatic relief of headache, facial pain, malaise, fever, nasal and sinus congestion often associated with acute and chronic sinusitis, allergic rhinitis, vasomotor rhinitis and the common cold.

Contraindications: Sensitivity to any of the components. Patients receiving MAO inhibitors.

Warnings: Massive acetaminophen overdose can be toxic and potentially fatal. In adults, hepatotoxicity from acetaminophen is unlikely to occur with overdoses of less than 10 g ingested at one time and fatalities are unlikely to occur with overdoses of less than 15 g ingested at one time.

Precautions: Recommended dose should not be exceeded without consulting a physician.

Pregnancy: Safety in pregnancy not yet established.

Use with caution in elderly, pregnant or nursing patients and patients with hyperthyroidism, hypertension, glaucoma, asthma, prostatic hypertrophy, diabetes mellitus or severe cardiovascular diseases.

Sinutab with Codeine Ⓝ: Codeine may be habit forming. Occupational Hazards: Patients should be cautioned not to operate vehicles or hazardous machinery until their response to the drug has been determined.

Since the depressant effects of antihistamines are additive to those of other drugs affecting the CNS, patients should be cautioned against drinking alcoholic beverages or taking hypnotics, sedatives, psychotherapeutic agents or other drugs with CNS depressant effects during antihistaminic therapy.

Adverse Effects: Acetaminophen may occasionally cause gastric upset. The incidence and severity of this adverse effect is less than that after ASA administration.

Pseudoephedrine may cause mild stimulation, particularly in patients sensitive to sympathomimetic drugs. Drowsiness, confusion and gastrointestinal upset may occur with antihistamines. Excitement may occur in children. Nausea, diarrhea, mild stimulation, and abdominal pain from sympathomimetic agents may occur.

Overdose: Symptoms: Symptoms of massive overdosage include gastric irritation, nausea and vomiting, chills, hyperthermia, tinnitus, hypotension, circulatory collapse, cyanosis, methemoglobinemia, jaundice, coma, disorientation, hallucinations, hyperreflexia, tremors, convulsions, respiratory failure and renal damage.

Treatment: Evacuate the stomach by emesis or gastric lavage and administer activated charcoal.

Dosage: Sinutab: Regular Strength: Adults: 2 caplets every 4 to 6 hours, not to exceed 4 doses/day (maximum 8 caplets/day). Children 6 to 12 years: 1 caplet every 4 to 6 hours, not to exceed 4 doses/day.

Extra Strength: Adults: 1 to 2 caplets every 4 to 6 hours, not to exceed 4 doses/day (maximum 8 caplets/day).

Sinutab with Codeine Ⓝ: Adults: 1 to 2 tablets every 4 to 6 hours, not to exceed 4 doses/day (maximum 8 tablets/day).

Sinutab Non Drowsy: Regular Strength: Adults: 2 caplets every 4 to 6 hours, not to exceed 4 doses/day (maximum 8 caplets/day). Children 6 to 12 years: 1 caplet every 4 to 6 hours, not to exceed 4 doses/day.

Extra Strength: Adults: 1 to 2 caplets every 4 to 6 hours. Do not exceed 8 caplets/day. Use only as directed by physician.

Sinutab SA: Adults: 1 tablet every 12 hours. Children 10 to 14 years: 1/2 tablet every 12 hours. Do not administer to children less than 10 years. Tablets should not be chewed. Do not exceed 2 doses/day.

Sinutab Nightime Extra Strength: Adults and children over 12 years of age: 2 caplets at bedtime. Do not exceed 2 caplets/day.

Supplied: Sinutab: Regular Strength: Each yellow caplet imprinted "Sinutab" on both sides contains: acetaminophen 325 mg, pseudoephedrine HCl 30 mg and chlorpheniramine maleate 2 mg. Nonmedicinal ingredients: celluloses, D&C Yellow No. 10, FD&C Yellow No. 6, polyethylene glycol, polysorbate, starch, titanium dioxide, wax and zinc stearate. Energy: 0.76 kJ (0.18 kcal). Boxes of 12 and 24 in blister packages and bottles of 36.

Extra Strength: Each yellow caplet imprinted "Sinutab" on both sides contains: acetaminophen 500 mg, pseudoephedrine HCl 30 mg and chlorpheniramine maleate 2 mg. Nonmedicinal ingredients: celluloses, D&C Yellow No. 10, FD&C Yellow No. 6, polyethylene glycol, polysorbate, starch, titanium dioxide, wax and zinc stearate. Energy: 0.76 kJ (0.18 kcal). Boxes of 12 and 24 in blister packages.

Sinutab with Codeine Ⓝ: Each blue, biconvex tablet contains: acetaminophen 325 mg, pseudoephedrine HCl 30 mg, chlorpheniramine maleate 2 mg and codeine 8 mg. Nonmedicinal ingredients: FD&C Blue No. 1, gelatin (pork), guar gum, hydrogenated vegetable oil, isopropyl alcohol, lactose, magnesium stearate, starch and stearic acid. Energy: 4.7 kJ (1.13 kcal). Sodium-free. Bottles of 16.

Sinutab Non Drowsy: Regular Strength: Each orange caplet imprinted "Sinutab" on both sides contains: acetaminophen 325 mg and pseudoephedrine HCl 30 mg. Nonmedicinal ingredients: celluloses, D&C Yellow No. 6, polyethylene glycol, polysorbate, starch, titanium dioxide, wax and zinc stearate. Energy: 0.8 kJ (0.19 kcal). Sodium: <1 mmol (0.01 mg). Boxes of 12 and 24 in blister packages.

Extra Strength: Each orange caplet imprinted "Sinutab" on both sides contains: acetaminophen 500 mg and pseudoephedrine HCl 30 mg. Nonmedicinal ingredients: celluloses, FD&C Yellow No. 6, polyethylene glycol, polysorbate, starch, titanium dioxide, wax and zinc stearate. Energy: 1.05 kJ (0.25 kcal). Sodium: 0.02 mg. Boxes of 12 and 24 in a blister package.

Sinutab SA: Each pink, bilayered, scored, sustained action tablet, contains: acetaminophen 600 mg, phenylpropanolamine HCl 100 mg and phenyltoloxamine citrate 66 mg. Nonmedicinal ingredients: calcium sulfate, celluloses, FD&C Red No. 2, FD&C Yellow No. 6, gelatin (pork), guar gum, lactose, magnesium stearate, starches, stearic acid, talc, titanium dioxide, vegetable oil and wax. Energy 2 kJ (0.48 kcal). Boxes of 10 in blister packages.

Sinutab Nightime Extra Strength: Each white caplet, printed "NIGHT/NUIT" on both sides, contains: acetaminophen 500 mg, pseudoephedrine HCl 30 mg and diphenhydramine HCl 25 mg. Nonmedicinal ingredients: celluloses, propylene glycol, silicon dioxide, titanium dioxide, wax and zinc stearate. Available as part of Sinutab Extra Strength Daytime/Nightime Combo Pack (see below).

Sinutab Extra Strength Daytime/Nightime Combo Pack: Each box contains: 18 caplets of Sinutab Non Drowsy Extra Strength and 6 caplets of Sinutab Nightime Extra Strength.

All preparations are gluten-, paraben-, sulfite- and tartrazine-free. Sinutab with Codeine and Sinutab SA tablets also contain lactose; others are lactose-free.

(Shown in Product Recognition Section)

692® TABLETS Ⓝ

Frosst

ASA—Caffeine—Propoxyphene HCl

Analgesic

Indications: For the relief of mild to moderate pain.

Contraindications: Hypersensitivity to propoxyphene or to any of the ingredients of 692 Tablets. Because of ASA content, 692 tablets are contraindicated in patients with peptic ulcer.

Warnings: Do not prescribe propoxyphene for patients who are suicidal or addiction-prone.

Prescribe propoxyphene with caution for patients taking tranquilizers or antidepressant drugs and patients who use alcohol in excess.

Tell patients not to exceed the recommended dose and to limit their intake of alcohol.

Excessive doses of propoxyphene, alone or in combination with other CNS depressants, including alcohol, have been recognized as a major cause of drug-related deaths. Fatalities not uncommonly occur within the first hour of overdosage.

Safe use of this drug requires judicious prescribing. Do not prescribe large amounts or doses larger than those recommended. Considerations should be given to the use of non-narcotic analgesics for patients who are depressed or suicidal. Patients should be cautioned about not taking doses higher than those recommended and about the potentially serious, additive CNS-depressant effects of propoxyphene products and alcohol. Prescribe propoxyphene with caution for patients whose medical condition requires concomitant administration of sedatives, tranquilizers, muscle-relaxants, antidepressants, or other CNS-depressant drugs. Advise the patients about the additive depressant effects of these combinations.

Many propoxyphene-related deaths have occurred in patients with previous histories of emotional disturbances or suicidal ideation or attempts, as well as histories of misuse of alcohol, tranquilizers, and other CNS-active drugs. Some deaths have occurred because of the accidental ingestion of excessive quantities of propoxyphene alone or in combination with other drugs.

Drug Dependence: Abuse of propoxyphene has been reported. Tolerance, psychologic dependence, and physical dependence have been reported. Appropriate caution should therefore be exercised in prescribing preparations containing propoxyphene. Propoxyphene will only partially suppress the withdrawal syndrome in individuals physically dependent on morphine or other narcotics. The abuse liability of propoxyphene is qualitatively similar to that of codeine although it is quantitatively less; therefore, propoxyphene should be prescribed with the same degree of caution.

Occupational Hazards: Propoxyphene may impair the mental and physical abilities required for the performance of potentially hazardous tasks such as driving a car, especially during the first few days of therapy; therefore, caution the patient accordingly.

Precautions: *Drug Interactions:* Advise patients that propoxyphene, in combination with alcohol, tranquilizers, sedative-hypnotics, and other CNS depressants, has an additive depressant effect.

Pregnancy: The safety of propoxyphene during pregnancy has not been established. Recent data indicate that neonates can experience propoxyphene withdrawal symptoms if the drug has been taken by their mothers during pregnancy. Therefore, propoxyphene should not be used in pregnant women unless the potential benefits outweigh the possible hazards.

Lactation: Propoxyphene is excreted in milk, and the infant of a mother taking maximal doses might receive a pharmacologically active dose.

Children: Propoxyphene should not be used in children because adequate data to establish safe conditions in this age group are not available.

Recent studies have suggested that ASA usage may be associated with the development of Reye's syndrome in children, teenagers and young adults with acute febrile illnesses, especially influenza and varicella. Although a direct causal relationship has not been established, it is recommended that salicylates be avoided when possible in children, teenagers and young adults with influenza or varicella until the nature of the possible association between ASA and Reye's syndrome has been clarified.

The concurrent use of orphenadrine and propoxyphene need not be avoided when indicated. If toxic CNS effects occur, they are probably due to either drug alone and require a reduction in the dose or discontinuation of one or both agents.

Salicylates should be administered with caution to patients with asthma and other allergic conditions, with a history of gastrointestinal ulcerations, with bleeding tendencies, with significant anemia, or with hypoprothrombinemia.

Salicylates increase the effects of oral anticoagulants. Caution is necessary when salicylates and anticoagulants are prescribed concurrently. Also salicylates may depress the concentration of prothrombin in the plasma.

Salicylates may potentiate sulfonylurea hypoglycemic agents. Large doses of salicylates may have a hypoglycemic action, and thus affect the insulin requirements of diabetics.

Salicylates can produce changes in thyroid function tests.

Sodium excretion produced by spironolactone may be decreased in the presence of salicylates.

Although salicylates in large doses are uricosuric agents, smaller amounts may depress uric acid clearance and thus decrease the uricosuric effects of probenecid, sulfinpyrazone and phenylbutazone.

Adverse Effects: The most frequently reported have been dizziness, sedation, nausea and vomiting. In general, the reactions are those of the components:

Propoxyphene: CNS: dizziness, drowsiness, sedation, headache, euphoria, paradoxical excitement and insomnia. The chronic ingestion of propoxyphene in doses exceeding 800 mg/day has caused toxic psychoses and convulsions.

Gastrointestinal: nausea, vomiting, gastrointestinal disturbances, abdominal pain, constipation and liver dysfunction.

Dermatologic and hypersensitivity reactions: itching and skin rashes.

Miscellaneous: minor visual disturbances, depression of urinary 17-hydroxy-corticoids, and 17-ketosteroids.

ASA: Gastrointestinal: dyspepsia, heartburn, nausea, vomiting, diarrhea, gastrointestinal ulceration and bleeding.

Ear reactions: tinnitus, hearing loss.

Hematologic: anemia, leukopenia, thrombocytopenia, purpura.

Dermatologic and hypersensitivity reactions: urticaria, angioedema, pruritus, various skin eruptions, asthma and anaphylaxis.

Miscellaneous: mental confusion, drowsiness, sweating and thirst.

Caffeine: Caffeine may cause nausea, nervousness, insomnia, headache, vomiting, palpitation, vertigo, muscle tremor, sensory disturbances, excessive diuresis in sensitive patients. Large doses may cause gastric ulceration.

Overdose: Symptoms: The manifestations of serious overdosage with propoxyphene are similar to those of narcotic overdosage and include respiratory depression (a decrease in respiratory rate and/or tidal volume, Cheyne-Stokes respiration, cyanosis), extreme somnolence progressing to stupor or coma, initial pupillary constriction followed by dilation as hypoxia progresses, and circulatory collapse. In addition to these characteristics typical of narcotic poisoning, focal and generalized convulsions constitute a prominent feature in most cases of severe propoxyphene poisoning. Cardiac arrhythmias and conduction delay may be present. Pulmonary edema has occasionally been reported. Apnea, cardiac arrest and death have occurred. A combined respiratory-metabolic acidosis occurs owing to retained CO_2 and formation of lactic acid. Acidosis may be severe if large amounts of salicylates also have been ingested.

In addition, nephrogenic diabetes insipidus, and electro-cardiographic abnormalities may occur with propoxyphene poisoning. As many of the combinations of propoxyphene contain acetylsalicylic acid, the clinical picture may be complicated by the added features of salicylism (central nausea and vomiting, tinnitus and deafness, vertigo and headaches, mental dullness and confusion, diaphoresis, rapid pulse, increased respiration and respiratory alkalosis).

After ingestion of a therapeutic quantity (65 mg) of propoxyphene HCl, the maximal plasma concentration is about 6 μg/100 mL in the adult. The minimal lethal dose of propoxyphene HCl in man has been reported to be from 500 to 800 mg. This would correspond to between 7 and 12 doses of 65 mg each, and could result in a blood concentration of 46 to 74 μg/100 mL. Blood concentration of 200 μg/100 mL or higher is diagnostic of severe propoxyphene intoxication in non-tolerant individuals. The average blood concentrations in patients dying from ingestion of propoxyphene HCl alone is 472 μg/100 mL, suggesting an average absorbed quantity of 5 120 mg.

Treatment: Primary attention should be given to the re-establishment of adequate respiratory exchange through provision of a patent airway and institution of assisted or controlled ventilation.

The narcotic antagonist naloxone, given i.v., will reverse the signs of propoxyphene intoxication. It should be repeated as necessary. In addition to the use of a narcotic antagonist, the patient may require careful titration with an anticonvulsant to control convulsions.

The stomach should be emptied as soon as possible after ingestion of larger than therapeutic amounts. However, induction of emesis is contraindicated in a comatose patient, and induction of emesis and gastric lavage are contraindicated in a patient who is convulsing. The oral administration of activated charcoal may be an effective means for treating excessive ingestions of propoxyphene. It is suggested that a slurry of 10 g of activated charcoal be administered by mouth when the patient is first seen, before induction of emesis or gastric lavage. Following stomach emptying, another 10 g dose should be given to prevent the systemic absorption of propoxyphene remaining in the gastrointestinal tract.

Blood gases, pH and electrolytes should be monitored in order that acidosis and any electrolytic disturbance present may be promptly corrected. Acidosis, hypoxia, and generalized CNS depression predispose to the development of cardiac arrhythmias. Ventricular fibrillation or cardiac arrest may occur and necessitate full cardiopulmonary resuscitative (CPR) measures. Respiratory acidosis quickly subsides as ventilation is restored and hypercapnea is eliminated, however, lactic acidosis may require i.v. bicarbonate for prompt correction.

Electrocardiographic monitoring is essential. Prompt correction of hypoxia, acidosis, and electrolytic disturbances (when present) will help prevent cardiac complications and will increase the efficacy of agents administered to restore cardiac function. Oxygen, i.v. fluids, vasopressors, and other supportive measures should be employed as indicated.

Analeptic agents should not be used, since CNS stimulants may precipitate fatal convulsions. Dialysis is of little value in poisoning by propoxyphene alone.

Efforts should be made to determine whether other CNS depressants were taken concomitantly, since these increase CNS depression and cause other specific toxic effects.

Treatment of acute salicylate intoxication includes minimizing drug absorption, promoting elimination through the kidneys, and correcting metabolic derangements. If the patient is seen within 4 hours, the stomach should be emptied, when possible, by inducing emesis or by gastric lavage. Intermittent peritoneal dialysis is useful for adult cases of moderate severity. Alkaline i.v. fluids are helpful. Hemodialysis with an artificial kidney is the most effective means of removing salicylate and is indicated for very severe cases.

Dosage: Adults: One tablet orally, 3 or 4 times daily, as required.

Information for the Patient: See Blue Section—Information for the Patient "692 Tablets".

Supplied: Each oval, salmon colored, film-coated tablet, engraved ϕ on one side and plain on the other, contains: propoxyphene hydrochloride 65 mg, ASA 375 mg and caffeine 30 mg. Also contains sucrose. Gluten-, lactose- and tartrazine-free. Bottles of 500.

(Shown in Product Recognition Section)

SLO-BID® Ⓟ

Rhône-Poulenc Rorer

Theophylline

Bronchodilator

Pharmacology: Theophylline relaxes the smooth muscle of the bronchial airways and pulmonary blood vessels to relieve bronchospasm and increases flow rates and vital capacity. It also produces other actions typical of the xanthine derivatives: coronary vasodilation, diuresis, increase in gastric secretion and cardiac, cerebral, and skeletal muscle stimulation. The action of theophylline may be mediated through inhibition of phosphodiesterase and a resultant increase in intracellular cyclic adenosine monophosphate, but the exact mechanism(s) has not been determined. Theophylline distributes in all body compartments. Protein binding accounts for some 50%. Liver is the primary site of metabolism.

The therapeutic serum concentrations of theophylline are accepted as 56 to 110 μmol/L (10 to 20 mg/L), levels above 20 μg/mL are associated with toxic reactions. The pharmacokinetics of theophylline are influenced by a number of variables such as: age, disease state, smoking, concomitant medication. Therefore, the optimum therapeutic maintenance dose should be determined by individual titration.

Slo-Bid (cont'd)

Slo-Bid is a controlled release formulation which produces peak blood levels between 5 and 8 hours post dose. Once the steady state has been achieved, therapeutic blood levels persist for 12 hours in most adult patients. The degree of fluctuation between blood peak and through theophylline levels is 37.2%.

Degree of Fluctuation is= $\frac{(C_{max}-C_{min})}{C_{min}} \times 100.$

Indications: For the symptomatic treatment of reversible bronchoconstriction associated with bronchial asthma, chronic obstructive pulmonary emphysema, chronic bronchitis, and related bronchospastic disorders.

Contraindications: Should not be administered to patients with hypersensitivity to xanthines, to patients with coronary artery disease where cardiac stimulation might prove harmful, or to patients with an active peptic ulcer.

Warnings: In clinical situations where immediate bronchodilatation is required, such as status asthmaticus, sustained release theophylline is not suitable.

Theophylline has a narrow therapeutic index, the margin of safety above therapeutic doses is small.

In patients showing intolerance to theophylline, the therapy should be reassessed.

Theophylline clearance can be changed by various disease states, as well as by the age of the patient, concomitant use of other medications and life-style habits (see Precautions).

Children: Dosage schedule in pediatric population has not been established. Use of sustained release theophylline in children under 12 years of age is not recommended.

Precautions: There is a marked variation in serum levels achieved in different patients, given the same dose of theophylline, resulting from individual differences in the rate of theophylline clearance. This may lead to serious adverse effects in some patients. Dosage regimen should, therefore, be individualized. The incidence of adverse reactions increases at serum theophylline levels above 82.5 μmol/L (15 mg/L) and levels in excess of 110 μmol/L (20 mg/L) are usually toxic.

Periodic monitoring of serum theophylline levels is recommended in order to assure maximal benefit without excessive risk.

In individuals in whom theophylline plasma clearance is reduced for any reason, even conventional doses of theophylline may result in increased serum levels and potential toxicity.

Reduced theophylline clearance has been documented in the following readily identifiable groups: patients with impaired renal or liver function; patients over 55 years of age, particularly males and those with chronic lung disease; those with cardiac failure from any cause; neonates; and those patients taking certain drugs (macrolide antibiotics and cimetidine). Decreased clearance of theophylline may be associated with either influenza immunization or active infection with influenza.

Laboratory monitoring of serum theophylline is especially appropriate in the above individuals in order to maintain appropriate theophylline dosage.

Many patients who require theophylline may exhibit tachycardia due to their underlying disease process so that the cause/effect relationship to elevated serum theophylline concentration may not be appreciated.

Theophylline products may cause dysrhythmia and/or worsen pre-existing arrhythmia and any significant change in cardiac rate and/or rhythm warrants monitoring and further investigation.

Serious side effects such as tachycardia, arrhythmia, seizures, vascular collapse and even death may occur without warning and may not be preceded by less severe symptoms such as nausea and restlessness.

Use with caution in patients with severe cardiac disease, severe hypoxemia, hypertension, hyperthyroidism, acute myocardial injury, cor pulmonale, congestive heart failure, liver disease, in the elderly (especially males).

Patients with congestive heart failure frequently have markedly prolonged serum levels with theophylline persisting in serum for long periods following discontinuation of the drug.

Theophylline may occasionally act as a local irritant to the gastrointestinal tract although gastrointestinal symptoms are more commonly centrally mediated and associated with serum drug concentrations over 20μg/mL.

Theophylline increases gastric secretion, caution should be exercised in patients with a history of peptic ulcer.

Sustained release theophylline should not be administered concurrently with other xanthine medications.

Theophylline half-life is shorter in smokers than in nonsmokers. Smokers may require larger or more frequent doses of theophylline.

Although Slo-Bid has pharmacokinetic properties similar to other controlled release theophylline products, it is not possible to ensure interchangeability between different products. Careful clinical monitoring is required when changing from one drug product to another.

The equivalent content of anhydrous theophylline is the active ingredient that determines blood concentration and clinical response. If a change in theophylline product is made and it involves a change in anhydrous theophylline equivalence, the dose should be adjusted accordingly.

Laboratory Test Interactions: Theophylline may cause elevation of urine catecholamines and plasma free fatty acids. This should be taken into consideration when interpreting biochemistry tests.

When plasma levels of theophylline are measured by spectrophotometric methods, coffee, tea, cola beverages, chocolate and acetaminophen contribute to falsely high values.

When high pressure liquid chromatography (HPLC) method is used, plasma theophylline concentration may be falsely increased by caffeine, some cephalosporine and sulfa medications.

Food Interactions: Taking sustained release theophylline immediately after a high-fat content meal such as 240 mL whole milk, 2 fried eggs, 2 strips of bacon, one bran muffin with butter, 2 ounces hash brown potatoes (about 3 303 kJ (789 kcal) including approximately 49 g of fat) may result in a decrease in the rate of absorption, but with no significant difference in the extent of absorption. The influence of the type and amount of other foods, as well as time interval between drug and food has not been studied.

Pregnancy and *Lactation:* Theophylline crosses the placental barrier, it also passes into breast milk. Safe use of theophylline in pregnancy and in lactation has not been established. The risk of uncontrolled asthma should be balanced against potential effects on the fetus or on the nursing newborn.

Drug Interactions: Theophylline pharmacokinetics are altered by the concurrent use of various drugs as listed in Table I.

Table I—Slo-Bid

Effect of Various Drugs on Theophylline Pharmacokinetics

Drug	Effect on Theophylline Clearance and Elimination Half-life	
Cimetidine, propranolol, allopurinol, macrolide antibiotics (erythromycin, troleandomycin), oral contraceptives	↑ t½,	↓clearance
Alkalinizing agents	↑ t½,	↓clearance
Influenza vaccine	↑ t½,	clearance reported to be decreased or no change
Phenytoin, barbiturates, carbamazepine, isoproterenol, rifampin	↓ t½,	↑clearance
Tobacco	↓ t½,	↑clearance
Acidifying agents	↓ t½,	↑clearance

Concurrent use of theophylline influences the effects of certain drugs, see Table II.

Table II—Slo-Bid

Effect of Theophylline on Certain Drugs

Drug	Influence of Theophylline
Digitalis glycosides	↑ cardiac effect
Thiazides	↑ diuresis
Nephrotoxic drugs	↑ nephrotoxicity
Lithium	↑ ratio of lithium/creatinine clearance, thus a decrease in lithium
Sympathomimetic amines	↑ toxicity ↑ CNS stimulation
Coumarin anticoagulants	↓ anticoagulant activity ↑ prothrombin and fibrinogen blood concentrations ↓ prothrombin time
Allopurinol	↓ antihyperuricemic action
Probenecid and pyrazolon derivatives	↓ uricosuric action

Adverse Effects: The most common adverse effects are gastric irritation, nausea, vomiting, epigastric pain, and tremor. These are usually early signs of toxicity. However, with high doses ventricular arrhythmias or seizures may be the first signs to appear.

Adverse reactions include: Gastrointestinal: nausea, vomiting, epigastric pain, hematemesis, diarrhea, anorexia, intestinal bleeding, reactivation of peptic ulcer.

CNS: headache, irritability, restlessness, insomnia, twitching, convulsions, reflex hyperexcitability.

Cardiovascular: palpitations, tachycardia, hypotension, circulatory failure, ventricular arrhythmias, extrasystoles, flushing.

Renal: albuminuria, diuresis and hematuria.

Others: hyperglycemia, tachypnea and inappropriate ADH syndrome.

Overdose: Symptoms: Insomnia, restlessness, mild excitement or irritability, and rapid pulse are the early symptoms, which may progress to mild delirium. Sensory disturbances such as tinnitus or flashes of light are common. Anorexia, nausea and vomiting are also frequently early observations of theophylline overdosage.

Fever, diuresis, dehydration and extreme thirst may be seen. Severe overdosage results in bloody, syrup-like "coffeeground" vomitus, tremors, tonic extensor spasm interrupted by clonic convulsions, extrasystoles, quickened respiration, stupor and finally coma. Cardiovascular disorders and respiratory collapse, leading to shock, cyanosis and death follow gross overdosages.

Treatment: Monitoring serum theophylline levels: Following intake of Slo-Bid, the blood theophylline peak levels may not show until 5 hours post-ingestion. Patients ingesting overdoses of sustained release theophylline formulations may have after the initial rise in blood theophylline also a secondary increase in theophylline levels. One report on fatal self-poisoning has attributed this to compacted tablet masses in the gastrointestinal tract. Careful clinical and laboratory monitoring of stabilized patient is advisable.

If potential oral overdose is established and seizure has not occurred: Induce emesis. Administer a cathartic (this is particularly important when a sustained release preparation has been taken). Administer activated charcoal.

If patient is having a seizure, establish an airway. Administer oxygen. Treat the seizure with i.v. diazepam, 0.1 to 0.3 mg/kg up to 10 mg. Monitor vital signs, maintain blood pressure and provide adequate hydration.

Post-Seizure Coma: Maintain airway and oxygenation. If a result of oral medication, follow above recommendations to prevent absorption of drug, but intubation and lavage will have to be performed instead of inducing emesis, and the cathartic and charcoal will need to be introduced via a large bore gastric lavage tube. Continue to provide full supportive care and adequate hydration while waiting for the drug to be metabolized. In general, the drug is metabolized sufficiently rapidly so as not to warrant consideration of dialysis. However, if serum levels exceed 257 μmol/L (50 mg/L) charcoal hemoperfusion may be indicated.

Dosage: Dosing of theophylline should be individual in respect of the patients clinical response and serum theophylline levels. There is considerable patient-to-patient variation in the daily theophylline dose required to achieve optimal therapeutic levels. Ideally, all patients should have serum theophylline levels measured to ensure desired clinical response and avoid toxicity.

Therapeutic serum levels are generally considered to be between 55 to 110 μmol/L (10 and 20 μg/mL).

Dosage calculations should be based on lean body mass (ideal body weight).

Monitoring of serum theophylline concentrations is important. When peak concentrations need to be determined, blood samples should be drawn 4 to 8 hours after dosing.

In bioavailability studies conducted with Slo-Bid, the time to achieve steady state with Slo-Bid was usually 5 days.

If dosage increase is not tolerated, reduce the dose to previously acceptable level.

The contents of the capsules should not be chewed or crushed.

Adults: Usual dose is 200 to 300 mg every 12 hours. This dose may be increased by 50 to 100 mg every 12 hours at 3 day intervals until a satisfactory response is obtained or toxic effects appear.

Dosage adjustments should be based on theophylline concentration and/or upon the patients clinical response. However, doses of 400 mg every 12 hours or higher should not be given unless serum theophylline concentration can be monitored. It should not be necessary to exceed a daily dose of 18 mg/kg in adult patients. Even with serum level monitoring, this dose may lead to side effects because of day-to-day variations in blood levels within individual patients.

Dividing the daily dosage into 3 doses administered at 8 hour intervals may be indicated if symptoms repeatedly occur at the end of 12 hour dosing intervals.

Sprinkle Technique Method of Administration: Administration of Slo-Bid by the sprinkle technique does not alter the rate or extent of absorption of Slo-Bid. This is particularly useful if you are unable to swallow whole capsules.

Instructions for Use by the Sprinkle Technique:

1. Hold the capsule horizontally above a spoonful of cool soft food that is easy to swallow such as apple sauce, pudding, fruit puree or ice cream.
2. Rotate the capsule ends slightly in opposite directions to loosen them and gently pull apart, sprinkling the beads onto the food.
3. Do not chew the drug/food mixture, but swallow immediately.
4. Do not save or reuse any medicine that has already been sprinkled on food.
5. If the beads are spilled while sprinkling, start over to make sure you get the proper dose.

Children: The use of Slo-Bid in children under the age of 12 years is not recommended, as dose schedule in this age group with this time release product, has not been established.

Information for the Patient: See Blue Section—Information for the Patient "Slo-Bid".

Supplied: 50 mg: Each size 4 capsule, opaque white cap and body, with on cap and "Slo-Bid 50 mg" on body printed in red, contains: anhydrous theophylline timed release 50 mg. Nonmedicinal ingredients: ethyl cellulose, gelatin, methylene chloride, methylparaben, propylene glycol, propylparaben, shellac, starch, sucrose and titanium dioxide. Bottles of 100.

100 mg: Each size 3 capsule, opaque white cap and body, with on cap and "Slo-Bid 100 mg" on body printed in red, contains: anhydrous theophylline timed release 100 mg. Nonmedicinal ingredients: ethyl cellulose, gelatin, methylene chloride, methylparaben, propylene glycol, propylparaben, shellac, starch, sucrose and titanium dioxide. Bottles of 100.

200 mg: Each size 1 capsule, opaque white cap and body, with on cap and "Slo-Bid 200 mg" on body printed in red, contains: anhydrous theophylline timed release 200 mg. Nonmedicinal ingredients: ethyl cellulose, gelatin, methylene chloride, methylparaben, propylene glycol, propylparaben, shellac, starch, sucrose and titanium dioxide. Bottles of 100.

300 mg: Each size 0 capsule, opaque white cap and body, with on cap and "Slo-Bid 300 mg" on body printed in red, contains: anhydrous theophylline timed release 300 mg. Nonmedicinal ingredients: ethyl cellulose, gelatin, methylene chloride, methylparaben, propylene glycol, propylparaben, shellac, starch, sucrose and titanium dioxide. Bottles of 100.

Store at room temperature. Dispense in a light-resistant container with tight closure. Protect from excessive heat, light and moisture.

(Shown in Product Recognition Section)

SLOW-FE®

Novartis Consumer Health

Ferrous Sulfate

Management of Iron Deficiency States

Pharmacology: Iron enters into the body metabolism as an essential component of hemoglobin, myoglobin and a number of enzymes.

Ferrous sulfate has long been the preferred salt for treating iron deficiencies. Yet it is inherently astringent and irritant to mucous membranes—high concentrations of the salt in the gastrointestinal tract often cause discomfort and intolerance.

Slow-Fe is formulated to be better tolerated than ordinary ferrous sulfate tablets, being suitable for prolonged administration. The minimizing of nausea and gastrointestinal disorder is advantageous in pregnancy, convalescence and in old age, all of which may be associated with simple iron deficiency anemias.

In normal volunteers, monitoring by serial x-rays indicated that Slow-Fe tablets had lost their ferrous sulfate and disappeared over a period of 90 to 150 minutes. In vitro studies utilizing artificial gastric juice (B.P. disintegration apparatus) show that the 160 mg of dried ferrous sulfate was released over a period of 1½ to 2 hours. Maximum effective absorption is achieved during this optimum release period with iron release in the duodenum and upper small intestine. By way of comparison, standard ferrous sulfate tablets B.P. release the total iron content in 36 minutes. Clinical trials demonstrated that the hemoglobin response showed an average rise comparable with the rise described as a standard response by Swan and Jowett (1959). Under conditions of controlled trial Slow-Fe given once daily adequately maintained the hemoglobin levels of pregnant women through gestation. Regardless of their initial hemoglobin it was found that Slow-Fe produced a statistically significant increase in hemoglobin. Assessment of 2 343 patient records, under conditions of general practice showed a low incidence of side effects (comparable to the expected level with placebo) indicating good tolerability on both 1 and 2 tablets daily.

Indications: Iron deficiency anemias. Iron deficiency states without anemia.

Contraindications: Hemochromatosis, hemosiderosis and hemolytic anemia.

Warnings: Keep out of reach of children.

Precautions: May aggravate existing peptic ulcer, regional enteritis and ulcerative colitis.

Drug Interactions: Oral administration of iron preparations will inhibit absorption of tetracyclines from the gastrointestinal tract and vice versa, which will therefore lead to decreased serum concentrations of both tetracycline and iron. Orally administered iron may also decrease the absorption of penicillamine. Therefore, a period of at least 2 hours should separate the administration of iron and either tetracycline or penicillamine. The concurrent administration of antacids with oral iron preparations may decrease the absorption of iron. Administration of antacids and oral iron preparations should therefore be separated as far apart as possible.

Adverse Effects: The tolerance of ferrous sulfate was demonstrated in the multicentre investigation (Parrot, 1969) by 258 general practitioners, which involved over 2 300 patients. Of 1 797 patients given 1 tablet daily, 92.5% reported that it was well tolerated. 436 patients were given 2 tablets daily, and 90.3% of these reported no side effects. The incidence of individual side effects is, in most cases, comparable to the expected level with placebo (see Table I).

Table I—Slow-Fe

Percentage Side Effects*

	Slow-Fe Dosage	
	1 tablet daily	**2 tablets daily**
Total patients	1 889	454
Total with completed forms	1 797	436
Nausea and/or vomiting	2.4%	4.0%
Constipation	1.4%	1.1%
Diarrhea	1.4%	2.3%
Abdominal pain	0.8%	1.1%
Skin rash	0.3%	0.4%
Other	0.8%	0.4%

*Calculated as percentages of the total group including patients whose record forms were in some way incomplete.

Overdose: Symptoms and Treatment: Iron poisoning is rare in adults but serious acute poisoning in children can result from ingestion of doses in excess of 1 g. Doses of 1 g should be considered as toxic in children and therapy instituted as soon as possible. Serum iron levels above 300 µg/100 mL can be taken as presumptive evidence of poisoning requiring treatment; severe poisoning is usually associated with concentrations well above 500 µg/100 mL.

Symptoms may occur within 10 to 60 minutes or may be delayed several hours. They are largely those of gastrointestinal irritation and necrosis with vomiting, diarrhea, tarry stools, hematemesis, fast and weak pulse, lethargy, low blood pressure, coma and signs of peripheral circulatory collapse. Local erosion of the stomach and small intestine might result in a further increase in iron absorption. If poisoning is not immediately fatal, there may be a transient period of apparent recovery after 4 to 6 hours lasting up to 24 hours. This may be followed by a phase characterized by CNS abnormalities, cyanosis, pulmonary edema, shock, convulsions, metabolic acidosis and hyperthermia and may progress to circulatory collapse, coma and death within 12 to 48 hours.

If patient is not in shock or coma, ipecac syrup should be given immediately and vomiting induced. Gastric lavage should be performed with 1 to 5% sodium bicarbonate solution within the first hour after ingestion of iron. Administration of a saline cathartic or surgical removal of iron tablets (visible in abdominal radiographs) may be needed if other methods of removing iron have been unsuccessfully attempted. If an iron-chelating agent such as deferoxamine mesylate is available it should be utilized as soon as possible, especially if (a) serum iron (SI) is greater than total iron binding capacity (TIBC), (b) SI is greater than 350 µg/100 mL (if TIBC is unavailable), or (c) SI is not readily available and the patient is symptomatic. (Note: Leukocytosis [WBC > 15 000/mm³], hyperglycemia [blood sugar > 150 mg/dL] or diarrhea strongly suggest that SI will be in the toxic range.) Shock and dehydration may be combatted with i.v. fluids or blood, oxygen and vasopressor agents.

Dosage: Prophylaxis: A single tablet daily is sufficient to maintain an adequate iron intake both during pregnancy and in patients with simple iron deficiency.

Iron Deficiency: Depending on the severity, 1 or 2 tablets daily, usually in 1 dose.

Mild anemias (e.g. hemoglobin above 75%): 1 tablet daily will usually suffice.

Moderate or severe anemias: 2 tablets daily should be given until hemoglobin levels return to normal. In severe cases to a maximum of 4 tablets daily.

Children: 1 tablet daily is a suitable dose for children able to swallow a small tablet.

The physiological process of hemoglobin levels returning to normal may require up to approximately 8 weeks. In most patients the dose can then be reduced to 1 tablet daily for maintenance, to build up iron reserves over a further 12 to 16 weeks.

Supplied: Each off-white, film-coated tablet, imprinted CG 503 on one side and plain on the other, contains: dried ferrous sulfate 160 mg (equivalent to elemental iron 50 mg) in a slow release inert wax core. Nonmedicinal ingredients: cetostearyl alcohol, FD&C Blue No. 2, hydroxypropyl methylcellulose, lactose, magnesium stearate, polysorbate, talc, titanium dioxide, and yellow iron oxide. Energy: 2.1 kJ (0.5 kcal). Alcohol-, bisulfite-, gluten-, parabens-, sodium- and tartrazine-free. Push-through blister-packs of 30 and high density plastic bottles of 120 with child resistant caps.

SLOW-FE FOLIC®

Novartis Consumer Health

Ferrous Sulfate—Folic Acid

Hematinic—Hematopoietic

Pharmacology: Iron is utilized chiefly in the synthesis of hemoglobin, myoglobin and certain respiratory enzymes; unless it is supplied in appropriate amounts, the maturation of the red cells is retarded and the numbers discarded from the bone marrow into the general circulation are reduced.

Folic acid exerts important effects on hemapoiesis. It is essential in the synthesis of the cell's nucleoproteins. The reactions in which folic acid participates are important in the synthesis of DNA. As a consequence, deficiency of folic acid leads to damage in those tissues in which DNA synthesis and turnover are rapid. This includes the hematopoietic tissues, the mucosa of the gastrointestinal tract and the developing embryo.

The controlled-release base of Slow-Fe Folic tablets is specially formulated to release the tablet's contents evenly over an average period of 2 hours, the optimum time for maximum effective absorption. Furthermore, high concentrations of iron during the tablet's passage through the stomach and upper small intestine are avoided thus minimizing the incidence of gastrointestinal side effects.

Indications: Prophylaxis of iron and folic acid deficiencies and treatment of megaloblastic anemia, during pregnancy, puerperium and lactation.

Contraindications: Hemochromatosis, hemosiderosis and hemolytic anemia.

Warnings: Keep out of reach of children.

Precautions: The use of folic acid in the treatment of pernicious (Addisonian) anemia, in which vitamin B_{12} is deficient, may return the peripheral blood picture to normal while neurological manifestations remain progressive.

Oral iron preparations may aggravate existing peptic ulcer, regional enteritis and ulcerative colitis.

Oral administration of iron preparations will inhibit absorption of tetracyclines from the gastrointestinal tract and vice versa, which will therefore lead to decreased serum concentrations of both tetracycline and iron. Orally administered iron may also decrease the absorption of penicillamine. Therefore, a period of at least 2 hours should separate the administration of iron and either tetracycline or penicillamine. The concurrent administration of antacids with oral iron preparations may decrease the absorption of iron. Administration of antacids and oral iron preparations should therefore be separated as far apart as possible.

Slow-Fe Folic (cont'd)

Adverse Effects: Nausea, diarrhea, constipation, vomiting, dizziness, abdominal pain, skin rash, headache.

Overdose: Symptoms and Treatment: See Slow-Fe. Signs of toxicity from folic acid have not been observed even with doses several times higher than the usual therapeutic levels.

Dosage: Prophylaxis: 1 tablet daily throughout pregnancy, puerperium and lactation.
Treatment of megaloblastic anemia: during pregnancy, puerperium and lactation; and, in multiple pregnancy: 2 tablets, in a single dose, should be swallowed daily.

Tablets to be swallowed whole.

Supplied: Each pale yellow, film-coated tablet, imprinted CIBA on one side and TP on the other, contains: dried ferrous sulfate 160 mg (equivalent to 50 mg elemental iron) and folic acid 400 μg in a specially formulated slow-release base. Nonmedicinal ingredients: cetostearyl alcohol, FD&C Blue No. 2, hydroxypropyl methylcellulose, lactose, magnesium stearate, polysorbate, talc, titanium dioxide and yellow iron oxide. Energy: 2.1 kJ (0.5 kcal). Alcohol-, bisulfite-, gluten-, parabens-, sodium and tartrazine-free. Push-through foil packs of 30 tablets per sheet. High density plastic bottles of 120 with child-resistant caps. Protect from heat and moisture.

SLOW-K®

Novartis Pharmaceuticals

Potassium Chloride

Potassium Supplement

Pharmacology: Potassium ions participate in a number of essential physiological processes. Depletion may occur whenever the rate of potassium loss through renal excretion and/or loss from the gastrointestinal tract exceeds the rate of potassium intake. Although there is no uniform correlation between plasma concentrations of potassium and total body stores, clinical signs of potassium deficiency are usually observed whenever the plasma potassium concentration falls below 3.5 mEq/L (hypokalemia).

Hypokalemia can be prevented and/or corrected by giving supplementary potassium. Administration of potassium salts is an alternative to increasing dietary intake of potassium-rich foods, which may not always be practical. In view of the frequency with which deficits of K^+ and Cl^- coexist, potassium chloride is the preferred salt for most of the clinical conditions associated with hypokalemia (see Warnings).

Slow-K is a sugar-coated (not enteric-coated) tablet containing 600 mg potassium chloride in a wax matrix. This formulation is intended to provide a controlled release of potassium chloride from the matrix, thereby minimizing the likelihood of producing high localized concentration of potassium within the gastrointestinal tract. The release of potassium chloride is largely pH-independent and occurs at a rate sufficient to permit complete absorption during its transit through the gastrointestinal tract.

Indications: The treatment of potassium depletion found in patients with hypokalemia and metabolic alkalosis.

Slow-K is also indicated for the prevention of potassium depletion when the dietary intake of potassium is inadequate for this purpose. The prophylactic administration of potassium ion may be indicated in patients receiving digitalis and/or diuretics for the treatment of congestive heart failure and hepatic cirrhosis with ascites. Slow-K may be indicated in selected patients with hypertension on long-term diuretic therapy, hyperaldosteronism states with normal renal function, the nephrotic syndrome and certain diarrheal states.

Contraindications: Hypersensitivity to potassium administration, e.g., in adynamia episodica hereditaria or congenital paramyotonia.

Hyperkalemia of any etiology, since a further increase in the serum potassium concentration in such patients can produce cardiac arrhythmia and cardiac arrest. Hyperkalemia may complicate any of the following conditions: marked renal failure, untreated Addison's disease, hyperadrenalism associated with adrenogenital syndrome, hyporeninemic hypoaldosteronism, extensive tissue breakdown (as in severe burns, trauma, massive hemolysis, rhabdomyolysis, tumour lysis), acute dehydration, heat cramps, metabolic acidosis.

Renal impairment with oliguria or azotemia.

Concomitant administration of Slow-K and potassium-sparing diuretics (e.g. spironolactone, triamterene or amiloride).

Patients in whom there is cause for arrest or delay in tablet passage through the gastrointestinal tract. These states include: partial or complete esophageal obstruction, for example by carcinomas (esophageal, post-cricoidal, thyroidal), aortic aneurysm, left-atrial enlargement, inflammatory stricture due to reflux esophagitis, and esophageal displacement due to cardiac surgery (e.g. valve replacement); stenosis or atony in any part of the gastrointestinal tract (e.g. pyloric stenosis, intestinal strictures). In these instances, potassium supplementation should be with a liquid preparation.

Warnings: In patients with impaired mechanisms for excreting potassium, administration of potassium salts can produce hyperkalemia and cardiac arrest. This occurs most commonly in patients given potassium by the i.v. route but may also occur in patients given potassium orally. Potentially fatal hyperkalemia can develop rapidly and be asymptomatic. The use of potassium salts in patients with chronic renal disease, or any other condition which impairs potassium excretion, requires particularly careful monitoring of the serum potassium concentration and appropriate dosage adjustment.

ACE inhibitors (e.g. captopril, enalapril) will produce some potassium retention by inhibiting aldosterone production. In patients receiving ACE inhibitors, therefore, potassium supplements should only be given under close monitoring.

Hypokalemia in patients with metabolic acidosis should be treated with an alkalinizing potassium salt such as potassium acetate, potassium bicarbonate or potassium citrate.

A probable association exists between the use of coated tablets containing potassium salts, with or without thiazide diuretics, and the incidence of serious small bowel ulceration. Such preparations should be used only when adequate dietary supplementation is not practical, and should be discontinued if abdominal pain, distention, nausea, vomiting or gastrointestinal bleeding occurs.

Slow-K is a wax matrix tablet formulated to provide a controlled rate of release of potassium chloride and thus to minimize the possibility of a high local concentration of potassium near the bowel wall. While the reported frequency of small bowel lesions is very much less with wax matrix tablets (less than 1/100 000 patient years) than with enteric coated potassium chloride tablets (40 to 50/100 000 patient years), a few cases associated with wax matrix tablets have been reported.

Slow-K should be discontinued immediately and the possibility of bowel obstruction or perforation considered if pronounced nausea, severe vomiting, diarrhea, abdominal pain, distention or gastrointestinal bleeding occurs.

Such risks may be increased in patients with esophageal stasis, known peptic and/or gastric ulcers, delayed intestinal transit, or intestinal ischemia due to generalized atherosclerotic vascular disease.

Precautions: Periodic serum potassium determinations are recommended during long-term potassium supplementation. When blood samples are taken for the analysis of plasma potassium, it is important to remember that artifactual elevations can occur after an improper venipuncture technique or as a result of in vitro hemolysis of the sample.

The correction of hypokalemia, particularly in the presence of cardiac disease, renal disease or acidosis requires careful attention to acid-base balance and appropriate monitoring of serum electrolytes, the electrocardiogram and the clinical status of the patient.

Potassium supplements should be used with caution in diseases associated with heart block since increased serum potassium may increase the degree of block.

Patients with ostomies may have an altered intestinal transit time and are better treated with other forms of potassium salt.

In some patients, diuretic-induced magnesium deficiency will prevent the restoration of intracellular deficits of potassium, so that hypomagnesemia should be corrected at the same time as hypokalemia.

Pregnancy: In general, no drug should be taken during the first trimester, and the benefits and risks of drug administration should be carefully considered throughout pregnancy.

Pregnancy is associated with gastrointestinal hypomotility. Solid oral potassium supplements should therefore only be given to pregnant women if such therapy is considered essential.

Lactation: The normal K^+ content of human milk is approximately 13 mEq/L. Since oral potassium becomes part of the body's potassium pool, provided the body potassium is not excessive, the contribution of Slow-K can be expected to have little or no effect on the potassium level in human milk.

Drug Interactions: Concomitant treatment with potassium sparing diuretics is contraindicated.

Slow-K should be used with caution in patients receiving agents known to have a potential for hyperkalemia, such as ACE inhibitors (e.g. captopril, enalapril; see Warnings), NSAIDs (e.g. indomethacin), beta-blockers, heparin and digoxin.

Since anticholinergic agents have the potential to reduce gastrointestinal motility, they should be prescribed with caution when given concomitantly with solid oral potassium preparations, particularly in high doses.

Children: Safety and effectiveness in children have not been established.

Geriatrics: As renal function, and hence the potential for maintaining potassium balance may decrease with age, serum potassium levels should be monitored regularly and dosage adjusted as appropriate. As gastrointestinal motility may also be affected by age, elderly patients should be reminded to swallow solid oral potassium salts with adequate amounts of fluid.

Adverse Effects: The most common adverse reactions to oral potassium salts are nausea, vomiting, flatulence, abdominal discomfort and diarrhea. These symptoms are due to irritation of the gastrointestinal tract and are best avoided by increasing fluid intake when possible, taking the dose with meals or reducing the dose.

One of the most severe adverse effects is hyperkalemia (see Warnings).

There have also been reports of esophageal and gastrointestinal obstruction, bleeding, ulceration or perforation (see Warnings). Small bowel lesions have been reported following the administration of Slow-K. The incidence is much lower than that reported for enteric-coated potassium chloride tablets (see Warnings).

Pruritus and/or skin rash, as well as urticaria, have been reported rarely.

Overdose: Overdosage from therapeutic doses of solid oral potassium salts in persons with normal excretory mechanisms rarely occurs. However, if excretory mechanisms are impaired, potentially fatal hyperkalemia may occur. Acute (accidental or intentional) overdosages of solid oral potassium salts have resulted in severe and/or fatal hyperkalemia.

Symptoms: Overdosage with potassium is characterized chiefly by cardiovascular, neuromuscular and gastrointestinal disturbances.

Cardiovascular: ECG changes, hypotension and shock, bundle-branch block, ventricular arrhythmias, ventricular fibrillation leading possibly to cardiac arrest.

Neuromuscular: paresthesia, areflexia, convulsions, flaccid paralysis of striated muscle leading possibly to respiratory paralysis.

Gastrointestinal: nausea, vomiting, diarrhea and abdominal cramp.

It is important to recognize that hyperkalemia is usually asymptomatic and may be manifested only by an increased serum potassium concentration and characteristic electrocardiographic changes which include increased amplitude and peaking of the T-wave, and flattening or absence of P-wave. As hyperkalemia worsens prolongation of the P-R interval, widening of the QRS complex with ST segment depression, and arrhythmias may develop.

Widening of the QRS complex is one of the most ominous signs and indicates the need for aggressive treatment.

Treatment: The plasma concentration and electrocardiogram must be monitored in every case of potassium overdosage, as well as serum electrolytes, BUN, glucose and arterial blood gases.

Electrocardiographic signs of hyperkalemia (tall peaked T waves, P-R prolongation, disappearance of P waves, QRS widening, heart block) are indications for immediate treatment.

In severe hyperkalemia (plasma potassium exceeds 8 mEq/L or ECG abnormalities include absence of P wave, presence of widened QRS complex or ventricular arrhythmia): Administer i.v. 300 to 500 mL/hour of 10% dextrose solution containing 10 to 20 units of insulin/1 000 mL. Correct acidosis, if present, with i.v. sodium bicarbonate (44 to 132 mEq/L of glucose solution). Administer 10 to 30 mL of 10% calcium gluconate i.v. over 1 to 5 minutes under continuous ECG monitoring. Administer cation exchange resin by high retention enema. Thirty to 50 g sodium polystyrene sulfonate suspended in 100 mL warm aqueous sorbitol solution should be kept in the sigmoid colon for several hours, if possible. The colon is then irrigated with a non-sodium containing solution to remove the resin. Repeated enemas can be administered, or the resin given repeatedly by mouth to maintain a physiologic potassium concentration. Hemodialysis or peritoneal dialysis may be of use, particularly in patients with renal failure.

In moderately severe hyperkalemia (plasma potassium between 6.5 and 8 mEq/L or ECG peaking of T wave): Administer i.v. 300 to 500 mL/hour of 10% dextrose solution containing 10 to 20 units of insulin/1 000 mL. Correct acidosis, if present, with i.v. sodium bicarbonate (44 to 132 mEq/L of glucose solution). Correct hyponatremia and hypovolemia, if present.

Once the patient's cardiac state has been stabilized, in the case of a recent acute ingestion of Slow-K, consideration should be given to the evacuation of the stomach. When overdosage is the result of chronic therapeutic ingestion, Slow-K should be discontinued immediately as well as potassium containing foods and medications and also potassium-sparing diuretics.

In treating hyperkalemia, it should be recalled that in patients who have been stabilized on digitalis, lowering the serum potassium concentration too rapidly can produce digitalis toxicity.

Dosage: The usual dietary intake of potassium by the average adult is 50 to 100 mEq/day. Potassium depletion sufficient to cause hypokalemia usually requires the loss of 200 or more mEq of potassium from the total body store.

Dosage must be adjusted to the individual needs of each patient, and to the cause and degree of the manifest or potential hypokalemic state. Where intermittent diuretic therapy is being used, Slow-K should preferably be given on days other than those on which diuretic is administered.

Prevention of hypokalemia: Typically in the range of 20 mEq/day.

Correction of Hypokalemia: Typically in the range of 40 to a maximum of 100 mEq/day, depending on initial plasma K^+ concentrations. The response to treatment should preferably be monitored by repeated plasma K^+ determinations, and Slow-K continued until the hypokalemia has been corrected.

The usual dosage range is 2 to 6 Slow-K tablets daily. It is recommended not to exceed 12 tablets daily. If the daily requirement exceeds 20 mEq K^+, it should be taken in divided doses, so that not more than 20 mEq K^+ is given in a single dose.

Slow-K is preferably administered after meals. The tablets must not be crushed, chewed or sucked but should be swallowed whole with fluids while the patient is upright.

The insoluble wax matrix is excreted in a softened form and may be found in the feces.

Supplied: Each light orange, round, biconvex, sugar-coated tablet, branded SLOW-K in black, contains: potassium chloride 600 mg (equivalent to 8 mEq of potassium) in a slow-release wax core. Nonmedicinal ingredients: acacia, cetostearyl alcohol, carnauba wax, dispersed buff 1715, gelatin, magnesium stearate, sucrose, talc, titanium dioxide, trichloroethane and white beeswax. Energy: 1.7 kJ (0.4 kcal). Alcohol-, bisulfite-, gluten-, lactose-, parabens-, sodium- and tartrazine-free. Bottles of 100 and 1 000. Protect from heat (i.e. store below 30°C) and humidity.

(Shown in Product Recognition Section)

SLOW-MAG™
Roberts

Magnesium Chloride
Magnesium Supplement

Supplied: Each white, round, biconvex, enteric-coated tablet, imprinted "Slow-Mag" in blue on one side, contains: magnesium 64 mg (5.26 mEq) as magnesium chloride hexahydrate 535 mg. Nonmedicinal ingredients: calcium carbonate, cellulose acetate phthalate, diethyl phthalate, FD&C Blue No. 2 lake, hydroxypropyl cellulose, magnesium stearate, povidone, talc and titanium dioxide. Bottles of 60.

(Shown in Product Recognition Section)

New Product 1998

Abbreviations used in the *CPS* are listed in the front of the WHITE SECTION.

SLOW-TRASICOR® Pr
Novartis Pharmaceuticals

Oxprenolol HCl
Antihypertensive

Pharmacology: Oxprenolol is a noncardioselective beta-adrenergic receptor blocking agent which possesses partial agonist activity. It is used in the treatment of hypertension.

The mechanism of the antihypertensive effect has not been established. Among the factors which may be involved are: a) competitive ability to antagonize catecholamine induced tachycardia at the beta-receptor sites in the heart, thus decreasing cardiac output; b) inhibition of renin release by the kidneys; c) inhibition of the vasomotor centres.

Oxprenolol is rapidly and well absorbed from the gastrointestinal tract. Peak plasma concentrations are reached approximately 0.5 to 1.5 hours after ingestion of the conventional oxprenolol tablet and 2 to 4 hours after the slow-release tablet.

There is a variable hepatic first-pass effect. The systemic bioavailability of oxprenolol hydrochloride ranges from 20 to 70%.

Oxprenolol is 80% bound to plasma proteins, and has a calculated distribution volume of 1.3 L/kg.

The mean plasma half-life for oral doses of the conventional tablet is 1.3 to 1.5 hours. The time taken for mean plasma levels to decrease from the peak value to half that value were approximately 4.5 hours for the 80 mg slow-release tablet and 7 hours for the 160 mg slow-release tablet.

Oxprenolol is primarily excreted in the urine in the form of inactive metabolites. Less than 5% is excreted unchanged and the major metabolite is a glucuronide.

β-blocking effects continue for at least 8 hours and up to 12 hours after a conventional tablet and for up to 24 hours after a slow-release tablet.

Indications: In patients with mild or moderate hypertension. It is usually used in combination with other drugs, particularly thiazide or thiazide-related diuretics. However, it may be tried alone as an initial agent in those patients in whom, in the judgment of the physician, treatment should be started with a beta-blocker rather than a diuretic. Therapy should start using Trasicor (regular formulation), and once the maintenance dose has been established, Slow-Trasicor may be substituted (see Dosage).

The combination of oxprenolol with a thiazide-related diuretic and/or peripheral vasodilator has been found to be compatible and generally more effective than oxprenolol alone. Experience with other antihypertensive agents has not shown evidence of incompatibility.

Oxprenolol is not recommended for the emergency treatment of hypertensive crisis.

Contraindications: Bronchospasm (including bronchial asthma); allergic rhinitis during the pollen season; sinus bradycardia and greater than first degree AV block; sick sinus syndrome; right ventricular failure secondary to pulmonary hypertension; congestive heart failure; cardiogenic shock; anesthesia with agents that produce myocardial depression, e.g. ether; known hypersensitivity to oxprenolol and related derivatives.

Warnings: Cardiac Failure: Special caution should be exercised when administering oxprenolol to patients with a history of heart failure. Sympathetic stimulation is a vital component supporting circulatory function in congestive heart failure, and inhibition with beta-blockade always carries the potential hazard of further depressing myocardial contractility and precipitating cardiac failure.

Oxprenolol acts selectively without abolishing the inotropic action of digitalis on the heart muscle. However, the positive inotropic action of digitalis may be reduced by the negative inotropic effect of oxprenolol when the 2 drugs are used concomitantly. The effects of beta-blockers and digitalis are additive in depressing AV conduction.

In patients without a history of cardiac failure, continued depression of the myocardium over a period of time can, in some cases, lead to cardiac failure. Therefore, at the first sign or symptom of impending cardiac failure, patients should be fully digitalized and/or given a diuretic, and the response observed closely. If cardiac failure continues, despite adequate digitalization and diuretic therapy, oxprenolol therapy should be immediately withdrawn.

In rare cases, preexisting AV conduction disorders may become aggravated (possibly leading to AV block). As a rule, no worsening of peripheral conduction disorders (left and/or right bundle-branch block) occur.

Abrupt Cessation of Therapy with Trasicor: Patients with angina should be warned against abrupt discontinuation of oxprenolol. There have been reports of severe exacerbation of angina and of myocardial infarction or ventricular arrhythmias occurring in patients with angina pectoris following abrupt discontinuation of beta-blocker therapy. The last 2 complications may occur with or without preceding exacerbation of angina pectoris. Therefore, when discontinuation of oxprenolol is planned in patients with angina pectoris, Trasicor should be substituted for Slow-Trasicor and then the dosage should be gradually reduced over a period of about 2 weeks and the patient should be carefully observed. The same frequency of administration should be maintained. In situations of greater urgency, oxprenolol therapy should be discontinued in a stepwise manner and the patient observed closely. If angina markedly worsens or acute coronary insufficiency develops, it is recommended that treatment with oxprenolol be reinstituted promptly, at least temporarily.

Various skin rashes and conjunctival xerosis have been reported with beta-blockers, including oxprenolol. A severe syndrome (oculo-muco-cutaneous syndrome) whose signs include conjunctivitis sicca and psoriasiform rashes, otitis, and sclerosing serositis has occurred with the chronic use of β-adrenergic-blocking agent, practolol. This syndrome has not been observed with oxprenolol or any other such agent. However, physicians should be alert to the possibility of such reactions and should discontinue treatment in the event that they occur.

Severe sinus bradycardia due to unopposed vagal activity may occur with the use of oxprenolol; in such cases, dosage should be reduced or withdrawn and the use of atropine and isoproterenol considered.

In patients with thyrotoxicosis, oxprenolol may give a false impression of improvement by masking the clinical signs of continuing hyperthyroidism or its complications. Therefore, abrupt withdrawal of oxprenolol may be followed by an exacerbation of the symptoms of hyperthyroidism, including thyroid storm. Oxprenolol does not alter thyroid function tests.

Precautions: In patients prone to nonallergic bronchospasm (e.g., chronic bronchitis, emphysema), oxprenolol should be administered with caution since it may block the bronchodilation produced by endogenous and exogenous catecholamine stimulation of $beta_2$-receptors.

Oxprenolol should be administered with caution to patients subject to spontaneous hypoglycemia or to diabetic patients (especially those with labile diabetes) who are receiving insulin or oral hypoglycemic agents. β-adrenergic blockers may mask the premonitory signs and symptoms of acute hypoglycemia. As β-blockade also reduces the release of insulin in response to hyperglycemia, it may be necessary to adjust the dosage of antidiabetic drugs.

Appropriate laboratory tests should be performed at regular intervals during long-term treatment.

There may be increased difficulty in treating an allergic type reaction in patients on β-blockers. In these patients, the reaction may be more severe due to pharmacologic effects of the β-blockers and problems with fluid changes. Epinephrine should be administered with caution since it may not have its usual effects in the treatment of anaphylaxis. On the one hand, larger doses of epinephrine may be needed to overcome the bronchospasm, while on the other, these doses can be associated with excessive α-adrenergic stimulation with consequent hypertension, reflex bradycardia and heart block and possible potentiation of bronchospasm. Alternatives to the use of large doses of epinephrine include vigorous supportive care such as fluids and the use of β-agonists including parenteral salbutamol or isoproterenol to overcome bronchospasm and norepinephrine to overcome hypotension.

In Patients Undergoing Elective or Emergency Surgery: The management of patients being treated with β-blockers and undergoing elective or emergency surgery is controversial. Although β-adrenergic receptor blockade impairs the ability of the heart to respond to beta-adrenergically mediated reflex stimuli, abrupt discontinuation of therapy with oxprenolol may be followed by severe complications (see Warnings). Some patients receiving β-adrenergic blocking agents have been subject to protracted severe hypotension during anesthesia. Difficulty in restarting and maintaining the heartbeat has also been reported.

For these reasons, in patients with angina undergoing elective surgery, Trasicor should be withdrawn gradually following

Slow-Trasicor (cont'd)

the recommendation given under Abrupt Cessation of Therapy (see Warnings). According to available evidence, all clinical and physiological effects of β-blockade are no longer present 48 hours after cessation of medication.

In emergency surgery, since oxprenolol is a competitive inhibitor of β-adrenergic receptor agonists, its effects may be reversed if necessary, by sufficient doses of such agonists as isoproterenol or levarterenol. The anesthetic selected should be one exhibiting as little negative inotropic activity as possible (see Contraindications).

In patients with acute or chronic inflammatory diseases an increase in the plasma levels of oxprenolol has been observed.

Plasma levels may also increase in the presence of severe hepatic insufficiency associated with a reduced metabolic rate.

Impaired renal function generally leads to an increase in the blood levels of oxprenolol, but the area under the concentration-time curve remains within (although at the upper limit of) the range recorded in subjects with healthy kidneys. The apparent elimination half-life for unchanged oxprenolol in patients with renal failure is comparable to the corresponding half-life values determined in subjects with no renal disease. Hence, there is no need to readjust the dosage in the presence of impaired renal function.

In patients with pheochromocytoma, a β-blocker should only be given together with an α-blocker.

Occupational Hazards: β-blockers may adversely affect the patient's reactions when driving or operating machinery.

Pregnancy: Oxprenolol crosses the placental barrier. It is not recommended that oxprenolol be given to pregnant women. The use of any drug in patients of childbearing potential requires that the anticipated benefit be weighed against possible hazards. β-blockers may possibly cause undesirable side effects (especially bradycardia) in the fetus and newborn infants.

Lactation: Oxprenolol passes into breast milk. If use of the drug is deemed essential, the patient should stop nursing.

Children: Although there is limited experience with oxprenolol in children, it is not recommended for pediatric use.

After the active substance has diffused out of the insoluble core of the Slow-Trasicor tablet, the empty matrix is excreted in a softened form and may be found in the feces.

Drug Interactions: As the antihypertensive effect of oxprenolol is enhanced by concomitant treatment with other antihypertensive agents, dosage should be adjusted appropriately.

Calcium antagonists of the verapamil-type must not be administered i.v. to patients receiving β-blocker therapy because of the danger of hypotension, cardiac arrhythmias and cardiac arrest.

β-blockers may potentiate the negative-inotropic and negative-dromotropic effect of antiarrhythmic agents such as quinidine and amiodarone.

Epinephrine or other substances displaying sympathomimetic activity (e.g., antitussives or nose and eye drops) may lead to hypertensive reactions under treatment with oxprenolol and other non-cardioselective β-blockers.

The hypertensive crisis which may follow the withdrawal of clonidine may be accentuated in the presence of β-blockade. It has been proposed that withdrawal of the β-blocker several days before the clonidine may reduce the danger of rebound effects.

The hypoglycemic effect of insulin or oral antidiabetic agents may be potentiated (see above).

Concurrent treatment with indomethacin may decrease the antihypertensive effect of β-blockers.

Since cimetidine increases the bioavailability of β-blockers which are mainly metabolized in the liver, the effect of oxprenolol may become potentiated during concomitant treatment with cimetidine.

When oxprenolol is used concomitantly with catecholamine-depleting drugs (such as reserpine or guanethidine) or MAO inhibitors, patients should be observed closely. The added β-adrenergic blocking action of this drug may produce an excessive reduction of sympathetic activity.

A deterioration in peripheral blood flow has been reported in predisposed patients receiving concomitant treatment with ergot alkaloids and β-blockers.

Attention should be paid to the cardiodepressant effect of inhalation anesthetics in patients receiving beta-blocker therapy (see above).

The central depressant effect of alcohol, analgesics, antihistamines, and psycho-active drugs (e.g., tricyclic antidepressants) may be potentiated.

β-blockers may diminish liver function and thus affect the metabolism of other drugs.

Adverse Effects: Cardiovascular: congestive heart failure (see Warnings), pulmonary edema, cardiac enlargement, secondary effects of decreased cardiac output which include: syncope, vertigo, lightheadedness and postural hypotension, severe bradycardia, lengthening of PR interval, second and third degree AV block, sinus arrest, palpitations, chest pains, peripheral vascular disorders (cold/tingling extremities) Raynaud's phenomenon, claudication, hot flushes.
Respiratory: shortness of breath, wheezing, bronchospasm, status asthmaticus.
CNS: headache, dizziness, anxiety, mental depression, nervousness, irritability, hallucinations, sleep disturbances including nightmares and insomnia, tinnitus, weakness, sedation, vivid dreams, vertigo, paresthesia and slurred speech.
Gastrointestinal: diarrhea, constipation, flatulence, heartburn, anorexia, nausea and vomiting, abdominal pain, dryness of mouth.
Allergic/Dermatological: (see Warnings), rash (psoriasiform and exanthematic), dry skin, pruritus, sweating.
Ophthalmological: keratoconjunctivitis, dry eyes, itching eyes, blurred vision.
Miscellaneous: impotence, decreased libido, nasal stuffiness, weight gain, exertional tiredness.
Clinical Laboratory: elevated transaminases, BUN, alkaline phosphatase and bilirubin have occurred in some patients. Thrombocytopenia and leukopenia, and hypoglycemia have also been reported rarely.

Overdose: Symptoms: The most common signs to be expected with overdosage of a β-adrenergic blocking agent are hypotension, bradycardia, congestive heart failure, bronchospasm, and hypoglycemia. Cardiogenic shock and cardiac arrest may develop. Impairment of consciousness and generalized convulsions may occur.

Treatment: If overdosage occurs, in all cases therapy with oxprenolol should be discontinued and the patient observed closely. In addition, if required, the following therapeutic measures are suggested:
Bradycardia and hypotension: Initially 1 to 2 mg atropine sulfate should be given i.v. If a satisfactory effect is not achieved a pressor agent such as norepinephrine may be administered after preceding treatment with atropine. Glucagon in a dose of 1 to 10 mg can also be administered.
Heart block: (second or third degree): isoproterenol or transvenous cardiac pacemaker.
Congestive heart failure: conventional therapy.
Bronchospasm: i.v. aminophylline or a β_2-agonist (e.g., salbutamol, terbutaline).
Hypoglycemia: i.v. glucose.
Convulsions: i.v. diazepam.

It should be remembered that oxprenolol is a competitive antagonist of isoproterenol and hence large doses of isoproterenol can be expected to reverse many of the effects of excessive doses of oxprenolol. However, the complications of excess isoproterenol should not be overlooked.

Dosage: Oxprenolol is usually used in conjunction with other antihypertensive agents, particularly thiazide diuretics, but may be used alone (see Indications).

Dosage must always be adjusted according to the individual requirements of the patient, within the following guidelines:
Initial Dosage: Treatment should be initiated with Trasicor (regular formulation), 20 mg 3 times a day, followed by upward titration of the dose 3 times a day, with increases of 60 mg/day at 1 to 2 week intervals until adequate control of blood pressure is obtained.
Maintenance Dosage: Once the optimal dose has been established, the total daily dose of Trasicor (regular formulation) may be given twice a day although no comparison studies between the 3 and 2 times daily regimen have been carried out. Alternatively, an equivalent single daily dose of Slow-Trasicor may be substituted, and should be taken in the morning. Slow-Trasicor tablets should be swallowed whole. The usual effective dose range is 120 to 320 mg/day, and the daily dosage should not exceed 480 mg.

Supplied: 80 mg: Each light red, round, biconvex, film-coated, slow-release tablet, imprinted CG on one side and BEB on the other, contains: oxprenolol HCl 80 mg. Nonmedicinal ingredients: calcium stearate, cellulose compounds, colloidal silicon dioxide, iron oxide red, glycerin esters of palmitic acid and stearic acid, lactose, magnesium stearate, methacrylic acid, polysorbate, talc and titanium dioxide. Energy: 1.4 kJ (0.33 kcal). Alcohol-, bisulfite-, gluten-, parabens-, sodium- and tartrazine-free. Bottles of 100.

160 mg: Each white, round, biconvex, film-coated, slow-release tablet, imprinted CG on one side and BNB on the other, contains: oxprenolol HCl 160 mg. Nonmedicinal ingredients: calcium stearate, cellulose compounds, colloidal silicon dioxide, glycerin esters of palmitic acid and stearic acid, lactose, magnesium stearate, methacrylic acid, polysorbate, talc and titanium dioxide. Energy: 2.8 kJ (0.67 kcal). Alcohol-, bisulfite-, gluten-, parabens-, sodium- and tartrazine-free. Bottles of 100.

Protect from heat (i.e., store below 30°C).

(Shown in Product Recognition Section)

Reviewed 1997

SMA®, PREEMIE
Wyeth-Ayerst

Low Birthweight Infant Formula

Supplied: Each bottle contains: water; skim milk; whey protein concentrate; lactose; malto-dextrins; oleo (beef), coconut, high monounsaturated safflower and soybean oils; medium chain triglycerides (coconut oil origin); soy lecithin; calcium carrageenan; potassium bicarbonate and chloride; calcium carbonate and chloride, magnesium chloride; sodium citrate; ferrous, manganese, zinc and cupric sulfates; ascorbic acid; alpha tocopheryl acetate; niacinamide; vitamin A palmitate; calcium pantothenate; dibasic calcium phosphate; biotin, thiamine hydrochloride; riboflavin; pyridoxine hydrochloride; beta-carotene; folic acid; phytonadione; cholecalciferol; cyanocobalamin; taurine.

SMA, Preemie 20 kcal (84 kJ)/30 mL: Ready-to-feed presterilized disposable bottles (hospital use only) of 100 mL, cases of 48.

SMA, Preemie 24 kcal (100 kJ)/30 mL: Ready-to-feed presterilized disposable bottles (hospital use only) of 100 mL, cases of 48.

Preemie SMA 20 kcal (84 kJ)/30 mL is **not a dilution** of Preemie SMA 24 kcal (100 kJ)/30 mL. It is reformulated and yields the same essential proteins, vitamins and minerals.

SMA® Preparations
Wyeth-Ayerst

Milk Protein (Whey Predominant)
Infant Formula

Indications: A nutritionally complete cow's milk-based infant formula for routine feeding of infants for the first year of life if breast-feeding is not an option or if a supplement is required. Contains vitamin A in the form of beta-carotene and the 5 major nucleotides found in breast milk.

Supplied: Protein: whey-predominant (60% lactalbumin: 40% casein). Carbohydrate: lactose. Fat: polyunsaturated 18.7%, monounsaturated 37.3%, saturated 44.1%. Vitamins and Minerals: at recommended levels.

SMA Iron-fortified concentrated liquid contains (by decreasing quantity): skim milk; water; reduced minerals whey; oleo (beef), coconut and soybean oils; lactose; high monounsaturate safflower or sunflower oil; soy lecithin; potassium bicarbonate; calcium chloride; ascorbic acid; sodium bicarbonate; potassium chloride; sodium citrate; ferrous sulfate; taurine; calcium citrate; cytidine-5′-monophosphate; zinc sulfate; calcium carrageenan; alpha-tocopheryl acetate; disodium uridine-5′-monophosphate; adenosine-5′-monophosphate; niacinamide; disodium inosine-5′-monophosphate; disodium guanosine-5′-monophosphate; cupric sulfate; vitamin A palmitate; calcium pantothenate; thiamine hydrochloride; riboflavin; pyridoxine hydrochloride; manganese sulfate; beta-carotene; folic acid; phytonadione; potassium iodide; biotin; cholecalciferol; cyanocobalamin. Note:

Composition of powder, ready-to-serve and ready-to-feed formulas may vary slightly. See Table I.

Table I—SMA Preparations

SMA Iron-fortified Concentrated Liquid

Analysis	Normal Dilution 100 mL	
Energy		
Calories	67	kcal
Kilojoules	280	kJ
Carbohydrate	7.2	g
Fat	3.6	g
Linoleic acid	0.33	g
Protein	1.5	g
60% lactalbumin: 40% casein		
Ash	0.25	g
Vitamin A	200	IU
Vitamin D	40	IU
Vitamin E	0.95	IU
Vitamin K_1	0.0055	mg
Vitamin C	5.5	mg
Thiamine	0.067	mg
Riboflavin	0.1	mg
Niacin	0.5	mg
Vitamin B_6	0.042	mg
Folic acid	0.005	mg
Vitamin B_{12}	0.00013	mg
Biotin	0.0015	mg
d-Pantothenic acid	0.21	mg
Calcium	42	mg
Phosphorus	28	mg
Magnesium	4.5	mg
Iron	1.2	mg
Iodine	0.006	mg
Zinc	0.5	mg
Copper	0.047	mg
Manganese	0.01	mg
Sodium	15	mg
Potassium	56	mg
Chloride	37.5	mg
Choline	10	mg
Taurine	3.76	mg
Nucleotides	3	mg

Concentrated Liquid: Normal dilution: equal parts SMA concentrated liquid and water. Available as regular (0.15 mg iron/100 mL) and iron-fortified (1.2 mg iron/100 mL). Cans of 385 mL, cases of 12.

Powder: Normal dilution: 1 scoop SMA powder and 60 mL water. Scoop provided in each can. Available as regular (0.15 mg iron/100 mL) and iron-fortified (1.2 mg iron/100 mL). Cans of 450 g, cases of 6.

Ready-to-Serve: No dilution required: 20 kcal/30 mL (280 kJ/100 mL). Available as regular (0.15 mg iron/100 mL) and iron-fortified (1.2 mg iron/100 mL). Cans of 385 mL, cases of 12.

Ready-to-Feed: No dilution required. For hospital use only. Presterilized, disposable bottles of SMA 20 kcal/30 mL (280 kJ/100 mL) available as regular (0.15 mg iron/100 mL) and iron-fortified (1.2 mg iron/100 mL) and SMA 24 kcal/30 mL (335 kJ/100 mL) available as iron-fortified (1.44 mg iron/100 mL). Bottles of 100 mL, cases of 48.

SNAKE BITE ANTISERUM

Wyeth-Ayerst

see ANTIVENIN

SODIUM BICARBONATE

General Monograph, CPhA

Alkalinizer

> This monograph has been compiled by CPhA. It may contain information different from that approved by Therapeutic Products Programme, Health Canada, and the pharmaceutical manufacturers' approval has not been requested.

Pharmacology: Sodium bicarbonate is an alkalinizing agent. It increases plasma bicarbonate, buffers excess hydrogen ions, raises blood pH and reverses the clinical signs of acidosis. Sodium bicarbonate dissociates to sodium and bicarbonate ions in water. Sodium is the principal cation of the extracellular fluid. Bicarbonate is found in body fluids and plasma. The normal plasma level of bicarbonate ranges from 24 to 31 mmol/L. Bicarbonate is a component of the principal extracellular buffer in the body, the bicarbonate-carbonic acid buffer. Bicarbonate buffers excess hydrogen ions by converting to carbonic acid or carbon dioxide and water. Plasma bicarbonate is regulated by the kidney. In a healthy adult with normal renal function, less than 1% of bicarbonate is excreted in the urine, most of the glomerular filtered bicarbonate ion is reabsorbed.

Indications: Oral: A gastric, systemic and urinary alkalinizer. Sodium bicarbonate is also used in conditions (e.g., chronic renal failure) requiring prolonged therapy with an alkalinizing agent.

Parenteral: Sodium bicarbonate i.v. is indicated for the treatment of metabolic acidosis which may occur in severe renal disease, uncontrolled diabetes, shock or severe dehydration, extracorporeal circulation of blood, cardiac arrest and severe primary lactic acidosis. The underlying cause of the acidosis must be treated in addition to sodium bicarbonate therapy.

For the treatment of certain drug intoxications, including long-acting barbiturates, salicylates, tricyclic antidepressants or methyl alcohol and in hemolytic reactions requiring alkalinization of the urine to diminish nephrotoxicity of blood pigments.

Used in severe diarrhea when loss of bicarbonate has been significant.

Sodium bicarbonate is also used as an adjunct in the treatment of hyperkalemia.

Vigorous bicarbonate therapy is required in any form of metabolic acidosis where a rapid increase in plasma CO_2 content is crucial (e.g., cardiac arrest, circulatory insufficiency due to shock or severe dehydration, and in severe primary lactic acidosis or severe diabetic acidosis).

Contraindications: Patients with: metabolic or respiratory alkalosis, hypocalcemia (because of an increased risk of alkalosis-induced tetany), excessive chloride loss from vomiting or from continuous gastrointestinal suction, states of hypoventilation or a risk of developing diuretic-induced hypochloremic alkalosis.

Precautions: Routine use during cardiopulmonary resuscitation (CPR) is not recommended. In certain circumstances such as pre-existing metabolic acidosis, hyperkalemia, tricyclic or phenobarbital overdose or prolonged cardiac arrest, bicarbonate may be useful in CPR. For more information on the use of drugs during CPR, see Drugs Used in Cardiac Arrest in the Clin-Info section.

Sodium bicarbonate should be used with caution, due to the potentially large sodium load, in edematous or sodium-retaining conditions (e.g., congestive heart failure), in renal insufficiency (e.g., oliguria or anuria), in patients receiving corticosteroids or corticotropin.

Administration of i.v. sodium bicarbonate may cause fluid or solute overload. This results in the dilution of serum electrolytes, overhydration, congestive states or pulmonary edema. Hypertonic solutions may cause phlebitis. Avoid extravasation.

Metabolic alkalosis from excessive sodium bicarbonate therapy may cause hypokalemia (due to an intracellular potassium shift) and decreased ionized serum calcium concentrations (which may result in tetany and carpopedal spasm as the plasma pH rises). To minimize the risks of bicarbonate administration in preexisting hypokalemia and/or hypocalcemia, these electrolyte disturbances should be corrected before or during sodium bicarbonate therapy.

The use of sodium bicarbonate in the treatment of diabetic ketoacidosis is controversial. Sodium bicarbonate may produce paradoxical cerebrospinal fluid acidosis which may result in decreased CNS function and increased stupor. Severe hypokalemia may result due to an intracellular shift of potassium mediated by both insulin and bicarbonate therapy. In addition, sodium bicarbonate has the potential of causing rebound alkalosis, impaired oxygen delivery to tissues, lactic acidosis and sodium overload. In general, sodium bicarbonate should be reserved for severe acidosis (e.g., arterial pH < 7), and its benefits in the management of diabetic ketoacidosis must be weighed against the complications of bicarbonate therapy.

Sodium bicarbonate should not be used as an antidote in the treatment of acute ingestion of strong acids.

Children under 2 years: I.V. administration of sodium bicarbonate in neonates and children under 2 years should not exceed 8 mmol/kg/day. Slow administration rates using less concentrated solutions (e.g., 0.5 mmol/mL or 4.2%) are recommended to reduce the possibility of producing hypernatremia, decreasing cerebrospinal fluid pressure or inducing intracranial hemorrhage.

Drug Interactions: Sodium bicarbonate is physically and/or chemically incompatible with many drugs. Specialized references should be consulted for specific compatibility information.

Pregnancy: It is not known whether sodium bicarbonate can cause fetal harm when administered during pregnancy. It should be used during pregnancy only when clearly needed.

Adverse Effects: Oral sodium bicarbonate may cause gastric distention and flatulence.

Extravasation of hypertonic solutions of sodium bicarbonate has been reported to cause chemical cellulitis resulting in tissue necrosis, ulceration, and/or sloughing at the site of injection.

Excessive parenteral doses may cause hypokalemia, accompanied by dry mouth, increased thirst, irregular heart beat, mood or mental changes, muscle cramps or pain, or weak pulse.

Administration of large doses or administration to patients with renal impairment may cause metabolic alkalosis which may be accompanied by hyperirritability or tetany.

Rapid alkalinization with sodium bicarbonate, in patients with ketoacidosis, may result in clouding consciousness, cerebral dysfunction, obtundation, seizures, and peripheral tissue hypoxia and lactic acidosis.

Hypernatremia, hyperosmolality and peripheral or pulmonary edema may occur when sodium bicarbonate is administered in large doses or in patients with renal insufficiency, congestive heart failure or those predisposed to sodium retention and edema.

Overdose: Symptoms and Treatment: Should alkalosis result, the bicarbonate should be stopped and the patient managed according to the degree of alkalosis present. Sodium chloride 0.9% injection may be given i.v. Potassium chloride may also be indicated if hypokalemia is present. Severe alkalosis may be accompanied by hyperirritability or tetany and these symptoms may be controlled by calcium gluconate. An acidifying agent such as ammonium chloride may also be indicated in severe alkalosis.

Dosage: To aid in converting: 84 mg of sodium bicarbonate = 1 mmol (1 mEq) of sodium bicarbonate = 1 mmol (1 mEq) each of sodium and bicarbonate ions. An 8.4% sodium bicarbonate solution = 84 mg/mL of sodium bicarbonate = 1 mmol (1 mEq)/mL of sodium bicarbonate.

Oral: Urinary Alkalinizer: Adults: 4 g initially, then 1 to 2 g every 4 hours. Some patients may require up to 16 g daily. Dosage should be titrated to maintain desired urinary pH.

Acidosis Associated with Chronic Renal Failure: Adults: Initial dose is 1.7 to 3 g daily in divided doses, with subsequent adjustment according to plasma bicarbonate concentration; fluid and electrolyte balance must be carefully monitored in these patients because of the potentially large sodium load associated with bicarbonate therapy.

Parenteral: Acidosis: Adults and children over 2 years: The dosage of sodium bicarbonate can be based on the severity of the condition, laboratory determinations and the patient's weight.

Frequent evaluations of the patient are required during therapy to monitor acid-base and fluid and electrolyte balance. Full correction of acid-base balance should not be attempted during the first 24 hours because of the risk of delayed compensation and alkalosis. The initial dose is usually 2 to 5 mmol/kg administered as an i.v. infusion over 4 to 8 hours. Repeated dosage will be dependent on response to the initial dose and the clinical condition of the patient with respect to the cause of acidosis. Generally, the magnitude and frequency of subsequent doses should decrease once symptoms of severe acidosis have ameliorated.

Children: The initial dose for infants and children under 2 years is usually 1 mmol/kg administered slowly in a concentration of 0.5 mmol/mL (see Precautions). Subsequent dosage will depend on the clinical status of the patient. A maximum daily dose of 8 mmol/kg has been recommended.

Cardiac Arrest: Sodium bicarbonate is not recommended for routine use during CPR. It is only used when clearly indicated and where adequte ventilation can be ensured (see Precautions). For more information on the use of drugs during CPR, see Drugs Used in Cardiac Arrest in the Clin-Info Section.

Adults: An initial dose of 1 mmol/kg (1 mL of sodium bicarbonate 8.4% solution per kg body weight) may be given by rapid i.v. injection with repeated doses of 0.5 mmol/kg (0.5 mL sodium bicarbonate 8.4%/kg) every 10 minutes during continued cardiac arrest.

Children: an initial dose of 1 mmol/kg may be given slowly i.v. in a concentration of 1 mmol/mL (8.4% solution) to children 2 years of age and older. Subsequent doses of 1 mmol/kg may be considered at 10-minute intervals during continued cardiac arrest. Infants and children under 2 years may receive the above dosage, but a lower solution concentration is recommended (e.g., 0.5 mmol/mL or 4.2%).

Reviewed 1997

SODIUM BICARBONATE INJECTION
Abbott
Alkalizer

Supplied: 4.2%: Each mL contains: sodium bicarbonate 42 mg (0.5 mEq). Abboject syringes of 10 mL, boxes of 10.

7.5%: Each mL contains: sodium bicarbonate 75 mg (0.9 mEq). Abboject syringes of 50 mL, boxes of 10.

8.4%: Each mL contains: sodium bicarbonate 84 mg (1 mEq). Vials of 50 mL, trays of 25. Abboject syringes of 10 and 50 mL, boxes of 10.

SODIUM BICARBONATE INJECTION USP
Astra
Alkalizer

Pharmacology: I.V. sodium bicarbonate therapy increases plasma bicarbonate, buffers excess hydrogen ion concentration, raises blood pH and reverses the clinical manifestations of acidosis.

Sodium bicarbonate in water dissociates to provide sodium and bicarbonate ions. Sodium is the principal cation of the extracellular fluid and plays a large part in the therapy of fluid and electrolyte disturbances. Bicarbonate is a normal constituent of body fluids and the normal plasma level ranges from 24 to 31 mmol/L. Plasma concentration is regulated by the kidney through acidification of the urine when there is a deficit or by alkalinization of the urine when there is an excess. Bicarbonate anion is considered labile since at a proper concentration of hydrogen ion it may be converted to carbonic acid and thence to its volatile form, carbon dioxide which is excreted by the lung. Normally a ratio of 1:20 (carbonic acid: bicarbonate) is present in the extracellular fluid. In a healthy adult with normal kidney function, practically all the glomerular filtered bicarbonate ion is reabsorbed; less than 1% is excreted in the urine.

Indications: In the treatment of metabolic acidosis which may occur in severe renal disease, uncontrolled diabetes, circulatory insufficiency due to shock or severe dehydration, extracorporeal circulation of blood, cardiac arrest and severe primary lactic acidosis.

In the treatment of certain drug intoxications, including barbiturates (where dissociation of the barbiturate-protein complex is desired), in poisoning by salicylates or methyl alcohol and in hemolytic reactions requiring alkalinization of the urine to diminish nephrotoxicity of blood pigments.

In severe diarrhea which is often accompanied by a significant loss of bicarbonate.

Treatment of metabolic acidosis should, if possible, be superimposed on measures designed to control the basic cause of the acidosis, e.g. insulin in uncomplicated diabetes, blood volume restoration in shock. Since an appreciable time interval may elapse before all of the ancillary effects are brought about, bicarbonate therapy is indicated to minimize risks inherent to the acidosis itself.

Vigorous bicarbonate therapy is required in any form of metabolic acidosis where a rapid increase in plasma total CO_2 content is crucial, e.g., cardiac arrest, circulatory insufficiency due to shock or severe dehydration, and in severe primary lactic acidosis or severe diabetic acidosis.

Contraindications: In patients who are losing chloride by vomiting or from continuous gastrointestinal suction, and in patients receiving diuretics known to produce a hypochloremic alkalosis.

Warnings: Caution: Sodium Bicarbonate Injection is under pressure (see Dosage).

Solutions containing sodium ions should be used with great care, if at all, in patients with congestive heart failure, severe renal insufficiency and in clinical states in which there exists edema with sodium retention.

In patients with diminished renal function, administration of solutions containing sodium ions may result in sodium retention.

The i.v. administration of these solutions can cause fluid and/or solute overloading resulting in dilution of serum electrolyte concentrations, overhydration, congested states or pulmonary edema.

The risk of dilutional states is inversely proportional to the electrolyte concentrations of administered parenteral solutions. The risk of solute overload causing congested states with peripheral and pulmonary edema is directly proportional to the electrolyte concentrations of such solutions.

Extravascular infiltration should be avoided (see Adverse Effects).

Precautions: The aim of all bicarbonate therapy is to produce a substantial correction of the low total CO_2 content and blood pH, but the risks of overdosage and alkalosis should be avoided. Hence, repeated fractional doses and periodic monitoring by appropriate laboratory tests are recommended to minimize the possibility of overdosage.

The potentially large loads of sodium given with bicarbonate require that caution be exercised in the use of sodium bicarbonate injection in patients with congestive heart failure or other edematous or sodium-retaining states, as well as in patients with oliguria or anuria. See Supplied section for amounts of sodium present in solutions. Caution must be exercised in the administration of parenteral fluids, especially those containing sodium ions, to patients receiving corticosteroids or corticotropin.

Potassium depletion may predispose to metabolic alkalosis and coexistent hypocalcemia may be associated with carpopedal spasm as the plasma pH rises. These dangers can be minimized if such electrolyte imbalances are appropriately treated prior to or concomitantly with bicarbonate infusion.

The addition of sodium bicarbonate to parenteral solutions containing calcium should be avoided, except where compatibility has been previously established. Precipitation or haze may result from sodium bicarbonate-calcium admixtures.

Children under 2 Years: Rapid injection (10 mL/min) of hypertonic sodium bicarbonate solutions into neonates and children under 2 years of age may produce hypernatremia, a decrease in cerebrospinal fluid pressure and possible intracranial hemorrhage. The rate of administration in such patients should therefore be limited to no more than 8 mmol/kg/day. In emergencies such as cardiac arrest, the risk of rapid infusion must be weighed against the potential for fatality due to acidosis.

Pregnancy: Animal reproduction studies have not been conducted with sodium bicarbonate. It is also not known whether sodium bicarbonate can cause fetal harm when administered to a pregnant woman or can affect reproduction capacity. Sodium bicarbonate injection should be given to a pregnant woman only if clearly needed.

Adverse Effects: Inadvertent extravasation of i.v. administered hypertonic solutions of sodium bicarbonate have been reported to cause chemical cellulitis because of their alkalinity. Tissue necrosis, ulceration or sloughing at the site of infiltration may occur. Prompt elevation of the area, warmth and local injection of lidocaine or hyaluronidase are recommended to prevent sloughing of extravasated i.v. infusions.

Overdose: Symptoms and Treatment: Should alkalosis result, the bicarbonate should be stopped and the patient managed according to the degree of alkalosis present. Sodium chloride injection 0.9% may be given i.v. Potassium chloride may also be indicated if there is hypokalemia. Severe alkalosis may be accompanied by hyperirritability or tetany and these symptoms may be controlled by calcium gluconate. An acidifying agent such as ammonium chloride may also be indicated in severe alkalosis (see Warnings and Precautions).

Dosage: Caution: Sodium Bicarbonate Injection is under pressure. The vial should be at room temperature when inserting the needle into the rubber stopper. Do not shake before use.

Sodium bicarbonate injection is for single use only. Discard unused portion.

Sodium bicarbonate injection is administered by the i.v. route.

Adults: In cardiac arrest, a rapid i.v. dose of 200 to 300 mmol of bicarbonate is suggested for adults. Caution should be observed in emergencies where very rapid infusion of large quantities of bicarbonate is indicated. Bicarbonate solutions are hypertonic and may produce an undesirable rise in plasma sodium concentration in the process of correcting the metabolic acidosis. In cardiac arrest, however, the risks from acidosis exceed those of hypernatremia.

Children under 2 Years: In infants (up to 2 years of age) i.v. administration of a dose not to exceed 8 mmol/kg/day is recommended. Slow administration rates are recommended in neonates, to guard against the possibility of producing hypernatremia, decreasing cerebrospinal fluid pressure and inducing intracranial hemorrhage.

In less urgent forms of metabolic acidosis, sodium bicarbonate injection may be added to other i.v. fluids. The amount of bicarbonate to be given to older children and adults over a 4 to 8 hour period is approximately 2 to 5 mmol/kg of body-weight, depending upon the severity of the acidosis as judged by the lowering of total CO_2 content, blood pH and clinical condition of the patient. Bicarbonate therapy should always be planned in a stepwise fashion since the degree of response from a given dose is not precisely predictable. Initially an infusion of 2 to 5 mmol/kg body weight over a period of 4 to 8 hours will produce a measurable improvement in the abnormal acid-base status of the blood. The next step of therapy is dependent upon the clinical response of the patient. If severe symptoms have abated, then the frequency of administration and the size of the dose may be reduced.

In general, it is unwise to attempt full correction of a low total CO_2 content during the first 24 hours of therapy, since this may be accompanied by an unrecognized alkalosis because of a delay in the readjustment of ventilation to normal. Owing to this lag, the achievement of total CO_2 content of about 20 mmol/L at the end of the first day of therapy will usually be associated with a normal blood pH. Further modification of the acidosis to completely normal values usually occurs in the presence of normal kidney function when and if the cause of the acidosis can be controlled. Values for total CO_2 which are brought to normal or above normal within the first day of therapy are very likely to be associated with grossly alkaline values for blood pH, with ensuing undesired side effects.

Supplied: 7.5%: Each mL of sterile, nonpyrogenic, hypertonic solution contains: sodium bicarbonate 75 mg (0.9 mmol) in water for injection. Single use vials of 50 mL.

8.4%: Each mL of sterile, nonpyrogenic, hypertonic solution contains: sodium bicarbonate 84 mg (1 mmol) in water for injection. Single use vials of 50 mL.

The solutions contain no bacteriostat, antimicrobial agent or added buffer and are intended only for use as a single-dose injection. Discard unused portion. Do not use if the solutions are colored or contain a precipitate. pH: 7.0 to 8.5. Store at controlled room temperature (15 to 30°C).

Reviewed 1999

SODIUM CHLORIDE INHALATION SOLUTION
BDH
Sodium Chloride
Diluent

Supplied: 0.45% (Hypotonic): Each plastic vial contains: sodium chloride 0.45% w/v. Vials of 3 and 5 mL, cartons of 100.

0.9% (Isotonic): Each plastic vial contains: sodium chloride 0.9% w/v. Dey-Pak vials of 3 and 5 mL, cartons of 100 (for respiratory therapy). Dey-Vial tapered vials of 3 and 5 mL with Leur tip, cartons of 250 (for tracheal lavage).

3% (Hypertonic): Each plastic vial contains: sodium chloride 3% w/v. Vials of 15 mL, cartons of 50.

10% (Hypertonic): Each plastic vial contains: sodium chloride 10% w/v. Vials of 15 mL, cartons of 50.

Contains no bacteriostatic agents or preservatives. **Not for injection.** Discard any unused portion of the contents. Store at controlled room temperature 15 to 30°C.

SODIUM CHLORIDE INJECTION, USP
Abbott
Isotonic Vehicle—Electrolyte Replenisher

Supplied: Bacteriostatic with Preservative: Each mL contains: sodium chloride 9 mg. Also contains benzyl alcohol and hydrochloric acid. Fliptop plastic vials of 10, 20, 30 and 100 mL. Boxes of 10 and 25.

Preservative-free: Each mL contains: sodium chloride 9 mg. Also contains hydrochloric acid and/or sodium hydroxide. Osmolarity: 0.3 mOsmol/mL. Fliptop plastic vials of 10 and 20 mL. Boxes of 25.

SODIUM CHLORIDE INJECTION USP
Astra
Isotonic Saline

Indications: Sodium chloride injection USP can be used as an isotonic vehicle for many parenteral drugs. Injections may also be administered s.c. to infants in conjunction with hyaluronidase, which facilitates the absorption of the fluid.

Precautions: Cardiovascular disease; patients receiving corticosteroids, corticotropin or drugs that may give rise to sodium retention.

Adverse Effects: Excessive amounts by any route may cause hypokalemia and acidosis.

Excessive amounts by the parenteral route may precipitate congestive heart failure and acute pulmonary edema, especially in patients with cardiovascular disease.

Dosage: Parenterally, 0.45 to 0.9% solution, amount and concentration varying with circumstances.

Supplied: Each mL contains: sodium chloride 9 mg in single use glass vials or plastic ampuls (Polyamp Duofit) (suitable for Luer fit and Luer lock syringes) of 10 mL. Preservative-free. The solution has an osmolarity of approximately 0.31 mOsm/mL (calc.). Do not use if solution is cloudy or contains a precipitate. Discard unused portion. Store at room temperature (15 to 30°C).

SODIUM CHLORIDE IRRIGATION SOLUTION USP

Astra

Sodium Chloride

Irrigation Solution

Indications: A sterile solution which exerts a mechanical cleansing action for: sterile irrigation of body cavities, tissues, wounds, indwelling urethral catheters, surgical drainage tubes; washing and rinsing purposes that allow use of a sterile nonpyrogenic electrolyte solution; soaking of surgical dressings, instruments and laboratory specimens.

Contraindications: Sodium chloride irrigation solution 0.9% is for topical use only and should never be administered by parenteral injection. Solutions containing electrolytes should not be used for irrigation during electrosurgical procedures. Irrigating solutions should not be used in situations where systemic absorption may occur.

Precautions: Sodium chloride irrigation solution should be used with caution in patients with severe renal or cardiac dysfunction, since systemic absorption may substantially alter cardiopulmonary or renal function. If adverse effects, overhydration or solute overload occur, the solution should be discontinued, the patient evaluated, and appropriate corrective therapy instituted if necessary.

Sodium chloride irrigation solution should not be used unless the solution is clear, and the ampul seal intact. Once opened, the solution should be used promptly to minimize the possibility of bacterial contamination. Any unused portion should be discarded.

Adverse Effects: Adverse effects resulting from irrigation of body cavities, tissues, or indwelling catheters are usually avoidable when appropriate procedures are followed. Displaced catheters or drainage tubes can lead to irrigation or infiltration of unintended structures. Excessive volume or pressure during irrigation of closed cavities may result in distention or disruption of tissues. Inadvertent contamination from careless technique may transmit infection.

Dosage: Sodium chloride irrigation solution is administered topically, or during urological irrigation via an administration set connected to an indwelling urethral catheter designed for intermittent or 2-way flow.

Dosage of the solution depends on the capacity or surface area of the structure to be irrigated, as well as on the nature of the procedure.

The use of aseptic technique is essential when irrigating solutions are used for irrigation of body cavities, wounds, and urethral catheters, or when used for wetting dressing which comes into contact with body tissues.

Supplied: Each mL of isotonic sterile solution contains: sodium chloride 9 mg in sterile water. Polyamp units (single use plastic ampuls) of 30 and 50 mL. Store at room temperature (15 to 30°C). Do not use if solution is cloudy or contains a precipitate. Discard unused portion.

SODIUM EDECRIN® Ⓟ

MSD

see EDECRIN

SODIUM SULAMYD® Ⓟ

Schering

Sulfacetamide Sodium

Ophthalmic Antibacterial

Indications: The treatment of conjunctivitis, corneal ulcer, and other superficial ocular infections due to susceptible microorganisms, and as adjunctive treatment in systemic therapy of trachoma.

Contraindications: Hypersensitivity to sulfonamide preparations.

Precautions: The solutions are incompatible with silver preparations. Ophthalmic ointments may retard corneal healing. Nonsusceptible organisms, including fungi, may proliferate with the use of these preparations. Do not use solutions if colored. Sulfonamides may be inactivated by the para-aminobenzoic acid present in purulent exudates. If sensitivity reactions occur, discontinue treatment.

Dosage: 30% Solution: Conjunctivitis or corneal ulcer: 1 drop into lower conjunctival sac every 2 hours or less frequently according to severity of infection. Trachoma (adjunctive treatment): 2 drops every 4 hours.

10% Solution with Methylcellulose: 1 or 2 drops into the lower conjunctival sac every 2 or 3 hours during the day and less often at night.

10% Ointment: Apply a small amount 4 times daily and at bedtime. The ointment may be used adjunctively with either of the solution forms.

Supplied: Ophthalmic Ointment: Sulfacetamide sodium USP 10% in a sterile petrolatum base. Nonmedicinal ingredients: benzalkonium chloride, methylparaben, propylparaben, sorbitan monolaurate and white petrolatum. Tubes of 3.5 g. Store away from heat.

Ophthalmic Solutions: Sulfacetamide sodium USP in sterile buffered 30% aqueous solution and 10% aqueous solution with methylcellulose USP. Nonmedicinal ingredients: 10%: hydroxypropyl methylcellulose, methylparaben, monobasic sodium phosphate, propylparaben, sodium thiosulfate and water. 30%: methylparaben, monobasic sodium phosphate, propylparaben, sodium thiosulfate and water. Plastic dropper bottles of 15 mL. Store between 2 and 30°C.

SODIUM THIOSULFATE INJECTION USP

Faulding

Antidote

Supplied: Each mL contains: sodium thiosulfate USP 25%. Vials of 10 mL, packages of 5. Store below 25°C. Protect from light.

SOFLAX™

Pharmascience

Docusate Sodium

Stool Softener

Supplied: 100 mg: Each orange, oval, soft gelatin capsule, identified PMS 100, contains: docusate sodium USP 100 mg. Unit dose packages of 30 and 100. Bottles of 60, 100 and 1 000.

200 mg: Each orange, oblong, soft gelatin capsule, imprinted P inside a triangle, contains: docusate sodium USP 200 mg. Bottles of 100 and 1 000.

New Product 1998

SOFLAX® EX

Pharmascience

Bisacodyl

Laxative

Supplied: Suppositories: Each rectal suppository contains: bisacodyl 10 mg. Boxes of 3 and 6. Store at room temperature less than 30°C.

Tablets: Each yellow, enteric-coated tablet contains: bisacodyl 5 mg. Unit dose packages of 10 and 30.

New Product 1998

SOFRACORT® Ⓟ

Hoechst Marion Roussel

Framycetin Sulfate—Gramicidin—Dexamethasone Compound

Antibiotic—Corticosteroid

Indications: Ear: Otitis externa (acute and chronic) and other inflammatory and seborrheic conditions of the external ear.

Eye: Blepharitis and infected eczema of the eyelid; allergic, infective and rosacea conjunctivitis; rosacea keratitis; scleritis and episcleritis; iridocyclitis, and other inflammatory conditions of the anterior segment of the eye.

Contraindications: Ear: Viral and fungal infections; acute purulent, untreated infections; perforation of the eardrum and known hypersensitivity to any of the ingredients.

Eye: Herpes simplex and other viral diseases of the cornea and conjunctiva; tuberculosis and fungal diseases of the eye; trachoma. Acute purulent, untreated infections of the eye, which, like other diseases caused by microorganisms, may be masked or enhanced by the presence of the steroid. Known hypersensitivity to any of the ingredients.

Precautions: Extended ophthalmic use of corticosteroids may increase intraocular pressure in some individuals in such cases, intraocular pressure should be checked regularly. In conditions causing thinning of the cornea, topical steroids may cause perforation. Cataract has occurred after prolonged treatment with topical steroids.

Pregnancy: The safety of prolonged use of topical steroids during pregnancy has not been substantiated. The benefits of use should be weighed against possible adverse effects on the fetus.

The drug should be discontinued if there are signs of sensitivity to any of its ingredients.

Patients are advised to inform the physicians of the prior use of corticosteroids.

Children: Although it is unlikely that infants will be treated with Sofracort for prolonged periods, there is a risk of adrenal suppression, even without occlusive dressings, after prolonged treatment of these patients with topical steroids.

Adverse Effects: See Precautions. Increased intraocular pressure; perforation of the cornea; hypersensitivity; burning or stinging of the eye.

Dosage: Drops: Ear: Instill 2 or 3 drops in the ear canal 3 or 4 times daily by tilting head to one side. Squeeze bottle carefully. To avoid possibility of reinfection later, do not touch ear with dropper. Alternatively, a saturated gauze wick may be inserted by the physician into the external auditory meatus.

Eye: In acute conditions, 1 or 2 drops every 1 to 2 hours may be instilled (generally for 2 or 3 days). Subsequently, 1 or 2 drops 3 or 4 times daily.

Ointment: Ear: Apply 2 or 3 times a day, including bedtime, to the outer portion of, and inside the ear canal and to adjacent areas if the infection has spread.

Eye: 2 or 3 times a day, or at bedtime if drops have been used during the day.

Supplied: Drops: Each mL of sterile drops contains: framycetin sulfate BP 5 mg, gramicidin 50 µg and dexamethasone 500 µg. pH is 4.5 to 5.0. Calibrated dropper bottles of 8 mL.

Ointment: Each g of sterile ointment contains: framycetin sulfate BP 5 mg, gramicidin 50 µg and dexamethasone 500 µg. Also contains Plastibase 30W. Tubes of 5 g.

Store at controlled room temperature. Use within 4 weeks of opening.

SOFRAMYCIN® Ointment Ⓟ
SOFRAMYCIN® Ophthalmic Ⓟ

Hoechst Marion Roussel

Framycetin Sulfate—Gramicidin

Framycetin Sulfate

Antibiotic

Pharmacology: Framycetin, a broad spectrum aminoglycoside antibiotic, is usually bactericidal in action. Although the exact mechanism of action has not been fully elucidated, the drug appears to inhibit protein synthesis in susceptible bacteria by binding to ribosomal subunits. In general, framycetin is active against many aerobic gram-negative bacteria and some aerobic gram-positive bacteria. The drug is inactive against fungi, viruses, and most anaerobic bacteria.

Soframycin (cont'd)

Indications: For local use in the treatment of infections caused by pyogenic organisms, in particular S. aureus, the proteus group of bacteria, coliforms and P. aeruginosa.
Ointment: The treatment of bacterial infections of the skin and mucous membrane caused by susceptible bacteria. These include such conditions as pyoderma, folliculitis, paronychia, sycosis barbae, and impetigo. Also useful in controlling secondary bacterial infections in skin carcinoma, burns, eczemas, contact dermatitis, seborrhea, acne, psoriasis, varicose ulcers, and neurodermatitis.
Ophthalmic Drops and Ointment: Treatment of bacterial blepharitis, conjunctivitis, styes, corneal abrasions and burns; prophylactically following removal of foreign bodies; corneal ulcers (sole treatment or as an adjunct to subconjunctival injection of framycetin).

Contraindications: Sensitivity to framycetin.

Framycetin should never be administered either i.v. or i.m. in view of the risk of irreversible ototoxicity or reversible nephrotoxicity.

Precautions: Cross sensitization may occur among the group of Streptomyces derived antibiotics (neomycin, paromomycin, kanamycin) of which framycetin is a member, but this is not invariable. Prolonged use of antibiotics may result in the overgrowth of nonsusceptible organisms, including fungi. Appropriate measures should be taken if this occurs.

Dosage: Ointment: Apply locally 2 to 4 times a day as prescribed.
Ophthalmic Drops and Ointment: Drops for rapid action: 1 or 2 drops every 1 or 2 hours in acute conditions (generally for 2 or 3 days), reducing to 1 or 2 drops, 3 or 4 times daily.

Ointment for continued effect: 2 or 3 applications daily, or at bedtime if drops have been used during the day.

Supplied: Ointment: Each g of ointment contains: framycetin sulfate BP 15 mg (1.5%), gramicidin 50 μg (0.005%) and anhydrous lanolin 10%. Tubes of 15 g.

Ophthalmic Drops and Ointment: Each mL of drops (pH is 5.8 to 6.8) or g of ointment contains: framycetin sulfate BP 5 mg in a sterile, buffered, isotonic aqueous solution or sterile, greasy ointment base, respectively. The ointment base is Plastibase 30W. Drops, bottles of 8 mL. Ointment, tubes of 5 g.

Store all Soframycin products at controlled room temperature.

SOFRA-TULLE® Ⓟ

Hoechst Marion Roussel

Framycetin Sulfate

Topical Antibiotic

Pharmacology: Framycetin, a broad spectrum aminoglycoside antibiotic, is usually bactericidal in action. Although the exact mechanism of action has not been fully elucidated, the drug appears to inhibit protein synthesis in susceptible bacteria by binding to ribosomal subunits. In general, framycetin is active against many aerobic gram-negative bacteria and some aerobic gram-positive bacteria, namely staphylococci including S. aureus. The drug is inactive against fungi, viruses, and most anaerobic bacteria.

Indications: Treatment of infected or potentially infected burns, wounds, ulcers and graft sites.

Contraindications: Known allergy to lanolin or framycetin. Organisms resistant to framycetin.

Precautions: In most cases, where small areas are covered with the tulle, absorption of the antibiotic is so slight that it can be discounted. However, where a very large body surface is involved (e.g., 30% or more body surface area), the possibility of eventual toxicity and nephrotoxicity must be considered. Prolonged use of antibiotics may result in the overgrowth of nonsusceptible organisms, including fungi. Appropriate measures should be taken if this occurs.

Cross sensitization may occur among the group of Streptomyces derived antibiotics (neomycin, paromomycin, kanamycin) of which framycetin is a member, but this is not invariable.

Dosage: A single layer to be applied directly to the wound and covered with an appropriate dressing. If exudative, dressings should be changed at least daily. In case of leg ulcers cut dressing accurately to size of ulcer to decrease the risk of sensitization and to avoid contact with surrounding healthy skin.

Supplied: A lightweight, lano-paraffin (anhydrous lanolin 9.95%) gauze dressing impregnated with 1% framycetin sulfate BP. Available in 2 sizes: 10 cm by 10 cm sterile single units, flow wrapped packages of 10 and 50; 10 cm by 30 cm sterile single units, cartons of 10. Store flat at cool temperature.

SOLAQUIN™
SOLAQUIN FORTE™

ICN

Hydroquinone

Demelanizing Agent

Supplied: Each g contains: hydroquinone USP 2% (Solaquin) or 4% (Solaquin Forte) in a vanishing, moisturizing sunscreen cream base, containing octyldimethyl PABA 5%, dioxybenzone 3% and oxybenzone 2%. Parabens-free. pH approximately 4. Tubes of 30 g.

SOLGANAL® Ⓟ

Schering

Aurothioglucose

Antirheumatic Agent

Pharmacology: Although the mechanism of action is not well understood, gold compounds have been reported to decrease synovial inflammation and retard cartilage and bone destruction.

Gold is absorbed from injection sites, reaching peak concentration in blood in 4 to 6 hours. Following a single i.m. injection of 50 mg aurothioglucose suspension in each of 2 patients, peak serum levels were about 235 μg/dL in one patient and 450 μg/dL in the other. In plasma, 95% is bound to the albumin fraction. Approximately 70% of the gold is eliminated in the urine and approximately 30% in the feces. When the standard weekly treatment schedule is followed, approximately 40% of the administered dose is excreted each week, and the remainder is excreted over a longer period. The biological half-life of gold salts following a single 50 mg dose has been reported to range from 3 to 27 days. Following successive weekly doses, the half-life increases and may be 14 to 40 days after the third dose and up to 168 days after the eleventh weekly dose.

After the initial injection, the serum level of gold rises sharply and declines over the next week. Peak levels with aqueous preparations are higher and decline faster than those with oily preparations. Weekly administration produces a continuous rise in the basal value for several months, after which the serum level becomes relatively stable. After a standard weekly dose, considerable individual variation in the levels of gold has been found. A steady decline in gold levels occurs when the interval between injections is lengthened, and small amounts may be found in the serum for months after discontinuance of therapy. The incidence of toxic reactions is apparently unrelated to the plasma level of gold, but it may be related to the cumulative body content of gold.

Storage of gold in human tissues is dependent upon organ mass as well as upon the concentration of gold. Therefore, tissues having the highest gold levels (w/w) do not necessarily contain the greatest total amounts of gold. The major depots, in decreasing order of total gold content are the bone marrow, liver, skin and bone, accounting for approximately 85% of body gold. The highest concentrations of gold are found in the lymph nodes, adrenal glands, liver, kidneys, bone marrow, and spleen. Relatively small concentrations are found in articular structures.

Gold passes the blood-brain barrier in hamsters.

Transfer of gold across the human placenta at the 20th week of pregnancy has been documented. The placenta showed numerous gold deposits and smaller amounts were detected in the fetal liver and kidneys; other tissues provided no evidence of gold deposition.

Gold is excreted into human milk in significant amounts and trace amounts can be demonstrated in the blood of nursing infants (see Precautions, Lactation).

Indications: For the adjunctive treatment of early active rheumatoid arthritis (both of the adult and juvenile types) not adequately controlled by other anti-inflammatory agents and conservative measures. In chronic, advanced cases of rheumatoid arthritis, gold therapy is less valuable.

Antirheumatic measures such as salicylates and other anti-inflammatory drugs (both steroidal and nonsteroidal) may be continued after initiation of gold therapy. After improvement commences, these measures may be discontinued slowly as symptoms permit.

See Precautions, Laboratory Tests and Dosage.

Contraindications: A history of known hypersensitivity to any component of aurothioglucose contraindicates its use. Gold therapy is contraindicated in patients with uncontrolled diabetes mellitus, severe debilitation, systemic lupus erythematosus, renal disease, hepatic dysfunction, uncontrolled congestive heart failure, marked hypertension, agranulocytosis, other blood dyscrasias or hemorrhagic diathesis; or if there is a history of infectious hepatitis. Patients who recently have had radiation, and those who have developed severe toxicity from previous exposure to gold or other heavy metals should not receive aurothioglucose.

Urticaria, eczema, and colitis are also contraindications.

Gold therapy is usually contraindicated in pregnancy (see Precautions, Pregnancy).

Gold salts should not be used with penicillamine (see Adverse Effects, Management of Adverse Effects), or antimalarials. The safety of coadministration with immunosuppressive agents other than corticosteroids has not been established.

Warnings: The following signs should be considered danger signals of gold toxicity, and no additional injection should be given unless further studies reveal some other cause for their presence: rapid reduction of hemoglobin, leukopenia (WBC below 4 000/mm³), eosinophilia above 5%, platelet count below 100 000/mm³, albuminuria, hematuria, pruritus, dermatitis, stomatitis, jaundice and petechiae.

Effects that may occur immediately following an injection, or at any time during gold therapy, include: anaphylactic shock, syncope, bradycardia, thickening of the tongue, difficulty in swallowing and breathing, and angioneurotic edema. If such effects are observed, treatment with aurothioglucose should be discontinued.

Tolerance to gold usually decreases with advancing age. Diabetes mellitus or congestive heart failure should be under control before gold therapy is instituted.

Aurothioglucose should be used with extreme caution in patients with: skin rash, hypersensitivity to other medications, or a history of renal or liver disease.

Precautions: General: Before each injection, the physician should personally check the patient for adverse reactions and inquiry should be made regarding pruritus, rash, sore mouth, indigestion and metallic taste. The patient should be observed for at least 15 minutes following each injection (see Laboratory Tests).

Patients with HLA-D locus histocompatibility antigens DRw2 and DRw3 may have a genetic predisposition to develop certain toxic reactions, such as proteinuria, during treatment with gold or D-penicillamine.

Aurothioglucose should be used with caution in patients with compromised cardiovascular or cerebral circulation.
Information for the Patient: 1. Promptly report to the physician any unusual symptoms such as pruritus (itching), rash, sore mouth, indigestion, or metallic taste.
2. Increased joint pain may occur for 1 or 2 days after an injection and usually subsides after the first few injections.
3. Exposure to sunlight or artificial ultraviolet light should be minimized.
4. Careful oral hygiene is recommended in conjunction with therapy.
5. Patients should be aware of potential hazards if they become pregnant while receiving gold therapy (see Pregnancy).
Laboratory Tests: Before treatment is started, a complete blood count, platelet count and urinalysis should be done to serve as reference points. Since gold therapy is usually contraindicated in pregnant patients, pregnancy should be ruled out before treatment is started. Throughout the treatment period, urinalysis should be repeated prior to each injection, and complete blood cell and platelet counts should be performed every 2 weeks. A platelet count is indicated any time that purpura or ecchymosis occurs.
Drug Interactions: Drug interactions have not been reported (see Contraindications).
Carcinogenesis, Mutagenesis, and Impairment of Fertility: Renal adenomas developed in rats receiving an injectable gold product similar to aurothioglucose at doses of 2 mg/kg weekly for 46 weeks, followed by 6 mg/kg daily for 47 weeks. These doses were higher and administered more frequently than the recommended human doses. The adenomas were similar histologically to those produced by chronic administration of other gold compounds and heavy metals, such as lead or nickel.

Renal tubular cell neoplasia consisting of renal adenoma and adenocarcinoma were noted in a dose-response relationship in another study in rats using daily i.m. doses of 3 mg/kg and 6 mg/kg for up to 2 years. These doses were higher and were administered more frequently than the recommended human doses. In this same study, sarcomas at the injection site occurred in some rats but their numbers were not sufficient to demonstrate a dose-response relationship.

No report of renal adenoma or sarcoma at the injection site in man in association with the use of aurothioglucose has been received.

Gold compounds have not been studied for evaluation of mutagenesis.

Gold sodium thiomalate given s.c. did not adversely affect fertility or reproductive performance.

Pregnancy: Gold therapy is usually contraindicated in pregnant patients. The patient should be warned about the hazards of becoming pregnant while on gold therapy. Rheumatoid arthritis frequently improves when the patient becomes pregnant, thereby eliminating the need for gold therapy. The potential nephrotoxicity of gold should not be superimposed on the increased renal burden which normally occurs in pregnancy and hence, gold therapy should be discontinued upon recognition of pregnancy unless continued use is required in an individual case. The slow excretion of gold and its persistence in body tissue after discontinuation of treatment should be kept in mind when a woman of child-bearing potential being treated with gold plans to become pregnant.

Pregnancy Category C: Gold sodium thiomalate administered s.c., a route not used clinically, has been shown to be teratogenic during the organogenic period in rats and rabbits when given in doses 140 and 175 times, respectively, the usual human dose. Hydrocephalus and microphthalmia were the malformations observed in rats when gold sodium thiomalate was administered at a dose of 25 mg/kg/day from day 6 through day 15 of gestation. In rabbits, limb defects and gastroschisis were the malformations observed when gold sodium thiomalate was administered at doses of 20 to 45 mg/kg/day from day 6 through day 18 of gestation.

Gold compounds administered orally to rabbits from days 6 through 18 of pregnancy resulted in the occurrence of abdominal defects such as gastroschisis and umbilical hernia; anomalies of the brain, heart, lung, and skeleton; and microphthalmia.

The administration of excessive doses of gold-containing compounds during pregnancy in the above studies was toxic to the mothers and their embryos; the embryotoxic effects probably were secondary to maternal toxicity. Therefore, the significance of these findings in relation to human use is unknown.

There are no adequate and well-controlled studies with aurothioglucose in pregnant women. Extensive clinical experience with aurothioglucose has not demonstrated human teratogenicity.

Lactation: Gold has been demonstrated in the milk of lactating mothers. In one patient, a total dose of 135 mg of gold thioglucose was given during the postpartum period. Samples of the maternal milk and urine, and samples of red blood cells and serum of the mother and child were evaluated by atomic absorption spectrophotometry. Trace amounts of gold appeared in the serum and red blood cells of the nursing offspring. It has been postulated that this may be the cause of unexplained rashes, nephritis, hepatitis, and hematologic aberrations in the nursing infants of mothers treated with gold. Because of the potential for serious adverse reactions in nursing infants, a decision should be made whether to discontinue nursing or to discontinue the gold therapy, taking into account the importance of the drug to the mother. The slow excretion of gold and its persistence in the mother after discontinuation of treatment should be kept in mind.

Children: Safety and effectiveness in children below the age of 6 years have not been established.

Adverse Effects: Adverse reactions to gold therapy may occur at any time during treatment or many months after therapy has been discontinued. The incidence of toxic reactions is apparently unrelated to the plasma level of gold, but it may be related to the cumulative body content of gold. Higher than conventional dosage schedules may increase the occurrence and severity of toxicity. Severe effects are most common after 300 to 500 mg have been administered.

Cutaneous: Dermatitis is the most common reaction. Pruritus should be considered a warning signal of an impending cutaneous reaction. Erythema and occasionally the more severe reactions such as papular, vesicular, and exfoliative dermatitis leading to alopecia and shedding of the nails may occur. Chrysiasis (gray-to-blue pigmentation) has been reported, especially on photoexposed areas. Gold dermatitis may be aggravated by exposure to sunlight, or an actinic rash may develop.

Mucous Membrane: Stomatitis is the second most common adverse reaction. Shallow ulcers on the buccal membranes, on the borders of the tongue and on the palate, diffuse glossitis or gingivitis may be preceded by the sensation of metallic taste. Careful oral hygiene is recommended. Inflammation of the upper respiratory tract, pharyngitis, gastritis, colitis, tracheitis, and vaginitis have also been reported. Conjunctivitis is rare.

Renal: Nephrotic syndrome or glomerulitis with hematuria, which is usually relatively mild, subsides completely if recognized early and treatment is discontinued. These reactions become severe and chronic if gold therapy is continued after their onset. Therefore, it is important to perform a urinalysis before each injection and to discontinue treatment promptly if proteinuria or hematuria develops.

Hematologic: Although rare, blood dyscrasias, including granulocytopenia, agranulocytosis, thrombocytopenia with or without purpura, leukopenia, eosinophilia, panmyelopathy, hemorrhagic diathesis, and hypoplastic and aplastic anemia, have been reported. These reactions may occur separately or in combination.

Nitritoid and Allergic: These reactions, which may rarely occur with aurothioglucose and which resemble anaphylactoid effects, include flushing, fainting, dizziness, sweating, malaise, weakness, nausea, and vomiting.

Miscellaneous: On rare occasions, gastrointestinal symptoms, i.e., nausea, vomiting, colic, anorexia, abdominal cramps, diarrhea, ulcerative enterocolitis, and headache have been reported.

There have been rare reports of iritis and corneal ulcers. Transient asymptomatic gold deposits in the cornea or conjunctiva may occur.

Other reported reactions include encephalitis, immunological destruction of the synovia, EEG abnormalities, intrahepatic cholestasis, hepatitis with jaundice, toxic hepatitis, acute yellow atrophy, peripheral neuritis, gold bronchitis, pulmonary injury manifested by interstitial pneumonitis or fibrosis, fever, and partial or complete hair loss.

Less common but more severe effects that may occur shortly after an injection or at any time during gold therapy include; anaphylactic shock, syncope, bradycardia, thickening of the tongue, difficulty in swallowing and breathing, and angioneurotic edema. If they are observed, treatment with aurothioglucose should be discontinued.

Arthralgia may occur for 1 or 2 days after an injection and usually subsides after the first few injections. The mechanism of the transient increase in rheumatic symptoms after injection of gold (the so-called nonvasomotor postinjection reaction) is unknown. These reactions are usually mild but occasionally may be so severe that treatment is stopped prematurely.

Management of Adverse Effects: In the event of toxic reactions, gold therapy should be discontinued immediately.

In the presence of mild reactions, it may be sufficient to discontinue the administration of aurothioglucose for a short period and then to resume treatment with smaller doses.

Dermatitis and pruritus may respond to soothing lotions, other appropriate antipruritic treatment, or topical glucocorticoids.

If dermatitis or stomatitis becomes severe or spreads, systemic glucocorticoid treatment may be indicated. For renal, hematologic, and most other adverse reactions, glucocorticoids may be required in larger doses and for a longer time than for dermatologic reactions. Often this treatment may be required for many months because of the slow elimination of gold from the body.

If severe adverse reactions do not improve with steroid treatment in patients who receive large doses of gold, a chelating agent, such as dimercaprol (BAL), may be used. In one case, it was reported that penicillamine was beneficial in the treatment of gold-induced thrombocytopenia. Adjunctive use of an anabolic steroid with other drugs (i.e., BAL, penicillamine, and corticosteroids) may contribute to recovery of bone marrow deficiency.

In the presence of severe or idiosyncratic reactions, treatment with aurothioglucose should not be reinstituted.

Overdose: Symptoms: Overdose resulting from too rapid increases in dosing with aurothioglucose will be manifested by rapid appearance of toxic reactions, particularly those relating to renal damage, such as hematuria, proteinuria, and to hematologic effects, such as thrombocytopenia and granulocytopenia. Other toxic effects, including fever, nausea, vomiting, diarrhea, and various skin disorders such as papulovesicular lesions, urticaria, and exfoliative dermatitis, all attended with severe pruritus, may develop.

Treatment: Treatment consists of prompt discontinuation of the medication and early administration of dimercaprol. Specific supportive therapy should be given for the renal and hematologic complications (see also Adverse Effects, Management of Adverse Effects).

Dosage: Adults: The usual dosage schedule for the i.m. administration of aurothioglucose is as follows: first dose, 10 mg; second and third doses, 25 mg; fourth and subsequent doses, 50 mg. The interval between doses is 1 week. The 50 mg dose is continued at weekly intervals until 0.8 to 1 g has been given. If the patient has improved and has exhibited no sign of toxicity, the 50 mg dose may be continued many months longer at 3 to 4 week intervals. A weekly dose above 50 mg is usually unnecessary and contraindicated; the tendency in gold therapy is toward lower dosage. With this in mind, it may eventually be established that a 25 mg dose is the one of choice. If no improvement has been demonstrated after a total administration of 1 g of aurothioglucose, the necessity for gold therapy should be reevaluated.

Children 6 to 12 years: one-fourth of the adult dose, governed chiefly by body weight, not to exceed 25 mg/dose.

Aurothioglucose should be injected **i.m.** (preferably intragluteally), **never i.v.** The patient should be lying down and should remain recumbent for approximately 10 minutes after the injection. The vial should be thoroughly shaken in order to suspend all of the active material. Heating the vial to body temperature (by immersion in warm water) will facilitate drawing the suspension into the syringe. An 18-gauge, 1½ inch needle is recommended for depositing the preparation deep into the muscular tissue. For obese patients, an 18-gauge, 2 inch needle may be used. The site usually selected for injection is the upper outer quadrant of the gluteal region.

Note: Shake the vial in horizontal position before the dose is withdrawn. Needle and syringe must be dry. The patient should be observed for at least 15 minutes following each injection.

Information for the Patient: See Blue Section—Information for the Patient "Solganal".

Supplied: Each mL of sterile suspension contains: aurothioglucose USP 50 mg (5%) in sesame oil. Nonmedicinal ingredients: aluminum monostearate 2% and propylparaben. Multiple-dose vials of 10 mL, boxes of 1. Shake well before using. Store between 0 and 30°C. Protect from light. Store in carton until contents are used.

SOLU-CORTEF® Ⓟ

Pharmacia & Upjohn

Hydrocortisone Sodium Succinate

Glucocorticoid

Pharmacology: Sterile Solu-Cortef—the highly water-soluble sodium succinate ester of hydrocortisone—permits the immediate i.v. administration of high doses of hydrocortisone in a small volume of diluent and is, therefore, particularly useful in situations where high blood levels of hydrocortisone are required rapidly.

Solu-Cortef has the same metabolic and anti-inflammatory actions as hydrocortisone. When given parenterally and in equimolar quantities, the 2 compounds are equivalent in biologic activity. Following the i.v. injection of hydrocortisone sodium succinate, experimental evidence of its effects has been noted within a few minutes and persists for a variable period. Excretion of the administered dose is nearly complete within 12 hours. Thus, if constantly high blood levels are required, hydrocortisone sodium succinate should be injected every 4 to 6 hours. Hydrocortisone sodium succinate may also be administered by i.v. infusion, or by i.m. injection. The preferred method for initial emergency use is i.v. injection.

Indications: Endocrine Disorders: Primary or secondary adrenocortical insufficiency (hydrocortisone or cortisone is the drug of choice; synthetic analogs may be used in conjunction with mineralocorticoids where applicable; in infancy, mineralocorticoid supplementation is of particular importance).

Acute adrenocortical insufficiency (hydrocortisone or cortisone is the drug of choice; mineralocorticoid supplementation may be necessary, particularly when synthetic analogs are used).

Preoperatively and in the event of serious trauma or illness, in patients with known adrenal insufficiency or when adrenocortical reserve is doubtful. Shock unresponsive to conventional therapy if adrenocortical insufficiency exists or is suspected.

Congenital adrenal hyperplasia.

Solu-Cortef (cont'd)

Nonsuppurative thyroiditis.

Hypercalcemia associated with cancer.

Rheumatic Disorders: As adjunctive therapy for short-term administration (to tide the patient over an acute episode or exacerbation) in: post-traumatic osteoarthritis, synovitis or osteoarthritis, rheumatoid arthritis, including juvenile rheumatoid arthritis, (selected cases may require low dose maintenance therapy), acute and subacute bursitis, epicondylitis, acute nonspecific tenosynovitis, acute gouty arthritis, psoriatic arthritis, ankylosing spondylitis.

Collagen Diseases: During an exacerbation or as maintenance therapy in selected cases of: systemic lupus erythematosus, acute rheumatic carditis, systemic dermatomyositis (polymyositis).

Dermatologic Diseases: pemphigus, severe erythema multiforme (Stevens-Johnson syndrome), exfoliative dermatitis, bullous dermatitis herpetiformis, severe seborrheic dermatitis, severe psoriasis, mycosis fungoides.

Allergic States: Control of severe or incapacitating allergic conditions intractable to adequate trials of conventional treatment in: bronchial asthma, contact dermatitis, atopic dermatitis, serum sickness, seasonal or perennial allergic rhinitis, drug hypersensitivity reactions, urticarial transfusion reactions, acute noninfectious laryngeal edema (epinephrine is the drug of first choice).

Ophthalmic Diseases: Severe acute and chronic allergic and inflammatory processes involving the eye, such as: herpes zoster ophthalmicus, iritis, iridocyclitis, chorioretinitis, diffuse posterior uveitis and choroiditis, optic neuritis, sympathetic ophthalmia, anterior segment inflammation, allergic conjunctivitis, allergic corneal marginal ulcers, keratitis.

Gastrointestinal Diseases: To tide the patient over a critical period of the disease in: ulcerative colitis (systemic therapy), regional enteritis (systemic therapy).

Respiratory Diseases: symptomatic sarcoidosis, berylliosis, fulminating or disseminated pulmonary tuberculosis when used concurrently with appropriate antituberculous chemotherapy, Löffler's syndrome not manageable by other means, aspiration pneumonitis.

Hematologic Disorders: acquired (autoimmune) hemolytic anemia, idiopathic thrombocytopenia purpura in adults (i.v. only; i.m. administration is contraindicated), erythroblastopenia (RBC anemia), congenial (erythoid) hypoplastic anemia, secondary thrombocytopenia in adults.

Neoplastic Diseases: for palliative management of: leukemias and lymphomas in adults, acute leukemia of childhood.

Edematous States: To induce diuresis or remission of proteinuria in the nephrotic syndrome, without uremia, or the iopathic type or that due to lupus erythematosus.

Medical Emergencies: Hydrocortisone is indicated in the treatment of 1) shock secondary to adrenocortical insufficiency or shock unresponsive to conventional therapy when adrenal cortical insufficiency may be present; and 2) acute allergic disorders (status asthmaticus, anaphylactic reactions, insect stings, etc.) following epinephrine.

Although there are no well controlled (double-blind, placebo) clinical trials, data from experimental animal models indicate that corticosteroids may be useful in hemorrhagic, traumatic and surgical shock in which standard therapy (e.g., fluid replacement, etc.) has not been effective. **Also see warning statement.**

Miscellaneous: Tuberculous meningitis with subarachnoid block or impending block when used concurrently with appropriate antituberculous chemotherapy. Trichinosis with neurologic or myocardial involvement.

Contraindications: In patients with known hypersensitivity to any components of the product and in patients with systemic fungal infections.

Warnings: In patients on corticosteroid therapy subjected to unusual stress, increased dosage or rapidly acting corticosteroids before, during and after the stressful situation is indicated.

Corticosteroids may mask some signs of infection, and new infections may appear during their use. There may be decreased resistance and inability to localize infection when corticosteroids are used. Infections with any pathogen including viral, bacterial, fungal, protozoan or helminthic infections, in any location in the body, may be associated with the use of corticosteroids alone or in combination with other immunosuppressive agents that affect cellular immunity, or neutrophil function. These infections may be mild, but can be severe and at times fatal. With increasing doses of corticosteroids, the rate of occurrence of infectious complication increases.

Average and large doses of hydrocortisone can cause elevation of blood pressure, salt and water retention, and increased excretion of potassium. These effects are less likely to occur with synthetic derivatives except when used in large doses. Dietary salt restriction and potassium supplementation may be necessary. All corticosteroids increase calcium excretion.

Administration of live or live, attenuated vaccines is contra-indicated in patients receiving immunosuppressive doses of corticosteroids. Killed or inactivated vaccines may be administered to patients receiving immunosuppressive doses of corticosteroids. However the response to such vaccines may be diminished. Indicated immunization procedures may be undertaken in patients receiving nonimmunosuppressive doses of corticosteroids.

The use of hydrocortisone in active tuberculosis should be restricted to those cases of fulminating or disseminated tuberculosis in which the corticosteroid is used for the management of the disease in conjunction with appropriate antituberculosis regimen.

If corticosteroids are indicated in patients with latent tuberculosis or tuberculin reactivity, close observation is necessary as reactivation of the disease may occur. During prolonged corticosteroid therapy, these patients should receive chemoprophylaxis.

Because rare instances of anaphylactoid reactions (e.g., bronchospasm) have occurred in patients receiving parenteral corticosteroid therapy, appropriate precautionary measures should be taken prior to administration, especially when the patient has a history of allergy to any drug.

This product contains benzyl alcohol. Benzyl alcohol has been reported to be associated with a fatal Gasping Syndrome in premature infants.

Although recent studies have not been conducted with hydrocortisone or other corticosteroids, studies of methylprednisolone sodium succinate in septic shock suggest that increased mortality may occur in some subgroups of patients at higher risk (i.e., elevated creatinine greater than 2.0 mg% or with secondary infections).

Pregnancy and *Lactation:* Some animal studies have shown that corticosteroids, when administered to the mother at high doses, may cause fetal malformations. Adequate human reproductive studies have not been done with corticosteroids. Therefore the use of this drug in pregnancy, nursing mothers, or women of childbearing potential requires that the benefits of the drug be carefully weighed against the potential risk to the mother and embryo or fetus. Since there is inadequate evidence of safety in human pregnancy, this drug should be used in pregnancy only if clearly needed.

Corticosteroids readily cross the placenta. Infants born of mothers who have received substantial doses of corticosteroids during pregnancy must be carefully observed and evaluated for signs of adrenal insufficiency. There are no known effects of corticosteroids on labor and delivery. Corticosteroids are excreted in breast milk.

Precautions: Corticosteroids should be used cautiously in patients with ocular herpes simplex for fear of corneal perforation.

Psychic derangements may appear when corticosteroids are used, ranging from euphoria, insomnia, mood swings, personality changes, and severe depression to frank psychotic manifestations. Also, existing emotional instability or psychotic tendencies may be aggravated by corticosteroids.

Steroids should be used with caution in nonspecific ulcerative colitis, if there is a probability of impending perforation, abscess or other pyogenic infections, also in diverticulitis, fresh intestinal anastomoses, active or latent peptic ulcer, renal insufficiency, hypertension, osteoporosis, and myasthenia gravis.

Although controlled clinical trials have shown corticosteroids to be effective in speeding the resolution of acute exacerbations of multiple sclerosis, they do not show that corticosteroids affect the ultimate outcome or natural history of the disease. The studies do show that relatively high doses of corticosteroids are necessary to demonstrate a significant effect (see Dosage).

An acute myopathy has been described with the use of high doses of corticosteroids, most often occurring in patients with disorders of neuromuscular transmission (e.g., myasthenia gravis), or in patients receiving concomitant therapy with neuromuscular blocking drugs (e.g., pancuronium). This acute myopathy is generalized, may involve ocular and respiratory muscles, and may result in quadriparesis. Elevations of creatine kinase may occur. Clinical improvement or recovery after stopping corticosteroids may require weeks to years.

Kaposi's sarcoma has been reported to occur in patients receiving corticosteroid therapy. Discontinuation of corticosteroids may result in clinical remission.

Carcinogenesis, Mutagenesis, Impairment of Fertility: There is no evidence that corticosteroids are carcinogenic, mutagenic or impair fertility.

Labor and Delivery: No effect known.

Lactation: Because prednisone is excreted in breast milk, it is reasonable to assume that all corticoids are. No data is known for hydrocortisone sodium succinate.

Children: Growth may be supressed in children receiving long-term, daily-divided dose glucocorticoid therapy. The use of such a regimen should be restricted to the most serious indications.

Drug Interactions: The pharmacokinetic interactions listed below are potentially clinically important.

Drugs that induce hepatic enzymes such as phenobarbital, phenytoin and rifampin may increase the clearance of corticosteroids and may require increases in corticosteroid dose to achieve the desired response.

Drugs such as troleandomycin and ketoconazole may inhibit the metabolism of corticosteroids and thus decrease their clearance. Therefore the dose of corticosteroids should be titrated to avoid steroid toxicity.

Corticosteroids may increase the clearance of chronic high dose ASA. This could lead to decreased salicylate serum levels or increase the risk of salicylate toxicity when corticosteroid is withdrawn. ASA should be used cautiously in conjunction with corticosteroids in patients suffering from hypoprothrombinemia.

The effect of corticosteroids on oral anticoagulants is variable. There are reports of enhanced as well as diminished effects of anticoagulant when given concurrently with corticosteroids. Therefore coagulation indices should be monitored to maintain the desired anticoagulant effect.

Adverse Effects: Note: The following are typical for all systemic corticosteroids. Their inclusion in this list does not necessarily indicate that the specific event has been observed with this particular formulation.

Fluid and Electrolyte Disturbances: congestive heart failure in susceptible patients, hypertension, hypokalemic alkalosis. Sodium retention, fluid retention and potassium loss which are correctable and largely preventable by restricting sodium intake to 500 mg/day and supplementing potassium intake.

Musculoskeletal: steroid myopathy, muscle weakness, osteoporosis, pathologic fractures, vertebral compression fractures, aseptic necrosis, loss of muscle mass, tendon rupture—particularly of the Achilles tendon.

Gastrointestinal: peptic ulceration with possible perforation and hemorrhage, gastric hemorrhage, pancreatitis, esophagitis, ulcerative esophagitis, perforation of the bowel, abdominal distention.

Increases in ALT, AST and alkaline phosphatase have been observed following corticosteroid treatment. These changes are usually small associated with any clinical syndrome and are reversible upon discontinuation.

Dermatologic: impaired wound healing (usually at high doses), petechiae and ecchymoses, thin fragile skin, facial erythema, increased sweating.

Metabolic: negative nitrogen balance due to protein catabolism.

Neurological: increased intracranial pressure, pseudotumor cerebri, psychic derangements, seizures, headache, vertigo.

Endocrine: menstrual irregularities, development of Cushingoid state, suppression of pituitary-adrenal axis leading to secondary adrenocortical and pituitary unresponsiveness, decreased carbohydrate tolerance, manifestation of latent diabetes mellitus, increased requirement for insulin or oral hypoglycemic agents in diabetics, suppression of growth in children.

Ophthalmic: posterior subcapsular cataracts (associated with prolonged, high dose systemic therapy), glaucoma, increased intraocular pressure, exophthalmos.

Immune System: masking of infections, latent infections becoming active, opportunistic infections, hypersensitivity reactions including anaphylaxis may, suppress reactions to skin tests.

The following additional reactions are related to parenteral corticosteroid therapy: hyperpigmentation or hypopigmentation, s.c. and cutaneous atrophy, sterile abscess, anaphylactoid reaction (e.g., bronchospasm, laryngeal edema, urticaria).

Overdose: Symptoms and Treatment: There is no clinical syndrome of acute overdosage with hydrocortisone. Hydrocortisone is dialyzable.

Dosage: This preparation may be administered by i.v. injection, by i.v. infusion, or by i.m. injection; the preferred method for initial emergency use being i.v. injection. Following the initial emergency period, consideration should be given to employing a longer-acting injectable preparation or an oral preparation.

Therapy is initiated by administering hydrocortisone sodium succinate i.v. over a period of 30 seconds (e.g., 100 mg) to 10 minutes (e.g., 500 mg or more). In general, high-dose corticosteroid therapy should be continued only until the patient's condition has stabilized—usually not beyond 48 to 72 hours. Although adverse effects associated with high dose, short-term corticoid therapy are uncommon, peptic ulceration may occur. Prophylactic antacid therapy may be indicated. When high-dose hydrocortisone therapy must be continued beyond 48 to 72 hours, hypernatremia may occur. Under such circumstances it may be desirable to replace hydrocortisone with a corticosteroid product such as methylprednisolone sodium succinate which causes little or no sodium retention.

The initial dose of hydrocortisone is 100 to 500 mg or more depending on the severity of the condition. This dose may be repeated at intervals of 2, 4, or 6 hours as indicated by the patient's response and clinical condition. While the dose may be reduced for infants and children, it is governed more by the severity of the condition and response of the patient than by age or body weight but should not be less than 25 mg daily.

Patients subjected to severe stress following corticosteroid therapy should be observed closely for signs and symptoms of adrenocortical insufficiency.

Corticosteroid therapy is an adjunct to, and not a replacement for, conventional therapy.

Preparation of Solutions: Parenteral drug products should be inspected visually for particulate matter and discoloration prior to administration, whenever solution and container permit.

I.V./I.M. Injection: To use Solu-Cortef Act-O-Vial reconstitute Act-O-Vial according to Directions For Using The Act-O-Vial System. Further dilution is not necessary for i.v. or i.m. injection.

I.V. Infusion: For i.v. infusion first reconstitute Act-O-Vials according to instructions. The 100 mg solution may then be added to 100 to 1 000 mL of 5% Dextrose in Water (or isotonic saline solution or 5% dextrose in isotonic saline solution if patient is not on sodium restriction). The 250 mg solution may be added to 250 to 1 000 mL, the 500 mg solution may be added to 500 to 1 000 mL and the 1 000 mg solution to 1 000 mL of the same diluents. In cases, where administration of a small volume of fluid is desirable, 100 mg to 3 000 mg of Solu-Cortef may be added to 50 mL of the above diluents. The resulting solutions are stable for at least 4 hours and may be administered either directly or by I.V. piggy back.

Table I provides the stability data of hydrocortisone in 5% Dextrose in Water, USP (D5W) or 0.9% Sodium Chloride Injection, UPS (NS), at room temperature.

Table I—Solu-Cortef

Hydrocortisone Sodium Succinate (HCSS) Stability

HCSS Concentration	Stability (time)
≤1 mg/mL	24 hours
1 mg/mL <x<25 mg/mL	unpredictable, 4 to 6 hours
≥25 mg/mL	3 days

Freezing: In-house studies have shown reconstituted hydrocortisone 50 mg/mL and 125 mg/mL to be physically and chemically stable after 1 month of freezing. Once thawed, the above guidelines should be followed for hydrocortisone.

Directions for Using the Act-O-Vial System: Press down on plastic activator to force diluent into the lower compartment. Gently agitate to effect solution. Remove plastic tab covering center of stopper. Sterilize top of stopper with a suitable germicide. Insert needle squarely through center of stopper until tip is just visible. Invert vial and withdraw dose.

Storage: Store unreconstituted product at controlled room temperature 15 to 30°C. Store solution at controlled room temperature 15 to 30°C and protect from light. Use solution only if it is clear. Discard unused solutions affter 3 days. The Act-O-Vial is a single dose vial and once reconstituted solution is used, any remaining portion should be discarded.

Supplied: Act-O-Vials: 100 mg: Each 2 mL (when mixed) contains: hydrocortisone (as hydrocortisone sodium succinate) 100 mg, monobasic sodium phosphate anhydrous 0.8 mg, dibasic sodium phosphate dried 8.76 mg and benzyl alcohol 18.1 mg. Sodium: <1 mmol. Vial packs of 5.

250 mg: Each 2 mL (when mixed) contains: hydrocortisone (as hydrocortisone sodium succinate) 250 mg, monobasic sodium phosphate anhydrous 2 mg, dibasic sodium phosphate dried 21.8 mg and benzyl alcohol 16.4 mg. Sodium: <1 mmol. Vial packs of 5.

500 mg: Each 4 mL (when mixed) contains: hydrocortisone (as hydrocortisone sodium succinate) 500 mg, monobasic sodium phosphate anhydrous 4 mg, dibasic sodium phosphate dried 44 mg and benzyl alcohol 33.4 mg. Sodium: <1 mmol. Vial packs of 5.

1 g: Each 8 mL (when mixed) contains: hydrocortisone (as hydrocortisone sodium succinate) 1 g, monobasic sodium phosphate anhydrous 8 mg, dibasic sodium phosphate dried 87.32 mg and benzyl alcohol 66.9 mg. Sodium: <1 mmol. Vial packs of 5.

Reviewed 1997

SOLUGEL® 4
SOLUGEL® 8 Ⓟ

Stiefel

Benzoyl Peroxide

Acne Therapy

Pharmacology: The topical use of benzoyl peroxide provides therapeutic control of acne through drying and desquamative action as well as antibacterial activity.

Indications: Acne vulgaris.

Contraindications: Patients with a known sensitivity to benzoyl peroxide or any of the components should not use this medication.

Precautions: For external use only. Do not permit product to come in contact with the eyes or mucous membranes. Very fair individuals should always be started with a single application. Benzoyl peroxide may bleach colored fabrics.

Dosage: Wash thoroughly with a non-medicated soap such as Acne-Aid and water. Apply once or twice daily to affected areas or according to the instructions of a physician.

Supplied: Each g of gel contains: benzoyl peroxide 4% (Solugel 4), or 8% (Solugel 8) in a unique patented hydrophase gel base. Nonmedicinal ingredients: cetyl alcohol, dimethyl isosorbide, fragrance X-23304 ungerer, promulgen G, purified water USP and simethicone. Tubes of 45 g. Store below 27°C.

SOLU-MEDROL® Ⓟ

Pharmacia & Upjohn

Methylprednisolone Sodium Succinate

Glucocorticoid

Pharmacology: Like other corticosteroids, methylprednisolone exerts its effect by its anti-inflammatory action.

Methylprednisolone is a potent anti-inflammatory steroid. It has a greater anti-inflammatory potency than prednisolone and has less tendency than prednisolone to induce sodium and water retention.

Methylprednisolone sodium succinate has the same metabolic and anti-inflammatory actions as methylprednisolone. When given parenterally and in equimolar quantities, the 2 compounds are equivalent in biologic activity. The relative potency of methylprednisolone and hydrocortisone, following i.v. administration, is at least 4 to 1. This is in good agreement with the relative oral potency of methylprednisolone and hydrocortisone.

The metabolism and excretion of methylprednisolone is similar to that of other corticosteroids. It influences carbohydrate, protein, fat and purine metabolism, electrolyte and water balance, and the functional capacities of the cardiovascular system, the kidney, skeletal muscle, the nervous system and other organs and tissues. Like other corticosteroids, methylprednisolone endows the organism with the capacity to resist not a few but all types of noxious stimuli and environmental change.

Indications: I.V. administration of methylprednisolone is indicated in situations in which a rapid and intense hormonal effect is required. These include the following:

Hypersensitivity and dermatologic conditions: status asthmaticus, anaphylactic reactions, drug reactions, contact dermatitis, urticaria, generalized neurodermatitis, reactions to insect bites, pemphigus foliaceous and vulgaris, exfoliative dermatitis, erythema multiforme.

As adjunctive therapy in: acute systemic lupus erythematosus, acute rheumatic fever, acute gout.

Ulcerative colitis: In addition to the above conditions, colonic instillations of methylprednisolone in retention enemas or by continuous drip, have been shown to be a useful adjunct in the treatment of patients with ulcerative colitis.

In anaphylactic reactions: Epinephrine or norepinephrine should be administered first for an immediate hemodynamic effect followed by i.v. injection of methylprednisolone and other accepted procedures. There is evidence that the corticoids through their prolonged hemodynamic effect are of value in preventing recurrent attacks of acute anaphylactic reactions.

In sensitivity reactions: Such as in serum sickness, allergic dermatosis (urticaria) and reactions to insect bites, methylprednisolone is capable of providing relief within ½ to 2 hours. In some asthmatic patients it may be advantageous to administer methylprednisolone by slow i.v. drip over a period of hours.

As adjunctive therapy in fulminating acute systemic lupus erythematosus and acute rheumatic fever, and to relieve pain during the acute manifestations of gout: Methylprednisolone may be given by slow i.v. administration over a period of several minutes. Thereafter, the patient should be placed on i.m. or oral therapy as required for continued relief of symptoms. In these conditions, other accepted measures of therapy should also be instituted.

Shock: In severe hemorrhagic or traumatic shock adjunctive use of i.v. methylprednisolone may aid in achieving hemodynamic restoration. [Although there are no well controlled (double-blind placebo) clinical trials, data from experimental animal models indicate that methylprednisolone may be useful in hemorrhagic and traumatic shock. See also Warnings regarding septic shock.] Corticoid therapy should not replace standard methods of combating shock, but present evidence indicates that concurrent use of large doses of corticoids with other measure may improve survival rates.

Organ transplants: Corticosteroids both parenterally and orally in high doses have been used following organ transplantation as part of multi-faceted attempts to reduce the rejection phenomenon. Methylprednisolone is suitable for such indications.

Cerebral edema: Corticosteroid therapy as an adjunct to the usual forms of therapy for cerebral edema has been used for many years. Cerebral edema associated with acute craniocerebral injuries and intracranial hematomas of traumatic origin, has been treated with methylprednisolone with some improvement in overall survival rate and reduction of permanent disability following such conditions. Administration of methylprednisolone immediately prior to intracranial surgery and in the immediate post-operative period has reduced the duration of post-operative complications related to cerebral edema.

Acute spinal cord injury: The use of methylprednisolone in high doses has resulted in improvement in motor and sensory recovery. Treatment should begin within 8 hours of injury.

Contraindications: Except when used for short-term or emergency therapy as in acute sensitivity reactions, methylprednisolone is contraindicated in patients with arrested tuberculosis, herpes simplex keratitis, acute psychoses, Cushing's syndrome, peptic ulcer, markedly elevated serum creatinine, vaccinia and varicella. Also contraindicated for systemic fungal infections and known hypersensitivity to the ingredients.

Warnings: Recent studies do not establish the efficacy of methylprednisolone in septic shock, and suggest that increased mortality may occur in some subgroups at higher risk (i.e., elevated serum creatinine greater than 2.0 mg% or secondary infections).

Administration of live or live, attenuated vaccines is contraindicated in patients receiving immunosuppressive doses of corticosteroids. Killed or inactivated vaccines may be administered to patients receiving immunosuppressive doses of corticosteroids. However the response to such vaccines may be diminished. Indicated immunization procedures may be undertaken in patients receiving nonimmunosuppressive doses of corticosteroids.

Because rare instances of anaphylactoid (e.g., bronchospasm) reactions have occurred in patients receiving parenteral corticosteroid therapy, appropriate precautionary measures should be taken prior to administration, especially when the patient has a history of allergy to any drug.

Bacteriostatic Water for Injection included in the Act-O-Vials contains benzyl alcohol. Benzyl alcohol has been reported to be associated with a fatal Gasping Syndrome in premature infants.

Precautions: The existence of diabetes, osteoporosis, renal insufficiency, chronic psychosis, diverticulitis, fresh intestinal anastomoses, active or latent peptic ulcer, hypertension, myasthenia gravis or predisposition to thrombophlebitis requires that methylprednisolone be administered with extreme caution. The same caution should also be used in non-specific ulcerative colitis, if there is a probability of impending perforation, abscess or other pyogenic infections.

Solu-Medrol (cont'd)

Psychic derangements may appear when corticosteroids are used, ranging from euphoria, insomnia, mood swings, personality changes, and severe depression to frank psychotic manifestations. Also, existing emotional instability or psychotic tendencies may be aggravated by corticosteroids, and therefore these patients should be treated with caution.

Since complications of treatment with glucocorticoids are dependent on the size of the dose and the duration of treatment, a risk/benefit decision must be made in each individual case as to dose and duration of treatment and as to whether daily or intermittent therapy should be used.

Corticosteroids may mask some signs of infection, and new infections may appear during their use. There may be decreased resistance and inability to localize infection when corticosteroids are used. Infections with any pathogen including viral, bacterial, fungal, protozoan or helminthic infections, in any location in the body, may be associated with the use of corticosteroids alone or in combination with other immunosuppressive agents that affect cellular immunity, or neutrophil function. These infections may be mild, but can be severe and at times fatal. With increasing doses of corticosteroids, the rate of occurrence of infectious complication increases.

Adequate adrenocortical supportive therapy including ACTH must be employed promptly if the patient is subjected to any unusual stress such as surgery, trauma or severe infection.

Since methylprednisolone, like prednisolone, suppresses endogenous adrenocortical activity, it is highly important that the patient receiving methylprednisolone be under careful observation, not only during the course of treatment but for some time after treatment is terminated.

There are reports of cardiac arrhythmias and/or circulatory collapse and/or cardiac arrest following the rapid administration or large i.v. doses of methylprednisolone (greater than 0.5 g administered over a period of less than 10 minutes). Bradycardia has been reported during or after the administration of large doses of methylprednisolone, and may be unrelated to the speed or duration of infusion.

Dosage must be decreased or discontinued gradually when the drug has been administered for more than a few days.

Patients should be advised to inform subsequent physicians of the prior use of methylprednisolone.

Convulsions have been reported with concurrent use of methylprednisolone and cyclosporine. Since concurrent administration of these agents results in a mutual inhibition of metabolism, it is possible that convulsions and other adverse events associated with the individual use of either drug may be more apt to occur.

An acute myopathy has been described with the use of high doses of corticosteroids, most often occurring in patients with disorders of neuromuscular transmission (e.g., myasthenia gravis), or in patients receiving concomitant therapy with neuromuscular blocking drugs (e.g., pancuronium). This acute myopathy is generalized, may involve ocular and respiratory muscles, and may result in quadriparesis. Elevations of creatine kinase may occur. Clinical improvement or recovery after stopping corticosteroids may require weeks to years.

Kaposi's sarcoma has been reported to occur in patients receiving corticosteroid therapy. Discontinuation of corticosteroids may result in clinical remission.

Drug Interactions: Table I includes the common interactions seen with Solu-Medrol and other drug products. Methylprednisolone, like all glucocorticoids, can cause the following effects when administered in combination with these products. This table is meant to serve as a guide to professionals when considering a rational course of therapy.

Pregnancy: Some animal studies have shown that corticosteroids, when administered to the mother at high doses, may cause fetal malformations. There are, however, no adequate and well-controlled studies in pregnant women. Because animal reproduction studies are not always predictive of human response, the use of this drug during pregnancy, in nursing mothers and women of childbearing potential, requires that the benefits of the drug be carefully weighed against the potential risk to the mother and embryo or fetus. Newborn infants of mothers who received such therapy during pregnancy should be observed for signs of hypoadrenalism and appropriate measures instituted if such signs are present. No effect is known upon labor and delivery.

Lactation: Because prednisolone is excreted in breast milk it is reasonable to assume that all corticosteroids are. No specific data are available for methylprednisolone sodium succinate.

Table I—Solu-Medrol

Common Interactions Seen with Solu-Medrol and Other Drug Products

Class of Drug	Drug(s) Involved	Affects Therapy of Drugs	Clinical Implication	Mechanism
Antibiotic/ Antifungal therapy	Troleandomycin Erythromycin Ketoconazole	Methylprednisolone	Enhanced clinical effects and side effects of methylprednisolone	Enzyme inhibition: Reduced MP elimination
	Rifampin	Methylprednisolone	May reduce efficacy; dosage adjustment may be required.	Enzyme induction, increased clearance
Anticholinesterase	Neostigmine, pyridostigmine	Anticholinesterase	Precipitation of myasthenic crisis	
Anticoagulants	Oral anticoagulants or heparin	Anticoagulant	Increased or decreased clotting. Monitor response. Adjust dose.	
Anticonvulsants	e.g., phenobarbital, phenytoin	Methylprednisolone	May reduce methylprednisolone efficacy. Monitor clinical response. Adjust dose if necessary.	Enzyme induction: increased clearance of methylprednisolone
Antidiabetic Drugs	e.g., insulin, glibenclamide, metformin	Antidiabetic	May impair glucose control. Monitor glucose levels and adjust dose of antidiabetic therapy.	Diabetogenic effects of corticosteroid
Antihypertensive Agents	All antihypertensives	Antihypertensive	May result in partial loss of hypertensive control.	Mineralocorticoid effect of corticosteroid leading to raised blood pressure
Diuretics	All potassium losing diuretics e.g., furosemide		Enhanced toxicity. Monitor K+ levels and supplement if necessary.	Potassium loss
Cardioactive drugs	Digoxin and related glycosides	Digoxin	Potentiation of digoxin toxicity	Corticosteroid induced potassium loss (mineralocorticoid effect)
Immunizing Agents	Live vaccine: poliomyelitis, BCG, mumps, measles, rubella, smallpox	Vaccine	May see increased toxicity from vaccine. Disseminated viral disease may occur.	Corticosteroid induced immunosuppression
	Killed Virulent Vaccines	Vaccine	Reduced response to vaccine	Impaired immune response
Immuno-suppressants	Methotrexate Azathioprine	Methylprednisolone	May allow reduced dose of corticosteroid.	Synergistic effect on disease state
	Cyclosporin (CYA)	Both	Monitor cyclosporin A levels. Adjust dose as necessary.	Mutual inhibition of metabolism
Neuromuscular Blocking Agents	Pancuronium	Pancuronium	Partial reversal of neuromuscular block	
Psychotherapeutic	Anxiolytics Antipsychotics	CNS active drug	Recurrence or poor control of CNS symptoms. May require dose adjustment.	CNS effects of corticosteroid
Salicylates		Salicylate	Apparent decrease in salicylate efficacy or salicylate toxicity upon reduction of corticosteroid dose.	Increased clearance and decreased plasma level
Sympathomimetic Agents	e.g., salbutamol		Increased efficacy and potentially increased toxicity	Increased response to sympathetic agents

Adverse Effects: The following adverse reactions have been reported with the systemic use of corticosteroid preparations (e.g., methylprednisolone). Their inclusion in this list does not necessarily indicate that the specific event has been observed with methylprednisolone.

Fluid and Electrolyte Disturbances: sodium retention, fluid retention, hypertension, potassium loss, hypokalemic alkalosis, diuresis, sodium excretion, congestive heart failure in susceptible patients.

Musculoskeletal: steroid myopathy, muscle weakness, osteoporosis, pathologic fractures, vertebral compression fractures, aseptic necrosis of femoral and humeral heads, tendon rupture—particularly of the Achilles tendon.

Gastrointestinal: peptic ulcer with possible perforation and hemorrhage, gastric hemorrhage, pancreatitis, esophagitis, perforation of the bowel, transient nausea, vomiting or dysgeusia (with rapid administration of large doses).

Increases in ALT, AST and alkaline phosphatase have been observed following corticosteroid treatment. These changes are usually small, not associated with any clinical syndrome and are reversible upon discontinuation.

Dermatologic: impaired wound healing, petechiae and ecchymoses, thin fragile skin.

Endocrine: decreased carbohydrate tolerance, manifestations of latent diabetes mellitus, increased requirements for insulin or oral hypoglycemic agents in diabetics, menstrual irregularities, development of Cushingoid State, suppression of pituitary-adrenal axis, suppression of growth in children.

Metabolic: negative nitrogen balance due to protein catabolism.

Neurological: increased intracranial pressure, pseudotumor cerebri, psychic derangements, seizures.

Ophthalmic: posterior subcapsular cataracts, increased intraocular pressure, exophthalmos.

Immunological: masking of infections, latent infections becoming active, opportunistic infections, hypersensitivity reactions including anaphylaxis, may suppress reactions to skin tests.

The following additional reactions are related to parenteral corticosteroid therapy: anaphylactic reaction with or without circulatory collapse, cardiac arrest, bronchospasm, cardiac arrhythmias, hypotension or hypertension.

The following additional reactions are related to parenteral corticosteroid therapy: anaphylactic reaction with or without circulatory collapse, cardiac arrest, bronchospasm, cardiac arrhythmias, hypotension or hypertension.

Overdose: Symptoms and Treatment: There is no clinical symptom of acute overdosage with this drug. Methylprednisolone is dialyzable. Continuous overdosage would require careful gradual reduction of dosage in order to prevent the occurrence of acute adrenal insufficiency.

Dosage: As adjunctive therapy in life-threatening conditions (e.g., shock states), the recommended dose of methylprednisolone is 30 mg/kg, given i.v. over a period of at least 30 minutes. The large doses may be repeated every 4 to 6 hours for up to 48 hours.

Acute Spinal Cord Injury: For treatment of acute spinal cord injury, administer i.v. 30 mg methylprednisolone/kg of body weight in a bolus dose over a 15 minute period, followed by a 45 minute pause, and then a continuous infusion of 5.4 mg/kg/hour for 23 hours. There should be a separate i.v. site for the infusion pump. The treatment should begin within 8 hours of injury.

In other indications, initial dosage will vary from 10 to 500 mg depending on the clinical problem being treated. Larger doses may be required for short-term management of severe, acute conditions. Therapy may be initiated by administering methylprednisolone i.v. over a period of at least 5 minutes (e.g., doses up to 250 mg) to at least 30 minutes (e.g., doses greater than 250 mg). Subsequent doses may be given i.v. or i.m. at intervals dictated by the patient's response and clinical condition. Corticosteroid therapy is an adjunct to, and not replacement for, conventional therapy.

Methylprednisolone in doses of 40 to 120 mg administered as retention enemas or by continuous drip 3 to 7 times weekly for periods of 2 or more weeks have been shown to be a useful adjunct in the treatment of some patients with ulcerative colitis. Many patients can be controlled with 40 mg administered in from 30 to 300 mL of water depending on the degree of involvement of the inflamed colonic mucosa. Other accepted therapeutic measures should, of course, be instituted.

Methylprednisolone may be administered by i.v. or i.m. injection or by i.v. infusion, the preferred method for initial emergency use being i.v. injection. To administer i.v. (or i.m.) injection, prepare solution as directed.

Compatibility and Stability: The compatibility and stability of methylprednisolone in solutions and with other drugs in i.v. admixtures is dependent on admixture pH, concentration, time, temperature, and the ability of methylprednisolone to solubilize itself. Thus, to avoid compatibility and stability problems, whenever possible it is recommended that methylprednisolone be administered separate from other drugs and as either I.V. push, through an I.V. medication chamber, or as an I.V. piggy-back solution.

Preparation of Solutions: To prepare solutions for i.v. infusion, first reconstitute methylprednisolone as directed. Therapy may be initiated by administering the drug i.v. over a period of at least 5 minutes (e.g., doses up to 250 mg) to at least 30 minutes (e.g., doses of 250 mg or more). Subsequent doses may be withdrawn and administered similarly. If desired, the medication may be administered in dilute solutions by admixing the reconstituted product with Dextrose 5% in Water, Normal Saline, Dextrose 5% in 0.45% Sodium Chloride. Dilute concentrations of 0.25 mg/mL or greater dilution are physically and chemically stable for 48 hours.

Each Act-O-Vial (AOV) or vial of Solu-Medrol delivers after reconstitution with the diluent supplied or as directed (see Table II).

When needed, the pH of each formula was adjusted with sodium hydroxide so that the pH of the reconstituted solution is within the range of 7 to 8.

Storage: Store unreconstituted product at controlled room temperature 15 to 25°C. Store reconstituted solution at controlled room temperature 15 to 25°C. Use solution within 48 hours after mixing. Protect unreconstituted sterile powder and reconstituted solution from light.

Reconstituted Solutions: Directions for using the Act-O-Vial system: Press down on plastic activator to force diluent into the lower compartment. Gently agitate to effect solution. Remove plastic tab covering centre of stopper. Sterilize top of stopper with suitable germicide. Insert needle squarely through centre of stopper until tip is just visible. Invert vial and withdraw dose. See Table III.

Parenteral drug products should be inspected visually for particulate matter and discoloration prior to administration, whenever solution and container permit.

Supplied: Act-O-Vials: 40 mg: Each mL (when mixed) contains: methylprednisolone (as methylprednisolone sodium succinate) 40 mg, monobasic sodium phosphate anhydrous 1.6 mg, dibasic sodium phosphate dried 17.5 mg, lactose hydrous 25 mg and bacteriostatic water for injection q.s. In diluent, benzyl alcohol 8.8 mg with sterile water for injection q.s. Vial packs of 5.

125 mg: Each 2 mL (when mixed) contains: methylprednisolone (as methylprednisolone sodium succinate) 125 mg, monobasic sodium phosphate 1.6 mg, dibasic sodium phosphate dried 17.4 mg, and bacteriostatic water for injection q.s. In diluent benzyl alcohol 17.6 mg with sterile water for injection q.s. Vial packs of 5.

500 mg: Each 4 mL (when mixed) contains: methylprednisolone (as methylprednisolone sodium succinate) 500 mg, monobasic sodium phosphate anhydrous 6.4 mg, dibasic sodium phosphate dried 69.6 mg and bacteriostatic water for injection q.s. In diluent benzyl alcohol 33.7 mg with sterile water for injection q.s. Vial packs of 5.

1 g: Each 8 mL (when mixed) contains: methylprednisolone (as methylprednisolone sodium succinate) 1 g, monobasic sodium phosphate anhydrous 12.8 mg, dibasic sodium phosphate dried 139.2 mg and bacteriostatic water for injection q.s. In diluent benzyl alcohol 66.8 mg with sterile water for injection q.s. Single vials.

Table II—Solu-Medrol

Composition

Solu-Medrol	40 mg AOV	125 mg AOV	500 mg AOV	1 g AOV	40 mg Vial	125 mg Vial	500 mg Vial	1 g Vial
Powder								
Deliverable Volume	1 mL	2 mL	4 mL	8 mL	1 mL	2 mL	8 mL	16 mL
Methylprednisolone (as sodium succinate)	40 mg	125 mg	500 mg	1 g	40 mg	125 mg	500 mg	1 g
Monobasic sodium phosphate anhydrous	1.6 mg	1.6 mg	6.4 mg	12.8 mg	1.84 mg	1.84 mg	7.7 mg	15.5 mg
Dibasic sodium phosphate dried	17.5 mg	17.4 mg	69.6 mg	139.2 mg	17.46 mg	17.4 mg	73.1 mg	146.2 mg
Lactose Hydrous	25 mg	—	—	—	25 mg	—	—	—
Diluent								
Benzyl Alcohol	8.8 mg	17.6 mg	33.7 mg	66.8 mg	—	—	—	—
Sterile Water for Injection	q.s.	q.s.	q.s.	q.s.				

Table III—Solu-Medrol

Reconstitution Table

Size	Volume of Diluent to be Added	Nominal Concentration per mL
40 mg AOV	Entire contents supplied	40 mg/mL
125 mg AOV	Entire contents supplied	62.5 mg/mL
500 mg AOV	Entire contents supplied	125 mg/mL
1 g AOV	Entire contents supplied	125 mg/mL
40 mg Vial	1 mL	40 mg/mL
125 mg Vial	2 mL	62.5 mg/mL
500 mg Vial	7.8 mL	62.5 mg/mL
1 g Vial	15.6 mL	62.5 mg/mL

Vials: 40 mg: Reconstitute with 1 mL Bacteriostatic Water for Injection USP (benzyl alcohol as preservative) or Sterile Water for Injection. Each mL (when mixed) contains: methylprednisolone (as methylprednisolone sodium succinate) 40 mg, monobasic sodium phosphate anhydrous 1.84 mg, dibasic sodium phosphate dried 17.46 mg, lactose hydrous 25 mg and diluent q.s. Vial packs of 25.

125 mg: Reconstitute with 2 mL Bacteriostatic Water for Injection USP (benzyl alcohol as preservative) or Sterile Water for Injection. Each 2 mL (when mixed) contains: methylprednisolone (as methylprednisolone sodium succinate) 125 mg, monobasic sodium phosphate anhydrous 1.84 mg, dibasic sodium phosphate dried 17.4 mg and diluent q.s. Vial packs of 25.

500 mg: Reconstitute with 7.8 mL Bacteriostatic Water for Injection USP (benzyl alcohol as preservative) or Sterile Water for Injection. Each 8 mL (when mixed) contains: methylprednisolone (as methylprednisolone sodium succinate) 500 mg, monobasic sodium phosphate anhydrous 6.4 mg, dibasic sodium phosphate dried 69.6 mg and diluent q.s. Vial packs of 5.

1 g: Reconstitute with 15.6 mL Bacteriostatic Water for Injection USP (benzyl alcohol as preservative) or Sterile Water for Injection. Each 16 mL (when mixed) contains: methylprednisolone (as methylprednisolone sodium succinate) 1 g, monobasic sodium phosphate anhydrous 12.8 mg, dibasic sodium phosphate dried 139.2 mg and diluent q.s. Single vials.

Reviewed 1998

SOLUVER®
Dermtek

Salicylic Acid

Verrucae Therapy

Supplied: Each bottle contains: salicylic acid USP 20% in an acrylic vehicle. Bottles of 15 mL with brush applicator.

SOLUVER® PLUS
Dermtek

Salicylic Acid

Verrucae Therapy

Supplied: Each bottle contains: salicylic acid USP 27% in an acrylic vehicle. Bottles of 10 mL with brush applicator.

SOMA® ℞
Carter Horner

Carisoprodol

Skeletal Muscle Relaxant

Pharmacology: Carisoprodol produces muscle relaxation in animals by blocking interneuronal activity in the descending reticular formation and spinal cord. There are no peripheral or autonomic effects. Clinically, carisoprodol relieves muscle spasm and associated pain in patients with painful musculoskeletal disorders. The onset of action is rapid; effects last 4 to 6 hours.

In dogs, no withdrawal symptoms occurred after abrupt cessation of carisoprodol in doses as high as 1 g/kg/day.

In a study in humans, abrupt cessation of 100 mg/kg/day (about 5 times the recommended daily adult dosage) was followed in some subjects by mild withdrawal symptoms such as abdominal cramps, insomnia, chilliness, headache, and nausea. Such signs are classified as mild to moderate by the World Health Organization and are not considered specific abstinence signs. Delirium and convulsions, which are considered specific, did not occur in this study. In clinical use, psychological dependence and abuse have been rare, and there have been no reports of significant abstinence signs. Nevertheless, the drug should be used with caution in addiction-prone individuals.

Carisoprodol is metabolized by the liver and excreted in the urine as metabolites. The half-life is approximately 8 hours.

Indications: As an adjunct to rest, physical therapy, and other measures for the relief of discomfort associated with acute, painful musculo-skeletal conditions. The mode of action of this drug has not been clearly identified, but may be related to its sedative properties. Carisoprodol does not directly relax tense skeletal muscles in humans.

Soma (cont'd)

Contraindications: Previous allergic or idiosyncratic reactions to carisoprodol or related compounds such as meprobamate.

Precautions: On very rare occasions, the first dose of carisoprodol has been followed by idiosyncratic symptoms appearing within minutes or hours. Symptoms reported include: extreme weakness, transient quadriplegia, dizziness, ataxia, temporary loss of vision, diplopia, mydriasis, dysarthria, agitation, euphoria, confusion, and disorientation. Symptoms usually subside over the course of the next several hours. Supportive and symptomatic therapy, including hospitalization, may be necessary.

Since the effects of carisoprodol and alcohol or carisoprodol and other CNS depressants may be additive, appropriate caution should be exercised. The drug should be used with caution in addiction prone individuals.

Since carisoprodol has a chemical structure similar to meprobamate, it should be used with caution in patients with known porphyria.

Occupational Hazards: Patients receiving carisoprodol should be cautioned about driving a motor vehicle or operating machinery or apparatus requiring alert attention.

Pregnancy and *Lactation:* Safe usage of this drug in pregnancy has not been established. Therefore, the expected benefits must be weighed against the potential hazards. Carisoprodol is present in breast milk of lactating mothers at concentrations two to four times that of maternal plasma. This factor should be taken into account when use of the drug is contemplated in nursing mothers.

Children: Because of limited clinical experience, carisoprodol is not recommended for use in patients under 12 years of age.

Adverse Effects: CNS: Drowsiness and other CNS effects may require dosage reduction. Also observed: dizziness, vertigo, ataxia, tremor, agitation, irritability, headache, depressive reactions, syncope, and insomnia (see also Precautions).

Allergic or idiosyncratic: Allergic or idiosyncratic reactions rarely develop. They are usually seen within the period of the first to fourth dose in patients having had no previous contact with the drug. Skin rash, erythema multiforme, pruritus, eosinophilia, and fixed drug eruption with cross reaction to meprobamate have been reported with carisoprodol. Severe reactions have been manifested by asthmatic episodes, fever, weakness, dizziness, angioneurotic edema, smarting eyes, hypotension, and anaphylactoid shock (see also Precautions).

Cardiovascular: tachycardia, postural hypotension, facial flushing.

Gastrointestinal: nausea, vomiting, hiccup, epigastric distress.

Hematologic: Leukopenia, in which other drugs or viral infection may have been responsible, and pancytopenia, attributed to phenylbutazone, have been reported. No serious blood dyscrasias have been attributed to carisoprodol.

Overdose: Symptoms: Drowsiness, dizziness, headache. Overdosage of carisoprodol has produced stupor, coma, shock, respiratory depression, and very rarely, death.

Treatment: Gastric lavage followed by the administration of activated charcoal. In children, induce emesis and if there is no immediate response, use gastric lavage. Symptomatic therapy. Should respiration or blood pressure become compromised, respiratory assistance, symptomatic cautious use of pressor amines is indicated. Although overdosage experience is limited, the following types of treatment have been used successfully with the related drug, meprobamate: forced diuresis, peritoneal dialysis and hemodialysis (carisoprodol is dialyzable). Careful monitoring of urinary output is necessary and caution should be taken to avoid overhydration. In treating severe reactions, discontinue carisoprodol and initiate appropriate symptomatic therapy.

Dosage: Usual adult dose is 350 mg 3 times daily and at bedtime; use in patients under age 12 is not recommended.

Supplied: Each white, round, biconvex, uncoated tablet, with 37-WALLACE 2001 imprinted on one side, contains: carisoprodol 350 mg. Nonmedicinal ingredients: alginic acid, magnesium stearate, potassium sorbate, starch (corn) and tribasic calcium phosphate. Gluten- and tartrazine-free. Bottles of 25 and 250.

Readers are encouraged to photocopy the cardiac arrest algorithms found in the CLIN-INFO SECTION.

SOMNOL® Ⓟ
Carter Horner

Flurazepam Monohydrochloride
Hypnotic

Supplied: 15 mg: Each white, oval, film-coated tablet, with one side imprinted Horner and the other side bisected, and imprinted 15 and mg on either side of the bisect, contains: flurazepam monohydrochloride equivalent to 15 mg of flurazepam dihydrochloride. Nonmedicinal ingredients: alumina, cellulose, FD&C Blue No. 2, lactose, magnesium stearate, polyethylene glycol, starch (corn), talc and titanium dioxide. Energy: 1.2 kJ (0.3 kcal). Gluten-, sodium- and tartrazine-free. Bottles of 100 and 500.

30 mg: Each light blue, oval, film-coated tablet, imprinted Horner on one side and the other side bisected and imprinted 30 and mg on either side of the bisect, contains: flurazepam monohydrochloride equivalent to 30 mg of flurazepam dihydrochloride. Nonmedicinal ingredients: alumina, cellulose, FD&C Blue No. 2 and Red No. 3, glycerin, lactose, magnesium stearate, starch (corn), talc and titanium dioxide. Energy: 2.5 kJ (0.6 kcal). Gluten-, sodium- and tartrazine-free. Bottles of 100 and 500.

(Shown in Product Recognition Section)

SONACIDE®
Wyeth-Ayerst

Glutaral
Chemical Sterilizer

Supplied: Each 4.5 L plastic container contains: an acidic aqueous 2% solution of glutaraldehyde potentiated with a nonionic surfactant. Nonmedicinal ingredients: antifoam, fragrance maskant 5A6, phosphoric acid, purified water and tergitol. pH range: 3.6 to 4.2. Preserve in tight, light-resistant containers. Avoid exposure to excessive heat. During aging under the influence of time or temperature, a slight yellow coloration may develop. This, however, does not affect the product's activity. One-week storage at −20°C does not modify the biocidal potency of sonacide.

SOPALAMINE/3B
SOPALAMINE/3B PLUS C
Technilab

Vitamin Supplement

Supplied: Sopalamine/3B: Each tablet contains: thiamine HCl 250 mg, pyridoxine HCl 125 mg and vitamin B_{12} 250 μg. Nonmedicinal ingredients: acetylated hydrogenated cottonseed glyceride, colloidal silicon dioxide, erythrosine aluminum lake, ethylcellulose, FD&C Blue #1 aluminum lake, FD&C Yellow #6 aluminum lake, lactose, magnesium stearate, microcrystalline cellulose, methylcellulose, povidone, sodium croscarmellose and starch. White plastic bottles of 500.

Sopalamine/3B Plus C: Each tablet contains: vitamin A (palmitate) 4 000 IU, vitamin D_3 400 IU, vitamin C 250 mg, thiamine mononitrate 250 mg, riboflavin 2 mg, pyridoxine HCl 125 mg, vitamin B_{12} 250 μg, niacinamide 20 mg, pantothenic acid 10 mg, folic acid 0.1 mg and vitamin E (as alpha tocopheryl acetate) 15 IU. Nonmedicinal ingredients: acetylated hydrogenated cottonseed glyceride, colloidal silicon dioxide, cornstarch, erythrosine aluminum lake, FD&C Blue #1 aluminum lake, FD&C Yellow #6 aluminum lake, hydroxypropylcellulose, hydroxypropyl methylcellulose, magnesium stearate, microcrystalline cellulose, povidone, sodium croscarmellose, sucrose and titanium dioxide. White plastic bottles of 100.

SORIATANE™ Ⓟ
Roche

Acitretin
Keratinization Disorder Therapy

Pharmacology: Acitretin is a retinoid, an aromatic analog of vitamin A. The mechanism of action is unknown; however, evidence exists for a wide range of actions at various cellular and subcellular levels. These include: regulation of RNA/DNA synthesis, modulation of factors which influence epidermal proliferation, modification of glycoprotein synthesis and modulation of the immune response. Whatever the exact mechanism of action, the most prominent effect of acitretin is a modulation of cellular differentiation in the epidermis, which re-establishes a more normal pattern of cell growth.

Use of acitretin in psoriatic patients results in improvement manifested by a decrease in scale, erythema and thickness of lesions, and decreased inflammation in the epidermis and dermis.

Oral absorption of acitretin was optimal when given with food. Following administration of a single oral dose of 50 mg acitretin to healthy volunteers, maximum plasma acitretin concentrations ranged from 196 to 728 ng/mL (mean 416 ng/mL) and were achieved in 2 to 5 hours (mean 2.7 hours). Following multiple doses, acitretin plasma concentrations reached steady-state conditions within 2 weeks. In psoriatic patients who received acitretin (10 to 50 mg/day) for 8 weeks, mean steady-state trough concentrations of acitretin ranged between 6 and 25 ng/mL in a dose-dependent manner. In patients administered multiple oral doses of acitretin for up to 9 months, the range of elimination half-life ($t^{1/2}$) values observed was 33 to 92 hours for acitretin (harmonic mean=48 hours) and 28 to 123 hours for cis-acitretin (harmonic mean=64 hours).

In a multiple-dose study in healthy young and elderly subjects, increased acitretin plasma concentrations were seen in elderly subjects. The range of terminal elimination half-lives observed for acitretin were 37 to 96 hours (harmonic mean=54 hours) in elderly and 39 to 70 hours (harmonic mean=53 hours) in young subjects.

Following oral absorption, acitretin undergoes metabolism and interconversion by simple isomerization to its 13-cis form. Both acitretin and its 13-cis isomer are eliminated from the body primarily by metabolism to chain-shortened breakdown products and conjugates. Acitretin is more than 98% bound to plasma proteins, primarily albumin.

Measurable levels of etretinate, of which acitretin is the active metabolite, have been detected in plasma samples of patients administered acitretin. The use of alcohol may have been a factor contributing to the presence of etretinate in these patients. In a 2-way crossover study in healthy volunteers, all 10 subjects formed etretinate following the ingestion of a single 100 mg oral dose of acitretin in the presence of alcohol (1.4 g/kg ethanol over approximately 3 hours). Peak concentrations of etretinate measured in these subjects ranged from 22 ng/mL to 105 ng/mL (mean: 55 ng/mL). When acitretin was administered in the absence of ethanol in this study, etretinate was not measurable. However, the formation of etretinate from acitretin in the absence of ethanol cannot be excluded. Etretinate has a long elimination phase. When etretinate has been used as primary therapy, etretinate has been found in the blood of some patients up to 2.9 years after discontinuation of treatment. Of 240 evaluated psoriatic patients who received treatment with acitretin (5 to 60 mg/day) with no restrictions on alcohol use, 7.5% were found to have measurable concentrations of etretinate (range: 5 to 62 ng/mL) and a further 27% had a trace of etretinate in the plasma which was not measurable.

Indications: For the treatment of severe psoriasis (includes erythrodermic and pustular types) and other disorders of keratinization.

Severe psoriasis is a condition that involves more than 10% of body surface area or is physically, occupationally or psychologically disabling.

Because of significant adverse effects associated with its use, acitretin should be reserved for patients with the diseases listed above when these are unresponsive to or intolerant of standard treatment. Acetretin should only be prescribed by physicians knowledgeable in the use of systemic retinoids. It is recommended that each acitretin prescription is limited to preferably a 1-month supply in order to encourage patients to return for their regular appointments.

Most patients experience a relapse after discontinuing therapy. Subsequent courses, when clinically indicated, have produced similar therapeutic results.

Contraindications: *Pregnancy:* Acitretin is contraindicated in pregnancy. Retinoids are known to cause severe birth defects in a very high percentage of infants exposed to them in utero (see Warnings; Pregnancy, Pregnancy Testing, Contraception).

Females must not become pregnant while taking acitretin and effective contraception must be practised for an undetermined period of time of at least 2 years following discontinuation of acitretin. Thereafter, the patient and physician should assess the risks and desirability of discontinuing effective contraception, based on the most current information available. Measurable levels of etretinate, the prodrug of acitretin, have been detected in plasma samples of patients administered acitretin. The use of alcohol appears to be a factor contributing to the interconversion of acitretin back to etretinate. Ethanol must not be ingested during treatment with acitretin as clinical evidence has shown that etretinate can be formed with concurrent ingestion of acitretin and alcohol. Ethanol should be avoided for 2 months after cessation of therapy. The length of time necessary to wait after termination of acitretin treatment to ensure that no etretinate will be detectable in the blood has not been determined. Etretinate has a long elimination phase. When etretinate has been used as primary therapy, etretinate has been found in the blood of some patients up to 2.9 years after discontinuation of treatment.

Acitretin is contraindicated in females of childbearing potential unless **all** of the following conditions apply:

1. The patient has severe psoriasis or other severe disorders of keratinization.
2. The patient is reliable in understanding and carrying out instructions.
3. The patient is able to comply with mandatory contraceptive measures.
4. The patient has received, and acknowledged understanding of, a careful oral and printed explanation of the hazards of fetal exposure to acitretin and the risk of possible contraception failure. This explanation may include showing a line drawing to the patient of an infant with the characteristic external deformities resulting from retinoid exposure during pregnancy.
5. The patient has had a serum or urine pregnancy test with a sensitivity of at least 50 mIU/mL with a negative result, performed in a licensed laboratory, within 2 weeks prior to initiating therapy. The patient has had 2 or 3 days of the next normal menstrual period before acitretin therapy is initiated.

(Regarding items 2 to 5, see Warnings; Pregnancy, Pregnancy Testing, Contraception.)

Acitretin is also contraindicated in patients with severely impaired hepatic or renal function, intractable hyperlipidemia, hypervitaminosis A or hypersensitivity to vitamin A or its metabolites.

Warnings: *Pregnancy,* Pregnancy Testing and Contraception: The use of systemic retinoids in humans has been associated with congenital abnormalities. There is an extremely high risk that major human fetal abnormalities will occur if pregnancy occurs during treatment with acitretin. Potentially any exposed fetus can be affected. Major fetal abnormalities associated with retinoid administration during pregnancy have been reported; including meningomyelocoele, meningoencephalocoele, multiple synostosis, facial dysmorphia, anophthalmia, syndactyly, absences of terminal phalanges, malformations of hip, ankle and forearm, low set ears, high palate, decreased cranial volume and alterations of the skull and cervical vertebrae on x-ray.

Female patients of childbearing potential must not be given acitretin until pregnancy is excluded. A serum or urine pregnancy test with a sensitivity of at least 50 mIU/mL must be performed within 2 weeks prior to starting acitretin treatment. Acitretin treatment should start on the second or third day of the next normal menstrual period following this negative pregnancy test.

Effective contraception must be used for at least 1 month before starting acitretin treatment, during treatment and for an undetermined period of time of at least 2 years duration after discontinuation of treatment (see Contraindications). Thereafter, the patient and physician should assess the risks and desirability of discontinuing effective contraception, based on the most current information available. It is recommended that two reliable forms of contraception be used simultaneously unless abstinence is the chosen method.

Pregnancy occurring during treatment with acitretin and for an undetermined period of time of at least 2 years duration after its discontinuation carries the risk of fetal malformation (see Warnings above). Females must be fully counselled on the serious risks to the fetus should they become pregnant whilst undergoing acitretin treatment or after discontinuation of acitretin treatment. If pregnancy does occur during this time the physician and patient should discuss the desirability of continuing the pregnancy.

It is strongly recommended that all female patients of childbearing potential treated with acitretin have monthly pregnancy tests during treatment and at regular intervals for an undetermined period of time of at least 2 years duration after the discontinuation of treatment. These pregnancy tests will: a) Serve primarily to reinforce to the patient the necessity of avoiding pregnancy. b) In the event of accidental pregnancy, provide the physician and patient an immediate opportunity to discuss the serious risk to the fetus from this exposure to acitretin and the desirability of continuing the pregnancy in view of the potential teratogenic effect of acitretin (see Warnings above).

Women of childbearing potential who have switched from etretinate therapy to acitretin must continue to follow the contraceptive recommendations for etretinate when on acitretin therapy.

Lactation: Clinical data indicate that acitretin is excreted in human milk. Therefore, nursing mothers should not receive acitretin because of the potential for serious adverse reactions in nursing infants. Women should not breast-feed for an undetermined period of time of at least 2 years following discontinuation of acitretin.

Hyperostosis: In clinical trials with acitretin, patients were prospectively evaluated for evidence of development or change in bony abnormalities of the vertebral column following 6 months of treatment. Of 262 patients treated with acitretin, 7% had pre-existing abnormalities of the spine which showed new changes or progression of pre-existing findings. Changes included degenerative spurs, anterior bridging of spinal vertebrae, diffuse idiopathic skeletal hyperostosis, and narrowing and destruction of cervical disc space. These existing abnormalities may be in some part attributable to the underlying psoriasis and/or the patient's age. During the 6-month period of observation, no bone changes were seen in patients who had normal pretreatment x-rays. Other retinoids including etretinate, of which acitretin is the active metabolite, have been associated with the development of extraosseous calcification and/or hyperostosis. Calcification of the ligaments of the spine, tendon insertions of the arms and legs, and intraosseous membranes of the arms and legs, have been reported. Hyperostotic changes of the vertebrae, forearms, hips, acetabula, legs and calcanei have also been reported. It is not clear whether the extraosseous calcification and/or hyperostosis are progressive. Pre-treatment radiographs of the cervical, thoracic and lumbar spine may be useful when monitoring patients on long-term acitretin therapy. Early recognition of musculoskeletal symptoms associated with acitretin therapy may be important. There is some evidence that scintigraphic changes appear before radiographic findings. Scintigraphic changes may disappear after discontinuation of acitretin treatment; however, radiographic changes may persist. Bone scintigraphy may be important in monitoring patients on acitretin therapy since scintigraphic changes seem to precede radiographic changes.

In adults receiving long-term treatment with acitretin, appropriate examinations should be periodically performed in view of possible ossification abnormalities. If such disorders arise, the continuation of therapy should be discussed with the patient on the basis of a careful risk/benefit analysis. In 1 patient, spinal hyperostosis and calcification of spinal ligaments, resulting in compression of the spinal chord, appeared after several years' therapy with Tegison.

Hepatotoxicity: Hepatic function should be checked before starting treatment with acitretin every 1 to 2 weeks for the first 2 months after commencement and then every 3 months during treatment. If abnormal results are obtained, weekly checks should be instituted. If hepatic function fails to return to normal or deteriorates further, acitretin must be withdrawn. In such cases it is advisable to continue monitoring hepatic function for at least 3 months. Elevations of AST, ALT or LDH have occurred in 20 to 28% of patients treated with acitretin. One of the 329 patients treated in clinical trials had clinical jaundice with elevated serum bilirubin and transaminases considered possibly related to acitretin treatment. Liver function test results in this patient returned to normal after acitretin was discontinued.

If hepatotoxicity is suspected during treatment with acitretin, the drug should be discontinued and the etiology further investigated.

Ten of 652 patients treated in clinical trials of etretinate, of which acitretin is the active metabolite, had clinical or histologic hepatitis considered to be possibly or probably related to etretinate treatment. There have been 4 reports of hepatitis-related deaths worldwide; 2 of these patients had received etretinate for a month or less before presenting with hepatic symptoms.

Precautions: General: Patients should be advised that a transient worsening of their psoriasis may occur during the initial acitretin treatment period.

Benign Intracranial Hypertension (Pseudotumor Cerebri): Acitretin and other retinoids have been associated with cases of pseudotumor cerebri (benign intracranial hypertension). Early symptoms and signs of benign intracranial hypertension include headache, nausea and vomiting and visual disturbances. Patients with these symptoms should be examined for papilledema and if present, they should discontinue acitretin immediately and be referred for neurological diagnosis and care.

As tetracyclines can also cause an increase in intracranial pressure, their combination with acitretin should be avoided.

Ophthalmic Effects: Drug-related ophthalmic effects (dry eyes, irritation of eyes, brow and lash loss, blepharitis and/or crusting of lids, photophobia, redness, recurrent styes, pannus and subepithelial corneal lesions) were noted during treatment with acitretin in 29% of 252 patients who were followed with ophthalmic examinations. Patients should be advised that they may experience decreased tolerance to contact lenses during the initial treatment period.

Overall in clinical studies, decreased night vision was reported by 2 patients and blurring of vision by 3 patients.

The following additional ophthalmic effects have occurred in patients taking etretinate, of which acitretin is the active metabolite: decreased visual acuity, minimal posterior subcapsular cataract, iritis, blot retinal hemorrhage and scotoma.

Any patient receiving acitretin therapy, experiencing visual difficulties should discontinue this drug and undergo ophthalmic evaluation.

Lipids: Blood lipid determinations should be performed before acitretin is administered and again at intervals of 1 or 2 weeks until the lipid response to the drug is established, which is usually within 4 to 8 weeks. Approximately 65% of patients receiving acitretin during clinical trials experienced an elevation in serum triglycerides. Approximately 30% developed a decrease in high density lipoproteins (HDL). Approximately 9% experienced elevated serum cholesterol levels. These effects of acitretin were reversible upon cessation of therapy.

Patients with an increased tendency to develop hypertriglyceridemia include those with diabetes mellitus, obesity, increased alcohol intake or a familial history of these conditions.

Hypertriglyceridemia and lowered HDL may increase a patient's cardiovascular risk status. In addition, elevation of serum triglycerides to greater than 800 mg/dL has been associated with acute pancreatitis. Therefore, every attempt should be made to control significant elevations of triglycerides or HDL decreases by reduction of weight or restriction of dietary fat and alcohol intake while continuing acitretin therapy.

If, despite these measures, hypertriglyceridemia and low HDL levels persist, the discontinuation of acitretin should be considered. An associated risk of atherogenesis cannot be ruled out if these conditions persist.

Vitamin A: Acitretin is a derivative of vitamin A. To avoid the risk of additive toxic effects, patients should be advised against taking other systemic retinoids or vitamin supplements containing vitamin A.

Methotrexate: Due to an increased hepatitis risk, the combined use of acitretin and methotrexate should be avoided.

Children: Safety and efficacy of acitretin in children have not been established. Ossification of interosseous ligaments and tendons of the extremities, skeletal hyperostosis and premature epiphyseal closure have been reported with other systemic retinoids, including etretinate of which acitretin is the active metabolite. Due to the uncertain effect of long-term acitretin therapy on growth and skeletal development, acitretin should only be used in pediatric patients with the most severe forms of keratinization disorders for which there are no effective alternative therapies. Pretreatment x-rays for bone age including x-rays of the knees are advised. Bone scans (scintigraphs) and/or x-rays should be considered at yearly intervals when monitoring children on long-term therapy. In addition pain or limitation of movement should be evaluated by appropriate radiological examination.

Soriatane (cont'd)

Blood Donation: It is recommended that blood donation for transfusion purposes be deferred during therapy with acitretin and for an undetermined period of time of at least 2 years duration after discontinuation of treatment. Theoretically, blood from such donors could present a small risk to the fetus if transfused to a pregnant mother during the first trimester of pregnancy (see Contraindications).

Drug Interactions: Concomitant administration of vitamin A and other systemic retinoids must be avoided due to the risk of possible additive toxic effects.

The concomitant administration of methotrexate and etretinate has been associated with hepatitis, a similar increased hepatitis risk may be expected with the combined use of acitretin and methotrexate.

Preliminary studies indicated that acitretin does not influence the endogenous progesterone plasma concentrations induced by oral contraceptives. The effect of microdosed progesterone preparations may be diminished by interaction with acitretin. Therefore, microdosed progesterone preparations or "minipills" should not be used.

Concomitant administration of phenprocoumon and acitretin does not alter the hypothrombinemic effect of phenprocoumon or the plasma disposition of acitretin.

The pharmacokinetics of acitretin and digoxin are not altered by concomitant multiple dose regimens of these 2 drugs.

Concomitant administration of cimetidine did not alter the oral bioavailability of acitretin or the isomerization to its 13-cis form. Single oral doses of acitretin did not affect the steady state plasma concentration or renal clearance of cimetidine.

Limited data which could not be duplicated, indicated that acitretin treatment either increased insulin sensitivity directly or interacted with glyburide to do so. Careful supervision of diabetic patients under treatment with acitretin is recommended.

Adverse Effects: Hypervitaminosis A produces a wide spectrum of signs and symptoms primarily of the mucocutaneous, musculoskeletal, hepatic and central nervous systems. Nearly all of the clinical adverse events reported to date with acitretin administration resemble those of the hypervitaminosis A syndrome. Table I and Table II (on following page) list, grouped by frequency, the adverse reactions reported during clinical trials in which patients were treated with acitretin for psoriasis.

Other reported laboratory abnormalities include: increased creatinine phosphokinase (37%), increased (21%) or decreased (7%) fasting blood sugar and increased (7%) or decreased (3%) iron.

Overdose: Symptoms and Treatment: To date, there has been no experience with acute overdose of acitretin. In the event of acute overdosage, evacuation of the stomach should be considered during the first few hours after this overdose. Signs and symptoms of overdosage with acitretin would probably be similar to acute vitamin A toxicity, i.e., severe headache, nausea or vomiting, drowsiness, irritability and pruritus. Elevated intracranial pressure has been reported with both acute and chronic vitamin A overdoses as well as in patients treated with therapeutic doses of acitretin. Patients with a acitretin overdose should be monitored closely for signs of increased intracranial pressure. If overdosage occurs in patients already receiving therapeutic doses of acitretin, the drug must be discontinued immediately.

All female patients of childbearing potential who have taken an overdose of acitretin must: 1. Have a pregnancy test at the time of the overdose. 2. Use an effective form of contraception for an undetermined period of time of at least 2 years duration after the overdose.

If the pregnancy test is positive, the patient should be fully counselled on the serious risk to the fetus from this exposure to acitretin and the physician and patient should discuss the desirability of continuing the pregnancy (see Contraindications and Warnings).

Dosage: There is intersubject variation in the pharmacokinetics, clinical efficacy, and incidence of side effects with acitretin. Individualization of dosage is required to achieve maximum therapeutic response while minimizing side effects.

Initial Therapy: Therapy should be initiated at 25 mg/day, given as a single dose with the main meal. If by 4 weeks the response is unsatisfactory, and in the absence of toxicity, the daily dose may be gradually increased to a maximum of 75 mg/day. The dose may be reduced if necesssary to minimize side effects.

Table I—Soriatane

Adverse Events

Body System	Most Frequent >10%	Less Frequent[a] 1-10%	Rare[a] <1%
Skin and Appendages	Skin peeling/scaling Alopecia Pruritus Sticky skin Nail disorder Dry skin Erythematous rash Skin atrophy Hyperesthesia	Paronychia Paresthesia Psoriaform rash Rash Photosensitivity reaction Pyogenic granuloma Bullous eruption Skin ulceration Cold/clammy skin Increased sweating Purpura Abnormal hair texture Skin fissures Hypoesthesia Infection Seborrhea	Dermatitis Abnormal skin odor Skin nodule Skin hypertrophy Skin disorder Impaired healing Eczema Otitis externa Flushing Acne
Mucous Membranes	Cheilitis Rhinitis Dry mouth	Thirst Stomatitis Gingivitis Increased saliva Gingival bleeding Epistaxis	Ulcerative stomatitis Pharyngitis Anal disorder Nose bleeds Altered saliva
Eye Disorders	Xerophthalmia	Conjunctivitis/irritation Abnormal/blurred vision Blepharitis[b] Eye pain Photophobia	Abnormal lacrimation Decreased night vision Cataract Eye abnormality Pannus[b] Recurrent styes[b] Subepithelial corneal lesions[b]
Musculoskeletal	Arthralgia	Myalgia Spinal hyperostosis[c] Back pain Hypertonia Arthritis	Arthrosis Leg cramps Olecranon bursitis
CNS	Rigors	Headache Pain	Abnormal gait Pseudotumor cerebri
Gastrointestinal		Nausea Abdominal pain	Constipation Diarrhea Tenesmus Dyspepsia Glossitis Melena Tongue ulceration Pancreatitis
Special Senses/Other		Tinnitus Taste perversion Earache Ceruminosis	Deafness Taste loss
Psychiatric		Insomnia Nervousness	Depression Somnolence Dysphonia
Respiratory			Coughing Laryngitis Sinusitis Increased sputum
Urinary			Dysuria Abnormal urine Balanoposthitis
Reproductive			Leukorrhea
Cardiovascular			Increased bleeding time Chest pain Angioedema Vasculitis[d]
Body as a Whole		Fatigue Anorexia Increased appetite Impotence Edema	Malaise Fever Moniliasis[e] Muscle weakness Alcohol intolerance Hot flashes Hepatitis[f] Icterus[f]

[a]Some may bear no relationship to therapy.
[b]Based on review of eye examination forms by consulting ophthalmologist (n=252).
[c]Incidence of 7% based on review of films by consulting radiologist (n=262).
[d]Vasculitis has not been documented with acitretin but has been seen with other retinoids.
[e]Increased incidence of vulvovaginitis due to C. albicans has been noted during treatment with Soriatane.
[f]Events observed and reported rarely.

Table II—Soriatane

Laboratory Abnormalities

Body System	**Laboratory Abnormality (%)**		**Comments**
Hepatic	**Increased**		
	ALT	(28%)	—In most patients, elevations were slight to moderate and returned to normal either during continuation of therapy or after cessation of treatment.
	AST	(23%)	
	LDH	(21%)	—**If hepatotoxicity is suspected, therapy should be discontinued (see Contraindications and Warnings).**
	Alkaline Phosphatase	(16%)	
	GGTP	(14%)	
	Direct Bilirubin	(11%)	
	Increased		
	Triglycerides	(65%)	—These changes are more common in patients who are predisposed to hypertriglyceridemia (see Precautions).
	Cholesterol	(9%)	
	Decreased		
	HDL	(30%)	—The effects on triglycerides, cholesterol and HDL were reversible upon cessation of acitretin therapy.
	Increased		
	Total Bilirubin	(2%)	
	Globulin	(2%)	
	Decreased		
	Serum Albumin	(1%)	
Renal	**Increased**		
	Uric Acid	(17%)	
	Creatinine	(5%)	
	BUN	(2%)	
Hematologic	**Increased**		
	Reticulocytes	(38%)	
	WBC	(11%)	
	Eosinophils	(8%)	
	Monocytes	(7%)	
	Bands	(4%)	
	Basophils	(3%)	
	Decreased		
	WBC	(7%)	
	Increased	**Decreased**	
	(16%) Neutrophils	(5%)	
	(2%) Lymphocytes	(11%)	
	(4%) Hemoglobin	(9%)	
	(2%) Platelets	(6%)	
	(3%) Hematocrit	(5%)	
	(2%) RBC	(3%)	
Urinary	RBC in urine	(10%)	
	WBC in urine	(7%)	
	Glycosuria	(4%)	
	Acetonuria	(3%)	
	Proteinuria	(2%)	
Electrolytes	**Increased**	**Decreased**	
	(16%) Phosphorus	(3%)	
	(12%) Potassium	(3%)	
	(12%) Magnesium	(12%)	
	(2%) Sodium	(1%)	
	(4%) Calcium	(2%)	
	(2%) Chloride	(3%)	

Maintenance Therapy: Psoriasis: Maintenance doses of 25 to 50 mg/day may be given after initial response to treatment. The maintenance dose should be based on clinical efficacy and tolerability. It may be necessary in some cases to increase the dose to a maximum of 75 mg/day.

In general, therapy should be terminated when lesions have resolved sufficiently. Relapses may be treated as outlined for initial therapy.

Other Keratinization Disorders: Maintenance doses of 10 mg to a maximum of 50 mg/day may be given for disorders of keratinization.

Information for the Patient: See Blue Section—Information for the Patient "Soriatane".

Supplied: 10 mg: Each brown and white, hard gelatin capsule (No. 4), marked ROCHE ROCHE, contains: acitretin 10 mg. Nonmedicinal ingredients: gelatin, maltodextrin, microcrystalline cellulose and sodium ascorbate; gelatin capsule shell: iron oxide (yellow, black and red) and titanium dioxide. Push-through blister packages of 30.

25 mg: Each brown and yellow, hard gelatin capsule (No. 1), marked ROCHE ROCHE, contains: acitretin 25 mg. Nonmedicinal ingredients: gelatin, maltodextrin, microcrystalline cellulose and sodium ascorbate; gelatin capsule shell: iron oxide (yellow, black and red) and titanium dioxide. Push-through blister packages of 30.

Store at 15 to 30°C. Protect from light.

(Shown in Product Recognition Section)

Reviewed 1998

SOROPON®
Purdue Frederick

Tyrothricin Compound
Shampoo

Supplied: Each mL of lemon colored, perfumed shampoo contains: triethanolamine polypeptide cocoate condensate 12%, tyrothricin 0.1%, propylene glycol 50% and parabens as preservatives. pH: 5.8 to 6.2. Bottles of 110 mL. Expiration period: 3 years from date of manufacture.

SOTACOR® ℞
Bristol

Sotalol HCl
Antiarrhythmic

Pharmacology: Sotalol has both beta-adrenoreceptor blocking (Vaughan Williams Class II) and cardiac action potential duration prolongation (Vaughan Williams Class III) antiarrhythmic properties. Sotalol is a racemic mixture of d-and l-sotalol. Both isomers have similar class III antiarrhythmic effects, while the l-isomer is responsible for virtually all of the beta-blocking activity. Sotalol is noncardioselective and is not associated with partial agonist or membrane stabilizing activity. Like other beta-blockers, sotalol inhibits renin release. The renin-suppressive effect of sotalol is significant both at rest and during exercise. Its beta-adrenergic activity causes a reduction in heart rate (negative chronotropic effect) and a limited reduction in the force of contraction (negative inotropic effect). These cardiac changes reduce myocardial oxygen consumption and cardiac work. The class II and III properties may be reflected on the surface electrocardiogram by a lengthening of the PR, QT and QT_c (QT corrected for heart rate) intervals with no significant alteration in the QRS duration. Whereas significant beta-blockade may occur at oral doses as low as 25 mg, Class III effects are seen at daily doses of 160 mg and above. The antiarrhythmic activity of sotalol appears to be primarily due to the drug's Class III property, based on animal models.

Pharmacologically, in addition to its antiarrhythmic properties, sotalol also has antihypertensive and anti-anginal properties.

Electrophysiology: Sotalol prolongs the plateau phase of the cardiac action potential in the isolated myocyte, as well as in isolated tissue preparations of ventricular and atrial muscle (class III activity). In intact animals it slows heart rate, decreases AV nodal conduction and increases the refractory periods of atrial and ventricular muscle and conduction tissue.

In man, the class II (beta-blockade) electrophysiological effects of sotalol are manifested by increased sinus cycle length (slowed heart rate), decreased AV nodal conduction and increased AV nodal refractoriness. The class III electrophysiological effects in man include prolongation of the atrial and ventricular monophasic action potentials, and effective refractory period prolongation of atrial muscle, ventricular muscle, and atrioventricular accessory pathways (where present) in both the anterograde and retrograde directions. With oral doses of 160 to 640 mg/day, the surface ECG shows dose-related mean increases of 40 to 100 msec in QT and 10 to 40 msec in QT_c (see Warnings). No significant alteration in QRS interval is observed.

In a small study (n=25) of patients with implanted defibrillators treated concurrently with sotalol, the average defibrillatory threshold was 6 joules (range 2 to 15 J) compared to a mean of 16 J for a nonrandomized comparative group primarily receiving amiodarone.

In a randomized clinical trial [Electrophysiologic Study Versus Electrocardiographic Monitoring (ESVEM) Trial] comparing choice of antiarrhythmic therapy by PES suppression versus Holter monitor selection (in each case followed by treadmill exercise testing) in patients with a history of sustained VT/VF who were also inducible by PES, the effectiveness acutely and chronically of sotalol was compared with 6 other drugs (procainamide, quinidine, mexiletine, propafenone, imipramine and pirmenol). Overall response, limited to first randomized drug, was 39% for sotalol and 30% for the pooled other drugs. Acute response rate for first drug randomized using suppression of PES induction was 36% for sotalol versus a mean of 13% for the other drugs. Using the Holter monitoring endpoint (complete suppression of sustained VT, 90% suppression of NSVT, 80% suppression of VPC pairs, and at least 70% suppression of VPCs), sotalol yielded 41% response versus 45% for the other drugs combined. Among responders placed on long-term therapy identified acutely as effective (by either PES or Holter), sotalol, when compared to the pool of other drugs, had the lowest 2-year mortality (13% versus 22%), the lowest 2-year VT recurrence rate (30% versus 60%), and the lowest withdrawal rate (38% versus about 75 to 80%). The most commonly used doses of sotalol in this trial were 320 to 480 mg/day (66% of patients), with 16% receiving 240 mg/day or less and 18% receiving 640 mg or more.

It cannot be determined, however, in the absence of a controlled comparison of sotalol versus no pharmacologic treatment (e.g., in patients with implanted defibrillators) whether

Sotacor (cont'd)

sotalol response causes improved survival or identifies a population with a good prognosis.

Hemodynamics: In a study of systemic hemodynamic function measured invasively in 12 patients with a mean left ventricular (LV) ejection fraction of 37% and ventricular tachycardia (9 sustained and 3 nonsustained), a median dose of 160 mg twice daily of sotalol produced a 28% reduction in heart rate and a 24% decrease in cardiac index at 2 hours postdosing at steady-state. Concurrently, systemic vascular resistance and stroke volume showed nonsignificant increases of 25% and 8%, respectively. Pulmonary capillary wedge pressure increased significantly from 6.4 mmHg to 11.8 mmHg in the 11 patients who completed the study. One patient was discontinued because of worsening congestive heart failure. Mean arterial pressure, mean pulmonary artery pressure and stroke work index did not significantly change. Exercise and isoproterenol induced tachycardia are antagonized by sotalol and total peripheral resistance increases by a small amount.

Sotalol causes little or no change in systemic blood pressure in normotensive patients, and no significant changes in pulmonary vascular pressures have been noted. In hypertensive patients, sotalol produces significant reductions in both systolic and diastolic blood pressures. Although sotalol is usually well-tolerated hemodynamically, caution should be exercised in patients with marginal cardiac compensation as deterioration in cardiac performance may occur (see Warnings: Congestive Heart Failure).

Pharmacokinetics: Healthy Subjects: The oral bioavailability of sotalol is 90 to 100%. After oral administration, peak plasma concentrations are reached in 2.5 to 4 hours, and steady-state plasma concentrations are attained within 2 to 3 days. Over the dosage range of 160 to 640 mg/day, sotalol displays dose proportionality with respect to plasma concentrations. Distribution occurs to a central (plasma) and to a peripheral compartment, with a mean elimination half-life of 10 to 20 hours.

Sotalol does not bind to plasma proteins and is not metabolized. The pharmacokinetics of the d and l enantiomers of sotalol are essentially identical. Sotalol crosses the blood brain barrier poorly. In one study, mean cerebrospinal fluid concentrations following a single oral dose ranged from 5 to 28% of those observed in plasma. The primary route of elimination is renal excretion. Approximately 80 to 90% of a dose is excreted unchanged in the urine, while the remainder is excreted in the feces.

Renally Impaired Patients: Lower doses are necessary in renal impairment (see Dosage and Precautions).

Hepatically Impaired Patients: Since sotalol is not subject to first-pass metabolism, patients with hepatic impairment show no alteration in clearance of sotalol.

Geriatrics: Age does not significantly alter the pharmacokinetics of sotalol, but impaired renal function in elderly patients can increase the terminal elimination half-life, resulting in increased drug accumulation.

Effect of Food: When sotalol was administered with a standard meal, the absorption of sotalol was reduced by approximately 20% compared to that in the fasting state.

Indications:

> No antiarrhythmic drug has been shown to reduce the incidence of sudden death in patients with **asymptomatic** ventricular arrhythmias. Most antiarrhythmic drugs have the potential to cause dangerous arrhythmias; some have been shown to be associated with an increased incidence of sudden death. In light of the above, physicians should carefully consider the risks and benefits of antiarrhythmic therapy for all patients with ventricular arrhythmias.

For the treatment of documented life-threatening ventricular arrhythmias such as sustained ventricular tachycardia. Sotalol may also be used for the treatment of patients with documented symptomatic ventricular arrhythmias when the symptoms are of sufficient severity to require treatment. Because of the proarrhythmic effects of sotalol, its use should be reserved for patients in whom, in the opinion of the physician, the benefit of treatment clearly outweighs the risks.

For patients with sustained ventricular tachycardia, sotalol therapy should be initiated in the hospital. Hospitalization may also be required for certain other patients depending on their cardiac status and underlying cardiac disease.

In view of the proarrhythmic effects of sotalol, its use in patients with hypertension or angina pectoris is not recommended unless they also require sotalol for the treatment of ventricular arrhythmias.

Contraindications: In patients with bronchial asthma or chronic obstructive airway disease, allergic rhinitis, severe sinus node dysfunction, symptomatic sinus bradycardia, sick sinus syndrome, second- and third-degree AV block (unless a functioning pacemaker is present), congenital or acquired long QT syndrome, cardiogenic shock, severe or uncontrolled congestive heart failure, hypokalemia, renal failure, anesthesia with agents that produce myocardial depression and previous evidence of hypersensitivity to sotalol.

Warnings: Mortality: The results of the Cardiac Arrhythmia Suppression Trial (CAST) in postmyocardial infarction patients with asymptomatic ventricular arrhythmias showed a significant increase in mortality and in nonfatal cardiac arrest rate in patients treated with encainide or flecainide compared with a matched placebo-treated group. CAST was continued using a revised protocol with the moricizine and placebo arms only. The trial was prematurely terminated because of a trend towards an increase in mortality in the moricizine treated group. The applicability of these results to other populations or other antiarrhythmic agents is uncertain, but at present it is prudent to consider these results when using any antiarrhythmic agent.

Proarrhythmia: Sotalol may cause new or worsen existing arrhythmias. Such proarrhythmic effects range from an increase in frequency of premature ventricular contractions to the development of more severe ventricular tachycardia, ventricular fibrillation or torsades de pointes. It is therefore essential that each patient administered sotalol be evaluated clinically and electrocardiographically prior to, and during therapy to determine whether the response to sotalol supports continued treatment. Sotalol, like some antiarrhythmic agents, has been associated with a specific form of arrhythmia, torsades de pointes, which is defined as a polymorphic ventricular tachycardia with prolongation of the QT interval and QRS complexes of changing amplitude that appear to twist around the isoelectric axis. Torsades have been observed more frequently in patients with an elevated baseline QT (>430 msec), on-therapy QT of >500 msec, bradycardia (heart rate <50 bpm), hypokalemia and hypomagnesemia (e.g., as a consequence of diuretic use) (see Warnings, Electrolyte Disturbances), high plasma drug concentrations (e.g., as a consequence of overdosage or renal insufficiency), with the concomitant use of sotalol and other medications such as antidepressants and Class I antiarrhythmics and congestive heart failure. ECG monitoring immediately prior to or following the episodes usually reveals a significantly prolonged QT interval and a significantly prolonged Qt_c interval. In clinical trials, sotalol generally has not been initiated to patients whose pretreatment Qt_c interval exceeded 450 msec. Sotalol should be titrated very cautiously in patients with prolonged QT intervals. Because of the variable temporal recurrence of arrhythmias, it is not always possible to distinguish between a new or aggravated arrhythmic event and lack of efficacy. Thus, the incidence of drug-related events cannot be precisely determined and the rates of occurrence provided below must be considered approximations. It should be noted that drug-induced arrhythmias may often not be identified until late after starting the drug because of infrequent monitoring. Due to the possibility of proarrhythmic effects, sotalol is not recommended for the treatment of patients with asymptomatic premature contractions (see Indications).

Torsades de pointes is dose dependent, usually occurs early after initiating therapy or escalation of the dose, and terminates spontaneously in the majority of patients. Although most episodes of torsades de pointes are self-limited or associated with symptoms (e.g., syncope), they can progress to ventricular fibrillation.

Overall in clinical trials with sotalol, 4.3% of 3 257 patients experienced a new or worsened ventricular arrhythmia. Of this 4.3%, new or worsened sustained ventricular tachycardia was reported in approximately 1% of patients, and torsades de pointes in 2.4%. Additionally, in approximately 1% of patients, deaths were considered possibly drug-related; such cases, although difficult to evaluate, may have been associated with proarrhythmic events. In patients with a history of sustained ventricular tachycardia, the incidence of torsades de pointes was 4%, and worsened VT was approximately 1%; in patients with other, less serious, ventricular arrhythmias and supraventricular arrhythmias, the incidence of torsades de pointes was 1% and 1.4%, respectively.

As shown in Table I, torsades de pointes arrhythmias as well as the prolongation of QT (QT_c) interval were dose related.

Table I—Sotacor

Percent Incidence of Torsades de pointes and Mean QT_c* Interval by Dose for Patients with Sustained VT/VF

Daily Dose (mg)	Incidence of Torsades de pointes	Mean QT_c* (msec)
80	0% (69)	463 (17)
160	0.5% (832)	467 (181)
320	1.6% (835)	473 (344)
480	4.4% (459)	483 (234)
640	3.7% (324)	490 (185)
>640	5.8% (103)	512 (62)

( ) Number of patients assessed.
*Highest on-therapy value.

In addition to dose and presence of sustained VT, other risk factors for torsades de pointes were gender (females had a higher incidence), excessive prolongation of the QT_c interval (see Table II) and history of cardiomegaly or congestive heart failure. Patients with sustained ventricular tachycardia and a history of congestive heart failure appear to have the highest risk for serious proarrhythmia (7%). Of the patients experiencing torsades de pointes, approximately two-thirds spontaneously reverted to their baseline rhythm. The others were either converted electrically (D/C cardioversion or overdrive pacing) or treated with other drugs (see Overdose: Symptoms and Treatment). It is not possible to determine whether some sudden deaths represented episodes of torsades de pointes, but in some instances sudden death did follow a documented episode of torsades de pointes. Although sotalol therapy was discontinued in most patients experiencing torsades de pointes, 17% were continued on a lower dose. Nonetheless, sotalol should be used with particular caution if the QT_c is greater than 500 msec on-therapy and serious consideration should be given to reducing the dose or discontinuing therapy when the QT_c exceeds 550 msec. Due to the multiple risk-factors associated with torsades de pointes, however, caution should be exercised regardless of the QT_c interval. Table II relates the incidence of torsades de pointes to on-therapy QT_c and change in QT_c from baseline. It should be noted, however, that the highest on-therapy QT_c was in many cases the one obtained at the time of the torsades de pointes event, so that the Table overstates the predictive value of a high QT_c.

Proarrhythmic events must be anticipated not only on initiating therapy, but with every upward dose adjustment. Proarrhythmic events most often occur within 7 days of initiating therapy or of an increase in dose; 75% of serious proarrhythmias (torsades de pointes and worsened VT) occurred within 7 days of initiating sotalol therapy, while 60% of such events occurred within 3 days of initiation or a dosage change. Initiating therapy at 80 mg b.i.d. with gradual upward dose titration and appropriate evaluations for efficacy (e.g., PES or Holter) and safety (e.g., QT interval, heart rate and electrolytes) prior to dose escalation, should reduce the risk of proarrhythmia. Avoiding excessive accumulation of sotalol in patients with diminished renal function, by appropriate dose reduction, should also reduce the risk of proarrhythmia (see Dosage).

Table II—Sotacor

Relationship between QT_c Interval Prolongation and Torsades de pointes

On-therapy QT_c Interval (msec)	Incidence of Torsades de pointes	Change in QT_c Interval from Baseline (msec)	Incidence of Torsades de pointes
<500	1.3% (1 787)	<65	1.6% (1 516)
500-525	3.4% (236)	65-80	3.2% (158)
525-550	5.6% (125)	80-100	4.1% (146)
>550	10.8% (157)	100-130	5.2% (115)
		>130	7.1% (99)

( ) Number of patients assessed.

Electrolyte Disturbances: Sotalol should not be used in patients with hypokalemia or hypomagnesemia prior to correction of such imbalance, as these conditions can exaggerate the degree of QT prolongation and increase the potential for torsades de pointes. The serum electrolytes must be monitored regularly and more frequently if diuretics are used concomitantly. Special attention should be given to electrolyte and acid-base balance in patients experiencing severe or prolonged diarrhea or patients receiving concomitant diuretics.

Congestive Heart Failure: Sympathetic stimulation is a vital component supporting circulatory function in congestive heart failure (CHF), and beta-blockade carries the potential hazard of further depressing myocardial contractility and precipitating more severe failure. Moreover, patients with CHF have a higher risk of torsades de pointes (see Warnings, Proarrhythmia).

In patients with controlled CHF, sotalol should be administered cautiously. The positive inotropic action of digitalis may be reduced when the 2 drugs are used concomitantly. Both digitalis and sotalol slow AV conduction. If cardiac failure continues despite adequate digitalization, sotalol should be discontinued. Caution is also advised when initiating therapy in patients with agents such as ACE inhibitors, diuretics etc.; a low initial dose and careful titration dose titration is appropriate.

In patients without a history of heart failure, continued depression of the myocardium over a period of time can, in some cases, lead to cardiac failure. At the first sign of impending heart failure, appropriate therapy must be established and consideration should be given to discontinuation of treatment with sotalol.

In clinical trials, new or worsened congestive heart failure (CHF) occurred in 3.3% (n=3 257) of patients and led to discontinuation in approximately 1% of patients receiving sotalol. The incidence was higher in patients presenting with sustained ventricular tachycardia/fibrillation (4.6%, n=1 363), or a prior history of heart failure (7.3%, n=696). Based on a life-table analysis, the one-year incidence of new or worsened CHF was 3% in patients without a prior history and 10% in patients with a prior history of CHF. NYHA Classification was also closely associated to the incidence of new or worsened heart failure in patients receiving sotalol (1.8% in 1 395 Class I patients, 4.9% in 1 254 Class II patients and 6.1% in 278 Class III or IV patients).

Conduction Disturbances: Excessive prolongation of the QT interval (>550 msec) can promote serious arrhythmias and should be avoided (see Proarrhythmia). Sinus bradycardia (heart rate less than 50 bpm) occurred in 13% of patients receiving sotalol in clinical trials, and led to discontinuation in about 3% of patients. Bradycardia itself increases the risk of torsades de pointes. Sinus pause, sinus arrest and sinus node dysfunction occur in less than 1% of patients. The incidence of second- or third-degree AV block is approximately 1%.

Recent Myocardial Infarction: Caution should be exercised when sotalol is given to patients with recent myocardial infarction. Experience in the use of sotalol in the early stage of recovery from acute myocardial infarction is limited and, at least at high initial doses, not reassuring. In patients with impaired left ventricular function, the risk versus benefit of sotalol administration must be considered. Careful monitoring and dose titration are critical during initiation and follow-up therapy.

The adverse results of clinical trials involving antiarrhythmic drugs (i.e., apparent increase in mortality) suggest that sotalol should be avoided in patients with left ventricular ejection fractions ≤40% without serious ventricular arrhythmias.

In a large controlled trial in patients with a recent myocardial infarction without heart failure, who did not necessarily have ventricular arrhythmias, oral sotalol treatment was associated with a nonstatistically significant risk reduction in mortality compared to the placebo group (18%). In this post-infarction study using a fixed dose of 320 mg once daily and in a second small randomized trial in high-risk postinfarction patients with left ventricular ejection fractions ≤40% treated with high doses (640 mg/day), there were suggestions of an excess of early sudden deaths.

In a double-blind, placebo-controlled secondary prevention trial in 1 456 postinfarction patients who did not necessarily have ventricular arrhythmias, sotalol was given as a non-titrated dose of 320 mg once daily. The results did not suggest an adverse effect on survival; however, there was a suggestion of excess mortality (3% on sotalol versus 2% on placebo) during the first 10 days of the trial. In another trial, where high doses of sotalol (320 mg twice daily) were given to a small number of high-risk postinfarction patients (n=17 randomized to sotalol), there were 4 fatalities and 3 serious hemodynamic/electrical adverse events within 2 weeks of initiating sotalol.

Abrupt Cessation of Therapy: Patients should be warned against abrupt interruption or discontinuation of sotalol. Hypersensitivity to catecholamines has been observed in patients withdrawn from beta-blocker therapy. There have been occasional reports of severe exacerbation of angina pectoris, ventricular arrhythmias and in some cases myocardial infarction following abrupt discontinuation of beta-blocker therapy. The last two complications may occur with or without preceding exacerbation of angina pectoris. Therefore, it is prudent when discontinuing chronically administered sotalol, particularly in patients with ischemic heart disease, to carefully monitor the patient and to discontinue sotalol in a stepwise manner or consider the temporary use of an alternate beta-blocker if appropriate. If possible, the dosage should be gradually reduced over a period of 1 to 2 weeks. The same frequency of administration should be maintained. If angina markedly worsens or acute coronary insufficiency develops, appropriate therapy should be instituted promptly. Because coronary artery disease is common and may be unrecognized in patients receiving sotalol, abrupt discontinuation in patients with arrhythmias may unmask latent coronary insufficiency.

Anaphylaxis: While taking beta-blockers, patients with a history of anaphylactic reactions to a variety of allergens may have a more severe reaction on repeated challenge, either accidental, diagnostic or therapeutic.

There may be increased difficulty in treating an allergic type reaction in patients on beta-blockers. In these patients, the reaction may be more severe due to pharmacologic effects of the beta-blockers and problems with fluid changes. Epinephrine should be administered with caution since it may not have its usual effects in the treatment of anaphylaxis. On the one hand, larger doses of epinephrine may be needed to overcome the bronchospasm, while on the other hand, these doses can be associated with excessive alpha adrenergic stimulation with consequent hypertension, reflex bradycardia and heart block and possible potentiation of bronchospasm. Alternatives to the use of large doses of epinephrine include vigorous supportive care such as fluids and the use of beta agonists including parenteral salbutamol or isoproterenol to overcome bronchospasm and norepinephrine to overcome hypotension.

Nonallergic Bronchospasm (e.g., chronic bronchitis and emphysema): Patients with bronchospastic diseases should in general not receive beta-blockers. It is prudent, if sotalol is to be administered, to use the smallest effective dose, so that inhibition of bronchodilation produced by endogenous or exogenous catecholamine stimulation of $beta_2$ receptors may be minimized.

Skin Rashes and Oculomucocutaneous Syndrome: Various skin rashes and conjunctival xerosis have been reported with beta-blockers, including sotalol. A severe syndrome (oculomucocutaneous syndrome) whose signs include conjunctivitis sicca and psoriasiform rashes, otitis, and sclerosing serositis has occurred with the chronic use of one beta-adrenergic-blocking agent (practolol). This syndrome has not been observed with sotalol. Physicians, however, should be alert to the possibility of such reactions and should discontinue treatment in the event that they occur.

Thyrotoxicosis: In patients with thyrotoxicosis, sotalol may mask the clinical signs of hyperthyroidism or its complications and give a false impression of improvement. Patients suspected of developing thyrotoxicosis should be managed carefully to avoid abrupt withdrawal of sotalol which might be followed by an exacerbation of the symptoms of hyperthyroidism, including thyroid storm.

Precautions: Renal Impairment: Renal function tests should be carried out at appropriate intervals. Caution should be observed in patients with impaired renal function since sotalol is eliminated mainly via the kidneys through glomerular filtration and to a small degree by tubular secretion. There is a direct relationship between renal function, as measured by serum creatinine or creatinine clearance, and the elimination rate of sotalol and its urinary excretion. Guidance for dosing in conditions of renal impairment can be found under Dosage.

Diabetes: Sotalol should be administered with caution to patients with history of spontaneous hypoglycemia or to patients with diabetes (especially labile diabetes) receiving insulin or oral hypoglycemic agents. Beta-adrenergic blockers may mask the premonitory signs and symptoms of acute hypoglycemia; e.g., tachycardia.

Anesthesia: It is not advisable to withdraw beta-adrenoceptor blocking drugs prior to surgery in the majority of patients. However, care should be taken when using sotalol with anesthetic agents such as cyclopropane or trichloroethylene which may depress the myocardium. Vagal dominance, if it occurs, may be corrected with atropine (1 to 2 mg i.v.).

Some patients receiving beta-adrenoceptor blocking agents have been subject to protracted severe hypotension during anesthesia. Difficulty in restarting the heart and maintaining the heartbeat has also been reported.

In emergency surgery, since sotalol is a competitive antagonist at beta-adrenoceptor sites, its effects may be reversed, if required, by sufficient doses of such agonists as isoproterenol or epinephrine.

Pregnancy: There are no studies in pregnant women. Sotalol has been shown to cross the placenta, and is found in amniotic fluid. There has been a report of subnormal birth weight with sotalol. Therefore, sotalol should be used during pregnancy only if the potential benefit outweighs the potential risk.

Lactation: Sotalol has been reported to be present in human milk. Because of the potential for adverse reactions from sotalol in nursing infants, a decision should be made whether to discontinue nursing or to discontinue the drug, taking into account the importance of the drug to the mother.

Children: The safety and effectiveness of sotalol in children under 18 have not been established.

Drug Interactions: Antiarrhythmics: Class Ia antiarrhythmic drugs, such as disopyramide, quinidine and procainamide, and Class III drugs (e.g., amiodarone) are not recommended as concomitant therapy with sotalol because of their potential to prolong refractoriness (see Warnings). There is only limited experience with the concomitant use of Class Ib or Ic antiarrhythmics. Additive class II effects would also be anticipated with the use of other beta-blocking agents concomitantly with sotalol.

Potassium-Depleting Diuretics: Hypokalemia or hypomagnesia may occur, increasing the potential for torsades de pointes (see Warnings, Electrolyte Disturbances).

Drugs Prolonging the QT Interval: Sotalol should also be given with extreme caution in conjunction with other drugs known to prolong the QT interval, such as Class I and Class III antiarrhythmics, phenothiazines, tricyclic antidepressants, terfenadine, astemizole, erythromycin, lithium and liquid protein diets.

Digoxin: Single and multiple doses of sotalol do not significantly affect serum digoxin levels. Proarrhythmic events were more common in sotalol treated patients also receiving digoxin. It is not clear whether this represents an interaction or is related to the presence of CHF, a known risk factor for proarrhythmia, in the patients receiving digoxin.

Calcium blocking drugs: Concurrent administration of beta-blocking agents and calcium channel blockers has resulted in hypotension, bradycardia, conduction defects, and cardiac failure. Beta-blockers should be avoided in combination with cardiodepressant calcium-channel blockers such as verapamil and diltiazem because of the additive effects of atrioventricular conduction and ventricular function.

Catecholamine-depleting Agents: Concomitant use of catecholamine-depleting drugs, such as reserpine and guanethidine, with a beta-blocker may produce an excessive reduction of resting sympathetic nervous tone. Patients should be closely monitored for evidence of hypotension and/or marked bradycardia, which may produce syncope.

Insulin and Oral Hypoglycemics: Hyperglycemia may occur and the dosage of antidiabetic drug may require adjustment. Symptoms of hypoglycemia may be masked by sotalol (see Precautions, Diabetes).

Clonidine: Beta-blocking drugs may potentiate the rebound hypertension sometimes observed after discontinuation of clonidine; therefore, the beta-blocker should be discontinued slowly several days before the gradual withdrawal of clonidine.

Beta-2-receptor Stimulants: Beta-agonists such as salbutamol, terbutaline and isoprenaline may have to be administered in increased dosages when used concomitantly with sotalol.

Drug/Laboratory Interaction: The presence of sotalol in the urine may result in falsely elevated levels of urinary metanephrine when measured by photometric methods. Patients suspected of having pheochromocytoma and who are treated with sotalol should have their urine screened utilizing the high performance liquid chromatographic assay with solid phase extraction.

Adverse Effects: Sotalol is well tolerated in the majority of patients, with the most frequent adverse events arising from its beta-blockade properties. Adverse events are usually transient in nature and rarely necessitate interruption of, or withdrawal from treatment. These include dyspnea, fatigue, dizziness, headache, fever, excessive bradycardia and/or hypotension. If they do occur, these side effects usually disappear when the dosage is reduced. The most significant adverse events, however, are those due to proarrhythmia, including torsades de pointes.

Sotacor (cont'd)

During premarketing trials, 3 186 patients with cardiac arrhythmias (1 363 with sustained ventricular tachycardia) received oral sotalol, of whom 2 451 received the drug for at least 2 weeks. The most important adverse effects are torsades de pointes and other serious new ventricular arrhythmias (see Warnings), occurring at rates of almost 4% and 1%, respectively, in the VT/VF population. Overall, discontinuation because of unacceptable side effects was necessary in 18% of all patients in clinical trials, and in 13% of patients treated for at least 2 weeks. The most common adverse reactions leading to discontinuation of sotalol are as follows: fatigue 4%, bradycardia (<50 bpm) 3%, dyspnea 3%, proarrhythmia 3%, asthenia 2%, and dizziness 2%.

Occasional reports of elevated serum liver enzymes have occurred with sotalol therapy but no cause and effect relationship has been established.

One case of peripheral neuropathy which resolved on discontinuation of sotalol and recurred when the patient was rechallenged with the drug was reported in an early dose tolerance study. Elevated blood glucose levels and increased insulin requirements can occur in diabetic patients.

Table III lists as a function of dosage the most common (incidence of 2% or greater) adverse events, regardless of relationship to therapy and the percent of patients discontinued due to the event, as collected from clinical trials involving 1 292 patients with sustained VT/VF.

Potential Adverse Effects: Marketing experience with sotalol shows an adverse experience profile similar to that described above from clinical trials. Voluntary reports since introduction include rare reports (less than one report per 10 000 patients) of: emotional lability, slightly clouded sensorium, incoordination, vertigo, paralysis, thrombocytopenia, eosinophilia, leukopenia, photosensitivity reaction, fever, pulmonary edema, hyperlipidemia, myalgia, pruritus, reversible alopecia.

Additional adverse effects have been reported with other beta-adrenergic blocking agents.

CNS: reversible mental depression progressing to catatonia; and acute reversible syndrome characterized by disorientation for time and place, short-term memory loss and decreased performance on neuropsychometrics.

Allergic: fever, combined with aching and sore throat, laryngospasm; respiratory distress.

Hematologic: agranulocytosis; thrombocytopenic or nonthrombocytopenia purpura.

Gastrointestinal: mesenteric arterial thrombosis; ischemic colitis.

Other: Peyronie's disease, Raynaud's phenomenon.

Overdose: Symptoms and Treatment: Intentional or accidental overdosage with sotalol has rarely resulted in death.

The most common signs to be expected are bradycardia, congestive heart failure, hypotension, bronchospasm and hypoglycemia. In cases of massive intentional overdosage (2 to 16 g) with sotalol the following clinical findings were seen: hypotension, bradycardia, prolongation of QT interval, torsades de pointes, ventricular tachycardia, and premature ventricular complexes. If overdosage occurs, therapy with sotalol should be discontinued. Close monitoring of the electrocardiogram in patients with suspected sotalol intoxication is essential. Because of the lack of protein binding, hemodialysis is useful for reducing sotalol plasma concentrations. Patients should be carefully observed until QTc intervals are normalized.

Every effort should be made to correct promptly metabolic and electrolyte imbalances which might contribute to the initiation of ventricular arrhythmias (see Warnings).

If required, the following therapeutic measures are suggested: Bradycardia: atropine, another anticholinergic drug, a beta-adrenergic agonist or transvenous cardiac pacing.

Heart Block (second- and third-degree): isoproterenol or transvenous cardiac pacemaker.

Congestive Heart Failure: conventional therapy.

Hypotension: Epinephrine rather than isoproterenol or norepinephrine may be useful, depending on associated factors, in addition to atropine and digitalis (see Precautions).

Bronchospasm: aerosolized beta-2-receptor stimulant or aminophylline.

Hypoglycemia: i.v glucose.

Torsades de pointes: epinephrine and/or magnesium sulfate, transvenous cardiac pacing, DC cardioversion.

It should be remembered that sotalol is a competitive antagonist of isoproterenol and, hence, large doses of isoproterenol can be expected to reverse many of the effects of excessive doses of sotalol. However, the complications of excess isoproterenol should not be overlooked.

Table III—Sotacor

Incidence (%) of Adverse Events and Discontinuations Associated with Daily Dose

Body System	160 mg (n=832)	240 mg (n=263)	320 mg (n=835)	480 mg (n=459)	640 mg (n=324)	Any Dose* (n=1 292)	% Patients Discont. (n=1 292)
Body as a Whole							
Infection	1	2	2	2	3	4	<1
Fever	1	2	3	2	2	4	<1
Localized pain	1	1	2	2	2	3	<1
Cardiovascular							
Dyspnea	5	8	11	15	15	21	2
Bradycardia	8	8	9	7	5	16	2
Chest pain	4	3	10	10	14	16	<1
Palpitation	3	3	8	9	12	14	<1
Edema	2	2	5	3	5	8	1
ECG abnormal	4	2	4	2	2	7	1
Hypotension	3	4	3	2	3	6	2
Proarrhythmia	<1	<1	2	4	5	5	3
Syncope	1	1	3	2	5	5	1
Heart failure	2	3	2	2	2	5	1
Presyncope	1	2	2	4	3	4	<1
Peripheral vascular disorder	1	2	1	1	2	3	<1
Cardiovascular disorder	1	<1	2	2	2	3	<1
Vasodilation	1	<1	1	2	1	3	<1
AICD discharge	<1	2	2	2	2	3	<1
Hypertension	<1	1	1	1	2	2	<1
Nervous							
Fatigue	5	8	12	12	13	20	2
Dizziness	7	6	11	11	14	20	1
Asthenia	4	5	7	8	10	13	1
Light-headed	4	3	6	6	9	12	1
Headache	3	2	4	4	4	8	<1
Sleep problem	1	1	5	5	6	8	<1
Perspiration	1	2	3	4	5	6	<1
Altered consciousness	2	3	1	2	3	4	<1
Depression	1	2	2	2	3	4	<1
Paresthesia	1	1	2	3	2	4	<1
Anxiety	2	2	2	3	2	4	<1
Mood change	<1	<1	1	3	2	3	<1
Appetite disorder	1	2	2	1	3	3	<1
Stroke	<1	<1	1	1	<1	1	<1
Digestive							
Nausea/Vomiting	5	4	4	6	6	10	1
Diarrhea	2	3	3	3	5	7	<1
Dyspepsia	2	3	3	3	3	6	<1
Abdominal pain	<1	<1	2	2	2	3	<1
Colon problem	2	1	1	<1	2	3	<1
Flatulence	1	<1	1	1	2	2	<1
Respiratory							
Pulmonary problem	3	3	5	3	4	8	<1
Upper respiratory tract problem	1	1	3	4	3	5	<1
Asthma	1	<1	1	1	1	2	<1
Urogenital							
Genitourinary disorder	1	0	1	1	2	3	<1
Sexual dysfunction	<1	1	1	1	3	2	<1
Metabolic							
Abnormal lab value	1	2	3	2	1	4	<1
Weight change	1	1	1	<1	2	2	<1
Musculoskeletal							
Extremity pain	2	2	4	5	3	7	<1
Back pain	1	<1	2	2	2	3	<1
Skin and Appendages							
Rash	2	3	2	3	4	5	<1
Hematologic							
Bleeding	1	<1	1	<1	2	2	<1
Special Senses							
Visual problem	1	1	2	4	5	5	<1

*Because patients are counted at each dose level tested, the "Any Dose" column cannot be determined by adding across the doses.

Dosage: Sotalol, when used for the treatment of documented life-threatening ventricular arrhythmias, should be initiated and dose increased in a hospital with facilities for cardiac rhythm monitoring and assessment (see Indications). Sotalol should be administered only after appropriate clinical assessment, and the dosage of sotalol must be individualized on the basis of therapeutic response and tolerance. The usefulness of monitoring plasma level for optimization of therapy has not been established. Proarrhythmic events can occur not only at the initiation of therapy, but also with each upward dosage adjustment.

Dosage of sotalol should be adjusted gradually, allowing 2 to 3 days between dosing increments in order to attain steady-state plasma concentrations and to allow monitoring of QT intervals. Graded dose adjustment will help prevent the use of doses which are higher than necessary to control the arrhythmia. The recommended initial dose is 160 mg daily, given in 2 divided doses at approximately 12-hour intervals and taken preferably 1 to 2 hours before meals. If needed, this dose may be increased, after appropriate evaluation, to 240 or 320 mg/day. In most patients, a therapeutic response is obtained at a total daily dose of 160 to 320 mg/day, given in

2 divided doses. Some patients with life-threatening refractory arrhythmias may require doses as high as 480 to 640 mg/day; however, these doses should only be prescribed when the potential benefit outweighs the increased risk of adverse events, in particular proarrhythmias. Because of the long elimination half-life of sotalol, dosing on more than a twice daily regimen is not usually necessary.

Patients experiencing bradycardia or hypotension on initial administration of sotalol should be removed from therapy; sotalol may be later reintroduced at a lower dose. A dose reduction may also be advisable to alleviate symptoms of weakness and dizziness in cases where blood pressure remains low after more than a month of therapy.

Renal Impairment: Because sotalol is excreted predominantly in urine and its terminal elimination half-life is prolonged in conditions of renal impairment, a longer duration of dosing is required to reach steady-state. The dosing of sotalol should then be modified, when creatinine clearance is <60 mL/min, as shown in Table IV.

Table IV—Sotacor

Dosing Intervals in Renal Impairment

Creatinine Clearance (mL/min)	Dosing Recommendation
> 60	usual Sotacar dose
30–60	½ usual Sotacar dose
10–30	¼ usual Sotacor dose
< 10	avoid or use with caution

Dose increases in renal impairment should only be done after administration of at least 5 or 6 doses at appropriate intervals.

Transfer to and from Sotalol: Based on theoretical considerations rather than experimental data, the following suggestion is made: under careful monitoring and if the patient's clinical condition permits, when transferring patients from another antiarrhythmic drug to sotalol or from sotalol to another antiarrhythmic agent, allow at least 3 to 4 half-lives to elapse for the drug being discontinued before starting the alternative drug at the usual dosage. In patients where withdrawal of a previous antiarrhythmic agent is likely to produce life-threatening arrhythmias, the physician should consider hospitalizing the patient. After discontinuation of amiodarone, sotalol should not be initiated until the Qtc interval is less than 450 msec (see Warnings). Treatment has been initiated in some patients receiving i.v. lidocaine without ill effect.

Supplied: 80 mg: Each light blue, biconvex, capsule-shaped tablet, engraved with SOTACOR on one side and a full bisect bar, BL and 80 on the other contains: sotalol HCl 80 mg. Nonmedicinal ingredients: colloidal silicon dioxide, FD&C Blue No. 2, lactose, magnesium stearate, microcrystalline cellulose, starch and stearic acid. Bottles of 100.

160 mg: Each light blue, biconvex, capsule-shaped tablet, engraved with SOTACOR on one side and a full bisect bar, BL and 160 on the other contains: sotalol HCl 160 mg. Nonmedicinal ingredients: colloidal silicon dioxide, FD&C Blue No. 2, lactose, magnesium stearate, microcrystalline cellulose, starch and stearic acid. Bottles of 100.

Store at room temperature (15 to 30°C).

(Shown in Product Recognition Section)

Reviewed 1998

SOTAMOL ℞

Technilab

Sotalol HCL

Antiarrhythmic

Supplied: 80 mg: Each scored, blue caplet, engraved with TEC on one side, contains: sotalol HCl 80 mg. Nonmedicinal ingredients: colloidal silicon dioxide, FD&C Blue #2 aluminum lake, lactose, magnesium stearate, microcrystalline cellulose, starch and stearic acid. Bottles of 100.

160 mg: Each scored, blue caplet, engraved with TEC on one side, contains: sotalol HCl 160 mg. Nonmedicinal ingredients: colloidal silicon dioxide, FD&C Blue #2 aluminum lake, lactose, magnesium stearate, microcrystalline cellulose, starch and stearic acid. Bottles of 100.

Store at room temperature (15 to 30°C). Protect from light.

New Product 1998

SPECTRO DERM®

Spectropharm Dermatology

Polysiloxane-Cellulose Complex—Triglycerides

Skin Cleanser

Supplied: Each mL of cleanser contains: carbomer, diazolidinylurea, glycerin, isopentyldiol, butylene glycol, dimethicone copolyol, polysorbate 20, sorbitan oleate, almond glycerides, cetyl alcohol, cellulose, hydrated silica, ethanol, trolamine and water. Fragrance-free. Squeeze bottles of 200 mL. Pump bottles of 500 mL.

SPECTRO GLUVS "19"®

Spectropharm Dermatology

Perfluoropolymethylisopropyl Ether—Tricontanyl PVP—Dimethicone

Skin Barrier—Emollient

Supplied: Each mL of barrier cream contains: polyoxyethylene stearyl stearate, glyceryl polyacrylate, tricontanyl PVP, dimethicone, PEG 100 stearate and glyceryl stearate, myristyl myristate, cetyl alcohol, perfluoropolymethylisopropyl ether, phytolipid/hyaluronic acid, tocopheryl linoleate, sodium hydroxymethylglycinate, disodium EDTA, diazolidinylurea, tocopheryl acetate, ascorbyl palminate and water. Fragrance-free. Tubes of 60 and 120 mL.

SPECTRO GRAM "2"™

Spectropharm Dermatology

Chlorhexidine Gluconate

Topical Antibacterial—Antifungal

Pharmacology: Effective antisepsis against a wide range of gram negative and gram positive bacteria. In vitro testing showed the following destruction percentage in the 0 seconds to 1 minute period: E. coli -approx. 100%, S. aureus -approx. 95%, B. subtilis -approx. 100%, P. aeruginosa -approx. 99%, C. albicans -approx. 100%.

Indications: Topical skin antisepsis for health professionals and patients who encounter skin problems caused by soap solutions and other strong antiseptics and disinfectants. Especially useful where frequent and long-term use of hand antiseptics is required. General hospital and clinical use, administration of medication and injections, bandage changing, baby formula preparation, etc.

Contraindications: Hypersensitivity to any of the ingredients.

Precautions: Patients with ear drum perforation should avoid use near ear canal. Avoid usage near the eyes.

Dosage: Apply approximately 5 mL to moistened hands and rub vigorously to achieve a foam. Rinses off easily even in cold, hard water. May be used as often as required.

Supplied: Each mL of solution contains: chlorhexidine gluconate 2% w/v in a foaming nonmedicinal lactated vehicle. Nonmedicinal ingredients: vegetable triglycerides. Alcohol-, parabens- and sodium lauryl sulfate-free. Pump dispenser of 500 mL. Squeeze bottles of 200 mL. Containers of 1 and 4 L (available to health professionals, hospitals, clinics and laboratories).

SPECTRO JEL "609"®

Spectropharm Dermatology

Polysiloxane Cellulose Complex

Skin Cleanser

Supplied: Each mL of cleanser contains: diazolidinylurea, carbomer, glycerin, butylene glycol, dimethicone copolyol, polysorbate, sorbitan, cetyl alcohol, cellulose, hydrated silica, triethanolamine, ethanol and water. Squeeze bottles of 200 mL. Pump bottles of 500 mL. Scented or fragrance-free formulations are available.

SPECTRO TAR™ Antiseptic Shampoo

Spectropharm Dermatology

Chlorhexidine Gluconate—Coal Tar

Psoriasis—Seborrhea Therapy

Pharmacology: Tar promotes normalization of the keratinization processes and impedes the vitality of the malpighian cells, thereby slowing the rate of epithelial cell formation. Chlorhexidene gluconate, combined with a special biodegradable surfactant at a controlled pH manifests potent antibacterial and antifungal activity. A nonmedicinal lactic/lactate buffering system provides gentle desquamation, and an amino-protein compound assists in the treatment of damaged hair. Naphthalene, cresol and xylenol content of the tar has been greatly reduced thereby diminishing potential for phototoxicity, skin irritancy and harsh odor. Contains antioxidant tocopherols.

In vitro testing (0 to 2 minutes) has confirmed the shampoo's efficacy against P. ovale, C. albicans and S. aureus.

Indications: Symptomatic relief of seborrheic dermatitis, dandruff, scaling and itchy scalp, psoriatic syndrome.

Contraindications: Hypersensitivity to any of the ingredients.

Precautions: Photosensitivity may occur occasionally. Patients with ear drum perforation should avoid use near ear canal. Avoid usage near the eyes.

Dosage: Moisten scalp with warm water and apply a liberal amount of shampoo. Massage into scalp using fingertips in a gentle circular motion. Allow lather to remain on scalp for 2 or 3 minutes. Rinse off using lukewarm or cool water. Use 2 or 3 times weekly or as directed by physician.

Supplied: Each mL of foaming shampoo, stainless and virtually devoid of tar odor after rinsing, contains: chlorhexidine gluconate 1% w/v, and a special solution of coal tar 7.5% w/v in a soapless, biodegradable vehicle. Plastic bottles of 200 mL.

SPECTRO TAR Skin Wash™

Spectropharm Dermatology

Coal Tar

Psoriasis—Eczema Therapy—Antipruritic

Pharmacology: A special solution of coal tar with reduced naphthalene, cresol and xylenol content may diminish both phototoxicity and irritancy in the treatment of psoriasis. Tar induces keratinization and impedes rate of epithelial cell formation. Nonmedicinal lactic and linoleic acids assist in desquamation and aid the restoration of skin barrier function in the stratum corneum. The gentle foaming action is easily rinsed away with warm water leaving a clean and soft skin surface. Contains antioxidant tocopherols.

Indications: Scaly psoriatic lesions requiring desquamation and skin cleansing. Pruritus associated with eczematous eruptions. May replace soap cleansers in frequent daily washing.

Contraindications: Hypersensitivity to any of the ingredients.

Precautions: Photosensitivity may occur occasionally.

Dosage: Apply directly to moistened skin lesions and rub in with a gentle circular motion adding more water if necessary to create a smooth foam. May be left on skin for several minutes prior to rinsing off with lukewarm or cool water. Pat dry with a soft towel. May be used 2 or 3 times daily instead of soap.

Supplied: Each mL of cleanser contains: a special solution of coal tar 7.5% w/v in a nonmedicinal foamy, lactic/linoleic emollient vehicle. Fragrance- and parabens-free. Plastic bottles of 200 mL.

SPORANOX® Capsules ℞

Janssen-Ortho

Itraconazole

Antifungal

Pharmacology: In vitro studies have demonstrated that itraconazole inhibits the cytochrome P450-dependent synthesis of ergosterol which is a vital component of fungal and yeast cell membranes. This inhibition leads to deteriorated membranes, disturbed enzyme activities and an uncoordinated synthesis of chitin, all together contributing to the antifungal activity. The

Sporanox Capsules (cont'd)

inhibition of ergosterol synthesis has been attributed to interference with the reactions involved in the removal of the 14-α-methyl group of the precursor of ergosterol, lanosterol. Itraconazole has a very low affinity for mammalian P450 enzymes in contrast to fungal P450 enzymes. Itraconazole is fungitoxic to dermatophytes and yeasts.

Indications: For the treatment of the following fungal infections in normal, predisposed or immunocompromised patients: dermatomycoses due to tinea corporis, tinea cruris, tinea pedis and pityriasis versicolor, where oral therapy is considered appropriate; onychomycosis; invasive and noninvasive pulmonary aspergillosis; oral and oral/esophageal candidiasis; chronic pulmonary histoplasmosis; cutaneous and lymphatic sporotrichosis; paracoccidioidomycosis; chromomycosis; blastomycosis.

The type of organism responsible for the infection should be isolated and identified and other relevant laboratory studies (wet mount, histopathology, serology) should be undertaken, as appropriate, to confirm diagnosis. Therapy may be initiated prior to obtaining these results when clinically warranted; however, once these results become available, antifungal therapy should be adjusted accordingly.

Since elimination of itraconazole from skin and nail tissues is slower than from plasma, optimal clinical and mycological responses are thus reached 2 to 4 weeks after the cessation of treatment for skin infections and 6 to 9 months after the cessation of treatment for nail infections.

Contraindications: Concurrent therapy of terfenadine with itraconazole is contraindicated. Rare cases of serious cardiovascular adverse events, including death, ventricular tachycardia and torsades de pointes have been observed in patients taking itraconazole concomitantly with terfenadine, due to increased terfenadine concentrations induced by itraconazole.

Pharmacokinetic data indicate that another oral antifungal, ketoconazole, inhibits the metabolism of astemizole, resulting in elevated plasma levels of astemizole and its active metabolite desmethylastemizole which may prolong QT intervals. In vitro data suggest that itraconazole, when compared to ketoconazole, has a less pronounced effect on the biotransformation system responsible for the metabolism of astemizole. **Based on the chemical resemblance of itraconazole and ketoconazole, coadministration of astemizole with itraconazole is contraindicated.**

Concomitant administration of cisapride with oral ketoconazole is contraindicated because it has resulted in markedly elevated cisapride plasma concentrations and prolonged QT interval, and has rarely been associated with ventricular arrhythmia and torsades de pointes. Due to potent in vitro inhibition of the hepatic enzyme system mainly responsible for the metabolism of cisapride (cytochrome P450 3A4), itraconazole is also expected to markedly raise cisapride plasma concentrations. **Therefore, concomitant use of cisapride with itraconazole is also contraindicated.**

Oral midazolam and triazolam should not be used by patients during treatment with itraconazole capsules. Pharmacokinetic data revealed higher and prolonged midazolam concentrations when oral midazolam was administered concomitantly with itraconazole versus placebo. A more pronounced and prolonged hypnotic effect of midazolam was also observed. Metabolism of both itraconazole and midazolam by the same cytochrome P450 3A isozyme may explain this interaction. Similar pharmacokinetic and pharmacodynamic effects have been observed for triazolam which is primarily metabolized by the same P450 3A isozyme (see Precautions, Drug Interactions).

Itraconazole inhibits the metabolism of HMG-CoA reductase inhibitors such as lovastatin. Coadministration of itraconazole and lovastatin resulted in elevated and prolonged plasma concentrations of lovastatin and its active metabolite, lovastatin acid, which may increase the risk of diffuse myalgia and rhabdomyolysis. **Therefore, HMG-CoA reductase inhibitors that are metabolized by the P450 3A enzyme system, such as lovastatin should not be used during treatment with itraconazole.**

Itraconazole is contraindicated in patients with known hypersensitivity to the drug or its excipients. There is no information regarding cross hypersensitivity between itraconazole and other azole antifungal agents. Caution should be used in prescribing itraconazole to patients with hypersensitivity to other azoles.

Pregnancy: Itraconazole should not be administered for the treatment of dermatomycoses (tinea corporis, tinea cruris, tinea pedis, pityriasis versicolor) to pregnant patients or to women contemplating pregnancy.

Warnings: During long-term therapy in patients, most of whom had major underlying pathology and multiple concomitant treatments, a few cases of hepatitis have been observed. Itraconazole is predominantly metabolized in the liver. For therapy longer than 30 days, liver function should be monitored by appropriate tests. Patients who develop abnormal liver function tests during itraconazole therapy should be monitored for the development of more severe hepatic injury. Although serious hepatic reactions have been rare and the causal relationship with itraconazole uncertain, if clinical signs and symptoms consistent with liver disease develop during itraconazole therapy, administration of itraconazole should be discontinued and the potential cause of the liver disease should be investigated. It is not advisable to give this drug to patients with a known history of liver disease or to patients who have experienced liver toxicity with other drugs.

Women of Childbearing Age: In women of childbearing potential, an effective form of contraception must be used during therapy and for 1 menstrual cycle (1 month) after stopping therapy with itraconazole.

Pregnancy: Itraconazole has been shown to produce teratogenic effects (major skeletal and secondary soft tissue defects) when administered at high doses (40 mg/kg/day or higher) to pregnant rats. When administered to pregnant mice at high doses (80 mg/kg/day or higher) itraconazole has been shown to produce encephaloceles and/or macroglossia. There are no studies available on the use of itraconazole in pregnant women; therefore, itraconazole should be used in pregnancy only if the benefit outweighs the potential risk. Itraconazole should not be used for the treatment of dermatomycoses in pregnant patients or in women contemplating pregnancy (see Contraindications).

Lactation: Itraconazole is excreted in human milk; therefore, the patient should be advised to discontinue nursing while taking itraconazole.

Precautions: General: Patients should be instructed to report any signs and symptoms which may suggest liver dysfunction so that appropriate biochemical testing can be done. Such signs and symptoms would include unusual fatigue, anorexia, nausea and/or vomiting, jaundice, dark urine or pale stools. Patients who receive itraconazole concomitantly with potentially hepatotoxic drugs, those who are expected to be on long-term (>30 days) therapy as well as those with a history of significant alcohol intake or suspicion of liver disorder should have liver function monitored (see Warnings).

Patients should be instructed to take itraconazole with food.

Patients with Decreased Gastric Acidity: Absorption of itraconazole is impaired when gastric acidity is decreased. In patients also receiving acid-neutralizing medicines (e.g., aluminum hydroxide), these should be administered at least 2 hours after the intake of itraconazole. In patients with achlorhydria such as certain AIDS patients on acid secretion suppressors (e.g., H_2-antagonists, proton pump inhibitors), it is advisable to administer itraconazole with a cola beverage.

Children: The efficacy and safety of itraconazole have not been established in children. No pharmacokinetic data are available in children. A small number of patients from age 3 to 16 years have been treated with 100 mg/day of itraconazole for systemic fungal infections and no serious adverse effects have been reported.

Toxicological studies have shown that itraconazole, when administered to rats, can produce bone toxicity. While no such toxicity has been reported in adult patients, the long-term effect of itraconazole in children is unknown.

Geriatrics: The pharmacokinetics of itraconazole after single and repeated dosing of 100 mg once daily in 12 elderly subjects were found to be similar to those in young and middle-aged adults. Therefore, no dose adjustments are required in elderly patients.

Patients with Hepatic Impairment: Itraconazole is predominantly metabolized in the liver. The oral bioavailability in cirrhotic patients is somewhat decreased. It is advisable to monitor itraconazole plasma concentrations and to adapt the dose when necessary (see also Warnings and Precautions [General]).

Patients with Renal Insufficiency: The absorption of itraconazole may be lower in patients with renal insufficiency. Since clinical experience is lacking in this patient population, dosage recommendations cannot be made at this time.

In a few patients, hypokalemia has been reported. Consequently, serum potassium should be monitored in patients at risk during high-dose itraconazole therapy.

Itraconazole cannot be removed by dialysis.

Acquired Immunodeficiency Syndrome (AIDS) and Neutropenic Patients: Studies with itraconazole in neutropenic and AIDS patients have indicated that itraconazole plasma concentrations are lower than those in healthy subjects (particularly in those patients who are achlorhydric); therefore, monitoring of the itraconazole plasma concentrations and a dose adjustment, if necessary, is recommended. In 1 study, adequate plasma concentrations of itraconazole (measured by HPLC) for antifungal prophylaxis in neutropenic patients were greater than 250 ng/mL.

Inadequate plasma concentrations were frequently found in patients whose antineoplastic therapy predisposed them to very poor oral absorption and frequent vomiting. In this case, antiemetics can be coadministered and it is particularly important that itraconazole be administered with meals.

There has been 1 report of reduced itraconazole absorption when taken with didanosine. Since the excipients in the didanosine formulation are known to have an acid-neutralizing effect, and since the absorption of itraconazole can be affected by the level of acidity in the stomach, it is recommended that didanosine be administered at least 2 hours after dosing with itraconazole.

The results from a study in which 8 HIV-infected individuals were treated with zidovudine, 8 ± 0.4 mg/kg/day, with or without itraconazole, 100 mg b.i.d., showed that the pharmacokinetics of zidovudine were not affected during concomitant administration of itraconazole.

Drug Interactions: Itraconazole can inhibit the metabolism of drugs metabolized by the cytochrome 3A family. This can result in an increase and/or prolongation of their effects:

Concurrent therapy of terfenadine with itraconazole has led to elevated plasma concentrations of terfenadine, resulting in rare instances of life-threatening cardiac dysrhythmias and 1 death (see Contraindications).

Pharmacokinetic data indicate that another oral antifungal, ketoconazole, inhibits the metabolism of astemizole, resulting in elevated plasma levels of astemizole and its active metabolite desmethylastemizole which may prolong QT intervals. In vitro data suggest that itraconazole, when compared to ketoconazole, has a less pronounced effect on the biotransformation system responsible for the metabolism of astemizole. Based on the chemical resemblance of itraconazole and ketoconazole, concurrent therapy of astemizole with itraconazole is contraindicated (see Contraindications).

Human pharmacokinetic data indicate that oral ketoconazole potently inhibits the metabolism of cisapride, resulting in a mean 8-fold increase in AUC of cisapride. Data suggest that coadministration of cisapride and oral ketoconazole can result in prolongation of the QT interval on the ECG. In vitro data suggest that itraconazole also markedly inhibits the biotransformation system mainly responsible for the metabolism of cisapride. Therefore, concomitant administration of itraconazole with cisapride is contraindicated (see Contraindications).

Pharmacokinetic data demonstrate that when coadministered, itraconazole inhibits the metabolism of lovastatin, resulting in increased plasma concentrations of lovastatin, and its active metabolite lovastatin acid, and a 20-fold increase in AUC for both compounds. These increased plasma levels potentially elevate the risk of skeletal muscle toxicity such as diffuse myalgia and rhabdomyolysis. Therefore, concomitant administration of itraconazole with HMG-CoA reductase inhibitors such as lovastatin is contraindicated (see Contraindications).

Pharmacokinetic data suggest that itraconazole may inhibit the metabolism of oral midazolam. In 9 subjects, pretreatment with 200 mg itraconazole once daily for 4 days resulted in a 10-fold increase in midazolam $AUC_{0\rightarrow\infty}$, an approximate 3-fold increase in C_{max}, and an approximate 3-fold increase in $t_{1/2}$. Enhanced and prolonged sedative effects were also observed. Similar pharmacokinetic and pharmacodynamic effects have been observed for triazolam which is primarily metabolized by the same P450 3A isozyme. In 9 subjects, pretreatment with 200 mg itraconazole for 4 days resulted in a 27-fold increase in triazolam $AUC_{0\rightarrow\infty}$, a 3-fold increase in C_{max} and a 7-fold increase in $t_{1/2}$. Midazolam and triazolam should not be used by patients during treatment with itraconazole (see Contraindications). If midazolam is administered i.v., special precaution is required since the sedative effect may be prolonged.

Concurrent therapy of itraconazole and cyclosporine or digoxin has led to increased plasma concentrations of the latter two drugs. When digoxin is given concurrently with itraconazole, the physician is advised to monitor digoxin concentrations and reduce the dosage as needed. Although no studies have been conducted, literature case reports suggest that the dose of cyclosporine should be reduced by 50% when itraconazole doses greater than 100 mg daily are given. Cyclosporine concentrations should be monitored frequently and the dose adjusted appropriately.

Itraconazole may inhibit the metabolism of methylprednisolone, vinca-alkaloids and possibly tacrolimus. The dosage of systemic methylprednisolone, vinca-alkaloids and tacrolimus, if coadministered with itraconazole, should be reduced if necessary.

It has been reported that itraconazole enhances the anticoagulant effect of coumarin-like drugs. Therefore, prothrombin time should be carefully monitored in patients receiving itraconazole and coumarin-like drugs simultaneously.

Patients receiving itraconazole concomitantly with dihydropyridine calcium channel blockers or quinidine, should be monitored for side effects, e.g., edema and tinnitus/decreased hearing, respectively. If necessary, the dose of these drugs should be reduced.

When itraconazole was coadministered with phenytoin, rifampin or H_2 antagonists, reduced plasma concentrations of itraconazole were reported. The physician is advised to monitor the plasma concentrations of itraconazole when any of these drugs is taken concurrently, and to increase the dose of itraconazole if necessary. Although no studies have been conducted, concomitant administration of itraconazole and phenytoin may alter the metabolism of phenytoin; therefore, plasma concentrations of phenytoin should also be monitored when it is given concurrently with itraconazole.

Plasma concentrations of azole antifungal agents are reduced when given concurrently with isoniazid. Itraconazole plasma concentrations should be monitored when itraconazole and isoniazid are coadministered.

Severe hypoglycemia has been reported in patients concomitantly receiving azole antifungal agents and oral hypoglycemic agents. Blood glucose concentrations should be carefully monitored when itraconazole and oral hypoglycemic agents are coadministered.

There has been 1 report of reduced itraconazole absorption when taken with didanosine. Since the excipients in the didanosine formulation are known to have an acid-neutralizing effect, and since the absorption of itraconazole can be affected by the level of acidity in the stomach, it is recommended that didanosine be administered at least 2 hours after dosing with itraconazole (see AIDS and Neutropenic Patients).

No interaction of itraconazole with AZT (zidovudine) has been observed (see AIDS and Neutropenic Patients).

No inducing effects of itraconazole on the metabolism of ethinylestradiol and norethisterone were observed.

Laboratory Tests: Plasma levels 3 to 4 hours after dosing with itraconazole should be monitored in patients requiring treatment for more than 1 month, in patients with systemic mycoses who have factors predisposing to poor absorption (such as achlorhydria, renal insufficiency, neutropenia, AIDS) or in those who are taking drugs which may alter itraconazole absorption or metabolism (such as rifampin and phenytoin).

Due to the presence of an active metabolite, monitoring of plasma levels by bioassay will indicate plasma levels roughly 3 times higher than will monitoring by high-pressure liquid chromatography, unless solvent conditions for the HPLC assay are adjusted to allow simultaneous detection of both the parent drug and this metabolite (hydroxy-itraconazole).

Adverse Effects: Adverse experiences during short-term therapy with itraconazole occurred in 7.8% of patients. During long-term therapy in patients, most of whom had underlying pathology and received multiple concomitant treatments, the incidence of adverse experiences was higher (20.6%). The most common adverse experiences (reported by at least 1% of patients) during short-term or long-term therapy with itraconazole are presented in Table I.

For 834 clinical trial patients receiving 2 to 4 cycles of 1-week therapy, the most frequently reported adverse events during the treatment and follow-up period were: abdominal pain (1.9%), nausea (1.6%) and headache (1.3%).

The following adverse experiences have been reported at an incidence greater than 0.05% and less than 1% during short-term therapy with itraconazole: dyspepsia/epigastric pain/upset stomach; abdominal pain/discomfort; vomiting; pyrosis; diarrhea; gastritis; flatulence/meteorism; constipation; decreased appetite; other gastric complaints; dizziness/faintness; sleepiness/somnolence; vertigo; pruritus; rash; pain; fatigue; fever; edema; allergic reaction. Allergic reactions (such as pruritus, rash, urticaria and angioedema) and reversible increases in hepatic enzymes and menstrual disorder have been reported from postmarketing experience. Isolated cases of peripheral neuropathy and of Stevens-Johnson syndrome have been reported; a causality for the latter has not been established. If neuropathy occurs that may be attributable to itraconazole, the treatment should be discontinued.

Table I—Sporanox Capsules

Adverse Effects

	Short-term Therapy	Long-term Therapy
Total Number of Patients	**12 889**	**916**
Body System/ Adverse Event	**Incidence (%)**	
Gastrointestinal	4.4	9.1
nausea	1.6	2.9
Dermatological	0.8	4.5
rash	<1.0	1.6
pruritus	<1.0	1.3
CNS	2.1	4.3
headache	1.0	1.1
Respiratory System	<1.0	3.9
Liver and Biliary System	0.11	2.7
Miscellaneous	0.7	5.6
edema	<1.0	1.0

The following adverse experiences have been reported at an incidence of greater than 0.5% but less than 1% of patients during long-term therapy with itraconazole: vomiting; dyspepsia/epigastralgia; diarrhea; abdominal pain; dizziness; bronchitis/bronchospasm; coughing; dyspnea; rhinitis; sinusitis; increase in liver enzymes; abnormal liver function tests; jaundice; hepatitis; cirrhosis; hepatocellular damage; abnormal hepatic function; pain; chest pain; hypertension; fatigue; fever; hypokalemia.

Postmarketing: Especially in patients receiving prolonged (approx. 1 month) treatment, most of whom had major underlying pathology and multiple concomitant medications, cases of hypokalemia, edema, hepatitis and hair loss have been observed.

Overdose: Symptoms and Treatment: There is no experience of overdosage with itraconazole; however, based on animal toxicity data, symptoms of a gastrointestinal or CNS nature may be expected to occur.

In the event of accidental overdosage, supportive measures, including gastric lavage with sodium bicarbonate should be employed. It has been reported that itraconazole cannot be removed by hemodialysis.

Dosage: When itraconazole therapy may be indicated, the type of organism responsible for the infection should be isolated and identified; however, therapy may be initiated prior to obtaining these results, when clinically warranted. **For maximal absorption, it is essential to administer itraconazole immediately after a full meal. The capsules must be swallowed whole.** For treatment of patients with decreased gastric acidity, see Precautions.

Itraconazole should be administered at a dose of 100 to 400 mg/day. Dosage recommendations vary according to the infection treated.

Oral and Oral/Esophageal Candidiasis: The recommended dose is 100 mg daily for 2 weeks. The dose should be increased to 200 mg/day in patients with AIDS and neutropenic patients. In patients with oral/esophageal candidiasis, treatment should last 4 weeks.

Blastomycosis and Chronic Pulmonary Histoplasmosis: The recommended dose is 200 mg once daily. If there is no obvious improvement or there is evidence of progressive fungal disease, the dose should be increased in 100 mg increments to a maximum of 400 mg daily. Doses above 200 mg/day should be given in 2 divided doses.

Treatment should be continued for a minimum of 3 months and until clinical parameters and laboratory tests indicate that the active fungal infection has subsided. An inadequate period of treatment may lead to recurrence of active infection.

Other Systemic Mycoses: See Table II.

Table II—Sporanox Capsules

Dosage—Other Systemic Mycoses

Indication	Dose	Median Duration
Aspergillosis		
Pulmonary	200 mg o.d.	3–4 months
Invasive pulmonary	200 mg b.i.d.	3–4 months
Sporotrichosis	100 mg o.d.	3 months
Paracoccidioidomycosis	100 mg o.d.	6 months
Chromomycosis		
due to Fonsecaea pedrosoi	200 mg o.d.	6 months
due to Cladosporium carrionii	100 mg o.d.	3 months

Dermatomycoses: Standard Dosages: Tinea Corporis/Tinea Cruris: The recommended dose is 100 mg once daily for 14 consecutive days.

Tinea Pedis: The recommended dose is 100 mg once daily for 28 consecutive days.

Pityriasis Versicolor: The recommended dose is 200 mg once daily for 7 consecutive days.

Alternative Dosages: Shorter dosing schedules have also been found to be effective in the treatment of tinea corporis/tinea cruris and tinea pedis. The shorter dosages are:

Tinea Corporis/Tinea Cruris: 200 mg o.d. for 7 consecutive days.

Tinea Pedis: 200 mg b.i.d. for 7 consecutive days.

Equivalency between standard and alternative dosages was not established. Patients with chronic recalcitrant tinea pedis may benefit from the standard dosage of lower daily dose (100 mg) for a longer period of time (4 weeks).

Onychomycosis: The recommended clinical dose for onychomycosis is: A 1-week treatment course consists of 200 mg twice daily for 7 days. Treatment with two 1-week courses is recommended for fingernail infections and three 1-week courses for toenail infections. The 1-week courses are always separated by a 3-week drug-free interval. Clinical response will become evident as the nail regrows, following discontinuation of the treatment. See Table III.

Tissue Elimination of Itraconazole: Elimination of itraconazole from skin and nail tissues is slower than from plasma. Optimal clinical and mycological responses are thus reached 2 to 4 weeks after the cessation of treatment for skin infections and 6 to 9 months after the cessation of treatment for nail infections.

Supplied: Each pink and blue capsule, imprinted in white with JANSSEN on the cap and SPORANOX 100 on the body, contains: itraconazole 100 mg in a pellet formulation. Nonmedicinal ingredients: D&C Red No. 22, D&C Red No. 28, FD&C Blue No. 1, FD&C Blue No. 2, gelatin, hydroxypropylmethylcellulose, polyethylene glycol, sugar spheres and titanium dioxide. Bisulfite-, gluten- and tartrazine-free. HDPE bottles of 30. Store at room temperature (15 to 30°C). Protect from light and moisture.

(Shown in Product Recognition Section)

Reviewed 1999

Table III—Sporanox Capsules

Dosage—Onychomycosis

Site of onychomycosis	Week 1	Week 2	Week 3	Week 4	Week 5	Week 6	Week 7	Week 8	Week 9
Toenails with or without fingernail involvement	200 mg b.i.d. for 7 days	itraconazole free weeks			200 mg b.i.d. for 7 days	itraconazole free weeks			200 mg b.i.d. for 7 days
Fingernails only	200 mg b.i.d. for 7 days	itraconazole free weeks			200 mg b.i.d. for 7 days				

SPORANOX® Oral Solution Ⓟ

Janssen-Ortho

Itraconazole

Antifungal

Pharmacology: Mode of Action: Itraconazole, a triazole derivative, has a broad-spectrum activity; with respect to Candida spp., its activity includes C. albicans, C. glabrata and C. krusei.

In vitro studies have demonstrated that itraconazole impairs the synthesis of ergosterol in fungal cells. Ergosterol is a vital cell membrane component in fungi. Impairment of its synthesis ultimately results in an antifungal effect.

Pharmacokinetics: The oral bioavailability of itraconazole oral solution is maximal when it is taken without food. During chronic administration, steady-state is reached after 1 to 2 weeks. Peak plasma levels are observed 2 hours (fasting) to 5 hours (with food) following the oral administration. After repeated once-a-day administration of itraconazole 200 mg in fasting condition, steady-state plasma concentrations of itraconazole fluctuate between 1 and 2 μg/mL (trough to peak). When the oral solution is taken with food, steady-state plasma concentrations of itraconazole are about 25% lower.

The plasma protein binding of itraconazole is 99.8%. Itraconazole is extensively distributed into tissues which are prone to fungal invasion. Concentrations in lung, kidney, liver, bone, stomach, spleen and muscle were found to be 2 to 3 times higher than the corresponding plasma concentration.

Itraconazole is extensively metabolized by the liver into a large number of metabolites. One of the metabolites is hydroxy-itraconazole, which has in vitro a comparable antifungal activity to itraconazole. Plasma levels of hydroxy-itraconazole are about 2 times higher than those of itraconazole.

After repeated oral administration, elimination of itraconazole from plasma is biphasic with a terminal half-life of 1.5 days. Fecal excretion of the parent drug varies between 3 to 18% of the dose. Renal excretion of the parent drug is less than 0.03% of the dose. About 35% of the dose is excreted as metabolites in the urine within 1 week.

Indications: For the treatment of oral and/or esophageal candidiasis in adult HIV-positive or other immunocompromised patients.

Note: Itraconazole oral solution and itraconazole capsules should not be used interchangeably.

Contraindications: Concurrent therapy of terfenadine with itraconazole is contraindicated. Rare cases of serious cardiovascular adverse events, including death, ventricular tachycardia and torsades de pointes have been observed in patients taking itraconazole concomitantly with terfenadine, due to increased terfenadine concentrations induced by itraconazole.

Coadministration of astemizole with itraconazole has led to elevated plasma concentrations of astemizole and its active metabolite desmethylastemizole which may prolong the QT intervals. Therefore, **concomitant administration of itraconazole with astemizole is contraindicated.**

Concomitant administration of cisapride with oral ketoconazole is contraindicated because it has resulted in markedly elevated cisapride plasma concentrations and prolonged QT interval, and has rarely been associated with ventricular arrhythmia and torsades de pointes. Due to potent in vitro inhibition of the hepatic enzyme system mainly responsible for the metabolism of cisapride (cytochrome P450 3A4), itraconazole is also expected to markedly raise cisapride plasma concentrations. **Therefore, concomitant use of cisapride with itraconazole is also contraindicated.**

Oral midazolam and triazolam should not be used by patients during treatment with itraconazole. Pharmacokinetic data revealed higher and prolonged midazolam concentrations when oral midazolam was administered concomitantly with itraconazole versus placebo. A more pronounced and prolonged hypnotic effect of midazolam was also observed. Metabolism of both itraconazole and midazolam by the same cytochrome P450 3A isozyme may explain this interaction. Similar pharmacokinetic and pharmacodynamic effects have been observed for triazolam which is primarily metabolized by the same P450 3A isozyme.

Itraconazole inhibits the metabolism of HMG-CoA reductase inhibitors such as lovastatin. Coadministration of itraconazole and lovastatin resulted in elevated and prolonged plasma concentrations of lovastatin and its active metabolite, lovastatin acid, which may increase the risk of diffuse myalgia and rhabdomyolysis. **Therefore, HMG-CoA reductase inhibitors that are metabolized by the P450 3A enzyme system, such as lovastatin should not be used during treatment with itraconazole.**

Itraconazole is contraindicated in patients with known hypersensitivity to the drug or its excipients. There is no information regarding cross hypersensitivity between itraconazole and other azole antifungal agents. Caution should be used in prescribing itraconazole to patients with hypersensitivity to other azoles.

Warnings: Itraconazole oral solution and itraconazole capsules should not be used interchangeably. Itraconazole oral solution has been demonstrated to be effective in the treatment of oropharyngeal and/or esophageal candidiasis. The efficacy of oral solution for other indications is unknown. The two dosage forms have different absorption profiles. Itraconazole oral solution contains the excipient hydroxypropyl-β-cyclodextrin which produced adenocarcinomas of the exocrine pancreas in a rat but not in a similar mouse carcinogenicity study. The clinical relevance of these findings is unknown.

It is advisable to monitor liver function in patients receiving continuous treatment of more than 1 month and promptly in patients developing symptoms suggestive of hepatitis such as anorexia, nausea, vomiting, fatigue, abdominal pain or dark urine. If abnormal, treatment should be terminated. In patients with raised liver enzymes or an active liver disease or who have experienced liver toxicity with other drugs, treatment should not be started unless the expected benefit exceeds the risk of hepatic injury. In such cases, liver enzyme monitoring is necessary.

Women of Childbearing Age: In women of childbearing potential, an effective form of contraception must be used during therapy and for one menstrual cycle (1 month) after stopping therapy with itraconazole.

Pregnancy: Itraconazole has been shown to produce teratogenic effects (major skeletal and secondary soft tissue defects) when administered at high doses (40 mg/kg/day or higher) to pregnant rats. When administered to pregnant mice at high doses (80 mg/kg/day or higher), itraconazole has been shown to produce encephaloceles and/or macroglossia. There are no studies available on the use of itraconazole in pregnant women. Itraconazole oral solution should only be given to pregnant women in life-threatening cases and when in these cases the potential benefit outweighs the potential harm to the fetus.

Lactation: Itraconazole is excreted in human milk; therefore, the patient should be advised to discontinue nursing while taking itraconazole.

Precautions: General: Patients should be instructed to report any signs and symptoms which may suggest liver dysfunction. Such signs and symptoms include unusual fatigue, anorexia, nausea and/or vomiting, jaundice, abdominal pain, dark urine or pale stools. Patients who receive itraconazole concomitantly with potentially hepatotoxic drugs, those who are expected to be on long-term (>30 days) therapy as well as those with a history of significant alcohol intake or suspicion of liver disorder should have liver function monitored (see Warnings).

Itraconazole binds to plasma proteins and cannot be removed by hemodialysis.

Children: The efficacy and safety of itraconazole have not been established in pediatric patients.

A pharmacokinetic study was conducted with itraconazole oral solution in 26 pediatric patients, aged 6 months to 12 years, requiring systemic antifungal treatment. Itraconazole was dosed at 5 mg/kg once daily for 2 weeks and no serious unexpected adverse events were reported.

Toxicological studies have shown that itraconazole, when administered to rats, can produce bone toxicity. While no such toxicity has been reported in adult patients, the long-term effect of itraconazole in children is unknown.

Geriatrics: Since clinical data on the use of itraconazole oral solution in elderly patients is limited, it is advised to use itraconazole oral solution in these patients only if the potential benefit outweighs the potential risks.

Patients with Hepatic Impairment: Itraconazole is predominantly metabolized in the liver. The terminal half-life of itraconazole in cirrhotic patients is somewhat prolonged. A decrease in the oral bioavailability of itraconazole from Sporanox capsules was observed in cirrhotic patients. This can also be expected with Sporanox oral solution. Therefore, it is advisable to monitor itraconazole plasma concentrations and to adapt the dose when necessary. Itraconazole treatment should not be started in patients with raised liver enzymes unless the expected benefit exceeds the risk of hepatic injury (see Warnings and Precautions, General).

Patients with Renal Insufficiency: A decrease in the oral bioavailability of itraconazole from Sporanox capsules was observed in some patients with renal insufficiency. This can also be expected with itraconazole oral solution. It is advised to monitor the itraconazole plasma concentration and to adapt the dose when necessary.

In a few patients, hypokalemia has been reported. Consequently serum potassium should be monitored in patients at risk during high-dose itraconazole therapy.

Acquired Immunodeficiency Syndrome (AIDS) and Neutropenic Patients: Studies with itraconazole capsules in neutropenic and AIDS patients have indicated that itraconazole plasma concentrations are lower than those in healthy subjects (particularly in those patients who are achlorhydric). However, the bioavailability of itraconazole oral solution, when tested in AIDS patients, was found satisfactory and not altered by the stage of HIV infection.

Patients on Continuous Treatment: In patients receiving continuous treatment of more than 1 month and in patients developing symptoms such as anorexia, nausea, vomiting, fatigue, abdominal pain or dark urine, it is advisable to monitor liver function. If tests are abnormal, treatment should be terminated.

If neuropathy occurs that may be attributable to itraconazole oral solution, the treatment should be discontinued.

Drug Interactions: Both itraconazole and its major metabolite, hydroxy-itraconazole, are inhibitors of the cytochrome P450 3A enzyme system. Coadministration of itraconazole and drugs primarily metabolized by the cytochrome P450 3A enzyme system may result in increased plasma concentrations of the other drug that could increase or prolong both its therapeutic and adverse effects. Tables I and II provide selected drugs that are predicted to have altered plasma concentrations by itraconazole.

Table I—Sporanox Oral Solution

Table of Selected Drugs That Are Predicted to Have Plasma Concentrations Increased by Itraconazole[a]

Anticoagulants: warfarin
Antihistamines: terfenadine[b], astemizole[b]
Anti-HIV protease inhibitors: ritonavir, indinavir
Antineoplastic agents: vinca alkaloids
Benzodiazepines: midazolam[b,c], triazolam[b], diazepam
Calcium channel blockers: dihydropyridines
Cholesterol-lowering agents: lovastatin[b], simvastatin[b]
Gastrointestinal motility agents: cisapride[b]
Immunosuppressive agents: cyclosporine, tacrolimus
Steroids: methylprednisolone
Other: digoxin, quinidine

[a] This table is not all inclusive.
[b] Specifically contraindicated with Sporanox based on clinical and/or pharmacokinetics studies (see Contraindications and below).
[c] See paragraph below on benzodiazepines for information on parenteral administration.

Table II—Sporanox Oral Solution

Table of Selected Drugs That Are Predicted to Decrease Itraconazole Plasma Concentrations[a,b]

Anticonvulsants: phenytoin, phenobarbital, carbamazepine
Antimycobacterial agents: isoniazid, rifampin, rifabutin

[a] This table is not all inclusive.
[b] Sporanox may not be effective due to decreased itraconazole plasma concentrations in patients using these agents concomitantly.

Anticoagulants: It has been reported that itraconazole enhances the anticoagulant effect of coumarin-like drugs. Therefore, prothrombin time should be carefully monitored in patients receiving itraconazole and coumarin-like drugs simultaneously.

Anticonvulsants: Reduced plasma concentrations of itraconazole were reported when itraconazole was coadministered with phenytoin. The physician is advised to monitor the plasma concentrations of itraconazole when phenytoin is taken concurrently, and to increase the dose of itraconazole if necessary.

Antihistamines: Coadministration of terfenadine with itraconazole has led to elevated plasma concentrations of terfenadine, resulting in rare instances of life-threatening cardiac dysrhythmia and death. Coadministration of astemizole with itraconazole has led to elevated plasma concentrations of astemizole and desmethylastemizole which may prolong the QT intervals. Therefore, concomitant administration of itraconazole with astemizole is contraindicated (see Contraindications).

Anti-HIV Protease Inhibitors: Coadministration of itraconazole with protease inhibitors primarily metabolized by the cytochrome P450 3A enzyme system, such as ritonavir or indinavir, may result in changes in plasma concentrations of both drugs. Caution is advised when these drugs are used concomitantly.

Anti-HIV Reverse Transcriptase Inhibitors: The results from a study in which 8 HIV-infected individuals were treated with zidovudine, 8±0.4 mg/kg/day, showed that the pharmacokinetics of zidovudine were not affected during concomitant administration of itraconazole capsules, 100 mg b.i.d. Other agents have not been studied.

Antimycobacterial Agents: Plasma concentrations of azole antifungal agents are reduced when given concurrently with isoniazid or rifampin. Itraconazole plasma concentrations should be monitored when itraconazole and isoniazid/rifampin are coadministered. A similar effect may be expected with rifabutin.

Antineoplastic Agents: The metabolism of vinca alkaloids may be inhibited by itraconazole. Therefore, patients receiving itraconazole concomitantly with vinca alkaloids should be monitored for an increase and/or prolongation of the effects of the latter drug product, including adverse effects such as peripheral neuropathy and ileus, and the dose of the vinca alkaloid should be adjusted appropriately.

Benzodiazepines: Coadministration of itraconazole with oral midazolam or triazolam has resulted in elevated plasma concentrations of the latter two drugs. This may potentiate and prolong hypnotic and sedative effects. These agents should not be used during treatment with itraconazole. If midazolam is administered parenterally, special precaution and patient monitoring is required since the sedative effect may be prolonged (see Contraindications).

Calcium Channel Blockers: Edema has been reported in patients concomitantly receiving itraconazole and dihydropyridine calcium channel blockers. Appropriate dosage adjustments may be necessary.

Cholesterol-Lowering Agents: Human pharmacokinetic data indicate that itraconazole inhibits the metabolism of lovastatin resulting in significantly elevated plasma concentrations of lovastatin or lovastatin acid, which have been associated with rhabdomyolysis. Use of HMG-CoA reductase inhibitors metabolized by the P450 3A enzyme system, such as lovastatin or simvastatin, should be temporarily discontinued during itraconazole therapy (see Contraindications).

Digoxin: Coadministration of itraconazole and digoxin has led to increased plasma concentrations of digoxin. Digoxin concentrations should be monitored at the initiation of itraconazole therapy and frequently thereafter, and the dose of digoxin should be adjusted appropriately.

Gastrointestinal Motility Agents: Human pharmacokinetic data indicate that oral ketoconazole potently inhibits the metabolism of cisapride resulting in significantly elevated plasma concentrations of cisapride. Data suggest that coadministration of oral ketoconazole and cisapride can result in prolongation of the QT interval on the ECG. In vitro data suggest that itraconazole also markedly inhibits the biotransformation system mainly responsible for the metabolism of cisapride; therefore, concomitant administration of itraconazole with cisapride is contraindicated (see Contraindications).

H_2 Antagonists: Reduced plasma concentrations of itraconazole were reported when itraconazole capsules were coadministered with H_2 antagonists. However, as itraconazole is already dissolved in itraconazole oral solution, the effect of H_2 antagonists is expected to be substantially less than with the capsules. Nevertheless, caution is advised when the two drugs are coadministered.

Immunosuppressive Agents: Coadministration of itraconazole and cyclosporine or tacrolimus has led to increased plasma concentrations of the latter 2 agents. Cyclosporine and tacrolimus concentrations should be monitored at the initiation of itraconazole therapy and frequently thereafter, and the dose of cyclosporine or tacrolimus should be adjusted appropriately.

Oral Hypoglycemic Agents: Severe hypoglycemia has been reported in patients concomitantly receiving azole antifungal agents and oral hypoglycemic agents. Blood glucose concentrations should be carefully monitored when itraconazole and oral hypoglycemic agents are coadministered.

Quinidine: Tinnitus and decreased hearing have been reported in patients concomitantly receiving itraconazole and quinidine.

Steroids: The metabolism of methylprednisolone may be inhibited by itraconazole. Therefore, patients receiving itraconazole concomitantly with methylprednisolone should be monitored for an increase and/or prolongation of the effects of the latter drug product, including adverse effects, and the dose of methylprednisolone should be adjusted appropriately.

No inducing effects of itraconazole on the metabolism of ethinylestradiol and norethisterone were observed.

In vitro studies have shown that there are no interactions on the plasma protein binding between itraconazole and imipramine, propranolol, diazepam, cimetidine, indomethacin, tolbutamide and sulfamethazine.

Laboratory Tests: Due to the presence of an active metabolite, hydroxy-itraconazole, plasma levels monitored by bioassay will yield plasma levels roughly 3 times higher than that obtained by high-pressure liquid chromatography (HPLC), unless solvent conditions for the HPLC assay are adjusted to allow simultaneous detection of both the parent drug and the metabolite

Adverse Effects: Oral Solution: The adverse event profile was analyzed for 889 HIV-positive and other immunocompromised patients receiving itraconazole oral solution for the treatment of oral and esophageal candidiasis. The most frequently reported adverse events were of gastrointestinal origin. The total observed incidence of adverse events that are possibly or directly drug-related, during treatment or within 14 days post-treatment for itraconazole oral solution is 18.2%. A listing of adverse events reported with a frequency ≥1% for itraconazole in all worldwide studies of oropharyngeal and esophageal candidiasis is presented in Table III.

Table III—Sporanox Oral Solution

Adverse Experience Incidence ≥1.0% in Worldwide Trials of Oropharyngeal and Esophageal Candidiasis, by Body System

Body System/Adverse Event	Itraconazole n=889
Gastrointestinal	12.3%
Nausea	5.3%
Diarrhea	4.5%
Vomiting	3.4%
Abdominal pain	2.5%
Skin and Appendages	2.4%
Rash	1.3%
Central and Peripheral Nervous System	1.7%
Headache	1.1%
Liver and Biliary System	1.3%
Special senses	1.1%
Taste perversion	1.0%
Body as a Whole	1.0%

Capsules: Adverse experiences reported in association with the use of itraconazole capsules: the most frequently reported are of gastrointestinal origin, such as dyspepsia, nausea, abdominal pain and constipation. Less frequently reported adverse experiences include headache, reversible increases in hepatic enzymes, menstrual disorder, dizziness and allergic reactions (such as pruritus, rash, urticaria and angioedema). Isolated cases of peripheral neuropathy and of Stevens-Johnson syndrome have also been reported: a causality for the latter was not established.

Especially in patients receiving prolonged (≥1 month) treatment, most of whom had major underlying pathology and multiple concomitant medications, cases of hypokalemia, edema, hepatitis and hair loss have been observed.

Overdose: Symptoms and Treatment: There is no experience of overdosage with itraconazole; however, based on animal toxicity data, symptoms of a gastrointestinal or CNS nature may be expected to occur.

In the event of accidental overdosage, supportive measures including gastric lavage with sodium bicarbonate should be employed. It has been reported that itraconazole cannot be removed by hemodialysis.

Dosage: When itraconazole may be indicated, the type of organism responsible for the infection should be isolated and identified; however, therapy may be initiated prior to obtaining these results, when clinically warranted.

For optimal absorption, itraconazole oral solution should be taken without food. The solution should be swished in the oral cavity and swallowed. There should be no rinsing after swallowing.

Oropharyngeal Candidiasis: The recommended dosage of itraconazole oral solution for oropharyngeal candidiasis is 200 mg daily in a single dose or divided doses; treatment should continue for 1 to 2 weeks to decrease the likelihood of relapse.

Esophageal Candidiasis: The recommended dosage for esophageal candidiasis is 100 mg daily for a minimum treatment of 3 weeks. Treatment should continue for 2 weeks following resolution of symptoms. Doses up to 200 mg/day may be used based on medical judgment of the patient's response to therapy.

Supplied: Each mL contains: itraconazole 10 mg. Nonmedicinal ingredients: caramel flavor, cherry flavor 1 and 2, hydrochloric acid, hydroxypropyl-β-cyclodextrin, propylene glycol, purified water, sodium hydroxide, sodium saccharin and sorbitol. Amber glass bottles of 150 mL. Store at 15 to 25°C. Discard remaining unused product 3 months after opening bottle.

(Shown in Product Recognition Section)

Reviewed 1999

SSD™ ®
Knoll

Silver Sulfadiazine

Topical Antibacterial

Pharmacology: The mechanism of silver sulfadiazine's antimicrobial action has not been fully elucidated. The dominant manifestation of the reaction of silver sulfadiazine with sensitive organisms may result from the displacement of hydrogen bonds within the bacterial DNA. Once these bonds that serve to connect the 2 strands of the DNA double helix are displaced, bacterial replication and cell viability are effectively reduced.

Mammalian cells have approximately 100 times more DNA than bacterial cells. Thus, the ratio of inhibitory concentrations of silver sulfadiazine to bacterial DNA is high enough to prevent bacterial division. However, the resulting ratio of silver sulfadiazine to epithelial DNA is sufficiently low that epithelial cell regeneration is not impaired.

Indications: For the adjunctive treatment of burns, skin grafts, incisions, leg ulcers and other clean lesions, abrasions, minor cuts and wounds. It is especially indicated in the treatment and prophylaxis of infection in serious burn victims.

Contraindications: In patients with a history of hypersensitivity to silver sulfadiazine.

Since sulfonamide derivatives are known to increase the possibility of kernicterus, silver sulfadiazine cream should not be used in pregnant women approaching or at term, in premature infants, or in neonates less than 2 months of age.

Warnings: Silver sulfadiazine cream should be administered with caution to patients with a history of hypersensitivity to silver sulfadiazine. It is not known whether prior sensitivity to other sulfonamides will precipitate an allergic response to silver sulfadiazine cream.

Silver sulfadiazine cream should be used with caution in patients with a history of G-6-PD deficiency, as hemolysis may occur.

When treatment with silver sulfadiazine cream involves prolonged administration and/or large burn surfaces, considerable amounts of silver sulfadiazine are absorbed. Serum concentrations of sulfadiazine may approach adult therapeutic levels (8 to 12 mg %).

Precautions: Following administration of silver sulfadiazine cream, absorption of sulfadiazine has been reported. In addition, small amounts of silver are absorbed over the course of repeated application of silver sulfadiazine cream. In extensively burned patients, serum sulfa concentrations and renal functions should be closely monitored.

Silver sulfadiazine cream should be used with caution in patients with significant hepatic or renal impairment.

Leukopenia has been reported following the use of silver sulfadiazine cream, especially in patients with large burn areas (see Adverse Effects).

<u>*Drug Interactions:*</u> Enzymatic Debridement: Silver sulfadiazine cream may inactivate topical enzymatic preparations used for debridement. Therefore, the use of concomitant systemic or alternative topical antimicrobial therapy should be considered.

Oral Hypoglycemic Agents and Phenytoin: Sulfa drugs may compete for the same degradation pathways utilized by some oral hypoglycemic agents and phenytoin. There is a possibility of half-life prolongation and decreased plasma clearance of these drugs, which may potentiate their activity.

Cimetidine: An increased incidence of leukopenia has been observed in patients receiving concomitant treatment with silver sulfadiazine cream and cimetidine.

Pregnancy: The safe use of silver sulfadiazine cream has not been established in pregnancy. The cream should be administered to pregnant women only when the physician decides that the potentially life-saving benefits of silver sulfadiazine therapy in the larger burn (extent greater than 20% body surface area) outweigh possible hazard to the fetus (see Contraindications).

Adverse Effects: Leukopenia: Several cases of transient leukopenia have been reported in patients receiving silver sulfadiazine therapy. Leukopenia associated with silver sulfadiazine administration is primarily characterized by a decreased neutrophil count. Maximal white blood cell depression occurs within 2 to 4 days of initiation of therapy. Rebound to normal leukocyte levels follow onset of leukopenia within 2 to 3 days.

SSD (cont'd)

Recovery is not influenced by continuation of silver sulfadiazine therapy. The incidence of leukopenia in various reports averages about 20% although an incidence as high as 55% has been noted.
Sulfonamides: During the treatment of burns over large body surfaces (greater than 20% body surface area), significant amounts of silver sulfadiazine are systemically absorbed. Therefore, it is possible that any adverse reactions associated with sulfonamides may occur.
Miscellaneous: A low incidence of other adverse reactions has been reported. This includes local burning sensation, rashes and pruritus, and rarely, interstitial nephritis.

Overdose: Symptoms and Treatment: In extensively burned patients or in patients suspected of showing symptoms of excessive absorption, it is important to optimally maintain fluid balance to prevent dehydration and the associated possibility of renal impairment.

Dosage: The cream should be applied to a thickness of at least 3 to 5 mm to burned surfaces once or twice daily. It is recommended that a protocol for management of the burn wound using accepted principles and techniques of debridement be followed. Silver sulfadiazine cream should be applied with sterile gloves. Silver sulfadiazine cream will provide antimicrobial activity when used with either open treatment or an occlusive dressing regimen. When treating patients using the open method, care must be taken to promptly reapply silver sulfadiazine cream whenever it is removed by patient movement.

The cream application should continue until either spontaneous healing or grafting of the burn wound is achieved.

Supplied: Each g of nonsterile cream contains: micronized silver sulfadiazine 1%. Nonmedicinal ingredients: isopropyl myristate, methylparaben, polyoxyl 40 stearate, propylene glycol, purified water, sodium hydroxide, sorbitan monooleate, stearyl alcohol and white petrolatum. Jars of 50, 400 and 1 000 g. Store between 15 and 30°C.

ST. JOHN'S WORT
Swiss Herbal

St. John's Wort Herbal Extract (Hypercin perforatum)
Herbal Sedative

Indications: To help relieve restlessness due to overwork, tiredness and fatigue.

Precautions: Avoid excessive exposure to sunlight as this medication may cause increased photosensitivity. Do not take in conjunction with other sedative medication. May cause drowsiness.
Pregnancy and *Lactation*: Not recommended for pregnant or lactating women.
Children: Keep out of reach of children.

Dosage: Adults: 1 to 3 capsules daily with food. Do not exceed recommended dose except on the advice of a physician.

Supplied: Each capsule contains: St. John's Wort powdered extract 300 mg, standardized to active substance hypericin 0.3%. Nonmedicinal ingredients: magnesium stearate and rice flour. Bottles of 60 and 120.
New Product 1998

STADOL NS™ ⊕
Bristol-Myers Squibb

Butorphanol Tartrate
Analgesic

Pharmacology: Butorphanol acts as an agonist at kappa-opioid receptors and a mixed agonist-antagonist at mu-opioid receptors in the CNS to alter the perception of pain. The drug is believed to act at sites in the periventricular and periaqueductal gray matter, and at sites in the spinal cord.

In an animal model, the dose of butorphanol required to antagonize morphine analgesia by 50% was similar to that for nalorphine, less than that for pentazocine and more than that for naloxone.

The analgesic activity of 2 mg of butorphanol administered parenterally is approximately equivalent to 10 mg morphine sulfate, 80 mg meperidine HCl or 40 mg pentazocine. In normal volunteers, the same doses of these drugs produced nearly equivalent respiratory depression. Butorphanol, in contrast to morphine or meperidine, produces respiratory depression in a limited dose range, reaching a plateau at approximately 4 mg. The magnitude of respiratory depression with butorphanol is not appreciably increased at a dose of 4 mg; however, the duration of respiratory depression appears to be dose-related. Respiratory rates were monitored in controlled clinical studies with therapeutic doses of butorphanol and no untoward effects were observed. Respiratory depression noted after administration of butorphanol by any route is reversed by treatment with naloxone, a specific opioid antagonist (see Overdose: Symptoms and Treatment).

Butorphanol has a marked sedative effect that is dose-related and this property should be considered in its clinical application (see Precautions).

The hemodynamic changes after the i.v. administration of butorphanol are similar to those produced by pentazocine. These include increased pulmonary artery pressure, pulmonary wedge pressure, left ventricular end diastolic pressure, systemic arterial pressure and pulmonary vascular resistance. Although smaller than those associated with pentazocine, these changes are nevertheless in a direction that increases the work of the heart, especially in the pulmonary circuit.

Butorphanol, like other mixed agonist-antagonists with a high affinity for the kappa receptor, produced unpleasant psychotomimetic effects in some individuals.
Pharmacokinetics: The pharmacokinetics (including absorption times and peak blood levels) of a nasal spray dose and an i.m. dose of butorphanol are similar. In addition, after an initial absorption phase, the pharmacokinetics of a nasal spray dose are also similar to those of an i.v. dose.

Butorphanol is rapidly absorbed without significant biotransformation following nasal administration. In both young and elderly normal volunteers, peak blood levels occur around one-half hour following nasal administration. Peak plasma concentrations after a 1 mg dose vary from a mean of 0.9 to 1.04 ng/mL (see Table I). Elderly subjects may have a somewhat decreased ability to eliminate butorphanol, with an apparent elimination half-life of 6.6 hours as opposed to 4.7 hours for younger subjects. The mean absolute bioavailability may be somewhat less for elderly women (48%) than for elderly men or younger subjects (75% and 69% respectively).

The mean plasma half-life of butorphanol is 5.1 hours after a 2 mg intranasal administration.

Serum protein binding is independent of concentration over the range achieved in clinical practice (up to 7 ng/mL) with a bound fraction of approximately 80%. Butorphanol crosses the blood brain and placental barriers and is found in human milk (see Precautions).

The volumes of distribution of butorphanol varies from 305 to 901 L and total body clearance from 52 to 154 L/h.

Table I—Stadol NS

Mean Pharmacokinetic Parameters of Stadol Nasal Spray in Young and Elderly Subjects[a]

Parameter	Young	Elderly
T_{max}[b] (h)	0.62 (0.50–2.00)[e]	0.75 (0.25–3.00)
C_{max}[c] (ng/mL)	1.04 (0.35–1.97)	0.90 (0.10–2.68)
AUC (inf)[d] (h·ng/mL)	4.93 (2.16–7.27)	5.24 (0.30–10.34)
Half-life (h)	4.7 (2.89–8.79)	6.6 (3.75–9.17)
Absolute Bioavailability (%)	69 (44–113)	62 (3–121)
Volume of Distribution[f] (L)	487 (305–901)	552 (305–737)
Clearance[f] (L/h)	98 (70–154)	82 (52–143)

[a] Young subjects (n=24) are from 20 to 40 years old (mean M/F, 25/30 years) and elderly subjects (n=24) are from 65 to 83 years old (mean M/F, 71 years).
[b] Time to peak plasma concentration, median values.
[c] Peak plasma concentration normalized to 1 mg dose.
[d] Area under the plasma concentration time curve after a 1 mg dose.
[e] (range of observed values).
[f] Derived from i.v. data.

Intranasal butorphanol pharmacokinetics studies determined that steady-state plasma levels of butorphanol were dose proportional (in doses up to 4 mg every 6 hours). Steady-state is achieved within 2 days, and plasma concentrations are approximately 1.8 times those following a single dose.

Butorphanol is extensively metabolized in the liver and is eliminated as oxidized and conjugated metabolites. Metabolism is qualitatively and quantitatively similar with nasal, i.v., or i.m. administration. Less than 5% of an i.v. dose is recovered in the urine as unchanged drug. Because of extensive first-pass metabolism, the bioavailability of oral butorphanol is less than 10%.

Hydroxybutorphanol is the main urinary metabolite of butorphanol (49% of dose); small amounts of norbutorphanol (<5%) are also excreted in urine. The analgesic activity of these two metabolites has not been determined in humans.
Patients with Renal Insufficiency: Eighteen female volunteers (age 30 to 65 years) with normal or varying degrees of renal impairment were given single 1 mg intranasal doses of butorphanol. As shown in Table II, the elimination half-life of butorphanol was prolonged, and the AUC increased, in patients with reduced creatinine clearance (CrCl). No effect, however, was observed on C_{max} or T_{max}.

Table II—Stadol NS

Pharmacokinetics in Patients with Renal Insufficiency

	CrCl (mL/min)	$t_{1/2}$ (h)	AUC (h·ng/mL)
Normal	>70	5.75	4.32 (1.63)*
Moderately Impaired	30–60	8.55	6.49 (1.32)
Severely Impaired	<30	10.48	7.41 (2.64)

*Standard deviation.

Patients with Hepatic Disease: The pharmacokinetics and absolute bioavailability of a 1 mg dose of transnasal butorphanol was studied in 12 (8M, 4F) subjects with hepatic impairment, and 12 normal subjects matched for sex, age and weight. Compared to normal subjects, patients with hepatic impairment had on average a 3-fold increase in $t_{1/2}$ and a 2- to 3-fold increase in AUC. Absolute bioavailability was 99% in the subjects with hepatic impairment compared to 73% in controls. C_{max} and T_{max}, however, remained unaltered regardless of the liver conditions.
Pharmacodynamics: Following intranasal administration of butorphanol, onset of analgesia is within 15 to 30 minutes, and peak analgesic activity generally occurs within 1 to 2 hours. The duration of analgesia varies depending on the pain model but is generally 3 to 6 hours with intranasal doses of 1 to 2 mg.
Clinical Studies: Migraine Headache Pain: The analgesic efficacy of two 1 mg doses 1 hour apart of butorphanol in migraine headache pain was compared with a single dose of 10 mg i.m. methadone or placebo (32 patients per treatment group). Significant onset of analgesia occurred within 15 minutes for both butorphanol and i.m. methadone. Peak analgesic effect occurred at 2 hours for butorphanol and 1.5 hours for methadone. The median duration of pain relief was 6 hours with butorphanol and 4 hours with methadone as judged by the time when approximately half of the patients remedicated.

In the two other trials in patients with migraine headache pain, a 2 mg initial dose of butorphanol followed by an additional 1 mg dose 1 hour later (76 patients) was compared with either 75 mg i.m. meperidine (24 patients) or placebo (72 patients). Onset peak activity and duration were similar with both active treatments; however, the incidence of adverse experiences (nausea, vomiting, dizziness) was higher in these two trials with the 2 mg initial dose of butorphanol than in the trial with the 1 mg initial dose.
Postoperative Analgesia: The analgesic efficacy of butorphanol was investigated in placebo-controlled studies in postoperative surgical pain (abdominal, orthopedic, gynecologic) and in postoperative caesarian section pain. Patients had moderate to severe pain at baseline.

In the general surgery study, a single 1 or 2 mg dose of butorphanol (33 to 36 patients per treatment group) was compared to a single dose of 37.5 or 75 mg i.m. meperidine. In this blinded study, the effects of the lower doses of each drug could be distinguished from those of the higher doses. Analgesia provided by the 1 and 2 mg doses of butorphanol was equivalent to that of 37.5 and 75 mg meperidine respectively. The duration of pain relief was 2 to 3 hours with 1 mg butorphanol and 3 to 4 hours with 2 mg butorphanol, as judged by the time when approximately half of the patients required a repeat dose.

In the caesarian section study, a single dose of 2 mg butorphanol nasal spray (37 patients) or two 1 mg doses butorphanol nasal spray given 1 hour apart (35 patients), were compared to a single dose of 2 mg i.v. butorphanol (37 patients) or placebo (37 patients). Significant pain relief began within 5 minutes for i.v. butorphanol, 15 minutes for 2 mg butorphanol nasal spray, and 30 minutes for the two 1 mg doses of butorphanol nasal spray. Peak analgesic effects were similar for the 3 butorphanol treatments. The duration of pain relief, as judged by this time when approximately half of the patients required a repeat dose, was 2 to 3 hours for 2 mg i.v. butorphanol and 4 to 5 hours for 2 mg butorphanol nasal spray administered either as a single dose or two 1 mg doses given 1 hour apart.

Indications: For the relief of moderate to severe acute pain. The efficacy of butorphanol for periods longer than 3 days has not been established.

Contraindications: Patients hypersensitive to butorphanol or to any component of the preparation.

Warnings: Patients Dependent on Narcotics: Because of the opioid antagonist properties of butorphanol, patients who are physically dependent on narcotics should not be given butorphanol as they may experience withdrawal symptoms. Such patients should have an adequate period of withdrawal from opioid drugs prior to beginning butorphanol therapy.

Butorphanol has precipitated opioid withdrawal symptoms in patients taking opioid analgesics chronically. Adverse experiences include those of the CNS (anxiety, agitation, mood changes, hallucinations, and dysphoria) more frequently than typical somatic opioid withdrawal symptoms. Because of the difficulty in assessing opioid tolerance in patients who have recently received repeated doses of narcotic analgesic medication, caution should be used in the administration of butorphanol to such patients.

Precautions: General: Hypotension associated with syncope during the first hour of dosing with butorphanol has been reported rarely, particularly in patients with past history of similar reactions to opioid analgesics. Therefore, patients should be advised to avoid activities with potential risks.

The sedative property should be considered in the clinical use of butorphanol. In addition, patients receiving recommended therapeutic doses may experience severe dizziness, nausea and vomiting and confusion. Infrequently, hallucinations have also occurred at 2 mg. The patient should be advised accordingly (see Adverse Effects).

Limited clinical experience appears to suggest that patients with migraine headache may be more susceptible to certain adverse reactions associated with butorphanol (see Adverse Effects).

Head Injury and Increased Intracranial Pressure: As with other opioids, butorphanol used in patients with head injury may be associated with carbon dioxide retention and secondary elevation of cerebrospinal fluid pressure, miosis, and alterations in mental state that would obscure the interpretation of the clinical course of head injuries. In such patients, butorphanol should be used only if the benefits of use outweigh the risks.

Respiratory Depression: As a class, the mixed agonist-antagonist opioid drugs are less likely than morphine to produce significant respiratory depression. Nevertheless, drugs of this class may produce respiratory depression in susceptible individuals, especially patients receiving other CNS-active agents or suffering from CNS diseases or respiratory impairment.

Hepatic Disease: Butorphanol should be administered with caution to patients with liver disease (see Pharmacology, Pharmacokinetics, and Dosage, Dosage Adjustments).

Renal Disease: Impaired renal function necessitates alterations in dosing schedule (see Pharmacology, Pharmacokinetics and Dosage, Dosage Adjustments).

Cardiovascular Effects: Because butorphanol increases the work of the heart, especially the pulmonary circuit, the use of this drug in acute myocardial infarction or in cardiac patients with ventricular dysfunction or coronary insufficiency should be limited to those patients for whom the benefits clearly outweigh the risk.

Severe hypertension has been reported rarely during parenteral administration of butorphanol. Because of the similarity in pharmacokinetics (see Pharmacology), this adverse event could potentially occur during use of butorphanol nasal spray. In such cases, butorphanol should be discontinued and the hypertension treated with antihypertensive drugs. In patients who are not opioid dependent, naloxone has also been reported to be effective.

Anesthesia: Butorphanol has not been evaluated for use in anesthesia.

Occupational Hazards: Ambulatory Patients: Drowsiness and dizziness related to the use of butorphanol may impair mental and/or physical abilities required for the performance of potentially hazardous tasks (e.g., driving, operating machinery, etc.). Patients should be told to use caution in such activities until their individual response to butorphanol has been well characterized.

Pregnancy: There are no adequate and well-controlled studies of butorphanol in pregnant women before 37 weeks of gestation. The use of butorphanol in women of childbearing potential requires that the expected benefit of the drug be weighed against the potential risk to the mother and fetus.

Reproduction studies in mice, rats and rabbits during organogenesis did not reveal any teratogenic potential of butorphanol. Pregnant rats treated s.c. with butorphanol at 1 mg/kg (5.9 mg/m²) had a higher frequency of stillbirths than controls. Butorphanol administered orally at 30 mg/kg (5.1 mg/m²) and 60 mg/kg (10.2 mg/m²) also showed higher incidences of postimplantation loss in rabbits.

Labor and Delivery: Butorphanol is not recommended during labor or delivery because there is no clinical experience with its use in this setting. Butorphanol injection has been used during labor, and there have been rare reports of neonatal respiratory depression of the newborn occurring after delivery.

Lactation: There is no clinical experience with the use of butorphanol in nursing mothers. If butorphanol is administered to a nursing mother, consideration should be given to the possibility that pharmacologically active drug could be available to a nursing infant. Butorphanol administered i.v. or i.m. is secreted in low concentrations in human milk; however, the clinical significance of this finding has not been systematically evaluated.

Children: Safety and efficacy in patients under 18 years of age have not been established.

Geriatrics: The mean half-life of butorphanol is increased to 6 hours in patients over the age of 65 (see Pharmacology). In addition to having a somewhat reduced ability to eliminate butorphanol, elderly patients may be more sensitive to its side effects, particularly dizziness (see Dosage).

Dependence Liability: Although, as a class, the mixed agonist-antagonist opioid analgesics have a much lower abuse potential than morphine, all such drugs have been reported to be abused.

Among 161 patients who used butorphanol for 2 months or longer, during a controlled clinical trial, there were 5 reports suggestive of possible abuse, including 3 reports of clinically significant overuse. Post-treatment symptoms such as anxiety, agitation and diarrhea were observed in 6 patients. Symptoms suggestive of opioid withdrawal occurred in 2 patients who stopped the drug abruptly after using 16 mg a day or more for longer than 3 months. Neither withdrawal nor symptoms suggestive of withdrawal occurred when the drug was used for less than a week or when the dose was tapered if use exceeded 1 to 2 weeks. Special care should be exercised in administering butorphanol to emotionally unstable patients and to those with a history of drug abuse.

Drug Interactions: Concurrent use of butorphanol with CNS depressants (e.g., alcohol, barbiturates, tranquilizers and antihistamines) may result in additive CNS depressant effects. The dose of butorphanol should be minimized and the frequency of dosing reduced when it is administered concomitantly with drugs that potentiate the action of opioids.

It is not known if the effects of butorphanol are altered by concomitant medications that affect hepatic metabolism of drugs (erythromycin, theophylline, etc.), but physicians should be alert to the possibility that longer intervals between doses may be needed.

Caution should be exercised in using butorphanol concomitantly with MAO inhibitors, as the latter have been associated with severe and sometimes fatal adverse reactions in certain susceptible individuals when used with meperidine and other narcotic analgesics.

Administration of a single 2 mg dose of butorphanol to 18 subjects with allergic rhinitis resulted in a higher C_{max} and shorter T_{max} compared to healthy subjects, although bioavailabilities were similar. When these 18 subjects were pretreated with the nasal vasoconstrictor, oxymetazoline, bioavailability of butorphanol was not affected, however, C_{max} was reduced and T_{max} was increased to values similar to those observed in healthy subjects.

No significant pharmacokinetic interactions between butorphanol (1 mg) and sumatriptan (6 mg s.c.) were observed in a single dose clinical trial involving 24 healthy volunteers. However, the safety and efficacy of butorphanol in the treatment of migraine headache pain refractory to sumatriptan has not been established.

In another study among 16 healthy male volunteers, the plasma concentrations of a 1 mg dose of butorphanol nasal spray (q.i.d. for 4 days) were not affected when cimetidine was coadministered (300 mg q.i.d. for 4 days). Conversely, the pharmacokinetics of cimetidine (300 mg q.i.d. for 4 days) were not altered when butorphanol nasal spray (1 mg q.i.d.) was coadministered for 4 days.

Adverse Effects: Commonly Observed: Across all controlled and uncontrolled acute treatment clinical trials (799 patients exposed to butorphanol) the most commonly observed adverse experiences (with incidence of at least 10%) regardless of relationship to butorphanol were: drowsiness (35%), somnolence (17%), dizziness (25%) and nausea and vomiting (11%). These adverse events appeared dose-related. They also occurred more frequently in patients given butorphanol for migraine. In nearly all cases, the type and incidence of side effects were those expected of a potent opioid analgesic, and no unforseen or unusual toxicity was reported.

Severe Adverse Reactions: During controlled and uncontrolled acute clinical trials involving 799 patients exposed to butorphanol, the following adverse events regardless of relationship (incidence in parentheses) were rated as severe in greater than 1% of patients: drowsiness and somnolence (7.7%), dizziness (4.4%), nausea and vomiting (3.4%) and confusion (1%).

Controlled Clinical Studies: The incidences of adverse reactions (>3%) to butorphanol (see Table III on following page) are derived from placebo-controlled trials (N=662) in a variety of postoperative pain models at doses of 1 or 2 mg, and from two placebo-controlled trials involving the treatment of migraine pain at doses of 2 to 3 mg.

Other adverse reactions (≤3%) that were reported with butorphanol in all acute (controlled and non-controlled) clinical trials (N=799) are listed below.

These adverse events, regardless of relationship to butorphanol, are listed in order of decreasing frequency according to the following definitions: Frequent events were reported on one or more occasions by at least 1/100 individuals; Infrequent events by 1/100 to 1/1 000 individuals. (All events **except those already listed in Table III** [on following page] **are included.)**

Body as a Whole: Infrequent: sensation of cold, fever, edema, accidental injury, back pain.

Gastrointestinal: Infrequent: pharyngitis, stomach pain, abdominal pain, dysphagia, flatulence.

Cardiovascular: Frequent: hypotension. Infrequent: blood pressure elevated, hypertension, tachycardia, pallor, arrhythmia.

Musculoskeletal: Infrequent: muscle relaxation, leg pain.

Nervous System: Infrequent: hallucinations, feel calm, insomnia, abnormal dreams, agitation, abnormal gait, dysarthria, ataxia, tremor, derealization, intoxication, spasms, stupor, hyperesthesia, motor retardation, vivid imagination, abnormal involuntary movement, slowed movement.

Respiratory: Infrequent: dyspnea, cough, hypoventilation, respiratory disorder, sinus congestion, nasal congestion.

Dermatological: Infrequent: rash, erythema.

Genitourinary: Infrequent: impaired urination, libido increased.

Nasal Experiences: Infrequent: nasal symptoms, nose pain.

Special Senses: Infrequent: visual disturbance, photophobia, hyperacusia, eye pain, ear pain, tinnitus, eye disorder, taste loss.

Hemic and Lymphatic: Infrequent: petechiae.

Postmarketing Experience: The following adverse events also have occurred in less than 1% of patients in short-term butorphanol trials and postmarketing experience.

Body as a Whole: excessive drug effect associated with transient difficulty speaking and/or executing purposeful movements.

Cardiovascular: chest pain, hypertension, tachycardia.

Nervous System: convulsions, drug dependence.

Overdose: Symptoms: Based on its pharmacology, butorphanol overdosage could produce signs of respiratory depression, cardiovascular failure (especially in predisposed patients), or CNS depression. There have been no clinical reports of fatal overdosage of butorphanol as a single drug in healthy individuals, but the injectable product has been reported in a fatal overdose in combination with other drugs or alcohol.

Treatment: The specific treatment of suspected butorphanol overdosage is immediate establishment of adequate airway and ventilation, followed (if necessary) by an opioid antagonist such as i.v. naloxone. Physicians are reminded that the duration of butorphanol action exceeds the duration of action of naloxone, and repeated dosing of naloxone may be required. The patient should be carefully monitored, especially the respiratory and cardiac status, and appropriate supportive measures, such as oxygen, i.v. fluids and/or vasopressors, should be instituted if necessary.

Dosage: Butorphanol has an onset of effect within 15 to 30 minutes and requires individualization of dosage based on clinical response.

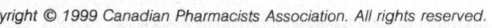

Stadol NS (cont'd)

Table III—Stadol NS

Summary of Adverse Events in Patients Receiving Stadol NS or Placebo in Postoperative Pain and Migraine Trials (only adverse events reported by >3% of patients treated with Stadol NS at the specified dose are included)

	Migraine Pain Trials				Postoperative Pain			
	Stadol NS (% of Patients)			Placebo (% of Patients)	Stadol NS (% of Patients)			Placebo (% of Patients)
	1+1 mg N=32	2 mg N=33	2+1 mg N=16	N=78	1 mg N=128	1+1 mg N=70	2 mg N=149	N=156
Body as a Whole								
Asthenia	9	18	6	3				
Chills	—	6	—	3				
Headache					4	4	—	3
Pain	—	6	—	1				
Sensation of Heat	6	12	6	3	—	—	5	1
Cardiovascular								
Chest Pain	—	6	—	—				
Palpitation	6	—	—	—				
Syncope	—	9	—	—				
Vasodilation	6	—	6	1				
Digestive								
Dry Mouth	6	21	12	—				
Increased Appetite	—	6	—	—				
Nausea/Vomiting	22	61	37	4	—	—	8	1
Thirst	—	—	6	—				
Nervous System								
Abnormal Feelings	6	12	6	—				
Abnormal Thinking	—	6	—	—				
Anxiety	—	6	—	—				
Confusion	9	24	6	—	—	6	—	—
Dizziness	50	85	75	10	23	6	25	1
Drowsiness	41	51	50	5	26	33	40	16
Euphoria	—	3	6	—				
Incoordination	—	6	—	—				
Nervousness	16	9	6	—				
Paresis	—	15	6	—				
Paresthesia	6	21		—				
Somnolence					23	36	39	12
Vertigo	9	6	—	1				
Respiratory								
Epistaxis	—	—	6	—				
Nasal Irritation	—	6	6	1				
Dermatological								
Pruritus	6	12	6	—				
Sweating	6	30	19	—	—	4	—	1
Special Senses								
Blurred Vision	12	9	12	1				
Diplopia	6	—	—	—				
Ear Disorder	—	6	—	—				
Hearing Loss	—	—	6	—				
Unpleasant Taste	12	9	6	—				

Adults: The usual recommended dose for initial nasal administration is 1 spray in one nostril (1 mg). Adherence to this dose may reduce the likelihood of drowsiness, dizziness, and nausea and vomiting. If adequate pain relief is not achieved within 60 to 90 minutes, an additional 1 mg dose may be given.

The initial dose sequence may be repeated in 3 to 4 hours as needed. Due to limited clinical experience with higher doses, total daily doses of more than 16 mg are not recommended.

Depending on the severity of the pain, an initial dose of 2 mg (1 spray in each nostril) may be used in patients who will be able to remain recumbent in the event drowsiness or dizziness occur. In such patients, additional doses should not be given for 3 to 4 hours.

Dosage Adjustments: Patients with Hepatic Impairment: The elimination half-life of butorphanol is prolonged in patients with impaired hepatic function (see Pharmacology, Pharmacokinetics). Butorphanol should thus be used with caution in this population. The initial dosage interval should be increased to 6 to 12 hours until the response is well characterized. Subsequent dosings should be determined by patient response rather than being scheduled at fixed intervals.

Patients with Renal Impairment: The elimination half-life of butorphanol is prolonged in patients with impaired renal function (see Pharmacology, Pharmacokinetics). Dosage adjustments may thus be necessary. In patients with severe renal disease (i.e., creatinine clearance <30 mL/min), the initial dosage interval should be increased to 6 to 8 hours until the response has been well characterized. Subsequent dosings of butorphanol should be determined by patient response rather than being scheduled at fixed intervals.

Geriatrics: Because elderly patients may have a somewhat decreased ability to eliminate butorphanol (see Pharmacology, Pharmacokinetics) and may be more sensitive to butorphanol's side effects, the effects of the initial dose should be carefully assessed, and it may be appropriate to modify the frequency of subsequent dosing.

Initially a 1 mg dose of butorphanol should generally be used in elderly patients, and 90 to 120 minutes should elapse before deciding whether a second 1 mg dose is needed. The repeat dose sequence should be determined by the patient's response rather than at fixed times, but will generally be no less than at 6-hour intervals (see Precautions).

Special Instructions: Stadol NS is an open delivery system that has a risk of accidental exposure to health care workers. In the priming process, a certain amount of butorphanol may be aerosolized; therefore, the pump sprayer should be aimed away from the patient or animals.

Significant absorption from accidental dermal exposure is unlikely, and the contents of a spilled system should be washed from the skin by rinsing with cool water.

The best way to dispose of the unit safely is to unscrew the cap, rinse the bottle and spray assembly under the water faucet, then dispose of the parts in a waste can where children cannot get to them easily.

Information for the Pharmacist: Instructions for Assembly of Nasal Spray Unit: Assemble Stadol NS prior to dispensing to the patient, according to the following instructions.

1. Open the container and remove the spray pump and solution bottle.
2. Assemble by first unscrewing the white cap from the solution bottle and screwing the pump unit tightly onto the bottle. Make sure the clear cover is on the pump unit.
3. Return bottle to the container for dispensing to the patient. Patients should be instructed in the proper use of Stadol NS.

Information for the Patient: See Blue Section—Information for the Patient "Stadol NS".

Supplied: Each mL of aqueous solution contains: butorphanol tartrate 10 mg. Nonmedicinal ingredients: benzethonium chloride as a preservative, citric acid, sodium chloride, in purified water with sodium hydroxide and/or hydrochloric acid added to adjust the pH to 5.0. Bottles of 2.5 mL with a metered-dose spray pump with protective clip and dust cover and a patient instruction leaflet. After priming, each metered spray delivers 1.0 mg of butorphanol tartrate. The 2.5 mL bottle will deliver on average 14 to 15 metered doses, if no repriming is necessary. Store at room temperature (15 to 30°C).

(Shown in Product Recognition Section)

Reviewed 1999

STATEX® Ⓝ

Pharmascience

Morphine Sulfate

Analgesic

Supplied: Drops: Each mL of clear, unflavored, colorless liquid contains: morphine sulfate 20 or 50 mg. Graduated bottles of 25 and 100 mL (20 mg/mL) and graduated bottles of 50 mL (50 mg/mL) with calibrated dropper.

Suppositories: Each white, cone shaped suppository contains: morphine sulfate 5, 10, 20 or 30 mg. Boxes of 10.

The suppository should be placed against the rectal mucosa. The drug is not absorbed if pushed into a mass of stool or if it is placed in the anal canal.

Syrup: 1 mg: Each mL of unflavored (clear) syrup contains: morphine sulfate 1 mg. Energy: 3.3 kJ (0.8 kcal/mL). Pet-G plastic graduated bottles of 250 and 500 mL.

5 mg: Each mL of unflavored (clear), syrup contains: morphine sulfate 5 mg. Energy: 6.8 kJ (1.6 kcal/mL). Pet-G plastic graduated bottles of 250 and 500 mL.

10 mg: Each mL of unflavored (clear) syrup contains: morphine sulfate 10 mg. Energy: 5.1 kJ (1.2 kcal/mL). Pet-G plastic graduated bottles of 250 mL.

Tablets: Each round, scored tablet contains: morphine sulfate 5 mg (green), 10 mg (blue), 25 mg (pink) or 50 mg (orange). Control packs of 4×25. Bottles of 100.

STATICIN® Ⓟ

Westwood-Squibb

Erythromycin—Ethyl Alcohol—Laureth-4

Acne Therapy

Indications: The treatment of acne vulgaris. For use primarily in the treatment of the inflammatory papular lesions of acne.

Contraindications: Hypersensitivity to any of the components.

Warnings: Eye contact should be avoided since Staticin is irritating to the eyes. Instillation in the rabbit eye is known to provoke corneal damage. Concomitant topical antiacne therapy should be avoided because a cumulative irritancy effect may occur, particularly with those preparations containing peeling, desquamating or abrasive agents.

Precautions: For external use only. Avoid contact with the eyes, nostrils, mouth and other mucous membranes. Contains drying and peeling agents that are potential irritants, therefore reduction in frequency of application may be necessary to avoid excessive irritation.

The use of preparations containing antibiotics may be associated with overgrowth of antibiotic resistant organisms. Cross resistance between erythromycin and macrolide antibiotics can occur. If this should occur, therapy should be discontinued and appropriate measures taken.

Adverse Effects: Symptoms of irritation: erythema, desquamation, tenderness and excessive dryness.

Mild to moderate symptoms of irritation were observed in 70% of Staticin treated patients, while severe irritation was seen in 12%.
Others: pruritus, urticaria, oiliness and fissuring around the mouth.

Overdose: Symptoms: Accidental ingestion could result in alcoholic intoxication and/or intestinal tract irritation manifested by vomiting, cramping, diarrhea.

Treatment: Treat with a demulcent. If eye contact with Staticin should occur, wash with copious amounts of water for at least 5 minutes. If discomfort persists, a physician should be contacted.

Excessive frequency of application can cause erythema, excessive scaling and sensations of burning and tenderness. Appropriate anti-inflammatory measures (e.g. compresses or topical corticosteroids) may be employed.

Dosage: Apply each morning and evening to the areas affected by acne. Before applying, areas should be washed with mild soap, rinsed well, and patted dry. Use fingertips to apply medication. Wash hands after use. Because the drying and peeling agents in Staticin are potentially irritating, the frequency of application may require adjustment to once a day or less. Ethyl alcohol and Laureth-4 contribute significantly to the effectiveness of Staticin due to their drying and peeling properties. The erythromycin component significantly reduces the number of papular lesions after four weeks of treatment. Staticin reduced the total acne lesion count (closed and open comedones, papules and pustules) to a significant degree by 12 weeks of therapy.

Supplied: Each bottle contains: erythromycin base 1.5% w/v, ethyl alcohol 55% v/v and 6% w/v laureth-4. Nonmedicinal ingredients: fragrance and propylene glycol. Plastic bottles of 60 and 120 mL, with optional applicator. Store tightly closed in a cool, dry place, and avoid contact with open flame.

STELABID® Preparations

SmithKline Beecham

Trifluoperazine HCl—Isopropamide Iodide

Adjuvant Therapy in Gastrointestinal Disorders

Pharmacology: Isopropamide is an inherently long-acting synthetic anticholinergic agent that provides 12-hour antisecretory-antispasmodic activity.

Trifluoperazine is a piperazine phenothiazine derivative with antipsychotic and antiemetic properties. The mode of action of phenothiazines has not been definitely established. Like most phenothiazines, trifluoperazine possesses weak anticholinergic and possibly alpha-adrenergic blocking activities.

Indications: Stelabid may be employed to advantage in the treatment of a wide range of gastrointestinal disorders, including such conditions as peptic ulcer, gastritis, hyperchlorhydria, functional diarrhea, irritable or spastic colon, pyloroduodenal irritability, pylorospasm, acute nonspecific gastroenteritis, biliary dyskinesia and chronic cholelithiasis, duodenitis, gastrointestinal spasm; it may also be used to treat genitourinary spasm.

Stelabid is particularly indicated where anxiety, tension, worry, or other emotional factors are thought to be wholly or partially responsible for the digestive dysfunction. Since both components of Stelabid are inherently long-acting, a single tablet twice daily (every 12 hours) can provide continuous 24-hour control of symptoms of ulcer and other gastrointestinal disorders.

In addition to the convenience of twice-daily dosage, Stelabid tablets can provide these significant therapeutic advantages: continuous reduction of gastric secretion; continuous inhibition of spasm and motility; continuous relief of anxiety and tension; continuous control of nausea and vomiting.

Contraindications: In comatose states and in the presence of glaucoma, cardiospasm, obstructive uropathy (e.g., bladder neck obstruction due to prostatic hypertrophy) or obstructive lesions of the gastrointestinal tract (as in achalasia, obstructive or paralytic ileus, pyloroduodenal stenosis, etc.), intestinal atony of the elderly or debilitated patient, severe ulcerative colitis, toxic megacolon complicating ulcerative colitis.

Because of the antiemetic action of the trifluoperazine component, Stelabid should not be used where nausea and vomiting are believed to be evidence of intestinal obstruction or brain tumor.

Precautions: Use with caution in elderly patients, in patients with cardiac impairment, hyperthyroidism, or hiatal hernia associated with reflux esophagitis (anticholinergic drugs may aggravate this condition).

Since the iodine in isopropamide iodide may alter PBI test results, and will suppress ^{131}I uptake, it is suggested that therapy be discontinued 1 week prior to these tests.

Clinical experience has demonstrated that trifluoperazine has a wide margin of safety and that there is little likelihood of blood or liver toxicity. However, such adverse effects have been reported, and the physician should be aware of their possible occurrence.

Hypotension has not been a problem with trifluoperazine. Nevertheless, adequate precautions should be taken when the drug is administered to patients with impaired cardiovascular function.

Trifluoperazine therapy may produce an increase in mental and physical activity. In certain instances, this effect may not be desirable. For example, some patients with angina pectoris have complained of increased pain while taking trifluoperazine. Therefore, if Stelabid is used in angina patients, they should be observed carefully and, if an unfavorable response is noted, the drug should be withdrawn.

Trifluoperazine's potent antiemetic action may mask signs of overdosage of toxic drugs or may obscure the diagnosis of conditions such as intestinal obstruction, and brain tumor.

Pregnancy and *Lactation:* Use during pregnancy should be restricted to those cases where the potential benefit to the mother outweighs the potential risk to the fetus.

Adequate human data on use during lactation and adequate animal reproduction studies are not available.

Adverse Effects: May be those of either component. The usual anticholinergic side effects—dry mouth, blurred vision, urinary hesitancy and retention, and constipation—have been encountered with Stelabid. Iodine skin rash may occur rarely. A few patients sensitive to phenothiazine compounds may experience a transient unpleasant agitation, or jitteriness, characterized by restlessness and sometimes by insomnia. These symptoms often disappear spontaneously. Where the effect is particularly bothersome, the concomitant administration of a mild sedative may be helpful.

Phenothiazines can, in some patients on long-term therapy, cause tardive dyskinesia which can last for months or years; the risk appears greater in elderly patients.

Overdose: Symptoms: Symptoms may be those of either isopropamide or trifluoperazine overdosage.
Isopropamide: May include dryness of mouth, dysphagia, thirst, blurred vision, dilated pupils, photophobia, fever, rapid pulse and respiration, disorientation. Depression and circulatory collapse may result from severe overdosage.
Trifluoperazine: Primarily, involvement of the extrapyramidal mechanism(s) producing some of the dystonic reactions to a more marked degree. Lesser degrees of overdosage may cause muscular twitching, drowsiness or dizziness. Symptoms of gross overdosage may include CNS depression, weakness, tremor, torticollis and dystonia. Agitation and restlessness may occur. Salivation, dysphagia, or disturbances of gait may also be present.

Treatment: Essentially symptomatic and supportive. Early gastric lavage is helpful. **Do not attempt to induce emesis because a dystonic reaction of the head or neck may develop that could result in aspiration of vomitus.**

Force fluids by mouth or, if necessary, by i.v. administration of glucose 10% in water.

Respiratory depression should be treated promptly by the use of oxygen and stimulants.

If marked excitement is present, one of the short-acting barbiturates or chloral hydrate may be used. Otherwise, do not administer sedation.

Hyperpyrexia may be treated with physical cooling measures.

If hypotension occurs, the standard measures for managing circulatory shock should be initiated, e.g., i.v. fluids and/or vasoconstrictors. If it is desirable to administer a vasoconstrictor, norepinephrine or phenylephrine is most suitable. Other pressor agents, including epinephrine, are not recommended because phenothiazine derivatives may reverse the usual elevating action of these agents and cause a further lowering of blood pressure. If administration of a stimulant is desirable, amphetamine or caffeine and sodium benzoate is recommended. Stimulants that may cause convulsions (e.g., picrotoxin or pentylenetetrazol) should be avoided. Extrapyramidal symptoms may be treated with antiparkinsonism drugs (except levodopa), barbiturates or diphenhydramine.

While pilocarpine or similar drugs are sometimes recommended for the relief of dry mouth, many authorities feel that these drugs are not indicated, since they relieve the minor peripheral effect but do not influence the more serious central effects, and thus may merely mask signs of drug activity.

If photophobia occurs, the patient should be kept in a darkened room.

It is not known whether isopropamide is dialyzable. Limited experience indicates that phenothiazines are **not** dialyzable.

Dosage: Adults: 1 tablet twice daily (every 12 hours). The No. 2 strength is recommended for the majority of patients. Where there is relatively little psychic distress, the No. 1 strength may be preferred. Stelabid Forte will be especially useful for those patients in whom a greater degree of antispasmodic and antisecretory action is desired.

Supplied: No. 1: Each round, biconvex, maize-colored, film-coated tablet, monogrammed SKF P90, contains: trifluoperazine 1 mg (present as trifluoperazine HCl 1.18 mg) and isopropamide 5 mg (present as isopropamide iodide 6.8 mg). Nonmedicinal ingredients: candelilla wax, cellulose, cosmetic ochre no. 3506, lactose, magnesium stearate, Opadry clear, Opadry yellow, sodium starch glycolate and talc. Energy: 1.63 kJ (0.39 kcal). Lactose: 94.5 mg. Sodium: <1 mmol (0.0875 mg). Bottles of 100.

No. 2: Each round, biconvex, maize-colored, film-coated tablet, monogrammed SKF P91, contains: trifluoperazine 2 mg (present as trifluoperazine HCl 2.36 mg) and isopropamide 5 mg (present as isopropamide iodide 6.8 mg). Nonmedicinal ingredients: candelilla wax, cellulose, cosmetic ochre no. 3506, lactose, magnesium stearate, Opadry clear, Opadry yellow, sodium starch glycolate and talc. Energy: 2.24 kJ (0.53 kcal). Lactose: 129.7 mg. Sodium: <1 mmol (0.105 mg). Bottles of 100.

Forte: Each round, biconvex, maize-colored, film-coated tablet, monogrammed SKF P92, contains: trifluoperazine 2 mg (present as trifluoperazine HCl 2.36 mg) and isopropamide 7.5 mg (present as isopropamide iodide 10.2 mg). Nonmedicinal ingredients: candelilla wax, cellulose, cosmetic ochre no. 3506, lactose, magnesium stearate, Opadry clear, Opadry yellow, sodium starch glycolate and talc. Energy: 2.99 kJ (0.712 kcal). Lactose: 173.3 mg. Sodium: <1 mmol (0.175 mg). Bottles of 100.

(Shown in Product Recognition Section)

Reviewed 1999

STELAZINE®

SmithKline Beecham

Trifluoperazine HCl

Antianxiety—Antiemetic—Antipsychotic

Pharmacology: The mode of action of the phenothiazines has not yet been definitely established. Existing information suggests the following possibilities: Antipsychotic/antianxiety effects: Observations suggest that the primary action is to depress the physiologic accompaniments of the emotional factors of the personality which are believed to be basically evoked by the limbic system and its connections with the hypothalamus.

Experimental and clinical evidence indicates that the phenothiazines act on the subcortical areas of the CNS which influence the affective functions. Trifluoperazine is more specific than other phenothiazines in its activity. Its effects seem limited to parts of the basal ganglia, such as the amygdaloid nucleus.

The fact that trifluoperazine modifies behavior of opposite extremes toward more normal activity suggests that the drug is not working on behavior per se but on some factor or factors underlying behavior. Its rapidity of action, increased potency and effectiveness in chronic regressed patients in whom other agents were less effective are believed due to its specificity of action.
Antiemetic effect: The phenothiazines (including trifluoperazine) inhibit indirect stimulation of the vomiting centre, but do not inhibit indirect stimulation of the centre by gastrointestinal stimulants. Because of this, it is believed that their site of action is the chemoreceptor trigger zone.

Stelazine (cont'd)

Onset of action occurs normally within 0.5 to 1 hour following tablet administration. Onset is slightly more rapid with the concentrate form because no disintegration time is involved. Onset usually occurs within 10 to 15 minutes when trifluoperazine is administered i.m., and within 5 to 15 minutes following i.v. administration. Peak activity occurs within 2 hours in animals.

Clinical observations indicate that disappearance of, or marked reduction in psychomotor activity and hallucinations, occurs within hours after i.m. administration of trifluoperazine.

Indications: Anxiety states: It controls excessive anxiety, tension and agitation seen in neuroses or associated with somatic conditions.

The treatment or prevention of nausea and vomiting of various causes.

The management of psychotic disorders, such as acute or chronic catatonic, hebephrenic and paranoid schizophrenia; psychosis due to organic brain damage, toxic psychosis, and the manic phase of manic-depressive illness.

Contraindications: Comatose or greatly depressed states due to CNS depressants; blood dyscrasias, bone marrow depression; liver damage.

Warnings: Patients who have demonstrated a hypersensitivity reaction (e.g., blood dyscrasias, jaundice) with a phenothiazine should not be re-exposed to any phenothiazine, including trifluoperazine, unless, in the judgment of the physician, the potential benefits of treatment outweigh the possible hazard.

Trifluoperazine may impair mental and/or physical abilities, especially during the first few days of therapy. Therefore, patients should be cautioned about activities requiring alertness (e.g., operating vehicles or machinery).

If agents such as sedatives, narcotics, anesthetics, tranquilizers or alcohol are used either simultaneously or successively with trifluoperazine, the possibility of an undesirable additive depressant effect should be considered.

Precautions: Clinical experience has demonstrated that trifluoperazine has a wide margin of safety. However, rare cases of blood dyscrasias (agranulocytosis, anemia, leukopenia, neutropenia, pancytopenia, thrombocytopenia) and jaundice of the cholestatic type have been reported in patients receiving high doses of trifluoperazine. Therefore, the physician should bear in mind the possibility of such reactions.

Geriatrics and Debilitated Patients: Care should be exercised in treating elderly or debilitated patients as some appear prone to neurological adverse reactions.

Phenothiazines can produce alpha-adrenergic blockade. Because hypotension has occurred, large doses and parenteral administration should be avoided in patients with impaired cardiovascular systems. To further minimize the occurrence of hypotension after initial injection, keep patient lying down and observe for at least 0.5 hour. If hypotension occurs from parenteral or oral dosing, place patient in head-low position with legs raised. If a vasoconstrictor is required, norepinephrine or phenylephrine is suitable. Other pressor agents, including epinephrine, should not be used as they may cause a paradoxical further lowering of blood pressure (see Overdose: Symptoms and Treatment).

Trifluoperazine therapy may produce an increase in mental and physical activity. In certain instances, this effect may not be desirable. For example, some patients with angina pectoris have complained of increased pain while taking trifluoperazine; therefore, if trifluoperazine is used in angina patients, such patients should be observed carefully and if an unfavorable response is noted, the drug should be withdrawn.

As with all drugs which exert an anticholinergic effect or cause mydriasis, trifluoperazine should be used with caution in patients with glaucoma.

Certain phenothiazines have been reported to produce retinopathy, especially with long-term treatment at high dosage. Should ophthalmoscopic examination or visual field studies demonstrate retinal changes in patients on trifluoperazine, the drug should be discontinued.

Skin pigmentation and ocular changes have been reported in a few hospitalized mental patients taking substantial doses of some phenothiazine derivatives for prolonged periods. Present evidence suggests that these changes may be reversible.

The antiemetic action of trifluoperazine may mask signs and symptoms of toxicity or overdosage of other drugs or may obscure the diagnosis of conditions such as intestinal obstruction, brain tumor and Reye's syndrome.

With prolonged administration at high dosages, the possibility of cumulative effects, with sudden onset of severe CNS or vasomotor symptoms, should be kept in mind. To lessen the likelihood of adverse reactions related to drug accumulation, patients on long-term therapy, particularly on high doses, should be evaluated periodically to decide whether the maintenance dosage could be lowered or drug therapy discontinued.

Although phenothiazines cause neither psychic nor physical dependence, sudden discontinuance in long-term psychiatric patients may cause temporary symptoms, e.g., nausea and vomiting, dizziness, tremulousness.

Phenothiazines have been found to be mutagenic with in vivo administration to rodents and in vitro administration to human cells and bacteria. No clinical relevance has been established.

Drug Interactions: Phenothiazines may diminish the effect of oral anticoagulants.

Concomitant administration of propranolol with phenothiazines results in increased plasma levels of both drugs.

Phenothiazines may lower the convulsive threshold; dosage adjustment of anticonvulsants may be necessary. Potentiation of anticonvulsant effects does not occur. However, it has been reported that phenothiazines may interfere with the metabolism of phenytoin and thus precipitate phenytoin toxicity.

Drugs that lower the seizure threshold, including phenothiazine derivatives, should not be used with metrizamide. As with other phenothiazine derivatives, trifluoperazine should be discontinued at least 48 hours before myelography, should not be resumed for at least 24 hours post procedure, and should not be used for the control of nausea and vomiting occurring either prior to myelography or post procedure.

Pregnancy: Animal reproduction studies and follow-up studies in 819 women in Canada and Great Britain, who had taken trifluoperazine during pregnancy, showed no causal relationship between the drug and congenital malformations.

While it is generally recognized that caution should always be observed when prescribing for the pregnant patient, especially during the first trimester, if the physician considers that antiemetic or tranquilizer therapy is necessary for the welfare of the patient, then trifluoperazine is indicated.

Lactation: There is evidence that phenothiazines are excreted in the milk of nursing mothers.

Adverse Effects: At therapeutic dosage levels, adverse reactions are infrequent, usually mild and transient, and unlikely to affect the course of treatment. Drowsiness, dizziness, skin reactions, dry mouth, stimulation, insomnia, fatigue, weakness, anorexia, amenorrhea, lactation and blurred vision may be seen occasionally. Extrapyramidal symptoms may occur but are rare at dosages of 6 mg or less. Tardive dyskinesia has been reported.

Extrapyramidal Symptoms: These symptoms are seen in a significant number of hospitalized mental patients receiving higher dosages of trifluoperazine (10 mg to 40 mg or more daily). They may be characterized by motor restlessness, may be of the dystonic type, or may resemble parkinsonism. Depending on the severity of symptoms, dosage should be reduced or discontinued. If therapy is reinstituted, it should be a lower dosage. Should these symptoms occur in children or pregnant patients, the drug should be stopped and not reinstated. In most cases, barbiturates by suitable route of administration will suffice. In more severe cases the administration of an antiparkinsonism agent (**except levodopa**) usually produces rapid reversal of symptoms. Suitable supportive measures such as maintaining a clear airway and adequate hydration should be employed.

Motor Restlessness: Symptoms may include agitation or jitteriness and sometimes insomnia. These symptoms often disappear spontaneously. At times these symptoms may be similar to the original neurotic or psychotic symptoms. Dosage should not be increased until these side effects have subsided. If this condition becomes too troublesome, the symptoms can be controlled by dosage reduction or concomitant administration of a barbiturate.

Dystonias: Symptoms may include spasm of the neck muscles, sometimes progressing to torticollis; extensor rigidity of back muscles; sometimes progressing to opisthotonos; carpopedal spasm, trismus, swallowing difficulty, oculogyric crises and protrusion of the tongue. The onset of the dystonias may be sudden. They may last several minutes, disappear and then recur. There is typically no loss of consciousness and definite prodromata are usually present. They usually subside within a few hours, and almost always within 24 to 48 hours after the drug has been discontinued.

In mild cases, reassurance or a barbiturate is often sufficient. In moderate cases, barbiturates will usually bring rapid relief. In more severe adult cases, the administration of an antiparkinsonism agent, **except levodopa**, usually produces rapid reversal of symptoms. Also, i.v. diphenhydramine or caffeine with sodium benzoate seems to be effective. In children, reassurance and barbiturates will usually control symptoms.

Neuroleptic Malignant Syndrome: As with other neuroleptic drugs, a symptom complex sometimes referred to as neuroleptic malignant syndrome (NMS) has been reported. Cardinal features of NMS are hyperpyrexia, muscle rigidity, altered mental status (including catatonic signs), and evidence of autonomic instability (irregular pulse or blood pressure). Additional signs may include elevated CPK, myoglobinuria (rhabdomyolysis), and acute renal failure. NMS is potentially fatal and requires symptomatic treatment and immediate discontinuation of neuroleptic treatment.

Pseudoparkinsonism: Symptoms may include mask-like facies, drooling, tremor, pillrolling motion, cogwheel rigidity and shuffling gait. Reassurance and sedation are important. In most cases these symptoms are readily reversible when an antiparkinsonism agent is administered concomitantly. (Note: Antiparkinsonism agents should be used only when required. Levodopa has not been found effective in pseudoparkinsonism.) Occasionally it is necessary to lower the dosage or to discontinue the drug temporarily.

Tardive Dyskinesia: In rare instances, this syndrome may occur on long-term therapy with phenothiazines, including trifluoperazine, or may appear after drug treatment has been discontinued. The risk appears to be greater in elderly patients, especially females, on high-dose therapy. The syndrome is characterized by rhythmical involuntary movements of the tongue and facial muscles (e.g., protrusion of the tongue, puffing of cheeks, puckering of mouth, chewing movements) and sometimes of the extremities. The symptoms may persist for many months or even years, and while they gradually disappear in some patients, they appear to be irreversible in others.

There is no known effective treatment for tardive dyskinesia; antiparkinsonism agents usually do not alleviate the symptoms of this syndrome. It is suggested that all antipsychotic agents be discontinued if these symptoms appear. If there is a reinstitution of treatment, or an increase in the dosage of the drug, or a switch to a different antipsychotic agent, the syndrome may be masked. It has been reported that fine vermicular movements of the tongue may be an early sign of the syndrome and if the medication is stopped at that time, the syndrome may not develop.

ECG Changes: ECG changes, particularly nonspecific, usually reversible Q and T wave distortions, have been observed in some patients receiving phenothiazine tranquilizers. This relationship to myocardial damage has not been confirmed.

Overdose: Symptoms: Primarily involvement of the extrapyramidal mechanism producing some of the dystonic reactions to a more marked degree. Lesser degrees of overdosage may case muscular twitching, drowsiness or dizziness. Symptoms of gross overdosage may include CNS depression, weakness, tremor, torticollis and dystonia. Agitation and restlessness may occur. Salivation, dysphagia, or disturbances of gait may also be present.

Treatment: Treatment is essentially symptomatic and supportive. Gastric lavage is helpful if performed early. **Do not attempt to induce emesis because a dystonic reaction of the head or neck may develop that could result in aspiration of vomitus.**

The patient should be kept under careful observation and particular attention should be directed to maintaining an open airway, since involvement of the extrapyramidal mechanism may produce dysphagia and respiratory difficulty in severe cases of overdosage.

If hypotension occurs, the standard measures for managing circulatory shock should be initiated, e.g., i.v. fluids and/or vasoconstrictors. If it is desirable to administer a vasoconstrictor, norepinephrine or phenylephrine is most suitable. Other pressor agents, including epinephrine, are not recommended because phenothiazine derivatives may reverse the usual elevating action of these agents and cause a further lowering of blood pressure.

If administration of a stimulant is desirable, amphetamine or caffeine with sodium benzoate is recommended. Stimulants that may cause convulsions (e.g., picrotoxin or pentylenetetrazol) should be avoided. Extrapyramidal symptoms may be treated with antiparkinsonism drugs (except levodopa), barbiturates or diphenhydramine.

Limited experience indicates that phenothiazines are **not** dialyzable.

Dosage: Trifluoperazine dosage must be adjusted to the severity of the symptoms under treatment, and to the response of the individual. Particularly in psychiatric patients, dosage should be titrated carefully in order to achieve maximum therapeutic effect with the lowest possible dose, thereby minimizing the occurrence of unwanted side effects.

General Practice: Oral: The usual starting dosage is a 1 mg or 2 mg tablet twice daily. In everyday practice it is seldom necessary to exceed 6 mg daily. Because of the inherent long action of trifluoperazine most patients can be effectively controlled on a convenient twice-a-day dosage regimen, and some have been maintained on once-a-day administration.

Office Psychiatric Practice: Neurotics and other patients with symptoms of anxiety: The dosage information given for the use of trifluoperazine in everyday practice is, generally speaking, applicable to the treatment of nonhospitalized psychiatric patients with relatively mild mental and emotional disturbances.

Released Patients: Psychiatric patients recently discharged from the hospital or on convalescent leave should continue with the maintenance dosage determined during hospitalization.

Patients with Moderate to Severe Symptoms: In borderline psychotics and in other nonhospitalized psychiatric patients with moderate to severe symptoms, the recommended starting dose is 2 to 4 mg twice daily. (Small or emaciated patients should always be started on the lower dosage.) The dosage should be increased gradually, as necessary, until symptoms are controlled. The majority of patients will show optimum response on 15 to 20 mg daily, although a few patients will require 40 mg or more per day. In most cases, optimum dosage levels are reached within 2 or 3 weeks after the start of therapy.

If side effects become bothersome during the period of dosage adjustment, they can usually be controlled promptly by concomitant administration of an antiparkinsonism agent (not levodopa). Some physicians prefer to administer an antiparkinsonism agent prophylactically in all patients whose daily dosage level reaches 10 mg or more.

Behavior Disorders in Children: The usual dose is a 1 mg tablet administered once or twice a day, depending on the size of the child (see also Dosage, Psychotic children).

Hospitalized Adult Psychiatric Patients: The usual starting dose is a 5 mg tablet administered orally 2 or 3 times daily. (Small or emaciated patients should be started on a 2 mg tablet 2 or 3 times daily.) Dosage should be increased gradually. The majority of patients will show optimum response on 15 to 20 mg/day, although a few may require 40 mg or more. Although some patients have been given 80 mg or more daily, there is now every evidence that such high dosages are rarely necessary. Optimum dosage levels are usually reached within 2 or 3 weeks after the start of therapy. It is important to maintain therapeutic dosage levels for a sufficient time to produce maximum improvement. In most hospitalized acute cases, 2 to 3 weeks at optimum dosage will suffice before gradual reduction to maintenance dosage levels is begun. In some chronic refractory patients, this period may extend from several months to a year.

Psychotic Children: The dosages given below apply to children ages 6 to 12, who are either hospitalized or under adequate supervision.

The usual starting dose is a 1 mg tablet administered once or twice daily, depending on the size of the child. Dosage may be gradually increased until symptoms are controlled or until side effects become troublesome.

Both the rate and the amount of dosage increases should be carefully adjusted to the size of the child and the severity of the symptoms, and the lowest effective dosage should always be used. Once control is achieved, it is usually possible to reduce dosage to a satisfactory maintenance level. In most cases, it is not necessary to exceed 15 mg of trifluoperazine daily. However, some older children with severe symptoms may require, and be able to tolerate, higher dosages.

Supplied: 1 mg: Each blue, round, biconvex, film-coated tablet, debossed $^{SKF}_{1}$, contains: trifluoperazine 1 mg (present as trifluoperazine HCl 1.18 mg). Nonmedicinal ingredients: candelilla wax, cellulose, FD&C blue no. 2 lake, lactose, magnesium stearate, Opadry blue, Opadry clear, sodium starch glycolate and talc. Energy: 1.88 kJ (0.45 kcal). Lactose: 109.3 mg. Sodium: <1 mmol (0.002 mg). Plastic securitainers of 100.

2 mg: Each blue, round, binconvex, film-coated tablet, debossed $^{SKF}_{2}$, contains: trifluoperazine 2 mg (present as trifluoperazine HCl 2.36 mg). Nonmedicinal ingredients: candelilla wax, cellulose, FD&C blue no. 2 lake, lactose, magnesium stearate, Opadry blue, Opadry clear, sodium starch glycolate and talc. Energy: 2.96 kJ (0.71 kcal). Lactose: 141.6 mg. Sodium: <1 mmol (0.002 mg). Plastic securitainers of 100.

5 mg: Each blue, round, binconvex, film-coated tablet, debossed $^{SKF}_{5}$, contains: trifluoperazine 5 mg (present as trifluoperazine HCl 5.90 mg). Nonmedicinal ingredients: candelilla wax, cellulose, FD&C blue no. 2 lake, lactose, magnesium stearate, Opadry blue, Opadry clear, sodium starch glycolate and talc. Energy: 3.19 kJ (0.76 kcal). Lactose: 185.1 mg. Sodium: <1 mmol (0.002 mg). Plastic securitainers of 100.

10 mg: Each blue, round, biconvex, film-coated tablet, debossed $^{SKF}_{10}$, contains: trifluoperazine 10 mg (present as trifluoperazine HCl 11.8 mg). Nonmedicinal ingredients: candelilla wax, cellulose, FD&C blue no. 2 lake, lactose, magnesium stearate, Opadry blue, Opadry clear, sodium starch glycolate and talc. Energy: 4.20 (1.00 kcal). Lactose: 243.7 mg. Sodium: 1 mmol (0.004 mg). Plastic securitainers of 100.

(Shown in Product Recognition Section)

Reviewed 1999

STEMETIL® ℞

Rhône-Poulenc Rorer

Prochlorperazine

Antipsychotic—Antiemetic

Pharmacology: Prochlorperazine is a piperazine phenothiazine derivative with antipsychotic, antiemetic and weak sedative activity.

Prochlorperazine has actions similar to those of other phenothiazine derivatives but appears to be less sedating and to have a weak propensity for causing hypotension or potentiating the effects of CNS depressants and anesthetics. However, it produces a high incidence of extrapyramidal reactions.

Prochlorperazine is well absorbed from the gastrointestinal tract. Onset of action following oral administration is 30 to 40 minutes; 60 minutes for suppositories and 10 to 20 minutes after i.m. administration. Duration of action for all routes is 3 to 4 hours. Prochlorperazine distributes to most body tissues with high concentrations being distributed into liver and spleen. Prochlorperazine enters the enterohepatic circulation and is excreted chiefly in the feces.

Indications: In the management of manifestations of psychotic disorders such as agitation, confusion, delusion, tension and anxiety.

It is also effective in controlling nausea and vomiting due to stimulation of the chemoreceptor trigger zone.

In selected patients, prochlorperazine may be of value for the relief of excessive anxiety, accompanied by severe tension and agitation, associated with psychoneurotic or somatic conditions.

Contraindications: Should not be administered in the presence of circulatory collapse, altered states of consciousness or comatose states, particularly when these are due to intoxication with central depressant drugs (alcohol, hypnotics, narcotics). It is contraindicated in severely depressed patients, in the presence of blood dyscrasias, liver disease, renal insufficiency, pheochromocytoma, or in patients with severe cardiovascular disorders or a history of hypersensitivity to phenothiazine derivatives.

As with other phenothiazines, prochlorperazine is contraindicated in patients with suspected or established subcortical brain damage, with or without hypothalamic damage, since a hyperthermic reaction with temperatures above 40°C may occur, sometimes not until 14 to 16 hours after drug administration.

Phenothiazine compounds should not be used in patients receiving large doses of hypnotics, due to the possibility of potentiation.

Prochlorperazine is contraindicated in children undergoing surgery.

Warnings: The antiemetic action of prochlorperazine may mask the signs and symptoms of overdosage of other drugs and may obscure the diagnosis and treatment of other conditions such as brain tumor or intestinal obstruction. Therefore the etiology of nausea and vomiting should be established before using the drug.

Occupational Hazards: The use of this drug may impair the mental and physical abilities required for the performance of potentially hazardous tasks, such as driving a car or operating machinery.

Potentiation of the effects of alcohol may also occur.

Pregnancy: Safety during pregnancy has not been established. Therefore, it is recommended that the drug be given to pregnant patients only when, in the judgment of the physician, the potential benefit to the patient outweighs the possible risk to the fetus.

Children: The drug should not be used in children under 2 years unless potentially lifesaving.

The extrapyramidal symptoms which can occur secondary to prochlorperazine may be confused with the CNS signs of an undiagnosed primary disease responsible for the vomiting, e.g. Reye's syndrome or other encephalopathy. The use of prochlorperazine should be avoided in children and adolescents whose signs and symptoms suggest Reye's syndrome.

Precautions: The increased incidence of seizures, which occasionally occur in epileptics started on antipsychotic medication, may be controlled by increasing the dosage of their anticonvulsant. Patients with a familial history of seizures or febrile convulsions are more likely to develop seizures than those who have no such history.

Phenothiazines may increase the effects of general anesthetics, opiates, barbiturates, and other CNS depressants and the doses of these drugs should be reduced if administered concomitantly with prochlorperazine.

On long-term therapy, particularly during the first 2 or 3 months, it is advisable to perform periodic liver function tests and blood counts as cholestatic jaundice and blood dyscrasias may occur, necessitating discontinuation of treatment. Renal function should be monitored and, if BUN becomes abnormal, treatment should be discontinued.

To lessen the likelihood of adverse reactions related to drug accumulation, patients on long-term therapy, particularly on high doses, should be evaluated periodically to decide whether the maintenance dosage could be lowered or drug therapy discontinued.

Because of its anticholinergic action, prochlorperazine should be used with great caution in patients with glaucoma or prostatic hypertrophy.

The effects of anticholinergic drugs may be potentiated by prochlorperazine. Paralytic ileus, even resulting in death, may occur, especially in the elderly. Caution should be observed if constipation develops.

Retinal changes, lenticular and corneal deposits and abnormal skin pigmentation have been observed with other phenothiazines and may occur after prolonged therapy. The possibility of persistent tardive dyskinesia should also be borne in mind when patients are under long-term treatment.

Patients receiving prochlorperazine should be cautioned against exposure to extreme heat or organophosphorous insecticides.

Hypotension and ECG changes, particularly non-specific and usually reversible Q and T wave distortions, have been associated with the administration of phenothiazines. Therefore, prochlorperazine should be used with caution in patients with compensated cardiovascular and cerebrovascular disorders.

Unexpected, sudden deaths have occurred in hospitalized patients treated with phenothiazines. Previous brain damage or seizures may predispose. High doses should be avoided in known seizure patients. Sudden exacerbations of psychotic behavior patterns occurred in several patients shortly before death. Acute fulminating pneumonia or pneumonitis and aspiration of gastric contents also were observed. Therefore, the physician also should keep in mind the possible development of silent pneumonias.

Neuroleptic drugs elevate prolactin levels; the elevation persists during chronic administration. Tissue culture experiments indicate that approximately one-third of human breast cancers are prolactin-dependent in vitro, a factor of potential importance if the prescription of these drugs is contemplated in a patient with a previously detected breast cancer. Although disturbances such as galactorrhea, amenorrhea, gynecomastia and impotence have been reported, the clinical significance of elevated serum prolactin levels is unknown for most

Stemetil (cont'd)

patients. An increase in mammary neoplasms has been found in rodents after chronic administration of neuroleptic drugs. Neither clinical studies, nor epidemiologic studies conducted to date, however, have shown an association between chronic administration of these drugs and mammary tumorogenesis; the available evidence is considered too limited to be conclusive at this time.

Withdrawal Emergent Neurological Signs: Abrupt withdrawal after short term administration of antipsychotic drugs does not generally pose problems. However, transient dyskinetic signs are experienced by some patients on maintenance therapy after abrupt withdrawal. The signs are very similar to those described under Tardive Dyskinesia, except for duration. Although it is not known whether gradual withdrawal of antipsychotic drugs will decrease the incidence of withdrawal emergent neurological signs, gradual withdrawal would appear to be advisable.

Older Patients: The incidence of adverse reactions may be greater in patients over 55 years of age, since the half-lives of antipsychotic drugs are often prolonged. To minimize this possibility, the maintenance dosage should be reduced to the lowest effective level as soon as possible after initial titration and periodically reviewed.

Since psychiatric syndromes in the elderly can be caused by drugs or organic disease, withdrawal of the precipitating drug or treatment of the medical condition should supersede initiation of antipsychotic medication. These agents should not be used for non-psychiatric conditions for which other drugs are available, since the elderly are especially prone to develop adverse effects from antipsychotic drugs.

Children: Children with an acute febrile illness or suffering from dehydration seem to be much more susceptible than adults to neuromuscular reactions, particularly dystonias. In such patients, the drug should be used under close supervision and at low doses.

Adverse Effects: Adverse reactions with different phenothiazines vary in type, frequency, and mechanism of occurrence, i.e., some are dose-related, while others involve individual patient sensitivity. Some adverse reactions may be more likely to occur with greater intensity, in patients with special medical problems.

Not all of the following adverse reactions have been observed with every phenothiazine derivative, but they have been reported with one or more and should be borne in mind when drugs of this class are administered.

Neurological: Extrapyramidal reactions including tremor, rigidity, akathisia, dystonia, dyskinesia, oculogyric crises, opisthotonos, hyperreflexia and sialorrhea. EEG changes, disturbed temperature regulation and seizures have also been encountered.

Persistent Tardive Dyskinesia: As with other antipsychotic agents, tardive dyskinesia may occur in patients on long term therapy or may be observed after drug therapy has been discontinued. The risk seems to be greater in elderly patients on high doses, especially females. The symptoms are persistent and in some patients appear to be irreversible. The syndrome is characterized by rhythmical involuntary movements of the tongue, face, mouth or jaw (e.g., protusion of tongue, puffing of cheeks, puckering of mouth, chewing movements). Sometimes, these may be accompanied by involuntary movements of the extremities.

There is no known effective treatment for tardive dyskinesia; antiparkinsonian agents usually do not alleviate the symptoms of this syndrome. It is suggested that all antipsychotic agents be discontinued if these symptoms appear. Should it be necessary to reinstitute treatment, or increase the dosage of the agent, or switch to a different antipsychotic agent, the syndrome may be masked. It has been reported that fine vermicular movements of the tongue may be an early sign of the syndrome and if the medication is stopped at that time, the syndrome may not develop. The physician may be able to reduce the risk of this syndrome by minimizing the unnecessary use of neuroleptic drugs and reducing the dose or discontinuing the drug, if possible, when manifestations of this syndrome are recognized, particularly in patients over the age of 50.

Behavioral: Sleep disturbances, drowsiness, fatigue, insomnia, and depression have been reported and may, in severe cases, necessitate reduction in dosage. As with other phenothiazine derivatives, reactivation or aggravation of psychotic processes may be encountered. Paradoxical effects such as agitation, anxiety, restlessness, excitement and bizarre dreams, have been observed.

Autonomic Nervous System: Dry mouth, nasal congestion, headache, nausea, constipation, tachycardia, hypotension, syncope, dizziness, blurred vision, vomiting, sweating and urinary incontinence have been observed.

Patients with pheochromocytoma, cerebral vascular or renal insufficiency, or a severe cardiac reserve deficiency such as mitral insufficiency appear to be particularly prone to hypotensive reactions with phenothiazine compounds, and should therefore be observed closely when the drug is administered. Should hypotension occur in patients receiving prochlorperazine and a vasopressor agent be required, i.v. levarterenol or phenylephrine should be used, and **not** epinephrine, since phenothiazine derivatives can reverse the pressor effect of the latter drug.

Other autonomic reactions which have occurred with phenothiazines are salivation, polyuria, glaucoma, bladder paralysis, adynamic ileus, and fecal compaction.

Metabolic and Endocrine: Anorexia, menstrual irregularities, impotence, and increased thirst, weight changes, increased appetite, peripheral edema, galactorrhea, gynecomastia, false positive pregnancy tests, and changes in libido have also occurred in patients receiving phenothiazine therapy.

Allergic or Toxic: Pruritus, dermatitis, rash, erythema, urticaria, seborrhea, eczema, exfoliative dermatitis, and photosensitivity. The possibility of an anaphylactoid reaction should be borne in mind.

Blood dyscrasias including leukopenia, agranulocytosis, pancytopenia, thrombocytopenic or non-thrombocytopenic purpura, eosinophilia, and anemia, have been associated with phenothiazine therapy. Routine blood counts are therefore advisable during prolonged therapy. If any soreness of the mouth, gums or throat or any symptoms of upper respiratory infection occur and confirmatory leukocyte count indicates cellular depression, therapy should be discontinued and other appropriate measures instituted immediately.

Cholestatic jaundice and biliary stasis may be encountered, particularly during the first months of therapy, and require immediate discontinuation of treatment.

Miscellaneous: The following adverse reactions have been reported in patients receiving phenothiazine derivatives: headache, asthma, laryngeal, cerebral and angioneurotic edema, altered cerebrospinal fluid proteins, systemic lupus erythematosus-like syndrome. hyperpyrexia, ECG and EEG changes and hypotension severe enough to cause fatal cardiac arrest. Skin pigmentation, epithelial keratopathy, lenticular and corneal deposits have been associated with long-term administration.

Sudden, unexpected and unexplained deaths have been reported in hospitalized psychotic patients receiving phenothiazines. Previous brain damage or seizures may be predisposing factors; high doses should be avoided in known seizure patients. Several patients have shown flare-ups of psychotic behaviour patterns shortly before deaths. Autopsy findings have usually revealed acute fulminating pneumonia or pneumonitis, aspiration of gastric contents or intramyocardial lesions.

Potentiation of CNS depressants (barbiturates, narcotics, analgesics, alcohol, antihistamines) may occur.

Neuroleptic Malignant Syndrome: As with other neuroleptic drugs, a symptom complex sometimes referred to as neuroleptic malignant syndrome (NMS) may occur. Cardinal features of NMS are hyperpyrexia, muscle rigidity, altered mental status (including catatonic signs), and evidence of autonomic instability (irregular pulse or blood pressure). Additional signs may include elevated CPK, myoglobinuria (rhabdomyolysis), and acute renal failure. NMS is potentially fatal and requires symptomatic treatment and immediate discontinuation of neuroleptic treatment.

Overdose: Symptoms: Primarily extrapyramidal reactions, CNS depression which may vary from simple lethargy to coma. Agitation and restlessness may also occur. Other possible manifestations include convulsions, fever and autonomic reactions such as hypotension, dry mouth and ileus.

Treatment: Essentially symptomatic and supportive. Early gastric lavage may be helpful.

Maintain an open airway. If hypotension occurs, the standard measures for managing circulatory shock should be initiated; if a pressor agent is required give levarterenol or phenylephrine and **not** epinephrine as it may further depress the blood pressure. Extrapyramidal reactions should be treated with an antiparkinsonian agent.

Centrally acting emetics will be ineffective because of prochlorperazine antiemetic action. Limited experience indicates that phenothiazines are not dialyzable.

Dosage: Begin with the lowest recommended dosage. Adjust to response of the individual.

Adults: Oral and rectal route: To control nausea, vomiting or excessive anxiety: usually 5 to 10 mg, 3 or 4 times daily; in mild cases, a single dose of 5 to 10 mg is often adequate. In psychiatry for moderate to severe conditions, the usual starting dosage is 10 mg 3 or 4 times a day; increase dosage gradually by 5 to 10 mg every 2 or 3 days until symptoms are controlled or adverse reactions intervene. Some patients respond satisfactorily on 50 to 75 mg per day. In more severe disturbances it may reach 100 to 150 mg a day. For maintenance therapy, the dosage should be reduced to the minimum effective dose.

Parenteral route: I.M. Dosage: The drug is given by deep i.m. injection. Total daily dosage rarely exceeds 40 mg, except in severe psychiatric cases. When control is achieved, the oral route should be substituted. To control nausea, vomiting or excessive anxiety: 5 to 10 mg, 2 or 3 times a day. In psychiatry: for the immediate control of severely disturbed patients, 10 to 20 mg initially, repeated every 2 to 4 hours until control is obtained. More than 3 or 4 doses are seldom necessary. The patients should be kept in bed and under medical supervision. In surgery: 5 to 10 mg i.m., 1 to 2 hours before anesthesia. Repeat once during surgery if necessary. Postoperatively, the same dose of 5 to 10 mg i.m. may be given to control acute symptoms and repeated, if necessary, every 3 to 4 hours (maximum, 40 mg daily).

I.V. Infusion: During and after surgery, may be given i.v. in the infusion solution at a concentration of 20 mg/L. Total daily dose rarely exceeds 30 mg.

Children: Daily dosage, administered in divided doses, should be based on body weight rather than on age, and should not be exceeded. Do not administer to children under 2 years of age or 9 kg of body weight. Occasionally the patient may react to the drug with signs of restlessness and excitement; if this occurs, treatment should be discontinued.

Oral and rectal routes: From 9 to 14 kg: 2.5 mg, 1 or 2 times a day, maximum 7.5 mg/day. From 14 to 18 kg: 2.5 mg, 2 or 3 times a day, maximum 10 mg/day. From 18 to 39 kg: 2.5 mg, 3 times a day, or 5 mg 2 times a day, maximum 15 mg/day. Vomiting usually subsides after a single day of treatment. In psychiatry: on the first day of treatment a dosage of 10 mg, in divided doses, should not be exceeded. The maximum total daily dosage reached by gradual increments should not exceed 20 mg for children of 2 to 5 years, and 25 mg for children of 6 to 12 years.

Parenteral route: For severe nausea and vomiting and in child psychiatry: calculate each dose on the basis of 0.13 mg/kg of body weight and give by deep i.m. injection. Control is usually obtained with one dose. When further therapy is needed, transfer the patient to an oral form at an equal or higher dose.

Supplied: Injectable: Each mL contains: prochlorperazine base 5 mg (as the mesylate). Nonmedicinal ingredients: sodium chloride, sodium citrate, sodium sulfite and water for injection. Ampuls of 2 mL, boxes of 10. Protect from light or discoloration may occur. Discard if markedly discolored.

Liquid: Each 5 mL of red liquid contains: prochlorperazine base 5 mg (as the mesylate). Nonmedicinal ingredients: artificial butterscotch flavor, artificial chocolate flavor, artificial cognac flavor, poloxamer, purified water, sodium chloride, sodium citrate and sucrose. Sucrose: 4.0 g/5 mL. Energy: 65.0 kJ (15.5 kcal)/5 mL. Tartrazine-free. Bottles of 100 mL. Protect from light.

Suppositories: Each rectal suppository contains: prochlorperazine base 10 mg. Nonmedicinal ingredients: hydrogenated vegetable glycerides. Tartrazine-free. Boxes of 10. Store in a cool place.

Tablets: Each varnished, peach colored tablet contains: prochlorperazine base 5 or 10 mg (as the bimaleate). Nonmedicinal ingredients: acetic anhydride, carnauba wax, cellulose, colloidal silicon dioxide, D&C Yellow No 10, dicalcium phosphate, diethyl phthalate, FD&C Yellow No 6, magnesium stearate, sodium croscarmellose, sodium oleate, titanium oxide and zein. Tartrazine-free. Bottles of 100 and 500.

(Shown in Product Recognition Section)

STERI/SOL®
Warner-Lambert Consumer Healthcare

Hexetidine

Therapeutic Oral Rinse

Indications: The symptomatic treatment of "strep" throat, tonsillitis, pharyngitis, laryngitis, gingivitis, ulcerative stomatitis, oral thrush and Vincent's angina; postoperative hygiene following tonsillectomy, throat or oral surgery.

Precautions: Avoid swallowing. Do not give to children under 12 years of age.

Dosage: As a mouthwash, gargle or spray, use full strength. Apply by swab to local lesions; for buccal and pharyngeal lesions, swish in mouth and gargle for 30 seconds, using 15 mL morning and night.

Supplied: Each mL of clear, red liquid with modified mint flavor contains: hexetidine 0.1%. Nonmedicinal ingredients: alcohol, citric acid, D&C Red No. 33, FD&C Red No. 2, FD&C Yellow No. 6, flavors, polysorbate, sodium cyclamate, sorbitol and water. Alcohol: 9%. Bottles of 100, 250 and 500 mL.

STIEVA-A® Preparations Ⓟ
STIEVA-A® FORTE Ⓟ
Stiefel

Tretinoin

Acne Therapy

Supplied: Cream: Each g of cream contains: tretinoin USP 0.01%, 0.025% or 0.05% in an emollient cream base. Nonmedicinal ingredients: butylated hydroxyanisole, butylated hydroxytoluene, cetyl alcohol, edetate disodium, isopropyl palmitate, methyl paraben, polyoxyl 40 stearate, propyl paraben, propylene glycol, purified water USP, stearic acid, stearyl alcohol NF and white petrolatum. Tubes of 25 g.

Forte Cream: Each g of cream contains: tretinoin USP 0.1%. Nonmedicinal ingredients: butylated hydroxyanisole, butylated hydroxytoluene, cetyl alcohol, edetate disodium, isopropyl palmitate, methyl paraben, polyoxyl 40 stearate, propyl paraben, propylene glycol, purified water USP, stearic acid, stearyl alcohol NF, titanium oxide and white petrolatum. Tubes of 25 g.

Gel: Each g of gel contains: tretinoin USP 0.01%, 0.025% or 0.05% in an alcohol base gel. Nonmedicinal ingredients: alcohol anhydrous, butylated hydroxytoluene and hydroxypropyl cellulose. Tubes of 25 g.

Solution: Each mL of solution contains: tretinoin USP 0.025% or 0.05%. Nonmedicinal ingredients: butylated hydroxytoluene, ethyl alcohol 95% and hydroxypropylcellulose. Bottles of 50 mL with snap-on Dab-O-Matic applicator.

Store at 15 to 30°C.

STIEVAMYCIN® Preparations Ⓟ
Stiefel

Erythromycin—Tretinoin

Topical Acne Therapy

Pharmacology: Tretinoin: The precise mechanism of action of tretinoin on the skin is not fully understood. It is known that tretinoin is both pharmacologically and structurally related to vitamin A which regulates epithelial cell growth and differentiation. Tretinoin itself is known to have an irritant and keratolytic effect on the skin. These two actions which occur simultaneously have been shown histologically in both animal and man to be associated with an increased growth rate and with a decrease in the cohesiveness of the epidermal cells. The result is a slightly thickened epidermis with an accelerated turnover rate and shedding of keratinized cells as very fine barely perceptible scales.

In acne vulgaris, the induced fine scaling of the skin surface is accompanied by an increased production of less cohesive epidermal sebaceous cells which consequently flow out of the follicle at a more rapid rate. The thickened mass of sebaceous cellular debris, the comedones, appear to be initially extruded and then prevented from recurring by these actions. Histopathologically, acne is the impaction plus distention of the sebaceous follicles by tightly packed horny cells and disruption of the follicular epithelium. It has been postulated that tretinoin inhibits the synthesis or quality of the substance which binds the horny cells within the sebaceous follicle.

Erythromycin: Erythromycin exerts its antibacterial action by binding to the 50S ribosomal subunit of susceptible bacteria and suppressing protein synthesis. Erythromycin is usually bacteriostatic but may be bactericidal in high concentrations or against highly susceptible organisms.

The precise mechanism of action of erythromycin in the treatment of acne has not been established.

Indications: In the treatment of acne vulgaris, primarily where comedones, papules and pustules predominate. Not effective in most cases of severe pustular and deep cystic nodular varieties (acne conglobata). Not indicated in Stage IV acne.

Contraindications: In patients with known hypersensitivity to retinoids and/or erythromycin or any of the components of the preparations.

Warnings: Topical gels are intended for external use only and should be kept away from eyes, nose, mouth, and other mucous membranes because of its irritant effect. Do not apply to eyelids or to the skin at the corners of the eyes and mouth. Avoid the angles of the nose and nasolabial fold (if treatment in these areas is necessary, apply very sparingly). Topical use may induce severe local erythema and peeling at the site of application. If the degree of local irritation warrants, patients should be directed to use the medication less frequently, discontinue use temporarily or discontinue use altogether. Tretinoin has been reported to cause severe irritation of eczematous skin and should only be used with utmost caution in patients with this condition.

Pregnancy: **Topical tretinoin should be used by women of childbearing years only after contraceptive counselling. It is recommended that topical tretinoin should not be used by pregnant women.**

There have been rare reports of birth defects among babies born to women exposed to **topical** tretinoin during pregnancy. However, there are no well controlled prospective studies of the use of topical tretinoin in pregnant women. A retrospective study of mothers exposed to topical tretinoin during the first trimester of pregnancy found no increase in the incidence of birth defects.

Topical retinoid teratology studies in rats and rabbits have been inconclusive. As with all retinoids, tretinoin administered **orally** at high doses is teratogenic.

The safety of erythromycin during pregnancy has not been established. Erythromycin crosses the placental barrier.

Lactation: **It is unknown whether tretinoin is excreted in human milk but erythromycin is so excreted. Nevertheless, a decision should be made whether to discontinue nursing or to discontinue the drug taking into account the importance of the drug to the mother.**

Precautions: The use of preparations containing antibiotics may be associated with overgrowth of antibiotic resistant organisms, including those initially sensitive to the drug. Cross-resistance between erythromycin and macrolide antibiotics can occur. If this should occur, therapy should be discontinued and appropriate measures taken. A cross-resistance between erythromycin and clindamycin has rarely been reported.

Excessive exposure to sunlight or ultraviolet rays (sun lamps) should be avoided during treatment with Stievamycin topical gels because the additional irradiation may lead to a more intense action.

If a sunburn occurs, it is advisable to interrupt therapy until the severe erythema and peeling subside. Patients whose occupations require considerable exposure to the sun should exercise particular caution.

Drug Interactions: Concomitant topical medications should be used with caution during therapy with Stievamycin topical gels because of possible intensified reactions. Particular caution should be exercised when using preparations containing a peeling agent concomitantly (such as sulfur, resorcinol, benzoyl peroxide or salicylic acid) with Stievamycin. It may be advisable to "rest" a patient's skin until the effects of previously used peeling agents subside before initiating Stievamycin therapy. Concurrent use of abrasive or medicated soaps, or cosmetic products containing alcohol, such as astringents and after-shave lotions, may also result in a cumulative drying or irritant effect in patients using Stievamycin topical gels.

Adverse Effects: The skin of certain sensitive individuals, particularly those with fair complexion, may become excessively red, edematous, blistered or crusted when exposed to Stievamycin topical gels. Pain, burning sensation, tenderness, irritation or pruritus have also been occasionally reported. If any of these effects occur, the medication should be discontinued until the integrity of the skin has been restored or the treatment schedule adjusted to the level the patient can tolerate. Temporary hyper- or hypopigmentation has been reported with repeated application of tretinoin. To date, all adverse clinical effects of tretinoin encountered have been reversible upon discontinuance of therapy. In many instances, reinstitution of therapy with tretinoin failed to produce the adverse effect previously experienced.

Topical erythromycin may cause desquamation and excessive dryness. Mild to moderate irritation has been observed in many patients, but severe irritation is generally less frequent. Urticaria, oiliness, coriaceousness and fissuring around the mouth may occur.

Overdose: Symptoms and Treatment: Topical: If medication is applied excessively, marked redness, peeling or discomfort may occur.

Accidental Ingestion: In oral doses of over 2 g erythromycin per day, abdominal discomfort, nausea or diarrhea may occur. There is no specific treatment. Gastric lavage should be considered, otherwise, the treatment should be symptomatic.

Dosage: Stievamycin topical gels should be applied to the affected area once a day, preferably before retiring. The area under treatment (not just clinical lesions) should be thoroughly cleansed with a mild soap, and dried, followed by application of the gel in a gentle rubbing motion, using fingertips to apply medication. Application may be accompanied by a transitory feeling of warmth or a stinging sensation. Treatment should be discontinued if a severe local inflammatory response is experienced.

In cases where it may be necessary to discontinue therapy or reduce the frequency of applications, therapy may be resumed, when the adverse effects have ceased. In some patients, during the early weeks of therapy, an apparent exacerbation of the acne lesions may occur.

Therapeutic results may be noticed after 2 to 3 weeks of therapy; however, results may not be optimal until after 8 to 10 weeks of treatment. Once the acne lesions have responded satisfactorily, it may be possible to maintain the improved state with less frequent applications.

Patients being treated with Stievamycin topical gels may continue to use cosmetics; however, astringents may produce exacerbation when used concurrently with Stievamycin topical gels. The area of skin to be treated should be thoroughly cleansed and dried before Stievamycin topical gels are applied.

Information for the Patient: See Blue Section—Information for the Patient "Stievamycin Preparations".

Supplied: Forte: Each g of gel contains: tretinoin USP 0.05% and erythromycin USP 4.0% in an alcohol gel base. Nonmedicinal ingredients: BHT, ethyl alcohol and hydroxypropyl cellulose. Tubes of 25 g.

Mild: Each g of gel contains: tretinoin USP 0.01% and erythromycin USP 4.0% in an alcohol gel base. Nonmedicinal ingredients: BHT, ethyl alcohol and hydroxypropyl cellulose. Tubes of 25 g.

Regular: Each g of gel contains: tretinoin USP 0.025% and erythromycin USP 4.0% in an alcohol gel base. Nonmedicinal ingredients: BHT, ethyl alcohol and hydroxypropyl cellulose. Tubes of 25 g.

Store between 15 and 30°C.

STILAMIN® Ⓟ
Serono

Somatostatin

Treatment of Acute Variceal Bleeding

Pharmacology: Somatostatin is a synthetic cyclic 14 amino acid peptide (identical in structure and activity to naturally occurring somatostatin) which decreases splanchnic blood flow and portal venous pressure in man, possibly through a direct action on the unstriated muscle cells mediated by a calcium-dependent mechanism. In anesthetized healthy volunteers, somatostatin—dosed as a 250 μg i.v. bolus followed by a 250 μg/hour continuous infusion—also reduced blood flow in the common hepatic artery (56%), in the splenic artery (26%) and in the upper and lower mesenteric branches. In cirrhotic patients, wedged hepatic pressure and estimated liver

Stilamin (cont'd)

blood flow were decreased with the administration of somatostatin.

Somatostatin is rapidly metabolized by the liver (plasma half-life of 1.1 to 3 minutes in healthy subjects) and cleared (50.3±7.0 mL/kg/min) from the body. Consequently, its pharmacological effects are transient, and a return to basal levels is generally seen shortly after the cessation of an i.v. infusion. In cirrhotic patients, the plasma half-life (1.2 to 4.8 minutes) approximates that of healthy volunteers while in patients with chronic renal failure, the plasma half-life is prolonged (2.6 to 4.9 minutes, see Precautions and Dosage). Somatostatin is excreted renally, with excretion 70% complete within 24 hours after dosing.

Indications: For the symptomatic treatment of acute bleeding from esophageal varices. Other treatment options for long-term management of the condition may be considered if necessary, once initial control has been established.

Contraindications: Cases of known hypersensitivity to the product, its excipients or recommended diluents.

Pregnancy and *Lactation:* The use of somatostatin in known or suspected pregnancy and during the immediate post partum period is contraindicated.

During preclinical studies in the rabbit, somatostatin doses of 0.2 mg/kg/day and higher were found to interfere with the early stages of embryonal development (e.g., implantation). Studies performed in pregnant women during labor indicated that somatostatin (500 µg infused over 30 minutes) crossed the placental barrier, with effects on fetal levels of growth hormone and thyrotrophin.

In the absence of data concerning the effects of somatostatin on human pregnancy, its use is not recommended.

There is no information from animal or human studies concerning the passage of somatostatin in breast milk. As somatostatin has a wide variety of potential pharmacological effects, its use during lactation is contraindicated until further information can be obtained.

Warnings: Somatostatin has an inhibitory effect on the secretion of insulin and glucagon. Therefore, at the outset of treatment, somatostatin can lead to a transient fall in blood glucose levels. Caution should therefore be used in administering the product to insulin-dependent diabetics in whom blood glucose should be measured every 3 to 4 hours. Simultaneous administration of insulin-requiring sugars should be avoided if possible. Insulin should be administered as necessary.

Children: There is no information concerning the use of somatostatin in children. Use in this patient population should only be considered if the potential benefits outweigh the possible risks.

Precautions: General: As somatostatin has a short plasma half-life, it is essential that the infusion be maintained continuously once it has been initiated. In the event that any interruption in the infusion occurs, a repeat bolus dose may be given to the patient, followed by resumption of the continuous infusion (see Dosage).

Patients with Renal Disease: The plasma half-life of somatostatin is increased in patients with chronic renal disease, and its rate of clearance is reduced (see Pharmacology). Somatostatin should therefore be administered to such patients with caution.

Drug Interactions: Somatostatin has been demonstrated to prolong or enhance the effects of barbiturates such as hexobarbital and pentetrazole, in preclinical studies. Caution should be used in administering such agents concomitantly with somatostatin.

The glucoregulatory properties of somatostatin may cause it to interfere with the insulin requirements of insulin-dependent diabetics (see Warnings).

Laboratory Tests: Somatostatin has produced transient hyperglycemia and thrombocytopenia in some patients (see Adverse Effects).

Adverse Effects: The adverse reactions which were reported by more than one patient during the clinical trials with the product in 278 patients included: nausea (4.0%); vomiting (2.1%); hyperglycemia (generally transient) (1.8%); pyrexia (1.8%); hypocalcemia (0.7%); headache (0.7%); thrombocytopenia (0.7%) and ventricular extrasystoles (0.7%).

Overdose: Symptoms: Transient bradycardia and hypotension were observed in some preclinical studies and may be a sign of overdosage in humans. Cramping and vomiting have been reported as the result of an accidental overdosage with somatostatin.

Treatment: The infusion should be stopped immediately if overdosage is suspected. Given the short half-life of somatostatin, symptoms should resolve rapidly with the cessation of the infusion. Other treatment would consist of standard supportive measures until the symptoms have been resolved.

Dosage: Somatostatin should be given as a slow 250 µg i.v. bolus injection over 3 to 5 minutes, followed by a continuous infusion at a rate of 250 µg/hr until bleeding from the varices has stopped (usually within 12 to 24 hours). Once bleeding has been controlled, it is recommended that the infusion be continued for at least another 48 to 72 hours, or out to a maximum of 120 hours to prevent recurrent bleeding.

The short plasma half-life of somatostatin makes it essential that the infusion be maintained continuously. It has therefore been the practice in some clinical trials to establish the continuous infusion line prior to administering the bolus dose to ensure that the administration of the drug is uninterrupted. If the continuous infusion is interrupted for any reason, a second bolus dose may be given to rapidly re-establish circulating levels of the drug.

Patients with decreased renal function should be closely monitored since the plasma half-life is prolonged.

Immediately prior to administration, the 250 µg lyophilized product should be reconstituted with the sterile normal saline solution provided. Storage of the reconstituted product is not recommended.

The 3 mg lyophilized powder for continuous infusion should be reconstituted in either sterile normal (0.9%) saline or in 5% dextrose to provide sufficient solution for a 12-hour infusion of somatostatin at a rate of 250 µg/hr (approximately 3.5 µg/kg/hr). Once reconstituted it should be used within 24 hours and should be protected from light during this time.

Parenteral Products: Stilamin must be reconstituted before use.

Direct I.V. Injection: The 250 µg ampul is accompanied by a 1 mL ampul of sterile, normal (0.9%) saline for reconstitution. Immediately before use, the sodium chloride solution should be added to the lyophilized material under aseptic conditions (creating a 250 µg/mL solution) and swirled gently until all particles have been dissolved. Only clear solutions should be administered.

Continuous Infusion: The 3 mg ampul is not provided with diluent. It should be reconstituted with either sterile normal saline (0.9%) or in 5% dextrose prior to administration. The 3 mg ampul contains sufficient somatostatin to deliver a 12-hour continuous infusion at a rate of 250 µg/hr. The volume of dilution will depend on the infusion system used and should be adjusted to ensure a continuous rate of infusion over 12 hours.

As with all parenteral drug products, i.v. admixtures should be inspected visually for clarity, particulate matter, precipitation, discoloration and leakage prior to administration whenever solution and container permit.

Stability and Storage Recommendations: The ampuls are stable when stored refrigerated (2 to 8°C). The product should be protected from light.

The Sodium Chloride diluent can be stored either at room temperature (15 to 30°C) or at refrigerated temperatures (2 to 8°C).

Reconstituted Solutions: Stilamin, reconstituted with sterile, normal (0.9%) saline or 5% dextrose to a concentration of 250 µg/mL, is stable for 24 hours when refrigerated and protected from light.

Supplied: 250 µg: Each ampul of white, lyophilized, sterile, pyrogen-free powder contains: somatostatin 250 µg (present as acetate hydrate) and mannitol 5 mg. Intended for reconstitution and administration as an i.v. bolus dose. Each ampul of Stilamin 250 µg is accompanied by its diluent, a 3 mL ampul which contains 1 mL of sterile normal (0.9%) Sodium Chloride Injection. Cartons of 1 ampul of diluent and 1 ampul of somatostatin. Cartons of 5 ampuls of diluent and 5 ampuls of somatostatin.

3 mg: Each ampul of white, lyophilized, sterile, pyrogen-free powder contains: somatostatin 3 mg (present as acetate hydrate) and mannitol 5 mg. Intended for reconstitution and administration as a 12-hour continuous infusion (delivery 250 µg/hour). Cartons of 1.

STILBESTROL ℞

Roberts

Diethylstilbestrol

Estrogen

Pharmacology: Similar to those of natural estrogens, i.e., stimulation of proliferative development of endometrium; development of secondary female sex characteristics; suppression of pituitary gonadotropin secretion; stimulation of protein synthesis; lowering of serum lipids; suppression of function of male target organs.

Indications: The palliative treatment of advanced cancer of the prostate.

Contraindications: Diethylstilbestrol should not be administered to patients with active hepatic disease, especially of the obstructive type. The drug is also contraindicated in the following situations: children or young adults; a recent history of cerebrovascular accident or coronary thrombosis; thrombophlebitis and thromboembolic disease; partial or complete loss of vision or diplopia from ophthalmic vascular disease; porphyria; severe hypertension.

Warnings: Before diethylstilbestrol is administered, the patient should have a complete physical examination, including a blood pressure determination.

If any surgical procedures are performed, the pathologist should be advised of the patient's therapy when specimens are sent for examination.

Alternative therapy should be considered in patients who develop visual disturbances, classical migraine, transient aphasia, paralysis, loss of consciousness, or sudden elevation of blood pressure.

If the patient develops any sign of phlebitis or thromboembolic complications, medication should be discontinued.

Precautions: Estrogen may cause fluid retention therefore particular caution is indicated in patients with cardiac or renal dysfunction, epilepsy, or asthma.

Diabetic patients or those with a predisposition to diabetes should be observed closely to detect any alterations in carbohydrate metabolism. When liver or endocrine function tests are indicated, the results should not be considered reliable unless therapy has been discontinued for 2 to 4 months.

Elevation of blood pressure in previously normotensive or hypertensive patients may necessitate cessation of medication. Caution is indicated in patients with depression and in patients using contact lenses.

Adverse Effects: Although not all of the reactions listed below have been specifically associated with diethylstilbestrol tablets, they have been reported following estrogen therapy generally, and may be encountered when giving any product containing an estrogenic drug.

Gastrointestinal: nausea, anorexia, vomiting, abdominal cramps, bloating, cholestatic jaundice, cholelithiasis and increase or decrease in body weight.

Genitourinary: cystitis-like syndrome.

Endocrine and Metabolic: breast swelling and tenderness, testicular atrophy, increased blood sugar levels, and decreased glucose tolerance. Gynecomastia, reduced potency and feminization are expected adverse effects.

CNS: headaches, mental depression, increase or decrease of libido, nervousness, dizziness, fatigue, irritability.

Dermatologic: hypersensitivity reactions, loss of scalp hair, allergic reactions and rashes, hemorrhagic eruptions, itching, erythema nodosum, erythema multiforme, pigmentation of the skin.

Cardiovascular: sodium and water retention, increased blood pressure in susceptible individuals and aggravation of migraine headaches.

Hematologic: A statistically significant association has been demonstrated between the use of certain preparations containing estrogen and the following serious reactions: thrombophlebitis, pulmonary embolism and cerebral thrombosis.

Available evidence is suggestive of an association with the following reactions: coronary thrombosis and neuro-ocular lesions (e.g., retinal thrombosis and optic neuritis); altered coagulation tests (increase in prothrombin and Factors VII, VIII, IX, X).

Miscellaneous: precipitation or aggravation of porphyria cutanea tarda in predisposed individuals.

Overdose: Symptoms and Treatment: Excessive doses may result in nausea, vomiting and abdominal cramps, headache, dizziness and general malaise. Gastric lavage may be considered if ingestion of the drug is recent and symptomatic treatment should be given. If the transient hyperestrogenic effects include severe sodium and water retention, administer diuretics.

Dosage: Carcinoma of the prostate: Initial dose: 1 mg/day. Maximum dose: 3 mg/day. Maintenance dose: 1 mg/day.

Supplied: 0.1 mg: Each round, white tablet contains: diethylstilbestrol 0.1 mg. Bottles of 100.

0.5 mg: Each round, light pink tablet contains: diethylstilbestrol 0.5 mg. Bottles of 100.

1 mg: Each round, dark pink tablet contains: diethylstilbestrol 1 mg. Bottles of 100.

STREPTASE® Ⓟ

Hoechst Marion Roussel

Streptokinase

Fibrinolytic Agent

Pharmacology: Streptokinase acts with plasminogen (or plasmin) to produce an "activator complex" that converts residual plasminogen into the proteolytic enzyme, plasmin. Plasmin is capable of hydrolysing fibrin into polypeptides; it also hydrolyses fibrinogen and other plasma proteins. Since plasminogen is present in the thrombus/embolus, activation by streptokinase occurs within the thrombus/embolus as well as on its surface.

The activity of streptokinase is expressed in International Units (IU) and is a measure of its ability to cause lysis of a fibrin clot via the plasmin system in vitro. The effect on coagulation after i.v. administration may persist for 12 to 24 hours after discontinuation due to a decrease in plasma levels of fibrinogen and an increase in the amount of circulating fibrin (ogen) degradation products (FDP). Studies with radioactive streptokinase indicate 2 disappearance rates: a fast half-life of approximately 18 minutes due to the action of antibodies, and a slow half-life, operative in the absence of antibodies, of approximately 83 minutes. Effective blood level and disappearance rate are dependent upon availability of substrates and, thus, are only relative indices of the pharmacologic effects of the drug. The efficacy of streptokinase in the lysis of venous thrombi and massive pulmonary emboli has been established in clinical studies by angiographic evaluations, before and after treatment.

Two large, randomized, multicentre, placebo-controlled studies involving almost 30 000 patients have demonstrated that a 60-minute i.v. infusion of 1 500 000 IU of streptokinase significantly reduces mortality rates following a myocardial infarction. Concomitant oral administration of low-dose ASA (160 mg/day) over a period of 1 month was shown to significantly enhance this beneficial effect.

Indications: Acute Myocardial Infarction: For use in the management of suspected acute myocardial infarction, for the lysis of acute thrombi obstructing coronary arteries associated with evolving transmural myocardial infarction, for the improvement of ventricular function, and for the reduction of infarct size and mortality associated with acute myocardial infarction, when administered by the i.v. or intracoronary route, as well as for the reduction of congestive heart failure associated with AMI when administered by the i.v. route. In the high risk group with anterior myocardial infarction, 1 year mortality was significantly reduced in those patients who reperfused in response to streptokinase.

Thrombolysis following i.v. streptokinase is usually achieved within less than 1 hour. Early administration is correlated with greater clinical benefit.

Pulmonary Embolism: In adults for the lysis of acute massive pulmonary emboli, defined as obstruction or significant filling defects involving 2 or more lobar pulmonary arteries or an equivalent amount of emboli in other vessels. It is also indicated for embolization accompanied by unstable hemodynamics i.e., failure to maintain blood pressure without supportive measures. The diagnosis should be confirmed by objective means, preferably by pulmonary arteriography via an upper extremity vein, or noninvasive procedures such as lung scanning.

Deep Vein Thrombosis: For lysis of acute, extensive thrombi of the deep veins in adults such as those involving the popliteal and more proximal vessels. Diagnosis should be confirmed by ascending venography or other equally objective methods.

Studies have demonstrated a better salvage of valvular function and prevention of postphlebitic syndrome by the combined usage of streptokinase and heparin than by heparin alone.

Arterial Thrombosis and Embolism: For the lysis of acute arterial thrombi and for the lysis of arterial emboli. However, the use of streptokinase in arterial emboli originating from the left side of the heart (e.g., in mitral stenosis accompanied by atrial fibrillation) should be avoided due to the danger of new embolic phenomena including those to cerebral vessels.

Arteriovenous Cannula Occlusion: For clearing of totally or partially occluded arteriovenous cannulae as an alternative to surgical intervention when acceptable flow cannot otherwise be achieved.

Contraindications: Because thrombolytic therapy increases the risk of bleeding, streptokinase is contraindicated in the following conditions: active internal bleeding; recent (within 2 months) cerebrovascular accident, intracranial or intraspinal surgery (see Warnings); intracranial neoplasm; severe uncontrollable hypertension; uncontrollable clotting disorders.

Streptokinase should not be administered to patients having experienced severe allergic reaction to the product.

Warnings: Bleeding: The aim of streptokinase therapy is the production of sufficient amounts of plasmin for the lysis of intravascular deposits of fibrin; however, fibrin deposits which provide hemostasis, for example at sites of needle punctures, are also lysed and bleeding from such sites may occur.

Following i.v. high-dose brief-duration streptokinase therapy (1 500 000 IU over 60 minutes), in acute myocardial infarction, severe bleeding complications requiring transfusion are extremely rare (0.3 to 0.5%), and combined therapy with low-dose ASA (160 mg/day over a period of 1 month) does not appear to increase the risk of major bleeding. The addition of ASA to streptokinase may cause a slight increase in the risk of minor bleeding (3.1% without ASA vs 3.9% with ASA).

I.M. injections and nonessential handling of the patient must be avoided during treatment with streptokinase. Venipunctures should be performed carefully and as infrequently as possible.

Should an arterial puncture be necessary, upper extremity vessels are preferable. Pressure should be applied for at least 30 minutes, a pressure dressing applied and the puncture site checked frequently for evidence of bleeding. When internal bleeding occurs, it may be more difficult to manage than that which occurs with conventional anticoagulant therapy.

In the following conditions, the risks of therapy may be increased and should be weighed against the anticipated benefits: recent (within 10 days) major surgery, obstetrical delivery, organ biopsy, previous puncture of noncompressible vessels; recent (within 10 days) serious gastrointestinal bleeding; recent (within 10 days) trauma including cardiopulmonary resuscitation; severe hypertension (systolic BP > 200 mmHg, or diastolic BP > 100 mmHg, or hypertensive retinal changes Grades III/IV); high likelihood of left heart thrombus, e.g., mitral stenosis with atrial fibrillation; subacute bacterial endocarditis; hemostatic defects including those secondary to severe hepatic or renal disease; pregnancy; cerebrovascular disease; pulmonary diseases with cavitation (e.g., open tuberculosis) or severe bronchitis; acute pancreatitis or severe diabetes mellitus; diseases of the urogenital tract with potential sources of bleeding; diabetic hemorrhagic retinopathy; septic thrombophlebitis or occluded AV cannula at seriously infected site; suspicion of severe artherosclerotic degeneration; any other condition in which bleeding constitutes a significant hazard or would be particularly difficult to manage because of its location.

Should serious spontaneous bleeding (not controllable by local pressure) occur, the infusion of streptokinase should be terminated immediately and treatment instituted as described under Adverse Effects.

Arrhythmias: Rapid lysis of coronary thrombi may cause reperfusion atrial or ventricular dysrhythmia requiring immediate treatment. Careful monitoring for arrhythmia should be maintained during and immediately following administration of streptokinase.

Hypotension: Hypotension, sometimes severe, not secondary to bleeding or anaphylaxis has been observed during i.v. streptokinase infusion in 1 to 10% of patients. Patients should be monitored closely and should symptomatic or alarming hypotension occur, appropriate treatment should be administered. This treatment may include a decrease in the i.v. streptokinase infusion rate. Smaller hypotensive effects are common and have not required treatment.

Precautions: General: Streptokinase should be used in hospitals where the recommended diagnostic and monitoring techniques are available.

Noncardiogenic pulmonary edema has been reported rarely in patients treated with streptokinase. The risk of this appears greatest in patients who have large myocardial infarctions and are undergoing thrombolytic therapy by the intracoronary route.

Rarely, polyneuropathy has been temporally related to the use of streptokinase.

Should pulmonary embolism or recurrent pulmonary embolism occur during streptokinase therapy, the originally planned course of treatment should be completed in an attempt to lyse these emboli. While pulmonary embolism may occasionally occur during streptokinase treatment, the incidence is no greater than when patients are treated with heparin alone.

Repeated Administration: Because of the increased likelihood of resistance due to antistreptokinase antibody, streptokinase may not be effective if administered between 5 days and 6 months of a prior streptokinase administration or streptococcal infection (e.g., streptococcal pharyngitis, acute rheumatic fever or acute glomerulonephritis secondary to a streptococcal infection).

Pregnancy: Experience in pregnant women has not shown that streptokinase increases the risk of fetal abnormalities if administered during pregnancy. If this drug is used during pregnancy, the possibility of fetal harm appears remote. Because studies cannot rule out the possibility of harm, however, streptokinase should be used during pregnancy only if clearly needed.

Children: Safety and effectiveness in children have not been established.

Lactation: It is not known whether streptokinase is excreted in the breast milk nor whether it has harmful effects on the newborn. In the absence of further information, it is recommended that breast-feeding be discontinued in a woman who is to receive streptokinase.

Drug Interactions: The potential for an additive hypotensive effect should be borne in mind when streptokinase therapy is combined with antihypertensive agents, such as β-blockers and glyceryl trinitrate.

Until information regarding the interaction between streptokinase and tissue plasminogen activator (tPA) is available, special care should be taken if such a combination is considered.

There is an increased risk of hemorrhage in:

—Patients previously receiving heparin or coumarin derivatives. The effect of heparin can, however, be rapidly neutralized by administering protamine sulfate. In the case of prior treatment with coumarin derivatives, the Quick value must be more than 50% before the beginning of lysis.

—Patients receiving simultaneous treatment with platelet-aggregation inhibitors, e.g., ASA (see below also), phenylbutazone, dipyridamole and nonsteroidal anti-inflammatory drugs (NSAIDs).

—Patients receiving simultaneous or previous treatment with dextrans.

Combination of Streptokinase with ASA for Treatment of Myocardial Infarction: In the treatment of acute myocardial infarction with i.v. streptokinase (1 500 000 IU over 1 hour) combined with enteric-coated ASA (160 mg/day for 1 month), it was shown that the combined treatment results in a further reduction in mortality rate, as well as a decreased risk of reinfarction and stroke in comparison to treatment with each of the drugs alone. The addition of ASA to streptokinase may cause a slight increase in the risk of minor bleeding, but does not appear to increase the incidence of major bleeding. Unless contraindicated, concomitant administration of ASA is recommended (see Dosage).

Anticoagulation Treatment Following Streptokinase: Anticoagulation Following Treatment for Myocardial Infarction: The use of anticoagulants following administration of streptokinase treatment for acute myocardial infarction increases the risk of bleeding, and has not been shown to be of unequivocal clinical benefit. Therefore, their use should be decided upon at the discretion of the treating physician.

Anticoagulation Following I.V. Treatment for Other Indications: To prevent rethrombosis following termination of streptokinase infusion treatment for pulmonary embolism or deep vein thrombosis, continuous i.v. infusion of heparin without a loading dose is recommended (see Patient Monitoring).

Patient Monitoring: I.V. or Intracoronary Artery Infusion for Myocardial Infarction: I.V. administration of streptokinase will cause marked decreases in plasminogen and fibrinogen levels and increases in thrombin time (TT), activated partial thromboplastin time (APTT), and prothrombin time (PT), which usually normalize within 12 to 24 hours. These changes may also occur in some patients with intracoronary administration of the drug.

Streptase (cont'd)

I.V. Infusion for Other Indications: Before commencing thrombolytic therapy, it is desirable to obtain a thrombin time (TT), activated partial thromboplastin time (APTT), prothrombin time (PT), and hematocrit and platelet count to obtain hemostatic status of the patient.

If heparin has been given, it should be discontinued and the TT or APTT should be less than twice the normal control value before thrombolytic therapy is started.

During the infusion, decreases in the plasminogen and fibrinogen levels and an increase in the level of FDP (the latter two serving to prolong the clotting times of coagulation tests) will generally confirm the existence of a lytic state. Therefore, therapy can be monitored by performing the TT, or APTT or PT, approximately 4 hours after initiation of therapy.

To prevent rethrombosis following the streptokinase infusion, continuous i.v. heparin infusion without a loading dose is recommended. The effect of streptokinase on thrombin time (TT) and activated partical thromboplastin time (APTT) will usually diminish within 3 to 4 hours after streptokinase therapy. A thrombin time value should be obtained during this period, and heparin therapy without a loading dose can be initiated when TT or APTT is less than twice the normal control value. (See manufacturer's prescribing information for proper use of heparin.) This should be followed by conventional oral anticoagulation therapy.

Adverse Effects: The following adverse reactions have been frequently associated with i.v. therapy but may also occur with intracoronary artery infusion.

Bleeding: The reported incidence of bleeding (major or minor) has varied widely depending on the indication, dose, route and duration of administration and concomitant therapy.

Minor bleeding occurs often with thrombolytic therapy mainly at invaded or disturbed sites. When lytic therapy is continued while local measures are used to control minor bleeding, **do not** reduce the dose as this will increase the conversion of plasminogen to plasmin which may increase bleeding.

Severe internal bleeding involving gastrointestinal, genitourinary, retroperitoneal or intracerebral sites, may occur. Intracerebral bleeding in connection with the treatment of myocardial infarction has been reported with an incidence of 0.1 to 0.3%. Several fatalities due to cerebral and other serious internal hemorrhage have occurred during thrombolytic therapy.

In the treatment of acute myocardial infarction with i.v. streptokinase, the GISSI and ISIS-2 studies reported a rate of major bleeding (requiring transfusion) of 0.3 to 0.5%. In the TIMI study, which required both invasive techniques and administration of anticoagulants, a frequency of 15.6% for major bleeding (intracranial, or decrease in hemoglobin > 5 g/dL, or decrease in hematocrit > 15%) was reported.

Should uncontrollable bleeding occur, streptokinase infusion should be terminated immediately; slowing the rate of administration may increase the bleeding. If necessary, bleeding can be reversed and blood loss effectively managed with appropriate replacement therapy (see Overdose: Symptoms and Treatment).

Allergic Reactions: Reactions attributed to possible anaphylaxis have been observed rarely in patients treated with streptokinase. These ranged in severity from minor breathing difficulty to bronchospasm, periorbital swelling or angioneurotic edema. Other, milder allergic effects such as urticaria, itching, flushing, nausea, headache and musculoskeletal pain have also been observed as have delayed hypersensitivity reactions such as vasculitis and interstitial nephritis. Anaphylactoid shock is very rare, having been reported in 0 to 0.1% of patients.

An anaphylactic reaction has been reported in a patient following a second course of streptokinase within 1 month for clearance of an occluded arteriovenous shunt. Therefore, the possibility of systemic absorption of streptokinase following its use for this purpose must be considered.

Mild or moderate reactions may be managed with concomitant antihistamine and/or corticosteroid therapy. Severe allergic reactions require immediate discontinuation of streptokinase with adrenergics, antihistamines, or corticosteroids administered i.v. as required.

Fever: Although streptokinase is nonpyrogenic in standard animal tests, approximately 33% of patients treated with streptokinase have shown increases in body temperature of > 0.83°C. Symptomatic treatment is usually sufficient to alleviate discomfort.

Other: Transient elevations of serum transaminases may occur.

A few cases of cholesterol embolism have been described in temporal coincidence with thrombolytic therapy, particularly in patients undergoing angiography.

During local lysis of occluded peripheral arteries, distal embolization cannot be excluded.

Hemorrhagic myocardial infarction has been reported.

Overdose: Symptoms and Treatment: Minor bleeding complications with streptokinase are usually overcome by increasing the dosage. Should serious uncontrollable bleeding occur as a result of overdosage, the infusion of streptokinase and any other concomitant anticoagulant should be discontinued immediately. If necessary, blood loss and reversal of the bleeding tendency can be effectively managed with whole blood (fresh blood preferable), packed red cells and cryoprecipitate or fresh frozen plasma. Although the use of aminocaproic acid (or aprotinin) in humans as an antidote for streptokinase has not been documented, it may be considered in an emergency situation.

Dosage: Streptokinase should be administered by volumetric infusion pump. Do not use drop-counting infusion methods since streptokinase may alter droplet size.

Acute Myocardial Infarction: Streptokinase treatment of coronary thrombosis should be instituted as soon as possible after the onset of symptoms of acute myocardial infarction. The greatest benefit in mortality reduction was observed when streptokinase was administered within 4 hours, but statistically significant benefit has been reported when administered up to 24 hours (see Table I).

Table I—Streptase

Dosage—Acute Myocardial Infarction

Route	Dosage/Duration
I.V. infusion (see below)	1 500 000 IU within 60 min
Intracoronary infusion (see below)	20 000 IU by bolus followed by 2 000-4 000 IU/min for 30-90 min (average 60 min)

I.V. Administration: With the above regimen, 1 500 000 IU within 60 minutes, no coagulation tests are necessary to monitor streptokinase therapy. Unless contraindicated, the concomitant use of ASA at a dose of 160 mg/day orally, starting prior to streptokinase infusion and continued for 1 month is recommended.

Intracoronary Administration: Streptokinase treatment of coronary thrombosis should be undertaken only in medical centres where coronary arteriography is an established routine and appropriate after-treatment available. Streptokinase is administered selectively into the thrombosed coronary artery via coronary catheter positioned by the Judkins or Sones technique.

Deep Vein Thrombosis, Pulmonary or Arterial Embolism or Arterial Thrombosis: Streptokinase treatment should be instituted as soon as possible after onset of thrombotic event, preferably within 7 days. Any delay in instituting lytic therapy to evaluate the effect of heparin therapy decreases the potential for optimal efficacy, although slight enhancement of clot lysis has been shown with initiation of thrombolytic therapy up to 2 weeks after the onset of symptoms of deep vein thrombosis.

Since human exposure to streptococci is common, antibodies to streptokinase are prevalent. Thus, a loading dose of streptokinase sufficient to neutralize these antibodies is required. A dose of 250 000 IU infused into a peripheral vein over 30 minutes has been found appropriate in over 90% of patients. If the thrombin time or any other parameter of fibrinolysis after 4 hours of treatment is not significantly different from the normal control level, discontinue streptokinase because excessive resistance to streptokinase is present. Furthermore, if the thrombin time after 16 hours is still prolonged to more than fourfold the control level, the streptokinase dosage should be doubled for several hours until the thrombin time recedes.

The dosage schedule in Table II is recommended.

A continuous i.v. infusion of heparin, without a loading dose, is recommended to prevent rethrombosis following termination of streptokinase infusion. (see Precautions, Patient Monitoring).

Arteriovenous Cannula Occlusion: Before Treatment: Before using streptokinase, an attempt should be made to clear the cannula by careful syringe technique, using heparinized saline solution. If adequate flow is not re-established, streptokinase may be employed. Allow the effect of any pretreatment anticoagulants to diminish.

Streptokinase Administration: Instill 250 000 IU streptokinase in 2 mL i.v. solution into each occluded limb of the cannula slowly. Clamp off cannula limb(s) for 2 hours. Observe the patient closely for possible adverse effects.

After Treatment: Aspirate contents of infused cannula limb(s), flush with saline, reconnect cannula.

Reconstitution and Dilution: Intracoronary Artery and I.V. Administration: The protein nature and lyophilized form of streptokinase require careful reconstitution and dilution.

The following procedure is recommended: Add 5 mL Sodium Chloride Injection USP or Dextrose 5% Injection USP **slowly** to the vacuum packed Streptase container, directing the vehicle at the side of the container rather than into the lyophilized streptokinase powder.

Roll and tilt the container **gently** to reconstitute. **Avoid shaking.** (Shaking may cause foaming.)

Dilute the entire reconstituted contents of the container with Sodium Chloride Injection USP or Dextrose 5% Injection USP, to a total volume of approximately 45 mL (see Table III on following page). Dilute slowly and carefully; avoid shaking and agitation. (If necessary, total volume may be increased to a maximum of 500 mL with the infusion pump setting in Table III [on following page] increased accordingly.) To facilitate setting the infusion pump rate, a total volume of approximately 45 mL, or multiples thereof, is suggested.

Solutions of Streptokinase reconstituted and diluted to 500 mL or 50 mL with Sodium Chloride Injection, USP, in glass containers, irrespective of which potency is used (250 000 IU; 750 000 IU; 1 500 000 IU), can be drawn through in-line filters without a reduction in drug potency providing the filter is of 0.80 μm or greater pore size (if of cellulose construct) or of 0.22 μm or greater pore size (if of PVC—acrylic polymer construct). Flocculated product should be discarded if filters of the above mentioned construct and/or pore size are not available.

Parenteral drug products should be inspected visually for particulate matter and discoloration prior to administration whenever solution and container permit. (The Albumin (Human) may impart a slightly yellow color to the solution.)

Do not add other medication to the container of reconstituted streptokinase.

For Use in Arteriovenous Cannulae: Slowly reconstitute the contents of 250 000 IU/streptokinase vial with 2 mL Sodium Chloride Injection USP or Dextrose 5% Injection USP.

The suggested dilutions and infusion rates provided in Table III (on following page) represent a practical means of streptokinase administration without compromise of safety and efficacy considerations. Depending on the type of available infusion pump/bags, the solution/volumes/rates cited may be adjusted to correspond with the particular dosage rate to be administered.

Stability and Storage of Reconstituted and Diluted Solutions: Reconstituted Solutions: Streptase reconstituted with 5 mL of saline (Sodium Chloride Injection USP, 0.9%) or dextrose (Dextrose Injection USP, 5%) is stable for 24 hours at room temperature (15 to 30°C) and refrigeration (2 to 4°C). For the recommended total period of use of the product, from reconstitution and dilution to the end of patient administration, see Diluted Solutions.

Diluted Solutions: Stability studies have been carried out on the 3 potencies, reconstituted and diluted with saline (Sodium Chloride Injection USP, 0.9%) or dextrose (Dextrose Injection USP, 5%), to 50 or 500 mL, in glass or plastic containers. The total period of use of the product, from reconstitution and dilution to end of patient administration, should not exceed the specific stability time indicated in Table IV (on following page).

Table II—Streptase

Dosage Schedule

Indication	Loading Dose	I.V. Infusion Dosage/Duration
Pulmonary Embolism	250 000 IU/30 min	100 000 IU/h for 24 h (72 h if concurrent deep vein thrombosis suspected)
Deep Vein Thrombosis	250 000 IU/30 min	100 000 IU/h for 72 h
Arterial Thrombosis or Embolism	250 000 IU/30 min	100 000 IU/h for 24 h

Table III—Streptase

Suggested Dilution and Infusion Rates

Indication/Dosage Route	Total dosage to be administered (IU)	Total vials or bottles of Streptase required	Volume of dilution/ vial or bottle (mL)	Loading Dose (IU)	Loading Infusion Rate (mL/hr)	Maintenance Dose (IU)	Maintenance Infusion Rate (mL/hr)
I. Acute Myocardial Infarction							
A. Intracoronary artery administration	140 000 IU	1 vial 250 000 IU	125	20 000 IU	10 mL bolus injection	2 000 IU/min	60 mL/h
B. I.V. administration	1 500 000 IU	i) 1 vial 1 500 000 IU	50[a]	—	—	1 500 000 IU	i) 50 mL/h
		ii) 1 bottle 1 500 000 IU	50[a]			1 500 000 IU	ii) 50 mL/h
		iii) 2 vials 750 000 IU	50[a]			1 500 000 IU	iii) 100 mL/h
II. Deep Vein Thrombosis, Pulmonary Embolism, Arterial Thrombosis							
A. I.V. infusion	2 650 000 to 7 450 000 IU	i) 11 to 30 vials 250 000 IU	45[b]	250 000 IU	i) 90 mL/h for 30 min	100 000 IU/h for 24 to 72 h	i) 18 mL/h
		ii) 4 to 10 vials 750 000 IU	45[b]	250 000 IU	ii) 30 mL/h for 30 min	100 000 IU/h for 24 to 72 h	ii) 6 mL/h
		iii) 2 to 5 vials 1 500 000 IU	45[b]	250 000 IU	iii) 15 mL/h for 30 min	100 000 IU/h for 24 to 72 h	iii) 3 mL/h
		iv) 2 to 5 bottles 1 500 000 IU	45[b]	250 000 IU	iv) 15 mL/h for 30 min	100 000 IU/h for 24 to 72 h	iv) 3 mL/h

[a] Volumes of solution of 50 to 250 mL have been used.

[b] If necessary, total volume may be increased, in increments of approximately 45 mL, to a maximum of 500 mL with the infusion pump rate adjusted accordingly. The total volume of approximately 45 mL or multiple thereof is recommended to facilitate setting the infusion pump for hourly dosage.

Table IV—Streptase

Stability of Reconstituted/Diluted Solutions

Dosage (IU)	Final Volume (mL)	Diluent	Container	Temperature	Stable (hours)
250 000	50	saline or dextrose	plastic	RT*	24
	500	dextrose	glass	RT	12
	500	dextrose	glass	5°C	24
	500	dextrose	plastic	RT	12
	500	dextrose	plastic	5°C	24
750 000	50	dextrose	glass or plastic	RT	24
	50	dextrose	glass or plastic	5°C	24
	50	saline	plastic	RT	24
1 500 000	50	saline or dextrose	glass or plastic	RT	24
	500	saline or dextrose	glass	RT	24

*Room temperature.

Supplied: Each 6.5 mL vial of sterile, lyophilized white powder contains: 250 000 IU (green labels), 750 000 IU (blue labels) or 1 500 000 IU (red labels) of purified streptokinase, 25 mg crosslinked gelatin polypeptides, 25 mg sodium L-glutamate, sodium hydroxide to adjust pH and 100 mg albumin (human) as stabilizer. Packages of 10. Streptokinase 1 500 000 IU is also available in infusion bottles of 68 mL, individually packaged.

When stored at room temperature below 25°C, the dried product is stable up to the expiration date indicated on the package.

Reviewed 1999

STREPTOMYCIN Ⓟ

General Monograph, CPhA

Antibiotic

This monograph has been compiled by CPhA. It may contain information different from that approved by Therapeutic Products Programme, Health Canada, and the pharmaceutical manufacturers' approval has not been requested.

Pharmacology: Streptomycin is an aminoglycoside antibiotic obtained from cultures of Streptomyces griseus. It is used in conjunction with other agents in the treatment of infections caused by M. tuberculosis. Streptomycin also has activity against H. ducreyi (chancroid), M. leprae (leprosy), Y. pestis (plague), C. granulomatosis (granuloma inguinale), F. tularensis (tularemia), Brucella, enterococci and some Enterobacteriaceae.

Pharmacokinetics: Streptomycin is not absorbed from the gastrointestinal tract and is administered i.m. for systemic action.

Following i.m. injection of 1 g of the drug, a peak serum concentration of 25 to 50 μg/mL is reached within 1 to 2 hours. The elimination half-life in adults with normal renal function is usually 2 to 3 hours. In newborns and premature infants the half-life may range from 4 to 10 hours. Adults with severe renal impairment may have half-lives of up to 110 hours. Appreciable concentrations are found in all organ tissues except the brain. Significant amounts have been found in pleural fluid and tuberculous cavities. The drug has a reported protein binding of up to 35%. Streptomycin passes through the placenta with serum concentrations in the cord blood similar to maternal levels. Small amounts are excreted in milk, saliva, and sweat. It is excreted rapidly in the urine by glomerular filtration. In patients with normal kidney function, between 29 and 89% of a single 600 mg dose is excreted within 24 hours. Any reduction of glomerular activity results in decreased excretion of the drug and concurrent rise in serum and tissue concentrations.

Indications: M. tuberculosis: The treatment of tuberculosis in conjunction with other antituberculosis agents, when the infecting organisms are susceptible.

Nontuberculosis Infections: Used in combination with other drugs or antibiotics in the treatment of tularemia, plague, streptococcal and enterococcal endocarditis and brucellosis, when caused by susceptible organisms.

Note: The use of streptomycin should be limited to the treatment of infections caused by bacteria which have been shown to be susceptible to the antibacterial effects of streptomycin and which are not amenable to therapy with less potentially toxic agents.

Contraindications: Patients with a history of ototoxic reactions or hypersensitivity reactions to streptomycin or other aminoglycosides.

Warnings: Extreme caution is advised in people with preexisting eighth cranial nerve impairment. The risk of severe neurotoxic reactions is sharply increased in patients with impaired kidney function or prerenal azotemia. These include disturbances of the auditory nerve, optic nerve, peripheral neuritis, arachnoiditis and encephalopathy. Renal function should be carefully determined and patients with renal impairment should be given reduced dosages. The peak serum concentration in individuals with kidney damage should not exceed 20 to 25 μg/mL.

Ototoxicity: Streptomycin-induced eighth cranial nerve damage may result in permanent loss of inner ear function. Aminoglycoside-induced ototoxicity is usually irreversible, although some adaptation may occur. Ototoxicity may be manifested by vestibular and/or auditory dysfunction. Vestibular symptoms are more common and may include nausea, vomiting, vertigo, nystagmus and ataxia. Auditory symptoms include tinnitus, roaring noises, a sense of fullness in the ears and varying degrees of hearing impairment. Loss of high-frequency perception, which can be detected by audiometric testing, usually occurs before clinical hearing loss. Loss of hearing may be permanent if damage is extensive.

The incidence of ototoxicity is directly proportional to duration and amount of the drug administered. Advanced age, dehydration, and renal impairment predispose to ototoxicity.

Periodic assessment of eighth cranial nerve function may avert ototoxicity. Tinnitus, roaring noises or a sense of fullness in the ears indicates the need for audiometric examination or termination of therapy or both. Patients should be warned to immediately report any of the above signs and symptoms of toxicity.

Pregnancy: Aminoglycosides should be used during pregnancy only for severe infections when safer drugs cannot be used or are ineffective. Aminoglycosides have been shown to cross the placenta and there have been several reports of total irreversible bilateral congenital deafness in children whose mothers received streptomycin during pregnancy.

Precautions: Although streptomycin is thought to be less nephrotoxic than other aminoglycosides, impairment of renal function may occur. Adverse effects on kidneys may include tubular necrosis, reduced glomerular filtration rate, decreased creatinine clearance, and rarely, electrolyte disturbances. Monitor patients for increased serum creatinine, proteinuria and the presence of casts or cells in the urine. Aminoglycoside-induced nephrotoxicity is usually reversible when the drug is discontinued.

Since streptomycin may aggravate muscle weakness, use with caution in patients with neuromuscular disorders (e.g., myasthenia gravis).

Special care should be taken by individuals handling or preparing streptomycin for injection to avoid contact with or inhalation of this antibiotic. Hypersensitivity reactions have been reported.

Streptomycin should be administered by deep i.m. injection. The i.v. route is not recommended but may be used if i.m. injections are contraindicated.

As with other antibiotics, use of this drug may result in overgrowth of nonsusceptible organisms, including fungi. If superinfection occurs, institute appropriate therapy.

Drug Interactions: Since neurotoxic, ototoxic, or nephrotoxic effects may be additive, avoid concurrent or sequential administration of other drugs with similar toxic potential, particularly other aminoglycosides, amphotericin B, cephalosporins, colistin (polymyxin E), cisplatin, methoxyflurane, vancomycin and potent diuretics (ethacrynic acid, furosemide, mannitol).

General anesthetics and neuromuscular blocking agents (e.g., succinylcholine, tubocurarine): The neurotoxicity of streptomycin can result in respiratory paralysis from neuromuscular blockade, especially when the drug is given concurrently with or soon after anesthesia and the use of muscle relaxants.

The combination of streptomycin and penicillin is synergistic against some organisms, and may be used to treat infections

Streptomycin (cont'd)

due to organisms resistant to either drug along (e.g., enterococci, Viridans streptococci).
Lactation: Small amounts of streptomycin are excreted in breast milk. Since the oral absorption of this antibiotic is poor, it is unlikely that renal or ototoxicity would occur in the infant.
Children: Use with caution and in reduced dosage in premature infants and in neonates younger than 6 weeks of age because of their renal immaturity and resulting prolongation of serum half-life of streptomycin.
Geriatrics: Elderly patients may be at greater risk for renal and ototoxicity due to decreased kidney function. Use reduced dosages and monitor serum drug concentrations, renal status and eighth cranial nerve function.

Adverse Effects: Commonly noted are ototoxicity manifested by nausea, vomiting, and vertigo; paresthesia of the face; rash; fever; urticaria, angioneurotic edema; and eosinophilia. Less frequent are deafness, exfoliative dermatitis, anaphylaxis, azotemia, oliguria, proteinuria, leukopenia, thrombocytopenia, pancytopenia, hemolytic anemia, muscular weakness, and amblyopia.

Dosage: Streptomycin should be administered by deep i.m. injection into a large muscle mass such as the gluteus maximus or the mid-lateral thigh. Injection site should be rotated to decrease irritation.
Tuberculosis: As part of a multidrug regimen for active pulmonary tuberculosis, the usual adult dose is 1 g or 15 mg/kg daily during the early months of therapy. Dosage can be reduced to 1 g or 25 mg/kg 2 or 3 times weekly as soon as clinically possible after the disease is controlled. Therapy with streptomycin may be discontinued when toxic symptoms have appeared or impending toxicity is feared, when organisms become resistant, or when full treatment has been obtained.

For elderly patients or those with auditory or renal function impairment, lower daily doses based on age, renal function and eighth cranial nerve function are recommended. A geriatric dose of 10 mg/kg daily to a maximum of 750 mg has been suggested.
Brucellosis: 1 to 2 g daily in divided doses for 2 weeks in conjunction with a tetracycline or sulfamethoxazole-trimethoprim.
Tularemia: 1 to 2 g daily in divided doses for 7 to 14 days or until the patient has been afebrile for 5 to 7 days.
Enterococcal Endocarditis: 1 g twice daily for 2 weeks followed by 0.5 g twice daily for 4 weeks. A penicillin or vancomycin is given in conjunction with streptomycin.
Plague: Doses of 2 to 4 g daily may be required, continued until the patient has been afebrile for at least 3 days.

In selected patients with renal disease, serum concentrations should be determined. Peak concentrations should be 15 to 25 µg/mL and trough concentrations should be below 5 µg/mL. If serum concentrations are not available, creatinine clearance (mL/s) can be used to adjust dosage in renal failure as follows (for calculation of creatinine clearance see Serum Drug Concentration Monitoring in the Clin-Info section): If 0.85 to 1.33 mL/s, give 7.5 mg/kg every 24 hours; if 0.17 to 0.85 mL/s, 7.5 mg/kg every 24 to 72 hours; and if less than 0.17 mL/s, 7.5 mg/kg every 72 to 96 hours.
Children: The individual dose of streptomycin for children may be calculated as 20 to 40 mg/kg to a maximum of 1g daily in equally divided doses at 6- to 12-hour intervals. Particular care should be taken to avoid excessive dosage in children (see also Precautions).

Reviewed 1999

STREPTOMYCIN SULFATE™ Ⓟ

Pfizer

Aminoglycoside Antibiotic

Pharmacology: Streptomycin is a bactericidal antibiotic in therapeutic dosage. The mode of action is the interference with normal protein synthesis and production of "faulty proteins".

In recommended doses, Streptomycin is active against susceptible strains of many gram-negative and gram-positive organisms, and M. tuberculosis. When used alone, bacterial resistance has been shown to develop rapidly. Therefore, in the treatment of tuberculosis, it should be used in combination with other antitubercular drugs.
Pharmacokinetics: Streptomycin is not absorbed from the gastrointestinal tract when given orally, and therefore should be administered parenterally for systemic action.

Following i.m. injection of 1 g of the drug, a peak serum level of 25 to 50 µg/mL is reached within 1 hour, diminishing slowly to about 50% after 5 to 6 hours. Appreciable concentrations are found in all organ tissues except the brain. Significant amounts have been found in pleural fluid and tuberculous cavities. Streptomycin passes through the placenta with serum levels in the cord blood similar to maternal levels. Small amounts are excreted in milk, saliva, and sweat.

Streptomycin is excreted rapidly in the urine by glomerular filtration. In patients with normal kidney function, between 29 and 89% of a single 0.6 g dose is excreted within 24 hours. Any reduction of glomerular activity results in decreased excretion of the drug and concurrent rise in serum and tissue levels.
Sensitivity Plate Testing: If the Kirby-Bauer method of disc sensitivity is used, a 10 µg streptomycin disc should give a zone of over 15 mm when tested against a streptomycin-sensitive bacterial strain.

Indications: M. tuberculosis: Streptomycin may be indicated for all forms of this infection when the infecting organisms are susceptible. It should be used only in combination with other antituberculosis drugs. The common combined drug therapy is streptomycin, PAS and isoniazid; this combination is effective only where the organisms are susceptible to the drugs being used in combination.
Nontuberculosis infections: Streptomycin should be used only in those serious nontuberculosis infections caused by organisms shown by in vitro sensitivity studies to be susceptible to it and when less potentially hazardous therapeutic agents are ineffective or contraindicated. a. Y. pestis (plague). b. P. tularensis (tularemia). c. Brucella. d. Donovanosis (granuloma inguinale). e. H. ducreyi (chancroid). f. H. influenzae (in respiratory, endocardial and meningeal infections-concomitantly with another antibacterial agent). g. K. pneumoniae pneumonia (concomitantly with another antibacterial agent). h. E. coli, Proteus, A. aerogenes, K. pneumoniae, and S. faecalis in urinary tract infections. i. S. viridans, E. faecalis (in endocardial infections-concomitantly with penicillin). j. Gram-negative bacillary bacteremia (concomitantly with another antibacterial agent).
Note: The use of streptomycin should be limited to the treatment of infections caused by bacteria which have been shown to be susceptible to the antibacterial effects of streptomycin and which are not amenable to therapy with less potentially toxic agents.

Contraindications: In those patients who have shown previous toxic or hypersensitivity reactions to streptomycin.

Warnings: Extreme caution is advised in people with VIII cranial nerve impairment. The risk of severe neurotoxic reactions is sharply increased in patients with impaired kidney function or prerenal azotemia. These include disturbances of the auditory nerve, optic nerve, peripheral neuritis, arachnoiditis, and encephalopathy. Renal function should be carefully determined and patients with renal damage and nitrogen retention should have reduced dosage. The peak serum concentration in individuals with kidney damage should not exceed 20 to 25 µg/mL.

The concurrent or sequential use of other neurotoxic and/or nephrotoxic drugs with streptomycin, particularly neomycin, kanamycin, gentamicin, cephaloridine, paromomycin, viomycin, polymyxin B, colistin, and tobramycin should be avoided.

The neurotoxicity of streptomycin can result in respiratory paralysis from neuromuscular blockade, especially when the drug is given soon after anesthesia and the use of muscle relaxants.

The administration of streptomycin in parenteral form should be reserved for patients where adequate laboratory facilities are available and constant supervision of patient is possible.
Ototoxicity: Streptomycin may frequently affect the vestibular branch of the auditory nerve causing severe nausea, vomiting, and vertigo. The incidence is directly proportional to duration and amount of drug administered. Advanced age and renal impairment predispose to ototoxicity. Symptoms subside and recovery is usually complete following discontinuance of the drug.

Loss of hearing has been reported following long-term therapy; however, ototoxic effect on the auditory branch of the eighth nerve is infrequent and is usually preceded by vestibular symptoms. Hearing loss, when extensive is usually permanent.

Streptomycin contains sodium metabisulfite, a sulfite that may cause allergic-type reactions including anaphylactic symptoms and life-threatening or less severe asthmatic episodes in certain susceptible people. The over-all prevalence of sulfite sensitivity in the general population is unknown. Sulfite sensitivity is seen more frequently in asthmatic than nonasthmatic people.
Pregnancy: Streptomycin should be used during pregnancy only if the potential benefit outweighs the potential risk to the mother and fetus. Since streptomycin readily crosses the placental barrier, caution in use of the drug is important to prevent ototoxicity in the fetus.

Precautions: Baseline and periodic caloric stimulation tests and audiometric tests are advisable with extended streptomycin therapy. Tinnitus, roaring noises, or a sense of fullness in the ears indicates need for audiometric examinations or termination of streptomycin therapy or both (see Adverse Effects).

Care should be taken by individuals handling or preparing streptomycin for injection to avoid skin sensitivity reactions.

As with all i.m. preparations, streptomycin injection should be injected well within the body of a relatively large muscle.
Adults: The preferred site is the upper outer quadrant of the buttock, (i.e., gluteus maximus), or the mid-lateral thigh.
Children: It is recommended that i.m. injections be given preferably in the mid-lateral muscles of the thigh. In infants and small children the periphery of the upper outer quadrant of the gluteal region should be used only when necessary, such as in burn patients, in order to minimize the possibility of damage to the sciatic nerve.

The deltoid area should be used only if well developed such as in certain adults and older children, and then only with caution to avoid radial nerve injury. I.M. injections should not be made into the lower and mid-third of the upper arm. As with all i.m. injections, aspiration is necessary to help avoid inadvertent injection into a blood vessel.

Injection sites should be alternated, and solutions of concentration greater than 500 mg/mL are not recommended.

As higher doses or more prolonged therapy with streptomycin may be indicated for more severe or fulminating infections (endocarditis, meningitis, etc.) the physician should always take adequate measure to be immediately aware of any toxic signs or symptoms occurring in the patient as a result of streptomycin therapy.

While disturbances in renal function due to streptomycin have been reported in the past, purification of the drug has minimized this side effect. In the presence of pre-existing renal insufficiency, however, extreme caution must be exercised in the administration of streptomycin. Since in severely uremic patients a single dose may produce reasonably high blood levels for several days, the cumulative effect may produce ototoxic sequelae. When streptomycin must be given for prolonged periods of time, alkalinization of the urine may minimize or prevent renal irritation.

A syndrome of apparent CNS depression, characterized by stupor and flaccidity, at times to the extent of coma and deep respiratory depression, has been reported in very young infants in whom streptomycin dosage had materially exceeded the recommended limits. Thus, infants should not receive streptomycin in excess of the recommended dosage.

In the treatment of venereal infections such as granuloma inguinale, and chancroid, if concomitant syphilis is suspected, suitable laboratory procedures such as a dark field examination should be performed before the start of treatment, and monthly serologic tests should be done for at least 4 months.

As with other antibiotics, use of this drug may result in overgrowth of nonsusceptible organisms, including fungi. If superinfection occurs, appropriate therapy should be instituted.

Adverse Effects: The following reactions are common: ototoxicity-nausea, vomiting and vertigo; paresthesia of face; rash; fever; urticaria; angioneurotic edema; and eosinophilia.

The following reactions are less frequent: deafness, exfoliative dermatitis, anaphylaxis, azotemia, leukopenia, thrombocytopenia, pancytopenia, hemolytic anemia, muscular weakness, and amblyopia.

Vestibular dysfunction resulting from the parenteral administration of streptomycin is cumulatively related to the total daily dose. When 1.8 to 2.0 g/day are given, symptoms are likely to develop in the large percentage of patients, especially in the elderly or patients with impaired renal function, within 4 weeks. Therefore, it is recommended that caloric and audiometric tests be done prior to, during, and following intensive therapy with streptomycin in order to facilitate detection of any vestibular dysfunction and/or impairment of hearing which may occur.

Vestibular symptoms generally appear early and usually are reversible with early detection and cessation of administration of the drug. After 2 to 3 months, gross vestibular symptoms usually disappear, except for the relative inability to walk in total darkness or on very rough terrain.

Clinical judgment as to termination of therapy must be exercised when side effects occur.

Dosage: I.M. Route Only. Tuberculosis: All forms when organisms are known or believed to be drug susceptible.
Adult, combined therapy: streptomycin, 1 g daily with PAS 5 g t.i.d. and isoniazid 200 to 300 mg daily. Elderly patients should have a smaller daily dose of streptomycin, based on age, renal function, and eighth nerve function. Ultimately the streptomycin should be discontinued or reduced in dosage to 1 g, 2 to 3 times weekly. Therapy with streptomycin may be terminated when toxic symptoms have appeared, when impending toxicity is feared, when organisms become resistant, or when full treatment effect has been obtained. The total period of drug treatment of tuberculosis is a minimum of 1 year; however, indications of terminating therapy with streptomycin may occur at any time as noted above.
Tularemia: 1 to 2 g daily in divided doses for 7 to 10 days until the patient is afebrile for 5 to 7 days.
Plague: 2 to 4 g daily in divided doses until the patient is afebrile for at least 3 days.
Bacterial Endocarditis: In penicillin-sensitive alpha and nonhemolytic streptococcal endocarditis (penicillin sensitive to 0.1 μg/mL or less), streptomycin may be used for 2-week treatment concomitantly with penicillin. Streptomycin dosage is 1 g b.i.d. for 1 week, and 0.5 g b.i.d. for the 2nd week. If the patient is over 60 years of age, the dosage should be 0.5 g b.i.d. for the entire 2-week period.
Enterococcal Endocarditis: Streptomycin in doses of 1 g b.i.d. for 2 weeks and 0.5 g b.i.d. for 4 weeks is given in combination with penicillin. Ototoxicity may require termination of the streptomycin prior to completion of the 6-week course of treatment.

For use concomitantly with other agents to which the infecting organism is also sensitive. Streptomycin in these conditions is considered as a drug of secondary choice: gram-negative bacillary bacteremia, meningitis, and pneumonia; brucellosis; granuloma inguinale; chancroid, and urinary tract infection.
Adults: a. Severe fulminating infection: 2 to 4 g daily, administered i.m. in divided doses every 6 to 12 hours. b. With less severe infections and with highly susceptible organisms: 1 to 2 g daily.
Children: 20 to 40 mg/kg of body weight daily in divided doses every 6 to 12 hours. (Particular care should be taken to avoid excessive dosage in children.)

Supplied: Each ampul of sterile solution contains: streptomycin sulfate equivalent to streptomycin 1 g. Nonmedicinal ingredients: liquefied phenol (as preservative), sodium citrate (as antioxidant), sodium metabisulfite (as antioxidant) and water for injection. Ampuls of 2.5 mL. Packages of 10. Store under refrigeration at 2 to 8°C.

STRESSTABS®
STRESSTABS® PLUS
STRESSTABS® with IRON
STRESSTABS® with ZINC

Whitehall-Robins

Vitamin B Complex—Ascorbic Acid—Vitamin E
Vitamin B Complex—Ascorbic Acid—Vitamin E—Selenium—Zinc—Beta Carotene
Vitamin B Complex—Ascorbic Acid—Vitamin E—Iron
Vitamin B Complex—Ascorbic Acid—Vitamin E—Zinc—Copper

Dietary Supplement

Indications: Stresstabs: Dietary supplement in conditions responding to therapy with B complex factors.
Stresstabs Plus: When physiologic stress causes severe tissue depletion of the B Complex, vitamins C, A and E.
Stresstabs with Iron: Where physiologic stress causes severe tissue depletion of ascorbic acid and of the B complex factors.
Stresstabs with Zinc: Nutritional support during physiologic stress situations such as: alcoholism, burns, fractures, surgery and infection, inadequate diet.

Contraindications: Stresstabs with Iron: hemochromatosis, hemosiderosis, hemolytic anemia.

Precautions: Stresstabs with Iron: Not intended for the treatment of pernicious anemia. Folic acid may obscure pernicious anemia in that the peripheral blood picture may return to normal while neurological manifestations remain progressive.

Iron compounds taken orally can impair the absorption of tetracycline antibiotics. Antacids given concomitantly with iron compounds decrease iron absorption.

Adverse Effects: Stresstabs with Iron: Rarely, in iron-sensitive patients, mild gastrointestinal upsets may occur.

Dosage: Adults, 1 tablet daily.

Supplied: Stresstabs: Each oval, orange, film-coated, scored tablet, engraved "W-R" and "S1" contains: vitamin B_1 (as thiamine mononitrate) 15 mg, riboflavin 15 mg, pyridoxine HCl 5 mg, vitamin B_{12} 12 μg, ascorbic acid 500 mg, niacinamide 100 mg, vitamin E (from dl-alpha tocopheryl acetate) 30 IU, pantothenic acid (from calcium pantothenate) 20 mg, folic acid 0.4 mg, and biotin 45 μg. Nonmedicinal ingredients: cellulose, citric acid, cornstarch, dicalcium phosphate, FD&C Yellow No. 6, lactose, magnesium stearate, mineral oil, pregelatinized starch, silicon dioxide, sodium benzoate, sodium citrate, sorbic acid, stearic acid, titanium dioxide and vitacel. Energy: <4.2 kJ (1 kcal). Tartrazine-free. Bottles of 100.

Stresstabs Plus: Each oval, orange, scored tablet, engraved "W-R" and "S4", contains: beta carotene 10 000 IU, folic acid 0.4 mg, vitamin B_1 (from thiamine mononitrate) 15 mg, riboflavin 10.2 mg, niacinamide 100 mg, pyridoxine HCl 11 mg, vitamin B_{12} (from cyanocobalamin) 6 μg, pantothenic acid (from calcium pantothenate) 28.5 mg, ascorbic acid 600 mg, vitamin E (from dl-α tocopheryl acetate) 100 IU, selenium (from sodium selenate) 50 μg, zinc (from zinc oxide) 22.5 mg. Nonmedicinal ingredients: ascorbyl palmitate, calcium carbonate, calcium phosphate dibasic, cellulose, citric acid, cornstarch, FD&C yellow No. 6, gelatin, hydrolyzed protein, lactose, magnesium stearate, mineral oil, polysorbate, silicon dioxide, sodium ascorbate, sodium benzoate, sodium citrate, sodium lauryl sulfate, sorbic acid, starch pregelatinized, stearic acid, sugar, titanium dioxide and triethyl citrate. Energy: 0.7 kJ (0.16 kcal). Tartrazine-free. Bottles of 80.

Stresstabs with Iron: Each oval, red, film-coated, scored tablet, engraved "W-R" and "S2" contains: vitamin B_1 (from thiamine monohydrate) 15 mg, riboflavin 15 mg, pyridoxine HCl 5 mg, vitamin B_{12} 12 μg, ascorbic acid 500 mg, niacinamide 100 mg, vitamin E (from dl-alpha tocopheryl acetate) 30 IU, pantothenic acid (from calcium pantothenate) 20 mg, iron (from ferrous fumarate) 27 mg, folic acid 0.4 mg, biotin 45 μg. Nonmedicinal ingredients: cellulose, citric acid, cornstarch, dicalcium phosphate, FD&C Red No. 40, FD&C Yellow No. 6, lactose, magnesium stearate, mineral oil, pregelatinized starch, silicon dioxide, sodium benzoate, sodium citrate, sorbic acid, stearic acid, titanium dioxide, vitacel and wax. Energy: <4.2 kJ (1 kcal). Tartrazine-free. Bottles of 100.

Stresstabs with Zinc: Each oval, peach, film-coated, scored tablet, engraved "W-R" and "S3" contains: vitamin B_1 (as thiamine mononitrate) 15 mg, riboflavin 15 mg, pyridoxine HCl 5 mg, vitamin B_{12} 12 μg, ascorbic acid 500 mg, niacinamide 100 mg, vitamin E (from dl-alpha tocopheryl acetate) 30 IU, pantothenic acid (from calcium pantothenate) 20 mg, copper (from cupric oxide) 3 mg, zinc (from zinc oxide) 23.9 mg, folic acid 0.4 mg, biotin 45 μg. Nonmedicinal ingredients: cellulose, citric acid, cornstarch, dicalcium phosphate, FD&C Yellow No. 6, lactose, magnesium stearate, mineral oil, pregelatinized starch, silicon dioxide, sodium benzoate, sorbic acid, stearic acid, titanium dioxide and vitacel. Energy: <4.2 kJ (1 kcal). Tartrazine-free. Bottles of 100.

SUCCINYLCHOLINE CHLORIDE INJECTION Ⓟ

Bioniche

Neuromuscular Blocking Agent

Supplied: Each mL of sterile solution contains: succinylcholine chloride (anhydrous base) 20 mg equivalent to dihydrate 22 mg. Nonmedicinal ingredients: hydrochloric acid (to adjust pH) and sodium chloride (for isotonicity). Ampuls of 5 mL, boxes of 10. Multiple dose vials of 10 and 20 mL (also contains methylparaben and propylparaben), trays of 10. Refrigerate (2 to 8°C) to prevent a loss of potency.

...For assistance in the visual identification of drug dosage forms, refer to the PRODUCT RECOGNITION SECTION.

SUDAFED® COLD & COUGH EXTRA STRENGTH
SUDAFED® COLD & FLU
SUDAFED® DECONGESTANT
SUDAFED® DECONGESTANT EXTRA STRENGTH
SUDAFED® DECONGESTANT 12 HOUR
SUDAFED® HEAD COLD AND SINUS EXTRA STRENGTH

Warner-Lambert Consumer Healthcare

Pseudoephedrine HCl—Dextromethorphan HBr—Acetaminophen
Acetaminophen—Dextromethorphan HBr—Guaifenesin—Pseudoephedrine HCl
Pseudoephedrine HCl
Pseudoephedrine HCl
Pseudoephedrine HCl
Acetaminophen—Pseudoephedrine HCl

Nasal Decongestant—Antitussive—Analgesic
Analgesic—Antitussive—Expectorant—Nasal Decongestant
Nasal Decongestant
Nasal Decongestant
Nasal Decongestant
Analgesic—Nasal Decongestant

Indications: Cold & Cough Extra Strength: For relief of nasal congestion, dry cough, headache, bodyache, fever and sore throat pain.
Cold & Flu: For relief of nasal congestion, cough, headache, bodyache, fever and sore throat pain.
Decongestant: Relief of nasal congestion associated with allergic rhinitis, acute coryza, vasomotor rhinitis, acute and subacute sinusitis, acute otitis media, postnasal drip, acute eustachian salpingitis.
Head Cold and Sinus Extra Strength: For relief of nasal congestion, sinus pain, headache and body aches.

Contraindications: Sensitivity to pseudoephedrine or any of the other components. Patients receiving or having received MAO inhibitors in the preceding 2 weeks; known hypersensitivity to pressor amines. Patients with severe hypertension or severe coronary artery disease.
Dextromethorphan: Pre-existing respiratory depression.

Warnings: Massive acetaminophen overdose can be toxic and potentially fatal. In adults, hepatotoxicity from acetaminophen is unlikely to occur with overdoses of less than 10 g ingested at one time and fatalities are unlikely to occur with overdoses of less than 15 g ingested at one time.

Precautions: As pseudoephedrine is a sympathomimetic amine, it should be used with caution in hypertensive and diabetic patients; patients with latent or clinically recognized angle closure glaucoma, coronary artery disease, congestive heart failure, prostatic hypertrophy, hyperthyroidism, urinary retention.
Geriatrics: The elderly (60 years and older) are more likely to have adverse reactions to sympathomimetics. Overdosage of sympathomimetics in this age group may cause hallucinations, convulsions, CNS depression and death.

In severe hepatic or renal dysfunction, a single dose should be given and the patient's response used as a guide to the dosage requirement for further administration.

Drug Interactions: Concomitant use of pseudoephedrine with other sympathomimetic agents, such as decongestants, appetite suppressants, and amphetamine-like psychostimulants or with MAO inhibitors, which interfere with the catabolism of sympathomimetic amines, may occasionally cause a rise in blood pressure.

The antibacterial agent, furazolidone, is known to cause a dose-related inhibition of MAO. Although there are no reports of a hypertensive crisis caused by the concurrent administration of pseudoephedrine and furazolidone, they should not be taken together.

Sudafed (cont'd)

The effect of antihypertensive drugs which interfere with sympathetic activity may be partially reversed by pseudoephedrine (e.g., bretylium, bethanidine, guanethidine, debrisoquine, methyldopa, beta and/or alpha-adrenergic-blocking agents).

Hypertension and unconsciousness following the ingestion of one Sudafed tablet by a normotensive individual has been reported and should be regarded as an extremely rare example of pseudoephedrine intolerance.

Pregnancy and *Lactation:* Use with caution. Pseudoephedrine has been reported to be excreted into breast milk of lactating women. Consult a physician before using these products.

Adverse Effects: As with other sympathomimetic amines, headache, dizziness, insomnia, tremor, confusion, CNS stimulation, muscular weakness, dry mouth, nausea, vomiting, difficulty in micturition, palpitations, tightness in the chest and syncope may be encountered. Fixed drug eruption has been reported and rarely hallucinations.

Dextromethorphan: drowsiness, dizziness, constipation, nausea, vomiting and confusion.

Guaifenesin: Nausea, gastrointestinal upset and drowsiness occur infrequently.

Overdose: Symptoms: Pseudoephedrine: Increase in pulse and respiratory rate, CNS stimulation, disorientation, headache, dry mouth, nausea and vomiting.

Dextromethorphan: In severe cases, there may be respiratory depression due to the dextromethorphan component.

Treatment: Pseudoephedrine: Gastric lavage, repeated, if necessary. Acidify the urine and institute general supportive measures. If CNS excitement is prominent, a short-acting barbiturate may be used. Catheterization of the bladder may be necessary. Alpha-adrenergic blockade may be required to treat hypertensive crises and beta-adrenergic blockade for the control of supraventricular dysrhythmias. Elimination may be accelerated by dialysis.

Dextromethorphan: In severe cases of acute poisoning, where the respiratory depressive effects of dextromethorphan may be apparent, the following may be indicated: naloxone; Adults: 400 µg s.c. Children: 5 to 10 µg/kg s.c. Depending on the patient's response, the dose can be repeated at 2 to 3 minute intervals.

Dosage: Cold & Cough Extra Strength: Adults and children 12 years and over: 1 caplet every 4 to 6 hours. Do not exceed 4 doses in 24 hours. Persons over 65 or under 12 years: use only as directed by a physician.

Cold & Flu: Adults and children 12 years and over: 2 capsules every 4 hours. Maximum daily dose: 8 capsules. Persons over 65 or under 12 years: use only as directed by a physician.

Decongestant Regular Strength: Tablets: Adults and children 12 years and over: 1 to 2 tablets every 4 to 6 hours. Children 6 to 11 years: 1 tablet every 4 to 6 hours. Do not exceed 4 doses in 24 hours. Persons over 65 or under 2 years, use only as directed by a physician.

Syrup: Adults and children 12 years and over: 10 mL every 4 to 6 hours. Children 6 to 11 years: 5 mL every 4 to 6 hours. Children 2 to 5 years: 2.5 mL every 4 to 6 hours. Do not exceed 4 doses in 24 hours. Persons over 65 or under 2 years, use only as directed by a physician.

Note: The following dosage is not detailed on the products label. Children 4 months to under 2 years: 1.25 mL every 4 to 6 hours.

Decongestant Extra Strength: Adults and children 12 years and over: 1 tablet every 4 to 6 hours. Children 6 to 11 years: ½ tablet every 4 to 6 hours. Do not exceed 4 doses in 24 hours. Persons over 65 or under 2 years, use only as directed by a physician.

Decongestant 12 Hour: Adults and children 12 years and older: 1 caplet every 12 hours. Do not exceed 2 doses in 24 hours. Not recommended for children under 12 years of age. Persons over 65: use only as directed by a physician.

Head Cold and Sinus Extra Strength: Adults and children 12 years of age and over: 1 caplet every 4 to 6 hours. Do not exceed 4 doses in 24 hours. Persons over 65 or under 12 years: use as directed by a physician.

Supplied: Cold & Cough Extra Strength: Each white, biconvex caplet, with code number "WELLCOME X2F" and score mark on reverse side, contains: pseudoephedrine HCl 60 mg, dextromethorphan HBr 30 mg and acetaminophen 500 mg. Nonmedicinal ingredients: cellulose, magnesium stearate, povidone and sodium starch glycolate. Blister packages of 12 and 24.

Cold & Flu: Each liquid filled gel cap, imprinted "SMS", contains: acetaminophen 250 mg, dextromethorphan HBr 10 mg, guaifenesin 100 mg and pseudoephedrine HCl 30 mg. Nonmedicinal ingredients: D&C yellow No. 10, FD&C red No. 40, gelatin, glycerin, polyethylene glycol, povidone, propylene glycol, sorbitol and water. Blister packages of 10.

Decongestant Regular Strength: Tablets: Each red sugar-coated tablet imprinted "SU" on one side, contains: pseudoephedrine HCl 30 mg. Nonmedicinal ingredients: acacia, calcium phosphate, carnauba wax, edible black ink, FD&C red No. 40 Lake, FD&C yellow No. 6 Lake, magnesium stearate, polysorbate, povidone, propylene glycol, shellac, sodium benzoate, starch, stearic acid, sucrose, talc and titanium dioxide. Blister packages of 12.

Syrup: Each 5 mL of clear purplish-red, syrupy liquid with a sweet raspberry flavor and odor, contains: pseudoephedrine HCl 30 mg. Nonmedicinal ingredients: citric acid, FD&C Red No. 2, glycerin, methylparaben, raspberry flavor, sodium benzoate and sucrose. Energy: 69 kJ (16.5 kcal/5 mL). Alcohol-free. Bottles of 100 mL.

Decongestant Extra Strength: Each white, biconvex tablet with code number "SUDAFED S7A" on same side as score mark, contains: pseudoephedrine HCl 60 mg. Nonmedicinal ingredients: cornstarch, lactose, magnesium stearate, povidone and stearic acid NF. Blister packages of 12 and 24. Bottles of 100.

Decongestant 12 Hour: Each white, biconvex caplet, printed "SUDAFED 12 HOUR", contains: pseudoephedrine HCl 120 mg. Nonmedicinal ingredients: celluloses, edible blue ink, magnesium stearate, polyethylene glycol, povidone, titanium dioxide and wax. Blister packages of 10 and 20.

Head Cold and Sinus Extra Strength: Each white caplet coded "WELLCOME" on the top side and "A7C" on each side of the score on the reverse side contains: acetaminophen 500 mg and pseudoephedrine HCl 60 mg. Nonmedicinal ingredients: cellulose, magnesium stearate, povidone and sodium starch glycolate (potato). Blister packages of 12 and 24.

All preparations should be stored at 15 to 25°C and protected from light.

(Shown in Product Recognition Section)

SUFENTA® Ⓝ

Janssen-Ortho

Sufentanil Citrate

Opioid Analgesic—Adjunct to Anesthesia

Pharmacology: Sufentanil is an opioid analgesic. The analgesic potency of sufentanil is approximately 5 to 7 times that of fentanyl. Dosage requirements for equianalgesic effect will be ⅕ to ⅐ those of fentanyl on a mg/kg basis.

Assays of histamine in patients administered sufentanil have shown no elevation in plasma histamine levels and no indication of histamine release.

I.V. Use: At i.v. doses of up to 8 µg/kg, sufentanil provides profound analgesia; at doses ≥8 µg/kg, sufentanil produces a deep level of anesthesia. Sufentanil produces a dose related attenuation of catecholamine release, particularly norepinephrine.

I.V. sufentanil has an immediate onset of action, with a distribution of 0.72 minutes, redistribution of 13.7 minutes and an elimination half-life of 148 minutes. It is rapidly and extensively metabolized into a large number of inactive metabolites that are excreted with the urine and feces. The liver and small intestine are the major sites of biotransformation; oxidative O- and N-dealkylation are the primary metabolic pathways. Approximately 80% of the administered dose is excreted within 24 hours and only 2% of the dose is eliminated as unchanged drug. Plasma protein binding of sufentanil is approximately 92.5%. The pharmacokinetics of sufentanil can be described as a three-compartment model, with relatively limited accumulation and rapid elimination from tissue storage sites, allowing for relatively more rapid recovery than with fentanyl.

At i.v. dosages of ≥8 µg/kg, sufentanil produces hypnosis and anesthesia without the use of additional anesthetic induction agents. A deep level of anesthesia is maintained at these dosages, as demonstrated by EEG patterns. Dosages of up to 25 µg/kg attenuate the sympathetic response to surgical stress and maintain cardiovascular stability. The sympathetic response is blocked at doses of sufentanil of 25 to 30 µg/kg, with dependable cardiovascular stability, infrequent bradycardia and preservation of myocardial oxygen balance.

Pancuronium may produce a dose-dependent elevation in heart rate and blood pressure during sufentanil-oxygen anesthesia that is not suppressed by the minimal effects of high doses of sufentanil on cardiac function, heart rate or blood pressure. The vagolytic effect of pancuronium may be reduced in patients administered nitrous oxide together with sufentanil. The use of moderate doses of pancuronium or of a less vagolytic neuromuscular blocking agent should maintain stable lower heart rate and blood pressure.

In patients administered high doses of sufentanil, dosage requirements for neuromuscular blocking agents are generally lower as compared to patients given fentanyl or halothane, and comparable to patients given enflurane or isoflurane.

Bradycardia is seen infrequently in patients administered sufentanil-oxygen anesthesia. The use of nitrous oxide with high doses of sufentanil may decrease mean arterial pressure, heart rate and cardiac output.

In one study of patients undergoing craniotomy, sufentanil at 20 µg/kg has been shown to provide more adequate reduction in intracranial volume than equivalent doses of fentanyl, based upon requirements for furosemide and anesthesia supplementation. During carotid endarterectomy, sufentanil produced EEG patterns and reductions in cerebral blood flow and oxygen utilization comparable to those of fentanyl.

The intraoperative use of sufentanil at anesthetic dosages maintains cardiac output, with a slight reduction in systemic vascular resistance during the initial postoperative period. Requirements for postoperative analgesics are generally reduced in patients administered moderate or high doses of sufentanil as compared to patients given inhalation agents.

Decreased respiratory drive and increased airway resistance occur with increased doses of sufentanil. The duration and degree of respiratory depression are dose-related when sufentanil is used at subanesthetic dosages. At high doses, a pronounced decrease in pulmonary exchange and apnea may be produced.

Epidural Use: Epidural sufentanil produces spinal analgesia of rapid onset, within 5 to 10 minutes and moderate duration, generally 4 to 6 hours. The onset and duration of analgesia appear to be dose-related.

Peak plasma concentrations following single epidural doses of sufentanil are reached within 10 minutes and are 4 to 6 times lower than those after i.v. administration. Systemic absorption within the first 3 hours after epidural administration is approximately ⅓ to ½ that of an i.v. bolus. Vascular uptake of sufentanil after high thoracic (T3-4) administration is 3 to 4 times lower than after mid-thoracic to lumbar epidural injection. Coadministration of epinephrine reduces systemic availability of sufentanil, especially in the first hours after injection. Time to peak plasma concentrations and maximum plasma concentrations increase with repeated epidural doses of sufentanil.

Mean sufentanil concentrations in CSF exceeded 2 ng/mL within a few minutes after an epidural injection of 75 µg; peak concentrations in the CSF occurred within 5 to 90 minutes. Thereafter, the decay of sufentanil concentrations in the CSF was biphasic with an average sufentanil terminal half-life of 165 minutes compared to 355 minutes in plasma.

During labor and vaginal delivery, the addition of 10 to 30 µg sufentanil to bupivacaine (0.125% to 0.25%) provided analgesia of better quality and longer duration versus bupivacaine (0.25%) alone. Apgar scores and neurobehavioral scores of neonates were not affected by the epidural administration of sufentanil to women in labor.

Placental transfer of sufentanil was investigated in women undergoing caesarean section. Within 30 to 55 minutes of epidural doses of 22 to 38 µg sufentanil, maternal plasma concentrations varied from ≤0.02 to 0.16 ng/mL; neonatal concentrations were generally below 0.02 ng/mL with measurable levels up to 0.9 ng/mL found in only a few neonates. Fetal plasma concentrations rapidly equilibrate with maternal concentrations. Individual umbilical vein:maternal plasma concentration ratios averaged 0.4. Plasma protein binding of sufentanil, related to the α_1 acid glycoprotein level, was 90.7% in mothers and 79.3% in neonates.

Indications: I.V. Administration: As a primary anesthetic agent for the induction and maintenance of anesthesia with 100% oxygen in patients undergoing major surgical procedures, such as cardiovascular surgery or neurosurgical procedures in the sitting position, for whom myocardial or cerebral oxygen imbalance would be particularly detrimental or for whom extended postoperative ventilation is anticipated.

As an analgesic adjunct at doses up to 8 µg/kg in the maintenance of balanced general anesthesia for major surgical procedures.

Epidural Administration: For the postoperative management of pain following general surgery, thoracic or orthopedic procedures and caesarean section. As an analgesic adjunct to epidural bupivacaine during labor and vaginal delivery.

Contraindications: In patients with known hypersensitivity to fentanyl or to other morphinomimetics.

I.V. use in labor or before clamping of the cord during caesarian section is not recommended due to the possibility of respiratory depression in the newborn infant. This, in contrast to the epidural use in labor, during which sufentanil in doses up to 30 μg does not influence the condition of the mother or the newborn.

As with other opiates administered epidurally, sufentanil should not be given to patients exhibiting the following: severe hemorrhage or shock; septicemia; local infection at the site of proposed puncture; disturbances in blood morphology and/or anticoagulant therapy or other concomitant drug therapy or medical conditions which could contraindicate the technique of epidural administration.

Warnings: Sufentanil should be administered only by persons specifically trained in the use of i.v. anesthetics and management of the respiratory effects of potent opioids and, when administered epidurally, persons specifically trained in the techniques and patient management associated with epidural administration.

Complete resuscitation equipment and an opioid antagonist should be readily available whenever sufentanil is used.

I.V. administration or inadvertent intravascular injection during epidural administration of sufentanil may cause skeletal muscle rigidity, particularly of the truncal muscles. The incidence of muscular rigidity associated with i.v. sufentanil can be reduced by: administration of up to ¼ of the full paralyzing dose of a nondepolarizing neuromuscular blocking agent just prior to administration at dosages of up to 8 μg/kg; incremental administration in divided doses of a full paralyzing dose of a neuromuscular blocking agent following loss of the eyelash reflex during induction with thiopental when sufentanil has been used in doses up to 8 μg/kg in major surgical procedures; simultaneous administration of sufentanil and a full paralyzing dose of a neuromuscular blocking agent when sufentanil is used in anesthetic doses (above 8 μg/kg).

The neuromuscular blocking agent used should be compatible with the patient's cardiovascular status. Adequate facilities should be available for postoperative monitoring and ventilation of patients administered anesthetic doses of sufentanil. It is essential that these facilities be fully equipped to handle all degrees of respiratory depression. Dosages above 1 μg/kg sufentanil/hour of surgery frequently produce respiratory depression. In a clinical study involving 616 patients, 69 of the 86 patients (80%) who required naloxone in the immediate postoperative period had received a sufentanil dosage in excess of 1 μg/kg/hour.

Nonepileptic myoclonic movements can occur.

Precautions: General: The initial dose should be appropriately reduced in elderly and debilitated patients. The effect of the initial dose should be considered in determining supplemental doses.

Vital signs should be monitored routinely.

Nitrous oxide may produce cardiovascular depression when given with high doses of sufentanil (see Pharmacology).

High doses of pancuronium may produce increases in heart rate during sufentanil-oxygen anesthesia. Bradycardia and possibly asystole can occur if the patient has received an insufficient amount of anticholinergic or when sufentanil is combined with nonvagolytic muscle relaxants. Bradycardia can be treated with atropine.

Head Injuries: Sufentanil may obscure the clinical course of patients with head injuries. In patients with compromised intracerebral compliance, the use of rapid bolus injections should be avoided; in such patients the transient decrease in mean arterial pressure has occasionally been accompanied by a short-lasting reduction of the cerebral perfusion pressure.

Impaired Respiration: Sufentanil should be used with caution in patients with pulmonary disease, decreased respiratory reserve or potentially compromised respiration. In such patients, opioids may additionally decrease respiratory drive and increase airway resistance.

During anesthesia, impaired respiration can be managed by assisted or controlled respiration. As with all potent opioids, profound analgesia is accompanied by respiratory depression and diminished sensitivity to CO_2 stimulation which may persist into or recur in the postoperative period. Appropriate postoperative monitoring should be employed to ensure that adequate spontaneous breathing is established and maintained prior to patient discharge from the recovery area.

Respiratory depression caused by opioid analgesics can be reversed by opioid antagonists such as naloxone. Because the duration of respiratory depression produced by sufentanil may last longer than the duration of the opioid antagonist action, appropriate surveillance should be maintained.

Patients should be closely monitored for at least 2 hours following each administration of an epidural injection of sufentanil as early respiratory depression may occur.

Opioids may induce hypotension, especially in hypovolemic patients. Appropriate measures to maintain a stable arterial pressure should be taken.

Patients on chronic opioid therapy or with a history of opioid abuse, may require increased amounts of sufentanil.

Careful titration of dosage may be required in patients with conditions such as uncontrolled hypothyroidism or alcoholism (see Drug Interactions; alcohol can potentiate the respiratory depression of opioids). In such cases, prolonged postoperative monitoring is required.

Drug Interactions: Interactions with other CNS Depressants: An additive effect with sufentanil may be exhibited in patients receiving barbiturates, tranquilizers, opioids, general anesthetics or other CNS depressants (e.g., alcohol). In such cases of combined treatment, the dose of sufentanil and/or these agents should be reduced.

MAO Inhibitors: It is usually recommended to discontinue MAO inhibitors 2 weeks prior to any surgical or anesthetic procedure.

Interactions with Beta-Blockers: As with all opioids, a decrease in heart rate and/or blood pressure may be seen when sufentanil is administered to patients on beta-blocker medication.

Table I—Sufenta

I.V. Use: Adult Dosage Range Chart

Administration with Nitrous Oxide/Oxygen

Indication	Approximate Duration of Anesthesia	Initial Dosage	Maintenance Increments (included in total dosage)	Total Dosage (A cumulative dosage in the range of 0.5-1.0 μg/kg/hour is recommended)
As an adjunct to major surgery	at least 1 hour	A minimum of 0.5 μg/kg is necessary to control or abolish cardiovascular responses to laryngoscopy and intubation. The initial dosage should represent at least 75% of the total dosage administered during the case.	**10-25 μg** as needed when movement and/or changes in vital signs indicate surgical stress or lightening of analgesia. Supplemental doses should be individualized and adjusted to the remaining operative time anticipated.	**0.5-2 μg/kg** administered as an analgesic adjunct with nitrous oxide/oxygen in patients undergoing general surgery in which endotracheal intubation and mechanical ventilation are required.
As an adjunct to more complicated major surgery	at least 2 hours		**25-50 μg** as determined by changes in vital signs that indicate stress or lightening of analgesia. Supplemental dosages should be individualized and adjusted to the remaining operative time anticipated.	**2-8 μg/kg** administered as an analgesic adjunct with nitrous oxide/oxygen in patients undergoing more complicated major surgical procedures. At dosages in this range, sufentanil has been shown to attenuate sympathetic reflex activity in response to surgical stimuli, maintain cardiovascular stability and provide relatively rapid recovery.

Administration with 100% Oxygen

Indication	Initial Dosage	Maintenance Increments (included in total dosage)	Total Dosage
As a primary anesthetic agent	The initial dosage should be individualized with due consideration given to patient status, concomitant medications, and anticipated level of surgical stimulation. See total dosage guidelines.	**25-50 μg** as determined by changes in vital signs that indicate stress and lightening of anesthesia.	**8-30 μg/kg** (anesthetic dosages) administered with 100% oxygen and a muscle relaxant. Sufentanil has been found to produce sleep at dosages ≥8 μg/kg and to maintain a deep level of anesthesia without the use of additional anesthetic agents. At dosages in this range of up to 25 μg/kg, catecholamine release is attenuated. High dosages are indicated in patients undergoing surgical procedures such as cardiovascular surgery and neurosurgery in the sitting position, in whom myocardial or cerebral oxygen Imbalance would be detrimental. Postoperative mechanical ventilation and observation are essential at these dosages due to extended postoperative respiratory depression.

Note: The suggested i.v. administration rate is 250 to 300 μg/min.

Hepatic or Renal Impairment: In patients with liver or kidney dysfunction, sufentanil should be administered with caution due to the importance of these organs in its metabolism and excretion of sufentanil.

Pregnancy: Sufentanil has been shown to have an embryocidal effect in rats and rabbits when given in doses 2.5 times the upper human dose for a period of 10 days to over 30 days. These effects were probably due to maternal toxicity (decreased food consumption with increased mortality) following prolonged administration of the drug. No evidence of teratogenic effects have been observed after its administration of sufentanil in rats or rabbits. Since the safety of sufentanil in pregnant women has not been established, this drug should be used in pregnancy only if the expected benefits are considered to outweigh any potential risks.

Labor and Delivery: Although the use of epidurally administered sufentanil is indicated for labor and delivery (see Indications and Dosage), caution should be exercised in the presence of fetal distress. The use of i.v. sufentanil in labor and delivery is not recommended (see Contraindications).

Lactation: It is not known whether this drug is excreted in human milk. Because fentanyl analogues are excreted in human milk, caution should be exercised when sufentanil is administered to a nursing woman.

Children: The safety and efficacy of sufentanil in children, particularly under 2 years of age, has been documented only in a limited number of cases. Likewise, documented use of epidural sufentanil in pediatric cases is limited.

Sufenta (cont'd)

Drug Abuse and Dependence: Sufentanil can produce drug dependence of the morphine type and, therefore, has the potential for being abused.

Occupational Hazards: Patients should be advised to allow sufficient time to elapse before operating a car or heavy machinery.

Adverse Effects: I.V. Use: The most frequent adverse reactions in 320 patients administered sufentanil i.v. were: hypotension (7%), hypertension (3%), chest wall rigidity (3%), bradycardia (3%).

Other adverse reactions that may occur (reported incidence of less than 1%) are:

Cardiovascular: tachycardia, arrhythmia.

Gastrointestinal: nausea, vomiting.

Respiratory: apnea, postoperative respiratory depression, bronchospasm.

Dermatological: itching.

CNS: chills.

Miscellaneous: intraoperative muscle movement.

Postmarketing adverse reports include: laryngospasm, dizziness, myoclonic movements, and respiratory depression.

Allergic reactions and asystole have been reported; but since several drugs were co-administered during anesthesia, it is uncertain whether there is a causal relationship to the drug.

Epidural Use: The frequency of adverse experiences associated with the use of epidural sufentanil was evaluated in 1 478 postoperative patients and 14 467 parturients. The most frequently reported adverse experiences were somnolence or sedation, pruritus, nausea, vomiting and urinary retention.

During clinical trials, slow respiratory rate (<10 breaths/min) and apneic periods were noted in 3.5% and 2.5% of postoperative patients, respectively. These episodes developed early after drug administration and were resolved within 1 hour. Concomitant use of epinephrine may reduce the incidence and severity of respiratory depression. No respiratory depressive episodes were observed in patients receiving epidural sufentanil during labor and delivery.

Other observed adverse experiences include:

Cardiovascular: hypotension (2%).

CNS: motor block (18%, labor patients only), dizziness (2%), euphoria (2%).

Urinary system disorders: urinary incontinence (1%).

Miscellaneous: fever (1%), shivering (2%), pain at injection site (1%), miosis (1%).

Adverse experiences that occurred in less than 1% of patients are: bradycardia, hypopnea, rash, headache, confusion.

Overdose: Symptoms: Overdosage would be manifested by an extension of the pharmacological actions (see Pharmacology) as with other potent opioid analgesics. Depending on the individual sensitivity, the clinical picture is determined primarily by the degree of respiratory depression, which varies from bradypnea to apnea. The i.v. LD_{50} of sufentanil in male rats is 12.5 mg/kg.

Treatment: I.V. administration of an opioid antagonist such as naloxone should be employed as a specific antidote to manage respiratory depression. The duration of respiratory depression following overdosage with sufentanil may be longer than the duration of action of the opioid antagonist. Additional doses of the latter may therefore be required.

Administration of an opioid antagonist should not preclude more immediate countermeasures. In the event of overdosage, oxygen should be administered and ventilation assisted or controlled as indicated for hypoventilation or apnea. A patent airway must be maintained, and a nasopharyngeal airway or endotracheal tube may be indicated. If depressed respiration is associated with muscular rigidity, a neuromuscular blocking agent may be required to facilitate assisted or controlled respiration. I.V. fluids and vasopressors for the treatment of hypotension and other supportive measures may be employed.

Dosage: The dosage should be individualized in each case according to body weight, physical status, underlying pathological condition, use of other drugs, and type of surgical procedure and anesthesia. In obese patients (more than 20% above ideal total body weight), the dosage should be determined on the basis of lean body weight. Dosage should be reduced in elderly and debilitated patients (see Precautions). Vital signs should be monitored routinely.

I.V. Use: See Table I (on previous page) for use by i.v. injection: 1) in doses of up to 8 μg/kg as an analgesic adjunct to general anesthesia. 2) in doses ≥8 μg/kg as a primary anesthetic agent for induction and maintenance of anesthesia with 100% oxygen.

Children: For induction and maintenance of anesthesia in children less than 12 years undergoing cardiovascular surgery, an anesthetic dose of 10 to 25 μg/kg administered with 100% oxygen is generally recommended. Supplemental dosages of 25 to 50 μg are recommended for maintenance based on response to initial dose and as determined by changes in vital signs indicating surgical stress or lightening of anesthesia. Since experience with the use of sufentanil particularly in the young age group is limited, anesthetists should be guided by progressive experience with the use of the drug in children.

Premedication: The selection of preanesthetic medications should be based upon the needs of the individual patient.

Neuromuscular Blocking Agents: The neuromuscular blocking agent selected should be compatible with the patient's condition, taking into account the hemodynamic effects of a particular muscle relaxant and the degree of skeletal muscle relaxation required (see Pharmacology, Warnings and Precautions).

In patients administered high (anesthetic) doses of sufentanil, it is essential that qualified personnel and adequate facilities are available for the management of postoperative respiratory depression (see Warnings and Precautions).

Epidural Use: Proper placement of the needle or catheter in the epidural space should be verified prior to sufentanil injection to preclude inadvertent intravascular or intrathecal administration. If analgesia is inadequate, the placement and integrity of the catheter should be verified prior to the administration of any additional epidural medication.

Postoperative Management of Pain: An initial dose of 30 to 60 μg sufentanil in 10 mL normal saline may be expected to provide adequate pain relief for up to 4 to 6 hours. Additional boluses of up to 25 μg sufentanil may be administered at not less than 1 hour intervals if there is evidence of lightening of analgesia.

Analgesic Adjunct during Labor and Delivery: The recommended initial dose for sufentanil, administered with 0.125% to 0.25% bupivacaine, is 10 μg in 10 mL normal saline. If required, 2 subsequent injections of the combination may be given; supplemental doses should be separated by intervals of at least 1 hour. It is recommended that the total sufentanil dose administered not exceed 30 μg.

Supplied: Each mL of sterile, preservative-free aqueous solution contains: sufentanil citrate equivalent to 50 μg of sufentanil base and water for i.v. and epidural injection. pH range of 3.5 to 6.0. Ampuls of 1 mL and 5 mL. Packages of 10. Store at controlled room temperature (15 to 25°C). Protect from light.

Reviewed 1999

SULCRATE® Ⓟ
SULCRATE® SUSPENSION PLUS Ⓟ

Hoechst Marion Roussel

Sucralfate

Gastroduodenal Cytoprotective Agent

Pharmacology: Sucralfate exerts a generalized gastric cytoprotective effect by enhancing natural mucosal defense mechanisms. Studies conducted in animals and clinical trials in humans have demonstrated that sucralfate can protect the gastric mucosa against various irritants such as alcohol, ASA, hydrochloric acid, sodium hydroxide or sodium taurocholate.

In addition, sucralfate has been demonstrated to have a greater affinity for ulcerated gastric or duodenal mucosa than for nonulcerated mucosa.

Sucralfate produces an adherent and cytoprotective barrier at the ulcer site. This barrier protects the ulcer site from the potential ulcerogenic properties of acid, pepsin and bile. Furthermore, sucralfate blocks acid diffusion across the sucralfate protein barrier and also complexes directly with pepsin and bile.

Pharmacokinetics: The action of sucralfate is nonsystemic as the drug is only minimally absorbed from the gastrointestinal tract. The minute amounts of the sulfated disaccharide which are absorbed are primarily excreted in the urine.

Each g of sucralfate contains approximately 200 mg of aluminum. The aluminum moiety can dissociate at low pH and aluminum release in the stomach can be expected; however, aluminum is poorly absorbed from the intact gastrointestinal tract. Following administration of 1 g of sucralfate (tablets or suspension) 4 times a day to individuals with normal renal function, approximately 0.001% to 0.017% of sucralfate's aluminum content is absorbed and excreted in the urine. This results in an aluminum load of between 0.008 and 0.136 mg following a 4 g daily dose. Individuals with normal renal function excrete absorbed aluminum and can respond to an increased aluminum load by increasing urinary excretion. These values were determined in individuals with intact gastrointestinal mucosa. Available evidence does not indicate that absorption of aluminum would be different in individuals with ulcerated gastrointestinal mucosa.

Experiments have shown that sucralfate is not an antacid.

Indications: Tablets: For the treatment of duodenal and nonmalignant gastric ulcer.

Also indicated for the prophylaxis of duodenal ulcer recurrence.

Suspension: For the treatment of duodenal ulcer and for the prophylaxis of gastrointestinal hemorrhage due to stress ulceration in critically ill patients.

Contraindications: There are no known contraindications to the use of sucralfate. However, the physician should read the Warnings section when considering the use of this drug in pregnant or pediatric patients, or patients of childbearing potential.

Warnings: *Pregnancy:* There has been no experience to date with the use of sucralfate in pregnant women. Therefore, sucralfate should not be used in pregnant women or women of childbearing potential unless, in the judgment of the physician, the anticipated benefits outweigh the potential risk.

Children: Clinical experience in children is limited. Therefore, sucralfate therapy cannot be recommended for children under 18 unless, in the judgment of the physician, anticipated benefits outweigh the potential risk.

Precautions: General: The following should be taken into account before treating patients with sucralfate:

Recurrence may be observed in patients after a successful course of treatment for gastric or duodenal ulcers. While treatment with sucralfate can result in complete healing of the ulcer, a successful course of treatment with sucralfate should not be expected to alter the underlying cause of ulcer disease.

Proper diagnosis is important since symptomatic response to sucralfate therapy does not rule out the presence of a gastric malignancy.

Drug Interactions: Antacids should not be taken within half an hour before or after sucralfate intake because of the possibility of decreased binding of sucralfate with the gastroduodenal mucosa as a consequence of a change of intragastric pH.

Animal studies have shown that simultaneous administration of sucralfate with tetracycline, phenytoin or cimetidine results in a statistically significant reduction in the bioavailability of these agents. Cimetidine absorption was not reduced in humans. In clinical trials, the concomitant administration of sucralfate reduced the bioavailability of digoxin.

These interactions appear to be nonsystemic and to result from the binding of sucralfate to the concomitantly administered drug in the gastrointestinal tract. In all cases, complete bioavailability was restored by separating the administration of sucralfate from that of the other agent by 2 hours.

Sucralfate, administered respectively 30 and 60 minutes before ASA or ibuprofen did not alter the bioavailability of these agents. In a study comparing the prior administration of a single dose of sucralfate tablets on the bioavailability of naproxen, indomethacin or ketoprofen versus administration in the absence of sucralfate, it was shown that the total amount of these drugs absorbed was not altered; however, the peak concentration of each was reduced, and the time to reach peak concentration was delayed. A single dose of the Sulcrate Suspension Plus administered one-half hour before naproxen had a similar effect on the bioavailability of naproxen.

The physician should consider the possible clinical implications of these interactions. It is recommended to separate the administration of any drug from that of sucralfate when the potential for altered bioavailability is felt to be critical to the effectiveness of that drug.

Unless specified, the above data are based on studies carried out with Sulcrate tablets.

Chronic Renal Failure: Dialyzed Patients: Sucralfate should be used with caution in patients with chronic renal failure. When sucralfate is administered orally, small amounts of aluminum are absorbed from the gastrointestinal tract (see Pharmacology). Existing evidence indicates that patients with normal renal function receiving the recommended doses of sucralfate adequately excrete aluminum in the urine; however, patients with chronic renal failure or those receiving dialysis have impaired excretion of absorbed aluminum, and in these individuals, aluminum is known to accumulate in serum and in tissues. In particular, dialysis patients are at greater risk as aluminum does not cross dialysis membranes of the dialysis machine since it is bound to plasma proteins, most notably albumin and transferrin.

In patients with chronic renal failure undergoing dialysis, aluminum-related toxicity (encephalopathy and aluminum-related bone disease), associated with the administration of sucralfate and/or other sources of aluminum has been reported. Consideration should therefore be given to the total daily load of aluminum before administering sucralfate in combination with other aluminum-containing medications, such as aluminum-containing antacids.

Nondialyzed Patients: In a study of 6 nondialyzed chronic renal failure patients with glomerular filtration rates ranging from approximately 10 to 40% of normal, sucralfate administered at a dose of 1 g 4 times daily for 3 weeks resulted in elevated serum aluminum concentrations which plateaued at approximately 23 μg/L after 1 week of treatment from a pretreatment level of 3 μg/L. Renal aluminum clearance increased in relation to the increase in serum levels and returned to baseline within 2 weeks following discontinuation of sucralfate as did serum aluminum concentrations. No adverse events were reported in these patients.

These data indicate that the use of sucralfate in nondialyzed chronic renal failure patients requires physician discretion since the excretion of absorbed aluminum may be impaired in these individuals.

Adverse Effects: Tablets: Very few side effects have been reported. They are mild in nature and have only exceptionally led to discontinuation of therapy.

The main complaint has been constipation ranging from 1.7 to 3.3% of patients.

Other side effects reported included diarrhea, nausea, gastric discomfort, indigestion, dry mouth, skin rash, pruritus, back pain, dizziness, sleepiness and vertigo.

Suspension Plus: In a placebo-controlled clinical trial involving 184 patients, the adverse event rates were similar to that seen in the placebo group (Sulcrate Suspension Plus 10.2% vs placebo 7.4%). The most common adverse event was headache (3.4%), followed by nausea (2.3%), abdominal pain (2.3%), constipation (1.1%), diarrhea (1.1%), and urticaria (1.1%). Only headache, abdominal pain and nausea had a higher incidence in the Sulcrate Suspension Plus group relative to placebo.

See Precautions for information on the potential for aluminum toxicity in dialyzed chronic renal failure patients.

Overdose: Symptoms and Treatment: Overdosage has never been observed and appears to be unlikely since, using maximal doses of up to 12 g/kg/body weight in a variety of animal species, a lethal dose could not be established.

Overdosage is likely to be associated with symptoms similar to those described in Adverse Effects, such as constipation. These should be treated symptomatically.

Dosage: Tablets: Duodenal and gastric ulcers: Adults: 1 g 4 times daily, 1 hour before meals and at bedtime, on an empty stomach. For duodenal ulcer, sulcralfate may also be administered as 2 g twice daily, on waking and at bedtime on an empty stomach.

In duodenal ulcers, while healing with sucralfate often occurs within 2 to 4 weeks, treatment should be continued for a maximum of 8 to 12 weeks unless healing has been demonstrated by x-ray and/or endoscopic examination.

In the case of gastric ulcers, an alternative treatment should be considered if no objective improvement is observed following 6 weeks of sucralfate therapy. However, patients with a large gastric ulcer that has demonstrated a progressive healing tendency may require an additional 6 weeks of treatment.

For the prophylaxis of duodenal ulcer recurrence, the recommended dosage is 1 g twice daily, on an empty stomach. Treatment may be continued for up to 1 year.

For relief of pain, antacids may be added to the treatment. However, antacids should not be taken within ½ hour before or after sucralfate intake.

Suspension Plus (1 g/5 mL): Adults: (Acute) duodenal ulcer: 2 g (10 mL) twice a day on waking and at bedtime on an empty stomach.

Prophylaxis of gastrointestinal hemorrhage due to stress ulceration: 1 g (5 mL) orally or via nasogastric tube 4 to 6 times a day. To prevent clogging of the nasogastric tube flush with 10 mL of water following each administration.

The duration of treatment for prophylaxis of stress ulceration must be individually determined. Treatment should be continued for as long as one or more of the risk factors for stress ulceration is present but normally not for more than 14 days.

Duration of continuous treatment in patients with chronic renal failure receiving dialysis should be evaluated by periodic monitoring of serum aluminum levels, due to the possibility of aluminum accumulation in these patients (see Precautions). According to information widely available in the literature, patients with serum aluminum concentrations that approach 100 μg/L should be carefully monitored for symptoms of aluminum toxicity and treatment should be discontinued if such symptoms appear.

There is no evidence to indicate that patients with chronic renal failure, who do not require dialysis, are at risk of developing aluminum toxicity while receiving the recommended doses of sucralfate. Physician discretion should be exercised when considering the duration of treatment (see Precautions).

Supplied: Tablets: Each white, capsule-shaped, compressed, biconvex tablet, embossed on one side with SULCRATE and the other side with HMR, contains: sucralfate 1 g. Nonmedicinal ingredients: carboxymethylcellulose, cellulose, hydrogenated vegetable oil and magnesium stearate. Gluten-free. Bottles of 100 and 500. Store and dispense in well-closed containers.

Suspension Plus: Each 5 mL of white, creamy, caramel-flavored suspension contains: sucralfate 1 g. Nonmedicinal ingredients: artificial caramel flavor, glycerin, purified water, sodium methylparaben, sodium phosphate, sodium propylparaben and xanthan gum. Bottles of 500 mL. Shake well before using. Store at room temperature. Avoid freezing.

(Shown in Product Recognition Section)

SULFACET-R® 🅿

Dermik Laboratories Canada

Sulfacetamide Sodium—Sulfur

Acne Therapy

Indications: Severe acne vulgaris, seborrheic dermatitis, bacterial folliculitis and related conditions.

Contraindications: Hypersensitivity to the sulfonamides as indicated by a previous toxic reaction to them (e.g. agranulocytosis, acute hemolytic anemia, purpura hemorrhagica, drug fever, jaundice, or contact dermatitis).

Precautions: Sulfur may cause reddening and scaling of the epidermis, but if undue skin irritation develops or increases, discontinue use and consult a physician. Keep away from eyes.

Dosage: For external use only. Keep away from eyes. Shake lotion well. Apply a small quantity with fingertips 2 or 3 times daily.

Supplied: Each mL of lotion contains: Sodium sulfacetamide 10% w/v, colloidal sulfur 5% w/v. Nonmedicinal ingredients: 2-bromo-2-nitropropane-1,3-diol (Bronopol), attapulgite, butylparaben, diethanolamine, hydroxyethyl cellulose, iron oxides, lauric myristic, methylparaben, naphthalene sulfonic acid, polyethylene glycol, polyethylene glycol monolaurate, precipitated sulfur, propylene glycol, purified water, silicone emulsion, sodium chloride, sodium metabisulfite, talc, titanium dioxide, xanthan gum and zinc oxide. Bottles of 25 g with color blender.

SULFAPYRIDINE 🅿

General Monograph, CPhA

Antibacterial Sulfonamide

> This monograph has been compiled by CPhA. It may contain information different from that approved by Therapeutic Products Programme, Health Canada, and the pharmaceutical manufacturers' approval has not been requested.

Pharmacology: Sulfapyridine is a sulfonamide antibacterial agent. Sulfonamides are structural analogs of para-aminobenzoic acid and exert their bacteriostatic activity by interfering with folic acid metabolism and ultimately with DNA synthesis in susceptible bacteria. Because of its toxicity (see Warnings), sulfapyridine is used only for dermatitis herpetiformis and related skin disorders when alternate treatment cannot be used.

Pharmacokinetics: Sulfapyridine is slowly and incompletely absorbed from the gastrointestinal tract. It is metabolized in the liver and excreted renally with up to 80% being reabsorbed by the renal tubules. Sulfapyridine readily crosses the placenta and is distributed into CSF and breast milk. It reaches its peak concentration within 4 to 6 hours, has a half-life of 6 to 14 hours and is approximately 50% protein bound.

Indications: As a second-line agent in the treatment of dermatitis herpetiformis in patients who fail to respond to dapsone.

Sulfapyridine is also used as a second-line agent in the treatment of subcorneal pustular dermatosis, bullous pemphigoid and pyoderma gangrenosum.

Contraindications: History of hypersensitivity to sulfonamides, furosemide, thiazide diuretics, sulfonylureas or carbonic anhydrase inhibitors.

Sulfapyridine should not be used in: patients with glucose-6-dehydrogenase (G6PD) deficiency as it may cause hemolytic anemia in this group; patients with porphyria as sulfapyridine may precipitate an acute attack; patients with blood dyscrasias.

Warnings: Fatalities have occurred due to severe reactions such as Stevens-Johnson syndrome, toxic epidermal necrolysis, fulminant hepatic necrosis, anaphylaxis and blood dyscrasias such as agranulocytosis and aplastic anemia. Therapy should be stopped at the first sign of skin rash or any serious adverse effect.

Sulfapyridine is known to cause oligospermia and infertility in men.

Precautions: Patients taking sulfapyridine should be advised to maintain adequate fluid intake to prevent crystalluria.

Periodic CBCs may be required for patients on long-term therapy, because of the risk of blood dyscrasias.

Sulfapyridine should be used with caution in patients with impaired renal or hepatic function.

Patients taking sulfapyridine should be monitored for early signs of serious reactions (e.g., sore throat, rash, arthralgia, purpura, shortness of breath).

Drug Interactions: Anticoagulants, anticonvulsants, methotrexate or sulfonylureas may be displaced from plasma proteins and their metabolism may be inhibited by sulfapyridine, leading to increased or prolonged therapeutic and toxic effects. Dosage adjustments may be necessary.

Bone Marrow Depressants or Hepatotoxic Drugs: Concurrent use with sulfapyridine may lead to increased toxic effects.

Drug-Laboratory Test Interactions: Administration of sulfapyridine within 3 days prior to a bentiromide test (for pancreatic insufficiency) may invalidate the results as sulfapyridine is also metabolized to arylamines.

Pregnancy: Sulfapyridine readily crosses the placenta and is known to cause kernicterus in neonates. Its use is not recommended during pregnancy.

Lactation: Sulfapyridine is excreted in breast milk in significant amounts (30 to 60% of serum concentrations). Its use in nursing mothers is not recommended due to the risk of kernicterus in the infant; there is also a risk of hemolytic anemia in infants with G6PD deficiency.

Adverse Effects: Gastrointestinal: Diarrhea, anorexia, nausea and vomiting are common. Hypersensitivity: Skin rash, pruritis, fever and photosensitivity occur more frequently. Hypersensitivity reactions reported less frequently include urticaria, erythema nodosum, Stevens-Johnson syndrome, Lyell's syndrome, Behcet's syndrome, toxic epidermal necrolysis, serum sickness syndrome and hepatitis. Anaphylaxis has been reported rarely (see Warnings).

Endocrine: goiter or thyroid function disturbance.

Hematologic: leukopenia, thrombocytopenia, agranulocytosis, aplastic anemia.

Renal: crystalluria, hematuria.

Overdose: Symptoms: Gastrointestinal symptoms such as nausea and vomiting are likely to occur. Hypersenstivity reactions may also occur (see Adverse Effects).

Treatment: If anaphylaxis occurs, management includes establishment of an open airway, administration of epinephrine and diphenhydramine, cardiac monitoring. Bronchodilators or inotropes may also be required.

Induction of emesis is indicated if the patient is conscious. Activated charcoal combined with a cathartic may prevent further absorption.

Other measures may be required depending on the patient's symptoms.

Dosage: Dermatitis Herpetiformis: Adults: 250 to 1 000 mg 4 times daily until improvement occurs. Reduce daily dose by 250 to 500 mg at 3-day intervals until a symptom-free maintenance dose is achieved.

Subcorneal Pustular Dermatosis: Adults: 500 mg twice daily to 750 mg 4 times daily.

Pemphigoid: Adults: 500 mg twice daily to 750 mg 4 times daily.

Reviewed 1999

SULFONYLUREAS

General Monograph, CPhA

Acetohexamide
Chlorpropamide
Gliclazide
Glyburide
Tolbutamide

Oral Hypoglycemic

This monograph has been compiled by CPhA. It may contain information different from that approved by Therapeutic Products Programme, Health Canada, and the pharmaceutical manufacturers' approval has not been requested.

Pharmacology: The sulfonylureas (see Table I) are orally active hypoglycemic agents which appear to act in part by stimulating insulin secretion from the beta cells of the pancreas. They are, therefore, ineffective in the absence of functioning beta cells.

With long-term administration, extrapancreatic effects appear to contribute to the hypoglycemic effect of sulfonylureas. These effects may include enhanced peripheral sensitivity to insulin and decreased hepatic glucose production.

At usual therapeutic doses gliclazide has been shown in man to reduce abnormal platelet adhesiveness and aggregation.

Glyburide may produce a mild diuresis by enhancing renal free water clearance. The exact mechanism by which glyburide enhances renal free water clearance is not known but it does not appear to be mediated through the release or action of antidiuretic hormone (ADH).

Chlorpropamide has antidiuretic activity possibly due to potentiating activity on ADH in the renal tubules and there is some evidence that chlorpropamide may actually stimulate ADH secretion.

Pharmacokinetics: See Table I. Sulfonylureas are readily absorbed from the gastrointestinal tract and are highly bound to plasma proteins (>90%). Sulfonylureas are metabolized in the liver and excreted in the urine and feces. Hydroxyhexamide, the pharmacologically active metabolite of acetohexamide, has an average half-life of 5 hours. Metabolites of the other sulfonylureas do not appear to have clinically significant hypoglycemic effects. The metabolism and excretion of sulfonylureas may be slowed in patients with impaired renal or hepatic function.

Table I—Sulfonylureas

Pharmacokinetics

Drug	Half-life (hours)	Time to Peak Concentration (hours)	Duration of Action (hours)
Acetohexamide	1.3	1.5–2	12–24
Chlorpropamide	36	2–4	24–72
Gliclazide	10	4–6	12–24
Glyburide	10	2–4	18–24
Tolbutamide	4.5–6.5	3–4	6–12

Indications: In noninsulin-dependent diabetes mellitus (NIDDM or Type II) to control hyperglycemia responsive to the drug. Sulfonylureas should not be used in those patients who are prone to ketosis or who can be controlled by dietary management and exercise alone or for whom insulin therapy is more appropriate.

Contraindications: Known hypersensitivity or allergy to any of the sulfonylureas. Insulin-dependent diabetes mellitus (IDDM); ketoacidosis; coma; during stress conditions such as severe infections, trauma or surgery; in the presence of severe liver, thyroid or renal impairment.

Pregnancy: Oral hypoglycemic drugs should not be given during pregnancy. Insulin should be used to maintain strict control of blood sugar.

Warnings: Use of sulfonylureas must be considered as treatment additional to a proper diet and exercise regimen and not as a substitute for diet. Sulfonylureas will not prevent the development of complications peculiar to diabetes mellitus.

Over a period of time, patients may become progressively less responsive to therapy with oral hypoglycemic agents. Therefore, patients should be monitored with regular clinical and laboratory evaluations, including blood glucose and glycosylated hemoglobin (Hgb AIC) determinations, to determine the minimum effective dosage and to detect primary failure (inadequate lowering of blood glucose concentrations at the maximum recommended dosage) or secondary failure (progressive deterioration in blood sugar control following an initial period of effectiveness). The rate of primary failure will vary greatly depending upon patient selection and adherence to diet and exercise. The etiology of secondary failure is multifactorial and may involve progressive beta cell failure as well as exogenous diabetogenic factors such as obesity, illness or drugs, or tachyphylaxis to the sulfonylurea. If a loss of adequate blood glucose lowering response to a sulfonylurea is detected, the addition of a different type of oral antidiabetic may be considered, although insulin is often required. Certain patients who demonstrate an inadequate response or true primary or secondary failure to one sulfonylurea may benefit from a switch to another sulfonylurea.

Precautions: Patient Selection and Follow-up: Careful selection of patients is important. Patients most likely to respond to sulfonylurea therapy are those with noninsulin-dependent diabetes mellitus (NIDDM); obese or normal body weight; duration of diabetes less than 5 to 10 years before initiation of therapy; absence of ketoacidosis; fasting serum glucose less than <11.2 mmol/L; insulin requirement less than 40 units/day. It is imperative that there be careful attention to diet, careful adjustment of dosage, instruction of the patient on hypoglycemic reactions and their treatment, as well as regular, thorough follow-up examinations.

In patients stabilized on sulfonylurea therapy, loss of blood sugar control may occur in cases of acute intercurrent disease or in stressful situations such as trauma or surgery. Under these conditions, consider discontinuation of the sulfonylurea and administration of insulin.

Sustained hyperglycemia is a risk factor for the development of microvascular diabetic complications. Controlling blood glucose levels helps to protect against the development and slow the progression of nephropathy, neuropathy and retinopathy. Hyperglycemia may contribute to the development of atherosclerosis.

Hypoglycemic Reactions: Severe hypoglycemia can be induced by all sulfonylureas (see Overdose). Particularly susceptible are the elderly, lean or underweight individuals and those with impaired hepatic or renal function. Also at risk are those who are debilitated or malnourished, and patients with primary or secondary adrenal insufficiency (Addison's disease). Hypoglycemia is more likely to occur when caloric intake is inadequate or after strenuous or prolonged exercise. Because of the long biological half-life of chlorpropamide, if the patient becomes hypoglycemic during therapy, the drug should be withdrawn and the patient should be kept under close supervision for 5 to 6 days. Subsequent reinstitution of the drug at lower dose levels may be considered.

Drug Interactions: Sulfonylureas can potentially interact with numerous other drugs. Mechanisms include displacement from plasma proteins, increased or decreased metabolism or urinary excretion, and hyperglycemic or hypoglycemic effects of other drugs. Enhanced glycemic monitoring should be instituted when therapy with other drugs is initiated, discontinued, or the dosages are changed.

Hypoglycemia: Hypoglycemia may be potentiated when sulfonylureas are used concurrently with agents such as: sulfonamides, salicylates, NSAIDs, H_2-antagonists, MAO inhibitors, fluconazole, anabolic steroids and allopurinol.

Hyperglycemia: Drugs which may cause hyperglycemia when used with sulfonylureas include: thiazide diuretics, corticosteroids, estrogens, rifampin and oral contraceptives.

Beta-adrenergic blocking agents may delay recovery from hypoglycemia and suppress hypoglycemic symptoms (with the exception of sweating). They may also inhibit insulin secretion. Cardioselective beta-blockers in low doses may be safer than nonselective beta-blockers.

Coumarin derivatives, when administered with sulfonylureas, may initially result in increased plasma concentrations of both drugs. With continued therapy, decreased anticoagulant concentrations and increased hepatic metabolism of sulfonylureas may occur. Adjustment in dosage for both drugs may be required.

Intolerance to alcohol (disulfiram-like reaction: flushing, sensation of warmth, giddiness, nausea and occasionally tachycardia) may occur in patients treated with sulfonylureas. This reaction occurs more frequently with chlorpropamide. Unpredictable fluctuations in serum glucose levels, most commonly hypoglycemia, may also occur following alcohol ingestion.

Pregnancy: See Contraindications.

Lactation: Chlorpropamide and tolbutamide enter breast milk and should not be administered during lactation. It is not known whether acetohexamide, gliclazide and glyburide enter breast milk. Because of the potential for hypoglycemia in nursing infants, a decision should be made whether to discontinue nursing or the drug, taking into account the importance of the drug to the mother.

Children: Sulfonylureas are not effective in insulin-dependent diabetes mellitus (IDDM or Type I).

Adverse Effects: The majority of side effects associated with sulfonylureas have been dose-related, transient and have responded to dose reduction or withdrawl of the drug.

Hypoglycemia: See Precautions and Overdose. Severe hypoglycemia, which mimics acute CNS disorders, may occur. Hepatic and/or renal disease, malnutrition, debility, advanced age, alcoholism, adrenal or pituitary insufficiency may be predisposing factors.

Gastrointestinal: Nausea, epigastric fullness and heartburn are common reactions. These tend to be dose-related and may disappear when dosage is reduced or the total daily dose is administered in divided doses.

Hepatic: Jaundice has been reported rarely. Discontinue therapy. Abnormalities in liver function tests have occasionally occurred.

Dermatologic: Allergic skin reactions such as pruritus, erythema, urticaria, morbiliform or maculopapular eruptions have been observed. These may subside on continued use of sulfonylureas but if they persist, discontinue the drug. Porphyria cutanea tarda and photosensitivity reactions have been reported.

Hematologic: Leukopenia, thrombocytopenia, agranulocytosis, hemolytic anemia and aplastic anemia have been noted.

Metabolic: The syndrome of inappropriate secretion of antidiuretic hormone (SIADH) has occasionally occurred with chlorpropamide. This is characterized by excessive water retention and hyponatremia, low serum osmolality and high urine osmolality. These adverse effects have occurred especially in the elderly and patients with congestive heart failure or hepatic cirrhosis or those taking diuretics.

Hepatic porphyria and disulfiram-like reactions have been observed.

Endocrine: Reduced RAI uptake by the thyroid gland has been reported.

Overdose: Symptoms: Sulfonylurea overdosage is manifested principally as hypoglycemia, which may be severe. The dosage which causes hypoglycemia varies widely, and may be within normal doses in sensitive individuals. Hypoglycemic episodes may last for several days, especially in susceptible individuals (e.g., the elderly, malnourished, those with renal or hepatic impairment or those on chlorpropamide). Relapse may occur after apparent recovery.

The manifestations of hypoglycemia include sweating, increased pulse rate, headache, drowsiness, dizziness, flushing or pallor, numbness, chilliness, hunger, trembling, weakness, palpitations, increase in blood pressure and apprehensiveness in mild cases. Severe hypoglycemia may result in altered behavior, confusion, seizures and coma, with resultant neurologic sequalae or death. However, symptoms of hypoglycemia are not necessarily as typical as described above and sulfonylureas may cause insidious development of symptoms mimicking cerebrovascular insufficiency.

Treatment: Discontinue medication. Treat hypoglycemia by administering dextrose promptly (e.g., 50% dextrose by rapid i.v. injection) and provide supportive therapy. In mild overdose, immediate ingestion of a source of sugar may be sufficient.

In severe cases of acute overdose, administration of repeated doses of activated charcoal with a cathartic combined with a dextrose infusion to maintain blood glucose levels may be necessary. This should be accompanied by careful monitoring of blood glucose, vital signs, arterial blood gases, and serum electrolytes. Continuous dextrose infusions for hours to days have been necessary. In cases refractory to dextrose, glucagon, steroids, or diazoxide have been used to control hypoglycemia. Dialysis is of little benefit; hemoperfusion may be useful.

Patients must be closely monitored for at least 24 to 72 hours (or longer with chlorpropamide) after apparent recovery, as relapse can occur.

Dosage: Sulfonylureas are generally administered with or before a meal (e.g., breakfast). For patients requiring higher doses, divided doses should be administered usually before the morning and evening meals. This regimen may improve gastrointestinal tolerance and improve glycemic control in some patients.

In diabetic subjects there is no fixed dosage regimen for management of blood glucose concentrations. Individual determination of the minimum dose that will lower the blood glucose adequately should be made (see Table II on following page). Since lean or elderly diabetic patients appear to be more sensitive to the effects of sulfonylureas, these patients should be started on smaller initial doses with dosage adjustments being

Table II—Sulfonylureas

Dosage

Drug	Daily Dose (mg)	Usual Initial Dose (mg)	Equivalent Dose (mg)	Doses/Day
Acetohexamide	250–1 500	250	500	1–2
Chlorpropamide	100–500	250	250	1
Gliclazide	40–320	160	80	1–2
Glyburide	2.5–20	5	5	1–2
Tolbutamide	500–3 000	1 000	1 000	1–3

made cautiously. Patients with renal or hepatic impairment may require dosage reduction. Overweight patients or those with symptomatic hyperglycemia (polyuria and polydipsia) may be started on higher initial doses.

The response to a sulfonylurea will generally be evident within an initial trial period of 1 week; nevertheless, 4 weeks of therapy should be attempted before determining whether the patient is responding.

In patients where, on initial trial, the maximal recommended dose fails to lower blood glucose adequately, the drug should be discontinued, or a trial of dual therapy with a biguanide or an alpha-glucosidase inhibitor can be considered. During the course of therapy a loss of effectiveness may occur (secondary failure). Some clinicians recommend ascertaining the contribution of the drug to the control of blood glucose by discontinuing the medication periodically (at least annually) with careful patient monitoring. If the need for the drug is not evident, therapy should not be resumed. In some diabetic subjects, short-term administration of the drug may be sufficient during periods of transient loss of blood sugar control.

Blood glucose levels can sometimes be lowered further through addition of metformin or acarbose to sulfonylurea monotherapy. This type of combination therapy in NIDDM patients may achieve satisfactory glycemic control and delay the need for introduction of insulin therapy in patients refractory to monotherapy. Combined therapy with insulin and a sulfonylurea may be effective in some individuals.

Changeover from Other Oral Hypoglycemic Agents: Discontinue previous medication and start sulfonylurea at usual initial dose. Determine maintenance dosage as in newly diagnosed diabetics. Because of its prolonged half-life, when transferring from chlorpropamide, monitor closely for 1 to 2 weeks.

Patients Receiving Insulin: Maturity onset diabetics with no ketoacidosis or history of metabolic decompensation and whose insulin requirements are less than 40 units/day may be considered for sulfonylurea therapy. If a change from insulin to a sulfonylurea is contemplated in such a patient, discontinue insulin for a period of 2 or 3 days to determine whether any therapy other than dietary regulation and exercise is needed. During this insulin-free interval, test the patient's blood and urine at least 3 times daily for glucose and ketone bodies. The appearance of progressive hyperglycemia with significant ketonuria within 12 to 24 hours after the withdrawal of insulin strongly suggests that the patient is ketosis prone and precludes the change from insulin to sulfonylurea therapy. Alternatively, measurement of C-peptide levels will assist in determining endogenous insulin secretion capability.

The reader is referred to individual product monographs for more specific prescribing information.

Reviewed 1997

SULFOXYL® Ⓟ

Stiefel

Sulfur—Benzoyl Peroxide

Acne Vulgaris Therapy

Supplied: Each mL of lotion contains: sulfur 2% and benzoyl peroxide 5% in a vanishing lotion base. Nonmedicinal ingredients: glyceryl monostearate, imidurea NF, isopropyl palmitate, PEG 1000 monostearate, propylene glycol, purified water USP, stearic acid, xantham gum and zinc stearate. Plastic bottles of 60 mL. Protect from heat.

SULFUR SOAP

Stiefel

Acne Therapy

Supplied: Each g of neutral soap contains: precipitated sulfur USP 10%. Nonmedicinal ingredients: butylated hydroxytoluene, fragrance, purified water USP, soap chips and trisodium HEDTA. Bars of 75 g.

SULTRIN® Ⓟ

Janssen-Ortho

Triple Sulfa

Vaginitis Therapy

Indications: Postoperative vaginitis or cervicitis, nonspecific vaginitis, ulcerative vaginitis and related gynecological conditions.

Contraindications: Sulfonamide sensitivity; kidney disease.

Precautions: Although some absorption of sulfonamide may occur through the vaginal mucosa, systemic reactions attributable to this are infrequent, as are local sensitivity reactions such as increased discomfort or a burning sensation following the use of this product. However, as with all sulfonamides, the usual precautions apply. Patients should be observed for manifestations such as skin rash, or other evidence of systemic toxicity and if these develop, the medication should be discontinued.

Pregnancy: Teratogenic Effects: Category C: The safe use of sulfonamides in pregnancy has not been established. The teratogenicity potential of most sulfonamides has not been thoroughly investigated in either animals or humans. However, significant increase in the incidence of cleft palate and other bony adnormalities of offspring has been observed when certain sulfonamides of the short, intermediate and long-acting types were given to pregnant rats and mice at high oral doses (7 to 25 times the human therapeutic dose).

Lactation: Because of the potential for serious adverse reactions in nursing infants from triple sulfa, a decision should be made whether to discontinue nursing or to discontinue the drug, taking into account the importance of the drug to the mother. See Contraindications.

Children: Safety and effectiveness in children have not been established.

Dosage: 1 applicatorful (approximately 5 mL) intravaginally before retiring and again in the morning, decreasing to 50 or 25% after a period of 4 to 6 days if desired. Course of treatment may be repeated if necessary.

Supplied: Each g of white, water dispersible, absorptive vaginal cream contains: sulfabenzamide 3.7%, sulfathiazole 3.42%, sulfacetamide 2.86%, compounded with cetyl alcohol, cholesterol, diethylaminoethyl stearamide, glyceryl monostearate, lanolin, lecithin, methylparaben, peanut oil, phosphoric acid, propylene glycol, propylparaben, purified water, stearic acid and urea. Tubes of 78 g with applicator.

Reviewed 1999

SUN-BENZ Ⓟ

Sun

Benzydamine HCl

Local Analgesic

Pharmacology: In animal studies by parenteral route, benzydamine appears to possess the properties of an analgesic-anti-inflammatory agent. In studies by topical route, benzydamine appears to have local anesthetic properties. In humans with radiation induced oropharyngeal mucositis, benzydamine has provided relief by reducing pain and edema. In similar studies, patients with acute sore throat, benzydamine has demonstrated relief from pain.

Benzydamine has been detected in blood and urine after gargling 4 times for 20 seconds, in rapid succession, each time with a volume equivalent to 25.5 mg benzydamine/70 kg body weight (approximately 17 mL per gargle). The average maximum plasma level of 59 ng/mL (range 17 to 173) was obtained 2 hours after gargling. For comparison, 1 dose of 17 mL, when swallowed, yielded an average maximum plasma level of 180 ng/mL (range 102 to 324), also at 2 hours after ingestion. Benzydamine was still detected 24 hours later in 7 out of 10 subjects after the gargling (average plasma level of 7 ng/mL) and in 9 out of 10 subjects after ingestion (average 32 ng/mL).

A systemic dose is usually excreted within 3 to 4 days. Amounts recovered depended on the amount of drug reaching the systemic circulation.

Indications: For relief of pain in acute sore throat and for the symptomatic relief of oropharyngeal mucositis due to radiation therapy.

Contraindications: Subjects with a history of hypersensitivity to any of its components.

Precautions: The use of undiluted benzydamine may produce local irritation manifested by burning sensation in patients with mucosal defects. If necessary, it may be diluted (1:1) with lukewarm water.

Since benzydamine is absorbed from oral mucosa and then excreted mostly unchanged in the urine, a possibility of its systemic action has to be considered in patients with renal impairment.

Pregnancy: The safety of benzydamine has not been established in pregnant patients. Risks to benefit ratio should be established if benzydamine is to be used in these patients.

Children: Safety and dose directions have not been established for children 6 years of age and younger.

Adverse Effects: The most frequent adverse reactions reported are: local numbness (9.7%), local burning or stinging sensation (8.2%), nausea and/or vomiting (2.1%).

The least frequent were reports of throat irritation, cough, dryness of the mouth associated with thirst, drowsiness, and headache.

Overdose: Symptoms and Treatment: There are no known cases of overdosage with benzydamine gargle. Since no specific antidote for benzydamine is available, cases of excessive ingestion of the liquid should receive supportive symptomatic treatment aimed at rapid elimination of the drug.

Dosage: Not less than 15 mL of the liquid should be used for each gargle or rinse and repeated 3 or 4 times a day, depending on the severity of the treated condition. The liquid should be kept in contact with the inflamed mucosa for at least 30 seconds and then expelled from the mouth. Administration should begin the day prior to commencement of radiation therapy and continue daily during the treatment period as well as after cessation of radiation applications until desired improvement is obtained.

In acute sore throat gargle with 15 mL every 1½ to 3 hours. The solution should be expelled from mouth after use.

Supplied: Each bottle of clear yellow-green liquid contains: benzydamine HCl 0.15% in a solvent consisting of water, glycerin and ethanol 10%. Nonmedicinal ingredients: D&C yellow #10, ethyl alcohol, FD&C blue #1, flavor, methyl- and propylparaben (as preservatives), polysorbate-80 and purified water. pH of 4.0 to 6.0. Tartrazine-free. Bottles of 250 mL. Store between 15 and 30°C.

Reviewed 1997

SUPEUDOL® Ⓝ

Sabex

Oxycodone HCl

Opioid Analgesic

Indications: Relief of moderate to severe pain.

Contraindications: Any situation where there is significant decrease of respiratory reserve, as in emphysema, kyphoscoliosis, bronchial asthma, cor pulmonale; in patients with head injury; in patients with elevated cerebral spinal fluid pressure; in patients hypersensitive to oxycodone.

Precautions: Oxycodone can produce drug dependence of the morphine type and, therefore, has the potential for being abused. Psychic dependence, physical dependence and tolerance may develop upon repeated administration of this product and should be prescribed and administered with the same degree of caution appropriate to the use of other opioid-containing medications.

Occupational Hazards: Oxycodone may impair the mental and/or physical abilities required for the performance of potentially hazardous tasks such as driving a car or operating machinery. Therefore, caution the patient accordingly.

Patients receiving other opioid analgesics, general anesthetics, MAO inhibitors, tricyclic antidepressants, phenothiazines, other tranquilizers, sedative-hypnotics or other CNS depressants (including alcohol) concomitantly with this product may exhibit an additive CNS depression. When such

Supeudol (cont'd)

combined therapy is contemplated, reduce the dose of one or both agents.

Should not be used for the management of opioid dependence.

The respiratory depressant effects of opioids and their capacity to elevate cerebrospinal fluid pressure may be markedly exaggerated in the presence of head injury, other intracranial lesions or a preexisting increase in intracranial pressure. Furthermore, opioids may produce adverse reactions which can obscure the clinical course of patients with head injuries.

The administration of this product or other opioids may obscure the diagnosis or clinical course in patients with acute abdominal conditions.

Because of the danger of cardiac or respiratory depression, administer with caution to certain patients such as the elderly or debilitated, and those with hemorrhage, severe impairment of hepatic, respiratory or renal function, hypothyroidism, Addison's disease and prostatic hypertrophy or urethral stricture.

Because headache often involves a significant psychological component, an opioid analgesic should only be employed for the treatment of headache when no other treatment is effective, in order to minimize the risk of psychological and physical dependence.

Pregnancy: Safe use in pregnancy has not been established relative to possible adverse effects on fetal development. Therefore, this product should not be used in pregnant women unless the potential benefits outweigh the possible hazards. The administration of Supeudol to obstetrical patients in labor may be associated with respiratory depression of the newborn.

Children: Not recommended for use in children.

Adverse Effects: Light headedness, dizziness, sedation, nausea and vomiting, euphoria, dysphoria, constipation, dry mouth, blurred vision, respiratory depression, mental clouding or depression, agitation, restlessness, nervousness, convulsion, pruritus and rarely delirium and insomnia may occur.

Dosage: Suppositories: Adults, 1 to 2 suppositories, 3 to 4 times per day as prescribed.

Tablets: 1 to 2 tablets, 3 to 4 times per day as prescribed.

Supplied: Suppositories: Each suppository contains: oxycodone HCl 10 mg or 20 mg. Nonmedicinal ingredients: semisynthetic glyceride. Boxes of 12. Store in a cool place.

Tablets: 5 mg: Each tablet contains: oxycodone HCl 5 mg. Nonmedicinal ingredients: brilliant blue sodium salt (FD&C Blue No. 1), calcium phosphate dibasic, croscarmellose sodium, magnesium stearate and microcrystalline cellulose. Gluten-, lactose-, sulfite- and tartrazine-free. Bottles of 100.

10 mg: Each tablet contains: oxycodone HCl 10 mg. Nonmedicinal ingredients: calcium phosphate dibasic, croscarmellose sodium, magnesium stearate, microcrystalline cellulose. Gluten-, lactose-, sulfite- and tartrazine-free. Bottles of 100.

(Shown in Product Recognition Section)

SUPLASYN®
Bioniche

Sodium Hyaluronate
Synovial Fluid Replacement

Pharmacology: Hyaluronic acid is a naturally occurring mucopolysaccharide present in the connective tissue of all animals. It is a biological polymer composed of repeating units of two sugars, D-glucuronic acid and N-acetylglycosamine, linked by glycosidic bonds. This configuration for hyaluronic acid is the same for all living species from bacteria to man. High concentrations are found in synovial fluid, the vitreous humor of the eye, cartilage, connective tissue and the umbilical cord. Hyaluronic acid functions as a viscoelastic support to maintain separation between tissues, as a tissue and joint lubricant, and is thought to play an important role in modulating the interactions between adjacent tissues.

Suplasyn is a highly purified sodium salt of hyaluronic acid, with a defined molecular chain length (2 500 to 3 500 saccharide units) and molecular weight (500 to 730 kDa). Suplasyn is nonantigenic, nonpyrogenic and does not cause inflammation of foreign body reactions. The viscoelastic properties of Suplasyn are similar to that of synovial fluid. The introduction of Suplasyn into the synovial space will assist in the normalization of the function and rheological properties of the joint.

Indications: As a replacement for synovial fluid following arthrocentesis.

Contraindications: When used as indicated, there are no known contraindications to the use of sodium hyaluronate.

Precautions: Do not administer to patients with known hypersensitivity reactions. Transient, short duration pain or swelling may occur following intra-articular injections of sodium hyaluronate.

Adverse Effects: Sodium hyaluronate is the salt of a natural component of many of the tissues of the body. It is extremely well tolerated when injected into the intra-articular space. Reports of minor inflammation have been reported but are generally considered to be due to the method of administration. Each batch of Suplasyn is tested in vivo to confirm its essential noninflammatory properties.

Dosage: Depending upon joint size, up to 2 mL may be administered intra-articularly. The recommended schedule is 3 weekly injections, but up to 6 may be given in chronic conditions. Using aseptic technique, introduce up to 2 mL intra-articularly into the affected joint. More than one joint may be treated at the same time. Discard any unused portion of the vial.

Supplied: Each mL of sterile, viscoelastic solution for intra-articular injection contains: sodium hyaluronate 10 mg (hyaluronic acid sodium salt). Vials of 2 mL, boxes of 3. Store at room temperature (15 to 30°C). Do not freeze.

Reviewed 1997

SUPLEVIT
Riva

Multiple Vitamins—Minerals
Vitamin and Mineral Supplement

Supplied: Each red tablet embossed Riva contains: vitamin A 5 000 IU, vitamin B_1 (thiamine mononitrate) 20 mg, vitamin B_2 (riboflavin) 5 mg, niacinamide 15 mg, vitamin B_6 (pyridoxine HCl) 20 mg, vitamin B_{12} (cyanocobalamin) 5 μg, folic acid 0.4 mg, vitamin C 150 mg, vitamin D 400 IU, vitamin E 100 IU, biotin 10 μg, calcium (as dibasic phosphate and carbonate) 100 mg, magnesium (as gluconate and oxide) 100 mg, iron (as ferrous fumarate) 15 mg, manganese (as sulfate) 0.5 mg, zinc (as sulfate) 15 mg, iodine (as potassium iodide) 0.075 mg, betaine HCl 10 mg. Nonmedicinal ingredients: carnauba wax, cellulose, FD&C Red, FD&C Yellow, hydroxypropyl methylcellulose, magnesium stearate, polyethylene glycol, polysorbate 80, polyvinylpyrrolidone, sodium croscarmellose, starch, sugar and titanium dioxide. Gluten-, tartrazine-free. Bottles of 60.

SUPRACAINE®
Hoechst Marion Roussel

Tetracaine
Oral Topical Anesthetic

Pharmacology: Tetracaine topical aerosol is a local anesthetic of the ester type (para-amino benzoic acid derivative) for use as a topical anesthetic in clinical dentistry. The medicinal ingredient is tetracaine base.

Tetracaine prevents the generation and conduction of sensory nerve impulses at the site of its application by an inhibition of the nerve cell depolarization process; onset of action is approximately 2 minutes.

Indications: For the prevention and treatment of pain in the soft tissues arising from minor oral surgical procedures (needle puncture; removal of dental calculus; prosthetic adjustments; clamp or crown placement; removal of primary teeth).

Tetracaine is also indicated for the reduction of the pharyngeal (gag) reflex associated with the placement into the oral cavity of various dental materials (impression trays, x-ray films, x-ray plate holders).

Contraindications: In patients with a recognized para group allergy, or other known hypersensitivity to local anesthetics of the ester type or any of the nonmedicinal ingredients (see Precautions).

Tetracaine is contraindicated for inhalation (see Warnings).

Tetracaine is contraindicated for internal use, use on the skin or in and around the eyes, or for vaginal use.

Local anesthetics of the ester type are contraindicated in patients with low plasma cholinesterase concentrations, or in those patients receiving anticholinesterase therapy.

Warnings: Inhalation of topical anesthetics in sufficient quantities may be harmful or fatal.

Resuscitative facilities should be readily available during administration of any local anesthetic.

Dental practitioners known to have a para group allergy, or to be hypersensitive to local anesthetics of the ester type, or to any of the nonmedicinal ingredients, must avoid contact (skin, inhalation) with the anesthetic during administration to the patient.

Container may explode if heated. Contents under pressure. Do not place in hot water or near radiators, stoves or other sources of heat. Do not puncture or incinerate container or store at temperature over 50°C.

Precautions: Should tetracaine topical aerosol be sprayed into the eyes, it must be washed out immediately.

To reduce seepage into the pharynx, the direction of spray should not be towards the back of the throat.

The teeth should be shielded from the anesthetic spray to prevent a sudden sensation of cold; appropriate shielding should be undertaken to prevent spraying into any undesirable area.

To avoid undue systemic absorption, patients should be instructed to expectorate any excessive anesthetic solution. Cautious use of topical anesthetics is advised on severely traumatized oral mucosa because of the possibility of increased systemic absorption and/or sensitization. Cautious use is also advised given evidence of secondary bacterial infection (sepsis) in the area of treatment.

Because of potential interference with the pharyngeal reflex, food should not be ingested for approximately 1 hour after the use of an oral topical aerosol anesthetic.

Drug Sensitivity: Cross sensitivity between ester derivatives, particularly para-amino benzoic acid (PABA) derivatives, is known to occur. Cross sensitivity has not been demonstrated between amide and ester derivatives. Cautious use of any local anesthetic is advised in patients with known drug sensitivities; skin tests to predict possible hypersensitivity may be of dubious value.

Repeated and prolonged application may potentiate hypersensitivity.

Pregnancy: Safe use has not been determined with respect to adverse effects upon fetal development. Careful consideration of the risk/benefit ratio should be given before administering tetracaine to patients of childbearing potential, and especially during early pregnancy.

General: Topical anesthetics of the ester type may interfere with the antibacterial activity of sulfonamides.

Any local anesthetic should be administered with caution to patients with epilepsy, impaired hepatic, renal, cardiac, or respiratory function, and particularly to patients with myasthenia gravis.

Tetracaine may damage lacquer finishes; an inadvertent spray on such surfaces should be immediately wiped clean.

Adverse Effects: Local: Tetracaine topical aerosol may cause transient reactions of stinging (burning), swelling, and/or sensation of tenderness.

Tetracaine may induce contact sensitization, characterized by rash, erythema, pruritus, swelling or urticaria. Topical benzalkonium chloride and aerosol refrigerant-propellant ingredients may induce contact sensitization.

Systemic: Though rare, systemic adverse effects generally occur as a result of high plasma levels caused either by rapid absorption, excessive dosage, idiosyncratic reaction or decreased patient tolerance. Systemic toxicity may first manifest itself through symptoms of numbness of the tongue and/or perioral regions. For tetracaine, CNS or cardiovascular effects are generally seen. CNS reactions may be excitatory and/or depressive; excitatory symptomatology is characterized by nervousness, excitement, dizziness, nystagmus, blurred vision, tinnitus, nausea, vomiting, muscle twitching and convulsions. If transient, the excitatory phase is followed by the depressive phase, manifested by drowsiness, respiratory failure and coma. Simultaneous cardiovascular effects may be observed, with myocardial depression and peripheral vasodilatation, leading to bradycardia, hypotension, increased perspiration, arrhythmia and possible cardiac arrest. The excitatory phase may be absent, in which case only the symptoms of the depressive phase present.

Systemic adverse effects of benzalkonium chloride may include nausea, vomiting, dyspnea, cyanosis, asphyxia, CNS depression (possibly preceded by CNS activation and convulsions), hypotension and coma.

Aerosol refrigerant-propellant ingredients may induce symptoms of excitement, headache, dizziness, stupor, convulsions, euphoria, bronchoconstriction, asphyxia and cardiac arrhythmia.

Overdose: Symptoms and Treatment: To treat systemic toxicity reactions to topical anesthetics, it is imperative that a patent airway be maintained, oxygen be administered and, if necessary, respiration be aided.

Convulsions may be treated with a benzodiazepine (e.g. diazepam) or, in persistent cases, with ultrashort-acting i.v. barbiturates (e.g. thiopental, thiamylal), or with short-acting barbiturates (e.g. pentobarbital or secobarbital). Administration of neuromuscular blocking agents is acceptable, but in such cases artificial respiration is required.

Dosage: 2 metered dose sprays (0.7 mg/spray) are sufficient for most procedures; the maximum daily adult dose is 20 mg of tetracaine (approximately 28 sprays).

A safe pediatric dose has not been established.

Administration: It is unnecessary to dry the application site prior to administration of tetracaine topical aerosol. To administer, the bottle cap is first removed, exposing the metered dose spray valve. The supplied plastic grooved valve cap, with its attached angled cannula, is then snugly fitted onto the metered dose spray valve. (The wire stylet must be removed from the lumen of the cannula.) To actuate the valve, it may be necessary to depress the valve cap several times. The angled cannula can be freely rotated, thus optimizing the direction of spray to be delivered. Upon delivery of one spray, sustained depression of the valve cap will not release more anesthetic; a safeguard against possible drug overdose. For resumption of spraying, the valve cap must first be released.

The grooved valve cap and cannula may be autoclaved for up to 30 minutes at 120°C; the wire stylet, accompanying the cannula, is designed to clear manually the lumen of the cannula.

Supplied: Each 65 g of topical aerosol contains: tetracaine 754 mg. Nonmedicinal ingredients: benzalkonium chloride (antimicrobial preservative), dehydrated ethanol 4.44% w/w (preservative-solvent), trichlorotrifluoroethane (FC113, refrigerant-solvent), and the refrigerant-propellant mixture dichlorodifluoromethane (FC12) and dichlorotetrafluoroethane (FC114). Individually boxed clear glass bottles of 65 g enveloped in a white plastic sheath.

Container may explode if heated. Contents under pressure. Do not place in hot water or near radiators, stove, or other sources of heat. Do not puncture or incinerate container or store at temperatures over 50°C. Store in original container at room temperature, below 25°C.

SUPRANE® ℞

Zeneca

Desflurane

Inhalation Anesthetic

Pharmacology: Desflurane is a volatile inhalational anesthetic whose low solubility (blood/gas partition coefficient equals 0.42) permits rapid variation in anesthetic depth. If anesthesia is maintained with inflow rates of greater than 2 L/min, the alveolar concentration is usually within 10% of the inspired concentration. It is not necessary to deliver concentrations of desflurane far in excess of the desired end-tidal concentration ("overpressurization" technique) due to the low blood and tissue solubilities of desflurane and the resulting rapid equilibrium of alveolar concentration with inspired and delivered concentrations (see Warnings).

Since awakening is rapid, care should be taken that appropriate analgesia has been administered to the patient at the end of the procedure or early in the postanesthesia care unit.

MAC varies widely with age. In 45 year old patients, MAC is 6% in 100% oxygen and 2.8% in 60% nitrous oxide (see Dosage, Table II).

Desflurane is not useful for mask induction as it causes an unacceptably high incidence of laryngospasm, coughing, secretions, breath holding and apnea (see Adverse Effects).

Approximately 0.02% of absorbed desflurane is metabolized. In normal volunteers, there was no increase in serum or urine fluoride concentrations. Studies in patients with chronic renal insufficiency and patients undergoing renal transplantation showed no effects on renal function. Hepatic dysfunction has been reported after desflurane use. A causal relationship may or may not exist.

Desflurane is a profound respiratory depressant, producing a progressive decrease in tidal volume and increase in arterial carbon dioxide tension. Apnea is common at concentrations above 1.5 MAC (Minimum Alveolar Concentration). This depression may be partly reversed by surgical stimulation. Nitrous oxide diminishes the inspired concentration of desflurane required to reach a desired level of anesthesia (see Dosage, Table II).

Desflurane potentiates the effect of depolarizing and nondepolarizing neuromuscular relaxants. When compared to nitrous oxide/opioid anesthesia, the requirements for depolarizing and nondepolarizing agents are reduced by 30% and 50%, respectively.

Desflurane, like other volatile anesthetics, induces malignant hyperthermia in genetically susceptible swine (see Precautions).

Hemodynamic Effects: Cardiovascular Effects: In healthy male volunteers, desflurane produced a progressive decrease in blood pressure (15% at 1.2 MAC), due mainly to vasodilation, and an increase in heart rate (15% at 1.2 MAC) when administered in oxygen or 60% nitrous oxide during controlled ventilation at normocapnia. The cardiac output was unchanged at 1.7 MAC in oxygen, but decreased 20% at 1.2 MAC in 60% nitrous oxide. Similar changes were seen during spontaneous ventilation.

Effect on Sympathetic Activity: Constant or slowly increasing concentrations of desflurane blunt or block sympathetic responses to noxious stimuli. The increased heart rate response to hypotension is reduced in this setting. However, rapid changes to concentrations above 6%, as well as rapid changes above 6% can result in tachycardia and hypertension. The physiology of this response is unknown. In unpremedicated volunteers, desflurane can unpredictably induce transient (approximately 4 minutes) increases in sympathetic activity, heart rate and blood pressure. The hemodynamic changes are more common at concentrations ≥6% and more severe with large (≥1%), sudden increments. A single clinical study of CABG patients showed similar effects (see Clinical Studies, Cardiovascular Surgery). This transient cardiovascular response can be blunted substantially by fentanyl (1.5 μg/kg), alfentanil (10 or 20 μg/kg), or clonidine 4 μg/kg as a premedication. Esmolol decreases the heart rate, but not blood pressure. The sympathetic stimulation is not obtunded by i.v. or endotracheal lidocaine or by i.v. propofol.

Desflurane does not alter the human myocardial arrhythmogenic threshold for epinephrine (approximately 7 μg/kg).

Clinical Studies: The safety and efficacy of desflurane have been established in large, multicentre clinical trials in adult outpatients (ASA I, II and III), in cardiovascular surgery (ASA II, III and IV) patients, in elderly (ASA II and III) patients and in pediatric (ASA I and II) patients.

Ambulatory Surgery: Desflurane was compared to isoflurane in multicentre studies (21 sites) of 792 ASA physical status I, II or III patients aged 18 to 76 years (median 32). Desflurane with or without nitrous oxide or other anesthetics was generally well tolerated. Patients receiving desflurane emerged significantly faster than those receiving isoflurane, and there were no differences in the incidence of nausea and vomiting.

Cardiovascular Surgery: Desflurane was compared to isoflurane, sufentanil or fentanyl for the anesthetic management of coronary artery bypass graft (CABG), abdominal aortic aneurysm, peripheral vascular and carotid endarterectomy surgery in 7 studies at 15 centres involving a total of 558 patients (ASA physical status II, III and IV).

Cardiac Studies: The effects of desflurane in patients undergoing CABG surgery were investigated in 3 studies.

Using echocardiography in addition to Holter monitoring to detect myocardial ischemia, 1 study compared desflurane with sufentanil in groups of 100 patients each. The opioid group received a small dose of thiopental, and sufentanil, 5 to 10 μg/kg followed by an infusion of 0.07 μg/kg/min, and no halogenated inhaled anesthetic. The desflurane group received no opioid for induction of anesthesia, and after i.v. thiopental had a rapid inhaled induction of anesthesia with desflurane concentrations exceeding 10% end-tidal. The desflurane group had increases in heart rate (HR) and mean arterial pressure (MAP) during induction of anesthesia and a 13% incidence of myocardial ischemia during induction of anesthesia which was greater than the zero incidence during induction in the sufentanil group. During the precardiopulmonary bypass period, more desflurane patients required cardiovascular adjuvants to control hemodynamics than the sufentanil patients. During maintenance of anesthesia, the sufentanil group had myocardial ischemia of greater duration and intensity than did the desflurane group. There were no differences in incidence of myocardial infarction or death between the 2 groups.

The second study compared desflurane with fentanyl in groups of 26 and 25 patients, respectively. The fentanyl group received 50 μg/kg and no halogenated inhaled anesthetic. The desflurane group received fentanyl 10 μg/kg and a maximum desflurane concentration of 6%. The groups did not differ in the incidence of ECG changes suggestive of ischemia, myocardial infarction, or death.

In the third study, investigators compared desflurane with isoflurane in groups of 57 and 58 patients, respectively. Both groups were given up to 10 μg/kg fentanyl during induction of anesthesia. The mean end-tidal anesthetic concentrations prior to coronary bypass were 6% desflurane or 0.9% isoflurane. Desflurane and isoflurane provided clinically acceptable anesthesia prior to and after coronary bypass. A subanalysis was performed for data collected at one of the study centres. At this centre desflurane was administered to 21 patients and 20 patients received isoflurane. Both groups were given fentanyl 10 μg/kg; during induction of anesthesia the maximum end-tidal anesthetic concentrations were 6% desflurane or 1.4% isoflurane. The groups had similar incidences of ischemia (as detected by Holter monitoring), myocardial infarction and death.

In the desflurane vs sufentanil study, investigators increased desflurane concentration rapidly to 10.2% end-tidal, without having administered any opioid, thereby increasing HR and MAP and observing a 13% incidence of myocardial ischemia in their patients with coronary artery disease. These rapid increases in desflurane concentration without pretreatment with an opioid, have been demonstrated to increase sympathetic activity, HR and MAP in volunteers. The other studies avoided these increases in HR and MAP by applying lower desflurane concentrations (less than 1 MAC), and by administering substantial doses of fentanyl (10 and 50 μg/kg) as part of the induction technique.

Peripheral Vascular Studies: Four randomized, open-label trials were conducted to assess the hemodynamic stability of patients administered desflurane vs isoflurane for maintenance anesthesia in peripheral vascular surgeries. These studies are summarized in Table I.

Table I—Suprane

Peripheral Vascular Studies

	Desflurane/O_2		Isoflurane/O_2	
Type of Surgery	**# of patients**	**mean dose (%)**	**# of patients**	**mean dose (%)**
Abdominal Aorta	25	5.2	29	0.74
Peripheral Vascular	24	2.9*	24	0.43*
Carotid	31	4.4	30	0.7
Endarterectomy	15	6.1	15	0.65

*Desflurane and isoflurane administered with 60% N_2O.

In all patients, the volatile anesthetics were supplemented with fentanyl. Blood pressure and heart rate were controlled by changes in concentrations of the volatile anesthetics or opioids and cardiovascular drugs, if necessary. No differences were found in cardiovascular outcome (death, myocardial infarction, ventricular tachycardia or fibrillation, heart failure) for desflurane and isoflurane in these studies.

Desflurane should not be used as the sole anesthetic in patients with coronary artery disease or in patients where increases in the heart rate or blood pressure are undesirable (see Warnings).

Geriatric Surgery: Desflurane plus nitrous oxide was compared to isoflurane plus nitrous oxide in a multicentre study (6 sites) of 203 ASA physical status II or III elderly patients, aged 57 to 91 years (median 71). Heart rate and arterial blood pressure remained within 20% of preinduction baseline values during administration of desflurane 0.5 to 7.7% (average 3.6%) with 50 to 60% nitrous oxide. Maintenance and recovery cardiovascular measurements did not differ from those during isoflurane plus nitrous oxide administration, nor did the postoperative incidence of nausea and vomiting. The most common cardiovascular adverse event was hypotension for both isoflurane (6%) as well as desflurane (8%).

Neurosurgery: Desflurane was studied in 38 patients aged 26 to 76 years (median 48 years), ASA physical status II or III undergoing neurosurgical procedures for intracranial lesions. Due to the limited number of patients studied, the safety of desflurane has not been established and is not recommended for use in neurosurgical procedures.

Pediatric Surgery: Desflurane was compared to halothane, with or without nitrous oxide, in 235 patients aged 2 weeks to 12 years (median 2 years), ASA physical status I or II. The concentration of desflurane required for maintenance of anesthesia is age dependent (see Dosage, Table II). Changes in blood pressure during maintenance of and recovery from anesthesia were similar between desflurane N_2O/O_2 and halothane/N_2O/O_2. Heart rate during maintenance of anesthesia was approximately 10 beats/min faster with desflurane than with halothane. There were no differences in the incidences of nausea and vomiting between desflurane and halothane.

Suprane (cont'd)

Indications: As an inhalation agent for maintenance of general anesthesia.

Desflurane is not recommended for mask induction of anaesthesia because of a high incidence of moderate to severe upper airway adverse events (see Adverse Effects).

Contraindications: Should not be used when general anesthesia is contraindicated, in patients with a known sensitivity to desflurane or other halogenated agents and in patients with a known or suspected genetic susceptibility to malignant hyperthermia.

Warnings: Desflurane should be administered only by persons trained in the administration of general anesthesia, using a vaporizer specifically designed and designated for use with desflurane. Facilities for maintenance of a patient airway, artificial ventilation, oxygen enrichment and circulatory resuscitation must be immediately available. Hypotension and respiratory depression increase as anesthesia is deepened.

Respiration must be monitored closely and supported when necessary.

Desflurane is not recommended for mask induction as it causes a high incidence of laryngospasm, coughing, breath holding, apnea, increase in secretions and oxyhemoglobin desaturation (see Adverse Effects).

Since awakening is rapid, care should be taken that appropriate analgesia has been administered to the patient at the end of the procedure or early in the postanesthesia care unit. Rapid awakening with pain may be associated with agitation, particularly in pediatric patients.

In healthy volunteers, in the absence of concomitant N_2O and/or opioid administration, sudden step increases in the end-tidal concentration of desflurane may cause transient increases in sympathetic activity with associated increases in heart rate and blood pressure. The hemodynamic changes are more common at concentrations $\geq$6% and more severe with large ($\geq$1%), sudden increments. Without treatment, and without further increases in desflurane concentration, these increases in heart rate and blood pressure resolve in approximately 4 minutes. At the new, higher end-tidal desflurane concentration blood pressure is likely to be lower and heart rate higher than at the previous, lower steady-state desflurane concentration. The transient increases of heart rate and blood pressure are less if the end-tidal concentration of desflurane is increased in increments of 1% or less. However, if during the transiently increased heart rate and blood pressure the end-tidal concentration of desflurane is again rapidly increased, further increase of heart rate and blood pressure may result. Administration of sympatholytic drugs (fentanyl, alfentanil, esmolol, clonidine) prior to a sudden step increase of desflurane blunts or blocks the increase in heart rate and blood pressure. The sympathetic response is not obtunded by i.v. or endotracheal lidocaine or by i.v. propofol (see Pharmacology).

When desflurane is used in the clinical setting, the following should be considered:

Desflurane should not be used as the sole anesthetic in patients with coronary artery disease or in patients where increases in heart rate or blood pressure are undesirable. Rapid inhaled induction of anesthesia with desflurane alone, without concomitant administration of an opioid, in patients with coronary artery disease, has been associated with an increased incidence of myocardial ischemia. Desflurane, when given in conjunction with opioids for maintenance of anesthesia in patients with coronary artery disease, has not produced an incidence of ischemia different from that produced by other anesthetics. Thus, when desflurane is to be used in patients with coronary artery disease, it should always be used in combination with other medications, such as i.v. opioids or hypnotics and it should not be used for induction (see Pharmacology).

When changing the depth of anesthesia, rapid increases in the end-tidal concentration of desflurane should be avoided and the end-tidal concentration increased in small increments of 1% or less. It is not necessary to deliver concentrations of desflurane far in excess of the desired end-tidal concentration ("overpressurization" technique) due to the low blood and tissue solubilities of desflurane and the resulting rapid equilibrium of alveolar concentration with inspired and delivered concentrations; thus the transient and self-limiting increases in heart rate and blood pressure may be avoided.

During maintenance of anesthesia, increases in heart rate and blood pressure occurring after rapid incremental increases in end-tidal concentration of desflurane may not represent inadequate anesthesia. The changes due to sympathetic activation resolve in approximately 4 minutes. Increases in heart rate and blood pressure occurring before or in the absence of a rapid increase in desflurane concentration, may be interpreted as light anesthesia. Thus, in such patients, incremental increases of 0.5 to 1% end-tidal desflurane may attenuate these signs of light anesthesia, as may concomitant administration of analgesics. Should raised heart rate and blood pressure persist, then other causes should be sought.

There are no data regarding the cardiovascular effects of desflurane in hypovolemic and hypotensive patients.

Precautions: General: As with any inhalation agent, the use of desflurane proportionately decreases the concentration of all other gases administered concurrently, including O_2. For example, the addition of 10% desflurane to 70% N_2O and 30% O_2 reduces the O_2 concentration to 27%.

Nitrous oxide diminishes the inspired concentration of desflurane required to reach a desired level of anesthesia (see Dosage, Table II following page).

As with other rapidly-acting anesthetic agents, rapid emergence with desflurane should be taken into account in cases where postanesthesia pain is anticipated. Care should be taken that appropriate analgesia has been administered to the patient at the end of the procedure or early in the postanesthesia care unit stay (see Warnings).

As with other halogenated anesthetic agents, there is some elevation of glucose intraoperatively. Glucose elevation should be considered in diabetic patients.

Desflurane can react with desiccated carbon dioxide (CO_2) absorbents to produce carbon monoxide which may result in elevated levels of carboxyhemoglobin in some patients. In clinical practice, cases of elevated carboxyhemoglobin have been reported in association with desflurane. Case reports suggest that barium hydroxide lime and sodalime become desiccated when fresh gases are passed through the CO_2 absorber cannister at high flow rates over many hours or days. When a clinician suspects that CO_2 absorbent may be desiccated, it should be replaced before the administration of desflurane.

Geriatrics: The MAC in geriatric patients is approximately 70% of the adult dose in 100% oxygen and 40% the adult dose in 60% nitrous oxide (see Dosage).

Pregnancy: There are no adequate and well-controlled studies in pregnant women. Desflurane should be used during pregnancy only if the potential benefit justifies the potential risk to the fetus.

Obstetrics: Due to the limited number of patients studied, safety of desflurane in obstetrics has not been established at this time.

Children: The MAC of desflurane in pediatric patients is higher than that in young adults (see Dosage). Several publications in the literature have reported frequent agitation upon emergence from desflurane anesthesia in children. It is unknown whether this is related to desflurane or to the rapid transition from anesthesia to consciousness.

Renal and Hepatic Impairment: No dosage adjustments are required in these patients. Hepatic dysfunction has been reported after desflurane use. A causal relationship may or may not exist.

Neurosurgery: Due to the limited number of patients studied, the safety of desflurane has not been established and is not recommended for use in neurosurgical procedures (see Pharmacology, Clinical Studies).

Drug Interactions: Benzodiazepines: Midazolam (25 to 50 μg/kg) decreases the MAC of desflurane by 16%.

Opioids: Immediately following the administration of fentanyl (3 to 6 μg/kg) the MAC of desflurane decreases by 50%.

Neuromuscular Relaxants: Desflurane potentiates the effect of depolarizing and nondepolarizing neuromuscular relaxants. When compared to nitrous oxide/opioid anesthesia, the requirements for depolarizing and nondepolarizing agents are reduced by 30% and 50%, respectively.

Other Drugs: The effects of desflurane on the disposition of other drugs has not been determined.

Pheochromocytoma/Neuroblastoma: There are insufficient data on the use of desflurane in patients with pheochromocytoma and neuroblastoma. Since desflurane can cause stimulation of the sympathetic nervous system, its use is not recommended in patients with these conditions (see Warnings).

Malignant Hyperthermia: In susceptible individuals, desflurane anesthesia may trigger a skeletal muscle hypermetabolic state leading to high oxygen demand and the clinical syndrome known as malignant hyperthermia. The clinical syndrome includes nonspecific features such as muscle rigidity, tachycardia, tachypnea, cyanosis, arrhythmias and unstable blood pressure. Some of these nonspecific signs may also appear during light anesthesia, acute hypoxia, hypercapnia and hypovolemia. An increase in overall metabolism may be reflected in an elevated temperature (which may rise rapidly early or late in the case, but usually is not the first sign of augmented metabolism) and an increased usage of the CO_2 absorption system (hot canister). PaO_2 and pH may decrease, and hyperkalemia and a base deficit may appear. Treatment includes discontinuation of desflurane, administration of i.v. dantrolene sodium, and application of supportive therapy. Such therapy includes vigorous efforts to restore body temperature to normal, respiratory and circulatory support as indicated, and management of electrolyte-fluid-acid-base derangements. (Consult prescribing information for dantrolene sodium i.v. for additional information on patient management.) Renal failure may appear later, and urine flow should be sustained if possible.

Adverse Effects: Adverse event information is derived from controlled clinical trials. The studies were conducted using a variety of premedications, other anesthetics, and surgical procedures of varying length. Of the 1 843 patients exposed to desflurane in clinical trials, 1 209 were used in estimating the incidence of adverse reactions below. Of these, 370 adults and 152 children were induced with desflurane alone and 687 patients were maintained principally with desflurane. Frequencies reflect the percent of patients with the event and each patient was counted once for each type of adverse event. They are presented in alphabetical order within each body system.

Probably Causally Related: Incidence Greater than 1%. Induction (Use as a Mask Inhalation Agent): Adult Patients (n=370): coughing 34%, breath holding 27%, apnea 15%, increased secretions 9%, laryngospasm 8%, oxyhemoglobin desaturation (SpO_2 <90%) 8%, pharyngitis 4% (see Warnings). Pediatric patients (n=152): coughing 72%, breath holding 63%, laryngospasm 50%, oxyhemoglobin desaturation (SpO_2 <90%) 26%, increased secretions 21%, bronchospasm 3% (see Warnings).

Maintenance or Recovery: Adult and Pediatric Patients (n=687): Body as a Whole: headache 1%.

Cardiovascular: bradycardia 1%, hypertension 1%, nodal arrhythmia 1%, tachycardia 1%.

Digestive: nausea 27%, vomiting 16%.

Nervous System: increased salivation 1%.

Respiratory: apnea 7%, breath holding 2%, cough increased 4%, laryngospasm 3%, pharyngitis 1%.

Special Senses: conjunctivitis (conjunctival hyperemia) 2%.

Probably Causally Related: Incidence Less than 1% and Reported in 3 or More Patients, Regardless of Severity (n=1 843): Cardiovascular: arrhythmia, bigeminy, ECG abnormal, myocardial ischemia, vasodilation.

Nervous System: agitation, dizziness.

Respiratory: asthma, dyspnea, hypoxia.

Causal Relationship Unknown: Incidence Less than 1% and Reported in 3 or More Patients, Regardless of Severity (n=1 843): Body as a Whole: fever.

Cardiovascular: hemorrhage, myocardial infarct.

Metabolic and Nutrition: creatinine phosphokinase increased.

Musculoskeletal System: myalgia.

Skin and Appendages: pruritus.

See Precautions for information regarding pediatric use and malignant hyperthermia.

Laboratory Findings: Transient elevations in glucose and white blood cell count may occur as with the use of other anesthetic agents. Abnormal liver function tests were observed in <1% of patients. Hepatitis has been reported very rarely.

Overdose: Symptoms: Marked hypotension, tachycardia and apnea.

Treatment: Stop drug administration. Support respiration and circulation as required.

Dosage: General: Deliver from a vaporizer specifically designed and designated for use with desflurane.

Premedication should be selected according to the need of the individual patient. There is no evidence of interaction between desflurane and commonly used anticholinergic drugs. Desflurane is potentiated by benzodiazepines and opioids (see Precautions, Drug Interactions).

Desflurane is not recommended for mask induction as it causes a high incidence of laryngospasm, coughing, secretions, breath holding, apnea, and increase in secretions and oxyhemoglobin desaturation (see Adverse Effects).

Maintenance: Adults: Surgical levels of anesthesia in adults may be maintained with concentrations of 2.5 to 8.5% desflurane with or without the concomitant use of nitrous oxide.

Children: Surgical anesthesia is maintained with concentrations of 5.2 to 10% desflurane in children with or without the concomitant use of nitrous oxide.

Geriatrics: Geriatric patients require approximately 70% the adult dose in 100% oxygen and approximately 40% the adult dose in 60% nitrous oxide.

Table II provides mean relative potency based on age in ASA physical status I and II patients.

Table II—Suprane

Effect of Age on MAC of Suprane; Mean ± SD (Percent Atmospheres)

Age	N	100% O_2	N	60% N_2O
2 weeks	6	9.2±0.0	—	—
10 weeks	5	9.4±0.4	—	—
9 months	4	10.0±0.7	5	7.5±0.8
2 years	3	9.1±0.6	—	—
3 years	—	—	5	6.4±0.4
4 years	4	8.6±0.6	—	—
7 years	5	8.1±0.6	—	—
25 years	4	7.3±0.0	4	4.0±0.3
45 years	4	6.0±0.3	6	2.8±0.6
70 years	6	5.2±0.6	6	1.7±0.4

*N=Number of cross over pairs (using up-and-down method of quantal response).

Desflurane should not be used as the sole anesthetic in patients with coronary artery disease or in patients where increases in heart rate or blood pressure are undesirable. Rapid inhaled induction of anesthesia with desflurane alone, without concomitant administration of an opioid, in patients with coronary artery disease, has been associated with an increased incidence of myocardial ischemia. Desflurane, when given in conjunction with opioids for maintenance of anesthesia in patients with coronary artery disease, has not produced an incidence of ischemia different from that produced by other anaesthetics. Thus, when desflurane is to be used in patients with coronary artery disease, it should always be used in combination with other medications, such as i.v. opioids or hypnotics and it should not be used for induction (see Pharmacology).

When changing the depth of anesthesia, rapid increases in the end-tidal concentration of desflurane should be avoided and the end-tidal concentration increased in small increments of 1% or less. It is not necessary to deliver concentrations far in excess of the desired end-tidal concentration ("overpressurization" technique) due to the low blood and tissue solubilities of desflurane and the resulting rapid equilibrium of alveolar concentration with inspired and delivered concentrations; thus the transient and self-limiting increases in heart rate and blood pressure may be avoided.

During maintenance of anesthesia, increases in heart rate and blood pressure occurring after rapid incremental increases in end-tidal concentration of desflurane may not represent inadequate anesthesia. The changes due to sympathetic activation resolve in approximately 4 minutes. Increases in heart rate and blood pressure occurring before or in the absence of a rapid increase in desflurane concentration may be interpreted as light anesthesia. Thus, in such patients, incremental increases of 0.5 to 1% end-tidal desflurane may attenuate these signs of light anaesthesia, as may concomitant administration of analgesics. Should raised heart rate and blood pressure persist, then other causes should be sought.

Supplied: Each bottle contains: desflurane 240 mL. Amber glass bottles of 250 mL. Store at or below 30°C.

Reviewed 1999

SUPRAX® Ⓟ

Rhône-Poulenc Rorer

Cefixime

Antibiotic

Pharmacology: Cefixime exerts its bactericidal effect by attaching to penicillin-binding proteins and inhibiting peptidoglycan synthesis, thus causing damage to the bacterial cell wall.

Pharmacokinetics: Following oral dosing, cefixime attains peak serum levels in approximately 4 hours. The half-life is about 3 to 4 hours and is not dose dependent. Cefixime is excreted by renal and biliary mechanisms. About 50% of the absorbed dose is excreted unchanged in the urine within 24 hours. There is no evidence of metabolism of cefixime in vivo.

Indications: Treatment of the following infections caused by susceptible strains of the designated microorganisms:

Middle Ear: Otitis media caused by S. pneumoniae, H. influenzae (beta-lactamase positive and negative strains), B. catarrhalis (beta-lactamase positive and negative strains) and S. pyogenes.

Paranasal Sinuses: Sinusitis caused by S. pneumoniae, H. influenzae (beta-lactamase positive and negative strains), and B. catarrhalis (beta-lactamase positive and negative strains).

Urinary Tract: Acute uncomplicated cystitis and urethritis caused by E. coli, P. mirabilis, and Klebsiella species.

Upper Respiratory Tract: Pharyngitis and tonsillitis caused by S. pyogenes.

Lower Respiratory Tract: Acute bronchitis caused by S. pneumoniae, B. catarrhalis (beta-lactamase positive and negative strains) and H. influenzae (beta-lactamase positive and negative strains).

Uncomplicated Gonorrhea: Uncomplicated gonorrhea (cervical/urethral and rectal) caused by N. gonorrhoeae, including penicillinase (beta-lactamase-positive) and nonpenicillinase (beta-lactamase-negative) producing strains.

Appropriate cultures should be taken for susceptibility testing before initiating treatment with cefixime. If warranted, therapy may be instituted before susceptibility results are known; however, once these are obtained, therapy may need to be adjusted.

Contraindications: Patients with known allergies to the cephalosporin or penicillin antibiotics.

Warnings: In penicillin-sensitive patients, cefixime should be administered cautiously. Patients may be sensitive to penicillins and not to cephalosporins such as cefixime or be sensitive to both. Medical literature indicates that patients sensitive to cephalosporins are very likely to be penicillin sensitive.

Antibiotics, including cefixime, should be administered cautiously to any patient who has demonstrated some form of allergy, particularly to drugs.

Treatment with broad-spectrum antibiotics such as cefixime alters the normal flora of the colon and may permit overgrowth of clostridia. Studies indicate that a toxin produced by C. difficile is a primary cause of antibiotic-associated diarrhea. Pseudomembranous colitis is associated with the use of broad-spectrum antibiotics (including macrolides, semisynthetic penicillins, and cephalosporins); therefore, it is important to consider its diagnosis in patients who develop diarrhea in association with the use of antibiotics. Symptoms of pseudomembranous colitis may occur during or after antibiotic treatment. Such colitis may range in severity from mild to life-threatening.

Mild cases of pseudomembranous colitis usually respond to drug discontinuation alone. In moderate to severe cases, management should include sigmoidoscopy, appropriate bacteriologic studies, fluids, electrolytes, and protein supplementation. If the colitis does not improve after the drug has been discontinued, or if the symptoms are severe, oral vancomycin should be considered for antibiotic-associated pseudomembranous colitis produced by C. difficile. Other causes of colitis should be excluded.

Precautions: General: If an allergic reaction to cefixime occurs, the drug should be discontinued, and, if necessary, the patient should be treated with appropriate agents, e.g., pressor amines, antihistamines, or corticosteroids. The possibility of the emergence of resistant organisms which might result in overgrowth should be kept in mind, particularly during prolonged treatment. In such use, careful observation of the patient is essential. If superinfection occurs during therapy, appropriate measures should be taken.

Broad-spectrum antibiotics such as cefixime should be prescribed with caution in individuals with a history of gastrointestinal disease.

Once daily dosing only must be used for urinary tract infections, since twice daily dosing was shown to be not as effective in clinical studies.

Do not use cefixime to treat S. aureus as this strain of staphylococci is resistant to cefixime.

Renal Impairment: Cefixime may be administered in the presence of impaired renal function, but dose modification is recommended for patients with moderate or severe renal impairment (i.e., creatinine clearance of <40 mL/min) (see Dosage).

Bioavailability Differences Between Tablet and Suspension: The area under the time versus concentration curve is greater by approximately 26.4% and the C_{max} is greater by approximately 20.7% with the oral suspension when compared to the tablet after doses of 400 mg. This increased absorption should be taken into consideration if the oral suspension is to be substituted for the tablet. Because of the lack of bioequivalence, tablets should not be substituted for oral suspension particularly in the treatment of otitis media where clinical trial experience with the suspension only is available (see Dosage).

Drug/Laboratory Interactions: A false-positive reaction for ketones in the urine may occur with tests using nitroprusside but not with those using nitroferricyanide.

The administration of beta-lactams may result in a false-positive reaction for glucose in the urine using Clinitest, Benedict's solution, or Fehling's solution. It is recommended that glucose tests based on enzymatic glucose oxidase reactions (such as Clinistix or Testape) be used. A false-positive direct Coombs test has been reported during treatment with cephalosporin antibiotics; therefore, it should be recognized that a positive Coombs test may be due to the drug.

Pregnancy: The safety of cefixime in the treatment of infection in pregnant women has not been established.

Reproduction studies have been performed in mice and rats at doses up to 400 times the human dose and have revealed no evidence of impaired fertility or harm to the fetus due to cefixime. Because animal reproduction studies are not always predictive of human response, this drug should be used during pregnancy only if the likely benefits of using cefixime outweighs the potential risk to the fetus and/or the mother.

Labor and Delivery: Cefixime has not been studied for use during labor and delivery.

Lactation: It is not known whether cefixime is excreted in human milk. Because many drugs are excreted in human milk, caution should be exercised when cefixime is administered to a nursing woman.

Children: Safety and effectiveness of cefixime in children less than 6 months old have not been established.

Adverse Effects: Five percent of patients in the clinical trials discontinued therapy because of drug-related adverse reactions. Thirty-six percent of the pediatric patient population experienced at least one adverse reaction (mild 25%, moderate 9%, severe 2%). Forty-seven percent of the adult patients experienced at least one adverse reaction (mild 24%, moderate 19%, severe 4%). The most commonly seen adverse reactions in the clinical trials of the tablet formulation were gastrointestinal events, which were reported in 37% of all adult patients treated (mild 21%, moderate 13%, severe 3%). The predominant adverse events seen in adults in clinical trials with cefixime were diarrhea 15%, (mild 7.2%, moderate 6.2%, severe 1.5%), headache 11%, stool changes 12%, nausea 9%, abdominal pain 5%, and dyspepsia 3%. The rates of the most prevalent adverse reactions were similar in the once a day and twice a day dosing regimens with the exception of headache which appears slightly more frequently in adults dosed once a day (12.9%) versus twice a day (8%). Other than for generally mild rashes or emesis which were each observed in 5% of children treated, the incidence of adverse reactions in pediatric patients receiving the suspension was generally comparable to the incidence seen in adult patients receiving tablets. These symptoms usually responded to symptomatic therapy or ceased when cefixime was discontinued.

Several patients developed severe diarrhea and/or documented pseudomembranous colitis, and a few required hospitalization.

The following adverse reactions have been reported following the use of cefixime. Incidence rates were less than 1 in 50 (less than 2%), except as otherwise noted.

CNS: headaches (11%) and dizziness (3%).

Gastrointestinal: diarrhea (15%), stool changes (12%), nausea (9%), abdominal pain (5%), dyspepsia (3%), flatulence (3%) and vomiting (2%). Pseudomembranous colitis has been reported rarely.

Hepatic: transient elevations of AST, ALT and alkaline phosphatase.

Renal: transient elevations in BUN or creatinine.

Hemic and Lymphatic: transient thrombocytopenia, leukopenia, and eosinophilia. Prolongation in prothrombin time was seen rarely.

Hypersensitivity: skin rashes, urticaria, drug fever and pruritus.

Other: genital pruritus, vaginitis and candidiasis.

When cefixime was used as single 400 mg dose therapy in clinical trials in the treatment of uncomplicated gonorrhea,

Suprax (cont'd)

adverse reactions which were considered to be related to cefixime therapy, were reported for 5.9% (21/358) of patients. Clinically mild gastrointestinal side effects occurred in 3.7% of all patients, moderate events occurred in 0.9% of all patients and no adverse reactions were reported as severe. Individual event rates included diarrhea 1% and loose or frequent stools 1%. Incidence rates for all other adverse reactions reported for adults in these trials were less than 1%.

In addition to the adverse reactions listed above which have been observed in patients treated with cefixime, the following adverse reactions and altered laboratory tests have been reported for cephalosporin-class antibiotics. Allergic reactions were reported including anaphylaxis, Stevens-Johnson syndrome, erythema multiforme, toxic epidermal necrolysis, superinfection, renal dysfunction, toxic nephropathy, hepatic dysfunction including cholestasis, aplastic anemia, hemolytic anemia, and hemorrhage. Abnormal laboratory tests were reported including positive Coombs test, elevated bilirubin, elevated LDH, pancytopenia, neutropenia and agranulocytosis.

Several cephalosporins have been implicated in triggering seizures, particularly in patients with renal impairment when the dosage was not reduced (see Dosage and Overdose). If seizures associated with cefixime occur, the drug should be discontinued. Anticonvulsant therapy can be given if clinically indicated.

Overdose: Symptoms and Treatment: Gastric lavage may be indicated; otherwise, no specific antidote exists. Cefixime is not removed in significant quantities from the circulation by hemodialysis or peritoneal dialysis.

Dosage: Adults: The recommended dose is 400 mg once daily. When necessary, a dose of 200 mg given twice daily may be considered except for urinary tract infections where once daily dosing must be used. For treatment of uncomplicated gonococcal infections, a single oral dose of 400 mg is recommended.

Children: The recommended dose is 8 mg/kg/day once daily (see Table I). When necessary, a dose of 4 mg/kg given twice daily may be considered except for urinary tract infections where once daily dosing must be used.

Table I—Suprax

Pediatric Dosage Chart

Weight kg	Dose/Day mg	Dose/Day tsp of suspension	Dose/Day mL
6	48	0.5	2.4
12.5	100	1.0	5.0
19	152	1.5	7.6
25	200	2.0	10.0
35	280	3.0	14.0

Children weighing more than 50 kg or older than 12 years should be treated with the recommended adult dose. Safety and effectiveness in infants aged less than 6 months have not been established.

Otitis media should be treated with the suspension. Clinical studies of otitis media were conducted with the suspension only and the suspension results in higher peak blood levels than the tablet when administered at the same dose. Therefore, the tablet should not be substituted for the suspension in the treatment of otitis media (see Precautions).

Duration of Therapy: Duration of dosage in clinical trials was 10 to 14 days. The duration of treatment should be guided by the patient's clinical and bacteriological response.

In the treatment of infections due to S. pyogenes, a therapeutic dose of cefixime should be administered for at least 10 days.

Renal Impairment: Cefixime may be administered in the presence of impaired renal function. Normal dose and schedule may be employed in patients with creatinine clearances of 40 mL/min or greater. Patients whose clearance is between 20 and 40 mL/min should be given 75% of the standard daily dosage. Patients whose creatinine clearance is less than 20 mL/min should be given 50% of the standard daily dosage. Experience in children with renal impairment is very limited.

Note: Neither hemodialysis, nor peritoneal dialysis remove significant amounts of cefixime from the body.

Reconstitution Directions for Oral Suspensions: see Table II.

After mixing, the suspension may be kept for 14 days at room temperature or under refrigeration without significant loss of potency. Keep container tightly closed. Shake well before using. Discard unused portion after 14 days.

Table II—Suprax

Reconstitution Directions for Oral Suspensions

Bottle Size	Reconstitution Directions
100 mL	Suspend with 69 mL water

Method: Tap the bottle several times to loosen powder contents prior to reconstitution. Add 69 mL of water in **2 portions.** Mix well after each addition. Provides 20 mg/mL.

Bottle Size	Reconstitution Directions
75 mL	Suspend with 52 mL water

Method: Tap the bottle several times to loosen powder contents prior to reconstitution. Add 52 mL of water in **2 portions.** Mix well after each addition. Provides 20 mg/mL.

Bottle Size	Reconstitution Directions
50 mL	Suspend with 36 mL water

Method: Tap the bottle several times to loosen powder contents prior to reconstitution. Add 36 mL of water in **2 portions.** Mix well after each addition. Provides 20 mg/mL.

Supplied: Powder for Oral Suspension: Each 5 mL of reconstituted suspension contains: cefixime 100 mg. Nonmedicinal ingredients: artificial strawberry flavor, sodium benzoate, sucrose and xanthan gum. Gluten- and lactose-free. Bottles of 50, 75 and 100 mL.

Tablets: Each rectangular, white, film-coated tablet, with rounded corners and beveled edges and a divided break line on each side, contains: cefixime 400 mg. Nonmedicinal ingredients: dibasic calcium phosphate, hydroxypropyl methylcellulose 2910, light mineral oil, magnesium stearate, microcrystalline cellulose, pregelatinized starch, sodium lauryl sulfate and titanium dioxide. Gluten- and lactose-free. Bottles of 50.

Store at controlled room temperature 15 to 30°C.

(Shown in Product Recognition Section)

SUPREFACT® Ⓟ
SUPREFACT® DEPOT Ⓟ

Hoechst Marion Roussel

Buserelin Acetate

Luteinizing Hormone-Releasing Hormone (LH-RH) Analog

Pharmacology: Buserelin is a synthetic peptide analog of the natural gonadotropin releasing hormone (GnRH/LHRH). The substitution of glycine in position 6 by D-serine, and that of glycinamide in position 10 by ethylamide, leads to a nonapeptide with a greatly enhanced LHRH effect. The effects of buserelin on follicle stimulating hormone (FSH) and luteinizing hormone (LH) release are 20 to 170 times greater than those of LHRH. Buserelin also has a longer duration of action than natural LHRH.

Investigations in healthy adult males and females have demonstrated that the increase in plasma LH and FSH levels persist for at least 7 hours and that a return to basal values requires about 24 hours.

Clinical inhibition of gonadotropin release, and subsequent reduction of serum testosterone or estradiol to castration level, was found when large pharmacologic doses (50 to 500 μg s.c./day or 300 to 1 200 μg intranasal/day) were administered for periods greater than 1 to 3 months. Chronic administration of such doses of buserelin results in sustained inhibition of gonadotropin production, suppression of ovarian and testicular steroidogenesis and, ultimately, reduced circulating levels of gonadotropin and gonadal steroids. These effects form the basis for buserelin use in patients with hormone-dependent metastatic carcinoma of the prostate gland as well as in patients with endometriosis.

In the clinical pharmacology studies with the buserelin implant, the time-concentration curves of buserelin release from implants were reproducible and similar to those observed in preclinical studies. Maximum release on day 1 was followed by an extended plateau phase which lasted for 8 weeks. After this period, an accelerated biodegradation of the implant material was observed with a terminal half-life of release of 20 to 30 days. The single dose studies performed in healthy male subjects and in patients with benign prostatic hypertrophy showed a therapeutic release rate for 8 weeks (dosage interval); a minimum therapeutic release rate of 4.95 μg/day after 8 weeks was fully effective in maintaining testosterone levels in the surgical castration range by controlled release of buserelin. At the end of the dosage interval, the average fraction of the buserelin dose released from the implants based on urinary excretion data was 84% (in healthy subjects) and 92% (in patients with benign prostatic hypertrophy). Chronic administration of the implant every 8 weeks ensures continuous suppression of testosterone secretion with no cumulation of buserelin release after repeated dosing.

Indications: For the palliative treatment of patients with hormone-dependent advanced carcinoma of the prostate gland (Stage D).

Buserelin is also indicated for the treatement of endometriosis in patients who do not require surgery as primary therapy. The duration of treatment is usually 6 months and should not exceed 9 months. Experience with buserelin for the management of endometriosis has been limited to women 18 years of age and older.

Contraindications: Patients with known hypersensitivity to buserelin or any other formulation component (see Supplied). In patients with prostatic cancer, buserelin is also contraindicated in patients who do not present with hormone-dependent carcinoma; and in patients who have undergone orchiectomy (in these patients, no further reduction of testosterone level is to be expected with buserelin therapy).

Pregnancy: Buserelin is contraindicated in women who are pregnant. As with other LHRH agonists, it is not known whether buserelin caused fetal abnormalities in humans. Women of childbearing potential should be carefully examined before treatment to exclude pregnancy.

Lactation: The use of buserelin in patients who are breast-feeding is not recommended. Buserelin should not be administered to females having undiagnosed abnormal vaginal bleeding.

Warnings: General: Initially, buserelin transiently increases serum testosterone in males, serum estradiol in females and other gonadal hormones.

Cases of early, transient exacerbation of disease signs and symptoms have been reported during treatment with LHRH agonists (see Precautions).

Prostatic Cancer: General: The majority of clinical studies demonstrating the efficacy of buserelin were completed without concomitant therapy with antiandrogens during the first weeks of treatment. For the clinical studies with the buserelin implant, however, an antiandrogen was administered as initial concurrent treatment for a duration of 5 weeks, starting 7 days before the start of buserelin implant therapy. At the start of treatment, there is a temporary rise in male sex hormones. In a few patients, this rise may be associated with isolated cases of short-term worsening of signs and symptoms such as bone pain, urinary signs and symptoms (usually occurring in patients with a previous history of obstructive uropathy) or muscular weakness in the legs.

Patients with Vertebral Metastases: Due to the possibility of early, transient, lesion exacerbation, and consequent possible spinal cord compression, these patients should be closely monitored when LHRH agonist treatment is initiated.

Patients with Genitourinary Tract Symptoms: Patients with genitourinary symptoms may experience a transient increase in such symptoms early in LHRH agonist treatment. These patients should be particularly closely observed for events indicative of obstruction.

Reversibility of LHRH Agonist-Induced Hypogonadism: While hypogonadism is a pharmacologic consequence of long-term LHRH agonist treatment, its reversibility has not been established in patients suffering with prostatic carcinoma.

Endometriosis: Oral contraceptives must be discontinued before starting LHRH treatment; and nonhormonal methods of contraception should be employed during therapy (see Precautions).

Worsening of clinical conditions may occasionally require discontinuation of therapy and/or surgical intervention.

Precautions: Transient Exacerbation of Disease Signs and Symptoms: The administration of LHRH agonists is occasionally related with early, transient (less than 10-days duration usually) exacerbation of the signs and symptoms of metastatic prostatic cancer or endometriosis which are sometimes but not necessarily, associated with a transient rise in serum testosterone or estradiol. Special precautions are recommended in the following patients with prostatic cancer since symptoms may progress to warrant, in rare cases, additional or alternate interventions: patients with metastatic vertebral lesions or patients with history of obstructive uropathy (see Warnings).

From clinical trials with the buserelin implant, administration of an antiandrogen before and concurrently at the start of buserelin implant therapy may avoid the occurrence of such signs and symptoms of the disease (in clinical trials, the antiandrogen was primarily given for the first 5 weeks, beginning 7 days prior to the first buserelin implant injection).

Monitoring of Patients: **Prostatic Cancer:** Regular clinical assessment of patients is recommended and should include clinical laboratory determinations of serum testosterone, prostatic acid phosphatase or acid phosphatase and prostate-specific antigen (PSA). If cancer is responsive to buserelin therapy, the prostate cancer tumor markers (PAP and PSA), if elevated prior to the commencement of treatment, are usually reduced by the end of the first month.

The status of bone lesions may be monitored by bone scans and that of the prostate lesions may be followed by ultrasonography and/or CT scan in addition to digital rectal examination.

Evaluation for obstructive uropathy may be undertaken by ultrasonography, i.v. pyelogram or CT scan in addition to clinical examination. In addition, it is recommended that serum testosterone levels be determined after 4 to 6 weeks of treatment with LHRH agonists and then at 3-monthly intervals. Inadequate serum testosterone suppression should lead to evaluation of patient compliance.

Patients with a history of depression or depressed moods should be observed closely for evidence of mood changes and treated accordingly.

In treated hypertensive patients, hypertensive crisis may occur. It is recommended that blood pressure be monitored regularly in these patients.

Isolated cases of loss of diabetic control have been observed. Blood glucose levels should be checked regularly in diabetic patients.

Effect on Clinical Laboratory Tests: LHRH agonist treatment will affect selected hormonal and other serum/urine parameters in the first week of treatment: elevation of testosterone and dihydrotestosterone, as well as acid phosphatase can be expected. With chronic drug administration, these elevated values of these variables will fall below baseline.

Renal function tests, blood urea nitrogen and creatinine may rarely be elevated during the first few days of LHRH agonist therapy in prostate cancer patients before returning to normal.

Drug Interactions: During treatment with buserelin, the effect of antidiabetic agents may be attenuated (see also Adverse Effects).

Allergic Reactions: Allergic asthma with dyspnea as well as in isolated cases, anaphylactic/anaphylactoid shock have been observed in patients treated with buserelin, necessitating early treatment of such conditions. For patients experiencing anaphylactic/anaphylactoid reactions who were given the buserelin implant, it may be necessary to surgically remove it.

Endometriosis: *Pregnancy:* Safe use of the drug in pregnancy has not been established; therefore, a nonhormonal method of contraception should be used during treatment. Patients should be advised that if they miss or postpone a dose of buserelin, ovulation may occur with the potential for conception. If a patient becomes pregnant during treatment, she should discontinue treatment and consult her physician.

Diagnostic Interference: Administration of buserelin in therapeutic doses results in suppression of the pituitary-gonadal system. Normal function is usually restored after a few weeks of the last dose of buserelin. Diagnostic tests of pituitary-gonadal function conducted during the treatment and within a few weeks after discontinuation of buserelin therapy may therefore be misleading.

General: Changes in Bone Density: Bone loss can be expected as part of natural aging and of natural menopause and can also be anticipated during medically induced hypogonadic status caused by long-term use of LHRH agonists such as buserelin. In patients with significant risk factors for decreased bone mineral content and/or bone mass such as family history of osteoporosis, chronic use of corticosteroids or anticonvulsants or chronic abuse of alcohol or tobacco, LHRH agonists may pose additional risk. In these patients, risk and benefits must be weighed carefully before initiation of LHRH agonist therapy. In patients with endometriosis, use of buserelin for longer than the recommended 6 months or in the presence of other known risk factors for decreased bone mineral content may cause additional bone loss.

Adverse Effects: The adverse effects observed in patients treated with buserelin and buserelin implant are, principally, directly related to its anticipated pharmacologic action, i.e., suppression of pituitary (gonadotropin) and gonadal (testosterone or estradiol) hormone production with resulting clinical signs and symptoms of hypogonadism.

Long-term treatment with LHRH agonists may, in isolated cases, lead to development of pituitary adenomas; in humans, however, this has not yet been observed with buserelin therapy.

Prostatic Cancer: Injection and Nasal Solution: An early in treatment transient increase in serum testosterone levels usually occurs. Occasionally, this may be associated with transient worsening of clinical status and secondary reactions such as: occurrence or exacerbation of bone pain in patients with bone metastases, signs of neurological deficit due to tumor compression, impaired micturition, hydronephrosis, lymphostasis or thrombosis with pulmonary embolism. This transient initial rise in serum androgen will be followed by a progressive decrease to castration levels (see Warnings and Precautions).

In patients treated with the buserelin implant, such reactions can be avoided when an antiandrogen is given concomitantly in the initial phase of buserelin treatment (see Precautions). Some of these patients may, nevertheless, develop a mild, transient increase in tumor pain and a deterioration in general well-being.

Injection and Nasal Solution: Serious clinical flare reactions were reported in approximately 1% of patients in buserelin efficacy trials.

In a large, North American multicenter study of buserelin, the following reactions were encountered: patients receiving daily s.c. buserelin: 71.6% reported hot flushes, 84.8% reported loss of libido, 79.4% reported impotence. However, more than 50% of all buserelin subjects reported loss of libido and impotence at admission.

For patients receiving intranasal buserelin: 66.1% reported hot flushes, 75% reported loss of libido, 75% reported impotence, 12.5% reported nasal irritation and 28.5% reported headache. Not all cases were considered to be buserelin related.

Other adverse reactions considered to be buserelin related and occurring in more than 1% of patients were: gynecomastia, pruritus and gastrointestinal disturbances.

Of patients who received maintenance buserelin therapy by daily s.c. injection, 11.9% reported one or more generally transient injection site reactions: pain (4.6%), irritation (3.3%), swelling (3.3%), urticaria (2%) and other (4.6%). None of the reactions were severe or required discontinuation of therapy.

Other adverse effects arranged by body system possibly or probably related to the administration of buserelin (individual signs/symptoms not marked with an asterisk occurred at an incidence below 1%; *=incidence between 1 and 2%) included: Body as a Whole* (s.c. use only): clinical flare reaction*, fever, pain.

Digestive* (s.c. use only): diarrhea, nausea.

Endocrine (s.c. use only): feminization.

Nervous System* (s.c. and intranasal* use): dry mouth* (intranasal use only), increased sweating* (intranasal use only), hot flushes (*intranasal use, <1% s.c. use).

Respiratory (intranasal use only): dry nose*.

Skin and Appendages (s.c. use only): gynecomastia*, hirsutism.

Urogenital (s.c. use only): urinary retention.

Implant: No serious clinical flare reactions were reported in patients (n=297) enrolled in clinical studies with the buserelin implant.

In an open-label, noncomparative, international multicenter study of the buserelin implant comprising a total of 241 patients, the following adverse reactions considered to be remotely, possibly or probably related to the buserelin implant were encountered during 1 year of treatment: 15.8% reported hot flushes, 2.5% reported libido decreased, 1.2% reported impotence, 1.2% reported injection site pain, hypertension [including hypertensive crises in treated hypertensive patients] (2.9%), depression (2.9%) and edema of the ankles and calves (2.1%).

Other adverse reactions, arranged by body system, and remotely, possibly or probably related to the administration of the buserelin implant (individual signs/symptoms occurred at an incidence of less than 1%) were: Body as a Whole: nonserious clinical flare reaction, fever, pain.

Cardiovascular: heart failure, palpitations, tachycardia, thrombosis.

Digestive: constipation, nausea.

Endocrine: exacerbation of a pre-existing diabetes mellitus, hyperglycemia.

Musculoskeletal: arthritis.

Metabolic and Nutritional Disorders: weight gain, weight loss.

Nervous: headache, hyperalgesia, sleep disorder (insomnia), sweating increased.

Respiratory: pharyngitis.

Skin and Appendages: eczema, gynecomastia, injection site pain, injection site reaction, pruritus, rash.

Special Senses: blindness in one eye (temporary).

Urogenital: abnormal ejaculation.

Miscellaneous: In the international database, other adverse events, including events which were observed only in females (excluding female gender-specific events) or for other unlabelled indications, have been observed in patients treated with buserelin, as itemized below (not all events were considered to be related to buserelin therapy):

Digestive: changes in appetite (e.g., anorexia), increased thirst, vomiting.

Hemic and Lymphatic: leukopenia, thrombopenia.

Laboratory Values: changes in blood lipids (e.g., hypercholesterolemia, hyperlipidemia), increase in bilirubin levels, increase in serum liver enzymes levels (e.g., transaminases).

Nervous: concentration and memory disturbances, dizziness, drowsiness, emotional instability, feelings of anxiety, mood changes, nervousness, tiredness.

Skin and Appendages: articular pains, irritation of the mucosa in the nasopharynx due to nasal solution administration (which may lead to nosebleeds, hoarseness, disturbances of smell or taste), rhinorrhea, skin reaction (wheal) allergy.

Special Senses: eye dryness and irritation, feeling of pressure behind the eyes, impaired vision (e.g., blurred vision), hearing disorders, tinnitus.

Endometriosis: During the first 2 weeks of treatment with intranasal buserelin, estradiol levels may increase but, thereafter decrease to basal or lower levels. This transient increase in estradiol may result in a temporary exacerbation of signs and symptoms (see Warnings and Precautions).

In two multicenter, open-label, randomized clinical trials, buserelin was compared to danazol in the treatment of patients with mild to severe endometriosis. Reported adverse reactions which were considered by the treating physician to have a possible or probable relationship to treatment and which occurred in 5% or more of patients are listed in Table I.

Table I—Suprefact

Adverse Reactions—Endometriosis

Adverse Reaction	Suprefact (n=168) n (%)	Danazol (n=109) n (%)
Hot flushes[a]	121 (72.0)	42 (38.5)
Vaginal dryness[a]	48 (28.6)	8 (7.3)
Menorrhagia[a]	40 (23.8)	24 (22.0)
Headache[a]	34 (20.2)	18 (16.5)
Libido decreased[a]	20 (11.9)	8 (7.3)
Dizziness	15 (8.9)	6 (5.5)
Application site reaction	13 (7.7)	0 (0.0)
Depression[a]	13 (7.7)	6 (5.5)
Emotional lability[a]	12 (7.1)	15 (13.8)
Asthenia	12 (7.1)	24 (22.0)
Nausea	11 (6.5)	9 (8.3)
Acne[b]	9 (5.4)	35 (32.1)

[a] Physiological effects of decreased estrogen.
[b] Androgenic-like effects.

In addition, in these same studies, other adverse reactions possibly or probably related to buserelin therapy reported in less than 5% of patients included (those marked with an asterick occurred between 1 and 5% of patients): Body as a Whole: abdominal pain, allergic reaction, neck rigidity*, pain, pain in extremity*, photosensitivity.

Cardiovascular: migraine*, palpitation*, syncope, vasodilatation.

Digestive: constipation*, gastrointestinal disorder, gastrointestinal fullness*, gastrointestinal pain, increased appetite, mouth ulceration.

Hemic and Lymphatic: purpura*.

Metabolic and Nutritional: edema*, weight gain*, weight loss*.

Musculoskeletal: arthralgia*, myalgia*.

Nervous System: amnesia, anxiety*, hostility*, insomnia*, nervousness*, paresthesia*, somnolence, sweating increased, thinking abnormal, tremor, vertigo.

Respiratory: epistaxis, rhinitis*, upper respiratory infection*.

Skin and Appendages: breast atrophy, breast enlargement, breast pain*, dry skin*, hirsutism*, rash, skin disorder*.

Special Senses: abnormality of accommodation, dry eyes, ear disorder, ear pain, eye disorder, parosmia, taste perversion*, tinnitus.

Urogenital: dyspareunia*, menstrual disorder*, vaginal hemorrhage, vaginitis*.

In other clinical trials comprising a total of 968 patients with endometriosis treated with buserelin, adverse events not listed above which occurred in 1% or more of patients included (not all cases were assessed for causality to buserelin): Body as a Whole: back pain, ill-defined symptoms, pelvic pain, infection, malaise, premenstrual syndrome.

Digestive: diarrhea, flatulence, sore throat, vomiting.

Suprefact (cont'd)

Metabolic and Nutritional: peripheral edema, generalized edema.
Nervous system: sleep disorder, dry mouth.
Skin and Appendages: pruritus.
Urogenital: leukorrhea, vaginal discharge, vaginal discomfort.
Miscellaneous: In the international database, other adverse events have been observed in patients treated with buserelin, as itemized below (not all events were considered to be related to buserelin therapy): Digestive: increased thirst.
Hemic and Lymphatic: leukopenia, thrombopenia.
Laboratory Values: changes in blood lipids, increase in bilirubin levels, increase in serum liver enzymes levels (e.g., transaminases).
Nervous System: concentration and memory distrubances, drowsiness, tiredness.
Skin and Appendages: articular pains, application site pain, irritation of the mucosa in the nasopharynx due to nasal solution administration (which may lead to nosebleeds, hoarseness, disturbances of smell or taste), brittle finger nails, female lactation, decrease or increase in scalp hair, decrease in body hair.
Special Senses: feeling of pressure behind the eyes, impaired vision (e.g., blurred vision).
Urogenital: ovarian cysts (during the initial phase of therapy).

Overdose: Symptoms and Treatment: There have been no clinical reports of acute overdosage with buserelin or buserelin implant.

From acute studies of buserelin acetate in rodents, neither 0.5 mg/kg/IV (mouse) nor 1 mg/kg/IV (rat) produced evidence of toxic signs.

Two groups of 6 and 4 healthy volunteers, aged 26 to 40 years and 31 to 40 years respectively, were given 1 mg buserelin or 5 mg buserelin **orally** as a single dose. No LH or FSH release was observed. No clinical effects were observed.

Dosage: Buserelin injection and nasal solution and buserelin implant should be administered at approximately equal time intervals to ensure that the desired therapeutic effect is maintained.

Prostatic Cancer: Injection and Nasal Solution: Initial Treatment: For the first 7 days of treatment give buserelin 500 μg (0.5 mL) every 8 hours by s.c. injection. For patient comfort, vary the injection site (see Information for the Patient).
Maintenance Treatment: Depending upon patient preference, or physician recommendation, maintenance treatment may be by daily s.c. injection or by intranasal administration 3 times daily.

During maintenance dosing by the s.c. route, the buserelin dose is 200 μg (0.2 mL) daily. For patient comfort, vary the site of injection (see Information for the Patient).

During maintenance dosing by the intranasal administration route, the buserelin dose is 400 μg (200 μg into each nostril) 3 times daily using the metered-dose pump (nebulizer) provided. Each pump action delivers 100 μg buserelin acetate or 0.1 mL solution (see Information for the Patient).
Suprefact Depot: Implant Dosing: The contents of 1 applicator, consisting of 2 implant rods, equivalent to a total of 6.3 mg buserelin, is injected s.c. every 8 weeks into the lateral abdominal wall. Before injection, a local anesthetic may be used if desired. It is important to maintain a regular, 8-week rhythm for the dosage interval. In exceptional cases, the dosage interval may be shortened or extended by a few days.

The applicator containing the implant rods should be kept horizontal before injection (see Manufacturer's Package Insert).

Suprefact Depot is intended for the long-term treatment of prostatic carcinoma.
Initial Antiandrogen Comedication: About 7 days before the first injection of the buserelin implant, an antiandrogen should be administered in accordance with the manufacturer's directions. This comedication is to be continued for 4 weeks after the first buserelin implant injection, when testosterone levels can be expected to have entered the surgical castration range.
Instructions for Using the Applicator (see package insert for illustrations): Please note: To prevent the implant rods from falling out of the injection needle, hold the applicator in a vertical position until immediately prior to puncture, with the needle pointing upwards.

After removing the applicator from the foil wrapping, check that both implant rods are located in the window of the handle. If necessary, tap the protective cap of the needle lightly to reposition them in the window.

Disinfect the injection site of the lateral abdominal wall and administer a local anesthetic, if desired. After removing the protective case from the plunger, remove the cap from the injection needle.

Lift a fold of skin and insert the needle approximately 3 cm (somewhat more than 1 inch) into the s.c. tissue, with the tip of the needle pointed slightly upwards. Withdraw the applicator about 1 to 2 cm prior to injection of the implant rods.

While fully depressing the plunger, inject the implant rods into the s.c. tissue. Compress the puncture channel while withdrawing the needle so that the implant rods are retained in the tissue.

To ensure that both implant rods have been injected, check the tip of the plunger to see if it is visible at the tip of the needle.

Endometriosis: Nasal Solution: The dose of buserelin in patients with endometriosis is 400 μg (200 μg into each nostril) 3 times daily using the metered-dose pump (nebulizer) provided. Each pump action delivers 100 μg or 0.1 mL solution (see Information for the Patient). The treatment duration is usually 6 months and should not exceed 9 months.

Information for the Patient: See Blue Section—Information for the Patient "Suprefact/Suprefact Depot".

Supplied: Suprefact: Injection: Each mL of sterile aqueous injection solution contains: buserelin acetate 1.05 mg (equivalent to 1 mg pure anhydrous buserelin free base). Nonmedicinal ingredients: benzyl alcohol, monobasic sodium phosphate buffer, sodium chloride for tonicity adjustment and sodium hydroxide for pH adjustment. Clear glass, multidose vials of 5.5 mL. Ready for administration direct from the container. Cartons of 2. Store at room temperature, below 25°C in the original container. **Do not freeze, do not expose to sources of heat** and do not use beyond the expiration date printed on the container label.

Nasal Solution: Each mL of aqueous intranasal solution contains: buserelin acetate 1.05 mg (equivalent to 1 mg pure anhydrous buserelin free base). Nonmedicinal ingredients: benzalkonium chloride 0.1 mg as preservative, sodium chloride for tonicity adjustment and citric acid/sodium citrate buffer. Provided ready for intranasal administration direct from the container. Amber glass bottles of 10 mL with metered-dose pumps (nebulizers) provided. Cartons of 4. Store at room temperature, below 25°C in the original container. **Do not freeze, do not expose to sources of heat** and do not use beyond the expiration date printed on the container label. The metered-dose pump (nebulizer) provided has a mechanical action and contains no propellants. Refer to Information for the Patient for details on pump operation.

There is no information available on possible incompatibilities between buserelin injection and nasal solution and other agents.

Suprefact Depot: A sterile, ready to use, disposable, for s.c. injection, applicator with an integrated needle (internal needle diameter of 1.4 mm). Each carton is supplied with 1 sterile foil bag containing 1 applicator prefilled with 1 implant dose consisting of 2 identical cream-colored, biodegradable and biocompatible rods, each of 3.3 mg buserelin acetate. Each implant dose contains a total of 6.6 mg buserelin acetate, equivalent to 6.3 mg buserelin base, 26.4 mg poly-(D,L-lactide-co-glycolide) in a 75:25 molar ratio. Cartons of 1. Store intact package between 15 and 30°C. **Do not freeze, protect from heat** and do not use beyond the expiration date printed on the container label.

Reviewed 1999

SUPRES® Ⓟ

Frosst

Methyldopa—Chlorothiazide

Antihypertensive

Pharmacology: Methyldopa: Methyldopa, an antihypertensive agent, is an aromatic-amino-acid decarboxylase inhibitor in animals and in man. Although the mechanism of action has yet to be conclusively demonstrated, the antihypertensive effect of methyldopa probably is due to its metabolism to alpha-methylnorepinephrine, which then lowers arterial pressure by stimulation of central inhibitory alpha-adrenergic receptors, false neurotransmission, and/or reduction of plasma renin activity. Methyldopa has been shown to cause a net reduction in the tissue concentration of serotonin, dopamine, norepinephrine and epinephrine.

In man the antihypertensive activity appears to be due solely to the L-isomer.

Methyldopa usually does not reduce glomerular filtration rate, renal blood flow, or filtration fraction. Cardiac output usually is maintained without cardiac acceleration. In some patients the heart rate is slowed.

Normal or elevated plasma renin activity may decrease in the course of methyldopa therapy.

Methyldopa reduces both supine and standing blood pressure. Methyldopa usually produces highly effective lowering of the supine pressure with infrequent symptomatic postural hypotension.

Exercise hypotension and diurnal blood pressure variations rarely occur.

Since methyldopa has a relatively short duration of action, withdrawal is followed by a gradual return to previous blood pressure levels, usually within 48 hours. This is not complicated by an overshoot of blood pressure.
Chlorothiazide: Chlorothiazide, when given orally is an effective diuretic and antihypertensive agent. Chlorothiazide interferes with the renal tubular mechanism of electrolyte reabsorption. This compound increases excretion of sodium and chloride in approximately equivalent amounts. Natriuresis may be accompanied by some loss of potassium and bicarbonate.

While this compound is predominantly a saluretic agent, in vitro studies have shown that it has a carbonic anhydrase inhibitory action which seems to be relatively specific for the renal tubular mechanism. It does not appear to be concentrated in erythrocytes or the brain in sufficient amounts to influence the activity of carbonic anhydrase in those tissues.

Chlorothiazide is useful in the treatment of hypertension. It may be used alone or as an adjunct to other antihypertensive drugs.

Chlorothiazide does not affect normal blood pressure. The mechanism of its antihypertensive action is not known. Lowering of the sodium content of arteriolar smooth muscle cells and diminished response to norepinephrine have been postulated.

Onset of the diuretic action following oral administration occurs in 2 hours and the peak action in about 4 hours. Diuretic activity lasts about 6 to 12 hours.

Indications: For maintenance therapy of patients with essential hypertension.

Fixed-dose combination drugs are not indicated for initial therapy. Patients should be titrated on the individual drugs. If the fixed combination represents the dosage so determined, its use may be more convenient in patient management. If during maintenance therapy dosage adjustment is necessary it is advisable to use the individual drugs.

Contraindications: Active hepatic disease, such as acute hepatitis and active cirrhosis. If previous methyldopa therapy has been associated with liver disorders or hemolytic anemia (see Warnings).

Because of the diuretic action of chlorothiazide, Supres is contraindicated in anuria. See also usage in Pregnancy and Lactation under Warnings.

This product is contraindicated in persons known to be sensitive to chlorothiazide or methyldopa.

Warnings: Methyldopa: A positive Coombs' test, hemolytic anemia, and liver disorders may occur with methyldopa therapy. The rare occurrences of hemolytic anemia or liver disorders could lead to potentially fatal complications unless properly recognized and managed.

With prolonged methyldopa therapy, 10 to 20% of patients develop a positive direct Coombs' test which usually occurs between 6 and 12 months of methyldopa therapy. Lowest incidence is at a daily dosage of 1 g or less. This on rare occasions may be associated with hemolytic anemia, which could lead to potentially fatal complications. One cannot predict which patients with a positive direct Coombs' test may develop hemolytic anemia.

Prior existence or development of a positive direct Coombs' test is not in itself a contraindication to use of methyldopa. If a positive Coombs' test develops during methyldopa therapy, the physician should determine whether hemolytic anemia exists and whether the positive Coombs' test may be a problem. For example, in addition to a positive direct Coombs' test there is less often a positive indirect Coombs' test which may interfere with cross matching of blood.

At the start of methyldopa therapy, it is desirable to do a blood count (hematocrit, hemoglobin, or red cell count) for a baseline or to establish whether there is anemia. Periodic blood counts should be done during therapy to detect hemolytic anemia. It may be useful to do a direct Coombs' test before therapy and at 6 and 12 months after the start of therapy.

If Coombs'-positive hemolytic anemia occurs, the cause may be methyldopa and the drug should be discontinued. Usually the anemia remits promptly. If not, corticosteroids may be given and other causes of anemia should be considered. If hemolytic anemia occurs the drug should not be reinstituted.

When methyldopa causes Coombs' positively alone or with hemolytic anemia, the red cell is usually coated with gamma globulin of the IgG (gamma G) class only. The positive Coombs' test may not revert to normal until weeks to months after methyldopa is stopped.

Should the need for transfusion arise in a patient receiving methyldopa, both a direct and an indirect Coombs' test should be performed on his blood. In the absence of hemolytic anemia, usually only the direct Coombs' test will be positive. A positive direct Coombs' test alone will not interfere with typing or cross matching. If the indirect Coombs' test is also positive, problems may arise in the major cross match and the assistance of a hematologist or transfusion expert will be needed.

Occasionally, fever has occurred within the first 3 weeks of methyldopa therapy, associated in some cases with eosinophilia or abnormalities in one or more liver function tests, such as serum alkaline phosphatase, serum transaminases [AST, ALT], bilirubin, cephalin cholesterol flocculation, prothrombin time, and bromsulphalein retention. Jaundice, with or without fever, may occur with onset usually within the first 2 to 3 months of therapy. In some patients the findings are consistent with those of cholestasis.

Rarely fatal hepatic necrosis has been reported after use of methyldopa. These hepatic changes may represent hypersensitivity reactions. Periodic determination of hepatic function should be done particularly during the first 6 to 12 weeks of therapy or whenever an unexplained fever occurs. If fever, abnormalities in liver function tests, or jaundice appear, stop therapy with methyldopa. If caused by methyldopa, the temperature and abnormalities in liver function characteristically have reverted to normal when the drug was discontinued. Methyldopa should not be reinstituted in such patients. Methyldopa should be used with caution in patients with a history of previous liver disease or dysfunction.

Rarely, a reversible reduction of the white blood cell count with a primary effect on the granulocytes has been seen. The granulocyte count returned promptly to normal on discontinuance of the drug. Rare cases of granulocytopenia have been reported. In each instance, upon stopping the drug, the white cell count returned to normal. Reversible thrombocytopenia has occurred rarely.

When methyldopa is used with other antihypertensive drugs, potentiation of antihypertensive effect may occur. Patients should be followed carefully to detect side reactions or unusual manifestations of drug idiosyncrasy. A paradoxical pressor response has been reported with i.v. methyldopate HCl.

Chlorothiazide: Azotemia may be precipitated or increased by chlorothiazide. Cumulative effects of the drug may develop in patients with impaired renal function. If increasing azotemia and oliguria occur during treatment of severe progressive renal disease, the diuretic should be discontinued.

Thiazides should be used with caution in patients with impaired hepatic function or progressive liver disease, since minor alterations of fluid and electrolyte balance may precipitate hepatic coma.

Sensitivity reactions may occur in patients with or without a history of allergy or bronchial asthma.

Chlorothiazide may add to or potentiate the action of other antihypertensive drugs.

The possibility of exacerbation or activation of systemic lupus erythematosus has been reported.

Non-specific small bowel lesions consisting of stenosis with or without ulceration may occur in association with the administration of enteric-coated potassium salts alone or with oral diuretics. These small bowel lesions have caused obstruction, hemorrhage and perforation. Surgery was frequently required and deaths have occurred. Available information tends to implicate enteric-coated potassium salts, although lesions of this type also occur spontaneously. Such preparations should be used only when adequate dietary supplementation is not practical, and should be discontinued immediately if abdominal pain, distension, nausea, vomiting or gastrointestinal bleeding occur.

Pregnancy: Use of any drug in women who are or may become pregnant requires that anticipated benefits be weighed against possible risks. Methyldopa crosses the placental barrier and appears in cord blood. No unusual adverse reactions have been reported in association with the use of methyldopa during pregnancy. Though no obvious teratogenic effects have been reported, the possibility of fetal injury cannot be excluded.

Thiazides cross the placental barrier and appear in cord blood. When chlorothiazide is used in pregnancy or in women of child-bearing age, the potential benefits of the drug should be weighed against the possible hazards to the fetus. These hazards include fetal or neonatal jaundice, thrombocytopenia, and possibly other adverse reactions which have occurred in the adult.

Lactation: Methyldopa and chlorothiazide appear in breast milk. Patients taking Supres should stop nursing.

Precautions: Methyldopa: Methyldopa should be used with caution in patients with a history of previous liver disease or dysfunction (see Warnings).

Methyldopa may interfere with measurement of: urinary uric acid by the phosphotungstate method, serum creatinine by the alkaline picrate method, and AST by colorimetric methods. Interference with spectrophotometric methods for AST analysis has not been reported.

Since methyldopa causes fluorescence in urine samples at the same wave lengths as catecholamines, falsely high levels of urinary catecholamines may be reported. This will interfere with the diagnosis of pheochromocytoma. It is important to recognize this phenomenon before a patient with a possible pheochromocytoma is subjected to surgery. Methyldopa does not interfere with measurement of VMA (vanillylmandelic acid), a test for pheochromocytoma, by those methods which convert VMA to vanillin. Methyldopa is not recommended for the treatment of patients with pheochromocytoma. Rarely, when urine is exposed to air after voiding, it may darken because of breakdown of methyldopa or its metabolites.

Rarely involuntary choreoathetotic movements have been observed during therapy with methyldopa in patients with severe bilateral cerebrovascular disease. Should these movements occur, stop therapy.

Methyldopa is largely excreted by the kidney and patients with impaired renal function may respond to smaller doses. Syncope in older patients may be related to an increased sensitivity and advanced arteriosclerotic vascular disease. This may be avoided by lower doses.

Patients may require reduced doses of anesthetics when on methyldopa. If hypotension does occur during anesthesia, it usually can be controlled by vasopressors. The adrenergic receptors remain sensitive during treatment with methyldopa.

Hypertension has recurred occasionally after dialysis in patients given methyldopa because the drug is removed by this procedure.

Chlorothiazide: Careful check should be kept for signs of fluid and electrolyte imbalance; namely, hyponatremia, hypochloremic alkalosis, hypokalemia and hypomagnesemia. Serum and urine electrolyte determinations are particularly important when the patient is vomiting excessively or receiving parenteral fluids. Warning signs or symptoms of fluid and electrolyte imbalance include dryness of mouth, thirst, weakness, lethargy, drowsiness, restlessness, muscle pains or cramps, muscular fatigue, hypotension, oliguria, tachycardia, and gastrointestinal disturbances.

Hypokalemia may develop with chlorothiazide, as with any other potent diuretic, especially with brisk diuresis, when severe cirrhosis is present, during concomitant steroid or ACTH administration, or after prolonged therapy. Interference with adequate electrolyte intake will contribute to hypokalemia. Hypokalemia can sensitize or exaggerate the response of the heart to the toxic effect of digitalis (e.g., increased ventricular irritability).

Although any chloride deficit is generally mild and usually does not require specific treatment except under extraordinary circumstances (as in liver disease or renal disease), chloride replacement may be required in the treatment of metabolic alkalosis.

Dilutional hyponatremia may occur in edematous patients in hot weather; appropriate therapy is water restriction, rather than administration of salt, except in rare instances when the hyponatremia is life threatening. In actual salt depletion, appropriate replacement is the therapy of choice.

Thiazide drugs may increase the responsiveness to tubocurarine.

The antihypertensive effects of the drug may be enhanced in the postsympathectomy patient. Chlorothiazide may decrease arterial responsiveness to norepinephrine. This diminution is not sufficient to preclude effectiveness of the pressor agent for therapeutic use. Orthostatic hypotension may occur and may be potentiated by alcohol, barbiturates or narcotics.

Thiazides may decrease serum PBI levels without signs of thyroid disturbance.

Thiazides may decrease urinary calcium excretion. Thiazides may cause intermittent and slight elevation of serum calcium in the absence of known disorders of calcium metabolism. Marked hypercalcemia may be evidence of hidden hyperparathyroidism. Thiazides should be discontinued before carrying out tests for parathyroid function.

Hyperuricemia may occur or acute gout may be precipitated in certain patients receiving thiazide therapy.

Insulin requirements in diabetic patients may be increased, decreased or unchanged. Diabetes mellitus which has been latent may become manifest during thiazide administration.

Lithium should generally not be given to patients receiving diuretics, since the risk of lithium toxicity is very high in such patients.

Adverse Effects: Methyldopa: Sedation, usually transient, may occur during the initial period of therapy or whenever the dose is increased. Headache, asthenia, or weakness may be noted as early and transient symptoms.

CNS: sedation, headache, asthenia or weakness, dizziness, lightheadedness, symptoms of cerebrovascular insufficiency, paresthesias, parkinsonism, Bell's palsy, decreased mental acuity, involuntary choreoathetotic movements. Psychic disturbances including nightmares and reversible mild psychoses or depression. Toxic encephalopathy.

Cardiovascular: bradycardia, prolonged carotid sinus hypersensitivity, aggravation of angina pectoris. Orthostatic hypotension (decrease daily dosage). Edema (and weight gain) usually relieved by use of a diuretic. (Discontinue methyldopa if edema progresses or signs of heart failure appear.)

Gastrointestinal: nausea, vomiting, distention, constipation, flatus, diarrhea, colitis, mild dryness of mouth, sore or "black" tongue, pancreatitis, sialadenitis.

Hepatic: abnormal liver function tests, jaundice, hepatocellular damage.

Hematologic: positive Coombs' test, hemolytic anemia, bone marrow depression, leukopenia, granulocytopenia, thrombocytopenia. Positive tests for antinuclear antibody, LE cells, and rheumatoid factor.

Allergic: drug-related fever, lupus-like syndrome, myocarditis.

Dermatologic: rash as in eczema or lichenoid eruption, toxic epidermal necrolysis.

Others: nasal stuffiness, rise in BUN, breast enlargement, gynecomastia, lactation, hyperprolactinemia, amenorrhea, impotence, decreased libido, mild arthralgia, myalgia.

Chlorothiazide: Gastrointestinal: anorexia, gastric irritation, nausea, vomiting, cramping, diarrhea, constipation, jaundice (intrahepatic cholestatic jaundice), pancreatitis, sialadenitis.

CNS: dizziness, vertigo, paresthesias, headache, xanthopsia.

Hematologic: leukopenia, agranulocytosis, thrombocytopenia, aplastic anemia, hemolytic anemia.

Cardiovascular: orthostatic hypotension (may be aggravated by alcohol, barbiturates or narcotics).

Hypersensitivity: purpura, photosensitivity, rash, urticaria, necrotizing angiitis (vasculitis, cutaneous vasculitis), fever, respiratory distress including pneumonitis and pulmonary edema, anaphylactic reactions.

Others: hyperglycemia, glycosuria, hyperuricemia, muscle spasm, weakness, restlessness, transient blurred vision.

Whenever adverse reactions are moderate or severe, dosage should be reduced or therapy withdrawn.

Overdose: Symptoms: Methyldopa: Acute overdosage may produce acute hypotension with other major responses attributable to brain and gastrointestinal malfunction (excessive sedation, weakness, bradycardia, dizziness, lightheadedness, constipation, distention, flatus, diarrhea, nausea, vomiting).

Potentiation of antihypertensive action may occur in combination therapy with other antihypertensives.

Chronic overdosage may produce hypotension and syncope, especially in presence of advanced arteriosclerosis.

Chlorothiazide: Overdosage may lead to excessive diuresis with electrolyte depletion (hypokalemia, hypochloremia, hyponatremia) and dehydration.

Signs are dryness of the mouth, thirst, weakness, lethargy, drowsiness, restlessness, muscle pains or cramps, muscular fatigue, hypotension, oliguria, tachycardia, gastrointestinal disturbances, mental confusion, delirium, convulsions, shock, coma.

If digitalis has also been administered, hypokalemia may accentuate myocardial abnormalities (e.g. cardiac arrhythmias).

Chlorothiazide may precipitate hepatic coma in cirrhotics, potentiate other antihypertensive agents, and decrease responsiveness to norepinephrine.

Treatment: There is no specific antidote.

If ingestion is recent, gastric lavage or emesis may reduce absorption; when ingestion has been earlier, infusions may be helpful to promote urinary excretion. Otherwise, management includes symptomatic treatment with special attention to cardiac rate and output, blood volume, electrolyte balance, dehydration, paralytic ileus, urinary function, hepatic coma, and cerebral activity. Administration of sympathomimetic drugs (e.g. norepinephrine, epinephrine) may be indicated. Administer oxygen or artificial respiration for respiratory impairment.

Supres (cont'd)

When chronic overdosage is suspected, the drug should be discontinued.

Dosage: Therapy is usually begun by administering 1 tablet twice daily during the first 48 hours. Thereafter, the daily dosage may be adjusted by the deletion of 1 or addition of 1 or 2 tablets, preferably at intervals of not less than two days, until an adequate response has been achieved. Once the effective dosage range has been attained, a smooth blood pressure response occurs in most patients in 12 to 24 hours. Although occasional patients have responded to higher doses, the maximal recommended daily dose is 3 g of methyldopa and 1 to 2 g of chlorothiazide. Where maximum doses have provided inadequate blood pressure control, it is suggested that additional methyldopa be given as the single drug to obtain the maximal blood pressure response.

Transfer from other Antihypertensive Agents: Supres may be introduced into the antihypertensive regimen of patients on treatment with thiazides by stopping the thiazides.

Therapy with Supres may be initiated in patients on ganglion-blocking agents or guanethidine by initially decreasing their dosage by 50% and by subsequent gradual withdrawal as Supres is gradually added. The gradual addition of Supres will provide a smooth transition with optimal control of blood pressure.

Therapy with Supres may be initiated in most other patients already on treatment with other antihypertensive agents (e.g., reserpine, other rauwolfia derivatives, hydralazine and antihypertensive agents of the monoamine oxidase inhibitor group) by terminating these antihypertensive medications. Following such previous antihypertensive therapy, Supres should be limited to an initial dose of one tablet daily and increased as required at intervals of not less than 2 days.

General Treatment Considerations: Methyldopa is largely excreted by the kidney. Therefore, patients with impaired kidney function may respond to smaller doses of the drug than patients with normal kidney function. Syncope in older patients has been related to an increased sensitivity in those patients with advanced arteriosclerotic vascular disease; this may be avoided by lower doses of Supres.

Many patients experience sedation for 2 or 3 days when therapy with Supres is started or when the dose is increased. The sedation can be expected to disappear after an effective maintenance dosage has been achieved. When increasing the dosage, it may be desirable to start with the evening dose to minimize the sedative effect without exaggerating morning postural hypotension.

Tolerance to Supres may occur occasionally as either an early or late event in treatment, but it is more likely to occur between the second and third month after initiation of therapy. Increasing the dosage of Supres or either methyldopa or chlorothiazide independently frequently will restore effective blood pressure control.

Since methyldopa and chlorothiazide have a relatively short duration of antihypertensive effect, withdrawal of Supres is followed by a gradual return to pretreatment blood pressure levels, usually within 48 hours. This is not complicated by an overshoot of blood pressure.

Supplied: Supres-150: Each oval, biconvex shaped, beige film-coated tablet, with a phi mark on one side, contains: methyldopa 250 mg and chlorothiazide 150 mg. Gluten-, lactose- and tartrazine-free. Bottles of 100.

Supres-250: Each oval, biconvex shaped, green film-coated tablet, with a phi mark on one side, contains: methyldopa 250 mg and chlorothiazide 250 mg. Gluten-, lactose- and tartrazine-free. Bottles of 100.

(Shown in Product Recognition Section)

SURFAK®
Hoechst Marion Roussel
Docusate Calcium
Stool Softener

Indications: For short-term use in the relief of occasional constipation caused by hard, dry stools. Stool softening generally occurs within 24 to 48 hours post-dosing.

Dosage: In adults, the dose is 1 capsule daily. The capsules are to be swallowed whole. Do not exceed the recommended dose.

Information for the Patient: See Blue Section—Information for the Patient "Surfak".

Supplied: Each soft, red, gelatin capsule contains: docusate calcium, USP 240 mg. Unit pack boxes of 30 (blister packs of 3×10) and 300 (10×30). Plastic bottles of 1 000.

(Shown in Product Recognition Section)

SURGAM®
SURGAM® SR
Hoechst Marion Roussel
Tiaprofenic Acid
Anti-inflammatory—Analgesic

Pharmacology: Tiaprofenic acid, a propionic acid derivative, is a nonsteroidal anti-inflammatory agent with analgesic and antipyretic properties. Its mechanism of action, as with other nonsteroidal anti-inflammatory agents, is not yet completely known. Tiaprofenic acid is an inhibitor of prostaglandin synthetase enzymes which are known to be associated with inflammation and pain. The therapeutic effect of tiaprofenic acid does not result from pituitary-adrenal stimulation.

In vitro and ex vivo studies in different experimental models with cartilage and cultures of human chondrocytes obtained from biopsy specimens have shown that exposure to tiaprofenic acid did not depress the biosynthesis of proteoglycans nor alter the differentiation of proteoglycans secreted. The degradation of proteoglycan aggregates was inhibited. In vivo data in osteoarthritis patients showed a significant reduction in stromelysin (proteoglycanase) activity further to pretreatment with tiaprofenic acid. These results support tiaprofenic acid as an effective inhibitor of stromelysin and also suggest a positive effect on the joint cartilage under experimental conditions in patients receiving therapeutic doses. The clinical significance of these findings is under further investigation.

Pharmacokinetics: Tiaprofenic acid given orally is rapidly absorbed at the gastric and duodenal levels. Peak serum levels are achieved in 30 to 90 minutes. It is extensively plasma protein bound (98%). Following a single dose of 200 mg the plasma half-life is approximately 1.7 hours. Food delays the absorption and the time to reach peak plasma concentrations by 10%.

Tiaprofenic acid is largely eliminated in the urine as unaltered tiaprofenic acid with its 2 metabolites (II & III) accounting for less than 10%; these metabolites have almost no activity.

Chronic administration of tiaprofenic acid at the dosage of 200 mg t.i.d. confirmed rapid elimination and absence of accumulation. Steady state was reached after one day's treatment and plasma levels approached zero within 24 hours of the last dose.

In 2 groups of arthritic patients treated with tiaprofenic acid 200 mg t.i.d. and 300 mg b.i.d. receiving the drug for 7 days or more, the times to reach mean peak serum levels were respectively 78 and 50 minutes; in synovial fluid, the mean time to peak levels was approximately 4 hours for both dosages. Following a 200 mg dose, peak serum and synovial fluid levels reached 26 μg/mL and 5.3 μg/mL respectively and 50 μg/mL and 7.7 μg/mL after a 300 mg dose. At 8 hours the serum blood levels were lower than those of synovial fluid but by 11 hours these levels were approximately the same.

In another study, rheumatoid arthritis patients were given tiaprofenic acid 200 mg t.i.d. for 7 days. After the first dose, a fall in the synovial PGE_2 level occurred inversely to a rise in drug level. The level of PGE_2 remained low after 1 week's continuous medication. These results indicate that tiaprofenic acid reaches its target organ and is retained within the joint. It also suggests that reduction in PGE_2 production is one of the ways in which tiaprofenic acid acts. The clinical significance of the relative serum and synovial fluid levels has, however, not been elucidated.

The results of a 3-month study in elderly osteoarthritis patients receiving tiaprofenic acid 300 mg b.i.d. showed no significant differences for all pharmacokinetic parameters (C_{max}, T_{max}, C_9, $AUC_{0\text{-}9h}$, t½) measured at weeks 0, 4, 8 and 12, thus suggesting a lack of accumulation.

Fecal blood loss at usual clinical doses was less than with usual clinical doses of ASA.

Following repeated administration of 2 capsules of tiaprofenic acid sustained release 300 mg once daily, C_{max} was reached 4 to 8 hours later, with a significantly higher concentration at 6 hours than that obtained with the regular tablets. Steady state was reached 12 hours after the first dose. There were no significant differences in C_{max}, C_{min} and $AUC_{0\text{-}24h}$ between the regular and the sustained release formulations.

In patients with rheumatoid arthritis treated with repeated doses of tiaprofenic acid sustained release 600 mg once daily, the time to synovial fluid C_{max} was 8 hours and the synovial fluid $AUC_{0\text{-}24h}$ was approximately 36% of the plasma $AUC_{0\text{-}24h}$. Twenty-four hours after the last dose, the tiaprofenic acid concentration was higher in the synovial fluid than in the plasma. The elimination half-life from synovial fluid (median: 8.6 hours) was at least twice that from plasma (median: 4.2 hours).

In a pharmacokinetics study in elderly patients, no accumulation of tiaprofenic acid was found following repeated once daily administration of sustained-release capsules. The mean half-life was 4.4 hours.

The effect of food on the bioavailability of tiaprofenic acid sustained-release capsules is not known as no studies have been carried out.

Indications: For the relief of signs and symptoms of rheumatoid arthritis and osteoarthritis (degenerative joint disease).

Contraindications: Active peptic ulcer, a history of recurrent ulceration or active inflammatory disease of the gastrointestinal system.

Known or suspected hypersensitivity to the drug or other nonsteroidal anti-inflammatory drugs (NSAIDs). The potential for cross-reactivity between different NSAIDs must be kept in mind.

Tiaprofenic acid is contraindicated in patients with a history of asthma, whether or not induced by ASA or NSAIDs.

Tiaprofenic acid should not be used in patients with the complete or partial syndrome of nasal polyps, or in whom asthma, anaphylaxis, urticaria, rhinitis or other allergic manifestations are precipitated by ASA or other NSAIDs. Fatal anaphylactoid reactions have occurred in such individuals. As well, individuals with the above medical problems are at risk of a severe reaction even if they have taken NSAIDs in the past without any adverse effects.

Significant hepatic impairment or active liver disease.

Severely impaired or deteriorating renal function (creatinine clearance <30 mL/minute). Individuals with lesser degrees of renal impairment are at risk of deterioration of their renal function when prescribed NSAIDs and must be monitored.

Tiaprofenic acid is not recommended for use with other NSAIDs because of the absence of any evidence demonstrating synergistic benefits and the potential for additive side effects.

Pregnancy (See Warnings).

Warnings: Gastrointestinal System: Serious gastrointestinal toxicity, such as peptic ulceration, perforation and gastrointestinal bleeding, **sometimes severe and occasionally fatal** can occur at any time, with or without symptoms in patients treated with NSAIDs including tiaprofenic acid.

Minor upper gastrointestinal problems, such as dyspepsia, are common, usually developing early in therapy. Physicians should remain alert for ulceration and bleeding in patients treated with NSAIDs, even in the absence of previous gastrointestinal tract symptoms.

In patients observed in clinical trials of such agents, symptomatic upper gastrointestinal ulcers, gross bleeding, or perforation appear to occur in approximately 1% of patients treated for 3 to 6 months and in about 2 to 4% of patients treated for 1 year. The risk continues beyond 1 year and possibly increases.

The incidence of these complications increases with increasing dose.

Tiaprofenic acid should be given under close medical supervision to patients prone to gastrointestinal tract irritation particularly those with a history of peptic ulcer, diverticulosis or other inflammatory disease of the gastrointestinal tract such as ulcerative colitis and Crohn's disease. In these cases the physician must weigh the benefits of treatment against the possible hazards.

Physicians should inform patients about the signs and/or symptoms of serious gastrointestinal toxicity and instruct them to contact a physician immediately if they experience persistent dyspepsia or other symptoms or signs suggestive of gastrointestinal ulceration or bleeding.

Because serious gastrointestinal tract ulceration and bleeding can occur without warning symptoms, physicians should follow chronically treated patients by checking their hemoglobin periodically and by being vigilant for the signs and symptoms of ulceration and bleeding and should inform the patients of the importance of this follow-up.

If ulceration is suspected or confirmed, or if gastrointestinal bleeding occurs, tiaprofenic acid should be discontinued immediately, appropriate treatment instituted and the patient monitored closely.

No studies, to date, have identified any group of patients **not** at risk of developing ulceration and bleeding. A prior history of serious gastrointestinal events and other factors such as excess alcohol intake, smoking, age, female gender and concomitant oral steroid and anticoagulant use have been associated with increased risk.

Studies to date show that all NSAIDs can cause gastrointestinal tract adverse events. Although existing data does not clearly identify differences in risk between various NSAIDs, this may be shown in the future.

Genitourinary Tract: Some NSAIDs are known to cause persistent urinary symptoms (bladder pain, dysuria, urinary frequency), hematuria or cystitis. The onset of these symptoms may occur at any time after the initiation of therapy with a NSAID. Some cases have become severe on continued treatment. Tiaprofenic acid appears to have a greater propensity than other NSAIDs to generate reports of cystitis. Although the reaction is generally reversible, nonrecognition has led to extensive investigations and even surgical intervention, in some patients. Should urinary symptoms occur, treatment with tiaprofenic acid **must be stopped immediately** to obtain recovery. This should be done before any urological investigations or treatments are carried out. Before starting treatment with tiaprofenic acid, the patient should be asked to inform his/her physician of any urinary symptoms, even if the patient is familiar with these symptoms from the patient's medical history.

Geriatrics: Patients older than 65 years and frail or debilitated patients are most susceptible to a variety of adverse reactions from NSAIDs: the incidence of these adverse reactions increases with dose and duration of treatment. In addition, these patients are less tolerant to ulceration and bleeding. Most reports of fatal gastrointestinal events are in this population. Older patients are also at risk of lower esophageal ulceration and bleeding.

For such patients, consideration should be given to a starting dose lower than the one usually recommended, with individual adjustment when necessary and under close supervision (see Precautions for further advice).

Cross-sensitivity: Patients sensitive to any of the NSAIDs may be sensitive to any one of the other NSAIDs also. There is a risk of cross-sensitivity among ASA and NSAIDs, including the group to which tiaprofenic acid belongs. These pseudoallergic reactions may include symptoms such as rash, urticaria, angiodema or more potentially severe manifestations (e.g., laryngeal edema, bronchoconstriction, shock). The risk of pseudoallergic reactions is greater in patients with recurrent rhino sinusitis, nasal polyposis or chronic urticaria. Asthmatic patients are particularly at risk of dangerous reactions. Therefore, tiaprofenic acid must not be administered to patients with asthma.

Aseptic Meningitis: In occasional cases, with some NSAIDs, the symptoms of aseptic meningitis (stiff neck, severe headaches, nausea and vomiting, fever or clouding of consciousness) have been observed. Patients with autoimmune disorders (systemic lupus erythematosus, mixed connective tissues diseases, etc.) seem to be predisposed. Therefore, in such patients, the physician must be vigilant to the development of this complication.

Pregnancy and *Lactation:* The safe use of tiaprofenic acid in pregnancy and lactation has not been established. Although no teratogenic effects were seen in animal studies, parturition was delayed and prolonged, and there was an increase in the number of stillbirths. There is also the possible risk of premature closure of the ductus arteriosus, and development of a bleeding tendency or renal risk in the neonate. Tiaprofenic acid crosses the placental barrier and is secreted in breast milk. The use of this drug is not, therefore, recommended during pregnancy and lactation.

Children: The safety and efficacy of tiaprofenic acid has not been established in children and its use in this age group is therefore not recommended.

Infection: In common with other anti-inflammatory drugs, tiaprofenic acid may mask the usual signs of infection. If tiaprofenic acid is used against symptoms of inflammation accompanying infectious disorders, effective anti-infective therapy is mandatory.

Fluid Balance: Tiaprofenic acid may cause sodium and water retention with edema. At the start of therapy, urine volume and renal function should be carefully monitored in patients with cardiac insufficiency, liver cirrhosis, or nephrotic syndrome and in patients on diuretics (see also Precautions).

Precautions: Gastrointestinal System: There is no definitive evidence that the concomitant administration of histamine H_2-receptor antagonists and/or antacids will either prevent the occurrence of gastrointestinal side effects or allow the continuation of tiaprofenic acid therapy when and if these adverse reactions appear.

Renal Function: Long-term administration of NSAIDs to animals has resulted in renal papillary necrosis and other abnormal renal pathology. In humans, there have been reports of acute interstitial nephritis with hematuria, proteinuria, and occasionally nephrotic syndrome.

A second form of renal toxicity has been seen in patients with prerenal conditions leading to the reduction in renal blood flow or blood volume, where the renal prostaglandins have a supportive role in the maintenance of renal perfusion. In these patients, administration of a NSAID may cause a dose-dependent reduction in prostaglandin formation and may precipitate overt renal decompensation. Patients at greatest risk of this reaction are those with impaired renal function, heart failure, liver dysfunction, those taking diuretics, and the elderly. Discontinuation of nonsteroidal anti-inflammatory therapy is usually followed by recovery to the pretreatment state.

Tiaprofenic acid and its metabolites are eliminated primarily by the kidneys, therefore the drug should be used with great caution in patients with impaired renal function. In these cases utilization of lower doses of tiaprofenic acid should be considered and patients carefully monitored.

During long-term therapy kidney function should be monitored periodically.

Hepatic Function: As with other NSAIDs, borderline elevations of one or more liver function tests may occur. Though these have been seen in up to 15% of patients treated with other NSAIDs, they have been reported in less than 1% of patients treated with tiaprofenic acid during clinical trials (see Adverse Effects). These abnormalities may progress, may remain essentially unchanged, or may be transient with continued therapy. A patient with symptoms and/or signs suggesting liver dysfunction, or in whom an abnormal liver test has occurred, should be evaluated for evidence of the development of more severe hepatic reaction while on therapy with this drug. Severe hepatic reactions including jaundice and cases of fatal hepatitis have been reported with NSAIDs.

Although such reactions are rare, if abnormal liver tests persist or worsen, if clinical signs and symptoms consistent with liver disease develop, or if systemic manifestations occur (e.g., eosinophilia, rash, etc.), this drug should be discontinued.

During long-term therapy, liver function tests should be monitored periodically. If there is a need to prescribe this drug in the presence of impaired liver function, it must be done under strict observation.

Fluid and Electrolyte Balance: Fluid retention and edema have been observed in patients treated with tiaprofenic acid. Therefore, as with many other NSAIDs, the possibility of precipitating congestive heart failure in elderly patients or those with compromised cardiac function should be borne in mind. Tiaprofenic acid should be used with caution in patients with heart failure, hypertension or other conditions predisposing to fluid retention.

With NSAID treatment, there is a potential risk of hyperkalemia particularly in patients with conditions such as diabetes mellitus or renal failure; elderly patients; or in patients receiving concomitant therapy with beta-adrenergic blockers, angiotensin-converting-enzyme inhibitors or some diuretics. Serum electrolytes should be monitored periodically during long-term therapy, especially in those patients who are at risk.

Hematology: Drugs inhibiting prostaglandin biosynthesis do interfere with platelet function to varying degrees; therefore, patients who may be adversely affected by such an action should be carefully observed when tiaprofenic acid is administered.

Blood dyscrasias (such as neutropenia, leukopenia, thrombocytopenia, aplastic anemia and agranulocytosis) associated with the use of NSAIDs are rare, but could occur with severe consequences.

Ophthalmology: Blurred and/or diminished vision has been reported with the use of tiaprofenic acid and other NSAIDs. If such symptoms develop this drug should be discontinued and an ophthalmologic examination performed; ophthalmologic examination should be carried out at periodic intervals in any patient receiving this drug for an extended period of time.

CNS: Some patients may experience drowsiness, dizziness, vertigo, insomnia or depression with the use of tiaprofenic acid. If patients experience these side effects, they should exercise caution in carrying out activities that require alertness.

Geriatrics: Tiaprofenic acid should be used with caution in the elderly, and the dosage adjusted individually.

<u>*Drug interactions:*</u> ASA or other NSAIDs: The use of tiaprofenic acid in addition to any other NSAID, including those over-the-counter ones (such as ASA and ibuprofen) is not recommended due to the possibility of additive side effects.

Concomitant administration of ASA results in decreased peak serum concentrations of tiaprofenic acid and slight increases in both clearance and apparent half-life. The clinical significance of these changes is unknown.

Drugs Affecting Blood Formation and Coagulation: Numerous studies have shown that the concomitant use of NSAIDs and anticoagulants increases the risk of gastrointestinal adverse events such as ulceration and bleeding.

Because prostaglandins play an important role in hemostasis, and NSAIDs affect platelet function, concurrent therapy of tiaprofenic acid with warfarin requires close monitoring to be certain that no change in anticoagulant dosage is necessary.

Tiaprofenic acid is not recommended for coadministration with vitamin K antagonists, ticlopidine, and heparin due to increased risk of hemorrhage. The possibility of interaction with thrombolytics must be taken into account.

Diuretics: Tiaprofenic acid may reduce the activity of diuretics (i.e., both their diuretic and antihypertensive effects).

Antihypertensives: NSAIDs can reduce the antihypertensive effect of propranolol and other beta-blockers as well as other antihypertensive agents. Coadministration of NSAIDs and ACE-inhibitors can promote impairment of renal function and/or hyperkalemia.

Glucocorticoids: Numerous studies have shown that the concomitant use of NSAIDs and oral glucocorticoids increases the risk of GI side effects such as ulceration and bleeding. This is especially the case in older (>65 years of age) individuals.

In patients receiving concomitant steroid therapy, any reduction in steroid dosage should be gradual to avoid the possible complications of sudden steroid withdrawal.

Lithium: Tiaprofenic acid can reduce the renal excretion of lithium.

Methothrexate: Tiaprofenic acid can interfere with the plasma protein binding and renal clearance of methothrexate.

Other Drug Interactions: Tiaprofenic acid is extensively bound to serum albumin (98%). This may lead to interaction with sulfonylurea, hypoglycemic agents, sulfonamides, phenytoin. Therefore, caution should be observed when these drugs are used concurrently.

Laboratory and Diagnostic Tests: No interference known.

Adverse Effects: The most common adverse reactions encountered with NSAIDs are gastrointestinal, of which peptic ulcer, with or without bleeding, is the most severe. Fatalities have occurred, particularly in the elderly.

In clinical trials with tiaprofenic acid encompassing 1 361 patients, the detailed breakdown of side effects is shown in Table I (on following page).

Laboratory and Biochemical Tolerance: Combined decrease of hematocrit and hemoglobin: 2.8% of patients. Decrease of hemoglobin: 2.8% of patients. Increased white blood cell count 0.6%; decreased count 0.3%.

Increased GGT and AST: less than 1%. Increased alkaline phosphatase from previously normal levels: less than 1%. In patients with initially high alkaline phosphatase the levels remained high or increased.

Increase in blood urea nitrogen (BUN): 2.5% of total patients (11.8% in the elderly). Increase in BUN and creatinine: 0.4% of patients.

Hyperkalemia: 2.4% of patients.

In addition, the following side effects have been reported in clinical and postmarket use of tiaprofenic acid: Gastrointestinal: disorders of intestinal transit, ulcer, perforation, overt or occult gastrointestinal hemorrhage resulting in anemia.

Muco-cutaneous: purpura, urticaria, very rarely erythema multiforme and bulbous eruptions (Stevens-Johnson syndrome or exceptionally toxic epidermal necrolysis); very rarely photosensitivity reactions.

Hypersensitivity Reactions: asthmatic attacks, especially in subjects allergic to ASA and other NSAIDs, angioedema, anaphylactic shock.

Hematological: thrombocytopenia, prolongation of bleeding time.

Urinary System: Urinary symptoms (bladder pain, dysuria, and frequency), hematuria or cystitis may occur. When treatment with tiaprofenic acid has been continued for months after onset of the urinary symptoms, inflammatory changes to the urinary tract, sometimes severe, have been observed and a few patients have undergone surgical procedures. Therefore, should any urinary symptom occur, treatment with tiaprofenic acid must be discontinued immediately. Complete recovery after discontinuation is the rule (see Warnings).

Nervous System: vertigo, tinnitus, tremor.

Renal: sodium and water retention (see Warnings). As with other NSAIDs, isolated cases of acute interstitial nephritis have been reported with tiaprofenic acid.

Hepatic: liver test abnormalities.

Other: palpebral edema, palpitations.

Surgam (cont'd)

Table I—Surgam

Clinical Tolerance

	Percentage of Incidence	
Adverse Effects	**Short-term (up to 8 wks)**	**Long-term (3 to 36 mths)**
Gastrointestinal (16%)		
Indigestion	3.1	13.5
Nausea	5.8	8.2
Heartburn	3.3	6.0
Epigastric pain	2.5	5.3
Vomiting	1.1	4.1
Abdominal pain	2.4	3.1
Constipation	2.9	2.7
Flatulence	1.5	2.2
Diarrhea	2.9	2.2
Less than 1%		
Enterocolitis	0.4	0.2
Melena	0.4	0.0
Although not seen in this series there have been rare incidents of gastric or duodenal ulceration.		
CNS (6.2%)		
Dizziness	2.4	3.9
Drowsiness	0.4	3.1
Headache	2.9	3.4
Depression	0.8	1.9
Less than 1% (range 0.2 to 0.7%)		
Disorientation, tinnitus, insomnia, anxiety, tiredness/weakness		
Cutaneous (2.1%)		
Rash, erythema, pruritus	1.7	7.2
Less than 1% (range 0.2 to 0.8%)		
Dry skin, onycholysis		
Cardiovascular (1.1%)		
Hot flushes	1.0	1.4
Less than 1% (range 0.3 to 0.5%)		
Chest pain, angina, bruising		
Renal (1.1%)		
Edema	1.2	1.9
Less than 1% (range 0.1 to 0.5%)		
Incontinence, polyuria, oliguria		
Hepatic (less than 1%) (see Laboratory and Biochemical Tolerance)		
Miscellaneous (2.2%)		
Dry mouth/tongue, stomatitis	1.1	2.4
Nosebleeds	0.1	1.4
Less than 1% (range 0.1 to 0.5%)		
Eye itching/conjunctivitis/red eyes, minor eye ulcers, blurred vision, anorexia, weight gain, cramps, dyspnea, intermenstrual bleeding/vaginal spotting, paresthesia of fingers, sneezing, sweating		

Overdose: Symptoms and Treatment: There have been no reports of overdosage. No specific antidote is known, therefore treatment should be symptomatic and supportive. Early gastric lavage is indicated.

Dosage: Sustained-Release Capsules: Rheumatoid Arthritis or Osteoarthritis: The initial and maintenance dose is 2 sustained release capsules of 300 mg once daily. Capsules should be swallowed whole.

Tablets: Rheumatoid Arthritis: The usual initial and maintenance dose is 600 mg daily in 3 divided doses. Some patients may do well on 300 mg twice daily. The maximum daily dose is 600 mg.

Osteoarthritis: The usual initial and maintenance dose is 600 mg daily in 2 or 3 divided doses. In rare instances patients may be maintained on 300 mg daily in divided doses. The maximum maintenance daily dose is 600 mg.

Information for the Patient: See Blue Section—Information for the Patient "Surgam/Surgam/SR".

Supplied: Capsules: Each hard gelatin, sustained-release capsule, with a transparent pink body and opaque maroon cap printed with "SURGAM SR" on one side and the Roussel logo on the other, each containing off-white spheroidal pellets, contains: tiaprofenic acid 300 mg. Nonmedicinal ingredients: glyceryl monostearate, microcrystalline cellulose and talc. Shell: gelatin. Cap: FD&C Blue No. 2, FD&C Red No. 3, titanium dioxide. Body: FD&C Blue No. 2, FD&C Red No. 3. White opaque polyethylene bottles of 60 and 500.

Tablets: 200 mg: Each white, biconvex tablet, marked with the Roussel logo on one side, the reverse side scored with a break-line, one half embossed "SURGAM" and the other half "200", contains: tiaprofenic acid 200 mg. Nonmedicinal ingredients: magnesium stearate, maize starch, Pluronic F68 and talc. Amber glass bottles of 100.

300 mg: Each white, biconvex tablet, marked with the Roussel logo on one side, the reverse side scored with a break-line, one half embossed "SURGAM" and the other half "300", contains: tiaprofenic acid 300 mg. Nonmedicinal ingredients: magnesium stearate, maize starch, Pluronic F68 and talc. Amber glass bottles of 100 and 500.

Store between 15 and 30°C. Protect from excessive heat, light and humidity.

(Shown in Product Recognition Section)

Reviewed 1999

SURMONTIL® Pr

Rhône-Poulenc Rorer

Trimipramine

Antidepressant

Pharmacology: Trimipramine is a tricyclic antidepressant with sedative properties. It also has anticholinergic properties and potentiates the sympathetic response, presumably by blocking the reuptake of norepinephrine which has been released by the presynaptic neurons. It has a quinidine-like effect on the heart and an EEG activity similar to that of other tricyclic antidepressants.

Indications: The drug treatment of depressive illness. Effective in endogenous depression and may also be useful in some patients with neurotic depression.

Contraindications: Trimipramine should not be given in conjunction with or within 2 weeks of, treatment with a MAO inhibitor drug; hyperpyretic crises, severe convulsions and death have occurred in patients receiving MAO inhibitors and tricyclic antidepressants. When substituting trimipramine for an MAOI, wait at least 2 weeks after discontinuing the MAOI, then start trimipramine cautiously and increase gradually.

The drug is contraindicated in the acute recovery period following myocardial infarction. It should not be used in those who have shown prior hypersensitivity to the drug nor in cases of drug induced CNS depression. Cross sensitivity between this and other dibenzazepines is a possibility.

Precautions: Extreme caution should be used when this drug is given in the following situations: a. In patients with cardiovascular disease, because of the possibility of conduction defects, arrhythmias, tachycardia, strokes and acute myocardial infarction. In such cases, treatment should be initiated with low doses, with progressive increases only if required and well tolerated. b. In patients with a history of urinary retention or glaucoma because of the anticholinergic properties of the drug. c. In patients with thyroid disease or those on thyroid medication, because of the possibility of cardiovascular toxicity, including arrhythmias. d. In patients with a history of seizure disorder, because this drug has been shown to lower the seizure threshold.

This drug is capable of blocking the antihypertensive effect of guanethidine and similarly acting compounds.

Pregnancy and *Lactation:* Safe use of trimipramine during pregnancy and lactation has not been established; therefore, if it is to be administered to pregnant patients, nursing mothers, or women of childbearing potential, the possible benefits must be weighed against the possible hazards to mother and child.

Occupational Hazards: This drug may impair the mental and/or physical abilities required for the performance of potentially hazardous tasks such as driving a car or operating machinery; therefore, the patient should be cautioned accordingly.

Reduce dosage, or alter treatment, if serious adverse effects occur.

Trimipramine therapy in patients with manic-depressive illness may induce a hypomanic state after the depressive phase terminates.

The drug may cause exacerbation of psychosis in schizophrenic patients.

Close supervision and careful adjustment of dosage are required when this drug is administered concomitantly with anticholinergic or sympathomimetic drugs.

Patients should be warned that while taking this drug their response to alcoholic beverages may be exaggerated.

Discontinue as soon as possible prior to elective surgery because of the possible cardiovascular effects. Hypertensive episodes have been observed during surgery in patients on tricyclic antidepressants.

The possibility of suicide in seriously depressed patients may remain until significant remission occurs. Such patients should be closely supervised throughout therapy and consideration should be given to the possible need for hospitalization and/or concomitant ECT.

Periodic blood counts and liver function tests should be performed when patients receive trimipramine in large doses or over prolonged periods.

Adverse Effects: Note: Included in the listing which follows are a few adverse reactions which have not been reported with this specific drug. However, the pharmacological similarities among the tricyclic antidepressant drugs require that each of the reactions be considered when trimipramine is administered.

Cardiovascular: orthostatic hypotension, hypertension, tachycardia, palpitation, arrhythmias, heart block, myocardial infarction, stroke. A few instances of unexpected death have been reported in patients with cardiovascular disorders.

Psychiatric: confusional states (especially in the elderly) with hallucinations, disorientation, delusions; anxiety, restlessness, agitation; insomnia and nightmares; hypomania; exacerbation of psychosis.

Neurological: numbness, tingling, paresthesias of extremities; incoordination, ataxia, tremors; peripheral neuropathy; extrapyramidal symptoms; seizures; alteration in EEG patterns; tinnitus.

Anticholinergic: dry mouth, and rarely associated sublingual adenitis; blurred vision, disturbance of accommodation, mydriasis; constipation, paralytic ileus; urinary retention, delayed micturition, dilatation of urinary tract.

Allergic: skin rash, petechiae, urticaria, itching, photosensitization (avoid excessive exposure to sunlight), edema (of face and tongue or general), drug fever, cross sensitivity with other tricyclic drugs.

Hematologic: bone marrow depressions including agranulocytosis, eosinophilia, purpura, thrombocytopenia.

Gastrointestinal: anorexia, nausea and vomiting, epigastric distress, peculiar taste, abdominal cramps, diarrhea, stomatitis, black tongue.

Endocrine: gynecomastia in the male, breast enlargement and galactorrhea in the female; increased or decreased libido, impotence, testicular swelling; elevation or depression of blood sugar levels.

Other: jaundice (simulating obstructive), altered liver function; weight gain or loss; perspiration, flushing; urinary frequency, nocturia; parotid swelling; drowsiness, dizziness, weakness and fatigue, headache; alopecia.

Withdrawal Symptoms: Though not indicative of addiction, abrupt cessation of treatment after prolonged therapy may produce nausea, headache and malaise.

Overdose: Symptoms: drowsiness, mydriasis, dysarthria, excitement, muscle spasms, convulsions, disturbances of cardiac conduction, arrhythmia, circulatory collapse, respiratory depression and coma. Cardiac arrhythmias and CNS involvement pose the greatest threat and may occur suddenly even when initial symptoms appear mild.

Treatment: There is no specific antidote and treatment must be symptomatic. Gastric lavage or, in the absence of coma, induction of emesis may be beneficial.

Administration of activated charcoal may help reduce absorption of trimipramine. In cases of severe intoxication dialysis may be undertaken, although the efficacy of such a procedure in tricyclic poisoning is doubtful due to low plasma concentrations of these drugs.

ECG monitoring in an intensive care unit is recommended in all patients, particularly in the presence of ECG abnormalities, and should be maintained for several days after the cardiac rhythm has returned to normal. Because of its effect on cardiac conduction, digitalis should be used only with caution. If rapid digitalization is required for the treatment of congestive heart failure, special care should be exercised in using the drug.

External stimulation should be minimized to reduce the tendency to convulsions. If an anticonvulsant is necessary, administer i.v. diazepam; barbiturates should be avoided since they intensify respiratory depression, particularly in children, and aggravate hypotension and coma.

Shock should be treated with supportive measures such as i.v. fluids, oxygen and corticosteroids. Pressor agents, such as levarterenol (but **not** epinephrine), are rarely indicated and should be given only after careful consideration and under continuous monitoring.

The slow i.v. administration of physostigmine salicylate has been reported to reverse most of the cardiovascular and CNS anticholinergic manifestations of tricyclic overdosage. The recommended dosage in adults has been 1 to 2 mg in **very slow** i.v. injection. In children, the initial dosage should not exceed 500 μg and should be adjusted to age and response. Since physostigmine has a short duration of action, administration may have to be repeated at 30 to 60 minute intervals.

Dosage: Treatment should be initiated at the lowest recommended dose and increased gradually, noting carefully the clinical response and any evidence of intolerance. It should be kept in mind that a lag in therapeutic response usually occurs at the onset of therapy, lasting from several days to a few weeks. Increasing the dosage does not normally shorten this latent period and may increase the incidence of side effects. All doses are expressed in terms of trimipramine base.

Initial Dosage: Adults: The recommended initial dose is 75 mg daily in two or three divided doses. Initial tolerance may be tested by giving the patient 25 mg on the evening of the first day. The initial dose should be increased by 25 mg increments, usually up to 150 mg daily, preferably by adding to the late afternoon and/or bedtime doses. In the case of severely depressed patients, a higher initial dose of 100 mg daily in two or three divided doses may be indicated. The usual optimal dose is 150 mg to 200 mg daily, but some patients may require up to 300 mg daily, depending on tolerance and response of each individual patient.

Elderly or Debilitated Patients: In these patients it is advisable to give a test dose of 12.5 to 25 mg and after 45 minutes examine the patient sitting and standing to check for orthostatic hypotension. Initial doses should usually be no more than 50 mg a day in divided doses, with weekly increments of no more than 25 mg a week, leading to a usual therapeutic dose range of 50 to 150 mg a day. Blood pressure and cardiac rhythm must be checked frequently, particularly in patients who have unstable cardiovascular function.

Maintenance Dosage: Once a satisfactory response has been obtained, the dosage should be adjusted to the lowest level required to maintain symptomatic relief. Medication should be continued for the expected duration of the depressive episode in order to minimize the possibility of relapse following clinical improvement.

When a maintenance dosage has been established as described above, trimipramine may be administered in a single dose before bedtime, provided such a dosage regimen is well tolerated.

Supplied: Capsules: Each capsule contains: trimipramine base 75 mg (as the maleate). Nonmedicinal ingredients: calcium phosphate dibasic, D&C Yellow No 10, FD&C Blue No 1, FD&C Red No 3, gelatin, magnesium stearate, polacrilin potassium and titanium dioxide. Tartrazine-free. Bottles of 100.

Tablets: Each tablet contains: trimipramine base 12.5 mg, 25 mg, 50 mg and 100 mg (as the maleate). Nonmedicinal ingredients: acetic anhydride, carnauba wax, cellulose, colloidal silicon dioxide, diethyl phthalate, erythrosine, FD&C Red No 3, lactose, magnesium stearate, sodium croscarmellose, talc, titanium dioxide and zein. Tartrazine-free. Bottles of 100 and 500.

(Shown in Product Recognition Section)

SURVANTA® P

Abbott

Beractant

Lung Surfactant

Pharmacology: Deficiency of pulmonary surfactant is an important factor in the development of Respiratory Distress Syndrome (RDS) in premature infants. Beractant replenishes surfactant and restores surface activity to the lungs of these infants. It reduces surface tension and concomitantly increases lung compliance.

Intratracheally administered beractant distributes rapidly to the alveolar surfaces and stabilizes the alveoli against collapse during respiration thereby increasing alveolar ventilation.

In clinical studies of premature infants with RDS, a significant improvement in oxygenation was demonstrated after treatment with a single dose of beractant. These infants showed a decreased need for supplemental oxygen and an increase in the arterial/alveolar oxygen ratio (a/ApO_2). Significantly decreased need for respiratory support, as indicated by a lower mean airway pressure, was also observed.

In prophylactic studies of premature infants at high risk of RDS, multiple doses (up to 4 doses within 48 hours) of beractant reduced the incidence and mortality of RDS, reduced the incidence of pulmonary air leaks and pulmonary interstitial emphysema, improved a/ApO_2 and FiO_2 (Fraction of inspired oxygen) at 72 hours of age, and reduced mortality from any cause.

No information is available about the metabolic fate of the surfactant-associated proteins in beractant. The metabolic disposition in humans has not been studied.

Indications: For prevention (prophylaxis) and treatment (rescue) of Respiratory Distress Syndrome (RDS/Hyaline Membrane Disease) in premature infants.

For **prophylactic** treatment of infants at risk of developing RDS or who have evidence of pulmonary immaturity.

In premature infants less than 1 250 g birthweight or with evidence of surfactant deficiency, give beractant as soon as possible after an airway has been established, preferably within 15 minutes of birth.

For **rescue** treatment of infants who have developed RDS. To treat infants with RDS confirmed by x-ray and who require mechanical ventilation, give beractant as soon as possible after an airway has been established, preferably by 8 hours of age.

Beractant significantly reduces the incidence of RDS, mortality due to RDS and air leak complications.

The use of beractant in infants less than 600 g birthweight or greater than 1 750 g birthweight has not been evaluated in controlled trials. There is no controlled experience with the use of beractant in conjunction with experimental therapies for RDS (e.g., high frequency ventilation or extra-corporeal membrane oxygenation).

Contraindications: There are no known contraindications to treatment with beractant.

Warnings: Beractant is intended for intratracheal use only (see Dosage).

General: Usage of beractant should be restricted to a highly supervised clinical setting with immediate availability of experienced neonatologists and other clinicians experienced with intubation, ventilator management, and general care of premature infants. Vigilant clinical attention should be given to all infants prior to, during, and after administration of beractant. Infants receiving beractant should be frequently monitored with arterial or transcutaneous measurement of systemic oxygen and carbon dioxide.

Beractant can rapidly affect oxygenation and lung compliance. In some infants, hyperoxia may occur within minutes of administration of beractant. If hyperoxia develops, and transcutaneous oxygen saturation is in excess of 95%, FiO_2 should be reduced until saturation is 90 to 95%. If the improvement in chest expansion seems excessive, peak ventilator inspiratory pressures should be immediately reduced. Failure to reduce inspiratory ventilatory pressures rapidly can result in lung overdistention and fatal pulmonary air leaks.

During the dosing procedure, transient episodes of bradycardia and decreased oxygen saturation have been reported (see Adverse Effects). If these occur, stop the dosing procedure and initiate appropriate measures to alleviate the condition. After stabilization, resume the dosing procedure.

Hyperoxia, cyanosis and reflux through the endotracheal tube, additionally to bradycardia and decreased oxygen saturation, have been the most frequently reported complications in clinical trials. If reflux occurs, drug administration should be stopped and if necessary, peak inspiratory pressure on the ventilator should be increased by 4 to 5 cm H_2O until clearing of the endotracheal tube occurs.

Increased probability of post-treatment nosocomial sepsis in beractant-treated infants was observed in clinical trials (see Table II on following page). The increased risk for sepsis among beractant-treated infants was not associated with increased mortality among these infants.

Mucous Plugs: Infants whose ventilation becomes markedly impaired during or shortly after dosing may have mucous plugging of the endotracheal tube, particularly if pulmonary secretions were prominent prior to drug administration. Suctioning of all infants prior to dosing may lessen the change of mucous plugs obstructing the endotracheal tube. If endotracheal tube obstruction from such plugs is suspected, and suctioning is unsuccessful in removing the obstruction, the blocked endotracheal tube should be replaced immediately. In the multiple-dose studies performed with beractant, there were 4 reports of endotracheal tube blockage out of 1 691 doses (0.2%).

Precautions: General: Rales and moist breath sounds can occur transiently after administration. Endotracheal suctioning or other remedial action is necessary if clear-cut signs of airway obstruction are present.

Table I—Survanta

Number of Infants with Adverse Events (All Controlled Studies) (Events with an Incidence ≥0.2% are Specified)

Body System/Event	Survanta n=840	(%)	Sham Air n=851	(%)
Respiratory				
Decreased oxygenation	9	(1.1)	3	(0.4)
Problems with ET tube	4	(0.5)	1	(0.1)
Blood from ET tube	3	(0.4)	0	(0.0)
Pulmonary hemorrhage	2	(0.9)	1	(0.1)
n=225 for Survanta				
n=238 for Sham Air				
Other respiratory adverse events	4	(0.5)	3	(0.4)
Cardiovascular				
Aortic thrombosis	3	(0.4)	0	(0.0)
Hypotension	3	(0.4)	0	(0.0)
Bradycardia	2	(0.2)	1	(0.1)
Other cardiovascular adverse events	7	(0.8)	9	(1.0)
Gastrointestinal				
Intestinal perforations	2	(0.2)	5	(0.6)
Volvulus	2	(0.2)	0	(0.0)
Other gastrointestinal adverse events	4	(0.5)	5	(0.6)
Renal				
Renal failure	2	(0.2)	2	(0.2)
Other renal adverse events	2	(0.2)	1	(0.1)
Hematologic				
Coagulopathy	2	(0.2)	0	(0.0)
Other hematologic adverse events	0	(0.0)	3	(0.4)
CNS				
Seizure	6	(0.7)	6	(0.7)
Other CNS adverse events	0	(0.0)	1	(0.1)
Systemic				
Sepsis	2	(0.2)	1	(0.1)
Other systemic adverse events	2	(0.2)	3	(0.4)
Other Adverse Events	3	(0.4)	3	(0.4)
At Least 1 Event	49	(5.8)	40	(4.7)

Survanta (cont'd)

In one of the single-dose rescue studies and one of the multi-dose prevention studies, the rate of intracranial hemorrhage was significantly higher in beractant patients than in control patients (63.3% vs 30.8%, p=0.001 and 48.8% vs 34.2%, p=0.047, respectively). However, when all controlled studies were pooled, there was no difference between treatment groups in incidences of intracranial hemorrhage.

The use of beractant in infants less than 600 g birthweight or greater than 1 750 g birthweight has not been evaluated in controlled trials. There is no controlled experience with the use of beractant in conjunction with experimental therapies for RDS (e.g., high frequency ventilation or extra-corporeal membrane oxygenation).

Carcinogenesis, Mutagenesis, Impairment of Fertility: Reproduction studies in animals have not been performed. Mutagenicity studies were negative. Carcinogenicity studies were not conducted with beractant.

Adverse Effects: The most commonly reported adverse experiences were associated with the dosing procedure. In the multiple-dose controlled clinical trials, each dose of beractant was divided into 4 quarter-doses. Each quarter dose was instilled through a catheter inserted into the endotracheal tube by briefly disconnecting the endotracheal tube from the ventilator.

Transient bradycardia occurred with 11.9% of doses. Oxygen desaturation occurred with 9.8% of doses. Other reactions during the dosing procedure occurred with fewer than 1% of doses and included endotracheal tube reflux, pallor, vasoconstriction, hypotension, endotracheal tube blockage, hypertension, hypocarbia, hypercarbia, and apnea. No deaths occurred during the dosing procedure, and all reactions resolved with symptomatic treatment.

Table I (on previous page) summarizes all adverse experiences reported during controlled clinical trials.

There were no statistically significant differences between treatments in the type or number of events reported.

A clinical study compared the above quarter-dose administration regimen to the same procedure using 2 half-doses and another 2 half-dose procedure with uninterrupted ventilation accomplished by passing the catheter through a neonatal suction valve in the endotracheal tube. With the first dose there was significantly less endotracheal tube reflux observed in the group with the quarter-dose regimen (p=.007) than in the group with uninterrupted ventilation. With the first dose there was significantly less oxygen desaturation in the group with uninterrupted ventilation (p=.008) than in the other group receiving 2 half-doses. There were no differences in these events after later doses and no differences in heart rate after any doses (see Dosage, Dosing Procedures).

The occurrence of concurrent illnesses common in premature infants was evaluated in the controlled trials. The rates in all controlled studies are in Table II.

Table II—Survanta

Percentage of Infants with Concurrent Events

	Survanta (%)	Control (%)
Patent ductus arteriosus	46.9	47.1
Intracranial hemorrhage	48.1	45.2
Severe intracranial hemorrhage	24.1	23.3
Pulmonary air leaks	10.9	24.7[a]
Pulmonary interstitial emphysema	20.2	38.4[a]
Necrotizing enterocolitis	6.1	5.3
Apnea	65.4	59.6
Severe apnea	46.1	42.5
Post-treatment sepsis	20.7	16.1[b]
Post-treatment infection	10.2	9.1
Pulmonary hemorrhage	7.2	5.3

[a] $p < 0.001$.
[b] $p < 0.05$.

In the controlled clinical trials, there was no effect of beractant on results of common laboratory tests: WBC count and serum sodium, potassium, bilirubin, creatinine. IgG or IgM antibodies to surfactant-associated proteins SP-B and SP-C were not detected.

Follow-up Evaluations: To date, no long-term complications or sequelae of beractant therapy have been found.

Single-Dose Studies: Six-month adjusted-age follow-up evaluations of 232 infants (115 treated) demonstrated no clinically important differences between treatment groups in pulmonary and neurologic sequelae, incidence or severity of retinopathy of prematurity, rehospitalizations, growth, or allergic manifestations.

Multiple-Dose Studies: Six-month adjusted-age follow-up evaluations have been completed in 631 (345 treated) of 916 surviving infants. There was significantly less cerebral palsy and need for supplemental oxygen in beractant infants. Wheezing at the time of examination was more frequent among beractant infants, although there was no difference in bronchodilator therapy.

Final 12-month follow-up data from the multiple-dose studies are available from 521 (272 treated) of 909 surviving infants. There was significantly less wheezing in beractant infants in contrast to the 6-month results. There was no difference in the incidence of cerebral palsy at 12 months.

Twenty-four month adjusted-age evaluations were completed in 429 (226 treated) of 906 surviving infants. There were significantly fewer beractant infants with rhonchi, wheezing, tachypnea or neurological findings, compared to infants treated with Sham-Air, at the time of examination. No other differences were found.

Overdose: Symptoms and Treatment: Overdosage with beractant has not been reported. Based on animal data, overdosage might result in acute airway obstruction. Treatment should be symptomatic and supportive.

Dosage: For intratracheal administration only.

Beractant should be administered by or under the supervision of clinicians experienced in intubation, ventilator management, and general care of premature infants.

Marked improvements in oxygenation may occur within minutes of administration of beractant. Therefore, **frequent** and careful clinical observation and monitoring of systemic oxygenation are essential to avoid hyperoxia.

Review of audiovisual instructional materials describing dosage and administration procedures is recommended before using beractant. Materials are available upon request from Ross Laboratories.

No information is available on the effects of doses other than 100 mg phospholipids/kg, more than 4 doses, dosing more frequently than every 6 hours, or administration after 48 hours of age.

Each dose of beractant is 100 mg of phospholipids/kg birthweight (4 mL/kg). The Survanta Dosing Chart (see Table III) shows the total dosage for a range of birthweights.

Table III—Survanta

Survanta Dosing Chart

Weight (g)	Total Dose (mL)	Weight (g)	Total Dose (mL)
600-650	2.6	1 301-1 350	5.4
651-700	2.8	1 351-1 400	5.6
701-750	3.0	1 401-1 450	5.8
751-800	3.2	1 451-1 500	6.0
801-850	3.4	1 501-1 550	6.2
851-900	3.6	1 551-1 600	6.4
901-950	3.8	1 601-1 650	6.6
951-1 000	4.0	1 651-1 700	6.8
1 001-1 050	4.2	1 701-1 750	7.0
1 051-1 100	4.4	1 751-1 800	7.2*
1 101-1 150	4.6	1 801-1 850	7.4*
1 151-1 200	4.8	1 851-1 900	7.6*
1 201-1 250	5.0	1 901-1 950	7.8*
1 251-1 300	5.2	1 951-2 000	8.0*

* Suggested dosages based on limited clinical experience in uncontrolled trials.

Four doses of beractant can be administered in the first 48 hours of life. Doses should be given no more frequently than every 6 hours.

Directions for Use: Beractant should be inspected visually for discoloration prior to administration. The color of beractant is off-white to light brown. If settling occurs during storage, swirl the vial gently **(do not shake)** to redisperse. Some foaming at the surface may occur during handling and is inherent to the nature of the product.

Beractant is stored refrigerated (2 to 8°C). Before administration, beractant should be warmed by standing at room temperature for at least 20 minutes or warmed in the hand for at least 8 minutes.

Artificial warming methods should not be used. If a prevention dose is to be given, preparation of beractant should begin before the infant's birth.

Beractant does not require reconstitution or sonication before use.

Dosing Procedures: General: Beractant is administered intratracheally. It can be instilled through a No. 5 French end-hole catheter inserted into the infant's endotracheal tube by briefly disconnecting the endotracheal tube from the ventilator **or** by inserting the catheter through a neonatal suction valve **without disconnecting the endotracheal tube from the ventilator** or by instillation through the secondary lumen of a double lumen endotracheal tube.

If the drug is instilled through an end-hole catheter, the length of the catheter should be shortened so that the tip of the catheter protrudes just beyond the endotracheal tube above the infant's carina. Beractant should not be instilled into a mainstem bronchus.

To ensure homogeneous distribution of beractant throughout the lungs, each dose is divided into fractional doses. Each dose can be administered in **2 half-doses** or **in 4 quarter-doses.** Each fractional dose is administered with the infant in a different position. To administer beractant in 2 half-doses, the recommended positions are: head and body turned approximately 45° to the right; head and body turned approximately 45° to the left.

To administer beractant in 4 quarter-doses, the recommended positions are: head and body inclined 5 to 10° down, head and body turned to the right; head and body inclined 5 to 10° down, head and body turned to the left; head and body inclined 5 to 10° up, head and body turned to the right; head and body inclined 5 to 10° up, head and body turned to the left (see package insert for illustrations).

The dosing procedure is facilitated if one person administers the dose while another person positions and monitors the baby.

The different methods of administering beractant were evaluated in clinical trials. In the 6 single-dose and 4 multiple-dose controlled clinical trials that established safety and efficacy, beractant was instilled through a catheter that was inserted into the infant's endotracheal tube by briefly disconnecting the endotracheal tube from the ventilator. Each dose was administered in 4 quarter-doses as described above.

This method of administering beractant was compared to 2 other methods in a multi-centre, randomized clinical study involving 299 infants weighing 600 g or more with RDS requiring mechanical ventilation. The other methods evaluated were: (1) Two half-doses administered by inserting the catheter through the endotracheal tube while the endotracheal tube was briefly disconnected from the ventilator. The half-doses were administered in the 2 positions described above. (2) Two half-doses administered without disconnecting the endotracheal tube from the ventilator by inserting the catheter through a neonatal suction valve into the endotracheal tube. The half-doses were administered in the 2 positions described above.

There were no significant differences among the three groups in average FiO_2, a/APO_2, or MAP at 72 hours of age, or in the incidence of pulmonary air leaks, pulmonary interstitial emphysema, patent ductus arteriosus, or mortality at 72 hours of age.

Administration of beractant using a double-lumen endotracheal tube is functionally equivalent to the use of the neonatal suction valve; i.e., delivery of beractant at the distal end of the endotracheal tube without interrupting mechanical ventilation. If an infant is already intubated with a single-lumen endotracheal tube, the infant should not be reintubated with a double-lumen endotracheal tube solely for the purpose of administering beractant.

First Dose: Instillation Through End-hole Catheter: Determine the total dose of beractant from the Survanta Dosing Chart (Table III) based on the infant's birthweight. Slowly withdraw the entire contents of the vial into a plastic syringe through a large gauge needle (e.g., at least 20 gauge). **Do not filter beractant and avoid shaking.**

Attach the premeasured No. 5 French end-hole catheter to the syringe. Fill the catheter with beractant. Discard excess beractant through the catheter so that only the total dose to be given remains in the syringe.

Before administering beractant, assure proper placement and patency of the endotracheal tube. At the discretion of the clinician, the endotracheal tube may be suctioned before administering beractant. The infant should be allowed to stabilize before proceeding with dosing.

First Fractional Dose: Prevention Strategy: Weigh, intubate and stabilize the infant. Administer the dose as soon as possible after birth, preferably within 15 minutes. Position the infant appropriately and gently inject the first quarter-dose through the catheter over 2 to 3 seconds.

After administration of the first fractional dose, remove the catheter from the endotracheal tube.

Manually ventilate with a hand-bag with sufficient oxygen to prevent cyanosis, at a rate of 60 breaths/minute, and sufficient positive pressure to provide adequate air exchange and chest wall excursion.

First Fractional Dose: Rescue Strategy: The first dose should be given as soon as possible after the infant is placed on a ventilator for management of RDS. In the clinical trials, immediately before instilling the first fractional dose, the infant's ventilator settings were changed to the rate of 60/minute, inspiratory time 0.5 second, and FiO_2 1.0.

Position the infant appropriately and gently inject the first fractional dose through the catheter over 2 to 3 seconds. After administration of the first fractional dose, remove the catheter from the endotracheal tube. Return the infant to the mechanical ventilator.

Remaining Fractional Doses: Prevention and Rescue Strategies: Ventilate the infant for at least 30 seconds or until stable. Reposition the infant for instillation of the next fractional dose.

Instill the remaining fractional doses using the same procedures. After instillation of each fractional dose, remove the catheter and ventilate for at least 30 seconds or until the infant is stabilized. After instillation of the final fractional dose, remove the catheter without flushing it.

Do not suction the infant for 1 hour after dosing unless signs of significant airway obstruction occur.

After completion of the dosing procedure, resume usual ventilator management and clinical care.

Instillation Through Secondary Lumen of a Double-Lumen Endotracheal Tube: Ensure that the infant is intubated with the appropriate size double-lumen endotracheal tube. Determine the total dose of beractant from the Survanta Dosing Chart (Table III) based on the infant's birthweight. Slowly withdraw the total dose from the vial into a plastic syringe through a large-gauge needle (e.g., at least 20 gauge). **Do not filter beractant and avoid shaking.**

Before administering beractant, assure proper placement and patency of the endotracheal tube. At the discretion of the clinician, the endotracheal tube may be suctioned before administering beractant. The infant should be allowed to stabilize before proceeding with dosing.

First Fractional Dose: Prevention Strategy: Weigh, intubate and stabilize the infant. Administer the dose as soon as possible after birth, preferably within 15 minutes. Attach the syringe containing beractant to the secondary lumen. Position the infant appropriately and gently inject the first fractional dose through the secondary lumen over 2 to 3 seconds without interrupting ventilation. If manually ventilated, ventilate with a hand-bag with sufficient oxygen to prevent cyanosis, at a rate of 60 breaths/minute, and sufficient positive pressure to provide adequate air exchange and chest wall excursion.

First Fractional Dose: Rescue Strategy: The first dose should be given as soon as possible after the infant is placed on a ventilator for management of RDS. Immediately before instilling the first fractional dose, change the infant's ventilator settings to the rate of 60/minute, inspiratory time 0.5 second, and FiO_2 1.0.

Position the infant appropriately and gently inject the first fractional dose through the secondary lumen over 2-3 seconds without interrupting mechanical ventilation.

Remaining Fractional Doses: Prevention and Rescue Strategies: Ventilate the infant for at least 30 seconds or until stable. Reposition the infant for instillation of the next fractional dose.

Instill the remaining fractional doses using the same procedures. After instillation of each fractional dose, ventilate for at least 30 seconds or until the infant is stabilized. After instillation of the final fractional dose, remove the syringe from the secondary lumen, **inject 0.5 mL of air to flush the secondary lumen and cap it.**

After completion of the dosing procedure, resume usual ventilator management and clinical care.

Repeat Doses: The need for additional doses of beractant is determined by evidence of continuing respiratory distress. Dose no sooner than 6 hours after the preceding dose if the infant remains intubated and requires at least 30% inspired oxygen to maintain a PaO_2 less than or equal to 80 torr. In controlled clinical trials, 60% of patients (prevention) and 79% of patients (rescue) required more than 1 dose of beractant. 34.8% of patients (prevention) and 52.2% of patients (rescue) required 4 doses. Radiographic confirmation of RDS should be obtained before administering additional doses to those who received a prevention dose.

The dosage of beractant for each repeat dose is also 100 mg phospholipids/kg and is based on the infant's birthweight. The infant should not be reweighed for determination of the beractant dosage. Use the Survanta Dosing Chart (Table III) to determine the total dosage.

Prepare beractant and position the infant for administration of each fractional dose as previously described. After instillation of each fractional dose, remove the dosing catheter from the endotracheal tube and ventilate the infant for at least 30 seconds or until stable.

In the clinical studies, ventilator settings used to administer repeat doses were different than those used for the first dose. For repeat doses, the FiO_2 was increased by 0.20 or an amount sufficient to prevent cyanosis. The ventilator delivered a rate of 30/minute with an inspiratory time less than 1.0 second. If the infant's pretreatment rate was 30 or greater, it was left unchanged during beractant instillation.

Manual hand-bag ventilation should not be used to administer repeat doses. **During the dosing procedure, ventilator settings may be adjusted at the discretion of the clinician to maintain appropriate oxygenation and ventilation.**

After completion of the dosing procedure, resume usual ventilator management and clinical care.

Dosing Precautions: If an infant experiences bradycardia or oxygen desaturation during the dosing procedure, stop the dosing procedure and initiate appropriate measures to alleviate the condition. After the infant has stabilized, resume the dosing procedure.

Rales and moist breath sounds can occur transiently after administration of beractant. Endotracheal suctioning or other remedial action is necessary if clear-cut signs of airway obstruction are present.

Supplied: Each mL of sterile, aqueous, off-white to light brown opaque, intratracheal solution, isolated from bovine lung extracts, contains: phospholipids 25 mg (200 mg phospholipids/8 mL) (including 11.0 to 15.5 mg/mL disaturated phosphatidylcholine), 0.5 to 1.75 mg/mL triglycerides; 1.4 to 3.5 mg/mL free fatty acids, and less than 1.0 mg/mL protein. It is suspended in 0.9% sodium chloride solution, and heat-sterilized. Its protein content includes two hydrophobic, low molecular weight, surfactant-associated proteins commonly known as SP-B and SP-C. It does not contain the hydrophilic, large molecular weight surfactant-associated protein known as SP-A. Preservative-free. Single glass vials of 8 mL.

Store unopened vials at refrigeration temperature (2 to 8°C). Protect from light. Store vials in carton until ready for use. Unopened, unused vials that have been warmed to room temperature may be returned to the refrigerator within 8 hours of warming, and stored for future use. Drug should not be warmed and returned to the refrigerator more than once. Each single use vial should be entered with a needle only once. Used vials with residual drug should be discarded.

Reviewed 1997

SUSTACAL®
Mead Johnson

Therapeutic Oral Supplement

Supplied: Sustacal is a pleasant tasting, high protein, lactose-free, nutritionally balanced oral feeding. It provides 100% Canadian adult RNI for vitamins, minerals and protein in just 1 100 mL. Each 235 mL can supplying 1 005 kJ (240 kcal) contains water, sugar, corn syrup solids, calcium caseinate, partially hydrogenated soya oil, soy protein isolate, sodium caseinate, lecithin, carrageenan, natural and artificial vanilla flavor and essential vitamins and minerals. Gluten- and tartrazine-free. Chocolate, strawberry and vanilla flavored Sustacal in cans of 235 mL, boxes of 24. Sustacal vanilla liquid in cans of 945 mL (4 053 kJ (965 kcal)). Cases of 12.

SWISS ONE
Swiss Herbal

Vitamin—Mineral Supplement

Supplied: Each caplet contains: vitamin A 8 000 IU, beta carotene 2 000 IU, vitamin D 400 IU, vitamin C 100 mg, vitamin E 10 IU, vitamin B_1 4.5 mg, vitamin B_2 2.5 mg, vitamin B_6 2.5 mg, vitamin B_{12} 5 μg, folic acid 0.05 mg, niacinamide 20 mg, D'pantothenic acid 5 mg, biotin 10 μg, calcium 125 mg, iron 4 mg, magnesium 50 mg, manganese 1 mg, copper 1 mg, zinc 1 mg, iodine 0.10 mg, potassium 10 mg, choline bitartrate 15 mg, inositol 15 mg and methionine 20 mg. Nonmedicinal ingredients: calcium carbonate, cellulose, magnesium stearate and stearic acid. Bottles of 50, 90, 180 and 500.

SYMMETREL® (Antiparkinson)
DuPont Pharma

Amantadine HCl

Antiparkinson

Pharmacology: While the mechanism of action of amantadine in the treatment of Parkinson's syndrome and drug-induced extrapyramidal reactions is not known, it is believed to release brain dopamine from nerve endings making it more available to activate dopaminergic receptors. The drug does not possess anticholinergic activity in animal tests at doses similar to those used clinically.

The antiviral activity of amantadine for the prophylaxis of Asian (A_2) influenza in humans appears not to be related to the possible mode of action of this drug in Parkinson's syndrome.

Pharmacokinetics: In man, amantadine is readily absorbed, passes the blood-brain barrier and appears in the saliva and nasal secretions. The drug can be detected in the blood and cerebrospinal fluid at relatively low, but dose-related, levels. No evidence of metabolites has been found and 90% or more of the dose can be recovered in the urine unchanged.

After oral administration of a single dose of 100 mg, maximum blood levels are reached in approximately 4 hours, based on mean time of the peak urinary excretion rate; the peak excretion rate is approximately 5 mg/hour; the mean half-life of the excretion rate approximates 15 hours.

Compared with otherwise healthy adult individuals, the clearance of amantadine is significantly reduced in adult patients with renal insufficiency. The elimination half-life increases 2 to 3 fold when creatinine clearance is less than 40 mL/min/1.73m² and averages 8 days in patients on chronic maintenance hemodialysis.

The renal clearance of amantadine is reduced and plasma levels are increased in otherwise healthy elderly patients age 65 years and older. The drug plasma levels in elderly patients receiving 100 mg daily have been reported to approximate those determined in younger adults taking 200 mg daily. Whether these changes are due to the normal decline in renal function or other age factors is not known.

Indications: Amandatine is useful in the treatment of Parkinson's syndrome and in the short-term management of drug-induced extrapyramidal symptoms.

In Parkinson's syndrome, amantadine has been used alone and in combination with anticholinergic antiparkinson drugs and with levodopa. The final therapeutic benefit seen with amantadine is significantly less than that seen with levodopa. The maximal therapeutic benefit to be obtained with amantadine is usually seen within 1 week. However, initial benefits may diminish with continued dosing.

Amantadine is useful as an adjunct in patients who do not tolerate optimal doses of levodopa alone or in combined therapy with a decarboxylase inhibitor. In these patients, the addition of amantadine may result in better control of Parkinson's syndrome and may help to smooth out fluctuations in performance.

The comparative efficacy of amantadine and anticholinergic antiparkinson drugs has not yet been established. When amantadine or anticholinergic antiparkinson drugs are each used with marginal benefit, concomitant use may permit the same degree of control, often with a lower dose of the anticholinergic medication.

Amantadine is effective in reducing severity or abolishing drug-induced extrapyramidal reactions including parkinsonism syndrome, dystonia and akathisia. It is not effective in the management of tardive dyskinesia.

Although anticholinergic-type side effects have been noted when used in patients with drug-induced extrapyramidal reactions, there appears to be a lower incidence of these side effects than that observed with anticholinergic antiparkinson drugs.

Antiparkinsonian agents should not usually be used prophylactically during neuroleptic administration. However, they may be given when needed to suppress extrapyramidal symptoms. Therefore, amantadine may be used in the management of extrapyramidal symptoms which cannot be controlled by reduction of neuroleptic dosage, but should be discontinued as soon as it is no longer required. Amantadine should be withdrawn after a period of time to determine whether there is recrudescence of extrapyramidal symptoms.

Contraindications: Known hypersensitivity to amantadine.

Warnings: A small number of suicidal attempts, some of which have been fatal, have been reported in patients treated with amantadine. The incidence of suicidal attempts is not known and the pathophysiologic mechanism is not understood. Suicidal attempts and suicidal ideation have been

Symmetrel (Antiparkinson) (cont'd)

reported in patients with and without prior history of psychiatric illness. Amantadine can exacerbate mental problems in patients with a history of psychiatric disorders or substance abuse.

Patients who attempt suicide may exhibit abnormal mental states which include disorientation, confusion, depression, personality changes, agitation, aggressive behavior, hallucinations, paranoia, other psychotic reactions, and somnolence or insomnia. Because of the possibility of serious adverse effects, caution should be observed when prescribing amantadine to patients being treated with drugs having CNS effects, or for whom the potential risks outweigh the benefit of treatment. Because some patients have attempted suicide by overdosing with amantadine, prescriptions should be written for the smallest quantity consistent with good patient management.

Patients with a history of epilepsy or other seizures should be observed closely for possible increased seizure activity.

Patients with a history of CHF or peripheral edema should be followed closely as there are patients who developed congestive heart failure while receiving amantadine.

Patients with Parkinson's disease improving on amantadine should resume normal activities gradually and cautiously, consistent with other medical considerations, such as the presence of osteoporosis or phlebothrombosis.

Occupational Hazards: Patients receiving amantadine who note CNS effects or blurring of vision should be cautioned against driving or working in situations where alertness and adequate motor coordination are important.

Precautions: General: Amantadine should not be discontinued abruptly since a few patients with Parkinson's syndrome experienced a parkinsonian crisis, i.e., sudden marked clinical deterioration, when this medication was suddenly stopped.

Neuroleptic Malignant Syndrome (NMS): Sporadic cases of possible Neuroleptic Malignant Syndrome (NMS) have been reported in association with dose reduction or withdrawal of amantadine therapy. NMS is an uncommon but life-threatening syndrome characterized by fever or hyperthermia; neurologic findings including muscle rigidity, involuntary movements, altered consciousness; other disturbances such as autonomic dysfunction, tachycardia, tachypnea, hyper- or hypotension; laboratory findings such as creatinine phosphokinase elevation, leukocytosis, and increased serum myoglobin.

The diagnostic evaluation of patients with this syndrome is complicated. In arriving at a diagnosis, it is important to identify cases where the clinical presentation includes both serious medical illness (e.g., pneumonia, systemic infection, etc.) and untreated or inadequately treated extrapyramidal signs and symptoms (EPS). Other important considerations in the differential diagnosis include central anticholinergic toxicity, heat stroke, drug fever, and primary CNS pathology.

The management of NMS should include: intensive symptomatic treatment and medical monitoring; and treatment of any concomitant serious medical problems for which specific treatments are available. There is no general agreement about specific pharmacological treatment regimens for uncomplicated NMS.

Patients with Special Diseases and Conditions: Because amantadine is not metabolized and is mainly excreted in the urine, it may accumulate in the plasma and in the body when renal function declines. The dose of amantadine should be reduced in patients with renal impairment and in patients who are 65 years of age or older (see Dosage). The dose of amantadine may need careful adjustment in patients with congestive heart failure, peripheral edema, or orthostatic hypotension.

Care shoud be exercised when administering amantadine to patients with liver disease, a history of recurrent eczematoid rash, or to patients with psychosis or severe psychoneurosis not controlled by chemotherapeutic agents. Rare instances of reversible elevation of liver enzyme levels have been reported in patients receiving amantadine, though a specific relationship between the drug and such changes has not been established.

Pregnancy: Amantadine has been shown to be embryotoxic and teratogenic in rats at 50 mg/kg/day, approximately 12 times the recommended human dose, but not at 37 mg/kg/day. Embryotoxic and teratogenic drug effects were not seen in rabbits that received up to 25 times the recommended human dose.

There are no adequate and well controlled studies in pregnant women. Therefore, amantadine should not be used in women with childbearing potential, unless in the opinion of the physician, the expected benefit to the patient outweighs the possible risk to the fetus.

Lactation: Since amantadine is secreted in human milk, its use is not recommended in nursing mothers.

Children: The safety and efficacy of use of amantadine in neonates and infants less than 1 year old have not been established.

Drug Interactions: The dose of anticholinergic drugs or of amantadine should be reduced if atropine-like effects appear when these drugs are used concurrently.

Careful observation is required when amantadine is administered concurrently with CNS stimulants.

Adverse Effects: Adverse reactions reported below have occurred in patients while receiving amantadine alone or in combination with anticholinergic antiparkinsonian drugs and/or levodopa.

The adverse reactions reported most frequently (5 to 10%) are: nausea, dizziness (lightheadedness) and insomnia.

Less frequently reported (1 to 5%) are: depression, anxiety and irritability, hallucinations, confusion, anorexia, dry mouth, constipation, ataxia, livedo reticularis, peripheral edema, orthostatic hypotension, headache, somnolence, nervousness, dream abnormality, agitation, dry nose, diarrhea and fatigue.

Infrequently occurring adverse reaction (0.1 to 1%) are: CHF, psychosis, urinary retention, dyspnea, skin rash, vomiting, weakness, slurred speech, euphoria, confusion, thinking abnormality, amnesia, hyperkinesia, hypertension, decreased libido, and visual disturbance, including punctuate subepithelial or other corneal opacity, corneal edema, decreased visual acuity, sensitivity to light, and optic nerve palsy.

Rarely occurring adverse reactions (less than 0.1%) are: instances of convulsion, leukopenia, neutropenia, ezcematoid dermatitis and oculogyric episodes. Other rare occurring adverse reactions are: suicidal attempt, suicide, and suicidal ideation (see Warnings).

Overdose: Symptoms: Deaths have been reported from overdose with amantadine. The lowest reported acute lethal dose was 2 g. An elderly patient with Parkinson's syndrome who took an overdose of 2.8 g of amantadine in a suicidal attempt, developed acute toxic psychosis, urinary retention, and a mixed acid-base disturbance. The toxic psychosis was manifested by disorientation, confusion, visual hallucinations and aggressive behavior. Convulsions did not occur, possibly because the patient had been receiving phenytoin prior to the acute ingestion of amantadine.

Treatment: There is no specific antidote. Slowly administered i.v. physostigmine in 1 and 2 mg doses at 1 to 2 hour intervals in an adult, and 0.5 mg doses at 5 to 10 minute intervals in a child up to a maximum of 2 mg/hour, have been reported to be effective in the control of CNS toxicity caused by amantadine. For acute overdosing, general supportive measures should be employed, along with immediate gastric lavage or induction of emesis. Fluids should be forced, and if necessary, given i.v.

Hemodialysis does not remove significant amounts of amantadine in patients with renal failure; a 4 hour hemodialysis removed 7 to 15 mg after a single 300 mg oral dose.

The pH of the urine has been reported to influence the excretion rate of amantadine. Since the excretion rate of the drug increases rapidly when the urine is acidic, the administration of urine-acidifying fluids may increase the elimination of the drug from the body. The blood pressure, pulse, respiration and temperature should be monitored. The patient should be observed for the possible development of arrhythmias, hypotension, hyperactivity, and convulsions; if required, appropriate therapy should be administered. The blood electrolytes, urine pH and urinary output should be monitored. If there is no record of recent voiding, catheterization should be done. The possibility of multiple drug ingestion by the patient should be considered.

Dosage: Parkinson's Syndrome: The initial dose of amantadine is 100 mg daily for patients with serious associated medical illnesses or who are receiving high doses of other antiparkinson drugs. After one to several weeks at 100 mg once daily, the dose may be increased to 100 mg twice daily. When amantadine and levodopa are initiated concurrently, amantadine should be held constant at 100 mg daily or twice daily while the daily dose of levodopa is gradually increased to optimal dose. When used alone, the usual dose of amantadine is 100 mg twice a day.

Patients whose responses are not optimal with amantadine at 200 mg daily may benefit from an increase to 300 mg daily in divided doses. Patients who experience a fall-off of effectiveness may regain benefit by increasing the dose to 300 mg daily; such patients should be supervised closely by their physicians.

Drug-Induced Extrapyramidal Symptoms: The usual dose of amantadine is 100 mg twice a day. Occasionally, patients whose responses are not optimal with amantadine at 200 mg daily may benefit from an increase up to 300 mg daily in divided doses.

In the presence of impaired renal function, see Table I.

Table I—Symmetrel (Antiparkinson)

Recommended Dosage Adjustments Dependent Upon Creatinine Clearance, Based Upon the Current National Advisory Committee on Immunization (NACI) Canada Communicable Disease Report, May 29, 1992

Creatinine Clearance (mL/min/1.73m²)	Dosage
≥80	100 mg twice daily
60–79	Alternating daily doses of 100 and 200 mg
40–59	100 mg once daily
30–39	200 mg twice weekly
20–29	100 mg thrice weekly
10–19	Alternating weekly doses of 100 and 200 mg

The recommended dosage for patients on hemodialysis is 200 mg every 7 days.

Supplied: Capsules: Each red, soft gelatin capsule contains: amantadine HCl USP 100 mg. Nonmedicinal ingredients: hydrogenated vegetable oil, lecithin unbleached, soybean oil, vegetable shortening and yellow wax; capsule shell: FD&C Red No. 40, gelatin, glycerin, methylparaben, propylparaben, purified water, titanium dioxide and white coloring "Ink Opacode". Alcohol-, lactose-, sodium-, sulfite- and tartrazine-free. Bottles of 100.

Syrup: Each 5 mL of clear colorless syrup contains: amantadine HCl USP 50 mg. Nonmedicinal ingredients: citric acid, methylparaben, propylparaben, purified water, raspberry flavor and sorbitol solution. Alcohol-, lactose-, sodium-, sulfite- and tartrazine-free. Bottles of 500 mL.

Store at controlled room temperature (15 to 30°C) in a tightly closed container.

(Shown in Product Recognition Section)

SYMMETREL® (Antiviral) Ⓟ

DuPont Pharma

Amantadine HCl

Antiviral

Pharmacology: The antiviral activity of amantadine against influenza A virus in humans is not completely understood. The mode of action appears to be the prevention of the release of infectious viral nucleic acid into the host cell.

Pharmacokinetics: In man, amantadine is readily absorbed, passes the blood-brain barrier and appears in the saliva and nasal secretions. The drug can be detected in the blood and cerebrospinal fluid at relatively low, but dose-related, levels. No evidence of metabolites has been found and 90% or more of the dose can be recovered in the urine unchanged.

After oral administration of a single dose of 100 mg, maximum blood levels are reached in approximately 4 hours, based on mean time of the peak urinary excretion rate; the peak excretion rate is approximately 5 mg/hour; the mean half-life of the excretion rate approximates 15 hours.

Compared with otherwise healthy adult individuals, the clearance of amantadine is significantly reduced in adult patients with renal insufficiency. The elimination half-life increases 2 to 3 fold when creatinine clearance is less than 40 mL/min/1.73m² and averages 8 days in patients on chronic maintenance hemodialysis.

The renal clearance of amantadine is reduced and plasma levels are increased in otherwise healthy elderly patients age 65 years and older. The drug plasma levels in elderly patients receiving 100 mg daily have been reported to approximate those determined in younger adults taking 200 mg daily. Whether these changes are due to the normal decline in renal function or other age factors is not known.

Indications: Influenza A virus respiratory infections: Prophylaxis: In the prevention of respiratory infections caused by influenza A virus strains. In the prophylaxis of influenza, early vaccination as periodically recommended by the National Advisory Committee on Immunization is the method of choice.

May be used for the control of influenza A outbreaks in institutions where high risk patients, close household or hospital ward contacts of index cases, and health care and community services personnel are exposed.

Can be used as the sole agent for prophylaxis against influenza A virus illness when early vaccination is not feasible or when the vaccine is contraindicated or not available.

May be used as an adjunct to late vaccination of people at risk, and as a supplement to vaccination in people at high risk expected to have an impaired immune response to vaccine.

Because amantadine does not appear to suppress antibody response, it can be used chemoprophylactically in conjunction with inactivated influenza A virus vaccine until protective antibody responses develop.

Amantadine can also be used for unvaccinated people who provide home care for high risk patients during the course of an outbreak.

Treatment: Amantadine is also indicated for the treatment of respiratory infections caused by influenza A virus strains.

There is no clinical evidence that this drug has efficacy in the prophylaxis or treatment of viral respiratory infections other than those caused by influenza A virus strains.

Contraindications: Known hypersensitivity to amantadine.

Warnings: A small number of suicidal attempts, some of which have been fatal, have been reported in patients treated with amantadine. The incidence of suicidal attempts is not known and the pathophysiologic mechanism is not understood. Suicidal attempts and suicidal ideation have been reported in patients with and without prior history of psychiatric illness. Amantadine can exacerbate mental problems in patients with a history of psychiatric disorders or substance abuse.

Patients who attempt suicide may exhibit abnormal mental states which include disorientation, confusion, depression, personality changes, agitation, aggressive behavior, hallucinations, paranoia, other psychotic reactions, and somnolence or insomnia. Because of the possibility of serious adverse effects, caution should be observed when prescribing amantadine to patients being treated with drugs having CNS effects, or for whom the potential risks outweigh the benefit of treatment. Because some patients have attempted suicide by overdosing with amantadine, prescriptions should be written for the smallest quantity consistent with good patient management.

Patients with a history of epilepsy or other seizures should be observed closely for possible increased seizure activity.

Patients with a history of CHF or peripheral edema should be followed closely as there are patients who developed congestive heart failure while receiving amantadine.

Occupational Hazards: Patients receiving amantadine who note CNS effects or blurring of vision should be cautioned against driving or working in situations where alertness and adequate motor coordination are important.

Precautions: Neuroleptic Malignant Syndrome (NMS): Sporadic cases of possible Neuroleptic Malignant Syndrome (NMS) have been reported in association with dose reduction or withdrawal of amantadine therapy. NMS is an uncommon but life-threatening syndrome characterized by fever or hyperthermia; neurologic findings including muscle rigidity, involuntary movements, altered consciousness; other disturbances such as autonomic dysfunction, tachycardia, tachypnea, hyper- or hypotension; laboratory findings such as creatinine phosphokinase elevation, leukocytosis, and increased serum myoglobin.

The diagnostic evaluation of patients with this syndrome is complicated. In arriving at a diagnosis, it is important to identify cases where the clinical presentation includes both serious medical illness (e.g., pneumonia, systemic infection, etc.) and untreated or inadequately treated extrapyramidal signs and symptoms (EPS). Other important considerations in the differential diagnosis include central anticholinergic toxicity, heat stroke, drug fever, and primary CNS pathology.

The management of NMS should include: intensive symptomatic treatment and medical monitoring; and treatment of any concomitant serious medical problems for which specific treatments are available. There is no general agreement about specific pharmacological treatment regimens for uncomplicated NMS.

Patients with Special Diseases and Conditions: Because amantadine is not metabolized and is mainly excreted in the urine, it may accumulate in the plasma and in the body when renal function declines. The dose of amantadine should be reduced in patients with renal impairment and in patients who are 65 years of age or older (see Dosage). The dose of amantadine may need careful adjustment in patients with congestive heart failure, peripheral edema, or orthostatic hypotension.

Care should be exercised when administering amantadine to patients with liver disease, a history of recurrent eczematoid rash, or to patients with psychosis or severe psychoneurosis not controlled by chemotherapeutic agents. Rare instances of reversible elevation of liver enzyme levels have been reported in patients receiving amantadine, though a specific relationship between the drug and such changes has not been established.

Pregnancy: Amantadine has been shown to be embryotoxic and teratogenic in rats at 50 mg/kg/day, approximately 12 times the recommended human dose, but not at 37 mg/kg/day. Embryotoxic and teratogenic drug effects were not seen in rabbits that received up to 25 times the recommended human dose.

There are no adequate and well controlled studies in pregnant women. Therefore, amantadine should not be used in women with childbearing potential, unless in the opinion of the physician, the expected benefit to the patient outweighs the possible risk to the fetus.

Lactation: Since amantadine is secreted in human milk, its use is not recommended in nursing mothers.

Children: The safety and efficacy of use of amantadine in neonates and infants less than 1 year old have not been established.

Drug Interactions: The dose of anticholinergic drugs or of amantadine should be reduced if atropine-like effects appear when these drugs are used concurrently.

Careful observation is required when amantadine is administered concurrently with CNS stimulants.

Adverse Effects: Adverse reactions reported below have occurred in patients while receiving amantadine alone or in combination with anticholinergic antiparkinsonian drugs and/or levodopa.

The adverse reactions reported most frequently (5 to 10%) are: nausea, dizziness (lightheadedness) and insomnia.

Less frequently reported (1 to 5%) are: depression, anxiety and irritability, hallucinations, confusion, anorexia, dry mouth, constipation, ataxia, livedo reticularis, peripheral edema, orthostatic hypotension, headache, somnolence, nervousness, dream abnormality, agitation, dry nose, diarrhea and fatigue.

Infrequently occurring adverse reactions (0.1 to 1%) are: congestive heart failure, psychosis, urinary retention, dyspnea, skin rash, vomiting, weakness, slurred speech, euphoria, confusion, thinking abnormality, amnesia, hyperkinesia, hypertension, decreased libido, and visual disturbance, including punctuate subepithelial or other corneal opacity, corneal edema, decreased visual acuity, sensitivity to light, and optic nerve palsy.

Rarely occurring adverse reactions (less than 0.1%) are: instances of convulsion, leukopenia, neutropenia, eczematoid dermatitis and oculogyric episodes. Other rare occurring adverse reactions are: suicidal attempt, suicide, and suicidal ideation (see Warnings).

Overdose: Symptoms: Deaths have been reported from overdose with amantadine. The lowest reported acute lethal dose was 2 g. An elderly patient with Parkinson's syndrome who took an overdose of 2.8 g of amantadine in a suicidal attempt, developed acute toxic psychosis, urinary retention, and a mixed acid-base disturbance. The toxic psychosis was manifested by disorientation, confusion, visual hallucinations and aggressive behavior. Convulsions did not occur, possibly because the patient had been receiving phenytoin prior to the acute ingestion of amantadine.

Treatment: There is no specific antidote. Slowly administered i.v. physostigmine in 1 and 2 mg doses at 1 to 2 hour intervals in an adult, and 0.5 mg doses at 5 to 10 minute intervals in a child up to a maximum of 2 mg/hour, have been reported to be effective in the control of CNS toxicity caused by amantadine. For acute overdosing, general supportive measures should be employed, along with immediate gastric lavage or induction of emesis. Fluids should be forced, and if necessary, given i.v.

Hemodialysis does not remove significant amounts of amantadine in patients with renal failure; a 4 hour hemodialysis removed 7 to 15 mg after a single 300 mg oral dose.

The pH of the urine has been reported to influence the excretion rate of amantadine. Since the excretion rate of the drug increases rapidly when the urine is acidic, the administration of urine-acidifying fluids may increase the elimination of the drug from the body. The blood pressure, pulse, respiration and temperature should be monitored. The patient should be observed for the possible development of arrhythmias, hypotension, hyperactivity, and convulsions; if required, appropriate therapy should be administered. The blood electrolytes, urine pH and urinary output should be monitored. If there is no record of recent voiding, catheterization should be done. The possibility of multiple drug ingestion by the patient should be considered.

Dosage: Dosage for Prophylaxis and Treatment of Influenza A Respiratory Infections: Adults: 200 mg: 2 capsules of 100 mg each or 20 mL of syrup as a single daily dose, or the daily dosage may be split into 1 capsule of 100 mg or 10 mL of syrup twice a day. If CNS effects develop on once-a-day dosage, a split dosage schedule may reduce such complaints.

Geriatrics: In persons 65 years of age or older, the daily dosage is 100 mg.

Children: 1 to 9 years: The total daily dose should be calculated on the basis of 4.5 to 9.0 mg/kg of body weight/day (but not to exceed 150 mg/day). The daily dose, given as the syrup, should be given in 2 or 3 equal portions. 9 to 12 years: The total daily dose is 200 mg given as 1 capsule of 100 mg or 10 mL of syrup twice a day.

In the presence of impaired renal function, see Table I.

Table I—Symmetrel (Antiviral)

Recommended Dosage Adjustments Dependent Upon Creatinine Clearance, Based Upon the Current National Advisory Committee on Immunization (NACI) Canada Communicable Disease Report, May 29, 1992

Creatinine Clearance (mL/min/1.73m²)	Dosage
≥80	100 mg twice daily
60–79	Alternating daily doses of 100 and 200 mg
40–59	100 mg once daily
30–39	200 mg twice weekly
20–29	100 mg thrice weekly
10–19	Alternating weekly doses of 100 and 200 mg

The recommended dosage for patients on hemodialysis is 200 mg every 7 days.

Supplied: Capsules: Each red, soft gelatin capsule contains: amantadine HCl USP 100 mg. Nonmedicinal ingredients: FD&C Red No. 40, gelatin, glycerin, hydrogenated vegetable oil, lecithin unbleached, methylparaben, propylparaben, purified water, soybean oil, titanium dioxide, vegetable shortening and yellow wax. Alcohol-, lactose-, sodium-, sulfite- and tartrazine-free. Bottles of 100.

Syrup: Each 5 mL of clear colorless syrup contains: amantadine HCl 50 mg. Nonmedicinal ingredients: citric acid, methylparaben, propylparaben, purified water, raspberry flavor and sorbitol solution. Alcohol-, lactose-, sodium-, sulfite- and tartrazine-free. Bottles of 500 mL.

Store at controlled room temperature (15 to 30°C) in a tightly closed container.

(Shown in Product Recognition Section)

SYNACTHEN® DEPOT ℞

Novartis Pharmaceuticals

Cosyntropin—Zinc Hydroxide

Adrenocorticotropic Hormone

Pharmacology: Natural adrenocorticotropin is a straight-chain polypeptide containing 39 amino acids which, by convention, are numbered from the N-terminal end of the molecule. The sequence of amino-acid occupying positions 25 to 33 varies among species and it is this part of the molecule which is most antigenic when ACTH of foreign origin is administered to man. In contrast, the N-terminal 24 amino-acid sequence is common to all species and is relatively non-antigenic, and it is only these amino-acids which are involved in its biological activities.

The most important physiological effects of ACTH involve the adrenal cortex and include the maintenance of adrenal weight and the control of adrenal corticosteroid synthesis and release. In its absence, adrenal blood flow is diminished, adrenal atrophy invariably ensues and cortisol secretion is markedly reduced. In addition to controlling corticosteroid secretion, ACTH also increases the synthesis and release of the other adrenal steroids, namely aldosterone and the adrenal androgens. It also has some degree of melanotropic activity and lipolytic effect.

Synacthen Depot, a long-acting synthetic β1-24-corticotropin, exhibits the same activity as natural ACTH with regard to all its biological activities. The complex results in a product whose absorption in man is effected over a longer period of time as compared to corticotropin. Therefore, therapy may be maintained with less frequent administration.

Synacthen Depot (cont'd)

The long-term administration produces the same effects as those produced by cortisone, cortisol and their synthetic analogues. In addition, there is also hypertrophy and hyperplasia of the adrenal cortex, in contrast to the effect of the exogenous corticoids.

Indications: Adrenal Function Test: The assessment of adrenocortical function based on its response to exogenous ACTH is well established. Nuki, G., et al. (1969) found that there was no significant difference in plasma 11-hydroxycorticosteroid response over 4 hours after a cosyntropin infusion or a single i.m. injection of 1 mg of depot cosyntropin in a group of patients with varying degrees of adrenocortical insufficiency secondary to corticosteroid therapy; suggesting its use to test for adrenocortical insufficiency without recourse of i.v. infusion, which is frequently unpleasant for both patient and clinician. Grant, J.K. (1969) found that the speed of response in the first 20 to 30 minutes is also virtually the same after cosyntropin i.v. as after cosyntropin depot i.m.; reasonably inferring that, except perhaps in states of extreme collapse, little advantage is to be gained in speed of response by giving cosyntropin (short acting) i.v. rather than cosyntropin depot i.m.

Galvao-Teles, A., et al. (1971) proposed as a test of adrenal function that plasma-cortisol be estimated before and 4 to 6 hours after an i.m. injection of 1 mg Synacthen Depot, generally recommended to be given at about 10 a.m. The results may be interpreted as shown in Table I.

Table I—Synacthen Depot

Interpretation of Plasma Cortisol Levels and Urinary Free Cortisol Excretion after injection of 1 mg Synacthen Depot

	Normal Subjects	Steroid Treated or Hypopituitary Patients with Abnormal Reserve: Moderately Impaired	Severely Impaired	Addisonian Subjects
Plasma-cortisol* 4-6 h after injection				
(μg/100 mL):	≥35	20–35	<20	<10
(nmol/L):	≥0.97	0.55–0.97	<0.55	<0.28
Urinary-free cortisol				
1st day				
(μg/day):	>700	—	<350	<150
(nmol/L):	>19.3	—	<9.66	<4.14
2nd day				
(μg/day):	Less than 1st day	—	More than 1st day	<150
(nmol/L):	—	—	—	<4.14

* By specific method; add one-third if plasma 11-OHCS is measured.

In hypoadrenal subjects, a further sample at 12 to 16 hours is indicated. Intermediate responses may then be clarified by measuring plasma-cortisol after 3 further injections of cosyntropin depot at 48-hour intervals during which period secondary hypoadrenalism may be expected to show recovery. The response to the first injection indicates the extent of adrenal atrophy or destruction, and that to the subsequent injections its recoverability.

Synacthen Depot offers two advantages: first, the longer duration of action might help to provide stronger adrenal stimulation; second, the delay in response to corticotropin in cases of secondary adrenal atrophy which can be shown by prolonged corticotropin stimulation might be elicited by a single injection of Synacthen Depot.

Performance of Adrenal Function Tests:

1. The 30-Minute Synacthen Depot Screening Test: Preparation: The subject need not be fasted. The procedure should be started at about 10:00 a.m. and can be performed as an out-patient procedure.

Procedure: i) A 5 to 7 mL blood sample is taken for determination of plasma cortisol levels at time 0. This will serve as a base against which to compare later values. ii) 1 mg of Synacthen Depot is given by i.m. injection immediately after the blood sample has been taken. iii) A further 5 to 7 mL blood sample is taken exactly 30 minutes after the injection.

Note: Some clinicians take an additional sample 45 to 60 minutes after the injection (in case the 30-minute sample is lost or the assay is invalid for any reason).

Interpretation of Results: In normal subjects the plasma cortisol level at 30 minutes reaches at least 20 μg/100 mL (0.55 nmol/L) with an increment which exceeds 7 μg/100 mL (0.19 nmol/L).

Note: This simple procedure should be used only for screening purposes with any abnormal results requiring confirmation by more prolonged ACTH stimulation. However, a normal response does exclude primary adrenocortical insufficiency, and may also be of value in the serial assessment of adrenocortical function in patients who are, or were, receiving corticosteroid therapy.

2. The 5-Hour Synacthen Depot Test: Preparation: The subject need not be fasted. The procedure should be started at about 10:00 a.m., at least 30 minutes after the insertion of an indwelling needle.

Procedure: i) A 5 to 7 mL blood sample is taken for determination of plasma cortisol levels at time 0. This will serve as a base against which to compare later values. ii) 1 mg of Synacthen Depot is given by i.m. injection immediately after the blood sample has been taken. iii) Further samples are taken after 0.5, 1, 2, 3, 4 and 5 hours for plasma cortisol assay. This assay of several samples avoids a single, possibly inaccurate result which might lead to an erroneous conclusion.

Note: The amount of Synacthen Depot used exceeds the amount required to induce a maximum adrenocortical response, ensuring an accurate assessment of the reserve capacity of the adrenal cortex.

Interpretation of Results: In normal subjects, plasma cortisol levels more than double in the first hour, and then rise more slowly. After 5 hours normal values lie within the range of 37 to 66 μg/100 mL (1.02-1.82 nmol/L).

3. The 3-Day Synacthen Depot Test: Preparation: For procedure A, hospitalization is not required, nor does the patient need to be fasted. Admission to hospital is usually required for procedure B, however, the patient can eat a normal diet and remain ambulant during his in-patient stay.

Procedure A: A 30-minute Synacthen Depot test (see section on 30-Minute Synacthen Depot Test) is performed at 9:00 a.m. on day 1. The patient then receives 1 mg of Synacthen Depot injected i.m. on days 2 and 3. On day 4 a second 30-minute Synacthen Depot test is performed at 10:00 a.m.

Procedure B: Urinary cortisol levels are determined on complete 24-hour collections for 5 consecutive days. The first 2 days serve as a control period. Starting on day 3 the patient is given, once daily, i.m. injections of 1 mg Synacthen Depot. See Table II.

Table II—Synacthen Depot

The 3-Day Synacthen Depot Test: Procedure B

Day 1	Day 2	Day 3	Day 4	Day 5
Daily Urinary Cortisol Determinations				
		← 1 mg i.m. daily Synacthen Depot at 9:30 a.m. →		

Interpretation of Results: Note: Prolonged ACTH stimulation tests offer advantages over the shorter tests only in differentiating between primary and secondary adrenocortical insufficiency. No response is found in patients with the primary type (Addison's disease) whereas, with prolonged stimulation, in the great majority of patients there is a marked but delayed corticosteroid response in secondary adrenal atrophy. Procedure A provides this information, i.e. a marked improvement in the second 30-minute Synacthen Depot test is consistent with secondary adrenocortical insufficiency whereas no improvement is found in the primary type. As concerns procedure B, in normal subjects, urinary cortisol excretion at least doubles on the first day of Synacthen Depot stimulation (i.e. day 3) and continues to increase during the remainder of the test.

Caution: The administration of ACTH for 3 consecutive days may rarely cause sodium and water retention with the risk of edema while the marked and prolonged increase in circulating corticosteroid levels, that may occur in patients with bilateral adrenal hyperplasia, can cause a severe exacerbation of the symptoms of Cushing's syndrome. On extremely rare occasions, adrenal crisis has supervened during prolonged ACTH stimulation in patients with marked adrenal insufficiency. For this reason, some clinicians give 1 mg of dexamethasone daily through the 3 days on which Synacthen Depot is given to provide steroid cover. This does not interfere with the test.

Synacthen Depot has been used in the following: Collagen Diseases: acute rheumatic fever; rheumatoid arthritis; lupus erythematosus; periarteritis nodosa; psoriatic arthritis; scleroderma; rheumatoid spondylitis; Still's disease.

Dermatologic Diseases: exfoliative dermatitis; dermatomyositis; pemphigus.

Endocrine Diseases: panhypopituitarism.

Eye Diseases: choroiditis; conjunctivitis; iritis; keratitis; optic neuritis; sympathetic ophthalmia; uveitis.

Hemolytic Diseases: acquired hemolytic jaundice.

Other Diseases: nephrotic syndrome; ulcerative colitis; Bell's palsy; acute exacerbations of multiple sclerosis, and as adjuvant treatment in cases of acute gout.

Contraindications: Known or suspected hypersensitivity to cosyntropin and or ACTH of animal origin or to any of the excipients of Synacthen Depot; pregnancy and lactation; untreated bacterial, fungal and viral infections; Cushing's syndrome; refractory congestive heart failure; active or latent peptic ulcer; acute psychosis; primary adrenocortical insufficiency; adrenogenital syndrome.

In view of the increased risk of anaphylactic reactions, Synacthen Depot must not be employed to treat asthma or other allergic affections. Since Synacthen Depot contains benzyl alcohol, it is contraindicated in neonates (especially premature infants), in whom benzyl alcohol can cause severe poisoning.

Warnings: Synacthen Depot must not be given i.v.

In rare cases, particularly in patients subject to asthma and/or other forms of allergy, severe anaphylactic reactions may occur. Such reactions set in usually within 30 minutes after administration.

If Synacthen Depot is used in any of the following conditions, the risks should be weighed against the possible benefits: non-specific ulcerative colitis; diverticulitis; recent intestinal anastomosis; renal insufficiency; hypertension; thromboembolic tendencies; acute or chronic infections, especially varicella or vaccinia; exanthematous and fungal diseases, osteoporosis; and myasthenia gravis.

Precautions: Before employing Synacthen Depot, the physician must ascertain whether the patient is suffering from an allergic disorder (especially asthma) or is susceptible in general to allergies (see Contraindications and Warnings). The physician should also enquire whether the patient has been treated with ACTH preparations in the past, and, if so, make sure that the treatment gave rise to no hypersensitivity reactions (see Contraindications).

Allergic reactions may occur in response to Synacthen Depot, which tend to be more severe in patients susceptible to allergies (especially asthma) (see Contraindications). Because of the possibility of an allergic reaction occurring with Synacthen Depot, the injection should be given under medical supervision and the patient kept under observation for about 1 hour. Self-injection by patients is not recommended. Should any prodromal signs occur, stop further treatment. Allergic reactions of this type include: marked redness and pain at the injection site, dizziness, nausea, vomiting, urticaria, pruritus, flushings, severe malaise, dyspnea, or angioneurotic edema or Quincke's edema. If local or systemic hypersensitivity reactions occur during or after an injection, treatment with cosyntropin must be discontinued and all use of ACTH preparations avoided in the future.

Treatment of Anaphylactic Reactions: Severe anaphylactic reactions usually can be avoided by discontinuing the use of the drug at the earliest sign of local or systemic hypersensitivity. In the rare event of a serious incident occurring despite these precautions, initiate the following emergency measures as treatment for shock: Initial treatment or for less severe reactions: 0.3 to 0.5 mL s.c. or i.m. of a 1 mg/mL aqueous solution of epinephrine. For more severe or life threatening reactions, or if no response to s.c. or i.m. route: 1 to 5 mL i.v. **slowly** of a 1 mg/mL aqueous epinephrine solution diluted in 10 mL physiologic saline. As well, consider administering a large i.v. dose of a corticosteroid, e.g. hydrocortisone or methylprednisolone.

Prolonged repeated cosyntropin administration may increase the risk of hypersensitivity reaction.

The blood pressure and weight should be carefully observed. Urinalysis should be done at intervals; if sugar is present the fasting blood glucose should be determined. Salt and water retention in response to Synacthen Depot can often be avoided or eliminated by prescribing a low-sodium diet; diuretics may be employed when strict sodium restriction is impossible.

Potassium supplement should be administered in cases of prolonged use.

Psychological disturbances such as euphoria, depression, insomnia, psychosis, mood swings, personality changes may occur during therapy. Existing emotional disorders or psychoses may be aggravated.

Prolonged use of cosyntropin may be associated with development of posterior subcapsular cataracts and glaucoma.

Infections must be treated simultaneously with appropriate antibiotics; the signs and symptoms of inflammation may be masked by the anti-inflammatory effects of cortisol produced by the over-active adrenal glands.

Vaccination: Patients on therapy with cosyntropin should not be vaccinated against smallpox. If other immunization procedures are considered, these should be undertaken with caution because of decrease in antibody response and possible hazard of neurological complications.

Surgery: Patients who are subjected to the stress of surgical operations or trauma while being treated, or within 1 year after treatment has been terminated, should have their Synacthen Depot therapy augmented or reinstated and continued for the duration of the stress period and immediately following it. In stressful conditions, additional use of rapidly acting corticosteroids may be required.

Although the action of cosyntropin is similar to that of exogenous adrenocortical steroids, the quantity of endogenous corticosteroids produced by the adrenal glands may be variable.

The lowest effective dose of cosyntropin should be used to control the condition under treatment. When reduction of the dosage is indicated, this should be gradual. Relative insufficiency of the pituitary-adrenal axis is induced by prolonged administration, therefore gradual reduction of cosyntropin dosage is essential. On discontinuation of therapy this type of insufficiency may persist for several months. During this period in case of stressful conditions appropriate adrenocortical therapy should be considered.

It is advisable to verify the adrenal responsiveness before and during cosyntropin therapy.

Patients with Special Diseases and Conditions: Patients already receiving medication for diabetes mellitus or for moderate to severe hypertension must have the dosage of their medication readjusted if treatment with Synacthen Depot is instituted.

An enhanced effect of corticotropin therapy has been observed in patients with hypothyroidism and in those with cirrhosis of the liver.

Synacthen Depot should be used cautiously in patients with ocular herpes simplex owing to possible corneal perforation.

Synacthen Depot may activate latent amoebiasis. It is therfore recommended that latent or active amoebiasis be ruled out before initiating therapy.

If Synacthen Depot is indicated in patients with latent tuberculosis or tuberculin reactivity, close observation is necessary because the disease may be reactivated. During prolonged therapy, such patients should receive chemoprophylaxis.

Children: Provided the dosage is carefully individualized Synacthen Depot is unlikely to inhibit growth in children. Nevertheless, in children undergoing long-term treatment, growth should be monitored.

In infants and small children treated with Synacthen Depot, echocardiographic recordings should be made regularly, because during long-term treatment with high doses reversible myocardial hypertrophy may occur.

Synacthen Depot is contraindicated in neonates.

Adverse Effects: Allergic reaction may develop (see Contraindications and Warnings) which in rare instances can lead to life-threatening anaphylactic shock. In rare cases the benzyl alcohol contained in Synacthen Depot may also give rise to hypersensitivity reactions.

In infants and small children treated over a prolonged period with high dosages, reversible myocardial hypertrophy may occur in isolated instances.

Fluid and Electrolyte Disturbances: sodium retention, fluid retention, potassium loss, hypokalemic alkalosis, calcium loss.

Musculoskeletal: muscle weakness, steroid myopathy, loss of muscle mass, osteoporosis, vertebral compression fractures, aseptic necrosis of femoral and humeral heads, pathologic fracture of long bones, tendon rupture.

Gastrointestinal: peptic ulcer with possible perforation and hemorrhage, pancreatitis, abdominal distension, ulcerative esophagitis.

Dermatologic: impaired wound healing, thin fragile skin, petechiae and ecchymoses, facial erythema, increased sweating, suppression of skin test reactions, acne, hyperpigmentation.

Cardiovascular: hypertension, necrotizing angiitis, congestive heart failure.

Neurological: convulsions, increased intracranial pressure with papilledema (pseudotumor cerebri) usually after treatment; headache; vertigo; psychic changes.

Endocrine: menstrual irregularities; development of Cushingoid state; suppression of growth in children; secondary adrenocortical and pituitary unresponsiveness, particularly in times of stress, as in trauma, surgery or illness; decreased carbohydrate tolerance; hyperglycemia; manifestations of latent diabetes mellitus; increased requirements for insulin or oral hypoglycemic agents in diabetics; hirsutism.

Ophthalmic: posterior subcapsular cataracts, increased intraocular pressure, glaucoma, exophthalmos.

Metabolic: negative nitrogen balance due to protein catabolism.

Allergic: especially in patients with allergic responses to proteins manifesting as dizziness, nausea and vomiting, anaphylactic shock, skin reactions.

Miscellaneous: Increased susceptibility to infection; abscess; thromboembolism; weight gain; increased appetite; leukocytosis; prolonged ACTH may result in antibodies and loss of stimulatory effect.

Overdose: Symptoms: Edema, hypertension or signs of excessive adrenocortical activity (Cushing's syndrome) during therapy usually indicate overdosage. In such cases the dosage should be reduced, frequency of administration decreased (i.e. to 5 to 7 days) or the drug withdrawn according to the severity of the condition.

Treatment: There is no known antidote for cosyntropin. Toxic effects should be treated symptomatically.

Dosage: Test of Adrenal Function: 1 mg Synacthen Depot, injected i.m. at about 10 a.m. Plasma 11-hydroxycorticosteroids to be measured before and 4 to 6 hours after the injection. For interpretation of results, and further measurement and caution in certain cases, refer to Indications.

Dosage for Other Clinical Disorders: In general, the correct dose is the smallest one given at the longest possible interval necessary to produce control of the clinical disorder.

The average dose is 0.5 to 1 mg i.m. twice a week, tailoring the dose according to the individual requirements. In acute cases, or after prolonged steroid therapy, 1 mg i.m. daily for 3 days. However, the interval should be extended as soon as an adequate response is obtained.

Once the acute manifestations have subsided, or for chronic conditions, the dose should be adjusted according to the patient's needs. Some may be best maintained on a dose of 0.5 to 1 mg every 2 or 3 days while others may respond better to 2 mg at weekly, or even longer intervals.

Based on a number of clinical studies, the dosage schedule in Table III is suggested for babies and children.

Table III—Synacthen Depot

Dosage Schedule for Babies and Children

Age	Initial Dosage	Maintenance Dosage
Under 1 year	0.25 mg/day	0.25 mg every 2nd day
1 to 6 years	0.25 to 0.5 mg/day	0.25 to 0.5 mg every 2 to 8 days
6 to 15 years	0.5 to 1 mg/day	0.25 to 1 mg every 2 to 8 days

Route of administration: The preferred route of administration is by i.m. injection, slowly and deeply into the gluteal region.

The ampuls should be slightly shaken until the suspension shows a uniform appearance.

Transferring from Corticoids: Administer 1 mg Synacthen Depot daily to elicit full adrenal response. At the same time withdraw the steroid gradually, reducing by a quarter the original dose on successive days. Once the steroid has been withdrawn, adjust Synacthen Depot dosage to individual patient's requirements.

Transferring from ACTH of Animal Origin: 1 mg of Synacthen has approximately the same corticotrophic activity as 100 IU of ACTH (as defined in the 3rd International Working Standard). This equivalence is not, however, valid for depot preparations since the effect of Synacthen Depot lasts appreciably longer than ACTH gel and considerably longer than ACTH in carboxymethyl cellulose. To transfer a patient receiving, for example, 40 units ACTH gel daily, give 0.5 mg Synacthen Depot i.m. instead on alternate days. The response should then be assessed and the dosage adjusted, preferably by lengthening the interval between injections.

Supplied: Each ampul of milky-white, sterile suspension contains: cosyntropin 1 mg as zinc hydroxide complex. Nonmedicinal ingredients: benzyl alcohol, sodium chloride, sodium hydroxide (to adjust pH), sodium phosphate and sterile water for injection. Alcohol: 1% w/v. Sodium: <1 mmol (1.13 mg)/mL. Bisulfite-, gluten-, lactose-, parabens- and tartrazine-free. Cartons of 1 ampul. Store in a refrigerator (2 to 8°C). Protect from light.

Reviewed 1997

SYNALAR® Ⓟ

Roche

Fluocinolone Acetonide

Topical Corticosteroid

Indications: For topical therapy of corticosteroid responsive acute and chronic skin eruptions where an anti-inflammatory, anti-allergenic, and antipruritic activity in the topical management is required.

Topical solution (0.01%) is more appropriate than the fluocinolone acetonide ointment formulation for use in locations such as the scalp.

Contraindications: Untreated bacterial, tubercular, fungal and most viral lesions of the skin (including herpes simplex, vaccinia, and varicella). Contraindicated in individuals with a history of hypersensitivity to any of the components.

Warnings: *Pregnancy* and *Lactation:* The safety of topical corticosteroids during pregnancy or lactation has not been established. The potential benefit of topical corticosteroids, if used during pregnancy or lactation, should be weighed against possible hazard to the fetus or the nursing infant.

Not for ophthalmic use.

Precautions: Not recommended for use under occlusive dressings.

Apply cautiously on lesions close to the eye. Severe irritation is possible if these formulations contact the eye. Should this occur, immediate flushings of the eye with a large volume of water is recommended.

Prolonged use of topical corticosteroid products may produce atrophy of the skin and of subcutaneous tissues, particularly on flexor surfaces and on the face. If this is noted, discontinue its use.

Use with caution in patients with stasis dermatitis and other skin diseases associated with impaired circulation.

If a symptomatic response is not noted within a few days to a week, the local applications of corticosteroids should be discontinued and the patient reevaluated.

During the use of topical corticosteroids secondary infections may occur.

Although hypersensitivity reactions have been rare with topically applied steroid products, the drug should be discontinued and appropriate therapy instituted if there are signs of reaction.

In cases of bacterial infections of the skin, appropriate antibacterial agents should be used as primary therapy. If it is considered necessary, the topical corticosteroid product may be used as an adjunct to control inflammation, erythema and itching.

Patients should be advised to inform subsequent physicians of the prior use of corticosteroids.

Significant systemic absorption may result when steroids are applied over large areas of the body. To minimize the possibility, when long-term therapy is anticipated, interrupt treatment periodically or treat one area of the body at a time.

Laboratory Tests: Urinary free cortisol test and ACTH stimulation test may be helpful in evaluating HPA axis suppression.

Adverse Effects: The following adverse skin reactions have been reported with the use of topical steroids: dryness, burning, itching, local irritation, striae, skin atrophy, atrophy of subcutaneous tissues, telangiectasia, hypertrichosis, change in pigmentation and secondary infection. Adrenal suppression has also been reported following topical corticosteroid therapy. Posterior subcapsular cataracts have been reported following systemic use of corticosteroids.

Overdose: Symptoms and Treatment: There is no specific antidote, but gastric lavage should be performed.

In case of hypercorticism and/or adrenal suppression, discontinue therapy.

Dosage: Synalar ointment is suitable when an emollient effect is desired. A small amount of ointment should be applied gently on the affected skin area, 2 or 3 times daily, as needed.

Synalar (cont'd)

Topical solution, 0.01% should be applied to the affected area as thin film, from 2 to 4 times daily, depending on the severity of the condition. On hairy sites, the hair should be parted to allow direct contact with the lesion.

It is recommended that ointment or solution not be used under occlusive conditions.

Supplied: Ointment: Each g of ointment contains: fluocinolone acetonide 0.025% in a petrolatum base without preservatives. Collapsible tubes of 60 g.

Solution: Each bottle contains: fluocinolone acetonide 0.01% in a propylene glycol vehicle without preservatives. Plastic squeeze bottles with controlled drop tip of 60 mL.

Store at room temperature (15 to 30°C).

SYNAREL® Ⓟ

Searle

Nafarelin Acetate

Gonadotropin Releasing Hormone (GnRH) Analogue

Pharmacology: Nafarelin is an agonistic analogue of the gonadotropin releasing hormone (GnRH). Given as a single intranasal dose, nafarelin stimulates release of the pituitary gonadotropins, LH and FSH, with consequent increase of ovarian steroidogenesis. Repeated intranasal dosing abolishes the stimulatory effect on the pituitary gland. Twice daily administration of 200 µg, as a nasal spray, leads to decreased secretion of gonadal steroids by about 4 weeks. Consequently, tissues and functions that depend on gonadal steroids for their maintenance become quiescent.

Pharmacokinetics: Nafarelin is rapidly absorbed from the nasal mucosa into the systemic circulation after intranasal administration. The relative bioavailability of intranasally administered nafarelin averaged 2.8% (range 1.2 to 5.6%). This was determined by comparing nafarelin AUC values after a single 400 µg intranasal dose and a 25 µg i.v. dose and adjusting for the lower i.v. dose administered. The low relative bioavailability results from the drug not being well absorbed by the nasal mucosa. Maximum plasma concentrations are achieved 10 to 40 minutes after dosing. Following a single intranasal dose of 200 µg base, the observed average peak concentration of nafarelin is 0.6 ng/mL, whereas following a single dose of 400 µg base, the observed average peak concentration is 1.8 ng/mL (range 1.52 to 2.0 ng/mL). The average serum half-life of nafarelin following intranasal administration is 3 hours (range 2 to 4 hours).

The effect of rhinitis or a topical decongestant on intranasally administered Synarel has not yet been determined with the presently available formulation.

Clinical Use: In controlled clinical studies, nafarelin at doses of 400 and 800 µg/day for 6 months was shown to relieve the clinical symptoms of endometriosis (pelvic pain, dysmenorrhea, and dyspareunia) and to reduce the size of endometrial implants as determined by laparoscopy. The clinical significance of a decrease in endometriotic lesions is not known at this time. Laparoscopic staging of endometriosis did not necessarily correlate with severity of symptoms.

In 73 patients, Synarel 400 µg daily induced amenorrhea in approximately 65%, 80% and 90% of the patients after 60, 90 and 120 days, respectively. Most of the remaining patients reported episodes of only light bleeding or spotting. In the first, second and third post-treatment months normal menstrual cycles resumed in 4%, 82% and 100%, respectively, of those patients who did not become pregnant.

The distribution of patients, treated with 400 µg/day, by symptom severity at admission, end of treatment and 6 months after treatment is shown in Table I.

Indications: For hormonal management of endometriosis, including pain relief and reduction of endometriotic lesions. Experience with nafarelin for the management of endometriosis has been limited to women 18 years of age and older and treated for 6 months. There is no evidence that pregnancy rates are enhanced or adversely affected by its use.

Contraindications: Should not be administered to patients who: are hypersensitive to GnRH, GnRH agonist analogues or any of the excipients in this product; have undiagnosed abnormal vaginal bleeding; are pregnant or who may become pregnant while receiving the drug (see Warnings). It is not known whether nafarelin causes fetal abnormalities in humans; are breast feeding (see Warnings).

Warnings: General: Isolated cases of short-term worsening of signs and symptoms or enlargement of ovarian cysts have been reported during initiation of nafarelin therapy: they are sometimes, but not necessarily, associated with a stimulation of the pituitary gland and an initial increase in the levels of circulating gonadal hormones.

Worsening of the clinical condition may occasionally require discontinuation of therapy and/or surgical intervention.

Pregnancy and *Lactation:* Safe use of nafarelin in pregnancy has not been established clinically. Before starting treatment, pregnancy must be excluded.

When used regularly at the recommended dose, nafarelin usually inhibits ovulation and stops menstruation. Contraception is not ensured, however, by taking nafarelin, particularly if patients miss successive drug doses. Therefore, **patients should use nonhormonal methods of contraception.** Patients should be advised to see their physician if they believe they may be pregnant. If a patient becomes pregnant during treatment, the drug must be discontinued. There is no experience with nafarelin in pregnant women.

It is not known whether or to what extent nafarelin is excreted into human breast milk. The effects, if any, on the breast-fed child have not been determined and therefore, nafarelin should not be used in breast feeding women.

Children: The safety and effectiveness in children have not been established and therefore, nafarelin should not be used.

Precautions: Information for the Patient: An information pamphlet for patients is included with the product and should be read carefully before initiating treatment with nafarelin. Patients should be made aware of the following information.

Menstruation: Since menstruation should stop with effective doses of nafarelin, the patient should notify her physician, if regular menstruation persists. Patients missing successive doses of the drug may experience break through vaginal bleeding.

Pregnancy and *Lactation:* Patients should not use nafarelin if they are pregnant, breast-feeding, have undiagnosed abnormal vaginal bleeding or are allergic to any of the ingredients in the product.

Use in Women of Childbearing Potential: Safe use of the drug in pregnancy has not been established clinically. Therefore, **a nonhormonal method of contraception should be used during treatment.** Patients should be advised that if they miss successive doses of nafarelin, ovulation may occur with the potential for conception. If a patient becomes pregnant during treatment, she should discontinue treatment and consult her physician.

Adverse Events: Adverse events associated with the hypoestrogenic state induced by nafarelin, occurred in clinical studies. The most frequently reported adverse events were hot flashes (90%), decrease in libido (22%), headache (19%), vaginal dryness (19%), emotional lability (15%), acne (13%), myalgia (10%) and reduction in breast size (10%). Estrogen levels returned to normal after treatment was discontinued with resolution of the hypoestrogenic effects. Nasal irritation occurred in about 10% of all patients who used intranasal nafarelin.

Bone Density: The induced hypoestrogenic state caused by nafarelin results in a small loss in bone density over the course of treatment, some of which may not be reversible. During one 6-month treatment period, this bone loss should not be important. In patients with major risk factors for decreased bone mineral content such as chronic alcohol and/or tobacco use, strong family history of osteoporosis or chronic use of drugs that can reduce bone mass such as anticonvulsants or corticosteroids, nafarelin therapy may pose an additional risk. In these patients, the risks and benefits must be weighed carefully before therapy is instituted. Repeated courses of treatment with gonadotropin releasing hormone analogues are not advisable in patients with major risk factors for loss of bone mineral content.

Retreatment: The safety of retreatment as well as of treatment beyond 6 months with nafarelin has not yet been established.

Drug Interactions: No pharmacokinetic drug interaction studies have been conducted with nafarelin. However, because nafarelin is a peptide that is primarily degraded by peptidases and not by cytochrome P-450 enzymes, and because the drug is only about 80% bound to plasma proteins at 4°C, drug interactions would not be expected to occur.

Patients with intercurrent rhinitis should consult with their physician before the use of a topical nasal decongestant. If the use of a topical nasal decongestant is required during treatment with nafarelin, the decongestant must be used at least 30 minutes after dosing to decrease the possibility of reducing drug absorption. The effect of rhinitis or a topical decongestant on nafarelin absorption by the nasal mucosa has not yet been determined.

Diagnostic Interference: Administration of nafarelin in therapeutic doses results in suppression of the pituitary-gonadal system. Normal function is usually restored within 4 to 8 weeks after treatment is discontinued. Diagnostic tests of pituitary-gonadal function conducted during the treatment and within 8 weeks after discontinuation of nafarelin therapy may therefore be misleading.

Fertility Studies: Use of nafarelin in human pregnancy has not been studied. After 6 months of therapy, 56 patients, who were treated with 400 µg/day, desired and attempted pregnancy. By the end of 18 months post treatment, 17 (30%) patients became pregnant. In the 800 µg/day group, out of 48 patients attempting pregnancy, 25 of them (52%) became pregnant within 18 months post treatment. Full term delivery occurred in 82% and 68% of patients in the 400 and 800 µg/day groups respectively. All newborns were normal except for one male baby who had hydrocele. The mother of the baby was in the 400 µg/day group.

The serum concentration of gonadotropins and estradiol returned promptly to normal after cessation of therapy.

Mutagenicity and Carcinogenicity: As seen with other GnRH agonists, high parenteral doses (up to 100 µg/kg/day in mice for 18 months and 500 µg/kg/day in rats for 24 months) induced hyperplasia and/or neoplasia (without metastasis) of endocrine organs including the pituitary (adenoma/carcinoma). Rodents are particularly sensitive to hormonal stimulation when tested for tumorigenicity. No evidence of tumorigenicity has been reported in monkeys or man. No indication of a mutagenic potential for nafarelin has been reported.

Adverse Effects: As would be expected with a drug which lowers serum estradiol levels, the most frequently reported adverse reactions were those related to hypoestrogenism.

Controlled studies included 203 evaluable women (mean age 32 years) treated on average for 170 days with nafarelin 400 µg/day. The adverse reactions most frequently reported and thought to be drug related are listed below (% incidence (n=203)).

CNS: headache 19%, emotional lability 15%, nervousness 9%, insomnia 8%, depression 2%, dizziness 1%, vertigo 1%, incoordination 0.5%, neurosis 0.5%, increased sweating 0.5%.

Skin and Appendages: acne 13%, breast atrophy 10%, seborrhea 8%, hirsutism 2%, dry skin 2%, alopecia 0.5%, chloasma 0.5%, gynecomastia 0.5%, herpes simplex 0.5%, maculopapular rash 0.5%.

Urogenital: vaginal dryness 19%, dyspareunia 1%, menstrual disorder 0.5%, cystitis 0.5%, dysuria 0.5%, urinary incontinence 0.5%, vaginal hemorrhage 0.5%.

Metabolic and Nutritional Disorders: weight gain 8%, edema 8%, weight loss 1%.

Musculoskeletal: myalgia 10%, arthralgia 1%, myasthenia 0.5%.

Digestive: nausea 7%, gastrointestinal fullness 5%, increased appetite 1%, anorexia 1%, constipation 0.5%, diarrhea 0.5%, gastritis 0.5%, vomiting 0.5%.

Respiratory: rhinitis 10%, epistaxis 1%, dry nose 0.5%, sinusitis 0.5%, voice alteration 0.5%.

Special Senses: taste perversion 3%, conjunctivitis 1%, ear pain 0.5%, eye pain 0.5%.

Body as a Whole: asthenia 1%, mucous membrane disorder 0.5%.

Cardiovascular: hot flashes 90.0%, palpitation 0.5%.

Others: breast pain 3%, decreased libido 22%, increased libido 1%.

Changes in Bone Density: After 6 months of treatment, vertebral trabecular bone density and total vertebral bone mass, measured by quantitative computed tomography (QCT), decreased by an average of 8.7% and 4.3%, respectively,

Table I—Synarel

Symptom Severity Score	N	0 None	1–2 Mild	3–5 Moderate	6–9 Severe
At Admission	73	6 (8%)	26 (36%)	28 (38%)	13 (19%)
End of treatment	73	44 (60%)	23 (32%)	5 (7%)	1 (1%)
6 months after treatment	73	37 (50%)	24 (33%)	12 (17%)	—

compared to pretreatment levels. There was partial recovery of bone density, when assessed 6 months after end of treatment, the average trabecular bone density and total bone mass were 4.9% and 3.3% less than the pretreatment levels, respectively. Total vertebral bone mass, measured by dual photon absorptiometry (DPA), decreased by a mean of 5.9% at the end of treatment. Mean total vertebral mass, re-examined by DPA 6 months after completion of treatment, was 1.4% below pretreatment levels. There was little, if any, decrease in the mineral content in compact bone of the distal radius and second metacarpal. Use of nafarelin for longer than the recommended 6 months or in the presence of other known risk factors for decreased bone mineral content may cause additional bone loss.

Changes in Laboratory Values: Plasma Enzymes: After 6 months of therapy with 400 μg/day of nafarelin, elevations in AST outside the normal range were observed in 5 (3%) of 180 patients with normal baseline values. Post- treatment evaluations were available for 4 of these patients: the level of AST was within the normal range. For ALT, 2 (3 %) of 68 patients with normal baseline had increases outside the normal range. 1 patient, for which data are available, returned to normal during the post-treatment observation. For alkaline phosphatase, 10 (5%) out of 182 patients with normal baseline level had increases outside the normal range at the end of treatment. Post-treatment evaluations were available for 8 of these patients: 4 patients were within the normal range, the other 4 patients were above the normal range but this was not considered clinically significant.

Lipids: At enrollment, 9% of the patients receiving nafarelin 400 μg/day had total cholesterol values above 250 mg/dL. These patients also had cholesterol values above 250 mg/dL at the end of treatment.

Of those patients whose pretreatment cholesterol values were below 250 mg/dL, 6% in the nafarelin group, had post-treatment values above 250 mg/dL.

The mean (±SEM) pretreatment values for total cholesterol from all nafarelin patients were 191.8 (4.3) mg/dL. At the end of the treatment period, the mean values for total cholesterol from all patients in the nafarelin group were 204.5 (4.8) mg/dL. The increase from the pretreatment value was statistically significant ($p < 0.05$).

Triglycerides were increased above the upper limit of 150 mg/dL in 12% of the patients who received nafarelin.

Following completion of treatment, no patients receiving nafarelin had abnormally low HDL cholesterol fractions (less than 30 mg/dL) and none of the patients receiving nafarelin had abnormally high LDL cholesterol fractions (greater than 190 mg/dL). There was no increase in the LDL/HDL ratio in patients receiving nafarelin.

Other Changes: In comparative studies, the following changes were seen in approximately 10% to 15% of patients. Nafarelin treatment was associated with elevations of plasma phosphorus and eosinophil counts, and decreases in serum calcium and WBC counts.

Overdose: Symptoms and Treatment: In experimental animals a single s.c. administration of up to 60 times the recommended human dose (expressed on a μg/kg basis not adjusted for bioavailability) had no adverse effects. Orally administered nafarelin is subject to enzymatic degradation in the gastrointestinal tract and is therefore inactive. At present, there is no clinical evidence of adverse effects following overdosage of GnRH analogues.

Dosage: For the management of endometriosis, the recommended daily dose is 400 μg. This is achieved by 1 spray (200 μg of nafarelin free base) into 1 nostril in the morning and 1 spray into the other nostril in the evening. Treatment should be started between days 2 and 4 of the menstrual cycle.

In an occasional patient, the 400 μg daily dose may not produce amenorrhea. For these patients with persistent regular menstruation after 2 months of treatment, the dose may be increased to 800 μg daily. The 800 μg dose is administered as 1 spray into each nostril in the morning (a total of 2 sprays) and again in the evening.

The recommended duration of administration is 6 months. The safety of retreatment as well as of treatment beyond 6 months with nafarelin has not yet been established. If the symptoms of endometriosis recur after a course of therapy, and further treatment is contemplated, it is recommended that bone density be assessed before retreatment begins to ensure that values are within normal limits.

If the use of a topical nasal decongestant is necessary during treatment with this product, the decongestant should not be used until at least 30 minutes after nafarelin dosing (see Precautions).

At 400 μg/day, a 10 mL bottle of nafarelin provides a 30-day (about 60 sprays) supply while a 6.5 mL bottle provides enough drug for 15 days (about 30 sprays). If the daily dose is increased, increase the supply to the patient to ensure uninterrupted treatment for the recommended duration of therapy.

Information for the Patient: See Blue Section—Information for the Patient "Synarel".

Supplied: Each mL of nasal solution contains: nafarelin acetate 2 mg (as nafarelin base). Nonmedicinal ingredients: benzalkonium chloride, glacial acetic acid, hydrochloric acid or sodium hydroxide, sorbitol and purified water. Bottles of 6.5 or 10 mL. Each bottle is supplied with a metered spray pump. A dust cover and a leaflet of patient instructions are also included.

After priming the pump unit, each actuation of the unit delivers approximately 100 μL of the metered droplet spray containing approximately 200 μg nafarelin base. The contents of one 10 mL spray bottle are intended to deliver at least 60 sprays. The contents of one 6.5 mL spray bottle are intended to deliver at least 30 sprays.

Store upright at room temperature. Avoid heat above 30°C. Protect from light. Do not freeze.

(Shown in Product Recognition Section)

SYNFLEX® Ⓟ
SYNFLEX® DS Ⓟ
AltiMed

Naproxen Sodium
Analgesic—Anti-inflammatory

Supplied: Synflex: Each oval-shaped, blue, film-coated tablet, with SYNFLEX engraved on one side, contains: naproxen sodium 275 mg. Nonmedicinal ingredients: FD&C Blue #2 aluminum lake, hydroxypropyl methylcellulose, magnesium stearate, microcrystalline cellulose, polyethylene glycol, povidone, talc and titanium dioxide. Bisulfite-, erythrosine-, gluten-, lactose-, sorbitol-, tartrazine- and xylitol-free. Bottles of 100 and 500.

Synflex DS: Each oval-shaped, blue, film-coated tablet, with SYNFLEX DS engraved on one side and single scored on the other, contains: naproxen sodium 550 mg. Nonmedicinal ingredients: FD&C Blue #2 aluminum lake, hydroxypropyl methylcellulose, magnesium stearate, microcrystalline cellulose, polyethylene glycol, povidone, talc and titanium dioxide. Bisulfite-, erythrosine-, gluten-, lactose-, sorbitol-, tartrazine- and xylitol-free. Bottles of 100 and 500.

Store at room temperature (15 to 30°C) in a well-closed container, protected from light.

SYNPHASIC® Ⓟ
Searle

Norethindrone—Ethinyl Estradiol
Oral Contraceptive

Pharmacology: Estrogen-progestogen combinations act primarily through the mechanism of gonadotropin suppression due to the estrogenic and progestational activity of their components. Although the primary mechanism of action is inhibition of ovulation, alterations in the cervical mucus and the endometrium may also contribute to effectiveness.

Indications: Prevention of pregnancy.

Contraindications: History of or actual thrombophlebitis or thromboembolic disorders; history of or actual cerebrovascular disorders; history of or actual myocardial infarction or coronary arterial disease; active liver disease or history of or actual benign or malignant liver tumors; history of or known or suspected carcinoma of the breast; history of or known or suspected estrogen-dependent neoplasia; undiagnosed abnormal vaginal bleeding; any ocular lesion arising from ophthalmic vascular disease, such as partial or complete loss of vision or defect in visual fields; when pregnancy is suspected or diagnosed.

Warnings: Predisposing Factors for Coronary Artery Disease: Cigarette smoking increases the risk of serious cardiovascular side effects and mortality. Birth control pills increase this risk, especially with increasing age. Convincing data are available to support an upper age limit of 35 years for oral contraceptive use in women who smoke.

Other women who are independently at high risk for cardiovascular disease include those with diabetes, hypertension, abnormal lipid profile, or a family history of these. Whether oral contraceptives accentuate this risk is unclear.

In low risk, nonsmoking women of any age, the benefits of oral contraceptive use outweigh the possible cardiovascular risks associated with low-dose formulations. Consequently, oral contraceptives may be prescribed for these women up to the age of menopause.

> Cigarette smoking increases the risk of serious adverse effects on the heart and blood vessels. This risk increases with age and becomes significant in oral contraceptive users over 35 years of age. Women should be counselled not to smoke.

Discontinue Medication at the Earliest Manifestation of the Following:

A. Thromboembolic and cardiovascular disorders such as: thrombophlebitis, pulmonary embolism, cerebrovascular disorders, myocardial ischemia, mesenteric thrombosis and retinal thrombosis.

B. Conditions that predispose to venous stasis and to vascular thrombosis, e.g., immobilization after accidents or confinement to bed during long-term illness. Other nonhormonal methods of contraception should be used until regular activities are resumed. For use of oral contraceptives when surgery is contemplated, see Precautions.

C. Visual defects, partial or complete.

D. Papilledema or ophthalmic vascular lesions.

E. Severe headache of unknown etiology or worsening of pre-existing migraine headache.

Precautions: Physical Examination and Followup: Before oral contraceptives are used, a thorough history and physical examination should be performed, including a blood pressure determination. Breasts, liver, extremities and pelvic organs should be examined and a Papanicolaou smear should be taken if the patient has been sexually active.

The first followup visit should be done 3 months after oral contraceptives are prescribed. Thereafter, examinations should be performed at least once a year or more frequently if indicated. At each annual visit, examination should include those procedures that were done at the initial visit as outlined above or per recommendations of the Canadian Workshop on Screening for Cancer of the Cervix. Their suggestion was that, for women who had 2 consecutive negative Pap smears, screening could be continued every 3 years up to the age of 69.

Pregnancy: Fetal abnormalities have been reported to occur in the offspring of women who have taken estrogen-progestogen combinations in early pregnancy. Rule out pregnancy as soon as it is suspected.

Lactation: The use of oral contraceptives during the period a mother is breast-feeding her infant may not be advisable. The hormonal components are excreted in breast milk and may reduce its quantity and quality. The long-term effects on the developing child are not known.

Hepatic Function: Patients who have had jaundice including a history of cholestatic jaundice during pregnancy should be given oral contraceptives with great care and under close observation.

The development of severe generalized pruritus or icterus requires that the medication be withdrawn until the problem is resolved.

If a patient develops jaundice that proves to be cholestatic in type, the use of oral contraceptives should not be resumed. In patients taking oral contraceptives, changes in the composition of the bile may occur and an increased incidence of gallstones has been reported.

Hepatic nodules have been reported to be associated with use of oral contraceptives, particularly in long-term users of oral contraceptives. These nodules include benign hepatic adenomas, focal nodular hyperplasia and other hepatic lesions. In addition, hepatocellular carcinoma has been reported. Although these lesions are extremely rare, they have caused fatal intra-abdominal hemorrhage and should be considered in women presenting with an abdominal mass, acute abdominal pain, or evidence of intra-abdominal bleeding.

Hypertension: Patients with essential hypertension whose blood pressure is well-controlled may be given oral contraceptives but only under close supervision. If a significant elevation of blood pressure in previously normotensive or hypertensive subjects occurs at any time during the administration of the drug, cessation of medication is necessary.

Migraine and Headache: The onset or exacerbation of migraine or the development of headache of a new pattern which is recurrent, persistent or severe, requires discontinuation of oral contraceptives and evaluation of the cause.

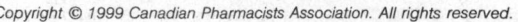

Synphasic (cont'd)

Diabetes: Current low dose oral contraceptives exert minimal impact on glucose metabolism. Diabetic patients, or those with a family history of diabetes, should be observed closely to detect any worsening of carbohydrate metabolism. Patients predisposed to diabetes who can be kept under close supervision may be given oral contraceptives. Young diabetic patients whose disease is of recent origin, well-controlled, and not associated with hypertension or other signs of vascular disease such as ocular fundal changes should be monitored more frequently while using oral contraceptives.

Ocular Disorders: Patients who are pregnant or are taking oral contraceptives may experience corneal edema that may cause visual disturbances and changes in tolerance to contact lenses, especially of the rigid type. Soft contact lenses usually do not cause disturbances. If visual changes or alterations in tolerance to contact lenses occur, temporary or permanent cessation of wear may be advised.

Breasts: Increasing age and a strong family history are the most significant risk factors for the development of breast cancer. Other established risk factors include obesity, nulliparity and late age at first full-term pregnancy. The identified groups of women that may be at increased risk of developing breast cancer before menopause are long-term users of oral contraceptives (more than 8 years) and starters at early age. In a few women, the use of oral contraceptives may accelerate the growth of an existing but undiagnosed breast cancer. Since any potential increased risk related to oral contraceptive use is small, there is no reason to change prescribing habits at present.

Women receiving oral contraceptives should be instructed in self-examination of their breasts. Their physicians should be notified whenever any masses are detected. A yearly clinical breast examination is also recommended because, if a breast cancer should develop, drugs that contain estrogen may cause a rapid progression.

Vaginal Bleeding: Persistent irregular vaginal bleeding requires assessment to exclude underlying pathology.

Fibroids: Patients with fibroids (leiomyomata) should be carefully observed. Sudden enlargement, pain, or tenderness requires discontinuance of the use of oral contraceptives.

Emotional Disorders: Patients with a history of emotional disturbances, especially the depressive type, may be more prone to have a recurrence of depression while taking oral contraceptives. In cases of a serious recurrence, a trial of an alternate method of contraception should be made which may help to clarify the possible relationship. Women with premenstrual syndrome (PMS) may have a varied response to oral contraceptives, ranging from symptomatic improvement to worsening of the condition.

Metabolic and Endocrine Diseases: In metabolic or endocrine diseases and when metabolism of calcium and phosphorus is abnormal, careful clinical evaluation should precede medication and a regular followup is recommended.

Connective Tissue Disease: The use of oral contraceptives in some women has been associated with positive lupus erythematous cell tests and with clinical lupus erythematous. In some instances exacerbation of rheumatoid arthritis and synovitis have been observed.

Laboratory Tests: Results of laboratory tests should be interpreted in the light of the fact that the patient is on oral contraceptives. The laboratory tests listed below are modified.

A. Liver function tests: Aspartate serum transaminase (AST): variously reported elevations. Alkaline phosphatase and gamma glutamine transaminase (GGT): slightly elevated.

B. Coagulation tests: Minimal elevation of test values reported for such parameters as Factors VII, VIII, IX and X. Increased platelet aggregation. Decreased antithrombin III.

C. Thyroid function tests: Protein binding of thyroxine is increased as indicated by increased total serum thyroxine concentrations and decreased T_3 resin uptake.

D. Lipoproteins: Small changes of unproven clinical significance may occur in lipoprotein cholesterol fractions.

E. Gonadotropins: LH and FSH levels are suppressed by the use of oral contraceptives. Wait 2 weeks after discontinuing the use of oral contraceptives before measurements are made.

Tissue Specimens: Pathologists should be advised of oral contraceptive therapy when specimens obtained from surgical procedures and Pap smears are submitted for examination.

Return to Fertility: After discontinuing oral contraceptive therapy, the patient should delay pregnancy until at least 1 normal spontaneous cycle has occurred in order to date the pregnancy. An alternative contraceptive method should be used during this time.

Amenorrhea: Women having a history of oligomenorrhea, secondary amenorrhea, or irregular cycles may remain anovulatory or become amenorrheic following discontinuation of estrogen-progestin combination therapy.

Amenorrhea, especially if associated with breast secretion, that continues for 6 months or more after withdrawal, warrants a careful assessment of hypothalamic-pituitary function.

Thromboembolic Complications—Postsurgery: There is an increased risk of postsurgery thromboembolic complications in oral contraceptive users, after major surgery. If feasible, oral contraceptives should be discontinued and an alternative method substituted at least 1 month prior to **major** elective surgery. Oral contraceptives should not be resumed until the first menstrual period after hospital discharge following surgery.

Drug Interactions: The concurrent administration of oral contraceptives with other drugs may result in an altered response to either agent. Reduced effectiveness of the oral contraceptive, should it occur, is more likely with the low dose formulations. It is important to ascertain all drugs that a patient is taking, both prescription and nonprescription, before oral contraceptives are prescribed.

Refer to the revised 1994 Report on Oral Contraceptives, Health Canada, for possible drug interactions with oral contraceptives.

Noncontraceptive Benefits of Oral Contraceptives: Several health advantages other than contraception have been reported.

Effects on menses: Increased menstrual cycle regularity; decreased menstrual blood loss; decreased incidence of iron deficiency anemia secondary to reduced menstrual blood loss; decreased incidence of dysmenorrhea.

Effects related to ovulation inhibition: Decreased incidence of functional ovarian cysts; decreased incidence of ectopic pregnancy.

Effects on other organs of the reproductive tract: Decreased incidence of acute salpingitis; decreased incidence of endometrial cancer (50%); decreased incidence of ovarian cancer (40%); potential beneficial effects on endometriosis; improvement of acne vulgaris, hirsutism, and other androgen-mediated disorders.

Effects on breasts: Decreased incidence of benign breast disease (fibroadenomas and fibrocystic breast disease); decreased incidence of breast biopsies.

The noncontraceptive benefits of oral contraceptives should be considered in addition to the efficacy of these preparations when counselling patients regarding contraceptive method selection.

> Oral contraceptives **do not protect** against sexually transmitted diseases (STDs) including HIV/AIDS. For protection against STDs, it is advisable to use latex condoms **in combination with** oral contraceptives.

Adverse Effects: An increased risk of the following serious adverse reactions has been associated with the use of oral contraceptives: thrombophlebitis; pulmonary embolism; mesenteric thrombosis; neuro-ocular lesions, e.g., retinal thrombosis; myocardial infarction; cerebral thrombosis; cerebral hemorrhage; hypertension; benign hepatic tumors; gallbladder disease.

The following adverse reactions also have been reported in patients receiving oral contraceptives: Nausea and vomiting, usually the most common adverse reaction, occurs in approximately 10% or less of patients during the first cycle. Other reactions, as a general rule, are seen less frequently or only occasionally.

Other adverse reactions: gastrointestinal symptoms (such as abdominal cramps and bloating); breakthrough bleeding; spotting; change in menstrual flow; dysmenorrhea; amenorrhea during and after treatment; infertility after discontinuance of treatment; edema; chloasma or melasma which may persist; breast changes: tenderness, enlargement, and secretion; change in weight (increase or decrease); endocervical hyperplasias; possible diminution in lactation when given immediately post-partum; cholestatic jaundice; migraine; increase in size of uterine leiomyomata; rash (allergic); mental depression; reduced tolerance to carbohydrates; vaginal candidiasis; premenstrual-like syndrome; intolerance to contact lenses; change in corneal curvature (steepening); cataracts; optic neuritis; retinal thrombosis; changes in libido; chorea; changes in appetite; cystitis-like syndrome; rhinitis; headache; nervousness; dizziness; hirsutism; loss of scalp hair; erythema multiforme; erythema nodosum; hemorrhagic eruption; vaginitis; porphyria; impaired renal function; Raynaud's phenomenon; auditory disturbances; hemolytic uremic syndrome; pancreatitis; arterial thromboembolism.

Overdose: Symptoms and Treatment: Numerous cases of the ingestion, by children, of estrogen-progestogen combinations have been reported. Although mild nausea may occur, there appears to be no other reaction. Treatment should be limited to a laxative such as citrate of magnesia with the aim of removing unabsorbed material as rapidly as possible.

Dosage: Information for the Patient on How to Take the Birth Control Pill:

1. **Read these directions:**
   - before you start taking your pills, and
   - any time you are not sure what to do.
2. **Look at your pill pack** to see if it has 21 or 28 pills:
   - 21-Pill Pack: 21 active pills (with hormones) taken daily for 3 weeks, and then take no pills for 1 week

   or
   - 28-Pill Pack: 21 active pills (with hormones) taken daily for 3 weeks, and then 7 "reminder" pills (no hormones) taken daily for 1 week.

   Also check the pill pack for instructions on (1) where to start and (2) directions to take pills (see package insert for illustrations).
3. It is recommended that you use a second method of birth control (e.g., latex condoms and spermicidal foam or gel) for the first 7 days of the first cycle of pill use. This will provide a back-up in case pills are forgotten while you are getting used to taking them.
4. **When receiving any medical treatment, be sure to tell your doctor that you are using birth control pills.**
5. **Many women have spotting or light bleeding or may feel sick to their stomach during the first 3 months on the pill.** If you do feel sick, do not stop taking the pill. The problem will usually go away. If it does not go away, check with your doctor or clinic.
6. **Missing pills also can cause some spotting or light bleeding,** even if you make up the missed pills. You also could feel a little sick to your stomach on the days you take 2 pills to make up for missed pills.
7. **If you miss pills at any time, you could get pregnant. The greatest risks for pregnancy are:**
   - when you start a pack late, or
   - when you miss pills at the beginning or at the very end of the pack.
8. **Always be sure you have ready:**
   - **another kind of birth control** (such as latex condoms and spermicidal foam or gel) to use as a backup in case you miss pills, and
   - **an extra, full pack of pills.**
9. **If you experience vomiting or diarrhea, or if you take certain medicines,** such as antibiotics, your pills may not work as well. Use a backup method, such as latex condoms and spermicidal foam or gel, until you can check with your doctor or clinic.
10. **If you forget more than 1 pill 2 months in a row,** talk to your doctor or clinic about how to make pill-taking easier or about using another method of birth control.
11. **If your questions are not answered here, call your doctor or clinic.**

When to start the first pack of pills: Be sure to read these instructions:

- before you start taking your pills, and
- any time you are not sure what to do.

Decide with your doctor or clinic what is the best day for you to start taking your first pack of pills. Your pills may be either a 21-day or a 28-day type.

A. 21-Day Combination: With this type of birth control pill, you are on pills for 21 days and off pills for 7 days. You must not be off the pills for more than 7 days in a row.

1. **The first day of your menstrual period (bleeding) is Day 1 of your cycle.** Your doctor may advise you to start taking the pills on Day 1, on Day 5, or on the first Sunday after your period begins. If your period starts on Sunday, start that same day.
2. Take 1 pill at approximately the same time every day for 21 days; **then take no pills for 7 days.** Start a new pack on the 8th day. You will probably have a period during the 7 days off the pill. (This bleeding may be lighter and shorter than your usual period.)

B. 28-Day Combination: With this type of birth control pill, you take 21 pills which contain hormones and 7 pills which contain no hormones.

1. **The first day of your menstrual period (bleeding) is Day 1 of your cycle.** Your doctor may advise you to start taking the pills on Day 1, on Day 5, or on the first Sunday after your period begins. If your period starts on Sunday, start that same day.
2. Take 1 pill at approximately the same time every day for 28 days. Begin a new pack the next day, **not missing any**

Table I—Synphasic

What to Do if You Miss Pills

Sunday Start	**Other Than Sunday Start**
Miss 1 pill	**Miss 1 pill**
Take it as soon as you remember, and take the next pill at the usual time. This means that you might take 2 pills in one day.	Take it as soon as you remember, and take the next pill at the usual time. This means that you might take 2 pills in one day.
Miss 2 pills in a row	**Miss 2 pills in a row**
First 2 Weeks: 1. Take 2 pills the day you remember and 2 pills the next day. 2. Then take 1 pill a day until you finish the pack. 3. Use a backup method of birth control if you have sex in the 7 days after you miss the pills.	**First 2 Weeks:** 1. Take 2 pills the day you remember and 2 pills the next day. 2. Then take 1 pill a day until you finish the pack. 3. Use a backup method of birth control if you have sex in the 7 days after you miss the pills.
Third Week: 1. Keep taking 1 pill a day until Sunday. 2. On Sunday, safely discard the rest of the pack and start a new pack that day. 3. Use a backup method of birth control if you have sex in the 7 days after you miss the pills. 4. You may not have a period this month. **If you miss 2 periods in a row, call your doctor or clinic.**	**Third Week:** 1. Safely dispose of the rest of the pill pack and start a new pack that same day. 2. Use a backup method of birth control if you have sex in the 7 days after you miss the pills. 3. You may not have a period this month. **If you miss 2 periods in a row, call your doctor or clinic.**
Miss 3 or more pills in a row	**Miss 3 or more pills in a row**
Anytime in the Cycle: 1. Keep taking 1 pill a day until Sunday. 2. On Sunday, safely discard the rest of the pack and start a new pack that day. 3. Use a backup method of birth control if you have sex in the 7 days after you miss the pills. 4. You may not have a period this month. **If you miss 2 periods in a row, call your doctor or clinic.**	**Anytime in the Cycle:** 1. Safely dispose of the rest of the pill pack and start a new pack that same day. 2. Use a backup method of birth control if you have sex in the 7 days after you miss the pills. 3. You may not have a period this month. **If you miss 2 periods in a row, call your doctor or clinic.**

days. Your period should occur during the last 7 days of using that pill pack.

What to do during the month:

1. **Take a pill at approximately the same time every day until the pack is empty.**
   - Try to associate taking your pill with some regular activity like eating a meal or going to bed.
   - Do not skip pills even if you have bleeding between monthly periods or feel sick to your stomach (nausea).
   - Do not skip pills even if you do not have sex very often.
2. **When you finish a pack:**
   - **21 pills: Wait 7 days** to start the next pack. You will have your period during that week.
   - **28 pills:** Start the next pack **on the next day.** Take 1 pill every day. Do not wait any days between packs.

What to do if you miss pills: Table I outlines the actions you should take if you miss 1 or more of your birth control pills. Match the number of pills missed with the appropriate starting time for your type of pill pack.

Note: 28-Day Pack: If you forget any of the 7 orange "reminder" pills (without hormones) in Week 4, just safely dispose of the pills you missed. Then keep taking 1 pill each day until the pack is empty. You do not need to use a backup method.

Always be sure you have on hand:

- a backup method of birth control (such as latex condoms and spermicidal foam or gel) in case you miss pills, and
- an extra, full pack of pills.

If you forget more than 1 pill 2 months in a row, talk to your doctor or clinic about ways to make pill-taking easier or about using another method of birth control.

Dosage: **A. 21-Day Pack:** With this type of birth control pill, the patient is 21 days on pills with 7 days off pills. The patient must not be off the pills for more than 7 days in a row.

1. **The first day of the patient's menstrual period (bleeding) is day 1 of a cycle.** The doctor may advise the patient to start taking the pills on Day 1, on Day 5, or on the first Sunday after a period begins. If a period starts on Sunday, the patient starts that same day.
2. The pack must be labelled correctly before starting. The pack is pre-printed with a Sunday starting day. If the patient is starting on a day other than a Sunday, she should use the Flexi-start sticker labels provided. The patient peels off the label with the chosen starting day and applies it over the pre-printed days on top of the card.
3. The patient takes 1 pill at approximately the same time every day for 21 days; **then she takes no pills for 7 days.** She starts a new pack on the 8th day. She will probably have a period during the 7 days off the pill. (This bleeding may be lighter and shorter than a usual period.)

B. 28-Day Pack: With this type of birth control pill, the patient takes 21 pills which contain hormones and 7 pills which contain no hormones.

1. **The first day of the patient's menstrual period (bleeding) is day 1 of a cycle.** The doctor may advise the patient to start taking the pills on Day 1, on Day 5, or on the first Sunday after a period begins. If a period starts on Sunday, the patient starts that same day.
2. The pack must be labelled correctly before starting. The pack is pre-printed with a Sunday starting day. If the patient is starting on a day other than a Sunday, she should use the Flexi-start sticker labels provided. The patient peels off the label with the chosen starting day and applies it over the pre-printed days on top of the card.
3. The patient takes 1 pill at approximately the same time every day for 28 days. She begins a new pack the next day, **not missing any days on the pills.** The patient's period should occur during the last 7 days of using that pill pack.

What to do during the month:

1. **The patient takes a pill at approximately the same time every day until the pack is empty.**
   - The patient should try to associate taking the pill with some regular activity like eating a meal or going to bed.
   - The patient must not skip pills even if she has bleeding between monthly periods or feels sick to her stomach (nausea).
   - The patient must not skip pills even if she does not have sex very often.
2. **When a pack is finished:**
   - **21 Pills: The patient must wait 7 days** to start the next pack. A period will begin during that week.
   - **28 Pills:** The patient starts the next pack **on the next day.** She takes 1 pill every day. She does not wait any days between packs.

Information for the Patient: See Blue Section—Information for the Patient "Oral Contraceptives".

Supplied: Each white circular tablet, imprinted "SEARLE" on one side and "BX" on the side, contains: norethindrone 1 mg and ethinyl estradiol 0.035 mg, and each blue circular tablet, imprinted "SEARLE" on one side and "BX" on the side, contains: norethindrone 0.5 mg and ethinyl estradiol 0.035 mg. Inert orange tablets are imprinted "SEARLE" on one side and P on the other, and contain inert ingredients. Nonmedicinal ingredients: Active tablets: cornstarch, FD&C Blue No. 2, lactose hydrous, magnesium stearate and polyvidone. Placebo tablets: FD&C Yellow No. 6 Lake, lactose, lactose monohydrate, magnesium stearate and microcrystalline cellulose. Available in 21-day and 28-day dispensers.

(Shown in Product Recognition Section)

Reviewed 1998

SYNTHROID® ℞

Knoll

Levothyroxine Sodium

Thyroid Hormone

Pharmacology: The synthesis and secretion of the major thyroid hormones, L-thyroxine (T_4) and L-triiodothyronine (T_3), from the normally functioning thyroid gland are regulated by complex feedback mechanisms of the hypothalamic-pituitary-thyroid axis. The thyroid gland is stimulated to secrete thyroid hormones by the action of thyrotropin (thyroid stimulating hormone, TSH), which is produced in the anterior pituitary gland. TSH secretion is in turn controlled by thyrotropin-releasing hormone (TRH) produced in the hypothalamus, circulating thyroid hormones, and possibly other mechanisms. Thyroid hormones circulating in the blood act as feedback inhibitors of both TSH and TRH secretion. Thus, when serum concentrations of T_3 and T_4 are increased, secretion of TSH and TRH decreases. Conversely, when serum thyroid hormone concentrations are decreased, secretion of TSH and TRH is increased. Administration of exogenous thyroid hormones to euthyroid individuals results in suppression of endogenous thyroid hormone secretion.

The mechanisms by which thyroid hormones exert their physiologic actions have not been completely elucidated. T_4 and T_3 are transported into cells by passive and active mechanisms. T_3 in cell cytoplasm and T_3 generated from T_4 within the cell diffuse into the nucleus and bind to thyroid receptor proteins, which appear to be primarily attached to DNA. Receptor binding leads to activation or repression of DNA transcription, thereby altering the amounts of mRNA and resultant proteins. Changes in protein concentrations are responsible for the metabolic changes observed in organs and tissues.

Thyroid hormones enhance oxygen consumption of most body tissues and increase the basal metabolic rate and metabolism of carbohydrates, lipids, and proteins. Thus, they exert a profound influence on every organ system and are of particular importance in the development of the CNS. Thyroid hormones also appear to have direct effects on tissues, such as increased myocardial contractility and decreased systemic vascular resistance.

The physiologic effects of thyroid hormones are produced primarily by T_3, a large portion of which is derived from the deiodination of T_4 in peripheral tissues. About 70 to 90% of peripheral T_3 is produced by monodeiodination of T_4 at the 5′ position (outer ring). Peripheral monodeiodination of T_4 at the 5 position (inner ring) results in the formation of reverse triiodothyronine (rT_3), which is calorigenically inactive.

Pharmacokinetics: Few clinical studies have evaluated the kinetics of orally administered thyroid hormone. In animals, the most active sites of absorption appear to be the proximal and mid-jejunum. T_4 is not absorbed from the stomach and little, if any, drug is absorbed from the duodenum. There seems to be no absorption of T_4 from the distal colon in animals. A number of human studies have confirmed the importance of an intact jejunum and ileum for T_4 absorption and have shown some absorption from the duodenum. Studies involving radioiodinated T_4 fecal tracer excretion methods, equilibration, and AUC methods have shown that absorption varies from 48 to 80% of the administered dose. The extent of absorption is increased in the fasting state and decreased in malabsorption syndromes, such as sprue. Absorption may also decrease with age. The degree of T_4 absorption is dependent on the product formulation as well as on the character of the intestinal contents, the intestinal flora, including plasma protein and soluble dietary factors, which bind thyroid hormone, making it unavailable for diffusion. Decreased absorption may result from administration of infant soybean formula, ferrous sulfate, sodium polystyrene sulfonate, aluminum hydroxide, sucralfate, or bile acid sequestrants. T_4 absorption following i.m. administration is variable.

Distribution of thyroid hormones in human body tissues and fluids has not been fully elucidated. More than 99% of circulating hormones is bound to serum proteins, including thyroxine-binding globulin (TBG), thyroxine-binding prealbumin (TBPA), and albumin (TBA). T_4 is more extensively and firmly bound to serum proteins than is T_3. Only unbound thyroid hormone is metabolically active. The higher affinity of TBG and TBPA for T_4 partly explains the higher serum levels, slower metabolic clearance, and longer serum elimination half-life of this hormone.

Certain drugs and physiologic conditions can alter the binding of thyroid hormones to serum proteins and/or the

Synthroid (cont'd)

concentrations of the serum proteins available for thyroid hormone binding. These effects must be considered when interpreting the results of thyroid function tests (see Precautions, Drug Interactions and Laboratory Test Interactions).

T_4 is eliminated slowly from the body, with a half-life of 6 to 7 days. T_3 has a half-life of 1 to 2 days. The liver is the major site of degradation for both hormones. T_4 and T_3 are conjugated with glucuronic and sulfuric acids and excreted in the bile. There is an enterohepatic circulation of thyroid hormones, as they are liberated by hydrolysis in the intestine and reabsorbed. A portion of the conjugated material reaches the colon unchanged, is hydrolyzed there, and is eliminated as free compounds in the feces. In man, approximately 20 to 40% of T_4 is eliminated in the stool. About 70% of the T_4 secreted daily is deiodinated to yield equal amounts of T_3 and rT_3. Subsequent deiodination of T_3 and rT_3 yields multiple forms of diiodothyronine. A number of other minor T_4 metabolites have also been identified. Although some of these metabolites have biologic activity, their overall contribution to the therapeutic effect of T_4 is minimal.

Indications: As replacement or supplemental therapy in patients of any age or state (including pregnancy) with hypothyroidism of any etiology except transient hypothyroidism during the recovery phase of subacute thyroiditis; primary hypothyroidism resulting from thyroid dysfunction, primary atrophy, or partial or total absence of the thyroid gland, or from the effects of surgery, radiation or drugs, with or without the presence of goiter, including subclinical hypothyroidism; secondary (pituitary) hypothyroidism; and tertiary (hypothalamic) hypothyroidism (see Contraindications and Precautions). Levothyroxine injection can be used i.v. when rapid repletion is required, and either i.v. or i.m. when the oral route is precluded.

As a pituitary TSH suppressant in the treatment or prevention of various types of euthyroid goiters, including thyroid nodules, subacute or chronic lymphocytic thyroiditis (Hashimoto's), multinodular goiter, and in conjunction with surgery and radioactive iodine therapy in the management of thyrotropin-dependent well-differentiated papillary or follicular carcinoma of the thyroid.

Contraindications: In patients with untreated thyrotoxicosis of any etiology, acute myocardial infarction, or an apparent hypersensitivity to thyroid hormones or any of the inactive product constituents. (Note: The 50 μg tablet is formulated without color additives for patients who are sensitive to dyes.) There is no well-documented evidence of true allergic or idiosyncratic reactions to thyroid hormone. Levothyroxine is also contraindicated in patients with uncorrected adrenal insufficiency, as thyroid hormones increase tissue demands for adrenocortical hormones and may thereby precipitate acute adrenal crisis (see Precautions).

Warnings: Thyroid hormones, either alone or together with other therapeutic agents, should not be used for the treatment of obesity. In euthyroid patients, doses within the range of daily hormonal requirements are ineffective for weight reduction. Larger doses may produce serious or even life threatening manifestations of toxicity, particularly when given in association with sympathomimetic amines such as those used for their anorectic effects.

The use of levothyroxine in the treatment of obesity, either alone or in combination with other drugs, is unjustified. The use of levothyroxine is also unjustified in the treatment of male or female infertility unless this condition is associated with hypothyroidism.

Precautions: General: Levothyroxine should be used with caution in patients with cardiovascular disorders, including angina, coronary artery disease, and hypertension, and in the elderly who have a greater likelihood of occult cardiac disease. Concomitant administration of thyroid hormone and sympathomimetic agents to patients with coronary artery disease may increase the risk of coronary insufficiency.

Use of levothyroxine in patients with concomitant diabetes mellitus, diabetes insipidus or adrenal cortical insufficiency may aggravate the intensity of their symptoms. Appropriate adjustments of the various therapeutic measures directed at these concomitant endocrine diseases may therefore be required. Treatment of myxedema coma may require simultaneous administration of glucocorticoids (see Dosage).

T_4 enhances the response to anticoagulant therapy. Prothrombin time should be closely monitored in patients taking both levothyroxine and oral anticoagulants, and the dosage of anticoagulant adjusted accordingly.

The bioavailability of levothyroxine may differ to some extent among marketed brands. Once the patient is stabilized on a particular brand of levothyroxine sodium, caution should be exercised when a change in drug product brand is implemented.

It has been shown that differences in formulations of levothyroxine, despite an identical content of active ingredient, may be associated with differences in fractional gastrointestinal absorption. These differences may not be observed through measurement of total T_3 and T_4 serum levels. It is therefore, recommended that patients who are switched from one levothyroxine formulation to another be retitrated to the desired thyroid function. Accuracy in retitration can best be achieved by using sensitive thyrotropin assays.

The intestinal absorption of levothyroxine may be impaired in patients with absorption disorder; in such patients, higher dosage levels of levothyroxine may be required.

Seizures have been reported rarely in association with the initiation of levothyroxine therapy, and may be related to the effect of thyroid hormone on seizure threshold.

Lithium blocks the TSH-mediated release of T_4 and T_3. Thyroid function should therefore be carefully monitored during lithium initiation, stabilization, and maintenance. If hypothyroidism occurs during lithium treatment, a higher than usual levothyroxine dose may be required.

Laboratory Tests: Treatment of patients with levothyroxine requires periodic assessment of thyroid status by appropriate laboratory tests and clinical evaluation. Selection of appropriate tests for the diagnosis and management of thyroid disorders depends on patient variables such as presenting signs and symptoms, pregnancy, and concomitant medications. A combination of sensitive TSH assay and free T_4 estimate (free T_4 index, FT_4I) are recommended to confirm a diagnosis of thyroid disease. Normal ranges for these parameters are age-specific in newborns and younger children.

TSH alone or initially may be useful for thyroid disease screening and for monitoring therapy for primary hypothyroidism as a linear inverse correlation exists between serum TSH and free T_4. Measurement of total serum T_4 and T_3, resin T_3 uptake, and free T_3 concentrations may also be useful. Antithyroid microsomal antibodies are an indicator of autoimmune thyroid disease. Positive microsomal antibody presence in an euthyroid patient is a major risk factor for the development of hypothyroidism. An elevated serum TSH in the presence of a normal T_4 may indicate subclinical hypothyroidism. Intracellular resistance to thyroid hormone is quite rare, and is suggested by clinical signs and symptoms of hypothyroidism in the presence of high serum T_4 levels. Adequacy of levothyroxine therapy for hypothyroidism of pituitary or hypothalamic origin should be assessed by measuring FT_4I, which should be maintained in the upper half of the normal range. Measurement of TSH is not a reliable indicator of response to therapy for this condition. Adequacy of levothyroxine therapy for congenital and acquired pediatric hypothyroidism should be assessed by measuring serum total T_4 or free T_4; these should be maintained in the upper half of the normal range. In congenital hypothyroidism, serum TSH normalization may lag behind serum T_4 normalization by 2 to 3 months or longer. In rare patients, serum TSH remains relatively elevated despite clinical euthyroidism and age-specific normal T_4 or free T_4 levels (see Children).

<u>Drug Interactions:</u> The magnitude and relative clinical importance of the effects noted below are likely to be patient-specific and may vary by such factors as age, gender, race, intercurrent illnesses, dose of either agents, additional concomitant medications, and timing of drug administration. Any agent that alters thyroid hormone synthesis, secretion, distribution, effect on target tissues, metabolism, or elimination may alter the optimal therapeutic dose of levothyroxine.

Levothyroxine Absorption: The following agents may bind and decrease absorption of levothyroxine from the gastrointestinal tract: aluminum hydroxide, cholestyramine resin, colestipol HCl, ferrous sulfate, sodium polystyrene sulfonate, soybean flour (e.g., infant formula), sucralfate.

Binding to Serum Proteins: The following agents may either inhibit levothyroxine binding to serum proteins or alter the concentrations of serum binding proteins: androgens and related anabolic hormones, asparaginase, clofibrate, estrogens and estrogen-containing compounds, 5-fluorouracil, furosemide, glucocorticoids, meclofenamic acid, mefenamic acid, methadone, perphenazine, phenylbutazone, phenytoin, salicylates, tamoxifen.

Thyroid Physiology: The following agents may alter thyroid hormone or TSH levels, generally by effects on thyroid hormone synthesis, secretion, distribution, metabolism, hormone action, or elimination, or altered TSH secretion: aminoglutethimide, p-aminosalicylic acid, amiodarone, androgens and related anabolic hormones, complex anions (thiocyanate, perchlorate, pertechnetate), antithyroid drugs, β-adrenergic blocking agents, carbamazepine, chloral hydrate, diazepam, dopamine and dopamine agonists, ethionamide, glucocorticoids, heparin, hepatic enzyme inducers, insulin, iodinated cholestographic agents, iodine-containing compounds, levodopa, lovastatin, lithium, 6-mercaptopurine, metoclopramide, mitotane, nitroprusside, phenobarbital, phenytoin, resorcinol, rifampin, somatostatin analogs, sulfonamides, sulfonylureas, thiazide diuretics.

Adrenocorticoids: Metabolic clearance of adrenocorticoids is decreased in hypothyroid patients and increased in hyperthyroid patients, and may therefore change with changing thyroid status.

Amiodarone: Amiodarone therapy alone can cause hypothyroidism or hyperthyroidism.

Anticoagulants (oral): The hypoprothrombinemic effect of anticoagulants may be potentiated, apparently by increased catabolism of vitamin K-dependent clotting factors.

Antidiabetic agents (insulin, sulfonylureas): Requirements for insulin or oral antidiabetic agents may be reduced in hypothyroid patients with diabetes mellitus, and may subsequently increase with the initiation of thyroid hormone replacement therapy.

β-adrenergic Blocking Agents: Actions of some beta-blocking agents may be impaired when hypothyroid patients become euthyroid.

Cytokines (interferon, interleukin): Cytokines have been reported to induce both hyperthyroidism and hypothyroidism.

Digitalis Glycosides: Therapeutic effects of digitalis glycosides may be reduced. Serum digitalis levels may be decreased in hyperthyroidism or when a hypothyroid patient becomes euthyroid.

Ketamine: Marked hypertension and tachycardia have been reported in association with concomitant administration of levothyroxine and ketamine.

Maprotiline: Risk of cardiac arrhythmias may increase.

Sodium iodide (^{123}I and ^{131}I), sodium pertechnetate Tc99m: Uptake of radiolabeled ions may be decreased.

Somatrem/Somatropin: Excessive concurrent use of thyroid hormone may accelerate epiphyseal closure. Untreated hypothyroidism may interfere with the growth response to somatrem or somatropin.

Theophylline: Theophylline clearance may decrease in hypothyroid patients and returns toward normal when the euthyroid state is achieved.

Tricyclic Antidepressants: Concurrent use may increase the therapeutic and toxic effects of both drugs, possibly due to increased catecholamine sensitivity. Onset of action of tricyclics may be accelerated.

Sympathomimetic Agents: Possible increased risk of coronary insufficiency in patients with coronary artery disease.

Laboratory Test Interactions: A number of drugs or moieties are known to alter serum levels of TSH, T_4 and T_3 and may thereby influence the interpretation of laboratory tests of thyroid function (see Drug Interactions).

Changes in TBG concentration should be taken into consideration when interpreting T_4 and T_3 values. Drugs such as estrogens and estrogen-containing oral contraceptives increase serum TBG concentrations. TBG concentrations may also be increased during pregnancy and in infectious hepatitis. Decreases in TBG concentrations are observed in nephrosis, acromegaly, and after androgen or corticosteroid therapy. Familial hyper- or hypo-thyroxine-binding- globulinemias have been described. The incidence of TBG deficiency is approximately 1 in 9 000. Certain drugs such as salicylates inhibit the protein-binding of T_4. In such cases, the unbound (free) hormone should be measured. Alternatively, an indirect measure of free thyroxine, such as the FT_4I, may be used.

Medicinal or dietary iodine interferes with in vivo tests of radioiodine uptake, producing low uptakes which may not indicate a true decrease in hormone synthesis.

Persistent clinical and laboratory evidence of hypothyroidism despite an adequate replacement dose suggests either poor patient compliance, impaired absorption, drug interactions, or decreased potency of the preparation due to improper storage.

Carcinogenesis, Mutagenesis, and Impairment of Fertility: Although animal studies to determine the mutagenic or carcinogenic potential of thyroid hormones have not been performed, synthetic T_4 is identical to that produced by the human thyroid gland. A reported association between prolonged thyroid hormone therapy and breast cancer has not been confirmed and patients receiving levothyroxine for established indications should not discontinue therapy.

Pregnancy: Studies in pregnant women have not shown that levothyroxine increases the risk of fetal abnormalities if administered during pregnancy. If levothyroxine is used during pregnancy, the possibility of fetal harm appears remote. Because studies cannot rule out the possibility of harm, levothyroxine should be used during pregnancy only if clearly needed.

Thyroid hormones cross the placental barrier to some extent. T_4 levels in the cord blood of athyroid fetuses have been shown to be about one-third of maternal levels. Nevertheless, maternal-fetal transfer of T_4 may not prevent in utero hypothyroidism.

Hypothyroidism during pregnancy is associated with a higher rate of complications, including spontaneous abortion and pre-eclampsia, and has been reported to have an adverse effect on fetal and childhood development. On the basis of current knowledge, levothyroxine should therefore not be discontinued during pregnancy, and hypothyroidism diagnosed during pregnancy should be treated. Studies have shown that during pregnancy T_4 concentrations may decrease and TSH concentrations may increase to values outside normal ranges. Postpartum values are similar to preconception values. Elevations in TSH may occur as early as 4 weeks gestation.

Pregnant women who are maintained on levothyroxine should have their TSH measured periodically. An elevated TSH should be corrected by an increase in levothyroxine dose. After pregnancy, the dose can be decreased to the optimal preconception dose.

Lactation: Minimal amounts of thyroid hormones are excreted in human milk. Thyroid hormones are not associated with serious adverse reactions and do not have known tumorigenic potential. While caution should be exercised when levothyroxine is administered to a nursing woman, adequate replacement doses of levothyroxine are generally needed to maintain normal lactation.

Children: Congenital hypothyroidism: Rapid restoration of normal serum T_4 concentrations is essential to prevent deleterious neonatal thyroid hormone deficiency effects on intelligence, overall growth, and development. Treatment should be initiated immediately upon diagnosis and generally maintained for life. The therapeutic goal is to maintain serum total T_4 or FT_4 in the upper half of the normal range and serum TSH in the normal range.

An initial starting dose of 10 to 15 μg/kg/day (ages 0 to 3 months) will generally increase serum T_4 concentrations to the upper half of the normal range in less than 3 weeks. Clinical assessment of growth, development, and thyroid status should be monitored frequently. In most cases, the levothyroxine dose per body weight will decrease as the patient grows through infancy and childhood (see Dosage, Children, Table I). Prolonged use of large doses in infants may be associated with temperament problems, which appear to be transient.

Thyroid function tests (serum total T_4 or FT_4, and TSH) should be monitored closely and used to determine the adequacy of levothyroxine therapy. Serum T_4 normalization is usually followed by a rapid decline in TSH. Nevertheless, TSH normalization may lag behind T_4 normalization by 2 to 3 months or longer. The relative serum TSH elevation is more marked in the early months, but can persist to some degree throughout life. In rare patients TSH remains relatively elevated despite clinical euthyroidism and age-specific normal total T_4 or FT_4 levels. Increasing the levothyroxine dosage to suppress TSH into the normal range may produce overtreatment, with an elevated serum T_4 and clinical features of hyperthyroidism including: irritability, increased appetite with diarrhea, and sleeplessness. Another risk of prolonged overtreatment in infants is premature cranial synostosis.

Hypothyroidism permanence may be assessed when transient hypothyroidism is suspected. Levothyroxine therapy may be interrupted for 30 days after 3 years of age and serum T_4 and TSH measured. Low T_4 and elevated TSH confirms permanent hypothyroidism; therapy should be re-instituted. If T_4 and TSH remain in the normal range, a presumptive diagnosis of transient hypothyroidism can be made. In this instance, continued clinical monitoring and periodic thyroid function test reevaluation may be warranted.

Acquired hypothyroidism: The initial levothyroxine dose varies with age and body weight, and should be adjusted to maintain serum total T_4 or free T_4 levels in the upper half of the normal range. In general, unless there are overriding clinical concerns, children should be started on a full replacement dose. Children with underlying heart disease should be started at lower dosages, with careful upward titration. Children with severe, longstanding hypothyroidism may also be started on a lower initial dose followed by an upward titration, attempting to avoid premature epiphyseal closure. The recommended dose per body weight decreases with age (see Dosage, Children, Table I on following page).

Treated children may resume growth at a greater than normal rate (period of transient catch-up growth). In some cases the catch-up may be adequate to normalize growth. However, severe and prolonged hypothyroidism may reduce adult height. Excessive thyroxine replacement may initiate accelerated bone maturation, producing disproportionate skeletal age advancement and shortened adult stature.

Hypothyroidism permanence may be assessed when transient hypothyroidism is suspected. Levothyroxine therapy may be interrupted for 30 days and serum T_4 and TSH measured. Low T_4 and elevated TSH confirms permanent hypothyroidism; therapy should be re-instituted. If T_4 and TSH remain in the normal range, a presumptive diagnosis of transient hypothyroidism can be made. In this instance, continued clinical monitoring and periodic thyroid function test reevaluation may be warranted.

Adverse Effects: Adverse reactions other than those indicative of thyrotoxicosis as a result of therapeutic overdosage, either initially or during the maintenance periods, are rare (see Overdose: Symptoms and Treatment). Craniosynostosis has been associated with iatrogenic hyperthyroidism in infants receiving thyroid hormone replacement therapy. Inadequate doses of levothyroxine sodium may produce or fail to resolve symptoms of hypothyroidism. Hypersensitivity reactions to the product excipients, such as rash and urticaria, may occur. Partial hair loss may occur during the initial months of therapy, but is generally transient. The incidence of continued hair loss is unknown. Pseudotumor cerebri has been reported in pediatric patients receiving thyroid hormone replacement therapy.

Overdose: Symptoms: Excessive doses of levothyroxine result in a hypermetabolic state indistinguishable from thyrotoxicosis of endogenous origin. Signs and symptoms of thyrotoxicosis include exophthalmic goiter, weight loss, increased appetite, palpitations, nervousness, diarrhea, abdominal cramps, sweating, tachycardia, increased pulse and blood pressure, cardiac arrhythmias, angina pectoris, tremors, insomnia, heat intolerance, fever, and menstrual irregularities. Symptoms are not always evident or may not appear until several days after ingestion.

Treatment: Levothyroxine should be reduced in dose or temporarily discontinued if signs and symptoms of overdosage appear.

In the treatment of acute massive levothyroxine overdosage, symptomatic and supportive therapy should be instituted immediately. Treatment is aimed at reducing gastrointestinal absorption and counteracting central and peripheral effects, mainly those of increased sympathetic activity. The stomach should be emptied immediately by emesis or gastric lavage if not otherwise contraindicated (e.g., by coma, convulsions or loss of gag reflex). Cholestyramine and activated charcoal have also been used to decrease levothyroxine absorption. Oxygen should be administered and ventilation maintained as necessary. β-receptor antagonists, particularly propranolol, are useful in counteracting many of the effects of increased sympathetic activity. Propranolol may be administered i.v. at a dosage of 1 to 3 mg over a 10 minute period or orally, 80 to 160 mg/day, especially when no contraindications exist for its use. Cardiac glycosides may be administered if congestive heart failure develops. Measures to control fever, hypoglycemia, or fluid loss should be initiated as necessary. Glucocorticoids may be administered to inhibit the conversion of T_4 to T_3.

Since T_4 is extensively protein bound, very little drug will be removed by dialysis.

Dosage: The dosage and rate of administration of levothyroxine is determined by the indication, and must in every case be individualized according to patient response and laboratory findings.

Adults: Hypothyroidism: The goal of therapy for primary hypothyroidism is to achieve and maintain a clinical and biochemical euthyroid state with consequent resolution of hypothyroid signs and symptoms. The starting dose of levothyroxine, the frequency of dose titration, and the optimal full replacement dose must be individualized for every patient, and will be influenced by such factors as age, weight, cardiovascular status, presence of other illness, and the severity and duration of hypothyroid symptoms.

The usual full replacement dose of levothyroxine for younger, healthy adults is approximately 1.6 μg/kg/day administered once daily. In the elderly, the full replacement dose may be altered by decreases in T_4 metabolism and levothyroxine sodium absorption. Older patients may require less than 1 μg/kg/day. Children generally require higher doses (see Children). Women who are maintained on levothyroxine during pregnancy may require increased doses (see Precautions, Pregnancy).

Therapy is usually initiated in younger, healthy adults at the anticipated full replacement dose. Clinical and laboratory evaluations should be performed at 6 to 8 week intervals (2 to 3 weeks in severely hypothyroid patients), and the dosage adjusted by 12.5 to 25 μg increments until the serum TSH concentration is normalized and signs and symptoms resolve. In older patients or in younger patients with a history of cardiovascular disease, the starting dose should be 12.5 to 50 μg once daily with adjustments of 12.5 to 25 μg every 3 to 6 weeks until TSH is normalized. If cardiac symptoms develop or worsen, the cardiac disease should be evaluated and the dose of levothyroxine reduced. Rarely, worsening angina or other signs of cardiac ischemia may prevent achieving a TSH in the normal range.

Treatment of subclinical hypothyroidism may require lower than usual replacement doses, e.g., 1 μg/kg/day. Patients for whom treatment is not initiated should be monitored yearly for changes in clinical status, TSH, and thyroid antibodies.

In patients with hypothyroidism resulting from pituitary or hypothalamic disease, the possibility of secondary adrenal insufficiency should be considered, and if present, treated with glucocorticoids prior to initiation of levothyroxine. The adequacy of levothyroxine therapy should be assessed in these patients by measuring FT_4I, which should be maintained in the upper half of the normal range, in addition to clinical assessment. Measurement of TSH is not a reliable indicator of response to therapy for this condition.

Few patients require doses greater than 200 μg/day. An inadequate response to daily doses of 300 to 400 μg/day is rare, and may suggest malabsorption, poor patient compliance, and/or drug interactions.

Once optimal replacement is achieved, clinical and laboratory evaluations should be conducted at least annually or whenever warranted by a change in patient status. Levothyroxine products from different manufacturers should not be used interchangeably unless retesting of the patient and retitration of the dosage, as necessary, accompanies the product switch.

Levothyroxine injection by the I.v. or i.m. route can be substituted for the oral dosage form when rapid repletion is required or oral administration is precluded. The initial parenteral dosage should be approximately one-half the previously established oral dosage of levothyroxine tablets. Close observation of the patient is recommended, with adjustment of the dosage as needed. Administration of levothyroxine injection by the s.c. route is not recommended as studies have shown that the influx of T_4 from the s.c. site is very slow, and depends on many factors such as volume of injection, the anatomic site of injection, ambient temperature, and presence of venospasm.

Myxedema Coma: Myxedema coma represents the extreme expression of severe hypothyroidism and is considered a medical emergency. It is characterized by hypothermia, hypotension, hypoventilation, hyponatremia, and bradycardia. In addition to restoration of normal thyroid hormone levels, therapy should be directed at the correction of electrolyte disturbances and possible infection. Because the mortality rate of patients with untreated myxedema coma is high, treatment must be started immediately, and should include appropriate supportive therapy and corticosteroids to prevent adrenal insufficiency. Possible precipitating factors should also be identified and treated. Levothyroxine may be given via nasogastric tube, but the preferred route of administration is i.v. A bolus dose of levothyroxine is given immediately to replete the peripheral pool of T_4, usually 300 to 500 μg. Although such a dose is usually well-tolerated even in the elderly, the rapid i.v. administration of large doses of levothyroxine to patients with cardiovascular disease is clearly not without risks. Under such circumstances, i.v. therapy should not be undertaken without weighing the alternate risks of myxedema coma and the cardiovascular disease. Clinical judgment in this situation may dictate smaller i.v. doses of levothyroxine. The initial dose is followed by daily i.v. doses of 75 to 100 μg until the patient is stable and oral administration is feasible. Normal T_4 levels are usually achieved in 24 hours, followed by progressive increases in T_3. Improvement in cardiac output, blood pressure, temperature, and mental status generally occur within 24 hours, with improvement in many manifestations of hypothyroidism in 4 to 7 days.

TSH Suppression in Thyroid Cancer and Thyroid Nodules: The rationale for TSH suppression therapy is that a reduction in TSH secretion may decrease the growth and function of abnormal thyroid tissue. Exogenous thyroid hormone may

Synthroid (cont'd)

inhibit recurrence of tumor growth and may produce regression of metastases from well-differentiated (follicular and papillary) carcinoma of the thyroid. It is used as ancillary therapy of these conditions following surgery or radioactive iodine therapy. Medullary and anaplastic carcinoma of the thyroid is unresponsive to TSH suppression therapy. TSH suppression is also used in treating nontoxic solitary nodules and multinodular goiters.

No controlled studies have compared the various degrees of TSH suppression in the treatment of either benign or malignant thyroid nodular disease. Further, the effectiveness of TSH suppression for benign nodular disease is controversial. The dose of levothyroxine used for TSH suppression should therefore be individualized by the nature of the disease, the patient being treated, and the desired clinical response, weighing the potential benefits of therapy against the risks of iatrogenic thyrotoxicosis. In general, levothyroxine should be given in the smallest dose that will achieve the desired clinical response.

For well-differentiated thyroid cancer, TSH is generally suppressed to less than 0.1 mU/L. Doses of levothyroxine greater than 2 μg/kg/day are usually required. The efficacy of TSH suppression in reducing the size of benign thyroid nodules and in preventing nodule regrowth after surgery is controversial. Nevertheless, when treatment with levothyroxine is warranted, TSH is generally suppressed to a higher target range (e.g., 0.1 to 0.3 mU/L) than that employed for the treatment of thyroid cancer. Levothyroxine therapy may also be considered for patients with nontoxic multinodular goiter who have a TSH in the normal range, to moderately suppress TSH (e.g., 0.1 to 0.3 mU/L).

Levothyroxine should be administered with caution to patients in whom there is a suspicion of thyroid gland autonomy, in view of the fact that the effects of exogenous hormone administration will be additive to endogenous thyroid hormone production.

Pediatric Dosage: Congenital or acquired hypothyroidism: The levothyroxine pediatric dosage varies with age and body weight. Levothyroxine should be given at a dose that maintains T_4 or free T_4 in the upper half of the normal range and serum TSH in the normal range (See Precautions, Children). Normalization of TSH may lag significantly behind T_4 in some infants. In general, despite the smaller body size of children, the dosage (on a weight basis) required to sustain full development and general thriving is higher than in adults. See Table I.

Therapy is usually initiated at the full replacement dose (see Table I). Infants and neonates with very low (<5 μg/dL) or undetectable serum T_4 levels should be started at higher end of the dosage range (e.g., 50 μg daily). A lower dose (e.g., 25 μg daily) should be considered for neonates at risk of cardiac failure, increasing every few days until a full maintenance dose is reached. In children with severe, longstanding hypothyroidism, levothyroxine should be initiated gradually, with an initial 25 μg dose for 2 weeks, then increasing by 25 μg every 2 to 4 weeks until the desired dose, based on serum T_4 and TSH levels, is achieved.

Table I—Synthroid

Dosage Guidelines for Pediatric Hypothyroidism

Age	**Daily dose/kg of body weight (μg)***
0-3 months	10-15
3-6 months	8-10
6-12 months	6-8
1-5 years	5-6
6-12 years	4-5
>12 years	2-3
Growth and puberty complete	1.6

*To be adjusted on the basis of clinical response and laboratory tests (see Precautions, Children).

Serum T_4 and TSH measurements should be evaluated at the following intervals, with subsequent dosage adjustments to normalize serum total T_4 or FT_4 and TSH: 2 and 4 weeks after therapy initiation, every 1 to 2 months during the first year of life, every 2 to 3 months between 1 and 3 years of age, every 3 to 12 months thereafter until growth is completed.

Evaluation at more frequent intervals is indicated when compliance is questioned or abnormal laboratory values are obtained. Patient evaluation is also advisable approximately 6 to 8 weeks after any change in levothyroxine dose.

Levothyroxine tablets may be given to infants and children who cannot swallow intact tablets by crushing the tablet and suspending the freshly crushed tablet in a small amount of water (5 to 10 mL), breast milk or non-soybean based formula. The suspension can be given by spoon or dropper. **Do not store the suspension for any period of time.** The crushed tablet may also be sprinkled over a small amount of food, such as apple sauce. Foods or formula containing large amounts of soybean, fibre, or iron should not be used for administering levothyroxine.

Injection: Directions for Reconstitution: Reconstitute the lyophilized levothyroxine sodium by aseptically adding 5 mL of 0.9% Sodium Chloride Injection, USP only. **Do not use bacteriostatic sodium chloride injection, USP, as the bacteriostatic agent may interfere with complete reconstitution.** Shake vial to ensure complete mixing. **Use immediately** after reconstitution. Do not add to other fluids. Discard any unused portion.

Supplied: Injection: Each vial of sterile lyophilized powder contains: levothyroxine sodium, USP 500 μg. Nonmedicinal ingredients: mannitol USP, sodium hydroxide and tribasic sodium phosphate (anhydrous). Single dose color-coded (yellow) vials of 10 mL. Store at controlled room temperature 15 to 30°C.

Tablets: 25 μg: Each orange, round, color-coded, scored tablet, debossed with "FLINT" and potency contains: levothyroxine sodium 25 μg. Nonmedicinal ingredients: acacia, confectioner's sugar, FD&C Yellow No. 6, lactose, magnesium stearate, povidone and talc. Bottles of 100.

50 μg: Each white, round, color-coded, scored tablet, debossed with "FLINT" and potency contains: levothyroxine sodium 50 μg. Nonmedicinal ingredients: acacia, confectioner's sugar, lactose, magnesium stearate, povidone and talc. Bottles of 100 and 1 000.

75 μg: Each violet, round, color-coded, scored tablet, debossed with "FLINT" and potency contains: levothyroxine sodium 75 μg. Nonmedicinal ingredients: acacia, confectioner's sugar, FD&C Blue No. 2, FD&C Red No. 40, lactose, magnesium stearate, povidone and talc. Bottles of 100 and 1 000.

88 μg: Each olive, round, color-coded, scored tablet, debossed with "FLINT" and potency contains: levothyroxine sodium 88 μg. Nonmedicinal ingredients: acacia, confectioner's sugar, FD&C Yellow No. 10, FD&C Blue No. 1, FD&C Yellow No. 6, lactose, magnesium stearate, povidone and talc. Bottles of 100 and 1 000.

100 μg: Each yellow, round, color-coded, scored tablet, debossed with "FLINT" and potency contains: levothyroxine sodium 100 μg. Nonmedicinal ingredients: acacia, confectioner's sugar, FD&C Yellow No. 10, FD&C Yellow No. 6, lactose, magnesium stearate, povidone and talc. Bottles of 100 and 1 000.

112 μg: Each rose, round, color-coded, scored tablet, debossed with "FLINT" and potency contains: levothyroxine sodium 112 μg. Nonmedicinal ingredients: acacia, confectioner's sugar, D&C Red No. 27 & 30, lactose, magnesium stearate, povidone and talc. Bottles of 100.

125 μg: Each brown, round, color-coded, scored tablet, debossed with "FLINT" and potency contains: levothyroxine sodium 125 μg. Nonmedicinal ingredients: acacia, confectioner's sugar, FD&C Blue No. 1, FD&C Red No. 40, FD&C Yellow No. 6, lactose, magnesium stearate, povidone and talc. Bottles of 100 and 1 000.

150 μg: Each blue, round, color-coded, scored tablet, debossed with "FLINT" and potency contains: levothyroxine sodium 150 μg. Nonmedicinal ingredients: acacia, confectioner's sugar, FD&C Blue No. 2, lactose, magnesium stearate, povidone and talc. Bottles of 100 and 1 000.

175 μg: Each lilac, round, color-coded, scored tablet, debossed with "FLINT" and potency contains: levothyroxine sodium 175 μg. Nonmedicinal ingredients: acacia, confectioner's sugar, D&C Red No. 27 & 30, FD&C Blue No. 1, lactose, magnesium stearate, povidone and talc. Bottles of 100.

200 μg: Each pink, round, color-coded, scored tablet, debossed with "FLINT" and potency contains: levothyroxine sodium 200 μg. Nonmedicinal ingredients: acacia, confectioner's sugar, FD&C Red No. 40, lactose, magnesium stearate, povidone and talc. Bottles of 100 and 1 000.

300 μg: Each green, round, color-coded, scored tablet, debossed with "FLINT" and potency contains: levothyroxine sodium 300 μg. Nonmedicinal ingredients: acacia, confectioner's sugar, D&C Yellow No. 10, FD&C Blue No. 1, FD&C Yellow No. 6, lactose, magnesium stearate, povidone and talc. Bottles of 100 and 1 000.

Store at controlled room temperature 15 to 30°C. Protect from light and moisture.

(Shown in Product Recognition Section)

Reviewed 1998

SYNVISC®

Biomatrix/Rhône-Poulenc Rorer

Hylan G-F 20

Viscosupplementation

Description: Synvisc (hylan G-F 20) is a sterile, nonpyrogenic, elastoviscous fluid containing hylans. Hylans are derivatives of hyaluronan (sodium salt of hyaluronic acid) and consist of repeating disaccharide units of N-acetylglucosamine and sodium glucuronate. Synvisc contains hylan fluid and hylan gel slurry (8 mg±2 mg/mL) in buffered physiological sodium chloride solution (pH 7.2±0.3).

Synvisc is biologically similar to hyaluronan. Hyaluronan is a component of synovial fluid which is responsible for its viscoelasticity. The mechanical (elastoviscous) properties of Synvisc are, however, superior to those of synovial fluid and hyaluronan solutions of comparable concentration. Hylans are degraded in the body by the same pathway as hyaluronan, and breakdown products are nontoxic.

Indications: A temporary replacement and supplement for synovial fluid. Synvisc is intended only for intra-articular use to treat pain associated with osteoarthritis of the knee. Synvisc is most effective in patients who are actively and regularly using the affected joint. Synvisc is most beneficial in patients with early stage joint pathology.

Synvisc achieves its therapeutic effect through viscosupplementation, a process whereby the physiological and rheological states of the arthritic joint tissues are restored. Viscosupplementation with Synvisc is a treatment to decrease pain and discomfort, allowing more extensive movement of the joint. In vitro studies have shown that Synvisc protects cartilage cells against certain physical and chemical damage.

Contraindications: If venous or lymphatic stasis is present in the leg, Synvisc should not be injected into the knee. Synvisc should not be used in infected or severely inflamed joints.

Warnings: Do not inject intravascularly.

Precautions: Transient pain and swelling may occur with intra-articular injections.

Synvisc should not be used if there is a large intra-articular effusion.

Synvisc has not been tested in pregnant women or children under 18 years of age.

Synvisc contains small amounts of avian protein and should not be used in patients with related hypersensitivities.

Dosage: Do not use Synvisc if package is opened or damaged. Do not resterilize Synvisc. The syringe contents are for single use only. Administer using aseptic procedures, taking particular care in removing the tip cap. Use an appropriate size needle (e.g., 18 to 22 gauge). Remove effusion, if present, before injecting Synvisc. Inject into the synovial space only.

The recommended treatment regimen for Synvisc is 3 injections in the knee, 1 week apart. To achieve maximum effect, it is essential to administer all 3 injections. The maximum recommended dosage is 6 injections within 6 months, with a minimum of 4 weeks between treatment regimens. The duration of effect for those patients who respond to treatment is generally 12 to 26 weeks, although shorter and longer periods have also been observed. Synvisc does not produce a general systemic effect.

Supplied: Each mL contains: hylan 8 mg. Nonmedicinal ingredients: disodium hydrogen phosphate, sodium chloride, sodium dihydrogen phosphate hydrate and sterile water for injection. Glass syringes of 2.25 mL containing 2 mL Synvisc, packed aseptically in a blisterpack. The contents of the syringe are sterile and nonpyrogenic. Store at room temperature. Do not freeze.

This is your typical *H. influenzae.*

Tough.

Menacing.

That's *H. influenzae*, a key pathogen in today's bronchitis. With Biaxin,* you can fight back. It has potent bactericidal activity versus *H. influenzae*,[1,2†] and is virtually unaffected by β-lactamase.[3] It has proven clinical success in acute exacerbations of chronic bronchitis.[3,4] And tolerability[‡] comparable to cephalosporins[5] – with no cross allergenicity with penicillins or cephalosporins.

Even a sumo-pathogen will find Biaxin very hard to defeat.

For today's bronchitis.

BIAXIN® 250

CLARITHROMYCIN *mg tablets*

*Biaxin is indicated for Acute Exacerbation of Chronic Bronchitis (AECB) caused by *S. pneumoniae*, *H. influenzae* and *M. catarrhalis*.

†In vitro activity does not necessarily correlate with clinical success.

‡Adverse reactions were mild and transient. The most frequent were nausea (4%) and diarrhea (3%).

COMMITTED TO THE APPROPRIATE USE OF ANTIBIOTICS

Product Monograph available upon request.

PAAB

T

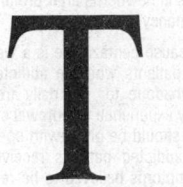

222®, 222® AF, 282® MEP, 292® Tablets
Frosst

see "Two ..." in monographs

TAGAMET®
SmithKline Beecham

Cimetidine

Histamine H_2 Receptor Antagonist

Pharmacology: Cimetidine competitively inhibits the action of histamine at the histamine H_2 receptor and thus represents a new class of pharmacological agents, the histamine H_2 receptor antagonists.

Cimetidine is not an anticholingeric agent. Studies have shown that cimetidine inhibits both daytime and nocturnal basal gastric acid secretion. Cimetidine also inhibits gastric acid secretion stimulated by food, histamine, pentagastrin, caffeine and insulin. Its ability to inhibit gastric acid secretion via this unique mechanism of action permits a new approach to the treatment of acid-related gastrointestinal disorders. In addition to its antisecretory effects, cimetidine also has cytoprotective properties.

In therapeutic studies, patients with NSAID-induced lesions or ulcers had symptomatic relief and healing when cimetidine was coadministered with the existing NSAID therapy.

Cimetidine is absorbed rapidly after oral administration. The plasma half-life is approximately 2 hours. The principal route of excretion is the urine.

The degree and duration of inhibition of basal and stimulated gastric acid secretion are dose related; the data suggest that 80% or higher inhibition throughout a 24 hour period can be achieved by a dosage regimen of 1.2 g daily given in divided doses. Cimetidine 300 mg reduced total pepsin output as a result of the decrease in volume of gastric juice. The drug had no effect on the rate of gastric emptying or lower esophageal sphincter (LES) pressure.

Indications: Primary therapy for conditions where the inhibition of gastric acid secretion is likely to be beneficial such as: Duodenal ulcer therapy. Non-malignant gastric ulcer therapy. Prophylaxis of recurrent duodenal or gastric ulcer. Gastroesophageal reflux disease. Management of upper gastrointestinal hemorrhage. Pathological hypersecretion associated with Zollinger-Ellison Syndrome, systemic mastocytosis and multiple endocrine adenomas. Prophylaxis of stress ulceration. Prophylaxis of acid aspiration pneumonitis. Adjunctive therapy in the management of cystic fibrosis in children. Treatment of NSAID-induced lesions (ulcers, erosions) and gastrointestinal symptoms and prevention of their recurrence.

Contraindications: In any patients who are known to have hypersensitivity to the drug.

Precautions: *Pregnancy* and *Lactation*: Experience to date with use of cimetidine in pregnant patients is limited. **No significant adversities have been reported.** Reproduction studies performed in rats, mice and rabbits have revealed no evidence of impaired fertility or harm to the fetus due to cimetidine. Studies have demonstrated that cimetidine crosses the placental barrier. It is also secreted in human milk. Cimetidine should be used in pregnant or lactating patients or women of child-bearing potential only when, in the judgement of the physician, the anticipated benefits outweigh the potential risks.

Cimetidine has been used in clinical trials for the prevention of acid aspiration pneumonitis in women undergoing cesarean section or vaginal delivery without harm to the fetus.

Impaired Renal Function: Because cimetidine is excreted by the kidney, a reduced dosage should normally be administered to patients with impaired renal function (see Dosage).

Drug Interactions: Cimetidine, apparently through an effect on certain microsomal enzyme systems, has been reported to reduce the hepatic metabolism of warfarin-type anticoagulants, phenytoin, propranolol, chlordiazepoxide, lidocaine, diazepam, theophylline, and nifedipine; thereby delaying elimination and increasing blood levels of these drugs. Benzodiazepines that are metabolized other than via the hepatic system do not exhibit this effect. Since clinically significant effects have been reported with the warfarin anticoagulants, close monitoring of prothrombin time is recommended, and adjustment of the anticoagulant dose may be necessary when cimetidine is administered concomitantly. Interaction with phenytoin has also been reported to produce adverse clinical effects.

Dosage of the drugs mentioned above and other similarly metabolized drugs, may require adjustment when starting or stopping concomitantly administered cimetidine, to maintain safe, optimum therapeutic blood levels.

The concomitant administration of cimetidine and NSAIDs does not result in any impairment of the efficacy of a number of NSAIDs; however, not all currently marketed NSAIDS were tested.

Gastric Ulcer: Symptomatic response to cimetidine does not preclude the presence of a gastric malignancy. Cimetidine treatment can mask the symptoms and allow transient healing of gastric cancer. The potential delay in diagnosis should be borne in mind in patients of middle age or older with new or recently changed dyspeptic symptoms.

Rapid I.V. Injection: Should be avoided as there have been rare cases of cardiac arrhythmias and hypotension reported (see Dosage).

Adverse Effects: Mild and transient diarrhea, tiredness, and dizziness have been reported in a small number of patients during treatment with cimetidine. Skin rashes, sometimes severe, including Stevens-Johnson syndrome, epidermal necrolysis, erythema multiforme, exfoliative dermatitis and generalized exfoliative erythroderma have been reported with H_2 receptor antagonists. Reversible alopecia has also been reported.

There have been reports that a few patients have developed reversible nonprogressive gynecomastia during prolonged treatment. No evidence of induced endocrine dysfunction was found, and the condition remained unchanged or returned toward normal with continuing cimetidine treatment. No effect of cimetidine (in recommended doses) on spermatogenesis, sperm count, motility or morphology has been found in double blind controlled studies. Fertilizing capacity has not been affected in vitro. Blood levels of androgen and gonadotropin were unchanged. Reversible impotence has been reported in rare instances.

H_2 antagonist administration has been associated with the occurrence of leukopenia (including agranulocytosis), thrombocytopenia, pancytopenia, and aplastic anemia, as well as extremely rare reports of immune hemolytic anemia.

A few cases of reversible confusional states have been reported, usually in elderly and/or severely ill patients, such as those with renal insufficiency or organic brain syndrome. These confusional states generally cleared within a few days of drug withdrawal.

Small increases of plasma creatinine have been reported. These did not progress with continued therapy and disappeared at the end of therapy. Some increases in serum transaminase and rare cases of hepatitis, fever, hypersensitivity vasculitis, interstitial nephritis, urinary retention and pancreatitis, which cleared on withdrawal of the drug, have been reported. Rare occurrences of sinus bradycardia, tachycardia, heart block and anaphylaxis have been reported in patients treated with H_2 antagonists.

Concomitant NSAID administration does not alter the incidence of adverse reactions resulting from therapy with cimetidine for those NSAIDs that have been tested.

Reported adverse reactions in children include neurotoxicity, and inhibition of hepatic microsomal metabolism. No change in adenohypophyseal secretion has been noted in studies in children receiving cimetidine. Cimetidine may produce transient cholestasis.

There have been rare reports of reversible arthralgia and myalgia; exacerbation of joint symptoms in patients with preexisting arthritis has also been reported. Such symptoms have usually been alleviated by a reduction in cimetidine dosage. Rare cases of polymyositis have been reported, but no causal relationship has been established.

Overdose: Symptoms: In cases reported to date, involving oral ingestion of up to 20 g of cimetidine, no untoward effects have been noted and recovery has been uneventful.

Treatment: The usual measures to remove unabsorbed material from the gastrointestinal tract, clinical monitoring and supportive therapy should be employed. Studies in animals indicate that assisted respiration may be of value.

Dosage: Adults: (for cimetidine administration in children see Pediatric Dosage): In clinical studies Tagament has been used in divided doses of up to 2 400 mg/day.

Duodenal Ulcer and Nonmalignant Gastric Ulcer: Active Ulcer: The recommended adult oral dose is 800 to 1 200 mg/day. This may be given as follows: 2 Tagamet 400 once daily at bedtime or 1 Tagamet 600 twice daily, at breakfast and bedtime or 1 Tagamet 300 4 times a day, with meals and at bedtime.

In some patients 400 mg twice daily has been shown to be effective.

While healing with cimetidine may occur during the first week or two, treatment should be continued for at least 4 weeks for duodenal ulcer and at least 6 weeks for nonmalignant gastric ulcer unless healing has been demonstrated by endoscopic examination.

While some patients may require concomitant antacids initially, cimetidine alone has been shown to promote rapid relief of symptoms.

Prophylaxis of Recurrent Duodenal or Gastric Ulcer: For most patients the following regimens have been shown to be effective: 1 Tagamet 400 at bedtime or 1 Tagamet 300 twice daily, at breakfast and bedtime.

Daily maintenance therapy may be used for those patients who would benefit from a reduction of gastric acid secretion, as well as those patients who are known to suffer frequent recurrence of duodenal or gastric ulcers, and should be continued for at least 6 to 12 months. Re-evaluation of the gastric ulcer patient should be undertaken at regular time intervals.

NSAID-induced Lesions and Symptoms: The recommended adult dose of Tagamet is 800 mg/day, either as 800 mg at bedtime or 400 mg twice daily, for 8 weeks. In patients with NSAID-induced lesions who have responded to an initial course of treatment and who require ongoing NSAID therapy, recurrence of lesions may be prevented by continual concomitant **maintenance treatment** with cimetidine. The recommended dosage for **maintenance treatment** is 400 mg of cimetidine at bedtime.

Gastroesophageal Reflux Disease: The recommended adult oral dose for gastroesophageal reflux disease is 1.2 g/day which may be given as follows: 2 Tagamet 400 once daily at bedtime or 1 Tagamet 600 twice daily at breakfast and bedtime or 1 Tagamet 300 four times daily with meals and at bedtime for 8 to 12 weeks.

While some patients may require concomitant antacids initially, cimetidine alone has been shown to promote rapid relief of symptoms.

Management of Upper Gastrointestinal Hemorrhage: In patients with upper gastrointestinal bleeding of sufficient magnitude as to require blood transfusions, cimetidine should be administered parenterally, preferably by i.v. injection or intermittent infusion until 48 hours after active bleeding has stopped. At this time an oral dosage regimen may be instituted.

Recommended Dosage for Oral Administration: 1 Tagamet 600 twice daily, at breakfast and bedtime or 1 Tagamet 300 every 6 hours.

Recommended Dosage for I.M. Injection Administration: 300 mg every 6 hours.

Recommended Dosage for I.V. Injection Administration: 300 mg every 6 hours. Dilute 300 mg cimetidine in Sodium Chloride Injection 0.9%, or other compatible i.v. solution to a total volume of 20 mL and inject **slowly** over a period of not less than 2 minutes. This method of administration should be avoided in patients with cardiovascular disease.

Recommended Dosage for Intermittent I.V. Infusion Administration: Vial: 300 mg every 6 hours. Dilute Tagamet 300 mg in 50 or 100 mL of Dextrose Injection 5%, Sodium Chloride Injection 0.9% or other compatible i.v. solution and infuse over 15 to 20 minutes.

Viaflex Plus Single Dose Container: 300 mg every 6 hours. Infuse over 15 to 20 minutes. Contains 300 mg cimetidine in 50 mL Sodium Chloride Injection 0.9%. Do not add supplementary medication or diluent (see detailed instructions at the end of this section).

In some patients it may be necessary to increase dosage. When this is necessary, the increases should be made by more frequent administration of a 300 mg dose, but total daily dosage should not exceed 2 400 mg.

Prophylaxis of Stress Ulceration: Recommended Adult Dosage: 300 mg i.v. every 6 hours, or more frequently to maintain a gastric pH above 4 (see recommendation for i.v. administration under Management of Upper Gastrointestinal Hemorrhage).

Pathological Hypersecretory Conditions: (e.g., Zollinger-Ellison Syndrome): Recommended Adult Oral Dosage: 300 mg 4 times a day, with meals and at bedtime. In some patients,

Tagamet (cont'd)

it may be necessary to administer higher and/or more frequent doses to control symptoms. Dosage should be adjusted to individual patient's needs, but usually should not exceed 2 400 mg/day. If i.v. administration is required, the dosage schedule should be the same as that recommended for control of upper gastrointestinal bleeding.

Prophylaxis of Acid Aspiration Pneumonitis: Recommended Adult Dosage: In emergency surgery, including emergency cesarean section, 300 mg i.m. 1 hour before induction of anesthesia and 300 mg i.v. or i.m. every 4 hours until patient responds to verbal commands.

In elective surgery, including elective cesarean section, same dosage as in emergency surgery, but oral cimetidine 300 mg may be started the night before the operation. For i.v. administration, see recommendation under Management of Upper Gastrointestinal Hemorrhage.

Dosage Adjustment for Patients With Impaired Renal Function: Patients with severely impaired renal function have been treated with cimetidine, however, such usage has been very limited. On the basis of this experience the recommended dosage is 300 mg every 12 hours orally or by i.v. injection. Should the patient's condition require, the frequency of dosing may be increased to every 8 hours or even further with caution. In severe renal failure accumulation may occur and the lowest frequency of dosing compatible with an adequate patient response should be used. When liver impairment is also present, further reductions in dosage may be necessary.

Hemodialysis: Hemodialysis reduces the level of circulating cimetidine. Greater than 80% of a 300 mg i.v. dose is cleared in a single 4-hour period of hemodialysis. It is completely cleared in an 8-hour period. Ideally, the dosage schedule should be adjusted so that the timing of a scheduled dose coincides with the end of hemodialysis.

Peritoneal Dialysis: Peritoneal dialysis does not appear to remove cimetidine to any appreciable extent.

Pediatric Dosage: I.V. or Oral Administration: When cimetidine is given i.v. to children, it should be injected or infused slowly over 10 to 20 minutes. 1 to 12 years: 20 to 25 mg/kg/day in divided doses every 4 to 6 hours.

Under 1 Year: Data for use of cimetidine in children under 1 year of age are limited; 20 mg/kg/day may be used in the absence of renal impairment.

In neonates under 1 week of age and in patients with moderate renal impairment the suggested dose is 10 to 15 mg/kg/day in divided doses. The dosage may need to be reduced further in the presence of additional liver impairment or with severe renal impairment.

Stability of Injectable Form: Cimetidine injection, when added to or diluted with most i.v. solutions, such as Sodium Chloride Injection 0.9%, or Dextrose Injection 5% or 10%, is stable for 48 hours at normal room temperature.

Cimetidine injection in vials should not be refrigerated.

Cimetidine infusion in Viaflex Plus containers is stable for the period indicated by the expiry date on the label.

Cimetidine infusion should be stored at room temperature.

Instructions for Administration of Tagamet Infusion in Viaflex Plus Containers: Containers should be replaced at least every 24 hours. Do not remove unit from overwrap until ready for use. Remove unit from cover using aseptic technique and check for leaks by squeezing bag firmly. Discard solution if leaks are found.

Preparation for administration: 1) Suspend container from eyelet support. 2) Remove plastic protector from outlet port at bottom of container. 3) Attach administration set. Refer to complete directions accompanying set.

Store at room temperature.

Warning: To avoid air embolism, do not use plastic containers in series connections. Do not add supplementary medication.

Supplied: Infusion: Each Viaflex Plus single dose polyvinyl chloride bag contains: cimetidine 300 mg (present as the hydrochloride). Nonmedicinal ingredients: sodium chloride injection 0.9%. Sodium: 7.7 mmol (177 mg). Boxes of 24. Do not add supplementary medication or diluent.

Liquid: Each 5 mL of light orange, bittersweet melon-pineapple flavored, sugar-free liquid contains: cimetidine 300 mg (present as the hydrochloride). Nonmedicinal ingredients: alcohol, artificial casaba melon flavor, artificial pineapple flavor, dibasic sodium phosphate, FD&C yellow no. 6, glycerin, hydrochloric acid (to adjust pH), methylparaben, propylene glycol, propylparaben, sodium chloride, sodium cyclamate, sorbitol solution and water. Sodium: <1 mmol (20.885 mg). Energy: 40.03 kJ (9.53 kcal). Bottles of 250 mL.

Tablets: Tagamet 300: Each pale green, circular, biconvex, film-coated tablet, engraved Tagamet on one face and SK&F 300 on the other, contains: cimetidine 300 mg. Nonmedicinal ingredients: carnauba wax, cornstarch, FD&C blue no. 2, iron oxide, magnesium stearate, microcrystalline cellulose, Opadry Green, povidone, sodium lauryl sulfate, sodium starch glycolate and talc. Sodium: <1 mmol (0.615 mg). Energy: 0.26 kJ (0.06 kcal). Bottles of 100 and 1 000.

Tagamet 400: Each pale green, ovoid, biconvex, film-coated tablet, engraved Tagamet on one face and SK&F 400 on the other face, contains: cimetidine 400 mg. Nonmedicinal ingredients: carnauba wax, cornstarch, FD&C blue no. 2, iron oxide, magnesium stearate, microcrystalline cellulose, Opadry Green, povidone, sodium lauryl sulfate, sodium starch glycolate and talc. Sodium: <1 mmol (0.780 mg). Energy: 0.38 kJ (0.09 kcal). Bottles of 100.

Tagamet 600: Each pale green, ovoid, biconvex, film-coated tablet, engraved Tagamet on one face and SK&F 600 on the other face, contains: cimetidine 600 mg. Nonmedicinal ingredients: carnauba wax, cornstarch, FD&C blue no. 2, iron oxide, magnesium stearate, microcrystalline cellulose, Opadry Green, povidone, sodium lauryl sulfate, sodium starch glycolate and talc. Sodium: <1 mmol (1.17 mg). Energy: 0.57 kJ (0.14 kcal). Bottles of 100.

All tablets are gluten-, lactose-, paraben-, sucrose-, sulfite- and tartrazine-free.

Reviewed 1999

TALWIN® Injection Ⓝ

Sanofi

Pentazocine Lactate

Analgesic

Pharmacology: Analgesic effects: Pentazocine relieves pain of all degrees, from mild to severe, in patients with acute and chronic disorders, regardless of age or sex. Analgesia usually occurs within 15 to 30 minutes after i.m. or s.c. injection, or 2 to 3 minutes after i.v. injection, and lasts for 3 to 4 hours. A dose of 30 mg administered parenterally is approximately equal in analgesic activity to 10 mg of morphine or 75 to 100 mg of meperidine. Pentazocine weakly antagonizes the analgesic effects of morphine, meperidine and phenazocine; in addition, it produces incomplete reversal of cardiovascular, respiratory, and behavioral depression induced by morphine and meperidine. Pentazocine has about 1/50 the antagonistic activity of nalorphine. It also has sedative activity.

Most authors agree that respiratory depression with pentazocine is equal to or less than opiates after a single dose. With repeated doses, however, the respiratory depressive effects are not cumulative, there being a ceiling effect at a dose of 30 to 60 mg.

Pentazocine does not significantly affect maternal blood pressure or heart rate, nor does it interfere with the progress of labor or uterine contractions. Generally there is minimal effect on Apgar ratings or fetal heart rate.

Indications: For the relief of moderate to severe pain. Also for preoperative or preanesthetic medication, and as a supplement to surgical anesthesia.

Contraindications: Should not be administered to patients who are hypersensitive to pentazocine.

Warnings: Drug Dependence: Special care should be exercised in prescribing pentazocine for emotionally unstable patients and for those with a history of drug misuse. Such patients should be closely supervised when long-term therapy is contemplated. There have been instances of psychological and physical dependence on pentazocine in patients with such a history and, rarely, in patients without such a history. Abrupt discontinuance following the extended use of parenteral pentazocine has resulted in symptoms such as abdominal cramps, elevated temperature, rhinorrhea, restlessness, anxiety, and lacrimation. Even when these occurred, discontinuance has been accomplished with minimal difficulty. In the rare patient in whom more than minor difficulty has been encountered, reinstitution of parenteral pentazocine with gradual withdrawal has ameliorated the patient's symptoms. Substituting methadone or other narcotics for pentazocine in the treatment of the pentazocine abstinence syndrome should be avoided.

In prescribing parenteral pentazocine for chronic use, particularly if the drug is to be self-administered, the physician should take precautions to avoid increases in dose and frequency of injection by the patient and to prevent the use of the drug in anticipation of pain rather than for the relief of pain. Just as with all medication, the oral form of pentazocine is preferable for chronic administration.

Pregnancy: There have been rare reports of possible abstinence syndromes in newborns after prolonged use of pentazocine during pregnancy.

Precautions: Because pentazocine is a weak narcotic antagonist, occasional patients who are addicted to narcotics and those given methadone for the daily treatment of narcotic dependence, may experience withdrawal symptoms and therefore pentazocine should be given with special caution to such persons. In nonaddicted patients receiving narcotics for a short period, symptoms believed to be related to antagonism may be observed. Intolerance or untoward reactions are usually not observed following administration of pentazocine to patients who have received single doses or who have had limited exposure to narcotics.

Occupational Hazards: Since sedation, dizziness and occasional euphoria have been noted, ambulatory patients should be warned not to operate machinery, drive cars or unnecessarily expose themselves to hazards.

Impaired Renal or Hepatic Function: Although laboratory tests have not indicated that pentazocine causes or increases renal or hepatic impairment, the drug should be administered with caution to patients with such impairment. Extensive liver disease appears to predispose to a higher incidence of side effects (e.g., marked apprehension, anxiety, dizziness, sleepiness) from the usual clinical dose, and may be the result of decreased metabolism of the drug by the liver.

Biliary Surgery: The drug should be used with caution in patients with acute cholecystitis or pancreatitis or in those about to undergo surgery of the biliary tract. Narcotic drug products are generally considered to elevate biliary tract pressure for varying periods following their administration. Some evidence suggests that pentazocine may differ from other marked narcotics in this respect (i.e., it causes little or no elevation in biliary tract pressures). The clinical significance of these findings, however, is not yet known.

Obstructive Uropathy: Because urinary retention has been observed in a few patients receiving pentazocine, caution is advised in administration of the drug to patients with obstructive uropathy.

Children: Since clinical experience in children under 12 years of age is limited, the use of pentazocine in this age group is not recommended.

Pregnancy: Safe use of pentazocine during pregnancy (other than labor) has not been established. Animal reproduction studies have not demonstrated teratogenic or embryotoxic effects. However, pentazocine should be administered to pregnant patients (other than labor) only when, in the judgment of the physician, the potential benefits outweigh the possible hazards. Patients receiving pentazocine during labor have experienced no adverse effects other than those that occur with commonly used analgesics. Pentazocine should be used with caution in women delivering premature infants.

Tissue Damage at Injection Sites: Severe sclerosis of the skin, s.c. tissues and underlying muscle have occurred at the injection sites of patients who have received multiple doses of pentazocine lactate. Constant rotation of injection sites is, therefore, essential. In addition, animal studies have demonstrated that pentazocine is tolerated less well s.c. than i.m.

Myocardial Infarction: Caution should be exercised in the i.v. use of pentazocine for patients with acute myocardial infarction accompanied by hypertension or left ventricular failure. Data suggest that i.v. administration of pentazocine increases systemic and pulmonary arterial pressure and systemic vascular resistance in patients with acute myocardial infarction.

Head Injury and Increased Intracranial Pressure: As in the case of other potent analgesics, the potential of pentazocine for elevating cerebrospinal fluid pressure may be attributed to CO_2 retention due to the respiratory depressant effects of the drug. These effects may be markedly exaggerated in the presence of head injury, other intracranial lesions, or a preexisting increase in intracranial pressure. Furthermore, pentazocine can produce effects which may obscure the clinical course of patients with head injuries. In such patients, pentazocine must be used with extreme caution and only if its use is deemed essential.

Certain Respiratory Conditions: Pentazocine should be administered only with caution and in low dosage to patients with respiratory depression (e.g., from other medication, uremia, or severe infection), severely limited respiratory reserve, obstructive respiratory conditions, or cyanosis.

Acute CNS Manifestations: Patients receiving therapeutic doses have experienced, in rare instances, hallucinations (usually visual), disorientation, and confusion which have cleared spontaneously within a period of hours. The mechanism of this reaction is not known. Such patients should be very closely observed and vital signs checked. If the drug is reinstituted, it should be done with caution since the acute CNS manifestations may recur. Due to the potential for increased CNS depressant effects, alcohol should be used with caution in patients who are currently receiving pentazocine. Caution should be used when pentazocine is administered to patients prone to seizures; seizures have occurred in a few such patients in association with the use of pentazocine although no cause and effect relationship has been established.

Anesthesia: Concomitant use of CNS depressants with parenteral pentazocine may produce additive CNS depression. Adequate equipment and facilities should be available to identify and treat systemic emergencies should they occur.

Adverse Effects: The most commonly occurring reactions are: nausea, dizziness or lightheadedness, vomiting, euphoria.

Dermatologic: Soft tissue induration, nodules, and cutaneous depression can occur at injection sites. Ulceration (sloughing) and severe sclerosis of the skin and s.c. tissues (and, rarely, underlying muscle) have been reported after multiple doses. Others include diaphoresis, sting on injection, flushed skin including plethora, dermatitis including pruritus.

Infrequently occurring reactions are: Respiratory: respiratory depression, dyspnea, transient apnea in a small number of newborn infants whose mothers received pentazocine during labor.

Cardiovascular: circulatory depression, shock, hypertension.

CNS: dizziness, lightheadedness, hallucinations, sedation, euphoria, headache, confusion, disorientation, infrequently weakness, disturbed dreams, insomnia, syncope, visual blurring and focusing difficulty, depression, and rarely tremor, irritability, excitement, tinnitus.

Gastrointestinal: constipation, dry mouth.

Other: urinary retention, headache, paresthesia, alterations in rate or strength of uterine contractions during labor.

Rarely reported reactions include: Neuromuscular and Psychiatric: muscle tremor, insomnia, disorientation, hallucinations.

Gastrointestinal: taste alteration, diarrhea and cramps.

Ophthalmic: blurred vision, nystagmus, diplopia, miosis.

Hematologic: depression of white blood cells (especially granulocytes), which is usually reversible, moderate transient eosinophilia.

Other: tachycardia, weakness or faintness, chills, allergic reactions including edema of the face, toxic epidermal necrolysis (see Acute CNS Manifestations under Precautions, and Drug Dependence under Warnings).

Overdose: Symptoms and Treatment: Like all potent analgesics, pentazocine exhibits some degree of respiratory depression although this has not proved to be a problem clinically. Pentazocine has not produced severe respiratory embarrassment in adults (never apnea), even when large amounts of the drug were used. However, moderate depression of respiration may occur occasionally. Should depression of respiration occur, oxygen, i.v. fluids, vasopressors, and other supportive measures should be employed as indicated. Assisted or controlled ventilation should also be considered. Although nalorphine and levallorphan are not effective antidotes for respiratory depression due to overdosage, parenteral naloxone (Narcan, available through Du Pont Pharma) is a specific and effective antagonist. The recommended adult dose of naloxone is 0.4 mg (1 mL) administered by i.v., i.m. or s.c routes. If the desired degree of counteraction and improvement in respiratory function is not obtained immediately, naloxone may be repeated at 2 to 3 minute intervals. Failure to obtain significant improvement after 2 to 3 doses suggests that causes other than pentazocine overdose may be responsible for the patient's condition. Apart from this there is no specific treatment for overdosage and the patient should be treated symptomatically.

Pentazocine shares with the narcotic analgesics and narcotic antagonists the potential, at high doses, of producing convulsions in animals and electrocortical dysrhythmia in man or animals.

Dosage: Adults, Excluding Patients in Labor: the average recommended single dose for adults is 30 mg depending on the needs of the patient. This dose, administered by i.m., s.c. or i.v. injection, may be repeated every 3 to 4 hours. Pain has been controlled in most patients with not more than 3 doses daily. In selected patients, 45 to 60 mg may be administered s.c. or i.m. as required. Total daily dosage should not exceed 360 mg.

Pentazocine has been administered to patients with chronic pain for over 300 days with absence of withdrawal symptoms, even when administration was stopped abruptly. However, since in a few patients, withdrawal symptoms have occurred after frequent, prolonged use (see Warnings, Drug Dependence), it may be of value to reduce the dose gradually when the drug is no longer needed.

Patients in Labor: Although most patients in labor have received a single injection of 30 mg i.m., some have obtained adequate pain relief with an i.v. injection of 20 mg. This latter dose may be repeated 1 or 2 times at 2 to 3 hour intervals as needed.

Compatibility with Other Drugs: Pentazocine has been compatible with other concurrently administered medication, such as diazepoxides, phenothiazines, meprobamate, barbiturates, chloral hydrate, digitalis, digitoxin, aminophylline, antibiotics and oncolytic drugs. Pentazocine did not alter insulin requirements in 5 diabetic patients.

Pentazocine should not be mixed in the same syringe with soluble barbiturates, chlordiazepoxide or diazepam since precipitation will occur.

Supplied: Each mL contains: pentazocine 30 mg as pentazocine lactate. Also contains sodium chloride in water for injection. Alcohol-, bisulfite-, parabens- and tartrazine-free. Ampuls of 1 mL, boxes of 25.

TALWIN® Tablets Ⓝ

Sanofi

Pentazocine HCl

Analgesic

Pharmacology: Pentazocine is a member of the benzazocine series of synthetic benzomorphans. It produces both analgesic (agonist) and narcotic antagonist effects. The analgesic effect of 50 mg pentazocine administered orally is approximately equivalent to 60 mg codeine. Pentazocine also produces a sedative effect.

The onset of analgesia following oral administration of pentazocine can occur within 15 to 30 minutes and the duration of effect is usually 3 hours or longer. The onset and duration of analgesia are, in part, related to the dose and severity of pretreatment pain. Peak serum levels of pentazocine occur between 1 and 3 hours after oral administration. Approximately 60% of an oral dose is eliminated in the urine within 24 hours. There is considerable variability between individuals in terms of the rate of pentazocine metabolism which may also account for the variability in analgesic response.

Indications: For the relief of chronic or acute pain of moderate to severe degree.

Contraindications: Pentazocine should not be administered to patients with known hypersensitivity to pentazocine.

Pregnancy: The use of pentazocine in women of childbearing potential requires that the expected benefit of the drug be weighed against the potential risk to the mother and fetus.

Children: Clinical experience in children under 12 years of age is limited, therefore, use of pentazocine is not recommended in this age group.

Warnings: Drug Dependence: There have been reported instances of psychological and physical dependence upon parenteral pentazocine. These reports have primarily concerned patients with a previous history of drug abuse, although there have been instances reported in patients without such a history. Usually there was a description of an increase in the dose and frequency of administration by the patient. In these patients abrupt discontinuance of the drug often resulted in withdrawal symptoms including abdominal cramps, elevated temperatures, rhinorrhoea, restlessness, anxiety and lacrimation. There have been reports of dependence upon oral pentazocine. Consequently, patients who may be prone to excessive usage of drugs should be supervised carefully during oral pentazocine therapy. During chronic use of pentazocine, the physician should avoid unnecessary escalation of the dose and should take precautions to avoid increases in dose by the patient. Physicians should warn the patient against the use of pentazocine in anticipation of pain.

Head Injury and Increased Intracranial Pressure: The respiratory depressant effects of pentazocine and its potential for elevating cerebrospinal fluid pressure may be markedly exaggerated in the presence of head injury, other intracranial lesions or a pre-existing increase in intracranial pressure. Pentazocine can produce effects which may obscure the clinical course of patients with head injuries. Pentazocine must be used with caution in such patients, and only if its use is deemed essential.

Acute CNS Manifestations: There have been reported instances of the acute onset of hallucinations (usually visual), disorientation, and confusion in patients receiving therapeutic doses. These manifestations have cleared spontaneously within hours upon discontinuation of the drug. The mechanism responsible for this reaction is not known. Patients demonstrating this reaction should be closely observed and if therapy with pentazocine is to be restarted, administration should proceed cautiously since the acute CNS manifestations may recur.

Precautions: Occupational Hazards: Since CNS effects have been noted with the use of pentazocine ambulatory patients should be warned not to operate machinery, drive cars or unnecessarily expose themselves to hazards.

Patients Dependent on Narcotics: Because pentazocine is a weak **narcotic antagonist,** patients who are addicted to narcotics may experience withdrawal symptoms and therefore it should be given with special caution to such persons. In non-addicted patients receiving narcotics for a short period, symptoms believed to be related to antagonism may be observed. Intolerance or untoward reactions are usually not observed following administration of pentazocine to patients who have received single doses of, or who have had limited exposure to narcotics.

Impaired Renal or Hepatic Function: Although laboratory tests have not indicated that pentazocine causes or increases renal or hepatic impairment, the drug should be administered with caution to patients with such impairment. Extensive liver disease appears to predispose to a higher incidence of side effects (e.g., marked apprehension, anxiety, dizziness, sleepiness) with the usual clinical dose, and may be the result of decreased metabolism of the drug by the liver.

Sphincter of Oddi: Until further experience is gained with the effects of pentazocine on the sphincter of Oddi, the drug should be used with caution in patients with acute cholecystitis or pancreatitis or in those about to undergo surgery of the biliary tract.

Obstructive Uropathy: Because urinary retention has been observed in a few patients receiving pentazocine, caution is advised in administration of the drug to patients with obstructive uropathy.

Respiratory Conditions: Respiratory depression has rarely been reported after oral administration, however, pentazocine, should be administered cautiously to patients with respiratory depression due to any cause, severely limited respiratory reserve, severe bronchial asthma, other obstructive respiratory conditions or cyanosis.

Myocardial Infarction: As with all drugs, pentazocine should be used with caution in patients with myocardial infarction who have nausea or vomiting.

Adverse Effects: The most frequently observed reactions after oral administration of pentazocine are sedation or somnolence, vertigo, nausea and vomiting, each of which may occur in approximately 15% of patients. Sedation may be more marked in the elderly.

Less frequent reactions have been: Gastrointestinal: constipation, abdominal distress, anorexia and diarrhea.

CNS: euphoria, lightheadedness, headache, dizziness, weakness, disturbed dreams, hallucinations (see Acute CNS effects in Warnings), visual disturbances, insomnia, tinnitus, irritability, excitement.

Autonomic: sweating, infrequently flushing or chills.

Cardiovascular: infrequently fall in blood pressure, tachycardia.

Allergic: infrequently rash and rarely urticaria, erythema and edema.

Hematologic: rarely depression of white blood cells (especially granulocytes), which is usually reversible, moderate transient eosinophilia.

Other: pruritus, alterations in maturation. Scattered reports of abnormal liver function of questionable significance were noted during the clinical trials. Hallucinations were noted to occur more frequently when doses exceeding that recommended were employed.

Overdose: Symptoms and Treatment: The clinical picture of overdose has not been well defined but high doses will cause respiratory depression, increased blood pressure and tachycardia.

Should depression of respiration occur, oxygen, i.v. fluids, vasopressors, and other supportive measures should be employed as indicated. Assisted or controlled ventilation should also be considered. Although nalorphine and levallorphan are not effective antidotes for respiratory depression due to overdosage, parenteral naloxone is a specific and effective antagonist.

The recommended adult dose of naloxone is 0.4 mg (1 mL) administered i.v., i.m. or s.c. If the desired degree of counteraction and improvement in respiratory function is not obtained

Talwin Tablets (cont'd)

immediately, naloxone may be repeated at 2 to 3 minute intervals. Failure to obtain significant improvement after 2 to 3 doses suggests that causes other than pentazocine overdose may be responsible for the patient's condition.

Dosage: Adults: Usual starting dose is 50 mg every 4 hours after meals. Dosage should be adjusted to individual requirements and tolerance within the range of 50 to 100 mg every 3 to 4 hours.

Concomitant Medication: When anti-inflammatory or antipyretic effects are desired in addition to analgesia, ASA can be administered concomitantly with pentazocine.

In light of the tendency to marked sedation among the elderly, dosage should be kept low in this group of patients.

Duration of Therapy: There have been rare reports of withdrawal symptoms upon abrupt discontinuance of therapy after prolonged administration of the product for chronic pain. Therefore, it would be prudent to reduce the dose gradually when the drug is no longer required.

Supplied: Each scored peach tablet with a stylized "W" on one side and scored on the other with "T" above and "21" below the score, contains: pentazocine HCl equivalent to 50 mg base. Nonmedicinal ingredients: calcium phosphate (dibasic), colloidal silicon dioxide, FD and C Yellow lake #6, magnesium stearate, microcrystalline cellulose, sodium lauryl sulfate, sodium metabisulfite and starch. Gluten-, lactose- and tartrazine-free. Bottles of 100 and 500.

(Shown in Product Recognition Section)

TAMBOCOR™ ℞

3M Pharmaceuticals

Flecainide Acetate

Antiarrhythmic Agent

Pharmacology: Flecainide belongs to the membrane stabilizing group of antiarrhythmic agents; it has electrophysiologic effects characteristic of the 1C class of the modified Vaughan-Williams classification. It also possesses local anesthetic properties.

In single cell preparations from canine cardiac tissue (Purkinje fibres) flecainide decreased the rate of rise (Vmax, Phase 0) of the action potential without greatly affecting its duration; the duration of the effective refractory period was lengthened and a small change was observed in the slope of Phase 4 depolarization. In ventricular muscle, some lengthening of the action potential duration has been observed.

Flecainide produces a dose-related decrease in intracardiac conduction in all parts of the heart with the greatest effect on the His-Purkinje system (H-V conduction). Effects upon atrioventricular (AV) nodal conduction time and intra-atrial conduction times, although present, are less pronounced than those on ventricular conduction velocity. Significant effects on refractory periods were observed only in the ventricle. Sinus node recovery times (corrected) following pacing and spontaneous cycle lengths are somewhat increased. This latter effect may become significant in patients with sinus node dysfunction (see Warnings).

Decreases in ejection fraction, consistent with a negative inotropic effect, have been observed after single administration of 200 to 250 mg flecainide; both increases and decreases in ejection fraction have been encountered during multidose therapy in patients at usual therapeutic doses (see Warnings).

During long-term clinical studies, some patients have developed congestive heart failure (CHF) while taking flecainide (see Warnings and Adverse Effects).

Flecainide does not usually alter heart rate, although bradycardia and tachycardia have been reported. In clinical studies, systolic and diastolic blood pressures increased slightly during therapy. A few patients have required changes in antihypertensive medication.

Following oral administration, flecainide is nearly completely absorbed with bioavailability of 90 to 95%. Peak plasma levels are attained at about 3 hours in most individuals (range, 1 to 6 hours). Food and antacids do not affect absorption. Flecainide does not undergo any consequential presystemic biotransformation.

The plasma half-life averages about 20 hours (range, 12 to 27 hours) after multiple oral doses in patients with premature ventricular complexes and normal renal function; this is similar to that in patients with CHF (mean, 19 hours), but it is moderately longer than for healthy subjects (mean, 14 hours). In patients with renal impairment the plasma half-life of flecainide is often prolonged and ranges from about 14 to 190 hours. Flecainide elimination from plasma is somewhat slower in healthy elderly subjects ($t_{1/2}$=18 hours) than in young healthy subjects.

Steady state plasma levels are reached within 3 to 5 days; once steady state is attained, no additional drug accumulation in plasma occurs. Therapeutic plasma concentrations of flecainide range from 0.2 to 1.0 μg/mL. The plasma levels are not directly proportional to dose. Within the usual therapeutic dose range, plasma levels deviate upwards from direct proportionality (average deviation about 10 to 15% per 100 mg).

The extent of flecainide binding to plasma proteins is about 40% and is independent of plasma drug level over the range of 0.015 to 3.4 μg/mL.

In healthy subjects, about 30% of a single oral dose (range, 10% to 50%) is excreted in urine as unchanged flecainide. The two major metabolites are meta-O-dealkylated flecainide (active, but about one fifth as potent) and the meta-O-dealkylated lactam of flecainide (non-active metabolite). These two metabolites (primarily conjugated) account for most of the remaining portion of the dose in urine. Several minor metabolites (3% of the dose or less) are also found in urine; only 5% of an oral dose is excreted in feces. In patients, free (unconjugated) plasma levels of the 2 major metabolites are very low (less than 0.05 μg/mL).

With increasing renal impairment, the extent of unchanged drug excretion in urine is reduced. Since flecainide is also extensively metabolized, there is no simple relationship between creatinine clearance and the rate of flecainide elimination from plasma (see Dosage). When urine is very alkaline (pH 8 or higher), as may occur in rare conditions (e.g., renal tubular acidosis, strict vegetarian diet), flecainide elimination from plasma is much slower.

Hemodialysis removes only about 1% of an oral dose as unchanged flecainide.

Indications:

> No antiarrhythmic drug has been shown to reduce the incidence of sudden death in patients with asymptomatic ventricular arrhythmias. Most antiarrhythmic drugs have the potential to cause dangerous arrhythmias; some have been shown to be associated with an increased incidence of sudden death. In light of the above, physicians should carefully consider the risks and benefits of antiarrhythmic therapy for all patients with ventricular arrhythmias.

In patients without structural heart disease and with disabling symptoms, flecainide is indicated for the prevention of: paroxysmal supraventricular tachycardias (PSVT), including AV nodal reentrant tachycardia, AV reentrant tachycardia and other supraventricular tachycardias of unspecified mechanism; paroxysmal atrial fibrillation/flutter (PAF).

Patients treated with flecainide for supraventricular arrhythmias having impaired left ventricular function (ejection fraction < 40) and/or ischemic heart disease may be at increased risk for cardiac adverse reactions. Use of flecainide in chronic atrial fibrillation has not been adequately studied and is not recommended (see Warnings).

Flecainide is also indicated for the treatment of documented ventricular arrhythmias, such as sustained ventricular tachycardia (sustained VT), that in the judgment of the physician, are life-threatening.

Because of the proarrhythmic effects of flecainide, its use should be reserved for patients in whom, in the opinion of the physician, the benefits of treatment outweigh the risks. The use of flecainide is not recommended in patients with less severe ventricular arrhythmias, even if the patients are symptomatic (see Warnings). Use of flecainide for treatment of sustained ventricular tachycardia should be initiated in the hospital.

Tambocor should not be used in patients with recent myocardial infarction (see Warnings).

Contraindications: In patients with: second or third degree AV block, unless a pacemaker is present to sustain rhythm; bifascicular or trifascicular bundle branch block unless a pacemaker is present to sustain rhythm; cardiogenic shock; and hypersensitivity to the drug.

Warnings:

> Mortality: The results of the Cardiac Arrhythmia Suppression Trial (CAST) in post-myocardial infarction patients with asymptomatic ventricular arrhythmias showed a significant increase in mortality and in non-fatal cardiac arrest rate in patients treated with encainide or flecainide compared with a matched placebo-treated group. This rate was 19/323 (5.8%) for flecainide and 7/318 (2.2%) for its matched placebo. The average duration of treatment with flecainide was 10 months. CAST was continued using a revised protocol with the moricizine and placebo arms only. The trial was prematurely terminated because of a trend towards an increase in mortality in the moricizine treated group.
>
> The applicability of these results to other populations or other antiarrhythmic agents is uncertain, but at present it is prudent to consider these results when using any antiarrhythmic agent.
>
> Ventricular Proarrhythmic Effects in Patients with Atrial Fibrillation/Flutter: A review of the world literature revealed reports of 568 patients treated with flecainide for paroxysmal atrial fibrillation/flutter (PAF). Ventricular tachycardia was experienced in 0.4% (2/568) of these patients. Of 19 patients in the literature with chronic atrial fibrillation, 10.5% (2/19) experienced ventricular tachycardia or ventricular fibrillation. **Flecainide is not recommended for use in patients with chronic atrial fibrillation.** Case reports of ventricular proarrhythmic effects in patients treated with flecainide for atrial fibrillation/flutter have included increased premature ventricular contractions (PVCs), ventricular tachycardia (VT), ventricular fibrillation (VF), and death.
>
> As with other class I agents, patients treated with flecainide atrial flutter have been reported with 1:1 AV conduction due to slowing of the atrial rate. A paradoxical increase in the ventricular rate also may occur in patients with atrial fibrillation who receive flecainide. Concomitant negative chronotropic therapy such as digoxin or beta-blockers may lower the risk of this complication.

Proarrhythmic Effects: Flecainide, like other antiarrhythmic agents, can cause new or worsened arrhythmias. Such proarrhythmic effects range from an increase in frequency of PVCs to the development of more severe ventricular tachycardia, e.g., tachycardia that is more sustained or more resistant to conversion to sinus rhythm, with potentially fatal consequences. In studies of 225 patients with supraventricular arrhythmia (108 with paroxysmal supraventricular tachycardia and 117 with paroxysmal atrial fibrillation), there were nine (4%) proarrhythmic events, eight of them in patients with paroxysmal atrial fibrillation. Of the nine, seven (including the one in a PSVT patient) were exacerbations of supraventricular arrhythmias (longer duration, more rapid rate, harder to reverse). Two were ventricular arrhythmias, including one fatal case of VT/VF and one wide complex VT (the patient showed inducible VT, however, after withdrawal of flecainide), both in patients with paroxysmal atrial fibrillation and known coronary artery disease.

In studies of patients with ventricular arrhythmias, flecainide proarrhythmic effects were reported in 6.8% of patients. Three fourths of the proarrhythmic events were new or worsened ventricular tachyarrhythmias, the remainder being increased frequency of PVCs or new supraventricular arrhythmias.

In patients with complex ventricular arrhythmias, it is often difficult to distinguish a spontaneous variation in the patient's underlying rhythm disorder from drug-induced worsening, so that the following occurrence rates must be considered approximations. Their frequency appears to be related to dose and to the underlying cardiac disease. Among patients treated for sustained VT (who frequently also had heart failure, a low ejection fraction, a history of myocardial infarction and/or an episode of cardiac arrest), the incidence of proarrhythmic events was 13% when dosage was initiated at 200 mg/day with slow upward titration, and did not exceed 300 mg/day in most patients. In early studies in patients with sustained VT utilizing a higher initial dose (400 mg/day) the incidence of proarrhythmic events was 26%; moreover, in about 10% of the patients treated, proarrhythmic events resulted in death, despite prompt medical attention. With lower initial doses, the incidence of proarrhythmic events resulting in death decreased to 0.5% of these patients. Accordingly, it is extremely important to follow the recommended dosage schedule (see Dosage).

The relatively high frequency of proarrhythmic events in patients with sustained ventricular tachycardia and serious underlying heart disease, and the need for careful titration and monitoring, requires that flecainide therapy be started in the hospital (see Dosage).

Heart Failure: Because flecainide has a negative inotropic effect, it may cause or worsen congestive heart failure, particularly in patients with cardiomyopathy, pre-existing severe heart failure (NYHA functional class III or IV) or low ejection fractions (less than 40%). In patients with supraventricular arrhythmias new or worsened CHF developed in 0.4% (1/225) of patients. New or worsened CHF which might be attributed to flecainide treatment occurred in approximately 5% of patients studied in various trials. CHF developed rarely (1%) in patients who had no previous history of CHF. Flecainide should be used cautiously in patients who are known to have a history of CHF or myocardial dysfunction. The initial dose should be no more than 100 mg twice daily in such patients (see Dosage) and they should be carefully monitored. Careful attention must be given to maintenance of cardiac function, including optimization of digitalis, diuretic or other therapy. In the cases where CHF has occurred or worsened during flecainide therapy, the onset has ranged from a few hours to several months after starting therapy. Patients who develop evidence of reduced myocardial function while on flecainide should have their dose reduced or discontinued. It is recommended that plasma flecainide levels be monitored. Attempts should be made to keep trough plasma levels below 0.7 to 1 μg/mL.

Effects on Cardiac Conduction: In most patients flecainide slows cardiac conduction sufficiently to produce dose-related increases in the duration of the PR, QRS and QT intervals on the ECG.

PR interval increases on average about 25% (0.04 seconds) and as much as 118% in some patients. Approximately one-third of patients may develop new first degree AV heart block (PR interval 0.20 seconds). The QRS complex increases on average about 25% (0.2 seconds) and as much as 150% in some patients. Many patient develop QRS complexes with a duration of 0.12 seconds or more. In one study, 4% of patients developed new bundle branch block while on flecainide. The degree of lengthening of PR and QRS intervals does not predict either efficacy or the development of cardiac adverse effects. In clinical trials, it was unusual for PR intervals to increase to 0.30 seconds or more, or for QRS intervals to increase to 0.18 seconds or more. Thus, caution should be used when such intervals occur, and dose reductions may be considered. The QT interval widens about 8%, but most of this widening (about 60% to 90%) is due to widening of the QRS duration. The JT interval (QT minus QRS) only widens about 4% on the average. Significant JT prolongation occurs in less than 2% of patients. There have been a few cases of Torsades de Pointes-type arrhythmia associated with flecainide-induced QT prolongation and bradycardia.

Clinically significant conduction changes have been observed with these incidences: sinus node dysfunction such as sinus pause, sinus arrest and symptomatic bradycardia (1.2%); second degree AV block (0.5%); and third degree AV block (0.4%). An attempt should be made to manage the patient on the lowest effective dose in an effort to minimize these effects (see Dosage). If second or third degree AV block, or right bundle branch block associated with a left hemiblock occurs, therapy should be discontinued unless a temporary or implanted ventricular pacemaker is in place to ensure an adequate ventricular rate.

Sinus Node Dysfunction: In patients with sinus node dysfunction (eg, sick sinus syndrome), flecainide should be used with extreme caution because it may cause sinus bradycardia, sinus pause or sinus arrest.

Digitalis Intoxication: Flecainide has not been evaluated in the treatment of arrhythmias secondary to digitalis intoxication, and it increases the plasma level of digoxin. Therefore, it is not recommended for such use.

Electrolyte Disturbances: The presence of potassium excess or deficit may alter the effects of antiarrhythmic drugs. Any pre-existing hypokalemia or hyperkalemia should be corrected before drug administration.

Effects of Pacemaker Thresholds: Flecainide is known to increase endocardial pacing thresholds and may suppress ventricular escape rhythms. These effects are reversible if flecainide is discontinued. It should be used with caution in patients with permanent pacemakers or temporary pacing electrodes and should not be administered to patients with existing poor thresholds or nonprogrammable pacemakers unless suitable pacing rescue is available.

The pacing threshold in patients with pacemakers should be determined prior to instituting therapy with flecainide, again after 1 week of administration and at regular intervals thereafter. Generally threshold changes are within the range of multiprogrammable pacemakers and, when these occur, a doubling of either voltage or pulse width is usually sufficient to regain capture.

Concomitant Antiarrhythmic Therapy: Due to limited experience, the concomitant use of flecainide and other antiarrhythmic agents is not recommended.

Both disopyramide and verapamil have negative inotropic properties and the effects of giving them with flecainide are unknown. Therefore, neither disopyramide or verapamil should be administered concurrently with flecainide unless, in the judgment of the physician, the possible benefit of this combination therapy clearly outweighs the risks.

When flecainide and amiodarone are coadministered, plasma flecainide levels may increase two-fold or more. If the combination therapy is required, the dose should be reduced (see Dosage).

Lidocaine has been used occasionally with flecainide while awaiting the therapeutic effect of flecainide. No adverse drug interactions were apparent. However, no studies have been performed to demonstrate the usefulness of this regimen.

Pregnancy: Flecainide has been shown to have teratogenic effects (club paws, sternebrae and vertebrae abnormalities, pale hearts with contracted ventricular septum) and an embryotoxic effect (increased resorptions) in one breed of rabbit (New Zealand White) but not in another breed of rabbit (Dutch Belted) when given in doses about 4 times (but not 3 times) the usual human dose (assuming a patient weight of 50 kg). No teratogenic effects were observed in rats and mice given doses up to 50 to 80 mg/kg/day, respectively; however, delayed sternebral and vertebral ossification was observed at the high dose in rats. There is no information about the effect on human fetus. Flecainide should not be used during pregnancy unless as a drug of last resort in life-threatening arrhythmias.

Labor and Delivery: It is not known whether the use of flecainide during labor or delivery has immediate or delayed adverse effects on the mother or fetus, affects the duration of labor or delivery, or increases the possibility of forceps delivery or other obstetrical intervention.

Precautions: Hepatic Impairment: Since flecainide elimination from plasma can be markedly slower in patients with significant hepatic impairment, it should not be used in such patients unless the potential benefits clearly outweigh the risks. If used, frequent and early plasma level monitoring is required to guide dosage (see Dosage); dosage increases should be made very cautiously when plasma levels have plateaued (after more than 4 days).

Abnormalities of liver function have rarely occurred in patients treated with flecainide (see Adverse Effects). In foreign post-marketing surveillance studies, there have been rare reports of hepatic dysfunction including reports of cholestasis and hepatic failure. Although no causal relationship has been established, periodic monitoring of liver function tests should be carried out during flecainide therapy. In patients who develop unexplained jaundice or signs of hepatic dysfunction, it is advisable to discontinue flecainide in order to eliminate the drug as the possible causative agent.

Renal Impairment: The elimination of flecainide from the body depends on renal function (ie, 10 to 50% appears in urine as unchanged drug). With increasing renal impairment, the extent of unchanged drug excretion in urine is reduced and the plasma half-life of flecainide is prolonged. Different dosage regimens are recommended for patients with various degrees of renal insufficiency (see Pharmacology and Dosage).

Blood Dyscrasias: There have been extremely rare reports of blood dyscrasias (pancytopenia, anemia, thrombocytopenia, leukopenia, granulocytopenia). Although no causal relationship has been established, it is advisable to discontinue flecainide in patients who develop blood dyscrasia in order to eliminate it as the possible causative agent.

Occupational Hazards: Since flecainide can cause dizziness, light headedness, faintness and visual disturbance, patients should be cautioned about engaging in activities requiring judgment and physical co-ordination (such as driving an automobile or operating dangerous machinery) when these effects occur.

Geriatrics: Flecainide elimination from plasma is somewhat slower in this age group (see Dosage).

Lactation: Flecainide is excreted in human milk. Because of the drug's potential for serious adverse reactions in nursing infants, a decision should be made whether to discontinue nursing or discontinue the drug, taking into account the importance of the drug to the mother.

Children: The safety and effectiveness in children below the age of 18 years have not been established.

Drug Interactions: Flecainide has been administered to patients receiving digitalis preparations or beta-adrenergic blocking agents without adverse effects. During multiple oral doses to healthy subjects stabilized on a maintenance dose of digoxin, a 13 to 19% increase in plasma digoxin levels occurred at 6 hours postdose.

In a study involving healthy subjects receiving flecainide and propranolol concurrently, plasma flecainide levels were increased about 20% and propranolol levels were increased about 30% compared with control values. In this study, flecainide and propranolol were each found to have negative inotropic effects; when the drugs were administered together, the effects were additive. The effects of concomitant administration on the PR interval were less than additive. In flecainide clinical trials, patients who were receiving beta blockers concurrently did not experience an increased incidence of side effects. Nevertheless, the possibility of additive negative inotropic effects of beta blockers and flecainide should be recognized.

Flecainide has been used in a large number of patients receiving diuretics without apparent interaction.

Interactions with antiarrhythmics, see Warnings.

Limited data in patients receiving known enzyme inducers (phenytoin, phenobarbital, carbamazepine) indicate a 30% increase in the rate of flecainide elimination.

In healthy subjects receiving cimetidine (1 g daily) for 1 week, plasma flecainide levels increased by about 30% and half-life increased by about 10%.

Flecainide is not extensively bound to plasma proteins. In vitro studies with several drugs which may be administered concomitantly showed that the extent of flecainide binding to human plasma proteins is either unchanged or only slightly less.

Adverse Effects: In postmyocardial infarction patients, flecainide was found to be associated with a 5.8% rate of mortality and nonfatal cardiac arrest (see Warnings).

Flecainide has been evaluated in 225 patients with supraventricular arrhythmias. The most serious adverse reaction reported for flecainide patients with supraventricular arrhythmias were new or worsened supraventricular or ventricular arrhythmias which were reported in 4% of patients (see Warnings), conduction disturbance which occurred in 2% of patients, and new or worsened CHF occurred in 0.4% of patients.

The most commonly reported non-cardiac adverse reactions for supraventricular patients remain consistent with those known for patients treated with flecainide for ventricular arrhythmias: vision disturbance 38%, dizziness 37%, headache 18%, nausea 18%, dyspnea 13%, fatigue 13%, chest pain 12%, palpitations 11%. Although these incidences are higher than those reported in ventricular patients it is difficult to compare supraventricular and ventricular data bases because many of the supraventricular patients were dosed to tolerance in the clinical trials.

Flecainide has been evaluated in 1 224 patients which included both life threatening and non life threatening ventricular arrhythmias. The separate figures for these 2 groups of patients are not available at this time. The possibility exist that the incidences of adverse reactions in patients with life threatening ventricular arrhythmias for which this drug is indicated, might be different than that listed below. The most serious adverse reactions reported were new or exacerbated ventricular arrhythmias which occurred in 6.8% of patients, and new or worsened congestive heart failure which occurred in 3.9% of patients (or 5% of 717 patients in controlled clinical studies).

In some patients, treatment has been associated with episodes of unresuscitatable ventricular tachycardia or ventricular fibrillation. There have also been instances of second (0.5%) or third degree (0.4%) AV block. A total of 1.2% of patients developed sinus bradycardia, sinus pause, or sinus arrest (see Warnings). The frequency of most of these serious adverse reactions probably increases with higher trough plasma levels, especially when these trough levels exceed 0.7 mg/mL.

The most commonly reported non-cardiac adverse reactions experienced by patients with ventricular arrhythmias participating in clinical trials were dizziness 26.6%, visual disturbance 25.9% (includes blurred vision, doplopia, visual field effects, photophobia), headache 10.4%, nausea 10.1%, and dyspnea 8.6%. Other adverse reactions occurring in over 3% of the patients in clinical trials:

Body as a Whole: fatigue 7.4%, asthenia 4.7%.

Cardiovascular: palpitations 6.0%, chest pain 6.0%.

Gastrointestinal: constipation 4.2%, abdominal pain 3.3%.

Tambocor (cont'd)

Nervous System: tremor 5.6%, nervousness 3.1%, paresthesia 3.1%.
Skin: rash 4.1%.

The following additional adverse reactions, possibly related to flecainide therapy and occurring in 1 to less than 3% of patients have been reported in clinical trials:
Body as a Whole: pain, increased sweating, flushing, dry mouth, arthralgia, fever, myalgia.
Cardiovascular: edema, syncope, tachycardia, angina pectoris, conduction disturbance.
Gastrointestinal: vomiting, diarrhea, anorexia.
Nervous System: hypoesthesia, somnolence, insomnia, ataxia.
Respiratory: coughing.
Skin: pruritus.
Special Senses: tinnitus.
Urinary System: micturition disorder (includes urinary retention, frequency, polyuria, dysuria).

The following additional adverse experiences, possibly related to flecainide, have been reported in less than 1% of patients:
Body as a Whole: impotence, decreased libido, gynecomastia, malaise.
Cardiovascular: bradycardia, EC abnormality, hypertension, hypotension, heart disorder, myocardial infarction, peripheral ischemia, pulmonary edema.
Gastrointestinal: dyspepsia, flatulence, gastrointestinal hemorrhage.
Nervous System: anxiety, twitching, convulsions, nystagmus, stupor, dysphonia, speech disorder, coma, amnesia, confusion, depersonalization, hallucination, paranoid reaction, euphoria, apathy.
Respiratory: bronchospasm, laryngismus.
Skin: dermatitis, hypertrichosis, photosensitivity reaction, skin discoloration.
Special Senses: deafness, parosmia, loss of taste, taste perversion.
Urinary System: renal failure, hematuria.
Laboratory Abnormalities: hyperglycemia, increased nonprotein in nitrogen, increased serum alkaline phosphatase, increased serum ALT and AST. Patients with elevations of liver function tests have been asymptomatic and no cause and effect relationship with flecainide has been established.

Adverse reactions leading to discontinuation of therapy occurred in 18.5% of the patients. The two most common were non-cardiac adverse reactions 9.0% and new or worsened arrhythmias 6.8%.

Overdose: Symptoms and Treatment: No specific antidote has been identified for the treatment of flecainide overdosage. Animal studies suggest the following events might occur with overdosage: lengthening of the PR interval; increase in the QRS duration, QT interval and amplitude of the T-wave; a reduction in myocardial rate and contractility; conduction disturbances; hypotension; and death from respiratory failure or asystole. Treatment of overdosage should be supportive and may include the following: removal of unabsorbed drug from the gastrointestinal tract, administration of inotropic agents or cardiac stimulants such as dopamine, dobutamine or isoproterenol; mechanically assisted respiration; circulatory assists such as intra-aortic balloon pumping; and transvenous pacing in the event of conduction block. Because of the long plasma half-life of flecainide (range from 12 to 27 hours in patients), and the possibility of markedly non-linear elimination kinetics at very high doses, these supportive treatments may need to be continued for extended periods of time.

Hemodialysis is not an effective means of removing flecainide from the body.

Since flecainide elimination is much slower when urine is very alkaline (pH 8 or higher), acidification of urine to promote drug excretion may, theoretically, be beneficial in overdose cases with very alkaline urine. There is no evidence that acidification from normal urinary pH increases excretion.

Dosage: Supraventricular Arrhythmias: The recommended starting dose for patients with paraoxysmal supraventricular tachycardias or patients with paroxysmal atrial fibrillation/flutter is 50 mg every 12 hrs. Flecainide may be increased in increments of 50 mg b.i.d. every 4 days until efficacy is achieved. The maximum recommended dose is 300 mg/day.
Ventricular Arrhythmias: For patients with sustained ventricular tachycardia, flecainide should be started in the hospital with rhythm monitoring. The recommended starting dose for patients with ventricular arrhythmias is 100 mg every 12 hours. Flecainide may be increased in increments of 50 g b.i.d. every 4 days until efficacy is achieved. Most patients do not require more than 150 mg every 12 hours (300 mg/day). The maximum dose is 400 g/day.

Use of higher initial doses and more rapid dosage adjustments has resulted in an increased incidence of proarrhythmic events and congestive heart failure, particularly during the first few days of dosing (see Warnings). Therefore, a loading dose is not recommended.

An occasional patient not adequately controlled by (or intolerant to) a dose given at 12-hour intervals may be given flecainide at 8 hour intervals.

Once adequate control of the arrhythmia has been achieved, it may be possible in some patients to reduce the dose as necessary to minimize side effects or effects on conduction. In such patients, efficacy at the lower dose should be evaluated.

In patients with a history of CHF or myocardial dysfunction, the initial dose should be no more than 100 mg every 12 hours. If needed to achieve efficacy, the dosage may be increased cautiously in increments of 50 mg twice a day every 4 days, and the maximum dosage should not exceed 200 mg every 12 hours (400 mg/day), because higher doses are associated with a greater incidence of worsened CHF (see Warnings).

In patients with severe renal impairment (creatinine clearance of 35 mL/min/1.73 m^2 or less), the initial dosage should be 50 mg to 100 mg once daily; when used in such patients, daily plasma level monitoring is required to guide dosage adjustments (see Plasma Level Monitoring). In patients with less severe renal disease, the initial dosage should be 100 mg every 12 hours; plasma level monitoring is also recommended in these patients during dosage adjustment. In both groups of patients, dosage increases should be made very cautiously when plasma levels have plateaued, observing the patient closely for signs of adverse cardiac effects or other toxicity. It should be borne in mind that in these patients it is likely to take longer than 4 days before a new steady state plasma level is reached following a dosage change. Therefore the interval between dose increases should be longer than the 4 days recommended for patients with normal renal function.

In elderly patients flecainide elimination from plasma is somewhat slower. The initial dosage need not be adjusted, however, daily trough plasma flecainide level monitoring is recommended during dosage adjustment.

Plasma Level Monitoring: Therapeutic trough plasma flecainide levels were found to range between 0.2 and 1.0 μg/mL. The probability of adverse experiences, especially cardiac, may increase with higher trough plasma levels, especially when these exceed 0.7 μg/mL. Periodic monitoring of trough plasma levels may be useful in patient management. Because elimination of flecainide from plasma may be markedly slower in patients with severe chronic renal failure or severe hepatic disease, plasma level monitoring is required in these patients. Plasma level monitoring is recommended in patients with congestive heart failure, moderate renal disease, and the elderly.

Based on theoretical considerations, rather than experimental data, the following suggestion is made: when transferring patients from another antiarrhythmic drug to flecainide or from flecainide to another antiarrhythmic, allow at least 2 to 4 plasma half-lives to elapse for the drug being discontinued before starting the alternative at the usual dosage. In patients where withdrawal of a previous antiarrhythmic agent is likely to produce life-threatening arrhythmias, the physician should consider hospitalizing the patient.

If flecainide is given in the presence of amiodarone (see Warnings) the usual dose of flecainide should be reduced by 50% and the patient should be monitored closely for adverse reactions. Plasma level monitoring is strongly recommended to guide dosage with such combination therapy.

Supplied: 50 mg: Each white, round, unscored tablet, imprinted with 3M on one side and TR 50 on the other side, contains: flecainide acetate 50 mg. Nonmedicinal ingredients: croscarmellose sodium, hydrogenated vegetable oil, magnesium stearate, microcrystalline cellulose and starch. Tartrazine-free. Bottles of 100.

100 mg: Each white, round, scored tablet, embossed with 3M on one side and TR 100 on the other side, contains: flecainide acetate 100 mg. Nonmedicinal ingredients: croscarmellose sodium, hydrogenated vegetable oil, magnesium stearate, microcrystalline cellulose and starch. Tartrazine-free. Bottles of 100.

Store between 15 to 30°C. Protect from light.

TAMOFEN® Ⓟ
Rhône-Poulenc Rorer
Tamoxifen Citrate
Antineoplastic

Pharmacology: Tamoxifen is a nonsteroidal agent which has demonstrated potent antiestrogenic properties in animal test systems. The antiestrogenic effects are related to is ability to compete with estrogen for binding sites in target tissues such as breast and uterus. Tamoxifen inhibits the induction of rat mammary carcinoma induced by dimethylbenzanthracene (DMBA) and causes the regression of already established DMBA-induced tumors. In this rat model tamoxifen appears to exert its antitumor effects by binding to estrogen receptors.

In cytosols derived from human endometrium and human breast and uterine adenocarcinomas tamoxifen competes with estradiol for estrogen receptor protein.

Reports of advanced breast cancer trials conducted worldwide, however, indicate that, using established criteria, there is an objective response rate (complete and partial remission) to tamoxifen of approximately 10% in patients with estrogen receptor negative tumors which may indicate other mechanisms of action. A further small percentage of patients show positive benefit in that they are reported to have disease stabilization. This may be explained by the shortcomings of the assay procedure or by actions of tamoxifen at loci other than the estrogen receptor.

Ranges as large as 0 to 300 fmoL/mg protein have been reported in histologically comparable portions of the same tumor. In addition, the collection, transport and storage of tumor specimens can affect the validity of current estrogen receptor assays.

The apparent discrepancy in correlation between estrogen receptor status and clinical response may also be explained by recent in vitro evidence indicating that not all of the growth inhibiting effects of tamoxifen are mediated through the estrogen receptor. Tamoxifen has been shown to have a low affinity for the androgen receptor and on a binding site distinct from the estrogen receptor. The possibility also exists that tamoxifen interferes with the action of hormonal steroids on cell growth, that it could modulate the action of peptide hormones at their receptors by effects on cell membranes, and that it inhibits prostaglandin synthetase thereby having the potential to limit tumor growth.

It is recognized that tamoxifen also displays estrogenic-like effects on several body systems including the endometrium, bone and blood lipids.

Therefore, although evidence suggests that patients with estrogen receptor positive tumors are more likely to respond, tamoxifen therapy may be considered in patients whose estrogen receptor status is unknown, in doubt or negative.

Indications: The treatment of breast cancer in estrogen receptor positive tumors.

Contraindications: *Pregnancy:* Tamoxifen must not be given during pregnancy. There have been a small number of reports of spontaneous abortions, birth defects and fetal deaths after women have taken tamoxifen, although no causal relationship has been established.

Reproductive toxicology studies in rats, rabbits and monkeys have shown no teratogenic potential.

In rodent models of fetal reproductive tract development, tamoxifen was associated with changes similar to those caused by estradiol, ethynylestradiol, clomiphene and diethylstilboestrol (DES). Although the clinical relevance of these changes is unknown, some of them, especially vaginal adenosis, are similar to those seen in young women who were exposed to DES in utero and who have a 1 in 1 000 risk of developing clear-cell carcinoma of the vagina or cervix. Only a small number of pregnant women have been exposed to tamoxifen. Such exposure has not been reported to cause subsequent vaginal adenosis or clear-cell carcinoma of the vagina or cervix in young women exposed in utero to tamoxifen.

Women should be advised not to become pregnant while taking tamoxifen and should use barrier or other nonhormonal contraceptive methods if sexually active. Premenopausal patients must be carefully examined before treatment to exclude the possibility of pregnancy. Women should be appraised of the potential risks to the fetus, should they become pregnant while taking tamoxifen or within 2 months of cessation of therapy.

Hypersensitivity to tamoxifen.

Warnings: In rats, tamoxifen can induce preneoplastic and neoplastic changes of the liver including hepatocellular carcinomas when administered at high doses for prolonged periods. In that species tamoxifen behaves as a partial agonist whereas it is primarily an antiestrogen in humans. For this reason and considering the high dosage used in the rat studies (up to 100 times the normal human therapeutic dose), the relevance of these findings to human use is unknown.

Gonadal tumors have been reported in mice receiving tamoxifen. To date, no case of hepatocellular carcinoma has been reported in patients receiving tamoxifen. However, the possibility of potential carcinogenicity in humans should be considered. Cataracts have also been found in chronic toxicity studies in rats. Tests conducted in various in vitro and in vivo systems have demonstrated that tamoxifen possesses genotoxic potential following hepatic metabolism. The significance of these results for man is at present unclear.

A number of second primary tumors, occurring at sites other than the endometrium and the opposite breast, have been reported in clinical trials, following the treatment of breast cancer patients with tamoxifen. No causal link has been established and the clinical significance of these observations remains unclear.

Precautions: Use tamoxifen cautiously in patients with existing thrombocytopenia or leukopenia. Transient decreases in platelet counts usually to 50 000 to 100 000/mm^3, have been observed occasionally during treatment. However, no hemorrhagic tendency was reported and platelet counts returned to normal even though treatment was continued.

Transient decreases in leukocytes also have been observed occasionally during treatment. Although it was uncertain that these incidences of leukopenia and thrombocytopenia were due to tamoxifen therapy, complete blood counts, including platelet counts, should be obtained periodically.

As with other additive hormonal therapy (estrogens and androgens) hypercalcemia has been reported in some breast cancer patients with bone metastases within a few weeks of starting treatment with tamoxifen. Patient who have metastatic bone disease should have periodic serum calcium determinations during the first few weeks of tamoxifen therapy and any symptoms suggestive of hypercalcemia should be evaluated promptly. If hypercalcemia is present, appropriate measures should be taken, and, if severe, tamoxifen should be discontinued.

The first patient follow-up should be done within 1 month following initiation of treatment. Thereafter, examinations may be performed at 1- to 2-month intervals. If adverse reactions such as hot flushes, nausea or vomiting occur, and are severe, they may be controlled in some patients by a dosage reduction without loss of effect on the disease.

Bone pain, if it should occur, may require analgesics.

Any patients receiving tamoxifen or having previously received tamoxifen who report abnormal vaginal bleeding should be promptly investigated.

In clinical studies, the median duration of treatment before the onset of a definite objective response has been 2 months. However, approximately 25% of patients who eventually responded were treated for 4 or more months before a definite objective response was recorded.

The duration of tamoxifen treatment will depend on the patient's response. The drug should be continued as long as there is a favorable response.

With obvious disease progression, discontinue tamoxifen. However, because an occasional patient will have a local disease flare (see Adverse Effects) or an increase in bone pain shortly after starting tamoxifen, it is sometimes difficult during the first few weeks of treatment to determine whether the patient's disease is progressing, or whether it will stabilize or respond to continued treatment. There are data to suggest that, if possible, treatment should not be discontinued before a minimum of 3 to 4 weeks.

Drug Interactions: When tamoxifen is used in combination with cytotoxic agents, there is increased risk of thromboembolic events occurring

Adverse Effects: The most frequent adverse reactions to tamoxifen are hot flushes, nausea and vomiting. These may occur in up to 25% of patients and are rarely severe enough to require discontinuation of treatment.

Less frequently reported adverse reactions are vaginal bleeding, vaginal discharge and skin rash. Usually these have not been severe enough to require dosage reduction or discontinuation of treatment.

Increased bone and tumor pain and also local disease flare have occurred. These are sometimes associated with good tumor response. Patients with soft tissue disease may have sudden increases in the size of pre-existing lesions, sometimes associated with marked erythema within and surrounding the lesions, and/or the development of new lesions. When they occur, the bone pain or disease flare are seen shortly after starting tamoxifen and generally subside rapidly.

Ocular changes have been reported in a few patients treated for periods longer than 1 year with doses that were at least 4 times the highest recommended daily dose of 40 mg. The ocular changes consisted of retinopathy and, in a few patients, there were also corneal changes and decreased visual acuity. There were multiple light refractive opacities in the paramacular area, and macular edema. The corneal lesions consisted of whorl-like superficial opacities. Ophthalmological examinations of selected patients on long-term tamoxifen therapy in the recommended doses revealed no ocular pathology attributable to the drug.

In addition, a few cases of ocular changes including visual disturbance, cataracts, and/or corneal changes and/or retinopathy have been reported in patients treated with tamoxifen at recommended doses. It is uncertain if these effects are due to the drug.

Leukopenia has been observed following the administration of tamoxifen, sometimes in association with anemia and/or thrombocytopenia. Neutropenia has been reported on rare occasions; this can sometimes be severe.

Elevations of ALT, AST and GGT levels have been reported on rare occasions in association with tamoxifen therapy. The incidence of overt cholestasis appears to be very low (<1%) but it should be kept in mind while administering tamoxifen over the long-term.

There have been infrequent reports of thromboembolic events occurring during tamoxifen therapy. As an increased incidence of these events is known to occur in patients with malignant disease, a causal relationship with tamoxifen has not been established.

Other adverse reactions noted infrequently are hypercalcemia, peripheral edema, benign symptomatic hepatic cysts, peliosis hepatitis, distaste for food, pruritus vulvae, depression, dizziness, lightheadedness and headache.

Tamoxifen therapy has been associated with an increased incidence of endometrial carcinoma. Uterine fibroids have been reported.

Overdose: Symptoms: Acute overdosage in humans has not been reported. Possible overdosage effects might include hot flushes, nausea, vomiting and vaginal bleeding.

Treatment: Symptomatic treatment. In the case of childhood accidental ingestion, gastric emptying is suggested.

Dosage: The usual dose is 20 to 40 mg/day in a single or 2 divided doses. Use the lowest effective dose.

Information for the Patient: See Blue Section—Information for the Patient "Tamofen".

Supplied: 10 mg: Each white, round, scored, biconvex tablet, marked $\frac{T}{10}$ on one side and scored on the other contains: tamoxifen citrate 15.2 mg equivalent to tamoxifen base 10 mg. Nonmedicinal ingredients: colloidal silicon dioxide, cornstarch, lactose, magnesium stearate, povidone and talc. Plastic containers of 60 and 250. Boxes of 30 and 60 in aluminum film strips (unit dose packages).

20 mg: Each white, round, biconvex tablet, marked $\frac{T}{20}$ on one side, contains: tamoxifen citrate 30.4 mg equivalent to tamoxifen base 20 mg. Nonmedicinal ingredients: colloidal silicon dioxide, cornstarch, lactose, magnesium stearate, povidone and talc. Plastic containers of 60. Boxes of 30 and 60 in aluminum film strips (unit dose packages).

Store at room temperature (between 15 and 30°C) in a well closed container. Protect from light.

(Shown in Product Recognition Section)

Reviewed 1998

TAMONE® Ⓟ

Pharmacia & Upjohn

Tamoxifen Citrate

Antineoplastic

Pharmacology: Tamoxifen is a nonsteroidal agent which has demonstrated potent antiestrogenic properties in animal test systems. The antiestrogenic effects are related to its ability to compete with estrogen for binding sites in target tissues such as breast and uterus. Tamoxifen inhibits the induction of rat mammary carcinoma induced by dimethylbenzanthracene (DMBA), and causes the regression of already established DMBA-induced tumors. In this rat model, tamoxifen appears to exert its antitumor effects by binding to estrogen receptors.

In cytosols derived from human endometrium and human breast and uterine adenocarcinomas, tamoxifen competes with estradiol for estrogen receptor protein.

Reports of advanced breast cancer trials conducted worldwide, however, indicate that, using established criteria, there is an objective response rate (complete and partial remission) to tamoxifen of approximately 10% in patients with estrogen receptor negative tumors. A further small percentage of patients show positive benefit in that they are reported to fall into the disease stabilization category. This may be explained by the shortcomings of the assay procedure or by actions of tamoxifen at loci other than the estrogen receptor.

Ranges as large as 0 to 300 fmol/mg protein have been reported in histologically comparable portions of the same tumor. In addition, the collection, transport and storage of tumor specimens can affect the validity of current estrogen receptor assays.

The apparent discrepancy in correlation between estrogen receptor status and clinical response may also be explained by recent in vitro evidence indicating that not all of the growth inhibiting effects of tamoxifen are mediated through the estrogen receptor. Tamoxifen has been shown to have a low affinity for the androgen receptor and on a binding site distinct from the estrogen receptor. The possibility also exists that tamoxifen interferes with the action of hormonal steroids on cell growth, that it could modulate the action of peptide hormones at their receptors by effects on cell membranes, and that it inhibits prostaglandin synthetase thereby having the potential to limit tumor growth.

Therefore, although evidence suggests that patients with estrogen receptor positive tumors are more likely to respond, tamoxifen therapy may be considered in patients whose estrogen receptor status is unknown, in doubt or negative.

Indications: In the treatment of breast cancer in estrogen receptor positive tumors.

Tamoxifen, alone or in combination with cytotoxic agents, is effective in significantly lowering recurrences of breast cancer in estrogen receptor positive tumors.

Contraindications: Hypersensitivity to tamoxifen.

Pregnancy: Tamoxifen must not be given during pregnancy. Premenopausal patients must be carefully examined before treatment to exclude the possibility of pregnancy.

Warnings: Tamoxifen should be used only for the conditions listed under Indications.

Disturbances of menstrual function, including oligomenorrhea and amenorrhea, have been reported in a proportion of premenopausal women receiving tamoxifen for the treatment of breast cancer. Available information indicates that in those women receiving tamoxifen for up to 2 years for the treatment of early breast cancer who develop disturbances of menstrual function on treatment, a proportion returns to normal cyclical bleeding on cessation of therapy.

Hepatocellular carcinomas as well as cataracts have been reported in the 2-year oncogenicity study in rats receiving tamoxifen. Gonadal tumors have been reported in mice receiving tamoxifen in long-term studies. The clinical relevance of these findings has not been established.

Precautions: Tamoxifen should be used cautiously in patients with existing thrombocytopenia or leukopenia. Transient decreases in platelet counts, usually to 50 000 to 100 000/mm^3, infrequently lower, have been observed occasionally during treatment with tamoxifen. However, no hemorrhagic tendency has been reported, and the platelet counts returned to normal levels even though treatment with tamoxifen was continued.

Transient decreases in leukocytes also have been observed occasionally during treatment. Although it was uncertain if these occasional incidences of leukopenia and thrombocytopenia were due to tamoxifen therapy, complete blood counts, including platelet counts, should be obtained periodically.

As with other additive hormonal therapy (estrogens and androgens), hypercalcemia has been reported in some breast cancer patients with bone metastases within a few weeks of starting treatment with tamoxifen. Any symptoms suggestive of hypercalcemia should be evaluated promptly. Patients who have metastatic bone disease should have periodic serum calcium determinations during the first few weeks of tamoxifen therapy. If hypercalcemia is present, appropriate measures should be taken and, if severe, tamoxifen should be discontinued.

The first patient follow-up should be done within 1 month following initiation of treatment. Thereafter, examinations may be performed at 1- to 2-month intervals. If adverse reactions such as hot flashes, nausea or vomiting occur, and are severe, they may be controlled in some patients by a reduction of dosage without loss of effect on the disease.

Bone pain, if it should occur, may require the use of analgesics.

If abnormal vaginal bleeding occurs during therapy, appropriate examinations should be performed to rule out a genital tract malignancy.

Tamone (cont'd)

In clinical studies, the median duration of treatment before the onset of a definite objective response has been 2 months. However, approximately one-quarter of patients who eventually responded were treated for 4 or more months before a definite objective response was recorded.

The duration of treatment with tamoxifen will depend on the patient's response. The drug should be continued as long as there is a favorable response.

With obvious disease progression, tamoxifen should be discontinued. However, because an occasional patient will have a local disease flare (see Adverse Effects) or an increase in bone pain shortly after starting tamoxifen, it is sometimes difficult during the first few weeks of treatment to determine whether the patient's disease is progressing, or whether it will stabilize or respond to continued treatment. There are data to suggest that, if possible, treatment should not be discontinued before a minimum of 3 to 4 weeks.

Adverse Effects: The most frequent adverse reactions to tamoxifen are hot flashes, nausea and vomiting. These may occur in up to one-quarter of all patients and are rarely severe enough to require discontinuation of treatment.

Less frequently reported adverse reactions are vaginal bleeding, vaginal discharge and skin rash. Usually these have not been of sufficient severity to require dosage reduction or discontinuation of treatment.

Increased bone and tumor pain and also local disease flare have occurred. These are sometimes associated with a good tumor response. Patients with soft tissue disease may have sudden increases in the size of pre-existing lesions, sometimes associated with marked erythema within and surrounding the lesions, and/or the development of new lesions. When they occur, the bone pain or disease flare are seen shortly after starting tamoxifen and generally subside rapidly.

Other adverse reactions noted infrequently are hypercalcemia, peripheral edema, distaste for food, pruritus vulvae, depression, dizziness, lightheadedness and headache.

Elevation of ALT, AST and GGT levels have been reported infrequently during therapy. Overt cholestasis has occurred less frequently and, in addition, there have been rare reports of benign, symptomatic hepatic cyst and peliosis hepatitis.

Ocular changes have been reported in a few breast cancer patients who, as part of a clinical trial, were treated for periods longer than 1 year with doses of tamoxifen that were at least 4 times the highest recommended daily dose of 40 mg. In each instance, the total amount of drug exceeded 100 g. These changes were a retinopathy and, in a few patients, corneal changes and decreased visual acuity. There were multiple light refractile opacities in the paramacular area, and macular edema. The corneal lesions consist of whorl-like superficial opacities. Ophthalmologic examinations of selected patients who received long-term therapy with tamoxifen at recommended doses did not detect any ocular pathology attributable to the drug.

In addition, a few cases of ocular changes including visual disturbance, cataracts and/or corneal changes and/or retinopathy have been reported in patients treated with tamoxifen at recommended doses. It is uncertain if these effects are due to tamoxifen; however, cataracts have been seen in an ongoing 2-year oncogenicity study in rats.

There have been infrequent reports of thromboembolic events occurring during tamoxifen therapy. As an increased incidence of these events is known to occur in patients with malignant disease, a causal relationship with tamoxifen has not been established.

Overdose: Symptoms and Treatment: Acute overdosage in humans has not been reported. Possible overdosage effects might include hot flashes, nausea, vomiting and vaginal bleeding. No specific treatment for overdosage is known and treatment must be symptomatic.

In case of accidental ingestion by a child, gastric emptying is suggested.

Dosage: The recommended daily dose of tamoxifen is 20 to 40 mg. The lowest effective dose should be used.
10 mg: 1 or 2 tablets twice a day, morning and evening. The lowest effective dose should be used.
20 mg: 1 or 2 tablets once a day. The lowest effective dose should be used.

Supplied: 10 mg: Each white, round, biconvex tablet, impressed with F on one face and 10 on the reverse, contains: tamoxifen citrate 15.2 mg (equivalent to tamoxifen 10 mg). Nonmedicinal ingredients: maize starch, magnesium stearate, lactose, povidone and sodium starch glycolate. Containers of 60 and 250. Blister packs of 10 strips of 10 tablets.

20 mg: Each white, round, biconvex tablet, impressed with F on one face and 20 on the reverse, contains: tamoxifen citrate 30.4 mg (equivalent to tamoxifen 20 mg). Nonmedicinal ingredients: maize starch, magnesium stearate, lactose, povidone and sodium starch glycolate. Containers of 30 and 100. Blister packs of 10 strips of 10 tablets.

Store at room temperature (15 to 30°C), protected from light.

Reviewed 1998

TANACET 125®
Ashbury Biologicals/Herbal Laboratories

Standardized Feverfew

Migraine Prophylaxis

Pharmacology: Clinical trials conducted in the United Kingdom have established the effectiveness of feverfew (Tanacetum parthenium) when taken daily over a 2-month period in reducing the frequency and intensity of migraine attacks.

Tanacet 125 contains specially prepared and standardized feverfew leaf (Tanacetum parthenium) which is a recognized traditional herbal remedy for several conditions, including the prevention of migraine headache. As with most migraine preventative therapies, the exact method of action remains to be defined; however, clinical trials have demonstrated that the drug reduces the frequency and severity of migraine attacks. Additionally, the drug reduces the severity of migraine associated gastro-intestinal upset (nausea, vomiting).

Although the interrelated role of several biological principles may be important, a sesquiterpene lactone, parthenolide, has been accepted as a biological marker for antimigraine activity of the herbal product. Only a product that has a minimum of 0.2% parthenolide demonstrates a correlation with biological activity. This product is certified to contain 125 mg of feverfew leaf material per tablet with a minimum parthenolide assay equal to or exceeding the 0.2% parthenolide requirement. This differentiates Tanacet 125 from other feverfew products.

In vitro studies have demonstrated that parthenolide acts to inhibit the release of serotonin from platelets and white blood cells. The clinical significance of this observation is not presently understood.

Indications: Prophylaxis of migraine.

Precautions: *Pregnancy* and *Lactation:* Tanacet 125 should not be taken during pregnancy or when breast-feeding.

Patients should be instructed to consult a doctor to evaluate progress before continuing to use Tanacet 125 beyond 4 months. Discontinue use if sore mouth develops. Keep out of reach of children.

Adverse Effects: Mild pruritus and occasional mouth sores have been reported in less than 7% of consumers; these reactions promptly cease with the reduction or discontinuation of Tanacet 125.

Dosage: Take 1 or 2 tablets daily with water after meals, preferably the first tablet after breakfast and the second after the evening meal. If mouth sores are experienced, discontinue use.

Supplied: Each compressed tablet contains: specially selected standardized certified feverfew leaf powder 125 mg (provides a minimum of 0.2% parthenolide). Nonmedicinal ingredients: dicalcium phosphate, microcrystalline cellulose, silicon dioxide and vegetable magnesium stearate. Packages of 60.

TANTA ORCIPRENALINE Ⓟ
Tanta

Orciprenaline Sulfate

β_2-Adrenergic Stimulant—Bronchodilator

Supplied: Each 5 mL of sugar-free, natural black cherry-flavored syrup contains: orciprenaline sulfate 10 mg. Bottles of 473 mL. Information for the consumer enclosed.

TANTUM™ Ⓟ
3M Pharmaceuticals

Benzydamine HCl

Local Analgesic

Supplied: Each mL of clear yellow-green liquid contains: benzydamine HCl 0.15%. Nonmedicinal ingredients: D & C yellow #10, ethyl alcohol, FD & C blue #1, flavor, glycerin, methyl- and propylparabens (as preservatives), polysorbate 80 and purified water. Alcohol: 10%. Tartrazine-free. Bottles of 100 and 250 mL.

TAPAZOLE® Ⓟ
Lilly

Methimazole

Antithyroid

Pharmacology: Methimazole inhibits the synthesis of thyroid hormones and thus is effective in the treatment of hyperthyroidism. The drug does not inactivate existing thyroxine and triiodothyronine that are stored in colloid or are circulating in the blood, nor does it interfere with the effectiveness of thyroid hormones given by mouth or by injection.

The actions and use of methimazole are similar to those of propylthiouracil. On a weight basis, the drug is at least 10 times as potent as propylthiouracil, but methimazole may be less consistent in action.

Methimazole is readily absorbed from the gastrointestinal tract. It is metabolized rapidly and requires frequent administration. Methimazole is excreted in the urine.

Indications: The medical treatment of hyperthyroidism. Long-term therapy may lead to remission of the disease. May be used to ameliorate hyperthyroidism in preparation for subtotal thyroidectomy or radioactive iodine therapy. When thyroidectomy is contraindicated or not advisable.

Contraindications: Hypersensitivity to methimazole.
Lactation: In nursing mothers, since the drug is excreted in breast milk.

Warnings: Agranulocytosis is potentially the most serious side effect of therapy with methimazole. Patients should be instructed to report to their physicians any symptoms of agranulocytosis, such as fever or sore throat. Leukopenia, thrombocytopenia, and aplastic anemia (pancytopenia) may also occur. The drug should be discontinued in the presence of agranulocytosis, aplastic anemia (pancytopenia), hepatitis, or exfoliative dermatitis. The patient's bone marrow function should be monitored.

Due to the similar hepatic toxicity profiles of methimazole and propylthiouracil, attention is drawn to the severe hepatic reactions which have occurred with both drugs. There have been rare reports of fulminant hepatitis, hepatic necrosis, encephalopathy, and death. Symptoms suggestive of hepatic dysfunction (anorexia, pruritus, right upper quadrant pain, etc) should prompt evaluation of liver function. Drug treatment should be discontinued promptly in the event of clinically significant evidence of liver abnormality, including hepatic transaminase values exceeding 3 times the upper limit of normal.
Pregnancy: Methimazole can cause fetal harm when administered to a pregnant woman. It readily crosses the placental membranes and can induce goiter and even cretinism in the developing fetus. In addition, rare instances of aplasia cutis, as manifested by scalp defects, have occurred in infants born to mothers who received methimazole during pregnancy. If methimazole is used during pregnancy, or if the patient becomes pregnant while taking this drug, the patient should be warned of the potential hazard to the fetus.

Since scalp defects have not been reported in offspring of patients treated with propylthiouracil, that agent may be preferable to methimazole in pregnant women requiring treatment with antithyroid drugs.
Lactation: Postpartum patients receiving methimazole should not nurse their babies.

Precautions: General: Patients who receive methimazole should be under close surveillance and should be cautioned to report immediately any evidence of illness, particularly sore throat, skin eruptions, fever, headache, or general malaise. In such cases, white-blood-cell and differential counts should be made to determine whether agranulocytosis has developed. Particular care should be exercised with patients who are receiving additional drugs known to cause agranulocytosis.
Laboratory Tests: Because methimazole may cause hypoprothrombinemia and bleeding, prothrombin time should be monitored during therapy with the drug, especially before surgical procedures. Periodic monitoring of thyroid function is warranted, and the finding of an elevated TSH warrants a decrease in the dosage of methimazole.
<u>*Drug Interactions:*</u> The activity of anticoagulants may be potentiated by anti-vitamin-K activity attributed to methimazole.
Carcinogenesis, Mutagenesis, Impairment of Fertility: Such effects have not been observed or reported. However, in a 2 year study, rats were given doses of 0.5, 3 and

18 mg/kg/day. These doses were 0.3, 2 and 12 times the 15 mg/day maximum human maintenance dose (when calculated on the basis of surface area). Thyroid hyperplasia, adenoma and carcinoma developed in rats at the 2 higher doses. The clinical significance of these findings is unclear.

Pregnancy: Methimazole, used judiciously, is an effective drug in hyperthyroidism complicated by pregnancy. In many pregnant women, the thyroid dysfunction diminishes as the pregnancy proceeds; consequently, a reduction in dosage may be possible. In some instances, use of methimazole can be discontinued 2 or 3 weeks before delivery.

If this drug is used during pregnancy, or if the patient becomes pregnant while taking this drug, the patient should be apprised of the potential hazard to the fetus.

Lactation: The drug appears in human breast milk and its use is contraindicated in nursing mothers.

Children: See Dosage.

Adverse Effects: Major adverse reactions (which occur with much less frequency than the minor adverse reactions) include inhibition of myelopoiesis (agranulocytosis, granulopenia, and thrombocytopenia), aplastic anemia, drug fever, a lupus-like syndrome, hepatitis (jaundice may persist for several weeks after discontinuation of the drug), periarteritis, and hypoprothrombinemia, nephritis (very rarely) and insulin autoimmune syndrome (which may result in hypoglycemic coma).

Minor adverse reactions include skin rash, urticaria, nausea, vomiting, epigastric distress, arthralgia, paresthesia, loss of taste, abnormal loss of hair, myalgia, headache, pruritus, drowsiness, neuritis, edema, vertigo, skin pigmentation, jaundice, sialadenopathy, and lymphadenopathy.

About 10% of patients with untreated hyperthyroidism have leukopenia (WBC count of less than 4 000/mm^3), often with relative granulopenia.

Overdose: Symptoms: May include nausea, vomiting, epigastric distress, headache, fever, joint pain, pruritus, and edema. Aplastic anemia (pancytopenia) or agranulocytosis may be manifested in hours to days. Less frequent events are hepatitis, nephrotic syndrome, exfoliative dermatitis, neuropathies, and CNS stimulation or depression. Although not well studied, methimazole-induced agranulocytosis is generally associated with doses greater than 40 mg in patients older than 40 years of age.

No information is available on the LD_{50} of the drug or the concentration of methimazole in biologic fluids associated with toxicity and/or death.

Treatment: In managing overdosage, consider the possibility of multiple drug overdoses, interaction among drugs, and unusual drug kinetics in your patient.

Protect the patient's airway and support ventilation and perfusion. Meticulously monitor and maintain, within acceptable limits, the patient's vital signs, blood gases, serum electrolytes, etc. The patient's bone marrow function should be monitored. Absorption of drugs from the gastrointestinal tract may be decreased by giving activated charcoal, which, in many cases, is more effective than emesis or lavage; consider charcoal instead of or in addition to gastric emptying. Repeated doses of charcoal over time may hasten elimination of some drugs that have been absorbed. Safeguard the patient's airway when employing gastric emptying or charcoal.

Forced diuresis, peritoneal dialysis, hemodialysis, or charcoal hemoperfusion have not been established as beneficial for an overdose of methimazole.

Dosage: Methimazole is administered orally. It is usually given in 3 equal doses at approximately 8-hour intervals.

Adults: The initial daily dosage is 15 mg for mild hyperthyroidism, 30 to 40 mg for moderately severe hyperthyroidism, and 60 mg for severe hyperthyroidism, divided into 3 doses at 8 hour intervals. The maintenance dosage is 5 to 15 mg daily.

Children: Initially, the daily dosage is 0.4 mg/kg of body weight divided into 3 doses and given at 8 hour intervals. The maintenance dosage is approximately one half of the initial dose.

Supplied: Each scored tablet contains: methimazole USP 5 mg. Identi-Code: J 94. Nonmedicinal ingredients: lactose, magnesium stearate, starch and talc. Tartrazine-free. Bottles of 100.

TARDAN

Odan

Salicylic Acid—Tar Shampoo

Antiseborrheic

Supplied: Each bottle contains: salicylic acid 2%, liquor carbonis detergens 5% and triclosan 0.3% dispersed in a blend of anionic and amphoteric surfactants, fatty acid alcanolamide and protein conditioning agents. Nonmedicinal ingredients: cocoamide DEA, disodium cocoamphodipropionate, hydrolized protein, methylcellulose, perfume, purified water and sodium lauryl sulfate. Acid pH. Plastic bottles of 250 and 500 mL.

TARGEL Preparations

Odan

Tar Compound

Antipsoriatic

Supplied: Targel: Each g contains: liquor carbonis detergens 10% in a water washable gel base. Nonmedicinal ingredients: carbomer, perfume, propylene glycol, purified water and trolamine. Plastic jars of 100 g.

Targel S.A.: Each g contains: liquor carbonis detergens 10% and salicylic acid 3% in a water washable gel base. Nonmedicinal ingredients: carbomer, perfume, propylene glycol, purified water and trolamine. Plastic jars of 100 g.

TARKA® Ⓟ

Knoll

Trandolapril—Verapamil HCl

Antihypertensive

Pharmacology: Tarka is a formulation containing slow-release verapamil, a phenylalkylamine calcium channel blocker, along with immediate-release trandolapril, an angiotensin converting enzyme (ACE) inhibitor.

Verapamil is a calcium channel blocker that exerts its pharmacologic effects by modulating the influx of ionic calcium across the cell membrane of the arterial smooth muscle as well as in conductile and contractile myocardial cells. Verapamil exerts antihypertensive effects by decreasing systemic vascular resistance, usually without reflex tachycardia. During isometric or dynamic exercise, verapamil does not blunt hemodynamic response in patients with normal ventricular function. Verapamil does not alter total serum calcium levels.

Trandolapril is a pro-drug. Trandolaprilat, its major active metabolite, inhibits ACE in human subjects and in animals. ACE is a peptidyl dipeptidase that catalyzes the conversion of angiotensin I to the more pharmacologically active substance, angiotensin II. Angiotensin II has vasoconstrictor activity and also stimulates aldosterone secretion by the adrenal cortex.

Inhibition of ACE results in decreased plasma angiotensin II, which leads to decreased vasopressor activity. Removal of angiotensin II negative feedback on renin secretion leads to increased plasma renin activity.

ACE is identical to kininase II, an enzyme that degrades bradykinin. Whether increased levels of bradykinin, a potent vasodepressor, play a role in the therapeutic effect of Tarka remains to be elucidated.

Pharmacokinetics and Metabolism: Following a single oral dose of Tarka in healthy subjects, peak plasma concentrations are reached within 0.5 to 2 hours for trandolapril and within 4 to 15 hours for verapamil. Peak plasma concentrations of the active desmethyl metabolite of verapamil, norverapamil, are reached within 5 to 15 hours. Cleavage of the ester group by hydrolysis converts trandolapril to its active diacid metabolite, trandolaprilat, which reaches peak plasma concentrations within 2 to 12 hours.

Trandolaprilat has an effective elimination half-life of approximately 10 hours while that of verapamil, as verapamil SR, is 6 to 11 hours. Steady-state plasma concentrations of the two components are achieved after about a week of once-daily dosing of Tarka. At steady-state, plasma concentrations of verapamil and trandolaprilat are up to 2-fold higher than those observed after a single oral Tarka dose.

Verapamil SR is a racemic mixture consisting of equal portions of the R enantiomer and the S enantiomer. More than 90% of the orally administered dose of verapamil SR is absorbed. Upon oral administration, there is rapid stereo selective biotransformation during the first pass of verapamil through the portal circulation. The S enantiomer is pharmacologically more active than the R enantiomer. There is a non-linear correlation between the verapamil dose administered and verapamil plasma levels.

In healthy men, orally administered verapamil undergoes extensive metabolism by the cytochrome P450 system. The particular isoenzymes involved are CYP3A4, CYP1A2, and CYP2C family. Thirteen metabolites have been identified in urine. Norverapamil can reach steady-state plasma concentrations approximately equal to those of verapamil itself. The cardiovascular activity of norverapamil appears to be approximately 20% that of verapamil. Approximately 70% of an administered dose is excreted as metabolites in the urine and 16% or more in the feces within 5 days. About 3 to 4% is excreted in the urine as unchanged drug. R-verapamil is 94% bound to plasma albumin, while S-verapamil is 88% bound. In addition, R-verapamil is 92% and S-verapamil 86% bound to alpha-1 acid glycoprotein. The degree of biotransformation during the first pass of verapamil may vary according to the status of the liver in different patient populations. In patients with hepatic insufficiency, metabolism is delayed and elimination half-life prolonged up to 14-16 hours (see Warnings, Hepatic Insufficiency and Dosage).

Verapamil crosses the placental barrier and can be detected in umbilical vein blood at delivery. Verapamil is excreted in human milk.

Approximately 40 to 60% of an administered oral dose of trandolapril is absorbed. Trandolapril undergoes extensive first-pass metabolism in the liver, and this is the reason that its bioavailability is low: 7.5% (ranging from 4 to 14%). Minor metabolic pathways lead to the formation of diketopiperazine derivatives of trandolapril and trandolaprilat. These molecules have no ACE inhibitory activity. Glucuronide conjugated derivatives of trandolapril and trandolaprilat are also produced.

Effect of Food: Administration of Tarka with a high-fat meal does not alter the bioavailability of trandolapril, whereas verapamil peak concentrations and area under the curve (AUC) decrease 42% and 27%, respectively, relative to administration in the fasting state. Norverapamil values are also decreased 22% and 17%, respectively, in the fed state. Food thus decreases verapamil bioavailability, and results in a narrower peak to trough ratio.

Geriatrics: The pharmacokinetics of verapamil and trandolaprilat are significantly different in the elderly (≥65 years), compared to younger subjects. AUCs are increased approximately 80% with verapamil and 35% with trandolaprilat. In the elderly, verapamil clearance is reduced resulting in increases in elimination half-life (see Precautions, Geriatrics).

Patients with Hepatic Impairment: In patients with hepatic insufficiency, verapamil clearance is reduced by 30% and the elimination half-life is prolonged up to 14 to 16 hours (see Precautions, Patients with Hepatic Impairment and Dosage).

In patients with moderate to severe impairment of liver function, plasma trandolapril levels were approximately 10 times higher than in healthy subjects. The plasma concentrations of trandolaprilat and the quantities excreted in the urine were also increased, although to a lesser degree. The dose should therefore be reduced in these patients.

In 1 study, cirrhotic patients who received a single dose of trandolapril 2 mg exhibited a 9-fold increase in trandolapril C_{max} and AUC values. The C_{max} and AUC values of trandolaprilat were about doubled.

Patients With Renal Impairment: The results of an i.v. pharmacokinetic study suggest that renal clearance of verapamil may be decreased in patients with renal disease (see Dosage).

In patients with creatinine clearance ≤30 mL/min/1.73m^2, the C_{max} and AUC of trandolaprilat were approximately doubled after repeated oral administration of trandolapril, as compared to those of normal subjects.

Pharmacodynamics: Controlled clinical studies have shown that the effects of concurrent use of verapamil SR and trandolapril are additive with respect to lowering systolic and diastolic blood pressure.

The antihypertensive effect of angiotensin converting enzyme inhibitors is generally lower in black patients than in non-blacks.

Indications: For the treatment of mild to moderate essential hypertension in patients for whom combination therapy is appropriate.

Tarka is not indicated for initial therapy. Patients in whom trandolapril and verapamil SR are initiated simultaneously can develop symptomatic hypotension (see Warnings, Hypotension).

Patients should be titrated with the individual drugs. If the fixed combination represents the dosage determined by this titration, the use of Tarka may be more convenient in the management of patients. If during maintenance therapy dosage adjustment is necessary, it is advisable to use individual drugs.

Both trandolapril and verapamil SR should normally be used in those patients in whom treatment with a diuretic or a β-blocker were found to be ineffective or were associated with unacceptable adverse effects. They can be tried as initial

Tarka (cont'd)

agents in those patients in whom diuretics and/or β-blockers are contraindicated or in patients with medical conditions in which these drugs frequently cause serious adverse effects.

In using trandolapril, consideration should be given to the risk of angioedema (see Warnings).

When used in pregnancy during the second and third trimesters, ACE inhibitors can cause injury to or even death of the developing fetus. When pregnancy is detected, Tarka should be discontinued as soon as possible (see Warnings, Pregnancy).

Contraindications: Tarka is contraindicated due to the verapamil component, in patients with: Complicated myocardial infarction (patients who have ventricular failure manifested by pulmonary congestion). Severe left ventricular dysfunction (see Warnings, Heart Failure). Hypotension (systolic pressure less than 90 mm Hg) or cardiogenic shock. Second or third degree AV block (except in patients with a functioning artificial ventricular pacemaker). Sick sinus syndrome (except in patients with a functioning artificial ventricular pacemaker). Marked bradycardia. Patients with atrial flutter or atrial fibrillation and an accessory bypass tract (e.g., Wolff-Parkinson-White, Lown-Ganong-Levine syndromes) (see Warnings, Accessory Bypass Tract). Known hypersensitivity to verapamil.

Tarka is contraindicated due to the trandolapril component, in patients with: A history of angioedema associated with prior angiotensin converting enzyme inhibitor (ACE) therapy. Known hypersensitivity to any angiotensin converting enzyme inhibitor.

Warnings: Hypotension: Concomitant therapy with ACE inhibitors and verapamil may result in hypotension. In controlled studies, hypotension was observed in 0.6% of uncomplicated hypertensive patients receiving Tarka. Dizziness occurred more frequently than with placebo (see Adverse Effects). In patients with angina or arrhythmias using antihypertensive drugs, the additional antihypertensive effect of Tarka should be taken into consideration.

Verapamil: Hypotensive symptoms of lethargy and weakness with faintness have been reported following single oral doses of verapamil and even after some months of treatment. In some patients it may be necessary to reduce the dose.

Trandolapril: Symptomatic hypotension has occurred after administration of trandolapril, usually after the first or second dose, or when the dose was increased. It is more likely to occur in patients who are volume depleted as a result of diuretic therapy, dietary salt restriction, dialysis, diarrhea or vomiting. In patients with ischemic heart disease or cerebrovascular disease, an excessive fall in blood pressure could result in a myocardial infarction or cerebrovascular accident. Because of the potential fall in blood pressure in these patients, therapy with trandolapril should be started under close medical supervision. Such patients should be followed closely for the first weeks of treatment and whenever the dose of trandolapril is increased. In patients with severe congestive heart failure, with or without associated renal insufficiency, ACE inhibitor therapy may cause excessive hypotension and has been associated with oliguria, and/or progressive azotemia, and rarely, with acute renal failure and/or death.

If hypotension occurs, the patient should be placed in a supine position and, if necessary, receive an i.v. infusion of 0.9% sodium chloride. A transient hypotensive response is not a contraindication to further doses which can be given usually without difficulty once the blood pressure has increased after volume expansion. If symptoms persist, the dosage should be reduced or the drug discontinued.

Heart Failure: Verapamil: Because of the drug's negative inotropic effect, verapamil should not be used in patients with poorly compensated congestive heart failure, unless the failure is complicated by or caused by a dysrhythmia. If verapamil is used in such patients, they must be digitalized prior to treatment.

It has been reported that digoxin plasma levels may increase with chronic verapamil administration (see Precautions, Drug Interactions: Digitalis) The use of verapamil in the treatment of hypertension is not recommended in patients with heart failure caused by systolic dysfunction.

Trandolapril: Trandolapril, as an ACE inhibitor, may cause excessive hypotension in patients with congestive heart failure (see Warnings, Hypotension).

Conduction Disturbance: Verapamil: Verapamil slows conduction across the AV node and rarely may produce second or third degree AV block, bradycardia and in extreme cases, asystole.

Verapamil causes dose-related suppression of the SA node. In some patients, sinus bradycardia may occur, especially in patients with a sick sinus syndrome (SA nodal disease), which is more common in older patients (see Contraindications).

Bradycardia: Verapamil: The total incidence of bradycardia with verapamil (ventricular rate less than 50 beats/min) was 1.4% in controlled studies. Asystole in patients other than those with sick sinus syndrome is usually of short duration (few seconds or less), with spontaneous return to AV nodal or normal sinus rhythm. If this does not occur promptly, appropriate treatment should be initiated immediately (see Overdose: Symptoms and Treatment).

Accessory Bypass Tract (Wolff-Parkinson-White or Lown-Ganong-Levine): Verapamil: Verapamil may result in significant acceleration of ventricular response during atrial fibrillation or atrial flutter in the Wolff-Parkinson-White (WPW) or Lown-Ganong-Levine syndromes after receiving i.v. verapamil. Although a risk of this occurring with oral verapamil has not been established, such patients receiving oral verapamil may be at risk and its use in these patients is contraindicated (see Contraindications).

Concomitant Use With β-blockers: Verapamil: Generally, oral verapamil should not be given to patients receiving β-blockers since the depressant effects on myocardial contractility, heart rate and AV conduction may be additive. However, in exceptional cases when in the opinion of the physician concomitant use in angina and arrhythmias is considered essential, such use should be instituted gradually under careful supervision. If combined therapy is used, close surveillance of vital signs and clinical status should be carried out and the need for continued concomitant treatment periodically assessed.

Verapamil gives no protection against the dangers of abrupt β-blocker withdrawal and such withdrawal should be done by the gradual reduction of the dose of β-blocker. Then verapamil may be started with the usual dose.

Patients with Hypertrophic Cardiomyopathy: Verapamil: In 120 patients with hypertrophic cardiomyopathy (most of them refractory or intolerant to propranolol) who received therapy with verapamil at doses up to 720 mg/day, a variety of serious adverse effects were seen. Three patients died in pulmonary edema; all had severe left ventricular outflow obstruction and a past history of left ventricular dysfunction. Eight other patients had pulmonary edema and/or severe hypotension; abnormally high (over 20 mm Hg) capillary wedge pressure and a marked left ventricular outflow obstruction were present in most of these patients. Sinus bradycardia occurred in 11% of the patients, second-degree AV block in 4% and sinus arrest in 2%. It must be appreciated that this group of patients had a serious disease with a high mortality rate. Most adverse effects responded well to dose reduction, but in some cases verapamil use had to be discontinued.

Angioedema: Trandolapril: Angioedema has been reported in patients taking ACE inhibitors, including trandolapril. Angioedema associated with laryngeal involvement may be fatal. If laryngeal stridor or angioedema of the face, tongue, or glottis occurs, trandolapril should be discontinued immediately, the patient treated appropriately in accordance with accepted medical care, and carefully observed until the swelling disappears. In instances where swelling is confined to the face and lips, the condition generally resolves without treatment. Where there is involvement of tongue, glottis, or larynx, likely to cause airway obstruction, appropriate therapy (including, but not limited to 0.3 to 0.5 mL of s.c. epinephrine solution 1:1 000) should be administered promptly (see Adverse Effects).

Patients with a history of angioedema unrelated to ACE inhibitor therapy may be at increased risk of angioedema while receiving an ACE inhibitor (see Contraindications).

The incidence of angioedema during ACE inhibition therapy has been reported to be higher in black than in non-black patients.

Neutropenia/Agranulocytosis: Trandolapril: Agranulocytosis and bone marrow depression have been caused by ACE inhibitors. Current experience with trandolapril shows the incidence to be rare. Periodic monitoring of white blood cell counts should be considered, especially in patients with collagen vascular disease and/or renal disease.

Pregnancy: Trandolapril: ACE inhibitors can cause fetal and neonatal morbidity and death when administered to pregnant women. Several dozen cases have been reported in the world literature. When pregnancy is detected, Tarka should be discontinued as soon as possible.

The use of ACE inhibitors during the second and third trimesters of pregnancy has been associated with fetal and neonatal injury, including hypotension, neonatal skull hypoplasia, anuria, reversible or irreversible renal failure, and death. Oligohydramnios has also been reported, presumably resulting from decreased fetal renal function; oligohydramnios in this setting has been associated with fetal limb contractures, craniofacial deformation, and hypoplastic lung development. Prematurity, intrauterine growth retardation, and patent ductus arteriosus have also been reported, although it is not clear whether these occurrences were due to the ACE-inhibitor exposure.

Rarely (probably less often than once in every thousand pregnancies), no alternative to ACE inhibitors will be found. In these rare cases, the mothers should be apprised of the potential hazards to their fetuses, and serial ultrasound examinations should be performed to assess the intra-amniotic environment.

If oligohydramnios is observed, trandolapril should be discontinued unless it is considered lifesaving for the mother. Contraction stress testing (CST), a nonstress test (NST), or biophysical profiling (BPP) may be appropriate, depending upon the week of pregnancy. Patients and physicians should be aware, however, that oligohydramnios may not appear until after the fetus has sustained irreversible injury.

Infants with histories of in utero exposure to ACE inhibitors should be closely observed for hypotension, oliguria and hyperkalemia. If oliguria occurs, attention should be directed toward support of blood pressure and renal perfusion. Exchange transfusion or dialysis may be required as a means of reversing hypotension and/or substituting for disordered renal function; however, limited experience with these procedures has not been associated with significant clinical benefits. It is not known if trandolapril, or trandolaprilat can be removed from the body by hemodialysis.

Elevated Liver Enzymes/Hepatic Failure: Verapamil: Elevations of transaminases, with and without concomitant elevations in alkaline phosphatase and bilirubin, have been reported. Several cases of hepatocellular injury related to verapamil have been proven by rechallenge. Clinical symptoms of malaise, fever, and/or right upper quadrant pain, in addition to elevations of AST, ALT, and alkaline phosphatase have been reported. Periodic monitoring of liver function in patients receiving Tarka is, therefore, prudent.

Trandolapril: In rare instances, ACE inhibitors have been associated with a syndrome of cholestatic jaundice, fulminant hepatic necrosis and death. The mechanism of this syndrome is not understood.

Patients receiving Tarka who develop jaundice should discontinue therapy and receive appropriate medical follow-up.

Precautions: Patients with Hepatic Impairment: In patients with impaired liver function, the elimination half-life of verapamil is prolonged four-fold and the plasma concentrations of trandolapril and, to a lesser extent, of its principle active metabolite, trandolaprilat, are increased (see Pharmacology, Pharmacokinetics and Metabolism). Accordingly, a decreased dosage of Tarka should be used in these patients (see Dosage).

In these patients, careful monitoring for abnormal prolongation of the PR interval or other signs of excessive pharmacologic effects should be carried out during Tarka therapy.

Patients with Renal Impairment: Verapamil: About 70% of an administered dose of verapamil is excreted as metabolites in the urine. In 1 study in healthy volunteers, the total body clearance after i.v. administration of verapamil was 12.08 mL/min/kg, while in patients with advanced renal disease it was reduced to 5.33 mL/min/kg. This pharmacokinetic finding suggests that renal clearance of verapamil in patients with renal disease is decreased. In 2 studies with oral verapamil no difference in pharmacokinetics could be demonstrated. Therefore, until further data are available, verapamil should be used with caution in patients with impaired renal function. These patients should be carefully monitored for abnormal prolongation of the PR interval or other signs of excessive pharmacologic effect (see Dosage).

Trandolapril: As a consequence of inhibiting the renin-angiotensin-aldosterone system, changes in renal function have been seen in susceptible individuals. In patients whose renal function may depend on the activity of the renin-angiotensin-aldosterone system, such as patients with bilateral renal artery stenosis, unilateral renal artery stenosis to a solitary kidney, or severe congestive heart failure, treatment with agents that inhibit this system has been associated with oliguria, progressive azotemia, and rarely, acute renal failure and/or death. In susceptible patients, concomitant diuretic use may further increase risk.

Use of trandolapril should include appropriate assessment of renal function.

Anaphylactoid Reactions During Membrane Exposure: Trandolapril: Anaphylactoid reactions have been reported in patients dialyzed with high-flux membranes (e.g., polyacrylonitrile [PAN]) and treated concomitantly with an ACE inhibitor. Dialysis should be stopped immediately if symptoms such as nausea, abdominal cramps, burning, angioedema, shortness of breath and severe hypotension occur. Symptoms are not relieved by antihistamines. In these patients consideration should be given to using a different type of dialysis membrane or a different class of antihypertensive agents.

Anaphylactoid Reactions During LDL Apheresis: Trandolapril: Rarely, patients receiving ACE inhibitors during low density lipoprotein apheresis with dextran sulfate have experienced life-threatening anaphylactoid reactions. These reactions were avoided by temporarily withholding ACE inhibitor therapy prior to each apheresis.

Anaphylactoid Reactions During Desensitization: Trandolapril: There have been isolated reports of patients experiencing sustained life-threatening anaphylactoid reactions while receiving ACE inhibitors during desensitization treatment with hymenoptera (bees, wasps) venom. In the same patients, these reactions have been avoided when ACE inhibitors were temporarily withheld for at least 24 hours, but they have reappeared upon inadvertent rechallenge.

Patients with Attenuated (Decreased) Neuromuscular Transmission: Verapamil: It has been reported that verapamil decreases neuromuscular transmission in patients with Duchenne's muscular dystrophy, and that verapamil prolongs recovery from the neuromuscular blocking agent vecuronium. Accordingly, it may be necessary to decrease the dosage of verapamil when it is administered to patients with attenuated neuromuscular transmission (see Precautions, Surgery/Anesthesia).

Surgery/Anesthesia: Trandolapril: In patients undergoing major surgery or during anesthesia with agents that produce hypotension, trandolapril will block angiotensin II formation secondary to compensatory renin release. If hypotension occurs and is considered to be due to this mechanism, it can be corrected by volume expansion (see Precautions, Patients with Attenuated (Decreased) Neuromuscular Transmission).

Hyperkalemia and Potassium-sparing Diuretics: In clinical trials, hyperkalemia (serum potassium >6 mEq/L) occurred in approximately 0.4% of hypertensive patients receiving trandolapril and in 0.8% of patients receiving trandolapril concurrently with verapamil SR. In most cases, elevated serum potassium levels were isolated values, which resolved despite continued therapy. None of these patients were discontinued from the trials because of hyperkalemia.

Risk factors for the development of hyperkalemia include renal insufficiency, diabetes mellitus, and the concomitant use of potassium-sparing diuretics, potassium supplements, and/or potassium-containing salt substitutes (see Precautions, Drug Interactions: Agents Increasing Serum Potassium).

Cough: Trandolapril: As with other ACE inhibitors, dry, persistent cough, which usually disappears only after withdrawal or lowering of the dose of trandolapril, has been reported. Such possibility should be considered as part of the differential diagnosis of cough.

Geriatrics: Although clinical experience has not identified differences in response between the elderly (≥65 years) and younger patients (<65 years), greater sensitivity of some older individuals to Tarka cannot be ruled out (see Pharmacology, Pharmacokinetics and Metabolism).

Caution should be exercised when verapamil is administered to elderly patients (≥65 years) especially those prone to developing hypotension or those with a history of cerebrovascular insufficiency (see Dosage). The adverse reactions occurring more frequently include dizziness and constipation. Serious adverse events associated with heart block have occurred in the elderly.

Children: The safety and effectiveness of Tarka in children below the age of 18 have not been established. Therefore, use in this group is not recommended.

Lactation: Tarka is not recommended in these patients because of the potential for adverse reactions in nursing infants. The verapamil component of Tarka is secreted in human milk. Following administration of radio-labeled trandolapril to lactating rats, radioactivity has been detected in the milk.

Labor and Delivery: It is not known whether the use of verapamil during labor or delivery has immediate or delayed adverse effects on the fetus, or whether it prolongs the duration of labor or increases the need for forceps delivery or other obstetric intervention.

Drug Interactions: As with all drugs, care should be exercised when treating patients with multiple medications. Calcium channel blockers undergo biotransformation by the cytochrome P450 system. Coadministration of verapamil with other drugs which follow the same route of biotransformation may result in altered bioavailability of verapamil or these drugs. Dosages of similarly metabolized drugs, particularly those of low therapeutic ratio, and especially in patients with renal and/or hepatic impairment, may require adjustment when starting or stopping concomitantly administered verapamil to maintain optimum therapeutic blood levels.

Drugs known to be inhibitors of the cytochrome P450 system include: azole antifungals, cimetidine, cyclosporine, erythromycin, quinidine, terfenadine, warfarin.

Drugs known to be inducers of the cytochrome P450 system include: phenobarbital, phenytoin, rifampin.

Drugs known to be biotransformed via P450 include: benzodiazepines, flecainide, imipramine, propafenone, theophylline.

Alcohol: Verapamil may increase blood alcohol concentrations and prolong its effects. Alcohol enhances the bioavailability of ACE inhibitors.

Agents Causing Renin Release: The antihypertensive effect of trandolapril is augmented by antihypertensive agents that cause renin release (e.g., diuretics).

Agents Increasing Serum Potassium: Since trandolapril decreases aldosterone production, elevation of serum potassium may occur. Potassium sparing diuretics such as spironolactone, triamterene or amiloride, or potassium supplements should be given only for documented hypokalemia and with caution and frequent monitoring of serum potassium, since a significant increase in serum potassium could occur.

Salt substitutes which contain potassium should be used with caution.

Allopurinol, Cytostatic, Immunosuppressive Agents, Systemic Corticosteroids or Procainamide: Concomitant administration with ACE-inhibitors may lead to an increased risk of leukopenia.

Antacids: Antacids decrease the bioavailability of ACE inhibitors (it is recommended to ingest these products separately).

Antidepressants/Major Tranquilizers: As with all antihypertensive agents, there is an elevated risk of orthostatic hypotension when combining Tarka with major tranquilizers or tricyclic antidepressants, such as imipramine.

Antineoplastic Agents: Verapamil inhibits P-glycoprotein mediated transport of antineoplastic agents out of tumor cells, resulting in their decreased metabolic clearance. Dosage adjustments of antineoplastic agents should be considered when verapamil is administered concomitantly.

ASA: Potential adverse reactions in terms of bleeding due to synergistic antiplatelet effects of ASA and verapamil should be taken into consideration in patients taking the 2 agents concomitantly.

β-Blockers: Concomitant therapy with β-adrenergic blockers and verapamil may result in additive negative effects on heart rate, atrioventricular conduction, and/or cardiac contractility.

Asymptomatic bradycardia (<36 beats/min) with a wandering atrial pacemaker has been observed in a patient receiving concomitant timolol (a β-adrenergic blocker) eye drops and oral verapamil.

Carbamazepine: The concomitant oral administration of verapamil and carbamazepine may potentiate the effects of carbamazepine neurotoxicity. Symptoms include nausea, diplopia, headache, ataxia or dizziness.

Cimetidine: The interaction between cimetidine and chronically administered verapamil has not been studied. Variable results on clearance have been obtained in acute studies of healthy volunteers; clearance of verapamil was either reduced or unchanged.

Concomitant Diuretic Therapy: Patients concomitantly taking antihypertensive therapy with diuretics, especially those on recently instituted diuretic therapy, may occasionally experience an excessive reduction of blood pressure after initiation of nondiuretic therapy. The possibility of hypotensive effects after initiation of antihypertensive therapy can be minimized by either discontinuing the diuretic or increasing salt intake (except in patients with heart failure) prior to initiation of antihypertensive therapy. If it is not possible to discontinue the diuretic, the initial dose of antihypertensive therapy should be reduced and the patient observed closely for several hours following initiation of therapy (see Warnings, Hypotension and Dosage).

Cyclosporine: Verapamil therapy may increase serum levels of cyclosporine.

Digoxin: Chronic verapamil treatment can increase serum digoxin levels by 50 to 75% during the first week of therapy, and this can result in digoxin toxicity. In patients with hepatic cirrhosis, the influence of verapamil on digoxin kinetics is magnified. Verapamil may reduce total body clearance and extrarenal clearance of digitoxin by 27% and 29%, respectively.

Maintenance digoxin doses should be reduced when verapamil is administered, and the patient should be carefully monitored to avoid over-or underdigitalization. Whenever overdigitalization is suspected, the daily dose of digoxin should be reduced or temporarily discontinued. Upon discontinuation of Tarka, the patient should be reassessed to avoid underdigitalization.

In one open-label study conducted in 8 healthy male volunteers, in which multiple therapeutic doses of both trandolapril and digoxin were administered, no changes were found in serum levels of trandolapril, trandolaprilat and digoxin. Pharmacodynamically, the combination had a synergistic effect on left ventricular functions, as evidenced by the improvement in systolic time-intervals.

Disopyramide: Data on possible interactions between verapamil and disopyramide are not available. Therefore, disopyramide should not be administered within 48 hours before or 24 hours after Tarka administration.

Flecainide: A study of healthy volunteers showed that the concomitant administration of flecainide and verapamil may have additive effects on myocardial contractility, AV conduction, and repolarization. Concomitant therapy with flecainide and Tarka may result in additive negative inotropic effect and prolongation of AV conduction.

Inhalation Anesthetics: Animal experiments have shown that inhalation anesthetics depress cardiovascular activity by decreasing the inward movement of calcium ions. When used concomitantly, inhalation anesthetics and calcium antagonists, such as verapamil, should be titrated carefully to avoid excessive hemodynamic effects.

Lithium: Increased sensitivity to the effects of lithium (neurotoxicity) has been reported during concomitant verapamil-lithium therapy with either no change or an increase in serum lithium levels.

Increased serum lithium levels and symptoms of lithium toxicity have been reported in patients receiving concurrently ACE inhibitors and lithium.

Lithium based drugs should be administered with caution, and frequent monitoring of serum lithium levels is recommended. If a diuretic is also used, the risk of lithium toxicity may be further increased.

Neuromuscular Blocking Agents: Clinical data and animal studies suggest that verapamil may potentiate the activity of neuromuscular blocking agents (curare-like and depolarizing). It may, therefore, be necessary to decrease the dose of verapamil and/or the dose of the neuromuscular blocking agent when the drugs are used concomitantly.

Nitrates: No cardiovascular adverse events have been attributed to any interaction between nitrates and verapamil.

Nonsteroidal Anti-inflammatory Agents: The antihypertensive effects of ACE inhibitors may be reduced with concomitant administration of nonsteroidal anti-inflammatory agents. The combination of trandolapril with nonsteroidal anti-inflammatory agents predisposes to a risk of hyperkalemia particularly in cases of renal failure.

Phenobarbital: Phenobarbital therapy may increase the clearance of verapamil.

Quinidine: In a small number of patients with hypertrophic cardiomyopathy, concomitant use of verapamil and quinidine resulted in significant hypotension. Until further data are obtained, combined therapy of Tarka and quinidine in patients with hypertrophic cardiomyopathy should be avoided.

The electrophysiological effects of quinidine and verapamil on AV conduction were studied in 8 patients. Verapamil significantly counteracted the effects of quinidine on AV conduction. There has been a report of increased quinidine levels during verapamil therapy.

Rifampin: Therapy with rifampin may markedly reduce oral verapamil bioavailability.

Sulfinpyrazone: Increased clearance and decreased bioavailability of verapamil may occur when administered concomitantly with sulfinpyrazone.

Theophylline: Tarka therapy may inhibit the clearance and increase the plasma levels of theophylline, due to verapamil.

Tarka (cont'd)

Warfarin: In a multi-dose placebo-controlled pharmacodynamic study in healthy volunteers, the anticoagulant effect of warfarin was not significantly changed by trandolapril.

Adverse Effects: The combination of trandolapril and verapamil SR has been evaluated in over 1 957 subjects and patients. Of these, 541 patients (including 23% elderly patients) participated in North American placebo-controlled clinical trials, and 251 were studied in European placebo-controlled clinical trials. This combination has been evaluated for long-term safety in 272 patients treated for 1 year or more.

The most frequent adverse events in controlled clinical trials conducted in North America with trandolapril and verapamil SR were (n=541): first degree AV block (3.9%); cough (4.6%); constipation (3.3%) and dizziness (3.1%).

The most serious adverse reactions with Tarka are second degree AV block, angina, hypotension and angioedema.

Discontinuation of therapy because of adverse events in North American placebo-controlled hypertension studies was required in 2.6% and 1.9% of patients treated with Tarka and placebo, respectively.

Hypotension: In hypertensive patients in North American controlled and uncontrolled trials, hypotension occurred in 0.6% and near syncope occurred in 0.1% (possibly, probably or definitely related to combination treatment). Hypotension or syncope was a cause for discontinuation of therapy in 0.4% of hypertensive patients in North American controlled studies (see Warnings, Hypotension).

Adverse experiences occurring more commonly with combination therapy than placebo in 1% or more of the 541 patients in North American placebo-controlled hypertension trials are shown in Table I.

Table I—Tarka

Adverse Events in North American Placebo-controlled Trials

	Tarka (N=541) % Incidence (% Discontinuance)	Placebo (N=206) % Incidence (% Discontinuance)
AV Block, First Degree	3.9 (0.2)	0.5 (0.0)
Bradycardia	1.8 (0.0)	0.0 (0.0)
Bronchitis	1.5 (0.0)	0.5 (0.0)
Chest Pain	2.2 (0.0)	1.0 (0.0)
Constipation	3.3 (0.0)	1.0 (0.0)
Cough	4.6 (0.0)	2.4 (0.0)
Diarrhea	1.5 (0.2)	1.0 (0.0)
Dizziness	3.1 (0.0)	1.9 (0.5)
Dyspnea	1.3 (0.4)	0.0 (0.0)
Edema	1.3 (0.0)	2.4 (0.0)
Fatigue	2.8 (0.4)	2.4 (0.0)
Increased Liver Enzymes*	2.8 (0.2)	1.0 (0.0)
Nausea	1.5 (0.2)	0.5 (0.0)
Pain Extremity(ies)	1.1 (0.2)	0.5 (0.0)
Pain Joint(s)	1.7 (0.0)	1.0 (0.0)

* Also includes increase in ALT, AST, alkaline phosphatase.

Other clinical adverse experiences possibly, probably, or definitely related to drug treatment, occurring in 0.3% or more of patients treated with Tarka in controlled, or uncontrolled trials (N=990) and less frequent, clinically significant events (in italics) include the following: Cardiovascular: angina, *second degree AV block, bundle branch block*, edema, flushing, hypotension, *myocardial infarction*, palpitations, premature ventricular contractions, nonspecific ST-T changes, near syncope, tachycardia.

CNS: drowsiness, *hypesthesia, insomnia, loss of balance, paresthesia, vertigo*.

Dermatologic: *pruritus*, rash.

Emotional, Mental, Sexual States: anxiety, impotence, *abnormal mentation*.

Eye, Ear, Nose, Throat: *epistaxis, tinnitus*, upper respiratory tract infection, *blurred vision*.

Gastrointestinal: dyspepsia, dry mouth, nausea.

General Body Function: chest pain, malaise, weakness.

Genitourinary: *endometriosis, hematuria, nocturia, polyuria, proteinuria*.

Hemopoietic: decreased leukocytes, *decreased neutrophils*.

Metabolism and Endocrine Function: increased alkaline phophatase, increased liver enzymes, increased potassium, increased AST.

Musculoskeletal System: arthralgia, myalgia, *gout, increased uric acid*.

Pulmonary: dyspnea.

Angioedema: Angioedema and/or facial edema has been reported in 3 (0.15%) patients receiving Tarka in North American and European studies (N=1 957). Angioedema associated with laryngeal edema may be fatal. If angioedema of the face, extremities, lips, tongue, glottis, and/or larynx occurs, treatment with Tarka should be discontinued and appropriate therapy instituted immediately (see Warnings, Angioedema).

In addition to those reported above, other adverse experiences have previously been reported with the individual components, verapamil and trandolapril: Verapamil Component Adverse Reactions: Cardiovascular: CHF/pulmonary edema, third degree AV block, atrioventricular dissociation, claudication, syncope (see Warnings, Hypotension).

Digestive: nausea, gingival hyperplasia, reversible paralytic ileus.

Hemic and Lymphatic: ecchymosis or bruising.

Nervous System: cerebrovascular accident, confusion, psychotic symptoms, shakiness, somnolence.

Skin: exanthema, hair loss, hyperkeratosis, purpura (vasculitis), sweating, urticaria, Stevens-Johnson syndrome, erythema multiforme.

Urogenital: gynecomastia, galactorrhea/hyperprolactinemia, increased urination, spotty menstruation.

Trandolapril Component Adverse Reactions: Body as a Whole: asthenia, abnormal feeling, abdominal pain, pain in extremities.

Cardiovascular: hypertension, migraine, syncope.

Dermatology: urticaria, pemphigus, Stevens-Johnson syndrome.

Gastrointestinal: gastrointestinal pain, gastrointestinal disorder, anorexia, abnormal liver function test, vomiting.

Nervous System: depression, sleep disorder, decreased libido, hot flushes.

Respiratory: bronchitis, pharyngitis.

Other: cramps, increased urinary frequency, edema, taste disorders, anaphylactoid reaction.

A symptom complex has been reported which may include fever, vasculitis, myalgia, arthralgia/arthritis, a positive ANA, elevated ESR, eosinophilia and leukocytosis. Rash, photosensitivity or other dermatologic manifestations may also occur.

Clinical Laboratory Testing Findings: Hematology: leukopenia, neutropenia, lymphopenia, thrombocytopenia (see Warnings, Neutropenia/Agranulocytosis).

Serum Electrolytes: hyperkalemia (see Precautions, Hyperkalemia and Potassium-sparing Diuretics), hyponatremia.

Renal Function Tests: Increases in creatinine and blood urea nitrogen levels occurred in 1.1% and 0.3%, respectively, of patients receiving Tarka with or without hydrochlorothiazide therapy. None of these increases required discontinuation of treatment. Increases in these laboratory values are more likely to occur in patients with renal insufficiency or those pretreated with a diuretic and, based on experience with other ACE inhibitors, would be expected to be especially likely in patients with renal artery stenosis (see Precautions, Patients with Renal Impairment).

Liver Function Tests: Elevations of liver enzymes (AST, ALT, LDH, and alkaline phosphatase) and/or serum bilirubin occurred. Discontinuation for elevated liver enzymes occurred in 0.9% of patients (see Warnings, Elevated Liver Enzymes/Hepatic Failure).

Overdose: Symptoms and Treatment: To date, there have been no reports of overdosage of Tarka in humans. Given this absence of practical experience with overdosage, the following is a synopsis of experiences gained with the individual monocomponents; mainly with verapamil.

Verapamil Overdosage: Based on reports of intentional overdosage of verapamil, the following symptoms have been observed. Hypotension occurs, varying from transient to severe. Conduction disturbances seen included: prolongation of AV conduction time, AV dissociation, nodal rhythm, ventricular fibrillation and ventricular asystole.

Treatment of overdosage should be supportive. Gastric lavage should be undertaken, even later than 12 hours after ingestion, if no gastrointestinal motility is present. β-adrenergic stimulation or parenteral administration of calcium solutions may increase calcium ion influx across the slow channel.

These pharmacologic interventions have been effectively used in treatment of overdosage with verapamil. Clinically significant hypotensive reactions should be treated with vasopressor agents. AV block is treated with atropine and cardiac pacing. Asystole should be handled by the usual Advanced Cardiac Life Support measures including the use of vasopressor agents, e.g., isoproterenol HCl. Verapamil is not removed by hemodialysis.

In case of overdosage with large amounts of verapamil SR it should be noted that the release of the active drug and the absorption in the intestine may take more than 48 hours. Depending on the time of ingestion, incompletely dissolved tablets may be present along the entire length of the gastrointestinal tract which function as active drug depots. Extensive elimination measures are indicated, such as induced vomiting, removal of the contents of the stomach and the small intestine under endoscopy, intestinal lavage and high enemas.

Actual treatment and dosage should depend on the severity of the clinical situation and the judgment of the treating physician. Patients with hypertrophic cardiomyopathy treated with verapamil should not be administered positive inotropic agents marked by asterisks in Table II.

Trandolapril Overdosage: The most likely clinical manifestations of overdosage of trandolapril would be symptoms attributable to severe hypotension, which should normally be treated by i.v. volume expansion with normal saline. It is not known if trandolapril or trandolaprilat can be removed from the body by hemodialysis.

No data are available to suggest that physiological maneuvers (e.g., maneuvers to change pH of the urine) might accelerate elimination of trandolapril and its metabolites.

Dosage: Dosage must be individualized. The fixed combination is not for initial therapy. The dose of Tarka should be determined by titration of the individual components.

Tarka tablets should not be divided, crushed or chewed. Tarka should be taken with food (see Pharmacology, Effect of Food).

Once the patient has been successfully titrated with the individual components as described below, Tarka may be substituted if the titrated doses and dosing schedule can be achieved by the fixed combination (see Indications and Warnings, Hypotension). Tarka is available at doses of 1/180 mg, 2/180 mg and 4/240 mg of trandolapril and verapamil SR, respectively.

For Verapamil Monotherapy: The dosage should be individualized by titration depending on patient tolerance and responsiveness to verapamil. Titration should be based on therapeutic efficacy and safety, evaluated weekly and approximately 24 hours after the previous dose.

The usual initial adult dose is 180 to 240 mg/day. If required, the dose may be increased up to 240 mg twice a day. A maximum daily dose of 480 mg should not be exceeded.

Recommended dosing intervals for specific daily dosages are given in Table III (on following page).

Table II—Tarka

Suggested Treatment of Acute Cardiovascular Adverse Effects

Adverse Reaction	Proven Effective Treatment	Treatment with Good Theoretical Rationale	Supportive Treatment
Shock, cardiac failure, severe hypotension	Calcium salt e.g., calcium gluconate i.v.; i.v. metaraminol bitartrate*	I.V. dopamine HCl* I.V. dobutamine HCl*	I.V. fluids; Trendelenburg position
Bradycardia, AV block, asystole	I.V. isoproterenol HCl*; i.v. atropine sulfate; cardiac pacing		I.V. fluids (slow drip)
Rapid ventricular rate (due to antegrade conduction in flutter/fibrillation with WPW or LGL syndrome)	D.C. cardioversion (high energy may be required); i.v. procainamide; i.v. lidocaine HCl		I.V. fluids (slow drip)

Table III—Tarka

Recommended Dosing Intervals

Total Daily Verapamil SR Dose	**Recommended Dosing Intervals**
180 mg	Once each morning with food
240 mg	Once each morning with food
360 mg	180 mg each morning plus 180 mg each evening, with food or 240 mg each morning plus 120 mg each evening, with food
480 mg	240 mg each morning plus 240 mg each evening with food

The antihypertensive effects of verapamil SR are evident within the first week of therapy. Optimal doses are usually lower in patients also receiving diuretics since additive antihypertensive effects can be expected.

Geriatrics: Lower dosages of verapamil SR, i.e., 120 mg a day, may be warranted in elderly patients (i.e., 65 years and older). The dosage should be carefully and gradually adjusted depending on patient tolerability and response.

Patients with Hepatic and Renal Impairment: Verapamil SR should be administered cautiously to patients with liver or renal function impairment. The dosage should be carefully and gradually adjusted depending on patient tolerance and response. These patients should be monitored carefully for abnormal prolongation of the PR interval or other signs of overdosage. Verapamil SR should not be used in severe hepatic dysfunction (see Precautions, Patients with Hepatic Impairment).

Switching from Verapamil Tablets to Verapamil SR: When switching from verapamil tablets to verapamil SR, the total daily dose in mg may remain the same.

For Trandolapril Monotherapy: The recommended initial dosage for trandolapril is 1 mg once daily. Dosage should be adjusted according to blood pressure response at intervals of 2 to 4 weeks up to a maximum of 4 mg once daily. The usual maintenance dose is 1 to 2 mg once daily.

In some patients treated once daily, the antihypertensive effect may diminish toward the end of the dosing interval. This can be evaluated by measuring blood pressure just prior to dosing to determine whether satisfactory control is being maintained for 24 hours. If it is not, an increase in dose should be considered. If blood pressure is not controlled alone, a diuretic may be added.

Diuretic-treated Patients: Symptomatic hypotension occasionally may occur following the initial dose of trandolapril and is more likely in patients who are currently being treated with a diuretic. The diuretic should, if possible, be discontinued for 2 to 3 days before beginning therapy with trandolapril to reduce the likelihood of hypotension. If the diuretic cannot be discontinued, an initial dose of 0.5 mg trandolapril should be used with careful medical supervision for several hours and until blood pressure has stabilized. The dosage of trandolapril should subsequently be titrated to the optimal response.

Dosage in Renal Impairment: For patients with a creatinine clearance below 30 mL/min/1.73 m^2, the recommended initial dose is 0.5 mg trandolapril once daily. Dosage may be titrated upward until blood pressure is controlled or to a maximum total daily dose of 1 mg.

In patients with severe renal impairment (creatinine clearance below 10 mL/min/1.73 m^2) a daily dosage of 0.5 mg in a single dose should not be exceeded.

Hepatic Impairment: The recommended initial dose is 0.5 mg trandolapril once daily.

Geriatrics: In elderly patients with normal renal and hepatic function, no dosage adjustment is necessary.

However, as some elderly patients may be particularly susceptible to ACE inhibitors, administration of low initial doses and evaluation of the blood pressure response and of the renal function at the beginning of the treatment is recommended.

Supplied: 1/180 mg: Each yellow, oval, film-coated tablet embossed with the Knoll triangle mark and "181" on one side and "TARKA" on the other side, contains: trandolapril 1 mg in an immediate release form and verapamil HCl 180 mg in a sustained release form. Nonmedicinal ingredients: cornstarch, dioctyl sodium sulfosuccinate, ethanol, hydroxypropyl cellulose, hydroxypropyl methylcellulose, lactose, magnesium stearate, microcrystalline cellulose, polyethylene glycol, povidone, purified water, silicon dioxide, sodium alginate, sodium stearyl fumarate, synthetic iron oxides, talc and titanium dioxide. Bottles of 100.

2/180 mg: Each salmon, oval, film-coated tablet embossed with the Knoll triangle and "182" on one side and "TARKA" on the other side, contains: trandolapril 2 mg in an immediate release form and verapamil HCl 180 mg in a sustained release form. Nonmedicinal ingredients: cornstarch, dioctyl sodium sulfosuccinate, ethanol, hydroxypropyl cellulose, hydroxypropyl methylcellulose, lactose, magnesium stearate, microcrystalline cellulose, polyethylene glycol, povidone, purified water, silicon dioxide, sodium alginate, sodium stearyl fumarate, synthetic iron oxides, talc and titanium dioxide. Bottles of 100.

4/240 mg : Each reddish-brown, oval, film-coated tablet embossed with the Knoll triangle and "244" on one side and "TARKA" on the other side, contains: trandolapril 4 mg in an immediate release form and verapamil HCl 240 mg in a sustained release form. Nonmedicinal ingredients: cornstarch, dioctyl sodium sulfosuccinate, ethanol, hydroxypropyl cellulose, hydroxypropyl methylcellulose, lactose, magnesium stearate, microcrystalline cellulose, polyethylene glycol, povidone, purified water, silicon dioxide, sodium alginate, sodium stearyl fumarate, synthetic iron oxides, talc and titanium dioxide. Bottles of 100.

Store at 15 to 25°C. Protect from light and moisture. Do not use beyond the expiry date indicated on the label.

New Product 1998

TARO-CARBAMAZEPINE Ⓟ
Taro

Carbamazepine

Anticonvulsant—Trigeminal Neuralgia Therapy

Supplied: Taro-Carbamazepine: 200 mg: Each white, round, quadrisected, immediate-release tablet, engraved "TARO", contains: carbamazepine 200 mg. Nonmedicinal ingredients: magnesium stearate, microcrystalline cellulose, povidone, sodium lauryl sulfate and sodium starch glycolate. Gluten- and tartrazine-free. Bottles of 100 and 500.

Taro-Carbamazepine CR: 200 mg: Each white to off white, capsule shaped, controlled-release tablet, engraved "T12" on one side, scored on both sides, contains: carbamazepine 200 mg. Nonmedicinal ingredients: diethyl phthalate, lactose monohydrate, magnesium stearate, maize starch, microcrystalline cellulose and sodium starch glycolate. Gluten- and tartrazine-free. Bottles of 100 and 500.

400 mg: Each white to off white, capsule shaped, controlled-release tablet, engraved "T17" on one side, scored on both sides, contains: carbamazepine 400 mg. Nonmedicinal ingredients: diethyl phthalate, lactose monohydrate, magnesium stearate, maize starch, microcrystalline cellulose and sodium starch glycolate. Gluten- and tartrazine-free. Bottles of 100 and 500.

Protect from heat and humidity.

TARO GEL
Taro

Lubricant

Supplied: Non-Sterile: Each g contains: lubricating jelly composed of purified water, glycerin, propylene glycol, carbomer and sodium hydroxide to adjust pH. Tubes of 60 g.

Sterile: Each g contains: sterile lubricating jelly composed of purified water, glycerin, propylene glycol, carbomer and sodium hydroxide to adjust pH. Tubes of 125 g. Sterility is guaranteed unless tubes are damaged or opened.

Store at room temperature (15 to 30°C).

TARO-SONE Ⓟ
Taro

Betamethasone Dipropionate

Topical Corticosteroid

Supplied: Cream: Each g of cream contains: betamethasone 0.5 mg (as dipropionate USP) in a water miscible base of white petrolatum, mineral oil, cetostearyl alcohol, cetomacrogol 1 000, purified water, sodium phosphate monobasic, chlorocresol and propylene glycol with sodium hydroxide and phosphoric acid for pH correction. Tubes of 15 and 50 g. Jars of 450 g.

Lotion: Each g of lotion contains: betamethasone 0.5 mg (as dipropionate USP) in a lotion base of isopropyl alcohol, purified water, carbomer and sodium hydroxide. Squeeze bottles of 30 and 75 mL.

Ointment: Each g of ointment contains: betamethasone 0.5 mg (as dipropionate USP) in an ointment base of white petrolatum and mineral oil. Tubes of 15 and 50 g. Jars of 450 g.

TASMAR™ Ⓟ
Roche

Tolcapone

Antiparkinsonian—COMT-inhibitor

Pharmacology: Tolcapone is a selective and reversible inhibitor of catechol-O-methyltransferase (COMT).

COMT catalyzes the transfer of the methyl group of S-adenosyl-L-methionine to the phenolic group of substrates that contain a catechol structure. Physiological substrates of COMT include dopa, catecholamines (dopamine, norepinephrine, epinephrine) and their hydroxylated metabolites. The function of COMT is the elimination of biologically active catechols and some other hydroxylated metabolites. In the presence of a decarboxylase inhibitor, COMT becomes the major enzyme which is responsible for the metabolism of levodopa to 3-methoxy-4-hydroxy-L-phenylalanine (3-OMD).

The mechanism of action of tolcapone is believed to be related to its ability to inhibit COMT and thereby alter the plasma pharmacokinetics of levodopa. When tolcapone is given in conjunction with levodopa and an aromatic amino acid decarboxylase inhibitor (AADC-I), such as carbidopa or benserazide, plasma levels of levodopa are more sustained than after the administration of levodopa and an AADC-I alone. The sustained plasma levels of levodopa result in more constant dopaminergic stimulation in the brain, leading to greater effects on the signs and symptoms of Parkinson's disease as well as increased levodopa adverse effects, requiring a decrease in the daily dose of levodopa.

There is some evidence that high levels of plasma 3-OMD are associated with poor response to levodopa in patients with Parkinson's disease. Tolcapone markedly reduces the plasma levels of 3-OMD.

Pharmacodynamics: Effect of Tolcapone on Erythrocyte COMT Activity: Studies in healthy volunteers have shown that tolcapone reversibly inhibits human erythrocyte COMT activity after oral administration. The inhibition is dose-related and tolerance does not develop to this effect. With a 200 mg single dose of tolcapone, maximum inhibition of erythrocyte COMT activity was approximately 80%. During repeated dosing with tolcapone (200 mg t.i.d.), erythrocyte COMT inhibition was 30 to 45% at trough tolcapone plasma concentrations.

Effect of Tolcapone on the Pharmacokinetics of Levodopa and 3-OMD: When tolcapone is administered together with levodopa/AADC-I (carbidopa or benserazide), it increases the relative bioavailability (AUC) of levodopa by approximately 2-fold. This is due to a decrease in levodopa clearance resulting in a prolongation of its terminal elimination half-life ($t_{1/2\beta}$). In healthy, elderly volunteers (n=36, age: 55 to 75 years), the terminal elimination half-life of levodopa increased from 1.9 hours in placebo-treated subjects to 3.2 hours in subjects treated with tolcapone, 200 mg t.i.d. Average peak levodopa plasma concentration (C_{max}) and the time of its occurrence (t_{max}) were unaffected. The onset of effect of tolcapone occurred after its first administration.

Population pharmacokinetic analyses in patients with Parkinson's disease have corroborated the effects of tolcapone on the pharmacokinetics of levodopa shown in healthy volunteers. During long-term clinical trials, tolcapone increased the relative bioavailability of levodopa, prolonged its elimination half-life, and thus, reduced the fluctuations in levodopa plasma concentrations (C_{max}-C_{min}).

Studies in healthy volunteers and in patients with Parkinson's disease have confirmed that (a) maximal effects occur with the 100 and 200 mg doses of tolcapone, given t.i.d., and (b) tolcapone given in combination with levodopa/AADC-I, decreases markedly and dose-dependently the plasma levels of 3-OMD.

The effect of tolcapone, on the pharmacokinetics of levodopa, was similar with all pharmaceutical formulations of levodopa/carbidopa and levodopa/benserazide, and was independent of the dose of levodopa.

Tasmar (cont'd)

Pharmacokinetics: Volunteers: The pharmacokinetics of tolcapone were linear in young volunteers over the single dose range of 50 to 400 mg and in elderly volunteers at the therapeutic doses (100 and 200 mg t.i.d.), and were independent of levodopa/AADC-I (carbidopa or benserazide) coadministration. The elimination half-life was 2 to 3 hours. Accumulation was not seen during t.i.d. dosing.

Patients With Parkinson's Disease: Population pharmacokinetic analyses indicated that the pharmacokinetics of tolcapone in patients with Parkinson's disease were in agreement with those observed in healthy volunteers. In a dose range of 50 to 400 mg t.i.d., the exposure to tolcapone was dose proportional. The mean C_{max} and AUC values at the 200 mg t.i.d. dose were 6 μg/mL and 25.1 μg•h/mL, respectively. The pharmacokinetic behavior of tolcapone was stable during long-term treatment. AUC values were similar in fluctuating and nonfluctuating patients. The elimination half-life of tolcapone was somewhat longer in patients than in volunteers, i.e., approximately 4 to 8 hours. Gender and age did not seem to affect the pharmacokinetics of tolcapone.

Absorption: Tolcapone is rapidly absorbed with a t_{max} of approximately 2 hours. The absolute bioavailability following oral administration is about 65%. In clinical trials, there were no restrictions as to how the drug was taken in relation to meals. Population pharmacokinetic studies indicated that while food delayed the absorption of tolcapone, its relative bioavailability was still 80 to 90% when the drug was taken within 1 hour before and 2 hours after meals.

Distribution and Protein Binding: The volume of distribution (V_{ss}) of tolcapone in healthy volunteers after i.v. administration was small (9 L). In patients, a higher volume of distribution (15 to 35 L) was estimated after oral dosing. Tolcapone does not distribute widely into tissues due to its high plasma protein binding. The plasma protein binding of tolcapone is >99.9% over the concentration range of 0.32 to 30 μg/mL. At clinical doses, mean C_{max} values were <10 μg/mL at the 200 mg dose. In vitro experiments have shown that tolcapone binds mainly to serum albumin.

Metabolism/Elimination: Tolcapone is almost completely metabolized prior to excretion, with only a very small amount (0.5% of dose) found unchanged in urine. The main metabolic pathway of tolcapone is conjugation to its inactive glucuronide. In addition, the compound is methylated by COMT to 3-O-methyl-tolcapone and metabolized by cytochromes P450 3A4 and P450 2A6 to a primary alcohol (hydroxylation of the 4' methyl group), which is subsequently oxidized to the carboxylic acid. Reduction to a putative amine, as well as the subsequent N-acetylation, occur to a minor extent. After oral administration of ^{14}C-labeled tolcapone, 60% of the labeled material is excreted in urine, and 40% in feces. More than 50% of the labeled dose of tolcapone is identified as 8 metabolites. Numerous additional metabolites account for the rest, none of them exceeding 5% of dose.

Tolcapone is a low-extraction-ratio drug (extraction ratio = 0.15), with a moderate systemic clearance of about 7 L/hour.

Hepatic Impairment: A study in patients with hepatic impairment has shown that moderate noncirrhotic liver disease did not affect the pharmacokinetics of tolcapone. However, in patients with moderate cirrhotic liver disease, clearance and volume of distribution of unbound tolcapone were reduced by 44% and 35%, respectively, when compared to values seen in demographically matched healthy volunteers. Since the reduction in clearance may increase the average concentration of unbound tolcapone approximately 2-fold, special dosing recommendations are given for patients with moderate cirrhotic liver disease (see Dosage).

In patients with moderate liver cirrhosis, the C_{max} and AUC of tolcapone glucuronide increased substantially (AUC values were 7.4 μg•h/mL in healthy volunteers, 20 μg•h/mL in subjects with noncirrhotic liver disease, and 52 μg•h/mL in subjects with cirrhotic liver disease). However, since tolcapone glucuronide is inactive and since this metabolic pathway is irreversible, it is unlikely that the changes will be clinically significant.

Renal Impairment: A specific study to evaluate the pharmacokinetics of tolcapone in patients with renal impairment has not been carried out. However, population pharmacokinetic analysis has shown in more than 400 patients that the clearance of tolcapone was not affected in a clinically meaningful way when creatinine clearance was > 30 mL/min. This could be explained by the fact that only a negligible amount of unchanged tolcapone is excreted in the urine, and the main metabolite, tolcapone-glucuronide, is excreted both in urine and bile (feces).

Drug Interactions: Studies Assessing Potential Drug Interactions: Effect of Tolcapone on the Pharmacokinetics of Other Drugs: Protein Binding: Although tolcapone is highly protein-bound, in vitro studies have shown that tolcapone, at 50 μg/mL (approximately 5-fold higher than therapeutic concentrations) did not displace other highly protein-bound drugs at therapeutic concentrations, like warfarin (0.5 to 7.2 μg/mL), phenytoin (7.9 to 38.7 μg/mL), tolbutamide (24.5 to 96.1 μg/mL), or digitoxin (9.0 to 27.0 μg/mL) from their binding sites.

Cytochrome P450 Metabolism: The effect of tolcapone on the metabolism of various drugs has been investigated utilizing human liver microsome preparations. Although tolcapone is not metabolized via CYP2C9, its affinity for the enzyme was greater than those of tolbutamide and diclofenac; consequently, tolcapone decreased the formation of their hydroxy metabolites in vitro. However, in a clinical study in healthy volunteers tolcapone did not affect either the pharmacokinetics or the hypoglycemic effect of tolbutamide. In vitro interaction between tolcapone and warfarin, a substrate of CYP2C9 was not evaluated. Since clinical information is limited regarding a potential interaction between these two drugs, coagulation parameters should be monitored when they are given concomitantly (see Precautions).

No relevant interactions were observed in vitro between tolcapone and substrates of CYP2A6 (coumarin), CYP1A2 (caffeine), CYP3A4 (midazolam, terfenadine, cyclosporin), CYP2C19 (S-mephenytoin) and CYP2D6 (desipramine).

Effect of Drugs on the Metabolism of Tolcapone: Glucuronidation: The major route of elimination of tolcapone is by glucuronidation. In vitro studies with desipramine and naproxen, drugs which are highly protein-bound and are metabolized via glucuronidation, did not indicate interference with tolcapone glucuronidation.

Cytochrome P450 Metabolism: Although under in vitro conditions midazolam, which is metabolized by CYP3A4, competed with the formation of the hydroxy metabolite of tolcapone, the fraction of tolcapone, which is metabolized by this isozyme, represents a minor metabolic pathway and no significant interactions are expected under clinical conditions.

Clinical Trials: Up to April 1, 1996, 1 685 patients have been exposed to tolcapone, with 647 patients being exposed for over a year and 117 patients being exposed for over 2 years.

The effectiveness of tolcapone, as an adjunct to levodopa/AADC-I (carbidopa or benserazide) therapy in the treatment of Parkinson's disease, was demonstrated in randomized placebo-controlled trials in patients who experienced end of dose wearing off phenomena (fluctuating patients) and in patients whose response to levodopa was relatively stable (nonfluctuating patients). The majority of the patients in the clinical trials were at stages 1.5 to 2.5 on the Hoehn and Yahr scale and only limited experience is available in patients who were at stage 4 on the Hoehn and Yahr scale.

Adjunct Therapy in Fluctuating Patients: In three phase III multicentre placebo-controlled studies, patients with documented episodes of wearing off phenomena, despite optimal levodopa therapy, were randomized to receive placebo (n=196) or tolcapone at doses of 100 mg t.i.d. (n=198) or 200 mg t.i.d. (n=200). The primary outcome measure was a comparison between treatments in the change from baseline in the amount of time spent off/on (based upon patient diaries recording time "on" and "off"). The formal double-blind portion of the trial was 3 months (2 of the studies) or 6 weeks (1 study). Based on a 16-hour waking day, the decreases in off time versus baseline ranged between 0.3 to 1.2, 1.9 to 2.1 and 1.6 to 2.9 hours in the placebo, 100 mg t.i.d. and 200 mg t.i.d. groups, respectively. Expressed as percentages, the decreases in off time ranged between 5 to 19%, 29 to 34% and 27 to 49% in the placebo, 100 mg t.i.d. and 200 mg t.i.d. groups, respectively. The difference between the placebo and Tasmar groups was significant. The Investigator's Global Assessment of Change also showed a statistically significant improvement in tolcapone-treated patients. In addition, the total daily dose of levodopa was significantly reduced in the tolcapone groups.

The improvement in off time, due to tolcapone treatment, was independent of the concomitant use of selegiline or dopamine agonist, the amount of slow-release-levodopa as a proportion of the total daily dose of levodopa, and the duration of levodopa therapy. There were no gender or age-related differences in effectiveness.

Adjunct Therapy in Nonfluctuating Patients: In a phase III multicentre study, 298 patients with Parkinson's disease on stable doses of levodopa/carbidopa, who were not experiencing wearing off phenomena, were randomized to placebo, tolcapone 100 mg t.i.d., or tolcapone 200 mg t.i.d. for 6 months. The primary measure of efficacy was the Activities of Daily Living (ADL) subscale of the UPDRS (Unified Parkinson's Disease Rating Scale). Mean ADL scores did not change in the placebo group while they decreased by 18 and 21% in patients treated with 100 mg t.i.d. or 200 mg t.i.d. of tolcapone, respectively. The differences between the placebo and tolcapone groups were significant. In nonfluctuating patients, the mean daily doses of levodopa at baseline were relatively low, namely 364 mg, 370 mg, and 382 mg in the placebo, 100 mg t.i.d. and 200 mg t.i.d. tolcapone groups, respectively. At 6 months, the mean daily dose of levodopa increased by 46.6 mg in the placebo group while it decreased in the tolcapone groups (100 mg t.i.d.: -20.8 mg; 200 mg t.i.d.: -32.3 mg). The difference between the placebo and tolcapone groups was significant. In tolcapone-treated patients the total scores and motor scores (subscale III) of the UPDRS decreased by 11 to 13%, while decreases in the placebo-treated patients ranged between one to two percent. The difference was statistically significant.

The improvement in ADL, due to tolcapone treatment, was independent of concomitant use of selegiline and duration of levodopa therapy. There were no gender or age-related differences in effectiveness.

Indications: As an adjunct to levodopa/carbidopa and levodopa/benserazide for the treatment of the signs and symptoms of idiopathic Parkinson's disease. Since tolcapone should be used in combination with levodopa, the prescribing information for levodopa/carbidopa and levodopa/benserazide are also applicable when tolcapone is added to the treatment regimen.

Contraindications: Patients with known hypersensitivity to tolcapone or the excipients of the drug product.

Tolcapone should not be given in conjunction with nonselective monoamine oxidase (MAO) inhibitors (e.g., phenelzine and tranylcypromine). The combination of MAO-A and MAO-B inhibitors is equivalent to nonselective MAO inhibition; therefore, they should not both be given concomitantly with tolcapone and levodopa preparations. Selective MAO-B inhibitors should not be used at higher than recommended doses (e.g., selegiline 10 mg/day) when coadministered with tolcapone.

Precautions: Orthostatic Hypotension: The incidence of orthostatic hypotension was slightly higher in the tolcapone treatment groups than in the placebo group. Orthostatic hypotension at baseline was a predisposing factor; however, this was true for tolcapone and placebo-treated patients alike. Concomitant treatment with a dopamine agonist increased slightly the incidence of orthostatic hypotension in the 200 mg t.i.d. tolcapone group (17% versus 11% in the presence and absence of a dopamine agonist, respectively). Syncope and falling occurred with a higher incidence in patients who had orthostatic hypotension (at the 200 mg t.i.d. dose, syncope was 10.3% versus 4.2%, falling was 10.3% versus 5.4% in patients with or without orthostatic hypotension, respectively). Gender and age had no apparent effect on the rates of orthostatic hypotension.

Dyskinesia: In patients treated with tolcapone, dyskinesia was the most common adverse event. Dyskinesia was dose-related and much more prevalent in fluctuating than nonfluctuating patients (see Adverse Effects). Concomitant treatment with selegiline, dopamine agonists and controlled-release levodopa (>70% of the daily dose) increased the incidence of dyskinesia. Although decreasing the dose of levodopa may ameliorate this adverse event, many patients in the controlled clinical trials continued to experience dyskinesia.

Hallucinations: The incidence of hallucinations was higher in the tolcapone groups than in the placebo group, it occurred in a dose-related manner and was more prevalent in the fluctuating than nonfluctuating patients (see Adverse Effects). Patients who had this adverse event prior to initiating tolcapone treatment and those with a pretreatment levodopa dose of >750 mg/day, had a higher rate of hallucinations. Hallucinations were commonly accompanied by confusion.

Diarrhea: Diarrhea was the most common nondopaminergic adverse reaction associated with tolcapone treatment. In the clinical trials, diarrhea developed in 16% and 18% of patients receiving tolcapone, at 100 and 200 mg t.i.d. doses, respectively, compared to 8% of patients receiving placebo. In some of the patients diarrhea was persistent and severe. Diarrhea was also the adverse reaction which most commonly led to discontinuation of treatment with 1.0, 5.4 and 6% of patients treated with placebo, 100 mg and 200 mg tolcapone t.i.d., respectively, withdrawing from the trials prematurely. Diarrhea usually started during the second, third or fourth month of treatment but may appear as early as 2 weeks and as late as many months after the initiation of treatment. Tolcapone-induced diarrhea was generally described as watery. The mechanism underlying the diarrhea has not yet been elucidated. In the clinical trials, diarrhea observed during tolcapone treatment was sometimes associated with anorexia (decreased appetite).

Elevated Liver Transaminases: An increase of liver transaminases (ALT and/or AST) to more than 3 times the upper limit of normal (ULN) occurred in 1.7 and 3.1% of patients receiving tolcapone at 100 mg and 200 mg t.i.d. doses, respectively. Increases to more than 8 times the ULN occurred in 0.3 and 0.7% of patients at the 100 mg and 200 mg t.i.d. doses, respectively. The incidence of elevated liver transaminases was higher in females than males (4.8% versus 1.5%). Approximately one third of patients with elevated enzymes had diarrhea. Elevated liver enzymes led to discontinuation of treatment in 0.3 and 1.7% of patients treated with tolcapone, 100 mg and 200 mg t.i.d., respectively. The majority of cases of elevated liver transaminases occurred 1 to 6 months after starting treatment, although elevated levels were seen at earlier times as well. In about half of the cases, transaminase levels returned to pretreatment levels within 1 to 3 months while patients continued treatment with tolcapone. In patients who discontinued treatment, transaminase levels generally declined within 2 to 3 weeks but it may take as long as 1 to 2 months to return to normal.

Liver transaminase levels should be determined prior to initiating treatment with tolcapone and monitored approximately every 6 weeks for the first 6 months. If elevations occur during this period, and the decision is made to continue treatment, monitoring of liver enzymes is recommended at approximately 2-week intervals. If transaminase levels keep on increasing or if clinical jaundice develops, treatment should be discontinued.

Neuroleptic Malignant Syndrome (NMS): This rare and potentially life-threatening syndrome is characterized by muscular rigidity, elevated temperature and altered consciousness associated with elevated serum creatine phosphokinase (CPK). The syndrome has been reported in association with rapid dose reduction, withdrawal of, or changes in treatment with dopaminergic antiparkinson therapy.

There have been 4 cases of NMS during tolcapone treatment. Three of the cases involved females (aged 74, 65 and 54 years), all these patients were Japanese. The fourth case involved a Caucasian male, aged 64 years. All patients were receiving levodopa/AADC-I and dopamine agonist treatment. The time of NMS, with respect to treatment with tolcapone, varied greatly, namely it occurred after 153, 99, 15 and 362 days. In all cases, CPK levels and WBC counts were markedly elevated, mild to moderate fever was also present. Two of the 4 patients had muscle rigidity. One of the female patients died due to respiratory failure, the other patients recovered. The investigators considered all cases to be probably related to tolcapone treatment.

If tolcapone is discontinued, physicians should consider increasing the patient's daily levodopa dose (see Dosage).

Urine Discoloration: Tolcapone and its metabolites are yellow and can cause a harmless intensification in the color of the patient's urine.

Special Populations: Renal/Hepatic Impairment: No information is available on the tolerability of tolcapone in patients with severe renal impairment (creatinine clearance <30 mL/min) (see Pharmacology, Pharmacokinetics and Metabolism). These patients should be treated with caution.

In patients with moderate cirrhotic liver disease, the clearance of unbound tolcapone is substantially reduced and the concentration of unbound drug increased approximately 2-fold (see Pharmacology, Pharmacokinetics and Metabolism). These patients should receive only the lower recommended dose of tolcapone (see Dosage).

Women: During tolcapone treatment, some adverse events occurred with a higher incidence in women than men. They included nausea, anorexia, diarrhea and elevated liver transaminases.

Geriatrics: During tolcapone treatment, some adverse events occurred with a higher incidence in patients over 75 years of age (n=95) compared to younger patients. They included diarrhea and hallucinations.

Carcinogenesis: Carcinogenicity studies, in which tolcapone was administered in the diet for 104 weeks, were conducted in rats. The doses were approximately 50, 250 and 450 mg/kg/day. In male rats, tolcapone exposures (in terms of AUC) were 1, 6.3 and 13 times the maximal human exposure; in female rats, tolcapone exposures (in terms of AUC) were 1.7, 11.8 and 26.4 times the maximal human exposure. There was evidence of renal tubular injury and renal tubular tumor formation. Minimal to marked damage to renal tubules, consisting of proximal tubule cell degeneration, single cell necrosis, hyperplasia and karyocytomegaly, occurred at the doses that were associated with renal tumors. A low incidence of renal tubular cell adenomas occurred in middle-and high-dose females and in high-dose males. The incidence of uterine adenocarcinomas was increased in high-dose female rats. In a 1-year toxicity study in rats, administered tolcapone at 150 and 450 mg/kg/day doses, renal tubule damage, characterized by proximal tubule cell degeneration and the presence of atypical nuclei, were observed. One adenocarcinoma in a high-dose male rat was also seen.

The carcinogenic potential of tolcapone in combination with levodopa/AADC-I has not been examined.

Pregnancy: The use of tolcapone during pregnancy is not recommended.

Tolcapone will always be given concomitantly with levodopa/AADC-I preparations which are known to cause visceral and skeletal malformations in the rabbit. The combination of tolcapone (100 mg/kg/day) with levodopa–carbidopa (80/20 mg/kg/day), produced an increased incidence of fetal malformations (primarily external and skeletal digit defects) compared to levodopa/carbidopa alone when pregnant rabbits were treated throughout organogenesis.

Tolcapone, when administered alone during organogenesis, was not teratogenic in rats at doses up to 300 mg/kg/day (5.7 times the recommended daily clinical dose of 600 mg on a mg/m² basis) or in rabbits at doses up to 400 mg/kg/day (15 times the recommended daily clinical dose of 600 mg on a mg/m² basis).

Lactation: In animal studies, tolcapone was excreted in maternal milk. It is not known whether tolcapone is excreted in human milk. Since the safety of tolcapone in infants is unknown, women should not breast-feed during treatment with tolcapone.

Children: Safety and efficacy of tolcapone have not been established in the pediatric population and use in patients below the age of 18 is not recommended.

Drug Interactions: Protein Binding: Although tolcapone is highly protein bound, in vitro studies have shown that at 50 μg/mL (approximately 5-fold higher than therapeutic concentrations), it did not displace warfarin, tolbutamide, digitoxin and phenytoin from their binding sites (see Pharmacology, Drug Interactions).

Drugs Metabolized by Catechol-O-methyltransferase (COMT): Tolcapone may influence the pharmacokinetics of drugs metabolized by COMT. No effects were seen on the pharmacokinetics of the COMT substrate carbidopa. However, an interaction was observed with benserazide, which may lead to increased levels of benserazide and its active metabolite. The magnitude of the effect depended upon the dose of benserazide. Plasma concentrations of benserazide, observed after co-administration of tolcapone and levodopa/benserazide, 100/25 mg, were still within the range of values observed with levodopa/benserazide alone. However, after the coadministration of tolcapone and levodopa/benserazide, 200/50 mg, benserazide plasma concentrations could be increased above the levels usually observed with levodopa/benserazide alone. The most prominent sign of benserazide toxicity is fatty liver degeneration in dogs. However, pharmacokinetic data indicate that the median AUC values of benserazide in dogs, at subtoxic doses, were considerably higher than AUC values seen in humans. A subanalysis of tolcapone safety in patients, receiving 25 mg versus 50 mg doses of benserazide, did not indicate different rates of occurrence of liver transaminase elevations.

The effect of tolcapone on the pharmacokinetics of other drugs metabolized by COMT, such as α-methyldopa, dobutamine, apomorphine, epinephrine and isoproterenol has not been evaluated. A dose reduction of such compounds should be considered when they are coadministered with tolcapone.

Effect of Tolcapone on the Metabolism of Other Drugs: Due to its in vitro affinity for cytochrome P450 2C9, tolcapone may interfere with drugs whose clearance is dependent on this metabolic pathway, such as tolbutamide and warfarin. In an interaction study (n=12 male volunteers, aged 21 to 39 years), tolcapone did not affect either the pharmacokinetics or the hypoglycemic effect of tolbutamide.

During clinical trials, 23 patients received a combination of warfarin and tolcapone and no particular pattern of adverse events was observed. However, since clinical experience is limited, coagulation parameters should be monitored when these drugs are coadministered.

Drugs that Increase Catecholamines: Tolcapone, in combination with Sinemet (n=12 male and female volunteers, aged 19 to 39 years), did not affect the pharmacokinetics of desipramine, a drug metabolized by cytochrome P450 2D6. While there were no significant changes in blood pressure or pulse rate, the frequency of adverse events, particularly dizziness, nausea and vomiting, increased. Therefore, caution should be exercised when potent norepinephrine reuptake inhibitors, such as desipramine, maprotiline or venlafaxine are administered to patients with Parkinson's disease who are being treated with tolcapone and levodopa preparations.

Tolcapone in combination with Sinemet (n=12 male and female volunteers, aged 21 to 30 years) had no effect on the hemodynamic parameters of ephedrine, an indirect acting sympathomimetic drug, either at rest or during exercise. Plasma levels of epinephrine and norepinephrine remained unchanged. Since tolcapone did not affect the tolerability of ephedrine, these drugs may be given concomitantly.

In clinical trials, patients receiving tolcapone/levodopa preparations reported a similar adverse event profile independent of whether or not they were also concomitantly administered selegiline (a selective MAO-B inhibitor).

Adverse Effects: Of the 1 685 patients, who received tolcapone during the premarketing clinical trials, 18.8% discontinued treatment due to adverse events. At the clinically recommended doses of tolcapone, in the placebo-controlled, phase III trials, 16.2% (48/296) and 15.4% (46/298) of patients discontinued treatment at the 100 and 200 mg t.i.d. doses, respectively, compared to 10.1% (30/298) of patients receiving placebo. The most common reason for withdrawal in the tolcapone groups was diarrhea, with 5% and 6% of patients withdrawing at the 100 and 200 mg t.i.d. doses, respectively, compared to 1% of patients receiving placebo.

Other adverse events which led to discontinuation of treatment in ≥1% of patients (placebo, 100 and 200 mg t.i.d., respectively) included nausea (2%, 1.7%, 2%), elevated liver transaminases (0%, 0.3%, 1.7%), hallucinations (0.3%, 1.4%, 1%), dyskinesia (0%, 0.3%, 1%), confusion (1%, 1.4%, 0.7%) and muscle cramps (1%, 1.4%, 0.3%).

The most commonly reported serious adverse events, defined as those requiring hospitalization (placebo, 100 and 200 mg t.i.d., respectively), included diarrhea (0.3%, 0.7%, 1.7%), dyskinesia (0.3%, 0.3%, 1.3%), and hallucinations (0%, 1.7%, 0%).

Of the 1 685 patients who received tolcapone, 4 patients experienced symptoms suggestive of Neuroleptic Malignant Syndrome (see Precautions and Dosage).

Incidence of Adverse Events in Placebo Controlled Trials: The most frequently observed adverse events, associated with the use of tolcapone were dyskinesia, nausea, sleep disorders, anorexia, dystonia and diarrhea (see Table I). Incidences were somewhat higher at the 200 mg t.i.d. dose. The incidence of dyskinesia, hallucination and confusion was considerably higher in fluctuating patients, while the incidence of nausea, vomiting and anorexia was higher in nonfluctuating patients (see Table II on following page). Orthostatic complaints and diarrhea occurred with similar frequencies in fluctuating and nonfluctuating patients.

Table I—Tasmar

Treatment Emergent Adverse Events (Rates ≥2% Higher During Tasmar Treatment Than During Placebo Treatment)

		Tasmar t.i.d.	
	Placebo N=298	**100 mg N=296**	**200 mg N=298**
Adverse Events	**%**	**%**	**%**
Dyskinesia	19.8	41.9	51.3
Nausea	17.8	30.4	34.9
Sleep Disorder	18.1	23.6	24.8
Anorexia	12.8	18.9	22.8
Dystonia	17.1	18.6	22.1
Diarrhea	7.7	15.5	18.1
Orthostatic Complaints*	13.8	16.6	16.8
Dreaming Excessive	17.1	21.3	16.4
Somnolence	13.4	17.9	14.4
Headache	7.4	9.8	11.4
Confusion	8.7	10.5	10.4
Hallucination	5.4	8.4	10.4
Vomiting	3.7	8.4	9.7
Constipation	5.0	6.4	8.4
Urine Discoloration	0.7	2.4	7.4
Upper Respiratory Tract Infection	3.4	4.7	7.4
Sweating Increased	2.3	4.4	7.4
Xerostomia	2.3	4.7	6.4
Dizziness	9.7	13.2	6.4
Abdominal Pain	2.7	4.7	5.7
Syncope	2.7	4.1	5.0
Influenza	1.7	3.0	4.0
Dyspepsia	1.7	4.1	3.0
Hypokinesia	0.7	0.7	2.7
Chest Pain	1.3	3.4	1.0

*Orthostatic complaints refer to experiences of dizziness and lightheadedness when standing.

Tasmar (cont'd)

Table II—Tasmar

Rates of Some Key Adverse Events in Fluctuating and Nonfluctuating Patients

Adverse Events	Fluctuating Placebo N=196 %	Fluctuating Tasmar t.i.d. 100 mg N=198 %	Fluctuating Tasmar t.i.d. 200 mg N=200 %	Nonfluctuating Placebo N=102 %	Nonfluctuating Tasmar t.i.d. 100 mg N=98 %	Nonfluctuating Tasmar t.i.d. 200 mg N=98 %
Dyskinesia	19.4	50.5	61.5	20.6	24.5	30.6
Hallucinations	7.7	11.1	14.0	1.0	3.1	3.1
Orthostatic Complaints	15.3	19.2	17.5	10.8	11.2	15.3
Confusion	10.7	12.1	14.0	4.9	7.1	3.1
Nausea	16.3	28.8	31.0	20.6	33.7	42.9
Vomiting	2.0	8.1	7.5	6.9	9.2	14.3
Anorexia	9.7	16.7	20.0	18.6	23.5	28.6
Diarrhea	9.7	10.6	18.0	3.9	25.5	18.4

Some of the most frequently reported adverse events (e.g., dyskinesia, nausea, orthostatic complaints, hallucinations, vomiting), which are considered levodopa-related, become enhanced in the presence of tolcapone. The highest risk of experiencing these dopaminergic adverse events occurred when tolcapone was first added to levodopa/AADC-I therapy, i.e., during the first few weeks of treatment. The prevalence rates tended to drop during the first 2 months, probably reflecting re-optimization of levodopa therapy. Therefore, a reduction in the dosage of levodopa may be necessary when initiating tolcapone treatment (see Dosage).

Laboratory Tests: Liver transaminases, ALT and AST, increased in a dose-dependent manner in tolcapone treated patients (see Precautions). The increases were observed within the first 6 months of treatment. In clinical trials, 0.3% and 1.7% of patients receiving tolcapone, at 100 and 200 mg t.i.d. doses, respectively, withdrew due to elevated liver transaminases. Slight increases in alkaline phosphatase or total bilirubin occurred in 20% and 10% of patients, respectively.

Liver transaminase levels should be monitored approximately every 6 weeks for the first 6 months of treatment with tolcapone. If elevations occur during this period, and the decision is made to continue treatment, monitoring of liver enzymes is recommended at approximately 2-week intervals. If transaminase levels keep on increasing or if clinical jaundice develops, treatment should be discontinued (see Precautions).

ECGs: In the course of the clinical trials, ventricular premature contractions were recorded in tolcapone treated patients but not in placebo treated patients. The incidence of ventricular premature contractions was 0.3 and 1.7% in patients treated with the 100 mg and 200 mg t.i.d. doses, respectively.

Adverse events reported by ≥1% of patients treated with tolcapone: Body as a Whole: fatigue, lethargy, peripheral edema, malaise, weight decrease, trauma, fever.

Nervous System: falling, tremor, loss of balance, hypoesthesia, hyperkinesia, paresthesia, paresis, speech disorder, burning, gait abnormal, vertigo, hyperactivity.

Psychiatric: depression, agitation, asthenia, emotional lability, anxiety, impotence, irritability, mental deficiency, panic reaction, hypertonia, euphoria.

Gastrointestinal: flatulence, abdominal discomfort.

Cardiovascular: hypotension, chest discomfort, palpitation.

Musculoskeletal: muscle cramps, back pain, arthralgia, pain in limbs, stiffness, neck pain, myalgia, arthritis.

Urogenital: urinary tract infection, micturition disorder, micturition frequency, urinary incontinence.

Skin and Appendages: rash, alopecia.

Respiratory: pneumonia, dyspnea, bronchitis, pharyngitis, sinusitis, sinus congestion.

Special Senses: tinnitus, taste alteration, cataract, vision blurred, eye inflamed.

Miscellaneous: tooth disorder, dermal bleeding, fractures, skin tumor, tumor of the uterus.

Additional adverse events are listed below. They include all adverse events that were reported in the overall clinical program for tolcapone. The events are enumerated using the following criteria: Infrequent: adverse events occur in less than 1% but at least 1/1 000 patients; Rare: adverse events occur in less than 1/1 000 patients.

Body as a Whole: Infrequent: hernia, pain, allergic reaction, cellulitis, fungal infection, viral infection, carcinoma, chills, abscess, face edema, joint edema.

Nervous System: Infrequent: neuralgia, memory disturbance, aggravated parkinsonism, sensory disturbance, migraine, neuropathy, cerebral ischemia, stroke. Rare: dementia, spasms.

Psychiatric: Infrequent: asthenia, aggressive reaction, paranoid reaction, delusion, nervousness. Rare: behavioral disturbances, libido disorder, compulsive reaction, personality disorder.

Gastrointestinal: Infrequent: dysphagia, gastrointestinal hemorrhage, gastrointestinal inflammation, oral canker sores, hernia inguinal, frequent bowel movements, esophagitis, hernia hiatal, tongue discoloration. Rare: appetite disturbances, tongue dryness.

Cardiovascular: Infrequent: hypertension, vasodilation, angina pectoris, heart failure, atrial fibrillation, tachycardia, aortic stenosis, arrythmia, arteriospasm, bradycardia, cerebral hemorrhage, coronary artery disorder, heart arrest, myocardial infarct, myocardial ischemia, pulmonary embolus. Rare: arteriosclerosis, cardiovascular disorder, pericardial effusion, thrombosis.

Musculoskeletal: Infrequent: sprains and strains, carpal tunnel syndrome, intervertebral disc disorder, bone spur, tendinitis. Rare: pathological fracture, leg discomfort, muscle disorder.

Urogenital: Infrequent: prostatic disorder, hematuria, urinary retention, urinary tract bleeding, dysuria, nocturia, polyuria, kidney calculus, vaginitis, enlarged prostate, bladder disorder. Rare: bladder calculus, ovarian carcinoma, uterine hemorrhage, kidney failure, abnormal renal function.

Skin and Appendages: Infrequent: herpes zoster, skin disorder, herpes simplex, erythema multiforme, pruritus, skin discoloration, cellulitis, seborrhea, eczema, furunculosis, urticaria.

Respiratory: Infrequent: increased cough, asthma, epistaxis, hyperventilation, rhinitis, laryngitis, dryness of pharynx, hiccup. Rare: lung edema, apnea, wheezing, hypoxia.

Special Senses: Infrequent: diplopia, ear pain, eye hemorrhage, eye pain, lacrimation disorder, otitis media, parosmia. Rare: glaucoma.

Metabolic and Nutritional: Infrequent: edema, hypercholesteremia, thirst, dehydration.

Miscellaneous: Infrequent: anemia, surgical procedure.

Overdose: Symptoms and Treatment: The highest dose of tolcapone administered to humans was 800 mg t.i.d., with and without levodopa coadministration. This was in a 1-week study in elderly, healthy volunteers. The peak plasma concentrations of tolcapone at this dose were on average 30 μg/mL (compared to 3 and 6 μg/mL with the 100 mg and 200 mg t.i.d. doses of tolcapone, respectively). Nausea, vomiting and dizziness were observed, particularly in combination with levodopa.

The threshold for the lethal plasma concentration for tolcapone based on animal data is >100 μg/mL. Respiratory difficulties were observed in rats at high oral (gavage) and i.v. doses and in dogs with rapidly injected i.v. doses.

Management of Overdose: Hospitalization is advised. General supportive care is indicated. Based on the physicochemical properties of the compound, hemodialysis is unlikely to be of benefit.

Dosage: Tolcapone is administered orally 3 times a day, as an adjunct to levodopa/AADC-I (carbidopa or benserazide) therapy. The first dose of the day should be taken together with the first dose of the day of a levodopa/AADC-I preparation, and the subsequent doses should be given approximately 6 and 12 hours later.

Tolcapone may be taken with or without food (see Pharmacology, Pharmacokinetics and Metabolism).

Tolcapone can be combined with all pharmaceutical formulations of levodopa/carbidopa and levodopa/benserazide.

Therapy with tolcapone should be initiated with 100 mg t.i.d. In clinical trials, the majority of patients required a decrease in daily levodopa dose if their daily dose of levodopa was >600 mg or if patients had moderate or severe dyskinesias.

After adjustment of levodopa dose, an increase to 200 mg tolcapone t.i.d. is recommended, if in the opinion of the physician further benefit may be expected without excessive dopaminergic adverse reactions. After increasing the dose of tolcapone to 200 mg t.i.d., a further readjustment of the dose of levodopa may be needed. In clinical trials, the average reduction in daily levodopa dose was about 30% in those patients who required a levodopa dose reduction. (Greater than 70% of patients with levodopa doses above 600 mg daily required such a reduction.)

The maximum therapeutic dose of 200 mg t.i.d. (600 mg/day) should not be exceeded since the safety and efficacy of higher doses have not been evaluated systematically and there is no evidence that higher doses provide any additional benefit.

Patients with Impaired Hepatic or Renal Function (see Pharmacology and Precautions): In patients with moderate to severe cirrhosis, the dose of tolcapone should be kept at 100 mg t.i.d. and not escalated to 200 mg t.i.d.

No dose adjustment of tolcapone is recommended for patients with mild to moderate renal impairment (creatinine clearance ≥30 mL/min). The safety of tolcapone has not been evaluated in patients whose creatinine clearance was <30 mL/min.

Discontinuation of Tolcapone: Due to the possibility for the occurrence of Neuroleptic Malignant Syndrome (NMS) upon a sudden decrease in the dose of dopaminergic drugs, including tolcapone (see Precautions), physicians should consider increasing the patient's levodopa dose if tolcapone is discontinued.

Information for the Patient: See Blue Section—Information for the Patient "Tasmar".

Supplied: 100 mg: Each pale to light yellow, hexagonal, biconvex, film-coated tablet, with "ROCHE" and "100" engraved on one side, contains: tolcapone 100 mg. Nonmedicinal ingredients: calcium hydrogen phosphate, ethylcellulose, hydroxypropyl methylcellulose, iron oxide, lactose, magnesium stearate, microcrystalline cellulose, povidone K30, sodium lauryl sulfate, sodium starch glycolate, talc, titanium dioxide and triacetin. Blisters of 30 and 60. Glass bottles of 100.

200 mg: Each brown to orange yellow, hexagonal, biconvex, film-coated tablet, with "ROCHE" and "200" engraved on one side, contains: tolcapone 200 mg. Nonmedicinal ingredients: calcium hydrogen phosphate, ethylcellulose, hydroxypropyl methylcellulose, iron oxide, lactose, magnesium stearate, microcrystalline cellulose, povidone K30, sodium lauryl sulfate, sodium starch glycolate, talc, titanium dioxide and triacetin. Blisters of 30 and 60. Glass bottles of 100.

Store at room temperature (15 to 30°C).

(Shown in Product Recognition Section)

New Product 1998

TAVIST®

Novartis Consumer Health

Clemastine

Antihistamine

Indications: The symptomatic relief of seasonal and nonseasonal allergic manifestations such as sneezing, rhinorrhea, nasal congestion, tearing, itching, urticaria, and angioedema in conditions generally responsive to antihistamines. These include seasonal allergic rhinitis and other respiratory allergies, allergic dermatoses (acute and chronic urticaria, angioedema), pruritides (atopic and contact dermatitis, neurodermatitis, pruritus ani, pruritus vulvae, insect bites), drug reactions, and in some cases, bronchial asthma.

Precautions: While in vitro and in vivo studies demonstrated that clemastine, a benzhydryl ether compound, had very weak anticholinergic activity, it should be used with caution in patients with glaucoma or prostatic hypertrophy.

Occupational Hazards: Since drowsiness may occur, caution sensitive patients against engaging in activities requiring rapid and precise responses, such as driving an automobile or operating dangerous machinery until their response has been determined.

Rarely, prolonged therapy with antihistamines can produce blood dyscrasias.

Children: Clemastine should not be given to children below 1 year of age, and should be kept out of the reach of children.

Pregnancy: Clemastine at relatively high doses in animals may have an adverse effect on the pregnant female and fetus. Clemastine should not be given during pregnancy unless the benefits outweigh the potential risks.

Lactation: Since some antihistamines may inhibit lactation and small amounts may appear in milk, clemastine should not be used by nursing mothers.

Special Diseases and Conditions: Clemastine should be used with caution in patients with epilepsy, narrow-angle glaucoma, stenosing peptic ulcer, pyloroduodenal obstruction, prostatic hypertrophy with urinary retention and bladder neck obstruction.

Drug Interactions: Antihistamines potentiate the effects of sedatives, hypnotics, MAO inhibitors and alcohol.

Adverse Effects: Weakness, dizziness, drowsiness, fatigue and dry mouth have been reported. Palpitations, anxiety states, vague gastrointestinal symptoms, heartburn, irregularity of menses, impotence, and skin rash have been reported rarely. Most of the adverse effects can be controlled by diminution in dosage or discontinuation of therapy.

Overdose: Symptoms: The effects of antihistamine overdosage may vary from CNS depression to stimulation. Anticholinergic symptoms such as dry mouth, fixed dilated pupils or flushing and gastrointestinal reactions may occur. Other symptoms of overdosage are dizziness, drowsiness, irritability and anxiety, fatigue, nausea, headache and tachycardia.

Treatment: Should overdosage be suspected, treatment is symptomatic and supportive, and may include induction of emesis or gastric lavage and administration of activated charcoal.

Good nursing care and supportive measures should be initiated in order to maintain respiration in the presence of CNS depression.

Dosage: The tablets should be taken with water before morning and evening meals.

Adults and children over 12 years: 2 mg (2 tablets) daily in divided doses. In refractory cases up to 6 tablets daily.

Children: 1 to 3 years: 0.25 to 0.5 mg morning and evening; 3 to 6 years: 0.5 mg morning and evening; 6 to 12 years: 0.5 to 1 mg morning and evening.

In all cases the dose should be individualized to the needs of the patient.

Clemastine should not be given to children under 1 year of age.

Supplied: Each white, scored tablet contains: clemastine 1 mg as clemastine hydrogen fumarate 1.34 mg. Nonmedicinal Ingredients: cornstarch, lactose, magnesium stearate, povidone and talc. Cartons of 16 and 32.

TAVIST-D®

Novartis Consumer Health

Clemastine—Phenylpropanolamine

Antihistamine—Decongestant

Supplied: Each tablet contains: clemastine 1 mg (equivalent to clemastine hydrogen fumarate 1.34 mg), phenylpropanolamine HCl (in sustained release form) 75 mg. Nonmedicinal ingredients: calcium phosphate, cellulose acetate phthalate, D&C yellow No. 10, lactose, magnesium stearate, polyvinyl acetate, povidone and starch. Blister packs, boxes of 12.

New Product 1998

Nonmedicinal ingredients are listed alphabetically within the supplied information of product monographs. Refer to the WHITE SECTION.

TAXOL™ Ⓟ

Bristol-Myers Squibb

Paclitaxel

Antineoplastic Agent

Caution: Paclitaxel should be administered under the supervision of a physician experienced in the use of cancer chemotherapeutic agents.

Patients receiving paclitaxel should be pretreated with corticosteroids, antihistamines, and H_2 antagonists (such as dexamethasone, diphenhydramine and cimetidine or ranitidine) to minimize hypersensitivity reactions (see Dosage). Severe hypersensitivity reactions characterized by dyspnea and hypotension requiring treatment, angioedema, and generalized urticaria have occurred in patients receiving paclitaxel. These reactions are probably histamine mediated. One of these reactions was fatal in a patient treated without premedication in a phase I study. Patients who experience severe hypersensitivity reactions to paclitaxel should not be rechallenged with the drug.

Pharmacology: Paclitaxel is a novel antimicrotubule agent that promotes the assembly of microtubules from tubulin dimers and stabilizes microtubules by preventing depolymerization.

In vitro, paclitaxel exhibits cytotoxic activity against a wide variety of both human and rodent tumor cell lines including leukemia, non-small cell lung carcinoma, small cell lung carcinoma, colon carcinoma, CNS carcinoma, melanoma, renal carcinoma, ovarian carcinoma and breast carcinoma.

Pharmacokinetics: The pharmacokinetics of paclitaxel have been evaluated over a wide range of doses, up to 300 mg/m², and infusion schedules ranging from 3 to 24 hours. Following i.v. administration of paclitaxel, the drug exhibited a biphasic decline in plasma concentrations. The initial rapid decline represents distribution to the peripheral compartment and elimination of the drug. The later phase is due, in part, to a relatively slow efflux of paclitaxel from the peripheral compartment. In patients treated with doses of 135 and 175 mg/m² given as 3 and 24 hour infusions, mean terminal half-life has ranged from 3 to 52.7 hours, and total body clearance has ranged from 11.6 to 24.0 L/h/m². Mean steady-state volume of distribution has ranged from 198 to 688 L/m², indicating extensive extravascular distribution and/or tissue binding.

Following 3 hour infusions of 175 mg/m², mean terminal half-life was estimated to be 9.9 hours; mean total body clearance was 12.4 L/h/m².

Variability in systemic paclitaxel exposure, as measured by $AUC_{0-\infty}$ for successive treatment courses was minimal; there was no evidence of accumulation of paclitaxel with multiple treatment courses.

The pharmacokinetics of paclitaxel have been shown to be nonlinear. There is a disproportionately large increase in C_{max} and AUC with increasing dose, accompanied by an apparent dose-related decrease in total body clearance. These findings are most readily observed in patients in whom high plasma concentrations of paclitaxel are achieved. Saturable processes in distribution and elimination/metabolism may account for these findings.

In vitro studies of binding to human serum proteins, using paclitaxel concentrations ranging from 0.1 to 50 µg/mL, indicated that on average 89% of drug is bound; the presence of cimetidine, ranitidine, dexamethasone, or diphenhydramine did not affect protein binding of paclitaxel.

The disposition of paclitaxel has not been fully elucidated in humans. After i.v. administration of paclitaxel, mean values for cumulative urinary recovery of unchanged drug ranged from 1.3 to 12.7% of the dose, indicating extensive nonrenal clearance. Hydroxylated metabolites isolated in bile have been demonstrated to be the principal metabolites. In 1 patient, approximately 20% of an administered dose of paclitaxel was recovered in bile as the parent compound and metabolites, in the 24-hour period following treatment. Hepatic metabolism and biliary clearance may be the principal mechanism for disposition of paclitaxel. The effect of renal or hepatic dysfunction on the disposition of paclitaxel has not been investigated.

The effect of cimetidine premedication on the metabolism of paclitaxel has been investigated; the clearance of paclitaxel was not affected by cimetidine pretreatment.

Preliminary animal/ex vivo data indicate that ketoconazole may inhibit the metabolism of paclitaxel. Likewise, preliminary reports suggest that plasma levels of doxorubicin (and its active metabolite doxorubicinol) may be increased when paclitaxel and doxorubicin are used in combination. The mechanism for this interaction is unknown. The pharmacodynamic consequences of this interaction are unclear (see Precautions, Drug Interactions).

Indications: Alone or in combination, for the treatment of carcinoma of the ovary or breast or lung.

Ovarian Carcinoma: First-line therapy in combination with other chemotherapeutic agents. Second-line treatment of metastatic carcinoma of the ovary after failure of standard therapy.

Breast Carcinoma: Second-line treatment of metastatic carcinoma of the breast after failure of standard therapy.

Lung Carcinoma: First-line treatment of advanced non-small cell lung cancer.

Contraindications: In patients who have a history of severe hypersensitivity reactions to paclitaxel or other drugs formulated in Cremophor EL (polyethoxylated castor oil).

Paclitaxel should not be used in patients with severe baseline neutropenia (<1 500 cells/mm³).

Warnings: Paclitaxel should be administered under the supervision of a physician experienced in the use of cancer chemotherapeutic agents.

Paclitaxel should be administered as a diluted infusion. Patients receiving paclitaxel should be pretreated with corticosteroids, antihistamines, and H_2 antagonists (such as dexamethasone, diphenhydramine and cimetidine or ranitidine) to minimize hypersensitivity reactions (see Dosage). Severe hypersensitivity reactions characterized by dyspnea, flushing, chest pain, tachycardia, hypotension requiring treatment, angioedema, and generalized urticaria have occurred in patients receiving paclitaxel. These reactions are probably histamine mediated. One of these reactions was fatal in a patient treated without premedication in a phase I study. In case of a severe hypersensitivity reaction, infusion should be discontinued immediately and the patient should not be rechallenged with the drug.

Paclitaxel should not be administered to patients with baseline neutrophil counts of less than 1 500 cells/mm³. Bone marrow suppression (primarily neutropenia) is dose dependent and is the dose-limiting toxicity. Neutrophil nadirs occurred at a median of 11 days. Frequent monitoring of blood counts should be instituted during paclitaxel treatment. Patients should not be retreated with subsequent cycles of paclitaxel until neutrophils recover to a level >1 500 cells/mm³ and platelets recover to a level >100 000 cells/mm³ (see Dosage).

Severe cardiac conduction abnormalities have been reported rarely during paclitaxel therapy. If patients develop significant conduction abnormalities during administration, appropriate therapy should be administered and continuous electrocardiographic monitoring should be performed during subsequent therapy with paclitaxel (see Adverse Effects).

Pregnancy: Paclitaxel may cause fetal harm when administered to a pregnant woman. Paclitaxel has been shown to be embryotoxic and fetotoxic in rabbits and to decrease fertility in rats. There are no studies in pregnant women. Women of childbearing potential should be advised to avoid becoming pregnant during therapy with paclitaxel.

Lactation: Paclitaxel should not be administered to nursing mothers.

Precautions: Contact of the undiluted concentrate with plasticized polyvinyl chloride (PVC) equipment or devices used to prepare solutions for infusion is not recommended. In order to minimize patient exposure to the plasticizer DEHP [di-(2-ethylhexyl)phthalate], which may be leached from PVC infusion bags or sets, diluted paclitaxel solutions should preferably be stored in bottles (glass, polypropylene) or plastic bags (polypropylene, polyolefin) and administered through polyethylene-lined administration sets.

Drug Interactions: In a Phase 1 trial in which paclitaxel was administered as a 24-hour infusion and cisplatin was administered as a 1 mg/min infusion, myelosuppression was more profound when paclitaxel was given after cisplatin than with the alternate sequence (i.e., paclitaxel before cisplatin). When paclitaxel is given before cisplatin, the safety profile of paclitaxel is consistent with that reported for single-agent use. Pharmacokinetic data from these patients demonstrated a decrease in paclitaxel clearance of approximately 33% when paclitaxel was administered following cisplatin. Therefore, paclitaxel should be given before cisplatin when used in combination.

Preliminary animal/ex vivo data indicate that ketoconazole may inhibit the metabolism of paclitaxel; caution should be

Taxol (cont'd)

exercised when treating patients with paclitaxel if they are receiving ketoconazole.

Preliminary reports suggest that plasma levels of doxorubicin (and its active metabolite doxorubicinol) may be increased when paclitaxel and doxorubicin are used in combination (see Pharmacology).

Hematology: Paclitaxel should not be administered to patients with baseline neutrophil counts of less than 1 500 cells/mm^3 (see Warnings and Contraindications). In order to monitor the occurrence of myelotoxicity, it is recommended that frequent peripheral blood cell counts be performed on all patients receiving paclitaxel. Patients should not be retreated with subsequent cycles of paclitaxel until neutrophils recover to a level >1 500 cells/mm^3 and platelets recover to a level >100 000 cells/mm^3. In the case of severe neutropenia (<500 cells/mm^3) during a course of paclitaxel therapy, a 20% reduction in dose for subsequent courses of therapy is recommended (see Dosage).

Hypersensitivity Reactions: Patients with a history of severe hypersensitivity reactions to products containing Cremophor EL should not be treated with paclitaxel (see Warnings and Contraindications). Minor symptoms such as flushing, skin reactions, dyspnea, hypotension or tachycardia do not require interruption of therapy. However, severe reactions, such as hypotension requiring treatment, dyspnea requiring bronchodilators, angioedema or generalized urticaria require immediate discontinuation of paclitaxel and aggressive symptomatic therapy. Patients who have developed severe hypersensitivity reactions should not be rechallenged with paclitaxel.

Cardiovascular: Hypotension and bradycardia have been observed during administration of paclitaxel; patients are usually asymptomatic and generally do not require treatment. Frequent monitoring of vital signs, particularly during the first hour of paclitaxel infusion, is recommended. Continuous cardiac monitoring is not required except for patients who develop serious conduction abnormalities (see Warnings and Adverse Effects).

Nervous System: Although the occurrence of peripheral neuropathy is frequent, the development of severe symptomatology is unusual. A dose reduction of 20% is recommended for all subsequent courses of paclitaxel for moderate to severe neuropathy (see Adverse Effects and Dosage).

Paclitaxel contains dehydrated alcohol, 396 mg/mL; consideration should be given to possible CNS and other effects of alcohol.

Hepatic: There is no evidence that the toxicity of paclitaxel is increased when given as a 3-hour infusion to patients with mildly abnormal liver function. No data are available for patients with severe baseline cholestasis (see Adverse Effects).

When paclitaxel is given as a 24-hour infusion to patients with moderate to severe hepatic impairment, increased myelosuppression may be seen as compared to patients with mildly elevated liver function tests given 24-hour infusions.

Adverse Effects: The incidences of adverse reactions in Table I are derived from 10 clinical trials in carcinoma of the ovary and of the breast involving 812 patients treated at doses ranging from 135 to 300 mg/m^2/day and schedules of 3 or 24 hours. In addition, toxicities which were observed in non-small cell lung carcinoma patients or were noted to have occurred with greater severity in this population are also described.

Data from a subset of 181 patients treated at the recommended dose of 175 mg/m^2 and a 3-hour infusion schedule is also included in Table I.

Safety referring to a large randomized trial of paclitaxel (135 mg/m^2 over 24 hours)/cisplatin (75 mg/m^2) versus cyclophosphamide/cisplatin, including 410 patients (196 receiving paclitaxel), has been evaluated. The combination of paclitaxel with platinum agents has not resulted in any clinically relevant changes to the safety profile of the drug when used at the recommended dosage. The frequency and severity of adverse events are generally similar between patients receiving paclitaxel for the treatment of ovarian, breast or non-small cell lung carcinoma.

Summary of 3-hour infusion data at a dose of 175 mg/m^2: Unless otherwise stated, the following safety data relate to 62 patients with ovarian cancer and 119 patients with breast cancer treated at a dose of 175 mg/m^2 and a 3-hour infusion schedule, in phase III clinical trials. All patients were premedicated to minimize hypersensitivity reactions. Data from these clinical trials demonstrate that paclitaxel given at this dose and schedule is well tolerated. Bone marrow suppression and peripheral neuropathy were the principal dose-related adverse effects associated with paclitaxel. Compared to 24-hour infusion schedules, neutropenia was less common when paclitaxel was given as a 3-hour infusion. Neutropenia was generally rapidly reversible and did not worsen with cumulative exposure. The frequency of neurologic symptoms increases with repeated exposure.

Table I—Taxol

Summary of Adverse Events

	135-300 mg/m^2 % of Patients N=812	175 mg/m^2 % of Patients N=181
Bone Marrow		
Neutropenia <2 000/mm^3	90	87
< 500/mm^3	52	27
Leukopenia <4 000/mm^3	90	86
<1 000/mm^3	17	4
Thrombocytopenia <100 000/mm^3	20	6
< 50 000/mm^3	7	1
Anemia <11 g/dL	78	62
< 8 g/dL	16	6
Infections	30	18
Bleeding	14	9
Red Cell Transfusions	25	13
Red Cell Transfusions (normal baseline)	12	6
Platelet Transfusions	2	0
Hypersensitivity Reaction		
All	41	40
Severe	2	1
Cardiovascular		
Bradycardia (first 3 hours of infusion)	3	3
Hypotension (first 3 hours of infusion)	12	11
Severe events	1	2
Abnormal ECG		
All Patients	23	13
Patients with normal baseline	14	8
Peripheral Neuropathy		
Any symptoms	60	64
Severe symptoms	3	4
Myalgia/Arthralgia		
Any symptoms	60	54
Severe symptoms	8	12
Gastrointestinal		
Nausea and vomiting	52	44
Diarrhea	38	25
Mucositis	31	20
Alopecia	87	93
Hepatic (Patients with normal baseline)		
Bilirubin elevations	7	4
Alkaline phosphatase elevations	22	18
AST elevations	19	18
Injection site reactions	13	4

None of the observed toxicities were influenced by age.

Hematologic: The most frequent significant undesirable effect of paclitaxel was bone marrow suppression. Severe neutropenia (<500 cells/mm^3) occurred in 27% of patients, but was not associated with febrile episodes. Only 1% of patients experienced severe neutropenia for 7 days or more. Neutropenia was not more frequent or severe in patients who received prior radiation therapy, nor did it appear to be affected by treatment duration or cumulative exposure. Eighteen percent of patients had an infectious episode, none resulting in fatality. Although severe septic episodes associated with severe neutropenia attributable to paclitaxel were reported in early clinical trials, no severe infections or septic episodes were seen at the recommended dose and infusion schedule. In the overall 812 patient experience, 5 septic episodes associated with severe neutropenia attributable to paclitaxel had a fatal outcome.

Thrombocytopenia with platelet counts below 100 000 cells/mm^3 and 50 000 cells/mm^3 occurred in 6% and 1% of patients, respectively. Severe thrombocytopenia (<50 000 cells/mm^3) was observed only during the first 2 courses. Bleeding episodes occurred in 9% of patients; no patient required platelet transfusion.

Anemia was observed in 62% of patients, but was severe (Hb<8 g/dL) in only 6% of patients. Incidence and severity of anemia are related to baseline hemoglobin status. Red cell transfusions were required in 13% of patients (6% of those with normal baseline hemoglobin levels).

When paclitaxel was administered in combination with cisplatin to patients with advanced NSCLC in the ECOG study, the incidence of neutropenia (Grade IV) was 74% (paclitaxel 135 mg/m^2/24 hours plus cisplatin) and 65% (paclitaxel 250 mg/m^2/24 hours plus cisplatin and G-CSF). Considerably less Grade IV neutropenia was observed in the EORTC study for paclitaxel 175 mg/m^2/3 hours plus cisplatin (28%), which was comparable to Grade IV neutropenia observed in patients with ovarian cancer (27%) or breast cancer (28%) receiving single-agent paclitaxel administered at a dose of 175 mg/m^2/3 hours.

Hypersensitivity Reactions: Despite premedication, severe hypersensitivity reactions occurred in 1% of patients. These reactions generally occurred in early treatment courses and within the first hour of infusion. Dyspnea, flushing, chest pain and tachycardia were the most frequent manifestations.

Paclitaxel dosage or schedule had no effect on the frequency of hypersensitivity reactions. In patients who received the recommended dose of paclitaxel at the recommended schedule, 21% of courses were associated with hypersensitivity reactions. The majority of reactions were of minor significance. The most frequent manifestations were flushing (28%), rash (14%) and hypotension (3%).

Cardiovascular: During paclitaxel infusion, hypotension or bradycardia were experienced by 24% and 4% of patients, respectively. Bradycardia and hypotension did not usually occur during the same course and the majority of episodes were asymptomatic and did not require treatment.

One patient experienced transient hypertension during the second paclitaxel cycle. In addition, 2 patients presented severe cardiovascular events (tachycardia and thrombophlebitis), possibly related to paclitaxel. None of these patients required discontinuation of treatment. In the same studies at a lower dose or longer infusion, 3 severe cardiovascular events (AV block, syncope and hypotension associated with coronary stenosis resulting in death) possibly related to paclitaxel administration were reported. In the overall 812 patients experience, 10 severe cardiovascular events occurred, including cardiac rhythm disturbance and syncope (see Warnings).

Thirteen percent of patients had an abnormal ECG during the clinical trials utilizing 175 mg/m^2 dose and a 3-hour infusion schedule. Eight percent of the patients with a normal ECG prior to study entry developed an abnormal tracing while on study. (In the overall 812 patient experience, the most frequently reported ECG changes were nonspecific repolarization abnormalities, sinus tachycardia and premature beats. In most cases, no clear relationship between paclitaxel administration and ECG alterations could be defined and these alterations were of no or minimal clinical relevance).

Since the above summary, cases of myocardial infarction have been reported rarely. Congestive heart failure has been reported typically in patients who have received other chemotherapy, notably anthracyclines.

The incidence of Grade III or greater cardiovascular events was 13% (paclitaxel 135 mg/m^2/24 hours plus cisplatin), 12% (paclitaxel 250 mg/m^2/24 hours plus cisplatin and G-CSF), and 6% (paclitaxel 175 mg/m^2/3 hours plus cisplatin) when paclitaxel followed by cisplatin was administered to patients with advanced NSCLC, with a similar incidence in the non-paclitaxel-containing control arms. The apparent increase in these cardiovascular events in patients with NSCLC compared to patients with breast or ovarian cancer is possibly related to the difference in cardiovascular risk factors among these patient groups.

Neurologic: Peripheral neuropathy, mainly manifested by paresthesia, affected 64% of patients, but was severe in only 4% of patients. Neurologic symptoms may occur following the first course and the frequency of symptoms may increase with increasing exposure to paclitaxel. Peripheral neuropathy was the cause of paclitaxel discontinuation in 3 cases. Sensory symptoms have usually improved or resolved within several months of paclitaxel discontinuation. Pre-existing neuropathies resulting from prior therapies are not a contraindication for paclitaxel therapy. Rare neurologic events reported after paclitaxel administration include grand mal seizures and encephalopathy. Reports of motor neuropathy with resultant minor distal weakness and autonomic neuropathy resulting in paralytic ileus and orthostatic hypotension have also appeared. Optic nerve and/or visual disturbances (scintillation scotomata) have also been reported, particularly in patients who have received higher doses than recommended. These effects generally have been reversible.

The administration of paclitaxel in combination with cisplatin compared with single-agent paclitaxel, regardless of the infusion duration, resulted in greater incidence of neurotoxicity in patients with NSCLC.

Arthralgia/Myalgia: Arthralgia or myalgia usually consisting of pain in the large joints of the arms and legs occurred in 54% of patients; severe symptoms were seen in 12% of patients. The symptoms were usually transient occurring 2 to 3 days after paclitaxel administration and resolving within a few days.

Alopecia: Alopecia was observed in almost all patients.

Gastrointestinal: Gastrointestinal side effects were usually mild to moderate: nausea/vomiting, diarrhea and mucositis were reported by 44%, 25% and 20% of patients, respectively. Other gastrointestinal events included anorexia (25% of patients), constipation (18%) and intestinal obstruction (4%). Neutropenic enterocolitis, bowel obstruction/perforation and ischemic colitis and pancreatitis have been reported.

The incidence of nausea and vomiting was greater when paclitaxel was administered with cisplatin as compared to single-agent paclitaxel.

Hepatic: In patients with normal baseline liver function, 4% experienced elevated bilirubin, 18% had elevated alkaline phosphatase, and 18% had elevated AST. Severe elevations (>5 x normal values) bilirubin, alkaline phosphatase or AST were seen in 1%, 5% and 5% of patients, respectively. Hepatic necrosis and hepatic encephalopathy leading to death have been reported rarely.

Injection Site Reactions: Phlebitis may occur following the i.v. administration of paclitaxel. Extravasation during i.v. administration may lead to edema, pain, erythema and induration; on occasion, extravasation can result in cellulitis. Skin discoloration may also occur. Recurrence of skin reactions at a site of previous extravasation following administration of paclitaxel at a different site, i.e., recall, has been reported rarely. A specific treatment for extravasation reactions is unknown at this time, however treatment with a s.c. injection of hyaluronidase diluted in saline has been demonstrated to be effective in a mouse skin model.

Other: Transient and mild nail and skin changes have been observed. Radiation pneumonitis has been reported in patients receiving concurrent radiotherapy.

Overdose: Symptoms and Treatment: There is no known antidote for paclitaxel overdosage. The primary anticipated complications of overdosage would consist of bone marrow suppression, peripheral neurotoxicity and mucositis.

Dosage: Note: Undiluted concentrate should not come in contact with plasticized PVC equipment. In order to minimize patients exposure to the plasticizer DEHP [di-(2-ethylhexyl)phthalate], which may be leached from PVC infusion bags or sets, diluted paclitaxel solutions should preferably be stored in bottles (glass, polypropylene) or plastic bags (polypropylene, polyolefin) and administered through polyethylene-lined administration sets.

Paclitaxel should be administered through an in-line filter with a microporous membrane not greater than 0.22 microns. Use of filter devices such as IVEX-2 filters which incorporate short inlet and outlet PVC-coated tubing has not resulted in significant leaching of DEHP.

All patients should be premedicated prior to paclitaxel administration in order to minimize severe hypersensitivity reactions. Such premedication may consist of dexamethasone 20 mg orally (or its equivalent) approximately 12 and 6 hours before paclitaxel, diphenhydramine 50 mg (or its equivalent) i.v. 30 to 60 minutes prior to paclitaxel, and cimetidine (300 mg) or ranitidine (50 mg) i.v. 30 to 60 minutes before paclitaxel.

Paclitaxel at a dose of 175 mg/m² administered i.v. over 3 hours every 3 weeks has been shown to be effective in patients with metastatic carcinoma of the ovary or breast who have failed standard therapy. For patients with non-small cell lung carcinoma, the recommended regimen, given every 3 weeks, is paclitaxel administered i.v. over 3 hours at a dose of 175 mg/m² followed by cisplatin. Single courses of paclitaxel should not be repeated until the neutrophil count is at least 1 500 cells/mm³ and the platelet count is at least 100 000 cells/mm³. Patients who experience severe neutropenia (neutrophil <500 cells/mm³) or moderate to severe peripheral neuropathy during paclitaxel therapy should have the dosage reduced by 20% for subsequent courses of paclitaxel.

Preparation and Administration Precautions: Paclitaxel is a cytotoxic anticancer drug and, as with other potentially toxic compounds, caution should be exercised in handling paclitaxel. The use of gloves is recommended. Following topical exposure, tingling, burning, redness have been observed. If paclitaxel solution contacts the skin, wash the skin immediately and thoroughly with soap and water.

If paclitaxel contacts mucous membranes, the membranes should be flushed thoroughly with water. Upon inhalation, dyspnea, chest pain, burning eyes, sore throat and nausea have been reported.

The administration of paclitaxel at a dose of 175 mg/m² over 3 hours in combination with cisplatin 75 mg/m² every 3 weeks is recommended for the primary treatment of patients with advanced carcinoma of the ovary. Paclitaxel should be given before cisplatin when used in combination.

Preparation for I.V. Administration: Paclitaxel for Injection must be diluted prior to infusion. Paclitaxel should be diluted in 0.9% Sodium Chloride Injection, 5% Dextrose Injection, 5% Dextrose and 0.9% Sodium Chloride Injection, or 5% Dextrose in Ringer's Injection to a final concentration of 0.3 to 1.2 mg/mL. The solutions are physically and chemically stable for up to 27 hours at ambient temperature (15 to 30°C).

Upon preparation, solutions may show haziness, which is attributed to the formulation vehicle. No significant loss in potency has been noted following simulated delivery of the solution through i.v. tubing containing an in-line (0.22 micron) filter.

Data collected for the presence of the extractable plasticizer DEHP [di-(2-ethylhexyl)phthalate] show that levels increase with time and concentration when dilutions are prepared in PVC containers. Consequently, the use of plasticized PVC containers and administration sets is not recommended. Paclitaxel solutions should be prepared and stored in glass, polypropylene, or polyolefin containers. Non-PVC containing administration sets, such as those which are polyethylene-lined, should be used.

As with all parenteral drug products, i.v. admixtures should be inspected visually for clarity, particulate matter, precipitate, discoloration and leakage prior to administration, whenever solution and container permit.

Paclitaxel should be administered through an in-line filter with a microporous membrane not greater than 0.22 microns.

Special Instructions: Preparation of paclitaxel should be done in a vertical laminar flow hood (Biological Safety Cabinet—Class II).

Personnel preparing paclitaxel should wear PVC gloves, safety glasses, disposable gowns and masks.

All needles, syringes, vials and other materials which have come in contact with paclitaxel should be segregated and incinerated at 1 000°C or more. Sealed containers may explode. Intact vials should be returned to the manufacturer for destruction. Proper precautions should be taken in packaging these materials for transport.

Personnel regularly involved in the preparation and handling of paclitaxel should have biannual blood examinations.

Directions for Dispensing from Pharmacy Bulk Vial: The use of Pharmacy Bulk Vial is restricted to hospitals with a recognized i.v. admixture program. The Pharmacy Bulk Vial is intended for single puncture, multiple dispensing and for i.v. use only. Dispensing from the Pharmacy Bulk Vial should be completed within 24 hours after initial entry.

Solutions for infusion prepared as recommended may be stored at room temperature (15 to 30°C) only if necessary. However, the infusion should be initiated within 24 hours of reconstitution.

Supplied: Each mL contains: paclitaxel 6 mg. Nonmedicinal ingredients: dehydrated alcool 49.7% v/v and polyethoxyethylated castor oil. Multidose vials of 5 and 16.7 mL and pharmacy bulk vials of 50 mL. Store at room temperature (15 to 30°C). Retain in the original package and protect from light. Once punctured, the 5 and 16.7 mL vials are stable for 28 days at room temperature. The 50 mL pharmacy bulk vial should be used within 24 hours after initial entry.

Reviewed 1999

TAXOTERE® ℞

Rhône-Poulenc Rorer

Docetaxel

Antineoplastic

Pharmacology: Docetaxel is an antineoplastic agent which acts by disrupting the microtubular network in cells that is essential for vital mitotic and interphase cellular functions. Docetaxel promotes the assembly of tubulin into stable microtubules while simultaneously inhibiting their disassembly. Docetaxel binds to free tubulin thereby decreasing the critical intracellular concentration of tubulin. The promoted polymerization of microtubules leads to the production of microtubule bundles without normal function and to the stabilization of microtubules, resulting in the inhibition of mitosis in cells. The binding of docetaxel to microtubules does not alter the number of protofilaments in the bound microtubules; in that, it differs from other spindle poisons.

Docetaxel was found to be cytotoxic in vitro against various murine and human tumor cell lines, and against freshly excised human tumor cells in clonogenic assays.

In addition, docetaxel was found to be active on a number of cell lines overexpressing the p-glycoprotein which is encoded by the multidrug resistant gene.

At doses of 70 to 115 mg/m², the kinetic profile of docetaxel is dose independent and consistent with a 3-compartment pharmacokinetic model, with half lives for the α, β and γ phases of 4 minutes, 36 minutes and 11.1 hours, respectively. Mean values for total body clearance and steady-state volume of distribution were 21 L/h/m² and 113 L, respectively.

A population pharmacokinetic analysis has been performed in patients receiving docetaxel. Pharmacokinetic parameters estimated by the model were very close to those estimated from Phase I studies. The pharmacokinetics of docetaxel were not altered by the age or sex of the patient. In a small number of patients with clinical chemistry data suggestive of mild to moderate liver function impairment (ALT, AST ≥1.5 times the upper limit of normal associated with alkaline phosphatase ≥2.5 times the upper limit of normal), total clearance was lowered by 27% on average (see Dosage).

Based on in vitro studies, isoenzymes of the cytochrome P450-3A subfamily appear to be involved in docetaxel metabolism.

Docetaxel is more than 95% protein bound. Dexamethasone does not affect the protein binding of docetaxel.

Indications: Breast Cancer: Treatment of patients with locally advanced or metastatic breast carcinoma in whom previous therapy has failed. Prior therapy should have included an anthracycline unless clinically contraindicated.

Non-Small Cell Lung Cancer: Treatment of patients with locally advanced or metastatic non-small cell lung cancer after failure of platinum-based chemotherapy.

Contraindications: In patients who have a history of hypersensitivity reactions to docetaxel or to other drugs formulated with polysorbate 80.

Docetaxel should not be used in patients with neutrophil counts of <1 500 cells/mm³.

Docetaxel is contraindicated in patients with severe liver impairment.

Warnings: Docetaxel concentrate for injection should be administered under the supervision of a physician experienced in the use of antineoplastic agents. Appropriate management of complications is possible only when adequate diagnostic and treatment facilities are readily available.

Docetaxel therapy should not be given to patients with neutrophil counts of less than 1 500 cells/mm³. In order to monitor the occurrence of neutropenia, which may be severe and result in infection, it is recommended that frequent blood cell counts be performed on all patients receiving docetaxel.

Severe hypersensitivity reactions resulting in immediate discontinuations occurred in 0.4% (5 of 1 260) of patients. Docetaxel must not be given to patients who have a history of severe hypersensitivity reactions to docetaxel or to other drugs formulated with polysorbate 80.

Hematologic Effects: Neutropenia is the most frequently reported adverse event. Neutrophil nadirs occurred at a median of 8 days. Frequent monitoring of blood counts should be conducted during docetaxel treatment. Patients should not be retreated with docetaxel until neutrophils recover to a level ≥1 500 cells/mm³ (see Dosage).

Hypersensitivity Reactions: Severe hypersensitivity reactions characterized by hypotension, bronchospasm and generalized rash/erythema have occurred. These reactions resulted in immediate discontinuation in approximately 0.4% (5 of 1 260) of patients. Severe symptoms resolve after discontinuation of the infusion and administration of appropriate therapy. Patients with a history of severe hypersensitivity reactions should not be rechallenged with docetaxel.

Pregnancy: Docetaxel may cause fetal harm when administered to a pregnant woman. There are no studies in pregnant women. No evidence of teratogenic effect was found when docetaxel was administered at 1.8 or 1.2 mg/m²/day, in rats or rabbits, respectively. However, these studies have shown that docetaxel, is also embryo or fetotoxic, characterized by

Taxotere (cont'd)

intrauterine mortality, reduced fetal weight and fetal ossification delays. These effects are consistent with maternal toxicity. If docetaxel is used during pregnancy, or if the patient becomes pregnant while receiving this drug, the patient should be apprised of the potential hazard to the fetus.

Children: The safety and effectiveness of docetaxel in children have not been established.

Precautions: Hematology: Docetaxel therapy should not be administered until the neutrophil count is over 1 500 cells/mm³. In order to monitor the occurrence of myelotoxicity, it is recommended that frequent blood cell counts be performed on all patients receiving docetaxel (see Warnings). Patients should not be retreated with subsequent cycles of docetaxel until neutrophils recover to a level of >1 500 cells/mm³. In cases of severe neutropenia (<500 cells/mm³) for 7 days or more during a course of docetaxel therapy, a reduction in dose for subsequent courses of therapy is recommended (see Dosage).

Hypersensitivity Reactions: Hypersensitivity reactions may occur within a few minutes following the initiation of the infusion of docetaxel. If minor reactions such as flushing or localized skin reactions occur, therapy with docetaxel does not have to be discontinued. However, severe reactions, such as hypotension requiring treatment, bronchospasm, or generalized rash/erythema require immediate discontinuation of docetaxel and aggressive therapy. Patients who have developed severe hypersensitivity reactions should not be rechallenged with docetaxel. All patients should be premedicated with an oral corticosteroid prior to the initiation of the infusion of docetaxel (see Dosage).

Cutaneous: Localized erythema of the extremities (palm of the hands and soles of the feet) with edema, followed by desquamation has been observed. In case of severe skin toxicity during a course of docetaxel therapy, a reduction in dose for subsequent courses of therapy is recommended (see Dosage).

Fluid Retention: Severe fluid retention has been reported following docetaxel therapy. Therefore, patients should be premedicated with oral corticosteroids prior to each docetaxel administration to reduce the incidence and severity of fluid retention (see Dosage). Patients with pre-existing effusion should be closely monitored from the first dose for the possible exacerbation of the effusions.

Patients with Liver Impairment: In patients treated with docetaxel at 100 mg/m² who have transaminase (ALT and/or AST) greater than 1.5 times the upper limit of normal concurrent with alkaline phosphatase greater than 2.5 times the ULN, there is a higher risk of developing severe adverse reactions such as toxic deaths including sepsis and gastrointestinal hemorrage which can be fatal, febrile neutropenia, infections, thrombocytopenia, stomatitis and asthenia. If docetaxel is considered essential for a patient with above specified hepatic function impairment, the recommended dose of docetaxel in patients with elevated liver function test (LFTs) is 75 mg/m² and LFTs should be measured at baseline and before each cycle (see Dosage).

Neurologic: The development of severe peripheral neurotoxicity is infrequent and requires a reduction in dose (see Dosage). If symptoms persist, treatment should be discontinued.

Carcinogenicity, Mutagenicity, Impairment of Fertility: The carcinogenic potential of docetaxel has not been studied. Docetaxel has been shown to be mutagenic in the in vitro chromosome aberration test in CHO-K_1 cells and in the in vivo micronucleus test in the mouse. However, it did not induce mutagenicity in the Ames test or the CHO/HGPRT gene mutation assay. These results are consistent with the pharmacological activity of docetaxel.

Lactation: It is not known whether docetaxel is excreted in human milk. Because many drugs are excreted in human milk, and because of the potential for serious adverse reactions in nursing infants from docetaxel, it is recommended that women be advised not to breast-feed during docetaxel therapy.

Drug Interactions: There have been no formal clinical studies to evaluate the drug interactions of docetaxel with other medications. In vitro studies have shown that the metabolism of docetaxel may be modified by the concomitant administration of compounds which induce, inhibit or are metabolized by (and thus may inhibit the enzyme competitively) cytochrome P450-3A such as cyclosporine, terfenadine, ketoconazole, erythromycin and troleandomycin. As a result, caution should be exercised when treating patients with these drugs as concomitant therapy since there is a potential for a significant interaction.

Adverse Effects: There were 1 312 patients with normal liver function tests (LFTs) at baseline who received an initial planned dose of 100 mg/m² over a 1-hour infusion independently of the premedication. The patients were enrolled in 36 clinical trials conducted in North America and Europe (breast carcinoma, n=535; non-small cell lung cancer, n=365). Table I lists adverse reaction data from 1 312 patients with normal LFTs at baseline and 54 patients with elevated LFTs at baseline. These reactions were considered possibly or probably related to docetaxel. The safety profile is generally similar in all patients whether they were treated for breast carcinoma or for other tumor types.

Table I—Taxotere

Summary of Adverse Events in 1 366 Patients Receiving Taxotere at 100 mg/m²

	Normal LFTs* at Baseline n=1 312 (%)	Elevated LFTs at Baseline n=54 (%)
Hematologic		
Neutropenia <2 000 cells/mm³	96.5	95.9
<500 cells/mm³	76.4	85.7
Leukopenia <4 000 cells/mm³	96.6	98.0
<1 000 cells/mm³	30.3	43.1
Thrombocytopenia <100 000 cells/mm³	7.8	27.8
Anemia <11 g/dL	90.4	92.6
<8 g/dL	8.9	31.5
Febrile Neutropenia	11.8	24.5
Septic Death	1.7	3.7
Nonseptic Death	0.5	7.4
Fever in Absence of Infection		
All	30.2	50.9
Severe	1.7	9.1
Hypersensitivity Reactions		
All	25.9	22.2
Severe	5.3	11.1
Fluid Retention		
All	48.4	35.2
Severe	8.3	7.4
Neurosensory		
All	50.0	33.3
Severe	4.1	0
Neuromotor		
All	13.8	3.7
Severe	4.0	1.9
Cutaneous		
All	56.6	57.4
Severe	5.9	11.1
Nail Changes		
All	27.9	16.7
Severe	2.6	3.7
Gastrointestinal		
Nausea	40.5	38.9
Diarrhea	40.6	33.3
Vomiting	24.5	25.9
Alopecia	79.0	61.1
Asthenia		
All	62.6	53.7
Severe	11.2	24.1
Stomatitis		
All	41.8	46.3
Severe	5.3	13.0
Myalgia		
All	20.0	18.5
Severe	1.4	1.9
Arthralgia		
All	8.6	7.4
Severe	0.5	0

*Normal liver function (LFTs): transaminase ≤1.5 times upper limit of normal or alkaline phosphatase ≤2.5 times upper limit of normal or isolated elevations of transaminase or alkaline phosphatase up to 5 times upper limit of normal.

Hematologic: Neutropenia was the most frequent adverse reaction associated with docetaxel; it was reversible and not cumulative. The median time to nadir was 8 days, while the median duration of severe neutropenia (<500 cells/mm³) was 7 days. Severe neutropenia occurred in 76% of the patients treated with docetaxel and lasted for more than 7 days in 3.5% of evaluable cycles.

Fever was associated with neutropenia (<500 cells/mm³) in 11.8% of the patients with normal liver function (3% of the cycles). The incidence of infections associated with neutrophil counts <500 cells/mm³ was 4.6% of the patients (1.2% of the cycles). Infectious episodes which included sepsis and pneumonia occurred in 20% of the patients (6% of the cycles) and were fatal in approximately 1.7% of those treated with docetaxel.

Thrombocytopenia (<100 000 cells/mm³) has been reported in 7.8% of the patients. Bleeding episodes were reported in 2% of the patients; this was associated with severe thrombocytopenia (<50 000 cells/mm³) in only 2 patients. A fatal gastrointestinal hemorrhage due to thrombocytopenia was reported in 1 patient.

Anemia (<11 g/dL) was observed in 90% of the patients and was severe (<8 g/dL) in 8.9% of the cases.

Hypersensitivity Reactions: Hypersensitivity reactions occurred in 26% of the patients (9.4% of the cycles) generally within a few minutes following the start of the infusion of docetaxel and were usually mild to moderate. The most frequent minor manifestations were flushing, rash with or without pruritus, chest tightness, back pain, dyspnea, drug fever, or chills.

Severe reactions characterized by hypotension, bronchospasm, or generalized rash/erythema have occurred within a few minutes following the initiation of infusion of docetaxel. Severe symptoms were observed in 5% of the patients; however, less than 0.4% (5 of 1 260) had immediate discontinuation of treatment. All hypersensitivity reactions resolved after discontinuation of the infusion and appropriate therapy.

Fluid Retention: Fluid retention has been reported in 50% of the patients (receiving premedication) which includes edema, and less frequently, pleural effusion, ascites, pericardial effusion, and weight gain. Fluid retention usually begins at the lower extremities and may become generalized with a weight gain of 3 kg or more.

The incidence of fluid retention in patients without premedication was 81.6%; of these 22.4% were severe. In patients premedicated up to 4 to 5 days with oral corticosteroids, the incidence of fluid retention was 50%; of these 5.3% were severe. Table II describes the effect on fluid retention with corticosteroid premedication (see Dosage for treatment regimen).

Table II—Taxotere

Effect of Corticosteroid Premedication of the Incidence of Fluid Retention

	Incidence	Severe
Without premedication	81.6%	22.4%
Premedication	50.0%	5.3%

Fluid retention has not been accompanied by acute episodes of dehydration, oliguria or hypotension, and was slowly reversible after docetaxel treatment was stopped.

Cutaneous: Cutaneous reactions have been observed in 57% of the patients treated with docetaxel. These reactions were characterized by a rash, including localized eruptions mainly on feet and hands, but also on arms, face or thorax. They were occasionally associated with pruritus. Eruptions generally occurred within 1 week following the docetaxel infusion, resolved before the next infusion, and were not disabling. Severe symptoms such as eruptions followed by desquamation occurred less frequently (5.6%). These reactions rarely lead to interruption or discontinuation of docetaxel treatment.

Severe nail disorders occurred in 2.6% of the patients. These reactions were characterized by hypo- or hyperpigmentation, and infrequently onycholysis and pain (0.8%).

Neurologic: Neurosensory symptoms characterized by paresthesia, dysthenia or pain (including burning sensation) were reported in 46% of all patients. Severe reactions were observed in less than 4% of the patients.

Neuromotor events were reported in 14% of patients. These reactions were severe in 4% of patients.

Gastrointestinal: Nausea (41%), diarrhea (41%), and vomiting (25%), were observed in patients treated with docetaxel. These reactions were generally mild to moderate. Severe gastrointestinal reactions generally occurred in less than 5% of the cases reported. Rare occurrences of gastrointestinal perforation have been reported.

Cardiovascular: Hypotension occurred in 4% of the patients and required therapy in 0.7% of the patients. Dysrhythmia occurred in 4% of the patients and was severe in 0.7% of the patients. Clinically meaningful events occurred in less than 3% of patients. These events included: heart failure (0.5%), paroxysmal atrial tachycardia, atrial flutter, and hypertension (2.4%).

Infusion Site Reactions: Infusion site reactions occurred in 5.6% of the patients treated with docetaxel and were generally mild. These reactions included skin sensitivities such as hyperpigmentation, inflammation, local erythema, dryness of the skin, or swelling of the vein. Phlebitis or extravasation were observed less frequently.

Hepatic: Increases ALT, AST, bilirubin, and alkaline phosphatase which were greater than 2.5 times the upper limit of normal were observed in less than 5% of patients.

Other: Alopecia was observed in 79% of patients and was reversible in 13% of the patients. Asthenia was reported by 63% of patients and was considered severe in 11.2% of these patients. Stomatitis was reported by 42% of patients. Arthralgias (9%) and myalgias (20%) were reported by patients but were generally considered to be mild to moderate.

Overdose: Symptoms and Treatment: There is no known antidote for docetaxel overdosage. In case of overdosage, the patient should be kept in a specialized unit where vital functions can be closely monitored and supportive treatment administered as necessary. Anticipated complications of overdosage include: bone marrow suppression, peripheral neurotoxicity, and mucositis.

There were 2 reports of overdose. One patient received 150 mg/m² and the other received 200 mg/m² as 1-hour infusions. Both patients experienced severe neutropenia, mild asthenia, cutaneous reactions, and mild paresthesia, and recovered without incident.

Dosage: Recommended Dosage: The recommended dosage of docetaxel is 100 mg/m² administered as a 1-hour infusion every 3 weeks.

Premedication Regimen: In order to reduce the incidence and severity of fluid retention, all patients should be pretreated with oral corticosteroids. The recommended premedication should consist only of oral corticosteroids, such as dexamethasone 16 mg/day (e.g., 8 mg b.i.d.), for 3 days starting 1 day prior to each docetaxel administration. Antihistamines have not been shown to be useful in controlling fluid retention.

Geriatrics: Based on the population pharmacokinetics, there are no special instructions for the use in the elderly.

Dosage Adjustments: Patients with Neutropenia, Cutaneous Reactions or Peripheral Neuropathy: Like many other chemotherapeutic agents, careful monitoring of neutrophil counts are an essential part of docetaxel therapy. Docetaxel should not be administered until the neutrophil count is at least 1 500 cells/mm³. Patients who experience either febrile neutropenia, severe neutropenia (neutrophil <500 cells/mm³ for more than 1 week), severe or cumulative cutaneous reaction, or severe peripheral neuropathy during docetaxel therapy should have the dosage of docetaxel reduced from 100 mg/m² to 75 mg/m². If these reactions persist, the dosage should be decreased from 75 mg/m² to 55 mg/m².

Patients with Hepatic Impairment: Based on pharmacokinetic data, in patients who have both elevations of transaminase values (ALT and/or AST) greater than 1.5 times the upper limit of the normal (ULN) and increases in alkaline phosphatase greater than 2.5 times the ULN, the recommended dose of docetaxel is 75 mg/m². For those patients with serum bilirubin greater than ULN and/or ALT and AST greater than 3.5 times ULN associated with alkaline phosphatase greater than 6 times ULN, docetaxel should not be used unless strictly indicated.

Administration Precautions: Docetaxel must be administered i.v. It is extremely important that the i.v. needle or catheter be properly positioned before any docetaxel is injected. Leakage into surrounding tissue during i.v. administration of docetaxel may cause considerable irritation, local tissue necrosis and/or thrombophlebitis. If extravasation occurs, the injection should be discontinued immediately, and any remaining portion of the dose should be introduced into another vein.

Stability and Storage Recommendations: Stability: Unopened vials of docetaxel are stable until the expiration date indicated on the package when stored under refrigeration at 2 to 8°C and protected from bright light. Freezing does not adversely affect the product.

Storage: Store the unopened vials under refrigeration, 2 to 8°C. Retain in the original package to protect from bright light.

Taxotere premix solution (10 mg docetaxel/mL) and fully prepared Taxotere infusion solution (in either 0.9% Sodium Chloride solution or 5% Dextrose solution) should be used a soon as possible after preparation. However, they are stable for 8 hours at room temperature, 15 to 25°C or under refrigeration, 2 to 8°C.

Reconstitution of Solutions: Preparation and Administration Precautions: Taxotere Concentrate for Injection requires dilution prior to administration. Please follow the preparation instructions provided below.

A. Preparation of the Premix Solution: 1. Remove the appropriate number of vials of Taxotere Concentrate for Injection and diluent from the refrigerator. Allow the vials to stand at room temperature for approximately 5 minutes.

2. Aseptically withdraw the entire contents of the diluent vial into a syringe and transfer it to the vial of Taxotere Concentrate for Injection.

3. Gently rotate each premix solution vial for approximately 15 seconds to assure full mixture of the concentrate and diluent.

4. The Taxotere premix solution (10 mg docetaxel/mL) should be clear; however, there may be some foam on top of the solution due to the polysorbate 80. Allow the premix solution to stand for a few minutes to allow any foam to dissipate. It is not required that all foam dissipate prior to continuing the preparation process.

B. Preparation of the Infusion Solution: 1. Aseptically withdraw the required amount of Taxotere premix with a calibrated syringe and inject the required volume of premix solution into a 250 mL infusion bag or bottle of either 0.9% Sodium Chloride solution or 5% Dextrose solution to produce a final concentration of 0.3 to 0.9 mg/mL. If a dose greater than 200 mg of Taxotere is required, use a larger volume of the infusion vehicle so that a concentration of 0.74 mg/mL Taxotere is not exceeded.

2. Thoroughly mix the infusion by manual rotation.

3. As with all parenteral products, Taxotere should be inspected visually for particulate matter or discoloration prior to administration whenever the solution and container permit. If the Taxotere for Injection premix solution or infusion solution is not clear or appears to have precipitation, the solution should be discarded.

Taxotere infusion solution should be administered i.v. as a 1-hour infusion under ambient room temperature and lighting conditions.

Contact of the undiluted concentrate with plasticized PVC equipment or devices used to prepare solution for infusion is not recommended. In order to minimize patient exposure to plasticizer DEHP (di-2-ethylhexyl phthalate), which may be leached from PVC infusion bags or sets, Taxotere infusion solution should be stored in bottles (glass, polypropylene) or plastic bags (polypropylene, polyolefin) and administered through polyethylene-lined administration sets.

Special Instructions: Docetaxel is a cytotoxic anticancer drug and, as with other potentially toxic compounds, caution should be exercised when handling and preparing docetaxel solutions. The use of gloves is recommended. Please refer to Handling and Disposal section.

If docetaxel concentrate, premix solution or infusion solution should come into contact with the skin, immediately and thoroughly wash with soap and water. If docetaxel concentrate, premix solution, or infusion solution should come into contact with mucosa, immediately and thoroughly wash with water.

Handling and Disposal: Procedures for proper handling and disposal of anticancer drugs should be considered. Several guidelines on this subject have been published. There is no general agreement that all of the procedures recommended in the guidelines are necessary or appropriate.

Information for the Patient: See Blue Section—Information for the Patient "Taxotere".

Supplied: 20 mg/0.5 mL: Single-dose vial of sterile, pyrogen-free, nonaqueous, clear yellow to brownish-yellow viscous solution contains: docetaxel (anhydrous) 20 mg in 0.5 mL polysorbate 80 (Fill: docetaxel 23.6 mg in 0.59 mL polysorbate 80) with an accompanying sterile, nonpyrogenic diluent vial containing 1.83 mL of ethanol 13% in water for injection. This overfill ensures that there is a minimal extractable premix volume of 2 mL containing 10 mg/mL docetaxel which corresponds to the labelled amount of 20 mg/vial. Nonmedicinal ingredients: ethyl alcohol, polysorbate 80 and water for injection. Both items are in blister pack in 1 carton.

80 mg/2 mL: Single-dose vial of sterile, pyrogen-free, nonaqueous, clear yellow to brownish-yellow viscous solution contains: docetaxel (anhydrous) 80 mg in 2 mL polysorbate 80 (Fill: docetaxel 94.4 mg in 2.36 mL polysorbate 80) with an accompanying sterile, nonpyrogenic diluent vial containing 7.33 mL of ethanol 13% in water for injection. This overfill ensures that there is a minimal extractable premix volume of 8 mL containing 10 mg/mL docetaxel which corresponds to the labelled amount of 80 mg/vial. Nonmedicinal ingredients: ethyl alcohol, polysorbate 80 and water for injection. Both items are in blister pack in 1 carton.

Reviewed 1999

TAZIDIME® Ⓟ

Lilly

Ceftazidime

Antibiotic

Pharmacology: In vitro studies indicate that the bactericidal action of ceftazidime results from inhibition of bacterial cell wall synthesis.

Indications: For the treatment of infections caused by susceptible strains of the designated organisms in the diseases listed below:

Pneumonia caused by P. aeruginosa, H. influenzae (including ampicillin-resistant strains), Klebsiella species, Enterobacter species, P. mirabilis, E. coli, Serratia species, S. pneumoniae and S. aureus (methicillin-susceptible strains).

Skin and skin-structure infections caused by P. aeruginosa, Klebsiella species, E. coli, P. mirabilis, Enterobacter species, S. aureus (methicillin-susceptible strains) and S. pyogenes.

Urinary tract infections caused by P. aeruginosa, Enterobacter species, Proteus species (indole positive and negative), Klebsiella species and E. coli.

Bacteremia/Septicemia caused by P. aeruginosa, Klebsiella species, E. coli, Serratia species, S. pneumoniae, S. aureus (methicillin-susceptible strains) and S. epidermidis.

Bone infections caused by P. aeruginosa, P. mirabilis, Enterobacter species, and S. aureus (methicillin-susceptible strains).

Peritonitis caused by E. coli, Klebsiella species, Peptostreptococcus species and Bacteroides species (most strains of B. fragilis are resistant).

Specimens for bacteriologic cultures should be obtained prior to therapy in order to isolate and identify causative organisms and to determine their susceptibilities to ceftazidime. Therapy may be instituted before results of susceptibility studies are known; however, once these results become available, the antibiotic treatment should be adjusted accordingly.

Due to the nature of the underlying conditions which usually predispose patients to Pseudomonas infections of the lower respiratory and urinary tracts, a good clinical response accompanied by bacterial eradication may not be achieved despite evidence of in vitro sensitivity.

Contraindications: Patients who have shown hypersensitivity to ceftazidime or the cephalosporin group of antibiotics.

Warnings: Before therapy with ceftazidime is instituted, careful inquiry should be made to determine whether the patient has had previous hypersensitivity reactions to ceftazidime, cephalosporins, penicillins or other drugs. Ceftazidime should be administered with caution to any patient who has demonstrated some form of allergy, particularly to drugs. This product should be given with caution to patients with type I hypersensitivity reactions to penicillin. If an allergic reaction to ceftazidime occurs, discontinue treatment with the drug. Serious acute hypersensitivity reactions may require epinephrine and other emergency measures.

Pseudomembranous colitis has been reported with virtually all broad-spectrum antibiotics, including ceftazidime. Therefore, it is important to consider its diagnosis in patients administered ceftazidime who develop diarrhea. Such colitis may range in severity from mild to life-threatening.

Treatment with broad-spectrum antibiotics including ceftazidime may alter the normal flora of the colon and may permit overgrowth of clostridia. Studies indicate that a toxin produced by C. difficile is one primary cause of antibiotic-associated colitis.

Mild cases of pseudomembranous colitis usually respond to drug discontinuance alone. In moderate to severe cases, management should include sigmoidoscopy, appropriate bacteriologic studies and fluid, electrolyte and protein supplementation. When the colitis does not improve after the administration of ceftazidime has been discontinued, or when it is severe, consideration should be given to the administration of oral vancomycin or other suitable therapy.

Precautions: Ceftazidime dosage should be reduced in patients with impaired renal function (see Dosage). High and

Tazidime (cont'd)

prolonged serum antibiotic concentrations can occur from normal dosages in patients with transient or persistent reduction of urinary output because of renal insufficiency. The total daily dosage should be reduced when ceftazidime is administered to such patients to avoid the clinical consequences, e.g., seizures due to elevated levels of antibiotics (see Dosage). Continued dosage should be determined by degree of renal impairment, severity of infection and susceptibility of the causative organism.

As with other antibiotics, prolonged use of ceftazidime may result in the overgrowth of non-susceptible organisms including species originally sensitive to the drug. Repeated evaluation of the patient's condition is essential. If superinfection occurs during therapy, appropriate measures should be taken. Resistance has developed during therapy with ceftazidime by S. aureus, Enterobacteriaceae, Acinetobacter species and Pseudomonas species.

Ceftazidime should be prescribed with caution in individuals with a history of gastrointestinal disease, particularly colitis.

Nephrotoxicity has been reported following concomitant administration of cephalosporins and aminoglycoside antibiotics or potent diuretics, such as furosemide. Although transient elevations of BUN and serum creatinine have been observed in clinical studies, there is no evidence that ceftazidime, when administered alone, is significantly nephrotoxic.

Pregnancy: The safety of ceftazidime in the treatment of infections during pregnancy has not been established. If the administration to pregnant patients is considered necessary, its use requires that the potential benefits be weighed against the possible hazards to the fetus.

Lactation: Ceftazidime is excreted in human milk in low concentrations (3.8 to 5.2 mg/mL). Caution should be exercised when ceftazidime is administered to a nursing woman.

Neonates: Safety in infants 1 month of age or younger has not been established.

Geriatrics: The elimination of ceftazidime may be reduced due to impairment of renal function.

Laboratory Test Changes: A false-positive reaction for glucose in the urine may occur with Benedict's or Fehling's solution or with Clinitest tablets but not with Tes-Tape (Glucose Enzymatic Test Strip, USP).

Adverse Effects: The most common adverse reactions associated with the administration of ceftazidime in clinical trials are listed below.

Local effects, reported in 2.8% of patients, were phlebitis, thrombophlebitis, pain and inflammation at the site of injection or infusion.

Hypersensitivity reactions, reported in 2.7% of patients, were pruritus, urticaria, rash and fever. Immediate reactions, generally manifested by rash and/or pruritus, occurred in 1 in 285 patients. Angioedema and anaphylaxis (0.2% of patients; bronchospasm and/or hypotension) have been reported very rarely.

Gastrointestinal symptoms, reported in <4% of patients, were diarrhea, colitis, nausea, vomiting, and abdominal pain. Pseudomembranous colitis has been reported (see Warnings).

CNS reactions (less than 1%) included headache, dizziness, and paresthesia. Seizures have been reported with several cephalosporins including ceftazidime (see Precautions).

Less frequent adverse events (<1%) were candidiasis (including oral thrush) and vaginitis.

Hepatic: <4% of patients experienced transient elevations of hepatic values, these included: AST, ALT, LDH and alkaline phosphatase.

Renal: transient elevations of blood urea, blood urea nitrogen and/or serum creatinine were noted in <1% of patients.

Hematopoietic effects were noted and included eosinophilia (3.4%), positive Coombs' test without hemolysis (5.1%). Transient leukopenia, neutropenia, agranulocytosis, thrombocytopenia, thrombocytosis and lymphocytosis were seen in <1% of patients.

Overdose: Symptoms: No case of overdosage has been reported to date with ceftazidime, no specific information on symptoms or treatment are available. It is reported that the administration of large doses of parenteral cephalosporins may cause dizziness, paresthesias and headaches. Seizures may occur following overdosage with some cephalosporins, particularly in patients with renal impairment in whom accumulation is likely to occur.

Laboratory abnormalities that may occur after an overdose include elevations in creatinine, BUN, liver enzymes and bilirubin, a positive Coombs' test, thrombocytosis, thrombocytopenia, eosinophilia, leukopenia and prolongation of the prothrombin time.

Treatment: If seizures occur, the drug should be discontinued promptly and anticonvulsant therapy may be administered if clinically indicated. The patient's airway should be protected and ventilation and perfusion supported. The patient's vital signs, blood gases, serum electrolytes, etc. should be meticulously monitored and maintained, within acceptable limits.

In cases of severe overdosage, especially in a patient with renal failure, combined hemodialysis and hemoperfusion may be considered if response to more conservative therapy fails. However, no clinical data supporting such therapy of ceftazidime overdosage are available.

Dosage: Ceftazidime may be administered i.v. or i.m. after reconstitution. Dosage and route of administration should be determined by the severity of infection, susceptibility of the causative organisms and condition and renal function of the patient.

Adults: The usual recommended daily dose is 1 to 6 g in divided doses; 250 mg to 2 g every 8 to 12 hours (see Table I).

Table I—Tazidime

Dosage Guide—Adults

Type of Infection	Dosage	Frequency and Route
Uncomplicated urinary tract infections	250 mg	q 12 h i.m. or i.v.
Skin and skin structure infections and uncomplicated pneumonia	500 mg–1 g	q 8 h i.m. or i.v.
Bone infections	2 g	q 12 h i.v.
Life-threatening infections (those commonly needing antibiotics in higher doses e.g., peritonitis or septicemia) or infections due to less susceptible organisms	2 g	q 8 h i.v.

A normal course of treatment should continue until 48 to 72 hours after the patient defervesces or after bacterial eradication has been obtained, usually 10 to 14 days, except for bone infections where treatment can continue for 6 weeks. In the treatment of beta-hemolytic streptococcal infections, ceftazidime should be administered for at least 10 days.

Adults with Impaired Renal Function: A reduced dosage must be employed and the serum levels closely monitored. After an initial dose of 1 g, a maintenance dosage schedule should be followed (see Table II). The maintenance dosage should be determined by degree of renal impairment, severity of infection and susceptibility of the causative organism.

When only serum creatinine is available, the following formula (based on sex, weight and age of the patient) may be used to convert this value into creatinine clearance. The serum creatinine should represent a steady state of renal function.

Males:

$$\text{Creatinine Clearance (mL/min)} = \frac{\text{Weight (kg)} \times (140 - \text{age})}{72 \times \text{serum creatinine (mg/dL)}}$$

Females: 0.85×above value.

Table II—Tazidime

Maintenance Dosage Guide for Patients with Renal Impairment

Creatinine Clearance (mL/min)	Recommended Dose of Tazidime	Frequency
50-31	1 g	q 12 h
30-16	1 g	q 24 h
15-6	500 mg	q 24 h
≤5	500 mg	q 48 h

In patients with severe infections who would normally receive 6 g of ceftazidime daily were it not for renal insufficiency, the dose given in Table II may be increased by 50% or the dosing frequency increased appropriately. Continued dosage should be determined by therapeutic monitoring, severity of the infection, and susceptibility of the causative organism.

In patients undergoing hemodialysis, a loading dose of 0.5 to 1 g is recommended, followed by 0.5 to 1 g after each hemodialysis period. Ceftazidime can also be used in patients undergoing intraperitoneal dialysis (IPD) and continuous ambulatory peritoneal dialysis (CAPD). In such patients, a loading dose of 1 g may be given, followed by 500 mg every 24 hours. In addition to i.v. use, ceftazidime can be incorporated in the dialysis fluid at a concentration of 250 mg/2 L of dialysis fluid.

Impaired Hepatic Function: No adjustment in dosage is required for patients with hepatic dysfunction provided renal function is not impaired.

Infants and Children:* The dosage schedule (not to exceed the maximum adult dose) in Table III is recommended, although renal status and seriousness of infection must be considered.

Table III—Tazidime

Dosage Guide—Infants and Children

Age	Dosage	Frequency
1 month—2 months	12.5–25 mg/kg	q 12 h i.v.
2 months—12 years	10–33 mg/kg	q 8 h i.v.

*Safety and efficacy has not been established in infants less than 1 month of age.

Due to the nature of the underlying conditions which usually predispose patients to Pseudomonas infections of the lower respiratory and urinary tracts, a good clinical response accompanied by bacterial eradication may not be achieved despite evidence of in vitro sensitivity.

Administration: I.M.: Ceftazidime should be injected well within the body of a large muscle mass such as the upper outer quadrant of the gluteus maximus or lateral part of the thigh.

I.V.: The i.v. route is preferable for patients with septicemia, peritonitis or other severe or life-threatening infections.

Intermittent I.V. Administration: The reconstituted solution may be slowly injected into the vein over a period of 3 to 5 minutes or given through the tubing of an administration set. During the infusion of the solution containing ceftazidime, the administration of other solutions should be discontinued temporarily.

Continuous I.V. Infusion: Ceftazidime may also be administered over a longer period of time.

Note: If therapy with ceftazidime is carried out in combination with an aminoglycoside antibiotic, either, each of these antibiotics should be administered at different sites, or ceftazidime and aminoglycosides may be administered sequentially by intermittent i.v. infusion. After the administration of 1 of the 2 drugs, the tubing is carefully and thoroughly flushed with an approved solution for reconstitution and then the other drug solution is administered. An aminoglycoside should not be mixed with ceftazidime in the same container.

Reconstitution: I.M.: Solutions for Reconstitution: Sterile Water for Injection or, if required, Bacteriostatic Water for Injection, 0.5 to 1.0% Lidocaine Hydrochloride Injection.

Reconstitute as directed in Table IV.

Table IV—Tazidime

Reconstitution Table—I.M.

Vial Size	Volume to Be Added to Vial	Approximate Available Volume	Approximate Average Concentration
1.0 g	3.0 mL	3.6 mL	280 mg/mL

Shake well until dissolved.

I.V.: Solutions for Reconstitution; Sterile Water for Injection.

Reconstitute as directed in Table V.

Table V—Tazidime

Reconstitution Table—I.V.

Vial Size	Diluent to Be Added to Vial	Approximate Available Volume	Approximate Average Concentration
1 g, Vial No. 7231	5 or 10 mL	5.6 or 10.6 mL	180 or 95 mg/mL
2 g, Vial No. 7234	10 mL	11.2 mL	180 mg/mL

Shake well until dissolved. The prepared solution may be further diluted to the desired volume with any of the solutions for i.v. infusion listed below.

Direct I.V. Injection: Reconstitute as directed in Table V.

For Intermittent I.V. Infusion: Reconstitute as directed in Table V for 1 or 2 g vials.

Continuous I.V. Infusion: Reconstitute 1 or 2 g vials with 10 mL Sterile Water for Injection. The appropriate quantity of the reconstituted solution may be added to an i.v. bottle containing any of the solutions listed below.

Pharmacy Bulk Vial: The availability of the bulk pharmacy vial is restricted to hospitals with a recognized i.v. admixture program.

Tazidime for Injection does not contain any preservatives. The Pharmacy Bulk Vial is intended for multiple dispensing for i.v. use only, employing a single puncture (see Table VI).

Table VI—Tazidime

Reconstitution Table—Pharmacy Bulk Vial

Vial Size	Diluent to Be Added to Vial	Approximate Available Volume	Approximate Average Concentration
6 g (100 mL) Vial No. 7241	26 mL 56 mL	30 mL 60 mL	200 or 100 mg/mL

Following reconstitution with Sterile Water for Injection, the solution should be dispensed and diluted for use within 8 hours. Any unused reconstituted solution should be discarded after 8 hours.

Solutions for I.V. Infusion: 0.9% Sodium Chloride Injection, M/6 Sodium Lactate Injection, Ringers Injection USP, Lactated Ringers Injection USP, 5% Dextrose Injection, 5% Dextrose and 0.45% Sodium Chloride Injection, 5% Dextrose and 0.9% Sodium Chloride Injection, 10% Dextrose Injection, Normosol-M in 5% Dextrose Injection.

When ceftazidime is dissolved, carbon dioxide is released and a positive pressure develops. For ease of use, please follow the recommended techniques of reconstitution described below.

Solutions of ceftazidime, like those of most beta-lactam antibiotics, should not be added to solutions of aminoglycoside antibiotics because of potential interaction. However, if concurrent therapy with ceftazidime and an aminoglycoside is indicated, each of these antibiotics should be administered in different sites.

Instructions for Reconstitution: For 1 g i.m./i.v. and 2 g i.v. vials:

1. Inject the diluent and shake well to dissolve.
2. Carbon dioxide is released as the antibiotic dissolves, generating pressure within the vial. The solution will become clear within 1 to 2 minutes.
3. Invert the vial, and completely depress the syringe plunger prior to insertion.
4. Insert the needle through the vial stopper. Be sure the needle remains within the solution, and withdraw contents of the vial in the usual maner. Pressure in the vial may aid withdrawal.
5. The withdrawn solution may contain carbon dioxide bubbles which should be expelled from the syringe before injection.

For 6 g pharmacy bulk package:

1. When diluent is being added, the vial must be vented to prevent buildup of pressure due to release of carbon dioxide formed as the antibiotic dissolves. Use standard venting procedures outlined in the venting card for Tazidime.
2. Inject 26 mL of diluent to provide a solution containing approximately 1 g of ceftazidime activity per 5 mL. Inject 56 mL of diluent to provide a solution containing approximately 1 g of ceftazidime activity per 10 mL.
3. Dissolve the antibiotic by gently agitating the solution.
4. Allow sufficient time (1 to 2 minutes) for carbon dioxide to vent before dispensing solution.
5. After storage, relieve any additional pressure which may develop in the vial before dispensing.

Storage: Ceftazidime in the dry state should be stored at room temperature and protected from light.

Reconstituted solutions should be administered within 12 hours when stored at room temperature (not exceeding 25°C), and within 48 hours when refrigerated, from the time of reconstitution.

Incompatibility: Ceftazidime should not be added to blood products, protein hydrolysates or amino acids. It should not be mixed together with an aminoglycoside.

Supplied: ADD-Vantage Vials: 1 g (No. 7290): Each vial contains: ceftazidime 1 g and sodium carbonate 118 mg.

2 g (No. 7291): Each vial contains: ceftazidime 2 g and sodium carbonate 236 mg.

Pharmacy Bulk Vial (No. 7241): Each vial of dry powder contains: ceftazidime 6 g and sodium carbonate 708 mg. Rubber-stoppered vials of 100 mL.

Vials: 1 g (No. 7231): Each vial of dry powder contains: ceftazidime 1 g and sodium carbonate 118 mg. Rubber-stoppered vials of 20 mL.

2 g (No. 7234): Each vial of dry powder contains: ceftazidime 2 g and sodium carbonate 236 mg. Rubber-stoppered vials of 50 mL.

The above ADD-Vantage Vials are to be used with Abbott Laboratories' ADD-Vantage Diluent Container containing: 0.9% Sodium Chloride Injection, USP, 50 mL, 100 mL or 5% Dextrose Injection, USP, 50 mL, 100 mL.

TAZOCIN® Ⓟ

Wyeth-Ayerst

Piperacillin Sodium—Tazobactam Sodium

Antibiotic—β-lactamase Inhibitor

Pharmacology: Tazocin is an injectable antibacterial combination consisting of the semisynthetic antibiotic piperacillin sodium and the ß-lactamase inhibitor tazobactam sodium for i.v. administration.

Piperacillin exerts bactericidal activity by inhibiting septum formation and cell wall synthesis. In vitro, piperacillin is active against a variety of gram-positive and gram-negative aerobic and anaerobic bacteria. Tazobactam is a β-lactamase inhibitor. Tazobactam, in combination with piperacillin enhances and extends the antibiotic spectrum of piperacillin to include β-lactamase producing bacteria normally resistant to piperacillin.

Piperacillin is metabolized to a minor microbiologically active desethyl metabolite. Tazobactam is metabolized to a single metabolite which lacks pharmacological and antibacterial activities. Both tazobactam and piperacillin are eliminated by the kidney via glomerular filtration and tubular secretion. Tazobactam and its metabolite are eliminated primarily by renal excretion with 80% of the dose as unchanged drug and the remainder as the single metabolite. Piperacillin is excreted rapidly as unchanged drug, with 68% of the dose in the urine. Piperacillin from Tazocin is excreted in the bile to a small extent (<1%) and no tazobactam or desethyl metabolite is excreted in the bile.

Tazobactam and piperacillin are widely distributed into tissues and body fluids including, but not limited to, intestinal mucosa, gallbladder, lung, female reproductive tissues (uterus, ovary and fallopian tube) interstitial fluid and bile. Mean tissue concentrations were generally 50 to 100% of those in plasma. Distribution of tazobactam and piperacillin into cerebrospinal fluid is low in subjects with non-inflamed meninges, as with other penicillins.

In subjects with renal impairment, the half-lives of tazobactam and piperacillin, after single doses, increase with decreasing creatinine clearance. At creatinine clearance below 20 mL/min, the increase in half-life is 4-fold for tazobactam and 2-fold for piperacillin compared to subjects with normal renal function. Dosage adjustments for Tazocin are recommended when creatinine clearance is below 40 mL/min in patients receiving the recommended daily dose of Tazocin (see Dosage).

Hemodialysis removes 30 to 40% of a Tazocin dose with an additional 5% of the tazobactam dose removed as the tazobactam metabolite. Peritoneal dialysis removes approximately 21% and 6% of the tazobactam and piperacillin doses, respectively, with up to 16% of the tazobactam dose removed as the tazobactam metabolite. For dosage recommendations for patients undergoing hemodialysis see Dosage.

Tazobactam and piperacillin half-lives increase by approximately 18 to 25% in patients with hepatic cirrhosis compared to healthy subjects. However, dosage adjustment of Tazocin due to hepatic cirrhosis is not necessary.

Indications: For the treatment of patients with systemic and/or local bacterial infections, caused by piperacillin resistant, piperacillin/tazobactam susceptible, β-lactamase producing strains of the designated microorganisms in the specified conditions listed below.

Intra-Abdominal Infections: Appendicitis (complicated by rupture or abscess) and peritonitis caused by piperacillin resistant, β-lactamase producing strains of E. coli or members of the B. fragilis group.

Skin and Skin Structure Infections: Uncomplicated and complicated skin and skin structure infections, including cellulitis, cutaneous abscess, acute ischemic/diabetic foot infections caused by piperacillin resistant ß-lactamase producing strains of S. aureus (not methicillin-resistant strains).

Gynecological Infections: Postpartum endometritis or pelvic inflammatory disease caused by piperacillin resistant, β-lactamase producing strains of E. coli.

Community-Acquired Lower Respiratory Tract Infections: Community-acquired pneumonia (moderate severity only) caused by piperacillin resistant, β-lactamase producing strains of H. influenzae.

While Tazocin is indicated only for the conditions listed above, infections caused by piperacillin susceptible organisms are also amenable to Tazocin treatment due to its piperacillin content. The tazobactam component of this combination product does not decrease the activity of the piperacillin component against piperacillin susceptible organisms. Therefore, the treatment of polymicrobial infections caused by piperacillin susceptible organisms and β-lactamase producing organisms susceptible to Tazocin should not require the addition of another antibiotic.

Tazocin may be useful as presumptive therapy in the indicated conditions prior to identification of causative organisms because of its broad spectrum of bactericidal activity against gram-positive and gram-negative aerobic and anaerobic organisms. Appropriate cultures should usually be performed before initiating antimicrobial treatment in order to isolate and identify the organisms causing infection and to determine their susceptibility to Tazocin. Antimicrobial therapy should be adjusted, if appropriate, once results of culture(s) and antimicrobial susceptibility testing are known.

Contraindications: Patients with a history of allergic reactions to any of the penicillins and/or cephalosporins or β-lactamase inhibitors.

Warnings: Serious and occasionally fatal hypersensitivity (anaphylactic) reactions have been reported in individuals receiving therapy with penicillins. These reactions are more apt to occur in individuals with a history of sensitivity to multiple allergens. There have been reports of individuals with a history of penicillin hypersensitivity who have experienced severe hypersensitivity reactions when treated with cephalosporins. Before initiating therapy with Tazocin, careful inquiry should be made concerning previous hypersensitivity reactions to penicillins, cephalosporins or other allergens. If an allergic reaction occurs during therapy with Tazocin, the antibiotic should be discontinued and appropriate therapy instituted. Serious anaphylactoid reactions require immediate emergency treatment with epinephrine, oxygen and i.v. steroids and airway management, including intubation, should also be administered as indicated.

Pseudomembranous colitis has been reported with nearly all antibacterial agents, including piperacillin/tazobactam and may range in severity from mild to life-threatening. Therefore, it is important to consider this diagnosis in patients who present with diarrhea subsequent to the administration of antibacterial agents.

Treatment with antibacterial agents alters the normal flora of the colon and may permit overgrowth of clostridia. Studies indicate that a toxin produced by C. difficile is one primary cause of "antibiotic-associated colitis".

After the diagnosis of pseudomembranous colitis has been established, therapeutic measures should be initiated. Mild cases of pseudomembranous colitis usually respond to drug discontinuation alone. In moderate to severe cases, consideration should be given to management with fluids and electrolytes, protein supplementation and treatment with an oral antibacterial drug effective against C. difficile colitis.

Precautions: General: Bleeding manifestations or significant leukopenia following prolonged administration have occurred in some patients receiving ß-lactam antibiotics, including piperacillin. These reactions have sometimes been associated with abnormalities of coagulation tests such as clotting time, platelet aggregation and prothrombin time and are more likely to occur in patients with renal failure. If bleeding manifestations occur, the antibiotic should be discontinued and appropriate therapy instituted.

The possibility of the emergence of resistant organisms that might cause superinfections should be kept in mind. If this occurs, appropriate measures should be taken.

As with other penicillins, patients may experience neuromuscular excitability or convulsions if higher than recommended doses are given i.v. (particularly in the presence of renal failure).

Tazocin is a monosodium salt of piperacillin and a monosodium salt of tazobactam containing a total of 2.35 mmol (54 mg) of Na^+/g of piperacillin in the combination product. This should be considered when treating patients requiring restricted salt intake. Periodic electrolyte determinations should be performed in patients with low potassium reserves, and the possibility of hypokalemia should be kept in mind with patients who have potentially low potassium reserves and who are receiving cytotoxic therapy or diuretics.

As with other semisynthetic penicillins, piperacillin therapy has been associated with an increased incidence of fever and rash in cystic fibrosis patients.

Tazocin (cont'd)

Because of chemical instability, Tazocin should not be used for i.v. administration with solutions containing **only** sodium bicarbonate (see Dosage, Incompatibility).

Tazocin should not be added to blood products.

Children: Safety and efficacy in children below the age of 12 have not been established.

Pregnancy and Teratology: Reproduction studies have been performed in rats and have revealed no evidence of impaired fertility due to piperacillin/tazobactam administered up to a dose which is similar to the maximum recommended human daily dose based on body-surface area (mg/m²). Teratology studies have been performed in mice and rats and have revealed no evidence of harm to the fetus due to piperacillin/tazobactam at doses 1 to 2 and 2 to 3 times the human dose of piperacillin and tazobactam, respectively, based on body-surface area (mg/m²).

Piperacillin: Reproduction and teratology studies have been performed in mice and rats and have revealed no evidence of impaired fertility or harm to the fetus due to piperacillin administered up to a dose which is half (mice) or similar (rats) to the human dose based on body-surface area (mg/m²).

Tazobactam: Reproduction studies have been performed in rats and have revealed no evidence of impaired fertility due to tazobactam administered up to a dose 3 times the human dose based on body-surface area (mg/m²). Teratology studies have been performed in mice and rats and have revealed no evidence of harm to the fetus due to tazobactam up to a dose which is 6 (mice) and 14 (rats) times the human dose based on body-surface area (mg/m²). In rats, tazobactam crosses the placenta. Concentrations in the fetus are less than or equal to 10% of that found in maternal plasma.

There are however, no adequate and well-controlled studies with the piperacillin/tazobactam combination or with piperacillin or tazobactam alone in pregnant women. Because animal reproduction studies are not always predictive of human response, this drug should be used during pregnancy only if clearly needed.

Lactation: Caution should be exercised when Tazocin is administered to nursing mothers. Piperacillin is excreted in low concentrations in human milk; tazobactam concentrations in milk have not been studied.

Geriatrics: Patients over 65 years of age are not at an increased risk of developing adverse effects solely because of age. However, dosage should be adjusted in the presence of renal insufficiency (see Dosage).

Drug Interactions: Aminoglycosides: The mixing of Tazocin with an aminoglycoside in vitro can result in substantial inactivation of the aminoglycoside.

When Tazocin is co-administered with tobramycin, the area under the curve, renal clearance, and urinary recovery of tobramycin were decreased by 11%, 32% and 38%, respectively. The alterations in the pharmacokinetics of tobramycin when administered in combination with piperacillin/tazobactam may be due to in vivo and in vitro inactivation of tobramycin in the presence of piperacillin/tazobactam. The inactivation of aminoglycosides in the presence of penicillin class drugs has been recognized. It has been postulated that penicillin-aminoglycoside complexes form; these complexes are microbiologically inactive and of unknown toxicity. In patients with severe renal dysfunction (i.e., chronic hemodialysis patients), the pharmacokinetics of tobramycin are significantly altered when tobramycin is administered in combination with piperacillin. The alteration of tobramycin pharmacokinetics and the potential toxicity of the penicillin-aminoglycoside complexes in patients with mild to moderate renal dysfunction who are administered an aminoglycoside in combination with piperacillin/tazobactam is unknown.

Probenecid: Concomitant administration of Tazocin and probenecid results in prolonged half-life of piperacillin (21%) and tazobactam (71%).

Vancomycin: No pharmacokinetic interactions are found between Tazocin and vancomycin.

Heparin: Coagulation parameters should be tested more frequently and monitored regularly, during simultaneous administration of high doses of heparin, oral anticoagulants and other drugs that may affect the blood coagulation system and/or the thrombocyte function.

Vecuronium: Piperacillin used concomitantly with vecuronium has been implicated in the prolongation of the neuromuscular blockade of vecuronium. Tazocin could produce the same phenomenon if given along with vecuronium. Due to their similar mechanism of action, it is expected that the neuromuscular blockade produced by any of the non-depolarizing muscle relaxants could be prolonged in the presence of piperacillin (see prescribing information for vecuronium bromide).

Lactated Ringers solution is not compatible with Tazocin (see Table III on following page).

Where Tazocin is administered concurrently with another antibiotic the drugs should **not** be mixed in the same solution but must be administered separately.

Drug/Laboratory Test Interactions: As with other penicillins, the administration of Tazocin may result in a false-positive reaction for glucose in the urine using a copper-reduction method (Clinitest). It is recommended that glucose tests based on enzymatic glucose oxidase reactions (such as Diastix or Tes-Tape) be used.

Adverse Effects: During the clinical investigations, 2 621 patients worldwide were treated with Tazocin in phase 3 trials. In the key North America clinical trials (n=830 patients), 90% of the adverse events reported were mild to moderate in severity and transient in nature. However, in 3.2% of the patients treated worldwide, Tazocin was discontinued because of adverse events primarily involving the skin (1.3%), including rash and pruritus; the gastrointestinal system (0.9%), including diarrhea, nausea, and vomiting; and allergic reactions (0.5%).

Adverse local reactions that were reported, irrespective of relationship to therapy with Tazocin, were phlebitis (1.3%), injection site reaction (0.5%), pain (0.2%), inflammation (0.2%), thrombophlebitis (0.2%) and edema (0.1%).

Adverse Clinical Events: Based on patients from the North American trials (n=1 063), the events with the highest incidence in patients, irrespective of relationship to Tazocin therapy, were diarrhea (11.3%); headache (7.7%); constipation (7.7%); nausea (6.9%); insomnia (6.6%); rash (4.2%), including maculopapular, bullous, urticarial, and eczematoid; vomiting (3.3%); dyspepsia (3.3%); pruritus (3.1%); stool changes (2.4%); fever (2.4%); agitation (2.1%); pain (1.7%); moniliasis (1.6%); hypertension (1.6%); dizziness (1.4%); abdominal pain (1.3%); chest pain (1.3%); edema (1.2%); anxiety (1.2%); rhinitis (1.2%); and dyspnea (1.1%).

Additional adverse systemic clinical events reported in 1% or less of the patients are listed below within each body system: Autonomic Nervous System: hypotension, ileus, syncope.

Body as a Whole: rigors, back pain, malaise.

Cardiovascular: tachycardia, including supraventricular and ventricular; bradycardia; arrhythmia, including atrial fibrillation, ventricular fibrillation, cardiac arrest, cardiac failure, circulatory failure, myocardial infarction.

CNS: tremor, convulsions, vertigo.

Gastrointestinal: melena, flatulence, hemorrhage, gastritis, hiccough, ulcerative stomatitis.

Pseudomembranous colitis was reported in 1 patient during the clinical trials. The onset of pseudomembranous colitis symptoms may occur during or after antibacterial treatment (see Warnings).

Hearing: tinnitus.

Hypersensitivity: anaphylaxis. Incidence of rash and fever is higher in patients with cystic fibrosis.

Metabolic and Nutritional: symptomatic hypoglycemia, thirst.

Musculoskeletal: myalgia, arthralgia.

Platelet, Bleeding, Clotting: mesenteric embolism, purpura, epistaxis, pulmonary embolism (see Precautions, General).

Psychiatric: confusion, hallucination, depression.

Reproduction, Female: leukorrhea, vaginitis.

Respiratory: pharyngitis, pulmonary edema, bronchospasm, coughing.

Skin and Appendages: genital pruritus, diaphoresis.

Special Senses: taste perversion.

Urinary: retention, dysuria, oliguria, hematuria, incontinence.

Vision: photophobia.

Vascular (extracardiac): flushing.

Adverse Laboratory Events: Changes in laboratory parameters, without regard to drug relationship, include: Hematologic: decreases in hemoglobin and hematocrit, thrombocytopenia, increases in platelet count, eosinophilia, leukopenia, neutropenia. The leukopenia/neutropenia associated with Tazocin administration appears to be reversible and most frequently associated with prolonged administration, i.e., ≥21 days of therapy. These patients were withdrawn from therapy; some had accompanying systemic symptoms (e.g., fever, rigors, chills).

Coagulation: positive direct Coombs' test, prolonged prothrombin time, prolonged partial thromboplastin time.

Hepatic: transient elevations of AST, ALT, alkaline phosphatase, bilirubin.

Renal: increases in serum creatinine, blood urea nitrogen.

Urinalysis: proteinuria, hematuria, pyuria.

Additional laboratory events include abnormalities in electrolytes (i.e., increases and decreases in sodium, potassium and calcium), hyperglycemia, decreases in total protein or albumin. In individuals with liver disease or those receiving cytotoxic therapy or diuretics, Tazocin has been reported rarely to produce a decrease in serum potassium levels at high doses of piperacillin.

The following adverse reactions have also been reported for Pipracil: Skin and Appendages: erythema multiforme and Stevens-Johnson syndrome, rarely reported.

Gastrointestinal: cholestatic hepatitis.

Renal: rarely, interstitial nephritis.

Skeletal: prolonged muscle relaxation (see Precautions, Drug Interactions).

Overdose: Symptoms and Treatment: Information on overdosage of Tazocin in humans in not available.

Excessive serum levels of either tazobactam or piperacillin may be reduced by hemodialysis, although no specific antidote is known. As with other penicillins, neuromuscular excitability or convulsions have occurred following large i.v. doses, primarily in patients with impaired renal function.

In the case of motor excitability or convulsions, general supportive measures, including administration of anticonvulsive agents (e.g., diazepam or barbiturates) may be considered.

Dosage: The usual total daily dose for adults is 12 g/1.5 g, given as 3 g/0.375 g every 6 hours.

Clinical trial data in the treatment of intra-abdominal infections support the efficacy of 4 g/0.5 g given every 8 hours.

Renal Insufficiency: In patients with renal insufficiency, the i.v. dose should be adjusted to the degree of actual renal function impairment. The suggested daily doses are shown in Table I.

Table I—Tazocin

Dosage Recommendations

Creatinine Clearance (mL/min)	Recommended Dosage Regimen
>40	12 g/1.5 g/day in divided doses of 3 g/0.375 g q6h
20–40	8 g/1 g/day in divided doses of 2 g/0.25 g q6h
<20	6 g/0.75 g/day in divided doses of 2 g/0.25 g q8h

For patients on hemodialysis, the maximum dose is 2 g/0.25 g piperacillin/tazobactam given every 8 hours. In addition, because hemodialysis removes 30 to 40% of Tazocin dose in 4 hours, one additional dose of 0.75 g piperacillin/tazobactam should be administered following each dialysis period. For patients with renal failure, measurement of serum levels of Tazocin will provide additional guidance for adjusting dosage.

Duration of Therapy: The usual duration of treatment is from 7 to 10 days. The duration should be guided by the severity of the infection and the patient's clinical and bacteriological progress.

Administration: Tazocin should be administered by i.v. infusion over 30 minutes (see Pharmacology).

Reconstituted Solutions: Reconstitute Tazocin with at least 5 mL of a suitable diluent per g of piperacillin from the list of diluents provided below. Shake well until dissolved. It should be further diluted to the desired final volume with an acceptable diluent (see Tables II and III on following page).

Intermittent I.V. Infusion: Reconstitute as previously described, with 5 mL of an acceptable diluent per 1 g of piperacillin and then further dilute in the desired volume (at least 50 mL). This diluted solution must be used immediately. Administer by infusion over a period of at least 30 minutes. During the infusion it is desirable to discontinue the primary infusion solution.

When concomitant therapy with aminoglycosides is indicated, Tazocin and the aminoglycoside should be reconstituted and administered separately, due to the in vitro inactivation of the aminoglycoside (see Precautions, Drug Interactions).

Stability of Tazocin following Reconstitution: Tazocin is stable in glass and plastic containers (plastic syringes, i.v. bags and tubing) when reconstituted with acceptable diluents.

Stability studies have demonstrated chemical stability [potency, pH of reconstituted solution, and clarity of solution] for up to 12 hours at room temperature and up to 48 hours at refrigerated temperatures in glass vials. Discard unused portions after storage for 12 hours at room temperature or 48 hours when refrigerated.

Table II—Tazocin

Reconstitution

Vial Size (piperacillin/ tazobactam)	Volume of Diluent to be Added to Vial	Approximate Available Volume	Nominal Concentration per mL
2.25 g (2 g/0.25 g)	10 mL	11.60 mL	0.194 g/mL (0.172 g/mL/0.022 g/mL
3.375 g (3 g/0.375 g)	15 mL	17.36 mL	0.194 g/mL (0.172 g/mL/0.022 g/mL
4.5 g (4 g/0.5 g)	20 mL	23.15 mL	0.194 g/mL (0.172 g/mL/0.022 g/mL)

Table III—Tazocin

Reconstitute Tazocin per gram of piperacillin with 5 mL of a **Compatible Reconstitution Diluent** (listed below)	**Further dilute** the reconstituted Tazocin with 50 mL to 150 mL of a **Compatible I.V. Diluent Solution** (listed below)
0.9% Sodium Chloride for Injection	0.9% Sodium Chloride for Injection
Sterile Water for Injection	Sterile Water for Injection*
Dextrose 5%	Dextran 6% in Saline
Bacteriostatic Saline/Parabens	Dextrose 5%
Bacteriostatic Water/Parabens	
Bacteriostatic Saline/Benzyl Alcohol	
Bacteriostatic Water/Benzyl Alcohol	

*Maximum recommended volume per dose of Sterile Water for Injection is 50 mL.
Lactated Ringers solution is not compatible with Tazocin.

Parenteral drug products should be inspected visually for particulate matter and discoloration prior to administration, whenever solution and container permit.

Incompatibilities: Not to be added to blood products.

Because of chemical instability, Tazocin should not be used for i.v. administration with solutions containing sodium bicarbonate alone. It may be used with i.v. admixtures containing other ingredients as well as sodium bicarbonate for up to 24 hours at room temperature and 48 hours refrigerated.

Solutions containing Tazocin and protein hydrolysates or amino acids should be used within 12 hours if stored at room temperature and 24 hours if refrigerated.

Supplied: 2.25 g Vial: Each vial contains: piperacillin sodium equivalent to piperacillin 2 g and tazobactam sodium equivalent to tazobactam 0.25 g. Sodium: 4.69 mmol (108 mg). Vials of 2.25 g, boxes of 10.

3.375 g Vial: Each vial contains: piperacillin sodium equivalent to piperacillin 3 g and tazobactam sodium equivalent to tazobactam 0.375 g. Sodium: 7.03 mmol (162 mg). Vials of 3.375 g, boxes of 10.

4.5 g Vial: Each vial contains: piperacillin sodium equivalent to piperacillin 4 g and tazobactam sodium equivalent to tazobactam 0.5 g. Sodium: 9.37 mmol (216 mg). Vials of 4.5 g, boxes of 10.

Store at controlled room temperature 15 to 30°C.

Sensitivity Discs: Tazocin 110 μg sensitivity discs (piperacillin 100 μg + tazobactam 10 μg) are available and must be refrigerated upon receipt.

TAZORAC™ Ⓟ

Allergan

Tazarotene

Antipsoriasis—Antiacne

Pharmacology: Tazarotene is a retinoid prodrug which is converted to its active form, M1 ("tazarotenic acid", or AGN 190299), by rapid de-esterification in most biological systems. "Tazarotenic acid" binds to and regulates gene expression through all three members of the RAR family of retinoid nuclear receptors, RARα, RARβ, and RARγ, but shows selectivity for RARβ and RARγ.

Psoriasis: The exact mechanisms of tazarotene action in psoriasis are not completely defined. Among its specific pharmacological activities, demonstrated in cellular and in in vivo studies, topical tazarotene blocks induction of epidermal ornithine decarboxylase (ODC) activity, which is associated with cell proliferation and hyperplasia, suppresses expression of MRP8, an inflammatory marker present in psoriatic epidermis at high levels, and inhibits cornified envelope formation and build-up, which is an element of psoriatic scale. Improvement in psoriatic patients appears to occur in association with restoration of normal cutaneous morphology and reduction of the inflammatory markers ICAM-1 and HLA-DR. There is also a diminution of markers of epidermal hyperplasia and abnormal differentiation such as keratinocyte transglutaminase, involucrin and keratin 16.

In 2 large vehicle-controlled clinical studies, tazarotene 0.1 and 0.05% gels applied once daily were significantly more effective than vehicle in reducing the severity of the clinical signs of plaque psoriasis. Tazarotene gels demonstrated effectiveness as early as 1 week after starting treatment, with initial treatment success (good or excellent response or complete clearing) reached significantly earlier than with vehicle. The 0.1% gel was more effective than the 0.05% gel, but the 0.05% gel was associated with less local irritation than the 0.1% gel. In one of these studies, patients were also evaluated for 12 weeks following cessation of therapy, and it was found that subjects treated with the 0.1 and 0.05% tazarotene gels continued to show a therapeutic effect during the 12-week post-treatment period.

Acne: Tazarotene is thought to act against several of the factors that contribute to acne vulgaris. Animal and in vitro studies show that tazarotene inhibits corneocyte accumulation in rhino mouse skin (in vivo) and cross-linked envelope formation in cultured human keratinocytes (in vitro). The primary mechanisms of action in humans are believed to be the normalizing of keratinization and a decrease in the coherence of follicular keratinocytes. Both mechanisms contribute to a comedolytic effect against existing comedones and prevention of the development of new microcomedones. Tazarotene also exhibits activity against inflammatory acne.

In 2 large vehicle-controlled studies, tazarotene 0.1 and 0.05% gels applied once daily were significantly more effective than their vehicle in the treatment of acne vulgaris. The 0.1% gel was more effective than the 0.05% gel, but the 0.05% gel was associated with less local irritation than the 0.1% gel.

Pharmacokinetics: Controlled clinical pharmacokinetic studies with 0.1% ^{14}C-tazarotene gel indicate that less than 1% of the dose is systemically absorbed when applied topically (unoccluded) to psoriatic plaques, and approximately 5% of the dose is absorbed after application to normal skin under occlusion. After a 7-day topical dosing period with tazarotene 0.1% gel to normal skin over 20% of the body surface area (0.1 mg/kg/day), the mean maximum plasma concentration was 0.72±0.58 ng/mL at 9 hours, and the area under the plasma concentration time curve over a 24-hour time period was 10.1±7.2 ng·hr/mL. A clinical pharmacokinetic study conducted in 5 psoriatic patients where treatment conditions were maximized to ensure sufficiently high plasma concentrations, showed that tazarotene absorption through the skin increased over the 2-week course of the study. The maximal plasma concentration was 12.0±7.6 ng/mL at 6 hours, and the area under the plasma concentration time curve over a 24-hour time period was 105±55 ng·hr/mL. This increased absorption through the skin in psoriatic may be due not only to a reduction of thick scale prior to normalization of indurated plaques, but also in part to a possible thinning of the stratum corneum. Following topical dosing of tazarotene, the half-life of "tazarotenic acid", the primary active metabolite, was approximately 18 hours. The terminal half-lives of tazarotene and "tazarotenic acid" were 6 and 14 hours respectively, following i.v. dosing to normal volunteers.

Following application, the drug undergoes esterase hydrolysis to its primary active metabolite, tazarotenic acid (the only metabolite of tazarotene known to have retinoid activity), and oxidative metabolism to inactive sulfoxide and sulfone derivatives. Following topical dosing with ^{14}C-tazarotene under occlusion to healthy subjects, 2.6 and 2.7% of the dose were excreted in urine and feces, respectively, over a 7-day period. Following a topical unoccluded dose to psoriatic patients, 0.3% of the dose was excreted in the urine and 0.4% excreted in the feces. Greater than 75% of total drug excretion was completed within 72 hours after drug removal, with equal excretion of radioactivity in urine and feces. The drug's rapid systemic metabolism limits the propensity for tissue distribution and body exposure to tazarotene.

Indications: For topical application in the treatment of plaque psoriasis and acne vulgaris.

Contraindications: Individuals who have shown hypersensitivity to retinoic compounds, or to any of the product excipients (see Supplied). Topical retinoids should not be used in the presence of seborrheic dermatitis.

Warnings: Topical retinoids should not be used on eczematous skin.

Keep away from the eyes, nose, mouth, and other mucous membranes. In the event of contact with the eye, flush with cold water.

In some patients, temporary skin irritation may occur, especially during the early weeks of treatment. If excessive pruritus, burning, skin redness or peeling occur, the medication should either be discontinued until the integrity of the skin is restored, or the dosing should be adjusted to a level or interval the patient can tolerate.

Pregnancy: **Topical tazarotene should be used by females of childbearing age only after contraceptive counselling. It is recommended that topical tazarotene should not be used by pregnant females.**

Tazarotene 0.05% gel, administered topically during gestation days 6 through 17 in rats and days 6 through 18 in rabbits, has been shown to be nonteratogenic and nonfetotoxic at maximum tolerated doses of 0.25 mg/kg/day. However, at these doses, slightly reduced fetal body weights and reduced skeletal ossification occurred in rats. These changes may be considered variants of normal development and were usually corrected after weaning. As with other retinoids, teratogenic effects were seen when tazarotene was given orally to rats and rabbits at doses of 0.25 and 0.2 mg/kg/day, respectively. Very low drug exposure to the fetus was observed after oral administration of ^{14}C-tazarotene to pregnant rats and rabbits. Multiple topical dosing to pregnant rats at 0.2 mg/kg daily resulted in undetectable radioactivity in the fetus. These finding indicate very little drug exposure to the rat fetus via placental transfer after topical treatment with tazarotene. There are no adequate and well-controlled studies in pregnant women.

Precautions: General: For external use only. Excessive use should be avoided.

Excessive exposure to sun or ultraviolet light should be minimized or avoided. Sunscreen and protective clothing should be used when exposed to sunlight.

The safety of use over more than 20% of body surface area has not been established.

The treatment area should not be covered with dressings or bandages.

In patients with psoriasis, application to normal skin should be avoided.

Drug Interactions: Concomitant dermatologic medications and cosmetics that have a strong drying effect should be avoided. It is also advisable to "rest" a patient's skin until the effects of such preparations subside before use of tazarotene gels begins.

Carcinogenesis, Mutagenesis, Impairment of Fertility: Long-term studies of tazarotene following topical application in mice and oral administration to rats showed no indications of increased carcinogenic risks related to treatment. Marked skin irritation, possibly contributing to enhancement of photocarcinogenesis, was observed in hairless mice following chronic topical dosing with intercurrent exposure to ultraviolet radiation at tazarotene concentrations of 0.001, 0.005, and 0.01% for up to 40 weeks. Relevance of these studies to use in humans has not been established, but patients should minimize exposure to sun or ultraviolet light.

Tazarotene was found to be nonmutagenic and nonclastogenic in a standard battery of in vitro and in vivo tests.

No impairment of fertility occurred in rats when male animals were treated for 70 days prior to mating and female

Tazorac (cont'd)

animals were treated for 14 days prior to mating and continuing through gestation and lactation with topical doses of tazarotene gel.

Reproductive capabilities of F1 animals, including F2 survival and development, were not affected by topical administration of tazarotene gel to female F0 parental rats from gestation day 16 through lactation day 20 at the maximum tolerated dose of 0.125 mg/kg/day.

Lactation: After single topical doses of ^{14}C-tazarotene to the skin of lactating rats, secretion of radioactivity at very low levels was detected in milk, suggesting that there would be limited transfer of drug-related material to the offspring via milk. It is not known whether this drug is excreted in human milk. Because many drugs are excreted in human milk, caution should be exercised when tazarotene is administered to a nursing woman.

Children: The safety and efficacy of tazarotene have not been established in pediatric patients under the age of 12 years.

Adverse Effects: Psoriasis: The most frequent adverse reactions (≥5%) reported during clinical trials with tazarotene gel included pruritus, burning, erythema, skin irritation, skin pain, and worsening of psoriasis. Reported less frequently (1 to <5%) were desquamation, rash, contact irritant dermatitis, skin inflammation, stinging, and dry skin. Rarely reported reactions (<1%) included fissuring of the skin, bleeding, skin discharge, increased skin fragility, and localized edema. The incidence and severity of adverse reactions appeared to be dose related.

Acne: The most frequent adverse reactions (≥5%) reported during clinical trials with tazarotene gels in the treatment of acne included burning, desquamation, dry skin, erythema, and pruritus. Reported less frequently (1 to <5%) were skin irritation, and stinging. The following reactions were reported rarely (<1%) by study subjects: skin pain, skin tightness, fissuring of the skin, cheilitis, skin discoloration, worsening of acne, contact irritant dermatitis, and localized edema. The incidence and severity of adverse reactions appeared to be dose related.

In human topical safety studies, tazarotene 0.1% and 0.05% gels did not induce contact sensitization, phototoxicity or photoallergy.

Overdose: Symptoms and Treatment: Excessive topical use of tazarotene may lead to marked redness, peeling, or discomfort (see Warnings). Inadvertent oral ingestion of tazarotene may lead to the same adverse effects as those associated with excessive oral intake of vitamin A including teratogenesis in women of childbearing age. If accidental oral ingestion occurs, the patient should be monitored, and appropriate supportive measures should be administered as necessary, including pregnancy testing in women of childbearing age.

Dosage: General: Application may cause a transitory feeling of burning or stinging. If irritation becomes problematic, the dosage may be altered by choosing the lower drug concentration or temporarily reducing the frequency of application.

Excessive exposure to sun or ultraviolet light should be minimized or avoided. Sunscreen and protective clothing should be used when exposed to sunlight.

Psoriasis: Apply once a day, in the evening, to psoriatic lesions, using enough to cover only the lesion with a thin film. If a bath or shower is taken prior to application, the skin should be dry before applying the gel. If emollients are used, they should be applied and allowed to absorb into the skin before application. Because unaffected skin may be more susceptible to irritation, application to these areas should be carefully avoided.

Acne: Cleanse the skin gently. After the skin is dry, apply a thin film once a day, in the evening, to the skin where acne lesions appear. Use enough to cover the entire affected area.

Information for the Patient: See Blue Section—Information for the Patient "Tazorac".

Supplied: Each g of colorless to light yellow, translucent homogeneous gel contains: tazarotene 0.05% or 0.1% (w/w). Nonmedicinal ingredients: ascorbic acid, benzyl alcohol, butylated hydroxyanisole, butylated hydroxytoluene, carbomer 934P, edetate disodium, hexylene glycol, poloxamer 407, polyethylene glycol, polysorbate 40, purified water and tromethamine. Collapsible aluminum tubes of 10, 30 and 100 g. Sample sizes of 3.5 g for physicians. Store at room temperature (15 to 25°C).

Reviewed 1998

Td POLIO ADSORBED (Tetanus and Diphtheria Toxoids Adsorbed and Inactivated Poliomyelitis Vaccine)

Connaught

Active Immunizing Agent

Pharmacology: Tetanus is an acute and often fatal disease caused by an extremely potent neurotoxin produced by C. tetani. The organism is ubiquitous and its occurrence in nature cannot be controlled. Immunization is highly effective, produces long-lasting protection and is recommended for the whole population. Only 2 to 3 cases of tetanus are now reported annually in Canada. Two deaths have been recorded in the past 5 years.

Diphtheria is a serious communicable disease caused by toxigenic strains of C. diphtheriae. The case-fatality rate remains 5 to 10%, with highest death rates in the very young and the elderly. The organism may be harbored in the nasopharynx, skin and other sites of asymptomatic carriers, making eradication of the disease difficult.

Routine immunization against diphtheria in infancy and childhood has been widely practised in Canada since 1930. This has resulted in a remarkable decline in the morbidity and mortality of this disease. In 1924, there were 9 000 cases reported, but less than 5 annually in recent years and no deaths since 1983. However, toxigenic strains of diphtheria bacilli are still detected each year in diphtheria carriers (pharyngeal, skin and ear) in Northern and Western Canada. Asymptomatic carriage of C. diphtheriae is far more common than clinical diphtheria. The disease occurs most frequently in unimmunized or partially immunized individuals. Although occasional cases of mild clinical diphtheria do occur in apparently fully immunized persons, antitoxin stimulated by immunization persists at protective levels for 10 years or more.

Poliomyelitis is caused by infection with 1 of 3 antigenic types of poliovirus. The last major epidemic occurred in 1959 when 1 887 paralytic cases occurred. Following the introduction of inactivated poliovirus vaccines (IPV) in Canada in 1955 and of trivalent oral poliovirus vaccine (OPV) in 1962, the indigenous disease has been virtually eliminated. In the 1970s an average of only 3 cases was reported each year.

The last significant outbreak of poliomyelitis in Canada occurred in 1978-1979 when there were 11 cases of paralytic disease among unimmunized contacts of imported cases in Ontario, Alberta and British Columbia. All had declined vaccination on religious grounds. In spite of the potential for spread in the community at large, this did not occur because of appropriate and prompt outbreak control measures and high levels of immunity induced earlier by IPV in Ontario, by OPV in British Columbia and by the combined use of IPV followed by OPV in Alberta.

Since 1980, 10 cases of poliomyelitis have been reported in Canada, 9 of which were determined to be vaccine-associated. The last reported case of paralytic disease caused by wild poliovirus occurred in 1988 and was caused by a strain imported from Pakistan. Circulation of wild polioviruses no longer occurs in the Canadian population except in rare circumstances. Thus, unapparent infections with these strains do not contribute to the maintenance of immunity in the population. It therefore remains crucial that the highest possible level of vaccine-induced immunity be maintained in the population by systematic immunization of infants and children.

In a clinical trial involving 276 individuals previously immunized against tetanus, diphtheria and poliomyelitis, a single (0.5 mL) injection of Td Polio Adsorbed, of any of the 3 vaccine lots tested, stimulated a prompt antibody response to each of the antigens -tetanus diphtheria and poliovirus types 1, 2, and 3. See Table I.

Response to the reinforcement injection was equally satisfactory in those whose most recent previous injection had been received more than 10 years previously as in those with a shorter interval since the last previous injection.

The immunogenicity of the tetanus and diphtheria components of Td Polio Adsorbed administered as a series of 3 (0.5 mL) injections for primary immunization has been demonstrated in a small number (17) of individuals whose ages ranged from 6 to 56 years. These individuals were all confirmed unimmunized to both tetanus and diphtheria. Four weeks following the second injection of vaccine, given 2 months after the first, all had responded with serum tetanus antitoxin levels ranging from 0.11 to 14.0 IU/mL and with diphtheria antitoxin levels ranging from 0.01 to 1.28 IU/mL. Following the third injection of vaccine 6 to 8 months after second, the 8 individuals tested developed antitoxin titres to tetanus of 0.56 to 14.0 IU/mL and to diphtheria of 0.16 to 5.12 IU/mL.

Inclusion of inactivated poliomyelitis vaccine with the tetanus and diphtheria toxoids adsorbed and the spacing of the 3 injections at 0, 2 and 6 to 12 months, produced an adequate neutralizing antibody response to all 3 types of poliovirus.

Indications: For secondary immunization in children 7 years of age and older and adults who have been previously immunized against tetanus, diphtheria and poliomyelitis.

Td Polio Adsorbed may also be used for primary immunization of older children (7 years of age and over) and of adults who have not been immunized previously against tetanus, diphtheria and poliomyelitis.

Contraindications: General: Immunization with Td Polio Adsorbed should be deferred in the presence of any acute illness, including febrile illness (to avoid superimposing any adverse effects from the vaccine on the underlying illness or mistakenly attributing a manifestation of the underlying illness as a complication of vaccine use). A minor afebrile illness such as mild upper respiratory infection is not usually reason to defer immunization.

Absolute: Allergy to any component of Td Polio Adsorbed (see Supplied) or an allergic or anaphylactic reaction to a previous dose of Td Polio Adsorbed are contraindications to vaccination.

Elective immunization of persons over 6 months of age should be deferred during an outbreak of poliomyelitis because of the risk of provocation paralysis.

Warnings: I.M. injections should be given with care in persons suffering from coagulation disorders or on anticoagulant therapy because of the risk of hemorrhage.

If Td Polio Adsorbed is used in persons with malignancies, persons receiving immunosuppressive therapies, including irradiation, antimetabolites, alkylating agents, cytotoxic drugs, or persons who are otherwise immunocompromised (including HIV infected individuals transplant recipients, persons suffering from autoimmune disorders), the expected immune response may not be obtained.

Corticosteroid therapy can result in immunosuppression although the exact dose and duration of therapy required to suppress the immune system is not well defined. Persons treated with high doses of systemic steroids, e.g., ≥2 mg/kg/day of prednisone orally for more than 2 weeks, should be considered to have a compromised immune system.

As with any vaccine, immunization with Td Polio Adsorbed may not protect 100% of susceptible individuals.

Precautions: General: The possibility of allergic reactions in individuals sensitive to components of the vaccine should be evaluated. Epinephrine HCl solution (1:1 000) and other appropriate agents should be available for immediate use in case an anaphylactic or acute hypersensitivity reaction occurs. Health care providers should be familiar with current recommendations for the initial management of anaphylaxis in nonhospital settings, including proper airway management.

Table I—Td Polio Adsorbed

Antibody Titres in Recipients of a Single (0.5 mL) Injection of Td Polio Adsorbed

	Pre-injection		28 Days Post Injection	
	Range	**G.M.T.***	**Range**	**G.M.T.***
Tetanus Antitoxin IU/mL	0.01-14.0	0.72	0.56-14.0	2.78
Diphtheria Antitoxin IU/mL	0.005-10.24	0.17	0.04-40.96	1.34
Poliovirus Neutralizing Antibody				
Type 1	1:4-1:2048	1:69.8	1:8-1:16384	1:383.9
Type 2	1:4-1:2048	1:67.2	1:16-1:16384	1:573.0
Type 3	1:4-1:2048	1:44.4	1:16-1:32768	1:1007.4

*G.M.T.=Geometric Mean Titre.

Before administration of any vaccine, all appropriate precautions should be taken to prevent adverse reactions. This includes a review of the patient's history with respect to possible hypersensitivity to the vaccine or similar vaccine, determination of previous immunization history, and the presence of any contraindications to immunization, current health status, and a current knowledge of the literature concerning the use of the vaccine under consideration.

Frequent booster doses of tetanus toxoid in the presence of adequate or excessive serum levels of tetanus antitoxin have been associated with increased incidence and severity of reactions and should be avoided. If hypersensitivity to the diphtheria component is suspected, tetanus toxoid should be used for reinforcing doses.

Special care should be taken to ensure that the product is not injected into a blood vessel.

Caution: A separate sterile needle and syringe, or a sterile disposable unit, must be used for each individual patient to prevent the transmission of infectious agents.

There have been case reports of transmission of HIV and hepatitis by failure to scrupulously observe sterile technique. In particular, the same needle and/or syringe must never be used to re-enter a multidose vial to withdraw vaccine even when it is to be used for inoculation of the same patient. This may lead to contamination of the vial contents and infection of patients who subsequently receive vaccine from the vial.

Needles should not be recapped and should be disposed of properly.

Before administration of Td Polio Adsorbed, health-care personnel should inform the parent (or guardian) or the patient to be immunized of the benefits and risks of immunization, inquire about the recent health status of the patient and comply with any local requirements with respect to information to be provided to the patient before immunization.

Adverse Effects: During the clinical trial of Td Polio Adsorbed, the vaccinees experienced only a low level of reactions associated with the injections. Discomfort at the injection site was usually of short duration. Systemic complaints included mild fever (none exceeded 37.6°C), headache, malaise, tiredness and dizziness. No side effects of major significance were noted.

Localized reactions consisting of discomfort, pain, swelling and redness at the injection site may be associated with the toxoids. These are usually of low frequency and transient in duration. Following booster doses, local erythema and swelling are not uncommon and Arthus-type sensitivity may occur. Persistent nodules at the site of injection have occurred following the use of adsorbed vaccine, but this complication is unusual.

Generalized reactions may develop following immunization and may take the form of allergic reactions including urticaria and less commonly, angioneurotic edema. Influenza-like symptoms have been reported and usually occur within 12 hours of vaccination. Neurological complications such as peripheral neuropathies and demyelinating diseases of the CNS following tetanus toxoid or diphtheria toxoid have been documented but are rare.

It has been shown that the incidence of reactions to toxoids (especially to tetanus toxoid) rises according to the number of previously administered doses. This incidence in adults is unlikely to exceed 1% and occurs mainly in the overimmunized.

Nervous System: The following neurologic illnesses have been reported as temporally associated with vaccine containing tetanus toxoid: neurological complications including cochlear lesion, brachial plexus neuropathies, paralysis of the radial nerve, paralysis of the recurrent nerve, accommodation paresis, and EEG disturbances with encephalopathy. In the differential diagnosis of polyradiculoneuropathies following administration of a vaccine containing tetanus toxoid, tetanus toxoid should be considered as a possible etiology.

On the basis of a case report and evidence that a vaccine-induced immunologic response can cause Guillain Barre Syndrome (GBS), the Institute of Medicine concluded that tetanus toxoid-containing vaccines can trigger GBS in adults. No increased risk for GBS has been observed with the use of DTP in children.

Physicians, nurses, and pharmacists should report any adverse occurrences temporally related to the administration of the product in accordance with local requirements and to the Medical Director, Connaught Laboratories Limited, 1755 Steeles Avenue West, Toronto, Ontario, Canada, M2R 3T4.

Dosage: For persons who have previously been immunized against tetanus, diphtheria and poliomyelitis, a dose of 0.5 mL should be administered as a reinforcing dose at approximately 10 year intervals.

For primary immunization of persons 7 years or older a series of three (0.5 mL) injections is required. The first 2 doses should be given 4 to 8 weeks apart and the third 6 to 12 months later.

Tetanus Prophylaxis in Wound Management: Table II summarizes the recommended use of immunizing agents in wound management. It is important to ascertain the number of doses of toxoid previously given and the interval since the last dose. If not clearly documented, a history of immunization should be regarded as "uncertain". If a tetanus booster is required it is preferred to choose a combined preparation such as Tetanus and Diphtheria Toxoids Adsorbed For 7 Years and Older, containing 5 Lf tetanus toxoid and 2 Lf diphtheria toxoid per 0.5 mL dose. Appropriate cleansing and debridement of the wound is imperative. Booster doses given more frequently than recommended above may lead to adverse local and systemic reactions.

Note: Diphtheria and Tetanus Toxoids Adsorbed and Poliomyelitis Vaccine, containing 25 Lf of diphtheria toxoid and 5 Lf of the tetanus toxoid per 0.5 mL dose, should not be administered as a tetanus booster to children over 7 years of age or adults due to the risk of reaction to the higher content of diphtheria toxoid in this vaccine.

Table II—Td Polio Adsorbed (Tetanus and Diphtheria Toxoids and Inactivated Poliomyelitis Vaccine)

Immunizing Agents in Wound Management

History of Tetanus Immunization (doses)	Clean, Minor Wounds		All Other Wounds	
	Td Polio[a]	TIG[b]	Td Polio[a]	TIG[b]
Uncertain or less than 3	Yes	No	Yes	Yes
3 or more	No[c]	No	No[d]	No

[a] Adult type tetanus and diphtheria toxoids and poliomyelitis vaccine adsorbed (for 7 years and older). If the patient is less than 7 years old, DT or DPT or DPT Polio is given (see text).
[b] Tetanus immune globulin.
[c] Yes if more than 10 years since the last dose.
[d] Yes if more than 5 years since last dose.

Note: Tetanus toxoid, or a combined vaccine containing tetanus toxoid, and tetanus immune globulin should be administered in separate syringes at different sites.

Parenteral biological products should be inspected visually for extraneous particulate matter and/or discoloration before administration. If these conditions exist, the product should not be administered.

Shake the vial or ampul well to distribute uniformly the suspension before withdrawing each dose. Before withdrawing a dose from an ampul, tap the container first to ensure that any vaccine in the ampul neck falls to the lower portion of the ampul. Once the ampul has been opened, any of its contents not used immediately should be discarded. When administering a dose from a rubber-stoppered vial, do not remove either the rubber stopper or the metal seal holding it in place. Aseptic technique must be used for withdrawal of each dose (see Precautions).

Before injection, the skin over the site to be injected should be cleansed with a suitable germicide.

Administer the vaccine **i.m.** The preferred site is into the deltoid muscle.

After insertion of the needle, aspirate to ensure that the needle has not entered a blood vessel.

Do not inject I.v.

Each person who is immunized should be given a permanent personal immunization record. In addition, it is essential that the physician or nurse record the immunization history in the permanent medical record of each patient. This permanent office record should contain the name of the vaccine, date given, dose, manufacturer and lot number.

Supplied: Td Polio Adsorbed is a sterile cloudy uniform suspension of diphtheria and tetanus toxoids adsorbed on aluminum phosphate and combined with inactivated poliomyelitis vaccine. Each dose of 0.5 mL contains: purified inactivated poliomyelitis vaccine (Type I (Mahoney), Type 2 (M.E.F.1) and Type 3 (Saukett)), tetanus toxoid (5 Lf), diphtheria toxoid (2 Lf) and aluminum phosphate (1.5 mg). Albumin (Human) is present at a concentration of $\leq 0.05\%$. Trace amounts of neomycin and polymyxin B may be present from the cell growth medium. 2-phenoxyethanol 0.5% is added as a preservative.

Ready for use multiple dose rubber-stoppered vials of 5 mL. Single-dose glass ampuls of 0.5 mL, packages of 5. Store between 2 and 8°C. **Do not freeze.** Product which has been exposed to freezing should not be used. Do not use vaccine after expiration date.

Reviewed 1999

TEARDROPS®
CIBA Vision

Polyvinyl Alcohol—Povidone

Artificial Tears

Supplied: Each mL contains: polyvinyl alcohol 14 mg and povidone 6 mg in a sterile, aqueous vehicle with chlorobutanol as preservative. Plastic squeeze bottles of 15 mL with dropper tips.

TEARS ENCORE®
Dioptic

Polysorbate 80

Eye Lubricant

Supplied: Each mL of sterile, aqueous solution contains: 0.4% polysorbate 80. Nonmedicinal ingredients: disodium edetate, purified water, retinyl palmitate and sodium chloride. If solution changes color or becomes cloudy do not use. Plastic dropper bottles of 10 mL. Discard the bottle 30 days after opening.

TEARS NATURALE®
Alcon

Dextran 70—Hydroxypropyl Methylcellulose

Artificial Tears

Supplied: Each Drop-Tainer dispenser contains: a sterile, buffered, isotonic solution of dextran 70 0.1% and hydroxypropyl methylcellulose 0.3%. Preservative: benzalkonium chloride. Nonmedicinal ingredients: edetate disodium, hydrochloric acid, potassium chloride, purified water, sodium chloride and sodium hydroxide. Drop-Tainer dispensers of 15 or 30 mL.

TEARS NATURALE® FREE
Alcon

Dextran 70—Hydroxypropyl Methylcellulose

Artificial Tears

Supplied: Each mL of sterile, isotonic solution contains: 0.1% dextran 70 and hydroxypropyl methylcellulose 0.3%. Preservative-free. Nonmedicinal ingredients: hydrochloric acid, potassium chloride, purified water, sodium borate, sodium chloride and sodium hydroxide. Unit dose containers of 0.6 mL. Boxes of 24, packs of 6.

TEARS NATURALE® II
Alcon

Dextran 70—Hydroxypropyl Methylcellulose

Artificial Tears

Supplied: Each mL of sterile, isotonic solution contains: Duasorb (0.1% dextran 70 and hydroxypropyl methylcellulose 0.3%) with Polyquad 0.001% as a preservative. Nonmedicinal ingredients: hydrochloric acid, potassium chloride, purified water, sodium borate, sodium chloride and sodium hydroxide. Drop-Tainer dispensers of 15 and 30 mL.

TEARS PLUS®
Allergan

Polyvinyl Alcohol—Povidone

Ocular Lubricant

Supplied: Each mL of an aqueous, sterile, non-buffered isotonic solution contains: polyvinyl alcohol 1.4% and povidone with chlorobutanol (preservative). Plastic dropper bottles of 15 and 30 mL.

TEBRAZID™ ℞
ICN

Pyrazinamide

Tuberculosis Therapy

Supplied: Each white, scored, compressed tablet imprinted ICN T11 contains: pyrazinamide USP 500 mg. Nonmedicinal ingredients: cornstarch, silicone dioxide and talc. Bottles of 120 and 500.

TECNAL® ◈
TECNAL® C¼, C½ Ⓝ
Technilab

ASA—Caffeine—Butalbital
ASA—Caffeine—Codeine Phosphate—Butalbital

Analgesic—Sedative

Supplied: Tecnal: Capsules: Each blue and purple capsule contains: butalbital USP 50 mg, caffeine USP 40 mg and ASA USP 330 mg. Nonmedicinal ingredients: FD&C Blue #1 aluminum lake, FD&C Red #3, gelatin, microcrystalline cellulose, pregelatinized cornstarch, propylene glycol, shellac, silicon dioxide, sodium chloride, sodium lauryl sulfate and titanium dioxide. Bottles of 100 and 500.

Tablets: Each white tablet contains: butalbital USP 50 mg, caffeine USP 40 mg and ASA USP 330 mg. Nonmedicinal ingredients: microcrystalline cellulose, povidone, simethicone, sodium croscarmellose and stearic acid. Bottles of 100 and 500.

Tecnal C¼: Each dark blue and white capsule contains: butalbital USP 50 mg, caffeine USP 40 mg, ASA USP 330 mg and codeine phosphate USP 15 mg. Nonmedicinal ingredients: black iron oxide, FD&C Blue #1 aluminum lake, FD&C Blue #2 aluminum lake, FD&C Red #3, FD&C Red #40 aluminum lake, FD&C Yellow #40 aluminum lake, gelatin, microcrystalline cellulose, pregelatinized cornstarch, shellac, silicon dioxide, sodium chloride, sodium lauryl sulfate and titanium dioxide. Bottles of 100 and 500.

Tecnal C½: Each light blue and dark blue capsule contains: butalbital USP 50 mg, caffeine USP 40 mg, ASA USP 330 mg and codeine phosphate USP 30 mg. Nonmedicinal ingredients: black iron oxide, FD&C Blue #1 aluminum lake, FD&C Blue #2 aluminum lake, FD&C Red #3, FD&C Red #40 aluminum lake, FD&C Yellow #10 aluminum lake, gelatin, microcrystalline cellulose, pregelatinized cornstarch, shellac, silicon dioxide, sodium chloride, sodium lauryl sulfate and titanium dioxide. Bottles of 100 and 500.

TEEJEL®
Purdue Frederick

Choline Salicylate Compound

Topical Oral Analgesic

Pharmacology: Choline salicylate, a topical analgesic, acts to reduce and relieve the pain and discomfort of sore, tender, inflamed gums.

Indications: For relief of teething pain, denture irritations and gum and mouth sores; also used postoperatively following oral procedures.

Contraindications: Known hypersensitivity to salicylates.

Precautions: Discontinue use if excessive irritation develops, or pain or discomfort persists. Do not administer to children under 2 years of age except on the advice of a physician or dentist.

Adverse Effects: One case of probable salicylate hypersensitivity was reported in a series of 728 patients.

Dosage: Spread an adequate amount (1 cm) of gel on finger and apply to the tender, painful area, without rubbing vigorously or using pressure. The gel may be applied every 3 to 4 hours as needed, including just before bedtime.

Supplied: Each g of clear, liquorice flavored, sugar-free gel contains: choline salicylate 87 mg (equivalent to salicylate content of 65 mg of ASA), cetyl dimethyl benzyl-ammonium chloride 100 µg, flavoring agents and vehicles. Alcohol: 39%. Sodium: <1 mmol/g. pH: 5.5. Tubes of 7 g.

TEGOPEN® ℞
Bristol

Cloxacillin Sodium

Antibiotic

Pharmacology: Cloxacillin is a penicillinase-resistant, acid resistant, semi-synthetic penicillin. Cloxacillin exerts a bactericidal action against susceptible microorganisms during the stage of active multiplication. It acts through the inhibition of biosynthesis of cell wall mucopeptides.

Cloxacillin is readily absorbed following i.m. administration and rapidly reaches therapeutically effective blood levels. Serum levels are approximately proportional to dosage. Peak plasma concentrations of 15 µg/mL have been observed 30 minutes after an i.m. injection of cloxacillin 500 mg; plasma concentrations may be doubled by administration of a doubled dose.

At the end of a 3-hour i.v. infusion of cloxacillin 250 mg given to normal subjects, plasma concentrations of the drug were 15 µg/mL. After 2 hours, plasma concentrations were 0.6 µg/mL.

Approximately 94% of cloxacillin binds to circulating plasma proteins, mainly albumin. It is distributed in therapeutic concentrations into the pleural, synovial, bile and amniotic fluids and attains insignificant concentrations in cerebrospinal and ascitic fluids.

The plasma half-life of cloxacillin is between 0.5 and 1.5 hours. Cloxacillin is partially metabolized to microbiologically active and inactive metabolites. Cloxacillin and its metabolites are rapidly excreted in the urine by glomerular filtration and active tubular secretion. The urinary clearance rate was 162.2 mL/minute and a total of 62% of the dose was excreted in the urine in a study of normal subjects receiving an i.v. infusion of 250 mg of cloxacillin. The drug is also partly eliminated in the feces via biliary excretion.

Reduced plasma concentrations of cloxacillin seen in patients with cystic fibrosis have been attributed to enhanced nonrenal clearance of the drug.

Cloxacillin demonstrates activity against strains of beta-hemolytic streptococci, pneumococci, penicillin G sensitive staphylococci and, due to its resistance to penicillinase, penicillin G resistant (penicillinase producing) staphylococci, cloxacillin displays less intrinsic antibacterial activity and a narrower spectrum than penicillin G.

Indications: In the treatment of beta-hemolytic streptococcal and pneumococcal infections as well as staphylococcal infections (including those caused by penicillinase producing organisms). It is not effective against the so-called methicillin-resistant strains of staphylococcus. In severe staphylococcal infections (septicemia, osteomyelitis, endocarditis, pneumonia) or when staphylococci are suspected and treatment is required before sensitivity results are available, parenteral cloxacillin should be administered at once, followed by cloxacillin orally, when indicated. If the results of identification and susceptibility testing indicate that the infection is due to an organism other than a penicillinase producing staphylococcus susceptible to cloxacillin sodium, treatment should be discontinued and therapy with an alternative agent instituted.

Contraindications: Persons who have shown hypersensitivity to any of the penicillins or any component of the formulation.

Warnings: Serious and occasionally fatal anaphylactic reactions have been reported in patients receiving penicillin or cephalosporin therapy. These reactions are more apt to occur in individuals with a history of sensitivity to multiple allergens. Careful inquiry should be made concerning previous hypersensitivity reactions to penicillins, cephalosporins or other allergens. Serious anaphylactic reactions require immediate emergency treatment with epinephrine, i.v. fluids and steroids, oxygen and airway management, including intubation, as indicated.

Precautions: Before therapy with a penicillin, careful inquiry should be made concerning previous hypersensitivity reactions to penicillins, cephalosporins, and other allergens. There is clinical and laboratory evidence of cross-allergenicity among the penicillins and partial cross-allergenicity among bicyclic β-lactam antibiotics including penicillins, cephalosporins, cepharmycins, 1-oxa-β-lactams, and carbapenems. If an allergic reaction occurs, the drug should be discontinued and appropriate measures taken.

Candidiasis and other superinfections may occur, especially in debilitated and malnourished patients, or those with low resistance to infection due to corticosteroids, immunosuppressors or irradiation. If superinfection occurs, institute appropriate measures.

Pseudomembranous colitis has been reported with nearly all antibacterial agents, and may range from mild to life-threatening. Therefore, it is important to consider this diagnosis in patients who present with diarrhea subsequent to the administration of antimicrobial agents. After the diagnosis of colitis has been established, therapeutic measures should be initiated.

Bacteriologic studies to determine the causative organisms and their susceptibility to the penicillinase-resistant penicillins should be performed. In the treatment of suspected staphylococcal infections, therapy should be changed to another active agent if culture tests fail to demonstrate the presence of staphylococci.

Periodic assessment of organ system function including renal, hepatic and hematopoietic should be made during prolonged therapy with the penicillinase-resistant penicillins.

White blood cell counts and differential cell counts should be obtained prior to initiation of therapy and at least weekly during therapy with penicillinase-resistant penicillins.

Periodic urinalysis should be performed, and blood urea nitrogen, creatinine, AST and ALT concentrations should be determined during therapy with the penicillinase-resistant penicillins. Dosage alterations should be considered if these values become elevated.

Drug Interactions: Probenecid administered concomitantly with penicillins increases and prolongs serum penicillin levels. Probenecid slows the rate of excretion by competitively inhibiting renal tubular secretion of penicillins.

Aminoglycosides and penicillins are physically and/or chemically incompatible and can mutually inactivate each other in vitro. In vitro mixing of penicillinase-resistant penicillins and aminoglycosides should be avoided during concomitant therapy, and the drugs should be administered separately. Penicillins can also inactivate aminoglycosides in vitro in serum samples from patients receiving both drugs, which could produce falsely decreased results in serum aminoglycoside assays of the serum samples.

Pregnancy: Safety in pregnancy has not been established. Cloxacillin passes through the placenta into the fetal circulation. This drug should be used in pregnancy only if clearly needed.

Lactation: Cloxacillin is distributed into human milk. Therefore, caution should be exercised when cloxacillin is administered to a nursing woman.

Children: Because of incompletely developed renal function in newborns, penicillinase-resistant penicillins (especially methicillin) may not be completely excreted, resulting in abnormally high blood levels. Frequent blood levels determinations and dosage adjustments when necessary are advisable in these patients. All newborns treated with penicillins should be monitored closely for clinical and laboratory evidence of toxic or adverse effects.

Adverse Effects: Hypersensitivity: Two types of allergic reactions to penicillins are noted clinically, immediate and delayed.

Immediate reactions usually occur within 20 minutes of administration and range in severity from urticaria and pruritus to angioedema, laryngospasm, bronchospasm, hypotension, vascular collapse, and death. Such events are very rare. They usually occur after parenteral therapy but have occurred in patients receiving oral therapy. Another type of immediate reaction, an accelerated reaction, may occur 20 minutes to 48 hours after administration and include urticaria, pruritus, wheezing, sneezing and fever. Although laryngeal edema, laryngospasm and hypotension occasionally occur, fatality is uncommon.

Delayed allergic reactions to penicillin therapy usually occur after 48 hours and sometimes as late as 2 to 4 weeks after initiation of therapy. Manifestations of this type of reaction include serum sickness-like symptoms (i.e., fever, malaise, urticaria, myalgia, arthralgia, abdominal pain) and various skin rashes.

Gastrointestinal: Nausea, vomiting, diarrhea, stomatitis, black or hairy tongue, and other symptoms of gastrointestinal irritation may occur. Antibiotic-associated pseudomembranous colitis has been reported rarely with penicillinase-resistant penicillins.

Neurologic: Neurotoxicity similar to that observed with penicillin G (e.g., lethargy, confusion, twitching, multifocal myoclonus, localized or generalized epileptiform seizures) may occur with large i.v. doses of the penicillinase-resistant penicillins especially in patients with renal insufficiency.

Renal: Renal tubular damage and interstitial nephritis have been associated with the administration of methicillin sodium and infrequently with the administration of nafcillin and oxacillin and cloxacillin. Manifestations of this may include rash,

fever, eosinophilia, hematuria, proteinuria, and renal insufficiency. Nephropathy does not appear to be dose-related and is generally reversible upon prompt discontinuation of therapy.
Hematologic: Eosinophilia, hemolytic anemia, agranulocytosis, neutropenia, leukopenia, granulocytopenia, thrombocytopenia, and bone marrow depression have been associated with the use of penicillinase-resistant penicillins.
Hepatic: Hepatotoxicity, characterized by fever, nausea, and vomiting associated with abnormal liver function tests, mainly elevated AST levels, has been associated with the use of penicillinase-resistant penicillins. Asymptomatic, transient increases in serum concentrations of alkaline phosphatase, AST, and ALT have been reported.

Overdose: Symptoms and Treatment: Treatment is likely needed only in patients with severely impaired renal function, since patients with normal kidneys excrete penicillins at a fast rate. No specific treatment can be recommended.

In patients with severe allergic reactions, general supportive measures (if the patient is in shock) or symptomatic therapy similar to that applied in all cases of hypersensitivity are recommended.

Cloxacillin is only minimally removed by hemodialysis and peritoneal dialysis up to 5%.

Dosage: Bacteriologic studies to determine the causative organisms and their susceptibility to the penicillinase-resistant penicillins should be performed. Duration of therapy varies with the type and severity of infection as well as the overall condition of the patient. Therefore, it should be determined by the clinical and bacteriological response of the patient. Therapy should be continued for at least 48 to 72 hours after the patient has become afebrile, asymptomatic, and cultures are negative. In severe staphylococcal infections, therapy with penicillinase-resistant penicillins should be continued for at least 14 days. The treatment of endocarditis and osteomyelitis requires a longer term of therapy.
Adults and Children weighing >20 kg: 250 to 500 mg every 6 hours, depending on severity of infection. Children <20 kg: 25 to 50 mg/kg/day in 4 equal doses administered every 6 hours. For severe infections, the dosage may be increased. Maximum dosage for adults is 6 g/day.
Renal Impairment: Adjustment of dosage is generally unnecessary in patients with renal impairment.
Preparation of Solution: Prepare solution for parenteral use with Sterile Water for Injection. The reconstituted solution is stable for 24 hours at room temperature (25°C) and for 96 hours under refrigeration (2 to 10°C).
I.M. Administration: see Table I.

Table I—Tegopen

I.M. Administration

Dosage Form mg/vial	Amount of Diluent mL	Concentration mg/mL
500	2.0	250
2 000	6.8	250

A 0.5% lidocaine HCl solution may be used, if necessary, as a diluent for the i.m. administration.
I.V. Administration: see Table II.

Table II—Tegopen

I.V. Administration

Dosage Form mg/vial	Amount of Diluent mL	Concentration mg/mL
500	10.0	50
2 000	20.0	100

When i.v. therapy is required, cloxacillin should be given by slow injection (3 to 4 minutes) or infusion (30 to 40 minutes). The equivalent of 500 mg in 10 mL of water for injection may be given by slow i.v. injection over 3 to 4 minutes every 4 to 6 hours or by i.v. infusion.

Caution: More rapid administration may result in convulsive seizures.
Administration by I.V. Drip: The 2 000 mg vial should be reconstituted by adding 20 mL of Sterile Water for Injection.

Stability studies at concentrations of 1 and 2 mg/mL in the following various i.v. solutions indicate that the drug will lose less than 10% activity at 25°C during 8 hours: Normal Saline Solution; 5% Dextrose in Water w/v; 10% D-Fructose in Water w/v; 10% D-Fructose in Normal Saline w/v; M/6 Sodium-Lactate Solution; Lactate Ringer Injection; 10% Invert Sugar in Water w/v; 10% Invert Sugar in Normal Saline w/v.

Cloxacillin should not be mixed with an aminoglycoside in the syringe, i.v. fluid or administration set because mutual inactivation and loss of antibacterial activity can occur (see Precautions, Drug Interactions). In general, it is advisable to administer these antibiotics separately.

Supplied: 500 mg: Each dry filled vial contains: cloxacillin (as the sodium salt) 500 mg. Nonmedicinal ingredients: none. Sodium: <1.1 mmol (25 mg)/500 mg.

2 000 mg: Each dry filled vial contains: cloxacillin (as the sodium salt) 2 000 mg. Nonmedicinal ingredients: none. Sodium: <4.3 mmol (100 mg)/2 000 mg.

Store at controlled room temperature not exceeding 25°C.

Reviewed 1997

TEGRETOL® ℞

Novartis Pharmaceuticals

Carbamazepine

Anticonvulsant—Symptomatic Relief of Trigeminal Neuralgia—Antimanic

Pharmacology: Carbamazepine has anticonvulsant properties which have been found useful in the treatment of partial seizures (simple or complex) with and without secondary generalization, and generalized tonic clonic seizures. A mild psychotropic effect has been observed in some patients, which seems related to the effect of carbamazepine in localization-related epilepsies and syndromes.
Clinical Trials: Evidence supporting the efficacy of carbamazepine as an anticonvulsant was derived from active drug-controlled studies that enrolled patients with the following seizure types: partial seizures with simple or complex symptomatology; generalized tonic-clonic seizures; mixed seizure patterns which include the above, or other partial or generalized seizures.

Carbamazepine relieves or diminishes the pain associated with trigeminal neuralgia often within 24 to 48 hours.

Carbamazepine given as a monotherapy or in combination with lithium or neuroleptics has been found useful in the treatment of acute mania and the prophylactic treatment of bipolar (manic-depressive) disorders.

Like other tricyclic compounds, carbamazepine has a moderate anticholinergic action which is responsible for some of its side effects. A tolerance may develop to the action of carbamazepine after a few months of treatment and should be watched for.

Carbamazepine may suppress ventricular automaticity due to its membrane-depressant effect, similar to that of quinidine and procainamide, associated with suppression of phase 4 depolarization of the heart muscle fibre.

A number of investigators have reported a deterioration of EEG abnormalities with regard to focal alterations and a higher incidence of records with nil β-activity during carbamazepine-combined treatment.

The absorption of carbamazepine in man is relatively slow. When taken in a single oral dose, the carbamazepine tablets and chewable tablets yield peak plasma concentrations of unchanged carbamazepine within 4 to 24 hours. With respect to the quantity of carbamazepine absorbed, there is no clinically relevant difference between the various dosage forms. However, carbamazepine suspension is absorbed somewhat faster than the tablet; peak plasma levels are reached within 2 hours. Following b.i.d. dosage regimens, higher peak levels and lower trough levels are obtained with the suspension than with the tablets. Steady-state plasma levels are comparable for carbamazepine suspension given t.i.d. and carbamazepine tablets given b.i.d., when administered at the same total daily dose.

Ingestion of food has no significant influence on the rate and extent of absorption regardless of the dosage form of carbamazepine.

When carbamazepine controlled-release tablets are administered repeatedly, they yield a lower average maximal concentration of carbamazepine in the plasma, without a reduction in the average minimal concentration. This tends to result in a lower incidence of intermittent concentration-dependent adverse drug reactions. It also ensures that the plasma concentrations remain largely stable throughout the day, thereby making it possible to manage with a twice-daily dosage.

Carbamazepine becomes bound to serum proteins to the extent of 70 to 80%. The concentration of unchanged substance in the saliva reflects the nonprotein-bound portion present in the serum (20 to 30%).

The elimination half-life of unchanged carbamazepine in the plasma averages approximately 36 hours following a single oral dose, whereas after repeated administration, which leads to autoinduction of hepatic enzymes, it averages only 16 to 24 hours, depending on the duration of the medication. In patients receiving concomitant treatment with other enzyme-inducing antiepileptic agents, half-life values averaging 9 to 10 hours have been found. One study in 39 children (aged 3 to 10 years) and 79 adults (aged 15 to 65 years) has indicated that carbamazepine elimination may be slightly enhanced in children. This data suggests that children may require higher doses of carbamazepine (in mg/kg) than adults.

Only 2 to 3% of the dose, whether given singly or repeatedly, is excreted in the urine in unchanged form. Approximately 30% of carbamazepine is renally eliminated via the epoxide pathway. The primary metabolite is the pharmacologically active 10, 11-epoxide. The mean elimination half-life of this active metabolite in the plasma is about 6 hours following single oral doses of the epoxide itself.

In man, the main urinary metabolite of carbamazepine is the trans-diol derivative originating from the 10,11-epoxide; a small portion of the epoxide is converted into 9-hydroxy-methyl-10-carbamoyl-acridan. Other important biotransformation products are various monohydroxylated compounds, as well as the N-glucuronide of carbamazepine.

In patients with epilepsy, the therapeutic range for the steady-state plasma concentration of carbamazepine generally lies between 4 and 10 μg/mL.

Indications: Epilepsy: For use as an anticonvulsant drug either alone or in combination with other anticonvulsant drugs.

Carbamazepine is not effective in controlling absence, myoclonic or atonic seizures, and does not prevent the generalization of epileptic discharge. Moreover, exacerbation of seizures may occasionally occur in patients with atypical absences.
Trigeminal Neuralgia: Carbamazepine is indicated for the symptomatic relief of pain of trigeminal neuralgia only during periods of exacerbation of true or primary trigeminal neuralgia (tic douloureux). It should not be used preventively during periods of remission. In some patients, carbamazepine has relieved glossopharyngeal neuralgia. For patients who fail to respond to carbamazepine, or who are sensitive to the drug, recourse to other accepted measures must be considered.

Carbamazepine is not a simple analgesic and should not be used to relieve trivial facial pains or headaches.
Treatment of Acute Mania and Prophylaxis in Bipolar (Manic-Depressive) Disorders: Carbamazepine may be used as a monotherapy or as an adjunct to lithium in the treatment of acute mania or prophylaxis of bipolar (manic-depressive) disorders in patients who are resistant to or intolerant of conventional antimanic drugs. Carbamazepine may be a useful alternative to neuroleptics in such patients. Patients with severe mania, dysphoric mania or rapid cycling who are non-responsive to lithium may show a positive response when treated with carbamazepine.

It is important to note that these recommendations are based on extensive clinical experience and some clinical trials vs active comparison agents.

Contraindications: Should not be administered to patients with hepatic disease, a history of acute intermittent porphyria or serious blood disorder.

The drug should not be administered immediately before, in conjunction with, or immediately after an MAO inhibitor. When it seems desirable to administer carbamazepine to a patient who has been receiving an MAO inhibitor, there should be as long a drug free interval as the clinical condition allows, but in no case should this be less than 14 days. Then the dosage of carbamazepine should be low initially, and increased very gradually.

Carbamazepine should not be administered to patients presenting AV heart block (see Pharmacology and Precautions).

Carbamazepine should not be administered to patients with known hypersensitivity to carbamazepine, to any of the components of the tablets or suspension, or to any of the tricyclic compounds, such as amitriptyline, trimipramine, imipramine, or their analogues or metabolites, because of the similarity in chemical structure.

Warnings: Although reported infrequently, serious adverse effects have been observed during the use of carbamazepine. Agranulocytosis and aplastic anemia have occurred in a few instances with a fatal outcome. Leukopenia, thrombocytopenia, hepatocellular and cholestatic jaundice, and hepatitis have also been reported. However, in the majority of cases, leukopenia and thrombocytopenia were transient and did not signal the onset of either aplastic anemia or agranulocytosis. It is important that carbamazepine should be used carefully and close clinical and frequent laboratory supervision should be maintained throughout treatment in order to detect as early as possible signs and symptoms of a possible blood dyscrasia. Carbamazepine should be discontinued if any evidence of significant bone marrow depression appears (see Precautions).

Tegretol (cont'd)

Should signs and symptoms suggest a severe skin reaction such as Stevens-Johnson syndrome or Lyell's syndrome, carbamazepine should be withdrawn at once.

Long-term toxicity studies in rats indicated a potential carcinogenic risk. Therefore, the possible risk of the drug must be weighed against the potential benefits before prescribing carbamazepine to individual patients.

Pregnancy: **Women with epilepsy who are pregnant, or intend to become pregnant, should be treated with special care.**

In women of childbearing potential, carbamazepine should, whenever possible, be prescribed as monotherapy, because the incidence of congenital abnormalities in the offspring of women treated with more than one antiepileptic drug (e.g., valproic acid plus carbamazepine plus phenobarbital and/or phenytoin) is greater than in those of women receiving a single antiepileptic.

Minimum effective doses should be given and the plasma levels monitored.

If pregnancy occurs in a woman receiving carbamazepine, or if the problem of initiating carbamazepine arises during pregnancy, the drug's potential benefits must be weighed against its hazards, particularly during the first 3 months of pregnancy. Carbamazepine should not be discontinued or withheld from patients if required to prevent major seizures because of the risks posed, to both mother and fetus, by status epilepticus with attendant hypoxia.

The possibility that carbamazepine, like all major antiepileptic drugs, increases the risk of malformations has been reported. There are rare reports on developmental disorders and malformations, including spina bifida, in association with carbamazepine. Conclusive evidence from controlled studies with carbamazepine monotherapy is lacking. Patients should be counselled regarding the possibility of an increased risk of malformations and given the opportunity of antenatal screening.

Folic acid deficiency is known to occur in pregnancy. Antiepileptic drugs have been reported to aggravate folic acid deficiency. This deficiency may contribute to the increased incidence of birth defects in the offspring of treated epileptic women. Folic acid supplementation has therefore been recommended before and during pregnancy.

To prevent neonatal bleeding disorders, Vitamin K_1 administration to the mother during the last weeks of pregnancy, as well as to the newborn, has been recommended.

Lactation: **Carbamazepine passes into breast milk in concentrations of about 25 to 60% of the plasma level. No reports are available on the long-term effect of breast-feeding. The benefits of breast-feeding should be weighed against the possible risks to the infant. Should the mother taking carbamazepine nurse her infant, the infant must be observed for possible adverse reactions, e.g., somnolence.**

A severe hypersensitivity skin reaction in a breast-fed baby has been reported.

It should be noted that the reliability of oral contraceptives may be adversely affected by carbamazepine (see Precautions, Drug Interactions).

Precautions: Clinical Monitoring of Adverse Reactions: Carbamazepine should be prescribed only after a critical risk-benefit appraisal in patients with a history of cardiac, hepatic or renal damage, adverse hematological reactions to other drugs, or interrupted courses of therapy with carbamazepine. **Careful clinical and laboratory supervision should be maintained throughout treatment.** Should any signs or symptoms or abnormal laboratory findings be suggestive of blood dyscrasia or liver disorder, carbamazepine should be immediately discontinued until the case is carefully reassessed.

Bone Marrow Function: Complete blood counts, including platelets and possibly reticulocytes and serum iron, should be carried out before treatment is instituted. Suggested guidelines for monitoring are weekly for the first month, then monthly for the next 5 months, thereafter 2 to 4 times a year.

If definitely low or decreased white blood cell or platelet counts are observed during treatment, the patient and the complete blood count should be monitored closely. Nonprogressive fluctuating asymptomatic leukopenia, which is encountered, does not generally call for the withdrawal of carbamazepine. However, treatment with carbamazepine should be discontinued if the patient develops leukopenia which is progressive or accompanied by clinical manifestations, e.g., fever or sore throat, as this could indicate the onset of significant bone marrow depression.

Because the onset of potentially serious blood dyscrasias may be rapid, patients should be made aware of early toxic signs and symptoms of a potential hematological problem, as well as symptoms of dermatological or hepatic reactions. If reactions such as fever, sore throat, rash, ulcers in the mouth, easy bruising, petechial or purpuric hemorrhage appear, the patient should be advised to consult his/her physician immediately.

Hepatic Function: Baseline and periodic evaluations of hepatic function must be performed, particularly in elderly patients and patients with a history of liver disease. Carbamazepine should be withdrawn immediately in cases of aggravated liver dysfunction or active liver disease.

Kidney Function: Pretreatment and periodic complete urinalysis and BUN determinations should be performed.

Ophthalmic Examinations: Carbamazepine has been associated with pathological eye changes. Periodic eye examinations, including slit-lamp funduscopy and tonometry, are recommended.

Plasma Levels: Although correlations between dosage and plasma levels of carbamazepine, and between plasma levels and clinical efficacy or tolerability, are rather tenuous, monitoring plasma levels may be useful in the following conditions: dramatic increase in seizure frequency/verification of patient compliance; during pregnancy; when treating children or adolescents; in suspected absorption disorders; in suspected toxicity, especially where more than one drug is being used (see Drug Interactions).

Increased Seizure Frequency: Carbamazepine should be used with caution in patients with a mixed seizure disorder that includes atypical absence seizures, since its use has been associated with increased frequency of generalized convulsions. In case of exacerbation of seizures, carbamazepine should be discontinued.

Dermatologic: Mild skin reactions, e.g., isolated macular or maculopapular exanthema, usually disappear within a few days or weeks, either during a continued course of treatment or following a decrease in dosage. However, the patient should be kept under close surveillance because of the rare possibility of Stevens-Johnson syndrome or Lyell's syndrome occurring (see Warnings).

Urinary Retention and Increased Intraocular Pressure: Because of its anticholinergic action, carbamazepine should be given cautiously, if at all, to patients with increased intraocular pressure or urinary retention. Such patients should be followed closely while taking the drug.

Occurrence of Behavioral Disorders: Because it is closely related to the other tricyclic drugs, there is some possibility that carbamazepine might activate a latent psychosis, or, in elderly patients, produce agitation or confusion, especially when combined with other drugs. Caution should also be exercised in alcoholics.

Patients with Cardiovascular Disorders: Carbamazepine should be used cautiously in patients with a history of coronary artery disease, organic heart disease or congestive heart failure. If a defective conductive system is suspected, an ECG should be performed before administering carbamazepine in order to exclude patients with AV block.

Occupational Hazards: Driving and Operating Hazardous Machinery: Because dizziness and drowsiness are possible side effects of carbamazepine, patients should be warned about the possible hazards of operating machinery or driving automobiles.

Drug Interactions: Induction of hepatic enzymes in response to carbamazepine may have the effect of diminishing or abolishing the activity of certain drugs that are also metabolized in the liver. The dosage of the following drugs may have to be adjusted when administered with carbamazepine: clobazam, clonazepam, ethosuximide, primidone, valproic acid, alprazolam, corticosteroids (e.g., prednisolone, dexamethasone), cyclosporin, digoxin, doxycycline, felodipine, haloperidol, thioridazine, imipramine, methadone, oral contraceptives, theophylline and oral anticoagulants (warfarin, phenprocoumon, dicumarol).

Phenytoin plasma levels have been reported both to be raised and to be lowered by carbamazepine, and mephenytoin plasma levels have been reported in rare instances to increase.

The following drugs have been shown to raise plasma carbamazepine levels: erythromycin, troleandomycin, possibly josamycin, isoniazid, verapamil, diltiazem, propoxyphene, viloxazine, fluoxetine, cimetidine, acetazolamide, danazol and possibly desipramine. Nicotinamide raises carbamazepine plasma levels in children, but only at high dosage in adults. Since an increase in carbamazepine plasma levels may result in unwanted effects (e.g., dizziness, drowsiness, ataxia, diplopia and nystagmus), the dosage of carbamazepine should be adjusted accordingly and the blood levels monitored.

The plasma levels of carbamazepine may be reduced by phenobarbitone, phenytoin, primidone, progabide or theophylline and possibly by clonazepam. On the other hand, valproic acid, valpromide and primidone have been reported to raise plasma levels of the pharmacologically active metabolite, carbamazepine-10,11 epoxide. The dose of carbamazepine may consequently have to be adjusted.

Combined use of carbamazepine with lithium, metoclopramide or haloperidol may increase the risk of neurotoxic side effects (even in the presence of "therapeutic plasma levels").

Concomitant use of carbamazepine and isoniazid has been reported to increase isoniazid-induced hepatotoxicity.

Carbamazepine, like other anticonvulsants, may adversely affect the reliability of oral contraceptives; breakthrough bleeding may occur. Patients should accordingly be advised to use some alternative, nonhormonal method of contraception.

Concomitant medication with carbamazepine and some diuretics (hydrochlorothiazide, furosemide) may lead to symptomatic hyponatremia.

Carbamazepine may antagonize the effects of nondepolarizing muscle relaxants (e.g., pancuronium); their dosage may need to be raised and patients should be monitored closely for more rapid recovery from neuromuscular blockade than expected.

Isotretinoin has been reported to alter the bioavailability and/or clearance of carbamazepine and its active 10,11-epoxide; carbamazepine plasma levels should be monitored.

Carbamazepine, like other psychoactive drugs, may reduce the patient's alcohol tolerance; it is therefore advisable to abstain from alcohol consumption during treatment.

Carbamazepine should not be administered in conjunction with an MAO inhibitor (see Contraindications).

Adverse Effects: The reactions which have been most frequently reported with carbamazepine are CNS (e.g., drowsiness, headache, unsteadiness on the feet, diplopia, dizziness), gastrointestinal disturbances (nausea, vomiting), as well as allergic skin reactions. These reactions usually occur only during the initial phase of therapy, if the initial dose is too high, or when treating elderly patients. They have rarely necessitated discontinuing carbamazepine therapy and can be minimized by initiating treatment at a low dosage.

The occurrence of CNS adverse reactions may be a manifestation of relative overdosage or significant fluctuation in plasma levels. In such cases it is advisable to monitor the plasma levels and possibly lower the daily dose and/or divide it into 3 to 4 fractional doses.

The more serious adverse reactions observed are the hematologic, hepatic, cardiovascular and dermatologic reactions, which require discontinuation of therapy. If treatment with carbamazepine has to be withdrawn abruptly, the change-over to another antiepileptic drug should be effected under cover of diazepam.

The following adverse reactions have been reported:

Hematologic: Occasional or frequent: leukopenia, occasional eosinophilia, thrombocytopenia. Rare: leukocytosis, lymphadenopathy. Isolated cases: agranulocytosis, aplastic anemia, pure red cell aplasia, macrocytic anemia, megaloblastic anemia, acute intermittent porphyria, reticulocytosis, folic acid deficiency, thrombocytopenic purpura, and possibly hemolytic anemia. In a few instances, deaths have occurred.

Hepatic: Frequent: elevated gamma-GT (due to hepatic enzyme induction), usually not clinically relevant. Occasional: elevated alkaline phosphatase. Rare: elevated transaminases, jaundice, hepatitis of a cholestatic, parenchymal (hepatocellular), or mixed type. Isolated cases: granulomatous hepatitis.

Dermatologic: Occasional or frequent: skin sensitivity reactions and rashes, erythematous rashes, urticaria. Rare: exfoliative dermatitis and erythroderma, Stevens-Johnson syndrome, systemic lupus erythematosus-like syndrome. Isolated cases: toxic epidermal necrolysis (Lyell's syndrome), photosensitivity, erythema multiforme and nodosum, skin pigmentation changes, pruritus, purpura, acne, diaphoresis, alopecia and neurodermatitis. Isolated cases of hirsutism have been reported, however the causal relationship is not clear.

Neurologic: Frequent: vertigo, somnolence, ataxia and fatigue. Occasional: an increase in motor seizures (see Indications), headache, diplopia, nystagmus, accommodation disorders (e.g., blurred vision). Rare: abnormal involuntary disorders (e.g., tremor, asterixis, orofacial dyskinesia, choreoathetosis disorders, dystonia, tics). Isolated cases: oculomotor disturbances, speech disorders (e.g., dysarthria or slurred speech), peripheral neuritis, paresthesia, muscle weakness. There have been some reports of paralysis and other symptoms of cerebral arterial insufficiency but no conclusive relationship to the administration of carbamazepine could be established.

Cardiovascular: Rare: disturbances of cardiac conduction. Isolated cases: bradycardia, arrhythmias, Stokes-Adams in

patients with AV block, collapse, congestive heart failure, hypertension or hypotension, aggravation of coronary artery disease, thrombophlebitis, thromboembolism. Some of these complications (including myocardial infarction and arrhythmia) have been associated with other tricyclic compounds.
Psychiatric: Isolated cases: hallucinations (visual or acoustic), depression, sometimes with talkativeness, agitation, loss of appetite, restlessness, aggressive behavior, confusion, activation of psychosis.
Genitourinary: Isolated cases: interstitial nephritis and renal failure, as well as signs of renal dysfunction (e.g., albuminuria, glycosuria, hematuria, oliguria sometimes associated with elevated blood pressure, and elevated BUN/azotemia), urinary frequency, urinary retention and sexual disturbances/impotence.
Gastrointestinal: Frequent: nausea, vomiting. Occasional: dryness of the mouth and throat. Rare: diarrhea or constipation. Isolated cases: abdominal pain, glossitis, stomatitis, anorexia.
Sense Organs: Isolated cases: lens opacities, conjunctivitis, retinal changes, tinnitus, hyperacusis, taste disturbances.
Endocrine System and Metabolism: Occasional: edema, fluid retention, weight increase, hyponatremia and reduced plasma osmolality due to antidiuretic hormone (ADH)-like effect occurs, leading in isolated cases to water intoxication accompanied by lethargy, vomiting, headache, mental confusion and neurological abnormalities. Isolated cases: gynecomastia, galactorrhea, abnormal thyroid function tests (decreased L-thyroxine, i.e., FT_4, T_4, T_3, and increased TSH, usually without clinical manifestations), disturbances of bone metabolism (decrease in plasma calcium and 25-OH-calciferol), leading in isolated cases to osteomalacia, as well as reports of elevated levels of cholesterol, including HDL cholesterol and triglycerides.
Musculoskeletal: Isolated cases: arthralgia, muscle pain or cramp.
Respiratory: Isolated cases: pulmonary hypersensitivity characterized by fever, dyspnea, pneumonitis or pneumonia.
Hypersensitivity: Rare: delayed multi-organ hypersensitivity disorder with fever, skin rashes, vasculitis, lymphadenopathy, disorders mimicking lymphoma, arthralgia, leukopenia, eosinophilia, hepatosplenomegaly and abnormal liver function tests, occurring in various combinations. Other organs may also be affected (e.g., lungs, kidneys, pancreas, myocardium). Isolated cases: aseptic meningitis with myoclonus and eosinophilia; anaphylactic reaction. Treatment should be discontinued should such hypersensitivity reactions occur.

Overdose: Lowest known lethal dose: estimated 3.2 g (24-year-old-woman). Highest known doses survived: 80 g (34-year-old-man); 34 g (13-year-old-girl); 1.4 g (23-month-old-girl).

Symptoms: The presenting signs and symptoms of overdosage usually involve the central nervous, cardiovascular and respiratory systems.
CNS: CNS depression, disorientation, tremor, restlessness, somnolence, agitation, hallucination, coma, blurred vision, nystagmus, mydriasis, slurred speech, dysarthria, ataxia, dyskinesia, abnormal reflexes (slowed/hyperactive), convulsions, psychomotor disturbances, myoclonus, opisthotonia, hypothermia/hyperthermia, flushed skin/cyanosis, EEG changes.
Respiratory: respiratory depression, pulmonary edema.
Cardiovascular: tachycardia, hypotension/hypertension, conduction disturbance with widening of QRS complex, syncope in association with cardiac arrest.
Gastrointestinal: nausea, vomiting, delayed gastric emptying, reduced bowel motility.
Renal function: urinary retention, oliguria or anuria; fluid retention, and water intoxication.
Laboratory findings: hyponatremia, hypokalemia, leukocytosis, reduced white cell count, metabolic acidosis, hyperglycemia, glycosuria, acetonuria, increased muscle creatinine phosphokinase.

Treatment: There is no known specific antidote to carbamazepine.

Evacuate the stomach, with an emetic or by gastric lavage, then administer activated charcoal.

Vital signs should be watched and symptomatic treatment should be administered as required. Hyperirritability or convulsions may be controlled by the administration of parenteral diazepam or barbiturates but they may induce respiratory depression, particularly in children. Paraldehyde may be used to counteract muscular hypertonus without producing respiratory depression.

When barbiturates are employed, it is advisable to have equipment available for artificial ventilation and resuscitation. Barbiturates should not be used if drugs that inhibit monoamine oxidase have been taken by the patient, either in overdosage or in recent therapy (within 2 weeks).

Hyponatremia should be treated by restricting fluids and a slow and careful NaCl 0.9% infusion i.v. These measures may be useful in preventing brain damage.

Shock (circulatory collapse) should be treated with supportive measures, including i.v. fluids, oxygen and corticosteroids. For hypotension unresponsive to measures taken to increase plasma volume, dopamine or dobutamine i.v. may be administered.

It is recommended that the ECG be monitored, particularly in children, to detect any cardiac arrhythmias or conduction defects.

Charcoal hemoperfusion has been recommended. Forced diuresis, hemodialysis and peritoneal dialysis have been reported to be ineffective.

Relapse and aggravation of the symptomatology on the 2nd or 3rd day after overdose, due to delayed absorption, should be anticipated.

Dosage: Epilepsy (see Indications): Carbamazepine may be used alone or with other anticonvulsants. A low initial daily dosage of carbamazepine with a gradual increase in dosage is advised. Dosage should be adjusted to the needs of the individual patient. Carbamazepine should be taken with meals whenever possible.

Tegretol tablets, Chewtabs and suspension should be taken in 2 to 4 divided doses daily.

Tegretol suspension should be well shaken before use since improper re-suspension may lead to administering an incorrect dose. Since a given dose of Tegretol suspension produces higher peak carbamazepine levels than the same dose in tablet form, it is advisable to start with low doses and to increase slowly to avoid adverse reactions. When switching a patient from Tegretol tablets to Tegretol suspension, the same number of mg/day should be given in smaller, more frequent doses (i.e., b.i.d. tablets to t.i.d. suspension).

Tegretol Chewtabs and the suspension are particularly suitable for patients who have difficulty swallowing tablets or who need initial careful adjustment of dosage.

The controlled release characteristics of Tegretol CR reduce the daily fluctuations of plasma carbamazepine. Tegretol CR tablets (either whole or, if so prescribed, only half a tablet) should be swallowed unchewed with a little liquid during or after a meal. These controlled release tablets should be prescribed as a twice-daily dosage. If necessary, 3 divided doses may be prescribed. Some patients have been reported to require a dosage increase when switching from tablets to CR tablets. Dosage adjustments should be individualized based on clinical response and, if necessary, plasma carbamazepine levels.
Adults and Children Over 12 Years of Age: Initially: 100 to 200 mg once or twice a day depending on the severity of the case and previous therapeutic history. The initial dosage is progressively increased, in divided doses, until the best response is obtained. The usual optimal dosage is 800 to 1 200 mg daily. In rare instances, some adult patients have received 1 600 mg. As soon as disappearance of seizures has been obtained and maintained, dosage should be reduced very gradually until a minimum effective dose is reached.
Children 6 to 12 Years of Age: Initially: 100 mg in divided doses on the first day. Increase gradually by adding 100 mg/day until the best response is obtained. Dosage should generally not exceed 1 000 mg daily. As soon as disappearance of seizures has been obtained and maintained, dosage should be reduced very gradually until a minimum effective dose is reached.
Combination Therapy: When added to existing anticonvulsant therapy, the drug should be added gradually while the other anticonvulsants are maintained or gradually decreased, except for phenytoin, which may be increased (See Precautions, Drug Interactions and Warnings, Pregnancy and Lactation).
Trigeminal Neuralgia: The initial daily dosage should be small; 200 mg taken in 2 doses of 100 mg each is recommended. Total daily dosage can be increased by 200 mg/day until relief of pain is obtained. This is usually achieved at dosage between 200 and 800 mg daily, but occasionally up to 1 200 mg/day may be necessary. As soon as relief of pain has been obtained and maintained, progressive reduction in dosage should be attempted until a minimal effective dosage is reached. Because trigeminal neuralgia is characterized by periods of remission, attempts should be made to reduce or discontinue the use of carbamazepine at intervals of not more than 3 months, depending upon the individual clinical course.

Prophylactic use of the drug in trigeminal neuralgia is not recommended.
Mania and Bipolar (Manic-Depressive) Disorders: The initial daily dosage should be low, 200 to 400 mg/day, administered in divided doses, although higher starting doses of 400 to 600 mg/day may be used in acute mania. This dose may be gradually increased until patient symptomatology is controlled or a total daily dose of 1 600 mg is achieved. Increments in dosage should be adjusted to provide optimal patient tolerability. The usual dose range is 400 to 1 200 mg/day administered in divided doses. Doses used to achieve optimal acute responses and tolerability should be continued during maintenance treatment. When given in combination with lithium and neuroleptics, the initial dosage should be low, 100 to 200 mg daily, and then increased gradually. A dose higher than 800 mg/day is rarely required when given in combination with neuroleptics and lithium, or with other psychotropic drugs such as benzodiazepines. Plasma levels are probably not helpful for guiding therapy in bipolar disorders.

Information for the Patient: See Blue Section—Information for the Patient "Tegretol".

Supplied: Tegretol: Chewtabs: 100 mg: Each white with red specks, round, flat-faced, beveled-edge tablet, engraved GEIGY on one side and M/R with bisect on the other, contains: carbamazepine 100 mg. Nonmedicinal ingredients: cherry-mint flavor, cornstarch, erythrosine, gelatin, glycerin, magnesium stearate, silicon dioxide, sodium starch glycolate, stearic acid and sugar. Energy: 4.5 kJ (1.08 kcal). Sodium: <1 mmol (0.12 mg). Bottles of 100. Store below 30°C. Protect from humidity and light.

200 mg: Each white with red specks, oval, biconvex tablet, engraved GEIGY on one side and P/U with bisect on the other, contains: carbamazepine 200 mg. Nonmedicinal ingredients: cherry-mint flavor, cornstarch, erythrosine, gelatin, glycerin, magnesium stearate, silicon dioxide, sodium starch glycolate, stearic acid and sugar. Energy: 8.9 kJ (2.12 kcal). Sodium: <1 mmol (0.12 mg). Bottles of 100. Store below 30°C. Protect from humidity and light.

Suspension: Each 5 mL of orange suspension contains: carbamazepine 100 mg. Nonmedicinal ingredients: citric acid, citrus-vanilla flavor, FD&C Yellow No. 6, pluronic polyol, potassium sorbate, propylene glycol, sucrose, sorbitol, water and xanthan gum. Energy: 37.63 kJ (8.96 kcal)/5 mL. Bottles of 450 mL. Store below 30°C. Protect from humidity and light.

Tablets: Each white, round, flat-faced and beveled-edge tablet, engraved GEIGY on one side, and quadrisected on the other, contains: carbamazepine 200 mg. Nonmedicinal ingredients: cellulose compounds, magnesium stearate and silicon dioxide. Energy: nil. Sodium: <1 mmol (0.3 mg). Bottles of 100 and 500. Store below 30°C. Protect from humidity.

Tegretol CR: 200 mg: Each beige-orange, oval, slightly biconvex, controlled-release tablet, C/G engraved on one side and H/C engraved on the other, fully bisected on both sides, contains: carbamazepine 200 mg. Nonmedicinal ingredients: acrylic esters, castor oil derivative, cellulose compounds, iron oxides, magnesium stearate, silicon dioxide, talc and titanium dioxide. Energy: nil. Sodium: <1 mmol (2.1 mg). Bottles of 100. Store below 25°C. Protect from humidity.

400 mg: Each brown-orange, oval, slightly biconvex, controlled-release tablet, CG/CG engraved on one side and ENE/ENE engraved on the other, fully bisected on both sides, contains: carbamazepine 400 mg. Nonmedicinal ingredients: acrylic esters, castor oil derivative, cellulose compounds, iron oxides, magnesium stearate, silicon dioxide, talc and titanium dioxide. Energy: nil. Sodium: <1 mmol (4.3 mg). Bottles of 100. Store below 25°C. Protect from humidity.

All Tegretol products are alcohol-, bisulfite-, gluten-, lactose-, parabens- and tartrazine-free. Keep out of reach of children.

(Shown in Product Recognition Section)

Reviewed 1997

TELEBRIX® 38 ORAL

Mallinckrodt

Meglumine Ioxitalamate—Sodium Ioxitalamate

Radiopaque Contrast Medium

Indications: As a bowel opacifier during CT scanning of the abdomen and pelvis.

Contraindications: Hypersensitivity to ioxitalamate acid salts. Severe oliguria or anuria.

Warnings: Although there have been no reports to date of adverse effects arising from the use of Telebrix 38 Oral, the possibility of an allergic reaction due to iodine sensitivity should be kept in mind.

Telebrix 38 Oral (cont'd)

Sensitivity to iodine per se, or to other contrast media is not an absolute contraindication to ioxitalamates, but extreme caution is called for.

Precautions: General: Diagnostic procedures which involve the use of iodinated contrast agents should be carried out under the direction of radiologists skilled and experienced in the particular procedure to be performed.

The possibility of an idiosyncratic reaction occurring in patients who have previously received a contrast medium without ill effect should always be considered.

A positive history of bronchial asthma or allergy, a family history of allergy, or a previous reaction or hypersensitivity to a contrast agent implies a greater than usual risk. Such a history may be more accurate than pre-testing in predicting the potential for reaction, although not necessarily the severity or type of reaction in the individual case. A positive history of this type does not absolutely contraindicate the use of a contrast agent, when a diagnostic procedure is deemed essential, but does call for extreme caution. Premedication with antihistamines or corticosteroids as a means of avoiding or at least decreasing possible allergic reactions in such patients should be considered.

Pregnancy: Safety of the use of Telebrix 38 during pregnancy has not been established, therefore the product should be used during pregnancy only if the benefit to the mother clearly outweighs the risk to the fetus.

Lactation: It is not known whether Telebrix 38 is excreted in human milk. Because of possible adverse effects in the nursing infant, bottle feeding should be substituted for at least 24 hours following administration of Telebrix 38.

Adverse Effects: There have been no reports of adverse reactions to date following the use of oral ioxitalamate.

Overdose: Symptoms and Treatment: Treatment of an overdose should be directed towards the support of all vital functions and prompt institution of specific therapy. As much as possible of the contrast medium should be removed from the stomach by gastric suction and lavage.

Dosage: Telebrix 38 Oral has to be diluted to a 2% w/v salt solution before use. This can be accomplished, for example, by adding 12 mL of Telebrix 38 Oral to 450 mL of water (see Directions for Dilution).

The diluted solution is used orally for opacification of the bowel lumen in individual patients in the following doses, taken in small aliquots over a period of time.

Adults: For opacification of the colon: 450 mL of the diluted solution may be given several hours before the examination and 450 mL at least 1/2 hour before.

For small bowel opacification: 450 mL is given several hours before the examination followed by 450 mL at least 1/2 hour before and 150 mL immediately before the examination. The maximum total dose is 1 050 mL.

Children: The oral dose of the diluted solution, for children 1 to 12 years of age, will be limited to 8 mL/kg or 400 mL total dose, whichever is less. For opacification of the colon, one half of the dose may be ingested several hours before the examination and the other half at least 1/2 hour before the examination.

Directions for Dilution: Telebrix 38 Oral may be diluted with tap water. Twelve mL of Telebrix 38 Oral is added to 450 mL of water. This will produce 462 mL of a 2% salt solution. This solution has been found to be stable for 2 weeks at room temperature (15 to 30°C). However, the solution should be kept at room temperature and discarded within 48 hours of preparation to avoid the risk of microbial growth.

Supplied: Telebrix 38 Oral is an aqueous solution for oral use subsequent to dilution. Each mL contains: meglumine ioxitalamate 513 mg and sodium ioxitalamate 255 mg, equivalent to a combined content of 38% w/v organically bound iodine. Nonmedicinal ingredients: edetate calcium disodium and monobasic sodium phosphate. The pH is approximately 7.0. Bottles of 30 and 120 mL.

Store at 15 to 30°C. Do not freeze. If product is frozen or if crystallization of the salt has occurred, examine the container for physical damage. If no damage has occurred, the container should be brought to room temperature. Intermittent shaking may be necessary to completely redissolve the crystals. Before use, examine the product to ensure that all solids are redissolved. This preparation is sensitive to light and must be protected from strong daylight or direct exposure to the sun.

TEMAZEPAM ℞
General Monograph, CPhA
see BENZODIAZEPINES

TEMPRA®
Mead Johnson

Acetaminophen

Antipyretic—Analgesic

Indications: As a non-salicylate analgesic-antipyretic for the temporary relief of pain from headache, muscle strain, bursitis, sprains, menstrual cramps. Also effective in relieving fever due to the common cold and other viral or bacterial infections.

Precautions: When used as directed, acetaminophen is virtually free of severe toxicity or side effects. The incidence of gastrointestinal upset is less than after salicylate administration. If a rare sensitivity reaction occurs, discontinue the drug. Hypersensitivity to acetaminophen is usually manifested by a rash or urticaria.

Regular use of acetaminophen has been shown to produce a slight increase in prothrombin time in patients receiving oral anticoagulants but the clinical significance of this effect is not clear.

Acetaminophen poisoning can result in severe hepatic damage. Phenobarbital increases the activity of microsomal enzymes which produce a toxic metabolite and therefore acetaminophen's hepatotoxicity may be enhanced. Thus, concomitant ingestion of phenobarbital may increase the likelihood of liver necrosis in acetaminophen overdose. The chronic ingestion of alcohol may be implicated in the increasing potential for hepatic toxicity.

Overdose: Symptoms and Treatment: In adults, hepatotoxicity may occur after ingestion of a single dose of 10 to 15 g (200 to 250 mg/kg) of acetaminophen; a dose of 25 g or more is potentially fatal. Reports have indicated hepatic necrosis with a single dose of 6 g and death occurring with a single dose of 13 g. Non-fatal overdoses of 12.5 to 31.5 g have also been reported. It is generally agreed that consumption of more than 50% of the toxic dose, i.e., 7.5 g in adults and 140 to 150 mg/kg in children could initiate liver damage.

The earliest symptoms of overdose with acetaminophen are nausea, vomiting, sweating and pallor. This may be followed in cases of large overdoses by liver damage which may lead to coma and death. In any suspected case of acetaminophen overdose, it is strongly advised that the patient be seen immediately by a physician.

Dosage: Adults: 650 to 1 000 mg every 4 to 6 hours, not to exceed 4 000 mg in 24 hours. Children: 10 to 15 mg/kg every 4 to 6 hours, not to exceed 65 mg/kg/24 hours; or according to age (see Table I).

Table I—Tempra

Age	Maximum Single Dose
0 to 3 months	40 mg
4 to 11 months	80 mg
12 to 23 months	120 mg
2 to 3 years	160 mg
4 to 5 years	240 mg
6 to 8 years	320 mg
9 to 10 years	400 mg
11 to 12 years	480 mg

Supplied: Drops: Each 1 mL of wild cherry- or banana-flavored liquid contains: acetaminophen 80 mg. Nonmedicinal ingredients: artificial flavoring, citric acid, glycerin, polyethylene glycol, propylene glycol, purified water, sodium citrate and sodium saccharin. Energy: 5.88 kJ (1.4 kcal)/mL. Sodium: <1 mmol (1.5 mg)/mL. Alcohol- and sucrose-free. Bottles of 15 and 24 mL with calibrated dropper.

Syrup: 80 mg/5 mL: Each 5 mL of cherry-flavored syrup contains: acetaminophen 80 mg. Nonmedicinal ingredients: artificial flavors and coloring, butylated hydroxyanisol, citric acid, polyethylene glycol, purified water, sodium benzoate, sodium chloride, sodium citrate and sucrose. Energy: 37.38 kJ (8.9 kcal)/5 mL. Sodium: <1 mmol (3.6 mg)/5 mL. Alcohol-free. Bottles of 100 mL.

160 mg/5 mL: Each 5 mL of cherry- or banana-flavored syrup contains: acetaminophen 160 mg. Nonmedicinal ingredients: artificial flavors and coloring, butylated hydroxyanisol, citric acid, polyethylene glycol, purified water, sodium benzoate, sodium chloride, sodium citrate and sucrose. Energy: 37.38 kJ (8.9 kcal)/5 mL. Sodium: <1 mmol (3.6 mg)/5 mL. Alcohol-free. Bottles of 100 mL.

Chewable Tablets: 80 mg: Each purple tablet, engraved 80 on one side and engraved Tempra on the other, contains: acetaminophen 80 mg. Nonmedicinal ingredients: artificial flavor and coloring, aspartame, croscarmellose sodium, glycine, magnesium stearate, mannitol, microcrystalline cellulose, sodium chloride and stearic acid. Bottles of 24.

160 mg: Each purple tablet, engraved 160 on one side and engraved Tempra on the other, contains: acetaminophen 160 mg. Nonmedicinal ingredients: artificial flavor and flavoring, aspartame, croscarmellose sodium, glycine, magnesium stearate, mannitol, microcrystalline cellulose, sodium chloride and stearic acid. Bottles of 20.

TENOLIN ℞
Technilab

Atenolol

Beta-adrenergic Receptor Blocking Agent

Supplied: 50 mg: Each white to off-white biconvex, scored, film-coated tablet, embossed with Tenolin 50 on one face, contains: atenolol 50 mg. Nonmedicinal ingredients: hydroxypropylcellulose, hydroxypropyl methylcellulose, magnesium stearate, magnesium trisilicate, microcrystalline cellulose, polyethylene glycol, sodium croscarmellose, talc and titanium dioxide. Compliance packs of 30. Bottles of 100 and 500.

100 mg: Each white to off-white biconvex, scored, film-coated tablet, embossed with Tenolin 100 on one face, contains: atenolol 100 mg. Nonmedicinal ingredients: hydroxypropylcellulose, hydroxypropyl methylcellulose, magnesium stearate, magnesium trisilicate, microcrystalline cellulose, polyethylene glycol, sodium croscarmellose, talc and titanium dioxide. Compliance packs of 30. Bottles of 100 and 500.

Store at room temperature (15 to 30°C). Protect from light and moisture.

TENORETIC® ℞
Zeneca

Atenolol—Chlorthalidone

Antihypertensive Agent

Pharmacology: Tenoretic combines the antihypertensive activity of 2 agents, a β-adrenergic receptor blocking agent (atenolol) and diuretic (chlorthalidone).

Atenolol is a β_1-selective, β-adrenergic blocking agent, devoid of membrane stabilizing or intrinsic sympathomimetic (partial agonist) activities. It is a racemic mixture and the β_1 properties reside in the S(-) enantiomer. β_1-selectivity decreases with increasing dose.

The mechanism of the antihypertensive effect of atenolol has not been established. Among the factors that may be involved are: competitive ability to antagonize catecholamine-induced tachycardia at the β-receptor sites in the heart, thus decreasing cardiac output; inhibition of renin release by the kidneys; inhibition of the vasomotor centres.

In man atenolol reduces both isoproterenol-and exercise-induced increases in heart rate over the dose range of 50 to 200 mg. At an oral dose of 100 mg the β_1-blocking effects persist for at least 24 hours; the reduction in exercise-induced heart rate increase being about 32% and 13%, 2 and 24 hours after dosing, respectively. The logarithm of the plasma atenolol level correlates with the degree of β_1-blockade but not with the antihypertensive effect.

Chlorthalidone, a monosulfonamyl diuretic, increases excretion of sodium and chloride. Natriuresis is accompanied by some loss of potassium. The mechanism by which chlorthalidone reduces blood pressure is not fully known but may be related to the excretion and redistribution of body sodium. Chlorthalidone usually does not decrease normal blood pressure.

The combination of atenolol with thiazide-like diuretics has been shown to be compatible and generally more effective than either drug used alone as an antihypertensive agent.

Pharmacokinetics: Approximately 40 to 50% of an oral dose of atenolol is absorbed from the gastrointestinal tract, the remainder being excreted unchanged in the feces. Peak plasma concentrations occur 2 to 4 hours after dosing and are subject to a 4-fold variability. The plasma levels are proportional to dose over the range 50 to 400 mg and 6 to 16% of atenolol is bound to plasma proteins. The plasma half-life is approximately 6 to 7 hours.

Approximately 60% of an oral dose of chlorthalidone is absorbed from the gastrointestinal tract and excreted unchanged in the urine. Following a single dose, the peak blood concentration of chlorthalidone occurs after approximately 12 hours and decreases thereafter according to first-order kinetics; the disposition half-life is approximately 50 hours. Approximately 75% of chlorthalidone is bound in plasma.

Indications: This fixed combination is not indicated for initial therapy of hypertension. Hypertension requires therapy titrated to the individual patient. It is always better to adjust the dosage of each antihypertensive drug separately, but when the fixed combination corresponds to the optimum drug and dose requirements of the patient, its use may be more convenient in patient management. For further adjustment of dosage, however, it is best to use the individual drugs again. The treatment of hypertension is not static, but must be reevaluated as conditions in each patient warrant.

Tenoretic is indicated for the maintenance therapy of patients with hypertension who require atenolol and chlorthalidone in the dosage and ratios present in Tenoretic.

Contraindications: Sinus bradycardia, or bradycardia of other origin; second and third degree AV block; sick sinus syndrome; right ventricular failure secondary to pulmonary hypertension; congestive heart failure; cardiogenic shock; hypotension; severe peripheral arterial disorders; anesthesia with agents that produce myocardial depression; pheochromocytoma, in the absence of α-blockade; metabolic acidosis; anuria; hypersensitivity to atenolol, chlorthalidone or to sulfonamide-derived drugs.

Warnings: Cardiac Failure: Special caution should be exercised when administering Tenoretic to patients with a history of cardiac failure. Sympathetic stimulation is a vital component supporting circulatory function in congestive heart failure and inhibition with β-blockade always carries the potential hazard of further depressing myocardial contractility and precipitating cardiac failure.

In patients without a history of cardiac failure, continued depression of the myocardium with β-blocking agents over a period of time can, in some cases, lead to cardiac failure. Therefore, at the first sign or symptom of impending cardiac failure, patients should be fully digitalized and/or given additional diuretic and the response observed closely.

Atenolol acts selectively without blocking the inotropic action of digitalis on the heart muscle. However, the positive inotropic action of digitalis may be reduced by the negative inotropic effect of atenolol when the two drugs are used concomitantly. The effects of β-blockers and digitalis are additive in depressing AV conduction. If cardiac failure continues, despite adequate digitalization, Tenoretic therapy should be withdrawn immediately and diuretic therapy maintained (see below).

Abrupt Cessation of Therapy: Patients with angina should be warned against abrupt discontinuation of Tenoretic. There have been reports of severe exacerbation of angina and of myocardial infarction or ventricular arrhythmias occurring in patients with angina pectoris, following abrupt discontinuation of β-blocker therapy. The last two complications may occur with or without preceding exacerbation of angina pectoris. Therefore, when discontinuation of Tenoretic is planned in patients with angina pectoris, the drug should be stopped and immediately replaced with atenolol and a diuretic given separately, so that the dose of atenolol may be gradually reduced over a period of about 2 weeks while the dose of diuretic is maintained. The same frequency of administration of both drugs should be maintained. The patient should be carefully observed.

In situations of greater urgency, Tenoretic should be discontinued stepwise over a shorter time and under closer observation. If angina markedly worsens or acute coronary insufficiency develops, it is recommended that treatment with Tenoretic be reinstituted promptly, at least temporarily.

Since ischemic heart disease may be unrecognized, the above advice should be followed in patients considered to be at risk of having asymptomatic ischemic heart disease.

Oculomucocutaneous Syndrome: Various skin rashes and conjunctival xerosis have been reported with β-blockers, including atenolol. A severe syndrome (oculomucocutaneous syndrome) whose signs include conjunctivitis sicca and psoriasiform rashes, otitis, and sclerosing serositis has occurred with the chronic use of one β-adrenergic blocking agent (practolol). This syndrome has not been observed with atenolol or any other such agent. However, physicians should be alert to the possibility of such reactions and should discontinue treatment with Tenoretic in the event that they occur.

Prinzmetal's Angina: Atenolol may increase the number and duration of angina attacks in patients with Prinzmetal's angina due to unopposed α-receptor mediated coronary artery vasoconstriction. Tenoretic, therefore, should only be used in these patients with the utmost care.

Sinus Bradycardia: Severe sinus bradycardia may occur with the use of atenolol from unopposed vagal activity remaining after blockade of β_1-adrenergic receptors; in such cases, the dose should be reduced.

Thyrotoxicosis: In patients with thyrotoxicosis, possible deleterious effects from long-term use of atenolol have not been adequately appraised. β-blockade may mask the clinical signs of continuing hyperthyroidism or its complications and give a false impression of improvement. Therefore, abrupt withdrawal of atenolol may be followed by an exacerbation of the symptoms of hyperthyroidism, including thyroid storm. Thiazides may decrease serum PBI levels without signs of thyroid disturbance.

Impaired Renal Function: Tenoretic should be used with caution since chlorthalidone may precipitate or increase azotemia. Cumulative effects may develop since both components of Tenoretic are excreted by the kidney. If progressive renal impairment becomes evident, Tenoretic should be discontinued.

When renal function is impaired, clearance of atenolol is closely related to the glomerular filtration rate. However, significant accumulation does not occur until the creatinine clearance falls below 35 mL/min/1.73m^2.

Impaired Hepatic Function: In patients with impaired hepatic function or progressive liver disease, even minor alterations in fluid and electrolyte balance may precipitate hepatic coma. Hepatic encephalopathy, manifested by tremors, confusion and coma, has been reported in association with diuretic therapy, including chlorthalidone.

Hypersensitivity Reactions: In patients receiving chlorthalidone, sensitivity reactions may occur with or without a history of allergy or bronchial asthma.

Systemic Lupus Erythematosus: Possible exacerbation of systemic lupus erythematosus has been reported with thiazide-like diuretics.

Precautions: Bronchospastic Disorders: Patients with bronchospastic diseases should, in general, not receive β-blockers. Due to the relative β_1-selectivity of atenolol, atenolol may be used with caution in patients with bronchospastic disease who do not respond to, or cannot tolerate, other antihypertensive treatment. Since β_1-selectivity is not absolute, a β_2-stimulating agent should be administered concomitantly and the lowest possible dose of atenolol should be used. Despite these precautions, the respiratory status of some patients may worsen, and, in such cases, Tenoretic should be withdrawn.

First Degree Heart Block: Due to atenolol's negative effect on AV conduction time, Tenoretic should be used with caution in patients with first degree block.

Peripheral Arterial Circulatory Disorders: Tenoretic may aggravate less severe peripheral arterial circulatory disorders (see Contraindications).

Anaphylaxis–Epinephrine and β-blockers: There may be increased difficulty in treating an allergic type reaction in patients on β-blockers. In these patients, the reaction may be more severe due to pharmacological effects of β-blockers and problems with fluid changes. Epinephrine should be administered with caution since it may not have its usual effects in the treatment of anaphylaxis. On the one hand, larger doses of epinephrine may be needed to overcome the bronchospasm, while on the other, these doses can be associated with excessive α-adrenergic stimulation with consequent hypertension, reflex bradycardia and heart-block and possible potentiation of bronchospasm. Alternatives to the use of large doses of epinephrine include vigorous supportive care such as fluids and the use of β-agonists including parenteral salbutamol or isoproterenol to overcome bronchospasm and norepinephrine to overcome hypotension.

Diabetes and Patients Subject to Hypoglycemia: Tenoretic should be administered with caution to patients subject to spontaneous hypoglycemia, or to diabetic patients (especially those with labile diabetes) who are receiving insulin or oral hypoglycemic agents. β-adrenergic receptor blocking agents may mask the premonitory signs (e.g., tachycardia) and symptoms of acute hypoglycemia. Insulin requirements in diabetic patients may be increased, decreased, or unchanged by chlorthalidone. Diabetes mellitus which has been latent may become manifest during chlorthalidone administration.

Elective or Emergency Surgery: It is not advisable to withdraw β-adrenoceptor blocking drugs prior to surgery in the majority of patients. However, care should be taken when using Tenoretic with anesthetic agents such as those which may depress the myocardium. Vagal dominance, if it occurs, may be corrected with atropine (1 to 2 mg i.v.).

Some patients receiving β-adrenergic blocking agents have been subject to protracted severe hypotension during anesthesia. Difficulty in restarting and maintaining the heartbeat has also been reported.

In emergency surgery, since atenolol is a competitive inhibitor of β-adrenergic receptor agonists, its effects may be reversed, if necessary, by sufficient doses of such agonists as isoproterenol or norepinephrine.

Fluid or Electrolyte Imbalance: Patients receiving chlorthalidone should be carefully observed for clinical signs of fluid or electrolyte imbalance (hyponatremia, hypochloremic alkalosis and hypokalemia). Periodic determination of serum electrolytes should be performed at appropriate intervals. Serum and urine electrolyte determinations are particularly important when the patient is vomiting excessively or receiving parenteral fluids. Warning signs or symptoms of fluid and electrolyte imbalance include dryness of the mouth, thirst, weakness, lethargy, drowsiness, restlessness, muscle pains or cramps, muscular fatigue, hypotension, oliguria, tachycardia and gastrointestinal disturbances.

Hypokalemia may develop, especially with brisk diuresis, when severe cirrhosis is present, or during concomitant use of corticosteroids or ACTH. Interference with adequate oral electrolyte intake will also contribute to hypokalemia. Hypokalemia can sensitize or exaggerate the response of the heart to the toxic effects of digitalis (e.g., increased ventricular irritability). Hypokalemia may be avoided or treated by use of potassium supplements, potassium-sparing agents or foods with a high potassium content.

Any chloride deficit during chlorthalidone therapy is generally mild and usually does not require specific treatment except under extraordinary circumstances (as in liver disease or renal disease). Dilutional hyponatremia may occur in edematous patients in hot weather; appropriate therapy is water restriction rather than administration of salt except in rare instances when the hyponatremia is life threatening. In actual salt depletion, appropriate replacement is the therapy of choice.

Because calcium excretion is decreased by chlorthalidone, Tenoretic should be discontinued before carrying out tests for parathyroid function. Pathologic changes in the parathyroid glands, with hypercalcemia and hypophosphatemia, have been observed in a few patients on prolonged thiazide therapy; however, the common complications of hyperparathyroidism such as renal lithiasis, bone resorption and peptic ulceration have not been seen.

Postsympathectomy Patients: The antihypertensive effects of thiazides may be enhanced in the postsympathectomy patient.

Hyperuricemia: Hyperuricemia may occur or acute gout may be precipitated in certain patients receiving chlorthalidone.

Ethnic Populations: Atenolol appears to be effective and well-tolerated in most ethnic populations, although the response may be less in black patients than in Caucasians.

Pregnancy: Atenolol has been shown to produce a dose-related increase in embryo-fetal resorptions in rats at doses equal to or greater than 50 mg/kg or 25 or more times the maximum recommended human dose. Studies in humans have shown that transplacental passage of atenolol does occur in pregnant women with fetal drug serum levels equal to those of the mother. Thiazides also cross the placental barrier and appear in cord blood.

The safe use of Tenoretic in pregnancy has not been established. The use of Tenoretic in pregnancy or in women of childbearing potential requires that the anticipated benefit be weighed against possible risk to mother and/or fetus. These hazards include fetal or neonatal jaundice, thrombocytopenia and, possibly, other adverse reactions which have occurred in the adult.

Lactation: In humans, there is a significant accumulation of atenolol in the breast milk of lactating women. Chlorthalidone also appears in human milk. If the use of Tenoretic is deemed essential, the patient should stop nursing.

Children: The safety of use of atenolol in children has not been established; therefore, Tenoretic is not recommended in the pediatric age group.

Occupational Hazards: Use of Tenoretic is unlikely to result in any impairment of the ability of patients to drive or operate machinery. However, it should be taken into account that dizziness or fatigue may occur.

Drug Interactions: Clonidine: β-blockers may exacerbate the rebound hypertension which can follow the withdrawal of clonidine. If the two drugs are coadministered, the β-blocker

Tenoretic (cont'd)

should be withdrawn several days before discontinuing clonidine. If replacing clonidine by β-blocker therapy, the introduction of β-blockers should be delayed for several days after clonidine administration has stopped. (Also see prescribing information for clonidine.)
Reserpine or Guanethidine: Patients receiving catecholamine-depleting drugs, such as reserpine or guanethidine, should be closely monitored because the added β-adrenergic blocking action of atenolol may produce an excessive reduction of sympathetic activity. Tenoretic should not be combined with other drugs containing β-blockers.
Antihypertensive Peripheral Vasodilator: The combination of Tenoretic with an antihypertensive peripheral vasodilator produces a greater fall in blood pressure than either drug alone. The same degree of blood pressure control can be achieved by lower than usual doses of each drug. Therefore, when using such concomitant therapy, careful monitoring of the doses is required until the patient is stabilized.
Norepinephrine: Thiazides may decrease arterial responsiveness to norepinephrine. This diminution is not sufficient to preclude the therapeutic effectiveness of the pressor agent in therapy.
Tubocurarine: Thiazide diuretics may increase the responsiveness to tubocurarine.
Lithium: Lithium generally should not be given with diuretics because they reduce its renal clearance and add a high risk of lithium toxicity. The Prescribing Information for lithium preparations should be read before use of such preparations with Tenoretic.
Alcohol, Barbiturates or Narcotics: Orthostatic hypotension may occur and may be potentiated by alcohol, barbiturates or narcotics.
Antiarrhythmic Agents: Care should be taken when atenolol is used concomitantly with Class I antiarrhythmic agents since these drugs may potentiate the cardiac depressing activity of atenolol. On rare occasions the concomitant administration of i.v. beta-adrenergic blocking agents with i.v. verapamil has resulted in serious adverse effects, especially in patients with severe cardiomyopathy, congestive heart failure or recent myocardial infarction.
Calcium Channel Blockers: Combined use of β-blockers and calcium channel blockers with negative inotropic effects can lead to prolongation of SA and AV conduction, particularly in patients with impaired ventricular function, conduction abnormalities, or diminished cardiac output. This may result in severe hypotension, bradycardia and cardiac failure. Concomitant therapy with dihydropyridines, e.g., nifedipine, may increase the risk of hypotension, and cardiac failure may occur in patients with latent cardiac insufficiency.
Digitalis Glycosides: Digitalis glycosides may potentiate the bradycardia of β-blockade.
Nonsteroidal Anti-inflammatory Agents: The concomitant use of nonsteroidal anti-inflammatory agents may blunt the antihypertensive effects of β-blockers.
Anesthetic Agents: Anesthetics can produce a hypotensive state with associated reflex tachycardia. Since β blockade will inhibit reflex tachycardia, the hypotensive potential of anesthetic agents is increased with concomitant use of Tenoretic (see Contraindications and Precautions).

Adverse Effects: Adverse reactions that have been reported with the individual components are listed below.
Atenolol: The most serious adverse reactions encountered are congestive heart failure, AV block and bronchospasm.

The most common adverse reactions reported in clinical trials with atenolol in 2 500 patients are bradycardia (3%), dizziness (3%), vertigo (2%), fatigue (3%), diarrhea (2%) and nausea (3%).

Adverse reactions, occurring with an incidence of less than 1%, grouped by system, are as follows: Cardiovascular: congestive heart failure (see Warnings), heart block, palpitations, lengthening of PR interval, chest pain, lightheadedness, postural hypotension which may be associated with syncope, Raynaud's phenomenon, intermittent claudication, or worsening of pre-existing intermittent claudication, leg pain and cold extremities, edema.
Respiratory: dyspnea, wheeziness, cough, bronchospasm.
CNS: faintness, ataxia, tiredness, lethargy, nervousness, depression, drowsiness, vivid dreams, insomnia, paresthesia, headache, tinnitus, mood changes, visual disturbances, psychoses and hallucinations.
Gastrointestinal: abdominal discomfort, indigestion, constipation, anorexia.
Miscellaneous: skin rash, itchy and/or dry eyes, psoriasiform skin reactions, exacerbation of psoriasis, decreased exercise tolerance, alopecia, epistaxis, flushes, impotence, decreased libido, sweating, general body aches, thrombocytopenia and purpura.
Postmarketing Experience: During postmarketing experience with atenolol, the following have been reported in temporal relationship to the use of the drug: elevated liver enzymes and/or bilirubin, headache, confusion, nightmares, impotence, Peyronie's disease, psoriasiform rash or exacerbation of psoriasis, purpura, reversible alopecia and thrombocytopenia. Rare cases of hepatic toxicity including intrahepatic cholestasis have been reported. Atenolol, like other β blockers, has been associated with the development of antinuclear antibodies (ANA) and lupus syndrome.

In a long-term, well controlled trial of 1 627 elderly patients with systolic hypertension, the incidence of dry mouth was significantly higher in patients taking atenolol (12.2%).
Potential Adverse Reactions: The following adverse reactions have occurred with other β-blockers but have not been reported with atenolol:
Cardiovascular: pulmonary edema, cardiac enlargement, hot flushes and sinus arrest.
CNS: aggressiveness, anxiety, short-term memory loss, and emotional lability with slightly clouded sensorium.
Allergic: laryngospasm, status asthmaticus and fever combined with aching and sore throat.
Dermatological: exfoliative dermatitis.
Ophthalmological: blurred vision, burning, and grittiness.
Hematological: agranulocytosis.
Gastrointestinal: mesenteric arterial thrombosis and ischemic colitis.
Chlorthalidone: The following adverse reactions have been reported:
Gastrointestinal: anorexia, gastric irritation, nausea, vomiting, cramping, diarrhea, constipation, jaundice (intrahepatic cholestatic jaundice), pancreatitis.
CNS: dizziness, vertigo, paresthesias, headache, xanthopsia.
Hematologic: leukopenia, agranulocytosis, thrombocytopenia, aplastic anemia.
Dermatologic-Hypersensitivity: purpura, photosensitivity, rash, urticaria, necrotizing angiitis (vasculitis) (cutaneous vasculitis), Lyell's syndrome (toxic epidermal necrolysis).
Cardiovascular: Orthostatic hypotension may occur and may be aggravated by alcohol, barbiturates or narcotics.
Other: hyperglycemia, glycosuria, hyperuricemia, hyponatremia, muscle spasm, weakness, restlessness, impotence.

Overdose: Symptoms and Treatment: No specific information is available with regard to overdosage of Tenoretic in humans.
Atenolol: Overdosage with atenolol has been reported with patients surviving acute doses as high as 5 g. One death was reported in a man who may have taken as much as 10 g acutely.

The predominant symptoms reported following atenolol overdosage are lethargy, disorder of respiratory drive, wheezing, sinus pause, and bradycardia. Additionally, common effects associated with overdosage of any β-adrenergic blocking agent are congestive heart failure, hypotension, bronchospasm and/or hypoglycemia.

Treatment should be symptomatic and supportive and directed to the removal of any unabsorbed drug by induced emesis, or administration of activated charcoal. Atenolol can be removed from the general circulation by hemodialysis. Further consideration should be given to dehydration, electrolyte imbalance and hypotension by established procedures.

Other treatment modalities should be employed at the physician's discretion and may include:
Bradycardia: Atropine 1 to 2 mg i.v. If there is no response to vagal blockade, give isoproterenol cautiously. In refractory cases, a transvenous cardiac pacemaker may be indicated. Glucagon in a 10 mg i.v. bolus has been reported to be useful. If required, this may be repeated or followed by an i.v. infusion of glucagon 1 to 10 mg/h depending on response. If no response to glucagon occurs or if glucagon is unavailable, a β-adrenoceptor stimulant such as dobutamine 2.5 to 10 μg/kg/min by i.v. infusion or isoproterenol 10 to 25 μg given as an infusion at a rate not exceeding 5 μg/min may be given, although larger doses may be required.
Heart Block (second or third degree): Isoproterenol or transvenous pacemaker.
Congestive Heart Failure: Digitalize the patient and administer a diuretic. Glucagon has been reported to be useful.
Hypotension: Vasopressors such as dopamine or norepinephrine. Monitor blood pressure continuously.
Bronchospasm: A β_2-stimulant such as isoproterenol or terbutaline, and/or i.v. aminophylline.
Hypoglycemia: I.V. glucose.
Electrolyte Disturbance: Monitor electrolyte levels and renal function. Institute measures to maintain hydration and electrolytes.

Based on the severity of symptoms, management may require intensive support care and facilities for applying cardiac and respiratory support.
Chlorthalidone: Symptoms of chlorthalidone overdose include nausea, weakness, dizziness and disturbances of electrolyte balance.

Dosage: Dosage must be determined for individual patients by titration of each component separately. Where the fixed combination in Tenoretic supplies the dosage so determined, the combination product may be used for maintenance therapy. One tablet once daily can be used to administer up to 100 mg of atenolol and 25 mg of chlorthalidone.

If further lowering of the blood pressure is required, another antihypertensive agent may be added to the regimen.

In patients with renal impairment, the dose of the components should be carefully individualized. Recommendations for dosage adjustments for atenolol and chlorthalidone in renal disease are found in the Tenormin and Hygroton prescribing information.

If dosage adjustment is necessary during maintenance therapy, it is advisable to use the individual drugs.

Supplied: Tablets 50/25: Each white, round, biconvex tablet, scored and embossed 50/25 on one face and plain on the other, contains: atenolol 50 mg and chlorthalidone 25 mg. Nonmedicinal ingredients: magnesium stearate, microcrystalline cellulose, povidone and sodium starch glycolate. Calendar packs of 28.

Tablets 100/25: Each white, round, biconvex tablet, scored and embossed with 100/25 on one face and plain on the other, contains: atenolol 100 mg and chlorthalidone 25 mg. Nonmedicinal ingredients: magnesium stearate, microcrystalline cellulose, povidone and sodium starch glycolate. Calendar packs of 28.

Protect from light and moisture. Store at room temperature.

Reviewed 1999

TENORMIN® Ⓟ

Zeneca

Atenolol

β-adrenergic Receptor Blocking Agent

Pharmacology: Atenolol is a β_1-selective, β-adrenergic blocking agent, devoid of membrane stabilizing or intrinsic sympathomimetic (partial agonist) activities. It is a racemic mixture and the β_1-properties reside in the S(-) enantiomer. β_1-selectivity decreases with increasing dose.

The mechanism of the antihypertensive effect has not been established. Among the factors that may be involved are: competitive ability to antagonize catecholamine-induced tachycardia at the β-receptor sites in the heart, thus decreasing cardiac output; inhibition of renin release by the kidneys; inhibition of the vasomotor centres.

The mechanism of the antianginal effect is also uncertain. An important factor may be the reduction of myocardial oxygen requirements by blocking catecholamine-induced increases in heart rate, systolic blood pressure, and the velocity and extent of myocardial contraction.

In man atenolol reduces both isoproterenol- and exercise-induced increases in heart rate over the dose range of 50 to 200 mg. At an oral dose of 100 mg the β_1-blocking effects persist for at least 24 hours; the reduction in exercise-induced heart rate increase being about 32% and 13%, 2 and 24 hours after dosing, respectively. The logarithm of the plasma atenolol level correlates with the degree of β_1-blockade but not with the antihypertensive effect.

Pharmacokinetics: Approximately 40 to 50% of an oral dose of atenolol is absorbed from the gastrointestinal tract, the remainder being excreted unchanged in the feces. Peak plasma concentrations occur 2 to 4 hours after dosing and are subject to a 4-fold variability. The plasma levels are proportional to dose over the range 50 to 400 mg and 6 to 16% of atenolol is bound to plasma proteins. The mean peak plasma concentrations of atenolol were approximately 300 and 700 ng/mL following 50 and 100 mg, respectively. The plasma half-life is approximately 6 to 7 hours. Atenolol is extensively distributed to extravascular tissues, but only a small amount is found in the CNS.

There is no significant hepatic metabolism of atenolol in man and more than 90% of the absorbed dose reaches the systemic circulation unaltered. Small quantities of a hydroxy metabolite and a glucuronide are produced but neither has major pharmacological activity. As a consequence no accumulation occurs in patients with liver disease and no dosage adjustment is required. Approximately 47% and 53% of the oral dose is eliminated in the urine and feces, respectively. Recovery is complete after 72 hours.

Atenolol is primarily eliminated by the kidney, predominantly by glomerular filtration. The normal elimination half-life may increase in severe renal impairment but no significant accumulation occurs in patients who have creatinine clearance greater than 35 mL/min. The oral dose should be reduced in patients with a creatinine clearance less than 35 mL/min (see Dosage).

Atenolol is excreted in human breast milk and crosses the placental barrier–the maternal to cord blood ratio being about unity.

Indications: Hypertension: In patients with mild or moderate hypertension. It is usually used in combination with other drugs, particularly a thiazide diuretic. However, it may be tried alone as an initial agent in those patients in whom, in the judgement of the physician, treatment should be started with a β-blocker rather than a diuretic. Atenolol may be used in combination with diuretics and/or vasodilators to treat severe hypertension.

The combination of atenolol with a diuretic or peripheral vasodilator has been found to be compatible. Limited experience with other antihypertensive agents has not shown evidence of incompatibility with atenolol.

Atenolol is not recommended for the emergency treatment of hypertensive crises.

Angina Pectoris: In the long-term management of patients with angina pectoris due to ischemic heart disease.

Contraindications: Sinus bradycardia, or bradycardia of other origin; second and third degree AV block; sick sinus syndrome; right ventricular failure secondary to pulmonary hypertension; congestive heart failure; cardiogenic shock; hypotension; severe peripheral arterial disorders; anesthesia with agents that produce myocardial depression; pheochromocytoma, in the absence of α-blockade; metabolic acidosis; known hypersensitivity to the product.

Warnings: Cardiac Failure: Special caution should be exercised when administering atenolol to patients with a history of heart failure. Sympathetic stimulation is a vital component supporting circulatory function in congestive heart failure and inhibition with β-blockade always carries the potential hazard of further depressing myocardial contractility and precipitating cardiac failure. Atenolol acts selectively without abolishing the inotropic action of digitalis on the heart muscle. However, the positive inotropic action of digitalis may be reduced by the negative inotropic effect of atenolol when the two drugs are used concomitantly. The effects of β-blockers and digitalis are additive in depressing AV conduction. In patients without a history of cardiac failure, continued depression of the myocardium over a period of time can, in some cases, lead to cardiac failure. Therefore, at the first sign or symptom of impending cardiac failure, patients should be fully digitalized and/or given a diuretic and the response observed closely. If cardiac failure continues, despite adequate digitalization and diuretic therapy, atenolol therapy should be immediately withdrawn.

Abrupt Cessation of Therapy: Patients with angina should be warned against abrupt discontinuation of atenolol. There have been reports of severe exacerbation of angina and of myocardial infarction or ventricular arrhythmias occurring in patients with angina pectoris, following abrupt discontinuation of β-blocker therapy. The last two complications may occur with or without preceding exacerbation of angina pectoris. Therefore, when discontinuation of atenolol is planned in patients with angina pectoris, the dosage should be gradually reduced over a period of about 2 weeks and the patient should be carefully observed and advised to limit physical activity to a minimum. The same frequency of administration should be maintained. In situations of greater urgency, atenolol should be discontinued stepwise over a shorter time and under closer observation. If angina markedly worsens or acute coronary insufficiency develops, it is recommended that treatment with atenolol be reinstituted promptly, at least temporarily.

Oculomucocutaneous Syndrome: Various skin rashes and conjunctival xerosis have been reported with β-blockers, including atenolol. A severe syndrome (oculomucocutaneous syndrome) whose signs include conjunctivitis sicca and psoriasiform rashes, otitis, and sclerosing serositis has occurred with the chronic use of one β-adrenergic blocking agent (practolol). This syndrome has not been observed with atenolol or any other such agent. However, physicians should be alert to the possibility of such reactions and should discontinue treatment in the event that they occur.

Prinzmetal's Angina: Atenolol may increase the number and duration of angina attacks in patients with Prinzmetal's angina due to unopposed α-receptor mediated coronary artery vasoconstriction. Atenolol, therefore, should only be used in these patients with the utmost care.

Sinus Bradycardia: Severe sinus bradycardia may occur with the use of atenolol from unopposed vagal activity remaining after blockade of β_1-adrenergic receptors; in such cases, dosage should be reduced.

Thyrotoxicosis: In patients with thyrotoxicosis, possible deleterious effects from long-term use of atenolol have not been adequately appraised. β-blockade may mask the clinical signs of continuing hyperthyroidism or its complications and give a false impression of improvement. Therefore, abrupt withdrawal of atenolol may be followed by an exacerbation of the symptoms of hyperthyroidism, including thyroid storm.

Precautions: Bronchospastic Disorders: Patients with bronchospastic diseases should, in general, not receive β-blockers. Due to the relative β_1-selectivity of atenolol, atenolol may be used with caution in patients with bronchospastic disease who do not respond to, or cannot tolerate, other antihypertensive treatment. Since β_1-selectivity is not absolute, a β_2-stimulating agent should be administered concomitantly and the lowest possible dose of atenolol should be used. Despite these precautions, the respiratory status of some patients may worsen, and, in such cases, atenolol should be withdrawn.

First Degree Heart Block: Due to its negative effect on AV conduction time, atenolol should be used with caution in patients with first degree block.

Peripheral Arterial Circulatory Disorders: Atenolol may aggravate less severe peripheral arterial circulatory disorders (see Contraindications).

Anaphylaxis–Epinephrine and β-blockers: There may be increased difficulty in treating an allergic type reaction in patients on β-blockers. In these patients, the reaction may be more severe due to pharmacologic effects of β-blockers and problems with fluid changes. Epinephrine should be administered with caution since it may not have its usual effects in the treatment of anaphylaxis. On the one hand, larger doses of epinephrine may be needed to overcome the bronchospasm, while on the other, these doses can be associated with excessive α-adrenergic stimulation with consequent hypertension, reflex bradycardia and heart block and possible potentiation of bronchospasm. Alternatives to the use of large doses of epinephrine include vigorous supportive care such as fluids and the use of β-agonists including parenteral salbutamol or isoproterenol to overcome bronchospasm and norepinephrine to overcome hypotension.

Diabetes and Patients Subject to Hypoglycemia: Atenolol should be administered with caution to patients subject to spontaneous hypoglycemia, or to diabetic patients (especially those with labile diabetes) who are receiving insulin or oral hypoglycemic agents. β-adrenergic blockers may mask the premonitory signs (e.g., tachycardia) and symptoms of acute hypoglycemia.

Impaired Renal Function: Atenolol should be used with caution in patients with impaired renal function (see Dosage).

When renal function is impaired, clearance of atenolol is closely related to the glomerular filtration rate; however, significant accumulation does not occur until the creatinine clearance falls below 35 ml /min/1.73 m^2.

Elective or Emergency Surgery: It is not advisable to withdraw β-adrenoceptor blocking drugs prior to surgery in the majority of patients. However, care should be taken when using atenolol with anesthetic agents such as those which may depress the myocardium. Vagal dominance, if it occurs, may be corrected with atropine (1 to 2 mg i.v.).

Some patients receiving β-adrenergic blocking agents have been subject to protracted severe hypotension during anesthesia. Difficulty in restarting and maintaining the heartbeat has also been reported.

In emergency surgery, since atenolol is a competitive inhibitor of β-adrenergic receptor agonists, its effects may be reversed, if necessary, by sufficient doses of such agonists as isoproterenol or norepinephrine.

Ethnic Populations: Atenolol appears to be effective and well-tolerated in most ethnic populations, although the responses may be less in black patients than in Caucasians.

Pregnancy: Atenolol has been shown to produce a dose-related increase in embryo/fetal resorptions in rats at doses equal to or greater than 50 mg/kg/day. Although similar effects were not seen in rabbits, the compound was not evaluated in rabbits at doses above 25 mg/kg/day. There are no adequate and well-controlled studies in pregnant women. Studies in humans have shown that transplacental passage of atenolol does occur in pregnant women with fetal drug serum levels equal to those of the mother. In a limited number of patients who were given the drug during the last trimester of pregnancy, low birth weight, neonatal hypoglycemia, bradycardia in the fetus/newborn, and placental insufficiency were observed. Atenolol should be used during pregnancy only if the potential benefit justifies the potential risk to the fetus.

Lactation: In humans, there is a significant accumulation of atenolol in the breast milk of lactating women. If use of atenolol is considered essential, then mothers should stop nursing.

Children: There is no experience with atenolol in the treatment of pediatric age groups.

Occupational Hazards: Use of atenolol is unlikely to result in any impairment of the ability of patients to drive or operate machinery. However, it should be taken into account that dizziness or fatigue may occur.

Drug Interactions: Clonidine: β-blockers may exacerbate the rebound hypertension which can follow the withdrawal of clonidine. If the two drugs are coadministered, the β-blocker should be withdrawn several days before discontinuing clonidine. If replacing clonidine by β-blocker therapy, the introduction of β-blockers should be delayed for several days after clonidine administration has stopped (see also prescribing information for clonidine).

Reserpine or Guanethidine: Patients receiving catecholamine-depleting drugs, such as reserpine or guanethidine, should be closely monitored because the added β-adrenergic blocking action of atenolol may produce an excessive reduction of sympathetic activity. Atenolol should not be combined with other β-blockers.

Antiarrhythmic Agents: Care should be taken when atenolol is used concomitantly with Class I antiarrhythmic agents since these drugs may potentiate the cardiac depressing activity of atenolol. On rare occasions the concomitant administration of i.v. β-adrenergic blocking agents with i.v. verapamil has resulted in serious adverse effects, especially in patients with severe cardiomyopathy, congestive heart failure or recent myocardial infarction.

Calcium Channel Blockers: Combined use of β-blockers and calcium channel blockers with negative inotropic effects can lead to prolongation of SA and AV conduction, particularly in patients with impaired ventricular function, conduction abnormalities, or diminished cardiac output. This may result in severe hypotension, bradycardia and cardiac failure. Concomitant therapy with dihydropyridines, e.g., nifedipine, may increase the risk of hypotension, and cardiac failure may occur in patients with latent cardiac insufficiency.

Digitalis Glycosides: Digitalis glycosides may potentiate the bradycardia of β_1-blockade.

Nonsteroidal Anti-inflammatory Agents: The concomitant use of nonsteroidal anti-inflammatory agents may blunt the antihypertensive effects of β-blockers.

Anesthetic Agents: Anesthetics can produce a hypotensive state with associated reflex tachycardia. Since β-blockade will inhibit reflex tachycardia, the hypotensive potential of anesthetic agents is increased with concomitant use of atenolol (see Contraindications and Precautions).

Adverse Effects: The most serious adverse reactions encountered are congestive heart failure, AV block and bronchospasm.

The most common adverse reactions reported in clinical trials with oral Tenormin in 2 500 patients are bradycardia (3%), dizziness (3%), vertigo (2%), fatigue (3%), diarrhea (2%) and nausea (3%).

Adverse reactions occurring with an incidence of less than 1%, grouped by system, are as follows:

Cardiovascular: congestive heart failure (see Warnings), heart block, palpitations, lengthening of PR interval, chest pain, lightheadedness, postural hypotension which may be associated with syncope, Raynaud's phenomenon, intermittent claudication, or worsening of pre-existing intermittent claudication, leg pain and cold extremities, edema.

Respiratory: dyspnea, wheeziness, cough, bronchospasm.

CNS: faintness, ataxia, tiredness, lethargy, nervousness, depression, drowsiness, vivid dreams, insommnia, paresthesia, headache, tinnitus, mood changes, visual disturbances, psychoses and hallucinations.

Gastrointestinal: constipation, anorexia, abdominal discomfort, indigestion.

Miscellaneous: skin rash, itchy and/or dry eyes, psoriasiform skin reactions, exacerbation of psoriasis, decreased exercise tolerance, alopecia, epistaxis, flushes, impotence, decreased libido, sweating, general body aches, thrombocytopenia and purpura.

Postmarketing Experience: During the postmarketing experience with Tenormin, the following have been reported in temporal relationship to the use of the drug: elevated liver enzymes and/or bilirubin, headache, confusion, nightmares, impotence, Peyronie's disease, psoriasisform rash or exacerbation of psoriasis, purpura, reversible alopecia and thrombocytopenia. Rare cases of hepatic toxicity including intrahepatic

Tenormin (cont'd)

cholestasis have been reported. Tenormin, like other β-blockers, has been associated with the development of antinuclear antibodies (ANA) and lupus syndrome.

In a long-term, well-controlled trial of 1 627 elderly patients with systolic hypertension, the incidence of dry mouth was significantly higher in patients taking atenolol (12.2%).

Potential Adverse Reactions: The following adverse reactions have occurred with other β-blockers but have not been reported with atenolol:

Cardiovascular: pulmonary edema, cardiac enlargement, hot flushes and sinus arrest.

CNS: aggressiveness, anxiety, short-term memory loss, and emotional lability with slightly clouded sensorium.

Allergic: laryngospasm, status asthmaticus and fever combined with aching and sore throat.

Dermatological: exfoliative dermatitis.

Ophthalmological: blurred vision, burning, and grittiness.

Hematological: agranulocytosis.

Gastrointestinal: mesenteric arterial thrombosis and ischemic colitis.

Overdose: Symptoms and Treatment: Limited information is available with regard to overdosage with atenolol in humans. Overdosage with atenolol has been reported with patients surviving acute doses as high as 5 g. One death was reported in a man who may have taken as much as 10 g acutely.

The predominant symptoms reported following atenolol overdosage are lethargy, disorder of respiratory drive, wheezing, sinus pause and bradycardia. Additionally, common effects associated with overdosage of any β-adrenergic blocking agent are congestive heart failure, hypotension, bronchospasm and/or hypoglycemia.

Treatment should be symptomatic and supportive and directed to the removal of any unabsorbed drug by induced emesis, or administration of activated charcoal. Atenolol can be removed from the general circulation by hemodialysis. Further consideration should be given to dehydration, electrolyte imbalance and hypotension by established procedures.

Other treatment modalities should be employed at the physician's discretion and may include:

Bradycardia: Atropine 1 to 2 mg i.v. If there is no response to vagal blockade, give isoproterenol cautiously. In refractory cases, a transvenous cardiac pacemaker may be indicated. Glucagon in a 10 mg i.v. bolus has been reported to be useful. If required, this may be repeated or followed by an i.v. infusion of glucagon 1 to 10 mg/h depending on response. If no response to glucagon occurs or if glucagon is unavailable, a β-adrenoceptor stimulant such as dobutamine 2.5 to 10 μg/kg/min by i.v. infusion or isoproterenol 10 to 25 μg given as an infusion at a rate not exceeding 5 μg/min may be given, although larger doses may be required.

Heart Block (second or third degree): Isoproterenol or transvenous pacemaker.

Congestive Heart Failure: Digitalize the patient and administer a diuretic. Glucagon has been reported to be useful.

Hypotension: Vasopressors such as dopamine or norepinephrine. Monitor blood pressure continuously.

Bronchospasm: A β_2-stimulant such as isoproterenol or terbutaline and/or i.v. aminophylline.

Hypoglycemia: I.V. glucose.

Based on the severity of symptoms, management may require intensive support care and facilities for applying cardiac and respiratory support.

Dosage: Hypertension: Atenolol is usually used in conjunction with other antihypertensive agents, particularly a thiazide diuretic, but may be used alone (see Indications).

The dose of atenolol should be administered in accordance with individual patient's needs.

The following guidelines are recommended: Initial dose: 50 mg administered as 1 tablet a day either added to diuretic therapy or alone. The full effect of this dose will usually be seen within 1 to 2 weeks. If an adequate response is not achieved, the dose should be increased to 100 mg once daily. Increasing the dose beyond 100 mg a day is unlikely to produce any further benefit.

If further lowering of the blood pressure is required, another antihypertensive agent should be added to the regimen.

Angina Pectoris: Initial dose: 50 mg given as 1 tablet a day. The full effect of this dose will usually be seen within 1 or 2 weeks. If an optimal response is not achieved within 1 week, the dosage should be increased to 100 mg given as 1 tablet a day. Some patients may require a dosage of 200 mg a day for optimal effect.

Renal Impairment: Since atenolol is eliminated predominantly via the kidneys, dosage should be adjusted in patients with severe renal impairment. Significant accumulation of atenolol occurs when creatinine clearance falls below 35 mL/min/1.73 m² (normal range is 100 to 150 mL/min/1.73 m²).

The maximum dosages recommended for patients with renal impairment are found in Table I.

Table I—Tenormin

Dosage in Renal Impairment

Creatinine Clearance (mL/min/1.73 m²)	Atenolol Elimination Half-life (h)	Maximum Dosage
15–35	16–27	50 mg daily
<15	>27	50 mg every other day

Patients on hemodialysis should be given 50 mg after each dialysis; this should be done under hospital supervision as marked falls in blood pressure can occur.

Supplied: 50 mg: Each scored, white to off-white biconvex, film-coated tablet embossed with TENORMIN 50 on one face, contains: atenolol 50 mg. Nonmedicinal ingredients: gelatin, glycerol, heavy magnesium carbonate, hydroxypropyl methylcellulose, magnesium stearate, maize starch, sodium lauryl sulfate and titanium dioxide. Energy: 1.26 kJ (0.3 kcal). Sodium: <1 mmol (0.3 mg). Calendar packs of 28.

100 mg: Each scored, white to off-white biconvex, film-coated tablet embossed with TENORMIN on one face, contains: atenolol 100 mg. Nonmedicinal ingredients: gelatin, glycerol, heavy magnesium carbonate, hydroxypropyl methylcellulose, magnesium stearate, maize starch, sodium lauryl sulfate and titanium dioxide. Energy: 2.1 kJ (0.5 kcal). Sodium: <1 mmol (0.6 mg). Calendar packs of 28.

Store at room temperature. Protect from light and moisture.

Reviewed 1999

TENSILON® Ⓟ

ICN

Edrophonium Chloride

Nondepolarizing Neuromuscular Antagonist

Pharmacology: The curare antagonizing effect of edrophonium appears to be predominantly the result of inhibiting effect on cholinesterase present at the myoneural junction. It may also displace curare-like drugs from their attachment to the muscle cell, thus permitting resumption of the normal transmission of neuromuscular impulses over the myoneural junction. Edrophonium acts within 0.5 to 1 minute and its effect lasts for an average of 10 minutes. The terminal elimination half life is approximately 33 minutes.

Indications: For the differential diagnosis of myasthenia gravis and as an adjunct in the evaluation of treatment requirements in this disease; for evaluating emergency treatment in myasthenic crises. Because of its short duration of action, edrophonium is not recommended for maintenance therapy in myasthenia gravis.

Also useful whenever a curare antagonist is needed to reverse the neuromuscular block produced by curare, tubocurarine, gallamine triethiodide or dimethyltubocurarine; not effective against decamethonium bromide or succinylcholine chloride. May be used adjunctively in the treatment of respiratory depression caused by curare overdosage.

Contraindications: Known hypersensitivity to anticholinesterase agents; intestinal and urinary obstruction of mechanical type.

Warnings: Whenever anticholinesterase drugs are used for testing, a syringe containing 1 mg atropine sulfate should be immediately available to be given in aliquots intravenously to counteract severe cholinergic reactions which may occur in the hypersensitive individual, whether the patient is normal or myasthenic.

Use edrophonium with caution in patients with bronchial asthma or cardiac dysrhythmias. The transient bradycardia which sometimes occurs can be relieved by atropine sulfate.

Isolated instances of cardiac and respiratory arrest following edrophonium administration have been reported; possibly, these are vagotonic effects.

Note: This product is packaged in a multiple dose vial. Single injection of the entire contents of one vial (100 mg) could be fatal.

Precautions: Patients may develop anticholinesterase insensitivity for brief or prolonged periods. During these periods, patients should be carefully monitored and may need respiratory assistance. Reduce or withhold dosage of anticholinesterase drugs until patients again become sensitive to them.

Pregnancy and *Lactation:* The safety of edrophonium during human pregnancy or lactation has not been established. Therefore, weigh the potential benefits of therapy against the possible hazards to mother and child before using the drug in women of childbearing potential.

Adverse Effects: Careful observation should be made for severe cholinergic reactions in the hyperreactive individual. The myasthenic patient in crisis who is being tested with edrophonium should be observed for bradycardia or cardiac standstill and cholinergic reactions if an overdose is given. The following reactions common to anticholinesterase agents may occur, although not all of these reactions have been reported with the administration of edrophonium, probably because of the short duration of action and limited indications:

Eye: increased lacrimation, pupillary constriction, spasm of accommodation, diplopia, conjunctival hyperemia.

CNS: convulsions, dysarthria, dysphonia, dysphagia.

Respiratory: increased tracheobronchial secretions, laryngospasm, bronchiolar constriction, paralysis of muscles of respiration, central respiratory paralysis.

Cardiac: arrhythmias (especially bradycardia), fall in cardiac output leading to hypotension.

Gastrointestinal: increased salivary, gastric and intestinal secretion, nausea, vomiting, increased gastrointestinal peristalsis, diarrhea, abdominal cramps.

Skeletal muscle: weakness, fasciculations.

Miscellaneous: increased urinary frequency and incontinence, diaphoresis.

Overdose: Symptoms: With large doses, curariform effects; generalized cholinergic activity: bradycardia, arrhythmias, hypotension, bronchiolar spasm.

Treatment: Artificial respiration; 400 to 500 μg atropine i.v., repeated every 3 to 10 minutes. Because of the short duration of action of edrophonium, atropine requirement seldom exceeds 2 mg; general supportive measures.

Dosage: Diagnosis of myasthenia gravis: 2 mg i.v., leaving needle in situ; if no reaction in 30 seconds, remaining 8 mg injected. Positive test shows marked increase of muscle strength within 1 minute followed by relapse within 5 to 30 minutes.

Differentiation of myasthenic and cholinergic crises: 1 mg to 2 mg i.v. 1 hour after last dose of cholinergic compound. Inadequate therapy causes transient increase of muscle strength; over treatment causes transient increase of muscle weakness. Do not perform this test unless respiratory exchange is adequate. Artificial ventilation may be necessary.

Antidote to curare: 10 mg i.v. May be necessary to repeat dose. Maximum dose for any patient is 40 mg.

Suspected dual block: to elicit presence of dual block in case of prolonged apnea following use of depolarizing drugs such as succinylcholine during anesthesia, 10 mg i.v.; if block is due to depolarization it is briefly potentiated, whereas dual block is completely reversed. May be necessary to repeat dose.

Supplied: Each mL contains: edrophonium chloride 10 mg with 4.5 mg phenol as preservative, 2 mg sodium sulfite, and buffered with sodium citrate and citric acid. pH of solution is 5.4. Sodium: <1 mmol/mL. Paraben-free. Vials of 10 mL, packs of 10. Store at 15 to 30°C. Stability not guaranteed if diluted with other solutions or drugs.

TENUATE® ♦
TENUATE® DOSPAN® ♦

Hoechst Marion Roussel

Diethylpropion HCl

Anorexiant

Pharmacology: Diethylpropion is a psychomotor stimulant with anorectic, sympathomimetic and other effects similar to those of amphetamines. As with all other drugs of this class in which the phenomenon has been studied, the initial rate of weight loss decreases until a plateau is reached; a regain of weight thereafter even though drug administration is continued has been reported. As with similar drugs, rebound weight gain also may occur after discontinuation of diethylpropion.

Indications: A psychomotor stimulant used as an adjunct in the short-term (i.e., a few weeks) to continued dietary treatment in the medical management of obesity, in patients who have not responded to an appropriate weight reducing diet alone. Diethylpropion is recommended only for obese patients with an initial body mass index ≥30 kg/m², or ≥27 kg/m² in the presence of other risk factors (e.g., hypertension, diabetes, hyperlipidemia). See Table I.

Table I—Tenuate/Tenuate Dospan

Body Mass Index (BMI), kg/m²

Weight (pounds)	Height (feet, inches) 5′0″	5′3″	5′6″	5′9″	6′0″	6′3″
140	**27**	25	23	21	19	18
150	**29**	**27**	24	22	20	19
160	31	**28**	26	24	22	20
170	33	30	**28**	25	23	21
180	35	32	**29**	**27**	25	23
190	37	34	31	**28**	26	24
200	39	36	32	30	**27**	25
210	41	37	34	31	**29**	26
220	43	39	36	33	30	**28**
230	45	41	37	34	31	**29**
240	47	43	39	36	33	30
250	49	44	40	37	34	31

When prescribing anorectic agents it should be borne in mind that the role of these drugs in the management of obesity is strictly limited, since patients treated with anorectics lose, on average, only a fraction of a pound per week more than those who are on a weight reducing diet alone. Furthermore, the rate of weight loss tends to decrease within a few weeks and a plateau is reached. Prolonged administration of diethylpropion should also be strictly avoided since it can lead to drug dependence and abuse (see Warnings). Therefore, even short-term use of an anorectic drug is not recommended unless a carefully supervised weight reduction regimen by itself is not successful.

Contraindications: Diethylpropion should not be administered during therapy with MAO inhibitors or within 14 days following withdrawal of these agents. Diethylpropion is contraindicated in patients with glaucoma, hyperthyroidism, advanced arteriosclerosis, agitated states, known hypersensitivity to sympathomimetic amines and in emotionally unstable individuals who are known to be susceptible to or have a history of drug abuse.

Warnings: Primary Pulmonary Hypertension: **Anorexigens, including diethylpropion, increase the risk of developing primary pulmonary hypertension, an often fatal disorder.**

An epidemiological study has indicated that use of anorexigens, including diethylpropion, for longer than 3 months was associated with a 23-fold increase in the risk of developing Primary Pulmonary Hypertension (PPH). There was no significant increase in risk for persons who had used these agents for 3 months or less. Obesity itself (body mass index ≥30 kg/m²) was also independently associated with an increase of about 2-fold in the risk of developing PPH. In the general population, the yearly occurrence of PPH is estimated to be about 1 to 2 cases per 1 000 000 persons. Therefore, the estimated risk associated with the long-term use of anorexigen drugs is about 23 to 46 cases per million persons exposed per year. The study further suggested that the risk of PPH rises with increasing duration of use of these drugs. The effect of intermittent compared to continuous use of anorexigens on the risk of PPH has not been determined.

The onset or aggravation of exertional dyspnea, or unexplained symptoms of angina pectoris, syncope, or lower extremity edema suggest the possibility of occurrence of pulmonary hypertension. Under these circumstances, treatment should be immediately discontinued, and the patient should be evaluated for the possible presence of PPH.

Drug Dependence: There is a good correlation between a drug's ability to act as a positive reinforcer in animals and its abuse potential in man. Diethylpropion has been shown to serve as a positive reinforcer in various self-administration studies performed in animals.

Furthermore, experience with anorectic drugs with amphetamine-like properties such as diethylpropion has established that prolonged use of these drugs can produce tolerance, severe psychological dependence and may lead to extensive abuse. There have been a significant number of reports of abuse of diethylpropion in the last several years. This should be kept in mind when assessing the desirability of using the drug and caution should be exercised not to use the drug in individuals whose histories suggest they may develop dependence or increase the dosage on their own initiative.

If psychological dependence occurs, gradual withdrawal of the medication is recommended. Abrupt cessation following prolonged high dosage may result in extreme fatigue and mental depression and changes in the sleep EEG. Drug abuse may lead to moderate to severe manifestations of chronic intoxication including marked insomnia, irritability, hyperactivity, personality changes and even psychosis.

Tolerance: In most patients, weight loss during treatment with diethylpropion plateaus after a few weeks. If this occurs, discontinuation of medication is indicated rather than an increase in the dose.

Pregnancy: Diethylpropion should not be used in women of childbearing potential unless in the opinion of the prescribing physician the potential benefits of drug therapy outweigh the possible risks to mother and fetus.

Children: Diethylpropion is not recommended for use in children under 12 years of age.

Precautions: Diethylpropion should be used with caution in patients with mild cardiovascular disease or hypertension, and regular monitoring of cardiovascular function and blood pressure is indicated in such patients receiving diethylpropion. Diethylpropion should not be used in patients with severe cardiovascular disease including arrhythmias or hypertension.

Diethylpropion may alter the effect of other drugs which act on the CNS. Insulin requirements in diabetes mellitus may be altered in association with the use of diethylpropion and the concomitant dietary regimen. Diethylpropion may decrease the hypotensive effect of guanethidine. In addition, drugs of this class may potentiate the pressor effects of exogenous catecholamines.

Reports also suggest that diethylpropion may increase the incidence of convulsions in some epileptic patients. Therefore, caution is required if the drug is administered to epileptic patients.

Adverse Effects: The most frequently encountered side effects of diethylpropion are insomnia, nervousness, dizziness, anxiety, agitation and dry mouth. An epidemiological study has indicated that use of anorexigens for longer than 3 months was associated with an increase in the risk of developing Primary Pulmonary Hypertension (PPH) (see Warnings).

CNS: Overstimulation, nervousness, restlessness, dizziness, jitteriness, insomnia, anxiety, euphoria, dysphoria and occasionally depression, tremor, mydriasis, drowsiness, headache and psychotic episodes. Increase in convulsive disorders has been reported.

Cardiovascular: Tachycardia, precordial pain, arrhythmias, palpitation, increased blood pressure. One published report described T wave changes in the ECG of a healthy young male after ingestion of diethylpropion. There have been reports of primary pulmonary hypertension associated with the use of diethylpropion (see Warnings).

Gastrointestinal: diarrhea, constipation, nausea, vomiting and abdominal discomfort and dryness of the mouth.

Allergic: urticaria, rash, ecchymosis and erythema.

Endocrine: dysmenorrhea, decreased libido and gynecomastia.

Other: dyspnea, hair loss, muscle pain, dysuria, polyuria, bone marrow depression, leukopenia, agranulocytosis.

Overdose: Symptoms and Treatment: Clinical manifestations of diethylpropion intoxication are as follows: nervousness and irritability, insomnia, rapid respiration, confusion, assaultiveness, hallucinations, and panic states. Convulsions and tachycardia are frequently present. Exhaustion, drowsiness or depression usually follow central stimulation, and coma may occur. Cardiovascular effects may include arrhythmias, changes in blood pressure and circulatory collapse. Gastrointestinal symptoms include nausea, vomiting, diarrhea and abdominal cramps.

Management of acute intoxication is largely symptomatic. It includes gastric lavage if possible, and sedation with a barbiturate may be desirable. Experience with peritoneal dialysis or hemodialysis is not sufficient to permit a recommendation at this time.

Dosage: Adults: One 25 mg tablet may be administered 3 times daily, 1 hour before meals. Alternatively, one 75 mg sustained release tablet may be given once daily, in midmorning. Administration should not be extended beyond a period of 4 weeks. The least amount feasible should be prescribed or dispensed at one time (not to exceed a 2-week supply) in order to minimize the possibility of abuse.

Diethylpropion should be used for a duration of no more than a few weeks (see Warnings).

Supplied: Tenuate: Each white tablet contains: diethylpropion HCl USP 25 mg. Nonmedicinal ingredients: lactose, magnesium stearate, talc and tartaric acid. Bottles of 100.

Tenuate Dospan: Each capsule shaped, continuous release, white tablet contains: diethylpropion HCl USP 75 mg. Nonmedicinal ingredients: carboxypolymethylene, mannitol, povidone, tartaric acid and zinc stearate. Bottles of 100 and 250. Cartons of 30 strip packed tablets.

Store between 15 and 30°C.

(Shown in Product Recognition Section)

Reviewed 1998

TERAZOL® 🄿

Janssen-Ortho

Terconazole

Antifungal

Pharmacology: The exact pharmacologic mode of action of terconazole is uncertain; however, it may exert its antifungal activity by disruption of normal fungal cell membrane permeability. Terconazole exhibits fungicidal activity in vitro against the genus Candida. Both the yeast and mycelial forms of C. albicans are sensitive to terconazole.

Following intravaginal administration of terconazole in humans, absorption ranged from 5 to 8% in 3 hysterectomized patients and 12 to 16% in 2 nonhysterectomized subjects with tubal ligations. After single and multiple doses of terconazole 0.4% (20 mg) vaginal cream, the mean peak plasma concentration for both treatments was 0.004 μg, indicating no accumulation of terconazole following repeated intravaginal dosing.

Indications: For the local treatment of vulvovaginal candidiasis (moniliasis). The diagnosis of monilial infection should be confirmed by microscopic examination of KOH smear and/or by culture.

The ovules and cream may be used in pregnant patients during the second and third trimesters if the physician considers it essential to the welfare of the patient (see Precautions, Pregnancy). The therapeutic effect of terconazole is not affected by oral contraceptive usage, menstruation or previous monilial infection.

Contraindications: Patients known to be hypersensitive to terconazole or to any components of the ovule or cream.

Warnings: None.

Precautions: General: Terconazole cream and ovules should be discontinued and patients should not be retreated if sensitization, vulvovaginal irritation, fever, chills or flu-like symptoms are reported during use.

Photosensitivity reactions were observed in some normal volunteers following repeated dermal application of terconazole 2.0% and 0.8% creams under conditions of filtered artificial ultraviolet light. Photosensitivity reactions have not been observed in clinical trials in patients who were treated vaginally with terconazole 0.4%, 0.8% or 1.6% vaginal cream.

The base contained in the ovule formulation may interact with certain natural rubber products, such as those used in vaginal contraceptive diaphragms or condoms. Concurrent use is not recommended. The cream may be considered for use under these conditions.

If there is a lack of response to terconazole therapy, appropriate microbiological studies (standard KOH smear and/or cultures) should be repeated to confirm the diagnosis and rule out other pathogens.

Intractable candidiasis may be the presenting symptom of unrecognized diabetes mellitus. In these cases appropriate diagnostic tests for diabetes should be done.

Children: Safety and efficacy in children have not been established.

Pregnancy: Terconazole should not be used in the first trimester of pregnancy.

In studies, over 600 pregnant patients have used terconazole during the second and third trimesters with no apparent adverse effect on the course of pregnancy. These studies have not shown increased risk of abnormalities when administered during this period.

Pregnant patients should be advised to exercise caution in the use of the vaginal applicator.

Lactation: It is not known whether terconazole is excreted in human milk. Should the decision be made to use this drug, nursing should be discontinued during therapy.

Adverse Effects: During controlled clinical studies conducted in the U.S., 284 patients with vulvovaginal candidiasis were treated with terconazole 80 mg vaginal ovules and 521 patients were treated with terconazole 0.4% vaginal cream and 297 patients were treated with terconazole 0.8% vaginal cream.

Terazol (cont'd)

Terazol 3 Vaginal Ovules (terconazole 80 mg): Based on comparative analyses with placebo and a standard agent, the adverse experiences considered adverse reactions most likely related to terconazole 80 mg vaginal ovules are shown in Table I.

Table I—Terazol

Adverse Effects—Terazol 3 Vaginal Ovules

Event	Terazol	Placebo
Headache	30.3%	20.7%
Pain (female genitalia)	4.2%	0.7%
Burning	15.2%*	11.2%
Body Pain	3.9%*	1.7%
Fever	2.8%	1.4%
Chills	1.8%	0.75%

* Not statistically significantly different from placebo.

The adverse drug experience on terconazole 80 mg ovules most frequently causing discontinuation was burning (2.5% vs 1.4% with placebo) and pruritus (1.8% vs 1.4% with placebo). The terconazole therapy-related dropout rate was 3.5% and the placebo therapy-related dropout rate was 2.7%.

Terazol 7 Vaginal Cream (terconazole 0.4%): Based on comparative analyses with placebo and a standard agent, the adverse experiences considered to be most likely related to terconazole 0.4% vaginal cream are shown in Table II.

Table II—Terazol

Adverse Effects—Terazol 7 Vaginal Cream

Event	Terazol	Placebo
Headache	26.0%	17.0%
Body Pain	2.1%	0.0%
Fever	1.75%	0.5%
Chills	0.4%	0.0%

Vulvovaginal burning (5.2%), itching (2.3%) or irritation (3.1%) occurred less frequently with terconazole 0.4% vaginal cream than with the vehicle placebo. The adverse drug experience most frequently causing discontinuation of treatment with terconazole cream was vulvovaginal itching (0.6%) which was lower than the incidence for placebo (0.9%). The terconazole therapy and the placebo therapy-related dropout rate was 1.9%.

Terazol 3 Vaginal Cream (terconazole 0.8%): Based on comparative analyses with placebo and a standard agent, the only adverse experiences considered adverse reactions to terconazole 0.8% vaginal cream are shown in Table III.

Table III—Terazol

Adverse Effects—Terazol 3 Vaginal Cream

Event	Terazol	Placebo
Headache	21.0%	16.0%
Dysmenorrhea	6.0%	2.0%

Fever (1.0% vs. 0.3% with placebo) has been reported. The therapy related dropout rate was 2.0%. The adverse drug experience on terconazole 0.8% most frequently causing discontinuation was vulvovaginal itching (0.7%) which was similar to the incidence for placebo (0.3%).

Overdose: Symptoms and Treatment: Overdose of terconazole in humans has not been reported to date.

Dosage: Terazol 3 Vaginal Ovules: 1 ovule is administered intravaginally once daily at bedtime for 3 consecutive days.

Terazol 7 Vaginal Cream: One applicatorful (5 g) of vaginal cream (20 mg terconazole) is administered intravaginally once daily at bedtime for 7 consecutive days. In addition, a thin layer of vaginal cream is applied for 7 consecutive days directly to the vulva and (0.8% terconazole) massaged in gently.

Terazol 3 Vaginal Cream: One applicatorful (5 g) of vaginal cream (40 mg terconazole) is administered intravaginally once daily at bedtime for 3 consecutive days. In addition, a thin layer of vaginal cream (0.8% terconazole) is applied for 3 consecutive days directly to the vulva and massaged in gently.

Terazol 3 Dual-Pak Package: One vaginal ovule is administered intravaginally once daily at bedtime for 3 consecutive days. In addition, a thin layer of vaginal cream is applied for 3 consecutive days directly to the vulva and massaged in gently.

Before prescribing another course of therapy of terconazole, the diagnosis of monilial infection should be confirmed by microscopic examination of KOH smear and/or by culture. Intractable candidiasis may be the presenting symptom of unrecognized diabetes mellitus. In these cases appropriate diagnostic tests for diabetes should be done. The therapeutic effect of terconazole products is not affected by oral contraceptive usage or menstruation.

Information for the Patient: See Blue Section—Information for the Patient "Terazol".

Supplied: Terazol 3 Vaginal Ovules: Each elliptically-shaped, white to off-white, 2.5 g ovule contains: terconazole 80 mg. Nonmedicinal ingredients: butylated hydroxyanisol, cetyl alcohol, hydrogenated vegetable oils, isopropyl myristate, polysorbate 60, polysorbate 80, purified water and stearyl alcohol. Packages of 3 with an Ortho vaginal applicator.

Terazol 7 Vaginal Cream: Each g of white to off-white, water washable cream contains: terconazole 0.4%. Nonmedicinal ingredients: butylated hydroxyanisol, cetyl alcohol, isopropyl myristate, polysorbate 60, polysorbate 80, propylene glycol, purified water and stearyl alcohol. Tubes of 45 g with an Ortho vaginal applicator.

Terazol 3 Vaginal Cream: Each g of white to off-white, water washable cream contains: terconazole 0.8%. Nonmedicinal ingredients: butylated hydroxyanisol, cetyl alcohol, isopropyl myristate, polysorbate 60, polysorbate 80, propylene glycol, purified water and stearyl alcohol. Tubes of 20 g with an Ortho vaginal applicator.

Terazol 3 Dual-Pack Package: 3 Terazol 3 vaginal ovules, an Ortho vaginal applicator and a 9 g tube of Terazol 3 vaginal cream.

Store at controlled room temperature (15 to 30°C).

(Shown in Product Recognition Section)

Reviewed 1999

TERSAC®

TCD

Salicylic Acid—Triclosan

Acne Therapy

Supplied: Each 120 g tube contains: salicylic acid USP 2% and triclosan 0.5% in an aqueous lathering gel base. Nonmedicinal ingredients: cocamido propyl betaine, coco betaine, glycerin, methylparaben, purified water, salicylic acid, sodium laureth sulfate, sodium metabisulfite, tetra sodium EDTA and triclosan.

TERSASEPTIC®

TCD

Triclosan

Antibacterial

Supplied: Each 150 or 450 mL bottle contains: triclosan 0.5% in a liquid soapless detergent anionic base and emollients. Nonmedicinal ingredients: citric acid anhydrous, diethanolamine alcohol sulfate, diethylene glycol and ethylene glycol, EDTA, FD&C yellow, fragrance, lauramide and propylene glycol and PEG 6000 distearate. Preservative-free. pH 6.5.

TERSA-TAR®

TCD

Tar Distillate

Psoriasis—Seborrhea Therapy

Supplied: Tersa-Tar: Each mL of shampoo contains: tar distillate "Doak" 3% in a soapless alkaline free solvent and emulsifying base. Nonmedicinal ingredients: diethylglycol mono ethyl ether, EDTA, isopropyl alcohol, lauramide DEA and propylene glycol, PEG 6000 distearate, perfume, phosphoric acid, propylparaben, purified water and sodium lauryl sulfate. Bottles of 150 and 450 mL.

Tersa-Tar Mild: Each mL of shampoo contains: tar distillate "Doak" 1% in a soapless alkaline free solvent and emulsifying base with protein and an oil free conditioner. Nonmedicinal ingredients: diethylglycol mono ethyl ether, EDTA, isopropyl alcohol, lauramide DEA and propylene glycol, PEG 6000 distearate, perfume, phosphoric acid, propylparaben, purified water and sodium lauryl sulfate. pH 6.5. Bottles of 150 and 450 mL.

TES-TAPE®

Lilly

Glucose Enzymatic Test Strip

Diagnostic Aid

Description: Tes-Tape is impregnated with the enzymes glucose oxidase and peroxidase and an oxidizable substrate, orthotolidine. When the tape is dipped into urine containing glucose, the glucose oxidase catalyzes the reaction of glucose in the urine with oxygen from the air to form gluconic acid and hydrogen peroxide. The enzyme peroxidase (from horseradish) then catalyzes the reaction of hydrogen peroxide and orthotolidine to form a blue color. With the addition of a yellow dye (FDC Yellow No. 5) to the paper, the possible color range of the test is extended from yellow to light green to deep blue. If no glucose is present, the tape maintains its yellow color. See Table I.

Table I—Tes-Tape

Reactive Ingredients

Reactive Ingredients	Approximate Amount per 4 cm of Tape
Glucose oxidase	3.78 units
Horseradish peroxidase	2.82 PZ units
o-tolidine	0.136 mg

Nonreactive ingredients include filter paper, FDC Yellow No. 5 coloring, buffers, stabilizers, and wetting agents.

Indications: For in vitro diagnostic use in testing for the presence of glucose in human urine.

Precautions: Do not use if the tape turns dark yellow or brown or if, after being tested in distilled water, it does not match the negative color bar.

The urine should be fresh, collected in a container free of chemicals and glucose, and clear in appearance.

If the freshly voided specimen is not to be tested within 4 hours, it should be refrigerated or preserved in up to 0.37 % formaldehyde.

Drugs that are known to have an inhibitory effect on the enzyme reactions include ascorbic acid (vitamin C), dipyrone, gentisic acid (a metabolite of ASA), homogentisic acid (present in alkaptonuria), levodopa, meralluride injection and methyldopa. The inhibiting effect is notable on the dipped part of the tape, but accurate readings may be obtained by observing the narrow band of color at the junction of the dry and wet portions. A separation of glucose from the inhibitory substances occurs as the urine travels along the dry portion of the tape. Ingestion of more than 1.5 g of ascorbic acid may produce urine with inhibitory action on Tes-Tape.

Specimens for storage or shipment should be refrigerated or preserved with up to 0.37 % formaldehyde.

All materials are provided for the test and include dispenser, tape and color chart.

Results on the color chart are expressed as positive or negative.

After dipping Tes-Tape into urine, do not place it on the lavatory or on paper. Small amounts of glucose in paper or perspiration will affect the test.

Patients who are receiving high doses of ascorbic acid or whose urine contains dipyrone, meralluride, homogentisic acid, gentisic acid, levodopa or methyldopa should read only the very narrow band of color in the moist part of the tape above the level to which it was dipped into the specimen.

Very high doses of ascorbic acid may cause a false negative test even with the above precaution. (Urinary levels of ascorbic acid in excess of 0.1% are necessary to block the test completely. This concentration is most likely to appear within 3 to 7 hours after a single dose of 1.5 g or more.)

Normal urine should test negative with Tes-Tape. Persons using Tes-Tape for a screening test should report all positive readings to their physician. The color chart provided is based on the average color perception of many observers. Patients who have difficulty in differentiating color should seek the advice of their physician before using Tes-Tape.

Numerous other clinical and laboratory studies have shown that Tes-Tape is accurate in qualitative determinations of urine sugar. Tes-Tape is specific for glucose in urine sugar testing. Except for instances involving contamination of the tape or urine receptacle with glucose from other sources (e.g., perspiration, tears, and saliva) or with a residue of chlorine from cleansing agents, there is no known clinical situation in which a false-positive test for glucose occurs with Tes-Tape. The sensitivity of Tes-Tape is such that it will react with concentrations of 0.05 % glucose or more. Trace reactions shown by the development of a very light yellow-green color may be observed with less than this amount of glucose.

Directions: See Blue Section—Information for the Patient "Tes-Tape".

Information for the Patient: See Blue Section—Information for the Patient "Tes-Tape".

Supplied: Individual dispenser packages of approximately 100 tests. Materials included for tests include dispenser, tape and color chart. Store at controlled room temperature, 15 to 30°C. Protect from high humidity and light.

TESTOSTERONE ENANTHATE INJECTION, USP ◈

Taro

Androgen

Supplied: Each mL of solution contains: testosterone enanthate 200 mg. Nonmedicinal ingredients: chlorobutanol (chloral derivative) and sesame oil. Multiple dose vials of 10 mL, individually boxed. Store at room temperature. Shaking the vial will dissolve any crystals that may have formed during storage at low temperatures.

New Product 1998

TESTOSTERONE PROPIONATE INJECTION, USP ◈

Taro

Androgen

Supplied: Each mL of solution contains: testosterone propionate 100 mg. Nonmedicinal ingredients: benzyl alcohol and sesame oil. Multiple dose vials of 10 mL, individually boxed. Store at room temperature. Shaking the vial will dissolve any crystals that may have formed during storage at low temperatures.

New Product 1998

TETANUS AND DIPHTHERIA TOXOIDS ADSORBED (Td Adsorbed)

Connaught

Active Immunizing Agent

Pharmacology: Tetanus is an acute and often fatal disease caused by an extremely potent neurotoxin produced by C. tetani. The organism is ubiquitous and its occurrence in nature cannot be controlled. Immunization is highly effective, produces long-lasting protection and is recommended for the whole population. Only 2 to 3 cases of tetanus are now reported annually in Canada. Two deaths have been recorded in the past 5 years.

Diphtheria is a serious communicable disease caused by toxigenic strains of C. diphtheriae. The case-fatality rate remains 5 to 10%, with highest death rates in the very young and the elderly. The organism may be harbored in the nasopharynx, skin and other sites of asymptomatic carriers, making eradication of the disease difficult.

Routine immunization against diphtheria in infancy and childhood has been widely practised in Canada since 1930. This has resulted in a remarkable decline in the morbidity and mortality of this disease. In 1924, there were 9 000 cases reported, but less than 5 annually in recent years and no deaths since 1983. However, toxigenic strains of diphtheria bacilli are still detected each year in diphtheria carriers (pharyngeal, skin and ear) in Northern and Western Canada. Asymptomatic carriage of C. diphtheriae is far more common than clinical diphtheria. The disease occurs most frequently in unimmunized or partially immunized individuals. Although occasional cases of mild clinical diphtheria do occur in apparently fully immunized persons, antitoxin stimulated by immunization persists at protective levels for 10 years or more.

In a clinical trial involving 347 individuals ranging in age from 17 to 29 years, previously immunized against diphtheria and tetanus, a single 0.5 mL dose of any of the three clinical trial lots of Tetanus and Diphtheria Toxoids Adsorbed stimulated a prompt antibody response to both antigens.

Four weeks following a single 0.5 mL injection, of 245 individuals tested, 100% had tetanus antitoxin titers ≥0.02 IU/mL with a geometric mean titer of 3.91 IU/mL; 98% of 244 individuals treated had diphtheria antitoxin titers ≥0.02 IU/mL with a geometric mean titer of 1.12 IU/mL.

The immunogenicity of Tetanus and Diphtheria Toxoids Adsorbed administered as a series of 3 (0.5 mL) injections for primary immunization has been demonstrated in a small number (17) of individuals whose ages ranged from 6 to 56 years. These individuals were all confirmed unimmunized to both tetanus and diphtheria. Four weeks following the second injection of vaccine, given 2 months after the first, all had responded with serum tetanus antitoxin levels ranging from 0.11 to 14.0 IU/mL and with diphtheria antitoxin levels ranging from 0.01 to 1.28 IU/mL. Following the third injection of vaccine 6 to 8 months after second, the 8 individuals tested developed antitoxin titers to tetanus of 0.56 to 14.0 IU/mL and to diphtheria of 0.16 to 5.12 IU/mL.

During clinical trials, reactions associated with the injection of Td Adsorbed occurred at a low level of frequency, were usually transient in duration and consisted largely of discomfort, pain, swelling and redness at the injection site (see Table I).

Table I—Tetanus and Diphtheria Toxoids Adsorbed (Td Adsorbed)

Reactivity in 346 Young Adults Following Single Injection of Td Adsorbed Vaccine

Reactions (%)	Day 1	Day 2	Day 3	Day 4
Discomfort	19.1	15.1	3.8	1.9
Pain	2.2	2.4	1.4	1.1
Swelling	1.1	0.5	0	0.2
Redness	0.5	0.6	0.3	0.3
Induration	0	1.1	0	0.3
Lymphadenopathy	0	0.3	0	0
Fever 37-38°C	0.3	0	0	0
38-39°C	0.5	0.5	0.3	0.3
≥39°C	0	0	0	0.3
Chills	1.6	1.1	0.3	0.5
Headache	4.4	2.7	0.8	1.1
Malaise	3.0	1.4	0.8	1.1
Muscle Ache	5.9	3.8	1.4	0.3
Nausea	1.9	0.7	0.5	0.3
Abdominal Pain	0.5	0.8	0.8	0.3
Joint Pain	1.6	1.9	0.8	0.5

Indications: For secondary immunization **in children aged 7 years and older and adults who have been previously immunized against tetanus and diphtheria.**

Tetanus and Diphtheria Toxoids Adsorbed may also be used for primary immunization of older children (7 years of age and older) and of adults who have not been previously immunized against tetanus and diphtheria.

Contraindications: General: Immunization with Tetanus and Diphtheria Toxoids Adsorbed should be deferred in the presence of any acute illness, including febrile illness (to avoid superimposing adverse effects from the vaccine on the underlying illness or mistakenly identifying a manifestation of the underlying illness as a complication of vaccine use). A minor afebrile illness such as mild upper respiratory infection is not usually reason to defer immunization.

Absolute Contraindications: Allergy to any component of Td Adsorbed (see Supplied), an anaphylactic or other allergic reaction to a previous dose of Td Adsorbed are contraindications to vaccination.

Elective immunization of persons over 6 months of age should be deferred during an outbreak of poliomyelitis because of the risk of provocation paralysis.

Warnings: I.M. injections should be given with care in persons suffering from coagulation disorders or on anticoagulant therapy because of the risk of hemorrhage.

If Tetanus and Diphtheria Toxoids Adsorbed is used in persons with malignancies, persons receiving immunosuppressive therapies, including irradiation, antimetabolites, alkylating agents, cytotoxic drugs, or persons who are otherwise immunocompromised (including HIV-infected individuals, transplant recipients, persons suffering from autoimmune disorders), the expected immune response may not be obtained.

Corticosteroid therapy can result in immunosuppression although the exact dose and duration of therapy required to suppress the immune system is not well defined. Persons treated with high doses of systemic steroids, e.g., ≥2 mg/kg/day of prednisone orally for more than 2 weeks, should be considered to have a compromised immune system.

As with any vaccine, immunization with Td Adsorbed may not protect 100% of susceptible individuals.

Precautions: General: The possibility of allergic reactions in individuals sensitive to components of the vaccine should be evaluated. Epinephrine HCl solution (1:1 000) and other appropriate agents should be available for immediate use in case an anaphylactic or acute hypersensitivity reaction occurs. Health care providers should be familiar with current recommendations for the initial management of anaphylaxis in non-hospital settings, including proper airway management.

Before administration of any vaccine, all appropriate precautions should be taken to prevent adverse reactions. This includes a review of the patient's history with respect to possible hypersensitivity to the vaccine or similar vaccine, determination of previous immunization history, and the presence of any contraindications to immunization, current health status, and a current knowledge of the literature concerning the use of the vaccine under consideration.

Frequent booster doses of tetanus toxoid in the presence of adequate or excessive serum levels of tetanus antitoxin have been associated with increased incidence and severity of reactions and should be avoided. If hypersensitivity to the diphtheria component is suspected, tetanus toxoid should be used for reinforcing doses.

Special care should be taken to ensure that the product is not injected into a blood vessel.

Caution: A separate sterile needle and syringe, or a sterile disposable unit, must be used for each individual patient to prevent the transmission of infectious agents.

There have been case reports of transmission of HIV and hepatitis by failure to scrupulously observe sterile technique. In particular, the same needle and/or syringe must never be used to re-enter a multidose vial to withdraw vaccine even when it is to be used for inoculation of the same patient. This may lead to contamination of the vial contents and infection of patients who subsequently receive vaccine from the vial.

Needles should not be recapped and should be disposed of properly.

Before administration of Tetanus and Diphtheria Toxoids Adsorbed health care personnel should inform the parent or guardian or the patient to be immunized of the benefits and risks of immunization, inquire about the recent health status of the patient and comply with any local requirements with respect to information to be provided to the patient before immunization.

Adverse Effects: Localized reactions consisting of discomfort, pain, swelling and redness at the injection site may be associated with the toxoids. These are usually of low frequency and transient in duration. Following booster doses, local erythema and swelling are not uncommon and Arthus-type sensitivity may occur. Persistent nodules at the site of injection have occurred following the use of adsorbed vaccine, but this complication is unusual.

Generalized reactions may develop following immunization and may take the form of allergic reactions including urticaria and, less commonly, angioneurotic edema. Influenza-like symptoms have been reported and usually occur within 12 hours of vaccination. Neurological complications such as peripheral neuropathies following tetanus toxoid or diphtheria toxoid have been documented but are rare.

Nervous System: The following neurologic illnesses have been reported as temporally associated with vaccine containing tetanus toxoid: neurological complications including cochlear lesion, brachial plexus neuropathies, paralysis of the radial nerve, paralysis of the recurrent nerve, accommodation paresis, and EEG disturbances with encephalopathy. In the differential diagnosis of polyradiculoneuropathies following administration of a vaccine containing tetanus toxoid, tetanus toxoid should be considered as a possible etiology.

On the basis of a case report and evidence that a vaccine-induced immunologic response can cause Guillain Barre Syndrome (GBS), the Institute of Medicine concluded that tetanus toxoid-containing vaccines can trigger GBS in adults. No increased risk for GBS has been observed with the use of DTP in children.

Physicians, nurses, and pharmacists should report any adverse occurrences temporally related to the administration of the product in accordance with local requirements and to the Medical Director, Connaught Laboratories Limited, 1755 Steeles Avenue West, Toronto, Ontario, Canada M2R 3T4.

Dosage: For persons who have previously been immunized against tetanus and diphtheria, a dose of 0.5 mL should be administered as a reinforcing dose at approximately 10 year intervals.

For primary immunization of individuals 7 years or older a series of 3 (0.5 mL) injections is required with the first 2 injections being administered 2 months apart followed by the third injection 6 to 12 months later. Thereafter reinforcing doses are recommended at approximately 10 year intervals.

Tetanus and Diphtheria Toxoids Adsorbed (Td Adsorbed) (cont'd)

Tetanus Prophylaxis in Wound Management: Table II summarizes the recommended use of immunizing agents in wound management. If not clearly documented, a history of immunization should be regarded as "uncertain". If a tetanus booster is required it is preferred to choose a combined preparation such as this product containing 5 Lf of tetanus toxoid and 2 Lf of diphtheria toxoid per 0.5 mL dose. Appropriate cleansing and debridement of the wound is imperative. Booster doses given more frequently than recommended above may lead to adverse local and systemic reactions.
Note: Diphtheria and Tetanus Toxoids Adsorbed, containing 25 Lf of diphtheria toxoid and 5 Lf of tetanus toxoid per 0.5 mL dose, should not be administered as a tetanus booster to children over 7 years of age or adults due to the risk of reaction to the high diphtheria toxoid component in this vaccine.

Table II—Tetanus and Diphtheria Toxoids Adsorbed (Td Adsorbed)

Tetanus Prophylaxis in Wound Management

History of Tetanus Immunization (doses)	Clean, Minor Wounds Td[a]	Clean, Minor Wounds TIG[b]	All Other Wounds Td[a]	All Other Wounds TIG[b]
Uncertain or less than 3	Yes	No	Yes	Yes
3 or more	No[c]	No	No[d]	No

[a]Adult type tetanus and diphtheria toxoids. If the patient is less than 7 years old, DT or DPT is given (see text).
[b]Tetanus immune globulin.
[c]Yes if more than 10 years since the last dose.
[d]Yes if more than 5 years since last dose.

Note: Tetanus toxoid, or a combined vaccine containing tetanus toxoid, and tetanus immune globulin should be administered in separate syringes at different sites.

Parenteral biological products should be inspected visually for extraneous particulate matter and/or discoloration before administration. If these conditions exist, the product should not be administered.

Shake the vial or ampul well to distribute uniformly the suspension before withdrawing each dose. Before withdrawing a dose from an ampul, tap the container first to ensure that any vaccine in the ampul neck falls to the lower portion of the ampul. Once the ampul has been opened, any of its contents not used immediately should be discarded. When administering a dose from a rubber-stoppered vial, do not remove either the rubber stopper or the metal seal holding it in place. Aseptic technique must be used for withdrawal of each dose (see Precautions)

Before injection, the skin over the site to be injected should be cleansed with a suitable germicide.

Administer the vaccine **i.m.** The preferred site is into the deltoid muscle.

After insertion of the needle, aspirate to ensure that the needle has not entered a blood vessel.

Do not inject i.v.

Each person who is immunized should be given a permanent personal immunization record. In addition, it is essential that the physician or nurse record the immunization history in the permanent medical record of each patient. This permanent office record should contain the name of the vaccine, date given, dose, manufacturer and lot number.

Supplied: Tetanus and Diphtheria Toxoids Adsorbed is a sterile, cloudy, uniform suspenison of diphtheria and tetanus toxoids adsorbed on aluminum phosphate and suspended in isotonic sodium chloride solution. Each dose (0.5 mL) contains: tetanus toxoid (5 Lf), diphtheria toxoid (2 Lf) and aluminum phosphate 1.5 mg. Thimerosal 0.01% is added as a preservative. Ready for use rubber stoppered multiple-dose vials of 5 mL, and glass ampuls of 0.5 mL (1 dose). Store at 2 to 8°C. **Do not freeze.** Product exposed to freezing should not be used. Do not use vaccine after expiry date.

Reviewed 1999

The database, reporting form and procedures for monitoring adverse events from vaccines are separate from those of other drug products. See the CLIN-INFO SECTION for a description of the program and a copy of the reporting form.

TETANUS IMMUNE GLOBULIN (HUMAN)

General Monograph, CPhA

TIG

Tetanus Prophylaxis

This monograph has been compiled by CPhA. It may contain information different from that approved by Therapeutic Products Programme, Health Canada, and the pharmaceutical manufacturers' approval has not been requested.

Description: Tetanus immune globulin (human) (TIG) is a sterile solution of immunoglobulins (≥90% immunoglobulin G (IgG)), containing 15 to 18% protein, prepared from plasma of individuals immunized with tetanus toxoid. The method of preparation ensures that TIG is free from hepatitis B, C and HIV. The product is standardized to contain 250 units per vial or syringe. Store at 2 to 8°C. Discard if frozen. **TIG must be administered i.m.**

Pharmacology: Tetanus immune globulin (TIG) provides passive immunity to those individuals who have low or no immunity to tetanus. The tetanus antitoxin antibodies act to neutralize the exotoxin produced by the causative tetanus organism, C. tetani. Passive immunization with TIG may be undertaken concomitantly with active immunization using tetanus toxoid.
Pharmacokinetics: Peak blood levels of IgG are obtained approximately 2 days after i.m. injection. The half-life of IgG in the circulation of individuals with normal IgG levels is 23 days. Adequate serum titres (0.01 antitoxin units/mL) persist for approximately 4 to 6 weeks after i.m. administration of 250 units of TIG.

Indications: For tetanus prophylaxis following injury in patients whose immunization is incomplete or uncertain (see Table I). Administration of TIG provides only short-term, passive immunity and does not prevent the spread of C. tetani. Long-lasting, active immunity requires administration of tetanus toxoid. Table I is a summary guide to tetanus prophylaxis in wound management. For more information on recommended childhood immunizations, see Immunization Schedules for Infants and Children in the Clin-Info section.

Table I—Tetanus Immune Globulin (Human)

Prophylaxis in Wound Management

History of tetanus immunization	Clean, minor wounds Td[a]	Clean, minor wounds TIG	All other wounds Td[a]	All other wounds TIG
Uncertain or <3 doses	Yes	No	Yes	Yes
≥3 doses	No[b]	No	No[c]	No

[a]Adult type tetanus and diphtheria toxoids. For children <7 years of age, DT, DPT or DPT-polio is given as part of the routine childhood immunization.
[b]Yes, if >10 years since the last dose of tetanus toxoid.
[c]Yes, if >5 years since the last dose of tetanus toxoid.

TIG is also indicated, although evidence of effectiveness is limited, in the treatment of active tetanus infection in conjunction with appropriate antibiotics (e.g., penicillin), muscle relaxants and sedatives.

Warnings: Tetanus immune globulin (TIG) should be given with caution to patients with a history of prior systemic allergic reactions following the administration of human immunoglobulin preparations, or in patients who are hypersensitive to thimerosal (used as preservative).

Risk versus benefit should be weighed before i.m. injections are administered to patients with thrombocytopenia or coagulation disorders.

Immune serums should not be administered to persons with isolated immunoglobulin A (IgA) deficiency. These persons may develop antibodies to IgA and have anaphylactic reactions to subsequent administratin of blood products containing IgA.

Precautions: Tetanus immune globulin (TIG) **must not be given i.v.** Severe systemic reactions (e.g. severe fever, precipitous fall in blood pressure, fatal cardiovascular reactions, anaphylactoid reactions) have occurred following i.v. injection of immunoglobulin intended for i.m. use. I.M. injections are preferably administered in the anterolateral aspects of the upper thigh and the deltoid muscle of the upper arm.

Skin tests should not be performed prior to the administration of TIG. The intradermal injection of concentrated IgG solutions often causes a localized area of inflammation due to tissue irritation, which can be misinterpreted as a positive allergic reaction. True allergic responses to human IgG are rare as this is a product of human origin; however, severe systemic reactions to immune serum globulin have occurred, and epinephrine should be available.

Since tetanus is actually a local infection, proper initial wound care is of paramount importance. The use of TIG is adjunctive to this procedure.
Drug Interactions: Antibodies in immunoglobulin preparations may interfere with the response to live virus vaccines such as measles, mumps, polio and rubella. Therefore, use of such vaccines should be deferred until 3 months after TIG administration.

TIG does not interfere with the immune response to tetanus toxoid, although they should not be given in the same syringe nor injected at the same site, as neutralization of the toxoid may occur.

No interactions with other products are known.
Pregnancy: Animal reproduction studies have not been conducted with tetanus immune globulin. It is not known whether TIG can cause fetal harm or can affect reproduction capacity, although no risk to the fetus has been reported. TIG should be given during pregnancy only if clearly needed.
Lactation: It is not known if TIG antibodies are excreted in breast milk. Problems in humans have not been documented.

Adverse Effects: Reactions are usually of a mild nature. Soreness at the injection site is common. Some patients may react more strongly with localized tenderness, muscle stiffness and erythema, persisting for several hours. Low grade fever may occur. Hives, local inflammation and angioedema occur occasionally. Nephrotic syndrome and anaphylactic reactions are rare.

Sensitization to tetanus immune globulin (TIG), with severe local and systemic responses, has occurred after repeated injections of TIG, especially in individuals with previous history of allergy.

Overdose: Symptoms and Treatment: Although few data are available, clinical experience with other immunoglobulin preparations suggests that the only manifestations would be pain and tenderness at the injection site.

Dosage: Adults and children ≥3 years of age should receive i.m. injections into the deltoid muscle. I.M. injections in infants and children <3 years should be made into the antero-lateral aspect of the thigh. The plunger of the syringe should be drawn back before injection to ensure that the needle is not in a blood vessel. 250 units tetanus immune globulin (TIG) should be given by deep i.m. injection. In cases of severe or grossly contaminated wounds, or when treatment is delayed > 24 hours, a dose of 500 units may be required. If the threat of tetanus infection persists, repeat doses of TIG can be given at 4-week intervals.

At the same time, but in a different extremity and with a separate syringe, tetanus toxoid should be administered (see Table I). Further injections are required to complete the series for producing active immunity.
Children (<7 years of age): The pediatric dose is the same as for adults. Alternatively, in small children, 4 units/kg can be given.
Immunocompromised Patients: Current recommendations on the use of TIG in patients with altered immunocompetence, including those with HIV infection, are the same as those for patients who are not immunocompromised.
Treatment of Tetanus: Standard therapy for the treatment of active tetanus, including the use of tetanus immune globulin, must be implemented immediately. Although the optimum therapeutic dose and effectiveness is not established, recommended dosage of TIG for treatment is 3 000 to 6 000 units. Intrathecal administration of TIG should not be used as it is not superior to the i.m. route.

Reviewed 1997

TETANUS TOXOID ADSORBED

BioChem Vaccines

Vaccine

Indications: For active immunization against tetanus. It may be used for primary immunization and reinforcing doses against tetanus, as well as in the event of injury for which tetanus prophylaxis is indicated.

Contraindications: Immunization with Tetanus Toxoid Adsorbed should be postponed in the presence of any acute illness, including febrile illness.

It is a contraindication to administer this vaccine to individuals known to be sensitive to thimerosal.

Warnings: If the vaccine is administered to persons receiving immunosuppressive therapy, it should be borne in mind that the expected antigenic response may not be obtained.

Precautions: Individuals who are hypersensitive to the components of the vaccine may develop allergic reactions. Sterile epinephrine HCl solution 1:1 000 should always be readily available in case an acute anaphylactic reaction should occur.

Frequent reinforcing (booster) doses of tetanus toxoid in the presence of adequate or excessive serum levels of tetanus antitoxin have been associated with increased incidence and severity of reactions and should be avoided.

Caution: A separate **sterile** syringe and needle or a **sterile** disposable unit should always be used for each patient to prevent transmission of hepatitis B virus, HIV virus or other infectious agent from one person to another.

Pregnancy: When indications for their use are present, toxoids may be given to pregnant women. It is preferable, however, to defer immunization until after delivery unless immediate risk is involved.

Adverse Effects: Mild local reactions such as pain, erythema, tenderness and induration at the injection site are common, and may be associated with systemic reactions including mild to moderate transient fever, chills, malaise and irritability. Persistent nodules at the injection site have occurred following the use of adsorbed vaccine, but this reaction is unusual.

Systemic reactions may develop and take the form of allergic reactions including urticaria and, less commonly, angioneurotic edema. Influenza-like symptoms have been reported and usually occur within 12 hours of vaccination. Neurological complications such as peripheral neuropathies following tetanus toxoid administration have been reported but are rare.

It has been shown that the incidence of reactions to tetanus toxoid rises according to the number of previously administered doses and occurs mainly in the over-immunized.

Notification of Reactions: It is desirable that all unusual reactions occurring immediately or shortly after any vaccination be reported to the manufacturer of the product and to the provincial epidemiologist.

Dosage: Primary Immunization: To establish active immunity against tetanus, it is recommended that 2 doses of 0.5 ml each of Tetanus Toxoid Adsorbed be administered **i.m.** with an interval of 4 weeks between doses. A third dose of 0.5 mL, which is essential for primary immunization, should be given approximately 6 months to 1 year after the second injection. Active immunization may also be accomplished by the administration of a combined vaccine containing tetanus toxoid.

Reinforcing (Booster) Doses: For persons who have completed the primary immunization course against tetanus, a single dose of 0.5 mL of Tetanus Toxoid Adsorbed should be administered **i.m.** as a reinforcing (booster) dose, at approximately 10-year intervals. A reinforcing dose may also be given with a combined vaccine containing tetanus toxoid.

Procedure at Time of Injury: No additional dose of tetanus toxoid is recommended, at the time of injury, for those who, within the previous 5 years, have received the complete primary immunization course of injections or a reinforcing dose against tetanus.

If more than 5 years have elapsed since the completion of a primary course of immunization or receipt of the last reinforcing dose against tetanus, a single dose of Tetanus Toxoid Adsorbed or of an appropriate combined vaccine containing tetanus toxoid should be administered.

Should information about previous administration of tetanus toxoid be inadequate or missing, a prophylactic dose of 250 U of tetanus immune globulin of human origin (TIG) should be administered **in addition to** Tetanus Toxoid Adsorbed in cases of clean, minor wounds. If the wounds are severe or grossly contaminated, a dose of 500 U of human tetanus immune globulin (TIG) is recommended **along with** Tetanus Toxoid Adsorbed.

Should human tetanus immune globulin (TIG) and Tetanus Toxoid Adsorbed, or a combined vaccine containing tetanus toxoid, be required simultaneously, the 2 preparations should never be mixed together in the same syringe: they should be administered in separate syringes and at different sites.

Administration: The skin at the injection site should be cleaned with a suitable antiseptic and dried with a piece of dry sterile cotton. The vaccine should be administered **i.m.** into the deltoid muscle or the mid-lateral aspect of the thigh.

Do not inject i.v. or s.c.

In order to avoid i.v. injection, the plunger of the syringe should be pulled back to ensure that no blood is withdrawn before injecting the desired dose.

Withdrawal from an Ampul: **Shake** the ampul to disperse the contents thoroughly **immediately before** withdrawing the dose of vaccine.

Tap the ampul to ensure that the suspension is in the lower portion rather than in the neck of the ampul.

Using a sterile piece of cotton or a sterile towel, break off the top of the ampul at the colored line (no file is required). Then, following an aseptic technique to prevent contamination, and using a **sterile** needle affixed to a **sterile** syringe, withdraw the contents of the ampul into the syringe, holding the ampul in such a way that the tip of the needle is kept immersed throughout the withdrawal.

Once the ampul has been opened, any of its unused contents should immediately be discarded.

Each person who is immunized should be given a permanent personal immunization record. In addition, it is essential that the physician or nurse record the immunization history in the permanent medical record of each patient. This permanent office record should contain the name of the vaccine, date given, dose, manufacturer and lot number.

Supplied: Tetanus Toxoid Adsorbed is a sterile, cloudy, uniform suspension of tetanus toxoid, adsorbed on aluminum phosphate, in an isotonic sodium chloride solution. Each dose (0.5 mL) contains: tetanus toxoid 5 Lf, aluminum phosphate 1.5 mg and thimerosal 0.01% as a preservative. Ampuls of 0.5 mL. Boxes of 5.

Store in the refrigerator between 2 and 8°C. **Do not freeze.** Carefully check the expiry date. An outdated vaccine should never be used.

Reviewed 1998

TETANUS TOXOID ADSORBED

Connaught

Vaccine

Indications: For primary and secondary immunization against tetanus.

Contraindications: Immunization with Tetanus Toxoid Adsorbed should be deferred in the presence of any acute illness, including febrile illness.

Elective immunization should be deferred during an outbreak of poliomyelitis.

Warnings: Individuals receiving corticosteroids or other immunosuppressive drugs may not develop an optimum immunologic response.

Precautions: The possibility of allergic reactions in individuals sensitive to the components of the vaccine should be borne in mind.

Epinephrine HCl solution 1:1 000 should be available for immediate use in case an anaphylactic or acute hypersensitivity reaction occurs. Frequent booster doses of tetanus toxoid in the presence of adequate or excessive serum levels of tetanus antitoxin have been associated with increased incidence and severity of reactions and should be avoided.

Caution: A separate **sterile** syringe and needle or a **sterile** disposable unit should be used for each individual patient to prevent the transmission of hepatitis or other infectious agents.

Adverse Effects: Mild local reactions consisting of pain, erythema, tenderness and induration at the injection site are common and may be associated with systemic reactions including mild to moderate transient fever, chills, malaise and irritability. Persistent nodules at the site of injection have occurred following the use of adsorbed vaccine, but this complication is unusual.

Generalized reactions may develop following injection and may take the form of allergic reactions including urticaria and, less commonly, angioneurotic edema. Influenza-like symptoms have been reported and usually occur within 12 hours of vaccination. Neurological complications such as peripheral neuropathies following tetanus toxoid have been documented but are rare. It has been shown that the incidence of reactions to tetanus toxoid rises according to the number of previously administered doses and occurs mainly in the over-immunized.

Dosage: Primary Immunization: To establish active immunity against tetanus it is recommended that 2 doses of 0.5 mL each of Tetanus Toxoid Adsorbed be administered i.m. with an interval of 4 weeks between doses. A third dose of 0.5 mL which is required for primary immunization should be given approximately 6 months to 1 year after the second injection. Active immunization may also be accomplished by the administration of combined vaccines containing tetanus toxoid.

Secondary Immunization: For individuals who have previously been immunized against tetanus, a dose of 0.5 mL should be administered i.m. as a reinforcing dose at approximately 10 year intervals.

Tetanus Prophylaxis in Wound Management: Table I summarizes the recommended use of immunizing agents in wound management. If not clearly documented, a history of immunization should be regarded as "uncertain". If a tetanus booster is required it is often appropriate to choose a combined preparation such as Tetanus and Diphtheria Toxoids Adsorbed For 7 years and Older containing 5 Lf of tetanus toxoid and 2 Lf of diphtheria toxoid per 0.5 mL dose. Appropriate cleansing and debridement of the wound is imperative. Booster doses given more frequently than recommended above may lead to adverse local and systemic reactions.

Note: Diphtheria and Tetanus Toxoids Adsorbed, containing 25 Lf of diphtheria toxoid and 5 Lf of tetanus toxoid per 0.5 mL dose, should not be administered as a tetanus booster to children over 7 years of age or adults due to the risk of reaction to the high diphtheria toxoid component in this vaccine.

Table I—Tetanus Toxoid Adsorbed

Tetanus Prophylaxis in Wound Management

History of Tetanus Immunization (doses)	Clean, Minor Wounds		All Other Wounds	
	Td[a]	TIG[b]	Td[a]	TIG[b]
Uncertain or less than 3	Yes	No	Yes	Yes
3 or more	No[c]	No	No[d]	No

[a]Adult type tetanus and diphtheria toxoids. If the patient is less than 7 years old, DT or DPT is given (see text).
[b]Tetanus immune globulin.
[c]Yes if more than 10 years since the last dose.
[d]Yes if more than 5 years since last dose.

Note: Tetanus toxoid, or a combined vaccine containing tetanus toxoid, and tetanus immune globulin should be administered in separate syringes at different sites.

Administration: The vaccine should be administered **i.m.** into the deltoid muscle or the mid-lateral aspect of the thigh. The site of the injection should be prepared by a suitable antiseptic. **Do not inject s.c. or i.v.**

Withdrawing the Preparation from a Sealed Glass Ampul: Shake the ampul to disperse the contents thoroughly immediately before withdrawing the dose. **Tap the ampul to ensure that the solution is in the lower portion rather than in the neck of the ampul.** Wipe the neck of the ampul with a suitable antiseptic. Using a sterile piece of cotton or a sterile towel, break off the top of the ampul at the scored line (no file is required). Then, with the sterile syringe and needle withdraw the contents of the ampul into the syringe, holding the ampul in such a way that the point of the needle is kept immersed throughout the withdrawal. **Once the ampul has been opened, any of its contents not used immediately should be discarded.**

Withdrawing the Preparation from a Rubber-stoppered Vial: **Do not remove the rubber stopper from the vial.** Shake the vial to disperse the contents thoroughly immediately before withdrawing each dose of vaccine. Apply a sterile piece of cotton moistened with a suitable antiseptic to the surface of the rubber stopper and allow to dry. Draw into the **sterile** syringe a volume of air equal to the amount of preparation to be withdrawn from the vial. Pierce the centre of the rubber stopper with the **sterile** needle of the syringe, invert the vial, slowly inject into it the air contained in the syringe, and, keeping the point of the needle immersed, withdraw into the syringe the required amount of the preparation. Then hold the syringe plunger steady and withdraw the needle from the vial. Carefully insert the needle **i.m.** at the prepared injection site. **In order to avoid i.v. injection,** pull back the plunger of the syringe to make certain that no blood is withdrawn before injecting the desired dose.

Supplied: Tetanus Toxoid Adsorbed, as supplied by Connaught Laboratories Limited, is a sterile, cloudy, uniform suspension of tetanus toxoid adsorbed on aluminum phosphate and suspended in isotonic sodium chloride solution. Each dose (0.5 mL) contains: tetanus toxoid (5Lf) and aluminum phosphate (1.5 mg). Thimerosal 0.01% is added as a preservative. Ready for use, rubber-stoppered vials of 5 mL. Glass ampuls of 0.5 mL. Store between 2 and 8°C. **Do not freeze.** Do not use product exposed to freezing.

Reviewed 1998

...Canada's Poison Control Centres are listed in the CLIN-INFO SECTION.

TETRACYCLINES

General Monograph, CPhA

Chlortetracycline
Demeclocycline
Doxycycline
Minocycline
Tetracycline

Antibiotic

This monograph has been compiled by CPhA. It may contain information different from that approved by Therapeutic Products Programme, Health Canada, and the pharmaceutical manufacturers' approval has not been requested.

Pharmacology: The tetracyclines are semisynthetic derivatives obtained form Streptomyces cultures. They contain the tetracycline nucleus with various substitutions which impart different degrees of antibacterial activity, gastrointestinal absorption, affinity for divalent or trivalent cations and protein binding. Tetracyclines are mainly bacteriostatic agents which inhibit bacterial protein synthesis by binding to the 30S and to some extent the 50S ribosomal subunits. They may also alter the cytoplasmic membrane leading to leakage of intracellular components such as nucleotides from the cell.

Members of the tetracycline class have similar spectra of activity. They are active against a wide variety of organisms including Rickettsia, Chlamydia and Mycoplasma species, gram-positive bacteria such as B. anthracis, C. perfringens, C. tetani, L. monocytogenes, Nocardia, P. acnes, some strains of staphylococci and streptococci (although resistance is increasing) and gram-negative bacteria including B. pertussis, Brucella, Campylobacter, H. ducreyi, H. influenzae, N. gonorrhoea (increasingly resistant), N. meningitidis, Shigella, V. cholerae and Y. pestis. Although susceptible in vitro, most strains of Acinetobacter, Bacteroides, E. aerogenes, E. Coli and Klebsiella are resistant to tetracyclines.

Spirochetes including Borrelia, Leptospira and Treponema species are generally inhibited in vivo by tetracyclines. B. burgdorferi (Lyme disease) has a higher minimum bactericidal concentration than other organisms.

Resistance to tetracyclines may be natural or acquired and usually results in decreased permeability of the organism's cell wall to tetracycline. Complete cross-resistance occurs among members of the tetracycline class, with the exception of minocycline which exhibits only partial cross-resistance.

Pharmacokinetics (see Table I): With the exception of rolitetracycline which is not absorbed from the gastrointestinal tract, the tetracyclines are between 60 and 90% absorbed after oral administration. Absorption takes place mainly in the stomach and upper small intestine. The presence of food, milk or cations may significantly decrease the extent of absorption. Tetracyclines are poorly and erratically absorbed after i.m. injection.

Tetracyclines are distributed into most body tissues and fluids. They are distributed into the bile and undergo varying degrees of enterohepatic recirculation. The tetracyclines tend to localize in tumors, necrotic or ischemic tissue, liver and spleen and form tetracycline-calcium orthophosphate complexes at sites of new bone formation or tooth development.

Tetracyclines readily cross the placenta and are excreted in high amounts in breast milk.

For the most part, the tetracyclines are excreted unchanged in the urine and bile or secreted into the gastrointestinal tract. Only minocycline is significantly metabolized in the liver.

Hemodialysis removes 20 to 30% of tetracycline but has little effect on doxycycline or minocycline. Peritoneal dialysis has no effect on any of the tetracyclines.

Table I—Tetracyclines

Pharmacokinetics of Tetracyclines[a]

Drug	Protein Binding (approx. %)	Normal Serum Half-life (hours)	Half-life in Anuric Patients (hours)	% Excreted Unchanged in Urine
Demeclocycline	36 to 91	10 to 17	40 to 60	39
Doxycycline	25 to 93	12 to 22	12 to 22	30 to 42
Minocycline	55 to 88	11 to 26	11 to 23	6 to 12
Tetracycline	20 to 67	6 to 12	57 to 108	60

[a] Chlortetracycline is available as an ophthalmic or topical ointment only.

Indications: Tetracyclines are indicated in the treatment of infections caused by susceptible strains of Rickettsiae (e.g., Rocky Mountain spotted fever, typhus fever, Q fever, rickettsialpox and Brill-Zinsser disease), Chlamydiae (psittacosis, lymphogranuloma venereum, uncomplicated sexually transmitted diseases in adults or adolescents), M. pneumoniae, B. burgdorferi (Lyme disease), certain uncommon gram-negative infections such as brucellosis, bartonellosis, granuloma inguinale caused by C. granulomatis, cholera.

Although not the drugs of first choice, tetracyclines are sometimes used alternatively in the treatment of plague, tularemia, Campylobacter fetus infections, Leptotrichia buccalis (Vincent's) infection, chancroid, pertussis, anthrax and actinomycosis.

Oral doxycycline is indicated for the acute treatment of pelvic inflammatory disease following initial treatment with i.v. antibiotics. Doxycycline or tetracycline may be used to treat syphilis (except neurosyphilis) in penicillin-allergic patients.

Tetracycline has been used in multiple-drug regimens with bismuth, metronidazole and a proton pump inhibitor for treatment of H. pylori infection.

Doxycycline is used for chemoprophylaxis of malaria caused by chloroquine-resistant and/or sulfadoxine and pyrimethamine-resistant P. falciparum in patients travelling for less than 4 months. It provides substantial but incomplete suppression, as it is active only against the asexual erythrocytic forms of P. falciparum. Tetracycline with quinine sulfate is used for treatment of malaria when the drugs of choice are contraindicated or ineffective.

Demeclocycline has been effective in the treatment of the syndrome of inappropriate antidiuretic hormone secretion (SIADH).

Minocycline and tetracycline have been used in some mycobacterial infections.

Due to an increasingly high level of resistance, tetracyclines should not be used empirically to treat the more common gram-negative or gram-positive bacterial infections such as Acinetobacter, Bacteroides species, E. aerogenes, E. coli, H. influenzae, Shigella, K. pneumoniae, streptococci or staphylococci. They should only be used to treat susceptible strains of these infections when other appropriate anti-infectives are ineffective or contraindicated.

Tetracyclines have been used as sclerosing agents in the treatment of malignant pleural effusions. They have also been used in the treatment of moderate to severe inflammatory acne vulgaris.

Topical chlortetracycline is indicated for treatment of minor bacterial infections caused by susceptible organisms.

Ophthalmic chlortetracycline and tetracycline are indicated for treatment of superficial ocular infections caused by: S. aureus, S. epidermicus (S. pyogenes), S. pneumoniae, N. gonorrhoea or E. coli, and for prophylaxis of ophthalmia neonatorum caused by N. gonorrhoea or C. trachomatis. Ophthalmic chlortetracycline is also indicated for treatment of ocular infections caused by H. influenzae, H. ducreyi, K. pneumoniae, F. tularensis, Y. pestis, B. anthracis or L. venereum.

Contraindications: Hypersensitivity to any of the tetracyclines; severe renal or hepatic dysfunction; during pregnancy or lactation unless the potential benefit to the patient outweighs the risk to the fetus or child (see Precautions); therapy of common infections in children under 9 years.

Doxycycline is contraindicated in patients with myasthenia gravis because of a possible association with muscle weakness.

Precautions: If renal impairment exists, even usual oral or parenteral doses may lead to excessive systemic accumulation of the drug and possible liver toxicity. Under such conditions, lower doses are indicated and if therapy is prolonged, serum level determinations of the drug may be advisable. Usual doses of doxycycline may be used in patients with impaired renal function.

The antianabolic action of the tetracyclines, with the exception of doxycycline, may cause an increase in BUN, which is not problematic in patients with normal renal function. However, in patients with significantly impaired renal function, higher serum levels of tetracycline may lead to azotemia, hyperphosphatemia and acidosis. Consequently, increasing levels of BUN may not accurately reflect changes in renal function; the serum creatinine will provide a more reliable index.

Commercial preparations of tetracyclines may contain sulfites which may cause hypersensitivity reactions including anaphylaxis, with a higher incidence among asthmatic individuals.

Photosensitivity manifested by an exaggerated sunburn reaction has been observed in some individuals taking tetracyclines. Patients should be warned to avoid exposure to direct sunlight or ultraviolet light while taking tetracycline drugs and treatment should be discontinued at the first sign of skin discomfort.

Tetracyclines form a stable calcium complex in any bone-forming tissue. A decrease in the fibula growth rate has been observed in premature infants receiving oral tetracycline in doses of 25 mg/kg every 6 hours. This reaction was shown to be reversible when the drug was discontinued.

Tetracycline administration may result in overgrowth of nonsusceptible organisms. Suprainfections due to staphylococci and other organisms may occur. If suprainfections are encountered, tetracyclines should be discontinued and appropriate therapy started. Although rare, suprainfection of the bowel involving staphylococci may be life threatening.

It is important to adhere closely to expiration dates; ingestion of outdated or deteriorated tetracylines has produced kidney damage corresponding clinically to the acute Fanconi syndrome (nausea, vomiting, polyuria, polydipsia, albuminuria, glycosuria, aminoaciduria, hypophosphatemia, hypokalemia, and acidosis). Such damage is usually reversed slowly after withdrawal of the deteriorated tetracycline, although fatal reactions have been reported.

In rare instances, oral tetracyclines have caused esophagitis and esophageal ulceration. Patients should be advised not to take tetracyclines at bedtime and to take each dose with a large glass of water, while standing or sitting upright.

During long-term therapy, periodic laboratory evaluation of organ systems, including hematopoietic, renal and hepatic studies should be performed.

Since sensitivity reactions are more likely to occur in persons with a history of allergy, asthma, hay fever, or urticaria, tetracyclines should be used with caution in such individuals.

Drug Interactions: Anticoagulants: Tetracyclines may potentiate the effects of oral anticoagulants; INR or prothrombin times should be monitored more frequently in patients receiving concomitant anticoagulant therapy and dosage of the anticoagulant should be adjusted as required.

Cations: Antacids containing aluminum, calcium, or magnesium and laxatives containing magnesium may impair the absorption of oral tetracyclines and should be given 1 to 2 hours before or after the anti-infective.

Digoxin: Bioavailability of digoxin may be increased by tetracyclines in a small subset of patients (<10%) who metabolize significant amounts of digoxin in the gut, apparently by altering the gastrointestinal flora. Increased serum digoxin may result and may occur up to several months after the discontinuation of tetracyclines. If both drugs are used together, it is recommended to monitor for potential increases in the response to digoxin; a lower dose of digoxin may be needed in certain patients.

Hepatotoxic drugs: Other potentially hepatotoxic drugs should be avoided, if possible.

Insulin: Tetracyclines may reduce insulin requirements. Controlled studies are needed. Monitor blood glucose.

Iron: Iron salts may impair the gastrointestinal absorption of tetracyclines. It is also possible that tetracyclines may reduce iron absorption. If concurrent use cannot be avoided, give iron 3 hours before or 2 hours after the tetracycline.

Methoxyflurane: Concurrent use of methoxyflurane anesthesia and tetracyclines has been reported to seriously impair renal function, leading in some cases to death. Extreme caution is advised if the concurrent use of these drugs is contemplated.

Oral contraceptives: Concomitant use of oral contraceptives and tetracyclines may decrease the pharmacologic effects of oral contraceptives; breakthrough bleeding or pregnancy may occur.

Penicillin: Since bacteriostatic drugs may interfere with the bactericidal action of penicillin, it is advisable to avoid giving tetracycline in conjunction with penicillin.

Antidiarrhea agents containing kaolin and pectin or bismuth subsalicylate may impair absorption of oral tetracyclines and it is recommended to avoid concurrent use.

Barbiturates, carbamazepine and phenytoin may increase the rate of metabolism, and therefore, decrease the half-life of doxycycline. Adjustment of doxycycline dosage or substitution of another tetracycline may be necessary.

Pregnancy: Tetracyclines may cause fetal toxicity and should not be used in pregnant women unless in the judgement of the clinician the potential benefit to the mother outweighs the possible risk to the fetus.

Food Interactions: Food and dairy products containing high concentrations of cations may decrease the absorption of tetracyclines due to chelate formation in the gut. Tetracyclines should generally be administered on an empty stomach, 1 hour before or 2 hours after food or milk ingestion.

Lactation: Tetracyclines are distributed into breast milk and should not be used in lactating mothers unless the potential benefit to the mother outweighs the potential risk to the infant.

Children: The use of tetracyclines during tooth development may cause permanent tooth discoloration (yellow/ gray/ brown). This reaction is more common during long-term use of the tetracyclines but has been observed following repeated short-term courses. Enamel hypoplasia has also been reported. Tetracyclines should be avoided in children before the formation of dental enamel is complete in most permanent teeth, unless other drugs are not likely to be effective, are contraindicated, or are more toxic.

Geriatrics: Because of the greater prevalence of renal impairment in the elderly, renal function should be evaluated and dosage should be reduced or dosing intervals increased accordingly.

Occupational Hazards: Patients receiving minocycline may experience headache, light-headedness, dizziness or vertigo and should be cautioned about the operation of hazardous machinery or motor vehicles.

Adverse Effects: CNS: Lightheadedness, dizziness, vertigo, ataxia, drowsiness and fatigue may occur with minocycline and are often associated with nausea and vomiting. These reactions may occur in 30 to 90% of patients treated with minocycline. Tinnitus, hearing loss and visual disturbances have also been reported with tetracycline.

Increased intracranial pressure (pseudotumor cerebri) has been reported rarely in adults receiving tetracycline. Bulging fontanels have occurred in infants taking the drug. While both conditions tend to resolve when tetracycline is discontinued, the possibility of permanent sequelae exists.

Gastrointestinal: anorexia, epigastric distress, nausea, vomiting, diarrhea, bulky loose stools, stomatitis, sore throat, glossitis, black hairy tongue, dysphagia, hoarseness, enterocolitis and inflammatory lesions with candidal overgrowth in the anogenital region, including proctitis and pruritus ani. Rarely, esophagitis and esophageal ulceration have occurred. See Precautions.

Hematologic: Anemia, hemolytic anemia, thrombocytopenia, thrombocytopenic purpura, neutropenia and eosinophilia have been reported.

Hepatic: Hepatic cholestasis has been reported rarely and is associated primarily with high serum levels of tetracycline. Hepatic toxicity, associated with pancreatitis in some cases, has been attributed to the long-term use of doses larger than those recommended in patients with renal insufficiency or to the concomitant administration of other potentially hepatotoxic drugs. This serious reaction has occurred most often in pregnant or in postpartum patients with pyelonephritis. Fatty infiltration of the liver has been associated primarily with i.v. tetracycline and appears to be particularly significant in pregnant women who were given large doses (≥2 g/day).

Hypersensitivity Reactions: urticaria, angioneurotic edema, anaphylaxis, anaphylactoid purpura, pericarditis, exacerbation of systemic lupus erythematosus, serum sickness like reactions such as fever, rash and arthralgia. When given over prolonged periods, tetracyclines have been reported to produce brown-black microscopic discoloration of thyroid glands. No abnormalities of thyroid function studies are known to occur.

A Jarisch-Herxheimer reaction has occurred occasionally when tetracyclines were used to treat brucellosis or spirochetal infections. It is presumably caused by pyrogen and/or endotoxin release from phagocytized organisms and occurs 12 to 24 hours after initiation of treatment.

Renal: Rise in BUN with or without increased serum creatinine concentrations has been reported and is apparently dose-related (see Precautions).

Skin: maculopapular and erythematous rashes. Exfoliative dermatitis has been reported but is uncommon. Onycholysis and discoloration of the nails have been reported rarely. Photosensitivity has occurred (see Precautions).

Overdose: Symptoms: Severe toxicity following acute overdose is unlikely. Symptoms may include nausea and vomiting, esophagitis or esophageal ulceration, hypersensitivity reactions including anaphylaxis.

Treatment: Dilute well with water or milk due to the possibility of esophageal ulceration. Antacids may relieve nausea and abdominal pain (e.g., calcium carbonate or lactate, milk of magnesia, aluminum hydroxide). Measures to reduce absorption such as induction of emesis or use of cathartic may be beneficial in certain patients.

Dosage: Antacids containing aluminum, calcium, or magnesium and iron salts impair absorption (see Precautions). Foods and some dairy products also interfere with absorption. Oral forms of most tetracyclines should be given 1 hour before or 2 hours after meals. Doxycycline and minocycline preparations may be given orally with food and/or milk without a clinically important reduction in gastrointestinal absorption. To reduce the risk of esophageal irritation and ulceration, tetracyclines should not be given at bedtime and should be taken with a full glass of water, while standing or sitting upright.

Tetracycline: Adults: 250 mg 4 times daily. Higher dosages such as 500 mg 4 times daily may be required for severe infections.

Children (9 years of age and older): 25 mg/kg/day up to a maximum of 50 mg/kg/day for severe infections, administered in 2 to 4 divided doses (see Precautions).

Brucellosis: 500 mg every 6 hours for 3 weeks, with concurrent streptomycin.

Syphilis: 500 mg every 6 hours for 15 to 30 days.

Uncomplicated nongonococcal sexually transmitted diseases: 500 mg 4 times daily for at least 7 days.

Lyme disease: 500 mg 4 times daily.

Doxycycline: Adults: 100 mg every 12 hours the first day, then 100 to 200 mg once daily or 50 to 100 mg every 12 hours.

Children (9 years of age and older): 2.2 mg/kg every 12 hours or 2.2 to 4.4 mg/kg every 12 hours.

Malaria prophylaxis: 100 mg once daily, beginning 1 or 2 days before travel to the malarious area and continuing for 4 weeks after leaving the area.

Nongonococcal urethritis and uncomplicated chlamydial infections: 100 mg twice daily for at least 7 days.

Syphilis: 150 mg once daily for 3 weeks.

Lyme disease: 100 mg twice daily.

Minocycline: Adults: 200 mg initially, then 100 mg every 12 hours.

Children (9 years of age and older): 4 mg/kg initially, then 2 mg/kg every 12 hours.

Demeclocycline: Adults: SIADH: 3.25 to 3.75 mg/kg every 6 hours.

Topical: Chlortetracycline 3% ointment: Apply 2 to 3 times daily to cleansed affected area.

Reviewed 1999

THALARIS
Technilab

Hypertonic Sea Salt Solution
Decongestant—Antibacterial

Supplied: Each mL of gargle and oral rinse contains: sodium chloride 2.98% (as hypertonic sea salt solution) with benzalkonium chloride as preservative. Bottles of 500 mL.

THEO-BRONC Ⓟ
Rougier

Theophylline—Potassium Iodide—Guaifenesin—Mepyramine Maleate
Bronchodilator—Expectorant

Indications: For the symptomatic relief of reversible bronchoconstriction associated with chronic obstructive pulmonary emphysema, bronchial asthma, chronic bronchitis and related bronchospastic disorders and where expectoration is required.

Contraindications: Hyperthyroidism, active peptic ulcer, sensitivity to any of the components, pregnancy, in coronary artery diseasе where myocardial stimulation might prove harmful.

Precautions: Inquire before administration, particularly in young children (less than 7 years old), if a derivative of theophylline has been administered (parenteral or rectal route) in the previous 12 hours. It is strongly recommended to maintain an 8 to 12 hour interval between doses because of possible accumulation. In some patients prolonged iodide therapy may lead to hypothyroidism.

Use with caution in cases of hypertension, severe organic diseases or known sensitivity to guaifenesin.

A metabolite of guaifenesin has been found to produce an apparent increase in urinary 5-hydroxyindoleacetic acid, and guaifenesin could thus interfere with the diagnosis of the carcinoid syndrome. Asthmatic patients being evaluated for the carcinoid syndrome should therefore discontinue any preparation containing guaifenesin for 24 hours before the collection of urine specimens for the determination of 5-hydroxyindoleacetic acid.

Adverse Effects: Gastric upset, drowsiness, dizziness may occur.

Dosage: Adults: 10 mL 4 times/day. Children under 6 years: 2.5 mL/6.8 kg; 6 years and over: 5 mL 3 times a day, at 8 hour intervals.

The following mg equivalents facilitate changing from one xanthine preparation to another: theophylline anhydrous 100 mg=aminophylline 118 mg=diprophylline 141 mg=oxtriphylline 156 mg=theophylline sodium glycinate 200 mg.

Supplied: Each 5 mL of clear, colorless, bitter tasting solution contains: guaifenesin 50 mg, potassium iodide 80 mg, theophylline (base) 35 mg and mepyramine maleate 6 mg. Energy: 56.6 kJ (13.5 kcal). Bottles of 250 and 2 000 mL.

THEOCHRON® SR Ⓟ
Riva

Theophylline
Bronchodilator

Pharmacology: Theophylline is a bronchodilator which directly relaxes the smooth muscle of the bronchial airways and pulmonary and coronary blood vessels. These actions may be mediated through inhibition of phosphodiesterase and a resultant increase in intracellular cyclic AMP.

Theophylline sustained release tablets produce peak blood levels of theophylline between 5 and 8 hours following dosing in adults. Once a steady state level has been reached, the therapeutic blood levels of theophylline persist for 12 hours in most adult patients.

Theophylline is usually well absorbed following oral administration. In the therapeutic blood range of between 5 and 20 μg/mL (28 to 111 μmol/L), about 55 to 65% of theophylline is found bound to plasma protein. The half-life of theophylline is influenced by a number of known variables. In adult nonsmokers with uncomplicated asthma the half-life ranges from 3 to 9 hours. In older adults (over 55 years of age), patients with chronic obstructive lung disease, impaired hepatic or renal function, or chronic alcoholism, the half-life is usually longer, sometimes exceeding 24 hours. The half-life of theophylline in smokers and young children is, on the other hand, shorter. Between 3 months and 2 years may be necessary to reverse the effect of smoking on theophylline pharmacokinetics. The time required to reach steady state varies between subjects but is related to the half-life for theophylline in that subject. Steady state is generally reached within 5 half-lives.

Theophylline is metabolized by the liver to 3-methyl-xanthine, 1-methyl-uric acid and 1,3-dimethyluric acid. About 10% of a dose is excreted unchanged in the urine.

Biliary excretion, with subsequent reabsorption, may occur but has not been demonstrated in man.

Indications: For the symptomatic treatment of reversible bronchospasm associated with asthma, chronic bronchitis, emphysema and related bronchospastic disorders.

Contraindications: In patients with hypersensitivity to theophylline or xanthine derivatives; peptic ulcer; coronary artery disease (when, in the physician's judgment, myocardial stimulation might prove harmful).

Warnings: Children: The margin of safety above the therapeutic dose is small. The use of theophylline sustained release tablets in children under the age of 12 years is not recommended as a dose schedule in this age group has not been established.

Precautions: Marked differences in serum levels may be seen in patients receiving the same theophylline dose. This may be explained by differences between patients in the rate of metabolism. Dosage regimens should therefore be individualized.

Ideally, serum theophylline levels should be monitored in all patients and a theophylline half-life calculated which would enable doses and dosing regimens to be tailored to each patient to maintain a therapeutic level, to ensure optimal clinical response and to avoid toxicity.

The incidence of toxicity increases at serum theophylline levels greater than 15 μg/mL (83 μmol/L) and levels above 20 μg/mL (111 μmol/L) are usually quite toxic in most patients (adults). High serum levels may be seen in some patients receiving doses considered to be conventional. The possibility of overdose should therefore not be considered with large doses only. Overdosage of theophylline may cause peripheral vascular collapse.

Careful monitoring of serum levels is particularly advisable in patients with hepatic dysfunction since theophylline metabolism may be impaired, resulting in toxic levels.

Theophylline should also be used with caution in elderly patients, and patients with severe hypoxemia, uncompensated cardiac failure, cor pulmonale, or hyperthyroidism.

Theochron SR (cont'd)

Theophylline may also worsen pre-existing arrhythmias.

Caution should be exercised when theophylline is used concurrently with sympathomimetic amines, since the incidence and severity of adverse reactions may be increased. The concurrent administration of other theophylline derivatives along with theophylline sustained release tablets is not recommended.

In the interpretation of biochemistry tests, it should be remembered that theophylline may cause an elevation of urine catecholamines and plasma free fatty acids.

Pregnancy: Theophylline crosses the placental barrier and also passes freely into breast milk, where concentrations are similar to plasma levels. Safe use in pregnancy has not been established relative to possible adverse effects on fetal development, but neither have adverse effects on fetal development been established. Therefore, use of theophylline in pregnant women should be balanced against the risk of uncontrolled asthma.

Lactation: It has been reported that theophylline distributes readily into breast milk and may cause adverse effects in the infant. Caution must be used if prescribing xanthines to a mother who is nursing, taking into account the risk-benefit of this therapy.

Drug Interactions: Cimetidine, erythromycin, influenza vaccine and propranolol may increase the effect of theophylline by decreasing theophylline clearance.

Smoking may decrease theophylline effect by increasing clearance.

Acidifying agents, by increasing urinary excretion of weak bases such as xanthines, may inhibit theophylline action. Alkalinizing agents, by decreasing urinary excretion, may potentiate the action of theophylline.

The actions of thiazide diuretics and digitalis glycosides may be potentiated by xanthine derivatives such as theophylline.

The effects of coumarin anticoagulants may be antagonized by methylxanthine-induced increases of prothrombin and fibrinogen.

Theophylline has been shown to increase the ratio of clearance of lithium/creatinine and may thus decrease serum lithium to ineffective levels.

Xanthines may antagonize the antihyperuricemic action of allopurinol; the uricosuric action of probenecid may also be antagonized.

Xanthines have been shown to be nephrotoxic with prolonged use at high dosage. Coincident toxicity should therefore be borne in mind when other potentially nephrotoxic drugs are administered concurrently. Combined use of several xanthines, or the concurrent use of sympathomimetics, may cause excessive CNS stimulation.

Adverse Effects: The most common adverse reactions are nausea, vomiting, epigastric pain, headache and tremor. These are usually early signs of toxicity; however, with high doses, ventricular arrhythmias or seizures may be the first signs to appear. Adverse reactions reported with theophylline preparations include: Gastrointestinal: nausea, vomiting, epigastric pain, hematemesis, diarrhea, anorexia, reactivation of peptic ulcer, intestinal bleeding.

CNS: headaches, irritability, restlessness, insomnia, hyperactivity, reflex hyperexcitability, muscle twitching, clonic and tonic generalized convulsions.

Cardiovascular: palpitation, tachycardia, extrasystoles, flushing, hypotension, circulatory failure, life-threatening ventricular arrhythmias.

Respiratory: tachypnea.

Renal: albuminuria, diuresis and hematuria.

Others: hyperglycemia and inappropriate ADH syndrome.

Overdose: Symptoms: Insomnia, restlessness, mild excitement or irritability, and rapid pulse, are early symptoms which may progress to mild delirium.

Sensory disturbances such as tinnitus or flashes of light are common. Anorexia, nausea and vomiting are frequently early observations of theophylline overdosage.

Fever, diuresis, dehydration and extreme thirst may be seen. Severe poisoning results in bloody, syrup-like "coffee-ground" vomitus, tremors, tonic extensor spasm interrupted by clonic convulsions, extrasystoles, quickened respiration, stupor and finally coma. Cardiovascular disorders and respiratory collapse, leading to shock, cyanosis and death follow gross overdosages.

Treatment: If potential oral overdose is established and seizure has not occurred, induce vomiting. Administer a cathartic (this is particularly important when a sustained release preparation has been taken). Administer activated charcoal.

If patient is having a seizure, establish an airway. Administer oxygen. Treat the seizure with i.v. diazepam, 100 to 300 μg/kg up to a total dose of 10 mg. Monitor vital signs, maintain blood pressure and provide adequate hydration.

Post-Seizure Coma: Maintain airway and oxygenation. If a result of oral medication, follow above recommendations to prevent absorption of drug, but intubation and lavage will have to be performed instead of inducing emesis, and the cathartic and charcoal will need to be introduced via a large bore gastric lavage tube. Continue to provide full supportive care and adequate hydration while waiting for the drug to be metabolized. In general, the drug is metabolized sufficiently rapidly so as not to warrant consideration of dialysis. However, charcoal or resin hemoperfusion should be considered if serum level monitoring indicates dose-dependent kinetics.

Dosage: Therapeutic serum levels are generally considered to be between 10 and 20 μg/mL (56 to 111 μmol/L). Due to variable rates of elimination, there is patient-to-patient variation in dosage needed to achieve a therapeutic serum level. Because of the variation from patient-to-patient, the variation within the same patient, and the relatively narrow therapeutic range, dosage should be individualized. Monitoring of serum theophylline concentrations is also extremely important especially in the initial stages of therapy (see Precautions).

It is preferable to monitor peak concentrations rather than trough concentrations. Therefore, blood samples should be drawn 5 hours after dosing with theophylline sustained release tablets. It should be ascertained that all doses have been taken for 60 hours prior to blood sampling. Depending on the sensitivity of the assay method used, dietary xanthines may interfere with assay results.

If a dosage increase is not tolerated, dosage should be reduced to the previously tolerated level. Do not attempt to maintain a dosage which is not tolerated or which produces serum concentrations above the therapeutic range.

Theophylline sustained release tablets should not be chewed or crushed, but may be halved.

Adults: Usual Initial Dose: 200 to 300 mg every 12 hours. This dose may be increased by 50 to 100 mg every 12 hours at 3 day intervals until a satisfactory response is obtained or toxic effects appear. Dosage adjustments should be based upon serum theophylline concentration and/or upon the patient's clinical response. However, doses of 400 mg every 12 hours or higher should not be given unless serum theophylline concentration can be monitored. It should not be necessary to exceed a daily dose of 18 mg/kg in adult patients. Even with serum level monitoring, this dose may lead to side effects because of day-to-day variations in blood levels within individual patients.

Supplied: 100 mg: Each round, concave-shaped, white, bisected tablet, imprinted IL/3584, contains: sustained release theophylline anhydrous 100 mg. Bottles of 100, 500 and 1 000.

200 mg: Each oval, concave-shaped, white, bisected tablet, imprinted IL/3583, contains: sustained release theophylline anhydrous 200 mg. Bottles of 100, 500 and 1 000.

300 mg: Each capsule-shaped, white, scored tablet, imprinted IL/3581, contains: sustained release theophylline anhydrous 300 mg. Bottles of 100 and 500.

Store at controlled room temperature 15 to 30°C. Dispense in tight containers.

THEO-DUR® Ⓟ

Astra

Theophylline

Bronchodilator

Pharmacology: Theophylline relaxes the smooth muscle of the bronchial airways and pulmonary blood vessels to relieve bronchospasm and increase flow rates and vital capacity. It also produces other actions typical of the xanthine derivatives: coronary vasodilation, diuresis, increase in gastric secretion, and cardiac, cerebral, and skeletal muscle stimulation. The actions of theophylline may be mediated through inhibition of phosphodiesterase and a resultant increase in intracellular cyclic adenosine monophosphate, but the exact mechanism(s) has not been determined. Theophylline is usually readily absorbed and distributed into all body compartments. Protein binding accounts for some 55 to 65%. The liver is the primary site of metabolism.

The therapeutic serum concentration of theophylline is accepted as 55 to 110 μmol/L (10 to 20 mg/L); levels above 20 mg/L are associated with toxic reactions. The pharmacokinetics of theophylline are influenced by a number of variables such as: age, disease state, smoking, concomitant medication. Therefore the optimum therapeutic maintenance dose should be determined by individual titration.

The sustained-release tablets produce peak blood levels between 5 to 8 hours after dosing in adults, and between 4 to 6 hours after dosing in children 6 years of age and older. Once the steady state level has been reached (3 days) the therapeutic blood levels persist for 12 hours in most adult patients. The mean elimination half-life of theophylline in children is about 4 hours and in nonsmoking adults, about 8 hours. The degree of fluctuation between peak and trough theophylline levels are listed in Table I.

$$\% \text{ fluctuation} = \frac{C_{max} - C_{min}}{C_{min}} \times 100$$

Table I—Theo-Dur

% Theophylline Fluctuation

	Children (%)	Nonsmoking Adults (%)
Theo-Dur 200, 300, 450 mg	38	16
Theo-Dur 100 mg	87	34

Indications: For the symptomatic treatment of reversible bronchospasm associated with asthma, chronic bronchitis, emphysema and related bronchospastic disorders.

Contraindications: Hypersensitivity to theophylline or xanthine derivatives; peptic ulcer; coronary artery disease (when, in the physician's judgment, myocardial stimulation might prove harmful).

Warnings: In clinical situations where immediate bronchodilatation is required, such as status asthmaticus, Theo-Dur is not suitable. Theophylline has a narrow therapeutic range; the margin of safety above therapeutic doses is small. In patients showing intolerance to theophylline, the therapy should be reassessed. Theophylline clearance can be changed by various disease states, as well as by the age of the patient, concomitant use of other medications and lifestyle habits (see Precautions).

The use of Theo-Dur in children under the age of 6 years is not recommended as a dose schedule in this age group has not been established.

Precautions: Theo-Dur tablets should not be chewed or crushed, but may be halved.

Marked differences in serum levels may be seen in patients receiving the same theophylline dose. This may be explained by differences between patients in the rate of metabolism. Smokers and children are usually high metabolizers. Dosage regimens should therefore be individualized.

Theophylline half-life is shorter in smokers than in nonsmokers. Smokers may require larger or more frequent doses of theophylline.

Ideally, serum theophylline should be monitored in all patients and a theophylline half-life calculated which would enable doses and dosing regimens to be tailored to each patient to maintain a therapeutic level, to ensure optimal clinical response and to avoid toxicity.

The incidence of toxicity increases at serum theophylline levels greater than 82.5 μmol/L (15 mg/L) and levels above 110 μmol/L (20 mg/L) may produce toxic effects in most adult patients. High serum levels may be seen in some patients receiving doses considered to be conventional. The possibility of overdose should therefore not be considered with large doses only. Overdosage of theophylline may cause peripheral vascular collapse.

Reduced theophylline clearance has been documented in the following readily identifiable groups: patients with impaired renal or hepatic function; patients over 55 years of age, particularly males and those with chronic lung disease; those with cardiac failure from any cause; patients taking certain drugs (i.e., macrolide antibiotics, cimetidine or fluvoxamine). Decreased clearance may be associated with either influenza immunization or active infection with influenza; those with acute viral infections or other conditions with fever.

Laboratory monitoring of serum theophylline is especially appropriate in the above individuals to maintain an appropriate theophylline dosage and to avoid accumulation of theophylline to potentially toxic serum concentrations (greater than 110 μmol/L=20 mg/L).

Serious side effects such as tachycardia, arrhythmia, seizures, vascular collapse and even death may occur without warning and may not be preceded by less severe symptoms such as nausea and restlessness. These serious side effects usually appear in patients at high plasma concentrations of theophylline (above 25 mg/L).

Use with caution in patients with severe cardiac disease, severe hypoxemia, hypertension, hyperthyroidism, acute myocardial injury, cor pulmonale, congestive heart failure, liver disease, in the elderly (especially males).

Patients with congestive heart failure frequently have markedly prolonged serum levels with theophylline persisting in serum for long periods following discontinuation of the drug.

Theophylline may occasionally act as a local irritant to the gastrointestinal tract although gastrointestinal symptoms are more commonly centrally mediated and associated with serum drug concentrations over 110 μmol/L (20 mg/L).

Theophylline increases gastric secretion, and caution should be exercised in patients with a history of peptic ulcer.

Theophylline may potentiate hypokalemia if administered concomitantly with β_2-agonists, steroids, diuretics or in hypoxic and severe asthmatic patients. Serum potassium levels should be monitored in these situations.

Although Theo-Dur has pharmacokinetic properties similar to other controlled-release theophylline products, it is not possible to ensure interchangeability between different products. Careful clinical monitoring is required when changing from one drug product to another.

The concurrent administration of other theophylline derivatives along with Theo-Dur is not recommended.

Laboratory Test Interactions: In the interpretation of biochemistry tests, it should be remembered that theophylline may cause an elevation of urine catecholamines and serum free fatty acids. When serum levels of theophylline are measured by spectrophotometric methods, coffee, tea, cola beverages, chocolate and acetaminophen contribute to falsely high values.

When high pressure liquid chromatography (HPLC) method is used, serum theophylline concentration may be falsely increased by caffeine, some cephalosporin and sulfa medications.

Food Interactions: Theophylline clearance is increased when diet includes a low carbohydrate, high protein intake, or a high carbohydrate, low protein intake and there is a chronic ingestion of charcoal broiled meats. However, the administration of Theo-Dur with meals appears not to significantly affect the release of theophylline from Theo-Dur tablets.

Pregnancy and *Lactation:* Theophylline crosses the placental barrier and also passes freely into breast milk, where concentrations are similar to serum levels. Safe use in pregnancy has not been established relative to possible adverse effects on fetal development but neither have adverse effects on fetal development been established. Therefore, use of theophylline for uncontrolled asthma in pregnant women and nursing mothers, should be balanced against the risk of potential effects on the fetus or on the nursing newborn.

Drug Interactions: Theophylline pharmacokinetics are altered by the concurrent use of various drugs as listed in Table II.

Table II—Theo-Dur

Effect of Various Drugs on Theophylline Pharmacokinetics

Drugs	Theophylline	
Cimetidine, propranolol, allopurinol, macrolide antibiotics (i.e., troleandomycin, erythromycin), oral contraceptives	↑ t½,	↓ clearance
Alkalinizing agents	↑ t½,	↓ clearance
Influenza vaccine	↑ t½,	clearance reported to be decreased or no change
Phenytoin, barbiturates, carbamazepine, isoproterenol, rifampin	↓ t½,	↑ clearance
Smoking (tobacco)	↓ t½,	↑ clearance
Acidifying agents	↓ t½,	↑ clearance
Quinolones (ciprofloxacin, norfloxacin)	↑ t½,	↓ clearance
Disulfiram	↑ t½,	↓ clearance
Aminoglutethimide	↑ t½,	↓ clearance
Mexiletine	↑ t½,	↓ clearance
Serotonin reuptake inhibitors (e.g., fluvoxamine	↑ t½,	↓ clearance
Ranitidine, thiabendazole		↓ clearance
Nifedipine, verapamil		↑ plasma levels

For how concurrent use of theophylline influences effects of certain drugs, see Table III.

Table III—Theo-Dur

Effect of Theophylline on Certain Drugs

Drug	Effects
Digitalis glycosides	↑ cardiac effect
Thiazides	↑ diuresis
Nephrotoxic drugs	↑ nephrotoxicity
Lithium	↑ ratio of lithium/creatinine clearance, thus decrease serum lithium
Sympathomimetic amines	↑ toxicity, ↑CNS stimulation
Coumarin anticoagulants	↓ anticoagulant activity, increase prothrombin and fibrinogen blood concentrations, shorten prothrombin time
Allopurinol	↓ antihyperuricemic action
Probenecid and pyrazolon derivatives	↓ uricosuric action
Ketamine	↓ threshold value for inducing convulsions

Adverse Effects: The most common adverse reactions are nausea, vomiting, epigastric pain, headache and tremor. These are usually early signs of toxicity; however, with high doses, cardiac arrhythmias or seizures may be the first signs to appear. Adverse reactions reported with theophylline preparations include:

Gastrointestinal: nausea, vomiting, epigastric pain, hematemesis, diarrhea, anorexia, reactivation of peptic ulcer, intestinal bleeding.

CNS: headaches, irritability, restlessness, insomnia, hyperactivity, reflex hyperexcitability, muscle twitching, clonic and tonic generalized convulsions. In rare cases, theophylline has been reported to adversely affect the behavior and school performance of children.

Cardiovascular: palpitation, tachycardia, extrasystoles, flushing, hypotension, circulatory failure, life-threatening ventricular arrhythmias.

Respiratory: tachypnea.

Renal: albuminuria, diuresis, hematuria.

Others: exanthema, urticaria, hyperglycemia, inappropriate ADH syndrome.

Overdose: Symptoms: Insomnia, restlessness, mild excitement or irritability, and rapid pulse are the early symptoms, which may progress to mild delirium. Sensory disturbances such as tinnitus or flashes of light are common. Anorexia, nausea and vomiting are frequently early observations of theophylline overdosage.

Fever, diuresis, dehydration and extreme thirst may be seen. Severe poisoning results in bloody, syrup-like "coffee ground" vomitus, tremors, tonic extensor spasm interrupted by clonic convulsions, extrasystoles, quickened respiration, stupor and finally, coma.

Cardiovascular disorders and respiratory collapse, leading to shock, cyanosis and death follow gross overdosages.

Treatment: A. Monitoring Serum Theophylline Levels: Following intake of Theo-Dur, the blood theophylline peak levels may not show until 5 to 8 hours post-ingestion in adults and 4 to 6 hours in children. Patients ingesting overdoses of sustained-release theophylline formulations may have, after the initial rise in blood theophylline, also a secondary increase in theophylline levels. One report on fatal self-poisoning has attributed this to compacted tablet masses in the gastrointestinal tract. Careful clinical and laboratory monitoring of stabilized patients is advisable.

B. If potential oral overdose is established and seizure has not occurred: Induce vomiting. Administer a cathartic (this is particularly important when a sustained-release preparation has been taken). Administer activated charcoal.

C. If patient is having a seizure: Establish an airway. Administer oxygen. Treat the seizure with i.v. diazepam, 0.1 to 0.3 mg/kg up to a total dose of 10 mg. Monitor vital signs, maintain blood pressure and provide adequate hydration.

D. Post-seizure Coma: Maintain airway and oxygenation. If a result of oral medication, follow above recommendations to prevent drug absorption, but intubation and lavage will have to be performed instead of inducing vomiting, and the cathartic and charcoal will need to be introduced via a large bore gastric lavage tube. Continue to provide full supportive care and adequate hydration while waiting for the drug to be metabolized. In general, the drug is metabolized sufficiently rapidly so as not to warrant consideration of dialysis. However, if serum levels exceed 257 μmol/L (50 mg/L), charcoal hemoperfusion may be indicated.

Dosage: Therapeutic serum levels are generally considered to be between 55 and 110 μmol/L (10 and 20 mg/L). Due to variable rates of elimination, there is patient-to-patient variation in dosage needed to achieve a therapeutic serum level. Because of the variation from patient to patient, the variation within the same patient, and the relatively narrow therapeutic range, dosage should be individualized. Monitoring of serum theophylline concentrations is also extremely important, especially in the initial stages of therapy (see Precautions).

It is preferable to monitor peak concentrations rather than trough concentrations. Therefore, blood samples should be drawn 4 to 8 hours after Theo-Dur dosing. It should be ascertained that all doses have been taken for 60 hours prior to blood sampling (steady state is usually achieved within 3 days). Depending on the sensitivity of the assay method used, dietary xanthines may interfere with assay results. If a dosage increase is not tolerated, dosage should be reduced to the previously tolerated level. Do not attempt to maintain a dosage which is not tolerated or which produces serum concentrations above the therapeutic range.

Theo-Dur tablets should not be chewed or crushed but may be halved.

Adults: The usual initial dose is 200 to 300 mg every 12 hours. This dose may be increased by 50 to 100 mg every 12 hours at 3-day intervals until a satisfactory response is obtained or toxic effects appear.

Dosage adjustments should be based upon serum theophylline concentration and/or upon the patient's clinical response. However, doses of 450 mg every 12 hours or higher (900 mg/day) should not be given unless serum theophylline concentration can be monitored. It should not be necessary to exceed a daily dose of 16 mg/kg in adult patients. Even with serum level monitoring, this dose may lead to side effects because of day-to-day variations in blood levels within individual patients.

Children: The usual initial dose (age 6 to 12 years) is 6 mg/kg given every 12 hours (12 mg/kg/day).

If the desired response is not obtained after 3 days, and there are no adverse effects, dosage may be increased to 8 mg/kg every 12 hours (16 mg/kg/day). This dose should be considered the maximum unless serum theophylline concentrations can be monitored to guide further dose increases.

If serum concentrations are monitored, and there are no adverse effects, the dosage may be increased by 2 to 3 mg/kg/day at intervals of not less than 3 days, until the desired response is obtained, or until side effects appear. It should not be necessary to exceed a daily dose of 21 mg/kg to obtain an adequate response in children. Even with serum theophylline concentration monitoring, this dose (21 mg/kg/day) may lead to side effects because of day-to-day variations of blood levels within individual patients.

Dividing the daily dosage into 3 doses administered at 8-hour intervals may be indicated if symptoms repeatedly occur at the end of 12 hour dosing intervals.

Information for the Patient: See Blue Section—Information for the Patient "Theo-Dur".

Supplied: 100 mg: Each white, round, biconvex, sustained-release tablet, engraved THEO-DUR/100 on one side and scored in the transverse direction on the opposite side, contains: anhydrous theophylline 100 mg. Nonmedicinal ingredients: acacia, cellulose acetate phthalate, cetyl alcohol, cornstarch, diethyl phthalate, glycerol monostearate, lactose powder, magnesium stearate, myristyl alcohol, nonpareil seeds, sodium lauryl sulfate, sucrose, talc and white wax. Energy: 0.42 kJ (0.1 kcal). Gluten- and tartrazine-free. Bottles of 100

200 mg: Each white, slightly convex, sustained-release, elliptical tablet with bevelled edges, engraved THEO-DUR/200 on one side and scored in the transverse direction on the opposite side, contains: anhydrous theophylline 200 mg. Nonmedicinal ingredients: cellulose acetate phthalate, cetyl alcohol, diethyl phthalate, glycerol monostearate, hydroxypropyl methylcellulose, lactose anhydrous, magnesium stearate, myristyl alcohol, nonpareil seeds and white wax. Energy: 0.84 kJ (0.2 kcal). Gluten-, sodium- and tartrazine-free. Bottles of 100 and 500.

Theo-Dur (cont'd)

300 mg: Each white, biconvex, staff-shaped, sustained-release tablet, with parallel sides and rounded ends, engraved THEO-DUR/300 on one side and scored in the transverse direction on the opposite side, contains: anhydrous theophylline 300 mg. Nonmedicinal ingredients: cellulose acetate phthalate, cetyl alcohol, diethyl phthalate, glycerol monostearate, hydroxypropyl methylcellulose, lactose anhydrous, magnesium stearate, myristyl alcohol, nonpareil seeds and white wax. Energy: 1.26 kJ (0.3 kcal). Gluten-, sodium- and tartrazine-free. Bottles of 100 and 500.

450 mg: Each white, biconvex, staff-shaped, sustained-release tablet, with parallel sides and rounded ends, engraved THEO-DUR/450 on one side and scored in the transverse direction on the opposite side, contains: anhydrous theophylline 450 mg. Nonmedicinal ingredients: cellulose acetate phthalate, cetyl alcohol, diethyl phthalate, glycerol monostearate, hydroxypropyl methylcellulose, lactose anhydrous, magnesium stearate, myristyl alcohol, nonpareil seeds and white wax. Energy: 1.89 kJ (0.45 kcal). Gluten-, sodium- and tartrazine-free. Bottles of 100.

(Shown in Product Recognition Section)

THEOLAIR™
THEOLAIR™ LIQUID
3M Pharmaceuticals

Theophylline

Bronchodilator

Supplied: Liquid: Each 15 mL of alcohol free, citrus berry flavored liquid contains: theophylline (anhydrous) 80 mg. Nonmedicinal ingredients: flavor, methyl- and propylparabens, purified water, sorbitol and sucrose. Tartrazine-free. Bottles of 500 mL.

Tablets: 125 mg: Each white, round tablet, "3M" imprint on one face, "342" bisect score on the other face contains: theophylline (anhydrous) 125 mg. Nonmedicinal ingredients: colloidal silicon dioxide, lactose, magnesium stearate and pregelatinized starch. Tartrazine-free. Bottles of 100.

250 mg: Each white, capsule-shaped tablet, "3M" imprint on one face, "THEOLAIR 250" bisect score on the other face, contains: theophylline (anhydrous) 250 mg. Nonmedicinal ingredients: colloidal silicon dioxide, lactose, magnesium stearate and pregelatinized starch. Tartrazine-free. Bottles of 100.

THEOLAIR™-SR
3M Pharmaceuticals

Theophylline

Bronchodilator

Supplied: 250 mg: Each white, round, sustained-release tablet, "3M" imprint on one face, "SR-250" bisect score on the other face, contains: theophylline (anhydrous) 250 mg. Nonmedicinal ingredients: cellulose acetate phthalate, lactose and magnesium stearate. Tartrazine-free. Bottles of 100.

300 mg: Each white, oval-shaped, sustained-release tablet, "3M" imprint on one face, "SR-300" bisect bar on the other face, contains: theophylline (anhydrous) 300 mg. Nonmedicinal ingredients: cellulose acetate phthalate, lactose and magnesium stearate. Tartrazine-free. Bottles of 100.

THEOPHYLLINE
Technilab

Bronchodilator

Supplied: Each 15 mL of fruit-flavored elixir contains: theophylline anhydrous 80 mg. Nonmedicinal ingredients: alcohol, artificial coloring and flavoring, FD&C Yellow #6, methylparaben, propylparaben, purified water, sodium benzoate, sorbitol and sucrose. Bottles of 500 mL.

THEOPHYLLINE AND ITS SALTS
General Monograph, CPhA

Aminophylline
Oxtriphylline
Theophylline

Bronchodilator

This monograph has been compiled by CPhA. It may contain information different from that approved by Therapeutic Products Programme, Health Canada, and the pharmaceutical manufacturers' approval has not been requested.

Pharmacology: Theophylline is an alkaloid of the methylxanthine group. Aminophylline and oxtriphylline are complexes of theophylline with ethylenediamine and choline respectively. Both aminophylline and oxtriphylline dissociate in biological fluids to yield theophylline.

Theophylline's principle pharmacologic actions include stimulation of the CNS, stimulation of cardiac muscle, relaxation of bronchial smooth muscle and diuresis. The mechanism of action is still unknown; however, the three basic cellular effects of theophylline are translocation of intracellular calcium, accumulation of cyclic AMP and adenosine receptor blockade. The accumulation of cyclic AMP increases the release of endogenous epinephrine resulting in increased beta-adrenergic stimulation. The methylxanthines have also been reported to potentiate inhibition of the synthesis of contractile prostaglandins.

Pharmacokinetics: Theophylline is well absorbed orally. Maximal plasma concentrations occur approximately 2 hours after ingestion of oral liquids and nonsustained-release tablets. Maximal plasma concentrations occur within 3 to 7 hours after ingestion of most sustained-release preparations; however, this varies with the individual preparation. Food delays but does not reduce absorption of uncoated tablets and liquids, however it may affect absorption of extended-release preparations. The product manufacturers guidelines on administration should be consulted.

The absorption of theophylline administered i.m. is usually slow and incomplete. I.M. theophylline is extremely painful and is not recommended. Absorption of theophylline from rectal suppositories is not dependable; a retention enema may be more reliable, but no preparation is currently available in Canada. I.V. theophylline produces the highest and most rapidly achieved serum theophylline concentrations, reaching peak serum levels within 30 minutes.

Theophylline is distributed throughout extracellular fluids and body tissues. It does not distribute into adipose tissue. Theophylline readily crosses the placenta and is secreted into breast milk in concentrations approaching 70% those in maternal serum. The average volume of distribution (Vd) is reported to be 0.45 L/kg for children and adults. At therapeutic concentrations plasma protein binding is approximately 60% in adults compared to 35% in neonates and in patients with hepatic cirrhosis.

Theophylline undergoes hepatic biotransformation via the cytochrome P-450 component of the microsomal oxidative enzyme system, to 1,3 dimethyluric acid, 1-methyluric acid and 3-methylxanthine. Theophylline and its metabolites are excreted mainly by the kidneys. Metabolites account for approximately 85%, renal elimination of unchanged drug being less than 15% of the overall plasma clearance of theophylline.

Table I—Theophylline and Its Salts

Average Plasma Half-Life of Theophylline	
Adults (healthy, nonsmokers)	7–9 hours
Adults (smokers)	4–5 hours
Elderly (nonsmokers)	10 hours
Children	3–5 hours
Neonates (premature)	20–30 hours

Theophylline clearance is markedly reduced in neonates. Neonates excrete a larger proportion of unchanged theophylline in the urine and dosage must be adjusted in the presence of renal failure in this group. Theophylline half-life is much longer in neonates which allows for dosing intervals of every 12 hours (see Table I for information on half-life of theophylline). Theophylline clearance increases during the first year of life and remains relatively constant during the first 9 years, thereafter decreasing to adult values by age 16. Clearance is decreased in hepatic cirrhosis, acute hepatitis, cholestasis, heart failure, cor pulmonale, febrile respiratory tract infections and in the elderly. Cigarette or marijuana smokers have a more rapid clearance. Diets low in carbohydrates and high in protein or charcoal broiled meats may contribute to an increased ability to clear theophylline.

There is significant interpatient variability in theophylline pharmacokinetics. Steady state is usually achieved within 48 hours with a consistent dosage schedule. Serum concentrations should be monitored more closely, regardless of steady state, in patients with acute respiratory illness, in neonates or in patients at risk of decreased theophylline clearance. The therapeutic plasma concentration range is 55 to 110 μmol/L in children and adults. The upper end of the range for neonates is generally closer to 55 μmol/L but must be individualized depending on the condition treated and individual tolerance. Generally the peak concentration should be monitored for clinical guidance. The peak level yields information about efficacy and potential for toxicity of the dosage regimen. Sampling time for peak concentration will vary depending on the route of administration and dosage form. If the patient becomes symptomatic at the end of the dosing interval, a trough concentration may be taken to determine whether or not the patient's dosing interval is appropriate.

Saliva concentrations are not a reliable indicator of serum concentrations.

Concurrent administration of other drugs and xanthine-containing beverages can affect some assay results measured by spectrophotometric methods. These substances do not interfere with results when measured by high-pressure liquid chromatography or EMIT (enzyme multiplied immunoassay technique).

Indications: The symptomatic treatment of reversible bronchoconstriction associated with chronic obstructive pulmonary disease, bronchial asthma, chronic bronchitis and related bronchospastic disorders. According to current Canadian guidelines, theophylline is advocated as adjunctive therapy in patients in whom β_2-agonists cannot provide suficient bronchodilation and inhaled corticosteroid therapy is inadequate.

Contraindications: Hypersensitivity to xanthines; active peptic ulcer; coronary artery disease when myocardial stimulation might prove harmful.

Warnings: Children: Parents or other caregivers should be cautioned against overdosing children; children are very sensitive to xanthines, especially the CNS stimulant effects. The margin of safety above therapeutic doses is small. It is important to ensure that children receiving oral theophylline are not also receiving the drug by the rectal route.

Long-acting dosage forms are not recommended in children under 6 years of age as safety and efficacy have not been established.

For once-a-day dosage forms, dosage has not been established for children up to 12 years of age.

Precautions: There is a marked variation in blood concentrations achieved in different patients given the same dose of theophylline which may lead to serious adverse effects in some patients. It is advisable to individualize dosage regimens. Ideally, all individuals should have serum theophylline concentrations measured. Theophylline clearance is decreased in certain situations, which can lead to toxicity: in premature or neonatal infants; in patients over 60 years old; if the intake of carbohydrates is high; if there is concurrent methylxanthine intake; where drug interactions are present (see Table II); where the patient has a concurrent disease such as, hepatic cirrhosis, congestive heart failure, acute pulmonary edema, chronic obstructive lung disease, pneumonia, severe pulmonary obstruction, acute febrile episodes.

I.V. injections must be given slowly and cautiously, especially in patients with pronounced myocardial injury. Rapid i.v. injection may cause sudden and severe hypotension, or cardiac arrest.

Theophylline should be used with caution in patients having or suspected of having a peptic ulcer.

Extended release preparations should be taken with adequate liquids to ensure swallowing and to prevent esophageal erosion and ulceration.

Drug Interactions: Tobacco and marijuana induce the hepatic metabolism of theophylline resulting in increased clearance and decreased serum concentrations.

The drug interactions represented in Table II are clinically significant interactions. Monitoring of serum theophylline concentrations and/or dosage adjustments are recommended when concurrent use of these medications with theophylline is initiated or discontinued.

Table II—Theophylline and its Salts

Drug Interactions

Interacting Drug	↑ [THP][a]	↓ [THP][b]
Adenosine	↓ cardiac effects of adenosine	
Allopurinol (≥600 mg/day)	•	
Barbiturates[c]		•
Benzodiazepines	↓ sedative effects of benzodiazepines	
β-Blockers (nonselective)	•	
Calcium Channel Blockers[d]	•	
Carbamazepine		•
Cimetidine	•	
Contraceptives, Oral	•	
Disulfiram	•	
Fluvoxamine	•	
Halothane	arrhythmias	
Interferon α, Recombinant	•	
Lithium	↓ serum lithium concentrations	
Macrolides[e]	•	
Mexiletine	•	
Nondepolarizing Muscle Relaxants	↓ neuromuscular blockade	
Phenytoin[f]		•
Propafenone	•	
Quinolones[g]	•	
Rifampin		•
Thiabendazole	•	
Thioamines[h]		•
Thyroid Hormones[i]	•	
Ticlopidine	•	

[a]↑ [THP]=increased serum theophylline concentrations.
[b]↓ [THP]=decreased serum theophylline concentrations.
[c]Includes primidone and its major metabolite, phenobarbital.
[d]Includes diltiazem and verapamil.
[e]Includes clarithromycin and erythromycin.
[f]Decreased phenytoin levels may also occur.
[g]Includes ciprofloxacin and norfloxacin. Ofloxacin is not considered to decrease theophylline clearance significantly.
[h]Methimazole and PTU may increase THP clearance in hyperthyroid patients.
[i]Levothyroxine and dextrothyroxine may increase THP clearance in hypothyroid patients.

Pregnancy: Theophylline readily crosses the placenta. Transient tachycardia, irritability and vomiting have been reported in newborns exposed to theophylline in utero. Theophylline has not been associated with an increased risk of fetal malformations. Because of the risk of uncontrolled asthma, the use of theophylline when clearly needed during pregnancy is generally not seriously questioned.

Lactation: Theophylline is excreted in breast milk and may occasionally cause irritability in nursing infants.

Adverse Effects: Side effects most frequently experienced include: anorexia, nausea, vomiting, headache, abdominal discomfort, nervousness, insomnia, irritability and tremor. Tolerance to these effects may develop with continued dosing or a small reduction in dosage may alleviate the symptoms. About 5 to 15% of patients do not tolerate oral theophylline even if serum concentrations are less than 83 μmol/L.

Theophylline toxicity is frequently associated with large doses and high plasma concentrations of theophylline; severe effects are rare at concentrations below 110 μmol/L. Atrial and ventricular arrhythmias may occur with serum theophylline concentrations greater than 110 μmol/L, or at therapeutic concentrations in patients with heart disease. Focal or generalized seizures have occurred over 222 μmol/L, as well as with lower concentrations. Toxicity of theophylline and its derivatives may present as follows:
Gastrointestinal: nausea, vomiting, diarrhea, abdominal cramps, epigastric pain, anorexia, reactivation of peptic ulcer, intestinal bleeding.
CNS: headache, nervousness, insomnia, dizziness, lightheadedness, excitement, irritability, restlessness, fever, convulsions.
Cardiovascular: palpitations, sinus tachycardia, atrial or ventricular arrhythmias, increased pulse rate, peripheral vascular constriction and/or collapse.
Urinary Tract: albuminuria.
Skin: rarely urticaria, generalized pruritus, angioedema, contact dermatitis.

Overdose: Symptoms: Patients, especially children, who are chronically overmedicated may develop severe toxicity with serum levels lower than those seen in an acute intoxication.

Seizures and death have occurred following large overdoses without prior symptoms of toxicity. The most common reactions observed with toxic overdoses of theophylline are:
Gastrointestinal: nausea, vomiting, epigastric pain, hematemesis, diarrhea.
CNS: Hyperreflexia, fasciculations and tonic-clonic convulsions.
Cardiovascular: fatal arrhythmia or shock; marked hypotension and circulatory failure.
Respiratory: tachypnea and respiratory arrest.
Renal: Albuminuria and microhematuria. Increased excretion of renal tubular cells.
General Systemic Events: syncope, collapse, fever and dehydration.

Treatment: If theophylline was orally ingested, the stomach should be emptied using ipecac syrup or by gastric lavage. Emesis should not be induced if the patient is exhibiting seizures, which may be treated with diazepam; if diazepam is ineffective, phenytoin or phenobarbital may be used. Seizures should be treated or the patient sedated before attempting gastric lavage. Treatment should be followed with activated charcoal and a cathartic. Multiple doses of activated charcoal may speed elimination whether theophylline was given orally or i.v. Activated charcoal may be repeated every 4 to 6 hours until serum level is within the therapeutic range. Treatment also involves support of cardiac and respiratory functions, maintenance of fluid and electrolyte balance and ECG monitoring. Charcoal hemoperfusion and hemodialysis are effective in removing theophylline. Hemoperfusion is more effective than hemodialysis.

Dosage: Theophylline has a low therapeutic index; therefore, cautious dosage determination is essential. Individuals metabolize theophylline at different rates, appropriate dosages must be determined for each patient by carefully monitoring patient response and tolerance, pulmonary function and serum theophylline concentrations. Dosage adjustments are based on clinical response with careful monitoring for manifestations of toxicity. Symptoms of toxicity may even occur when serum concentrations are within the upper end of the therapeutic range (85 to 110 μmol/L), particularly during initiation of therapy.

All dosages should be calculated based on **lean** or **ideal** body weight.

Regardless of the salt used, dosages should be based on equivalent anhydrous theophylline content (see Table III).

Table III—Theophylline and Its Salts

Theophylline Content

Xanthine	Percent Theophylline
Aminophylline	85%
Oxtriphylline	65%
Theophylline Sodium Glycinate	50%

Parenteral: Acute: The loading dose does not generally require adjustment in the presence of various disease states. The following loading doses are designed to achieve serum theophylline concentrations at the lower end of the therapeutic range (55 to 65 μmol/L).

If it has been established that the patient has not taken any theophylline preparation within the preceding 24 hours, the following loading dose is appropriate: Load: Theophylline 5 mg/kg i.v. over 20 to 30 minutes (Aminophylline 6 mg/kg i.v. over 20 to 30 minutes).

If there is a strong suspicion that the patient has ingested some form of theophylline within the last 24 hours, then ideally, the loading dose should be deferred until a serum theophylline determination is made. Since this is usually not possible, the use of other nonxanthine bronchodilators should be considered. If there is sufficient respiratory distress to warrant a small risk, a partial loading dose may be administered. Partial Loading Dose: Theophylline 2.5 mg/kg i.v. over 20 to 30 minutes (aminophylline 3 mg/kg i.v. over 20 to 30 minutes).

This dose should produce an increase in serum theophylline concentration of approximately 25 to 30 μmol/L.

Alternatively, an increase in dosage of 1 mg/kg for every desired 10 μmol/L increase in serum theophylline concentration may be used at the discretion of the clinician.

Maintenance: These recommendations are not designed to replace serum theophylline concentrations as a guide for dosage adjustment, and should be used only until serum concentrations are available (see Table IV).

The infusion is most accurately given by a constant infusion pump, but a minidrip set is adequate for clinical use if carefully adjusted.

Oral: Chronic therapy: Adults and children (over 1 year); Starting dose: the lesser of: 16 mg/kg/day or 400 mg/day administered in 3 to 4 divided doses at 6- to 8-hour intervals.

The above dosage may be increased, if tolerated, in approximately 25% increments at 2- to 3-day intervals, up to the maximum doses indicated in Table V. When the recommended maximum dosage is exceeded, dosage adjustment should be based on measurement of peak serum theophylline concentration.

Use ideal body weight.

Table V—Theophylline and Its Salts

Maximum Dosage in the Absence of Serum Level Determinations

Age (years)	Dose of Theophylline
1–9	24 mg/kg/day
9–12	20 mg/kg/day
12–16	18 mg/kg/day
Adults >16	13 mg/kg/day or 900 mg/day (whichever is less)

Table IV—Theophylline and Its Salts

Parenteral Maintenance Dosage[a]

Group	Dose of Theophylline I.V. (mg/kg/h)[b]	Aminophylline I.V. (mg/kg/h)[b]
Children 6 months to 9 years	0.79	1
Children 9 to 16 years and adults, otherwise healthy, smoker	0.63	0.8
Adults, otherwise healthy, nonsmoker	0.39	0.5
Elderly (>60 years) and patients with cor pulmonale	0.24	0.3
Patients with cardiac decompensation and/or significant liver disease	0.08–0.16	0.1–0.2

[a]To be used only until serum level determinations are available to guide further dosage adjustment.
[b]Doses are designed to achieve a serum concentration of 55 μmol/L in most patients. Lean body weight should be used in obese patients.

Theophylline (cont'd)

Table VI—Theophylline and Its Salts

Dosage Adjustment after Peak Serum Theophylline Measurement

If serum theophylline is:		Directions
Within normal limits	55–110 µmol/L	Maintain dosage if tolerated. Check serum theophylline concentration at 6- to 12-month intervals.[a]
Too high	110–138 µmol/L	Decrease dose by about 10%. Recheck serum theophylline at 48–72 hours. Check serum theophylline concentration at 6- to 12-month intervals.[a]
	138–165 µmol/L	Skip next dose and decrease subsequent doses by 25%. Recheck serum theophylline at 48–72 hours.
	Over 165 µmol/L	Skip next 2 doses and decrease subsequent doses by 50%. Recheck serum theophylline at 48–72 hours.
Too low	42–56 µmol/L	Increase dose by about 25%.[b] Recheck serum theophylline at 48–72 hours. Check serum theophylline concentration at 6- to 12-month intervals.[a]
	28–42 µmol/L	Increase dose by about 25% to the nearest dose increment[b] and recheck serum theophylline for guidance in further dosage adjustment (another increase will probably be needed, but this provides a safety check).

[a] Finer adjustments in dosage may be needed for some patients.
[b] Dividing the daily dose into 3 doses administered at 8-hour intervals may be indicated if symptoms occur repeatedly at the end of a dosing interval.

Infants: Elimination of the drug in children younger than 1 year of age, especially in neonates, generally appears to be reduced. Due to potential for toxicity, use of the drug in children younger than 1 year of age should be carefully considered and, if used, the initial and maintenance dosages (particularly the latter) should be conservative. The maintenance dose and dosing interval must be guided by monitoring of serum theophylline concentrations. It is recommended that serum theophylline concentrations be maintained below 55 µmol/L in neonates and 110 µmol/L in older infants. Therapy with the drug should not be continued unless the drug is well tolerated and clinically beneficial.

Caution in younger children who cannot complain of minor side effects is recommended.

Extended-release Preparations: Although extended-release preparations have been formulated to release the drug at various rates suitable for dosing every 8 to 12, 12 or 24 hours, the actual dosing frequency for a given patient and preparation depends on the patient's individual pharmacokinetic parameters.

Extended-release preparations are not indicated for the relief of acute conditions.

When extended-release preparations are to be administered, some clinicians may recommend that the daily dosage requirement first be established by monitoring serum theophylline concentrations while the patient is receiving a rapidly absorbed dosage form; then, therapy with an extended-release preparation may be started by administering one-half of the total daily dose every 12 hours. When initiating or transferring a patient to once daily extended-release preparations, the manufacturer's specific dosage and administration directions should be followed.

Extended-release preparations should not be chewed or crushed; the contents of extended-release capsules may be mixed with soft food and taken without chewing in patients who have difficulty swallowing solid dosage forms. For administration information with respect to meals, see the pharmacokinetics section.

Dosage adjustments may be based on peak serum theophylline concentrations and the clinical response and tolerance of the patient, as indicated in Table VI.

When adjusting dosage in this manner, it is important that dosage in the previous 48 hours be reasonably typical of the prescribed regimen and that the patient not have missed a dose nor taken an extra dose in this period. It is important that serum levels are obtained at steady state. If laboratory results appear questionable, serum levels should be repeated.

Reviewed 1997

THEOPHYLLINE SOLUTION ℞

Desbergers

Bronchodilator

Supplied: Each 15 mL of red-orange, raspberry-flavored syrup contains: theophylline 80 mg. Energy: 37.1 kJ (8.7 kcal)/5 mL. Alcohol-, bisulfite-, gluten-, lactose-, parabens-, sucrose- and tartrazine-free. Bottles of 500 mL.

THEO-SR® ℞

Rhône-Poulenc Rorer

Theophylline

Bronchodilator

Pharmacology: Theophylline relaxes the smooth muscles of the bronchial airways and pulmonary blood vessels to relieve bronchospasm and increase flow rates and vital capacity. It also produces other actions typical of the xanthine derivatives: coronary vasodilation, diuresis, increase in gastric secretion, and cardiac, cerebral, and skeletal muscle stimulation. The actions of theophylline may be mediated through inhibition of phosphodiesterase and a resultant increase in intracellular cyclic adenosine monophosphate, but the exact mechanism(s) has not been determined. Theophylline distributes in all body compartments. Protein binding accounts for some 50%. Liver is the primary site of metabolism.

The accepted therapeutic serum concentrations range of theophylline are within 55 to 110 µmol/L (10 and 20 mg/L); levels above 110 µmol/L are associated with toxic reactions. The pharmacokinetics of theophylline are influenced by a number of variables such as: age, disease state, smoking, concomitant medication. Therefore, the optimum therapeutic maintenance dose should be determined by individual titration.

Theo-SR is a controlled-release formulation which produces peak blood levels between 4 and 6 hours post-dose. Once the steady state has been achieved, therapeutic blood levels persist for 12 hours in most adult patients.

The percentage of fluctuation in plasma concentrations, on average, is 63%.

Indications: For the symptomatic treatment of reversible bronchospasm associated with asthma, chronic bronchitis, emphysema and related bronchospastic disorders.

Contraindications: Patients with hypersensitivity to xanthines, patients with coronary artery disease where cardiac stimulation might prove harmful, or patients with an active peptic ulcer.

Warnings: In clinical situations where immediate bronchodilation is required, such as status asthmaticus, sustained-release theophylline is not suitable.

Theophylline has a narrow therapeutic index; the margin of safety above therapeutic doses is small.

In patients showing intolerance to theophylline, the therapy should be reassessed.

Dosage schedule in pediatric population has not been established. Use in children under 12 years of age is not recommended.

Theophylline clearance can be affected by various disease states, the age of patient, concomitant use of other medication and lifestyle habits (see Precautions).

Precautions: There is a marked variation in serum levels achieved in different patients, given the same dose of theophylline, resulting from individual differences in the rate of theophylline clearance. This may lead to serious adverse effects in some patients. Dosage regimen should therefore be individualized. The incidence of adverse reactions increases at serum theophylline levels above 82.5 µmol/L (15 mg/L) and levels in excess of 110 µmol/L (20 mg/L) are usually toxic.

Periodic monitoring of serum theophylline levels is recommended in order to assure maximal benefit without excessive risk.

In individuals in whom theophylline plasma clearance is reduced for any reason, even conventional doses of theophylline may result in increased serum levels and potential toxicity.

Reduced theophylline clearance has been documented in the following readily identifiable groups: patients with impaired renal or liver function; patients over 55 years of age, particularly males and those with chronic lung disease; those with cardiac failure from any cause; neonates; those patients taking certain drugs (macrolide antibiotics and cimetidine). Decreased clearance of theophylline may be associated with either influenza immunization or active infection with influenza.

Laboratory monitoring of serum theophylline is especially appropriate in the above individuals in order to maintain appropriate theophylline dosage.

Many patients who require theophylline may exhibit tachycardia due to their underlying disease process so that the cause/effect relationship to elevated serum theophylline concentrations may not be appreciated.

Theophylline products may cause dysrhythmia and/or worsen preexisting arrhythmia and any significant change in cardiac rate and/or rhythm warrants monitoring and further investigation.

Use with caution in patients with severe cardiac disease, severe hypoxemia, hypertension, hyperthyroidism, acute myocardial injury, cor pulmonale, congestive heart failure, liver disease, in the elderly (especially males).

Patients with congestive heart failure frequently have markedly prolonged serum levels with theophylline persisting in serum for long periods following discontinuation of the drug.

Theophylline may occasionally act as a local irritant to the gastrointestinal tract although gastrointestinal symptoms are more commonly centrally mediated and associated with serum drug concentrations over 110 µmol/L.

Theophylline increases gastric secretion; caution should be exercised in patients with a history of peptic ulcer.

Theophylline-SR should not be administered concurrently with other xanthine medications.

Theophylline half-life is shorter in smokers than in nonsmokers. Smokers may require larger or more frequent doses of theophylline.

Although Theo-SR has pharmacokinetic properties similar to other controlled-release theophylline products, it is not possible to ensure interchangeability between different products. Careful clinical monitoring is required when changing from one formulation to another.

The equivalent content of anhydrous theophylline is the active ingredient that determines blood concentration and clinical response. If a change in theophylline product is made and it involves a change in anhydrous theophylline equivalence, the dose should be adjusted accordingly.

Laboratory Test Interactions: Theophylline may cause elevation of urine catecholamines and plasma free fatty acids. This should be taken into consideration when interpreting biochemistry tests.

When plasma levels of theophylline are measured by spectrophotometric methods, coffee, tea, cola beverages, chocolate and acetaminophen contribute to falsely high values.

When high pressure liquid chromatography (HPLC) method is used, plasma theophylline concentration may be falsely increased by caffeine, some cephalosporine and sulfa medications.

Food Interactions: Food does not affect the extent of theophylline absorption but slightly increases the peak plasma of theophylline following a single dose. Therefore, theophylline should be administered consistently with respect to food: either with or without meals.

Pregnancy and *Lactation:* Theophylline crosses the placental barrier; it also passes into breast milk. Safe use of theophylline in pregnancy and in lactation has not been established. The risk of uncontrolled asthma should be balanced against potential effects on the fetus or on the nursing newborn.

Drug Interactions: Theophylline pharmacokinetics are altered by the concurrent use of various drugs as listed in Table I.

Concurrent use of theophylline influences effects of certain drugs, see Table II.

Table I—Theo-SR

Effect of Various Drugs on Theophylline Pharmacokinetics

Drug	Effect on theophylline clearance and elimination half-life
Cimetidine, propranolol, allopurinol, macrolide antibiotics (erythromycin, troleandomycin), oral contraceptives	↑ t½, ↓ clearance
Alkalinizing agents	↑ t½, ↓ clearance
Influenza vaccine	↑ t½, clearance reported to be decreased or no change
Phenytoin, barbiturates, carbamazepine, isoproterenol, rifampin	↓ t½, ↑ clearance
Tobacco	↓ t½, ↑ clearance
Acidifying agents	↓ t½, ↑ clearance

Table II—Theo-SR

Effect of Theophylline on Certain Drugs

Drug	Influence of theophylline
Digitalis glycosides	↑ cardiac effect
Thiazides	↑ diuresis
Nephrotoxic drugs	↑ nephrotoxicity
Lithium	↑ ratio of lithium/creatinine clearance, thus decrease serum lithium
Sympathomimetic amines	↑ toxicity, ↑ CNS stimulation
Coumarin anticoagulants	↓ anticoagulant activity ↑ prothrombin and fibrinogen blood concentrations ↓ prothrombin time
Allopurinol	↓ antihyperuricemic action
Probenecid and pyrazolon derivatives	↓ uricosuric action

Adverse Effects: The most common adverse reactions are gastric irritation, nausea, vomiting, epigastric pain and tremor. These are usually early signs of toxicity; however, with high doses, ventricular arrhythmias or seizures may be the first signs to appear.

Gastrointestinal: nausea, vomiting, epigastric pain, hematemesis, diarrhea, anorexia, intestinal bleeding and reactivation of peptic ulcer.

CNS: headache, irritability, restlessness, insomnia, twitching convulsions and reflex hyperexcitability.

Cardiovascular: palpitations, tachycardia, hypotension, circulatory failure, ventricular arrhythmias, extrasystoles and flushing.

Renal: albuminuria, diuresis and hematuria.

Others: hyperglycemia, tachypnea and inappropriate ADH syndrome.

Overdose: Symptoms: Insomnia, restlessness, mild excitement or irritability and rapid pulse are the early symptoms, which may progress to mild delirium.

Sensory disturbances such as tinnitus or flashes of light are common. Anorexia, nausea and vomiting are frequently early observations of theophylline overdosage.

Fever, diuresis, dehydration and extreme thirst may be seen. Severe poisoning results in bloody, syrup-like coffee-grounds vomitus, tremors, tonic extensor spasm interrupted by clonic convulsions, extrasystoles, quickened respiration, stupor and finally coma. Cardiovascular disorders and respiratory collapse, leading to shock, cyanosis and death follow gross overdosage.

Treatment: Monitoring Serum Theophylline Levels: It is important to note that, following the intake of Theo-SR tablets, the blood theophylline peak levels may not occur until 4 to 6 hours post-ingestion. Moreover, patients ingesting overdoses of sustained-release theophylline formulations may have, after the initial rise in blood theophylline, also a secondary increase in theophylline levels (one report on fatal self-poisoning has attributed this to compacted tablet masses in the gastrointestinal tract). **Therefore, following initial treatment, longer careful clinical and laboratory monitoring is advisable after patient's stabilization.**

If potential oral overdose is established and seizure has not occurred: induce vomiting; administer a cathartic (this is particularly important when a sustained-release preparation has been taken); administer activated charcoal.

If patient is having a seizure: establish an airway; administer oxygen; treat the seizure with i.v. diazepam, 0.1 to 0.2 mg/kg up to 10 mg; monitor vital signs, maintain blood pressure and provide adequate hydration.

Post-seizure coma: maintain airway and oxygenation; if a result of oral medication, follow above recommendations to prevent absorption of drug, but intubation and lavage will have to be performed instead of inducing emesis, and the cathartic and charcoal will need to be introduced via a large bore gastric lavage tube; continue to provide full supportive care and adequate hydration while waiting for drug to be metabolized. In general, the drug is metabolized sufficiently rapidly so as not to warrant consideration of dialysis. However, if serum levels exceed 275 µmol/L (50 mg/L), charcoal hemoperfusion may be indicated.

Dosage: Therapeutic theophylline serum levels are generally in the range of 55 to 110 µmol/L (10 to 20 mg/L). Because of the large intersubject variability, monitoring of plasma theophylline concentrations is extremely important, especially in the initial stages of therapy, and dosage should be individualized (see Precautions). Dosage should be based on lean body mass (ideal body weight).

It is preferable to **monitor peak concentrations** rather than trough concentrations, hence blood samples should be drawn 4 to 6 hours after administration. Steady state is usually achieved within 3 days of initiating therapy.

If dosage increase is not tolerated, dosage should be reduced to previously acceptable level.

Theo-SR scored tablets may be broken in 2 and still retain their sustained-release properties. **The tablets should not be chewed or crushed.**

Adults (including adolescents 12 years and over): The average starting dose is one 200 or 300 mg tablet every 12 hours. Total daily dose should be individually titrated based on the patient's clinical response and/or plasma theophylline level which should be in the range of 55 to 110 µmol/L. Usually the dose is between 600 to 900 mg of anhydrous theophylline per 24 hours. Within any 24 hours, a maximum dose of 13 mg/kg or 900 mg (whichever is less) should not be exceeded.

If the maximum dose is used in chronic therapy, theophylline serum levels should be closely monitored.

Note: Exceptions for elderly patients, patients with relatively low body weight or with severe hepatic, cardiac or renal impairment: the initial starting dose should be 450 mg daily, and dosage adjustment should be based upon theophylline plasma levels.

Doses should be taken with a glass of water. If gastrointestinal irritation is experienced, tablets may be taken consistently with meals.

Food does not affect the extent of theophylline absorption from Theo-SR but slightly increases the peak plasma level of theophylline following a single dose. Therefore, theophylline should be administered consistently with respect to food: either with, or without meals.

Information for the Patient: See Blue Section—Information for the Patient "Theo-SR".

Supplied: Each white, oblong, sustained release tablet, engraved 300 on one side; identified with and scored on the opposite side, contains: theophylline anhydrous 300 mg. Nonmedicinal ingredients: colloidal silicon dioxide, hydroxypropyl cellulose, lactose and magnesium stearate. Tartrazine-free. Bottles of 100.

(Shown in Product Recognition Section)

THIAMINE
General Monograph, CPhA

see VITAMIN B₁

THIAMINE HCl INJECTION
Bioniche

Vitamin B_1

Vitamin

Supplied: Each mL of sterile solution for i.m. or i.v. use contains: thiamine HCl 100 mg. Ampuls of 1 mL, boxes of 10. Store at room temperature (15 to 30°C). Protect from light.

THIAMINE HCl INJECTION USP
Faulding

Vitamin Supplement

Supplied: Each mL contains: thiamine HCl USP 100 mg. Ampuls of 1 mL, packages of 5. Store below 25°C. Protect from light.

THIOTEPA
Wyeth-Ayerst

Cytotoxic Agent

Pharmacology: Thiotepa is a cytotoxic agent of the polyfunctional alkylating type (more than one reactive ethylenimine group) related chemically and pharmacologically to nitrogen mustard. Its radiomimetic action is believed to occur through the release of ethylenimine radicals which, like irradiation, disrupt the bonds of DNA. One of the principal bond disruptions is initiated by alkylation of guanine at the N-7 position, which severs the linkage between the purine base and the sugar and liberates alkylated guanines.

On the basis of tissue concentration studies, it is reported that thiotepa has no differential affinity for neoplasms. Thiotepa and triethylenephosphoramide (TEPA) in urine each accounts for less than 2% of the administered dose.

Indications: Thiotepa has been tried with varying results in the palliation of a wide variety of neoplastic diseases. However, the most consistent results have been seen in the following tumors: adenocarcinoma of the breast; adenocarcinoma of the ovary; for controlling intracavitary effusions secondary to diffuse or localized neoplastic diseases of various serosal cavities; and for the treatment of superficial papillary carcinoma of the urinary bladder. While now largely superseded by other treatments, thiotepa has been effective against other lymphomas, such as lymphosarcoma and Hodgkin's disease.

Contraindications: Therapy is probably contraindicated in cases of existing hepatic, renal or bone marrow damage. However, if the need outweighs the risk in such patients, thiotepa may be used in low dosage, and accompanied by hepatic, renal and hemopoietic function tests.

Thiotepa is contraindicated in patients with a known hypersensitivity (allergy) to this preparation.

Warnings: *Pregnancy:* The administration of thiotepa to pregnant women is not recommended except in cases where the benefit to be gained outweighs the risk of teratogenicity involved.

Death has occurred after intravesical administration, caused by bone-marrow depression from systemically absorbed drug.

Thiotepa is highly toxic to the hematopoietic system. A rapidly falling white blood cell or platelet count indicates the necessity for discontinuing or reducing the dosage of thiotepa. Weekly blood and platelet counts are recommended during therapy and for at least 3 weeks after therapy has been discontinued.

Thiotepa is a polyfunctional alkylating agent, capable of cross-linking the DNA within a cell and changing its nature. The replication of the cell is, therefore, altered, and thiotepa may be described as mutagenic. An in vitro study has shown that it causes chromosomal aberrations of the chromatid type and that the frequency of induced aberrations increases with the age of the subject.

Like many alkylating agents, thiotepa has been reported to be carcinogenic when administered to laboratory animals. Carcinogenicity is shown most clearly in studies using mice but there is strong circumstantial evidence of carcinogenicity in man. In patients treated with thiotepa, cases of myelodysplastic syndromes and acute nonlymphocytic leukemia have been reported.

Precautions: The serious complication of excessive thiotepa therapy, or sensitivity to the effects of thiotepa, is bone

Thiotepa (cont'd)

marrow depression. If proper precautions are not observed thiotepa may cause leukopenia, thrombocytopenia and anemia. Death from septicemia and hemorrhage has occurred as a direct result of hematopoietic depression by thiotepa.

The patient should notify the physician in the case of any sign of bleeding (epistaxis, easy bruising, change in color of urine, black stool) or infection (fever, chills) or for possible pregnancy to patient or partner. Effective contraception should be used during thiotepa therapy if either the patient or the partner is of childbearing potential. Thiotepa impaired fertility, inhibited implantation and interfered with spermatogenesis in animal studies. There are no adequate and well-controlled studies in pregnant women. If thiotepa is used during pregnancy, or if pregnancy occurs during thiotepa therapy, the patient and partner should be apprised of the potential hazard to the fetus.

It is not advisable to combine simultaneously or sequentially cancer chemotherapeutic agents or a cancer chemotherapeutic agent and a therapeutic modality having the same mechanism of action. Therefore, thiotepa combined with other alkylating agents such as nitrogen mustard or cyclophosphamide or thiotepa combined with irradiation would serve to intensify toxicity rather than to enhance therapeutic response. If these agents must follow each other, it is important that recovery from the first agent, as indicated by white blood cell count, be complete before therapy with the second agent is instituted.

The most reliable guide to thiotepa toxicity is the white blood cell count. If this falls to 3 000/mm³ or less, the dose should be discontinued. Another good index of thiotepa toxicity is the platelet count; if this falls to 150 000/mm³, therapy should be discontinued. Red blood cell count is a less accurate indicator of thiotepa toxicity. If the drug is used in patients with hepatic or renal damage (see Contraindications), regular assessment of hepatic and renal function tests are indicated.

Other drugs which are known to produce bone marrow depression should be avoided.

There is no known antidote for overdosage with thiotepa. Transfusions of whole blood or platelets or leukocytes have proved beneficial to the patient in combatting hematopoietic toxicity.

Lactation: It is not known whether thiotepa is excreted in human milk. Because many drugs are excreted in human milk and because of the potential for tumorigenicity shown for thiotepa in animal studies, a decision should be made whether to discontinue nursing or to discontinue the drug, taking into account the importance of the drug to the mother.

Children: Safety and effectiveness in children have not been established.

Adverse Effects: In addition to its effect on the blood-forming elements (see Warnings and Precautions), thiotepa may cause other adverse reactions.

General: fatigue, weakness. Febrile reaction and discharge from a s.c. lesion may occur as the result of breakdown of tumor tissue.

Hypersensitivity Reactions: Allergic Reactions: rash, urticaria, laryngeal edema, asthma, anaphylactic shock, wheezing.

Local Reactions: contact dermatitis, pain at the injection site.

Gastrointestinal: nausea, vomiting, abdominal pain, anorexia.

Renal: dysuria, urinary retention. There have been rare reports of chemical cystitis or hemorrhagic cystitis following intravesical, but not parenteral administration of thiotepa.

Respiratory: Prolonged apnea has been reported when succinylcholine was administered prior to surgery, following combined use of thiotepa and other anticancer agents. It was theorized that this was caused by decrease of pseudocholinesterase activity caused by the anticancer drugs.

Neurologic: dizziness, headache, blurred vision.

Skin: dermatitis, alopecia. Skin depigmentation has been reported following topical use.

Special Senses: conjunctivitis.

Reproductive: amenorrhea, interference with spermatogenesis.

Overdose: Symptoms and Treatment: Hematopoietic toxicity can occur following overdose, manifested by a decrease in the white cell count and/or platelets. Red blood cell count is a less accurate indicator of thiotepa toxicity. Bleeding manifestations may develop. The patient may become more vulnerable to infection, and less able to combat such infection.

Dosages within and minimally above the recommended therapeutic doses have been associated with potentially life-threatening hematopoietic toxicity. Thiotepa has a toxic effect on the hematopoietic system that is dose related.

Thiotepa is dialyzable.

There is no known antidote for overdosage with thiotepa. Transfusions of whole blood or platelets have proven beneficial to the patient in combatting hematopoietic toxicity.

Dosage: Parenteral routes of administration are most reliable since absorption of thiotepa from the gastrointestinal tract is variable.

Since thiotepa is nonvesicant, i.v. doses may be given directly and rapidly without need for slow drip or large volumes of diluent.

Dosage must be carefully individualized. A slow response to thiotepa may be deceptive and may occasion unwarranted frequency of administration with subsequent signs of toxicity. After maximum benefit is obtained by initial therapy, it is necessary to continue the patient on maintenance therapy (1 to 4 week intervals). In order to continue optimal effect, maintenance doses should be no more frequent than weekly in order to preserve correlation between dose and blood counts.

Initial and Maintenance Doses: Initially the higher dose in the given range is commonly administered. The maintenance dose should be adjusted weekly on the basis of pretreatment control blood counts and subsequent blood counts.

I.V. Administration: Thiotepa may be given by rapid i.v. administration in doses of 0.3 to 0.4 mg/kg. Doses should be given at 1 to 4 week intervals.

For conversion of mg/kg of body weight to mg/m² of body surface or the reverse, a ratio of 1:30 is given as a guideline. The conversion factor varies between 1:20 and 1:40 depending on age and body build.

Intracavitary Administration: The dosage recommended is 0.6 to 0.8 mg/kg. Administration is usually effected through the same tubing which is used to remove the fluid from the cavity involved.

Intravesical Administration: Patients with papillary carcinoma of the bladder are dehydrated for 8 to 12 hours prior to treatment. Then 60 mg of thiotepa in 30 to 60 mL of 0.9% sodium chloride injection is instilled into the bladder by catheter. For maximum effect, the solution should be retained for 2 hours.

If the patient finds it impossible to retain 60 mL for 2 hours, the dose may be given in a volume of 30 mL. If desired, the patient may be positioned every 15 minutes for maximum area contact. The usual course of treatment is once a week for 4 weeks. The course may be repeated if necessary, but second and third courses must be given with caution since bone marrow depression may be increased. Deaths have occurred after intravesical administration, caused by bone marrow depression from systemically absorbed drug.

Stability and Storage: When in its original powder form, thiotepa must be stored in the refrigerator at 2 to 8°C. Protect from light.

Reconstituted Solutions: The powder should be reconstituted preferably in Sterile Water for Injection. The amount of diluent most often used is 1.5 mL resulting in a drug concentration of 5 mg in each 0.5 mL of solution. The reconstituted solution is hypotonic and should be further diluted with 0.9% sodium chloride injection before use.

When reconstituted with Sterile Water for Injection, solutions of thiotepa should be stored in a refrigerator and used within 8 hours. Reconstituted solutions further diluted with 0.9% sodium chloride injection should be used immediately.

In order to eliminate haze, solutions should be filtered through a 0.22 μ filter* prior to administration. Filtering does not alter solution potency. Reconstituted solutions should be clear. Solutions that remain opaque or precipitate after filtration should not be used.

*Polysulfone membrane (Gelman's Sterile Aerodisc, Single Use) or triton-free mixed ester of cellulose/PVC (Millipore's Millex-GS Filter Unit).

Parenteral drug products should be inspected visually for particulate matter and discoloration prior to administration, whenever solution and container permit.

Larger volumes are usually employed for intracavitary use, i.v. drip or perfusion therapy. The 1.5 mL reconstituted preparation may be added to larger volumes of 0.9% sodium chloride injection. Reconstituted solutions should be clear to slightly opaque but solutions that are grossly opaque or precipitated should not be used.

Parenteral Products: The actual withdrawable quantities and concentration achieved are illustrated in Table I.

Special Instructions: Preparation and Administration Precautions: Thiotepa is a cytotoxic anticancer drug and as with other potentially toxic compounds, caution should be exercised in handling and preparation of thiotepa. Skin reactions associated with accidental exposure to thiotepa may occur. The use of gloves is recommended. If thiotepa solution contacts the skin, immediately wash the skin thoroughly with soap and water. If thiotepa contacts mucous membranes, the membranes should be flushed thoroughly with water.

Procedures for proper handling and disposal of anticancer drugs should be considered. Several guidelines on this subject have been published. There is no general agreement that all of the procedures recommended in the guidelines are necessary or appropriate.

Trained personnel should reconstitute thiotepa in a designated area. Adequate protective gloves and goggles should be worn and the work surface should be covered with disposable plastic-backed absorbent paper. Thiotepa is not vesicant and should not cause harm if it comes in contact with the skin. It should, of course, be washed off with water immediately. Any transient stinging may be treated with a bland cream.

The cytotoxic preparation should not be handled by pregnant staff.

Supplied: Vials of 15 mg (sterile cryodesiccated powder), boxes of 10.

Reviewed 1998

Table I—Thiotepa

Actual Withdrawable Quantities and Concentration

Label Claim (mg/vial)	Actual Content (mg/vial)	Amount of Diluent to be Added (mL)	Approximate Withdrawable Volume (mL)	Approximate Withdrawable Amount (mg/mL)	Approximate Reconstituted Concentration (mg/mL)
15.0	15.6	1.5	1.4	14.7	10.4

3TC® Pr

Glaxo Wellcome

Lamivudine

Antiretroviral Agent

Pharmacology: Lamivudine is a potent, selective inhibitor of HIV-1 and HIV-2 replication in vitro. Lamivudine is the (-) enantiomer of a dideoxy analogue of cytidine. The sugar ring of lamivudine is novel in that it contains a sulphur at the 3′ position as a second heteroatom. Intracellularly, lamivudine is phosphorylated to its active 5′-triphosphate metabolite (lamivudine triphosphate or L-TP), which has an intracellular half-life of approximately 10.5 to 15.5 hours. The principal mode of action of lamivudine is inhibition of HIV reverse transcription via viral DNA chain termination. In addition, L-TP inhibits both the RNA- and DNA-dependent DNA polymerase activities of reverse transcriptase (RT), and is a weak inhibitor of mammalian α, β, and γ DNA polymerases.

Pharmacokinetics: The pharmacokinetic properties of lamivudine have been studied in asymptomatic, HIV-infected adult patients after administration of single oral, multiple oral and i.v. doses ranging from 0.25 to 10 mg/kg. After oral administration of 2 mg/kg, the peak plasma lamivudine concentration (C_{max}) was 1.5 ± 0.5 μg/mL (mean$\pm$S.D.) and half-life was 2.6 ± 0.5 hours. There were no significant differences in half-life across the range of single doses (0.25 to 8 mg/kg). The area under the plasma concentration versus time curve (AUC) and C_{max} increased in proportion to dose over the range from 0.25 to 10 mg/kg.

Lamivudine is well absorbed from the gut, and the bioavailability of oral lamivudine in adults is normally between 80 and 85%. Following oral administration, the mean time (t_{max}) to maximal serum concentrations (C_{max}) is about 1 hour.

No dose adjustment is needed when co-administered with food as lamivudine bioavailability is not altered, although a delay in t_{max} and reduction in C_{max} have been observed. Lamivudine exhibits linear pharmacokinetics over the therapeutic dose range and displays limited binding to the major plasma protein albumin.

Coadministration of zidovudine results in a 13% increase in AUC_∞ for zidovudine and a 28% increase in peak plasma levels. This is not considered to be of significance to patient safety and therefore no dosage adjustments are necessary.

Indications: Lamivudine in combination with zidovudine is indicated for the treatment of HIV-infection when therapy is warranted based on clinical and/or immunological evidence of disease progression. This indication is based on the analysis of surrogate endpoints. At present, there are no results from controlled trials evaluating the effect of lamivudine plus zidovudine on clinical progression of HIV infection, such as the incidence of opportunistic infections or survival.

Contraindications: In patients with previously demonstrated clinically significant hypersensitivity to any of the components of the products.

Warnings: Pancreatitis in Pediatric Patients: **In pediatric patients with a history of pancreatitis or other significant risk factors for the development of pancreatitis, the combination of lamivudine and zidovudine should be used with extreme caution and only if there is no satisfactory alternative therapy. Treatment with lamivudine should be stopped immediately if clinical signs, symptoms, or laboratory abnormalities suggestive of pancreatitis occur (see Adverse Effects).**

Lactic Acidosis/Severe Hepatomegaly With Steatosis: Lactic acidosis and severe hepatomegaly with steatosis, including fatal cases, have been reported with the use of antiretroviral nucleoside analogues alone or in combination, including lamivudine, in the treatment of HIV infection. A majority of these cases have been in women. Caution should be exercised when administering lamivudine to any patient, and particularly to those with known risk factors for liver disease. Treatment with lamivudine should be suspended in any patient who develops clinical or laboratory findings suggestive of lactic acidosis or hepatotoxicity.

The safety profile of combination therapy with lamivudine and zidovudine reflects the individual safety profile of each component. The complete prescribing information for zidovudine should be consulted before combination therapy with lamivudine and zidovudine is initiated.

Precautions: General: Patients receiving lamivudine or any other antiretroviral therapy may continue to develop opportunistic infections and other complications of HIV infection. Therefore, patients should remain under close observation by physicians experienced in the treatment of patients with HIV-associated diseases.

Patients should be advised that current antiretroviral therapy, including lamivudine, has not been proven to reduce the risk of transmission of HIV to others through sexual contact or blood contamination.

Diabetic patients should be advised that an adult dose of lamivudine oral solution contains 3 g of sucrose.

Patients should be advised that lamivudine oral solution contains alcohol.

Pancreatitis in Pediatric Patients: Pediatric patients with a history of pancreatitis or known risk factors for the development of pancreatitis (e.g., concurrent treatment with a drug known to cause pancreatitis such as i.v. pentamidine) should be followed closely while on combination therapy with lamivudine and zidovudine. Treatment with lamivudine should be stopped immediately if clinical signs or symptoms (e.g., nausea, vomiting, abdominal pain) or if abnormalities in laboratory values (hyperamylasemia, rising triglyceride level, decreasing serum calcium) suggestive of pancreatitis occur (see Adverse Effects).

Patients with Impaired Renal Function: Patients with impaired renal function may be at a greater risk of toxicity from lamivudine due to decreased renal clearance of the drug. Consideration should be given to appropriate reduction in the dose of lamivudine (see Dosage).

Patients Coinfected With Hepatitis B Virus: Clinical trials and marketed use of lamivudine have shown that some patients with chronic hepatitis B virus (HBV) disease may experience clinical or laboratory evidence of recurrent hepatitis upon discontinuation of lamivudine, which may have more severe consequences in patients with decompensated liver disease. If lamivudine is discontinued in a patient with HIV and HBV coinfection, periodic monitoring of both liver function tests and markers of HBV replication should be considered.

Children: There are no data on the use of lamivudine in combination with zidovudine in pediatric patients (see Pharmacokinetics).

Pregnancy: The safety of lamivudine in human pregnancy has not been established. Reproductive studies in animals have not shown evidence of teratogenicity, and showed no effect on male or female fertility. There was some evidence of early embryolethality when administered to pregnant rabbits at exposure levels comparable to those achieved in man. Lamivudine crosses the placenta in animals but there is no information on placental transfer in humans.

Because animal reproduction studies are not always predictive of the human response, administration during pregnancy should only be considered if the expected benefit outweighs any possible risk.

To monitor maternal-fetal outcomes of pregnant women exposed to lamivudine, an Antiretroviral Pregnancy Registry has been established. Physicians are encouraged to register patients by calling Glaxo Wellcome's Drug Surveillance Department (1-800-668-6051).

Lactation: It is not known if lamivudine is excreted in human breast milk. A study in lactating rats showed that, following oral administration, lamivudine was excreted in the milk.

Because of the uncertainties related to the transmission of the virus and to excretion of lamivudine in breast milk, it is advisable to caution mothers against breast-feeding.

Drug Interactions: Zidovudine plasma levels are not significantly altered when co-administered with lamivudine. Zidovudine has no effect on the pharmacokinetics of lamivudine (see Pharmacology).

Administration of trimethoprim, a constituent of co-trimoxazole causes a 40% increase in lamivudine plasma levels. However, unless the patient has renal impairment, no dosage adjustment of lamivudine is necessary. Lamivudine has no effect on the pharmacokinetics of co-trimoxazole. Administration of co-trimoxazole with the lamivudine/zidovudine combination in patients with renal impairment should be carefully assessed.

The possibility of interactions with other drugs administered concurrently should be considered, particularly when the main route of elimination is renal.

Information for the Patient: Lamivudine is not a cure for HIV infection and patients may continue to experience illnesses associated with HIV infection, including opportunistic infections. Treatment with lamivudine has not been shown to reduce the frequency of such illnesses and patients should remain under the care of a physician when using lamivudine. Patients should be advised that the use of lamivudine has not been shown to reduce the risk of transmission of HIV to others through sexual contact or blood contamination.

Patients should be advised that the long-term effects of lamivudine are unknown at this time.

Lamivudine tablets and oral solution are for oral ingestion only.

Patients should be advised of the importance of taking lamivudine exactly as it is prescribed.

Parents or guardians should be advised to monitor pediatric patients for signs and symptoms of pancreatitis.

Adverse Effects: The combination of lamivudine 150 mg b.i.d. with zidovudine 600 mg/day is not associated with a significant change in the frequencies of clinical or laboratory adverse events from those associated with zidovudine.

Adults: The most frequent clinical adverse events (≥5% frequency) reported during therapy with lamivudine 150 mg b.i.d. plus zidovudine 600 mg/day compared with zidovudine are listed in Table I.

Other clinical adverse events reported in controlled clinical trials in association with lamivudine 150 mg b.i.d. plus zidovudine 600 mg/day in at least 1% of patients were:

Gastrointestinal: gastrointestinal gas (4%), abdominal discomfort and pain (3%), abdominal distention (3%), gastrointestinal discomfort and pain (3%), dyspepsia (2%), hyposalivation (2%), oral ulceration (1%).

Neurological: sleep disorders (4%), taste disturbances (1%), mood disorders (1%).

Musculoskeletal: muscle pain (2%), muscle atrophy/weakness/tiredness (1%).

Skin: skin rashes (1%), pruritus (1%); sweating (1%).

Other: breathing disorders (2%), temperature regulation disturbance (1%), pain (2%), general signs and symptoms (1%), sexual function disturbances (1%).

Pancreatitis was observed in 3 of 656 adult patients (<0.5%) in controlled clinical trials. One patient received lamivudine 150 mg b.i.d. plus zidovudine and 2 patients received lamivudine 300 mg b.i.d. plus zidovudine.

Six percent of patients treated with lamivudine 150 mg b.i.d. plus zidovudine 200 mg t.i.d. in controlled clinical trials permanently discontinued treatment due to an investigator-attributed drug-related adverse event, compared with 7% of patients receiving monotherapy with zidovudine and 13% of patients receiving zidovudine plus zalcitabine. The most frequent adverse events necessitating such permanent discontinuation of therapy with lamivudine 150 mg b.i.d. plus zidovudine 200 mg t.i.d. were nausea (2%), malaise and fatigue (1%), and anemia (1%).

Table I—3TC

Most Frequent Clinical Adverse Events (≥5% Frequency) Reported in Four Controlled Clinical Trials

Adverse Event	3TC 150 mg b.i.d. Plus Zidovudine (n=251) %	Zidovudine (n=230) %
Body as a Whole		
Headache	35	27
Malaise and fatigue	27	23
Fever or chills	10	12
Digestive		
Nausea	33	29
Diarrhea	18	22
Nausea and vomiting	13	12
Anorexia and/or decreased appetite	10	7
Abdominal pain	9	11
Abdominal cramps	6	3
Dyspepsia	5	5
Nervous		
Neuropathy	12	10
Dizziness	10	4
Insomnia and other sleep disorders	11	7
Depressive disorders	9	4
Respiratory		
Nasal signs and symptoms	20	11
Cough	18	13
Skin and Appendages		
Skin rashes	9	6
Musculoskeletal		
Musculoskeletal pain	12	10
Myalgia	8	6
Arthralgia	5	5

The frequencies of selected laboratory abnormalities (Grades 3 and 4) during therapy are listed in Table II.

Table II—3TC

Percentages of Patients with Selected Laboratory Abnormalities (Grades 3 and 4) During Therapy in Four Controlled Clinical Trials in Patients with Normal Baseline Values

Test (Abnormal Level)	3TC 150 mg b.i.d. Plus Zidovudine % (n)	Zidovudine % (n)
Neutropenia (ANC<750/mm^3)	4.9 (202)	4.0 (196)
Anemia (Hgb<8.0 g/dL)	2.9 (239)	1.8 (218)
ALT (>5.0×ULN)	2.4 (204)	1.6 (187)
AST (>5.0×ULN)	1.9 (215)	1.0 (194)
Thrombocytopenia (<50,000/mm^3)	0.4 (236)	0.4 (220)
Bilirubin (>2.5×ULN)	0.4 (235)	0.4 (220)
Amylase (>2.0×ULN)	2.8 (71)	0 (119)

Legend: ULN=Upper Limit of Normal.
n=Number of patients assessed.
ANC=Absolute Neutrophil Count.
Hgb=Hemoglobin.

Children: No double-blind, controlled clinical trials have been done to assess the incidences of adverse events associated with therapy with lamivudine in pediatric patients. However, clinical adverse events are available from pediatric patients in one open-label, uncontrolled Phase I/II clinical study. Approximately 81% of these patients had received previous antiretroviral therapy with a median duration of 132 weeks. The most frequent clinical adverse events (≥5% frequency) during therapy with lamivudine in pediatric patients receiving doses ranging from 1 to 20 mg/kg/day are listed in Table III (on following page).

Seven percent of pediatric patients treated with lamivudine 4 mg/kg b.i.d. discontinued treatment due to an investigator-attributed drug-related adverse event. The most frequent adverse events necessitating discontinuation of therapy were pancreatitis (6%), neuropathy (2%) and psychomotor disorders (2%).

Of pediatric patients (age range, 4.8 months to 17 years) enrolled in this open-label, dose-escalation study (A2002), 14 patients (14%) developed clinical pancreatitis while receiving monotherapy with lamivudine. All 14 pediatric patients had previously received antiretroviral therapy and 4 patients had experienced a previous episode of pancreatitis.

3TC (cont'd)

Table III—3TC

Most Frequent Clinical Adverse Events (≥5% Frequency) Reported in Association with 3TC in an Uncontrolled Phase I/II Clinical Trial in 97 Pediatric Patients

Adverse Event	Frequency (%)
Gastrointestinal	
Feeding problems	19
Pancreatitis	14
Abdominal discomfort and pain	10
Diarrhea	8
Neurological	
Psychomotor disturbances	15
Headache	10
Neuropathy	6
Sleep disorders	6
Lower Respiratory	
Cough	8
Chest sounds	7
Pneumonia	6
Breathing disorders	5
Upper Respiratory	
Nasal signs and symptoms	7
Ear, nose and throat infection	6
Sinusitis	5
Other	
Fever and chills	9
Malaise and fatigue	8
Musculoskeletal pain	8
Spleen disorders	7
Lymphatic signs and symptoms	6
Fungal Infection	5
Skin rashes	5

No therapy-naive pediatric patient receiving lamivudine developed pancreatitis. Of 47 pediatric patients (age range, 3 months to 18 years) enrolled in an open-label evaluation of lamivudine/didanosine, lamivudine/zidovudine, and lamivudine/zidovudine/didanosine, 7 patients (15%) who received lamivudine in combination with didanosine or didanosine/zidovudine developed pancreatitis. Paresthesias and peripheral neuropathies were reported in 13 patients (13%) in study A2002 and resulted in treatment discontinuation in 3 patients (see Warnings).

The frequencies of laboratory abnormalities in these pediatric patients are listed in Table IV.

Table IV—3TC

Frequencies of Selected Laboratory Abnormalities in an Uncontrolled Phase I/II Clinical Trial of 3TC in 97 Pediatric Patients

Test (Abnormal Level)	Patients with Normal Baselines % (n)	Patients with Abnormal Baselines % (n)
Neutropenia (ANC<750/mm³)	22 (55)	45 (33)
Anemia (Hgb<8.0 g/dL)	2 (50)	24 (46)
Thrombocytopenia (platelets<40 000/mm³)	0 (68)	25 (12)
ALT (>5.0×ULN)	4 (51)	29 (42)
AST (>5.0×ULN)	0 (29)	19 (57)
Amylase (>2.0×ULN)	3 (69)	23 (13)

Legend: ULN=Upper Limit of Normal.
n=Number of patients assessed.
ANC=Absolute Neutrophil Count.
Hgb=Hemoglobin.

Postmarketing Experience: The following additional adverse experiences have been reported in postmarketing experience without regard to causality: Body as a Whole: anaphylaxis, weakness.

Endocrine/Metabolic: hyperglycemia; lactic acidosis and hepatic steatosis (see Warnings).

Musculoskeletal: muscle disorders including rarely rhabdomyolosis.

Nervous: peripheral neuropathy.

Skin: pruritus, rash, urticaria.

Other: alopecia.

Overdose: Symptoms and Treatment: There is no known antidote for lamivudine. Lamivudine has very low acute toxicity in laboratory animals. The maximum tolerated dose in the mouse and rat is in excess of 4 000 mg/kg/day by the oral route (approximately 65 and 130 times the exposure due to the recommended adult dose based on body surface area comparisons).

One case of acute overdose in an adult ingesting 6 g of lamivudine was reported; there were no clinical signs or symptoms noted and hematologic tests remained normal. One other adult patient in error ingested lamivudine 1 200 mg/day plus zidovudine 1 200 mg/day for approximately 2 weeks; he had a Grade 3 decrease in absolute neutrophil count that resolved upon reduction of doses of lamivudine and zidovudine. In Phase I studies, lamivudine was administered at doses up to 20 mg/kg/day (i.e., approximately 5 times the usual recommended dose in adults) without serious consequences. It is not known whether lamivudine can be removed by peritoneal dialysis or hemodialysis.

Dosage: Adults and Adolescents: The recommended oral dose of lamivudine for adults and adolescents who are at least 12 years old is 150 mg twice daily, administered with zidovudine 600 mg daily in 3 divided doses.

Dose Adjustment: Patients with impaired renal function have increases in C_{max} and half-life of lamivudine with diminishing creatinine clearance. In addition, apparent total oral clearance of lamivudine decreases as creatinine clearance decreases. Doses of lamivudine may be adjusted, as shown in Table V, in accordance with creatinine clearance in adults.

For adults with low body weights (less than 50 kg), the recommended oral dose of lamivudine is 2 mg/kg twice daily administered in combination with zidovudine.

The dose used for pediatric patients in one study (A2005), was 4 mg/kg twice daily (up to a maximum of 150 mg twice a day) administered with zidovudine 180 mg/m² every 6 hours (720 mg/m²/day) (see Pharmacology and Precautions).

Table V—3TC

Adjustment of Dosage of 3TC in Accordance with Creatinine Clearance

Creatinine Clearance (mL/min)	Recommended Dosage
≥50	150 mg twice daily
30–50	150 mg once daily
15–29	150 mg first dose, then 100 mg once daily
5–14	150 mg first dose, then 50 mg once daily
<5	50 mg first dose, then 25 mg once daily

Information for the Patient: See Blue Section—Information for the Patient "3TC".

Supplied: Oral Solution: Each mL of colorless to pale yellow, strawberry-banana flavored, clear liquid contains: lamivudine 10 mg. Nonmedicinal ingredients: artificial strawberry and banana flavors, citric acid (anhydrous), edetate disodium, ethanol (6% v/v), methylparaben, propylene glycol, propylparaben, and sucrose. Plastic bottles of 240 mL. Store between 2 and 25°C.

Tablets: Each, white, modified diamond-shaped, film-coated tablet, imprinted with GX CJ7 on one face, contains: lamivudine 150 mg. Nonmedicinal ingredients: hydroxypropyl methylcellulose, magnesium stearate, microcrystalline cellulose, polyethylene glycol, polysorbate 80, sodium starch glycollate and titanium dioxide. Plastic bottles of 60. Store between 2 and 30°C.

(Shown in Product Recognition Section)

Reviewed 1999

THROMBATE III®

Bayer

Antithrombin III (Human)

Anticoagulant

Pharmacology: Antithrombin III (AT-III), an alpha$_2$-glycoprotein of molecular weight 58 000, is normally present in human plasma at a concentration of approximately 12.5 mg/dL and is the major plasma inhibitor of thrombin. Inactivation of thrombin by AT-III occurs by formation of a covalent bond resulting in an inactive 1:1 stoichiometric complex between the two, involving an interaction of the active serine of thrombin and an arginine reactive site on AT-III. AT-III is also capable of inactivating other components of the coagulation cascade including factors IXa, Xa, XIa, and XIIa, as well as plasmin.

The neutralization rate of serine proteases by AT-III proceeds slowly in the absence of heparin, but is greatly accelerated in the presence of heparin. As the therapeutic antithrombotic effect in vivo of heparin is mediated by AT-IIII, heparin is ineffective in the absence or near absence of AT-III.

The prevalence of the hereditary deficiency of AT-III is estimated to be 1 per 2 000 to 5 000 in the general population. The pattern of inheritance is autosomal dominant. In affected individuals, spontaneous episodes of thrombosis and pulmonary embolism may be associated with AT-III levels of 40–60% of normal. These episodes usually appear after the age of 20, the risk increasing with age and in association with surgery, pregnancy and delivery. The frequency of thromboembolic events in hereditary antithrombin III (AT-III) deficiency during pregnancy has been reported to be 70% and several studies of the beneficial use of antithrombin III (human) concentrates during pregnancy in women with hereditary deficiency have been reported. In many cases, however, no precipitating factor can be identified for venous thrombosis or pulmonary embolism. Greater than 85% of individuals with hereditary AT-III deficiency have had at least one thrombotic episode by the age of 50 years. In about 60% of patients thrombosis is recurrent. Clinical signs of pulmonary embolism occur in 40% of affected individuals. In some individuals, treatment with oral anticoagulants leads to an increase in the endogenous levels of AT-III, and treatment with oral anticoagulants may be effective in the prevention of thrombosis in such individuals.

In clinical studies of Thrombate III conducted in 10 asymptomatic subjects with hereditary deficiency at AT-III, the mean in vivo recovery of AT-III was 1.6% per unit per kg administered based on immunologic AT-III assays, and 1.4% per unit per kg administered based on functional AT-III assays. The mean 50% disappearance time (the time to fall to 50% of the peak plasma level following an initial administration) was approximately 22 hours and the biologic half-life was 2.5 days based on immunologic assays and 3.8 days based on functional assays of AT-III. These values are similar to the half-life for radiolabeled antithrombin III (human) reported in the literature of 2.8 to 4.8 days.

In clinical studies of Thrombate III, none of 13 patients with hereditary AT-III deficiency and histories of thromboembolism treated prophylactically on 16 separate occasions with Thrombate III for high thrombotic risk situations (11 surgical procedures, 5 deliveries) developed a thrombotic complication. Heparin was also administered in 3 of the 11 surgical procedures and all 5 deliveries. Eight patients with hereditary AT-III deficiency were treated with Thrombate III as well as heparin for major thrombotic or thromboembolic complications, with 7 patients recovering. Treatment with Thrombate III reversed heparin resistance in two patients with hereditary AT-III deficiency being treated for thrombosis or thromboembolism.

During clinical investigation of Thrombate III, none of 12 subjects monitored for a median of 8 months (range 2 to 19 months) after receiving Thrombate III, became antibody positive to human immunodeficiency virus (HIV-1). None of 14 subjects monitored for ≥3 months demonstrated any evidence of hepatitis B, or hepatitis C.

Indications: For the treatment of patients with hereditary antithrombin III deficiency in connection with surgical or obstetrical procedures or when they suffer from thromboembolism.

Subjects with AT-III deficiency should be informed about the risk of thrombosis in connection with pregnancy and surgery and about the inheritance of the disease.

Diagnosis: See Precautions.

Contraindications: None known.

Warnings: This product is prepared from pooled human plasma which may contain the causative agents of hepatitis and other viral diseases. Prescribed manufacturing procedures utilized at the plasma collection centres, plasma testing laboratories and the fractionation facilities are designed to reduce the risk of transmitting viral infection. However, the risk of viral infectivity from this product cannot be totally eliminated. Each unit used in the manufacture of this product has been found to have an alanine aminotransferase (ALT) level less than two times the upper limit of normal for the test. Thrombate III has been heat-treated in solution at 60°C±0.5°C for not less than 10 hours in order to reduce the potential for transmission of infectious agents.

Individuals who receive infusions of blood or plasma products may develop signs and/or symptoms of some viral infections, particularly hepatitis C.

The anticoagulant effect of heparin is enhanced by concurrent treatment with antithrombin III (human) in patients with hereditary AT-III deficiency. Thus, in order to avoid bleeding, reduced dosage of heparin is recommended during treatment with antithrombin III (human).

Precautions: General: 1. Administer within 3 hours after reconstitution. Do not refrigerate after reconstitution.

2. Administer only by the i.v. route. 3. Antithrombin III (human) should be given alone, without mixing with other agents or diluting solutions. 4. Product administration and handling of the needles must be done with caution. Percutaneous puncture with a needle contaminated with blood can transmit infectious virus including HIV (AIDS) and hepatitis. Obtain immediate medical attention if injury occurs.

Place needles in sharps container after single use. Discard all equipment including any reconstituted product in accordance with biohazard procedures.

Diagnosis: The diagnosis of hereditary antithrombin III (AT-III) deficiency should be based on a clear family history of venous thrombosis as well as decreased plasma AT-III levels, and the exclusion of acquired deficiency.

AT-III in plasma may be measured by amidolytic assays using synthetic chromogenic substrates, by clotting assays, or by immunoassays. The latter does not detect all hereditary AT-III deficiencies.

The AT-III level in neonates of parents with hereditary AT-III deficiency should be measured immediately after birth. (Fatal neonatal thromboembolism, such as aortic thrombi in children of women with hereditary antithrombin III deficiency, has been reported.)

Plasma levels of AT-III are lower in neonates than adults, averaging approximately 60% in normal term infants. AT-III levels in premature infants may be much lower. Low plasma AT-III levels, especially in a premature infant, therefore, do not necessarily indicate hereditary deficiency. It is recommended that testing and treatment with antithrombin III (human), of neonates be discussed with an expert on coagulation.

It is recommended that AT-III plasma levels be monitored during the treatment period.

Drug Interactions: The anticoagulant effect of heparin is enhanced by concurrent treatment with antithrombin III (human) in patients with hereditary AT-III deficiency. Thus, in order to avoid bleeding, reduced dosage of heparin is recommended during treatment with antithrombin III (human).

Pregnancy: Reproduction studies have been performed in rats and rabbits at doses up to 4 times the human dose and have revealed no evidence of harm to the fetus due to antithrombin III (human). It is not known whether antithrombin III (human) can cause fetal harm when administered to a pregnant woman or can affect reproduction capacity. Because animal reproduction studies are not always predictive of human response, this drug should be used during pregnancy only if clearly needed.

Children: Only a few neonates and children have so far been treated with antithrombin III (human). Safety and effectiveness in children have not been established.

Adverse Effects: In clinical studies involving antithrombin III (human) adverse reactions have been reported in association with 17 of 340 infusions (5%). Reported adverse reactions include: dizziness 7, nausea 3, foul taste 3, chest tightness 3, abdominal cramps 2, chills 2, fever 1, hives 1, chest pain 1, shortness of breath 1, bowel fullness 1, oozing and hematoma formation 1, film over eye 1 and light-headedness 1.

If adverse reactions are experienced, the infusion rate should be decreased, or if indicated, the infusion should be interrupted until symptoms abate.

Dosage: Each bottle has the functional activity, in international units (IU), stated on the label of the bottle. The potency assignment has been determined with a standard calibrated against a World Health Organization antithrombin III reference preparation.

Dosage should be determined on an individual basis based on the pre-therapy plasma antithrombin III (AT-III) level, in order to increase plasma AT-III levels to the level found in normal human plasma (100%). Dosage of antithrombin III (human) can be calculated from the following formula:

$$\text{units required (IU)} = \frac{[\text{desired level} - \text{baseline AT-III level}^{*}] \times \text{weight (kg)}}{1.4}$$

*Expressed as % normal level based on functional AT-III assay.

The above formula is based on an expected incremental in vivo recovery above baseline levels for antithrombin III (human) of 1.4% per IU per kg administered. Thus, if a 70 kg individual has a baseline AT-III level of 57%, in order to increase plasma AT-III to 120%, the initial antithrombin III (human) dose would be $[(120-57)\times 70]/1.4 = 3\,150$ IU total.

However, recovery may vary, and initially levels should be drawn at baseline and 20 minutes post infusion. Subsequent doses can be calculated based on the recovery of the first dose. These recommendations are intended only as a guide for therapy. The exact loading dose and maintenance intervals should be individualized for each patient.

It is recommended that following an initial dose of antithrombin III (human), plasma levels of AT-III be initially monitored at least every 12 hours and before the next infusion of antithrombin III (human) to maintain plasma AT-III levels greater than 80%. In some situations, e.g., following surgery, hemorrhage or acute thrombosis, and during i.v. heparin administration, the half-life of antithrombin III (human) has been reported to be shortened, and in such conditions, plasma AT-III levels should be monitored more frequently, administering antithrombin III (human) as necessary.

When an infusion of antithrombin III (human) is indicated for a patient with hereditary deficiency to control an acute thrombotic episode or prevent thrombosis following surgical or obstetrical procedures, it is desirable to raise the AT-III level to normal and maintain this level for 2 to 8 days, depending on the indication for treatment, type and extent of surgery, patient's medical condition, past history and physician's judgment. Concomitant administration of heparin in each of these situations should be based on the medical judgment of the physician.

As a general recommendation, the following therapeutic program may be utilized as a starting program for treatment, modifying the program based on the actual plasma AT-III levels achieved.

a) An initial loading dose of antithrombin III (human) calculated to elevate the plasma AT-III level to 120%, assuming an expected rise over the baseline plasma AT-III level of 1.4% (functional activity) per IU per kg of antithrombin III (human) administered. Thus, if an individual has a baseline AT-III level of 57%, the initial dose would be $(120-57)/1.4=45$ IU/kg.

b) Measure pre- and 20 minutes post-infusion (peak) plasma antithrombin III levels following the initial loading dose, plasma antithrombin III level after 12 hours, then preceding the next infusion (trough level). Subsequently measure antithrombin III levels preceding and 20 minutes after each infusion until predictable peak and trough levels have been achieved, generally between 80 to 120%. Plasma levels between 80 to 120% may be maintained by administration of maintenance doses of 60% of the initial loading dose, administered every 24 hours. Adjustments in the maintenance dose and/or interval between doses should be made based on actual plasma AT-III levels achieved.

The above recommendations for dosing are provided as a general guideline for therapy only. The exact loading and maintenance dosages and dosing intervals should be individualized for each subject, based on the individual clinical conditions, response to therapy, and actual plasma AT-III levels achieved. In some situations, e.g., following surgery, with hemorrhage or acute thrombosis and during i.v. heparin administration, in vivo survival of infused antithrombin III (human) has been reported to be shortened, resulting in the need to administer antithrombin III (human) more frequently.

Antithrombin III (human) should be reconstituted with sterile water for injection, USP and brought to room temperature prior to administration. It should be filtered through a sterile filter needle as supplied in the package prior to use, and should be administered within 3 hours following reconstitution. It may be infused over 10 to 20 minutes.

Antithrombin III (human) must be administered i.v.

Parenteral drug products should be inspected visually for particulate matter and discoloration prior to administration, whenever solution and container permit.

Reconstitution: Vacuum Transfer (see package insert for illustrations): 1. Warm the unopened diluent and the concentrate to room temperature (NMT 37°C). 2. After removing the plastic flip-top caps, aseptically cleanse the rubber stoppers of both bottles. 3. Remove the protective cover from the plastic transfer-needle cartridge with tamper-proof seal and penetrate the stopper of the diluent bottle. 4. Remove the remaining portion of the plastic cartridge, invert the diluent bottle and penetrate the rubber seal on the concentrate bottle with the needle at an angle. (Alternate Method of Transferring Sterile Water: With a sterile needle and syringe, withdraw the appropriate volume of diluent and transfer to the bottle of lyophilized concentrate.) 5. The vacuum will draw the diluent into the concentrate bottle. Hold the diluent bottle at an angle to the concentrate bottle in order to direct the jet of diluent against the wall of the concentrate bottle. Avoid excessive foaming. 6. After removing the diluent bottle and transfer needle, swirl continuously until completely dissolved. 7. After the concentrate powder is completely dissolved, withdraw solution into the syringe through the filter needle which is supplied in the package. Replace the filter needle with the administration set provided and inject i.v. 8. If the same patient is to receive more than one bottle, the contents of 2 bottles may be drawn into the same syringe through a separate unused filter needle before attaching the vein needle.

Rate of Administration: The rate of administration should be adapted to the response of the individual patient, but administration of the entire dose in 10 to 20 minutes is generally well tolerated.

Supplied: Each vial of sterile, stable, nonpyrogenic, lyophilized preparation contains: antithrombin III (human) 500 IU or 1 000 IU. A suitable volume of sterile water for injection, USP, a sterile double ended transfer needle and a sterile filter needle are provided. Each vial contains the labeled amount of antithrombin III in international units (IU) per vial. The potency assignment has been determined with a standard calibrated against a World Health Organization (WHO) antithrombin III reference preparation. It is prepared from pooled units of human plasma from normal donors by modifications and refinements of the cold ethanol method of Cohn. In addition, antithrombin III (human) has been heat-treated in solution at 60.0 ± 0.5°C for not less than 10 hours. When reconstituted, the final product has a pH of 6.0 to 7.5, a sodium content of 110 to 210 mEq/L, a chloride content of 110 to 210 mEq/L, an alanine content of 0.075 to 0.125 M and a heparin content of NMT 0.004 unit/IU AT-III. Must be administered by the i.v. route. Preservative-free. Store under refrigeration (2 to 8°C). Freezing should be avoided as breakage of the diluent bottle might occur.

THROMBOSTAT™

Parke-Davis

Thrombin (Bovine Origin)

Topical Hemostatic

Pharmacology: Thrombostat is a protein substance produced through a conversion reaction in which prothrombin of bovine origin is activated by tissue thromboplastin in the presence of calcium chloride. Thrombin requires no intermediate physiological agent for its action. It clots the fibrinogen of the blood directly. **Failure to clot blood occurs in the rare case where the primary clotting defect is the absence of fibrinogen itself.** The speed with which thrombin clots blood is dependent upon its concentration. For example, the contents of a 5 000 unit vial dissolved in 5 mL of saline diluent is capable of clotting an equal volume of blood in less than a second, or 1 000 mL in less than a minute.

Indications: As an aid in hemostasis wherever oozing blood from capillaries and small venules is accessible.

In various types of surgery, solutions of thrombin may be used in conjunction with absorbable gelatin sponge for hemostasis.

Contraindications: In persons known to be sensitive to any of its components and/or to material of bovine origin.

Warnings:

> The use of topical bovine thrombin preparations has occasionally been associated with abnormalities in hemostasis ranging from asymptomatic alterations in laboratory determinations such as prothrombin time (PT), and partial thromboplastin time (PTT) to mild to severe bleeding or thrombosis which rarely have been fatal. These hemostatic effects appear to be related to the formation of antibodies against bovine thrombin and/or factor V which in some cases may cross react with human factor V potentially resulting in factor V deficiency. Repeated clinical applications of topical bovine thrombin increase the likelihood that antibodies against thrombin and/or factor V may be formed. Consultation with an expert in coagulation disorders is recommended if a patient exhibits abnormal coagulation laboratory values, abnormal bleeding, or abnormal thrombosis following the use of topical thrombin. Any interventions should consider the immunologic basis of this condition. Patients with antibodies to bovine thrombin preparations should not be re-exposed to these products.

Because of its action in the clotting mechanism, thrombin must not be injected or otherwise allowed to enter large blood vessels. Extensive intravascular clotting and even death may result. Thrombin is an antigenic substance and has caused sensitivity and allergic reactions, including anaphylaxis.

Thrombostat (cont'd)

Precautions: General: Consult the absorbable gelatin sponge product labeling for complete information for use prior to utilizing the thrombin-saturated sponge procedure.

Pregnancy and *Lactation:* Animal reproduction studies have not been conducted with thrombin. It is also not known whether thrombin can cause fetal harm when used in nursing mothers or pregnant women, or if it can affect reproduction capacity. There are no adequate and well-controlled studies in pregnant women or nursing mothers; therefore, thrombin should not be given to these patients unless clearly indicated.

Children: Safety and effectiveness in children have not been established.

Adverse Effects: Allergic reactions may be encountered in persons known to be sensitive to bovine materials.

An allergic type reaction following the use of thrombin for treatment of epistaxis has been reported. Febrile reactions have also been observed following the use of thrombin in certain surgical procedures, but no cause-effect relationship has been established.

Anaphylaxis (see Warnings).

Hematologic (see Warnings).

Dosage: Solutions of thrombin may be prepared in sterile distilled water or isotonic saline. The intended use determines the strength of the solution to prepare. For general use in plastic surgery, dental extractions, skin grafting, neurosurgery, etc., solutions containing approximately 100 u/mL are frequently used. For this, an appropriate dilution of Thrombostat should be prepared to yield a concentration of 100 units/mL. Where bleeding is profuse, as from cut surfaces of liver and spleen, concentrations as high as 1 000 to 2 000 u/mL may be required. For this, the 5 000 unit vial dissolved in 5 or 2.5 mL respectively, of the diluent supplied in the package is convenient. Intermediate strengths to suit the needs of the case may be prepared by selecting the proper strength package and dissolving the contents in an appropriate volume of diluent. In many situations, it may be advantageous to use thrombin in dry form on oozing surfaces.

Caution: Solutions should be used immediately upon reconstitution. If necessary, refrigerate the solution and use within 3 hours of reconstitution.

The following techniques are suggested for topical application:

1. The recipient surface should be sponged (not wiped) free of blood before thrombin is applied.
2. A spray may be used or the surface may be flooded using a sterile syringe and small gauge needle. The most effective hemostasis results when the thrombin mixes freely with the blood as soon as it reaches the surface.
3. In instances where thrombin in dry form is needed, the vial is opened by removing the metal ring by flipping up the plastic cap and tearing counterclockwise. The rubber-diaphragm cap may be easily removed and the dried thrombin is then broken up into a powder by means of a sterile glass rod or other suitable sterile instrument.
4. Sponging of treated surfaces should be avoided in order that the clot remain securely in place.

Thrombostat may be used in conjunction with Absorbable Gelatin Sponge, USP as follows:

1. Prepare thrombin solution of the desired strength.
2. Immerse sponge strips of the desired size in the thrombin solution. Knead the sponge strips vigorously with moistened gloved fingers to remove trapped air, thereby facilitating saturation of the sponge.
3. Apply saturated sponge to bleeding area. Hold in place for 10 to 15 seconds with a pledget of cotton or a small gauze sponge.

Supplied: Thrombostat is supplied as a sterile powder that has been freeze-dried in the final container. It is prepared under rigid assay control against US Standard Thrombin. Each package contains: one 5 000 unit vial of Thrombostat (nonmedicinal ingredients: amino acetic acid, calcium chloride and sodium chloride) and one 5 mL vial of isotonic saline diluent (nonmedicinal ingredients: benzethonium chloride, sodium chloride and water for injection). Ten mL vials of 10 000 units (nonmedicinal ingredients: amino acetic acid, calcium chloride and sodium chloride). Store between 2 and 10°C.

Reviewed 1997

...How to obtain emergency drugs—refer to the CLIN-INFO SECTION.

THYRO-BLOCK®

Carter Horner

Potassium Iodide

Thyroid Blocking Agent

Pharmacology: Potassium iodide, an ionic thyroid blocking agent, acts on the transport of iodide into and out of the thyroid. When given in sufficient amounts, entry of radioiodide into the gland can be virtually prevented.

The onset of inhibition is rapid and is readily demonstrated 30 minutes after oral administration. An important factor in obtaining satisfactory acute block of radioiodine uptake is the speed of iodide administration after exposure to radioiodine. It is clear from standard uptake curves that, after a single pulse of radioiodine, the bulk of it has entered the gland by 10 to 12 hours and little benefit may be expected by blocking beyond this time. A substantial benefit (e.g. a block of 50%) is attainable only during the first 3 to 4 hours.

For more prolonged iodine 131 exposure, iodide will be useful at any time during the exposure and hence should still be given even if the drug was not given shortly after the release of radioactivity.

Indications: Prevention of thyroid uptake of radioiodine in a nuclear emergency situation.

Contraindications: Iodide sensitivity.

Warnings: Potassium iodide should not be used by people allergic to iodide.

In case of overdose or allergic reaction, a physician should be contacted.

Adverse Effects: Thyrotoxicosis is unlikely to occur in iodine sufficient areas. Patients with nodular goiter have an increased risk of thyrotoxicosis if they receive large doses of iodides for several weeks or longer. Monitor at 4 week intervals if the treatment is prolonged.

Iodide goiter is rare after only a few weeks of iodide administration for limited periods of blocking.

Pregnancy: Respiratory obstruction of the infant by an enlarged thyroid should be looked for during delivery of women treated with iodide for any substantial period during pregnancy.

Patients with thyroiditis or other known parenchymal tissue damage or with low thyroid reserve for unknown reasons, should be watched for a propensity to suffer iodide myxedema.

Hypothyroidism with goiter is a rare complication of iodide ingestion. It is a distinct risk in patients who have been treated for thyrotoxicosis with radioiodine or surgery in the past or who have had Hashimoto's thyroiditis and in addition received iodide for several weeks or longer.

Iodide parotitis is an uncommon complication, characterized by swelling of the salivary gland.

Cutaneous iodine occurs rarely in individuals who ingest large doses of iodine over long periods. It takes the appearance of a pustular acneform eruption.

Systemic manifestations rarely encountered; fever, generalized skin rash, arthralgia, inflammatory joint involvement and changes in the hair and nails. The appearance of these manifestations indicate that the iodine therapy should be discontinued.

Dosage: Adults and children one year of age or older: One tablet once a day. Crush for small children.

Children under one year of age: One half tablet once a day. Crush first.

To be taken for 10 days unless otherwise directed.

Supplied: Each white round flat tablet, one side bisected and the other side plain contains: potassium iodide 130 mg. Nonmedicinal ingredients: cellulose, magnesium stearate, silica gel and sodium thiosulfate. Gluten- and tartrazine-free. Special order only.

THYROID HORMONE ℞

Parke-Davis

Desiccated Thyroid

Hypothyroidism Therapy

Pharmacology: The principal pharmacologic effect of exogenous thyroid hormones is to increase the metabolic rate of body tissues.

The normal thyroid gland contains approximately 200 µg of levothyroxine (T_4)/g of gland, and 15 µg of triiodothyronine (T_3)/g. The ratio of these two hormones in the circulation does not represent the ratio in the thyroid gland, since about 80% of peripheral triiodothyronine comes from monodeiodination of the outer ring of levothyroxine. Peripheral monodeiodination of levothyroxine at the 5 position (inner ring) also results in the formation of reverse triiodothyronine (r T_3), which is calorigenically inactive. These facts would seem to advocate levothyroxine as the treatment of choice for the hypothyroid patient and to mitigate against the administration of hormone combinations, which, while normalizing thyroxine levels, may produce triiodothyronine levels in the thyrotoxic range.

Triiodothyronine (T_3) level is low in the fetus and newborn, in old age, in chronic caloric deprivation, hepatic cirrhosis, renal failure, surgical stress, and chronic illnesses representing what has been called the "low triiodothyronine syndrome."

Pharmacokinetics: Animal studies have shown that T_4 is only partially absorbed from the gastrointestinal tract. The degree of absorption is dependent on the vehicle used for its administration and by the character of the intestinal contents, the intestinal flora, including plasma protein, soluble dietary factors, all of which bind thyroid and thereby make it unavailable for diffusion. Only 41% is absorbed when given in a gelatin capsule as opposed to a 74 percent absorption when given with an albumin carrier.

Depending on other factors, absorption has varied from 48 to 79% of the administered dose.

Fasting increases absorption. Malabsorption syndromes, as well as dietary factors (children's soybean formula, concomitant use of anionic exchange resins such as cholestyramine), cause excessive fecal loss. T_3 is almost totally absorbed, (95% in 4 hours). The hormones contained in the natural preparations are absorbed in a manner similar to the synthetic hormones.

More than 99% of circulating hormones are bound to serum proteins, including thyroid-binding globulin (TB_g), thyroid-binding prealbumin (TBPA), and albumin (TB_a), whose capacities and affinities vary for the hormones. The higher affinity of levothyroxine (T_4) for both TB_g and TBPA as compared to triiodothyronine (T_3) partially explains the higher serum levels and longer half-life of the former hormone. Both protein-bound hormones exist in reverse equilibrium with minute amounts of free hormone, the latter accounting for the metabolic activity.

Deiodination of levothyroxine (T_4) occurs at a number of sites, including liver, kidney, and other tissues. The conjugated hormone, in the form of glucuronide or sulfate, is found in the bile and gut where it may complete an enterohepatic circulation. Eighty-five percent of levothyroxine (T_4) metabolized daily is deiodinated.

Indications: Specific replacement therapy for decreased or absent thyroid function.

Contraindications: Thyroid hormone preparations are generally contraindicated in patients with diagnosed, but as yet uncorrected, adrenal cortical insufficiency, untreated thyrotoxicosis, and apparent hypersensitivity to any of their active or extraneous constituents. There is no well documented evidence from the literature, however, of true allergic or idiosyncratic reactions to thyroid hormone.

Warnings: Drugs with thyroid hormone activity, alone or together with other therapeutic agents, have been used for the treatment of obesity. In euthyroid patients, doses within the range of daily hormonal requirements are ineffective for weight reduction. Larger doses may produce serious or even life-threatening manifestations of toxicity, particularly when given in association with sympathomimetic amines such as those used for their anorectic effects.

The use of thyroid hormones in the therapy of obesity, alone or combined with other drugs, is not justified and has been shown to be ineffective. Neither is their use justified for the treatment of male or female infertility unless this condition is accompanied by hypothyroidism.

Precautions: General: Thyroid hormones should be used with great caution in a number of circumstances where the integrity of the cardiovascular system, particularly the coronary arteries, is suspect. These include patients with angina pectoris, hypertension, other cardiac conditions, or the elderly, in whom there is a greater likelihood of occult cardiac disease. In these patients, therapy should be initiated with low doses, i.e., 25 to 50 µg levothyroxine (T_4) or its isocaloric equivalent (16 to 32 mg, or 0.25 to 0.5 grain of desiccated thyroid). When, in such patients, a euthyroid state can only be reached at the expense of an aggravation of the cardiovascular disease, thyroid hormone dosage should be reduced. Thyroid hormone therapy in patients with concomitant diabetes mellitus or insipidus or adrenal cortical insufficiency aggravates the intensity of their symptoms. Appropriate adjustments of the various therapeutic measures directed at these concomitant endocrine diseases are required. The therapy of myxedema coma requires simultaneous administration of glucocorticoids (see Dosage).

Hypothyroidism decreases and hyperthyroidism increases the sensitivity to oral anticoagulants. Prothrombin time should be closely monitored in thyroid-treated patients on oral anticoagulants and dosage of the latter agents adjusted on the basis of frequent prothrombin time determination. In infants, excessive doses of thyroid hormone preparations may produce craniosynostosis.

Information for the Patient: Patients on thyroid hormone preparations and parents of children on thyroid therapy should be informed that:

1. Replacement therapy is to be taken essentially for life, with the exception of cases of transient hypothyroidism, usually associated with thyroiditis, and in those patients receiving a therapeutic trial of the drug.
2. They should immediately report during the course of therapy any signs or symptoms of thyroid hormone toxicity, e.g., chest pain, increased pulse rate, palpitations, excessive sweating, heat intolerance, nervousness, or any other unusual event.
3. In case of concomitant diabetes mellitus, the daily dosage of antidiabetic medication may need readjustment as thyroid hormone replacement is achieved. If thyroid medication is stopped, a downward readjustment of the dosage of insulin or oral hypoglycemic agent may be necessary to avoid hypoglycemia. At all times, close monitoring of glucose levels is mandatory in such patients.
4. In case of concomitant oral anticoagulant therapy, the prothrombin time should be measured frequently to determine if the dosage of oral anticoagulants is to be readjusted.
5. Partial loss of hair may be experienced by children in the first few months of thyroid therapy, but this is usually a transient phenomenon and later recovery is usually the rule.

Laboratory Tests: Treatment of patients with thyroid hormones requires the periodic assessment of thyroid status by means of appropriate laboratory tests in addition to the full clinical evaluation. The TSH suppression test can be used to test the effectiveness of any thyroid preparation, bearing in mind the relative insensitivity of the infant pituitary to the negative feedback effect of thyroid hormones. Serum T_4 levels can be used to test the effectiveness of all thyroid medications except T_3.

When the total serum T_4 is low but TSH is normal, a test specific to assess unbound (free) T_4 levels is warranted. Specific measurements of T_4 and T_3 by competitive protein binding or radioimmunoassay are not influenced by blood levels or organic or inorganic iodine and have essentially replaced older tests of thyroid hormone measurements, i.e., PBI, BEI, and T_4 by column.

Drug Interactions: Oral Anticoagulants: Thyroid hormones appear to increase catabolism of vitamin K-dependent clotting factors. If oral anticoagulants are also being given, compensatory increases in clotting factor synthesis are impaired. Patients stabilized on oral anticoagulants who are found to require thyroid replacement therapy should be watched very closely when thyroid is started. If a patient is truly hypothyroid, it is likely that a reduction in anticoagulant dosage will be required. No special precautions appear to be necessary when oral anticoagulant therapy is begun in a patient already stabilized on maintenance thyroid replacement therapy.

Insulin or Oral Hypoglycemics: Initiating thyroid replacement therapy may cause increases in insulin or oral hypoglycemic requirements. The effects seen are poorly understood and depend upon a variety of factors such as dosage and type of thyroid preparations and endocrine status of the patient. Patients receiving insulin or oral hypoglycemics should be closely watched during initiation of thyroid replacement therapy.

Cholestyramine: Cholestyramine binds both T_4 and T_3 in the intestine, thus impairing absorption of these thyroid hormones. In vitro studies indicate that the binding is not easily released from the cholestyramine. Therefore, 4 to 5 hours should elapse between administration of cholestyramine or similar resins, such as colestipol, and thyroid hormones.

Estrogen, Oral Contraceptives: Estrogens tend to increase serum thyroxine-binding globulin (TBg). In a patient with a nonfunctioning thyroid gland who is receiving thyroid replacement therapy, free levothyroxine may be decreased when estrogens are started thus increasing thyroid requirements. However, if the patient's thyroid gland has sufficient function, the decreased free thyroxine will result in a compensatory increase in thyroxine output by the thyroid. Therefore, patients without a functioning thyroid gland who are on thyroid replacement therapy may need to increase their thyroid dose if estrogens or estrogen-containing oral contraceptives are given.

Drug/Laboratory Test Interactions: The following drugs or moieties are known to interfere with laboratory tests performed in patients on thyroid hormone therapy: androgens, corticosteroids, estrogens, oral contraceptives containing estrogens, iodine-containing preparations, and the numerous preparations containing salicylates.

Changes in TBg concentration should be taken into consideration in the interpretation of T_4 and T_3 values. In such cases, the unbound (free) hormone should be measured. Pregnancy, estrogens, and estrogen-containing oral contraceptives increase TBg concentrations. TBg may also be increased during infectious hepatitis. Decreases in TBg concentrations are observed in nephrosis, acromegaly, and after androgen or corticosteroid therapy. Familial hyper or hypothyroxinebinding-globulinemias have been described. The incidence of TBg deficiency approximates 1 in 9 000. The binding of thyroxine by TBPA is inhibited by salicylates.

Medicinal or dietary iodine interferes with all in vivo tests of radioiodine uptake, producing low uptakes which may not be reflective of a true decrease in hormone synthesis.

The persistence of clinical and laboratory evidence of hypothyroidism in spite of adequate dosage replacement indicates poor patient compliance, poor absorption, excessive fecal loss, or inactivity of the preparation. Intracellular resistance to thyroid hormone is quite rare.

Carcinogenesis, Mutagenesis, and Impairment of Fertility: No confirmatory long-term studies in animals have been performed to evaluate carcinogenic potential, mutagenicity, or impairment of fertility in either males or females. A reportedly apparent association between prolonged thyroid therapy and breast cancer has not been confirmed and patients on thyroid for established indications should not discontinue therapy.

Pregnancy: Thyroid hormones do not readily cross the placental barrier. The clinical experience to date does not indicate any adverse effect on fetuses when the thyroid hormones are administered to pregnant women. On the basis of current knowledge, thyroid replacement therapy to hypothyroid women should be continued during pregnancy. However, the physician should be aware that pregnancy increases TBg concentrations (see Drug/Laboratory Test Interactions).

Lactation: Minimal amounts of thyroid hormones are excreted in human milk. Thyroid is not associated with serious adverse reactions and does not have a known tumorigenic potential. However, caution should be exercised when thyroid is administered to a nursing mother.

Children: Pregnant mothers provide little or no thyroid hormone to the fetus. The incidence of congenital hypothyroidism is relatively high (1:4 000) and the hypothyroid fetus would not derive any benefit from the small amounts of hormone crossing the placental barrier. Routine determinations of serum (T_4) and/or TSH are strongly advised in neonates in view of the deleterious effects of thyroid deficiency on growth and development.

Treatment should be initiated immediately upon diagnosis and maintained for life, unless transient hypothyroidism is suspected. In this case, therapy may be interrupted for 2 to 8 weeks after the age of 3 years to reassess the condition. Cessation of therapy is justified in patients who have maintained a normal TSH during those 2 to 8 weeks.

Adverse Effects: Except in rare instances of intolerance, possibly due to the development of hypersensitivity to animal protein in whole thyroid, adverse effects are generally infrequent at physiologic doses.

Neurological: nervousness, tremors, headache, insomnia.

Cardiovascular: palpitation, tachycardia, cardiac arrhythmias, angina pectoris.

Gastrointestinal: diarrhea, abdominal cramps.

Miscellaneous: sweating, heat intolerance, fever, weight loss.

Overdose: Symptoms and Treatment: Signs and symptoms of excessive doses of thyroid hormone result in a hypermetabolic state resembling in every respect the condition of endogenous origin. The condition may be self-induced.

Dosage should be reduced or therapy temporarily discontinued if signs and symptoms of overdosage appear. Treatment may be reinstituted at a lower dosage. In normal individuals, normal hypothalamic-pituitary-thyroid axis function is restored in 6 to 8 weeks after thyroid suppression.

Treatment of acute massive thyroid hormone overdosage is aimed at reducing gastrointestinal absorption of the drugs and counteracting central and peripheral effects, mainly those of increased sympathetic activity. Vomiting may be induced initially if further gastrointestinal absorption can reasonably be prevented and barring contraindications such as coma, convulsions, or loss of the gag reflex. Treatment is symptomatic and supportive. Oxygen may be administered and ventilation maintained. Cardiac glycosides may be indicated if congestive heart failure develops. Measures to control fever, hypoglycemia, or fluid loss should be instituted if needed. Antiadrenergic agents, particularly propranolol, have been used advantageously in the treatment of increased sympathetic activity. Propranolol may be administered i.v. at a dosage of 1 to 3 mg over a 10 minute period or orally, 80 to 160 mg/day initially, especially when no contraindications exist for its use. Other adjunctive measures include administration of cholestyramine to interfere with thyroxine absorption, and/or the administration of glucocorticoids to partially inhibit conversion of T_4 to T_3.

Dosage: The dosage of thyroid hormones is determined by the indication and must in every case be individualized according to patient response and laboratory findings. There are wide variations in individual responses. The effects of daily thyroid reach a therapeutic maximum usually in 4 to 6 weeks.

Initial dose for myxedema is usually 30 to 180 mg daily; other hypothyroid states, 60 to 300 mg daily. Usual maintenance dose is 30 to 125 mg daily.

Note: Desiccated thyroid 60 mg is usually considered equivalent to thyroglobulin 60 mg, levothyroxine sodium (T4) 0.1 mg or liothyronine sodium (T3) 25 μg.

Pediatric Dosage: Pediatric dosage should follow the recommendations summarized in Table I. In infants with congenital hypothyroidism, therapy with full doses should be instituted as soon as the diagnosis has been made.

Table I—Thyroid

Recommended Pediatric Dosage for Congenital Hypothyroidism

	Tetraiodothyronine (T_4, levothyroxine sodium)	
Age	**Dose per day**	**Daily Dose/kg of Body Weight**
0-6 months	25-50 μg	8-10 μg
6-12 months	50-75 μg	6-8 μg
1-5 years	75-100 μg	5-6 μg
6-12 years	100-150 μg	4-5 μg
over 12 years	over 150 μg	2-3 μg

Instructions for Use: Table II lists the approximate equivalents of other thyroid preparations, when changing medication from desiccated thyroid, T_4 (levothyroxine sodium), or T_3 (liothyronine sodium).

Table II—Thyroid

Conversion Table

Dose of Thyroglobulin (grain)	mg Equivalents	Dose of Desiccated Thyroid (grain)	Dose of T_4 (levothyroxine) mg	Dose of T_3 (liothyronine) μg
0.5	32	0.5	0.05	12.5
1	65	1	0.1	25
2	130	2	0.2	50
3	200	3	0.3	75
4	260	4	0.4	100
5	325	5	0.5	125

Supplied: Each tan-colored tablet, embossed PD, contains: desiccated thyroid 30 mg, 60 mg or 125 mg. Nonmedicinal ingredients: cornstarch, magnesium stearate, sugar and talc. Energy: 1.2 kJ (0.28 kcal)/30 mg tablet; 1.1 kJ (0.26 kcal)/60 mg tablet; 2.2 kJ (0.52 kcal)/125 mg tablet. Gluten-, lactose-, paraben-, sodium-, sulfite- and tartrazine-free. Bottles of 500. Store at controlled room temperature 15 to 30°C.

Reviewed 1997

TIAMOL® Pr

Spectropharm Dermatology

Fluocinonide

Topical Corticosteroid

Pharmacology: Fluocinonide is effective because of the anti-inflammatory, antipruritic and vasoconstrictor actions of fluocinonide.

Indications: For topical use in the management of acute or chronic dermatoses responsive to corticosteroids.

Contraindications: Topical corticosteroids are contraindicated in tuberculosis, fungal, most viral lesions of the skin (including herpes simplex, vaccinia and varicella), untreated bacterial infections and also contraindicated in individuals with a history

Tiamol (cont'd)

of hypersensitivity to its components. This preparation is not for ophthalmic use.

Warnings: Adrenal suppression and other systemic effects may occur after applications to extensive areas and prolonged usage. Fluocinonide should not be used under occlusive dressings. Not for ophthalmic use.

Dilution of a physical topical, commercially formulated corticosteroid preparation may result in a physical incompatibility or an unstability of the active ingredients. Manipulation of the preparation may cause bacterial contamination or alter the release of active ingredients from the base.

Pregnancy and *Lactation*: The safety of topical corticosteroid preparations during pregnancy and lactation has not been established; therefore, they should not be used on pregnant patients.

Precautions: Although side effects are not ordinarily encountered with topically applied corticosteroids, as with all drugs, a few patients may react unfavorably under certain conditions. Should symptoms of hypersensitivity or idiosyncrasy occur, the medication should be discontinued and appropriate steps taken.

If the lesion is infected the use of an appropriate antifungal or antibacterial agent should be instituted. If a favorable response does not occur promptly, the corticosteroid cream should be discontinued until the infection has been adequately controlled.

If extensive areas are treated, the possibility exists of increased systemic absorption requiring that the amount applied and frequency of application be suitably adjusted.

Patients should be advised to inform other physicians attending them of their use of corticosteroids.

Causal factors of dermatoses should be eliminated whenever possible.

It is recommended that rotation of sites of application and intermittent therapy should be considered.

Application in or near the eye should be avoided.

Prolonged use of topical corticosteroid products may produce atrophy of the skin and of subcutaneous tissues, particularly on flexor surfaces and on the face. If this is noted, discontinue the use of this product.

Fluocinonide should be used with caution in patients with stasis dermatitis and other skin diseases associated with impaired circulation.

During the use of topical corticosteroids secondary infections may occur.

Adverse Effects: The following adverse skin reactions have been reported with the use of topical steroids: dryness, itching, burning, local irritation, striae, skin atrophy, atrophy of the subcutaneous tissues, telangiectasia, hypertrichosis, change in the pigmentation and secondary infection.

Adrenal suppression has also been reported following topical corticosteroid therapy.

Posterior subcapsular cataracts have been reported following systemic use of corticosteroids.

Dosage: Suitable when an emollient effect is desired. A small amount is applied lightly to affected skin area 2 to 4 times daily with gentle but thorough massage.

Supplied: Each g of cream contains: fluocinonide 0.05% in an emollient base. Nonmedicinal ingredients: cetyl alcohol, citric acid, mineral oil, polysorbate-60, propylene glycol, sorbitan monostearate, stearyl alcohol and white petrolatum. Jars of 100 g. Tubes of 25 g.

TIAZAC® Ⓟ

Crystaal

Diltiazem HCl

Antihypertensive—Antianginal

Pharmacology: Diltiazem is a calcium ion cellular influx inhibitor (calcium entry blocker or calcium ion antagonist).

Mechanism of Action: The therapeutic effect of this group of drugs is believed to be related to their specific cellular action of selectively inhibiting transmembrane influx of calcium ions into cardiac muscle and vascular smooth muscle. The contractile processes of these tissues are dependent upon the movement of extracellular calcium into the cells through specific ion channels. Diltiazem blocks transmembrane influx of calcium through the slow channel without affecting, to any significant degree, the transmembrane influx of sodium through the fast channel. This results in a reduction of free calcium ions available within cells of the above tissues. Diltiazem does not alter total serum calcium.

Hypertension: The antihypertensive effect of diltiazem is believed to be brought about largely by its vasodilatory action on peripheral blood vessels with resultant decrease in peripheral vascular resistance.

Angina: The precise mechanism by which diltiazem relieves angina has not been fully determined, but it is believed to be brought about largely by its vasodilatory action.

In angina of effort it appears that the action of diltiazem is related to the reduction of myocardial oxygen demand. This is probably caused by a decrease in blood pressure brought about by the reduction of peripheral resistance and of heart rate.

Hemodynamic and Electrophysiologic Effects: Diltiazem produces antihypertensive effects both in the supine and standing positions. Resting heart rate is usually slightly reduced. During dynamic exercise, increases in diastolic pressure are inhibited while maximum achievable systolic pressure is usually unaffected. Heart rate at maximum exercise is reduced. Studies to date, primarily in patients with normal ventricular function, have shown that cardiac output, ejection fraction and left ventricular end-diastolic pressure have not been affected.

Chronic therapy with diltiazem produces no change, or an increase, in circulating plasma catecholamines. However, no increased activity of the renin-angiotensin-aldosterone axis has been observed. Diltiazem inhibits the renal and peripheral effects of angiotensin II.

In man, i.v. diltiazem in doses of 20 mg prolongs AH conduction time and AV node functional and effective refractory periods by approximately 20%. Chronic oral administration of diltiazem in doses up to 540 mg/day has resulted in small increases in PR interval. Second-degree and third-degree AV block have been observed (see Warnings). In patients with sick sinus syndrome, diltiazem significantly prolongs sinus cycle length (up to 50% in some cases).

Pharmacokinetics: Diltiazem is well absorbed from the gastrointestinal tract and is subject to an extensive first-pass effect giving absolute bioavailability (compared to i.v. dosing) of about 40%. Therapeutic blood levels appear to be in the range of 50 to 200 ng/mL range and the plasma elimination half-life (beta-phase) following single or multiple drug administration is approximately 3.5 to 6 hours. In-vitro human serum binding studies revealed that 70 to 80% of diltiazem is bound to plasma proteins. Following extensive hepatic metabolism, only 2 to 4% of the drug appears unchanged in the urine and 6 to 7% appears as metabolites.

The metabolic pathways of diltiazem include N-and O-demethylation (via cytochrome P450), deacetylation (via plasma and tissue esterases), in addition to conjugation (via sulfation and glucuridonation). In vitro studies have demonstrated that CYP 3A4 is the principal CYP isoenzyme involved in N-demethylation. The major metabolite, desacetyl diltiazem, is present in the plasma at levels 10 to 20% of the parent drug and is 25 to 50% as potent as diltiazem in terms of coronary vasodilation.

Tiazac Capsules: When compared to a regimen of immediate-release tablets at steady-state, approximately 93% of drug is absorbed from the Tiazac formulation. When Tiazac was coadministered with a high fat content breakfast, the extent of diltiazem absorption was not affected; T_{max}, however, occurred slightly earlier. Dose-dumping does not occur. The apparent elimination half-life after single or multiple dosing is 4 to 9.5 hours (mean 6.5 hours).

Diltiazem extended-release demonstrates nonlinear pharmacokinetics. As the dose of Tiazac is increased from a daily dose of 120 to 240 mg, there is an increase in the AUC of 2.4 times. When the dose is increased from 240 mg to 360 mg there is an increase in AUC of 1.5 times.

In a study with 14 healthy subjects, the steady-state pharmacokinetics of Tiazac were compared with Cardizem CD at a dose of 240 mg/day. The bioavailability of Tiazac relative to Cardizem CD based on mean diltiazem AUC was 124% (90% C.I. 111 to 139%). The relative mean C_{max} was 121%.

Pharmacodynamics: Hypertension: In a parallel-group, double-blind placebo-controlled study of 198 patients with mild to moderate essential hypertension, diltiazem extended-release was given for 4 weeks. The changes in diastolic blood pressure measured at trough (24 hours after the dose) for placebo, 90 mg, 180 mg and 360 mg were -5.4, -6.3, -6.2, -8.2 mm Hg, respectively.

Another double-blind placebo-controlled clinical trial in 56 patients with mild to moderate essential hypertension treated for 8 weeks, followed a dose-escalation design. Supine diastolic blood pressure measured at trough following 2-week intervals of treatment with diltiazem extended-release was reduced by -3.7 mm Hg with 120 mg/day vs -2.0 mm Hg with placebo, by -7.6 mm Hg after escalation to 240 mg/day vs -2.3 mm Hg with placebo, by -8.1 mm Hg after escalation to 360 mg/day versus -0.9 mm Hg with placebo.

In a double-blind, multicentre study, 181 patients with mild to moderate essential hypertension controlled with Cardizem CD monotherapy, were randomized to the same dose of either Cardizem CD or Tiazac. The least squares mean for the difference in diastolic blood pressure at trough between Tiazac and Cardizem CD groups pooled was 0.19 mm Hg (90% confidence interval -1.2 to 1.6 mm Hg). Data based on same dose comparisons were supportive of this result.

Angina: In a double-blind, parallel group placebo-controlled trial, 158 patients with chronic stable angina were, after titration, treated for 2 weeks on their target maintenance dose of diltiazem.

Diltiazem increased exercise tolerance times in a Bruce exercise protocol, at trough, 24 hours after dosing. Exercise tolerance times increased by 14, 26, 41 and 33 seconds for placebo, 120 mg, 240 mg, and 360 mg/day treated patient groups respectively. At peak, 8 hours after dosing, exercise tolerance times were increased by 13, 38, 64 and 53 seconds for placebo, 120 mg, 240 mg and 360 mg/day treated groups, respectively.

Indications: Essential Hypertension: For the treatment of mild to moderate essential hypertension. Diltiazem should normally be used in those patients in whom treatment with diuretics or beta-blockers has been ineffective, or has been associated with unacceptable adverse effects.

Diltiazem can be tried as an initial agent in those patients in whom the use of diuretics and/or beta-blockers is contraindicated, or in patients with medical conditions in which these drugs frequently cause serious adverse effects.

Safety of concurrent use of diltiazem with other antihypertensive agents has not been established.

Chronic Stable Angina: For the management of chronic stable angina (effort-associated angina) without evidence of vasospasm in patients who remain symptomatic despite adequate doses of beta-blockers and/or organic nitrates or who cannot tolerate these agents.

Diltiazem may be tried in combination with beta-blockers in chronic stable angina patients with normal ventricular function. When such concomitant therapy is introduced, patients must be monitored closely (see Warnings, Use with Beta-blockers).

Since the safety and efficacy of diltiazem in the management of unstable or vasospastic angina has not been substantiated, its use for these indications is not recommended.

Contraindications: Patients with sick sinus syndrome except in the presence of an implanted pacemaker; patients with second- or third-degree AV block except in the presence of an implanted pacemaker; patients with known hypersensitivity to diltiazem; patients with severe hypotension (less than 90 mm Hg systolic); myocardial infarction patients, who have left ventricular failure manifested by congestion.

Pregnancy: In pregnancy and in women of childbearing potential. Fetal malformations and adverse effects on pregnancy have been reported in animals. In repeated dose studies a high incidence of vertebral column malformations were present in the offspring of mice receiving more than 50 mg/kg of diltiazem orally.

In the offspring of mice receiving a single oral dose of 50 or 100 mg/kg on day 12 of gestation, the incidence of cleft palate and malformed extremities was significantly higher. Vertebral malformations were most prevalent when they received the drug on day 9. In rats, a significantly higher fetal death rate was present when 200 and 400 mg/kg were given orally on days 9 to 14 of gestation. Single oral dose studies in rats resulted in a significant incidence of skeletal malformations in the offspring of the group receiving 400 mg/kg on day 11. In rabbits, all pregnant dams receiving 70 mg/kg orally from day 6 to 18 of gestation aborted; at 35 mg/kg, a significant increase in skeletal malformations was recorded in the offspring.

Warnings: Cardiac Conduction: Diltiazem prolongs AV node refractory periods without significantly prolonging sinus node recovery time, except in patients with sick sinus syndrome. This effect may rarely result in abnormally slow heart rates (particularly in patients with sick sinus syndrome) or second- or third-degree AV block (13 of 3 007 patients or 0.43%). Concomitant use of diltiazem with beta-blockers or digitalis may result in additive effects on cardiac conduction.

Congestive Heart Failure: Because diltiazem has a negative inotropic effect in vitro and it affects cardiac conduction, the drug should only be used with caution and under careful medical supervision in patients with congestive cardiac failure (see also Contraindications).

Use with Beta-blockers: The combination of diltiazem and beta-blockers warrants caution since in some patients additive effects on heart rate, cardiac conduction, blood pressure or left ventricular function have been observed. Close medical supervision is recommended.

Generally diltiazem should not be given to patients with impaired left ventricular function while they receive beta-blockers. However in exceptional cases, when in the opinion of the physician, concomitant use is considered essential, such use should be instituted gradually in a hospital setting.

Diltiazem gives no protection against the dangers of abrupt beta-blocker withdrawal and such withdrawal should be done by the gradual reduction of the dose of beta-blocker.

Hypotension: Decreases in blood pressure associated with diltiazem therapy may occasionally result in symptomatic hypotension.

Patients With Myocardial Infarction: Use of immediate release diltiazem at 240 mg/day started 3 to 15 days after a myocardial infarction was associated with an increase in cardiac events in patients with pulmonary congestion with no overall effect on mortality. Although there has not been a study of sustained release formulations of diltiazem in acute myocardial infarction, their use may have effects similar to those of immediate release diltiazem in acute myocardial infarction.

Acute Hepatic Injury: In rare instances, significant elevations in alkaline phosphatase, CPK, LDH, AST, ALT and symptoms consistent with acute hepatic injury have been observed. These reactions have been reversible upon discontinuation of drug therapy. Although a causal relationship to diltiazem has not been established in all cases, a drug induced hypersensitivity reaction is suspected (see Adverse Effects). As with any drug given over prolonged periods, laboratory parameters should be monitored at regular intervals.

Precautions: Impaired Hepatic or Renal Function: Because diltiazem is extensively metabolized by the liver and excreted by the kidney and in bile, monitoring of laboratory parameters and cautious dosage titration are recommended in patients with impaired hepatic or renal function (see Adverse Effects).

Children: Safety and effectiveness in children have not been established.

Lactation: Diltiazem is excreted in human milk. One report suggests that concentrations in breast milk may approximate serum levels. If use of diltiazem is deemed essential, an alternative method of infant feeding should be instituted.

Geriatrics: Administration of diltiazem to elderly patients (over or equal to 65 years of age) requires caution. The incidence of adverse reactions is approximately 13% higher in this group. Those adverse reactions which occur more frequently include: peripheral edema, bradycardia, palpitation, dizziness, rash and polyuria. Therefore particular care in titration is advisable.

Drug Interactions: As with all drugs, care should be exercised when treating patients with multiple medications. Calcium channel blockers undergo biotransformation by the cytochrome P450 system. Coadministration of diltiazem with other drugs which follow the same route of biotransformation may result in altered bioavailability. Dosages of similarly metabolized drugs, particularly those of low therapeutic ratio, and especially in patients with renal and/or hepatic impairment, may require adjustment when starting or stopping concomitantly administered diltiazem to maintain optimum therapeutic blood levels.

Drugs known to be inhibitors of the cytochrome P450 system include: azole antifungals, cimetidine, cyclosporine, erythromycin, quinidine, warfarin.

Drugs known to be inducers of the cytochrome P450 system include: phenobarbital, phenytoin, rifampin.

Drugs known to be biotransformed via P450 include: benzodiazepines, flecainide, imipramine, propafenone, terfenadine, theophylline.

Anesthetics: The depression of cardiac contractility, conductivity, and automaticity as well as the vascular dilation associated with anesthetics may be potentiated by calcium channel blockers. When used concomitantly, anesthetics and calcium blockers should be titrated carefully.

Benzodiazepines: Diltiazem significantly increases peak plasma levels and the elimination half-life of triazolam and midazolam.

Beta-blockers: The concomitant administration of diltiazem with beta adrenergic blocking drugs warrants caution and careful monitoring. Such an association may have an additive effect on heart rate, on AV conduction or on blood pressure (see Warnings). Appropriate dosage adjustments may be necessary. A study in 5 normal subjects showed that diltiazem increased propranolol bioavailability by approximately 50%.

Carbamazepine: Concomitant administration of diltiazem with carbamazepine has been reported to result in elevated serum levels of carbamazepine (40 to 72% increase), resulting in toxicity in some cases. Patients receiving these drugs concurrently should be monitored for a potential drug interaction.

Cimetidine: A study in 6 healthy volunteers has shown a significant increase in peak diltiazem plasma levels (58%) and AUC (53%) after a 1-week course of cimetidine 1 200 mg/day and a single dose of diltiazem 60 mg. Ranitidine produced smaller, nonsignificant increases. The effect may be mediated by cimetidine's known inhibition of hepatic cytochrome P450, the enzyme system responsible for the first-pass metabolism of diltiazem. Patients currently receiving diltiazem therapy should be carefully monitored for a change in pharmacological effect when initiating and discontinuing therapy with cimetidine. An adjustment in the diltiazem dose may be warranted.

Cyclosporine: A pharmacokinetic interaction between diltiazem and cyclosporine has been observed during studies involving renal and cardiac transplant patients. In renal and cardiac transplant recipients, a reduction of cyclosporine dose ranging from 15 to 48% was necessary to maintain cyclosporine trough concentrations similar to those seen prior to the addition of diltiazem. If these agents are to be administered concurrently, cyclosporine concentrations should be monitored, especially when diltiazem therapy is initiated, adjusted, or discontinued. The effect of cyclosporine on diltiazem plasma concentrations has not been evaluated.

Digitalis: Diltiazem and digitalis glycosides may have an additive effect in prolonging AV conduction. In clinical trials, concurrent administration of diltiazem and digoxin have resulted in increases in serum digoxin levels with prolongation of AV conduction. This increase may result from a decrease in renal clearance of digoxin. Patients on concomitant therapy, especially those with renal impairment, should be carefully monitored. The dose of digoxin may need downward adjustment.

Rifampin: Administration of diltiazem with rifampin markedly reduced plasma diltiazem concentrations and the therapeutic effect of diltiazem.

Short- and Long-Acting Nitrates: Diltiazem may be safely coadministered with nitrates.

Other Calcium Antagonists: Limited clinical experience suggests that in certain severe conditions not responding adequately to verapamil or to nifedipine, using diltiazem in conjunction with either of these drugs may be beneficial.

Adverse Effects: Overall Diltiazem Safety Profile: In clinical trials with diltiazem involving over 3 300 patients, the most common adverse reactions were headache (4.6%), edema (4.6%), dizziness (3.5%), asthenia (2.7%), first degree AV block (2.4%), bradycardia (1.7%), flushing (1.5%), nausea (1.4%), rash (1.2%) and dyspepsia (1.0%).

In addition, the following events were reported with a frequency of less than 1%:

Cardiovascular: angina, arrhythmia, AV block (second-or third-degree), bundle branch block, congestive heart failure, ECG abnormalities, hypotension, palpitations, syncope, tachycardia, ventricular extrasystoles.

Nervous System: abnormal dreams, amnesia, depression, gait abnormality, hallucinations, insomnia, nervousness, paresthesia, personality change, somnolence, tinnitus, tremor.

Gastrointestinal: anorexia, constipation, diarrhea, dry mouth, dysgeusia, mild evelations of AST, ALT, LDH, and alkaline phosphatase (see Warnings), thirst, vomiting, weight increase.

Dermatological: petechiae, photosensitivity, pruritus.

Other: amblyopia, CPK increase, dyspnea, epistaxis, eye irritation, hyperglycemia, hyperuricemia, impotence, nasal congestion, nocturia, osteoarticular pain, polyuria, sexual difficulties, dry mouth.

The following postmarketing events have been reported infrequently in patients receiving diltiazem: alopecia, erythema multiforme, exfoliative dermatitis, Stevens-Johnson syndrome, angioedema, toxic epidermal necrolysis, extrapyramidal symptoms, gingival hyperplasia, hemolytic anemia, increased bleeding time, leukopenia, purpura, retinopathy, and thrombocytopenia. In addition, events such as myocardial infarction have been observed which are not readily distinguishable from the natural history of the disease in these patients. A number of well-documented cases of generalized rash, characterized as leukocytoclastic vasculitis, have been reported. However, a definitive cause and effect relationship between these events and diltiazem therapy is yet to be established.

Hypertension: A safety evaluation was carried out in placebo-controlled studies in which 345 hypertensive patients (diltiazem extended-release n=243; placebo n=102) were treated with diltiazem extended-release at doses up to 360 mg/day. The most common adverse effects were: headache (13%); edema (5%); gastrointestinal disease (5%); pain (4%); vasodilation (3%); asthenia (3%); dizziness (3%) and palpitations (2%).

The following percentage of adverse effects, divided by system, were reported: Cardiovascular: edema, including peripheral edema (5%), vasodilation, including hypotension, syncope and flushing (3%), palpitations (2%) and tachycardia (1%).

CNS: headache (13%), asthenia (3%), dizziness (3%), neck rigidity (1%), nervousness (1%), paresthesia (1%).

Gastrointestinal: gastrointestinal disease, including dyspepsia, nausea (5%), constipation (1%), anorexia (1%), dry mouth (1%).

Other: pain (4%), pharyngitis (2%), rhinitis (1%), dyspnea (1%), allergic reaction (1%), polyuria (1%), rash (1%).

The most common adverse effects for placebo treated patients in the above mentioned trials were: headache (17%), edema (3%), gastrointestinal disease (2%), pain (5%), vasodilation (1%), asthenia (6%), dizziness (4%), palpitations (2%), pharyngitis (2%), rhinitis (2%), dyspnea (1%), nervousness (2%), paresthesia (2%), tachycardia (2%).

Angina: The safety of diltiazem was evaluated in 158 patients with chronic stable angina pectoris treated with diltiazem at doses from 120 to 360 mg/day and in 50 patients treated with placebo. Thirty three percent of the diltiazem treated patients had one or more adverse event compared to 18% in the placebo group. Discontinuation due to adverse events was required in 3 patients who were on diltiazem 240 mg/day. The most common adverse events were: headache (8%), pain (4%), dizziness (3%) and peripheral edema (2%).

The following percentage of adverse effects, divided by system, were reported: Cardiovascular: edema, peripheral (1.8%), palpitations (1.2%), arrhythmia (1.2%).

CNS: headache (8.2%), asthenia (0.6%), dizziness (3.1%).

Gastrointestinal: constipation (1.2%), dyspepsia (1.2%).

Other: pain (3.7%), pharyngitis (1.8%), cough increase (1.2%), gout (1.2%), rash (1.2%), hyperglycemia (1.2%), albuminuria (1.2%), crystalluria (1.2%), dyspnea (0.6%), infection (0.6%).

Overdose: Symptoms and Treatment: There have been reports of diltiazem overdose in doses ranging from less than 1 to 18 g. In cases with fatal outcome, the majority involved multiple drug ingestion.

Events observed following diltiazem overdose included bradycardia, hypotension, heart block and cardiac failure. Most reports of overdose described some supportive medical measure and/or drug treatment. Bradycardia frequently responded favorably to atropine as did heart block, although cardiac pacing was also frequently utilized to treat heart block. Fluids and vasopressors were used to maintain blood pressure, and in cases of cardiac failure, inotropic agents were administered. In addition, some patients received treatment with ventilatory support, gastric lavage, activated charcoal, and i.v. calcium.

The effectiveness of i.v. calcium administration to reverse the pharmacological effects of diltiazem overdose has been inconsistent. In a few reported cases, overdose with calcium channel blockers associated with hypotension and bradycardia that was initially refractory to atropine became more responsive to atropine after the patients received i.v. calcium. In some cases i.v. calcium has been administered (1 g calcium chloride or 3 g calcium gluconate) over 5 minutes, and repeated every 10 to 20 minutes as necessary. Calcium gluconate has also been administered as a continuous infusion at a rate of 2 g/hour for 10 hours. Infusions of calcium for 24 hours or more may be required. Patients should be monitored for signs of hypercalcemia.

In the event of overdosage or exaggerated response, appropriate supportive measures should be employed in addition to gastric lavage. The following measures may be considered:

Bradycardia: Administer atropine. If there is no response to vagal blockage, administer isoproterenol cautiously.

High-degree AV Block: Treat as for bradycardia above. Fixed high-degree AV block should be treated with cardiac pacing.

Cardiac Failure: Administer inotropic agents (isoproterenol, dopamine or dobutamine) and diuretics.

Hypotension: Vasopressors (e.g., dopamine or norepinephrine bitartrate). Actual treatment and dosage should depend on the severity of the clinical situation and the judgment and experience of the treating physician.

Dosage: Diltiazem should not be chewed or crushed. Diltiazem has not been shown to be bioequivalent to other diltiazem formulations (see Pharmacology, Pharmacokinetics).

Hypertension: When used as monotherapy, usual starting doses are 180 to 240 mg once daily, although some patients may respond to 120 mg once daily. Maximum antihypertensive effect is usually observed after approximately 2 to 4 weeks of therapy; therefore, dosage adjustments should be scheduled accordingly.

A maximum daily dose of 360 mg should not be exceeded.

Tiazac (cont'd)

The dosage of diltiazem or concomitant antihypertensive agents may need to be adjusted when adding one to the other. See Warnings and Precautions regarding use with beta-blockers.

Angina: Dosages for the treatment of angina should be adjusted to each patient's needs, starting with a dose of 120 mg to 180 mg once daily. Individual patients may respond to higher doses of up to 360 mg once daily. When necessary, titration should be carried out over a 7- to 14-day period.

There is limited experience with doses above 360 mg. However, the incidence of adverse events increases as the dose increases with first-degree AV block, dizziness, and sinus bradycardia bearing the strongest realtionship to dose. Therefore, doses greater than 360 mg are not recommended.

Information for the Patient: See Blue Section—Information for the Patient "Tiazac".

Supplied: 120 mg: Each lavender/lavender extended-release capsule, imprinted, in white ink, with a maple leaf on one end and "BVF 120" on the other, contains: diltiazem HCl 120 mg. Nonmedicinal ingredients: black iron oxide, D&C Red #28, eudragit, FD&C Blue #1, FD&C Green #3, FD&C Red #40, gelatin, hydroxypropylmethylcellulose, magnesium stearate, microcrystalline cellulose, polysorbate, povidone, simethicone, sucrose stearate, talc and titanium dioxide. Bottles of 100.

180 mg: Each bluish green/white extended-release capsule imprinted, in black ink, with a maple leaf on one end and "BVF 180" on the other, contains: diltiazem HCl 180 mg. Nonmedicinal ingredients: black iron oxide, D&C Red #28, eudragit, FD&C Blue #1, FD&C Green #3, FD&C Red #40, gelatin, hydroxypropylmethylcellulose, magnesium stearate, microcrystalline cellulose, polysorbate, povidone, simethicone, sucrose stearate, talc and titanium dioxide. Bottles of 100.

240 mg: Each lavender/bluish green extended-release capsule imprinted, in white ink, with a maple leaf on one end and "BVF 240" on the other, contains: diltiazem HCl 240 mg. Nonmedicinal ingredients: black iron oxide, D&C Red #28, eudragit, FD&C Blue #1, FD&C Green #3, FD&C Red #40, gelatin, hydroxypropylmethylcellulose, magnesium stearate, microcrystalline cellulose, polysorbate, povidone, simethicone, sucrose stearate, talc and titanium dioxide. Bottles of 100.

300 mg: Each lavender/white extended-release capsule imprinted, in black ink, with a maple leaf on one end and "BVF 300" on the other, contains: diltiazem HCl 300 mg. Nonmedicinal ingredients: black iron oxide, D&C Red #28, eudragit, FD&C Blue #1, FD&C Green #3, FD&C Red #40, gelatin, hydroxypropylmethylcellulose, magnesium stearate, microcrystalline cellulose, polysorbate, povidone, simethicone, sucrose stearate, talc and titanium dioxide. Bottles of 100.

360 mg: Each bluish green/bluish green extended-release capsule imprinted, in white ink, with a maple leaf on one end and "BVF 360" on the other, contains: diltiazem HCl 360 mg. Nonmedicinal ingredients: black iron oxide, D&C Red #28, eudragit, FD&C Blue #1, FD&C Green #3, FD&C Red #40, gelatin, hydroxypropylmethylcellulose, magnesium stearate, microcrystalline cellulose, polysorbate, povidone, simethicone, sucrose stearate, talc and titanium dioxide. Bottles of 100.

Store between 15 to 30°C. Avoid excessive humidity.

(Shown in Product Recognition Section)

Reviewed 1999

TICLID® ℞

Roche

Ticlopidine HCl

Inhibitor of Platelet Function

Pharmacology: Ticlopidine is an inhibitor of platelet aggregation. It causes a time and dose-dependent inhibition of platelet aggregation and release of platelet factors, as well as a prolongation of bleeding time. The drug has no significant in vitro activity.

The exact mechanism of action is not fully characterized, but does not involve inhibition of the prostacyclin/thromboxane pathways or platelet CAMP.

Ticlopidine interferes with platelet membrane function by inhibiting ADP-induced platelet-fibrinogen binding and subsequent platelet-platelet interactions. The effect of ticlopidine on platelet function is irreversible.

Template bleeding time is usually prolonged by 2- to 5-fold of baseline values with the therapeutic dose of ticlopidine.

Upon discontinuation of ticlopidine dosing, bleeding time and other platelet function tests return to normal within 1 week in the majority of patients.

The correlation between ticlopidine plasma levels and activity is still under investigation. Much of the following data was obtained from older patients corresponding to the age of patients participating in clinical trials (mean age: 63 years).

After oral administration of the therapeutic dose of ticlopidine, rapid absorption occurs, with peak plasma levels occurring at approximately 2 hours after dosing. Absorption is at least 80% complete. Administration of ticlopidine after meals results in an increased (20%) level of ticlopidine in plasma.

Steady-state plasma levels of ticlopidine in plasma are obtained after approximately 14 days of dosing at 250 mg b.i.d. The terminal elimination half-life is 4 to 5 days. However, inhibition of platelet aggregation is not correlated with plasma drug levels.

Ticlopidine binds reversibly (98%) to plasma proteins, mainly to serum albumin and lipoproteins in a nonsaturable manner.

Ticlopidine is metabolized extensively by the liver; no intact ticlopidine is detected in the urine. Unmetabolized ticlopidine is a minor component in plasma after a single dose, but at steady state, ticlopidine is the major component.

Impaired hepatic function resulted in higher than normal plasma levels of unchanged ticlopidine after single doses or after multiple doses.

Inhibition of platelet aggregation is detected within 2 days of administration with 250 mg b.i.d. Maximum platelet aggregation inhibition is achieved 8 to 11 days following dosing with 250 mg b.i.d.

Indications: For reduction of the risk of first or recurrent stroke for patients who have experienced at least one of the following events: complete thromboembolic stroke, minor stroke, reversible ischemic neurological deficit (RIND), or transient ischemic attack (TIA) including transient monocular blindness (TMB).

Considerations in the selection of stroke prevention therapy should include the patients' current medical status and history, and their ability to comply with the required blood monitoring instructions concerning the use of ticlopidine.

Contraindications: The following conditions: known hypersensitivity to drug or its excipients; presence of hematopoietic disorders (such as neutropenia and/or thrombocytopenia); presence of hemostatic disorder; conditions associated with active bleeding, such as bleeding peptic ulcer or intracranial bleeding; severe liver dysfunction.

Warnings: The following warnings were developed from clinical trial experience with over 2 000 patients with cerebrovascular disease who were treated with ticlopidine for as long as 5.8 years.

Hematological Complications: About 2.4% of ticlopidine treated patients in clinical trials developed neutropenia (defined as an absolute neutrophil count (ANC) below 1.2×10^9 cells/L). The incidence of severe neutropenia (ANC $< 0.45 \times 10^9$ cells/L) was 0.8%. Severe neutropenia occurs during the first 3 to 12 weeks of therapy, and may develop quickly over a few days. The bone marrow shows a reduction in myeloid precursors. The condition may be life-threatening. The condition is usually reversible, and recovery usually occurs within 1 to 3 weeks after discontinuation of the drug but may take longer on occasion.

In clinical trials, thrombocytopenia (defined as a platelet count of $< 0.8 \times 10^{11}$ cells/L) has been observed in 0.4% of ticlopidine patients. The incidence of thrombocytopenia in patients on ASA or placebo was 0.3 or 0.4% respectively. The thrombocytopenia may occur as an isolated finding or in combination with neutropenia. Thrombocytopenia occurs during the first 3 to 12 weeks of therapy, and recovery usually occurs after drug discontinuation.

All patients should have a white blood cell count with a differential and platelet count performed every 2 weeks starting at baseline, before treatment is initiated, to the end of the third month of therapy with ticlopidine. When the neutrophil count shows a declining trend or the neutrophil numbers have fallen below 30% of the baseline, the values should be confirmed. If the presence of neutropenia (ANC $< 1.2 \times 10^9$ cells/L) or thrombocytopenia ($< 0.8 \times 10^{11}$ cells/L), are confirmed, the drug should be discontinued. Because of the long plasma half-life of ticlopidine, it is recommended that any patient who discontinues ticlopidine for any reason within the first 90 days have an additional CBC with white cell differential count obtained 2 weeks after discontinuation of therapy (see Precautions).

All forms of hematological adverse reactions are potentially fatal. Rarely, cases of pancytopenia, aplastic anemia or thrombocytopenia have been reported. Most cases were reversible, but some of them have been fatal. Thrombocytopenia may occur in isolation or together with neutropenia. Thrombotic thrombocytopenic purpura (TTP) has been reported, therefore careful attention to diagnosis should be made to guide treatment, platelet transfusion may be harmful in these patients.

Hemorrhagic Complications: Prolongation of bleeding time occurs in subjects treated with ticlopidine. Purpura and a few cases of more serious hemorrhagic events such as hematemesis, melena, hemothorax and intracranial bleeding have been reported. Patients must be instructed to watch for signs of bleeding disorders and to report any abnormality to their physician immediately. Ticlopidine therapy has to be stopped by the patient if a physician is not immediately available for consultation.

Anticoagulant Drugs: Should be avoided as tolerance and safety of simultaneous administration with ticlopidine has not been established.

Hepatic Abnormalities: Most patients receiving ticlopidine showed some increase of their alkaline phosphatase values above their baseline and in one-third the increase exceeded the upper reference range. In 6% the value was greater than twice the upper reference range. These increases in alkaline phosphatase were nonprogressive and asymptomatic. In clinical trials, 2 cases (0.1%) of cholestatic jaundice accompanied by elevated transaminases alkaline phosphatase, and bilirubin levels above 43 μmol/L have been observed. Both patients recovered promptly upon drug discontinuation.

Pregnancy: The safety of ticlopidine in pregnancy has not been established. It should not be used in pregnant patients.

Children: Safety in children has not been studied. Do not use in pediatric patients.

Precautions: Selection of Patients: Ticlopidine should be used only for the established indications (see Indications) and should not be given to patients with hematopoietic disorders, hemostatic disorders, patients suffering from conditions associated with active bleeding (see Contraindications) and patients anticipating elective surgery. In clinical trials elderly patients tolerated the drug well, but safety in children and pregnant women have not been established.

Clinical Monitoring: All patients have to be carefully monitored for clinical signs and symptoms of adverse drug reactions (see Adverse Effects). The signs and symptoms possibly related to neutropenia (fever, chills, sore throat, ulcerations in oral cavity), thrombocytopenia and abnormal hemostasis (prolonged or unusual bleeding, bruising, purpura, dark stool), jaundice (including dark urine, light colored stool) and allergic reactions should be explained to the patients who should be advised to stop medication and consult their physician immediately if any of these occur.

Laboratory Monitoring: All patients should have a white blood cell count with a differential and platelet count performed every 2 weeks starting at baseline, before treatment is initiated, to the end of the third month of therapy with ticlopidine. When the neutrophil count shows a declining trend or the neutrophil numbers have fallen below 30% of the baseline, the value should be confirmed. If the presence of neutropenia (ANC $< 1.2 \times 10^9$ cells/L) or thrombocytopenia ($< 0.8 \times 10^{11}$ cells/L) are confirmed, the drug should be discontinued. Because of the long plasma half-life of ticlopidine, it is recommended that any patient who discontinues ticlopidine for any reason within the first 90 days, have an additional CBC with white cell differential obtained 2 weeks after discontinuation of therapy (see Warnings). Thereafter, the WBC counts need only be repeated for symptoms or signs suggestive of neutropenia.

Liver function tests should be conducted during therapy with ticlopidine in response to signs and symptoms suggestive of hepatic dysfunction.

Elective Surgery: Ticlopidine should be discontinued 10 to 14 days prior to elective surgery or dental extraction and bleeding time and thrombocyte count performed before the procedure if clinically indicated.

Emergency Surgery: Prolonged bleeding during surgery may be a problem in ticlopidine treated patients. Transfusions of fresh platelets would be expected to improve hemostasis in such patients, but there are no data from clinical trials to confirm this expectation. There are data from clinical pharmacology trials that indicate treatment with glucocorticosteroids can normalize bleeding time in ticlopidine treated subjects, but there is no experience with ticlopidine treated surgical patients to show that such treatment improves hemostasis.

Specific Precautions: Liver: Ticlopidine is contraindicated in patients with severe liver dysfunction or cholestatic jaundice. Mild increase of alkaline phosphatase may be seen for the duration of the treatment and is inconsequential in the majority of patients (see Warnings and Contraindications).

Kidneys: Ticlopidine has been well tolerated in patients with moderately decreased renal function. In severe renal disease, caution and close monitoring are recommended.

Gastrointestinal: Conditions associated with active bleeding, such as bleeding ulcers, constitute contraindication for ticlopidine. Clinical judgment and monitoring of stool for occult blood are required for patients with a history of ulcerative lesions.

Trauma: Ticlopidine should be discontinued temporarily until the danger of abnormal bleeding is eliminated. A single fatal case of intracranial bleeding following head trauma has been reported. The extent to which ticlopidine may have contributed to the severity of the bleeding is unknown.

Drug Interactions: Since ticlopidine is metabolized by the liver, dosing of ticlopidine or other drugs metabolized in the liver may require adjustment upon starting or stopping therapy.

Table I outlines the agents which have been concomitantly administered with ticlopidine and the observed interaction if any.

Other Concomitant Therapy: Although specific interaction studies were not performed, in clinical studies, ticlopidine was used concomitantly with beta-blockers, calcium channel blockers and diuretics without evidence of clinically significant adverse interactions.

Adverse Effects: Most adverse effects are mild, transient and occur early in the course of treatment.

In controlled clinical trials of 1 to 5 years' duration, discontinuation of ticlopidine due to one or more adverse effects was required in 20.9% of patients. In these same trials, ASA and placebo led to discontinuation in 14.5 and 6.7% of patients respectively.

The incidence rates of adverse reactions listed in Table II were derived from multicentre, controlled clinical trials comparing ticlopidine, placebo and ASA over study periods of up to 5 years. The rates are based on adverse reactions considered probably drug-related by the investigator. Adverse experiences occurring in greater than 1% of patients treated with ticlopidine in controlled clinical trials are shown in Table II.

The incidence of thrombocytopenia in these controlled studies was 0.4% in the ticlopidine and placebo groups of patients and 0.3% in the ASA patient population.

The following rare events have been reported and their relationship to ticlopidine is uncertain.

Pancytopenia, hemolytic anemia with reticulocytosis, thrombocytopenic thrombotic purpura, jaundice, allergic pneumonitis, systemic lupus (positive ANA), peripheral neuropathy, vasculitis, serum sickness, arthropathy, hepatitis, nephrotic syndrome, myositis angioedema, fever, hyponatremia, bleeding increased (spontaneous, post-traumatic or postoperative), cholestatic jaundice, colitis, erythema multiforme, hepatic necrosis, hepatocellular jaundice, peptic ulcer, Stevens-Johnson syndrome, renal failure, and sepsis.

Table II—Ticlid

Adverse Effects

Event	Ticlid (n=2 048) Incidence	ASA (n=1 527) Incidence	Placebo (n=536) Incidence
	Percent of Patients in Controlled Studies		
Diarrhea	12.5(6.3)*	5.2(1.8)	4.5(1.7)
Nausea	7.0(2.6)	6.2(1.9)	1.7(0.9)
Dyspepsia	7.0(1.1)	9.0(2.0)	0.9(0.2)
Rash	5.1(3.4)	1.5(0.8)	0.6(0.9)
Gastrointestinal Pain	3.7(1.9)	5.6(2.7)	1.3(0.4)
Neutropenia	2.4(1.3)	0.8(0.1)	1.4(0.4)
Purpura	2.2(0.2)	1.6(0.1)	0.0(0.0)
Vomiting	1.9(1.4)	1.4(0.9)	0.9(0.4)
Flatulence	1.5(0.1)	1.4(0.3)	0.0(0.0)
Pruritus	1.3(0.8)	0.3(0.1)	0.0(0.0)
Dizziness	1.1(0.4)	0.5(0.4)	0.0(0.0)
Anorexia	1.0(0.4)	0.5(0.4)	0.0(0.0)

*Percent of patients (in parentheses) discontinuing clinical trials due to event.

Gastrointestinal: Ticlopidine therapy has been associated with a variety of gastrointestinal complaints including diarrhea and nausea. The majority of cases are mild and transient in nature and occur within 3 months of initiation of therapy. Typically, events are resolved within 1 to 2 weeks without discontinuation of therapy. If the effect is severe or persistent, therapy should be discontinued.

Hemorrhagic: Ticlopidine has been associated with a number of bleeding complications such as ecchymosis, epistaxis, hematuria, conjunctival hemorrhage, gastrointestinal bleeding and postoperative bleeding.

Intracerebral bleeding was rare in clinical trials with ticlopidine and was no more than that seen with comparator agents (ASA, placebo).

Rash: Ticlopidine has been associated with a maculopapular or urticarial rash (often with pruritus). Rash usually occurs within 3 months of initiation of therapy, with a mean time to onset of 11 days. If drug is discontinued, recovery should occur within several days. Many rashes do not recur on drug rechallenge. There have been rare reports of more severe rashes.

Altered Laboratory Findings: Hematological: agranulocytosis, eosinophilia, neutropenia, pancytopenia, thrombocytopenia, and thrombocytosis have been associated with ticlopidine administration (see Warnings).

Liver: Ticlopidine therapy has been associated with elevations of alkaline phosphatase (see Warnings). Maximal changes occur within 1 to 4 months of therapy initiation. No further progressive increases are seen with continuous therapy. Occasionally patients developed deviations in bilirubin, AST, ALT and GGTP.

Cholesterol: Chronic ticlopidine therapy has been associated with increased serum cholesterol and triglycerides. Serum levels of HDL-C, LDL-C, VLDL-C, and triglycerides are increased 8 to 10% after 1 to 4 months of therapy. No further progressive elevations are seen with continuous therapy. The ratios of the lipoprotein subfractions are unchanged. The effect is not correlated with age, sex, alcohol use or diabetes.

Table I—Ticlid

Drug Interactions

Agents	Observed Interaction
NSAIDs including ASA	Ticlopidine potentiates the effect of ASA or NSAIDs on platelet aggregation. The safety of use of ticlopidine with ASA or NSAIDs is not established.
Antipyrine and products metabolized by hepatic microsomal enzymes	30% increase in t½ of antipyrine. Dose of products metabolized by hepatic microsomal enzymes to be adjusted when starting or stopping concomitant therapy with ticlopidine.
Theophylline	t½ of theophylline increased from 8.6 to 12.2 hours along with a comparable reduction in its total plasma clearance.
Digoxin	Approximately 15% reduction in digoxin plasma levels, (little or no change in digoxin's efficacy expected).
Cimetidine	Chronic administration of cimetidine induced a 50% reduction in clearance of a single dose of ticlopidine.
Antacids	20% decrease in ticlopidine plasma level when administered after antacids.
Phenobarbital	No interaction reported.

Overdose: Symptoms and Treatment: One case of deliberate overdosage with ticlopidine has been reported in a foreign postmarketing surveillance program. A 38-year-old male took a single 6 000 mg dose of ticlopidine (equivalent to 24 standard 250 mg tablets). The only abnormalities reported were increased bleeding time and increased ALT. No special therapy was instituted and the patient recovered without sequelae. Based on animal studies, overdosage may result in severe gastrointestinal intolerance.

In the case of excessive bleeding after injury or surgery, standard supportive measures should be carried out if indicated, including gastric lavage, platelet transfusion and use of corticosteroids.

Dosage: The recommended dose is 250 mg twice daily with food.

Ticlopidine should be taken with meals to minimize gastrointestinal intolerance.

Information for the Patient: See Blue Section—Information for the Patient "Ticlid".

Supplied: Each oval, white, film-coated tablet, printed using blue ink with Ticlid above half an arrow on one side, "250" above half an arrow on the other side, contains: ticlopidine HCl 250 mg. Nonmedicinal ingredients: citric acid, cornstarch, FD&C blue No. 1 aluminum lake, hydroxypropyl methylcellulose, magnesium stearate, microcrystalline cellulose, povidone, stearic acid powder, titanium dioxide, polyethylene glycol and water. Gluten- and tartrazine-free. Fold-over cards of 28 (2 blisters of 14 tablets). Boxes of 56 (4×14).

For the first 3 months of therapy, only request or dispense the 14 days' supply of tablets (see Precautions).

Store at room temperature. Dispense in light-resistant containers. Blister packs should not be exposed to light.

(Shown in Product Recognition Section)

TILADE® Ⓟ

Rhône-Poulenc Rorer

Nedocromil Sodium

Bronchial Anti-inflammatory Agent

Pharmacology: Nedocromil sodium is a new chemical entity that inhibits the release of inflammatory mediators from a variety of cell types occurring in the lumen and in the mucosa of the bronchial tree. When it is administered topically to the bronchi, it displays specific anti-inflammatory properties. Laboratory experiments have shown that nedocromil sodium prevents the release of inflammatory chemotactic and smooth muscle contracting mediators, which are preformed or derived from arachidonic acid metabolism by both the lipoxygenase and cyclo-oxygenase pathways, in a range of human and animal leukocytes. Nedocromil sodium prevents the release of mediators, such as, histamine, leukotriene C_4 (LTC_4) and prostaglandin D_2 (PGD_2) from the cellular population of the chronically inflamed bronchus, especially from mast cells of the mucosal type. There is growing evidence that these mediators are important in human lung disease, and nedocromil sodium may, therefore, be expected to have more scope in the management of chronic reversible obstructive airways disease in which allergy, inflammation and bronchial hyperresponsiveness are significant pathophysiological factors.

After inhalation, nedocromil sodium is deposited throughout the respiratory tract where about 5% of the dose is absorbed. Because nedocromil sodium is inhaled, much of the delivered dose is either swallowed directly or subsequently due to mucociliary clearance from the large airways. A small amount of nedocromil sodium (2 to 3%) is then absorbed from the gastrointestinal tract. Since the absorption rate constant from the respiratory tract is lower than the elimination rate constant in bile and urine, the terminal half-life (1.5 to 2 hours) reflects the absorption rate of the lungs. The drug is cleared rapidly enough from the circulation so that successive doses in the recommended dosing regimen do not accumulate.

Nedocromil sodium is bound reversibly (80%) to human plasma proteins and to a lesser extent in animals. It is not metabolized in man or in animals. In man it is excreted unchanged in the urine (approximately 70%) and in feces (approximately 30%). While the plasma concentration falls rapidly (i.e., to 10% of peak levels in 8 hours) and urinary excretion is 90% complete within 12 hours, fecal elimination may take up to 3 days to be completed.

The pharmacokinetic profile of nedocromil sodium is similar in healthy volunteers and in patients with reversible obstructive airways disease. In challenge studies, a single dose of nedocromil provided protection against bronchospasm provoked

Tilade (cont'd)

by stimulants such as, inhaled allergens, cold air, exercise and atmospheric pollutants.

There is limited data on the pharmacokinetic profile of nedocromil sodium in children.

Indications: As an adjunctive in the treatment of mild to moderate reversible obstructive airways disease, including bronchial asthma and bronchitis, particularly where allergic factors may be present.

Nedocromil sodium can also be used on a maintenance or on an occasional basis in the prevention of bronchospasm provoked by stimulants, such as, inhaled allergens, cold air, exercise and atmospheric pollutants.

Nedocromil sodium may be used safely with other antiasthma drugs. The addition of nedocromil sodium may permit reduction of concomitant therapy.

Contraindications: Known hypersensitivity to nedocromil sodium, to sorbitan trioleate or to propellants, such as, dichlorotetrafluoroethane and dichlorodifluoromethane.

Warnings: Nedocromil sodium should not be used for the relief of an acute attack of bronchospasm.

Precautions: In the treatment of asthma, nedocromil sodium should not be used as an alternative to bronchodilators. However, addition of nedocromil sodium to the treatment regimen can reduce the need for concomitant medications. **This reduction should be done slowly and under close supervision. The requirements for the reduction of corticosteroids have not been established.**

To ensure optimal delivery to the bronchial tree patients should be carefully instructed in the proper use of the inhaler. For maximum benefit, patients should be reminded of the necessity to take nedocromil sodium regularly, as prescribed.

Physicians should advise patients that to relieve or prevent throat irritation and the unpleasant taste caused by nedocromil sodium, they may gargle or rinse their mouth after use.

Abuse of fluorocarbon propellants may be hazardous. Deliberate inhalation of propellants in high concentrations, particularly under conditions of hypoxia, has resulted in toxic cardiovascular effects, severe CNS disturbances, and death. Acute toxic effects of nedocromil sodium would be restricted to propellant overdose or to aerosol-induced bronchoconstriction. Nedocromil sodium itself has an extremely low acute toxicity.

Pregnancy: Safety in human pregnancy and the absence of adverse effects on the human reproductive process have not been established. Small amounts are known to cross the placenta but without effect in animals. In fact, in reproductive studies, nedocromil sodium at up to 100 mg/kg (more than 800 times the human maintenance dose) has shown no teratogenic or embryotoxic effects, nor has it interfered with reproductive performance, gestation, parturition, or suckling. Nedocromil sodium did not affect male or female fertility nor did it alter the development of progeny.

Although there is no reason to suspect that nedocromil sodium affects the fetus or mother, as with any drug, caution must be exercised. The benefits of treatment to the mother must be weighed against the potential risk to the fetus before proposing its use.

Lactation: Safety in breast-fed infants has not been established. Animal studies have indicated no toxicity of nedocromil sodium in suckling newborns receiving drug from the parent or directly by injection. The concentrations of nedocromil sodium in milk of animals were very low but have not been measured in human milk. The benefits of treating a nursing mother must be weighed against potential risk to the infant.

Children: The safety and efficacy in children under 6 years of age has not yet been established.

Drug Interactions: Nedocromil sodium has been used in association with other antiasthmatic drugs in man including β-adrenergic agonists, inhaled and oral corticosteroids, theophylline and other methylxanthines and, with ipratropium bromide. No drug-drug interactions have been observed in humans or in animals.

Children: There is limited data on drug interactions with nedocromil sodium use in children under 12 years of age.

Adverse Effects: Few side effects have been reported, principally headache and upper gastrointestinal tract symptoms, (nausea, vomiting, dyspepsia and abdominal pain). These have been mild and transient and insufficient to require discontinuation of treatment in nearly all cases. Some patients have reported an unpleasant taste. In common with other inhaled medications nedocromil sodium may produce cough or bronchospasm. There have been reports of a generalized sensation of warmth with nedocromil sodium use.

Specific side effects and their frequencies of occurrence with chronic dosing are unpleasant taste (12.2%), headache (5.98%), nausea (3.77%), vomiting (1.77%), dyspepsia (1.21%) and abdominal pain (0.94%).

In pediatric clinical trials, specific side effects and their occurrence were unpleasant taste (5.86%), headache (12.02%), nausea (1.69%), vomiting (2.93%) and abdominal pain (3.08%).

Overdose: Symptoms and Treatment: There have been no reported cases of overdose in humans. Animal studies have not shown evidence of toxic effects of nedocromil sodium, even at high dosage. If overdosage is suspected, treatment should be supportive and directed to the control of the relevant symptoms.

Dosage: Nedocromil sodium is intended for regular daily usage and should not be used for relief of symptoms during an acute attack.

The therapeutic benefits of repeated doses will be apparent in most patients within 1 week of starting treatment, but it may take longer on occasion.

Adults and children over 6 years of age: In initial and maintenance therapy, 2 actuations (4 mg of nedocromil sodium) 4 times daily. In patients under good control on 4 times daily dosing, a lower dose of nedocromil sodium can be tried. This reduction should first be to 3 times daily. Then, after several weeks of continued good control, administration can be changed to twice daily dosing. Data on the effectiveness of 2 actuations twice daily is limited in patients under 12 years of age.

Nedocromil sodium in a single dose of 2 actuations (4 mg) up to 30 minutes before exposure may provide protection against bronchospasm provoked by stimulants, such as, inhaled allergens, cold air, exercise and atmospheric pollutants.

It is essential that patients be properly instructed in the use of the inhaler, and that the correct method be reinforced periodically.

Information for the Patient: See Blue Section—Information for the Patient "Tilade".

Supplied: Each metered actuation contains: nedocromil sodium 2 mg. Nonmedicinal ingredients: dichlorodifluoromethane, dichlorotetrafluoroethane and sorbitan trioleate. Pressurized, aluminum canisters of 17 mL. Units are filled with material to provide a minimum of 112 metered actuations. The pack consists of an aerosol canister with a plastic adapter and a patient instruction sheet. Store at 15 to 30°C. Contents under pressure. Do not place in hot water or near radiators, stoves or other sources of heat. Do not puncture or incinerate container even when empty. Do not store at temperatures over 30°C.

Reviewed 1997

TIM-AK Ⓟ
Dioptic
Timolol Maleate
Elevated Intraocular Pressure Therapy

Supplied: Each mL of sterile ophthalmic solution contains: timolol maleate equivalent to timolol 0.5%. Nonmedicinal ingredients: benzalkonium chloride, dibasic sodium phosphate, monobasic sodium phosphate, purified water, sodium chloride and sodium hydroxide. Plastic dropper bottles of 5 and 10 mL. Store between 15 and 30°C. Protect from light and freezing.

TIMED RELEASE SWISS ONE "50"
Swiss Herbal
Multivitamins—Minerals

Supplied: Each timed release caplet contains: beta carotene 10 000 IU, vitamin D 400 IU, vitamin E 75 IU, vitamin C 100 mg, vitamin B_1 50 mg, vitamin B_2 50 mg, vitamin B_6 50 mg, vitamin B_{12} 75 μg, niacinamide 50 mg, biotin 50 μg, folic acid 0.4 mg and D'pantothenic acid 50 mg. Chelated minerals: calcium 125 mg, magnesium 100 mg, potassium 25 mg, iron 18 mg, manganese 5 mg, zinc 10 mg, copper 2 mg, iodine 0.225 mg, selenium 25 μg and chromium 25 μg. Choline bitartrate 50 mg, inositol 50 mg and dl methionine 50 mg. In a food and herbal matrix base: acerola, alfalfa, camomile, green cabbage, kelp, papaya, parsley, protein hydrolysates, rice bran, rosehips, sarsaparilla and watercress. Nonmedicinal ingredients: betaine HCl, cellulose, co-enzyme Q10, dried barley crass juice powder, echinacea, glutamic acid, hesperidin, lemon bio-flavonoids, magnesium stearate, papain, para amino benzoic acid, peppermint oil, rosehips, rutin, unsaturated fatty acids and vanilla. Bottles of 30, 60 and 90.

TIMED RELEASE VITAMIN C 500 mg
Swiss Herbal
Vitamin

Supplied: Each timed released capsule contains: vitamin C 500 mg. Nonmedicinal ingredients: cellulose, magnesium stearate and stearic acid. Bottles of 90 and 180.

TIMED RELEASE VITAMIN C 1 000 mg
Swiss Herbal
Vitamin

Supplied: Each timed release caplet contains: vitamin C 1 000 mg. Nonmedicinal ingredients: cellulose, magnesium stearate and stearic acid. Bottles of 50, 90 and 180.

TIMENTIN® Ⓟ
SmithKline Beecham
Ticarcillin Disodium—Potassium Clavulanate
Antibiotic—β-Lactamase Inhibitor

Pharmacology: Ticarcillin exerts a bactericidal action against sensitive organisms during the stage of active multiplication through the inhibition of the biosynthesis of bacterial cell wall mucopeptides. Clavulanic acid inhibits specific β-lactamases of some microorganisms and allows ticarcillin to inhibit ticarcillin resistant organisms which produce clavulanic acid sensitive β-lactamases.

Indications: For the treatment of the following infections when caused by Timentin-susceptible strains of the designated bacteria: Bacterial septicemia when caused by β-lactamase (excluding Type I) producing strains of E. coli, S. aureus, and Klebsiella species.

Lower respiratory infections when caused by β-lactamase (excluding Type I) producing strains of S. aureus, H. influenzae and Klebsiella species.

Bone infections when caused by β-lactamase producing strains of S. aureus.

Skin structure infections when caused by β-lactamase (excluding Type I) producing strains of S. aureus, E. coli and Klebsiella species.

Urinary tract infections when caused by β-lactamase (excluding Type I) producing strains of E. coli and Klebsiella species.

Gynecologic infections when caused by β-lactamase (excluding Type I) producing strains of Bacteroides species, E. coli, S. aureus, S. epidermidis and Klebsiella species.

Intra-abdominal infections including peritonitis and intra-abdominal abscess, when caused by β-lactamase (excluding Type 1) producing strains of E. coli, K. pneumoniae, B. fragilis, and P. aeruginosa. The efficacy and safety of Timentin for the treatment of intra-abdominal infections in infants and children under the age of 12 have not been established.

Appropriate culture and susceptibility tests should be performed before treatment in order to isolate and identify organisms causing infection and to determine their susceptibilities to Timentin. Therapy may, however, be initiated before results of such tests are known when there is reason to believe the infection may involve any of the β-lactamase (excluding Type I) producing organisms listed above. Modification of the treatment may be required once these results become available or if there is no clinical response.

The treatment of mixed infections caused by ticarcillin susceptible organisms and β-lactamase (excluding Type 1) producing organisms susceptible to Timentin should not require the addition of another antibiotic due to the ticarcillin content of Timentin.

Prophylaxis: The administration of Timentin perioperatively (preoperatively, intraoperatively and postoperatively) may reduce the incidence of certain infections in patients undergoing elective surgical procedures (i.e. colorectal surgery and abdominal hysterectomy) that may be classified as contaminated or potentially contaminated.

In patients undergoing cesarean section, who are considered to be at increased risk of infection, intraoperative (after clamping the umbilical cord) and postoperative use of Timentin may reduce the incidence of surgery related postoperative infections.

The data from all the surgical prophylaxis trials were combined to obtain a sufficient number of patients to suggest that Timentin may be of value in reducing infection following colorectal surgery, abdominal hysterectomy or high risk cesarean section.

If signs of postsurgical infection should appear, specimens for culture should be obtained for identification of the causative organism(s) so that appropriate therapy may be instituted.

Contraindications: Patients with a history of hypersensitivity to the penicillin, clavam, or cephalosporin, group of β-lactams.

Warnings: Serious and occasionally fatal hypersensitivity (anaphylactoid) reactions have been reported in patients on penicillin therapy. These reactions are more apt to occur in individuals with a history of penicillin hypersensitivity and/or a history of sensitivity to multiple allergens. There have been reports of individuals with a history of cephalosporin hypersensitivity who have experienced severe reactions when treated with penicillins. Before initiating therapy with Timentin, careful inquiry should be made concerning previous hypersensitivity reactions to penicillins, cephalosporins, clavams or other allergens. If an allergic reaction occurs, the administration of Timentin should be discontinued and appropriate therapy should be instituted. Serious anaphylactoid reactions require immediate emergency treatment with epinephrine. Oxygen, i.v. steroids and airway management, including intubation, should also be used as indicated.

Patients with renal impairment or underlying hemostatic problems should be observed for bleeding manifestations. Such patients should be dosed strictly according to recommendations (see Dosage). If bleeding occurs the administration of Timentin should be discontinued and appropriate therapy instituted.

Patients receiving Timentin may develop hemorrhagic manifestations associated with coagulation abnormalities, such as changes in bleeding time and platelet function, particularly if co-administered with drugs such as ASA or anticoagulants. If these occur, the administration of Timentin should be discontinued and appropriate therapy instituted. On withdrawal of the drug, the bleeding time and coagulation abnormalities should revert to normal after approximately 7 days. Other causes of abnormal bleeding should also be considered.

Precautions: The total daily dosage should be reduced when Timentin is administered to patients with transient or persistent reduction of urinary output due to renal insufficiency (see Dosage) because high and prolonged serum antibiotic concentrations can occur from usual doses.

Periodic assessment of organ system functions, including renal, hepatic and hematopoietic function should be made during prolonged therapy with Timentin.

The passage of any penicillin from blood into brain is facilitated by inflamed meninges and during cardiopulmonary bypass. In the presence of these conditions and particularly when accompanied by renal failure, sufficiently high serum ticarcillin concentration can be attained to produce CNS adverse effects: these include myoclonia, convulsive seizures and depressed consciousness.

Timentin has been reported to cause hypokalemia; therefore, the possibility of this occurring should be kept in mind particularly when treating patients with fluid and electrolyte imbalance. Periodic monitoring of serum potassium is advisable and, when necessary, corrective therapy implemented.

The theoretical sodium content is 4.83 mmol (111 mg)/g of Timentin. Therefore, electrolyte levels and cardiac status should be monitored carefully during treatment, particularly in patients with hypertension or congestive heart failure.

The possibility of overgrowth by non-susceptible organisms and species originally sensitive to Timentin should be kept in mind, particularly during prolonged treatment. If superinfection occurs during therapy, appropriate measures should be taken.

Children: The safety and efficacy for the treatment of infections in infants from birth to 1 month of age have not been established.

Pregnancy: Safety in the treatment of infections during human pregnancy is unknown. Timentin should only be used during pregnancy if the anticipated benefit to the mother justifies the potential risk to the fetus.

Lactation: Penicillins have been shown to be excreted in human breast milk. It is not known whether clavulanic acid is excreted in breast milk. Nursing should be avoided during treatment with Timentin.

Drug/Laboratory Test Interactions: Timentin should not be mixed with an aminoglycoside in the same container. Penicillins can cause substantial inactivation of aminoglycosides.

Probenecid interferes with the renal tubular secretion of ticarcillin, thereby increasing serum concentrations and prolonging serum half-life of the antibiotic. However, probenecid has no effect on the renal clearance or serum concentrations of clavulanic acid.

High urine concentrations of ticarcillin (>1 500 mg/L 2 hours after an i.v. injection of 3.1 g Timentin) may produce false positive protein reactions (pseudoproteinuria) with the following methods: sulfosalicylic acid and boiling test, acetic acid test, biuret reaction, and nitric acid test. The bromphenol blue (Multi-stix) reagent strip test has been reported to be reliable.

The presence of clavulanic acid in Timentin may cause a non-specific binding of IgG and albumin by red cell membranes leading to a false positive Coombs test.

Adverse Effects: The following adverse reactions may occur during therapy: Hypersensitivity: skin rash, pruritus, urticaria, arthralgia, myalgia, drug fever, chills, chest discomfort, bronchospasm, wheezing, and anaphylactic reactions.

CNS: headache, giddiness, neuromuscular hyperirritability or convulsive seizures.

Gastrointestinal: disturbances of taste and smell, stomatitis, flatulence, nausea, vomiting and diarrhea, epigastric pain.

Hemic and Lymphatic: thrombocytopenia, leukopenia, neutropenia, eosinophilia and reduction of hemoglobin or hematocrit. Prolongation of prothrombin time and bleeding time.

Abnormalities of Hepatic and Renal Function Tests: elevation of serum aspartate aminotransferase AST, serum alanine aminotransferase ALT, serum alkaline phosphatase, serum LDH, serum bilirubin. Elevation of serum creatinine and/or BUN, hypernatremia. Reduction in serum potassium and uric acid.

Local: pain, burning, erythema, swelling and induration at the injection site and phlebitis and thrombophlebitis with i.v. administration.

Other: Increased muscle weakness in patients with myasthenia gravis has been reported.

Overdose: Symptoms and Treatment: Timentin overdosage has the potential to cause neuromuscular hyperirritability or convulsive seizures. Ticarcillin may be removed from circulation by hemodialysis. The molecular weight, degree of protein binding and pharmacokinetic profile of clavulanic acid together with information from a single patient with renal insufficiency all suggest that this compound may also be removed by hemodialysis.

Dosage: Timentin should be administered only by i.v. infusion over 30 minutes.

Adults: Dosage for any individual patient must take into consideration the site and severity of infection, the susceptibility of the organisms causing infection, and the status of the patient's host defense mechanisms.

The recommended dosage for adults (60 kg or greater) is 3.1 g every 4 to 6 hours.

For patients weighing less than 60 kg, the recommended dosage is 200 to 300 mg/kg/day, based on ticarcillin content, given in divided doses every 4 to 6 hours.

The duration of therapy depends upon the severity of infection. Generally, Timentin should be continued for at least 2 days after signs and symptoms of infection have disappeared. The usual duration is 10 to 14 days; however, in difficult and complicated infections, more prolonged therapy may be required. In certain infections, involving abscess formation, appropriate surgical drainage should be performed in conjunction with antimicrobial therapy.

Adults with Impaired Renal Function: The serum half-life of Timentin in patients with renal insufficiency is prolonged, consequently, the dosage regimen must be adjusted. Clinical efficacy data are insufficient at present to establish an appropriate dosage regimen for Timentin in patients with renal dysfunction. However, on the basis of theoretical pharmacokinetic considerations (namely absence of any change in the pharmacokinetics of ticarcillin due to clavulanic acid and the apparent greater tissue clearance of clavulanic acid as compared to ticarcillin) it is suggested that for infections complicated by renal dysfunction, the dosage regimen as used currently for ticarcillin alone may generally be adopted (see below).

An initial loading dose of 3.1 g Timentin followed by doses indicated in Table I.

Table I—Timentin

Dosage in Adults with Impaired Renal Function

Creatinine clearance mL/min	Dosage (based on ticarcillin content)
Over 60	3 g every 4 hours
30–60	2 g every 4 hours
10–30	2 g every 8 hours
less than 10	2 g every 12 hours
less than 10 with hepatic dysfunction	2 g every 24 hours
patients on peritoneal dialysis	3 g every 12 hours
patients on hemodialysis	2 g every 12 hours supplemented with 3 g after each dialysis

The half-lives of ticarcillin and clavulanic acid in patients with renal dysfunction (creatinine clearance <10 mL/min) is 8.5 and 2.9 hours, respectively.

To calculate creatinine clearance from a serum creatinine value use the following formula:

$$C_{cr} = \frac{(140-\text{age})\ (\text{wt in kg})}{72 \times S_{cr}(\text{mg/dL})}$$

This is the calculated creatinine clearance for adult males, for females it is 15% less. To convert calculated creatinine clearance to SI units (mL/second), multiply result by 0.0167.

Prophylaxis: For surgical prophylaxis, administration should not exceed the recommended dosage regimen, since the continued administration of any antibiotic increases the risk of adverse reactions while, in the majority of surgical procedures, does not reduce the incidence of subsequent infection.

A 3 dosage regimen is recommended as follows: Patients undergoing cesarean section: Administer the first dose of 3.1 g Timentin as soon as the umbilical cord is clamped. The second and third dosage of 3.1 g should be administered at 4 hour intervals after the initial dose for a total of 3 doses.

Patients undergoing Abdominal Hysterectomy or Colorectal Surgery: Administer the first dose of 3.1 g Timentin one-half to 1 hour prior to the initial incision. The second and third dosage of 3.1 g should be administered at 4 hour intervals after the initial dose for a total of 3 doses.

Infants and Children (Under 40 kg, 1 month to 12 years of age): Clinical and pharmacokinetic data are limited in these age groups. However, the dosages in Table II based on the ticarcillin content, have been used. These daily dosages should not exceed the adult dose.

Neonates: The safety and efficacy for the treatment of infections in neonates (birth to 1 month of age) have not been established.

Administration: Timentin must not be administered by bolus i.v. injection or by i.m. injection. The dissolved drug should be further diluted to the desired volume using a suitable solution listed below. The further diluted i.v. solution of Timentin should be administered over a period of 30 minutes by direct infusion or through a Y-type i.v. infusion set which may already be in place. If this method or the piggyback method of administration is used, it is advisable to discontinue temporarily the administration of any other solutions during the infusion of Timentin.

Timentin should not be physically mixed or administered at the same site with any other antimicrobial agent such as an aminoglycoside.

Reconstitution: For I.V. Infusion: **3.1 g:** Reconstitute each vial with 13 mL Sterile Water for Injection USP; when dissolved,

Table II—Timentin

Dosage in Infants and Children

Infections		Dosage Schedule (mg/kg)*	Total Daily Dosage (mg/kg/day)*
Non U.T.I.	severe	50mg/kg every 4 hours	300
	mild-moderate	50mg/kg every 6 hours	200
U.T.I.	complicated	50mg/kg every 4 hours	300
	uncomplicated	50mg/kg every 6 hours	200

* based on ticarcillin content.

Timentin (cont'd)

the concentration of ticarcillin will be approximately 200 mg/mL with a corresponding concentration of 6.7 mg/mL for clavulanic acid (stock solution). Conversely, each 5 mL of the 3.1 g dose reconstituted with approximately 13 mL of diluent will contain approximately 1 g of ticarcillin and 33 mg of clavulanic acid.

31 g: Reconstitute each vial with 76 mL Sterile Water for Injection USP; when dissolved, concentration of ticarcillin will be approximately 300 mg/mL with a corresponding concentration of 10 mg/mL for clavulanic acid (stock solution). Conversely, each 5.0 mL of the 31 g dose reconstituted with approximately 76 mL of diluent will contain approximately 1.5 g of ticarcillin and 50 mg of clavulanic acid.

Solutions of I.V. Infusion: Sodium Chloride Injection USP, Dextrose Injection 5% USP, sterile water for injection USP and Lactated Ringer's Injection.

Note: When Timentin is given in combination with another antimicrobial such as an aminoglycoside, each drug should be given separately in accordance with the recommended dosage and routes of administration for each drug.

After reconstitution and prior to administration, Timentin, as with other parenteral drugs, should be inspected visually for particulate matter and discoloration.

Stability of Solutions: Timentin stock solution at 200 mg/mL or 300 mg/mL (ticarcillin) is stable for up to 6 hours at room temperature (21 to 24°C) or up to 72 hours under refrigeration (4°C).

Further diluted solutions of 200 mg/mL Timentin stock solution should be used within the stated time periods as shown in Table III.

Table III—Timentin

Stability Period

I.V. Solution	Room Temp. 21-24°C	Refrigeration 4°C
Sodium Chloride Injection USP	16 hours	48 hours
Dextrose Injection USP	8 hours	24 hours
Lactated Ringer's Injection USP	16 hours	48 hours

Further diluted solutions of 300 mg/mL Timentin stock solution should be used within the stated time periods as shown in Table IV.

Table IV—Timentin

Stability Period

I.V. Solution	Room Temp. (21-24°C)	Refrigeration (4°C)
Sodium Chloride Injection USP	24 hours	3 days
Dextrose Injection 5% USP	24 hours	3 days
Lactated Ringer's Injection USP	24 hours	3 days
Sterile Water for Injection USP	24 hours	3 days

Supplied: Discs: Each susceptibility disc is impregnated with ticarcillin 75 μg and clavulanic acid 10 μg. Cartridges of 50.

Vials: 3.1 g: Each vial contains: sterile ticarcillin disodium equivalent to ticarcillin 3 g and sterile potassium clavulanate equivalent to clavulanic acid 0.1 g.

31 g: Each vial contains: sterile ticarcillin disodium equivalent to ticarcillin 30 g and sterile potassium clavulanate equivalent to clavulanic acid 1 g.

Store at or below 24°C.

Reviewed 1999

TIMOLIDE®

Frosst

Timolol Maleate—Hydrochlorothiazide

Antihypertensive

Pharmacology: Timolide combines the antihypertensive activity of 2 agents: a beta-adrenergic receptor blocking agent (timolol maleate) and a diuretic (hydrochlorothiazide).

Timolol is a non-selective beta-adrenergic receptor blocking agent that does not have significant intrinsic sympathomimetic, direct myocardial depressant, or local anesthetic (membrane stabilizing) activity in humans.

The mechanism of the antihypertensive effect of beta-adrenergic receptor blocking agents has not yet been established. Among the factors that may be involved are: (i) competitive ability to antagonize catecholamine-induced tachycardia at the beta-receptor sites in the heart, thus decreasing cardiac output, (ii) inhibition of renin release by the kidneys, (iii) inhibition of the vasomotor centres.

Hydrochlorothiazide increases excretion of sodium and chloride in approximately equivalent amounts, and may cause a simultaneous, usually minimal, loss of bicarbonate. Natriuresis is usually accompanied by some loss of potassium. The mechanism of the antihypertensive effect of thiazides may be related to the excretion and redistribution of body sodium. Hydrochlorothiazide usually does not decrease normal blood pressure.

The combination of timolol with thiazide-like diuretics has been shown to be compatible and generally more effective than timolol alone in reducing elevated blood pressure.

Timolol is rapidly absorbed following oral ingestion. Detectable plasma levels of timolol occur within one-half hour and persist for about 8 to 12 hours. Peak plasma levels occur in about 1 to 2 hours. The drug half-life in plasma is approximately 3 to 4 hours. Timolol and its metabolites are excreted principally by the kidney. Plasma levels following oral administration are about half those following i.v. administration indicating approximately 50% first pass metabolism.

The onset of the diuretic action of hydrochlorothiazide occurs in 2 hours and the peak action in about 4 hours. Diuretic activity lasts about 6 to 12 hours. Hydrochlorothiazide is eliminated rapidly by the kidney.

Indications: This fixed combination is not indicated for initial therapy of hypertension. Hypertension requires therapy titrated to the individual patient. It is always better to adjust the dosage of each antihypertensive drug separately, but when the fixed combination corresponds to the optimum drug and dose requirements of the patient its use may be convenient in patient management. For further adjustment of dosage, however, it is best to use the individual drugs again. The treatment of hypertension is not static, but must be re-evaluated as conditions in each patient warrant.

Timolide is indicated for maintenance therapy of patients with hypertension who require timolol maleate and hydrochlorothiazide as part of their treatment in the dosage and ratio present in Timolide.

Contraindications: Congestive heart failure (see Warnings), right ventricular failure secondary to pulmonary hypertension, significant cardiomegaly, sinus bradycardia, second and third degree AV block, cardiogenic shock, allergic rhinitis, bronchospasm (including bronchial asthma), or severe chronic obstructive pulmonary disease (see Precautions), anesthesia with agents that produce myocardial depression, e.g., ether, anuria, hypersensitivity to timolol maleate, hydrochlorothiazide or to sulfonamide-derived drugs.

Warnings: Cardiac Failure: Special caution should be exercised when administering Timolide to patients with a history of heart failure. Sympathetic stimulation is a vital component supporting circulatory function in congestive heart failure, and inhibition with beta blockade always carries a potential hazard of further depressing myocardial contractility and precipitating cardiac failure.

In patients without a history of cardiac failure, continued depression of the myocardium over a period of time can, in some cases, lead to cardiac failure. In rare instances this has been observed during timolol maleate therapy. Therefore, at the first sign or symptom of impending cardiac failure occurring during therapy with Timolide, patients should be fully digitalized and/or given additional diuretic therapy, and the response observed closely.

Timolol acts selectively without blocking the inotropic action of digitalis on the heart muscle. However, the positive inotropic action of digitalis may be reduced by the negative inotropic effects of timolol when the 2 drugs are used concomitantly. The effects of timolol maleate and digitalis are additive in depressing AV conduction. If cardiac failure persists, therapy with Timolide should be discontinued (see below).

Abrupt Cessation of Therapy: Patients with angina should be warned against abrupt discontinuation of Timolide. There have been reports of severe exacerbation of angina and of myocardial infarction or ventricular arrhythmias occurring in patients with angina pectoris, following abrupt discontinuation of beta blocker therapy including timolol maleate. The last two complications may occur with or without preceding exacerbation of angina pectoris. Therefore, when discontinuation of Timolide is planned in patients with angina pectoris, the dosage should be gradually reduced over a period of about 2 weeks and the patient should continue to be carefully observed. The same frequency of administration should be maintained. In situations of greater urgency, therapy with Timolide should be discontinued stepwise and under conditions of closer observation. If angina markedly worsens or acute coronary insufficiency develops, it is recommended that treatment with Timolide be reinstituted promptly at least temporarily.

Since ischemic heart disease may be unrecognized, the above advice should be followed in patients considered to be at risk of having asymptomatic ischemic heart disease.

Severe sinus bradycardia due to unopposed vagal activity may result from the administration of timolol; in such cases, consider the use of i.v. atropine, and, if no improvement is seen, i.v. isoproterenol.

Various skin rashes and conjunctival xerosis have been reported with beta blockers including timolol maleate. A severe syndrome (oculo-muco-cutaneous syndrome) whose signs include conjunctivitis sicca and psoriasiform rashes, otitis and sclerosing serositis have occurred with the chronic use of one beta-adrenergic blocking agent. This syndrome has not been observed with timolol. However physicians should be alert to the possibility of such reactions and should discontinue treatment in the event that this occurs.

In patients with thyrotoxicosis, timolol may give a false impression of improvement by diminishing peripheral manifestations of hyperthyroidism without improving thyroid function. Special considerations should be given to the potential of timolol to aggravate congestive heart failure. Timolol does not alter thyroid function tests. Patients suspected of developing thyrotoxicosis should be managed carefully to avoid abrupt withdrawal of beta blockade which might precipitate a thyroid storm. Thiazides may decrease serum PBI levels without signs of thyroid disturbance.

In patients with renal disease, thiazides may precipitate azotemia, and cumulative effects may develop in the presence of impaired renal function. If progressive renal impairment becomes evident, Timolide should be discontinued.

In patients with impaired hepatic function or progressive liver disease, even minor alterations in fluid and electrolyte balance may precipitate hepatic coma. Hepatic encephalopathy, manifested by tremors, confusion, and coma, has been reported in association with diuretic therapy including hydrochlorothiazide.

In patients receiving thiazides, sensitivity reactions may occur with or without a history of allergy or bronchial asthma.

The possible exacerbation or activation of systemic lupus erythematosus has been reported with thiazides.

Precautions: Timolide should be administered with caution to patients prone to non-allergic bronchospasm (e.g., chronic bronchitis, emphysema) since beta-blockade may block bronchodilatation produced by endogenous and exogenous catecholamine stimulation of beta receptors.

Elective or emergency surgery: Beta-adrenergic receptor blockade impairs the ability of the heart to respond to beta-adrenergically mediated reflex stimuli. Some patients receiving beta-adrenergic receptor blocking agents have been subject to protracted severe hypotension during anesthesia. Difficulty in restarting and maintaining the heartbeat has also been reported.

For these reasons, in patients with angina pectoris undergoing elective surgery, some authorities recommend gradual withdrawal of beta-adrenergic receptor blocking agents (see recommendations given under Warnings—Abrupt cessation of therapy).

In emergency surgery, since timolol is a competitive inhibitor of beta-adrenergic receptor agonists its effects may be reversed, if necessary, by sufficient doses of such agonists as isoproterenol or levarterenol.

Beta-adrenergic receptor blocking agents may mask the premonitory signs and symptoms of acute hypoglycemia. Therefore, Timolide should be administered with caution to patients subject to spontaneous hypoglycemia, or to diabetic patients (especially those with labile diabetes) who are receiving insulin or oral hypoglycemic agents. Insulin requirements in diabetic patients may be increased, decreased, or unchanged by thiazides. Diabetes mellitus which has been latent may become manifest during administration of thiazide diuretics.

Since timolol is excreted mainly by the kidneys, dosage reduction may be necessary when renal insufficiency is present. Marked hypotension has been observed in patients with severe renal insufficiency undergoing renal hemodialysis following oral administration of 20 mg of timolol.

Patients receiving thiazides should be carefully observed for clinical signs of fluid or electrolyte imbalance (hyponatremia, hypochloremic alkalosis, and hypokalemia). Periodic determination of serum electrolytes should be performed at appropriate intervals. Serum and urine electrolyte determinations are particularly important when the patient is vomiting excessively or receiving parenteral fluids. Warning signs or symptoms of fluid and electrolyte imbalance include dryness of the mouth, thirst, weakness, lethargy, drowsiness, restlessness, muscle pains or cramps, muscular fatigue, hypotension, oliguria, tachycardia, and gastrointestinal disturbances such as nausea and vomiting.

Hypokalemia may develop, especially with brisk diuresis, when severe cirrhosis is present, or during concomitant use of corticosteroids or ACTH. Interference with adequate oral electrolyte intake will also contribute to hypokalemia. Hypokalemia can sensitize or exaggerate the response of the heart to the toxic effects of digitalis (e.g., increased ventricular irritability). Hypokalemia may be avoided or treated by use of potassium supplements, potassium sparing agents or foods with a high postassium content.

Any chloride deficit during thiazide therapy is generally mild and usually does not require specific treatment except under extraordinary circumstances (as in liver disease or renal disease). Dilutional hyponatremia may occur in edematous patients in hot weather; appropriate therapy is water restriction rather than administration of salt except in rare instances when the hyponatremia is life threatening. In actual salt depletion, appropriate replacement is the therapy of choice.

Because calcium excretion is decreased by thiazides, Timolide should be discontinued before carrying out tests for parathyroid function. Pathologic changes in the parathyroid glands, with hypercalcemia and hypophosphatemia, have been observed in a few patients on prolonged thiazide therapy; however, the common complications of hyperparathyroidism such as renal lithiasis, bone resorption, and peptic ulceration have not been seen.

The antihypertensive effects of thiazides may be enhanced in the postsympathectomy patient.

Hyperuricemia may occur or acute gout may be precipitated in certain patients receiving thiazide therapy.

Pregnancy: Thiazides cross the placental barrier and appear in cord blood. Timolol has not been studied in human pregnancy. The use of Timolide in pregnancy or in women of childbearing potential requires that the anticipated benefit be weighed against possible risk to mother and/or fetus. These hazards include fetal or neonatal jaundice, thrombocytopenia, and possibly other adverse reactions which have occurred in the adult.

Lactation: Although timolol is excreted in the milk of the rat, it is not known whether it is excreted in human milk. Thiazides appear in human milk. If use of the drug is deemed essential, the patient should stop nursing.

Children: The safety for use of timolol in children has not been established; therefore, Timolide is not recommended in the pediatric age group.

Drug Interactions: The combination of Timolide with an antihypertensive peripheral vasodilator produces a greater fall in blood pressure than either drug alone. The same degree of blood pressure control can be achieved by lower than usual dosages of each drug. Therefore, when using such combined therapy, careful monitoring of the dosages is required until the patient is stabilized.

Close observation of the patient is recommended when Timolide is administered to patients receiving catecholamine-depleting drugs such as reserpine because of possible additive effects and the production of hypotension and/or marked bradycardia which may produce vertigo, syncope, or postural hypotension.

Thiazides may decrease arterial responsiveness to norepinephrine. This diminution is not sufficient to preclude the therapeutic effectiveness of the pressor agent in therapy.

Thiazides may increase the responsiveness to tubocurarine.

Lithium generally should not be given with diuretics because they reduce its renal clearance and add a high risk of lithium toxicity. Read Prescribing Information for lithium preparations before use of such preparations with Timolide.

Orthostatic hypotension may occur and may be potentiated by alcohol, barbiturates or narcotics.

The rate of elimination of hydrochlorothiazide is decreased somewhat by the coadministration of probenecid without, however, an accompanying reduction in diuresis.

Adverse Effects: In clinical trials of 257 patients treated with Timolide the following incidence of adverse reactions was determined (see Table I).

Table I—Timolide Adverse Effects

	Incidence ≥3%	Incidence >1%–<3%	Incidence ≤1%
Respiratory	dyspnea (3.5%) bronchial spasm (3.1%)	cough	rales
CNS	dizziness (3.8%)	headache insomnia	local weakness paresthesia vertigo anxiety depression nervousness confusion decreased libido somnolence
Cardiovascular		bradycardia hypotension cardiac failure	arrhythmia syncope worsening of angina pectoris
Gastrointestinal		diarrhea abdominal pain dyspepsia nausea constipation	vomiting
Allergic/ Dermatologic			pruritus dry mucous membrane pigmentation rash sweating
Genitourinary			renal colic urinary frequency
Others	fatigue/ tiredness (4.2%)	asthenia back pain chest pain edema extremity pain	myalgia

Clinical Laboratory Test Findings: Clinically important changes in standard laboratory parameters were rarely associated with the administration of Timolide. The changes in laboratory parameters were not progressive and usually were not associated with clinical manifestations. The most common changes were increases in serum triglycerides and uric acid and decreases in serum potassium and chloride.

Other adverse reactions that have been reported with the individual components are: Respiratory: laryngospasm, epistaxis; CNS: lightheadedness, drowsiness, vivid dreams, abnormal gait, abnormal sensations, agitation, neurosis; Cardiovascular: hypertension, palpitation, orthostatic hypotension (may be aggravated by alcohol, barbiturates, or narcotics), decreased renal perfusion, lengthening of the PR interval, 2nd and 3rd degree AV block, sinus arrest (if SA node previously diseased), cold extremities, Raynaud's phenomenon; Gastrointestinal: anorexia, gastric irritation, cramping, intrahepatic cholestatic jaundice, pancreatitis, sialadenitis, fecal incontinence, hepatomegaly; Hematologic: leukopenia, agranulocytosis, thrombocytopenia, aplastic anemia, hemolytic anemia; Urogenital: impotence; Hypersensitivity: purpura, photosensitivity, urticaria, exfoliative dermatitis, necrotizing angiitis (vasculitis, cutaneous vasculitis), fever, respiratory distress including pneumonitis, anaphylactic reactions; Special Senses: visual disturbances, including xanthopsia and transient blurred vision, dry eyes, conjunctivitis, itching eyes, tinnitus, vestibular disorder; Other: hyperglycemia, glycosuria, hyperuricemia, muscle cramps, weakness, restlessness, weight loss.

Overdose: Symptoms: The timolol component may cause bradycardia, hypotension, bronchospasm or acute cardiac failure.

The hydrochlorothiazide component may cause excessive diuresis with electrolyte depletion and dehydration. Signs are dry mouth, thirst, weakness, lethargy, drowsiness, restlessness, muscle pains or cramps, muscular fatigue, hypotension, oliguria, tachycardia, gastrointestinal disturbances, mental confusion, delirium, convulsions, shock and coma.

If digitalis has also been administered, hypokalemia may accentuate myocardial abnormalities (e.g. cardiac arrhythmias).

Hydrochlorothiazide may precipitate hepatic coma in cirrhotics, potentiate other antihypertensive agents and decrease responsiveness to norepinephrine.

Treatment: There is no specific antidote. If ingestion is, or may have been, recent, gastric lavage or emesis may reduce absorption; when ingestion has been earlier, infusions may be helpful to promote urinary excretion.

Symptomatic Bradycardia: Use atropine sulfate i.v. in a dosage of 0.25 mg to 2 mg to induce vagal blockade. If bradycardia persists, intravenous isoproterenol hydrochloride should be administered cautiously. In refractory cases the use of a cardiac pacemaker may be considered.

Acute Cardiac Failure: Conventional therapy with digitalis, diuretics, and oxygen should be instituted immediately. In refractory cases the use of intravenous aminophylline is suggested. This may be followed, if necessary, by glucagon hydrochloride which has been reported to be useful.

Hypotension: Use sympathomimetic pressor drug therapy, such as levarterenol or epinephrine. In refractory cases the use of glucagon hydrochloride has been reported to be useful.

Bronchospasm: Use isoproterenol hydrochloride. Additional therapy with aminophylline may be considered.

Stupor or Coma: Administer supportive therapy as clinically warranted.

Gastrointestinal Effects: Though usually of short duration, these may require symptomatic treatment.

Abnormalities in BUN and/or Serum Electrolytes: Monitor serum electrolyte levels and renal function; institute supportive measures as required individually to maintain hydration, electrolyte balance, respiration and cardiovascular-renal function.

Dosage: Dosage must be determined for individual patients by titration of each component separately. Where the fixed combination in Timolide supplies the dosage so determined, the combination product may be used for maintenance therapy.

One tablet of Timolide given once or twice daily can be used to administer 10 to 20 mg timolol and 25 to 50 mg hydrochlorothiazide/day. Giving the 2 tablets in the morning may be tried provided the patient is carefully monitored to assure that the blood pressure remains controlled.

If higher doses of either ingredient are needed the individual components should be used.

When necessary, another antihypertensive agent may be added gradually, beginning with 50% of the usual recommended starting dose to avoid excessive reduction in blood pressure. If during maintenance therapy dosage adjustment is necessary, it is advisable to use the individual drugs.

Supplied: Each light blue, bevelled edge, hexagonal shaped tablet, marked Frosst 67, contains: timolol maleate 10 mg and hydrochlorothiazide 25 mg. Gluten-, lactose- and tartrazine-free. Bottles of 100.

(Shown in Product Recognition Section)

TIMOLOL Ⓟ

BDH

Glaucoma Therapy

Supplied: Each mL of clear, colorless ophthalmic solution contains: timolol maleate equivalent to 2.5 mg (0.25%) or 5 mg (0.5%) timolol. Nonmedicinal ingredients: benzalkonium chloride, dibasic sodium phosphate anhydrous, monobasic sodium phosphate monohydrate and water for injection. White opaque plastic ophthalmic dispensers of 5 and 10 mL with controlled drop tip. Store between 15 and 30°C in a tight, light resistant container. Protect from freezing.

New Product 1998

TIMOPTIC® Ⓡ
TIMOPTIC-XE® Ⓡ
MSD

Timolol Maleate

Elevated Intraocular Pressure Therapy

Pharmacology: Timolol is a general beta-adrenergic receptor blocking agent that does not have significant intrinsic sympathomimetic, direct myocardial depressant or local anesthetic (membrane-stabilizing) activity. Timolol combines reversibly with a part of the cell membrane, the beta-adrenergic receptor, and thus inhibits the usual biologic response that would occur with stimulation of that receptor. This specific competitive antagonism blocks stimulation of the beta-adrenergic receptors by catecholamines having beta-adrenergic stimulating (agonist) activity, whether these originate from an endogenous or exogenous source. Reversal of this blockade can be accomplished by increasing the concentration of the agonist, which will restore the usual biologic response.

Indications: The reduction of elevated intraocular pressure.

In clinical trials it has been shown to reduce intraocular pressure in patients with chronic open-angle glaucoma; patients with ocular hypertension; aphakic patients having glaucoma, including those wearing contact lenses; patients with narrow angles and a history of spontaneous or iatrogenically-induced narrow-angle closure in the opposite eye in whom reduction of intraocular pressure is necessary (see Precautions).

Contraindications: Bronchospasm, including bronchial asthma or a history of bronchial asthma or chronic obstructive pulmonary disease.

Sinus bradycardia; second and third degree atrioventricular block; overt cardiac failure; cardiogenic shock.

Hypersensitivity to any component of this product.

Warnings: As with other topically applied ophthalmic drugs, this drug may be absorbed systemically. The same adverse reactions reported with oral beta-adrenergic blocking agents may occur with topical administration.

Use with caution in patients subject to spontaneous hypoglycemia or in diabetic patients (especially those with labile diabetes) who are receiving insulin or oral hypoglycemic agents. Beta-adrenergic blocking agents may mask the signs and symptoms of acute hypoglycemia.

Cardiac failure should be adequately controlled before beginning therapy with Timoptic and Timoptic-XE. In patients with a history of severe cardiac disease, signs of cardiac failure should be watched for and pulse rates should be checked.

Respiratory reactions and cardiac reactions, including death due to bronchospasm in patients with asthma and rarely death in association with cardiac failure, have been reported following administration of Timoptic. These are also potential complications of therapy with Timoptic-XE.

Precautions: Patients who are already receiving a beta-adrenergic blocking agent orally and who are given Timoptic and Timoptic-XE should be observed for a potential additive effect either on the intraocular pressure or on the known systemic effects of beta blockade.

In patients with angle-closure glaucoma, the immediate objective of treatment is to reopen the angle. This requires constricting the pupil with a miotic. Timolol has little or no effect on the pupil. When Timoptic or Timoptic-XE is used to reduce elevated intraocular pressure in angle-closure glaucoma they should be used with a miotic and not alone.

As with the use of other antiglaucoma drugs, diminished responsiveness to timolol after prolonged therapy has been reported in some patients. However, in clinical studies in which 164 patients have been followed for at least 3 years, no significant difference in mean intraocular pressure has been observed after initial stabilization.

The preservative in Timoptic is benzalkonium chloride and in Timoptic-XE benzododecinium bromide. Both preservatives are quaternary ammonium compounds that may be absorbed by soft contact lenses. For Timoptic, the lenses should be removed before application of the drops and not re-inserted earlier than 15 minutes after use. For Timoptic-XE, studies have not been done in patients wearing contact lenses. However, in a clinical study, the time required to eliminate 50% of the gellan solution from the eye was up to 30 minutes.

Risk from Anaphylactic Reaction: While taking beta-blockers, patients with a history of atopy or a history of severe anaphylactic reaction to a variety of allergens may be more reactive to repeated challenge with such allergens, either accidental, diagnostic, or therapeutic. These patients may be more resistant to treatment of anaphylactic reactions with the usual doses of epinephrine since timolol may blunt the beta agonist effect of epinephrine. In such cases, alternatives to epinephrine should be considered.

Pregnancy: Timolol has not been studied in human pregnancy. The use of timolol requires that the anticipated benefit be weighed against possible hazards.

Lactation: Timolol is detectable in human milk. Because of the potential for serious adverse reactions from timolol in nursing infants, a decision should be made whether to discontinue nursing or to discontinue the drug, taking into account the importance of the drug to the mother.

Children: Timolol is not currently recommended for use in children.

Drug Interactions: Although timolol used alone has little or no effect on pupil size, mydriasis resulting from concomitant therapy with Timoptic and epinephrine has been reported occasionally.

The potential for mydriasis also exists from concomitant therapy with Timoptic-XE and epinephrine.

The potential exists for additive effects and production of hypotension and/or marked bradycardia when Timoptic or Timoptic-XE is administered together with an oral calcium entry blocker, quinidine, catecholamine-depleting drugs or beta-adrenergic blocking agents.

Information for the Patient: Patients should be instructed to avoid allowing the tip of the dispensing container to contact the eye or surrounding structures. Ocular solutions, if handled improperly, can become contaminated by common bacteria known to cause ocular infections. Serious damage to the eye and subsequent loss of vision may result from using contaminated solutions.

The contents should not be used for more than 1 month after the date on which the container is first opened.

Patients Wearing Contact Lenses: Timoptic: Patients should be instructed to remove their lenses before application of the drops and not to re-insert the lenses earlier than 15 minutes after use.

Timoptic-XE: Patients should be instructed to consult their physician before using.

The contents should not be used for more than 1 month after the date on which the container is first opened.

Adverse Effects: Timoptic is usually well tolerated.

Special Senses: Signs and symptoms of ocular irritation, including conjunctivitis, blepharitis, keratitis, blepharoptosis and decreased corneal sensitivity have been reported occasionally. Visual disturbances including refractive changes (due to withdrawal of miotic therapy in some cases), diplopia and ptosis have been reported infrequently.

Integumentary: Hypersensitivity reactions, including localized and generalized rash, urticaria and alopecia.

Cardiovascular: Aggravation or precipitation of certain cardiovascular, pulmonary and other disorders presumably related to effects of systemic beta blockade has been reported (see Contraindications and Precautions). These include bradycardia, arrhythmia, hypotension, syncope, heart block, cerebrovascular accident, cerebral ischemia, palpitation, cardiac arrest, congestive heart failure, and in insulin-dependent diabetics masked symptoms of hypoglycemia have been reported rarely. In clinical trials, slight reduction of the resting heart rate in some patients (mean reduction 2.9 beats/minute, standard deviation 10.2) has been observed.

Respiratory: bronchospasm (predominantly in patients with pre-existing bronchospastic disease), respiratory failure, dyspnea.

Body as a Whole: headache, asthenia, fatigue, chest pain.

Nervous System/Psychiatric: dizziness, depression, increase in signs and symptoms of myasthenia gravis.

Digestive: nausea.

Causal Relationship Unknown: The following adverse reactions have been reported but a causal relationship to therapy with timolol has not been established: aphakic cystoid macular edema, dry mouth, nasal congestion, anorexia, dyspepsia, CNS effects (e.g. behavioral changes including confusion, hallucinations, anxiety, disorientation, nervousness, somnolence, and other psychic disturbances), hypertension and retroperitoneal fibrosis.

Timoptic-XE: Timolol maleate ophthalmic gellan solution is usually well tolerated. The most frequent (6%) drug-related complaint in clinical studies was transient blurred vision, lasting from 30 seconds to 5 minutes, following instillation.

The following possibly, probably, or definitely drug-related adverse reactions occurred with frequency of at least 1% in parallel active treatment controlled clinical trials: Ocular: Burning and stinging, discharge, foreign body sensation, itching.

Potential Adverse Reactions: The adverse reactions listed above under Timoptic are potential adverse reactions for Timoptic-XE.

Adverse reactions reported in clinical experience with oral timolol may be considered potential side effects of ophthalmic timolol.

Overdose: Symptoms and Treatment: No data are available in regard to overdosage in humans.

The most common signs and symptoms to be expected with overdosage with administration of a systemic beta-adrenergic receptor blocking agent are symptomatic bradycardia, hypotension, bronchospasm, and acute cardiac failure.

The following additional therapeutic measures should be considered: (1) Gastric lavage: if ingested. Studies have shown that timolol does not dialyze readily. (2) Symptomatic bradycardia: use atropine sulfate i.v. in a dosage of 0.25 to 2 mg to induce vagal blockade. If bradycardia persists, i.v. isoproterenol hydrochloride should be administered cautiously. In refractory cases the use of a transvenous cardiac pacemaker may be considered. (3) Hypotension: use sympathomimetic pressor drug therapy, such as dopamine, dobutamine or levarterenol. In refractory cases the use of glucagon hydrochloride has been reported to be useful. (4) Bronchospasm: use isoproterenol hydrochloride. Additional therapy with aminophylline may be considered. (5) Acute cardiac failure: conventional therapy with digitalis, diuretics and oxygen should be instituted immediately. In refractory cases the use of i.v. aminophylline is suggested. This may be followed if necessary by glucagon hydrochloride which has been reported to be useful. (6) Heart block (second or third degree): use isoproterenol hydrochloride or a transvenous cardiac pacemaker.

Dosage: Timoptic: 1 drop of 0.25% solution in the affected eye twice a day.

If clinical response is not adequate, dosage may be changed to 1 drop of 0.5% solution in each affected eye twice a day. If needed, concomitant therapy with miotics, epinephrine and systemically administered carbonic anhydrase inhibitors may be given with timolol.

Since in some patients the pressure-lowering response to timolol may require a few weeks to stabilize, evaluation should include a determination of intraocular pressure after approximately 4 weeks of treatment.

If the intraocular pressure is maintained at satisfactory levels, many patients can be placed on once-a-day therapy. Because of naturally occurring diurnal variations in intraocular pressure, satisfactory response is best determined by measuring the intraocular pressure at different times during the day.

How to Transfer Patients from Other Therapy: When a patient is transferred from another topical ophthalmic beta-adrenergic blocking agent, that agent should be discontinued after proper dosing on one day and treatment with timolol started on the following day with 1 drop of 0.25% timolol in the affected eye(s) twice a day. The dose may be increased to 1 drop of 0.5% timolol twice a day if the clinical response is not adequate.

When a patient is transferred from a single antiglaucoma agent, other than a topical ophthalmic beta-adrenergic blocking agent, continue the agent already being used and add 1 drop of 0.25% timolol in each affected eye twice a day. On the following day, discontinue the previously used antiglaucoma agent completely and continue with timolol. If a higher dosage is required, substitute 1 drop of 0.5% solution in each affected eye twice a day.

When a patient is transferred from several concomitantly administered antiglaucoma agents, individualization is required. The physician may be able to discontinue some or all of the other antiglaucoma agents. Adjustments should involve one agent at a time.

Clinical trials have shown the addition of timolol to be useful in patients who respond inadequately to the maximum tolerable antiglaucoma drug therapy.

Timoptic-XE: The usual starting dose is one drop of 0.25% in the affected eye(s) once a day. If the clinical response is not adequate, the dosage may be changed to one drop of 0.5% in the affected eye(s) once a day.

Invert the closed container and shake once before each use. It is not necessary to shake the container more than once.

If needed, concomitant therapy with miotics, epinephrine and systemically administered carbonic anhydrase inhibitors may be given with Timoptic-XE. Other topically applied medications should be administered no less than 10 minutes before Timoptic-XE.

How to Transfer Patients from Other Therapy: When a patient is transferred from Timoptic to Timoptic-XE, Timoptic should be discontinued after proper dosing on one day, and treatment with the same concentration of Timoptic-XE started on the following day.

When a patient is transferred from another topical ophthalmic beta-adrenergic blocking agent, that agent should be discontinued after proper dosing on one day and treatment with Timoptic-XE started on the following day with one drop of 0.25% Timoptic-XE in the affected eye(s) once a day. The dose may be increased to one drop of 0.5% once a day if the clinical response is not adequate.

When a patient is transferred from a single antiglaucoma agent, other than a topical ophthalmic beta-adrenergic blocking agent, continue the agent and add one drop of 0.25% Timoptic-XE to each affected eye once a day. On the following day, discontinue the previously used antiglaucoma agent and continue Timoptic-XE. If a greater response is required, substitute one drop of 0.5% for the 0.25% dosage.

Gellan gum used in this formulation contains a highly purified anionic heteropolysaccharide. Aqueous solutions of gellan gum form a clear transparent gel at low polymer concentrations in the presence of cations. The concentration of sodium cation in tears is ideally suited to cause gelation of the material when topically instilled in the conjunctival sac. When Timoptic-XE contacts the pre-corneal tear film, it becomes a gel. The vehicle of Timoptic-XE, gellan gum, increases the contact time of the drug with the eye.

Supplied: Timoptic: Each mL of clear, colorless to light yellow, sterile, isotonic, buffered, aqueous ophthalmic solution contains: timolol maleate equivalent to 2.5 mg (0.25%) or 5 mg (0.5%) timolol. Nonmedicinal ingredients: benzalkonium chloride, monobasic and dibasic sodium phosphate, sodium hydroxide and water for injection. White, opaque, plastic Ocumeter ophthalmic dispensers, color-coded with light blue (2.5 mg) or yellow (5 mg) cap and label, of 10 mL with controlled drop tip. Store at room temperature (15 to 25°C). Protect from light.

Timoptic-XE: Each mL of sterile, colorless to nearly colorless, slightly opalescent, slightly viscous, aqueous ophthalmic solution contains: timolol maleate equivalent to 2.5 mg (0.25%) or 5 mg (0.5%). Nonmedicinal ingredients: benzododecinium bromide, gellan gum, mannitol, tromethamine. Dispensers, color-coded with light blue (2.5 mg) or yellow (5 mg) cap and label, of 2.5 and 5 mL. Store at room temperature (15 to 25°C). Protect from light and freezing.

The contents of timolol should not be used for more than 1 month after the date on which the container is first opened.

TIMPILO® ℞

MSD

Timolol Maleate—Pilocarpine HCl

Elevated Intraocular Pressure Therapy

Pharmacology: Timolol is a non-selective beta-adrenergic receptor blocking agent that does not have significant intrinsic sympathomimetic, direct myocardial depressant, or local anesthetic (membrane-stabilizing) activity. Timolol combines reversibly with a part of the cell membrane, the beta-adrenergic receptor, and thus inhibits the usual biologic response that would occur with stimulation of that receptor. This specific competitive antagonism blocks stimulation of the beta-adrenergic receptors by catecholamines having beta-adrenergic stimulating (agonist) activity, whether these originate from an endogenous or exogenous source. Reversal of this blockade can be accomplished by increasing the concentration of the agonist, which will restore the usual biologic response.

Pilocarpine is a parasympathomimetic that directly stimulates cholinergic receptors. It produces contraction of the iris sphincter muscle, resulting in pupillary constriction (miosis); constriction of the ciliary muscle (resulting in increased accommodation) and a reduction in intraocular pressure associated with decreased resistance of aqueous humor outflow. Pilocarpine may also inhibit aqueous humor secretion.

Each of the two components decreases elevated intraocular pressure (IOP) by different but complementary mechanisms. Timolol lowers IOP primarily by reducing aqueous humor production. Pilocarpine lowers IOP primarily by enhancing the outflow of aqueous humor from the anterior chamber of the eye. Although pilocarpine, given alone requires administration 4 times a day, it has been shown that when formulated with timolol in Timpilo, administration twice daily is adequate.

Indications: For the reduction of elevated intraocular pressure in patients whose IOP is not adequately controlled on monotherapy with a beta-adrenergic receptor blocking agent or pilocarpine or when concomitant therapy is appropriate.

In clinical trials, it has been shown to reduce intraocular pressure in patients with ocular hypertension when miosis is not a contraindication and in patients with chronic open-angle glaucoma.

Contraindications: Bronchospasm, including bronchial asthma, or a history of these conditions, or chronic obstructive pulmonary disease.

Sinus bradycardia, second and third degree atrioventricular block, overt congestive cardiac failure, cardiogenic shock.

Conditions in which miosis is undesirable: malignant glaucoma, peripheral anterior synechia, trauma, acute-inflammatory disease of anterior chamber, glaucoma occurring or persisting after extracapsular cataract extraction when posterior synechia may occur, etc.

Hypersensitivity to any component of this product.

Warnings: As with other topically applied ophthalmic drugs, this drug may be absorbed systemically.

Timpilo should be used with caution in patients with diabetes, especially labile diabetes (see Precautions).

Following administration of timolol ophthalmic solution, severe respiratory reactions and cardiac reactions have been reported, including death due to bronchospasm in patients with asthma, and rarely death in association with cardiac failure.

Precautions: Cardiovascular Function: Cardiac failure should be controlled before beginning therapy with Timpilo. In patients with a history of cardiac disease, signs of cardiac failure should be watched for and pulse rate should be checked.

Because of potential effects of beta-adrenergic blocking agents relative to blood pressure and pulse, these agents should be used with caution in patients with cerebrovascular insufficiency. If signs or symptoms suggesting reduced cerebral blood flow develop following initiation of therapy with Timpilo, alternative therapy should be considered.

Patients should not receive two topical ophthalmic beta-blockers concurrently (see Dosage). Patients already receiving a beta-blocker orally and who are given Timpilo should be observed for a potential additive effect on the intraocular pressure or on the known systemic effects of beta-blockers.

Eye Accommodation: Miosis usually causes difficulty in dark adaptation. Caution should be exercised in night driving and other hazardous activities in poor illumination.

The preservative in Timpilo may be deposited in soft contact lenses; therefore, Timpilo should not be used while wearing these lenses. The lenses should be removed before application of the drops and not be reinserted earlier than 15 minutes after use.

Risk from Anaphylactic Reaction: While taking beta-blockers, patients with a history of atopy or a history of severe anaphylactic reaction to a variety of allergens may be more reactive to repeated challenge with such allergens, either accidental, diagnostic, or therapeutic. These patients may be more resistant to treatment of anaphylactic reactions with the usual doses of epinephrine since timolol may blunt the beta agonist effect of epinephrine. In such cases, alternatives to epinephrine should be considered.

Major Surgery: The necessity or desirability of withdrawal of beta-adrenergic blocking agents prior to major surgery is controversial. If necessary during surgery, the effects of beta-adrenergic blocking agents may be reversed by sufficient doses of such agonists as isoproterenol, dopamine, dobutamine or norepinephrine.

Diabetes Mellitus: Beta-adrenergic blocking agents should be administered with caution in patients subject to spontaneous hypoglycemia or to diabetic patients (especially those with labile diabetes) who are receiving insulin or oral hypoglycemic agents. Beta-adrenergic receptor blocking agents may mask the signs and symptoms of acute hypoglycemia.

Thyrotoxicosis: Beta-adrenergic blocking agents may mask certain clinical signs of hyperthyroidism (e.g., tachycardia). Patients suspected of developing thyrotoxicosis should be managed carefully to avoid abrupt withdrawal of beta-adrenergic blocking agents which might precipitate a thyroid storm.

Muscle Weakness: Beta-adrenergic blockage has been reported to increase muscle weakness consistent with certain myasthenic symptoms (e.g., diplopia, ptosis and generalized weakness). Timolol has been reported rarely to increase muscle weakness in some patients with myasthenic symptoms.

Pregnancy: Timpilo has not been studied in human pregnancy. The use of Timpilo in pregnancy requires that the anticipated benefit be weighed against potential hazards.

The use of systemic beta-blockers is not recommended during pregnancy.

Lactation: Timolol is detectable in human milk. Because of the potential for serious adverse reactions in nursing infants, a decision should be made whether to discontinue nursing or to discontinue the drug, taking into account the importance of the drug to the mother.

Children: Since clinical studies in children have not been conducted, Timpilo is not currently recommended for use in children.

<u>*Drug Interactions:*</u> Oral beta-blockers or calcium blockers or catecholamine-depleting drugs such as reserpine, may produce additive effects, hypotension and/or marked bradycardia, with possible vertigo, syncope or postural hypotension. I.V. calcium blockers should be used with caution in patients receiving beta-blockers.

Adverse Effects: Timpilo is generally well-tolerated. In clinical studies the adverse experiences reported were mainly well-known pilocarpine side effects: blurring of vision, difficulty with dark adaptation, headache/brow-ache and ocular irritation (see below).

Potential Side Effects: Side effects reported in clinical experience with Timoptic ophthalmic solution, Blocadren and pilocarpine ophthalmic solution may be considered potential side effects of Timpilo ophthalmic solution.

The side effects reported for Timoptic and pilocarpine HCl ophthalmic solutions are listed below.

Timolol Maleate Ophthalmic Solution: Ocular: Signs and symptoms of ocular irritation, including conjunctivitis, blepharitis, keratitis, blepharoptosis, and decreased corneal sensitivity have been reported occasionally. Visual disturbances, diplopia, and ptosis have been reported infrequently.

Cardiovascular: Aggravation or precipitation of certain cardiovascular pulmonary and other disorders presumably related to effects of systemic beta blockade has been reported (see Contraindications and Precautions). These include bradycardia, arrhythmia, hypotension, syncope, heart block, cerebrovascular accident, cerebral ischemia, palpitation, cardiac arrest. Congestive heart failure, and in insulin-dependent diabetics masked symptoms of hypoglycemia have been reported rarely. In clinical trials, slight reduction of the resting heart rate in some patients (mean reduction 2.9 beats/minute, standard deviation 10.2) has been observed.

Respiratory: bronchospasm (predominantly in patients with pre-existing bronchospastic disease), respiratory failure, dyspnea.

Miscellaneous: headache, asthenia, fatigue, chest pain.

Integumentary: hypersensitivity reactions, including localized and generalized rash and urticaria, alopecia.

Nervous System/Psychiatric: dizziness, depression, increase in signs and symptoms of myasthenia gravis.

Digestive: nausea.

Clinical Laboratory Tests: Clinically important changes in standard laboratory parameters were rarely associated with the administration of oral timolol. Slight increases in blood urea nitrogen, serum potassium, serum uric acid and triglycerides, and slight decreases in hemoglobin, hematocrit and HDL-cholesterol occurred, but were not progressive or associated with clinical manifestations.

Pilocarpine HCl Ophthalmic Solution: Ocular: ciliary spasm, conjunctival vascular congestion, lacrimation, temporal or supra-orbital headache, induced myopia, reduced visual acuity in poor illumination (especially in the elderly and in patients with lens opacities), retinal detachment (especially in young myopic patients). Lens opacity may occur with prolonged use of pilocarpine.

Systemic: Extremely rare, but have included hypertension, tachycardia, bronchospasm, pulmonary edema, salivation, sweating, nausea, vomiting and diarrhea.

Overdose: Symptoms and Treatment: No data are available in regard to overdosage in humans with Timpilo.

Timolol Maleate: The most common signs and symptoms to be expected with overdosage with administration of a systemic beta-adrenergic receptor blocking agent are symptomatic bradycardia, hypotension, bronchospasm, and acute cardiac failure.

The following therapeutic measures should be considered: 1) Gastric lavage: If ingested. 2) Symptomatic bradycardia: Use atropine sulfate i.v. in a dosage of 0.25 to 2 mg to induce vagal blockade. If bradycardia persists, i.v. isoproterenol HCl should be administered cautiously. In refractory cases the use of a transvenous cardiac pacemaker may be considered. 3) Hypotension: Use sympathomimetic pressor drug therapy, such as dopamine, dobutamine or norepinephrine. In refractory cases the use of glucagon HCl has been reported to be useful. 4) Bronchospasm: Use isoproterenol HCl. Additional therapy with aminophylline may be considered. 5) Acute cardiac failure: Conventional therapy with digitalis, diuretics and oxygen should be instituted immediately. In refractory cases the use of i.v. aminophylline is suggested. This may be followed if necessary by glucagon HCl which has been reported

Timpilo (cont'd)

to be useful. 6) Heart block (second or third degree): Use isoproterenol HCl or a transvenous cardiac pacemaker.
Pilocarpine: Cholinergic systemic effects are extremely rare with ocular use of pilocarpine (see Adverse Effects). If accidentally swallowed, pilocarpine is readily absorbed from the alimentary tract, and if a large amount is ingested cholinergic symptoms may appear, including salivation, lacrimation, nausea, vomiting, headache, mental confusion, visual disturbances, abdominal colic, diarrhea, bronchospasm and hypotension. Dehydration and shock may develop. Respiratory depression has been reported in severe cases of pilocarpine poisoning.

Treatment is with general measures and atropine.

Dosage: Recommended dosing is as follows: Instill 1 drop of Timpilo 2 twice daily in the affected eye. If the clinical response is inadequate the dosage may be increased by using 1 drop of Timpilo 4 twice daily.

When a patient is transferred from prior therapy, the previously-administered agents should be discontinued after proper dosing on one day, and treatment with Timpilo started on the following day.
Stability and Storage: Prior to mixing solutions, avoid temperatures above 30°C. After mixing, Timpilo 2 and Timpilo 4 are stable for 28 days when stored at room temperature (15 to 25°C). Protect from light and freezing.

Information for the Patient: See Blue Section—Information for the Patient ''Timpilo''.

Supplied: Timpilo 2: Each mL of sterile, aqueous ophthalmic solution contains: timolol maleate 6.8 mg, equivalent to timolol 5.0 mg (0.5%) and pilocarpine HCl 20.0 mg (2.0%). White, opaque, polyethylene ophthalmic dispensers of 5 mL after reconstitution.

Timpilo 4: Each mL of sterile, aqueous ophthalmic solution contains: timolol maleate 6.8 mg, equivalent to timolol 5.0 mg (0.5%) and pilocarpine HCl 40.0 mg (4.0%). White, opaque, polyethylene ophthalmic dispensers of 5 mL after reconstitution.

Dispensed in a unique, 2-chambered vial system. One of the chambers contains a concentrated solution of timolol and pilocarpine at a pH of approximately 3.7. This low pH prevents the hydrolysis of pilocarpine prior to dispensing. The other chamber contains a diluent solution with a pH of approximately 8.0 for Timpilo 2 and approximately 9.0 for Timpilo 4. The two solutions are separated by an internal plug.

Prior to use, the two solutions are mixed together. The resulting solution for administration has a pH of 6.4 to 6.8.

TINACTIN®
TINACTIN® JOCK ITCH
TINACTIN® PLUS
Schering

Tolnaftate

Topical Antifungal

Indications: Topical treatment for tinea pedis, tinea cruris, tinea corporis, and tinea manuum due to infection with T. rubrum, T. mentagrophytes, T. tonsurans, M. audouini, E. floccosum, and for tinea versicolor due to M. furfur. Good results can be anticipated in patients with recent, mild fungus infection of the scalp (tinea capitis) treated with Tinactin solution. An oral antifungal agent such as griseofulvin is required in (1) onychomycosis; and (2) chronic infections of the scalp in which fungi are numerous and widely distributed in the skin and hair follicles, and where kerion formation has occurred. Similarly, an oral antifungal agent may be required in chronic refractory fungus infections of the palms and soles which have not responded to Tinactin. Powder or Solution may be used concurrently for adjunctive local benefit in the treatment of these lesions. Tolnaftate is ineffective in vitro against C. albicans and against gram-negative and gram-positive bacteria.

Contraindications: Known hypersensitivity to any of the components of this preparation.

Precautions: If no improvement in 4 weeks, diagnosis should be reviewed. In mixed infections where bacteria or nonsusceptible fungi are present, supplementary topical or systemic anti-infective therapy is indicated. In mixed infections of yeasts and susceptible fungi, the yeasts frequently do not survive when the fungus infection is cured. Treatment should be discontinued if patient's skin disease becomes worse. If sensitization or irritation due to tolnaftate occurs, treatment with the drug should be discontinued.

Keep away from eyes and mucous membranes. Do not inhale powder preparations.
Aerosols: Contents under pressure. Do not place in hot water or near radiators, stoves or other sources of heat. Do not puncture or incinerate container or store at temperature above 50°C. Do not use in the presence of open flame or spark. For external use only. Avoid inhalation. Keep out of eyes and reach of children.

Adverse Effects: Tolnaftate preparations are essentially nonsensitizing and do not ordinarily sting or irritate intact or broken skin in either exposed or intertriginous areas. A few cases of mild irritation possibly due to the drug have been reported but not confirmed. One case of sensitization to butylated hydroxytoluene has been confirmed.

Dosage: Tinactin: Aerosol Liquid: Apply liberally to the infected area.

Aerosol Powder: Spray liberally from a distance of 15 to 25 cm between toes and on feet, in shoes, socks or on affected area.

Cream: Apply a small amount on the affected area and massage gently until it disappears.

Powder: Apply a small amount to the affected area, rubbing it gently into the lesions.

Solution: 1 or 2 drops are sufficient for an area as large as the hand; 2 or 3 drops cover the toes and interdigital webs of 1 foot. Apply to each lesion and massage gently, then allow to dry.

Treatment twice a day for 2 or 3 weeks is usually adequate, although treatment for 4 to 6 weeks might be required, particularly if some thickening of the skin has occurred. As the primary lesions regress, dermatophytid reactions disappear. In patients with lesions in intertriginous areas or on the pressure points of the feet, a keratolytic agent and longer treatment with tolnaftate might be required. Surgical debridement of dead skin and treatment of callosities on the feet may also be advisable in some cases. Moist compresses promote healing of exudative lesions and do not interfere with the fungicidal action of Tinactin Solution. Any two forms may be used in conjunction, especially in cases of tinea pedis. The aerosol spray or powder dusted periodically into socks and shoes may assist in preventing recurrence of infection.

Tinactin Plus: Aerosol Powder/Powder: These products contain a light fresh fragrance to control odor and starch to absorb moisture.

Supplied: Tinactin: Aerosol Liquid: Aerosol container contains: tolnaftate USP 0.72 mg/g. Nonmedicinal ingredients: alcohol, butylated hydroxytoluene, polyethylene-polypropylene monobutyl ether and propellant—isobutane. Aerosol containers of 70 g.

Aerosol Powder: Aerosol container contains: tolnaftate USP 10 mg (1%)/g. Nonmedicinal ingredients: alcohol, butylated hydroxytoluene, polyethylene-polypropylene glycol monobutyl ether, propellant—isobutane and talc. Aerosol containers of 120 g.

Cream: Each g contains: tolnaftate USP 10 mg (1%). Nonmedicinal ingredients: butylated hydroxytoluene, carbomer 934P, monoamylamine, polyethylene glycol, propylene glycol and titanium dioxide. Tubes of 15 and 30 g.

Powder: Each g contains: tolnaftate USP 10 mg (1%). Nonmedicinal ingredients: cornstarch and talc. Shaker bottles of 30 g.

Solution: Each mL contains: tolnaftate USP 10 mg. Nonmedicinal ingredients: butylated hydroxytoluene and propylene glycol 400. Plastic dropper bottle of 15 mL.

Tinactin Jock Itch: Aerosol Powder: Aerosol container contains: tolnaftate USP 10 mg (1%)/g. Nonmedicinal ingredients: alcohol, butylated hydroxytoluene, polyethylene-polypropylene glycol monobutyl ether, propellant—isobutane and talc. Aerosol Powder: Each 120 g aerosol container contains: tolnaftate USP 10 mg (1%)/g. Nonmedicinal ingredients: alcohol, butylated hydroxytoluene, polyethylene-polypropylene glycol monobutyl ether, propellant—isobutane and talc. Aerosol containers of 120 g.

Cream: Each g contains: tolnaftate USP 10 mg (1%) in a bland cream base. Nonmedicinal ingredients: cetostearyl alcohol, chlorocresol, mineral oil, phosphoric acid, polyethylene glycol 1000 monocetyl ether, propylene glycol, sodium hydroxide, sodium phosphate monobasic, water and white petrolatum. Tubes of 15 g.

Tinactin Plus: Aerosol Powder: Aerosol container contains: tolnaftate USP 10 mg (1% w/w)/g. Nonmedicinal ingredients: alcohol, butylated hydroxytoluene, fragrance, PE-PPG monobutyl ether, propellant—isobutane, silica and talc. Aerosol containers of 120 g.

Powder: Each g contains: tolnaftate USP 10 mg (1% w/w). Nonmedicinal ingredients: cellulose, fragrance, starch/acrylates/acylamide copolymer and talc. Shaker bottles of 30 g.

Aerosol preparations do not contain CFCs.

TINZAPARIN Ⓟ
General Monograph, CPhA

see HEPARINS: LOW MOLECULAR WEIGHT

TISSEEL® KIT VH
Baxter

Fibrin Sealant

Description: Tisseel's action simulates key features of the physiological process of wound closure. A highly concentrated fibrinogen aprotinin solution, which among other ingredients contains Factor XIII, and a solution of thrombin and calcium chloride are applied to the wound area, where the mixture coagulates. The presence of Factor XIII causes the fibrin to crosslink, which gives the coagulum additional resilience.

Tisseel-sealant is a tissue glue with sealing, hemostyptic and gluing properties, which does not interfere with but may enhance wound healing.

Numerous clinical studies investigating the safety and efficacy of the product as a hemostyptic and biodegradable tissue glue in various fields of surgery have been performed. A number of these were controlled studies in fields including orthopedic surgery, abdominal surgery, urology, vascular and cardiovascular surgery. The recently concluded cardiovascular safety study using the heat treated product has shown that Tisseel transmits neither hepatitis viruses nor HIV. Preclinical studies have shown that the vapor heated product is at least as effective as the heat treated product.

Use of the sealant has invariably shown superior results in the groups treated as against the untreated controls who underwent the same types of surgery. These results were attributable to an improved hemostasis and, therefore, reduced blood loss, a tighter sealing of sutures preventing leakages or a faster and uncomplicated healing of the surgical wound.

In none of the studies have systemic side effects been seen nor has any product related transmission of viral hepatitis or HIV occurred in any of the patients treated.

Indications: Used to achieve hemostasis, to seal or glue tissue, and to support wound healing. Indications include: abdominal surgery, cardiovascular surgery, orthopedic surgery, thoracic surgery, urology.

Contraindications: None known.

Warnings: Since Tisseel is a plasma derivative, a risk of it transmitting viral hepatitis cannot be entirely ruled out. A recently concluded study with the heat treated product documented the safety of Tisseel with regard to a transmission of HIV-1 and hepatitis viruses. Today, Tisseel comes vapor heated, which further reduces any potential risk.

Neither of the 2 components, separately or combined, should be administered by the intravascular route, or thromboembolic complications will occur.

This product must not be used in animals.
<u>Drug Interactions:</u> Are not known. The sealant may be applied in fully heparinized patients (e.g. extracorporeal circulation).

Adverse Effects: Are not known.

Dosage: The required dose of Tisseel solution depends on the size of the surface to be sealed or coated or on the size of the defect to be packed (see Table I).

Table I—Tisseel Kit VH

Required Dose of Tisseel Solution

Maximum size of the area to be sealed	Required package sizes of Tisseel Kit VH	
	Application with spray head	Other application methods
4 cm²		Tisseel Kit VH 0.5
8 cm²	Tisseel Kit VH 0.5	Tisseel Kit VH 1.0
16 cm²	Tisseel Kit VH 1.0	Tisseel Kit VH 2.0
40 cm²	Tisseel Kit VH 2.0	Tisseel Kit VH 5.0
100 cm²	Tisseel Kit VH 5.0	

It is desirable for the Tisseel-sealant to be absorbed slowly during the wound healing process. For that reason, aprotinin solution is used for reconstitution of the freeze-dried Tisseel. The concentration of the aprotinin solution supplied with the kit may be varied to control the rate at which the sealant will be absorbed. If the aprotinin solution is diluted with sterile water for injection, the sealant will be absorbed faster. This may also be desirable if a recipient surface is known to have a low fibrinolytic activity of its own.

The setting rate of the sealant, on the other hand, depends on the concentration of the thrombin solution used. While the sealant may take up to 1 minute to set with a thrombin concentration of 4 IU/mL, this setting process will be complete within seconds if the higher thrombin concentration of 500 IU/mL is used. The higher thrombin concentration may be advantageous to achieve hemostasis, while the lower thrombin concentration is better apt to seal tissue because it allows time for approximation of the wound areas.

Various methods can be used to apply the two components of the sealant:

Simultaneous application: a) using Duploject and application needle; b) using Duploject and spray head; c) premixing.

Consecutive application.

Note: Simultaneous application by premixing requires a low thrombin concentration of 4 IU/mL while 500 IU/mL are recommended for the consecutive application method. Either concentration is suitable for applications using Duploject.

How to Prepare Tisseel Solution: Freeze-dried Tisseel is reconstituted in the Aprotinin Solution of 3 000 KIU/mL. To obtain lower concentrations, dilute the Solution with Sterile Water for Injection. For example, to obtain a concentration of 100 KIU/mL dilute 0.1 mL (0.2 mL if Tisseel Kit VH 5.0 is used) with 3 mL (5 mL) of Sterile Water for Injection using the blue-scaled syringe.

Reconstitution of Freeze-Dried Tisseel Using Fibrinotherm: For ease of handling, a combined heating and stirring device, Fibrinotherm, has been developed to meet the specific requirements of reconstituting freeze-dried Tisseel. Fibrinotherm is a thermoblock with a magnetic stirrer (the vials for freeze-dried Tisseel contain a magnetic spin propeller to stir the contents). Heating and stirring can be operated independently. In a first step, Fibrinotherm heats up to 37°C and then maintains that temperature constantly with minimum variation. Fibrinotherm has been designed to hold the various vial sizes of freeze-dried Tisseel and Aprotinin Solution.

Place vials containing freeze-dried Tisseel and Aprotinin Solution into the appropriate openings of Fibrinotherm and operate red flip switch. Wait until signal lamp goes out. Fibrinotherm has now reached 37°C. Preheat vials for 10 minutes.

Transfer Aprotinin Solution into vial containing freeze-dried Tisseel using blue-scaled syringe of corresponding size (or syringe that has been used for dilution of Aprotinin Solution).

Place vial into largest opening of Fibrinotherm (if necessary, use adaptors). Turn on stirrer with green flip switch and stir contents for 8 to 10 minutes.

Reconstitution of freeze-dried Tisseel is complete as soon as no undissolved particles are detectable in transparent light. Otherwise, replace into Fibrinotherm and agitate for another few minutes until the solution appears homogeneous.

Note: If not used immediately, keep Tisseel Solution at 37°C without stirring. To ensure homogeneity switch on stirrer of Fibrinotherm shortly before drawing up the solution.

Reconstitution of Freeze-Dried Tisseel Using a Water-Bath: Preheat the vial with freeze-dried Tisseel and the vial with the Aprotinin solution to about 37°C (but not beyond 40°C).

Transfer Aprotinin Solution into vial containing freeze-dried Tisseel using blue-scaled syringe of corresponding size (or syringe that has been used for dilution of Aprotinin Solution).

Allow vial to stand at 37°C for 1 minute.

Swirl briefly and vigorously with a circular motion (avoid excessive frothing) and replace vial into water-bath for another 10 to 15 minutes.

Reconstitution of freeze-dried Tisseel is complete as soon as no undissolved particles are detectable in transparent light. Otherwise, swirl again briefly and keep bottle at 37°C for a few more minutes.

Draw up reconstituted Tisseel Solution into a sterile blue-scaled syringe using aseptic precautions (insert a needle through the rubber stopper at its center to allow access of air).

Note: If not used immediately, keep Tisseel Solution at 37°C. To ensure homogeneity, swirl with a circular motion (avoiding frothing) before drawing up the solution.

How to Prepare Thrombin Solution: Depending on the desired Thrombin concentration, either transfer the contents of the vial with Calcium Chloride Solution into the vial containing freeze-dried Thrombin 500 (quick solidification) or Thrombin 4 (slow solidification).

Use one of the sterile black-scaled syringes for preparing Thrombin Solution.

Swirl briefly. Keep Thrombin Solution at 37°C until used. Draw up an amount of Thrombin Solution equal to the amount of Tisseel Solution that will be used into a sterile black-scaled syringe using aseptic precautions.

Note: Do not use the syringes and needles previously used for reconstitution of freeze-dried Tisseel to prevent premature setting.

Simultaneous Application Using Duploject-System: The Duploject-System allows simultaneous application of the 2 components and ensures that they are quickly and thoroughly mixed, which is essential for the Sealant to gain the optimum strength. Either Thrombin concentration can be used.

Simultaneous Application Using Duploject and Application Needle: The sterile Duploject-System consists of a clip for 2 identical disposable syringes and a common plunger which ensures that equal volumes of the 2 components are fed over a common adjoining piece before mixed in the application needle and ejected.

Operating Instructions: Place syringes filled with Tisseel and Thrombin Solutions into the clip. Both syringes should be filled with equal amounts and should not contain any air bubbles.

Connect the nozzles of the 2 syringes with the joining piece. Ensure firm hold. Secure the joining piece by fastening the strap to the clip.

Fit application needle onto the joining piece. Do not remove remaining air from inside the joining piece or application needle. Otherwise the apertures of the needle may clog before application of the Sealant.

Apply Sealant onto the recipient surface or surfaces if 2 parts of tissue need to be glued together.

Note: Only the syringes contained in the Kit for reconstitution and application are designed to perfectly fit into the Duploject clip. Any other syringe may cause problems since exact and firm adaptation to the joining piece cannot be granted for. If the procedure of applying the 2 components with Duploject is interrupted, replace application needle by a new one when sealing is resumed (three spare needles come with the Kit). Only replace application needle immediately prior to resuming sealing. Otherwise, the apertures of the joining piece will clog, which requires it to be also replaced (one spare joining piece comes with the Kit).

Simultaneous Application Using Duploject and Spray Head: The spray head is particularly suitable for spraying of larger areas, e.g., to control oozing of parenchymateous organs.

Duploject is used for this method of application except that a spray head is used instead of the joining piece. Spray the 2 components simultaneously using sterile propellant gas and control the volume of the Solutions ejected with the Duploject plunger. Spray at a distance of 10 to 20 cm.

Note: A detailed description of this application method is included in the leaflet of the Spray Set.

Simultaneous Application by Premixing: Mix equal volumes of the 2 components and immediately apply them to the recipient surface or surfaces. When the low Thrombin concentration of 4IU/ mL is used, approximately 1 minute is allowed for mixing the components, applying the Sealant, and approximating the wound areas. If desired, the Sealant can be mixed with spongiosa to pack bone defects.

Consecutive Application: Apply the 2 components in 2 layers. Apply Tisseel Solution to the recipient surface or surfaces first, then top with an equal amount of Thrombin Solution (500 IU/mL). Alternatively, when 2 parts are to be glued, apply one component to 1 surface, the other component to the opposite surface.

Note: To prevent the Sealant from adhering to gloves and instruments, wet these with saline before contact with Sealant.

Gluing of Tissue: After the 2 components have been applied, approximate the wound areas. Fix or hold the glued parts in the desired position for 3 or 5 minutes to ensure that the setting Sealant adheres firmly to the surrounding tissue. Solidified Sealant reaches its ultimate strength after about 2 hours (70% after about 10 minutes).

Note: In order to avoid excess formation of granulation tissue and slow absorption of the Sealant, only apply thin layers of the 2 components.

Supplied: The kit contains the following substances in 5 separate vials: 1. Sealer Protein Concentrate (Human)*, freeze dried, vapor treated. Reconstituted solution contains: total protein, 100–130 mg/mL; including fibrinogen, 70–110 mg/mL; Plasma fibronectin (cold insoluble globulin), 2–9 mg/mL; Factor XIII, 10–50 U/mL; plasminogen, 40–120 μg/mL. 2. Aprotinin solution, bovine 3 000 KIU/mL. 3. Thrombin 4 (bovine), freeze dried reconstituted contains: 4 IU/mL. 4. Thrombin 500 (bovine), freeze dried reconstituted contains: 500 IU/mL. 5. Calcium chloride solution, 40 mmol/L.

In addition each kit contains a sealant application set consisting of a Duploject applicator, disposable syringes, 2 joining pieces and 4 application needles.

In addition to the kit, a spray set is available.

Tisseel sealer protein concentrate is made from pooled fresh frozen human plasma. Donors of this plasma are tested at every donation for HB_s-antigenemia, anti-HIV-1 or with elevated ALT levels are irrevocably excluded from the plasmapheresis program. In addition, Tisseel is subjected to a product-specific vapor heat treatment. Preclinical data show that this treatment produces a decrease in HIV-1 titer of 10^6 or more infectious units/mL.

*Each vial contains a magnetic spin propeller to facilitate reconstitution when placed in the Fibrinotherm warming and stirring device.

Tisseel Kit 0.5 for 0.5 mL of reconstituted Tisseel solution and 0.5 mL Thrombin solution.

Tisseel Kit 1.0 for 1.0 mL of reconstituted Tisseel solution and 1.0 mL Thrombin solution.

Tisseel Kit 2.0 for 2.0 mL of reconstituted Tisseel solution and 2.0 mL Thrombin solution.

Tisseel Kit 5.0 for 5.0 mL of reconstituted Tisseel solution and 5.0 mL Thrombin solution.

Store between 2 and 8°C. Reconstituted solutions must be used within 4 hours.

TI-U-LAC® HC Ⓟ

Spectropharm Dermatology

Hydrocortisone—Urea

Topical Corticosteroid

Pharmacology: Topical corticosteroids are synthetic derivatives of cortisone which are effective when applied locally to control many types of inflammatory, allergic and pruritic dermatoses.

They are thought to act by controlling the rate of synthesis of proteins. The primary action of the corticosteroid is to interfere with the synthesis of arachidonic acid by inhibiting the phospholipase A_2 synthesis. The overall effect of corticosteroids is a catabolic one.

Corticosteroid responsive dermatoses may be divided into those which are very responsive and those which require higher concentrations of corticosteroids, occlusion of the drug under a plastic film or intralesional administration. Attention must be paid to the concentration of topical corticosteroid used.

Although effectiveness is enhanced by the application of the corticosteroid preparation under a transparent plastic wrapping, systemic absorption is also enhanced, occasionally sufficient to suppress the pituitary-adrenal axis.

Indications: For inflammatory manifestations of corticosteroid responsive dermatoses, where an anti-inflammatory, anti-allergenic and antipruritic activity in topical management is required.

Contraindications: Untreated tubercular, bacterial and fungal infections involving the skin and in certain viral diseases such as herpes simplex, chickenpox and vaccinia. Hypersensitivity to any of the components of the preparation. Not for ophthalmic use.

Warnings: *Pregnancy* and *Lactation:* The safety of topical corticosteroids during pregnancy and lactation has not been established. The potential benefit should be weighed in these conditions against possible hazard to the fetus or the nursing infant.

Adrenal suppression and other systemic effects may occur after application to extensive areas and prolonged usage.

Should not be used under occlusive dressings. If used under an occlusive dressing, particularly over extensive areas, sufficient absorption may take place to give rise to adrenal suppression and other systemic effects.

Precautions: Topical corticosteroids should be used with caution on lesions close to the eye.

Although hypersensitivity reactions have been rare with topically applied steroid products, the drug should be discontinued and appropriate therapy initiated if there are signs of reaction.

Prolonged use of topical corticosteroid products may produce atrophy of the skin and subcutaneous tissues, particularly on flexor surfaces and on the face. If this is noted, discontinue the use of these products. In cases of bacterial infections of the skin appropriate antibacterial agents should

Ti-U-Lac HC (cont'd)

be used as primary therapy. If necessary, the topical corticosteroid may be used as an adjunct to control inflammation, erythema and itching.

These products should be used with caution in patients with stasis dermatitis and other skin diseases associated with impaired circulation. If a symptomatic response is not noted within a few days to a week, the local applications of corticosteroid should be discontinued and the patient re-evaluated.

During the use of topical corticosteroids secondary infections may occur.

Significant systemic absorption may occur when corticosteroids are applied over large areas of the body. To minimize this possibility, when long-term therapy is anticipated, interrupt treatment periodically or treat one area of the body at a time.

Advise patients to inform subsequent physicians of the prior use of corticosteroids.

Not for ophthalmic use.

Adverse Effects: The following adverse skin reactions have been reported with the use of topical corticosteroids; dryness, itching, burning, local irritation, striae, skin atrophy, atrophy of subcutaneous tissues, telangiectasia, hypertrichosis, change in pigmentation and secondary infection.

Adrenal suppression has also been reported following topical corticosteroid therapy.

Posterior subcapsular cataracts have been reported following use of corticosteroids.

These side effects have been very rarely observed, even under occlusive conditions, with low potency topical glucocorticosteroid preparations such as hydrocortisone.

Dosage: Apply sparingly to affected areas 2 or 3 times daily. When favorable response is obtained, reduce frequency of application and eventually discontinue altogether.

Supplied: Each mL of white, odorless, washable lotion contains: hydrocortisone 2.5% and urea 10%. Nonmedicinal ingredients: arlacel, cetyl glycol, Germall, lactic acid, mineral oil, lauryl sulfate, propylene glycol, Veegum, water and white petrolatum. Plastic bottles of 60 mL. Protect from excessive heat. Store at room temperature. Avoid freezing.

TOBRADEX® ℞

Alcon

Tobramycin—Dexamethasone

Antibiotic—Corticosteroid

Pharmacology: Dexamethasone, a potent corticosteroid, suppresses the inflammatory response to chemical, immunological or mechanical irritants. The bactericidal activity of tobramycin is accomplished by specific inhibition of normal protein synthesis in susceptible bacteria.

Indications: For steroid-responsive inflammatory ocular conditions for which a corticosteroid is indicated and where bacterial infection or a risk of bacterial ocular infection exist.

Ocular steroids are indicated in inflammatory conditions of the palpebral and bulbar conjunctiva, cornea and anterior segment of the globe where the inherent risk of steroid use in certain infective conjunctivitides is accepted to obtain a diminution in edema and inflammation. They are also indicated in chronic anterior uveitis and corneal injury from chemical, radiation, thermal burns or penetration of foreign bodies.

Contraindications: Vaccinia, varicella, herpes simplex and other viral diseases of the cornea and conjunctiva; tuberculosis of the eye; fungal diseases of the eye; acute purulent untreated infections of the eye, which, like other diseases caused by microorganisms may be masked or enhanced by the presence of the steroid.

Hypersensitivity to a component of the medication. Partial cross-allergenicity to other aminoglycosides has been established.

The use of this combination is always contraindicated after uncomplicated removal of a corneal foreign body.

Warnings: Not for injection into the eye.

Sensitivity to topically applied aminoglycosides may occur in some patients. If a sensitivity reaction does occur, discontinue use.

Prolonged use of corticosteroids may result in glaucoma, with damage to the optic nerve, defects in visual acuity and fields of vision, and posterior subcapsular cataract formation.

Prolonged use may suppress the host response and thus increase the hazard of secondary ocular infections.

Extended ophthalmic use of corticosteroid drugs may cause increased intraocular pressure in certain individuals and in those diseases causing thinning of the cornea, perforation has been known to occur. If treatment exceeds 9 days, intraocular pressure should be routinely monitored.

Precautions: General: Fungal infections of the cornea are particularly prone to develop coincidentally with long-term local steroid application; fungus invasion must be considered in any persistent corneal ulceration where a steroid has been used or is in use. As with other antibiotics, prolonged use may result in overgrowth of nonsusceptible organisms. As with all steroids, heating may be delayed if used in the uncomplicated removal of foreign bodies.

Ophthalmic examinations are recommended during long-term therapy. If there is no improvement after 5 or 7 days of therapy or if the condition worsens, the medication should be discontinued.

If topical ocular tobramycin is administered concomitantly with systemic aminoglycoside antibiotics, care should be taken to monitor the total serum concentration.

Patients should be advised to inform their physicians of any prior use of corticosteroids.

Patients should be advised regarding the use of contact lenses while on therapy.

Pregnancy: Animal reproduction studies have not been conducted with this product. It is not known whether the drug can cause fetal harm when administered to a pregnant woman or can affect reproduction capacity. TobraDex should be given to a pregnant woman only if clearly needed.

Lactation: It is not known whether this drug is excreted in human milk. Because many drugs are excreted in human milk, caution should be exercised when this product is administered to a nursing woman.

Children: Safety and effectiveness in children have not been established.

Adverse Effects: Adverse reactions have occurred with steroid/anti-infective combination drugs which can be attributed to the steroid component, the anti-infective component, or the combination. Exact incidence figures are not available.

The most frequent adverse reactions to topical ocular tobramycin are localized ocular toxicity and hypersensitivity, including lid itching and swelling, and conjunctival erythema. These reactions occur in less than 4% of patients. Other adverse reactions have not been reported from ocular tobramycin therapy.

The reactions due to the steroid component in decreasing order of frequency are: elevation of intraocular pressure (IOP) with possible development of glaucoma, and infrequent optic nerve damage; posterior subcapsular cataract formation; and delayed wound healing.

The development of secondary infection has occurred after use of combinations containing steroids and antimicrobials. Fungal infections of the cornea are particularly prone to develop coincidentally with long-term applications of steroid. The possibility of fungal invasion must be considered in any persistent corneal ulceration where steroid treatment has been used.

Overdose: Symptoms and Treatment: There is no known treatment of overdosage since overdosage in the use of topical ophthalmic preparations is a remote possibility. Discontinue medication when heavy or protracted use is suspected.

Dosage: Suspension: 1 to 2 drops instilled into the conjunctival sac every 4 hours. During the initial 24 to 48 hours the dosage may be increased to 1 or 2 drops every 2 hours. Frequency should be decreased gradually as warranted by improvement in clinical signs. Care should be taken not to discontinue therapy prematurely.

Ointment: Apply a 1.25 cm ribbon into the conjunctival sac(s) up to 3 or 4 times daily or may be used adjunctively with drops at bedtime.

Special Instructions: Patients should be instructed to avoid contamination of dispensing tip.

Supplied: Ointment: Each g of sterile ophthalmic ointment contains: tobramycin 3 mg and dexamethasone 0.1% with chlorobutanol 0.5% as a preservative in a mineral oil and petrolatum base. Tubes of 3.5 g.

Suspension: Each mL of sterile, isotonic, aqueous suspension contains: tobramycin 3 mg and dexamethasone 0.1% with benzalkonium chloride 0.01% as a preservative. Nonmedicinal ingredients: edetate disodium, hyroxyethyl cellulose, purified water, sodium chloride, sodium hydroxide, sodium sulfate, sulfuric acid and tyloxapol. Drop-Tainer dispensers of 5 mL. Shake well before use. Store in an upright position. Store at room temperature.

TOBREX® Ophthalmic ℞

Alcon

Tobramycin

Topical Antibiotic

Pharmacology: Like other aminoglycosides, the bactericidal activity of tobramycin is accomplished by specific inhibition of normal protein synthesis in susceptible bacteria, but at the present time, very little is known about this action. It is thought that inhibition of synthesis is due to an action on ribosomes that, in turn, causes bacterial misreading of messenger RNA.

Because the ocular concentrations of tobramycin achieved after topical application are higher than those which can be safely used in systemic therapy, standardized susceptibility tests may not be appropriate to predict its effectiveness.

The gram-positive bacteria against which tobramycin solution is clinically effective include the coagulase-positive and coagulase-negative staphylococci, including penicillin-resistant strains, S. pneumoniae, other alpha-hemolytic streptococci, Group A beta-hemolytic and non-hemolytic streptococci. The gram-negative bacteria against which tobramycin ophthalmic solution has been shown to have clinical effectiveness includes most strains of P. aeruginosa, E. coli, K. pneumoniae, E. aerogenes, P. mirabilis (indole-negative) and indole-positive Proteus species, as well as Haemophilus, Moraxella, and A. calcoacetius. Bacterial susceptibility studies show that many microorganisms resistant to gentamicin retain susceptibility to tobramycin. A significant bacterial population resistant to tobramycin has not yet emerged; however, bacterial resistance may develop upon prolonged use.

Indications: For the treatment of external infections of the eye and its adnexa caused by susceptible bacteria. Appropriate monitoring of bacterial response to topical antibiotic therapy should accompany its use.

Contraindications: Patients with known hypersensitivity to any of its components. Partial cross-allergenicity to other aminoglycosides has been established.

Warnings: Not for injection into the eye. Sensitivity to topically applied aminoglycosides may occur in some patients. If a sensitivity reaction to tobramycin occurs, discontinue use.

Pregnancy: Reproduction studies in 3 types of animals at doses up to 33 times the normal systemic dose have revealed no evidence of impaired fertility or harm to the fetus due to tobramycin. There are, however, no adequate and well-controlled studies in pregnant women. Because animal studies are not always predictive of human response, this drug should be used during pregnancy only if clearly needed.

Lactation: Because of the potential for adverse reactions in nursing infants from tobramycin, a decision should be made whether to discontinue nursing the infant or discontinue the drug, taking into account the importance of the drug to the mother.

Precautions: As with other antibiotic preparations, prolonged use may result in overgrowth of nonsusceptible organisms, including fungi. If superinfection or drug resistance occurs, or irritation or sensitization to any of the components of this preparation develops, treatment should be discontinued and appropriate therapy should be initiated. The patient should be advised to consult a physician if improvement fails to occur, or if signs of superinfection should occur. The patient should also be advised to avoid contamination of the dropper tip by the eye, or other objects.

If tobramycin is administered concomitantly with systemic aminoglycoside antibiotics, care should be taken to monitor the total serum concentration.

Adverse Effects: The most frequent adverse reactions to tobramycin are localized ocular toxicity and hypersensitivity, including lid itching and swelling and conjunctival erythema. These reactions occur in less than 3% of patients treated. Other adverse reactions have not been reported.

Overdose: Symptoms and Treatment: Clinically apparent signs and symptoms of an overdose e.g., punctate keratitis, erythema, increased lacrimation, edema and lid itching, may be similar to adverse reaction effects in some patients. In case of dramatic systemic overdose, serum concentrations should be monitored and prolonged levels above 12 μg/mL avoided. Hemodialysis will help remove tobramycin from the blood. Such reactions and the necessity for counter measures are not expected from the use of Tobrex.

Dosage: Solution: In mild to moderate disease, instill 1 or 2 drops into the affected eye(s) every 4 hours. In severe infections, instill 2 drops into the eye(s) hourly until improvement, following which treatment should be reduced prior to discontinuation.

Ointment: For mild to moderate disease instill a 1.25 cm ribbon into the conjunctival sac of the affected eye(s) 2 to 3 times per day. For severe infections instill a 1.25 cm ribbon into the conjunctival sac of the affected eye(s) every 3 to 4 hours until improvement is detected. Following improvement, treatment should be reduced prior to discontinuation.

Children: Clinical studies have shown tobramycin to be safe and effective for use in children.

Supplied: Solution: Each mL of sterile solution contains: tobramycin 0.3% (3 mg) and benzalkonium chloride 0.01% as preservative. Nonmedicinal ingredients: boric acid, purified water, sodium chloride, sodium hydroxide and/or sulfuric acid (to adjust pH), sodium sulfate and tyloxapol. Drop-Tainer dispensers of 5 mL. Keep tightly closed.

Ointment: Each g of sterile, ophthalmic ointment contains: tobramycin 3 mg and chlorobutanol 0.5% as preservative, in a mineral oil and petrolatum base. Tubes of 3.5 g. Keep tightly closed.

TOFRANIL® Ⓟ
Novartis Pharmaceuticals

Imipramine HCl
Antidepressant

Pharmacology: Imipramine is a tricyclic antidepressant with general pharmacological properties similar to those of structurally related tricyclic antidepressant drugs such as amitriptyline and doxepin.

It possesses anticholinergic properties which are responsible for certain of its side effects. The mechanism of action of imipramine and other tricyclic antidepressants is not well established, but it is thought that it might be related to their action on the transmitter-uptake mechanism of monoaminergic neurons. The mechanism of action in childhood nocturnal enuresis is not fully known.

Imipramine is rapidly and almost completely absorbed from the gastrointestinal tract. Peak plasma levels are reached in 2 to 5 hours, and plasma half-life ranges from 9 to 20 hours. After oral administration of 50 mg 3 times daily for 10 days, the mean steady-state plasma concentration was 33 to 85 ng/mL for imipramine and 43 to 109 ng/mL for desmethylimipramine, an active metabolite. Approximately 86% of imipramine is bound to plasma proteins. It is excreted primarily as inactive metabolites, up to 80% in the urine and up to 20% in the feces.

Owing to the lower clearance of imipramine in plasma, elderly patients require lower doses of imipramine than patients in younger age groups.

Indications: For the relief of symptoms of depression.

Imipramine may also be useful as temporary adjunctive therapy in reducing enuresis in children aged 5 years and older, after possible organic causes have been excluded by appropriate tests. In patients having daytime symptoms of frequency and urgency, examination should include voiding cystourethrography and cytoscopy, as necessary. The effectiveness of treatment may decrease with continued drug administration.

Contraindications: In patients who have known or suspected hypersensitivity to the drug or its excipients, or have known or suspected hypersensitivity to tricyclic antidepressants belonging to the dibenzazepine group.

Imipramine should not be given in conjunction with, or within 14 days before or after treatment with a MAO inhibitor (see Precautions, Drug Interactions). The concomitant treatment with selective reversible MAO-A inhibitors, such as moclobemide, is also contraindicated. Hypertensive crises, hyperactivity, hyperpyrexia, spasticity, severe convulsions or coma, and death have been reported in patients receiving such combinations.

Imipramine is contraindicated for use during the acute recovery phase following a myocardial infarction and in the presence of acute congestive heart failure.

Imipramine is contraindicated in patients with existing liver or kidney damage and should not be administered to patients with a history of blood dyscrasias.

Imipramine is contraindicated in patients with glaucoma, as the condition may be aggravated due to the atropine-like effects of the drug.

Warnings: Seizures: Tricyclic agents are known to lower the convulsive threshold and imipramine should, therefore, be used with extreme caution in patients with a history of convulsive disorders and other predisposing factors, e.g., brain damage of varying etiology, concomitant use of neuroleptics, alcoholism and withdrawal from alcohol, and concomitant use with other drugs that lower the seizure threshold. It appears that the occurrence of seizures is dose dependent. Therefore, the recommended total daily doses should not be exceeded (see Dosage).

Concurrent administration of electroconvulsive therapy and imipramine may be hazardous and such treatment should be limited to patients for whom it is essential. Physicians should discuss with patients the risk of taking imipramine while engaging in activities in which a sudden loss of consciousness could result in serious injury to the patient or others e.g., the operation of complex machinery, driving, swimming, or climbing.

Cardiovascular: Tricyclic antidepressants particularly in high doses, have been reported to produce sinus tachycardia, changes in conduction time and arrhythmias. A few instances of unexpected death have been reported in patients with cardiovascular disorders. Myocardial infarction and stroke have also been reported with drugs of this class. Therefore, imipramine should be administered with extreme caution to patients with a history of cardiovascular disorders, especially those with cardiovascular insufficiency, conduction disorders (e.g., atrioventricular block grades I to III) or other arrhythmias, those with circulatory lability and elderly patients. Imipramine also has a hypotensive action which may be detrimental in these circumstances. In such cases, treatment should be initiated at low doses with progressive increases only if required and tolerated, and the patients should be under close surveillance at all dosage levels. Monitoring of cardiac function and the ECG is indicated in such patients as well as in the elderly.

Concomitant Illness: Caution should be observed when prescribing imipramine for hyperthyroid patients or for patients receiving thyroid medication. Transient cardiac arrhythmias have occurred in rare instances in patients who have been receiving other tricyclic compounds concomitantly with thyroid medication.

Because of its anticholinergic properties, imipramine should be used with caution in patients wiith increased intraocular pressure, narrow angle glaucoma or urinary retention, particularly in the presence of prostatic hypertrophy.

Tricyclic antidepressants may give rise to paralytic ileus, particularly in the elderly and in hospitalized patients. Therefore, appropriate measures should be taken if constipation occurs.

Caution is called for when employing imipramine in patients with tumors of the adrenal medulla (e.g., pheochromocytoma, neuroblastoma), in whom the drug may provoke hypertensive crisis.

Children: Effectiveness of imipramine in children for conditions other than nocturnal enuresis has not been established. The safety and effectiveness of the drug as temporary adjunctive therapy for nocturnal enuresis in children under 5 years of age has not been established.

The safety of imipramine for long-term chronic use as adjunctive therapy for nocturnal enuresis in children 5 years of age or older has not been established; consideration should be given to establishing a drug free period following an adequate therapeutic trial with a favorable response. Recommended doses should not be exceeded in childhood, because ECG changes of unknown significance have been reported with higher doses in pediatric patients. To guard against possible cardiotoxic effects, a daily dosage of 2.5 mg/kg should not be exceeded in children.

Imipramine should be kept in a safe place, well out of the reach of children.

Pregnancy: The safety of use in pregnant women has not been established. Therefore, imipramine should not be administered to women of childbearing potential, or during pregnancy, unless in the opinion of the physician the expected benefit to the patient outweighs the potential risk to the fetus. Withdrawal symptoms including: tremors, dyspnea, lethargy, colic, irritability, hypotonia/hypertonia, convulsions and respiratory depression have been reported in neonates whose mothers received tricyclic antidepressants during the third trimester of pregnancy. To avoid such symptoms, imipramine should, if possible, be gradually withdrawn at least 7 weeks before the calculated date of confinement.

Lactation: Since imipramine passes into the breast milk, imipramine should be gradually withdrawn or the infant should be weaned if the patient is breast-feeding.

Precautions: Suicide: The possibility of a suicide attempt is inherent in depression. These patients should be carefully supervised during treatment with imipramine and hospitalization or concomitant electroconvulsive therapy may be required. To minimize the risk of an intentional overdose by a depressed patient, prescriptions for imipramine should be written for the smallest possible quantity of the drug consistent with good patient management.

Psychosis, Mania-Hypomania and Other Neuropsychiatric Phenomena: In patients treated with tricyclic antidepressants, activation of latent schizophrenia or aggravation of existing psychotic manifestations in schizophrenic patients may occur. Patients with manic-depressive tendencies may experience hypomanic or manic shifts. Hyperactive or agitated patients may become over stimulated. A reduction in dose or discontinuation of imipramine should be considered under these circumstances.

In predisposed and elderly patients, tricyclic antidepressants may, particularly at night, provoke pharmacogenic (delirious) psychoses that disappear within a few days of withdrawing the drug.

Occupational Hazards: Since imipramine may produce sedation, particularly during the initial phase of therapy, patients should be cautioned about the danger of engaging in activities requiring mental alertness, judgment and physical coordination.

Cardiovascular: Before initiating treatment, it is advisable to check the patient's blood pressure, because individuals with hypotension or a labile circulation may react to the drug with a fall in blood pressure. Regular measurements of blood pressure should be performed in susceptible patients.

Postural hypotension may be controlled by reducing the dosage or administering circulatory stimulants.

ECG abnormalities have been observed in patients treated with imipramine. The most common ECG changes were premature ventricular contractions (PVCs), ST-T wave changes, and abnormalities in intraventricular conduction. These changes were rarely associated with significant clinical symptoms. Nevertheless, caution is necessary when treating patients with heart disease, as well as elderly subjects. In these patients cardiac function should be monitored and ECG examinations performed during long-term therapy. Gradual dose titration is also recommended.

Hepatic Changes: Isolated cases of obstructive jaundice have been reported. Caution is indicated in treating patients with known liver disease and periodic monitoring of hepatic function is recommended in such patients.

Hematological Changes: Isolated cases of bone marrow depression with agranulocytosis have been reported. Leukocyte and differential blood cell counts are recommended in patients receiving treatment with imipramine over prolonged periods, and should be performed for patients who develop fever, an influenzal infection or sore throat. In the event of an allergic skin reaction, imipramine should be withdrawn.

Withdrawal Symptoms: A variety of withdrawal symptoms have been reported in association with abrupt discontinuation of imipramine, including dizziness, nausea, vomiting, headache, malaise, sleep disturbance, hyperthermia and irritability. In addition, such patients may experience a worsening of psychiatric status. While the withdrawal effects of imipramine have not been systematically evaluated in controlled trials, they are well known with closely related tricyclic antidepressants, and it is recommended that the dosage be tapered gradually and the patient monitored carefully during discontinuation.

Metabolic Effects: Tricyclic antidepressants have been associated with porphyrinogenicity in susceptible patients.

Renal Function: It is advisable to monitor renal function during long-term therapy with tricyclic antidepressants.

Dental Effects: Lengthy treatment with tricyclic antidepressants can lead to an increased incidence of dental caries.

Lacrimation: Decreased lacrimation and accumulation of mucoid secretions due to the anticholinergic properties of tricyclic antidepressants may cause damage to the corneal epithelium in patients with contact lenses.

Drug Interactions: Patients should be warned that, while taking imipramine their responses to alcoholic beverages, other CNS depressants (e.g., barbiturates, benzodiazepines or general anesthetics) or anticholinergic agents (e.g., atropine, biperiden, levodopa) may be exaggerated. When tricyclic antidepressants are given in combination with anticholinergics or neuroleptics with an anticholinergic action, hyperexcitation states or delirium may occur, as well as attacks of glaucoma.

Tricyclic antidepressants should not be employed in combination with antiarrhythmic agents of the quinidine type (see Warnings, Cardiovascular).

Since imipramine may diminish or abolish the antihypertensive effects of guanethidine, bethanidine, clonidine, reserpine, or alpha-methyldopa, patients requiring concomitant treatment for hypertension should be given antihypertensives of a different type (e.g., diuretics, vasodilators, beta-blockers).

Tofranil (cont'd)

Imipramine may potentiate the cardiovascular effects of norepinephrine or epinephrine, amphetamine, as well as nasal drops and local anesthetics containing sympathomimetics (e.g., isoprenaline, ephedrine, phenylephrine).

Fluoxetine, fluvoxamine and other selective serotonin reuptake inhibitors (SSRIs) may increase the activity and plasma concentrations of tricyclic antidepressants with corresponding adverse effects.

Caution should be exercised if imipramine is administered together with cimetidine or methylphenidate since these drugs have been shown to inhibit the metabolism of several tricyclic antidepressants. Clinically significant increases in plasma levels of imipramine may occur, necessitating a dosage reduction.

Substances which activate the hepatic mono-oxygenase enzyme system (e.g., barbiturates, carbamazepine, phenytoin, nicotine and oral contraceptives) may lower plasma concentrations of tricyclic antidepressants and so reduce their antidepressive effects. In addition, imipramine may increase plasma levels of phenytoin and carbamazepine, therefore, it may be necessary to adjust the dosage of these drugs.

Imipramine should not be administered for a period of at least 14 days after the discontinuation of treatment with MAO inhibitors due to the potential for severe interactions (see Contraindications). The same caution should also be observed when administering a MAO inhibitor after previous treatment with imipramine.

Imipramine should be discontinued prior to elective surgery for as long as clinically feasible, since little is known about the interaction between imipramine and general anesthetics.

Concomitant treatment with neuroleptic agents (e.g., phenothiazines and butyrophenones) may result in increased plasma concentrations of imipramine, a lowered convulsion threshold and seizures. Combination with thioridazine may produce severe cardiac arrhythmias. No such effects are known to occur in combination with diazepam, but it might be necessary to lower the dosage of imipramine if administered concomitantly with alprazolam or disulfiram.

Tricyclic antidepressants may potentiate the anticoagulant effect of coumarin drugs by inhibiting hepatic metabolism of these drugs. Careful monitoring of plasma prothrombin is therefore advised.

If administered concomitantly with estrogens, the dose of imipramine should be reduced since steroid hormones inhibit the metabolism of imipramine.

Adverse Effects: If severe neurological or psychiatric reactions occur, imipramine should be withdrawn.

Elderly patients are particularly susceptible to anticholinergic, psychiatric, neurological and cardiovascular effects.

The following adverse reactions have been reported with imipramine or other tricyclic antidepressants. (Frequency estimates: Frequent: $>10\%$; Occasional: between 1 to 10%; Rare: between 0.01 to 1%; Isolated cases: $<0.01\%$.)

Neurological: Frequent: tremors. Occasional: drowsiness, headache, paresthesia (numbness, tingling sensation, symptoms suggestive of peripheral neuropathy), delirium. Rare: epileptic seizures. Isolated cases: tinnitus, incoordination, ataxia, alterations in EEG patterns, extrapyramidal symptoms, myoclonus, speech disorders, weakness.

Behavioral: Occasional: drowsiness, fatigue, insomnia, confusional states with hallucinations (particularly in geriatric patients suffering from Parkinson's disease), anxiety, agitation, restlessness, nightmares, hypomania, mania, decrease in memory, feeling of unreality. Rare: activation of latent psychosis. Isolated cases: aggressiveness.

Anticholinergic: dry mouth and rarely associated sublingual adenitis, blurred vision, disturbances of visual accommodation, constipation, perspiration, hot flushes. Occasional: delayed micturition, dilation of the urinary tract. Isolated cases: mydriasis, glaucoma, paralytic ileus.

Cardiovascular: Frequent: hypotension, particularly orthostatic hypotension with associated vertigo, sinus tachycardia, ECG changes (including flattening or inversion of T wave, depressed S-T segments) in patients of normal cardiac status. Occasional: arrhythmia, disturbances in cardiac conduction (e.g., widening of QRS complex, PQ changes, bundle-branch block), palpitation, syncope. Isolated cases: hypertension, congestive heart failure, myocardial infarction, heart block, asystole, stroke, peripheral vasospastic reactions.

Hematologic: Isolated cases: agranulocytosis, eosinophilia, leukopenia, purpura and thrombocytopenia may occur as an idiosyncratic response.

Gastrointestinal: Occasional: nausea, vomiting, anorexia, abdominal cramps. Rare: diarrhea, elevated transaminases. Isolated cases: bitter taste, stomatitis, epigastric distress, black tongue, dysphagia, increased salivation, hepatitis with or without jaundice.

Respiratory: Isolated cases: bronchospasm.

Endocrine: Frequent: weight gain. Occasional: increased or decreased libido, impotence. Isolated cases: gynecomastia in the male, breast enlargement and galactorrhea in the female, testicular swelling, elevation or depression of blood sugar levels, weight loss, inappropriate antidiuretic hormone (SIADH) secretion syndrome.

Allergic or Toxic: Occasional: skin rash, urticaria. Isolated cases: petechiae, itching, photosensitization (avoid excessive exposure to sunlight), edema (general or of face and tongue), drug fever, obstructive jaundice, nasal congestion, alopecia, cross-sensitivity with desipramine, allergic alveolitis (pneumonia) with or without eosinophilia, systemic anaphylactic/anaphylactoid reactions including hypotension.

Withdrawal Symptoms: Abrupt cessation of treatment with tricyclic antidepressants after prolonged administration may occasionally produce nausea, vomiting, abdominal pain, diarrhea, insomnia, nervousness, anxiety, headache and malaise. These symptoms are not indicative of addiction.

Overdose: Since children may be more sensitive than adults to acute overdosage with tricyclic antidepressants, and since fatalities in children have been reported, effort should be made to avoid potential ovedose, particularly in this age group.

Symptoms: These may vary in severity depending upon factors such as the amount of drug absorbed, the interval between drug ingestion and the start of treatment and the age of the patient. Accidental ingestion in children should be regarded as serious and potentially fatal.

Symptoms generally appear within 4 hours of ingestion and reach maximum severity after 24 hours. Owing to delayed absorption (increased anticholinergic effect due to overdose), long half-life and enterohepatic recycling of the drug, the patient may be at risk for up to 4 to 6 days.

Symptoms may include drowsiness, stupor, ataxia, vomiting, cyanosis, restlessness, agitation, delirium, severe perspiration, hyperactive reflexes, muscle rigidity, athetoid and choreiform movements and/or convulsions. Hyperpyrexia, mydriasis, bowel and bladder paralysis, oliguria or anuria and respiratory depression may occur.

Hypotension and initial hypertension may occur. However, the usual finding is increasing hypotension which may eventually lead to shock. Serious cardiovascular disturbances are frequently present, including tachycardia, cardiac arrhythmias (flutter, atriofibrillation, premature ventricular beats and ventricular tachycardia), as well as impaired myocardial conduction, atrioventricular and intraventricular block, ECG abnormalities (such as widened QRS complexes and marked S-T shifts), signs of congestive heart failure and cardiac arrest. Coma may ensue.

Treatment: Patients in whom overdosage is suspected should be admitted to hospital without delay. No specific antidote is available and treatment is essentially symptomatic and supportive.

Gastric lavage or aspiration should be performed promptly and is recommended up to 12 hours or even more after the overdose, since the anticholinergic effect of the drug may delay gastric emptying. Administration of activated charcoal may help reduce absorption of the drug. As imipramine is largely protein bound, forced diuresis, peritoneal dialysis and hemodialysis are unlikely to be of value.

Treatment should be designed to insure maintenance of the vital functions. An open airway should be maintained in comatose patients and assisted ventilation instituted, if necessary, but respiratory stimulants should not be used. Hyperpyrexia should be controlled by external measures, such as ice packs and cooling sponge baths. Acidosis may be treated by cautious administration of sodium bicarbonate. Adequate renal function should be maintained.

ECG monitoring in an intensive care unit is recommended in all patients, particularly in the presence of ECG abnormalities, and should be maintained for several days after the cardiac rhythm has returned to normal. Unexpected deaths attributed to cardiac arrhythmias have been reported several days following an apparent recovery from tricyclic antidepressant overdose. Correction of hypoxia and acidosis, if present, may be beneficial. Correction of metabolic acidosis and low potassium concentrations by means of bicarbonate i.v. and potassium substitution may also be effective for treatment of arrhythmias. If bradyarrhythmia or AV-block ocur, consider temporary insertion of a cardiac pacemaker. Because of its effect on cardiac conduction, digitalis should be used only, with caution. If rapid digitalization is required for the treatment of congestive heart failure, special care should be exercised in using the drug.

External stimulation should be minimized to reduce the tendency to convulsions. If convulsions occur, anticonvulsants (preferably i.v. diazepam) should be administered. Barbiturates may intensify respiratory depression, particularly in children, and aggravate hypotension and coma. Paraldehyde may be used in some children to counteract muscular hypertonus and convulsions with less likelihood of causing respiratory depression. If the patient fails to respond rapidly to anticonvulsants, artificial ventilation should be instituted. Prompt control of convulsions is essential since they aggravate hypoxia and acidosis and may thereby precipitate cardiac arrhythmias and arrest.

Shock should be treated with supportive measures such as i.v. fluids, plasma expanders, and oxygen. The use of corticosteroids in shock is controversial and may be contraindicated in tricyclic antidepressant overdose. Hypotension usually responds to elevation of the foot of the bed. Pressor agents, (but **not** epinephrine) should be given cautiously, if indicated. In the event of a reduced myocardial function, consider recourse to treatment with dopamine or dobutamine by i.v. drip.

Since it has been reported that physostigmine may cause severe bradycardia, asystole and seizures, its use is not recommended in cases of overdosage with imipramine.

Deaths by deliberate or accidental overdosage have occurred with this class of drugs. Since the propensity for suicide is high in depressed patients, a suicide attempt by other means may occur during the recovery phase. The possibility of simultaneous ingestion of other drugs should also be considered.

Dosage: Depression: The dosage should be individualized according to the requirements of each patient. Treatment should be initiated at the lowest recommended dose and increased gradually noting carefully the clinical response and any evidence of intolerance, particularly when treating elderly and adolescent patients. It should be kept in mind that a lag in therapeutic response usually occurs at the onset of therapy, lasting from several days to a few weeks. Increasing the dosage does not normally shorten this latent period and may increase the incidence of side effects.

Initial Dosage: Adults: 25 mg 3 times daily. This should be increased gradually as required and tolerated, up to 150 mg/day. Dosages over 200 mg/day are not recommended. In severely ill, hospitalized patients, initially 100 mg/day in divided doses, gradually increasing to 200 mg/day, if required. If no significant response is observed after 3 weeks, dosage may be increased up to 250 to 300 mg/day.

Elderly and Debilitated Patients: 30 to 40 mg/day, in divided doses, gradually increasing dosage if necessary, and tolerated; it is generally not necessary to exceed 100 mg/day.

Maintenance Dosage: Dosage during maintenance therapy should be kept at the lowest effective level. Medication should be continued for the expected duration of the depressive episode in order to minimize the possibility of relapse following clinical improvement.

When a maintenance dosage has been established as described above, imipramine may be administered in a single daily dose at bedtime, provided such a dosage regimen is well tolerated.

Childhood Enuresis: For persistent functional enuresis which has not responded to other forms of management, a therapeutic trial with imipramine may be considered for children between 5 and 15 years of age, who are not mentally defective, and in whom organic causes of enuresis have been excluded.

The recommended dosage is 10 to 25 mg/day for children 5 years of age and older. If a satisfactory response does not occur within 1 week, the dosage may be increased up to 75 mg/day in children over 12 years of age. A daily dose greater than 75 mg does not enhance efficacy and tends to increase side effects. ECG changes of unknown significance have been reported with doses higher than those recommended in pediatric patients. The trial period should be 2 to 4 weeks. Medication should be given in a single dose 1 hour before bedtime, however, in children subject to enuresis early on in the night, part of the dose should be taken between 15 and 17 h.

Consideration should be given to instituting a drug free period following an adequate therapeutic trial with a favorable response, in order to assess the need for further drug treatment.

Dosage should be tapered off gradually rather than abruptly discontinued; this may reduce the tendency to relapse.

Children who relapse when the drug is discontinued do not always respond to a subsequent course of treatment.

The safety and effectiveness of imipramine as temporary adjunctive treatment for nocturnal enuresis in children less than 5 years of age has not been established.

Supplied: 25 mg: Each reddish brown, sugar-coated, round, biconvex tablet, contains: imipramine HCl 25 mg. Energy: 1 kJ (0.25 kcal). Bottles of 100 and 1 000.

50 mg: Each reddish brown, sugar-coated, round, biconvex tablet, branded Geigy on one side and LB on the other side in white, contains: imipramine HCl 50 mg. Energy: 3.77 kJ (0.90 kcal). Bottles of 100 and 500.

75 mg: Each reddish brown, sugar-coated, round, biconvex tablet, branded Geigy on one side and ATA on the other side in white, contains: imipramine HCl 75 mg. Energy: 3.3 kJ (0.8 kcal). Bottles of 30.

Nonmedicinal ingredients: cellulose compounds, colloidal silicon dioxide, cornstarch, glycerin, iron oxides, lactose, magnesium stearate, polyethylene glycol, povidone, stearic acid, sucrose, talc and titanium dioxide. All are alcohol-, bisulfite-, gluten-, parabens-, sodium- and tartrazine-free.

Protect from heat (store between 2 and 30°C) and humidity. Keep out of reach of children.

(Shown in Product Recognition Section)

Reviewed 1997

TOLBUTAMIDE

General Monograph, CPhA

see SULFONYLUREAS

TOLECTIN®

Janssen-Ortho

Tolmetin Sodium

Anti-inflammatory—Analgesic—Antipyretic

Pharmacology: Tolmetin has demonstrated anti-inflammatory, analgesic and antipyretic properties in classical animal test systems. In patients with rheumatoid arthritis the anti-inflammatory action has been shown by a reduction in joint swelling, pain and duration of morning stiffness, as well as by enhanced grip strength, increased mobility and increased delay in the onset of fatigue.

Studies in laboratory animals and man have demonstrated that the anti-inflammatory action of tolmetin is not due to pituitary-adrenal stimulation.

Tolmetin inhibits prostaglandin synthetase in vitro and lowers the plasma level of prostaglandin E in man. This inhibition of prostaglandin synthesis may be responsible for the anti-inflammatory action of the drug.

Clinical trials in human subjects have shown that the administration of tolmetin, in daily doses of 1 200 mg, is similar in alleviating arthritis symptomatology to ASA, in daily doses of 3 900 mg. It has been shown that gastrointestinal bleeding is less severe with tolmetin than with ASA.

Pharmacokinetics: In man, tolmetin is rapidly and completely absorbed with attainment of peak plasma levels within 20 to 60 minutes following an oral dose. The drug is eliminated from the plasma with a mean half-life of 1 to 3 hours. Peak plasma levels of about 40 μg/mL are obtained with an oral dose of 400 mg. Essentially all of the administered dose is recovered in the urine in 24 hours either as an inactive oxidative metabolite or as conjugates of tolmetin free acid.

Tolmetin is extensively (>99%) bound to plasma albumin (see Precautions, Drug Interactions).

Indications: The treatment of rheumatoid arthritis, juvenile rheumatoid arthritis, osteoarthritis, and ankylosing spondylitis.

Contraindications: Peptic ulcer or active inflammatory disease of the gastrointestinal system. Known or suspected hypersensitivity to the drug. Tolmetin should not be used in patients in whom acute asthmatic attacks, urticaria, rhinitis or other allergic manifestations are precipitated by ASA or other NSAIDs. Fatal anaphylactoid reactions have occurred in such individuals.

Warnings: Peptic ulceration, perforation and gastrointestinal bleeding, sometimes severe and occasionally fatal, have been reported during therapy with NSAIDs including tolmetin.

Tolmetin should be given under close medical supervision to patients prone to gastrointestinal tract irritation particularly those with a history of peptic ulcer, diverticulosis or other inflammatory disease of the gastrointestinal tract. In these cases the physician must weigh the benefits of treatment against the possible hazards.

Patients taking any NSAID including this drug should be instructed to contact a physician immediately if they experience symptoms or signs suggestive of peptic ulceration or gastrointestinal bleeding. These reactions can occur without warning symptoms or signs and at any time during the treatment.

Elderly, frail and debilitated patients appear to be at higher risk from a variety of adverse reactions from NSAIDs. For such patients, consideration should be given to a starting dose lower than usual, with individual adjustment when necessary and under close supervision (see Precautions).

Pregnancy: Safe conditions for the use of tolmetin in pregnancy have not been determined and, therefore, such use is not recommended. Rats treated with 10 to 50 mg/kg/day during the last part of pregnancy demonstrated prolonged parturition which increased hemorrhage and increased pup mortality.

Lactation: Tolmetin has been shown to be secreted in human milk. Therefore, because of the possible adverse effects of prostaglandin inhibiting drugs on neonates, use in nursing mothers should be avoided.

Precautions: Gastrointestinal: If peptic ulceration is suspected or confirmed, or if gastrointestinal bleeding or perforation occurs, tolmetin should be discontinued, an appropriate treatment instituted and the patient closely monitored.

There is no definitive evidence that the concomitant administration of histamine H_2-receptor antagonists and/or antacids will either prevent the occurrence of gastrointestinal side effects or allow continuation of tolmetin therapy when and if these adverse reactions appear.

Hypersensitivity Reactions: Anaphylactoid reactions have been reported with tolmetin. Because of the possibility of cross-sensitivity to other NSAIDs, particularly zomepirac, anaphylactoid reactions may be more likely to occur in patients who have exhibited allergic reactions to these compounds (see Contraindications).

Renal Function: As with other NSAIDs, long-term administration of tolmetin to animals has resulted in renal papillary necrosis and other abnormal renal pathology. In humans, there have been reports of renal failure, acute interstitial nephritis with hematuria, proteinuria, and occasionally nephrotic syndrome.

A second form of renal toxicity has been seen in patients with prerenal conditions leading to the reduction in renal blood flow or blood volume, where the renal prostaglandins have a supportive role in the maintenance of renal perfusion. In these patients, administration of a NSAID may cause a dose-dependent reduction in prostaglandin formation and may precipitate overt renal decompensation. Patients at greatest risk of this reaction are those with impaired renal function, heart failure, liver dysfunction, those taking diuretics, and the elderly. Discontinuation of NSAID therapy is usually followed by recovery to the pre-treatment state.

Tolmetin and its metabolites are eliminated primarily by the kidneys; therefore, the drug should be used with great caution in patients with impaired renal function. In these cases lower doses of tolmetin should be anticipated and patients carefully monitored.

The metabolites of tolmetin in urine have been found to give false positive tests for proteinuria using any test which relies on acid precipitation as its endpoint (e.g. sulfosalicylic acid). No interference is seen in the test for proteinuria using Albustix Reagent Strips.

During long-term therapy kidney function should be monitored periodically.

Hepatic Function: As with other NSAIDs, borderline elevations of one or more liver tests may occur. These abnormalities may progress, may remain essentially unchanged, or may be transient with continued therapy. A patient with symptoms and/or signs suggesting liver dysfunction, or in whom an abnormal liver test has occurred, should be evaluated for evidence of the development of more severe hepatic reaction while on therapy with this drug. Severe hepatic reactions including jaundice and cases of fatal hepatitis have been reported with this drug as with other NSAIDs. Although such reactions are rare, if abnormal liver tests persist, or worse, if clinical signs and symptoms consistent with liver disease develop, or if systemic manifestations occur (e.g., eosinophilia, rash, etc.), this drug should be discontinued.

During long-term therapy, liver function tests should be monitored periodically. If this drug is to be used in the presence of impaired liver function, it must be done under strict observation.

Fluid and Electrolyte Balance: Fluid retention and edema have been reported in about 7% of patients treated with tolmetin. Therefore, as with many other NSAIDs, the possibility of precipitating congestive heart failure in elderly patients or those with compromised cardiac function should be borne in mind. Tolmetin should be used with caution in patients with heart failure, hypertension or other conditions predisposing to fluid retention.

Serum electrolytes should be monitored periodically during long-term therapy, especially in those patients at risk.

Hematology: Drugs inhibiting prostaglandin biosynthesis do interfere with platelet function to some degree; therefore, patients who may be adversely affected by such an action should be carefully observed when tolmetin is administered.

Blood dyscrasias associated with the use of NSAIDs are rare, but can have severe consequences.

Infection: In common with other anti-inflammatory drugs, tolmetin may mask the usual signs of infection.

Ophthalmology: Blurred and/or diminished vision has been reported with the use of tolmetin and other NSAIDs. If such symptoms develop this drug should be discontinued and an ophthalmologic examination performed; ophthalmic examination should be carried out at periodic intervals in any patient receiving this drug for an extended period of time.

Geriatrics: As with other anti-inflammatory drugs, tolmetin should be used with caution in elderly patients, and the dosage should be adjusted individually. No data on pharmacokinetic studies involving elderly patients are available.

Children: The safety and effectiveness of tolmetin have not been established in infants under 2 years of age.

Drug Interactions: Tolmetin is highly bound to plasma proteins. This may lead to interaction with anticoagulants, sulfonylurea hypoglycemic agents, sulfonamides, phenytoin, lithium and certain chemotherapeutic agents such as methotrexate.

Concomitant administration of ASA results in decreased peak serum concentrations of tolmetin and slight increases in both clearance and apparent half-life. The clinical significance of these changes is unknown.

In clinical use, cases of increased prothrombin time and bleeding have been reported in patients taking anticoagulants. Therefore, such patients should be carefully monitored when tolmetin is administered. The in vitro binding of warfarin to human plasma proteins is unaffected by tolmetin, and tolmetin did not alter the prothrombin time of normal volunteers.

In a study in adult diabetic patients under treatment with either sulfonylureas or insulin there was no change in the clinical effects of either tolmetin or the hypoglycemic agents. However, if there are side effects such as nausea, anorexia or vomiting, the dose of the antidiabetic used may have to be reduced to prevent hypoglycemic reaction.

Tolmetin causes water retention and therefore may interfere with diuretics in the treatment of hypertension.

In patients receiving concomitant steroid therapy, any reduction in steroid dosage should be gradual to avoid the possible complications of sudden steroid withdrawal.

Drug-Food Interaction: In a controlled single dose study, administration of tolmetin with milk had no effect on peak plasma tolmetin concentrations but decreased total tolmetin bioavailability by 16%. When tolmetin was taken immediately after a meal, peak plasma tolmetin concentrations were reduced by 50% while total bioavailability was again decreased by 16%.

Adverse Effects: The most common adverse reactions encountered with NSAIDs are gastrointestinal, of which peptic ulcer, with or without bleeding, is the most severe. Fatalities have occurred on occasion, particularly in the elderly.

The following adverse reactions were reported in controlled clinical trials and/or since the drug has been marketed.

Gastrointestinal: nausea (11%), dyspepsia*, gastrointestinal distress*, abdominal pain*, diarrhea*, flatulence*, vomiting*, constipation, gastritis, peptic ulcer, gastrointestinal bleeding with or without evidence of peptic ulcer, glossitis, stomatitis, hepatitis.

Borderline elevations of liver function tests may occur in up to 15% of patients; less than 1% of patients had clinically significant elevations.

Hypersensitivity: anaphylactoid reactions, fever, lymphadenopathy, serum sickness.

Tolectin (cont'd)

Cardiovascular: elevated blood pressure*, edema*, congestive heart failure in patients with marginal cardiac function, palpitations.
CNS: headache*, dizziness*, drowsiness, depression, aseptic meningitis (causal relationship unknown).
Metabolic/Nutritional: asthenia*, weight gain*, weight loss*.
Dermatologic: skin irritation, urticaria, purpura, erythema multiforme, toxic epidermal necrolysis.
Special Senses: tinnitus, visual disturbance, optic neuropathy, retinal and macular changes.
Hematologic: small and transient decreases in hemoglobin and hematocrit not associated with gastrointestinal bleeding, hemolytic anemia, thrombocytopenia, granulocytopenia, agranulocytosis, leukopenia.
Renal: elevated BUN, urinary tract infection, hematuria, proteinuria, dysuria, interstitial nephritis, hyperuricemia, renal failure.
Miscellaneous: chest pain, epistaxis (causal relationship unknown).
*Reactions occurring in 3 to 9% of patients treated with tolmetin. Reactions occurring in fewer than 3% of the patients are unmarked.

Overdose: Symptoms and Treatment: In the event of overdosage, the stomach should be emptied by inducing vomiting or by gastric lavage, followed by the administration of activated charcoal.

Dosage: Adults: Rheumatoid Arthritis and Ankylosing Spondylitis: The recommended starting dose of tolmetin is 1 200 mg/day, in 3 doses. The dose should be individualized to achieve the minimum effective maintenance dose which lies between 600 and 1 800 mg/day given t.i.d. or q.i.d. Doses larger than 2 000 mg/day have not been studied and are not recommended. A 600 mg tablet is available for patients who require 1 800 mg/day in 3 divided doses.
Osteoarthritis: The recommended starting dose of tolmetin is 800 to 1 200 mg*/day given t.i.d. or q.i.d. The dose should be adjusted either upwards or downwards to achieve the minimum effective maintenance dose. The maintenance dose usually lies between 600 and 1 600 mg*/day given t.i.d. or q.i.d. Doses larger than 1 600 mg*/day have not been studied and are not recommended.
*Expressed as tolmetin-free acid.
Children (2 years and older): The recommended starting dose in juvenile rheumatoid arthritis is 20 mg/kg/day in divided doses (t.i.d. or q.i.d.). When control has been achieved the usual dose ranges from 15 to 30 mg/kg/day. Doses higher than 30 mg/kg/day have not been studied and, therefore, are not recommended.

Abdominal discomfort which may occur with tolmetin can be minimized by the administration of the drug with meals, milk (see Precautions, Drug-Food Interaction) or antacids other than sodium bicarbonate.

Tolmetin should not be used in conjunction with salicylates since greater benefit from the combination is not likely, but the potential for adverse effects is increased.

Tolmetin may also be added to the treatment regimen of patients receiving gold or corticosteroids.

Information for the Patient: See Blue Section—Information for the Patient "Tolectin".

Supplied: Tolectin 200: Each round, hard, flat-faced, beveled, scored, cream-colored tablet, engraved "TOLECTIN" and "200" on one side and engraved "McNEIL" on the other, contains: tolmetin sodium dihydrate equivalent to 200 mg of tolmetin (free acid). Nonmedicinal ingredients: cellulose, cornstarch, magnesium stearate, silicon dioxide and talc. Energy: 0.560 kJ (0.133 kcal). Sodium: <1 mmol (18 mg). Gluten-, lactose-, sodium metabisulfite- and tartrazine-free. Bottles of 100.

Tolectin 400: Each hard, orange-opaque, gelatin capsule containing a granular cream colored powder with a ring of grey-blue color located around the cap and body of the capsule, spin-printed grey-blue "McNEIL" and "TOLECTIN-DS" on one side, contains: tolmetin sodium dihydrate equivalent to 400 mg of tolmetin (free acid). Nonmedicinal ingredients: cornstarch, FD&C Red No. 3, FD&C Yellow No. 6, gelatin, magnesium stearate, talc and titanium dioxide. Energy: 1.405 kJ (0.334 kcal). Sodium: 1.568 mmol (36 mg). Gluten-, lactose-, sodium metabisulfite- and tartrazine-free. Bottles of 100.

Tolectin 600: Each orange, film-coated oval, biconvex tablet, printed "McNEIL", "TOLECTIN" and "600" on one side, contains: tolmetin sodium dihydrate equivalent to 600 mg of tolmetin (free acid). Nonmedicinal ingredients: cellulose, colloidal silicon dioxide, crospovidone, D&C Yellow No. 10, hydroxypropyl methylcellulose and polyethylene glycol. Energy: 3.017 kJ (0.721 kcal). Sodium: 2.35 mmol (54 mg). Gluten-, lactose-, sodium metabisulfite- and tartrazine-free. Bottles of 100.

Tolectin tablets, capsules and caplets should be stored at controlled room temperature (15 to 30°C) in well-closed containers. Tolectin 600 caplets should be protected from light.

(Shown in Product Recognition Section)

Reviewed 1999

TOLEREX®
Novartis Nutrition

Elemental Diet

Indications: A nutritionally complete elemental diet formulated for the nutritional management of patients with impaired digestion and absorption. May include those with inflammatory bowel disease, intestinal atresia, pancreatitis, fistula, partial obstruction, short-gut syndrome. Malnutrition and cachexia. Bowel preparation prior to diagnostic and surgical procedures. Transition diet between parenteral and normal oral feeding. Food sensitivities.

Precautions: Do not administer parenterally. For use only under medical supervision. Nausea, vomiting, abdominal cramps, distention, and diarrhea are possible. Nausea and diarrhea are usually due to feeding rate or diet concentration. Local water conditions may be implicated in instances of diarrhea. Preparing diet with deionized or distilled water may be effective in this circumstance.

Aspiration is an uncommon complication. However, radiologically confirm the anatomic position of the feeding tube, elevate head of the bed 30° while the patient is receiving diet intragastrically, and control the administration to 150 mL/hour or less, depending upon patient tolerance. Jejunal administration should also be considered.

Diabetics, and patients with renal insufficiency receiving this diet should be closely monitored.
Children: Use in children may require adjusting the daily consumption to meet the Recommended Daily Allowance for the age group involved.

Dosage: 3 100 mL or 13 000 kJ (10.3 servings or 3 100 kcal) provides at least 100% of the Canadian RNI (adult males, 25 to 49) for protein and essential vitamins and minerals. May be administered by nasogastric, nasointestinal, esophagostomy, gastrostomy or jejunostomy feeding tube (see Table I).

Oral: For oral use, the product may be flavored and chilled over ice. Flavoring agents may be used if their contribution to the elemental and nutritional qualities of the diet are kept in mind. It should be sipped slowly, perferably through a straw, when served as a beverage.

Table I—Tolerex

Day	Strength	Approx. Rate mL/hr	Kilojoules (kJ)/24 hrs	Nitrogen (g)/24 hrs
Gastric Administration:				
1	½	50	2 510	2.4
2	Full	50	5 020	4.8
3	Full	100	10 041	9.6
4	Full	125	12 552	12.0
Intestinal Administration:				
1	½	50	2 510	2.4
2	½	100	5 020	4.8
3	¾	100	7 531	7.2
4	Full	100	10 041	9.6
5	Full	125	12 552	12.0

Tolerex is a perishable liquid food when in solution. A full day's supply may be prepared at one time and stored in the refrigerator for up to 48 hours, shake the liquid before serving. Do not leave at room temperature for more than 8 hours.

Supplied: Each 80 g packet contains: Ⓓ-D maltodextrin, magnesium gluconate, L-glutamine, calcium glycerophosphate, L-arginine acetate, modified cornstarch, L-aspartic acid, glycine, L-lysine acetate, L-leucine, safflower oil, potassium chloride, L-proline, L-phenylalanine, L-valine, L-alanine, L-methionine, L-threonine, L-isoleucine, sodium phosphate dibasic, L-serine, potassium sorbate, potassium citrate, L-histidine monohydrochloride monohydrate, sodium citrate, L-tryptophan, L-tyrosine, choline bitartrate, polyoxyethylene sorbitan monooleate, ascorbic acid, ferrous sulfate, alpha tocopheryl acetate, zinc sulfate, niacinamide, copper gluconate, calcium pantothenate, manganese sulfate, ascorbyl palmitate (to preserve freshness), vitamin A palmitate, alpha tocopherol (to preserve freshness), pyridoxine HCl, riboflavin, thiamine HCl, chromic acetate, folic acid, BHA/BHT (to preserve freshness), biotin, potassium iodide, sodium molybdate, sodium selenite, phytonadione (vitamin K_1), cholecalciferol (vitamin D_3), cyanocobalamin (vitamin B_{12}). See Table II.

Table II—Tolerex

Analysis	100 mL	
Energy	418 (100)	kJ (kcal)
Protein	2.1	g
Carbohydrate	23	g
Fat	0.15	g
Linoleic Acid	0.12	g
Sodium	47	mg
Potassium	120	mg
Vitamin A	280	IU
Vitamin C	3.3	mg
Thiamine	0.083	mg
Riboflavin	0.094	mg
Niacin	1.1	mg
Calcium	56	mg
Iron	1.0	mg
Vitamin D	22	IU
Vitamin E	1.7	IU
Vitamin B_6	0.11	mg
Folic Acid	0.022	mg
Vitamin B_{12}	0.0003	mg
Phosphorus	56	mg
Iodine	0.009	mg
Magnesium	22	mg
Zinc	0.83	mg
Copper	0.11	mg
Biotin	0.017	mg
Pantothenic Acid	0.56	mg
Vitamin K	0.0037	mg
Choline	4.1	mg
Chloride	95	mg
Manganese	0.11	mg
Selenium	0.004	mg
Chromium	0.007	mg
Molybdenum	0.004	mg

The standard dilution of 4.2 kJ (1 kcal)/mL has a pH of approximately 5.5 and an average osmolality of 550 mOsm/kg/water. Pouches of 80 g, cartons of 6, cases of 10 cartons. Store unopened powder below 30°C.

Reviewed 1999

TOMUDEX® Ⓟ
Zeneca

Raltitrexed Disodium

Antineoplastic

Caution: Raltitrexed should be administered only by, or under the supervision of, a physician who is experienced in cancer chemotherapy and in the management of related toxicities. This includes myelosuppression, hepatic and renal impairment. Raltitrexed should not be administered to patients with severe hepatic impairment.

Pharmacology: Raltitrexed is a quinazoline folate analogue that selectively inhibits thymidylate synthase (TS). Thymidylate synthase is a key enzyme in the de novo synthesis of thymidine triphosphate (TTP), a nucleotide required exclusively for deoxyribonucleic acid (DNA) synthesis. Inhibition of thymidylate synthase leads to DNA fragmentation and cell death.

Raltitrexed is transported into cells via a reduced folate carrier (RFC) and is then extensively polyglutamated by the enzyme folyl polyglutamate synthetase (FPGS) to polyglutamate forms that are retained in cells and are even more potent inhibitors of thymidylate synthase. Raltitrexed polyglutamation enhances thymidylate synthase inhibitory potency and increases the duration of thymidylate synthase inhibition in cells which may improve antitumor activity. Polyglutamation could also contribute to increased toxicity due to drug retention in normal tissues.

Raltitrexed is 93% protein bound in humans.

Table I—Tomudex

Pharmacokinetic Parameters

C_{max} (ng/mL)	$AUC_{0-\infty}$ (ng·h/mL)	CL (mL/min)	CL_r (mL/min)	V_{ss} (L)	$t_{1/2}\beta$ (h)	$t_{1/2}\gamma$ (h)
656	1 056	51.6	25.1	548	1.79	198

Legend:
C_{max}: peak plasma concentration.
CL: clearance.
CL_r: renal clearance.
$t_{1/2}\beta$: half-life of the second phase.
$t_{1/2}\gamma$: terminal half-life.
AUC: area under plasma concentration-time curve.
V_{ss}: volume of distribution at steady state.

Pharmacokinetics: Following i.v. administration at 3 mg/m², the concentration-time profile in patients is triphasic. Peak concentrations, at the end of infusion, are followed by a rapid initial decline in concentration. This is followed by a slow elimination phase. The key pharmacokinetic parameters are presented in Table I.

The maximum concentrations of raltitrexed increased linearly with dose over the clinical dose range tested.

There is no clinically significant plasma accumulation of raltitrexed in patients with normal renal function during repeat administration at 3-week intervals.

Apart from the expected intracellular polyglutamation, raltitrexed was mainly (approximately 50%) excreted unchanged in the urine. It is also excreted in the feces with approximately 15% of the dose being eliminated over a 10-day period. In the study following [^{14}C] labelled raltitrexed, approximately half of the radiolabel was not recovered during the study period suggesting that a proportion (50%) of the raltitrexed dose is retained within tissues, perhaps as raltitrexed polyglutamates, beyond the end of the measurement period. Trace levels of radiolabel were detected in red blood cells on Day 29.

Raltitrexed pharmacokinetics are independent of age and gender. Pharmacokinetics have not been evaluated in children.

Mild (WHO grade 2) to moderate (WHO grade 3) hepatic impairment led to a reduction in plasma clearance of less than 25%.

Mild to moderate renal impairment (creatinine clearance of 25 to 65 mL/min) led to a significant reduction (approximately 50%) in raltitrexed plasma clearance.

Clinical Experience: In clinical trials raltitrexed, administered as a single 3 mg/m² i.v. dose every 3 weeks, demonstrated clinical antitumor activity with an acceptable toxicity profile in patients with advanced colorectal cancer.

Four large clinical trials have been conducted with raltitrexed in advanced colorectal cancer. Of the 3 comparative trials, 2 showed no statistical difference between raltitrexed and the combination of 5-fluorouracil plus leucovorin for survival, while 1 trial showed a statistically significant difference in favor of the combination of 5-fluorouracil plus leucovorin. Raltitrexed as a single agent was as effective as the combination of 5-fluorouracil in terms of objective response rate in all trials.

Indications: In the treatment of advanced colorectal cancer.

Contraindications: In patients with hypersensitivity to the drug or any of its components.

Pregnancy and *Lactation*: Raltitrexed is contraindicated in pregnant women, in women who may become pregnant during treatment or women who are breast-feeding. Teratology studies in the rat indicate that raltitrexed caused embryolethality and fetal abnormalities in pregnant rats. Pregnancy should be excluded before treatment with raltitrexed is commenced and should be avoided during treatment and for at least 6 months after cessation of treatment if either partner is receiving raltitrexed.

Children: Raltitrexed is not recommended for use in children as safety and efficacy have not been established in this group of patients.

Raltitrexed is contraindicated in patients with severe renal and/or hepatic impairment.

Warnings: Raltitrexed should be administered only by or under the supervision of a physician who is experienced in cancer chemotherapy and in the management of chemotherapy-related toxicity. Patients undergoing therapy should be subject to appropriate supervision so that signs of possible toxic effects or adverse reactions may be detected and treated promptly (see Dosage).

As with other cytotoxic agents of this type, caution is necessary in patients with depressed bone marrow function, poor general condition, or prior radiotherapy.

A proportion of raltitrexed is excreted via the fecal route (see Pharmacology) therefore, patients with mild (WHO grade 2) to moderate (WHO grade 3) hepatic impairment should be treated with caution.

Precautions: Raltitrexed is a cytotoxic agent and should be handled according to normal procedures adopted for such agents (see Dosage, Special Instructions).

Raltitrexed may cause malaise or asthenia following infusion and the ability to drive or use machinery could be impaired while symptoms continue.

Geriatrics: Elderly patients are more vulnerable to the toxic effects of raltitrexed. Extreme care should be taken to ensure adequate monitoring of adverse reactions, especially signs of gastrointestinal toxicity (diarrhea or mucositis).

Drug Interactions: No specific clinical drug-drug interaction studies have been conducted.

Leucovorin (folinic acid), folic acid or vitamin preparations containing these agents must not be given immediately prior to or during administration of raltitrexed, since they may interfere with its action.

There is no experience to date in relation to the combined use of raltitrexed with other cytotoxic agents.

Raltitrexed is 93% protein bound and while it has the potential to interact with other highly protein bound drugs, no interactions due to displacement between raltitrexed and warfarin has been observed in vitro. Active tubular secretion may contribute to the renal excretion of raltitrexed, indicating a potential interaction with other actively secreted drugs such as NSAIDs. However, a review of the clinical trial safety database does not reveal evidence of clinically significant interaction in patients treated with raltitrexed who also received concomitant NSAIDs, warfarin and other commonly prescribed drugs.

Adverse Effects: As with other cytotoxic drugs, the administration of raltitrexed is associated with certain adverse reactions; these mainly include reversible effects on the gastrointestinal tract, hematopoietic system and liver enzymes.

Gastrointestinal System: Diarrhea is usually mild or moderate in intensity. However, severe diarrhea can occur, and may be associated with concurrent hematological suppression, especially leukopenia. Subsequent treatment may need to be discontinued or the dose reduced depending on the grade of toxicity (see Dosage).

Nausea and vomiting are usually mild to moderate and responsive to antiemetics.

Hematopoietic System: Leukopenia, anemia and thrombocytopenia are usually mild to moderate, reaching a nadir in the first or second week after treatment and recovering by the third week. Severe leukopenia and thrombocytopenia of WHO grade 4 can occur and may be life-threatening or fatal, especially if associated with gastrointestinal toxicity.

Hepatic: Reversible increases in AST and ALT have been commonly reported as adverse drug reactions in clinical trials. Such changes have usually been asymptomatic and self-limiting.

Cardiovascular System: A number of cardiac rhythm or cardiac function abnormalities have been reported in clinical trials in advanced colorectal cancer. These ranged from sinus tachycardia and supraventricular tachycardia to atrial fibrillation and congestive heart failure. The incidence of disorders of rhythm and function in patients treated with raltitrexed was 2.8% and 1.8% respectively compared to 1.9% and 1.4% for patients on the comparator treatment. A causal relationship could not be established since many of the abnormalities were concurrent with the underlying conditions such as sepsis and dehydration and more than one third of the patients reported cardiovascular abnormalities prior to treatment.

Whole Body: The most frequent effects in clinical trials were asthenia and fever which were usually mild to moderate and reversible. Severe asthenia can occur and may be associated with malaise and a flu-like syndrome. There have been infrequent reports, including those from postmarketing surveillance, of desquamation.

The following effects (see Table II on following page) were reported as possible adverse drug reactions occurring with an incidence of 2% or more in patients with colorectal cancer treated with raltitrexed in clinical trials.

Overdose: Symptoms and Treatment: The expected manifestations of overdose are likely to be an exaggerated form of the adverse drug reactions anticipated with the administration of the drug. Patients should, therefore, be monitored carefully for signs of gastrointestinal and hematological toxicity. Symptomatic treatment and standard supportive care measures for the management of this toxicity should be applied.

There is no clinically proven antidote available. In the case of inadvertent or accidental administration of an overdose, consideration should be given to the administration of leucovorin. From clinical experience with other antifolates, leucovorin may be given at a dose of 25 mg/m² i.v. every 6 hours. As the time interval between raltitrexed administration and leucovorin rescue increases, its effectiveness in counteracting toxicity may decrease. Data in animals show that delayed administration of leucovorin after raltitrexed produced earlier recovery from weight loss and some improvement to intestinal damage and neutrophil and platelet numbers.

Dosage: The dose of raltitrexed is calculated on the basis of body surface area. The recommended dose is 3 mg/m² given i.v., as a single short, i.v. infusion in 50 to 250 mL diluted in 0.9% sodium chloride or 5% dextrose (glucose) solution. It is recommended that the infusion be given over a 15-minute period. In the absence of toxicity, treatment may be repeated every 3 weeks.

Other drugs should not be mixed with raltitrexed in the same infusion container.

Dose escalation above 3 mg/m² is not recommended, since higher doses have been associated with an increased incidence of life-threatening or fatal toxicity.

Prior to the initiation of treatment and before each subsequent treatment, a full blood count (including a differential count and platelets), liver transaminases, serum bilirubin and serum creatinine measurements should be performed. The total white cell count should be greater than 4 000/mm³, the neutrophil count greater than 2 000/mm³ and the platelet count greater than 100 000/mm³ prior to treatment.

In the event of toxicity the next scheduled dose should be withheld until signs of toxic effects regress. In particular, signs of gastrointestinal toxicity (diarrhea or mucositis) and hematological toxicity (neutropenia or thrombocytopenia) should have resolved completely before subsequent treatment is allowed. Patients who develop signs of gastrointestinal toxicity should have their full blood counts monitored at least weekly for signs of hematological toxicity. Treatment in patients with suspected drug-related rises in liver enzymes should be deferred until they show evidence of reversibility to at least WHO grade 2.

Based on the worst grade of gastrointestinal and hematological toxicity observed on the previous treatment and provided that such toxicity has resolved completely, the following dose reductions are recommended for subsequent treatment:

25% Dose Reduction: In patients with WHO grade 3 hematological toxicity (neutropenia or thrombocytopenia) or WHO grade 2 gastrointestinal toxicity (diarrhea or mucositis).

50% Dose Reduction: In patients with WHO grade 4 hematological toxicity (neutropenia or thrombocytopenia) or WHO grade 3 gastrointestinal toxicity (diarrhea or mucositis).

Once a dose reduction has been made, all subsequent doses should be given at the reduced dose level.

Treatment should be discontinued in the event of any WHO grade 4 gastrointestinal toxicity (diarrhea or mucositis) or in the event of a WHO grade 3 gastrointestinal toxicity associated with WHO grade 4 hematological toxicity. Patients with such toxicity should be managed promptly with standard supportive care measures including i.v. hydration and bone marrow support to help neutrophil and platelet recovery thus reducing the likelihood of fatal sepsis or hemorrhage. Based on data in animals where delayed administration of leucovorin after raltitrexed produced earlier recovery from weight loss and some improvement to intestinal damage and recovery of neutrophil and platelet numbers, consideration should be given to the administration of leucovorin (folinic acid). From clinical experience with other antifolates leucovorin may be given at a dose of 25 mg/m² i.v. every 6 hours until the resolution of symptoms. Further use of raltitrexed in such patients is not recommended.

It is essential that the dose reduction scheme be adhered to since the potential for life threatening and fatal toxicity increases if the dose is not reduced or treatment not stopped as appropriate.

Geriatrics: Dosage and administration as for adults. However, as with other cytotoxics, raltitrexed should be used with caution in elderly patients (see Precautions).

Tomudex (cont'd)

Table II—Tomudex

Drug-Related Adverse Events Reported for at Least 2% of Patients in Either Treatment Group of Both Colorectal Cancer Trials

	Number and Percentage of Patients		
	Both Colorectal Cancer Trials	Controlled Colorectal Cancer Trial	
Body System and COSTART Term	**Tomudex (N=399)**	**Tomudex (N=222)**	**5-FU-LV (N=212)**
Whole Body			
Asthenia	167 (42%)	64 (29%)	34 (16%)
Fever	79 (20%)	45 (20%)	19 (9%)
Mucous Membrane Disorder	42 (11%)	24 (11%)	72 (34%)
Flu Syndrome	43 (11%)	11 (5%)	1 (<1%)
Abdominal Pain	33 (8%)	13 (6%)	19 (9%)
Headache	12 (3%)	5 (2%)	0 (0%)
Cellulitis	13 (3%)	4 (2%)	0 (0%)
Pain	10 (3%)	4 (2%)	2 (<1%)
Malaise	9 (2%)	4 (2%)	1 (<1%)
Sepsis	8 (2%)	6 (3%)	3 (1%)
Digestive			
Nausea	217 (54%)	105 (47%)	82 (39%)
Diarrhea	134 (34%)	66 (30%)	102 (48%)
Vomiting	127 (32%)	64 (29%)	40 (19%)
Anorexia	97 (24%)	39 (18%)	13 (6%)
Stomatitis	34 (9%)	19 (9%)	56 (26%)
Constipation	24 (6%)	13 (6%)	9 (4%)
Dyspepsia	22 (6%)	5 (2%)	5 (2%)
Mouth ulceration	7 (2%)	5 (2%)	9 (4%)
Hemic and Lymphatic			
Leukopenia	91 (23%)	42 (18%)	71 (34%)
Anemia	75 (19%)	26 (12%)	16 (8%)
Thrombocytopenia	14 (4%)	8 (4%)	4 (2%)
Metabolic and Nutritional			
AST Increased	56 (14%)	41 (19%)	4 (2%)
ALT Increased	47 (12%)	34 (15%)	4 (2%)
Peripheral Edema	20 (5%)	7 (3%)	2 (<1%)
Weight Loss	18 (5%)	6 (3%)	4 (2%)
Dehydration	12 (3%)	8 (4%)	6 (3%)
Alkaline Phosphatase Increased	8 (2%)	5 (2%)	2 (<1%)
Musculoskeletal			
Arthralgia	8 (2%)	4 (2%)	0 (0%)
Nervous System			
Hypertonia	9 (2%)	5 (2%)	0 (0%)
Respiratory			
Cough Increased	9 (2%)	4 (2%)	2 (<1%)
Skin and Appendages			
Rash	53 (13%)	28 (13%)	22 (10%)
Alopecia	19 (5%)	9 (4%)	25 (12%)
Pruritus	9 (2%)	4 (2%)	0 (0%)
Sweating	8 (2%)	6 (3%)	3 (1%)
Special Senses			
Taste Perversion	13 (3%)	5 (2%)	1 (<1%)
Conjunctivitis	8 (2%)	4 (2%)	7 (3%)

Legend: 5-FU-LV=5-fluorouracil and leucovorin.

Renal Impairment: For patients with abnormal serum creatinine, before the first or any subsequent treatment, a creatinine clearance should be performed or calculated. For patients with a normal serum creatinine when the serum creatinine may not correlate well with the creatinine clearance due to factors such as age or weight loss, the same procedure should be followed. If creatinine clearance is ≤65 mL/min, the following dose modifications are recommended (see Table III).

Table III—Tomudex

Dose Modifications Recommended in Renal Impairment

Creatinine Clearance	Dose as % of 3 mg/m²	Dosing Interval
>65 mL/min	Full dose	3-weekly
55 to 65 mL/min	75%	4-weekly
25 to 54 mL/min	% equivalent to mL/min*	4-weekly
<25 mL/min	No therapy	Not applicable

* For example, if the creatinine clearance=30 mL/min, 30% of the full dose should be given.

Patients with renal impairment may have an increased propensity for side-effects and should be monitored appropriately.

Hepatic Impairment: No dosage adjustment is necessary for patients with mild (WHO grade 2) to moderate (WHO grade 3) hepatic impairment. However, given that a proportion of the drug is excreted via the fecal route (see Pharmacology) and that these patients usually form a poor prognosis group, patients with mild (WHO grade 2) to moderate (WHO grade 3) hepatic impairment need to be treated with caution.

Treatment in patients with suspected drug-related rises in liver enzymes should be deferred until they show evidence of reversibility to at least WHO grade 2. Raltitrexed has not been studied in patients with severe hepatic impairment, clinical jaundice or decompensated liver disease and its use in such patients is not recommended.

Special Instructions: Raltitrexed is a cytotoxic agent and should be handled according to the normal procedures adopted for such agents in each institution. At minimum the following are recommended:

Any unused injection or reconstituted solution should be discarded in a suitable manner for cytotoxics.

Raltitrexed should be reconstituted for injection by trained personnel in a designated area for the reconstitution of cytotoxic agents. Cytotoxic preparations such as raltitrexed should not be handled by pregnant women.

Reconstitution should normally be carried out in a partial containment facility with extraction capabilities, e.g., a laminar air-flow cabinet, and work surfaces should be covered with disposable plastic-backed absorbent paper.

Appropriate protective clothing, including surgical gloves and goggles, should be worn. In case of contact with skin, wash immediately with water. For splashes in the eyes irrigate with clean water, holding the eyelids apart, for at least 10 minutes. Seek medical attention.

Any spillage should be cleared up using standard procedures consistent with the handling of chemotherapeutic agents.

Waste material should be disposed of by incineration in a manner consistent with the handling of cytotoxic agents.

Stability and Storage Recommendations: Store at 2 to 25°C protected from light. Once reconstituted, raltitrexed is chemically stable for 24 hours at 25°C exposed to ambient light, however, it is recommended that raltitrexed should be refrigerated to avoid bacterial contamination (for further information see Reconstituted Solutions).

Reconstituted Solutions: Each vial, containing 2 mg of raltitrexed, should be reconstituted with 4 mL of sterile water for injection to produce a 0.5 mg/mL solution. The appropriate dose of solution, calculated on the basis of body surface area, is diluted in 50 to 250 mL of either 0.9% sodium chloride or 5% glucose (dextrose) injection and administered by a short i.v. infusion over a period of 15 minutes.

There is no preservative or bacteriostatic agent present in raltitrexed or the materials specified for reconstitution or dilution. Raltitrexed must therefore be reconstituted and diluted under aseptic conditions (see Special Instructions) and it is recommended that solutions of raltitrexed should be used as soon as possible. Reconstituted raltitrexed solution may be stored refrigerated (2 to 8°C) for up to 24 hours. The admixed solution must be completely used or discarded within 24 hours of reconstitution of raltitrexed i.v. injection.

Reconstituted and diluted solutions do not need to be protected from light.

Do not store partially used vials or admixed solutions for future patient use.

Parenteral Products: Continuous i.v. infusion (see Table IV).

Table IV—Tomudex

Reconstitution

Vial Size	Volume of Diluent to be Added to Vial	Approximate Available Volume	Nominal Concentration /mL
2 mg raltitrexed/ vial*	4 mL sterile water for injection	4 mL	0.5 mg/mL

*as the disodium salt.

There is no information on incompatibilities at present and therefore raltitrexed should not be mixed with any other drug.

As with all parenteral drug products, i.v. admixtures should be inspected visually for clarity, particulate matter, precipitate, discoloration and leakage prior to administration whenever solutions and containers permit.

Supplied: Each vial of sterile, lyophilized powder without preservative or bacteriostatic agent contains: raltitrexed 2 mg (as the disodium salt). Nonmedicinal ingredients: dibasic sodium phosphate, mannitol, nitrogen and sodium hydroxide. Single dose vials of 2 mg.

Reviewed 1999

TONOCARD® Ⓟ

Astra

Tocainide HCl

Antiarrhythmic Agent

Pharmacology: Tocainide is a primary amine analog of lidocaine. Its electrophysiologic properties are similar to those of lidocaine. It possesses class IB properties in the modified electrophysiological classification of antiarrhythmic drugs proposed by Vaughan-Williams. In studies of isolated dog Purkinje fibres, tocainide in concentrations of 1 to 50 μg/mL had no significant effect on resting membrane potential, but reduced the amplitude and rate of depolarization (dv/dt) of the action potential. Tocainide decreased the effective refractory period (ERP) to a lesser extent than the action potential duration (APD) resulting in an increase in the ERP/APD ratio. In patients with cardiac disease, tocainide produced no clinically significant changes in sinus nodal function, effective refractory periods, or intracardiac conduction times when studied under electrophysiologic testing procedures. Tocainide does not prolong ventricular depolarization (QRS duration) or repolarization (QT intervals) as measured by electrocardiography.

Pharmacokinetics: The absorption of tocainide from the gastrointestinal tract is almost complete and peak plasma levels occur within 1 to 2 hours after an oral dose. Tocainide shows insignificant first-pass elimination and its bioavailability is exceeding 95%. The extent of bioavailability is unaffected by food.

The half-life is 15.6±3.8 hours. This is increased to about 27 hours in patients with end stage renal failure. At antiarrhythmic concentrations, tocainide is approximately 10% bound to plasma proteins. The optimal plasma range for tocainide is approximately 4 to 10 μg/mL (18 to 45 μmol/L). Elimination occurs by both renal excretion and metabolic degradation and is not dose dependent. The principal metabolite of tocainide in urine was found to be N-carboxytocainide glucuronide (25% of dose after repeated oral administration).

The amount of tocainide excreted unchanged in urine is about 40% of the given dose and is independent of the route of administration. Alkalinization of the urine significantly reduces the amount of tocainide excreted.

Hemodynamics: Cardiac catheterization studies in man utilizing i.v. tocainide infusions (0.5 to 0.75 mg/kg/min over 15 min) have shown that tocainide usually produces a small degree of depression of parameters of left ventricular function, such as left ventricular dP/dt, and left ventricular end diastolic pressure. There were usually no changes in cardiac output or clinical evidence of increasing congestive heart failure in the well compensated patients studied. Small but statistically significant increases in aortic and pulmonary arterial pressures have been consistently observed and are probably related to small increases in vascular resistance. When used concomitantly with a beta-blocking drug, tocainide further reduced cardiac index and left ventricular dP/dt and further increased pulmonary wedge pressure.

No clinically significant changes in heart rate, blood pressure, or signs of myocardial depression were observed in a study of 72 post-myocardial infarction patients receiving long-term therapy with oral tocainide at usual doses (400 mg every 8 hours). Tocainide has been used safely in patients with acute myocardial infarction and various degrees of congestive heart failure. It has, however, a small negative inotropic effect and can increase peripheral resistance slightly. It therefore should be used cautiously in patients with known heart failure, particularly if a beta-blocker is given as well (see Precautions).

Indications:

> No antiarrhythmic drug has been shown to reduce the incidence of sudden death in patients with asymptomatic ventricular arrhythmias. Most antiarrhythmic drugs have the potential to cause dangerous arrhythmias; some have been shown to be associated with an increased incidence of sudden death. In light of the above, physicians should carefully consider the risks and benefits of antiarrhythmic therapy for all patients with ventricular arrhythmias.

For the treatment of documented life-threatening ventricular arrhythmias, such as sustained ventricular tachycardia. Tocainide may also be used for the treatment of patients with documented symptomatic ventricular arrhythmias when the symptoms are of sufficient severity to require treatment. Due to its adverse reaction profile (blood dyscrasias, pulmonary fibrosis, proarrhythmic effects), tocainide should be used only in patients not responding to other therapy, or when other therapy is not tolerated. Tocainide should be reserved for patients in whom, in the opinion of the physician, the benefit of treatment clearly outweighs the risks.

For patients with sustained ventricular tachycardia, tocainide therapy should be initiated in the hospital. Hospitalization may also be required for certain other patients depending on their cardiac status and underlying cardiac disease.

The effects of tocainide in patients with recent myocardial infarction have not been adequately studied and, therefore, its use in this condition cannot be recommended.

Contraindications: In patients with known hypersensitivity to local anesthetics of the amide type and in patients with second or third degree AV block in the absence of a pacemaker.

Warnings: Mortality: The results of the Cardiac Arrhythmia Suppression Trial (CAST) in post-myocardial infarction patients with asymptomatic ventricular arrhythmias showed a significant increase in mortality and in non-fatal cardiac arrest rate in patients treated with encainide or flecainide compared with a matched placebo-treated group. CAST was continued using a revised protocol with moricizine and placebo arms only. The trial was prematurely terminated because of a trend towards an increase in mortality in the moricizine treated group. The applicability of these results to other populations or other antiarrhythmic agents is uncertain, but at present it is prudent to consider these results when using any antiarrhythmic agent.

Proarrhythmic Effects: Tocainide has been reported to aggravate or induce arrhythmias in some patients (see Adverse Effects).

Blood Dyscrasias: Tocainide therapy should only be instituted when facilities are available for regular monitoring of blood counts. Agranulocytosis, bone marrow depression, leukopenia, neutropenia, aplastic/hypoplastic anemia and thrombocytopenia have been reported in patients receiving tocainide; concomitant septicemia and/or fatalities have occurred. A complete hemogram (hematocrit, hemoglobin, RBC count, and morphology if appropriate, complete WBC with differential and platelet count) should be performed before the patient is started on tocainide. Patients should be instructed to promptly report the development of bruising, bleeding, unusual tiredness or any signs of infection such as fever, sore throat or chills. Since most of these events have been noted during the first 12 weeks of therapy, it is recommended that blood counts be performed weekly during this period, and frequently thereafter. If any of these hematological disorders is identified, tocainide should be discontinued, and appropriate treatment instituted.

Pulmonary Toxicity: Pulmonary fibrosis, interstitial pneumonitis, fibrosing alveolitis, pulmonary edema, and pneumonia, possibly drug related, have been reported in patients receiving tocainide.

Many of these events occurred in patients who were seriously ill. The experiences are usually characterized by bilateral infiltrates on x-ray and are frequently associated with dyspnea and cough. Fever may or may not be present. Patients should be instructed to promptly report the development of any pulmonary symptoms such as exertional dyspnea, cough or wheezing. Chest x-rays are advisable at that time. If these pulmonary disorders develop, tocainide should be discontinued.

Ventricular Rate: Acceleration of ventricular rate occurs infrequently when antiarrhythmic agents are administered to patients with atrial flutter or fibrillation (see Adverse Effects).

Pregnancy: Fetal abnormalities were reported in all test groups in a rabbit teratogenicity study. At the highest dose level (100 mg/kg) the incidence differed significantly from the control group. Although maternal toxicity was observed at these doses, a drug effect on the fetus cannot be excluded. The safety of tocainide in pregnancy has not been established and therefore tocainide should not be administered unless the expected benefits outweigh the potential risks.

Precautions: Tocainide should be used with caution in patients with heart failure or with minimal cardiac reserve because of the potential for aggravating the degree of heart failure. It should also be used with caution in patients who are receiving beta-blockers and/or other antiarrhythmic drugs.

Tocainide has been reported to aggravate or induce arrhythmias in some patients (see Adverse Effects).

Since antiarrhythmic drugs may be ineffective in patients with hypokalemia, any potassium deficit should be corrected.

Caution should be used in the institution or continuation of antiarrhythmic therapy in the presence of signs of increasing depression of cardiac conductivity.

Occupational Hazards: Because tocainide can cause CNS effects such as lightheadedness/dizziness/vertigo/giddiness, tremor/quivering/tremulousness, confusion/disorientation, patients should be cautioned about engaging in activities requiring mental alertness, judgment and physical coordination (such as driving an automobile or operating dangerous machinery) when these effects occur.

Tocainide should be used with caution in patients with severe renal disease because of the risk of accumulation (see Dosage).

Patients receiving tocainide should have periodic testing of liver function, as hepatitis and abnormal liver test have been reported. Because of risk of accumulation, patients with preexisting severe hepatic disease should be treated with caution (see Dosage).

A lupus-erythematous-like syndrome has been reported in a few patients receiving tocainide. While a causal relationship has not been established, it is recommended that patients on long-term treatment be monitored for this possibility.

In epilepsy, tocainide should be used with caution because of the risk of precipitating convulsions.

Lactation: It is not known whether tocainide is secreted into breast milk. Therefore the drug is not recommended for use in lactating mothers unless the expected benefits outweigh the potential risks.

Children: The use of tocainide in children is not recommended since the safety and efficacy in children have not been established.

Geriatrics: Because of the possible risk of impaired elimination or increased sensitivity in the elderly, tocainide should be used with caution (see Dosage).

Drug Interactions: Caution should be exercised in the use of multiple drug therapy. Specific interaction studies with a beta-blocker have been carried out and showed no clinically significant interactions. However, in patients with sick sinus syndrome and patients with impaired atrioventricular conduction, the small depression of myocardial contractility resulting from the administration of tocainide may become significant when a beta-blocker and tocainide are administered concomitantly.

Tocainide has been used clinically with digitalis and other antiarrhythmic agents (quinidine, disopyramide, procainamide), anticoagulants and diuretics without evidence of untoward effects. Concurrent use of tocainide and lidocaine leads to potentiation of adverse effects involving the CNS.

There is no evidence of pharmacokinetic interaction between tocainide and phenobarbital, clofibrate or salicylamide.

Because of the limited plasma protein binding and the relatively large apparent volume of distribution of tocainide, significant interactions involving plasma protein binding displacement are unlikely.

Adverse Effects: Tocainide has been evaluated in both short-term and long-term controlled studies as well as an emergency use program. Dosages were lower in most of the controlled studies (1 200 mg/day) and higher in the emergency use program (1 800 mg/day and more). In long-term (2 to 6 months) controlled studies, the most frequent adverse reactions were lightheadedness/dizziness (15.3%), nausea (14.5%), paresthesia/numbness (9.2%), and tremor (8.5%). These reactions were generally mild, transient, dose-related and reversible with a reduction in dosage, by taking the drug with food, or by therapy discontinuation. Tremor, when present, may be useful as a clinical indicator that the maximum dose is being approached. Adverse reactions leading to therapy discontinuation occurred in 21% of patients in long-term controlled trials and were usually related to the CNS or gastrointestinal system.

Adverse reactions occurring in greater than 1% of patients from the short-term and long-term controlled studies appear in Table I (on following page).

An additional group of about 2 000 patients has been treated in a program allowing for the use of tocainide under emergency use circumstances. These patients were seriously ill with the large majority on multiple drug therapy, and comparatively high doses of tocainide were used. Fifty-four percent of the patients continued in the program for 1 year or longer, and 12% were treated for longer than 3 years, with the longest duration of therapy being 9 years. Adverse reactions leading to therapy discontinuation occurred in 12% of patients (usually CNS effects or rash).

A tabulation of adverse reactions occurring in 1% or more of patients is shown in Table II (on following page).

Adverse reactions occurring in less than 1% of patients in either the controlled studies or the emergency use program or those reported from marketed use are as follows:

Hematopoietic: agranulocytosis, hypoplastic anemia, leukopenia, thrombocytopenia, anemia. These have been reported in 0.18% of patients and continue to be reported in countries where the drug is on the market. These hematologic disorders usually occurred after 2 to 12 weeks of therapy (see Warnings).

CNS: coma, convulsions/seizures, depression, psychosis, mental change, agitation, altered taste/smell, difficulty concentrating, diplopia, dysarthria, impaired memory, increased stuttering/slurred speech, insomnia/sleeping disturbance, local anesthesia, nightmares, thirst, weakness, myasthenia gravis.

Gastrointestinal: abdominal pain/discomfort, constipation, dysphagia, gastrointestinal symptoms (including dyspepsia), abnormal liver function tests, hepatitis, jaundice.

Cardiovascular: ventricular fibrillation, extension of acute myocardial infarction, cardiogenic shock, angina, AV block, hypertension, increased QRS duration, pleurisy/pericarditis, prolonged QT interval, right bundle branch block, syncope, vaso-vagal episodes, cardiomegaly, sinus arrest.

Pulmonary: respiratory arrest, pulmonary edema, pulmonary embolism, pulmonary fibrosis, alveolitis, pneumonia, pneumonitis, dyspnea.

Other: increased ANA, urinary retention, polyuria/increased diuresis, alopecia, cinchonism, claudication, cold extremities, dry mouth, earache, edema, fever, hiccups, itching, leg cramps, malaise, metallic/menthol taste, muscle twitching/spasm, neck pain, pain radiating from neck, pallor/flushed face, pressure on shoulder, yawning, vasculitis.

Tonocard (cont'd)

Table I—Tonocard

Adverse Reactions Occurring in Greater than 1% of Patients

	Percentage of Patients Controlled Studies	
	Short-Term (n=1 358)	Long-Term (n=262)
CNS		
Lightheadedness/dizziness/ vertigo/giddiness	8.0	15.3
Paresthesia/numbness	3.5	9.2
Tremor/quivering/ tremulousness	2.9	8.4
Confusion/disorientation/ hallucinations	2.1	2.7
Altered mood/awareness	1.5	3.4
Restlessness/shakiness/ nervousness	1.5	0.4
Blurred vision/visual disturbances	1.3	1.5
Discoordination/unsteadiness/ walking disturbances	1.2	0.0
Anxiety	1.1	1.5
Tinnitus/hearing loss	0.4	1.5
Ataxia	0.2	3.0
Nystagmus	0.0	1.1
Gastrointestinal		
Nausea	15.2	14.5
Vomiting	8.3	4.6
Anorexia	1.2	1.9
Diarrhea/loose stools	0.0	3.8
Cardiovascular		
Hypotension	3.4	2.7
Bradycardia	1.8	0.4
Palpitations	1.8	0.4
Chest pain	1.6	0.4
Conduction disturbances	1.5	0.0
Left ventricular failure	1.4	0.0
Other		
Sweating/cold sweat/night sweats/clammy	5.1	2.3
Headache	2.1	4.6
Tiredness/drowsiness/fatigue/ lethargy/lassitude/ sleepiness	1.6	0.8
Hot/cold feelings	0.5	1.5
Rash/skin lesions	0.4	8.4

Pulmonary fibrosis, pneumonitis, alveolitis, pulmonary edema, and pneumonia, possibly drug related, have been reported in patients receiving tocainide. The incidence of pulmonary fibrosis was 0.03% in controlled trials and the emergency use program. These events usually occurred in seriously ill patients. Symptoms of these pulmonary disorders and/or x-ray changes usually occurred following 3 to 18 weeks of therapy and 2 patients died (see Warnings).

Overdose: Symptoms: Overdosage of tocainide can result in signs of CNS toxicity, including convulsions and respiratory depression.

Treatment: Should convulsions, signs of respiratory depression or respiratory arrest develop, the patency of the airway and adequacy of ventilation must be assured immediately. Should convulsions persist despite ventilation with oxygen, small increments of anticonvulsive agents may be given i.v.

Examples of such agents include a benzodiazepine (e.g., diazepam), an ultrashort-acting barbiturate (e.g., thiopental or thioamylal), or a short-acting barbiturate (e.g., pentobarbital or secobarbital).

Studies to date indicate that tocainide has a hemodialysis clearance approximately equivalent to its renal clearance in normal individuals.

Dosage: The dosage of tocainide should be adjusted individually, based on therapeutic response and tolerance.

Initiation of treatment, as with other antiarrhythmic agents used to treat life-threatening ventricular arrhythmias, should be carried out in hospital.

The following dose regimens can be used as guidelines: The recommended initial dosage is 1 200 mg daily (400 mg every 8 hours).

Table II—Tonocard

Adverse Reactions Occurring in 1% or More of Patients

	Percentage of Patients Emergency Use (n=1 927)
CNS	
Lightheadedness/dizziness/ vertigo/giddiness	25.3
Tremor/quivering/ tremulousness	21.6
Restlessness/shakiness/ nervousness	11.5
Confusion/disorientation/ hallucinations	11.2
Altered mood/awareness	11.0
Ataxia	10.8
Blurred vision/visual disturbances	10.0
Paresthesia/numbness	9.2
Nystagmus	1.1
Gastrointestinal	
Nausea	24.6
Anorexia	11.3
Vomiting	9.0
Diarrhea/loose stools	6.8
Cardiovascular	
Increased ventricular arrhythmias/PVCs	10.9
CHF/progression of CHF	4.0
Tachycardia	3.2
Hypotension	1.8
Conduction disturbances	1.3
Bradycardia	1.0
Other	
Rash/skin lesion	12.2
Sweating/cold sweat/night sweats/clammy	8.3
Arthritis/arthralgia	4.7
Myalgia	1.7
Lupus	1.6

Adults: The usual adult dosage of tocainide is between 1 200 to 1 800 mg/day, given in divided doses every 6 to 8 hours. Higher doses up to 2 400 mg/day divided into 4 doses every 6 hours should be used only in patients with refractory ventricular arrhythmias who failed to respond to other available therapy.

Six-hour dosing intervals generally are better tolerated than 8-hour intervals.

Geriatrics: The initial dosage for elderly patients should be reduced to 800 mg/day (400 mg every 12 hours). Because of the possible risk of impaired elimination or increased sensitivity in the elderly, any dose increase should be monitored. A 6- to 8-hour dosing regimen should be employed for higher dosage.

In patients with severe hepatic or renal insufficiency (creatinine clearance less than 30 mL/min) the initial dose should be reduced to 800 mg/day (400 mg every 12 hours).

With total renal failure the initial dose should be reduced to 400 mg daily. Monitoring of plasma concentrations is recommended in renal or hepatic diseases.

Conversion from Lidocaine: Adequate information on the most appropriate regimen for conversion from i.v. lidocaine to oral tocainide is lacking. Based on pharmacokinetic considerations, at present the following regimen can be used as a guideline: Initiate oral therapy with a 400 mg dose of tocainide upon cessation of the lidocaine infusion.

Follow with a 400 mg dose of tocainide every 4 hours during the first 8 hours.

Continue therapy with a regimen of 400 mg every 8 hours. During the first 24 hours of conversion, ECG and blood pressure monitoring is mandatory.

Supplied: Each yellow, biconvex, circular, film-coated tablet, engraved A, contains: tocainide HCl 400 mg. Nonmedicinal ingredients: hydroxypropyl methylcellulose, iron oxide, magnesium stearate, methylcellulose, paraffin, polyethylene glycol and titanium dioxide. Gluten-, lactose-, sodium- and tartrazine-free. Bottles of 100. Store at room temperature 15 to 30°C.

(Shown in Product Recognition Section)

***...CPS* is also available on CD-ROM.**

TOPAMAX® Ⓟ
Janssen-Ortho

Topiramate

Antiepileptic

Pharmacology: Pharmacodynamics: Topiramate is a novel antiepileptic agent classified as a sulfamate substituted monosaccharide. Three pharmacological properties of topiramate are believed to contribute to its anticonvulsant activity. First, topiramate reduces the frequency at which action potentials are generated when neurons are subjected to a sustained depolarization indicative of a state-dependent blockade of voltage-sensitive sodium channels. Second, topiramate markedly enhances the activity of GABA at some types of GABA receptors. Because the antiepileptic profile of topiramate differs markedly from that of the benzodiazepines, it may modulate a benzodiazepine-insensitive subtype of $GABA_A$ receptor. Third, topiramate antagonizes the ability of kainate to activate the kainate/AMPA subtype of excitatory amino acid (glutamate) receptors but has no apparent effect on the activity of N-methyl-D-aspartate (NMDA) at the NMDA receptor subtype.

In addition, topiramate inhibits some isoenzymes of carbonic anhydrase. This pharmacologic effect is much weaker than that of acetazolamide, a known carbonic anhydrase inhibitor, and is not thought to be a major component of topiramate's antiepileptic activity.

Pharmacokinetics: Absorption and Distribution: Topiramate is rapidly and well-absorbed. Following oral administration of 100 mg topiramate to healthy subjects, a mean peak plasma concentration (Cmax) of 1.5 μg/mL was achieved within 2 to 3 hours (Tmax). The mean extent of absorption from a 100 mg oral dose of ^{14}C-topiramate was at least 81% based on the recovery of radioactivity from the urine.

Topiramate exhibits low intersubject variability in plasma concentrations and, therefore, has predictable pharmacokinetics. The pharmacokinetics of topiramate are linear with plasma clearance remaining constant and area under the plasma concentration curve increasing in a dose-proportional manner over a 100 to 400 mg single oral dose range in healthy subjects. Patients with normal renal function may take 4 to 8 days to reach steady-state plasma concentrations. The mean Cmax following multiple, twice-a-day oral doses of 100 mg to healthy subjects was 6.76 μg/mL. The mean plasma elimination half-lives from multiple 50 and 100 mg q12h doses of topiramate were approximately 21 hours. The elimination half-life did not significantly change when switching from single dose to multiple dose.

Concomitant multiple-dose administration of topiramate, 100 to 400 mg q12h, with phenytoin or carbamazepine shows dose proportional increases in plasma concentrations of topiramate.

There was no clinically significant effect of food on the bioavailability of topiramate.

Approximately 13 to 17% of topiramate is bound to plasma proteins. A low capacity binding site for topiramate in/on erythrocytes that is saturable above plasma concentrations of 4 μg/mL has been observed.

The volume of distribution varied inversely with the dose. The mean apparent volume of distribution was 0.80 to 0.55 L/kg for a single dose range of 100 to 1 200 mg.

Metabolism and Excretion: Topiramate is not extensively metabolized (approximately 20%) in healthy volunteers. It is metabolized up to 50% in patients receiving concomitant antiepileptic therapy with known inducers of drug metabolizing enzymes. Six metabolites formed through hydroxylation, hydrolysis and glucuronidation, have been isolated, characterized and identified from plasma, urine and feces of humans. Each metabolite represents less than 3% of the total radioactivity excreted following administration of ^{14}C-topiramate.

Two metabolites, which retained most of the structure of topiramate, were tested and found to have little or no pharmacological activity.

In humans, the major route of elimination of unchanged topiramate and its metabolites is via the kidney (at least 81% of the dose). Approximately 66% of a dose of ^{14}C-topiramate was excreted unchanged in the urine within 4 days. The mean renal clearance for 50 and 100 mg of topiramate, following q12h dosing, was approximately 18 mL/min and 17 mL/min, respectively. Evidence exists for renal tubular reabsorption of topiramate. This is supported by studies in rats where topiramate was coadministered with probenecid, and a significant increase in renal clearance of topiramate was observed. This interaction has not been evaluated in humans. Overall, plasma clearance is approximately 20 to 30 mL/min in humans following oral administration.

Special Populations: Renal Impairment: The plasma and renal clearance of topiramate are decreased in patients with impaired renal function (CL_{cr} ≤60 mL/min), and the plasma clearance is decreased in patients with end-stage renal disease. As a result, higher steady-state topiramate plasma concentrations are expected for a given dose in renally-impaired patients as compared to those with normal renal function. Plasma clearance of topiramate is unchanged in elderly subjects in the absence of underlying renal disease.

Hemodialysis: Topiramate is effectively removed from plasma by hemodialysis (see Dosage).

Hepatic Impairment: The plasma clearance of topiramate is decreased in patients with moderate to severe hepatic impairment.

Age and Gender: Age (18 to 67) and gender appear to have no effect on the plasma clearance of topiramate.

In well-controlled add-on trials, no correlation has been demonstrated between trough plasma concentrations and its clinical efficacy.

No evidence of tolerance requiring increased dosage has been demonstrated in man during 4 years of use.

Pediatric Pharmacokinetics: Pharmacokinetics of topiramate were evaluated in patients ages 4 to 17 years receiving 1 or 2 other antiepileptic drugs. Pharmacokinetic profiles were obtained after 1 week at doses of 1, 3 and 9 mg/kg/day. As in adults, topiramate pharmacokinetics were linear with clearance independent of dose and steady-state plasma concentrations increasing in proportion to dose. Compared with adult epileptic patients, mean topiramate clearance is approximately 50% higher in pediatric patients. Steady-state plasma topiramate concentrations for the same mg/kg dose are expected to be approximately 33% lower in children compared to adults. As with adults, hepatic enzyme-inducing antiepileptic drugs (AEDs) decrease the plasma concentration of topiramate.

Clinical Experience: The results of clinical trials established the efficacy of topiramate as adjunctive therapy in patients with refractory partial onset seizures with or without secondarily generalized seizures. Six multicenter, outpatient, randomized, double-blind, placebo controlled trials were completed. Patients in all 6 studies were permitted a maximum of 2 antiepileptic drugs (AEDs) in addition to topiramate therapy (target doses of 200, 400, 600, 800 or 1 000 mg/day) or placebo.

In all 6 add-on trials, the primary efficacy measurement was reduction in seizure rate from baseline during the entire double-blind phase; responder rate (fraction of patients with a 50% reduction) was also measured. The median percent reductions in seizure rates and the responder rates by treatment group for each study are shown in Table I.

Across the 6 efficacy trials, 232 of the 527 topiramate patients (44%) responded to treatment with at least a 50% seizure reduction during the double-blind phase; by comparison, only 25 of the 216 placebo-treated patients (12%) showed the same level of treatment response. When the treatment response was defined more rigorously as a 75% or greater decrease from baseline in seizure rate during double-blind treatment, 111 of the 527 topiramate patients (21%) in the 200 to 1 000 mg/day groups, but only 8 of the 216 placebo patients (4%), demonstrated this level of efficacy. At target dosages of 400 mg/day and higher, the percent of treatment responders was statistically greater for topiramate-treated than placebo-treated patients.

Pooled analyses of secondarily generalized seizure rates for all patients who had this seizure type during the studies show statistically significant percent reductions in the topiramate groups when compared with placebo. The median percent reduction in the rate of generalized seizures was 57% for topiramate-treated patients compared with −4% for placebo-treated patients. Among topiramate-treated patients, 109 (55%) of 198 had at least a 50% reduction in generalized seizure rate compared with 24 (27%) of 88 placebo-treated patients.

The dose titration in the original clinical trials was 100 mg/day the first week, 100 mg b.i.d./day the second week, and 200 mg b.i.d./day the third week. In a 12-week, double-blind trial, this titration rate was compared to a less rapid rate beginning at 50 mg/day. There were significantly fewer adverse experiences leading to discontinuation and/or dosage adjustment in the group titrated at the less rapid rate. Seizure rate reductions were comparable between the groups at all time points measured.

Indications: As adjunctive therapy for the management of patients with epilepsy who are not satisfactorily controlled with conventional therapy. There is limited information on the use of topiramate in monotherapy at this time.

Contraindications: In patients with a history of hypersensitivity to any components of this product.

Warnings: Antiepileptic drugs, including topiramate, should be withdrawn gradually to minimize the potential of increased seizure frequency. In clinical trials, dosages were decreased by 100 mg/day at weekly intervals.

CNS Effects: Adverse events most often associated with the use of topiramate were CNS-related. The most significant of these can be classified into 2 general categories: psychomotor slowing: difficulty with concentration, and speech or language problems, in particular, word-finding difficulties; and somnolence or fatigue.

Additional nonspecific CNS effects occasionally observed with topiramate as add-on therapy include dizziness or imbalance, confusion, memory problems, and exacerbation of mood disturbances (e.g., irritability and depression).

These events were generally mild to moderate, and generally occurred early in therapy. While the incidence of psychomotor slowing does not appear to be dose-related, both language problems and difficulty with concentration or attention increased in frequency with increasing dosage in the 6 double-blind trials suggesting that these events are dose-related (see Adverse Effects).

Precautions: Effects Related to Carbonic Anhydrase Inhibition: Kidney Stones: A total of 32/1 715 (1.5%) of patients exposed to topiramate during its development reported the occurrence of kidney stones, an incidence about 10 times that expected in a similar, untreated population (M/F ratio; 27/1 092 male; 5/623 female). In the general population, risk factors for kidney stone formation include gender (male), ages between 20 to 50 years, prior stone formation, family history of nephrolithiasis and hypercalciuria. Based on logistic regression analysis of the clinical trial data, no correlation between mean topiramate dosage, duration of topiramate therapy, or age and the occurrence of kidney stones was established; of the risk factors evaluated, only gender (male) showed a correlation with the occurrence of kidney stones.

Carbonic anhydrase inhibitors, e.g., acetazolamide or dichlorphenamide, promote stone formation by reducing urinary citrate excretion and by increasing urinary pH. Concomitant use of topiramate, a weak carbonic anhydrase inhibitor, with other carbonic anhydrase inhibitors may create a physiological environment that increases the risk of kidney stone formation, and should therefore be avoided.

Patients, especially those with a predisposition to nephrolithiasis, may have an increased risk of renal stone formation. Increased fluid intake increases the urinary output lowering the concentration of substances involved in stone formation. Therefore, adequate hydration is recommended to reduce this risk. None of the risk factors for nephrolithiasis can reliably predict stone formation during topiramate treatment.

Paresthesia: Paresthesia, an effect associated with the use of other carbonic anhydrase inhibitors, appears to be a common effect of topiramate. These events were usually intermittent and mild and not necessarily related to the dosage of topiramate.

Adjustment of Dose in Renal Failure: The major route of elimination of unchanged topiramate and its metabolites is via the kidney. Renal elimination is dependent on renal function and is independent of age. Patients with impaired renal function (CL_{cr} ≤60 mL/min) or with end-stage renal disease receiving hemodialysis treatments may take 10 to 15 days to reach steady-state plasma concentrations as compared to 4 to 8 days in patients with normal renal function. As with all patients, the titration schedule should be guided by clinical outcome (i.e., seizure control, avoidance of side effects) with the knowledge that patients with known renal impairment may require a longer time to reach steady-state at each dose (see Dosage).

Decreased Hepatic Function: In hepatically impaired patients, topiramate should be administered with caution as the clearance of topiramate was decreased compared with normal subjects.

Information for the Patient: Adequate Hydration: Patients, especially those with predisposing factors, should be instructed to maintain an adequate fluid intake in order to minimize the risk of renal stone formation.

Occupational Hazards: Effects on Ability to Drive and Use Machines: Patients should be warned about the potential for somnolence, dizziness, confusion, and difficulty concentrating and advised not to drive or operate machinery until they have gained sufficient experience on topiramate to gauge whether it adversely affects their mental and/or motor performance.

Drug Interactions: Antiepileptic Drugs: Potential interactions between topiramate and standard antiepileptic drugs (AEDs) were measured in controlled clinical pharmacokinetic studies in patients with epilepsy. The effect of these interactions on plasma concentrations are summarized in Table II.

Table II—Topamax

Drug Interactions with Topamax Therapy

AED Coadministered	AED Concentration	Topamax Concentration
Phenytoin	↔[b]	↓59%
Carbamazepine (CBZ)	↔	↓40%
CBZ epoxide[a]	↔	NS
Valproic acid	↓11%	↓14%
Phenobarbital	↔	NS
Primidone	↔	NS

[a] Is not administered but is an active metabolite of carbamazepine.

[b] Plasma concentrations increased 25% in some patients, generally those on a b.i.d. dosing regimen of phenytoin.

Legend:

↔: No effect on plasma concentration.

↓: Plasma concentrations decrease in individual patients.

NS: Not studied.

AED: Antiepileptic drug.

The effect of topiramate on steady-state pharmacokinetics of phenytoin may be related to the frequency of phenytoin dosing. A slight increase in steady-state phenytoin plasma concentrations was observed, primarily in patients receiving phenytoin in 2 divided doses. The slight increase may be due to the saturable nature of phenytoin pharmacokinetics and inhibition of phenytoin metabolism.

The addition of topiramate therapy to phenytoin should be guided by clinical outcome. In general, as evidenced in clinical trials, patients do not require dose adjustments. However, any patient on phenytoin showing clinical signs or symptoms of toxicity should have phenytoin levels monitored.

Table I—Topamax

Median Percent Seizure Rate Reduction and Percent Responders in 6 Double-Blind, Placebo-Controlled, Add-On Trials

Protocol	Efficacy results	Placebo	Target Topiramate Dosage (mg/day) 200	400	600	800	1 000
YD	N	45	45	45	46	–	–
	Median % Reduction	13.1	29.6[a]	47.8[c]	44.7[d]	–	–
	% Responders	18	27	47[b]	46[b]	–	–
YE	N	47	–	–	48	48	47
	Median % Reduction	1.2	–	–	40.7[d]	41.0[d]	37.5[d]
	% Responders	9	–	–	44[d]	40[c]	38[c]
Y1	N	24	–	23	–	–	–
	Median % Reduction	1.1	–	40.7[f]	–	–	–
	% Responders	8	–	35[b]	–	–	–
Y2	N	30	–	–	30	–	–
	Median % Reduction	−12.2	–	–	46.4[c]	–	–
	% Responders	10	–	–	47[c]	–	–
Y3	N	28	–	–	–	28	–
	Median % Reduction	−17.8	–	–	–	35.8[c]	–
	% Responders	0	–	–	–	43[c]	–
YF/YG	N	42	–	–	–	–	167
	Median % Reduction	1.2	–	–	–	–	50.8[d]
	% Responders	19	–	–	–	–	52[d]

Comparisons with Placebo: [a] $p=0.051$; [b] $p<0.05$; [c] $p\leq0.01$; [d] $p\leq0.001$; [e] $p=0.053$; [f] $p=0.065$.

Topamax (cont'd)

Other Drug Interactions: Digoxin: In a single-dose study, serum digoxin AUC decreased 12% due to concomitant topiramate administration. Multiple dose studies have not been performed. When topiramate is added or withdrawn in patients on digoxin therapy, careful attention should be given to the routine monitoring of serum digoxin.

CNS Depressants: Concomitant administration of topiramate and alcohol or other CNS depressant drugs has not been evaluated in clinical studies. It is recommended that topiramate not be used concomitantly with alcohol or other CNS depressant drugs.

Oral Contraceptives: In an interaction study with oral contraceptives using a combination product containing norethindrone plus ethinyl estradiol, topiramate did not significantly affect the oral clearance of norethindrone. The serum levels of the estrogenic component decreased by 18, 21, and 30% at daily doses of 200, 400 and 800 mg, respectively. Consequently, the efficacy of low dose (e.g., 20 μg) oral contraceptives may be reduced in this situation. Patients taking oral contraceptives should receive a preparation containing not less than 50 μg of estrogen. Patients taking oral contraceptives should be asked to report any change in their bleeding patterns.

Others: Concomitant use of topiramate, a weak carbonic anhydrase inhibitor, with other carbonic anhydrase inhibitors, e.g., acetazolamide, may create a physiological environment that increases the risk of renal stone formation, and should therefore be avoided if possible.

Laboratory Tests: There are no known interactions of topiramate with commonly used laboratory tests.

Pregnancy: Like other antiepileptic drugs, topiramate was teratogenic in mice, rats and rabbits. In rats, topiramate crosses the placental barrier.

There are no studies using topiramate in pregnant women. However, topiramate therapy should be used during pregnancy only if the potential benefit outweighs the potential risk to the fetus.

Lactation: Topiramate is excreted in the milk of lactating rats. It is not known if topiramate is excreted in human milk. Since many drugs are excreted in human milk, and because the potential for serious adverse reactions in nursing infants to topiramate exists, the prescriber should decide whether to discontinue nursing or discontinue the drug, taking into account the risk benefit ratio of the importance of the drug to the mother and the risks to the infant.

The effect of topiramate on labor and delivery in humans is unknown.

Children: Safety and effectiveness in children under 18 years of age have not been established.

Geriatrics: There is limited information in patients over 65 years of age. The possibility of age-associated renal function abnormalities should be considered when using topiramate.

Race and Gender Effects: Although direct comparison studies of pharmacokinetics have not been conducted, analysis of plasma concentration data from clinical efficacy trials have shown that race and gender appear to have no effect on the plasma clearance of topiramate. In addition, based on pooled analyses, race and gender appear to have no effect on the efficacy of topiramate.

Adverse Effects: The most commonly observed adverse events associated with the adjunctive use of topiramate at dosages of 200 to 400 mg/day in controlled trials that were seen at greater frequency in topiramate-treated patients and did not appear to be dose-related within this dosage range were: somnolence, dizziness, ataxia, speech disorders and related speech problems, psychomotor slowing, nystagmus, and paresthesia (see Table III).

The most common dose-related adverse events at dosages of 200 to 1 000 mg/day were: nervousness, difficulty with concentration or attention, confusion, depression, anorexia, language and mood problems (see Table IV on following page).

In double-blind clinical trials, 10.6% of subjects (N=113) assigned to a topiramate dosage of 200 to 400 mg/day in addition to their standard AED therapy discontinued due to adverse events compared to 5.8% of subjects (N=69) receiving placebo. The percentage of subjects discontinuing due to adverse events appeared to increase at dosages above 400 mg/day. Overall, approximately 17% of all subjects (N=527) who received topiramate in the double-blind trials, discontinued due to adverse events compared to 4% of the subjects (N=216) receiving placebo.

Table III—Topamax

Incidence of Treatment-Emergent Adverse Events in Placebo-Controlled, Add-On Trials [a, b] (Events that occurred in ≥2% of Topiramate-treated patients and occurred more frequently in Topiramate-treated than placebo-treated patients)

Body System/ Adverse Event	Placebo (N=216)	Topamax Dosage (mg/day) 200-400 (N=113)	600-1 000 (N=414)
Body as a Whole			
Asthenia	1.4	8.0	3.1
Back Pain	4.2	6.2	2.9
Chest Pain	2.8	4.4	2.4
Influenza-Like Symptoms	3.2	3.5	3.6
Leg Pain	2.3	3.5	3.6
Hot Flushes	1.9	2.7	0.7
Nervous System			
Dizziness	15.3	28.3	32.1
Ataxia	6.9	21.2	14.5
Speech Disorders/Related Speech Problems	2.3	16.8	11.4
Nystagmus	9.3	15.0	11.1
Paresthesia	4.6	15.0	19.1
Tremor	6.0	10.6	8.9
Language Problems	0.5	6.2	10.4
Coordination Abnormal	1.9	5.3	3.6
Hypoaesthesia	0.9	2.7	1.2
Abnormal Gait	1.4	1.8	2.2
Gastrointestinal			
Nausea	7.4	11.5	12.1
Dyspepsia	6.5	8.0	6.3
Abdominal Pain	3.7	5.3	7.0
Constipation	2.3	5.3	3.4
Dry Mouth	0.9	2.7	3.9
Metabolic and Nutritional			
Weight Decrease	2.8	7.1	12.8
Neuropsychiatric			
Somnolence	9.7	30.1	27.8
Psychomotor Slowing	2.3	16.8	20.8
Nervousness	7.4	15.9	19.3
Difficulty with Memory	3.2	12.4	14.5
Confusion	4.2	9.7	13.8
Depression	5.6	8.0	13.0
Difficulty with Concentration/Attention	1.4	8.0	14.5
Anorexia	3.7	5.3	12.3
Agitation	1.4	4.4	3.4
Mood Problems	1.9	3.5	9.2
Aggressive Reaction	0.5	2.7	2.9
Apathy	0	1.8	3.1
Depersonalization	0.9	1.8	2.2
Emotional Lability	0.9	1.8	2.7
Reproductive, Female	**(N=59)**	**(N=24)**	**(N=128)**
Breast Pain, Female	1.7	8.3	0
Dysmenorrhea	6.8	8.3	3.1
Menstrual Disorder	0	4.2	0.8
Reproductive, Male	**(N=157)**	**(N=89)**	**(N=286)**
Prostatic Disorder	0.6	2.2	0
Respiratory			
Pharyngitis	2.3	7.1	3.1
Rhinitis	6.9	7.1	6.3
Sinusitis	4.2	4.4	5.6
Dyspnea	0.9	1.8	2.4
Skin and Appendages			
Pruritus	1.4	1.8	3.1
Vision			
Diplopia	5.6	14.2	10.4
Vision Abnormal	2.8	14.2	10.1
White Cell and RES			
Leukopenia	0.5	2.7	1.2

[a] Patients in these add-on trials were receiving 1 to 2 concomitant antiepileptic drugs in addition to topiramate or placebo.
[b] Values represent the percentage of patients reporting a given adverse event. Patients may have reported more than 1 adverse event during the study and can be included in more than 1 adverse event category.
Legend: RES=reticulo endothelial system.

Nephrolithiasis was reported rarely. Isolated cases of thromboembolic events have also been reported, a causal association with the drug has not been established.

When the safety experience of patients receiving topiramate as adjunctive therapy in both double-blind and open-label trials (n=1 446) was analyzed, a similar pattern of adverse events emerged.

Overdose: Symptoms and Treatment: In acute topiramate overdose, if the ingestion is recent, the stomach should be emptied immediately by lavage or by induction of emesis. Activated charcoal has not been shown to adsorb topiramate in vitro. Therefore, its use in overdosage is not recommended. Treatment should be appropriately supportive.

Hemodialysis is an effective means of removing topiramate from the body. However, in the few cases of acute overdosage reported, including doses of over 20 g in one individual, hemodialysis has not been necessary.

Dosage: Adults: The recommended total daily dose as adjunctive therapy is 200 to 400 mg/day in 2 divided doses. It is recommended that therapy be initiated at 50 mg/day, followed by titration to an effective dose. Doses above 400 mg/day have not been shown to improve responses and have been associated with a greater incidence of adverse events. The maximum recommended dose is 800 mg/day. Daily doses above 1 600 mg have not been studied.

Table IV—Topamax

Dose-Related Adverse Events From 6 Placebo-Controlled, Add-On Trials

Adverse Event	Placebo (N=216)	Topamax Dosage (mg/day) 200 (N=45)	400 (N=68)	600-1 000 (N=414)
Fatigue	13.4	11.1	11.8	29.7
Nervousness	7.4	13.3	17.6	19.3
Difficulty with Concentration/Attention	1.4	6.7	8.8	14.5
Confusion	4.2	8.9	10.3	13.8
Depression	5.6	8.9	7.4	13.0
Anorexia	3.7	4.4	5.9	12.3
Language Problem	0.5	2.2	8.8	10.1
Anxiety	6.0	2.2	2.9	10.4
Mood Problems	1.9	0.0	5.9	9.2

Titration should begin at 50 mg/day. At weekly intervals, the dose should be increased by 50 mg/day and taken in 2 divided doses. Dose titration should be guided by clinical outcome. Some patients may achieve efficacy with once-a-day dosing.

The recommended titration rate is shown in Table V.

Table V—Topamax

Titration Rate

	AM Dose	PM Dose
Week 1	none	50 mg
Week 2	50 mg	50 mg
Week 3	50 mg	100 mg
Week 4	100 mg	100 mg
Week 5	100 mg	150 mg
Week 6	150 mg	150 mg
Week 7	150 mg	200 mg
Week 8	200 mg	200 mg

Topiramate can be taken without regard to meals. Tablets should not be broken.

Geriatrics: See Precautions.

Children: As yet there is limited experience on the use of topiramate in children aged 18 years and under and dosing recommendations cannot be made for this patient population.

Patients with Renal Impairment: In renally impaired subjects (creatinine clearance less than 70 mL/min/1.73m²), one half of the usual adult dose is recommended. Such patients will require a longer time to reach steady-state at each dose.

Patients Undergoing Hemodialysis: Topiramate is cleared by hemodialysis at a rate that is 4 to 6 times greater than a normal individual. Accordingly, a prolonged period of dialysis may cause topiramate concentration to fall below that required to maintain an anti-seizure effect. To avoid rapid drops in topiramate plasma concentration during hemodialysis a supplemental dose of topiramate may be required. The actual adjustment should take into account 1) the duration of dialysis period, 2) the clearance rate of the dialysis system being used, and 3) the effective renal clearance of topiramate in the patient being dialyzed.

Patients with Hepatic Disease: In hepatically impaired patients topiramate plasma concentrations are increased approximately 30%. This moderate increase is not considered to warrant adjustment of the topiramate dosing regimen. Initiate topiramate therapy with the same dose and regimen as for patients with normal hepatic function. The dose titration in these patients should be guided by clinical outcome, i.e., seizure control and avoidance of adverse effects. Such patients will require a longer time to reach steady-state at each dose.

Information for the Patient: See Blue Section—Information for the Patient "Topamax".

Supplied: 25 mg: Each white, round, embossed, coated tablet contains: topiramate 25 mg. Nonmedicinal ingredients: carnauba wax, hydroxypropyl methylcellulose, lactose monohydrate, magnesium stearate, microcrystalline cellulose, polyethylene glycol, polysorbate 80, pregelatinized starch, purified water, sodium starch glycolate and titanium dioxide. Bottles of 60 (with desiccant).

100 mg: Each yellow, round, embossed, coated tablet contains: topiramate 100 mg. Nonmedicinal ingredients: carnauba wax, hydroxypropyl methylcellulose, lactose monohydrate, magnesium stearate, microcrystalline cellulose, polyethylene glycol, polysorbate 80, pregelatinized starch, purified water, sodium starch glycolate, synthetic yellow iron oxide and titanium dioxide. Bottles of 60 (with desiccant).

200 mg: Each salmon-colored, round, embossed, coated tablet contains: topiramate 200 mg. Nonmedicinal ingredients: carnauba wax, hydroxypropyl methylcellulose, lactose monohydrate, magnesium stearate, microcrystalline cellulose, polyethylene glycol, polysorbate 80, pregelatinized starch, purified water, sodium starch glycolate, synthetic red iron oxide and titanium dioxide. Bottles of 60 (with desiccant).

Store in tightly-closed containers at controlled room temperature (15 to 30°C). Protect from moisture.

(Shown in Product Recognition Section)

Reviewed 1999

TOPICAINE®

Hoechst Marion Roussel

Benzocaine

Oral Topical Anesthetic

Pharmacology: Benzocaine topical gel is a local anesthetic of the ester type for topical application to mucous membranes in clinical dentistry. Benzocaine rapidly produces topical anesthesia within 30 to 90 seconds of application to mucosal tissue. It has a short duration of action and is ineffective when applied to intact skin.

Indications: To minimize the pain of ulcers, needle puncture, deep scaling procedures, application of matrix bands and extraction of loose deciduous teeth.

It is also indicated for the reduction of the pharyngeal (gag) reflex associated with the placement into the oral cavity of various dental materials (impression trays, x-ray films, x-ray plate holders).

Contraindications: In patients with a known hypersensitivity to local anesthetics of the ester type or any of the nonmedicinal ingredients (see Precautions).

Benzocaine is contraindicated for use in or around the eye, for internal use, or for vaginal use.

Precautions: Application to severely traumatized areas which are infected or areas of the posterior pharynx that might dull protective reflexes should be avoided. Local anesthetics should be used with caution in patients with known drug sensitivities, particularly those known to be allergic to ester-type anesthetics (procaine, benzocaine, tetracaine).

Repeated and prolonged application may potentiate hypersensitivity.

Dosage: Area where benzocaine is to be applied must be dry prior to application. Removal of excess saliva with cotton rolls or saliva ejector will minimize dilution of the local anesthetic. Sterile cotton or gauze should be used in applying the anesthetic.

Care must be taken to avoid cross-contamination between patients. It is suggested that the benzocaine gel be transferred to a separate dish or plate for each patient with unused portion being discarded after each patient's visit.

When used with new dentures, it is important that patients consult their dentist regularly during the fitting period and that the total dose be limited to no more than 3 applications a day.

Total dose not to exceed the amount required for anesthesia.

Supplied: Each g of topical anesthetic gel contains: benzocaine USP 20%. Nonmedicinal ingredients: aspartame (contains phenylalanine); FD&C Red #40 (dye); flavorant and polyethylene glycol. Individual plastic containers of 30 g. Store at room temperature, below 25°C.

TOPICORT® Preparations ℞

Hoechst Marion Roussel

Desoximetasone

Topical Corticosteroid

Pharmacology: Topicort preparations are primarily effective because of their anti-inflammatory, antipruritic and vasoconstrictive actions.

Indications: For the relief of acute or chronic corticosteroid-responsive dermatoses.

Contraindications: Topical corticosteroids are contraindicated in untreated bacterial, tubercular, fungal and most viral lesions of the skin (including herpes simplex, vaccinia and varicella) and in those patients with a history of hypersensitivity to any of the components of the preparation.

Topicort preparations are not for ophthalmic use.

Warnings: Systemic side effects may occur with topical corticosteroid preparations, particularly when these preparations are used over large areas or for an extended period of time or with occlusive dressings. A patient who has been on prolonged therapy, especially occlusive therapy, may develop adrenal suppression due to sufficient absorption of the steroid.

Pregnancy and *Lactation:* The safety of topical corticosteroid preparations during pregnancy and lactation has not been established. The potential benefit should be weighed in these conditions against possible hazard to the fetus or the nursing infant. When indicated, they should not be used extensively, in large amounts or for prolonged periods of time in pregnant patients or nursing mothers.

Precautions: General: Children may absorb proportionally larger amounts of topical corticosteroids and thus be more susceptible to systemic toxicity (see Children).

If local infection exists, suitable concomitant antimicrobial or antifungal therapy should be administered as primary therapy. If it is considered necessary, the topical corticosteroid may be used as an adjunct to control inflammation, erythema and itching. If a favorable response does not occur promptly, application of the corticosteroid should be discontinued until the infection is adequately controlled.

If local irritation or sensitization develops, desoximetasone creams, gel and ointment should be discontinued and appropriate therapy instituted.

The use of occlusive dressings increases the percutaneous absorption of corticosteroids; their extensive use increases the possibility of systemic effects and is therefore not advisable. For patients with extensive lesions it may be preferable to use a sequential approach, treating one portion of the body at a time. The patient should be kept under close observation if treated with large amounts of topical corticosteroid or with the occlusive technique over a prolonged period of time.

Occlusive dressings should not be applied if there is an elevation of body temperature.

Patients should be advised to inform subsequent physicians of the prior use of corticosteroids.

Topical corticosteroids should be used with caution on lesions close to the eyes.

Prolonged use of topical corticosteroid products may produce atrophy of skin and s.c. tissues, particularly on flexor surfaces and on the face. If this is noted, discontinue the use of this product.

The product should be used with caution in patients with stasis dermatitis and other skin diseases associated with impaired circulation.

Children: **Pediatric patients may demonstrate greater susceptibility to topical corticosteroid induced HPA axis suppression and Cushing's syndrome than mature patients because of a larger skin surface area to body weight ratio.**

Hypothalamic-pituitary-adrenal [HPA] axis suppression, Cushing's syndrome and intracranial hypertension have been reported in children receiving topical corticosteroids. Manifestations of adrenal suppression in children include linear growth retardation, delayed weight gain, low plasma cortisol levels and absence of response to ACTH stimulation. Manifestations of intracranial hypertension include bulging fontanelles, headaches and bilateral papilledema.

Administration of topical corticosteroids to children should be limited to the least amount compatible with an effective therapeutic regimen. Chronic corticosteroid therapy may interfere with the growth and development of children.

Adverse Effects: Topicort preparations are well tolerated. Side effects have been rare. Similar to other topical corticosteroid preparations, they may cause: burning sensation, dryness, itching, erythema, change in skin pigmentation, folliculitis,

Topicort Preparations (cont'd)

pyoderma, striae, telangiectasia and skin atrophy. The following reactions are reported when corticosteroid preparations are used extensively on intertriginous areas or under occlusive dressings: maceration of the skin, secondary infection, striae, miliaria, hypertrichosis and localized skin atrophy.

Adrenal suppression has been shown to occur with prolonged use of large doses of topical corticosteroids, particularly under occlusion, due to increased percutaneous absorption.

Posterior subcapsular cataracts have been reported following systemic use of corticosteroids.

Overdose: Symptoms: Toxic effects due to prolonged percutaneous absorption of large amounts of corticosteroids may include: reversible suppression of adrenal function, skin striae, ecchymoses, discoloration or atrophy, acneiform eruptions, hirsutism, infection. Prolonged systemic corticosteroid action may cause hypertension, peptic ulceration, hypokalemia, muscle weakness and wastage and subcapsular cataracts.

Treatment: Treatment should include symptomatic therapy and discontinuation of corticosteroid administration. In chronically affected patients, a gradual discontinuation may prevent the development of steroid withdrawal symptoms.

Dosage: Apply a thin film to the affected skin areas twice daily. Rub in gently.

Supplied: Topicort: Each tube contains: desoximetasone USP, 0.25%. Nonmedicinal ingredients: isopropyl myristate, methylparaben, propylparaben, water, wool alcohols and wool alcohols ointment. Tubes of 20 and 60 g.

Topicort Mild: Each tube contains: desoximetasone USP, 0.05%. Nonmedicinal ingredients: edetate disodium, isopropyl myristate, lactic acid, methylparaben, propylparaben, water, wool alcohols and wool alcohols ointment. Tubes of 20 and 60 g.

Topicort Gel: Each tube contains: desoximetasone USP, 0.05%. Nonmedicinal ingredients: alcohol, carbopol 940 (carboxypolymethylene), docusate sodium, edetate disodium, isopropyl myristate, trolamine and water. Extended-tip tubes of 20 and 60 g.

Topicort Ointment: Each tube contains: desoximetasone USP, 0.25%. Nonmedicinal ingredients: aluminum stearate, beeswax, butylated hydroxyanisole, citric acid, fatty acid pentaerythritol ester, fatty alcohol citrate, propylene glycol USP, sorbitan sesquioleate and white petrolatum USP. Tubes of 20 and 60 g.

Store at room temperature, below 25°C.

TOPILENE® Ⓟ
Technilab

Betamethasone Dipropionate
Topical Corticosteroid

Supplied: Cream: Each g contains: betamethasone (as dipropionate USP) 0.5 mg (0.05%) in a propylene glycol base. Nonmedicinal ingredients: ceteareth-20, cetyl alcohol, glyceryl stearate, light mineral oil, methylparaben, petrolatum, polysorbate 60, propylene glycol, propylene glycol monostearate, propylparaben and purified water. Tubes of 15 and 50 g.

Lotion: Each g contains: betamethasone (as dipropionate USP) 0.5 mg (0.05%). Nonmedicinal ingredients: carbomer, isopropyl alcohol, propylene glycol, purified water, sodium phosphate monobasic and triethanolamine. Plastic squeeze bottles of 30 and 60 mL.

Ointment: Each g contains: betamethasone (as dipropionate USP) 0.5 mg (0.05%). Nonmedicinal ingredients: petrolatum, propylene glycol and propylene glycol monostearate. Tubes of 15 and 50 g.

Store between 15 and 30°C.

TOPISONE Ⓟ
Technilab

Betamethasone Dipropionate
Topical Corticosteroid

Supplied: Cream: Each g contains: betamethasone 0.5 mg (0.05%) (as dipropionate USP). Nonmedicinal ingredients: ceteareth-20, cetyl alcohol, glyceryl stearate, light mineral oil, methylparaben, petrolatum, polysorbate 60, propylene glycol, propylparaben and purified water. Tubes of 15 and 50 g. Plastic jars of 450 g.

Lotion: Each g contains: betamethasone 0.5 mg (0.05%) (as dipropionate USP). Nonmedicinal ingredients: carbomer, isopropyl alcohol, purified water and triethanolamine. Plastic bottles of 30 and 75 mL.

Ointment: Each g contains: betamethasone 0.5 mg (0.05%) (as dipropionate USP). Nonmedicinal ingredients: light mineral oil and petrolatum. Tubes of 15 and 50 g. Plastic jars of 450 g.

Store between 15 and 30°C.

TOPSYN® Ⓟ
Medicis

Fluocinonide
Topical Corticosteroid

Indications: For topical therapy of corticosteroid-responsive acute and chronic skin eruptions, where an anti-inflammatory, anti-allergenic and antipruritic activity in the topical management is required.

Contraindications: Untreated bacterial, tubercular, fungal and most viral lesions of skin (including herpes simplex, vaccinia and varicella). Hypersensitivity to any of the components.

Warnings: *Pregnancy* and *Lactation:* The safety of topical corticosteroids during pregnancy or lactation has not been established. The potential benefit of topical corticosteroids, if used during pregnancy or lactation, should be weighed against possible hazard to the fetus or the nursing infant.

Not for ophthalmic use.

Precautions: Not recommended for use under occlusive dressings.

Apply cautiously on lesions close to the eye. Severe irritation is possible if these formulations contact the eye. Should this occur, immediate flushing of the eye with a large volume of water is recommended.

Prolonged use of topical corticosteroid products may produce atrophy of the skin and of s.c. tissues, particularly on flexor surfaces and on the face. If this is noted, discontinue its use.

Use with caution in patients with stasis dermatitis and other skin diseases associated with impaired circulation.

If a symptomatic response is not noted within a few days to a week, the local applications of corticosteroids should be discontinued and the patient re-evaluated.

During the use of topical corticosteroids, secondary infections may occur.

Although hypersensitivity reactions have been rare with topically applied steroid products, the drug should be discontinued and appropriate therapy instituted if there are signs of reaction.

In cases of bacterial infections of the skin, appropriate antibacterial agents should be used as primary therapy. If it is considered necessary, the topical corticosteroid product may be used as an adjunct to control inflammation, erythema and itching.

Patients should be advised to inform subsequent physicians of the prior use of corticosteroids.

Significant systemic absorption may result when steroids are applied over large areas of the body. To minimize the possibility, when long-term therapy is anticipated, interrupt treatment periodically or treat one area of the body at a time. Laboratory Tests: Urinary free cortisol test and ACTH stimulation test may be helpful in evaluating HPA axis suppression.

Adverse Effects: The following adverse skin reactions have been reported with the use of topical steroids: dryness, burning, itching, local irritation, striae, skin atrophy, atrophy of s.c. tissues, telangiectasia, hypertrichosis, change in pigmentation and secondary infection. Adrenal suppression has also been reported following topical corticosteroid therapy. Posterior subcapsular cataracts have been reported following systemic use of corticosteroids.

Overdose: Symptoms and Treatment: There is no specific antidote, but gastric lavage should be performed.

In the case of hypercorticism and/or adrenal suppression, discontinue therapy.

Dosage: Gently apply a small amount onto the affected area 2 to 4 times daily depending on the severity of the condition.

The gel may be more appropriate for lesions of the scalp. It is recommended that the gel not be used under occlusive conditions.

Supplied: Each collapsible tube contains: fluocinonide 0.05% in a clear, colorless, water miscible, thixotropic gel base. Nonmedicinal ingredients: Carbopol 940 (carboxypolymethylene), disodium edetate, propyl gallate, propylene glycol and sodium hydroxide and/or hydrochloric acid to adjust the pH. Lanolin-, phenolic compounds-, parabens- and preservatives-free. Tubes of 60 g.

TORADOL® Ⓟ
TORADOL® IM Ⓟ
Roche

Ketorolac Tromethamine
NSAID Analgesic

Pharmacology: Ketorolac is a nonsteroidal anti-inflammatory drug (NSAID) that exhibits analgesic activity mediated by peripheral effects. Ketorolac inhibits the synthesis of prostaglandins through inhibition of the cyclo-oxygenase enzyme system. At analgesic doses it has minimal anti-inflammatory and antipyretic activity.

Pain relief is comparable following the administration of ketorolac by i.m. or oral routes. The peak analgesic effect occurs at 2 to 3 hours post-dosing with no evidence of a statistically significant difference over the recommended dosage range. The greatest difference between large and small doses of ketorolac administered by either route is in the duration of analgesia.

Ketorolac is rapidly and completely absorbed when administered by either the oral or the i.m. route. The pharmacokinetics are linear following single and multiple dosing. Steady-state plasma levels are attained after 1 day of q.i.d. dosing.

Following oral administration, peak plasma concentrations of 0.7 to 1.1 μg/mL occur at an average of 44 minutes after a single 10 mg dose. The terminal plasma elimination half-life ranges between 2.4 and 9 hours in healthy adults, and between 4.3 and 7.6 hours in elderly subjects (mean age 72 years). A high fat meal decreases the rate, but not the extent, of absorption of oral ketorolac. The use of an antacid has not been demonstrated to affect the pharmacokinetics of ketorolac.

Following i.m. administration, peak plasma concentrations of 2.2 to 3.0 μg/mL occur an average of 50 minutes after a single 30 mg dose. The terminal plasma half-life ranges between 3.5 and 9.2 hours in young adults and between 4.7 and 8.6 hours in elderly subjects (mean age=72 years).

In renally impaired patients there is a reduction in clearance and an increase in the terminal half-life of ketorolac (see Table I on following page).

The primary route of excretion of ketorolac and its metabolites (conjugates and the p-hydroxy metabolite) is in the urine (91.4%) with the remainder (6.1%) being excreted in the feces.

More than 99% of the ketorolac in plasma is protein bound over a wide concentration range.

The parenteral administration of ketorolac has not been demonstrated to affect the hemodynamics of anesthetized patients.

Indications: Oral: For the short-term management (not to exceed 5 days for post-surgical patients or 7 days for patients with musculoskeletal pain) of moderate to moderately severe acute pain, including post-surgical pain (such as general, orthopedic and dental surgery), acute musculoskeletal trauma pain and post-partum uterine cramping pain. (See Warnings and Dosage).

I.M.: For the short-term management (not to exceed 2 days) of moderate to severe acute pain, including pain following major abdominal, orthopedic and gynecological operative procedures. The total duration of combined i.m. and oral treatment should not exceed 5 days.

Contraindications: Hypersensitivity: Like other NSAIDs, ketorolac has been associated with hypersensitivity reactions. Ketorolac should not be used when there is a known or suspected hypersensitivity to the drug and should be discontinued in patients who develop symptoms of hypersensitivity during therapy. Because of the possibility of cross-sensitivity, ketorolac should not be used in patients with the complete or partial syndrome of nasal polyps, angioedema, bronchospastic reactivity (e.g., asthma) or other allergic manifestations to ASA or other NSAIDs. Severe and fatal anaphylactoid reactions have occurred in such individuals.

Gastrointestinal: Ketorolac should not be used in patients with suspected or confirmed peptic ulcer disease, gastrointestinal bleeding or perforation, or active inflammatory disease of the gastrointestinal system or in patients who have a history of

Table I—Toradol

Influence of Age, Liver and Kidney Function on the Clearance and Terminal Half-life of Toradol I.M.[a] and Oral[b]

Types of Subjects	Total Clearance (in L/h/kg)[c] I.M. mean (range)	Total Clearance (in L/h/kg)[c] Oral mean (range)	Terminal Half-life (in hours) I.M. mean (range)	Terminal Half-life (in hours) Oral mean (range)
Normal Subjects I.M. (n=54) Oral (n=77)	0.023 (0.010-0.046)	0.025 (0.013-0.050)	5.3 (3.5-9.2)	5.3 (2.4-9.0)
Healthy Elderly Subjects I.M. (n=13), Oral (n=12) (mean age=72, range=65-78)	0.019 (0.013-0.034)	0.024 (0.018-0.034)	7.0 (4.7-8.6)	6.1 (4.3-7.6)
Patients with Hepatic Dysfunction I.M. and Oral (n=7)	0.029 (0.013-0.066)	0.033 (0.019-0.051)	5.4 (2.2-6.9)	4.5 (1.6-7.6)
Patients with Renal Impairment I.M. and Oral (n=9) (serum creatinine 1.9-5.0 mg/dL)	0.014 (0.007-0.043)	0.016 (0.007-0.052)	10.3 (8.1-15.7)	10.8 (3.4-18.9)
Renal Dialysis Patients I.M. (n=9)	0.016 (0.003-0.036)		13.6 (8.0-39.1)	

[a]Estimated from 30 mg single i.m. doses of ketorolac tromethamine.
[b]Estimated from 10 mg single oral doses of ketorolac tromethamine.
[c]Litres/hour/kilogram.

these disorders. Severe and fatal reactions have occurred in such individuals.

Renal Impairment: Ketorolac is contraindicated in patients with moderate to severe renal impairment or in patients at risk for renal failure due to volume depletion.

Hemorrhagic Risk: Ketorolac is contraindicated immediately before any major surgery, and is contraindicated intraoperatively when hemostasis is critical because of the increased risk of bleeding. Ketorolac is also contraindicated in patients with coagulation disorders, postoperative patients with high hemorrhagic risk or incomplete hemostasis, and in patients with suspected or confirmed cerebrovascular bleeding.

Pregnancy: Ketorolac is contraindicated in labor and delivery because, through its prostaglandin synthesis inhibitory effect, ketorolac may adversely affect fetal circulation and inhibit uterine musculature, thus increasing the risk of uterine hemorrhage.

Neuraxial Administration: Ketorolac is contraindicated for neuraxial (epidural or intrathecal) administration due to its alcohol content.

Drug Interactions: Ketorolac is contraindicated in patients currently receiving ASA or NSAIDs because of the cumulative risks of inducing serious NSAID-related adverse events. The concomitant use of ketorolac and probenecid is also contraindicated.

Warnings: The long-term administration of ketorolac is not recommended as the incidence of side effects increases with the duration of treatment (see Indications and Dosage).

The most serious risks associated with NSAIDs including ketorolac are: Gastrointestinal Ulcerations, Bleeding and Perforation: Serious gastrointestinal toxicity, such as bleeding, ulceration, and perforation, can occur at any time, with or without warning symptoms, during therapy with NSAIDs. The incidence of gastrointestinal complications increases with dosage and duration of treatment. Elderly and debilitated patients are more susceptible to these complications.

To date, studies with NSAIDs have not identified any subset of patients not at risk for developing peptic ulceration and bleeding.

Postmarketing experience with Toradol suggests that there may be a greater risk of gastrointestinal ulcerations, bleeding, and perforation in the elderly, and most spontaneous reports of fatal gastrointestinal events are in the aged population.

The long-term use of ketorolac is not recommended.

Renal Toxicity: The following renal abnormalities have been associated with ketorolac and other drugs that inhibit renal prostaglandin biosynthesis: acute renal failure, nephrotic syndrome, interstitial nephritis, renal papillary necrosis. Elevations of BUN and creatinine have been reported in clinical trials with ketorolac. Ketorolac is contraindicated in patients with moderate to severe renal impairment.

Hypovolemia should be corrected before treatment with ketorolac is initiated. Patients who are volume-depleted may be dependent on renal prostaglandin production to maintain renal perfusion and, therefore, glomerular filtration rate. In such patients, the use of drugs which inhibit prostaglandin synthesis has been associated with further decreases in renal blood flow and may precipitate acute renal failure. Predisposing factors include dehydration (e.g., as a result of extreme exercise, vomiting or diarrhea associated with the loss of at least 5 to 10% of total body weight, unreplenished blood loss of approximately 500 mL), sepsis, impaired renal function, heart failure, liver dysfunction, diuretic therapy, and advanced age. Caution is advised if ketorolac is used in such circumstances. Close monitoring of urine output, serum urea and serum creatinine is recommended until renal function recovers.

Fluid Retention and Edema: Fluid retention, edema, NaCl retention, oliguria, elevations of serum urea nitrogen and creatinine have been observed in patients treated with ketorolac. Therefore, the possibility of precipitating congestive heart failure in elderly patients or those with compromised cardiac function should be considered. Ketorolac should be used with caution in patients with cardiac decompensation, hypertension or other conditions which cause a predisposition to fluid retention.

Hemorrhage: Postoperative hematomas and other symptoms of wound bleeding have been reported in association with the perioperative use of i.m. ketorolac. Ketorolac is contraindicated in patients who have coagulation disorders. If this drug is to be administered to patients who are receiving drug therapy that interferes with hemostasis, careful observation is advised.

Use of ketorolac in patients who are receiving therapy that affects hemostasis should be undertaken with caution, including close monitoring. The concurrent use of ketorolac and prophylactic, low dose heparin (2 500 to 5 000 units q12h), warfarin and dextrans may also be associated with an increased risk of bleeding (see Drug Interactions).

In patients receiving anticoagulants, the risk of i.m. hematoma formation from ketorolac i.m. injections is increased.

Hypersensitivity Reactions: The possibility of severe or fatal hypersensitivity reactions should be considered, even for patients with no known history of previous exposure or hypersensitivity to ketorolac or other NSAIDs. Counteractive measures must be available when administering the first dose of ketorolac i.m. As with other NSAIDs, patients should be questioned for history of allergy to NSAIDs or ASA or for the syndrome consisting of nasal polyps, ASA allergy and asthma before being prescribed ketorolac. Asthmatic patients with triad asthma (the syndrome of nasal polyps, asthma and hypersensitivity to ASA or other NSAIDs) may be at particular risk for severe hypersensitivity reactions.

Pregnancy and *Lactation*: The administration of ketorolac is not recommended during pregnancy or lactation. After 1 day at 10 mg q.i.d. oral dosing, ketorolac has been detected in the milk of lactating women at a maximum concentration of 7.9 ng/mL.

Children: Safety and efficacy in children have not been established. Therefore, ketorolac is not recommended for use in children under age 16.

Geriatrics: Because ketorolac is cleared somewhat more slowly by the elderly (see Pharmacokinetics) who are also more sensitive to the gastrointestinal and renal effects of NSAIDs (see Warnings and Precautions), extra caution and the lowest effective dose (see Dosage) should be used.

Precautions: Physicians should be alert to the pharmacologic similarity of ketorolac to other NSAIDs that inhibit cyclo-oxygenase.

Gastrointestinal Effects: Close medical supervision is recommended in patients prone to gastrointestinal tract irritation. In these cases, the physician must weigh the benefits of treatment against the possible hazards.

Patients taking any NSAID including ketorolac should be instructed to contact a physician immediately if they experience symptoms or signs suggestive of peptic ulceration or gastrointestinal bleeding. These reactions can occur at any time during the treatment. If peptic ulceration is suspected or confirmed, or if gastrointestinal bleeding occurs, ketorolac should be discontinued and appropriate treatment instituted with close patient monitoring.

Hepatic Effects: Caution should be observed if ketorolac is to be used in patients with impaired hepatic function, or a history of liver disease. Treatment with ketorolac may cause elevations of liver enzymes, and in patients with pre-existing liver dysfunction, it may lead to the development of a more severe hepatic reaction. Meaningful elevations (greater than 3 times normal) of serum transaminases (glutamate pyruvate [ALT] and glutamic oxalacetic [AST]) occurred in controlled clinical trials in less than 1% of patients. If clinical signs and symptoms consistent with liver disease develop, or if systemic manifestations occur (e.g., eosinophilia, rash, etc.), ketorolac should be discontinued. Patients with impaired hepatic function from cirrhosis do not have any clinically important changes in ketorolac clearance. Studies in patients with active hepatitis or cholestasis have not been performed.

Hematologic Effects: Ketorolac inhibits platelet function and may prolong bleeding time. It does not affect platelet count, prothrombin time (PT) or partial thromboplastin time (PTT). Unlike the prolonged effects from ASA the inhibition of platelet function by ketorolac is normalized within 24 to 48 hours after the drug is discontinued.

Blood dyscrasias associated with the use of NSAIDs are rare, but could occur with severe consequences.

Infection: In common with other NSAIDs, ketorolac may mask the usual signs of infection.

Drug Interactions: Protein Binding: Ketorolac is highly bound to human plasma protein (mean 99.2%) and binding is independent of concentration. As ketorolac is a highly potent drug and present in low concentrations in plasma, it would not be expected to displace other protein-bound drugs significantly. Therapeutic concentrations of digoxin, warfarin, acetaminophen, phenytoin, and tolbutamide did not alter ketorolac protein binding.

Anticoagulant Therapy: Prothrombin time should be carefully monitored in all patients receiving oral anticoagulant therapy concomitantly with ketorolac.

Ketorolac i.m. given with 2 doses of 5 000 U of heparin to 11 healthy volunteers, resulted in a mean template bleeding time of 6.4 min (3.2 to 11.4 min) compared to a mean of 6.0 min (3.4 to 7.5 min) for heparin alone and 5.1 min (3.5 to 8.5 min) for placebo.

The in vitro binding of warfarin to plasma proteins is only slightly reduced by ketorolac (99.5% control vs. 99.3%) at plasma concentrations of 5 to 10 μg/mL.

Digoxin: Ketorolac does not alter digoxin protein binding.

Salicylates: In vitro studies indicated that, at therapeutic concentrations of salicylates (300 μg/mL), the binding of ketorolac was reduced from approximately 99.2 to 97.5% representing a potential 2-fold increase in unbound ketorolac plasma levels.

Enzyme Induction: There is no evidence, in animal or human studies, that ketorolac induces or inhibits the hepatic enzymes capable of metabolizing itself or other drugs. Hence, it would not be expected to alter the pharmacokinetics of other drugs due to enzyme induction or inhibition mechanisms.

Probenecid: Concomitant administration of ketorolac and probenecid results in the decreased clearance of ketorolac and a significant increase in ketorolac plasma levels (approximately 3-fold increase) and terminal half-life (approximately 2-fold increase). The concomitant use of ketorolac and probenecid is, therefore, contraindicated.

Furosemide: Ketorolac reduces the diuretic response to furosemide by approximately 20% in normovolemic subjects.

Lithium: Some NSAIDs have been reported to inhibit renal lithium clearance, leading to an increase in plasma lithium concentrations and potential lithium toxicity. The effect of ketorolac on lithium plasma levels has not been studied.

Methotrexate: The concomitant administration of methotrexate and some NSAIDs has been reported to reduce the clearance of methotrexate, thus enhancing its toxicity. The effect of ketorolac on methotrexate clearance has not been studied.

ACE Inhibitors: Concomitant use of ACE inhibitors and other NSAIDs may increase the risk of renal impairment, particularly in volume depleted patients.

Morphine: I.M. ketorolac has been administered concurrently with morphine in several clinical trials of postoperative pain without evidence of adverse interactions.

Toradol (cont'd)

Adverse Effects: Oral: Short-Term Patient Studies: The incidence of adverse reactions in 371 patients receiving multiple 10 mg doses of ketorolac for pain resulting from surgery or dental extraction during the postoperative period (less than 2 weeks) is listed below. These reactions may or may not be drug related.

Incidence Between 4 and 9%: Nervous System: somnolence, insomnia.

Digestive: nausea.

Incidence Between 2 and 3%: Nervous System: nervousness, headache, dizziness.

Digestive: diarrhea, dyspepsia, gastrointestinal pain, constipation.

Body as a Whole: fever.

Incidence 1% or Less: Nervous System: abnormal dreams, anxiety, dry mouth, hyperkinesia, paresthesia, increased sweating, euphoria, hallucinations.

Digestive: anorexia, flatulence, vomiting, stomatitis, gastritis, gastrointestinal disorder, sore throat.

Body as a Whole: asthenia, pain, back pain.

Cardiovascular: vasodilatation, palpitation, migraine, hypertension.

Respiratory: cough increased, rhinitis, dry nose.

Musculoskeletal: myalgia, arthralgia.

Skin and Appendages: rash, urticaria.

Special Senses: blurred vision, ear pain.

Urogenital: dysuria.

Long-Term Patient Study: The adverse reactions listed below were reported to be probably related to study drug in 553 patients receiving long-term oral therapy (approximately 1 year) with ketorolac.

Incidence Between 10 and 12%: Digestive: dyspepsia, gastrointestinal pain.

Incidence Between 4 and 9%: Digestive: nausea, constipation.

Nervous System: headache.

Incidence Between 2 and 3%: Digestive: diarrhea, flatulence, gastrointestinal fullness, peptic ulcers.

Nervous System: dizziness, somnolence.

Metabolic/Nutritional Disorder: edema.

Incidence 1% or Less: Digestive: eructation, stomatitis, vomiting, anorexia, duodenal ulcer, gastritis, gastrointestinal hemorrhage, increased appetite, melena, mouth ulceration, rectal bleeding, sore mouth.

Nervous System: abnormal dreams, anxiety, depression, dry mouth, insomnia, nervousness, paresthesia.

Special Senses: tinnitus, taste perversion, abnormal vision, blurred vision, deafness, lacrimation disorder.

Metabolic/Nutritional Disorder: weight gain, alkaline phosphatase increase, BUN increased, excessive thirst, generalized edema, hyperuricemia.

Skin and Appendages: pruritus, rash, burning sensation skin.

Body as a Whole: asthenia, pain, back pain, face edema, hernia.

Musculoskeletal: arthralgia, myalgia, joint disorder.

Cardiovascular: chest pain, chest pain substernal, migraine.

Respiratory: dyspnea, asthma, epistaxis.

Urogenital: hematuria, increased urinary frequency, oliguria, polyuria.

Hemic and Lymphatic: anemia, purpura.

I.M.: The adverse reactions listed below are reported in ketorolac i.m. clinical efficacy trials. In these trials patients (n=660) received either single 30 mg doses (n=151) or multiple 30 mg doses (n=509) over a time period of 5 days or less for pain resulting from surgery. These reactions may or may not be drug related.

Incidence Between 10 and 13%: Nervous System: somnolence.

Digestive: nausea.

Incidence Between 4 and 9%: Nervous System: headache.

Digestive: vomiting.

Injection Site: injection site pain.

Incidence Between 2 and 3%: Nervous System: sweating, dizziness.

Cardiovascular: vasodilatation.

Incidence 1% or Less: Nervous System: insomnia, increased dry mouth, abnormal dreams, anxiety, depression, paresthesia, nervousness, paranoid reaction, speech disorder, euphoria, libido increased, excessive thirst, inability to concentrate, stimulation.

Digestive: flatulence, anorexia, constipation, diarrhea, dyspepsia, gastrointestinal fullness, gastrointestinal hemorrhage, gastrointestinal pain, melena, sore throat, liver function abnormalities, rectal bleeding, stomatitis.

Cardiovascular: hypertension, chest pain, tachycardia, hemorrhage, palpitation, pulmonary embolus, syncope, ventricular tachycardia, pallor, flushing.

Injection Site: injection site reaction.

Body as a Whole: asthenia, fever, back pain, chills, pain, neck pain.

Special Senses: taste perversion, tinnitus, blurred vision, diplopia, retinal hemorrhage.

Musculoskeletal: myalgia, twitching.

Respiratory: asthma, cough increased, dyspnea, epistaxis, hiccup, rhinitis.

Skin and Appendages: pruritus, rash, s.c. hematoma, skin disorder.

Urogenital: dysuria, urinary retention, oliguria, increased urinary frequency, vaginitis.

Metabolic/Nutritional Disorders: edema, hypokalemia, hypovolemia.

Hemic and Lymphatic: anemia, coagulation disorder, purpura.

Postmarketing Experience: The following postmarketing adverse experiences have been reported for patients who have received either formulation of Toradol: Renal Events: acute renal failure, flank pain with or without hematuria and/or azotemia, nephritis, hyponatremia, hyperkalemia, hemolytic uremic syndrome, urinary retention.

Hypersensitivity Reactions: bronchospasm, laryngeal edema, asthma, hypotension, flushing, rash, anaphylaxis and anaphylactoid reactions. Such reactions have occurred in patients with no prior history of hypersensitivity.

Gastrointestinal Events: gastrointestinal hemorrhage, peptic ulceration, gastrointestinal perforation, pancreatitis, melena.

Hematologic Events: postoperative wound hemorrhage, rarely requiring blood transfusion (see Precautions), thrombocytopenia, epistaxis, leukopenia.

CNS: convulsions, abnormal dreams, hallucinations, hyperkinesia, hearing loss, aseptic meningitis, extrapyramidal symptoms.

Hepatic Events: hepatitis, liver failure, cholestatic jaundice.

Cardiovascular: pulmonary edema, hypotension, flushing.

Dermatology: Lyell's syndrome, Stevens-Johnson syndrome, exfoliative dermatitis, maculopapular rash, uticaria.

Body as Whole: infection.

Overdose: Symptoms and Treatment: In a gastroscopic study of healthy subjects, daily doses of 360 mg given over an 8-hour interval for each of 5 consecutive days (3 times the highest recommended dose) caused pain and peptic ulcers which resolved after discontinuation of dosing.

Metabolic acidosis has been reported following intentional overdosage. Single oral doses of 200 mg have been administered to patients with no apparent serious side effects. Dialysis does not appreciably clear ketorolac from the blood stream.

Dosage: Adults: Dosage should be adjusted according to the severity of the pain and the response of the patient.

Oral: The usual oral dose is 10 mg every 4 to 6 hours for pain as required. Doses exceeding 40 mg/day are not recommended. The maximum duration of treatment with oral formulation is 5 days for post-surgical patients and 7 days for patients with musculoskeletal pain.

I.M.: The recommended usual initial dose is 10 to 30 mg, according to pain severity. Subsequent dosing may be 10 to 30 mg every 4 to 6 hours as needed to control pain. The lowest effective dose should be administered.

The administration of ketorolac i.m. should be limited to short-term therapy (not over 2 days). The total daily dose should not exceed 120 mg because the risk of toxicity appears to increase with longer use at recommended doses (see Warnings and Precautions). The administration of continuous multiple daily doses of ketorolac i.m. has not been extensively studied. There has been limited experience with i.m. dosing for more than 3 days since the vast majority of patients have transferred to oral medication or no longer required analgesic therapy after this time.

If supplementary analgesia is required, a concomitant low dose of opiate can be used.

Patients Under 50 kg, Over Age 65 years, or With Less Severe Pain at Baseline: Oral: The lowest effective dose is recommended. Parenteral: The lower end of the dosage range is recommended. The initial dose should be 10 mg. The total daily dose of ketorolac i.m. in the elderly should not exceed 60 mg.

Impaired Renal Function: Ketorolac is not recommended for patients with moderate to severe renal impairment.

Conversion from Parenteral to Oral Therapy: Tablets may be used either as monotherapy or as follow-on therapy to parenteral ketorolac.

When ketorolac tablets are used as a follow-on therapy to parenteral ketorolac, the total combined daily dose of ketorolac (oral + parenteral) should not exceed 120 mg in younger adult patients or 60 mg in elderly patients on the day the change of formulation is made. On subsequent days, oral dosing should not exceed the recommended daily maximum of 40 mg. Ketorolac i.m. should be replaced by an oral analgesic as soon as feasible.

The total duration of combined i.m. and oral treatment should not exceed 5 days.

Parenteral drug products should be inspected visually for particulate material and discoloration prior to use.

Information for the Patient: See Blue Section—Information for the Patient "Toradol/Toradol IM".

Supplied: Tablets: Each white, round, film-coated tablet, with one side printed in black ink with KET/10 on one side, contains: ketorolac tromethamine 10 mg. Nonmedicinal ingredients: hydroxypropyl-methylcellulose, lactose, magnesium stearate, microcrystalline cellulose, polyethylene glycol and titanium dioxide. Bottles of 100 and 500. Store at room temperature with protection from light.

Parenteral: 10 mg/mL: Each mL of clear, slightly yellow, sterile solution contains: ketorolac tromethamine 10 mg. Nonmedicinal ingredients: alcohol 10% w/w and sodium chloride in sterile water. The pH is adjusted with sodium hydroxide or hydrochloric acid. Ampuls of 1 mL, trays of 5. Store at room temperature with protection from light.

30 mg/mL: Each mL of clear, slightly yellow, sterile solution contains: ketorolac tromethamine 30 mg. Nonmedicinal ingredients: alcohol 10% w/w and sodium chloride in sterile water. The pH is adjusted with sodium hydroxide or hydrochloric acid. Ampuls of 1 mL, trays of 5. Store at room temperature with protection from light.

(Shown in Product Recognition Section)

TRACE ELEMENTS SOLUTION

Faulding

Electrolyte Replacement

Supplied: Each 5 mL ampul of trace elements concentrated solution contains: zinc chloride 10.42 mg (zinc 5 mg=76.5 μmol); copper chloride 2.68 mg (copper 1 mg=15.7 μmol); manganese chloride 1.44 mg (manganese 0.4 mg=7.3 μmol); chromium chloride 0.102 mg (chromium 0.02 mg=0.39 μmol) in water for injection. Contains no preservative. pH 1.8 to 2.2. Packages of 5. Store below 25°C.

TRACRIUM®

Glaxo Wellcome

Atracurium Besylate

Skeletal Neuromuscular Blocking Agent

Pharmacology: Atracurium is a nondepolarizing, intermediate-duration, skeletal neuromuscular blocking agent. Nondepolarizing agents antagonize the neurotransmitter action of acetylcholine by binding competitively to cholinergic receptor sites on the motor endplate. This antagonism is inhibited, and neuromuscular block reversed by acetylcholinesterase inhibitors such as neostigmine, edrophonium and pyridostigmine.

The duration of neuromuscular blockade produced by atracurium is approximately one-third to one-half the duration seen with d-tubocurarine, metocurine and pancuronium at equipotent doses. As with other nondepolarizing neuromuscular blockers, the time to onset of paralysis decreases and the duration of maximum effect increases with increasing atracurium doses.

The ED_{95} (dose required to produce 95% suppression of the muscle twitch response) averaged 0.23 mg/kg. An initial dose of 0.4 to 0.5 mg/kg generally produces complete neuromuscular blockade within 3 to 5 minutes of injection, with good or excellent intubation conditions within 2 to 2.5 minutes. Recovery from neuromuscular blockade (under balanced anesthesia) can be expected to begin approximately 20 to 35 minutes after injection. Recovery to 25% of control is achieved approximately 35 to 45 minutes after injection, and recovery is usually 95% complete approximately 60 to 70 minutes after injection. The neuromuscular blocking action of atracurium is enhanced in the presence of potent inhalation anesthetics. Isoflurane and enflurane increase the potency of atracurium and prolong neuromuscular blockade by approximately 35%; however, halothane's potentiating effect (approximately 20%) is marginal (see Dosage).

Repeatedly administered maintenance doses have no cumulative effect on the duration of neuromuscular blockade; therefore, doses can be administered at regular intervals with predictable results. After an initial dose of 0.4 to 0.5 mg/kg under balanced anesthesia, the first maintenance dose (suggested maintenance dose is 0.08 to 0.10 mg/kg) is generally required within 20 to 45 minutes, and subsequent maintenance doses are usually required at approximately 15- to 25-minute intervals.

Once recovery from the neuromuscular blocking effects begins, it proceeds more rapidly than recovery from d-tubocurarine, metocurine, and pancuronium. Regardless of dose, the time from start of recovery (from complete block) to complete (95%) recovery is approximately 30 minutes under balanced anesthesia, and approximately 40 minutes under halothane, enflurane or isoflurane. Repeated doses have no cumulative effect on recovery rate.

Reversal of neuromuscular blockade produced by atracurium can be achieved with an anticholinesterase agent such as neostigmine, edrophonium, or pyridostigmine, in conjunction with an anticholinergic agent such as atropine or glycopyrrolate. Under balanced anesthesia, reversal can usually be attempted approximately 20 to 35 minutes after an initial dose of 0.4 to 0.5 mg/kg, or approximately 10 to 30 minutes after a 0.08 to 0.10 mg/kg maintenance dose, when recovery of muscle twitch has started. Complete reversal is usually accomplished within 8 to 10 minutes of the administration of reversing agents. Rare incidences of breathing difficulties, possibly related to incomplete reversal, have been reported following attempted pharmacologic antagonism of atracurium-induced neuromuscular blockade. As with other agents in this class, the tendency for residual neuromuscular block is increased if reversal is attempted at deep levels of blockade or if inadequate doses of reversal agents are employed.

Pharmacokinetics: The pharmacokinetics of atracurium in man are essentially linear within the 0.3 to 0.6 mg/kg dose range. The elimination half-life is approximately 20 minutes. The duration of neuromuscular blockade produced by the drug does not correlate with plasma pseudocholinesterase levels and is not altered by the absence of renal function. This is consistent with the results of in vitro studies which have shown that the drug is inactivated in plasma via 2 nonoxidative pathways: ester hydrolysis, catalyzed by nonspecific esterases; and Hofmann elimination, a nonenzymatic chemical process which occurs at physiological pH. Some placental transfer occurs in humans.

Radiolabel studies demonstrated that atracurium undergoes extensive degradation in cats, and neither kidney nor liver plays a major role in its elimination. Biliary and urinary excretion were the major routes of excretion of radioactivity (totaling >90% of the labeled dose within 7 hours of dosing), of which atracurium represented only a minor fraction. The metabolites in bile and urine were similar, including products of Hofmann elimination and ester hydrolysis.

Histamine release and hemodynamic changes are minimal with initial atracurium doses up to 0.4 mg/kg. A moderate histamine release following 0.6 mg/kg has been shown to correlate with a transient (<5 minutes) decrease in blood pressure and a brief (2 to 3 minutes) episode of skin flushing. This is of little clinical significance in most patients; however, the possibility of substantial histamine release in sensitive individuals or in patients in whom substantial histamine release would be especially hazardous (e.g., patients with significant cardiovascular disease) must be considered.

It is not known whether the prior use of other nondepolarizing neuromuscular blocking agents has any effect on the activity of atracurium. The prior use of succinylcholine decreases by approximately 2 to 3 minutes the time to maximum blockade induced by the drug, and may increase the depth of blockade. Atracurium should be administered only after a patient recovers from succinylcholine-induced neuromuscular blockade.

Indications: As an adjunct to general anesthesia, to facilitate endotracheal intubation and to provide skeletal muscle relaxation during surgery or mechanical ventilation. It can be used most advantageously if muscle twitch response to peripheral nerve stimulation is monitored.

Contraindications: In patients known to have a hypersensitivity to it.

Warnings: Atracurium should be used only by those skilled in the management of artificial respiration and only when facilities are instantly available for endotracheal intubation and for providing adequate ventilation of the patient, including the administration of oxygen under positive pressure and the elimination of carbon dioxide. The clinician must be prepared to assist or control respiration and anticholinesterase reversal agents should be immediately available. Do not give atracurium i.m.

Atracurium has no known effect on consciousness, pain threshold, or cerebration. It should be used only with adequate anesthesia.

The injection, which has an acid pH, should not be mixed with alkaline solutions (e.g., barbiturate solutions) in the same syringe or administered simultaneously during i.v. infusion through the same needle. In such mixtures, the resultant pH may cause inactivation of the drug and precipitation of the free acid.

Atracurium is also hypotonic and must not be administered into the infusion line of a blood transfusion.

Tracrium 10 mL multiple-dose vials contain benzyl alcohol. Benzyl alcohol has been associated with an increased incidence of neurological and other complications in newborn infants which are sometimes fatal.

The 5 mL vial do not contain benzyl alcohol.

The 5 mL ampuls and vials do not contain benzyl alcohol.

Precautions: Histamine Release: The possibility of substantial histamine release with consequent bronchospasm or anaphylaxis in sensitive individuals must be considered. Special caution should be exercised in administering atracurium to those patients in whom substantial histamine release would be especially hazardous (e.g., patients with clinically significant cardiovascular disease) and in patients with any history (e.g., severe anaphylactoid reactions or asthma) suggesting a greater risk of histamine release. In these patients, the recommended initial dose is lower (0.3 to 0.4 mg/kg) than for other patients and should be administered slowly or in divided doses over 1 minute. Limited clinical experience indicates that mean arterial pressure decreases in a substantial percentage of patients with a history of cardiovascular disease even at these doses.

Pregnancy: Atracurium has been shown to be potentially teratogenic at up to half the human dose when given to nonventilated rabbits by the s.c. route at sub-paralyzing doses. Therefore, atracurium should not be used during pregnancy unless, in the opinion of the physician, the potential benefits outweigh the unknown hazards.

Obstetrics: It is not known whether muscle relaxants administered during vaginal delivery have immediate or delayed adverse effects on the fetus or increase the likelihood that resuscitation of the newborn will be necessary. The possibility that a forceps delivery will be necessary may increase.

In an open study, atracurium has been administered (0.3 mg/kg) to 26 pregnant women during delivery by cesarean section. No harmful effects were attributable to the drug in any of the newborn infants, although small amounts were shown to cross the placental barrier. The possibility of respiratory depression in the newborn infant should always be considered following cesarean section during which a neuromuscular blocking agent has been administered. In patients receiving magnesium sulfate, the reversal of neuromuscular blockade may be unsatisfactory and atracurium dose should be lowered as indicated.

Lactation: It is not known whether this drug is excreted in human milk. Because many drugs are excreted in human milk, caution should be exercised when atracurium is administered to a nursing woman.

Children: Safety and effectiveness in children below the age of 1 month have not been established.

Patients with Special Disease and Conditions: Atracurium may have profound effects in patients with myasthenia gravis, Eaton-Lambert syndrome, or other neuromuscular diseases in which potentiation of nondepolarizing agents has been noted. The use of a peripheral nerve stimulator is especially important for assessing neuromuscular blockade in these patients. Similar precautions should be taken in patients with severe electrolyte disorders or carcinomatosis.

The safety of atracurium has not been established in patients with bronchial asthma.

Obesity: Ideal body weight should be considered in dosage calculations for obese patients with appropriate attention to the attendant risk of underdosing. Severe obesity may pose airway or ventilatory problems before, during, or after the use of nondepolarizing neuromuscular blockers.

Hypothermia: Hypothermia (25 to 28°C) has been associated with a decreased requirement for nondepolarizing blocking agents.

Cardiovascular Effects: Since atracurium has no clinically significant effects on heart rate at the recommended dosage range, it will not counteract the bradycardia produced by many anesthetic agents or vagal stimulation.

Malignant Hyperthermia: Multiple factors in anesthesia practice are suspected of triggering malignant hyperthermia (MH), a potentially fatal hypermetabolic state of skeletal muscle. Halogenated anesthetic agents and succinylcholine are recognized as the principal pharmacologic triggering agents in MH-susceptible patients; however, since MH can develop in the absence of established triggering agents, the clinician should be prepared to recognize and treat MH in any patient scheduled for general anesthesia. Reports of MH have been rare in cases in which atracurium has been used. In a clinical study of MH-susceptible patients, atracurium did not trigger this syndrome.

Burns: Resistance to nondepolarizing neuromuscular blocking agents may develop in burn patients. Increased doses of nondepolarizing muscle relaxants may be required in burn patients and are dependent on the time elapsed since the burn injury and the size of the burn.

Electrolyte Abnormalities: Electrolyte abnormalities may antagonize or potentiate the action of neuromuscular blocking agents. For example, hyperkalemia has been reported to antagonize nondepolarizing agents, while hypokalemia has been associated with an enhancement of their activity.

The action of neuromuscular blocking agents may be enhanced by magnesium salts administered for the management of toxemia of pregnancy.

Long-Term Use in Intensive Care Unit (ICU): There is only limited information available on the efficacy and safety of long-term (days to weeks) i.v. atracurium infusion to facilitate mechanical ventilation in the ICU. These data suggest that dosage requirements show wide interpatient variability and may decrease or increase with time. When there is a need for long-term mechanical ventilation, the benefits-to-risk ratio of neuromuscular blockade must be considered.

Little information is available on the plasma levels or clinical consequences of atracurium metabolites that may accumulate during days to weeks of atracurium administration in ICU patients. Concentrations of metabolites are higher in ICU patients with abnormal renal and/or hepatic function. These metabolites do not contribute to neuromuscular block.

Laudanosine, a major biologically active metabolite of atracurium without neuromuscular blocking activity, produces transient hypotension and, in higher doses, cerebral excitatory effects (generalized muscle twitching and seizures) when administered to several species of animals. There have been rare reports of seizures in ICU patients who have received atracurium or other agents. These patients usually had predisposing causes (such as head trauma, cerebral edema, hypoxic encephalopathy, viral encephalitis, uremia). There are insufficient data to determine whether or not laudanosine contributes to seizures in ICU patients.

Whenever the use of atracurium or any neuromuscular blocking agent is contemplated in the ICU, it is recommended that neuromuscular transmission be monitored continuosly during administration with the help of a nerve stimulator. Additional doses of atracurium or any other neuromuscular blocking agent should not be given before there is a definite response to T_1 or to the first twitch. If no response is elicited, infusion administration should be discontinued until a response returns.

The effects of hemodialysis, hemoperfusion and hemofiltration on plasma levels of atracurium and its metabolites are unknown.

Drug Interactions: Atracurium is potentiated by isoflurane and by enflurane anesthesia, and marginally potentiated by halothane (see Dosage).

Drugs which may enhance the neuromuscular blocking action of atracurium include: certain antibiotics, especially the aminoglycosides and polymyxins; lithium; magnesium salts; procainamide and quinidine.

If other muscle relaxants are used during the same procedure, the possibility of a synergistic or antagonistic effect should be considered.

The prior administration of succinylcholine does not enhance the duration, but quickens the onset and may increase the depth of neuromuscular blockade induced by atracurium. Atracurium should not be administered until a patient has recovered from succinylcholine-induced neuromuscular blockade.

Adverse Effects: Atracurium was well tolerated and produced few adverse reactions during extensive clinical trials and as observed in clinical practice. Most adverse reactions were suggestive of histamine release. Fully developed anaphylactic or anaphylactoid reactions have been reported, and in rare instances these were severe (e.g., cardiac arrest). Skin flush and decreases in mean arterial pressure were the most common reactions seen in the recommended dose range. The incidences of decreases in mean arterial pressure were substantially increased in patients with a history of cardiovascular disease.

Tracrium (cont'd)

Observed in Controlled Clinical Studies: In 27 studies including 875 patients, atracurium was discontinued in 1 patient (who required treatment for bronchial secretions). Six other patients required treatment for adverse reactions attributable to the drug (wheezing in 1, hypotension in 5). Of the 5 patients who required treatment for hypotension, three had a history of significant cardiovascular disease. The overall incidence rate for clinically important adverse reactions, therefore, was 7 in 875 or 0.8%. Table I includes all adverse reactions reported attributable to atracurium during clinical trials with 875 patients.

Table I—Tracrium

% of Patients Reporting Adverse Reactions

Adverse Reaction	Initial Dose (mg/kg) (Total=875 Patients) 0.00–0.30 n=485	0.31–0.40 n=236	0.46–0.50 n=127	≥0.56 n=27
Skin Flush	0.8%	5.5	15.0	26.0
Erythema	0.4%	0.0	2.4	0.0
Itching	0.4%	0.0	0.0	0.0
Wheezing/ Bronchial Secretions	0.2%	0.0	0.8	0.0
Hives	0.2%	0.0	0.0	0.0

Most adverse reactions were of little clinical significance unless they were associated with significant hemodynamic changes. Table II summarizes the incidences of substantial vital sign changes noted during atracurium clinical trials with 530 patients in whom these parameters were assessed.

Table II—Tracrium

% of Patients with Vital Sign Changes (ASA 1 and 2)*

Vital Sign Change		Initial Dose (mg/kg) 0.00–0.30 n=365	0.36–0.40 n=124	0.50 n=20	≥0.60 n=21
Mean Arterial Pressure					
Decrease	≥40%	0.3	0.0	10.0	5.0
Decrease	≥30%	1.1	0.0	15.0	15.0
Decrease	≥20%	2.5	2.4	15.0	30.0
Increase	≥20%	7.4	7.3	5.0	0.0
Increase	≥30%	1.9	3.2	0.0	0.0
Increase	≥40%	0.8	1.6	0.0	0.0
Heart Rate					
Decrease	≥40%	0.3	0.0	0.0	0.0
Decrease	≥30%	0.8	0.0	0.0	0.0
Decrease	≥20%	3.0	1.6	0.0	5.0
Increase	≥20%	4.9	4.0	5.0	10.0
Increase	≥30%	1.6	2.4	5.0	5.0
Increase	≥40%	1.4	1.6	0.0	0.0

* American Society of Anesthesiologists Classification of Physical Status:
1. A normal healthy patient.
2. A patient with a mild systemic disease.

In a small group of patients with cardiovascular disease (n=34) the changes in vital signs were more predominant, even at the lower doses (see Table III).

Table III—Tracrium

Patients with Cardiovascular Disease with Vital Sign Changes (%)

Vital Sign Change		Initial Dose (mg/kg) 0.00–0.30 n=18	0.36–0.40 n=16
Mean Arterial Pressure			
Decrease	≥40%	0.0	1 (6.3)
Decrease	≥30%	2 (11.1)	6 (37.5)
Decrease	≥20%	7 (38.9)	11 (68.8)
Increase	≥20%	0.0	2 (12.5)
Increase	≥30%	0.0	0.0
Heart Rate			
Decrease	≥30%	0.0	0.0
Decrease	≥20%	2 (11.0)	1 (6.3)
Increase	≥20%	2 (11.0)	0.0
Increase	≥30%	0.0	0.0

Three large prospective postmarketing surveillance studies have been reported, tabulating the incidence of adverse reactions associated with atracurium; they did not uncover any new events attributable to the drug.

Observed in Clinical Practice: Based on initial clinical practice experience in approximately 11 million patients who received atracurium, spontaneously reported adverse reactions were uncommon (0.006%). The following adverse reactions are among the most frequently reported, but there are insufficient data to support an estimate of their incidence.

General: Allergic reactions (anaphylactic or anaphylactoid responses) which, in rare instances, were severe (e.g. cardiac arrest).

Musculoskeletal: inadequate block, prolonged block.

Cardiovascular: hypotension, vasodilatation (flushing), tachycardia, bradycardia.

Respiratory: dyspnea, bronchospasm, laryngospasm.

Integumentary: rash, urticaria, reaction at injection site.

There have been rare reports of seizures in ICU patients following long-term infusion of atracurium to support mechanical ventilation. There are insufficient data to define the contribution, if any, of atracurium and/or its metabolite laudanosine (see Precautions: Long-Term Use in the Intensive Care Unit). There have been some reports of muscle weakness and/or myopathy following prolonged use of muscle relaxants in severely ill patients in the ICU. Most patients were receiving concomitant corticosteroids. These events have been seen infrequently in association with atracurium and a causal relationship has not been established.

Overdose: Symptoms and Treatment: There has been limited experience with atracurium overdosage. The possibility of limited iatrogenic overdosage can be minimized by carefully monitoring muscle twitch response to peripheral nerve stimulation. Excessive doses can be expected to produce enhanced pharmacological effects. Overdosage may increase the risk of histamine release and cardiovascular effects, especially hypotension. If cardiovascular support is necessary, this should include proper positioning, fluid administration, and the use of vasopressor agents if necessary. The patient's airway should be assured, with manual or mechanical ventilation maintained as necessary. A longer duration of neuromuscular blockade may result from overdosage and a peripheral nerve stimulator should be used to monitor recovery. Recovery may be facilitated by administration of an anticholinesterase-reversing agent such as neostigmine, edrophonium, or pyridostigmine, in conjunction with an anticholinergic agent such as atropine or glycopyrrolate.

Three pediatric patients (3 weeks, 4 and 5 months of age) unintentionally received doses of 0.8 mg/kg to 1 mg/kg of atracurium. The time to 25% recovery (50 to 55 minutes) following these doses, which were 5 to 6 times the ED_{95} dose, was moderately longer than the corresponding time observed following doses 2 to 2.5 times the atracurium ED_{95} dose in infants (22 to 36 minutes). Cardiovascular changes were minimal. Nonetheless, the possibility of cardiovascular changes must be considered in the case of overdose.

An adult patient (17 years of age) unintentionally received an initial dose of 1.3 mg/kg of atracurium. The time from injection to 25% recovery (83 minutes) was approximately twice that observed following maximum recommended doses in adults (35 to 45 minutes). The patient experienced moderate hemodynamic changes (13% increase in mean arterial pressure and 27% increase in heart rate) which persisted for 40 minutes and did not require treatment.

Dosage: To avoid distress to the patient, atracurium should not be administered before unconsciousness has been induced. It should not be mixed in the same syringe, or administered simultaneously through the same needle, with alkaline solutions (e.g., barbiturate solutions).

Atracurium should be administered i.v. **Do not give Tracrium i.m.** I.M. administration may result in tissue irritation and there are no clinical data to support this route of administration.

The use of a peripheral nerve stimulator to monitor muscle twitch suppression and recovery will permit the most advantageous use of the drug and minimize the possibility of overdosage.

Bolus Injections for intubation and maintenance of neuromuscular blockade: Adults: A dose of 0.4 to 0.5 mg/kg (1.7 to 2.2 times the ED_{95}), given as an i.v. bolus injection, is the recommended initial dose for most patients. With this dose, good or excellent conditions for nonemergency intubation can be expected in 2 to 2.5 minutes in most patients, with maximum neuromuscular blockade being achieved approximately 3 to 5 minutes after injection. Clinically effective neuromuscular blockade generally lasts 20 to 35 minutes under balanced anesthesia. Recovery to 25% of control is achieved approximately 35 to 45 minutes after injection, and recovery is usually 95% complete 60 minutes after injection.

Atracurium is potentiated by isoflurane or enflurane anesthesia. The same initial dose of 0.4 to 0.5 mg/kg may be used for intubation prior to administration of these inhalation agents; however, if atracurium is first administered under steady state isoflurane or enflurane anesthesia, the initial dose may be reduced by approximately one-third, i.e., to 0.25 to 0.35 mg/kg, to adjust for the potentiating effects of these anesthetic agents. With halothane, which has only a marginal (approximately 20%) potentiating effect on atracurium, smaller dosage reductions may be considered.

Doses of 0.08 to 0.10 mg/kg are recommended for maintenance of neuromuscular blockade during prolonged surgical procedures. The first maintenance dose will generally be required 20 to 45 minutes after the initial atracurium injection, but the need for maintenance doses should be determined by clinical criteria. Because atracurium lacks cumulative effects, maintenance doses may be administered at relatively regular intervals for each patient, ranging approximately from 15 to 25 minutes under balanced anesthesia, slightly longer under isoflurane or enflurane. Higher doses (up to 0.2 mg/kg) permit maintenance dosing at longer intervals.

Children: No dosage adjustments are required for pediatric patients 2 years of age or older. A dose of 0.3 to 0.4 mg/kg is recommended as the initial dose for infants (1 month to 2 years of age) under halothane anesthesia. Maintenance doses may be required with slightly greater frequency in children than in adults.

Reversal: Reversal of neuromuscular blockade produced by atracurium can be achieved with an anticholinesterase agent such as neostigmine, edrophonium, or pyridostigmine, in conjunction with an anticholinergic agent such as atropine or glycopyrrolate. Under balanced anesthesia, reversal can usually be attempted approximately 20 to 35 minutes after an initial dose of 0.4 to 0.5 mg/kg, or approximately 10 to 30 minutes after a 0.08 to 0.10 mg/kg maintenance dose, when recovery of muscle twitch has started. Complete reversal is usually accomplished within 8 to 10 minutes of the administration of reversing agents. Rare incidences of breathing difficulties, possibly related to incomplete reversal, have been reported following attempted pharmacologic antagonism of atracurium-induced neuromuscular blockade. As with other agents in this class, the tendency for residual neuromuscular block is increased if reversal is attempted at deep levels of blockade or if inadequate doses of reversal agents are employed.

Special Considerations: An initial dose of 0.3 to 0.4 mg/kg, given slowly or in divided doses over 1 minute, is recommended for adults or children with significant cardiovascular disease (an increased incidence of hypotensive episodes has been seen in these patients) and for adults or children with any history (e.g., severe anaphylactoid reactions or asthma) suggesting a greater risk of histamine release.

Dosage reductions must be considered also in patients with neuromuscular disease, severe electrolyte disorders, or carcinomatosis in which potentiation of neuromuscular blockade or difficulties with reversal have been demonstrated. There has been no clinical experience with atracurium in these patients, and no specific dosage adjustments can be recommended.

No atracurium dosage adjustments are required for patients with renal disease.

An initial dose of 0.3 to 0.4 mg/kg is recommended for adults following the use of succinylcholine for intubation under balanced anesthesia. Further reductions may be desirable with the use of potent inhalation anesthetics. The patient should be permitted to recover from the effects of succinylcholine prior to atracurium administration. Insufficient data are available for recommendation of a specific initial atracurium dose for administration following the use of succinylcholine in children and infants.

As with other parenteral drug products, atracurium should be inspected visually for particulate matter and discoloration prior to administration, whenever solution and container permit.

Use by Infusion: After administration of a recommended initial bolus dose of atracurium (0.3 to 0.5 mg/kg), a diluted solution can be administered by continuous infusion to adults and children aged 2 or more years for maintenance of neuromuscular blockade during extended surgical procedures.

Long-term i.v. infusion to support mechanical ventilation in the intensive care unit has not been studied sufficiently to support dosage recommendations (see Precautions: Long-Term Use in Intensive Care Unit).

Infusion should be individualized for each patient. The rate of administration should be adjusted according to the patient's response as determined by peripheral nerve stimulation. Accurate dosing is best achieved using a precision infusion pump.

Infusion should be initiated only after evidence of spontaneous recovery from the bolus dose. An initial infusion rate of 9 to 10 μg/kg/minute may be required to rapidly counteract the spontaneous recovery of neuromuscular function. Thereafter, a rate of 5 to 9 μg/kg/minute should be adequate to maintain continuous neuromuscular blockade in the range of 89 to 99% in most pediatric and adult patients under balanced anesthesia. Occasional patients may require infusion rates as low as 2 μg/kg/minute or as high as 15 μg/kg/minute.

The neuromuscular blocking effect of atracurium administered by infusion is potentiated by enflurane or isoflurane and, to a lesser extent, by halothane. Reduction in the infusion rate of atracurium should, therefore, be considered for patients receiving inhalation anesthesia. The rate of infusion should be reduced by approximately one-third in the presence of steady-state enflurane or isoflurane anesthesia; smaller reductions should be considered in the presence of halothane.

In patients undergoing cardiopulmonary bypass with induced hypothermia, the rate of infusion required to maintain adequate surgical relaxation during hypothermia (25 to 28°C) has been shown to be approximately half the rate required during normothermia.

Spontaneous recovery from neuromuscular blockage following discontinuation of infusion may be expected to proceed at a rate comparable to that following administration of a single bolus dose.

The amount of infusion solution required per minute will depend upon the concentration of atracurium in the infusion solution, the desired dose and the patient's weight. Tables IV and V provide guidelines for delivery in mL/hour (equivalent to microdrops/minute when 60 microdrops=1 mL) of drug solutions in concentrations of 0.2 mg/mL (20 mg in 100 mL) or 0.5 mg/mL (50 mg in 100 mL) with an infusion pump or a gravity flow device.

Table IV—Tracrium

Tracrium Infusion Rates for a Concentration of 0.2 mg/mL

Patient Weight (kg)	Drug Delivery Rate (μg/kg/min) 5	6	7	8	9	10
	Infusion Delivery Rate (mL/hr)					
30	45	54	63	72	81	90
35	53	63	74	84	95	105
40	60	72	84	96	108	120
45	68	81	95	108	122	135
50	75	90	105	120	135	150
55	83	99	116	132	149	165
60	90	108	126	144	162	180
65	98	117	137	156	176	195
70	105	126	147	168	189	210
75	113	135	158	180	203	225
80	120	144	168	192	216	240
90	135	162	189	216	243	270
100	150	180	210	240	270	300

Table V—Tracrium

Tracrium Infusion Rates for a Concentration of 0.5 mg/mL

Patient Weight (kg)	Drug Delivery Rate (μg/kg/min) 5	6	7	8	9	10
	Infusion Delivery Rate (mL/hr)					
30	18	22	25	29	32	36
35	21	25	29	34	38	42
40	24	29	34	38	43	48
45	27	32	38	43	49	54
50	30	36	42	48	54	60
55	33	40	46	53	59	66
60	36	43	50	58	65	72
65	39	47	55	62	70	78
70	42	50	59	67	76	84
75	45	54	63	72	81	90
80	48	58	67	77	86	96
90	54	65	76	86	97	108
100	60	72	84	96	108	120

Stability and Storage: Atracurium slowly loses potency with time at the rate of approximately 6% per year under refrigeration (2 to 8°C). Rate of loss in potency increases to approximately 5%/month at 25°C. The injection **should be stored under refrigeration (2 to 8°C)** to preserve potency. **Protect from freezing.** Stable for up to 14 days at room temperature up to 25°C without significant loss of potency.

Continuous Infusions: Infusion solutions may be prepared by admixing atracurium injection with an appropriate diluent such as 5% Dextrose Injection USP, 0.9% Sodium Chloride Injection USP, or 5% Dextrose and 0.9% Sodium Chloride Injection USP. Solutions containing 0.2 mg/mL or 0.5 mg/mL atracurium in these diluents may be stored either under refrigeration or at room temperature for 24 hours without significant loss of potency. Infusion solutions should be used within 24 hours of preparation. Unused solutions should be discarded.

Spontaneous degradation of atracurium has been demonstrated to occur more rapidly in Lactated Ringer's solution than in 0.9% Sodium Chloride Solution. Therefore, it is recommended that Lactated Ringer's Injection USP not be used as a diluent in preparing solutions for infusion.

Care should be taken during admixture to prevent inadvertent contamination. Visually inspect prior to administration.

Supplied: Single Use Vials: Each mL of sterile, nonpyrogenic aqueous solution contains: atracurium besylate 10 mg. Also contains water for injection. pH adjusted to 3.4 to 3.7 with benzene sulfonic acid. Single use vials of 5 mL.

Multiple-Dose Vials: Each mL of sterile, nonpyrogenic aqueous solution contains: atracurium besylate 10 mg. Also contains water for injection. Nonmedicinal ingredients: benzyl alcohol and water for injection. pH adjusted to 3.4 to 3.7 with benzene sulfonic acid. Multiple-dose vials of 10 mL.

TRANDATE® Ⓟ

Roberts

Labetalol HCl

Antihypertensive

Pharmacology: Labetalol is an adrenergic receptor blocking agent possessing both $alpha_1$-(post-synaptic) and beta-receptor blocking activity. Its action on beta-receptors is 4 times stronger than that on alpha-receptors. It antagonizes $beta_1$- and $beta_2$-receptors equally.

The mechanism of the antihypertensive action of labetalol has not been fully established. It is considered that labetalol lowers blood pressure by partially blocking the alpha-adrenoceptors in the peripheral arterioles, thus causing vasodilation and a resulting reduction of peripheral resistance. At the same time, blockade of the beta-adrenoceptors in the myocardium prevents reflex tachycardia and subsequent elevation of cardiac output. Peripheral vasodilation is achieved with incomplete blockade of alpha-adrenoceptors in the arterioles and the barostatic reflexes remain sufficiently active to reduce the incidence of postural hypotension.

At rest labetalol slightly reduces the heart rate, increases the stroke volume but does not significantly affect cardiac output. It reduces exercise-induced increases in systolic pressure and heart rate, again without significantly influencing cardiac output.

Following oral administration to hypertensive patients, labetalol decreases plasma renin activity and aldosterone levels, both at rest and during exercise, particularly when these were elevated prior to treatment. It is significantly more efficacious in hypertensive patients with high baseline plasma noradrenaline levels.

Labetalol is well absorbed from the gastrointestinal tract with peak blood levels occurring 1 to 2 hours after oral dosing. A single oral dose of 200 mg produced average peak plasma levels of 360 μg/100 mL. The drug undergoes extensive first pass metabolism following oral administration. The bioavailability of oral compared to i.v. labetalol is approximately 25%. When taken with food, the bioavailability of unchanged drug is increased although peak plasma levels remain the same. The drug is metabolized mostly by conjugation with glucuronic acid, the resulting metabolite is inactive. Rapid and extensive distribution within tissue compartments occurs after i.v. administration. The drug is approximately 50% bound to plasma proteins. Labetalol and its metabolites are rapidly excreted in urine, and via bile into the feces. The plasma half-life of labetalol is approximately 6 to 8 hours following oral administration, and 5.5 hours after i.v. administration.

Labetalol produces a significant fall in blood pressure in 1 to 4 hours after the first oral dose. The maximum blood pressure lowering effect at any particular dose level is usually achieved within 24 to 72 hours. Following a bolus i.v. injection, the maximum antihypertensive effect occurs within 5 to 10 minutes in the majority of patients. However, in some patients the peak effect occurs considerably later.

In a clinical pharmacologic study in severe hypertensives, an initial 0.25 mg/kg injection of labetalol administered to patients in the supine position decreased blood pressure by an average of 11/7 mm Hg. Additional injections of 0.5 mg/kg at 15-minute intervals up to a total cumulative dose of 1.75 mg/kg of labetalol caused further dose-related decreases in blood pressure. Some patients required cumulative doses of up to 3.25 mg/kg. The maximal effect of each dose level occurred within 5 minutes. Following discontinuation of i.v. treatment with labetalol, the blood pressure rose gradually and progressively, approaching pretreatment baseline values within an average of 16 to 18 hours in the majority of patients.

Similar results were obtained in the treatment of patients with severe hypertension requiring urgent blood pressure reduction with an initial dose of 20 mg (which corresponds to 0.25 mg/kg for an 80 kg patient) followed by additional doses of either 40 mg or 80 mg at 10-minute intervals to achieve the desired effect or up to a cumulative dose of 300 mg.

Labetalol administered as a continuous i.v. infusion, with a mean dose of 136 mg (27 to 300 mg) over a period of 2 to 3 hours (mean of 2 hours and 39 minutes) lowered the blood pressure by an average of 60/35 mm Hg.

Indications: Tablets: For treatment of hypertension. It is usually used in combination with other drugs, particularly a thiazide diuretic. However, it may be tried alone as an initial agent in those patients in whom, in the judgement of the physician, treatment should be started with an alpha-beta-blocker rather than with a diuretic. Labetalol may be used in combination with diuretics and/or other antihypertensive agents to treat severe hypertension.

The combination of labetalol tablets with a diuretic has been found to be compatible. Limited experience with other antihypertensive agents has not shown evidence of incompatibility with labetalol.

I.V. Injection: For the emergency treatment of severe hypertension when prompt and urgent reduction of blood pressure is essential.

Contraindications: Uncontrolled congestive heart failure (see Warnings); asthma or a history of obstructive airway disease; greater than first degree AV block; cardiogenic shock and states of hypoperfusion; sinus bradycardia; known sensitivity to labetalol.

Warnings: Cardiac failure should be controlled with digitalis and diuretics before labetalol treatment is initiated. Labetalol should not be given to patients with digitalis-resistant heart failure. Sympathetic stimulation is a vital component supporting circulatory function in congestive heart failure and inhibition with beta-blockade always carries the potential hazard of further depressing myocardial contractibility and precipitating cardiac failure. A few patients developed heart failure while on labetalol. Therefore, administration of labetalol to patients with controlled failure or those likely to develop such failure, must be carried out under careful supervision. The drug does not abolish the inotropic action of digitalis on heart muscle.

Patients with angina should be warned against abrupt discontinuation of beta-adrenergic blocking agents. There have been reports of severe exacerbation of angina, and of myocardial infarction or ventricular arrhythmias occurring in patients with angina pectoris, following abrupt discontinuation of therapy. The last two complications may occur with or without preceeding exacerbation of angina pectoris. Therefore, when discontinuation of labetalol is planned in patients with angina pectoris, the dosage should be gradually reduced over a period of about 2 weeks and the patient should be carefully observed. The same frequency of administration should be maintained. In situations of greater urgency, labetalol therapy should be discontinued stepwise and under conditions of closer observation. If angina markedly worsens or acute coronary insufficiency develops, it is recommended that treatment with the drug be re-instituted promptly, at least temporarily.

Various skin rashes and conjunctival xerosis have been reported with beta-blockers. A severe syndrome (oculomucocutaneous syndrome) whose signs include conjunctivitis sicca and psoriasiform rashes, otitis, and sclerosing serositis has occurred with the chronic use of one beta-adrenergic blocking agent (practolol). This syndrome has not been observed in association with labetalol or any other such agent. However, physicians should be alert to the possibility of such reactions and should discontinue treatment in the event that they occur.

Animal studies have shown that labetalol binds to the melanin of the uveal tract. The significance of this in humans is not known but periodic ophthalmic examinations are advisable while the patient is taking labetalol.

There have been rare reports of severe hepatocellular injury with labetalol therapy. Injury has occurred after both short-term and long-term treatment and may be slowly progressive despite minimal symptomatology. The hepatic injury is usually reversible but rare cases of hepatic necrosis and death have been reported. Appropriate laboratory testing should be performed at regular intervals during labetalol therapy. Tests should also be done at the first sign or symptom of liver dysfunction (e.g., pruritus, dark urine, persistent anorexia, jaundice, right upper quadrant tenderness or unexplained flu-like symptoms). If there is laboratory evidence of liver injury or the patient is jaundiced, labetalol should be stopped and not restarted.

Trandate (cont'd)

Severe sinus bradycardia may occur with the use of labetalol from unopposed vagal activity remaining after blockade of beta$_1$-adrenergic receptors; in such cases, dosage should be reduced.

In patients with thyrotoxicosis, possible deleterious effects from long-term use of labetalol have not been adequately appraised. Beta-blockade may mask the clinical signs of continuing hyperthyroidism or complications, and give a false impression of improvement. Therefore, abrupt withdrawal of labetalol may be followed by an exacerbation of the symptoms of hyperthyroidism, including thyroid storm.

While labetalol has been shown to be effective in lowering the blood pressure and relieving symptoms in patients with pheochromocytoma, paradoxical hypertensive responses have been reported in a few patients with this tumor. Use caution when administering labetalol to patients with pheochromocytoma.

During treatment with labetalol injection, signs of cerebral hypoperfusion may occur if blood pressure is reduced too rapidly. Signs include confusion, somnolence, light headedness, dizziness, nausea, vomiting, pallor, sweating, blurred vision, headache, hallucinations and loss of consciousness. Symptoms and signs of myocardial hypoperfusion include chest pain and ischemic changes in the ECG. Although they have not been seen with the use of i.v. labetalol, a number of other adverse reactions including cerebral infarction and optic nerve infarction have been reported with other agents when severely elevated blood pressure was reduced over time-courses or from several hours to as long as 1 or 2 days. The desired blood pressure lowering should therefore be achieved over as long a period of time as is compatible with the patient's status.

Precautions: Postural hypotension and syncope may occur in patients treated with labetalol tablets, particularly if the initial dose is too high or if dose titration is too rapid (see Dosage). Treatment should start with small doses without additional alpha- or beta-adrenergic blocking drugs.

Symptomatic postural hypotension (incidence 58%) is likely to occur if patients are tilted or allowed to assume the upright position within 3 hours of receiving labetalol injection. Therefore, the patient's ability to tolerate the upright position should be established before permitting any ambulation.

Beta-receptor blocking drugs may enhance hypoglycemia in patients prone to this condition. Also, diabetics on insulin or oral hypoglycemic medication may have an increased tendency towards hypoglycemia when treated with these drugs.

Care should be taken if labetalol is used concomitantly with either Class I antiarrhythmic agents or calcium antagonists of the verapamil class since these drugs may potentiate the cardiac depressant activities of labetalol.

In patients with chronic liver disease the oral bioavailability of labetalol is enhanced due to reduced first pass metabolism. Lower doses of labetalol tablets are likely to be required in these patients.

There may be increased difficulty in treating an allergic-type reaction in patients on beta-blockers. In these patients, the reaction may be more severe due to pharmacological effects of beta blockers and problems with fluid changes. Epinephrine should be administered with caution since it may not have its usual effects in the treatment of anaphylaxis. On the one hand, larger doses of epinephrine may be needed to overcome the bronchospasm, while on the other, these doses can be associated with excessive alpha adrenergic stimulation with consequent hypertension, reflex bradycardia and heart block and possible potentiation of bronchospasm. Alternatives to the use of large doses of epinephrine include vigorous supportive care such as fluids and the use of beta agonists including parenteral salbutamol or isoproterenol to overcome bronchospasm and norepinephrine to overcome hypotension.

Geriatrics: The bioavailability and half-life of labetalol are increased in the elderly. In addition, the hypotensive response is greater in this age group following oral or i.v. administration. Therefore, lower doses of labetalol are likely to be required in elderly patients.

Pregnancy: Although no teratogenic effects were seen in animal testing, the safety of the use of labetalol during pregnancy has not been established. Labetalol crosses the placental barrier in women and has been found to bind to the eyes of fetal animals. Labetalol should be used in pregnant women only if the expected benefit to the mother justifies the potential risk to the fetus.

Lactation: Labetalol has been found in the breast milk of lactating women. If the use of the drug is considered essential, then mothers should stop nursing.

Children: Safety and effectiveness in children have not been established.

Drug Interactions: When used with diuretics and/or other antihypertensive agents the dose of labetalol must be appropriately adjusted (see Dosage).

Labetalol and halothane have additive hypotensive effects. High doses of halothane (3%) with labetalol predispose the patient to the myocardial depressant effects of halothane and an undesirable reduction in myocardial performance. The anaesthesiologist should be informed when a patient is receiving labetalol.

Labetalol blunts the reflex tachycardia produced by nitroglycerin without preventing its hypotensive effect. When it is used with nitroglycerin in patients with angina pectoris, additional antihypertensive effects may occur.

Cimetidine has been shown to increase the bioavailability of labetalol. As cimetidine might be given to patients with hypertension also receiving labetalol tablets, special care should be used in establishing the dose required for blood pressure control in such patients.

In one survey, 2.3% of patients taking labetalol in combination with tricyclic antidepressants experienced tremor as compared to 0.7% reported to occur with labetalol alone. The contribution of each of the treatments to this adverse reaction is unknown, but the possibility of a drug interaction cannot be excluded.

Drug/Laboratory Test Interactions: The presence of a metabolite of labetalol in the urine may result in falsely elevated levels of urinary catecholamines when measured by a nonspecific trihydroxyindole (THI) reaction. In screening patients suspected of having a pheochromocytoma and being treated with labetalol, specific radioenzymatic or high performance liquid chromatographic assay techniques should be used to determine levels of catecholamines or their metabolites.

Adverse Effects: The most serious reported adverse effects of labetalol are severe postural hypotension, jaundice and bronchospasm.

Tablets: In well-controlled clinical trials, the most common transient adverse reactions reported at routinely administered therapeutic doses, were postural hypotension and/or dizziness (16.9%), fatigue/malaise (13.1%), and headache (8.0%). Other transient effects include acute retention of urine and difficulty in micturition. The following summarizes the adverse effects reported.

Cardiovascular: postural hypotension/dizziness (16.9%), angina pectoris (3.2%), Raynaud's phenomenon (3.2%), pedal edema (1.9%), palpitations (1.3%), bradycardia (<1.0%).

Gastrointestinal: nausea/vomiting (6.1%), dyspepsia (1.9%), constipation (1.6%), dry mouth/sore throat (1.6%).

Respiratory: dyspnea (3.8%), nasal congestion (1.3%).

Dermatological: drug rash (3.2%), paresthesia (especially "scalp tingling") (3.8%), pruritus (0.6%) and angioedema.

Urogenital: impotence (2.2%), failure of ejaculation (0.6%), dysuria (0.6%).

Musculoskeletal: aches/pains (3.5%), muscle cramps (1.3%).

CNS: fatigue/malaise (13.1%), headache (8.0%), depression (2.6%), loss of libido (1.3%), dreaming (1.3%).

Miscellaneous: visual blurring (4.2%), epistaxis (1.6%).

In addition, in the more extensive trials, bronchospasm, severe bradycardia were reported with the incidence less than 1%. There are rare reports of raised liver function tests, jaundice (both hepatic and cholestatic), and hepatic necrosis (see Warnings).

I.V. Injection: In well controlled clinical trials of 92 patients treated with labetalol injection the most common adverse reactions reported were postural hypotension and/or dizziness (58%), nausea/vomiting (13%), and tingling of the scalp/skin (7%). The following table summarizes the adverse effects reported.

Cardiovascular: postural hypotension/dizziness (58%), ventricular arrhythmia (1%), bradycardia (<1%).

Gastrointestinal: nausea/vomiting (13%), dyspepsia (1%), taste distortion (1%).

Respiratory: dyspnea (1%).

Dermatological: paresthesia (especially "scalp tingling") (7%), hypoesthesia (1%), pruritus (1%).

CNS: somnolence/yawning (3%), vertigo (1%).

Other published or unpublished reports describe other rare, isolated adverse events in patients who were taking labetalol, as follows: bronchospasm and reduction in PEFR, difficulty in micturition including acute urinary retention, ejaculatory failure, Peyronie's disease, toxic myopathy, tremor, hypersensitivity, rashes of various types, such as generalized maculopapular, lichenoid, urticarial, bullous lichen planus, psoriasiform, facial erythema and reversible alopecia and very rarely drug fever. A skin lesion resembling disseminated lupus erythematosus occurred in one patient receiving a high dose of labetalol. There are rare reports of patients who developed lupus-like syndromes while on labetalol which cleared upon discontinuation of treatment. Positive antinuclear factor and antimitochondrial antibodies have been reported in patients receiving the drug, but the significance of these findings is not clear. There is a report of hemiparesis following a rapid fall in blood pressure in a patient who was given a single dose of labetalol i.v. Clinical laboratory tests: Occasional elevations of serum transaminases and blood urea have been reported following oral administration. Elevations of BUN and serum creatinine following bolus injections were reported in 6.8% of patients.

Overdose: Symptoms: Excessive hypotension which is posture-sensitive, and sometimes, excessive bradycardia.

Treatment: Patients should be laid supine and their legs raised, if necessary.

Gastric lavage or pharmacologically-induced emesis (using syrup of ipecac) is useful for removal of the drug shortly after ingestion. Hemodialysis removes less than 1% of circulating labetalol, and is therefore not recommended.

The following additional measures should be employed if necessary:

Excessive bradycardia: Administer atropine to induce vagal blockade. If bradycardia persists, isoproterenol may be administered cautiously. In refractory cases, the use of a cardiac pacemaker may be considered.

Congestive heart failure: Conventional therapy with cardiac glycosides and diuretics.

Hypotension: Administer vasopressors, e.g. norepinephrine.

Bronchospasm: Administer a beta$_2$-stimulating agent and/or a theophylline preparation.

Oliguric renal failure has been reported after massive overdosage of labetalol orally. In one case, the use of dopamine to increase blood pressure may have aggravated the renal failure.

Dosage: Tablets: Labetalol should be taken preferably after food. The dosage must always be adjusted in accordance with the individual requirements of the patient. The recommended initial dose is 100 mg twice daily whether used alone or with a diuretic. Thereafter, the dose should be adjusted semiweekly or weekly according to the response.

The usual maintenance dose is 200 to 400 mg twice daily. Patients may require up to 1 200 mg/day, in 2 divided doses.

Optimal doses are usually lower in patients also receiving a diuretic since an additive antihypertensive effect can be expected.

Geriatrics: Lower doses of labetalol are likely to be required in elderly patients (see Precautions).

Children: Safe and effective use of labetalol tablets in children has not presently been elucidated.

Patients with liver function impairment will likely require lower doses since metabolism of the drug will be diminished.

I.V. Injection: The administration of i.v. labetalol should be restricted to hospitalized patients. **Dosage must be individualized** according to the severity of the hypertension, to the nature and duration of previous therapy and to the response of the patient during dosing.

Patients should be kept supine during the period of i.v. drug administration because a substantial fall in blood pressure on standing may be anticipated in these patients. The patient's ability to tolerate the upright position (e.g. use of toilet facilities) should be established, especially during the 3 hours post injection.

The blood pressure should be monitored during and after completion of the infusion or i.v. injections. Rapid or excessive falls in either systolic or diastolic blood pressure during i.v. treatment should be avoided. In patients with excessive systolic hypertension, the decrease in systolic pressure should be used as an indicator of effectiveness in addition to the response of the diastolic pressure.

Lower doses of labetalol are likely to be required in elderly patients (see Precautions).

Either of 2 methods of administration of labetalol injection may be used: repeated i.v. injection or slow continuous infusion.

Repeated i.v. injection: Initially, labetalol injection should be given in a dose of 20 mg labetalol (which corresponds to 0.25 mg/kg for an 80 kg patient) by slow i.v. injection over a 2-minute period.

Immediately before the injection and at 5 and 10 minutes after injection, supine blood pressure should be measured to evaluate response. Additional injections of 40 mg can be given at 10-minute intervals until a desired supine blood pressure is achieved or a total of 300 mg labetalol has been injected. The maximum effect usually occurs within 5 to 10 minutes of each injection but may be longer.

Slow continuous infusion: Labetalol is prepared for i.v. continuous infusion by diluting the vial contents with commonly used i.v. fluids (see below). Two methods of preparing the infusion solution: The contents of 2 vials (40mL) are added to 160 mL of a commonly used i.v. fluid such that the resultant 200 mL of solution contains 200 mg of labetalol, 1 mg/mL. The diluted solution should be administered at a rate of 2 mL/min to deliver 2 mg/min. Alternatively, the contents of 2 vials (40 mL) of labetalol injection can be added to 250 mL of a commonly used i.v. fluid. The resultant solution will contain 200 mg of labetalol, approximately 2 mg/3 mL. The diluted solution should be administered at a rate of 3 mL/min to deliver approximately 2 mg/min.

The rate of infusion of the diluted solution may be adjusted downward according to the blood pressure response, at the discretion of the physician. To facilitate a desired rate of infusion, the diluted solution can be infused using a controlled administration mechanism, e.g. graduated burette or mechanically driven infusion pump.

Since the half-life of labetalol is 5 to 8 hours, steady-state blood levels (in the face of a constant rate of infusion) would not be reached during the usual infusion time period. The infusion should be continued until a satisfactory response is obtained and should then be stopped and oral medication started when it has been established that the supine diastolic blood pressure has begun to rise. The effective i.v. dose is usually in the range of 50 to 200 mg. A total dose of up to 300 mg may be required in some patients.

Compatibility with commonly used i.v. fluids: Parenteral drug products should be inspected visually for particulate matter and discoloration prior to administration, whenever solution and container permit.

Labetalol injection was tested for compatibility with commonly used i.v. fluids at final concentrations of 1.25 mg to 3.75 mg labetalol/mL of the mixture. Labetalol injection was found to be compatible with and stable (**for 24 hours refrigerated or at room temperature**) in mixtures with the following solutions: Ringer's Injection USP, Lactated Ringer's Injection USP, 5% Dextrose and Ringer's Injection, 5% Lactated Ringer's and 5% Dextrose Injection, 5% Dextrose Injection USP, 0.9% Sodium Chloride Injection USP, 5% Dextrose and 0.2% Sodium Chloride Injection USP, 2.5% Dextrose and 0.45% Sodium Chloride Injection USP, 5% Dextrose and 0.9% Sodium Chloride Injection USP, and 5% Dextrose and 0.33% Sodium Chloride Injection USP. **Labetalol injection was not compatible with 5% Sodium Bicarbonate Injection USP.**

Supplied: Tablets: 100 mg: Each capsule-shaped, orange, film-coated tablet, engraved TRANDATE 100 on one side, scored and engraved RP on the other side, contains: labetalol HCl USP 100 mg. Also contains lactose. Tartrazine-free. Bottles of 100.

200 mg: Each capsule-shaped, white, film-coated tablet, engraved TRANDATE 200 on one side, scored and engraved RP on the other side, contains: labetalol HCl USP 200 mg. Also contains lactose. Tartrazine-free. Bottles of 100.

Injection: Each mL contains: labetalol HCl 5 mg. Also contains methylparaben and propylparaben. Multidose vials of 20 mL, boxes of 6.

(Shown in Product Recognition Section)

TRANDOLAPRIL Ⓟ

General Monograph, CPhA

see ACE INHIBITORS

TRANSDERM-NITRO®

Novartis Pharmaceuticals

Nitroglycerin

Transdermal Antianginal

Pharmacology: The principal pharmacological action of nitroglycerin is relaxation of vascular smooth muscle, producing a vasodilator effect on both peripheral arteries and veins, with more prominent effects on the latter. Dilation of the postcapillary vessels, including large veins, promotes peripheral pooling of blood and decreases venous return to the heart, thereby reducing left ventricular end-diastolic pressure (preload). Arteriolar relaxation reduces system vascular resistance and arterial pressure (afterload). Dilation of the coronary arteries also occurs. The relative importance of preload reduction, afterload reduction, and coronary dilation remains undefined.

When Transderm-Nitro is applied to the skin, nitroglycerin is absorbed directly into the systemic circulation. Thus, the active drug reaches target organs before inactivation by the liver. The transdermal absorption of nitroglycerin occurs in a continuous and well-controlled manner. Nitroglycerin is rapidly metabolized, principally by a liver reductase, to form glycerol nitrate metabolites and inorganic nitrate. Two active major metabolites, the 1,2-and 1,3-dinitroglycerols, the products of hydrolysis, appear to be less potent than nitroglycerin as vasodilators but have longer plasma half-lives. The dinitrates are further metabolized to mononitrates (biologically inactive with respect to cardiovascular effects) and ultimately to glycerol and carbon dioxide. There is extensive first-pass deactivation by the liver following gastrointestinal absorption.

Single-blind, placebo-controlled studies in healthy volunteers revealed that uniform steady state plasma concentrations were reached within 2 hours after application of the patch and remained at the same level until removal of the patch at 24 hours. Between 2 and 24 hours, the mean concentration was 0.16 ± 0.03 ng/mL (1×10 cm^2 patch), 0.25 ± 0.04 ng/mL (2×10 cm^2 patch), and 0.57 ± 0.11 ng/mL (4×10 cm^2 patch), the area under the curve showing a linear correlation between drug-release area and plasma concentration. Within 1 hour of removal of the patch, the plasma concentration declines to about 50% of steady state concentration and to undetectable concentrations by 2 hours.

Although dosing regimens for most chronically used drugs are designed to provide plasma concentrations that are continuously greater than a minimally effective concentration, such a strategy is probably inappropriate for organic nitrates. Some controlled clinical trials using exercise tolerance testing have shown maintenance of effectiveness when patches are worn continuously. The large majority of such controlled trials, however, have shown the development of tolerance (i.e., complete loss of effect as measured by exercise testing) within the first day. Tolerance has appeared even when doses greater than 4 mg/hour were delivered continuously. This dose is far in excess of the effective dose 0.2 to 0.8 mg/hour applied intermittently.

Efficacy of organic nitrates is restored after a period of absence of nitrates from the body. Drug-free intervals of 10 to 12 hours are known to be sufficient to restore response. Several studies have demonstrated that when nitroglycerin is administered according to an intermittent regimen, doses of Transderm-Nitro 0.4 to 0.8 mg/hour (20 to 40 cm^2) have increased exercise capacity for up to 8 hours, with a trend of increased exercise capacity to 12 hours. One controlled clinical trial suggested that the intermittent use of nitrates may be associated with a decreased, in comparison to placebo, exercise tolerance during the last part of the nitrate-free interval; the clinical relevance of this observation is unknown. In another clinical trial there was an increase in nocturnal angina attacks during the drug-free period in some patients treated with nitroglycerin as compared to placebo. Therefore the possibility of increased frequency or severity of angina during the nitrate-free interval should be considered.

Indications: Used intermittently (see Pharmacology) for the prevention of anginal attacks in patients with stable angina pectoris associated with coronary artery disease. It can be used in conjunction with other antianginal agents such as beta-blockers and/or calcium channel blockers.

Transderm-Nitro is not intended for the immediate relief of acute attacks of angina pectoris. Sublingual nitroglycerin preparations should be used for this purpose.

Contraindications: Known hypersensitivity to nitroglycerin and related organic nitrate compounds, known or suspected hypersensitivity to components of the patch, acute circulatory failure associated with marked hypotension (shock and states of collapse), postural hypotension, myocardial insufficiency due to obstruction (e.g., in the presence of aortic or mitral stenosis or of constrictive pericarditis), increased intracranial pressure, increased intraocular pressure, severe anemia.

Warnings: Transderm-Nitro must be removed before cardioversion or DC defibrillation is attempted, as well as before applying diathermy treatment, since it may be associated with damage to the paddles and burns to the patient.

The benefits and safety of transdermal nitroglycerin in angina patients with acute myocardial infarction or congestive heart failure have not been established. If one elects to use Transderm-Nitro in these conditions, careful clinical or hemodynamic monitoring must be used to avoid the potentially deleterious effects of induced hypotension and tachycardia.

Precautions: Headaches, or symptoms of hypotension, such as weakness or dizziness, particularly when arising suddenly from a recumbent position, may occur. A reduction in dose or discontinuation of treatment may be necessary.

Caution should be exercised when using nitroglycerin in patients prone to, or who might be affected by hypotension. The drug therefore should be used with caution in patients who may have volume depletion from diuretic therapy or in patients who have low systolic blood pressure (e.g., below 90 mmHg). Paradoxical bradycardia and increased angina pectoris may accompany nitroglycerin-induced hypotension.

Nitrate therapy may aggravate the angina caused by hypertrophic cardiomyopathy.

In industrial workers who have had long-term exposure to unknown (presumably high) doses of nitroglycerin, tolerance clearly occurs. There is moreover, physical dependence since chest pain, acute myocardial infarction, and even sudden death have occurred during temporary withdrawal of nitroglycerin from these workers. In clinical trials of angina patients, there are reports of anginal attacks being more easily provoked and of rebound in the hemodynamic effects soon after nitrate withdrawal. The importance of these observations to the routine clinical use of nitroglycerin has not been fully elucidated, but patients should be monitored closely for increased anginal symptoms during drug-free periods.

Caution should be exercised in patients with arterial hypoxemia due to anemia (see Contraindications), because in such patients the biotransformation of nitroglycerin is reduced. Similarly, caution is called for in patients with hypoxemia and a ventilation/perfusion imbalance due to lung disease or ischemic heart failure. Patients with angina pectoris, myocardial infarction, or cerebral ischemia frequently suffer from abnormalities of the small airways (especially alveolar hypoxia). Under these circumstances vasoconstriction occurs within the lung to shift perfusion from areas of alveolar hypoxia to better ventilated regions of the lung. As a potent vasodilator, nitroglycerin could reverse this protective vasoconstriction and thus result in increased perfusion to poorly ventilated areas, worsening of the ventilation/perfusion imbalance, and a further decrease in the arterial partial pressure of oxygen.

Tolerance to nitroglycerin with cross tolerance to other nitrates or nitrites may occur (see Pharmacology). Co-administration of other long-acting nitrates could jeopardize the integrity of the nitrate-free interval and therefore must be avoided. As tolerance to nitroglycerin patches develops, the effect of sublingual nitroglycerin on exercise tolerance, although still observable, is somewhat blunted.

Occupations Hazards: As patients may experience faintness and/or dizziness, reaction time when driving or operating machinery may be impaired, especially at the start of treatment.

Pregnancy: It is not known whether nitroglycerin can cause fetal harm when administered to a pregnant woman. Therefore use only if the potential benefit justifies the risk to the fetus.

Lactation: It is not known whether nitroglycerin is excreted into breast milk. Benefits to the mother must be weighed against the risks to the child.

Children: Safety and effectiveness have not been established in children.

Drug Interactions: Concomitant treatment with other vasodilators, calcium channel blockers, ACE inhibitors, beta-blockers, diuretics, antihypertensives, tricyclic antidepressants, and major tranquilizers may potentiate the blood pressure lowering effect of Transderm-Nitro. Dose adjustment may be necessary.

Marked symptomatic orthostatic hypotension has been reported when calcium channel blockers and organic nitrates were used in combination. Dosage adjustments of either class of agents may be necessary.

Alcohol may enhance sensitivity to the hypotensive effects of nitrates.

Concurrent administration of Transderm-Nitro with dihydroergotamine may increase the bioavailability of dihydroergotamine. Special attention should be paid to this point in patients with coronary artery disease, because dihydroergotamine antagonizes the effect of nitroglycerin and may lead to coronary vasoconstriction.

The possibility that the ingestion of ASA and nonsteroidal anti-inflammatory drugs might diminish the therapeutic response to nitrates and nitroglycerin cannot be excluded.

Information for the Patient: Daily headaches sometimes accompany treatment with nitroglycerin. In patients who get these headaches, the headaches may be a marker of the activity of the drug. Patients should resist the temptation to avoid headaches by altering the schedule of their treatment with nitroglycerin, since loss of headache may be associated with simultaneous loss of antianginal efficacy.

Treatment with nitroglycerin may be associated with lightheadedness on standing, especially just after rising from a recumbent or seated postion. This effect may be more frequent in patients who have also consumed alcohol.

After normal use, there is enough residual nitroglycerin in discarded patches that they are a potential hazard to children and pets.

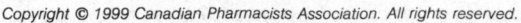

Transderm-Nitro (cont'd)

A patient leaflet is supplied with the patches (see Blue Section—Information for the Patient "Transderm-Nitro").

Adverse Effects: Headache, which may be severe, is the most commonly reported side effect. Headache may be recurrent with each daily dose, especially at higher doses of nitroglycerin. Headaches may be treated with concomitant administration of mild analgesics. If such headaches are unresponsive to treatment, the nitroglycerin dosage should be reduced or the product discontinued. Transient episodes of lightheadedness, occasionally related to blood pressure changes, may also occur. Hypotension occurs infrequently, but in some patients it may be severe enough to warrant discontinuation of therapy.

Reddening of the skin, with or without a mild local itching or burning sensation, as well as allergic contact dermatitis may occasionally occur. Upon removal of the patch, any slight reddening of the skin will usually disappear within a few hours. The application site should be changed regularly to prevent local irritation.

Less frequently reported adverse reactions include dizziness, faintness, facial flushing, postural hypotension which may be associated with reflex tachycardia. Syncope, crescendo angina and rebound hypertension have been reported but are uncommon. Rarely, nausea and vomiting.

Overdose: Symptoms: Nitroglycerin overdose may result in severe hypotension, persistent throbbing headache, vertigo, palpitations, visual disturbances, flushing and perspiring skin (later becoming cold and cyanotic), anorexia, nausea and vomiting (possibly with colic and even bloody diarrhea), syncope (especially in the upright posture), methemoglobinemia with cyanosis, hyperpnea, dyspnea and slow breathing, slow pulse (dicrotic and intermittent), heart block and bradycardia, increased intracranial pressure with cerebral symptoms of fever, confusion, and coma possibly followed by paralysis, clonic convulsions and death due to circulatory collapse.

Treatment: Keep the patient recumbent in a shock position and comfortably warm. Remove the Transderm-Nitro patch.

Passive movement of the extremities may aid venous return. Administer oxygen and artificial ventilation if necessary.

I.V. infusion of normal saline or similar fluid may also be required to produce sufficient central volume expansion. However, in patients with renal disease or congestive heart failure, therapy resulting in central volume expansion is not without hazard. Treatment of nitroglycerin overdose in these patients may be subtle and difficult, and invasive monitoring may be required.

Epinephrine is ineffective in reversing the severe hypotensive events associated with overdose; it and related compounds are contraindicated in this situation.

Methemoglobinemia: Case reports of clinically significant methemoglobinemia are rare at conventional doses of nitroglycerin. The formation of methemoglobin is dose-related, and in the case of genetic abnormalities of hemoglobin that favor methemoglobin formation, even conventional doses of organic nitrates can produce harmful concentrations of methemoglobin. Methemoglobin levels are available from most clinical laboratories. The diagnosis should be suspected in patients who exhibit signs of impaired oxygen delivery despite adequate cardiac output and adequate arterial pO_2. Classically, methemoglobinemic blood is described as chocolate brown, without color change on exposure to air. If methemoglobinemia is present, administration of methylene blue (1% solution), 1 to 2 mg/kg i.v., may be required.

Dosage: Daily Dosage Schedule: The daily dosage schedule is based on intermittent therapy to prevent the development of tolerance to nitroglycerin. The optimal dose should be selected based upon the clinical response, side effects, and the effects of therapy on blood pressure.

Starting dose: One 0.2 patch (10 cm²), usually applied in the morning. If 0.2 mg/hour (10 cm²) is well tolerated, the dose can be increased to 0.4 mg/hour (20 cm²) if required. A maximum of 0.8 mg/hour (40 cm²) may be used.

Prevention of Tolerance: Although some controlled clinical trials using exercise tolerance testing have shown maintenance of effectiveness when patches are worn continuously, the large majority of such controlled trials have shown the development of tolerance (i.e., complete loss of effect) within the first 24 hours after therapy was initiated. Dose adjustments even to levels much higher than generally used did not prevent the development of tolerance.

Table I—Transderm-Nitro

Rate of Nitroglycerin Release

	Transderm-Nitro 0.2	Transderm-Nitro 0.4	Transderm-Nitro 0.6
Rated Release of Nitroglycerin in vivo	0.2 mg/hour	0.4/hour	0.6 mg/hour
Nitroglycerin Content	25 mg	50 mg	75 mg
Drug Releasing Area	10 cm²	20 cm²	30 cm²
Printed Code	Transderm-Nitro 0.2 mg/hour CG DOD	Transderm-Nitro 0.4 mg/hour CG DPD	Transderm-Nitro 0.6 mg/hour CG EJE
Color of Protective Liner (peel off and discard)	off-white	off-white	off-white

Tolerance can be prevented or attenuated by use of an intermittent dosage schedule. Although the minimum nitrate-free interval has not been defined, clinical trials have demonstrated that an appropriate dosing schedule for nitroglycerin patches would provide for a daily patch-on period of 12 to 14 hours and a daily patch-off period of 10 to 12 hours. The patch-free time should coincide with the period in which angina pectoris is least likely to occur (usually at night). Patients should be watched carefully for an increase of angina pectoris during the patch-free period. Adjustment of background medication may be required.

The dose of Transderm-Nitro should be periodically reviewed in relation to continuing antianginal control.

Site of Patch Application: Transderm-Nitro can be applied to any area of skin **except** the distal extremities. Many patients prefer the chest. Each successive application should be to a different site to mimimize local irritation.

The area should be clean, dry and preferably hairless. If hair is likely to interfere with patch adhesion or removal, clipping may be necessary prior to application. Take care to avoid areas with cuts or irritations.

Information for the Patient: See Blue Section—Information for the Patient "Transderm-Nitro".

Supplied: Transderm-Nitro transdermal therapeutic system, is a flat multilayer unit designed to release nitroglycerin continuously through a semipermeable membrane following its application to intact skin. In cases where permeability of the skin is excessive, drug release is limited by this release membrane.

The rate of nitroglycerin release is linearly dependent upon the drug releasing area of the applied patch (see Table I). The nominal rate of nitroglycerin release in vivo is approximately 0.02 mg/cm²/hour. Nitroglycerin remaining in the patch serves as a thermodynamic energy source to keep the pattern of drug delivery constant.

The patch comprises 5 layers: a tan-colored backing layer (aluminized plastic) impermeable to nitroglycerin; a drug reservoir containing nitroglycerin adsorbed on lactose, colloidal silicon dioxide and silicone medical fluid; an ethylene/vinyl acetate copolymer membrane that is permeable to nitroglycerin; a layer of hypoallergenic silicone adhesive; a protective liner (peel strip) which is removed prior to use to expose the adhesive surface.

Store patches below 25°C. Do not freeze. Each patch is individually sealed in a separate pouch. Do not store out of the pouch. Keep Transderm-Nitro out of reach of children and pets both before use and when disposing of used patches.

(Shown in Product Recognition Section)

TRANSDERM-V®

Novartis Pharmaceuticals

Scopolamine

Anti-Motion Sickness Agent

Pharmacology: Scopolamine is a naturally occurring belladonna alkaloid. As a parasympatholytic agent it competitively antagonizes acetylcholine (or other direct parasympathomimetics) at the muscarinic receptor. This means that its effect can be abolished by high doses of a parasympathomimetic agent. The effect of scopolamine depends on the sensitivity of the target organs and on the size of the dose employed.

The principal actions of scopolamine are related to anticholinergic effects which include depressed motor function, decreased salivation and sweating, mydriasis, inhibition of visual accommodation, and tachycardia. Drowsiness may also occur at therapeutic doses.

The mechanism of action of scopolamine in the CNS is not well known but may include anticholinergic effects. The ability of scopolamine to prevent motion-induced nausea is believed to be associated with inhibition of vestibular input to the CNS, which results in inhibition of the vomiting reflex. In addition, scopolamine may have a direct action on the vomiting centre within the reticular formation of the brain stem.

After transdermal administration of scopolamine, the time necessary to reach maximum blood levels (estimated by urinary excretion of scopolamine) is approximately 12 hours. The disc is designed for continuous release of scopolamine over the 3-day functional lifetime. Scopolamine excretion continues for up to 12 hours after removal of the system. Approximately 5 to 8% of the administered drug is excreted unchanged.

Indications: For prevention of symptoms of motion sickness such as nausea and vomiting.

Contraindications: Known hypersensitivity to scopolamine or any components of the system.

Glaucoma or a predisposition to angle-closure glaucoma (see Warnings).

Warnings: Occupational Hazards: Since drowsiness, disorientation and confusion may occasionally occur with the use of scopolamine, patients should be cautioned about engaging in activities that require mental alertness, such as driving a motor vehicle or operating dangerous machinery.

Potentially alarming idiosyncratic reactions may occur with ordinary therapeutic doses of scopolamine.

In patients with a history of possible raised intraocular pressure (pressure pain, blurred vision, glaucomatous halo), scopolamine should be employed only after ophthalmological examination excludes glaucoma (see Contraindications).

Scopolamine should be discontinued if it causes blurring of vision with pressure pain within the eye (see Contraindications).

Precautions: Scopolamine should be used with caution in patients with dysuria, e.g., due to urinary bladder neck obstruction. Caution should be exercised when administering an antiemetic or antimuscarinic drug to patients suspected of having intestinal obstruction, e.g., pyloric stenosis.

Scopolamine should be used with caution in the elderly or in individuals with impaired metabolic, liver or kidney functions.

In certain cases, especially in the elderly, confusional states and/or visual hallucinations may occur. Should this occur, scopolamine should be removed at once. If severe symptoms persist, appropriate countermeasures should be taken (see Overdose: Symptoms and Treatment).

In epileptic patients, isolated cases of increased seizure frequency have been reported.

Children: Children are particularly susceptible to the side effects of belladonna alkaloids. Transderm-V should not be used in children because it is not known whether the amount of scopolamine released could produce serious adverse effects in children.

Pregnancy: Scopolamine should be used during pregnancy only if the anticipated benefit justifies the potential risk to the mother and fetus.

Lactation: Scopolamine should not be administered to nursing mothers since it is excreted into breast milk.

Drug Interactions: Scopolamine should be employed with caution in patients taking drugs which act on the CNS. This applies particularly to patients under treatment with drugs displaying anticholinergic properties, for example, belladonna alkaloids, antihistamines, antidepressants (tricyclics and MAO inhibitors), phenothiazines, amantadine and quinidine.

Any parasympatholytic or sympathomimetic agent or barbiturate should be administered with caution to persons wearing scopolamine.

Patients should refrain from consuming alcohol while using scopolamine. Alcohol may interfere with the metabolism of the drug and could thus cause plasma levels to become elevated, which could intensify the side effects.

Information for the Patient: Since scopolamine can cause temporary dilation of the pupils and blurred vision if it comes in contact with the eyes, patients should be strongly advised to wash their hands thoroughly with soap and water immediately after handling the disc and to avoid touching the disc while in place behind the ear.

Patients should be advised to remove the disc and contact a physician promptly in the unlikely event that they experience symptoms of angle-closure glaucoma (pain in and reddening of the eyes accompanied by dilated pupils).

Patients should be instructed to remove the disc if they develop difficulty urinating.

Patients should be advised to refrain from consuming alcohol while using scopolamine.

Patients should be warned against driving a motor vehicle or operating dangerous machinery.

A patient leaflet is supplied with the discs (see Blue Section—Information for the Patient "Transderm-V").

Adverse Effects: Gastrointestinal: Frequent: transient dryness of the mouth.

Ophthalmic: Frequent: transient impairment of eye accommodation (cycloplegia), including blurred (near) vision and dilatation of the pupils (sometimes in one eye only), especially if traces of active substance on the hands enter the eyes. Occasional: irritation of the eyelids. Isolated cases: dilatation of the pupils may provoke acute glaucoma, especially angle-closure glaucoma.

CNS: Occasional: drowsiness. Rare: impairment of memory and concentration, restlessness, giddiness, dizziness, disorientation, confusion and hallucinations.

Dermatological: Occasional: local irritation of the skin. Isolated cases: generalized skin rash.

Genitourinary: Rare: disturbances of micturition (retention of urine).

Cardiovascular: Isolated cases: slight variations in blood pressure.

Adverse Effects after Withdrawal of Scopolamine: In certain instances, there have been complaints of transient dizziness, nausea, vomiting, headache and disturbances of balance following discontinuation of scopolamine, usually after several days of use.

Overdose: Symptoms: The central actions of scopolamine in high doses are similar to those of atropine. They begin with restlessness, excitation states, disorientation and confusion. In response to higher doses, delirium, hallucinations and convulsions set in. At very high doses coma and respiratory paralysis occur.

Treatment: Remove the disc immediately.

Treatment of acute antimuscarinic overdose consists mainly of symptomatic and supportive treatments. Patients should be hospitalized and closely monitored, including continuous ECG monitoring.

The most effective antidote is physostigmine, which, depending on the severity of the poisoning, should be injected slowly i.v. in doses of 1 to 4 mg (0.5 mg in children). Since physostigmine is rapidly metabolized, the patients may lapse into coma again within 1 to 2 hours, thus necessitating renewed injections. It should, however, be noted that physostigmine has the potential for producing severe adverse effects (for instance, seizures, asystole). **The use of physostigmine should, therefore, be reserved for life-threatening situations only.**

Fairly small doses of diazepam may prove useful in the presence of excitation states and convulsions. Larger doses should be avoided in view of the possibility of additional respiratory depression. In severe cases artificial respiration may be necessary.

In the event of hyperthermia, urgent action should be taken to dissipate heat (e.g., cold baths).

Dosage: Adults: To obtain optimum effect, Transderm-V should be applied to a dry, hairless area of post-auricular skin approximately 12 hours before the antiemetic effect is required. Only 1 disc should be worn at any time. Should the disc become displaced, it should be discarded and a fresh one placed on a different skin site.

Scopolamine provides protection over a 3-day period. If the disc is only needed for a shorter time, it should be removed at the end of the journey.

If therapy is required for longer periods, the first disc should be removed after 72 hours and a second disc applied behind the other ear.

Children: Scopolamine should not be used in children (see Precautions).

Transderm-V is designed to deliver in vitro 1 mg scopolamine at a constant rate over the 3-day functional lifetime. An initial priming dose of scopolamine, released from the adhesive layer of the system, saturates the skin binding sites for the drug and brings the plasma concentration to the required steady state level. Subsequently, there is continuous controlled release of scopolamine, from the drug reservoir through the rate-controlling membrane.

Handling: After the disc is applied on dry skin behind the ear, the hands should be washed thoroughly with soap and water, then dried. Once the disc has been affixed, it should not be touched again while it is being worn. Upon removal, the disc should be carefully discarded, and the hands and application site washed thoroughly with soap and water to prevent traces of scopolamine from coming in direct contact with the eyes. If scopolamine were to contact the eyes it could cause slight temporary blurring of vision and dilation of the pupils (sometimes in one eye only).

Information for the Patient: See Blue Section—Information for the Patient "Transderm-V".

Supplied: Each flat, circular, multilayer, tan-colored, adhesive disc (contact surface 2.5 cm²), attached to a clear, oversized, hexagonal, protective liner (peel strip), contains: scopolamine 1.5 mg and is programmed to release in vitro 1 mg scopolamine over 3 days. Cartons of 2.

Transderm-V is a 0.2 mm-thick film with 5 layers. Proceeding from the visible surface towards the surface attached to the skin, these layers are: (1) a **backing layer** of tan-colored, aluminized polyester film; (2) a drug **reservoir** of scopolamine, mineral oil and polyisobutylene; (3) a microporous polypropylene **membrane** that controls the rate of delivery of scopolamine from the system to the skin surface; (4) an **adhesive** formulation of mineral oil, polyisobutylene and a priming dose of scopolamine; (5) a clear hexagonal **protective liner** (peel strip) of siliconized polyester, which is removed before applying the disc.

Store below 25°C. Do not freeze. Each disc is individually sealed in a separate pouch. Do not store out of the pouch. Apply immediately upon removal from the protective pouch. Keep out of the reach of children and pets both before use and when disposing of used discs.

TRANS-PLANTAR®
TRANS•VER•SAL®

Westwood-Squibb

Salicylic Acid

Plantar Wart Therapy
Verrucae Therapy

Indications: Trans-Plantar: For the treatment of plantar warts. Trans•Ver•Sal: For the treatment of common wart infections.

Contraindications: Should not be used by patients with diabetes or impaired blood circulation unless directed by physician. Do not use on moles, birthmarks, uro-genital warts and warts with hair. It is contraindicated for patients with a known sensitivity to any of the ingredients.

Warnings: For external use only. Avoid contact with eyes or mucous membranes. The pads should be trimmed so as not to come in contact with normal skin surrounding warts. Treatment should be discontinued if excessive irritation of surrounding skin occurs. Do not use on irritated skin or on any area that is infected or reddened. If symptoms persist, consult a physician.

Adverse Effects: Localized irritation will occur if salicylic acid comes in contact with normal skin. If this occurs the irritation should be allowed to subside by temporarily discontinuing treatment. Upon resuming treatment, trim the pads to contact wart tissue only.

Dosage: The pads are applied once each day before retiring. When necessary, the wart should first be cleared of debris with the emery file provided, taking care to avoid contact with healthy skin. Do not file to the point where bleeding occurs. The wart should then be moistened with warm water using a cotton tipped applicator.

The pad is then removed from the clear strip, trimmed to size (if necessary), and applied to the wart with the occlusive top film facing up. The pad is then secured with the adhesive strip provided.

The pad should be left in place overnight and discarded in the morning. This procedure is repeated daily until wart resolution is complete. Generally, visible clinical improvement will occur during the first 2 to 4 weeks of treatment. Complete resolution may be expected after 6 to 12 weeks. As the wart is diminishing it is important that the pad be trimmed accordingly to avoid contact with normal skin.

Supplied: Trans-Plantar: Each 20 mm pad contains: salicylic acid 15% w/w. Nonmedicinal ingredients: karaya gum, polyethylene glycol-300, propylene glycol and quaternium-15. Cartons of 20. Each carton also contains securing tapes and one emery file.

Trans•Ver•Sal: Each 6 mm pad contains: salicylic acid 15% w/w. Nonmedicinal indredients: karaya gum, polyethylene glycol-300, propylene glycol and quaternium-15. 6 mm Kit: 30 pads, tapes and 1 file.

Store between 4 and 37°C.

TRANXENE® Ⓟ

Abbott

Clorazepate Dipotassium

Anxiolytic—Sedative

Supplied: Each capsule contains: clorazepate dipotassium 3.75 mg (gray with white cap) or 7.5 mg (gray with maroon cap). Also contains: cellulose microcrystalline, magnesium stearate, potassium carbonate, potassium chloride and talcum powder. Alcohol-, gluten-, lactose-, paraben-, sodium-, sucrose-, sulfite- and tartrazine-free. Bottles of 100.

TRASICOR® Ⓟ

Novartis Pharmaceuticals

Oxprenolol HCl

Antihypertensive

Pharmacology: Oxprenolol is a noncardioselective beta-adrenergic receptor blocking agent which possesses partial agonist activity. It is used in the treatment of hypertension.

The mechanism of the antihypertensive effect has not been established. Among the factors which may be involved are: a) competitive ability to antagonize catecholamine induced tachycardia at the beta-receptor sites in the heart, thus decreasing cardiac output; b) inhibition of renin release by the kidneys; c) inhibition of the vasomotor centres.

Oxprenolol is rapidly and well absorbed from the gastrointestinal tract. Peak plasma concentrations are reached approximately 0.5 to 1.5 hours after ingestion of the conventional oxprenolol tablet and 2 to 4 hours after the slow-release tablet.

There is a variable hepatic first-pass effect. The systemic bioavailability of oxprenolol hydrochloride ranges from 20 to 70%.

Oxprenolol is 80% bound to plasma proteins, and has a calculated distribution volume of 1.3 L/kg.

The mean plasma half-life for oral doses of the conventional tablet is 1.3 to 1.5 hours. The time taken for mean plasma levels to decrease from the peak value to half that value were approximately 4.5 hours for the 80 mg slow-release tablet and 7 hours for the 160 mg slow-release tablet.

Oxprenolol is primarily excreted in the urine in the form of inactive metabolites. Less than 5% is excreted unchanged and the major metabolite is a glucuronide.

β-blocking effects continue for at least 8 hours and up to 12 hours after a conventional tablet and for up to 24 hours after a slow-release tablet.

Indications: In patients with mild or moderate hypertension. It is usually used in combination with other drugs, particularly thiazide or thiazide-related diuretics. However, it may be tried alone as an initial agent in those patients in whom, in the judgment of the physician, treatment should be started with a beta-blocker rather than a diuretic. Therapy should start using Trasicor (regular formulation), and once the maintenance dose has been established, Slow-Trasicor may be substituted (see Dosage).

The combination of oxprenolol with a thiazide-related diuretic and/or peripheral vasodilator has been found to be compatible and generally more effective than oxprenolol alone. Experience with other antihypertensive agents has not shown evidence of incompatibility.

Oxprenolol is not recommended for the emergency treatment of hypertensive crisis.

Contraindications: Bronchospasm (including bronchial asthma); allergic rhinitis during the pollen season; sinus bradycardia and greater than first degree AV block; sick sinus syndrome; right ventricular failure secondary to pulmonary hypertension; congestive heart failure; cardiogenic shock; anesthesia with agents that produce myocardial depression,

Trasicor (cont'd)

e.g. ether known hypersensitivity to oxprenolol and related derivatives.

Warnings: Cardiac Failure: Special caution should be exercised when administering oxprenolol to patients with a history of heart failure. Sympathetic stimulation is a vital component supporting circulatory function in congestive heart failure, and inhibition with beta-blockade always carries the potential hazard of further depressing myocardial contractility and precipitating cardiac failure.

Oxprenolol acts selectively without abolishing the inotropic action of digitalis on the heart muscle. However, the positive inotropic action of digitalis may be reduced by the negative inotropic effect of oxprenolol when the 2 drugs are used concomitantly. The effects of beta-blockers and digitalis are additive in depressing AV conduction.

In patients without a history of cardiac failure, continued depression of the myocardium over a period of time can, in some cases, lead to cardiac failure. Therefore, at the first sign or symptom of impending cardiac failure, patients should be fully digitalized and/or given a diuretic, and the response observed closely. If cardiac failure continues, despite adequate digitalization and diuretic therapy, oxprenolol therapy should be immediately withdrawn.

In rare cases, pre-existing AV conduction disorders may become aggravated (possibly leading to AV block). As a rule, no worsening of peripheral conduction disorders (left and/or right bundle-branch block) occur.

Abrupt Cessation of Therapy with Trasicor: Patients with angina should be warned against abrupt discontinuation of oxprenolol. There have been reports of severe exacerbation of angina and of myocardial infarction or ventricular arrhythmias occurring in patients with angina pectoris following abrupt discontinuation of beta-blocker therapy. The last 2 complications may occur with or without preceding exacerbation of angina pectoris. Therefore, when discontinuation of oxprenolol is planned in patients with angina pectoris, Trasicor should be substituted for Slow-Trasicor and then the dosage should be gradually reduced over a period of about 2 weeks and the patient should be carefully observed. The same frequency of administration should be maintained. In situations of greater urgency, oxprenolol therapy should be discontinued in a stepwise manner and the patient observed closely. If angina markedly worsens or acute coronary insufficiency develops, it is recommended that treatment with oxprenolol be reinstituted promptly, at least temporarily.

Various skin rashes and conjunctival xerosis have been reported with beta-blockers, including oxprenolol. A severe syndrome (oculo-muco-cutaneous syndrome) whose signs include conjunctivitis sicca and psoriasiform rashes, otitis, and sclerosing serositis has occurred with the chronic use of β-adrenergic-blocking agent, practolol. This syndrome has not been observed with oxprenolol or any other such agent. However, physicians should be alert to the possibility of such reactions and should discontinue treatment in the event that they occur.

Severe sinus bradycardia due to unopposed vagal activity may occur with the use of oxprenolol; in such cases, dosage should be reduced or withdrawn and the use of atropine and isoproterenol considered.

In patients with thyrotoxicosis, oxprenolol may give a false impression of improvement by masking the clinical signs of continuing hyperthyroidism or its complications. Therefore, abrupt withdrawal of oxprenolol may be followed by an exacerbation of the symptoms of hyperthyroidism, including thyroid storm. Oxprenolol does not alter thyroid function tests.

Precautions: In patients prone to nonallergic bronchospasm (e.g., chronic bronchitis, emphysema), oxprenolol should be administered with caution since it may block the bronchodilation produced by endogenous and exogenous catecholamine stimulation of beta$_2$-receptors.

Oxprenolol should be administered with caution to patients subject to spontaneous hypoglycemia or to diabetic patients (especially those with labile diabetes) who are receiving insulin or oral hypoglycemic agents. β-adrenergic blockers may mask the premonitory signs and symptoms of acute hypoglycemia. As β-blockade also reduces the release of insulin in response to hyperglycemia, it may be necessary to adjust the dosage of antidiabetic drugs.

Appropriate laboratory tests should be performed at regular intervals during long-term treatment.

There may be increased difficulty in treating an allergic type reaction in patients on β-blockers. In these patients, the reaction may be more severe due to pharmacologic effects of the β-blockers and problems with fluid changes. Epinephrine should be administered with caution since it may not have its usual effects in the treatment of anaphylaxis. On the one hand, larger doses of epinephrine may be needed to overcome the bronchospasm, while on the other, these doses can be associated with excessive α-adrenergic stimulation with consequent hypertension, reflex bradycardia and heart block and possible potentiation of bronchospasm. Alternatives to the use of large doses of epinephrine include vigorous supportive care such as fluids and the use of β-agonists including parenteral salbutamol or isoproterenol to overcome bronchospasm and norepinephrine to overcome hypotension.

In Patients Undergoing Elective or Emergency Surgery: The management of patients being treated with β-blockers and undergoing elective or emergency surgery is controversial. Although β-adrenergic receptor blockade impairs the ability of the heart to respond to β-adrenergically mediated reflex stimuli, abrupt discontinuation of therapy with oxprenolol may be followed by severe complications (see Warnings). Some patients receiving β-adrenergic blocking agents have been subject to protracted severe hypotension during anesthesia. Difficulty in restarting and maintaining the heartbeat has also been reported.

For these reasons, in patients with angina undergoing elective surgery, Trasicor should be withdrawn gradually following the recommendation given under Abrupt Cessation of Therapy (see Warnings). According to available evidence, all clinical and physiological effects of β-blockade are no longer present 48 hours after cessation of medication.

In emergency surgery, since oxprenolol is a competitive inhibitor of β-adrenergic receptor agonists, its effects may be reversed if necessary, by sufficient doses of such agonists as isoproterenol or levarterenol. The anesthetic selected should be one exhibiting as little negative inotropic activity as possible (see Contraindications).

In patients with acute or chronic inflammatory diseases an increase in the plasma levels of oxprenolol has been observed.

Plasma levels may also increase in the presence of severe hepatic insufficiency associated with a reduced metabolic rate.

Impaired renal function generally leads to an increase in the blood levels of oxprenolol, but the area under the concentration-time curve remains within (although at the upper limit of) the range recorded in subjects with healthy kidneys. The apparent elimination half-life for unchanged oxprenolol in patients with renal failure is comparable to the corresponding half-life values determined in subjects with no renal disease. Hence, there is no need to readjust the dosage in the presence of impaired renal function.

In patients with pheochromocytoma, a β-blocker should only be given together with an α-blocker.

Occupational Hazards: β-blockers may adversely affect the patients reactions when driving or operating machinery.

Pregnancy: Oxprenolol crosses the placental barrier. It is not recommended that oxprenolol be given to pregnant women. The use of any drug in patients of childbearing potential requires that the anticipated benefit be weighed against possible hazards. β-blockers may possibly cause undesirable side effects (especially bradycardia) in the fetus and newborn infants.

Lactation: Oxprenolol passes into breast milk. If use of the drug is deemed essential the patient should stop nursing.

Children: Although there is limited experience with oxprenolol in children, it is not recommended for pediatric use.

After the active substance has diffused out of the insoluble core of the Slow-Trasicor tablet, the empty matrix is excreted in a softened form and may be found in the feces.

Drug Interactions: As the antihypertensive effect of oxprenolol is enhanced by concomitant treatment with other antihypertensive agents, dosage should be adjusted appropriately.

Calcium antagonists of the verapamil-type must not be administered i.v. to patients receiving β-blocker therapy because of the danger of hypotension, cardiac arrhythmias and cardiac arrest.

β-blockers may potentiate the negative-inotropic and negative-dromotropic effect of anti-arrhythmic agents such as quinidine and amiodarone.

Epinephrine or other substances displaying sympathomimetic activity (e.g., antitussives or nose and eye drops) may lead to hypertensive reactions under treatment with oxprenolol and other non-cardioselective β-blockers.

The hypertensive crisis which may follow the withdrawal of clonidine may be accentuated in the presence of β-blockade. It has been proposed that withdrawal of the β-blocker several days before the clonidine may reduce the danger of rebound effects.

The hypoglycemic effect of insulin or oral antidiabetic agents may be potentiated (see above).

Concurrent treatment with indomethacin may decrease the antihypertensive effect of β-blockers.

Since cimetidine increases the bioavailability of β-blockers which are mainly metabolized in the liver, the effect of oxprenolol may become potentiated during concomitant treatment with cimetidine.

When oxprenolol is used concomitantly with catecholamine-depleting drugs (such as reserpine or guanethidine) or MAO inhibitors, patients should be observed closely. The added β-adrenergic blocking action of this drug may produce an excessive reduction of sympathetic activity.

A deterioration in peripheral blood flow has been reported in predisposed patients receiving concomitant treatment with ergot alkaloids and β-blockers.

Attention should be paid to the cardiodepressant effect of inhalation anesthetics in patients receiving beta-blocker therapy (see above).

The central depressant effect of alcohol, analgesics, antihistamines, and psycho-active drugs (e.g., tricyclic antidepressants) may be potentiated.

β-blockers may diminish liver function and thus affect the metabolism of other drugs.

Adverse Effects: Cardiovascular: congestive heart failure (see Warnings), pulmonary edema, cardiac enlargement, secondary effects of decreased cardiac output which include: syncope, vertigo, lightheadedness and postural hypotension, severe bradycardia, lengthening of PR interval, second and third degree AV block, sinus arrest, palpitations, chest pains, peripheral vascular disorders (cold/tingling extremities) Raynaud's phenomenon, claudication, hot flushes.

Respiratory: shortness of breath, wheezing, bronchospasm, status asthmaticus.

CNS: headache, dizziness, anxiety, mental depression, nervousness, irritability, hallucinations, sleep disturbances including nightmares and insomnia, tinnitus, weakness, sedation, vivid dreams, vertigo, paresthesia and slurred speech.

Gastrointestinal: diarrhea, constipation, flatulence, heartburn, anorexia, nausea and vomiting, abdominal pain, dryness of mouth.

Allergic/Dermatological: (see Warnings), rash (psoriasiform and exanthematic), dry skin, pruritus, sweating.

Ophthalmological: keratoconjunctivitis, dry eyes, itching eyes, blurred vision.

Miscellaneous: impotence, decreased libido, nasal stuffiness, weight gain, exertional tiredness.

Clinical Laboratory: elevated transaminases, BUN, alkaline phosphatase and bilirubin have occurred in some patients. Thrombocytopenia and leukopenia, and hypoglycemia have also been reported rarely.

Overdose: Symptoms: The most common signs to be expected with overdosage of a β-adrenergic blocking agent are hypotension, bradycardia, congestive heart failure, bronchospasm, and hypoglycemia. Cardiogenic shock and cardiac arrest may develop. Impairment of consciousness and generalized convulsions may occur.

Treatment: If overdosage occurs, in all cases therapy with oxprenolol should be discontinued and the patient observed closely. In addition, if required, the following therapeutic measures are suggested:

Bradycardia and hypotension: Initially 1 to 2 mg atropine sulfate should be given i.v. If a satisfactory effect is not achieved a pressor agent such as norepinephrine may be administered after preceding treatment with atropine. Glucagon in a dose of 1 to 10 mg can also be administered.

Heart block: (second or third degree): isoproterenol or transvenous cardiac pacemaker.

Congestive heart failure: conventional therapy.

Bronchospasm: i.v. aminophylline or a β_2-agonist. (e.g., salbutamol, terbutaline).

Hypoglycemia: i.v. glucose.

Convulsions: i.v. diazepam.

It should be remembered that oxprenolol is a competitive antagonist of isoproterenol and hence large doses of isoproterenol can be expected to reverse many of the effects of excessive doses of oxprenolol. However, the complications of excess isoproterenol should not be overlooked.

Dosage: Oxprenolol is usually used in conjunction with other antihypertensive agents, particularly thiazide diuretics, but may be used alone (see Indications).

Dosage must always be adjusted according to the individual requirements of the patient, within the following guidelines:

Initial Dosage: Treatment should be initiated with Trasicor (regular formulation), 20 mg 3 times a day, followed by upward titration of the dose 3 times a day, with increases of 60 mg/day at 1 to 2 week intervals until adequate control of blood pressure is obtained.

Maintenance Dosage: Once the optimal dose has been established, the total daily dose of Trasicor (regular formulation) may be given on a b.i.d. schedule, although no comparison studies between the t.i.d. and b.i.d. regimen have been carried out. Alternatively, an equivalent single daily dose of Slow-Trasicor may be substituted, and should be taken in the morning. Slow-Trasicor tablets should be swallowed whole.

The usual effective dose range is 120 to 320 mg/day, and the daily dosage should not exceed 480 mg.

Supplied: 40 mg: Each white, round, biconvex, film-coated tablet, imprinted CIBA on one side and AI, separated by a score on the other, contains: oxprenolol HCl 40 mg. Nonmedicinal ingredients: calcium phosphate, cellulose compounds, magnesium stearate, polyvinylpyrrolidone, wheat starch, sucrose, talc and titanium dioxide. Energy: 2.8 kJ (0.67 kcal). Also contains gluten. Alcohol-, bisulfite-, lactose-, parabens-, sodium- and tartrazine-free. Bottles of 100.

80 mg: Each light yellow, round, biconvex, film coated tablet, imprinted "CG" on one side and CG separated by a score on the other, contains: oxprenolol 80 mg. Nonmedicinal ingredients: calcium phosphate, cellulose compounds, colloidal silicon dioxide, iron oxide yellow, magnesium stearate, maize starch, polysorbate, polyvinylpyrrolidone, sodium carboxymethyl starch, talc and titanium dioxide. Energy: 1.2 kJ (0.29 kcal). Sodium: <1 mmol (0.64 mg). Alcohol-, bisulfite-, gluten-, lactose-, parabens- and tartrazine-free. Bottles of 100.

Protect from heat (i.e. store below 30°C.)

(Shown in Product Recognition Section)

TRASYLOL® Ⓟ

Bayer

Aprotinin

Polypeptide Proteinase Inhibitor—Hemostatic Agent

Pharmacology: Aprotinin is a potent and effective proteinase inhibitor obtained by extraction from bovine lung tissue. It inhibits a wide variety of proteinases (estero-proteinases) including trypsin, chymotrypsin, cathepsin, plasmin and kallikrein from plasma, tissue and urine. Aprotinin is rapidly excreted from the body. In humans, a biphasic elimination pattern with an initial half-life of 0.7 hour and a terminal half-life of 7 hours is observed.

Hemorrhages which are caused by a primary or secondary hyperfibrinolysis, due to an increased activation of plasmin or plasmin activator, or by a lack of the natural inhibitors of these enzymes, can be reduced or arrested by aprotinin.

Indications: Hyperfibrinolysis: The treatment of patients suffering from conditions due to excessive fibrinolysis. These conditions occur in surgery, including open heart surgery, prostatic surgery and pathological obstetrical bleeding conditions, such as in abruptio placentae.

Contraindications: During the course of clinical investigations, as well as during its wide use for several years abroad, no contraindications other than hypersensitivity to aprotinin have emerged.

Aprotinin is contraindicated in individuals who have shown hypersensitivity to aprotinin.

Warnings: Aprotinin is a polypeptide and thus may act as an antigen. Although adverse reactions due to hypersensitivity have been observed infrequently, this possibility should always be kept in mind.

Hypersensitive reactions, when they occur, will generally be seen at the onset of treatment. In such instances, administration of aprotinin should be discontinued. Animal experiments have shown that aprotinin at very high concentrations has a histamine releasing effect. In patients with a history of hypersensitivity or in cases of known or suspected reexposure to aprotinin, the following prophylactic measures are strongly recommended: i.v. administration of an H_1-antagonist (e.g., diphenhydramine) and an H_2-antagonist (e.g., cimetidine) 15 minutes before aprotinin. Additionally, 1 mL (10 000 KIU) of aprotinin should be administered with an observation time of at least 10 minutes before the main dose of aprotinin is given. Even after the uneventful administration of the initial 1 mL dose, the therapeutic dose may cause an anaphylactic reaction. If this happens, the infusion of aprotinin should immediately be stopped, and the standard emergency treatment for anaphylaxis should be applied.

In open heart surgery, an i.v. test using 1 mL (10 000 KIU) of aprotinin given at a rate of 5 mL/min at least 10 minutes prior to the remainder of the dose may be helpful in detecting hypersensitivity in some cases. When aprotinin is used in hemorrhagic conditions in which a severe depletion of fibrinogen has occurred, fibrinogen may be given together with aprotinin.

An increase in renal failure and mortality has been suggested in a preliminary study of patients undergoing deep hypothermia and circulatory arrest preparatory to surgery of the aortic arch as compared to age matched historical controls. The strength of this association is uncertain because there are no data from randomized studies to confirm or deny these findings. Caution should be exercised and a careful risk/benefit assessment made before aprotinin is used in this setting. Specifically, adequate anticoagulation with heparin must be assured.

Pregnancy: No evidence of teratogenic or embryotoxic effects has been seen in animals. Experience in human pregnancy is limited and inadequate to assess safety. Use of aprotinin in the first 3 months of pregnancy should only occur after a careful risk/benefit assessment is made.

Lactation: No studies are available on the passage of aprotinin into the mother's milk. However, since aprotinin is not absorbed after oral administration, if the milk did contain any of the drug it would have no effect on the baby.

Precautions: Children: Experience with the use of aprotinin in hyperfibrinolytic hemorrhages in children is limited. In most cases, the dose used was approximately half of the recommended adult dose.

Drug Interactions: Aprotinin has a dose-dependent inhibitory effect on the action of thrombolytic agents (i.e., streptokinase, tPA and urokinase).

An in vitro method for determining the degree of anticoagulation in heparinized blood is confounded in the presence of aprotinin, when celite is used as the contact activator resulting in a much longer activated clotting time (ACT). No prolongation of the ACT is seen when kaolin is used as the contact activating agent.

Therefore, prior to open heart surgery (OHS), the standard loading dose of heparin should be given, and during OHS additional heparin should be administered either at fixed intervals or on the basis of heparin levels measured by a method that is not affected by aprotinin, such as protamine titration. Likewise, protamine reversal of heparin should not be based on Activated Clotting Time (ACT) values measured using the Hemochron System but should be determined by the amount of heparin administered. It is recommended to keep the ACT greater than 750 seconds during extracorporeal circulation in patients receiving aprotinin.

Adverse Effects: Aprotinin is well tolerated at the recommended dosages. However, allergic reactions such as flushing, tachycardia, itching, rash and urticaria have been reported, as well as dyspnea, sweating, palpitations and nausea. Administration should be stopped at the onset of such symptoms.

Anaphylactic or anaphylactoid reactions are possible when aprotinin is administered. In case of reexposure the incidence of allergic/anaphylactic reactions - without any prophylactic premedication - may reach the 5% level. Even when a second administration has been tolerated, subsequent aprotinin therapy may result in severe anaphylaxis. This risk is higher in patients receiving aprotinin several times.

In single cases, anaphylactoid reactions have been observed during first-time administration.

The symptoms of anaphylactic/anaphylactoid reactions range from skin eruptions, itching, dyspnea, nausea, drop in blood pressure, tachycardia or bradycardia and airway obstruction to severe hypotension and anaphylactic shock with circulatory failure; this may develop into the complete picture of life-threatening-shock reaction leading to death in severe cases.

If hypersensitivity reactions occur during injection or infusion, administration should be stopped immediately. Standard emergency treatment may be required, e.g., epinephrine, corticosteroids and volume infusion.

Transient increases in serum creatinine have been observed in clinical studies with no clinical relevance in most cases.

As with all repeated venipunctures, local thrombophlebitic reactions may occur after aprotinin infusions.

Overdose: Symptoms and Treatment: Although aprotinin has been used extensively in clinical medicine, no symptoms of overdosing have come to our knowledge.

Dosage: Owing to the slight risk of allergic reactions, a 1 mL (10 000 KIU) initial dose should always be administered at least 10 minutes prior to the remainder of the dose. After the uneventful administration of the initial 1 mL dose, the therapeutic dose may be given.

Aprotinin must be given only to patients in the supine position and must be given slowly (maximum 5 mL/minute) as an i.v. injection or a short infusion, due to the possibility of a hypotensive response.

Hemorrhage Due to Hyperfibrinolysis: Initial Dosage: 200 000 to 500 000 KIU of which 200 000 KIU should be given by i.v. injection (at a rate not to exceed 5 mL/min); the rest, if necessary, by slow infusion. Administration should be continued up to 1 000 000 KIU/day until the hemorrhage has been arrested. Before infusion, aprotinin may be diluted with 5% glucose or physiologic saline solution. The duration of treatment should not be longer than 5 days.

Clinical experience so far suggests that patients with decreased renal function do not require special dose adjustment.

Stability and Storage Recommendations: Aprotinin is stable when stored in sealed vials at room temperature. Store below 30°C. Avoid freezing. If a precipitate or particulate matter is present, or if the contents are cloudy, the drug should not be used. Once a vial has been opened, it should be used immediately.

Parenteral Products: Direct I.V. Injection: No dilution is required. Should be given by slow i.v. injection (maximum rate 5 mL/min). Once a vial is opened, it should be used immediately.

Intermittent I.V. Infusions: Aprotinin may be diluted with 5% glucose or physiologic saline solution. It should be administered by slow infusion (at a rate not to exceed 50 000 KIU/min). Diluted product should be used immediately.

Continuous i.v. infusions: Aprotinin may be diluted with 5% glucose or physiologic saline solution. It should be administered by slow infusion (at a rate not to exceed 50 000 KIU/min). Diluted product should be used immediately.

Aprotinin is compatible with glucose 20% solution, hydroxyethyl starch solution and Ringer's lactate solution.

Aprotinin has been shown to be physically incompatible with corticosteroids, heparin, nutrient solutions containing amino acids or fat emulsions, and tetracyclines.

Administration of aprotinin in mixed infusions (particularly with beta-lactam antibiotics), should be avoided.

Precautions: Although aprotinin has been found to prolong the Activated Clotting Time (ACT) as measured using the Hemochron system, it should not be considered a heparin-sparing agent. When aprotinin is administered during open heart surgery, the ACT measured using the Hemochron system should not be used to determine either the dose of heparin or the dose of protamine for heparin reversal.

Repeated withdrawals should not be made from the 50 mL vial.

Solubility: The concentrate is infinitely miscible with water and dilute salt or buffer solutions. It dissolves without precipitation in methanol (max 70%, v/v), ethanol (max 70%, v/v) and acetone (max 50%, v/v).

Supplied: Each mL of clear almost colorless aqueous, isotonic solution contains: aprotinin 10 000 KIU (Kallikrein Inhibitory Units). Nonmedicinal ingredients: sodium chloride and water for injection. pH of the concentrate is adjusted to 5 to 7 during manufacture. Preservative-free. Single dose vials of 50, 100 and 200 mL. Store at room temperature.

TRAVASOL®

Clintec

Amino Acids

I.V. Nutritive Supplement

Supplied: Travasol Amino Acid Injection Blend B and Blend C, is available in 3.5%, 5.0%, 5.5%, 7.5%, 8.5% and 10% concentrations with Electrolytes in glass containers as well as in Viaflex plastic containers.

Travasol Amino Acid Injection Blend B and Blend C, is available in 3.5%, 5.0%, 5.5%, 7.5%, 8.5% and 10% concentrations without Electrolytes in glass containers as well as in Viaflex plastic containers.

Travasol (cont'd)

Travasol Amino Acid Injection with Electrolytes and Dextrose Injection USP are also available in a closed transfer system Quick Mix Dual Chamber Viaflex plastic container in the following range of concentrations: See Table I.

Table I—Travasol

Travasol with Electrolytes and Dextrose Injection USP

Product Code	Travasol Amino Acid Injection with Electrolytes Lower Chamber (Vol/%)	Dextrose Injection USP Upper Chamber (Vol/%)
JB6761	500 mL 10%	500 mL 50%
JB6763	500 mL 10%	500 mL 40%
JB6767	500 mL 10%	500 mL 20%
JB6771	500 mL 10%	500 mL 33.3%
JB6751	500 mL 8.5%	500 mL 50%
JB6753	500 mL 8.5%	500 mL 40%
JB6757	500 mL 8.5%	500 mL 20%
JB6759	500 mL 8.5%	500 mL 10%
JB6741	500 mL 5.5%	500 mL 50%
JB6749	500 mL 5.5%	500 mL 10%
JB6731	500 mL 5%	500 mL 50%
JB6737	500 mL 5%	500 mL 20%

Travasol Amino Acid Injection without Electrolytes and Dextrose Injection USP are available in a closed transfer system Quick Mix Dual Chamber Viaflex plastic container in the following range of concentrations: See Table II.

Table II—Travasol

Travasol without Electrolytes and Dextrose Injection USP

Product Code	Travasol Amino Acid Injection without Electrolytes Lower Chamber (Vol/%)	Dextrose Injection USP Upper Chamber (Vol/%)
JB6760	500 mL 10%	500 mL 50%
JB6762	500 mL 10%	500 mL 40%
JB6766	500 mL 10%	500 mL 20%
JB6770	500 mL 10%	500 mL 33.3%
JB6756	500 mL 8.5%	500 mL 20%
JB6750	500 mL 8.5%	500 mL 50%
JB6752	500 mL 8.5%	500 mL 40%
JB6758	500 mL 8.5%	500 mL 10%
JB6768	500 mL 10%	500 mL 10%
JB6736	500 mL 5%	500 mL 20%

Storage Conditions: The dosage forms packaged in dual-chamber Viaflex plastic containers should be stored at temperatures between 15 and 25°C protected from light and kept from freezing. The prepared amino acids/dextrose admixture should be administered immediately. If not, it should be stored under refrigeration (2 to 8°C) and used within 24 hours.

TRAVELTABS
Stanley

Dimenhydrinate
Antiemetic

Supplied: Each peach-colored, double-bisected tablet contains: dimenhydrinate 50 mg. Nonmedicinal ingredients: D&C Red No. 27, dextrose, FD&C Red No. 40, FD&C Yellow No. 6, magnesium stearate, microcrystalline cellulose and sodium starch glycolate. Bottles of 25 and 100.

TRAVEL TABS
WestCan

Dimenhydrinate
Antiemetic

Supplied: Each tablet contains: dimenhydrinate USP 50 mg. Blister packs of 25 and bottles of 100.

For information on drug interactions and their management, see the CLIN-INFO SECTION.

TRAZOREL ℞
ICN

Trazodone HCl
Antidepressant

Supplied: 50 mg: Each orange, biconvex, scored tablet, embossed ICN T21, contains: trazodone HCl 50 mg, USP. Nonmedicinal ingredients: cellulose, croscarmellose sodium, lactose, magnesium stearate and povidone. Bottles of 100, 250 and 500.

100 mg: Each white, biconvex, scored tablet, embossed ICN T22, contains: trazodone HCl 100 mg, USP. Nonmedicinal ingredients: cellulose, croscarmellose sodium, lactose, magnesium stearate and povidone. Bottles of 100 and 500.

150 mg: Each orange, biconvex, scored tablet, embossed ICN T23, contains: trazodone HCl 150 mg, USP. Nonmedicinal ingredients: cellulose, croscarmellose sodium, lactose, magnesium stearate and povidone. Bottles of 100 and 500.

TRENTAL® ℞
Hoechst Marion Roussel

Pentoxifylline
Vasoactive Agent

Pharmacology: Pentoxifylline is a xanthine derivative. It belongs to a group of vasoactive drugs which improve peripheral blood flow and thus enhance peripheral tissue oxygenation. The mechanism by which pentoxifylline achieves this effect has not been determined, but it is likely that the following factors are involved: pentoxifylline, as other xanthine derivatives, relaxes certain smooth muscles including those of the peripheral vessels, thus causing vasodilation or preventing spasm. This action, however, may have a limited role in patients with chronic obstructive arterial disease when peripheral vessels are already maximally dilated.

Pentoxifylline improves flexibility of red blood cells. This increase in the flexibility of red blood cells probably contributes to the improvement of the ability of blood to flow through peripheral vessels (hemorheologic action). This property was seen during in vitro and in vivo experiments. The correlation of this property and the clinical improvement of patients with peripheral vascular diseases has not been determined.

Pentoxifylline promotes platelet deaggregation.

Improvement of red blood cell flexibility and platelet deaggregation contribute to the decrease in blood viscosity.

Pentoxifylline is almost completely absorbed after oral administration. The Trental 400 mg sustained release tablet showed an initial peak plasma pentoxifylline concentration 2 to 3 hours post-administration. The drug is extensively metabolized. Biotransformation products are almost exclusively eliminated by the kidneys.

Food intake before the administration of pentoxifylline delayed the absorption but did not decrease it.

Indications: For the symptomatic treatment of patients with chronic occlusive peripheral vascular disorders of the extremities. In such patients pentoxifylline may give relief of signs and symptoms of impaired blood flow, such as intermittent claudication or trophic ulcers.

Contraindications: In patients with acute myocardial infarction, patients with severe coronary artery disease when, in the physician's judgement, myocardial stimulation might prove harmful, patients with hemorrhage, patients who have previously exhibited intolerance to pentoxifylline or other xanthines such as caffeine, theophylline and theobromine, patients with peptic ulcers or recent history thereof.

Warnings: Since pentoxifylline is extensively metabolized in the liver and eliminated through the kidneys, the use of this drug is not recommended in patients with marked impairment of kidney or liver function. Patients with less severe impairment of liver and patients with impaired renal function (creatinine clearance below 30 mL/min) should be closely monitored during drug therapy and they may require lower doses.

The administration of pentoxifylline has been associated with bleeding and/or prolonged prothrombin time (see Precautions, Drug Interactions). The risk of bleeding may be increased by combined treatment with anticoagulant agents. Therefore, in patients on anticoagulant therapy, pentoxifylline should be used with caution and only when in the physician's judgment the potential benefit outweighs the risk.

Children: The use of pentoxifylline in patients below the age of 18 years is not recommended as safety and effectiveness have not been established in this age group.

Precautions: Low, labile blood pressure: Caution should be exercised when administering pentoxifylline to patients with low, labile blood pressure. In such patients any dose increase should be done gradually.

Geriatrics: Pentoxifylline should be used with caution in elderly patients as peak plasma levels of pentoxifylline and its metabolites are moderately higher in this age group. Elderly patients had a slight increase in the incidence of some adverse effects. Careful dose adjustment is therefore recommended.

Pregnancy: Reproduction studies have been performed in rats, mice and rabbits at doses up to 23, 2 and 11 times the maximum recommended daily human dose and have revealed no evidence of impaired fertility or harm to the fetus due to pentoxifylline. The drug has been shown to cross the blood-placenta barrier in mice. There is no adequate experience in pregnant women. Therefore, pentoxifylline is not recommended for women who are, or may become, pregnant unless the expected benefits for the mother outweigh the potential risk to the fetus.

Lactation: Pentoxifylline and its major metabolites are excreted in human milk, following a 400 mg single oral dose of Trental. The patient should be advised to discontinue nursing or to discontinue taking the drug depending on the importance of the drug to the mother.

Drug Interactions: Antihypertensive Agents: Pentoxifylline may potentiate the action of antihypertensive agents. Patients receiving these agents require blood pressure monitoring and possibly a dose reduction of the antihypertensive agents.

Sympathomimetics: Combined use with other xanthines or with sympathomimetics may cause excessive CNS stimulation.

Theophylline: Although causality has not been established, concurrent use of pentoxifylline with theophylline has resulted in elevated theophylline plasma levels, which may enhance the possibility of adverse effects.

Erythromycin: No data are available on the possible interaction of pentoxifylline and erythromycin. However concurrent administration of erythromycin and theophylline has resulted in significant elevation of serum theophylline levels with toxic reactions.

Hypoglycemic agents: In patients treated with hypoglycemic agents, a moderate adjustment in the dose of these agents may be required when pentoxifylline is prescribed.

Anticoagulants: There have been reports of bleeding and/or prolonged prothrombin time in patients treated with pentoxifylline with and without anticoagulants or platelet aggregation inhibitors. Patients on warfarin should have more frequent monitoring of prothrombin time, while patients with other risk factors complicated by hemorrhage (e.g., recent surgery) should have periodic examinations for signs of bleeding, including hematocrit and hemoglobin.

Antacids: In patients with digestive side effects, antacids may be administered with pentoxifylline. In a comparative bioavailability study, no interference with absorption of pentoxifylline by antacids was observed.

Cimetidine: During concurrent use of cimetidine and pentoxifylline, cimetidine has been shown to significantly increase the steady-state plasma concentration of pentoxifylline, which may enhance the possibility of adverse effects.

Adverse Effects: The most frequent adverse effect reported with pentoxifylline is nausea (14%). Individual signs/symptoms not marked with an asterisk occurred at an incidence below 1% (* = incidence between 1 and 3%).

Cardiovascular: flushing*, chest pain, arrhythmia, hypertension, dyspnea, edema, hypotension, angina, tachycardia.

CNS: dizziness/lightheadedness (9.4%), headache (4.9%), drowsiness/sleepiness, tremor, agitation, anxiety, confusion, insomnia, restlessness.

Gastrointestinal: nausea (14%), vomiting (3.4%), abdominal discomfort*, bloating*, diarrhea*, dyspepsia*, abdominal burning, abdominal pain, anorexia, flatus, constipation, hemorrhage, heartburn, salivation, dry mouth/throat, hepatitis, jaundice, increased liver enzymes.

Hemic and lymphatic: decreased serum fibrinogen, pancytopenia, purpura, thrombocytopenia, leukopenia, anemia, aplastic anemia.

Hypersensitivity: pruritus, rash, urticaria, angioedema.

Organs of Special Sense: blurred vision, scotoma, lacrimation, epistaxis.

Miscellaneous: malaise*, muscle aches/spasms, weight change, backache, bad taste in mouth, leg cramps, fever, weakness, sweating.

Overdose: Has been reported in children and adults.

Symptoms: Symptoms appear to be dose related and usually occurred 4 to 5 hours after ingestion and lasted about 12 hours. The highest amount ingested was 80 mg/kg;

flushing, hypotension, convulsions, somnolence, loss of consciousness, fever, and agitation occurred. All patients recovered.

Treatment: In addition to symptomatic treatment and gastric lavage, special attention must be given to supporting respiration, maintaining systemic blood pressure, and controlling convulsions with i.v. diazepam. Activated charcoal has been used to adsorb pentoxifylline in patients who have overdosed.

Dosage: The recommended starting dosage of pentoxifylline is 400 mg twice daily after meals. The usual maintenance dose is 400 mg 2 or 3 times daily. A maximum dose of 400 mg 3 times daily should not be exceeded.

It may take up to 2 months to obtain full results.

Tablets must be swallowed whole.

Supplied: Each pink, oblong, film-coated, sustained release tablet contains: pentoxifylline 400 mg. Nonmedicinal ingredients: FD&C red No. 3, hydroxyethyl cellulose, hydroxypropyl methylcellulose, magnesium stearate, polyethylene glycol, povidone, talc, titanium dioxide and water. Unit pack cartons of 6 × 10 blister-packed tablets. Plastic bottles of 500. Store between 15 and 30°C not beyond the date indicated on the container.

(Shown in Product Recognition Section)

TRIACOMB® ℞

Technilab

Triamcinolone Acetonide—Nystatin—Neomycin Sulfate—Gramicidin

Corticosteroid—Antifungal—Antibacterial

Supplied: Each g of cream contains: triamcinolone acetonide USP 1 mg, nystatin USP 100 000 units, neomycin base (in sulfate) USP 2.5 mg and gramicidin USP 0.25 mg. Nonmedicinal ingredients: aluminum hydroxide, ceteareth-20, cetearyl alcohol, glyceryl monostearate, glyceryl stearate, methylparaben, petrolatum, polysorbate 60, propylene glycol, propylene glycol monostearate, propylparaben, purified water, sorbitol and titanium dioxide. Jars of 450 g. Tubes of 15, 30 and 60 g. Keep tube tightly closed. Keep from freezing and store away from heat and direct light.

TRIADERM ℞

Taro

Triamcinolone Acetonide

Topical Corticosteroid

Supplied: Cream: Each g contains: triamcinolone acetonide USP 0.1% (regular) or 0.025% (mild) in an aqueous vanishing cream base containing cetyl alcohol, propylene glycol, glyceryl monostearate, isopropyl palmitate, cetyl esters wax, polysorbates and purified water. Paraben-free. Tubes of 15 g and jars of 500 g.

Ointment: Each g contains: triamcinolone acetonide USP 0.1% (regular) or 0.025% (mild) in a petrolatum base with fractionated coconut oil and methylparaben and propylparaben as preservatives. Tubes of 15 g and jars of 454 g.

TRIAMCINOLONE ℞

General Monograph, CPhA

see CORTICOSTEROIDS: EYE EAR NOSE
see CORTICOSTEROIDS: INHALED
see CORTICOSTEROIDS: SYSTEMIC
see CORTICOSTEROIDS: TOPICAL

TRIAMCINOLONE DIACETATE INJECTABLE SUSPENSION, USP ℞

Taro

Corticosteroid

Supplied: Each mL of injectable suspension contains: triamcinolone diacetate 40 mg. Nonmedicinal ingredients: benzyl alcohol, polyethylene glycol, polysorbate, sodium chloride and water for injection. Multiple dose vials of 5 mL. **Shake well.** Store at room temperature. Do not permit to freeze.

New Product 1998

TRIAMINIC® Cold and Allergy Syrup
TRIAMINIC® Tablets

Novartis Consumer Health

Phenylpropanolamine HCl—Chlorpheniramine Maleate

Phenylpropanolamine HCl—Pheniramine Maleate—Pyrilamine Maleate

Antihistamine—Decongestant

Indications: To relieve nasal and sinus congestion in colds, allergies, sinusitis, rhinitis and postnasal drip.

Contraindications: Hypersensitivity to antihistamines, sympathomimetics, or patients receiving MAO inhibitors.

Precautions: Patients with hypertension, heart or lung diseases, glaucoma, diabetes mellitus, hyperthyroidism, or prostatic enlargement, should use only as directed by a physician.

Elderly patients should use only as directed by a physician. Occupational Hazards: May cause drowsiness. Patients should be cautioned not to operate vehicles or hazardous machinery until their response to the drug has been determined.

Pregnancy and *Lactation:* Pregnant women and nursing mothers should use only as directed by a physician.

Drug Interactions: The depressant effect of antihistamines is additive to those of other drugs affecting the CNS. During antihistaminic therapy, patients should avoid alcoholic beverages or hypnotics, sedatives, psychotherapeutic agents or other drugs with CNS depressant effects. Use with caution in patients receiving methyldopa or beta adrenergic blockers.

Adverse Effects: Drowsiness, blurred vision, cardiac palpitations, flushing, dizziness, nervousness, fatigue or gastrointestinal upsets may occur occasionally.

Dosage: Syrup: Adults: 10 mL. Children: 6 to 12 years: 5 mL; 2 to 6 years: 2.5 mL. Do not administer to children under 2, unless directed by a physician. Repeat every 4 hours as required. Do not exceed 6 doses/day.

Tablets: Adults: 1 tablet, swallowed whole in the morning, mid afternoon, and in the evening.

Supplied: Syrup: Each 5 mL contains: phenylpropanolamine HCl 12.5 mg and chlorpheniramine maleate 2.0 mg. Nonmedicinal ingredients: amaranth, benzoic acid, FD&C Yellow No. 6, flavors, sorbitol, sucrose and water. Energy: 62.59 kJ (14.96 kcal)/5 mL. Alcohol- and tartrazine-free. Bottles of 100 mL.

Tablets: Each yellow timed release tablet contains: phenylpropanolamine HCl 50 mg, pheniramine maleate 25 mg and pyrilamine maleate 25 mg. Nonmedicinal ingredients: lactose, sucrose, cornstarch, acacia, D&C Yellow No. 10, FD&C Yellow No. 6, sodium alginate, magnesium stearate, stearic acid, shellac and talc. Sodium: <1 mmol (16.33 mg). Tartrazine-free. Half of each ingredient is released promptly and the balance in 3 to 4 hours. Boxes of 12.

TRIAMINIC® COLD & FEVER

Novartis Consumer Health

Acetaminophen—Dextromethorphan HBr—Pseudoephedrine HCl

Analgesic—Antipyretic—Antitussive—Decongestant

Supplied: Each 5 mL of grape-flavored, purple syrup contains: acetaminophen 160 mg, dextromethorphan HBr 7.5 mg and pseudoephedrine HCl 15 mg. Nonmedicinal ingredients: benzoic acid, D&C Red No. 33, edetate disodium, FD&C Blue No. 1, FD&C Red No. 40, flavors, glycerin, polyethylene glycol, propylene glycol, sodium phosphate, sucrose, tartaric acid and water. Bottles of 100 mL.

Do you need quick access to a list of alcohol-free or low alcohol content products? Refer to the CLIN-INFO SECTION.

TRIAMINIC® DM DAYTIME

Novartis Consumer Health

Dextromethorphan HBr—Guaifenesin—Phenylpropanolamine HCl

Antitussive—Expectorant—Decongestant

Indications: For temporary relief of coughs and nasal congestion due to the common cold in children and infants.

Contraindications: Hypersensitivity to any of the components, patients receiving MAO inhibitors.

Precautions: Use with caution in patients with hypertension, coronary artery disease, diabetes mellitus, glaucoma, lung diseases, prostatic enlargement and hyperthyroidism. See also guaifenesin monograph.

Adverse Effects: Occasional dizziness, blurred vision, cardiac palpitations, flushing, nervousness, gastrointestinal upsets, nausea may occur.

Dosage: Children: 6 to 12 years: 10 mL; 2 to 6 years: 5 mL; under 2 years: consult a physician. Administer 3 or 4 times daily. Do not exceed 4 doses in 24 hours.

Supplied: Each 5 mL of syrup contains: dextromethorphan HBr 7.5 mg, phenylpropanolamine HCl 8.75 mg, guaifenesin 37.5 mg. Nonmedicinal ingredients: amaranth, benzoic acid, FD&C Blue No. 1, ethanol (5.5% v/v), flavor, maltol, sorbitol, sucrose, tartaric acid and water. Energy: 70.7 kJ (16.9 kcal)/5 mL. Tartrazine-free. Bottles of 100 mL.

TRIAMINIC® DM EXPECTORANT

Novartis Consumer Health

Dextromethorphan HBr—Guaifenesin—Chlorpheniramine Maleate—Pseudoephedrine HCl

Antihistaminic—Antitussive—Decongestant—Expectorant

Indications: Temporary relief of coughs and nasal congestion due to the common cold.

Contraindications, Precautions and Adverse Effects: See Triaminic Expectorant.

A persistent cough may be a sign of a serious condition. If symptoms persist for more than a week, or are accompanied by high fever or tend to recur, consult a physician.

Do not take this product for persistent or chronic cough or if you have chronic lung disease or shortness of breath, unless directed by a physician.

Dosage: Administer 4 times daily. Do not exceed 4 doses in 24 hours. Adults: 10 mL; children 6 to 12 years: 5 mL; children 2 to 6 years: 2.5 mL. Do not administer to children under 2 years unless directed by a physician.

Supplied: Each 5 mL of green, mint-flavored liquid contains: dextromethorphan HBr 15 mg, pseudoephedrine HCl 30 mg, chlorpheniramine maleate 2 mg and guaifenesin 100 mg. Nonmedicinal ingredients: benzoic acid, citric acid, D&C Yellow No. 10, ethanol (7.1% v/v), ethyl maltol, ethyl vanillin, FD&C Blue No. 1, flavor, menthol, sodium citrate, sodium cyclamate, sorbitol, sucrose and water. Tartrazine-free. Bottles of 100 and 200 mL.

TRIAMINIC® DM LONG LASTING FOR CHILDREN

Novartis Consumer Health

Dextromethorphan Polistirex

Antitussive

Pharmacology: Dextromethorphan is a centrally acting antitussive which is comparable to codeine on a mg basis for cough suppression but lacking analgesic or addictive properties.

Antitussive efficacy in adults is seen after 10 to 20 mg doses every 4 hours or 30 mg every 6 to 8 hours. With the usual therapeutic dosage, no effect has been noted on respiratory, cardiovascular or gastrointestinal function. Respiratory depression has been noted following ingestion of very large doses.

Dextromethorphan polistirex is a controlled-release preparation. Clinical bioavailability studies have shown that a single

Triaminic DM Long Lasting for Children (cont'd)

60 mg dose provides plasma concentrations of dextromethorphan similar to those obtained with two 30 mg doses of dextromethorphan HBr given at 6 hour intervals. After repeated doses at steady state, equivalent plasma concentrations are maintained when dextromethorphan polistirex is taken every 12 hours as compared to dextromethorphan HBr every 6 hours.

Indications: For the temporary relief of cough due to minor throat and bronchial irritation as may occur with the common cold or with inhaled irritants.

Warnings: As with all antitussives, do not use this product if cough persists for more than 1 week, tends to recur, or is accompanied by excessive secretions or high fever; if patient is an asthmatic; or during pregnancy, unless advised by a physician.

Keep out of reach of children.

Do not give this product to children under 2 years of age except under the advice and supervision of a physician.

Drug Interactions: Two fatalities have been reported following ingestion of dextromethorphan in patients treated with phenelzine. Do not use in patients receiving MAO inhibitors.

Pregnancy and *Lactation:* Do not administer to women who are pregnant or nursing unless, in the opinion of a physician, the potential benefits of the drug outweigh the possible risks.

Precautions: A persistent cough may be a sign of a serious condition. The patient should be advised to consult a physician if cough persists for more than 1 week or if cough tends to recur or is accompanied by high fever, rash or persistent headache.

Dependence Liability: Substitution studies in morphine addicts indicate that dextromethorphan is devoid of dependence liability. Intoxication and bizarre behavior have occurred after ingestion of 300 to 1 500 mg several times daily.

Adverse Effects: Rarely drowsiness, dizziness, headache, nausea or vomiting may occur.

Overdose: Symptoms and Treatment: Respiratory depression has been noted with very large doses. Ataxia and hyperactivity have also been reported following ingestion of 360 mg of dextromethorphan HBr in a 22-month old child. Administration of 5 μg/kg naloxone HCl i.v. produced rapid resolution of ataxia.

Dosage: Children 6 to 12 years: 5 mL every 12 hours; do not exceed 10 mL in 24 hours. 2 to 5 years: 2.5 mL every 12 hours; do not exceed 5 mL in 24 hours. Under 2 years: Use only under the advice of a physician. **Shake well before use.**

Supplied: Each 5 mL of controlled-release suspension contains: dextromethorphan polistirex equivalent to dextromethorphan HBr 30 mg. Nonmedicinal ingredients: citric acid, corn syrup, EDTA, ethylcellulose, FD&C yellow No. 6, gum tragacanth, methylparaben, orange flavor, polyethylene glycol, polysorbate 80, propylene glycol, propylparaben, sugar, vegetable oil, water and xanthan gum. Energy: 27.6 kJ (6.6 kcal)/5 mL. Sodium: <1 mmol (6.5 mg)/5 mL. Alcohol-, lactose-, gluten- and tartrazine-free. Bottles of 100 and 200 mL (child resistant cap and seal on bottle cap). Store at room temperature.

Reviewed 1998

TRIAMINIC® DM NIGHTTIME

Novartis Consumer Health

Dextromethorphan HBr—Chlorpheniramine Maleate—Pseudoephedrine HCl

Antitussive—Antihistamine—Decongestant

Indications: Temporary relief of coughs and nasal congestion due to the common cold and enabling children to sleep.

Contraindications, Precautions and Adverse Effects: See Triaminic Expectorant.

Dosage: Administer 3 to 4 times daily. Adults: 20 mL. Children: 6 to 12 years: 10 mL; 2 to 6 years: 5 mL. For children under 2 years, consult a physician. Do not exceed 4 doses in 24 hours.

Supplied: Each 5 mL of purple, grape-flavored syrup contains: dextromethorphan HBr 7.5 mg, chlorpheniramine maleate 1 mg and pseudoephedrine HCl 15 mg. Nonmedicinal ingredients: benzoic acid, citric acid, D&C Red No. 33, FD&C Blue No. 1, FD&C Red No. 40, flavors, propylene glycol, sodium phosphate, sorbitol, sucrose and water. Alcohol- and tartrazine-free. Bottles of 100 and 200 mL.

TRIAMINIC® EXPECTORANT

Novartis Consumer Health

Guaifenesin—Chlorpheniramine Maleate—Pseudoephedrine HCl

Decongestant—Expectorant—Antihistaminic

Indications: Temporary relief of coughs and nasal congestion due to the common cold.

Contraindications: Hypersensitivity to any of the components, marked hypertension, patients receiving MAO inhibitors.

Precautions: Patients with hypertension, heart or lung diseases, peripheral vascular disease, glaucoma, diabetes mellitus, hyperthyroidism, or prostatic enlargement, should use only as directed by a physician.

Elderly patients should use only as directed by a physician. Occupational Hazards: May cause drowsiness. Caution patients not to operate vehicles or hazardous machinery until their response to the drug has been determined.

Pregnancy and *Lactation:* Pregnant women and nursing mothers should use only as directed by a physician.

Drug Interactions: The depressant effect of antihistamines is additive to those of other drugs affecting the CNS. During antihistaminic therapy, patients should avoid alcoholic beverages or hypnotics, sedatives, psychotherapeutic agents or other drugs with CNS depressant effects. Use with caution in patients receiving methyldopa or beta adrenergic blockers.

See also guaifenesin monograph.

Adverse Effects: Drowsiness, blurred vision, cardiac palpitation, flushing, dizziness, nervousness, fatigue or gastrointestinal upsets may occur occasionally.

Dosage: Adults: 10 mL. Children 6 to 12 years: 5 mL; 2 to 6 years: 2.5 mL. Do not administer to children under 2 years unless directed by a physician. Administer 4 times daily. Do not exceed 4 doses in 24 hours.

Supplied: Each 5 mL of citrus-flavored, yellow liquid contains: pseudoephedrine HCl 30 mg, chlorpheniramine maleate 2 mg and guaifenesin 100 mg. Nonmedicinal ingredients: benzoic acid, citric acid, D&C Yellow No. 10, ethanol (7.8% v/v), ethyl maltol, flavor, glycerin, sodium chloride, sodium citrate, sodium cyclamate, sodium hydroxide, sorbitol, sucrose and water. Energy: ≤64.31 kJ (15.37 kcal)/5mL. Sodium: <1 mmol (20.2 mg). Tartrazine-free. Bottles of 100 mL.

TRIAMINIC® EXPECTORANT DH Ⓝ

Novartis Consumer Health

Guaifenesin—Hydrocodone Bitartrate—Pheniramine Maleate—Phenylpropanolamine HCl—Pyrilamine Maleate

Antihistaminic—Antitussive—Decongestant—Expectorant

Indications: To facilitate expectoration and control cough associated with inflamed mucosa and tenacious sputum which does not respond to products of lesser potency.

Contraindications, Precautions and Adverse Effects: See Triaminic Expectorant monograph. Hydrocodone is a narcotic and may be habit-forming.

Before prescribing medication to suppress or modify cough, it is important to ascertain that the underlying cause of the cough is identified, that modification of the cough does not increase the risk of clinical or physiologic complications, and that appropriate therapy for the primary disease is provided.

In young children the respiratory centre is especially susceptible to the depressant action of narcotic cough suppressants. Benefit to risk ratio should be carefully considered, especially in children with respiratory embarrassment, e.g., croup. Estimation of dosage relative to the child's age and weight is of great importance.

Pregnancy: Since hydrocodone crosses the placental barrier, its use in pregnancy is not recommended.

As hydrocodone may inhibit peristalsis, patients with chronic constipation should be given Triaminic Expectorant DH only after weighing the potential therapeutic benefit against the hazards involved.

Dosage: Adults: 10 mL. Children 6 to 12 years: 5 mL; 2 to 6 years: 2.5 mL. Dosage is administered every 4 hours. **Triaminic Expectorant DH is not recommended for children under 2 years of age.**

Supplied: Each 5 mL of mint green elixir contains: hydrocodone bitartrate 1.67 mg, phenylpropanolamine HCl 12.5 mg, pheniramine maleate 6.25 mg, pyrilamine maleate 6.25 mg, guaifenesin 100 mg. Nonmedicinal ingredients: benzoic acid, D&C Yellow No. 10, ethanol (5% v/v), ethyl vanillin, FD&C Blue No. 1, FD&C Yellow No. 6, flavor, glycerin, menthol, sorbitol, sucrose and water. Energy: 59.79 kJ (14.29 kcal)/5 mL. Tartrazine-free. Bottles of 500 mL.

TRIAMINIC® ORAL PEDIATRIC DROPS

Novartis Consumer Health

Pseudoephedrine HCl

Decongestant

Supplied: Each 0.8 mL (dropperful) of grape-flavored, dye-free and alcohol-free syrup contains: pseudoephedrine HCl 7.5 mg. Nonmedicinal ingredients: benzoic acid, disodium edetate, ethyl maltol, flavors, glycerin, sodium hydroxide, sorbitol, sucrose and water. Bottles of 40 mL.

TRIAMINICIN®

Novartis Consumer Health

Acetaminophen—Caffeine—Pheniramine Maleate—Phenylpropanolamine HCl—Pyrilamine Maleate

Decongestant—Analgesic—Antihistamine—Antipyretic

Indications: For temporary relief of nasal congestion, rhinorrhea, postnasal drip, pain, headache and fever associated with the common cold.

Contraindications, Precautions and Adverse Effects: See Triaminic and acetaminophen.

Dosage: Adults, 1 tablet 3 times a day, or as prescribed.

Supplied: Each yellow, capsule-shaped tablet contains: phenylpropanolamine HCl 25 mg, pyrilamine maleate 12.5 mg, pheniramine maleate 12.5 mg, acetaminophen 325 mg, caffeine 30 mg. Nonmedicinal ingredients: calcium sulfate, calcium stearate, cellulose, D&C Yellow No. 6, D&C Yellow No. 10 and starch. Tartrazine-free. Cartons of 12.

TRIAMINICOL® DM

Novartis Consumer Health

Dextromethorphan HBr—Chlorpheniramine Maleate—Pseudoephedrine HCl

Antihistaminic—Antitussive—Decongestant

Indications: A non-narcotic antitussive, decongestant, anti-allergic formulation for relief of cough and nasal congestion due to the common cold.

Contraindications: Hypersensitivity to any of the components, marked hypertension, patients receiving MAO inhibitors.

Precautions: Patients with hypertension, heart or lung diseases, glaucoma, diabetes mellitus, thyrotoxicosis, hyperthyroidism, or prostatic enlargement, should use only as directed by a physician.

Elderly patients should use only as directed by a physician. Occupational Hazards: May cause drowsiness. Patients should be cautioned not to operate vehicles or hazardous machinery until their response to the drug has been determined.

Pregnancy and *Lactation:* Pregnant women and nursing mothers should use only as directed by a physician.

Drug Interactions: The depressant effect of antihistamines is additive to those of other drugs affecting the CNS. During antihistaminic therapy, patients should avoid alcoholic beverages or hypnotics, sedatives, psychotherapeutic agents or other drugs with CNS depressant effects. Use with caution in patients receiving methyldopa or beta-adrenergic-blockers.

Adverse Effects: Drowsiness, blurred vision, cardiac palpitations, flushing, dizziness, nervousness, fatigue or gastrointestinal upsets may occur.

Dosage: Adults: 10 mL. Children: 6 to 12 years: 5 mL; 2 to 6 years: 2.5 mL. Children under 2 years, consult a physician. Administer 4 times daily. Do not exceed 4 doses in 24 hours.

Supplied: Each 5 mL of syrup contains: pseudoephedrine HCl 30 mg, chlorpheniramine maleate 2 mg and dextromethorphan

HBr 15 mg, in a cherry flavored, nonalcoholic vehicle. Nonmedicinal ingredients: benzoic acid, D&C Red No. 33, FD&C Red No. 40, ethyl maltol, flavors, glycerin, propylene glycol, sodium chloride, sodium citrate, sorbitol, sucrose and water. Tartrazine-free. Bottles of 100 and 200 mL.

TRIANAL ◈

Trianon

ASA—Caffeine—Butalbital

Analgesic—Sedative

Supplied: Capsules: Each hard gelatin, oblong capsule, blue opaque cap printed "TRIANAL" and purple insert part printed "△", contains: butalbital USP 50 mg, caffeine USP 40 mg and ASA USP 330 mg. Nonmedicinal ingredients: cellulose and stearic acid. Alcohol-, gluten-, lactose-, sulfite- and tartrazine-free. Bottles of 100 and 500.

Tablets: Each white compressed tablet embossed "TRIANAL" on one side and "△" on the other, contains: butalbital USP 50 mg, caffeine USP 40 mg and ASA USP 330 mg. Nonmedicinal ingredients: cellulose, croscarmellose sodium, sodium lauryl sulfate and stearic acid. Alcohol-, gluten-, lactose-, sulfite- and tartrazine-free. Bottles of 100 and 500.

TRIANAL C¼, C½ Ⓝ

Trianon

ASA—Caffeine—Codeine Phosphate—Butalbital

Analgesic—Sedative

Supplied: Trianal C¼: Each hard gelatin, oblong capsule, blue opaque cap printed "TRIANAL C¼" and white insert part printed "△", contains: butalbital USP 50 mg, caffeine USP 40 mg, ASA USP 330 mg and codeine phosphate USP 15 mg. Nonmedicinal ingredients: cellulose, croscarmellose sodium and stearic acid. Alcohol-, gluten-, lactose-, sulfite- and tartrazine-free. Bottles of 100 and 500.

Trianal C½: Each hard gelatin, oblong capsule, blue opaque cap printed "TRIANAL C½" and pale blue insert part printed "△", contains: butalbital USP 50 mg, caffeine USP 40 mg, ASA USP 330 mg and codeine phosphate USP 30 mg. Nonmedicinal ingredients: cellulose, starch and stearic acid. Alcohol-, gluten-, lactose-, sulfite- and tartrazine-free. Bottles of 100 and 500.

TRIATEC-8 Ⓝ
TRIATEC-8 STRONG Ⓝ
TRIATEC-30 Ⓝ

Trianon

Acetaminophen—Codeine Phosphate—Caffeine Citrate

Acetaminophen—Codeine Phosphate—Caffeine Citrate

Acetaminophen—Codeine Phosphate

Analgesic—Antipyretic—Antitussive

Supplied: Triatec-8: Each tablet contains: acetaminophen 325 mg, codeine phosphate 8 mg and caffeine citrate 30 mg. Nonmedicinal ingredients: cellulose, citric acid, croscarmellose sodium, magnesium stearate and stearic acid. Alcohol-, gluten-, lactose-, sulfite- and tartrazine-free. Bottles of 30, 100 and 200.

Triatec-8 Strong: Each tablet contains: acetaminophen 500 mg, codeine phosphate 8 mg and caffeine citrate 30 mg. Nonmedicinal ingredients: cellulose, citric acid, croscarmellose sodium, magnesium stearate and stearic acid. Alcohol-, gluten-, lactose-, sulfite- and tartrazine-free. Bottles of 50.

Triatec-30: Each tablet contains: acetaminophen 300 mg and codeine phosphate 30 mg. Nonmedicinal ingredients: cellulose, colloidal silicon dioxide FD&C yellow #6 aluminum lake, lactose, sodium starch glycolate, stearic acid and talc. Alcohol-, gluten-, sulfite- and tartrazine-free. Bottles of 100 and 500.

TRIAVIL® Ⓟ

MSD

Amitriptyline HCl—Perphenazine

Antidepressant—Neuroleptic

Pharmacology: Triavil exerts the actions of its components. Perphenazine is a potent tranquilizer and also a potent antiemetic. Perphenazine has a non-hypnotic depressant activity on the CNS and is capable of relieving anxiety, tension, psychomotor excitement and other psychotic symptoms. Perphenazine has also widespread effects which include central and peripheral adrenergic blocking effects, anticholinergic action and loss of inhibitory control of the basal ganglia, which may result in extrapyramidal symptoms.

In addition, perphenazine has endocrine, antihistaminic, antiserotonin, metabolic and other effects. Its central adrenergic blocking action is believed to result from interference with norepinephrine uptake at the nerve cell endings, and appears to act principally in the subcortical area.

Amitriptyline is an antidepressant with sedative properties. Its mechanism of action in man is not known. It is not a MAO inhibitor and it does not act primarily by stimulation of the CNS.

Amitriptyline inhibits the membrane pump mechanism responsible for uptake of norepinephrine and serotonin in adrenergic and serotonergic neurons. Pharmacologically this action may potentiate or prolong neuronal activity since reuptake of these biogenic amines is important physiologically in terminating transmitting activity. This interference with the re-uptake of norepinephrine and/or serotonin is believed by some to underlie the antidepressant activity of amitriptyline. It has also anticholinergic properties.

Indications: In patients with agitated depression. It is particularly indicated in patients with depression associated with marked psychomotor unrest.

It has also been found useful in some schizophrenic patients who have associated symptoms of depression.

Triavil has been used in depressed patients, suffering from marked agitation, anxiety and tension, who may respond to the combination of a phenothiazine with amitriptyline.

Contraindications: In depression of the CNS caused by drugs (barbiturates, alcohol, narcotics, analgesics, antihistamines); in the presence of evidence of bone marrow depression; and in patients known to be hypersensitive to phenothiazines or amitriptyline.

This drug is not recommended for use during the acute recovery phase following myocardial infarction, and in the presence of acute congestive heart failure.

Triavil should not be given concomitantly with guanethidine or similarly acting compounds, since amitriptyline, like other tricyclic antidepressants, is capable of blocking the antihypertensive effect of these compounds.

Monoamine oxidase (MAO) inhibitor drugs may potentiate other drug effects and such potentiation may even cause death. Accordingly, Triavil should not be given to patients who have been receiving an MAO inhibitor, for at least 2 weeks after stopping the MAO inhibitor. In such patients, it is recommended that therapy with Triavil be initiated cautiously with gradual increase in the dosage required to obtain a satisfactory response.

Warnings: Tricyclic antidepressant drugs, including amitriptyline, particularly when given in high doses, have been reported to produce arrhythmias, sinus tachycardia and prolongation of conduction time. A few instances of unexpected death have been reported in patients with cardiovascular disorders. Myocardial infarction and stroke have also been reported with drugs of this class. Therefore, these drugs should be used with caution in patients with a history of cardiovascular disease, such as myocardial infarction and congestive heart failure.

Because of the anticholinergic activity of amitriptyline, Triavil should be used with caution in patients with glaucoma and in those who may be expected to experience problems of urinary retention.

Occupational Hazards: The drug may impair alertness in some patients; operation of automobiles and other activities made hazardous by diminished alertness should be avoided.

Perphenazine can lower the convulsive threshold in susceptible individuals. It should be given with caution to patients with convulsive disorders. Dosage of the anticonvulsive agent may have to be increased.

Tardive Dyskinesia: Tardive dyskinesia, a syndrome consisting of potentially irreversible, involuntary dyskinetic movements may develop in patients treated with neuroleptic (antipsychotic) drugs. Although the prevalence of the syndrome appears to be highest among the elderly, especially elderly women, it is impossible to predict, at the inception of neuroleptic treatment, which patients are likely to develop the syndrome.

If signs and symptoms of tardive dyskinesia appear in a patient on Triavil, drug discontinuation should be considered, as the syndrome may remit, partially or completely. However, some patients may require treatment despite the presence of the syndrome.

Neuroleptic Malignant Syndrome: A potentially fatal syndrome complex, sometimes referred to as neuroleptic malignant syndrome (NMS), has been reported in association with antipsychotic drugs. Clinical manifestations of NMS are muscle rigidity, altered mental status, and evidence of autonomic instability (labile pulse and blood pressure, hyperpyrexia, diaphoresis and cardiac dysrhythmias).

If a patient manifests evidence of NMS, therapy with Triavil should be discontinued immediately. If a patient requires antipsychotic therapy after recovery from NMS, the potential reintroduction of Triavil should be carefully considered. The patient should be carefully monitored, since recurrences of NMS have been reported.

Precautions: General: The possibility of suicide in seriously depressed patients is inherent in the illness and may remain until significant remission occurs. Patients should be closely supervised during the early phase of therapy with Triavil in case they may require hospitalization or concomitant electroshock therapy in addition to therapy with Triavil.

As with any psychotherapeutic agent, patients should be cautioned by the physician against errors of judgment attributable to change in mood.

As with all phenothiazine compounds, perphenazine should not be used indiscriminantly. Caution should be observed in giving it to patients who have previously exhibited severe adverse reactions to other phenothiazines.

Some of the untoward actions of perphenazine tend to appear more frequently when high doses are used. However, as with other phenothiazine compounds, patients receiving perphenazine in any dosage should be kept under close supervision.

The antiemetic effect of perphenazine may obscure signs of toxicity due to overdosage of other drugs, or render more difficult the diagnosis of disorders such as brain tumors or intestinal obstruction.

A significant, not otherwise explained, rise in body temperature may suggest individual intolerance to perphenazine, in which case Triavil should be discontinued.

The tendency for antidepressant medication to provoke mania or hypomania in manic-depressive patients has been reported in the literature. The tranquilizing effect of Triavil has seemed to reduce the likelihood of this effect.

Poor Metabolizers of Debrisoquine/Sparteine: Like other tricyclic antidepressants, Triavil is metabolized by the specific hepatic cytochrome P450 isozyme (IID6), which is responsible for the metabolism of debrisoquine and sparteine. Poor metabolizers of debrisoquine/sparteine represent approximately 5 to 10% of the white North American population.

Following usual doses of tricyclic antidepressants, plasma concentrations may be higher than expected in these patients. Cautious dose titration is recommended if Triavil is to be administered to patients known to be poor metabolizers of debrisoquine/sparteine. Monitoring of drug plasma levels should be considered.

Drug Interactions: Phenothiazines may potentiate the action of CNS depressants (opiates, analgesics, antihistamines, barbiturates, alcohol) and atropine. In concurrent therapy with any of these, Triavil should be given in reduced dosage. Patients should be cautioned that the response to alcohol may be increased. Phenothiazines also may potentiate the action of heat and phosphorus insecticides.

If hypotension develops, epinephrine should not be employed, as its action is blocked and partially reversed by perphenazine.

Cimetidine is reported to reduce hepatic metabolism of certain tricyclic antidepressants.

When amitriptyline is given with anticholinergic agents or sympathomimetic drugs, including epinephrine combined with local anesthetics, close supervision and careful adjustment of dosage are required. Paralytic ileus may occur in patients taking tricyclic antidepressants in combination with anticholinergic-type drugs.

Delirium has been reported with concurrent administration of amitriptyline and disulfiram.

Caution is advised if patients receive large doses of ethchlorvynol concurrently. Transient delirium has been reported in patients who were treated with 1 g of ethchlorvynol and 75 to 100 mg of amitriptyline.

Triavil (cont'd)

Interactions Mediated through Cytochrome P450 Isozyme IID6: Like other tricyclic antidepressants, Triavil is metabolized by the hepatic cytochrome P450 isozyme, P450 IID6, which is responsible for the metabolism of debrisoquine and sparteine. Elevated levels of Triavil may result when the drug is co-administered with agents which compete for metabolism by P450 IID6 such as selective serotonin reuptake inhibitors (e.g. paroxetine, fluoxetine, sertraline, and fluvoxamine), phenothiazines (e.g. fluphenazine, thioridazine, perphenazine), and Type 1c antiarrhythmics (e.g. propafenone, flecainide). Agents (e.g. quinidine) which inhibit the isozyme may exert a similar effect. Dosage adjustments and monitoring of drug levels should be considered if Triavil is to be used in combination with these agents.

Children: Since a children's dosage has not been established, Triavil is not recommended for use in children.

Pregnancy: Triavil is not recommended for use in pregnant patients. Reproduction studies in rats have shown no fetal abnormalities; however, clinical experience and follow-up in pregnancy have been limited, and the possibility of adverse effects on fetal development must be considered.

Lactation: Amitriptyline is detectable in breast milk. Because of the potential for serious adverse reactions in infants from amitriptyline, a decision should be made whether to discontinue nursing or discontinue the drug.

Adverse Effects: Clinical evaluation of Triavil has not revealed any adverse reactions peculiar to the combination. The adverse reactions that occurred were limited to those that have been reported previously for perphenazine and amitriptyline.

Perphenazine: Behavioral: Oversedation, impaired psychomotor function, paradoxical agitation or excitement and aggravation of psychotic symptoms. Catatonic like states, lassitude, insomnia, bizarre dreams and toxic confusional states have also been described.

Neurologic: Extrapyramidal symptoms (opisthotonos, oculogyric crisis, hyperreflexia, dystonia, akathisia, dyskinesia, parkinsonism) have been reported. Their incidence and severity usually increase with an increase in dosage, but there is considerable individual variation in the tendency to develop such symptoms. Extrapyramidal symptoms can usually be controlled by the concomitant use of effective antiparkinsonian drugs, such as benztropine mesylate, and/or by reduction in dosage. In some instances, they may persist after discontinuation of the drug. Paresthesias, slowing of the EEG, disturbed body temperature, muscle weakness and convulsions have also been reported.

Autonomic: dry mouth, constipation, urinary frequency, blurred vision, and nasal congestion may occur.

Cardiovascular: Severe, acute hypotension has occurred with phenothiazines, and is of particular concern in patients with mitral insufficiency or pheochromocytoma. ECG abnormalities (quinidine-like effect) have also occurred with phenothiazine compounds. Changes in pulse rate and cutaneous vasodilation have been reported.

Toxic and Allergic: The phenothiazine compounds have produced blood dyscrasias (pancytopenia, thrombocytopenic purpura, leukopenia, agranulocytosis, eosinophilia); and liver damage (jaundice, biliary stasis). These have not been observed with perphenazine.

Skin disorders have occurred with phenothiazine compounds (photosensitivity, itching, contact dermatitis, erythema, urticaria, eczema, up to exfoliative dermatitis), as well as other allergic reactions (asthma, laryngeal edema, angioneurotic edema, anaphylactoid reactions).

Endocrine and Metabolic: disturbances in the menstrual cycle, lactation, swollen breasts, failure of ejaculation, reduced sexual urge in the male, increased sexual urge in the female, pseudopregnancy, infertility, and glycosuria, increased appetite, weight gain, hyperglycemia, altered cerebrospinal fluid proteins, peripheral edema.

Ophthalmologic: Centrally located stellate cataracts, corneal opacities, pigmentation of the conjunctiva, cornea or lens, lacrimation, and kerato-conjunctivitis have been reported following the use of phenothiazines. Pigmentary retinopathy has been reported with some phenothiazines with a piperidyl-ethyl side chain.

Miscellaneous: Other adverse reactions reported with various phenothiazine compounds include gastrointestinal effects such as nausea, vomiting and heartburn; potentiation of CNS depressants; headache; and cerebral edema.

Amitriptyline: Behavioral: Confusional states, disturbed concentration, disorientation, delusions, hallucinations, excitement, anxiety, restlessness, drowsiness, insomnia, nightmares.

Neurological: epileptiform seizures, coma, dizziness, tremors, numbness, tingling, paresthesias of the limbs, peripheral neuropathy, headache, ataxia, alteration in EEG patterns, extrapyramidal symptoms including abnormal involuntary movements and tardive dyskinesia, dysarthria, tinnitus, incoordination, and slurred speech.

Anticholinergic: urinary retention, dilatation of the urinary tract, constipation, paralytic ileus, especially in the elderly, hyperpyrexia, dry mouth, blurred vision, disturbance of accommodation, increase intraocular pressure, precipitation of latent glaucoma, aggravation of existing glaucoma, and mydriasis.

Cardiovascular: Quinidine-like effect and other non-specific ECG changes and changes in AV conduction, prolonged conduction time, asystole, hypotension, syncope, hypertension, palpitation, arrhythmias, heart block, ventricular tachycardia, fibrillation, myocardial infarction, stroke, unexpected death in patients with cardiovascular disorders.

Allergic: skin rash, urticaria, photosensitization, edema of face and tongue.

Hematologic: bone marrow depression including agranulocytosis, leukopenia, eosinophilia, purpura, thrombocytopenia.

Gastrointestinal: nausea, epigastric distress, vomiting, anorexia stomatitis, peculiar taste, diarrhea, parotid swelling, black tongue, rarely hepatitis (including altered liver function and jaundice).

Endocrine: testicular swelling and gynecomastia in the male, breast enlargement and galactorrhea in the female, increased or decreased libido, impotence, elevation or lowering of blood sugar levels, syndrome of inappropriate ADH (antidiuretic hormone) secretion.

Miscellaneous: Other adverse reactions that may occur include fainting, weakness, urinary frequency, alopecia and increased perspiration.

Overdose: Symptoms: Deliberate and accidental overdoses with tricyclic antidepressants have been associated with fatalities. Depression of the level of consciousness and marked anticholinergic reactions are the most common manifestations of tricyclic antidepressant overdose. Agitation, confusion, extrapyramidal signs, and hallucinations may also be present. Patients may progress rapidly from lethargy to coma and respiratory failure. Severe hypotension, ventricular arrhythmias, seizures, and respiratory arrest are the major causes of morbidity and mortality. Treatment is essentially supportive.

Treatment: If overdosage with a tricyclic antidepressant is suspected, the patient should be admitted to the Emergency Department without delay. Gastric lavage should be performed promptly. In the obtunded patient, a cuffed endotracheal tube should be used to secure the airway before beginning lavage. Because the anticholinergic effect of these drugs may delay gastric emptying, lavage is recommended for 12 hours or more after the overdose. Activated charcoal with a cathartic such as sorbitol should be given after lavage. Repeated doses of activated charcoal every 6 hours can be given if bowel peristalsis is not suppressed. Persistent unconsciousness (>48 hours) in the absence of hypoxic brain injury should prompt a search for a pill bezoar. The induction of emesis is not indicated as consciousness can be lost precipitously in tricyclic overdose, and aspiration is a frequent complication.

Maintenance of oxygenation and ventilation is crucial. As seizures, coma, and arrhythmias are exacerbated by acidosis, metabolic or respiratory alkalosis should be induced. Intubation should be undertaken early if there is a decreased level of consciousness. Mechanical ventilation can be used to induce an alkalosis. Arrhythmias and seizures may be abolished when the pH has been titrated to a level within a range of 7.45 to 7.55; however, a pH of 7.60 should not be exceeded. An infusion of sodium bicarbonate is often helpful in maintaining the alkalosis.

ICU admission with ECG monitoring is required for all patients with neurological abnormalities, anticholinergic manifestations of overdose, or symptoms of cardiac toxicity (incl. a QRS duration greater than 100 msec). If overdose is suspected, but these abnormalities are not present at admission to the Emergency Department, the patient should be observed for 6 hours. If no such abnormalities develop, the likelihood of significant toxicity is low. ECG monitoring should be continued for a period of 24 hours after full consciousness has been regained and cardiac conduction normalized. Late deaths due to arrhythmias have been reported, but in almost all cases the patients had persistent neurological changes or ECG abnormalities at the time of discharge.

Arrhythmias are usually responsive to aggressive alkalinization. Recalcitrant arrhythmias may respond to lidocaine or phenytoin, but these drugs should be given cautiously since they may induce bradyarrhythmias. Class IA anti-arrhythmics (quinidine, procainamide, disopyramide) are contraindicated. Beta-blockers may control tachyarrhythmias, but frequently induce sever hypotension, bradyarrhythmias or third degree atrioventricular block. Overdrive pacing has been used successfully to control tachyarrhythmias. Cardiac pacing is sometimes effective in severe bradycardia or asystole. Potassium replacements should be undertaken cautiously since hyperkalemia may induce or worsen arrhythmias. Because of its effect on cardiac conduction, digitalis should be used only with caution. If rapid digitalization is required for the treatment of congestive heart failure, special care should be exercised in using the drug. Close monitoring of cardiac function of not less than 5 days is advisable.

Hypotension is usually responsive to i.v. fluids. If hypotension persists after 2 to 3 L of normal saline in Ringer's lactate has been infused, right heart catheterization should be considered since the tricyclic antidepressants can cause direct myocardial depression. Inotropes such as dopamine and dobutamine should be used cautiously, since they may induce, or worsen, arrhythmias. Some authorities suggest norepinephrine as the inotrope of choice.

Seizures must be treated aggressively, as they compromise ventilation and induce acidosis. I.V. benzodiazepines are frequently effective, but the control of seizures is often transient. Early intubation should be undertaken and an alkalosis induced. To prevent the recurrence of convulsions, phenytoin (18 mg/kg at 25 to 50 mg/hr) should be given to all patients who experience seizures. As bradyarrhythmias and atrioventricular block have been reported with phenytoin administration, continuous ECG monitoring should be performed. Barbiturates may be used to control seizures, but they may produce profound hypotension. Refractory seizures are sometimes responsive to physostigmine. However, the use of physostigmine is controversial and should be reserved for life-threatening situations. Physostigmine is not innocuous and carries a risk of inducing seizures, bronchospasm, increased respiratory secretions, muscle weakness, bradycardia, and asystole. Physostigmine is the only drug of this class which may be used. If symptoms of cholinergic toxicity develop, physostigmine should be discontinued. Atropine should be available for the treatment of toxic cholinergic effects such as bronchoconstriction which may be induced by physostigmine.

Severe hyperthermia has been sporadically reported in association with tricyclic antidepressant overdose. Aggressive treatment with cooling blankets and ice packs is recommended in the event of hyperthermia.

As tricyclic antidepressants exhibit high protein binding and rapid tissue fixation, hemodialysis, peritoneal dialysis, exchange transfusions, and forced diuresis have not proved to be effective in the treatment of overdosage with these drugs.

Dosage: In prescribing Triavil the recommended indications, management considerations, dosage schedules and attention to tolerance and response that are normal practice in using each one of the combined drugs, perphenazine and amitriptyline, should be borne in mind at all times.

Initial Dosage: In ambulatory depressed patients with anxiety and/or agitation of such degree as to warrant combined therapy rather than amitriptyline HCl alone, 1 tablet 3 or 4 times a day as an initial dosage, depending on the severity of the agitation and anxiety.

The dosage should be individualized according to the need and response of the patient. The total daily dosage should not exceed 10 tablets. As a dosage for children has not been established, Triavil is not recommended for use in children.

Maintenance Dosage: Depending on the condition being treated, the onset of therapeutic response may vary from a few days to a few weeks or even longer. The sedative effect of Triavil is more rapidly apparent, while the antidepressant effect is usually delayed. After a satisfactory response is noted, dosage should be reduced to the smallest amount necessary to obtain relief from the symptoms for which Triavil is being administered.

A useful maintenance dosage is 1 tablet 2 to 4 times/day. In some patients, maintenance dosage is required for many months.

Supplied: Each film-coated, capsule shaped, salmon pink tablet, contains: perphenazine 3 mg and amitriptyline HCl 15 mg. Nonmedicinal ingredients: calcium phosphate dibasic, cornstarch, hydroxypropyl cellulose, hydroxypropyl methylcellulose, lactose, magnesium stearate, powdered cellulose, red iron oxide, talc and titanium dioxide. Gluten- and tartrazine-free. Bottles of 100. Keep container tightly closed. Protect from light.

(Shown in Product Recognition Section)

TRIAZOLAM ℞
General Monograph, CPhA
see BENZODIAZEPINES

TRI-CYCLEN® ℞
Janssen-Ortho
Norgestimate—Ethinyl Estradiol
Oral Contraceptive

Pharmacology: The primary mechanism of action of Tri-Cyclen is an inhibition of ovulation. Additionally, other effects caused by the treatment (for example, alteration of the endometrium and the thickening of the cervical mucus) appear to interfere with implantation and conception.

Indications: Treatment of moderate acne vulgaris in females who have no known contraindications to oral contraceptive therapy. Conception control.

Contraindications: History of/or actual thrombophlebitis or thromboembolic disorders. History of/or actual cerebrovascular disorders. History of/or actual myocardial infarction or coronary arterial disease. Active liver disease or history of/or actual benign or malignant liver tumors. Known or suspected carcinoma of the breast. Known or suspected estrogen-dependent neoplasia. Undiagnosed abnormal vaginal bleeding. Any ocular lesion arising from ophthalmic vascular disease, such as partial or complete loss of vision or defect in visual fields. When *pregnancy* is suspected or diagnosed.

Warnings: Predisposing Factors for Coronary Artery Diseases: Cigarette smoking increases the risk of serious cardiovascular side effects and mortality. Birth control pills increase this risk, especially with increasing age. Convincing data are available to support an upper age limit of 35 years for oral contraceptive use in women who smoke.

Other women who are independently at high risk for cardiovascular disease include those with diabetes, hypertension, abnormal lipid profile, or a family history of these. Whether oral contraceptives accentuate this risk is unclear.

In low-risk, nonsmoking women of any age, the benefits of oral contraceptive use outweigh the possible cardiovascular risks associated with low dose formulations. Consequently, oral contraceptives may be prescribed for these women up to the age of menopause.

> Cigarette smoking increases the risk of serious adverse effects on the heart and blood vessels. This risk increases with age and becomes significant in oral contraceptive users over 35 years of age. Women should be counselled not to smoke.

Discontinue medication at the earliest manifestation of the following:

A. Thromboembolic and cardiovascular disorders such as: thrombophlebitis, pulmonary embolism, cerebrovascular disorders, myocardial ischemia, mesenteric thrombosis and retinal thrombosis.

B. Conditions that predispose to venous stasis and to vascular thrombosis, e.g., immobilization after accidents or confinement to bed during long-term illness. Other nonhormonal methods of contraception should be used until regular activities are resumed. For use of oral contraceptives when surgery is contemplated, see Precautions.

C. Visual defects, partial or complete.

D. Papilledema, or ophthalmic vascular lesions.

E. Severe headache of unknown etiology or worsening of pre-existing migraine headache.

Precautions: Physical Examination and Follow-up: Before oral contraceptives are used, a thorough history and physical examination should be performed, including a blood pressure determination. Breasts, liver, extremities and pelvic organs should be examined. A Papanicolaou smear should be taken if the patient has been sexually active.

The first follow-up visit should be done 3 months after oral contraceptives are prescribed. Thereafter, examinations should be performed at least once a year, or more frequently if indicated. At each annual visit, examination should include those procedures that were done at the initial visit as outlined above or per recommendations of the Canadian Workshop on Screening for Cancer of the Cervix. Their suggestion was that, for women who had 2 consecutive negative Pap smears, screening could be continued every 3 years up to the age of 69.

> *Pregnancy:* Oral contraceptives should not be taken by pregnant women. However, if conception accidentally occurs while taking the pill, there is no conclusive evidence that the estrogen and progestin contained in the oral contraceptive will damage the developing child.
>
> *Lactation:* In breastfeeding women, the use of oral contraceptives results in the hormonal components being excreted in breast milk and may reduce its quantity and quality. If the use of oral contraceptives is initiated after the establishment of lactation, there does not appear to be any effect on the quantity and quality of the milk. There is no evidence that low dose oral contraceptives are harmful to the nursing infant.

Hepatic Function: Patients who have had jaundice including a history of cholestatic jaundice during pregnancy should be given oral contraceptives with great care and under close observation.

The development of severe generalized pruritus or icterus requires that the medication be withdrawn until the problem is resolved.

If the patient develops jaundice that proves to be cholestatic in type, the use of oral contraceptives should not be resumed. In patients taking oral contraceptives, changes in the composition of the bile may occur and an increased incidence of gallstones has been reported. Hepatic nodules (adenoma and focal nodular hyperplasia) have been reported, particularly in long-term users of oral contraceptives. Although these lesions are extremely rare they have caused fatal intra-abdominal hemorrhage and should be considered in women with an abdominal mass, acute abdominal pain or evidence of intra-abdominal bleeding.

Hypertension: Patients with essential hypertension whose blood pressure is well controlled may be given oral contraceptives but only under close supervision. If a significant elevation of blood pressure in previously normotensive or hypertensive subjects occurs at any time during the administration of the drug, cessation of medication is necessary.

Migraine and Headache: The onset or exacerbation of migraine or the development of headache of a new pattern that is recurrent, persistent or severe requires discontinuation of oral contraceptives and evaluation of the cause.

Diabetes: Current low dose oral contraceptives exert minimal impact on glucose metabolism. Diabetic patients, or those with a family history of diabetes, should be observed closely to detect worsening of carbohydrate metabolism. Patients predisposed to diabetes who can be kept under close supervision may be given oral contraceptives. Young diabetic patients whose disease is of recent origin, well-controlled and not associated with hypertension or other signs of vascular disease such as ocular fundal changes should be monitored more frequently while using oral contraceptives.

Ocular Disease: Patients who are pregnant or are taking oral contraceptives may experience corneal edema that may cause visual disturbances and changes in tolerance to contact lenses, especially of the rigid type. Soft contact lenses usually do not cause disturbances. If visual changes or alterations in tolerance to contact lenses occur, temporary or permanent cessation of wear may be advised.

Breasts: Increasing age and a strong family history are the most significant risk factors for the development of breast cancer. Other established risk factors include obesity, nulliparity and late age at first full-term pregnancy. The identified groups of women that may be at increased risk of developing breast cancer before menopause are long-term users of oral contraceptives (more than 8 years) and starters at early age. In a few women, the use of oral contraceptives may accelerate the growth of an existing but undiagnosed breast cancer. Since any potential increased risk related to oral contraceptive use is small, there is no reason to change prescribing habits at present.

Women receiving oral contraceptives should be instructed in self-examination of their breasts. Their physicians should be notified whenever any masses are detected. A yearly clinical breast examination is also recommended because, if a

Table I—Tri-Cyclen

Drugs Which May Decrease the Efficacy of Oral Contraceptives

Class of Compound	Drug	Proposed Mechanism	Suggested Management
Anticonvulsants	Carbamazepine Ethosuximide Phenobarbital Phenytoin Primidone	Induction of hepatic microsomal enzymes: Rapid metabolism of estrogen and increased binding of progestin and ethinyl estradiol to SHBG.	Use higher dose OCs (50 μg ethinyl estradiol), another drug or another method.
Antibiotics	Ampicillin Cotrimoxazole Penicillin	Enterohepatic circulation disturbance, intestinal hurry.	For short course, use additional method or use another drug. For long course, use another method.
	Rifampin	Increased metabolism of progestins. Suspected acceleration of estrogen metabolism.	Use another method.
	Chloramphenicol Metronidazole Neomycin Nitrofurantoin Sulfonamides Tetracyclines	Induction of hepatic microsomal enzymes. Also disturbance of enterohepatic circulation.	For short course, use additional method or use another drug. For long course, use another method.
	Troleandomycin	May retard metabolism of OCs, increasing the risk of cholestatic jaundice.	
Antifungal	Griseofulvin	Stimulation of hepatic metabolism of contraceptive steroids may occur.	Use another method.
Cholesterol Lowering agents	Clofibrate	Reduces elevated serum triglycerides and cholesterol; this reduces OC efficacy.	Use another method.
Sedatives and Hypnotics	Benzodiazepines Barbiturates Chloral hydrate Glutethimide Meprobamate	Induction of hepatic microsomal enzymes.	For short course, use additional method or another drug. For long course, use another method or higher dose OCs.
Antacids		Decreased intestinal absorption of progestins.	Dose 2 hours apart.
Other Drugs	Phenylbutazone Antihistamines Analgesics Antimigraine preparations Vitamin E	Reduced OC efficacy has been reported. Remains to be confirmed.	

Tri-Cyclen (cont'd)

breast cancer should develop, drugs that contain estrogen may cause a rapid progression.

Vaginal Bleeding: Persistent irregular vaginal bleeding requires assessment to exclude underlying pathology.

Fibroids: Patients with fibroids (leiomyomata) should be carefully observed. Sudden enlargement, pain or tenderness require discontinuation of the use of oral contraceptives.

Emotional Disorders: Patients with a history of emotional disturbances, especially the depressive type, may be more prone to have a recurrence of depression while taking oral contraceptives. In cases of a serious recurrence, a trial of an alternate method of contraception should be made which may help to clarify the possible relationship. Women with premenstrual syndrome (PMS) may have a varied response to oral contraceptives, ranging from symptomatic improvement to worsening of the condition.

Laboratory Tests: Results of laboratory tests should be interpreted in the light that the patient is on oral contraceptives. The following laboratory tests are modified.

Liver Function Tests: Bromsulphthalein Retention Test (BSP), moderate increase; AST and GGT, minor increase; akaline phosphatase, variable increase; serum bilirubin, increased, particularly in conditions predisposing to or associated with hyperbilirubinemia.

Coagulation Tests: Factors II, VII, IX, X, XII and XIII, increased; Factor VIII, mild increase; platelet aggregation and adhesiveness, mild increase in response to common aggregating agents; fibrinogen, increased; plasminogen, mild increase; antithrombin III, mild decrease; prothrombin time, increased.

Thyroid Function Tests: Protein-bound Iodine (PBI), increased; Total Serum Thyroxine (T_4), increased; Thyroid Stimulating Hormone (TSH), unchanged.

Adrenocortical Function Tests: plasma cortisol, increased.

Miscellaneous Tests: serum folate, occasionally decreased; glucose tolerance test, variable increase with return to normal after 6 to 12 months; insulin response, mild to moderate increase; c-peptide response, mild to moderate increase.

Tissue Specimens: Pathologists should be advised of oral contraceptive therapy when specimens obtained from surgical procedures and Pap smears are submitted for examination.

Return to Fertility: After discontinuing oral contraceptive therapy, the patient should delay pregnancy until at least 1 normal spontaneous cycle has occurred in order to date the pregnancy. An alternative contraceptive method should be used during this time.

Amenorrhea: Women having a history of oligomenorrhea, secondary amenorrhea or irregular cycles may remain anovulatory or become amenorrheic following discontinuation of estrogen-progestin combination therapy. Amenorrhea, especially if associated with breast secretion, that continues for 6 months or more after withdrawal warrants a careful assessment of hypothalamic-pituitary function.

Thromboembolic Complications—Post-surgery: There is an increased risk of thromboembolic complications in oral contraceptive users after major surgery. If feasible, oral contraceptives should be discontinued and an alternative method substituted at least 1 month prior to **major** elective surgery. Oral contraceptives should not be resumed until the first menstrual period after hospital discharge following surgery.

Drug Interactions: The concurrent administration of oral contraceptives with other drugs may result in an altered response to either agent (see Table I (on previous page) and Table II). Reduced effectiveness of the oral contraceptive, should it occur, is more likely with the low-dose formulations. It is important to ascertain all drugs that a patient is taking, both prescription and nonprescription, before oral contraceptives are prescribed.

Non-contraceptive Benefits of Oral Contraceptives: Several health advantages other than contraception have been reported.

1. Combination oral contraceptives reduce the incidence of cancer of the endometrium and ovaries.
2. Oral contraceptives reduce the likelihood of developing benign breast disease and, as a result, decrease the incidence of breast biopsies.
3. Oral contraceptives reduce the likelihood of development of functional ovarian cysts.
4. Pill users have less menstrual blood loss and have more regular cycles, thereby reducing the chance of developing iron-deficiency anemia.
5. The use of oral contraceptives may decrease the severity of dysmenorrhea and premenstrual syndrome, and may improve acne vulgaris, hirsutism and other androgen-mediated disorders. Tri-Cyclen tablets are also used to treat moderate acne in females who are able to take oral contraceptives.
6. Oral contraceptives decrease the incidence of acute pelvic inflammatory disease and, thereby reduce as well the incidence of ectopic pregnancy.
7. Oral contraceptives have potential beneficial effects on endometriosis.

Table II—Tri-Cyclen

Modification of Other Drug Action by Oral Contraceptives

Class of Compound	Drug	Modification of Other Drug Action	Suggested Management
Alcohol		Possible increased levels of ethanol or acetaldehyde.	Use with caution.
Alpha-II Adrenoreceptor Agents	Clonidine	Sedation effect increased.	Use with caution.
Anticoagulants	All	OCs increase clotting factors, decrease efficacy. However, OCs may potentiate action in some patients.	Use another method.
Anticonvulsants	All	Fluid retention may increase risk of seizures.	Use another method.
Antidiabetic Drugs	Oral hypoglycemics and insulin	OCs may impair glucose tolerance and increase blood glucose.	Use low dose estrogen and progestin OC or another method. Monitor blood glucose.
Antihypertensive Agents	Guanethidine and methyldopa	Estrogen component causes sodium retention, progestin has no effect.	Use low dose estrogen OC or use another method.
	Beta-blockers	Increased drug effect (decreased metabolism).	Adjust dose of drug if necessary. Monitor cardiovascular status.
Antipyretics	Acetaminophen	Increased metabolism and renal clearance.	Dose of drug may have to be increased.
	Antipyridine	Impaired metabolism.	Decrease dose of drug.
	ASA	Effects of ASA may be decreased by the short-term use of OCs.	Patients on chronic ASA therapy may require an increase in ASA dosage.
Aminocaproic Acid		Theoretically, a hypercoagulable state may occur because OCs augment clotting factors.	Avoid concomitant use.
Betamimetic Agents	Isoproterenol	Estrogen causes decreased response to these drugs.	Adjust dose of drug as necessary. Discontinuing OCs can result in excessive drug activity.
Caffeine		The actions of caffeine may be enhanced as OCs may impair the hepatic metabolism of caffeine.	Use with caution.
Cholesterol Lowering Agents	Clofibrate	Their action may be antagonized by OCs. OCs may also increase metabolism of clofibrate.	May need to increase dose of clofibrate.
Corticosteroids	Prednisone	Markedly increased serum levels.	Possible need for decrease in dose.
Cyclosporine		May lead to an increase in cyclosporine levels and hepatotoxicity.	Monitor hepatic function. The cyclosporine dose may have to be decreased.
Folic Acid		OCs have been reported to impair folate metabolism.	May need to increase dietary intake, or supplement.
Meperedine		Possible increased analgesia and CNS depression due to decreased metabolism of meperidine.	Use combination with caution.
Phenothiazine Tranquilizers	All phenothiazines, reserpine and similar drugs	Estrogen potentiates the hyperprolactinemia effect of these drugs.	Use other drugs or lower dose OCs. If galactorrhea or hyperprolactinemia occurs, use other method.
Sedatives and Hypnotics	Chlordiazepoxide Lorazepam Oxazepam Diazepam	Increased effect (increased metabolism).	Use with caution.
Theophylline	All	Decreased oxidation, leading to possible toxicity.	Use with caution. Monitor theophylline levels.
Tricyclic Antidepressants	Clomipramine (possibly others)	Increased side effects; i.e., depression.	Use with caution.
Vitamin B_{12}		OCs have been reported to reduce serum levels of Vitamin B_{12}.	May need to increase dietary intake, or supplement.

> Oral contraceptives **do not protect** against sexually transmitted diseases (STDs) including HIV/AIDS. For protection against STDs, it is advisable to use latex condoms **in combination with** oral contraceptives.

Adverse Effects: An increased risk of the following serious adverse reactions has been associated with the use of oral contraceptives: thrombophlebitis, pulmonary embolism, mesenteric thrombosis, neuro-ocular lesions, e.g., retinal thrombosis, myocardial infarction, cerebral thrombosis, cerebral hemorrhage, hypertension, benign hepatic tumors, gallbladder disease.

The following adverse reactions also have been reported in patients receiving oral contraceptives: Nausea and vomiting, usually the most common adverse reaction, occurs in approximately 10% or less of patients during the first cycle. Other reactions, as a general rule, are seen less frequently or only occasionally, as follows: gastrointestinal symptoms (such as abdominal cramps and bloating), breakthrough bleeding, spotting, change in menstrual flow, dysmenorrhea, amenorrhea during and after treatment, temporary infertility after discontinuance of treatment, edema, chloasma or melasma which may persist, breast changes (tenderness, enlargement and secretion), change in weight (increase or decrease), endocervical hyperplasias, possible diminution in lactation when given immediately postpartum, cholestatic jaundice, migraine, increase in size of uterine leiomyomata, rash (allergic), depression, reduced tolerance to carbohydrates, vaginal candidiasis, premenstrual-like syndrome, intolerance to contact lenses, change in corneal curvature (steepening), cataracts, optic neuritis, retinal thrombosis, changes in libido, chorea, changes in appetite, cystitis-like syndrome, rhinitis, headache, nervousness, dizziness, hirsutism, loss of scalp hair, erythema multiforme, erythema nodosum, hemorrhagic eruption, vaginitis, porphyria, impaired renal function, Raynaud's phenomenon, auditory disturbances, hemolytic uremic syndrome, pancreatitis.

Overdose: Symptoms and Treatment: In case of overdose or accidental ingestion by children, the physician should observe the patient closely although generally no treatment is required. Gastric lavage may be utilized if considered necessary.

Dosage: Information for the Patient on How to Take the Birth Control Pill:

1. **Read these directions:**
   - before you start taking your pills, and
   - any time you are not sure what to do.
2. **Look at your pill pack** to see if it has 21 or 28 pills:
   - 21-Pill Pack: 21 active pills (with hormones) taken daily for 3 weeks, and then take no pills for 1 week

     or
   - 28-Pill Pack: 21 active pills (with hormones) taken daily for 3 weeks, and then 7 "reminder" pills (no hormones) taken daily for 1 week.

   Also check the pill pack for instructions on (1) where to start and (2) directions to take pills (see package insert for illustrations).
3. You may wish to use a second method of birth control (e.g., latex condoms and spermicidal foam or gel) for the first 7 days of the first cycle of pill use. This will provide a back-up in case pills are forgotten while you are getting used to taking them.
4. **When receiving any medical treatment, be sure to tell your doctor that you are using birth control pills.**
5. **Many women have spotting or light bleeding or may feel sick to their stomach during the first 3 months on the pill.** If you do feel sick, do not stop taking the pill. The problem will usually go away. If it does not go away, check with your doctor or clinic.
6. **Missing pills also can cause some spotting or light bleeding,** even if you make up the missed pills. You also could feel a little sick to your stomach on the days you take 2 pills to make up for missed pills.
7. **If you miss pills at any time, you could get pregnant. The greatest risks for pregnancy are:**
   - when you start a pack late, and
   - when you miss pills at the beginning or at the very end of the pack.
8. **Always be sure you have ready:**
   - **another kind of birth control** (such as latex condoms and spermicidal foam or gel) to use as a back-up in case you miss pills, and
   - **an extra, full pack of pills.**
9. **If you have vomiting or diarrhea, or if you take some medicines,** such as antibiotics, your pills may not work as well. Use a back-up method, such as latex condoms and spermicidal foam or gel, until you can check with your doctor or clinic.
10. **If you forget more than 1 pill 2 months in a row,** talk to your doctor or clinic about how to make pill-taking easier or about using another method of birth control.
11. **If your questions are not answered here, call your doctor or clinic.**

When to Start the First Pack of Pills: Be sure to read these instructions:

- before you start taking your pills, and
- any time you are not sure what to do.

Decide with your doctor or clinic what is the best day for you to start taking your first pack of pills. Your pills may be either a 21-day or a 28-day type.

Directions for 21-Day and 28-Day Pill Packs:

1. **The first day of your menstrual period (bleeding) is Day 1 of your cycle.** The pills may be started up to Day 6 of your cycle. Your starting day will be chosen in discussion with your doctor. You will **always** begin taking your pill on this day of the week. Your doctor may advise you to start taking the pills on Day 1, on Day 5, or on the first Sunday after your period begins. If your period starts on Sunday, start that same day.
2. **If you are using a: 21-Day Pill Pack:** With this type of birth control pill, you are on pills for 21 days and off pills for 7 days. You must not be off the pills for more than 7 days in a row.

   Take 1 pill at approximately the same time every day for 21 days. **Then do not take a pill for 7 days.** Start a new pack on the 8th day. You will probably have a period during the 7 days off the pill. (This bleeding may be lighter and shorter than your usual period.)

Table III—Tri-Cyclen

What To Do if you Miss Pills

Sunday Start	Other Than Sunday Start
Miss 1 pill	**Miss 1 pill**
Take it as soon as you remember, and take the next pill at the usual time. This means that you might take 2 pills in one day.	Take it as soon as you remember, and take the next pill at the usual time. This means that you might take 2 pills in one day.
Miss 2 pills in a row	**Miss 2 pills in a row**
First 2 Weeks: 1. Take 2 pills the day you remember and 2 pills the next day. 2. Then take 1 pill a day until you finish the pack. 3. Use a back-up method of birth control if you have sex in the 7 days after you miss the pills.	**First 2 Weeks:** 1. Take 2 pills the day you remember and 2 pills the next day. 2. Then take 1 pill a day until you finish the pack. 3. Use a back-up method of birth control if you have sex in the 7 days after you miss the pills.
Third Week: 1. Keep taking 1 pill a day until Sunday. 2. On Sunday, safely discard the rest of the pack and start a new pack that day. 3. Use a back-up method of birth control if you have sex in the 7 days after you miss the pills. 4. You may not have a period this month. **If you miss 2 periods in a row, call your doctor or clinic.**	**Third Week:** 1. Safely dispose of the rest of the pill pack and start a new pack that same day. 2. Use a back-up method of birth control if you have sex in the 7 days after you miss the pills. 3. You may not have a period this month. **If you miss 2 periods in a row, call your doctor or clinic.**
Miss 3 or more pills in a row	**Miss 3 or more pills in a row**
Anytime in the Cycle: 1. Keep taking 1 pill a day until Sunday. 2. On Sunday, safely discard the rest of the pack and start a new pack that day. 3. Use a back-up method of birth control if you have sex in the 7 days after you miss the pills. 4. You may not have a period this month. **If you miss 2 periods in a row, call your doctor or clinic.**	**Anytime in the Cycle:** 1. Safely dispose of the rest of the pill pack and start a new pack that same day. 2. Use a back-up method of birth control if you have sex in the 7 days after you miss the pills. 3. You may not have a period this month. **If you miss 2 periods in a row, call your doctor or clinic.**

28-Day Pill Pack: With this type of birth control pill, you take 21 pills that contain hormones and seven pills that contain no hormones.

Take 1 pill at approximately the same time every day for 28 days. Begin a new pack the next day, **not missing any days on the pills.** Your period should occur during the last 7 days of using that pill pack.

Instructions for Using Your Dialpak Tablet Dispenser: Follow these instructions carefully: 21-Day Regimen: Always complete white and light blue tablets before blue tablets (see package insert for illustrations): Your starting day will be chosen in discussion with your doctor. You should **always** begin taking your tablets on this day of the week. To set the package to the day you and your physician selected, insert a coin into the middle slot and turn the inner wheel counterclockwise until that day appears in the window. The example shown is for a **Sunday** start. Your first white tablet is immediately to the right of the blue tablets and below the "V" notch as shown. Ensure that the tab marked "Lift Out" is set over this white tablet. Break off the tab and begin tablet taking. To take your second and all subsequent tablets, turn the clear outer cover clockwise to the next available tablet. Take 1 tablet every day for 21 days, first completing all 7 white tablets, then all 7 light blue tablets, then all 7 blue tablets. After you have taken all of your tablets, wait 7 days and begin your next package on your chosen starting day, whether you have finished menstruating or not. Always remember to set the starting day of each new package to the day chosen by you and your doctor.

Your first pill of each package is always under the "V" notch.

28-Day Regimen: Always complete white, light blue and blue tablets before green tablets (see package insert for illustrations): Your starting day will be chosen in discussion with your doctor. You should **always** begin taking your tablets on this day of the week. To set the package to the day you and your physician selected, insert a coin into the middle slot and turn the inner wheel counterclockwise until that day appears in the window. The example shown is for a **Sunday** start. Your first white tablet is immediately to the right of the green tablets and below the "V" notch as shown. Ensure that the tab marked "Lift Out" is set over this white tablet. Break off the tab and begin tablet taking. To take your second and all subsequent tablets, turn the clear outer cover clockwise to the next available tablet. Take 1 tablet every day for 28 days, first completing all 7 white tablets, then all 7 light blue tablets, then all 7 blue tablets and finally the 7 green tablets. After you have taken all of your tablets, begin your next package the very next day, on your chosen starting day, whether you have finished menstruating or not. Always remember to set the starting day of each new package to the day chosen by you and your doctor.

Your first pill of each package is always under the "V" notch.

Instructions for Using Your Discreet Package for Both 21-Day and 28-Day Packs: Follow these instructions carefully:

1. **For Day 1 start:** Label the Discreet package by selecting the day label that starts with Day 1 of your menstrual period (the first day of menstruation is Day 1). For example, if your first day of menstruation is Tuesday, attach the day label that begins with **TUE** in the space provided.

   or

   For Day 5 start: Label the Discreet package by selecting the day label that starts with the day that is 5 days after your period begins. (Count 5 days **including,** the first day of menstruation.) For example, if your first day of menstruation is Saturday, place the day label that starts with **WED** in the space provided.

   or

   For Sunday start: Label the Discreet package by selecting the day label that starts with **SUN**. (The first Sunday **after** your period begins, or, if your period starts on Sunday, start that **same day.**)
2. Place the day label in the space where you see the words "Place day label here". Having the Discreet Package labelled with the days of the week will help remind you to take your pill every day.
3. To begin taking your pills, start with the first pill in top row (where you see the word **Start**). This pill should correspond to the day of the week that you are taking your first pill. To remove the pill, push through the back of the Discreet Package.
4. On the following day, take the next pill in the same row, always proceeding from left to right (→). Each row will always begin on the same day of the week.

What to Do During the Month:

1. **Take a pill at approximately the same time every day until the pack is empty.**
   - Try to associate taking your pill with some regular activity like eating a meal or going to bed.
   - Do not skip pills even if you have bleeding between monthly periods or feel sick to your stomach (nausea).
   - Do not skip pills even if you do not have sex very often.
2. **When you finish a pack:**
   - **21 pills: Wait 7 days** to start the next pack. You will have your period during that week.

Tri-Cyclen (cont'd)

- **28 pills:** Start the next pack **on the next day.** Take 1 pill every day. Do not wait any days between packs.

What to Do if You Miss Pills: Table III (on previous page) outlines the actions you should take if you miss 1 or more of your birth control pills. Match the number of pills missed with the appropriate starting time for your type of pill pack.

Note: 28-Day Pack: If you forgot any of the 7 "reminder" pills (without hormones) in Week 4, just safely dispose of the pills you missed. Then keep taking 1 pill each day until the pack is empty. You do not need to use a back-up method.

Always be sure you have on hand:

- a back-up method of birth control (such as latex condoms and spermicidal foam or gel) in case you miss pills, and
- an extra full pack of pills.

If you forget more than 1 pill 2 months in a row, talk to your doctor or clinic about ways to make pill-taking easier or about using another method of birth control.

Information for the Patient: See Blue Section—Information for the Patient "Oral Contraceptives".

Supplied: Each white tablet, unscored with ORTHO 180 engraved on each side, contains: norgestimate 0.18 mg and ethinyl estradiol 0.035 mg. Each light blue tablet, unscored with ORTHO 215 engraved on each side, contains: norgestimate 0.215 mg and ethinyl estradiol 0.035 mg. Each blue tablet, unscored with ORTHO 250 engraved on each side, contains: norgestimate 0.25 mg and ethinyl estradiol 0.035 mg. Nonmedicinal ingredients: white, light blue, and blue tablets: lactose, magnesium stearate and starch. Light blue and blue tablets also contain FD&C Blue #2 Aluminum Lake. In the 28-day regimen the green tablets, embossed on each side with ORTHO, contain inert ingredients. Nonmedicinal ingredients: D&C Yellow #10 Aluminum Lake, FD&C Blue #2 Aluminum Lake, lactose, magnesium stearate, microcrystalline cellulose and starch. VARIDATE DIALPAK Tablet Dispenser Units and Discreet Packages of 21-day and 28-day. Store between 15 and 25°C. Leave contents in protective packaging until time of use.

(Shown in Product Recognition Section)

Reviewed 1999

TRIDESILON® Ⓟ

Bayer

Desonide

Topical Corticosteroid

Supplied: Cream: Each tube and jar contains: desonide 0.05% in Acid Mantle vehicle formulated with glycerin, methylparaben, sodium lauryl sulfate, aluminum acetate, purified water, cetyl stearyl alcohol, synthetic B-wax, white petrolatum and mineral oil. Tubes of 60 g. Jars of 454 g.

Ointment: Each tube contains: desonide 0.05% in white petrolatum. Tubes of 60 g.

Store below 30°C. Avoid freezing.

TRIDIL®

DuPont Pharma

Nitroglycerin

Vasodilator

Supplied: Each 10 mL ampul or vial contains: nitroglycerin 50 mg in propylene glycol, alcohol and water for injection. Boxes of 10. Store between 15 and 30°C. Protect from freezing and excessive light.

TRIHEXYPHENIDYL HCl Ⓟ

General Monograph, CPhA

Antiparkinsonian

> This monograph has been compiled by CPhA. It may contain information different from that approved by Therapeutic Products Programme, Health Canada, and the pharmaceutical manufacturers' approval has not been requested.

Pharmacology: Trihexyphenidyl is a synthetic tertiary amine with antimuscarinic and antiparkinsonian effects. Its exact mechanism of action as an antiparkinsonian agent is unknown but may involve inhibition of central motor centers and blockade of efferent impulses.

Trihexyphenidyl also exhibits a direct antispasmodic effect on smooth muscle. In small doses, trihexyphenidyl causes CNS depression while in larger doses it may cause CNS stimulation.

Pharmacokinetics: Following oral administration, trihexyphenidyl is rapidly absorbed from the gastrointestinal tract. Onset of action is within 1 hour of administration. Peak effects of the drug last for 2 to 3 hours and the duration of action is 6 to 12 hours. Trihexyphenidyl is excreted in the urine, probably as unchanged drug.

Indications: Adjunctive therapy in the symptomatic treatment of parkinsonism and drug-induced extrapyramidal reactions.

Contraindications: In patients with a known hypersensitivity to trihexyphenidyl or to any of its excipients. Antimuscarinic agents are contraindicated in patients with angle-closure glaucoma.

Precautions: Closely observe patients with cardiac, liver, kidney or hypertensive disorders. Patients undergoing prolonged therapy should be monitored periodically for signs of adverse reactions. Gonioscope evaluation and monitoring of intraocular pressures should take place at regular intervals. Trihexyphenidyl should be used with caution in patients with obstructive disease of the gastrointestinal or genitourinary tracts, and in elderly males with possible prostatic hypertrophy. Trihexyphenidyl may cause anhidrosis. Caution should be exercised during hot weather, especially if trihexiphenidyl is taken concurrently with other anticholinergic drugs.

Drug Interactions: CNS depressants: Trihexyphenidyl in small doses, may enhance the CNS depressant effects of drugs including alcohol, anticonvulsants, barbiturates, MAO inhibitors, narcotic analgesics, phenothiazines and tricyclic antidepressants.

Anticholinergics: Trihexyphenidyl may enhance the anticholinergic effects of drugs including atropine, MAO inhibitors, tricyclic antidepressants and phenothiazines. Paralytic ileus (sometimes fatal), hyperthermia and heat stroke may occur. Advise patients to report gastrointestinal problems, fever or heat intolerance promptly.

Levodopa: When trihexyphenidyl is used in combination with levodopa, the dosage of each drug may have to be reduced.

Occupational Hazards: Trihexyphenidyl may impair mental and/or physical abilities required for performance of hazardous tasks such as operating machinery or driving a motor vehicle.

Pregnancy, Lactation and Children: Safe use in children, or pregnant or lactating women has not been established.

Geriatrics: Geriatric patients, particularly over the age of 60, frequently develop increased sensitivity to parasympatholytic drugs and hence, require strict dosage regulation.

Adverse Effects: Dry mouth, blurred vision, dizziness, mild nausea or anxiety will be experienced by 30 to 50% of patients. Isolated instances of suppurative parotitis secondary to excessive dryness of the mouth, skin rashes, dilatation of the colon, paralytic ileus, certain psychiatric manifestations such as delusions and hallucinations and one possible case of paranoia have been reported with trihexyphenidyl.

Older patients, particularly those with underlying cognitive impairment, are especially prone to reactions such as mental confusion, agitation, disturbed behavior, or nausea and vomiting. Such patients should receive lower initial doses, with gradual increases until an effective level is reached.

If a severe reaction should occur, the drug should be discontinued for a few days and then resumed at a lower dosage.

Withdrawal symptoms may occur in patients who were receiving large doses.

Potential untoward effects associated with the use of any atropine-like drug include constipation, drowsiness, urinary hesitancy or retention, tachycardia, postural hypotension, dilatation of the pupils, increased intraocular pressure, weakness, vomiting and headache.

Overdose: Symptoms: Symptoms of trihexyphenidyl overdosage are related to an extension of its pharmacologic action. Severe anticholinergic side effects may include: clumsiness; unsteadiness; severe dry mouth, nose or throat; tachycardia; shortness of breath; warmth, dryness and flushing of the skin. CNS depression or severe drowsiness may be preceded or followed by CNS stimulation including hallucinations, seizures and confusion. Toxic psychosis may occur in patients with psychiatric illness being treated with neuroleptic drugs. Other symptoms may include: nausea, vomiting, blurred vision, mydriasis, seizures, respiratory and circulatory failure.

Treatment: For oral overdoses, perform gastric lavage followed by administration of activated charcoal and a cathartic. Cathartics should not be administered to patients with an ileus or impaired renal function. Treatment is symptomatic and supportive. Monitor the patient for development of seizures, hypertension and arrhythmias. Maintain respiration, fluid and electrolyte balance. A local miotic for mydriasis and cycloplegia may be used and ice bags or sponging with tepid water for hyperpyrexia. Physostigmine is not routinely recommended for the treatment of anticholinergic toxicity because of its potential for adverse effects. Peritoneal dialysis and hemodialysis are of no value in the management of trihexiphenidyl overdose.

Dosage: Should be individualized. The initial dosage should be low and then increased gradually, especially in patients over 60 years of age.

Parkinsonism: 1 mg orally the first day; increased by 2 mg daily at intervals of 3 to 5 days, up to 6 to 10 mg daily. The total daily dose is best tolerated if divided into 3 doses and taken at mealtimes; however, controlled release-formulations should be taken as a single dose after breakfast or in 2 divided doses 12 hours apart.

Drug-induced Parkinsonism: The size and frequency of doses of trihexyphenidyl needed to control drug-induced extrapyramidal reactions, attributable especially to neuroleptics, must be determined empirically. The total daily dosage usually ranges between 5 and 15 mg; however, in some cases, these reactions have been satisfactorily controlled with as little as 1 mg daily. It may be advisable to commence therapy with a single 1 mg dose. If the extrapyramidal manifestations are not controlled in a few hours, the subsequent doses may be progressively increased until satisfactory control is achieved. Satisfactory control may sometimes be more rapidly achieved by temporarily reducing the dosage of the neuroleptic or instituting trihexyphenidyl therapy and then adjusting the dosage of both drugs until the desired antipsychotic effect is retained without onset of the extrapyramidal reactions.

It is sometimes possible to maintain the patient on a reduced trihexyphenidyl dosage after the reactions have remained under control for several days. In the majority of patients, the use of anticholinergic agents is not required after 3 months of neuroleptic therapy. Instances have been reported in which these reactions have remained in remission for long periods after therapy was discontinued.

Reviewed 1999

TRILAFON® Ⓟ

Schering

Perphenazine

Anxiolytic—Antipsychotic—Antiemetic

Indications: For use in the management of the manifestations of psychotic disorders and for the control of severe nausea and vomiting in adults.

Perphenazine has not been shown effective for the management of behavioral complications in patients with mental retardation.

Contraindications: In comatose or greatly obtunded patients and in patients receiving large doses of CNS depressants (barbiturates, alcohol, analgesics or antihistamines); in the presence of blood dyscrasias, bone marrow depression or liver damage; and in patients who have shown hypersensitivity to the components of the injection or related compounds.

It is also contraindicated in patients with suspected or established subcortical brain damage, with or without hypothalamic damage, since a hyperthermic reaction with temperatures in excess of 40°C may occur in such patients, sometimes not until 14 to 16 hours after drug administration. Total body ice packing is recommended for such a reaction; antipyretics may also be useful.

Warnings: Tardive dyskinesia, a syndrome consisting of potentially irreversible, involuntary dyskinetic movements, may develop in patients treated with neuroleptic (antipsychotic) drugs. Although the prevalence of the syndrome appears to be highest among the elderly, especially elderly women, it is impossible to rely upon prevalence estimates to predict, at the inception of neuroleptic treatment, which patients are likely to develop the syndrome. Whether neuroleptic drug products differ in their potential to cause tardive dyskinesia is unknown.

Both the risk of developing the syndrome and the likelihood that it will become irreversible are believed to increase as the duration of treatment and the total cumulative dose of neuroleptic drugs administered to the patient increase. However, the syndrome can develop, although much less commonly, after relatively brief treatment periods at low doses. There is no known treatment for established cases of tardive dyskinesia, although the syndrome may remit, partially or completely, if neuroleptic treatment is withdrawn. Neuroleptic treatment itself, however, may suppress (or partially suppress) the signs and symptoms of the syndrome, and thereby may possibly mask the underlying disease process. The effect that symptomatic suppression has upon the long-term course of the syndrome is unknown.

Given these considerations, neuroleptics should be prescribed in a manner that is most likely to minimize the occurrence of tardive dyskinesia. Chronic neuroleptic treatment should generally be reserved for patients who suffer from a chronic illness that, 1) is known to respond to neuroleptic drugs, and 2) for whom alternative, equally effective, but potentially less harmful treatments are not available or appropriate. In patients who do require chronic treatment, the smallest dose and the shortest duration of treatment should be reassessed periodically.

If signs and symptoms of tardive dyskinesia appear in a patient on neuroleptics, drug discontinuation should be considered. However, some patients may require treatment despite the presence of the syndrome.

Neuroleptic malignant syndrome, a potentially fatal symptom complex sometimes referred to as Neuroleptic Malignant Syndrome (NMS) has been reported in association with antipsychotic drugs. Clinical manifestations of NMS are hyperpyrexia, muscle rigidity, altered mental status and evidence of autonomic instability (irregular pulse or blood pressure, tachycardia, diaphoresis, and cardiac dysrhythmias).

In arriving at a diagnosis, it is important to identify cases where the clinical presentation includes both serious medical illness (e.g., pneumonia, systemic infection) and untreated or inadequately treated extrapyramidal signs and symptoms (EPS). Other important considerations in the differential diagnosis include central anticholinergic toxicity, heat stroke, drug fever and primary CNS pathology.

The management of NMS should include immediate discontinuation of antipsychotic drugs and other drugs not essential to concurrent therapy, intensive symptomatic treatment and medical monitoring; and treatment of any concomitant serious medical problems for which specific treatments are available. There is no general agreement about specific pharmacological treatment regimens for uncomplicated NMS. If a patient requires antipsychotic drug treatment after recovery from NMS, the potential reintroduction of drug therapy should be carefully considered. The patient should be carefully monitored, since recurrences of NMS have been reported.

If hypotension develops, epinephrine should **not** be administered. If a vasopressor is needed, norepinephrine or phenylephrine may be used. Severe, acute hypotension has occurred with the use of phenothiazines and is particularly likely to occur in patients with mitral insufficiency or pheochromocytoma patients.

Perphenazine can lower the convulsive threshold in susceptible individuals; therefore, it should be used with caution in alcohol withdrawal and in patients with convulsive disorders. If the patient is being treated with an anticonvulsive agent, increased dosage of that agent may be required when perphenazine is used concomitantly.

Occupational Hazards: Perphenazine may impair the mental and/or physical abilities required for the performance of potentially hazardous tasks, such as driving a car or operating machinery. Therefore, the patient should be warned accordingly.

Pregnancy and *Lactation:* No adequate or well-controlled studies in pregnant women have been conducted. Perphenazine should be used during pregnancy, in nursing mothers or women of childbearing age only if the potential benefits to the mother justify the potential risks to the fetus or infant (see Precautions).

Precautions: When perphenazine is given by i.m. or i.v. injection, the more rapid and greater degree of drug effects as compared to oral forms should be kept in mind.

Perphenazine should be used with caution in patients with psychic depression.

The possibility of suicide in depressed patients continues during treatment until significant remission occurs. Potentially suicidal patients should not have access to large quantities of perphenazine.

As with all phenothiazines, perphenazine should not be used indiscriminately. Some of the untoward actions to perphenazine tend to appear more frequently when high doses are used. However, as with other phenothiazines, patients receiving perphenazine in any dosage should be kept under close supervision.

Since perphenazine treatment increases serum prolactin levels, caution is suggested in the use of phenothiazine derivatives in breast cancer patients.

The antiemetic effort of perphenazine may obscure signs of toxicity due to overdosage of other drugs, or render more difficult the diagnosis of disorders such as intestinal obstruction, Reye's Syndrome, brain tumor or other encephalopathies.

Aspiration of vomitus has occurred in a few post-surgical patients who received phenothiazines. Although a causal relationship has not been established, this possible occurrence should be considered during post-surgical care.

Patients on large doses of a phenothiazine who are undergoing surgery should be watched carefully for possible hypotensive phenomena. Moreover, reduced amounts of anesthetics or CNS depressants may be necessary.

Phenothiazines depress the mechanism for regulation of temperature and, depending upon the environmental temperature, may cause hyperthermia and heat prostration or hypothermia and respiratory distress. Therefore, perphenazine should be used with great caution in persons exposed to extreme heat or extreme cold.

A significant rise in body temperature, not otherwise explained, may suggest intolerance to perphenazine, in which case therapy should be discontinued.

Because photosensitivity reactions to phenothiazines have been reported, patients being treated with these medications should avoid undue exposure to sunlight.

Phenothiazines should be used cautiously in patients with diminished renal function; and in patients with respiratory impairment due to acute pulmonary infections, or to chronic respiratory disorders, such as severe asthma or emphysema.

The use of alcohol should be avoided, since it may potentiate drug effects, including hypotension. The risk of suicide and the danger of overdosage may be increased in patients who use alcohol excessively.

The possible occurrence of liver damage, corneal and lenticular deposits, retinal changes and irreversible dyskinesia should be considered when patients are on long-term therapy.

Trilafon injection contains sodium bisulfite as a preservative, a sulfite that may cause allergic-type reactions including anaphylactic symptoms and life-threatening or less severe asthmatic episodes in certain susceptible people. The overall prevalence of sulfite sensitivity is seen more frequently in asthmatic than in non-asthmatic people.

Drug Interactions: Concurrent administration of phenothiazines may potentiate CNS depressant effects of opiates, barbiturates or other sedatives, anesthetics, tranquilizers and alcohol (ethanol).

Respiratory depressant effects of meperidine (and other opioid analgesics) may be increased. When phenothiazines are used concomitantly with CNS depressant drugs, overdosage must be avoided.

Phenothiazines do not appear to potentiate the anticonvulsant activity of barbiturates or other anticonvulsant medications. Rather, they can lower the seizure threshold in susceptible individuals. Therefore, the dosage of anticonvulsant agents should not be reduced and may have to be increased if a phenothiazine is added to the therapeutic regimen of a patient with a convulsive disorder; phenothiazine therapy should be initiated at a low dosage.

Concurrent phenothiazine administration may potentiate anticholinergic effects of atropine, tricyclic antidepressant drugs and antihistamines.

When phenothiazines are used concomitantly with these medications, caution should be observed to avoid overdosage. Potentiation of anticholinergic effects of organophosphorus insecticides can occur in patients concurrently receiving phenothiazines and exposed to these insecticides.

Barbiturates and other sedatives and anticonvulsant agents that induce microsomal drug-metabolizing enzymes can enhance phenothiazine metabolism. The phenothiazine dose may require adjustment to maintain efficacy. Rare clinical cases of phenothiazine induced inhibition of phenytoin metabolism have been reported. Caution should be observed in the concomitant administration of perphenazine and phenytoin.

Concurrent phenothiazine use with guanethidine in controlled hypertensive patients may result in exacerbation of hypertension after several days of dosing. This interaction may not be as great with perphenazine as with some other phenothiazines. If guanethidine antagonism is noted, increasing the guanethidine dose or substituting another antihypertensive agent may be appropriate.

Conversely, concurrent phenothiazine use with methyldopa and beta-adrenergic receptor blocking agents administered for hypertension may result in additive hypotensive effects. Phenothiazines should be given with caution to patients receiving these medications to avoid excessive hypotension.

Phenothiazines can block or reverse the pressor effects of epinephrine. Norepinephrine or phenylephrine should be used to treat significant phenothiazine-induced hypotension.

Concurrent phenothiazine administration with levodopa to patients with Parkinson's disease may result in a decreased antiparkinsonian response. Phenothiazines should be avoided or used with caution in these patients.

Laboratory Tests: Since phenothiazines affect many organ functions, their safe and effective use requires pretreatment and periodic laboratory tests, especially during high-dose or prolonged therapy. Blood counts and hepatic and renal functions should be checked periodically. If drug-induced cardiovascular effects are suspected, ECGs should be done. If abnormalities in hepatic or renal function tests occur, perphenazine treatment should be discontinued.

Patients should be watched closely for hematologic effects, especially between the fourth and tenth weeks of therapy, for the sudden appearance of sore throat or other signs of infection. If white blood cell counts are depressed and differential cell counts show significant cellular depression of granulocytes, the drug should be discontinued and appropriate therapy started. However, a slightly lowered white cell count is not in itself an indication to discontinue medication.

Laboratory Test Interactions: Urinary metabolites of phenothiazines may cause urine to darken, resulting in false-positive tests for urobilinogen, amylase, uroporphyrins, porphobilinogens and 5-hydroxy-indoleacetic acid.

Patients receiving therapeutic doses of phenothiazines may show electrocardiographic changes, such as lengthening of the QT interval, accompanied by widening, blunting and notching of the T wave. At higher doses, lowering and inversion of the T wave may occur.

Phenothiazines may increase serum protein-bound iodine levels without clinical thyrotoxicosis.

Since phenothiazines may cause a decrease in adrenocorticosteroid secretion as a result of diminished release of corticotropin, perphenazine may interfere with metyrapone testing of the hypothalamic-pituitary complex.

Depending on the urine pregnancy test being used, false-positive or false-negative results may be reported in phenothiazine treated patients.

Children: Safety and effectiveness of perphenazine in children less than 12 years of age have not been established.

Pregnancy and *Lactation:* In newborn infants of mothers treated with phenothiazines during pregnancy, extrapyramidal reactions, including agitation, hypertonicity, opisthotonus, tremors, hyperreflexia and bizarre motor activity have been reported. In rare cases the movement disorders persisted for 3 to 12 months. Respiratory depression persisting for several days occurred in a newborn whose mother had received a phenothiazine for schizophrenia. Congenital cataracts occurred in an infant whose mother had been treated with promazine during pregnancy.

Phenothiazines cross the human placental barrier and enter the fetal circulation easily. Chlorpromazine and promethazine, administered to the mother just prior to delivery, were excreted by the newborn infant within the first 48 to 60 hours after birth.

Perphenazine should not be used in pregnant women prior to labor unless in the judgment of the physician the potential benefits to the mother outweigh the potential risks to the infant. Since both the usual drugs given to the woman in labor and phenothiazine drugs cross the placental barrier, the infant may be exposed to unwanted individual and combined effects of therapy.

Perphenazine is excreted rapidly in breast milk and could cause unwanted effects in the breast-fed infant. Because of the potential for serious adverse effects in nursing infants from perphenazine injection, a decision should be made whether to discontinue nursing or to discontinue the medication, taking into account the importance of therapy to the mother.

Drug Abuse and Dependence: In general, phenothiazines do not produce psychic dependence. However, following abrupt cessation of high-dose therapy, gastritis, nausea, vomiting, dizziness, tremulousness and motor hyperactivity have been reported. These symptoms may be reduced by continuing concomitant antiparkinsonian agents for several weeks after phenothiazine withdrawal.

Adverse Effects: Side effects with i.m. perphenazine injection have been infrequent and transient. Dizziness or significant hypotension after treatment with the injection is a rare occurrence.

Not all of the following adverse reactions have been reported with perphenazine use; however, pharmacologic similarities among various phenothiazine derivatives require that each be considered. With the piperazine group (of which perphenazine is an example), the extrapyramidal symptoms are more

Trilafon (cont'd)

common, and others (e.g., sedation, jaundice, blood dyscrasias) are less frequent.

CNS: Extrapyramidal Reactions: opisthotonus, trismus, torticollis, retrocollis, aching and numbness of the limbs, motor restlessness, oculogyric crisis, hyperreflexia, dystonia, including protrusion, discoloration, aching and rounding of the tongue, tonic spasm of the masticatory muscles, tight feeling in the throat, slurred speech, dysphagia, akathisia, dyskinesia, parkinsonism and ataxia. Extrapyramidal symptoms can usually be controlled by concomitant use of antiparkinsonian agents, such as benztropine mesylate, and/or reduction in dosage. In some instances, however, extrapyramidal reactions may persist after discontinuation of perphenazine treatment.

Persistent Tardive Dyskinesia: As with all antipsychotic agents, tardive dyskinesia may appear in some patients on long-term therapy or may appear after therapy has been discontinued. Although the risk appears to be greater in elderly patients on high-dose therapy, especially females, it may occur in either sex and in children. Symptoms are persistent and in some patients appear to be irreversible. If these symptoms appear, it is suggested that all antipsychotic agents be discontinued. Should it be necessary to reinstitute treatment, increase dosage, or switch to a different antipsychotic agent, the syndrome may be masked. Fine vermicular movements of the tongue may be an early sign of the syndrome. If the medication is stopped at that time, the complete syndrome may not develop.

Other CNS effects include cerebral edema; abnormality of cerebrospinal fluid proteins; convulsive seizures, particularly in patients with EEG abnormalities or a history of such disorders; and headaches. Neuroleptic malignant syndrome has been reported in patients treated with neuroleptic drugs. It is a relatively uncommon, potentially lethal syndrome, characterized by severe extrapyramidal dysfunction, with rigidity and eventual stupor or coma, hyperthermia and autonomic disturbances, including cardiovascular effects. There is no specific treatment; the neuroleptic drug should be stopped immediately.

Drowsiness may occur, particularly during the first or second week, after which it typically disappears. Hypnotic effects appear to be minimal, especially in patients who are permitted to remain active.

Adverse behavioral effects include paradoxical exacerbation of psychotic symptoms; catatonic-like states; paranoid reactions; lethargy; paradoxical excitement; restlessness; hyperactivity; nocturnal confusion; bizarre dreams; and insomnia. Hyperreflexia has been reported in the newborn when a phenothiazine was used during pregnancy.

Autonomic: dry mouth or salivation, nausea, vomiting, gastric retention, diarrhea, anorexia, constipation, obstipation, fecal impaction, urinary retention, frequency or incontinence, bladder paralysis, polyuria, nasal congestion, pallor, miosis, mydriasis, blurred vision, glaucoma, perspiration, hypertension, hypotension and change in pulse rate occasionally may occur. Significant autonomic effects have been infrequent in patients receiving less than 24 mg perphenazine daily.

A dynamic ileus occasionally occurs with phenothiazine therapy and if severe can result in complications and death. It is of particular concern in psychiatric patients, who may fail to seek treatment of the condition.

Allergic: urticaria, erythma, eczema, exfoliative dermatitis, pruritus, photosensitivity, asthma, fever, anaphylactoid reactions and laryngeal edema may occur. Angioneurotic edema and contact dermatitis have been reported in nursing personnel administering phenothiazines. In extremely rare instances, individual idiosyncrasy or hypersensitivity to phenothiazines has resulted in cerebral edema, circulatory collapse and death.

Endocrine: lactation, galactorrhea, moderate breast enlargement in females and gynecomastia in males on large doses, disturbances in the menstrual cycle, amenorrhea, changes in libido, inhibition of ejaculation, hyperglycemia, hypoglycemia, glycosuria, syndrome of inappropriate antidiuretic hormone (ADH) secretion.

Cardiovascular: postural hypotension, tachycardia (especially with sudden marked increase in dosage), bradycardia, cardiac arrest, faintness and dizziness. Occasionally the hypotensive effect may produce a shock-like condition.

Sudden death has occasionally been reported in patients who have received phenothiazines. In some cases the death was apparently due to cardiac arrest; in others, the cause appeared to be asphyxia due to failure of the cough reflex.

Hematologic: agranulocytosis, eosinophilia, leukopenia, hemolytic anemia, thrombocytopenic purpura and pancytopenia. Most cases of agranulocytosis have occurred between the fourth and tenth weeks of therapy.

Hepatic: Liver damage (biliary stasis) may occur. Jaundice, usually between the second and fourth treatment weeks, is regarded as a hypersensitivity reaction. The incidence is low. The clinical picture resembles infectious hepatitis but with laboratory features of obstructive jaundice. It is usually reversible; however, chronic jaundice has been reported.

Other: Special considerations with long-term therapy include: skin pigmentation, occurring chiefly in the exposed areas; ocular changes consisting of deposition of fine particulate matter in the cornea and lens, progressing in more severe cases to star-shaped lenticular opacities; epithelial keratopathies; retinal changes; and pigmentary retinopathy.

Also noted: peripheral edema; reversed epinephrine effect; parotid swelling (rare); hyperpyrexia; systemic lupus erythematosus-like syndrome; increases in appetite and weight; polyphagia; photophobia; and muscle weakness.

Overdose: Emergency treatment should be started immediately. Patients should be hospitalized as soon as possible. Concurrent ingestion of alcohol or other drugs or some medical explanation for the patient's condition should be considered.

Symptoms: Perphenazine overdosage primarily involves the extrapyramidal system. Overdosage symptomatology is generally an extension of the many pharmacologic effects of perphenazine.

CNS depression progressing from drowsiness to stupor or coma with areflexia may occur. Patients with early or mild intoxication may experience restlessness, confusion and excitement. Other symptoms include hypotension, tachycardia, hypothermia, miosis, tremor, muscle twitching, spasm, rigidity or hypotonia, convulsions, difficulty in swallowing and breathing, cyanosis and respiratory and/or vasomotor collapse, possibly with sudden apnea.

Treatment: Treatment is symptomatic and supportive. There is no specific antidote. The patient should be induced to vomit even if emesis has occurred spontaneously. Pharmacologic vomiting by the administration of ipecac syrup is a preferred method. It should be noted that ipecac has central mode of action in addition to its local gastric irritant properties, and the central mode of action may be blocked by the antiemetic effect of perphenazine products. Vomiting should not be induced in patients with impaired consciousness. The action of ipecac is facilitated by physical activity and by the administration of 240 to 350 mL of water. If emesis does not occur within 15 minutes, the dose of ipecac should be repeated. Precautions against aspiration must be taken, especially in infants and children. Following emesis any drug remaining in the stomach may be adsorbed by activated charcoal administered as a slurry with water. If vomiting is unsuccessful or contraindicated, gastric lavage should be performed. Isotonic and one-half isotonic saline are the lavage solutions of choice. Saline cathartics, such as milk of magnesia, draw water into the bowel by osmosis and therefore may be valuable for their action in rapid dilution of bowel content.

Standard measures (oxygen, i.v. fluids, corticosteroids) should be used to manage circulatory shock or metabolic acidosis. An open airway and adequate fluid intake should be maintained. Body temperature should be regulated. Hypothermia is expected, but severe hyperthermia may occur and must be treated vigorously.

An ECG should be taken and close monitoring of cardiac function instituted for not less than 5 days. Cardiac arrhythmias may be treated with neostigmine, pyridostigmine or propranolol. Digitalis should be considered for cardiac failure.

Vasopressors, such as norepinephrine or phenylephrine, may be used to treat hypotension, but epinephrine should **not** be used.

Anticonvulsant agents, such as an inhalation anesthetic, diazepam or paraldehyde, are recommended for control of seizures, but not barbiturates, since perphenazine increases the CNS depressant action but not the anticonvulsant action of barbiturates. Since phenothiazines lower the convulsive threshold, convulsant stimulants such as picrotoxin or pentylenetetrazol should not be given.

If acute parkinson-like symptoms result from perphenazine intoxication, benztropine mesylate, trihexyphenidyl or diphenhydramine may be administered.

Arousal may not occur for 48 hours following toxic overdose, despite supportive and contra-active measures.

Dialysis is of no value in treatment.

Dosage: Must be individualized and adjusted according to the severity of the disorder and the response obtained. Since extrapyramidal symptoms increase in frequency and severity with increased dosage, the lowest effective dose should be administered. These symptoms have disappeared upon reduction of dosage, withdrawal of medication or administration of an antiparkinsonian agent. After maximum therapeutic response is obtained, dosage may be decreased gradually to a minimum effective maintenance dose.

Prolonged administration of doses exceeding 24 mg daily should be reserved for hospitalized patients or patients under continued observation.

Injection: I.M.: Perphenazine injection should be administered by deep i.m. injection, with the patient seated or recumbent. Following administration, the patient should be observed for a short time for possible occurrence of acute adverse effects. Therapeutic effect is seen usually within 10 minutes and is maximal within 1 to 2 hours. The average duration of effect may be 12 to 24 hours.

Psychotic Conditions: The usual initial dose is 5 mg (1 mL), which may be repeated every 6 hours. When required for satisfactory control of symptoms in severe conditions, an initial 10 mg i.m. dose may be given. Total daily dosage should not exceed 15 mg in ambulatory patients or 30 mg in hospitalized patients.

Patients should be placed on oral therapy as soon as feasible. Generally, this may be achieved within 24 to 48 hours. In some instances, however, patients have been maintained on parenteral therapy for several months.

Since perphenazine injection is more potent than oral formulations, equal or higher dosages should be used when the patient is transferred to oral therapy. A gradual reduction to the minimum effective maintenance oral dose is recommended.

Acute conditions often respond well to a single injection; in chronic conditions several injections may be required.

Severe Nausea and Vomiting in Adults: The usual dose for rapid control of vomiting is 5 mg (1 mL). Rarely, a 10 mg (2 mL) dose is necessary. Higher doses should be given only to hospitalized patients.

I.V.: Administration of perphenazine injection is seldom required. This route of administration should be used with particular caution and care and only when absolutely necessary to control severe vomiting, intractable hiccoughs, or acute conditions, such as violent retching during surgery. Its use should be limited to recumbent hospitalized patients in doses not exceeding 5 mg. When so employed, i.v. injection ordinarily should be administered as a diluted solution by either fractional injection or as a slow drip infusion. In the surgical patient, slow infusion or not more than 5 mg is preferred. When administered in divided doses, perphenazine injection should be diluted to 0.5 mg/mL (1 mL mixed with 9 mL of physiologic saline solution), and not more than 1 mg/injection given at not less than 1 to 2 minute intervals.

I.V. injection should be discontinued as soon as symptoms are controlled. Vital signs should be monitored continuously during i.v. administration.

The possibility of hypotensive and extrapyramidal side effects should be considered and appropriate means for management kept available. Pharmacologic and clinical studies indicate that i.v. administration of norepinephrine or phenylephrine should be useful in alleviating the hypotensive effect.

Tablets: Suggested dosages for various conditions follow: Moderately disturbed non-hospitalized patients: 4 to 8 mg t.i.d., initially; reduce as soon as possible to minimum effective dosage. Total daily dose in ambulatory patients should not exceed 24 mg.

Severely disturbed hospitalized psychiatric patients or those with resistant mental and emotional disorders may temporarily require more than 24 mg daily, especially during early management. It is very important to employ the lowest effective dose since extrapyramidal symptoms increase in frequency and severity with increased dosage.

Severe Nausea and Vomiting in Adults: 8 to 16 mg daily in divided doses; 24 mg occasionally may be necessary; early dosage reduction is desirable.

Supplied: Injection: Each mL of aqueous solution contains: perphenazine 5 mg. Nonmedicinal ingredients: citric acid, sodium bisulfite, sodium hydroxide and water. Ampuls of 1 mL.

Tablets: 2 mg: Each tablet, stamped black, contains: perphenazine 2 mg. Nonmedicinal ingredients: cornstarch, lactose, magnesium stearate, povidone and Velvetine Black (dye); coating: carnauba wax, dye (Opalux Gray), gelatin, sucrose, talc, terra alba and white wax. Tartrazine-free. Bottles of 100.

4 mg: Each tablet, stamped black, contains: perphenazine 4 mg. Nonmedicinal ingredients: cornstarch, lactose, magnesium stearate and povidone; coating: acacia, carnauba wax, dye (Opalux Gray), gelatin, sucrose, talc, terra alba and white wax. Tartrazine-free. Bottles of 100.

(*Shown in Product Recognition Section*)

TRILISATE® Ⓟ

Purdue Frederick

Choline Magnesium Trisalicylate

Anti-inflammatory—Analgesic

Pharmacology: Choline magnesium trisalicylate is a combination of choline salicylate and magnesium salicylate.

Choline magnesium trisalicylate is a nonsteroidal anti-inflammatory drug (NSAID) which possesses the anti-inflammatory, analgesic and antipyretic activities characteristic of salicylates. It is, however, longer acting than acetylsalicylic acid and is less likely to cause gastrointestinal bleeding.

In clinical trials 6 Trilisate tablets (containing 3 g of salicylate) showed similar efficacy to a dose of ASA containing 3 g of salicylate and to indomethacin (100 mg/day), ibuprofen (2 400 mg/day) and naproxen (500 to 750 mg/day).

Choline magnesium trisalicylate is well absorbed. Maximum salicylate levels are reached within 2 hours. The half-life of the drug is 9 to 17 hours.

In a multi-dose bioavailability study, subjects who received 1 g (2 tablets) b.i.d. reached a mean steady-state serum salicylate level of 8.77 mg/100 mL, with a lower limit of 5.09 mg/100 mL and an upper limit of 12.45 mg/100 mL. Steady-state concentration was achieved at 55 hours after the first dose. Subjects who received 1.5 g (3 tablets) b.i.d. reached a mean steady-state serum salicylate level of 20.18 mg/100 mL, with a lower limit of 16.44 mg/100 mL and an upper limit of 23.93 mg/100 mL. Steady-state serum concentration was achieved at 85 hours after the first dose.

As with other salicylates the primary route of excretion is through the kidneys.

As for other salicylates, the pharmacologic profile of choline magnesium trisalicylate is a function of the salicylate blood level. Choline magnesium trisalicylate has been shown to be an effective anti-arthritic agent. Like other salicylates it has analgesic and antipyretic properties.

In contrast to ASA, nonacetylated salicylates, such as choline magnesium trisalicylate, do not irreversibly acetylate the enzyme cyclo-oxygenase and therefore would be expected to differ from ASA in their effects on a number of functions dependent on prostaglandin and thromboxane biosynthesis, such as platelet aggregation, renal blood flow and the integrity of the gastrointestinal mucosa.

Effects on Platelet Aggregation: Using in vitro methods, Trilisate did not inhibit platelet aggregation at salicylate concentrations forty-fold higher than those at which ASA did so. Also in contrast to results with ASA, in vivo studies have shown that single oral doses of Trilisate did not affect bleeding time, platelet aggregation, platelet 5HT release or plasma thromboxane levels. These results were confirmed in a parallel design multiple dose study in which 30 healthy volunteers were administered Trilisate (2×750 mg salicylate, q12h) or ASA (2×325 mg, q4h) for 5 days. Trilisate produced a statistically significant decrease in bleeding time on the second treatment day, whereas ASA significantly increased bleeding time over the 5-day treatment period and for 3 days thereafter. During the study, significantly more subjects in the ASA group showed changes in platelet aggregation from normal to abnormal than in the Trilisate group (8 subjects versus 1 subject). In 9 patients (7 of whom had rheumatoid or osteoarthritis) administered Trilisate for 7 to 15 months, 5 showed no abnormalities and 3 showed only minimal effects on platelet aggregation. The remaining patient showed a pattern of platelet aggregation abnormalities consistent with inadvertent use of ASA.

Indications: For the relief of the signs and symptoms of rheumatoid arthritis and osteoarthritis. The safety and efficacy of Trilisate have not been established in patients designated as functional class IV.

Contraindications: Should not be administered to patients with peptic ulcer or active inflammatory disease of the gastrointestinal tract or to patients with known or suspected hypersensitivity to salicylates including those in whom acute asthmatic attacks, urticaria, rhinitis or other allergic manifestation are precipitated by ASA or other nonsteroidal anti-inflammatory agents.

Warnings: Should be given under close medical supervision to patients prone to gastrointestinal tract irritation particularly those with a history of peptic ulcer, diverticulosis or other inflammatory disease of the gastrointestinal tract. In these cases the physician must weigh the benefits of treatment against the possible hazards.

Since peptic ulceration, perforation and gastrointestinal bleeding, sometimes severe and occasionally fatal have been reported during therapy with other NSAIDs patients taking any NSAID including Trilisate should be instructed to contact a physician immediately if they experience symptoms or signs suggestive of peptic ulceration or gastrointestinal bleeding. These reactions can occur without warning symptoms or signs and at any time during treatment.

Elderly, frail and debilitated patients appear to be at higher risk from a variety of adverse reactions from NSAIDs. For such patients, consideration should be given to a starting dose lower than usual, with individual adjustment when necessary and under close supervision (see Precautions).

Pregnancy and *Lactation:* The safety of this drug in pregnancy and lactation has not been established and its use is therefore not recommended. Due to the inhibition of prostaglandin synthesis by salicylates (including Trilisate) parturition may be prolonged.

Children: A possible association between Reye's syndrome and the use of salicylates has been suggested but not established. Reye's syndrome has also occurred in many patients not exposed to salicylates. However, caution is advised when prescribing salicylate-containing medications for children and teenagers with influenza or chickenpox. Trilisate is not recommended for use in patients under 12 years of age.

Precautions: Precautions Specific to Trilisate: When salicylates are given with steroids, alcohol or the butazones, the risk of gastrointestinal ulceration is increased.

Trilisate is excreted primarily in the urine and adequate precautions including dose reduction and/or increasing the time interval between doses, together with careful monitoring, should be employed when it is administered to patients with renal insufficiency.

General Precautions for NSAIDs: Gastrointestinal: If peptic ulceration is suspected or confirmed, or if gastrointestinal bleeding or perforation occurs, Trilisate should be discontinued, an appropriate treatment instituted and the patient closely monitored.

There is no definitive evidence that the concomitant administration of histamine H_2-receptor antagonists and/or antacids will either prevent the occurrence of gastrointestinal side effects or allow continuation of therapy with NSAIDs when and if these adverse reactions appear.

Renal: Long-term administration of NSAIDs to animals has resulted in renal papillary necrosis and other abnormal renal pathology. In humans, there have been reports of acute interstitial nephritis with hematuria, proteinuria, and occasionally nephrotic syndrome.

A second form of renal toxicity has been seen in patients with prerenal conditions leading to reduction in renal blood flow or blood volume, where the renal prostaglandins have a supportive role in the maintenance of renal perfusion. In these patients, administration of a NSAID may cause a dose-dependent reduction in prostaglandin formation and may precipitate overt renal decompensation. Patients at greatest risk of this reaction are those with impaired renal function, heart failure, liver dysfunction, those taking diuretics and the elderly. Discontinuation of nonsteroidal anti-inflammatory therapy is usually followed by recovery to the pretreatment state.

During long-term therapy, kidney function should be monitored periodically.

Hepatic Function: Disturbances of hepatic function ranging from jaundice and cases of fatal hepatitis to borderline elevations of one or more liver tests have occurred with NSAIDs. These abnormalities may progress, may remain essentially unchanged, or may be transient with continued therapy. During long-term therapy, liver function tests should be monitored periodically especially in patients with pre-existing liver dysfunction. A patient with symptoms and/or signs suggesting liver dysfunction, or in whom an abnormal liver test has occurred while receiving Trilisate, should be evaluated for evidence of the development of a more severe hepatic reaction. If abnormal liver tests persist or worsen, if clinical signs and symptoms consistent with liver disease develop or if systemic manifestations occur (e.g. eosinophilia, rash, etc.), Trilisate should be discontinued.

Fluid and Electrolyte Balance: Trilisate should be used with caution in patients with heart failure, hypertension or other conditions predisposing to fluid retention. The possibility of precipitating congestive heart failure in elderly patients or those with compromised cardiac function should be borne in mind.

Serum electrolytes should be monitored periodically during long-term therapy, especially in those patients at risk.

Hematology: As with other anti-inflammatory drugs that inhibit prostaglandin biosynthesis, caution should be used in the event that Trilisate tablets are administered to persons with intrinsic coagulation defects or those on anticoagulant therapy.

The rare association of NSAIDs with blood dyscrasias (possibly serious) should be borne in mind.

Infection: As with other anti-inflammatory drugs, Trilisate may mask the usual signs of infection.

Ophthalmology: Blurred and/or diminished vision has been reported with other nonsteroidal anti-inflammatory drugs. If such symptoms develop with Trilisate it should be discontinued and an ophthalmologic examination performed; ophthalmic examination should be carried out at periodic intervals in any patient receiving this drug for an extended period of time.

Drug Interactions: Salicylates compete for protein binding sites with a large number of drugs eg. penicillin, thiopental, phenytoin, sulfinpyrazone, warfarin and other NSAIDs as well as endogenous substances such as thyroxine, triiodothyronine and bilirubin.

In addition to displacement of other agents from protein binding, salicylates also diminish the renal excretion of methotrexate, may reduce plasma concentrations of prothrombin and may counteract the effect of uricosuric agents.

Adverse Effects: The most common adverse reactions encountered with most nonsteroidal anti-inflammatory drugs are gastrointestinal, of which peptic ulcer, with or without bleeding, is the most severe. Fatalities have occurred on occasion, particularly in the elderly.

In clinical studies with Trilisate the most frequently reported side effect was tinnitus with an incidence of 10.2%. Should tinnitus occur it is recommended that dosage be reduced. Other side effects reported in Trilisate clinical studies are listed below: Gastrointestinal: nausea (3.4%), heartburn (1.5%), cramps (1.1%). Less than 1% incidence: abdominal pain, indigestion, stomach ache and constipation.

CNS: Less than 1% incidence: headache, lightheadedness and dizziness.

Dermatologic: Less than 1% incidence: skin rash.

Hematologic: Less than 1% incidence: positive fecal occult blood.

Special Senses: Less than 1% incidence: hearing loss.

Overdose: Symptoms: There are no reports to date of Trilisate overdosage in man. Signs of salicylate toxicity would be anticipated. Mild salicylate intoxication is characterized by headache, dizziness, tinnitus, hearing impairment, dimness of vision, mental confusion, lassitude, drowsiness, thirst, hyperventilation, nausea, vomiting and diarrhea. In more severe cases, CNS disturbances including EEG abnormalities, generalized convulsions and coma, skin eruption, alterations in acid-base balance, fever, hemorrhage, hypoglycemia or hyperglycemia and dehydration may also occur. In extreme cases death may result from respiratory and cardiovascular failure.

Treatment: Treatment of salicylate intoxication is largely symptomatic. Absorption of salicylate from the gastrointestinal tract can be reduced by emesis, gastric lavage, or administration of activated charcoal. Hyperthermia and dehydration are the immediate threat to life and treatment should be directed at their correction together with correction of acid-base disturbances. Renal clearance of salicylate may be increased by alkaline diuresis, as consistent with the patient's acid-base status. Hemorrhagic phenomena are treated with vitamin K.

Dosage: For rheumatoid arthritis and more severe osteoarthritis, the recommended dose is 2 to 3 tablets (containing a total of 1 to 1.5 g salicylate content) b.i.d. or 1 to 2 tablets (total of 0.5 to 1 g salicylate) t.i.d.

For less severe osteoarthritis the recommended dose is 2 tablets (1 g salicylate) b.i.d. In some cases doses less than 2 tablets b.i.d. may achieve the desired results.

It is recommended that therapy be initiated at the lower dosage level then titrated upwards as required for optimal results. The maximum recommended daily dose is 6 tablets (3 g expressed as salicylate). The safety of doses above 3 g/day has not been investigated.

Information for the Patient: See Blue Section—Information for the Patient "Trilisate".

Supplied: Each scored, capsule-shaped, pale pink tablet contains: choline salicylate 293 mg combined with magnesium salicylate 362 mg to provide 500 mg of salicylate content. Tartrazine-free. Bottles of 100.

TRINALIN® ℞

Schering

Azatadine Maleate—Pseudoephedrine Sulfate

Antihistamine—Decongestant

Pharmacology: Azatadine is an antihistamine, related to cyproheptadine, with antiserotonin, anticholinergic, and sedative effects. Antihistamines appear to compete with histamine for histamine H1-receptor sites on effector cells and antagonize the vasodilator effect of endogenously released histamine. Consequently antihistamines antagonize the physiological manifestations of histamine release in the nose following antigen-antibody interaction, such as congestion related to vascular engorgement, mucosal edema, and profuse, watery secretion, and irritation and sneezing resulting from histamine action on afferent nerve terminals.

Pseudoephedrine is an orally effective nasal decongestant. In effective recommended oral dosage, pseudoephedrine produces minimal other sympathomimetic effects, such as pressor activity and CNS stimulation. Use of an orally administered vasoconstrictor for shrinkage of congested nasal mucosa produces a gradual but sustained decongestant effect, causing little, if any "rebound" congestion; it facilitates shrinkage of swollen mucosa in upper respiratory areas that are relatively inaccessible to topically applied sprays or drops and it relieves nasal obstruction without the additional irritation that may result from local medication.

The apparent elimination half-life of pseudoephedrine was approximately 6.5 hours while the apparent elimination half-life of azatadine available from the outer layer of the tablets was approximately 12 hours.

Indications: The relief of the symptoms of upper respiratory mucosal congestion in perennial and allergic rhinitis, and for the relief of nasal congestion and eustachian tube congestion.

Contraindications: Antihistamines should not be used to treat lower respiratory tract symptoms.

Patients with narrow-angle glaucoma, urinary retention and patients receiving MAO inhibitor therapy or within 10 days of stopping such treatment (see Precautions, Drug Interactions), patients with severe hypertension, severe coronary artery disease, hyperthyroidism, and those who have shown hypersensitivity or idiosyncrasy to its components.

Precautions: Trinalin should be used with caution in patients with glaucoma, stenosing peptic ulcer, pyloroduodenal obstruction, prostatic hypertrophy or bladder neck obstruction, cardiovascular disease, those with increased intraocular pressure or diabetes mellitus. Because of the atropine-like action of antihistamines, this product should be used with caution in patients with a history of bronchial asthma.

Drug Interactions: MAO inhibitors prolong and intensify the effects of antihistamines. Concomitant use of antihistamines with alcohol, tricyclic antidepressants, barbiturates, or other CNS depressants may have an additive effect. The action of oral anticoagulants may be inhibited by antihistamines.

When sympathomimetic drugs are given to patients receiving MAO inhibitors, hypertensive reactions, including hypertensive crises, may occur. Beta-adrenergic blocking agents may also interact with sympathomimetics. Increased ectopic pacemaker activity can occur when pseudoephedrine is used concomitantly with digitalis. Antacids increase the rate of absorption of pseudoephedrine, while kaolin decreases it.

Occupational Hazards: Patients should be warned about engaging in activities requiring mental alertness, such as driving a car or operating appliances, or machinery.

Antihistamines are more likely to cause dizziness, sedation, and hypotension in patients over 60 years of age. In these patients, sympathomimetics are also more likely to cause adverse reactions, such as confusion, hallucinations, convulsions, CNS depression and death.

Overdosage of antihistamines, particularly in infants and children may produce convulsions and death.

Antihistamines should be discontinued approximately 4 days prior to skin testing procedures since these may prevent or diminish otherwise positive reactions to dermal reactivity indicators.

Pregnancy and *Lactation:* The safe use of this product during pregnancy and lactation has not been established and therefore the compound should be used only if the potential benefit justifies the potential risk to the fetus or infant.

Children: Safety and effectiveness in children below the age of 12 years have not been established.

Adverse Effects: Trinalin has caused no serious or unusual adverse reaction. Drowsiness was the most frequently reported side effect.

Adverse effects with antihistamines vary in incidence and severity. Among them are cardiovascular, hematologic (pancytopenia, thrombocytopenia, hemolytic anemia), neurologic (confusion, hallucinations, tremor), gastrointestinal, genitourinary (urinary retention), respiratory adverse reactions and mood changes. The most common include sedation, sleepiness, dizziness, disturbed coordination, epigastric distress, rash, dry mouth and thickening of bronchial secretions.

Sympathomimetic drugs have been associated with fear, anxiety, tenseness, weakness, pallor, respiratory difficulty, dysuria, insomnia, CNS stimulation and depression, convulsions, arrhythmias, and cardiovascular collapse with accompanying hypotension. Ephedrine-like reactions in hyperreactive individuals include: palpitations, tachycardia, hypertension, headache, dizziness or nausea.

Overdose: Symptoms: Manifestations of overdosage may vary from CNS depression (sedation, apnea, diminished mental alertness, cyanosis, coma, cardiovascular collapse) to stimulation (insomnia, hallucinations, tremors, or convulsions) to death. Other signs and symptoms may be euphoria, excitement, tachycardia, palpitations, thirst, perspiration, nausea, dizziness, tinnitus, ataxia, blurred vision, and hypertension or hypotension. Stimulation is particularly likely in children as are atropine-like signs and symptoms (dry mouth; fixed, dilated pupils, flushing; hyperthermia; and gastrointestinal symptoms).

In large doses, sympathomimetics may give rise to giddiness, headache, nausea, vomiting, sweating, thirst, tachycardia, precordial pain, palpitations, difficulty in micturition, muscular weakness and tenseness, anxiety, restlessness, and insomnia. Many patients can present a toxic psychosis with arrhythmias, circulatory collapse, convulsions, coma, and respiratory failure.

Treatment: Emergency treatment should be started immediately. The patient should be induced to vomit, even if emesis has occurred spontaneously. Pharmacologically induced vomiting by the administration of ipecac syrup is a preferred method. However, vomiting should not be induced in patients with impaired consciousness. Following emesis, any drug remaining in the stomach may be absorbed by activated charcoal administered as a slurry with water. If vomiting is unsuccessful or contraindicated, gastric lavage should be performed. Dialysis is of little value in antihistamine poisoning. After emergency treatment the patient should continue to be medically monitored.

Treatment of the signs of symptoms of overdosage is symptomatic and supportive. Stimulants (analeptic agents) should not be used. Vasopressors may be used to treat hypotension. Short-acting barbiturates, diazepam, or paraldehyde may be administered to control seizures. Hyperpyrexia, especially in children, may require treatment with tepid water sponge baths or a hypothermic blanket. Apnea is treated with ventilatory support.

Dosage: Trinalin tablets are not intended for use in children under 12 years of age. The usual adult dosage is 1 tablet twice a day.

Supplied: Each light grey, sugar-coated tablet, branded in black with the Schering trademark on both sides, contains: azatadine maleate 1 mg and pseudoephedrine sulfate USP 60 mg in the outer layer for immediate action and pseudoephedrine sulfate USP 60 mg in the tablet core for repeat action 4 to 6 hours later. Nonmedicinal ingredients: cornstarch, lactose, magnesium stearate and povidone; coating: acacia, calcium sulfate, carnauba wax, dye, Opalux Gray, gelatin, gum rosin, oleic acid, soap powder, White Neutral, sucrose, talc, white wax and zein. Tartrazine-free. Bottles of 100. Store between 2 and 30°C.

(Shown in Product Recognition Section)

TRINIPATCH® 0.2
TRINIPATCH® 0.4
TRINIPATCH® 0.6

Sanofi

Nitroglycerin Transdermal Delivery System

Antianginal

Pharmacology: The principal pharmacological action of nitroglycerin is relaxation of vascular smooth muscle, producing a vasodilator effect on both peripheral arteries and veins, with more prominent effects on the latter. Dilation of the postcapillary vessels, including large veins, promotes peripheral pooling of blood and decreases venous return to the heart, thereby reducing left ventricular end-diastolic pressure (preload). Arteriolar relaxation reduces system vascular resistance and arterial pressure (afterload). Dilation of the coronary arteries also occurs. The relative importance of preload reduction, afterload reduction, and coronary dilation remains undefined.

When Trinipatch is applied to the skin, nitroglycerin is absorbed directly into the systemic circulation. Thus, the active drug reaches target organs before inactivation by the liver. The transdermal absorption of nitroglycerin occurs in a continuous and well-controlled manner. Nitroglycerin is rapidly metabolized, principally by a liver reductase, to form glycerol nitrate metabolites and inorganic nitrate. Two active major metabolites, the 1,2- and 1,3-dinitroglycerols, the products of hydrolysis, appear to be less potent than nitroglycerin as vasodilators but have longer plasma half-lives. The dinitrates are further metabolized to mononitrates (biologically inactive with respect to cardiovascular effects) and ultimately to glycerol and carbon dioxide. There is extensive first-pass deactivation by the liver following gastrointestinal absorption.

The volume of distribution of nitroglycerin is about 3 L/kg, and nitroglycerin is cleared from this volume at extremely rapid rates, with a resulting serum half-life of about 3 minutes. The observed clearance rates (close to 1 L/kg/min) greatly exceed hepatic blood flow, known sites of extrahepatic metabolism include red blood cells and vascular walls.

In healthy volunteers, after the application of the system in different dosages (2×7 cm^2 patch, 1×14 cm^2 patch and 1×21 cm^2 patch), the concentrations of nitroglycerin reached in the plasma were uniform and dose-related, i.e., dependent on drug-release area. They remained constant as long as the system is in contact with the skin. Upon removal of the patch, the plasma concentrations declined with a half-life of about an hour.

Although dosing regimens for most chronically used drugs are designed to provide plasma concentrations that are continuously greater than a minimally effective concentration, such a strategy is probably inappropriate for organic nitrates. Some controlled clinical trials using exercise tolerance testing have shown maintenance of effectiveness when patches are worn continuously. The large majority of such controlled trials, however, have shown the development of tolerance (i.e., complete loss of effect as measured by exercise testing) within the first day. Tolerance has appeared even when doses greater than 4 mg/hour were delivered continuously. This dose is far in excess of the effective dose 0.2 to 0.8 mg/hour applied intermittently.

Efficacy of organic nitrates is restored after a period of absence of nitrates from the body. Drug-free intervals of 10 to 12 hours are known to be sufficient to restore response. Several studies have demonstrated that when nitroglycerin is administered according to an intermittent regimen, doses of 0.4 to 0.8 mg/hour have increased exercise capacity for up to 8 hours, with a trend of increased exercise capacity to 12 hours. One controlled clinical trial suggested that the intermittent use of nitrates may be associated with a decreased exercise tolerance, in comparison to placebo, during the last part of the nitrate-free interval; the clinical relevance of this observation is unknown, but the possibility of increased frequency or severity of angina during the nitrate-free interval should be considered.

Indications: Nitroglycerin used intermittently (see Pharmacology) for the prevention of anginal attacks in patients with stable angina pectoris associated with coronary artery disease. It can be used in conjunction with other antianginal agents such as beta-blockers and/or calcium antagonists.

Not intended for the immediate relief of acute attacks of angina pectoris. Sublingual nitroglycerin preparations should be used for this purpose.

Contraindications: Known hypersensitivity to nitroglycerin and related organic nitrate compounds. Known or suspected hypersensitivity to components of the patch. Acute circulatory failure associated with marked hypotension (shock and states of collapse). Postural hypotension. Myocardial insufficiency due to obstruction (e.g., in the presence of aortic or mitral stenosis or of constrictive pericarditis). Increased intracranial pressure. Increased intraocular pressure. Severe anemia.

Warnings: Trinipatch must be removed before cardioversion or DC defibrillation is attempted, as well as before applying diathermy treatment, since it may be associated with damage to the paddles and burns to the patient.

The benefits and safety of transdermal nitroglycerin in angina patients with acute myocardial infarction or congestive heart failure have not been established. If one elects to use transdermal nitroglycerin in these conditions, careful clinical or hemodynamic monitoring must be used to avoid the potentially deleterious effects of induced hypotension and tachycardia.

Precautions: Headaches or symptoms of hypotension, such as weakness or dizziness, particularly when arising suddenly from a recumbent position, may occur. A reduction in dose or discontinuation of treatment may be necessary.

Caution should be exercised when using nitroglycerin in patients prone to, or who might be affected by hypotension. The drug therefore should be used with caution in patients who may have volume depletion from diuretic therapy or in patients who have low systolic blood pressure (e.g., below 90 mm Hg). Paradoxical bradycardia and increased angina pectoris may accompany nitroglycerin-induced hypotension.

Nitrate therapy may aggravate the angina caused by hypertrophic cardiomyopathy.

In industrial workers who have had long-term exposure to unknown (presumably high) doses of nitroglycerin, tolerance clearly occurs. There is moreover, physical dependence since chest pain, acute myocardial infarction, and even sudden death have occurred during temporary withdrawal of nitroglycerin from these workers. In clinical trials of angina patients, there are reports of anginal attacks being more easily provoked and of rebound in the hemodynamic effects soon after nitrate withdrawal. The importance of these observations to the routine clinical use of nitroglycerin has not been fully elucidated, but patients should be monitored closely for increased anginal symptoms during drug-free periods.

Caution should be exercised in patients with arterial hypoxemia due to anemia (see Contraindications), because in such patients the biotransformation of nitroglycerin is reduced. Similarly, caution is called for in patients with hypoxemia and a ventilation/perfusion imbalance due to lung disease or ischemic heart failure. Patients with angina pectoris, myocardial infarction, or cerebral ischemia frequently suffer from abnormalities of the small airways (especially alveolar hypoxia). Under these circumstances vasoconstriction occurs within the lung to shift perfusion from areas of alveolar hypoxia to better ventilated regions of the lung. As a potent vasodilator, nitroglycerin could reverse this protective vasoconstriction and thus result in increased perfusion to poorly ventilated areas, worsening of the ventilation/perfusion imbalance, and a further decrease in the arterial partial pressure of oxygen.

Tolerance to nitroglycerin with cross tolerance to other nitrates or nitrites may occur (see Pharmacology). Coadministration of other long-acting nitrates could jeopardize the integrity of the nitrate-free interval and therefore must be avoided. As tolerance to nitroglycerin patches develops, the effect of sublingual nitroglycerin on exercise tolerance, although still observable, is somewhat blunted.

As patients may experience faintness and/or dizziness, reaction time when driving or operating machinery may be impaired, especially at the start of treatment.

Pregnancy: Animal reproduction studies have not been conducted with nitroglycerin. It is not known whether nitroglycerin can cause fetal harm when administered to a pregnant woman. Therefore use nitroglycerin only if the potential benefit justifies the risk to the fetus.

Lactation: It is not known whether nitroglycerin is excreted into breast milk. Benefits to the mother must be weighed against the risks to the child.

Children: Safety and effectiveness have not been established in children.

Drug Interactions: Concomitant treatment with other vasodilators, calcium channel blockers, ACE inhibitors, beta-blockers, diuretics, antihypertensives, tricyclic antidepressants, and major tranquilizers may potentiate the blood pressure lowering effect of nitroglycerin. Dose adjustment may be necessary.

Marked symptomatic orthostatic hypotension has been reported when calcium channel blockers and organic nitrates were used in combination. Dosage adjustments of either class of agents may be necessary.

Alcohol may enhance sensitivity to the hypotensive effects of nitrates.

Concurrent administration of nitroglycerin with dihydroergotamine may increase the bioavailability of dihydroergotamine. Special attention should be paid to this point in patients with coronary artery disease, because dihydroergotamine antagonizes the effect of nitroglycerin and may lead to coronary vasoconstriction.

The possibility that the ingestion of ASA and nonsteroidal anti-inflammatory drugs might diminish the therapeutic response to nitrates and nitroglycerin cannot be excluded.

Information to be Provided to the Patient: Daily headaches sometimes accompany treatment with nitroglycerin. In patients who get these headaches, the headaches may be a marker of the activity of the drug. Patients should resist the temptation to avoid headaches by altering the schedule of their treatment with nitroglycerin, since loss of headache may be associated with simultaneous loss of antianginal efficacy.

Treatment with nitroglycerin may be associated with lightheadedness on standing, especially just after rising from a recumbent or seated position. This effect may be more frequent in patients who have also consumed alcohol.

After normal use, there is enough residual nitroglycerin in discarded patches that they are a potential hazard to children and pets.

A patient leaflet is supplied with the patches (see Blue Section—Information for the Patient).

Adverse Effects: Headache, which may be severe, is the most commonly reported side effect. Headache may be recurrent with each daily dose, especially at higher doses of nitroglycerin. Headaches may be treated with concomitant administration of mild analgesics. If such headaches are unresponsive to treatment, the nitroglycerin dosage should be reduced or the product discontinued. Transient episodes of lightheadedness, occasionally related to blood pressure changes, may also occur. Hypotension occurs infrequently, but in some patients it may be severe enough to warrant discontinuation of therapy.

Reddening of the skin, with or without a mild local itching or burning sensation, as well as allergic contact dermatitis may occasionally occur. Upon removal of the patch, any slight reddening of the skin will usually disappear within a few hours. The application site should be changed regularly to prevent local irritation.

Less frequently reported adverse reactions include dizziness, faintness, facial flushing, postural hypotension which may be associated with reflex tachycardia. Syncope, crescendo angina, and rebound hypertension have been reported but are uncommon. Rarely nausea, and vomiting.

Overdose: Symptoms: Nitroglycerin overdose may result in severe hypotension, persistent throbbing headache, vertigo, palpitations, visual disturbances, flushing and perspiring skin (later becoming cold and cyanotic), anorexia, nausea and vomiting (possibly with colic and even bloody diarrhea), syncope (especially in the upright posture), methemoglobinemia with cyanosis, hyperpnea, dyspnea and slow breathing, slow pulse (dicrotic and intermittent), heart block and bradycardia, increased intracranial pressure with cerebral symptoms of fever, confusion, and coma possibly followed by paralysis, clonic convulsions and death due to circulatory collapse.

Treatment: Keep the patient recumbent in a shock position and comfortably warm. Remove the patch.

Passive movement of the extremities may aid venous return. Administer oxygen and artificial ventilation if necessary.

I.V. infusion of normal saline or similar fluid may also be required to produce sufficient central volume expansion. However, in patients with renal disease or congestive heart failure, therapy resulting in central volume expansion is not without hazard. Treatment of nitroglycerin overdose in these patients may be subtle and difficult, and invasive monitoring may be required.

Epinephrine is ineffective in reversing the severe hypotensive events associated with overdose; it and related compounds are contraindicated in this situation.

Methemoglobinemia: Case reports of clinically significant methemoglobinemia are rare at conventional doses of nitroglycerin. The formation of methemoglobin is dose-related, and in the case of genetic abnormalities of hemoglobin that favor methemoglobin formation, even conventional doses of organic nitrates can produce harmful concentrations of methemoglobin. Methemoglobin levels are available from most clinical laboratories. The diagnosis should be suspected in patients who exhibit signs of impaired oxygen delivery despite adequate cardiac output and adequate arterial pO_2. Classically, methemoglobinemic blood is described as chocolate brown, without color change on exposure to air. If methemoglobinemia is present, administration of methylene blue (1% solution), 1 to 2 mg/kg i.v., may be required.

Dosage: Daily Dosage Schedule: The daily dosage schedule is based on intermittent therapy to prevent the development of tolerance to nitroglycerin. The optimal dose should be selected based upon the clinical response, side effects, and the effects of therapy on blood pressure.

Starting dose is one 0.2 patch (7 cm^2), usually applied in the morning. If 0.2 mg/hour (7 cm^2) is well tolerated, the dose can be increased to 0.4 mg/hour (14 cm^2) if required. A maximum of 0.8 mg/hour may be used.

Prevention of Tolerance: Although some controlled clinical trials using exercise tolerance testing have shown maintenance of effectiveness when patches are worn continuously, the large majority of such controlled trials have shown the development of tolerance (i.e., complete loss of effect) within the first 24 hours after therapy was initiated. Dose adjustments even to levels much higher than generally used did not prevent the development of tolerance.

Tolerance can be prevented or attenuated by use of an intermittent dosage schedule. Although the minimum nitrate-free interval has not been defined, clinical trials have demonstrated that an appropriate dosing schedule for nitroglycerin patches would provide for a daily patch-on period of 12 to 14 hours and a daily patch-off period of 10 to 12 hours. The patch-free time should coincide with the period in which angina pectoris is least likely to occur (usually at night). Patients should be watched carefully for an increase of angina pectoris during the patch-free period. Adjustment of background medication may be required.

The dose of transdermal nitroglycerin should be periodically reviewed in relation to continuing antianginal control.

Site of Application: The patch can be applied to any area of skin **except** the distal extremities. Many patients prefer the chest. Each successive application should be to a different site.

The area should be clean, dry, and preferably hairless. If hair is likely to interfere with patch adhesion or removal, clipping may be necessary prior to application. Take care to avoid areas with cuts or irritations.

Information for the Patient: See Blue Section—Information for the Patient "Trinipatch".

Supplied: The Trinipatch (nitroglycerin) transdermal system is a flat unit designed to provide continuous controlled release of nitroglycerin through intact skin. The rate of release of nitroglycerin is linearly dependent upon the area of the applied system; each cm^2 of applied system delivers approximately 0.03 mg of nitroglycerin per hour. Thus, the 7, 14 and 21 cm^2 systems deliver approximately 0.2, 0.4 and 0.6 mg of nitroglycerin per hour, respectively. The remainder of the nitroglycerin in each system serves as a reservoir and is not delivered in normal use. After 12 hours, for example, each system has delivered approximately 10% of its original content of nitroglycerin.

The Trinipatch system comprises three layers: a thin, occlusive, LDBE backing film layer, an acrylic adhesive matrix/drug reservoir layer and a layer of siliconized polyester release liner comprised of overlapped liner strips that form an easy-opening tab.

Trinipatch 0.2: Each 7 cm^2 patch contains: nitroglycerin 22.4 mg and delivers approximately 0.2 mg of active substance per hour.

Trinipatch 0.4: Each 14 cm^2 patch contains: nitroglycerin 44.8 mg and delivers approximately 0.4 mg of active substance per hour.

Trinipatch 0.6: Each 21 cm^2 patch contains: nitroglycerin 67.2 mg and delivers approximately 0.6 mg of active substance per hour.

Nonmedicinal Ingredients: sorbitan mono-oleate and DuroTak 80-1196. Each system is individually sealed in a separate pouch. Boxes of 30 and 100. Store under controlled room temperature (between 15 and 30°C). Shelf-life: 2 years. Do not store out of the pouch. Keep out of reach of children and pets before use and when disposing of used patches.

New Product 1998

TRIPHASIL® 21 Ⓟ
TRIPHASIL® 28 Ⓟ

Wyeth-Ayerst

Levonorgestrel—Ethinyl Estradiol

Oral Contraceptive

Pharmacology: Although the primary mechanism of action is inhibition of ovulation, the effectiveness of Triphasil may also result from other mechanisms of action, such as hostility of the cervical mucus to sperm penetration and migration.

Indications: Conception control.

Contraindications: History of/or actual thrombophlebitis or thromboembolic disorders; history of/or actual cerebrovascular disorders; history of/or actual myocardial infarction or coronary arterial disease; active liver disease or history of/or actual benign or malignant liver tumors; known or suspected

Triphasil (cont'd)

carcinoma of the breast; known or suspected estrogen-dependent neoplasia; undiagnosed abnormal vaginal bleeding; any ocular lesion arising from ophthalmic vascular disease, such as partial or complete loss of vision or defect in visual fields; when pregnancy is suspected or diagnosed.

Warnings: Predisposing Factors for Coronary Artery Disease: Cigarette smoking increases the risk of serious cardiovascular side effects and mortality. Birth control pills increase this risk, especially with increasing age. Convincing data are available to support an upper age limit of 35 years for oral contraceptive use by women who smoke.

Other women who are independently at high risk for cardiovascular disease include those with diabetes, hypertension, abnormal lipid profile, or a family history of these. Whether oral contraceptives accentuate this risk is unclear.

In low-risk, nonsmoking women of any age, the benefits of oral contraceptive use outweigh the possible cardiovascular risks associated with low-dose formulations. Consequently, oral contraceptives may be prescribed for these women up to the age of menopause.

> Cigarette smoking increases the risk of serious adverse effects on the heart and blood vessels. This risk increases with age and becomes significant in oral contraceptive users older than 35 years of age. Women should be counselled not to smoke.

Discontinue medication at the earliest manifestation of:

A. Thromboembolic and cardiovascular disorders such as: thrombophlebitis, pulmonary embolism, cerebrovascular disorders, myocardial ischemia, mesenteric thrombosis, and retinal thrombosis.

B. Conditions that predispose to venous stasis and to vascular thrombosis, (e.g., immobilization after accidents or confinement to bed during long-term illness). Other nonhormonal methods of contraception should be used until regular activities are resumed. For use of oral contraceptives when surgery is contemplated, see Precautions.

C. Visual defects, partial or complete.

D. Papilledema, or ophthalmic vascular lesions.

E. Severe headache of unknown etiology or worsening of pre-existing migraine headache.

A meta-analysis from 54 epidemiological studies reported that there is a slightly increased relative risk (RR=1.24) of having breast cancer diagnosed in women who are currently using combined oral contraceptives. The increased risk gradually disappears during the course of the 10 years after cessation of combined oral contraceptive use. Because breast cancer is rare in women under 40 years of age, the excess number of breast cancer diagnoses in current and recent combined oral contraceptive use is small in relation to the lifetime risk of breast cancer. These studies do not provide evidence of causation. The observed pattern of increased risk maybe due to an earlier diagnosis of breast cancer in combined oral contraceptive users, the biological effects of combined oral contraceptives or a combination of both. The breast cancers diagnosed in ever-users tend to be less advanced clinically than the cancers diagnosed in the never-users.

Precautions: Physical Examination and Follow-up: Before oral contraceptives are used, a thorough history and physical examination should be performed, including a blood pressure determination. Breasts, liver, extremities and pelvic organs should be examined and a Papanicolaou smear should be taken if the patient has been sexually active.

The first follow-up visit should be done 3 months after oral contraceptives are prescribed. Thereafter, examinations should be performed at least once a year or more frequently if indicated. At each annual visit, examination should include those procedures that were done at the initial visit as outlined above or per recommendations of the Canadian Workshop on Screening for Cancer of the Cervix. Their suggestion was that, for women who had 2 consecutive negative Pap smears, screening could be continued every 3 years to the age of 69.

Pregnancy: Oral contraceptives should not be taken by pregnant women. However, if conception accidently occurs while taking the pill, there is no conclusive evidence that the estrogen and progestin contained in the oral contraceptive will damage the developing child.

Lactation: In breast-feeding women, the use of oral contraceptives results in the hormonal components being excreted in breast milk and may reduce its quantity and quality. If the use of oral contraceptives is initiated after the establishment of lactation, there does not appear to be any effect on the quantity and quality of the milk. There is no evidence that low-dose oral contraceptives are harmful to the nursing infant.

Hepatic Function: Patients who have had jaundice, including a history of cholestatic jaundice during pregnancy, should be given oral contraceptives with great care and under close observation.

The development of severe generalized pruritus or icterus requires that the medication be withdrawn until the problem is resolved.

If a patient develops jaundice that proves to be cholestatic in type, the use of oral contraceptives should not be resumed. In patients taking oral contraceptives, changes in the composition of the bile may occur and an increased incidence of gallstones has been reported.

Hepatic nodules (adenoma and focal nodular hyperplasia) have been reported, particularly in long-term users of oral contraceptives. Although these lesions are extremely rare, they have caused fatal intra-abdominal hemorrhage and should be considered in women with an abdominal mass, acute abdominal pain, or evidence of intra-abdominal bleeding.

Hypertension: Patients with essential hypertension whose blood pressure is well-controlled may be given oral contraceptives but only under close supervision. If a significant elevation of blood pressure in previously normotensive or hypertensive subjects occurs at any time during the administration of the drug, cessation of medication is necessary.

Migraine and Headache: The onset or exacerbation of migraine or the development of headache of a new pattern that is recurrent, persistent or severe, requires discontinuation of oral contraceptives and evaluation of the cause.

Diabetes: Current low-dose oral contraceptives exert minimal impact on glucose metabolism. Diabetic patients, or those with a family history of diabetes, should be observed closely to detect any worsening of carbohydrate metabolism. Patients predisposed to diabetes who can be kept under close supervision may be given oral contraceptives. Young diabetic patients whose disease is of recent origin, well-controlled, and not associated with hypertension or other signs of vascular disease such as ocular fundal changes, should be monitored more frequently while using oral contraceptives.

Ocular Disease: Patients who are pregnant or are taking oral contraceptives, may experience corneal edema that may cause visual disturbances and changes in tolerance to contact lenses, especially of the rigid type. Soft contact lenses usually do not cause disturbances. If visual changes or alterations in tolerance to contact lenses occur, temporary or permanent cessation of wear may be advised.

Breasts: Increasing age and a strong family history are the most significant risk factors for the development of breast cancer. Other established risk factors include obesity, nulliparity and late age at first full-term pregnancy. The identified groups of women that may be at increased risk of developing breast cancer before menopause are long-term users of oral contraceptives (more than 8 years) and starters at early age. In a few women, the use of oral contraceptives may accelerate the growth of an existing but undiagnosed breast cancer. Since any potential increased risk related to oral contraceptive use is small, there is no reason to change prescribing habits at present (see Warnings).

Women receiving oral contraceptives should be instructed in self-examination of their breasts. Their physicians should be notified whenever any masses are detected. A yearly clinical breast examination is also recommended because, if a breast cancer should develop, drugs that contain estrogen may cause a rapid progression.

Vaginal Bleeding: Persistent irregular vaginal bleeding requires assessment to exclude underlying pathology.

Table I[a]—Triphasil

Drugs that May Decrease the Efficacy of Oral Contraceptives

Class of Compound	Drug	Proposed Mechanism	Suggested Management
Anticonvulsants	Carbamazepine Ethosuximide Phenobarbital Phenytoin Primidone	Induction of hepatic microsomal enzymes. Rapid metabolism of estrogen and increased binding of progestin and ethinyl estradiol to SHBG.	Use higher-dose OCs (50 μg ethinyl estradiol), another drug or another method.
Antibiotics	Ampicillin Cotrimoxazole Penicillin	Enterohepatic circulation disturbance, intestinal hurry.	For short course, use additional method or use another drug. For long course, use another method.
	Rifampin	Increased metabolism of progestins. Suspected acceleration of estrogen metabolism.	Use another method.
	Chloramphenicol Metronidazole Neomycin Nitrofurantoin Sulfonamides Tetracyclines	Induction of hepatic microsomal enzymes. Also disturbance of enterohepatic circulation.	For short course, use additional method or use another drug. For long course, use another method.
	Troleandomycin	May retard metabolism of OCs, increasing the risk of cholestatic jaundice.	
Antifungals	Griseofulvin	Stimulation of hepatic metabolism of contraceptive steroids may occur.	Use another method.
Cholesterol-lowering Agents	Clofibrate	Reduces elevated serum triglycerides and cholesterol; this reduces OC efficacy.	Use another method.
Sedatives and Hypnotics	Benzodiazepines Barbiturates Chloral Hydrate Glutethimide Meprobamate	Induction of hepatic microsomal enzymes.	For short course, use additional method or another drug. For long course, use another method or higher-dose OCs.
Antacids		Decreased intestinal absorption of progestins.	Dose 2 hours apart.
Other Drugs	Phenylbutazone[b] Antihistamines[b] Analgesics[b] Antimigraine preparations[b] Vitamin E	Reduced OC efficacy has been reported. Remains to be confirmed.	

[a]Adapted from Dickey, R.P., ed.: Managing Contraceptive Pill Patients, 5th edition Creative Informatics Inc., Durant, OK, 1987.

[b]Refer to Oral Contraceptives 1994, A report by the Special Advisory Committee on Reproductive Physiology to the Drugs Directorate, Health Protection Branch, Health Canada.

Fibroids: Patients with fibroids (leiomyomata) should be carefully observed. Sudden enlargement, pain, or tenderness requires discontinuation of the use of oral contraceptives.

Emotional Disorders: Patients with a history of emotional disturbances, especially the depressive type, may be more prone to have a recurrence of depression while taking oral contraceptives. In cases of a serious recurrence, a trial of an alternate method of contraception should be made which may help to clarify the possible relationship. Women with premenstrual syndrome (PMS) may have a varied response to oral contraceptives, ranging from symptomatic improvement to worsening of the condition.

Laboratory Tests: Results of laboratory tests should be interpreted in the light that the patient is on oral contraceptives. The following laboratory tests are modified.

A. Liver Function Tests: Bromsulphthalein Retention Test (BSP): moderate increase. AST and GGT: minor increase. Alkaline phosphatase: variable increase. Serum bilirubin: increased, particularly in conditions predisposing to or associated with hyperbilirubinemia.

B. Coagulation Tests: Factors II, VII, IX, X, XII and XIII: increased. Factor VIII: mild increase. Platelet aggregation and adhesiveness: mild increase in response to common aggregating agents. Fibrinogen: increased. Plasminogen: mild increase. Antithrombin III: mild decrease. Prothrombin Time: increased.

C. Thyroid Function Tests: Protein-bound Iodine (PBI): increased. Total Serum Thyroxine (T_4): increased. Thyroid Stimulating Hormone (TSH): unchanged.

D. Adrenocortical function tests: Plasma Cortisol: increased.

E. Miscellaneous Tests: Serum Folate: occasionally decreased. Glucose Tolerance Test: variable increase with return to normal after 6 to 12 months. Insulin Response: mild to moderate increase. c-Peptide Response: mild to moderate increase.

Tissue Specimens: Pathologists should be advised of oral contraceptive therapy when specimens obtained from surgical procedures and Pap smears are submitted for examination.

Return to Fertility: After discontinuing oral contraceptive therapy, the patient should delay pregnancy until at least 1 normal spontaneous cycle has occurred in order to date the pregnancy. An alternative contraceptive method should be used during this time.

Amenorrhea: Women having a history of oligomenorrhea, secondary amenorrhea, or irregular cycles may remain anovulatory or become amenorrheic following discontinuation of estrogen-progestin combination therapy.

Amenorrhea, especially if associated with breast secretion, that continues for 6 months or more after withdrawal, warrants a careful assessment of hypothalamic-pituitary function.

Thromboembolic Complications—Postsurgery: There is an increased risk of thromboembolic complications in oral contraceptive users, after major surgery. If feasible, oral contraceptives should be discontinued and an alternative method substituted at least 1 month prior to **major** elective surgery. Oral contraceptive use should not be resumed until the first menstrual period after hospital discharge following surgery.

Drug Interactions: The concurrent administration of oral contraceptives with other drugs may result in an altered response to either agent. Reduced effectiveness of the oral contraceptive, should it occur, is more likely with the low dose formulations. It is important to ascertain all drugs that a patient is taking, both prescription and nonprescription, before oral contraceptives are prescribed.

For possible drug interactions with oral contraceptives see Table I (on previous page) and Table II.

Noncontraceptive Benefits of Oral Contraceptives: Several health advantages other than contraception have been reported.

1. Combination oral contraceptives reduce the incidence of cancer of the endometrium and ovaries.
2. Oral contraceptives reduce the likelihood of developing benign breast disease.
3. Oral contraceptives reduce the likelihood of development of functional ovarian cysts.
4. Pill users have less menstrual blood loss and have more regular cycles, thereby reducing the chance of developing iron-deficiency anemia.
5. The use of oral contraceptives may decrease the severity of dysmenorrhea and premenstrual syndrome, and may improve acne vulgaris, hirsutism, and other androgen-mediated disorders.
6. Other noncontraceptive benefits are outlined in Oral Contraceptives 1994, Health Canada.

Table II*—Triphasil

Modification of Other Drug Action by Oral Contraceptives

Class of Compound	Drug	Modification of Other Drug Action	Suggested Management
Alcohol		Possible increased levels of ethanol or acetaldehyde.	Use with caution.
Alpha-II Adrenoreceptor Agents	Clonidine	Sedation effect increased.	Use with caution.
Anticoagulants	All	OCs increase clotting factors, decrease efficacy. However, OCs may potentiate action in some patients.	Use another method.
Anticonvulsants	All	Fluid retention may increase risk of seizures.	Use another method.
Antidiabetic Drugs	Oral hypoglycemics and insulin	OCs may impair glucose tolerance and increase blood glucose.	Use low-dose estrogen and progestin OC or another method. Monitor blood glucose.
Antihypertensive Agents	Guanethidine and methyldopa	Estrogen component causes sodium retention, progestin has no effect.	Use low-dose estrogen OC or use another method.
	Beta-blockers	Increased drug effect (decreased metabolism).	Adjust dose of drug if necessary. Monitor cardiovascular status.
Antipyretics	Acetaminophen	Increased metabolism and renal clearance.	Dose of drug may have to be increased.
	Antipyridine	Impaired metabolism.	Decrease dose of drug.
	ASA	Effects of ASA may be decreased by the short-term use of OCs.	Patients on chronic ASA therapy may require an increase in ASA dosage.
Aminocaproic Acid		Theoretically, a hypercoagulable state may occur because OCs augment clotting factors.	Avoid concomitant use.
Betamimetic Agents	Isoproterenol	Estrogen causes decreased response to these drugs.	Adjust dose of drug as necessary. Discontinuing OCs can result in excessive drug activity.
Caffeine		The actions of caffeine may be enhanced as OCs may impair the hepatic metabolism of caffeine.	Use with caution.
Cholesterol-lowering Agents	Clofibrate	Their action may be antagonized by OCs. OCs may also increase metabolism of clofibrate.	May need to increase dose of clofibrate.
Corticosteroids	Prednisone	Markedly increased serum levels.	Possible need for decrease in dose.
Cyclosporine		May lead to an increase in cyclosporine levels and hepatotoxicity.	Monitor hepatic function. The cyclosporine dose may have to be decreased.
Folic Acid		OCs have been reported to impair folate metabolism.	May need to increase dietary intake, or supplement.
Meperedine		Possible increased analgesia and CNS depression due to decreased metabolism of meperidine.	Use combination with caution.
Phenothiazine Tranquilizers	All phenothiazines, reserpine and similar drugs	Estrogen potentiates the hyperprolactinemia effect of these drugs.	Use other drugs or lower dose OCs. If galactorrhea or hyperprolactinemia occurs, use other method.
Sedatives and Hypnotics	Chlordiazepoxide Lorazepam Oxazepam Diazepam	Increased effect (increased metabolism).	Use with caution.
Theophylline	All	Decreased oxidation, leading to possible toxicity.	Use with caution. Monitor theophylline levels.
Tricyclic Antidepressants	Clomipramine (possibly others)	Increased side effects; i.e., depression.	Use with caution.
Vitamin B_{12}		OCs have been reported to reduce serum levels of Vitamin B_{12}.	May need to increase dietary intake, or supplement.

*Adapted from Dickey, R.P., ed.: Managing Contraceptive Pill Patients, 5th edition Creative Informatics Inc., Durant, OK, 1987.

Oral contraceptives **do not protect** against sexually transmitted diseases including HIV/AIDS. For protection against STDs, it is advisable to use latex condoms **in combination with** oral contraceptives.

Adverse Effects: An increased risk of the following serious adverse reactions has been associated with the use of oral contraceptives: thrombophlebitis; pulmonary embolism; mesenteric thrombosis; neuro-ocular lesions, e.g., retinal thrombosis; myocardial infarction; cerebral thrombosis; cerebral hemorrhage, hypertension; benign hepatic tumors; gallbladder disease.

The following adverse reactions also have been reported in patients receiving oral contraceptives: nausea and vomiting, usually the most common adverse reaction, occurs in approximately 10% or fewer of patients during the first cycle. Other reactions, as a general rule, are seen less frequently or only occasionally.

Other Adverse Reactions: gastrointestinal symptoms (such as abdominal cramps and bloating); change in menstrual flow; temporary infertility after discontinuation of treatment; edema; melasma which may persist; breast changes: tenderness, enlargement, secretion; change in weight (increase or decrease); change in cervical erosion and secretion; cholestatic jaundice; rash (allergic); vaginal candidiasis; change in corneal curvature (steepening).

The following adverse reactions have been reported in users of oral contraceptives, and the association has been neither confirmed nor refuted: congenital anomalies, premenstrual syndrome, cataracts, optic neuritis, changes in appetite,

Triphasil (cont'd)

cystitis-like syndrome, headache, nervousness, dizziness, hirsutism, loss of scalp hair, erythema multiforme, erythema nodosum, hemorrhagic eruption, vaginitis, porphyria, impaired renal function, hemolytic uremic syndrome, Budd-Chiari syndrome, acne, changes in libido, colitis, sickle-cell disease, cerebral-vascular disease with mitral valve prolapse, lupus-like syndrome.

Overdose: Symptoms: With levonorgestrel and ethinyl estradiol, acute doses in excess of clinical levels when administered to experimental animals, have been shown to have a minimal deleterious effect. The LD_{50} values for the combination of norgestrel and ethinyl estradiol in acute oral administration approximates 500 000 times the equivalent human oral dose. In humans, however, the extent of ill effects to be expected following accidental ingestion of a large dose of any oral contraceptive has not been firmly established.

Depending upon the amount ingested, liver toxicity, temporary interference with the function of the seminiferous tubules, or in the case of females, possible withdrawal bleeding within a few days of consumption, are theoretically possible. However, case histories of both male and female children, some of whom ingested more than half a month's supply of oral contraceptive tablets, indicate that the effects are asymptomatic and without immediate consequence. Despite the frequency of nausea and vomiting in adult females during the first few cycles of use, none of these children presented such symptoms.

Treatment: Although the physiologic effects of oral contraceptives may be theoretically offset by concomitant administration of gonadotrophin preparations, there are no known chemotherapeutic agents which will neutralize their effects subsequent to accidental ingestion. In the practical management of an acute overdosage, gastric lavage may be of value if the offending agent has recently been swallowed. The general rules for observation and symptomatic resolution should be followed. Liver function tests should be conducted, particularly transaminase levels, 2 to 3 weeks after consumption.

Dosage: Triphasil 21: Each cycle consists of 21 days on medication and a 7-day interval without medication (3 weeks on, 1 week off).

The 21-day regimen is comprised of the first 6 days of pale brown tablets, followed by 5 days of white tablets, followed by 10 days of yellow tablets.

For the first cycle of medication, the patient is instructed to take 1 Triphasil tablet daily for 21 consecutive days beginning on Day 1 of her menstrual cycle, on Day 5, or on the first Sunday after her period begins. (For the first cycle only, the first day of menstrual flow is considered Day 1.) The tablets are then discontinued for 7 days (1 week). Withdrawal bleeding should usually occur during the period that the patient is off the tablets.

The patient begins her next and all subsequent 21-day courses of Triphasil tablets (following the same 21 days on, 7 days off) on the same day of the week that she began her first course. She begins taking her tablets 7 days after discontinuation regardless of whether or not withdrawal bleeding is still in progress.

Triphasil 28: Each cycle consists of 21 days of Triphasil followed by 7 days of inert tablets (3 weeks on Triphasil, 1 week on inert tablets).

The 28-day regimen is comprised of the first 6 days of pale brown tablets, followed by 5 days of white tablets, followed by 10 days of yellow tablets, followed by 7 days of inert green tablets.

For the first cycle of medication, the patient is instructed to take 1 tablet for 28 consecutive days beginning on Day 1 of her menstrual cycle, on Day 5, or on the first Sunday after her period begins. (For the first cycle only, the first day of menstrual flow is considered Day 1.) Withdrawal bleeding should usually occur during the week the patient is taking the green inert tablets.

The patient begins her next and all subsequent 28-day courses of tablets on the same day of the week that she began her first course. She continues her next course of 28 tablets immediately after the last course, regardless of whether or not a period of withdrawal bleeding is still in progress. There is no need for the patient to count days between cycles because there are no "off-tablet days".

Special Notes on Administration: It is recommended that Triphasil tablets be taken at the same time each day, preferably after the evening meal or at bedtime.

Table III—Triphasil

What To Do If You Miss Pills

Sunday Start	Other Than Sunday Start
Miss 1 pill	**Miss 1 pill**
Take it as soon as you remember, and take the next pill at the usual time. This means that you might take 2 pills in one day.	Take it as soon as you remember, and take the next pill at the usual time. This means that you might take 2 pills in one day.
Miss 2 pills in a row	**Miss 2 pills in a row**
First 2 Weeks: 1. Take 2 pills the day you remember and 2 pills the next day. 2. Then take 1 pill a day until you finish the pack. 3. Use a back-up method of birth control if you have sex in the 7 days after you miss the pills.	**First 2 Weeks:** 1. Take 2 pills the day you remember and 2 pills the next day. 2. Then take 1 pill a day until you finish the pack. 3. Use a back-up method of birth control if you have sex in the 7 days after you miss the pills.
Third Week: 1. Keep taking 1 pill a day until Sunday. 2. On Sunday, safely discard the rest of the pack and start a new pack that day. 3. Use a back-up method of birth control if you have sex in the 7 days after you miss the pills. 4. You may not have a period this month. **If you miss 2 periods in a row, call your doctor or clinic.**	**Third Week:** 1. Safely dispose of the rest of the pill pack and start a new pack that same day. 2. Use a back-up method of birth control if you have sex in the 7 days after you miss the pills. 3. You may not have a period this month. **If you miss 2 periods in a row, call your doctor or clinic.**
Miss 3 or more pills in a row	**Miss 3 or more pills in a row**
Anytime in the Cycle: 1. Keep taking 1 pill a day until Sunday. 2. On Sunday, safely discard the rest of the pack and start a new pack that day. 3. Use a back-up method of birth control if you have sex in the 7 days after you miss the pills. 4. You may not have a period this month. **If you miss 2 periods in a row, call your doctor or clinic.**	**Anytime in the Cycle:** 1. Safely dispose of the rest of the pill pack and start a new pack that same day. 2. Use a back-up method of birth control if you have sex in the 7 days after you miss the pills. 3. You may not have a period this month. **If you miss 2 periods in a row, call your doctor or clinic.**

Triphasil is effective from the first day of therapy if tablets are begun as described under Dosage.

If Triphasil administration is initiated later than the fifth day of the first menstrual cycle of medication or postpartum, contraceptive reliance should not be placed on Triphasil until after the first 7 consecutive days of administration. The possibility of ovulation and conception prior to initiation of medication should be considered. In the nonlactating mother, Triphasil may be prescribed in the postpartum period either immediately or at the first postpartum examination, whether or not menstruation has resumed.

If spotting or breakthrough bleeding occurs, the patient is instructed to continue on the same regimen. This type of bleeding usually is transient and without significance; however, if the bleeding is persistent or prolonged, the patient is advised to consult her physician.

The patient should be instructed to use Table III if she misses one or more of her birth control pills. She should be told to match the number of pills with the appropriate starting time for her type of pill.

Information for the Patient: See Blue Section—Information for the Patient "Oral Contraceptives".

Supplied: Triphasil 21: Each Cyclette dispenser contains: 6 pale brown tablets of 50 µg levonorgestrel plus 30 µg ethinyl estradiol (Days 1–6), 5 white tablets of 75 µg levonorgestrel plus 40 µg ethinyl estradiol (Days 7–11), and 10 yellow tablets of 125 µg levonorgestrel plus 30 µg ethinyl estradiol (Days 12-21). Nonmedicinal ingredients: hydroxypropyl methylcellulose, iron oxide (yellow tablets), lactose, magnesium stearate, microcrystalline cellulose, polacrilin potassium, polyethylene glycol, red iron oxide (brown tablets), titanium dioxide, wax and yellow iron oxide (brown and yellow tablets). Energy: 1.13 kJ (0.27 kcal). Gluten- and tartrazine-free.

Triphasil 28: Each Cyclette dispenser contains: the same as Triphasil 21 plus 7 green inert tablets (Days 22-28). Nonmedicinal ingredients: FD&C Blue No. 1 aluminum lake (green tablets), hydroxypropyl methylcellulose, iron oxide (yellow tablets), lactose, magnesium stearate, microcrystalline cellulose, polacrilin potassium, polyethylene glycol, red iron oxide (brown tablets), titanium dioxide, wax and yellow iron oxide (brown, green and yellow tablets). Energy: 1.13 kJ (0.27 kcal). Gluten- and tartrazine-free.

(Shown in Product Recognition Section)

Reviewed 1997

For comparative information on Tetracyclines, see the CPhA General Monograph in the WHITE SECTION.

TRIPTIL® ℞

MSD

Protriptyline HCl

Antidepressant

Indications: In the treatment of depression that is a manifestation of psychosis or neurosis, whether endogenous or reactive in nature. Endogenous depression is more likely to respond than other depressive states. It is especially recommended for apathetic, withdrawn patients because it promptly relieves anergia and lacks sedative activity. These qualities make it useful also in ambulatory depressed patients.

When used in anergic schizophrenic patients, protriptyline has been reported to markedly improve hypoactivity and accessibility, resulting in increased participation in concurrent psychotherapeutic and milieu therapy. However, as with all potent antidepressant agents, the schizophrenic symptomatology may be activated and require a major tranquilizer.

The symptoms of depression that may be helped by this drug include depressed mood, excessive crying, apathy, withdrawal, psychomotor retardation, loss of interest, fatigue, lassitude, feelings of guilt, anorexia, headache, insomnia, and functional somatic complaints, for example gastrointestinal symptoms.

Contraindications: Cases of known hypersensitivity to tricyclic antidepressants or to any of the nonmedicinal ingredients of the tablets.

Protriptyline should not be given concomitantly with a MAO inhibiting compound. Hyperpyretic crises, severe convulsions, and deaths have occurred in patients receiving tricyclic antidepressant and MAO inhibiting drugs simultaneously.

When it is desired to substitute protriptyline for a MAO inhibitor, a minimum of 14 days should be allowed to elapse after the latter is discontinued. Protriptyline should then be initiated cautiously with gradual increase in dosage until optimum response is achieved.

This drug should not be used during the acute recovery phase following myocardial infarction.

Pregnancy and *Lactation:* see Precautions.

Warnings: The drug is to be used with caution in patients with a history of seizures, impaired liver function, urinary retention or increased intraocular pressure.

Tachycardia and postural hypotension may occur more frequently with protriptyline than with other antidepressant drugs. Protriptyline should be used with caution in elderly patients and patients with cardiovascular disorders; such patients should be observed closely because of the tendency of the drug to produce tachycardia, hypotension, arrhythmias, and prolongation of the conduction time.

Myocardial infarction and stroke have been reported with drugs of this class. Therefore, these drugs should be used with caution in patients with a history of cardiovascular diseases such as myocardial infarction and congestive heart failure.

Due to an infrequent risk of arrhythmias, close supervision is required for hyperthyroid patients or those receiving thyroid medication.

Precautions: When protriptyline is used to treat the depressive component of schizophrenia, psychotic symptoms may be aggravated. Likewise, in manic depressive psychosis, depressed patients may experience a shift toward the manic phase if they are treated with an antidepressant drug. Paranoid delusions, with or without associated hostility, may be exaggerated. In any of these circumstances, it may be advisable to reduce the dose of protriptyline or to use a major tranquilizing drug, such as perphenazine, concurrently.

Symptoms, such as anxiety or agitation, may be aggravated in overactive or agitated patients.

The possibility of suicide in depressed patients remains during treatment. Patients should not have access to large quantities of the drug during treatment. It is advisable to initiate therapy with the concurrent administration of a tranquilizer and preventive supervision in suicidal patients since they usually have a high level of anxiety, and especially as protriptyline may relieve anergia before there is complete recovery from the depressive state.

Discontinue the drug several days before elective surgery if possible.

Occupational Hazards: The drug may impair mental and/or physical abilities required for performance of hazardous tasks, such as operating machinery or driving a motor vehicle.

In patients using alcohol excessively, potentiation may increase the inherent danger of suicide attempt or overdosage.

Pregnancy and *Lactation*: Safe use in pregnancy and lactation has not been established; therefore, use in pregnant women, nursing mothers or women who may become pregnant requires that possible benefits be weighed against possible hazards to mother and child.

Children: This drug is not recommended for use in children (under 12 years of age) because safety and effectiveness in the pediatric age group have not been established.

Drug Interactions: Protriptyline may block the antihypertensive effect of guanethidine or similarly acting compounds.

When protriptyline is given with anticholinergic agents or sympathomimetic drugs, including epinephrine combined with local anesthetics, close supervision and careful adjustment of dosages are required.

Cimetidine is reported to reduce hepatic metabolism of certain tricyclic antidepressants.

Protriptyline may enhance the response to alcohol and the effects of barbiturates and other CNS depressants.

Concurrent administration of protriptyline and electroshock therapy may increase the hazards of therapy. Such treatment should be limited to patients for whom it is essential.

Patients receiving thyroid medication may develop arrhythmias when protriptyline is given.

Adverse Effects: Note: Included in the listing which follows are a few adverse reactions which have not been reported with this specific drug. However, the pharmacological similarities among the tricyclic antidepressant drugs require that each of the reactions be considered when protriptyline is administered. Protriptyline is more likely to aggravate agitation and anxiety and produce cardiovascular reactions such as tachycardia and hypotension.

Cardiovascular: hypotension (particularly orthostatic hypotension), hypertension, tachycardia, palpitation, myocardial infarction, arrhythmias, heart block, stroke.

Psychiatric: confusion states (especially in the elderly) with hallucinations, disorientation, delusions, anxiety, restlessness, agitation; insomnia, panic, and nightmares; hypomania; exacerbation of psychosis.

Neurological: numbness, tingling, and paresthesias of extremities; incoordination; ataxia; tremors; peripheral neuropathy; extrapyramidal symptoms; seizures; alteration in EEG patterns; tinnitus; drowsiness, dizziness, weakness and fatigue; headache.

Anticholinergic: dry mouth and rarely associated sublingual adenitis; blurred vision, disturbance of accommodation, mydriasis; constipation; paralytic ileus; hyperpyrexia; urinary retention, delayed micturition, dilation of the urinary tract.

Allergic: skin rash, petechiae, urticaria, itching, photosensitization (avoid excessive exposure to sunlight), edema (general, or of face and tongue), drug fever.

Hematologic: bone marrow depression; agranulocytosis; leukopenia; eosinophilia; purpura; thrombocytopenia.

Gastrointestinal: nausea and vomiting; anorexia; epigastric distress; diarrhea; peculiar taste; stomatitis; abdominal cramps; black tongue.

Endocrine: gynecomastia in the male, breast enlargement and galactorrhea in the female; increased or decreased libido, impotence; testicular swelling; elevation or depression of blood sugar levels; syndrome of inappropriate ADH secretion.

Other: jaundice (stimulating obstructive); altered liver function; weight gain or loss; perspiration; flushing; urinary frequency, nocturia; parotid swelling; alopecia.

Abrupt cessation of treatment after prolonged administration may produce nausea, headache, and malaise. Gradual dosage reduction has been reported to produce, within 2 weeks, transient symptoms including irritability, restlessness, and dream and sleep disturbance. These symptoms are not indicative of addiction. Rare instances have been reported of mania or hypomania occurring within 2 to 7 days following cessation of chronic therapy with tricyclic antidepressants.

Overdose: Symptoms: High doses may cause temporary confusion, disturbed concentration, or transient visual hallucinations. Overdosage may cause drowsiness; hypothermia; tachycardia and other arrhythmic abnormalities, for example, bundle branch block; ECG evidence of impaired conduction; congestive heart failure; dilated pupils; convulsions; severe hypotension; stupor; and coma. Other symptoms may be agitation, hyperactive reflexes, muscle rigidity, vomiting, hyperpyrexia, or any of those listed under Adverse Effects.

Treatment: Experience in the management of overdosage with protriptyline is limited. The following recommendations are based on the management of overdosage with other tricyclic antidepressants.

All patients suspected of having taken an overdosage should be admitted to a hospital. Treatment is symptomatic and supportive. If ingestion is recent, empty the stomach as quickly as possible by emesis followed by gastric lavage. Following gastric lavage, activated charcoal may be administered. Twenty to 30 g of activated charcoal may be given every 4 to 6 hours during the first 24 to 48 hours after ingestion. An ECG should be taken and close monitoring of cardiac function instituted if there is any sign of abnormality. Maintain an open airway and adequate fluid intake; regulate body temperature.

The i.v. administration of 1 to 3 mg of physostigmine salicylate is reported to reverse the symptoms of other tricyclic antidepressant poisoning in humans. Because physostigmine is rapidly metabolized, the dosage of physostigmine should be repeated as required particularly if life-threatening signs such as arrhythmias, convulsions, and deep coma recur or persist after the initial dosage of physostigmine. Because physostigmine itself may be toxic, it is not recommended for routine use.

Standard measures should be used to manage circulatory shock and metabolic acidosis. Close monitoring of cardiac function for not less than 5 days is advisable.

Anticonvulsants may be given to control convulsions.

Dialysis is of no value because of low plasma concentrations of the drug.

Since overdosage is often deliberate, patients may attempt suicide by other means during the recovery phase.

Deaths by deliberate or accidental overdosage have occurred with this class of drugs.

Dosage: Depression tends to be cyclical in nature and varying in severity. Therefore, dosage must be individualized, bearing in mind the possibility of spontaneous remission in certain instances, regardless of therapy, as well as the danger of relapse.

The natural course of depression is often many months in duration. Accordingly, it is suggested that maintenance therapy should be continued for at least 3 months after there is satisfactory improvement. This will reduce the chance of relapse, which may occur if the depressive cycle is not complete. If relapse does occur after discontinuation of protriptyline, therapy with the drug may be reinstituted.

Daily dosage ranges between 20 and 60 mg orally depending on the severity of the condition and should preferably be divided into 2 or 4 doses a day. If insomnia is present, the last dose of the day should be given no later than midafternoon. Required increases in dosage should be added to the morning dose. When a satisfactory response is obtained, dosage should be reduced to the smallest amount required for maintenance therapy.

If dosage required to maintain adequate response produces overstimulation, concomitant use of a tranquilizer will usually provide effective control. If dosage can be kept below 20 mg daily, overstimulation may not occur.

Outpatients: An initial dosage of 20 to 30 mg a day, orally, is recommended.

Hospitalized Patients: A dosage of 30 to 60 mg a day, orally, may be necessary to obtain adequate initial dosage.

Elderly Patients and Adolescents: These patients often respond to lower doses, and may not tolerate higher doses as well as other patients. Ten mg twice a day may be given to them as initial therapy. In the elderly patients, the cardiovascular system should be closely monitored if the daily dose exceeds 20 mg.

Supplied: Each white, round, film-coated tablet, with MSD 47 printed on one side, contains: protriptyline HCl 10 mg. Nonmedicinal ingredients: calcium phosphate, carnauba wax, cellulose derivatives, guar gum, magnesium stearate, silica, starch, talc and titanium dioxide. Gluten-, lactose- and tartrazine-free. High density polyethylene bottles of 100. Store at controlled room temperature (between 15 and 30°C).

(Shown in Product Recognition Section)

Reviewed 1997

TRIQUILAR® 21 Ⓟ
TRIQUILAR® 28 Ⓟ

Berlex Canada

Levonorgestrel—Ethinyl Estradiol

Oral Contraceptive

Pharmacology: Although the primary mechanism of action is inhibition of ovulation, the effectiveness of Triquilar may also result from other mechanisms of action, such as hostility of the cervical mucus to sperm penetration and migration.

Triquilar, a triphasic oral contraceptive, contains as active ingredients levonorgestrel and ethinyl estradiol. It acts primarily through the mechanism of gonadotrophin suppression by the estrogenic and progestational activity of the active ingredients. Although the primary activity is inhibition of ovulation, alterations in the genital tract, including changes in the cervical mucus (which make sperm penetration more difficult), and the endometrium (which reduce the likelihood of implantation) may also contribute to contraceptive effectiveness.

Levonorgestrel has been evaluated extensively in women to assess its progestational activity.

In women, the endometrium is transformed by the oral administration of 2.5 mg levonorgestrel given over a period of 10 days (total dose after pretreatment with estrogen). The endometrial transformation dose is 250 µg/day, corresponding to 5 µg/kg.

Levonorgestrel at a dose of 125 µg/day was also shown to be twice as potent as norethindrone in the delay of menstruation test by "Swyer and Greenblatt".

Ovulation is inhibited and a distinct antifertile effect is exerted in the peripheral cycle function during therapy with Triquilar.

Endometrial Biopsy: Endometrial biopsies obtained at variable times during the cycle were assessed according to the criteria of Noyes. Overall it was shown that this triphasic contraceptive causes a moderate degree of endometrial proliferation during the first phase, followed by premature secretory changes in the second phase, and minimal but continued development and maturation in the third phase that do not approach those seen in a normal cycle.

The overall Pearl Index and Lifetable analysis for the clinical trials were 0.3 and 0.4 respectively.

Indications: Prevention of pregnancy or conception control.

Contraindications: History of/or actual thrombophlebitis or thromboembolic disorders in arteries or veins and states which predispose to such disorders. History of/or actual cerebrovascular disorders. History of/or actual myocardial infarction or coronary arterial disease. Active liver disease or history of/or actual benign or malignant liver tumors. Known or suspected carcinoma of the breast. Known or suspected estrogen-dependent neoplasia. Undiagnosed abnormal vaginal bleeding. Any ocular lesion arising from ophthalmic vascular disease, such as partial or complete loss of vision or defect in visual fields. When pregnancy is suspected or diagnosed.

Warnings: Predisposing Factors for Coronary Artery Disease: Cigarette smoking increases the risk of serious cardiovascular side effects and mortality. Birth control pills increase this risk, especially with increasing age. Convincing data are available to support an upper age limit of 35 years for oral contraceptive use in women who smoke.

Other women who are independently at high risk for cardiovascular disease include those with diabetes, hypertension, abnormal lipid profile, or a family history of these. Whether oral contraceptives accentuate this risk is unclear.

Triquilar (cont'd)

In low-risk, nonsmoking women of any age, the benefits of oral contraceptive use outweigh the possible cardiovascular risks associated with low-dose formulations. Consequently, oral contraceptives may be prescribed for these women up to the age of menopause.

> Cigarette smoking increases the risk of serious adverse effects on the heart and blood vessels. The risk increases with age and becomes significant in oral contraceptive users over 35 years of age. Women should be counselled not to smoke.

Discontinue medication at the earliest manifestation of:
A. Thromboembolic and cardiovascular disorders such as: thrombophlebitis, pulmonary embolism, cerebrovascular disorders, myocardial ischemia, mesenteric thrombosis and retinal thrombosis.
B. Conditions which predispose to venous stasis and to vascular thrombosis (e.g., immobilization after accidents or confinement to bed during long-term illness). Other nonhormonal methods of contraception should be used until regular activities are resumed. For use of oral contraceptives when surgery is contemplated, see Precautions.
C. Visual defects, partial or complete.
D. Papilledema, or ophthalmic vascular lesions.
E. Severe headache of unknown etiology or worsening of preexisting migraine headache.
F. Increase in epileptic seizures.

Precautions: Physical Examination and Follow-up: Before oral contraceptives are used, a thorough history and physical examination should be performed, including a blood pressure determination and the family case history carefully noted. In addition, disturbances of the clotting system must be ruled out if any members of the family have suffered from thromboembolic diseases (e.g., deep vein thrombosis, stroke, myocardial infarction) at a young age. Breasts, liver, extremities and pelvic organs should be examined. A Papanicolaou smear should be taken if the patient has been sexually active.

The first follow-up visit should be done 3 months after oral contraceptives are prescribed. Thereafter, examinations should be performed at least once a year, or more frequently if indicated. At each annual visit, examination should include those procedures that were done at the initial visit as outlined above or per recommendations of the Canadian Workshop on Screening for Cancer of the Cervix. Their suggestion was that, for women who had 2 consecutive negative Pap smears, screening could be continued every 3 years to up to age 69.

Pregnancy: Oral contraceptives should not be taken by pregnant women. However, if conception accidentally occurs while taking the pill, there is no conclusive evidence that the estrogen and progestin contained in the oral contraceptive will damage the developing child.

Lactation: In breast-feeding women, the use of oral contraceptives results in the hormonal components being excreted in breast milk and may reduce its quantity and quality. If the use of oral contraceptives is initiated after the establishment of lactation, there does not appear to be any effect on the quantity and quality of milk. There is no evidence that low-dose oral contraceptives are harmful to the nursing infant.

Hepatic Function: Patients who have had jaundice, including a history of cholestatic jaundice during pregnancy, should be given oral contraceptives with great care and under close observation.

The development of severe generalized pruritus or icterus requires that the medication be withdrawn until the problem is resolved.

If a patient develops jaundice which proves to be cholestatic in type, the use of oral contraceptives should not be resumed. In patients taking oral contraceptives, changes in the composition of the bile may occur and an increased incidence of gallstones has been reported.

Hepatic nodules (adenoma and focal nodular hyperplasia) have been reported, particularly in long-term users of oral contraceptives. Although these lesions are extremely rare, they have caused fatal intra-abdominal hemorrhage and should be considered in women with an abdominal mass, acute abdominal pain, or evidence of intra-abdominal bleeding.

Hypertension: Patients with essential hypertension whose blood pressure is well-controlled may be given oral contraceptives but only under close supervision. If a significant elevation of blood pressure in previously normotensive or hypertensive subjects occurs at any time during the administration of the drug, cessation of medication is necessary.

Migraine and Headache: The onset or exacerbation of migraine or the development of headache of a new pattern which is recurrent, persistent or severe requires discontinuation of oral contraceptives and evaluation of the cause.

Diabetes: Current low-dose oral contraceptives exert minimal impact on glucose metabolism. Diabetic patients, or those with a family history of diabetes, should be observed closely to detect any worsening of carbohydrate metabolism. Patients predisposed to diabetes who can be kept under close supervision may be given oral contraceptives. Young diabetic patients whose disease is of recent origin, well-controlled and not associated with hypertension or other signs of vascular disease such as ocular fundal changes should be monitored more frequently while using oral contraceptives.

Ocular Disease: Patients who are pregnant or are taking oral contraceptives, may experience corneal edema that may cause visual disturbances and changes in tolerance to contact lenses, especially of the rigid type. Soft contact lenses usually do not cause disturbances. If visual changes or alterations in tolerance to contact lenses occur, temporary or permanent cessation of wear may be advised.

Breasts: Increasing age and a strong family history are the most significant risk factors for the development of breast cancer. Other established risk factors include obesity, nulliparity and late age at first full-term pregnancy. The identified groups of women that may be at increased risk of developing breast cancer before menopause are long-term users of oral contraceptives (more than 8 years) and starters at early age. In a few women, the use of oral contraceptives may accelerate the growth of an existing but undiagnosed breast cancer. Since any potential increased risk related to oral contraceptives use is small, there is no reason to change prescribing habits at present.

Women receiving oral contraceptives should be instructed in self-examination of their breasts. Their physicians should be notified whenever any masses are detected. A yearly clinical breast examination is also recommended because, if a breast cancer should develop, estrogen-containing drugs may cause a rapid progression.

Vaginal Bleeding: Persistent irregular vaginal bleeding requires assessment to exclude underlying pathology.

Fibroids: Patients with fibroids (leiomyomata) should be carefully observed. Sudden enlargement, pain, or tenderness requires discontinuation of the use of oral contraceptives.

Emotional Disorders: Patients with a history of emotional disturbances, especially the depressive type, may be more prone to have a recurrence of depression while taking oral contraceptives. In cases of a serious recurrence, a trial of an alternative method of contraception should be made which may help to clarify the possible relationship. Women with premenstrual syndrome (PMS) may have a varied response to oral contraceptives, ranging from symptomatic improvement to worsening of the condition.

Laboratory Tests: Results of laboratory tests should be interpreted in the light that the patient is on oral contraceptives. The following laboratory tests are modified.
A. Liver Function Tests: Aspartate serum transaminase (AST): variously reported elevations. Alkaline phosphatase and gamma glutamine transaminase (GGT): slightly elevated.
B. Coagulation Tests: Minimal elevation of test values reported for such parameters as Factors VII, VIII, IX and X.
C. Thyroid Function Tests: Protein binding of thyroxine is increased as indicated by increased total serum thyroxine concentrations and decreased T_3 resin uptake.
D. Lipoproteins: Small changes of unproven clinical significance may occur in lipoprotein cholesterol fractions.
E. Gonadotrophins: LH and FSH levels are suppressed by the use of oral contraceptives. Wait 2 weeks after discontinuing the use of oral contraceptives before measurements are made.

Tissue Specimens: Pathologists should be advised of oral contraceptive therapy when specimens obtained from surgical procedures and Papanicolaou smears are submitted for examination.

Return to Fertility: After discontinuing oral contraceptive therapy, the patient should delay pregnancy until at least 1 normal spontaneous cycle has occurred in order to date the pregnancy. An alternative contraceptive method should be used during this time.

Amenorrhea: Women having a history of oligomenorrhea, secondary amenorrhea, or irregular cycles, may remain

Table I—Triquilar

Drugs Which May Decrease the Efficacy of Oral Contraceptives

Class of Compound	Drug	Proposed Mechanism	Suggested Management
Anticonvulsants	Carbamazepine Ethosuximide Phenobarbital Phenytoin Primidone	Induction of hepatic microsomal enzymes. Rapid metabolism of estrogen and increased binding of progestin and ethinyl estradiol to SHBG.	Use higher dose OCs (50 μg ethinyl estradiol), another drug, or another method.
Antibiotics	Ampicillin Cotrimoxazole Penicillin	Enterohepatic circulation disturbance, intestinal hurry.	For short course, use additional method or use another drug. For long course, use another method.
	Rifampin	Increased metabolism of progestins. Suspected acceleration of estrogen metabolism.	Use another method.
	Chloramphenicol Metronidazole Neomycin Nitrofurantoin Sulfonamides Tetracyclines	Induction of hepatic microsomal enzymes. Also disturbance of enterohepatic circulation.	For short course, use additional method or use another drug. For long course, use another method.
	Troleandomycin	May retard metabolism of OCs, increasing the risk of cholestatic jaundice.	
Antifungals	Griseofulvin	Stimulation of hepatic metabolism of contraceptive steroids may occur.	Use another method.
Sedatives and Hypnotics	Benzodiazepines Barbiturates Chloral Hydrate Glutethimide Meprobamate	Induction of hepatic microsomal enzymes.	For short course, use additional method or another drug. For long course, use another method or higher dose OCs.
Antacids		Decreased intestinal absorption of progestins.	Dose 2 hours apart.
Other Drugs	Phenylbutazone Antihistamines Analgesics Antimigraine preparations Vitamin E	Reduced OC efficacy has been reported. Remains to be confirmed.	

anovulatory or become amenorrheic following discontinuation of estrogen-progestogen combination therapy.

Amenorrhea, especially if associated with breast secretion, that continues for 6 months or more after withdrawal, warrants a careful assessment of hypothalamic-pituitary function.

Thromboembolic Complications—Postsurgery: There is an increased risk of thromboembolic complications in oral contraceptive users, after major surgery. If feasible, oral contraceptives should be discontinued and an alternative method substituted at least 1 month prior to **major** elective surgery. Oral contraceptive use should not be resumed until the first menstrual period after hospital discharge following surgery.

Drug Interactions: The concurrent administration of oral contraceptives with other drugs may result in an altered response to either agent (see Table I (on previous page) and Table II). Reduced effectiveness of the oral contraceptive, should it occur, is more likely with the low-dose formulations. It is important to ascertain all drugs that a patient is taking, both prescription and nonprescription, before oral contraceptives are prescribed.

Noncontraceptive Benefits of Oral Contraceptives: Several health advantages other than contraception have been reported.

1. Combination oral contraceptives reduce the incidence of cancer of the endometrium and ovaries.
2. Oral contraceptives reduce the likelihood of developing benign breast disease.
3. Oral contraceptives reduce the likelihood of development of functional ovarian cysts.
4. Pill-users have less menstrual blood loss and have more regular cycles, thereby reducing the chance of developing iron-deficiency anemia.
5. The use of oral contraceptives may decrease the severity of dysmenorrhea and premenstrual syndrome, and may improve acne vulgaris, hirsutism, and other androgen-mediated disorders.
6. Oral contraceptives decrease the incidence of ectopic pregnancy.
7. Oral contraceptives have potential beneficial effects on endometriosis.

> Oral contraceptives **do not protect against** sexually transmitted diseases (STDs) including HIV/AIDS. For protection against STDs, it is advisable to use latex condoms **in combination with** oral contraceptives.

Adverse Effects: An increased risk of the following serious adverse reactions has been associated with the use of oral contraceptives: thrombophlebitis; pulmonary embolism; mesenteric thrombosis; neuro-ocular lesions (e.g., retinal thrombosis); myocardial infarction; cerebral thrombosis; cerebral hemorrhage; hypertension; benign hepatic tumors; gallbladder disease.

The following adverse reactions have also been reported in patients receiving oral contraceptives: nausea and vomiting, usually the most common adverse reaction, occurs in approximately 10% or fewer of patients during the first cycle. Other reactions, as a general rule, are seen less frequently or only occasionally.

The most frequently reported adverse events in the 8 748 patients (50 793 cycles) monitored during the registration clinical trials have been tabulated in Table III (on following page).

There was a decline in the incidence of symptoms with time. Most adverse effects were observed in the first 3 months of therapy. From cycle 4 to 24, the frequencies of all symptoms were lower than the pretreatment values.

Overdose: Symptoms: With levonorgestrel and ethinyl estradiol, acute doses in excess of clinical levels when administered to experimental animals, have been shown to have a minimal deleterious effect. In humans, however, the extent of ill effects to be expected following accidental ingestion of a large dose of any oral contraceptive has not been firmly established.

Depending upon the amount ingested, liver toxicity, temporary interference with the function of the seminiferous tubules, or in the case of females, possible withdrawal bleeding within a few days of consumption, are theoretically possible. However, case histories of both male and female children, some of whom ingested more than half a month's supply of oral contraceptive tablets, indicate that the effects are asymptomatic and without immediate consequence. Despite the frequency of nausea and vomiting in adult females during the first few cycles of use, none of these children presented such symptoms.

Table II—Triquilar

Modification of Other Drug Action by Oral Contraceptives

Class of Compound	Drug	Modification of Other Drug Action	Suggested Management
Alcohol		Possible increased levels of ethanol or acetaldehyde.	Use with caution.
Alpha-II Adrenoreceptor Agents	Clonidine	Sedation effect increased.	Use with caution.
Anticoagulants	All	OCs increase clotting factors, decrease efficacy. However, OCs may potentiate action in some patients.	Use another method.
Anticonvulsants	All	Fluid retention may increase risk of seizures.	Use another method.
Antidiabetic Drugs	Oral Hypoglycemics and Insulin	OCs may impair glucose tolerance and increase blood glucose.	Use low-dose estrogen and progestin OC or another method. Monitor blood glucose.
Antihypertensive Agents	Guanethidine and Methyldopa	Estrogen component causes sodium retention, progestin has no effect.	Use low-dose estrogen OC or use another method.
	Beta-blockers	Increased drug effect (decreased metabolism).	Adjust dose of drug if necessary. Monitor cardiovascular status.
Antipyretics	Acetaminophen	Increased metabolism and renal clearance.	Dose of drug may have to be increased.
	Antipyrine	Impaired metabolism.	Decrease dose of drug.
	ASA	Effects of ASA may be decreased by the short-term use of OCs.	Patients on chronic ASA therapy may require an increase in ASA dosage.
Aminocaproic Acid		Theoretically, a hypercoagulable state may occur because OCs augment clotting factors.	Avoid concomitant use
Betamimetic Agents	Isoproterenol	Estrogen causes decreased response to these drugs.	Adjust dose of drug as necessary. Discontinuing OCs can result in excessive drug activity.
Caffeine		The actions of caffeine may be enhanced as OCs may impair the hepatic metabolism of caffeine.	Use with caution.
Cholesterol Lowering Agents	Clofibrate	Their action may be antagonized by OCs. OCs may also increase metabolism of clofibrate.	May need to increase dose of clofibrate.
Corticosteroids	Prednisone	Markedly increased serum levels.	Possible need for decrease in dose.
Cyclosporine		May lead to an increase in cyclosporine levels and hepatotoxicity.	Monitor hepatic function. The cyclosporine dose may have to be decreased.
Folic Acid		OCs have been reported to impair folate metabolism.	
Meperedine		Possible increased analgesia and CNS depression due to decreased metabolism of meperidine.	Use combination with caution.
Phenothiazine Tranquilizers	All Phenothiazines, Reserpine and similar drugs	Estrogen potentiates the hyperprolactinemia effect of these drugs.	Use other drugs or lower dose OCs. If galactorrhea or hyperprolactinemia occurs, use other method.
Sedatives and Hypnotics	Chlordiazepoxide Lorazepam Oxazepam Diazepam	Increased effect (increased metabolism).	Use with caution.
Theophylline	All	Decreased oxidation, leading to possible toxicity.	Use with caution. Monitor theophylline levels.
Tricyclic Antidepressants	Clomipramine (possibly others)	Increased side effects; i.e., depression.	Use with caution.
Vitamin B_{12}		OCs have been reported to reduce serum levels of Vitamin B_{12}.	May need to increase dietary intake, or supplement.

Treatment: Although the physiologic effects of oral contraceptives may be theoretically offset by concomitant administration of gonadotrophin preparations, there are no known chemotherapeutic agents which will neutralize their effects subsequent to accidental ingestion. In the practical management of an acute overdosage, gastric lavage may be of value if the offending agent has recently been swallowed. The general rules for observation and symptomatic resolution should be followed. Liver function tests should be conducted, particularly transaminase levels, 2 to 3 weeks after consumption.

Dosage: Information for the Patient on How to Take the Birth Control Pill:

1. **Read these directions:**
   - before you start taking your pills, and
   - any time you are not sure what to do.
2. **Look at your pill pack to see if it has 21 or 28 pills:**
   - 21-Pill Pack: 21 active pills (with hormones) taken daily for 3 weeks, and then no pills taken for 1 week.

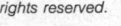

   or
   - 28-Pill Pack: 21 active pills (with hormones) taken daily for 3 weeks, and then seven "reminder" pills (no hormones) taken daily for 1 week.
3. You may wish to use a second method of birth control (e.g., latex condoms and spermicidal foam or gel) for the first 7 days of the first cycle of pill use. This will provide a back-up in case pills are forgotten while you are getting used to taking them.
4. **When receiving any medical treatment, be sure to tell your doctor that you are using birth control pills.**
5. **Many women have spotting or light bleeding, or may feel sick to their stomach during the first 3 months on the**

Triquilar (cont'd)

Table III—Triquilar

Adverse Effects

Adverse Events	Frequency of Observations per Cycle (%)
Gynecological	
Dysmenorrhea	6.5%
Spotting	5.8%
Breast tension or pain	4.2%
Libido, increase - decrease	2.0%
Breakthrough bleeding	1.8%
Chloasma	1.8%
Amenorrhea	0.8%
Gastrointestinal	
Nausea and/or vomiting	4.2%
Increased appetite	0.5%
CNS	
Headache	5.6%
Migraine	2.0%
Depression	2.0%
Cardiovascular	
Varicose veins	3.5%
Edema	0.4%
Thrombophlebitis	0.2%
Dermatological	
Acne	2.3%
Miscellaneous Symptoms	
Weight gain	0.3%

pill. If you do feel sick, do not stop taking the pill. The problem will usually go away. If it does not go away, check with your doctor or clinic.

6. **Missing pills also can cause some spotting or light bleeding,** even if you make up the missed pills. You also could feel a little sick to your stomach on the days you take 2 pills to make up for missed pills.
7. **If you miss pills at any time, you could get pregnant. The greatest risks for pregnancy are:**
   - when you start a pack late, or
   - when you miss pills at the beginning or at the very end of the pack.
8. **Always be sure you have ready:**
   - **another kind of birth control** (such as latex condoms and spermicidal foam or gel) to use as a back-up in case you miss pills, and
   - **an extra, full pack of pills.**
9. **If you experience vomiting or diarrhea, or if you take certain medicines,** such as antibiotics, your pills may not work as well. Use a back-up method, such as latex condoms and spermicidal foam or gel, until you can check with your doctor or clinic.
10. **If you forget more than 1 pill 2 months in a row, talk to your doctor or clinic** about how to make pill-taking easier or about using another method of birth control.
11. **If your questions are not answered here, call your doctor or clinic.**

When to start the first pack of pills: Be sure to read these instructions:

- before you start taking your pills, and
- any time you are not sure what to do

Start taking your pills on day one of your menstrual cycle. Your pills may be either a 21-day or a 28-day type.

A. **21-Day Combination:** With this type of birth control pill, you are on pills for 21 days and off pills for 7 days. You must not be off the pills for more than 7 days in a row.

1. **The first day of your menstrual period (bleeding) is Day 1 of your cycle.** Your doctor will advise you to start taking the pills on Day 1 of your period.
2. Take 1 pill at approximately the same time every day for 21 days; **then take no pills for 7 days.** Start a new pack on the eighth day. You will probably have a period during the 7 days off the pill. (This bleeding may be lighter and shorter than your usual period.)

B. **28-Day Combination:** With this type of birth control pill, you take 21 pills which contain hormones and 7 pills which contain no hormones.

1. **The first day of your menstrual period (bleeding) is Day 1 of your cycle.** Your doctor will advise you to start taking the pills on Day 1 of your period.
2. Take 1 pill at approximately the same time every day for 28 days. Begin a new pack the next day, **not missing any days.** Your period should occur during the last 7 days of using that pill pack.

What to do during the month:

1. **Take a pill at approximately the same time every day until the pack is empty.**
   - Try to associate taking your pills with some regular activity such as eating a meal or going to bed.
   - Do not skip pills even if you have bleeding between monthly periods or feel sick to your stomach (nausea).
   - Do not skip pills even if you do not have sex very often.
2. **When you finish a pack**
   - **21 pills: Wait 7 days** to start the next pack. You will have your period during that week.
   - **28 pills: Start the next pack on the next day.** Take 1 pill every day. Do not wait any days between packs.

What to do if you miss pills: Table IV outlines the actions you should take if you miss one or more of your birth control pills.

Table IV—Triquilar

Miss 1 pill

Take it as soon as you remember, and take the next pill at the usual time. This means that you might take 2 pills in one day.

Miss 2 pills in a row

First 2 Weeks:

1. Take 2 pills the day you remember and 2 pills the next day.
2. Then take 1 pill a day until you finish the pack.
3. Use a back-up method of birth control if you have sex in the 7 days after you miss the pills.

Third Week:

1. Safely dispose of the rest of the pill pack and start a new pack that same day.
2. Use a back-up method of birth control if you have sex in the 7 days after you miss the pills.
3. You may not have a period this month.

If you miss 2 periods in a row, call your doctor or clinic.

Miss 3 or more pills in a row

Anytime in the Cycle:

1. Safely dispose of the rest of the pill pack and start a new pack that same day.
2. Use a back-up method of birth control if you have sex in the 7 days after you miss the pills.
3. You may not have a period this month.

If you miss 2 periods in a row, call your doctor or clinic.

Note: 28-Day Pack: If you forget any of the 7 "reminder" pills (without hormones) in Week 4, just safely dispose of the pills you missed. Then keep taking one pill each day until the pack is empty. You do not need to use a back-up method.

Always be sure you have on hand:

- a back-up method of birth control (such as latex condoms and spermicidal foam or gel) in case you miss pills, and
- an extra, full pack of pills.

If you forget more than 1 pill 2 months in a row, talk to your doctor or clinic about ways to make pill-taking easier or about using another method of birth control.

Information for the Patient: See Blue Section—Information for the Patient "Oral Contraceptives".

Supplied: Triquilar 21: Days 1–6: Each light brown tablet contains: levonorgestrel 50 μg and ethinyl estradiol 30 μg. Days 7–11: Each white tablet contains: levonorgestrel 75 μg and ethinyl estradiol 40 μg. Days 12–21: Each ochreous tablet contains: levonorgestrel 125 μg and ethinyl estradiol 30 μg. Nonmedicinal ingredients: calcium carbonate, cornstarch, glycerin, lactose, magnesium stearate, polyethylene glycol, polyvinylpyrrolidone, red ferric oxide, sucrose, talc, titanium dioxide, wax E and yellow ferric oxide. Gluten- and tartrazine-free.

Triquilar 28: Package contains the same tablets as Triquilar 21 plus seven slightly larger inert white tablets, containing no active ingredients. Nonmedicinal ingredients: calcium carbonate, cornstarch, glycerin, lactose, magnesium stearate, polyethylene glycol, polyvinylpyrrolidone, red ferric oxide, sucrose, talc, titanium dioxide, wax E and yellow ferric oxide. Gluten- and tartrazine-free.

(Shown in Product Recognition Section)

Reviewed 1997

...Drug identification problem? Consult the PRODUCT RECOGNITION SECTION.

TRISORALEN™ Ⓟ

ICN

Trioxsalen

Melanizing Agent

Pharmacology: Trioxsalen is a synthetic melanizing agent structurally and pharmacologically related to methoxsalen. The normal pigmentation of the skin is due to melanin, which is produced in the cytoplasm of the melanocytes located in the basal layers of the epidermis at its junction with the dermis. Melanin is formed by the oxidation of tyrosine to DOPA (dihydroxyphenylalanine) with tyrosinase as catalyst. This enzymatic reaction, however, must be activated by radiant energy in the form of ultraviolet (UV) light, preferably between 2 900 and 3 800 angstroms (black light).

The exact mechanism of the action of psoralens in the process of melanogenesis is not known. One group of investigators feels that the psoralens have a specific effect on the epidermis or, more specifically, on the melanocytes. Another group feels that the primary response to the psoralens is an inflammatory one and that the process of melanogenesis is secondary.

Indications: Taken approximately 2 hours before measured periods of exposure to UV light, trioxsalen facilitates:

Repigmentation of idiopathic vitiligo: Repigmentation, not equally reversible in every patient, will vary in completeness, time of onset, and duration. The rate of completeness of pigmentation with respect to locations of lesions, occurs more rapidly on fleshy regions, such as the face, abdomen, and buttocks, and less rapidly over bony areas such as the dorsum of the hands and feet. Repigmentation may begin after a few weeks; however, significant results may take as long as 6 to 9 months, and repigmentation, at the optimum level, may, in some cases, require maintenance dosage to retain the new pigment. If follicular repigmentation is not apparent after 3 months of daily treatment, treatment should be discontinued as a failure.

Increasing tolerance to sunlight: In blond persons and those with fair complexions who suffer painful reactions when exposed to sunlight, trioxsalen aids in increasing resistance to solar damage. Certain persons who are allergic to sunlight or exhibit sun sensitivity may be benefited by trioxsalen's protective action.

In albinism, trioxsalen will increase the tolerance of the skin to sunlight, although no pigment is formed. This protective action seems to be related to the thickening of the horny layer and retention of melanin which produces a thickened, melanized stratum corneum and formation of a stratum lucidum.

Contraindications: Diseases associated with photosensitivity such as porphyria, acute lupus erythematosus or leukoderma of infectious origin. Safety for use in children 12 years and under has not been established. Do not use photosensitizing preparations, internal or external, concomitantly with trioxsalen.

Precautions: Trioxsalen is a potent drug. Dosage and exposure time should not be increased. Overdosage and/or overexposure may result in serious burning and blistering. When used to increase tolerance to sunlight, the total trioxsalen dosage should not exceed 28 tablets (140 mg), taken in daily single 10 mg doses on a continuous or interrupted regimen. To prevent harmful effects, the patient must be carefully instructed to adhere to the prescribed dosage schedule and procedure.

Pregnancy: Safe use in human pregnancy has not been established, although animal reproduction studies (mice, rats) demonstrated no teratogenic effect. Therefore, use trioxsalen during pregnancy only when the probable benefits outweigh the possible risks.

Although there are no clinical reports or tests to verify that more severe reactions may result from the concomitant ingestion of food containing furocoumarin while on trioxsalen therapy, the patient should be warned that eating limes, figs, parsley, parsnips, mustard, carrots and celery, might be dangerous. Use trioxsalen with caution in patients with defective coagulation or in patients receiving anticoagulants.

Sunglasses should be worn during exposure and the lips protected with a light-screening lipstick. Initiate sunlamp exposure according to the sunlamp manufacturer's directions.

Adverse Effects: Severe burns can result from excessive sunlight or sunlamp UV exposure. Occasionally, gastric discomfort may occur, which can be minimized by taking the medication with milk or after a meal. Some patients who cannot tolerate 10 mg will tolerate 5 mg. This dosage produces the same therapeutic effect but more slowly. In a small percentage of cases, abnormal liver function tests have been reported, as measured by increased thymol turbidity (Thymol Turbidity Test); by increased BSP retention; or by elevated values following the Ceph-Floc test (Cephalin-Cholesterol Flocculation Test).

Overdose: Symptoms and Treatment: If an overdose of trioxsalen or UV light has been taken, encourage emesis. Keep the individual in a darkened room for 8 hours or until cutaneous reactions subside. The treatment for severe reactions resulting from overdosage or overexposure should follow accepted procedures for treatment of severe burns.

Dosage: Adults and children over 12 years: Vitiligo: 10 mg 2 to 4 hours before measured periods of UV exposure or fluorescent black light. See suggested sun exposure guide.
To ensure tolerance to sunlight: 10 mg daily 2 hours before measured periods of exposure to sun or UV irradiation. Not to be continued for longer than 14 days. The dosage should **not** be increased, as severe burning may occur. See suggested sun exposure guide.
Subsequent Exposure: Gradually increase exposure based on erythema and tenderness (see Table I).

Table I—Trisoralen

Suggested Sun Exposure Guide
The exposure time to sunlight should be limited according to the following plan:

	Basic Skin Color	
Exposure	**Light**	**Medium**
Initial	15 min.	20 min.
Second	20 min.	25 min.
Third	25 min.	30 min.
Fourth	30 min.	35 min.

Supplied: Each white, round, sugar-coated tablet, printed ICN on one side and 303 on the other side contains: trioxsalen USP 5 mg. Nonmedicinal ingredients: lactose, magnesium stearate, starch, sucrose and talc. Bottles of 100.

TRISULFAMINIC ℞
Shepherd

Triple Sulfas—Phenylpropanolamine HCl Compound—Pheniramine Maleate

Decongestant—Antibacterial

Indications: Congestion and infection of upper respiratory tract caused by sulfa-susceptible organisms.

Contraindications: Sensitivity to any of the components, impaired renal function, pregnancy approaching term, and in premature infants and newborn infants during the first month of life. Do not use in patients with glaucoma, prostatic hypertrophy, stenosing peptic ulcer, pyloroduodenal or bladder neck obstruction or patients receiving MAO inhibitors.

Precautions: Use with caution in patients with histories of significant allergy or asthma or patients receiving methyldopa or beta adrenergic blockers. Assure an adequate fluid intake. Occupational Hazards: Patients should be cautioned not to operate vehicles or hazardous machinery until their response to the drug has been determined.

Since the depressant effects of antihistamines are additive to those of other drugs affecting the CNS, patients should be cautioned against drinking alcoholic beverages or taking hypnotics, sedatives, psychotherapeutic agents or other drugs with CNS depressant effects during antihistaminic therapy.

Use with caution in the presence of hypertension, hyperthyroidism, cardiovascular disease and diabetes mellitus. Use only after careful evaluation in patients with liver or renal damage, urinary obstruction, or blood dyscrasias. In intermittent or prolonged therapy, blood counts and liver and kidney function tests should be performed periodically. Sulfonamide therapy may potentiate the hypoglycemic action of sulfonylureas and induce hemolytic anemia in patients with a deficiency of glucose-6-phosphate dehydrogenase.

Adverse Effects: As in all sulfonamide therapy, the following reactions may occur: headache, nausea, vomiting, diarrhea, icterus, hepatitis, pancreatitis, urticaria, rash, fever, cyanosis, hematuria, crystalluria, proteinuria, blood dyscrasias, petechiae, purpura, neuropathy and injection of the conjunctiva and sclera. If any of these reactions occur, the drug should be discontinued.

With antihistaminic therapy there have been reports of sedation varying from mild drowsiness to deep sleep, dizziness, lassitude, inability to concentrate, fatigue, incoordination, tinnitus, blurred vision, diplopia, euphoria, nervousness, insomnia, tremors, palpitation, hypotension, headache, chest tightness, urinary frequency, dysuria, tingling of the hands, dryness of the mouth, throat, and nose, gastrointestinal disturbances such as epigastric distress, anorexia, nausea, vomiting, constipation and diarrhea and very rarely, leukopenia and agranulocytosis.

Adverse effects reported with the use of sympathomimetic amines include anxiety, tension, restlessness, nervousness, tremor, weakness, insomnia, headache, palpitation, tachycardia, angina, elevation of blood pressure, sweating, mydriasis, anorexia, nausea, vomiting, dizziness, constipation, and dysuria due to vesicle sphincter spasm.

Dosage: Adults: 10 to 20 mL or 2 to 4 tablets initially, followed by 10 mL or 2 tablets every 6 hours. Children: 8 to 12 years: 10 mL or 2 tablets initially, followed by 5 mL or 1 tablet every 6 hours; 3 to 7 years: 5 mL every 6 hours; 1 to 2 years: 2.5 mL every 6 hours.

Medication should be continued until patient has been afebrile for 3 days.

Supplied: Suspension: Each 5 mL of orange-colored suspension contains: phenylpropanolamine HCl 12.5 mg, pheniramine maleate 6.25 mg, pyrilamine maleate 6.25 mg, sulfadiazine 167 mg, sulfamerazine 167 mg and sulfamethazine 167 mg. Nonmedicinal ingredients: D&C Yellow, FD&C Red, menthol, methyl cellulose, orange concentrate, sodium benzoate, sorbitol, sucrose and water. Energy: 80.5 kJ (19.24 kcal)/5 mL. Sodium: <1 mmol (0.8 mg). Alcohol- and tartrazine-free. Bottles of 500 mL.

Tablets: Each capsule-shaped tablet contains: phenylpropanolamine HCl 12.5 mg, pheniramine maleate 6.25 mg, pyrilamine maleate 6.25 mg, sulfadiazine 167 mg, sulfamerazine 167 mg and sulfamethazine 167 mg. Nonmedicinal ingredients: acacia, cornstarch, D&C Yellow, guar gum, icing sugar, magnesium stearate, methylcellulose, sodium alginate, stearic acid and water. Sodium: <1 mmol (<5 mg). Tartrazine-free. Bottles of 100 and 500.

TROMBOVAR®
Therapex

Sodium Tetradecyl Sulfate

Sclerosing Agent

Indications: Sclerosing treatment of varicose veins in the legs, using compression sclerotherapy.

Contraindications: Incompetency of collateral deep veins in the legs; incompetency of the valves of the greater and lesser saphenous veins before ligation of those veins; thrombophlebitis, tuberculosis and hyperthyroidism, acute infections, prolonged recumbency; cardiac insufficiency, diabetes, arterial disease, varicosities caused by pelvic neoplasia, pregnancy. Hypersensitivity to sodium tetradecyl sulfate.

Warnings: Because of the danger of extension of thrombosis into the deep venous system, thorough pre-injection evaluation for valvular competency should be carried out. In particular, deep venous potency must be determined by angiography, Perthes test or Doppler test before sclerotherapy is undertaken. A complication of sloughing may occur if product is injected outside the vein. Allergic reactions have been reported, therefore, as a precaution, it is recommended that an injection of 0.5 mL of the 1% solution into a varicosity be followed by observance of the patient for a few hours before a second injection is administered. The possibility of an anaphylactic reaction should always be kept in mind and the physician should be prepared to treat it appropriately. In extreme emergency, 0.25 mL of a 1:1 000 solution of epinephrine (0.25 mg) i.v. should be used and side effects controlled with antihistamines.

An injection outside the vein may cause severe necrosis. A consequence of intra-arterial injection may be amputation of the limb. Injections must be carried out exclusively by an experienced physician, having thorough knowledge of the sclerotherapy technique.

Adverse Effects: Allergic reactions to the product are rare: In case of side effects such as pruritus of the face and extremities, redness of the conjunctiva, shortness of breath or irritating cough within minutes of injection, appropriate treatment must be carried out immediately. Hyperpigmentation at the injection site may occur, but disappears spontaneously in most cases.

Dosage: Dosage and concentration of the solution depend on the size of the veins to sclerose. Doses at site of injection and total dose given per visit must be increased progressively from one visit to the next according to the size of the vein segment to sclerose while taking into account variable individual sensitivity to the sclerosing agent. Normal dosage varies from 0.5 to 2 mL (max) per injection, in sites situated between 6 and 12 cm from each other. Several separate injections can be made in either leg, but do not exceed a total of 10 mL of 3% solution/week.

In the treatment of superficial s.c. varicose veins, great care must be taken. In this case, only the 1% solution should be used and is most effective when used as a froth prepared by vigorously shaking the syringe. It is important to use a syringe that is transparent to be able to check the venous return to avoid extravasation.

Supplied: Each 2 mL ampul contains: sodium tetradecyl sulfate 1% or 3% with benzyl alcohol 2% as preservative in a buffered solution. Packages of 10.

TROPICAMIDE ℞
Rivex Ophthalmics

Mydriatic—Cycloplegic

Supplied: Each mL of sterile ophthalmic solution contains: tropicamide 1%. Nonmedicinal ingredients: benzalkonium chloride, boric acid, edetate disodium, hydrochloric acid, purified water and sodium hydroxide. Plastic squeeze bottles of 15 mL with controlled tip applicators.

TROSYD™ AF
TROSYD™ J
Pfizer Consumer

Tioconazole

Antifungal Agent

Pharmacology: Tioconazole is a member of the imidazole class of antifungal agents. Although the mode of action of tioconazole has not as yet been determined, several studies have demonstrated that the imidazoles inhibit ergosterol synthesis in fungi by blocking C-14 demethylation. As a result, there is an accumulation of C-14 methyl sterol intermediates like langosterol, and a decrease in ergosterol. Langosterol cannot support yeast growth in the absence of ergosterol, and the inhibition of ergosterol synthesis or the accumulation of langosterol may be the primary antifungal mechanism of this class of drugs. At high drug concentrations the imidazoles have been postulated to exert a fungicidal effect by rapid membrane damage of the fungi.

Indications: Trosyd AF: For the topical treatment of patients with tinea pedis and tinea corporis caused by T. rubrum, T. mentagrophytes, E. floccosum; cutaneous candidiasis due to C. albicans; tinea (pityriasis) versicolor caused by M. furfur (P. orbiculare).
Trosyd J: For the topical treatment of patients with tinea cruris caused by T. rubrum, T. mentagrophytes, E. floccosum; cutaneous candidiasis due to C. albicans; tinea (pityriasis) versicolor caused by M. furfur (P. orbiculare).
Children: Clinical experience with tioconazole cream in children is very limited.

Contraindications: In those patients who have a history of sensitization to tioconazole or to any of the other components of the dermal cream, or to other imidazole antifungal agents.

Warnings: *Pregnancy:* There are no adequate and well controlled studies which establish the safety of tioconazole cream in pregnant women.

In limited uncontrolled clinical use, tioconazole vaginal ointment and ovule applied as a single dose to about 20 patients during various stages of pregnancy did not appear to interfere with the normal progress of the pregnancy and at delivery.

However, local and systemic administration to rats indicate that adverse effects of parturition and/or fetal development were observed.

Accordingly, tioconazole cream should be used during pregnancy only if in the opinion of the physician the potential benefit outweighs the potential risk to the fetus.
Lactation: It is not known whether this drug is excreted in human milk. Because many drugs are excreted in human milk, tioconazole cream should not be used by nursing women unless, in the judgment of a physician, the potential benefit outweighs the possible risk.

Trosyd AF (cont'd)

Precautions: Skin and mucosal sensitization may occur. Use of tioconazole cream should be discontinued should such reaction occur, and appropriate therapy instituted.

Tioconazole cream is not for ophthalmic use.

Adverse Effects: Tioconazole cream 1% w/w is well tolerated upon local application and no systemic adverse reactions have been observed with the dermal application of the drug.

Symptoms of local irritation have been reported by some patients (7.2%). They are usually seen during the first week of treatment and are most often transient. The most commonly observed symptoms of local irritation reported in clinical studies were burning sensation (3.2%), itching (2.8%), erythema (1.5%), rash (0.8%) and edema (0.2%).

Treatment was discontinued in 1.9% of the patients. The principal reason for termination of treatment was the development of eczematous reactions or dermatitis.

Overdose: Symptoms and Treatment: None known.

Dosage: Skin Infections: Trosyd AF or Trosyd J should be gently massaged into the affected and surrounding skin area twice a day, in the morning and evening. In intertriginous areas, the creams should be applied sparingly and smoothed in well to avoid macerating effects.

The duration of treatment and the success achieved will vary from patient to patient, depending on the infecting organism and the site of infection. On the basis of clinical studies the recommended length of treatment is: tinea versicolor, 7 to 28 days; tinea cruris, up to 14 days; tinea pedis, up to 6 weeks may be required in severe cases, especially the chronic hyperkeratotic type; dermatophyte infections and cutaneous candidiasis at other sites, 2 to 4 weeks.

Information for the Patient: See Blue Section—Information for the Patient "Trosyd AF/Trosyd J".

Supplied: Trosyd AF: Each g of white homogeneous cream contains: tioconazole 10 mg (1% w/w) in a vanishing cream base. Nonmedicinal ingredients: benzyl alcohol (as preservative), ethoxylated cetostearyl alcohol, mineral oil, propylene glycol, purified water, stearic acid, stearyl alcohol and white petrolatum. Tubes of 5, 15 and 30 g.

Trosyd J: Each g of white homogeneous cream contains: tioconazole 10 mg (1% w/w) in a vanishing cream base. Nonmedicinal ingredients: benzyl alcohol (as preservative), ethoxylated cetostearyl alcohol, mineral oil, propylene glycol, purified water, stearic acid, stearyl alcohol and white petrolatum. Tubes of 5, 15 and 30 g.

Store at 15 to 30°C; avoid freezing.

(Shown in Product Recognition Section)

Reviewed 1997

TRUSOPT® Ⓟ

MSD

Dorzolamide HCl

Elevated Intraocular Pressure Therapy—Topical Carbonic Anhydrase Inhibitor

Pharmacology: Dorzolamide is a carbonic anhydrase inhibitor formulated for topical ophthalmic use.

Inhibition of carbonic anhydrase in the ciliary processes of the eye decreases aqueous humor secretion, presumably by slowing the formation of bicarbonate ions with subsequent reduction in sodium and fluid transport. The result is a reduction in intraocular pressure (IOP).

Unlike oral carbonic anhydrase inhibitors, topically applied dorzolamide exerts its effects at substantially low doses and therefore with less systemic exposure.

When applied topically, dorzolamide reaches the systemic circulation. To assess the potential for systemic carbonic anhydrase inhibition following topical administration, drug and metabolite concentrations in RBCs and plasma and carbonic anhydrase inhibition in RBCs were measured. Dorzolamide accumulates in RBCs during chronic dosing as a result of selective binding to CA-II while extremely low concentrations of free drug in plasma are maintained. The parent drug forms a single N-desethyl metabolite that inhibits CA-II less potently than the parent drug but also inhibits a less active isoenzyme (CA-I). The metabolite also accumulates in RBCs where it binds primarily to CA-I. Dorzolamide binds moderately to plasma proteins (approximately 33%). Dorzolamide is excreted unchanged in the urine; the metabolite is also excreted in urine. After dosing ends, dorzolamide washes out of RBCs in a nonlinear manner, resulting in a rapid decline of drug concentration initially, followed by a slower elimination phase with a half-life of about 4 months.

To simulate the maximum systemic exposure after long-term topical ocular administration, dorzolamide was given orally to 8 healthy subjects for up to 20 weeks. The oral dose of 4 mg/day closely approximates the maximum amount of dorzolamide delivered by topical ocular administration of dorzolamide 2% t.i.d. Dorzolamide and metabolite reached steady-state by 4 and 13 weeks, respectively, and the following observations were noted:

In plasma, concentrations of dorzolamide and metabolite were generally below the assay limit of quantitation (15 nmol) indicating almost no free drug or metabolite;

In RBCs, dorzolamide concentrations approached the binding capacity of CA-II (20 to 25 μmol) and metabolite concentrations approached 12 to 15 μmol, well below the binding capacity of CA-I (125 to 155 μmol);

In RBCs, inhibition of CA-II activity and total carbonic anhydrase activity was below the degree of inhibition anticipated to be necessary for a pharmacological effect on renal function and respiration.

Indications: In the treatment of elevated intraocular pressure in patients with ocular hypertension, open-angle glaucoma.

Contraindications: In patients who are hypersensitive to any component of this product.

Dorzolamide has not been studied in patients with severe renal impairment (CrCl <30 mL/min). Because dorzolamide and its metabolite are excreted predominantly by the kidney, the drug is not recommended in such patients.

There is a potential for an additive effect with the known systemic effects of carbonic anhydrase inhibition in patients receiving an oral carbonic anhydrase inhibitor and dorzolamide. The concomitant administration of dorzolamide and oral carbonic anhydrase inhibitors has not been studied and is not recommended.

Warnings: Dorzolamide is a sulfonamide and although administered topically, is absorbed systemically. Therefore the same types of adverse reactions that are attributable to sulfonamides may occur with topical administration. If signs of serious reactions or hypersensitivity occur, discontinue the use of this preparation.

The management of patients with acute angle-closure glaucoma requires therapeutic interventions in addition to ocular hypotensive agents. Dorzolamide has not been studied in patients with acute angle-closure glaucoma.

Dorzolamide has not been studied in patients with hepatic impairment and should therefore be used with caution in such patients.

Dorzolamide has not been studied in patients wearing contact lenses. The preservative in Trusopt ophthalmic solution, benzalkonium chloride, may be absorbed by soft contact lenses. Patients should be instructed to remove their lenses before application of the drops and not to reinsert the lenses earlier than 15 minutes after use.

Children: Safety and effectiveness in children have not been established.

Pregnancy: There are no adequate and well-controlled studies in pregnant women. Dorzolamide should be used during pregnancy only if the potential benefit justifies the potential risk to the fetus.

Lactation: It is not known whether dorzolamide is excreted in human milk. Because many drugs are excreted in human milk and because of the potential for serious adverse reactions from dorzolamide in nursing infants, a decision should be made whether to discontinue nursing or to discontinue the drug, taking into account the importance of the drug to the mother.

In a study of dorzolamide in lactating rats, decreases in body weight gain of 5 to 7% in offspring at an oral dose of 7.5 mg/kg/day (94 times the maximum recommended human ophthalmic dose) were seen during lactation. A slight delay in postnatal development (incisor eruption, vaginal canalization and eye openings), secondary to lower fetal body weight, was noted at 7.5 mg/kg/day (94 times the maximum recommended human ophthalmic dose).

Precautions: In clinical studies, local ocular adverse effects, primarily conjunctivitis and eyelid reactions, were reported with chronic administration of dorzolamide. Some of these reactions had the clinical appearance and course of an allergic-type reaction that resolved upon discontinuation of drug therapy. If such reactions are observed, discontinuation of treatment with dorzolamide should be considered.

Patients should be advised that if serious or unusual reactions or signs of hypersensitivity occur, they should discontinue the use of the product and to communicate with the treating physician.

Patients should be advised that if they develop any ocular reactions, particularly conjunctivitis and lid reactions, they should immediately seek their physician's advice about continuing treatment with dorzolamide.

There have been reports of bacterial keratitis associated with the use of multiple dose containers of topical ophthalmic products. These containers had been inadvertently contaminated by patients who, in most cases, had a concurrent corneal disease or a disruption of the ocular epithelial surface.

Patients should be instructed to avoid allowing the tip of the dispensing container to contact the eye or surrounding structures.

Patients should also be instructed that ocular solutions, if handled improperly, can become contaminated by common bacteria known to cause ocular infections. Serious damage to the eye and subsequent loss of vision may result from using contaminated solutions.

Patients should also be advised that if they develop an intercurrent ocular condition (e.g., trauma, ocular surgery or infection), they should immediately seek their physician's advice concerning the continued use of the present multidose container.

If more than one topical ophthalmic drug is being utilized, the drugs should be administered at least 10 minutes apart.

Geriatrics: Of the total number of patients in clinical studies of dorzolamide, 44% were 65 years of age and over, while 10% were 75 years of age and over. No overall differences in effectiveness or safety were observed between these patients and younger patients, but greater sensitivity of some older individuals to the product cannot be ruled out.

Drug Interactions: Specific drug interaction studies have not been performed with dorzolamide ophthalmic solution. In clinical studies, dorzolamide was used concomitantly with the following medications without evidence of adverse interactions: timolol ophthalmic solution, betaxolol ophthalmic solution and systemic medications, including ACE inhibitors, calcium channel blockers, diuretics, nonsteroidal anti-inflammatory drugs including ASA, and hormones (e.g., estrogen, insulin, thyroxine).

Dorzolamide is a carbonic anhydrase inhibitor and although administered topically, is absorbed systemically. In clinical studies, dorzolamide was not associated with acid-base disturbances. However, these disturbances have been reported with oral carbonic anhydrase inhibitors and have, in some instances, resulted in drug interactions (e.g., toxicity associated with high-dose salicylate therapy). Therefore, the potential for such drug interactions should be considered in patients receiving dorzolamide.

Occupational Hazards: Effects on Ability to Drive and Use Machines: Possible side effects such as visual disturbances may affect the ability to drive and use machines.

Laboratory Tests: Dorzolamide was not associated with clinically meaningful electrolyte disturbances.

Adverse Effects: In long-term studies of 1 108 patients treated with dorzolamide as monotherapy or as adjunctive therapy with an ophthalmic beta-blocker, the most frequent cause of discontinuation (approximately 3%) from treatment with dorzolamide was drug-related ocular adverse effects, primarily conjunctivitis and eyelid reactions (see Precautions).

The most common ocular complaints were burning and stinging, blurred vision, itching and tearing. Bitter taste was also frequently reported. If these local symptoms were considered clinically important by investigators they also appear as adverse experiences in the listing below.

Adverse experiences that were reported as drug-related (possibly, probably or definitely) in 1 to 5% of patients on dorzolamide were in decreasing order of frequency:

Ocular: burning and stinging, conjunctivitis, eyelid inflammation, eye itching, eyelid irritation.

Systemic: headache, bitter taste, nausea, asthenia/fatigue.

Iridocyclitis and rash were each reported rarely. There was 1 report of urolithiasis.

Overdose: Symptoms and Treatment: No data are available in humans in regard to overdosage by accidental or deliberate ingestion.

Treatment should be symptomatic and supportive. Electrolyte imbalance, development of an acidotic state, and possible CNS effects may occur. Serum electrolyte levels (particularly potassium) and blood pH levels should be monitored.

Significant lethality was observed in female rats and mice after single oral doses of dorzolamide HCl of 11 369 mg/m² or 1 927 mg/kg (24 000 times the maximum recommended human ophthalmic dose) and 3 960 mg/m² or 1 320 mg/kg

(16 000 times the maximum recommended human ophthalmic dose), respectively.

Dosage: When used as monotherapy, the dose is 1 drop of ophthalmic solution 2% in the affected eye(s) 3 times daily.

When used as adjunctive therapy with an ophthalmic beta-blocker, the dose is 1 drop in the affected eye(s) 2 times daily.

When substituting dorzolamide for another ophthalmic antiglaucoma agent, discontinue the other agent after proper dosing on one day, and start dorzolamide on the next day.

If more than 1 topical ophthalmic drug is being used, the drugs should be administered at least 10 minutes apart.

Information for the Patient: See Blue Section—Information for the Patient "Trusopt".

Supplied: Each mL of sterile, clear, colorless to nearly colorless, isotonic, buffered, slightly viscous, aqueous ophthalmic solution contains: dorzolamide HCl 22.3 mg equivalent to dorzolamide 20 mg (2%). Nonmedicinal ingredients: benzalkonium chloride, hydroxyethyl cellulose, mannitol, sodium citrate dihydrate, sodium hydroxide and water for injection. White, opaque, plastic Ocumeter ophthalmic dispensers (with controlled drop tip) of 5 mL. Store at 15 to 25°C. Protect from light. The contents of the ophthalmic dispenser should not be used for more than 28 days after the date on which the container is first opened.

Reviewed 1998

TRYPTAN™ ℞

ICN

L-Tryptophan

Adjunct in the Management of Affective Disorders

Pharmacology: The rationale for the use of L-tryptophan in affective disorders is based on clinical findings more than 20 years ago, that L-tryptophan increases 5-HT (serotonin) synthesis in the CNS of humans. It has been demonstrated in clinical trials that oral ingestion of L-tryptophan in humans caused a significant increase in the level of the serotonin metabolite, 5-hydroxyindoleacetic acid (5-HIAA), in the lumbar cerebrospinal fluid, indicating an increased turnover of serotonin in the CNS.

L-tryptophan is 1 of the 8 essential amino acids. The minimum daily requirements are said to be 0.25 g for males and 0.15 g for females. It is present in the hydrolysates of most proteins, the average western diet containing between 1 and 3 g/day. There are 2 major metabolic pathways for L-tryptophan, the first to serotonin, the second to nicotinic acid. Approximately 98% of dietary L-tryptophan is metabolized into nicotinic acid and only a very small amount is being metabolized to serotonin via the intermediary stage of 5-hydroxy-tryptophan (5-HTP). Tryptophan hydroxylase, the enzyme responsible for this step, is the rate-limiting enzyme for serotonin production and is normally only about half-saturated. CNS serotonin is metabolized by monoamine oxidase to 5-HIAA.

Indications: As a valuable adjunct to antidepressant drug treatment in the management of patients suffering from depressive disorders (bipolar affective disorders). An adjunctive effect has been observed in some cases when L-tryptophan is given in combination with lithium in bipolar patients with mania or depression for whom lithium alone or in combination with neuroleptics or tricyclics has shown little or no effect. Clinical observations suggest the possibility that the combination of lithium and L-tryptophan may reduce the need for the higher, more toxic doses of lithium necessary in control acute mania.

Contraindications: In patients with known sensitivity to L-tryptophan or any other compound in the formulation.

Warnings: L-tryptophan should not be given to patients suffering from the following conditions or should be prescribed only under close supervison.

Bladder Cancer: To minimize the risk of bladder cancer, it may be recommended to give vitamin B_6 supplements if the L-tryptophan doses are many times in excess of those consumed normally in dietary protein. An increased incidence rate of bladder cancer has been observed in experimental animals after implantation of pellets containing any of the 7 tryptophan metabolites formed by tryptophan pyrrolase. Active metabolites included kynurenine, 3-hydroxykynurenine, 3-hydroxyanthranillic acid, and xanthurenic acid, but not tryptophan itself. Vitamin B_6 has been reported to correct the metabolism of L-tryptophan and to reduce the metabolites to normal levels. A large study carried out by the National Cancer Institute did not find L-tryptophan to produce cancer in either rats or mice. Elevated levels of L-tryptophan metabolites in the urine have been reported both in bladder cancer patients relative to controls, in patients who had a recurrence of cancer relative to those who did not, and in patients taking oral contraceptives or hormones.

Diabetes Mellitus: Xanthurenic acid, which is increased on L-tryptophan loading, has a diabetogenic action in animals, possibly due to its ability to bind insulin, suggesting caution in the use of tryptophan in patients with a family history of diabetes.

Achlorhydria/Malabsorption: In ruminants, oral L-tryptophan caused pulmonary edema and emphysema, mediated by bacterial conversion of L-tryptophan to skatole (3-methylindole). This is not normally of concern in humans except where bacteria exist high in the gastrointestinal tract due to conditions such as achlorhydria, or where L-tryptophan reaches the bacterial populations lower in the gastrointestinal tract due to malabsorption.

Cataract Formation: Animal data suggest that photooxidation of L-tryptophan and some of its metabolites, such as kynurenine, may be involved in cataract formation. Although there is no evidence that this occurs in humans, L-tryptophan administration is likely to raise lenticular tryptophan and kynurenine concentrations, and this might make subjects more susceptible to cataract formation, particularly if exposed to ultraviolet light.

Precautions: *Drug Interactions:* Drug interactions between tryptophan and other CNS affecting drugs have been reported. A higher occurrence of side effects was reported when tryptophan was given in combination with MAO inhibitors. The most common side effects caused by this drug combination were dizziness, nausea and headache. At a dosage of 20 to 50 mg/kg tryptophan in addition to MAO inhibitors, the following side effects have been reported: ethanol-like intoxication, drowsiness, hyperreflexia and clonus. Single case reports of adverse reactions to the drug combination include hypomanic behavior, ocular oscillation, ataxia, and myoclonus. Some of these reactions resemble the "serotonin syndrome" seen in experimental animals, which consists of tremor, hypertonus, myoclonus, and hyperreactivity. These symptoms disappear soon after cessation of tryptophan, and no detrimental long-term effects have been reported.

When tryptophan was given in combination with fluoxetine, the following side effects have been reported, but disappeared as soon as the medication was discontinued. Neither drug alone caused similar side effects: agitation, restlessness, poor concentration, nausea, diarrhea, and worsening of obsessive-compulsive disorder.

Patients taking high doses of L-tryptophan should not be protein deprived since an amino acid imbalance can ensue.

Adverse Effects: L-tryptophan, in doses below 5 g/day may cause dry mouth and drowsiness. In higher doses (9 to 12 g/day) nausea, anorexia, dizziness and headache have been reported.

Side effects disappear when medication is continued and in most cases only a light dizziness may persist.

Sexual disinhibition has been reported in some patients with emotional disorders.

L-tryptophan, when given with lithium, might increase some side effects associated with lithium therapy by potentiating the lithium effect (nausea, vomiting, dermatological eruptions, psoriasis, alopecia).

Overdose: Symptoms and Treatment: According to the toxicity described, symptoms of overdosage would include vomiting and might include serotonin syndrome symptoms. Treatment of overdosage would be symptomatic with close monitoring and support of vital systems as necessary.

Dosage: Clinical reports on the use of L-tryptophan as an adjunct in the management of affective disorders have indicated the dose of 8 to 12 g/day to be the most effective one. Lower doses have been reported to be effective in combination with other antidepressants. Some patients may not tolerate 12 g/day but might still benefit from doses reduced to 8 g/day.

The treatment might be initiated with 12 g/day of L-tryptophan, given in 3 to 4 equally divided doses. Administration with meals or snacks is recommended to reduce the incidence of nausea. The dose and frequency of administration may have to be adjusted to the patient's need and tolerance.

A small number of bipolar patients are particularly sensitive to L-tryptophan and will not tolerate higher doses than 1 or 2 g/day. Patients on concomitant medication should be monitored for possible reduction of the concomitant medication since L-tryptophan may enhance their efficacy.

If L-tryptophan is used in the acute treatment of mania in conjunction with lithium it will potentiate some of the side effects associated with lithium such as nausea and vomiting. Thus, often it will be necessary to decrease the lithium dosage especially when it is given in doses above 900 to 1 200 mg/day. In manic-depressive illness chronically treated with lithium, the lithium dose may need to be decreased when L-tryptophan is added because of increased side effects. In these patients L-tryptophan tends to produce an increase in lithium concentrations, thus it is important to monitor the lithium concentration closely for at least 2 weeks after the addition of L-tryptophan.

With some of the more sedative neuroleptics and antidepressants, if L-tryptophan is added, an increased incidence of sedation may occur.

Information for the Patient: For better results, L-tryptophan should be taken with a protein-low, carbohydrate-rich snack or meal.

Supplied: Capsules: Each opaque white capsule, size No. 00, imprinted with ICN T17, contains: L-tryptophan, USP 500 mg. Nonmedicinal ingredients: magnesium stearate and talc. Bottles of 100 and 250.

Tablets: 500 mg: Each white, oval, biconvex, film-coated tablet, contains: L-tryptophan, USP 500 mg. Nonmedicinal ingredients: calcium phosphate, croscarmellose sodium, film coating base solution (includes: acetylated monoglyceride, hydroxypropylmethyl cellulose, povidone, titanium dioxide), magnesium stearate, methylcellulose, opaspray white and wax solution. Bottles of 100 and 250.

1 g: Each white, oval, film-coated tablet, contains: L-tryptophan, USP 1 g. Nonmedicinal ingredients: calcium phosphate, croscarmellose sodium, film coating base solution (includes: acetylated monoglyceride, hydroxypropylmethyl cellulose, povidone, titanium dioxide), magnesium stearate, methylcellulose, opaspray white and wax solution. Bottles of 100 and 250.

Store at controlled room temperature (15 to 30°C). Protect from heat and light.

Reviewed 1997

T-STAT® ℞

Westwood-Squibb

Erythromycin—Ethyl Alcohol

Topical Anti-acne Therapy

Pharmacology: Ethyl alcohol is a drying and peeling agent. The mechanism of action of topically applied erythromycin in the treatment of acne vulgaris is not known.

Indications: For the treatment of the inflammatory papular lesions of acne vulgaris. Not indicated for Grade IV acne.

Contraindications: Individuals who have shown hypersensitivity to erythromycin or any of its other ingredients.

Warnings: Eye contact should be avoided since T-Stat is irritating to the eyes. Concomitant topical anti-acne therapy should be used with caution because a cumulative irritancy effect may occur, particularly with those preparations containing peeling, desquamating or abrasive agents.

Precautions: Recommended for external use only but care should be taken to avoid contact with the eyes, nostrils, mouth and other mucous membranes.

The use of preparations containing antibiotics, including T-Stat, may be associated with overgrowth of antibiotic-resistant organisms. If this should occur, the administration of T-Stat should be discontinued and appropriate measures taken. A recent report indicates that cross resistance between erythromycin and macrolide antibiotics can occur.

Pregnancy and *Lactation:* The safety of T-Stat during pregnancy or lactation has not been established.

Adverse Effects: Adverse reactions associated with the use of T-Stat include dryness, erythema, pruritus, desquamation, fissuring around the mouth, tenderness, scaling, skin irritation and burning sensation.

Overdose: Symptoms and Treatment: Accidental ingestion of T-Stat could result in alcoholic intoxication and/or intestinal tract irritation (manifested by vomiting, cramping, diarrhea). Treat with a demulcent.

If eye contact should occur, wash with copious amounts of water for at least 5 minutes. If discomfort persists, a physician should be contacted.

Excessive frequency of application can cause erythema, excessive scaling and sensations of burning and tenderness. Appropriate anti-inflammatory measures (e.g. compresses or topical corticosteroids) may be employed.

T-Stat (cont'd)

Dosage: The topical lotion should be applied twice a day to the areas affected by acne.

Before application, these area should be washed with mild soap, rinsed well, and patted dry. T-Stat should be applied with the applicator, the fingertips, or the pads carefully to avoid the eyes, nose, mouth and other mucous membranes. The hands should be washed thoroughly after applications.

Because ethyl alcohol is potentially irritating, the frequency of application may require adjustment to once a day.

Information for the Patient: See Blue Section—Information for the Patient "T-Stat".

Supplied: Each mL of topical lotion contains: erythromycin base 2% w/v and ethyl alcohol 75% v/v. Nonmedicinal ingredients: fragrance and propylene glycol, may contain citric acid. Plastic bottles of 60 mL with optional applicator. Premoistened nonwoven pads of 60 in round plastic jars. Store tightly closed, upright, at room temperature (15 to 25°C) and away from open flame.

TUBERCULIN, OLD, TINE TEST®

Wyeth-Ayerst

Diagnostic Test

Indications: For detection of tuberculin sensitive individuals, as a determinant for additional testing (i.e., chest x-rays), and in epidemiological surveys to identify those areas having high levels of infection. Also useful in mass tuberculosis screening programs.

In clinical studies covering various geographical areas and all age groups, with a total of 30 588 test subjects, there were 911 (4%) false positive reactors among 26 236 subjects who were Mantoux negative, and 342 (8%) false negative reactors among 4 352 subjects who were Mantoux positive.

The frequency of repeated tuberculin tests depends on risk of exposure of the individual and on the prevalence of tuberculosis in the population group. The repeated testing of uninfected individuals does not sensitize to tuberculin. Among individuals with waning sensitivity to homologous or heterologous mycobacterial antigens, however, the stimulus of a tuberculin test may boost or increase the size of the reaction to a second test, even causing an apparent development of sensitivity in some cases.

Contraindications: There are no known contraindications for use of Tuberculin, Old, TINE TEST. See Precautions for information regarding special care to be exercised for safe and effective use.

Warnings: There are no known serious adverse reactions or potential safety hazards associated with the use of Tuberculin, Old, TINE TEST. However, as with the use of any biological product, the possibility of anaphylactic reaction should be considered. See Precautions for information regarding special care to be exercised for safe and effective use.

Precautions: Individuals with active tuberculosis. Although activation of quiescent lesions is rare, if a patient has a history of vesiculation and necrosis with a previous tuberculin test by any method, testing should be avoided.

This product contains some acacia as stabilizer and should be used with caution in patients with known allergy to this component. In these instances, remedial measures for anaphylactoid reactions, including epinephrine injection (1:1 000), must be available for immediate use.

Reactivity to the test may be suppressed in patients who are receiving corticosteroids or immunosuppressive agents, or those who have been recently vaccinated with live virus vaccines such as measles, mumps, rubella and polio, etc.

Further diagnostic procedures must be considered with a positive reaction such as chest x-ray, microbiologic examinations of sputa and other specimens, and confirmation of the positive reaction (except vesiculation reactions) using the Mantoux method. In general, the Tine Test does not need to be repeated. Antituberculous chemotherapy should not be instituted solely on the basis of a single positive Tine Test.

When vesiculation occurs, the reaction is to be interpreted as strongly positive and a repeat Mantoux not attempted. Similar or more severe vesiculation with or without necrosis is likely to occur.

Pregnancy: Safe use during pregnancy is unknown and therefore should not be given to a pregnant woman unless clearly needed.

During pregnancy, known positive reactors may demonstrate a negative response to a Tuberculin Tine Test.

Never reuse Tuberculin, Old, Tine Test unit.

Adverse Effects: Vesiculation (positive reaction), ulceration, or necrosis may occur at the test site in highly sensitive persons. Localized pain, pruritus, and discomfort may be relieved by cold packs or by topical glucocorticoid ointment or cream. Transient bleeding may be observed at a puncture site and is of no significance.

Dosage: Standardized by clinical evaluation in humans the test is equivalent to, or more potent than 5 T.U.* of standard old tuberculin administered intradermally in the Mantoux test. However, all multiple puncture type devices must be regarded as screening tools and other appropriate diagnostic procedures such as the Mantoux test should be utilized for retesting reactors.

*U.S. (International) tuberculin units.

The volar surface of the upper one third of the forearm, over a muscle belly, is the preferred site. Hairy areas and areas without adequate subcutaneous tissue, e.g., concavities over a tendon or bone should be avoided.

Alcohol, acetone, ether, or soap and water may be used to cleanse the skin. The area must be clean and thoroughly dry before application.

Expose the 4 coated tines by removing the protective cap while holding the plastic handle. Grasp the patient's forearm firmly, since the sharp momentary sting may cause the patient to jerk his or her arm, resulting in scratching. Stretch the skin of the forearm tightly and apply the disc with the other hand. Sufficient pressure should be exerted so that the 4 puncture sites, and circular depression of the skin from the plastic base are visible. Hold at least 1 second. Release tension grip on forearm. Withdraw tine unit and discard. Local care of the skin is not necessary.

Reading and Interpretation: Read at 48 to 72 hours. Vesiculation or the extent of induration are the determining factors; erythema without induration is of no significance. Readings should be made in good light with the forearm slightly flexed. The size of the induration in millimeters should be determined by inspection, measuring, and palpation with gentle finger stroking. The site is easily identified because of the distinct 4 point pattern. The diameter of the largest single reaction around one of the puncture sites should be measured. With pronounced reactions, the areas of induration around the puncture sites may coalesce.

If vesiculation and induration of 2 mm or greater occurs, the test should be interpreted as positive. If induration is less than 2 mm the test reaction is negative. Unless the person is a contact of a patient with tuberculosis, or there is clinical evidence suggestive of the disease, there is no need for retesting.

Supplied: Each multiple puncture, disposable, intradermal test consists of a stainless steel disc attached to a plastic handle. Projecting from the disk are 4 triangular shaped prongs (tines) which are 2 mm long and approximately 4 mm apart. The tines have been mechanically dipped in a solution of old tuberculin, containing 7% acacia (gum arabic) and 8.5% lactose as stabilizers, and then dried. The entire unit has been sterilized by irradiation. No preservative has been added. Boxes of 25 individual tests. Tartrazine-free. Store unrefrigerated below 30°C.

TUBERCULIN PURIFIED PROTEIN DERIVATIVE (MANTOUX)—TUBERSOL®

Connaught

Tuberculin Test

Pharmacology: Intracutaneous tuberculin testing is an accepted aid in the diagnosis of tuberculosis infection.

The reaction to intracutaneously injected tuberculin is a delayed (cellular) hypersensitivity reaction. The reaction which characteristically shows a delayed course, reaching its peak more than 24 hours after administration, consists of induration due to cell infiltration and occasionally vesiculation and necrosis. Clinically, a delayed hypersensitivity reaction to tuberculin is a manifestation of previous infection with M. tuberculosis or a variety of nontuberculosis bacteria. In most cases sensitization is induced by natural mycobacterial infection or by vaccination with BCG vaccine.

The sensitization following infection with mycobacteria occurs primarily in the regional lymph nodes. Small lymphocytes (T lymphocytes) proliferate in response to the antigenic stimulus to give rise to specifically sensitized lymphocytes. After several weeks, these lymphocytes enter the blood stream and circulate for long periods of time. Subsequent restimulation of these sensitized lymphocytes with the same or a similar antigen, such as the intradermal injection of tuberculin, evokes a local reaction mediated by these cells.

The tuberculin reaction is characterized by the early predominance of mononuclear cells (small and medium sized lymphocytes and monocytes). Only a small proportion of these cells appear to be lymphocytes sensitized to tuberculin. Most cells are brought into the reaction through the release of biologically active substances by sensitized lymphocytes. An increase in vascular permeability leading to erythema and edema also occurs in tuberculin reactions.

Characteristically, delayed hypersensitivity reactions to tuberculin begin at 5 to 6 hours, are maximal at 48 to 72 hours and subside over a period of days. In those who are elderly or those who are being tested for the first time reactions may develop slowly and may not peak until after 72 hours. Immediate hypersensitivity reactions to tuberculin may occur.

Indications: As an aid in the detection of infection with M. tuberculosis.

Previous BCG vaccination is not a contraindication to tuberculin testing.

The repeated testing of uninfected persons does not sensitize them to tuberculin.

Contraindications: Allergy to any component of Tuberculin Purified Protein Derivative (Mantoux) (see Supplied) or an allergic or anaphylactic reaction to a previous test of Tuberculin Purified Protein Derivative (Mantoux).

Tuberculin Purified Protein Derivative (Mantoux) should not be administered to known tuberculin positive reactors because of the severity of reactions (e.g., vesiculation, ulceration or necrosis) that may occur at the test site in highly sensitive persons; to patients with severe blistering tuberculin reactions in the past; to patients with extensive burns or eczema or to persons with documented active TB or documented treatment (active or passive) in the past.

Warnings: Tuberculin Purified Protein Derivative (Mantoux) 250 U.S. units (TU) per test dose (0.1 mL) is not, under any circumstances, to be used for the initial injection.

Tuberculin PPD 250 U.S. units (TU) per test dose (0.1 mL) is to be used only after the individual has been tested with, and failed to respond to the 5 TU dose, but is suspected of being infected with M. tuberculosis.

Avoid injecting Tuberculin PPD s.c. If this occurs, no local reaction will develop, but a general febrile reaction and/or acute inflammation around old tuberculosis lesions may occur in highly sensitive individuals.

Do not inject i.v.

Precautions: General: Effective use of tuberculin testing requires an understanding of the characteristics inherent to the test and extrinsic factors relating that have influence on interpertation of the results. The utility of the tuberculin test depends on the prevalance of infection with M. tuberculosis and to relative prevalence of cross-reaction with nontuberculous mycobacteria.

The possibility of allergic reactions in individuals sensitive to components of Tuberculin Purified Protein Derivative should be evaluated. Epinephrine HCl solution (1:1 000) and other appropriate agents should be available for immediate use in case an anaphylactic or acute reaction occurs. Before the use of this product, all appropriate precautions should be taken to prevent adverse reactions. This includes a review of the patient's history with respect to possible hypersensitivity to the product or similar products, determination of previous testing history with Tuberculin Purified Protein Derivative, and the presence of any contraindications to the use of Tuberculin Purified Protein Derivative. Familiarity with the recommendations for the initial management of anaphylaxis in non-hospital settings is recommended before administering Tuberculin Purified Protein Derivative.

Reactivity to the test may be depressed or suppressed for as long as 4 to 6 weeks in individuals who have had viral infections (rubeola, influenza, mumps and probably others) or in those who are receiving corticosteroids or immunosuppressive agents.

Reactivity to PPD may be temporarily depressed by certain live virus vaccines (measles, mumps, rubella, oral polio). Therefore, if a tuberculin test is to be performed it should be administered either before or at the same time as the live virus vaccines (such as MMR), or wait at least 30 days before administering the test.

Anything that impairs or attenuates cell mediated immunity (CMI) potentially can cause a false negative tuberculin reaction (viral infections, particularly HIV; live virus vaccines; severe protein malnutrition; lymphoma; leukemia; sarcoidosis; use of glucocorticosteroids and other immunosuppressant drugs).

In HIV-infected individuals, tuberculin skin test results are less reliable as CD4 counts decline, and negative tuberculin reactions may occur in more than 40% of HIV-infected persons who have active tuberculosis. HIV-infected individuals should receive tuberculin skin testing as recommended.

Special care should be taken to ensure the product is not injected into a blood vessel.

A separate, **sterile** syringe and needle, or a **sterile** disposable unit, must be used for each individual patient to prevent the transmission of infectious agents. There have been case reports of transmission of HIV and hepatitis by failure to scrupulously observe sterile technique. In particular, the same needle and/or syringe must never be used to re-enter a multi-dose vial to withdraw product even when it is to be used for testing of the same patient. This may lead to contamination of the vial contents and infection of patients who subsequently receive product from the vial.

Needles should not be recapped and should be disposed of properly.

In those who are elderly or being tested for the first time, reactions may develop slowly and may not peak until after 72 hours.

Adverse Effects: Vesiculation, ulceration or necrosis may appear at the test site in highly sensitive persons. Pain, pruritus and discomfort at the test site may also occur.

Strongly positive reactions may result in scarring at the test site.

Immediate erythematous or other reactions may occur at the injection site. The reason(s) for these occurences are presently unknown.

There have been rare systemic allergic reactions reported that were manifested by immediate skin rash or generalized rash within 24 hours. Two of the reported cases had concurrent symptoms of upper respiratory stridor. These reactions were treated with epinephrine and steroids and resolved. No cause and effect was able to be established with a specific component of skin test.

Physicians, nurses, and pharmacists should report any adverse occurrences temporally related to the administration of the product in accordance with local requirements and to the Medical Director, Connaught Laboratories Limited, 1755 Steeles Avenue West, Toronto, Ontario, Canada, M2R 3T4.

Dosage: Parenteral biological products should be inspected visually for extraneous particulate matter and/or discoloration before administration. If these conditions exist, the product should not be administered.

The Test: For the initial intracutaneous (Mantoux) tuberculin test it is customary to use 5 TU (bioequivalent) per dose (0.1 mL).

Five Tuberculin units (TU) per test dose of 0.1 mL is the standard strength tuberculin test used for intracutaneous (Mantoux) testing. 1 TU per test (0.1 mL) and 250 TU per test dose (0.1 mL) are also available, however, these are not standardized and have limited clinical application in routine or serial (two-step) testing. Under no circumstances is the 250 TU per test dose (0.1 mL) to be used for the initial injection.

Method of Administration: The preferred site of the test is the flexor surface of the forearm.

The skin site is first cleansed with a suitable germicide and should be dry prior to injection of the antigen.

The rubber cap of the vial should be wiped with a suitable germicide and should be dry prior to needle insertion. The needle is then inserted gently through the cap and 0.1 mL of Tuberculin PPD is drawn into the syringe.

The test dose (0.1 mL) of Tuberculin PPD is administered with a 1 mL syringe calibrated in tenths and fitted with a short, ¼ to ½ inch, 26 or 27 gauge needle.

The point of the needle is inserted into the most superficial layers of the skin with the needle bevel pointing upward. If the intracutaneous injection is performed properly, a definite pale bleb will rise at the needle point, about 10 mm (⅜″) in diameter. This bleb will disperse within minutes. No dressing is required.

In the event of an improperly performed injection (i.e., no bleb formed), the test should be repeated immediately at another site.

Failure to store and handle Tuberculin PPD as recommended will result in a loss of potency and inaccurate test results.

Interpretation of the Test: Intracutaneous tuberculin testing is an accepted aid in the diagnosis of tuberculosis. Sensitivity to tuberculin, may be the result of a previous infection with mycobacteria. This infection, likely due to M. tuberculosis, may have occured years ago or may be of recent origin.

The test should be read 48 to 72 hours after administration of the Tuberculin. Sensitivity is indicated by induration, usually accompanied by erythema. Distinctly palpable induration should be measured at the widest diameter in millimeters (mm) and recorded. The tip of a ballpoint pen pushed at a 45° angle toward the site of injection will stop at the edge of induration. Presence and size of necrosis and edema (if present) should also be recorded. See Table I.

Table I—Tuberculin Purified Protein Derivative (Mantoux)—Tubersol

Interpretation of Tuberculin Test

Tuberculin reaction size, mm induration	Setting in which reaction considered significant
0-4	HIV infection and expected risk of tuberculosis infection is high (e.g., patient is an immigrant from a country where TB is endemic, is a household contact, or has an abnormal x-ray). Anergy testing, if done, should show anergy. This reaction size is not normally considered significant but in the presence of immune suppression may be important.
5-9	HIV infection Contact of active contagious case Abnormal chest x-ray with fibronodular disease
≥10	All others

BCG vaccination may produce a PPD reaction that cannot be distinguished reliably from a reaction caused by infection with M. tuberculosis. For a person who was vaccinated with BCG, the probability that a PPD reaction results from infection with M. tuberculosis increases as the size of the reaction increases, when the person is a contact of a person with TB, when the person's country of origin has a high prevalence of TB, and as the length of time between vaccination and PPD testing increases. For example, a PPD test reaction of ≥10 mm probably can be attributed to M. tuberculosis infection in an adult who was vaccinated with BCG as a child and who is from a country with high prevalence of TB.

Booster Effect: Infection of an individual with tubercle bacilli or other mycobacteria results in a delayed hypersensitivity response to tuberculin which is demonstrated by the skin test. The delayed hypersensitivity response may gradually wane over a period of years. If a person received a tuberculin test at this time (after several years) the response may be a reaction that is not significant. The stimulus of the test may boost or increase the size of the reaction to a second test, sometimes causing an apparent conversion or development of sensitivity.

Although the booster phenomenon may be documented at any age, its frequency increases with age and is highest among persons >55 years old. When the tuberculin skin testing of adults is to be repeated periodically, as in employee-health or institutional screening programs, a 2 step approach can reduce the likelihood that a boosted reaction will be incorrectly interpreted as representing a recent infection. If the first tuberculin test result is negative, a second 5-TU test should be given 1 to 3 weeks later. If the second result is positive, it probably indicates the boosting of a remote infection. Persons who have a boosting reaction should be classified as reactors, not converters. If the second result is negative, the person should be considered uninfected, and any positive reaction to subsequent skin test should be considered a true tuberculin skin test conversion.

Since a tuberculin reactivity may not necessarily indicate the presence of active tuberculous disease, individuals showing a tuberculin reaction should be further evaluated with other diagnostic procedures.

Those individuals giving a positive tuberculin reaction may or may not show evidence of tuberculous disease. Chest X-ray examination and microbiological examination of the sputum in these cases is recommended as a means of determining the presence or absence of pulmonary tuberculosis.

The possibility should not be excluded that the skin sensitivity is due to previous contact with atypical mycobacteria or previous BCG vaccination. In the absence of signs of tuberculous disease, differential diagnosis by means of intracutaneous skin tests with PPD derived from atypical mycobacteria may be indicated.

Each person who is tested with Tuberculin Purified Protein Derivative should be given a permanent personal record. In addition, it is essential that the physician or nurse record the testing history in the permanent medical record of each patient. This permanent office record should contain the name of the product, date given, dose, manufacturer and lot number.

Supplied: Tuberculin Purified Protein Derivative for intracutaneous (Mantoux) tuberculin testing is prepared by the Connaught Laboratories Limited from a large Master Batch Connaught Tuberculin (CT68) which has been obtained from a human strain of M. tuberculosis grown on a protein-free synthetic medium. The use of a standard preparation derived from a single batch (CT68) has been recommended in order to eliminate batch to batch variation by the same manufacturer.

It is estimated that this batch is large enough to provide solutions for many years. From this batch, Tuberculin PPD at 3 concentrations is available in sterile isotonic phosphate buffered saline containing Tween 80 (0.0005%) as a stabilizer. Phenol 0.28% is added as a preservative.

Independent studies conducted by the U.S. Public Health Service in humans have determined the amount of CT68 in stabilized solution necessary to produce bio-equivalency with Tuberculin PPD-S (in phosphate buffer without Tween 80) using 5 U.S. units (TU) Tuberculin PPD-S as the standard. Prior to release, each successive lot is tested for potency in comparison with a Standard.

Tuberculin PPD (Mantoux)—Tubersol bioequivalent to 5 U.S. units (TU) PPD-S per test dose (0.1 mL) is available in 1 and 5 mL vials. Tuberculin PPD (Mantoux)—Tubersol 1 TU and 250 TU per test dose (0.1 mL) are available in 1 mL vials. Tuberculin PPD (Mantoux)—Tubersol solutions do not require further dilution.

Store between 2 and 8°C. **Do not freeze.** Product which has been exposed to freezing should not be used. Tuberculin PPD solutions can be adversely affected by exposure to light. The product should be stored in the dark except when doses are actually being withdrawn from the vial. **A vial of Tuberculin PPD which has been entered and in use for 1 month should be discarded because oxidation and degradation may have reduced the potency.** Do not use product beyond the expiry date.

Reviewed 1998

TUSSAMINIC® C FORTE Ⓝ
TUSSAMINIC® C PED Ⓝ
TUSSAMINIC® DH FORTE Ⓝ
TUSSAMINIC® DH PED Ⓝ

Novartis Consumer Health

Codeine Phosphate or Hydrocodone Bitartrate—Pheniramine Maleate—Phenylpropanolamine HCl—Pyrilamine Maleate

Antihistaminic—Antitussive—Decongestant

Indications: The treatment of cough associated with inflamed mucosa, which does not respond to products of lesser potency.

Contraindications: Hypersensitivity to any of the components, marked hypertension, patients receiving MAO inhibitors.

Precautions: Since the depressant effects of antihistamines are additive to those of other drugs affecting the CNS, caution patients against drinking alcoholic beverages or taking hypnotics, sedatives, psychotherapeutic agents or other drugs with CNS-depressant effects during antihistaminic therapy.

Occupational Hazards: Caution patients not to operate vehicles or hazardous machinery until their response to the drug has been determined.

Use with caution in patients with hypertension, diabetes mellitus, thyrotoxicosis, glaucoma, cardiac disease, peripheral vascular disease and patients receiving methyldopa or beta adrenergic blockers.

The use of hydrocodone bitartrate and of codeine phosphate over a prolonged period may, in susceptible individuals, lead to habituation and, in some cases, true addiction.

Adverse Effects: Drowsiness, blurred vision, cardiac palpitation, flushing, dizziness, nervousness, or gastrointestinal upsets may occur occasionally.

Dosage: Tussaminic C Forte and Tussaminic DH Forte: Adults, 5 mL every 4 hours.

Tussaminic C Ped and Tussaminic DH Ped: Children 6 to12 years, 5 mL every 4 hours; 2 to 6 years, 2.5 mL every 4 hours; Under 2 years, as directed by physician.

Supplied: Tussaminic C Forte: Each 5 mL of clear, black currant-flavored liquid contains: codeine phosphate 15 mg, phenylpropanolamine HCl 25 mg, pyrilamine maleate 12.5 mg, pheniramine maleate 12.5 mg. Nonmedicinal ingredients: benzoic acid, flavor, menthol, sorbitol, sucrose and water. Energy: 44.35 kJ (10.6 kcal)/5 mL. Alcohol- and tartrazine-free. Bottles of 500 mL.

Tussaminic (cont'd)

Tussaminic C Ped: Each 5 mL of cherry raspberry-flavored liquid contains: codeine phosphate 5 mg, phenylpropanolamine HCl 12.5 mg, pyrilamine maleate 6.25 mg, pheniramine maleate 6.25 mg. Nonmedicinal ingredients: benzoic acid, FD&C Red No. 2, flavors, sorbitol, sucrose and water. Energy: 44.35 kJ (10.6 kcal)/5 mL. Alcohol- and tartrazine-free. Bottles of 500 mL.

Tussaminic DH Forte: Each 5 mL of clear, black currant-flavored liquid contains: hydrocodone bitartrate 5 mg, phenylpropanolamine HCl 25 mg, pyrilamine maleate 12.5 mg, pheniramine maleate 12.5 mg. Nonmedicinal ingredients: benzoic acid, flavor, menthol, sorbitol, sucrose and water. Energy: 44.2 kJ (10.56 kcal)/5 mL. Alcohol- and tartrazine-free. Bottles of 500 mL.

Tussaminic DH Ped: Each 5 mL of cherry raspberry-flavored liquid contains: hydrocodone bitartrate 1.67 mg, phenylpropanolamine HCl 12.5 mg, pyrilamine maleate 6.25 mg, pheniramine maleate 6.25 mg. Nonmedicinal ingredients: benzoic acid, FD&C Red No. 2, flavors, sorbitol, sucrose and water. Energy: 44.2 kJ (10.56 kcal)/5 mL. Alcohol- and tartrazine-free. Bottles of 500 mL.

TUSSIONEX® Ⓝ

Rhône-Poulenc Rorer

Hydrocodone (Resin Complex)—Phenyltoloxamine (Resin Complex)

Antitussive—Antihistamine

Pharmacology: Hydrocodone is a semi-synthetic narcotic antitussive and analgesic with multiple actions qualitatively similar to those of codeine. As an antitussive, hydrocodone is approximately 3 times as potent as codeine on a weight for weight basis. The precise mechanism of action of hydrocodone and other opiates is not known; however, hydrocodone is believed to inhibit coughing by interfering with the central modulation of afferent signals, thereby decreasing sensitivity of the cough centre to incoming stimuli. In excessive doses, hydrocodone, like other opium derivatives, will depress respiration. Hydrocodone can produce miosis, euphoria, physical and psychological dependence.

Phenyltoloxamine acts as competitive inhibitor of histamine. As with other antihistamines, it is possible that its sedative and tranquilizing characteristics may contribute to its antitussive action. In addition, phenyltoloxamine in a similar manner to other antihistamines has been shown to potentiate the effects of hydrocodone.

Both of the above active ingredients are complexed to an inert cation exchange resin. It has been shown that the resin itself does not impart any additional toxicity into the final product, and the drug-resin complex produces a higher LD_{50} in mice and rats for the drug substances than when they are administered in their free or common salt form. The time required to cause death in rats following a certain lethal dose of drug as an ion-exchange resin complex was longer than when the drug was administered as a soluble salt. These 2 factors combine to make these resin complexes less toxic and, hence, safer to administer orally than the soluble salt form of the drug.

The benefits derived from the sustained-release action resulting from this complexing and the apparent potentiation of the narcotic antitussive effect by phenyltoloxamine constitute the basic of action of this preparation.

Indications: The treatment of exhausting or non-productive cough; associated with cold or with upper respiratory allergic condition that does not respond to non-narcotic antitussives. It is an effective antitussive which acts for approximately 8 to 12 hours.

Contraindications: Hypersensitivity to any of the components, marked hypertension, patients receiving MAO inhibitors, pre-existing respiratory depression, intracranial lesions with increased intracranial pressure.

Warnings: It is important to provide appropriate therapy for the primary disease and to ensure that modification of the cough does not increase the risk of physical or psychological complications.

Children: In young children, the respiratory centre is especially susceptible to the depressant action of narcotic cough suppressants.

Pregnancy and *Lactation:* Since hydrocodone crosses the placenta, its use in pregnancy is not recommended. Babies of nursing mothers using opioids may become physically dependent.

Hydrocodone may inhibit peristalsis, and patients with chronic constipation should be given Tussionex only after weighing the potential therapeutic benefit against the hazards involved.

Occupational Hazards: Caution patients not to operate vehicles or hazardous machinery until their response to the drug has been determined.

Since the depressant effects of some antihistamines are additive to those of other drugs affecting the CNS, caution patients against drinking alcoholic beverages or taking hypnotics/sedatives, tricyclic antidepressants, benzodiazepines or other opiate agonists during antihistaminic therapy.

Tussionex contains hydrocodone: may be habit forming.

Tussionex suspension must not be diluted with fluids or mixed with other drugs because this alters the resin-binding and changes the absorption rate, possibly increasing the toxicity.

Precautions: Before prescribing medication to suppress or modify cough, it is important to identify the underlying cause of the cough.

In young children, the benefit-to-risk ratio should be carefully considered, especially in children with respiratory embarrassment (e.g., croup).

Use with caution in patients with hypertension, diabetes mellitus, thyrotoxicosis, glaucoma, cardiac disease and peripheral vascular disease and in patients receiving methyldopa or beta adrenergic blockers.

The use of hydrocodone bitartrate over a prolonged period may, in susceptible individuals, lead to habituation and, in some cases, true addiction.

Adverse Effects: Negligible, but when encountered may include mild constipation, nausea, facial pruritus, and drowsiness that disappear with adjustment of dose or discontinuance of treatment.

Overdose: Symptoms: are similar to those of codeine overdosage. Narcosis is usually present, sometimes associated with convulsions. Tachycardia, bradycardia, pupillary constriction, nausea and vomiting and respiratory depression can occur. The resinated formulation mitigates the immediate absorption of large quantities of hydrocodone; however, the absorption period may be prolonged.

Treatment: If respiration is severely depressed, administer the narcotic antagonist, naloxone. Adults: 0.4 mg to 2.0 mg by i.v., i.m. or s.c. routes and repeated at 2 to 3 minute intervals if necessary. Children: 0.01 mg/kg by i.v., i.m. or s.c. routes. Dosage may be repeated also at 2 to 3 minute intervals if necessary. Since the duration of action of hydrocodone in this formulation may exceed that of naloxone, the patient should be kept under surveillance and repeated doses of naloxone should be administered as needed. Failure to obtain significant improvement after 2 to 3 doses suggests that causes other than narcotic overdosage may be responsible for the patient's condition.

If naloxone is unsuccessful, institute intubation and respiratory support and conduct gastric lavage in the unconscious patient.

Convulsions, sometimes seen in children, can be controlled by i.v. administration of benzodiazepines (e.g., diazepam).

Dosage: Tussionex should not be diluted with fluids or mixed with other drugs. Shake well before using.

Adults: 5 mL of suspension or 1 tablet every 8 to 12 hours. Maximum daily dose is 10 mL of suspension or 2 tablets. May be adjusted to individual requirements.

Children (Suspension): From 1 to 5 years: 2.5 mL every 12 hours (maximum daily dose of 5 mL). Over 5 years: 5 mL every 12 hours (maximum daily dose of 10 mL). Tussionex is not recommended for children under the age of 1 year or weighing less than 9 kg.

Supplied: Suspension: Each 5 mL of neutral tasting, gold-colored, thixotropic suspension, contains: hydrocodone resin complex equivalent to hydrocodone bitartrate 5 mg and phenyltoloxamine resin complex equivalent to phenyltoloxamine citrate 10 mg. Nonmedicinal ingredients: alcohol 95%, D&C Yellow No 10, FD&C Yellow No 6, glycerin, methylparaben, natural and artificial pineapple flavor, natural peach flavor, polacrilin potassium, propylene glycol, propylparaben, purified water, sorbitol and xanthan gum. Ethyl alcohol: 0.03 mL/5 mL. Energy: 16 kJ (3.9 kcal)/5 mL. Sodium: <1 mmol (2.6 mg)/5 mL. Gluten-, lactose-, sucrose- and tartrazine-free. Bottles of 500 and 1 000 mL. Store at room temperature.

Tablets: Each light brown tablet, scored on one side and marked 0894 on the other, contains: hydrocodone resin complex equivalent to hydrocodone bitartrate 5 mg and phenyltoloxamine resin complex equivalent to phenyltoloxamine citrate 10 mg. Nonmedicinal ingredients: calcium phosphate dibasic, colloidal silicon dioxide, cornstarch, lactose, magnesium stearate, polacrilin potassium and sucrose. Energy: 5 kJ (1.23 kcal). Sodium: <1 mmol (2.6 mg). Gluten- and tartrazine-free. Bottles of 100. Store at room temperature.

(Shown in Product Recognition Section)

TWINRIX™

SmithKline Beecham

Combined Hepatitis A and Hepatitis B Vaccine

Active Immunizing Agent

Pharmacology: Twinrix confers immunity against HAV and HBV infection by inducing specific anti-HAV and anti-HBs antibodies.

Data has been obtained from clinical studies involving over 980 adults, adolescents, children and infants.

Anti-HAV Response: In clinical studies involving subjects 18 to 50 years of age, specific humoral antibodies against HAV were detected in more than 88% of vaccinees at day 15 and 99% of vaccinees 1 month after the second dose. One month after the third dose, 100% of subjects were anti-HAV seropositive. In clinical studies involving subjects 1 to 18 years of age, specific humoral antibodies against HAV were detected in more than 93% of the vaccinees at day 15, and 99% of vaccinees 1 month following vaccination.

Anti-HBV Response: The seroconversion rate 1 month after the second dose vaccine was >96.5% in adult subjects. At month 7, one month after dose 3, seroprotection was close to 100%. The seroconversion rate 1 month after the second dose of Twinrix Junior was >98%.

Immunogenicity of the vaccine was analyzed 1 month after the third vaccine dose. The seroprotection rate (>10 IU/L) for hepatitis B was 100%. An anti-HBs antibody titre above 10 IU/L correlates with protection to HBV infection.

Indications: For active immunization against hepatitis A and hepatitis B virus infection in adults, adolescents, children and infants.

The vaccine will not protect against infection caused by other agents such as hepatitis C, hepatitis E and other pathogens known to infect the liver. It can be expected that hepatitis D will also be prevented by immunization with Twinrix as hepatitis D (caused by the delta agent) does not occur in the absence of hepatitis B infection.

Twinrix is recommended in susceptible subjects at risk of hepatitis A and hepatitis B infection, including and not limited to: Travellers: Persons travelling to areas with a high endemicity of HBV and HAV. Persons originating from areas with a high endemicity of HBV and HAV. Armed Forces: Armed Forces personnel who travel to higher endemicity areas or to areas where hygiene is poor. Persons for whom hepatitis A and B are an occupational hazard: These include employees in day-care centres, nursing, medical and paramedical personnel in hospitals and institutions, especially gastroenterology and pediatric units, and sewage workers, among others. Personnel and residents of institutions. Patients frequently receiving blood products: hemophiliac patients. Patients who are candidates for organ transplantation. Anybody who through their work or personal lifestyle may be exposed to HBV and HAV: e.g., homosexuals, persons with multiple sexual partners, abusers of injectable drugs. Household contacts of any of the above groups and of patients with acute or chronic HBV infection. Specific population groups known to have higher incidence of hepatitis A and B.

Contraindications: Should not be administered to subjects with known hypersensitivity to any constituent of the vaccine, or to subjects having shown signs of hypersensitivity after previous administration of Twinrix or the monovalent hepatitis A or hepatitis B vaccine.

As with other vaccines, the administration of Twinrix should be postponed in subjects suffering from acute severe febrile illness. The presence of a minor infection, however, is not a contraindication for vaccination.

Precautions: General: As with all injectable vaccines, appropriate medication (e.g., epinephrine) should always be readily available in case of anaphylaxis or anaphylactoid reactions following administration of the vaccine. For this reason, the vaccinee should remain under medical supervision for 30 minutes after immunization.

Since there is a possibility that the vaccine may contain trace amounts of neomycin, the possibility of an allergic reaction in individuals sensitive to this substance should be kept in mind when considering the use of this vaccine.

Twinrix should be administered s.c. to subjects with thrombocytopenia or bleeding disorders since bleeding may occur following an i.m. administration to these subjects. S.C. injection may result in a less optimal antibody response.

It is possible that subjects may be in the incubation period of a hepatitis A or hepatitis B infection at the time of vaccination. It is not known whether Twinrix will prevent hepatitis A and hepatitis B in such cases.

Pregnancy: The effect of Twinrix on fetal development has not been assessed. However, as with all inactivated viral vaccines the risks to the fetus are considered to be negligible. Twinrix should be used during pregnancy only when clearly needed.

Lactation: The effect on breast-fed infants of the administration of Twinrix to their mothers has not been evaluated in clinical studies. Twinrix should therefore be used with caution in breast-feeding mothers.

Patients with Special Diseases and Conditions: As with other vaccines, hemodialysis patients and persons with an impaired immune system, adequate anti-HAV and anti-HBs antibody titres may not be obtained after the primary immunization course and such patients may therefore require administration of additional doses of vaccine. However, no specific dosing recommendations can be made at this time.

Drug Interactions: Although the concomitant administration of Twinrix and other vaccines has not specifically been studied, it is anticipated that, if different syringes and other injection sites are used, no interaction will be observed.

As with other vaccines, it may be expected that in patients receiving immunosuppressive treatment or patients with immunodeficiency, an adequate response may not be achieved.

Adverse Effects: In controlled clinical studies, signs and symptoms were actively monitored in all subjects for 4 days following the administration of the vaccine. A checklist was used for this purpose. The vaccinees were also requested to report any clinical events occurring during the study period.

Injection site reactions, such as redness and swelling of >3 cm for longer than 24 hours and severe pain were reported in only 1 child of all the administered doses, in both age groups of healthy children. In adults, injection site reactions were reported in 1.5% of administered doses.

The systemic solicited adverse events reported included fever, headache, malaise, fatigue, nausea and vomiting.

These events were reported with a frequency varying between 0.7 and 8.7% of administered doses given to children, and 0.3 and 10% of administered doses given to adults. The investigators considered these events to be possibly related or related to the administration of the vaccine.

No serious adverse events, considered related to vaccination, were reported during clinical trials.

Most solicited events were considered by the subjects as mild and were transient. In a comparative study it was noted that the frequency of solicited adverse events following the administration of Twinrix is not different from the frequency of solicited adverse events following the administration of the monovalent vaccine.

Dosage: Adults over 18 years of age: The recommended dose is 1 mL. Infants, children and adolescents 1 through 18 years of age: The recommended dose is 0.5 mL.

Primary Vaccination Schedule: The standard primary course of vaccination consists of 3 doses, the first administered at the elected date, the second 1 month later and the third 6 months after the first dose.

Booster Dose: The following information should be considered in establishing the timing of a booster dose.

Hepatitis B Component: It is not yet fully established whether immunocompetent individuals who have responded to hepatitis B vaccines will require booster doses to ensure long-term protection or whether natural boosting will occur when vaccinees are exposed to the virus.

Although the persistence of protection is still unknown, it is generally accepted that an antibody titre of ≥10 IU/L is protective for hepatitis B. It would seem advisable to recommend a booster dose for all people at risk when the anti-HBs titre falls below 10 IU/L.

The timing for a hepatitis B vaccine booster dose will depend upon the anti-HBs titre reached after completion of the primary immunization schedule. From available data, generated with the hepatitis B component, general guidelines for a booster dose can be made as follows: After the 0, 1, 6 month primary immunization schedule a booster dose will probably not be required earlier than 5 years following initiation of the primary vaccination course.

Hepatitis A Component: Persistence of hepatitis A antibodies has been followed for 4 years after the administration of a hepatitis A component. It is predicted, based upon extrapolation from the available data, that antibodies will persist for at least 10 years.

It is recommended that the booster dose be administered with Twinrix in order to ensure long-term protection against both diseases. However, the monovalent hepatitis A or hepatitis B vaccines can be used.

Method of Administration: Twinrix is for **i.m.** injection, preferably in the deltoid region, or in the anterolateral thigh in infants. The vaccine **should not** be administered i.m. in the gluteal region or s.c. or intradermally since administration by these routes may result in a less than optimal anti-HAV antibody response.

As with all parenterals, vaccines products should be inspected visually for any foreign particulate matter or discoloration prior to administration. Before use, the vaccine should be well shaken to obtain a slightly opaque, white suspension. Discard if the contents of the vial appear otherwise.

Twinrix should never be administered i.v.

Supplied: Twinrix Adult: Each 1 mL dose contains: hepatitis A 720 ELISA units and hepatitis B 20 μg. Single dose syringes of 1 mL, packages of 1, 10 and 25.

Twinrix Junior: Each 0.5 mL dose contains: hepatitis A 360 ELISA units and hepatitis B 10 μg. Single dose vials of 0.5 mL, packages of 1, 3 and 10. Single dose syringes of 0.5 mL, packages of 1 and 10.

Adsorbed onto aluminum, as aluminum hydroxide and aluminum phosphate. The liquid suspension is made isotonic with sodium chloride in water for injection. The vaccine contains 2-phenoxyethanol as a preservative agent. Residual compounds: formaldehyde, polysorbate 20, amino acids for injection and traces of neomycin sulfate.

Twinrix is a combined vaccine formulated of the purified, inactivated hepatitis A (HA) virus and purified hepatitis B surface antigen (HBsAg) (genetically engineered).

HA and HBsAg antigen bulk vaccines are identical to those used for the preparation of the licensed monovalent vaccines, respectively Havrix (SmithKline Beecham inactivated hepatitis A vaccine) and Engerix-B (recombinant DNA, yeast-derived hepatitis B vaccine).

Twinrix meets the World Health Organization requirements for the manufacture of biological substances.

The expiry date of the vaccine is indicated on the label and packaging. Store at +2 to +8°C. **Do not freeze;** discard if the vaccine has been frozen.

Reviewed 1999

222® AF

Johnson & Johnson • Merck

Acetaminophen

Analgesic—Antipyretic

Indications: For the relief of mild to moderate pain and the reduction of fever.

Acetaminophen is a nonsalicylate analgesic-antipyretic which could be used for the relief of pain in some arthritic and rheumatic conditions involving musculoskeletal pain as well as in myalgia and neuralgia. It has no useful anti-inflammatory properties. It is also used for mild to moderate pain associated with headache, toothache, dysmenorrhea and following tonsillectomy and adenoidectomy. It is also useful for the symptomatic reduction of fever due to the common cold, flu, inoculations or vaccination.

Acetaminophen is particularly useful when ASA is contraindicated or inadvisable, i.e. in patients receiving anticoagulants or uricosuric agents, patients with hemophilia or other bleeding problems, and those with upper gastrointestinal disease or intolerance or hypersensitivity to ASA.

Contraindications: Do not administer in presence of allergy to acetaminophen or to one of the ingredients of 222 AF.

Mild bronchospastic reactions with acetaminophen have been reported in some ASA-sensitive asthmatics. Acetaminophen should be given with care to patients with impaired kidney or liver function. It should be administered with care to patients taking other drugs that affect the liver.

Acetaminophen may be contraindicated in the patient with known glucose-6-phosphate dehydrogenase deficiency.

Precautions: Regular use of acetaminophen has been shown to produce a slight increase in prothrombin time in patients receiving oral anticoagulants but the clinical significance of this effect is not clear.

Renal damage has not been reported following the use of acetaminophen in therapeutic doses, but the chemical relationship of this drug to phenacetin cautions against its use in large amounts over protracted periods of time.

Acetaminophen overdosage can produce severe hepatic damage. Phenobarbital increases the activity of hepatic microsomal enzymes which produce hydroxylated metabolites of acetaminophen responsible for its hepatotoxicity. Thus, concomitant ingestion of phenobarbital may increase the likelihood of liver necrosis in acetaminophen overdose.

Adverse Effects: In recommended therapeutic doses, acetaminophen is usually well tolerated, though hematological reactions have been reported.

The incidence of gastrointestinal upset is less than after salicylate administration.

Skin rash and other allergic reactions occur occasionally. The rash is usually erythematous or urticarial.

Drug Interactions: Anticholinergic agents or opioid analgesics which decrease gastric emptying may delay gastrointestinal absorption of acetaminophen.

Enzyme-inducing agents such as alcohol and antiepileptic drugs may increase the likelihood of acetaminophen toxicity.

The anticoagulant response to coumarins may be increased by repeated doses of acetaminophen.

Chloramphenicol concentrations may be increased by acetaminophen.

Overdose: The toxic dose is estimated at 150 mg/kg or greater. In adults, hepatotoxicity may occur after ingestion of a single dose of 10 g (30 or more 325 mg tablets) of acetaminophen; a dose of 25 g or more is potentially fatal. In adults, nonfatal overdoses ranging from 12.5 to 31.5 g have been reported. A child of 13 is reported to have died after ingesting 15 g.

If the history indicates ingestion of a quantity possibly in excess of 7.5 g or if information on ingestion is unreliable, treatment should be instituted until the result of the initial plasma assay of acetaminophen is available.

Symptoms: Symptoms during the first 2 days of acute poisoning by acetaminophen do not reflect the potential seriousness of the intoxication.

The first 12 to 24 hours after ingestion: The patient may experience nausea, vomiting, diaphoresis, or lethargy; some patients with lower blood levels may be completely symptom-free. It is only during this stage that aggressive therapeutic intervention may prevent liver damage and even death.

The next 24 to 48 hours: The patient becomes— or remains— asymptomatic. At this time, however, liver injury may become manifest initially by elevation of serum transaminase and lactic dehydrogenase activity, increased serum bilirubin concentration and prolongation of prothrombin time, which ultimately peak at day 3 or 4. Unless there are problems associated with other medications taken along with the acetaminophen, glucose, electrolyte and creatinine levels are unchanged.

Days 3 to 5 postingestion: Liver abnormalities become symptomatic. Jaundice, hypoglycemia, prolongation of prothrombin time, seizures, and coma may culminate in hepatic failure. Secondary renal failure may occur. Liver biopsy reveals centrilobular necrosis with sparing of the periportal area. In nonfatal cases, the hepatic lesions are reversible over a period of weeks or months.

Determination of Acetaminophen Concentration in Plasma: Plasma assays should be taken no earlier than at 4 hours, and at 12 hours, after overdosage. A single determination is a less reliable predictor of hepatic injury. When accurate readings are available, plasma concentrations of 200 μg/mL at 4 hours after ingestion or above 50 μg/mL at 12 hours after ingestion forecast severe liver damage. However, only minimal liver damage has developed when the serum concentrations were below 150 μg/mL at 4 hours or less than 37 μg/mL at 12 hours after ingestion of the drug.

Acetaminophen can be measured in the plasma by methods described by the following authors: Thomas BH, Caldwell BB. J Pharm Pharmacol 1972;24:243. Prescott LF. J Pharm Pharmacol 1971;23:111-15. Glynn JP, Kendall SE. Lancet 1975;1147-48 (colorimetric method).

Treatment: Although acetaminophen is rapidly absorbed, induction of vomiting or gastric lavage may help reduce drug absorption, if done within a few hours of ingestion. Do not use charcoal lavage because of its interference with acetylcysteine absorption.

Acetylcysteine (Mucomyst) appears to be an appropriate antidote to counteract acetaminophen's hepatotoxicity. Start acetylcysteine therapy as soon as possible within the first 12 hours after drug ingestion.

For treatment of acetaminophen overdose, most clinicians give 20% acetylcysteine solution orally diluted 1:3 in cola

222 AF (cont'd)

drinks or grapefruit juice. For patients who still cannot tolerate the taste, the drug can be administered by gastric tube. A loading dose of 140 mg/kg has been given, followed by 70 mg/kg every 4 hours for 17 additional doses, since 2 to 3 days are required for acetaminophen blood levels to return to normal. If vomiting occurs within 1 hour after acetylcysteine, the dose is repeated.

In all cases of suspected overdose, immediately contact a Poison Control Centre or a physician, even if there are no symptoms.

Dosage: Adults and Children 12 years of age and over: 1 or 2 tablets (325 or 650 mg) at 4-hour intervals or 1 or 2 tablets (500 mg) at 4- to 6-hour intervals as needed.

Total daily dose should not exceed 4 g (12 Regular Strength tablets or 8 Extra Strength tablets).

Children and Infants: Regular Strength tablets (325 mg) should be used as directed by a physician.

Extra Strength tablets (500 mg) are not a standard dosage unit. Use only as directed by a physician. Not recommended for use in children under 12 years of age.

Supplied: Extra Strength: Each white, round, flat tablet, single-scored on one side, with engraved FROSST above and below score, and engraved 222AF-X on the other, contains: acetaminophen 500 mg. Nonmedicinal ingredients: colloidal silicon dioxide, microcrystalline cellulose, povidone, pregelatinized starch, stearic acid and talc. Plastic bottles of 30 with a safety seal under cap (child-resistant package) and 100.

Regular Strength: Each white, round, flat tablet, single-scored on one side with engraved FROSST above and below score, and engraved 222AF-R on the other, contains: acetaminophen 325 mg. Nonmedicinal ingredients: colloidal silicon dioxide, microcrystalline cellulose, povidone, pregelatinized starch, stearic acid and talc. Plastic bottles of 24 with a safety seal under cap (child-resistant package).

222® TABLETS Ⓝ

Johnson & Johnson • Merck

ASA—Caffeine—Codeine Phosphate

Analgesic—Antipyretic

Indications: For the symptomatic relief of mild to moderate pain, fever and inflammation such as headaches, pain due to cold symptoms, toothache, pain or menstrual cramps, arthritic pain and the pain caused by muscle strains and sprain.

Contraindications: Patients with a history of blood coagulation defects, or receiving anticoagulant drugs or with severe anemia.

Gastrointestinal ulceration and sensitivity to any of the components or to other nonsteroidal anti-inflammatory drugs (NSAIDs).

Patients who had a bronchospastic reaction, generalized urticaria, angioedema, severe rhinitis, laryngeal edema or shock precipitated by ASA or nonsteroidal anti-inflammatory drugs.

Pregnancy and *Lactation:* Because of the potential for increased maternal blood loss and possible adverse effects on the neonate, ASA should be avoided during the last 3 months of pregnancy or when nursing. Pregnant women should be advised not to take ASA during the last trimester of pregnancy unless prescribed and monitored by a physician.

Persons with hypersensitivity to caffeine (risk of allergic reaction).

Persons with hypersensitivity to codeine, pre-existing respiratory depression.

Warnings: This product has the potential for being abused and for being habit forming.

Excessive and prolonged therapy has been associated with nephropathy.

ASA is one of the most frequent causes of accidental poisoning in toddlers and infants. ASA containing preparations should therefore be kept well out of the reach of all children.

Precautions: ASA: General: Salicylates should be administered with caution to patients with asthma and other allergic conditions, with bleeding tendencies, or with hypoprothrombinemia or in patients prone to dyspepsia or known to have a lesion of the gastric mucosa. It should not be administered to patients with hemophilia or other hemorrhagic disorders or to those with an intolerance to ASA (especially ASA-sensitive asthmatics). Caution is necessary when renal or hepatic function is impaired.

Salicylates can produce changes in the thyroid function tests.

ASA may precipitate or worsen attacks of gout.

Discontinue use of 222 tablets 5 to 7 days prior to surgery.

Geriatrics: The elderly may be more susceptible to the toxic effects of salicylates, possibly because of decreased renal function. Inhibiting production of renal prostaglandins by ASA and other nonsteroidal anti-inflammatory agents can result in an acute reduction in renal blood flow with subsequent deterioration of renal function.

Certain prostaglandins may act as renal vasodilators if renal blood flow is reduced. Individuals at risk are those with preexisting renal dysfunction, heart failure, and liver cirrhosis and ascites. The first two conditions occur more commonly in the elderly and may also depend on renal prostaglandins to act as vasodilators.

Opioids may increase the risk of adverse effects especially respiratory depression.

Children: Salicylates: Use of ASA may be associated with the development of Reye's Syndrome in children and teenagers with acute febrile illnesses, especially influenza and varicella. Although a direct causal relationship has not been established, salicylates should not be administered to, or used by, children or teenagers who have chickenpox or manifest flu symptoms before a physician or pharmacist is consulted about Reye's Syndrome, a rare but serious illness.

Caffeine: Pediatric patients are especially susceptible to overdose of caffeine and its adverse CNS effects.

Pregnancy: ASA does not appear to have any teratogenic effects. High doses (3 g daily) of ASA during pregnancy may lengthen the gestation and parturition time. This effect has also been described with nonsteroidal anti-inflammatory agents which inhibit prostaglandin synthesis.

Labor and Delivery: Chronic, high-dose salicylate therapy late in pregnancy may result in prolonged labor, complicated deliveries, and increased risk of maternal or fetal hemorrhage.

Lactation: Salicylate is excreted in breast milk, in moderate amounts, with chronic high-dose use, intake by the infant may be high enough to cause adverse effects.

Drug Interactions: Salicylates increase the effects of oral anticoagulants. Caution is necessary when salicylates and anticoagulants are prescribed concurrently. Also, salicylates may depress the concentration of prothrombin in the plasma.

Salicylates may potentiate sulfonylurea hypoglycemic agents. Large doses of salicylates may have a hypoglycemic action, and thus, affect the insulin requirements of diabetics.

Although salicylates in large doses are uricosuric agents, smaller amounts may depress uric acid clearance, and thus, decrease the uricosuric effects of probenecid, sulfinpyrazone and phenylbutazone.

Sodium excretion produced by spironolactone may be decreased in the presence of salicylates.

Salicylates also retard the renal elimination of methotrexate.

Concomitant use of salicylates and alcohol or other nonsteroidal anti-inflammatory drugs (NSAIDs), may predispose to gastric bleeding, including ulceration.

Concurrent use of other NSAIDs with ASA may also increase the risk of bleeding at sites other than the gastrointestinal tract because of additive inhibition of platelet aggregation.

Caution is necessary when cefamandole, cefoperazone, cefotetan, moxalactam, plicamycin or, valproic acid are prescribed concurrently with ASA as these medications may cause hypoprothrombinemia.

Salicylates may potentiate ototoxic agents (vancomycin, others). Concurrent or sequential administration of these medications with a salicylate should be avoided because hearing loss may occur and may progress to deafness even after discontinuation of the medication; although these effects may be reversible, but usually are permanent.

Salicylates decrease the clearance of zidovudine, leading to potentiation of zidovudine toxicity; concurrent use of ASA and zidovudine should be avoided.

Codeine: Care should be observed in the use of codeine although tolerance and addiction to its use are rare.

Codeine should be given with caution to patients with severe respiratory depression. The depressant effect of codeine may be enhanced by the concurrent administration of sedatives and tranquilizers.

Adverse Effects: Gastrointestinal: dyspepsia, heartburn, nausea, vomiting, constipation, diarrhea, abdominal pain, gastrointestinal ulceration and bleeding.

Otic: tinnitus, hearing loss, dizziness.

Hematologic: anemia, leukopenia, thrombocytopenia, hypoprothrombinemia, purpura.

Dermatologic and Hypersensitivity: urticaria, angioedema, pruritus, various skin eruptions, asthma and anaphylaxis.

Hepatic: reversible hepatotoxicity particularly in patients with juvenile rheumatoid arthritis and systemic lupus erythematosus.

Miscellaneous: mental confusion, headache, drowsiness, sweating and thirst, palpitation, excessive diuresis.

CNS Depression: coma, cardiovascular collapse, respiratory failure, vertigo, muscle tremor, sensory disturbances, nervousness, insomnia.

The potential for habituation may occur.

Overdose: Symptoms: In mild overdosage, these may include rapid and deep breathing, severe drowsiness, nausea, vomiting (leading to alkalosis), stomach pain, diarrhea, headache, hyperpnea, vertigo, tinnitus, flushing, sweating, thirst and tachycardia. (High blood levels of ASA lead to acidosis.) Severe cases may show fever, hemorrhage, bloody urine, excitement, confusion, hallucinations, severe nervousness, convulsions or coma, and respiratory failure.

Codeine and related narcotic analgesics depress respiration by an action on the brain stem respiratory centres.

Other symptoms of overdose may include euphoria, dysphoria, and visual disturbances.

Treatment: Treatment is essentially symptomatic and supportive. Administer water, activated charcoal and ipecac syrup unless the patient is comatose, and remove by gastric lavage or emesis. Patients with mild intoxication should be encouraged to drink plenty of fluids. In patients with more severe intoxication, forced alkaline diuresis may be required. Plasma electrolytes, especially potassium, and the acid-base balance should be monitored regularly. In the presence of cardiac or renal impairment or in very severe intoxication, hemodialysis or hemoperfusion may need to be considered.

Respiratory depression may require intubation measures aimed at supporting respiration and the administration of a narcotic antagonist, e.g., naloxone.

Dosage: Adults: 1 or 2 tablet(s), 1 to 3 times daily (every 4 to 8 hours), as required. **Not recommended for use in children. Do not exceed** 4 g ASA (10 tablets) a day.

Children: **Warning: Do not administer** to children or teenagers who have chickenpox or flu symptoms before a physician or pharmacist is consulted about Reye's Syndrome, a rare and serious illness. When recommended by a physician or dentist: 10 to 14 years: 1 tablet, 1 to 3 times daily (every 4 to 8 hours); 5 to 10 years: one-half tablet, 1 to 3 times daily (every 4 to 8 hours).

Information for the Patient: See Blue Section—Information for the Patient "222 Tablets".

Supplied: Each white scored tablet, engraved 222 contains: ASA 375 mg, caffeine 15 mg (equivalent to 30 mg caffeine citrate) and codeine phosphate 8 mg. Nonmedicinal ingredients: cornstarch, disodium edetate, ethylcellulose, hydrogenated vegetable oil, microcrystalline cellulose, sodium carboxymethylcellulose and sodium lauryl sulfate. Blister packages of 24. Plastic bottles (with safety seal under cap) of 24 (child-resistant package) and 40 (child-resistant package), 100 and 250.

(Shown in Product Recognition Section)

282 MEP® Ⓝ

Frosst

ASA—Meprobamate Compound

Analgesic—Muscle Relaxant—Anxiolytic

Pharmacology: ASA has antipyretic, analgesic and anti-inflammatory activity.

Codeine is useful in the relief of mild to moderate pain from a variety of causes. It is probably the most useful mild analgesic because it has a wide effective dosage range.

The combination of codeine with ASA provides an additive analgesic effect thus giving a greater degree of pain relief than ASA alone and allowing reduced doses of codeine. The association of codeine with a drug of the analgesic-antipyretic group appears to be rational because the mechanism of action of the 2 groups differ. Results of controlled studies have shown that the analgesic effect of codeine and ASA are additive.

Meprobamate has been used extensively in the control of anxiety and various tension states, as well as in muscle spasm. As a tranquilizer-muscle relaxant, this compound acts by blocking the interneuronal passage of nerve impulses. It usually does not adversely affect alertness or psychomotor coordination.

Caffeine stimulates the CNS at all levels including the cortex. In addition, it acts on the kidney to produce diuresis, stimulates cardiac muscle and depresses smooth muscle.

Indications: For the relief of pain of various origins, accompanied by muscle spasm and anxiety. Meprobamate has been successful in relieving tension and emotional stress that are sometimes associated with pain. Symptoms such as nervousness, irritability, headache and malaise may be alleviated by the timely use of this compound. Although meprobamate is not a hypnotic, its tranquilizing and muscle relaxant properties may nevertheless relieve insomnia.

Tension headache, low back pain and neck pain, postpartum pain, dysmenorrhea, toothache, sprains and strains, fractures, myositis, neuralgia, synovitis, arthritis, bursitis, burns, injuries, following surgical and dental procedures, and cancer.

Contraindications: Gastrointestinal ulceration and hypersensitivity to any of the components. Patients with porphyria should not receive meprobamate, as this drug has been reported to precipitate an acute attack.

Warnings: Occupational Hazards: Patients should be warned that meprobamate may impair the mental or physical abilities required for performance of potentially hazardous tasks such as driving or operating machinery.

Since CNS suppressant effects of meprobamate and alcohol or meprobamate and other psychotropic drugs may be additive, appropriate caution should be exerted with patients who take more than one of these agents simultaneously.

Salicylates increase the effects of oral anticoagulants. Caution is necessary when salicylates and anticoagulants are prescribed concurrently. Also, salicylates may depress the concentration of prothrombin in the plasma.

Salicylates may potentiate sulfonylurea hypoglycemic agents. Large doses of salicylates may have a hypoglycemic action, and thus, affect the insulin requirements of diabetics.

Analgesic abuse (excessive and prolonged therapy) has been associated with nephropathy.

Today ASA is one of the most frequent causes of accidental poisoning in toddlers and infants. ASA containing preparations should therefore be kept well out of the reach of all children.

Pregnancy and *Lactation:* Safe use of meprobamate in pregnancy or lactation has not been established; therefore, use of the drug during pregnancy, in nursing mothers or in women of childbearing potential requires that the expected benefits of the drug be weighed against the possible hazards to the mother and child. In animal reproduction studies in mice, rats and rabbits, meprobamate administered at 5 times the maximum human dose has been shown to produce reduction in litter size due to resorption.

Meprobamate passes the placental barrier. It is present in umbilical cord blood at or near maternal plasma levels and in breast milk of lactating mothers at concentrations 2 to 4 times that of maternal plasma. When use of meprobamate is contemplated in breast feeding patients, the drug's higher concentration in breast milk as compared to maternal plasma levels should be considered.

Children: Meprobamate should not be administered to children under 6 years of age since there is a lack of documented evidence of safety and effectiveness.

Recent studies have suggested that ASA usage may be associated with the development of Reye's syndrome in children, teenagers and young adults with acute febrile illnesses, especially influenza and varicella. Although a direct causal relationship has not been established, it is recommended that salicylates be avoided when possible in children, teenagers and young adults with influenza or varicella until the nature of the possible association between ASA and Reye's syndrome has been clarified.

Precautions: Meprobamate: Physical dependence, psychological dependence and abuse have occurred. Chronic intoxication from prolonged ingestion of, usually, greater than recommended doses is manifested by ataxia, slurred speech and vertigo. Therefore, careful supervision of dose and amounts prescribed is advised, as well as avoidance of prolonged administration, especially for alcoholics and other patients with a known propensity for taking excessive quantities of drugs.

Sudden withdrawal of the drug after prolonged and excessive use may precipitate recurrence of pre-existing symptoms such as anxiety, anorexia or insomnia, or withdrawal reactions such as vomiting, ataxia, tremors, muscle twitching, confusional states, hallucinosis and, rarely, convulsive seizures. Such seizures are more likely to occur in persons with CNS damage or pre-existent or latent convulsive disorders. Onset of withdrawal symptoms occurs usually within 12 to 48 hours after discontinuation of meprobamate; symptoms usually cease within the next 12 to 48 hour-period.

When excessive dosage has continued for weeks or months, dosage should be reduced gradually over a period of 1 to 2 weeks rather than abruptly stopped. Alternatively, a short-acting barbiturate may be substituted then gradually withdrawn.

Meprobamate should be administered in its least effective dose, particularly to elderly and/or debilitated patients in order to preclude oversedation.

Meprobamate is metabolized in the liver and excreted by the kidney; to avoid its excess accumulation, caution should be exercised in the administration to patients with compromised liver or kidney function.

Meprobamate occasionally may precipitate seizures in epileptic patients.

Meprobamate should be prescribed cautiously and in small quantities to patients with suicidal tendencies.

Salicylate: Salicylates should be administered with caution to patients with asthma and other allergic conditions, with bleeding tendencies, or with hypoprothrombinemia.

Salicylates can produce changes in the thyroid function tests.

Codeine: Care should be observed in the use of codeine although tolerance and addiction to its use are rare.

Codeine should be given with caution to patients with severe respiratory depression. The depressant effect of codeine may be enhanced by the concurrent administration of sedatives and tranquilizers.

Adverse Effects: Meprobamate: CNS: Drowsiness, ataxia, dizziness, slurred speech, headache, vertigo, weakness, paresthesias, impairment of visual accommodation, euphoria, overstimulation, paradoxical excitement, fast EEG activity.

Gastrointestinal: nausea, vomiting, diarrhea.

Cardiovascular: palpitations, tachycardia, various forms of arrhythmia, transient ECG changes, syncope, hypotensive crisis.

Allergic or Idiosyncratic: Milder reactions are characterized by an itchy, urticarial or erythematous maculopapular rash which may be generalized or confined to the groin. Other reactions have included leukopenia, acute non-thrombocytopenic purpura, petechiae, ecchymoses, eosinophilia, peripheral edema, adenopathy, fever, fixed drug eruption with cross reaction to carisoprodol and cross sensitivity between meprobamate/mebutamate and meprobamate/carbromal.

More severe hypersensitivity reactions, rarely reported, include hyperpyrexia, chills, angioneurotic edema, bronchospasm, oliguria, and anuria. Anaphylaxis, exfoliative dermatitis, stomatitis and proctitis, Stevens-Johnson syndrome and bullous dermatitis have also occurred.

Hematologic: Agranulocytosis, aplastic anemia have been reported, although no causal relationship has been established, and thrombocytopenic purpura.

ASA: Gastrointestinal: dyspepsia, heartburn, nausea, vomiting, diarrhea, gastrointestinal ulceration and bleeding.

Ear: tinnitus, hearing loss.

Hematologic: anemia, leukopenia, thrombocytopenia, purpura.

Dermatologic and Hypersensitivity: urticaria, angioedema, pruritus, various skin eruptions, asthma and anaphylaxis.

Miscellaneous: mental confusion, drowsiness, sweating and thirst.

Codeine: Average or large doses of codeine may cause various gastrointestinal symptoms such as nausea, vomiting and constipation.

Caffeine: Caffeine may cause nausea, nervousness, insomnia, headache, vomiting, palpitation, vertigo, muscle tremor, sensory disturbances, excessive diuresis in sensitive patients. Large doses may cause gastric ulceration.

Overdose: Symptoms and Treatment: Meprobamate: Suicidal attempts with meprobamate have resulted in drowsiness, lethargy, stupor, ataxia, coma, shock, vasomotor and respiratory collapse. Some suicidal attempts have been fatal. The following data have been reported in the literature, and from other sources. These data are not expected to correlate with each case (considering factors such as individual susceptibility and length of time from ingestion to treatment) but represent the usual ranges reported.

Acute simple overdose (meprobamate alone): Death has been reported with ingestion of as little as 12 g meprobamate and survival with as much as 40 g.

Blood levels: 0.5 to 2.0 mg% represents the usual blood level range of meprobamate after therapeutic doses. The level may occasionally be as high as 3 mg%.

3 to 10 mg% usually corresponds to findings of mild to moderate symptoms of overdosage, such as stupor or light coma.

10 to 20 mg% usually corresponds to deeper coma, requiring more intensive treatment. Some fatalities occur.

At levels greater than 20 mg%, more fatalities than survivals can be expected.

Acute combined overdose (meprobamate with other psychotropic drugs or alcohol): Since effects can be additive, a history of ingestion of a low dose of meprobamate plus any of these compounds (or of a relatively low blood or tissue level) cannot be used as a prognostic indicator.

In cases where excessive doses have been taken, sleep ensues rapidly and blood pressure, pulse, and respiratory rates are reduced to basal levels. Any drug remaining in the stomach should be removed and symptomatic treatment given. Should respiration or blood pressure become compromised, respiratory assistance, CNS stimulants, and pressor agents should be administered cautiously as indicated. Meprobamate is metabolized in the liver and excreted by the kidney. Diuresis, osmotic (mannitol) diuresis, peritoneal dialysis and hemodialysis have been used successfully. Careful monitoring of urinary output is necessary and caution should be taken to avoid overhydration. Relapse and death, after initial recovery, have been attributed to incomplete gastric emptying and delayed absorption.

ASA: In mild overdosage these may include rapid and deep breathing, nausea, vomiting (leading to alkalosis), hyperpnea, vertigo, tinnitus, flushing, sweating, thirst and tachycardia. (High blood levels of ASA lead to acidosis.) Severe cases may show fever, hemorrhage, excitement, confusion, convulsions or coma, and respiratory failure.

Treatment is essentially symptomatic and supportive. Administer water, universal antidote and remove by gastric lavage or emesis. Force fluids (e.g. salty broth) to replace sodium loss. If the patient is unable to retain fluids orally, the alkalosis can be treated by hypertonic saline i.v. If salicylism acidosis is present, sodium bicarbonate i.v. is preferred because it increases the renal excretion of salicylates. Vitamin K is indicated if there is evidence of hemorrhage. Hemodialysis has been used with success.

Codeine: Codeine and related narcotics depress respiration by an action on the brain stem respiratory centers.

General supportive measures for depressed respiration e.g., oxygen and artificial respiration.

Dosage: Adults: 1 or 2 tablets 3 or 4 times a day.

Supplied: Each white, phi-marked tablet, with 282 MEP engraved obverse, contains: ASA 350 mg, caffeine citrate 30 mg, codeine phosphate 15 mg and meprobamate 200 mg. Gluten-, lactose- and tartrazine-free. Bottles of 50 and 500.

(Shown in Product Recognition Section)

292® TABLETS Ⓝ

Frosst

ASA—Caffeine—Codeine Phosphate

Analgesic—Antipyretic

Indications: For symptomatic relief of mild to severe pain, fever and Inflammation.

Contraindications: Patients with a history of blood coagulation defects, or receiving anticoagulant drugs or with severe anemia.

Gastrointestinal ulceration and sensitivity to ASA, codeine, caffeine or to other NSAIDs or any of the nonmedicinal ingredients. Patients who had generalized urticaria, angioedema, severe rhinitis, laryngeal edema or shock precipitated by ASA or other NSAIDs.

Pregnancy and *Lactation:* Because of the potential for increased maternal blood loss and possible adverse effects on the neonate, ASA should be avoided during the last 3 months of pregnancy, or when nursing.

Warnings: This product has the habit-forming potential of opioid analgesics and has potential for being abused.

Excessive and prolonged therapy has been associated with nephropathy.

ASA is one of the most frequent causes of accidental poisoning in toddlers and infants. ASA containing preparations should therefore be kept out of the reach of all children.

Pregnancy: High doses (3 g daily) of ASA during pregnancy may lengthen the gestation and parturition time. This effect has also been described with NSAIDs which inhibit prostaglandin synthesis. They may also prolong and complicate labor and delivery. Studies in animals have shown that ASA and caffeine causes birth defects. ASA and opioid analgesics cross the placenta.

292 Tablets (cont'd)

Precautions: General: Salicylates should be administered with caution to patients with asthma and other allergic conditions, with bleeding tendencies, or with hypoprothrombinemia or in patients prone to dyspepsia or known to have a lesion of the gastric mucosa. It should not be administered to patients with hemophilia or other hemorrhagic disorders or to those with an intolerance to ASA (especially ASA-sensitive asthmatics). Caution is necessary when renal or hepatic function is impaired.

Salicylates can produce changes in the thyroid function tests.

ASA may precipitate or worsen attacks of gout.

Opioid analgesics may cause dryness of the mouth. For temporary relief, use sugarless candy or gum, melt bits of ice in your mouth, or use a saliva substitute. If dry mouth continues for more than 2 weeks, check with your dentist.

Do not take this medicine for 5 to 7 days before any surgery, including dental surgery, unless otherwise directed by your physician or dentist.

Usage of this medication may cause drowsiness, dizziness or lightheadedness, or false sense of well being. If it occurs, lying down for a while may help reduce dizziness or lightheadedness. Getting up slowly may also help lessen these two side effects.

Occupational Hazards: Opioid containing preparations may impair mental and/or physical abilities required for the performance of potentially hazardous tasks such as driving a vehicle or operating machinery.

Geriatrics: The elderly may be more susceptible to the toxic effects of salicylates, possibly because of decreased renal function. Inhibiting production of renal prostaglandins by ASA and other NSAIDs can result in an acute reduction in renal blood flow with subsequent deterioration of renal function.

Certain prostaglandins may act as renal vasodilators if renal blood flow is reduced. Individuals at risk are those with preexisting renal dysfunction, heart failure, and liver cirrhosis and ascites. The first two conditions occur more commonly in the elderly and may also depend on renal prostaglandins to act as vasodilators.

Opioids may increase the risk of adverse effects especially respiratory depression.

Children: Use of ASA may be associated with the development of Reye's syndrome in children and teenagers with acute febrile illnesses, especially influenza and varicella. Although a direct causal relationship has not been established, salicylates should not be administered to, or used by, children or teenagers who have chickenpox or manifest flu symptoms before a physician or pharmacist is consulted about Reye's syndrome, a rare and serious illness.

Pediatric patients are especially susceptible to overdose of caffeine and its adverse CNS effects.

Pregnancy: ASA does not appear to have any teratogenic effects.

Chronic, high-dose salicylate therapy late in pregnancy may result in increased risk of maternal or fetal hemorrhage (see Warnings).

Lactation: Salicylate, caffeine and codeine are excreted in breast milk; and, with chronic high-dose use, intake by the infant may be high enough to cause adverse effects.

Regular use of opioids by pregnant women may cause withdrawal symptoms in the neonate.

Drug Interactions: Salicylates increase the effects of oral anticoagulants. Caution is necessary when salicylates and anticoagulants are prescribed concurrently. Also, salicylates may depress the concentration of prothrombin in the plasma.

Salicylates may potentiate sulfonylurea hypoglycemic agents. Large doses of salicylates may have a hypoglycemic action, and thus, affect the insulin requirements of diabetics.

Although salicylates in large doses are uricosuric agents, smaller amounts may depress uric acid clearance and thus decrease the uricosuric effects of probenecid, sulfinpyrazone and phenylbutazone.

Sodium excretion produced by spironolactone may be decreased in the presence of salicylates.

Salicylates also retard the renal elimination of methotrexate.

Concomitant use of salicylates and alcohol or other NSAIDs, may predispose to gastric bleeding, including ulceration.

Concurrent use of other NSAIDs with ASA may also increase the risk of bleeding at sites other than the gastrointestinal tract because of additive inhibition of platelet aggregation.

Caution is necessary when cefamandole, cefoperazone, cefotetan, moxalactam, plicamycin or, valproic acid are prescribed concurrently with ASA as these medications may cause hypoprothrombinemia.

Salicylates may potentiate ototoxic agents (vancomycin, others). Concurrent or sequential administration of these medications with a salicylate should be avoided because hearing loss may occur and may progress to deafness even after discontinuation of the medication; although these effects may be reversible, but usually are permanent.

Salicylates decrease the clearance of zidovudine, leading to potentiation of zidovudine toxicity; concurrent use of ASA and zidovudine should be avoided.

Care should be observed in the use of codeine although tolerance and addiction to its use are rare.

Codeine should be given with caution to patients with severe respiratory depression. The depressant effect of codeine may be enhanced by the concurrent administration of sedatives and tranquilizers.

Adverse Effects: Gastrointestinal: dyspepsia, heartburn, nausea, vomiting, constipation, diarrhea, abdominal pain, gastrointestinal ulceration and bleeding.

Otic: tinnitus, hearing loss, dizziness.

Hematologic: anemia, leukopenia, thrombocytopenia, hypoprothrombinemia, purpura.

Dermatologic and Hypersensitivity: urticaria, angioedema, pruritus, various skin eruptions, asthma and anaphylaxis.

Hepatic: reversible hepatotoxicity particularly in patients with juvenile rheumatoid arthritis and systemic lupus erythematosus.

Miscellaneous: mental confusion, headache, drowsiness, sweating and thirst, palpitation, excessive diuresis.

CNS Depression: coma, cardiovascular collapse, respiratory failure, vertigo, muscle tremor, sensory disturbances, nervousness, insomnia.

The potential for habituation may occur.

Overdose: Symptoms: In mild overdosage these may include rapid and deep breathing, severe drowsiness, nausea, vomiting (leading to alkalosis), stomach pain, diarrhea, headache, hyperpnea, vertigo, tinnitus, flushing, sweating, thirst and tachycardia. (High blood levels of ASA lead to acidosis.) Severe cases may show fever, hemorrhage, bloody urine, excitement, confusion, hallucinations, severe nervousness, convulsions or coma, and respiratory failure.

Codeine and related narcotic analgesics depress respiration by an action on the brain stem respiratory centres.

Other symptoms of overdose may include euphoria, dysphoria, and visual disturbances.

Treatment: Treatment is essentially symptomatic and supportive. Administer water, activated charcoal and ipecac syrup unless the patient is comatose and remove by gastric lavage or emesis. Patients with mild intoxication should be encouraged to drink plenty of fluids. In patients with more severe intoxication forced alkaline diuresis may be required. Plasma electrolytes, especially potassium, and the acid-base balance should be monitored regularly. In the presence of cardiac or renal impairment or in very severe intoxication, hemodialysis or hemoperfusion may need to be considered.

Respiratory depression may require intubation measures aimed at supporting respiration and the administration of a narcotic antagonist, e.g., naloxone.

Dosage: 1 tablet with a large glass of water (250 mL) every 4 hours, as required.

Supplied: Each round, biconvex, peach-colored tablet with the letter phi and one score line on one side and 292 on the other side, contains: ASA 375 mg, caffeine 15 mg (equivalent to 30 mg caffeine citrate) and codeine phosphate 30 mg. Nonmedicinal ingredients: cornstarch, disodium edetate, ethylcellulose, guar gum, hydrogenated vegetable oil, sunset yellow on aluminum substrate and sodium lauryl sulfate. Gluten-, lactose- and tartrazine-free. Bottles of 50 and 500. Store at 15 to 30°C. Protect from light and moisture.

(Shown in Product Recognition Section)

TYLENOL®

McNeil Consumer Products

Acetaminophen

Analgesic—Antipyretic

Pharmacology: The analgesic and antipyretic effects of acetaminophen are believed to be related to the inhibition of prostaglandin synthetase (a mechanism shared by ASA and related drugs). It is postulated that the analgesic effect is produced by elevation of the pain threshold and the antipyretic effect is produced through action on the hypothalamic heat-regulating center.

Acetaminophen is considered equipotent to ASA in its analgesic and antipyretic effects and is unlikely to produce many of the side effects associated with ASA and ASA containing products. Unlike these drugs, however, it has no anti-inflammatory effect at clincally relevant doses in humans.

Acetaminophen is metabolized in the liver. The major pathway involves glucuronyl transferase and the minor pathway involves the cytochrome P450 mixed function oxidase system.

Indications: As a nonsalicylate analgesic-antipyretic for the temporary relief of mild to moderate pain in a wide variety of conditions involving musculoskeletal pain, as well as in other painful disorders such as headache, earache, low back pain, dysmenorrhea, myalgias, neuralgias. Also indicated for the symptomatic reduction of fever due to the common cold, flu and other viral or bacterial infections.

Contraindications: Hypersensitivity to acetaminophen.

Precautions: As with any other nonprescription analgesic drug, physicians should be cognisant of and supervise the use of acetaminophen in patients with alcoholism, serious kidney or serious liver disease. Physicians should alert their patients who regularly consume large amounts of alcohol not to exceed the recommended doses of acetaminophen.

Patients should be counseled to consult a physician if redness or swelling is present in an area of pain, if symptoms do not improve or if they worsen, or if new symptoms such as high fever, rash or headache occur, as these may be signs of a condition which requires medical attention.

Acetaminophen should not be taken for pain for more than 5 days or for fever for more than 3 days, unless directed by a physician.

Pregnancy and *Lactation:* As with any drug, patients who are pregnant or nursing a baby should consult a physician before taking this product.

Do not use with other products containing acetaminophen. Keep out of the reach of children.

Adverse Effects: When used as directed, acetaminophen is virtually free of severe toxicity or side effects.

The classic gastrointestinal irritation associated with nonsteroidal anti-inflammatory drugs, including ASA does not occur with acetaminophen. Sensitivity reactions are rare. Cross-reactivity in ASA sensitive persons has been rarely reported. If sensitivity is suspected, discontinue use of the drug.

Patients who concomitantly medicate with warfarin-type anticoagulants and regular doses of acetaminophen have occasionally been reported to have unforeseen elevations in their INR. Physicians should be cognisant of this potential interaction and monitor the INR in such patients closely while therapy is established.

Overdose: Symptoms and Treatment: Acetaminophen: Typical Toxidrome: Significant overdoses of acetaminophen may result in potentially fatal hepatotoxicity. The physician should be mindful that there is no early presentation that is pathoneumonic for the overdose. A high degree of clinical suspicion must always be maintained.

Due to the wide availability of acetaminophen, it is commonly involved in single and mixed drug overdose situations and the practitioner should have a low threshold for screening for its presence in a patient's serum. Acute toxicity after single dose overdoses of acetaminophen can be anticipated when the overdose exceeds 150 mg/kg. Chronic alcohol abusers, cachectic individuals, and persons taking pharmacologic inducers of the hepatic P450 microsomal enzyme system may be at risk with lower exposures.

Chronic intoxication has rarely been reported in persons consuming in excess of 150 mg/kg of acetaminophen daily for several days.

Specific Antidote: NAC (N-acetylcysteine) administered by either the i.v. or the oral route is known to be a highly effective antidote for acetaminophen poisoning. It is most effective when administered within 8 hours of a significant overdose but reports have indicated benefits to treatment initiated well beyond this time period. It is imperative to administer the antidote as early as possible in the time course of acute intoxication to reap the full benefits of the antidote's protective effects.

General Management: When the possibility of acetaminophen overdose exists, treatment should begin immediately and include appropriate decontamination of the gastrointestinal tract, proper supportive care, careful assessment of appropriately timed serum acetaminophen estimations evaluated against the Matthew-Rumack nomogram, timely administration of NAC as required and appropriate follow-up care. Physicians unfamiliar with the current management of acetaminophen overdose should consult with a Poison Control

Centre immediately. Telephone numbers for local Poison Control Centres are available in the local phone directory. Delays in initiation of appropriate therapy may jeopardize the patient's chances for full recovery.

Dosage: Adults and children over 12 years of age: 650 to 1 000 mg every 4 hours, as required, not to exceed 4 000 mg acetaminophen in 24 hours. Doses may be administered with or without food.
Children: 10 to 15 mg/kg every 4 hours, as required, not to exceed 75 mg/kg/24 hours and never to exceed the maximum adult daily dose of 4 000 mg of acetaminophen. Alternatively, the following single doses (see Table I), may be given every 4 hours not to exceed 5 doses in 24 hours. Doses may be given with or without food (i.e., milk, formula, juices, etc).

Table I—Tylenol

Dosage in Children

Age	Weight kg	Single Dose
Newborn to under 4 months*	2.5-5.4	40 mg
4 months to under 12 months	5.5-7.9	80 mg
12 months to under 2 years	8.0-10.9	120 mg
2 and 3 years	11.0-15.9	160 mg
4 and 5 years	16.0-21.9	240 mg
6, 7 and 8 years	22.0-26.9	320 mg
9 and 10 years	27.0-31.9	400 mg
11 years	32.0-43.9	480 mg

*Consumer labelling for Infant's and Children's Tylenol brand of acetaminophen does not offer dosing information for children under 4 months of age; therefore, this dose is provided as a guideline for professional recommendations to the consumer.

Supplied: Caplets: 325 mg: Each elongated, capsule-shaped white tablet, engraved "TYLENOL" one side and "325" on the other, contains: acetaminophen 325 mg. Nonmedicinal ingredients: cellulose, cornstarch, hydroxypropyl methylcellulose, magnesium stearate, polyethylene glycol and sodium starch glycolate. Energy: 0.7 kJ (0.2 kcal). Sodium: <1 mmol (0.3 mg). Gluten-, lactose- and tartrazine-free. Plastic bottles of 24†, 50†, 100† and 200.

500 mg: Each elongated, capsule-shaped white tablet, engraved "TYLENOL" one side and "500" on the other, contains: acetaminophen 500 mg. Nonmedicinal ingredients: cellulose, cornstarch, hydroxypropyl methylcellulose, magnesium stearate, polyethylene glycol and sodium starch glycolate. Energy: 0.8 kJ (0.2 kcal). Sodium: <1 mmol (0.4 mg). Gluten-, lactose- and tartrazine-free. Vials of 10†, plastic bottles of 24†, 50†, 100†, 150 and 400 (for institutional use only).

Chewable Tablets (fruit): Each round, pink tablet, engraved "TYLENOL" one side and "80" with a partial score the other side, contains: acetaminophen 80 mg. Nonmedicinal ingredients: cellulose, citric acid, compressible sugar, D&C Red No. 7, ethylcellulose, flavoring, magnesium stearate, mannitol and sodium cyclamate. Energy: 5 kJ (1.2 kcal). Sodium: <1 mmol (0.6 mg). Gluten-, lactose- and tartrazine-free. Plastic bottles of 24†.

Chewable Tablets, sucrose-free (bubble gum): Each round, dark pink tablet engraved "TYLENOL" one side and "80" with a partial score the other side contains: acetaminophen 80 mg. Nonmedicinal ingredients: aspartame, cellulose, D&C Red No. 7, ethylcellulose, flavoring, magnesium stearate and mannitol. Phenylketonurics: contains phenylalanine (aspartame). Energy: 4.2 kJ (1 kcal). Gluten-, lactose-, sodium-, sugar- (as sucrose) and tartrazine-free. Plastic bottles of 24†.

Chewable Tablets, sucrose-free (grape): Each round, purple tablet, engraved "TYLENOL" one side and "80" with a partial score the other side, contains: acetaminophen 80 mg. Nonmedicinal ingredients: aspartame, cellulose, citric acid, D&C Red No. 7, ethylcellulose, FD&C Blue No. 1, flavoring, magnesium stearate and mannitol. Phenylketonurics: contains phenylalanine (aspartame). Energy: 4.2 kJ (1 kcal). Gluten-, lactose-, sodium-, sugar- (as sucrose) and tartrazine-free. Plastic bottles of 24† and 50† (for institutional use).

Children's Elixir: Each 5 mL contains: acetaminophen 160 mg in a cherry-flavored red vehicle. Nonmedicinal ingredients: benzoic acid, citric acid, D&C Red No. 33, FD&C Red No. 40, flavoring, glycerin, polyethylene glycol, propylene glycol, purified water, sodium benzoate, sorbitol and sucrose. Energy: 36.7 kJ (8.8 kcal). Sodium: <1 mmol (1.2 mg). Alcohol-, gluten-, lactose- and tartrazine-free. Plastic bottles of 100 mL† and amber glass bottles of 500 mL.

Children's Suspension Liquid (bubble gum): Each 5 mL contains: acetaminophen 160 mg in a dark pink liquid vehicle with a bubble gum-flavored taste. Nonmedicinal ingredients: butylparaben, cellulose, citric acid, corn syrup, D&C Red No. 33, FD&C Red No. 40, flavoring, glycerin, propylene glycol, purified water, sodium benzoate, sorbitol and xanthan gum. Energy: 51 kJ (12 kcal). Sodium: <1 mmol (1.6 mg). Alcohol-, gluten-, lactose- and tartrazine-free. Plastic bottles of 24† and 100 mL†.

Children's Suspension Liquid (grape): Each 5 mL contains: acetaminophen 160 mg in a purple liquid vehicle with a grape-flavored taste. Nonmedicinal ingredients: butylparaben, cellulose, citric acid, corn syrup, D&C Red No. 33, FD&C Blue No. 1, flavoring, glycerin, propylene glycol, purified water, sodium benzoate, sorbitol and xanthan gum. Energy: 46 kJ (11 kcal). Sodium: <1 mmol (1.6 mg). Alcohol-, gluten-, lactose- and tartrazine-free. Plastic bottles of 100 mL†.

Gelcaps: Each solid capsule-shaped tablet, coated with red gelatin on one end and yellow on the other, printed "TYLENOL/500" on each gelatin-coated end, contains: acetaminophen 500 mg. Nonmedicinal ingredients: benzyl alcohol, castor oil, cellulose, cornstarch, D&C yellow No. 10, edetate calcium disodium, FD&C Blue No. 1 and FD&C Blue No. 2, FD&C Red No. 40, gelatin, hydroxypropyl methylcellulose, magnesium stearate, parabens, sodium lauryl sulfate, sodium propionate, sodium starch glycolate and titanium dioxide. Energy: 1 kJ (0.2 kcal). Sodium: <1 mmol (0.42 mg). Gluten-, lactose- and tartrazine-free. Plastic bottles of 24† and 50.

Infants' Drops: Each mL contains: acetaminophen 80 mg in an orange liquid vehicle with a fruit-flavored taste. Nonmedicinal ingredients: citric acid, FD&C Yellow No. 6, flavoring, polyethylene glycol, propylene glycol, purified water, sodium benzoate, sodium cyclamate and sorbitol. Energy: 4.1 kJ (0.98 kcal). Sodium: <1 mmol (1.4 mg). Tartrazine-, gluten-, alcohol- and lactose-free. Plastic bottles of 15 mL† and 24 mL† with a calibrated dropper. Concentrated for dropper dosage only.

Infants' Suspension Drops (grape): Each mL contains: acetaminophen 80 mg in a purple liquid vehicle with a grape-flavored taste. Nonmedicinal ingredients: butylparaben, cellulose, citric acid, corn syrup, D&C Red No. 33, FD&C Blue No. 1, flavoring, glycerin, propylene glycol, purified water, sodium benzoate, sorbitol and xanthan gum. Energy: 8.8 kJ (2.1 kcal). Sodium: <1 mmol (0.3 mg). Alcohol-, gluten-, lactose- and tartrazine-free. Plastic bottles of 15 mL†, 24 mL† and 24 mL† (for institutional use only) with a calibrated dropper. Concentrated for dropper dosage only.

Infants' Suspension Drops (cherry): Each mL contains: acetaminophen 80 mg in a red liquid vehicle with a cherry-flavored taste. Nonmedicinal ingredients: butylparaben, cellulose, citric acid, corn syrup, FD&C Red No. 40, flavoring, glycerin, propylene glycol, purified water, sodium benzoate, sorbitol and xanthan gum. Energy: 12.9 kJ (3.1 kcal). Sodium: 0.04 mmol (0.95 mg). Alcohol-, gluten-, lactose-, sucrose-, sulfite- and tartrazine-free. Plastic bottles of 15 mL† and 24 mL† with a calibrated dropper. Concentrated for dropper dosage only.

Junior Strength Chewable Tablets, sucrose-free (bubble gum): Each round, dark pink tablet, scored one side and engraved "TYLENOL 160" the other side, contains: acetaminophen 160 mg. Nonmedicinal ingredients: aspartame, cellulose, D&C Red No. 7, ethylcellulose, flavoring, magnesium stearate and mannitol. Phenylketonurics: contains phenylalanine (aspartame). Energy: 8.4 kJ (2 kcal). Gluten-, lactose-, sodium-, sugar- (as sucrose) and tartrazine-free. Plastic bottles of 20†.

Junior Strength Chewable Tablets, sucrose-free (grape): Each round, purple tablet, scored on one side and engraved "TYLENOL 160" the other side, contains: acetaminophen 160 mg. Nonmedicinal ingredients: aspartame, cellulose, citric acid, D&C Red No. 7, ethylcellulose, FD&C Blue No. 1, flavoring, magnesium stearate and mannitol. Phenylketonurics: contains phenylalanine (aspartame). Energy: 8 kJ (2 kcal). Gluten-, lactose-, sodium-, sugar- (as sucrose) and tartrazine-free. Plastic bottles of 20†.

Junior Strength Chewable Tablets (fruit): Each round, pink tablet, scored on one side and engraved "TYLENOL 160" the other side, contains: acetaminophen 160 mg. Nonmedicinal ingredients: cellulose, citric acid, compressible sugar, D&C Red No. 7, ethylcellulose, flavoring, magnesium stearate, mannitol and sodium cyclamate. Energy: 10 kJ (2.5 kcal). Sodium: <1 mmol (1.1 mg). Gluten-, lactose- and tartrazine-free. Plastic bottles of 20†.

Tablets: 325 mg: Each round, white tablet, engraved "TYLENOL" one side and "325" the other side, contains: acetaminophen 325 mg. Nonmedicinal ingredients: cellulose, cornstarch, magnesium stearate and sodium starch glycolate. Energy: 0.8 kJ (0.2 kcal). Sodium: <1 mmol (0.1 mg). Gluten-, lactose- and tartrazine-free. Vials of 12†, plastic bottles of 24†, 50†, 100 and 500.

500 mg: Each round, white tablet, engraved "TYLENOL" one side and "500" other side, contains: acetaminophen 500 mg. Nonmedicinal ingredients: cellulose, cornstarch, magnesium stearate and sodium starch glycolate. Energy: 1.3 kJ (0.3 kcal). Sodium: <1 mmol (0.1 mg). Gluten-, lactose- and tartrazine-free. Vials of 10†, plastic bottles of 30†, 50 and 100†.

†Container provided with a child-resistant closure.
All packages are safety sealed.

(Shown in Product Recognition Section)

Reviewed 1999

TYLENOL® ACHES AND STRAINS MEDICATION

McNeil Consumer Products

Acetaminophen—Chlorzoxazone

Analgesic—Muscle Relaxant

Pharmacology: Tylenol Aches and Strains Medication combines the muscle-relaxant effect of chlorzoxazone with acetaminophen, a well known analgesic.

Chlorzoxazone is a centrally-acting agent for painful musculoskeletal conditions. Data available from animal experiments, as well as human study, indicate that chlorzoxazone acts primarily at the level of the spinal cord and subcortical areas of the brain where it inhibits multisynaptic reflex arcs involved in producing and maintaining skeletal muscle spasm of varied etiology. The clinical result is a reduction of the skeletal muscle spasm with relief of pain and increased mobility of the involved muscles.

Pharmacokinetics: Blood levels of chlorzoxazone can be detected in humans during the first 30 minutes after oral administration of Tylenol Aches and Strains Medication and peak levels may be reached in about 1 to 2 hours. Chlorzoxazone is rapidly metabolized and is excreted in the urine, primarily in a conjugated form as the glucuronide. Less than 1% of a dose of chlorzoxazone is excreted unchanged in the urine in 24 hours.

Acetaminophen provides analgesic action to supplement that which results secondarily from muscle relaxation. Acetaminophen is rapidly absorbed after oral administration, with peak plasma levels occurring in 1 to 2 hours. After 8 hours, only negligible amounts remain in the blood. Only 4% is excreted unchanged; 85% of the ingested dose is recovered in the urine in conjugated form as the glucuronide. Acetaminophen is distributed throughout most tissues of the body. Acetaminophen is metabolized primarily in the liver. Little unchanged drug is excreted in the urine, but most metabolic products appear in the urine within 24 hours.

The mode of action of chlorzoxazone has not been clearly identified, but may be related to its sedative properties. Chlorzoxazone does not directly relax tense skeletal muscles in man.

Following oral administration chlorzoxazone in combination with acetaminophen, both drugs are rapidly absorbed. Mean drug plasma concentrations reach a peak level in the majority of subjects in 45 to 90 minutes.

The plasma elimination half-life is about 1 hour for chlorzoxazone and ranges from 1.5 to 3.5 hours for acetaminophen.

Metabolism is rapid, the principal metabolites are conjugates of glucuronic acid which are excreted primarily in the urine. Less than 1% of an administered dose of chlorzoxazone and less than 4% of an administered dose of acetaminophen is excreted unchanged in the urine in 24 hours. Only traces of unchanged drug are excreted through the bile into the feces.

Indications: As an adjunct to rest, physical therapy and other measures for the relief of discomfort associated with acute musculoskeletal conditions. This may include skeletal muscle spasm and pain associated with sprains, strains and other traumatic muscle injuries; myalgias; arthritides; low back pain; tension headache; torticollis; fibrositis; spondylitis; and cervical root and disc syndromes.

Contraindications: Hypersensitivity to the components, hepatic impairment and acute porphyria.

Precautions: As with any other nonprescription analgesic drug, physicians should be cognisant of and supervise the use of acetaminophen in patients with alcoholism, serious kidney or serious liver disease. Physicians should alert their patients who regularly consume large amounts of alcohol not to exceed the recommended doses of acetaminophen.

Tylenol Aches and Strains Medication (cont'd)

Patients should be counseled to consult a physician if redness or swelling is present in an area of pain, if symptoms do not improve or if they worsen, or if new symptoms such as high fever, rash or headache occur, as these may be signs of a condition which requires medical attention.

Acetaminophen should not be taken for pain for more than 5 days unless directed by a physician.

Pregnancy and *Lactation:* As with any drug, patients who are pregnant or nursing a baby should consult a physician before taking this product.

Do not use with other products containing acetaminophen. Keep out of the reach of children.

There have been reports of liver damage associated with the use of chlorzoxazone-containing products. If any symptoms suggestive of liver dysfunction are observed, the drug should be discontinued. Tylenol Aches and Strains Medication should be used with caution in patients with severe impairment of renal function.

Drowsiness and dizziness can occur with use of this product.

Occupational Hazards: Patients using this drug should be cautioned about driving a car or operating potentially hazardous machinery if they become drowsy, dizzy or show impaired mental or physical abilities while taking this medication.

Drug Interactions: Patients receiving antipsychotics, anti-anxiety agents or other CNS depressants (including alcohol) concomitantly with this drug may exhibit an additive CNS depression. When such combined therapy is contemplated, the dose of one or both agents should be reduced. Avoid consumption of alcohol while using this product.

Pregnancy: Should be used during pregnancy only if the potential benefit justifies the potential risk to the fetus.

Lactation: Chlorzoxazone and acetaminophen is not recommended during lactation because safety in nursing mothers has not been established. It is not known if chlorzoxazone is excreted in breast milk. Acetaminophen passes into breast milk but is not likely to have an adverse effect on the infant at therapeutic doses.

Children: Because safety and effectiveness of chlorzoxazone and acetaminophen in combination have not been established in children such use is not recommended.

Adverse Effects: When used as directed, acetaminophen is virtually free of severe toxicity or side effects. The classic gastrointestinal irritation associated with nonsteroidal anti-inflammatory drugs, including ASA does not occur with acetaminophen. Sensitivity reactions are rare. Cross-reactivity in ASA sensitive persons has been rarely reported. If sensitivity is suspected, discontinue use of the drug.

Patients who concomitantly medicate with warfarin-type anticoagulants and regular doses of acetaminophen have occasionally been reported to have unforeseen elevations in their INR. Physicians should be cognisant of this potential interaction and monitor the INR in such patients closely while therapy is established.

Gastrointestinal: Occasional patients may develop gastrointestinal disturbances and abdominal pain. It is possible in rare instances that chlorzoxazone may have been associated with gastrointestinal bleeding.

CNS: Drowsiness, dizziness, lightheadedness, malaise, or overstimulation may be noted by an occasional patient.

Allergic: Rarely, allergic-type skin rashes, petechiae, or ecchymoses may develop during treatment. Angioneurotic edema or anaphylactic reactions are extremely rare.

Renal Toxicity: There is no evidence that Tylenol Aches and Strains Medication will cause renal damage. Rarely, a patient may note discoloration of the urine resulting from a phenolic metabolite of chlorzoxazone. This finding is of no known clinical significance.

Hepatotoxicity: Serious, including fatal, hepatocellular toxicity has been reported rarely in patients receiving chlorzoxazone. The mechanism is unknown but appears to be idiosyncratic and unpredictable. Factors predisposing patients to this rare event are not known. Patients should be instructed to report early signs and/or symptoms of hepatotoxicity such as fever, rash, anorexia, nausea, vomiting, fatigue, right upper quadrant pain, dark urine, or jaundice. Chlorzoxazone should be discontinued immediately and a physician consulted if any of these signs or symptoms develop. Chlorzoxazone use should also be discontinued if a patient develops abnormal liver enzymes (e.g., AST, ALT, alkaline phosphatase or bilirubin).

In a controlled multidose clinical trial with chlorzoxazone 500 mg, the following adverse events occurred in $\geq 1\%$ of patients receiving chlorzoxazone or occurred in $<1\%$ of patients but resulted in patient withdrawal from the study and were considered possibly, probably or definitely related to chlorzoxazone.

Body as a Whole: asthenia (2%), body pain, edema.

CNS: anxiety, dizziness (6%), drowsiness (9%), headache (5%), nervousness, paresthesia, vertigo.

Gastrointestinal: abnormal pain, anorexia, diarrhea (2%), dyspepsia (1%), flatulence, melena, nausea (3%).

Skin: pruritus, rash, skin discoloration.

Urogenital: polyuria.

The following adverse reports occurred with a frequency of $<1\%$ and the relationship to chlorzoxazone remains undetermined: chills, tachycardia, vasodilation, abnormal thinking, confusion, depression, emotional lability, hypotonia, insomnia, constipation, dry mouth, thirst, vomiting, cough increase, dyspnea, flu symptoms, rhinitis, sweating, increased urinary frequency, menorrhagia.

Overdose: Symptoms and Treatment: Acetaminophen: Typical Toxidrome: Significant overdoses of acetaminophen may result in potentially fatal hepatotoxicity. The physician should be mindful that there is no early presentation that is pathoneumonic for the overdose. A high degree of clinical suspicion must always be maintained.

Due to the wide availability of acetaminophen, it is commonly involved in single and mixed drug overdose situations and the practitioner should have a low threshold for screening for its presence in a patient's serum. Acute toxicity after single dose overdoses of acetaminophen can be anticipated when the overdose exceeds 150 mg/kg. Chronic alcohol abusers, cachectic individuals, and persons taking pharmacologic inducers of the hepatic P450 microsomal enzyme system may be at risk with lower exposures.

Chronic intoxication has rarely been reported in persons consuming in excess of 150 mg/kg of acetaminophen daily for several days.

Specific Antidote: NAC (N-acetylcysteine) administered by either the i.v. or the oral route is known to be a highly effective antidote for acetaminophen poisoning. It is most effective when administered within 8 hours of a significant overdose but reports have indicated benefits to treatment initiated well beyond this time period. It is imperative to administer the antidote as early as possible in the time course of acute intoxication to reap the full benefits of the antidote's protective effects.

General Management: When the possibility of acetaminophen overdose exists, treatment should begin immediately and include appropriate decontamination of the gastrointestinal tract, proper supportive care, careful assessment of appropriately timed serum acetaminophen estimations evaluated against the Matthew-Rumack nomogram, timely administration of NAC as required and appropriate follow-up care. Physicians unfamiliar with the current management of acetaminophen overdose should consult with a Poison Control Centre immediately. Telephone numbers for local Poison Control Centres are available in the local phone directory. Delays in initiation of appropriate therapy may jeopardize the patient's chances for full recovery.

Chlorzoxazone: Typical Toxidrome: extreme weakness (voluntary muscles), CNS depression, labored breathing.

Specific Antidote: none.

General Management: Stabilize the patient (A, B, C's), undertake appropriate gastrointestinal tract decontamination procedures, initiate supportive care, consult with a Regional Poison Control Centre regarding ongoing management, and arrange for appropriate follow-up care.

Dosage: Adults: 2 caplets every 4 hours as required. It is hazardous to exceed 8 caplets/day.

Supplied: Each capsule-shaped, blue tablet, engraved "ESTAC" one side and "500" the other side contains: chlorzoxazone 250 mg and acetaminophen 500 mg. Nonmedicinal ingredients: carnauba wax, cellulose, cornstarch, FD&C blue No. 1, hydroxypropyl methylcellulose, magnesium stearate, polyethylene glycol, polysorbate 80, sodium starch glycolate and titanium dioxide. Energy: 1.1 KJ (0.26 kcal). Sodium: <1 mmol (0.7 mg). Gluten-, lactose- and tartrazine-free. Plastic bottles of 18† and 40.

† Container provided with a child-resistant closure.

All packages are safety sealed.

(Shown in Product Recognition Section)

Reviewed 1999

Canadian manufacturers who do not use gluten in their products are listed in the CLIN-INFO SECTION.

TYLENOL® ALLERGY SINUS MEDICATION

McNeil Consumer Products

Acetaminophen—Chlorpheniramine Maleate—Pseudoephedrine HCl

Analgesic—Antihistamine—Decongestant

Indications: For the temporary relief of headache, sinus pain, nasal and sinus congestion, runny nose, sneezing and watery, itchy eyes due to hayfever or similar allergies.

Contraindications: Known hypersensitivity to acetaminophen and/or pressor amines. Patients receiving or having received MAO inhibitors in the preceding 3 weeks. Although pseudoephedrine is virtually without pressor effect in normotensive patients, it should be used with caution in hypertensives.

Precautions: As with any other nonprescription analgesic drug, physicians should be cognisant of and supervise the use of acetaminophen in patients with alcoholism, serious kidney or serious liver disease. Physicians should alert their patients who regularly consume large amounts of alcohol not to exceed the recommended doses of acetaminophen.

Patients should be counseled to consult a physician if redness or swelling is present in an area of pain, if symptoms do not improve or if they worsen, or if new symptoms such as high fever, rash or headache occur, as these may be signs of a condition which requires medical attention.

Acetaminophen should not be taken for pain for more than 5 days unless directed by a physician.

Pregnancy and *Lactation:* As with any drug, patients who are pregnant or nursing a baby should consult a physician before taking this product.

Do not use with other products containing acetaminophen. Keep out of the reach of children.

Adverse Effects: When used as directed, acetaminophen is virtually free of severe toxicity or side effects. The classic gastrointestinal irritation associated with nonsteroidal anti-inflammatory drugs, including ASA does not occur with acetaminophen. Sensitivity reactions are rare. Cross-reactivity in ASA sensitive persons has been rarely reported. If sensitivity is suspected, discontinue use of the drug.

Patients who concomitantly medicate with warfarin-type anticoagulants and regular doses of acetaminophen have occasionally been reported to have unforeseen elevations in their INR. Physicians should be cognisant of this potential interaction and monitor the INR in such patients closely while therapy is established.

In patients with high blood pressure, heart disease, diabetes, thyroid disease or difficulty in urination due to the enlargement of the prostate gland, pseudoephedrine HCl should be used with caution and only under close medical supervision. Patients with asthma, glaucoma, emphysema, chronic pulmonary disease, or shortness of breath should not use this medication unless directed by a physician.

Occupational Hazards: Preparations containing chlorpheniramine may cause drowsiness; alcoholic beverages may increase this effect and should be avoided. Advise caution when driving a motor vehicle or operating machinery or engaging in any activity requiring alertness.

Overdose: Symptoms and Treatment: Acetaminophen: Typical Toxidrome: Significant overdoses of acetaminophen may result in potentially fatal hepatotoxicity. The physician should be mindful that there is no early presentation that is pathoneumonic for the overdose. A high degree of clinical suspicion must always be maintained.

Due to the wide availability of acetaminophen, it is commonly involved in single and mixed drug overdose situations and the practitioner should have a low threshold for screening for its presence in a patient's serum. Acute toxicity after single dose overdoses of acetaminophen can be anticipated when the overdose exceeds 150 mg/kg. Chronic alcohol abusers, cachectic individuals, and persons taking pharmacologic inducers of the hepatic P450 microsomal enzyme system may be at risk with lower exposures.

Chronic intoxication has rarely been reported in persons consuming in excess of 150 mg/kg of acetaminophen daily for several days.

Specific Antidote: NAC (N-acetylcysteine) administered by either the i.v. or the oral route is known to be a highly effective antidote for acetaminophen poisoning. It is most effective when administered within 8 hours of a significant overdose but reports have indicated benefits to treatment initiated well beyond this time period. It is imperative to administer the antidote as early as possible in the time course of acute intoxication to reap the full benefits of the antidote's protective effects.

General Management: When the possibility of acetaminophen overdose exists, treatment should begin immediately and include appropriate decontamination of the gastrointestinal tract, proper supportive care, careful assessment of appropriately timed serum acetaminophen estimations evaluated against the Matthew-Rumack nomogram, timely administration of NAC as required and appropriate follow-up care. Physicians unfamiliar with the current management of acetaminophen overdose should consult with a Poison Control Centre immediately. Telephone numbers for local Poison Control Centres are available in the local phone directory. Delays in initiation of appropriate therapy may jeopardize the patient's chances for full recovery.

Pseudoephedrine HCl: Typical Toxidrome: sympathomimetic/stimulant.

Specific Antidote: none.

General Management: Stabilize the patient (A, B, C's), undertake appropriate gastrointestinal tract decontamination procedures, initiate supportive care, consult with a Regional Poison Control Centre regarding ongoing management, and arrange for appropriate follow-up care.

Chlorpheniramine Maleate: Typical Toxidrome: anticholinergic, CNS depressant (adult), CNS stimulant (child).

Specific Antidote: none.

General Management: Stabilize the patient (A, B, C's), undertake appropriate gastrointestinal tract decontamination procedures, initiate supportive care, consult with a Regional Poison Control Centre regarding ongoing management, and arrange for appropriate follow-up care.

Dosage: Adults: 2 caplets every 6 hours as required. Do not exceed 8 caplets in any 24 hour period. Reduce dosage if nervousness or sleeplessness occurs.

Supplied: Each capsule-shaped, hard, bright yellow, film-coated extra strength tablet, engraved "TAS" one side and "500" the other side, contains: acetaminophen 500 mg, pseudoephedrine HCl 30 mg and chlorpheniramine maleate 2 mg. Nonmedicinal ingredients: carnauba wax, cellulose, cornstarch, D&C yellow No. 10, FD&C blue No. 1, FD&C yellow No. 6, hydroxypropyl cellulose, hydroxypropyl methylcellulose, magnesium stearate, polyethylene glycol, sodium starch glycolate and titanium dioxide. Energy: 0.8 kJ (0.2 kcal). Sodium: <1 mmol (0.42 mg). Gluten-, lactose- and tartrazine-free. Blister packs of 12 and plastic bottles of 24† and 50†.

†Container provided with a child-resistant closure.

All packages are safety sealed.

(Shown in Product Recognition Section)

Reviewed 1999

TYLENOL® COLD MEDICATIONS

McNeil Consumer Products

Acetaminophen—Chlorpheniramine Maleate—Pseudoephedrine HCl—Dextromethorphan HBr

Analgesic—Antipyretic—Antihistamine—Decongestant—Antitussive

Indications: For the temporary relief of the symptoms associated with common colds and other upper respiratory infections, including: nasal and sinus congestion, cough, runny nose, sneezing, minor sore throat pain, fever, headache, aches, pains and general discomfort.

Contraindications: Known hypersensitivity to acetaminophen, pressor amines or other individual ingredients. Patients receiving or having received MAO inhibitors in the preceding 3 weeks. Although pseudoephedrine is virtually without pressor effect in normotensive patients, it should be used with caution in hypertensives.

Precautions: As with any other nonprescription analgesic drug, physicians should be cognisant of and supervise the use of acetaminophen in patients with alcoholism, serious kidney or serious liver disease. Physicians should alert their patients who regularly consume large amounts of alcohol not to exceed the recommended doses of acetaminophen.

Patients should be counseled to consult a physician if redness or swelling is present in an area of pain, if symptoms do not improve or if they worsen, or if new symptoms such as high fever, rash or headache occur, as these may be signs of a condition which requires medical attention.

Acetaminophen should not be taken for pain for more than 5 days or for fever for more than 3 days, unless directed by a physician.

Pregnancy and *Lactation:* As with any drug, patients who are pregnant or nursing a baby should consult a physician before taking this product.

Do not use with other products containing acetaminophen. Keep out of the reach of children.

Adverse Effects: When used as directed, acetaminophen is virtually free of severe toxicity or side effects. The classic gastrointestinal irritation associated with nonsteroidal anti-inflammatory drugs, including ASA does not occur with acetaminophen. Sensitivity reactions are rare. Cross-reactivity in ASA sensitive persons has been rarely reported. If sensitivity is suspected, discontinue use of the drug.

Patients who concomitantly medicate with warfarin-type anticoagulants and regular doses of acetaminophen have occasionally been reported to have unforeseen elevations in their INR. Physicians should be cognisant of this potential interaction and monitor the INR in such patients closely while therapy is established.

In patients with high blood pressure, heart disease, diabetes, thyroid disease, difficulty in urination due to enlargement of the prostate gland, or are taking a prescription drug for high blood pressure or depression, pseudoephedrine HCl should be used with caution and only under close medical supervision. Patients with asthma, glaucoma, emphysema, chronic pulmonary disease, or shortness of breath should not use this medication unless directed by a physician.

Occupational Hazards: Preparations containing chlorpheniramine may cause drowsiness; alcoholic beverages may increase this effect and should be avoided. Advise caution when driving a motor vehicle or operating machinery or engaging in any activity requiring alertness.

Overdose: Symptoms and Treatment: Acetaminophen: Typical Toxidrome: Significant overdoses of acetaminophen may result in potentially fatal hepatotoxicity. The physician should be mindful that there is no early presentation that is pathoneumonic for the overdose. A high degree of clinical suspicion must always be maintained.

Due to the wide availability of acetaminophen, it is commonly involved in single and mixed drug overdose situations and the practitioner should have a low threshold for screening for its presence in a patient's serum. Acute toxicity after single dose overdoses of acetaminophen can be anticipated when the overdose exceeds 150 mg/kg. Chronic alcohol abusers, cachectic individuals, and persons taking pharmacologic inducers of the hepatic P450 microsomal enzyme system may be at risk with lower exposures.

Chronic intoxication has rarely been reported in persons consuming in excess of 150 mg/kg of acetaminophen daily for several days.

Specific Antidote: NAC (N-acetylcysteine) administered by either the i.v. or the oral route is known to be a highly effective antidote for acetaminophen poisoning. It is most effective when administered within 8 hours of a significant overdose but reports have indicated benefits to treatment initiated well beyond this time period. It is imperative to administer the antidote as early as possible in the time course of acute intoxication to reap the full benefits of the antidote's protective effects.

General Management: When the possibility of acetaminophen overdose exists, treatment should begin immediately and include appropriate decontamination of the gastrointestinal tract, proper supportive care, careful assessment of appropriately timed serum acetaminophen estimations evaluated against the Matthew-Rumack nomogram, timely administration of NAC as required and appropriate follow-up care. Physicians unfamiliar with the current management of acetaminophen overdose should consult with a Poison Control Centre immediately. Telephone numbers for local Poison Control Centres are available in the local phone directory. Delays in initiation of appropriate therapy may jeopardize the patient's chances for full recovery.

Pseudoephedrine HCl: Typical Toxidrome: sympathomimetic/stimulant.

Specific Antidote: none.

General Management: Stabilize the patient (A, B, C's), undertake appropriate gastrointestinal tract decontamination procedures, initiate supportive care, consult with a Regional Poison Control Centre regarding ongoing management, and arrange for appropriate follow-up care.

Chlorpheniramine Maleate: Typical Toxidrome: anticholinergic, CNS depressant (adult), CNS stimulant (child).

Specific Antidote: none.

General Management: Stabilize the patient (A, B, C's), undertake appropriate gastrointestinal tract decontamination procedures, initiate supportive care, consult with a Regional Poison Control Centre regarding ongoing management, and arrange for appropriate follow-up care.

Dextromethorphan HBr: Typical Toxidrome: narcotic/opiate.

Specific Antidote: naloxone HCl.

General Management: Stabilize the patient (A, B, C's), undertake appropriate gastrointestinal tract decontamination procedures, initiate supportive care, consult with a Regional Poison Control Centre regarding ongoing management, and arrange for appropriate follow-up care.

Dosage: Children's Chewable Tablets/DM Chewable Tablets: Single dosage (see Table I) may be repeated every 4 to 6 hours as required, not to exceed 4 doses in 24 hours.

Table I—Tylenol Cold Medications

Dosage—Children's Chewable Tablets/DM Chewable Tablets

Age	Single Dose Tablets
2 and 3 years	2
4 and 5 years	3
6 to 11 years	4

Children's Liquid/DM Liquid: Single dosage (see Table II) may be repeated every 4 to 6 hours as required, not to exceed 4 doses in 24 hours.

Table II—Tylenol Cold Medications

Dosage—Children's Liquid/DM Liquid

Age	Single Dose mL	Single Dose Teaspoonful(s)
4 months to under 12 months	2.5	½
12 months to under 2 years	3.75	¾
2 and 3 years	5.0	1
4 and 5 years	7.5	1½
6 to 8 years	10.0	2
9 and 10 years	12.5	2½
11 and 12 years	15.0	3

Infants' Suspension: Single dosage (see Table III) may be repeated every 4 to 6 hours, as required, not to exceed 4 doses in 24 hours. Dose with dropper only.

Table III—Tylenol Cold Medications

Dosage—Infants' Suspension

Age	Single Dose mL	Single Dose Dropperful(s)
4 to 11 months	1.0	1
12 to 23 months	1.5	1½
2 and 3 years	2.0	2

Junior Strength DM Chewable Tablets: 6 to 11 years: 2 tablets; 2 to 5 years: 1 tablet; or as directed by a physician. Single dosage may be repeated every 4 to 6 hours as required, not to exceed 4 doses in 24 hours.

Extra-Strength (Nighttime): Adults: 1 to 2 caplets every 6 hours as required, not to exceed 8 caplets/day. Reduce dosage if nervousness or sleeplessness occurs.

Extra-Strength (Daytime): Adults: 1 to 2 caplets every 6 hours as required, not to exceed 8 caplets/day. Reduce dosage if nervousness or sleeplessness occurs.

Regular Strength (Nighttime): Adults: 1 to 2 caplets every 6 hours as required, not to exceed 8 caplets/day. Reduce dosage if nervousness or sleeplessness occurs.

Regular Strength (Daytime): Adults: 1 to 2 caplets every 6 hours as required, not to exceed 8 caplets/day. Reduce dosage if nervousness or sleeplessness occurs.

Extra-Strength Cold and Flu Powder: Dissolve the contents of 1 pouch in 225 mL of hot water. The single dosage may be repeated every 4 to 6 hours as required, not to exceed 4 times in 24 hours. Reduce dosage if nervousness or sleeplessness occurs.

Supplied: Caplets: Extra-Strength (Nighttime): Each yellow caplet, engraved "TCM" one side and "500" the other side, contains: chlorpheniramine maleate 2 mg, pseudoephedrine HCl 30 mg, dextromethorphan HBr 15 mg and acetaminophen 500 mg. Nonmedicinal ingredients: carnauba wax, cellulose, cornstarch, D&C Yellow No. 10, FD&C Yellow No. 6, hydroxypropyl methylcellulose, magnesium stearate, sodium starch glycolate, titanium dioxide and triacetin. Energy: 1.0 kJ (0.2 kcal). Sodium: <1 mmol (0.8 mg). Plastic bottles of 24†. Blister packs of 12.

Tylenol Cold Medications (cont'd)

Extra-Strength (Daytime): Each yellow caplet, engraved "TCM-ND" one side and "500" the other side, contains: pseudoephedrine HCl 30 mg, dextromethorphan HBr 15 mg and acetaminophen 500 mg. Nonmedicinal ingredients: carnauba wax, cellulose, cornstarch, D&C Yellow No. 10, FD&C Yellow No. 6, hydroxypropyl methylcellulose, magnesium stearate, sodium starch glycolate, titanium dioxide and triacetin. Energy: 1.0 kJ (0.2 kcal). Sodium: <1 mmol (0.8 mg). Plastic bottles of 24†. Blister packs of 12.

Regular Strength (Nighttime): Each yellow caplet, engraved "TCM" one side and "325" the other side, contains: chlorpheniramine maleate 2 mg, pseudoephedrine HCl 30 mg, dextromethorphan HBr 15 mg and acetaminophen 325 mg. Nonmedicinal ingredients: carnauba wax, cellulose, cornstarch, D&C Yellow No. 10, FD&C Yellow No. 6, hydroxypropyl methylcellulose, magnesium stearate, sodium starch glycolate, titanium dioxide and triacetin. Energy: 0.7 kJ (0.2 kcal). Sodium: <1 mmol (0.6 mg). Plastic bottles of 24†.

Regular Strength (Daytime): Each yellow caplet, engraved "TCM-ND" one side and "325" the other side, contains: pseudoephedrine HCl 30 mg, dextromethorphan HBr 15 mg and acetaminophen 325 mg. Nonmedicinal ingredients: carnauba wax, cellulose, cornstarch, D&C Yellow No. 10, FD&C Yellow No. 6, hydroxypropyl methylcellulose, magnesium stearate, sodium starch glycolate, titanium dioxide and triacetin. Energy: 0.7 kJ (0.2 kcal). Sodium: <1 mmol (0.6 mg). Plastic bottles of 24†.

Powder: Extra-Strength Cold and Flu (chicken soup): Each pouch of pale yellow powder contains: acetaminophen 1 000 mg, chlorpheniramine maleate 4 mg, pseudoephedrine HCl 60 mg and dextromethorphan HBr 30 mg. Nonmedicinal ingredients: cornstarch, flavor (contains monosodium glutamate) and sucrose. Energy: 82 kJ (20 kcal). Sodium: 1 200 mg. Boxes of 8.

Extra-Strength Cold and Flu (honey lemon): Each pouch of orange and white granular powder contains: acetaminophen 1 000 mg, chlorpheniramine maleate 4 mg, pseudoephedrine HCl 60 mg and dextromethorphan HBr 30 mg. Nonmedicinal ingredients: citric acid, cornstarch, D&C Yellow No. 10, FD&C Red No. 40, flavor, sodium citrate, sucralose and sucrose. Energy: 293 kJ (70 kcal). Boxes of 10.

Suspension: Children's (bubble gum): Each 5 mL contains: acetaminophen 160 mg, chlorpheniramine maleate 1 mg and pseudoephedrine HCl 15 mg in a bubble gum flavored pink vehicle. Nonmedicinal ingredients: butylparaben, cellulose, citric acid, corn syrup, FD&C red No. 40, flavor, glycerin, polysorbate 60, propylene glycol, purified water, sodium benzoate, sorbitol and xanthan gum. Energy: 71 kJ (17 kcal). Sodium: <1 mmol (1.6 mg). Alcohol- and sucrose-free. Plastic bottles of 100 mL†.

Children's DM (bubble gum): Each 5 mL contains: acetaminophen 160 mg, chlorpheniramine maleate 1 mg, pseudoephedrine HCl 15 mg and dextromethorphan HBr 7.5 mg in a bubble gum flavored pink vehicle. Nonmedicinal ingredients: butylparaben, cellulose, citric acid, corn syrup, FD&C red No. 40, flavor, glycerin, polysorbate 60, propylene glycol, purified water, sodium benzoate, sorbitol and xanthan gum. Energy: 71 kJ (17 kcal). Sodium: <1 mmol (1.6 mg). Alcohol- and sucrose-free. Plastic bottles of 100 mL†.

Infants' (bubble gum): Each mL contains: acetaminophen 80 mg, chlorpheniramine maleate 0.5 mg and pseudoephedrine HCl 7.5 mg in a bubble gum flavored pink vehicle. Nonmedicinal ingredients: butylparaben, cellulose, citric acid, corn syrup, FD&C red No. 40, flavor, glycerin, propylene glycol, purified water, sodium benzoate, sodium saccharin, sorbitol and xanthan gum. Energy: 12.7 kJ (3 kcal). Sodium: <1 mmol (0.95 mg). Alcohol- and sucrose-free. Plastic bottles of 24 mL†.

Tablets: Children's Chewable (fruit): Each orange chewable tablet, engraved "TYLENOL COLD" one side and "80" with a partial score the other side, contains: acetaminophen 80 mg, chlorpheniramine maleate 0.5 mg and pseudoephedrine HCl 7.5 mg. Phenylketonurics: contains phenylalanine (aspartame). Nonmedicinal ingredients: cellulose, citric acid, compressible sugar, cornstarch, ethylcellulose, FD&C Yellow No. 6, flavor, magnesium stearate and mannitol. Energy: 4.8 kJ (1.2 kcal). Gluten-, lactose-, sodium- and tartrazine-free. Plastic bottles of 24†.

Children's Chewable (bubble gum): Each pink chewable tablet, engraved "TYLENOL COLD" one side and "80" with a partial score the other side, contains: acetaminophen 80 mg, chlorpheniramine maleate 0.5 mg and pseudoephedrine HCl 7.5 mg. Nonmedicinal ingredients: cellulose, cornstarch, D&C red No. 7, ethylcellulose, flavor, magnesium stearate, sorbitol, sucralose and sucrose. Energy: 1.4 kJ (5.9 kcal). Gluten-, lactose-, sodium- and tartrazine-free. Plastic bottles of 24†.

Children's DM Chewable (grape): Each round, purple tablet engraved "TYLENOL COLD DM" one side and "80" with a partial score the other side, contains: acetaminophen 80 mg, chlorpheniramine maleate 0.5 mg, pseudoephedrine HCl 7.5 mg and dextromethorphan HBr 3.75 mg. Phenylketonurics: contains phenylalanine (aspartame). Nonmedicinal ingredients: cellulose, citric acid, cornstarch, D&C Red No. 7, ethylcellulose, FD&C Blue No. 1, flavor, magnesium stearate, magnesium trisilicate and mannitol. Energy: 4.2 kJ (1.0 kcal). Gluten-, lactose-, sodium- and tartrazine-free. Plastic bottles of 24†.

Children's DM Chewable (bubble gum): Each pink chewable tablet, engraved "TYLENOL COLD DM" one side and "80" with a partial bisect score the other side, contains: acetaminophen 80 mg, chlorpheniramine maleate 0.5 mg, pseudoephedrine HCl 7.5 mg and dextromethorphan HBr 3.75 mg. Nonmedicinal ingredients: cellulose, cornstarch, D&C red No. 7, ethylcellulose, flavor, magnesium stearate, magnesium trisilicate, mannitol, sucralose and sucrose. Energy: 1.4 kJ (5.9 kcal). Gluten-, lactose-, sodium- and tartrazine-free. Plastic bottles of 24†.

Junior Strength DM Chewable (grape): Each round, purple tablet, engraved "TCM DM" one side and "160" with a partial score the other side, contains: acetaminophen 160 mg, chlorpheniramine maleate 1 mg, pseudoephedrine HCl 15 mg and dextromethorphan HBr 7.5 mg. Phenylketonurics: contains phenylalanine (aspartame). Nonmedicinal ingredients: cellulose, citric acid, cornstarch, D&C Red No. 7, ethylcellulose, FD&C Blue No. 1, flavor, magnesium stearate, magnesium trisilicate and mannitol. Energy: 8.4 kJ (2.0 kcal). Plastic bottles of 20†.

† Container provided with a child-resistant closure.
All packages are safety sealed.

(Shown in Product Recognition Section)

Reviewed 1999

TYLENOL® COUGH MEDICATION

McNeil Consumer Products

Acetaminophen—Dextromethorphan HBr—Pseudoephedrine HCl

Analgesic—Antipyretic—Antitussive—Decongestant

Indications: For the temporary relief of dry cough, sore throat, aches, pains and fever.

Contraindications: Known hypersensitivity to acetaminophen and/or pressor amines. Patients receiving or having received MAO inhibitors in the preceding 3 weeks. Although pseudoephedrine is virtually without pressor effect in normotensive patients, it should be used with caution in hypertensive individuals.

Precautions: As with any other nonprescription analgesic drug, physicians should be cognisant of and supervise the use of acetaminophen in patients with alcoholism, serious kidney or serious liver disease. Physicians should alert their patients who regularly consume large amounts of alcohol not to exceed the recommended doses of acetaminophen.

Patients should be counseled to consult a physician if redness or swelling is present in an area of pain, if symptoms do not improve or if they worsen, or if new symptoms such as high fever, rash or headache occur, as these may be signs of a condition which requires medical attention.

Acetaminophen should not be taken for pain for more than 5 days or for fever for more than 3 days, unless directed by a physician.

Pregnancy and *Lactation:* As with any drug, patients who are pregnant or nursing a baby should consult a physician before taking this product.

Do not use with other products containing acetaminophen. Keep out of the reach of children.

Adverse Effects: When used as directed, acetaminophen is virtually free of severe toxicity or side effects. The classic gastrointestinal irritation associated with nonsteroidal anti-inflammatory drugs, including ASA does not occur with acetaminophen. Sensitivity reactions are rare. Cross-reactivity in ASA sensitive persons has been rarely reported. If sensitivity is suspected, discontinue use of the drug.

Patients who concomitantly medicate with warfarin-type anticoagulants and regular doses of acetaminophen have occasionally been reported to have unforeseen elevations in their INR. Physicians should be cognisant of this potential interaction and monitor the INR in such patients closely while therapy is established.

In patients with high blood pressure, heart disease, diabetes, thyroid disease or difficulty in urination due to the enlargement of the prostate gland, pseudoephedrine HCl should be used with caution and only under close medical supervision. Patients with asthma, glaucoma, emphysema, chronic pulmonary disease, or shortness of breath should not use this medication unless directed by a physician.

Overdose: Symptoms and Treatment: Acetaminophen: Typical Toxidrome: Significant overdoses of acetaminophen may result in potentially fatal hepatotoxicity. The physician should be mindful that there is no early presentation that is pathoneumonic for the overdose. A high degree of clinical suspicion must always be maintained.

Due to the wide availability of acetaminophen, it is commonly involved in single and mixed drug overdose situations and the practitioner should have a low threshold for screening for its presence in a patient's serum. Acute toxicity after single dose overdoses of acetaminophen can be anticipated when the overdose exceeds 150 mg/kg. Chronic alcohol abusers, cachectic individuals, and persons taking pharmacologic inducers of the hepatic P450 microsomal enzyme system may be at risk with lower exposures.

Chronic intoxication has rarely been reported in persons consuming in excess of 150 mg/kg of acetaminophen daily for several days.

Specific Antidote: NAC (N-acetylcysteine) administered by either the i.v. or the oral route is known to be a highly effective antidote for acetaminophen poisoning. It is most effective when administered within 8 hours of a significant overdose but reports have indicated benefits to treatment initiated well beyond this time period. It is imperative to administer the antidote as early as possible in the time course of acute intoxication to reap the full benefits of the antidote's protective effects.

General Management: When the possibility of acetaminophen overdose exists, treatment should begin immediately and include appropriate decontamination of the gastrointestinal tract, proper supportive care, careful assessment of appropriately timed serum acetaminophen estimations evaluated against the Matthew-Rumack nomogram, timely administration of NAC as required and appropriate follow-up care. Physicians unfamiliar with the current management of acetaminophen overdose should consult with a Poison Control Centre immediately. Telephone numbers for local Poison Control Centres are available in the local phone directory. Delays in initiation of appropriate therapy may jeopardize the patient's chances for full recovery.

Pseudoephedrine HCl: Typical Toxidrome: sympathomimetic/stimulant.

Specific Antidote: none.

General Management: Stabilize the patient (A, B, C's), undertake appropriate gastrointestinal tract decontamination procedures, initiate supportive care, consult with a Regional Poison Control Centre regarding ongoing management, and arrange for appropriate follow-up care.

Dextromethorphan HBr: Typical Toxidrome: narcotic/opiate.

Specific Antidote: naloxone HCl.

General Management: Stabilize the patient (A, B, C's), undertake appropriate gastrointestinal tract decontamination procedures, initiate supportive care, consult with a Regional Poison Control Centre regarding ongoing management, and arrange for appropriate follow-up care.

Dosage: Extra Strength Caplets: Adults: 2 caplets every 6 to 8 hours, as required. Do not exceed 8 caplets in any 24-hour period.

Regular Strength Liquid Suspension: Adults: 15 mL every 6 to 8 hours, as required. Do not exceed 4 doses in any 24-hour period.

Regular Strength Liquid Suspension with Decongestant: Adults: 15 mL every 6 to 8 hours, as required. Do not exceed 4 doses in any 24-hour period. Reduce dosage if nervousness or sleeplessness occurs.

Supplied: Extra Strength Caplets: Each capsule-shaped, hard, red film-coated tablet, engraved "TYCOF" on one side and "500" the other side, contains: acetaminophen 500 mg and dextromethorphan hydrobromide 15 mg. Nonmedicinal ingredients: carnauba wax, cellulose, cornstarch, FD&C red No. 40, FD&C yellow No. 6, hydroxypropyl methylcellulose, magnesium stearate, menthol flavor, polyethylene glycol, polysorbate 80, sodium starch glycolate and titanium dioxide. Energy: <5 kJ (<1 kcal). Sodium: <1 mmol (0.64 mg).

Gluten-, lactose- and tartrazine-free. Blister packs of 12 and plastic bottles of 24.†

Regular Strength Liquid Suspension: Each 15 mL contains: acetaminophen 650 mg and dextromethorphan HBr 30 mg in a red liquid vehicle with a cherry-flavored taste. Nonmedicinal ingredients: butylparaben, cellulose, citric acid, corn syrup, D&C Red No. 33, FD&C Red No. 40, flavoring, glycerin, polysorbate 60, propylene glycol, purified water, sodium benzoate, sodium saccharin, sorbitol and xanthan gum. Energy: 212 kJ (51 kcal). Sodium: <1 mmol (5.7 mg). Gluten-, lactose- and tartrazine-free. Plastic bottles of 100 mL†.

Regular Strength Liquid Suspension with Decongestant: Each 15 mL contains: acetaminophen 650 mg, pseudoephedrine HCl 60 mg and dextromethorphan HBr 30 mg in a red liquid vehicle with a cherry-flavored taste. Nonmedicinal ingredients: butylparaben, cellulose, citric acid, corn syrup, D&C Red No. 33, FD&C Red No. 40, flavoring, glycerin, polysorbate 60, propylene glycol, purified water, sodium benzoate, sodium saccharin, sorbitol and xanthan gum. Energy: 211 kJ (51 kcal). Sodium: <1 mmol (5.7 mg). Gluten-, lactose- and tartrazine-free. Plastic bottles of 100 mL.†

†Container provided with a child-resistant closure.

All packages are safety sealed.

(Shown in Product Recognition Section)

Reviewed 1999

TYLENOL® DECONGESTANT

McNeil Consumer Products

Acetaminophen—Pseudoephedrine HCl

Analgesic—Antipyretic—Decongestant

Indications: For the temporary relief of earache pain, nasal congestion, fever and other aches and pains associated with colds and flu.

Contraindications: Known hypersensitivity to acetaminophen and/or pressor amines. Patients receiving or having received MAO inhibitors in the preceding 3 weeks. Although pseudoephedrine is virtually without pressor effect in normotensive patients, it should be used with caution in hypertensives.

Precautions: As with any other nonprescription analgesic drug, physicians should be cognizant of and supervise the use of acetaminophen in patients with alcoholism, serious kidney or serious liver disease. Physicians should alert their patients who regularly consume large amounts of alcohol not to exceed the recommended doses of acetaminophen.

Patients should be counseled to consult a physician if redness or swelling is present in an area of pain, if symptoms do not improve or if they worsen, or if new symptoms such as high fever, rash or headache occur, as these may be signs of a condition which requires medical attention.

Acetaminophen should not be taken for pain for more than 5 days or for fever for more than 3 days, unless directed by a physician.

Pregnancy and *Lactation:* As with any drug, patients who are pregnant or nursing a baby should consult a physician before taking this product.

Do not use with other products containing acetaminophen. Keep out of the reach of children.

Adverse Effects: When used as directed, acetaminophen is virtually free of severe toxicity or side effects.

The classic gastrointestinal irritation associated with nonsteroidal anti-inflammatory drugs, including ASA does not occur with acetaminophen.

Sensitivity reactions are rare. Cross-reactivity in ASA sensitive persons has been rarely reported. If sensitivity is suspected, discontinue use of the drug.

Patients who concomitantly medicate with warfarin-type anticoagulants and regular doses of acetaminophen have occasionally been reported to have unforeseen elevations in their INR. Physicians should be cognizant of this potential interaction and monitor the INR in such patients closely while therapy is established.

In patients with high blood pressure, heart disease, diabetes, or thyroid disease, pseudoephedrine HCl should be used with caution and only under close medical supervision. Patients with glaucoma or on other medications should not use this medication unless directed by a physician. This preparation may, in some cases, cause excitability or dizziness.

Patients are advised to consult a physician if fever persists for more than 3 days or if symptoms, particularly earache, are severe, do not improve or new ones occur within 5 days or are accompanied by high fever or rash. A physician should be consulted if the illness lasts more than 5 days without response to treatment.

Overdose: Symptoms and Treatment: Acetaminophen: Typical Toxidrome: Significant overdoses of acetaminophen may result in potentially fatal hepatotoxicity. The physician should be mindful that there is no early presentation that is pathoneumonic for the overdose. A high degree of clinical suspicion must always be maintained.

Due to the wide availability of acetaminophen, it is commonly involved in single and mixed drug overdose situations and the practitioner should have a low threshold for screening for its presence in a patient's serum.

Acute toxicity after single dose overdoses of acetaminophen can be anticipated when the overdose exceeds 150 mg/kg. Chronic alcohol abusers, cachectic individuals, and persons taking pharmacologic inducers of the hepatic P450 microsomal enzyme system may be at risk with lower exposures.

Chronic intoxication has rarely been reported in persons consuming in excess of 150 mg/kg of acetaminophen daily for several days.

Specific Antidote: NAC (N-acetylcysteine) administered by either the i.v. or the oral route is known to be a highly effective antidote for acetaminophen poisoning. It is most effective when administered within 8 hours of a significant overdose but reports have indicated benefits to treatment initiated well beyond this time period. It is imperative to administer the antidote as early as possible in the time course of acute intoxication to reap the full benefits of the antidote's protective effects.

General Management: When the possibility of acetaminophen overdose exists, treatment should begin immediately and include appropriate decontamination of the gastrointestinal tract, proper supportive care, careful assessment of appropriately timed serum acetaminophen estimations evaluated against the Matthew-Rumack nomogram, timely administration of NAC as required and appropriate follow-up care. Physicians unfamiliar with the current management of acetaminophen overdose should consult with a poison control centre immediately. Telephone numbers for local poison control centres are available in the local phone directory. Delays in initiation of appropriate therapy may jeopardize the patient's chances for full recovery.

Pseudoephedrine HCl: Typical Toxidrome: Sympathomimetic/Stimulant.

Specific Antidote: None.

General Management: Stabilize the patient (ABC's), undertake appropriate gastrointestinal tract decontamination procedures, initiate supportive care, consult with a Regional Poison Control Centre regarding ongoing management, and arrange for appropriate follow-up care.

Dosage: Single dose (see Table I) may be repeated every 4 to 6 hours, as required, not to exceed 4 doses per day. Reduce dosage if nervousness or sleeplessness occurs.

Dose with measuring cup or measured teaspoon only.

Table I—Tylenol Decongestant Dosage

Age	Single Dose mL	Teaspoonful(s)
2 to 5 years	5	1
6 to 11 years	10	2

Supplied: Each 5 mL of bubble gum flavored, red liquid contains: acetaminophen 160 mg and pseudoephedrine HCl 15 mg. Nonmedicinal ingredients: butylparaben, cellulose, citric acid, corn syrup, FD&C red no. 40, flavor, glycerin, propylene glycol, purified water, sodium benzoate, sorbitol and xanthan gum. Energy: 68 kJ (16 kcal). Sodium: 0.069 mmol (1.6 mg). Alcohol-, gluten-, lactose-, sucrose-, sulfite- and tartrazine-free. Plastic bottles of 100 mL†.

†Container provided with a child-resistant closure.

All packages are safety sealed.

(Shown in Product Recognition Section)

New Product 1998

TYLENOL® FLU MEDICATION

McNeil Consumer Products

Acetaminophen—Diphenhydramine HCl—Pseudoephedrine HCl

Analgesic—Antipyretic—Antihistamine—Decongestant

Indications: For the temporary relief of runny nose, sneezing, watery and itchy eyes, nasal congestion, aches, pain and fever due to flu.

Contraindications: Known hypersensitivity to acetaminophen, pressor amines or other individual ingredients. Patients receiving or having received MAO inhibitors in the preceding 3 weeks. Although pseudoephedrine is virtually without pressor effect in normotensive patients, it should be used with caution in hypertensives.

Precautions: As with any other nonprescription analgesic drug, physicians should be cognisant of and supervise the use of acetaminophen in patients with alcoholism, serious kidney or serious liver disease. Physicians should alert their patients who regularly consume large amounts of alcohol not to exceed the recommended doses of acetaminophen.

Patients should be counseled to consult a physician if redness or swelling is present in an area of pain, if symptoms do not improve or if they worsen, or if new symptoms such as high fever, rash or headache occur, as these may be signs of a condition which requires medical attention.

Acetaminophen should not be taken for pain for more than 5 days or for fever for more than 3 days, unless directed by a physician.

Pregnancy and *Lactation:* As with any drug, patients who are pregnant or nursing a baby should consult a physician before taking this product.

Do not use with other products containing acetaminophen. Keep out of the reach of children.

Occupational Hazards: Preparations containing diphenhydramine may cause drowsiness: alcoholic beverages may increase this effect and should be avoided. Advise caution when driving a motor vehicle or operating machinery or engaging in any activity requiring alertness.

Adverse Effects: When used as directed, acetaminophen is virtually free of severe toxicity or side effects. The classic gastrointestinal irritation associated with nonsteroidal anti-inflammatory drugs, including ASA does not occur with acetaminophen. Sensitivity reactions are rare. Cross-reactivity in ASA sensitive persons has been rarely reported. If sensitivity is suspected, discontinue use of the drug.

Patients who concomitantly medicate with warfarin-type anticoagulants and regular doses of acetaminophen have occasionally been reported to have unforeseen elevations in their INR. Physicians should be cognisant of this potential interaction and monitor the INR in such patients closely while therapy is established.

In patients with high blood pressure, heart disease, diabetes, thyroid disease, difficulty in urination due to enlargement of the prostate gland or are taking a prescription drug for high blood pressure or depression, pseudoephedrine HCl should be used with caution and only under close medical supervision. Patients with asthma, glaucoma, emphysema, chronic pulmonary disease or shortness of breath should not use this medication unless directed by a physician.

Diphenhydramine has an atropine-like action and should be used with caution in patients with a history of bronchial asthma, increased intraocular pressure, hyperthydroidism, cardiovascular disease or hypertension. Drowsiness, dizziness, dryness of mouth, nausea and nervousness may occur with the use of diphenhydramine. Other infrequently reported effects include vertigo, palpitations, blurred vision, headache, restlessness, insomnia and thickening of bronchial secretions.

Overdose: Symptoms and Treatment: Acetaminophen: Typical Toxidrome: Significant overdoses of acetaminophen may result in potentially fatal hepatotoxicity. The physician should be mindful that there is no early presentation that is pathoneumonic for the overdose. A high degree of clinical suspicion must always be maintained.

Due to the wide availability of acetaminophen, it is commonly involved in single and mixed drug overdose situations and the practitioner should have a low threshold for screening for its presence in a patient's serum. Acute toxicity after single dose overdoses of acetaminophen can be anticipated when the overdose exceeds 150 mg/kg. Chronic alcohol abusers, cachectic individuals, and persons taking pharmacologic inducers of the hepatic P450 microsomal enzyme system may be at risk with lower exposures.

Chronic intoxication has rarely been reported in persons consuming in excess of 150 mg/kg of acetaminophen daily for several days.

Specific Antidote: NAC (N-acetylcysteine) administered by either the i.v. or the oral route is known to be a highly effective antidote for acetaminophen poisoning. It is most effective when administered within 8 hours of a significant overdose but reports have indicated benefits to treatment initiated well beyond this time period. It is imperative to administer the antidote as early as possible in the time course of acute intoxication to reap the full benefits of the antidote's protective effects.

Tylenol Flu Medication (cont'd)

General Management: When the possibility of acetaminophen overdose exists, treatment should begin immediately and include appropriate decontamination of the gastrointestinal tract, proper supportive care, careful assessment of appropriately timed serum acetaminophen estimations evaluated against the Matthew-Rumack nomogram, timely administration of NAC as required and appropriate follow-up care. Physicians unfamiliar with the current management of acetaminophen overdose should consult with a Poison Control Centre immediately. Telephone numbers for local Poison Control Centres are available in the local phone directory. Delays in initiation of appropriate therapy may jeopardize the patient's chances for full recovery.
Pseudoephedrine HCl: Typical Toxidrome: sympathomimetic/stimulant.
Specific Antidote: none.
General Management: Stabilize the patient (A, B, C's), undertake appropriate gastrointestinal tract decontamination procedures, initiate supportive care, consult with a Regional Poison Control Centre regarding ongoing management, and arrange for appropriate follow-up care.
Diphenhydramine HCl: Typical Toxidrome: anticholinergic, CNS depressant (adult), CNS stimulant (child).
Specific Antidote: none.
General Management: Stabilize the patient (A, B, C's), undertake appropriate gastrointestinal tract decontamination procedures, initiate supportive care, consult with a Regional Poison Control Centre regarding ongoing management, and arrange for appropriate follow-up care.

Dosage: Adults: 1 to 2 gelcaps every 6 hours as required. Do not exceed 8 gelcaps/day. Reduce dosage if nervousness or sleeplessness occurs.

Supplied: Each solid capsule-shaped tablet, coated with white gelatin on one end and blue gelatin on the other, with "Tylenol Flu NT" printed in grey, contains: acetaminophen 500 mg, diphenhydramine HCl 25 mg and pseudoephedrine HCl 30 mg. Nonmedicinal ingredients: benzyl alcohol, castor oil, cellulose, cornstarch, D&C red No. 28, edetate calcium disodium, FD&C blue No. 1, gelatin, hydroxypropyl methylcellulose, iron black oxide, magnesium stearate, parabens, sodium citrate, sodium lauryl sulfate, sodium propionate, sodium starch glycolate and titanium dioxide. Energy: 1.73 kJ (0.41 kcal). Sodium: <1 mmol (0.93 mg). Gluten-, lactose- and tartrazine- free. Blister packs of 10. Plastic bottles of 20†.

†Container provided with a child-resistant closure.

All packages are safety sealed.

(Shown in Product Recognition Section)

Reviewed 1999

TYLENOL® SINUS MEDICATION

McNeil Consumer Products

Acetaminophen—Pseudoephedrine HCl

Analgesic—Decongestant

Indications: For the temporary relief of sinus headache pain and congestion caused by sinusitis and common colds.

Contraindications: Known hypersensitivity to acetaminophen and/or pressor amines. Patients receiving or having received MAO inhibitors in the preceding 3 weeks. Although pseudoephedrine is virtually without pressor effect in normotensive patients, it should be used with caution in hypertensives.

Precautions: As with any other nonprescription analgesic drug, physicians should be cognisant of and supervise the use of acetaminophen in patients with alcoholism, serious kidney or serious liver disease. Physicians should alert their patients who regularly consume large amounts of alcohol not to exceed the recommended doses of acetaminophen.

Patients should be counseled to consult a physician if redness or swelling is present in an area of pain, if symptoms do not improve or if they worsen, or if new symptoms such as high fever, rash or headache occur, as these may be signs of a condition which requires medical attention.

Acetaminophen should not be taken for pain for more than 5 days unless directed by a physician.

Pregnancy and *Lactation:* As with any drug, patients who are pregnant or nursing a baby should consult a physician before taking this product.

Do not use with other products containing acetaminophen. Keep out of the reach of children.

Adverse Effects: When used as directed, acetaminophen is virtually free of severe toxicity or side effects. The classic gastrointestinal irritation associated with nonsteroidal anti-inflammatory drugs, including ASA does not occur with acetaminophen. Sensitivity reactions are rare. Cross-reactivity in ASA sensitive persons has been rarely reported. If sensitivity is suspected, discontinue use of the drug.

Patients who concomitantly medicate with warfarin-type anticoagulants and regular doses of acetaminophen have occasionally been reported to have unforeseen elevations in their INR. Physicians should be cognisant of this potential interaction and monitor the INR in such patients closely while therapy is established.

In patients with high blood pressure, heart disease, diabetes, thyroid disease or difficulty in urination due to enlargement of the prostate gland, pseudoephedrine HCl should be used with caution and only under close medical supervision. Patients with asthma, glaucoma, emphysema, chronic pulmonary disease, or shortness of breath should not use this medication unless directed by a physician.

Patients are advised to consult a physician if symptoms do not improve or new problems such as high fever, rash, excessive mucus, persistent cough or headache occur. A physician should be consulted if the illness lasts more than 5 days despite treatment.

Overdose: Symptoms and Treatment: Acetaminophen: Typical Toxidrome: Significant overdoses of acetaminophen may result in potentially fatal hepatotoxicity. The physician should be mindful that there is no early presentation that is pathoneumonic for the overdose. A high degree of clinical suspicion must always be maintained.

Due to the wide availability of acetaminophen, it is commonly involved in single and mixed drug overdose situations and the practitioner should have a low threshold for screening for its presence in a patient's serum. Acute toxicity after single dose overdoses of acetaminophen can be anticipated when the overdose exceeds 150 mg/kg. Chronic alcohol abusers, cachectic individuals, and persons taking pharmacologic inducers of the hepatic P450 microsomal enzyme system may be at risk with lower exposures.

Chronic intoxication has rarely been reported in persons consuming in excess of 150 mg/kg of acetaminophen daily for several days.
Specific Antidote: NAC (N-acetylcysteine) administered by either the i.v. or the oral route is known to be a highly effective antidote for acetaminophen poisoning. It is most effective when administered within 8 hours of a significant overdose but reports have indicated benefits to treatment initiated well beyond this time period. It is imperative to administer the antidote as early as possible in the time course of acute intoxication to reap the full benefits of the antidote's protective effects.
General Management: When the possibility of acetaminophen overdose exists, treatment should begin immediately and include appropriate decontamination of the gastrointestinal tract, proper supportive care, careful assessment of appropriately timed serum acetaminophen estimations evaluated against the Matthew-Rumack nomogram, timely administration of NAC as required and appropriate follow-up care. Physicians unfamiliar with the current management of acetaminophen overdose should consult with a Poison Control Centre immediately. Telephone numbers for local Poison Control Centres are available in the local phone directory. Delays in initiation of appropriate therapy may jeopardize the patient's chances for full recovery.
Pseudoephedrine HCl: Typical Toxidrome: sympathomimetic/stimulant.
Specific Antidote: none.
General Management: Stabilize the patient (A, B, C's), undertake appropriate gastrointestinal tract decontamination procedures, initiate supportive care, consult with a Regional Poison Control Centre regarding ongoing management, and arrange for appropriate follow-up care.

Dosage: Extra-Strength: Adults: 1 to 2 caplets every 4 hours as required, not to exceed 8 caplets in any 24-hour period. Reduce dosage if nervousness or sleeplessness occurs.
Regular Strength: Adults: 1 to 2 caplets every 4 hours as required, not to exceed 8 caplets in any 24-hour period. Reduce dosage if nervousness or sleeplessness occurs.

Supplied: Extra-Strength: Each green caplet, engraved "MSTSM" on one side and "500" on the other side, contains: acetaminophen 500 mg and pseudoephedrine HCl 30 mg. Nonmedicinal ingredients: carnauba wax, cellulose, cornstarch, D&C Yellow No. 10, FD&C Blue No. 1, FD&C Red No. 40, FD&C Yellow No. 6, hydroxypropyl methylcellulose, magnesium stearate, polyethylene glycol, polysorbate 80, sodium starch glycolate and titanium dioxide. Energy: 1.2 kJ (0.3 kcal). Sodium: <1 mmol (0.4 mg). Gluten-, lactose- and tartrazine-free. Blister packs of 12 and opaque plastic bottles of 24† and 50†.

Regular Strength: Each green caplet, engraved "RSTSM" on one side and "325" on the other side, contains: acetaminophen 325 mg and pseudoephedrine HCl 30 mg. Nonmedicinal ingredients: carnauba wax, cellulose, cornstarch, D&C Yellow No. 10, FD&C Blue No. 1, FD&C Red No. 40, FD&C Yellow No. 6, hydroxypropyl methylcellulose, magnesium stearate, polyethylene glycol, polysorbate 80, sodium starch glycolate and titanium dioxide. Energy: 0.8 kJ (0.2 kcal). Sodium: <1 mmol (0.3 mg). Gluten-, lactose- and tartrazine-free. Blister packs of 12 and opaque plastic bottles of 24†.

†Container provided with a child-resistant closure.

All packages are safety sealed.

(Shown in Product Recognition Section)

Reviewed 1999

TYLENOL® with CODEINE Preparations Ⓝ

Janssen-Ortho/
McNeil Consumer Products

Acetaminophen—Codeine Compound

Analgesic—Antipyretic

Pharmacology: Tylenol acetaminophen with codeine combines the analgesic effects of the centrally acting analgesic codeine, with a peripherally acting analgesic, acetaminophen. Caffeine stimulates the CNS at all levels including the cortex. In addition, it acts on the kidney to produce diuresis, stimulates cardiac muscle and depresses smooth muscle.

Both acetaminophen and codeine are well absorbed orally.

Acetaminophen is distributed throughout most tissues of the body. Acetaminophen is metabolized primarily in the liver. Little unchanged drug is excreted in the urine, but most metabolic products appear in the urine within 24 hours.

Codeine retains at least one-half of its analgesic activity when administered orally. A reduced first-pass metabolism of codeine by the liver accounts for the greater oral potency of codeine when compared to most other morphine-like narcotics. Following absorption, codeine is metabolized by the liver and metabolic products are excreted in the urine. Approximately 10% of the administered codeine is demethylated to morphine, which may account for its analgesic activity.

Caffeine is rapidly distributed and appears in all tissues within 5 minutes with peak plasma levels being reached in 30 minutes. It is almost completely metabolized via oxidation, demethylation and acetylation with only about 1% of caffeine excreted via the urine. The principal metabolites in man are methyluric acid, 1-methylxanthine, paraxanthine and theobromine.

Pharmacokinetics: Following oral administration of acetaminophen in combination with codeine, both drugs are rapidly absorbed with peak plasma levels occurring within 60 minutes. Given 2 tablets of Tylenol with codeine NO. 3, acetaminophen 600 mg produces a peak plasma level of 6.25 μg/mL within 40 minutes, codeine phosphate 60 mg produces a peak plasma level of 150 ng/mL within 60 minutes.

Following oral administration, caffeine is rapidly absorbed with a peak plasma level occurring within 60 minutes. Given an oral dose of 100 mg, peak plasma caffeine concentrations of 1.5 to 1.8 μg/mL are reached within 60 minutes.

The plasma elimination half-life ($t_{1/2}$) ranges from 1.5 to 3.5 hours for acetaminophen, 1.5 to 4 hours for codeine and from 2.5 to 4.5 hours for caffeine. Metabolism is rapid, the principle metabolites are conjugates of glucuronic acid which are excreted in the urine. Less than 1% of an administered dose of codeine or caffeine, and less than 4% of an administered dose of acetaminophen, is excreted unchanged in the urine.

Indications: For the relief of mild to moderate pain associated with conditions such as headache, dental pain, myalgia, dysmenorrhea, pain following trauma and pain following operative procedures. May also be effective in relieving the pain associated with various forms of arthritis, but is not indicated as primary therapy for rheumatoid arthritis and similar inflammatory conditions.

The elixir is useful as an analgesic/antipyretic in the symptomatic treatment of mild to moderate pain and fever in children. Tylenol with Codeine No. 4 tablets are indicated for the relief of moderate to severe pain in adults only.

Contraindications: Patients who have previously exhibited hypersensitivity to acetaminophen, codeine or caffeine.

Warnings and Precautions: As with any other nonprescription analgesic drug, physicians should be cognisant of and supervise the use of acetaminophen in patients with alcoholism, serious kidney or serious liver disease. Physicians should alert their patients who regularly consume large amounts of alcohol not to exceed the recommended doses of acetaminophen.

Patients should be counseled to consult a physician if redness or swelling is present in an area of pain, if symptoms do not improve or if they worsen, or if new symptoms such as high fever, rash or headache occur, as these may be signs of a condition which requires medical attention.

Acetaminophen should not be taken for pain for more than 5 days or for fever for more than 3 days, unless directed by a physician. As with any drug, patients who are pregnant or nursing a baby should consult a physician before taking this product.

Do not use with other products containing acetaminophen. Keep out of the reach of children.

General: Head Injury and Increased Intracranial Pressure: The respiratory depressant effects of narcotics and their capacity to elevate cerebrospinal fluid pressure may be markedly exaggerated in the presence of head injury, other intracranial lesions or a pre-existing increase in intracranial pressure. Furthermore, narcotics produce adverse reactions which may obscure the clinical course of patients with head injuries.

Acute Abdominal Conditions: The administration of these drugs or other narcotics may obscure the diagnosis or clinical course of patients with acute abdominal conditions.

Special Risk Patients: These drugs should be given with caution to certain patients such as the elderly or debilitated, and those with severe impairment of hepatic or renal function, hypothyroidism, Addison's disease, and prostatic hypertrophy or urethral stricture.

Occupational Hazards: Codeine may impair the mental and/or physical abilities required for the performance of potentially hazardous tasks. Patients using this drug should be cautioned about driving a car or operating potentially hazardous machinery if they become drowsy or show impaired mental or physical abilities while taking this medication.

The patient should understand the single-dose and 24-hour dose limits, and the time interval between doses. Like other narcotic-containing medications, these drugs are subject to the Controlled Drugs and Substances Act.

Drug Interactions: Patients receiving other narcotic analgesics, antipsychotics, anti-anxiety agents, or other CNS depressants (including alcohol) concomitantly with this drug may exhibit an additive CNS depression. When such combined therapy is contemplated, the dose of one or both agents should be reduced.

The concurrent use of anticholinergics with codeine may produce paralytic ileus.

Pregnancy: Teratogenic Effects: Codeine: A study in rats and rabbits reported no teratogenic effect of codeine administered during the period of organogenesis in doses ranging from 5 to 120 mg/kg. In the rat, doses at the 120 mg/kg level, in the toxic range for the adult animal, were associated with an increase in embryo resorption at the time of implantation. In another study, a single 100 mg/kg dose of codeine administered to pregnant mice reportedly resulted in delayed ossification in the offspring.

There are no studies in humans, and the significance of these findings to humans, if any, is not known.

Acetaminophen with codeine should be used during pregnancy only if the potential benefit justifies the potential risk to the fetus.

Nonteratogenic Effects: Dependence and withdrawal signs have been reported in newborns whose mothers took opiates regularly during pregnancy. These signs include irritability, excessive crying, tremors, hyperreflexia, fever, vomiting and diarrhea. Signs usually appear during the first few days of life.

Labor and Delivery: Narcotic analgesics cross the placental barrier. The closer to delivery and the larger the dose used, the greater the possibility of respiratory depression in the newborn. Narcotic analgesics should be avoided during labor if delivery of a premature infant is anticipated. If the mother has received narcotic analgesics during labor, newborn infants should be observed closely for signs of respiratory depression. Resuscitation may be required (see Overdose). The effects of codeine, if any, on the later growth, development, and functional maturation of the child is unknown.

Lactation: Acetaminophen with codeine is not recommended during lactation because safety in nursing mothers has not been established. Acetaminophen passes into breast milk but is not likely to have an adverse effect on the infant at therapeutic doses.

Some studies, but not others, have reported detectable amounts of codeine in breast milk. The levels are probably not clinically significant after usual therapeutic dosage. The possibility of clinically important amounts being excreted in breast milk in individuals abusing codeine should be considered.

Caffeine is found in breast milk following the consumption of tea or coffee. About 1% of the caffeine in these beverages is recovered in approximately 100 mL of breast milk at 4 hours.

Children: These products contain codeine and should not be administered to children except on the advice of a physician. Tablets and caplets should not be administered to children below the age of 12 years. Safe dosage of the elixir has not been established in infants below the age of 2 years.

Drug Abuse and Dependence: Codeine can produce drug dependence of the morphine type, and therefore has the potential for being abused. Psychic dependence, physical dependence and tolerance may develop upon repeated administration of this product. These drugs should be prescribed and administered with the same degree of caution appropriate to the use of other oral narcotic-containing medications.

Adverse Effects: The most frequently observed adverse effects include lightheadedness, dizziness, sedation, shortness of breath, nausea and vomiting. These effects seem to be more prominent in ambulatory than in nonambulatory patients, and some of these adverse reactions may be alleviated if the patient lies down. Other adverse reactions include allergic reactions, euphoria, dysphoria, constipation, abdominal pain, and pruritus. The incidence and severity of gastrointestinal upset is less than that after salicylate administration.

When used as directed, acetaminophen is virtually free of toxicity or side effects. The classic gastrointestinal irritation associated with NSAIDs, including ASA does not occur with acetaminophen. Sensitivity reactions are rare. Cross-reactivity in ASA-sensitive persons has been rarely reported. If sensitivity is suspected, discontinue use of the drug.

Patients who concomitantly medicate with warfarin-type anticoagulants and regular doses of acetaminophen have occasionally been reported to have unforeseen elevations in their INR. Physicians should be cognisant of this potential interaction and monitor the INR in such patients closely while therapy is established.

At higher doses, codeine has most of the disadvantages of morphine including respiratory depression.

Higher doses of caffeine lead to overstimulation of the higher centres of the CNS. Long-term use of caffeine may cause gastric disturbances and subsequent development of gastric ulcers.

Overdose: Symptoms: Acetaminophen: Typical Toxidrome: Significant overdoses of acetaminophen may result in potentially fatal hepatotoxicity. The physician should be mindful that there is no early presentation that is pathognomonic for the overdose. A high degree of clinical suspicion must always be maintained.

Due to the wide availability of acetaminophen, it is commonly involved in single and mixed drug overdose situations and the practitioner should have a low threshold for screening for its presence in a patient's serum. Acute toxicity after single dose overdoses of acetaminophen can be anticipated when the overdose exceeds 150 mg/kg. Chronic alcohol abusers, cachectic individuals, and persons taking pharmacologic inducers of the hepatic P450 microsomal enzyme system may be at risk with lower exposures. Chronic intoxication has rarely been reported in persons consuming in excess of 150 mg/kg of acetaminophen daily for several days.

Specific Antidote: NAC (N-acetylcysteine) administered by either the i.v. or the oral route is known to be a highly effective antidote for acetaminophen poisoning. It is most effective when administered within 8 hours of a significant overdose but reports have indicated benefits to treatment initiated well beyond this time period. It is imperative to administer the antidote as early as possible in the time course of acute intoxication to reap the full benefits of the antidote's protective effects.

General Management: When the possibility of acetaminophen overdose exists, treatment should begin immediately and include appropriate decontamination of the GI tract, proper supportive care, careful assessment of appropriately timed serum acetaminophen estimations evaluated against the Mathew-Rumack nomogram, timely administration of NAC as required and appropriate followup care. Physicians unfamiliar with the current management of acetaminophen overdose should consult with a poison control centre immediately. Telephone numbers for local poison control centres are available in the local phone directory. Delays in initiation of appropriate therapy may jeopardize the patient's chances for full recovery.

Codeine: Typical Toxidrome: Narcotic/Opiate.

Specific Antidote: Naloxone HCl.

General Management: Stabilize the patient (A, B, C's), undertake appropriate gastrointestinal tract decontamination procedures, initiate supportive care, administer antidote as needed (see manufacturer's product monograph), consult with a Regional Poison Control Centre regarding ongoing management, and arrange for appropriate followup care.

Caffeine: Typical Toxidrome: Xanthine (theophylline-like picture), CNS excitation, skeletal muscle irritability.

Specific Antidote: None.

General Management: Stabilize the patient (A, B, C's), undertake appropriate gastrointestinal tract decontamination procedures, initiate supportive care, consult with a Regional Poison Control Centre regarding ongoing management, and arrange for appropriate follow-up care.

Dosage: Dosage should be adjusted according to severity of pain and response of the patient. However, it should be kept in mind that tolerance to codeine can develop with continued use and that the incidence of untoward effects is dose related. Adult doses of codeine higher than 60 mg fail to give commensurate relief of pain but merely prolong analgesia and are associated with an appreciably increased incidence of undesirable side effects. Equivalently high doses in children would have similar effects.

Tablets, caplets and elixir are given orally.

Tylenol NO. 1: Adults: 1 to 2 caplets every 4 hours as required, not to exceed 12 caplets in 24 hours.

Children: when recommended by a physician or dentist: (12 to 14 years of age): 1 caplet 3 times daily. Not to exceed 1 caplet 4 times daily.

Tylenol NO. 1 Forte: Adults: 1 or 2 caplets 3 to 4 times daily as required, not to exceed 8 caplets in a 24-hour period.

Do not exceed the recommended dose unless advised by a physician. Use longer than 5 days only on the advice of a physician.

Tylenol NO. 2 and NO. 3: Adults: 1 or 2 tablets every 4 hours as required.

Tylenol NO. 4: Adults: 1 tablet every 4 hours as required.

Based on the dosage guidance, the number of tablets per dose, and the maximum number of tablets per 24 hours, should be conveyed in the prescription.

Tylenol Elixir with Codeine: Dosage should be adjusted according to severity of pain and response of the patient. As an analgesic-antipyretic, the dose is given every 4 hours as required. Not to exceed 5 doses in a 24-hour period.

Adults: 10 to 20 mL every 4 hours as required.

Children: 2 to 3 years: 3.75 to 5 mL; 4 to 5 years: 5 to 6.25 mL; 6 to 8 years: 6.25 to 8.75 mL; 9 to 10 years: 8.75 to 10 mL; 11 to 12 years: 10 to 12.5 mL.

Safe dosage of this elixir has not been established in children below the age of 2 years.

Note: The recommended dose of codeine in children is 0.5 mg/kg body weight.

Supplied: Tylenol NO. 1: Each hard, white, capsule-shaped tablet imprinted with stylized M and McNEIL on one face and imprinted NO. 1 on the other face, contains: acetaminophen 300 mg, caffeine 15 mg and codeine phosphate 8 mg. Nonmedicinal ingredients: cellulose, cornstarch, magnesium stearate and sodium starch glycolate. Energy: 0.761 kJ (0.182 kcal). Gluten-, lactose-, sodium metabisulfite- and tartrazine-free. Bottles of 30, 50 and 100 (supplied by McNeil Consumer Products).

Tylenol NO. 1 Forte: Each hard, white, capsule-shaped tablet imprinted with stylized M and McNEIL on one face and imprinted NO. 1 FORTE on the opposite face, contains: acetaminophen 500 mg, caffeine 15 mg and codeine phosphate 8 mg. Nonmedicinal ingredients: cellulose, cornstarch, magnesium stearate and sodium starch glycolate. Energy:

Tylenol with Codeine Preparations (cont'd)

1.645 kJ (0.391 kcal). Gluten-, lactose-, sodium metabisulfite- and tartrazine-free. Bottles of 50 (supplied by McNeil Consumer Products).

Tylenol NO. 2 and NO. 3 with Codeine: Each round, hard, white tablet, flat-faced, beveled, engraved 2 or 3, respectively, on one side and has a flat-faced, special design, beveled, engraved with McNEIL the other side, contains: acetaminophen 300 mg and caffeine 15 mg, in combination with codeine phosphate 15 mg and 30 mg, respectively. Nonmedicinal ingredients: cellulose, cornstarch and magnesium stearate. Energy: NO. 2: 0.949 kJ (0.224 kcal); NO. 3: 0.976 kJ (0.232 kcal). Gluten-, lactose-, sodium metabisulfite- and tartrazine-free. Bottles of 100 and 500 (supplied by Janssen-Ortho).

Tylenol NO. 4: Each round, hard, white tablet, flat-faced, beveled, engraved 4 one side and flat-faced special design, beveled, engraved McNEIL the other side contains: acetaminophen 300 mg and codeine phosphate 60 mg. Nonmedicinal ingredients: cellulose, cornstarch, magnesium stearate, sodium lauryl sulfate, sodium starch glycolate and talc. Energy: 1.704 kJ (0.405 kcal). Gluten-, lactose-, sodium metabisulfite- and tartrazine-free. Bottles of 100 (supplied by Janssen-Ortho).

Tylenol Elixir with Codeine: Each 5 mL of elixir contains: acetaminophen 160 mg and codeine phosphate 8 mg in a slightly viscous, clear red liquid that tastes and smells like cherry. Nonmedicinal ingredients: alcohol, citric acid, D&C Red No. 33, flavor, polyethylene glycol, sodium benzoate, sodium cyclamate, sorbitol and sucrose. Alcohol: 6% w/v (7% v/v). Energy: 45.93 kJ (10.98 kcal)/5 mL. Sucrose: 31% w/v. Gluten-, lactose-, sodium metabisulfite- and tartrazine-free. Dark amber glass bottles of 500 mL (supplied by Janssen-Ortho). Dispense in tight and light-resistant containers.

(Shown in Product Recognition Section)

Reviewed 1999

TYPHIM Vi™

Connaught

Salmonella typhi Vi Capsular Polysaccharide Vaccine

Active Immunizing Agent

Pharmacology: S. typhi is the etiological agent of typhoid fever, an acute, febrile enteric disease transmitted by contaminated water and food. The fatality rate ranges from 16% in untreated cases to less than 1% in those given appropriate antibiotic therapy.

The incidence of typhoid fever has declined steadily in Canada. Approximately 80 cases are reported annually. Most of these infections are contracted abroad, but a small number occur in Canada. Typhoid vaccination is not required for international travel, but it is recommended for travellers to areas where there is a recognized risk of exposure to S. typhi, the organism which causes typhoid fever. S. typhi is prevalent in many countries of Africa, Asia and Central and South America. Vaccination is particularly recommended for travellers who will have prolonged exposure to potentially contaminated food and water in smaller cities and villages, or rural areas off the usual tourist itineraries. However, even travellers who have been vaccinated should use caution in selecting food and water.

An increase in specific serum antibodies is the predominant immune response elicited by injection of capsular polysaccharides. The Vi vaccine confers significant protection against typhoid fever based on the production of measurable antibodies, predominantly of the IgG class. Both the seroconversion rate (≥4-fold rise in serum antibodies) and the protective efficacy induced by Vi in the Nepalese were similar (about 75%). The results of the immunogenicity and effectiveness studies in Nepal provide evidence that serum antibodies to the Vi antigen confer immunity to typhoid fever.

The protective efficacy against typhoid fever of a single i.m. injection of 25 μg of Typhim Vi was assessed in two randomized double-blind controlled trials.

A clinical trial was done in Nepal in a target population, 5 through 44 years of age, in 5 villages. There were 6 907 vaccinated subjects, of whom 6 438 were members of the target population; 3 457 received Vi and 3 450 received the control vaccine. There were 165 children under 5 years of age and 304 adults over 44. The protective efficacy of Typhim Vi is shown in Table I. The seroconversion rates (≥4-fold rise in serum antibodies), 76.9% in the 5 to 14 year age group, 79.1% in the 15 to 44 year age group and 62.5% in the over 45 to 55 year age group, were similar to the protective efficacy. This provides evidence that serum antibodies to the Vi antigen confer immunity to typhoid fever.

Table I—Typhim Vi

Protective Efficacy

Typhoid Fever Cases	Vaccine: Vi	Vaccine: Control	Efficacy %
Culture Positive	9	32	72
Clinically Suspected	5	25	80
Combined	14	57	75

In a second double blind, controlled efficacy trial conducted in South Africa 11 384 children ages 5 to 16 were immunized with Typhim Vi or a control vaccine, while a total of 23 075 children were followed. A total of 239 cases of blood-culture proven S. typhi infection occurred during the 21-month follow-up period among the 23 075 children participating, (5.9 cases per annum, per 1 000 children). There were 173 cases in the unvaccinated group (n=11 691) (8.5 cases per annum, per 1 000 children), 47 cases in the children immunized with control vaccine (4.7 cases per annum, per 1 000 children), and 19 cases in children immunized with the Vi vaccine (1.9 cases per annum, per 1 000 children). The incidence of typhoid in the Vi immunized children was significantly lower than in the control vaccinated children ($p<0.001$). Estimates of vaccine efficacy after 21 months ranged from 60% (comparison to control group, all cases from date of immunization) to 81% (comparison to untreated group, all cases after 6 weeks post-immunization). Serology in a random sample of 0.5% of vaccinees showed an increase in anti-Vi antibodies as measured by radioimmunoassay and enzyme-linked immunosorbent assay. Antibody levels remained significantly elevated at 6 and 12 months postvaccination. Follow-up for 3 years following immunization showed a Vi vaccine efficacy of 50% in the third year.

Immunogenicity trials performed in Houston, Texas, in a racially mixed adult American population showed seroconversion rates and antibody levels equal to or greater than those seen in South Africa or Nepal. A single dose of Vi capsular polysaccharide vaccine resulted in a 4-fold increase in antibody titre in between 83 and 96%. A 4-fold rise in antibody level occurred by 1 week in 60%, by 2 weeks in 80%, and by 1 month in 93%. A level of 4-fold rises persisted in 33% of 43 persons tested prior to a booster dose at 27 months following immunization, and 50% of 12 persons tested prior to a booster dose at 34 months following immunization. A second dose of Vi given at 27 to 34 months following initial immunization elicited antibody levels similar to those observed following the first dose.

A double blind, controlled safety and immunogenicity trial of Typhim Vi vaccine was performed in 268 Indonesian children. The overall seroconversion rate was 98.7% one month after vaccination. The seroconversion rates for the different age groups were: 100% for 12 to 24 months, 98% for 24 to 60 months and 99% for 60 to 144 months. Although antibody levels to Vi antigen are generally correlated with the protective levels, there are no specific data available to substantiate the efficacy in children 2 to 5 years old. No data are available on booster doses in children.

Indications: Active immunization against exposure to S. typhi the organism which causes typhoid fever.

For active immunization in persons 2 years of age and older in the following situations: travellers to endemic or epidemic areas or where sanitary conditions may be doubtful and where travellers may be exposed to potentially contaminated food and water (see Pharmacology and Warnings); persons with ongoing household or intimate exposure to an S. typhi carrier; laboratory workers who frequently handle cultures of S. typhi.

The optimum interval for booster doses has not been established, but a booster dose every 3 years under condition of repeated or continuous exposure to the S. typhi organism is recommended.

As with any vaccine, vaccination with Typhim Vi vaccine may not result in protection in all individuals. Travellers should take all necessary precautions to avoid contaminated food and water.

No data are available on the response to Typhim Vi in chronic carriers.

Contraindications: Patients with a history of hypersensitivity to any component of this vaccine (Vi antigen, isotonic buffer or phenol).

Immunization should be deferred during the course of any acute illness.

Warnings: It is advisable that vaccinees be warned that immunization is only one preventive measure and that care in selection of food and water is of primary importance. This is of particular concern when the vaccine is administered less than 2 weeks prior to departure as optimum antibody protection may not yet be reached.

If the vaccine is used in persons receiving immunosuppressive therapy or who are otherwise immunocompromised, the expected immune response may not be obtained.

This vaccine will not afford protection against species of Salmonella other than S. typhi or against other bacteria that cause enteric disease.

As with any vaccine, vaccination with Typhim Vi may not protect 100% of susceptible individuals.

Precautions: General: Epinephrine HCl solution (1:1 000) should be available for immediate use in case an anaphylactic or acute hypersensitivity reaction occurs.

Prior to an injection of any vaccine, all known precautions should be taken to prevent adverse reactions. This includes a review of the patient's history with respect to possible hypersensitivity to the vaccine or any component including phenol or similar vaccines.

Any febrile illness or acute infection likely to be accompanied by fever is reason to delay the use of Typhim Vi.

Special care should be taken to ensure that Typhim Vi vaccine is not injected into a blood vessel.

A separate sterile needle and syringe should be used for each individual patient to prevent transmission of hepatitis or other infectious agents from one person to another. **Do not recap needle.**

Drug Interactions: There are no known interactions of Typhim Vi vaccine with drugs or foods.

Typhim Vi vaccine may be administered simultaneously with vaccines against tetanus and inactivated poliomyelitis vaccine or with meningococcus (groups A and C) vaccine at separate sites with separate syringes. Data on simultaneous administration with other vaccines are not available. If any vaccines are administered at the same visit, they must be given at separate sites and with separate syringes.

Pregnancy: Animal reproduction studies have not been conducted with Typhim Vi vaccine. It is also not known whether Typhim Vi vaccine can cause fetal harm when administered to a pregnant woman or can affect reproduction capacity. Typhim Vi should be given to a pregnant women only if clearly needed.

Children: Safety and immunogenicity of Typhim Vi vaccine have been demonstrated in children 2 years of age and older (see Dosage).

Typhim Vi vaccine is not currently recommended for children under 2 years of age.

Adverse Effects: Health care providers should report any occurrences temporally related to the administration of the product in accordance with provincial and federal statutory requirements.

Tolerance has been studied in more than 10 000 subjects both in countries of high and low endemicity. The secondary effects are generally minor and transient.

No serious or life-threatening adverse events attributed to Typhim Vi have been reported (see Table II and Table III on following page).

Adverse reactions from trials in Houston, Texas (18 to 40 year-old adults) are summarized in Table II. No severe or unusual side effects were observed.

Adults who received a booster dose of Typhim Vi 27 to 34 months following the initial dose were more likely to develop erythema and/or induration (10/55) than those given a first dose (13/182), but the rate of systemic reactions was not increased.

Adverse reactions from a trial in Indonesia in children 1 to 7 years old are summarized in Table III (on following page). No severe or unusual side effects were observed.

Dosage: The immunizing dose is a single injection of 0.5 mL given i.m.

Table II—Typhim Vi

Percentage of 18 to 40 Year-Old Adults Presenting with Local or Systemic Reactions within the First 24 to 48 Hours after Immunization with Typhim Vi Vaccine

Reactions	(n=98) %	(n=54) %
Local		
Pain	26.5	40.7
Induration	5.1	14.8
Erythema	5.1	3.7
Tenderness	96.9	98
Systemic		
Malaise	8.3	24
Myalgia	3.1	7.4
Headache	16.3	20.3
Nausea	8.1	1.9
Vomiting	0	1.9
Diarrhea	3.0	0
Feverish	3.1	2

Table III—Typhim Vi

Percentage of Children 1 to 7 Years Presenting with Local or Systemic Reactions after Immunization with Typhim Vi Vaccine

	Children (Age in Months)		
Reactions	12-24 (n=21) %	24-60 (n=66) %	60-144 (n=88) %
Local			
Soreness	4.8	4.6	21
Pain	9.6	9.1	19
Erythema	0	4.6	10.2
Induration	4.8	3	2.3
Systemic			
Feverishness	0	3	3.4
Headache	0	0	0
Decreased Activity	0	4.6	0
Rash	0	0	0

The vaccine should be inspected visually for extraneous particulate matter and/or discoloration prior to administration. If either of these conditions exist, the vaccine should not be administered.

A separate, sterile syringe and needle or a sterile disposable unit should be used for each individual patient to prevent transmission of hepatitis or other infectious agents from one person to another.

The skin at the site of injection first should be cleansed and disinfected. Shake vial before use. Remove plastic tab of flip-off cap. Cleanse top of rubber stopper of the vial with a suitable antiseptic and wipe away all excess before withdrawing vaccine.

For the single dose presentation, shake the prefilled syringe well before administering dose.

Each person who is immunized should be given a permanent personal immunization record. In addition, it is essential that the health care provider also maintain a permanent record of the immunization history of each individual. This office record should contain the name of the vaccine, date given, dose, manufacturer and lot number.

Supplied: Each single dose (0.5 mL) of sterile, clear, colorless, isotonic buffered solution contains: purified Vi polysaccharide 25 μg. Phenol (0.25% w/v) is added as a preservative. Prefilled syringes of 0.5 mL (1 dose) and vials of 10 mL (20 doses). Store between 2 and 8°C. **Do not freeze.**

Reviewed 1997

Now indicated for angina

Smooth and Effective blood pressure *control.*

A bright idea.

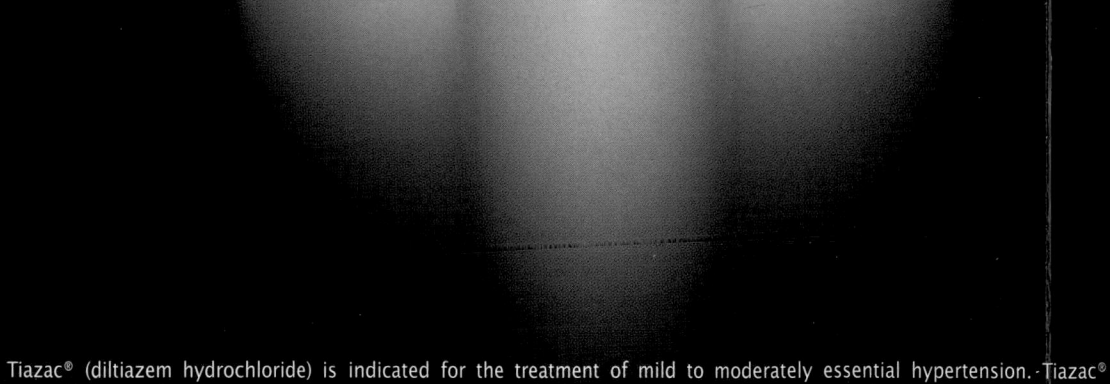

Tiazac® (diltiazem hydrochloride) is indicated for the treatment of mild to moderately essential hypertension. Tiazac® should normally be used in those patients in whom treatment with diuretics or beta-blockers has been ineffective, or has been associated with unacceptable adverse effects[1].

Tiazac® is also indicated for the management of chronic stable angina (effort-associated angina) without evidence of vasospasm in patients who remain symptomatic despite adequate doses of beta-blockers and/or organic nitrates or who cannot tolerate these agents[1].

Hypertension: The most common adverse effects were: headache (13%); edema (5%); GI disease (5%); pain (4%); vasodilation (3%); asthenia (3%); dizziness (3%); and palpitations (2%)[1].

Angina: The most common adverse events were: headache (8%); pain (4%); dizziness (3%); and peripheral edema (2%)[1].

TIAZAC®

DILTIAZEM HCI

Reference: 1 Tiazac® (diltiazem HCl) product monograph, August 21, 1998.

PAAB

98T001E

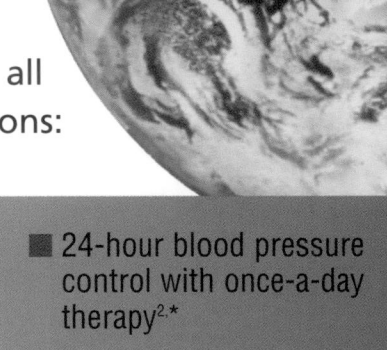

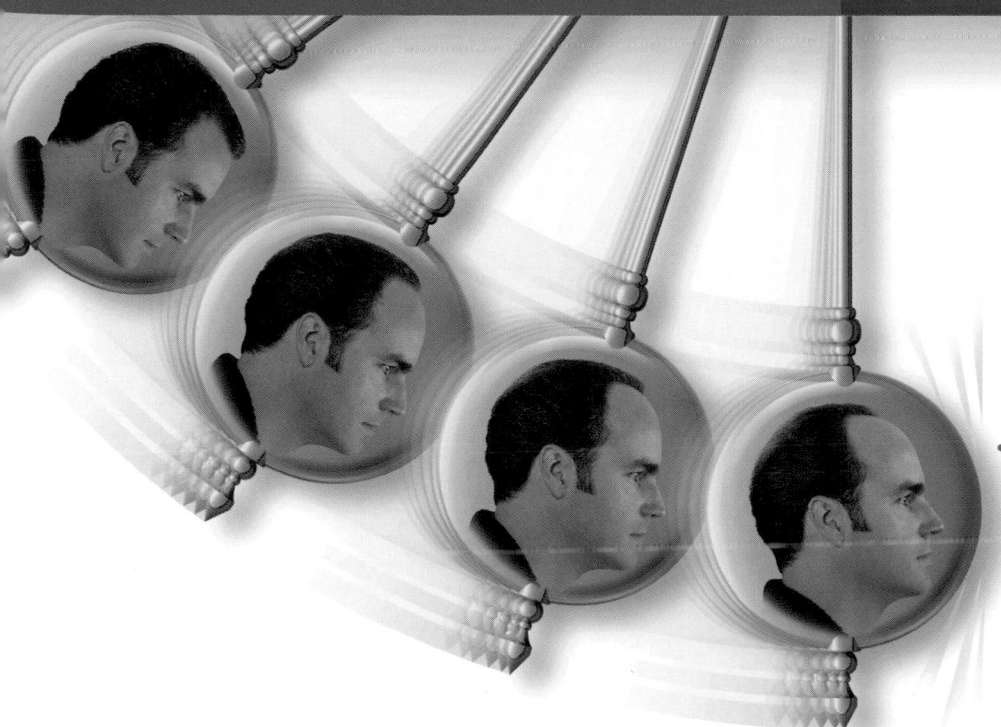

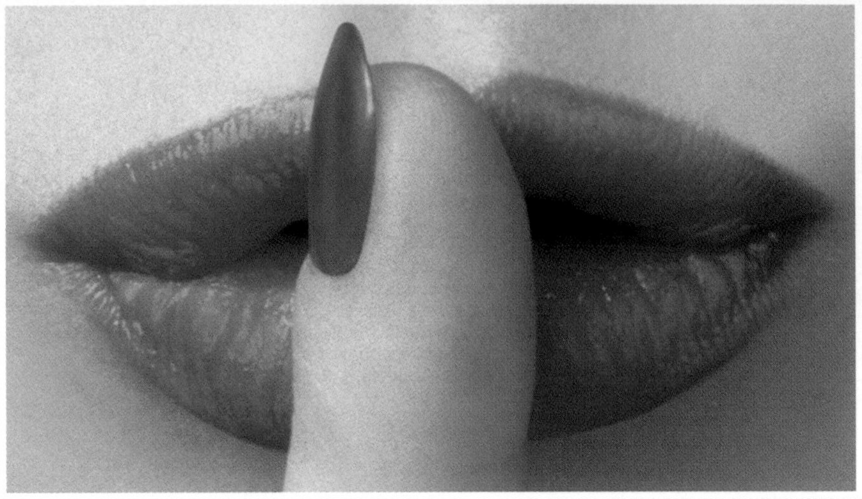

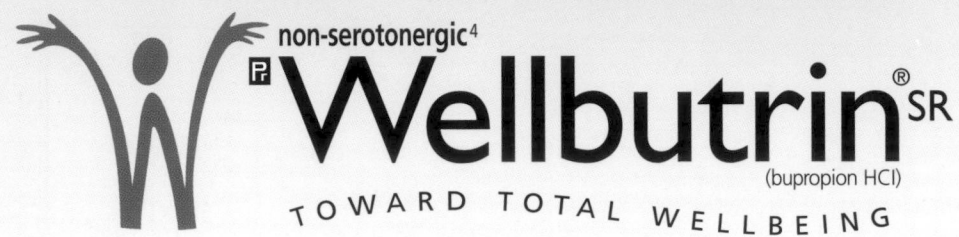

References: 1. Wells BG, Mandos LA, Hayes PE. Depressive disorders. In: *Pharmacotherapy: A pathophysiologic approach.* 3rd ed. Dipiro JT *et al*., eds. Stamford, Conn: Appleton & Lange, Stamford, 1997;1395-1418. 2. Crenshaw TL, Goldberg JP, eds. *Sexual pharmacology: Drugs that affect sexual function.* New York, N.Y.: W.W. Norton & Company Inc., 1996;23-25, 273-277, 285-295. 3. Kaplan HI, Sadock BJ. *Pocket handbook of psychiatric drug treatment.* 4th ed. Baltimore, Md: Williams & Wilkins, 1993;14-23. 4. Product Monograph of Wellbutrin®SR, Glaxo Wellcome Inc. April 17, 1998. 5. Lineberry CG *et al*. A fixed-dose (300 mg) efficacy study of bupropion and placebo in depressed outpatients. *J Clin Psychiatry* 1990;51:194-199. 6. Protocol #203, 205, 212. Data on file, Glaxo Wellcome Inc. 7. Stahl SM, ed. *Essential psychopharmacology. Neuroscientific basis and clinical applications.* Cambridge, U.K.: Cambridge University Press, 1996;149-150. 8. Ascher JA *et al*. Bupropion: A review of its mechanism of antidepressant activity. *J Clin Psychiatry* 1995;56:395-401. 9. Ferris RM, Cooper BR. Mechanism of antidepressant activity of bupropion. *J Clin Psychiatry* 1993;11:2-14. 10. Kavoussi RJ, Segraves RT *et al*. Double-blind comparison of bupropion sustained release and sertraline in depressed outpatients. *J Clin Psychiatry* 1997;58:532-537.

U

ULCIDINE® Ⓟ

ICN

Famotidine

Histamine H_2-Receptor Antagonist

Supplied: 20 mg: Each flesh-colored, film-coated, round tablet, embossed "ICN" on one side and "U11" on the other side, contains: famotidine 20 mg, USP. Nonmedicinal ingredients: microcrystalline cellulose, lactose, magnesium stearate, pregelatinized starch and talc; film-coating materials: Opaspray Tar K (alcohol, hydroxypropylcellulose, synthetic red iron oxide, synthetic yellow iron oxide, titanium dioxide); film-coating base solution: acetylated monoglycerides, alcohol, hydroxypropyl methylcellulose, methylene chloride and povidone. Bottles of 100 and 500.

40 mg: Each light brown-colored, film-coated, round tablet, embossed "ICN" on one side and "U12" on the other side, contains: famotidine 40 mg, USP. Nonmedicinal ingredients: lactose, magnesium stearate, pregelatinized starch and talc; film-coating materials: Opaspray Orange K (alcohol, hydroxypropycellulose, synthetic red iron oxide, synthetic yellow iron oxide, titanium dioxide) and carnauba wax; film-coating base solution: acetylated monoglycerides, alcohol, hydroxypropyl methylcellulose, methylene chloride and povidone. Bottles of 100 and 500.

New Product 1998

ULONE™

3M Pharmaceuticals

Chlophedianol HCl

Antitussive

Supplied: Each 5 mL contains: chlophedianol HCl 25 mg in a flavored syrup base. Nonmedicinal ingredients: citric acid, ethyl alcohol, FD&C yellow #6, flavoring, glycerin, menthol racemic, methyl- and propylparabens, sodium citrate, sucrose, water. Tartrazine-free. Bottles of 100 mL and 1 L.

ULTIVA® Ⓝ

Glaxo Wellcome

Remifentanil HCl

Opioid Component to Anesthesia

Pharmacology: Remifentanil is an opioid agonist with rapid onset and peak effect and ultra-short duration of action. The opioid activity of remifentanil is antagonized by opioid antagonists such as naloxone.

The analgesic effects of remifentanil are rapid in onset and offset. Its effects and side effects are dose dependent and similar to other opioids. Remifentanil in humans has a rapid blood-brain equilibration half-time of 1 ± 1 minutes (mean$\pm$SD) and a rapid onset of action. The pharmacodynamic effects of remifentanil closely follow the measured blood concentrations, allowing direct correlation between dose blood levels, and response. Blood concentration decreases 50% in 3 to 6 minutes after a 1-minute infusion or after prolonged continuous infusion due to rapid distribution and elimination processes and is independent of duration of drug administration. Recovery from the effects of remifentanil occurs rapidly (within 5 to 10 minutes). New steady-state concentrations occur within 5 to 10 minutes after changes in infusion rate. When used as a component of an anesthetic technique, remifentanil can be rapidly titrated to the desired depth of anesthesia/analgesia (e.g., as required by varying levels of intraoperative stress) by changing the continuous infusion rate or by administering an i.v. bolus injection.

Hemodynamics: In premedicated patients undergoing anesthesia, 1-minute infusions of <2 μg/kg of remifentanil caused dose-dependent hypotension and bradycardia. While additional doses >2 μg/kg (up to 30 μg/kg) do not produce any further decreases in heart rate or blood pressure, the duration of the hemodynamic change is increased in proportion to the blood concentrations achieved. Peak hemodynamic effects occur within 3 to 5 minutes of a single dose of remifentanil or an infusion rate increase. Glycopyrrolate, atropine and vagolytic neuromuscular blocking agents attenuate the hemodynamic effects associated with remifentanil. When appropriate, bradycardia and hypotension can be reversed by reduction of the rate of infusion of remifentanil, or the dose of concurrent anesthetics, or by the administration of fluids or vasopressors.

Respiration: Remifentanil depresses respiration in a dose-related fashion. Unlike other fentanyl analogs, the duration of action of remifentanil at a given dose does not increase with increasing duration of administration, due to lack of drug accumulation. When remifentanil and alfentanil were dosed to equal levels of respiratory depression, recovery of respiratory drive after 3-hour infusions was more rapid and less variable with remifentanil.

Spontaneous respiration occurs at blood concentrations of 4 to 5 ng/mL in the absence of other anesthetic agents; for example, after discontinuation of a 0.25-μg/kg/min infusion of remifentanil, these blood concentrations would be reached in 2 to 4 minutes. In patients undergoing general anesthesia, the rate of respiratory recovery depends upon the concurrent anesthetic; $N_2O <$ propofol $<$ isoflurane.

Muscle Rigidity: Skeletal muscle rigidity can be caused by remifentanil and is related to the dose and speed of administration. Remifentanil may cause chest wall rigidity (inability to ventilate) after single doses of >1 μg/kg administered over 30 to 60 seconds or infusion rates >0.1 μg/kg/min; peripheral muscle rigidity may occur at lower doses. Administration of doses <1 μg/kg may cause chest wall rigidity when given concurrently with a continuous infusion of remifentanil. Prior or concurrent administration of a hypnotic (propofol or thiopental) or a neuromuscular blocking agent may attenuate the development of muscle rigidity. Excessive muscle rigidity can be treated by decreasing the rate or discontinuing the infusion of remifentanil or by administering a neuromuscular blocking agent.

Histamine Release: Assays of histamine in patients and normal volunteers have shown no elevation in plasma histamine levels after administration of remifentanil in doses up to 30 μg/kg over 60 seconds.

Anesthesia: Remifentanil is synergistic with the activity of hypnotics (propofol and thiopental), inhaled anesthetics and benzodiazepines (see Precautions and Dosage).

Gender: No differences have been shown in the pharmacodynamic activity (as measured by the EEG) of remifentanil between men and women.

Pharmacokinetics: After i.v. doses administered over 60 seconds, the pharmacokinetics of remifentanil fit a 3-compartment model with a rapid distribution half-life of 1 minute, a slower distribution half-life of 6 minutes and a terminal elimination half-life of 10 to 20 minutes. Since the terminal elimination component contributes less than 10% of the overall area under the concentration versus time curve (AUC), the effective biological half-life of remifentanil is 3 to 10 minutes. This is similar to the 3- to 10-minute half-life measured after termination of prolonged infusions (up to 4 hours) and correlates with recovery times observed in the clinical setting after infusions up to 12 hours. Concentrations of remifentanil are proportional to the dose administered throughout the recommended dose range. The pharmacokinetics of remifentanil are unaffected by the presence of renal or hepatic impairment.

Distribution: The initial volume of distribution (V_d) of remifentanil is approximately 100 mL/kg and represents distribution throughout the blood and rapidly perfused tissues. Remifentanil subsequently distributes into peripheral tissues with a steady-state volume of distribution of approximately 350 mL/kg. These two distribution volumes generally correlate with total body weight (except in severely obese patients when they correlate better with ideal body weight [IBW]). Remifentanil is approximately 70% bound to plasma proteins of which two-thirds is binding to alpha-1-acid-glycoprotein.

Metabolism: Remifentanil is an esterase-metabolized opioid. A labile ester linkage renders this compound susceptible to hydrolysis by nonspecific esterases in blood and tissues. This hydrolysis results in production of the carboxylic acid metabolite (3-[4-methoxycarbonyl-4-[(1-oxopropyl)phenylamino]-1-piperidine]propanoic acid), and represents the principal metabolic pathway for remifentanil ($>$95%). The carboxylic acid metabolite is essentially inactive (1/4 600 as potent as remifentanil in dogs) and is excreted by the kidneys with an elimination half-life of approximately 90 minutes. Remifentanil is not metabolized by plasma cholinesterase (pseudocholinesterase) and is not appreciably metabolized by the liver or lung.

Elimination: The clearance of remifentanil in young, healthy adults is approximately 40 mL/min/kg. Clearance generally correlates with total body weight (except in severely obese patients when it correlates better with ideal body weight). The high clearance of remifentanil combined with a relatively small volume of distribution produces a short elimination half-life of approximately 3 to 10 minutes. This value is consistent with the time taken for blood or effect site concentrations to fall by 50% (context-sensitive half-times) which is approximately 3 to 6 minutes. Unlike other fentanyl analogs, the duration of action does not increase with prolonged administration.

Titration to Effect: The rapid elimination of remifentanil permits the titration of infusion rate without concern for prolonged duration. In general, every 0.1-μg/kg/min change in the i.v. infusion rate will lead to a corresponding 2.5-ng/mL change in blood remifentanil concentration within 5 to 10 minutes. In intubated patients only, a more rapid increase (within 3 to 5 minutes) to a new steady state can be achieved with a 1-μg/kg bolus dose in conjunction with an infusion rate increase.

Clinical Experience: Remifentanil was evaluated in 2 169 patients undergoing general anesthesia. Currently investigation of remifentanil is ongoing in the following areas: in spontaneous ventilation anesthesia, in monitored anesthesia care, for continuation as an analgesic in the immediate postoperative period, in neurosurgery, in cardiac surgery and in pediatric anesthesia. Currently there are insufficient safety and/or efficacy data to make dosage recommendations in these areas.

Indications: For i.v. administration as an analgesic agent for use during the induction and maintenance of general anesthesia for inpatient and outpatient procedures.

Due to insufficient safety and efficacy data, remifentanil is not recommended for use in spontaneous ventilation anesthesia, in monitored anesthesia care, for continuation as an analgesic in the immediate postoperative period, in neurosurgery, in cardiac surgery or in pediatric anesthesia.

Contraindications: Due to the presence of glycine in the formulation, remifentanil is contraindicated for epidural or intrathecal administration.

Remifentanil is also contraindicated in patients with known hypersensitivity to the drug or any component of its formulation/preparation or to other fentanyl analogs.

Warnings: Remifentanil is not recommended for use as the sole agent in general anesthesia because loss of consciousness cannot be assured and because of a high incidence of apnea, muscle rigidity and tachycardia.

Continuous infusions of remifentanil should be administered only by an infusion device. **I.V. bolus administration should only be used in intubated patients during the maintenance of general anesthesia.** For induction of anesthesia in nonintubated patients, a single dose of remifentanil, not exceeding 1 μg/kg, may be administered over 30 to 60 seconds.

Interruption of an infusion of remifentanil will result in rapid offset of effect. Rapid clearance and lack of drug accumulation result in rapid dissipation of respiratory depressant and analgesic effects upon discontinuation of remifentanil at recommended doses. However, delayed respiratory depression may occur in some patients up to 30 minutes after termination of remifentanil infusions due to residual effects of concomitant anesthetics. Discontinuation of an infusion of remifentanil should be preceded by the establishment of adequate postoperative analgesia (see Precautions and Dosage).

Injections of remifentanil should be made into i.v. tubing at or close to the venous cannula. Upon discontinuation of remifentanil, the i.v. tubing should be removed or cleared to prevent the inadvertent administration of remifentanil at a later point in time. **Failure to adequately clear the i.v. tubing to remove residual remifentanil has been associated with the appearance of respiratory depression, apnea and muscle rigidity upon the administration of additional fluids or medications through the same i.v. tubing.**

Use of remifentanil is associated with apnea and respiratory depression. Remifentanil should be administered only in a setting fully equipped for the monitoring and support of respiratory and cardiovascular function. Resuscitative and intubation equipment, oxygen and an opioid antagonist must be readily available.

Remifentanil should be administered only by persons specifically trained in the use of anesthetic drugs and the recognition and management of the expected adverse effects of potent opioids, including respiratory and cardiac resuscitation of patients in the age-group being treated. Such training must include the establishment and maintenance of a patent airway and assisted ventilation.

Ultiva (cont'd)

Skeletal muscle rigidity can be caused by remifentanil and is related to the dose and speed of administration. Remifentanil may cause chest wall rigidity (inability to ventilate) after single doses >1 μg/kg administered over 30 to 60 seconds, or after infusion rates >0.1 μg/kg/min. Single doses <1 μg/kg may cause chest wall rigidity when given concurrently with a continuous infusion of remifentanil.

Muscle rigidity induced by remifentanil should be managed in the context of the patient's clinical condition. Muscle rigidity occurring during the induction of anesthesia should be treated by the administration of a neuromuscular blocking agent and the concurrent induction medications.

Remifentanil should not be administered into the same i.v. tubing with blood/serum/plasma due to potential inactivation by nonspecific esterases in blood products.

Precautions: Rapid Offset of Action: **Within 5 to 10 minutes after the discontinuation of remifentanil, no residual analgesic activity will be present. However, respiratory depression may occur in some patients up to 30 minutes after termination of infusion due to residual effects of concomitant anesthetics.** Standard monitoring should be maintained in the postoperative period to ensure adequate recovery without stimulation. For patients undergoing surgical procedures where postoperative pain is generally anticipated, other analgesics should be administered prior to the discontinuation of remifentanil.

General: Vital Signs and oxygenation must be continually monitored during the administration of remifentanil.

Bradycardia has been reported with remifentanil and is responsive to ephedrine or anticholinergic drugs, such as atropine and glycopyrrolate.

Hypotension has been reported with remifentanil and is responsive to decreases in the administration of remifentanil or to i.v. fluids or catecholamine (ephedrine, epinephrine, norepinephrine, etc.) administration.

Intraoperative awareness has been reported in patients under 55 years of age when remifentanil has been administered with propofol infusion rates of ≤75 μg/kg/min. Therefore, propofol rates <100 μg/kg/min are not recommended for use with remifentanil for total i.v. anesthesia in patients <55 years of age.

Renal Impairment: The pharmacodynamic/pharmacokinetic profile of remifentanil is not changed in patients with end stage renal disease (creatinine clearance <10 mL/min). No dosage adjustment is necessary in this patient population.

In anephric patients, the half-life of the carboxylic acid metabolite increases from 90 minutes to approximately 30 hours. The metabolite is removed by hemodialysis with a dialysis extraction ratio of approximately 30%.

Hepatic Impairment: Remifentanil pharmacokinetic/pharmacodynamic profile is not changed in patients with severe hepatic impairment. However, these patients may be slightly more sensitive to respiratory depressant effects of remifentanil. Therefore, these patients should be closely monitored and the dose of remifentanil titrated to individual patient need.

Geriatrics: (>65 years): The clearance of remifentanil is reduced (approximately 25%) in the elderly (>65 years of age) compared to young adults (average 25 years of age). However, remifentanil blood concentrations fall as rapidly after termination of administration in the elderly as in young adults. The pharmacodynamic activity of remifentanil (as measured by the EC_{50} for development of delta waves on the EEG) increases with increasing age. The EC_{50} of remifentanil for this measure was 50% less in patients over 65 years of age when compared to healthy volunteers (25 years of age); therefore, the recommended starting dose of remifentanil should be decreased by 50% in elderly patients and then titrated to individual patient need (see Dosage).

Morbidly Obese Patients: As for all potent opioids, caution is required when used in morbidly obese patients because of alterations in cardiovascular and respiratory physiology (see Dosage).

Children (<12 years of age): Due to the limited number of patients studied, there are insufficient data to make dosage recommendations in the pediatric population.

Cardiovascular Surgery: Clinical experience with remifentanil in patients undergoing cardiac surgery is limited to coronary artery bypass graft procedures (CABG). There are insufficient data to make a dosage recommendation.

Neurosurgery: Due to the limited number of patients studied, there are insufficient data to make dosage recommendations.

Pregnancy, Labor and Delivery and *Lactation:* There are insufficient clinical data to support safety, and therefore, remifentanil is not recommended for use in these populations.

ASA III/IV Patients: Limited data are available from 65 ASA III and 1 ASA IV patients. As the hemodynamic effects of potent opioids can be expected to be more pronounced in ASA III/IV patients, caution should be exercised in the administration of remifentanil in this population. Initial dosage reduction and subsequent titration to effect is therefore recommended.

Dependence Liability: As with other opioids, remifentanil can produce drug dependence of the morphine type and therefore has the potential of being abused.

Drug Interactions: Remifentanil clearance is not altered by concomitant administration of thiopental, isoflurane, propofol or temazepam during anesthesia. In vitro studies with atracurium, mivacurium, esmolol, echothiophate, neostigmine, physostigmine and midazolam revealed no inhibition of remifentanil hydrolysis in whole human blood by these drugs. In animals the duration of muscle paralysis from succinylcholine is not prolonged by remifentanil.

Remifentanil is synergistic with other anesthetics and doses of thiopental, propofol, isoflurane and midazolam have been reduced by up to 75% with the coadministration of remifentanil. If doses of concomitantly administered CNS depressant drugs are not reduced, patients may experience an increased incidence of adverse effects associated with these agents.

Adverse Effects: Remifentanil produces adverse events that are characteristic of opioids, such as respiratory depression, bradycardia, hypotension and skeletal muscle rigidity. These adverse events dissipate within minutes of discontinuing or decreasing the infusion rate of remifentanil. See Pharmacology, Warnings and Precautions on the management of these events.

Adverse event information is derived from controlled clinical trials that were conducted in a variety of surgical procedures of varying duration, using a variety of premedications and other anesthetics, and in patient populations with diverse characteristics including underlying disease.

Approximately 2 492 patients were exposed to remifentanil in controlled clinical trials. The frequencies of adverse events during general anesthesia with the recommended doses of remifentanil are given in Table I.

In the elderly population (>65 years), the incidence of hypotension is higher, whereas the incidence of nausea and vomiting is lower (see Precautions).

Data from cardiac risk analysis in noncardiac general anesthesia studies indicate the incidence of hypotension in patients with cardiac risk factors (i.e., >65 years of age, concomitant use of cardiac medication) is higher with remifentanil than comparator drugs (27% vs 12%, respectively).

Other adverse events reported less frequently (<1%) include constipation and sedation.

Overdose: Symptoms and Treatment: As with all potent opioid analgesics, overdosage would be manifested by an extension of the pharmacological actions of remifentanil. Expected signs and symptoms of overdosage include: apnea, chest-wall rigidity, seizures, hypoxemia, hypotension and bradycardia.

In case of overdosage or suspected overdosage, discontinue administration of remifentanil, maintain a patent airway, initiate assisted or controlled ventilation with oxygen and maintain adequate cardiovascular function. If depressed respiration is associated with muscle rigidity, a neuromuscular blocking agent or an opioid antagonist may be required to facilitate assisted or controlled respiration. I.V. fluids and vasopressors for the treatment of hypotension and other supportive measures may be employed. Glycopyrrolate or atropine may be useful for the treatment of bradycardia and/or hypotension.

I.V. administration of an opioid antagonist such as naloxone may be employed as a specific antidote to manage severe respiratory depression or muscle rigidity. Respiratory depression following overdosage with remifentanil is not expected to last longer than the opioid antagonist, naloxone. Reversal of the opioid effects may lead to acute pain and sympathetic hyperactivity.

Dosage: Due to insufficient safety and efficacy data, remifentanil is not recommended for use in spontaneous ventilation anesthesia, in monitored anesthesia care, for continuation as an analgesic in the immediate postoperative period, in neurosurgery, in cardiac surgery, or in pediatric anesthesia.

Remifentanil is not recommended as the sole agent in general anesthesia because loss of consciousness cannot be assured and because of a high incidence of apnea, muscle rigidity and tachycardia.

Remifentanil should be administered only in a setting fully equipped for the monitoring and support of respiratory and

Table I—Ultiva

Adverse Events ≥1% of Patients in General Anesthesia Studies at the Recommended Doses of Remifentanil[a]

Adverse Event	Induction/Maintenance: Remifentanil (n=921)	Induction/Maintenance: Alfentanil/Fentanyl (n=466)	After Discontinuation: Remifentanil (n=929)	After Discontinuation: Alfentanil/Fentanyl (n=466)
Nausea	8 (<1%)	0	339 (36%)	202 (43%)
Hypotension	178 (19%)	30 (6%)	16 (2%)	9 (2%)
Vomiting	4 (<1%)	1 (<1%)	150 (16%)	91 (20%)
Muscle rigidity	98 (11%)[b]	37 (8%)	2 (<1%)	1 (<1%)
Bradycardia	62 (7%)	24 (5%)	11 (1%)	6 (1%)
Shivering	3 (<1%)	0	49 (5%)	10 (2%)
Fever	1 (<1%)	0	44 (5%)	9 (2%)
Dizziness	0	0	27 (3%)	9 (2%)
Visual disturbance	0	0	24 (3%)	14 (3%)
Headache	0	0	21 (2%)	8 (2%)
Respiratory depression	1 (<1%)	0	17 (2%)	20 (4%)
Apnea	0	1 (<1%)	2 (<1%)	1 (<1%)
Pruritus	2 (<1%)	0	22 (2%)	7 (2%)
Tachycardia	6 (<1%)	7 (2%)	10 (1%)	8 (2%)
Postoperative pain	0	0	4 (<1%)	5 (1%)
Hypertension	10 (1%)	7 (2%)	12 (1%)	8 (2%)
Agitation	2 (<1%)	0	6 (<1%)	1 (<1%)
Hypoxia	0	0	10 (1%)	7 (2%)

[a] **Not all doses of remifentanil were equipotent to the comparator opioid. Administration of remifentanil in excess of the recommended dose (i.e., doses >1 and up to 20 μg/kg) resulted in a higher incidence of some adverse events: muscle rigidity (37%), bradycardia (12%), hypertension (4%) and tachycardia (4%).**

[b] Included in the muscle rigidity incidence is chest wall rigidity (5%). The overall muscle rigidity incidence is reduced to <1% when remifentanil is administered concurrently with or after a hypnotic induction agent.

Table II—Ultiva

Dosing Guidelines

Phase	Continuous I.V. Infusion of Ultiva (μg/kg/min)	Infusion Dose Range of Ultiva (μg/kg/min)	Supplemental I.V. Bolus Dose of Ultiva (μg/kg)
Induction of Anesthesia (through intubation)	0.5-1*		
Maintenance of Anesthesia with:			
Nitrous oxide (66%)	0.4	0.1-2	0.5-1
Isoflurane (starting dose 0.5 MAC)	0.25	0.05-2	0.5-1
Propofol (starting dose 100 μg/kg/min)	0.25	0.05-2	0.5-1

*An initial dose of 1 μg/kg may be administered over 30 to 60 seconds.

cardiovascular function. Resuscitative and intubation equipment, oxygen and an opioid antagonist must be readily available.

Remifentanil should only be administered by persons specifically trained in the use of anesthetic drugs and the recognition and management of the expected adverse effects of potent opioids, including respiratory and cardiac resuscitation of patients in the age-group being treated. Such training must include the establishment and maintenance of a patent airway and assisted ventilation.

Remifentanil is for i.v. use only and must not be administered by epidural or intrathecal injection. Continuous infusions of remifentanil should be administered only by an infusion device. The injection site should be close to the venous cannula and all i.v. tubing should be cleared at the time of discontinuation of infusion.

Remifentanil is synergistic with other anesthetics and doses of thiopental, propofol, isoflurane and midazolam have been reduced by up to 75% with the coadministration of remifentanil. At the recommended doses shown in Table II (on previous page), remifentanil significantly reduces the amount of hypnotic agent required to maintain anesthesia. Therefore isoflurane and propofol should be administered as recommended below to avoid excessive depth of anesthesia.

Intraoperative awareness has been reported in patients under 55 years of age when remifentanil has been administered with propofol infusion rates of ≤75 µg/kg/min. Therefore, propofol rates <100 µg/kg/min are not recommended for use with remifentanil for total i.v. anesthesia in patients <55 years of age.

I.V. bolus administration should only be used in intubated patients during the maintenance of general anesthesia. For induction of anesthesia in nonintubated patients, a single dose of remifentanil, not exceeding 1 µg/kg, may be administered over 30 to 60 seconds.

Reconstituted solutions of remifentanil should be diluted prior to administration (see Reconstituted Solutions).

The administration of remifentanil must be individualized based on the patient's response. Table II (on previous page) summarizes the recommended doses in adult patients, predominately ASA physical status I, II, or III.

During Induction of Anesthesia: Remifentanil should be administered at an infusion rate of 0.5 to 1 µg/kg/min with a hypnotic or volatile agent for the induction of anesthesia. If endotracheal intubation is to occur less than 8 minutes after the start of the infusion of remifentanil, then an initial dose of 1 µg/kg may be administered over 30 to 60 seconds.

During Maintenance of Anesthesia: After endotracheal intubation, the infusion rate of remifentanil should be decreased in accordance with the dosing guidelines in Table II (on previous page). Due to the fast onset and short duration of action of remifentanil, the rate of administration during anesthesia can be titrated upward in 25 to 100% increments or downward in 25 to 50% decrements every 2 to 5 minutes to attain the desired level of µ-opioid effect. In response to light anesthesia or transient episodes of intense surgical stress, supplemental bolus doses of 0.5 to 1 µg/kg may be administered every 2 to 5 minutes. At infusion rates >1 µg/kg/min, increases in the concomitant anesthetic agents should be considered to increase the depth of anesthesia.

Guidelines for Discontinuation: **Upon discontinuation of remifentanil, the i.v. tubing should be cleared to prevent the inadvertent administration of remifentanil at a later time. Due to the rapid offset of action of remifentanil, no residual analgesic activity will be present within 5 to 10 minutes after discontinuation. However respiratory depression may occur in some patients up to 30 minutes after termination of infusion due to residual effects of concomitant anesthetics. Standard monitoring should be maintained in the postoperative period to ensure adequate recovery without stimulation. For those patients undergoing surgical procedures where postoperative pain is generally anticipated, alternative analgesics should be administered prior to discontinuation of remifentanil. Sufficient time must be allowed to reach the maximum effect of the longer acting analgesic.** The choice of analgesic should be appropriate for the patient's surgical procedure and the level of follow-up care.

Geriatrics: Due to the increased sensitivity to the pharmacological effects of remifentanil in this population (>65 years), the starting doses of remifentanil should be decreased by 50% and then be titrated to individual patient need.

Obese Patients: The starting doses of remifentanil should be based on ideal body weight in obese patients as the clearance and volume of distribution of remifentanil are better correlated with ideal body weight than actual body weight in this population.

Preanesthetic Medication: The need for premedication and the choice of anesthetic agents must be individualized. In clinical studies, patients who received remifentanil frequently received a benzodiazepine premedication.

Individualization of Infusion Rates: Infusion rates of remifentanil can be individualized for each patient using Table III.

Table III—Ultiva

Infusion Rates of Ultiva (mL/kg/h)

Drug Delivery Rate (µg/kg/min)	Infusion Delivery Rate (mL/kg/h) 25 µg/mL	50 µg/mL	250 µg/mL
0.05	0.12	0.06	0.012
0.075	0.18	0.09	0.018
0.1	0.24	0.12	0.024
0.15	0.36	0.18	0.036
0.2	0.48	0.24	0.048
0.25	0.6	0.3	0.06
0.5	1.2	0.6	0.12
0.75	1.8	0.9	0.18
1.0	2.4	1.2	0.24
1.25	3.0	1.5	0.3
1.5	3.6	1.8	0.36
1.75	4.2	2.1	0.42
2.0	4.8	2.4	0.48

Table IV is a guideline for mL/hour delivery for a solution of 25 µg/mL with an infusion device.

Table V is a guideline for mL/hour delivery for a solution of 50 µg/mL with an infusion device.

Table VI is a guideline for mL/hour delivery for a solution of 250 µg/mL with an infusion device.

Reconstituted Solutions: Preparation for Administration: To reconstitute solution, add 1 mL of diluent per mg of remifentanil. Shake well to dissolve. When reconstituted as directed, the solution contains approximately 1 mg of remifentanil activity per 1 mL. Ultiva should be reconstituted and diluted to a recommended final concentration of 25, 50, or 250 µg/mL prior to administration as indicated in Table VII and Table VIII (on following page). **Remifentanil should not be administered without dilution.** The product does not contain any antimicrobial preservatives and thus care must be taken to assure the sterility of prepared solutions.

Remifentanil can be reconstituted and diluted to concentrations of 20 to 250 µg/mL in any of the following i.v. fluids: Sterile Water for Injection, USP; 5% Dextrose Injection, USP; 5% Dextrose and 0.9% Sodium Chloride Injection, USP; 0.9% Sodium Chloride Injection, USP; 0.45% Sodium Chloride Injection, USP; Lactated Ringer's and 5% Dextrose Injection, USP; Lactated Ringer's Injection, USP.

Remifentanil has been shown to be compatible with these i.v. fluids when coadministered into a running i.v. administration set.

Table VII—Ultiva

Reconstitution of Ultiva

Vial Size (mg of remifentanil base)	Volume of Diluent to be Added to Vial	Approximate* Available Volume	Nominal Concentration
1 mg	1 mL	1 mL	1 mg/mL
2 mg	2 mL	2 mL	1 mg/mL
5 mg	5 mL	5 mL	1 mg/mL

*Densities for water and reconstituted Ultiva are not significantly different.

Compatibility With Other Therapeutic Agents: Remifentanil has been shown to be compatible with propofol injection when coadministered into a running i.v. administration set. The compatibility of remifentanil with other therapeutic agents has not been evaluated.

Incompatibilities: Nonspecific esterases in blood products may lead to the hydrolysis of remifentanil to its carboxylic acid metabolite. Therefore, administration of remifentanil into the same i.v. tubing with blood/serum/plasma is not recommended.

Table IV—Ultiva

Infusion Rates of Ultiva (mL/h) for a 25 µg/mL Solution

Infusion Rate (µg/kg/min)	Patient Weight (kg) 30	40	50	60	70	80	90	100
0.05	3.6	4.8	6.0	7.2	8.4	9.6	10.8	12.0
0.075	5.4	7.2	9.0	10.8	12.6	14.4	16.2	18.0
0.1	7.2	9.6	12.0	14.4	16.8	19.2	21.6	24.0
0.15	10.8	14.4	18.0	21.6	25.2	28.8	32.4	36.0
0.2	14.4	19.2	24.0	28.8	33.6	38.4	43.2	48.0

Table V—Ultiva

Infusion Rates of Ultiva (mL/h) for a 50 µg/mL Solution

Infusion Rate (µg/kg/min)	Patient Weight (kg) 30	40	50	60	70	80	90	100
0.05	1.8	2.4	3.0	3.6	4.2	4.8	5.4	6.0
0.075	2.7	3.6	4.5	5.4	6.3	7.2	8.1	9.0
0.1	3.6	4.8	6.0	7.2	8.4	9.6	10.8	12.0
0.15	5.4	7.2	9.0	10.8	12.6	14.4	16.2	18.0
0.2	7.2	9.6	12.0	14.4	16.8	19.2	21.6	24.0
0.25	9.0	12.0	15.0	18.0	21.0	24.0	27.0	30.0
0.5	18.0	24.0	30.0	36.0	42.0	48.0	54.0	60.0
0.75	27.0	36.0	45.0	54.0	63.0	72.0	81.0	90.0
1.0	36.0	48.0	60.0	72.0	84.0	96.0	108.0	120.0
1.25	45.0	60.0	75.0	90.0	105.0	120.0	135.0	150.0
1.5	54.0	72.0	90.0	108.0	126.0	144.0	162.0	180.0
1.75	63.0	84.0	105.0	126.0	147.0	168.0	189.0	210.0
2.0	72.0	96.0	120.0	144.0	168.0	192.0	216.0	240.0

Table VI—Ultiva

Infusion Rates of Ultiva (mL/h) for a 250 µg/mL Solution

Infusion Rate (µg/kg/min)	Patient Weight (kg) 30	40	50	60	70	80	90	100
0.1	0.72	0.96	1.20	1.44	1.68	1.92	2.16	2.40
0.15	1.08	1.44	1.80	2.16	2.52	2.88	3.24	3.60
0.2	1.44	1.92	2.40	2.88	3.36	3.84	4.32	4.80
0.25	1.80	2.40	3.00	3.60	4.20	4.80	5.40	6.00
0.5	3.60	4.80	6.00	7.20	8.40	9.60	10.80	12.00
0.75	5.40	7.20	9.00	10.80	12.60	14.40	16.20	18.00
1.0	7.20	9.60	12.00	14.40	16.80	19.20	21.60	24.00
1.25	9.00	12.00	15.00	18.00	21.00	24.00	27.00	30.00
1.5	10.80	14.40	18.00	21.60	25.20	28.80	32.40	36.00
1.75	12.60	16.80	21.00	25.20	29.40	33.60	37.80	42.00
2.0	14.40	19.20	24.00	28.80	33.60	38.40	43.20	48.00

Ultiva (cont'd)

Table VIII—Ultiva

Dilution of Ultiva

Final Concentration	Amount of Remifentanil in Each Vial	Volume to be Added to Dilute*	Final Volume after Dilution
	1 mg	39 mL	40 mL
25 μg/mL	2 mg	78 mL	80 mL
	5 mg	195 mL	200 mL
	1 mg	19 mL	20 mL
50 μg/mL	2 mg	38 mL	40 mL
	5 mg	95 mL	100 mL
250 μg/mL	5 mg	15 mL	20 mL

*Note amounts indicated are those to be added after Ultiva has been reconstituted to a 1 mg/mL solution as indicated in Table VII (on previous page).

Note: Parenteral drug products should be inspected visually for particulate matter and discoloration prior to administration whenever solution and container permit. Product should be a clear, colorless liquid after reconstitution and free of visible particulate matter.

Supplied: 1 mg: Each vial of lyophilized powder contains: remifentanil base (as the HCl salt) 1 mg. Nonmedicinal ingredients: glycine and hydrochloric acid (adjust pH). Vials of 3 mL, cartons of 5.

2 mg: Each vial of lyophilized powder contains: remifentanil base (as the HCl salt) 2 mg. Nonmedicinal ingredients: glycine and hydrochloric acid (adjust pH). Vials of 5 mL, cartons of 5.

5 mg: Each vial of lyophilized powder contains: remifentanil base (as the HCl salt) 5 mg. Nonmedicinal ingredients: glycine and hydrochloric acid (adjust pH). Vials of 10 mL, cartons of 5.

Store between 2 and 25°C. Reconstituted and diluted solutions (20 to 250 μg/mL) are stable for 24 hours at room temperature for all recommended i.v. fluids except those containing Lactated Ringer's Solution (stable for 4 hours).

Reviewed 1998

ULTRACAINE® DS
ULTRACAINE® DS FORTE

Hoechst Marion Roussel

Articaine HCl—Epinephrine

Local Anesthetic

Pharmacology: Ultracaine has been shown to block conduction by interfering with the process fundamental to the generation of the nerve action potential, namely, the large transient increase in the permeability of the membrane to sodium ions that is produced by a slight depolarization of the membrane.

Ultracaine kinetics were determined in man by radioassay following a single i.m. dose of 5 mg/kg and a single i.v. dose of 1 mg/kg of ^{35}S-labelled articaine HCl. The maximal blood concentration was reached 45 to 60 minutes after the i.m. injection. The elimination from the blood occurred in 2 phases with the following half-lives: 1.2 and 69.7 hours, and 2.0 and 31.5 hours after i.v. and i.m. injection, respectively. Ultracaine is excreted mainly via the kidneys, in 3 phases, with the following half-lives: 2.5, 4.4 and 210 hours, and 1.6, 4.6 and 39 hours after i.v. and i.m. injection, respectively. The total excretion of radioactivity, through the kidneys, was 89% after i.v. injection and 76% after i.m. injection while 1.5% (i.v.) and 1.3% (i.m.) were excreted with the feces. After the i.m. injection, 2 metabolites (M_1 and M_2) accounting for 87% and 2%, respectively, of the administered dose were found. No metabolite was detected in the blood following an i.v. injection. In the urine, only metabolites were found.

A study in male volunteers demonstrated that a single submucosal injection of 80 mg articaine 4% with epinephrine (1:200 000) resulted in a mean maximum serum concentration of 326±158 ng/mL. The C_{max} was reached an average of 17.7±6.6 minutes after injection. Articaine is rapidly hydrolysed to its primarily inactive principal metabolite, articaine carboxylic acid. Maximum concentrations of the metabolite were reached 46.2±9.2 minutes after injection.

Indications: For infiltration anesthesia and nerve block anesthesia in clinical dentistry.

Contraindications: Known hypersensitivity to any of its components (see Supplied) and/or local anesthetics of the amide group; in the presence of inflammation and/or sepsis near the proposed injection site; in patients with severe shock; in patients with any degree of heart block; in patients with paroxysmal tachycardia; in patients with known arrhythmia with rapid heart rate; in patients with narrow-angle glaucoma; in patients with cholinesterase deficiency; in patients with existing neurologic disease and in patients with severe hypertension.

When articaine with epinephrine is used, the caution required of any vasopressor drug is in order.

Warnings: As with other local anesthetics applied to the head and neck area, life-threatening or fatal shock, respiratory or cardiac arrest may rarely occur with Ultracaine.

Methemoglobinemia: As with any local anesthetic, articaine HCl with epinephrine may rarely produce methemoglobinemia: this has been observed when an i.v. regional anesthesia technique was used. When used as directed in dental procedures, Ultracaine was not associated with methemoglobinemia.

Methemoglobinemia values of less than 20% usually do not produce any clinical symptoms. The usual clinical signs of methemoglobinemia are cyanosis of the nail beds and lips. Although the possibility of methemoglobinemia occurring in dental patients is extremely rare it can be rapidly reversed by the use of 1 to 2 mg/kg body weight of methylene blue administered i.v. over a 5 minute period.

Pregnancy and *Lactation:* Animal studies have not demonstrated teratogenic or embryotoxic effects of Ultracaine. However, safe use in pregnant women has not been established. Ultracaine is unlikely to be transferred to the mother's milk since it is rapidly decomposed and eliminated.

As with other local anesthetics, Ultracaine has been shown to cross the placental barrier after peridural administration.

Precautions: General: Resuscitative equipment and drugs should be readily available when any local anesthetic is used. The safety and effectiveness of local anesthetics depend upon proper dosage, correct technique, adequate precautions, and readiness for emergencies. Ultracaine should be used cautiously in persons with known drug allergies or sensitivities, or suspected sensitivity to the amide-type local anesthetics.

The following precautions apply to all anesthetics: avoid excessive premedications with sedatives, tranquilizers, and anti-emetic agents, especially in infants, small children and elderly patients. Inject slowly with frequent aspirations and if blood is aspirated, relocate needle. Keep dosage, including the concentration and total volume of solution, as low as possible, with due regard to the age, weight, and physical status of the patient and the vascularity of the area injected. Absorption is greater when injections are made into a highly vascular tissue. The lowest dosage that gives effective anesthesia should be used to avoid high plasma levels and serious systemic side effects.

In children and elderly patients, as well as in patients of all ages with chronic or debilitating disease, the response to local anesthetics may be modified (see Dosage).

Patients with Special Diseases and Conditions: The use of a local anesthetic containing a vasoconstrictor in areas with a limited blood supply or in patients with peripheral vascular disease, will depend on an appraisal of the relative advantages and risks.

Ultracaine should be used with extreme caution in patients whose medical history and physical evaluation suggest the existence of thyrotoxicosis or diabetes.

Owing to the sulfite component, hypersensitivity reactions may occur occasionally in patients with bronchial asthma and, very rarely, in other patients (see Adverse Effects).

Drug Interactions: Solutions containing a vasoconstrictor, e.g. epinephrine, should be used with caution, if at all, in patients who are receiving MAO inhibitors or tricyclic antidepressants, because severe, prolonged hypertension may result.

Dose-related cardiac arrhythmias may occur if preparations containing epinephrine are employed in patients during, or immediately following, the administration of enflurane, halothane, or other halogenated anesthetics.

Adverse Effects: Persistent paresthesia of the lips and oral tissues have been reported after blocking the inferior alveolar nerve.

Reactions to Ultracaine are characteristic of those associated with amide-type local anesthetics and/or vasoconstrictors.

A major cause of adverse effects to this group of drugs is excessive plasma levels, which may be due to overdosage, inadvertent intravascular injection, or slow metabolic degradation. Other causes of reactions to these local anesthetics may be hypersensitivity, idiosyncrasy, or diminished tolerance.

Reactions at the site of injection may include swelling, a burning sensation, and in insolated cases, ischemic zones, sometimes progressing to tissue necrosis.

As with all local anesthetics of this type, excessive plasma levels cause systemic reactions involving the CNS and cardiovascular systems. The **CNS effects** are characterized by excitation and/or depression. The first manifestation may be nervousness, dizziness, headache, tremors, or temporary visual disturbances (blurred vision, blindness, double vision) followed by drowsiness, convulsions, unconsciousness and possibly life-threatening or fatal respiratory arrest. Since excitement may be transient or absent, the first manifestation may be drowsiness, sometimes merging into unconsciousness and rarely fatal respiratory arrest. Other CNS effects may be nausea, vomiting, chills, constriction of the pupils, or tinnitus. The **cardiovascular manifestations** of excessive plasma levels may include depression of the myocardium, cardiac arrhythmia, tachycardia, bradycardia, blood pressure changes (usually hypotension) and possibly fatal cardiac arrest.

Allergic reactions are characterized by cutaneous lesions (e.g., urticaria, edema, itching, reddening of the skin), nausea, diarrhea, wheezing respirations, acute asthmatic attacks, impaired consciousness and anaphylactic shock which may be life-threatening or fatal.

Overdose: The type of toxic reaction is unpredictable and depends on factors such as dosage, rate of absorption and clinical status of patient. These reactions call for extreme preparedness, symptoms occurring rapidly and with little warning.

Reactions due to systemic absorption are primarily of 2 types and related to stimulation and/or depression of the CNS.

Symptoms: CNS stimulation may include nervousness, dizziness, blurred vision, nausea, vomiting, tinnitus, tremor, generalized convulsions, hypertension with facial flushing and tachycardia.

CNS depression may include drowsiness, loss of consciousness, pallor, and dyspnea ranging to possibly fatal respiratory arrest.

Depression of cardiac and circulatory function can lead to cardiac arrhythmias, bradycardia, hypotension, cyanosis, cardiovascular collapse and possible fatal cardiac arrest.

Treatment: Toxic effects of local anesthetics require symptomatic treatment; there is no specific cure. 1) For all symptoms: resuscitate with oxygen 2) Circulatory collapse: immediately resuscitate with oxygen and maintain blood pressure with i.v. vasopressor agents; if cardiac arrest occurs, cardiac massage or external cardiac stimulation is indicated 3) Respiratory failure: resuscitate with oxygen, keep airway open and support respiration 4) Severe convulsions: the use of curare-like drugs, e.g. succinylcholine chloride, 40 mg, i.v. is preferred to i.v. administration of ultrashort-acting barbiturates, e.g. thiopental, 30 to 50 mg per minute, because of their depressant effect. I.V. muscle relaxants and barbiturates should only be administered by those familiar with their use.

Dosage: As with all local anesthetics, the dosage varies and depends upon the area to be anesthetized, the vascularity of the tissues, the number of neuronal segments to be blocked, individual tolerance and the technique of anesthesia. The lowest dosage needed to provide effective anesthesia should be administered. A test aspiration should always be performed before injection, in order to avoid intravascular injection. The pressure of the injection must be adapted to the sensitivity of the tissue. See Table I.

Table I—Ultracaine DS

Dosage

	Ultracaine DS Forte		Ultracaine DS	
Procedure	Volume (mL)	Total dose (mg)	Volume (mL)	Total dose (mg)
Infiltration	0.5–2.5	20–100	0.5–2.5	20–100
Nerve Block	0.5–3.4	20–136	0.5–3.4	20–136
Oral Surgery	1.0–5.1	40–204	1.0–5.1	40–204

It is recommended that the dosage should not exceed 7 mg/kg body weight in adults.

To date, Ultracaine has not been administered to children under 4 years of age, nor in doses greater than 5 mg/kg in children between the ages of 4 and 12.

Supplied: Ultracaine DS: Each cartridge contains: articaine HCl 4% with epinephrine 1/200 000. Nonmedicinal ingredients: sodium metabisulfite (0.50 mg/mL) as antioxidant and water for injection. Cartridges of 1.7 mL, boxes of 50.

Ultracaine DS Forte: Each cartridge contains: articaine 4% with epinephrine 1/100 000. Nonmedicinal ingredients: sodium metabisulfite (0.50 mg/mL) as antioxidant and water for injection. Cartridges of 1.7 mL, boxes of 50.

Store at room temperature, below 25°C. Protect from light. Do not freeze.

ULTRADOL™

Procter & Gamble Pharmaceuticals

Etodolac

Nonsteroidal Anti-inflammatory—Analgesic

Pharmacology: Etodolac is a nonsteroidal anti-inflammatory drug (NSAID) that exhibits anti-inflammatory analgesic and antipyretic properties in animal models. The pharmacological actions of etodolac are thought to be related to inhibition of prostaglandin biosynthesis at the site of inflammation.

Ultradol is a racemic mixture of R- and S-etodolac. As with other NSAIDs, it has been demonstrated in animals that the S-form is biologically active and the R-form is not. Both enantiomers are stable and there is no R-to-S conversion in vivo.

According to in vitro studies of human chondrocytes, etodolac may preserve collagen phenotype while still inhibiting prostaglandin (PGE_2) biosynthesis. The results demonstrated that normal chondrocyte function remained unaffected by etodolac, as assessed by the rate of DNA synthesis, proteoglycan synthesis, type II collagen production, and collagenase production. Etodolac maintained type II collagen synthesis and partially blocked the effects of interleukin-1 (IL-1). Nevertheless, PGE_2 synthesis was significantly decreased in the presence of etodolac. These results need to be verified through in vivo testing.

Pharmacokinetics: Etodolac is well absorbed following oral administration. The systemic availability of etodolac is at least 80%, and the drug does not undergo significant first-pass metabolism. The dose-proportionality based on AUC (the area under the plasma concentration-time curve) is linear following doses up to 600 mg every 12 hours. Etodolac is more than 99% bound to plasma proteins.

Mean peak plasma concentrations range from approximately 14±4 to 37±9 μg/mL after 200 to 600 mg single doses and are reached in 80±30 minutes. The mean plasma clearance of etodolac is 47(±16) mL/h/kg, and terminal disposition half-life is 7.3 (±4) hours (see Table I).

Table I—Ultradol

Etodolac Steady-State Pharmacokinetic Parameters (n=267)

Kinetic Parameters	Scientific Notation (units)	Mean±SD
Extent of oral absorption (bioavailability)	F (%)	≥80
Peak concentration time	t_{max} (h)	1.7±1.3
Oral-dose clearance	CL/F (mL/h/kg)	47±16
Central compartment volume	V_c/F (mL/kg)	132±47
Steady-state volume	V_{ss}/F (mL/kg)	362±129
Distribution half-life	$t_{1/2\alpha}$ (h)	0.71±0.50
Terminal half-life	$t_{1/2\beta}$ (h)	7.3±4.0

Etodolac is extensively metabolized in the liver, with renal elimination of etodolac and its metabolites being the primary route of excretion. Approximately 72% of the administered dose is recovered in the urine as the following, indicated as % of the administered dose: etodolac, unchanged 1%, etodolac glucuronide 13%, hydroxylated metabolites (6-, 7- and 8-OH) 5%, hydroxylated metabolite glucuronides 20% and unidentified metabolites 33%.

Fecal excretion accounted for 16% of the dose. Therefore, enterohepatic circulation, if present, is not extensive.

The extent of absorption of etodolac is not affected when it is administered after a meal or with an antacid. Food intake, however, reduces the peak concentration reached by approximately one-half, and increases the time-to-peak concentration by 1.4 to 3.8 hours. Coadministration with an antacid decreases the peak concentration reached by about 15 to 20%, with no measurable effect on time-to-peak.

In studies in the elderly, age was found to have no effect on etodolac half-life or protein binding, and there was no drug accumulation. Etodolac clearance was reduced by about 15%. Because the reduction in clearance is small, no dosage adjustment is generally necessary in the elderly on the basis of pharmacokinetics. The elderly may need dosage adjustment, however, on the basis of body size, and they may be more sensitive to antiprostaglandin effects than younger patients.

In studies of the effects of mild to moderate renal impairment, no significant differences in the disposition of total and free etodolac were observed. In patients undergoing hemodialysis, there was a 50% greater apparent clearance of total etodolac, due to a 50% greater unbound fraction. Free etodolac clearance was not altered, indicating the importance of protein binding in etodolac's disposition. Nevertheless, etodolac is not dialyzable. No dosage adjustment of etodolac is generally required in patients with mild to moderate renal impairment; however, etodolac should be used with caution in such patients because, as with other NSAIDs, it may further decrease renal function in some patients with impaired renal function.

In patients with compensated hepatic cirrhosis, the disposition of total and free etodolac is not altered. Although no dosage adjustment is generally required in this patient population, etodolac clearance is dependent on hepatic function and could be reduced in patients with severe hepatic failure.

Clinical Studies: Rheumatoid Arthritis and Osteoarthritis: Etodolac has been studied in double-blind, randomized, parallel-group, multicentre clinical trials in the treatment of rheumatoid arthritis and osteoarthritis. In rheumatoid arthritis studies, etodolac 200 mg twice a day was compared with naproxen 500 mg twice a day, piroxicam 20 mg once a day, or diclofenac 50 mg 3 times a day. In osteoarthritis studies, etodolac 200 mg 3 times a day was compared with diclofenac 50 mg 3 times a day, and etodolac 300 mg twice a day was compared with piroxicam 20 mg once a day, or naproxen 500 mg twice a day.

Results of these rheumatoid arthritis and osteoarthritis studies showed etodolac to be comparable to naproxen, piroxicam and diclofenac. Key efficacy parameters improved significantly ($p \leq 0.05$) in all treatment groups with no significant differences between therapies.

Analgesia: Clinical trials have demonstrated the effectiveness of etodolac when used as an analgesic. In well-controlled, double-blind, randomized, parallel, single-dose acute pain studies in 3 pain models (dental extractions, postgeneral surgery, and postepisiotomy pain), the onset of analgesia occurred approximately 30 minutes after oral administration with the peak effect occurring between 1 and 2 hours. The analgesic effective dose for etodolac established in these acute pain models was 200 to 400 mg. The duration of relief with these doses was generally 4 to 6 hours but persisted for up to 8 to 12 hours in some patients.

Special Studies: Etodolac was compared to other NSAIDs in studies focusing on gastrointestinal microbleeding, endoscopy, and gastroduodenal prostaglandin asseys. The clinical significance of these results is unknown.

In gastrointestinal microbleeding studies of healthy individuals, the GI blood loss observed with etodolac (600 mg to 1 200 mg/day) was similar to that seen with placebo and significantly less than that seen with ASA (2 600 mg/day), ibuprofen (2 400 mg/day), indomethacin (200 mg/day), or naproxen (750 mg/day). In a study of etodolac (600 and 1 000 mg/day) and piroxican (20 mg/day), gastrointestinal blood loss observed with etodolac was comparable with that seen with placebo and significnatly less than that seen with piroxicam.

With endoscopy studies in healthy volunteers, etodolac treatment (up to 1 200 mg/day) resulted in endoscopy scores which were similar to baseline and placebo, and significantly better than following treatment with ASA (3 900 mg/day), ibuprofen (2 400 mg/day), indomethacin (200 mg/day), or naproxen)1 000 mg/day). The effects of etodolac (600 mg to 1 200 mg/day) and diclofenac (150 mg/day) were not significantly different from each other or from baseline, as shown by endoscopy. Gastrointestinal microbleeding and endoscopy studies provide an objective measure of blood loss and lesions.

Prostaglandin assays of the gastroduodenal mucosa of patients with active rheumatoid arthritis were performed in a double-blind randomized study involving therapeutic doses of etodolac (600 mg/day) and naproxen (1 000 mg/day). Biopsies were taken at baseline and after 4 weeks of treatment. The results of this study indicate that etodolac does not appear to affect gastric or duodenal prostaglandin synthesis.

Indications: For acute or long-term use in the relief of signs and symptoms of rheumatoid arthritis and osteoarthritis (degenerative joint disease). Etodolac is also indicated for the short-term treatment of mild to moderate pain.

Contraindications: Active peptic ulcer, a history of recurrent ulceration or active inflammatory disease of the gastrointestinal system. Known or suspected hypersensitivity to the drug or other NSAIDs. The potential for cross-reactivity between different NSAIDs must be kept in mind.

Etodolac should not be used in patients with the complete or partial syndrome of nasal polyps, or in whom asthma, anaphylaxis, urticaria, rhinitis or other allergic manifestations are precipitated by ASA or other NSAIDs. Fatal anaphylactoid reactions have occurred in such individuals. As well, individuals with the above medical problems are at risk of a severe reaction even if they have taken NSAIDs in the past without any adverse effects.

Significant hepatic impairment or active liver disease. Severely impaired or deteriorating renal function (creatinine clearance <30 mL/min or <0.5 mL/sec). Individuals with lesser degrees of renal impairment are at risk of deterioration of their renal function when prescribed NSAIDs and must be monitored. Etodolac is not recommended for use with other NSAIDs because of the absence of any evidence demonstrating synergistic benefits and the potential for additive side effects.

Warnings: Gastrointestinal: Serious gastrointestinal toxicity, such as peptic ulceration, perforation and gastrointestinal bleeding, **sometimes severe and occasionally fatal** can occur at any time, with or without symptoms in patients treated with NSAIDs including etodolac.

Minor upper gastrointestinal problems, such as dyspepsia, are common, usually developing early in therapy. Physicians should remain alert for ulceration and bleeding in patients treated with NSAIDs, even in the absence of previous gastrointestinal tract symptoms.

In patients observed in clinical trials of such agents, symptomatic upper gastrointestinal ulcers, gross bleeding or perforation appear to occur in approximately 1 % of patients treated for 3 to 6 months and in about 2 to 4 % of patients treated for 1 year. The risk continues beyond 1 year and possibly increases.

The incidence of these complications increases with increasing dose.

In a 3-year double-blind, parallel group, multicentre study, evaluating the long-term effects of 300 mg/day and 1 000 mg/day etodolac vs ibuprofen in patients with rheumatoid arthritis, cumulative rates of less than 1 % for gastrointestinal ulcers and bleeding were reported in both the 300 mg/day and 1 000 mg/day etodolac groups compared to 4.74 % of patients in the 2 400 mg/day ibuprofen group over the 3-year study period.

Etodolac should be given under close medical supervision to patients prone to gastrointestinal tract irritation particularly those with a history of peptic ulcer, melena, diverticulosis or other inflammatory disease of the gastrointestinal tract such as ulcerative colitis or Crohn's disease. In these cases the physician must weigh the benefits of treatment against the possible hazards (see Contraindications and Adverse Effects).

Physicians should inform patients about the signs and/or symptoms of serious gastrointestinal toxicity and instruct them to contact a physician immediately if they experience persistent dyspepsia or other symptoms or signs suggestive of gastrointestinal ulceration or bleeding.

Because serious gastrointestinal tract ulceration and bleeding can occur without warning symptoms, physicians should follow chronically treated patients by checking their hemoglobin periodically and by being vigilant for the signs and symptoms of ulceration and bleeding and should inform the patients of the importance of this followup.

If ulceration is suspected or confirmed, or if gastrointestinal bleeding occurs, etodolac should be discontinued immediately, appropriate treatment instituted and the patient monitored closely.

No studies, to date, have identified any group of patients **not** at risk of developing ulceration and bleeding. A prior history of serious gastrointestinal events and other factors such as excess alcohol intake, smoking, age, female gender and concomitant oral steroid and anticoagulant use have been associated with increased risk.

Studies to date show that all NSAIDs can cause gastrointestinal tract adverse events. Although existing data does not clearly identify differences in risk between various NSAIDs, this may be shown in the future.

Geriatrics: Patients older than 65 years and frail or debilitated patients are most susceptible to a variety of adverse reactions from NSAIDs: the incidence of these adverse reactions increases with dose and duration of treatment. In addition, these patients are less tolerant to ulceration and bleeding. Most reports of fatal gastrointestinal events are in this population. Older patients are also at risk of lower esophageal ulceration and bleeding.

For such patients consideration should be given to a starting dose lower than the one usually recommended, with individual

Ultradol (cont'd)

adjustment when necessary and under close supervision. See "Precautions" for further advice.

Cross-sensitivity: Patients sensitive to any one of the NSAIDs may be sensitive to any of the other NSAIDs also.

Aseptic Meningitis: In occasional cases, with some NSAIDs, the symptoms of aseptic meningitis (stiff neck, severe headaches, nausea and vomiting, fever or clouding of consciousness) have been observed. Patients with autoimmune disorders (systemic lupus erythematosus, mixed connective tissues diseases, etc.) seem to be predisposed. Therefore, in such patients, the physician must be vigilant to the development of this complication.

Pregnancy, Labor and *Lactation:* The safety of etodolac during pregnancy and lactation has not been established and therefore, its use during pregnancy and lactation is not recommended.

In teratology studies, isolated occurrences of alterations in limb development were found and included polydactyly, oligodactyly, syndactyly, and unossified phalanges in rats and oligodactyly and synostosis of metatarsal in rabbits. These were observed at dose levels (2 to 14 mg/kg/day) close to human clinical doses. However, the frequency and the dosage group distribution of these findings in intial or repeated studies did not establish a clear drug- or dose-response relationship.

In rat studies with etodolac, as with other drugs known to inhibit prostaglandin synthesis, an increased incidence of dystocia, delayed parturition, and decreased pup survival occurred. The effects of etodolac on labor and delivery in pregnant women are unknown.

It is not known whether etodolac is excreted in human milk. Caution should be exercised if etodolac is administered to a nursing woman, because many drugs are excreted in human milk.

Children: The safety and effectiveness of etodolac in children have not been established and therefore, the drug is not recommended in this age group.

Precautions: Gastrointestinal: There is no definitive evidence that the concomitant administration of histamine H_2-receptor antagonists and/or antacids will either prevent the occurrence of gastrointestinal side effects or allow the continuation of etodolac therapy when and if the adverse reactions appear.

Renal Function: Long term administration of NSAIDs to animals has resulted in renal papillary necrosis and other abnormal renal pathology. In humans, there have been reports of acute interstitial nephritis with hematuria, proteinuria and occasionally nephrotic syndrome.

A second form of renal toxicity has been seen in patients with prerenal conditions leading to the reduction in renal blood flow or blood volume, where the renal prostaglandins have a supportive role in the maintenance of renal perfusion. In these patients, administration of a NSAID may cause a dose dependent reduction in prostaglandin formation and may precipitate overt renal decompensation. Patients at greatest risk of this reaction are those with impaired renal function, heart failure, liver dysfunction, those taking diuretics and the elderly. Discontinuation of nonsteroidal anti-inflammatory therapy is usually followed by recovery to the pretreatment state.

Etodolac and its metabolites are eliminated primarily by the kidneys; therefore, the drug should be used with great caution in patients with impaired renal function. In these cases, utilization of lower doses of etodolac should be considered and patients carefully monitored. During long-term therapy, kidney function should be monitored periodically.

Genitourinary Tract: Some NSAIDs are known to cause persistent urinary symptoms (bladder pain, dysuria, urinary frequency), hematuria or cystitis. The onset of these symptoms may occur at any time after the initiation of therapy with an NSAID. Some cases have become severe on continued treatment. Should urinary symptoms occur, treatment with etodolac **must be stopped immediately** to obtain recovery. This should be done before any urological investigations or treatments are carried out.

Hepatic Function: As with other NSAIDs, borderline elevations of one or more liver function tests may occur in up to 15% of patients. These abnormalities may progress, may remain essentially unchanged, or may be transient with continued therapy. Meaningful (3 times the upper limit of normal) elevations of ALT or AST occurred in controlled clinical trials with etodolac in approximately 1% of patients. A patient with symptoms and/or signs suggesting liver dysfunction, or in whom an abnormal liver test has occurred, should be evaluated for evidence of the development of more severe hepatic reaction while on therapy with this drug. Severe hepatic reactions including jaundice and cases of fatal hepatitis have been reported with NSAIDs. Although such reactions are rare, if abnormal liver tests persist or worsen, if clinical signs and symptoms consistent with liver disease develop, or if systemic manifestations occur (e.g., eosinophilia, rash, etc.), this drug should be discontinued.

During long-term therapy, liver function tests should be monitored periodically. If this drug is to be used in the presence of impaired liver function, it must be done under strict observation.

Fluid and Electrolyte Balance: Fluid retention and edema have been observed in patients treated with etodolac. Therefore, as with many other NSAIDs, the possibility of precipitating congestive heart failure in elderly patients or those with compromised cardiac function should be borne in mind. Etodolac should be used with caution in patients with heart failure, hypertension and renal diseases and in those recovering from surgical operations under general anesthesia and other conditions predisposing to fluid retention.

With NSAID treatment there is a potential risk of hyperkalemia, particularly in patients with conditions such as diabetes mellitus or renal failure, elderly patients or in patients receiving concomitant therapy with beta-adrenergic blockers, angiotensin converting enzyme inhibitors or some diuretics.

Serum electrolytes should be monitored periodically during long-term therapy, especially in those patients at risk.

Hematology: Drugs inhibiting prostaglandin biosynthesis do interfere with platelet function to varying degrees; therefore, patients who may be adversely affected by such an action should be carefully observed when etodolac is administered.

Blood dyscrasias (such as neutropenia, leukopenia, thrombocytopenia, aplastic anemia and agranulocytosis) associated with the use of NSAIDs are rare, but could be with severe consequences.

Anemia is commonly observed in rheumatoid arthritis and is sometimes aggravated by NSAIDs, which may produce fluid retention or minor gastrointestinal blood loss in some patients. Therefore, patients with initial hemoglobin values of 10 g/dL or less who are to receive long-term therapy, should have hemoglobin values determined frequently.

Infection: In common with other anti-inflammatory drugs, etodolac may mask the usual signs of infection.

Ophthalmology: Blurred and/or diminished vision has been reported with the use of etodolac and other NSAIDs. If such symptoms develop, this drug should be discontinued and an ophthalmologic examination performed; ophthalmic examination should be carried out at periodic intervals in any patient receiving this drug for an extended period of time.

CNS: Some patients may experience drowsiness, dizziness, vertigo, insomnia or depression with the use of etodolac. If patients experience these side effects, they should exercise caution in carrying out activities that require alertness.

Hypersensitivity: As with other nonsteroidal anti-inflammatory drugs, allergic reactions, including anaphylactic/anaphylactoid reactions, can occur without prior exposure to drug; therefore, careful questioning of patients for a history of asthma, nasal polyps, urticaria, and hypotension associated with NSAIDs before starting therapy is important.

Drug Interactions: ASA or other NSAIDs: When etodolac is administered with ASA, its protein binding is reduced although the clearance of free etodolac is not altered. The clinical significance of this interaction is not known; however, the use of etodolac in addition to any other NSAID, including those over the counter ones (such as ASA and ibuprofen), is not recommended due to the possibility of additive side effects.

Cyclosporine, Digoxin, Lithium, Methotrexate: Etodolac, like other NSAIDS, through effects on renal prostaglandins may cause changes in the elimination of these drugs leading to elevated serum levels of digoxin, lithium, and methotrexate and increased toxicity. Nephrotoxicity associated with cyclosporine may also be enhanced. Patients receiving these drugs who are given etodolac, or any other NSAID, and particularly those patients with altered renal function, should be observed for the development of the specific toxicities of these drugs (monitoring of plasma drug levels).

Anticoagulants: Numerous studies have shown that the concomitant use of NSAIDs and anticoagulants increases the risk of gastrointestinal adverse events such as ulceration and bleeding. Concomitant administration of warfarin and etodolac results in reduced protein binding of warfarin, but there is no change in the clearance of free warfarin. There is no significant difference in the pharmacodynamic effect of warfarin administered alone and warfarin administered with etodolac as measured by prothrombin time. Thus, concomitant therapy with warfarin and etodolac should not require dosage adjustment of either drug. However, in postmarketing experience there have been spontaneous reports of prolonged prothrombin times in etodolac-treated patients receiving concomitant warfarin therapy. As well, because prostaglandins play an important role in hemostasis, and NSAIDs affect platelet function, concurrent therapy of etodolac with warfarin requires close monitoring to be certain that no change in anticoagulant dosage is necessary.

Glyburide: Etodolac has no apparent pharmacokinetic or pharmacodynamic interaction when administered with glyburide.

Diuretics: Etodolac has no apparent pharmacokinetic interaction when administered with furosemide or hydrochlorothiazide, nor does etodolac attenuate the diuretic response of either of these drugs in normal volunteers. Etodolac, and other NSAIDs nevertheless, should be used with caution in patients receiving diuretics or who have cardiac, renal or hepatic failure (see Renal Function).

Antihypertensive Agents: NSAIDs can reduce the antihypertensive effect of propranolol and other β-blockers as well as other antihypertensive agents.

Glucocorticoids: Numerous studies have shown that the concomitant use of NSAIDs and oral glucocorticoids increases the risk of gastrointestinal side effects such as ulceration and bleeding. This is especially the case in older (>65 years of age) individuals.

Antacids: The concomitant administration of antacids has no apparent effect on the extent of absorption of etodolac. However, antacids can decrease the peak concentration reached by 15 to 20 % but have no detectable effect on the time-to-peak.

Phenytoin: Etodolac has no apparent pharmacokinetic interaction when administered with phenytoin.

Protein Binding: Data from in vitro studies, using peak serum concentrations at reported therapeutic doses in humans, show that the etodolac free fraction is not significantly altered by ibuprofen, acetaminophen, phenytoin, probenecid, indomethacin, chlorpropamide, glyburide, naproxen, glypizide or piroxicam.

In contrast, phenylbutazone causes an increase (by about 80 %) in the free fraction of etodolac. Although in vivo studies have not been done to see if etodolac clearance is changed by coadministration of phenylbutazone, it is not recommended that they be coadministered.

The following drug interactions have been identified for NSAIDs in general on the basis of their potential clinical significance: potassium supplements, insulin, bone marrow depressants, valproic acid, colchicine, nephrotoxic agents and platelet aggregation inhibitors.

These interactions have not been documented with all NSAIDs but have been reported for some NSAIDs and should be considered potential precautions to the use of any NSAID, especially with chronic administration.

Clinical Laboratory Tests: The urine of patients who take etodolac can give a false-positive reaction for urinary bilirubin (urorubin) due to the presence of phenolic metabolites of etodolac.

Diagnostic dip-stick methodology, used to detect ketone bodies in urine, has resulted in false-positive findings in some patients treated with etodolac. Generally, this phenomenon has not been associated with other clinically significant events. No dose-relationship has been observed.

Etodolac treatment is associated with a small decrease in serum uric acid levels. In clinical trials, mean decreases of 1 to 2 mg/dL were observed in arthritic patients receiving etodolac (600 to 1 000 mg/day) after 4 weeks of therapy. These levels then remained stable for up to 1 year of therapy.

Adverse Effects: The most common adverse reactions encountered with nonsteroidal anti-inflammatory drugs are gastrointestinal, of which peptic ulcer, with or without bleeding, is the most severe. Fatalities have occurred on occasion, particularly in the elderly.

Adverse reaction information for etodolac was derived from 2 629 arthritic patients treated with etodolac in double-blind and open-label clinical trials of 4 to 320 weeks in duration, 2 213 patients treated with etodolac in double-blind, single-dose analgesia clinical trials, and worldwide postmarketing surveillance studies in approximately 60 000 patients. Spontaneous postmarketing reports are also included.

In clinical studies, etodolac was generally well tolerated. Most adverse reactions were mild and transient. The discontinuation rate in controlled clinical trials because of adverse events, was 9% for arthritic patients and 0.6% for analgesic patients treated with etodolac.

Listed below are the patient complaints with an incidence of greater than, equal to, or less than 1% which occurred in clinical trials and postmarketing experience with etodolac at doses up to 1 000 mg/day.

Incidence ≥1%: Gastrointestinal: nausea, diarrhea, epigastric pain, heartburn, indigestion, flatulence, abdominal pain,

gastrointestinal cramps, abdominal distention, constipation, vomiting, dyspepsia, gastritis, melena.
CNS: headache, dizziness, drowsiness, insomnia, nervousness/anxiety, depression.
Dermatologic: dermatitis manifested as skin rash (erythematous, vesicular, maculopapular, morbilliform, petechial, or eczematous) or pruritus.
General Illness: fatigue, weakness/malaise, chills and fever.
Genitourinary: urinary frequency, dysuria, after-birth pain.
Metabolic: fluid retention/edema.
Eye, Ear, Nose and Throat: tinnitus, blurred vision.
Incidence < 1%: Gastrointestinal: dry mouth; peptic ulcer with/without gastrointestinal hemorrhage and/or perforation; hematemesis; rectal bleeding; stool changes (loose, with mucus, or increase in number and/or frequency); taste abnormalities including loss of taste; eructation; stomatitis (including ulcerative stomatitis); hepatitis (including cholestatic hepatitis); hepatic failure; intestinal ulceration; cholestasis; jaundice (including cholestatic jaundice); esophagitis with or without erosions or stricture or cardiospasm; colitis (including ischemic colitis); pancreatitis; duodenitis; enterocolitis, anorexia.
CNS: restlessness; confusion; vertigo; syncope; nightmares; listlessness; inability to concentrate, somnolence; paresthesia circumoral; emotional lability; hallucinations; minor hysteria; stupor; hypertonia.
Dermatologic: urticaria; angioedema; alopecia; sore, dry, inflamed or swollen mucous membranes including mouth, tongue, and lips; photosensitivity; peeling; easy bruising; brittle nails; exfoliative dermatitis; Stevens-Johnson syndrome, cutaneous vasculitis with purpura; erythema multiforme; hyperpigmentation; sweating; vesiculobullous rash.
Eye, Ear, Nose and Throat: hearing loss, visual disturbances including teichopsia; epistaxis; earache; pressure/throbbing in ears; burning sensation of eyes/nose; twinging behind eyes; photophobia; conjunctivitis; conjunctival ulcer; lacrimation disorders; edema of gums: gingivitis.
Extremities: paresthesias; muscle cramps; muscle pain; muscular fatigue; involuntary muscle movement; pain in arms/hands/shoulders/back; hand tremor, tenderness; s.c. nodulo/first metatarsophalangeal join; pain from fracture; heat at site of fracture; joint discomfort; myasthenia; myelitis.
General Illness: lethargy; vasculitis (including necrotizing and allergic); general deterioration; breast tenderness; infection; pain.
Genitourinary: dysuria; urinary urgency; hematuria; nocturia; vaginal bleeding; difficulty maintaining erection; recto-pubic pain; cystitis; leukorrhea; renal calculus; interstitial nephritis; papillary necrosis; renal insufficiency; renal failure; pyelonephritis; glomerulonephritis; uterine bleeding irregularities; rectal disorder; myomatous uterus; painful testicles; uterine cramps.
Metabolic: change in weight; change in appetite; flushing; excessive thirst; hot flashes; diaphoresis; elevated BUN; hyperglycemia in previously controlled diabetic patients; dehydration.
Cardiovascular: hypertension; congestive heart failure; palpitations; tachycardia; chest pain (costal, costochondral, or retrosternal); arrhythmias; myocardial infarction; and chest tightness or fullness; cerebrovascular accident; postural hypotension.
Respiratory: dyspnea; asthma; bronshospasm; hyperventilation; sneezing and sighing; bronchitis; pharyngitis; rhinitis; sinusitis.
Hypersensitivity: allergic/anaphylactic/anaphylactoid reaction; laryngeal edema.
Hematology: agranulocytosis; pancytopenia; decreased hemoglobin; decreased hematocrit; anemia; hemolytic anemia; thrombocytopenia; leukopenia; neutropenia; eosinophilia; atypical lymphocytes; increased bleeding time; ecchymosis.
Laboratory: elevated hepatic enzymes; increased serum creatinine.

Overdose: Symptoms: Symptoms following acute NSAID overdose are usually limited to lethargy, drowsiness, nausea, vomiting, and epigastric pain which are generally reversible with supportive care. Gastrointestinal bleeding can occur and coma has occurred following massive ibuprofen or mefenamic acid overdose. Hypertension, acute renal failure, and respiratory depression may occur, but are rare. Anaphylactoid reactions have been reported with therapeutic ingestion of NSAIDs, and may occur following overdose.

Treatment: Patients should be managed by symptomatic and supportive care following an NSAID overdose. There are no specific antidotes. Gut decontamination may be indicated in patients seen within 4 hours with symptoms or following a large overdose (5 to 10 times the usual dose). This should be accomplished via emesis and/or activated charcoal (60 to 100 g in adults, 1 to 2 g/kg in children) with an osmotic cathartic. Forced diuresis, alkalinization of the urine, hemodialysis or hemoperfusion would probably not be useful due to etodolac's high protein binding.

There have been infrequent reports of etodolac overdose. One case of intentional etodolac overdosage has been reported (Human Toxicol. 1988; 7: 203-204). This 53-year-old female ingested from 15 to 46 two hundred mg etodolac capsules (3 to 8.6 g). Plasma etodolac concentrations were measured frequently over the next 4 days. At 5 hours after ingestion (3 hours after gastric lavage) the plasma etodolac level was 22 μg/mL. These plasma levels and her subsequent recovery with no signs or symptoms of etodolac toxicity were consistent with systemic absorption of 600 to 800 mg. Her laboratory tests on admission showed a prolonged prothrombin time and a false-positive urine bilirubin (attributed to the phenolic etodolac metabolites).

Dosage: Rheumatoid Arthritis and Osteoarthritis: Adults: The recommended dosage of etodolac in the treatment of rheumatoid arthritis and osteoarthritis is 200 to 300 mg twice daily. Patients may also respond to single daily (400 or 600 mg) dose administered in the evening.
Geriatrics: As with any NSAID, caution should be exercised in treating the elderly, and when individualizing their dosage, extra care should be taken when increasing the dose because the elderly seem to tolerate NSAID side effects less well than younger patients. In otherwise healthy patients 65 years and older, no substantial differences in the side effects profile of etodolac were seen.
Analgesia: Adults: The usual recommended dose of etodolac in the treatment of short-term acute pain is 200 to 400 mg every 6 to 8 hours, as needed. For this indication, the maximum duration of treatment is 7 days. In some patients, adequate analgesic relief is provided with 12-hour dosing intervals.

The safety of doses in excess of 1 000 mg/day for extended periods has not been established. In order to maximize the effectiveness of therapy, the dosage must be individualized for each patient.

Information for the Patient: See Blue Section—Information for the Patient "Ultradol".

Supplied: 200 mg: Each light grey capsule with a wide red band printed "Ultradol 200"/dark grey with 2 narrow red bands, contains: etodolac 200 mg. Nonmedicinal ingredients: cellulose, lactose, magnesium stearate, povidone, sodium lauryl sulfate and sodium starch glycolate; capsule shell also contains black iron oxide, gelatin and silicon dioxide and titanium dioxide and may contain benzyl alcohol, butylparaben, carboxymethylcellulose sodium, edetate calcium disodium, methylparaben, propylparaben, sodium propionate and yellow iron oxide. Bottles of 100.

300 mg: Each light grey capsule with a wide red band printed "Ultradol 300" and 2 narrow red bands, contains: etodolac 300 mg. Nonmedicinal ingredients: cellulose, lactose, magnesium stearate, povidone, sodium lauryl sulfate and sodium starch glycolate; capsule shell also contains black iron oxide, gelatin and silicon dioxide and titanium dioxide and may contain benzyl alcohol, butylparaben, carboxymethylcellulose sodium, edetate calcium disodium, methylparaben, propylparaben, sodium propionate and yellow iron oxide. Bottles of 100.

Store at room temperature (25°C) and protect from moisture.

Reviewed 1999

ULTRAMOP™ Capsules ℞

Canderm Pharma

Methoxsalen

Melanin Repigmentation Photochemotherapy of Atopic Dermatitis and Psoriasis

Supplied: Each ivory-beige, soft gelatin capsule contains: methoxsalen USP 10 mg. Bottles of 100.

For comparative information on Corticosteroids: Inhaled, Topical, Systemic or Eye Ear Nose, see the CPhA General Monograph in the WHITE SECTION.

ULTRAMOP™ Lotion ℞

Canderm Pharma

Methoxsalen

Vitiliginous Lesion Repigmentation—Photochemotherapy of Psoriasis

Supplied: Each 25 mL amber glass bottle contains: methoxsalen topical solution USP 1%.

ULTRAQUIN™ Preparations

Canderm Pharma

Hydroquinone

Skin Bleacher

Supplied: Cream: Each tube contains: hydroquinone USP 4%, with sunblocks padimate O and oxybenzone USP in a nonmedicinal cream base. Tubes of 15 g.

Plain Cream: Each tube contains: hydroquinone USP 4% in a water washable, nonmedicinal cream base. Tubes of 15 g.

Gel: Each tube contains: hydroquinone USP 4%, with sunblocks padimate O and oxybenzone USP in a nonmedicinal alcoholic gel base. Tubes of 15 g.

ULTRASE®
ULTRASE® MT

Axcan Pharma

Pancrelipase

Digestive Enzymes

Pharmacology: Pancrelipase capsules are designed to prevent inactivation by gastric acid thereby resulting in the delivery of predictable, high levels of biologically active enzymes into the duodenum. The enzymes catalyze the hydrolysis of fats into glycerol and fatty acids, starch into dextrins and sugars, and protein into proteoses and derived substances.

Indications: For patients with partial or complete exocrine pancreatic insufficiency such as: cystic fibrosis, chronic pancreatitis, postpancreatectomy, postgastrointestinal bypass surgery (e.g., Billroth II gastroenterostomy), and ductal obstruction from neoplasm (e.g., of the pancreas or common bile duct).

Pancrelipase capsules are effective in controlling steatorrhea.

Contraindications: In patients known to be hypersensitive to pork protein.

Pancrelipase capsules are contraindicated in patients with acute pancreatitis or with acute exacerbations of chronic pancreatic diseases.

Warnings: Should hypersensitivity occur, discontinue medication and treat symptomatically.

Precautions: General: **To protect enteric coating, minitablets or microspheres must not be crushed or chewed.** Where swallowing of capsules is difficult, they may be opened and the minitablets or microspheres added to a small quantity of a soft food (e.g., applesauce, gelatin, etc.), which does not require chewing, and swallowed immediately. Contact of the minitablet with foods having a pH greater than 5.5 can dissolve the protective enteric shell.
Carcinogenesis, Mutagenesis, Impairment of Fertility: Long-term studies in animals have not been performed to evaluate carcinogenic potential. Methacrylic acid, a minor component of the methacrylic acid copolymer enteric-coating contained in Ultrase MT capsules, has been reported to act as a teratogen in rat embryo cultures. However, Ultrase MT capsules have been shown to contain < 0.001% of methacrylic acid, and the mammalian teratology studies in the rat and rabbit were negative.

The copolymer enteric-coating of Ultrase MT capsules was not mutagenic by the Ames test, and it did not produce chromosome damage in a test for unscheduled DNA synthesis in rat hepatocytes.
Pregnancy: Category C: Animal reproduction studies have not been conducted with pancrelipase. It is not known whether pancrelipase can cause fetal harm when administered to a pregnant woman or can affect reproduction capacity. Pancrelipase should be given to a pregnant woman only if the potential benefit outweighs the potential risk to the fetus.

Ultrase (cont'd)

Lactation: It is not known whether pancrelipase is excreted in human milk. Because many drugs are excreted in human milk, caution should be exercised when pancrelipase is administered to a nursing mother.

Adverse Effects: The most frequently reported adverse reactions to pancrelipase-containing products are gastrointestinal in nature. Less frequently, allergic-type reactions have also been observed.

Extremely high doses of exogenous pancreatic enzymes have been associated with hyperuricosuria and hyperuricemia when the preparations given were pancrelipase in powdered or capsule form, or pancreatin in tablet form.

In 2 clinical studies with Ultrase MT in 193 patients with cystic fibrosis, the adverse events described were all gastrointestinal in nature and may actually represent symptoms of the underlying disease, such as abdominal pain/cramps (5.7%), diarrhea (3.6%), and greasy stools and flatulence (1.5% each). In a postmarketing trial with another enteric-coated formulation, 160 adverse events occurred in the 15 711 patients (0.97%) evaluated. The most frequent events reported were diarrhea, skin reaction, and abdominal discomfort (0.2% each).

Colonic strictures have been reported in cystic fibrosis patients treated with both high- and lower-strength enzyme supplements. A causal relationship has not been established. The possibility of bowel stricture should be considered if symptoms suggestive of gastrointestinal obstruction occur. Since impaired fluid secretion may be a factor in the development of intestinal obstruction, care should be taken to maintain adequate hydration, particularly in warm weather.

''Fibrosing colonopathy'' is a term used to describe a condition seen in patients with CF who have taken high amounts of pancreatic enzyme supplements (>6 000 lipase U/kg/meal). At its most advanced, this condition leads to colonic strictures.

Dosage: The enzymatic activity of pancrelipase is expressed in USP units. Each capsule contains the labeled amount of lipase activity and an overage of not more than 25%.

The smallest effective dose should be used. Dosage should be adjusted according to the severity of the exocrine pancreatic insufficiency. Begin therapy with 1 or 2 capsules with meals or snacks and adjust dosage according to symptoms. The number of capsules or capsule strength given with meals and/or snacks should be estimated by assessing which dose minimizes steatorrhea and maintains good nutritional status.

Dosages should be adjusted according to the response of the patient. Where swallowing of capsules is difficult, they may be opened and the minitablets or microspheres added to a small quantity of a soft food (e.g., applesauce, gelatin, etc.), which does not require chewing, and swallowed immediately.

It is recommended that the total dose of pancrelipase being ingested for a meal or snack be dispersed equally (with fluids) before, during, and after the meal or snack.

Supplied: Ultrase: Each opaque white and opaque white capsule, printed ''ULTRASE'' and ''MS 4'' of enteric-coated microspheres contains: lipase 4 500 USP units, amylase 20 000 USP units and protease 25 000 USP units. Nonmedicinal ingredients: Eudragit L30D, neutral pellets, pancreatin, povidone, simethicone emulsion, talc and triethylcitrate. Bottles of 100.

Ultrase MT 12: Each white and yellow capsule, printed ''ULTRASE'' and ''MT 12'' of enteric-coated minitablets, contains: lipase 12 000 USP units, amylase 39 000 USP units and protease 39 000 USP units. Nomedicinal ingredients: cellulose microcrystalline, hydrogenated castor oil, iron oxides, magnesium stearate, silicone dioxide, simethicone, sodium carboxymethylcellulose, talc, titanium oxide, triethylcitrate and USP methacrylic acid copolymer (type C). Bottles of 100.

Ultrase MT 20: Each light grey and yellow capsule, printed ''ULTRASE'' and ''MT 20'' of enteric-coated minitablets, contains: lipase 20 000 USP units, amylase 65 000 USP units and protease 65 000 USP units. Nomedicinal ingredients: cellulose microcrystalline, hydrogenated castor oil, iron oxides, magnesium stearate, silicone dioxide, simethicone, sodium carboxymethylcellulose, talc, titanium oxide, triethylcitrate and USP methacrylic acid copolymer (type C). Bottles of 100.

(Shown in Product Recognition Section)

Reviewed 1997

For information on drug interactions and their management, see the CLIN-INFO SECTION.

ULTRAVATE™ Preparations ℞

Westwood-Squibb

Halobetasol Propionate

Topical Corticosteroid

Indications: Halobetasol cream and ointment are high to super-high potency topical corticosteroids indicated for the relief of inflammatory manifestations of resistant or severe psoriasis and corticosteroid-responsive dermatoses. These products are not recommended for use in children.

Contraindications: In patients who are hypersensitive to halobetasol, to other corticosteroids or to any of the ingredients in these products.

Halobetasol cream and ointment are contraindicated in viral diseases of the skin including herpes simplex, vaccinia and varicella. They are also contraindicated in untreated bacterial, tubercular and fungal infections involving the skin.

Warnings: *Pregnancy:* There are no clinical trials of halobetasol in pregnant women. Therefore, this product should be used during pregnancy only if the potential benefit justifies the potential risk to the fetus.

Corticosteroids have been shown to be teratogenic and embryotoxic in laboratory animals at low doses when administered systemically. Some corticosteroids have been shown to be teratogenic after topical application. Halobetasol has been shown to be teratogenic in rats and rabbits at low doses. The human topical dose of halobetasol was embryotoxic in rabbits.

Lactation: Systemically administered corticosteroids appear in human milk and can suppress growth, interfere with endogenous corticosteroid production, or cause other adverse effects. It is not known whether topical administration of corticosteroids could result in sufficient systemic absorption to produce detectable quantities in human milk. Because many drugs are excreted in human milk, caution should be exercised when administering halobetasol to a nursing woman.

Halobetasol cream or ointment is not to be used with occlusive dressing. These products are not formulated for ophthalmic use and should not be used in or near the eyes.

Halobetasol cream or ointment is for dermatological use only.

Precautions: General: In the presence of bacterial infections of the skin, an appropriate antibacterial agent should be used as primary therapy. If it is considered necessary, the topical corticosteroid may be used as an adjunct to control inflammation, erythema and itching. If a favorable response does not occur within a few days to a week, the steroid should be discontinued until the infection has been adequately controlled.

Significant systemic absorption may occur when steroids are applied over large areas of the body. To minimize this possibility, when long-term therapy is anticipated, interrupt treatment periodically or treat one area of the body at a time.

Halobetasol ointment produced HPA axis suppression when used at recommended doses of 7 g/day for 1 week in patients with psoriasis. These effects were reversible upon discontinuation of treatment.

Laboratory Tests: Patients receiving a large dose of a high potency topical steroid applied to a large surface area should be evaluated periodically for evidence of HPA axis suppression. This may be done by using the ACTH stimulation, A.M. plasma cortisol and urinary free-cortisol tests. Patients receiving super-potent corticosteroids should not be treated for more than 2 weeks at a time and it is recommended that only small areas be treated at any one time due to the increased risk of HPA suppression.

Prolonged use of topical corticosteroid products may produce atrophy of the skin and s.c. tissues. If this occurs, treatment should be discontinued.

Topical corticosteroids should be used with caution in patients with stasis dermatitis and other skin diseases associated with impaired circulation, hypersensitive patients and patients with glaucoma.

Patients should be advised to inform subsequent physician of the prior use of corticosteroids.

Carcinogenesis, Mutagenesis: Long-term animal studies have not been performed to evaluate the carcinogenic potential of halobetasol. Positive mutagenicity studies were observed in 2 genotoxicity assays. Halobetasol was positive in a Chinese hamster micronucleus test in vivo and in a mouse lymphoma gene mutation assay in vitro. In other genotoxicity tests including Ames/Salmonella assay, sister chromatid exchange test, chromosome aberration studies of germinal and somatic cells of rodents and mammalian spot test for point mutations, halobetasol was not found to be genotoxic.

Children: Halobetasol cream or ointment should not be used in children. Because of the higher ratio of skin surface area to body mass, children are at greater risk for HPA axis suppression, glucocorticoid insufficiency after withdrawal of treatment and Cushing's syndrome while on treatment.

Information for the Patient: Patients using halobetasol cream or ointment should receive the following information:

1. This medication is to be used as directed by the physician and should not be used longer than the prescribed time period. It is for external use only. Avoid contact with eyes.
2. The medication should not be used for any disorder other than for which it was prescribed.
3. The treated skin area should not be bandaged or otherwise covered or wrapped so as to be occlusive.
4. Any signs of local adverse reactions should be reported to your physician.

Adverse Effects: A total of 1 018 patients have been studied in halobetasol clinical trials, 596 received the ointment formulation, 341 received the cream formulation and 81 received both formulations. The incidence of adverse reactions with halobetasol cream and ointment were those commonly observed with topical corticosteroids.

The most frequently reported adverse reaction across all clinical trials with halobetasol was stinging (2%). Other adverse reactions related and probably related that were reported at less than 1% were: burning, erythema, acne, skin atrophy, pruritus, leukoderma, telangiectasia, pustulation, dry skin, bruise, rash, lichenified dermatitis, paresthesia, urticaria and fungal infection.

The most frequently reported adverse reaction across all clinical trials with halobetasol cream was also stinging (3%). Other adverse reactions related and probably related that were reported at less than 1% were: pruritus, burning skin, dry skin, leukoderma, erythema, skin atrophy, sore joint and eye pressure.

The following adverse skin reactions have been reported with the use of topical corticosteroids and may occur more frequently with high potency corticosteroids such as halobetasol cream and ointment. These reactions are listed in approximately decreasing order of occurrence: burning, itching, irritation, dryness, folliculitis, hypertrichosis, acneiform eruptions, hypopigmentation, perioral dermatitis, allergic contact dermatitis, maceration of the skin, secondary infection, skin atrophy, striae and miliaria. Systemic absorption of topical corticosteroids has produced reversible HPA axis suppression, manifestations of Cushing's syndrome, hyperglycemia and glucosuria in some patients. In rare instances, treatment (or withdrawal of treatment) of psoriasis with corticosteroids is thought to have provoked the pustular form of the disease.

Overdose: Symptoms and Treatment: Topically applied halobetasol can be absorbed in sufficient amounts to produce systemic effects including reversible HPA axis suppression with the potential for glucocorticosteroid insufficiency after withdrawal of treatment. If HPA axis suppression is noted, withdraw the drug gradually by reducing the amount and frequency of application. Recovery of HPA axis function is generally prompt and complete upon discontinuation of topical corticosteroids. Infrequently, signs and symptoms of glucocorticosteroid insufficiency may occur requiring supplemental systemic corticosteroids.

Dosage: Apply a thin layer of halobetasol cream or ointment to the affected skin and rub in gently and completely. Apply twice daily, or as directed by your physician. Treatment is to be discontinued when the dermatologic disorder is controlled.

Treatment with halobetasol cream or ointment should be limited to 50 g/week. The duration of therapy should not exceed 2 weeks without patient re-evaluation. Halobetasol cream and ointment are not to be used with occlusive dressing.

Information for the Patient: See Blue Section—Information for the Patient ''Ultravate''.

Supplied: Cream: Each g contains: halobetasol propionate 0.5 mg. Nonmedicinal ingredients: cetyl alcohol, diazolidinyl urea, glycerin, isopropyl isostearate, isopropyl palmitate, methylchloroisothiazolinone and methylisothiazolinone, steareth-21 and water. Aluminum tubes of 15 and 50 g. Store at controlled room temperature between 15 and 25°C.

Ointment: Each g contains: halobetasol propionate 0.5 mg. Nonmedicinal ingredients: beeswax, dehymuls E, petrolatum and propylene glycol. Aluminum tubes of 15 and 50 g. Store at controlled room temperature between 15 and 25°C.

ULTRAVIST®

Berlex Canada

Iopromide

Nonionic Iodinated Radiographic Contrast Medium

Pharmacology: Iopromide is a nonionic iodinated radiographic contrast medium which is available in 3 stable, ready-to-use solutions of different concentrations. Following intravascular injection, iopromide provides radiographic opacification of the vasculature and extracellular space allowing diagnostic assessment of the limbs and internal organs. For example, after i.v. injection, opacification of the renal parenchyma begins within 1 minute. Excretion of the contrast agent becomes apparent in 1 to 3 minutes with optimal contrast in the calyces and collecting system occurring between 5 and 15 minutes. In nephropathic conditions, particularly when excretory capacity has been altered, the excretion rate varies unpredictably and opacification may be delayed for several hours after injection.

Pharmacokinetics: The pharmacokinetics of iopromide are similar to those of other ionic and nonionic contrast media. Immediately following intravascular injection, iopromide reaches peak plasma concentrations and is then rapidly distributed throughout the extracellular fluid compartment. It is excreted unchanged by the kidneys mainly by glomerular filtration. About 90% of the injected dose is excreted unchanged by the kidneys during the first 24 hours with peak urine concentrations occurring in the first hour. In healthy volunteers, elimination half-life is approximately 2 hours and renal clearance is 93 ± 14 mL/min.

Iopromide does not cross the intact blood-brain barrier. It displays little tendency to bind to serum or plasma proteins, and there is no evidence of metabolism, deiodination or biotransformation in rats and humans.

In double blind clinical trials iopromide has shown diagnostic efficacy comparable to other nonionic and ionic radiographic contrast agents when studied in excretory urography (vs iopamidol, ioxithalamate, and ioxaglate); renal arteriography (vs amidotrizoate); cerebral arteriography (vs iopamidol); peripheral arteriography of the leg (vs ioxaglate); phlebography of the pelvis and leg (vs ioglicinate); coronary arteriography and ventriculography (vs iohexol and diatrizoate and amidotrizoate); and in computed tomography (vs ioglicinate). In these studies, iopromide has demonstrated properties comparable to other nonionic compounds with respect to neuroangiographic and cardiovascular tolerance and has demonstrated superiority over ionic agents particularly in causing less pain and warmth following injection.

The influence of iopromide on clotting, fibrinolysis, complement activation and erythrocyte morphology has been minimal (see Warnings).

Indications: For intravascular use to provide diagnostic information in a number of radiographic contrast procedures. It is also indicated for the visualization of various body cavities, e.g., arthrography and hysterosalpingography.

Ultravist 240: computed tomography (CT), peripheral arteriography (bifemoral pelvis/leg), phlebography of the extremities, cerebral arteriography, arthrography and hysterosalpingography.

Ultravist 300: computed tomography (CT), excretory urography, pediatric excretory urography, renal arteriography, peripheral arteriography (bifemoral pelvis/leg), cerebral arteriography, phlebography of the extremities and arthrography.

Ultravist 370: computed tomography (CT), excretory urography, coronary arteriography (including PTCA), with or without left ventriculography, pediatric angiocardiography and arthrography.

Contraindications: Iopromide is not indicated for use in myelography, cerebral ventriculography and cisternography.

Iopromide should not be administered to patients with known hypersensitivity to the drug, anuria or severe oliguria, clinically significant impairment of both renal and hepatic function or with manifest hyperthyroidism.

Hysterosalpingography must not be performed during pregnancy or in the presence of acute inflammatory process in the pelvic cavity.

Warnings: Nonionic iodinated contrast media inhibit blood coagulation less than ionic contrast media. Clotting has been reported in vivo and in vitro when blood remains in contact with syringes, catheters or tubes containing nonionic contrast media.

Serious, rarely fatal, thromboembolic events causing myocardial infarction and stroke have been reported during angiographic procedures with both nonionic and ionic contrast media. Therefore, meticulous intravascular administration technique is necessary, particularly during angiographic procedures, to minimize thromboembolic events. Numerous factors, including length of procedure, number of injections, catheter and syringe material, underlying disease state, and concomitant medication may contribute to the development of thromboembolic events. For these reasons, meticulous angiographic techniques are recommended including close attention to keeping guidewires, catheters and all angiographic equipment free of blood; use of manifold systems and/or 3-way stopcocks; frequent catheter flushing with heparinized saline solution; and minimizing the length of the procedure. The use of plastic syringes in place of glass syringes has been reported to decrease but not eliminate the likelihood of in vitro clotting. Nonionic contrast media are not suitable flush solutions.

Iopromide is related chemically to other tri-iodinated benzoic acid derivatives which have been associated with serious and fatal reactions. Therefore, clear indication and evaluation of the benefit/risk ratio for every patient should precede each examination with contrast media. Also, it is of utmost importance that adequate facilities and appropriate personnel be readily available and a course of action be planned in advance for the immediate treatment of any serious untoward reaction. Diagnostic procedures utilizing a radiopaque contrast agent should be conducted only by a physician with the requisite training and a thorough knowledge of the particular procedure to be performed. The physician must also be thoroughly familiar with the emergency treatment of all adverse effects.

Precautions: Before any contrast medium is injected, the patient should be questioned for a history of allergy (i.e., shellfish), sensitivity to iodine or to radiographic media and bronchial asthma, as the reported incidence of adverse reactions to contrast media are higher in patients with these conditions. Most adverse reactions to contrast agents appear within 30 minutes after the start of their injection, but a delayed reaction may occur. Premedication with corticoids may be considered in order to avoid or minimize possible allergic adverse reactions. However, antihistamines or corticosteroids should not be mixed in the same syringe with any contrast medium because of potential chemical incompatibility.

Caution is advised in patients with cardiac and circulatory insufficiency, hypertension, pheochromocytoma, cerebral arteriosclerosis, latent hyperthyroidism, severe impairment of hepatic or renal function, pulmonary emphysema, very poor general condition, diabetes with renal dysfunction requiring treatment, cerebral arterial spasm, bland nodular goiter and multiple myeloma, homocystinuria and other paraproteinemias and renal transplant.

An i.v. test dose of 0.5 to 1 mL of the contrast agent before injection of the full dose has been employed to predict severe or fatal reactions. These provocative tests may themselves cause severe, even fatal, reactions and are unreliable in predicting patients at special risk.

Renal function should be assessed before injecting iopromide since the drug is excreted largely by the kidney and may accumulate in the absence of normal renal function.

In patients with myeloma, diabetes mellitus, polyuria, oliguria or gout and in newborns, small children and in patients in poor general health, fluid intake should not be restricted even before the use of low-osmolar contrast media.

Assessment of thyroid function may be obscured for several weeks following the administration of iopromide.

Reports of thyroid storm after the intravascular use of iodinated radiopaque agents in patients with hyperthyroidism or with an autonomously functioning thyroid nodule suggest that this additional risk be evaluated in appropriate patients prior to the use of iopromide.

Administration of iopromide should be postponed in patients who have to undergo oral cholecystography.

Premedication with an α-blocker is recommended in patients having a pheochromocytoma because of the risk of hypertensive crises.

In patients with decreased renal function, 48 hours should elapse between 2 examinations. Special attention should be paid to patients with increased intracranial pressure, disrupted blood-brain barrier (tumor, meta supra-arachnoid hemorrhage, transient ischemic attack, cerebral thrombosis, ischemia) or any condition whereby the presence of contrast material in the vessels is prolonged. Serious neurological sequelae (stroke, aphasia, cortical blindness, convulsions) may occur following intra-arterial or intravascular infusion of contrast media. The benefit/risk ratio of the procedure has to be evaluated and the amount of contrast medium necessary to obtain a diagnostic picture kept to a minimum.

Iopromide should be administered intravascularly with caution to patients with known convulsive disorders.

Pregnancy: The safe use of iopromide during pregnancy has not been established. Therefore, it should not be used unless the benefits outweigh the risks.

Lactation: If the use of iopromide is considered necessary in a nursing mother, it is suggested to discontinue breast-feeding for 48 hours.

Geriatrics: Elderly patients may present a special risk in the use of radiographic contrast media. These patients may have compromised renal and cardiac function and may be taking medication (e.g., ß-blockers) which may make them more susceptible to the potentially harmful effects of procedures involving the use of contrast agents.

Intravascular Use: Iopromide produces less circulatory osmotic load than ionic contrast agents; however, it can produce significant hemodynamic disturbances especially in patients with reduced cardiac reserve. The volume of injection should be minimized and the patient's vital signs should be continuously monitored for several hours following the procedure to detect delayed hemodynamic disturbances. Hypotension should be corrected promptly as it can lead to serious arrhythmias. Special care regarding dosage should be observed in patients with right ventricular failure, pulmonary emphysema, pulmonary hypertension or a stenotic pulmonary vascular bed because serious hemodynamic changes may occur in these individuals.

Mesenteric necrosis, acute pancreatitis, renal shutdown and serious neurologic complications including spinal cord damage and hemiplegia have been reported following inadvertent injection of a large part of the aortic dose of an ionic contrast medium directly into an aortic branch or arterial trunk.

There are inherent dangers associated with catheter manipulation, contrast medium injection and angiographic procedures. Dislodging plaques or damaging, dissecting or perforating a vessel wall or causing injury to neighboring organs can lead to embolization. The possibility of these occurrences should be borne in mind during the procedure. Therefore, fluoroscope guidance is to be used to place the catheter.

Pulsation must be present in the artery to be injected. Extreme caution is therefore advised for the patients considered for angiography, particularly those suspected of having thromboangiitis obliterans (Buerger's disease), since vascular procedures may induce severe arterial spasm.

In intra-arterial administration, caution is advisable in patients with suspected thrombosis, ischemic disease, local infection, a totally obstructed vascular system or severe ischemia associated with ascending infection or advanced arteriosclerosis. With the use of conventional ionic contrast media, occasional serious neurologic complications, including paraplegia, have been reported in patients with aorto-iliac or femoral artery obstruction, abdominal compression, hypotension or hypertension and following the injection of vasopressors.

When large individual doses are administered, an appropriate time interval should elapse between injections to allow any hemodynamic disturbances to subside. Hemodynamic changes are likely to be more pronounced following repeated injections given in rapid succession.

Following arterial catheterization and injection, pressure hemostasis is advisable with immobilization of the limb for several hours to prevent hemorrhage from the site of arterial puncture.

Drug Interactions: Diabetic nephropathy may predispose to renal impairment following intravascular contrast media administration. Since biguanides may precipitate lactic acidosis in patients with renal impairment, they should be discontinued 48 hours prior to the contrast medium examination and reinstated only after adequate renal function has been regained.

The prevalence of delayed reactions (e.g., fever, rash, flu-like symptoms, joint pain and pruritus) to contrast media is higher in patients who received interleukins.

Treatment with β-blockers or general anesthesia increases the incidence of adverse reactions, particularly in people with asthma.

Ultravist (cont'd)

Adverse Effects: Adverse reactions reported with iopromide have generally been less frequent than with some commonly used iodinated compounds. However, all side effects and toxicity associated with this class of compound are possible during the use of iopromide.

Careful patient observation for adverse reactions is recommended in the use of all contrast media. Reactions accompanying use may vary with the dosage, the technique of administration, the procedure and the underlying condition of the patient. Adverse reactions generally occur within 30 minutes after injection but some may be delayed or of long-lasting nature. These reactions include: laryngospasm, bronchospasm, wheezing, dyspnea, and status asthmaticus; angioedema, subglottic edema and signs of airway obstruction; anaphylactic shock; cardiovascular collapse with peripheral vasodilation, hypotension, tachycardia, dyspnea, cyanosis, sweating, pallor, ventricular fibrillation and cardiac arrest; CNS stimulation or depression with agitation, convulsions, coma and death. Severe life-threatening reactions to iodinated contrast media require appropriate emergency measures.

Many life-threatening reactions begin with only mild symptoms such as nasal congestion, sneezing, watery eyes, skin erythema, or a vague sense of discomfort. It is therefore extremely important that all patients be watched closely until their symptoms have abated. The symptoms, which occur regardless of the amount of contrast medium administered and the mode of administration, can indicate incipient shock. Administration of the contrast medium must then be interrupted immediately and, if necessary, specific therapy initiated i.v. In the case of i.v. administration use of a flexible indwelling catheter is therefore recommended.

The most common adverse event following i.v. injection of iopromide is a sensation of warmth and/or pain especially in peripheral arteriography. This is generally less severe with iopromide than with ionic contrast media.

The list of adverse reactions and their incidence as shown in Table I is based on clinical studies of approximately 2 398 patients who have received iopromide.

Table I—Ultravist

Adverse Reactions

General Reactions		**Incidence (%)**
Warmth	(slight to moderate)	36.4
	(severe)	3.0
Pain	(slight to moderate)	6.1
	(severe)	0.4
Nausea/Vomiting/Diarrhea		2.3

Adverse Reactions Having an Incidence of <1%: Allergic/Cutaneous: urticaria (0.8%); respiratory symptoms (0.3%): sneezing, coughing, bronchospasm; angioedema and lip swelling (0.1%); Quinke's edema (0.1%).

Cardiovascular: hypotension (0.4%); tachycardia (0.3%); unconsciousness/collapse (0.3%); hypertension (0.1%); bradycardia (0.1%); extrasystoles (0.1%); left bundle branch heart block (0.1%); anginal symptoms (0.1%); arrhythmia (0.1%).

CNS: restlessness/anxiety (0.3%); paresthesia (0.2%): arm or face; vertigo (0.1%); blurred vision (0.1%).

Others: taste sensation (0.4%); headache (0.3%); knee swelling/pain (0.1%); shoulder pain (0.1%); venous pressure (0.1%); numbness (0.1%); shivers (0.1%); popliteal region tension (0.1%); pressure over eyes (0.1%); vegetative dystonia (0.1%); sore throat (0.1%); septicemia (0.1%); dizziness (0.1%).

The following additional adverse reactions have been reported postmarketing: allergic reactions, agitation, amnesia, anaphylactic and anaphylactoid reactions, blood pressure disturbances, cardiac arrest, cardiac rhythm or function disturbances, chills, confusion, conjunctivitis, convulsion, heart rate disturbances, cyanosis, dyspnea, fever, hearing disturbances, hypertonia, increased sweating, laryngeal spasm or edema, malaise, paralysis, paresis, photophobia, pruritus, renal impairment or failure, respiratory arrest, respiratory distress, rhinitis, shock, speech disturbances, Stevens-Johnson syndrome, thrombophlebitis, transient local pain and edema or local inflammation sometimes leading to tissue necrosis in the case of inadvertent paravascular administration, transient disturbances in respiratory rate, tremor, vasodilatation, venous thrombosis, vision disturbances.

Overdose: Symptoms and Treatment: An overdose of iopromide should be treated by support of vital functions and prompt institution of symptomatic therapy.

Dosage: General: Solutions of iopromide, like those of other radiopaque contrast agents, should be at or close to body temperature when injected. As with other sterile parenteral products, iopromide should not be withdrawn from the vial except immediately prior to use (see Warnings). Iopromide should not be mixed with other drugs. Any unused portion should be discarded.

Vials containing contrast medium solutions are not intended for the withdrawal of multiple doses. The rubber stopper should never be pierced more than once. The use of a cannula or needle with a long tip and a maximum diameter of 18 G is recommended for piercing the stopper and drawing up the contrast medium.

Patients should be in a fasted state (when this can be safely achieved) and adequately hydrated on the day of the examination. Disturbances of water and electrolyte balance must be corrected prior to the administration of iopromide.

In the case of abdominal angiography and urography, the diagnostic yield is increased if the bowels are empty of fecal matter and gas. It may be necessary to administer an enema or laxative in the evening prior to examination, provided purging of the bowels is not contraindicated.

However, in infants and young children, prolonged fasting, restriction of fluids and the administration of a laxative before the examination are contraindicated.

Experience shows that pronounced states of excitement, anxiety and pain can be the cause of side effects or intensified contrast medium-related reactions. They can be counteracted by calm management of the patients and the use of suitable drugs.

Intravascular administration of contrast media should, if possible, be done with the patient lying down. After the administration, the patient should be kept under observation for at least 30 minutes, since experience shows that the majority of all severe incidents occur within this time.

The recommended dosages of iopromide should not be exceeded. The volume of each individual injection is a more important consideration than the total dose used. When large individual volumes are administered, as in cardiac ventriculography, sufficient time should be permitted to elapse between injections to allow any hemodynamic disturbances to subside.

Excretory Urography: Adults: Recommended doses: Ultravist 300: 40 to 70 mL. Ultravist 370: 30 to 55 mL.

The dose may be adjusted in special indications (e.g., obese patients, impaired renal function), if necessary.

Children: The physiologically poor concentrating ability of the immature nephron necessitates the administration of relatively high doses of contrast medium in children.

The dose of Ultravist 300 should not exceed: Neonates: 4 mL/kg of body weight equivalent to 1.2 g I/kg. Infants: 3 mL/kg of body weight equivalent to about 1 g I/kg. Small Children: 1.5 mL/kg of body weight equivalent to about 0.5 g I/kg.

Computerized Tomography (CT): Cranial CT: The following doses are recommended and should not be exceeded: Ultravist 240: 105 to 175 mL. Ultravist 300: 70 to 140 mL. Ultravist 370: 70 to 105 mL.

Whole-body CT: In whole-body computerized tomography, the necessary doses of iopromide and the rates of administration depend on the organs under investigation, the diagnostic problem and, in particular, the different scan and image reconstruction times of the scanner. An infusion is preferred for slow scanners and a bolus injection, for fast scanners.

Recommended doses: Ultravist 240: 125 to 180 mL. Ultravist 300: 100 to 150 mL. Ultravist 370: 80 to 120 mL.

Angiography: The dosage depends on the age, weight, cardiac output and general condition of the patient, the clinical problem, examination technique, and the nature and volume of the vascular region to be investigated. The dosages in Table II may serve as a guide.

Arthrography: See Table III.

Intra-articular injections of contrast media should be monitored by fluoroscopy to ensure adequate injection technique and opacification while preventing over distention of the joint space. Excessive dilution of the contrast medium should be avoided.

Hysterosalpingography: Hysterosalpingographic contrast media should be instilled into the uterine cavity under controlled pressure with fluoroscopic monitoring of the dose to avoid excessive injection pressures and doses.

Usual recommended single dose of Ultravist 240 is 10 to 25 mL.

Table II—Ultravist

Dosage in Angiography

Procedure	**Ultravist Concentration (mg I/mL)**	**Usual Recommended Single Dose (mL/injection)**
Cerebral Arteriography		
Aortic arch angiography	300	40-80
Retrograde carotid angiography	300	30-40
Common carotid	300	6-12
Internal carotid	300	5-12
External carotid	300	4-8
Vertebral artery	300	6-10
Aortography		
Thoracic aortography	300	50-80
Abdominal aortography	300	40-60
Peripheral Angiography		
Selective arteriography	300	8-12
Aorto-femoral runoffs	300	40-80
Phlebography	240	60-100
	300	60-90
Angiocardiography		
Left ventriculography	370	30-60
Coronary arteriography	370	5-8

Table III—Ultravist

Dosage in Arthrography

Procedure	**Ultravist Concentration (mg I/mL)**	**Usual Recommended Single Dose (mL/injection)**
Knee	240	5-11
	300	5-11
	370	5-11

Supplied: See Table IV. **Ultravist 240** (iopromide 49.9%): Each mL of sterile, colorless to pale yellow aqueous solution contains: iopromide 499 mg equivalent to 240 mg of organically bound iodine. Nonmedicinal ingredients: calcium disodium edetate (EDTA), hydrochloric acid and tromethamine. Preservative-free. pH has been adjusted to 6.5 to 8 with hydrochloric acid. Vials of 50 and 200 mL.

Ultravist 300 (iopromide 62.3%): Each mL of sterile, colorless to pale yellow aqueous solution contains: iopromide 623 mg equivalent to 300 mg of organically bound iodine. Nonmedicinal ingredients: calcium disodium edetate (EDTA), hydrochloric acid and tromethamine. Preservative-free. pH has been adjusted to 6.5 to 8 with hydrochloric acid. Vials of 50, 100 and 150 mL.

Ultravist 370 (iopromide 76.9%): Each mL of sterile, colorless to pale yellow aqueous solution contains: iopromide 769 mg equivalent to 370 mg of organically bound iodine. Nonmedicinal ingredients: calcium disodium edetate (EDTA), hydrochloric acid and tromethamine. Preservative-free. pH has been adjusted to 6.5 to 8 with hydrochloric acid. Vials of 50, 100 and 200 mL.

Table IV—Ultravist

Physical Properties

	Ultravist 240	**Ultravist 300**	**Ultravist 370**
Iodine concentration (mg/mL)	240	300	370
Iopromide concentration (mg/mL)	499	623	769
Viscosity (mPa·s or cp)			
at 20°C	4.8	8.7	20.1
at 37°C	2.8	4.6	9.5
Osmotic Pressure at 37°C			
(MPa)	1.22	1.59	2.02
(atm)	12.1	15.7	19.9
Osmolality at 37°C (osm/kg H_2O)	0.48	0.61	0.77
Specific Gravity at 37°C	1.263	1.33	1.409

Store between 15 and 30°C and protect from light. It should be visually inspected and used only if clear and within the normal colorless to pale yellow range. Discard unused portions.

Reviewed 1998

UNIPHYL®
Purdue Frederick

Theophylline

Bronchodilator

Pharmacology: Theophylline relaxes bronchial smooth muscle (particularly when the muscles are constricted); produces vasodilation except in cerebral vessels; stimulates the CNS including the respiratory center; stimulates cardiac muscle; produces diuresis and increases gastric acid secretion. In addition to its activity as a bronchodilator, theophylline may also stimulate mucociliary clearance, inhibit anaphylactic mediator release, suppress mediator induced inflammation and improve contractility of the diaphragm.

Uniphyl tablets are a sustained release formulation of theophylline. The release system consists of a homogeneous matrix of aliphatic alcohol, cellulose, and active drug. The proportion of these components in the formulation has been chosen to provide gradual, measured release of theophylline by diffusion through the tablet matrix and dissolution. The rate of release of active drug is dependent upon the drug's partition coefficients between the components of the tablet matrix and the aqueous phase within the gastrointestinal tract. The controlled release of theophylline from these tablets has been demonstrated by both dissolution and pharmacokinetic studies.

Theophylline's mechanism of action is not fully known and evidence exists indicating that phosphodiesterase inhibition, prostaglandin inhibition, effects on calcium flux and intracellular calcium distribution, and antagonism of endogenous adenosine may all contribute to its pharmacological effects.

Theophylline is usually well absorbed from the gastrointestinal tract, although there are some differences in the pharmacokinetic behavior of various sustained release formulations. Theophylline distributes to all body compartments and is approximately 50% protein bound. Elimination is primarily by hepatic biotransformation with approximately 50% excreted as 1,3-dimethyluric acid. Unchanged theophylline, 3-methylxanthine and 1-methyluric acid each account for 10% to 15% and 1-methylxanthine is excreted in smaller amounts.

The generally accepted optimal therapeutic serum theophylline concentrations are 10 to 20 mg/L (55 to 110 μmol/L). Levels above 20 mg/L (110 μmol/L) are usually associated with toxic reactions. The pharmacokinetics of theophylline are influenced by a number of variables such as age, concomitant medications, disease state and smoking (see Precautions). Therefore, each patient's optimal therapeutic maintenance dosage should be determined by individual titration.

At steady state, Uniphyl tablets taken once daily produce peak theophylline levels between 8 and 12 hours post-dose, and trough levels almost always occur at the time of dosing. During once-daily dosing, the mean fluctuation between peak and trough theophylline levels is 130%.

$$\% \text{ Fluctuation} = \frac{C_{max} - C_{min}}{C_{min}} \times 100$$

Indications: The symptomatic treatment of reversible bronchoconstriction associated with bronchial asthma, chronic obstructive pulmonary emphysema, chronic bronchitis and related bronchospastic disorders.

Contraindications: Should not be administered to patients with hypersensitivity to xanthines, to patients with coronary artery disease where cardiac stimulation might prove harmful, or to patients with active peptic ulcer.

Warnings: In clinical situations where immediate bronchodilation is required, such as status asthmaticus, Uniphyl tablets (a sustained release preparation) are not appropriate.

Theophylline has a narrow therapeutic index, the margin of safety above therapeutic doses is small.

Whenever signs of intolerance to theophylline develop, the therapy should be reassessed.

Theophylline clearance can be affected by various disease states, the age of the patient, concomitant use of other medication and lifestyle habits (see Precautions).

Children: A dosage schedule in the pediatric population has not been established. Use in children under 12 years of age is not recommended.

Precautions: General: There is a marked variation in serum levels achieved in different patients given the same dose of theophylline. Therefore, high serum levels may occur in some patients receiving doses considered to be conventional. The possibility of theophylline overdose should always be considered. Overdoses of theophylline may cause serious side effects such as tachycardia, arrhythmias, seizures, vascular collapse and even death. These may occur without warning and may not be preceded by less severe side effects such as nausea or restlessness.

The variability in serum levels is primarily due to differences in the rate of metabolism. Therefore, it is advisable to individualize the dosage regimen. Ideally, all patients should have serum theophylline levels measured which would enable doses and dosing regimens to be tailored for each patient in order to maintain therapeutic levels, ensure optimal clinical response and avoid toxicity. The incidence of adverse reactions increases at theophylline levels greater than 15 mg/L (82.5 μmol/L) and levels above 20 mg/L (110 μmol/L) are usually quite toxic in most adults.

Although Uniphyl tablets have pharmacokinetic properties similar to other sustained release theophylline formulations, it is not possible to ensure interchangeability between different formulations. Careful clinical monitoring is required when changing from one formulation to another. The equivalent content of anhydrous theophylline is the active ingredient that determines the blood concentration and clinical response. If a change in theophylline product is made and it involves a change in anhydrous theophylline equivalence, the dose should be adjusted accordingly.

Patients with Special Diseases and Conditions: Theophylline clearance is decreased, which may result in increased serum levels and resultant toxicity in patients: with impaired liver or kidney function; over 55 years of age, particularly males and those with chronic lung disease; with cardiac failure from any cause; with active influenza or other viral disease or after influenza immunization; with a high carbohydrate, low protein diet; patients taking certain drugs such as cimetidine, ciprofloxacin, norfloxacin, erythromycin and troleandomycin.

Laboratory monitoring of serum theophylline levels is especially appropriate in the above individuals in order to maintain the appropriate theophylline dosage.

Patients who are rapid metabolizers of theophylline, such as the young, smokers and some nonsmoking adults may not be suitable candidates for once-daily dosing. In rapid metabolizers, peak to trough fluctuations in theophylline levels may be greater than desirable or result in side effects at the time of maximum levels and/or the recurrence of symptoms toward the end of the 24 hour dose interval when levels are lowest. In such patients, dividing the total daily theophylline dose into 2 equal doses may be indicated.

Theophylline is known to stimulate gastric acid secretion and may also act as a local gastrointestinal irritant. Therefore, the drug should only be used with caution in patients with a history of peptic ulcer disease.

Theophylline may cause arrhythmia and/or worsen preexisting arrhythmia. Any significant change in rate and/or rhythm warrants monitoring and further investigation.

Many patients who require theophylline may exhibit tachycardia due to their underlying disease process so that the cause/effect relationship to elevated serum theophylline concentrations may not be appreciated.

Use with caution in patients with severe cardiac disease, severe hypoxemia, hypertension, hyperthyroidism, acute myocardial injury, cor pulmonale, congestive heart failure, liver disease, in the elderly (especially males).

Drug Interactions: Theophylline pharmacokinetics are altered by the concurrent use of various drugs as listed in Table I.

Table I—Uniphyl

Effect of Various Drugs on Theophylline Pharmacokinetics

Drug	Effect on theophylline clearance and elimination half-life
Cimetidine, propranolol, allopurinol, macrolide antibiotics (erythromycin, troleandomycin), quinolone antibacterials (ciprofloxacin, norfloxacin), oral contraceptives	↑ T½, ↓ clearance
Alkalinizing agents	↑ T½, ↓ clearance
Influenza vaccine	↑ T½, ↓ clearance reported to be decreased or no change
Phenytoin, barbiturates, carbamazepine, isoproterenol, rifampin	↓ T½, ↑ clearance
Tobacco	↓ T½, ↑ clearance
Acidifying agents	↓ T½, ↑ clearance

Concurrent use of theophylline influences the actions of certain drugs (see Table II).

Table II—Uniphyl

Effect of Theophylline on Certain Drugs

Drug	Influence of theophylline
Digitalis glycosides	↑ cardiac effect
Thiazides	↑ diuresis
Nephrotoxic drugs	↑ nephrotoxicity
Lithium	↑ ratio of lithium/creatinine clearance, thus a decrease in serum lithium levels
Sympathomimetic amines	↑ toxicity ↑ CNS stimulation
Coumarin anticoagulants	↓ anticoagulant activity ↑ prothrombin and fibrinogen blood concentrations ↓ prothrombin time
Allopurinol	↓ antihyperuricemic action
Probenecid and pyrazolon derivatives	↓ uricosuric action

Pregnancy and *Lactation:* Theophylline crosses the placental barrier and also passes freely into breast milk, where concentrations are similar to plasma levels. Safe use in pregnancy has not been established relative to possible adverse effects on fetal development, but neither have adverse effects on fetal development been established. Therefore, use of theophylline in pregnant women and nursing mothers should be balanced against the risk of uncontrolled asthma.

Laboratory Test Interactions: When plasma levels are measured by spectrophotometric methods, coffee, tea, cola beverages, chocolate and acetaminophen contribute to falsely high values.

When high pressure liquid chromatography (HPLC) method is used, plasma theophylline concentration may be falsely increased by caffeine, some cephalosporins and sulfa medications.

Theophylline may cause elevation of urine catecholamines, plasma uric acid and free fatty acids.

Food Interaction: When immediate release theophylline formulations are administered with food, the rate of absorption is reduced but absorption remains complete. Various sustained release formulations, because of differences in their release mechanisms, may be affected in different ways by concomitant food intake.

Studies have shown that Uniphyl tablets are more completely absorbed when taken with food as opposed to under fasting conditions.

Adverse Effects: The most common adverse reactions are gastric irritation, nausea, vomiting, epigastric pain, and tremor. These are usually early signs of toxicity, however, with high doses ventricular arrhythmias or seizures may be the first signs to appear.

Gastrointestinal: nausea, vomiting, epigastric pain, hematemesis, diarrhea, anorexia, intestinal bleeding and reactivation of peptic ulcer.

CNS: headache, irritability, restlessness, insomnia, twitching, convulsions and reflex hyperexcitability.

Cardiovascular: palpitations, tachycardia, hypotension, circulatory failure, ventricular arrhythmias, extrasystoles and flushing.

Renal: albuminuria, diuresis and hematuria.

Other: hyperglycemia, tachypnea and inappropriate ADH syndrome.

Overdose: Symptoms: Insomnia, restlessness, mild excitement or irritability and rapid pulse are the early symptoms, which may progress to mild delirium. Sensory disturbances such as tinnitus or flashes of light are common. Anorexia, nausea and vomiting are also frequently early observations of theophylline overdosage.

Fever, diuresis, dehydration and extreme thirst may be seen. Severe overdosage results in bloody, syrup-like "coffeeground" vomitus, tremors, tonic extensor spasm interrupted by clonic convulsions, extrasystoles, quickened respiration, stupor and finally coma.

Cardiovascular disorders and respiratory collapse, leading to shock, cyanosis and death follow gross overdosages.

Treatment: Monitoring Serum Theophylline Levels: It is important to note that, following the intake of Uniphyl tablets, the peak theophylline levels may not occur until 8 to 12 hours post ingestion. Moreover, patients ingesting overdoses of sustained release theophylline formulations may also

Uniphyl (cont'd)

have, after the initial rise in the blood theophylline, a secondary increase in theophylline levels (1 report on lethal self-poisoning has attributed this to compacted tablets in the gastrointestinal tract). **Following initial treatment, longer careful clinical and laboratory monitoring is advisable after patients' stabilization.**

If a potential oral overdose is established and a seizure has not occurred, induce emesis. Administer a cathartic (this is particularly important when a sustained release preparation has been taken). Administer activated charcoal.

If patient is having a seizure, establish an airway. Administer oxygen. Treat the seizure with i.v. diazepam, 0.1 to 0.3 mg/kg up to 10 mg. Monitor vital signs, maintain blood pressure and provide adequate hydration.

Post Seizure Coma: Maintain airway and oxygenation. If a result of oral medication, follow the above recommendations to prevent absorption of the drug, but intubation and lavage will have to be performed instead of inducing emesis and the cathartic and charcoal will need to be introduced via a large bore gastric lavage tube. Continue to provide full supportive care and adequate hydration while waiting for the drug to be metabolized. In general, the drug is metabolized sufficiently rapidly so as not to warrant consideration of dialysis. However, if serum levels exceed 50 mg/L (275 μmol/L) charcoal hemoperfusion may be indicated.

Dosage: Administration and dosing of theophylline should be individualized in respect of the patient's clinical response and serum theophylline levels. There is considerable patient-to-patient variation in the daily theophylline dose required to achieve therapeutic and safe levels. Ideally, all patients should have serum theophylline levels measured which would enable doses and dosing regimens to be tailored in order to maintain therapeutic levels, ensure optimal clinical response and avoid toxicity. Therapeutic serum levels are generally considered to be between 10 and 20 mg/L (55 and 110 μmol/L). Dosage calculations should be based on lean body mass (ideal body weight). A serum level of 20 mg/L (110 μmol/L) is an important reference point in terms of toxicity (see Precautions).

Initial Adult Dose: For patients not currently receiving oral theophylline, the recommended initial dose is 400 to 600 mg once daily.

In patients currently controlled on oral theophylline, Uniphyl therapy should start at the same daily theophylline dosage (mg for mg basis) provided by the previous formulation. For example, a patient receiving 400 mg twice daily (800 mg daily dosage) would be given two 400 mg Uniphyl tablets once daily. A minimum of 12 hours should elapse between a patient's last dose of the previous oral theophylline formulation and the first dose of Uniphyl.

It is recommended that once daily Uniphyl be taken in the evening. Studies have demonstrated that while the bioavailability and pharmacokinetics of Uniphyl tablets were not significantly different between morning and evening dosing, a better clinical response was obtained with evening dosing. Subsequent studies indicate that the clinical advantages of evening dosing are likely a result of the maximum theophylline levels occurring in the early morning hours, a time of greatest bronchoconstriction and symptoms for many asthmatics.

It is advisable that Uniphyl be taken **with** food, or within 1 to 2 hours of mealtime, as studies have suggested that absorption may be incomplete if taken under conditions of prolonged fasting.

Overall, therefore, it is recommended that most patients should take once daily Uniphyl with, or shortly following, the evening meal.

Dose Titration: Dosage adjustments should be based on the patient's clinical response and/or serum theophylline levels, with increases of ½ tablet/day at 3 to 4 day intervals. Individual requirements vary considerably, therefore, the physician should be prepared to adjust each patient's dose. Do not attempt to maintain any dosage that is poorly tolerated.

Monitoring serum theophylline levels is important, especially during initiation of therapy and dosage adjustment. For serum levels to be most useful, it is important that the patient not have missed or added any doses during the previous 3 days and that the dose intervals remained relatively constant. At steady state, Uniphyl tablets produce peak theophylline levels between 8 and 12 hours post-dose, and trough levels almost always occur at the time of dosing. During once daily dosing, the mean fluctuation between peak and trough theophylline levels is 130%.

The generally accepted optimal therapeutic range is 10 to 20 mg/L (55 to 110 μmol/L), although some patients obtain a very good bronchodilator effect from serum levels less than 10 mg/L (55 μmol/L). In cases where it is not possible to monitor theophylline levels, patients should be closely observed for signs of toxicity and dosages greater than 13 mg/kg/day (or 900 mg/day, whichever is less) should not be given.

Uniphyl tablets should not be chewed or crushed, they may be halved.

Information for the Patient: See Blue Section—Information for the Patient "Uniphyl".

Supplied: 400 mg: Each round, flat-faced, white, scored tablet, engraved $\frac{U}{400}$ on one side and PF on the reverse, contains: theophylline 400 mg sustained release. Nonmedicinal ingredients: cetostearyl alcohol, hydroxyethyl cellulose, magnesium stearate, povidone and talc. Sodium- and tartrazine-free.

600 mg: Each capsule-shaped, concave-faced, white, scored tablet, engraved U 600 on one side and PF on the reverse, contains: theophylline 600 mg sustained release. Nonmedicinal ingredients: cetostearyl alcohol, hydroxyethyl cellulose, magnesium stearate, povidone and talc. Sodium- and tartrazine-free.

Opaque plastic bottles of 50. Dispense in amber or opaque containers. Store at room temperature, below 30°C.

(Shown in Product Recognition Section)

UNIVOL®
Carter Horner

Magnesium Hydroxide—Aluminum Hydroxide
Antacid

Indications: For the symptomatic relief of hyperacidity associated with peptic ulcer, gastritis, esophagitis, heartburn or hiatal hernia.

Contraindications: Not to be given to patients who are severely debilitated or suffering from renal failure. Alkalosis, hypermagnesemia.

Warnings: Do not take more than 80 mL during a 24-hour period. Do not take the maximum dosage for more than 2 weeks or if symptoms recur, unless directed by a physician. Do not take if you suffer from kidney disease, except under your physician's advice. Antacids can interfere with the absorption of iron preparations and/or tetracyclines.

Precautions: Avoid concomitant use with tetracycline antibiotics and/or iron preparations. Do not take within 2 hours of another medicine because the effectiveness of the other medicine may be altered.

Overdose: Symptoms: In the presence of renal insufficiency, accumulation of magnesium in circulation may cause CNS depression. Chronic ingestion may lead to phosphorus deficiency in presence of low phosphorus diet.

Treatment: Symptomatic.

Dosage: Adults: 10 to 20 mL taken 4 times daily as needed between meals and at bedtime or as directed.

Supplied: Each 5 mL of opaque, white suspension with a mint flavor and a peppermint and spearmint odor (pH: 7.3 to 8.5) contains: aluminum hydroxide 165 mg (as aluminum hydroxide compress gel), magnesium hydroxide 200 mg. Nonmedicinal ingredients: alcohol, calcium cyclamate, flavor, guar gum, hydrogen peroxide, parabens, simethicone and sorbitol. Alcohol: 1%. Energy: 9.6 kJ (2.3 kcal). Sodium: <1 mmol (1 mg). Gluten-, sucrose- and tartrazine-free. Bottles of 350 mL. Protect from freezing.

URASAL®
Carter Horner

Hexamine
Urinary Antiseptic

Indications: Mild and chronic urinary tract infections, especially cystitis, prostatitis, urethritis.

Overdose: Symptoms: Nausea, anorexia, pain on urination.

Treatment: Gastric lavage or emesis. In children, induce emesis and if there is no immediate response, use gastric lavage. No known antidote.

Dosage: 2 level teaspoonfuls in 240 mL of water 3 times a day before meals, or as prescribed.

Supplied: Each 2 level teaspoonfuls (approximately 10 g) of fine, white, effervescent granules contain: hexamine 500 mg. Nonmedicinal ingredients: silicon dioxide, sodium bicarbonate, sodium cyclamate and tartaric acid. Sodium: 6.2 mmol (145 mg). Gluten- and tartrazine-free. Bottles of 255 g.

URECHOLINE® Pr
Frosst

Bethanechol Chloride
Parasympathomimetic Agent

Pharmacology: Bethanechol acts principally by producing the effects of stimulation of the parasympathetic nervous system. It increases the tone of the detrusor urinae muscle, usually producing a contraction sufficiently strong to initiate micturition and empty the bladder. It stimulates gastric motility, increases gastric tone, and often restores rhythmic peristalsis.

Stimulation of the parasympathetic nervous system releases acetylcholine at the nerve endings. When spontaneous stimulation is reduced and therapeutic intervention is required, acetylcholine can be given, but it is rapidly hydrolyzed by cholinesterase, and its effects are transient. Bethanechol is not destroyed by cholinesterase and its effects are more prolonged and predictable than those of acetylcholine.

It has predominant muscarinic action and only feeble nicotinic action. Doses that stimulate micturition and defecation and increase peristalsis do not ordinarily stimulate ganglia or voluntary muscles. Therapeutic test doses in normal human subjects have little effect on heart rate, blood pressure, or peripheral circulation.

Indications: The treatment of acute postoperative and postpartum nonobstructive (functional) urinary retention and for neurogenic atony of the urinary bladder with retention.

As adjunctive therapy in the treatment of gastroesophageal reflux with pyrosis unresponsive to conventional therapy.

Contraindications: Hypersensitivity to bethanechol or to any component of the injection. Hyperthyroidism, pregnancy, lactation, peptic ulcer, latent or active bronchial asthma, pronounced bradycardia or hypotension, vasomotor instability, coronary artery disease, epilepsy, and parkinsonism.

Should not be employed when the strength or integrity of the gastrointestinal or bladder wall is in question, or in the presence of mechanical obstruction; when increased muscular activity of the gastrointestinal tract or urinary bladder might prove harmful, as following recent urinary bladder surgery, gastrointestinal resection and anastomosis, or when there is possible gastrointestinal obstruction; in bladder neck obstruction, spastic gastrointestinal disturbances, acute inflammatory lesions of the gastrointestinal tract, or peritonitis; or in marked vagotonia.

Precautions: The sterile solution is for s.c. use only. It should never be given i.m. or i.v. Violent symptoms of cholinergic over-stimulation, such as circulatory collapse, fall in blood pressure, abdominal cramps, bloody diarrhea, shock, or sudden cardiac arrest are likely to occur if the drug is given by either of these routes. Although rare, these same symptoms have occurred after s.c. injection, and may occur in cases of hypersensitivity or overdosage.

Special care is required when bethanechol is given to patients receiving ganglion blocking compounds because a critical fall in blood pressure may occur. Usually, severe abdominal symptoms appear before there is such a fall in the blood pressure.

In urinary retention, if the sphincter fails to relax as bethanechol contracts the bladder, urine may be forced up the ureter into the kidney pelvis. If there is bacteriuria, this may cause reflux infection.

Adverse Effects: Abdominal discomfort, salivation, flushing of the skin ("hot feeling"), sweating.

Large doses more commonly result in effects of parasympathetic stimulation, such as malaise, headache, sensation of heat about the face, flushing, colicky pain, diarrhea, nausea and belching, abdominal cramps, borborygmi, asthmatic attacks, and fall in blood pressure.

Atropine is a specific antidote. A syringe containing a dose, for adults, of 0.6 mg of atropine sulfate should always be available to treat symptoms of toxicity. Use proportionately smaller amounts for children. S.C. injection is preferred except in emergencies when the i.v. route may be employed.

Overdose: Symptoms: Overdosage, i.v., i.m. administration and hypersensitivity to the drug can cause violent symptoms of cholinergic over-stimulation including fall in blood pressure, circulatory collapse, cardiac arrest, shock, severe abdominal cramps with bloody diarrhea and possibly severe bronchospasm.

Treatment: Atropine is a specific antidote. Use a dose of 0.6 mg for adults and proportionately smaller doses for children. S.C. injection is the preferred route of administration, except in emergencies when the i.v. route may be used.

Administer the atropine first followed by standard treatment for cardiac arrest, circulatory collapse, shock and/or bronchospasm. Bloody diarrhea and other symptoms of violent cholinergic over-stimulation rarely require any additional treatment following adequate doses of atropine.

Dosage: Dosage and route of administration must be individualized, depending on the type and severity of the condition to be treated. Preferably give the drug when the stomach is empty. If taken soon after eating, nausea and vomiting may occur.

If necessary, the effects of the drug can be abolished promptly by atropine (see Adverse Effects).

Urinary Retention: Oral: The usual adult dosage is 10 to 50 mg 3 or 4 times a day. The minimum effective dose is determined by giving 5 to 10 mg initially and repeating the same amount at hourly intervals until a satisfactory response occurs or a maximum of 50 mg has been given. The effects of the drug sometimes appear within 30 minutes and usually within 60 to 90 minutes. They persist for about an hour.

S.C.: The usual dose is 5 mg, although some patients respond satisfactorily to as little as 2.5 mg. The minimum effective dose is determined by injecting 2.5 mg initially and repeating the same dose at 15 to 30 minute intervals to a maximum of 4 doses until satisfactory response is obtained, unless disturbing reactions appear. The minimum effective dose may be repeated thereafter 3 or 4 times a day as required. Rarely, single doses up to 10 mg may be required. Such large doses may cause severe reactions and should be used only after adequate trial of single doses of 2.5 to 5 mg has established that smaller doses are not sufficient.

Bethanechol is usually effective in 5 to 15 minutes after s.c. injection.

Gastroesophageal reflux with pyrosis: 25 mg 4 times a day, orally, one half hour before meals and at bedtime.

Supplied: Injection: Each mL of clear, colorless sterile solution contains: bethanechol chloride 5 mg. May be autoclaved at 120°C for 20 minutes without discoloration or loss of potency. Ampuls of 1 mL, boxes of 6.

Tablets: 10 mg: Each white, discoid, compressed tablet, with a beveled edge quadrisected on one side and engraved "FROSST 412" on the other, contains: bethanechol chloride 10 mg. Also contains lactose. Bottles of 100.

25 mg: Each yellow, discoid, compressed tablet, with a beveled edge, scored on one side, contains: bethanechol chloride 25 mg. Also contains lactose. Bottles of 50.

Both strengths gluten- and tartrazine-free.

(Shown in Product Recognition Section)

UREMOL® 10
TCD

Urea
Emollient—Moisturizer—Antipruritic

Supplied: Cream: Each tube or jar contains: urea 10% in a white emollient cream containing moisturizers and skin protectant. Nonmedicinal ingredients: cyclomethicone/dimethicone copolyol, germaben II, lauryl methicone copolyol, polyalpha olefin, polydimethyl cyclosiloxane, purified water and white petrolatum. Tubes of 75 g and jars of 120 g.

Lotion: Each bottle contains: urea 10% in an emollient, unscented lotion containing moisturizers and skin protectants. Nonmedicinal ingredients: ceteareth-12, ceteareth-20, decanoic acid triglyceride, germaben II, glycerin, glyceryl stearate, octyl dodecanol, potassium phosphate monobasic, purified water and sodium phosphate dibasic anhydrous. Plastic bottles of 250 mL. Protect from excessive heat.

UREMOL® 20
TCD

Urea Preparations
Emollient—Moisturizer—Antipruritic

Supplied: Each 100 g tube or 225 g jar of unscented cream contains: urea 20% in a white practically odorless emollient base. pH approximately 7. Nonmedicinal ingredients: ceteareth-12, ceteareth-20, citric acid anhydrous, decanoic acid triglyceride, germaben II, glyceryl monostearate, octyl dodecanol, potassium phosphate monobasic, purified water, sodium hydroxide and sodium phosphate dibasic. Protect from excessive heat.

UREMOL®-HC ℞
TCD

Hydrocortisone Acetate—Urea
Topical Corticosteroid—Emollient—Antipruritic

Supplied: Cream: Each tube or jar contains: micronised hydrocortisone acetate USP 1% in an aqueous emollient hydrating base consisting of urea USP 10%, pH approximately 7. Nonmedicinal ingredients: caprylic/capric triglyceride, ceteareth-12, ceteareth-20, cetyl alcohol, disodium EDTA, germaben II, glyceryl stearate, isopropyl myristate, mineral oil and lanolin alcohol, potassium phosphate monobasic, propylene glycol, purified water, sodium lauryl sulfate, sodium phosphate monobasic and xanthan gum. Plastic tubes of 50 g and plastic jars of 225 g.

Lotion: Each bottle contains: micronised hydrocortisone acetate USP 1% in an aqueous emollient hydrating base consisting of urea USP 10%. Nonmedicinal ingredients: acetylated lanolin and cetylacetate, ceteareth-12, ceteareth-20, citric acid anhydrous, citric acid monohydrated, decanoic acid triglyceride, disodium edetate, germaben II, glycerin, glyceryl monostearate, isopropyl myristate, octyl dodecanol, purified water, sodium hydroxide, sodium phosphate dibasic and xanthan gum. Plastic bottles of 150 mL.

Unscented, odorless. Store at room temperature. Protect from excessive heat and freezing.

URISEC®
Odan

Urea
Emollient—Moisturizer—Antipruritic

Supplied: Cream: Each tube or jar contains: urea USP 22% in an emollient base. Nonmedicinal ingredients: ceteareth, collagen, Germaben II, glyceryl stearate, glyceryl monostearate, mineral oil, menthyl lactate, octyldodecanol, perfume, propylene glycol, purified water and sodium lauryl sulfate. Tubes of 120 g and jars of 454 g. pH approximately 7. Protect from excessive heat.

Lotion: Each bottle contains: urea USP 12% in an emollient base. Nonmedicinal ingredients: ceteareth, cetaryl alcohol, collagen, Germaben II, glyceryl monostearate, mineral oil, menthyl lactate, methylparaben, octyldodecanol, perfume, propylparaben, propylene glycol and purified water. Plastic applicator bottles of 250 mL. pH approximately 7. Protect from excessive heat.

URISPAS® ℞
Pharmascience

Flavoxate HCl
Urinary Tract Antispasmodic

Pharmacology: Flavoxate is a papaverine-like smooth muscle relaxant. It exhibits, however, greater antispasmodic activity and is less toxic.

The basic action of flavoxate is the relaxation of smooth muscle fibres of the urinary tract through a mechanism not yet defined.

By counteracting smooth muscle spasms of the urinary tract, it relieves the pain and discomfort accompanying a variety of urological disorders, e.g., frequency, dysuria, urgency, nocturia and incontinence.

In addition, flavoxate has been shown to have analgesic and local anesthetic properties in laboratory animals (mouse).

Its pharmacological effects are considered to be due to a direct action on the smooth muscle of the urinary tract, rather than to indirect blocking of autonomic nervous system receptors, as elicited by anticholinergic medications. Inhibition of phosphodiesterase by the drug itself or a metabolite is regarded to codetermine its mechanism of action.

At therapeutic concentrations, flavoxate displays low protein affinity. Its major metabolites, 3-methyl-flavone-8-carboxylic acid (MFCA) is, however, almost completely protein bound (99.5%) under comparable experimental conditions.

Absorption, distribution and excretion were determined in rats and dogs following oral and i.v. administration of C^{14}-labeled flavoxate. The drug was found to be well absorbed from the gastrointestinal tract and rapidly metabolized. Oral administration produced peak blood levels within 20 minutes. Tissue distribution was low in the brain, but high in the liver, kidneys and bladder. Urinary and fecal excretion was practically complete within 24 hours, about 30 to 40% of C^{14} appearing in the urine and 50 to 60% concentrated in the feces. 3-Methyl-flavone-8-carboxylic acid was identified as the principal metabolite.

When administered i.v., peak blood levels were reached after 5 minutes (0.6 to 1.2 μg/mL) while those of the principal metabolite (1.9 to 4.0 μg/mL) were reached in 10 to 15 minutes. Appreciable amounts of the drug and its metabolite appeared in the urine within the first hour, but maximum excretion occurred between 2 and 3 hours. Collections made during 24 hours did not contain any free drug but had high concentrations of 3-methyl-flavone-8-carboxylic acid either free or as conjugated glucuronide. The experimental data confirmed earlier observations that the drug does not accumulate in the body.

Kohler and Morales observed that in rats, peak plasma levels were reached approximately 2 hours after oral or intraperitoneal administration, and that rabbits excreted about 76% of the administered dose (100 mg/kg) over a 24 hour period.

It is not indicated for the definitive treatment of urinary tract infections, but is compatible with drugs used for their management. Where evidence of such infection is present, appropriate anti-infective therapy should be instituted concomitantly. In non-infectious cases of bladder inflammation or irritation, flavoxate alone can provide symptomatic relief.

Flavoxate is also indicated for the relief of vesicourethral spasms due to catheterization, cystoscopy or indwelling catheters, prior to cystoscopy or catheterization, and sequelae of surgical intervention of the lower urinary tract.

Indications: The symptomatic relief of dysuria, urgency, nocturia, suprapubic pain, frequency and incontinence, as may occur in cystitis, prostatitis, urethritis, urethrocystitis and urethrotrigonitis.

Flavoxate is also indicated for the relief of vesicourethral spasms due to catheterization, cystoscopy or indwelling catheters, prior to cystoscopy or catheterization, and sequelae of surgical intervention of the lower urinary tract.

Contraindications: Pyloric or duodenal obstruction, obstructive intestinal lesions or ileus, achalasia, gastrointestinal hemorrhage and obstructive uropathies of the lower urinary tract. It is not yet recommended for infants and children under 12 years of age since safety and efficacy studies in this age group are not completed.

Warnings: Flavoxate should be given cautiously to patients with suspected glaucoma.

Pregnancy: Although studies in sensitive animals have not shown any potential for teratogenic effects, the drug should only be used during pregnancy if, in the opinion of the physician, the anticipated benefits outweigh any risks.

Precautions: Occupational Hazards: In the event of drowsiness or blurred vision, the patient should not operate a motor vehicle or any machinery, and refrain from participating in activities requiring alertness.

Adverse Effects: Adverse reactions reported include nausea and vomiting, dry mouth, nervousness, vertigo, headache, drowsiness, blurred vision, increased ocular tension, disturbance in eye accommodation, urticaria and other dermatoses, mental confusion, especially in the elderly patient, dysuria, tachycardia and palpitation, hyperpyrexia, eosinophilia and leukopenia (one case which was reversible upon discontinuation of the drug).

Overdose: Symptoms: Although no such experience has been reported to-date, it is considered likely that the following symptoms may be observed: nausea, vomiting, dryness of the mouth, blurred vision, disturbance in visual accommodation, tachycardia, tachypnea, mental confusion, excitement, convulsions, respiratory failure and coma.

Treatment: There is no known specific antidote. Treatment is, essentially, symptomatic with close monitoring of vital functions imperative.

In a conscious, alert patient prompt evacuation of the stomach should be performed. When evacuation is complete, observation and further treatment should be made according to the attending physician's assessment of the patient.

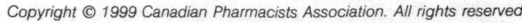

Urispas (cont'd)

If overdosage is extreme, or there is delay in removing the drug from the stomach, administration of a parasympathomimetic drug should be considered.

In the presence of severe anticholinergic reactions, slow i.v. injection of 1 to 4 mg of physostigmine is indicated, and in case of favorable response, repeated doses may be administered. If marked excitement is observed, diazepam may be given for sedation and control of convulsions. In a comatosed patient, a clear airway must be established immediately and artificial respiration instituted.

Dosage: Adults and children over 12 years of age: 1 tablet 3 or 4 times a day.

Flavoxate is rapidly absorbed. Clinical response will vary depending on the nature and severity of symptoms diagnosed and the patient's overall condition. Therapeutic effects on bladder musculature may be observed within 2 or 3 hours.

In patients with infection, treatment is usually continued for as long as antibacterial or anti-infective medications are administered (i.e., a week or so). In patients with chronic bladder symptoms, maintenance therapy for prolonged periods may be required for optimum results. With improvement of symptoms, the dose may be reduced.

It is recommended that tablets be taken after meals.

Supplied: Each white, sugar coated tablet contains: flavoxate HCl 200 mg. Bottles of 100.

Reviewed 1999

UROMITEXAN™ Ⓟ

Bristol

Mesna

Uroprotector

Pharmacology: Mesna is rapidly and easily converted by autooxidation to its only metabolite disodium 2,2′-dithio-bis ethane sulfonate (mesna disulfide, dimesna), forming a disulfide link. Following i.v. injection, only a small portion of the administered dose is detected in the blood as a reactive thiol compound (mesna). Mesna disulfide remains in the intravascular space and is rapidly forwarded to the kidney. In the renal tubular epithelium a considerable proportion of mesna disulfide is again reduced to a free thiol compound, presumably by mediation of glutathione reductase. It is then capable of chemically reacting with acrolein or other urotoxic oxazaphosphorine metabolites in the urine, thereby developing its detoxifying activity.

The first and most important step towards detoxification is the addition of mesna to the double bond of acrolein, resulting in the formation of a stable thio ether which could be detected in the urine by chromatography. In the second step, mesna reduces the speed of degradation of the 4-hydroxy metabolite in the urine. A relatively stable, non-urotoxic condensation product from 4-hydroxy cyclophosphamide or 4-hydroxy ifosfamide and mesna is formed. By such stabilization mesna inhibits the degradation of 4-hydroxy cyclophosphamide or 4-hydroxy ifosfamide and hence the formation of acrolein. This intermediate deactivated product could also be detected by chromatographic urinalysis.

Indications: For the reduction and prevention of urinary tract toxicity (hemorrhagic cystitis) of oxazaphosphorines (see Adverse Effects sections of the Cytoxan and Ifex product monographs).

Contraindications: In individuals with a known hypersensitivity to it.

Warnings: The protective effect of mesna applies only to the urotoxic effects of oxazaphosphorines. Additional prophylactic or accompanying measures recommended during treatment with oxazaphosphorines are thus not affected and should not be discontinued.

In vitro mesna is incompatible with cisplatin. The combination of an oxazaphosphorine cytostatic agent with mesna and cisplatin in the same infusion solution is not stable and is not to be used.

Precautions: Mesna treatment may cause false positive reactions in tests for ketone bodies in the urine. The color reaction is reddish purple rather than purple. The reddish purple color is less stable, and fades immediately by adding glacial acetic acid.

Children: Mesna has been administered to patients as young as 13 years of age.

Pregnancy: Although the use of mesna in pregnant women has not been established, animal studies have not revealed any embryotoxic or mutagenic effects. However, in view of the fact that oxazaphosphorines are not recommended during pregnancy, this would eliminate the need for mesna.

Adverse Effects: At recommended doses, side effects are not usually observed.

The following adverse reactions have been reported in a phase I trial in healthy volunteers: diarrhea, abdominal pain, headache, pain in limbs and joints, transient drop in blood pressure, increase in pulse rate. These reactions occurred at doses of 60 mg/kg or more, given as a single bolus.

Venous irritation may occur in rare instances. This reaction may be attributed to the physical properties of mesna (i.e., pH 6, and hypertonic solution). No venous complications were observed when the solution was given diluted with Sterile Water for Injection USP (1 part mesna solution to 3 parts water).

Overdose: Symptoms and Treatment: No specific antidote for mesna is known. Overdosage should be managed with supportive measures to sustain the patient through any period of toxicity. Mesna has been administered at doses from 70 to 100 mg/kg without any toxic effect on hematopoiesis, hepatic and renal function or the CNS.

Dosage: Mesna should be administered by i.v. injection, usually at 20% of the respective oxazaphosphorine dose at time 0 (=administration of the cytostatic agent), 4 hours and 8 hours. In the case of ifosfamide, the usual dose of mesna is 10 to 12 mg/kg i.v. at 0, 4 and 8 hours after the ifosfamide dose (see Dosage sections of Cytoxan and Ifex product monographs).

In the treatment of children, and particularly when administering very high doses, such as required when conditioning patients for bone-marrow transplantations, the mesna doses should be given at 0, 1, 3, 6, 9 and 12 hours or dosage increased to 30% of the respective oxazaphosphorine dose.

Oral administration of mesna, e.g., in patients with poor veins, is also feasible. Mesna is then given either at doses of 20% of the oxazaphosphorine dose at time 0 hours by the parenteral route, followed by oral doses of 40% of the oxazaphosphorine dose after 4 and 8 hours, taken in juice or cola, or in 3 oral doses of 40% of the oxazaphosphorine dose at time 0, 4 and 8 hours.

Solution for I.V. Infusion: 5% Dextrose Injection USP, 5% Dextrose Injection with 0.45% Sodium Chloride Injection USP, 0.9% Sodium Chloride Injection USP, Lactated Ringer's Injection USP. Solutions for infusion should be made up at a concentration of 1 mg/mL or greater.

Stability of Solution: Solutions for infusion should be used within 24 hours from the time of preparation.

Supplied: Each mL of solution contains: mesna 100 mg. Nonmedicinal ingredients: disodium edetate, sodium hydroxide (for pH adjustments) and water for injection. Ampuls of 4 and 10 mL.

URSOFALK® Ⓟ

Axcan Pharma

Ursodiol

Litholytic Agent—Cholestatic Liver Diseases

Pharmacology: Ursodiol, a naturally occurring bile acid, is present as a minor fraction of the total human bile acids. Oral administration of ursodiol increases this fraction in a dose related manner, to become the major biliary acid. Since in patients with gallstones, the total bile acid pool size is generally reduced, the exogenous supply of ursodiol helps to increase this bile acid pool size and increases the cholesterol saturation index. In addition, the fecal bile acid loss is increased and cholesterol secretion into the bile is reduced, without a concomitant reduction in phospholipids. Consequently, the cholesterol saturation of bile is reduced, allowing gradual solubilization of cholesterol from gallstones to occur.

The cholesterol-lowering effect observed following the administration of ursodiol in patients with primary biliary cirrhosis could be related to an improvement of cholestatis, modifications in cholesterol metabolism or both. Changes in the endogenous bile acid composition induced by ursodiol might be the common denominator of these two mechanisms.

Indications: Gallstone Dissolution: For the dissolution of gallstones and the treatment of associated symptoms in patients with radiolucent, noncalcified gallstones of less than 20 mm size in well opacifying gallbladders in whom cholecystectomy would be undertaken except: for patients who refuse surgery, for the presence of increased surgical risk due to systemic disease, advanced age and idiosyncratic reaction to general anesthesia.

Likelihood of therapeutic success with ursodiol is far greater if the stones are floatable or if the stone size is smaller since the dissolution rate is inversely proportional to the size of the stones. Safety of use of ursodiol beyond 24 months is not established.

Cholestatic Liver Diseases (PBC): Ursodiol is also indicated for the management of cholestatic liver diseases, such as primary biliary cirrhosis (PBC).

Cholestatic liver diseases are characterized by a decrease in bile secretion and bile flow.

The diagnosis of cholestatic liver diseases is based on the biochemical signs of cholestasis (such as an increase in alkaline phosphatase, γ-GT, bilirubin), and also an increase in IgM levels and the presence of antimitochondrial antibodies in PBC.

The monitoring of the efficacy of ursodiol in the management of cholestatic liver diseases should be based on the biochemical parameters of cholestasis, as described above, as well as on signs of hepatic cytolysis (such as AST, ALT) which are very often associated with cholestasis during the progression of the disease.

Therefore, liver function tests (γ-GT, alkaline phosphatase, AST, ALT), and bilirubin level should be monitored: every month for 3 months after start of therapy, and then every 6 months. Serum levels of these parameters usually decrease rapidly thus demonstrating efficacy. Treatment should be discontinued if the levels of above parameters increase (see Precautions).

Ursodiol is not indicated for the treatment of decompensated cirrhosis.

The long-term effect of ursodiol treatment for chronic cholestatic liver disease conditions have not been fully established. Results from clinical trials indicate that ursodiol treatment improves certain laboratory parameters, such as bilirubin level, and serum levels of alkaline phosphatase, AST, and ALT and IgM. Ursodiol may be effective in slowing down the progression of the disease.

Contraindications: Patients with compelling reasons for cholecystectomy including unremitting acute cholecystitis, cholangitis, biliary obstruction, gallstone pancreatitis or biliary-gastrointestinal fistula, and in patients with calcified cholesterol stones, radiopaque stones or radiolucent bile pigment stones.

Warnings: Gallstone Dissolution: Patients should be informed of the response rate, recurrence rate and the underlying cholecystectomy rate (4%) seen in patients while on the treatment.

Cholecystectomy as an alternative to therapy with ursodiol should be considered as it offers the advantages of immediate and permanent stone removal but carries a high risk in some patients.

Precautions: Gallstone Dissolution: Patient Monitoring: The following tests are important for patient monitoring: Liver Tests: Ursodiol therapy has not been associated with liver damage. Lithocholic acid, a naturally occurring bile acid, is known to be a liver-toxic metabolite of ursodiol. This bile acid is formed in the gut from ursodiol. Lithocholic acid is detoxified in the liver by sulfation and although man appears to be an efficient sulfater, it is possible that some patients may have a congenital or acquired deficiency in sulfation, thereby predisposing them to lithocholic acid-induced liver damage. For these reasons patients given ursodiol should have AST and ALT measured at the initiation of therapy, after 3 months of therapy and every 6 months thereafter. Therapy should be discontinued if increased levels persist.

Echogram: Recommended prior to treatment to determine the presence of gallbladder stones and gallbladder function, and at 6 month intervals during the first year of treatment to monitor stone dissolution; also recommended after gallstone dissolution to monitor for possible recurrence.

Cholecystogram: Prior to treatment to judge if the gallbladder is functional or not, and whether gallstones are translucent (mostly cholesterol stones) or radiopaque (calcified stones, pigment stones).

Patients should be counselled on the importance of periodic visits for liver function tests and oral radiograms or ultrasonograms for monitoring stone dissolution. They should be made aware of symptoms of gallstone complications and be warned to report immediately such symptoms to the physicians.

Patients should be instructed on ways to facilitate faithful compliance with the dosage regimen throughout the usual long-term therapy.

Cholestatic liver diseases (PBC): Patient Monitoring: Lithocholic acid, the metabolite of ursodeoxycholic acid (ursodiol), is hepatotoxic unless it is effectively detoxified in the liver. Therefore, the following tests are important for patient monitoring: Liver function tests (γ-GT, alkaline phosphatase, AST,

ALT), and bilirubin level should be monitored: every month for 3 months after start of therapy, and then every 6 months. Serum levels of these parameters usually decrease rapidly thus demonstrating efficacy. Treatment should be discontinued if the levels of above parameters increase.

Drug Interactions: Bile acid sequestrants such as cholestyramine or colestipol may interfere with the action of ursodiol by reducing its absorption. Aluminum based antacids have been shown to absorb bile acid in vitro and may be expected to interfere with ursodiol in the same manner as the sequestering agents. Estrogens, oral contraceptives and fibrates increase biliary cholesterol secretion and hence may counteract the effectiveness of ursodiol. Statins have been shown to induce a decrease of the cholesterol saturation index as a consequence of a depression of the biliary cholesterol secretion rate, which potentiates the similar effect of ursodiol, but does not seem to have an effect on gallstone dissolution.

Carcinogenesis, Mutagenesis and Impairment of Fertility: Ursodiol has no carcinogenic, mutagenic or teratogenic effects in laboratory animals treated at higher doses than those intended for therapy in human and after long-term treatment.

Pregnancy: Ursodiol should not be used in women who are or may become pregnant. If this drug is used during pregnancy, or if the patient becomes pregnant while taking this drug, the patient should be appraised of the potential hazard to the fetus. To date, no reports of adverse reactions have been filed. In pilot studies, ursodiol has been effectively used for the treatment of cholestatic of pregnancy during the last trimester without any side effects.

Lactation: It is not known whether ursodiol is excreted in human milk. Because many drugs are excreted in human milk, caution should be exercised when ursodiol is administered to a nursing mother.

Children: The safety and effectiveness of ursodiol in children has not been established.

Geriatrics: Appropriate studies with ursodiol have not been performed in the geriatric population. However, geriatric-specific problems that would limit the use or usefulness of ursodiol in the elderly are not expected.

Miscellaneous: Risk-benefit should be considered in the case of gallstone complications such as biliary gastrointestinal fistula, biliary obstruction, cholecystitis and pancreatitis.

Adverse Effects: Gallstone Dissolution: The following adverse reactions have been reported with the use of ursodiol in very rare cases: exacerbation of pre-existing psoriasis, rash, urticaria, dry skin, sweating, hair thinning, biliary pain, cholecystitis, constipation, stomatitis, flatulence, headache, fatigue, anxiety, depression, sleep disorder, arthralgia, myalgia, back pain, cough and rhinitis.

In various clinical trials in gallstone dissolution, 648 patients were treated with ursodiol. Six of 648 (1.0%) had gastrointestinal complaints: 4 had diarrhea (0.6%) and 2 dyspepsia (0.3%). In addition, 1 patient was thought to have pruritus, 1 foot swelling and 4 other miscellaneous complaints.

Cholestatic Liver Diseases (PBC): Five hundred and forty eight patients (275 ursodiol, 273 placebo) have been enrolled in the three main clinical trials in primary biliary cirrhosis. Only one patient on ursodiol complained that preexisting pruritus became aggravated and severe 1 hour after administration of the drug. Treatment was discontinued and cholestyramine was administered to restore the patient to her original condition.

The following symptoms were also reported by one patient in the ursodiol group: abdominal pain with postprandial distension, pruritus, dizziness, temporal pressure, in the third month of treatment, for 15 days. The symptoms disappeared despite continuation of treatment, thus making the causal relationship to the drug doubtful.

Overdose: Symptoms and Treatment: Accidental or intentional overdosage of ursodiol has not been reported and likely would result only in self-limiting acute diarrhea which should be treated symptomatically.

Dosage: Gallstone Dissolution: The recommended dose is 8 to 10 mg/kg/day which may be given in 2 divided doses, 1 capsule in the morning with breakfast and 2 to 3 capsules at bedtime with food.

Table I may be consulted to calculate the quantity of capsules to be taken per day. An incremental program of increasing dosage has not usually been employed. Dosage less than 8 mg/kg/day is relatively ineffective and is not recommended.

Ultrasound images of the gallbladder should be obtained at 6 month intervals for the first year of therapy to monitor gallstone response. If gallstones appear to have dissolved, ursodiol therapy should be continued another 3 months, and dissolution confirmed on a repeated ultrasound examination. Most patients who eventually achieve complete stone dissolution will show partial or complete dissolution at first treatment re-evaluation. If partial stone dissolution is not seen by 12 months of ursodiol therapy, the likelihood of success is greatly reduced, and therapy should be stopped.

Cholestatic Liver Diseases (PBC): The recommended dose is 13 to 15 mg/kg/day which may be given in 2 divided doses, i.e. in the morning and at bedtime, with food.

Patient Monitoring: Liver function tests (γ-GT, alkaline phosphatase, AST, ALT), and bilirubin level should be monitored: every month for 3 months after start of therapy, and then every 6 months. Serum levels of these parameters usually decrease rapidly thus demonstrating efficacy. Treatment should be discontinued if the levels of above parameters increase.

Information for the Patient: See Blue Section—Information for the Patient "Ursofalk".

Supplied: Each opaque, white, gelatin capsule, contains: ursodiol 250 mg. Nonmedicinal ingredients: cornstarch, colloidal silicon dioxide, gelatin, magnesium stearate, polysorbate, salt and titanium dioxide. High density polyethylene bottles of 100. Store at room temperature.

(Shown in Product Recognition Section)

Reviewed 1997

Table I—Ursofalk

Weight Dosage Guide

Gallstone Dissolution		Cholestatic Liver Diseases (PBC)	
Body Weight (kg)	**Recommended no. of capsule(s)/day**	**Body Weight (kg)**	**Recommended no. of capsule(s)/day**
45-48	2	40-50	3
59-75	3	51-60	3
76-90	3	61-70	4
91-107	4	71-80	5
108-125	5		

V

VALISONE-G® ℞
Schering

Betamethasone Valerate—Gentamicin Sulfate

Topical Corticosteroid—Antibiotic

Pharmacology: Valisone-G provides the combined anti-inflammatory, anti-allergic, and antipruritic actions of betamethasone valerate with the antibacterial topical effect of gentamicin.

Indications: The topical management of secondarily infected allergic or inflammatory dermatoses responsive to corticosteroid therapy, such as contact dermatitis, seborrheic dermatitis, neurodermatitis, intertrigo, exfoliative dermatitis, stasis dermatitis and psoriasis. Secondary infections caused by gram positive or gram negative bacteria including Streptococci, Staphylococci, and Pseudomonas, Aerobacter, Escherichia and Klebsiella, which are susceptible organisms to the topical action of gentamicin. The ointment may be preferred for the treatment of dry, scaling and fissured lesions.

Contraindications: Tuberculosis of the skin, chickenpox, herpes simplex, and vaccinia. Application in or near the eyes should be avoided.

Precautions: Gentamicin is not effective against fungi, yeasts or viruses. Patients with superficial fungus or yeast infections also must receive specific therapy and the use of the drug may have to be discontinued.

Corticosteroids and gentamicin are known to be absorbed percutaneously in patients under prolonged treatment, with extensive body surface treatment and particularly in those using the occlusive dressing technique on large areas of the body. In such cases, it is recommended that kidney function studies such as BUN be carried out prior to treatment and regularly throughout the course of the treatment.

Pregnancy and *Lactation:* The use of any drug during pregnancy and the lactation period or in women of childbearing age requires that the potential benefits of the drug be weighed against the possible hazards to the fetus or infant. Although topical steroids have not been reported to have had an adverse effect on the fetus, the safety of their use in pregnant patients has not been definitely established. Accordingly, they should not be used extensively or for prolonged periods of time in pregnant patients.

Children: Any of the side effects that have been reported following systemic use of corticosteroids, including adrenal suppression, may also occur with topical corticosteroids, especially in infants and children.

Systemic absorption of topical corticosteroids will be increased if extensive body surface areas are treated or if the occlusive technique is used. Suitable precautions should be taken under these conditions or when long-term use is anticipated, particularly in infants and children. Pediatric patients may demonstrate greater susceptibility to topical corticosteroid-induced HPA axis suppression and Cushing's syndrome than mature patients because of a larger skin surface area to body weight ratio. Use of topical corticosteroids in children should be limited to the least amount compatible with an effective therapeutic regimen. Chronic corticosteroid therapy may interfere with growth and development of children.

Causal factors should be sought and eliminated whenever possible and the sensitivity of an infecting organism to gentamicin should be verified.

Percutaneous absorption of the corticosteroid can produce systemic effects such as adrenal suppression, moon facies, striae, suppression of growth in children. When longterm topical treatment under occlusive dressings is necessary, small dosages, rotation of sites and intermittent therapy should be considered.

Patients should be advised to inform subsequent physicians of the prior use of corticosteroids.

While no systemic effects have been observed following the topical application of gentamicin, toxic systemic concentrations can cause permanent impairment of vestibular function in the presence of renal insufficiency or existing 8th cranial nerve damage.

Caution should be exercised if gentamicin is used in individuals who are known to be sensitive to topically applied antibacterials.

The possibility of sensitivity reactions to any of the product's components should be kept in mind.

Adverse Effects: The following local adverse reactions have been reported rarely with the use of topical corticosteroids: burning, itching, irritation, dryness, folliculitis, hypertrichosis, acneiform eruptions, hypopigmentation.

The following may occur more frequently with occlusive dressings: maceration of the skin, secondary infection, skin atrophy, striae, miliaria.

In patients with dermatoses treated with gentamicin, mild irritation (erythema and pruritus) that did not usually require discontinuance of treatment, has been reported in a small percentage of cases. There was no evidence of irritation or sensitization, however, in any of these patients patch tested subsequently with gentamicin on normal skin. Possible photosensitization has been reported in several patients but could not be elicited in these patients by reapplication of gentamicin followed by exposure to u.v. radiation.

Overdose: Symptoms and Treatment (accidental ingestion): No known antidote. Gastric lavage should be performed.

Dosage: Apply a small amount on the affected area 2 or 3 times daily. Refractory lesions of psoriasis and deep-seated dermatoses which have been secondarily infected may respond better to topical corticosteroids and antibiotics when used with the hydration technique or occlusive dressing method described as follows: Apply a thick layer of medication over the entire surface of the lesion under a light gauze dressing and cover it with a pliable, transparent, impermeable, plastic material well beyond the edges of the treated area. Seal the edges to the normal skin by adhesive tape or other means. Leave the dressing in place 1 to 3 days and repeat the procedure 3 or 4 times as needed. With this method of treatment, marked improvement often is seen in a few days. However, this technique requires closer supervision of the patient since occasionally miliary eruptions or folliculitis develop in the skin under an occlusive dressing, requiring removal of the plastic cover and/or discontinuance of this method of treatment.

Supplied: Cream: Each g of cream contains: betamethasone 1 mg (as valerate USP) and gentamicin 1 mg (as sulfate USP) in a water miscible base. Nonmedicinal ingredients: cetostearyl alcohol, chlorocresol, mineral oil, monobasic sodium phosphate, phosphoric acid, polyethylene glycol 1000 monocetyl ether, sodium hydroxide, water and white petrolatum. Tubes of 15 and 30 g.

Ointment: Each g of ointment contains: betamethasone 1 mg (as valerate USP) and gentamicin 1 mg (as sulfate USP) in a lanolin-free base. Nonmedicinal ingredients: petrolatum USP. Tubes of 15 and 30 g.

Store at 2 to 30°C.

VALISONE® Scalp Lotion ℞
Schering

Betamethasone Valerate

Topical Corticosteroid

Indications: The management of dermatoses of the scalp. May also be used in corticosteroid responsive dermatoses.

Contraindications: See Celestoderm-V.

Warnings: This lotion contains isopropyl alcohol, and may cause stinging or burning upon application to abraded or sunburned skin. Do not use in or near the eyes.

Precautions and Adverse Effects: See Celestoderm-V.

Dosage: Apply a small amount on the affected skin 2 to 3 times daily. Refractory lesions of psoriasis and other deep seated dermatoses such as lichen simplex chronicus, hypertrophic lichen planus, atopic dermatitis, chronic eczematous and lichenified hand eruptions, and recalcitrant pustular eruptions on the palms and soles will respond better to topical corticosteroids when used with the hydration technique of occlusive dressing as described in the Celestoderm-V monograph.

Supplied: Each mL of lotion contains: betamethasone 1 mg (as valerate USP). Nonmedicinal ingredients: carbomer 934P, isopropanol, sodium hydroxide and water. Plastic squeeze bottles of 30 and 75 mL. Store at a temperature not exceeding 30°C.

VALIUM® ROCHE® INJECTION ℞
Roche

Diazepam

Anxiolytic—Sedative

Pharmacology: Diazepam is an anxiolytic-sedative drug useful in the symptomatic relief of anxiety and tension states. It has also adjunctive value in the relief of certain neurospastic conditions and in certain cases, its anticonvulsant activity has been found useful in controlling status epilepticus.

Peak blood levels after the i.v. administration of diazepam injection are reached within 15 minutes as compared to 1 hour after a single oral dosing and are of the same magnitude. The acute half-life is 2 to 3 hours with a slower decline thereafter, possibly due to tissue storage. Repeated doses further increase blood levels. In humans, comparable blood levels of diazepam injection were obtained in maternal and cord blood indicating rapid placental transfer of the drug.

Indications: In the symptomatic management of mild to moderate degrees of anxiety in conditions dominated by tension, excitation, agitation, fear or aggressiveness, such as may occur in: psychoneurosis; anxiety reactions due to stressful conditions; and anxiety states with somatic expression.

Diazepam is indicated parenterally when a rapid response is desired and has been found useful: in acute anxiety or tension states related to stressful conditions or non-psychotic emotional disorders; to alleviate the symptoms of acute alcoholic withdrawal, including delirium tremens; as an adjunct in relieving anxiety states that may be present before minor surgical procedures or prior to esophagoscopy and gastroscopy (when used under conditions in which resuscitative measures are available); to control prolonged seizure activity (status epilepticus) including severe recurrent seizures (see Precautions); for the relief of muscle spasm in cerebral palsy, athetosis, the rare stiff man syndrome and adjunctively in tetanus; as premedication for relief of anxiety states prior to surgical procedures (i.m. route) or cardioversion (i.v. route).

Contraindications: Myasthenia gravis, infants, known hypersensitivity to the drug.

Warnings: Diazepam injection should not be administered to patients in shock or coma. Rare reports of apnea or cardiac arrest have been noted, usually following i.v. administration, especially in elderly or very ill patients and those with limited pulmonary reserve. Duration is generally brief. Resuscitative facilities should be available. Since lingual obstruction of the airway may occur, particularly in children and in the elderly, caution is required to maintain a free airway in patients receiving diazepam.

Rapid injection or the use of veins with too small a lumen carries the risk of thrombophlebitis. I.V. injection should be directly into a large lumen vessel, such as an antecubital vein, and the ampul solution should be administered slowly (e.g. 5 mg/minute).

Intra-arterial injection must be carefully avoided on account of the danger of necrosis.

Diazepam should not be diluted with parenteral fluids. One exception is when it is considered essential to administer it in a large volume of fluids (see i.v. Infusion under Dosage).

Do not mix or dilute diazepam injection with other solutions or drugs.

Precautions: Geriatrics: Elderly and debilitated patients and those with organic brain disorders have been found to be prone to CNS depression following even low doses. For these patients diazepam injection should be used with caution and in low doses to preclude development of ataxia, sedation or other possible adverse effects.

Emotional Disorders: Diazepam is not recommended in the treatment of psychotic or severely depressed patients. Precautions are indicated for severely depressed patients or those who show any evidence of impending depression, particularly the recognition that suicidal tendencies may be present and protective measures may be necessary.

Since excitement and other paradoxical reactions may result from the use of the drug in psychotic patients, it should not be used in ambulatory patients suspected of having psychotic tendencies.

Pregnancy: Diazepam injection should not be used during the first trimester of pregnancy except if absolutely necessary.

Obstetrics: The safety and efficacy in obstetrics have not yet been established.

Use before Bronchoscopy and Laryngoscopy: Since there are insufficient data available to establish the safety of diazepam

Valium Roche Injection (cont'd)

prior to bronchoscopy and laryngoscopy, its use is not recommended.

Use before Gastroscopy, Esophagoscopy, Cardioversion and Surgical Procedures: Diazepam should be used only under conditions in which safeguards are available should laryngospasm and circulatory or respiratory depression occur. Concurrent use of narcotics and barbiturates with diazepam may produce a potentiation of effect and, when such combinations are used, appropriate reduction of dosage is required.

Use in Status Epilepticus: Diazepam is not recommended as a substitute for standard anticonvulsant medication in the long-term control of epilepsy. Appropriate anticonvulsant therapy should be instituted or continued when necessary, as soon as possible after interruption of the status epilepticus. Although diazepam is used to control status epilepticus, it may occasionally induce or aggravate seizures in some patients with convulsive disorders.

Potentiation of Drug Effects: Careful consideration should be given if diazepam is to be combined with other psychotropic agents (phenothiazines, barbiturates, MAO inhibitors and other antidepressants) because the pharmacological action of these agents might potentiate the action of diazepam.

Patients should be advised to abstain from alcohol during treatment with diazepam.

In view of possible adverse reactions and potentiation of effects, patients should be advised to abstain from CNS depressant drugs during treatment with diazepam.

Drug Dependence: Abrupt cessation of large doses of diazepam after prolonged periods may precipitate acute withdrawal symptoms and, in these cases, the drug should be discontinued gradually. Caution should be exercised when it is considered necessary to administer diazepam to addiction-prone individuals.

Interference with Serum Creatinine Phosphokinase Determinations: As with a number of other i.m. dosage forms, i.m. administration of diazepam (but not oral or i.v. administration), can lead to a rise in serum creatinine phosphokinase activity. A maximum level is usually noticed between 12 and 24 hours after i.m. injection. These elevated readings should be taken into account in the event of differential diagnosis of myocardial infarction.

Occupational Hazards: General: After parenteral administration, ambulation should be delayed at least 1 or 2 hours or until complete alertness is restored. Patients receiving diazepam should be advised to proceed cautiously wherever mental alertness and physical co-ordination are required.

The usual precautions in treating patients with impaired renal and hepatic functions should be observed. If diazepam is administered for protracted periods, periodic blood counts and liver function tests may be advisable.

Adverse Effects: The most common adverse effects reported are drowsiness and ataxia.

Other reactions noted less frequently are fatigue, dizziness, nausea, blurred vision, diplopia, vertigo, headache, slurred speech, tremors, hypoactivity, dysarthria, euphoria, impairment of memory, confusion, depression, incontinence or urinary retention, constipation, skin rash, generalized exfoliative dermatitis, hypotension, tachycardia, flushing, hematuria, changes in libido, pain at the site of injection and phlebitis following i.v. administration.

The more serious adverse reactions occasionally reported are leukopenia, jaundice, hypersensitivity and paradoxical reactions. Circulatory and respiratory depression may follow rapid i.v. administration.

Paradoxical reactions such as hyperexcited states, anxiety, excitement, hallucinations, increased muscle spasticity, insomnia, rage, as well as sleep disturbances and stimulation, have been reported: should these occur, the drug should be discontinued.

Minor changes in EEG patterns have been observed in patients on diazepam therapy. These changes consist of low to moderate voltage fast activity, 20 to 30 cycles/second and are of no known significance.

In animals, i.m. administration has produced localized irritation of tissue at injection sites and some thickening of veins after i.v. use. A mild hemolytic effect was observed in in vitro and in vivo tests in dogs.

Overdose: Symptoms and Treatment: The main symptoms of overdosage are drowsiness, oversedation and ataxia. When the effects of the drug overdosage begin to wear off, the patient exhibits some jitteriness and overstimulation. The cardinal manifestations of overdosage are drowsiness and confusion, reduced reflexes and coma. There are minimum effects of respiration, pulse and blood pressure unless the overdosage is extreme.

Gastric lavage may be beneficial if performed soon after oral ingestion. If necessary, a CNS stimulant such as caffeine or methylphenidate may be administered with caution. Supportive measures should be instituted as indicated: maintenance of an adequate airway, levarterenol for hypotension. Dialysis appears to be of little value.

Dosage: Valium Roche Injection is used without diluent for both the i.m. and i.v. routes. The i.m. route should be preferred whenever the indication and urgency of the clinical situation permit. The i.m. route is indicated when diazepam injection is used as premedication to relieve anxiety states prior to surgical procedures (usually 30 to 45 minutes before the procedure. The i.v. route is indicated when diazepam injection is used prior to cardioversion.

While dosage should be individualized for maximum beneficial effect, as a general rule the usual dose for both the i.v. and i.m. routes is:

Acute anxiety or tension states related to stressful conditions or nonpsychotic emotional disorders: 2 to 10 mg i.m. or i.v. Repeat in 3 to 4 hours, if necessary.

Acute alcoholic withdrawal: To alleviate the symptoms of acute alcoholic withdrawal including delirium tremens: 10 mg i.m. or i.v. initially, then 5 to 10 mg in 3 to 4 hours, if necessary.

Minor surgical procedures including esophagoscopy and gastroscopy: As an adjunct in relieving anxiety states that may be present before these procedures: 5 to 10 mg i.m. or i.v. approximately 30 minutes prior to procedures.

For the relief of muscle spasm in cerebral palsy, athetosis, the rare "stiff man syndrome" and adjunctively in tetanus: 5 to 10 mg i.m. or i.v. initially; then 5 to 10 mg in 3 to 4 hours, if necessary. For tetanus, larger doses may be required.

Status epilepticus including severe recurrent seizures: For the control of prolonged seizure activity: 5 to 10 mg i.v. (preferred route) initially. Repeat in 2 to 4 hours if necessary.

Premedication to surgical procedures: For the relief of anxiety states (if atropine, scopolamine or other premedication are desired, they must be administered in separate syringes): 10 mg i.m. (preferred route), 1 to 2 hours before surgery.

Cardioversion: To relieve anxiety and tension: 5 to 15 mg i.v. within 5 to 10 minutes prior to the procedure.

Children: Depending on age and severity of symptoms, 2 to 10 mg i.m. or i.v. or 1 mg/4.5 kg.

Elderly and debilitated: (see Precautions and Adverse Effects) 2 to 5 mg i.m. or i.v.

I.M.: Diazepam injection should be injected deeply into the muscle.

I.V.: Diazepam injection should be administered slowly, i.e., 5 mg/minute.

In acute conditions, the injection may be repeated within 1 hour although an interval of 3 to 4 hours is usually satisfactory. Generally not more than 30 mg should be given in an 8 hour period.

I.V. Infusion: (see Warnings). Not more than 40 mg (8 mL of ampul solution) should be added to 500 mL of infusion solution (normal saline or 5% dextrose in water). The solution should be freshly made up and used within 6 hours.

Over 50% of the diazepam in the infusion solution may be adsorbed onto the walls of plastic containers. Therefore, only infusion solutions in glass containers can be administered.

Adsorption onto plastic drip tubing causes an initial significant and variable reduction (up to 40% or more) of delivered diazepam concentration which then gradually rises over the next few hours. The drip rate should be frequently titrated against the patient's condition.

Bolus allows a more accurate and rapid titration of dosage than slow i.v. infusion. It is therefore to be preferred in the management of acute problems.

Supplied: Each mL contains: diazepam 5 mg. Nonmedicinal ingredients: benzoic acid, benzyl alcohol, ethanol, propylene glycol, sodium benzoate and sodium hydroxide. Sodium: <1 mmol/mL. Paraben- and sulfite-free. Ampuls of 10 mg/2 mL, packages of 50. Protect from light.

VALIUM® ROCHE® ORAL Ⓟ

Roche

Diazepam

Anxiolytic—Sedative

Pharmacology: Diazepam is an anxiolytic-sedative drug useful in the symptomatic relief of anxiety and tension states. It has also adjunctive value in the relief of certain neurospastic conditions. Peak blood levels after oral administration of diazepam are reached within 1 to 2 hours after single oral dosing. The acute half-life is 6 to 8 hours with a slower decline thereafter, possibly due to tissue storage. However, after repeated doses, blood levels increase significantly over a period of 24 to 48 hours.

In humans, comparable blood levels of diazepam were obtained in maternal and cord blood indicating placental transfer of the drug.

Indications: The symptomatic management of mild to moderate degrees of anxiety in conditions dominated by tension, excitation, agitation, fear or aggressiveness, such as may occur in psychoneurosis, anxiety reactions due to stress conditions and anxiety states with somatic expression.

In acute alcoholic withdrawal, diazepam may be useful in the symptomatic relief of acute agitation, tremor and impending acute delirium tremens.

As an adjunct for the relief of skeletal muscle spasm due to reflex spasm to local pathology, such as inflammation of the muscle and joints or secondary to trauma; spasticity caused by upper motor neuron disorders, such as cerebral palsy and paraplegia; athetosis and the rare "stiff man syndrome".

Contraindications: Myasthenia gravis, known hypersensitivity to the drug and, because of lack of sufficient clinical experience, in children under 6 months of age.

Precautions: Geriatrics: Elderly and debilitated patients or those with organic brain disorders have been found to be prone to CNS depression following even low doses. For these patients it is recommended that the dosage be limited to the smallest effective amount to preclude development of ataxia, oversedation or other possible adverse effects.

Emotional Disorders: Diazepam is not recommended in the treatment of psychotic or severely depressed patients. Precautions are indicated for severely depressed patients or those who show evidence of impending depression, particularly the recognition that suicidal tendencies may be present and protective measures may be necessary. Since excitement and other paradoxical reactions may result from the use of the drug in psychotic patients, it should not be used in ambulatory patients suspected of having psychotic tendencies.

Epileptic Patients: Careful consideration should be given if diazepam is to be used in patients with epilepsy as the possibility of an increase in the frequency and/or severity of grand mal seizures may require an increase in the doses of standard anticonvulsant medication. An abrupt withdrawal of diazepam is such cases may also be associated with the temporary increase in the frequency and/or severity of seizures.

Pregnancy: Diazepam should not be used during the first trimester of pregnancy except if absolutely necessary.

Potentiation of Drug Effects: Careful consideration should be given if diazepam is to be combined with other psychotropic agents, phenothiazines, barbiturates, MAO inhibitors and other antidepressants because the pharmacological action of these agents might potentiate the action of diazepam. Since diazepam has a CNS depressant effect, patients should be advised against the simultaneous ingestion of alcohol and other CNS depressant drugs during diazepam therapy.

Drug Dependence: Abrupt cessation of large doses of diazepam after prolonged periods may precipitate acute withdrawal symptoms and, in these cases, the drug should be discontinued gradually. Caution should be exercised when it is considered necessary to administer diazepam to addiction prone individuals.

General: Patients receiving diazepam should be advised to proceed cautiously wherever mental alertness and physical coordination are required.

The usual precautions in treating patients with impaired renal and hepatic functions should be observed. If diazepam is administered for protracted periods, periodic blood counts and liver function tests would be highly advisable.

Adverse Effects: The most common adverse effects reported are drowsiness and ataxia. Other reactions noted less frequently are fatigue, dizziness, nausea, blurred vision, diplopia, vertigo, headache, slurred speech, tremors, hypoactivity, dysarthria, euphoria, impairment of memory, confusion, depression, incontinence or urinary retention, constipation, skin rash, generalized exfoliative dermatitis, hypotension and changes in libido.

The more serious adverse reactions occasionally reported are leukopenia, jaundice, hypersensitivity and paradoxical reactions (such as hyperexcited states, anxiety, excitement, hallucinations, increased muscle spasticity, insomnia, rage, as well as sleep disturbances and stimulation). Should these occur, the drug should be discontinued.

Minor changes in EEG patterns have been observed in patients on diazepam therapy. These changes consist of low to moderate voltage fast activity, 20 to 30 cycles/second and are of no known significance.

Overdose: Symptoms: Drowsiness, oversedation and ataxia. When the effects of drug overdosage begin to wear off, the patient exhibits some jitteriness and overstimulation. The cardinal manifestations of overdosage are drowsiness and confusion, reduced reflexes and coma. There are minimum effects on respiration, pulse and blood pressure unless the overdosage is extreme.

Treatment: Gastric lavage may be beneficial if performed soon after oral ingestion of diazepam. If necessary, a CNS stimulant such as caffeine or methylphenidate may be administered with caution. Supportive measures should be instituted as indicated, such as, maintenance of an adequate airway, levarterenol or metaraminol bitartrate for hypotension. Dialysis appears to be of little value.

Dosage: Should be individualized for maximal beneficial effect. While the usual daily dosages given below will meet the needs of most patients, there will be some who may require higher doses. In the first few days of administration a cumulative effect of the drug may occur, and therefore, the dosage should be increased only after stabilization is apparent.

Adults: Symptomatic relief of anxiety and tension in psychoneurosis and anxiety reactions: 2 to 10 mg, 2 to 4 times daily depending upon severity of symptoms.

Symptomatic relief in acute alcohol withdrawal: 10 mg, 3 or 4 times during the first 24 hours, reducing to 5 mg, 3 or 4 times daily as needed.

Adjunctively for relief of skeletal muscle spasms: 2 to 10 mg, 3 to 4 times daily.

Elderly and debilitated patients, or in the presence of debilitating disease: 2 mg, 1 or 2 times daily initially; increase gradually as needed and tolerated.

Children: Because of varied responses, initiate therapy with lowest dose and increase as required. Not for use in children under 6 months (see Contraindications): 1 to 2.5 mg, 3 or 4 times daily initially; increase gradually as needed and tolerated.

Supplied: 5 mg: Each pale yellow cylindrical, biplane beveled edged tablet, engraved ROCHE 5 on one side, single scored on both sides, contains: diazepam 5 mg. Nonmedicinal ingredients: iron oxide yellow, lactose and magnesium stearate. Energy: 2.8 kJ (0.7 kcal). Gluten-, paraben-, sodium-, sulfite- and tartrazine-free. Bottles of 100 and 1 000.

10 mg: Each light blue cylindrical, biplane beveled-edged, single scored on one side and engraved ROCHE 10 on unscored side contains: diazepam 10 mg. Nonmedicinal ingredients: cornstarch, indigotine, lactose and magnesium stearate. Energy: 2.8 kJ (0.7 kcal). Gluten-, paraben-, sodium-, sulfite- and tartrazine-free. Bottles of 100.

Store between 15 and 30°C. Keep in a tightly closed, light-resistant container.

(Shown in Product Recognition Section)

VALTREX® Ⓟ

Glaxo Wellcome

Valacyclovir HCl

Antiviral Agent

Pharmacology: Mechanism of Action: Valacyclovir is the L-valyl ester and a pro-drug of the antiviral drug acyclovir. Valacyclovir is rapidly converted to acyclovir, which has in vitro and in vivo inhibitory activity against human herpes viruses including herpes simplex virus types 1 (HSV-1) and 2 (HSV-2), and varicella-zoster virus (VZV).

The inhibitory activity of acyclovir is highly selective due to its unique affinity for the thymidine kinase (TK) encoded by HSV, and VZV. This viral enzyme converts acyclovir into acyclovir monophosphate, a nucleotide analogue. The monophosphate is further converted into diphosphate by cellular guanylate kinase and into triphosphate by a number of cellular enzymes. In vitro, acyclovir triphosphate terminates growing chains of viral DNA. Once incorporated, acyclovir irreversibly binds to viral DNA polymerase, effectively inactivating the enzyme. Acyclovir triphosphate is a potent inhibitor of all of the human herpes virus DNA polymerases studied.

Acyclovir is virtually inactive in uninfected cells, since it is preferentially taken up and selectively converted to the active triphosphate form by herpes virus-infected cells. Additionally, the enzyme thymidine kinase of uninfected cells does not effectively use acyclovir as a substrate and cellular α-DNA polymerase is less sensitive than viral DNA polymerase to the effects of acyclovir.

A combination of the thymidine kinase specificity, competitive inhibition of DNA polymerase and incorporation and termination of the growing viral DNA chain results in inhibition of herpes virus replication. No effect on latent nonreplicating virus has been demonstrated. Inhibition of viral replication reduces the period of viral shedding, limits the degree of spread and level of pathology, and thereby facilitates healing. The pain of shingles is related to viral damage to neurons which takes place during viral replication.

Pharmacokinetics: After oral administration, valacyclovir is rapidly absorbed from the gastrointestinal tract. Following absorption, valacyclovir is rapidly and nearly completely hydrolyzed to acyclovir and L-valine, an essential amino acid, by first-pass metabolism. This hydrolysis is mediated primarily by the enzyme valacyclovir hydrolase, and occurs predominantly in the liver. The absolute bioavailability of acyclovir after administration of valacyclovir is 54.5±9.1% as determined following a 1 g oral dose of valacyclovir and a 350 mg i.v. acyclovir dose to 12 healthy volunteers. The pharmacokinetic disposition of acyclovir delivered by valacyclovir is consistent with previous experience from i.v. and oral acyclovir.

Acyclovir is eliminated primarily by urinary excretion of unchanged drug. In all studies of valacyclovir, the half-life of acyclovir typically averages 2.5 to 3.3 hours in subjects with normal renal function. In a single-dose escalation study conducted in healthy volunteers with doses of 100 mg, 500 mg, and 1 g of valacyclovir, average (±SD) peak acyclovir concentrations (C_{max}) were 0.83 (±0.14) to 5.6 (±2.4) µg/mL, respectively. Area under the acyclovir concentration-time curve (AUC) was 2.3 (±0.4), 11.6 (±1.8), and 19.5 (±6.0) hr•µg/mL, respectively. Acyclovir pharmacokinetics are unaltered after multiple-dose administration.

Clinical Trials: Zoster: Two randomized double-blind clinical trials in 1 540 immunocompetent patients with localized herpes zoster were conducted. In patients less than 50 years of age, valacyclovir 1 000 mg 3 times daily for 7 days was compared to placebo. In patients greater than 50 years of age, valacyclovir 1 000 mg 3 times daily for 7 days or 14 days was compared to acyclovir 800 mg 5 times daily for 7 days. All patients were treated within 72 hours of appearance of zoster rash.

In patients less than 50 years of age, the median time to cessation of new lesion formation was shorter for those treated with valacyclovir (2 days) compared with those treated with placebo (3 days, p=0.03). In patients greater than 50 years of age, the median time to cessation of new lesion formation was 3 days in patients treated with either valacyclovir or acyclovir.

In both studies, the median time to at least 50% crusting or healing was 5 days for all treatment groups.

These trials also included assessment of pain. The primary endpoint for pain was time to complete cessation of zoster-associated pain. Zoster-associated pain, as defined in these trials, combined acute pain (pain associated with zoster lesions) and postherpetic neuralgia (pain after 100% crusting/healing of lesion rash), a definition that is not universally accepted; most experts consider each pain component to have different pathogenesis and different morbidity. The clinical trials were not designed to look specifically at postherpetic neuralgia. However, a posthoc analysis for postherpetic neuralgia was requested and carried out.

In patients greater than 50 years of age, the median time to resolution of postherpetic neuralgia for the study population (including those with zero postherpetic neuralgia) was significantly shorter in patients treated with valacyclovir compared with patients treated with acyclovir (9 and 4 days shorter for patients treated with valacyclovir for 7 and 14 days respectively, $p \leq 0.05$). In patients greater than 50 years of age, the incidence of chronic pain after 100% crusting/healing of lesion rash was not significantly different among the 3 treatment groups (79 and 80% in patients treated with valacyclovir for 7 or 14 days and 85% in patients treated with acyclovir). In patients less than 50 years of age, there was no statistically significant difference in the median time to cessation of postherpetic neuralgia between the recipients of valacyclovir and placebo.

There were no significant differences in secondary endpoints, such as use of analgesics or quality of life, for patients treated with valacyclovir compared to placebo or acyclovir. In addition, no significant differences were found among the 3 groups with respect to intensity of pain.

Genital Herpes: Two randomized, double-blind, placebo-controlled trials in 2 187 immunocompetent patients with recurrent genital herpes were conducted. In one study (004), patients were randomized to receive 5 days of treatment with either valacyclovir 1 000 mg bid, acyclovir 200 mg 5 times daily, or placebo. In a second study (028), patients were randomized to receive either valacyclovir 1 000 mg, valacyclovir 500 mg, or placebo, administered twice daily for 5 days. In both trials, patients self-initiated therapy within 24 hours of the first sign or symptom of a recurrent genital herpes episode.

Valacyclovir significantly accelerated lesion healing and resolved episodes faster compared to placebo in both studies (p=0.0001). The median time to lesion healing was 4.8 days and 4.1 days for the valacyclovir groups versus 6.0 days and 6.0 days for the placebo groups, for studies 004 and 028 respectively. The median length of an episode was 4.8 days and 4.0 days for the valacyclovir groups versus 5.9 days and 5.9 days for the placebo groups, for studies 004 and 028, respectively (p=0.0001). There were no differences between active treatments groups in both studies.

In study 028, there was a significantly higher proportion of patients with aborted episodes in the valacyclovir 1 000 mg group (28%) and 500 mg group (31%) compared to placebo (21%) (p=0.042 and p=0.005 respectively). In study 004, the proportion of patients with aborted episodes was higher in the valacyclovir group (25.9%) than in the placebo group (19.8%), although this was not statistically significant (p=0.097).

The duration of lesion pain/discomfort was significantly shorter in the valacyclovir treatment groups compared to placebo (p=0.0014 for study 004 and p=0.0001 for study 028). In study 028, the median time to cessation of pain was 2.8 days in the valacyclovir 500 mg group versus 3.9 days for the placebo group. There were no differences between active treatments groups in either study.

In both studies, valacyclovir significantly shorten the duration of viral shedding compared to placebo (p=0.0001). The median time to cessation of viral shedding in patients with at least one positive culture was 2 days in the valacyclovir treatment groups versus 4 days in the placebo group, for both studies. There were no differences between active treatments groups in either study.

Indications: For the treatment of herpes zoster (shingles) and recurrent genital herpes in immunocompetent adults.

Contraindications: In patients with a known hypersensitivity or intolerance to valacyclovir, acyclovir, or any component of the formulation.

Warnings: Thrombotic Thrombocytopenic Purpura/Hemolytic Uremic Syndrome (TTP/HUS), in some cases resulting in death, has been reported in patients with advanced HIV disease and also in bone marrow transplant and renal transplant patients participating in clinical trials of valacyclovir. Valacyclovir caplets are not indicated for the treatment of immunocompromised patients. This syndrome has not been observed in immunocompetent patients treated with valacyclovir caplets in clinical trials.

Precautions: General: Caution should be exercised when administering valacyclovir to patients with significant renal impairment or those receiving potentially nephrotoxic agents, since this may increase the risk of renal dysfunction (see Dosage) and/or the risk of reversible CNS symptoms such as those that occur infrequently in patients treated with i.v. acyclovir.

Efficacy has not been studied in immunocompromised patients or in those with disseminated herpes zoster.

Geriatrics: Of the total number of patients included in clinical studies of valacyclovir 799 were age 65 or older, and 338 were age 75 or older. A total of 34 volunteers age 65 or older completed a pharmacokinetic trial of valacyclovir. The pharmacokinetics of acyclovir following single- and multiple-dose oral administration of valacyclovir caplets in geriatric volunteers varied with renal function. Dosage reduction may be required in geriatric patients depending on the underlying renal status of the patient (see Pharmacology and Dosage). Adequate hydration should be maintained.

Children: Safety and effectiveness in children have not been adequately studied.

Pregnancy: There are no adequate and well-controlled studies with either acyclovir or valacyclovir in pregnant women. Valacyclovir caplets should be used during pregnancy only if the potential benefit justifies the potential risk to the fetus.

There has not been an increased incidence of birth defects in over 300 women exposed to acyclovir, during the first trimester of pregnancy, as compared with the incidence in the general population. Most women were exposed to acyclovir oral doses of 800 to 1 000 mg/day (approximately equivalent to the acyclovir exposure from 500 mg of valacyclovir once daily). The daily acyclovir area under the plasma concentration vs time curve (AUC) following valacyclovir 1 000 and 3 000 mg/day would be 2 to 4 times greater than that expected

Valtrex (cont'd)

with oral acyclovir. The reported defects show no uniqueness or pattern to suggest a common etiology. However, the small size of patients registered is insufficient to evaluate the risk of less common defects or to permit reliable and definitive conclusions regarding the safety of acyclovir in pregnant women and their developing fetuses.

Valacyclovir was not teratogenic in rats or rabbits given 400 mg/kg (which results in 10 and 7 times human plasma levels, respectively) during the period of major organogenesis. However, in a nonstandard test in rats given 3 s.c. doses of 100 mg/kg acyclovir (20 times human plasma levels) on gestation day 10, there were fetal abnormalities, such as head and tail anomalies, and maternal toxicity.

Lactation: There is no experience with valacyclovir. However, acyclovir concentrations have been documented in breast milk in 2 women following oral administration of acyclovir and ranged from 0.6 to 4.1 times corresponding plasma levels. These concentrations would potentially expose the nursing infant to a dose of acyclovir up to 0.3 mg/kg/day. Caution should be exercised when valacyclovir is administered to a nursing woman. Consideration should be given to temporary discontinuation of nursing, as the safety of valacyclovir has not been established in infants.

Drug Interactions: Coadministration of probenecid with i.v. acyclovir has been shown to increase the mean elimination half-life, and the AUC of acyclovir. Urinary excretion and renal clearance of acyclovir were correspondingly reduced. An additive increase in acyclovir AUC with concomitant administration of valacyclovir, cimetidine, and probenecid has also been observed. Acyclovir C_{max} was increased 8.4±27.8%, 22.5±25.3%, and 29.6±27.5% by cimetidine, probenecid, and combination treatment (concomitant cimetidine and probenecid administration), respectively. Acyclovir AUC (0 to 24 hours) was increased 31.9±22.9%, 49.0±27.9%, and 77.9±38.6% by cimetidine, probenecid, and combination treatment, respectively. There are no known drug interactions that require dosage adjustment in patients with normal renal function. Other drugs which affect renal physiology could affect plasma levels of acyclovir.

Hepatic Impairment: Dose modification is not required in patients with mild or moderate cirrhosis (hepatic synthetic function maintained). Pharmacokinetic data in patients with advance cirrhosis (impaired hepatic synthetic function and evidence of portal-systemic shunting) do not indicate the need for dosage adjustment. However, clinical experience is limited.

Information for the Patient: Patients should be informed that valacyclovir is not a cure for genital herpes.

Adverse Effects: Adverse events were not significantly different in recipients of valacyclovir (n=967) compared to placebo (n=195) or acyclovir (n=376) in the 2 double-blind, randomized clinical trials of treatment of herpes zoster (shingles). In addition, adverse events were not significantly different in recipients of valacyclovir (n=1 235) compared to placebo (n=439) in the two double-blind, randomized trials of treatment of recurrent genital herpes. The most frequent adverse events reported in recipients of valacyclovir are listed in Table I.

Overdose: Symptoms and Treatment: There have been no reports of overdosage from the administration of valacyclovir. However, it is known that precipitation of acyclovir in renal tubules may occur when the solubility (2.5 mg/mL) is exceeded in the intratubular fluid. In the event of acute renal failure and anuria, the patient may benefit from hemodialysis until renal function is restored (see Dosage).

Dosage: Caplets may be given without regard to meals.

Herpes Zoster: The recommended dosage is 1 g (2 caplets) orally 3 times daily for 7 days. Treatment with valacyclovir should be initiated within 72 hours of the onset of rash.

Recurrent Genital Herpes: The recommended dosage is 500 mg orally twice daily for 5 days. Therapy should be initiated at the earliest sign or symptom of recurrence. Valacyclovir can prevent lesion development when taken at the first signs and symptoms of a genital herpes recurrence.

Patients with Acute or Chronic Renal Impairment: Pharmacokinetic and safety evaluations following administration of oral valacyclovir have been performed in patients with renal impairment and volunteers with end-stage renal disease (ESRD) managed by hemodialysis. Based on these studies and extensive experience with acyclovir, the following dosage adjustments are recommended (see Table II).

Table II—Valtrex

Dosage Adjustments for Renal Impairment

Creatinine Clearance (mL/min)	Herpes Zoster	Genital Herpes
>30	1 g every 8 hours*	500 mg every 12 hours*
15 to 30	1 g every 12 hours	500 mg every 12 hours*
<15	1 g every 24 hours	500 mg every 24 hours

*Standard dose—adjustment not necessary.

Hemodialysis: During hemodialysis, the half-life of acyclovir after administration of valacyclovir is approximately 4 hours. About 1/3 of acyclovir in the body is removed by dialysis during a 4-hour hemodialysis session. These patients should receive the daily dose of valacyclovir recommended for patients with creatinine clearance of <15 mL/min, with the dose administered after hemodialysis on the days it is performed.

Peritoneal Dialysis: There is no information specific to administration of valacyclovir. The effect of chronic ambulatory peritoneal dialysis (CAPD) and continuous arteriovenous hemofiltration/dialysis (CAVHD) on acyclovir pharmacokinetics has been studied. The removal of acyclovir after CAPD and CAVHD is less pronounced than with hemodialysis, and the pharmacokinetic parameters closely resemble those observed in patients with ESRD not receiving hemodialysis. Therefore, supplemental doses of valacyclovir should not be required following CAPD or CAVHD.

Information for the Patient: See Blue Section—Information for the Patient "Valtrex".

Supplied: Each blue, film-coated, capsule-shaped tablet (caplet), printed with edible white ink with "VALTREX 500 mg", contains: valacyclovir HCl equivalent to 500 mg valacyclovir. Nonmedicinal ingredients: carnauba wax, cellulose, crospovidone, hydroxypropyl methylcellulose, Indigotine Aluminum Lake, magnesium stearate, polyethylene glycol, polysorbate 80, povidone, silicon dioxide and titanium dioxide. Bottles of 42, blister packs of 10. Store between 15 and 25°C and protect from light.

(Shown in Product Recognition Section)

Reviewed 1998

Table I—Valtrex

Incidence (%) of Adverse Events in Herpes Zoster and Genital Herpes Study Populations*

	Herpes Zoster				Genital Herpes	
	18-50 Years		≥50 Years		18-79 Years	
Adverse Event	Valtrex (n=202)	Placebo (n=195)	Valtrex (n=765)	Acyclovir (n=376)	Valtrex (n=1 235)	Placebo (n=439)
Nausea	10	8	16	19	6	8
Headache	17	12	13	13	17	14
Vomiting	4	3	7	8	<1	<1
Diarrhea	4	6	5	7	4	6
Constipation	1	3	5	5	<1	1
Asthenia	3	4	4	5	2	4
Dizziness	2	2	4	6	3	3
Abdominal Pain	2	2	3	3	2	3
Anorexia	<1	2	3	3	<1	<1
Dyspepsia	0	1	2	2	1	2
Dry Mouth	<1	0	2	1	1	<1

*Adverse events were not significantly different in recipients of Valtrex compared to placebo or acyclovir.

VAMIN® 18 ELECTROLYTE-FREE

Pharmacia & Upjohn

Amino Acids

Nutritive and Electrolyte Supplements for I.V. Infusion

Pharmacology: Vamin 18 Electrolyte-Free acts as a source for protein synthesis in patients with insufficient enteral supply of precursors for protein synthesis. The solution contains all 18 essential and nonessential amino acids. The balance between the amino acids is such that positive nitrogen balance can be achieved in the postoperative period. When the current needs of energy, electrolytes, trace elements and vitamins are covered, the infused amino acids will be utilized maximally for protein synthesis.

The metabolism of the Vamin preparations is the same as for amino acids and electrolytes obtained in food. The Vamin preparations are used in the body to maintain or restore body cell mass and electrolyte content and for the supply of energy.

They have no pharmacodynamic effects when administered at recommended rates. No effects were observed on blood pressure, heart rate and respiratory frequency in patients and healthy subjects when Vamin 18 Electrolyte-Free alone and with additional electrolytes were administered at and above the recommended dosage rates. Only negligible amounts of the infused amino acids were excreted in urine.

Plasma amino acid concentrations have been measured in patients receiving infusions of Vamin 18. The plasma concentration of valine, leucine, phenylalanine, lysine, glycine, alanine, histidine and arginine increased during a study period of 7 days. However, these increases are not considered to be clinically significant. Evaluation of amino acid concentration in patients is complicated by the derangement of the plasma aminogram which varies with the clinical situation.

Efficacy has been determined by nitrogen balance studies which indicate that the amino acid content of Vamin 18 Electrolyte-Free is used in minimizing losses of, maintaining or increasing the amount of body proteins.

The infusion of 18 g of nitrogen daily as Vamin 18 in patients with severe burns, an example of patients with a greatly increased protein requirement, led to significantly improved nitrogen balance when compared to similar patients receiving the same amount of energy but no amino acids. The nitrogen balance did not improve further when 24 g of nitrogen were administered.

Positive nitrogen balance was achieved in most surgical patients, an example of patients with a moderately increased protein requirement, by infusion of 18 g of nitrogen as Vamin 18. However, severely ill patients with highly increased excretion of nitrogen were not brought into positive nitrogen balance on all days.

To obtain a positive effect on protein metabolism there is an additional requirement. Amino acids should be infused as part of a complete nutritional regimen supplying sufficient amounts of energy and essential nutrients, e.g., essential fatty acids, electrolytes, trace elements and vitamins.

Indications: As a source of amino acids for protein synthesis in patients requiring i.v. nutrition. Vamin 18 Electrolyte-Free is suitable for patients with varying degrees of metabolic stress, from unstressed malnourished patients in an anabolic state to severely catabolic patients such as those who have experienced major surgery, severe trauma or burns.

Contraindications: Irreversible liver damage. Severe uremia when dialysis facilities are not available. Hypersensitivity to one or more amino acids.

Warnings: At the recommended rate of infusion single cases of nausea may occur. Vomiting, flushing and sweating may occur when the infusion rate is high.

Appropriate laboratory tests, especially those for monitoring of liver functions and renal functions, should be performed periodically during the course of use of the product.

The solutions are hypertonic and thrombophlebitis may occur when a hypertonic solution is infused into peripheral veins. Consequently, when it is infused peripherally care should be taken to select a vein so that blood flow is not reduced by the pressure of the needle or catheter. Furthermore, the risk of thrombophlebitis can be reduced if the solution is infused simultaneously with the almost isotonic fat emulsion Intralipid. A Y-connector should be employed to provide a dilution effect when using the peripheral technique.

Administration of Vamin 18 Electrolyte-Free simultaneously with blood through the same infusion apparatus can provoke pseudo-agglutination.

Vamin, like any other arginine containing amino acid solution, is an insulin secretagogue, and should be infused concomitantly with a glucose solution in order to avoid hypoglycemia.

Pregnancy and *Lactation:* Animal reproduction studies have not been carried out with Vamin 18 Electrolyte-Free. There are published reports on the successful and safe infusion of amino acid solutions during pregnancy. However, Vamin 18 Electrolyte-Free should be administered with caution to pregnant and lactating women and only when this is deemed essential to the patient's welfare, as judged by the physician.

Children: No controlled studies have been conducted to establish the mode of use of Vamin 18 Electrolyte-Free in children.

Precautions: Infusion by central venous catheter should be used only by those familiar with this technique and its complications.

In patients with risk of electrolyte retention, e.g., impaired renal function, Vamin 18 Electrolyte-Free is recommended.

Adverse Effects: Single cases of nausea may occur at the recommended rate of infusion. Vomiting, flushing, sweating may occur when the infusion rate is high. If these symptoms appear or are severe, reduce or discontinue the infusion.

Hypersensitivity Rarely, patients may exhibit hypersensitivity to one or more amino acids.

Symptoms of thrombophlebitis can appear at the site of a peripheral vein infusion. In such instances, the infusion site should be changed to another vein. Use of a larger peripheral vein and reducing the rate of infusion might be helpful. Alternatively, infusion by central venous catheter can be used (see Precautions).

Overdose: Symptoms and Treatment: If the solution is administered at a rate exceeding that recommended, there is an increased risk of nausea and vomiting as well as thrombophlebitis.

Dosage: Adults: Up to 1 L i.v./day depending upon the patient's requirement. The infusion time of 1 L Vamin 18 Electrolyte-Free should be 8 hours or longer.

Energy requirements should be met by infusing additional carbohydrate solution and lipid emulsion according to the individual energy requirements calculated for each patient (see Warnings). When Vamin 18 Electrolyte-Free is infused simultaneously with 500 mL of the fat emulsion Intralipid 20% over 8 hours, the drip rate should be adjusted to about 40 drops/minute of the amino acid solution and to about 20 drops/minute of the fat emulsion. This will reduce the risk for thrombophlebitis when infused into peripheral veins.

The nitrogen requirement for maintenance of body protein mass depends on the patient's condition, i.e., nutritional state and degree of metabolic stress. The requirements are: 0.10 to 0.15 g nitrogen/kg/day: no or minor metabolic stress and normal nutritional state; 0.15 to 0.20 g nitrogen/kg/day: moderate metabolic stress with or without malnutrition; 0.20 to 0.25 g nitrogen/kg/day: severe catabolism as in burns, sepsis and trauma; $\leq$0.40 g nitrogen/kg/day: pure malnutrition without metabolic stress (patient must be adequately monitored.

The dosage range of 0.10 to 0.25 g nitrogen/kg/day, corresponds to 6 to 14 mL Vamin 18 Electrolyte-Free/kg/day.

In obese patients, the dose should be based on the estimated ideal weight.

Vamin 18 Electrolyte-Free is particularly suitable for the most catabolic patients who require the highest doses and also for fluid restricted patients because it is the most concentrated solution.

Vamin 18 Electrolyte-Free allows individualized dosing of electrolytes.

Electrolytes can be added to the amino acid solution in amounts depending on the particular requirement of the patient.

1 000 mL of Vamin 18 Electrolyte-Free can be added without risk for precipitation together or separately $\leq$480 mmol Na^+ and $\leq$480 mmol K^+ as chlorides, $\leq$24 mmol Ca^{++} as glubionate and $\leq$48 mmol Mg^{++} as sulfate.

Additions should be performed aseptically immediately before the start of the infusion. Discard unused contents.

Supplied: Each 100 mL of sterile solution contains: see Table I.

Table I—Vamin 18 Electrolyte-Free

Composition	
Amino Acids	
Essential	
L-Isoleucine	560 mg
L-Leucine	790 mg
L-Lysine (as acetate)	900 mg
L-Methionine	560 mg
L-Phenylalanine	790 mg
L-Threonine	560 mg
L-Tryptophan	190 mg
L-Valine	730 mg
Nonessential	
L-Alanine	1 600 mg
L-Arginine	1 130 mg
L-Aspartic Acid	340 mg
L-Cysteine/L-Cystine	56 mg
L-Glutamic Acid	560 mg
Glycine	790 mg
L-Histidine	680 mg
L-Proline	680 mg
L-Serine	450 mg
L-Tyrosine	23 mg
Electrolytes	
Acetate	11 mEq
Water for Injection to 100 mL	
pH is adjusted with acetic acid to pH 5.6	
Amino acid concentration (% by weight)	11.4
Total nitrogen (g/L)	18.0
Energy (kcal/L)	460
Osmolality (mOsm/L)	1 035

Sulfite-free. Bottles of 500 and 1 000 mL. Store at 15 to 25°C. Do not freeze.

Reviewed 1997

VAMIN® N
Pharmacia & Upjohn
Amino Acids—Electrolytes
Nutritive and Electrolyte Supplements for I.V. Infusion

Pharmacology: Vamin N supplies electrolytes and essential, semi-essential and nonessential L-amino acids for synthesis of body proteins. Nitrogen retention can be promoted by adjusting the energy to nitrogen ratio with simultaneous administration of lipids and/or hypertonic sugar solutions according to the needs of the patient.

Indications: For parenteral nutrition in the following conditions: Pre- and postoperative nutritional disorders, in which an increased administration of amino acids is desired or necessary. In many cases this is synonymous with a disturbed nitrogen balance.

Nutritive disorders or nitrogen imbalance resulting from decreased or inhibited intestinal absorption. Such disorders may be due to tumors of the digestive tract, to acute or chronic intestinal diseases such as: peritonitis, ulcerative colitis or terminal ileitis.

Burns. In extensive burns the protein losses are often excessive. In these cases every amino acid and caloric supplement is of the utmost importance for reducing such losses.

Even if the patients are able to take nourishment by mouth, difficulties are often encountered in supplying sufficient amounts of protein and calories in the diet.

Prolonged states of unconsciousness, e.g., following trauma of the skull or intoxication and in such cases where tube feeding is inadvisable or impossible.

Cachexia due to serious diseases in organs other than the alimentary tract, e.g., metastasized tumors, systemic diseases.

As Vamin N does not contain sulfites, it can safely be used in patients with a known or suspected sulfite sensitivity.

Contraindications: Irreversible liver insufficiency and severe uremia when dialysis possibilities are lacking, and hypersensitivity to one or more amino acids are contraindications (see Warnings and Precautions).

Warnings: Clinical studies have shown that Vamin N is well tolerated both in the immediate postoperative period and in short-term i.v. nutrition. However, in isolated cases, nausea and hypersensitivity symptoms have been reported as was the possibility of liver malfunction.

Appropriate laboratory tests, especially those for the monitoring of liver functions and renal functions, should be performed periodically during the course of use of the product.

Infusion by central catheter should be used only by those familiar with this technique and its complications.

Compared to plasma, Vamin N is a hypertonic solution (665 mOsm/L). Consequently, when it is infused peripherally, care should be taken to select a vein such that blood flow is not reduced by the pressure of the needle or catheter. Furthermore, simultaneous infusion of isotonic nutrient solutions with a Y-connector should be employed to provide a dilution effect when using the peripheral technique.

Administration of Vamin N simultaneously with blood through the same infusion apparatus can provoke pseudo-agglutination.

Pregnancy and *Lactation* and Children: Safety to the fetus and the neonate has not been established. Vamin N should be administered with caution to neonates and to females during pregnancy and lactation and only when this is deemed essential to the patient's welfare, as judged by the physician.

Vamin N should be given with caution to very sick children, small and/or premature babies requiring neonatal intensive care due to the risk of inducing hyperphenylalaninemia. In such babies, it is advisable to monitor the plasma phenylalanine concentration.

Vamin N contains electrolytes including sodium ion and potassium ion. These electrolytes should be used with great care and with periodical monitoring using the appropriate laboratory tests.

Precautions: Vamin N should be used cautiously in severe hepatic diseases and acute renal impairment.

Vamin N should be given with caution to very sick children, small and/or premature babies requiring neonatal intensive care due to the risk of inducing hyperphenylalaninemia. In such babies, it is advisable to monitor the plasma phenylalanine concentration (see Warnings and Adverse Effects).

Infusion by central venous catheter should be used only by those familiar with this technique and its complications.

Adverse Effects: Nausea: If such symptoms appear or are of a severe degree, reduce or discontinue the infusion.

Hypersensitivity: Rarely, patients may exhibit hypersensitivity to 1 or more amino acids.

Symptoms of thrombophlebitis can appear at the site of a peripheral vein infusion. In such instances, the infusion site should be changed to another vein. Use of a larger peripheral vein and reducing the rate of infusion might be helpful. Alternatively, infusion by central venous catheter can be used (see Precautions).

Dosage: The dosage of parenteral nutrient solutions should be calculated separately for each patient in accordance with nutrient requirements and body weight.

Vamin N provides 70 g crystalline amino acids/L. The basal requirements of amino acids for adults (0.7 to 1 g/kg body weight/day) can be met with 10 to 15 mL/kg of Vamin/day (or 1 L/day for a 70 kg patient).

The basal energy requirement of 20 to 30 kcal/kg/day should be met by infusing additional carbohydrate solution and/or lipid emulsion. The actual amount of additional carbohydrate and/or lipid to be included in the dosage should be adjusted to meet individual patient requirements.

The basal dosage of Vamin N (10 to 15 mL/kg/day) should be adjusted to meet increased amino acid and caloric requirements such as with severely depleted or hypercatabolic patients.

An infusion rate of between 4 and 2 mL/min is usually most suitable, such that 1 L of solution is infused during 4 to 8 hours in adults. Higher or lower infusion rates may be desirable for practical reasons.

When Vamin N is infused simultaneously with other nutrient solutions using a Y-connector either peripherally or centrally, the drip rates of each solution should be reduced in keeping with the patient's tolerance for the total fluid volumes.

Infusion by central venous catheter should be used only by those familiar with this technique and its complications.

Symptoms of thrombophlebitis can appear at the site of peripheral vein infusion. In such instances, the infusion site should be changed to another vein. Use of a larger peripheral vein and reducing the rate of infusion may be helpful. Alternatively, infusion by central venous catheter can be used (see Warnings and Precautions).

Vamin N (cont'd)

Supplied: Each 100 mL of sterile, pyrogen-free solution contains: See Table I.

Table I—Vamin N

Composition	
Amino Acids	
Essential	
L-Isoleucine	390 mg
L-Leucine	530 mg
L-Lysine (as hydrochloride)	390 mg
L-Methionine	190 mg
L-Phenylalanine	550 mg
L-Threonine	300 mg
L-Tryptophan	100 mg
L-Valine	425 mg
Nonessential	
L-Alanine	300 mg
L-Arginine	330 mg
L-Aspartic Acid	410 mg
L-Cysteine/L-Cystine (as hydrochloride)	140 mg
L-Glutamic Acid	900 mg
Glycine	210 mg
L-Histidine	240 mg
L-Proline	810 mg
L-Serine	750 mg
L-Tyrosine	50 mg
Electrolytes	
Sodium	5.0 mEq (sodium hydroxide)
Potassium	2.0 mEq (potassium chloride and potassium hydroxide)
Calcium	0.5 mEq (calcium chloride)
Magnesium	0.3 mEq (magnesium sulfate)
Chloride Ion	5.0 mEq
Water for Injection to 100 mL	
Energy	250 kcal/L
Osmolarity	665 mOsm/L
pH	5.2
Nitrogen	9.4 g/L

Sulfite- and tartrazine-free. Bottles of 500 and 1 000 mL. Vamin N will remain stable for 2 years, when stored at 5 to 25°C.

Reviewed 1997

VANCENASE®

Schering

Beclomethasone Dipropionate

Rhinitis—Hay Fever Therapy

Indications: The treatment of perennial and seasonal rhinitis and hay fever symptoms when tolerance to, or effectiveness of, conventional treatment is unsatisfactory.

Contraindications: Active or quiescent untreated pulmonary tuberculosis; untreated bacterial, viral or fungal infections; hypersensitivity to any of the product's components; children under 6 years of age.

Precautions: See Vanceril Oral Inhaler. Vancenase is not recommended for patients with a history of recurrent nasal bleeding.

Patients receiving corticosteroids who are potentially immunosuppressed should be warned of the risk of exposure to certain infections (e.g., chickenpox, measles) and of the importance of obtaining medical advice if such exposure occurs. This is of particular importance in children.

During Vancenase therapy, the possibility of pharyngeal candidiasis, atrophic rhinitis or other changes in nasal mucosa should be kept in mind.

Instruct patients to use Vancenase for several days as the onset of action and full therapeutic effect may be somewhat slower than for topical or oral sympathomimetic amines or antihistamines. Patients should be reevaluated after several days.

Pregnancy and *Lactation:* The use of this product during pregnancy and lactation has not been established and therefore the compound should be used only if the potential benefit justifies the potential risk to the fetus or infant.

If hypersensitivity reactions occur during therapy, discontinue the drug.

Adverse Effects: The most frequently observed adverse effects are those consistent with what one would expect in applying a topical medication to an already inflamed membrane. These include mild transient burning and stinging which occasionally require discontinuance of therapy. Other possible adverse effects in patients treated with Vancenase are: nasal irritation, nosebleed, sneezing, throat irritation and sore throat.

Overdose: Symptoms and Treatment: Vancenase has the potential for causing hypercorticism and/or adrenal suppression which may respond to dosage reduction or symptomatic treatment respectively.

Dosage: The usual dose for adults and children over 6 years of age is 1 metered dose (50 μg) into each nostril 3 to 4 times daily. Maximum daily dose should not exceed 20 metered doses (1 000 μg) for adults and 10 doses (500 μg) for children. Subsequent dosage may be modified according to patient response. Insufficient information is available to warrant the safe use in children under 6 years of age.

When Vancenase is used concurrently with Vanceril, the combined total daily dose should not exceed the maximum daily recommended dose of beclomethasone dipropionate.

Emphasize to patients the need for the regular use and proper operation of the pressurized canister. The nasal passages must be clear before using Vancenase. This may be done simply by blowing the nose or by taking other appropriate medical measures when necessary.

Careful attention must be given to patients previously treated for prolonged periods with systemic corticosteroids when transferring them to Vancenase. Initially, Vancenase and the systemic corticosteroid must be given concomitantly for 10 to 14 days, followed by a gradual withdrawal of the systemic corticosteroids. Dose reductions should be at a rate not to exceed 1 mg (prednisone) every 10 to 14 days if close continuous medical supervision is not feasible. It may be possible to withdraw systemic corticosteroids more rapidly if the initial dosage was 7.5 mg daily of prednisone (or equivalent) or less, or if the patient is under close continuous medical supervision. In patients who are not able to completely discontinue the use of systemic corticosteroids, a minimum maintenance dose should be continued in addition to Vancenase.

Supplied: Each metered dose of nasal inhaler contains: beclomethasone dipropionate USP 50 μg. Nonmedicinal ingredients: oleic acid, trichloromonofluoromethane and dichlorodifluoromethane. Aerosol canisters filled to provide a minimum of 100 or 200 doses depending on dosage regimen utilized.

VANCERIL®

Schering

Beclomethasone Dipropionate

Asthma Prophylaxis

Pharmacology: Beclomethasone is a potent anti-inflammatory steroid with a strong topical and weak systemic activity. When inhaled at therapeutic doses it has a direct anti-inflammatory action on the bronchial mucosa with minimal systemic effect.

After administration by inhalation approximately 10 to 25% of a dose reaches the respiratory tract; the remainder is swallowed and absorbed from the gastrointestinal tract. Beclomethasone dipropionate is rapidly hydrolyzed by lung esterases to 17-monopropionate and more slowly to the free base. Orally absorbed drug is metabolized by the liver. After administration of labeled drug approximately 35 to 65% of the radioactivity is recovered in the feces and 10 to 15% in the urine.

Indications: Treatment of corticosteroid responsive asthma: 1) In asthmatic patients who do not respond adequately to conventional therapy. 2) In corticosteroid dependent asthmatics where a reduction of systemic corticosteroids is desirable.

Contraindications: Active or quiescent untreated pulmonary tuberculosis, or untreated fungal, bacterial and viral infections of the respiratory system. Do not use in children under the age of 6 years, in status asthmaticus, or in patients with moderate to severe bronchiectasis.

Precautions: In patients previously on high doses of systemic corticosteroids, transfer to beclomethasone aerosol may cause withdrawal symptoms such as tiredness, aches and pains and depression. In severe cases, acute adrenal insufficiency may occur necessitating the temporary resumption of systemic corticosteroids.

The development of pharyngeal and laryngeal candidiasis is cause for concern because the extent of its penetration of the respiratory tract is unknown. If candidiasis develops, discontinue beclomethasone aerosol and institute appropriate antifungal therapy. The incidence of candidiasis can generally be held to a minimum by having the patient rinse their mouth with water after each inhalation. The patient must be instructed not to swallow the water used for rinsing.

The replacement of a systemic steroid with beclomethasone aerosol must be gradual and supervised carefully. Follow the guidelines under Dosage in all such cases.

Pregnancy and *Lactation:* The safe use of this product during pregnancy and lactation has not been established and therefore the compound should be used only if the potential benefit justifies the potential risk to the fetus, particularly during the first trimester of pregnancy, or to the infant.

Patients receiving corticosteroids who are potentially immunosuppressed should be warned of the risk of exposure to certain infections (e.g., chickenpox, measles) and of the importance of obtaining medical advice if such exposure occurs. This is of particular importance in children.

A decreased resistance to localized infection has been observed during corticosteroid therapy. Corticosteroids may mask some signs of infection and new infections may appear.

During long-term therapy, pituitary-adrenal function and hematological status should be periodically assessed.

Fluorocarbon propellants may be hazardous if they are deliberately abused. Inhalation of high concentrations of aerosol sprays has brought about cardiovascular toxic effects and even death, especially under conditions of hypoxia. However, evidence attests to the relative safety of aerosols when used properly and with adequate ventilation.

Instruct patients that beclomethasone aerosol is a preventative agent which must be taken at regular intervals, and is not to be used during an asthmatic attack.

There is an enhanced effect of corticosteroids on patients with hypothyroidism and in those with cirrhosis.

Use ASA cautiously in conjunction with corticosteroids in hypoprothrombinemia.

Advise patients to inform subsequent physicians of the prior use of corticosteroids.

Adverse Effects: No major adverse effects attributable to the use of recommended doses have been reported. No significant systemic effects have been observed when the daily dose was below 1 mg (20 puffs). Above this dose, reduction of plasma cortisol, indicating adrenal cortical suppression, may occur. Immediate and delayed hypersensitivity reactions including bronchospasm, rash, urticaria, angioedema and localized infections with C. albicans or A. niger in the mouth, throat, larynx, bronchus and esophagus have been reported. In a few patients, the appearance of hoarseness, drymouth and pharyngeal irritation has been observed, occasionally necessitating withdrawal of treatment.

Rare cases of glaucoma have been reported with the use of inhaled corticosteroids.

The replacement of systemic steroids with the inhaler may unmask symptoms of allergies which were suppressed previously by the systemic drug. Conditions such as allergic rhinitis and eczema may thus become apparent during therapy after the withdrawal of systemic corticosteroids and should be treated appropriately.

Overdose: Symptoms and Treatment: Overdosage may cause systemic steroid effects resulting in symptoms of hypercorticism and/or adrenal suppression. Decreasing the dose will abolish some of these adverse effects, when due to excessive dosage. Treat adrenal suppression symptomatically.

Dosage: Optimum doses vary, but the total daily dose should not exceed 1 mg of beclomethasone (20 puffs), and should not be instituted until the severe attack has been controlled with systemic corticosteroids.

For adults, the usual maintenance dose is 2 inhalations (each 50 μg) 3 to 4 times/day. In severe cases, it is advisable to control the symptoms with systemic corticosteroids before starting treatment with beclomethasone inhaler. Insufficient information is available to warrant the safe use in children under age 6. For children over 6 years of age, 1 inhalation (50 μg) up to 4 times daily.

Maximum daily dose should not exceed 20 inhalations for adults and 10 inhalations for children under 12 years of age.

Since the effect of the inhaler depends on its regular use and on the proper inhalation technique, instruct patients to take inhalations at regular intervals. They should also be instructed in the correct method; to exhale completely, lips to be placed tightly around the mouth piece and actuate the aerosol in the next inspiratory period.

In the presence of excess mucus secretion, severe attacks of asthma, and/or infection or high atmospheric concentrations of appropriate antigens, the drug may fail to reach the bronchioles. Therefore, if an obvious response is not obtained after 7 days, institute appropriate therapy including a short course of systemic corticosteroids before returning to the use of inhaler, as well as the concomitant use of bronchodilator aerosol.

Careful attention must be given to patients treated previously for prolonged periods with systemic corticosteroids when transferring them to beclomethasone aerosol. Initially, beclomethasone aerosol and the systemic steroid must be given concomitantly for 10 to 14 days, followed by a gradual withdrawal of the systemic steroids. Dose reductions should be the equivalent of 1.0 mg of prednisone every 10 to 14 days if close continuous medical supervision is not feasible. It may be possible to withdraw systemic corticosteroids more rapidly if the initial dosage was 7.5 mg daily of prednisone (or equivalent) or less, or if the patient is under close continuous medical supervision. Some patients may not be able to completely discontinue the use of systemic steroids. In such cases, a minimum maintenance dose should be continued in addition to beclomethasone aerosol.

Supplied: Each metered dose of oral inhaler contains: beclomethasone dipropionate USP 50 μg. Nonmedicinal ingredients: oleic acid, trichlorofluoromethane and dichlorofluoromethane. Each canister provides 200 metered sprays. Canisters of 100 doses available to hospitals only.

VANCOCIN® Ⓟ

Lilly

Vancomycin HCl

Antibiotic

Pharmacology: In vitro studies indicate that the bactericidal action of vancomycin against many Gram-positive bacteria results from the inhibition of cell-wall synthesis. There is also evidence that vancomycin alters the permeability of the cell membrane and selectively inhibits RNA synthesis.

Vancomycin, a glycopeptide antibiotic derived from A. orientalis (formerly N. orientalis) is poorly absorbed by mouth, but a 1 g i.v. dose produces serum levels averaging 25 μg/mL at 2 hours. Its half-life in the circulation is about 6 hours.

Cross-resistance has not been demonstrated between vancomycin and other classes of antibiotics. Laboratory-induced resistance has been reported to occur in a slow stepwise fashion. The development of resistance to vancomycin by staphylococci has not been reported in clinical use. Its activity is not significantly altered by changes in pH or by the presence of serum. Vancomycin is active against most strains of the following organisms in vitro and in clinical infections: S. aureus (including heterogeneous methicillin-resistant strains), C. difficile, S. epidermidis (including heterogeneous methicillin-resistant strains), S. pneumoniae (including multiple-resistant strains), S. pyogenes (group A beta-hemolytic), S. agalactiae (group B beta-hemolytic), S. bovis, Alpha-hemolytic streptococci (viridans groups), Enterococci (e.g., E. faecalis), Bacillus species, L. monocytogenes, Lactobacillus species, Neisseria species, Diphtheroids, Actinomyces species.

Many strains of streptococci, staphylococci, C. difficile and other Gram-positive bacteria are sensitive in vitro to concentrations of 0.5 to 5 μg/mL. Staphylococci are generally susceptible to less than 5 μg/mL, but a small proportion of S. aureus strains requires 10 to 20 μg/mL for inhibition. Vancomycin is not effective in vitro against Gram-negative bacilli, mycobacteria or fungi.

Adults: I.V.: When a single i.v. injection of 500 mg of vancomycin was administered over 30 minutes to healthy volunteers, the mean serum peak concentration was 51 μg/mL, 18.6 μg/mL at 1 hour and 5.8 μg/mL at 6 hours post infusion. After a 1 g single dose i.v. over 30 minutes, the mean peak level was 85 μg/mL, 29 μg/mL at 1 hour, 11 μg/mL at 6 hours, and 5.1 μg/mL at 12 hours post infusion. Following multiple dosages of 500 mg every 6 hours infused over 30 minutes, the mean peak ranged from 41 to 57 μg/mL. Following multiple 60 minute 1 g i.v. infusions of vancomycin in healthy volunteers, mean peak plasma concentrations were 64 μg/mL, 12.5 μg/mL at 6 hours, and 7 μg/mL at 12 hours post infusion. The plasma half-life ranged from 3 to 8 hours with an overall mean of 4.5 hours.

Renal Insufficiency: Infusions of 1 g vancomycin in 250 mL D5-W were given over 30 minutes to 29 anephric patients. After 18 days with intermittent dialysis at 3-day intervals, the serum concentration was still 3.5 μg/mL. The elimination half-life was about 7.5 days.

Oral: Vancomycin is poorly absorbed after oral administration, only trace amounts being found in blood or urine. Following 125 mg orally 4 times daily, the mean concentration of vancomycin in stools was approximately 350 μg/g. Following up to 10 daily oral doses of 2 g, a mean level of 3 100 μg/g with a range of 905 to 8 760 μg/g was detected in feces of patients with pseudomembranous colitis.

Tissue Penetration and Distribution: CNS: Vancomycin does not readily diffuse across normal meninges into the spinal fluid; but, when the meninges are inflamed, penetration into the spinal fluid occurs.

Other Tissues and Fluids: Vancomycin concentration in human pericardial, pleural, bile, ascitic and synovial fluids reaches approximately one third of the equivalent serum level after single i.v. doses. A level of 7.6 μg/mL was achieved in the brain cyst of one infant following i.v. infusion of 40 mg/kg daily for 4 days.

Indications: I.V.: May be indicated in the therapy of severe or life-threatening staphylococcal infections in patients who cannot receive or who have failed to respond to the penicillins and cephalosporins or who have infections with staphylococci resistant to other antibiotics, including methicillin.

Vancomycin i.v. has been used successfully alone in the treatment of staphylococcal endocarditis.

Vancomycin i.v. has been reported to be effective alone or in combination with an aminoglycoside for endocarditis caused by S. viridans or S. bovis. For endocarditis caused by enterococci (e.g. E. faecalis), vancomycin i.v. has been reported to be effective only in combination with an aminoglycoside.

Vancomycin i.v. has been reported to be effective for the treatment of diphtheroid endocarditis. It has been used successfully in combination with either rifampin, an aminoglycoside, or both in early-onset prosthetic valve endocarditis caused by S. epidermidis or diphtheroids.

Specimens for bacteriologic cultures should be obtained in order to isolate and identify causative organisms and to determine their susceptibilities to vancomycin i.v.

Its effectiveness has been documented in other infections due to staphylococci, including osteomyelitis, pneumonia, septicemia, and soft-tissue infections. When staphylococcal infections are localized and purulent, antibiotics are used as adjuncts to appropriate surgical measures.

Although no controlled clinical efficacy trials have been conducted, vancomycin i.v. has been suggested by the American Heart Association and the American Dental Association for prophylaxis against bacterial endocarditis in patients allergic to penicillin who have congenital and/or rheumatic or other acquired valvular heart disease when they undergo dental procedures or surgical procedures of the upper respiratory tract. (Note: When selecting antibiotics for the prevention of bacterial endocarditis, the physician or dentist should read the full joint statement of the American Heart Association and the American Dental Association.)

Capsules: May be used orally for the treatment of staphylococcal enterocolitis and antibiotic associated pseudomembranous colitis produced by C. difficile. **Parenteral administration of vancomycin is not effective for these indications, therefore vancomycin must be given orally.**

Vancomycin is not effective by the oral route for the treatment of other types of infection. Vancomycin is not effective in vitro against Gram-negative bacilli, mycobacteria, or fungi.

Contraindications: Known hypersensitivity to vancomycin.

Warnings: Rapid bolus administration (e.g., over several minutes) may be associated with exaggerated hypotension, including shock, and, rarely, cardiac arrest.

When given i.v., toxic serum levels can occur. Vancomycin is excreted fairly rapidly by the kidney and blood levels increase markedly with decreased renal clearance. During parenteral therapy, the risk of toxicity appears appreciably increased by high blood concentrations or prolonged treatment. Vancomycin is poorly absorbed orally. Toxic serum levels are therefore not attained from oral dosage.

Clinically significant serum concentrations have been reported in some patients who have taken multiple oral doses of vancomycin for active C. difficile-induced pseudomembranous colitis; therefore, monitoring of serum concentrations may be appropriate in these patients.

Ototoxicity has occurred when serum levels exceeded 80 μg/mL. Deafness may be preceded by tinnitus. The elderly are more susceptible to auditory damage. Experience with other antibiotics suggests that deafness may be progressive despite cessation of treatment.

Concurrent and sequential use of other neurotoxic and/or nephrotoxic antibiotics, particularly ethacrynic acid, neuromuscular blocking agents, aminoglycoside antibiotics, polymyxin B, colistin, viomycin and cisplatin requires careful monitoring.

If parenteral and oral vancomycin are administered concomitantly an additive effect can occur. This should be taken into consideration when calculating the total dose. In this situation serum levels of the antibiotic should be monitored.

Precautions: Vancomycin i.v. should be administered in a dilute solution over a period of not less than 60 minutes to avoid rapid-infusion-related reactions. Stopping the infusion usually results in a prompt cessation of these reactions (see Dosage and Adverse Effects).

Because of its ototoxicity and nephrotoxicity, vancomycin should be used with care in patients with renal insufficiency. If it is necessary to use vancomycin parenterally in patients with renal impairment, the dose and/or dose intervals should be adjusted carefully and blood levels monitored.

Vancomycin should be avoided (if possible) in patients with previous hearing loss. If it is used in such patients, the dose of vancomycin should be regulated by periodic determination of drug levels in the blood. Patients with renal insufficiency and individuals over the age of 60 should be given serial tests of auditory function and of vancomycin blood levels. All patients receiving the drug should have periodic hematologic studies, urinalysis, and liver and renal function tests.

The prolonged use of vancomycin may result in overgrowth of nonsusceptible organisms. If new infections due to bacteria or fungi appear during therapy with this product, appropriate measures should be taken including withdrawal of vancomycin. In rare instances there have been reports of pseudomembranous colitis due to C. difficile developing in patients who received i.v. vancomycin.

Since vancomycin i.v. is irritating to tissue and causes drug fever, pain and possibly necrosis it should **never** be injected i.m.; it must be administered i.v. Pain and thrombophlebitis occur in many patients receiving vancomycin i.v. and are occasionally severe. The frequency and severity of thrombophlebitis can be minimized if the drug is administered in a volume of at least 200 mL of glucose or saline solution and if the injection sites are rotated.

There have been reports that the frequency of infusion-related events (including hypotension, flushing, erythema, urticaria, and pruritus) increases with concomitant administration of anesthetic agents. Infusion-related events may be minimized by the administration of vancomycin i.v. as a 60-minute infusion prior to anesthetic induction.

The safety and efficacy of vancomycin administration by the intrathecal (intralumbar or intraventricular) route have not been assessed.

Some patients with inflammatory disorders of the intestinal mucosa may have significant systemic absorption of oral vancomycin and, therefore, may be at risk for the development of adverse reactions associated with the parenteral administration of vancomycin. The risk is greater if renal impairment is present. It should be noted that the total systemic and renal clearances of vancomycin are reduced in the elderly.

When patients with underlying renal dysfunction or those receiving concomitant therapy with an aminoglycoside are being treated, serial monitoring of renal function should be performed.

Serial tests of auditory function may be helpful in order to minimize the risk of ototoxicity. Patients who will undergo prolonged therapy with vancomycin or those who are receiving concomitant drugs that may cause neutropenia should have periodic monitoring of their leukocyte count.

Concurrent and/or sequential systemic or topical use of other potentially neurotoxic and/or nephrotoxic drugs with vancomycin should be carefully monitored.

Pregnancy: Vancomycin should be given to a pregnant woman only if clearly needed. In a controlled clinical study, vancomycin was administered to 10 pregnant women for serious staphylococcal infections complicating i.v. drug abuse to evaluate potential ototoxic and nephrotoxic effects on the infant. Vancomycin levels of 13.2 and 16.6 μg/mL were measured in the cord blood of 2 patients. No sensorineural hearing loss or nephrotoxicity attributable to vancomycin was noted. One infant whose mother received vancomycin in the third trimester experienced conductive hearing loss that was not attributed to the administration of vancomycin. Because the

Vancocin (cont'd)

number of patients treated in this study was limited and vancomycin was administered only in the second and third trimesters, it is not known whether vancomycin causes fetal harm.

Lactation: Vancomycin is excreted in human milk. Caution should be exercised if vancomycin is to be administered to a nursing woman. Because of the potential for adverse events, a decision should be made whether to discontinue nursing or discontinue administration of the drug, taking into account the importance of the drug to the mother.

Children: In premature neonates and young infants, it may be appropriate to confirm desired vancomycin serum concentrations. Concomitant administration of vancomycin and anesthetic agents has been associated with erythema and histamine-like flushing in children.

Geriatrics: The natural decrement in glomerular filtration with increasing age may lead to elevated vancomycin serum concentrations if dosage is not adjusted. Vancomycin dosage schedules should be adjusted in elderly patients.

Adverse Effects: Infusion-related: During or soon after rapid infusion of vancomycin i.v., patients may develop anaphylactoid reactions, including hypotension, wheezing, dyspnea, urticaria, or pruritus. Rapid infusion may also cause flushing of the upper body (red neck) or pain and muscle spasm of the chest and back. These reactions usually resolve within 20 minutes but may persist for several hours. Such events are infrequent if vancomycin is given by slow infusion over 60 minutes. In studies in normal volunteers, infusion-related events did not occur when vancomycin was administered at a rate of 10 mg/minute or less.

Nephrotoxicity: Rarely, renal failure, principally manifested by increased serum creatinine or BUN concentrations, especially in patients given large doses of vancomycin, has been reported. Rare cases of interstitial nephritis have been reported. Most of these have occurred in patients who were given aminoglycosides concomitantly or who had pre-existing kidney dysfunction. When vancomycin was discontinued, azotemia resolved in most patients.

Ototoxicity: A few dozen cases of hearing loss, associated with vancomycin have been reported. Most of these patients had kidney dysfunction, pre-existing hearing loss, or concomitant treatment with an ototoxic drug. Vertigo, dizziness, and tinnitus have been reported rarely.

Hematopoietic: Reversible neutropenia, usually starting 1 week or more after onset of therapy with vancomycin or after a total dose of more than 25 g has been reported in several dozen patients. Neutropenia appears to be promptly reversible when vancomycin is discontinued. Thrombocytopenia has rarely been reported. Although a causal relationship has not been established, reversible agranulocytosis (granulocyte count less than 500/mm³) has been reported rarely.

Phlebitis: Inflammation at the injection site has been reported.

Miscellaneous: Anaphylaxis, drug fever, nausea, chills, eosinophilia, urticaria, and rashes, including exfoliative dermatitis, Stevens-Johnson syndrome, and rare cases of vasculitis, hypotension, wheezing, dyspnea, pruritus, flushing of the upper body ("red neck"), pain and muscle spasm of the chest and back have been associated with the administration of vancomycin.

Overdose: Symptoms and Treatment: Other than general supportive treatment, no specific antidote is known. Dialysis does not remove significant amounts of vancomycin. Hemofiltration and hemoperfusion with polysulfone resin have been reported to result in increased vancomycin clearance. In managing overdosage, consider the possibility of multiple drug overdoses, interaction among drugs, and unusual drug kinetics in the patient.

Dosage: Adults: The usual i.v. dose is 500 mg every 6 hours or 1 g every 12 hours. Each dose should be administered at no more than 10 mg/minute or over a period of at least 60 minutes, whichever is longer. Other patient factors, such as age or obesity, may call for modification of the usual i.v. daily dose.

Adults with impaired renal function: Dosage adjustment must be made in patients with impaired renal function to avoid toxic serum levels. Serum levels should be checked regularly, since accumulation in such patients has been reported to occur over several weeks of treatment.

For most patients with renal impairment or the elderly, the dosage calculation may be made by using the Figure I nomogram if the creatinine clearance value is known.

Figure I—Vancocin

Vancocin Dosing Nomogram

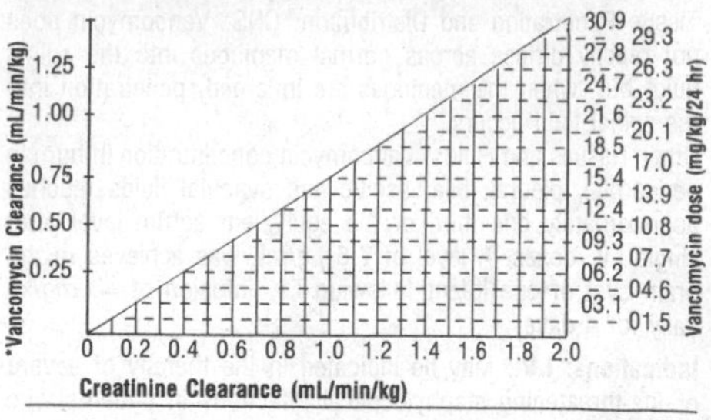

The nomogram is not valid for functionally anephric patients on dialysis. For such patients, a loading dose of 15 mg/kg of body weight should be given in order to achieve therapeutic serum levels promptly, and the dose required to maintain stable levels is 1.9 mg/kg/24 h.

When only serum creatinine is available, the following formula (based on sex, weight, and age of the patient) may be used to convert this value into estimated creatinine clearance. The serum creatinine should represent a steady state of renal function:

Males: $\dfrac{\text{Weight (kg)} \times (140-\text{age})}{72 \times \text{serum creatinine (mg/dL)}}$

Females: 0.85×above value.

Neonates, Infants and Children: The following dosage schedule has been used. Infusions should be over 60 minutes, and can be divided and incorporated in with the child's 24-hour fluid requirement.

Infants and Neonates: In both neonates and infants it is suggested that an initial dose of 15 mg/kg be given followed by 10 mg/kg every 12 hours for neonates in the first week of life and every 8 hours thereafter up to the age of one month. Each dose should be administered over 60 minutes. Close monitoring of serum concentrations of vancomycin may be warranted in these patients.

Children: The usual i.v. dosage of vancomycin is 10 mg/kg/dose given every 6 hours. The majority of patients with infections caused by organisms susceptible to the antibiotic show a therapeutic response by 48 to 72 hours. The total duration of therapy is determined by the type and severity of the infection and the clinical response of the patient. In staphylococcal endocarditis, therapy for 3 weeks or longer is recommended.

Oral: Adults: The usual daily dosage for antibiotic-associated pseudomembranous colitis and staphylococcal enterocolitis produced by C. difficile (orally administered vancomycin is not effective for other types of infection) is 125 to 500 mg administered orally every 6 to 8 hours for 7 to 10 days.

Children: The usual daily dosage is approximately 40 mg/kg in 3 or 4 divided doses for 7 to 10 days. The total daily dosage should not exceed 2 g.

Administration: Intermittent I.V. Infusion: The reconstituted solution must be **further diluted** with 100 to 200 mL Normal Saline or 5% dextrose in sterile water for injection. This should be infused over a period of at least 60 minutes. See instructions in the Reconstitution section.

Continuous I.V. Infusion: Should be used only when intermittent infusion is not practical.

Note: Infusion-related events are related to both concentration and rate of administration of vancomycin. Concentration of no more than 5 mg/mL and rates of no more than 10 mg/minute are recommended in adults (see age-specific recommendations). In selected patients in need of fluid restriction, a concentration up to 10 mg/mL may be used; use of such higher concentrations may increase risk of infusion-related events. Infusion related events may occur, however, at any rate or concentration.

Note: Vancomycin capsules are formulated in a matrix gel that prevents administration by a nasogastric tube; if this route of administration is being considered, the i.v. dosage form should be used.

Reconstitution: 500 mg vial: Reconstitute by adding 10 mL Sterile Water for Injection. This provides 10.3 mL of a solution containing 50 mg/mL of vancomycin base. Vancomycin solution has a low pH that may cause chemical or physical instability when it is mixed with other compounds. Prior to administration, parenteral drug products should be inspected visually for particulate matter and discoloration whenever solution or container permits.

1 g vial: Reconstitute by adding 20 mL Sterile Water for Injection. This provides 20.6 mL of solution containing 50 mg/mL of vancomycin base.

10 g Pharmacy Bulk Vial: Reconstitute by adding 95 mL Sterile Water for Injection. This provides 100 mL of solution containing 100 mg/mL of vancomycin base.

Note: Further dilution is required.

For intermittent i.v. infusion: 500 mg vial: Reconstituted solutions must be diluted with at least 100 mL of 0.9% Sodium Chloride Injection or D5W for Injection.

1 g vial: Reconstituted solutions must be diluted with at least 200 mL of 0.9% Sodium Injection or D5W for Injection.

For continuous i.v. infusion: The vials reconstituted according to the directions above should be further diluted to the desired volume with any of the solutions for i.v. infusion listed below: 5% Dextrose Injection; 5% Dextrose Injection and 0.9% Sodium Chloride Injection; Lactated Ringer's Injection; Lactated Ringer's in 5% Dextrose Injection; Normosol-M in D5W; 0.9% Sodium Chloride Injection; Isolyte E; Acetated Ringer's Injection.

Pharmacy Bulk Vial: The availability of the Pharmacy Bulk Vial is restricted to hospitals with a recognized i.v. admixture program. Vancocin does not contain any preservatives. The Pharmacy Bulk Vial is intended for multiple dispensing for i.v. use only, employing a single puncture.

Stability of Solutions: Storage: Reconstituted stock solution for Pharmacy Bulk vials should be used within 8 hours. All other reconstituted solutions and further diluted infusion mixtures should be used within 24 hours if kept at room temperatures or 96 hours if stored under refrigeration (5°C).

Incompatibility: Some of the specific substances found incompatible are aminophylline, chloramphenicol sodium succinate, dexamethasone phosphate, phenytoin sodium, methicillin, vitamin B_{12} complex with C, sulfisoxazole diethanolamine, heparin sodium, potassium penicillin G, hydrocortisone sodium succinate, amobarbital sodium, nitrofurantoin sodium, pentobarbital sodium, phenobarbital sodium, secobarbital sodium, sodium bicarbonate, and sulfadiazine sodium.

Note: Common flavoring syrups have been added to the solution to improve the taste for oral administration. There is no information to indicate that the potency or efficacy of the drug is affected by the addition of these agents.

Supplied: Vials: Each vial contains: vancomycin HCl equivalent to 500 mg and 1 g of vancomycin base. Rubber stoppered vials of 10 and 20 mL.

Pharmacy Bulk Vials: Each vial contains: vancomycin HCl equivalent to 10 g of vancomycin base, edetate calcium disodium equivalent to 0.2 mg edetate/g vancomycin, and ethanol equivalent to up to 30 mg/g vancomycin.

ADD-Vantage Vials: Each vial contains: vancomycin HCl equivalent to 500 mg and 1 g of vancomycin base.

The above ADD-Vantage Vials are to be used with Abbott Laboratories' ADD-Vantage Diluent Container containing 0.9% Sodium Chloride Injection USP 100 or 250 mL or 5% Dextrose Injection USP 100 or 250 mL.

The resulting solution should be used immediately.

Note: ADD-Vantage Vancocin should not be used in neonates, infants or young children who require doses of less than 500 mg.

The 1 g ADD-Vantage Vial should be joined only to a 250 mL ADD-Vantage Flexible Container. The desired dose diluted in this manner should be administered by i.v. infusion over a period of at least 60 minutes.

Capsules: 125 mg: Each peach and dark blue capsule contains: vancomycin HCl equivalent to vancomycin 125 mg. Nonmedicinal ingredients: polyethylene glycol; capsule shell: benzyl alcohol, butylparaben, carboxymethylcellulose sodium, edetate calcium disodium, FD&C Blue, gelatin, methylparaben, propylparaben, sodium lauryl sulfate, sodium propionate, synthetic iron oxide red, synthetic iron oxide yellow and titanium dioxide. Identi-Dose (unit dose) packages of 20.

250 mg: Each pale brown and dark blue capsule contains: vancomycin HCl equivalent to vancomycin 250 mg. Nonmedicinal ingredients: polyethylene glycol; capsule shell: benzyl alcohol, butylparaben, carboxymethylcellulose, edetate calcium disodium, FD&C Blue No 2, gelatin, methylparaben, propylparaben, sodium lauryl sulfate, sodium propionate, synthetic iron oxide black, synthetic iron oxide red and titanium dioxide. Identi-Dose (unit dose) packages of 20.

VANQUIN®

Warner-Lambert Consumer Healthcare

Pyrvinium Pamoate

Oxyuriasis Therapy

Indications: Treatment of pinworms.

Contraindications: In patients who have previously exhibited hypersensitivity to the drug.

Precautions: To forestall undue concern and help avoid accidental staining, patients and parents should be advised of the staining properties of pyrvinium. Parents and patients should be informed that pyrvinium will color the stool a bright red. This is not harmful to the patient. If emesis occurs, the vomitus will probably be colored red and will stain most materials. Because pinworm infections are easily transferred from person to person, meticulous hygiene is essential.

Pregnancy: Animal reproduction studies have not been conducted. It is also not known whether pyrvinium can cause fetal harm when administered to a pregnant woman or if it can affect reproduction capacity. Pyrvinium should be given to a pregnant woman only if the benefit clearly outweighs the risk.

Lactation: It is not known whether this drug is excreted in human milk. Because many drugs are excreted in human milk, a decision should be made to discontinue nursing or to discontinue the drug, taking into account the importance of drug therapy to the mother.

Children: Pyrvinium should not be used in children under 10 kg except on the advice of a physician.

Adverse Effects: Nausea, vomiting, cramping, diarrhea and hypersensitivity reactions (photosensitization and other allergic reactions) have been reported. The gastrointestinal reactions occur more often in older children and adults who have received large doses.

Dosage: A single dose of 50 mg/10 kg. Take immediately after a meal. If necessary, the dose may be repeated in 2 to 3 weeks. See Table I.

Table I—Vanquin

Dosage Schedule

Body weight (kg)	Dosage Suspension (mL)
10	5
15	7.5
20	10
25	12.5
30	15
40	20
50	25
60	30
70*	35

*Since the gastrointestinal tract of adults does not appreciably increase in size with increased weight gain, the dosage for adults need not exceed that recommended in a patient weighing 70 kg.

Supplied: Each 5 mL of pleasant-tasting, strawberry flavored, red suspension contains: pyrvinium pamoate 75.25 mg equivalent to pyrvinium base 50 mg. Nonmedicinal ingredients: benzoic acid, hydrochloric acid, methylcellulose, poloxamer, propylene glycol, strawberry flavor, sodium hydroxide, sodium phosphate, sorbitan monolaurate, sugar and water. Energy: 18.8 kJ (4.49 kcal)/5 mL. Sodium: <1 mmol (12.23 mg)/5 mL. Alcohol-, gluten-, lactose-, paraben-, sulfite- and tartrazine-free. Bottles of 50 mL.

VAPONEFRIN®

Rhône-Poulenc Rorer

Racemic Epinephrine HCl

Bronchodilator

Indications: For the symptomatic relief of bronchial obstruction due to bronchial spasm and mucous secretions associated with bronchial asthma, hay fever, chronic bronchitis, pulmonary emphysema, and other pulmonary diseases associated with bronchospasm.

Precautions: Use with caution in children under 12 years of age, in patients sensitive to sympathomimetic amines, in the presence of hypertension or cardiovascular disorders (including coronary insufficiency), in patients with a potential for cardiac arrhythmias and in those patients receiving MAO inhibitors. Do not use concurrently with other bronchodilators; may be used interchangeably with isoproterenol, but an interval of 4 hours should elapse before changing from one to the other. Do not exceed dose recommended by the physician. If difficulty in breathing persists or if the number of doses has to be increased to obtain the desired effect, a physician should be called immediately. Do not use solution if discolored or if it contains a precipitate.

Occasional patients have been reported to develop severe paradoxical airway resistance associated with the repeated, excessive use of bronchodilator inhalation preparations. The cause of this refractory state is unknown. It is advisable that in such instances the use of the solution be discontinued immediately and alternative therapy instituted, since in the reported cases the patients did not respond to other forms of therapy until the medication was withdrawn. Deaths have been reported following excessive use of bronchodilator inhalation preparations, the exact cause of which is unknown. Cardiac arrest was noted in several instances.

Adverse Effects: In excessive dosage, epinephrine may cause bronchial edema and inflammation, palpitation, precordial ache or anginal pain, tremor, nervousness, restlessness, sleeplessness, dizziness, headache, nausea and sweating. If any of these occur, dosage should be reduced by ordering fewer inhalations or less frequent use.

Dosage: Should be used at the first sign of wheezing or shortness of breath due to bronchospasm. Add 10 to 15 drops to nebulizer and inhale deeply with mouth wide open, while compressing the rubber bulb with a sharp, quick squeeze. Take 2 or 3 inhalations. If relief is not obtained after 5 minutes, repeat inhalation. Do not repeat again before 4 hours. If difficulty in breathing still persists, contact physician immediately.

Use the smallest amount which will bring relief from wheezing or bronchospasm. After inhalations, the sputum may be pink in color due to a chemical reaction between the mucous secretions and Vaponefrin solution.

After dilution, the solution should be used within 30 minutes. Do not use solution if discolored or if it contains a precipitate.

Supplied: Each mL of clear solution contains: racemic epinephrine base 2.25% as hydrochloride for inhalation therapy. Nonmedicinal ingredients: benzoic acid, chlorobutanol hemihydrate, glycerin, hydrochloric acid, purified water, sodium chloride and sodium metabisulfite. Bottles of 30 mL. Store solution in tight, light-resistant container at controlled room temperature (15 to 30°C).

VAQTA®

MSD

Hepatitis A Vaccine (Purified Inactivated)

Vaccine

Pharmacology: Hepatitis A vaccine, purified inactivated is an inactivated whole virus vaccine which has been shown to induce antibody to hepatitis A virus protein.

Disease Epidemiology: Hepatitis A virus is one of several hepatitis viruses that cause a systemic infection with pathology in the liver. The incubation period ranges from approximately 20 to 50 days. While the course of the disease is generally benign and does not result in chronic hepatitis, infection with hepatitis A virus remains an important cause of morbidity and occasional fulminant hepatitis and death.

Hepatitis A is transmitted most often by the fecal-oral route, with infection occurring primarily within private households, daycare centers, neonatal intensive care units, and chronic-care hospitals. Common-source outbreaks due to contaminated food and water supplies have occurred following consumption of certain foods such as raw shellfish, and uncooked foods prepared by an infected food-handler or otherwise contaminated prior to ingestion (salads, sandwiches, frozen raspberries, etc). Bloodborne transmission, while uncommon, is possible via blood transfusion, contaminated blood products, or from needles shared with an infected viremic individual. Sexual transmission has also been reported.

The disease burden due to hepatitis A in the U.S. has been estimated to be approximately 75 800 cases of clinical hepatitis each year, resulting in 11 400 hospitalizations, and 80 deaths due to fulminant hepatitis. Worldwide, it has been estimated that 1.4 million cases occur annually. The clinical manifestations of hepatitis A infection often pass unrecognized in children ≤2 years of age whereas overt hepatitis develops in the majority of infected older children and adults. Symptoms and signs of hepatitis A infection are similar to those associated with other types of viral hepatitis and include anorexia, nausea, fever/chills, jaundice, dark urine, light-colored stools, abdominal pain, malaise, and fatigue.

Clinical Evaluation: Clinical trials conducted worldwide with several formulations of the vaccine in 9 181 healthy individuals ranging from 2 to 85 years of age have demonstrated that Vaqta is highly immunogenic and generally well tolerated.

Protection from hepatitis A disease has been shown to be related to the presence of antibody; an anamnestic antibody response occurs in healthy individuals with a history of infection who are subsequently re-exposed to hepatitis A virus. Similarly, protection after vaccination with hepatitis A vaccine (purified inactivated) was associated with the onset of seroconversion with an anamnestic antibody response following booster vaccination with hepatitis A vaccine (purified inactivated).

Clinical Studies: In combined clinical studies, 97% of 1 214 children and adolescents 2 to 17 years of age seroconverted (≥10 mIU/mL of hepatitis A antibody, measured by a modification of the Havab radioimmunoassay [RIA]) within 4 weeks after a single approximately 25 U i.m. dose of hepatitis A vaccine (purified inactivated). Similarly, 95% of 1 428 adults ≥18 years of age seroconverted within 4 weeks after a single approximately 50 U i.m. dose of hepatitis A vaccine (purified inactivated). Immune memory was later demonstrated by an anamnestic antibody response in individuals who received a booster dose.

While a study evaluating hepatitis A vaccine (purified inactivated) alone in a postexposure setting has not been conducted, the concurrent use of hepatitis A vaccine (purified inactivated) (approximately 50 U) and immune globulin (IG, 0.06 mL/kg) was evaluated in a clinical study involving healthy adults 18 to 39 years of age. Table I provides seroconversion rates at 4 and 24 weeks after the first dose in each treatment group and at 1 month after a booster dose of hepatitis A vaccine (purified inactivated) (administered at 24 weeks).

Table I—Vaqta

Seroconversion Rates After Vaccination with Vaqta Plus IG, Vaqta Alone, and IG Alone

Weeks	Vaqta plus IG	Vaqta	IG
	Seroconversion Rate		
4	100% (n=129)	96% (n=135)	87% (n=30)
24	92% (n=125)	*97% (n=132)	0% (n=28)
28	100% (n=114)	100% (n=128)	N/A

*Seroconversion rate in the vaccine alone group significantly higher than that in the vaccine plus IG group (p=0.05).

Legend: N/A=Not applicable.

A very high degree of protection has been demonstrated after a single dose of hepatitis A vaccine (purified inactivated) in children and adolescents. The protective efficacy, immunogenicity, and safety of hepatitis A vaccine (purified inactivated) were evaluated in a randomized, double-blind placebo-controlled study involving 1 037 susceptible healthy children and adolescents 2 to 16 years of age in a U.S. community with recurrent outbreaks of hepatitis A (The Monroe Efficacy Study). Each child received a single i.m. dose of hepatitis A vaccine (purified inactivated) (approximately 25 U) or placebo. Among those individuals who were initially seronegative (by modified HAVAB), seroconversion was achieved in >99% of vaccine recipients within 4 weeks after vaccination. The onset of seroconversion following a single dose of hepatitis A vaccine (purified inactivated) was shown to parallel the onset of protection against clinical hepatitis A disease. Because of the long incubation period of the disease (approximately 20 to 50 days), analysis of protective efficacy was based on cases of hepatitis A occurring ≥50 days after vaccination in order to exclude any children incubating the infection before vaccination. In subjects who were initially seronegative, the protective efficacy of a single dose of hepatitis A vaccine (purified inactivated) was observed to be 100% with 25 cases of clinical hepatitis A occurring in the placebo group and none in the vaccine group (p<0.001). No cases of clinical hepatitis A disease occurred in the vaccine group after day 18. In addition, 9 cases of clinical hepatitis A occurred in the placebo group while none occurred in the vaccine group 19 to 49 days after vaccination. Following demonstration of protection with a single dose and termination of the study, a booster dose was administered to most vaccinees 6, 12, or 18 months after the primary dose. The effectiveness of hepatitis A vaccine (purified inactivated) for use in community outbreak control has been demonstrated by the fact that, to date, no cases of hepatitis A disease ≥19 days after vaccination have occurred in those vaccinees from The Monroe Efficacy Study monitored

Vaqta (cont'd)

for up to 4 years. In contrast, three nearby sister communities to Monroe have continued to experience outbreaks.

The total duration of the protective effect of hepatitis A vaccine (purified inactivated) in healthy vaccinees is unknown at present. However, seropositivity was shown to persist up to 18 months after a single approximately 25 U dose in most children and adolescents who participated in The Monroe Efficacy Study. In adults, seropositivity has been shown to persist up to 6 months after a single approximately 50 U dose (studies ongoing). Studies are ongoing to evaluate longer-term persistence and the need, if any, for additional booster doses. Persistence of immunologic memory was demonstrated with an anamnestic antibody response to a booster dose of approximately 25 U given 6 to 18 months after the primary dose in children and adolescents, and to a booster dose of approximately 50 U given 6 months after the primary dose to adults. In the absence of study data on antibody persistence for vaccine recipients over several decades, an extrapolation from a kinetic model of antibody decay was used to estimate the duration of antibody. Extrapolation of observed antibody titers from year 2 to 3 in 118 children and adults, most of whom had received 3 injections of 6, 13 or 25 U vaccine, suggests that detectable levels of antibody may persist after the booster dose for many years. The median duration based on this extrapolation was calculated to be 21 years [95% CI= (14 to 27 years)].

Indications: For vaccination against infection caused by hepatitis A virus.

Hepatitis A vaccine (purified inactivated) is indicated for active pre-exposure prophylaxis against disease caused by hepatitis A virus. Vaccination is recommended in children 2 years of age and older, adolescents, and adults who are at risk of contracting or spreading infection or who are at risk of life-threatening disease if infected, including but not limited to: A. Travelers to endemic or outbreak areas.

B. Frequently affected communities: members residing in any community with 1 or more recorded outbreaks within the last 5 years.

C. Daycare: Children and staff of daycare centers as well as their parents, siblings and other contacts.

D. Military personnel prior to departure for endemic or outbreak areas.

E. Persons for whom Hepatitis A is an occupational hazard: healthcare workers; staff and residents of orphanages, chronic care hospitals and mental healthcare facilities; sewage workers.

F. Hemophiliacs and other recipients of therapeutic blood products.

G. Food handlers.

H. Consumers of high-risk foods: e.g., raw shellfish.

I. Persons at increased risk of the disease due to their sexual practices: homosexually-active males; persons who repeatedly contract sexually transmitted diseases.

J. Users of illicit injectable drugs.

Hepatitis A vaccine (purified inactivated) will not prevent hepatitis caused by infectious agents other than hepatitis A virus.

Revaccination: see Dosage.

Contraindications: Hypersensitivity to any component of the vaccine.

Warnings: If hepatitis A vaccine (purified inactivated) is used in individuals with malignancies or those receiving immunosuppressive therapy or who are otherwise immunocompromised, the expected immune response may not be obtained.

Hepatitis A vaccine (purified inactivated) is not recommended for use in infants younger than 2 years of age since data on use in this age group are not currently available.

Precautions: General: Individuals who develop symptoms suggestive of hypersensitivity after an injection of hepatitis A vaccine (purified inactivated) should not receive further injections of the vaccine (see Contraindications).

As with any vaccine, adequate treatment provisions, including epinephrine, should be available for immediate use should an anaphylactic or anaphylactoid reaction occur.

Since there is a possibility that the vaccine may contain trace amounts of neomycin, the possibility of an allergic reaction in individuals sensitive to this substance should be kept in mind when considering the use of this vaccine (see Supplied).

As with any vaccine, vaccination with hepatitis A vaccine (purified inactivated) may not result in a protective response in all susceptible vaccinees.

Any acute infection or febrile illness is reason for delaying use of hepatitis A vaccine (purified inactivated) except when, in the opinion of the physician, withholding the vaccine entails a greater risk.

Hepatitis A vaccine (purified inactivated) will not prevent hepatitis caused by infectious agents other than hepatitis A virus. Because of the long incubation period (approximately 20 to 50 days) for hepatitis A, it is possible for unrecognized hepatitis A infection to be present at the time the vaccine is given. The vaccine may not prevent hepatitis A in such individuals.

Children: Hepatitis A vaccine (purified inactivated) has been shown to be generally well-tolerated and highly immunogenic in individuals 2 to 17 years of age. See Dosage for the recommended dosage schedule.

Safety and effectiveness in infants below 2 years of age have not been established.

Pregnancy: Animal reproduction studies have not been conducted with hepatitis A vaccine (purified inactivated). It is also not known whether hepatitis A vaccine (purified inactivated) can cause fetal harm when administered to a pregnant woman or can affect reproductive capacity. Hepatitis A vaccine (purified inactivated) should be given to a pregnant woman only if clearly needed.

Lactation: It is not known whether hepatitis A vaccine (purified inactivated) is excreted in human milk. Because many drugs are excreted in human milk, caution should be exercised when hepatitis A vaccine (purified inactivated) is administered to a woman who is breast-feeding.

Carcinogenesis, Mutagenesis, Reproduction: Hepatitis A vaccine (purified inactivated) has not been evaluated for its carcinogenic or mutagenic potential, or its potential to impair fertility.

Drug Interactions: Other Vaccines: Data are not yet available to recommend concurrent use with other vaccines.

Immune Globulin: For individuals requiring either postexposure prophylaxis or combined immediate and longer-term protection (e.g., travelers departing on short notice to endemic areas), hepatitis A vaccine (purified inactivated) may be administered concomitantly with IG using separate sites and syringes.

Adverse Effects: No serious vaccine-related adverse experiences were observed during clinical trials.

In The Monroe Efficacy Study, 1 037 healthy children and adolescents 2 to 16 years of age received either a primary dose of approximately 25 U of hepatitis A vaccine and a booster 6, 12 or 18 months later, or placebo. Subjects were observed during a 5-day period for fever and local complaints and during a 14-day period for systemic complaints. Injection-site complaints, generally mild and transient, were the most frequently reported complaints. Table II summarizes the local and systemic complaints (≥1%) reported in this study, without regard to causality. There were no significant differences in the rates of any complaint between vaccine and placebo recipients after dose 1.

Table II—Vaqta

Local and Systemic Complaints (≥1%) Healthy Children and Adolescents from The Monroe Efficacy Study

	Vaqta		
Reaction	**Dose 1[a]**	**Booster**	**Placebo[b]**
Injection-Site Complaints			
Pain	6.4% (33/515)	3.4% (16/475)	6.3% (32/510)
Tenderness	4.9% (25/515)	1.7% (8/475)	6.1% (31/510)
Erythema	1.9% (10/515)	0.8% (4/475)	1.8% (9/510)
Swelling	1.7% (9/515)	1.5% (7/475)	1.6% (8/510)
Warmth	1.7% (9/515)	0.6% (3/475)	1.6% (8/510)
Systemic Complaints			
Abdominal Pain	1.2% (6/519)	1.1% (5/475)	1.0% (5/518)
Pharyngitis	1.2% (6/519)	0% (0/475)	0.8% (4/518)
Headache	0.4% (2/519)	0.8% (4/475)	1.0% (5/518)

[a]No statistically significant differences between the 2 groups.
[b]Second injection of placebo not administered because code for the trial was broken.

Children/Adolescents 2 to 17 years of age: In combined clinical trials (including Monroe Efficacy Study participants) involving 2 595 healthy children and adolescents who received one or more approximately 25 U doses of hepatitis A vaccine, fever and local complaints were observed during a 5-day period following vaccination and systemic complaints during a 14-day period following vaccination. Injection-site complaints, generally mild and transient, were the most frequently reported complaints. Table III lists the complaints (≥1%) reported, without regard to causality, in decreasing order of frequency within each body system.

Table III—Vaqta

Local and Systemic Complaints (≥1%) in Healthy Children and Adolescents from Combined Clinical Trials

Localized Injection-Site Reactions (generally mild and transient)	**%**
Pain	18.7
Tenderness	16.8
Warmth	8.6
Erythema	7.5
Swelling	7.3
Ecchymosis	1.3
Body as a Whole	
Fever ≥38.9°C, Oral	3.1
Abdominal Pain	1.6
Digestive	
Diarrhea	1.0
Vomiting	1.0
Nervous System/Psychiatric	
Headache	2.3
Respiratory System	
Pharyngitis	1.5
Upper Respiratory Infection	1.1
Cough	1.0

Laboratory Findings: Very few laboratory abnormalities were reported and included isolated reports of elevated liver function tests, eosinophilia, and increased urine protein.

Adults 18 years of age and older: In combined clinical trials involving 1 529 healthy adults who received 1 or more approximately 50 U doses of hepatitis A vaccine, fever and local complaints were observed during a 5-day period following vaccination and systemic complaints during a 14-day period following vaccination. Injection-site complaints, generally mild and transient, were the most frequently reported complaints. Table IV lists the complaints (≥1%) reported, without regard to causality, in decreasing order of frequency within each body system.

Table IV—Vaqta

Local and Systemic Complaints (≥1%) in Healthy Adults from Combined Clinical Trials

Localized Injection-Site Reactions (generally mild and transient)	**%**
Tenderness	52.6
Pain	51.1
Warmth	17.3
Swelling	13.6
Erythema	12.9
Ecchymosis	1.5
Pain/Soreness	1.2
Body as a Whole	
Asthenia/Fatigue	3.9
Fever ≥38.3°C, Oral	2.6
Abdominal Pain	1.3
Digestive	
Diarrhea	2.4
Nausea	2.3
Musculoskeletal	
Myalgia	2.0
Arm Pain	1.3
Back Pain	1.1
Stiffness	1.0
Nervous System/Psychiatric	
Headache	16.1
Respiratory	
Pharyngitis	2.7
Upper Respiratory Infection	2.8
Nasal Congestion	1.1
Urogenital	
Menstruation Disorder	1.1

Dosage: For i.m. use only. The deltoid muscle is the preferred site for injection.

Do not inject i.v., intradermally, or s.c.

The vaccination series consists of 1 primary dose and 1 booster dose given according to the following schedule:

Children/Adolescent: Individuals 2 to 17 years of age should receive a single 0.5 mL (approximately 25 U) dose of vaccine at elected date and a booster dose of 0.5 mL (approximately 25 U) 6 to 18 months later.

Adults: Adults 18 years of age and older should receive a single 1.0 mL (approximately 50 U) dose of vaccine at an elected date and a booster dose of 1.0 mL (approximately 50 U) 6 months later.

Known or Presumed Exposure to Hepatitis A Virus, Travel to Endemic Areas, and Use With Immune Globulin: Hepatitis A vaccine (purified inactivated) may be administered concomitantly with IG using separate sites and syringes. The vaccination regimen for hepatitis A vaccine (purified inactivated) should be followed as stated above. Consult the manufacturers' Product Monograph for the appropriate dosage of IG. A booster dose of hepatitis A vaccine (purified inactivated) should be administered at the appropriate time as outlined above (see Pharmacology, Clinical Studies and Precautions, Drug Interactions).

The vaccine should be used as supplied; no reconstitution is necessary.

Shake well before withdrawal and use. Thorough agitation is necessary to maintain suspension of the vaccine.

Parenteral drug products should be inspected visually for extraneous particulate matter and discoloration prior to administration whenever solution and container permit. After thorough agitation, hepatitis A vaccine (purified inactivated) is a slightly opaque, white suspension.

It is important to use a separate, sterile syringe and needle for each individual to prevent transmission of infectious agents from one person to another.

Supplied: 0.5 mL: Each sterile, i.m. injection, 0.5 mL pediatric/adolescent suspension dose, contains: approximately 25 U of hepatitis A virus protein. Nonmedicinal ingredients: aluminum hydroxide, sodium borate and sodium chloride. Single use vials, packages of 1. Single use prefilled syringes, packages of 1.

1 mL: Each sterile, i.m. injection, 1 mL adult suspension dose, contains: approximately 50 U of hepatitis A virus protein. Nonmedicinal ingredients: aluminum hydroxide, sodium borate and sodium chloride. Single use vials, packages of 1 and 5. Single use prefilled syringes, packages of 1 and 5.

Vaqta is a highly purified inactivated whole virus vaccine derived from hepatitis A virus grown in cell culture in human MRC-5 diploid fibroblasts. It contains inactivated virus of a strain which was originally derived by further serial passage of a proven attenuated strain. The virus is grown, harvested, purified by a combination of physical and high performance liquid chromatographic techniques, formalin inactivated, and then adsorbed onto aluminum hydroxide. One mL of the vaccine contains approximately 50 U of hepatitis A antigen, equivalent to approximately 50 ng of virus protein per mL which is highly purified and is formulated without a preservative. Within the limits of current assay variability, the 50 U dose contains less than 0.1 μg of nonviral protein, less than 4×10^{-6} μg of DNA, less than 10^{-4} μg of bovine albumin, less than 0.8 μg of formaldehyde and a trace of neomycin B sulfate ($\leq$0.002 μg). Other process chemical residuals are less than 10 parts per billion (ppb).

Store vaccine at 2 to 8°C. **Do not freeze** since freezing destroys potency. Stability studies with Vaqta show that the potency of unopened vaccine is not significantly affected after exposure at 37°C for up to 6 months. This is **not,** however, a storage recommendation.

Reviewed 1999

VASERETIC® ℞

Frosst

Enalapril Maleate—Hydrochlorothiazide

Angiotensin Converting Enzyme Inhibitor—Diuretic

Pharmacology: Vaseretic combines the action of an angiotensin converting enzyme inhibitor, enalapril maleate, and that of a diuretic, hydrochlorothiazide.

Enalapril Maleate: Angiotensin converting enzyme (ACE) is a peptidyl dipeptidase which catalyzes the conversion of angiotensin I to the pressor substance, angiotensin II. After absorption, enalapril, a pro-drug, is hydrolyzed to enalaprilat, its active metabolite, which inhibits ACE. Inhibition of ACE results in decreased plasma angiotensin II, which leads to increased plasma renin activity (due to removal of negative feedback to renin release) and decreased aldosterone secretion. Although the latter decrease is small, it results in a small increase in serum potassium. In patients treated with enalapril and a thiazide diuretic there was essentially no change in serum potassium (see Precautions).

ACE is identical to kininase II. Thus, enalapril may also block the degradation of bradykinin, a potent vasodepressor peptide. However, the role that this plays in the therapeutic effects of enalapril is unknown.

While the mechanism through which enalapril lowers blood pressure is believed to be primarily the suppression of the renin-angiotensin-aldosterone system, enalapril also lowers blood pressure in patients with low-renin hypertension.

Administration of enalapril to patients with hypertension results in a reduction of both supine and standing blood pressure. Abrupt withdrawal of enalapril has not been associated with a rapid increase in blood pressure. In most patients studied, after oral administration of an individual dose of enalapril, the onset of antihypertensive activity is seen at 1 hour with peak reduction of blood pressure achieved by 4 to 6 hours. At recommended doses, the antihypertensive effect has been shown to be maintained for at least 24 hours. In some patients the effect may diminish towards the end of the dosing interval (see Dosage). On occasion, achievement of optimal blood pressure reduction may require several weeks of therapy.

In hemodynamic studies in patients with essential hypertension, blood pressure reduction was accompanied by a reduction in peripheral arterial resistance with an increase in cardiac output and little or no change in heart rate. Following administration of enalapril, there was an increase in renal blood flow; glomerular filtration rate was usually unchanged.

The antihypertensive effect of angiotensin converting enzyme inhibitors is generally lower in black than in nonblack patients.

Hydrochlorothiazide: Hydrochlorothiazide is a diuretic and antihypertensive which interferes with the renal tubular mechanism of electrolyte reabsorption. It increases excretion of sodium and chloride in approximately equivalent amounts. Natriuresis may be accompanied by some loss of potassium and bicarbonate. While this compound is predominantly a saluretic agent, in vitro studies have shown that it has a carbonic anhydrase inhibitory action which seems to be relatively specific for the renal tubular mechanism. It does not appear to be concentrated in erythrocytes or the brain in sufficient amounts to influence the activity of carbonic anhydrase in those tissues.

Hydrochlorothiazide is useful in the treatment of hypertension. It may be used alone or as an adjunct to other antihypertensive drugs. Hydrochlorothiazide does not affect normal blood pressure. The mechanism of its antihypertensive action is not known. Lowering of the sodium content of arteriolar smooth muscle cells and diminished response to norepinephrine have been postulated.

Onset of the diuretic action following oral administration occurs in 2 hours and the peak action in about 4 hours. Diuretic activity lasts about 6 to 12 hours.

Pharmacokinetics: Enalapril Maleate: Following oral administration, enalapril is rapidly absorbed with peak serum concentrations of enalapril occurring within 1 hour. Based on urinary recovery the extent of absorption of enalapril from enalapril maleate is approximately 60%.

Following absorption, enalapril is rapidly and extensively hydrolyzed to enalaprilat, a potent angiotensin converting enzyme inhibitor (which itself is poorly absorbed). Peak serum concentrations of enalaprilat occur 3 to 4 hours after an oral dose of enalapril maleate. Excretion of enalapril maleate is primarily renal. Approximately 94% of the dose is recovered in the urine and feces as enalaprilat or enalapril. The principal components in urine are enalaprilat, accounting for about 40% of the dose, and intact enalapril. Except for conversion to enalaprilat, there is no evidence of significant metabolism of enalapril. The serum concentration profile of enalaprilat exhibits a prolonged terminal phase, apparently associated with binding to ACE. The effective half-life for accumulation of enalaprilat following multiple doses of enalapril maleate is 11 hours. The absorption of enalapril is not influenced by the presence of food in the gastrointestinal tract.

Hydrochlorothiazide: Hydrochlorothiazide is not metabolized but is eliminated rapidly by the kidney. The plasma half-life is 5.6 to 14.8 hours when the plasma levels can be followed for at least 24 hours. At least 61% of the oral dose is eliminated unchanged within 24 hours. Hydrochlorothiazide crosses the placental but not the blood-brain barrier and is excreted in breast milk.

Enalapril Maleate—Hydrochlorothiazide: Concomitant administration of enalapril and hydrochlorothiazide has little, or no effect on the bioavailability of either drug. The combination tablet is bioequivalent to concomitant administration of the separate entities.

Pharmacodynamics: Enalapril Maleate: The disposition of enalapril and enalaprilat in patients with renal insufficiency is similar to that in patients with normal renal function until the glomerular filtration rate is 30 mL/min (0.50 mL/s) or less. With renal function $\leq$30 mL/min ($\leq$0.50 mL/s), peak and trough enalaprilat levels increase, time to peak concentration increases and time to steady state may be delayed. The effective half-life of enalaprilat following multiple doses of enalapril maleate is prolonged at this level of renal insufficiency (see Dosage). Enalaprilat is dialyzable at the rate of 62 mL/min (1.03 mL/s).

Studies in dogs indicate that enalapril crosses the blood brain barrier poorly, if at all; enalaprilat does not enter the brain.

Indications: In the treatment of essential hypertension in patients for whom this combination therapy is appropriate.

In using Vaseretic consideration should be given to the risk of angioedema (see Warnings).

Enalapril should normally be used in those patients in whom treatment with diuretic or beta blocker was found ineffective or has been associated with unacceptable adverse effects.

Vaseretic is not indicated for initial therapy. Patients in whom enalapril and diuretic are initiated simultaneously can develop symptomatic hypotension (see Precautions, Drug Interactions).

Patients should be titrated on individual drugs. If the fixed combination represents the dose and dosing frequency determined by this titration, the use of Vaseretic may be more convenient in the management of patients. If during maintenance therapy dosage adjustment is necessary it is advisable to use the individual drugs.

Pregnancy: **When used in pregnancy during the second and third trimesters, ACE inhibitors can cause injury or even death of the developing fetus. When pregnancy is detected Vaseretic should be discontinued as soon as possible (see Warnings: in Pregnancy, and Information for the Patient).**

Contraindications: Patients who are hypersensitive to any component of this product and in patients with a history of angioneurotic edema relating to previous treatment with an angiotensin converting enzyme inhibitor. Because of the hydrochlorothiazide component, this product is contraindicated in patients with anuria or hypersensitivity to other sulfonamide-derived drugs.

Warnings: Angioedema: Angioedema has been reported in patients treated with Vaseretic. Angioedema associated with laryngeal edema and/or shock may be fatal. This may occur at any time during treatment. If angioedema occurs, Vaseretic should be promptly discontinued and appropriate monitoring should be instituted to ensure complete resolution of symptoms prior to dismissing the patient. Where swelling is confined to the face, lips and mouth the condition will usually resolve without further treatment, although antihistamines may be useful in relieving symptoms. These patients should be followed carefully until the swelling has resolved. However, where there is involvement of the tongue, glottis or larynx, likely to cause airway obstruction, appropriate therapy such as s.c. epinephrine (0.5 mL 1:1 000) should be administered promptly when indicated.

The incidence of angioedema during ACE inhibitor therapy has been reported to be higher in black than in nonblack patients.

Patients with a history of angioedema unrelated to ACE inhibitor therapy may be at increased risk of angioedema while receiving an ACE inhibitor (see Contraindications).

Hypotension: Symptomatic hypotension has occurred after administration of enalapril, usually after the first or second dose or when the dose was increased. It is more likely to occur in patients who are volume depleted by diuretic therapy, dietary salt restriction, dialysis, diarrhea or vomiting. Therefore, Vaseretic should not be used to start therapy or when a dose change is needed. In patients with ischemic heart or cerebrovascular disease, an excessive fall in blood pressure could result in a myocardial infarction or cerebrovascular accident (see Adverse Effects). Because of the potential fall in blood pressure in these patients, therapy with enalapril should be started under very close medical supervision, usually in a hospital. Such patients should be followed closely for the first 2 weeks of treatment and whenever the dose of enalapril and/or hydrochlorothiazide is increased. In patients with severe congestive heart failure, with or without associated renal insufficiency, excessive hypotension has been observed and may be associated with oliguria and/or progressive azotemia, and rarely with acute renal failure and/or death.

If hypotension occurs, the patient should be placed in supine position and, if necessary, receive an i.v. infusion of normal saline. A transient hypotensive response is not a contraindication to further doses which usually can be given without difficulty once the blood pressure has increased after volume expansion.

Vaseretic (cont'd)

Neutropenia/Agranulocytosis: Agranulocytosis and bone marrow depression have been caused by angiotensin converting enzyme inhibitors. Several cases of agranulocytosis and neutropenia have been reported in which a causal relationship to enalapril cannot be excluded. Current experience with the drug shows the incidence to be rare. Periodic monitoring of white blood cell counts should be considered, especially in patients with collagen vascular disease and renal disease.

Azotemia: Azotemia may be precipitated or increased by hydrochlorothiazide. Cumulative effects of the drug may develop in patients with impaired renal function. If increasing azotemia and oliguria occur during treatment of severe progressive renal disease the diuretic should be discontinued.

Patients with Impaired Liver Function: Hepatitis, jaundice (hepatocellular and/or cholestatic), elevations of liver enzymes and/serum bilirubin have occurred during therapy with enalapril in patients with or without pre-existing liver abnormalities (see Adverse Effects). In most cases the changes were reversed on discontinuation of the drug.

Should the patient receiving Vaseretic experience any unexplained symptoms (see Information for the Patient), particularly during the first weeks or months of treatment, it is recommended that a full set of liver function tests and any other necessary investigation be carried out. Discontinuation of Vaseretic should be considered when appropriate.

There are no adequate studies in patients with cirrhosis and/or liver dysfunction. Enalapril should be used with particular caution in patients with pre-existing liver abnormalities. In such patients baseline liver function tests should be obtained before administration of the drug and close monitoring of response and metabolic effects should apply.

Thiazides should be used with caution in patients with impaired hepatic function or progressive liver disease, since minor alterations of fluid and electrolyte balance may precipitate hepatic coma.

Hypersensitivity Reactions: Sensitivity reactions to hydrochlorothiazide may occur in patients with or without a history of allergy or bronchial asthma.

The possibility of exacerbation or activation of systemic lupus erythematosus has been reported in patients treated with hydrochlorothiazide.

Pregnancy: ACE inhibitors can cause fetal and neonatal morbidity and mortality when administered to pregnant women. Several dozen cases have been reported in the world literature. When pregnancy is detected, Vaseretic should be discontinued as soon as possible.

In rare cases (probably less than once in every thousand) in which no alternative to ACE inhibitor therapy will be found, the mothers should be apprised of the potential hazards to their fetuses. Serial ultrasound examinations should be performed to assess fetal development and well-being and the volume of amniotic fluid.

If oligohydramnios is observed, Vaseretic should be discontinued unless it is considered life-saving for the mother. A nonstress test (NST), and/or a biophysical profiling (BPP) may be appropriate, depending upon the week of pregnancy. If concerns regarding fetal well-being still persist, a contraction stress testing (CST) should be considered. Patients and physicians should be aware, however, that oligohydramnios may not appear until after the fetus has sustained irreversible injury.

Infants with a history of in utero exposure to ACE inhibitors should be closely observed for hypotension, oliguria, and hyperkalemia. If oliguria occurs, attention should be directed toward support of blood pressure and renal perfusion. Exchange transfusion or dialysis may be required as a means of reversing hypotension and/or substituting for impaired renal function; however, experience with those procedures has been limited.

Enalapril has been removed from the neonatal circulation by peritoneal dialysis with some clinical benefit and may, theoretically, be removed by exchange transfusion, although there is no experience with the latter procedure.

Human Data: It is not known whether exposure limited to the first trimester of pregnancy can adversely affect fetal outcome. The use of ACE inhibitors during the second and third trimesters of pregnancy has been associated with fetal and neonatal injury including hypotension, neonatal skull hypoplasia, anuria, reversible or irreversible renal failure, and death. Oligohydramnios has also been reported, presumably resulting from decreased fetal renal function; oligohydramnios in this setting has been associated with fetal limb contractures, craniofacial deformation, and hypoplastic lung development. Prematurity and patent ductus arteriosus have also been reported, although it is not clear whether these occurrences were due to the ACE inhibitor exposure.

Animal Data: Maternal and fetal toxicity occurred in some rabbits given enalapril at doses of 1 mg/kg/day or more. Saline supplementation prevented the maternal and fetal toxicity seen at doses of 3 and 10 mg/kg/day, but not at 30 mg/kg/day (50 times the maximum human dose). Enalapril was not teratogenic in rabbits.

There was no fetotoxicity or teratogenicity in rats treated with enalapril at doses up to 200 mg/kg/day (333 times the maximum human dose). Fetotoxicity expressed as a decrease in average fetal weight, occurred in rats given 1 200 mg/kg/day of enalapril, but did not occur when these animals were supplemented with saline. The drug crosses the placental barrier in rats and hamsters.

Precautions: Renal Impairment: As a consequence of inhibiting the renin-angiotensin-aldosterone system, changes in renal function have been seen in susceptible individuals. In patients whose renal function may depend on the activity of the renin-angiotensin-aldosterone system, such as patients with bilateral renal artery stenosis, unilateral renal artery stenosis to a solitary kidney, or severe congestive heart failure, treatment with agents that inhibit this system has been associated with oliguria, progressive azotemia, and rarely, acute renal failure and/or death. In susceptible patients, concomitant diuretic use may further increase risk.

Use of Vaseretic should include appropriate assessment of renal function.

Thiazides may not be appropriate diuretics for use in patients with renal impairment and are inefffective at creatinine clearance values of 30 mL/min or below (i.e., moderate or severe renal insufficiency).

Hyperkalemia: Elevated serum potassium (greater than 5.7 mEq/L) was observed in approximately 1% of hypertensive patients in clinical trials with enalapril alone. In most cases these were isolated values which resolved despite continued therapy. Hyperkalemia was a cause of discontinuation of therapy in 0.28% of hypertensive patients. Risk factors for the development of hyperkalemia may include renal insufficiency, diabetes mellitus, and the concomitant use of agents to treat hypokalemia (see Drug Interactions, Agents Increasing Serum Potassium).

Valvular Stenosis: There is concern on theoretical grounds that patients with aortic stenosis might be at particular risk of decreased coronary perfusion when treated with vasodilators because they do not develop as much afterload reduction.

Metabolism: Hyperuricemia may occur or acute gout may be precipitated in certain patients receiving thiazide therapy.

Thiazides may decrease serum PBI levels without signs of thyroid disturbance.

Thiazides have been shown to increase excretion of magnesium; this may result in hypomagnesemia.

Thiazides may decrease urinary calcium excretion. Thiazides may cause intermittent and slight elevation of serum calcium in the absence of known disorders of calcium metabolism. Marked hypercalcemia may be evidence of hidden hyperparathyroidism. Thiazides should be discontinued before carrying out tests for parathyroid function.

Increases in cholesterol and triglyceride levels may be associated with thiazide diuretic therapy.

Surgery/Anesthesia: In patients undergoing major surgery or during anesthesia with agents that produce hypotension, enalapril blocks angiotensin II formation, secondary to compensatory renin release. If hypotension occurs and is considered to be due to this mechanism, it can be corrected by volume expansion.

Thiazides may increase the responsiveness to tubocurarine.

Cough: A dry, persistent cough, which usually disappears only after withdrawal or lowering of the dose of enalapril has been reported.

Such possibility should be considered as part of the differential diagnosis of the cough.

Lactation: Both enalapril and thiazides appear in human milk. In general, nursing hould be interrupted if Vaseretic is given to a nursing mother.

Children: Vaseretic has not been studied in children and, therefore, use in this age group is not recommended.

Anaphylactoid Reactions during Membrane Exposure: Anaphylactoid reactions have been reported in patients dialysed with high-flux membranes (e.g.: polyacrylonitrile [PAN]) and treated concomitantly with an ACE inhibitor. Dialysis should be stopped immediately if symptoms such as nausea, abdominal cramps, burning, angioedema, shortness of breath and severe hypotension occur. Symptoms are not relieved by antihistamines. In these patients consideration should be given to using a different type of dialysis membrane or a different class of antihypertensive agent.

Anaphylactoid Reactions during Desensitization: There have been isolated reports of patients experiencing life-threatening anaphylactoid reactions while receiving ACE inhibitors during desensitizing treatment with hymenoptera (bee, wasp) venom. In the same patients, these reactions have been avoided when ACE inhibitors were temporarily withheld for at least 24 hours, but they have reappeared upon inadvertent rechallenge.

Anaphylactoid Reactions during LDL Apheresis: Rarely, patients receiving ACE inhibitors during low density lipoprotein (LDL)-apheresis with dextran sulfate have experienced life-threatening anaphylactoid reactions. These reactions were avoided by temporarily withholding ACE inhibitor therapy prior to each apheresis.

<u>*Drug Interactions:*</u> Hypotension: Patients on Diuretic Therapy: Patients on diuretics and especially those in whom diuretic therapy was recently instituted, may occasionally experience an excessive reduction of blood pressure after initiation of therapy with enalapril. The possibility of hypotensive effects with enalapril can be minimized by either discontinuing the diuretic or increasing the salt intake prior to initiation of treatment with enalapril (see Warnings and Dosage).

Agents Increasing Serum Potassium: Since enalapril decreases aldosterone production, elevation of serum potassium may occur. Potassium sparing diuretics such as spironolactone, triamterene or amiloride, or potassium supplements should be given only for documented hypokalemia and with caution and frequent monitoring of serum potassium since they may lead to a significant increase in serum potassium. Salt substitutes which contain potassium should also be used with caution.

Agents Causing Renin Release: The antihypertensive effect of Vaseretic is augmented by antihypertensive agents that cause renin release (e.g., diuretics).

Agents Affecting Sympathetic Activity: Agents affecting sympathetic activity (e.g., ganglionic blocking agents or adrenergic neuron blocking agents) may be used with caution. β-adrenergic blocking drugs add some further antihypertensive effect to enalapril.

Lithium: Lithium generally should not be given with diuretics or ACE inhibitors. Diuretic agents and ACE inhibitors reduce the renal clearance of lithium and add a high risk of lithium toxicity.

d-tubocurarine: Thiazide drugs may increase the responsiveness to tubocurarine.

Insulin: Insulin requirements in diabetic patients treated with thiazide diuretics, may be increased. Diabetes mellitus which has been latent may become manifest during thiazide administration.

Alcohol, Barbiturates or Narcotics: In the presence of thiazide diuretics, potentiation of orthostatic hypotension may occur.

Corticosteroids, ACTH: Intensified electrolyte depletion, particularly hypokalemia may occur when given concomitantly with thiazide diuretics.

Pressor Amines (e.g., norepinephrine): In the presence of thiazide diuretics, possible decreased response to pressor amines may be seen but not sufficient to preclude their use.

Nonsteroidal Anti-inflammatory Drugs: In some patients, the administration of a nonsteroidal anti-inflammatory agent can reduce the diuretic, natriuretic and antihypertensive effects of loop, potassium-sparing and thiazide diuretics. Therefore, when Vaseretic and nonsteroidal anti-inflammatory agents are used concomitantly, the patient should be observed closely to determine if the desired effect of the diuretic is obtained.

Information for the Patient: Angioedema: Angioedema, including laryngeal edema, may occur during treatment with Vaseretic. Patients should be so advised and told to report immediately any signs or symptoms suggesting angioedema (swelling of face, extremities, eyes, lips, tongue, difficulty in breathing) and to take no more drug until they have consulted with the prescribing physician.

Hypotension: Patients should be cautioned to report lightheadedness especially during the first few days of therapy. If actual syncope occurs, the patients should be told to discontinue the drug until they have consulted with the prescribing physician.

All patients should be cautioned that excessive perspiration and dehydration may lead to an excessive fall in blood pressure because of reduction in fluid volume. Other causes of volume depletion such as vomiting or diarrhea may also lead to a fall in blood pressure; patients should be advised to consult with their physician.

Neutropenia: Patients should be told to report promptly any indication of infection (e.g., sore throat, fever) which may be a sign of neutropenia.

Impaired Liver Function: Patients should be advised to return to the physician if he/she experiences any symptoms possibly related to liver dysfunction. This would include viral-like symptoms in the first weeks to months of therapy (such as fever, malaise, muscle pain, rash or adenopathy which are possible indicators of hypersensitivity reactions), or if abdominal pain,

nausea or vomiting, loss of appetite, jaundice, itching or any other unexplained symptoms occur during therapy.
Hyperkalemia: Patients should be told not to use salt substitutes containing potassium without consulting their physician.
Pregnancy: Patients should be advised to report promptly to their physician if they become pregnant, since the use of Vaseretic during pregnancy can cause injury and even death of the developing fetus.
Note: As with many other drugs, certain advice to patients being treated with Vaseretic is warranted. This information is intended to aid in the safe and effective use of this medication. It is not a disclosure of all possible adverse or intended effects.

Adverse Effects: In clinical trials involving 1 580 hypertensive patients, including over 300 patients treated for 1 year or more, the most severe adverse reactions were: angioedema (0.3%), syncope (1.3%) and renal failure (0.1%).

The most frequent clinical adverse experiences in controlled trials were: dizziness (8.6%), headache (5.5%), fatigue (3.9%) and cough (3.5%).

Adverse experiences that have occurred, have been those that were previously reported with enalapril maleate or hydrochlorothiazide when used separately for the treatment of hypertension.

Adverse reactions occurring in patients treated with Vaseretic in controlled trials are shown in Table I.

Table I—Vaseretic

Adverse Effects	**Enalapril 2 314 Patients**	**Enalapril Plus Hydrochlorothiazide 1 580 Patients**
Cardiovascular		
Hypotension	0.9%	0.9%
Chest Pain	0.9%	1.1%
Palpitations	0.6%	1.0%
Syncope	0.5%	1.3%
Myocardial Infarction	0.2%	0.4%
Gastrointestinal		
Nausea	1.4%	2.5%
Vomiting	0.8%	1.6%
Dysphagia	0.1%	0.1%
Diarrhea	1.4%	2.1%
Abdominal Pain	0.7%	1.1%
Renal		
Renal Failure	0.1%	0.1%
Oliguria	1 case	2 cases
Proteinuria*	0.1%	0
Dermatologic		
Rash	1.4%	1.3%
Pruritus	0.4%	0.5%
Nervous System		
Headache	5.2%	5.5%
Dizziness	4.3%	8.6%
Insomnia	0.5%	0.9%
Nervousness	0.6%	0.5%
Somnolence	0.6%	0.5%
Paresthesia	0.6%	1.1%
Allergic		
Cough	1.3%	3.5%
Angioedema	0.2%	0.3%
Hematologic		
Anemia	0.1%	0.1%
Leukopenia	1 case	0
Miscellaneous		
Muscle Cramps	0.6%	2.7%
Dyspnea	0.6%	0.7%
Hyperhidrosis	0.7%	0.8%
Impotence	0.4%	2.2%
Fatigue	3.0%	3.9%
Taste Disturbance	0.4%	0.2%

* Defined as >1 g/24h or >0.5 g/12h on 2 consecutive measurements, at least 1 month apart.

Laboratory Test Findings: Hyperkalemia: (see Precautions).
Creatinine, Blood Urea Nitrogen: In controlled clinical trials minor increases in blood urea nitrogen and serum creatinine, reversible upon discontinuation of therapy, were observed in about 0.6% of patients with essential hypertension treated with Vaseretic.

In patients treated with enalapril alone, increases in serum creatinine and BUN were reported in about 20% of patients with renovascular hypertension and in about 0.2% of patients with essential hypertension.
Hemoglobin and Hematocrit: Decreases in hemoglobin and hematocrit (mean approximately 0.34 g% and 1 vol% respectively) occurred frequently in hypertensive patients treated with enalapril but were rarely of clinical importance. In clinical trials, less than 0.1% of patients discontinued therapy due to anemia.
Others: Elevations of liver enzymes and/or serum bilirubin have occurred (see Warnings).
Adverse Reactions Reported in Uncontrolled Trials and/or Marketing Experience: Vasotec: The following occurred in an incidence of 0.5 to 1.0%: insomnia, impotence, renal dysfunction, renal failure and oliguria.

The following occurred at an incidence of $<0.5\%$:
Cardiovascular: myocardial infarction or cerebrovascular accident, possibly secondary to excessive hypotension in high risk patients (see Warnings). Cardiac arrest, pulmonary embolism, rhythm disturbances, angina pectoris.
Dermatologic: pemphigus, erythema multiforme, exfoliative dermatitis, Stevens-Johnson syndrome, toxic epidermal necrosis, urticaria, photosensitivity, alopecia.
Gastrointestinal: anorexia, ileus, pancreatitis, dyspepsia, constipation, stomatitis.
Hematologic: hemolytic anemia, neutropenia, thrombocytopenia, bone marrow depression.
Hepatic: liver function abnormalities, hepatitis (hepatocellular and/or cholestatic, hepatic failure, jaundice
Nervous System/Psychiatric: vertigo, depression, confusion, ataxia.
Respiratory: bronchospasm/asthma, rhinorrhea, pulmonary infiltrates.
Other: flushing, tinnitus, hearing impairment, glossitis, blurred vision.

A symptom complex has been reported which may include fever, serositis, vasculitis, myalgia/myositis, arthralgia/arthritis, a positive ANA, elevated erythrocyte sedimentation rate, eosinophilia and leukocytosis. Rash, photosensitivity or other dermatologic manifestations may occur. These symptoms have disappeared after discontinuation of therapy.
Laboratory Test Findings: hyponatremia.
Vaseretic (Marketing Experience Only): arthralgia, asthenia, constipation, decreased libido, dry mouth, dyspepsia, flatulence, gout, hypotension, tachycardia, tinnitus, vertigo.

Overdose: Symptoms and Treatment: No specific information is available on the treatment of overdosage with Vaseretic. Treatment is symptomatic and supportive. Therapy with Vaseretic should be discontinued and the patient observed closely. Suggested measures include induction of emesis and/or gastric lavage, and correction of dehydration, electrolyte imbalance and hypotension by established procedures.

Enalaprilat may be removed from the general circulation by hemodialysis.
Enalapril Maleate: The most prominent feature of overdosage reported to date is marked hypotension, beginning some 6 hours after ingestion of tablets, concomitant with blockade of the renin-angiotensin system, and stupor. Serum enalaprilat levels 100 times and 200 times higher than usually seen after therapeutic doses have been reported after ingestion of 300 mg and 440 mg of enalapril maleate, respectively.
Hydrochlorothiazide: The most common signs and symptoms observed are those caused by electrolyte depletion (hypokalemia, hypochloremia, hyponatremia) and dehydration resulting from excessive diuresis. If digitalis has also been administered hypokalemia may accentuate cardiac arrhythmias.

Dosage: Dosage must be individualized. The fixed combination is not for initial therapy. The dose of Vaseretic should be determined by the titration of the individual components.

Once the patient has been successfully titrated with the individual components as described below, Vaseretic (1 or 2 tablets daily) may be substituted if the titrated doses and dosing schedule can be achieved by the fixed combination (see Indications and Warnings).

Patients usually do not require doses in excess of 50 mg of hydrochlorothiazide daily, particularly when combined with hypertensive agents. Therefore, since each tablet of Vaseretic includes 25 mg of hydrochlorothiazide, the daily dosage of Vaseretic should not exceed 2 tablets. If further blood pressure control is indicated, additional doses of enalapril or other nondiuretic, antihypertensive agents should be considered.

For enalapril monotherapy the recommended initial dose in patients not on diuretics is 5 mg of enalapril once a day. Dosage should be adjusted according to blood pressure response. The usual dosage range of enalapril is 10 to 40 mg/day administered in a single dose or 2 divided doses. In some patients treated once daily, the antihypertensive effects may diminish toward the end of the dosing interval. In such patients an increase in dosage or twice daily administration should be considered. If blood pressure is not controlled with enalapril alone, a diuretic may be added. In the elderly the starting dose of enalapril should be 2.5 mg since some elderly patients may be more responsive to enalapril than younger patients.

In patients who are currently being treated with a diuretic, symptomatic hypotension occasionally may occur following the initial dose of enalapril. The diuretic should, if possible, be discontinued for 2 to 3 days before beginning therapy with enalapril to reduce the likelihood of hypotension (see Warnings). If the patient's blood pressure is not controlled with enalapril alone, diuretic therapy may be resumed.

If the diuretic cannot be discontinued, an initial dose of 2.5 mg of enalapril should be used to determine whether excessive hypotension occurs.

In patients with mild to moderate renal impairment (creatinine clearance >30 mL/min.), the usual dose titration of the individual components is required. The recommended initial dose of enalapril maleate, when used alone in patients with mild renal impairment, is 5 mg. In patients with moderate renal impairment, the initial dose of enalapril, when used alone, is 2.5 mg.

When concomitant diuretic therapy is required in patients with severe renal impairment, a loop diuretic, rather than a thiazide diuretic is preferred for use with enalapril. Therefore, for patients with severe renal dysfunction, Vaseretic is not recommended (see Precautions—Anaphylactoid Reactions during Membrane Exposure).

Information for the Patient: See Blue Section—Information for the Patient "Vaseretic".

Supplied: Each red, squared capsule-shaped, compressed tablet, engraved 720 on one side and VASERETIC on the other, contains: enalapril maleate 10 mg and hydrochlorothiazide 25 mg. Nonmedicinal ingredients: cornstarch, lactose, magnesium stearate, red ferric oxide and sodium bicarbonate. Blister packages of 30. Store at controlled room temperature (15 to 30°C). Keep container tightly closed. Protect from moisture.

(Shown in Product Recognition Section)

Reviewed 1998

VASOCIDIN® ℞
CIBA Vision

Prednisolone Sodium Phosphate—Sulfacetamide Sodium
Ophthalmic Corticosteroid—Antibacterial

Supplied: Each mL of ophthalmic solution contains: prednisolone sodium phosphate 2.5 mg (equivalent to 2.3 mg of prednisolone phosphate or 2.0 mg prednisolone) and sulfacetamide sodium 100 mg. Nonmedicinal ingredients: benzalkonium chloride 0.0025% w/v (preservative), boric acid, disodium edetate, hydrochloric acid (to adjust pH), poloxamer 407 and purified water. Plastic squeeze bottles with dropper tips of 5 mL. Store at 15 to 30°C. Protect from light. Keep bottle tightly closed when not in use.

VASOCON®
CIBA Vision

Naphazoline HCl
Ophthalmic Decongestant

Supplied: Each 15 mL plastic squeeze bottle with dropper tip contains: naphazoline HCl 0.1% (w/v). Nonmedicinal ingredients: benzalkonium chloride 0.01% (w/v) (preservative), disodium edetate, hydrochloric acid and/or sodium hydroxide (to adjust pH), polyethylene glycol, polyvinyl alcohol, purified water and sodium chloride. Store at 15 to 30°C. Keep bottle tightly closed when not in use.

VASOCON-A®
CIBA Vision

Naphazoline HCl—Antazoline Phosphate
Ophthalmic Decongestant—Antihistaminic

Supplied: Each 15 mL plastic squeeze bottle with dropper tip contains naphazoline HCl 0.05% (w/v) and antazoline phosphate 0.5% (w/v). Nonmedicinal ingredients: benzalkonium chloride 0.01% (w/v) (preservative), disodium edetate, hydrochloric acid and/or sodium hydroxide (to adjust pH), polyethylene glycol, polyvinyl alcohol, purified water and sodium

Vasocon-A (cont'd)

chloride. Store at 15 to 30°C. Protect from light. Keep bottle tightly closed when not in use.

VASOPRESSIN INJECTION ℞

Pharmaceutical Partners

Antidiuretic Agent

Pharmacology: The antidiuretic action of vasopressin is ascribed to increasing reabsorption of water by the renal tubules.

Vasopressin can cause contraction of smooth muscle of the gastrointestinal tract and of all parts of the vascular bed especially the capillaries, small arterioles and venules with less effect on the smooth musculature of the large veins. The direct effect on the contractile elements is neither antagonized by adrenergic blocking agents nor prevented by vascular denervation.

Indications: Prevention and treatment of postoperative abdominal distention, in abdominal roentgenography to dispel interfering gas shadows, and in diabetes insipidus.

Contraindications: Anaphylaxis or hypersensitivity to the drug or its components.

Warnings: This drug should not be used in patients with vascular disease, especially disease of the coronary arteries, except with extreme caution. In such patients, even small doses may precipitate anginal pain, and with larger doses, the possibility of myocardial infarction should be considered.

Vasopressin may produce water intoxication. The early signs of drowsiness, listlessness, and headaches should be recognized to prevent terminal coma and convulsions.

Precautions: Vasopressin should be used cautiously in the presence of epilepsy, migraine, asthma, heart failure or any state in which a rapid addition to extracellular water may produce hazard for an already overburdened system.

Chronic nephritis with nitrogen retention contraindicates the use of vasopressin until reasonable nitrogen blood levels have been attained.

Adverse Effects: Local or systemic allergic reactions may occur in hypersensitive individuals. The following side effects have been reported following the administration of vasopressin: tremor, sweating, vertigo, circumoral pallor, "pounding" in head, abdominal cramps, passage of gas, nausea, vomiting, urticaria, bronchial constriction. Anaphylaxis (cardiac arrest and/or shock) have been observed shortly after injection of vasopressin.

Dosage: May be administered i.m. or s.c.

Ten units (0.5 mL) will usually elicit full physiologic response in adult patients: 5 units (0.25 mL) will be adequate in many cases. Should be given i.m. at 3- or 4-hour intervals as needed. The dosage should be proportionately reduced for children. (For an additional discussion of dosage, consult the sections below.)

When determining the dose of vasopressin injection for a given case, the following should be kept in mind: It is particularly desirable to give a dose not much larger than is just sufficient to elicit the desired physiologic response. Excessive doses may cause undesirable side actions–blanching of the skin, abdominal cramps, nausea–which, though not serious, may be alarming to the patient. Spontaneous recovery from such side actions occurs in a few minutes. It has been found that 1 or 2 glasses of water given at the time vasopressin injection is administered reduces such symptoms.

Abdominal Distention: In the average postoperative adult patient, give 5 units (0.25 mL) initially, increase to 10 units (0.5 mL) at subsequent injections if necessary. It is recommended that vasopressin injection be given i.m. and that injections be repeated at 3- or 4-hour intervals as required. Dosage to be reduced proportionately for children.

Vasopressin injection used in this manner will frequently prevent, or relieve, postoperative distention. These recommendations apply also to distention complicating pneumonia or other acute toxemias.

Abdominal Roentgenography: For the average case, 2 injections of 10 units (0.5 mL) each are suggested. These should be given 2 hours and ½ hour, respectively before films are exposed. Many roentgenologists advise giving an enema prior to the first dose of vasopressin injection.

Diabetes Insipidus: May be given by injection or administered intranasally on cotton pledgets, by nasal spray, or by dropper. The dose by injection is 5 to 10 units (0.25 to 0.5 mL) repeated 2 or 3 times daily as needed. When it is administered intranasally by spray or on pledgets, the dosage and interval between treatments must be determined for each patient.

Parenteral drug products should be inspected visually for particulate matter and discoloration prior to administration, whenever solution and container permit.

Supplied: Each mL of sterile, nonpyrogenic solution contains: vasopressin 20 USP pressor units, chlorobutanol 5 mg as preservative, water for injection q.s., glacial acetic acid and/or sodium hydroxide for pH adjustment (2.5 to 4.5). Flip-top vials of 1 mL (partially filled in 2 mL vial), packages of 25. Store at 15 to 30°C. Do not permit to freeze.

Reviewed 1997

VASOTEC® ℞
VASOTEC® I.V. ℞

Frosst

Enalapril Maleate
Enalaprilat

Angiotensin Converting Enzyme Inhibitor

Pharmacology: Enalapril is an ACE inhibitor which is used in the treatment of hypertension and heart failure. Enalaprilat is an active metabolite of enalapril and is used in the treatment of hypertension.

Angiotensin converting enzyme (ACE) is a peptidyl dipeptidase which catalyzes the conversion of angiotensin I to the pressor substance, angiotensin II. After absorption, enalapril, a pro-drug, is hydrolyzed to enalaprilat, its active metabolite, which inhibits ACE. Inhibition of ACE results in decreased plasma angiotensin II, which leads to increased plasma renin activity (due to removal of negative feedback of renin release) and decreased aldosterone secretion. Although the latter decrease is small, it results in a small increase in serum potassium. In patients treated with enalapril and a thiazide diuretic there was essentially no change in serum potassium (see Precautions).

ACE is identical to kininase II. Thus, both Vasotec and Vasotec I.V. may also block the degradation of bradykinin, a potent vasodepressor peptide. However, the role that this plays in the therapeutic effects of either drug is unknown.

While the mechanism through which Vasotec and Vasotec I.V. lowers blood pressure is believed to be primarily the suppression of the renin-angiotensin-aldosterone system, both Vasotec and Vasotec I.V. also lower blood pressure in patients with low-renin hypertension.

Administration of Vasotec or Vasotec I.V. to patients with hypertension results in a reduction of both supine and standing blood pressure. Abrupt withdrawal of Vasotec or Vasotec I.V. has not been associated with a rapid increase in blood pressure. Following administration of Vasotec I.V., the onset of action usually occurs within 15 minutes, with the maximum effect occurring within 1 to 4 hours. In most patients studied, after oral administration of an individual dose of enalapril, the onset of antihypertensive activity is seen at 1 hour with peak reduction of blood pressure achieved by 4 to 6 hours. At recommended doses, the antihypertensive effect has been shown to be maintained for a least 24 hours. In some patients the effect may diminish towards the end of the dosing interval (see Dosage). On occasion, achievement of optimal blood pressure reduction may require several weeks of therapy.

In hemodynamic studies in patients with essential hypertension, blood pressure reduction was accompanied by a reduction in peripheral arterial resistance with an increase in cardiac output and little or no change in heart rate. Following administration of Vasotec, there was an increase in renal blood flow; glomerular filtration rate was usually unchanged. The antihypertensive effect of angiotensin converting enzyme inhibitors is generally lower in black than in nonblack patients.

When Vasotec is given together with thiazide-type diuretics, its blood pressure lowering effect is approximately additive.

Administration of enalapril to patients with congestive heart failure reduces afterload and preload of the heart, resulting in an increase in cardiac output, without reflex tachycardia.

In a multi-centre, placebo-controlled, double-blind study (SOLVD), 2 569 patients with symptomatic heart failure (primarily New York Heart Association Class II and III and ejection fraction ≤35%), were randomized to placebo or enalapril given as an adjunct to conventional therapy. Diseases that excluded patients from enrolment in the study included severe stable angina, hemodynamically significant valvular or outflow tract obstruction, renal failure, cerebral vascular disease (e.g., significant carotid artery diseases), advanced pulmonary disease, malignancies, active myocarditis and constrictive pericarditis. The use of enalapril was associated with an 11% reduction in all-cause mortality (which corresponds to a 16% risk reduction in all-cause mortality) and a 30% reduction in hospitalization for heart failure (which corresponds to a 36% risk reduction in hospitalization for heart failure). The chief difference in mortality was in deaths due to progressive heart failure. There was no significant difference in the number of deaths classified as due to arrhythmia without worsening congestive heart failure.

A second multicenter trial used the SOLVD protocol for a study of asymptomatic or minimally symptomatic patients. SOLVD-Prevention patients, who had left ventricular ejection fraction ≤35% and no history of symptomatic heart failure, were randomized to placebo (n=2117) or enalapril (n=2111) and followed for up to 5 years. The majority of patients in the SOLVD-Prevention trial had a history of ischemic heart disease. A history of myocardial infarction was present in 80% of patients, current angina pectoris in 34%, and a history of hypertension in 37%. No statistically significant mortality effect was demonstrated in this population. Enalapril-treated subjects had 32% fewer first hospitalizations for heart failure, and 32% fewer total heart failure hospitalizations. Compared to placebo, 32% fever patients receiving enalapril developed symptoms of overt heart failure.

Hospitalizations for cardiovascular reasons were also reduced. There was an insignificant reduction in hospitalizations for any cause in the enalapril treatment group (for enalapril vs. placebo, respectively, 1 166 vs. 1 201 first hospitalizations, 2 649 vs. 2 840 total hospitalizations), although the study was not powered to look for such an effect.

The SOLVD-Prevention trial was not designed to determine whether treatment of asymptomatic patients with low ejection fraction would be superior, with respect to preventing hospitalization, to closer follow-up and use of enalapril at the earliest sign of heart failure. However, under the conditions of follow-up in the SOLVD-Prevention trial (every 4 months at the study clinic; personal physician as needed), 68% of patients on placebo who were hospitalized for heart failure had no prior symptoms recorded which would have signaled initiation of treatment.

The SOLVD-Prevention trial was also not designed to show whether enalapril modified the progression of underlying heart disease.

In another multi-centre, placebo-controlled trial (CONSENSUS), 253 patients with severe congestive heart failure (New York Heart Association Class IV) were randomized to placebo or enalapril given as an adjunct to conventional therapy. The use of enalapril was associated with an improvement of symptoms and a reduction in mortality from the progression of heart failure. No difference was seen in the incidence of sudden cardiac death.

Pharmacokinetics: Enalapril is rapidly absorbed with peak serum concentrations occurring within 1 hour. Based on urinary recovery the extent of absorption is approximately 60%.

Following absorption, enalapril is rapidly and extensively hydrolyzed to enalaprilat, a potent angiotensin-converting enzyme inhibitor (which itself is poorly absorbed). Peak serum concentrations of enalaprilat occur 3 to 4 hours after an oral dose of enalapril maleate. Excretion of enalapril is primarily renal. Approximately 94% of the dose is recovered in the urine and feces as enalaprilat or enalapril. The principal components in urine are enalaprilat, accounting for about 40% of the dose, and intact enalapril. Except for conversion to enalaprilat, there is no evidence of significant metabolism of enalapril. The serum concentration profile of enalaprilat exhibits a prolonged terminal phase, apparently associated with binding to ACE. The effective half-life for accumulation of enalaprilat following multiple doses of enalapril maleate is 11 hours. The absorption of enalapril is not influenced by the presence of food in the gastrointestinal tract.

Pharmacodynamics: The disposition of enalapril and enalaprilat in patients with renal insufficiency is similar to that in patients with normal renal function until the glomerular filtration rate is 0.50 mL/s (30 mL/min) or less. With renal function ≤0.50 mL/s (≤30 mL/min), peak and trough enalaprilat levels increase, time to peak concentration increases and time to steady state may be delayed. The effective half-life of enalaprilat following multiple doses of enalapril is prolonged at this level of renal insufficiency (see Dosage). Enalaprilat is dialyzable at the rate of 1.03 mL/s (62 mL/min).

When used in hypertensive, normolipidemic patients, enalapril had no effect on plasma lipoprotein fractions.

Studies in dogs indicate that enalapril crosses the blood brain barrier poorly, if at all; enalaprilat does not enter the brain.

Indications: Vasotec: In the treatment of essential or renovascular hypertension. It is usually administered in association with other drugs, particularly thiazide diuretics.

In using enalapril consideration should be given to the risk of angioedema (see Warnings).

Enalapril should normally be used in those patients in whom treatment with a diuretic or beta-blocker was found ineffective or has been associated with unacceptable adverse effects.

Enalapril can also be tried as an initial agent in those patients in whom use of diuretics and/or beta-blockers is contraindicated or in patients with medical conditions in which these drugs frequently cause serious adverse effects.

Enalapril is indicated in the treatment of symptomatic congestive heart failure usually in combination with diuretics and/or digitalis. In these patients, enalapril improves symptoms, increases survival, and decreases the frequency of hospitalization (see Pharmacology for details and limitations of survival trials). Treatment with enalapril should be initiated under close medical supervision.

In clinically stable asymptomatic patients with left ventricular dysfunction (ejection fraction ≤35%), enalapril decreases the rate of development of overt heart failure and decreases the incidence of hospitalization for heart failure (see Pharmacology for details and limitations of survival trials).

Pregnancy: **When used in pregnancy during the second and third trimesters, ACE inhibitors can cause injury or even death of the developing fetus. When pregnancy is detected enalapril should be discontinued as soon as possible (see Warnings, Pregnancy and Information for the Patient).**

Vasotec I.V.: For the treatment of hypertension when oral therapy is not practical.

Enalaprilat has been studied with only one other antihypertensive agent, furosemide, which showed approximately additive effects on blood pressure.

Due to insufficient experience with enalaprilat in the treatment of accelerated or malignant hypertension, this drug is not recommended in such situations (see Dosage).

Contraindications: Patients who are hypersensitive to these products or any of their components and in patients with a history of angioneurotic edema relating to previous treatment with an angiotensin converting enzyme inhibitor.

Warnings: Angioedema: Angioedema has been reported in patients treated with Vasotec and Vasotec I.V. This may occur at any time during treatment. Angioedema associated with laryngeal edema and/or shock may be fatal. If angioedema occurs, Vasotec or Vasotec I.V. should be discontinued and appropriate monitoring should be instituted to ensure complete resolution of symptoms prior to dismissing the patient. Where swelling is confined to the face, lips and mouth the condition will usually resolve without further treatment, although antihistamines may be useful in relieving symptoms. These patients should be followed carefully until the swelling has resolved. However, where there is involvement of the tongue, glottis or larynx, likely to cause airway obstruction, appropriate therapy such as s.c. epinephrine (0.5 mL 1:1 000) should be administered promptly when indicated.

The incidence of angioedema during ACE inhibitor therapy has been reported to be higher in black than in nonblack patients.

Patients with a history of angioedema unrelated to ACE inhibitor therapy may be at increased risk of angioedema while receiving an ACE inhibitor (see Contraindications).

Hypotension: Symptomatic hypotension has occurred after administration of both Vasotec and Vasotec I.V., usually after the first or second dose or when the dose was increased. It is more likely to occur in patients who are volume depleted by diuretic therapy, dietary salt restriction, dialysis, diarrhea, or vomiting. In patients with severe congestive heart failure, with or without associated renal insufficiency, excessive hypotension has been observed and may be associated with oliguria and/or progressive azotemia, and rarely with acute renal failure and/or death. Because of the potential fall in blood pressure in these patients, therapy should be started under very close medical supervision, usually in a hospital. Such patients should be followed closely for the first 2 weeks of treatment and whenever the dose of enalapril and/or diuretic is increased. Similar considerations may apply to patients with ischemic heart or cerebrovascular disease in whom an excessive fall in blood pressure could result in a myocardial infarction or cerebrovascular accident (see Adverse Effects).

If hypotension occurs, the patient should be placed in supine position and, if necessary, receive an i.v. infusion of normal saline. A transient hypotensive response is not a contraindication to further doses which usually can be given without difficulty once the blood pressure has increased after volume expansion.

Neutropenia/Agranulocytosis: Agranulocytosis and bone marrow depression have been caused by ACE inhibitors. Several cases of agranulocytosis and neutropenia have been reported in which a causal relationship to enalapril cannot be excluded. Current experience with the drug shows the incidence to be rare. Periodic monitoring of white blood cell counts should be considered, especially in patients with collagen vascular disease and renal disease.

Pregnancy: ACE inhibitors can cause fetal and neonatal morbidity and mortality when administered to pregnant women. Several dozen cases have been reported in the world literature. When pregnancy is detected, enalapril should be discontinued as soon as possible.

In rare cases (probably less than once in every 1 000) in which no alternative to ACE inhibitor therapy will be found, the mothers should be apprised of the potential hazards to their fetuses. Serial ultrasound examinations should be performed to assess fetal development and well-being and the volume of amniotic fluid.

If oligohydramnios is observed, enalapril should be discontinued unless it is considered life-saving for the mother. A non-stress test (NST), and/or a biophysical profiling (BPP) may be appropriate, depending upon the week of pregnancy. If concerns regarding fetal well-being still persist, a contraction stress testing (CST) should be considered. Patients and physicians should be aware, however, that oligohydramnios may not appear until after the fetus has sustained irreversible injury.

Infants with a history of in utero exposure to ACE inhibitors should be closely observed for hypotension, oliguria, and hyperkalemia. If oliguria occurs, attention should be directed toward support of blood pressure and renal perfusion. Exchange transfusion or dialysis may be required as a means of reversing hypotension and/or substituting for impaired renal function; however, experience with those procedures has been limited.

Enalapril has been removed from the neonatal circulation by peritoneal dialysis with some clinical benefit and may, theoretically, be removed by exchange transfusion, although there is no experience with the latter procedure.

Human Data: It is not known whether exposure limited to the first trimester of pregnancy can adversely affect fetal outcome. The use of ACE inhibitors during the second and third trimesters of pregnancy has been associated with fetal and neonatal injury including hypotension, neonatal skull hypoplasia, anuria, reversible or irreversible renal failure, and death. Oligohydramnios has also been reported, presumably resulting from decreased fetal renal function; oligohydramnios in this setting has been associated with fetal limb contractures, craniofacial deformation, and hypoplastic lung development. Prematurity and patent ductus arteriosus have also been reported, although it is not clear whether these occurrences were due to the ACE inhibitor exposure.

Animal Data: No reproductive or teratogenicity studies have been performed with enalaprilat.

Maternal and fetal toxicity occurred in some rabbits given enalapril at doses of 1 mg/kg/day or more. Saline supplementation prevented the maternal and fetal toxicity seen at doses of 3 and 10 mg/kg/day, but not at 30 mg/kg/day (50 times the maximum human dose). Enalapril was not teratogenic in rabbits.

There was no fetotoxicity or teratogenicity in rats treated with enalapril at doses up to 200 mg/kg/day (333 times the maximum human dose). Fetotoxicity expressed as a decrease in average fetal weight, occurred in rats given 1 200 mg/kg/day of enalapril, but did not occur when these animals were supplemented with saline. The drug crosses the placental barrier in rats and hamsters.

Precautions: Impaired Renal Function: As a consequence of inhibiting the renin-angiotensin-aldosterone system, changes in renal function have been seen in susceptible individuals. In patients whose renal function may depend on the activity of the renin-angiotensin-aldosterone system, such as patients with bilateral renal artery stenosis, unilateral renal artery stenosis to a solitary kidney, or severe congestive heart failure, treatment with agents that inhibit this system has been associated with oliguria, progressive azotemia, and rarely, acute renal failure and/or death. In susceptible patients, concomitant diuretic use may further increase risk.

Use of enalapril should include appropriate assessment of renal function.

Hyperkalemia: Elevated serum potassium (>5.7 mEq/L) was observed in approximately 1% of hypertensive patients in clinical trials with enalapril. In most cases these were isolated values which resolved despite continued therapy. Hyperkalemia was a cause of discontinuation of therapy in 0.28% of hypertensive patients. Risk factors for the development of hyperkalemia may include renal insufficiency, diabetes mellitus, and the concomitant use of agents to treat hypokalemia (see Drug Interactions, Agents Increasing Serum Potassium).

Valvular Stenosis: There is concern on theoretical grounds that patients with aortic stenosis might be at particular risk of decreased coronary perfusion when treated with vasodilators because they do not develop as much afterload reduction.

Surgery/Anesthesia: In patients undergoing major surgery or during anesthesia with agents that produce hypotension, enalapril blocks angiotensin II formation, secondary to compensatory renin release. If hypotension occurs and is considered to be due to this mechanism, it can be corrected by volume expansion.

Patients with Impaired Liver Function: Hepatitis, jaundice (hepatocellular and/or cholestatic), elevations of liver enzymes and/or serum bilirubin have occurred during therapy with Vasotec in patients with or without pre-existing liver abnormalities (see Adverse Effects). In most cases the changes were reversed on discontinuation of the drug.

Should the patient receiving Vasotec experience any unexplained symptoms (see Information for the Patient), particularly during the first weeks or months of treatment, it is recommended that a full set of liver function tests and any other necessary investigation be carried out. Discontinuation of Vasotec should be considered when appropriate.

There are no adequate studies in patients with cirrhosis and/or liver dysfunction. Both Vasotec and Vasotec I.V. should be used with particular caution in patients with pre-existing liver abnormalities. In such patients baseline liver function tests should be obtained before administration of the drug and close monitoring of response and metabolic effects should apply.

Cough: A dry, persistent cough, which usually disappears only after withdrawal or lowering of the dose of Vasotec has been reported.

Such possibility should be considered as part of the differential diagnosis of the cough.

Lactation: Enalapril and enalaprilat are secreted in human milk in trace amounts. In general, nursing should be interrupted if Vasotec is given to a nursing mother.

Children: Neither enalapril nor enalaprilat have been studied in children and, therefore, use in this age group is not recommended.

Anaphylactoid Reactions during Membrane Exposure: Anaphylactoid reactions have been reported in patients dialyzed with high-flux membranes (e.g., polyacrylonitrile [PAN]) and treated concomitantly with an ACE inhibitor. Dialysis should be stopped immediately if symptoms such as nausea, abdominal cramps, burning, angioedema, shortness of breath and severe hypotension occur. Symptoms are not relieved by antihistamines. In these patients consideration should be given to using a different type of dialysis membrane or a different class of antihypertensive agent.

Anaphylactoid Reactions during Desensitization: There have been isolated reports of patients experiencing sustained life-threatening anaphylactoid reactions while receiving ACE inhibitors during desensitizing treatment with hymenoptera (bees, wasp) venom. In the same patients, these reactions have been avoided when ACE inhibitors were temporarily withheld for at least 24 hours, but they have reappeared upon inadvertent rechallenge.

Anaphylactoid Reactions during LDL Apheresis: Rarely, patients receiving ACE inhibitors during low density lipoprotein (LDL)-apheresis with dextran sulfate have experienced life-threatening anaphylactoid reactions. These reactions were avoided by temporarily withholding ACE inhibitor therapy prior to each apheresis.

Drug Interactions: Hypotension—Patients on Diuretic Therapy: Patients on diuretics, and especially those in whom diuretic therapy was recently instituted, may occasionally experience an excessive reduction of blood pressure after initiation of therapy with enalapril or enalaprilat. The possibility of hypotensive effects with enalapril or enalaprilat can be minimized by either discontinuing the diuretic or increasing the salt intake prior to initiation of treatment with enalapril or enalaprilat (see Warnings and Dosage). If the diuretic cannot be discontinued, patients should be placed under close medical supervision for at least 1 hour after the initial dose of Vasotec I.V. (see Warnings).

Agents Increasing Serum Potassium: Since enalapril and enalaprilat decreases aldosterone production, elevation of serum potassium may occur. Potassium sparing diuretics such as spironolactone, triamterene or amiloride, or potassium supplements should be given only for documented hypokalemia and with caution and frequent monitoring of serum potassium

Vasotec (cont'd)

since they may lead to a significant increase in serum potassium. Salt substitutes which contain potassium should also be used with caution.

Agents Causing Renin Release: The antihypertensive effect of both Vasotec and Vasotec I.V. is augmented by antihypertensive agents that cause renin release (e.g., diuretics).

Agents Affecting Sympathetic Activity: Agents affecting sympathetic activity (e.g., ganglionic blocking agents or adrenergic neuron blocking agents) may be used with caution. Beta-adrenergic blocking drugs add some further antihypertensive effect to enalapril.

Lithium Salts: As with other drugs which eliminate sodium, lithium clearance may be reduced. Therefore, the serum lithium levels should be monitored carefully if lithium salts are to be administered.

Information for the Patient: Angioedema: Angioedema, including laryngeal edema, may occur especially following the first dose of enalapril or enalaprilat. Patients should be so advised and told to report immediately any signs or symptoms suggesting angioedema (swelling of face, extremities, eyes, lips, tongue, difficulty in breathing) and to take no more drug until they have consulted with the prescribing physician.

Hypotension: Patients should be cautioned to report lightheadedness especially during the first few days of therapy. If actual syncope occurs, the patients should be told to discontinue the drug until they have consulted with the prescribing physician.

All patients should be cautioned that excessive perspiration and dehydration may lead to an excessive fall in blood pressure because of reduction in fluid volume. Other causes of volume depletion such as vomiting or diarrhea may also lead to a fall in blood pressure; patients should be advised to consult with their physician.

Neutropenia: Patients should be told to report promptly any indication of infection (e.g., sore throat, fever) which may be a sign of neutropenia.

Impaired Liver Function: Patients should be advised to return to the physician if he/she experiences any symptoms possibly related to liver dysfunction. This would include "viral-like symptoms" in the first weeks to months of therapy (such as fever, malaise, muscle pain, rash or adenopathy which are possible indicators of hypersensitivity reactions), or if abdominal pain, nausea or vomiting, loss of appetite, jaundice, itching or any other unexplained symptoms occur during therapy.

Hyperkalemia: Patients should be told not to use salt substitutes containing potassium without consulting their physician.

Pregnancy: Patients should be advised to report promptly to their physician if they become pregnant, since the use of Vasotec during pregnancy can cause injury and even death of the developing fetus.

Note: As with many other drugs, certain advice to patients being treated with Vasotec is warranted. This information is intended to aid in the safe and effective use of this medication. It is not a disclosure of all possible adverse or intended effects.

Adverse Effects: Vasotec: In controlled clinical trials involving 2 314 hypertensive patients and 363 patients with congestive heart failure, the most severe adverse reactions were: angioedema (0.2%), hypotension (2.3%) and renal failure (5 cases).

In hypertensive patients, hypotension occurred in 0.9% and syncope in 0.5%, with a discontinuation rate of 0.1%.

In congestive heart failure patients, hypotension occurred in 4.4% and syncope 0.8%, with a discontinuation rate of 2.5%.

The most frequent clinical adverse reactions in controlled clinical trials were: headache (4.8%), dizziness (4.6%) and fatigue (2.8%). Discontinuation of therapy was required in 6% of the 2 677 patients.

Adverse reactions occurring in patients treated with Vasotec in controlled clinical trials are shown in Table I.

Laboratory Test Findings: Hyperkalemia: (see Precautions).

Creatinine, BUN: Increases in serum creatinine and BUN were reported in about 20% of patients with renovascular hypertension and in about 0.2% of patients with essential hypertension treated with enalapril alone.

In patients with congestive heart failure, who were also receiving diuretics and/or digitalis, increases in BUN and serum creatinine, usually reversible upon discontinuation of Vasotec and/or concomitant therapy, were observed in about 9.7% of patients.

Table I—Vasotec

Adverse Effects

	Hypertension (2 314 Patients)	Congestive Heart Failure (363 Patients)
Cardiovascular		
Hypotension	0.9%	4.4%
Chest Pain	0.9%	1.7%
Palpitations	0.6%	0.3%
Myocardial Infarction, acute	0.2%	0.6%
Myocardial Infarction, recurrent	—	0.3%
Gastrointestinal		
Nausea	1.4%	1.1%
Vomiting	0.8%	1.7%
Dysphagia	0.1%	—
Diarrhea	1.4%	3.0%
Abdominal Pain	0.7%	1.4%
Renal		
Renal Failure	0.1%	0.6%
Oliguria	1 case	—
Proteinuria*	0.1%	—
Dermatologic		
Rash	1.4%	1.9%
Pruritus	0.4%	1.4%
CNS		
Headache	5.2%	2.2%
Dizziness	4.3%	6.6%
Insomnia	0.5%	0.3%
Nervousness	0.6%	—
Somnolence	0.6%	—
Paresthesia	0.6%	—
Allergic		
Cough	1.3%	1.4%
Angioedema	0.2%	—
Hematologic		
Anemia	0.1%	—
Leukopenia	1 case	—
Miscellaneous		
Muscle Cramps	0.6%	0.3%
Dyspnea	0.6%	1.1%
Hyperhidrosis	0.7%	—
Impotence	0.4%	0.3%
Fatigue	3.0%	1.4%
Taste Disturbance	0.4%	0.3%

* Defined as >1 g/24h or >0.5 g/12h on 2 consecutive measurements, at least 1 month apart.

Hemoglobin and Hematocrit: Decreases in hemoglobin and hematocrit (mean approximately 0.34 g% and 1 vol% respectively) occurred frequently in either hypertensive or congestive heart failure patients treated with Vasotec, but were rarely of clinical importance. In clinical trials, less than 0.1% of patients discontinued therapy due to anemia.

Hepatic: Elevations of liver enzymes and/or serum bilirubin have occurred (see Precautions).

Adverse reactions reported in uncontrolled trials and/or marketing experience: The following occurred in an incidence of 0.5 to 1%: insomnia, impotence, renal dysfunction, renal failure and oliguria.

The following occurred at an incidence of $<0.5\%$:

Cardiovascular: myocardial infarction or cerebrovascular accident, possibly secondary to excessive hypotension in high risk patients (see Warnings). Cardiac arrest, pulmonary embolism, rhythm disturbances, angina pectoris.

Dermatologic: pemphigus, erythema multiforme, exfoliative dermatitis, Stevens-Johnson syndrome, toxic epidermal necrosis, urticaria, photosensitivity, alopecia.

Gastrointestinal: anorexia, ileus, pancreatitis, dyspepsia, constipation, stomatits.

Hematologic: hemolytic anemia, neutropenia, thrombocytopenia, bone marrow depression.

Hepatic: liver function abnormalities, hepatitis, jaundice, hepatic failure.

Nervous System/Psychiatric: vertigo, depression, confusion, ataxia.

Respiratory: bronchospasm/asthma, rhinorrhea, pulmonary infiltrates.

Other: flushing, tinnitus, hearing impairment, glossitis, blurred vision.

A symptom complex has been reported which may include fever, serositis, vasculitis, myalgia/myositis, arthralgia/arthritis, a positive ANA, elevated erythrocyte sedimentation rate, eosinophilia and leukocytosis. Rash, photosensitivity or other dermatologic manifestations may occur. These symptoms have disappeared after discontinuation of therapy.

Laboratory Test Findings: hyponatremia.

Vasotec I.V.: Since enalapril is converted to enalaprilat, those adverse reactions associated with Vasotec tablets might also be expected to occur with Vasotec I.V.

The incidence of symptomatic hypotension is 3.4% with Vasotec I.V. Other adverse experiences occurring in greater than 1% of patients were headache (2.9%) and nausea (1.1%).

Adverse reactions occurring in 0.5 to 1% of patients in controlled clinical trials include myocardial infarct, fatigue, dizziness, fever, rash and constipation.

Overdose: Symptoms and Treatment: Limited data are available for overdosage in humans. The most prominent features of overdosage reported to date are marked hypotension, beginning some 6 hours after ingestion of tablets, concomitant with blockade of the renin-angiotensin system, and stupor. Serum enalaprilat levels 100- and 200-fold higher than usually seen after therapeutic doses have been reported after ingestion of 300 mg and 440 mg of enalapril, respectively.

The recommended treatment of overdosage is i.v. infusion of normal saline solution. If ingestion is recent, induce emesis. Enalaprilat may be removed from the general circulation by hemodialysis.

Dosage: Vasotec: For oral administration only.

The absorption of enalapril is not affected by food.

Dosage must be individualized.

Hypertension: Initiation of therapy requires consideration of recent antihypertensive drug treatment, the extent of blood pressure elevation and salt restriction; the dosage of other antihypertensive agents being used with enalapril may need to be adjusted.

The recommended initial dose in patients not on diuretics is 5 mg once a day. Dosage should be adjusted according to blood pressure response. The usual dosage range is 10 to 40 mg/day administered in a single dose or 2 divided doses. In some patients treated once daily, the antihypertensive effect may diminish toward the end of the dosing interval. In such patients, an increase in dosage or twice daily administration should be considered. If blood pressure is not controlled, a diuretic may be added.

The maximum daily dose is 40 mg. Raising the dose above that level is not recommended because of the possibility of increased adverse reactions.

Symptomatic hypotension occasionally may occur following the initial dose of enalapril and is more likely in patients who are currently being treated with a diuretic. The diuretic should, if possible, be discontinued for 2 to 3 days before beginning therapy with enalapril to reduce the likelihood of hypotension (see Warnings).

If the diuretic cannot be discontinued, an initial dose of 2.5 mg should be used to determine whether excessive hypotension occurs.

To date there is insufficient experience with enalapril in the treatment of accelerated or malignant hypertension. Enalapril, therefore, is not recommended in such situations.

Geriatrics (over 65 years): The starting dose should be 2.5 mg. Some elderly patients may be more responsive to enalapril than younger patients.

Dosing Adjustment in Renal Impairment (see Precautions, Anaphylactoid Reactions during Membrane Exposure): The doses should be reduced in patients with hypertension according to the guidelines in Table II.

Table II—Vasotec

Dosing Adjustment in Renal Impairment

Renal Status	Creatinine Clearance mL/s (mL/min)	Initial Dose mg/day
Normal Renal Function	>1.33 mL/s (>80 mL/min)	5 mg
Mild Impairment	$\leq 1.33 > 0.50$ mL/s ($\leq 80 > 30$ mL/min)	5 mg
Moderate to Severe Impairment	≤ 0.50 mL/s (≤ 30 mL/min)	2.5 mg
Dialysis Patients	—	2.5 mg on dialysis days*

* Enalaprilat is dialyzable. Dosage on nondialysis days should be adjusted depending on the blood pressure response.

Congestive Heart Failure: Enalapril is generally used in conjunction with a diuretic and/or digitalis. Blood pressure and renal function should be monitored, both before and during treatment with enalapril, because severe hypotension and, more rarely, consequent renal failure have been reported (see Warnings and Precautions).

Initiation of therapy requires consideration of recent diuretic therapy and the possibility of severe salt/volume depletion. If possible, the dose of diuretic should be reduced before beginning treatment to reduce the likelihood of hypotension. Serum potassium also should be monitored (see Precautions, Drug Interactions).

The recommended initial dose in patients with symptomatic heart failure or asymptomatic left ventricular dysfunction (ejection fraction ≤35%) is 2.5 mg once a day, to be administered under close medical supervision to determine the initial effect on blood pressure. After the initial dose, the patient should be observed for at least 2 hours or until the pressure has stabilized for at least another additional hour (see Warnings, Hypotension).

In the absence of, or after effective management of symptomatic hypotension following initiation of therapy, the dose should be increased gradually depending on the patient's response. The usual therapeutic dosing range is 5 to 20 mg daily, given as a single dose or 2 divided doses.

This dose titration may be performed over a 2 to 4 week period, or more rapidly if indicated by the presence of residual signs and symptoms of heart failure. The dosage regimen, in patients with symptomatic heart failure, which was effective in reducing mortality and the need for hospitalization in multicentre studies ranged between 16.4 and 18.8 mg/day. The majority of patient experience in clinical studies has been with twice daily dosage.

The maximum daily dose is 40 mg.

Dosage Adjustment in Patients with Congestive Heart Failure and Renal Impairment or Hyponatremia: In patients with heart failure who have hyponatremia (serum sodium less than 130 mEq/L) or with serum creatinine greater than 1.6 mg/dL, therapy should be initiated at 2.5 mg daily under close medical supervision (see Dosage, Congestive Heart Failure, Warnings and Precautions, Drug Interactions).

The dose may be increased to 2.5 mg b.i.d. then 5 mg b.i.d. and higher as needed, usually at intervals of 4 days or more if at the time of dosage adjustment there is not excessive hypotension or significant deterioration of renal function. The maximum daily dose is 40 mg.

Vasotec I.V.: For i.v. administration only.

Enalaprilat vials should be inspected visually and should not be used if particulate matter or discoloration is observed.

Enalaprilat may be administered i.v. as supplied, or mixed with up to 50 mL of 1 of the following diluents: 5% Dextrose Injection, 0.9% Sodium Chloride Injection, 0.9% Sodium Chloride Injection in 5% Dextrose, 5% Dextrose in Lactated Ringer's Injection.

Diluted solutions should be used within 24 hours.

The dose is 1.25 mg every 6 hours administered i.v. over at least 5 minutes. A clinical response is usually seen within 15 minutes. Peak effects after the first dose may not occur for up to 4 hours after dosing. The peak effects of the second and subsequent doses may exceed those of the first.

No dosage regimen for enalaprilat has been clearly demonstrated to be more effective in treating hypertension than 1.25 mg every 6 hours. However, in controlled clinical studies in hypertension, doses as high as 5 mg every 6 hours were well tolerated for up to 36 hours. There has been inadequate experience with doses greater than 20 mg/day.

In studies of patients with hypertension, enalaprilat has not been administered for periods longer than 48 hours. In other studies, patients have received enalaprilat for as long as 7 days.

The dose for patients being converted to enalaprilat from oral therapy for hypertension with enalapril is 1.25 mg every 6 hours administered i.v. over at least 5 minutes. For conversion from i.v. to oral therapy, the recommended initial dose of enalapril tablets is 5 mg once a day with subsequent dosage adjustments as necessary.

Patients on Diuretic Therapy: For patients on diuretic therapy the recommended starting dose for hypertension is 0.625 mg administered i.v. over at least 5 minutes. A clinical response is usually seen within 15 minutes. Peak effects after the first dose may not occur for up to 4 hours after dosing, although most of the effect is usually apparent within the first hour. If after 1 hour there is an inadequate clinical response, the 0.625 mg dose may be repeated. Additional doses of 1.25 mg may be administered at 6-hour intervals.

For conversion from i.v. to oral therapy, the recommended initial dose of Vasotec tablets for patients who have responded to 0.625 mg of enalaprilat every 6 hours is 2.5 mg once a day with subsequent dosage adjustment as necessary.

Dosage Adjustment in Renal Impairment: The usual dose of 1.25 mg of enalaprilat every 6 hours is recommended for patients with a creatinine clearance >0.50 mL/s [>30 mL/min] (serum creatinine of up to approximately 265.2 μmol/L [3 mg/dL]). For patients with creatinine clearance ≤0.50 mL/s [≤30 mL/min] (serum creatinine ≥265.2 μmol/L [≥3 mg/dL]), the initial dose is 0.625 mg (see Warnings).

If after 1 hour there is an inadequate clinical response, the 0.625 mg dose may be repeated. Additional doses of 1.25 mg may be administered at 6-hour intervals.

For dialysis patients the initial dose should be 0.625 mg every 6 hours (see Precautions, Anaphylactoid Reactions during Membrane Exposure).

For conversion from i.v. to oral therapy, the recommended initial dose of Vasotec is 5 mg once a day for patients with creatinine clearance >0.50 mL/s [>30 mL/min] and 2.5 mg once daily for patients with creatinine clearance ≤0.50 mL/s [≤30 mL/min]. Dosage should then be adjusted according to blood pressure response.

Diluted Solutions: Vasotec I.V. may be used as supplied, or may be diluted with the diluents listed below (up to 50 mL). The diluted solutions are stable for 24 hours at room temperature. Diluents: 5% Dextrose Injection, 0.9% Sodium Chloride Injection, 0.9% Sodium Chloride Injection in 5% Dextrose, 5% Dextrose in Lactated Ringer's Injection.

Parenteral Products: As with all parenteral drug products, i.v. admixtures should be inspected visually for clarity, particulate matter, precipitate, discoloration and leakage prior to administration, whenever solution and container permit.

Information for the Patient: See Blue Section—Information for the Patient "Vasotec".

Supplied: Vasotec: 2.5 mg: Each yellow, barrel-shaped, biconvex, scored tablet, engraved 14 on one side and VASOTEC on the other, contains: enalapril maleate 2.5 mg. Nonmedicinal ingredients: cornstarch, lactose, magnesium stearate, pregelatinized starch, red and/or yellow iron oxides and sodium bicarbonate. Blisters of 30. Polyethylene bottles of 100 and 500.

5 mg: Each white, barrel-shaped, biconvex, scored tablet, engraved 712 on one side and VASOTEC on the other, contains: enalapril maleate 5 mg. Nonmedicinal ingredients: cornstarch, lactose, magnesium stearate, pregelatinized starch and sodium bicarbonate. Blisters of 30. Polyethylene bottles of 500.

10 mg: Each rust-red colored, barrel-shaped, biconvex tablet, engraved 713 on one side and VASOTEC on the other, contains: enalapril maleate 10 mg. Nonmedicinal ingredients: cornstarch, lactose, magnesium stearate, pregelatinized starch, red and/or yellow iron oxides and sodium bicarbonate. Blisters of 30. Polyethylene bottles of 500.

20 mg: Each peach-colored, barrel-shaped, biconvex tablet, engraved 714 on one side and VASOTEC on the other, contains: enalapril maleate 20 mg. Nonmedicinal ingredients: cornstarch, lactose, magnesium stearate, pregelatinized starch, red and/or yellow iron oxides and sodium bicarbonate. Blisters of 30. Polyethylene bottles of 100 and 500.

All strengths are gluten- and tartrazine-free. Store at controlled room temperature (15 to 30°C). Keep container tightly closed. Protect from moisture.

Note: Bottles of 500 mg tablets: Discard remaining tablets 6 months after opening bottle.

Vasotec I.V.: Each mL of clear, colorless solution contains: enalaprilat (anhydrous equivalent) 1.25 mg, sodium chloride 6.2 mg to adjust tonicity and sodium hydroxide to adjust pH (to approximately 7.0), water for injection, q.s.; with benzyl alcohol 9 mg as preservative. Vials of 2 mL.

Store at controlled room temperature (15 to 30°C).

(Shown in Product Recognition Section)

Reviewed 1998

VASOXYL® Ⓟ

Glaxo Wellcome

Methoxamine HCl

Vasopressor

Pharmacology: Methoxamine is an alpha-receptor stimulant which produces a prompt and prolonged rise in blood pressure following parenteral administration.

It acts by exclusively stimulating alpha-adrenergic receptors and hence causes vasoconstriction. Raised arterial pressure stimulates reflex vagal inhibitory effects on the heart, and it is by this effect that methoxamine curtails supraventricular tachycardia.

The major pharmacological effect of methoxamine is a potent, prolonged pressor action following parenteral administration. Methoxamine differs from most other sympathomimetic amines both in animals and in humans by having a predominantly peripheral action and lacking inotropic and chronotropic effects. Methoxamine has less arrhythmogenic potential than other sympathomimetic amines and rarely causes ventricular tachycardia, fibrillation, or increased sino-atrial rate. On occasion, a decrease in cardiac rate develops as the blood pressure increases. This bradycardia is apparently caused by a carotid sinus reflex mediated over the vagus nerve. It is abolished by atropine.

Evidence for direct action on blood vessels is provided by the observation of intense constriction along the course of a vein into which methoxamine has been injected. Methoxamine also increases central venous pressure and has the distinct advantage of being free of central stimulating action. Pressor action without central stimulation may be especially desirable in patients undergoing surgery under spinal anesthesia.

Methoxamine does not increase the irritability of the cyclopropane-sensitized heart. It is a safe pressor agent for use during cyclopropane anesthesia. It has already been noted that methoxamine tends to slow the ventricular rate; large doses may produce bradycardia, but do not cause ventricular tachycardia, fibrillation, or an increased sino-atrial rate.

Tachyphylaxis has not been a clinical problem.

Following i.v. administration of methoxamine in dogs and humans, the peak pressor effect occurs within 0.5 to 2 minutes. In a group of surgical patients, the duration of the pressor effect following a single i.v. dose of 2 to 4 mg of methoxamine was 10 to 15 minutes. No clinical pharmacology studies are available concerning the onset and duration of action after administration of recommended i.m. doses (10 to 15 mg). With administration of 10 to 40 mg methoxamine i.m. to patients, however, the peak effect occurs within 15 to 20 minutes, and the duration of action is approximately 1½ hours.

It has been shown by cardiac catheterization that methoxamine does not increase cardiac output or stroke volume, although it does increase right auricular and ventricular pressure by increasing venous pressure. It has been shown repeatedly that it does not affect cardiac irritability and that it tends to slow rather than to increase heart rate. Also, it has a marked power to raise total peripheral resistance. Studies have indicated that increased force of cardiac contractions can occur without direct stimulation of the heart, probably due to the general improvement in circulation resulting from the increase in arterial pressure. These actions contribute to the restoration of circulatory function, without unduly increasing the work of the cardiac musculature.

Indications: Intended for supporting, restoring or maintaining blood pressure during anesthesia (including cyclopropane anesthesia). It is especially useful to counteract the fall in blood pressure that commonly follows the administration of a spinal anesthetic. This pressor agent is particularly indicated just before surgery on patients who are poor risks and who have low blood pressure and where emergency operations are involved. It may also be helpful in treating postoperative collapse. The drug is not to be regarded as a substitute for blood, plasma, or other measures indicated in the treatment of shock.

Methoxamine is indicated in the treatment of shock due to traumatic, surgical or medical conditions, including acute myocardial infarction, in which it is desired to increase peripheral resistance without producing myocardial stimulation.

The i.v. administration of methoxamine promptly terminates episodes of paroxysmal supraventricular tachycardia. Normal rhythm of the heart is restored, usually in less than 1 minute. No adverse effect on the heart has been observed. The reversion from paroxysmal to normal rhythm following methoxamine administration is mediated through the baroreceptors in the carotid sinus and aortic arch. The stimulation of the vagus nerves in turn acts on the pacemaker of the heart to slow it down. Current practice, however, favors use of antiarrhythmic drugs such as verapamil, beta-blockers or adenosine for termination of paroxysmal supraventricular tachycardia.

Contraindications: In patients with severe hypertension, or in patients who are hypersensitive to methoxamine.

Warnings: The use of methoxamine in patients receiving MAO inhibitors, tricyclic antidepressants or oxytocic agents such as vasopressin or certain ergot alkaloids may result in potentiation of the pressor effect (see Precautions, Drug Interactions).

Contains potassium metabisulfite, a sulfite that may cause allergic-type reactions including anaphylactic symptoms and life-threatening or less severe asthmatic episodes in certain

Vasoxyl (cont'd)

susceptible people. The overall prevalence of sulfite sensitivity in the general population is unknown and probably low. Sulfite sensitivity is seen more frequently in asthmatic than in non-asthmatic people.

Pregnancy: Methoxamine has been shown to decrease uterine blood flow, decrease fetal heart rate and adversely affect the fetal acid-base status in pregnant ewes and monkeys at doses comparable to those used in humans. There are no adequate and well-controlled studies in pregnant women. There has been one report of a fetal death; the mother received methoxamine concomitantly with several other drugs. A direct causal relationship to methoxamine was not established. Methoxamine should be used during pregnancy only if the potential benefit justifies the potential risk to the fetus.

Precautions: General: Methoxamine, like other vasopressor agents, should be used with caution in patients with hyperthyroidism, bradycardia, partial heart block, myocardial disease, or severe arteriosclerosis. Caution should be exercised to avoid overdosage, preventing undesirable high blood pressure and/or bradycardia. Note: bradycardia may be abolished with atropine (see Overdose: Symptoms and Treatment). Also caution should be taken when methoxamine is used closely following the parenteral injection of ergot alkaloids to avoid an excessive rise in blood pressure.

Children: Safety and effectiveness in children have not been established.

Pregnancy: see Warnings, Pregnancy.

Labor and Delivery: If vasopressor drugs are used to correct hypotension or are added to the local anesthetic solution during labor and delivery, some oxytocic drugs (vasopressin, ergotamine, ergonovine, methylergonovine) may cause severe persistent hypertension (see Drug Interactions). Note: In pregnant animals, methoxamine has been shown to decrease uterine blood flow, possibly resulting in fetal asphyxia. Uterine hypertonus and fetal bradycardia may also be produced (see Adverse Effects and Warnings, Pregnancy).

Lactation: It is not known whether this drug is excreted in human milk. Because many drugs are excreted in human milk, caution should be exercised when methoxamine is administered to a nursing woman.

Drug Interactions: The pressor effect of methoxamine may be markedly potentiated when methoxamine is used in conjunction with MAO inhibitors, tricyclic antidepressants, vasopressin or ergot alkaloids such as ergotamine, ergonovine or methylergonovine, sympathomimetic agents such as decongestants, some appetite suppressants and amphetamine-like psychostimulants. Therefore, when initiating pressor therapy in patients receiving these drugs, the initial dose should be small and given with caution (see Warnings).

Cardiovascular: Methoxamine should not be administered unless facilities are available to measure systemic blood pressure frequently. The effect of increased arterial pressure on a patient with pre-existing vascular disease or impairment of myocardial function should be considered before administering methoxamine Injection.

Use methoxamine Injection with care in patients with poor left ventricular function as the increase in peripheral resistance, which is brought about by methoxamine, may cause or exacerbate cardiac failure.

The use of methoxamine injection is not a substitute for replacement of lost intravascular fluids and care should be taken to ensure adequate provision of i.v. fluid, plasma or blood before or during recourse to methoxamine injection.

Laboratory Tests: Methoxamine may increase plasma cortisol and ACTH levels. Caution should be used when interpreting plasma cortisol and ACTH levels in a patient concurrently receiving methoxamine.

Carcinogenesis, Mutagenesis, Impairment of Fertility: No long-term animal studies have been performed to evaluate the potential of methoxamine in these areas.

Adverse Effects: The following adverse reactions have been observed, but there are insufficient data to support an estimate of their frequency: Cardiovascular: excessive blood pressure elevations particularly with high dosage, ventricular ectopic beats, reflex bradycardia.

Gastrointestinal: nausea, vomiting (often projectile).

CNS: headache (often severe), anxiety.

Integumentary: sweating, pilomotor response; feeling of cold and other skin sensations resulting from piloerection.

Genitourinary: uterine hypertonus, fetal bradycardia (see Precautions, Labor and Delivery), urinary urgency.

Overdose: Symptoms and Treatment: Overdosage of methoxamine may be manifested as an undesirable elevation in blood pressure and/or bradycardia. Should a clinically significant elevation of blood pressure occur that requires treatment, it may be immediately reversed with an alpha-adrenergic blocking agent (e.g., phentolamine). Bradycardia may be abolished by atropine.

Dosage: Blood volume depletion should always be corrected before any vasopressor is administered.

Methoxamine is administered either i.m. or i.v. In emergencies or where a serious vasomotor collapse has occurred, i.v. injection is desirable. The i.m. route alone is recommended where there is no emergency.

When administered i.v., large veins are preferred to prevent extravasation of methoxamine injection. Extravasation may cause necrosis and sloughing of surrounding tissue. The infusion site should be monitored closely for free flow. The usual i.v. dose of methoxamine, for emergencies, is 3 to 5 mg, injected slowly. I.V. injection may be supplemented by i.m. injections to provide a more prolonged effect. The usual i.m. dose is 10 to 15 mg given shortly before or at the time of administering spinal anesthesia to prevent a fall in blood pressure. The tendency for the blood pressure to fall is greater with higher levels of spinal anesthesia, hence, the dosage may be adjusted accordingly; 10 mg may be adequate at lower spinal levels while 15 to 20 mg may be required at high levels of spinal anesthesia. Repeated doses may be given if necessary, but time should be allowed for the previous dose to act (about 15 minutes, see Pharmacology).

For purposes of correcting a fall in blood pressure, an i.m. injection of 10 to 15 mg may be given depending on the degree of fall. In cases where the systolic pressure falls to 60 mm Hg or less, or whenever an emergency exists, an i.v. injection of 3 to 5 mg is indicated. This i.v. dose may be accompanied by 10 to 15 mg i.m. to provide a more prolonged effect.

For preoperative and postoperative use in cases of only moderate hypotension, 5 to 10 mg i.m. may be adequate.

For the treatment of hypotension associated with acute myocardial infarction or prolonged shock due to other causes, methoxamine may be administered in dilute solution by slow i.v. infusion. A solution of dextrose 5% in 250 mL of distilled water containing methoxamine 35 to 40 mg is administered at the rate required to provide an optimal response.

For termination of episodes of supraventricular tachycardia not responsive to other modes of therapy, the usual dose of methoxamine is 10 mg i.v., administered by slow push (i.e., 3 to 5 minutes).

Supplied: Each mL of sterile aqueous solution contains: methoxamine HCl 20 mg. Nonmedicinal ingredients: citric acid anhydrous and sodium citrate (added as buffers), carbon dioxide, potassium metabisulfite (added as an antioxidant), sodium chloride and water for injection. Parenteral drug products should be inspected visually for particulate matter and discoloration prior to administration whenever solution and container permit. Store at controlled room temperature between 15 and 30°C, and protect from light. Ampuls of 1 mL, boxes of 10.

Reviewed 1997

VAXIGRIP®

Connaught

Inactivated Influenza Vaccine Trivalent Types A and B (Split Virion)

Influenza Prophylaxis

Pharmacology: The inoculation of antigen prepared from inactivated influenza virus stimulates the production of specific antibodies. Protection is afforded only against those strains of virus from which the vaccine is prepared or closely related strains.

Influenza A viruses are classified into subtypes on the basis of 2 surface antigens: hemagglutinin (H) and neuraminidase (N). Three subtypes of hemagglutinin (H1, H2, H3) and 2 subtypes of neuraminidase (N1, N2) are recognized among influenza A viruses that have caused widespread human disease. Immunity to these antigens—especially to the hemagglutinin—reduces the likelihood of infection and lessens the severity of disease if infection occurs. Infection with a virus of one subtype confers little or no protection against viruses of other subtypes. Furthermore, over time, antigenic variation (antigenic drift) within a subtype may be so marked that infection or vaccination with one strain may not induce immunity to distantly related strains of the same subtype. Although influenza B viruses have shown more antigenic stability than influenza A viruses, antigenic variation does occur. For these reasons, major epidemics of respiratory disease caused by new variants of influenza continue to occur. The antigenic characteristics of circulating strains provide the basis for selecting the virus strains included in each year's vaccine.

Each year's influenza vaccine contains 3 virus strains (usually 2 type A and 1 type B) representing the influenza viruses that are likely to circulate in Canada in the coming winter.

Most vaccinated children and young adults develop high postvaccination hemagglutination-inhibition antibody titres. These antibody titres are protective against illness caused by strains similar to those in the vaccine or the related variants that may emerge during outbreak periods. Elderly persons and persons with certain chronic diseases may develop lower postvaccination antibody titres than healthy young adults and thus may remain susceptible to influenza-related upper-respiratory-tract infection. However, even if such persons develop influenza illness despite vaccination, the vaccine can be effective in preventing lower-respiratory-tract involvement or other secondary complications, thereby reducing the risk for hospitalization and death.

The effectiveness of influenza vaccine in preventing or attenuating illness varies, depending primarily on the age and immunocompetence of the vaccine recipient and the degree of similarity between the virus strains included in the vaccine and those that circulate during the influenza season. When a good match exists between vaccine and circulating viruses, influenza vaccine has been shown to prevent illness in approximately 70 to 90% of healthy persons less than 65 years of age. In these circumstances, studies also have indicated that the effectiveness of influenza vaccine in preventing hospitalization for pneumonia and influenza among elderly persons living in settings other than nursing homes or similar chronic care facilities ranges from 30 to 70%.

Among elderly persons residing in nursing homes, influenza vaccine is most effective in preventing severe illness, secondary complications, and death. Studies of this population have indicated that the vaccine can be 50 to 60% effective in preventing hospitalization and pneumonia and 80% effective in preventing death, even though efficacy in preventing influenza illness may often be in the range of 30 to 40% among the frail elderly. Achieving a high rate of vaccination among nursing home residents and staff can reduce the spread of infection in a facility, thus preventing disease through herd immunity. Vaccination of health care workers in nursing homes also has been demonstrated to reduce the impact of influenza among residents.

Although the current influenza vaccine can contain 1 or more of the antigens administered in previous years, annual vaccination using the current vaccine is necessary because immunity declines in the year following vaccination.

Indications: For adults and children 6 months of age and older when influenza vaccine is recommended.

The National Advisory Committee on Immunization recommends annual vaccination for individuals in the following categories: People at High Risk: Vaccination of people at high risk is the single most important measure for reducing the impact of influenza. Priority should be given to ensure annual vaccination of people in the following groups:

Adults and children with chronic cardiac or pulmonary disorders (including bronchopulmonary dysplasia, cystic fibrosis, and asthma) severe enough to require regular medical follow-up or hospital care: Chronic cardiac and pulmonary disorders are by far the most important risk factors for influenza-related death.

People of any age who are residents of nursing homes and other chronic care facilities: Such residents generally have one or more of the medical conditions outlined in the first group. In addition, their institutional environment may promote spread of the disease. Studies have shown that the use of vaccine in this setting will decrease occurrence of illness and has an even greater impact in reducing the rates of hospitalization, pneumonia and death.

People 65 years of age and over: The risk of severe illness and death related to influenza is moderately increased in healthy people in this age group but is not nearly as great as in people with chronic underlying disease. Vaccination is effective in preventing hospitalization and death.

Adults and children with chronic conditions such as diabetes mellitus and other metabolic diseases, cancer, immunodeficiency, immunosuppression, renal disease, anemia, and hemoglobinopathy: The degree of risk associated with chronic renal and metabolic diseases in children is uncertain, but this uncertainty should not preclude consideration of vaccination.

Children and adolescents (age 6 months to 18 years) with conditions treated for long periods with ASA: ASA might increase the risk of Reye's syndrome after influenza.

Persons infected with Human Immunodeficiency Virus (HIV): Limited information exists regarding the frequency and severity of influenza illness among HIV-infected persons, but reports suggest that symptoms may be prolonged and the risk for complications increased for some HIV-infected persons. Because influenza can result in serious illness and complications, vaccination is a prudent precaution and will result in protective antibody levels in many recipients. However, the antibody response to vaccine may be low in persons with advanced HIV-related illnesses; giving a second dose of vaccine 4 or more weeks after the first does not improve the immune response for these persons. HIV load does not increase with influenza immunization according to a randomized, placebo-controlled trial.

Because influenza can result in serious illness and complications and because influenza vaccination may result in protective antibody titres, vaccination will benefit many HIV-infected patients.

People Capable of Transmitting Influenza to Those at High Risk: People who are potentially capable of transmitting influenza to those at high risk should receive annual vaccination.

Health care and other personnel who have significant contact with people in the high risk groups previously described: The potential for infecting people at high risk outlined above, particularly those in institutions, may be reduced through vaccination programs for health care personnel. Such personnel include: physicians, nurses and other personnel in both hospital and outpatient-care settings; employees of nursing homes and chronic care facilities who have contact with patients or residents; providers of home care to persons at high risk (e.g., visiting nurses and volunteer workers).

Household contacts (including children) of people at high risk who either cannot be vaccinated or may respond inadequately to vaccination: Because low antibody responses to influenza vaccine may occur in some people at high risk (e.g., the elderly, people with immunodeficiency), annual vaccination of their household contacts may reduce the risk of influenza exposure.

Other People: People who provide essential community services should be considered for vaccination to minimize disruption of routine activities in epidemics. Employers and their employees should consider yearly influenza immunization for healthy working adults as this has been shown to decrease work absenteeism because of respiratory and other illnesses.

Pregnant Women: Vaccination is recommended for pregnant women in high-risk groups (see above), regardless of their stage of pregnancy (see Precautions, Pregnancy).

Foreign Travellers: Predeparture influenza immunization for prevention of the disease in travellers should be considered for anyone leaving Canada during the local influenza transmission season and should be offered to anyone leaving Canada who will be exposed during the influenza transmission season at the destination.

General Population: Health care providers should administer influenza vaccine to any person who wishes to reduce the likelihood of becoming ill with influenza.

Students or other persons in institutional settings (e.g., those who reside in dormitories) should be encouraged to receive vaccine to minimize disruption of routine activities during epidemics.

Vaccine should be offered to both children and adults up to and even after influenza virus activity is documented in a community.

Contraindications: General: Influenza virus for Vaxigrip is propagated in eggs, therefore, this vaccine should not be administered to anyone with a history of hypersensitivity (allergy) and especially anaphylactic reactions, to eggs or egg products. It is also a contraindication to administer this vaccine to individuals known to be sensitive to thimerosal. In any case, epinephrine HCl solution (1:1 000) must be immediately available should an acute anaphylactic reaction occur due to any component of the vaccine.

Absolute Contraindication: Allergy to any component of Vaxigrip, (see Supplied) or an allergic or anaphylactic reaction to a previous dose of influenza vaccine are contraindications to vaccination.

The use of Vaxigrip in infants under 6 months of age is not recommended.

Immunization with Vaxigrip should be deferred in the presence of any acute illness, including febrile illness, or active infection to avoid superimposing adverse effect from the vaccine on the underlying illness or mistakenly identifying a manifestation of the underlying illness as a complication of vaccine use. A minor afebrile illness such as mild upper respiratory infection is not usually reason to defer immunization.

Immunization should be delayed in a patient with an active neurologic disorder, but should be considered when the disease process has been stabilized.

Warnings: I.M. injections should be given with care in persons suffering from coagulation disorders or on anticoagulant therapy because of the risk of hemmorrhage.

During recent decades, data on influenza vaccine immunogenicity and side effects have been obtained for i.m. administered vaccine. Because recent influenza vaccines have not been adequately evaluated when administered by other routes, the i.m. route is recommended.

If Vaxigrip is used in persons with malignancies, persons receiving immunosuppressive therapies, including irradiation, antimetabolites, alkylating agents, cytotoxic drugs, or who are otherwise immunocompromised, (including HIV-infected individuals, transplant recipients, persons suffering from autoimmune disorders), the expected immune response may not be obtained.

Corticosteroid therapy can result in immunosuppression although the exact dose and duration of therapy required to suppress the immune system is not well defined. Persons treated with high doses of systemic steroids, e.g., ≥2 mg/kg/day of prednisone orally for more than 2 weeks, should be considered to have a compromised immune system.

Although influenza vaccination can inhibit the clearance of warfarin, theophylline, and phenytoin, clinical studies have consistently failed to show any adverse effects attributable to these drugs in people receiving influenza vaccine.

Influenza virus is remarkably capricious in that significant antigenic changes may occur from time to time. It is known definitely that Vaxigrip, as now constituted, is not effective against all possible strains of influenza virus. Protection is afforded most people only against those strains of virus from which the vaccine is prepared or against closely related strains.

As with any vaccine, immunization with influenza vaccine may not protect 100% of susceptible individuals.

Precautions: General: The possibility of allergic reactions in individuals sensitive to the components of the vaccine should be evaluated. Epinephrine HCl solution (1:1 000) and other appropriate agents should be available for immediate use in case an anaphylactic or acute hypersensitivity reaction occurs. Health care providers should be familiar with current recommendations for the initial management of anaphylaxis in non-hospital settings including proper airway management.

Before administration of any vaccine, all appropriate precautions should be taken to prevent adverse reactions. This includes a review of the patient's history with respect to possible hypersensitivity to the vaccine or similar vaccine, determination of previous immunization history, and the presence of any contraindications to immunization, current health status, and a current knowledge of the literature concerning the use of the vaccine under consideration.

Special care should be taken to ensure that the product is not injected into a blood vessel.

A separate sterile needle and syringe, or a sterile disposable unit, must be used for each individual patient to prevent the transmission of infectious agents. There have been case reports of transmission of HIV and hepatitis by failure to scrupulously observe sterile technique. In particular, the same needle and/or syringe must never be used to re-enter a multi-dose vial to withdraw vaccine even when it is to be used for inoculation of the same patient. This may lead to contamination of the vial contents and infection of patients who subsequently receive vaccine from the vial.

Needles should not be recapped and should be disposed of as biohazardous waste.

Before administration of Vaxigrip, healthcare personnel should inform the parent or guardian or the patient to be immunized of the benefits and risks of immunization, inquire about the recent health status of the patient and comply with any local requirements with respect to information to be provided to the patient before immunization.

Pregnancy: Reproduction studies have not been conducted with Vaxigrip. Vaxigrip should be given to a pregnant woman only if clearly needed (see Indications).

Simultaneous Administration of other Vaccines: Pneumococcal vaccine and influenza vaccine can be given at the same visit at different sites with separate sterile needles and syringes without an increase in side effects, but it should be emphasized that, whereas influenza vaccine is given annually, pneumococcal vaccine should be given only once to adults. Detailed immunization records should be provided to each patient to help ensure that additional doses of pneumococcal vaccine are not given. Children at high risk may receive influenza vaccine at the same time as routine pediatric vaccines but at separate sites with separate sterile needles and syringes.

Adverse Effects: Split-virus vaccines, produced by chemically disrupting the influenza virus, are generally associated with somewhat fewer side effects in children and young adults than are whole-virus vaccines; consequently, only split-virus vaccines are recommended for persons under 13 years of age.

Because Vaxigrip contains only noninfectious viruses, it cannot cause influenza. Respiratory disease after vaccination represents coincidental illness unrelated to influenza vaccination. The most frequent side effects of vaccination are soreness, redness and induration at the vaccination site that last for up to 2 days; this is reported by fewer than one-third of vaccinees. In addition, 2 types of systemic reactions have occurred: 1. Fever, malaise, myalgia, and other systemic symptoms occur infrequently and most often affect persons who have had no exposure to the influenza virus antigens in the vaccine (e.g., young children). These reactions begin 6 to 12 hours after vaccination and can persist for 1 to 2 days. Recent placebo-controlled trials suggest that in elderly persons and healthy young adults, split-virus influenza vaccine is not associated with higher rates of systemic symptoms (e.g., fever, malaise, myalgia, and headache) when compared with placebo injections.

2. Immediate—presumably allergic—reactions (such as hives, angioedema, allergic asthma, or systemic anaphylaxis) occur rarely after influenza vaccination. These reactions probably result from hypersensitivity to some vaccine component—the majority are most likely related to residual egg protein. Although current influenza vaccines contain only a small quantity of egg protein, this protein may induce immediate hypersensitivity reactions among persons with severe egg allergy. Persons who have developed hives, have had swelling of the lips or tongue, or have experienced acute respiratory distress or collapse after eating eggs should consult a physician for appropriate evaluation to help determine if vaccine should be administered. Persons who have documented immunoglobulin E(IgE)-mediated hypersensitivity to eggs, including those who have had occupational asthma or other allergic responses due to exposure to egg protein, also might be at increased risk for reactions from influenza vaccine, and similar consultation should be considered.

The protocol for influenza vaccination developed by Murphy and Strunk may be considered for patients who have egg allergies and medical conditions that place them at increased risk for influenza-associated complications.

Prophylactic acetaminophen may decrease the frequency of some side effects in adults.

Thrombocytopenia has been observed rarely. Vasculitis with transient. renal involvement has been reported in very rare cases.

Unlike the 1976 swine influenza vaccine, subsequent vaccines prepared from other virus strains have not been clearly associated with an increased frequency of Guillain-Barré syndrome (GBS). However it is difficult to obtain strong evidence for a possible small increase in risk for a rare condition such as GBS, which has an annual background incidence of only 10 to 20 cases per million in the adult population. During 3 of 4 seasons studied between 1977 and 1991 in the USA, the point estimates of the overall relative risks of GBS after influenza vaccination were slightly elevated; but were not statistically significant in any of these studies. However, a recent U.S. study of the 1992-93 and 1993-94 seasons found an elevation in the overall relative risk of 1.83 (95% Confidence Interval 1.12 to 3.00) during the 6 weeks following vaccination, representing an excess of an estimated 1 to 2 cases per million persons vaccinated; the combined number of GBS cases peaked 2 weeks after vaccination. The increase in the relative risks and the increased number of cases in the second week after vaccination may be the result of vaccination but also could be due to other factors (e.g., confounding or diagnostic bias) rather than a true vaccine-related risk.

Among persons who received the swine influenza vaccine in 1976, the rate of GBS that exceeded the background rate was slightly less than 10 cases per million vaccinations. Even if GBS were a true side effect in subsequent years, the estimated risk for GBS of 1 to 2 cases per million vaccinations is substantially less than that for severe influenza, which could be prevented by vaccination among all age groups, especially among persons 65 years of age or more and those who have medical indications for influenza vaccination. Estimates of excess hospitalization rates during different influenza epidemics have ranged from approximately 200 to 300 hospitalizations per million previously healthy persons age 5 to 44 years to 2 000 to greater than 10 000 hospitalizations per million persons aged 65 and older. Estimates of influenza-associated death rates have ranged from approximately 300 to 1 500 per million persons aged 65 and older, which account for more than 90% of all influenza-associated deaths. The

Vaxigrip (cont'd)

average case-fatality ratio for GBS is approximately 6% and increases with age. There is no indication that the case-fatality ratio for GBS differs by influenza vaccination status. The potential benefits of influenza vaccination clearly outweigh the possible risks for vaccine-associated GBS.

Whereas the incidence of GBS in the general population is very low, persons with a history of GBS have a substantially greater likelihood of subsequently developing GBS than persons without such a history. Thus, the likelihood of coincidentally developing GBS after influenza vaccination is expected to be greater among persons with a history of GBS than among persons with no history of this syndrome. Whether influenza vaccination might be causally associated with this risk for recurrence is not known. Avoiding subsequent influenza vaccination of persons known to have developed GBS within 6 weeks of a previous influenza vaccination seems prudent. However, for most persons with a history of GBS who are at high risk for severe complications from influenza, many experts believe the established benefits of influenza vaccination justify yearly vaccination.

Influenza vaccine is not known to predispose to Reye's syndrome.

Neurological disorders temporally associated with influenza vaccination such as encephalopathy, optic neuritis, facial paralysis, labyrinthitis, and brachial plexus neuropathy have been reported. However, no cause and effect have been established. Almost all persons affected were adults, and the described clinical reactions began as soon as a few hours and as late as 2 weeks after vaccination. Full recovery was almost always reported.

Fatalities from a variety of other causes have been reported in the high-risk population following influenza vaccination without the establishment of a definite causal relationship.

Physicians, nurses, and pharmacists should report any adverse occurrences temporally related to the administration of the product in accordance with local requirements and to the Medical Director, Connaught Laboratories Limited, 1755 Steeles Avenue West, Toronto, Ontario, Canada M2R 3T4.

Dosage: Parenteral biological products should be inspected visually for extraneous particulate matter and/or discoloration before administration. If these conditions exist, the product should not be administered.

Shake the vial well to distribute uniformly the suspension before withdrawing each dose. When administering a dose from a rubber-stoppered vial, do not remove either the rubber stopper or the metal seal holding it in place. Aseptic technique must be used for withdrawal of each dose (see Precautions).

Before injection, the skin over the site to be injected should be cleansed with a suitable germicide.

Administer the vaccine **i.m.**, preferably in the region of the deltoid muscle, in adults and older children. The preferred site for infants and young children (< 1 year of age) is the anterolateral aspect of the thigh.

After insertion of the needle, aspirate to insure the needle has not entered a blood vessel.

Do not inject i.v.

Vaxigrip may be used for all age groups. **It is not recommended for infants under 6 months of age.** The dosage is as follows: See Table I.

Table I—Vaxigrip

Recommended Influenza Vaccine Dosage by Age 1998-1999

Age	Vaccine Type	Dose	Number of Doses
13 years and older	Whole-virus or split-virus	0.5 mL	1
9-12 years	Split-virus	0.5 mL	1
3-8 years	Split-virus	0.5 mL	1 or 2*
6-35 months	Split-virus	0.25 mL	1 or 2*

*Children under 9 years require 2 doses, with an interval of 4 weeks; the second dose is not needed if the child received 1 or more doses of influenza vaccine prepared for a previous season.

Each person who is immunized should be given a permanent personal immunization record. In addition, it is essential that the physician or nurse record the immunization history in the permanent medical record of each patient. This permanent office record should contain the name of the vaccine, date given, dose, manufacturer and lot number.

Supplied: Vaxigrip is prepared from the allantoic fluids of chicken embryos infected with a specific type of influenza virus. The virus containing fluids are harvested and the virus inactivated with formaldehyde and purified by zonal centrifugation. The virus is then chemically disrupted using glycol p-isooctylphenyl ether (Triton X-100) producing a "split-antigen". The split antigen is suspended in sodium phosphate buffered, isotonic sodium chloride solution. The type and amount of viral antigens contained in Vaxigrip conform to the current requirements of the World Health Organization (WHO).

For the 1998-99 season, the vaccine contains not less than 45 μg hemagglutinin (HA). Each dose (0.5 mL) contains the following 3 strains: A/Beijing/262/95 (H1N1)15 μg HA, A/Sydney/5/97 (H3N2)15 μg HA, B/Harbin/07/94 (a B/Beijing/184/93-like strain) 15 μg HA. The vaccine contains thimerosal 0.01% w/v (0.05 mg/dose) as a preservative. This vaccine may contain undetectable traces of neomycin, used during production. After shaking vial well, Vaxigrip is essentially clear and opalescent whitish in color. Vials of 5 mL (10 doses), boxes of 1.

Store between 2 and 8°C. **Do not freeze.** Product which has been exposed to freezing should not be used. Do not use after expiration.

Reviewed 1999

VELBE® Ⓟ

Lilly

Vinblastine Sulfate

Antineoplastic Agent

Pharmacology: Vinblastine has been used for the palliative treatment of a variety of malignant neoplastic conditions. In susceptible clinical cases, vinblastine sulfate has produced temporary reduction in the size or temporary disappearance of some tumors. It has relieved pain and other symptoms and allowed some patients to regain appetite and weight. Periods of remission have varied from patient to patient.

Experimental data indicate that vinblastine's action is different from that of other recognized antineoplastic agents. Tissue culture studies suggest an interference with metabolic pathways of amino acids leading from glutamic acid to the citric acid cycle and to urea. In vivo experiments tend to confirm the in vitro results. A number of studies in vitro and in vivo have demonstrated that vinblastine produces a stathmokinetic effect and various atypical mitotic figures. The therapeutic responses, however, are not fully explained by the cytological changes, since these changes are sometimes observed clinically and experimentally in the absence of any oncolytic effects.

Reversal of the antitumor effect of vinblastine by glutamic acid or tryptophan has been observed. In addition, glutamic acid and aspartic acid have protected mice from lethal doses of vinblastine sulfate. Aspartic acid was relatively ineffective in reversing the antitumor effect.

Other studies indicate that vinblastine has an effect on cell energy production required for mitosis and interferes with nucleic acid synthesis.

Pharmacokinetics: Pharmacokinetic studies in patients with cancer have shown a triphasic serum decay pattern following rapid i.v. injection. The initial, middle, and terminal half-lives are 3.7 minutes, 1.6 hours, and 24.8 hours respectively. The volume of the central compartment is 70% of body weight, probably reflecting very rapid tissue binding to formed elements of the blood. Extensive reversible tissue binding occurs. Low body stores are present at 48 and 72 hours after injection. Since the major route of excretion may be through the biliary system, toxicity from this drug may be increased when there is hepatic excretory insufficiency. Following injection of tritiated vinblastine in the human cancer patient,10% of the radioactivity was found in the feces and 14% in the urine; the remaining activity was not accounted for. Similar studies in dogs demonstrated that, over 9 days, 30 to 36% of radioactivity was found in the bile and 12 to 17% in the urine. A similar study in the rat demonstrated that the highest concentrations of radioactivity were found in the lung, liver, spleen, and kidney 2 hours after injection.

Hematologic Effects: Clinically, leukopenia is an expected effect of vinblastine and the level of the leukocyte count is an important guide to therapy with this drug. In general, the larger the dose employed, the more profound and longer lasting the leukopenia will be. The fact that the WBC count returns to normal levels after drug-induced leukopenia is an indication that the white cell producing mechanism is not permanently depressed. Usually, the white count has completely returned to normal after the virtual disappearance of white cells from the peripheral blood.

Following vinblastine therapy, the nadir in white blood cell count may be expected to occur 5 to 10 days after the last day of drug administration. Recovery of the white blood count is fairly rapid thereafter and is usually complete within another 7 to 14 days. With the smaller doses employed for maintenance therapy, leukopenia may not be a problem.

Although the thrombocyte count ordinarily is not significantly lowered by therapy with vinblastine, patients whose bone marrow has been recently impaired by prior therapy with radiation or with other oncolytic drugs may show thrombocytopenia (less than 200 000 platelets/mm^3). When other chemotherapy or radiation has not been employed previously, thrombocyte reduction below the level of 200 000/mm^3 is rarely encountered, even when vinblastine may be causing significant leukopenia. Rapid recovery from thrombocytopenia within a few days is the rule.

Vinblastine's effect upon the red cell count and hemoglobin is usually insignificant when other therapy does not complicate the picture. It should be remembered, however, that patients with malignant disease may exhibit anemia even in the absence of any therapy.

Indications: In the palliative treatment of the following:

I. Frequently Responsive Malignancies: Generalized Hodgkin's disease (Stages III and IV, Ann Arbor modification of Rye); lymphocytic lymphoma (nodular and diffuse, poorly and well differentiated); histiocytic lymphoma; mycosis fungoides (advanced stages); advanced carcinoma of the testis; Kaposi's sarcoma; Letterer-Siwe disease (histiocytosis X).

II. Less Frequently Responsive Malignancies: choriocarcinoma resistant to other chemotherapeutic agents; carcinoma of the breast, unresponsive to appropriate endocrine surgery and hormonal therapy.

Current principles of chemotherapy for many types of cancer include the concurrent administration of several antineoplastic agents. For enhanced therapeutic effect without additive toxicity, agents with different dose limiting clinical toxicities and different mechanisms of action are generally selected. Therefore, although vinblastine is effective as a single agent in the aforementioned indications, it is usually administered in combination with other antineoplastic drugs. Such combination therapy produces a greater percentage of response than does a single agent regimen. These principles have been applied, for example, in the chemotherapy of Hodgkin's disease.

Hodgkin's Disease: Vinblastine has been shown to be one of the most effective single agents for the treatment of Hodgkin's disease. Advanced Hodgkin's disease has also been successfully treated with several multiple drug regimens that included vinblastine. Patients who had relapses after treatment with the MOPP program-mechlorethamine hydrochloride (nitrogen mustard), vincristine sulfate (Oncovin), prednisone, and procarbazine—have likewise responded to combination drug therapy that included vinblastine. A protocol using cyclophosphamide in place of nitrogen mustard and vinblastine instead of vincristine is an alternative therapy for previously untreated patients with advanced Hodgkin's disease.

Advanced testicular germinal cell cancers (embryonal carcinoma, teratocarcinoma, and choriocarcinoma) are sensitive to vinblastine alone, but better clinical results are achieved when vinblastine is administered concomitantly with other antineoplastic agents. The effect of bleomycin is significantly enhanced if vinblastine is administered 6 to 8 hours prior to the administration of bleomycin; this schedule permits more cells to be arrested during metaphase, the stage of the cell cycle in which bleomycin is active.

Contraindications: Vinblastine is contraindicated in patients who have significant granulocytopenia, unless this is a result of the disease being treated with vinblastine. It should not be used in the presence of bacterial infection. Such infections must be brought under control with antiseptics or antibiotics prior to the initiation of vinblastine sulfate therapy.

Warnings: Caution: Vinblastine is a potent drug and should be used only by physicians experienced with cancer chemotherapeutic drugs. Blood counts should be taken once or twice weekly. Discontinue or reduce the dosage upon evidence of abnormal depression of the bone marrow. This product is for i.v. use only. The intrathecal administration of vinblastine has resulted in death. Syringes containing this product should be labeled: "Warning—For i.v. use only".

Extemporaneously prepared syringes containing this product must be packaged in an overwrap which is labeled **"Do not remove covering until moment of injection. Fatal if given intrathecally. For i.v. use only."**

The following treatment successfully arrested progressive paralysis in a single patient mistakenly given the related vinca alkaloid, vincristine sulfate, intrathecally. If vinblastine is mistakenly administered intrathecally, this treatment is recommended and should be initiated immediately after the intrathecal injection: 1. Remove as much spinal fluid as can be safely done through the lumbar access. 2. Insert a catheter in a lateral cerebral ventricle for the purpose of flushing the subarachnoid space from above with removal through a lumbar access. 3. Initiate flushing through the cerebral catheter with lactated Ringer's solution infused at the rate of 150 mL/h. Replace the lactated Ringer's solution with fresh frozen plasma as soon as it becomes available. 4. Infuse fresh frozen plasma, 25 mL, diluted in 1 L of lactated Ringer's solution at the rate of 75 mL/h with removal through the lumbar access. The rate of infusion should be adjusted to maintain a protein level in the spinal fluid of 150 mg/dL. 5. Administer 10 g of glutamic acid i.v. over 24 hours followed by 500 mg 3 times daily by mouth for 1 month or until neurological dysfunction stabilizes. The role of glutamic acid in this treatment is not certain and may not be essential.

The use of this treatment has not been reported following intrathecal vinblastine.

Pregnancy: Use oncolytic drugs cautiously during pregnancy. Information on the use of vinblastine during pregnancy is very limited. Although no abnormalities of the human fetus have been reported thus far, animal studies with vinblastine suggest that teratogenic effects may occur. Laboratory animals given this drug early in pregnancy suffer resorption of the conceptus; surviving fetuses demonstrate gross deformities. There are no adequate and well-controlled studies in pregnant women. If this drug is used during pregnancy, or if the patient becomes pregnant while receiving this drug, she should be informed of the potential hazard to the fetus. Women of childbearing potential should be advised to avoid becoming pregnant.

Aspermia has been reported in man. Animal studies show metaphase arrest and degenerative changes in germ cells.

Leukopenia and granulocytopenia may reach dangerously low levels following administration of the higher recommended doses. It is therefore important to follow the dosage technique recommended under the Dosage section. Stomatitis and neurologic toxicity, although not common or permanent, can be disabling.

Precautions: Toxicity may be enhanced in the presence of hepatic insufficiency. If leukopenia with less than 2 000 white blood cells/mm^3 occurs following a dose of vinblastine watch the patient carefully for evidence of infection until the WBC count has returned to a safe level.

When cachexia or ulcerated areas of the skin surface are present, there may be a more profound leukopenic response to the drug; therefore, avoid its use in older persons suffering from either of these conditions.

In patients with malignant cell infiltration of the bone marrow, the leukocyte and platelet counts have sometimes fallen precipitously after moderate doses of vinblastine. Further use of the drug in such patients is inadvisable.

The use of small amounts of vinblastine daily for long periods is not advisable, even though the resulting total weekly dosage may be similar to that recommended. Little or no added therapeutic effect has been demonstrated when such regimens have been used. **Strict adherence to the recommended dosage schedule is very important.** When amounts equal to several times the recommended weekly dosage were given in 7 daily installments for long periods, convulsions, severe and permanent CNS damage, and even death occurred.

Acute shortness of breath and severe bronchospasm have been reported following the administration of vinca alkaloids. These reactions have been encountered most frequently when the vinca alkaloid was used in combination with mitomycin-C. The onset may be within minutes or several hours after the vinca is injected.

Avoid contamination of the eye with concentrations of vinblastine used clinically. If accidental contamination occurs, severe irritation (or, if the drug was delivered under pressure, even corneal ulceration) may result. Wash the eye with water immediately and thoroughly.

It is not necessary to use preservative-containing solvents if unused portions of the remaining solutions are discarded immediately. Unused preservative-containing solutions should be refrigerated for future use.

Information for the Patient: The patient should be warned to report immediately the appearance of sore throat, fever, chills, or sore mouth. Advice should be given to avoid constipation, and the patient should be made aware that alopecia may occur and that jaw pain and pain in the organs containing tumor tissue may occur. The latter is thought possibly to result from swelling of tumor tissue during its response to treatment. Scalp hair will regrow to its pretreatment extent even with continued treatment with vinblastine. Nausea and vomiting, although not common, may occur. Any other serious medical event should be reported to the physician.

Laboratory Tests: Since the dose-limiting clinical toxicity is the result of depression of the white-blood-cell count, it is imperative that this count be obtained just before the planned dose of vinblastine. Following administration of vinblastine, a fall in the white-blood-cell count may occur. The nadir of this fall is observed from 5 to 10 days following a dose. Recovery to pretreatment levels is usually observed from 7 to 14 days after treatment. These effects will be exaggerated when preexisting bone marrow damage is present and also with the higher recommended doses (see Dosage). The presence of this drug or its metabolites in blood or body tissues is not known to interfere with clinical laboratory tests.

Drug Interactions: Vinblastine should not be diluted with solvents that raise or lower the pH of the resulting solution from between 3.5 and 5. Solutions should be made with normal saline (with or without preservative) and should not be combined in the same container with any other chemical.

The simultaneous oral or i.v. administration of phenytoin and antineoplastic chemotherapy combinations that include vinblastine have been reported to have reduced blood levels of the anticonvulsant and to have increased seizure activity. Dosage adjustment should be based on serial blood level monitoring. The contribution of vinblastine to this interaction is not certain. The interaction may result from either reduced absorption of phenytoin or an increase in the rate of its metabolism and elimination.

Pregnancy: Vinblastine should be given to a pregnant woman only if clearly needed. Animal studies suggest that teratogenic effects may occur.

Children: The dosage schedule for children is indicated under Dosage.

Lactation: It is not known whether this drug is excreted in human milk. Because many drugs are excreted in human milk and because of the potential for serious adverse reactions from vinblastine in nursing infants, a decision should be made whether to discontinue nursing or the drug, taking into account the importance of the drug to the mother.

Adverse Effects: Prior to the use of the drug, advise patients of the possibility of untoward symptoms.

In general, the incidence of side effects attending the use of vinblastine appears to be related to the size of the dosage employed. With the exception of epilation and leukopenia, adverse reactions usually have not persisted for longer than 24 hours. Leukopenia, the most common adverse reaction, is usually the dose-limiting factor.

The following are manifestations which have been reported as adverse reactions, the most common reactions are in bold face.

Hematologic: **leukopenia** (granulocytopenia), anemia, thrombocytopenia (myelosuppression).

Dermatologic: **alopecia** is common. A single case of light sensitivity associated with this product has been reported.

Gastrointestinal: **constipation** anorexia, nausea, vomiting, abdominal pain, ileus, vesiculation of the mouth, pharyngitis, diarrhea, hemorrhagic enterocolitis, bleeding from an old peptic ulcer, rectal bleeding.

Neurologic: numbness of digits (paresthesias), loss of deep-tendon reflexes, peripheral neuritis, mental depression, headache, convulsions.

Cardiovascular: **hypertension.** Cases of unexpected myocardial infarction and cerebrovascular accidents have occurred in patients undergoing combination chemotherapy with vinblastine, bleomycin, and cisplatin. Raynaud's phenomenon has also been reported with this combination.

Pulmonary: See Precautions.

Miscellaneous: **malaise, bone pain,** weakness, **pain in tumor-containing tissue,** dizziness, **jaw pain,** skin vesiculation, Raynaud's phenomenon when patients are being treated with vinblastine in combination with bleomycin and cis-platinum for testicular cancer. The syndrome of inappropriate secretion of antidiuretic hormone has occurred with higher than recommended doses.

Nausea and vomiting usually may be controlled easily by antiemetic agents. When epilation develops, it frequently is not total, and, in some cases, hair regrows while maintenance therapy continues.

Extravasation during i.v. injection may lead to cellulitis and phlebitis. If the amount of extravasation is great, sloughing may occur.

Overdose: Symptoms and Treatment: Side effects following the use of vinblastine are dose related. Therefore, following administration of more than the recommended dose, patients can be expected to experience these effects in an exaggerated fashion (see Pharmacology, Contraindications, Warnings, Precautions and Adverse Effects). There is no specific antidote. In addition, neurotoxicity similar to that with vincristine sulfate may be observed. Since the major route of excretion may be through the biliary system, toxicity from this drug may be increased when there is hepatic insufficiency.

In managing overdosage, consider the possibility of multiple drug overdoses, interaction among drugs, and unusual drug kinetics in your patient. Overdoses of vinblastine have been reported rarely. The following is provided to serve as a guide should such an overdose be encountered.

Supportive care should include the following: (1) prevention of side effects that result from the syndrome of inappropriate secretion of antidiuretic hormone (this would include restriction of the volume of daily fluid intake to that of the urine output plus insensible loss and perhaps the administration of a diuretic affecting the function of the loop of Henle and the distal tubule); (2) administration of an anticonvulsant; (3) prevention of ileus; (4) monitoring the cardiovascular system; and (5) determining daily blood counts for guidance in transfusion requirements and assessing the risk of infection. The major effect of excessive doses of vinblastine will be myelosuppression, which may be life-threatening. There is no information regarding the effectiveness of dialysis nor of cholestyramine for the treatment of overdosage.

Vinblastine in the dry state is irregularly and unpredictably absorbed from the gastrointestinal tract following oral administration. Absorption of the solution has not been studied. If vinblastine is swallowed, activated charcoal in a water slurry may be given by mouth along with a cathartic. The use of cholestyramine in this situation has not been reported. Symptoms of overdose will appear when greater-than-recommended doses are given. Any dose of vinblastine that results in elimination of platelets and neutrophils from blood and marrow and their precursors from marrow should be considered life-threatening. The exact dose that will do this in all patients is unknown. Overdoses occurring during prolonged, consecutive-day infusions may be more toxic than the same total dose given by rapid i.v. injection. The i.v. median lethal dose in mice is 10 mg/kg body weight; in rats, it is 2.9 mg/kg. The oral median lethal dose in rats is 7 mg/kg.

Protect the patient's airway and support ventilation and perfusion. Meticulously monitor and maintain, within acceptable limits, the patient's vital signs, blood gases, serum electrolytes, etc. Absorption of drugs from the gastrointestinal tract may be decreased by giving activated charcoal, which, in many cases, is more effective than emesis or lavage; consider charcoal instead of, or in addition to, gastric emptying if the drug has been swallowed. Repeated doses of charcoal over time may hasten elimination of some drugs that have been absorbed. Safeguard the patient's airway when employing gastric emptying or charcoal.

Dosage: Caution: It is extremely important that the needle be properly positioned in the vein before this product is injected.

If leakage into surrounding tissue should occur during i.v. administration of vinblastine, it may cause considerable irritation. The injection should be discontinued immediately, and any remaining portion of the dose should then be introduced into another vein. Local injection of hyaluronidase and the application of moderate heat to the area of leakage help disperse the drug and are thought to minimize discomfort and the possibility of cellulitis.

There are variations in the depth of the leukopenic response which follows therapy with vinblastine. For this reason, it is recommended that the drug be given no more frequently than **once every 7 days.** It is wise to initiate therapy for adults by administering a single i.v. dose of 3.7 mg/m^2 of body surface area (bsa). Thereafter, white-blood-cell counts should be made to determine the patient's sensitivity to vinblastine.

A simplified and conservative incremental approach to dosage **at weekly intervals** may be outlined as seen in Table I.

Table I—Velbe

Dosage	**Adults (bsa)**	**Children (bsa)**
First dose	3.7 mg/m^2	2.5 mg/m^2
Second dose	5.5 mg/m^2	3.75 mg/m^2
Third dose	7.4 mg/m^2	5 mg/m^2
Fourth dose	9.25 mg/m^2	6.25 mg/m^2
Fifth dose	11.1 mg/m^2	7.5 mg/m^2

The above mentioned increases may be used until a maximum dose (not exceeding 18.5 mg/m^2 bsa for adults and 12.5 mg/m^2 bsa for children) is reached. The dose should not be increased after that dose which reduces the white-cell count to approximately 3 000 cells/mm^3. In some adults,

Velbe (cont'd)

3.7 mg/m² bsa may produce this leukopenia; other adults may require more than 11.1 mg/m² bsa; and, very rarely, as much as 18.5 mg/m² bsa may be necessary. For most adult patients, however, the weekly dosage will prove to be 5.5 to 7.4 mg/m² bsa.

When the dose of vinblastine which will produce the above degree of leukopenia has been established, a dose **one increment smaller** than this should be administered at weekly intervals for maintenance. Thus, the patient is receiving the maximum dose that does not cause leukopenia. **It should be emphasized that, even though 7 days have elapsed, the next dose of vinblastine should not be given** until the white-cell count has returned to at least 4 000/mm³. In some cases, oncolytic activity may be encountered before leukopenic effect. When this occurs, there is no need to increase the size of subsequent doses.

The duration of maintenance therapy varies according to the disease being treated and the combination of antineoplastic agents being used. There are differences of opinion regarding the duration of maintenance therapy with the same protocol for a particular disease; for example, various durations have been used with the MOPP programme in treating Hodgkin's disease. Prolonged chemotherapy for maintaining remissions involves several risks, among which are life threatening infectious diseases, sterility, and possibly the appearance of other cancers through suppression of immune surveillance.

In some disorders, survival following complete remission may not be as prolonged as that achieved with shorter periods of maintenance therapy. On the other hand, failure to provide maintenance therapy in some patients may lead to unnecessary relapse; complete remission in patients with testicular cancer, unless maintained for at least 2 years, often result in early relapse.

To prepare a solution containing 1 mg of vinblastine/mL, add 10 mL of Sodium Chloride Injection (preserved with phenol or benzyl alcohol) to the 10 mg of vinblastine in the sterile vial. Other solutions are not recommended. The drug dissolves instantly to give a clear solution. After a solution has been made in this way and a portion of it has been removed from a vial, the remainder of the vial's contents may be stored in a refrigerator for 14 days without significant loss of potency.

The dose of vinblastine (calculated to provide the desired amount) may be injected either into the tubing of a running i.v. infusion or directly into a vein. The latter procedure is readily adaptable to outpatient therapy. In either case, the injection may be completed in about 1 minute. If care is taken to insure that the needle is securely within the vein and that no solution containing vinblastine is spilled extravascularly, cellulitis and/or phlebitis will not occur. To minimize further the possibility of extravascular spillage, it is suggested that the syringe and needle be rinsed with venous blood before withdrawal of the needle. The dose should not be diluted in large volumes of diluent (i.e., 100 to 250 mL) or given i.v. for prolonged periods (ranging from 30 to 60 minutes or more), since this frequently results in irritation of the vein and increases the chance of extravasation.

Because of the enhanced possibility of thrombosis, it is considered inadvisable to inject a solution of vinblastine into an extremity in which the circulation is impaired or potentially impaired by such conditions as compressing or invading neoplasm, phlebitis, or varicosity.

Special Dispensing Information: When dispensing vinblastine in other than the original container, e.g., a syringe containing a specific dose, it is imperative that it be packaged in an overwrap bearing the statement: **"Do not remove covering until moment of injection. Fatal if given intrathecally. For i.v. use only"** (see Warnings).

Supplied: Each 10 mL, dry powder vial contains: vinblastine sulfate USP 10 mg, without excipients. When sodium chloride solution is added prior to injection, the pH of the resulting solution lies in the range of 3.5 to 5. Refrigeration required.

The database, reporting form and procedures for monitoring adverse events from vaccines are separate from those of other drug products. See the CLIN-INFO SECTION for a description of the program and a copy of the reporting form.

VENTOLIN® Ⓟ
VENTODISK® Ⓟ
VENTODISK® DISKHALER®
VENTOLIN® ROTACAPS® Ⓟ
VENTOLIN® ROTAHALER®
VENTOLIN® RESPIRATOR SOLUTION Ⓟ
VENTOLIN® NEBULES P.F. Ⓟ

Glaxo Wellcome

Salbutamol

Bronchodilator—Beta₂-adrenergic Stimulant

Pharmacology: Salbutamol produces bronchodilation through stimulation of beta$_2$-adrenergic receptors in bronchial smooth muscle, thereby causing relaxation of bronchial muscle fibres. This action is manifested by an improvement in pulmonary function as demonstrated by spirometric measurements. At therapeutic doses, salbutamol has little action on the beta$_1$-adrenergic receptors in cardiac muscle (Ventolin, Ventodisk and Ventolin Rotacaps).

A measurable decrease in airway resistance is typically observed 5 to 15 minutes after inhalation of salbutamol. The maximum improvement in pulmonary function usually occurs 60 to 90 minutes after salbutamol treatment, and significant bronchodilator activity has been observed to persist for 3 to 6 hours.

Indications: Salbutamol inhalation aerosol and powder for inhalation are indicated for the symptomatic relief and prevention of bronchospasm due to bronchial asthma, chronic bronchitis and other chronic bronchopulmonary disorders in which bronchospasm is a complicating factor. In addition, salbutamol inhalation aerosol and powder for inhalation are indicated for the prevention of exercise-induced asthma.

Salbutamol respirator solutions are indicated for the treatment of severe bronchospasm associated with exacerbations of chronic bronchitis and bronchial asthma. They can be used by "wet" nebulization. When administered through a nebulizer, salbutamol respirator solutions should be used with compressed air or oxygen.

Contraindications: Patients with a hypersensitivity to any of the ingredients and in patients with tachyarrhythmias.

Warnings: Use of Anti-inflammatory Agents: In accordance with the present practice for asthma treatment, concomitant anti-inflammatory therapy (e.g., corticosteroids) should be part of the regimen if inhaled salbutamol needs to be used on a regular daily basis (see Dosage). It is essential that the physician instruct the patient in the need for further evaluation if the patient's asthma becomes worse.

Deterioration of Asthma: The management of asthma should normally follow a stepwise program and patient response should be monitored clinically and by lung function tests. The increasing use of fast-acting, short-duration inhaled beta$_2$-adrenergic agonists to control symptoms indicates deterioration of asthma control and the patient's therapy plan should be reassessed. Sudden or progressive deterioration in asthma control is potentially life-threatening; the treatment plan must be re-evaluted, and consideration be given to corticosteroid therapy.

Cardiovascular Effects: In individual patients, any beta$_2$-adrenergic agonist, including salbutamol, may have a clinically significant cardiac effect. Care should be taken with patients suffering from cardiovascular disorders, especially coronary insufficiency, cardiac arrhythmias and hypertension. Special care and supervision are required in patients with idiopathic hypertrophic subvalvular aortic stenosis, in whom an increase in the pressure gradient between the left ventricle and the aorta may occur, causing increased strain on the left ventricle.

Hypokalemia: In common with other beta-adrenergic agents, salbutamol can induce reversible metabolic changes such as potentially serious hypokalemia, particularly following nebulized or especially infused administration. Particular caution is advised in acute severe asthma since hypokalemia may be potentiated by concomitant treatment with xanthine derivatives, steroids and diuretics and by hypoxia. Hypokalemia will increase the susceptibility of digitalis-treated patients to cardiac arrhythmias. It is recommended that serum potassium levels be monitored in such situations.

Diabetes: Care should be taken with patients with diabetes mellitus. Salbutamol can induce reversible hyperglycemia during nebulized administration or especially during infusions of the drug. The diabetic patient may be unable to compensate for this and the development of ketoacidosis has been reported. Concurrent administration of corticosteroids can exaggerate this effect.

Paradoxical Bronchospasm: With repeated excessive use of sympathomimetic inhalation preparations, some patients have been reported to have developed severe paradoxical bronchospasm, occasionally leading to death. The cause of either the refractory state or death is unknown. However, it is suspected in the fatal episodes that cardiac arrest occurred following the unexpected development of a severe acute asthmatic crisis and subsequent hypoxia. Several cases have been reported in which intermittent positive pressure ventilation in acute asthma attacks was related to lethal episodes of hypoxia and pneumothorax. This method of drug administration may be ineffective in patients with severe obstruction and greatly increased airway resistance, and it may induce severe hypercapnia and hypoxia. During intermittent ventilation therapy, the monitoring of arterial blood gases is highly desirable. It is advisable that in the event of either hypoxia and pneumothorax or paradoxical bronchospasm the use of the preparation should be discontinued immediately and alternate therapy instituted, since in the reported cases the patients did not respond to other forms of therapy until the drug was withdrawn.

Care should be taken with patients with convulsive disorders, hyperthyroidism or in patients who are unusually responsive to sympathomimetic amines.

Do Not Exceed Recommended Dose: Fatalities have been reported in association with excessive use of inhaled sympathomimetic drugs in patients with asthma. The exact cause of death is unknown, but cardiac arrest following an unexpected development of a severe acute asthmatic crisis and subsequent hypoxia is suspected.

Immediate Hypersensitivity Reactions: Immediate hypersensitivity reactions may occur after administration of salbutamol or salbutamol sulfate, as demonstrated by rare cases of urticaria, angioedema, rash, bronchospasm, anaphylaxis, and oropharyngeal edema.

Precautions: General: If therapy does not produce a significant improvement or if the patient's condition worsens, medical advice must be sought to determine a new plan of treatment. In the case of acute or rapidly worsening dyspnea, a doctor should be consulted immediately.

Failure to respond for at least 3 hours to a previously effective dose of salbutamol indicates a deterioration of the condition and the physician should be contacted promptly. Patients should be warned not to exceed recommended dose. Increasing use of beta$_2$-agonists to control symptoms is usually a sign of worsening asthma. In worsening asthma it is inadequate to increase beta$_2$-agonist use only, especially over an extended period of time. Instead, a reassessment of the patient's therapy plan is required and concomitant anti-inflammatory therapy should be considered (see Dosage).

Patients should always carry their salbutamol aerosol or dry powder to use immediately if an episode of asthma is experienced.

To ensure administration of the proper dose of the drug, the patient should be instructed by the physician or other health professional in the proper use of the inhaler, Diskhaler, Rotahaler or nebulizer systems. The application of these inhalation systems in children depends on the ability of the individual child to learn the proper use of the devices. During inhalation, children should be assisted or supervised by an adult who knows the proper use of the devices.

Pregnancy: Salbutamol has been in widespread use for many years in human beings without apparent ill consequence. However, there are no adequate and well-controlled studies in pregnant women, and there is little published evidence of its safety in the early stages of human pregnancy. Administration of any drug to pregnant women should only be considered if the anticipated benefits to the expectant woman are greater than any possible risks to the fetus.

A reproducton study in CD-1 mice with salbutamol showed cleft palate formation in 5 of 111 (4.5%) fetuses at 0.25 mg/kg and in 10 of 108 (9.3%) fetuses at 2.5 mg/kg. None was observed at 0.025 mg/kg. Cleft palate also occurred in 22 of 72 (30.5%) fetuses treated with 2.5 mg/kg isoproterenol positive control. A reproduction study in Stride Dutch rabbits revealed cranioschisis in 7 of 19 (37%) fetuses at 50 mg/kg, corresponding to 78 times the maximum human oral dose of salbutamol.

Labor and Delivery: Although there have been no reports concerning the use of inhaled salbutamol formulations during labor and delivery, i.v. administered salbutamol given at high doses may inhibit uterine contractions. While this effect is extremely unlikely as a consequence of using inhaled formulations, it should be kept in mind. Oral salbutamol has been shown to delay preterm labor in some reports, but there are no well-controlled studies which demonstrate that it will stop preterm labor or prevent labor at term. When given to pregnant patients for relief of bronchospasm, cautious use of Ventolin products is required to avoid interference with uterine contractility.

Lactation: Since salbutamol is probably excreted in breast milk and because of its observed tumorigenicity in animal studies, a decision should be made whether to discontinue nursing or to discontinue the drug, taking into account the benefit of the drug to the mother. It is not known whether salbutamol in breast milk has a harmful effect on the neonate.

Drug Interactions: MAO Inhibitors or Tricyclic Antidepressants: Salbutamol should be administered with extreme caution to patients being treated with MAO inhibitors or tricyclic antidepressants since the action of salbutamol on the cardiovascular system may be potentiated.

Other Inhaled Sympathomimetic Bronchodilators or Epinephrine: Other inhaled sympathomimetic bronchodilators or epinephrine should not be used concomitantly with salbutamol. If additional adrenergic drugs are to be administered by any route to the patient using inhaled salbutamol, the adrenergic drugs should be used with caution to avoid deleterious cardiovascular effects. Such concomitant use must be individualized and not given on a routine basis. If regular coadministration is required then alternative therapy must be considered.

Beta-blockers: Beta-adrenergic blocking drugs, especially the noncardioselective ones, may effectively antagonize the action of salbutamol, and therefore, salbutamol and nonselective beta-blocking drugs, such as propranolol, should not usually be prescribed together.

Ipratropium Bromide: A small number of cases of acute angle closure glaucoma have been reported in patients treated with a combination of nebulized salbutamol and ipratropium bromide. Therefore, a combination of nebulized salbutamol with nebulized anticholinergics should be used cautiously. Patients should receive adequate instruction in correct administration and be warned not to let the solution or mist enter the eye.

Diuretics: The ECG changes and/or hypokalemia that may result from the administration of nonpotassium sparing diuretics (such as loop or thiazide diuretics) can be acutely worsened by beta-agonists, especially when the recommended dose of the beta-agonist is exceeded. Although the clinical significance of these effects is not known, caution is advised in the coadministration of beta-agonists with nonpotassium sparing diuretics.

Digoxin: Mean decreases of 16 to 22% in serum digoxin levels were demonstrated after single dose i.v. and oral administration of salbutamol, respectively, to normal volunteers who had received digoxin for 10 days. The clinical significance of these findings for patients with obstructive airways disease who are receiving salbutamol and digoxin on a chronic basis is unclear. Nevertheless, it would be prudent to carefully evaluate serum digoxin levels in patients who are currently receiving digoxin and salbutamol.

Adverse Effects: The most frequent adverse reactions associated with salbutamol inhalation aerosol, dry powder or respirator solution formulations are nervousness and tremor. In some patients inhaled salbutamol may cause a fine tremor of skeletal muscle, particularly in the hands. This effect is common to all beta$_2$-adrenergic stimulants. Adaptation occurs during the first few days of dosing, and the tremor usually disappears as treatment continues. Headache, palpitations, transient muscle cramps, insomnia, nausea, weakness and dizziness have been reported as untoward effects following salbutamol administration. Peripheral vasodilation and a compensatory small increase in heart rate may occur in some patients.

Cardiac arrhythmias (including atrial fibrillation, supraventricular tachycardia and extrasystoles) have been reported, usually in susceptible patients.

Rarely reported adverse effects include drowsiness, flushing, restlessness, irritability, chest discomfort, difficulty in micturition, hypertension, angina, vomiting, vertigo, CNS stimulation, hyperactivity in children, unusual taste and drying or irritation of the oropharynx.

Immediate hypersensitivity reactions including angioedema, urticaria, bronchospasm, hypotension, rash, oropharyngeal edema, anaphylaxis and collapse have been reported very rarely.

As with other bronchodilator inhalation therapy, the potential for paradoxical bronchospasm should be kept in mind. If it occurs, the preparation should be discontinued immediately and alternative therapy instituted.

Potentially serious hypokalemia may result from beta$_2$-agonist therapy, primarily from parenteral and nebulized routes of administration.

Overdose: Symptoms and Treatment: Overdosage may cause tachycardia, cardiac arrhythmia, hypokalemia, hypertension and, in extreme cases, sudden death. To antagonize the effect of salbutamol, the judicious use of a cardioselective beta-adrenergic blocking agent (e.g., metoprolol, atenolol) may be considered, bearing in mind the danger of inducing an asthmatic attack. Serum potassium levels should be monitored.

Dosage: Dosage should be individualized, and the patient's response should be monitored by the prescribing physician on an ongoing basis.

In accordance with the present practice for asthma treatment, if salbutamol is required for relief of symptoms more than twice a day on a regular daily basis or for an extended period of time, anti-inflammatory therapy (e.g., corticosteroid) should be part of the regimen.

Increasing demand for salbutamol preparations in bronchial asthma is usually a sign of worsening asthma and indicates that the treatment plan should be reviewed.

If a previously effective dose fails to provide the usual relief, or the effects of a dose last for less than 3 hours, patients should seek prompt medical advice since this is usually a sign of worsening asthma.

As there may be adverse effects associated with excessive dosing the dosage or frequency of administration should only be increased on medical advice. However, if a more severe attack has not been relieved by the usual dose, additional doses may be required. In these cases, patients should immediately consult their doctors or the nearest hospital.

Ventodisk blisters and Ventolin Rotacaps capsules are alternative inhalation forms of salbutamol to the metered-dose pressurized aerosol. The Ventodisk Diskhaler and Ventolin Rotacaps/Rotahaler systems are particularly useful in patients who are unable to use properly the pressurized aerosol form of salbutamol or who prefer an alternative delivery system. Ventodisk blisters and Ventolin Rotacaps capsules are for inhalation use only, using only a Ventodisk Diskhaler or Ventolin Rotahaler inhalation device, respectively.

Ventolin Respirator Solution may be preferred in the treatment of severe bronchospasm associated with exacerbations of chronic bronchitis and bronchial asthma.

Ventolin Inhalation Aerosol: Experience is insufficient for recommending the treatment of children under 6 years of age.

Acute Symptoms: Adults: 1 to 2 puffs (100 to 200 μg salbutamol).

Children (6 years or older): 1 puff (100 μg salbutamol).

If a more severe attack has not been relieved by the usual dose (1 to 2 puffs), further puffs may be required. In these cases, patients should immediately consult their doctors or the nearest hospital.

Intermittent and Long-term Treatment: If despite appropriate anti-inflammatory therapy (e.g., corticosteroid), regular daily use of the inhalation aerosol remains necessary for the control of bronchospasm, the recommended dose is: Adults: 1 or 2 puffs (100 to 200 μg salbutamol) 3 to 4 times daily, not exceeding 8 puffs (800 μg salbutamol)/day.

Children (6 years or older): 1 puff (100 μg salbutamol) 3 to 4 times daily, not exceeding 4 puffs (400 μg salbutamol)/day.

Prevention of Exercise-induced Asthma: Adults: 2 puffs (200 μg salbutamol) before exertion.

Children (6 years or older): 1 puff (100 μg salbutamol) before exertion.

Total Daily Dose Should Not Exceed: Adults: 8 puffs (800 μg salbutamol).

Children (6 years or older): 4 puffs (400 μg salbutamol).

Ventodisk Blisters/Diskhaler and Ventolin Rotacaps/Rotahaler: Experience is insufficient for recommending the treatment of children under 6 years of age.

Acute Symptoms: Adults: 200 to 400 μg salbutamol (1 to 2 Ventodisk blisters or Ventolin Rotacaps capsules).

Children (6 years or older): 200 μg salbutamol (1 Ventodisk blister or Ventolin Rotacaps capsule).

If a more severe attack has not been relieved by the usual dose (1 to 2 Ventodisk blisters or Ventolin Rotacaps capsules), additional blisters or capsules may be required. In these cases, patients should immediately consult their doctors or the nearest hospital.

Intermittent and Long-term Treatment: If despite appropriate anti-inflammatory therapy (e.g., corticosteroid) regular daily use of Ventodisk blisters remains necessary for the control of bronchospasm, the recommended dose is: Adults: 200 to 400 μg salbutamol (1 to 2 Ventodisk blisters or Ventolin Rotacaps capsules) 3 to 4 times daily, not exceeding 1 600 μg salbutamol daily.

Children (6 years or older): 200 μg salbutamol (1 Ventodisk blister or Ventolin Rotacaps capsule) 3 to 4 times daily, not exceeding 800 μg salbutamol daily.

Prevention of Exercise-induced Asthma: Adults: 200 to 400 μg salbutamol (1 or 2 Ventodisk blisters or Ventolin Rotacaps capsules) before exertion.

Children (6 years or older): 200 μg salbutamol (1 Ventodisk blister or Ventolin rotacaps capsule) before exertion.

Total Daily Dose Should Not Exceed: Adults: 1 600 μg salbutamol (8×200 μg Ventodisk blisters or 4×400 μg Ventodisk blisters or 8×200 μg Ventolin Rotacaps capsules or 4×400 μg Ventolin Rotacaps capsules).

Children (6 years or older): 800 μg salbutamol (4×200 μg Ventodisk blisters or 4×200 μg Ventolin Rotacaps capsules).

Ventolin Respirator Solution Regimens: Experience is insufficient for recommending the treatment of children under 5 years of age.

Ventolin Respirator Solution: Adults: In adults, 0.5 to 1 mL (2.5 to 5 mg of salbutamol) should be diluted in 2 to 5 mL or more of sterile normal saline. Treatment may be repeated 4 times a day if necessary.

Children (5 to 12 years): The average dose for a single treatment is 0.25 to 0.5 mL (1.25 to 2.5 mg of salbutamol) diluted in 2 to 5 mL or more of sterile normal saline. For more refractory cases, the single dose of Ventolin Respirator Solution may be increased to 1 mL (5 mg of salbutamol). Treatment may be repeated 4 times a day if necessary.

Ventolin Nebules P.F.: Adults: Patients requiring single doses of 2.5 mg or 5 mg may be administered the contents of a single unit dose (Ventolin Nebules P.F. 2.5 or 5 mg of salbutamol). Treatment may be repeated 4 times a day if necessary.

Children (5 to 12 years): Children requiring single doses of 1.25 mg or 2.5 mg may be administered the contents of a single unit dose (Ventolin Nebules P.F. 1.25 or 2.5 mg of salbutamol). For more refractory cases children may use a 5 mg unit dose (see dosage above). Treatment may be repeated 4 times a day if necessary.

If a more severe attack has not been relieved by a treatment, further treatments may be required. In these cases, patients should immediately consult their doctor or the nearest hospital.

Use of Ventolin Respirator Solution: Ventolin Respirator Solution is to be used only under the direction of a physician employing either a respirator or nebulizer. Ventolin Respirator Solution can be taken by either the nebulization or intermittent positive pressure ventilation method. When used in a nebulizer, a mouthpiece or a face mask may be applied. The nebulizer should be connected to a compressed air or oxygen pump. Gas flow should be in the range of 6 to 10 L/minute. With an average volume of 3 mL, a single treatment lasts approximately 10 minutes. It is advisable to prepare 1 dose at a time or to utilize the unit dose (Ventolin Nebules P.F.) presentation. When administered through intermittent positive pressure ventilation, the inspiratory pressure is usually 10 to 20 cm H_2O and the duration of administration varies from 5 to 20 minutes, depending upon the patient and the control of the apparatus. This length of administration provides a more gradual and more complete lysis of bronchospasm. In several cases it has been reported that the use of intermittent positive pressure ventilation in acute asthma attacks was related to lethal episodes of hypoxia and pneumothorax. This method of drug administration may be ineffective in patients with severe obstruction and may greatly increase airway resistance and possibly induce severe hypercapnia and hypoxia. It is highly desirable to monitor arterial blood gases during intermittent positive pressure ventilation therapy.

In hospitals, Ventolin Respirator Solution, diluted (1:5 or 1:10) with sterile normal saline, should be used within 24 hours from time of dilution when stored at room temperature or within 48 hours when stored under refrigeration.

Cleansing and maintenance of the nebulizer must be carefully exercised by strict adherence to the manufacturer's instructions.

The respirator solution must not be injected.

Supplied: Ventolin Inhalation Aerosol: Each metered-dose aerosol unit for oral inhalation contains: a microcrystalline suspension of salbutamol in propellants. Each actuation delivers to the patient salbutamol 100 μg. Nonmedicinal ingredients: dichlorodifluoromethane (propellant), oleic acid and trichloromonofluoromethane (propellant). Dose format of 200. Store at a temperature between 2 to 30°C. Protect from direct sunlight.

The canister should not be punctured, broken or burnt, even when apparently empty.

Ventodisk Blisters: Each blister contains: microfine salbutamol (as the sulfate) 200 μg (pale blue disk) or 400 μg (dark blue disk). Each double-foil disk contains 8 sealed blisters.

Ventolin (cont'd)

Also contains lactose. Disks of 8, cartons of 15. Store below 30°C, in a dry place.

The contents of each Ventodisk blister are inhaled using the specially designed plastic device called the Ventodisk Diskhaler. The Ventodisk Diskhaler is available separately from the Ventodisk disks.

Ventolin Rotacaps Capsules: Each Rotacaps capsule contains: microfine salbutamol sulfate 200 μg (pale blue) or 400 μg (dark blue). Also contains lactose. Polypropylene bottles of 100, closed with polythene snap caps. Store below 30°C, in a dry place.

The contents of each Ventolin Rotacaps capsule are inhaled using the specially designed plastic device called the Ventolin Rotahaler. The Ventolin Rotahaler comes in a plastic box and is available separately from the Ventolin Rotacaps capsules.

Ventolin Respirator Solution: Each mL of isotonic solution contains: salbutamol sulfate, equivalent to salbutamol base 5 mg. Adjusted to pH 3.4 to 4.4. Preserved with benzalkonium chloride 0.01% w/v. Bottles of 10 and 100 mL. Store below 25°C. Protect from light.

Ventolin Respirator Solution Unit Dose (Ventolin Nebules P.F.): Each unit dose of sterile, isotonic solution contains: salbutamol sulfate equivalent to salbutamol base 1.25, 2.5 or 5 mg in 2.5 mL. Adjusted to pH 3.5 to 4.5. Boxes of 20. Overwrapped nebule: Store below 25°C. Nebule removed from overwrap: Store below 25°C. Protect from light. Use within 3 months.

(Shown in Product Recognition Section)

Reviewed 1999

VENTOLIN® Injection Ⓟ

Glaxo Wellcome

Salbutamol Sulfate

Bronchodilator—Beta₂-adrenergic Stimulant

Pharmacology: Salbutamol produces bronchodilation through stimulation of beta$_2$-adrenergic receptors in bronchial smooth muscle, thereby causing relaxation of muscle fibers. This action is manifested by an improvement in pulmonary function as demonstrated by spirometric measurements.

Indications: For the relief of severe bronchospasm associated with acute exacerbations of chronic bronchitis and bronchial asthma, and for the treatment of status asthmaticus.

Continuous i.v. infusion, when practicable, is the preferred method of administration. If a more rapid response is required, an i.v. bolus should be given, which may be followed by a continuous infusion, if desired. I.M. injection may be employed when venipuncture is undesirable, inconvenient, or impossible.

In many patients, the injections will be no more effective, and likely less well tolerated, than salbutamol inhaler or respirator solution. However, patients who are severely ill with airway inflammation and mucus plugging may respond well to parenteral salbutamol after failing to benefit from the inhaled drug.

Contraindications: Patients who are hypersensitive to any of the ingredients and in patients with cardiac tachyarrhythmias or at risk of threatened abortion during the first or second trimester.

Warnings: Immediate hypersensitivity reactions may occur after administration of salbutamol, as demonstrated by rare cases of urticaria, angioedema, rash, bronchospasm, anaphylaxis and oropharyngeal edema.

In common with other beta-adrenergic agents, salbutamol can induce reversible metabolic changes. These are most pronounced during infusions of the drug and include hyperglycemia and hypokalemia. Potentially serious hypokalemia may result from beta$_2$-agonist therapy, mainly from parenteral and nebulized administration. Particular caution is advised in acute severe asthma as this effect may be potentiated by concomitant treatment with xanthine derivatives, steroids, diuretics and hypoxia. Hypokalemia will increase the susceptibility of digitalis-treated patients to cardiac arrhythmias (see Precautions). It is recommended that serum potassium levels be monitored in such situations.

Large doses of i.v. salbutamol have been reported to aggravate pre-existing diabetes mellitus and may precipitate ketoacidosis. Concurrent administration of corticosteroids can exaggerate this effect. Diabetic patients and those concurrently receiving corticosteroids should be monitored frequently during i.v. infusion of salbutamol i.v. infusion solution so that remedial steps (e.g. an increase in insulin dosage) can be taken to counter any metabolic change that is occurring. For these patients the i.v. infusion solution should be diluted with sodium chloride injection BP, rather than sodium chloride and dextrose injection BP. The relevance of these observations to the use of the injections is unknown.

Special care and supervision are required in patients with idiopathic hypertrophic subvalvular aortic stenosis, in whom an increase in the pressure gradient between the left ventricle and the aorta may occur, causing increased strain on the left ventricle.

Beta-adrenergic blocking drugs, especially the non-cardioselective ones, may effectively antagonize the action of salbutamol. Bronchospasm occurring in patients treated with such agents may prove resistant to treatment with salbutamol injections.

Fatalities have been reported following excessive use of inhaled sympathomimetic drugs, the exact cause of which is unknown; however, cardiac arrest was noted in several instances. Therefore, it is essential that the physician instruct the patient in the need of further evaluation in case of deterioration. In individual patients, any beta$_2$-adrenergic agonist, including salbutamol, may have a clinically significant cardiac effect.

Some patients have been reported to have developed severe paradoxical bronchospasm with repeated excessive use of sympathomimetic inhalation preparations. In this event, the use of the preparation should be discontinued immediately and alternate therapy instituted, since in the reported cases the patients did not respond to other forms of therapy until the drug was withdrawn.

Pregnancy and *Lactation:* The safety of salbutamol use in pregnancy and lactation has not been established.

Precautions: General: ECG and serum potassium and glucose should be monitored during continuous infusions of salbutamol.

Salbutamol i.v. infusion solution may be diluted with water for injection BP, sodium chloride injection BP, dextrose injection BP, or sodium chloride and dextrose injection BP (see Dosage). These are the only recommended diluents. Dextrose containing solutions may not be suitable for patients with diabetes mellitus, due to the possible danger of glucose overload (see also Warnings).

The use of salbutamol injections in the treatment of severe bronchospasm or status asthmaticus does not obviate the requirement for glucocorticoid steroid therapy as appropriate. When practicable, administration of oxygen, concurrently with the injections is recommended, particularly when salbutamol is given by i.v. infusion to hypoxic patients.

Children: The dosage of salbutamol injections in the pediatric age group has not been established. At present there are insufficient data to recommend a dosage regimen for use in children.

Patients with Special Diseases and Conditions: Parenteral salbutamol should always be administered with caution, particularly in patients suffering from cardiovascular disorders, especially coronary insufficiency, cardiac arrhythmias and hypertension; in patients with convulsive disorders, diabetes mellitus or hyperthyroidism; and in patients who are unusually responsive to sympathomimetic amines.

Pregnancy: Teratogenic Effects: Administration of drugs during pregnancy should only be considered if the expected benefit to the mother is greater than any possible risk to the fetus.

Salbutamol has been in widespread use for many years in human beings without apparent ill consequence; however, as with the majority of drugs, there is little published evidence of its safety in the early stages of human pregnancy. In animal studies there was evidence of some harmful effects on the fetus at very high dose levels.

Salbutamol has been shown to be teratogenic in mice when given in doses corresponding to 14 times the human aerosol dose; when given s.c. in doses corresponding to 0.2 times the maximum human (child weighing 21 kg) oral dose; and when given s.c. in doses corresponding to 0.4 times the maximum human oral dose.

There are no adequate and well-controlled studies in pregnant women. Salbutamol should be used during pregnancy only if the potential benefit to the mother justifies the potential risk to the fetus.

Labor and Delivery: Although there have been no reports concerning the use of salbutamol during labor and delivery, it has been reported that high doses of salbutamol, administered i.v., inhibit uterine contractions.

Some reports have shown that oral salbutamol has delayed preterm labor. There are no well-controlled studies which demonstrate that salbutamol will stop preterm labor or prevent labor at term. Therefore, cautious use of salbutamol injections is required in pregnant patients when it is given for relief of bronchospasm so as to avoid interference with uterine contractibility.

As maternal pulmonary edema has been reported during or following premature labor in patients receiving beta$_2$-agonists, careful attention should be given to fluid balance and cardiorespiratory function should be monitored.

Lactation: As salbutamol is probably secreted in breast milk and because of the potential for tumorigenicity of salbutamol shown in some animal studies, a decision should be made whether to discontinue nursing or to discontinue the drug, taking into account the importance of the drug to the mother. It is not known whether salbutamol has a harmful effect on the neonate.

Drug Interactions: The concomitant use of salbutamol and other sympathomimetic agents is not recommended since such combined use may lead to deleterious cardiovascular effects. If regular co-administration is required, then alternative therapy should be considered.

Salbutamol should be administered with extreme caution to patients being treated with MAO inhibitors or tricyclic antidepressants because the action of salbutamol on the vascular system may be potentiated.

Beta-receptor blocking agents and salbutamol inhibit the effect of each other.

Adverse Effects: I.M. injection of the undiluted preparation may produce slight local pain or stinging.

Fine muscle tremor is a common side effect of salbutamol injections. This is due to the direct beta$_2$-stimulation by salbutamol of skeletal muscle. There have been very rare reports of transient muscle cramps.

A dose-dependent increase in heart rate, secondary to a reduction in peripheral resistance, due to vasodilation, may occur with parenteral salbutamol, and may cause palpitations. This is most likely to occur in patients with normal heart rates. In patients with pre-existing sinus tachycardia, especially those in status asthmaticus, the heart rate tends to fall as the condition of the patient improves.

Other side effects which may occur with salbutamol are sweating, headache, dizziness, flushing, nausea, vomiting, muscle cramps, insomnia, drowsiness, restlessness, irritability, chest discomfort, difficulty in micturition, hypertension, angina, vertigo, central nervous stimulation, unusual taste and drying or irritation of the oropharynx.

Paradoxical bronchospasm has been reported to occur following salbutamol inhalation therapy, requiring the immediate discontinuation of the drug and the institution of alternative forms of therapy.

As with other beta$_2$-agonists hyperactivity has been reported rarely in children.

Potentially serious hypokalemia may result from beta$_2$-agonist therapy, mainly from parenteral and nebulized administration.

Hypersensitivity reactions including angioedema, urticaria, bronchospasm, hypotension and collapse have been reported very rarely.

Overdose: Symptoms and Treatment: Overdosage may cause tachycardia, cardiac arrhythmia, hypokalemia, hypertension and in extreme cases, sudden death. To antagonize the effect of salbutamol, the judicious use of a cardioselective beta-adrenergic blocking agent (e.g. metoprolol, atenolol) may be considered, bearing in mind the danger of inducing an asthmatic attack. Serum potassium levels should be monitored.

Dosage: Salbutamol injections are not to be administered in the same syringe or infusion as any other medication.

Adults: In severe bronchospasm and status asthmaticus: I.M. Injection: 500 μg (8 μg/kg body weight) every 4 hours as required. Maximum daily dose: 2 000 μg.

Bolus I.V. Injection: 250 μg (4 μg/kg body weight) over 2 to 5 minutes, repeated after 15 minutes, if necessary. Maximum daily dose: 1 000 μg.

Continuous I.V. Infusion: 5 μg/min, increased to 10 μg/min and 20 μg/min at 15 to 30 minute intervals, if necessary. A suitable solution for infusion may be prepared by diluting 5 mL of the i.v. infusion solution (1 mg/mL) in 500 mL of a chosen i.v. solution to provide a salbutamol concentration of 10 μg/mL. **The i.v. infusion solution must not be injected undiluted. The concentration should be reduced 50% before administration.** The injections are compatible in PVC bags and in glass bottles with water for injection BP, sodium chloride injection BP, dextrose injection BP, and sodium chloride and dextrose injection BP. Dextrose-containing solutions may not be suitable for patients with diabetes mellitus due to the possible danger of glucose overload (see also Warnings). All unused admixtures of the injections with infusion fluids should be discarded 24 hours after preparation.

Children: The dosage of the injections in the pediatric age group has not been established. At present, there are insufficient data to recommend a dosage regimen for children.

Supplied: I.M. Injection: Each mL of colorless or faintly straw-colored, sterile, isotonic solution contains: salbutamol 0.5 mg as salbutamol sulfate. Adjusted to pH 3.5 with sulfuric acid and/or sodium hydroxide. Ampuls of 1 mL.

I.V. Bolus Injection: Each mL of colorless or faintly straw-colored, sterile, isotonic solution contains: salbutamol 0.05 mg as salbutamol sulfate. Adjusted to pH 3.5 with sulfuric acid and/or sodium hydroxide. Ampuls of 5 mL.

I.V. Infusion Solution: Each mL of colorless or faintly straw-colored, sterile, isotonic solution contains: salbutamol 1 mg as salbutamol sulfate. Adjusted to pH 3.5 with sulfuric acid and/or sodium hydroxide. Ampuls of 5 mL.

Protect from light and store at controlled room temperature (15 to 30°C).

VENTOLIN® Oral Liquid ℞

Glaxo Wellcome

Salbutamol Sulfate

Bronchodilator

Pharmacology: Salbutamol produces bronchodilation through stimulation of beta$_2$-adrenergic receptors in bronchial smooth muscle, thereby causing relaxation of muscle fibers. This action is manifested by an increase in pulmonary function as demonstrated by spirometric measurements.

A measurable decrease in airway resistance is typically observed 30 minutes after an oral dose of salbutamol sulfate. The maximum improvement in pulmonary function usually occurs after 2 to 3 hours, and significant bronchodilator activity has been observed to persist for 6 hours or longer.

Indications: Prevention or relief of bronchospasm due to bronchial asthma, chronic bronchitis and other chronic bronchopulmonary disorders in which bronchospasm is a complicating factor.

Contraindications: Hypersensitivity to any of the ingredients and cardiac tachyarrhythmias. Not recommended for use in children under 2 years of age, until the dose regimen and evidence concerning its safety have been established.

Warnings: *Pregnancy* and *Lactation:* The safety of salbutamol in pregnancy and in lactation has not been established.

Immediate hypersensitivity reactions may occur after administration of salbutamol, as demonstrated by rare cases of urticaria, angioedema, rash, bronchospasm, anaphylaxis and oropharyngeal edema.

In common with other β-adrenergic agents, salbutamol can induce reversible metabolic changes; these are more pronounced during infusions of the drug and include hyperglycemia and hypokalemia. Potentially serious hypokalemia may result from β_2-agonist therapy, mainly from parenteral and nebulized administration. Particular caution is advised in acute severe asthma as this effect may be potentiated by concomitant treatment with xanthine derivatives, steroids, diuretics and hypoxia. It is recommended that serum potassium levels be monitored in such situations. Large doses of i.v. salbutamol have been reported to aggravate pre-existing diabetes mellitus and may precipitate ketoacidosis. The relevance of these observations to the use of salbutamol oral liquid is unknown.

Care should be taken with patients suffering from cardiovascular disorders, especially coronary insufficiency, cardiac arrhythmias and hypertension; in patients with convulsive disorders, diabetes mellitus or hyperthyroidism and in patients who are unusually responsive to sympathomimetic amines. Special care and supervision are required in patients with idiopathic hypertrophic subvalvular aortic stenosis, in whom an increase in the pressure gradient between the left ventricle and the aorta may occur, causing increased strain on the left ventricle.

Precautions: Salbutamol should be used with caution in patients sensitive to sympathomimetic amines.

The regular concomitant use of oral salbutamol and other sympathomimetic agents or epinephrine is not recommended since such combined use may lead to deleterious cardiovascular effects. This recommendation does not preclude the judicious use of an aerosol bronchodilator of the adrenergic stimulant type in patients receiving salbutamol oral liquid. Such concomitant use, however, should be individualized, and not given on a routine basis. If concomitant use is required, then this may indicate that disease control is suboptimal and other treatments such as anti-inflammatory therapy should be considered.

Salbutamol should be administered with extreme caution to patients being treated with MAO inhibitors or tricyclic antidepressants since the action of salbutamol on the cardiovascular system may be potentiated.

Beta-adrenergic blocking drugs, especially the non-cardioselective ones, may effectively antagonize the action of salbutamol. Therefore, salbutamol and non-selective beta-blocking drugs, such as propranolol, should not usually be prescribed together.

Pregnancy: Teratogenic Effects: Administration of drugs during pregnancy should only be considered if the expected benefit to the mother is greater than any possible risk to the fetus. Salbutamol has been in widespread use for many years in human beings without apparent ill consequence; however, as with the majority of drugs, there is little published evidence of its safety in the early stages of human pregnancy.

Labor and Delivery: There are no adequate and well-controlled studies in pregnant women. Salbutamol should be used during pregnancy only if the potential benefit justifies the potential risk to the fetus. Some reports have shown that oral salbutamol has delayed preterm labor. There are no well-controlled studies which demonstrate that salbutamol will stop preterm labor or prevent labor at term. Therefore, cautious use of salbutamol is required in pregnant patients when it is given for relief of bronchospasm so as to avoid interference with uterine contractibility.

Lactation: As salbutamol is probably secreted in breast milk and because of the potential for tumorigenicity shown in some animal studies, a decision should be made whether to discontinue nursing or to discontinue the drug, taking into account the importance of the drug to the mother. It is not known whether salbutamol in breast milk has a harmful effect on the neonate.

Adverse Effects: The most frequent adverse effects to oral salbutamol are nervousness and tremor. Salbutamol oral liquid may cause a fine tremor of skeletal muscle in some patients; usually the hands are the most obviously affected. This aspect is common to all beta-adrenergic stimulants. Adaption occurs in the first few days of dosing and in most cases tremor disappears as treatment continues. Headache, tension due to effects on skeletal muscle, tachycardia, palpitations, transient muscle cramps, insomnia, nausea, weakness, and dizziness have also been reported. Other rare adverse effects have been drowsiness, flushing, restlessness, irritability, chest discomfort, difficulty in micturition, hypertension, angina, vomiting, vertigo, CNS stimulation, unusual taste, and drying or irritation of the oropharynx.

Hypersensitivity reactions including angioedema, urticaria, bronchospasm, hypotension, rash, oropharyngeal edema and collapse have been reported very rarely.

Peripheral vasodilation and a compensatory small increase in heart rate may occur in some patients.

As with other β_2-agonists, hyperactivity has been reported rarely in children.

Potentially serious hypokalemia may result from β_2-agonist therapy, mainly from parenteral and nebulized administration.

Overdose: Symptoms and Treatment: Overdosage may cause peripheral vasodilation and increased irritability of skeletal muscle, hypokalemia, tachycardia, cardiac arrhythmia, hypertension and, in extreme cases, sudden death. In case of overdosage, gastric lavage should be performed. In order to antagonize the effect of salbutamol, the judicious use of a cardioselective beta-adrenergic blocking agent (e.g. metoprolol, atenolol) may be considered, bearing in mind the danger of inducing an asthmatic attack.

Dosage: Salbutamol oral liquid is not intended for patients experiencing an acute episode of bronchospasm.

Adults and children over 12 years of age: 5 to 10 mL (2 to 4 mg) 3 to 4 times daily.

In elderly patients or in those known to be unusually sensitive to beta-adrenergic stimulant drugs, it is advisable to initiate treatment with 2 mg 3 or 4 times/day.

Children between 6 and 12 years of age: 5 mL (2 mg) 3 to 4 times daily. Children aged 2 to 6 years: 0.25 mL (0.1 mg)/kg body weight 3 to 4 times daily. The safety and efficacy of salbutamol oral liquid in children under 2 years of age, and for chronic therapy in children 2 to 6 years of age, have not been established.

If a previously effective dosage regimen fails to provide the usual relief, medical advice should be sought immediately as this is often a sign of seriously worsening asthma that could require reassessment of therapy.

When prescribing salbutamol oral liquid, the patient should be advised that the action of this medication may last for 6 to 8 hours. As there may be adverse effects associated with excessive dosing, the dosage or frequency of administration should only be increased upon medical advice.

Supplied: Each mL of clear, colorless, orange-flavored liquid contains: salbutamol 0.4 mg (as the sulfate). Nonmedicinal ingredients: citric acid anhydrous, citric acid solution, hydroxypropyl methylcellulose, orange flavor, sodium benzoate, sodium chloride, sodium citrate dihydrate, sodium cyclamate and sodium hydroxide. Gluten- and tartrazine-free. Bottles of 250 mL. Store below 25°C.

(Shown in Product Recognition Section)

VEPESID® ℞

Bristol

Etoposide

Antineoplastic

Pharmacology: Etoposide is a semi-synthetic derivative of podophyllotoxin.

In vitro, etoposide has cytostatic action, which prevents the cells from entering mitosis or destroys them in the premitotic phase. Etoposide interferes with the synthesis of DNA and has a secondary effect on arresting cells in resting (G_2) phase in experiments with human lymphoblastic cell lines.

Etoposide has a marked action on human hemopoietic cells causing leukopenia and thrombocytopenia. Animal experiments have shown evidence of teratogenicity.

An i.v. dose (259 mg/m²) of tritium-labelled etoposide given over 1 hour in man, showed the mean volume of distribution to be 32% of body weight. The plasma decay was biphasic with a beta half-life of 11.5 hours. Urinary recovery was 44% of which 67% was unchanged drug. Recovery in feces was variable (1.5 to 16%) over a 3-day period.

A plasma decay with a beta half-life of 6.8 hours was observed following oral administration of etoposide. The t ½ for oral absorption was 0.44 hour and peak plasma concentrations were noted 0.5 to 3 hours after oral administration.

In a limited number of children, etoposide administered in a dose of 200 to 250 mg/m² produced a peak serum concentration between 17 and 88 μg/mL and showed a terminal half-life ($t_{1/2\beta}$) of 5.7±1.3 hours. Mean plasma clearance was 21.5 mL/min/m² and CSF concentrations 24 hours post-infusion ranged from less than 10 ng/mL to 45 μg/mL.

After either i.v. infusion or oral capsule administration of etoposide, the C_{max} and AUC values exhibit marked intra- and inter-subject variability. The overall mean value of oral capsule bioavailability is approximately 50% (range 25 to 75%).

Etoposide crosses the blood brain barrier in low concentrations.

Etoposide is cleared by both renal and nonrenal processes, i.e., metabolism and biliary excretion. Biliary excretion, however, appears to be a minor route of etoposide elimination.

Indications: Oral and I.V.: Small-cell Carcinoma of the Lung: First-line therapy in combination with other established antineoplastic agents. Second-line combination or single agent therapy in patients who have not responded or relapsed on other chemotherapeutic regimens.

Malignant Lymphoma (histiocytic type): First-line therapy in combination with other established antineoplastic agents.

Non-small Cell Carcinoma of the Lung: For patients considered ineligible for surgery, etoposide has been shown effective alone or in combination with cisplatin. For patients who require chemotherapy following surgery.

Testicular Malignancies (germ cell tumors including seminomas): In combination with other effective chemotherapeutic agents in patients who have already received appropriate therapy. **I.V. only:** In the first-line combination chemotherapeutic regimens with appropriate surgical and/or radiotherapeutic procedures.

Contraindications: Should not be given to individuals who have demonstrated hypersensitivity to etoposide or to any component of the formulation. Also, it is contraindicated in patients having severe leukopenia, thrombocytopenia and severe hepatic and/or renal impairment.

Warnings: Etoposide is a potent drug and should be used only by physicians experienced with cancer chemotherapeutic drugs (see Precautions). Blood counts as well as renal and hepatic function tests should be taken regularly. Discontinue the drug if abnormal depression of bone marrow or abnormal renal or hepatic function is seen. Vepesid injection contains polysorbate 80. In premature infants

Vepesid (cont'd)

a life-threatening syndrome of liver and renal failure, pulmonary deterioration, thrombocytopenia and ascites has been associated with injectable vitamin E product containing polysorbate 80.

Patients being treated with etoposide must be frequently observed for myelosuppression both during and after therapy. Dose-limiting bone marrow suppression is the most significant toxicity associated with etoposide therapy. Therefore, the following studies should be obtained at the start of therapy and prior to each subsequent dose of etoposide: platelet count, hemoglobin, white blood cell count and differential. The occurrence of a platelet count below 50 000/mm³ or an absolute neutrophil count below 500/mm³ is an indication to withhold further therapy until the blood counts have sufficiently recovered.

Bacterial infection must be brought under control before the administration of etoposide therapy because of the risk of septicemia.

Physicians should be aware of the possible occurrence of an anaphylactic reaction manifested by chills, fever, tachycardia, bronchospasm, dyspnea and/or hypotension (see Adverse Effects). Treatment is symptomatic. The administration of etoposide should be terminated immediately, followed by the administration of pressor agents, corticosteroids, antihistamines, or volume expanders at the discretion of the physician.

For parenteral administration, etoposide should be given only by slow i.v. infusion (usually over a 30-to 60-minute period) since hypotension has been reported as a possible side effect of rapid i.v. injection.

Pregnancy: Etoposide can cause fetal harm when administered to pregnant women.

Etoposide has been shown to be embryotoxic in rats and teratogenic in mice and rats. There are no adequate and well-controlled studies in pregnant women. If the drug is used during pregnancy, or if the patient becomes pregnant while receiving this drug, the patient should be apprised of the potential hazard to the fetus. Women of childbearing potential should be advised to avoid becoming pregnant and should exercise adequate contraceptive control.

Etoposide has caused reduced or absent spermatogenesis and reduced testes weights at autopsy in rats and dogs, as well as reduced weight of ovaries in female rats. Chronic toxicity studies in rats have shown etoposide to have an oncogenic potential (see Adverse Effects, Hematologic Toxicity).

Lactation: There has been evidence of etoposide being excreted in human milk.

Because of the potential for serious adverse reactions in nursing infants from etoposide, breast-feeding should be discontinued.

As with any potent antineoplastic drug, the benefit to patient versus the risk of toxicity must be carefully weighed.

Precautions: General: The physician must evaluate the need and usefulness of the drug against the risk of adverse reactions. Most such adverse reactions are reversible if detected early. If severe reactions occur, the drug should be reduced in dosage or discontinued and appropriate corrective measures should be taken according to the clinical judgment of the physician. Reinstitution of etoposide therapy should be carried out with caution, and with adequate consideration of the further need for the drug and **alertness** to the possible recurrence of toxicity.

Etoposide should be administered by individuals experienced in the use of antineoplastic therapy.

Neutropenia is at its lowest level 7 to 14 days after initial therapy. Thrombocytopenia is at its lowest level 9 to 16 days after initial therapy. Bone marrow recovery requires 20 days.

Liver and renal function should be regularly monitored.

Professional staff administering etoposide injection should exercise particular care to prevent spillage and self-contact with the drug. Skin reactions, at times severe, associated with accidental exposure to etoposide may occur. Gloves should be worn by anyone handling the drug. If etoposide solution contacts the skin, immediately wash thoroughly with soap and water. If etoposide solution contacts mucous membranes, flush thoroughly with water. Materials used for cleaning accidental spills should be disposed of by incineration.

Carcinogenesis: Carcinogenicity tests with etoposide have not been conducted in laboratory animals. Given its mechanism of action, it should be considered a possible carcinogen in humans.

The occurrence of acute leukemia, which can occur with or without a preleukemic phase, has been reported rarely in patients treated with etoposide in association with other antineoplastic drugs. Neither the cumulative risk, nor the predisposing factors related to the development of secondary leukemia are known. The roles of both administration schedules and cumulative doses of etoposide have been suggested, but have not been clearly defined.

An 11q23 chromosome abnormality has been observed in some cases of secondary leukemia in patients who have received epipodophyllotoxins. This abnormality has also been seen in patients developing secondary leukemia after being treated with chemotherapy regimens not containing epipodophyllotoxins and in leukemia occurring de novo. Another characteristic that has been associated with secondary leukemia in patients who have received epipodophyllotoxins appears to be a short latency period, with average median time to development of leukemia being approximately 32 months.

Drug Interactions: Severe cases of neuropathy have been reported in 0.7% of patients possibly due to an interaction of vincristine and etoposide.

Children: Clinical experience in childhood malignancies is very limited (see Warnings).

Adverse Effects: The following data on adverse reactions are based on both oral and i.v. administration of etoposide as a single agent, using several different dose schedules for treatment of a wide variety of malignancies.

Hematologic Toxicity: Since leukopenia and thrombocytopenia have been reported in patients on etoposide therapy, platelets and white blood cell counts should be performed prior to each cycle.

A white blood cell count of between 2 000 to 3 000 cells/mm³ suggests that the dose of etoposide should be reduced by 50%. Platelet counts between 75 000 to 100 000 cells/mm³ require a dosage reduction of 50%. Should the neutrophil count fall below 500 cells/mm³ or the platelet count fall below 50 000 cells/mm³, etoposide should be discontinued and should not be resumed until counts have returned to normal (see Warnings). Myelosuppression is dose related and dose limiting, with granulocyte nadirs occurring 7 to 14 days and platelet nadirs occurring 9 to 16 days after drug administration. Bone marrow recovery is usually complete by day 20, and no cumulative toxicity has been reported.

The occurrence of acute leukemia with or without a preleukemic phase has been reported in patients treated with etoposide in association with other antineoplastic agents.

Gastrointestinal Toxicity: Nausea and vomiting are the major gastrointestinal toxicities. The severity of such nausea and vomiting is generally mild to moderate with treatment discontinuation required in 1% of patients. Nausea and vomiting can usually be controlled with standard antiemetic therapy. Gastrointestinal toxicities are slightly more frequent after oral administration than after i.v. infusion. Mild to severe mucositis/eosophagitis may occur.

Hypotension: Transient hypotension following rapid i.v. administration has been reported in 1 to 2% of patients. It has not been associated with cardiac toxicity or ECG changes. No delayed hypotension has been noted. To prevent this occurrence, it is recommended that etoposide be administered by slow i.v. infusion over a 30-to 60-minute period. If hypotension occurs, it usually responds to cessation of the infusion and administration of fluids or other supportive therapy as appropriate. When restarting the infusion, a slower administration rate should be used.

Allergic Reactions: Anaphylactic-like reactions characterized by chills, fever, tachycardia, bronchospasm, dyspnea and/or hypotension have been reported to occur in 0.7 to 2% of patients during or immediately after etoposide administration. Higher rates of anaphylactic-like reactions have been reported in children who received etoposide infusions at concentrations higher than those recommended. The role that concentration of infusion (or rate of infusion) plays in the development of anaphylactic-like reactions is uncertain. Reactions have occurred very rarely in patients treated with oral capsules. Anaphylactic-like reactions have usually responded promptly to etoposide cessation, and subsequent administration of pressor agents, corticosteroids, antihistamines or volume expanders as appropriate. Acute fatal reactions associated with bronchospasm have been reported. Hypertension and/or flushing have also been reported. Blood pressure usually normalizes within a few hours after cessation of the infusion. Anaphylactic-like reactions can occur with the initial dose of etoposide. Apnea with spontaneous resumption of breathing following discontinuation has been described in patients receiving etoposide infusion.

Alopecia: Reversible alopecia, sometimes progressing to total baldness was observed in up to 66% of patients.

Neuropathy: The use of etoposide has been reported to cause peripheral neuropathy in 0.7% of patients. The associated use of vincristine sulfate can possibly enhance this neuropathy.

Other Toxicities: Weakness (3%), mouth ulceration (2%). The following have been reported in less than 1%: hyperuricemia, sepsis, numbness and tingling, dizziness, depression, nail pigmentation and moniliasis. The following adverse reactions have been infrequently reported: somnolence and fatigue, liver toxicity, fever, aftertaste, rash, pigmentation, pruritus, urticaria, constipation, dysphagia, transient cortical blindness and a single report of radiation recall dermatitis.

Occasionally following extravasation, soft tissue irritation and inflammation has occurred; ulceration is generally not seen.

The incidences of adverse reactions in Table I are derived from multiple data bases from studies in patients when etoposide was used either orally or by injection as a single agent.

Table I—Vepesid

Adverse Reactions

Adverse Drug Effect	Range of Reported Incidence (%)
Hematologic Toxicity	
Leukopenia (less than 1 000 WBC/mm³)	3–17
Leukopenia (less than 4 000 WBC/mm³)	60–91
Thrombocytopenia (less than 50 000 platelets/mm³)	1–20
Thrombocytopenia (less than 100 000 platelets/mm³)	22–41
Anemia	0–33
Gastrointestinal Toxicity	
Nausea and vomiting	31–43
Abdominal pain	0–2
Anorexia	10–13
Diarrhea	1–13
Stomatitis	1–6
Other	
Alopecia	8–66
Peripheral neurotoxicity	1–2
Hypotension	1–2
Allergic reaction	1–2
Hepatic	0–3

Legend: WBC=white blood cell.

Overdose: Symptoms and Treatment: The anticipated acute complications would be related to etoposide's hematotoxicity.

Total doses of 2.4 g/m² to 3.5 g/m² administered i.v. over 3 days resulted in severe mucositis and myelotoxicity.

Metabolic acidosis and cases of serious hepatic toxicity have been reported in patients receiving higher than recommended i.v. doses of etoposide.

There is no known antidote and therefore symptomatic measures should be taken to sustain the patient through any period of toxicity that might occur. Patients' renal and hepatic functions should be monitored for 3 to 4 weeks in case of delayed toxicity.

Dosage: Note: Plastic devices made of acrylic or ABS (a polymer composed of acrylonitrile, butadiene and styrene) have been reported to crack and leak when used with undiluted etoposide injection. This effect has not been reported with diluted etoposide.

I.V.: 50 to 100 mg/m² daily for 5 days.

Hypotension following rapid i.v. administration has been reported, hence, it is recommended that the etoposide solution be administered over a period of not less than 30 minutes (usually over 30 to 60 minutes). Longer infusion times may be required based on patient tolerance. **Etoposide should not be given by rapid i.v. injection.**

Oral: 100 to 200 mg/m² daily for 5 days.

The dose of etoposide capsules is based on the recommended i.v. dose with consideration given to the bioavailability of etoposide capsules appearing to be dependent upon the dose administered. A 100 mg oral dose would be comparable to a 75 mg i.v. dose; a 400 mg oral dose would be comparable to a 200 mg i.v. dose. The bioavailability also varies from patient to patient following any oral dose. This should be taken into consideration when prescribing this medication. In view of significant intra-patient variability, dose adjustment may be required to achieve the desired therapeutic effect.

Dosage should be modified to take into account the myelosuppressive effects of other drugs in the combination or the effects of prior x-ray therapy or chemotherapy which may have compromised bone marrow reserve.

Capsules should be taken on an empty stomach.

Preparation of I.V. Solutions: Etoposide injection must be diluted prior to use with either 5% Dextrose Injection USP or 0.9% Sodium Chloride Injection USP to give a final concentration of 0.2 or 0.4 mg/mL. **More concentrated solutions show crystal formation upon stirring or seeding within 5 minutes and should not be given i.v.** Etoposide diluted to 0.4 mg/mL and administered through tubing connected to a pump with peristaltic mechanism may precipitate out of solution in the tubing. Contact with buffered aqueous solutions above pH 8 should be avoided. Reconstitution results in a clear, colorless solution. Etoposide diluted with 0.9% Sodium Chloride Injection USP or 5% Dextrose Injection USP to a concentration of 0.2 to 0.4 mg/mL is stable for 96 and 24 hours respectively, at room temperature under room light in both glass and plastic containers. Etoposide should not be mixed with other antineoplastic drugs. Care should be taken to prevent spillage and self-contact with the drug. **If etoposide solution contacts the skin, immediately wash thoroughly with soap and water. If etoposide solution contacts mucous membranes, flush thoroughly with water.**

Preparation for I.V. Administration: Etoposide injection must be diluted with 5% Dextrose Injection USP or 0.9% Sodium Chloride Injection USP to give a concentration of 0.2 or 0.4 mg/mL.

As with all parenteral drug products, i.v. drug admixtures should be inspected visually for clarity, particulate matter, precipitate, discoloration and leakage prior to administration, whenever solution and container permit.

Stability: Injection: When diluted with 0.9% Sodium Chloride Injection USP or 5% Dextrose Injection USP to a concentration of 0.2 or 0.4 mg/mL, etoposide solutions are physically and chemically stable for 96 and 24 hours respectively, at room temperature (25°C) under room light in both glass and plastic containers.

Special Instructions: Handling and Disposal: 1. Preparation of etoposide should be done in a vertical laminar flow hood (Biological Safety Cabinet—Class II). 2. Personnel preparing etoposide should wear PVC gloves, safety glasses, disposable gowns and masks. 3. All needles, syringes, vials and other materials that have come in contact with etoposide should be segregated and incinerated at 1 000 °C or more. Sealed containers may explode. Intact vials should be returned to the manufacturer for destruction. Proper precautions should be taken in packaging these materials for transport. 4. Personnel regularly involved in the preparation and handling of etoposide should have biannual blood examinations.

Supplied: Capsules: Each pink, liquid-filled, soft gelatin capsule printed with edible ink, contains: etoposide 50 mg. Nonmedicinal ingredients: citric acid, glycerol, polyethylene glycol and water; capsule shell: gelatin, glycerol, iron oxide red, parabens (ethyl and propyl), purified water, sorbitol and titanium dioxide. Bottles of 20.

Injection: Each mL of clear yellow solution contains: etoposide 20 mg. Nonmedicinal ingredients: alcohol, benzyl alcohol, citric acid, polyethylene glycol and polysorbate 80. The pH is 3 to 4. Vials and ampuls of 5 mL. Vials of 25 and 50 mL.

Store at room temperature (15 to 25°C).

(Shown in Product Recognition Section)

Reviewed 1998

VERAPAMIL INJECTION ℞

Abbott

Verapamil HCl

Antiarrhythmic

Supplied: Each mL of sterile, nonpyrogenic solution contains: verapamil HCl 2.5 mg (equivalent to verapamil 2.3 mg) and sodium chloride in water for injection. The solution contains no bacteriostat or antimicrobial agent and is intended for single use only. May contain hydrochloric acid for pH adjustment; pH 4.9 (4.0 to 6.5). Ampuls of 2 and 4 mL, sleeves of 10. Fliptop vials of 2 and 4 mL, cartons of 5. Store at controlled room temperature (15 to 30°C). Protect from light and freezing. Retain in carton until ready for use.

VERELAN® ℞

Wyeth-Ayerst

Verapamil HCl

Antihypertensive

Pharmacology: Verapamil is a calcium ion influx inhibitor (calcium entry blocker or calcium ion antagonist) which exerts its pharmacologic effects by modulating the influx of ionic calcium across the cell membrane of the arterial smooth muscle as well as in conductile and contractile myocardial cells.

Verapamil exerts antihypertensive effects by inducing peripheral vasodilation and reducing peripheral vascular resistance usually without reflex tachycardia. These effects are mediated by inhibition of calcium ion influx into smooth muscle cells of the arteriolar wall. Verapamil does not blunt hemodynamic response to isometric or dynamic exercise. Compared to baseline, verapamil administration did not affect electrolytes, glucose and creatinine. The hypotensive effect of verapamil is not blunted by an increase in sodium intake.

Pharmacokinetics: Immediate Release Formulations of Verapamil: With the immediate release formulations, more than 90% of the orally administered dose of verapamil is absorbed. Because of rapid biotransformation during its first pass through the portal circulation, bioavailability ranges from 20 to 35%. Peak plasma concentrations are reached between 1 and 2 hours after oral administration. Chronic oral administration of 120 mg of verapamil every 6 hours resulted in plasma levels of verapamil ranging from 125 to 400 ng/mL, with higher values reported occasionally. A nonlinear correlation between the verapamil dose administered and verapamil plasma levels does exist. In initial dose titration with verapamil a relationship exists between verapamil plasma concentration and prolongation of the PR interval. After repetitive dosing, less than 10 consecutive doses given 6 hours apart, the mean elimination half-life ranged from 4.5 to 12 hours. Half-life of verapamil increases during titration due to saturation of hepatic enzyme systems as plasma verapamil levels rise.

Aging affects the pharmacokinetics of verapamil. Elimination half-life is prolonged in the elderly.

In healthy men, orally administered verapamil undergoes extensive metabolism in the liver through the cytochrome P450 system. The particular isoenzymes involved are: CYP-3A4, CYP-1A2, and the CYP-2C family. Twelve metabolites have been identified in plasma; all except norverapamil are present in trace amounts only. Norverapamil can reach steady-state plasma concentrations approximately equal to those of verapamil itself. The biologic activity of norverapamil appears to be approximately 20% that of verapamil. Approximately 70% of an administered dose is excreted as metabolites in the urine and 16% or more in the feces within 5 days. About 3 to 4% is excreted in the urine as unchanged drug. Approximately 90% is bound to plasma proteins. In patients with hepatic insufficiency, metabolism is delayed and elimination half-life prolonged up to 14 to 16 hours (see Warnings, Hepatic Insufficiency and Dosage).

After 4 weeks of oral dosing (120 mg q.i.d.) verapamil and norverapamil levels were noted in the cerebrospinal fluid with estimated partition coefficients of 0.06 for verapamil and 0.04 for norverapamil.

Verelan Sustained Release Capsules: In a multiple dose pharmacokinetic study, peak concentrations for a single daily dose of Verelan Sustained Release Capsule 240 mg were approximately 65% of those obtained with an 80 mg t.i.d. dose of the conventional immediate release tablets, and the 24 hours post-dose concentrations were approximately 30% higher. The steady-state pharmacokinetic data are summarized in Table I.

Food does not affect the extent or rate of the absorption of verapamil from the controlled release Verelan capsule. The Verelan 240 mg capsule when administered with food had a C_{max} of 77 ng/mL which occurred 9 hours after dosing and an AUC(0-inf) of 1 387 ng.hr/mL. Verelan 240 mg under fasting conditions had a C_{max} of 77 ng/mL which occurred 9.8 hours after dosing, and an AUC(0-inf) of 1 541 ng.hr/mL.

The time to reach maximum verapamil concentrations (T_{max}) with Verelan Sustained Release Capsules has been found to be approximately 7 to 9 hours in each of the single dose (fasting), single dose (fed), the multiple dose (steady state) studies and dose proportionality pharmacokinetic studies. Similarly the apparent half-life ($T_{1/2}$) has been found to be approximately 12 hours independent of dose.

Indications: In the treatment of mild to moderate essential hypertension. It should normally be used in those patients in whom treatment with diuretics or beta-blockers has been associated with unacceptable adverse effects.

Verelan can be tried as an initial agent in those patients in whom the use of diuretics and/or beta-blockers is contraindicated, or in patients with medical conditions in which these drugs frequently cause serious adverse effects.

Combination of verapamil with a diuretic has been found to be compatible and showed additive antihypertensive effect.

Verelan should not be used concurrently with beta-blockers in the treatment of hypertension (see Precautions, Drug Interactions).

Safety of concurrent use of Verelan Sustained Release Capsules with other antihypertensive agents has not been established and such use cannot be recommended at this time.

Contraindications: Severe hypotension or cardiogenic shock. Acute myocardial infarction; severe congestive heart failure and/or severe left ventricular dysfunction (unless secondary to a supraventricular tachycardia amenable to oral verapamil therapy); second- or third-degree AV block; sick sinus syndrome (see Warnings, Conduction Disturbance); marked bradycardia. Patients with atrial flutter or atrial fibrillation and an accessory bypass tract (e.g., Wolff-Parkinson-White, Lown-Ganong-Levine syndromes) (see Warnings, Accessory Bypass Tract). Hypersensitivity to the drug.

Warnings: General: In patients with angina or arrhythmias using antihypertensive drugs, the additional hypotensive effect of verapamil should be taken into consideration.

Heart Failure: Because of verapamil's negative inotropic effect, the drug should not be used in patients with poorly compensated congestive heart failure, unless the failure is complicated by or caused by a dysrhythmia. If verapamil is used in such patients, they must be digitalized prior to treatment. It has been reported that digoxin plasma levels may increase with chronic verapamil administration (see Precautions, Drug Interactions—Digitalis).

The use of verapamil in the treatment of hypertension is not recommended in patients with heart failure caused by systolic dysfunction.

Hypotension: Hypotensive symptoms of lethargy and weakness with faintness have been reported following single oral doses, and even after some months of treatment. In some patients it may be necessary to reduce the dose.

Conduction Disturbance: Verapamil slows conduction across the AV node and rarely may produce second- or third-degree AV block, bradycardia and in extreme cases, asystole.

Verapamil causes dose-related suppression of the SA node. In some patients, sinus bradycardia may occur, especially in patients with sick sinus syndrome (SA nodal disease), which is more common in older patients (see Contraindications).

Bradycardia: The total incidence of bradycardia (ventricular rate less than 50 beats/min) was 1.4% in controlled studies. Asystole in patients other than those with sick sinus syndrome is usually of short duration (few seconds or less), with spontaneous return to AV nodal or normal sinus rhythm. If this does not occur promptly, appropriate treatment should be initiated immediately (see Overdose: Symptoms and Treatment).

Accessory Bypass Tract: Verapamil may result in significant acceleration of ventricular response during atrial fibrillation or atrial flutter in the Wolff-Parkinson White (WPW) or Lown-Ganong-Levine Syndromes after receiving i.v. verapamil. Although a risk of this occurring with oral verapamil has not been established, such patients receiving oral verapamil may be at risk and its use in these patients is contraindicated (see Contraindications).

Concomitant Therapy with Beta-adrenergic Blockers: Generally, oral verapamil should not be given to patients receiving

Table I—Verelan

Comparison of Pharmacokinetic Parameters of Verelan Versus Immediate Release Formulations

Parameters	Immediate Release Tablets t.i.d.		Verelan Once Daily Dose		
	80 mg t.i.d. 240 mg/day	120 mg t.i.d. 360 mg/day	120 mg	240 mg	360 mg
C_{max} (ng/mL)	170.5	289.4	39.4	107.7	173.9
C_{min} (ng/mL)	25.5	80.1	10.8	32.8	61
T_{max} (hours)	0.96	1.4	8.2	7.9	7.1
$T_{1/2}$ (hours)	6.1	6.1	13.6	10.5	9.6
$AUC_{(0-24h)}$(ng.h/mL)	1 569		565	1 660	2 729
$AUC_{(0-36h)}$(ng.h/mL)		1 809			

Verelan (cont'd)

beta-blockers since the depressant effects on myocardial contractility, heart rate and atrioventricular conduction may be additive.

Verapamil gives no protection against the dangers of abrupt beta-blocker withdrawal and such withdrawal should be done by the gradual reduction of the dose of beta-blocker. Then verapamil may be started with the usual dose.

Patients with Hypertrophic Cardiomyopathy: In 120 patients with hypertrophic cardiomyopathy who received therapy with verapamil at doses up to 720 mg/day, a variety of serious adverse effects were seen. Three patients died due to pulmonary edema; all had severe left ventricular outflow obstruction and a past history of left ventricular dysfunction. Eight other patients had pulmonary edema and/or severe hypotension, abnormally high (greater than 20 mmHg) pulmonary wedge pressure and a marked left ventricular outlfow obstruction were present in most of these patients.

Concomitant administration of quinidine (see Precautions, Drug Interactions) preceded the severe hypotension in 3 of the 8 patients (2 of whom developed pulmonary edema). Sinus bradycardia occurred in 11% of the patients, second-degree AV block in 4%, and sinus arrest in 2%. It should be appreciated that this group of patients had a serious disease with high mortality rate. Most adverse effects responded well to dose reduction, but in some cases verapamil had to be discontinued.

Elevated Liver Enzymes: Elevations of transaminases with and without concomitant elevations in alkaline phosphatase and bilirubin have been reported. Several published cases of hepatocellular injury produced by verapamil have been proven by rechallenge. Clinical symptoms of malaise, fever, and/or right upper quadrant pain, in addition to elevation of AST, ALT and alkaline phosphatase have been reported. Periodic monitoring of liver function in patients receiving verapamil is therefore prudent.

Hepatic Insufficiency: Since verapamil is extensively metabolized by the liver, it should be administered cautiously to patients with impaired hepatic function. Impaired hepatic function prolongs the elimination half-life of immediate-release verapamil to about 14 to 16 hours. A decreased dosage should be used in patients with hepatic insufficiency and careful monitoring for abnormal prolongation of the PR interval or other signs of excessive, pharmacologic effect should be carried out (see Pharmacology, Pharmacokinetics and Dosage).

Renal Insufficiency: About 70% of an administered dose of verapamil is excreted as metabolites in the urine. In one study in healthy volunteers, the total body clearance after i.v. administration of verapamil was 12.08 mL/min/kg, while in patients with advanced renal disease it was reduced to 5.33 mL/min/kg. This pharmacokinetic finding suggests that renal clearance of verapamil in patients with renal disease is decreased. In 2 studies with oral verapamil no difference in pharmacokinetics could be demonstrated. Therefore, until further data are available, verapamil should be used with caution in patients with impaired renal function. These patients should be carefully monitored for abnormal prolongation of the PR interval or other signs of excessive pharmacologic effect (see Dosage).

Precautions: Atypical lens changes and cataracts were observed in beagle dog studies at high doses. This has been concluded to be species-specific for the beagle dog. (These ophthalmological changes were not seen in a second study.) No similar changes have been observed in long-term prospective human ophthalmological trials.

Verapamil does not alter total serum calcium levels. However, one report suggested that calcium levels above the normal range may decrease the therapeutic effect of verapamil.

Patients with Attenuated (Decreased) Neuromuscular Transmission: It has been reported that verapamil decreases neuromuscular transmission in patients with Duchenne's muscular dystrophy, and that verapamil prolongs recovery from the neuromuscular blocking agent vecuronium. It may be necessary to decrease the dosage of verapamil when it is administered to patients with attenuated neuromuscular transmission.

Geriatrics: Caution should be exercised when verapamil is administered to elderly patients (≥65 years) especially those prone to developing hypotension or those with a history of cerebrovascular insufficiency (see Pharmacology, Pharmacokinetics, and Dosage, Geriatrics). The incidence of adverse reactions is approximately 4% higher in the elderly. The adverse reactions occurring more frequently include dizziness and constipation. Serious adverse events associated with heart block have occurred in the elderly.

Pregnancy: Teratology and reproduction studies have been performed with verapamil in rabbits and rats at oral doses up to 1.5 (15 mg/kg/day) and 6 (60 mg/kg/day) times the human oral daily dose, respectively, and have revealed no evidence of teratogenicity or impaired fertility. In rat, however, this multiple of the human dose was embryocidal and retarded fetal growth and development, probably because of adverse maternal effects reflected in reduced weight gains of the dams. This oral dose has also been shown to cause hypotension in rats.

There are no studies in pregnant women. Verapamil crosses the placental barrier and can be detected in umbilical vein blood at delivery. Verelan Sustained Release Capsules are not recommended for use in pregnant women unless the anticipated benefits outweigh the potential risks to mother and fetus.

Labor and Delivery: It is not known whether the use of verapamil during labor or delivery has immediate or delayed adverse effects on the fetus, or whether it prolongs the duration of labor, increases the need for forceps delivery or other obstetric intervention.

Lactation: Verapamil is excreted in human milk. Because of the potential for adverse reactions in nursing infants from verapamil, nursing should be discontinued while the drug is administered.

Children: The safety and dosage regimen of verapamil in children has not yet been established.

Drug Interactions: As with all drugs, care should be exercised when treating patients with multiple medications.

Calcium channel blockers undergo biotransformation by the cytochrome P450 system. Coadministration of verapamil with other drugs which follow the same route of biotransformation may result in altered bioavailability of verapamil or these drugs.

Dosages of similarly metabolized drugs, particularly those of low therapeutic ratio, and especially in patients with renal and/or hepatic impairment, may require adjustment when starting or stopping concomitantly administered verapamil to maintain optimum therapeutic blood levels.

Drugs known to be inhibitors of the cytochrome P450 system include: asole antifungals cimetidine, cyclosporine, erythromycin, quinidine, terfenadine, warfarin.

Drugs known to be inducers of the cytochrome P450 system include: phenobarbital, penytoin, rifampin.

Drugs known to be biotransformed via P450 include: benzodiazepines, flecainide, imipramine, propafenone, theophylline.

Alcohol: Verapamil may increase blood alcohol concentrations and prolong its effects.

Antihypertensive Agents: Verapamil administered concomitantly with other antihypertensive agents may have an additive effect on lowering blood pressure. In patients with hypertension, combination with a diuretic has been found to be compatible; however, combination with other antihypertensive agents has not been established. Verapamil should not be combined with beta-blockers for the treatment of hypertension.

Antineoplastic Agents: Verapamil inhibits P-glycoprotein mediated transport of antineoplastic agents out of tumor cells, resulting in their decreased metabolic clearance. Dosage adjustments of antineoplastic agents should be considered when verapamil is administered concomitantly.

Concomitant administration of R-verapamil can decrease the clearance of paclitaxil.

ASA: Potential adverse reactions in terms of bleeding due to antiplatelet effects of the two agents should be taken into consideration in patients taking verapamil and ASA concomitantly.

Beta-Adrenergic Blockers: The concomitant administration of verapamil with beta-blockers can result in severe adverse effects (see Warnings).

Carbamazepine: The concomitant oral administration of verapamil and carbamazepine may potentiate the effects of carbamazepine neurotoxicity. Symptoms include nausea, diplopia, headache, ataxia or dizziness.

Cimetidine: The interaction between cimetidine and chronically administered verapamil has not been adequately studied. Variable results on clearance have been obtained in acute studies of healthy volunteers.

Cyclosporine: Verapamil therapy may increase serum levels of cyclosporine.

Digitalis: Verapamil treatment increases serum digoxin levels by 50 to 75% during the first week of therapy, and this can result in digitalis toxicity. In patients with hepatic cirrhosis the influence of verapamil on digoxin kinetics is magnified. Verapamil may reduce total body clearance and nonrenal clearance of digitoxin by 27 and 29% respectively. Maintenance and digitalization doses should be reduced when verapamil is administered, and the patient should be carefully monitored to avoid over- or underdigitalization. Whenever overdigitalization is suspected, the daily dose of digitalis should be reduced or temporarily discontinued. On discontinuation of verapamil use, the patient should be reassessed to avoid underdigitalization.

Disopyramide: Until data on possible interactions between verapamil and disopyramide are obtained, disopyramide should not be administered within 48 hours before or 24 hours after verapamil administration.

Flecainide: A study in healthy volunteers showed that the concomitant administration of flecainide and verapamil may have additive effects on myocardial contractility, AV conduction, and repolarization. Concomitant therapy with flecainide and verapamil may result in additive negative inotropic effect and prolongation of atrioventricular conduction.

Inhalation Anesthetics: When used concomitantly, inhalation anesthetics and calcium antagonists, such as verapamil, should be titrated carefully because additive hemodynamic depressive effects have been observed.

Lithium: Oral verapamil therapy may result in a lowering of serum lithium levels in patients receiving chronic, oral lithium therapy. A dose adjustment of the lithium may be necessary.

Neuromuscular Blocking Agents: Clinical data and animal studies suggest that verapamil may potentiate the activity of neuromuscular blocking agents (curare-like and depolarizing). It may be necessary to decrease the dose of verapamil and/or the dose of the neuromuscular blocking agent when the drugs are used concomitantly.

Nitrates, Diuretics: No cardiovascular adverse effects have been attributed to any interaction between these agents and verapamil.

Phenobarbital: Phenobarbital therapy may increase verapamil clearance.

Quinidine: In a small number of patients with hypertrophic cardiomyopathy, concomitant use of verapamil and quinidine resulted in significant hypotension. Until further data are obtained, combined therapy of verapamil and quinidine in patients with hypertrophic cardiomyopathy should probably be avoided.

The electrophysiologic effects of quinidine and verapamil on AV conduction were studied in 8 patients. Verapamil significantly counteracted the effects of quinidine on AV conduction. There has been a report of increased quinidine levels during verapamil therapy.

Rifampin: Therapy with rifampin may markedly reduce oral verapamil bioavailability.

Sulfinpyrazone: Oral clearance of verapamil following single and multiple doses in volunteers was increased, with an associated decrease in bioavailability.

Theophylline: Increased plasma theophylline concentrations due to verapamil administration have been reported.

Adverse Effects: In controlled clinical trials involving 285 hypertensive patients treated with Verelan sustained release capsules, the overall incidence of adverse events irrespective of causality was 26% and the rate of discontinuation from these trials due to adverse events was 2%. The following adverse reactions were reported in greater than 1% of the patients: constipation (7.4%), headache (5.3%), dizziness (4.2%), lethargy (3.2)%, dyspepsia (2.5%), rash (1.4%), ankle edema (1.4%), sleep disturbance (1.4%) and myalgia (1.1%).

In clinical trials with other formulations of verapamil HCl, (n=4 954), the following adverse reactions divided by body system have been reported. The most serious adverse reactions reported with verapamil are heart failure (1.8%), hypotension (2.5%), AV block (1.2%) and rapid ventricular response (see Warnings).

Cardiovascular: hypotension (2.5%), edema (2.1%) CHF/pulmonary edema (1.9%), bradycardia (1.4%), AV block, total (first, second and third degree) (1.2%) or second and third degree (0.8%).

CNS: dizziness (3.2%), headache (2.2%), fatigue (1.7%).

Gastrointestinal: constipation (7.3%), nausea (2.7%).

The following reactions were reported in 1% or less of patients: Cardiovascular: flushing, angina pectoris, atrioventricular dissociation, chest pain, claudication, myocardial infarction, palpitations, purpura, syncope, severe tachycardia, developing or worsening of heart failure, development of rhythm disturbances, ventricular dysrhythmias, painful coldness or numbness of extremities.

CNS: cerebrovascular accident, confusion, equilibrium disorders, insomnia, muscle cramps, paresthesia, psychotic symptoms, shakiness, somnolence, excitation, depression, rotary

nystagmus, vertigo, tremor, extrapyramidal disorders, muscle fatigue, hyperkinesis.
Gastrointestinal: diarrhea, dry mouth, gastrointestinal distress, gingival hyperplasia, vomiting.
Respiratory: dyspnea, bronchospasm.
Urogenital: gynecomastia, increased frequency of urination, spotty menstruation, oligomenorrhea, impotence.
Hematologic and Lymphatic: ecchymosis or bruising.
Skin: arthralgia and rash, exanthema, hair loss, hyperkeratosis, macules, sweating, urticaria, Stevens-Johnson Syndrome, erythema multiforme, pruritus.
Special Senses: blurred vision, diplopia.

Hepatotoxicity with elevated enzymes [AST, ALT, alkaline phosphatase] and bilirubin levels, jaundice and associated symptoms of hepatitis with cholestasis have been reported (see Warnings).

Isolated cases of angioedema have been reported. Angioedema may be accompanied by breathing difficulty.

In clinical trials related to the control of ventricular response in digitalized patients who had atrial fibrillation or flutter, ventricular rates below 50 at rest occurred in 15% of patients and asymptomatic hypotension occurred in 5% of patients.

Overdose: Symptoms: Based on reports of intentional overdosage with verapamil, the following symptoms have been observed. Hypotension occurs, varying from transient to severe. Conduction disturbances seen included: prolonged AV conduction time, AV dissociation, nodal rhythm, ventricular fibrillation and ventricular asystole.

Treatment: In case of overdosage with Verelan, it should be noted that the release rate and absorption of verapamil from Verelan is prolonged (see Table I) due to the sustained release characteristics of the formulation.

Treatment of overdosage should be supportive (see Table II). Gastric lavage should be undertaken even later than 12 hours after ingestion, if no gastrointestinal motility is present. Beta-adrenergic stimulation or parenteral administration of calcium solutions may increase calcium ion influx across the slow channel. These pharmacologic interventions have been effectively used in treatment of overdosage with verapamil. Clinically significant hypotensive reactions should be treated with vasopressor agents. AV block is treated with atropine and cardiac pacing. Asystole should be handled by the usual advanced cardiac life support measures including the use of vasopressor agents, e.g., isoproterenol HCl. Verapamil is not removed by hemodialysis.
Suggested Treatment of Acute Cardiovascular Adverse Effects: Actual treatment and dosage should depend on the severity of the clinical situation and the judgment of the treating physician. Patients with hypertrophic cardiomyopathy treated with verapamil should not be administered positive inotropic agents (marked by asterisks in Table II).

Dosage: Mild to Moderate Essential Hypertension: The dosage should be individualized by titration depending on patient tolerance and responsiveness to Verelan. Titration should be based on therapeutic efficacy and safety, evaluated weekly and approximately 24 hours after the previous dose.

The usual initial adult dose is 180 to 240 mg/day, taken once a day, in the morning. If adequate response is not obtained, the dose may be titrated upward to 360 mg or to 480 mg taken once a day in the morning. Optimal doses are usually lower in patients also receiving diuretics since additive antihypertensive effects can be expected.

The maximum daily dose of 480 mg should not be exceeded.

The antihypertensive effects are evident within the first week of therapy.
Geriatrics: Initial doses of 120 mg a day may be warranted in patients who may have an increased response to verapamil (see Precautions, Geriatrics). The dosage should be carefully and gradually adjusted depending on patient tolerability and response. Patients with Impaired Liver or Renal Function: Verelan should be administered cautiously to patients with impaired liver or renal function. The dosage should be adjusted gradually depending on patient tolerance and response. These patients should be monitored for abnormal prolongation of the PR interval or other signs of overdosage. Verelan should not be used in severe hepatic dysfunction (see Warnings, Hepatic Insufficiency).

Supplied: 120 mg: Each sustained release, pellet-filled capsule with yellow body and yellow cap contains: verapamil HCl 120 mg. Nonmedicinal ingredients: FD&C red #40, fumaric acid, gelatin, methylparaben, povidone, propylparaben, shellac, silicon dioxide, sodium lauryl sulfate, sugar spheres, talc, titanium dioxide and yellow iron oxide. High density polyethylene bottles of 100.

180 mg: Each sustained release, pellet-filled capsule with yellow body and grey cap contains: verapamil HCl 180 mg. Nonmedicinal ingredients: black iron oxide, FD&C red #40, fumaric acid, gelatin, methylparaben, povidone propylparaben, shellac, silicon dioxide, sodium lauryl sulfate, sugar spheres, talc, titanium dioxide and yellow iron oxide. High density polyethylene bottles of 100.

240 mg: Each sustained release, pellet-filled capsule with yellow body and blue cap contains: D&C red #28, FD&C blue #1, FD&C red #40, fumaric acid, gelatin, methylparaben, povidone, propylparaben, shellac, silicon dioxide, sodium lauryl sulfate, sugar spheres, talc, titanium dioxide and yellow iron oxide. High density polyethylene bottles of 100.

Store at 15 to 25°C. Protect from moisture and light.

Reviewed 1999

Table II—Verelan

Overdose: Treatment

Adverse Effects	Proven Effective Treatment	Treatment with Good Theoretical Rationale	Supportive Treatment
shock, cardiac failure, severe hypotension	calcium salts e.g., calcium gluconate i.v. metaraminol* bitartrate i.v.	dopamine HCl* i.v. dobutamine HCl* i.v.	i.v. fluids Trendelenburg position
bradycardia, AV block, asystole	isoproterenol HCl* i.v. atropine sulfate i.v. cardiac pacing		i.v. fluids (slow drip)
rapid ventricular rate (due to antegrade conduction in flutter/fibrillation with W-P-W or L-G-L syndrome	D.C. cardioversion (high energy may be required) procainamide i.v. lidocaine HCl i.v.		i.v. fluids (slow drip)

VERMOX®

Janssen-Ortho

Mebendazole

Anthelmintic

Pharmacology: Mebendazole induces in vitro and in vivo inhibition of the glucose uptake by parasitic helminths; this is associated with glycogen depletion and a decrease in the generation of ATP, leading to inhibition of larval development.

Mebendazole is poorly absorbed after oral administration. At the normal anthelmintic dosage, the bioavailability is poor due to a combination of high first-pass metabolism and the very low solubility of the drug.

Indications: Mebendazole has a broad spectrum of anthelmintic activity and is effective in the treatment of single or mixed helminthic infestations. Clinical studies have shown it effective in the treatment of Enterobius vermicularis (pinworm); Ascaris lumbricoides (roundworm); Trichuris trichiura (whipworm); Ankylostoma duodenale and Necator americanus (hookworm). It has also been used to treat infections due to Strongyloides stercoralis and Taenia solium (large tapeworms).

Contraindications: In persons who have shown hypersensitivity to the drug.

Warnings: *Pregnancy:* Animal trials conducted in a wide range of species revealed an embryotoxic and teratogenic effect in the rat. Also, the safety of use in pregnant women has not been established. Therefore, mebendazole should not be administered during pregnancy, particularly in the first trimester, unless the potential benefit to the patient outweighs the possible risk to the fetus.

Precautions: Patients should be carefully checked to detect any alteration in blood studies or hepatic or renal function tests following treatment with mebendazole. Special attention should be given to patients with intestinal pathology (e.g. Crohn's ileitis, ulcerative colitis).
Lactation: It is not known whether mebendazole is excreted in human milk. Therefore caution should be exercised when mebendazole is administered to nursing women.
Children (under age 2): Since mebendazole has not been extensively studied in infants under 2 years of age, its use in such individuals should only be implemented in cases where the potential therapeutic effects outweigh the possible hazard to the patient. There have been very exceptional reports of convulsions in infants less than 1 year old.
Drug Interactions: Concomitant treatment with cimetidine may inhibit the metabolism of mebendazole in the liver, resulting in increased plasma concentrations of the drug especially during prolonged treatment. In the latter case, determination of plasma concentrations are recommended in order to allow dose adjustments.

Adverse Effects: Mebendazole is generally well tolerated. However, patients with high parasitic burdens when treated with mebendazole have manifested diarrhea, vomiting and/or abdominal pain. Other adverse reactions reported were drowsiness, itching, headache and dizziness. Reports from clinical trials also mentioned increased AST, ALT, alkaline phosphatase and BUN. Eosinophilia and decreased hemoglobin and/or white cell count, hematuria and cylindruria have been reported. Hypersensitivity reactions such as exanthema, rash, urticaria and angioedema have rarely been observed.

Overdose: Symptoms: In the event of accidental overdosage, abdominal cramps, nausea, vomiting and diarrhea may occur. Although the recommended maximum treatment duration of mebendazole is limited to 3 days, there have been rare reports of reversible liver function disturbances, hepatitis and neutropenia described in patients who were treated for hydatid disease with massive doses for prolonged periods of time.

Treatment: There is no specific antidote. Gastric lavage with aqueous potassium permanganate at 20 mg/100 mL may be performed. Activated charcoal may be given.

Dosage: Adults and Children 2 Years and Older: Enterobiasis: One tablet (100 mg) given as a single dose. Since reinfections by Enterobius are known to be very frequent, it is recommended that treatment be repeated after 2 or 4 weeks, especially in eradication programs.
Trichuriasis, ascariasis, ankylostomiasis, strongyloidiasis, taeniasis and mixed infections: One tablet (100 mg) in the morning and evening for 3 consecutive days.

If the patient is not cured 3 weeks after treatment, a second course of treatment is advised.

No special procedures such as fasting or purgation are required.

Tablets must be chewed.
Children Under 2 Years: See Precautions.

Supplied: Each chewable, orange, scored, compressed tablet contains: mebendazole 100 mg. Nonmedicinal ingredients: colloidal silicon dioxide, dextrose, magnesium stearate, methylcellulose, natural orange flavor, sodium lauryl sulfate and sunset yellow (E110). Bisulfite-, gluten- and tartrazine-free. Amber glass bottles of 12. Store between 15 and 30°C. Protect from light

Reviewed 1999

VERSED®

Roche

Midazolam

Premedicant—Sedative—Anesthetic

Pharmacology: General: Adult and Pediatric: I.V. midazolam has been associated with respiratory depression and respiratory arrest, especially when used for sedation in noncritical care settings. In some cases, where this was not recognized promptly and treated effectively, death or hypoxic encephalopathy has resulted. I.V. midazolam should be used only in hospital or ambulatory care settings that provide for continuous monitoring of respiratory and cardiac function, i.e., pulse oximetry. Immediate availability of resuscitative drugs and age and size-appropriate equipment for bag/valve/mask ventilation and intubation, and personnel trained in their use and skilled in airway management should be assured (see Warnings). For deeply sedated patients, a dedicated individual, other than the practitioner performing the procedure, should monitor the patient throughout the procedure.

The initial i.v. dose for sedation in adult patients may be as little as 1 mg, but should not exceed 2.5 mg in a normal

Versed (cont'd)

healthy adult. Lower doses are necessary for older (over 60 years) or debilitated patients and in patients receiving concomitant narcotics or other CNS depressants. The initial dose and all subsequent doses should always be titrated slowly; administer over 2 to 3 minutes and allow about 2 minutes to fully evaluate the sedative effect. The use of the 1 mg/mL formulation or dilution of the 1 mg/mL or 5 mg/mL formulation is recommended to facilitate slower injection. Doses of sedative medications in pediatric patients must be calculated on a mg/kg basis, and initial doses and all subsequent doses should always be titrated slowly. The initial pediatric dose of midazolam for sedation/anxiolysis/amnesia is age, procedure, and route dependent (see Dosage for complete dosing information).

Neonates: Midazolam should not be administered by rapid injection in the neonatal population. Severe hypotension and seizures have been reported following rapid i.v. administration, particularly with concomitant use of fentanyl (see Dosage for complete information).

Midazolam injection is a short-acting, water soluble benzodiazepine which has CNS depressant effects. Depending on the route of administration and dose used, midazolam can produce sedative-hypnotic effects or induce anesthesia. The administration of midazolam may often be followed by anterograde amnesia.

Onset of sedative effects after i.m. administration is about 15 minutes, with peak sedation occurring 30 to 60 minutes following injection. Sedation (defined as drowsiness with the ability to respond to verbal commands) after i.v. injection is usually achieved within 3 to 6 minutes; the time of onset is affected by the dose administered, the concurrent administration of narcotic premedications and the condition of the patient. Induction of anesthesia can usually be achieved in 1.5 minutes when narcotic premedication has been administered and in 2 to 2.5 minutes without narcotic premedication. When used as directed, recovery after awakening from general anesthesia usually occurs within 2 hours, but recovery may take up to 6 hours in some cases. Recovery in patients receiving midazolam may be slightly slower than in patients who receive thiopental.

I.V. doses of midazolam depress the ventilatory response to CO_2 stimulation for 15 minutes or more beyond the duration of ventilatory depression following administration of thiopental. **The ventilatory response to CO_2 is markedly impaired in patients with chronic obstructive pulmonary disease.** I.V. sedation with midazolam in healthy volunteers does not adversely affect the mechanics of respiration (pulmonary resistance, static recoil, functional residual capacity or residual volume). However, total lung capacity (TLC) and peak expiratory flow decrease significantly, but static compliance and maximum expiratory flow at 50% of awake TLC (Vmax) increase. In healthy volunteers an i.m. premedicating dose of midazolam (0.07 mg/kg) did not depress the ventilatory response to CO_2 stimulation to a clinically significant extent. The i.v. administration of midazolam decreases in a dose dependent manner the minimum alveolar concentration (MAC) of halothane required for general anesthesia.

In cardiac hemodynamic studies, induction with midazolam was associated with a slight to moderate decrease in mean arterial pressure, cardiac output, stroke volume and systemic vascular resistance. When used in i.v. sedation midazolam produces a higher incidence of fall in mean arterial pressure than diazepam. Slow heart rates (less than 65/minute), particularly in patients taking propranolol for angina, tended to rise slightly while faster heart rates (e.g., 85/minute) tended to slow slightly.

In patients without any previous history of cerebrospinal diseases scheduled for elective surgery under lumbar spinal anesthesia, i.v. administration of midazolam at a dose of 0.15 mg/kg tended to reduce the cerebrospinal fluid pressure during the induction of anesthesia to an extent similar to 3.9 mg/kg i.v. thiopental. Measurements of intraocular pressure in patients without eye disease show a moderate lowering following induction with midazolam. Patients with glaucoma have not been studied. The increase in intraocular pressure after succinylcholine administration or endotracheal intubation is not prevented by midazolam, diazepam or thiopental.

Pharmacokinetics: Midazolam dosing should not be based on pharmacokinetic values; it should always be titrated to achieve a given clinical effect. This is especially important when used for long-term sedation in the Intensive Care Unit (ICU). Elimination half-life of midazolam is increased in congestive heart failure, hepatic cirrhosis, and chronic renal failure. It is markedly and unpredictably increased in critically ill patients with multiorgan failure. Table I summarizes the available data.

Table I—Versed

Pharmacokinetic Parameters

Patient Type	Dose range (mg/kg)	Elimination t½[a] (h)	Volume of distribution (Vdβ) (L/kg)	Total body clearance (TBC) (L/h/kg)
Normal Subjects 21–50 years	0.07–0.25	1.0[b]–2.8	0.80–1.64	0.24–0.43
Surgical (Elective) 30–54 years	0.15–0.45	3.0–3.9	1.67–3.21	0.37–0.51
Congestive Heart Failure 33–67 years	0.1	6.5	2.50	0.27
Hepatic Dysfunction 21–59 years	0.07	2.4	1.77	0.50
Severe Alcoholic Cirrhosis 39–54 years	0.075	3.9	1.49	0.32
Chronic Renal Failure[c] 24–68 years	0.20	3.3	3.40	0.60
Volunteers:				
Male:				
24–33 years	5 mg[d]	1.9	1.34	0.47
60–74 years	5 mg[d]	4.0	1.64	0.26
Female:				
23–37 years	5 mg[d]	2.3	2.00	0.56
64–79 years	5 mg[d]	3.0	2.11	0.45
Patients:				
Male:				
30 years[e]	0.2	2.3	1.44	0.49
82 years[e]	0.2	8.5	3.63	0.34
Female:				
31 years[e]	0.2	2.9	1.36	0.36
86 years[e]	0.2	3.0	2.30	0.55
Obese Volunteers 22–62 years	5 mg[d]	6.5	2.66	0.25

[a] Harmonic mean (h).
[b] Lower value of the range in the study (mean not reported).
[c] In 2 critically ill patients with impaired renal function and renal failure with impaired hepatic function, t½ values of 18 and 21 hours, respectively, were reported.
[d] Absolute dose.
[e] Mean age.

Following i.v. administration, midazolam is rapidly metabolized to 1-hydroxymethyl midazolam, which is the major metabolite, and to 4-hydroxy and 1,4-dihydroxy midazolam, which are minor metabolites. Mean peak plasma concentration of midazolam is several fold greater than that of 1-hydroxymethyl midazolam. The half-life of elimination of this metabolite is similar to that of the parent compound. Less than 0.03% of the dose is excreted in the urine as intact midazolam, 45 to 81% of the dose is excreted in urine as the conjugates of the metabolites. Midazolam is approximately 97% plasma protein-bound in normal subjects. In patients with chronic renal failure, the free fraction of drug in plasma can be significantly higher than in healthy subjects.

The mean relative bioavailability of midazolam following i.m administration is greater than 90%. Following i.m. administration, the mean time to peak midazolam plasma concentrations is 0.5 hour. Peak concentrations of midazolam as well as 1-hydroxymethyl midazolam after i.m. administration are about one-half of those achieved after equivalent i.v. doses. There is, however, no direct correlation between clinical effects and blood levels of midazolam. The elimination half-life of i.m. administered midazolam is comparable to that observed following i.v. administration.

In animals and humans, midazolam has been shown to cross the placenta and to enter the fetal circulation. Clinical data indicate that midazolam is excreted in human milk. Following oral intake, low concentrations of midazolam could be detected for short periods of time.

Pharmacokinetics in Adult Patients in Intensive Care Unit (ICU): The pharmacokinetics of midazolam following continuous i.v. infusion were determined in intubated, mechanically ventilated patients although not critically ill. The kinetics in critically ill patients with mutisystem dysfunction are unpredictable and it is recommended that midazolam be titrated to the desired effect (see Table II on following page).

The elimination half-life of midazolam was longer following continuous infusion in ICU patients than following the injection of single i.v. doses. The data were derived from studies in which midazolam was infused for less than 24 hours. Steady-state plasma levels increased with increasing rates of infusion.

In patients with acute renal failure (n=6, mean age 48 years), total body clearance was lower (132 mL/min versus 198 mL/min) and the elimination half-life of midazolam longer (13.2 hours versus 7.6 hours) than in patients with normal kidney function (n=33, mean age 62 years). In patients with impaired kidney function, the excretion of 1-hydroxymethyl midazolam glucuronide, the major metabolite of midazolam, is impaired. The de-glucuronidation of this metabolite may increase its plasma concentration which in turn may interfere with the hydroxylation of midazolam itself.

Pharmacokinetics in the Pediatric Population: In healthy children aged 1 year and older, the pharmacokinetic properties of midazolam are similar to those in adults. Weight-normalized clearance is similar to or higher than adult and elimination half-life is similar to or shorter than adult. As with adults, absolute bioavailability of i.m. midazolam is greater than 80%.

In seriously ill neonates and children the half-life of midazolam is substantially prolonged and the clearance reduced compared to healthy adults or other groups of children. It cannot be determined if these differences are due to age, immature organ function or immature metabolic pathways, underlying illness or debility.

In the literature, midazolam is reported to be administered orally and rectally in pediatric patients as well as via the recommended parenteral routes, i.v. and i.m. When administered via the nonparenteral routes, the elimination half-life is similar to that of the parenteral administration, however, the bioavailability is less than 50% versus greater than 80% when administered i.m.

Table III and Table IV (on following page) display pharmacokinetic data on midazolam in pediatric patients. This information was collected from published scientific literature.

Indications: Adult Population: As i.m. premedication prior to surgical or diagnostic procedures. As an i.v. agent for patients requiring sedation/anxiolysis/amnesia prior to and during short endoscopic or diagnostic procedures and direct-current cardioversion. As an alternative i.v. agent for the induction of anesthesia.

Midazolan may also be administered as a continuous i.v. infusion in intubated, mechanically ventilated patients requiring sedation in the ICU.

When used i.v. as an agent for sedation/anxiolysis/amnesia for short endoscopic or other short diagnostic procedures, the desired psychosedation can usually be attained within 3 to 6 minutes, depending on the dose administered and whether or not narcotic premedication is used concomitantly.

Induction of anesthesia with midazolam occurs in approximately 1.5 minutes when a narcotic premedicant has been administered and in 2 or more minutes with or without a nonnarcotic premedicant. Duration of effect when used for induction of anesthesia is generally dose-dependent.

Pediatric Patients: Midazolam has been clinically used for i.v. (including continuous infusion) or i.m. sedation of pediatric patients. Sedation, anxiolysis, and/or amnesia may be necessary for diagnostic or therapeutic procedures, preanesthesia, as a component of anesthesia during surgical procedures, or during treatment in critical care settings.

Contraindications: In patients with a known hypersensitivity to benzodiazepines, and acute pulmonary insufficiency, and also in patients with severe chronic obstructive pulmonary disease (see Warnings). Careful monitoring and slow administration is essential if the drug is used in elderly or debilitated patients. Marked hypoventilation is common if the patient is not responsive to verbal commands.

Outside the ICU setting, marked i.v. sedation must be avoided in elderly or debilitated patients. All patients receiving midazolam for i.v. sedation should, of course, remain sufficiently alert to respond appropriately to verbal requests.

Benzodiazepines are contraindicated in patients with acute narrow angle glaucoma. Midazolam lowered the intraocular pressure in subjects without eye disease, but did not prevent the increases elicited by succinylcholine or endotracheal intubation. Patients with glaucoma have not been studied.

Table II—Versed

Pharmacokinetics in the Intensive Care Unit

Patient Type	Dosing: Bolus* Doses (mg/kg)	Dosing: Maintenance Infusion Rate (mg/kg/h)	Pharmacokinetic Values: Css (ng/mL)	Pharmacokinetic Values: t½ (h)	Pharmacokinetic Values: Total Body Clearance (L/kg/h)
Coronary Artery Bypass	0.015	0.014			
Graft Surgery	0.03	to	66	9.3	0.26
(n=30)	0.05	0.017			
45–71 years					
Abdominal-Aortic Surgery	0.03	0.036	76	6.2	0.52
(n=30)	0.06	0.054	132	6.2	0.40
50–76 years	0.10	0.080	205	6.5	0.41

*Bolus doses of 0.05, 0.06 and 0.10 mg/kg administered in these studies are not recommended in clinical practice (see Dosage).

Table III—Versed I.V.

Kinetics of I.V. Midazolam in Pediatric Patients After Single I.V. Doses or Short I.V. Infusions

Number of Patients	Age (years)	Dose (mg/kg)	V_d, area method (L/kg)	Elimination t½ (h)	Clearance (mL/min/kg)
18	12.8[a]	0.08	—	1.45	8.0
20	8-17[b]	up to 0.1	0.6	0.78	10.0
21	3.8-7.3[c]	0.075-0.6	1.4-1.7[c]	1.4-1.7[c]	4.8-11.2[c]
6	2.5[a]	0.2	2.4	2.4	13.3
8	1-10[b]	0.15	—	1.2	9.1
12	5-9[b]	0.5	2.2	1.8	15.4
17	1.3-5.2[c]	0.3	2.4-2.7[c]	2.8-3.3[c]	8.5-12.0[c]
9	2-9[b]	0.2	—	0.6	7.6
6	5-7	0.1	—	1.8	3.2
10	2-5 days	0.2	—	6.5	2.0

a: Mean Value.
b: Actual Range.
c: Range of Mean Values for Subgroups.

Table IV—Versed

Kinetics of I.V. Midazolam in Pediatric Patients During and After Prolonged I.V. Infusion

Number of Patients	Age (years)	Infusion Rate (μg/kg/min)	Infusion Duration (h)	Elimination t½ (h)	Clearance (mL/min/kg)
10	0.5-8.8[b]	2-5	21-114	4.0 (n=5)	—
10	4.9[a]	0.8	16	3.1	9.6
15	1-5 days[b]	1.0	60	12.0	1.7
187	0-10 days[b]	1.15[a]	62[a]	—	1.17[a]

a: Mean Value.
b: Actual Mean.

Midazolam is not intended for intrathecal or epidural administration due to the presence of the preservative benzyl alcohol in the dosage form.

Warnings:

Midazolam injection must never be used without individualization of dose. The immediate availability of oxygen and other appropriate medication, and the equipment necessary for resuscitation, the maintenance of a patent airway, support of ventilation and cardiac function should be ensured prior to the use of i.v. midazolam in any dose.

Because i.v. midazolam depresses respiration and because opioid agonists and other sedatives can add to this depression, midazolam should be administered as an induction agent only by a person trained in general anesthesia and should be used for sedation/anxiolysis/amnesia only in the presence of personnel skilled in early detection of hypoventilation, maintenance of a patent airway and support of ventilation.

Patients should be continuously monitored for early signs of hypoventilation or apnea which can lead to hypoxia/cardiac arrest unless effective countermeasures are taken. This should include pulse oximetry. Vital signs should continue to be monitored during the recovery period. Opioid agonists and other sedatives add to the respiratory depression produced by midazolam.

Midazolam should be used for i.v. sedation only with caution and must not be administered by single bolus or rapid i.v. administration. Doses used for i.v. sedation should be always restricted to the special low levels recommended (see Dosage) and careful attention should be given in the selection and exclusion of patients that might be specially susceptible to adverse cardiac and respiratory reactions. Older chronically ill patients and those with concomitant use of other cardiorespiratory depressant agents are also especially susceptible to adverse reactions. It should be borne in mind that a fall in oxygen saturation will increase the probability of arrhythmias and other potentially fatal events in susceptible patients. Oxygen supplementation should be used in elderly patients with chronic respiratory or cardiac disease and patients who are seriously ill. Experience in the administration of drugs for i.v. sedation, continuous monitoring of patients to detect reversible adverse effects which may occur in individual patients and the means and setting required for immediate management of these patients are essential prior to the administration of midazolam for i.v. sedation.

Serious cardiorespiratory events have occurred. These have included respiratory depression, apnea, respiratory arrest and/or cardiac arrest, sometimes resulting in death. Strict adherence to the cautions and warnings recommended in the use of this drug is therefore required in order to minimize the incidence of these reactions.

Reactions such as agitation, involuntary movements (including tonic/clonic movements and muscle tremor), hyperactivity and combativeness have been reported. These reactions may be due to inadequate or excessive dosing or improper administration of midazolam; however, consideration should be given to the possibility of cerebral hypoxia or true paradoxical reactions. Should such reactions occur, the response to each dose of midazolam and all other drugs, including local anesthetics, should be evaluated before proceeding.

Outside the ICU setting, midazolam should not be administered to patients in shock, coma, acute alcoholic intoxication, renal failure, or with severe depression of vital signs. Extreme care must be used in administering midazolam, particularly by the i.v. route to the elderly, to very ill patients and to those with limited pulmonary reserve due to the possible occurrence of excessive sedation and/or of apnea or respiratory depression. Patients with chronic obstructive pulmonary disease are unusually sensitive to the respiratory depressant effect of midazolam (see Contraindications).

Myasthenic patients have the potential for respiratory decompensation if a substance with CNS-depressant and/or muscle-relaxant properties is administered. However, those myasthenic patients with established respiratory failure will need mechanical ventilation and for this sedation will be necessary. Careful monitoring of the patients is recommended should midazolam be used for sedation.

Concomitant use of barbiturates, alcohol, opiates or other CNS depressants increases the risk of apnea and may contribute, to excessive and/or prolonged drug effect.

Midazolam should not be given with a narcotic as an i.m. combination for premedication due to the risk of apnea. If a narcotic premedication is given, the subsequent i.v. dose of midazolam should be reduced.

The safety and efficacy of midazolam following non-i.v. and non-i.m. routes of administration have not been established. Midazolam should only be administered i.m. or i.v. The hazards of intra-arterial injection of midazolam solutions in humans are unknown; therefore, precautions against unintended intra-arterial injection should be taken. Extravasation should also be avoided.

Twenty-four months (life-time) toxicity studies in mice and rats indicate carcinogenic activity. The significance of these findings relative to the infrequent use of midazolam in humans is, at present, unknown. The physician should therefore take these findings into consideration when using midazolam.

Occupational Hazards: Patients receiving midazolam injection on an outpatient basis should not engage in hazardous activities requiring complete mental alertness (i.e., operating machinery or driving a motor vehicle) until the effects of the drug, such as drowsiness, have subsided or until 1 full day after anesthesia and surgery, whichever is longer. Patients should also be cautioned about the ingestion of alcohol or other CNS depressant drugs until the effects of midazolam have subsided.

Usage in Preterm Infants and Neonates: Versed contains 1% benzyl alcohol (based on volume). Exposure to excessive amounts of benzyl alcohol has been associated with toxicity (hypotension, metabolic acidosis) particularly in neonates and an increased incidence of kernicterus, particularly in small preterm infants. There have been rare reports of deaths, primarily in preterm infants, associated with exposure to excessive amounts of benzyl alcohol. The amount of benzyl alcohol from medications is usually considered negligible compared to that received in flush solutions containing benzyl alcohol. Administration of high dosages of medications (including Versed) containing this preservative must take into account the total amount of benzyl alcohol administered. The recommended dosage range of Versed for preterm and term infants includes amounts of benzyl alcohol well below that associated with toxicity; however, the amounts of benzyl alcohol at which toxicity may occur is not known. If the patient requires more than the recommended dosages of other medications containing this preservative, the practitioner must consider the daily metabolic load of benzyl alcohol from these combined sources.

Precautions: General: Since an increase in cough reflex and laryngospasm may occur with peroral endoscopic procedures, the use of a topical anesthetic agent and the availability of necessary countermeasures are recommended. During routine diagnostic bronchoscopies, in patients with CO_2 retention, the use of a narcotic premedication is recommended.

ICU Sedation: When administering midazolam injection as continuous infusion for ICU sedation, the changes in the rate of administration should be made slowly (at 30-minute intervals) in order to avoid hypotension and/or overdosage. The change in dose should be in increments of 25 to 50% of the original dose (see Dosage). Dosage should be titrated to a desired level of sedation; reliance on predicted kinetics may result in significant overdosage.

As with other sedative medications, there is wide interpatient variability in midazolam dosage requirements, and these requirements may change with time.

The infusion rate should be adjusted to achieve the required level of sedation according to the patient's age and clinical status. In patients who are still sedated and/or who received large doses of narcotics, a bolus dose may not be necessary and the initial infusion rate should be substantially decreased. The elimination half-life of midazolam is variable and may be considerably longer than seen during short-term administration (e.g., induction of anesthesia) (see Pharmacokinetics). Recovery may be dependent upon the duration of infusion and is more prolonged if the infusion exceeds 24 hours.

Versed (cont'd)

Physical and Psychological Dependence: Physical and psychological dependence may occur during benzodiazepine treatment. The risk is more pronounced in patients on long-term or high-dose treatment and in predisposed patients such as those with a history of alcoholism, drug abuse or marked psychiatric disorders.

In order to minimize the risk of dependence, midazolam should only be administered for the shortest possible duration. Should treatment need to be extended, a careful assessment of the risks and benefits should be made.

Withdrawal symptoms may occur from a few hours to over a week after discontinuing treatment. Symptoms may range from tremor, restlessness, insomnia, anxiety, headache and inability to concentrate to sweating, muscular/abdominal spasms and perceptual changes in more severe cases. In rare instances, delirium and convulsions may also occur. Consequently, abrupt discontinuation of midazolam should generally be avoided and a gradual tapering of dose followed.

Geriatrics and Debilitated Patients: Doses of midazolam injection should be decreased for elderly and debilitated patients (see Dosage). Complete recovery after midazolam administration in such patients may take longer.

Children: Based upon published literature, pediatric patients generally require higher doses of midazolam than adults (see Dosage). Convulsions have occurred in children, most frequently in premature infants and neonates (see Adverse Effects).

Pregnancy: Safety in pregnancy has not been established. Therefore, midazolam should not be used in women who may be pregnant. Several studies have suggested an increased risk of congenital malformations associated with the use of some of the benzodiazepines during the first trimester of pregnancy.

Obstetrics: The use of midazolam has not been evaluated in obstetric studies; therefore, it is not recommended for obstetrical use. Measurable levels of midazolam were found in maternal venous serum, umbilical venous and arterial serum and amniotic fluid, indicating placental transfer of the drug in humans. Fifteen to 60 minutes following i.m. administration of 0.05 mg/kg of midazolam, both the umbilical venous and the umbilical arterial serum concentrations were lower than maternal venous concentrations.

Pregnant women in active labor have significantly higher midazolam plasma levels, a smaller volume of distribution and a lower clearance than pregnant women undergoing cesarean section or nonpregnant gynecological patients. When given immediately before cesarean section, midazolam can cause depression of the infant.

Lactation: Midazolam is excreted in human milk. Therefore, midazolam is not recommended for use in nursing mothers.

Patients with Special Conditions: Higher risk surgical patients or debilitated patients require lower dosages, whether as a premedicant or for i.v. sedation or induction of anesthesia.

Patients with chronic obstructive pulmonary disease may experience prolonged sedation and prolonged respiratory depression (see Contraindications).

Patients with congestive heart failure and obese subjects have a substantially prolonged elimination half-life and an increased volume of distribution of midazolam. Patients with chronic renal failure or severe alcoholic cirrhosis exhibit changes in elimination half-life, volume of distribution and total body clearance (see Pharmacology). Caution should therefore be exercised in administrating midazolam to these patients.

Drug Interactions: The hypnotic effect of i.v. midazolam and the risk of apnea are accentuated by premedication, particularly narcotics (e.g., morphine, meperidine and fentanyl), secobarbital, and the droperidol-fentanyl combination. Consequently, the dosage of midazolam should be adjusted according to the type and amount of premedication administered.

A slight reduction in induction dosage requirements of thiopental (about 13%) has been noted following i.m. use of midazolam for premedication.

The administration of midazolam has resulted in a dose dependent reduction of the minimum alveolar concentration of halothane required during maintenance of anesthesia.

Preliminary data, with a small number of subjects, reveal that midazolam appears to potentiate the effect of pancuronium.

Midazolam injection does not cause a clinically significant change in onset or duration of action of a single intubating dose of succinylcholine. Midazolam does not protect against the characteristic circulatory changes noted after administration of succinylcholine or pancuronium.

Midazolam has been used as an induction agent in conjunction with commonly used premedicants or drugs used during anesthesia and surgery (including atropine, scopolamine, glycopyrrolate, diazepam, hydroxyzine, succinylcholine and d-tubocurarine and other nondepolarizing muscle relaxants) or topical anesthetics (e.g., lidocaine).

Data from spontaneous reports as well as kinetic studies in humans indicate that midazolam may interact with compounds which affect or are also metabolized by the cytochrome P450 3A4 hepatic enzymes. Data indicate that these compounds (cimetidine, erythromycin, diltiazem, verapamil, ketoconazole and itraconazole) influence the pharmacokinetics of midazolam (increased C_{max} and AUC) and may lead to prolonged sedation. Therefore patients receiving the above compounds or others which inhibit P450 3A4 enzymes together with midazolam should be monitored for the first few hours after administration of midazolam.

Adverse Effects: See Warnings concerning serious cardiorespiratory events and possible paradoxical reactions.

Adverse Reactions in Adults: Sedative effects and fluctuations in vital signs were the most frequent findings following parenteral administration of midazolam injection. These are affected by the lightening or deepening of anesthesia, instrumentation, intubation and use of concomitant drugs. The more frequently encountered fluctuations in vital signs included decreased tidal volume and/or decreased respiratory rate and apnea, as well as variations in blood pressure and pulse rate. When used in i.v. sedation, midazolam tends to produce a higher incidence of fall in mean arterial pressure than diazepam.

The most frequently reported adverse reactions observed in association with the use of midazolam in clinical research programs are reported in Table V. Although adverse reactions may not have been observed in all clinical research programs, the possibility of their occurrence with the different clinical uses of midazolam cannot be excluded.

Other adverse reactions (not reported in previous table) occurring at a lower incidence, usually < 1% are: Cardiovascular: premature ventricular contractions, bigeminy, vasovagal episode, bradycardia, tachycardia, and nodal rhythm.

Respiratory: laryngospasm, bronchospasm, dyspnea, shallow respiration, hyperventilation and wheezing.

CNS/Neuromuscular: nervousness, restlessness, anxiety, argumentativeness, aggression, insomnia, nightmares; deep sedation, prolonged sedation, oversedation, disorientation, slurred speech, emergence delirium, agitation during emergence, prolonged emergence from anesthesia, dreaming during emergence; dysphoria, euphoria, anterograde amnesia, lightheadedness, feeling faint; tremors, muscle contractions, twitches and abnormal spontaneous muscular activity, tonic/clonic movements, athetoid movements; ataxia.

Gastrointestinal: acid taste, excessive salivation and retching.

Special Senses: blurred vision, diplopia, nystagmus, visual disturbance, difficulty focusing eyes, pinpoint pupils, cyclic movement of eyelids, ears blocked and loss of balance.

Dermatological: erythema, rash, pruritus and hives.

Hypersensitivity: allergic reactions, including anaphylactic shock.

Miscellaneous: muscle stiffness, toothache, yawning, cold feeling when drug injected and cool sensation in arm during infusion.

Adverse Reactions in Pediatric Patients: Limited information is available from published literature regarding the use of midazolam in pediatric patients. However, based on information obtained from published literature and spontaneous adverse reaction reporting, the safety profile in children more than 1 month of age appears to be very similar to that observed in adults.

The most frequent acute events were airway compromise and hypoventilation. This most often occurred when used in conjunction with opiates or other anesthetic agents. The next most common adverse event with long-term use was withdrawal syndrome. The following list shows the other reported side effects. This list is not exhaustive.

Respiratory: respiratory arrest, respiratory failure, apnea, hypoxia, oxygen desaturation. Danger of respiratory disorders may increase when midazolam is administered with opioids. Therefore the dosage of both agents should be reduced (see Warnings and Dosage).

Psychiatric: withdrawal syndrome, combative reaction, agitation, hallucination.

Central and Peripheral Nervous System: convulsions, excessive sedation, tonic/clonic convulsions, cerebral convulsion, lethargy. Convulsions occurred primarily in neonates (under 4 months old) and/or children with history of seizures.

Cardiovascular: hypotension, bradycardia, cardiac/cardiopulmonary arrest.

Miscellaneous: lack of efficacy, paradoxical response, therapeutic response decreased.

Local and Vein Tolerance: The incidence of local and vein tolerance observed in the early adult experience with midazolam is listed in Table VI (on following page).

In the pediatric patients similar observations as in adults have been made. Some of the most frequently reported findings include: rash, urticaria, erythema, hives, skin necrosis and wheals.

Laboratory Abnormalities: Isolated elevations in certain parameters of liver function (AST, ALT, alkaline phosphatase and total bilirubin), as well as isolated changes in total protein and albumin, have been reported.

Overdose: Symptoms and Treatment: The manifestations of midazolam overdosage are sedation, somnolence, confusion, impaired coordination, diminished reflexes, untoward effects on vital signs, coma and possible cardio-respiratory arrest.

Table V—Versed

Clinical Adverse Effects More Frequently Observed

		%			
Organ System	**Adverse Effect**	**I.M. Premed N=380**	**I.V. Sedation N=512**	**I.V. Induction N=1 073**	**I.V. ICU Sedation N=115**
Cardiovascular	Increased Mean Arterial Pressure	2.6	8.0	16.7	6.9
	Decreased Mean Arterial Pressure	6.3	29.9	30.8	17.0
	Hypotension				26.0[c]
	Increased Pulse Rate	7.1	29.9	36.0	
	Decreased Pulse Rate	9.5	16.8	12.6	
Respiratory	Increased Respiratory Rate/Tachypnea	11.5[a]	36.9	0.1	
	Decreased Respiratory Rate	10.8[a]	25.6	0.1	
	Apnea		1.0	22.9	
	Coughing		0.2	2.0	
	Respiratory Depression		0.2	25.0	
	Airway Obstruction		0.2	1.0	
CNS	Headache	1.3	0.8	2.0	
	Drowsiness		0.5	1.7	
	Excessive Sedation		0.6	1.6	
	Dizziness		0.2	1.2	
	Hallucination				2.8
	Agitation				1.8
	Confusion	0.3	0.6	0.9	2.8
Gastrointestinal	Hiccoughs	0.3	0.4[b]	6.0	0.9
	Nausea	0.5	0.8[b]	4.0	
	Emesis/Vomiting	0.5	0.6[b]	3.5	

[a]N=130.
[b]N=500.
[c]Hypotension during ICU Sedation was defined as systolic blood pressure ≤ 90 mmHg or diastolic blood pressure ≤ 50 mmHg or a clinically significant fall in blood pressure.

Table VI—Versed

Local and Vein Tolerance

Adverse Effects on Local and Vein Tolerance	% Incidence: I.M. Premed N=380	% Incidence: I.V. Sedation N=512	% Incidence: I.V. Induction N=1 073
Local			
Pain at site of injection	3.7	—	—
Pain during injection of drug	0.0	0.4	7.5
Induration at site of injection	0.5	—	—
Swelling at site of injection	0.0	0.0	0.2
Erythema at site of injection	0.5	—	—
Hive-like elevation at injection site	—	—	0.2
Warmth at injection site	—	—	0.1
Burning at injection site	—	—	0.1
Hematoma at i.v. site	—	—	0.3
Vein			
Tenderness of vein	0.0	1.4	8.0
Induration of vein	—	1.6	2.1
Redness of vein	0.0	1.4	3.4
Red wheal/flare along vein	—	—	0.1
Pain in vein after injection	—	—	0.1
Phlebitis	—	—	0.6
Thrombophlebitis	—	—	0.1

Treatment of overdosage is the same as that followed for overdosage with other benzodiazepines. Continuous monitoring of vital signs including ECG, should be immediately instituted and general supportive measures should be employed. Immediate attention should be given to the maintenance of an adequate airway and support of ventilation. If not already present, an i.v. infusion line should be established and further measures should be taken to provide critical care. Should hypotension develop, treatment may include i.v. fluid therapy, repositioning, and other appropriate countermeasures. Cardiopulmonary resuscitation may be required. At present, there is no information as to whether peritoneal dialysis, forced diuresis or hemodialysis are of value in the treatment of midazolam overdosage.

The benzodiazepine antagonist, flumazenil is a specific antidote in known or suspected overdose (for conditions of use see flumazenil product monograph).

Dosage: Midazolam injection should only be administered i.m. or i.v. (see Warnings). The dosage of midazolam must be carefully individualized. In elderly and debilitated patients, lower doses are required. The dosage should further be adjusted according to the type and amount of premedication used. **Excess doses or rapid or single bolus i.v. administration may result in respiratory depression and/or arrest particularly in elderly or debilitated patients (see Warnings).** Clinical experience has shown midazolam to be more potent than diazepam on a mg/kg basis.

Midazolam injection has been shown to cause dose related anterograde amnesia, an impairment or a lack of recall of events following administration of the drug.

Midazolam does not protect against the circulatory effects of succinylcholine administration or against the heart rate rise and/or blood pressure rise associated with endotracheal intubation under light general anesthesia.

For **i.m.** use, midazolam should be injected deep in a large muscle mass. **I.V.** midazolam should be administered only by a person trained in general anesthesia and should be used for sedation/anxiolysis/amnesia only in the presence of personnel skilled in early detection of hypoventilation, maintenance of a patent airway and support of ventilation. The necessary equipment and medications must be immediately available to ensure the safety of the procedures and the maintenance of respiratory and cardiovascular functions (see Warnings).

Midazolam injection for i.v. sedation prior to and during short endoscopic or short diagnostic procedures and direct current cardioversion, should always be administered slowly (see Warnings and I.V. Sedation). Rapid i.v. injection may cause respiratory depression or apnea requiring respiratory assistance or controlled ventilation.

Reactions such as agitation, involuntary movements, hyperactivity and combativeness have been reported. Should such reactions occur, the response to each dose of midazolam and all other drugs, including local anesthetics, should be evaluated before proceeding with the administration of the drug (see Warnings).

For induction of general anesthesia in healthy patients, the initial dose should be administered over 20 to 30 seconds for optimal effect. About 2 minutes must pass to see the effect of the dose. Extreme care should be taken to avoid intraarterial injection or extravasation.

Midazolam may be mixed in the same syringe with frequently used premedicants: morphine sulfate, meperidine HCl, atropine sulfate or scopolamine hydrobromide. However, if an opioid is mixed with midazolam, the initial doses of both products should be reduced and constant monitoring is recommended. Midazolam is compatible with 5% dextrose in water, normal saline, and lactated Ringer's solution. Both the 1 mg/mL and 5 mg/mL formulations may be diluted with normal saline or 5% dextrose in water.

Usual Recommended Adult Dosage: I.M. Premedication: For preoperative sedation and to impair memory of perioperative events: For premedication, the recommended dose is 0.07 to 0.08 mg/kg i.m. (usual dose is about 5 mg i.m. for an average adult) administered 30 to 60 minutes preoperatively. Lower doses should be used in elderly or debilitated patients. In a study of patients 60 years or older who did not receive concomitant narcotics, 2 to 3 mg of midazolam produced adequate sedation during the preoperative period. Some patients responded to doses as low as 1 mg. As with any potential respiratory depressant, these patients require observation for signs of cardiorespiratory depression after receiving i.m. midazolam. Onset of action is within 15 minutes, with peak effect occurring 30 to 60 minutes following injection. Midazolam can be administered concomitantly with atropine sulfate or scopolamine hydrobromide. When administered concomitantly with a narcotic, the dose of midazolam should be reduced.

I.V. Sedation (see Warnings): See Table VII. For short endoscopic or short diagnostic procedures and direct current cardioversion: **Midazolam 1 mg/mL formulation is recommended for i.v. sedation to facilitate slow injection.**

Midazolam can be used either alone or combined with a narcotic immediately before the procedure, with supplemental doses to maintain the desired level of sedation throughout the procedure. For peroral procedures, the use of an appropriate topical anesthetic is recommended. During routine diagnostic bronchoscopies, with no compromise of respiratory function, the use of narcotic premedication is recommended.

Administration: When used for i.v. sedation, midazolam should not be administered by rapid or single bolus i.v. administration (see Warnings).

Midazolam should be administered immediately prior to the procedure in small increments and titrated slowly until the desired sedative effect is achieved. An initial titration with a small dose, such as 2 to 2.5 mg (see Table V on previous page) **administered over a 2 to 3 minute period** is suggested for an average healthy adult. After waiting about 2 minutes, the dosage may be further titrated **in small increments of the initial dose** if necessary to the desired sedative effect. Wait about 2 minutes after each increment to fully evaluate the sedative effect. Additional maintenance doses may be given in increments of 25% of the initial dose to maintain the desired level of sedation, only by slow titration. The desired end point can usually be attained within 3 to 6 minutes, depending on the total dose administered and whether or not it is preceded by narcotic premedication. Narcotic premedication when indicated, results in less variability of patient response.

The dosage should be lowered in the elderly and debilitated, and in patients with limited pulmonary reserve (see Table V on previous page). Because the danger of underventilation or apnea is greatest in these patients and because peak effect may take longer, increments should be smaller and the rate of injections slower.

I.V. Induction of Anesthesia: See Table VIII on following page. For induction of general anesthesia before administration of other anesthetic agents: Individual response to midazolam is variable, particularly when a narcotic premedicant is not used. The dosage should be titrated according to the patient's age and clinical status.

Doses are administered over 20 to 30 seconds, allowing 2 minutes for effect.

ICU Sedation: For initiation and maintenance of ICU sedation in intubated, mechanically ventilated patients (see Table IX on following page).

Dosage and rate of infusion should be individualized to achieve the required level of sedation according to the patient's age and clinical status. In patients who are still sedated and/or who received large doses of narcotics, a bolus dose may not be necessary and the initial infusion rate of midazolam should be substantially decreased.

Recommended Pediatric Dosage: As a group, pediatric patients generally require higher doses of midazolam than do adults and younger children may require higher doses than older children. In obese individuals, the dose should be calculated based on ideal body weight. When midazolam is given in conjunction with opioids or other sedatives, the potential for respiratory depression/airway obstruction is increased. For appropriate patient monitoring, see Warnings. Midazolam should be administered as an induction agent only by a person trained in general anesthesia and should be used for sedation/anxiolysis/amnesia only in the presence of personnel skilled in early detection of hypoventilation, maintenance of a patent airway and support of ventilation (see Warnings).

Patients should be discharged in the care of a responsible individual.

I.M. Usual Pediatric Dose: For sedation prior to anesthesia or procedures (for longer and/or more stimulating procedures, i.m. midazolam can be used to facilitate insertion of an i.v. catheter for titration of additional medication). Sedation with i.m. midazolam is age and dose dependent: higher doses may result in deeper and more prolonged sedation. Doses of 0.1 to 0.15 mg/kg are usually effective and do not prolong emergence from general anesthesia. For more anxious patients,

Table VII—Versed

I.V. Sedation

Patient Type	Unpremedicated Patient: Initial Dose	Unpremedicated Patient: Total Dose	Premedicated Patient (Narcotics or CNS Depressants)
Patients less than age 55	No more than 2 to 2.5 mg	- Some patients may respond to as little as a total dose of 1 mg - More than a total dose of 5 mg is not usually necessary - Do not exceed 0.1 mg/kg	Reduce dosage by about 30%
Patients age 55 or older; Debilitated patients; Chronically ill patients; Patients with limited pulmonary reserve	No more than 1 to 1.5 mg	- Some patients may respond to as little as a total dose of 1 mg - More than a total dose of 3.5 mg is not usually necessary - Do not exceed 0.07 mg/kg	Reduce dosage by about 30% (i.e., 60% less than for healthy young unpremedicated patients)

Versed (cont'd)

Table VIII—Versed

I.V. Induction of Anesthesia

Patient Type	Unpremedicated Patients: Initial Dose	Unpremedicated Patients: Increments	Premedicated Patients (Narcotics or CNS Depressants): Initial Dose	Premedicated Patients (Narcotics or CNS Depressants): Increments
Patients less than age 55	0.3–0.35 mg/kg	**If needed** to complete induction, increments of approximately 25% of the initial dose may be used	0.15–0.35 mg/kg 0.25 mg/kg will usually suffice	**If needed** to complete induction, increments of approximately 25% of the intitial dose may be used
Patients age 55 or older (ASA I or II surgical patients)	0.3 mg/kg		0.2 mg/kg	
Patients with severe systemic disease or other debilitation	0.2–0.25 mg/kg In some cases as little as 0.15 mg/kg will suffice	The need for increment doses to complete induction must be evaluated by the anesthesiologist	0.15–0.2 mg/kg In some cases as little as 0.15 mg/kg will suffice	The need for increment doses to complete induction must be evaluated by the anesthesiologist

Table IX—Versed

ICU Sedation

Patient Type	Bolus Dose	Initial Infusion Dose	Maximum Dose	Increments
No prior Narcotics or CNS Depressants	0.015–0.03 mg/kg	0.01–0.03 mg/kg/hr	0.07–0.15 mg/kg/hr	For optimal sedation the maintenance infusion rate may be increased or decreased by increments of 25–50% of the initial dose at intervals of 30 minutes
Prior/ Concomitant Narcotics or CNS Depressants	0.015–0.03 mg/kg	0.01–0.03 mg/kg/hr	0.07 mg/kg/hr	

doses up to 0.5 mg/kg may be needed. Midazolam and an opioid should not be mixed as a premedication, however if required then constant monitoring is recommended. Should both be required the inital dose of each must be reduced and the second agent of the two should be administered i.v. on arrival at the procedure area.

I.V. by Intermittent Injection: Usual Pediatric Dose: For sedation prior to and during procedures or prior to anesthesia: For all patients titrate slowly to the desired effect. The initial dose should be administered over 2 to 3 minutes. Wait an additional 2 to 3 minutes to fully evaluate the sedative effect before initiating a procedure or repeating a dose. If further sedation is necessary, continue to titrate with small increments until the appropriate level of sedation is achieved. See Table X.

The dose of midazolam must be reduced in patients premedicated with opioids or other sedative agents including midazolam.

Continuous I.V. Infusion: For sedation in critical care settings: Usual Pediatric Dose: To initiate sedation, an i.v. loading dose of 0.05 to 0.2 mg/kg administered over at least 2 to 3 minutes can be used to establish the desired clinical effect. **I.V. loading doses should not be used in neonates** (midazolam should not be administered as a rapid i.v. dose to preterm and term neonates. See below for Preterm and Neonatal Dosing Information). This loading dose may be followed by a continuous i.v. infusion to maintain the effect. Based on pharmacokinetic parameters and reported clinical experience, continuous i.v. infusions of midazolam should be initiated at a rate of 0.001 to 0.002 mg/kg/min (1 to 2 μg/kg/min). The rate of infusion can be increased or decreased as required, or supplemental i.v. doses of midazolam can be administered to increase or maintain the desired effect. Frequent assessment using standard pain/sedation scales is recommended. Drug elimination may be delayed in patients receiving erythromycin and/or other P450IIIa enzyme inhibitors (see Precautions, Drug Interactions) and in patients with liver dysfunction, renal dysfunction, low cardiac output (especially those requiring ionotropic support), and in neonates. Hypotension may be observed in patients who are critically ill, particularly those receiving opioids and/or when midazolam is rapidly administered.

When initiating an infusion with midazolam in hemodynamically compromised patients, the usual loading dose of midazolam should be titrated in small increments, separated by 2 to 3 minutes, and the patient monitored for hemodynamic instability, e.g., hypotension, respiratory rate and oxygen saturation.

The dose of midazolam must be reduced in patients premedicated with opioids or other sedative agents including midazolam.

Neonatal Dosage: Based on the pharmacokinetic parameters and reported clinical experience in preterm and term neonates, continuous i.v. infusion of midazolam should be initiated at a rate of 0.0005 to 0.001 mg/kg/min (0.5 to 1 μg/kg/min). I.V. loading doses should not be used in neonates, rather the infusion may be run more rapidly for the first several hours to establish therapeutic plasma levels. Hypotension may be observed in patients who are critically ill and in preterm and term infants, particularly those receiving fentanyl and/or when midazolam is administered rapidly. Due to an increased risk of apnea, extreme caution is advised when sedating preterm and former preterm patients in combination with regional anesthesia.

Stability and Storage: The recommended storage temperature for midazolam injection is 15 to 30°C. As with all parenteral drug products whenever solutions and container permit, midazolam injection should be inspected for particulate matter and discoloration prior to administration.

Reconstitution: None required.

Stability of Solutions: Midazolam injection may be mixed and is stable for 30 minutes in the same syringe with frequently used premedicants: morphine sulfate, meperidine HCl, atropine sulfate or scopolamine hydrobromide.

Table X—Versed

Pediatric Dosing Table

Age of Child	Initial Dose	Total Dose	Comments
6 months-5 years	0.05-0.1 mg/kg	0.6 mg/kg	The initial dose should be administered over 2-3 minutes, wait for an additional 2-3 minutes to fully evaluate the sedative effect before initiating a procedure or repeating a dose. If further sedation is necessary, continue to titrate with small increments until the appropriate level of sedation is achieved
6-12 years	0.025-0.05 mg/kg	0.4 mg/kg	
12-17 years	Dose as Adults		

Midazolam injection is compatible and stable for 24 hours with 5% dextrose in water, and normal saline. The potency of midazolam decreases when mixed with lactated Ringer's solution (or Hartmann's solution) and should be used within 4 hours.

There is no evidence of the adsorption of midazolam onto the plastic of infusion apparatus or syringes.

Supplied: 1 mg/mL: Each mL contains: midazolam HCl equivalent to midazolam 1 mg. Nonmedicinal ingredients: sodium chloride and disodium edetate, benzyl alcohol as preservative and hydrochloric acid or sodium hydroxide to adjust pH. Paraben- and sulfite-free. Vials of 2, 5 and 10 mL. Boxes of 10.

5 mg/mL: Each mL contains: midazolam HCl equivalent to midazolam 5 mg. Nonmedicinal ingredients: sodium chloride and disodium edetate, benzyl alcohol as preservative and hydrochloric acid or sodium hydroxide to adjust pH. Paraben- and sulfite-free. Vials of 1, 2 and 10 mL. Boxes of 10.

Reviewed 1999

VERSEL®

TCD

Selenium Sulfide

Tineacide

Supplied: Each bottle of lotion contains: selenium sulfide USP 2.5% w/v in a detergent-free, pH 5.0, water-washable lotion. Nonmedicinal ingredients: captan, citric acid anhydrous, fragrance, germaben II, glycerin, hydrated silica, magnesium aluminium silicate, PEG 400, polysorbate 80, purified water, sodium phosphate dibasic anhydrous, titanium dioxide and xantham gum. Bottles of 125 mL. Protect from heat.

VESANOID™ Ⓟ

Roche

All-trans Retinoic Acid
Tretinoin

Differentiation Inducing Agent

Caution: All-trans retinoic acid should be administered to patients with APL only under the strict supervision of a physician who is experienced in the treatment of hematological/oncological diseases.

Pharmacology: All-trans retinoic acid is a natural metabolite of retinol and belongs to the class of compounds known as retinoids, which are structurally related to vitamin A and comprise natural and synthetic analogs. In vitro studies with all-trans retinoic acid have demonstrated induction of differentiation and inhibition of cell proliferation in transformed hemopoietic cell lines, including human myeloid leukemia cell lines.

Acute promyelocytic leukemia (APL) is associated with a nonrandom chromosomal abnormality characterized by balanced and reciprocal translocations between the long arm of chromosomes 15 and 17 [t(15;17)(q22;q21)]. The gene encoding the retinoic acid receptor-alpha (RAR-α) is located on chromosome 17. A previously unidentified gene, PML, that may act as a transcription factor, is located on chromosome 15. The 15;17 translocation fuses the genes for PML and RAR-α, resulting in the synthesis of 2 reciprocal fusion transcripts, PML/RAR-α (found in all patients) and RAR-α/PML (found in about 2/3 of patients). PML/RAR-α may inhibit the differentiation of myeloid cells, resulting in carcinogenesis, an effect which may be overcome by the use of high doses of all-trans retinoic acid. Orally administered all-trans retinoic acid induces a high rate of complete remissions in patients with APL.

Pharmacokinetics: All-trans retinoic acid is an endogenous metabolite of vitamin A and is normally present in plasma at concentrations of 2 to 4 ng/mL. All-trans retinoic acid is transported directly via the portal system rather than through the lymphatics and thus absorption does not require specific transport mechanisms. All-trans retinoic acid is highly lipophilic with more than 95% of total drug concentration bound to plasma protein. All-trans retinoic acid is primarily metabolized by liver enzymes and is converted to the 13-cis isomer. Oxidation by P450 isoenzymes leads to the corresponding 4-hydroxy and 4-oxo-compounds. After glucuronidation, these metabolites are excreted in the urine and bile.

Following a single dose of radiolabelled all-trans retinoic acid, about 30% of the total radioactivity was recovered in the feces and about 60% in the urine. Nearly the entire dose was excreted within 3 to 6 days.

Single Dose: The pharmacokinetics of all-trans retinoic acid were investigated in healthy volunteers following a single oral dose of 40 mg of all-trans retinoic acid and in patients with acute promyelocytic leukemia (APL) treated with 45 mg/m^2. Maximum plasma concentrations of all-trans retinoic acid were reached within 1 to 2 hours in the APL patients and within 3 to 4 hours in the healthy volunteers. Large intersubject variability was observed. Plasma concentrations declined mono-exponentially with a mean elimination half-life of 0.71 hours. Endogenous levels (2 to 4 ng/mL) were reached 7 to 12 hours after dosing.

Multiple Doses: Multiple oral doses of all-trans retinoic acid were associated with a significant (about 2 fold) decrease in both the peak plasma levels and the AUC levels, after 2 to 6 weeks of treatment. These changes were associated with a 10 fold increase in urinary excretion of 4-oxo all-trans retinoic acid glucuronide.

The administration of ketoconazole, an inhibitor of the P450 enzyme system, after multiple doses of all-trans retinoic acid, resulted in a greater mean plasma all-trans retinoic acid AUC than after the administration of all-trans retinoic acid alone.

Pharmacokinetics in Pediatric Patients: A phase I trial of all-trans retinoic acid administered orally twice-daily for treatment courses of 28 days was performed in pediatrics. Cohorts of at least 3 patients were entered at successive all-trans retinoic acid dose levels (from 45 to 80 mg/m^2/day, with a twice a day dosing regimen) until dose-limiting toxicity was consistently observed. Twenty-one patients with a median age of 14 years and various types of tumors including 2 patients with APL were entered into the trial.

Pharmacokinetics were determined in 18 patients on day 1 and in 7 patients on day 1 and day 28. Time to peak plasma concentrations was between 1 and 4 hours after dosing. Peak plasma concentrations of all-trans retinoic acid of 0.59, 0.62 and 1.64 μM (180, 190 and 490 ng/mL) were observed following doses of 22.5, 30 and 40 mg/m^2. AUC values for these doses were 1.29, 1.13 and 3.35 μM (387, 339 and 1 005 ng.h/mL), respectively. Peak plasma concentrations and AUC values did not appear to increase in proportion to dose. A greater than 3 fold increase in AUC was observed following a 30% increase in dose (30 to 40 mg/m^2). The average terminal half-life was 0.7 hours. The AUC on day 1 was significantly greater than the AUC on day 28 (mean decrease 78%±30 SD). Quantifiable concentrations of 4-oxo metabolites of all-trans retinoic acid were not observed.

Pharmacokinetics in renal and hepatic impairment: The pharmacokinetics of all-trans retinoic acid in patients with compromised kidney or liver function have not been studied.

Indications: For the induction of remission in acute promyelocytic leukemia (APL; FAB classification AML-M3). Previously untreated patients, as well as patients who relapsed after, or were refractory to, standard chemotherapy (daunomycin and cytosine arabinoside or equivalent therapies) may be treated with all-trans retinoic acid. Upon achievement of complete remission, full-dose consolidation chemotherapy should be employed. Among patients maintained on all-trans retinoic acid, a loss of responsiveness to all-trans retinoic acid, has been reported, with a median time to relapse of 4 to 6 months.

Contraindications: *Pregnancy:* All-trans retinoic acid is highly teratogenic; therefore it is contraindicated during pregnancy. All-trans retinoic acid must not be used by women of child-bearing potential unless effective contraception is practiced for at least 1 month before beginning therapy, during therapy and at least 1 month following discontinuation of therapy.

All-trans retinoic acid is contraindicated in patients with a known hypersensitivity to all-trans retinoic acid or related compounds.

Warnings: All-trans retinoic acid should be administered to patients with APL only under the strict supervision of a physician who is experienced in the treatment of hematological/oncological diseases.

Retinoic Acid Syndrome: In many patients (20 to 25%) with acute promyelocytic leukemia (APL) treated with all-trans retinoic acid, a syndrome may occur characterized by some or all of the following symptoms: fever, dyspnea, shortness of breath, acute respiratory distress, pulmonary infiltrates, hyperleukocytosis, hypotension, pleural effusions, and hepatic, renal and multiorgan failure (Retinoic Acid syndrome). Untreated, this syndrome can be fatal. If symptoms of the Retinoic Acid syndrome become apparent, treatment with a short course of high doses of corticosteroids (i.e., dexamethasone) should be initiated immediately particularly in patients where the syndrome is suspected but hyperleukocytosis is not observed.

The Retinoic Acid syndrome may also be prevented by initiating treatment with concomitant full-dose chemotherapy if a significant increase in the leukocyte count is observed. The following therapeutic regimen is recommended: patients initiating all-trans retinoic acid therapy with a low leukocyte count ($<5\times10^9$/L), concomitant full-dose chemotherapy should be initiated: on day 5 of all-trans retinoic acid treatment when leukocyte count exceeds 6.0×10^9/L; on day 10 of all-trans retinoic acid treatment when leukocyte count exceeds 10.0×10^9/L; on day 15 of all-trans retinoic acid treatment when leukocyte count exceeds 15×10^9/L.

Patients initiating all-trans retinoic acid therapy with an elevated leukocyte count ($>10\times10^9$/L) concomitant chemotherapy should be started immediately.

Mortality and morbidity is reduced by following these treatment recommendations in patients with this syndrome. All-trans retinoic acid therapy can continue.

Pregnancy:

Pregnancy: All-trans retinoic acid is highly teratogenic. Its use is contraindicated in pregnant women and women who might become pregnant during or within 1 month of the cessation of treatment. There is an extremely high risk that a deformed infant will result if pregnancy occurs while taking all-trans retinoic acid in any amount even for short periods or within 1 month of its discontinuation. Potentially all exposed fetuses can be affected. Therapy with all-trans retinoic acid should only be started in female patients if each of the following conditions is met:

- The patient is suffering from life-threatening malignancies. She is informed by her physicians of the hazards of becoming pregnant during and within 1 month after treatment with all-trans retinoic acid.
- She is capable of complying with the mandatory contraception measures.
- Every woman of childbearing potential who is to undergo treatment with all-trans retinoic acid uses effective contraception for 4 weeks before, during and for 1 month after discontinuation of treatment with all-trans retinoic acid.
- Therapy should not begin until the second or third day of the next normal menstrual period.
- A negative pregnancy test result must be obtained within the 2 weeks before commencement of treatment. It is advisable to perform additional pregnancy tests at monthly intervals during therapy.

Should pregnancy occur in spite of these precautions, during treatment with all-trans retinoic acid or within 1 month after its discontinuation, there is a high risk of severe malformation of the fetus.

All these measures should be considered in relationship to the severity of the disease and the urgency of the treatment.

Lactation: Nursing should be discontinued if therapy with all-trans retinoic acid is initiated.

Precautions: Drug Interactions: Drugs affecting the hepatic cytochrome P450 enzyme system function may interact with all-trans retinoic acid, leading to a change of blood levels.

The administration of ketoconazole, an inhibitor of the P450 enzyme system, after multiple doses of all-trans retinoic acid, resulted in a greater mean plasma all-trans retinoic acid AUC than after the administration of all-trans retinoic acid alone. Cytochrome P450 inhibitors, such as ketoconazole, may potentially enhance the therapeutic efficacy of all-trans retinoic acid.

Renal and Hepatic Impairment: The pharmacokinetics of all-trans acid in patients with compromised kidney or liver function have not been studied. The need for dosage adjustments in patients with renal or hepatic impairment is unknown.

Adverse Effects: The safety profile of all-trans retinoic acid has been evaluated retrospectively in a small number of patients.

In persons treated with the recommended daily doses of all-trans retinoic acid, the following adverse events were observed frequently (in about 1/4 of the patients or more) signs and symptoms of the hypervitaminosis A syndrome (including xeroderma, lip and mouth dryness, cheilitis, rash, edema, nausea, vomiting and bone pain). Headache, fever, shivering, fatigue, back pain, chest pain, dyspnea, coughing, abdominal pain, dermal bleeding, and elevation in serum triglycerides, cholesterol and transaminases may also be observed.

The following adverse events, considered remotely, possibly or probably related to drug treatment have been reported in less than 1/4 of all APL patients treated with all-trans retinoic acid in the clinical trials:

Autonomic Nervous System: tachycardia, hypertension, hypotension, flushing, pallor, red extremities.

Body as a Whole: generalized pain, abdominal distention, post traumatic pain, chest discomfort, hypothermia.

Cardiovascular System: cardiac failure, cyanosis, heart enlarged.

Central and Peripheral Nervous System: dizziness, confusion, intracranial hypertension, light headed feeling, flank pain, numbness of extremities, abnormal gait, leg weakness, neurologic reaction, inguinal pain, visual field defects, hyporeflexia.

Dermatological: pruritus, increased sweating, alopecia, dry scalp, nasal dryness, nail disorder, photosensitivity reaction, xerophthalmia.

Gastrointestinal: abdominal pain, diarrhea, constipation, blisters in the mouth, stomach upset, dysphagia, buccal mucosa ulceration, stomatitis, flatulence, ulcer.

Metabolic and Nutritional Disorders: weight changes, edema of extremities, acidosis, gout, dehydration, fluid overload, moonface.

Musculoskeletal: musculoskeletal pain.

Platelet, Bleeding and Clotting: disseminated intravascular coagulation (DIC), nosebleed and other bleeding disorders.

Psychiatric: generalized weakness, anxiety, lethargy, depression, malaise, insomnia, anorexia, agitation, forgetfulness.

Resistance Mechanism Disorders: infection, septicemia, moniliasis.

Respiratory: pleural effusion, nasal congestion, pharyngitis, rale, respiratory insufficiency, wheezing expiratory, pneumonia, respiratory distress, tachypnea, pharynx irritation, pulmonary infiltration, hypoxia, sinusitis, bronchial asthma.

Special Senses: blurred vision, visual disturbance, photophobia, conjunctivitis, decreased vision, changes in visual acuity, ear fullness, earache, ear buzzing.

Urinary: dysuria, kidney failure, urinary tract infection, micturition frequency, renal insufficiency, cystitis.

Based on the information presently available, these adverse events do not represent permanent or irreversible hazards. It may be advisable to interrupt or discontinue the therapy, depending on the alternative options available to the patient.

Symptoms of the Retinoic Acid syndrome in APL have been frequently reported and may be life-threatening unless treated (see Warnings).

Overdose: Symptoms and Treatment: Cases of acute overdosage with all-trans retinoic acid have not been reported. Cases of overdose would be expected to show largely reversible effects characteristic of hypervitaminosis A. The recommended dose is one-third of the maximum tolerated dose in solid tumor patients and below the maximum tolerated dose in children.

Dosage: A total daily dose of 45 mg/m^2 body surface divided in 2 equal doses is recommended for oral administration to APL patients, including pediatric and geriatric patients. Treatment should be continued for 30 to 90 days until complete remission has been achieved. After complete remission, standard chemotherapy should be initiated immediately.

Supplied: Each oval shaped, soft gelatin capsule, one half reddish-brown opaque and the other half brownish-yellow opaque, contains: tretinoin 10 mg. Nonmedicinal ingredients: gelatin, glycerol, hydrogenated hydrolyzed starch, hydrogenated soybean oil, iron oxide, mannitol, partially hydrogenated soybean oil, sorbitol, soybean oil, titanium dioxide and yellow beeswax. Bottles of 100. Keep the bottle tightly closed. Store at 15 to 30°C. Protect from light.

(Shown in Product Recognition Section)

VEXOL™ Ⓟ

Alcon

Rimexolone

Corticosteroid

Pharmacology: Rimexolone is an anti-inflammatory corticosteroid. Corticosteroids suppress the inflammatory response to a variety of inciting agents of a mechanical, chemical, or immunological nature. They inhibit edema, cellular infiltration, capillary dilatation, fibroblastic proliferation, deposition of collagen and late cicatrization. Corticosteroids are capable of producing a rise in intraocular pressure in susceptible individuals.

Placebo-controlled clinical studies demonstrated that rimexolone ophthalmic suspension is efficacious for the treatment of anterior chamber inflammation following cataract surgery.

In 2 controlled clinical trials, rimexolone 1% ophthalmic suspension demonstrated clinical equivalence to 1% prednisolone acetate in reducing uveitic inflammation.

Vexol (cont'd)

In a controlled 6-week study of steroid responsive subjects, the time to raise intraocular pressure was similar for rimexolone 1% ophthalmic suspension and 0.1% fluorometholone given 4 times daily.

Pharmacokinetics: As with other topically administered ophthalmic drugs, rimexolone 1% ophthalmic suspension is absorbed systemically. Studies in normal volunteers dosed bilaterally once every hour during waking hours for 1 week have demonstrated serum concentrations ranging from less than 80 pg/mL to 470 pg/mL. The mean serum concentrations were approximately 130 pg/mL. Serum concentrations were at or near steady state after 5 to 7 hourly doses.

After decreasing the dosing frequency to once every 2 hours while awake during the second week of administration, mean serum concentrations were approximately 100 pg/mL. The serum half-life of rimexolone could not be reliably estimated due to the large number of samples below the quantitation limit of the assay (80 pg/mL). However, based on the time required to reach steady state, the half-life appears to be short (1 to 2 hours).

Based upon in vivo and in vitro preclinical metabolism studies, and on in vitro results with human liver preparations, rimexolone undergoes extensive metabolism.

Following i.v. administration of radio-labeled rimexolone to rats, greater than 80% of the dose is excreted via the feces as rimexolone and metabolites. Metabolites have been shown to be less active than parent drug, or inactive in human glucocorticoid receptor binding assays.

Indications: For the treatment of postoperative inflammation following ocular surgery and for the treatment of anterior uveitis.

Contraindications: Epithelial herpes simplex keratitis (dendritic keratitis), vaccinia, varicella, and most other viral diseases of cornea and conjunctiva; mycobacterial infection of the eye; fungal diseases of the eye; acute purulent untreated infections which, like other diseases caused by microorganisms, may be masked or enhanced by the presence of the steroid; and those persons with hypersensitivity to any component of the formulation.

Warnings: Not for injection. Use in the treatment of herpes simplex infection requires great caution and frequent slit-lamp examinations. Prolonged use may result in ocular hypertension/glaucoma, damage to the optic nerve, defects in visual acuity and visual fields, and posterior subcapsular cataract formation. Prolonged use may also result in secondary ocular infections due to suppression of host response. Acute purulent infections of the eye may be masked or exacerbated by the presence of corticosteroid medication. In those diseases causing thinning of the cornea or sclera, perforation has been known to occur with topical steroids. It is advisable that the intraocular pressure be checked frequently.

Precautions: General: Fungal infections of the cornea are particularly prone to develop coincidentally with long-term local steroid application. Fungus invasion must be considered in any persistent corneal ulceration where a steroid has been or is in use.

Information for the Patient: Do not touch dropper tip to any surface, as this may contaminate the suspension.

Carcinogenesis, Mutagenesis, Impairment of Fertility: Rimexolone has been shown to be nonmutagenic in a battery of in vitro and in vivo mutagenicity assays. Fertility and reproductive capability were not impaired in a study in rats with plasma levels (42 ng/mL) approximately 200 times those obtained in clinical studies after topical administration (<0.2 ng/mL). Long-term studies have not been conducted in animals or humans to evaluate the carcinogenic potential of rimexolone.

Pregnancy: Rimexolone has been shown to be teratogenic and embryotoxic in rabbits following s.c. administration at the lowest dose tested (0.5 mg/kg/day, approximately 2 times the recommended human ophthalmic dose). Corticosteroids are recognized to cause fetal resorptions and malformations in animals.

There are no adequate and well-controlled studies in pregnant women. Rimexolone ophthalmic suspension should be used in pregnant women only if the potential benefits to the mother justifies the potential risk to the fetus.

Lactation: It is not known whether topical ophthalmic administration of corticosteroids could result in sufficient systemic absorption to produce detectable quantities in human breast milk. Nevertheless, caution should be exercised when topical corticosteroids are administered to a nursing woman; a decision should be made whether to discontinue nursing or discontinue therapy, taking into consideration the importance of the drug to the mother.

Children: Safety and effectiveness in children have not been established.

Drug Interactions: No drug interactions or incompatibilities were identified during the clinical development program.

Adverse Effects: Reactions associated with ophthalmic steroids include elevated intraocular pressure which may be associated with optic nerve damage, visual acuity and field defects, posterior subcapsular cataract formation, secondary ocular infection from pathogens including herpes simplex, and perforation of the globe where there is thinning of the cornea or sclera.

Ocular adverse reactions occurring in 1 to 5% of patients in clinical studies of rimexolone ophthalmic suspension included blurred vision (2.9%), discharge (2.4%), discomfort (1.8%), ocular pain (1.4%), increased intraocular pressure (1.1%) and foreign body sensation (1.1%). Other ocular related adverse reactions occurring in less than 1% of patients included hyperemia, ocular pruritus, sticky sensation, increased fibrin, dry eye, conjunctival edema, corneal staining, keratitis, tearing, photophobia, edema, irritation, corneal ulcer, browache, lid margin crusting, corneal edema, infiltrate and corneal erosion.

Nonocular adverse reactions were rare and occurred in less than 2% of patients. These included headache, hypotension, rhinitis, pharyngitis and taste perversion.

Overdose: Symptoms and Treatment: Discontinue medication when heavy or protracted use is suspected. A topical overdosage may be flushed from the eye(s) with warm tap water.

Dosage: Postoperative Inflammation: Apply 1 to 2 drops of ophthalmic suspension into the conjunctival sac of the affected eye 4 times daily beginning 24 hours after surgery and continuing throughout the first 2 weeks of the postoperative period. Uveitis: Apply 1 to 2 drops of ophthalmic suspension into the conjunctival sac of the affected eye every hour during waking hours for the first week, 1 drop every 2 hours during waking hours of the second week, 4 times per day during the third week, then 3 times per day during the first 4 days of week 4 and then twice per day during the last 3 days of week 4.

Information for the Patient: See Blue Section—Information for the Patient "Vexol".

Supplied: Each mL of sterile, multidose topical ophthalmic suspension, contains: rimexolone 1%. Preservative: benzalkonium chloride 0.01%. Nonmedicinal ingredients: carbomer 934P, edetate disodium, mannitol, polysorbate 80, purified water, sodium chloride, sodium hydroxide and/or hydrochloric acid to adjust pH. Plastic Drop-Tainer dispensers of 5 and 10 mL. Store upright between 2 and 30°C.

Reviewed 1997

VIADERM-K.C. Pr

Taro

Triamcinolone Acetonide—Neomycin—Nystatin—Gramicidin

Topical Dermatoses Therapy

Supplied: Cream: Each g contains: triamcinolone acetonide 1 mg, neomycin base (as sulfate) 2.5 mg, gramicidin 250 μg, nystatin 100 000 units. It is formulated in a perfumed aqueous vanishing cream base which permits its use even in most intertriginous areas. Nonmedicinal ingredients: aluminum hydroxide wet gel, glyceryl monostearate, methylparaben, polyethylene glycol-400 monostearate, polyoxyethylene fatty alcohol ether, polysorbate 60, propylene glycol, propylparaben, simethicone emulsion, sorbic acid, sorbitol solution, titanium dioxide, white petrolatum and purified water. Tubes of 15, 30 and 60 g. Jars of 454 g.

Ointment: Each g contains: triamcinolone acetonide 1 mg, neomycin base (as sulfate) 2.5 mg, gramicidin 250 μg, nystatin 100 000 units. It is formulated in a protective emollient ointment base of petrolatum and mineral oil. Tubes of 15 and 30 g. Jars of 400 g.

VIASPAN™

DuPont Pharma

Cold Storage Solution

Indications: For the flushing and cold storage of organs including kidney, liver and pancreas at the time of their removal from the donor in preparation for storage, transportation and eventual transplantation into a recipient.

After precooling the solution to approximately 2 to 6°C in ice, the cold solution is used to flush the isolated organ immediately before removal from the donor and/or immediately after removal from the donor. The solution is then left in the organ vasculature during hypothermic storage and transportation. This solution is to be used for cold storage of the organ and not for continuous machine perfusion. Use of the solution at the recommended temperatures will effectively cool the organ and should reduce its metabolic requirements.

Contraindications: There are no known contraindications when used as directed.

Warnings: Not for direct injection or i.v. infusion.

Precautions: Before reperfusion is effected in the recipient, the donor organ **must be** flushed free of the cold storage solution using a physiological solution to prevent occurrence in the recipient of potentially serious cardiovascular complications such as hyperkalemic cardiac arrest or bradyarrythmia. Because of the high concentration of potassium in the solution, precautions must be taken during donor organ retrieval to avoid cardiac arrest.

Viaspan contains variable amounts of visible and subvisible particles (primarily 5 to 100 microns in size) which have been identified as stearate and palmitate fatty acid salts. Stearates and palmitates are used in manufacturing the bags in which Viaspan is distributed (see Dosage, Preparation and Administration for filtration instructions.)

Viaspan includes components (allopurinol and pentafraction) which individually have caused hypersensitivity reactions in patients. Additionally, the additives recommended for use with Viaspan (penicillin, insulin, and dexamethasone) have individually been associated with hypersensitivity reactions in patients. Physicians should consult individual drug labelling and be alert to treat possible reactions.

Adverse Effects: Cardiovascular complications such as bradyarrhythmia have been reported in cases where the organ has been reflushed with fresh solution within a short period (1 to 3 hours) prior to release of vascular anastomosis clamps in the recipient, or when inadequate flush out of the solution has occurred.

A few anecdotal reports when Viaspan was used in liver graft preservation described clinical problems including hepatic functional changes, poor outcomes including death, and biopsies showing ischemic damage in the liver with or without signs of mild rejection. Any relationship between these clinical problems and Viaspan is unknown.

Dosage: Preparation and Administration: Cool the solution between 2 and 6°C in ice. Remove overwrap prior to use. Check bags for leaks by squeezing containers firmly. If leaks are found, discard solution containers. With the overwrap removed, perform a visual inspection of the solution for particulate matter and do not use if obvious particulate matter, precipitates, or contamination is evident in the solution. Bags which pass visual inspection **must** be filtered at the time of use with an in-line Pall Blood Transfusion Filter (No. SQ40S) as instructed below. **Only this filter is recommended for use with Viaspan.**

Immediately prior to use, to formulate the final solution, aseptically add the following additives: 1) penicillin G 200 000 units, 2) regular insulin 40 units, 3) dexamethasone 16 mg.

Glutathione, one of the components of Viaspan, oxidizes during storage. If desired an additional 0.922 g/L of glutathione may be added as a freshly prepared solution of reduced glutathione immediately prior to use.

Remove protective cap from outlet port of filter and insert spike from the administration set into port with twisting motion. Open clamp on administration set. Remove twist-off plug from bag port designated "delivery set port." Hold the administration set vertically above the solution bag, then squeeze solution bag to fill filter and administration set. Close the clamp.

Prior to connection to the organ, the solution container should be suspended from a sufficient height to allow for a steady stream of solution and to produce flow rates of at least 30 mL/min during flushing. Open the clamp to begin flushing. Flushing should be continued until the organ is uniformly pale and the effluent is relatively clear. One filter should be used per bag, and filters must not be reused.

Suggested Minimum Volumes: In situ aortic flush: adults, 2 to 4 L; infants, 50 mL/kg.

Ex vivo infusion: Liver (via portal vein and biliary tree): adults, 1 200 mL; infants, 50 mL/kg. Pancreas or kidney: adults, 300 to 500 mL; infants, 150 to 250 mL.

Additional solution should be dispensed into the container holding the organ. Seal the container aseptically. The organ storage container should be maintained within a well-insulated transport container. Ice should be used to surround the organ storage container, but should not be used within the container, where the ice could come into direct contact with the organ. Donor organs must be flushed free of Viaspan prior to anastomosis (see Precautions). In order to minimize residues of the solution in the liver, just prior to anastomosis, flush 1 L of lactated Ringer's through the hepatic portal vein.

Supplied: Each L of clear, light yellow, sterile, nonpyrogenic solution for hypothermic flushing and storage of organs contains: pentafraction 50 g, lactobionic acid 35.83 g, potassium phosphate monobasic 3.4 g, magnesium sulfate heptahydrate 1.23 g, raffinose pentahydrate 17.83 g, adenosine 1.34 g, allopurinol 0.136 g, total glutathione 0.922 g, potassium hydroxide 5.61 g, sodium hydroxide and/or hydrochloric acid adjust to pH 7.4, water for injection q.s. The solution has an approximate calculated osmolarity of 320 mOsM, a sodium concentration of 29 mEq/L, and a potassium concentration of 125 mEq/L, and a pH of approximately 7.4 at room temperature. Litre bags of 1 000 mL.

Store product at refrigerated temperature (2 to 8°C) until use. Avoid excessive heat. Do not freeze the solution, and do not use if frozen. Do not use if discolored or if obvious particulate matter, precipitates, or contamination is evident in the solution.

VIBRA-TABS™ Ⓟ

Pfizer

Doxycycline Hyclate

Antibiotic

Pharmacology: Doxycycline hyclate is a broad-spectrum antibiotic and is active against a wide range of gram-negative and gram-positive organisms. Doxycycline exerts its bacteriostatic effect by the inhibition of protein synthesis.

Indications: For the treatment of: Pneumonia: single and multilobe pneumonia and bronchopneumonia due to susceptible strains of S. pneumoniae (formerly D. pneumoniae) and other Streptococci, Staphylococcus, H. influenzae and K. pneumoniae.

Other Respiratory Tract Infections: pharyngitis, tonsillitis, sinusitis, otitis media, bronchitis caused by susceptible strains of β-hemolytic Streptococcus, Staphylococcus, S. pneumoniae (formerly D. pneumoniae), and H. influenzae.

Genitourinary Tract Infections: pyelonephritis, cystitis, urethritis, gonococcal urethritis caused by susceptible strains of Klebsiella species, E. aerogenes, E. coli, Enterococcus, Staphylococcus, Streptococcus and N. gonorrhoeae.

In adult patients with urethritis, cervicitis and vaginitis with a positive test for C. trachomatis and/or U. urealyticum, clinical resolution and absence of detectable organisms have only been observed at completion of oral therapy. Relapses or reinfection can occur. In these cases, limited data suggest that some patients may derive clinical benefit from the oral administration of doxycycline or an alternative therapy. The effect on long-term morbidity has not been established.

Skin and Soft Tissue Infections: impetigo, furunculosis, cellulitis, abscess, wound sepsis, paronychia, caused by susceptible strains of S. aureus and epidermidis (formerly albus), Streptococcus, E. coli, Klebsiella species and E. aerogenes.

Gastrointestinal Infections: caused by susceptible strains of Shigella, Salmonella and E. coli.

Up to 44% of strains of S. pyogenes and 74% of S. faecalis have been found to be resistant to tetracycline drugs.

Appropriate culture and susceptibility studies should be carried out prior to initiation of therapy with doxycycline and if clinically indicated during treatment. Consideration may be given to the initiation of therapy before obtaining results of these tests, however modification of such treatment may be required once the results become available.

Contraindications: In individuals who have shown hypersensitivity to tetracyclines and in patients with myasthenia gravis.

Warnings: Doxycycline like other tetracyclines, may form a stable calcium complex in any bone-forming tissue, though in vitro it binds calcium less strongly than other tetracyclines. It should be anticipated that the use of doxycycline during tooth development (last trimester of pregnancy, during lactation, neonatal period and early childhood to the age of 8 years) may cause permanent discoloration of the teeth (yellow-gray-brown). Though more commonly associated with long-term use of tetracyclines, this effect has also been known to occur after short courses. Enamel hypoplasia has also been reported. Doxycycline should, therefore, not be used in these age groups unless other drugs are unlikely to be effective or are contraindicated.

Photosensitivity manifested by an exaggerated sunburn reaction has been observed in some individuals taking tetracyclines. Patients apt to be exposed to direct sunlight or ultraviolet light should be advised that this reaction can occur with doxycycline, and treatment should be discontinued at the first evidence of skin erythema.

Pregnancy: Doxycycline should not be administered to pregnant women, unless in the judgment of the physician the potential benefit to the mother outweighs the risk to the fetus. (See Warnings about use during tooth development.)

Results of animal studies indicate that tetracyclines cross the placenta, are found in fetal tissues and can have toxic effects on the developing fetus (often related to retardation of skeletal development). Evidence of embryotoxicity has also been noted in animals treated early in pregnancy.

Lactation: Tetracyclines are excreted in the milk of lactating women. Accordingly the use of doxycycline is not recommended in women while they are breast feeding. (See Warnings about use during tooth development.)

Children: The use of doxycycline in children under 8 years is not recommended because safe conditions for its use have not been established. (See Warnings about use during tooth development.)

Doxycycline, like other tetracyclines, forms a stable calcium complex in any bone-forming tissue. A decrease in the fibula growth rate has been observed in prematures given oral tetracycline in doses of 25 mg/kg every 6 hours. This reaction was shown to be reversible when the drug was discontinued.

Precautions: In clinical studies to date, administration of doxycycline did not lead to increased serum levels nor to an increase in the serum half-life of doxycycline in patients with impaired renal function. Modification of the dosage for these patients is not necessary. Although no evidence of increased toxicity has been observed in such patients, the potential for increased hepatic or other toxicity should be considered until further data on the metabolic fate of doxycycline under these conditions become available.

Concurrent administration of doxycycline with agents known to be hepatotoxic should be avoided.

The use of antibiotics may occasionally result in overgrowth of nonsusceptible organisms; thus, observation of the patient is essential. There is evidence to suggest that doxycycline may have less effect on the gut flora than other tetracyclines. Nevertheless, it is important to consider the possibility of pseudomembranous colitis due to toxins produced by the overgrowth of C. difficile. Mild cases of pseudomembraneous colitis may respond to drug discontinuance alone. Moderate to severe cases should be managed with fluid, electrolyte and protein supplementation as indicated. When the colitis is not relieved by the discontinuance of doxycycline or when it is severe, consideration should be given to the administration of oral Vancomycin.

Increased intracranial pressure with bulging fontanels has been observed in infants receiving therapeutic doses of tetracycline. Although the mechanism of this phenomenon is unknown the signs and symptoms have disappeared rapidly upon cessation of treatment with no sequelae.

Isolated cases of esophageal injury consisting of esophagitis and esophageal ulceration have been reported in patients receiving doxycycline orally. Most of these patients took medication immediately before going to bed and/or without adequate amount of fluid (see Dosage). If this should occur, doxycycline should be discontinued until healing occurs. Administration of antacids and/or cimetidine has provided relief in the treatment of such cases. **To reduce the risk of esophageal injury, patients should be advised to take doxycycline capsules or film-coated tablets with an adequate amount of fluid while standing or sitting upright.**

In long-term therapy with doxycycline, periodic laboratory evaluation of organ systems, including hematopoietic, renal and hepatic studies should be performed. Liver function tests should be carried out at regular intervals on patients receiving high doses for prolonged periods of time.

Drug Interactions: Doxycycline should be given with caution to patients receiving oral anticoagulants. Because the tetracyclines have been shown to depress plasma prothrombin activity, patients who are on anticoagulant therapy may require downward adjustment of their anticoagulant dosage.

Antacids containing aluminum, calcium or magnesium impair absorption and should not be given to patients taking doxycycline.

The concurrent use of doxycycline with alcohol, barbiturates, phenytoin and carbamazepine (hepatic enzyme inducers) has been reported to result in a reduction of plasma half-life of doxycycline, thereby reducing the antimicrobial effectiveness of doxycycline. This effect may last for several days after discontinuation of therapy with the interacting agent. Therefore, consideration should be given to re-adjustment of the daily dose of doxycycline when administered concomitantly with alcohol and with drugs known to be enzyme inducers.

It has been reported that concurrent administration of ferrous sulfate (iron) lowered serum concentrations of doxycycline given orally and shortened the serum half-life after a single i.v. injection. In the event that iron and iron-containing products have to be given during treatment with doxycycline, the interval between administration of each drug should be as wide as possible.

It has been reported that when subsalicylate bismuth was given simultaneously and as a multiple-dose regimen before oral doxycycline there was a reduced bioavailability of doxycycline. Also peak serum concentrations of doxycycline were significantly decreased when subsalicylate bismuth was given 2 hours before oral doxycycline but not when given 2 hours after oral doxycycline. Therefore subsalicylate bismuth should not be taken during therapy with oral doxycyline.

Since bacteriostatic drugs may interfere with the bactericidal action of penicillin, it is advisable to avoid giving doxycycline, or any other tetracycline, in conjunction with penicillin.

There have been anecdotal reports that concurrent use of tetracyclines may render oral contraceptives less effective.

Adverse Effects: Gastrointestinal: As with other broad spectrum antibiotics administered orally and parenterally, gastrointestinal disturbances such as anorexia, nausea, vomiting, diarrhea, glossitis, dysphagia, stomatitis, proctitis and enterocolitis, may occur, but have rarely been sufficiently troublesome to warrant discontinuation of therapy.

Isolated cases of esophagitis and esophageal ulcerations in patients receiving capsule and tablet form of doxycycline have been reported (see Precautions and Dosage).

Hypersensitivity: Hypersensitivity reactions consisting of urticaria, angioneurotic edema, anaphylaxis, anaphylactoid purpura, pericarditis, serum sickness, and exacerbation of systemic lupus erythematosus have been reported.

Maculopapular and erythematous rashes have been reported. Exfoliative dermatitis has also been reported but is uncommon.

Photosensitivity: Photosensitivity reaction is discussed under Warnings.

CNS: Bulging fontanels in infants and benign intracranial hypertension in adults have been reported in patients receiving full therapeutic dosages. These conditions disappeared rapidly when the drug was discontinued.

Hepatic and Renal: As with other tetracyclines, elevation of AST or ALT values, or elevated BUN (apparently dose related) have been reported, the significance of which is not known.

Hematologic: anemia, thrombocytopenia, neutropenia, eosinophilia, leukopenia.

Overdose: Symptoms and Treatment: Specific information on symptoms or treatment of overdosage with doxycycline is not available. Treatment, therefore, should be symptomatic and gastric lavage may be considered for overdosage with the oral preparation. Dialysis does not alter serum half-life and thus would not be of benefit in treating cases of overdosage.

Dosage: The preferred route of administration is oral. I.V. administration should ony be used for patients in whom oral administration is not feasible (e.g., patients with dysphagia, nausea, gastrointestinal intolerance, unconsciousness, traumatic or surgical wounds of the gastrointestinal tract or intestinal obstruction). Oral therapy should be substituted as soon as possible.

Capsules and film-coated tablets should be given with or after a meal in order to minimize the possibility of gastric upset. Antacids and iron preparations impair absorption and should not be given concomitantly to patients taking oral doxycycline.

Capsules and film-coated tablets should be given to patients with adequate amounts of fluid while standing or sitting upright to reduce the risk of esophageal injury.

Adults: The recommended dosage of oral doxycycline for the majority of susceptible infections is a single loading dose of 200 mg on the first day of treatment followed by a maintenance dosage of 100 mg once daily at the same time each day thereafter.

In severe infections a single daily dose of 200 mg may be used throughout.

Therapy should be continued for at least 24 to 48 hours after symptoms and fever have subsided. It should be noted, however, that effective antibacterial levels are usually present 24 to 36 hours following discontinuance of therapy.

When used in streptococcal infections, therapy should be continued for 10 days to prevent the development of rheumatic fever or glomerulonephritis.

Vibra-Tabs (cont'd)

For treatment of uncomplicated acute gonococcal infections, the recommended dosage is 200 mg starting and 100 mg at bedtime, the first day, followed by 100 mg b.i.d. for 3 days.

For treatment of uncomplicated urethral, endocervical, or vaginal infections in adults associated with C. trachomatis and U. urealyticum: 100 mg, by mouth, twice a day for at least 10 days.

No alteration in recommended dosage schedule need be made when treating patients with impaired renal function.

Supplied: Vibra-Tabs: Each orange, film-coated tablet contains: doxycycline hyclate equivalent to doxycycline 100 mg. Nonmedicinal ingredients: microcrystalline cellulose, ethylcellulose, hydroxypropylmethylcellulose, magnesium stearate/sodium lauryl sulfate, propylene glycol, talc, titanium dioxide, FD & C Yellow #6 and aluminum hydroxide. Bottles of 100 and 250.

Vibramycin Capsules: Each blue, hard gelatin capsule contains: doxycycline hyclate equivalent to doxycycline 100 mg. Nonmedicinal ingredients: microcrystalline cellulose, magnesium stearate/ sodium lauryl sulfate; capsule shell: gelatin, sulfur dioxide, titanium dioxide and FD & C Blue #1. Bottles of 50 and 200.

Store at a temperature 15 to 30°C. Protect from light.

(Shown in Product Recognition Section)

VIBRA-TABS™ C-PAK™ ℞
Pfizer

Doxycycline Hyclate
Antibiotic

Indications: In adult patients with urethritis, cervicitis and vaginitis with a positive test for C. trachomatis and/or U. urealyticum, clinical resolution and absence of detectable organisms have only been observed at completion of oral therapy with doxycycline. Relapses or reinfection can occur. In these cases, limited data suggest that some patients may derive clinical benefit from the oral administration of doxycycline or an alternative therapy. The effect on long-term morbidity has not been established.

Contraindications: See Vibra-Tabs.

Warnings: See Vibra-Tabs.

Precautions: See Vibra-Tabs.

Adverse Effects: See Vibra-Tabs.

Overdose: Symptoms and Treatment: Specific information on symptoms or treatment of overdosage with doxycycline is not available. Treatment, therefore, should be symptomatic and gastric lavage may be considered for overdosage with the oral preparation.

Dosage: Doxycycline should be given with or after a meal in order to minimize the possibility of gastric upset. Antacids and iron preparations impair absorption and should not be given concomitantly to patients taking doxycycline.

Doxycycline should be given to patients with adequate amounts of fluid while standing or sitting upright to reduce the risk of esophageal injury.

Adults: For treatment of uncomplicated urethral, endocervical, or vaginal infections in adults associated with C. trachomatis and U. urealyticum: 100 mg by mouth, twice a day for at least 10 days.

No alteration in recommended dosage schedule need be made when treating patients with impaired renal function.

Supplied: Each orange, film-coated tablet contains: doxycycline hyclate equivalent to doxycycline 100 mg. Nonmedicinal ingredients: ethylcellulose, FD&C Yellow No. 6, hydroxypropylmethylcellulose, magnesium stearate/sodium lauryl sulfate, microcrystalline cellulose, propylene glycol, talc and titanium dioxide. Sodium: <1 mmol (0.029 mg). Tartrazine-free. Packages of 20. Store at room temperature between 15 and 30°C. Protect from light.

(Shown in Product Recognition Section)

For comparative information on Sulfonylureas, see the CPhA General Monograph in the WHITE SECTION.

VIDEX™ ℞
Bristol

Didanosine
Antiretroviral Agent

Pharmacology: Didanosine is a synthetic, purine nucleoside analogue of deoxyadenosine, active against the Human Immunodeficiency Virus (HIV).

Didanosine inhibits the in vitro replication of HIV in human primary cells cultures and in established cell lines. The active antiviral metabolite, dideoxyadenosine-triphosphate (ddATP), is formed in several steps by phosphorylation of didanosine by cellular enzymes. Inhibition of HIV reverse transcriptase by ddATP is through competition with endogenous deoxyadenosine triphosphate (dATP) for binding to the active site of the enzyme. In addition, ddATP is a substrate for reverse transcriptase and is incorporated into the growing DNA chain. The resulting nucleoside, dideoxyadenosine (ddA) lacks a 3′-hydroxyl group, which normally is the acceptor for covalent attachment of subsequent nucleoside 5′-monophosphates in DNA chain extension. Thus, ddA incorporated in the DNA prevents further chain extension and aborts proviral DNA synthesis.

Indications: For the treatment of HIV infection when antiretroviral therapy is warranted.

Clinical benefit of didanosine was demonstrated in several important clinical trials.

The duration of clinical benefit from antiretroviral therapy may be limited. Alteration in antiretroviral therapy should be considered if disease progression occurs while receiving didanosine.

Contraindications: In patients with previously demonstrated hypersensitivity to any of the components of the formulations.

Warnings: The major clinical toxicity of didanosine is pancreatitis (see Adverse Effects).

Patients receiving didanosine or any antiretroviral therapy may continue to develop opportunistic infections and other complications of HIV infection, and therefore should remain under close clinical observation by physicians experienced in the treatment of patients with HIV-associated diseases.

Pancreatitis: **Pancreatitis, which has been fatal in some cases, is the major clinical toxicity of didanosine (see Adverse Effects).** Pancreatitis must be considered whenever a patient receiving didanosine develops abdominal pain and nausea, vomiting or elevated biochemical markers for pancreatitis. Under these circumstances, didanosine use should be suspended until the diagnosis of pancreatitis is excluded. Similarly, when treatment with other drugs known to cause pancreatic toxicity is required (for example, i.v. pentamidine), suspension of didanosine therapy should be considered. Didanosine should be used only with extreme caution in patients with a history of pancreatitis. Positive relationships have been found between the risk of pancreatitis and daily dose. Patients with a heightened risk of pancreatitis such as those with a history of pancreatitis, alcohol consumption, elevated triglycerides or evidence of advanced HIV infection should be followed closely for signs and symptoms of pancreatitis. Patients with renal impairment may be at greater risk for pancreatitis if treated without dose adjustment.

Peripheral Neuropathy: **Peripheral neuropathy occurs in patients treated with didanosine and the frequency appears to be dose related.** Patients should be monitored for the development of a neuropathy that is usually characterized by symmetrical distal numbness, tingling, or pain in the feet or hands. In the U.S. Expanded Access Program, neuropathy occurred more frequently in patients with a history of neuropathy or neurotoxic drug therapy. These patients may be at increased risk of neuropathy during didanosine therapy.

Neuropathy has been reported rarely in children treated with didanosine. However, because signs and symptoms of neuropathy are difficult to assess in children, physicians should be alerted to the possibility of this event.

Liver Failure: In the ACTG 116B/117 trial, which compared 2 doses of didanosine with zidovudine, there was no difference in the 1-year rates of grade 3 or 4 liver function test (LFT) abnormalities between didanosine buffered powder at the recommended dose (250 mg b.i.d.) and zidovudine (600 mg/day). However, the difference in LFT abnormalities were statistically significant at the high dose (375 mg b.i.d.) of didanosine. In the ACTG 116A trial, the difference in the 1-year rate of LFT abnormalities was statistically significant for didanosine buffered powder at the recommended dose compared with zidovudine, but not at the high dose. Fatal liver failure of unknown etiology occurred during didanosine therapy in 0.6% patients in the Phase I trials and 0.2% in the U.S. Expanded Access Program. There were 3 reports of patients who died of unexplained liver failure in the ACTG 116B/117 trial: no such events were reported in the ACTG 116A trial.

Retinal Depigmentation and Vision: Pediatric patients have demonstrated retinal depigmentation or optic neuritis on rare (<1%) occasions, particularly at doses above those recommended. There have been rare (<1%) reports of retinal depigmentation and optic neuritis in adult patients (see Adverse Effects). Children receiving didanosine should undergo dilated retinal examination every 6 months or if a change in vision occurs. Periodic retinal examinations should be considered for adult patients receiving didanosine.

Precautions: General: Patients receiving didanosine or any other antiretroviral therapy may continue to develop opportunistic infections and other complications of HIV infection. Therefore, these patients should remain under close clinical observation by physicians experienced in the treatment of patients with HIV disease.

Ingestion of didanosine with food or as long as 2 hours after a meal reduces the absorption of didanosine by as much as 55%. Didanosine should be administered at least 30 minutes before a meal.

Lactic Acidosis: Occurrences of lactic acidosis (in the absence of hypoxemia), usually associated with severe hepatomegaly and hepatic steatosis have been reported with the use of nucleoside analogues. Treatment with nucleoside analogues should be discontinued in the setting of rapidly elevating aminotransferase levels, progressive hepatomegaly or metabolic/lactic acidosis of unknown etiology. Caution should be exercised when administering nucleoside analogues to any patient (particularly obese women) with hepatomegaly, hepatitis or other known risk factors for liver disease. These patients should be followed closely.

Table I—Videx

Adult Clinical Adverse Events/Cumulative Incidences ≥5% at Videx Recommended Dose (Data From Controlled Studies)

	%					
	Videx				Zidovudine	
	High Dose[a]		Recommended Dose[b]			
Adverse Events	116B/117 N=311	116A N=208	116B/117 N=298	116A N=197	116B/117 N=304	116A N=212
Diarrhea	20	17	28	19	21	15
Neuropathy (all grades)	17	21	20	17	12	14
Chills/Fever	9	13	12	9	11	12
Rash/Pruritus	7	7	9	7	5	8
Abdominal Pain	10	11	7	13	8	8
Asthenia	5	6	7	4	9	8
Headache	10	9	7	6	7	12
Pain	7	7	7	6	3	6
Nausea and Vomiting	6	10	7	7	6	14
Infection	5	4	6	7	5	7
Pancreatitis	10	9	6	7	2	3
Pneumonia	6	5	5	8	5	8
Sarcoma	3	4	3	5	4	2

[a]375 mg buffered powder b.i.d. if ≥60 kg; 250 mg b.i.d. if <60 kg.
[b]250 mg buffered powder b.i.d. if ≥60 kg; 167 mg b.i.d. if <60 kg.

Children: Efficacy and safety have been demonstrated in a comparative clinical trial, ACTG 152, involving over 800 pediatric patients which compared didanosine, zidovudine and the combination of the 2 drugs. Additionally, the pharmacokinetics of didanosine have been evaluated in pediatric studies. Insufficient clinical experience exists to recommend a dosing regimen in infants under 3 months of age.

Pregnancy: There are no adequate and well-controlled studies in pregnant women and it is not known whether didanosine can cause fetal harm or affect reproductive capacity when administered to a pregnant woman.

Reproduction studies have been performed in rats and rabbits at doses up to 12 to 14.2 times the estimated human exposure (based upon plasma levels) respectively, and have revealed no evidence of impaired fertility or harm to the fetus due to didanosine. At approximately 12 times the estimated human exposure, didanosine was slightly toxic to female rats and their pups during mid and late lactation. These rats showed reduced food intake and body weight gains but the physical and functional development of the offspring was not impaired and there were no major changes in the F_2 generation. A study in rats showed that didanosine and/or its metabolites are transferred to the fetus through the placenta.

Because animal reproduction studies are not always predictive of human response, this drug should be used during pregnancy only if clearly needed.

Lactation: It is not known whether didanosine is excreted in human milk. A study in rats showed that, following oral administration, didanosine and/or its metabolites were excreted into the milk of lactating rats. Because of uncertainties related to transmission of virus and to excretion of didanosine in breast milk, it is advisable to caution mothers against breast-feeding.

Patients with Special Diseases and Conditions: Patients with Phenylketonuria: The chewable/dispersible buffered tablets contain the following quantities of phenylalanine: per 2-tablet dose: 73 mg (100 and 150 mg strengths), 45 mg (25 and 50 mg strengths); per tablet: 36.5 mg (100 and 150 mg strengths), 22.5 mg (25 and 50 mg strengths).

Patients with Renal Impairment: Patients with renal impairment (serum creatinine >1.5 mg/dL or creatinine clearance <60 mL/min) may be at greater risk for toxicity from didanosine due to decreased drug clearance. The elimination half-life of didanosine is increased in anuric patients requiring hemodialysis. Because of the potential for drug removal, didanosine should be administered after dialysis. Dose reductions should be considered in patients with renal impairment (see Dosage). The magnesium hydroxide content of each didanosine tablet is 8.6 mEq. This may present an excessive load of magnesium to patients with significant renal impairment, particularly after prolonged dosing.

Patients with Hepatic Impairment: Patients with hepatic impairment may be at greater risk for toxicity related to didanosine treatment due to altered metabolism; a dose reduction may be necessary.

Hyperuricemia: Didanosine has been associated with asymptomatic hyperuricemia; treatment suspension may be necessary if clinical measures aimed at reducing uric acid levels fail.

Drug Interactions: **Coadministration of didanosine with drugs that are known to cause peripheral neuropathy or pancreatitis may increase the risk of these toxicities (see Warnings) and should be done only with extreme caution.** Drug interaction studies have demonstrated that there are no clinically significant interactions with didanosine and the following: stavudine, foscarnet, trimethoprim, sulfamethoxazole, dapsone, ranitidine, loperamide, metoclopramide and rifabutin.

Drugs whose absorption can be affected by the level of acidity in the stomach (e.g., ketoconazole, itraconazole, dapsone), should be administered at least 2 hours prior to dosing with didanosine.

Combination studies of didanosine buffered powder (up to 500 mg/day) and zidovudine (up to 600 mg/day) have not revealed any unexpected toxicities or alteration of pharmacokinetics of either drug.

A study in 4 patients revealed that concomitant administration of ganciclovir does not significantly affect the pharmacokinetics of didanosine. There is no evidence that didanosine potentiates the myelosuppressive effects of ganciclovir or zidovudine.

As with other products containing magnesium and/or aluminum antacid components, the didanosine tablets should not be administered with a prescription antibiotic containing any form of tetracycline.

Plasma concentrations of some quinolone antibiotics are decreased when administered with antacids containing magnesium and/or aluminum. Therefore, doses of quinolone antibiotics should not be administered within 2 hours of taking didanosine tablets. Concomitant administration of antacids containing magnesium or aluminum with the didanosine tablets may potentiate adverse effects associated with the antacid component.

Information for Patients: Didanosine is not a cure for HIV infection, and patients may continue to develop HIV-associated illnesses including opportunistic infections. Therefore, patients should remain under the care of a physician when using didanosine.

The major toxicity of didanosine is pancreatitis, which has been fatal in some patients. Symptoms of pancreatitis include abdominal pain, and nausea and vomiting. Peripheral neuropathy occurs in patients treated with didanosine. Symptoms of peripheral neuropathy include tingling, burning, pain or numbness in the hands or feet. These symptoms should be reported to your physician. The above toxicities of didanosine occur with the greatest frequency in patients with a history of these events and dose modification and/or discontinuation of didanosine may be required if toxicity develops. There are other medications including alcohol which may exacerbate didanosine toxicity. You should consult your physician about such medications.

Table II—Videx

Adult Clinical Adverse Events/Cumulative Incidences ≥1% and <5% at Videx Recommended Dose (Data From Controlled Studies)

	%					
	Videx				Zidovudine	
	High Dose[a]		Recommended Dose[b]			
Adverse Events	116B/117 N=311	116A N=208	116B/117 N=298	116A N=197	116B/117 N=304	116A N=212
Body as a Whole						
Allergic Reaction	2	2	1	2	1	0
Chest Pain	0	2	1	1	1	1
Malaise	1	1	1	0	3	2
Cardiovascular						
Hemorrhage	0	1	1	1	0	0
Hypotension	1	2	1	4	0	1
Digestive						
Anorexia	1	2	2	1	2	2
Constipation	1	1	1	0	0	0
Dry Mouth	3	3	2	1	0	1
Dysphagia	1	1	0	1	2	0
Flatulence	1	0	0	2	1	1
Gastrointestinal Hemorrhage	0	0	0	2	0	1
Oral Moniliasis	0	0	1	2	0	0
Melena	0	0	0	1	0	0
Hemic/Lymphatic						
Lymphoma like Reaction	1	0	0	2	1	0
Metabolic/Nutritional						
Dehydration	1	1	1	1	1	1
Edema	1	0	0	2	0	0
Musculoskeletal						
Arthralgia	1	1	0	2	1	0
Myopathy	2	4	3	2	6	3
Nervous						
Agitation	0	0	0	1	0	0
Amnesia	1	1	1	1	0	0
Anxiety/Nervous/Twitch	2	1	1	0	2	0
Aphasia	0	0	1	0	0	0
Confusion	2	2	1	2	0	0
Convulsion	2	2	2	4	2	1
Depression	2	2	1	5	3	2
Dizziness	1	3	1	2	1	2
Emotional Lability	0	0	0	1	0	0
Hypertension	1	2	1	2	0	0
Thinking Abnormal	1	2	2	2	1	1
Respiratory						
Asthma	1	1	0	2	0	1
Dyspnea	3	4	2	3	3	4
Bronchitis	1	0	1	1	1	1
Cough Increased	1	2	1	1	1	2
Respiratory Disorder	1	0	0	2	0	0
Skin and Appendages						
Herpex Simplex	1	2	0	1	0	1
Herpes Zoster	0	2	1	1	0	0
Pruritus	0	1	1	2	1	0
Sweating	1	0	1	2	1	0
Special Senses						
Blurred Vision	0	2	1	1	1	1
Otitis Media	0	0	1	1	0	0
Retinitis	0	0	1	0	1	1

[a] 375 mg buffered powder b.i.d. if ≥60 kg; 250 mg b.i.d. if <60 kg.
[b] 250 mg buffered powder b.i.d. if ≥60 kg; 167 mg b.i.d. if <60 kg.

The long-term effects of didanosine are unknown at this time. Didanosine therapy has not been shown to reduce the risk of transmission of HIV to others through sexual contact or blood contamination.

Adverse Effects: The major clinical toxicity of didanosine is pancreatitis (see Warnings).

Adults: Table I (on previous page) lists all adverse events which occurred in at least 5% of adult patients participating in 2 controlled clinical trials (ACTG 116B /117 and 116A) comparing 2 doses of didanosine (buffered powder for oral solution) to zidovudine.

Clinical adverse events which occurred in at least 1% and up to 5% of patients enrolled in the 2 controlled clinical trials are listed, by body system, in Table II.

Other clinical adverse events which occurred with a cumulative incidence of <1% in patients treated with didanosine in the 2 controlled clinical trials are presented by body system: Body as a Whole: Recommended dose: abscess, cellulitis, cyst, flu syndrome, hernia, neck rigidity, numbness (hands and feet) and suicide attempt. High dose: abscess, anaphylac-

Videx (cont'd)

toid reaction, cyst, dementia, face edema, general debilitation, malaise and pilonidal cyst.

Cardiovascular: Recommended dose: angina pectoris, migraine, palpitation, peripheral vascular disorder, shock and syncope. High dose: aortic stenosis, arrhythmia, cardiovascular disorder, chest pain substernal, heart arrest, heart failure right, hypotension, intracranial aneurysm, migraine, myocardial infarct, palpitation and tachycardia.

Digestive: Recommended dose: aphthous stomatitis, colitis, dyspepsia, eructation, flatulence, gastritis, gastroenteritis, gastrointestinal hemorrhage, gum hemorrhage, rectal hemorrhage, sialadenitis and stomach ulcer hemorrhage. High dose: abnormal stools, cholecystitis, cholelithiasis, colitis, duodenitis, dyspepsia, esophagitis, flatulence, gastritis, gastrointestinal carcinoma, gingivitis, hemorrhagic pancreatitis, hepatomegaly, leukoplakia, oral moniliasis, parotid gland enlargement, pseudomembranous enterocolitis, rectal hemorrhage and tongue disorder.

Endocrine: High dose: inappropriate ADH.

Hemic/Lymphatic: Recommended dose: lymphoma-like reaction. High dose: lymphoma-like reaction.

Metabolic/Nutritional: Recommended dose: edema peripheral. High dose: acidosis, dehydration, generalized edema and thirst.

Musculoskeletal: Recommended dose: arthralgia, arthritis, hemiparesis, joint disorder, leg cramps and tenosynovitis. High dose: arthritis, bone disorder, joint disorder, myositis and pyogenic arthritis.

Nervous: Recommended dose: acute brain syndrome, ataxia, dementia, drug dependence, encephalitis, encephalopathy, grand mal convulsion, hyperesthesia, hypertonia, ileus, incoordination, insomnia, intracranial hemorrhage, libido decreased, paralysis, paranoid reaction, psychosis, sleep disorder, speech disorder, tremor and withdrawal syndrome. High dose: abnormal gait, agitation, amnesia, aphasia, CNS depression, dementia, drug dependence, emotional lability, encephalitis, encephalopathy, foot drop, grand mal convulsion, hyperesthesia, hypertonia, insomnia, manic reaction, neuralgia, psychosis, reflexes decreased, reflexes increased, speech disorder, tremor and withdrawal syndrome.

Respiratory: Recommended dose: apnea, asthma, bronchiectasis, espistaxis, hemoptysis, hypoxia, laryngitis, lung function decreased, pharyngitis, pneumonia interstitial, pneumothorax and respiratory disorder. High dose: asthma, bronchitis, epistaxis, hemoptysis, hypoventilation and pharyngitis.

Skin and Appendages: Recommended dose: acne, exfoliative dermatitis, Herpes simplex, skin disorder and skin ulcer. High dose: acne, angioedema, fungal dermatitis, Herpes zoster, pruritus, skin discoloration, skin hypertrophy, sweating, urticaria and vesiculobullous rash.

Special Senses: Recommended dose: conjunctivitis, deafness, diplopia, dry eye, ear disorder, glaucoma, otitis externa and tinnitus. High dose: abnormal vision, blurred vision, conjunctivitis, ear pain, eye disorder, eye pain, iritis, photophobia, retinal detachment, retinitis, taste perversion and visual field defect.

Urogenital: Recommended dose: bladder carcinoma, breast abscess, impotence, kidney calculus, kidney failure, kidney function abnormal, nocturia, urinary frequency and vaginal hemorrhage. High dose: acute kidney failure, bladder carcinoma, hematuria, kidney function abnormal, kidney pain, penis disorder, polyuria, prostatic disorder, urinary frequency and vaginal hemorrhage.

There have been rare (<1%) reports of retinal depigmentation or optic neuritis in pediatric and/or adult patients. Children receiving didanosine should undergo dilated retinal examination every 6 months or if a change in vision occurs. Periodic retinal examinations should be considered for adult patients receiving didanosine (see Warnings).

Reports of rhabdomyolysis, hepatitis, impaired glucose tolerance, diabetes mellitus and alopecia have been received as part of ongoing surveillance. A few cases of rhabdomyolysis were complicated by acute renal failure, which required hemodialysis.

Cases of lactic acidosis (in the absence of hypoxemia), usually associated with severe hepatomegaly and hepatic steatosis have been reported with the use of nucleoside analogues.

Children: Adverse events reported in more than 4% of 98 patients in pediatric phase I trials (which includes all signs and symptoms while on study) are listed by organ system in Table III. There are no controlled comparative data to assess the incidence of adverse effects from didanosine at this time. Therefore, the adverse events reported in these pediatric studies should be considered as potential hazards of didanosine treatment.

In pediatric studies, pancreatitis occurred in 2 of 60 (3%) patients treated at entry doses below 300 mg/m²/day and in 5 of 38 (13%) patients treated at higher doses.

Serious adverse events reported in the pediatric phase I trials were: neurologic (2%), seizure (1%), pneumonia (1%), diabetes mellitus (1%), diabetes insipidus (1%).

Table III—Videx

Pediatric Clinical Adverse Events (Cumulative Incidences)

Adverse Events	**% of Patients (n=98)**
Body as a Whole	
Chills/Fever	82
Anorexia	51
Asthenia	41
Pain	31
Malaise	29
Failure to Thrive	9
Weight Loss	8
Flu Syndrome	7
Change in Appetite	6
Alopecia	5
Dehydration	5
Gastrointestinal	
Diarrhea	81
Nausea/Vomiting	58
Liver Abnormalities	38
Abdominal Pain	35
Stomatitis/Mouth Sores	16
Constipation	12
Oral Thrush	9
Pancreatitis	7
Melena	7
Dry Mouth	4
Lympho-Hematologic	
Ecchymosis	15
Hemorrhage	10
Petechiae	7
Musculoskeletal	
Arthritis	11
Myalgia	9
Muscle Atrophy	8
Decreased Strength	6
Cardiovascular	
Vasodilation	22
Arrhythmia	6
Nervous System	
Headache	55
Nervousness	27
Insomnia	8
Dizziness	7
Poor Coordination	6
Lethargy	4
Respiratory System	
Cough	85
Rhinitis	48
Dyspnea	23
Asthma	21
Rhinorrhea	21
Epistaxis	14
Pharyngitis	14
Hypoventilation	8
Sinusitis	7
Rhonchi/Rales	6
Skin and Appendages	
Rash/Pruritus	70
Skin Disorder	13
Eczema	12
Sweating	7
Impetigo	6
Excoriation	4
Erythema	4
Special Senses	
Otalgia/Otitis Media	11
Photophobia	5
Strabismus	5
Visual Impairment	5
Urogenital System	
Urinary Frequency	4

Laboratory Test Abnormalities: Adults: The cumulative incidences of serious laboratory abnormalities in the 2 controlled clinical trials comparing 2 doses of Videx to zidovudine, are listed in Table IV (on following page).

Children: Serious laboratory abnormalities experienced by 60 pediatric patients who received didanosine at doses ≤300 mg/m²/day are listed in Table V (on following page). These laboratory abnormalities were observed more frequently among patients who began didanosine therapy with abnormal values.

Overdose: Symptoms and Treatment: There is no known antidote for didanosine overdosage. Experience in the Phase I studies in which didanosine was initially administered at doses 10 times the currently recommended doses indicates that the complications of chronic overdosage would include pancreatitis, peripheral neuropathy, diarrhea, hyperuricemia and hepatic dysfunction. Didanosine is not dialyzable by peritoneal dialysis, although there is some clearance by hemodialysis.

Dosage: Adults: The dosing interval should be 12 hours. All formulations should be administered at least 30 minutes before a meal. Adult patients should take 2 tablets at each dose so that adequate buffering is provided to prevent gastric degradation of didanosine.

The recommended dose in adults is dependent on weight as outlined in Table VI (on following page).

Dose Adjustment: Clinical signs suggestive of pancreatitis should prompt dose suspension and careful evaluation of the possibility of pancreatitis. Only after pancreatitis has been ruled out should dosing be resumed.

Patients who have presented with symptoms of neuropathy may tolerate a reduced dose of didanosine after resolution of these symptoms upon drug discontinuation.

In adult patients with impaired renal function, the dose of didanosine should be adjusted to compensate for the slower rate of elimination. See Table VII (on following page).

For patients undergoing dialysis, the daily dose of didanosine should be administered after dialysis. It is not necessary to administer a supplemental dose of didanosine following hemodialysis.

Since urinary excretion is also a major route of elimination of didanosine in pediatric patients, the clearance of didanosine may be altered in pediatric patients with renal impairment. Although there are insufficient data to recommend a specific dosage adjustment of didanosine in this patient population, a reduction in the dose and/or an increase in the interval between doses should be considered.

There are insufficient data to recommend a specific dose adjustment of didanosine in patients with hepatic impairment, but an adjustment in the dose in these patients should also be considered.

Method of Preparation: Adult Dosing: 2 tablets should be thoroughly chewed, manually crushed, or dispersed in at least 30 mL of water prior to consumption. To disperse tablets, add 2 tablets to at least 30 mL of drinking water. Stir until a uniform dispersion forms, and drink the entire dispersion immediately. If additional flavoring is desired, the aqueous dispersion may be further diluted with 30 mL of clear apple juice. Stir and drink the entire dispersion immediately.

Storage and Stability of Reconstituted Preparations: Chewable/dispersible buffered tablets dispersed in water may be held for up to 1 hour at ambient temperature. The aqueous dispersion further diluted with apple juice is also stable for up to 1 hour at ambient temperature.

Supplied: 25 mg: Each round, off-white to light orange/yellow with a mottled appearance, orange-flavored, chewable, dispersible buffered tablet, embossed with "VIDEX" on one side and 25 on the other, contains: didanosine 25 mg. Nonmedicinal ingredients: aspartame, calcium carbonate, magnesium hydroxide, magnesium stearate, mandarin-orange flavor, microcrystalline cellulose, polyplasdone and sorbitol. Bottles of 60.

50 mg: Each round, off-white to light orange/yellow with a mottled appearance, orange-flavored, chewable, dispersible buffered tablet, embossed with "VIDEX" on one side and 50 on the other, contains: didanosine 50 mg. Nonmedicinal ingredients: aspartame, calcium carbonate, magnesium hydroxide, magnesium stearate, mandarin-orange flavor, microcrystalline cellulose, polyplasdone and sorbitol. Bottles of 60.

100 mg: Each round, off-white to light orange/yellow with a mottled appearance, orange-flavored, chewable, dispersible buffered tablet, embossed with "VIDEX" on one side and 100 on the other, contains: didanosine 100 mg. Nonmedicinal ingredients: aspartame, calcium carbonate, magnesium hydroxide, magnesium stearate, mandarin-orange flavor, microcrystalline cellulose, polyplasdone and sorbitol. Bottles of 60.

Table IV—Videx

Controlled Clinical Trials/Cumulative Incidences of Adult Laboratory Abnormalities

	%					
	Videx				Zidovudine	
	High Dose		Recommended Dose			
Laboratory Tests (seriously abnormal level)	**116B/117 N=311**	**116A N=208**	**116B/117 N=298**	**116A N=197**	**116B/117 N=304**	**116A N=212**
Leukopenia (<2 000/μL)	13	16	16	13	22	26
Amylase (≥1.4 X ULN)	22	10	15	7	5	2
Granulocytopenia (<750/μL)	8	8	8	6	15	19
Thrombocytopenia (<50 000/μL)	2	1	2	2	3	4
ALT (>5 X ULN)	8	7	6	9	6	6
AST (>5 X ULN)	8	6	7	9	6	4
Alkaline phosphatase (>5 X ULN)	4	2	1	4	1	1
Hemoglobin (<8.0 g/dL)	2	9	3	6	5	8
Bilirubin (>5 X ULN)	2	1	1	1	1	1
Uric Acid (>12 mg/dL)	1	1	2	3	1	1

Table V—Videx

Pediatric Patient Serious Laboratory Abnormalities (Cumulative Incidences)

Laboratory Test (Seriously Abnormal Level)	Normal Baseline %	Abnormal Baseline %
Thrombocytopenia (<50 000/μL)	2	67
Granulocytopenia (<1 000/μL)	24	62
Leukopenia (<2 000/μL)	3	36
AST (>5×ULN)	0	36
Anemia (Hgb<8 g/dL)	4	27
ALT (>5×ULN)	3	25
Bilirubin (>5×ULN)	2	0

Table VI—Videx

Adult Dosing

Patient Weight	Tablets
≥60 kg	200 mg b.i.d.
<60 kg	125 mg b.i.d.

Table VII—Videx

Dosage—Renal Impairment

Creatinine Clearance (mL/min/1.73 m²)	Patient Weight >60 kg Tablets	<60 kg Tablets	Interval
>60 (normal dose)	200	125	every 12 hours
30-59	100	75	every 12 hours
10-29	150	100	every 24 hours
<10	100	75	every 24 hours

150 mg: Each round, off-white to light orange/yellow with a mottled appearance, orange-flavored, chewable, dispersible buffered tablet, embossed with "VIDEX" on one side and 150 on the other, contains: didanosine 150 mg. Nonmedicinal ingredients: aspartame, calcium carbonate, magnesium hydroxide, magnesium stearate, mandarin-orange flavor, microcrystalline cellulose, polyplasdone and sorbitol. Bottles of 60.

Store at room temperature (15 to 30°C).

(Shown in Product Recognition Section)

Reviewed 1999

VINBLASTINE SULFATE INJECTION

Faulding

Antineoplastic

Pharmacology: Tissue culture studies indicate that vinblastine is a selective mitotic inhibitor of certain malignant cells and as such appears to be different from other recognized antineoplastic drugs.

There is evidence that vinblastine interferes with cell metabolism and the entrance of glutamic acid into the citric acid cycle and to urea. There is also evidence that the anti-tumor effect of vinblastine may possibly be due to its effect on cell energy mechanisms, and a decreased adenosine diphosphate production resulting from retarded nucleotide production. It has been suggested that the therapeutic ratio may depend on the greater energy needs of cancer cells along with their decreased efficiency in generating energy because of their reliance on the glycolytic pathway. These energy related actions for vinblastine have been brought forward because although it has been demonstrated that vinblastine has a stathmokinetic effect and produces various atypical mitotic figures in treated cells it has been observed clinically and experimentally that these cytological changes may occur in the absence of oncolytic effects.

It has also been demonstrated in vitro that vinblastine can prevent the invasion of normal tissue by malignant cells thus preventing the spread of malignancy.

The relationship of vinblastine to amino acid metabolism has been shown by a reversal of the anti-tumor effect of vinblastine by glutamic acid or tryptophan. As well, aspartic and glutamic acids had protected mice from lethal doses of vinblastine, although aspartic acid was relatively ineffective in reversing the anti-tumor effect of vinblastine.

Vinblastine has been shown in clinical practice to provide palliative treatment for a variety of malignant neoplastic diseases and in susceptible tumors produced a temporary reduction in the size of some tumors. Its use has relieved pain and other symptoms associated with neoplasm and permitted some patients to regain appetite and weight. Remission periods have varied from patient to patient.

Leukopenia is an expected effect of vinblastine and the leukocyte count is an important guide to vinblastine therapy. In general, the larger the dose the longer lasting and more profound is the leukopenia. However, the white cell producing mechanism is not permanently depressed by vinblastine as it returns to normal on discontinuing treatment. Normally when the white cells have essentially disappeared from the peripheral blood, the white count would have returned to normal. The nadir in the white cell count usually occurs 5 to 10 days after the last treatment with vinblastine. Recovery is usually quite rapid and complete within another 7 to 14 days. If small doses are employed for maintenance therapy, leukopenia may not be clinically significant.

The thrombocyte count is not usually significantly reduced by vinblastine therapy, however, in patients whose bone marrow has been recently impaired by radiation therapy or other antineoplastic agents thrombocytopenia may develop (less than 200 000 platelets/mm³). Thrombocyte values below 200 000/mm³ are rarely encountered when other chemotherapeutic agents or radiation have not previously been used, even though a significant leukopenia may be present. If thrombocytopenia does occur, it usually reverses within a few days after termination of treatment.

Vinblastine generally has an insignificant effect on red cell count and hemoglobin. However, patients with a malignant disease may have anemia even in the absence of antineoplastic therapy.

Indications: In the palliative treatment of the following neoplastic diseases: Frequently Responsive Malignancies: generalized Hodgkin's disease (Stages III and IV, Ann Arbor modification of Rye), lymphocytic lymphoma (nodular and diffuse, poorly and well differentiated), histiocytic lymphoma, mycosis fungoides (advanced stages), advanced carcinoma of the testis, Kaposi's Sarcoma, Letterer-Siwe disease (histiocytosis-X).

Less Frequently Responsive Malignancies: choriocarcinoma resistant to other neoplastic drugs, cancer of the breast (unresponsive to endocrine surgery and hormonal therapy).

The simultaneous use of several cancer chemotherapy drugs is common practice. Generally drugs with different dose limiting clinical toxicities and different mechanisms of action are selected in order to obtain an increase in therapeutic response without added toxicity. Rarely is it possible to obtain equally as good a response with single antineoplastic treatment. Therefore, vinblastine is often part of polychemotherapy because at the recommended doses it does not cause significant suppression of bone marrow or neuropathy. This approach to multiple treatment has been used in the chemotherapy of Hodgkin's disease.

Hodgkin's Disease: Vinblastine has been found to be one of the most effective single antineoplastic agents for the treatment of Hodgkin's disease. Successful treatment of advanced Hodgkin's disease has been accomplished by the use of various multiple-drug regimens that have included vinblastine. In patients who have relapsed following treatment with the MOPP-regimen (mechlorethamine HCl [nitrogen mustard] vincristine sulfate, prednisone and procarbazine) have often responded to combination drug therapy that included vinblastine. An alternative therapy that has been used in previously untreated patients with advanced Hodgkin's disease employs cyclophosphamide in place of nitrogen mustard and vinblastine instead of vincristine.

Advanced testicular germinal-cell cancers such as embryonal carcinoma, teratocarcinoma, and choriocarcinoma have been shown to be sensitive to vinblastine alone but more satisfactory clinical response may be obtained by the concomitant administration of vinblastine with other antitumor drugs. The efficacy of bleomycin has been found to be enhanced if vinblastine is given 6 to 8 hours prior to bleomycin. This procedure appears to result in more cells being arrested during metaphase, the stage of cell division in which bleomycin is active.

Contraindications: Patients with leukopenia. Should not be administered to patients with bacterial infections. Such infections must be brought under control by the use of antibiotic or antiseptic therapy prior to the initiation of vinblastine treatment.

Pregnancy: Although no abnormalities of the human fetus have been associated with the use of vinblastine, information on its use during pregnancy is limited. Animal studies suggest that vinblastine may be teratogenic. Therefore the use of vinblastine during pregnancy is contraindicated unless the expected benefits clearly outweigh the risk of side effects.

Warnings: Caution: Vinblastine is a potent drug and should be used only by physicians experienced with cancer chemotherapeutic drugs. Blood counts should be taken once or twice weekly. Discontinue or reduce the dosage upon evidence of abnormal depression of the bone marrow. Vinblastine sulfate USP should not be given intrathecally.

Aspermia has been reported in man. Animal studies have demonstrated degenerative changes in germ cells and arrest of cell division in metaphase.

Precautions: If leukopenia with less than 2 000 WBC/mm³ develops following administration of vinblastine, the patient should be monitored carefully for evidence of infection until the WBC count returns to normal.

If cachexia or skin ulcers are present, a more profound leukopenia response to the drug may occur; therefore, the use of vinblastine should be avoided in elderly persons with either of these conditions.

In patients with malignant-cell infiltration of the bone marrow, the leukocyte and platelet counts have occasionally fallen precipitously after moderate doses of vinblastine and the administration of additional doses of vinblastine in such patients is not recommended.

The use of daily low doses of vinblastine for prolonged periods is not recommended, even though the total weekly dosage may be similar to the recommended treatment regimen. Little or no added therapeutic benefit has been demonstrated with the use of such low dose regimens. Strict adherence to the recommended dosage schedule is very important. When vinblastine was given in 7 daily injections at a total dose equal to several times the recommended weekly dosage for prolonged periods, convulsions, severe and permanent CNS damage and even death occurred.

Avoid contamination of the eye with vinblastine solutions. If accidental contamination does occur severe irritation may result and if the drug was given under pressure, corneal ulceration may result. The eye should be washed immediately with copious quantities of water.

Adverse Effects: Leukopenia: Bone-marrow depression, especially leukopenia, is the most common adverse effect with vinblastine and tends to be dose-limiting. Before administering the drug to patients they should be advised of the possibility of adverse reactions. Maximum depression occurs 4 to 10 days after administration with recovery in 1 to 3 weeks.

Vinblastine Sulfate Injection (cont'd)

Except for alopecia and leukopenia the adverse reactions seen with vinblastine usually do not persist for more than 24 hours.

Gastrointestinal: Nausea, vomiting, constipation, vesiculation of the mouth, ileus, diarrhea, anorexia, abdominal pain, rectal bleeding, pharyngitis, hemorrhagic enterocolitis and bleeding from a dormant peptic ulcer may occur.

Neurologic: Neurological effects can involve the autonomic nervous system and include malaise, headache, depression, psychoses, paresthesia, neuromyopathy, loss of deep tendon reflexes, peripheral neuritis, constipation, numbness and convulsions.

Miscellaneous: Alopecia, malaise, weakness, dizziness, pain at the site of the tumor, and vesiculation of the skin may occur. Epilation is frequently not complete and in some instances, hair re-growth will occur even though therapy continues.

Cellulitis and phlebitis may result if extravasation occurs during i.v. injection. If the extravasation is excessive, sloughing may occur.

Overdose: Symptoms and Treatment: Side effects are dose related. Thus, patients can expect to experience these effects in an exaggerated manner if more than the recommended dose of vinblastine is given. As well, neurotoxicity may occur similar to that seen with vincristine. Management of suspected overdosage of vinblastine should include the following: administer an antiemetic drug which usually controls nausea and vomiting; administer phenobarbital in anticonvulsant doses; be alert for the development of ileus which may necessitate non-surgical decompression of the gastrointestinal tract; monitor the patient's cardiovascular system; carry out daily blood counts as a guide for transfusion requirements. The most serious effect of an excessive dose of vinblastine, which may be life-threatening, is granulopoiesis.

Dosage: There are variations in the depth of the leukopenic response which follows therapy with vinblastine. For this reason, it is recommended that the drug be given no more frequently than once every 7 days. It is wise to initiate therapy with a single i.v. dose of 3.7 mg/m² of body surface area (bsa). Thereafter, WBC counts should be made to determine the patient's sensitivity to vinblastine.

A simplified and conservative incremental approach to dosage at weekly intervals may be outlined as shown in Table I.

Table I—Vinblastine Sulfate Injection

Dosage	Adults (bsa)	Children (bsa)
First dose	3.7 mg/m²	2.5 mg/m²
Second dose	5.5 mg/m²	3.75 mg/m²
Third dose	7.4 mg/m²	5.0 mg/m²
Fourth dose	9.25 mg/m²	6.25 mg/m²
Fifth dose	11.1 mg/m²	7.5 mg/m²

The increases mentioned in Table I may be used until a maximum dose (not exceeding 18.5 mg/m² bsa for adults and 12.5 mg/m² bsa for children) is reached. The dose should not be increased after that dose which has reduced the white cell count to approximately 3 000 cells/mm³. In some adults, 3.7 mg/m² bsa may produce this leukopenia; other adults may require more than 11.1 mg/m² bsa; and very rarely, as much as 18.5 mg/m² bsa may be necessary. For most adult patients, however, the weekly dosage will prove to be 5.5 to 7.4 mg/m² bsa.

When the dose of vinblastine, which will produce the above degree of leukopenia, has been established, a dose one increment smaller than this should be administered at weekly intervals for maintenance. Thus, the patient is receiving the maximum dose that does not cause leukopenia. It should be emphasized that, even though 7 days have elapsed, the next dose of vinblastine should not be given until the white cell count has returned to at least 4 000/mm³. In some cases, oncolytic activity may be encountered before leukopenic effect. When this occurs, there is no need to increase the size of subsequent doses.

The duration of maintenance therapy varies according to the disease being treated and the combination of antineoplastic agents being used. There are differences of opinion regarding the duration of maintenance therapy with the same protocol for a particular disease; for example, various durations have been used with the MOPP program in treating Hodgkin's disease. Prolonged chemotherapy for maintaining remissions involves several risks, among which are life-threatening infectious diseases, sterility, and possibly the appearance of other cancers through suppression of immune surveillance. In some disorders, survival following complete remission may not be as prolonged as that achieved with shorter periods of maintenance therapy. On the other hand failure to provide maintenance therapy in some patients may lead to unnecessary relapse. Failure to provide maintenance therapy for at least 2 years after complete remission in patients with testicular cancer, often results in early relapse.

The dose of vinblastine (calculated to provide the desired amount) may be injected either into the tubing of a running i.v. infusion or directly into a vein. The latter procedure is readily adaptable to outpatient therapy. In either case, the injection may be completed in about 1 minute. If care is taken to insure that the needle is securely within the vein and that no solution containing vinblastine is injected extravascularly, cellulitis and/or phlebitis will not occur.

To minimize further the possibility of extravascular spillage, it is suggested that the syringe and needle be rinsed with venous blood before withdrawal of the needle. The dose should not be diluted in large volumes of diluent (i.e., 100 to 250 mL) or given i.v. for prolonged periods (ranging from 30 to 60 minutes or more), since this frequently results in irritation of the vein and increases the chances of extravasation.

Because of the enhanced possibility of thrombosis, it is considered inadvisable to inject a solution of vinblastine into an extremity in which the circulation is impaired or potentially impaired by such conditions as compressing or invading neoplasm, phlebitis or varicosity.

Caution: If leakage into the surrounding tissue should occur during i.v. administration of vinblastine, it may cause considerable irritation. The injection should be discontinued immediately, and any remaining portion of the dose should then be introduced into another vein. Local injection of hyaluronidase and the application of moderate heat to the area of leakage help disperse the drug and are thought to minimize discomfort and the possibility of cellulitis.

Supplied: Each mL of sterile, unpreserved solution contains: vinblastine sulfate 1 mg with 0.9% Sodium Chloride in Water for Injection. Vials of 10 mL. Store solution at 2 to 8°C. Protect from light and from freezing.

VINCRISTINE SULFATE INJECTION USP Ⓟ

Faulding

Antineoplastic

Pharmacology: The mode of action of vincristine has not been completely delineated. Evidence is available from in vitro studies that vincristine inhibits spindle formation and is associated with the reversible binding of vincristine to spindle proteins in the S phase. Vincristine has also been found to interfere with RNA synthesis. It has also been shown to stop cell reproduction in metaphase, but it is not known if this effect is related to the above actions.

Following the rapid i.v. administration of vincristine, a triphasic elimination pattern is seen with half-lives of 5 minutes, 2.3 hours and 85±69 hours, respectively. Large interpatient variation occurs in both the terminal elimination half-life and the volume of distribution of vincristine. Vincristine is excreted mainly by way of the liver with about 80% of the dose being recovered in the feces and 10 to 20% in urine. Over 90% of vincristine is distributed into tissue within 15 to 30 minutes after injection, where it is tightly but not irreversibly bound.

Because some patients who are responding to vincristine therapy have CNS leukemia, it has been suggested that the drug dose does not penetrate into cerebrospinal fluid.

Vincristine has not been found to have a consistent or significant influence on platelet count or morphology or red blood cells. If thrombocytopenia is present when treatment with vincristine is initiated the condition may improve prior to the appearance of bone marrow remission.

At the recommended doses of vincristine patients with normal bone marrow function will not develop significant leukopenia.

Indications: In the treatment of acute leukemia. It has also been used in combination with other antineoplastic drugs in Hodgkin's disease, soft-tissue sarcoma, bony-tissue sarcoma, sarcomas of specialized structures, breast cancer, small cell cancer of the lung, cancer of the uterine cervix, malignant melanoma, colorectal cancer, non-Hodgkin's lymphoma and Wilms' tumor.

The simultaneous use of several cancer chemotherapy drugs is common practice. Generally drugs with different dose limiting clinical toxicities and different mechanisms of action are selected in order to obtain an increase in therapeutic response without added toxicity. Rarely is it possible to obtain equally as good a response with single antineoplastic agent treatment. Therefore, vincristine is often part of polychemotherapy because at the recommended doses it does not cause a significant suppression of bone marrow or neuropathy.

In children multiple-agent chemotherapy of malignant disease is also common. Vincristine should be considered for use with other oncolytic agents in the treatment of neuroblastoma, osteogenic sarcoma, Ewing's sarcoma, rhabdomyosarcoma, Wilms' tumor, Hodgkin's disease, non-Hodgkin's lymphomas, embryonal carcinoma of the ovaries and rhabdomyosarcoma of the uterus.

Although not recommended as a primary treatment, vincristine may be useful in the treatment of true idopathic thrombocytopenia purpura which has been shown to be refractory to splenectomy and treatment with steroids. Administration of the recommended dose of vincristine weekly for 3 to 4 weeks has resulted in permanent remission in some patients. However, if no response is obtained after 3 to 6 doses it is unlikely that there will be any beneficial effects with additional administration.

Contraindications: There are no contraindications to the administration of vincristine, but careful attention should be given to those conditions listed under Warnings and Precautions.

Warnings: Caution: Vincristine is a potent drug and should be used only by physicians experienced with cancer chemotherapeutic drugs. Blood counts should be taken once or twice weekly. Discontinue or reduce the dosage upon evidence of abnormal depression of the bone marrow. Vincristine is fatal if given intrathecally; vincristine is for i.v. use only.

Pregnancy: No human or animal data is available which provides information on whether vincristine affects fertility in humans or whether it has teratogenic effects in animals or other adverse effects on the fetus.

Therefore, the physician should weigh the relative benefits of the administration of vincristine against the potential risks before giving the drug to individuals of childbearing age.

Precautions: As with other oncolytics vincristine has been associated with the development of acute uric acid nephropathy. If leukopenia or infection develops the physician should carefully consider whether to administer additional doses of vincristine.

As vincristine does not cross the blood-brain barrier in significant quantities with pre-existing neuromuscular disease and when given with other drugs which have neuromuscular toxic potential, attention should be given to the dose of vincristine used and the development of neurologic side effects.

Avoid contamination of the eyes with vincristine. If accidental contamination occurs, severe irritation or corneal ulceration may result and the eye should immediately be rinsed with copious quantities of water.

Adverse Effects: Adverse reactions are generally reversible and dose related, with the most common being hair loss and the most troublesome being neuromuscular in origin.

Neuromuscular: There is often a sequence in the development of neuromuscular side effects, with sensory impairment and paresthesias developing initially. Neuritic pain and motor difficulties may develop with continued administration. No agent is known which can reverse the neuromuscular effects of vincristine. Vincristine may cause an exacerbation of the signs and symptoms of pre-existing neurologic disorders.

Convulsions, often with hypertension, have been observed in a few patients given vincristine. As well, ataxia, foot drop, paresthesia and numbness of the digits have been reported.

Gastrointestinal: Upper colon fecal impaction (constipation) may occur but on physical examination, the rectum may be empty. Colic and abdominal pain together with an empty rectum may mislead the clinician. A flat film of the abdomen is useful in diagnosing this condition. High enemas and laxatives are effective treatment for this side effect. It is recommended that routine treatment for constipation be used prophylactically in patients administered vincristine.

Paralytic ileus may also occur, particularly in young children and in the elderly. This condition will reverse itself if vincristine is temporarily discontinued and the patient is given symptomatic care.

Abdominal cramps, vomiting and diarrhea have also been reported.

Renal: In elderly patients with obstructive uropathy, increased urinary retention may occur. If such patients are receiving other medications which may enhance urinary retention, they should be temporarily withdrawn during the first few days of viscristine therapy.

Polyuria and dysuria have been reported.

Hematologic: No consistent or significant effects of vincristine on platelets or red blood cells have been observed. If thrombocytopenia is present when vincristine therapy is initiated, it may actually improve before the development of marrow remission.

At the recommended doses of vincristine, patients with normal bone marrow function will not develop significant leukopenia.

Other: Weight loss, fever, cranial nerve manifestations, oral ulceration and headache have all been reported.

The syndrome resulting from inappropriate antidiuretic hormone secretion has been observed in some patients treated with vincristine. This syndrome has been described in association with several disease states. It includes high urinary sodium excretion together with hyponatremia; renal or adrenal disease, hypotension, dehydration, azotemia, and clinical edema are absent. With fluid deprivation, improvement occurs in the hyponatremia and in the renal loss of sodium.

The side effects of leukopenia, neuritic pain, and constipation which may be associated with the single weekly administration of recommended doses of vincristine are usually of a short duration of less than 7 to 10 days. These reactions may lessen or disappear if the dosage is reduced. The side effects appear to increase when the drug is given in divided doses. Other side effects such as hair loss, sensory loss, paresthesia, slapping gait, difficulty in walking, loss of deep-tendon reflexes and muscle wasting may persist while vincristine therapy is continued. In most instances, these side effects disappear by about the sixth week after stopping vincristine therapy, but neuromuscular signs may persist for prolonged periods in some patients.

After i.v. administration of vincristine, the drug is primarily secreted in the bile after rapid tissue binding. Therefore, in patients with significant liver disease vincristine excretion may be decreased resulting in an increase in the severity of side effects. Hemodialysis is not likely to be of significant value in instances of overdosage as only small quantities of the drug appear in the dialysate.

Overdose: Symptoms and Treatment: Because the toxic effects of vincristine are dose related, exaggerated side effects will be experienced in those administered an overdose. Supportive care in the treatment of symptoms should include: prevention of side effects resulting from the syndrome of inappropriate secretion of antidiuretic hormone which would include restriction of fluid intake and possibly the administration of a diuretic with a mechanism of action on the loop of Henle and the distal tubes; administration of anticonvulsant doses of phenobarbital; use of cathartic type laxatives to prevent ileus; monitoring the cardiovascular system; daily blood counts for guidance in transfusion requirements.

Dosage: Extreme care must be used in calculating and administering the dose of vincristine, since overdosage may have a very serious or fatal outcome.

The drug is given **i.v. at weekly intervals.**

Adults: The usual dose of vincristine is 1.4 mg/m².

Children: The usual dose of vincristine is 2 mg/m².

Other dosage schedules have been used.

For children weighing 10 kg or less, the initial dose of vincristine should be 0.05 mg/kg once a week, with careful increasing of dosing thereafter based on effects.

Vincristine should not be administered to patients receiving radiation therapy through ports that include the liver.

When vincristine is used in combination with L-asparaginase, it should be given 12 to 24 hours prior to administration of the enzyme in order to minimize toxicity because L-asparaginase may reduce hepatic clearance of vincristine.

Administration: Vincristine solution may be injected either directly into a vein or into the tubing of an i.v. infusion. Injection of the solution may be completed in about 1 minute.

Caution: It is extremely important to be certain that the needle is properly positioned in the vein before any vincristine is injected. If leakage into the surrounding tissue should occur during i.v. administration of vincristine, it may cause considerable irritation. The injection should be discontinued immediately, and any remaining portion of the dose should then be introduced into another vein. Local injection of hyaluronidase and the application of moderate heat to the area of leakage help disperse the drug and are thought to minimize discomfort and the possibility of cellulitis.

Safe Handling: Preparation of Vinca alkaloids, including vincristine, should be done in a biological safety cabinet. Personnel preparing Vinca alkaloids should wear safety glasses. If accidental skin contact occurs, the skin should be washed thoroughly. Incineration temperatures of 1 000°C or more should be sufficient for Vinca alkaloid wastes. If for any reason, a Vinca alkaloid needs to be returned to Faulding (Canada) Inc., proper precautions should be taken in packing these materials for transport.

Vincristine solutions should be inspected visually for particulate matter and discoloration prior to administration, whenever solution and container permit.

Further dilution: The solution may be further diluted with 0.9% sodium chloride injection or 0.5% dextrose injection if desired.

Stability: The further diluted solution must be used within 6 hours if stored at room temperature or 24 hours if refrigerated and protected from light.

Dispensing of Pharmacy Bulk Vials: Pharmacy Bulk Vials contain 1 mg/mL vincristine sulfate in 5 mL of sterile, unpreserved solution (see Supplied).

The availability of Pharmacy Bulk Vials is restricted to hospitals with a recognized i.v. admixture program.

Pharmacy Bulk Vials are intended for multiple dispensing **for i.v. use only** employing a single puncture (see Safe Handling).

The Pharmacy Bulk Vial content should be dispensed within 8 hours. Any unused solution should be discarded. The diluted solutions prepared from the Pharmacy Bulk Vial should be used within 24 hours, when kept at room temperature, from the time of puncture of the Pharmacy Bulk Vial.

Pharmacy Bulk Vials contain no preservatives. Care must be taken to minimize the potential for inadvertent introduction of microorganisms during manipulation in the hospital environment.

Storage: Store in refrigerator between 2 and 8°C. Protect from light.

Supplied: Pharmacy Bulk Vials: Each mL of sterile, unpreserved solution contains: vincristine sulfate USP 1 mg and mannitol 100 mg. Vials of 5 mL.

Prefilled Syringes: Each mL of solution contains: vincristine sulfate USP 1 mg and mannitol 100 mg. Prefilled syringes of 2 mL.

Vials: Each mL of solution contains: vincristine sulfate USP 1 mg and mannitol 100 mg, with Water for Injection USP. Single-dose, rubber-stoppered vials of 1 and 2 mL.

VINCRISTINE SULFATE INJECTION USP Ⓟ

Novopharm

Antineoplastic

Supplied: Each mL of solution contains: vincristine sulfate 1 mg. Nonmedicinal ingredients: mannitol, methylparaben, propylparaben and water for injection. Sodium hydroxide and/or sulfuric acid for pH adjustment. Multiple dose amber glass vials of 1 and 2 mL, and pharmacy bulk vials of 5 mL, packaged individually. The availability of Pharmacy bulk vials is restricted to hospitals with a recognized i.v. admixture program.

VIOFORM®

Novartis Pharmaceuticals

Clioquinol

Antibacterial—Antifungal

Pharmacology: Clioquinol is active against a broad spectrum of pathogenic microorganisms, including fungi (e.g., Candida, Microsporum, Trichophyton) and gram-positive bacteria (e.g., Staphylococci). Clioquinol has only a slight inhibitory effect on gram-negative bacteria. Clioquinol exerts a bacteriostatic, rather than a bactericidal action.

The antibacterial and antifungal properties of clioquinol have long been clinically established. Topically, clioquinol has demonstrated effectiveness in secondary skin infections and is compatible with many drugs commonly prescribed in the treatment of skin disorders.

Indications: Antimycotic and/or antibacterial treatment for nonextensive superficial dermatomycoses, infected forms of eczema, pyoderma, and mild burns.

The ointment is indicated for dry, crusted lesions.

In serious skin infections, the use of concomitant systemic antibacterial or antifungal agents may be indicated.

Contraindications: Known hypersensitivity to hydroxyquinolines, clioquinol, or other quinoline derivatives, iodine, as well as to any other components of the preparation (see Supplied).

Children: Clioquinol should not be used in children under 2 years of age.

Warnings: *Pregnancy* and *Lactation:* As in the case of any form of drug therapy, clioquinol should be used with caution during pregnancy, especially during the first 3 months.

It is not known whether the active substance passes into the breast milk when applied topically. The potential benefit of using this medication during pregnancy or lactation must be weighed against the possible hazard to the fetus or nursing infant.

Precautions: Application of clioquinol to relatively large and/or eroded areas of skin, treatment for longer than 1 week, as well as use under occlusive dressings may lead to a marked increase in protein-bound iodine (PBI) and should be avoided (see Overdose: Symptoms and Treatment).

If no improvement occurs within 1 week, the therapy should be discontinued; it is then advisable to identify and treat the causative pathogens.

Clioquinol should not be allowed to come into contact with the conjunctiva.

In patients suffering from hepatic and/or renal failure, caution is indicated.

Clioquinol may turn yellow when exposed to air and may stain fabric, hair, skin or nails.

Interactions: Topical use of clioquinol, as well as other iodine-containing compounds, may increase the amount of protein-bound iodine (PBI) in patients with normal thyroid function and therefore may interfere with some thyroid function tests (such as PBI, radioactive iodine and butanol-extractable iodine). These tests should not be performed within a period shorter than 1 month following the use of clioquinol. Other thyroid function tests, such as the T_3 resin sponge test or the T_4 determination, are unaffected by clioquinol.

The ferric chloride test for phenylketonuria may yield a false positive test when trace amounts of clioquinol are present in the urine.

Adverse Effects: In rare cases, clioquinol may prove irritating to sensitized skins. If an exacerbation or allergic type reaction occurs, treatment should be discontinued.

Overdose: Symptoms and Treatment: Application to extensive or eroded areas of skin may lead to increased PBI values within 1 week. Elevated PBI values may also occur where relatively small areas of skin are treated for more than 1 week. If signs and symptoms resembling those of thyrotoxicosis occur, the preparation should be withdrawn at once.

Dosage: Apply clioquinol to the affected area in a thin layer 2 to 3 times daily.

Use of clioquinol under occlusive dressings is not recommended in view of the presence of skin infection and also the possibility of an increase in PBI.

Information for the Patient: See Blue Section—Information for the Patient "Vioform".

Supplied: Each tube of off-white ointment contains: clioquinol 3%. Nonmedicinal ingredients: petrolatum and sorbitan esters. Bisulfite- and tartrazine-free. Tubes of 30 g. Protect from heat (store between 15 and 30°C). May turn yellow when exposed to air and may cause staining of the skin, nails, hair or fabrics.

Reviewed 1999

VIOFORM® HYDROCORTISONE Ⓟ

Novartis Pharmaceuticals

Clioquinol—Hydrocortisone

Antibacterial—Antifungal—Topical Corticosteroid

Pharmacology: Clioquinol, the antimicrobial component of Vioform Hydrocortisone, is active against a broad spectrum of pathogenic microorganisms, including fungi (e.g., Candida, Microsporum, Trichophyton) and gram-positive bacteria (e.g., Staphylococci). Clioquinol has only a slight inhibitory effect on gram-negative bacteria. Clioquinol exerts a bacteriostatic, rather than a bactericidal action.

Hydrocortisone is a mild glucocorticoid with an anti-inflammatory, antiallergic and vasoconstrictive effect. In inflammatory skin diseases of widely varying type and origin it affords prompt relief and eliminates symptoms such as pruritus.

Vioform Hydrocortisone combines the antifungal and antibacterial actions of clioquinol with the anti-inflammatory and antipruritic effects of hydrocortisone for broad control of acute and chronic dermatologic disorders.

Vioform Hydrocortisone (cont'd)

Indications: The initial treatment of corticosteroid-responsive inflammatory skin diseases complicated by bacterial and/or fungal infections, with appropriate systemic antibiotics if necessary. For example: atopic dermatitis, seborrheic dermatitis, contact dermatitis (dermatitis venenata), superficial forms of intertrigo, and dermatomycosis in which acute inflammation is a prominent feature.

The cream has a slightly drying effect primarily useful for moist, weeping lesions and in intertriginous areas.

Contraindications: Viral infections of the skin (e.g., chickenpox, skin eruptions following vaccination, herpes simplex, herpes zoster), tuberculosis of the skin, syphilitic skin infections.

Known hypersensitivity to hydrocortisone or to corticosteroids in general, hydroxyquinolines, clioquinol, or other quinoline derivatives, iodine, as well as to any other components of Vioform Hydrocortisone (see Supplied).

Application to ulcerated areas.

Application to the eye.

Children: Do not use in children under 2 years of age.

Warnings: *Pregnancy* and *Lactation:* The safety of Vioform Hydrocortisone during pregnancy or lactation has not been established. Animal studies have shown that corticosteroids may induce fetal abnormalities in pregnant animals. The relevance of this finding to human use has not been elucidated. It is not known whether the active substance passes into the breast milk when applied topically. Therefore, the potential benefit of Vioform Hydrocortisone, if used during pregnancy (particularly in the first 3 months) or lactation, should be weighed against possible hazard to the fetus or the nursing infant.

Precautions: Application to relatively large and/or eroded areas, treatment for longer than 1 week, as well as use under occlusive dressings may lead to a marked increase in protein-bound iodine (PBI) and should be avoided.

Provided the preparation is used as recommended, unwanted systemic effects are unlikely to occur. On basic medical grounds, the possibility of a clinically important effect on adrenocortical function should nevertheless be borne in mind, particularly if the preparation is used under occlusion, over large areas of the body, in pediatrics and in patients undergoing prolonged therapy.

If no improvement occurs within 1 week, the therapy should be discontinued; it is then advisable to identify and treat the causative pathogens.

Vioform Hydrocortisone should not be used to treat bacterial or mycotic skin diseases in which acute inflammation is not present.

If in exceptional cases Vioform Hydrocortisone is applied in large amounts, the patient should be kept under regular medical supervision.

As a general rule, advise patients to inform subsequent physicians that they have been using corticosteroids.

Vioform Hydrocortisone should not be allowed to come into contact with the conjunctiva.

Vioform Hydrocortisone should not be used in the external auditory canal if the eardrum is perforated.

In patients suffering from hepatic and/or renal failure, caution is indicated.

Vioform Hydrocortisone may turn yellow when exposed to air and may cause staining of the skin, nails, hair or fabrics.

Interactions: Topical use of clioquinol, as well as other iodine-containing compounds, may increase the amount of protein-bound iodine (PBI) in patients with normal thyroid function and therefore may interfere with some thyroid function tests (such as PBI, radioactive iodine and butanol-extractable iodine). These tests should not be performed within a period shorter than 1 month following the use of Vioform Hydrocortisone. Other thyroid function tests, such as the T_3 resin sponge test or the T_4 determination, are unaffected by clioquinol.

The ferric chloride test for phenylketonuria may yield a false-positive result when clioquinol is present in the urine.

Adverse Effects: Occasionally: signs of irritation such as burning sensation, itching or skin rash at the site of application; hypersensitivity reactions.

If an exacerbation or allergic type reaction occurs, treatment with Vioform Hydrocortisone should be discontinued.

Local adverse reactions reported during topical treatment with glucocorticoids (predominantly with glucocorticoids more potent thant hydrocortisone) include contact allergy, changes in skin pigmentation, secondary infections. Topically applied glucocorticoids may give rise to striae rubrae distensae, telangiectasia, purpura, skin atrophy, or steroid acne, especially if applied for prolonged periods of time, under occlusive dressings, to large areas or to permeable areas (e.g., face, axillae). However, serious side effects caused by topically applied hydrocortisone are rare unless it is used excessively.

Overdose: Symptoms and Treatment: Application to extensive and/or eroded areas of skin may lead to increased PBI values within 1 week. Elevated PBI values may also occur where relatively small areas of skin are treated for more than 1 week. If signs and symptoms resembling those of thyrotoxicosis occur, the preparation should be withdrawn at once.

Dosage: Apply Vioform Hydrocortisone to affected area in a thin layer 2 to 3 times daily.

Use of Vioform Hydrocortisone under occlusive dressings is not recommended as the resulting humid conditions may promote secondary infections with nonsensitive organisms and also may increase the possibility of elevated PBI.

Information for the Patient: See Blue Section—Information for the Patient "Vioform Hydrocortisone".

Supplied: Each tube of off-white water soluble cream contains: clioquinol 3% and hydrocortisone 1%. Nonmedicinal ingredients: cetyl alcohol, cetyl palmitate, glycerin, petrolatum, phenoxyethanol, sodium lauryl sulfate, stearyl alcohol and water. Sodium: <1 mmol (0.8 mg)/g. Bisulfite- and tartrazine-free. Tubes of 20 and 50 g. Protect from heat (store between 15 and 30°C) and freezing. May turn yellow when exposed to air and may cause staining of the skin, nails, hair or fabrics.

Reviewed 1999

VIOKASE®

Axcan Pharma

Pancrelipase

Oral Enzyme Therapy

Pharmacology: The natural digestive enzymes in Viokase hydrolyse fats into fatty acids and glycerol, split protein into amino acids, and convert carbohydrates to dextrins and short chain sugars. Under conditions of the USP test method (in vitro), Viokase has the following total digestive capacity: See Table I.

Table I—Viokase

Total Digestive Capacity

	Each tablet	Each 0.7 g powder
Dietary fat (g)	28	59
Dietary protein (g)	30	70
Dietary starch (g)	30	70

The digestive capacity of a pancreatic enzyme concentrate depends on the amount that passes through the stomach unchanged and is available at the site of action in the small intestine.

Indications: As a digestive aid in the treatment of exocrine pancreatic insufficiency as associated with but not limited to cystic fibrosis, chronic pancreatitis, pancreatectomy, or obstruction of the pancreas ducts.

Contraindications: Should not be used in patients hypersensitive to pork protein.

Precautions: Individuals previously sensitized to trypsin, pancreatin or pancrelipase may have allergic manifestations.

Pancrelipase should not be held in the mouth as the proteolytic action may cause irritation of the mucosa.

Avoid inhalation of the powder when administering pancrelipase.

Carcinogenesis, Mutagenesis, Impairment of Fertility: Long-term studies in animals have not been performed to evaluate the carcinogenic or mutagenic potential of pancrelipase. The effect on human fertility is not known.

Pregnancy: Animal reproduction studies have not been conducted with pancrelipase. It is also not known whether pancrelipase can cause fetal harm when administered to a pregnant woman or can affect reproduction capacity. Pancrelipase should be given to a pregnant woman only if clearly needed.

Lactation: It is not known whether this drug is excreted in human milk. Because many drugs are excreted in human milk, caution should be exercised when pancrelipase is administered to a nursing mother.

Adverse Effects: The dust or finely powdered enzyme concentrate is irritating to the nasal mucosa and the respiratory tract. It has been documented that inhalation of the airborne powder can precipitate an asthma attack. The literature also contains several references to asthma due to inhalation in patients sensitized to pancreatic enzyme concentrates.

Extremely high doses of exogenous pancreatic enzymes have been associated with hyperuricemia and hyperuricosuria.

Overdose: Symptoms and Treatment: Acute toxicity determinations in animals have not been possible since the maximum dose that could be given orally produced no toxic reaction. In chronic feeding tests rats developed swollen salivary glands. This is believed due to the proteolytic activity and the mucosal irritation caused by tissue digestion.

Overdosage of pancreatic enzyme concentrate may cause diarrhea or transient intestinal upset.

No acute toxic reaction have been reported.

Dosage: Powder: Dosage for patients with cystic fibrosis: ¼ teaspoonful (0.7 g) with meals or as directed by a physician.

Tablets: Dosage for patients with cystic fibrosis or chronic pancreatitis: 1 to 3 tablets with meals or as directed by a physician.

As a digestive aid in patients with pancreatectomy or obstruction of pancreatic ducts: 1 to 2 tablets taken at 2-hour intervals or as directed by a physician.

Supplied: Powder: Tan-colored, each 0.7 g contains: lipase 16 800 USP units, protease 70 000 USP units, amylase 70 000 USP units and digests in vitro 59 g of fat, 70 g of protein and 70 g of starch. Also contains lactose. Energy: 5.4 kJ (1.3 kcal)/g. Bottles of 114 g.

Tablets: Each tan-colored, round, compressed tablet contains: lipase 8 000 USP units, protease 30 000 USP units, amylase 30 000 USP units and digests in vitro 28 g of fat, 30 g of protein and 30 g of starch. Also contains lactose. Energy: <1 kJ (<1 kcal). Bottles of 100 and 1 000.

Store at controlled room temperature (15 to 30°C). Protect from heat and moisture. Dispense tablets and powder in a tight container, preferably with a desiccant.

VIPRINEX®

Knoll

Ancrod

Anticoagulant

Pharmacology: Ancrod, a thrombin-like enzyme obtained from the venom of the Malayan Pit Viper (Agkistrodon rhodostoma), is highly specific for fibrinogen, producing anticoagulation by defibrinogenation.

Enzymatically, Ancrod cleaves fibrinogen to split off the A-fibrinopeptides (A, AY and AP), but not the B-fibrinopeptide. The resulting fibrin polymers are imperfectly formed and much smaller in size (1 to 2 μm long) than the fibrin polymers produced by the action of thrombin. These ancrod-induced microthrombi are friable, unstable, urea-soluble and have significantly degraded α-chains. They do not cross-link to form thrombi. They are markedly susceptible to digestion by plasmin and are rapidly removed from circulation by either reticuloendothelial phagocytosis or normal fibrinolysis, or both.

Anticoagulant Effects: Anticoagulation through the removal of fibrinogen from the blood is rapid, occurring within hours following ancrod administration.

The blood viscosity in patients receiving ancrod is progressively reduced by 30 to 40% of the pretreatment levels. The decreased viscosity is directly attributable to lowered fibrinogen levels and leads to important improvements in blood flow and perfusion of the microcirculation. Erythrocyte flexibility is not affected by normal doses of ancrod. The rheological changes are readily maintained and the viscosity approaches pretreatment values very slowly (within about 10 days) after stopping ancrod.

Fibrinolytic Effects: Ancrod does not activate plagminogen and does not degrade preformed, fully cross-linked thrombin fibrin. Consequently, unlike fibrinolytic agents, ancrod can be used postoperatively.

However, ancrod has been reported to reduce the level of plasminogen activator inhibitor (PAI) and may stimulate the release of tissue plasminogen activator (TPA) from the endothelium. The profibrinolytic effect of these 2 actions appears to be limited to local microthrombus degradation. However, the extent and clinical significance of these effects are uncertain.

Effects on Other Clotting Factors: Unlike thrombin, ancrod does not directly activate Factor XIII, nor does it produce platelet aggregation nor cause the release of ADP, ATP, potassium, nor serotonin from platelets.

Platelet counts and survival time remain normal during ancord therapy.

Although ancrod has no direct effect on platelet aggregation, the fibrinogen degradation products (FDP) do inhibit platelet aggregation. For this reason the initial (Induction) dose of ancrod must be administered sufficiently slowly to prevent undue accumulation of FDP and thus minimize platelet aggregation inhibition.

Clinical *Pharmacokinetics:* When the fate of ancrod labelled with ^{125}I is followed, half the label disappears from the plasma in 3 to 5 hours, and at about 4 days 10% remains.

Ancrod is partially bound to the α_2 macroglobulin. Once the state of hypofibrinogenaemia is achieved by the induction dose it can be maintained by i.v. injections at 12-hour intervals or by continuous i.v. infusions, or s.c. injections.

Indications: For the treatment of established deep vein thrombosis; central retinal and branch vein thrombosis; priapism; pulmonary hypertension of embolic origin; embolism after insertion of prosthetic cardiac valves; rethrombosis after thrombolytic therapy and rethrombosis after vascular surgery. It is also indicated for the prevention of deep venous thrombosis after repair of the fractured neck of a femur.

For the treatment of moderate and severe chronic circulatory disorders of peripheral arteries (e.g., arteriosclerosis obliterans, thromboangiitis obliterans, diabetic microangiopathy and Raynaud's phenomenon).

Ancrod has been shown to be useful for maintaining anticoagulation in the presence of heparin-induced thrombocytopenia and thrombosis (HIT).

Contraindications: There is some evidence that the ancrod effect may be dangerous in septicemic states with or without evidence of diffuse intravascular coagulation.

Plasma expanders: Artificial plasma expanders (e.g. dextran) may cause severe bleeding in defibrinated patients and should **not** be administered during or within 10 days of ancrod therapy.

Pregnancy: It was not found to be teratogenic in animal studies, but some fetal deaths occurred as a result of placental hemorrhages in animals given high doses; therefore, it should **not** be used during pregnancy as the defibrinogenation mechanism of ancrod might be expected to interfere with the normal implantation of the fertilized egg.

Gastrointestinal pathology: The presence of lesions liable to bleed, such as peptic ulcer, ulcerative colitis contraindicates its administration.

Ulcerogenic drugs: Similarly, patients on drug regimes known to cause gastrointestinal bleeding should **not** be given ancrod.

Hematological defects: Underlying defects interfering with hemostasis, such as a platelet count less than 100 000/mm³, are also contraindications, unless the defect is drug-induced and reversible (as is the case in patients with HIT).

Reticulo-endothelial and lytic systems: Drugs that block the reticuloendothelial system (e.g. dextran), or block the physiological lytic system (e.g. aminocaproic acid), should **not** be administered concurrently with or within 10 days of ancrod therapy.

Warnings: Medical Support Level: To-date, clinical experience with ancrod has been gained in situations where high medical support levels exist (i.e., within the hospital environment). Until more extensive experience has been gained, this practice should be continued (see Dosage).

Before initiating therapy with ancrod, a supply of fibrinogen-rich cryoprecipitate should be secured and available to the physician (see Overdose).

Cardiovascular disease: The following cardiovascular conditions may be complicated by defibrinogenation: malignant hypertension; acute pericarditis; sub-acute bacterial endocarditis; retinopathy, grade 3 or worse; diabetic retinopathy; resting diastolic pressure >120 mm Hg.

Other conditions: Similarly, defibrinogenation may cause bleeding in uremia >100 mg% (>35.7 mM/L), renal colic with calculus; cerebrovascular accidents; history of neurosurgery.

Coronary thrombosis: In view of some evidence of delay in wound healing in experimental animals, it is considered at the present time that ancrod should **not** be used in coronary thrombosis, until further data on safety are available.

Antibody Formation/Resistance: I.M. use is **not** recommended as an alternative to i.v. administration, owing to the possibility of inducing antibody formation.

The s.c. regime recommended under Dosage should **not** be continued beyond a period of 1 month owing to risk of inducing resistance.

ESR: During treatment with ancrod, the erythrocyte sedimentation rate falls to about 1 mm/hour and cannot be used as an index of pathological activity.

Major Surgery: I.V. administration of ancrod is **not** recommended before, during or within 48 hours of major surgery. An exception is to prevent rethrombosis after vascular surgery when the risk of bleeding does exist, in which case, ancrod can be administered immediately postoperatively.

Induction Dose Duration: The first dose of ancrod must be given slowly so that the physiological methods of dealing with the fibrinogen degradation products are not overloaded.

When using the intravenous regime, the first dose is termed the **Induction Dose** and should be given by i.v. drip over a period of a minimum of **12** hours for maximum benefit at minimum risk.

The Induction Dose must **not** be given faster than over a period of **8** hours (see Dosage).

Although faster rates have been employed, usually in emergency situations, the risks are considered to outweigh the benefits.

Where there is circulatory insufficiency, the period of administration must be at least **12** hours.

Precautions: Pretreatment investigations: It is recommended that a blood film, platelet count and fibrinogen estimation should be made before treatment.

Daily Control: The fibrinogen concentration should be measured at six hours into, and at the end of the infusion of the Induction Dose.

Fibrinogen should also be measured at regular intervals, at the same time of the day, during the maintenance dose infusions.

Migraine: A few patients with a history of migraine have experienced headaches after ancrod injections. Maintenance doses should be administered very slowly to these individuals.

Minor surgery: It is possible to carry out minor surgery (e.g., opening an abscess) while the patient is undergoing ancrod therapy, but each case must be judged carefully for risk of bleeding.

Transfusion: Whole blood, plasma or albumin may be given as needed, but artificial plasma expanders must not be used until fibrinogen levels have returned to normal.

Adverse Effects: Bleeding: Since ancrod has a highly specific effect upon fibrinogen, the risk of bleeding is low. Nevertheless, patients should be selected carefully in the light of the advice given under Warnings and Precautions.

Hemorrhaging may occur. If necessary, the effects of ancrod may be rapidly reversed by specific procedures described under Overdose.

Minor bleeding and oozing may occur and these are dealt with by pressure.

Skin reactions: Reactions such as skin rash are rare and have responded to antihistamine.

Local injection site reactions to s.c. injections are not common and may be cleared with an antihistamine.

Other: Transient chills and elevated temperatures have been infrequently reported.

Overdose: Symptoms and Treatment: In the event of severe hemorrhage, or if major surgery becomes necessary during the course of ancrod therapy cryoprecipitate can be administered to rapidly raise the plasma fibrinogen concentrations to safe levels.

The need for specific emergency procedures has been very rare. Following discontinuation of ancrod, fibrinogen levels rise slowly, reaching normal levels within a few days to 1 week. An infusion of human plasma will accelerate this process.

Nevertheless, it is recommended that cryoprecipitate is always available when ancrod is used.

Use of Cryoprecipitate: Cryoprecipitate can be administered to rapidly raise the plasma fibrinogen concentrations to safe levels.

The amount of cryoprecipitate required is dependent upon the level of ancrod circulating in the patient. It can be titrated against the circulating fibrinogen concentration, which should be measured within 1 hour of cryoprecipitate administration.

A single administration of 10 to 20 units is usually sufficient. (One bag enables the fibrinogen level to be raised by 0.2 g/L.)

Where cryoprecipitate is not available, plasma can be used.

Dosage: Medical Support Levels: ancrod can be injected s.c. or by i.v. infusion.

S.C. treatment should be carried out in a hospital; if there are adequate facilitites for the regular control of fibrinogen concentration it may also be undertaken in the Out-patient's Clinic.

Most frequently, ancrod is given i.v. The infusion should be done under close observation in a hospital.

I.M. use is **not** recommended owing to the possibility of inducing antibody formation.

S.C. Regimen: Peripheral Arterial Insufficiency: The dose of Arvin should be determined individually depending on the concentration of fibrinogen. This should be slowly reduced to 0.2 to 0.7 g/L of plasma. It should be kept within this range during the whole course of treatment. Under these conditions the rheological properties of the blood are sufficiently improved. The duration of therapy is generally 3 to 4 weeks, and may be prolonged if necessary.

The following alternative schemes will produce the desired fibrinogen concentration within 3 to 6 days: 70 units (1 ampul) daily for the first 4 days, followed by 70 to 140 units (1 to 2 ampuls) daily from the 5th day onwards depending on the fibrinogen concentration; or 140 units (2 ampuls) per day in the initial stage of treatment. When the fibrinogen concentration has fallen to a level within the therapeutic range, 210 to 280 units (3 to 4 ampuls) are given in one injection 2 to 3 times per week.

Prophylaxis of Deep Vein Thrombosis in patients undergoing surgery for the fractured neck of a femur: The dose should be determined individually. The concentration of fibrinogen should be slowly reduced to 0.5 g/L of plasma or lower and should be maintained within this range during treatment. This may be achieved by giving 4 units/kg body weight (e.g., 4 ampuls for 70 kg weight) as a single s.c. injection immediately after surgery, then 1 ampul (1 unit/kg body weight) daily for the next 4 days.

S.C. regimes should **not** be continued beyond a period of one month owing to the risk of inducing resistance.

I.V. regimen: Induction Dose Administration: The first dose of ancrod must be given slowly so that the physiological methods of dealing with the fibrinogen degradation products are not overloaded.

The first dose is termed the **Induction Dose** and should be given by i.v. drip over a period of at least **12** hours.

The Induction Dose must **not** be given faster than over a period of **8** hours. Although faster rates have been employed, usually in emergency situations, the risks are considered to outweigh the benefits (see Warnings).

Induction Doses: 1 to 2 units/kg body weight in sodium chloride injection or dextrose 5% injection, the volume being varied from 250 to 500 mL according to the patient's condition. The target endpoint is to lower fibrinogen levels to between 0.2 and 0.7 g/L.

Dextran must not be used.

Maintenance Dose Administration: Subsequent (maintenance) doses of ancrod may be administered by i.v. infusion over 24 hours, to maintain a fibrinogen level of between 0.2 and 0.7 g/L.

Maintenance Doses: 0.5 to 1.0 units/kg body weight in 250 to 500 mL sodium chloride injection, or dextrose 5% injection, the volume being varied according to the patient's condition.

It is considered that the ideal period of treatment in patients with conditions such as deep vein thrombosis, central retinal vein thrombosis, is of the order of 7 days. Some patients have been successfully treated for periods up to 28 days.

The margin of safety with overdosage in the maintenance period, e.g. in the defibrinogenated state, is very wide, by a factor of at least 10. The regime for the Induction Dose, however, must be adhered to, so that the rate of production of fibrin degradation products does not overload the system.

Control methods: The fibrinogen concentration should be measured at 6 hours into, and at the end of the infusion of the Induction Dose. Fibrinogen should also be measured at regular intervals at the same time of day, during Maintenance Dose infusions.

A target fibrinogen level of between 0.2 and 0.7 g/L should be maintained, in order to provide adequate anticoagulation.

Copies of the methods for estimating the effect of ancrod on the plasma fibrinogen are available on application to Knoll Pharma Inc.

Supplied: Each mL of sterile, clean, colorless, aqueous solution contains: 70 IU ancrod in isotonic saline. pH 6.8 containing approximately 0.0025 M phosphate. Ampuls of 1 mL, boxes of 5. Store between 2 and 8°C. Do not freeze. Protect from light.

VIQUIN FORTE®

ICN

Hydroquinone—Glycolic Acid

Depigmentation Agent—Moisturizer

Pharmacology: Hyperpigmentation refers to the brown skin spots caused by an excess of the skin pigment melanin in certain areas. It can be hereditary as are freckles, caused

Viquin Forte (cont'd)

by sun damage, occur with increasing age, or be related to pregnancy or the use of oral contraceptives.

Hyperpigmentation usually develops gradually and increases with sun exposure. Skin lightening can be achieved by using a hydroquinone cream on small dark areas of skin. Hydroquinone slows down the production of melanin on the area to which it is applied. This gradually lightens the spot. The fading process usually takes 1 to 2 months with twice daily applications. After the spot has faded, skin fading creams need only be applied often enough to maintain the effect. Makeup can be applied over the product after it has dried.

Indications: To lighten age spots or other dark areas of skin.

Warnings: For external use only. Do not use near eyes, nostrils, mouth, mucous membranes or open cuts. In case of contact, rinse thoroughly with water. Do not use on broken or irritated skin. Do not use for children under 18 years of age (unless on the advice of a physician). Keep out of reach of children. Store at controlled room temperature between 15 and 30°C.

Precautions: Since Viquin Forte with moisturizing AHA contains sunscreens to protect treated areas from sun, it is not necessary to use sunscreens. However, during and after treatment with Viquin Forte with moisturizing AHA, limit sun exposure.

Dosage: First apply a thin layer of cream to a small area of unbroken skin behind the ear. If no excessive irritation or rash develops within 24 hours begin the treatment.

Then apply a thin layer of cream to areas you want to lighten for a period of 5 to 6 hours (rinse with water) for 2 days. If irritation develops, discontinue use.

Apply 2 times/day i.e., in the morning and at bedtime to areas you want to lighten. If irritation develops, reduce application to once daily. If irritation persists, discontinue use.

If no improvement is seen after 12 weeks, discontinue use. Use only on the advice of a physician.

Supplied: Each g of cream contains: hydroquinone 4%, sunscreens with a sun protecting factor (SPF) of 19 in a nonmedicinal base including glycolic acid (AHA) 10% among others. Tubes of 30 g. Store at controlled room temperature between 15 and 30°C.

New Product 1998

VIRAZOLE™ (LYOPHILIZED) ℞

ICN

Ribavirin

Antiviral

Pharmacology: Ribavirin is active against respiratory syncytial virus (RSV). In cell cultures, the inhibitory activity of ribavirin for RSV is selective. The mechanism(s) of action is unknown, although evidence exists that inhibition of other RNA and DNA viruses may be due to ribavirin competition with guanosine in formation of viral mRNA cap structures and/or interference with enzymes responsible for functional methylation of these molecules which are critical for production of structural viral proteins.

Indications: RSV infection should be documented by a rapid diagnostic method such as demonstration of viral antigen in respiratory tract secretions by immunofluorescence or ELISA before or during the first 24 hours of treatment. Ribavirin aerosol is indicated only for lower respiratory tract infection due to RSV. Treatment may be initiated while awaiting rapid diagnostic test results. However, treatment should not be continued without documentation of RSV infection.

Limited clinical data indicate that ribavirin administered as a small particle aerosol may be beneficial in the treatment of severe respiratory syncytial virus infection in neonates and infants when associated with underlying cardiovascular, pulmonary or immune deficiency. Treatment should be confined to hospitalized patients and administration should be continuous during the period of therapy apart from the time required for ancillary care of the patient. Only severe RSV lower respiratory tract infection is to be treated with ribavirin aerosol.

Ribavirin aerosol treatment must be accompanied by and does not replace standard supportive respiratory and fluid management for infants and children with severe respiratory tract infection.

Contraindications: Ribavirin aerosol is contraindicated in women or girls who are or may become pregnant during exposure to the drug. Ribavirin may cause fetal harm, and respiratory syncytial virus infection is self-limited in this population. Ribavirin is not completely cleared from human blood even 4 weeks after administration. Although there are no pertinent human data, ribavirin has been found to be teratogenic and/or embryolethal in nearly all species in which it has been tested; however, pregnant baboons given up to 120 mg/kg/day of ribavirin over a 4 day period within the 20 days of organogenesis during gestation failed to exhibit any teratogenic effect.

Warnings: Close monitoring of patients and respiratory equipment must be guaranteed when ribavirin is used in infants requiring assisted ventilation. Precipitation of ribavirin powder in respiratory equipment may interfere with safe and effective patient ventilation.

Bronchospasm was observed in a tolerance study with ribavirin aerosol in adults with chronic obstructive pulmonary disease and asthma.

Respiratory function should be carefully monitored during treatment. If initiation of ribavirin aerosol treatment appears to produce sudden deterioration of respiratory function, treatment should be stopped and only reinstituted with caution and continuous monitoring.

Pregnancy: Although ribavirin is not indicated in adults, the physician should be aware that it is teratogenic in animals (see Contraindications).

Ribavirin administered by aerosol produced cardiac lesions in mice and rats after 30 and 36 mg/kg, respectively, for 4 weeks, and after oral administration in monkeys at 120 mg/kg and rats at 154 to 200 mg/kg for 1 to 6 months. Ribavirin aerosol administered to developing ferrets at 60 mg/kg for 10 or 30 days resulted in inflammatory and possibly emphysematous changes in the lungs. Proliferative changes were seen at 131 mg/kg for 30 days. The significance of these findings to human administration is unknown.

Ribavirin lyophilized in 6 g vials is intended for use as an aerosol only.

It has been noted that ribavirin has shown some evidence of mutagenesis in some in vitro test systems. Carcinogenicity studies are incomplete and inconclusive. Some evidence for the production of benign tumors has been shown.

Precautions: Ribavirin has been in use for many years in human beings without any reported adverse effects in human fetuses. However, there are no adequate and well-controlled studies in pregnant women, and there is little published evidence of its safety in the early stages of human pregnancy. Since ribavirin is delivered in aerosolized form and because of known teratogenic effects in animals, pregnant women should not care for patients receiving ribavirin, although human teratogenic effects have not been proven.

Patients with lower respiratory tract infections due to respiratory syncytial virus require optimum monitoring and attention to respiratory and fluid status.

Drug Interactions: Interactions of ribavirin with other drugs such as digoxin, bronchodilators, other antiviral agents, antibiotics, or antimetabolites have not been evaluated. Interference by ribavirin with laboratory tests has not been evaluated. Appropriate attention should be given to the possibility of such interactions.

Adverse Effects: The safety data from patients treated with ribavirin aerosol has been carefully evaluated in 26 studies. Bronchospasm was observed in a tolerance study with ribavirin aerosol (20 mg/mL) in adults. One of 6 adult patients with chronic obstructive pulmonary disease and 2 of 6 asthmatic adults became dyspneic during the period of ribavirin aerosol administration. These patients required chronic administration of bronchodilators which were discontinued 24 hours prior to ribavirin treatment. An inhalation of a bronchodilator by puffer produced symptomatic relief and return to baseline conditions.

Several serious adverse events occurred in severely ill infants with life-threatening underlying diseases, many of whom required assisted ventilation. These events include: worsening of respiratory status, bacterial pneumonia and pneumothorax. The role of ribavirin in these events is indeterminate.

There were 19 deaths during or shortly after treatment with ribavirin aerosol. No death was attributed to ribavirin aerosol by the investigators.

Some subjects requiring assisted ventilation have experienced serious difficulties, which may jeopardize adequate ventilation and gas exchange. Precipitation of drug within the ventilatory apparatus, including the endotracheal tube, has resulted in increased positive end expiratory pressure and increased positive inspiratory pressure. Accumulation of fluid in tubing "rain out" has also been noted.

Although anemia has not been reported with use of the aerosol, it occurs frequently with oral and i.v. ribavirin, and most infants treated with the aerosol have not been evaluated 1 to 2 weeks post-treatment when anemia is likely to occur. Reticulocytosis has been reported with aerosol use.

Conjunctivitis has been reported in controlled studies with ribavirin aerosol, however, no significant difference was observed between ribavirin treated and control groups.

Overdose: Symptoms and Treatment: No overdosage with ribavirin by aerosol administration has been reported in the human. In man, ribavirin is sequestered in red blood cells for weeks after dosing.

Dosage: Before use, read thoroughly the ICN Small Particle Aerosol Generator (SPAG) Model SPAG-2 Operator's Manual for small particle aerosol generator operating instructions.

Treatment should be instituted as early as possible within the first 3 days of respiratory syncytial virus lower respiratory tract infection. Treatment early in the course of severe lower respiratory tract infection may be necessary to achieve efficacy. Treatment is carried out continuously, apart from the time required for ancillary care, for at least 3 and no more than 7 days, and is part of a total treatment program.

The aerosol is delivered to an infant oxygen hood from the SPAG-2 aerosol generator. Administration by face mask or oxygen tent may be necessary if a hood cannot be employed (see SPAG-2 manual). However, the volume of distribution and condensation area are larger in a tent and efficacy of this method of administering the drug has been evaluated in only a small number of patients. Ribavirin aerosol is not to be administered with any other aerosol generating device or from the same reservoir with other aerosolized medications.

Aerosolized bronchodilators, when clinically indicated, should be administered with the ribavirin SPAG-2 generator shut down.

Using the recommended drug concentration of 20 mg/mL ribavirin as the starting solution in the drug reservoir of the SPAG unit, the average aerosol concentration for a 12 hour period is 190 μg/L (0.19 mg/L) of air.

Reconstitution: By sterile technique, reconstitute drug with a minimum of 70 mL sterile water USP for injection or inhalation in the original 100 mL glass vial. Shake well. Transfer to the clean, sterilized 500 mL widemouth Erlenmeyer flask (SPAG-2 Reservoir) and further dilute to a final volume of 300 mL with sterile USP water for injection or inhalation. The final concentration should be 20 mg/mL.

Important: This water should not have **any antimicrobial agent or other substance added.** The solution should be inspected visually for particulate matter and discoloration prior to administration. When the liquid level in the SPAG-2 unit is low, it should be discarded before adding newly reconstituted solution. Solutions that have been placed in the SPAG-2 unit should be discarded at least every 24 hours.

Stability and Storage of Solution: Reconstituted solutions should be prepared immediately before use or may be stored in 100 mL glass vials under sterile conditions at 2 to 6°C for 24 hours. Further diluted solutions should not be stored.

Supplied: Each 100 mL glass vial of sterile, lyophilized powder contains: ribavirin 6 g. The drug is administered only by a small particle aerosol generator (SPAG-2). Store in a dry place at 15 to 25°C. Packs of 4.

Reviewed 1997

VIROPTIC® ℞

Glaxo Wellcome

Trifluridine

Topical Antiviral

Pharmacology: Trifluridine is phosphorylated by a cellular thymidine kinase to its nucleotide monophosphate. Trifluridine monophosphate is an inhibitor of thymidylate synthetase, the target enzyme for the action of monofluorinated pyrimidines. Trifluridine has been demonstrated to combine slowly and irreversibly with thymidylate synthetase in a reaction that requires ATP.

Trifluridine monophosphate is further phosphorylated by cellular enzymes to the triphosphate which is incorporated into DNA (but not RNA) by competitively inhibiting the incorporation of the natural nucleotide, thymidine triphosphate (dTTP).

The inhibition of viral replication can be reversed by the addition of thymidine (thymidine rescue).

Viral DNA polymerase has a higher affinity for trifluridine triphosphate than does the DNA polymerase of uninfected cells, resulting in the preferential incorporation of the analogue into viral DNA.

Trifluridine is active against the following DNA viruses: herpes simplex types 1 and 2, varicella zoster, adenovirus and vaccinia virus.

Intraocular penetration of trifluridine was evaluated in 5 patients undergoing intraocular surgery. One drop of 1% trifluridine was instilled into the affected eye 4 times at 10-minute intervals, the last dose being administered 5 minutes before sterile preparation for surgery. Penetration of the drug was demonstrated in 4 of the 5 patients in concentrations ranging from 3.1 to 43.9 μM with a mean value of 16.75 μM which exceeds the ED_{50}'s for most clinical isolates of HSV-1. There appeared to be a correlation between the degree of corneal integrity and the degree of penetration of trifluridine into the aqueous humor as evidenced by the fact that patients with corneal thinning had higher drug levels (mean 21.3 μM) than did the single patient with an intact cornea (3.1 μM) The major metabolite of trifluridine (5-carboxy-2'-deoxyuridine) was not detected in any of the eyes.

Pharmacokinetics: The pharmacokinetics of trifluridine in humans is similar to that of animals. The plasma half-life in human cancer patients following i.v. administration of the drug is short and dose-independent. In 3 patients, doses of 5, 15 and 27 mg/kg produced half-lives of 14, 28 and 18 minutes, respectively.

Following i.v. administration trifluridine is excreted in the urine largely as 5-carboxy-2'-deoxyuridine, with trace amounts of its intermediates and unchanged drug. Evidence indicates minimal tissue protein binding both in animals and man.

Samples from 12 volunteers who received topical 1% trifluridine did not reveal detectable serum levels of the drug, indicating that systemic absorption from the eye is minimal.

Indications: For the treatment of primary keratoconjunctivitis and recurrent epithelial keratitis due to herpes simplex viruses, types 1 and 2.

Trifluridine is also effective in the treatment of epithelial keratitis that has not responded clinically to the topical administration of idoxuridine or when ocular toxicity or hypersensitivity to idoxuridine has occurred. In a smaller number of patients found to be resistant to topical vidarabine, trifluridine was also effective.

Note: Trifluridine is not indicated for the treatment of keratitis with deep stromal invasion and uveitis, ocular vaccinia, adenoviral ocular disease, prophylaxis of keratoconjunctivitis and/or recurrent epithelial keratitis, Epstein Barr virus keratitis, or ocular bacterial, fungal, or chlamydial infections.

Contraindications: For patients who are known to be hypersensitive or intolerant to trifluridine or any of its nonmedicinal ingredients.

Warnings: The recommended dosage and frequency of administration should not be exceeded (see Dosage).

Pregnancy and *Lactation:* Trifluridine should not be administered to pregnant women or nursing mothers unless the anticipated benefits outweigh the potential risks. The teratogenic potential of this compound in humans is unknown.

The topical application of trifluridine to the eyes of rabbits on days 6 to 18 of gestation produced no teratogenic effects. When administered s.c. to rabbits and rats, fetal toxicity has been observed at doses above 1 mg/kg/day.

The maximum dose anticipated in a human being based on the recommended dosage is approximately 0.1 mg/kg/day, assuming a body weight of 45 kg.

Precautions: General: Trifluridine should be prescribed only for patients who have a clinical diagnosis of herpetic keratitis.

Trifluridine may cause mild local irritation of the conjunctiva and cornea when instilled, but these effects are usually transient.

Caution should be exercised in the use of trifluridine in the treatment of infections caused by strains of herpes simplex virus resistant to other antivirals. Conflicting evidence has been presented on the issue of cross-resistance to other antiviral agents. Resistance of herpes simplex virus type 1 to trifluridine has been produced in vitro and these strains are able to produce trifluridine-resistant infections in vivo. HSV 1 strains insensitive to trifluridine were also resistant to idoxuridine and vidarabine (adenine arabinoside). On the other hand, it has been shown that viruses lacking thymidine kinase and/or DNA polymerase activity may retain complete or reduced sensitivity to trifluridine in vitro and that trifluridine is still of some benefit in rabbit eyes infected with acyclovir-resistant strains of HSV-1. Early work showed that rabbits infected with HSV-1 strains made resistant to idoxuridine could still be treated successfully with trifluridine.

Following re-epithelialization, trifluridine should not be used in an attempt to reduce the rate of recurrence of herpetic keratitis, as supporting experimental and clinical data are lacking, and toxicity may occur with prolonged use.

Children: There is no specific experience respecting efficacy and safety of use in children.

Drug Interactions: Trifluridine should not be applied to the eye simultaneously with other medications. However, the following ophthalmic drugs have been administered topically and concurrently with trifluridine in a limited number of patients without apparent evidence of adverse interaction: antibiotics: chloramphenicol, erythromycin, polymyxin B sulfate, bacitracin, gentamicin sulfate, tetracycline HCl, sodium sulfacetamide, neoymcin sulfate; steroids: dexamethasone sodium phosphate, dexamethasone, prednisolone acetate, prednisolone sodium phosphate, hydrocortisone, fluorometholone; and other ophthalmic drugs: atropine sulfate, scopolamine HBr, naphazoline HCl, cyclopentolate HCl, homatropine HBr, pilocarpine, l-epinephrine HCl and sodium chloride.

Pregnancy: There are no adequate and well-controlled studies in pregnant women. The product should be used during pregnancy only if the potential benefit justifies the potential risk to the fetus.

Lactation: It is unlikely that trifluridine is excreted in human milk after ophthalmic instillation because of the relatively small dosage ($\leq$5.0 mg/day), its dilution in body fluids and its extremely short half-life (approximately 12 minutes). The drug should not be prescribed for nursing mothers unless the potential benefit outweighs the potential risk.

Adverse Effects: The following adverse reactions were noted in controlled and open studies during the administration of trifluridine: 54 of 297 (18%) patients experienced adverse reactions: burning upon instillation (12%); superficial punctate keratitis (2%); and eyelid edema, irritation, epithelial keratopathy, allergic reaction, increased intraocular pressure, keratitis sicca, stromal edema, blurred vision and nausea each occurred in less than 1% of the patients.

Overdose: Symptoms and Treatment: Overdosage by ocular instillation is unlikely because any excess solution should be quickly expelled from the conjunctival sac.

Acute overdosage by accidental oral ingestion has not been reported. However, should such ingestion occur, the 75 mg of trifluridine in a single bottle of solution would not be expected to produce adverse effects.

Single i.v. doses of 1.5 to 30 mg/kg/day in children and adults with neoplastic disease produce reversible bone marrow depression as the only potentially serious toxic effect and only after at least 5 doses. The acute oral LD_{50} in the mouse and rat was 4 379 mg/kg or higher.

Dosage: Adults: Instill 1 drop onto the cornea of the affected eye every 2 hours while awake. The maximum daily dosage is 9 drops.

This therapeutic regimen should be continued until the herpetic lesion has completely re-epithelialized. At this time the dosage should be reduced to 1 drop every 4 hours for a maximum daily dosage of 5 drops. This regimen should be continued for 7 days post-re-epithelialization.

If there are no signs of improvement after 7 days of full therapy or complete re-epithelialization has not occurred after 14 days of full therapy, other forms of therapy should be considered.

Administration of a full dosage regimen for periods exceeding 21 days should be avoided because of potential ocular toxicity.

Children: There is no specific information relating to use in children.

Supplied: Each bottle of sterile, aqueous, ophthalmic solution contains: trifluridine 1%. Nonmedicinal ingredients: acetic acid, benzalkonium chloride (as preservative), sodium acetate and sodium chloride. Plastic drop-dose dispenser bottle of 7.5 mL. Store under refrigeration at 2 to 8°C.

Reviewed 1997

VISIPAQUE™

Nycomed Imaging A.S.

Iodixanol

Nonionic Radiographic Contrast Medium

Pharmacology: Immediately following rapid intravascular injection, iodixanol reaches peak plasma concentration and is then rapidly distributed throughout the extracellular fluid compartment. It will opacify those vessels in the path of flow of the contrast medium, permitting radiographic visualization of the vasculature of the internal structures until significant dilution and elimination occurs. The degree of density enhancement is directly related to the iodine content in an administered dose.

The lower osmolality of iodixanol (which is isotonic with blood) compared with conventional contrast media of similar iodine concentration can be expected to cause fewer and less severe osmolality-related disturbances, specifically, less pain, heat and burning sensation, upon injection. Iodixanol has approximately one third the osmolality of the nonionic media and one sixth that of the monomeric ionic media of equiiodine concentration (i.e., 290 mOsm/kg water vs 844 and 1 800 mOsm/kg water respectively) (see Table I).

Table I—Visipaque

Osmolality

	Concentration (mg I/mL)	
Parameter	320	270
Osmolality (mOsm/kg water) (vapor pressure at 37°C)	290	290

Pharmacokinetics of i.v. administered iodixanol are best described by a 2-compartment model with a rapid phase for drug distribution and a slower phase for drug elimination. Following i.v. administration of 0.3 to 1.2 g I/kg body weight iodixanol to healthy adult males, the distribution half-life (alpha phase) is 21 minutes, excretion half-life (beta phase) 123 minutes, volume of distribution 0.26 L/kg body weight (a volume consistent with extracellular fluid), and renal clearance 110 mL/min. These values were independent of dose.

Iodixanol is excreted by glomerular filtration: approximately 97% of the injected dose is excreted unchanged in urine in the first 24 hours, with peak urine concentrations occurring in the first hour. Less than 2% is excreted in feces within 5 days post-injection.

In patients with impaired renal function, prolonged blood levels of a contrast agent, including iodixanol, may be anticipated due to decreased renal elimination.

In persons with normal renal function, renal visualization with iodixanol occurs approximately 5 minutes after injection; with monomeric nonionic media visualization occurs after approximately 2 minutes.

Iodixanol produced renal vacuolation of the proximal convoluted tubule in rats at lower urinary concentrations than did nonionic monomers. In view of these findings, it is recommended that caution should be exercised in patients with compromised renal function, and that only the lowest dose necessary to obtain adequate visualization should be used.

Iodixanol showed no significant metabolism in humans.

Iodixanol did not cross the intact blood-brain barrier to any significant extent following intravascular administration in animal studies.

In vitro at human plasma levels of 1.2 mg I/mL, iodixanol did not display any notable protein binding.

In contrast enhanced computed tomographic head imaging, iodixanol does not accumulate in normal brain tissue due to the presence of the normal blood-brain barrier. The increase in x-ray absorption in normal brain is due to the presence of iodixanol within the blood pool. Peak iodine levels occur immediately following rapid i.v. injection. A break in the blood-brain barrier, such as occurs in malignant tumors of the brain allows for the accumulation of contrast medium within the interstitial tissue of the tumor. Diagnostic contrast enhancement images of the brain have been obtained up to 1 hour after i.v. bolus administration.

In contrast enhanced CT body imaging (non-neural tissue), iodixanol diffuses rapidly from the vascular into the extravascular space. Increase in x-ray absorption is related to blood flow, dose, concentration of the contrast medium, diffusion of the contrast medium into the interstitial space, and timing of the scan. Contrast enhancement is thus due to the relative differences in vascularity and extravascular diffusion between normal and abnormal tissue, quite different from that in the brain.

Indications: Angiocardiography: Iodixanol 320 mg I/mL: For use in angiocardiography (left ventriculography, aortic root injections and selective coronary arteriography) and can be used in the diagnosis of coronary artery disease as well as evaluation of the function of the chambers of the heart and heart valves.

Arteriography: Iodixanol 320 mg I/mL: For visualization of the aorta and its branches and for selective peripheral and visceral arteriography and in diagnosing arterial occlusive diseases, aneurysms, arteriovenous malformations and tumors. It may be used for both conventional radiography and digital subtraction angiography (DSA).

Iodixanol 270 mg I/mL: For visualization of the aorta and its branches and for selective visceral arteriography and in diagnosing arterial occlusive diseases and tumors.

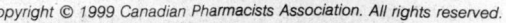

Visipaque (cont'd)

CT Scanning of the Head: Iodixanol 320 mg I/mL or 270 mg I/mL administered i.v. is indicated in refining diagnostic precision in areas of the brain that may not otherwise be satisfactorily visualized.

Iodixanol is useful in investigating the presence and extent of malignancies such as gliomas including malignant gliomas, glioblastomas, astrocytomas, oligodendrogliomas and gangliomas, ependymomas, medulloblastomas, meningiomas, neuromas, pinealomas, pituitary adenomas, craniopharyngiomas, geminomas and metastatic lesions. In calcified lesions there is less likelihood of enhancement; following therapy, tumors may show decreased or no enhancement.

Iodixanol may be beneficial in the enhancement of most non-neoplastic lesions, including many cerebral infarcts of recent onset, arteriovenous malformations and aneurysms.

Hematomas, intraparenchymal bleeding and clot seldom show enhancement; however, the administration of iodixanol may still help to rule out any associated arteriovenous malformation. Sites of active infection may be enhanced as well.

CT Scanning of the Body: Iodixanol 320 mg I/mL or 270 mg I/mL administered i.v. is indicated for enhancement of computed tomographic images for detection and evaluation of lesions in the liver, pancreas, kidney, aorta, mediastinum, pelvis, abdominal cavity, thoracic space and retroperitoneal space.

Excretory Urography: Iodixanol 320 mg I/mL or 270 mg I/mL administered i.v. is indicated in excretory urography to provide diagnostic contrast of the urinary tract and in the diagnosis of prostate enlargement, renal calculi, obstructive uropathy, urinary tract anomalies, neurogenic bladder and urinary tract malignancies.

Venography: Iodixanol 270 mg I/mL administered i.v. is indicated for venography and is useful in the diagnosis of thrombosis, phlebitis or obstructed venous system.

Contraindications: Iodixanol should not be administered to patients with known or suspected hypersensitivity to iodixanol.

Warnings: Use the recommended iodixanol concentration for the particular procedure to be undertaken.

Serious or fatal reactions have been associated with the administration of water-soluble contrast media. It is of utmost importance that a course of action be carefully planned in advance for immediate treatment of serious reactions, and that adequate facilities and appropriate personnel be readily available in case a severe reaction should occur.

There must be a clear indication for performing procedures involving the administration of contrast agents in all patients.

Diagnostic procedures which involve the use of radiopaque contrast agents should be carried out only by physicians with the prerequisite training and with a thorough knowledge of the particular procedure to be performed and who are thoroughly familiar with the emergency treatment of all adverse reactions to contrast media.

Generally accepted contraindications, warnings, precautions and adverse reactions commonly related to the use of radiopaque contrast media should be kept in mind during administration of iodixanol.

Pheochromocytoma: Administration of radiopaque media to patients known or suspected to have pheochromocytoma should be performed with extreme caution. If, in the opinion of the physician, the possible benefits of such procedures outweigh the considered risk, the amount of radiopaque material injected should be kept to a minimum. The blood pressure should be assessed throughout the procedure and measures for treatment of a hypertensive crisis should be available.

Sickle Cell: Contrast media, when injected i.v. or intra-arterially, may promote sickling in individuals who are homozygous for sickle cell disease.

Multiple Myeloma: Radiopaque contrast agents are potentially hazardous in patients with multiple myeloma or other paraproteinemias, particularly in those with therapeutically resistant anuria. Although neither the contrast agent nor dehydration has been proven separately to be the cause of anuria in myelomatous patients, it has been speculated that the combination of both may be causative. The risk in myelomatous patients is not a contraindication; however, they require special precautions (see Precautions).

Other Defined Patient Groups: Patients with a history of allergy, bronchial asthma or other allergic manifestations, combined renal and hepatic disease, the elderly, debilitated or severely ill patients, those with homocystinuria, endotoxemia, elevated body temperature, severe hypertension or congestive heart failure and other cardiovascular diseases, hyperthyroidism and recent renal transplant recipients, as well as patients sensitive to iodine, present an additional risk and call for careful benefit/risk ratio assessment. Patients with serum creatinine levels above 3 mg/dL should not undergo excretory urography or other radiological procedures unless the benefit clearly outweighs the risk.

Coagulation: Nonionic iodinated contrast media inhibit blood coagulation less than ionic contrast media in vitro. Clotting has been reported when blood remains in contact with syringes, catheters or tubes containing nonionic contrast media. Serious, rarely fatal, thromboembolic events causing myocardial infarction and stroke have been reported during angiographic procedures with nonionic and also with ionic contrast media. Therefore, meticulous intravascular administration technique is necessary, particularly during angiographic procedures, to minimize thromboembolic events. Numerous factors, including length of procedure, number of injections, catheter and syringe material, underlying disease state, and concomitant medications may contribute to the development of thromboembolic events. For these reasons, meticulous angiographic techniques are recommended including close attention to keeping guidewires, catheters and all angiographic equipment free of blood, use of manifold systems and/or three way stopcocks, frequent catheter flushing with heparinized saline solutions, and minimizing the length of the procedure. Nonionic iodinated contrast media are not recommended as flush solutions. The use of plastic syringes in place of glass syringes has been reported to decrease but not eliminate the likelihood of in vitro clotting.

Concurrent Medication: Extreme caution is advised should the injection of a contrast medium be indicated following the administration of vasopressors since they may strongly potentiate neurologic effects.

General anesthesia may be indicated in some procedures; however, one should be aware of possible increased incidence of adverse reactions in such circumstances.

Precautions: General: Patients should be well **hydrated** prior to and following administration of any contrast medium, including iodixanol. Preparatory dehydration is dangerous and may contribute to acute renal failure in patients with preexisting renal insufficiency, diabetes or advanced vascular disease. Dehydration in these patients seems to be enhanced by the osmotic diuretic action of urographic agents and by the decreased water clearance and uricosuria induced by cholangiographic agents. It is believed that overnight fluid restriction prior to excretory urography generally does not provide better visualization in normal patients.

Before any contrast medium is injected, the patient should be questioned for a history of allergy or bronchial **asthma.** The susceptible population includes, but is not limited to, patients with a known sensitivity to iodine per se, patients with a history of a previous reaction to contrast media, and patients with a known clinical hypersensitivity: bronchial asthma, hay fever and/or food allergies. Although a history of allergy or hypersensitivity may imply a greater than usual risk, it does not arbitrarily contraindicate the use of a contrast agent, but extreme caution should be exercised. Premedication with antihistamines or corticosteroids to avoid or minimize possible allergic reactions in such patients may be considered. Additionally, the possibility of an idiosyncratic reaction in patients who have previously received a contrast medium without ill effect should always be considered.

The i.v. injection of a test dose of 0.5 to 1 mL of the contrast agent, before injection of the full dose, has been employed in an attempt to predict severe or fatal adverse reactions. However, pretesting cannot be relied upon to predict severe reactions and may itself be hazardous for the patient. A history of allergy may be more useful in predicting reactions and warrants special attention when administering the drug. Since delayed severe reactions may occur, the patient should be kept under close observation following injection.

Unlike other iodinated contrast agents of comparable iodine concentration but with higher osmolality, iodixanol should not pull additional fluid into the blood because its osmolality is equivalent to the normal osmolality of whole blood. However, caution is required in patients with congestive heart failure since a transient increase in circulatory volume will occur with large injection volumes. These patients should be observed following the procedure to detect delayed hemodynamic disturbances.

Reports of thyroid storm occurring following the intravascular use of iodinated radiopaque agents in patients with hyperthyroidism or with an autonomously functioning thyroid nodule, suggest that this additional risk be evaluated in such patients prior to the use of iodixanol.

Caution should be exercised in performing contrast medium examination in patients with **endotoxemia** and in those with **elevated body temperature.**

Angiography should be avoided whenever possible in patients with **homocystinuria** because of the risk of inducing embolism.

In angiographic procedures, the possibility of dislodging **plaques,** rupturing **aneurysms,** or damaging (or perforating) the **vessel wall** should be borne in mind during catheter manipulations and contrast medium injection. Test injections to ensure proper catheter placement are recommended.

Special care is advised in patients with increased intracranial pressure, cerebral thrombosis or embolism, primary or metastatic cerebral lesions, subarachnoid hemorrhage, arterial spasm, transient ischemic attacks, and in any condition when the blood brain barrier is breached or the transit time of the contrast material through the cerebral vasculature is prolonged, since clinical deterioration, convulsions, and serious temporary or permanent neurological complications (including stroke, aphasia, cortical blindness, etc.) may occur following i.v. or intra-arterial injection of relatively large doses of contrast media. Such patients, and patients in clinically unstable or critical condition should undergo examinations with intravascular contrast media only if in the opinion of the physician the expected benefits outweigh the potential risks, and the dose should be kept to the absolute minimum.

Caution should be exercised in the administration of contrast media to severely debilitated patients, particularly those with severe hypertension and impaired renal function. Acute renal failure has been reported in patients with diabetic nephropathy and in susceptible nondiabetic patients (often elderly with preexisting renal disease) following administration of iodinated contrast agents. Careful consideration should be given to the potential risks before performing radiographic procedures in these patients.

When considering **aortic injections** the presence of a vigorous pulsatile flow should be established before using a catheter or pressure injection technique. A small "pilot" dose (about 2 mL) should be administered to locate the exact site of the needle or catheter tip to help prevent injection of the main dose into a branch of the aorta or intramurally.

Entry of a large concentrated bolus into an aortic branch should be avoided. Mesenteric necrosis, acute pancreatitis, renal shut-down, serious neurologic complications including spinal cord damage and hemiplegia or quadriplegia have been reported following inadvertent injection of a large part of the aortic dose of contrast media into an aortic branch or arterial trunks providing spinal or cerebral artery branches.

Pulsation must be present in the artery to be injected. Extreme caution is advised in considering peripheral angiography in patients suspected of having thromboangiitis obliterans (Buerger's disease) since any procedure (even insertion of a needle or catheter) may induce a severe arterial or venous spasm. Caution is also advisable in patients with severe ischemia associated with ascending infection. Special care is required in patients with suspected thrombosis, ischemic disease, local infection or a significantly obstructed vascular system. Occasional serious neurologic complications, including paraplegia have been reported in patients with aortoiliac or femoral artery bed obstruction, abdominal compression, hypotension, hypertension and following injection of vasopressors.

When large individual doses are administered, an appropriate time interval should be permitted to elapse between injections to allow for subsidence of hemodynamic disturbances.

Following catheter procedures gentle pressure hemostasis is advised followed by immobilization of the limb for several hours to prevent hemorrhage from the site of arterial puncture.

Special Precautions by Indication: Angiocardiography: Selective coronary arteriography should be performed only in those patients in whom the expected benefits outweigh the risk. The inherent risks of angiocardiography in patients with chronic obstructive pulmonary disease must be weighed against the necessity for performing this procedure.

During left ventriculography and coronary arteriography, vital signs and the ECG should be monitored routinely throughout the procedure. Caution is advised in the administration of large volumes to patients with incipient heart failure because of the possibility of aggravating the pre-existing condition. Hypotension should be corrected promptly.

Special care regarding dosage should be observed in patients with right ventricular failure, pulmonary hypertension, or stenotic pulmonary vascular beds, because of the hemodynamic changes that may occur after injection into the right heart outflow tract.

Depending on the injection site and the time of recording, significant changes include a drop in cardiac output, elevation or decrease in ventricular pressures (RVSP, LVSP, LVEDP,

RVEDP), systemic pressure, peripheral hypotension, brady- or tachycardia, ectopic beats and other arrhythmias.

The hemodynamic changes which occur during and after ventricular and coronary injections are, in general, less pronounced with the low-osmolality iodixanol than those seen with similar concentrations of conventional ionic contrast media, but serious and life-threatening hemodynamic disturbances can occur with the administration of all iodinated contrast media, including iodixanol. If repeat injections are made in rapid succession, all these changes are likely to be more pronounced.

After an initial rise, plasma volume may decrease and continue to fall below control levels, even beyond 30 minutes, probably due to diuresis.

The volume of each individual injection is a more important consideration than the total dose used. When large individual volumes are administered, as in ventriculography, sufficient time should be permitted to elapse between each injection to allow for subsidence of hemodynamic disturbances.

Due to increased risk of adverse reactions following recent acute myocardial infarction, careful patient selection is necessary, and the timing and performance of the examination should be carried out with extreme caution, if invasive radiographic procedures are considered necessary.

Cerebral Arteriography: Cerebral arteriography should be undertaken with extreme care, especially in elderly patients, patients in poor clinical condition, or patients with advanced arteriosclerosis, severe arterial hypertension, cardiac decompensation or recent cerebral embolism or thrombosis.

In patients with cerebral hemorrhage, a rare association between contrast administration and clinical deterioration, including severe headache and death, has been reported. Therefore, administration of intra-arterial iodinated contrast media in these patients should be undertaken with caution, and the lowest dose possible to achieve the necessary diagnostic information should be used.

Peripheral and Visceral Arteriography: Under conditions of slowed aortic circulation there is an increased likelihood for aortic injection to cause muscle spasm.

Entry of a large aortic dose into the renal artery may cause, even in the absence of symptoms, albuminuria, hematuria, elevated creatinine and urea nitrogen and possible renal damage.

Pulsation should be present in the artery to be injected. In thromboangiitis obliterans or ascending infection associated with severe ischemia, arteriography should be performed only if the benefits clearly outweigh the risks.

Venography: Special care is required when venography is performed in patients with suspected thrombosis, phlebitis, ischemic disease, local infection or a significantly obstructed venous system.

In thromboangiitis obliterans or ascending infection associated with severe ischemia, venography should be performed only if the benefits clearly outweigh the risks.

Excretory Urography: Urography should be performed with caution in patients with severely impaired renal function and patients with combined renal and hepatic disease. Preparatory dehydration is not recommended, especially in the elderly, diabetic or azotemic patients, or in patients with suspected myelomatosis. Caution is advised in patients with congestive heart failure and in cases of impaired renal function. In all these patients the individual's clinical status and renal function should be carefully monitored.

Since there is a possibility of temporary suppression of urine formation, it is recommended that an interval of at least 48 hours elapse before excretory urography is repeated in patients with unilateral or bilateral reduction in renal function.

Contrast Enhanced Computed Tomography: In patients where the blood-brain barrier is known or suspected to be disrupted, the use of any radiographic contrast medium must be assessed on an individual risk to benefit basis, since neurological complications are more likely to occur.

The decision to employ contrast enhancement should be based upon a careful evaluation of clinical, other radiological and unenhanced CT findings, because unenhanced scanning may provide adequate diagnostic information in the individual patient, and because contrast enhancement may be associated with risk, may obscure certain lesions and increases radiation exposure. I.V. CT scans of the head performed within 24 hours following myelography may yield false results due to the permeation of the brain by the contrast medium from adjacent CSF spaces. Therefore, if indicated, i.v. CT scan of the brain should be performed either before, or after a period of at least 24 hours following myelography.

The opacification of the inferior vermis following administration of contrast media has resulted in a false positive diagnosis in normal subjects.

Pregnancy: There are no studies on the use of iodixanol in pregnant women.

Reproduction studies have been performed in rats and rabbits with up to 1.6 times (cumulatively, 20 times) the maximum recommended human dose. No evidence of impaired fertility or definite harm to the fetus has been demonstrated due to iodixanol.

Animal reproduction studies are not always predictive of human response. Therefore, iodixanol should be used during pregnancy only if the benefit to the mother clearly outweighs the risk to the fetus.

Lactation: It is not known to what extent iodixanol is secreted in human milk.

If use of iodixanol is considered necessary, it is suggested that breast-feeding be discontinued for at least 48 hours following administration of iodixanol.

Children: The safety and effectiveness of iodixanol for use in children have not been established.

Drug Interactions: Administration of water soluble contrast media should be deferred for 48 hours in patients with hepatic or biliary disorders who have recently been administered **cholecystographic agents,** as renal toxicity has been reported in the literature in such patients who received conventional contrast agents.

There have been reports in the literature indicating that patients on **adrenergic beta-blockers** may be more prone to severe adverse reaction to contrast media. At the same time treatment of allergic-anaphylactoid reactions in these patients is more difficult. Epinephrine should be administered with caution since it may not exhibit its usual effects. On the one hand larger doses of epinephrine may be needed to overcome the bronchospasm, while on the other, these doses can be associated with excessive alpha adrenergic stimulation with consequent hypertension, reflex bradycardia and heart-block and possible potentiation of bronchospasm. Alternatives to the use of large doses of epinephrine include vigorous supportive care such as fluids and the use of beta agonists including parenteral salbutamol or isoproterenol to overcome bronchospasm and norepinephrine to overcome hypotension.

General **anesthesia** may be indicated in the performance of some procedures in selected adult patients. However, a higher incidence of adverse reactions following administration of contrast agents has been reported in anesthetized patients. This may be attributable either to the inability of the patient to identify untoward symptoms or to the hypotensive effect of anesthesia, which can reduce cardiac output and increase the duration of exposure to a contrast agent.

Addition of an **inotropic agent** to contrast agents may produce a paradoxical depressant response, which can be deleterious to the ischemic myocardium.

Do not mix contrast agents with any other drugs in the same syringe.

Laboratory Test Interactions: Radioactive iodine uptake studies if required, should be performed prior to the administration of iodixanol.

Iodixanol interferes with Multistix measurements of specific gravity and may produce a false-positive result for protein in the urine via Multistix. However, the Coomassie blue method has been shown to give accurate results for the measurement of urine protein in the presence of iodixanol. If a positive Multistix result is obtained, and it is clinically relevant, this method (Coomassie) should be used to check for the presence or absence of protein.

In vitro studies of human urine which tested negative for protein with Multistix, also showed a false positive reaction when iodixanol was added.

Adverse Effects: Since the reactions which are known to occur upon parenteral administration of iodinated contrast agents are possible with any nonionic agent, the same degree of careful patient observation for adverse reactions as with the use of conventional ionic contrast media should be strictly followed. Adequate equipment and appropriate personnel should be readily available in case a severe reaction should occur.

Adverse reactions following the use of iodixanol are usually of mild to moderate severity and of short duration, resolving spontaneously without treatment. However, serious, life-threatening and fatal adverse reactions have been associated with the administration of iodine-containing contrast agents.

Although most adverse reactions occur soon after the administration of the contrast medium, some adverse reactions may be delayed and could be of a long-lasting nature.

The reported incidence of adverse reactions to contrast media in patients with a history of allergy is twice that of the general population. Patients with a history of previous reactions to a contrast medium are 3 times more susceptible than other patients. However, sensitivity to contrast media does not appear to increase with repeated examinations.

The injection of contrast media is frequently associated with the sensation of warmth and pain, especially in peripheral arteriography. Patients receiving iodixanol have had less injection-associated discomfort than those receiving control nonionic contrast agents.

The following listing of adverse reactions is based upon clinical trials in over 2 100 patients, 1 246 of whom received iodixanol. This listing includes all adverse reactions that occurred following the administration of iodixanol, regardless of their attributability to the drug or to the procedure. The most frequent adverse reactions, which occurred in 1 to 3.4% of patients, were taste perversion (3.4%), nausea (2.8%), vertigo (2.4%), headache (2.3%), rash/erythematous rash (2.1%), pruritus (1.6%), chest pain (1.1%) and scotoma (1.1%).

The following adverse reactions occurred in less than 1% of patients. They appear in descending order of frequency. (However, significantly more severe experiences are listed before others in a system regardless of frequency.)

Injection Site: injection site pain, injection site reaction, injection site inflammation.

Body as a Whole: polymyalgia rheumatica, syncope, precordial chest pain, back pain, edema, pain, fatigue, malaise, rigors, peripheral edema, fever.

Cardiovascular (General): cardiac failure, myocardial infarction, angina pectoris.

Heart Rate and Rhythm: bradycardia, extrasystoles, atrial fibrillation.

Central and Peripheral Nervous System: amnesia, visual anosognosia, convulsions, stupor, paresthesia, sensory disturbance, dizziness, migraine, hypesthesia, leg cramps.

Gastrointestinal: vomiting, diarrhea, dry mouth, dyspepsia, abdominal pain, increased saliva, esophagitis.

Hearing and Vestibular: earache, tinnitus, hearing decreased.

Platelet, Bleeding and Clotting: hematoma.

Psychiatric: confusion, insomnia, nervousness, somnolence, agitation, anxiety, depression.

Respiratory: pharyngitis, rhinitis, sinusitis, upper respiratory tract infection, pulmonary edema, dyspnea, bronchitis, asthma.

Sensitivity: pharyngeal edema, facial edema, periorbital edema, urticaria, hypotension.

Skin and Appendage: increased sweating, dry skin.

Special Senses: parosmia.

Urinary: urinary tract infection, abnormal renal function, hematuria, BUN increased.

Vascular (Extracardiac): flushing, peripheral ischemia, cerebrovascular disorder.

Vision: abnormal vision, conjunctivitis, diplopia.

Adverse Reactions With Increased Frequency in Individual Indications: For certain procedures, the number of some adverse reactions was higher than the overall rate for all procedures. Following are the clinically relevant experiences occurring at a higher rate, listed by indication: Cerebral Arteriography: Central and Peripheral Nervous System: vertigo (28.3%), scotoma (12.3%), headache (11.3%), sensory disturbance (6.6%). Gastrointestinal System: nausea (5.7%). Psychiatric: confusion (3.8%).

CT Scanning of the Body: Central and Peripheral Nervous System: headache (5.1%). Gastrointestinal System: nausea (5.1%). Skin and Appendage: rash (6.1%), pruritus (4.2%). Special Senses: taste perversion (14.9%).

CT Scanning of the Head: Special Senses: parosmia (3%).

Venography: Body as a Whole: chest pain (4.3%).

Treatment of Adverse Reactions: Contrast media should be injected only by physicians thoroughly familiar with the emergency treatment of all adverse reactions to contrast media. The assistance of other trained personnel such as cardiologists, internists and anesthetists is required in the management of severe reactions.

A guideline for the treatment of adverse reactions is presented below. This outline is not intended to be a complete manual on the treatment of adverse reactions to contrast media or on cardiopulmonary resuscitation. The physician should refer to the appropriate texts on the subject.

It is also realized that institutions or individual practitioners will already have appropriate systems in effect and that circumstances may dictate the use of additional or different measures.

Minor Allergic Reactions (if considered necessary): The i.v. or i.m. administration of an antihistaminic such as diphenhydramine HCl 25 to 50 mg is generally sufficient (contraindicated in epileptics). The resulting drowsiness makes it imperative to ensure that out-patients do not drive or go home unaccompanied.

Visipaque (cont'd)

Major or Life-Threatening Reactions: A major reaction may be manifested by signs and symptoms of cardiovascular collapse, severe respiratory difficulty and nervous system dysfunction. Convulsions, coma and cardiorespiratory arrest may ensue.

The following measures should be considered: 1. Start emergency therapy immediately—carefully monitoring vital signs.
2. Have emergency resuscitation team summoned—do not leave patient unattended.
3. Ensure patent airway—guard against aspiration.
4. Commence artificial respiration if patient is not breathing.
5. Administer oxygen if necessary.
6. Start external cardiac massage in the event of cardiac arrest.
7. Establish route for i.v. medication by starting infusion of appropriate solution (5% Dextrose in Water).
8. Judiciously administer specific drug therapy as indicated by the type and severity of the reaction. Careful monitoring is mandatory to detect adverse reactions to all drugs administered.

Soluble hydrocortisone 500 to 1 000 mg i.v., for all acute allergic-anaphylactic reactions.

Epinephrine 1:1 000 solution (in the presence of anoxia it may cause ventricular fibrillation—**caution** in patients on adrenergic β-blockers, see Precautions): 0.2 to 0.4 mL s.c. for severe allergic reactions. In extreme emergency 0.1 mL per minute, appropriately diluted, may be given i.v. until desired effect is obtained. Do not exceed 0.4 mL. In case of cardiac arrest 0.1 to 0.2 mL appropriately diluted, may be given intracardially.

In hypotension (carefully monitoring blood pressure): phenylephrine HCl 0.1 to 0.5 mg appropriately diluted, by slow i.v. injection or infusion or norepinephrine bitartrate 4 mL of 0.2% solution in 1 000 mL of 5% Dextrose by slow drip infusion. Sodium bicarbonate 5%: 50 mL i.v., every 10 minutes as needed to combat post-arrest acidosis. Atropine 0.4 to 0.6 mg i.v., to increase heart rate in sinus bradycardia. May reverse 2nd or 3rd degree block.

To Control Convulsions: Diazepam 5 to 10 mg slowly i.v., titrating the dose to the response of the patient or **phenobarbital sodium** may be injected i.v., or i.m., at a rate not in excess of 30 to 60 mg/minute. Depending on the patient's response a total dose of 200 to 300 mg may be required. The dose may be repeated in 6 hours if necessary.
9. Defibrillation, administration of antiarrhythmics and additional emergency measures and drugs may be required.
10. Transfer patient to intensive care unit when feasible for further monitoring and treatment.

Overdose: Symptoms and Treatment: The adverse effects associated with overdosage of iodinated contrast media may be life-threatening; they affect mainly the pulmonary and cardiovascular systems. The symptoms include cyanosis, edema, bradycardia, acidosis, pulmonary hemorrhage, convulsions, coma and cardiac arrest. The symptoms of overdosage generally appear between 10 minutes and several hours after injection of the contrast medium. Treatment of an overdosage is directed toward the support of all vital functions and prompt institution of symptomatic therapy.

The minimum lethal dose of i.v. administered iodixanol in adult rats is approximately 14 g I/kg (over 10 times the maximum recommended human dose).

Dosage: Before use, iodixanol containers should be inspected visually for particulate matter and/or discoloration. If either is present, the containers should be discarded. Iodixanol should be injected at or close to body temperature and should be used immediately once the container seal has been punctured. Iodixanol should not be transferred from the original container to other delivery systems except immediately prior to use; nor should it be mixed with other drugs. Any unused portion should be discarded. Containers should be protected from exposure to light. Syringes, needles and catheter tips must be kept free of aspirated blood to prevent clotting from prolonged contact.

Do not use flexible container in series connections.

The combination of volume and concentration of iodixanol to be used should be carefully individualized accounting for factors such as age, body weight, size of the vessel, rate of blood flow within the vessel, indication for examination and timing of the x-ray or CT scan. Other factors to be considered are anticipated pathology, degree and extent of opacification required, structure or area to be examined, disease processes affecting the patient, and equipment and technique used (see Table II).

Table II—Visipaque

Dosage	Concentration (mg I/mL)	Usual Recommended Single Dose (mL)	Maximum Total Procedural Dosage (mL)
Intra-arterial[a]			
Angiocardiography	320		200
Left ventricle		20-45	
Left coronary artery		3-10	
Right coronary artery		3-8	
Cerebral Arteriography	320		
(A) Conventional			175
Carotid artery		10-14	
Vertebral artery		10-12	
(B) Digital Subtraction Angiography (DSA)			175
Carotid artery		5-8	
Vertebral artery		5-8	
Peripheral Arteriography	320		
(A) Conventional			250
Aortography		30-60	
Aortofemoral runoffs		20-90	
Peripheral arteries		15-30	
(B) Digital Subtraction Angiography (DSA)			250
Aortography/Aortofemoral runoffs		6-15	
Peripheral arteries		3-15	
Visceral Arteriography	320		
(A) Conventional			250
Aortography, including runoffs		30-70	
Major branches of aorta		10-70	
Renal arteries		8-18	
(B) Digital Substraction Angiography (DSA)	320		250
Aortography, including runoffs		10-50	
Major branches of aorta		2-10	
(C) Abdominal DSA	270		250
Aortography		20-50	
Major branches of aorta		5-30	
Renal arteries		10-25	
Intravenous			
Excretory Urography	270, 320	1/kg (0.27-0.32 g I/kg)	100
Computed Tomography (CT) of the Head	270, 320	100	—
Computed Tomography (CT) of the Body	270, 320	75-150	—
Venography	270	50-150/extremity[b]	

[a]These doses may be repeated as necessary, up to the procedural maximum dose shown.
[b]Volume depends on size, flow rate, and disease state of the injected vessel, on the size and condition of the patient, and on the imaging technique used.

Sterile technique must be used in all procedures involving vascular injections of contrast media. Withdrawal of contrast agents from their containers should be accomplished under aseptic conditions with sterile equipment.

Supplied: Visipaque 270: Each mL of sterile, pyrogen-free, colorless to pale yellow solution contains: iodixanol 550 mg. Iodine concentration: 270 mg I/mL. Nonmedicinal ingredients: calcium chloride and sodium chloride (providing a sodium/calcium ratio equivalent to blood), edetate calcium disodium and tromethamine. Osmolality: 290 mOsm/kg H_2O. Viscosity: 12.7 cps at 20°C; 6.3 cps at 37°C. Density (37°C): 1.303 g/mL.

Visipaque 320: Each mL of sterile, pyrogen-free, colorless to pale yellow solution contains: iodixanol 652 mg. Nonmedicinal ingredients: calcium chloride and sodium chloride (providing a sodium/calcium ratio equivalent to blood), edetate calcium disodium and tromethamine. Iodine concentration: 320 mg I/mL. Osmolality: 290 mOsm/kg H_2O. Viscosity: 26.6 cps at 20°C; 11.8 cps at 37°C. Density (37°C): 1.356 g/mL.

The pH is adjusted between 6.8 and 7.7 with hydrochloric acid and/or sodium hydroxide at 22°C. All solutions are terminally sterilized by autoclaving and contain no preservatives.

Vials of 50 mL, boxes of 10. Bottles of 100 mL, boxes of 10. Bottles of 200 mL with 150 mL fill, boxes of 10. Bottles of 200 mL, boxes of 10. Flexible containers of 100 mL, boxes of 10. Flexible containers of 150 mL, boxes of 10. Flexible containers of 200 mL, boxes of 10.

Protect vials, bottles and flexible containers from strong daylight and direct exposure to sunlight. Store at controlled room temperature, 15 to 30°C. Do not remove foil overwrap, which serves as a moisture and light barrier, from flexible containers until ready to use. It may be stored at 37°C for up to 1 month in a contrast agent warmer utilizing circulating air.

Do not freeze. Freezing may compromise the closure integrity of these packages. Do not use if the product is inadvertently frozen.

VISKAZIDE® ℞

Novartis Pharmaceuticals

Pindolol—Hydrochlorothiazide

Antihypertensive

Pharmacology: Viskazide contains the antihypertensive activity of 2 agents: a beta-adrenergic receptor blocking agent (pindolol) and a diuretic (hydrochlorothiazide).

Pindolol is a nonselective beta-adrenergic receptor blocking agent which possesses partial agonist activity (intrinsic sympathomimetic activity-ISA).

The mechanism of the antihypertensive effect of beta-adrenergic receptor blocking agents has not been established. Among the factors that may be involved are: (a) competitive ability to antagonize catecholamine induced tachycardia at the beta-receptor sites in the heart, thus decreasing cardiac output; (b) a reduction in total peripheral resistance; (c) inhibition of the vasomotor centres; (d) inhibition of renin release by the kidneys.

Hydrochlorothiazide increases excretion of sodium and chloride in approximately equivalent amounts, and may cause a simultaneous, usually minimal, loss of bicarbonate. Natriuresis is usually accompanied by some loss of potassium. The mechanism of the antihypertensive effect of thiazides may be related to the excretion and redistribution of body sodium. Hydrochlorothiazide usually does not decrease normal blood pressure.

The combination of pindolol with thiazide-like diuretics has been shown to be compatible and generally more effective than either of the drugs used alone in reducing elevated blood pressure.

In humans, orally administered pindolol is rapidly and completely absorbed. Because of negligible hepatic first pass effect, the bioavailability of oral pindolol is high and approaches 90% of the oral dose. Maximum plasma concentrations are reached within 2 hours after oral administration and the plasma half-life is approximately 3.5 hours. The elimination of pindolol is not dose dependent.

In man, pindolol is partially metabolized with approximately 40% of an oral dose being excreted unchanged in the urine. The principal metabolites of pindolol consist of the conjugated glucuronide and phenolic derivatives of pindolol conjugated with sulfuric or glucuronic acid.

Approximately 80% of an oral dose is accounted for in the urine within 24 hours.

The onset of the diuretic action of hydrochlorothiazide occurs in 2 hours and the peak action in about 4 hours. Diuretic activity lasts about 6 to 12 hours. Hydrochlorothiazide is eliminated rapidly by the kidney.

Indications: This fixed combination is not indicated for initial therapy of hypertension. Hypertension requires therapy titrated to the individual patient. It is always better to adjust the dosage of each antihypertensive drug separately, but when the fixed combination corresponds to the optimum drug and dose requirements of the patient, its use may be more convenient in patient management. For further adjustment of dosage, however, it is best to use the individual drugs again. The treatment of hypertension is not static, but must be reevaluated as conditions in each patient warrant.

Viskazide is indicated for the maintenance therapy of patients with hypertension who require pindolol and hydrochlorothiazide in the dosage and ratios present in Viskazide.

Contraindications: The presence of: congestive heart failure (see Warnings); right ventricular failure secondary to pulmonary hypertension; significant cardiomegaly; sinus bradycardia, second and third degree AV block; cardiogenic shock; bronchospasm (including bronchial asthma), or severe chronic obstructive pulmonary disease (see Precautions); anesthesia with agents that produce myocardial depression, e.g., ether; anuria; hypersensitivity to pindolol, hydrochlorothiazide, or to sulfonamide derived drugs.

Warnings: Cardiac Failure: Special caution should be exercised when administering Viskazide to patients with a history of heart failure. Sympathetic stimulation is a vital component supporting circulatory function in congestive heart failure, and inhibition with beta-blockade always carries the potential hazard of further depressing myocardial contractility and precipitating cardiac failure.

In patients without a history of cardiac failure, continued depression of the myocardium over a period of time can, in some cases, lead to cardiac failure. Therefore, at the first sign or symptom of impending cardiac failure occurring during therapy, patients should be fully digitalized and/or given additional diuretic therapy, and the response observed closely.

Pindolol acts selectively without blocking the inotropic action of digitalis on heart muscle. However, the positive inotropic action of digitalis may be reduced by the negative inotropic effect of pindolol when the 2 drugs are used concomitantly. The effects of pindolol and digitalis are additive in depressing AV conduction. If cardiac failure persists, therapy with Viskazide should be discontinued (see below).

Abrupt Cessation of Therapy in Angina Pectoris: Patients with angina should be warned against abrupt discontinuation of Viskazide. There have been reports of severe exacerbation of angina, and of myocardial infarction or ventricular arrhythmias occurring in patients with angina pectoris, following abrupt discontinuation of beta-blocker therapy. The last 2 complications may occur with or without preceding exacerbation of angina pectoris. Therefore, when discontinuation of Viskazide is planned in patients with angina pectoris, the dosage should be reduced over a period of about 2 weeks and the patient should continue to be observed. The same frequency of administration should be maintained.

In situations of greater urgency, therapy should be discontinued stepwise and under conditions of closer observation. If angina markedly worsens or acute coronary insufficiency develops, it is recommended that treatment be reinstituted promptly, at least temporarily.

Since ischemic heart disease may be unrecognized, the above advice should be followed in patients considered to be at risk of having asymptomatic ischemic heart disease.

Various skin rashes and conjunctival xerosis have been reported with beta-blockers, including pindolol. A severe syndrome (oculo-mucocutaneous syndrome) whose signs include conjunctivitis sicca and psoriasiform rashes, otitis, and sclerosing serositis has occurred with the chronic use of one beta-adrenergic blocking agent (practolol). This syndrome has not been observed with pindolol, however, physicians should be alert to the possibility of such reactions and should discontinue treatment in the event that they occur.

Sinus bradycardia may occur with the use of pindolol due to unopposed vagal activity remaining after blockade of beta$_1$-adrenergic receptors. Due to its intrinsic sympathomimetic activity (ISA), pindolol causes less bradycardia at rest than some other beta-adrenergic blocking agents. If excessive bradycardia occurs, the dosage should be reduced.

In patients with thyrotoxicosis, pindolol may give a false impression of improvement by diminishing peripheral manifestations of hyperthyroidism without improving thyroid function. Special considerations should be given to the potential of pindolol to aggravate congestive heart failure. Pindolol does not alter thyroid function tests. Patients suspected of developing thyrotoxicosis should be managed carefully to avoid abrupt withdrawal of beta-blockade which might precipitate a thyroid storm. Thiazides may decrease serum PBI levels without signs of thyroid disturbance.

In patients with renal disease, thiazides may precipitate azotemia, and cumulative effects may develop in the presence of impaired renal function. If progressive renal impairment becomes evident, Viskazide should be discontinued.

In patients with impaired hepatic function or progressive liver disease, even minor alterations in fluid and electrolyte balance may precipitate hepatic coma. Hepatic encephalopathy, manifested by tremors, confusion, and coma, has been reported in association with diuretic therapy including hydrochlorothiazide.

In patients receiving thiazides, sensitivity reactions may occur with or without a history of allergy or bronchial asthma.

The possible exacerbation or activation of systemic lupus erythematosus has been reported with thiazides.

Precautions: Viskazide should be administered with caution to patients prone to non allergic bronchospasm (e.g., chronic bronchitis, emphysema) since beta-blockade may block bronchodilatation produced by endogenous and exogenous catecholamine stimulation of beta-receptors.

Elective or Emergency Surgery: Beta-adrenergic receptor blockade impairs the ability of the heart to respond to beta-adrenergically mediated reflex stimuli. Some patients receiving beta-adrenergic receptor blocking agents have been subject to protracted severe hypotension during anesthesia. Difficulty in restarting and maintaining the heartbeat has also been reported.

For these reasons, in patients with angina pectoris undergoing elective surgery, some authorities recommend gradual withdrawal of beta-adrenergic receptor blocking agents (see recommendations given under Warnings—Abrupt Cessation of Therapy).

In emergency surgery, since pindolol is a competitive inhibitor of beta-adrenergic receptor agonists its effects may be reversed, if necessary, by sufficient doses of such agonists as isoproterenol or levarterenol.

Viskazide should be administered with caution to patients with allergic rhinitis prone to bronchospasm.

Beta-adrenergic receptor blocking agents may mask the premonitory signs and symptoms of acute hypoglycemia. Therefore, Viskazide should be administered with caution to patients subject to spontaneous hypoglycemia, or to diabetic patients (especialy those with labile diabetes) who are receiving insulin or oral hypoglycemic agents. Insulin requirements in diabetic patients may be increased, decreased, or unchanged by thiazides. Diabetes mellitus which has been latent may become manifest during administration of thiazide diuretics.

Epinephrine and Beta-blockers: There may be increased difficulty in treating an allergic type reaction in patients on beta-blockers. In these patients, the reaction may be more severe due to pharmacologic effects of the beta-blockers and problems with fluid changes. Epinephrine should be administered with caution since it may not have its usual effects in the treatment of anaphylaxis. On the one hand, larger doses of epinephrine may be needed to overcome the bronchospasm, while on the other hand, these doses can be associated with excessive alpha adrenergic stimulation with consequent hypertension, reflex bradycardia and heart block and possible potentiation of bronchospasm. Alternatives to the use of large doses of epinephrine include vigorous supportive care such as fluids and the use of beta agonists including parenteral salbutamol or isoproterenol to overcome bronchospasm and norepinephrine to overcome hypotension.

Patients receiving catecholamine depleting drugs, such as reserpine or guanethidine, should be closely monitored because the added beta-adrenergic blocking action of Viskazide may produce an excessive reduction of sympathetic activity. Viskazide should not be combined with other beta-blockers.

Patients receiving thiazides should be carefully observed for clinical signs of fluid and electrolyte imbalance (hyponatremia, hypochloremic alkalosis and hypokalemia). Periodic determination of serum electrolytes should be performed at appropriate intervals. Serum and urine electrolyte determinations are particularly important when the patient is vomiting excessively or receiving parenteral fluids. Warning signs or symptoms of fluid and electrolyte imbalance include dryness of the mouth, thirst, weakness, lethargy, drowsiness, restlessness, muscle pains or cramps, muscular fatigue, hypotension, oliguria, tachycardia, and gastrointestinal disturbances such as nausea and vomiting.

Hypokalemia may develop, especially with brisk diuresis, when severe cirrhosis is present, or during concomitant use of corticosteroids or ACTH. Interference with adequate oral electrolyte intake will also contribute to hypokalemia. Hypokalemia can sensitize or exaggerate the response of the heart to the toxic effects of digitalis (e.g., increased ventricular irritability). Hypokalemia may be avoided or treated by use of potassium supplements, potassium sparing agents or foods with a high potassium content.

Any chloride deficit during thiazide therapy is generally mild and usually does not require specific treatment except under extraordinary circumstances (as in liver disease or renal disease). Dilutional hyponatremia may occur in edematous patients in hot weather; appropriate therapy is water restriction rather than administration of salt, except in rare instances, when the hyponatremia is life threatening. In actual salt depletion, appropriate replacement is the therapy of choice.

Because calcium excretion is decreased by thiazides, Viskazide should be discontinued before carrying out tests for parathyroid function. Pathologic changes in the parathyroid glands, with hypercalcemia and hypophosphatemia, have been observed in a few patients on prolonged thiazide therapy; however, the common complications of hyperparathyroidism such as renal lithiasis, bone resorption, and peptic ulceration have not been seen.

The antihypertensive effects of thiazides may be enhanced in the postsympathectomy patient.

Hyperuricemia may occur or acute gout may be precipitated in certain patients receiving thiazide therapy.

The combination of Viskazide with an antihypertensive peripheral vasodilator produces a greater fall in blood pressure than either drug alone. The same degree of blood pressure control can be achieved by lower than usual doses of each drug. Therefore, when using such combined therapy, careful monitoring of the dosages is required until the patient is stabilized.

Thiazides may decrease arterial responsiveness to norepinephrine. This diminution is not sufficient to preclude the therapeutic effectiveness of the pressor agent in therapy.

Thiazides may increase the responsiveness to tubocurarine.

Lithium generally should not be given with diuretics because they reduce its renal clearance and add a high risk of lithium toxicity. Read prescribing information for lithium preparations before use of such preparations with Viskazide.

Orthostatic hypotension may occur and may be potentiated by alcohol, barbiturates or narcotics.

Pregnancy: Thiazides cross the placental barrier and appear in cord blood. The use of Viskazide in pregnancy or in women of child bearing potential requires that the anticipated benefit be weighed against possible risk to mother and/or fetus. These hazards include fetal or neonatal jaundice, thrombocytopenia, and possibly, other adverse reactions which have occurred in the adult.

Lactation: Thiazides appear in human milk. If use of Viskazide is deemed essential, the patient should stop nursing.

Children: The safety for use of pindolol in children has not been established; therefore, Viskazide is not recommended in the pediatric age group.

Adverse Effects: Cardiovascular: congestive heart failure (see Warnings), severe bradycardia (see Warnings) may occur as may syncope, lightheadedness, and postural hypotension. Lengthening of PR interval, second degree AV block, palpitation, chest pains, cold extremities, Raynaud's phenomenon, claudication, hot flushes, very rarely arrhythmia, coronary insufficiency. Orthostatic hypotension may be potentiated by alcohol, barbiturates or narcotics.

CNS: insomnia, nightmares, vivid dreams, fatigue, drowsiness, weakness, paresthesias, dizziness, vertigo, tinnitus, headache, mental depression, nervousness. Rarely have the following adverse reactions been reported: aggressiveness, motor disorders, confusion, xanthopsia.

Gastrointestinal: anorexia, gastric irritation, cramping, diarrhea, constipation, flatulence, heartburn, nausea and vomiting, abdominal pain, dry mouth, jaundice (intrahepatic, cholestatic), pancreatitis, sialadenitis.

Respiratory: shortness of breath and/or dyspnea, wheezing, bronchospasm (see Contraindications and Precautions).

Hematologic: leukopenia, agranulocytosis, thrombocytopenia, aplastic anemia, hemolytic anemia.

Urogenital: impotence.

Viskazide (cont'd)

Hypersensitivity: exanthema, sweating, pruritus, purpura, photosensitivity, urticaria, exfoliative dermatitis, psoriasiform rash, necrotizing angiitis vasculitis, cutaneous vasculitis, fever, respiratory distress, including pneumonitis, anaphylactic reactions.
Special Senses: visual disturbances, including xanthopsia and transient blurred vision, dry eyes, conjunctivitis, itching and/or burning eyes, tinnitus, vestibular disorder.
Other: hyperglycemia, glycosuria, hyperuricemia, muscle cramps, weakness, restlessness, weight gain or loss, urinary frequency, appetite stimulation.
Clinical Laboratory Test Findings: On rare occasions, changes in the following parameters were noted: elevations in transaminases, alkaline phosphate, LDH, serum uric acid; a reduction in bilirubin. The most common changes associated with the thiazide component are increases in uric acid and decreases in serum potassium and chloride.

Overdose: Symptoms: The pindolol component may cause bradycardia, hypotension, bronchospasm, hypoglycemia or acute cardiac failure.

The hydrochlorothiazide component may cause excessive diuresis with electrolyte depletion and dehydration. Signs are dry mouth, thirst, weakness, lethargy, drowsiness, restlessness, muscle pains or cramps, muscular fatigue, hypotension, oliguria, tachycardia, gastrointestinal disturbances, mental confusion, delirium, convulsions, shock and coma.

If digitalis has also been administered, hypokalemia may accentuate myocardial abnormalities (e.g., cardiac arrhythmias).

Hydrochlorothiazide may precipitate hepatic coma in cirrhotics, potentiate other antihypertensive agents and decrease responsiveness to norepinephrine.

Treatment: Discontinue Viskazide. There is no specific antidote. If ingestion is, or may have been, recent, gastric lavage or emesis may reduce absorption; when ingestion has been earlier, infusions may be helpful to promote urinary excretion.

If required the following therapeutic measures are suggested: Bradycardia: Atropine or another anticholinergic drug. Heart block: (second or third degree) Isoproterenol or transvenous cardiac pacemaker. Congestive heart failure: Conventional therapy. Hypotension: (depending on associated factors) Epinephrine rather than isoproterenol or norepinephrine may be useful in addition to atropine and digitalis. Bronchospasm: Aminophylline or isoproterenol. Hypoglycemia: I.V. glucose. Stupor or Coma: Supportive therapy as clinically warranted. Gastrointestinal Effects: Though usually of short duration, these may require symptomatic treatment.

Abnormalities in BUN and/or Serum Electrolytes: Monitor serum electrolyte levels and renal function; institute supportive measures as required individually to maintain hydration, electrolyte balance, respiration and cardiovascular-renal function.

It should be remembered that pindolol is a competitive antagonist of isoproterenol and hence large doses of isoproterenol can be expected to reverse many of the effects of excessive doses of Viskazide. However, the complications of excess isoproterenol should not be overlooked.

Dosage: Dosage must be determined for individual patients by titration of each component separately. Where the fixed combination in Viskazide supplies the dosage so determined, the combination product may be used for maintenance therapy. 1 or 2 Viskazide tablets once daily in the morning can be used to administer up to 20 mg pindolol and 100 mg hydrochlorothiazide.

If higher doses of either ingredient are needed, the individual components should be used.

When necessary, another antihypertensive agent may be added gradually, beginning with 50% of the usual recommended starting dose to avoid excessive reduction in blood pressure.

If dosage adjustment is necessary during maintenance therapy, it is advisable to use the individual drugs.

Supplied: Viskazide 10/25: Each peach, round, compressed tablet, 9 mm diameter, one side slope-faced and bisected with "10/25" embossed on each side of the bisect, reverse side flat-faced with beveled edge and embossed with "VISKAZIDE" around the circumference and '' centered, contains: pindolol 10 mg and hydrochlorothiazide 25 mg. Nonmedicinal ingredients: FD&C Yellow #6 Lake, magnesium stearate, microcrystalline cellulose, pregelatinized starch and silicon dioxide. Calendar packs of 35.

Viskazide 10/50: Each orange, round, compressed tablet, 9 mm diameter, one side slope-faced and bisected with "10/50" embossed on each side of the bisect, reverse side flat-faced with beveled edge and embossed with "VISKAZIDE" around the circumference and '' centered, contains: pindolol 10 mg and hydrochlorothiazide 50 mg. Nonmedicinal ingredients: FD&C Yellow #6 Lake, magnesium stearate, microcrystalline cellulose, pregelatinized starch and silicon dioxide. Calendar packs of 35.

(Shown in Product Recognition Section)

VISKEN® P

Novartis Pharmaceuticals

Pindolol

Antihypertensive—Antianginal

Pharmacology: Pindolol is a beta-adrenergic-receptor-blocking agent which possesses partial agonist activity (intrinsic sympathomimetic activity—I.S.A.).
Hypertension: The mechanism of the antihypertensive effect of pindolol has not been established. Among the factors that may be involved are: competitive ability to antagonize catecholamine-induced tachycardia at the beta-receptor sites in the heart, thus decreasing cardiac output; a reduction in total peripheral resistance; inhibition of the vasomotor centres; inhibition of renin release by the kidneys.
Angina Pectoris: The mechanism of the antianginal effect of pindolol has not been established. Pindolol may reduce the oxygen requirement of the heart at any level of effort by blocking catecholamine-induced increases in the heart rate, systolic blood pressure, and the velocity and extent of myocardial contraction. However, oxygen requirements may be increased by such actions as increases in left ventricular fibre length, end diastolic pressure and the systolic ejection period. When the net effect is beneficial in anginal patients, it manifests itself during exercise or stress by delaying the onset of pain and reducing the incidence and severity of anginal attacks.

In humans, orally-administered pindolol is rapidly and almost completely absorbed ($\geq$95%). Because of negligible hepatic first pass effect, the bioavailability of oral pindolol is high and approaches 90% of the oral dose. Maximum plasma concentrations are reached 1 to 2 hours after oral administration and the plasma half-life is approximately 3.5 hours. The elimination rate of pindolol is not dose dependent. Forty percent of pindolol is bound to plasma proteins. Pindolol has a volume of distribution of 2 to 3L/kg and a total clearance of 500 mL/min.

Pindolol is patially metabolized with approximately 40% of an oral dose being excreted unchanged in the urine. The remaining 60% is excreted in the urine and feces as inactive metabolites. The principle metabolites of pindolol consist of the conjugated glucuronide, and phenolic derivatives of pindolol conjugated with sulfuric or glucuronic acid.

Approximately 80% of an oral dose is accounted for in the urine within 24 hours.

Indications: a) Mild to moderate hypertension. Pindolol is usually used in combination with other drugs, particularly a thiazide diuretic. However, it may be used alone as an initial agent in those patients in whom, in the judgment of the physician, treatment should be started with a beta-blocker rather than a diuretic.

The combination of pindolol with a diuretic and/or peripheral vasodilator has been found to be compatible and generally more effective than pindolol alone. Limited experience with other antihypertensive agents, including methyldopa, has not shown evidence of incompatibility with pindolol.

Not recommended for the emergency treatment of hypertensive crises.
b) The prophylaxis of angina pectoris.

Contraindications: Sinus bradycardia; second and third degree AV block; right ventricular failure secondary to pulmonary hypertension; congestive heart failure (see Warnings); cardiogenic shock; anesthesia with agents that produce myocardial depression, e.g., ether; bronchospasm, including bronchial asthma or severe chronic obstructive pulmonary disease (see Precautions).

Warnings: Cardiac Failure: Special caution should be exercised when administering pindolol to patients with a history of heart failure. Sympathetic stimulation is a vital component supporting circulatory function in congestive heart failure, and inhibition with beta-blockade always carries the potential hazard of further depressing myocardial contractility and precipitating cardiac failure. Pindolol may reduce but does not abolish the inotropic action of digitalis on the heart muscle. However, the positive inotropic action of digitalis may be reduced by pindolol's negative inotropic effect when the 2 drugs are used concomitantly. The effects of beta-blockers and digitalis are additive in depressing AV conduction. In patients without a history of cardiac failure, continued depression of the myocardium over a period of time can, in some cases, lead to cardiac failure. Therefore, at the first sign or symptom of impending cardiac failure, patients should be fully digitalized and/or given a diuretic and the response observed closely. If cardiac failure continues, despite adequate digitalization and diuretic therapy, pindolol should be immediately withdrawn.
Abrupt Cessation of Therapy: Warn patients with angina against abrupt discontinuation of pindolol. There have been reports of severe exacerbation of angina, and of myocardial infarction or ventricular arrhythmias occurring in patients with angina pectoris, following abrupt discontinuation of beta-blocker therapy. The last 2 complications may occur with or without preceding exacerbation of angina pectoris. Therefore, when discontinuation of pindolol is planned in patients with angina pectoris, the dosage should be gradually reduced over a period of about 2 weeks and the patient should be observed carefully. The same frequency of administration should be maintained. In situations of greater urgency, discontinue pindolol therapy stepwise and under conditions of very close observation. If angina markedly worsens or acute coronary insufficiency develops, it is recommended that treatment with pindolol be reinstituted promptly, at least temporarily.

Various skin rashes and conjunctival xerosis have been reported with beta-blockers, including pindolol. A severe oculo-muco-cutaneous syndrome whose signs include conjunctivitis sicca and psoriasiform rashes, otitis and sclerosing serositis has occurred with the chronic use of one beta-adrenergic-blocking agent (practolol). This syndrome has not been observed with pindolol. However, physicians should be alert to the possibility of such reactions and should discontinue treatment in the event that they occur.

Sinus bradycardia may occur with the use of pindolol due to unopposed vagal activity remaining after blockade of $beta_1$-adrenergic receptors. Due to its intrinsic sympathomimetic activity, pindolol causes less bradycardia at rest than some other beta-adrenergic-blocking agents. If excessive bradycardia occurs, reduce the dosage.

In patients with thyrotoxicosis, possible deleterious effects from long-term use of pindolol have not been adequately appraised. Beta-blockade may mask the clinical signs of continuing hyperthyroidism or complications, and give a false impression of improvement. Therefore, abrupt withdrawal of pindolol may be followed by an exacerbation of the symptoms of hyperthyroidism, including thyroid storm.

Precautions: Caution should be exercised in patients prone to nonallergic bronchospasm (e.g., chronic bronchitis, emphysema) since pindolol may block bronchodilation produced by endogenous and exogenous catecholamine stimulation of beta–receptors.

Pindolol should be administered with caution to patients with allergic rhinitis prone to bronchospasm.

Epinephrine and Beta-blockers: There may be increased difficulty in treating an allergic type reaction in patients on beta-blockers. In these patients, the reaction may be more severe due to pharmacologic effects of the beta-blockers and problems with fluid changes. Epinephrine should be administered with caution since it may not have its usual effects in the treatment of anaphylaxis. On the one hand, larger doses of epinephrine may be needed to overcome the bronchospasm, while on the other hand, these doses can be associated with excessive alpha adrenergic stimulation with consequent hypertension, reflex bradycardia and heart block and possible potentiation of bronchospasm. Alternatives to the use of large doses of epinephrine include vigorous supportive care such as fluids and the use of beta agonists including parenteral salbutamol or isoproterenol to overcome bronchospasm and norepinephrine to overcome hypotension.

Pindolol should be administered with caution to patients subject to spontaneous hypoglycemia, or to diabetic patients (especially those with labile diabetes) who are receiving insulin or oral hypoglycemic agents. Beta-adrenergic-blockers may mask the premonitory signs and symptoms (tachycardia, tremor) of acute hypoglycemia.

Pindolol dosage should be individually adjusted when used concomitantly with other antihypertensive agents (see Dosage).

Patients receiving catecholamine depleting drugs, such as reserpine of guanethidine, should be closely monitored because the added beta-adrenergic-blocking action of pindolol may produce an excessive reduction of sympathetic activity. Do not combine pindolol with other beta-blockers.

Appropriate laboratory tests should be performed at regular intervals during long-term treatment.
Patients Undergoing Elective or Emergency Surgery: The management of patients being treated with beta-blockers and undergoing elective or emergency surgery is controversial. Although beta-adrenergic -receptor blockade impairs the ability of the heart to respond to beta-adrenergically-mediated reflex stimuli, abrupt discontinuation of pindolol therapy may be followed by severe complications (see Warnings). Some patients receiving beta-adrenergic-blocking agents have been subject to protracted severe hypotension during anesthesia. Difficulty in restarting and maintaining the heartbeat has also been reported.

For these reasons, in patients with angina undergoing elective surgery, withdraw pindolol gradually following the recommendation given under "Abrupt cessation of therapy" (see Warnings). According to available evidence, all clinical and physiological effects of beta-blockade are no longer present 48 hours after cessation of medication.

In emergency surgery, since pindolol is a competitive inhibitor of beta-adrenergic-receptor agoinsts, its effects may be reversed, if necessary, by sufficient doses of such agonists as isoproterenol or levarterenol.
Impaired Renal or Hepatic Function: β-blocking agents should be used with caution in patients with impaired hepatic or renal function. Poor renal function has only minor effects on pindolol clearance, but poor hepatic function may cause blood levels of pindolol to increase substantially.
Pregnancy: Since pindolol has not been studied in human pregnancy, it should not be given to pregnant women. The use of any drug in patients of child-bearing potential requires that the anticipated benefit be weighed against possible hazards. Pindolol crosses the placental barrier.
Lactation: Pindolol passes in small quantities into breast milk.
Children: There is no experience with pindolol in the treatment of pediatric age groups.
Occupational Hazards: Because dizziness or fatigue may occur during initiation of treatment with β-adrenoreceptor blocking drugs, patients driving vehicles or operating machinery should exercise caution until they have determined their individual response to treatment.

Adverse Effects: Cardiovascular: Congestive heart failure, severe bradycardia (see Warnings) may occur. Syncope, lightheadedness and postural hypotension. Lengthening of PR interval, second degree AV block, palpitation, chest pains, cold extremities, Raynaud's phenomenon, claudication, hot flushes. Very rarely: arrhythmia, coronary insufficiency.
CNS: insomnia, nightmares, vivid dreams, fatigue, drowsiness, weakness, dizziness, vertigo, tinnitus, headache, mental depression, nervousness. Rarely have the following adverse reactions been reported: aggressiveness, motor disorders, confusion.
Gastrointestinal: diarrhea, constipation, flatulence, heartburn, nausea and vomiting, abdominal pain and dry mouth.
Respiratory: shortness of breath and/or dyspnea, wheezing, bronchospasm.
Allergic, Dermatological (see Warnings): exanthema, sweating, pruritus, psoriasiform rash.
Eyes: itching, burning, grittiness, dryness.
Miscellaneous: muscle cramps, appetite stimulation, weight gain, urinary frequency.
Clinical Laboratory: The following parameters have been rarely elevated: transaminases, alkaline phosphatase, LDH, serum uric acid. Rarely reduction in bilirubin.

Overdose: Symptoms: The most common signs to be expected with overdosage of a beta-adrenergic-blocking agent are bradycardia, congestive heart failure, hypotension, bronchospasm, or hypoglycemia.

Treatment: If overdosage occurs, in all cases therapy with pindolol should be discontinued and the patient observed closely. In addition, if required, the following therapeutic measures are suggested:
1. Bradycardia: Atropine or another anticholinergic drug.
2. Heart block (second or third degree): Isoproterenol or transvenous cardiac pacemaker.
3. Congestive heart failure: Conventional therapy.
4. Hypotension: (depending on associated factors) Epinephrine rather than isoproterenol or norepinephrine may be useful in addition to atropine and digitalis (see Precautions concerning the use of epinephrine).
5. Bronchospasm: Aminophylline or isoproterenol.
6. Hypoglycemia: I.V. glucose.

It should be remembered that pindolol is a competitive antagonist of isoproterenol and hence large doses of isoproterenol can be expected to reverse many of the effects of excessive doses of pindolol. However, the complications of excess isoproterenol should not be overlooked.

Dosage: Hypertension: Pindolol is usually used in conjunction with other antihypertensive agents, particularly a thiazide diuretic but may be used alone (see Indications). Pindolol should be taken with meals.

The dosage of pindolol must always be adjusted to the individual requirements of the patients in accordance with the following guidelines: therapy should be initiated with doses of 5 mg in the morning with breakfast and 5 mg with the evening meal. If an adequate response is not achieved after 1 to 2 weeks, the dose should be increased to 10 mg twice daily.

If after 1 to 2 additional weeks an adequate response is not observed, dosage may be increased to 30 mg daily with 15 mg given in the morning with breakfast and 15 mg with the evening meal.

Doses greater than 30 mg daily must be given on a t.i.d. schedule.

Patients who show a satisfactory response to pindolol at daily doses of 10 to 20 mg may be maintained by giving the required total dose once daily in the morning with breakfast.

The usual maintenance dose is within the range of 15 to 45 mg daily which should not be exceeded. However, during long-term therapy, some patients may be maintained on smaller doses.
Angina Pectoris: The dosage must always be adjusted to the individual requirements of the patient.

In angina, pindolol should be administered on a 3 or 4 times per day dosing regimen. Therapy should be initiated with doses of 5 mg 3 times a day with meals. If after 1 to 2 weeks an adequate response is not observed dosage may be increased. The usual maintenance dose is 15 mg up to the maximum of 40 mg/day.

Supplied: 5 mg: Each whitish, compressed tablet, 7 mm diameter, slope faced, bisected with "LB" embossed on one side and flat faced, beveled edge with "VISKEN 5" embossed on reverse side, contains: pindolol 5 mg. Nonmedicinal ingredients: magnesium stearate, microcrystalline cellulose, silicon dioxide and starch. Bottles of 100.

10 mg: Each whitish, compressed tablet, 8 mm diameter, slope faced, bisected on one side and flat-faced, beveled edge with "VISKEN 10" embossed on reverse side, contains: pindolol 10 mg. Nonmedicinal ingredients: magnesium stearate, microcrystalline cellulose, silicon dioxide and starch. Bottles of 100.

15 mg: Each whitish, compressed tablet, 9 mm diameter, slope faced, bisected with "JU" embossed on one side and flat faced, beveled edge with "VISKEN 15" embossed on reverse side, contains: pindolol 15 mg. Nonmedicinal ingredients: magnesium stearate, microcrystalline cellulose, silicon dioxide and starch. Bottles of 100.

Protect from light.

(Shown in Product Recognition Section)

VITAMIN A

General Monograph, CPhA

Vitamin

This monograph has been compiled by CPhA. It may contain information different from that approved by Therapeutic Products Programme, Health Canada, and the pharmaceutical manufacturers' approval has not been requested.

Pharmacology: The term vitamin A is applied to a number of substances with very similar structure and similar activity. The principal and most active substance is all-trans retinol (vitamin A alcohol). Vitamin A activity is assayed biologically and 1 IU equals 1 USP unit which is equal to 0.3 μg of all-trans retinol or 0.6 μg of beta-carotene. One retinol equivalent (RE) is the specific biologic activity of 1 μg of all-trans retinol (3.33 IU) or 6 μg (10 IU) of beta-carotene.

Derivatives of vitamin A such as tretinoin (all trans-retinoic acid) and isotretinoin (13-cis-retinoic acid) are used in the treatment of acne and certain other skin disorders.

Beta-carotene, retinol and retinal (vitamin A aldehyde) possess effective and reliable vitamin A activity. Exogenous sources of vitamin A are required for growth and bone development, vision, reproduction and maintenance of the integrity of mucosal and epithelial surfaces. Beta-carotene has antioxidant activity. Although some studies have suggested that antioxidants may be beneficial in disease prevention, further studies are required before antioxidant vitamins can be recommended for the prevention of cancer and cardiovascular disease.

Retinal and retinol are in chemical equilibrium in the body and possess equivalent antixerophthalmic activity. Dietary vitamin A deficiency is a major cause of blindness in children in some developing countries. In developed areas, deficiency is rare in the absence of concurrent illness such as liver disease or intestinal malabsorption. Night blindness is the earliest symptom of deficiency, followed by degenerative changes in the retina such as xerophthalmia and keratomalacia.
Pharmacokinetics: Vitamin A is a fat soluble vitamin and is readily absorbed from the normal gastrointestinal tract. Plasma concentrations reach a peak level within 3 to 5 hours. Beta-carotene is converted to retinal, which is mostly reduced to retinol and conjugated with glucuronic acid and excreted in the urine and feces. Some retinol is esterified mainly to retinyl palmitate. Normal plasma concentration is approximately 1.4 μmol/L (130 units/100 mL). Retinyl palmitate and small amounts of retinol and retinal are stored in the liver. Body stores of vitamin A are normally sufficient to meet the body's needs for up to 2 years.

Indications: Prophylaxis and treatment of vitamin A deficiency.

Contraindications: Hypervitaminosis A; hypersensitivity to vitamin A or any component of a vitamin A containing pharmaceutical preparation.

Precautions: In physiologic doses, vitamin A is relatively nontoxic. Prolonged use of dosages greater than 7 500 RE (25 000 IU) may lead to symptoms of chronic toxicity such as bone and joint pain, hyperostosis, hair loss, anorexia and hepatosplenomegaly.

Excessive consumption of vitamin A supplements or foods rich in beta-carotene such as carrots may cause carotenemia and yellow discoloration of the skin. The same effect may result from defective utilisation of vitamin A precursors in diabetes mellitus and myxedema.
Drug Interactions: Excessive use of mineral oil as a laxative may reduce the utilization of the provitamin by carrying away large amounts in the feces. Cholestyramine and neomycin may affect drug absorption.

Vitamin A should not be used concurrently with isotretinoin since toxic effects may be additive.

Women on oral contraceptives have shown a significant increase in plasma vitamin A concentrations.
Pregnancy: Excessive intake of vitamin A during pregnancy may be a potential hazard to the mother and fetus. Effective measures to avoid pregnancy are necessary with high dose vitamin A therapy.

There is an extremely high risk that major fetal abnormalities will occur if pregnancy occurs during treatment with isotretinoin, which is contraindicated during pregnancy.
Lactation: Vitamin A is distributed into milk. Hypervitaminosis is a theoretical possibility.

Adverse Effects: See Overdose.

Overdose: Symptoms: The amount required to cause toxicity will vary among individuals. The manifestations of toxicity will depend on the patient's age and hepatic function, and on the dose and duration of administration.

Acute toxicity (single ingestion of 7 500 RE or 25 000 IU per kg or more): Signs and symptoms may be delayed for 8 to 24 hours and include: increased intracranial pressure, headache, irritability, drowsiness, dizziness, lethargy, vomiting, diarrhea, bulging of fontanels in infants, diplopia, papilledema. Peeling of skin around mouth may be observed from 1 to several days after ingestion and may spread to the rest of the body.

Chronic, excessive ingestion (1 200 RE or 4 000 IU/kg daily for 6 to 15 months) may produce symptoms of pseudotumor cerebri, anorexia, weakness, arthralgias, bone pain, bone demineralization, dry skin, cracked lips, brittle nails, hair loss, splenomegaly, hepatomegaly, hypoplastic anemia, leukopenia, optic neuropathy, and blindness. Increased plasma concentrations of vitamin A occur but do not necessarily correlate with toxicity.

Treatment: For an acute overdose, empty stomach and follow with activated charcoal and a cathartic. Treat symptomatically.

Intracranial pressure may be reduced with i.v. dexamethasone or i.v. mannitol. In untreated patients, increased intracranial pressure may persist for 4 weeks after discontinuation of vitamin A.

For chronic ingestions, discontinue vitamin A. Toxicity is slowly reversible but may persist for several weeks. Monitor blood pressure, fluids, electrolytes, CNS status, complete blood count and hepatic function.

Dosage: In preventing vitamin deficiency, adequate dietary intake is preferred over supplementation, whenever possible.

Vitamin A (cont'd)

For a listing of food sources of vitamin A, see Vitamin Food Sources in the Clin-Info section.

The recommended daily intake of vitamin A to prevent deficiency is 400 RE (1 300 IU) for infants, 400 to 900 RE (1 300 to 3 000 IU) for children and 800 to 1 000 RE (2 700 to 3 300 IU) for adolescents and adults. No additional vitamin A nutrient intake is recommended during pregnancy, however an additional 400 RE (1 300 IU)/day is recommended during lactation. For a complete listing of vitamin A and other nutrient requirements, see Recommended Nutrient Intake in the Clin-Info section.

Severe Deficiency with Xerophthalmia: Children 1 to 8 years: 1 500 to 3 000 RE (5 000 to 10 000 IU)/kg orally for 5 days or until recovery occurs.

Children >8 years and Adults: 150 000 RE (500 000 IU) orally for 3 days, followed by 15 000 RE (50 000 IU) daily for 2 weeks, then 3 000 to 6 000 RE (10 000 to 20 000 IU) daily for 2 months.

Deficiency without Corneal Changes: Infants <1 year: 3 000 RE (10 000 IU)/kg/day for 5 days, then 2 250 to 4 500 RE (7 500 to 15 000 IU)/day for 10 days.

Children 1 to 8 years: 1 500 to 3 000 RE (5 000 to 10 000 IU)/kg/day for 5 days, then 5 100 to 10 500 RE (17 000 to 35 000 IU)/day for 10 days.

Children >8 years and Adults: 30 000 RE (100 000 IU)/day for 3 days, then 7 500 to 15 000 RE (25 000 to 50 000 IU)/day for 14 days.

It has been suggested that infants and children (<8 years) with chronic intestinal malabsorption should be given about 600 RE (2 000 IU) of vitamin A daily in an aqueous preparation. Children >8 years and Adults: 3 000 to 15 000 RE (10 000 to 50 000 IU)/day of water-miscible products.

Reviewed 1998

VITAMIN A ACID ℞

Dermik Laboratories Canada

Tretinoin

Acne Therapy

Pharmacology: The interest in oral vitamin A in the treatment of acne started some 30 years ago following publication of a report by Straumfjord and theoretical support for the use of the vitamin in the reduction of hyperkeratosis came from basic science investigations. Hunter and Pinkus showed a reduction in the number of keratinocytes in the human stratum corneum during oral vitamin A therapy. Fell and Mellanby noticed a suppression of keratinization by excessive vitamin A in tissue culture. This led to the opinion that vitamin A is antikeratinizing.

Topical use of vitamin A was suggested as a means of reducing systemic toxicity from vitamin A taken orally and a number of topical forms of vitamin A were tried. Topical tretinoin was found to be the most potent because of its greater peeling action.

Topical tretinoin has a very pronounced keratolytic action according to both Von Beer and Von Stuttgen. This action has led to its use in a number of dermatological conditions. It was tried successfully by Kligman et al in the treatment of acne vulgaris since follicular hyperkeratosis is considered as being an initial stage of acne.

Indications: For topical application in the treatment of acne vulgaris, primarily Grades I, II and III in which comedones, papules and pustules predominate.

Contraindications: Use should be discontinued if hypersensitivity to any of the ingredients is noted.

Warnings: *Pregnancy:* **Topical tretinoin should be used by women of childbearing years only after contraceptive counseling. It is recommended that topical tretinoin not be used by pregnant women.** There have been rare reports of birth defects among babies born to women exposed to topical tretinoin during pregnancy. However, there are no well controlled prospective studies of the use of topical tretinoin in pregnant women. A retrospective study of mothers exposed to topical tretinoin during the first trimester of pregnancy found no increase in the incidence of birth defects. Topical retinoid teratology studies in rats and rabbits have been inconclusive. As with all retinoids, tretinoin administered orally at high doses is teratogenic.

When applying topical tretinoin, care should be taken not to apply near the eyes, mouth, angles of the nose and mucous membranes. Topical use may cause severe local redness and peeling at the site of the application. If the degree of local irritation warrants, use the medication less frequently, discontinue use temporarily, or discontinue use completely, and consult your physician.

Precautions: Concomitant topical medications and particularly other peeling agents should be used with caution. In case of a change of medications to topical tretinoin, it would be advisable to wait until peeling from previous medications has subsided.

Because of an increased susceptibility to sunlight in patients with sunburn, the use of a topical tretinoin is not advisable until the skin has fully recovered. Exposure to sunlight, including sunlamps, should be minimized during treatment with topical tretinoin.

Adverse Effects: In certain very sensitive patients, the skin may get to be very erythematous, edematous, blistered or crusted. In such cases, application of topical tretinoin should be discontinued until the skin has fully recovered; further application should be at a level that the individual can tolerate. Temporary hyper or hypopigmentation can occur with repeated application of topical tretinoin. Increased susceptibility to sunlight has been reported. All adverse reactions seem to be reversible when treatment is discontinued.

Overdose: Symptoms and Treatment: Topical tretinoin if used excessively, may cause marked erythema, severe peeling of the skin and discomfort; on the other hand, excessive application may not bring more rapid or better results. Amount or frequency of application should be reduced if undesirable reactions occur.

Inadvertent oral ingestion of topical tretinoin may lead to the same adverse effects as those associated with excessive oral intake of vitamin A including teratogenesis in women of childbearing years. Therefore, in such cases, pregnancy testing should be carried out in women of childbearing years.

Dosage: Apply daily, preferably before retiring, where acne lesions are present, using enough of the gel or cream to lightly cover the affected area. An exacerbation of the inflammatory lesions may take place during the early weeks of application. These result from the action of the topical tretinoin on deep and previously unseen comedones and papules. Therapeutic results should be seen after 2 to 4 weeks of treatment. Results may take 6 to 8 weeks before reaching optimal degree. Once the acne lesions have responded satisfactorily, improvement can be maintained with less frequent application.

In cases of severe erythema at an early stage of treatment, the frequency of application and amount may be reduced at the beginning of treatment and then increased progressively.

Information for the Patient: See Blue Section—Information for the Patient "Vitamin A Acid".

Supplied: Cream: Each g of cream contains: tretinoin USP 0.01%, 0.025%, 0.05% or 0.1%. Also contains 2-Bromo-2-nitropropane-1,3-diol. Tubes of 25 g (0.01, 0.025, 0.05 and 0.1%) and 50 g (0.05%).

Gel: Each g of gel contains: tretinoin USP 0.01%, 0.025% or 0.05%. Also contains methylparaben and propylparaben. Tubes of 25 and 50 g.

Store at controlled room temperature (15 to 30°C).

Reviewed 1998

VITAMIN B_1

General Monograph, CPhA

Thiamine

Vitamin

This monograph has been compiled by CPhA. It may contain information different from that approved by Therapeutic Products Programme, Health Canada, and the pharmaceutical manufacturers' approval has not been requested.

Pharmacology: Vitamin B_1 is a water soluble B complex vitamin. In vivo, vitamin B_1 combines with adenosine triphosphate (ATP) to form thiamine pyrophosphate, also known as cocarboxylase, a coenzyme. Its role in carbohydrate metabolism is the decarboxylation of pyruvic acid and alpha-ketoacids to acetaldehyde and carbon dioxide. Increased levels of pyruvic acid in the blood indicate vitamin B_1 deficiency.

Vitamin B_1 depletion can occur after approximately 3 weeks of total absence of the vitamin from the diet. Deficiency may occur in alcoholics and food faddists or in special clinical situations such as hemodialysis, chronic peritoneal dialysis, or after administration of glucose to a vitamin B_1-depleted patient. Requirements may be increased due to burns, chronic fever, gastrectomy, intestinal disease, liver disease and hyperthyroidism.

Deficiency of vitamin B_1 eventually leads to beriberi and Wernicke's encephalopathy. The cardiovascular or nervous system, or both, may be affected. Cardiovascular involvement is manifested by high output, biventricular heart failure and edema. CNS symptoms include peripheral neuropathy and an encephalopathy syndrome characterized by nystagmus, ophthalmoplegia, fever, ataxia and progressive mental deterioration which may ultimately result in coma and death.

Pharmacokinetics: Orally administered vitamin B_1 is absorbed mainly from duodenum, by both active and passive processes. The total amount which can be absorbed following administration of a large dose is 4 to 8 mg. Body stores are approximately 30 mg, with a 1 mg daily turnover. Storage is mainly in skeletal muscles, heart, liver, kidneys and brain.

Vitamin B_1 is metabolized in the liver and excreted in the urine. When large doses are administered, body stores may become saturated and unchanged vitamin B_1 may be excreted in the urine.

Indications: Prophylaxis and treatment of vitamin B_1 deficiency states including beriberi and Wernicke's encephalopathy.

Contraindications: Hypersensitivity to vitamin B_1 or any component of a product containing vitamin B_1.

Precautions: Serious sensitivity reactions can occur. Deaths have resulted from i.v. use. Some manufacturers recommend an intradermal test dose prior to i.v. administration in patients with suspected hypersensitivity.

Simple vitamin B_1 deficiency is rare. Multiple vitamin deficiencies should be suspected in any case of dietary inadequacy.

Pregnancy: No adverse effects have been reported with intake of normal daily requirements.

Lactation: No adverse effects have been reported with intake of normal daily requirements.

Adverse Effects: Feeling of warmth, pruritus, urticaria, weakness, sweating, nausea, restlessness, tightness of the throat, angioneurotic edema, cyanosis, pulmonary edema, hemorrhage into the gastrointestinal tract, collapse and death have been rarely reported, mainly following repeated i.v. administration of the drug.

Dosage: In preventing vitamin deficiencies, adequate dietary intake is preferred over supplementation whenever possible. For a listing of food sources of vitamin B_1, see Vitamin Food Sources in the Clin-Info section.

For a listing of the daily requirements of vitamin B_1, see Recommended Nutrient Intake in the Clin-Info section.

In the treatment of deficiency, vitamin B_1 is usually administered orally. When oral administration is not feasible, when malabsorption is suspected, or in patients with Wernicke's encephalopathy or high output heart failure secondary to beriberi, vitamin B_1 may be administered i.m. or i.v.

Oral: Usual adult dose to treat deficiency is 5 to 30 mg daily given as a single dose or in 3 divided doses.

Parenteral: Wernicke's encephalopathy and high output cardiac failure secondary to beriberi must be treated as emergencies. Critically ill patients or those with malabsorption syndromes should also be treated by the i.v. or i.m. route.

In the treatment of beriberi, 5 to 100 mg 3 times daily may be given by the i.v. or i.m. route. Dosage should then be reduced depending on patient response, followed by oral therapy for 1 month.

In Wernicke's encephalopathy 100 mg i.v. is given initially followed by 50 to 100 mg i.m. or i.v. daily until the patient is eating a well balanced diet. I.V. dextrose solutions increase thiamine requirements and thiamine should be given parenterally before administering these solutions to the patient with Wernicke's. Following clinical improvement and resumption of a regular diet, oral therapy may be instituted.

Reviewed 1998

The safety of immunization programs is in part maximized through monitoring vaccine-associated adverse events. To report a vaccine-associated adverse event, complete the form "Report of Vaccine-associated Adverse Event" found in the CLIN-INFO SECTION.

VITAMIN B_2

General Monograph, CPhA

Riboflavin

Vitamin

This monograph has been compiled by CPhA. It may contain information different from that approved by Therapeutic Products Programme, Health Canada, and the pharmaceutical manufacturers' approval has not been requested.

Pharmacology: Vitamin B_2 is a water-soluble, B complex vitamin. It is required for tissue respiration and is also indirectly involved in maintaining erythrocyte integrity.

Vitamin B_2 deficiency often accompanies pellagra and other B vitamin deficiency states and is also associated with conditions causing negative protein balance, such as chronic diarrhea, malabsorption syndrome, diabetes mellitus and chronic debilitating diseases. Deficiency is manifested by angular stomatitis, magenta tongue, fissuring of the lips and desquamation of mucous membranes, redness and scaling of the scrotum.

Pharmacokinetics: Vitamin B_2 is readily absorbed from the upper gastrointestinal tract, except in the presence of malabsorption syndromes. The extent of gastrointestinal absorption is increased when the drug is administered with food and is decreased in patients with hepatitis, cirrhosis, biliary obstruction.

Vitamin B_2 is inactive until phosphorylated to flavin mononucleotide (FMN) in gastrointestinal mucosal cells, erythrocytes and the liver; FMN is converted to another coenzyme, flavin adenine dinucleotide (FAD). Free vitamin B_2 is present in the retina. In blood, about 60% of FAD and FMN is protein bound.

The biologic half-life is about 66 to 84 minutes following oral or i.m. administration of a single large dose in healthy individuals.

Only about 9% of the drug is excreted unchanged; the fate of the remainder is unknown. Excretion appears to involve renal tubular secretion as well as glomerular filtration. Amounts in excess of the body's needs are excreted in urine.

Indications: Prophylaxis and treatment of vitamin B_2 deficiency.

Precautions: *Drug Interactions:* Alcohol impairs intestinal absorption of vitamin B_2.

Phenothiazines, Tricyclic Antidepressants: These drugs may inhibit the conversion of vitamin B_2 to the active coenzyme form. Requirements for vitamin B_2 may be increased in patients receiving these drugs.

Probenecid: The extent of gastrointestinal absorption of vitamin B_2 is decreased when it is used concomitantly with probenecid.

Pregnancy and *Lactation:* Vitamin B_2 crosses the placenta and is distributed in breast milk. Adverse effects have not been reported with intake of normal requirements.

Adverse Effects: Vitamin B_2 is usually well tolerated and nontoxic. Because of its fluorescent yellow color, large doses may cause yellow discoloration of urine.

Dosage: In preventing vitamin deficiencies, adequate dietary intake is preferred over supplementation whenever possible. For a listing of food sources of vitamin B_2, see Vitamin Food Sources in the Clin-Info section.

Vitamin B_2 is usually given orally. It may also be given by i.m. injection or i.v. infusion as a component of multivitamin injections.

For a detailed listing of vitamin B_2 and other nutrient requirements, see Recommended Nutrient Intake in the Clin-Info section.

The usual oral dose in the treatment of deficiency is 5 to 30 mg daily in divided doses for adults and 3 to 10 mg daily in divided doses for children.

Reviewed 1998

VITAMIN B_3

General Monograph, CPhA

see NIACIN/NIACINAMIDE

VITAMIN B_5

General Monograph, CPhA

see PANTOTHENIC ACID

VITAMIN B_6

General Monograph, CPhA

Pyridoxine

Vitamin

This monograph has been compiled by CPhA. It may contain information different from that approved by Therapeutic Products Programme, Health Canada, and the pharmaceutical manufacturers' approval has not been requested.

Pharmacology: Vitamin B_6 is a water soluble B complex vitamin which is present in many foods as pyridoxine, pyridoxal and pyridoxamine. These forms of vitamin B_6 are converted in vivo to pyridoxal phosphate and pyridoxamine phosphate, which are essential coenzymes in the metabolism of certain amino acids such as tryptophan, in carbohydrate and lipid metabolism, and in the synthesis of heme and GABA, an inhibitory neurotransmitter.

Vitamin B_6 deficiency is characterized by seizures, seborrheic dermatitis, glossitis, nausea and vomiting, and dizziness. There is also accumulation and urinary excretion of xanthurenic acid (an intermediary metabolite of tryptophan), which may be measured to aid in diagnosing vitamin B_6 deficiency. Certain drugs can act as vitamin B_6 antagonists, leading to secondary deficiency. These include hydrazines (e.g., isoniazid), cycloserine, pyrazinamide and penicillamine.

A hereditary vitamin B_6 dependency syndrome, in which large amounts are needed to prevent seizures, has been seen in infants in whom an apoenzyme for glutamic acid decarboxylase with decreased vitamin B_6 binding capacity leads to deficient production of GABA. Other vitamin B_6-responsive conditions have been identified such as a hereditary sideroblastic anemia and certain metabolic disorders caused by genetic abnormalities (e.g., xanthurenic aciduria, cystathioninuria, hyperoxaluria and homocystinuria).

Vitamin B_6 requirements are increased in pregnancy and lactation and in patients taking estrogens (e.g., oral contraceptives).

Pharmacokinetics: Pyridoxine, pyridoxal and pyridoxamine are readily absorbed from the gastrointestinal tract, converted to the active forms of vitamin B_6 and stored in the liver and brain. Total body stores amount to 16 to 27 mg. Vitamin B_6 is metabolized in the liver and excreted in the urine.

Vitamin B_6 crosses the placenta and is excreted in breast milk.

Indications: In the prevention and treatment of vitamin B_6 deficiency. Vitamin B_6 is also used in the management of acute isoniazid overdosage.

Contraindications: Hypersensitivity to vitamin B_6 or any component of a vitamin B_6-containing pharmaceutical preparation.

Precautions: Vitamin B_6 is relatively nontoxic in usual doses. However, chronic administration of high doses (e.g., 2 g or more daily for several months) has led to sensory neuropathy.

Drug Interactions: Vitamin B_6 increases the peripheral metabolism of levodopa. When levodopa is combined with carbidopa, this effect is prevented.

Isoniazid, cycloserine, pyrazinamide and penicillamine may antagonize the effects of vitamin B_6 and lead to a secondary deficiency.

Patients taking estrogens (e.g., oral contraceptives) have higher vitamin B_6 requirements.

Pregnancy: No adverse effects have been reported with the use of physiologic doses of vitamin B_6 during pregnancy. However, the use of high doses during pregnancy has been implicated in some cases of vitamin B_6 dependent syndrome in infants (see Pharmacology).

Lactation: Vitamin B_6 is excreted in breast milk; however, adverse effects have not been reported with the use of physiologic doses of vitamin B_6 during lactation.

Adverse Effects: Nausea, headache, paresthesia, somnolence and low serum folic acid concentrations have been reported. Sensory neuropathy can occur following long-term administration of large doses (2 g or more daily for 2 months or longer).

Transient dependency symptoms may occur upon withdrawal of vitamin B_6 therapy at a dose of 200 mg/day for 33 days. The significance of this is unknown; however, for patients on large doses for long periods of time, withdrawal of vitamin B_6 should probably be gradual.

Temporary burning or stinging and pain may be experienced at the site of s.c. or i.m. injection.

Dosage: In the prevention of vitamin deficiencies, adequate dietary intake is preferred over supplementation whenever possible. For information on food sources of vitamin B_6, see Vitamin Food Sources in the Clin-Info section.

For a listing of the daily requirements of vitamin B_6 and other nutrients, see Recommended Nutrient Intake in the Clin-Info section. Patients taking isoniazid, cycloserine, pyrazinamide, penicillamine or oral contraceptives may require higher daily intake. Requirements are also higher during pregnancy and lactation, and in patients with xanthurenic aciduria, hyperoxaluria, cystothioninuria or homocystinuria.

Vitamin B_6 is usually administered orally; however, it can be given by i.v., i.m. or s.c. injection when the oral route is not possible.

Treatment of Deficiency: 2.5 to 10 mg daily in adults. Once the clinical signs of deficiency have been corrected, the dose may be reduced to 2 to 5 mg daily for several weeks.

Vitamin B_6 Dependency in Infants: For the treatment of seizures in these infants, a single dose of 10 to 100 mg vitamin B_6 i.m. or i.v. has been recommended. Seizures usually stop within 2 to 3 minutes. Some infants may require lifelong supplementation with oral doses of 2 to 100 mg.

Hereditary Sideroblastic Anemia: An oral dose of 200 to 600 mg daily has been suggested. Lifelong supplementation may be required to prevent recurrence.

Treatment of Isoniazid Overdosage: For the treatment or prevention of seizures or coma following isoniazid poisoning, a dose of vitamin B_6 equal to the amount of isoniazid ingested is given by i.v. injection. Alternatively, if the amount ingested is unknown, a dose of 5 g vitamin B_6 may given i.v. initially and repeated at 30-minute intervals until seizures are controlled.

Reviewed 1998

VITAMIN B_{12}

General Monograph, CPhA

Cyanocobalamin

Hydroxocobalamin

Hematopoietic

This monograph has been compiled by CPhA. It may contain information different from that approved by Therapeutic Products Programme, Health Canada, and the pharmaceutical manufacturers' approval has not been requested.

Pharmacology: Vitamin B_{12} is a group of cobalt-containing B complex vitamins, also known as cobalamins, synthesized by microorganisms. Cyanocobalamin and hydroxocobalamin are the principal forms of vitamin B_{12} in clinical use. They have equivalent vitamin B_{12} activity. An exogenous source of vitamin B_{12} is required for nucleoprotein and myelin synthesis, cell production, normal growth, and for the maintenance of normal erythropoiesis.

Deficiency of vitamin B_{12} may be caused by dietary deficiency, malabsorption, or lack of sufficient intrinsic factor, and results in megaloblastic anemia, gastrointestinal lesions and neurologic damage characterized by demyelination and progressive axonal degeneration. Therapy with vitamin B_{12} reverses the anemia and gastrointestinal manifestations of deficiency, and halts the progression of neurologic damage. However, the existing nerve damage may not be completely reversible.

Pharmacokinetics: Vitamin B_{12} is irregularly absorbed from the distal small intestine following oral administration. Vitamin B_{12} absorption is an active process that requires gastric intrinsic factor. Intrinsic factor is a glycoprotein secreted by the gastric mucosa. Passive diffusion through the intestinal wall can occur but large amounts of B_{12} are required (i.e. >1 mg). Following oral doses less than 3 μg, peak plasma concentrations are not reached for 8 to 12 hours because the vitamin is transiently retained in the wall of the lower ileum. It is rapidly absorbed from i.m. and s.c. sites of injection; peak plasma concentrations are reached within 1 hour after i.m. injection.

Vitamin B_{12} is distributed into the liver, bone marrow, and other tissues, including the placenta. At birth, the blood concentration of vitamin B_{12} in neonates is 3 to 5 times that of the mother.

Total body stores of vitamin B_{12} in healthy individuals are estimated to range from 1 to 11 mg, with an average of 5 mg; 50 to 90% is stored in the liver. Vitamin B_{12} is believed to be converted to coenzyme form in the liver and is probably stored in tissues in this form.

Following i.v. or i.m. administration of 0.1 to 1 mg of cyanocobalamin, 50 to 90% of the dose may be excreted in urine by glomerular filtration within 48 hours, with the major portion

Vitamin B_{12} (cont'd)

being excreted in the first 8 hours. Hydroxocobalamin is more highly protein bound and is retained in the body longer than cyanocobalamin; however, it is not more effective in normalizing the hematocrit.

Because hydroxocobalamin may cause formation of antibodies to hydroxocobalamin-transcobalamin II complex, cyanocobalamin is usually the preferred form of vitamin B_{12}.

Indications: Vitamin B_{12} is used in the treatment of pernicious anemia and other vitamin B_{12} deficiency states. Vitamin B_{12} is also used to treat other macrocytic, megaloblastic anemias, in cases where malabsorption of vitamin B_{12} is suspected, e.g., gastric carcinoma, gastrectomy, sprue, ileal resection, strictures, or anastomoses involving the ileum.

Vitamin B_{12} deficiency requiring therapy may also be caused by lack of sufficient intrinsic factor which could have many causes, or by bacteria (blind loop syndrome), the fish tapeworm, or by certain drug therapies that may impair vitamin B_{12} absorption (see Precautions, Drug Interactions).

Vitamin B_{12} is used in conjunction with radiolabelled vitamin B_{12} in the study of vitamin B_{12} absorption and diagnosis of pernicious anemia (Schilling test).

Contraindications: Hypersensitivity to cobalamins.

Precautions: An intradermal sensitivity test may be performed in patients with suspected hypersensitivity to cobalamins.

In the treatment of megaloblastic anemia, erythrocyte potassium requirements may be increased as erythropoiesis normalizes, and potassium administration may be required.

It is important to accurately diagnose anemias prior to treatment, to ensure the proper therapy is initiated. If folic acid is used to treat pernicious anemia, for example, hematologic improvement may occur while neurologic complications continue to progress.

Vitamin B_{12} has been associated with accelerated optic nerve atrophy in patients with early Leber's disease (hereditary optic nerve atrophy).

Drug Interactions: Most antibiotics, methotrexate and pyrimethamine invalidate folic acid and vitamin B_{12} diagnostic microbiological blood assays. Chloramphenicol may antagonize the hematopoietic response to vitamin B_{12}.

Colchicine, aminoglycosides, certain anticonvulsants (e.g., phenytoin, phenobarbital, primidone), para-aminosalicylic acid or excessive alcohol intake for longer than 2 weeks may impair the absorption of vitamin B_{12}.

Histamine$_2$-Receptor Antagonists (cimetidine, ranitidine, nizatidine, famotidine): May potentially cause vitamin B_{12} deficiency by decreasing gastric acid cleavage of vitamin B_{12} from food sources. This may be important in patients with low stores of vitamin B_{12} or in patients taking H_2-antagonists for extended periods of time (>2 years).

Pregnancy: No adverse effects have been reported with ingestion of normal daily requirements during pregnancy.

Lactation: Vitamin B_{12} is distributed into the milk of nursing women in concentrations that approximate the maternal blood vitamin B_{12} concentration. No adverse effects have been reported with intake of normal daily requirements during lactation.

Adverse Effects: Vitamin B_{12} is usually non toxic even in large doses. However, some adverse effects have been reported such as mild, transient diarrhea, itch, urticaria.

Dosage: In the prevention of deficiency of any nutrient, adequate dietary intake is preferred over supplementation whenever possible. For a listing of dietary sources of vitamin B_{12}, see Vitamin Food Sources in the Clin-Info section. For a listing of the daily requirements of vitamin B_{12}, see Recommended Nutrient Intake in the Clin-Info section.

The preferred route of administration of vitamin B_{12} is parenteral, either i.m. or deep s.c. (avoiding the dermis and upper subcutaneous tissue). The preferred form of vitamin B_{12} is cyanocobalamin (see Pharmacology).

Treatment of Vitamin B_{12} Deficiency: Confirmatory diagnostic tests should be performed prior to initiation of therapy. Adults: The usual i.m. or s.c. dose is 30 to 100 μg daily for 5 to 10 days. A maintenance dose of 100 to 200 μg monthly is usually sufficient to maintain normal erythrocyte count.

Although the oral route is generally considered to be inferior to parenteral therapy in the treatment of vitamin B_{12} deficiencies, oral dosages of up to 1 000 μg daily have been used in patients who have refused parenteral therapy.

Children: 100 μg i.m. or s.c. daily until a total dose of 1 to 5 mg is given. The maintenance dose is 60 μg monthly.

It is important that patients understand their need for lifelong, regular maintenance therapy.

Reviewed 1998

VITAMIN B_{12}
Abbott

Cyanocobalamin

Hematopoietic

Supplied: Each mL contains: cyanocobalamin 100 or 1 000 μg. Nonmedicinal ingredients: acid acetic glacial, sodium acetate, sodium chloride, sodium hydroxide and water for injection. Ampuls of 1 mL, boxes of 50.

VITAMIN B_{12}
Taro

Cyanocobalamin

Hematopoietic

Supplied: Each mL contains: cyanocobalamin 1 000 μg. Also contains acetic acid, benzyl alcohol 1.5% as a preservative, sodium acetate, sodium chloride and water for injection. Hydrochloric acid or sodium hydroxide may be used to adjust pH. Multidose vials of 10 and 30 mL.

VITAMIN C
General Monograph, CPhA

Ascorbic Acid

Vitamin

> This monograph has been compiled by CPhA. It may contain information different from that approved by Therapeutic Products Programme, Health Canada, and the pharmaceutical manufacturers' approval has not been requested.

Pharmacology: Vitamin C is a water-soluble vitamin and is essential for the formation of collagen and intercellular material, and hence for the development of cartilage, bone and teeth, and for wound healing. Vitamin C influences the formation of hemoglobin, erythrocyte maturation, and certain immunological and biochemical reactions in the body. Vitamin C deficiency results in scurvy, which primarily affects collagen metabolism, but also blood vessels and bones.

Vitamin C has antioxidant properties. Although some studies have suggested that antioxidants may be beneficial in disease prevention, further study is required before antioxidant vitamins can be recommended for the prevention of cancer or cardiovascular disease.

Requirements for vitamin C may be increased in pregnancy, lactation, the elderly, hyperthyroidism, fever, cold exposure, stress, infection, trauma, burns, smoking and exposure to certain drugs (see Precautions, Drug Interactions).

Pharmacokinetics: Vitamin C is readily absorbed from the gastrointestinal tract by an active mechanism. It is widely distributed, with higher concentrations in liver, leukocytes, platelets, glandular tissue and the lens of the eye. Normal plasma concentrations range from 10 to 20 μg/mL; levels of 1 to 1.5 μg/mL are associated with scurvy.

Vitamin C is about 25% bound to plasma proteins. Its metabolism involves oxidation to dehydroascorbic acid and some other inactive compounds, all of which are renally excreted. With large doses, saturation occurs and unchanged vitamin C is excreted renally.

Vitamin C is removable by hemodialysis.

Indications: Vitamin C is used to prevent or treat scurvy.

Precautions: Large doses of vitamin C may lead to hyperoxaluria, or precipitation of urate, cystine, oxalate, or certain drugs in the urinary tract.

Vitamin C may cause transient mild pain at the site of s.c. or i.m. injection. Rapid i.v. injection may cause temporary faintness or dizziness.

Drug Interactions: Salicylates inhibit uptake of vitamin C into leukocytes and platelets. The clinical significance of this effect is variable. Patients on high dose salicylate therapy should be evaluated for possible vitamin C deficiency if they exhibit the related signs or symptoms.

Because vitamin C is a urinary acidifier in large doses, the excretion of drugs that are weak acids or bases may be decreased or increased respectively.

Drug-Laboratory Test Interactions: Because vitamin C is a potent reducing agent, it can interfere with the results of tests based on oxidation-reduction reactions. Because the degree of interference depends on many factors, specialized references should be consulted.

Pregnancy: Ingestion of large doses of vitamin C during pregnancy has resulted in scurvy in neonates.

Lactation: Vitamin C is excreted in breast milk. Adverse effects have not been reported with intake of normal daily requirements.

Adverse Effects: Vitamin C is generally well tolerated. Reported adverse effects include nausea, vomiting, heartburn, abdominal cramps, fatigue, flushing, headache, insomnia and sleepiness. Diarrhea may occur after oral dosage of 1 g/day or greater.

Dosage: In preventing vitamin deficiencies, adequate dietary intake is preferred over supplementation whenever possible. For information on dietary sources of vitamin C and other nutrients, see Vitamin Food Sources in the Clin-Info section. For a listing of recommended daily requirements of vitamin C, see Recommended Nutrient Intake in the Clin-Info section.

Vitamin C is usually administered orally. When the oral route is not feasible, it may be given by s.c., i.m. or i.v. injection.

Treatment of Scurvy: Adults: An oral or parenteral dose of 100 to 250 mg once or twice daily will successfully reverse the skeletal and vascular changes associated with scurvy within 2 days to 3 weeks.

Children: 100 to 300 mg daily in divided doses, orally or parenterally.

Reviewed 1998

VITAMIN C
Swiss Herbal

Vitamin

Supplied: Each black cherry, lemon, orange juice, raspberry juice or grape juice flavored chewable tablet contains: vitamin C 500 mg. Nonmedicinal ingredients: colors, dextrose, flavors and magnesium stearate. Bottles of 90 and 180.

VITAMIN D
General Monograph, CPhA

Vitamin

> This monograph has been compiled by CPhA. It may contain information different from that approved by Therapeutic Products Programme, Health Canada, and the pharmaceutical manufacturers' approval has not been requested.

Pharmacology: Vitamin D is a fat-soluble vitamin and has properties of both vitamins and minerals. The term vitamin D collectively refers to a group of structurally similar chemicals and their metabolites which includes alfacalcidol (1∝-hydroxycholecalciferol), calcitriol (1,25-dihydroxycholecalciferol), cholecalciferol (vitamin D_3), dihydrotachysterol (DHT) and ergocalciferol (vitamin D_2). These agents have antirachitic properties.

The biologic activity of 40 IU vitamin D equals that of 1 μg of ergocalciferol or cholecalciferol.

Vitamin D is essential for the absorption and utilization of calcium and phosphate and aids in the mobilization of bone calcium and maintenance of serum calcium concentrations.

Cholecalciferol (vitamin D_3) is synthesized in the skin on exposure to ultraviolet radiation. Cholecalciferol is also present in fish liver oils. Ergocalciferol (vitamin D_2) is produced by ultraviolet irradiation of a provitamin D sterol (ergosterol) which occurs in yeast and fungi. Both of these agents which have equal biologic activity are metabolized in the liver to calcifediol (25-hydroxycholecalciferol) which is then hydroxylated in the kidney to calcitriol (1,25-dihydroxycholecalciferol). Calcitriol is considered the most active form. Dihydrotachysterol is produced by synthetic reduction of ergocalciferol. Patients with chronic renal disease cannot convert calcifediol to calcitriol. Alfacalcidol (1∝ hydroxyvitamin D_3), a synthetic analogue of calcitriol, is rapidly converted in the liver to calcitriol, bypassing the renal conversion step.

Because alfacalcidol, calcitriol and dihydrotachysterol do not require renal hydroxylation, they are useful in patients with renal failure.

Pharmacokinetics: See Table I (on following page). Vitamin D analogs are readily absorbed from the small intestine if fat absorption is normal. Bile is required for absorption. Cholecalciferol and ergocalciferol are activated by the 2-step process described above. Dihydrotachysterol and alfacalcidol are activated by the liver. Vitamin D is eliminated renally and by biliary excretion.

Table I—Vitamin D

Pharmacokinetics

	t½ (hours)	Onset of Action[a] (hours)	Duration of Action
Alfacalcidol	3	6	up to 48 hours
Calcitriol	3–6	2–6	3–5 days
Dihydrotachysterol	N/A	several	up to 9 weeks
Ergocalciferol	19–48	12–24[b]	up to 6 months[c]

[a]Increase in serum calcium level.
[b]Therapeutic effect may require 10–14 days.
[c]Cumulative effect occurs with repeated dosing.

Indications: Vitamin D analogs are used in treatment of refractory rickets (vitamin D resistant rickets), familial hypophosphatemia and hypoparathyroidism, and in the management of hypocalcemia and renal osteodystrophy in patients with chronic renal failure undergoing dialysis. Vitamin D is used in conjunction with calcium in the management and prevention of primary or corticosteroid-induced osteoporosis. Vitamin D supplementation is indicated when dietary intake is insufficient, e.g., breast-fed infants.

Contraindications: Known hypersensitivity to vitamin D or any of its analogues and derivatives. Hypercalcemia, malabsorption syndrome, abnormal sensitivity to the toxic effects of vitamin D, hypervitaminosis D. The manufacture of ergocalciferol states that it is contraindicated in patients with decreased renal function.

Precautions: Vitamin D analogs are usually nontoxic in physiologic doses. Chronic or acute administration of excessive doses may lead to hypervitaminosis D, manifested by hypercalcemia and its sequelae.

The therapeutic index of vitamin D analogs is narrow, and there is great interindividual variation in the dose that will lead to chronic toxicity. Daily doses of ergocalciferol ranging from 1.25 to 2.5 mg in adults and 25 μg in children may result in hypervitaminosis. Other vitamin D analogs with shorter duration of action may have a lower propensity to accumulate and to cause hypercalcemia.

Early symptoms of hypercalcemia may include weakness, fatigue, somnolence, headache, anorexia, dry mouth, metallic taste, nausea, vomiting, vertigo, tinnitus, ataxia, hypotonia. Later and possibly more serious manifestations include nephrocalcinosis, renal dysfunction, osteoporosis in adults, impaired growth in children, anemia, metastatic calcification, pancreatitis, generalized vascular calcification and seizures.

Periodic monitoring of serum calcium, phosphate, magnesium, alkaline phosphatase is recommended for patients taking vitamin D analogs. Serum calcium should be maintainedin the range of 2.25 to 2.5 mmol/L and not allowed to exceed 2.75 mmol/L.

Drug Interactions: Antacids (Magnesium-containing): Hypermagnesemia may develop when these agents are used concurrently with vitamin D, particularly in patients with chronic renal failure.

Anticonvulsants (Phenytoin, Phenobarbital): Decreased vitamin D effects may occur when certain anticonvulsants are administered, as they may induce hepatic microsomal enzymes and accelerate the conversion of vitamin D to inactive metabolites.

Cholestyramine, Colestipol, Mineral Oil: Intestinal absorption of vitamin D may be impaired. Patients on cholestyramine or colestipol should be advised to allow as much time as possible between the ingestion of these drugs and vitamin D.

Digoxin: Vitamin D should be used with caution in patients on digoxin as hypercalcemia (which may result with vitamin D use) may precipitate cardiac arrhythmias.

Thiazide Diuretics: Concurrent administration of thiazide diuretics and vitamin D to hypoparathyroid patients may cause hypercalcemia which may be transient or may require discontinuation of vitamin D.

Different vitamin D analogs should be administered concurrently.

Pregnancy: Safety of doses in excess of 400 IU (10 μg) of vitamin D daily during pregnancy has not been established. Maternal hypercalcemia, possibly caused by excessive vitamin D intake during pregnancy, has been associated with hypercalcemia in neonates, which may lead to supravalvular aortic stenosis syndrome, the features of which may include retinopathy, mental or growth retardation, strabismus and other effects.

Hypercalcemia during pregnancy may also lead to suppression of parathyroid hormone release in the neonate, resulting in hypocalcemia, tetany and seizures.

Lactation: Vitamin D is deficient in maternal milk; therefore breast-fed infants may require supplementation. Use of excessive amounts of vitamin D in nursing mothers may result in hypercalcemia in infants. Doses of vitamin D analogs in excess of 10 μg daily should not be administered to nursing women.

Adverse Effects: Vitamin D analogs are well tolerated in normal daily doses. Chronic excessive dosing can lead to toxicity (see Precautions).

Overdose: Symptoms: Acute intoxication with vitamin D analogs may cuase hypervitaminosis D (See Precautions).

Treatment: Treatment of acute or chronic intoxication includes withdrawal of the vitamin D analog and any calcium supplements, administration of oral or i.v. fluids and possibly corticosteroids or calciuric diuretics such as furosemide and ethacrynic acid. Peritoneal or hemodialysis with calcium free dialysate will help remove calcium.

If acute ingestion is recent, gastric lavage or emesis may minimize further absorption. If the drug has already passed through the stomach, administration of mineral oil may promote fecal elimination.

Hypercalcemia is usually reversible; however if metastatic calcification has occurred, severe renal or cardiac failure or even death may result.

Dosage: In preventing vitamin deficiencies, adequate dietary intake is preferred over supplementation whenever possible. For a listing of dietary sources of vitamin D, see Vitamin Food Sources in the Clin-Info section.

For a listing of the daily requirements of vitamin D and other vitamins, see Recommended Nutrient Intake in the Clin-Info section. It should be noted that expert groups are now recommending a daily intake of 400 to 800 IU vitamin D to optimize calcium absorption and prevent primary or corticosteroid-induced osteoporosis. Daily doses of 400 to 800 IU and sometimes higher are used in conjunction with calcium and other measures in the treatment of osteoporosis.

At doses used for active treatment of deficiency, the range between therapeutic and toxic doses is narrow.

Dosage of vitamin D analogs must be individualized with careful monitoring of serum calcium levels. Careful titration is necessary to avoid overdosage. Dietary and other sources of vitamin D must be considered. Calcium intake should be adequate.

Ergocalciferol: For vitamin D deficiency, 5 000 IU (125 μg) daily until a biochemical and radiographic response is achieved.

For vitamin D resistant rickets, 12 000 to 500 000 IU (0.3 to 12.5 mg) daily.

For hypoparathyroidism, 50 000 to 200 000 IU (1.25 to 5 mg) daily. Calcium supplementation is also required.

Alfacalcidol: For hypocalcemia and osteodystrophy in patients with chronic renal failure undergoing dialysis: Initial: 1 μg daily, the dosage being increased in increments of 0.5 μg every 2 to 4 weeks as necessary, up to 2 μg daily. Rarely a dose of 3 μg/day is required. Maintenance: 0.25 μg to 1 μg/day.

Calcitriol: Adults: For management of hypocalcemia and osteodystrophy in patients with chronic renal failure on dialysis: Initial: 0.25 μg daily; the daily dose may be increased by 0.25 μg every 4 to 8 weeks as necessary.

Maintenance: 0.5 to 1 μg daily. Patients with normal or only slightly reduced serum calcium levels may respond to 0.25 μg every other day.

For hypoparathyroidism and vitamin D resistant rickets, initially, 0.25 μg daily; the dosage may be increased by 0.25 μg/day at 2- to 4-week intervals if necessary.

Children: Initiation of Treatment: For x-linked hypophosphatemic rickets, 0.01 to 0.02 μg/kg/day (mean 0.018 μg/kg/day). For vitamin D dependency rickets type I, 0.010 to 0.025 μg/kg/day (mean 0.017 μg/kg/day). For hypoparathyroidism, 0.03 to 0.05 μg/kg/day (mean 0.04 μg/kg/day). If biochemical improvement has not occurred in 2 weeks, the dose is increased by 25% and re-evaluated in 2 weeks. Maintenance: For x-linked hypophosphatemic rickets, 0.01 to 0.05 μg/kg/day (mean 0.022 μg/kg/day). For vitamin D dependency rickets type I, 0.0046 to 0.015 μg/kg/day. For hypoparathyroidism, 0.014 to 0.04 μg/kg/day (mean 0.025 μg/kg/day).

Dihydrotachysterol: For treatment of acute, chronic and latent forms of post-operative tetany, idiopathic tetany and hypoparathyroidism: Initial: 0.75 to 2.5 mg daily for several days. Maintenance: 0.25 mg weekly to 1 mg/day depending on serum calcium levels.

Reviewed 1998

VITAMIN E

General Monograph, CPhA

Vitamin

> This monograph has been compiled by CPhA. It may contain information different from that approved by Therapeutic Products Programme, Health Canada, and the pharmaceutical manufacturers' approval has not been requested.

Pharmacology: Vitamin E, a fat-soluble vitamin present in many foods, exists in a variety of forms, the most active of which is d-α-tocopherol. Table I lists the vitamin E activity of the many commerically available forms of the vitamin.

Table I—Vitamin E

Vitamin E Activity

Form of Vitamin E	Amount Containing 1 Unit of Vitamin E Activity (mg)
dl-α-tocopheryl acetate	1
dl-α-tocopheryl acid succinate	1.12
dl-α-tocopherol	0.91
d-α-tocopheryl acetate	0.74
d-α-tocopheryl acid succinate	0.83
d-α-tocopherol	0.67

Although the exact biological function of vitamin E in humans is unknown, it is considered an essential element of human nutrition. Many of its actions are related to its antioxidant properties. Although some studies have suggested that antioxidants may be beneficial in disease prevention, further investigation is required before antioxidant vitamins can be recommended for the prevention of cancer or cardiovascular disease.

Vitamin E deficiency rarely causes symptoms of clinical deficiency in adults; in premature neonates, irritability, edema, thrombosis, and hemolytic anemia may be caused by vitamin E deficiency. Creatinuria, ceroid deposition, muscle weakness, decreased erythrocyte survival or in vitro hemolysis by oxidizing agents has been identified in adults and children with low serum tocopherol concentrations. Administration of vitamin E completely reverses these signs.

Pharmacokinetics: Absorption of vitamin E from the gastrointestinal tract depends on the presence of bile and only 20 to 60% of the vitamin obtained from dietary sources is absorbed. As dosage increases, the fraction of vitamin E absorbed decreases. Chylomicrons and lipoproteins are involved in transporting vitamin E to the general circulation.

Plasma concentrations of the tocopherols vary widely among individuals but are highly correlated with plasma lipoprotein and total lipid concentrations. After large doses of vitamin E, plasma tocopherol concentrations may be elevated for 1 to 2 days.

Vitamin E is widely distributed after absorption and stored mainly in adipose tissue. It is believed that normal body stores, estimated to be 3 to 8 g, are sufficient to meet the body's needs for 4 years or more.

Vitamin E is metabolized in the liver and excreted primarily in the bile.

Indications: In the prevention and treatment of vitamin E deficiency.

Precautions: Vitamin E is usually nontoxic; however, prolonged use of high doses has caused symptoms and metabolic disturbances (see Adverse Effects).

Drug Interactions: Vitamin A absorption, utilization and storage may be increased.

Vitamin E may increase the hypoprothrombinemic response to oral anticoagulants. Doses in excess of recommended daily nutrient intakes should be avoided in patients on oral anticoagulants.

In dosages greater than 10 IU/kg daily, vitamin E may delay the response to iron therapy in children with iron-deficiency anemia, and low birth-weight infants treated with iron supplements may develop vitamin E deficiency hemolytic anemia.

Excessive use of mineral oil may decrease the absorption of vitamin E.

Pregnancy: No problems have been reported with intake of normal daily requirements.

Vitamin E (cont'd)

Lactation: No problems have been reported with intake of normal daily requirements.

Adverse Effects: Large doses (greater than 300 IU/day) have rarely caused nausea, diarrhea, intestinal cramps, fatigue, weakness, headache, blurred vision, rash, gonadal dysfunction, creatinuria, increased serum creatinine kinase, increased serum cholesterol and triglycerides, increased urinary estrogens and androgens, and decreased serum thyroxine and triiodothyronine. These effects disappear after discontinuing the vitamin.

Overdose: Symptoms: Acute toxicity not usually seen. Chronic excessive ingestion may produce symptoms. Gastrointestinal upset, lethargy and headache have been reported.

Treatment: Not usually required.

Dosage: In preventing nutrient deficiencies, adequate dietary intake is preferred over supplementation whenever possible. For a listing of dietary sources of vitamin E, see Vitamin Food Sources in the Clin-Info section. For a listing of vitamin E and other nutrient requirements, see Recommended Nutrient Intake in the Clin-Info section.

Vitamin E is usually administered orally, but may be given parenterally as a component of a multiple vitamin preparation. Treatment of Deficiency: Adults: 60 to 75 units orally, daily.

Reviewed 1998

VITAMIN E

Swiss Herbal

Vitamin Supplement

Supplied: Each capsule contains: natural source vitamin E 400 IU derived from d-alpha tocopherol 268 mg. Nonmedicinal ingredients: gelatin, glycerin and purified water. Bottles of 50, 90, 180 and 500.

VITAMIN K ℞

General Monograph, CPhA

Phytonadione

Hypoprothrombinemia Therapy

> This monograph has been compiled by CPhA. It may contain information different from that approved by Therapeutic Products Programme, Health Canada, and the pharmaceutical manufacturers' approval has not been requested.

Pharmacology: Vitamin K compounds are fat soluble naphthoquinones. Phytonadione (vitamin K_1) and vitamin K_2 occur in a variety of natural materials and are synthesized by certain bacteria in the gastrointestinal tract; however, commercially prepared phytonadione is synthetically produced. Phytonadione possesses essentially the same type and degree of activity as naturally occurring vitamin K_1.

Vitamin K is necessary for synthesis in the liver of factor II (prothrombin), factor VII (proconvertin), factor IX (thromboplastin), and factor X. Deficiency of vitamin K or disturbances of liver function may lead to deficiencies of these factors. When the prothrombin level falls to about 10 to 15% of normal, even slight trauma may cause bleeding; when the level is below 10%, spontaneous hemorrhage may occur, in the form of hematoma, hematemesis, hematuria or melena. The mechanism by which vitamin K promotes formation in the liver of clotting factors II, VII, IX, and X is not known.

Vitamin K deficiency may occur in patients with biliary obstruction or other conditions limiting absorption of vitamin K such as celiac disease, ulcerative colitis, sprue, regional enteritis, cystic fibrosis, intestinal resection, and in patients receiving drugs that may affect liver function or intestinal flora.

Pharmacokinetics: Phytonadione is absorbed from the gastrointestinal tract only in the presence of bile salts and pancreatic lipase. Once absorbed, vitamin K accumulates in the liver, spleen, and lungs, but significant amounts are not stored in the body for long periods.

The action of phytonadione, when administered parenterally, is generally detectable within 1 or 2 hours and hemorrhage is usually controlled within 3 to 8 hours. A normal prothrombin level may often be obtained in 12 to 14 hours.

Indications: Phytonadione is used in the prevention and treatment of hypoprothrombinemia caused by vitamin K deficiency, oral anticoagulants, or other factors which impair the absorption or synthesis of vitamin K. Phytonadione is also used in the prevention and treatment of hemorrhagic disease of the newborn.

Phytonadione may have a role in restoring normal clotting time in patients with hypoprothrombinemia induced by salicylates, sulfonamides, quinidine, quinine or broad-spectrum antibiotics, when interference with vitamin K activity is clearly the cause.

Contraindications: Hypersensitivity to vitamin K.

Warnings: Severe reactions, including fatalities, have occurred during and immediately after i.v. phytonadione injection even when precautions have been taken to dilute the phytonadione solution and to avoid rapid infusion. These severe reactions, which may occur in patients receiving phytonadione for the first time, resemble hypersensitivity or anaphylaxis, including shock and cardiac or respiratory arrest. Therefore, use of the i.v. route should be restricted to those situations where other routes are not feasible and the serious risk involved is considered justified.

Benzyl alcohol contained in some products has been associated with toxicity in newborns. Toxicity appears to have resulted from administration of large amounts (100 to 400 mg/kg daily) of benzyl alcohol in these neonates. Products containing benzyl alcohol should be used cautiously in newborns who are also receiving other benzyl alcohol-containing medications. In each case, the attending physician must weigh the potential benefits against the possible risks.

Precautions: Because the liver is the site of prothrombin biosynthesis, hypoprothrombinemia resulting from hepatocellular damage is not corrected by administration of vitamin K. Repeated large doses of vitamin K are not warranted in liver disease if the response to initial use of the vitamin is unsatisfactory. Failure to respond to vitamin K may indicate that a coagulation defect exists or that the condition is unresponsive to vitamin K.

Vitamin K does not counteract the anticoagulant effect of heparin. Dietary supplements high in vitamin K ($\geq$0.7 mg/day) can block the effect of oral anticoagulants.

Vitamin K_1 promotes the synthesis of prothrombin by the liver but does not directly reverse the effects of oral anticoagulants. Immediate coagulant effect should not be expected. It takes up to 2 hours for a measurable improvement in the prothrombin time. Whole blood or component therapy may also be necessary if bleeding is severe or if there is no response to phytonadione. Vitamin K_1 is not a clotting agent, but overzealous therapy with phytonadione may restore conditions which originally permitted thromboembolic phenomena. Keep dosage as low as possible, and check prothrombin time regularly as clinical conditions indicate.

Newborns should be observed for vitamin K deficiency. The incidence of vitamin K deficiency is higher in breast-fed infants. This increase may be partly due to lower concentrations of vitamin K in human milk than in cow's milk formula or it may be due to the smaller volume of milk infants may receive in their first few days of life, especially those exclusively breast-fed. Therefore, because an infant's milk intake cannot be predicted at birth, it is recommended that vitamin K prophylaxis be given to all newborns.

Drug Interactions: Anticoagulants (coumarin): Anticoagulant effects are antagonized by vitamin K. Temporary resistance to prothrombin depressing anticoagulants may result from vitamin K administration, especially when relatively large doses have been given. Therefore, when reinstituting anticoagulant therapy, it may be necessary to use larger doses of the prothrombin depressing anticoagulant or to use one that acts on a different principle, such as heparin.

Broad Spectrum Antibiotics, Quinidine, Quinine and High Dose Salicylates: Requirements for vitamin K may be increased. (see Indications).

Children: In newborns, particularly premature infants, hyperbilirubinemia and hemolytic anemia have been reported. The risk is much less with phytonadione than other vitamin K preparations unless high doses (10 to 20 mg) are given.

Pregnancy: Inadequate information exists as to whether vitamin K may affect fertility in human males or females or have a teratogenic potential or other adverse effect on the fetus. Large amounts of vitamin K in pregnancy, however, can cause jaundice in the newborn.

Lactation: Vitamin K may appear in human breast milk. Problems in humans have not been reported with the intake of normal daily requirements.

Adverse Effects: Deaths have occurred following i.v. administration of phytonadione (see Warnings).

Transient flushing sensations and peculiar sensations of taste have been observed following phytonadione injection as well as rare instances of dizziness, rapid and weak pulse, profuse sweating, brief hypotension, dyspnea, and cyanosis. Bronchospasm, shock, cardiac and/or respiratory arrest may also occur.

Pain, swelling, and tenderness at the injection site may occur. The possibility of allergic sensitivity (i.e., rash, urticaria), including an anaphylactoid reaction, should be kept in mind.

Large doses of vitamin K or its analogues may further depress liver function in patients with severe hepatic disease and thereby further decrease the concentration of prothrombin.

Neonates: In infants (particularly premature babies), excessive doses of vitamin K analogs during the first few days of life may cause hyperbilirubinemia; this in turn may result in severe hemolytic anemia, hemoglobinuria, kernicterus, leading to brain damage or even death. Immaturity is apparently an important factor in toxic reactions to vitamin K analogs, as full term and larger premature infants show greater tolerance than smaller premature infants.

Dosage: Minimum daily requirements of vitamin K have not been fully established. They have been estimated at 1 to 5 µg/kg for infants and 0.03 µg/kg for adults. Dietary abundance of vitamin K normally satisfies these requirements, except for a neonatal period of 5 to 8 days during which the intestinal flora is not yet fully established.

Dose, frequency of administration, and duration of treatment with vitamin K depend on the severity of the prothrombin deficiency and the response of the patient.

At present only an injectable form of vitamin K_1 (phytonadione) is available commercially. Phytonadione is intended for i.m., s.c. or i.v. injection, but has been administered orally. The i.v. route is indicated only when other routes of administration are not feasible (see Warnings).

In older children and adults, i.m. injection should be made in the upper outer quadrant of the buttocks. In infants and young children, the anterolateral aspect of the thigh or the deltoid region is preferred.

When i.v. administration is considered unavoidable, phytonadione should be injected very slowly, at a rate not exceeding 1 mg/minute.

Anticoagulant-Induced Hypoprothrombinemia: In less urgent situations, withdrawal or reduction of the dose of anticoagularnt may be sufficient. When phytonadione is used, it is important to use the lowest effective dose.

Adults: 2.5 to 10 mg i.m. or s.c. Rarely, higher doses of up to 25 to 50 mg have been required. The dose may be repeated if necessary after 6 to 8 hours. In cases of severe bleeding, higher doses may be required in conjunction with other measures such as replacement of clotting factors.

Children: 2.5 to 10 mg i.m. or s.c.; may be repeated in 6 to 8 hours.

Infants: 1 to 2 mg i.m. or s.c.; may be repeated in 4 to 8 hours.

Hemorrhagic Disease of the Newborn: Prophylaxis: In its 1997 clinical practice guidelines on vitamin K administration, the Canadian Paediatric Society recommends that vitamin K_1 be given as a single i.m. injection to all newborns within 6 hours of birth, at a dose of 1 mg for infants with a birthweight of >1 500 g and 0.5 mg if birthweight is $\leq$1 500 g. The guidelines recommend the oral route only when the parents refuse an i.m. injection for the newborn. The recommended oral dose is 2 mg, given at the time of first feeding, and again at 2 to 4 weeks and 6 to 8 weeks of age, for a total of 3 doses. The importance of the follow-up doses should be stressed with the parents.

At present, there is no commerically available oral formulation of vitamin K_1; however, the injectable formulation has been used orally.

Treatment: Vitamin K_1 1 mg i.m. or s.c.

Hypoprothrombinemia from Other Causes: When other drug therapy is the cause, discontinuation or reduction of the dosage of drug is suggested as an alternative to administering phytonadione. The severity of the coagulation disorder should determine whether the immediate administration of vitamin K is required in addition to discontinuation or reduction of dose of interfering drug(s).

Adults: A dosage of 2.5 to 25 mg or more (rarely up to 50 mg) is recommended; the dose and route of administration should be based on the severity of the condition and patient response.

Children: For the treatment of hypoprothrombinemia, the dose for infants is 2 mg and for older children, 5 to 10 mg.

Total Parenteral Nutrition: For prevention of hypoprothrombinemia, the adult dosage is 5 to 10 mg i.m. weekly, and the dosage for children is 2 to 5 mg i.m. weekly.

Reviewed 1998

VITAMIN K$_1$ ℞

Abbott

Phytonadione

Prothrombinogenic Vitamin

Supplied: Each mL contains: phytonadione 2 mg or 10 mg. Nonmedicinal ingredients: benzyl alcohol, dextrose, polysorbate 80, sodium hydroxide and water for injection. Ampuls of 0.5 mL or 1 mL of solution corresponding to phytonadione 1 mg and 10 mg. Boxes of 50. Keep under refrigeration.

VITATHION®-A.T.P.

Servier

Ascorbic Acid—Thiamine—Inositol

Stress Therapy

Indications: In the treatment of stress conditions (e.g. fatigue, asthenia, postpartum, postsurgical convalescence); for conditions in which supplements of ascorbic acid, glutathione, adenosine and thiamine are indicated.

Precautions: Do not use the contents of a sachet more than 8 days after the sachet has been opened.

Dosage: Adults: 1 to 2 sachets daily dissolved in 120 mL of water, to be taken preferably with breakfast. Children: 2 to 5 years, ½ sachet before breakfast; 5 to 15 years, ½ sachet before breakfast and ½ sachet before lunch.

Supplied: Each sachet contains: ascorbic acid 500 mg, thiamine 2 mg and inositol as a lipotrophic factor (from calcium and magnesium inositol hexaphosphate) 18 mg. Nonmedicinal ingredients: adenosine triphosphoric, glutathione (reduced form) and hemoglobin. One sachet also contains a sufficient quantity of excipients for 5 g of soluble effervescent granules and tartrazine. Boxes of 20.

(Shown in Product Recognition Section)

VITA 3B
VITA 3B + C

Riva

Vitamins B$_1$—B$_6$—B$_{12}$

Vitamins B$_1$—B$_6$—B$_{12}$—C

Vitamin Supplement

Supplied: Vita 3B: Each red tablet contains: thiamine HCl (B$_1$) 250 mg, pyridoxine HCl (B$_6$) 125 mg and cyanocobalamin (B$_{12}$) 250 μg. Nonmedicinal ingredients: carnauba wax, cellulose, colloidal silicone, FD&C Red, FD&C Yellow, hydroxypropyl methylcellulose, magnesium stearate, polyethylene glycol, polysorbate 80, polyvinylpyrrolidone, starch, stearic acid and titanium dioxide. Gluten-, sucrose-, tartrazine-free. Bottles of 50 and 300.

Vita 3B+C: Each yellow tablet contains: thiamine HCl (B$_1$) 250 mg, pyridoxine HCl (B$_6$) 125 mg, cyanocobalamin (B$_{12}$) 250 μg and ascorbic acid (C) 250 mg. Nonmedicinal ingredients: carnauba wax, cellulose, colloidal silicone, D&C Yellow, hydroxypropyl methylcellulose, iron oxide, magnesium stearate, polyethylene glycol, polysorbate 80, polyvinylpyrrolidone, starch and titanium dioxide. Gluten-, sucrose-, tartrazine-free. Bottles of 50 and 300.

VITINOIN™ ℞

Pharmascience

Tretinoin

Topical Acne Therapy

Supplied: Cream: Each g contains: tretinoin 0.025%, 0.05% or 0.1% in an emollient, topical cream vehicle. Tubes of 20 g.

Gel: Each g contains: tretinoin 0.025% in an emollient, topical alcoholic gel vehicle. Tubes of 20 g.

Keep container closed when not in use. Store in a cool dry place between 15 to 30°C.

VIVELLE® ℞

Novartis Pharmaceuticals

Estradiol-17β

Estrogen

Description: Vivelle is a thin, circular, multilayer, transparent transdermal therapeutic system, i.e., an adhesive patch, containing estradiol-17β that is designed for application to an area of intact skin.

The Vivelle patch comprises 3 layers. Proceeding from the visible surface toward the surface attached to the skin, these layers are: 1. A flexible semi-transparent **backing film** of polyurethane and ethylene vinyl alcohol polymer. 2. An **adhesive** formulation containing estradiol-17β, acrylic polymers, polyisobutylene, oleic acid, synthetic rubber based adhesive, vinyl acetate resin base, phosphatidylcholine, propylene glycol, bentonite, butylene glycol, mineral oil and dipropylene glycol. 3. A **protective liner** of polyester that is attached to the adhesive surface and must be removed before the patch can be used.

The active component of the patch is estradiol-17β. The matrix provides a source for continuous delivery of drug for up to 4 days. Vivelle is available in 4 strengths; the composition per unit area in each strength is identical.

Pharmacology: Vivelle is designed to deliver daily estradiol-17β, a physiologic hormone, transdermally into the systemic circulation. Due to the transdermal route of administration, the estradiol-17β does not undergo firstpass liver metabolism. Resultant estradiol-17β plasma levels are comparable to those seen in premenopausal women in the early follicular phase of the menstrual cycle. Estradiol-17β stimulates target tissues such as the uterus, breast and vagina.

Indications: For the relief of menopausal and postmenopausal symptoms occurring in naturally or surgically induced estrogen deficiency states.

In patients with an intact uterus, estradiol-17β should always be supplemented by sequential administration of a progestin whose role is to prevent endometrial hyperplasia.

Contraindications: Estradiol-17β should not be administered to patients with any of the following conditions: active hepatic dysfunction or disease, especially of the obstructive type; known or suspected breast cancer; known or suspected estrogen-dependent neoplasia; endometrial hyperplasia; undiagnosed abnormal vaginal bleeding; porphyria; known or suspected pregnancy; a history of cerebrovascular accident, coronary thrombosis, or in the presence of classical migraine; active thrombophlebitis, thrombosis or thromboembolic disorders; a history of thrombophlebitis, thrombosis or thromboembolic disorders associated with previous estrogen use; partial or complete loss of vision from ophthalmic vascular disease; known or suspected hypersensitivity to any component of the patch.

Warnings: There is evidence from several studies that estrogens, unopposed by progestins, increase the risk of carcinoma of the endometrium in humans. The incidence of endometrial hyperplasia is reported to be lowered with sequential coadministration of a progestin (see Dosage, Coadministration of Progestins).

Breast cancer is a multifactorial disease, which increases in frequency in older age. Much of the etiology of breast cancer is unknown. Several published epidemiological studies have documented an association between a modest increase in the risk of developing breast cancer and the use of hormone replacement therapy in menopause when given for periods exceeding 5 years. Information is still lacking to show whether the risks of combination estrogen-progestin therapy differ from those of estrogen used alone. It is recommended to avoid giving estrogens to women previously treated for breast cancer. There is a need for caution in prescribing estrogens for women with a strong family history of breast cancer or who present breast nodules, fibrocystic disease of the breast, or abnormal mammograms. Other known risk factors for the development of breast cancer such as nulliparity, obesity, early menarche, late age at first full term pregnancy and at menopause should also be evaluated. It is recommended that a mammography be performed before starting treatment and repeated at regular intervals in patients at high risk for breast cancer.

The overall benefits and possible risks of hormone replacement therapy should be fully considered and discussed with patients. Instructions for self-examination of the breasts should be included in this counselling.

Contact sensitization is known to occur with topical applications. Although it is extremely rare, patients who develop contact sensitization to any component of the patch should be warned that a severe hypersensitivity reaction may occur with continuing exposure to the causative agent.

Benign hepatic adenomas have been associated with the use of combined estrogen and progestin oral contraceptives. Although benign and rare, these tumors may rupture and cause death from intra-abdominal hemorrhage. Such lesions have not yet been reported in association with other estrogen or progestin preparations, but they should be considered if abdominal pain and tenderness, abdominal mass, or hypovolemic shock occurs in patients receiving estrogen. Hepatocellular carcinoma has also been reported in women taking estrogen-containing oral contraceptives. The causal relationship of this malignancy to these drugs is not known.

The relatively small number of epidemiological studies assessing the relation between hormone replacement therapy and risk of venous thromboembolism has led to conflicting results. While earlier studies have not shown an association, some epidemiological studies have suggested that, for healthy women, there is an increased relative risk of about 2 to 3.6 for developing deep vein thrombosis or pulmonary embolism for current users of hormone replacement therapy compared to nonusers.

The physician should be alert to the earliest manifestations of thrombotic disorders (thrombophlebitis, retinal thrombosis, cerebral embolism and pulmonary embolism). If these occur or are suspected, hormone therapy should be discontinued immediately. Women with severe varicose veins, severe obesity (Body Mass Index >30 kg/m²), or those undergoing immobilization for 3 weeks or more, trauma or surgery requiring bed rest, are generally considered to be at increased risk of venous thromboembolism. These women, and those with a past history of thromboembolic disorders during pregnancy or in association with estrogen use, should be kept under special observation while using hormone replacement therapy.

Precautions: Before estradiol-17β is administered, the patient should have a complete physical examination including a blood pressure determination. Breasts and pelvic organs should be appropriately examined and a Papanicolaou smear and endometrial biopsy should be performed. Baseline tests should include measurements of blood glucose, calcium, triglycerides and cholesterol, and liver function tests.

The first follow-up examination should be done within 6 months after initiation of treatment to assess response to treatment. Thereafter, examinations should be made once a year and should include at least those procedures outlined above. It is important that patients are encouraged to practice frequent self-examination of the breasts.

Abnormal vaginal bleeding due to its prolongation, irregularity or heaviness occurring during therapy should prompt diagnostic measures like endometrial biopsy or curettage to rule out the possibility of uterine malignancy and the treatment should be re-evaluated.

Pre-existing uterine leiomyoma may increase in size during estrogen use. Growth, pain or tenderness of uterine leiomyoma requires discontinuation of medication.

Symptoms and physical findings associated with a previous diagnosis of endometriosis may reappear or become aggravated with estrogen use.

Patients who develop visual disturbances, classical migraine, transient aphasia, paralysis, or loss of consciousness should discontinue medication.

If feasible, estrogens should also be discontinued at least 4 weeks before surgery which may be associated with an increased risk of thromboembolism or during periods of prolonged immobilization.

Women using oral estrogen and progestin contraceptives sometimes experience increased blood pressure which, in most cases, returns to normal upon discontinuing the drug. This may occur with use of oral estrogens during menopause and blood pressure should be monitored with estrogen use. Elevation of blood pressure in previously normotensive or hypertensive patients should be evaluated and estrogen therapy may have to be discontinued.

Estrogens may cause fluid retention. Therefore, particular caution is indicated in cardiac or renal dysfunction, epilepsy or asthma. Treatment should be stopped if there is an increase in epileptic seizures. If, in any of the above-mentioned conditions, a worsening of the underlying disease is diagnosed or suspected during treatment, the benefits and risks of treatment should be reassessed based on the individual case.

Because the prolonged use of estrogens influences the metabolism of calcium and phosphorus, estrogens should be used with caution in patients with metabolic and malignant

Vivelle (cont'd)

bone diseases associated with hypercalcemia and in patients with renal insufficiency.

A worsening of glucose tolerance has been observed in a significant percentage of patients on estrogen-containing oral contraceptives. Therefore, diabetic patients or those with a predisposition to diabetes should be observed closely to detect any alterations in carbohydrate or lipid metabolism, especially in triglyceride blood levels.

A 2- to 4-fold increase in the risk of surgically confirmed gallbladder disease has been reported in postmenopausal women receiving oral estrogens.

Caution is advised in patients with a history of estrogen-related jaundice and pruritus. If cholestatic jaundice develops during treatment, the treatment should be discontinued and appropriate investigations carried out.

Women with familial hypertriglyceridemia need special surveillance. Lipid-lowering measures are recommended additionally, before treatment is started.

Liver function tests should be done periodically in subjects who are suspected of having hepatic disease. For information on endocrine and liver function tests, see the section under Laboratory Tests.

Drug Interactions: Estrogens may diminish the effectiveness of anticoagulants and antidiabetic and antihypertensive agents.

Preparations inducing liver enzymes, (e.g., barbiturates, hydantoins, carbamazepine, meprobamate, phenylbutazone or rifampicin) may interfere with the activity of orally administered estrogens. The extent of interference with transdermally administered estradiol-17β is not known.

Laboraratory Tests: The results of certain endocrine and liver function tests may be affected by estrogen-containing products: increased sulfobromophthalein retention; increased prothrombin time and partial thromboplastin time; increased levels of fibrinogen and fibrinogen activity; increased coagulation factors VII, VIII, IX, X; increased norepinephrine-induced platelet aggregability; decreased antithrombin III; increased thyroxine-binding globulin (TBG), leading to increased circulating total thyroid hormone (T_4) as measured by column or radioimmunoassay; free T_3 resin uptake is decreased, reflecting the elevated TBG; free T_4 concentration is unaltered; other binding proteins may be elevated in serum, i.e., corticosteroid binding protein (CBG), sex-hormone binding globulin (SHBG), leading to increased circulating corticosteroids and sex steroids respectively; free or biologically active hormone concentrations are unchanged; reduced response to Metopirone test; reduced serum folate concentration; increased serum triglyceride and phospholipid concentration.

With transdermally administered estradiol-17β, no effect on fibrinogen, antithrombin III, TBG, CBG or SHBG and decreases in serum triglycerides have been observed.

The results of the above laboratory tests should not be considered reliable unless therapy has been discontinued for 2 to 4 months. The pathologist should be informed that the patient is receiving estrogen therapy when relevant specimens are submitted.

Adverse Effects: See Warnings and Precautions regarding potential induction of malignant neoplasms and adverse effects similar to those of oral contraceptives.

The most commonly reported adverse reaction to Vivelle in clinical trials was redness and irritation at the application site. This caused about 0.8% of the patients to discontinue therapy.

The following adverse reactions have been reported with estrogens in general.

Gastrointestinal: nausea; vomiting; abdominal discomfort (cramps, pressure, pain); bloating; gallbladder disorder; asymptomatic impaired liver function; cholestatic jaundice.

Genitourinary: breakthrough bleeding; spotting and vaginal bleeding; change in menstrual flow; dysmenorrhea; vaginal itching/discharge; dyspareunia; dysuria; endometrial hyperplasia; premenstrual-like syndrome; reactivation of endometriosis; cystitis; changes in cervical erosion and amount of cervical secretion.

Dermatological/Hypersensitivity: allergic contact dermatitis; reversible post-inflammatory pigmentation; general pruritus and exanthema; loss of scalp hair; chloasma; pigmentation of the skin; erythema nodosum; erythema multiforme; hemorrhagic skin eruptions; precipitation or aggravation of porphyria cutanea tarda in predisposed individuals.

Isolated cases of anaphylactoid reactions (some of the patients had a history of previous allergy or allergic disorders).

Endocrine: breast swelling and tenderness; increased blood sugar levels; decreased glucose tolerance; sodium retention.

Cardiovascular/Hematologic: palpitations; isolated cases of: thrombophlebitis; thromboembolic disorders; exacerbations of varicose veins; increase in blood pressure (see Precautions); coronary thrombosis; altered coagulation tests (see Precautions, Laboratory Tests).

CNS: aggravation of migraine headaches; headaches; mental depression; nervousness; dizziness; fatigue; irritability, neuro-ocular lesions (e.g., retinal thrombosis, optic neuritis).

Ophthalmic: visual disturbances; steepening of the corneal curvature; intolerance to contact lenses; neuro-ocular lesions (see CNS above).

Miscellaneous: changes in appetite; changes in body weight; edema; neuritis; change in libido; musculoskeletal pain [including leg pain not related to thromboembolic disease (usually transient, lasting 3 to 6 weeks). If symptoms persist, the dose of estrogen should be reduced].

Overdose: Symptoms: Numerous reports of ingestion of large doses of estrogen products and estrogen-containing oral contraceptives by young children have not revealed acute serious ill effects. Overdosage with estrogen may cause nausea, breast discomfort, fluid retention, bloating or vaginal bleeding in women.

Treatment: Owing to the mode of administration (transdermal), plasma levels of estradiol-17β can be rapidly reduced by removal of the patch. Symptomatic treatment should be given.

Dosage: In women who are not currently taking oral estrogens, treatment with estradiol-17β can be initiated at once. In women who are currently taking oral estrogens, treatment with Vivelle can be initiated on reappearance of menopausal symptoms, following discontinuation of oral therapy.

Vivelle should be applied twice weekly, i.e., the patch should be changed once every 3 to 4 days.

Cyclical administration is recommended (21 to 25 days of therapy followed by 5 to 7 days without). Continuous noncyclic therapy may be indicated in hysterectomized women or in cases where the signs and symptoms of estrogen deficiency become problematic during the treatment-free interval.

In women with an intact uterus, a progestin should be sequentially coadministered for a **minimum** of 10, but preferably 12 to 14 days/cycle to avoid overstimulation of the endometrium. The addition of sufficient progestin to induce secretory transformation of the endometrium during estrogen replacement therapy is mandatory.

Abnormal vaginal bleeding due to its prolongation, irregularity or heaviness in any patient receiving hormone replacement therapy requires institution of prompt diagnostic measures like endometrial biopsy or curettage to rule out the possibility of uterine malignancy.

The short term effects of progestin coadministration may include vaginal bleeding during or after progestin treatment, breast tenderness, and mood and weight changes. The long-term effects generally depend on the dosage and type of progestin used. The lowest effective dose of estrogen and progestin should be prescribed (see Coadministration of Progestins).

See the Precautions section on the examination of the patient before estradiol-17β administration.

Dose Adjustment: Treatment of menopausal symptoms is usually initiated with a patch that releases 50 μg estradiol-17β/day i.e., Vivelle 50. Thereafter the dosage should be adapted to the needs of the individual.

Breast discomfort, breakthrough or heavy vaginal bleeding, water retention, bloating or nausea (if persisting for more than 6 weeks), are generally signs that the estrogen dose is too high and needs to be lowered. If on the other hand, the selected dose fails to eliminate the signs and symptoms of estrogen deficiency, a higher dose may be considered.

For maintenance therapy one should always use the lowest dose that still proves effective. The requirement for hormone replacement therapy for menopausal symptoms should be reassessed periodically. Attempts to taper or discontinue the medication should be made at 3- to 6-month intervals.

Patch Application: The physician should discuss the most appropriate placement of the patch with the patient. Immediately after removal of a patch from the pouch and removal of the protective liner, the adhesive side of the Vivelle patch should be placed on a clean, dry area of intact skin. The area selected should not be oily, damaged or irritated, and not exposed to the sun. The site selected should also be one at which little wrinkling of the skin occurs during movement of the body, preferably the buttocks, lower abdomen or hip. The patch may also be placed on the side or lower back. The patch should be placed consistently on the same area of the body with each application (i.e., either the buttocks, lower abdomen, hip, side or lower back). Experience to date has shown that less irritation of the skin occurs on the buttocks than on other sites of application. Therefore, it is advisable to apply Vivelle to the buttocks. The waistline should be avoided, since tight clothing may dislodge the patch. The patch should be pressed firmly in place with the palm of the hand, making sure there is good contact, especially around the edges. In the event that a patch should fall off, it can be reapplied. If it fails to adhere then a new patch may be applied. In either case, the original treatment schedule should be continued. Patches should not be applied to the same skin site twice in succession.

Vivelle must not be applied to the breasts to avoid potentially harmful effects on the breast tissue.

Coadministration of Progestins: Studies have reported that the addition of a progestin for 10 or more days of a cycle of estrogen administration greatly lowers the incidence of endometrial hyperplasia, and thereby irregular bleeding and endometrial carcinoma, compared to estrogen treatment alone.

Wide interpatient variation in absorption occurs with progestins. The following regimens have been shown, in general, to produce histological and biochemical changes consistent with a uniform secretory pattern in the endometrium: norethindrone 0.7 mg/day orally, administered sequentially for 12 days each cycle; medroxyprogesterone acetate (MPA) 10 mg/day orally, administered sequentially for 12 days each cycle.

There are possible additional risks that may be associated with the inclusion of a progestin in estrogen replacement regimens. The potential risks include adverse effects on carbohydrate and lipid metabolism, mood changes and edema. The choice and dose of progestin may be important in minimizing these adverse effects and may differ among women.

Information for the Patient: See Blue Section—Information for the Patient "Vivelle".

Supplied: Vivelle 37.5: Each thin, circular, multilayer, transparent, 11 cm² transdermal therapeutic system, contains: estradiol-17β 3.28 mg for continuous delivery of estradiol-17β 37.5 μg/day. Nonmedicinal ingredients: acrylic adhesive, bentonite, butylene glycol, dipropylene glycol, ethylene vinyl acetate copolymer, lecithin, oleic acid, mineral oil, polyisobutylene, propylene glycol and styrene-butadiene rubber. Patient packs of 8 patches.

Vivelle 50: Each thin, circular, multilayer, transparent, 14.5 cm² transdermal therapeutic system, contains: estradiol-17β 4.33 mg for continuous delivery of estradiol-17β 50 μg/day. Nonmedicinal ingredients: acrylic adhesive, bentonite, butylene glycol, dipropylene glycol, ethylene vinyl acetate copolymer, lecithin, oleic acid, mineral oil, polyisobutylene, propylene glycol and styrene-butadiene rubber. Patient packs of 8 patches.

Vivelle 75: Each thin, circular, multilayer, transparent, 22 cm² transdermal therapeutic system, contains: estradiol-17β 6.56 mg for continuous delivery of estradiol-17β 75 μg/day. Nonmedicinal ingredients: acrylic adhesive, bentonite, butylene glycol, dipropylene glycol, ethylene vinyl acetate copolymer, lecithin, oleic acid, mineral oil, polyisobutylene, propylene glycol and styrene-butadiene rubber. Patient packs of 8 patches.

Vivelle 100: Each thin, circular, multilayer, transparent, 29 cm² transdermal therapeutic system, contains: estradiol-17β 8.66 mg for continuous delivery of estradiol-17β 100 μg/day. Nonmedicinal ingredients: acrylic adhesive, bentonite, butylene glycol, dipropylene glycol, ethylene vinyl acetate copolymer, lecithin, oleic acid, mineral oil, polyisobutylene, propylene glycol and styrene-butadiene rubber. Patient packs of 8 patches.

Store below 25°C. Do not freeze. Each patch is individually sealed in a separate pouch. Do not store out of the pouch. Apply immediately upon removal from the protective pouch. Keep out of the reach of children and pets both before use and when disposing of used patches.

(Shown in Product Recognition Section)

Reviewed 1999

VIVOL® ℞

Carter Horner

Diazepam

Anxiolytic—Sedative

Supplied: Each round, flat, uncoated tablet, quadrisected on one side, with a bevelled edge contains: diazepam 2 mg (light lime green, imprinted Horner 2), 5 mg (light green, imprinted Horner 5) or 10 mg (dark green, imprinted Horner 10). Nonmedicinal ingredients: alumina, cellulose, D&C Yellow No. 10, FD&C Green No. 3 & Yellow No. 6, lactose, magnesium stearate, silicon dioxide, starch (corn) and talc. Energy: 1.7 kJ (0.4 kcal). Sodium: <1 mmol (trace). Gluten- and tartrazine-free. Bottles of 100 and 1 000.

(Shown in Product Recognition Section)

VIVONEX® PEDIATRIC

Novartis Nutrition

Pediatric Elemental Diet

Indications: Use in the dietary management of children with clinical conditions of short bowel syndrome, inflammatory bowel disease, malabsorption syndrome, cow's milk protein enteropathy/sensitivity, select multiple trauma/major surgery, Crohn's disease, gastrointestinal fistula, select pre/post surgery, intractable diarrhea and gastrointestinal disorder related to HIV/AIDS.

Precautions: Do not administer parenterally. For use only under medical supervision. Nausea, vomiting, abdominal cramps, distention and diarrhea are possible. Nausea and diarrhea are usually due to feeding rate or diet concentrations. Local water conditions may be implicated in instances of diarrhea. Preparing diet with deionized or distilled water may be effective in this circumstance.

Aspiration is an uncommon complication. However, radiologically confirm the anatomic position of the feeding tube, elevate head of the bed 30° while the patient is receiving diet intragastrically, and control the administration to 150 mL/hour or less, depending upon patient tolerance. Jejunal administration should also be considered. Diabetics and patients with renal insufficiency receiving this diet should be closely monitored.

Dosage: 1 250 mL or 4 180 kJ (five 250 mL servings or 1 000 kcal) provides at least 100% of the 1990 Canadian RNI for protein and essential vitamins and minerals for children 1 to 9 years. May be administered by nasogastric, nasointestinal, esophagostomy, gastrostomy or jejunostomy feeding tube. Feed at room temperature. Follow a physician's or dietitian's direction. When initiating feeding, the flow rate, volume and dilution are dependent on the patient's condition and tolerance.

Feeding should be initiated at a slow rate. Rate and volume of feeding can be increased gradually over 48 hours if well tolerated. If intolerance develops, return to previously tolerated rate, or dilute formula to half strength until desired rate is achieved, then switch to full strength. Do not alter strength and volume at the same time. Rinse the tube with 20 to 30 mL water after each intermittent feeding or every 3 to 4 hours during continuous feeding to avoid clogging and provide additional water.

Vivonex Pediatric is a perishable liquid food when diluted in water. A full day's supply may be prepared at one time and stored in the refrigerator for up to 48 hours, shake the liquid before serving. Do not leave at room temperature for more than 8 hours.

Supplied: Each 48.7 g pouch contains: Ⓤ-D maltodextrin, modified cornstarch, modified coconut oil (medium chain triglycerides), soybean oil, calcium glycerophosphate, L-glutamine, magnesium gluconate, L-lysine acetate, L-leucine, L-arginine acetate, potassium chloride, L-valine, citric acid, L-isoleucine, L-aspartic acid, L-alanine, L-phenylalanine, L-serine, L-proline, L-threonine, L-tyrosine, L-glutamic acid, glycine, L-histidine monohydrochloride monohydrate, L-methionine, potassium citrate, L-cystine, choline bitartrate, polyglycerol esters of fatty acids, sodium citrate, sodium phosphate dibasic, L-tryptophan, potassium sorbate, ascorbic acid, taurine, zinc sulfate, ferrous sulfate, niacinamide, L-carnitine, alpha tocopheryl acetate, copper gluconate, d-calcium pantothenate, manganese sulfate, pyridoxine hydrochloride, riboflavin, thiamine HCl, BHA/BHT (to preserve freshness), vitamin A palmitate, beta carotene, folic acid, chromic acetate, sodium molybdate, potassium iodide, biotin, sodium selenite, vitamin K_1, vitamin D_3, cyanocobalamin. See Table I.

Table I—Vivonex Pediatric

Analysis	100 mL	
Energy	334 (80)	kJ (kcal)
Protein	2.4	g
Carbohydrate	13.0	g
Fat	2.4	g
Linoleic Acid	0.4	g
Sodium	40	mg
Potassium	120	mg
Vitamin A	250	IU
Vitamin C	8.0	mg
Thiamine	0.15	mg
Riboflavin	0.18	mg
Niacin	2.0	mg
Calcium	96.0	mg
Iron	1.0	mg
Vitamin D	32.0	IU
Vitamin E	1.2	IU
Vitamin B_6	0.2	mg
Folic Acid	0.02	mg
Vitamin B_{12}	0.00012	mg
Phosphorus	80	mg
Iodine	0.012	mg
Magnesium	16.0	mg
Zinc	1.2	mg
Copper	0.12	mg
Biotin	0.01	mg
Pantothenic Acid	0.5	mg
Vitamin K	0.004	mg
Choline	20	mg
Chloride	100	mg
Manganese	0.2	mg
Selenium	0.003	mg
Chromium	0.0045	mg
Molybdenum	0.0075	mg
L-carnitine	2.5	mg
Taurine	8.0	mg

The standard dilution of 3.3 kJ (0.8 kcal)/mL has a pH of approximately 5.0 and an average osmolality of 360 mOsm/kg water. Pouches of 48.7 g, cartons of 6, cases of 6 cartons. Store unopened powder below 30°C.

Reviewed 1998

VIVONEX® PLUS

Novartis Nutrition

High Nitrogen Elemental Diet

Indications: A high nitrogen, elemental (100% free amino acids) diet for patients with impaired digestion and absorption. Contains enhanced glutamine, arginine and branched chain amino acid content, especially useful in stressed catabolic patients. Suggested indications include: inflammatory bowel disease, intestinal atresia, pancreatitis, fistula, partial obstruction, short-gut syndrome. Malnutrition and cachexia. Bowel preparation prior to diagnostic and surgical procedures. Transition diet between parenteral and normal oral feeding. Food sensitivities.

Precautions: Do not administer parenterally. For use only under medical supervision. Nausea, vomiting, abdominal cramps, distention and diarrhea are possible. Nausea and diarrhea are usually due to feeding rate or diet concentration. Local water conditions may be implicated in instances of diarrhea. Preparing diet with deionized or distilled water may be effective in this circumstance.

Aspiration is an uncommon complication. However, radiologically confirm the anatomic position of the feeding tube, elevate head of the bed 30° while the patient is receiving diet intragastrically, and control the administration to 150 mL/hour or less, depending upon patient tolerance. Jejunal administration should also be considered.

Diabetics and patients with renal insufficiency receiving this diet should be closely monitored. Use in children may require adjusting the daily consumption to meet the Recommended Daily Allowance for the age group involved.

Dosage: 1 800 mL or 7 520 kJ (6 servings or 1 800 kcal) provides at least 100% of the Canadian RNI (adult males, 25 to 49) for protein and essential vitamins and minerals. May be administered by nasogastric, nasointestinal, esophagostomy, gastrostomy or jejunostomy feeding tube (see Table I). Oral: For oral use, the product should be flavored and chilled over ice. Flavoring agents may be used if their contribution to the elemental and nutritional qualities of the diet are kept in mind. It should be sipped slowly, preferably through a straw, when served as a beverage.

Table I—Vivonex Plus

Gastric Administration

Day	Strength	Approx. Rate (mL/h)	kJ/24 h	Nitrogen (g)/24 h
1	1/2	50	2 510	4.3
2	Full	50	5 020	8.6
3	Full	100	10 000	17.2
4	Full	125	12 500	21.5

Intestinal Administration

Day	Strength	Approx. Rate (mL/h)	kJ/24 h	Nitrogen (g)/24 h
1	1/2	50	2 510	4.3
2	1/2	100	5 020	8.6
3	3/4	100	7 520	12.9
4	Full	100	10 000	17.2
5	Full	125	12 500	21.5

Vivonex Plus is a perishable liquid food when in solution. A full day's supply may be prepared at one time and stored in the refrigerator for up to 48 hours, shake the liquid before serving. Do not leave at room temperature for more than 8 hours.

Supplied: Each 79.5 g packet contains: Ⓤ-D maltodextrin, L-glutamine, modified cornstarch, L-leucine, L-arginine acetate, soybean oil, L-lysine acetate, magnesium gluconate, L-isoleucine, L-valine, calcium glycerophosphate, L-phenylalanine, L-threonine, potassium citrate, L-cysteine HCl monohydrate, citric acid, L-methionine, L-tyrosine, L-histidine monohydrochloride monohydrate, L-aspartic acid, L-proline, sodium citrate, sodium phosphate dibasic, L-tryptophan, potassium chloride, choline bitartrate, L-serine, L-alanine, glycine, ascorbic acid, potassium sorbate, polyglycerol esters of fatty acids, L-carnitine, taurine, zinc sulfate, niacinamide, ferrous sulfate, alpha tocopheryl acetate, D-calcium pantothenate, BHA/BHT (to preserve freshness), alpha tocopherol (to preserve freshness), copper gluconate, pyridoxine HCl, manganese sulfate, vitamin A palmitate, riboflavin, thiamine HCl, folic acid, biotin, chromic acetate, potassium iodide, sodium molybdate, sodium selenite, phytonadione (vitamin K_1), cyanocobalamin (vitamin B_{12}), cholecalciferol (vitamin D_3). See table II.

Table II—Vivonex Plus

Analysis	100 mL	
Energy	418 (100)	kJ (kcal)
Protein	4.5	g
Carbohydrate	19.0	g
Fat	0.67	g
Linoleic Acid	0.34	g
Sodium	61	mg
Potassium	110	mg
Vitamin A	420	IU
Vitamin C	6.7	mg
Thiamine	0.17	mg
Riboflavin	0.19	mg
Niacin	2.2	mg
Calcium	56	mg
Iron	1.0	mg
Vitamin D	33	IU
Vitamin E	2.5	IU
Vitamin B_6	0.22	mg
Folic Acid	0.044	mg
Vitamin B_{12}	0.0007	mg
Phosphorus	56	mg
Iodine	0.0089	mg
Magnesium	22	mg
Zinc	1.3	mg
Copper	0.11	mg
Biotin	0.033	mg
Pantothenic Acid	1.1	mg
Vitamin K	0.0044	mg
Choline	22	mg
Chloride	94	mg
Manganese	0.17	mg
Selenium	0.0056	mg
Chromium	0.0083	mg
Molybdenum	0.014	mg
L-Carnitine	10	mg
Taurine	20	mg

Vivonex Plus (cont'd)

The standard dilution of 4.2 kJ (1 kcal)/mL has a pH of approximately 5.0 and an average osmolality of 650 mOsm/kg. Pouches of 79.5 g, cartons of 6, cases of 6 cartons. Store unopened powder below 30°C.

Reviewed 1999

VIVONEX® T.E.N.

Novartis Nutrition

Elemental Diet

Indications: A high nitrogen, elemental (100% free amino acids) diet enriched with glutamine for patients with impaired digestion or absorption. Suggested indications include: inflammatory bowel disease, intestinal atresia, pancreatitis, fistula, partial obstruction, short-gut syndrome. Malnutrition and cachexia. Bowel preparation prior to diagnostic and surgical procedures. Transition diet between parenteral and normal oral feeding. Food sensitivities.

Precautions: Do not administer parenterally. For use only under medical supervision. Nausea, vomiting, abdominal cramps, distention, and diarrhea are possible. Nausea and diarrhea are usually due to feeding rate or diet concentration. Local water conditions may be implicated in instances of diarrhea. Preparing diet with deionized or distilled water may be effective in this circumstance.

Aspiration is an uncommon complication. However, radiologically confirm the anatomic position of the feeding tube, elevate head of the bed 30° while the patient is receiving diet intragastrically, and control the administration to 150 mL/hour or less, depending upon patient tolerance. Jejunal administration should also be considered.

Diabetics, and patients with renal insufficiency receiving this diet should be closely monitored. Use in children may require adjusting the daily consumption to meet the Recommended Daily Allowance for the age group involved.

Dosage: 2 000 mL or 8 360 kJ (6.7 servings or 2 000 kcal) provides at least 100% of the Canadian RNI (adult males, 25 to 49) for protein and essential vitamins and minerals. May be administered by nasogastric, nasointestinal, esophagostomy, gastrostomy or jejunostomy feeding tube (see Table I). Oral: For oral use, the product should be flavored and chilled over ice. Flavoring agents may be used if their contribution to the elemental and nutritional qualities of the diet are kept in mind. It should be sipped slowly, preferably through a straw, when served as a beverage.

Table I—Vivonex T.E.N.

Gastric Administration

Day	Strength	Approx. Rate (mL/h)	Kilojoules (kJ)/24 h	Nitrogen (g)/24 h
1	½	50	2 510	3.4
2	Full	50	5 020	6.8
3	Full	100	10 040	13.7
4	Full	125	12 550	17.1

Intestinal Administration

Day	Strength	Approx. Rate (mL/h)	Kilojoules (kJ)/24 h	Nitrogen (g)/24 h
1	½	50	2 510	3.4
2	½	100	5 020	6.8
3	¾	100	7 530	10.3
4	Full	100	10 040	13.7
5	Full	125	12 550	17.1

Vivonex T.E.N. is a perishable liquid food when in solution. A full day's supply may be prepared at one time and stored in the refrigerator for up to 48 hours; shake the liquid before serving. Do not leave at room temperature for more than 8 hours.

Supplied: Each 80 g packet contains: Ⓤ-D maltodextrin, modified cornstarch, L-leucine, L-glutamine, L-arginine acetate, magnesium gluconate, L-valine, L-isoleucine, calcium glycerophosphate, safflower oil, L-lysine acetate, L-aspartic acid, L-alanine, L-phenylalanine, L-proline, glycine, L-threonine, L-methionine, L-histidine monohydrochloride monohydrate, potassium chloride, L-serine, L-tryptophan, sodium phosphate dibasic, potassium sorbate, sodium citrate, potassium citrate, L-tyrosine, ascorbic acid, choline bitartrate, ferrous gluconate, polyoxyethylene sorbitan monooleate, taurine, L-carnitine, niacinamide, zinc sulfate, alpha tocopheryl acetate, D-calcium pantothenate, ascorbyl palmitate (to preserve freshness) manganese glycerophosphate, alpha tocopherol (to preserve freshness), pyridoxine HCl, riboflavin phosphate sodium salt, cupric citrate, vitamin A palmitate, thiamine HCl, folic acid, BHA/BHT (to preserve freshness), biotin, sodium selenite, potassium iodide, sodium molybdate, chromic acetate, phytonadione (vitamin K_1), cyanocobalamin (vitamin B_{12}), cholecalciferol (vitamin D_3). See Table II.

Table II—Vivonex T.E.N.

Analysis	100 mL	
Energy	418 (100)	kJ (kcal)
Protein	3.8	g
Carbohydrate	21.0	g
Fat	0.28	g
Linoleic Acid	0.22	g
Sodium	46	mg
Potassium	78	mg
Vitamin A	250	IU
Vitamin C	6.0	mg
Thiamine	0.15	mg
Riboflavin	0.17	mg
Niacin	2.0	mg
Calcium	50	mg
Iron	0.9	mg
Vitamin D	20	IU
Vitamin E	1.5	IU
Vitamin B_6	0.2	mg
Folic Acid	0.04	mg
Vitamin B_{12}	0.0006	mg
Phosphorus	50	mg
Iodine	0.0075	mg
Magnesium	20	mg
Zinc	1	mg
Copper	0.1	mg
Biotin	0.03	mg
Pantothenic Acid	1.0	mg
Vitamin K	0.0022	mg
Choline	7.4	mg
Chloride	82	mg
Manganese	0.094	mg
Selenium	0.005	mg
Chromium	0.0017	mg
Molybdenum	0.005	mg
L-Carnitine	4.0	mg
Taurine	4.0	mg

The standard dilution of 4.2 kJ (1 kcal)/mL has a pH of approximately 5.3 and an average osmolality of 630 mOsm/kg. Cases of 6 cartons with 10 pouches of 80 g. Store unopened powder below 30°C.

Reviewed 1998

VIVOTIF BERNA™

Berna Products

Typhoid Vaccine Live Oral Attenuated Ty21a

Typhoid Prophylaxis

Pharmacology: S. typhi is the etiological agent of typhoid fever, an acute, febrile enteric disease. This vaccine will not afford protection against species of Salmonella other than S. typhi or other bacteria that cause enteric disease.

The incidence of typhoid fever has declined steadily in Canada. Approximately 70 cases are reported annually. Many of these infections were contracted abroad, but a small number occur in Canada, chiefly in areas where sanitation and hygiene are inadequate.

There are approximately 500 cases of typhoid fever per year diagnosed in the United States. In 62% of these patients (statistics from 1977 to 1979) the disease was acquired outside of the United States, while in 38% of the patients the disease was acquired within the United States. Of the disease acquired during foreign travel, 50% of the cases were contracted in Mexico, 20% in Asian countries and 15% in India. The majority of the remaining cases were acquired in the Caribbean basin, South and Central America, North Africa and Southern Europe. Typhoid fever is considered to be endemic in most areas of Central and South America, North and Central Africa, Southeast Asia and the Indian Subcontinent.

Of the disease acquired in the United States, 23% of the cases were associated with typhoid carriers, 24% were due to food outbreaks, 23% were associated with the ingestion of contaminated food or water, 6% due to household contact with an infected person, and 4% following exposure to S. typhi in a laboratory setting. The majority of typhoid cases respond favorably to antibiotic therapy. However, the emergence of chloramphenicol- or ampicillin-resistant strains has greatly complicated therapy. Even with appropriate antibiotic therapy there were 7 deaths among 901 acute typhoid cases reported in the United States from 1977 to 1979. Approximately 3 to 5% of acute typhoid cases result in the development of a chronic carrier state. These non-symptomatic carriers are the natural reservoir for S. typhi and can serve to maintain the disease in its endemic state or to directly infect individuals. Eradication of the carrier state by antibiotic therapy has been unsuccessful. The effect of immunization with Typhoid Vaccine Live Oral Attenuated Ty21a on the carrier state is unknown.

Upon ingestion, virulent strains of S. typhi are able to pass through the stomach acid barrier, colonize the intestinal tract, penetrate the lumen and enter the lymphatic system and bloodstream, thereby causing disease. The risk of severe illness is increased in the absence of gastric acid, e.g., prior gastrectomy, antacid therapy, H_2 antagonists, or in immunocompromised hosts. One possible mechanism by which disease may be prevented is by evoking a local immune response in the intestinal tract. Such local immunity may be induced by oral ingestion of a live attenuated strain of S. typhi undergoing an aborted infection.

The ability of S. typhi to cause disease and to induce a protective immune response is dependent upon the bacteria possessing a complete lipopolysaccharide. The S. typhi Ty21a vaccine strain, derived by chemical mutagenesis, is entirely deficient in activity of the gal E gene product, which restricts its ability to produce complete lipopolysaccharide. In addition, Ty21a has several nutritional auxotrophies, has approximately half the growth rate of the parent strain Ty2, does not produce H_2S, and lacks the Vi antigen (capsular acidic polysaccharide present on almost all virulent S. typhi strains). Ty21a, grown in the presence of low concentrations of galactose, is immunogenic, suggesting that the uptake of galactose by Ty21a enables production of lipopolysaccharide, leading to immunogenicity. It has been presumed that an oversupply of galactose results in accumulation of toxic metabolites within the bacterial cells leading to bacterial lysis. Attenuation and safety of Ty21a has been presumed to be due to the combination of gal E mutation and the lack of Vi antigen. However, an analogous mutant (Vi negative, gal E deletion mutant) of S. typhi prepared by recombinant DNA techniques has been shown to be virulent. In addition, galactose induced lysis of Ty21a is inhibited in vitro in the presence of glucose. Therefore, the combination of gal E and Vi mutations does not account for the safety of Ty21a or for the failure to recover vaccine organisms from people ingesting the usual dose. Ty21a is attenuated by an incompletely understood mechanism.

The efficacy of the S. typhi Ty21a strain has been evaluated in a series of double-blind field trials. The first trial was performed in Alexandria, Egypt with a study population of 32 388 children aged 6 to 7 years. Three doses of vaccine, in the form of a freshly reconstituted suspension administered after ingestion of 1 g of bicarbonate, were given on alternate days. Immunization resulted in a 95% decrease in the incidence of typhoid fever over a 3-year period of surveillance.

A series of field trials was subsequently performed in Santiago, Chile to evaluate efficacy when the vaccine strain was administered in the form of an acid-resistant enteric-coated capsule. The initial trial involved 91 954 school-aged children, and compared 1 or 2 doses of vaccine given 1 week apart. After 33 months of passive surveillance, vaccine efficacy was 21% for the single-dose schedule and 54% for the 2-dose schedule. A further field trial was performed in Santiago, Chile involving 109 594 school-aged children. Three doses of enteric-coated capsules were administered either on alternate days (short immunization schedule) or 21 days apart (long immunization schedule). Following 36 months of surveillance, vaccination resulted in a 67% decrease in the incidence of typhoid fever in the short immunization schedule group and a 49% reduction in the long immunization schedule group. After 48 months of surveillance, the short immunization schedule resulted in a 68% decrease in typhoid fever. Following 7 years of surveillance, vaccine efficacy was found to be 62.8% for the short immunization schedule. A field trial was next conducted in Santiago, Chile, to determine the relative efficacy of 2, 3 and 4 doses of enteric-coated vaccine administered on alternate days to school-aged children. Relative vaccine efficacy as determined by comparison of disease incidence within the 3 vaccinated groups was highest for the 4-dose regimen.

The efficacy of Typhoid Vaccine Live Oral Attenuated Ty21a has been demonstrated only in areas of the world where typhoid fever is endemic. Efficacy has not been demonstrated for individuals residing in a non-typhoid fever endemic area who then enter a typhoid fever endemic area. Ingestion of 3 doses of Typhoid Vaccine Live Oral Attenuated Ty21a induced comparable levels of anti-S. typhi lipopolysaccharide serum antibody levels in healthy young adults living in endemic (Chile) or non-endemic (United States and Switzerland) areas. However, the significance of this antibody response as relates to vaccine-induced protection against typhoid fever is not known.

Indications: For immunization of adults and children greater than 5 years of age against disease caused by S. typhi. Results from clinical studies indicate that adults and children greater than 5 years of age may be protected against typhoid fever following the oral ingestion of 4 doses of Typhoid Vaccine Live Oral Attenuated Ty21a. Immunization (ingestion of all 4 doses of Typhoid Vaccine Live Oral Attenuated Ty21a) should be completed at least 1 week prior to potential exposure to S. typhi.

Routine typhoid vaccination is not recommended in Canada but immunization should be considered in the following situations: 1) close continuing exposure to an S. typhi carrier such as occurs in members of a household or institution in which a carrier lives; 2) travel to countries where typhoid fever is endemic; 3) laboratory workers who frequently handle cultures of S. typhi.

Not all recipients of Typhoid Vaccine Live Oral Attenuated Ty21a will be fully protected against typhoid fever. Travelers should take all necessary precautions to avoid contact with or ingestion of potentially contaminated food or water sources.

There is no evidence to support the use of typhoid vaccine to control common source outbreaks, disease following natural disasters or in persons attending rural summer camps.

Typhoid Vaccine Live Oral Attenuated Ty21a will not afford protection against enteric organisms other than S. typhi.

There are no studies reported using Typhoid Vaccine Live Oral Attenuated Ty21a as a booster for persons previously vaccinated with the parenteral vaccine.

An optimal booster dose has not yet been established. However, it is recommended that a booster dose consisting of 4 vaccine capsules taken on alternate days be given every 7 years under conditions of repeated or continued exposure to typhoid fever (see Dosage).

Typhoid fever continues to be an important disease in many parts of the world. Travelers entering such areas are at risk to contracting typhoid fever following the ingestion of contaminated food or water. Parenterally administered typhoid vaccine has been shown to be effective at reducing the incidence of disease in such endemic areas. However, immunization with such vaccines is frequently accompanied by adverse reactions such as pain and/or swelling at the injection site, fever, malaise and headache.

Contraindications: Hypersensitivity to any component of the vaccine or the enteric-coated capsule.

Safety of the vaccine has not been demonstrated in persons deficient in their ability to mount a humoral or cell-mediated immune response due to either a congenital or acquired immunodeficient state including treatment with immunosuppressive or antimitotic drugs. The vaccine should not be administered to these persons regardless of benefits.

Warnings: Typhoid Vaccine Live Oral Attenuated Ty21a is not to be taken during an acute febrile illness or in the face of acute gastrointestinal illness or chronic inflammatory bowel disease. Postpone taking the vaccine if persistent diarrhea or vomiting is occurring (see Precautions, General).

Precautions: General: The vaccine should not be administered to persons during an acute febrile illness or acute gastrointestinal illness. The vaccine should not be administered to individuals receiving antibiotics (sulfonamides included) since these agents may be active against the vaccine strain and prevent a sufficient degree of multiplication to occur in order to induce a protective immune response. The vaccine should not be administered to persons with a known hypersensitivity to any vaccine component or medium component (see Supplied).

The antimalarial drug mefloquine does inhibit the growth of the Ty21a vaccine strain in vitro with a minimal inhibitory concentration (MIC) of 5 to 10 μg/mL. Mefloquine is rapidly absorbed from the intestinal tract ($T_{1/2}$ of 0.36 to 2 hours). It is reasonable to expect that the level of mefloquine would drop below the MIC for the vaccine strain by 8 hours after ingestion. It is therefore recommended that Thyphoid Vaccine Live Oral Attenuated Ty21a be administered at least 8 hours after mefloquine. No human studies are available to document that the above recommended dosing schedule does not adversely affect the immunogenicity of Typhoid Vaccine Live Oral Attenuated Ty21a. The MIC of chloroquine for the Ty21a vaccine strain is >200 μg/mL. While no in vitro inhibitory effect of chloroquine has been shown for the Ty21a vaccine strain, is is recommended that chloroquine be administered at least 8 hours prior to Typhoid Vaccine Live Oral Attenuated Ty21a.

Information for the Patient: It is essential that all 4 doses of vaccine be taken at the prescribed alternate day interval to obtain a maximal protective immune response. Vaccine potency is dependent upon storage under refrigeration (between 2 and 8°C). The vaccine should be stored under refrigeration at **all times**. It is essential to replace unused vaccine in the refrigerator between doses. The vaccine capsule should be swallowed approximately 1 hour before a meal with a cold or lukewarm drink (temperature not to exceed body temperature, i.e., 37°C). Care should be taken not to chew the vaccine capsule. After placing in the mouth, the vaccine capsule should be swallowed as soon as possible.

Carcinogenesis, Mutagenesis, Impairment of Fertility: Long-term studies in animals with Typhoid Vaccine Live Oral Attenuated Ty21a have not been performed to evaluate carcinogenic potential, mutagenic potential or impairment of fertility.

Pregnancy: Category C: Animal reproduction studies have not been conducted with Typhoid Vaccine Live Oral Attenuated Ty21a. It is not known whether Typhoid Vaccine Live Oral Attenuated Ty21a can cause fetal harm when administered to a pregnant woman or can affect reproduction capacity. Typhoid Vaccine Live Oral Attenuated Ty21a should be given to a pregnant woman only if clearly needed.

Lactation: There are no data to support the use of this product in nursing mothers. It is not known if Typhoid Vaccine Live Oral Attenuated Ty21a is excreted in human milk.

Children: The safety of Typhoid Vaccine Live Oral Attenuated Ty21a has not been established in children under 6 years of age. This product is therefore not recommended for use in children under 6 years of age.

Adverse Effects: Several lots of Typhoid Vaccine Live Oral Attenuated Ty21a have been evaluated in several field trials both in adults and in school-aged children. Objectively monitored side effects, e.g., abdominal pain, diarrhea, vomiting, fever, headache and skin rash, did not occur at a statistically higher frequency in the vaccinated group as compared to the placebo group. Postmarketing surveillance outside of the United States has found that side effects are infrequent, transient, and resolve of their own accord. Reported adverse reactions include nausea, abdominal cramps, vomiting, skin rash or urticaria in the trunk and/or extremities.

Overdose: Symptoms and Treatment: 5 to 8 doses of Typhoid Vaccine Live Oral Attenuated Ty21a containing between 3 to 10×10^{10} viable vaccine organisms were administered to 155 healthy adult males. This dosage was, at a minimum, 5-fold higher than the currently recommended dose. No significant reactions, e.g., vomiting, acute abdominal distress or fever, were observed. At the recommended dosage, the S. typhi Ty21a vaccine strain is not excreted in the feces. However, clinical studies in volunteers have shown that overdosing can increase the possibility of shedding the S. typhi Ty21a vaccine strain in the feces.

Dosage: 1 capsule is to be swallowed approximately 1 hour before a meal with a cold or lukewarm drink (temperature not to exceed body temperature, i.e., 37°C) on alternate days, e.g., days 1, 3, 5 and 7. The vaccine capsule should not be chewed and should be swallowed as soon as possible after placing in the mouth. A complete immunization schedule is the ingestion of 4 vaccine capsules as described above. Unless a complete immunization schedule is followed, an optimum immune response may not be achieved. Not all recipients of Typhoid Vaccine Live Oral Attenuated Ty21a will be fully protected against typhoid fever. Travelers should take all necessary precautions to avoid contact with or ingestion of potentially contaminated food or water.

Booster Use: The optimum booster schedule for Typhoid Vaccine Live Oral Attenuated Ty21a has not been determined. Efficacy has been shown to persist for at least 7 years. Further, there is no experience with Typhoid Vaccine Live Oral Attenuated Ty21a as a booster in persons previously immunized with parenteral typhoid vaccine. Despite these limitations, it is recommended that a booster dose consisting of 4 vaccine capsules taken on alternate days be given every 7 years under conditions of repeated or continued exposure to typhoid fever.

Supplied: Each enteric-coated capsule contains: viable S. typhi Ty21a 2 to 10×10^9 colony-forming units, non-viable S. typhi Ty21a 5 to 60×10^9 bacterial cells, sucrose 16.7 to 41.7 mg, ascorbic acid 0.6 to 1.6 mg, amino acid mixture 0.8 to 2.1 mg, lactose 135.8 to 166.6 mg and magnesium stearate 3.4 to 4.2 mg. Single foil blisters of 4. The blister containing the vaccine capsules should be inspected to ensure that the foil seal and the capsules are intact.

Typhoid Vaccine Live Oral Attenuated Ty21a is not stable when exposed to ambient temperatures. The vaccine should therefore be shipped and stored between 2 and 8°C. Each package of vaccine shows an expiration date. This expiration date is valid only if the product has been maintained between 2 and 8°C.

VIVOTIF BERNA® L VACCINE

Berna Products

Typhoid Vaccine Live Oral Attenuated Ty21a

Typhoid Prophylaxis

Pharmacology: S. typhi is the etiological agent of typhoid fever, an acute, febrile enteric disease. This vaccine will not afford protection against species of Salmonella other than S. typhi or other bacteria that cause enteric disease.

The incidence of typhoid fever has declined steadily in Canada. Approximately 70 cases are reported annually. Most of these infections were contracted abroad, but a small number occur in Canada, chiefly in areas where sanitation and hygiene are inadequate. There are approximately 500 cases of typhoid fever per year diagnosed in the United States. In 62% of these patients (statistics from 1977 to 1979) the disease was acquired outside of the United States, while in 38% of the patients the disease was acquired within the United States. Of the disease acquired during foreign travel, 50% of the cases were contracted in Mexico, 20% in Asian countries, and 15% in India. The majority of the remaining cases were acquired in the Caribbean basin, South and Central America, North Africa, and Southern Europe. Typhoid fever is considered to be endemic in most areas of Central and South America, the African continent, the Near East and the Middle East, Southeast Asia and the Indian subcontinent. Of the disease acquired in the United States, 23% of the cases were associated with typhoid carriers, 24% were due to food outbreaks, 23% were associated with the ingestion of contaminated food or water, 6% due to household contact with an infected person, and 4% following exposure to S. typhi in a laboratory setting.

The majority of typhoid cases respond favorably to antibiotic therapy. However, the emergence of chloramphenicol-or ampicillin-resistant strains has greatly complicated therapy. Even with appropriate antibiotic therapy, there were 7 deaths among 901 acute typhoid cases reported in the United States from 1977 to 1979. Approximately 3 to 5% of acute typhoid cases result in the development of a chronic carrier state. These nonsymptomatic carriers are the natural reservoir for S. typhi and can serve to maintain the disease in its endemic state or to directly infect individuals. Eradication of the carrier state by antibiotic therapy has been unsuccessful. The effect of immunization with Typhoid Vaccine Live Oral Attenuated Ty21a on the carrier state is unknown.

Upon ingestion, virulent strains of S. typhi are able to pass through the stomach acid barrier, colonize the intestinal tract, penetrate the lumen and enter the lymphatic system and blood stream, thereby causing disease. The risk of severe illness is increased in the absence of gastric acid, e.g., prior gastrectomy, antacid therapy, H_2 antagonist therapy, or in immunocompromised individuals. One possible mechanism by which disease may be prevented is by evoking a local immune response in the intestinal tract. Such local immunity may be induced by oral ingestion of a live attenuated strain of S. typhi which causes an aborted infection.

The ability of S. typhi to cause disease and to induce a protective immune response is dependent upon the bacteria possessing a complete lipopolysaccharide. The S. typhi Ty21a vaccine strain, derived by chemical mutagenesis, is entirely deficient in activity of the gal E gene product, which restricts its ability to produce complete lipopolysaccharide. In addition, Ty21a has several nutritional auxotrophies, has approximately half the growth rate of the parent strain Ty2, does not produce H_2S, and lacks the Vi antigen (capsular acidic polysaccharide present on almost all virulent S. typhi strains). Ty21a, grown in the presence of low concentrations of galactose, is immunogenic, suggesting that the uptake of galactose by Ty21a enables production of lipopolysaccharide, leading to immunogenicity. It has been presumed that an oversupply of galactose results in accumulation of toxic metabolites within the bacterial cells leading to bacterial lysis. Attenuation and safety of Ty21a have been presumed to be due to the combination of gal E

Vivotif Berna L Vaccine (cont'd)

mutation and the lack of Vi antigen. However, an analogous mutant (Vi negative, gal E deletion mutant) of S. typhi constructed by recombinant DNA techniques has been shown to be virulent. In addition, galactose induced lysis of Ty21a is inhibited in vitro in the presence of glucose. Therefore, the combination of gal E and Vi mutations does not account for the safety of Ty21a or for the failure to recover vaccine organisms from people ingesting the usual dose. Ty21a is attenuated by an incompletely understood mechanism.

The efficacy of the S. typhi Ty21a vaccine strain has been evaluated in a series of randomized, double-blind, placebo-controlled field trials. A trial was performed in Plaju, Indonesia, with a study population of 20 543 subjects aged 3 to 44 years. The subjects were randomized to receive either 3 doses of vaccine, either in sachets or enteric-coated capsules, or an identical appearing placebo. Each dose of vaccine was administered 1 week apart. After 30 months of passive surveillance, vaccine efficacy was determined to be 53% (95% confidence interval: 36 to 66%) for Vivotif Berna L Vaccine and 42% (95% confidence interval: 23 to 57%) for Vivotif Berna Vaccine (enteric-coated capsules). The difference in the overall degree of protection conferred against typhoid fever by the 2 different vaccine presentations was not statistically significant. A second trial of similar design was conducted in Santiago, Chile, with a study population of 81 621 school children aged 5 to 19 years. Protection against typhoid fever in all age groups after 36 months of passive surveillance was 76.9% (95% confidence interval: 60 to 87%) for Vivotif Berna L Vaccine versus 33.2% (95% confidence interval: 0 to 57%) for the enteric-coated Vivotif Berna Vaccine formulation. The difference in protection rates was highly significant ($p<0.0001$). This finding can be attributed to the fact that while Vivotif Berna L Vaccine afforded significant protection against disease in both young (5- to 9-year-old) and older children (>9 years of age), Vivotif Berna Vaccine was ineffective in younger children.

The efficacy of the S. typhi Ty21a vaccine strain has been evaluated in several additional double-blind, randomized field trials. The first was performed in Alexandria, Egypt, with a study population of 32 388 children 6.5 to 7 years of age. Three doses of vaccine, in the form of a freshly reconstituted suspension administered after ingestion of 1 g of bicarbonate, were given on alternate days. Immunization resulted in a 95% decrease in the incidence of typhoid fever over a 3-year period of surveillance. A further series of field trials was subsequently performed in Santiago, Chile, to evaluate efficacy where the vaccine was administered only in the form of an acid-resistant enteric-coated capsule. The initial trial involved 91 954 school-aged children, and compared 1 or 2 doses of vaccine given 1 week apart. After 33 months of passive surveillance, vaccine efficacy was 21% for the single dose schedule and 54% for the 2-dose schedule. A further field trial was performed in Santiago, Chile, involving 109 594 school-aged children. Three doses of vaccine were administered either on alternate days (short immunization schedule) or 21 days apart (long immunization schedule). Following 36 months of surveillance, vaccination resulted in a 67% decrease in the incidence of typhoid fever in the short immunization schedule group and a 49% reduction in the long immunization schedule group. Following 7 years of surveillance, vaccine efficacy was found to be 62.8% for the short immunization schedule. A field trial was next conducted in Santiago, Chile, to determine the relative efficacy of 2, 3 and 4 doses of enteric-coated vaccine administered on alternate days to school-aged children. Relative vaccine efficacy, as determined by comparison of disease incidence between the 3 vaccinated groups, was highest for the 4-dose schedule. The sum total of the above results indicates that 3 doses of Vivotif Berna L Vaccine provide a level of protection comparable to that obtained after vaccination with 4 doses of Vivotif Berna Vaccine (enteric-coated capsules).

The efficacy of the S. typhi Ty21a vaccine strain has been demonstrated only in areas of the world where typhoid fever is endemic. Efficacy has not been demonstrated for individuals residing in a nontyphoid fever endemic area who then enter a typhoid fever endemic area. Ingestion of 3 doses of Ty21a vaccine induced comparable levels of anti-S. typhi lipopolysaccharide serum antibody levels in healthy young adults living in endemic (Chile) or nonendemic (United States, Austria and Switzerland) areas. However, the significance of this antibody response as it relates to vaccine-induced protection against typhoid fever is not known.

Indications: For immunization of adults and children 3 years of age and older against disease caused by S. typhi. Results from clinical studies indicate that adults and children 3 years of age or older may be protected against typhoid fever following the oral ingestion of 3 doses of Vivotif Berna L Vaccine. Immunization (ingestion of all 3 doses) should be completed at least 1 week prior to potential exposure to S. typhi.

Routine typhoid vaccination is not recommended in Canada but immunization should be considered in the following situations: 1) travel in endemic areas for extended periods, or off the usual tourist tracks; 2) ongoing household or intimate exposure to a typhoid carrier; 3) laboratory workers who frequently handle cultures of S. typhi.

Not all recipients of Vivotif Berna L Vaccine will be fully protected against typhoid fever. Travelers should take all necessary precautions to avoid contact with or ingestion of potentially contaminated food or water. There is no evidence to support the use of typhoid vaccine to control common source outbreaks, disease following natural disasters or in persons attending rural summer camps. Vivotif Berna L Vaccine will not afford protection against enteric organisms other than S. typhi.

There are no studies reported using Vivotif Berna L Vaccine as a booster for persons previously vaccinated with the parenteral vaccine. An optimal booster dose has not yet been established. However, it is recommended that a booster dose consisting of 3 double-chambered sachets taken on alternate days be given every 7 years under conditions of repeated or continued exposure to typhoid fever (see Dosage).

Typhoid fever continues to be an important disease in many parts of the world. Travelers entering such areas are at risk of contracting typhoid fever following the ingestion of contaminated food or water. Parenterally administered typhoid vaccine has been shown to be effective at reducing the incidence of disease in endemic areas. However, immunization with such vaccines is frequently accompanied by adverse reactions such as pain and/or swelling at the injection site, fever, malaise and headache.

Contraindications: Hypersensitivity to any component of the vaccine or the buffer. Safety of the vaccine has not been demonstrated in persons deficient in their ability to mount a humoral or cell-mediated immune response due to either a congenital or acquired immunodeficient state, including treatment with immunosuppressive or antimitotic drugs. The vaccine should not be administered to these persons regardless of benefits.

Warnings: Typhoid Vaccine Live Oral Attenuated Ty21a is not to be taken during an acute febrile illness or in the face of acute gastrointestinal illness or chronic inflammatory bowel disease. Postpone taking the vaccine if persistent diarrhea or vomiting is occurring (see Precautions, General).

Phenylketonurics: contains phenylalanine (17 mg per double-chambered sachet). This is due to the fact that Vivotif Berna L Vaccine is sweetened by aspartame (a phenylalanine derivative).

Precautions: General: The vaccine should not be administered to persons during an acute febrile illness or acute gastrointestinal illness. The vaccine should not be administered to individuals receiving antibiotics (sulfonamides included) since these agents may be active against the vaccine strain and prevent a sufficient degree of multiplication to occur in order to induce a protective immune response. The vaccine should not be administered to persons with a known hypersensitivity to any vaccine, buffer or medium component (see Supplied). Several antimalaria drugs, such as mefloquine, chloroquine and proguanil possess antibacterial activity which may interfere with the immunogenicity of Vivotif Berna L Vaccine. To determine the effect of these antimalaria drugs on the humoral anti-S. typhi immune response, healthy adult subjects were given mefloquine (250 mg at weekly intervals; N=30) chloroquine (500 mg at weekly intervals; N=30) or proguanil (200 mg daily; N=30) together with Vivotif Berna L Vaccine. Concomitant treatment with mefloquine or chloroquine did not result in a significant ($p>0.05$) reduction in the serum anti-S. typhi immune response compared to subjects receiving vaccine only (N=45). The simultaneous administration of proguanil did effect a significant ($p=0.013$) decrease in the immune response rate. These findings indicate that mefloquine and chloroquine can be administered together with Vivotif Berna L Vaccine. Proguanil should be administered only if 10 days or more have elapsed since the final dose of Vivotif Berna L Vaccine was ingested. If Vivotif Berna L Vaccine and Mutacol Berna Vaccine (Cholera Vaccine Live Oral CVD 103-HgR) are taken together (see below) only mefloquine should be used for malaria prophylaxis due to the fact that chloroquine has been shown to suppress the immune response engendered by Mutacol Berna Vaccine.

The concomitant administration of oral polio vaccine or yellow fever vaccine did not suppress the immune response elicited by Vivotif Berna L Vaccine. There is no reason to believe that simultaneous administration of parenteral vaccines or immunoglobulins with Vivotif Berna L Vaccine will decrease vaccine efficacy. Vivotif Berna L Vaccine and Mutacol Berna Vaccine can be simultaneously administered safely without adversely affecting the immune response to either vaccine. Mutacol Berna Vaccine should be combined with the first dose of Vivotif Berna L Vaccine as this dosing schedule has been shown to elicit an optimal immune response to both vaccines. If taken together, a single sachet of Vivotif Berna L Vaccine and Mutacol Berna Vaccine should be reconstituted in the following way: The contents of the vaccine chamber (chamber B) of both vaccines are mixed with the contents of one buffer chamber (chamber A) in 100 mL of cold or lukewarm water (see Dosage). Alternatively, Vivotif Berna L Vaccine and Mutacol Berna Vaccine can be administered separately with an interval of greater than 4 hours between vaccinations. This is to allow the gastric acidity to return to normal levels between dosing.

Information to be Provided for the Patient: It is essential that all 3 doses of vaccine be taken at the prescribed alternate day interval to obtain a maximal protective immune response. Vaccine potency is dependent upon storage under refrigeration (between 2 and 8°C). The vaccine should be stored under refrigeration at all times. It is essential to replace unused vaccine in the refrigerator between doses. The vaccine is to be reconstituted and ingested in the following manner: First, gently shake or tap the sachet to ensure that the contents have settled to the bottom. Fold the sachet in half as depicted in step 1 shown on the reverse side of the sachet. Cut along the dotted line as shown in step 2. Carefully empty the entire contents of both sachet chambers into 100 mL of cold or lukewarm water (temperature not to exceed body temperature, i.e., 37°C). The vaccine is not to be reconstituted in carbonated beverages, fruit juices or milk. Gently stir (5 to 10 seconds) the mixture with a spoon or other appropriate utensil until a homogenous suspension is obtained. The vaccine should be swallowed as soon as possible thereafter.

Phenylketonurics: contains phenylalanine (17 mg per double-chambered sachet). This is due to the fact that Vivotif Berna L Vaccine is sweetened by aspartame (a phenylalanine derivative).

Carcinogenesis, Mutagenesis, Impairment of Fertility: Long-term studies in animals with Vivotif Berna L Vaccine have not been performed to evaluate carcinogenic potential, mutagenic potential or impairment of fertility.

Pregnancy: Animal reproduction studies have not been conducted with Vivotif Berna L Vaccine. It is not known whether Vivotif Berna L Vaccine can cause fetal harm when administered to a pregnant woman or can affect reproduction capacity. Vivotif Berna L Vaccine should be given to a pregnant woman only if clearly needed.

Lactation: There are no data to support the use of this product in nursing mothers. It is not known if Vivotif Berna L Vaccine is excreted in human milk.

Children: The safety of Vivotif Berna L Vaccine has not been established in children under 3 years of age. This product is therefore not recommended for use in children under 3 years of age.

Adverse Effects: Several lots of Vivotif Berna L Vaccine have been evaluated in field trials both in children and adults. There were no statistically significant differences for objectively monitored side effects, e.g., abdominal pain, diarrhea, vomiting, fever, nausea, except the higher incidence of skin rash in vaccine recipients versus placebo group. Objectively monitored side effects did not occur at a statistically higher frequency among 2- to 6-year-old Thai children or adult Europeans who received the vaccine as compared to a placebo group.

Overdose: Symptoms and Treatment: Five to 8 doses of the vaccine strain Ty21a containing between 3 to 10×10^{10} viable vaccine organisms were administered to 155 healthy adult males. This dosage was, at a minimum, 3-fold higher than the currently recommended dose. No significant reactions, e.g., vomiting, acute abdominal distress or fever, were observed. At the recommended dosage, the S. typhi Ty21a vaccine strain is not excreted in the feces. However, clinical studies in volunteers have shown that overdosing can increase the possibility of shedding the S. typhi Ty21a vaccine strain in the feces.

Dosage: The vaccine is to be taken approximately 1 hour before a meal as described below. A complete immunization schedule is the ingestion of 3 double-chambered sachets taken on alternate days. Unless a complete immunization schedule is followed, an optimum immune response may not be achieved. Not all recipients of Vivotif Berna L Vaccine will be fully protected against typhoid fever. Travelers should take all necessary precautions to avoid contact with or ingestion of potentially contaminated food or water.

The sachet containing the buffer (chamber A) and vaccine (chamber B) should be inspected to ensure that the foil is intact. Reconstitution of the vaccine is performed in the following manner: The sachet is to be folded along the solid black line and cut along the dotted line after insuring that the contents have been displaced to the bottom to prevent spillage. The contents of both chambers are to be emptied simultaneously into 100 mL of cold or lukewarm water (temperature not to exceed body temperature, e.g., 37°C). Do not resuspend in milk, juice or in a carbonated beverage. Resuspend the sachet contents by gently mixing for 5 to 10 seconds. The vaccine should be swallowed as soon after mixing as possible.

Booster Use: The optimum booster schedule for Vivotif Berna L Vaccine has not been determined. Efficacy has been shown to persist for at least 7 years. However, there is no experience with Vivotif Berna L Vaccine as a booster in persons previously immunized with parenteral typhoid vaccine. Despite these limitations, it is recommended that a booster dose consisting of 3 double-chambered sachets taken on alternate days be given every 7 years under conditions of repeated or continued exposure to typhoid fever.

Supplied: Vivotif Berna L Vaccine (Typhoid Vaccine Live Oral Attenuated Ty21a) is a live attenuated vaccine for oral administration. The vaccine contains the attenuated strain S. typhi Ty21a.

Vivotif Berna L Vaccine is manufactured by the Swiss Serum and Vaccine Institute Berne. The vaccine strain is grown under controlled conditions in a medium containing yeast extract, an acid digest of casein, dextrose and galactose. The bacteria are collected by centrifugation, mixed with a stabilizer containing sucrose, ascorbic acid and amino acids, and lyophilized. The lyophilized bacteria are mixed with lactose and aspartame and filled into 1 chamber of a double-chambered aluminum foil sachet. A sodium bicarbonate-ascorbic acid buffer is filled into the second chamber and the sachet is sealed. Each double-chambered sachet contains: buffer chamber A: sodium bicarbonate 2.4-2.9 g, ascorbic acid 1.5-1.8 g and lactose 0.18-0.22 g; vaccine chamber B: viable S. typhi Ty21a 2-10×10⁹ colony-forming units, nonviable S. typhi Ty21a 5-60×10⁹ bacterial cells, sucrose 15-250 mg, amino acid mixture 0.8-15 mg, ascorbic acid 0.6-10 mg, aspartame 20-30 mg and lactose 1.5-2.1 g.

Packages of 3 double-chambered aluminum foil sachets each containing 1 dose of vaccine. The contents of each chamber require simultaneous reconstitution prior to oral administration.

The vaccine is not stable when exposed to ambient temperatures. The vaccine should therefore be shipped and stored between 2 and 8°C. Each package of vaccine shows an expiration date. This expiration date is valid only if the product has been maintained between 2 and 8°C. Store in a dry place and protect from light.

New Product 1998

VOLTAREN® ℞
Novartis Pharmaceuticals

Diclofenac Sodium

Anti-inflammatory—Analgesic

Pharmacology: Diclofenac sodium is a nonsteroidal anti-inflammatory drug (NSAID) with analgesic and antipyretic properties. The mode of action is not fully known but it does not act through the pituitary-adrenal axis. Diclofenac inhibits prostaglandin synthesis by interfering with the action of prostaglandin synthetase. This inhibitory effect may partially explain its actions.

From a clinical efficacy standpoint, diclofenac sodium 75 mg has activity similar to 3.6 g of ASA.

Diclofenac sodium is similar in activity to equivalent dosages of indomethacin (75 to 150 mg daily), and causes less CNS side effects at these doses.

Although diclofenac sodium does not alter the course of the underlying disease, it has been found to relieve pain, reduce fever, swelling and tenderness, and increase mobility in patients with rheumatic disorders of the types listed.

Pharmacokinetics: Absorption: In humans, orally-administered diclofenac sodium is rapidly and almost completely absorbed and distributed to blood, liver, and kidneys. The plasma concentrations show a linear relationship to the amount of drug administered. No accumulation occurs provided the recommended dosage intervals are observed.

Enteric coating may delay the onset of absorption from 25 and 50 mg tablets. Absorption occurs more rapidly when the drug is administered on an empty stomach (T_{max} 2.5 hours), than with meals (T_{max} 6 hours). The bioavailability remains the same under both conditions. The mean peak plasma concentration of 1.5 μg/mL (5 μmol/L) is attained, on average, 2 hours after ingestion of one 50 mg enteric-coated tablet.

Following administration of slow-release (SR) diclofenac sodium, C_{max} is reached at approximately 4 hours or later. Significant drug plasma concentrations persist when levels would have dropped almost to baseline values following enteric-coated tablet administration. Mean plasma concentrations of 13 ng/mL (40 nmol/L) were produced 24 hours after diclofenac sodium slow release 100 mg, or 16 hours after diclofenac sodium slow release 75 mg (single dose). Trough levels are approximately 22 to 25 ng/mL (70 to 80 nmol/L) during treatment with diclofenac sodium slow release 100 mg once daily or diclofenac sodium slow release 75 mg twice daily. In pharmacokinetic studies no accumulation of diclofenac sodium was found following repeated once daily administration of diclofenac sodium slow release 100 mg tablets or repeated twice daily administration of diclofenac sodium slow release 75 mg tablets.

Suppositories have a more rapid onset, but slower rate of absorption than oral enteric-coated tablets. C_{max} is approximately ⅔ of that produced by an equivalent 50 mg enteric-coated tablet oral dose. T_{max} occurs within 1 hour. The unchanged diclofenac plasma AUC values for rectal administration are within the range of values produced by equivalent oral enteric-coated tablet doses. Since about half the active substance is metabolized during its first passage through the liver ("first pass" effect), the area under the concentration curve (AUC) following oral or rectal administration is about half as large as it is following a parenteral dose of equal size.

Distribution: Diclofenac sodium is extensively bound (99%) to serum albumin. The apparent volume of distribution is 0.12 to 0.17 L/kg. Single-dose (oral or i.m.) studies in rheumatoid patients with joint effusions have shown that diclofenac is distributed to the synovial fluid, where T_{max} occurs 2 to 4 hours after plasma T_{max}. Synovial fluid concentrations exceed plasma levels within 4 to 6 hours of administration. This elevation above plasma concentrations can be maintained for up to 12 hours. The synovial fluid elimination half-life is at least 3 times greater than that for plasma.

Biotransformation: Diclofenac undergoes single and multiple hydroxylation and methoxylation, producing 3'–, 4'–, 5–hydroxy, 4'–5–hydroxy and 3'–hydroxy–4'–methoxy derivatives of diclofenac. These phenolic metabolites are largely inactive, and (along with the parent compound) are mostly converted to glucuronide conjugates.

Elimination: Plasma clearance of diclofenac is 263±56 mL/minute. The mean terminal drug half-life in plasma is 1.8 hours after oral doses. In humans about 60% of the drug and its metabolites are eliminated in the urine and the balance through bile in the feces. More than 90% of an oral dose is accounted for in elimination products within 72 hours. About 1% of an oral dose is excreted unchanged in urine.

Special Populations: Renal Impairment: A single dose pharmacokinetic study in patients with varying degrees of renal dysfunction (creatinine clearance rates ranging from 3 to 42 mL/minute), suggests that moderate renal impairment does not affect the elimination rate of unchanged diclofenac from plasma but that it may reduce the elimination rate of the metabolites of the drug. In one patient with a creatinine clearance of <10 mL/minute, the theoretical steady-state plasma levels of metabolites (normally devoid of pharmacological activity) were about 4 times higher than those in normal subjects, with metabolites cleared through the bile. Although no accumulation of pharmacologically active substance seems to occur, caution is advised while administering diclofenac sodium to patients with impaired kidney function.

Hepatic Impairment: The kinetics and metabolism of diclofenac, as revealed in a study of 10 patients with impaired hepatic function (chronic hepatitis and nondecompensated cirrhosis) receiving a single oral dose of 100 mg, were the same as in patients without liver disease.

Geriatrics: The ability of elderly subjects to absorb, metabolize and excrete diclofenac sodium does not appear to differ significantly from those of young subjects.

Indications: The symptomatic treatment of rheumatoid arthritis and osteoarthritis, including degenerative joint disease of the hip.

Contraindications: Patients with active, or recent history of, inflammatory diseases of the gastrointestinal tract such as peptic ulcer, gastritis, regional enteritis, or ulcerative colitis.

Known or suspected hypersensitivity to the drug. Since cross sensitivity has been demonstrated, diclofenac sodium should not be given to patients in whom ASA or other nonsteroidal anti-inflammatory agents (NSAIDs) have induced asthma, rhinitis, urticaria or other allergic manifestations. Fatal anaphylactoid reactions have occurred in such individuals.

Suppositories are contraindicated in patients with any inflammatory lesions of rectum or anus and in patients with recent history of rectal or anal bleeding.

Warnings: Peptic ulceration, perforation and gastrointestinal bleeding, sometimes severe and occasionally fatal, in either the presence or absence of previous symptoms have been known to occur during therapy with nonsteroidal anti-inflammatory drugs (NSAIDs) including diclofenac sodium.

Diclofenac should be given under close medical supervision to patients prone to gastrointestinal tract irritation particularly those with a history of peptic ulcer, melena, diverticulosis or other inflammatory disease of the gastrointestinal tract (such as ulcerative colitis or Crohn's disease). In these cases the physician must weigh the benefits of treatment against the possible hazards (see Contraindications and Adverse Effects).

Patients should be instructed to contact their physician immediately if they experience symptoms or signs suggestive of peptic ulceration or gastrointestinal bleeding. These reactions can occur at any time during treatment, without warning symptoms or signs. If peptic ulceration is suspected or confirmed, or if gastrointestinal bleeding occurs, diclofenac sodium should be discontinued, appropriate treatment instituted and the patient closely monitored.

Diclofenac sodium is not recommended for routine use with other NSAIDs because of the potential for additive side effects.

Pregnancy and Lactation: Diclofenac sodium readily crosses the placental barrier. The safety in pregnancy and lactation has not been established and its use is therefore not recommended. It should only be used during pregnancy for the most compelling reasons, and then only at the lowest effective dose. As with other prostaglandin inhibitors, this applies particularly to the last 3 months of pregnancy, because of the possibility of uterine inertia and/or premature closing of the ductus arteriosus.

The highest diclofenac level observed in the breast milk of 6 patients receiving oral diclofenac sodium doses of 3×50 mg day 1, followed by 2×50 mg day 2, was smaller than 5 ng/g. By extrapolation, an infant of 3 kg, consuming 500 g/day (with a maximum concentration of 5 ng/g) of breast milk, would receive less than 0.83 μg/kg/day of diclofenac sodium. On the other hand, in 1 patient on long-term treatment with diclofenac sodium 150 mg daily, a level of 100 ng/mL (100 ng/g) was measured in breast milk; by extrapolation, an infant of 3 kg consuming 500 g/day of breast milk would receive less than 17 μg/kg/day of diclofenac sodium.

Geriatrics: When administering diclofenac to the elderly, frail, and debilitated, special care is indicated. These patients appear to have a higher risk for development of adverse reactions. The dosage should be reduced to the lowest level that will provide control of symptoms adjusted when necessary and closely supervised.

Children: Diclofenac sodium is not recommended in children under 16 years of age. Safety and dosages for the pediatric age group have not been established.

Occupational Hazards: CNS: Headache, dizziness, lightheadedness, and mental confusion have been reported following therapy. Patients experiencing these symptoms should be made aware that these side effects may occur, and be cautioned against operating machinery or motor vehicles should they experience any of these.

Precautions: Diclofenac sodium should not be used concomitantly with diclofenac potassium since both exist in plasma as the same active organic ion.

Gastrointestinal: If, during therapy, peptic ulceration is suspected or confirmed, or if gastrointestinal bleeding or perforation occurs, diclofenac sodium should be withdrawn immediately. Appropriate treatment should be instituted and the patient should be closely monitored.

There is no definitive evidence that the concomitant administration of histamine H_2-receptor antagonists and/or antacids will either prevent the occurrence of gastrointestinal side effects or allow continuation of diclofenac sodium therapy when and if these adverse reactions appear.

Hematology: Caution should be exercised in patients with a history of blood dyscrasias or coagulation disorders since drugs inhibiting prostaglandin biosynthesis do interfere with platelet function to some degree (see Adverse Effects).

Patients on long-term diclofenac sodium treatment should have their hemopoietic system evaluated periodically. Bone marrow functional abnormalities, although rare, could have severe consequences. Periodic hematologic examinations (CBC and blood film examination) can detect anemias or blood

Voltaren (cont'd)

dyscrasias secondary to possible gastrointestinal tract or bone marrow toxicity.

Fluid and Electrolyte Balance: As with many other nonsteroidal anti-inflammatory drugs (NSAIDs), fluid retention and edema have been reported; therefore the possibility of precipitating congestive heart failure in elderly patients or those with compromised cardiac function should be borne in mind. Diclofenac sodium should be used with caution in patients with cardiac decompensation, hypertension, renal diseases and in those recovering from surgical operations under general anesthesia and other conditions predisposing to fluid retention.

There is a risk of hyperkalemia with NSAID treatment. Patients most at risk are: the elderly, those having conditions such as diabetes mellitus or renal failure, or those receiving concomitant therapy with ß-adrenergic blockers, angiotensin converting enzyme inhibitors or some diuretics. Serum electrolytes should be monitored periodically during long-term therapy, especially in those patients at risk.

Renal Function: As with other NSAIDs, long-term administration of diclofenac sodium to animals has resulted in renal papillary necrosis and other abnormal renal pathology. In humans there have been reports of acute interstitial nephritis with hematuria, proteinuria, and occasionally nephrotic syndrome.

In patients with prerenal conditions leading to reduction in renal blood flow or blood volume, renal prostaglandins have a supportive role in the maintenance of renal perfusion. Administration of NSAIDS may precipitate overt renal decompensation due to a dose-dependent reduction in prostaglandin formation. Patients at greatest risk are those with impaired renal function, heart failure, liver dysfunction, those taking diuretics, and the elderly. Recovery to the pretreatment state usually follows discontinuation of NSAID therapy.

Diclofenac sodium and its metabolites are eliminated primarily (60%) by the kidneys; therefore, the drug should be used with great caution in patients with impaired renal function (see Pharmacology). In these cases lower doses of diclofenac should be considered. Urine output, serum urea, and serum creatinine should be carefully monitored.

During long-term therapy, kidney function should be monitored periodically.

Hepatic Function: As with other NSAIDs, borderline elevations of one or more liver tests may occur. These abnormalities may progress, may remain essentially unchanged, or may be transient with continued therapy. Patients manifesting abnormal liver function test results, or signs or symptoms that suggest liver dysfunction, should be evaluated for evidence of progression to a more severe hepatic reaction, while on therapy with diclofenac sodium. Severe hepatic reactions including jaundice and cases of fatal hepatitis have been reported with this drug as with other NSAIDs. If abnormal liver function test results persist or worsen, or if systemic manifestations or clinical signs consistent with liver disease develop, discontinue diclofenac sodium treatment. Liver function should be monitored during long-term treatment with this drug. Minimize hepatic injury risk by informing patients of hepatotoxicity symptoms. Patients will then be alerted that nausea, fatigue, lethargy, pruritus, jaundice, right upper quadrant tenderness and "flu-like" symptoms, are signs of possible liver injury.

If this drug is to be used in the presence of impaired liver function, it must be done under strict observation. Caution is called for when using diclofenac sodium in patients with hepatic porphyria, since diclofenac sodium may trigger an attack.

Infection: The anti-inflammatory, antipyretic, and analgesic effects of diclofenac sodium may mask the usual signs of infection. Physicians should be alert to the development of infection in patients receiving the drug.

Ophthalmology: Blurred and/or diminished vision has been reported with the use of diclofenac sodium and with other NSAIDs. If such symptoms develop, this drug should be discontinued and an ophthalmologic examination performed. Ophthalmic examination should be carried out at periodic intervals in any patient receiving this drug for an extended period of time.

Hypersensitivity: As with other NSAIDs, allergic reactions, including anaphylactic/anaphylactoid reactions, can occur without prior exposure to drug. Careful questioning for patient history of asthma, nasal polyps, urticaria, and hypotension associated with NSAIDs is important before starting therapy.

Drug Interactions: ASA: Serum levels of diclofenac may be reduced when the two drugs are taken simultaneously. The bioavailability of ASA is reduced by the presence of diclofenac. Although these pharmacokinetic interactions do not appear to be clinically relevant, there is no proven advantage in using these two medications together.

Digoxin: Diclofenac may increase the plasma concentration of digoxin. Dosage adjustment may be required.

Lithium: Lithium plasma concentrations will increase when administered concomitantly with diclofenac (which affects lithium renal clearance). Dosage adjustment of lithium may be required.

Oral hypoglycemic drugs: Pharmacodynamic studies have shown no potentiation of effect with concurrent administration with diclofenac; however, there are isolated reports of both hypoglycemic and hyperglycemic effects in the presence of diclofenac, which necessitated changes in the dosage of hypoglycemic agents.

Anticoagulants: Although clinical investigations would appear to indicate that diclofenac has no influence on the effect of anticoagulants, there have been isolated reports of an increased risk of hemorrhage with the combined use of diclofenac and acenocoumarol anticoagulant therapy. Special caution is therefore recommended and frequent laboratory tests should be performed to check that the desired response to the anticoagulant is being maintained. Although diclofenac, as with other NSAIDs, is an inhibitor of induced platelet aggregation in vitro and in vivo, it has little effect on spontaneous platelet aggregation at usual therapeutic dosages.

Diuretics: NSAIDs have been reported to decrease the activity of diuretics. Concomitant treatment with potassium-sparing diuretics may be associated with increased serum potassium, thus making it necessary to monitor levels.

Glucocorticoids: Concomitant administration may aggravate gastrointestinal side effects.

NSAIDs: Concurrent oral treatment with two or more NSAIDs may promote the occurrence of side effects (see Warnings).

Methotrexate: Caution should be exercised when NSAIDs are administered less than 24 hours before or after treatment with methotrexate. Elevated blood concentrations of methotrexate may occur, increasing toxicity.

Cyclosporine: Nephrotoxicity of cyclosporine may be increased because of the effect of NSAIDs on renal prostaglandins.

Quinolone antibacterials: There have been isolated reports of convulsions which may have been due to concomitant use of quinolones and NSAIDs.

Antihypertensive agents: Like other NSAIDs, diclofenac can reduce the antihypertensive effects of propranolol and other ß-blockers, as well as other antihypertensive agents.

Clinical Laboratory Tests: Diclofenac increases platelet aggregation time but does not affect bleeding time, plasma thrombin clotting time, plasma fibrinogen, or factors V and VII to XII. Statistically significant changes in prothrombin and partial thromboplastin times have been reported in normal volunteers. The mean changes were observed to be less than 1 second in both instances, and are unlikely to be clinically important.

Persistently abnormal or worsening renal, hepatic or hematological test values should be followed up carefully since they may be related to therapy.

Information to be Provided to the Patient. See Information for the Patient.

Adverse Effects: Gastrointestinal, dermatological and CNS adverse reactions are most commonly seen. The most severe gastrointestinal adverse reactions observed were ulceration and bleeding while the most severe dermatological albeit rare reactions observed were erythema multiforme (Stevens-Johnson syndrome and Lyell's syndrome). Fatalities have occurred on occasion, particularly in the elderly.

Adverse reactions reported in clinical trials and spontaneous reports are summarized below.

Frequency estimate: Frequent >10%, Occasional >1-10%, Rare >0.001-1%, isolated cases <0.001%.

Gastrointestinal: Occasional: epigastric, gastric, or abdominal pain, abdominal cramps, nausea, dyspepsia, anorexia, diarrhea, vomiting, flatulence. Rare: gastrointestinal bleeding (bloody diarrhea, melena, hematemesis) gastric and intestinal ulcerations with or without bleeding or perforation. Isolated: lower gut disorders (e.g., nonspecific hemorrhagic colitis and exacerbation of ulcerative colitis or Crohn's disease), diaphragm-like intestinal strictures, hyperacidity, stomatitis, glossitis, coated tongue, esophageal lesions, constipation, pancreatitis.

CNS: Occasional: dizziness, headache, vertigo. Rare: drowsiness, malaise, impaired concentration, tiredness. Isolated: sensory disturbances including paresthesia, memory disturbance, disorientation, insomnia, irritability, convulsions, depression, anxiety, nightmares, tremor, psychotic reactions, aseptic meningitis.

Special Senses: Isolated: vision disturbances (blurred vision, diplopia), impaired hearing, tinnitus, taste alteration disorders.

Cardiovascular: Rare: palpitation, angina, arrhythmias. Isolated: exacerbation of cardiac failure, hypertension.

Dermatologic: Occasional: rash, pruritus. Rare: urticaria. Isolated: bullous eruption, erythema, eczema, erythema multiforme, Stevens-Johnson syndrome, Lyell's syndrome (toxic epidermal necrolysis), erythroderma (exfoliative dermatitis), loss of hair, photosensitivity reactions, purpura including allergic purpura.

Renal System: Rare: edema (facial, general, peripheral). Isolated: acute renal failure, nephrotic syndrome, urinary abnormalities (e.g., hematuria and proteinuria), interstitial nephritis, papillary necrosis.

Hematologic: Isolated: thrombocytopenia, leukopenia, agranulocytosis, hemolytic anemia, aplastic anemia, anemia secondary to gastrointestinal bleeding.

Hepatic: Occasional: elevations (≥3 times the upper normal limit) of serum aminotransferase enzymes (AST, ALT). Rare: liver function disorders including hepatitis with or without jaundice. Isolated: fulminant hepatitis.

Hypersensitivity: Rare: hypersensitivity reactions such as asthma in patients sensitive to ASA e.g., bronchospasm; anaphylactic/anaphylactoid systemic reactions including hypotension. Isolated: vasculitis, pneumonitis.

Other: Administration of the suppositories may occasionally give rise to local irritation, rarely local bleeding and exacerbation of hemorrhoids.

Overdose: Symptoms and Treatment: There is no specific antidote. In cases of overdosage, absorption should be prevented as soon as possible by the induction of vomiting, gastric lavage or treatment with activated charcoal. Supportive and symptomatic treatment should be given for complications such as hypotension, renal failure, convulsions, gastrointestinal irritation and respiratory depression. Measures to accelerate elimination (forced diuresis, hemoperfusion, dialysis) may be considered, but may be of limited use because of the high protein-binding and extensive metabolism.

Dosage: Voltaren Tablets: In rheumatoid arthritic patients, treatment should be initiated with 75 to 150 mg/day in 3 divided doses, depending on the severity of the condition. For maintenance, the dose should be reduced to the minimum amount that will provide continuous control of symptoms, usually 75 to 100 mg daily in 3 divided doses.

In osteoarthritic patients, the starting and maintenance dose is usually 75 mg/day in 3 divided doses. The dose should be adjusted individually to the minimum dose that will provide control of symptoms.

The maximum recommended daily dose is 150 mg.

Diclofenac sodium should be taken with food and the tablets should be swallowed whole.

Voltaren SR Tablets: Treatment should be initiated and individual titration carried out using Voltaren enteric coated tablets.

Patients with rheumatoid arthritis or osteoarthritis on a maintenance dose of 75 mg per day may be changed to a once daily dose of Voltaren SR 75 mg administered morning or evening.

Patients on a maintenance dose of 100 mg/day may be changed to a once-daily dose of Voltaren SR 100 mg tablets, administered morning or evening.

Patients on a maintenance dose of 150 mg per day may be changed to a twice daily dose of one Voltaren SR 75 mg tablet administered morning and evening.

The maximum daily dose of Voltaren should not exceed 150 mg.

Voltaren SR tablets should be swallowed whole with liquid preferably at mealtime.

Voltaren Suppositories: 50 or 100 mg, may be given as substitute for the last of the 3 oral daily doses, to a total daily dose not greater than 150 mg.

Information for the Patient: See Blue Section—Information for the Patient "Voltaren".

Supplied: Voltaren Tablets: 25 mg: Each yellow, round, slightly biconvex, enteric-coated tablet, printed VOLTAREN on one side and 25 on the other, contains: diclofenac sodium 25 mg. Nonmedicinal ingredients: black ink, castor oil derivatives, cellulose compound, colloidal silicon dioxide, cornstarch, iron oxides, lactose, magnesium stearate, polymethacrylate, povidone, polyethylene glycol, sodium starch glycolate, talc and titanium dioxide. Energy: 1.1 kJ (0.26 kcal). Sodium: <1 mmol (2.03 mg). Alcohol-, bisulfite-, gluten-, parabens- and tartrazine-free. Bottles of 100.

50 mg: Each light brown, round, slightly biconvex, enteric-coated tablet, printed VOLTAREN on one side and 50 on the other, contains: diclofenac sodium 50 mg. Nonmedicinal ingredients: black ink, castor oil derivatives, cellulose compound, colloidal silicon dioxide, cornstarch, iron oxides, lactose, magnesium stearate, polymethacrylate, povidone, polyethylene glycol, sodium starch glycolate, talc and titanium dioxide. Energy: 1.6 kJ (0.39 kcal). Sodium: <1 mmol (4.06 mg). Alcohol-, bisulfite-, gluten-, parabens- and tartrazine-free. Bottles of 100.

Voltaren SR Tablets: 75 mg: Each light pink, triangular, biconvex, film-coated, slow-release tablet, printed VOLTAREN on one side and SR/75 on the other, contains: diclofenac sodium 75 mg. Nonmedicinal ingredients: black ink, carnauba wax, cellulose compounds, cetyl alcohol, colloidal silicon dioxide, iron oxides, magnesium stearate, povidone, sugar, talc and titanium dioxide. Energy: 1.56 kJ (0.37 kcal). Sodium: <1 mmol (6.1 mg). Alcohol-, bisulfite-, gluten-, lactose-, parabens- and tartrazine-free. Bottles of 100 and 500.

100 mg: Each pink, round, biconvex, film-coated, slow-release tablet, printed VOLTAREN SR on one side and 100 on the other, contains: diclofenac sodium 100 mg. Nonmedicinal ingredients: black ink, carnauba wax, cellulose compounds, cetyl alcohol, colloidal silicon dioxide, iron oxides, magnesium stearate, povidone, sugar, talc and titanium dioxide. Energy: 2.04 kJ (0.49 kcal). Sodium: <1 mmol (8.13 mg). Alcohol-, bisulfite-, gluten-, lactose-, parabens- and tartrazine-free. Bottles of 100 and 250.

Voltaren Suppositories: 50 mg: Each yellowish-white, torpedo-shaped suppository, with smooth surface, contains: diclofenac sodium 50 mg. Nonmedicinal ingredients: semisynthetic glycerides. Sodium: <1 mmol (4.06 mg). Cartons of 30.

100 mg: Each yellowish-white, torpedo-shaped suppository, with smooth surface, contains: diclofenac sodium 100 mg. Nonmedicinal ingredients: semi-synthetic glycerides. Sodium: <1 mmol (8.13 mg). Cartons of 30.

Protect the tablets from heat (store below 30°C) and humidity. Protect suppositories from heat (store below 30°C).

(Shown in Product Recognition Section)

VOLTAREN OPHTHA® P

CIBA Vision

Diclofenac Sodium

Anti-inflammatory—Analgesic

Pharmacology: Diclofenac is a nonsteroidal anti-inflammatory drug with analgesic properties. The mode of action is not fully known, but it does not act through the pituitary-adrenal axis, even when given systemically. Diclofenac inhibits prostaglandin synthesis by interfering with the action of prostaglandin synthetase. Prostaglandins play a critical role in many inflammatory processes of the eye and appear to play a role in the miotic response during ocular surgery. Topically applied diclofenac significantly reduces prostaglandin-synthetase activity in inflamed eyes, but does not appear to suppress the immune system.

In clinical studies diclofenac has been found to inhibit miosis during cataract surgery, to reduce inflammation following surgical interventions, trauma and in other non-infected inflammatory conditions. Diclofenac reduced the frequency and intensity of cystoid macular edema when administered prophylactically to patients undergoing cataract lens extraction with intraocular lens implantation.

Epithelialization was not adversely affected or delayed. A slight and transient elevation in the intraocular pressure (IOP) has been observed in some patients, following surgery, even with the use of diclofenac.

In man, the drug promptly passed into the aqueous humor following the topical application of 3 to 16 drops of 0.1% diclofenac to the eye. Levels of unchanged diclofenac in the aqueous humor were highly variable, ranging from 10 to 505 ng/g. There were no detectable levels of drug in plasma, indicating that no measurable systemic absorption occurs following a single instillation of the ophthalmic drops.

Indications: For the following conditions of the eye: pre- and postoperative cover (e.g., for cataract surgery); non-infected chronic conjunctivitis, keratoconjunctivitis; non-infected post-traumatic conditions of the cornea and conjunctiva.

Contraindications: Hypersensitivity to diclofenac or any component.

Since there exists the potential for cross-sensitivity, diclofenac should not be used in patients in whom acute asthmatic attacks, urticaria, rhinitis or other allergic manifestations are precipitated by ASA or other nonsteroidal anti-inflammatory agents.

Warnings: *Pregnancy* and *Lactation:* The safety of diclofenac in pregnancy and lactation has not been established and its use is therefore not recommended in pregnant or lactating women, unless the potential benefit to the mother outweighs the possible risk to the child.

Children: The safety and dosage ranges of diclofenac have not been established in children under 16 years of age; therefore, it is not recommended for pediatric use.

Precautions: The anti-inflammatory and analgesic effects of diclofenac may mask signs of infection and physicians should be alert to the development of infection in patients receiving the drug.

During prolonged use, it is recommended that physicians conduct periodic examinations of the eye, including measurement of intraocular pressure. Soft contact lenses should not be worn during treatment.

A slight and transient elevation in the intraocular pressure (IOP) has been observed in some patients, following surgery, even with the use of diclofenac.

Adverse Effects: When instilled into the eye, diclofenac has been associated with a mild to moderate burning sensation in 5 to 15% of patients studied. This symptom was transient in nature and almost never necessitated discontinuation of treatment. In addition, there has been one report each of the following symptoms: sensitivity to light, bad taste, feeling of pressure and a stainable cornea. There have also been 2 reports of an allergic reaction. The incidence of these latter 5 symptoms was 0.2 to 0.3% of all patients studied.

Overdose: Symptoms and Treatment: There has been limited experience with diclofenac overdosage, even when given systemically. The risk of an acute toxic response is highly remote as a 5 mL bottle of the ophthalmic drops contains a total of only 5 mg diclofenac, equivalent to just 3% of the normal recommended oral adult dose.

Dosage: Surgical Cover in Cataract Procedures: Pre-operatively: instill 1 drop in the conjunctival sac up to 5 times during the 3 hours preceding surgery. Post-operatively: instill 1 drop in the conjunctival sac 15, 30 and 45 minutes following surgery, then 3 to 5 times daily, for as long as required.

Inflammatory Conditions such as conjunctivitis, keratoconjunctivitis, and corneal ulcers: instill 1 drop in the conjunctival sac 4 to 5 times daily, depending upon the severity of the disease. Eye swab for culture should be taken before inititation of therapy.

Concomitant Therapy: Diclofenac may, if necessary, be safely combined with an ophthalmic corticosteroid. In clinical studies, an antihistamine and an adrenergic vasoconstrictor have been used concomitantly with the product.

In the presence of infection or if there is a risk of infection, appropriate therapy (antibiotics) should be given concurrently with diclofenac ophthalmic drops.

In surgery, diclofenac has been combined with such standard pretreatment measures as mydriatics and topical antibiotics.

Note: To prevent the active substances from being washed out when additional ophthalmic medication is used, leave an interval of at least 5 minutes between each application.

Information for the Patient: See Blue Section—Information for the Patient "Voltaren Ophtha".

Supplied: Each mL of ophthalmic solution contains: diclofenac sodium 0.1%. Nonmedicinal ingredients: preserved multi-dose bottles: boric acid, cremophor EL, edetate disodium, sorbic acid and tromethamine; single dose units: boric acid, cremophor EL, purified water and tromethamine (TRIS). Dropper bottles (preserved with sorbic acid) of 2.5, 5 and 10 mL. Single dose units (unpreserved) of 0.3 mL.

VOLTAREN RAPIDE® P

Novartis Pharmaceuticals

Diclofenac Potassium

Anti-inflammatory—Analgesic

Pharmacology: Diclofenac potassium, the active substance of Voltaren Rapide is a nonsteroidal anti-inflammatory drug (NSAID) with analgesic and antipyretic properties. Diclofenac inhibits prostaglandin synthesis by interfering with the action of prostaglandin synthetase. This inhibitory effect may partially explain its actions. It is considered to be a peripherally acting analgesic.

Diclofenac potassium tablets have a rapid onset of action, making them particularly suitable for the treatment of acute painful inflammatory conditions.

Pharmacokinetics: Absorption: In humans, diclofenac can be detected in the plasma within 10 minutes of oral administration of diclofenac potassium tablets. Absorption is virtually complete. The area under the plasma curve (AUC) is dose proportional. A 50-mg tablet produces a mean peak plasma concentration of 3.8 μmol/L, 20 to 60 minutes post dose. The amount of diclofenac absorbed from diclofenac potassium is the same as that obtained from an equivalent diclofenac enteric-coated tablet dose. Since diclofenac undergoes extensive first-pass metabolism, only half of an orally administered dose is systemically available. The rate and extent of absorption of diclofenac are insignificantly affected (slightly delayed) when diclofenac potassium tablets are taken with food. When given in a regimen of 50 mg t.i.d. for 8 days, diclofenac potassium did not produce plasma accumulation of diclofenac.

Distribution: Diclofenac sodium is extensively bound (99%) to serum albumin. The apparent volume of distribution is 0.12 to 0.17 L/kg. Single-dose (oral or i.m.) studies in rheumatoid patients with joint effusions have shown that diclofenac is distributed to the synovial fluid, where T_{max} occurs 2 to 4 hours after plasma T_{max}. Synovial fluid concentrations exceed plasma levels within 4 to 6 hours of administration. This elevation above plasma concentrations can be maintained for up to 12 hours. The synovial fluid elimination half-life is at least 3 times greater than that for plasma.

Biotransformation: The potassium salt of diclofenac yields the same active organic anion produced by the sodium salt found in diclofenac enteric coated tablets. Therefore, the fate of the systemically available anion is the same for both formulations.

Diclofenac undergoes single and multiple hydroxylation and methoxylation, producing 3'-, 4'-, 5-hydroxy, 4'-5-hydroxy and 3'-hydroxy-4'-methoxy derivatives of diclofenac. These phenolic metabolites are largely inactive, and (along with the parent compound) are mostly converted to glucuronide conjugates.

Elimination: Plasma clearance of diclofenac is 263±56 mL/min. The mean terminal drug half-life in plasma is 1.8 hours after oral doses. In humans, about 60% of the drug and its metabolites are eliminated in the urine and the balance through the bile in the feces. About 1% of an oral dose is excreted unchanged in urine.

Special Populations: Renal Impairment: A single study using the sodium salt in patients with varying degrees of renal dysfunction (creatinine clearance rates ranging from 3 to 42 mL/min), suggested that moderate renal impairment may not affect the elimination rate of unchanged diclofenac. It may reduce the elimination rate of metabolites. At a creatinine clearance of <10 mL/min, theoretical steady-state plasma levels of metabolites are about 4 times higher than those in normal subjects. The metabolites are ultimately cleared through the bile. Although no accumulation of pharmacologically active substance seems to occur, caution is advised while administering diclofenac to patients with imparied kidney function.

Hepatic Impairment: The kinetics and metabolism of diclofenac in 10 patients with impaired hepatic function (chronic hepatitis and nondecompensated cirrhosis) receiving a single 100 mg oral dose of diclofenac sodium were similar to patients without liver disease.

Geriatrics: No relevant age-dependant differences in the absorption, metabolism, or excretion of diclofenac have been observed.

Indications: For the short-term treatment of acute, mild to moderately severe pain that may be accompanied by inflammation, in conditions such as: musculoskeletal and/or soft tissue trauma including sprains, postoperative pain following dental extraction, episiotomy or dysmenorrhea.

Contraindications: Should not be used in patients with active, or recent history of, inflammatory diseases of the gastrointestinal tract such as: peptic ulcer, gastritis, regional enteritis, ulcerative colitis.

Diclofenac potassium is contraindicated in patients with known or suspected hypersensitivity to diclofenac. Since cross-sensitivity has been demonstrated, diclofenac potassium should not be given to patients in whom ASA or other NSAIDs have induced asthma, rhinitis, urticaria or other allergic manifestations. Fatal anaphylactoid reactions have occurred in such individuals.

Warnings: Peptic ulceration, perforation and gastrointestinal bleeding, sometimes severe and occasionally fatal, in either the presence or absence of previous symptoms, have been

Voltaren Rapide (cont'd)

known to occur during therapy with NSAIDs including diclofenac.

Diclofenac potassium should be given under close medical supervision to patients prone to gastrointestinal tract irritation, particularly those with a history of peptic ulcer, melena, diverticulosis or other inflammatory disease of the gastrointestinal tract (such as ulcerative colitis or Crohn's disease). In these cases the physician must weigh the benefits of treatment against the possible hazards (see Contraindications and Adverse Effects).

Patients should be instructed to contact their physician immediately if they experience symptoms or signs suggestive of peptic ulceration or gastrointestinal bleeding. These reactions can occur at any time during treatment, without warning symptoms or signs. If peptic ulceration is suspected or confirmed, or if gastrointestinal bleeding occurs, diclofenac potassium should be discontinued, appropriate treatment instituted and the patient closely monitored.

Diclofenac potassium is not recommended for routine use with other NSAIDs because of the potential for additive side effects.

Pregnancy: Diclofenac readily crosses the placental barrier and should only be used during pregnancy for the most compelling reasons and then only at the lowest effective dose. As with other prostaglandin inhibitors, this applies particularly to the last 3 months of pregnancy because of the possibility of uterine inertia and/or premature closing of the ductus arteriosus. Diclofenac potassium is not recommended for use in obstetrical analgesia, including preoperative medication, because of the known effects of NSAIDs on uterine contraction and fetal circulation.

Lactation: The administration of diclofenac potassium is not recommended during lactation, since its safety has not been established in this condition. The maximum diclofenac levels measured in the breast milk of 6 patients receiving oral doses of diclofenac sodium of 3×50 mg on day 1, followed by 2×50 mg on day 2, were smaller than 5 ng/g. In another patient on long-term treatment with diclofenac 150 mg daily, a level of 100 ng/g was measured. Extrapolating these 2 concentration estimates, a 3-kg infant, consuming 500 g/day of breast milk, would receive at most 0.83 to 17 μg/kg/day of diclofenac.

Elderly, Frail and Debilitated: When administering diclofenac potassium to the elderly, frail and debilitated, special care is indicated. These patients appear to have a higher risk for development of adverse reactions. The dosage should be reduced to the lowest level providing control of symptoms, adjusted when necessary and closely supervised.

Children: Diclofenac potassium is not recommended in children under 16 years of age. Safety and dosages for the pediatric age group have not been established.

CNS: Headache, dizziness, lightheadedness and mental confusion have been reported following therapy with diclofenac. Patients should be made aware that these side effects may occur, and be cautioned against operating machinery or motor vehicles should they experience any of these.

Precautions: Diclofenac potassium should not be used concomitantly with diclofenac sodium since both exist in plasma as the same active organic anion.

Gastrointestinal: If, during therapy, peptic ulcer is suspected or confirmed, or if gastrointestinal bleeding or perforation occurs, diclofenac potassium should be withdrawn immediately. Appropriate treatment should be instituted, and the patient should be monitored closely.

There is no definitive evidence that concomitant administration of histamine H_2-receptor antagonists and/or antacids will either prevent the occurrence of gastrointestinal side effects, or allow the continuation of diclofenac potassium therapy should adverse gastrointestinal reactions appear.

Hematology: Caution should be exercised in patients with a history of blood dyscrasias or coagulation disorders since drugs inhibiting prostaglandin biosynthesis interfere with platelet function to some degree (see Adverse Effects). When patients are on long-term treatment with diclofenac, a periodic evaluation of their hemopoietic system is advised. Bone marrow functional abnormalities, although rare, could have severe consequences. Periodic hematologic examinations (CBC and blood film examination) can detect anemias or blood dyscrasias secondary to possible gastrointestinal tract or bone marrow toxicity. However, diclofenac potassium is indicated for short-term treatment only.

Fluid and Electrolyte Balance: As with many other NSAIDs, fluid retention and edema have been reported; therefore, the possibility of precipitating congestive heart failure in elderly patients or those with compromised cardiac function should be borne in mind. Diclofenac potassium should be used with caution in patients with cardiac decompensation, hypertension, renal diseases and in those recovering from surgical operations under general anesthesia and other conditions predisposing to fluid retention.

There is a risk of hyperkalemia with NSAID treatment. Patients most at risk are: the elderly, those having conditions such as diabetes mellitus or renal failure, or those receiving concomitant therapy with beta-adrenergic blockers, angiotensin converting enzyme inhibitors or some diuretics. Serum electrolytes should be monitored periodically during long-term therapy, especially in those patients at risk. Diclofenac potassium is indicated for short-term therapy only.

Renal Function: As with other NSAIDs, long-term administration of diclofenac to animals has resulted in renal papillary necrosis and other abnormal renal pathology. In humans there have been reports of acute interstitial nephritis with hematuria, proteinuria and occasionally nephrotic syndrome.

In patients with prerenal conditions leading to reduction in renal blood flow or blood volume, renal prostaglandins have a supportive role in the maintenance of renal perfusion. Administration of NSAIDs may precipitate overt renal decompensation due to a dose-dependent reduction in prostaglandin formation. Patients at greatest risk are those with impaired renal function, heart failure, liver dysfunction, those taking diuretics, and the elderly. Recovery to the pretreatment state usually follows discontinuation of NSAID therapy.

Diclofenac and its metabolites are eliminated primarily (60%) by the kidneys; therefore, the drug should be used with great caution in patients with impaired renal function (see Pharmacology). In these cases lower doses of diclofenac potassium should be considered. Urine output, serum urea and serum creatinine should be carefully monitored.

Hepatic Function: As with other NSAIDs, borderline elevations of one or more liver tests may occur. These abnormalities may progress, may remain essentially unchanged or may be transient with continued therapy. Patients manifesting abnormal liver function test results, or signs or symptoms that suggest liver dysfunction, should be evaluated for evidence of progression to a more severe hepatic reaction while on therapy with diclofenac potassium. Severe hepatic reactions including jaundice and cases of fatal hepatitis have been reported with diclofenac as with other NSAIDs. The incidence of transaminase elevations during long-term treatment is similar to that for diclofenac sodium. If abnormal liver function test results persist or worsen, or if systemic manifestations or clinical signs consistent with liver disease develop, discontinue diclofenac potassium treatment. Minimize hepatic injury risk by informing patients of hepatotoxicity symptoms. Patients will then be alerted that nausea, fatigue, lethargy, pruritus, jaundice, right upper quadrant tenderness and "flu-like" symptoms, are signs of possible liver injury.

If this drug is to be used in the presence of impaired liver function, it must be done under strict observation. Caution is called for when using diclofenac potassium in patients with hepatic porphyria, since diclofenac potassium may trigger an attack.

Infection: The anti-inflammatory, antipyretic and analgesic effects of diclofenac potassium may mask the usual signs of infection. Physicians should be alert to the development of infection in patients receiving the drug.

Ophthalmology: Blurred and/or diminished vision has been reported with the use of diclofenac potassium and with other NSAIDs. If such symptoms develop, this drug should be discontinued and an ophthalmologic examination performed.

Hypersensitivity Reactions: As with other NSAIDs, allergic reactions, including anaphylactic/anaphylactoid reactions, can occur without prior exposure to the drug. Careful questioning for patient history of asthma, nasal polyps, urticaria and hypotension associated with NSAIDs is important before starting therapy.

Drug Interactions: ASA: Serum levels of diclofenac may be reduced when the 2 drugs are taken simultaneously. The bioavailability of ASA is reduced by the presence of diclofenac. Although these pharmacokinetic interactions do not appear to be clinically relevant, there is no proven advantage in using these 2 medications together.

Digoxin: Diclofenac may increase the plasma concentration of digoxin. Dosage adjustment may be required.

Lithium: Plasma concentrations will increase when administered concomitantly with diclofenac (which affects lithium renal clearance). Dosage adjustment of lithium may be required.

Oral Hypoglycemic Drugs: Pharmacodynamic studies have shown no potentiation of effect with concurrent administration with diclofenac; however there are isolated reports of both hypoglycemic and hyperglycemic effects in the presence of diclofenac, which necessitated changes in the dosage of hypoglycemic agents.

Anticoagulants: Although clinical investigations would appear to indicate that diclofenac has no influence on the effect of anticoagulants, there have been isolated reports of an increased risk of hemorrhage with the combined use of diclofenac and acenocoumarol anticoagulant therapy. Special caution is therefore recommended and frequent laboratory tests should be performed to check that the desired response to the anticoagulant is being maintained. Although diclofenac, as with other NSAIDs, is an inhibitor of induced platelet aggregation in vitro and in vivo, it has little effect on spontaneous platelet aggregation at usual therapeutic dosages.

Diuretics: NSAIDs have been reported to decrease the activity of diuretics. Concomitant treatment with potassium-sparing diuretics may be associated with increased serum potassium, thus making it necessary to monitor levels.

Glucocorticoids: Concomitant administration may aggravate gastrointestinal side effects.

NSAIDs: Concurrent oral treatment with 2 or more NSAIDs may promote the occurrence of side effects (see Warnings).

Methotrexate: Caution should be exercised when NSAIDs are administered less than 24 hours before or after treatment with methotrexate. Elevated blood concentrations of methotrexate may occur, increasing toxicity.

Cyclosporin: Nephrotoxicity of this compound may be increased because of the effect of NSAIDs on renal prostaglandins.

Quinolone Antibacterials: There have been isolated reports of convulsions which may have been due to concomitant use of quinolones and NSAIDs.

Antihypertensive Agents: Like other NSAIDs, diclofenac can reduce the antihypertensive effects of propranolol and other β-blockers, as well as other antihypertensive agents.

Clinical Laboratory Tests: Diclofenac increases platelet aggregation time but does not affect bleeding time, plasma thrombin clotting time, plasma fibrinogen, or factors V and VII to XII. Statistically significant changes in prothrombin and partial thromboplastin times have been reported in normal volunteers. The mean changes were observed to be less than 1 second in both instances and are unlikely to be clinically important.

Persistently abnormal or worsening renal, hepatic or hematological test values should be followed up carefully since they may be related to therapy.

Adverse Effects: Although not all adverse drug reactions have been reported with diclofenac potassium, the types of adverse drug reactions are expected to be similar to those of diclofenac sodium since both formulations exist in the plasma as the same active organic anion.

Gastrointestinal, dermatological and CNS adverse reactions are the most commonly seen with diclofenac. The most severe gastrointestinal adverse reactions are ulceration and bleeding, while the most severe dermatological, albeit rare, reaction observed with diclofenac is erythema multiforme (Stevens-Johnson syndrome and Lyell's syndrome); fatalities have occurred on occasion, particularly in the elderly.

Adverse reactions reported in clinical trials and spontaneous reports with diclofenac dosage forms are summarized below (frequency estimate: frequent >10%, occasional >1-10%, rare >0.001-1%, isolated cases <0.001%):

Gastrointestinal: Occasional: epigastric, gastric, or abdominal pain, abdominal cramps, nausea, dyspepsia, anorexia, diarrhea, vomiting, flatulence. Rare: gastrointestinal bleeding (bloody diarrhea, melena, hematemesis) gastric and intestinal ulcerations with or without bleeding or perforation. Isolated: lower gut disorders (e.g., nonspecific hemorrhagic colitis and exacerbation of ulcerative colitis or Crohn's disease), diaphragm-like intestinal strictures, hyperacidity, stomatitis, glossitis, coated tongue, esophageal lesions, constipation, pancreatitis.

CNS: Occasional: dizziness, headache, vertigo. Rare: drowsiness, malaise, impaired concentration, tiredness. Isolated:

sensory disturbances including paresthesia, memory disturbance, disorientation, insomnia, irritability, convulsions, depression, anxiety, nightmares, tremor, psychotic reactions, aseptic meningitis.

Special Senses: Isolated: vision disturbances (blurred vision, diplopia), impaired hearing, tinnitus, taste alteration disorders.

Cardiovascular: Rare: palpitation, angina, arrhythmias. Isolated: exacerbation of cardiac failure, hypertension.

Dermatologic: Occasional: rash, pruritus. Rare: urticaria. Isolated: bullous eruption, erythema, eczema, erythema multiforme, Stevens-Johnson syndrome, Lyell's syndrome (toxic epidermal necrolysis), erythroderma (exfoliative dermatitis), loss of hair, photosensitivity reactions, purpura including allergic purpura.

Renal: Rare: edema (facial, general, peripheral). Isolated: acute renal failure, nephrotic syndrome, urinary abnormalities (e.g., hematuria and proteinuria), interstitial nephritis, papillary necrosis.

Hematologic: Isolated: thrombocytopenia, leukopenia, agranulocytosis, hemolytic anemia, aplastic anemia, anemia secondary to gastrointestinal bleeding.

Hepatic: Occasional: elevations ($\geq$3 times the upper normal limit) of serum aminotransferase enzymes (AST, ALT). Rare: liver function disorders including hepatitis with or without jaundice. Isolated: fulminant hepatitis.

Hypersensitivity: Rare: hypersensitivity reactions such as asthma in patients sensitive to ASA, e.g., bronchospasm; anaphylactic/anaphylactoid systemic reactions including hypotension. Isolated: vasculitis, pneumonitis.

Other: Administration of the suppositories may occasionally give rise to local irritation, rarely local bleeding and exacerbation of hemorrhoids.

Overdose: Symptoms and Treatment: There is no specific antidote for diclofenac potassium. In an overdose, absorption should be prevented as soon as possible by the induction of vomiting, gastric lavage or treatment with activated charcoal. Supportive and symptomatic treatment should be given for complications such as hypotension, renal failure, convulsions, gastrointestinal irritation and respiratory depression. Measures to accelerate elimination (forced diuresis, hemoperfusion, dialysis) may be considered, but may be of limited value because of the high protein-binding and extensive metabolism.

Dosage: Diclofenac potassium is indicated for short-term treatment only, i.e., for a maximum of a few weeks only.

Diclofenac potassium should be taken with food.

The recommended daily dose for diclofenac potassium is 50 mg every 6 to 8 hours as required for a total daily maximum amount of 150 mg. For primary dysmenorrhea, treatment may be initiated with a loading dose of 100 mg, followed by 50 mg every 6 to 8 hours, when required. When a loading dose is necessary, the first-day maximum total amount is 200 mg.

Patients should be maintained on the lowest effective dose.

Diclofenac potassium is not recommended for use in patients under 16 years of age.

Lower doses of diclofenac potassium should be considered in patients with impaired renal function (see Precautions).

In the elderly, frail and debilitated, the dosage should be reduced to the lowest level providing control of symptoms, and adjusted when necessary (see Precautions).

Information for the Patient: See Blue Section—Information for the Patient "Voltaren Rapide".

Supplied: Each reddish-brown, round, biconvex, sugar-coated tablet, VOLTAREN printed in white on one side and RAPIDE 50 on the other, contains: diclofenac potassium 50 mg. Nonmedicinal ingredients: carnauba wax, cellulose, colloidal silicon dioxide, cornstarch, ferric oxide, magnesium stearate, polyethylene glycol, povidone, sodium carboxymethyl starch, sucrose, talc, titanium dioxide, tribasic calcium phosphate and white ink. Bottles of 100 or 500. Protect from heat (store below 30°C) and humidity.

Did you know that the *CPS* provides information on certain drugs or drug classes in the shaded monographs in the WHITE SECTION? Check out the index at the beginning of the section.

VōSoL®
VōSoL® HC ℞

Carter Horner

Benzethonium Chloride Compound

Otitis Therapy

Indications: VōSoL: For the treatment and prevention of otitis externa.

VōSoL HC: Treatment of otitis externa complicated by severe inflammation or when associated with seborrheic dermatitis, allergic eczema or other non-infectious conditions.

Contraindications: Sensitivity to any of the components. Perforated tympanic membranes are frequently considered a contraindication to the use of external ear canal medication.

VōSoL HC is contraindicated in the presence of pre-existing tuberculosis, fungal and viral lesions and acute purulent untreated infections.

Precautions: VōSoL HC: *Pregnancy:* As the safety of topical steroids during pregnancy has not been confirmed, they should not be used for an extended period during pregnancy.

Systemic adverse effects may occur with extensive use of steroids.

Dosage: Remove cerumen and debris. Instill 2 to 5 drops 3 or 4 times daily. To promote continuous contact, a saturated wick may be used for the first 24 to 48 hours to initiate therapy. For prophylaxis, 2 drops in each ear morning and evening.

Supplied: VōSoL Otic Solution: Each mL contains: 1, 2-propanediol diacetate 3%, acetic acid 2% and benzethonium chloride 0.02%. Nonmedicinal ingredients: propylene glycol and sodium acetate. Gluten- and tartrazine-free. Measured drop, safety tip plastic dropper bottles of 15 mL.

VōSoL HC: Each mL contains: 1, 2-propanediol diacetate 3%, acetic acid 2%, benzethonium chloride 0.02% and hydrocortisone 1%. Nonmedicinal ingredients: citric acid, propylene glycol and sodium acetate. Gluten- and tartrazine-free. Measured drop, safety tip plastic dropper bottles of 10 mL.

VUMON® PARENTERAL ℞

Bristol

Teniposide

Antineoplastic

Pharmacology: Teniposide is a semi-synthetic derivative of podophyllotoxin.

In vitro, teniposide exerts a powerful cytostatic effect by first arresting cells in metaphase. Its main effect, however, is preventing cells from entering mitosis (arrest of G2 phase of cell cycle) within 1 to 2 hours after drug addition. At higher concentrations, a third effect can be observed, disintegration of part of interphase cells (those preparing for mitosis). Unlike other podophyllum compounds and spindle poisons such as colchicine, the effect of teniposide on fibroblasts is virtually irreversible.

Teniposide produces a dose dependent inhibition of thymidine uptake after 2.5 hours. This, however, is not accompanied by a comparable reduction in DNA synthesis.

An i.v. dose of 67 to 90 mg/m² given over ½ to 1 hour in man, showed the mean volume of distribution to be 28.45% of body weight. An i.v. dose of 67 mg/m² administered over ½ hour produced a triexponential plasma decay with a terminal phase half-life of 21.2 hours in adults and 9.6 hours in children. Urinary recovery was 44.45% after 72 hours of which 21.3% was unchanged drug. Recovery in feces was variable (0 to 10.05%) over a 3-day period. Studies in rats show the major route of excretion to be the bile.

Indications: Neuroblastoma: Second-line single agent or combination therapy in patients who have not responded or who have relapsed on other chemotherapeutic regimens.

Non-Hodgkin's Lymphoma: Second-line combination or as a single agent in patients who are or have become refractory to other chemotherapeutic regimens.

Acute Lymphocytic Leukemia: Second-line combination therapy with cytosine arabinoside in patients who have not responded or relapsed on other chemotherapeutic regimens.

Contraindications: Teniposide should not be given to individuals who have demonstrated a previous hypersensitivity to it. Also, it is contraindicated in patients having severe leukopenia, thrombocytopenia and severe hepatic and/or renal impairment.

Warnings: Teniposide is a potent drug and should be used only by physicians experienced with cancer chemotherapeutic drugs (see Precautions). Blood counts as well as renal and hepatic function tests must be done regularly. Discontinue the drug if abnormal depression of bone marrow or abnormal renal or hepatic function is seen.

Teniposide should be given cautiously to individuals with pre-existing hepatic and/or renal impairment.

Bacterial infection must be brought under control before therapy due to the risk of septicemia. Near fatal anaphylactic reactions have occurred following teniposide administration.

Pregnancy: Use in pregnancy is not recommended.

Conception Control: It is also recommended that patients with childbearing or conceiving potential, who are receiving teniposide, exercise adequate conception control.

Although embryotoxic and teratogenic effects have not been seen in pregnant rats given teniposide, the possibility of these effects cannot be ruled out. Teniposide has caused reduced spermiogenesis in monkeys and dogs, and reduced testicular and ovarian weights in dogs.

As with any potent antineoplastic drug, the benefit to patient versus the risk of toxicity must be carefully weighed. Chronic toxicity studies in dogs have shown teniposide to have an oncogenetic potential.

Precautions: Teniposide should be administered by individuals experienced in the use of antineoplastic therapy.

Since leukopenia and thrombocytopenia have been reported, platelets and white blood cell counts should be performed prior to each subsequent cycle.

A white blood cell count of between 2 000 to 3 000 cells/mm³ suggests that the dose should be reduced by 50%. Platelet counts between 75 000 to 100 000 cells/mm³ require a dosage reduction of 50%. Should the white blood cell count fall below 2 000 cells/mm³ or the platelet count fall below 75 000 cells/mm³ consideration should be given to discontinuation of treatment until bone marrow recovery occurs. Leukopenia and thrombocytopenia are at their lowest level between 7 and 14 days after initial therapy. Bone marrow recovery requires 2 to 3 weeks.

Liver and renal function should be regularly monitored.

Care should be taken to ensure infusions are given i.v. with indwelling catheter in proper position prior to infusion, as extravasation necrosis and/or thrombophlebitis may result with improper administration.

Instances of hypotension have been reported during infusion. Therefore, vital signs should be monitored during first 30 minutes.

Adverse Effects: The most serious toxicity is bone marrow depression, notably leukopenia and thrombocytopenia, which occurs 7 to 14 days after treatment.

The most frequently reported side effects were immunosuppression, alopecia and nausea and/or vomiting. Gastrointestinal: nausea and vomiting (11%), vomiting (10%), nausea (4%), anorexia (1%), diarrhea (1%), pain (<1%).

Skin: alopecia (31%), stomatitis (3%), skin (2%).

Hematopoietic System: leukopenia (39%), thrombocytopenia (32%), low hemoglobin (9%), neutropenia (8%), pancytopenia (3%), sepsis (2%) and granulocytopenia (1%).

Cardiac: hypotension (1%), tachycardia (1%), heart failure (1%), tachypnea (<1%), vascular collapse (<1%).

Hepatotoxicity: 2%.

Nephrotoxicity: 2%.

Miscellaneous: fever and/or chills (3%), oral ulceration (2%), anaphylaxis (1%), and the following less than one percent: cystitis, lethargy, flushing, burning sensation in mouth, oesophagitis, aphasia, confusion and agitation, microscopic hematuria, peripheral neuropathy and asthenia.

Overdose: Symptoms and Treatment: No overdosage occurred during clinical trials, but should it occur, symptomatic measures should be taken to sustain the patient through any period of toxicity that might occur. The anticipated complications would be hematotoxicity, nephrotoxicity, hepatotoxicity, and cardiotoxicity. Patients should be monitored for 3 to 4 weeks in case of delayed toxicity.

Dosage: Table I (see following page) is given to provide a guideline for dosage schedules in neuroblastoma, non-Hodgkin's lymphoma, and acute lymphocytic leukemia.

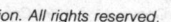

Vumon Parenteral (cont'd)

Doses should be adjusted according to individual patient variability and toxicity when employed as a single agent or in combination with other antineoplastic agents.

Teniposide has been employed in combinations with other antineoplastic agents as discussed in the medical literature. References are available from the manufacturer.

To avoid the possibility of hypotensive reactions, it should not be administered by bolus injection or rapid infusion.

Table I—Vumon Parenteral

Guidelines for Dosage Schedules

Indication	**Vumon Dose and Schedule**
Neuroblastoma	Single Agent: 130 to 180 mg/m²/day once weekly given in normal saline or 5% dextrose in water i.v. at a concentration of 0.2 mg/mL over a minimum of 30 minutes. Combination: 100 mg/m²/day every 21 days given in normal saline or 5% dextrose in water i.v. at a concentration of 0.2 mg/mL over a minimum of 30 minutes.
Non-Hodgkin's Lymphoma	Single Agent: The following regimens have been used: 30 mg/m²/day for 10 days given in normal saline or 5% dextrose in water i.v. at a concentration of 0.2 mg/mL over a minimum of 30 minutes. 30 mg/m²/day every 5 days given in normal saline or 5% dextrose in water i.v. at a concentration of 0.2 mg/mL over a minimum of 30 minutes. 50 to 100 mg/m²/day once weekly given in normal saline or 5% dextrose in water i.v. at a concentration of 0.2 mg/mL over a minimum of 30 minutes. Combination: 60 to 70 mg/m²/day once weekly given in normal saline or 5% dextrose in water i.v. at a concentration of 0.2 mg/mL over a minimum of 30 minutes.
Acute Lymphocytic Leukemia	Combination: 165 mg/m²/day twice weekly given in normal saline or 5% dextrose in water i.v. at a concentration of 0.2 mg/mL over a minimum of 30 minutes.

Preparation of I.V. Solutions: Add required dose of teniposide in normal saline or 5% dextrose in water at a concentration not exceeding 0.2 mg/mL. Contact with buffered aqueous solutions above pH 8 should be avoided. Reconstitution results in a clear, colorless solution which is stable for 4 hours at room temperature at concentrations of 0.1 to 0.2 mg/mL. Vumon mixed with normal saline or 5% dextrose in water should be administered immediately by the i.v. route over a period of not less than 30 minutes. It should not be mixed with other antineoplastic drugs.

Handling and Disposal: Preparation should be done in a vertical laminar flow hood (Biological Safety Cabinet—Class II).

Personnel preparing solutions should wear PVC gloves, safety glasses, disposable gowns, and masks.

All needles, syringes, vials and other materials which have come in contact with the drug should be segregated and incinerated at 1 000°C or more. Sealed containers may explode. Intact vials should be returned to the manufacturer for destruction. Proper precautions should be taken in packaging these materials for transport.

Personnel regularly involved in the preparation and handling of teniposide should have bi-annual blood examinations.

Supplied: Each 5 mL clear, glass ampul contains: teniposide 50 mg (10 mg/mL). Nonmedicinal ingredients: benzyl alcohol 3% w/v, ethanol, maleic acid, N.N. dimethylacetamide and polyoxyethylated castor oil.

W

WARFILONE® ℞

Frosst

Warfarin Sodium

Oral Anticoagulant

Indications: The prophylaxis and treatment of venous thrombosis and its extension, the treatment of atrial fibrillation with embolization, heart valve prosthesis and acute peripheral arterial embolism. Also in the prophylaxis and treatment of pulmonary embolism.

In acute myocardial infarction for patients with high risk factors for thromboembolic complications and as an adjunct in the treatment of coronary occlusion. It is also recommended as an adjunct in the treatment of transient cerebral ischemic attacks and cerebral embolism.

Contraindications: In any localized or general physical condition or personal circumstances in which the hazard of hemorrhage might be greater than the potential clinical benefits of anticoagulation, such as:

Pregnancy: Warfarin passes through the placental barrier and may cause fatal hemorrhage to the fetus in utero. Furthermore, there have been reports of birth malformations in children born to mothers who have been treated with warfarin during pregnancy.

Embryopathy characterized by nasal hypoplasia with or without stippled epiphyses (chondrodysplasia punctata) has been reported in pregnant women exposed to warfarin during the first trimester. CNS abnormalities also have been reported, including dorsal midline dysplasia characterized by agenesis of the corpus callosum, Dandy-Walker malformation, and midline cerebellar atrophy. Ventral midline dysplasia, characterized by optic atrophy, and eye abnormalities have been observed. Mental retardation, blindness, and other CNS abnormalities have been reported in association with second and third trimester exposure. Although rare, teratogenic reports following in utero exposure to warfarin include urinary tract anomalies such as single kidney, asplenia, anencephaly, spina bifida, cranial nerve palsy, hydrocephalus, cardiac defects and congenital heart disease, polydactyly, deformities of toes, diaphragmatic hernia and corneal leukoma.

Spontaneous abortion and stillbirth are known to occur and higher risk of fetal mortality is associated with the use of warfarin.

Women of childbearing potential who are candidates for anticoagulant therapy should be carefully evaluated and the indications critically reviewed with the patient. If the patient becomes pregnant while taking this drug, she should be apprised of the potential risks to the fetus, and the possibility of termination of the pregnancy should be discussed in light of those risks.

Hemorrhagic tendencies or blood dyscrasias.

Recent or contemplated surgery of CNS; eye; traumatic surgery resulting in large open surfaces.

Bleeding tendencies associated with active ulceration or overt bleeding of: gastrointestinal, genitourinary or respiratory tracts; cerebrovascular hemorrhage; aneurysm—cerebral, dissecting aorta; pericarditis and pericardial effusions; bacterial endocarditis.

Threatened abortion, eclampsia and preeclampsia.

Inadequate laboratory facilities or unsupervised senility, alcoholism, psychosis or lack of patient cooperation.

Spinal puncture and other diagnostic or therapeutic procedures with potential for uncontrollable bleeding.

Miscellaneous: Major regional, lumbar block anesthesia, and malignant hypertension.

Warnings: The most serious risks associated with anticoagulant therapy with warfarin are hemorrhage in any tissue or organ and, less frequently, necrosis and/or gangrene of skin and other tissues. The risk of hemorrhage is related to the level of intensity and the duration of anticoagulant therapy. Hemorrhage and necrosis have in some cases been reported to result in death or permanent disability. Necrosis appears to be associated with local thrombosis and usually appears within a few days of the start of anticoagulant therapy. In severe cases of necrosis treatment through debridement or amputation of the affected tissue, limb, breast or penis has been reported. Careful diagnosis is required to determine whether necrosis is caused by an underlying disease. Warfarin therapy should be discontinued when warfarin is suspected to be the cause of developing necrosis and heparin therapy may be considered for anticoagulation.

Although various treatments have been attempted, no treatment for necrosis has been considered uniformly effective. See below for information on predisposing conditions. These and other risks associated with anticoagulant therapy must be weighed against the risk of thrombosis or embolization in untreated cases.

Warfarin is a potent drug with a half-life of 2.5 days; therefore, its effects may become more pronounced as daily maintenance doses overlap. It cannot be emphasized too strongly that treatment of each patient is a highly individualized matter. Dosage should be controlled by periodic determinations of PT or other suitable coagulation tests. Determinations of whole blood clotting and bleeding times are not effective measures for control of therapy. Heparin prolongs the one-stage PT. When heparin and warfarin are administered concomitantly, refer to Dosage—Conversion from Heparin Therapy, for recommendations.

Caution should be observed when warfarin is administered in any situation or in the presence of any predisposing condition where added risk of hemorrhage or necrosis is present.

Anticoagulation therapy with warfarin may enhance the release of atheromatous plaque emboli, thereby increasing the risk of complications from systemic cholesterol microembolization, including the "purple toe syndrome". Discontinuation of warfarin therapy is recommended when such phenomena are observed. While the "purple toe syndrome" is reported to be reversible, other complications of microembolization may not be reversible.

Administration of anticoagulants in the following conditions will be based upon clinical judgment in which the risks of anticoagulant therapy are weighed against the risk of thrombosis or embolization in untreated cases. The following may be associated with these increased risks:

Lactation: Warfarin appears in the milk of nursing mothers in an inactive form. Infants nursed by warfarin treated mothers had no change in PT. Effects in premature infants have not been evaluated.

Severe to moderate hepatic or renal insufficiency.

Infectious diseases or disturbances of intestinal flora: sprue, antibiotic therapy.

Trauma which may result in internal bleeding.

Surgery or trauma resulting in large exposed raw surfaces.

Indwelling catheters.

Severe to moderate hypertension.

Known or suspected deficiency in protein C. This hereditary or acquired condition, which should be suspected if there is a history of recurrent episodes of thromboembolic disorders in the patient or in the family, has been associated with an increased risk of developing necrosis following warfarin administration. Tissue necrosis may occur in the absence of protein C deficiency. It has been reported that concurrent anticoagulant therapy with heparin for 5 to 7 days during initiation of therapy with warfarin may minimize the incidence of this reaction. Warfarin therapy should be discontinued when warfarin is suspected to be the cause of developing necrosis and heparin therapy may be considered for anticoagulation.

Miscellaneous: polycythemia vera, vasculitis, severe diabetes, severe allergic and anaphylactic disorders.

Patients with congestive heart failure may become more sensitive to warfarin, thereby requiring more frequent laboratory monitoring, and reduced doses of warfarin.

Concurrent use of anticoagulants with streptokinase or urokinase is not recommended and may be hazardous. (Please note recommendations accompanying these preparations.)

Precautions: Periodic determination of PT or other suitable coagulation test is essential. Numerous factors, alone or in combination, including travel, changes in diet, environment, physical state and medication may influence response of the patient to anticoagulants.

It is generally good practice to monitor the patient's response with additional PT determinations in the period immediately after discharge from the hospital, and whenever other medications are initiated, discontinued or taken haphazardly. Table I and Table II (on following page) provide a listing of factors, alone or in combination, which may affect the PT. However, other factors may also affect the anticoagulant response and the tables are provided for your reference only. **Because a patient may be exposed to a combination of listed factors, the net effect of warfarin on PT responses may be unpredictable.** More frequent PT monitoring is therefore advisable. Medications of unknown interaction with coumarins are best regarded with caution. When these medications are started or stopped, more frequent PT monitoring is advisable.

Table I—Warfilone

Factors which may be Responsible for Increased PT Response

Endogenous Factors

cancer	hyperthyroidism
collagen disease	poor nutritional state
congestive heart failure	steatorrhea
diarrhea	vitamin K deficiency
elevated temperature	
hepatic disorders	
infectious hepatitis	
jaundice	

Exogenous Factors

acetaminophen	diuretics*	naproxen
alcohol*	disulfiram	narcotics, prolonged
allopurinol	ethacrynic acid	pentoxifylline
aminosalicylic acid	fenoprofen	phenylbutazone
amiodarone HCl	fluoroquinolone antibiotics	phenytoin
anabolic steroids	glucagon	propafenone
anesthetics, inhalation	hepatotoxic drugs	pyrazolones
antibiotics	ibuprofen	quinidine
bromelains	indomethacin	quinine
chenodiol	influenza virus vaccine	ranitidine*
chloral hydrate*	lovastatin	salicylates
chlorpropamide	mefenamic acid	sulfinpyrazone
chymotrypsin	methyldopa	sulfonamides, long-acting
cimetidine	methylphenidate	sulindac
clofibrate	metronidazole	tamoxifen
Coumadin overdose	miconazole	thyroid drugs
dextran	monoamine oxidase inhibitors	tolbutamide
dextrothyroxine		trimethoprim/sulfamethoxazole
diazoxide	moricizine hydrochloride*	warfarin overdose
diflunisal	nalidixic acid	

also: other medications affecting blood elements which may modify hemostasis
- dietary deficiencies
- prolonged hot weather
- unreliable PT determinations

* Increased and decreased PT responses have been reported.

Warfilone (cont'd)

Coumarins may also affect the action of other drugs. Hypoglycemic agents (chlorpropamide and tolbutamide) and anticonvulsants (phenytoin and phenobarbital) may accumulate in the body as a result of interference with either their metabolism or excretion.

It has been reported that concomitant administration of warfarin and ticlopidine may be associated with cholestatic hepatitis.

Special Risk Patients: Caution should be observed when warfarin is administered to certain patients such as elderly or debilitated or when administered in any situation or physical condition where added risk of hemorrhage is present.

I.M. injections of concomitant medications should be confined to the upper extremities which permits easy access for manual compression, inspections for bleeding and use of pressure bandages.

Close monitoring of patients receiving nonsteroidal anti-inflammatory agents (NSAIDs) is recommended to be certain that no change in anticoagulation dosage is required. In addition to specific drug interactions that might affect prothrombin time, NSAIDs can inhibit platelet aggregation, and can cause gastrointestinal bleeding, peptic ulceration and/or perforation.

Information for the Patient: The objective of anticoagulant therapy is to control the coagulation mechanism so that thrombosis is prevented, while avoiding spontaneous bleeding. Effective therapeutic levels with minimal complications are in part dependent upon cooperative and well-instructed patients who communicate effectively with their physicians. Patients should be advised. Strict adherence to the prescribed dosage schedule is necessary; do not take or discontinue any other medication, except on the advice of the physician; avoid alcohol, salicylates (e.g. ASA), large amounts of green leafy vegetables, and/or drastic changes in dietary habits which may affect warfarin therapy; warfarin may cause a red-orange discoloration of alkaline urine; the patient should notify the physician: if any illness such as diarrhea, infection or fever develops; or if any unusual symptoms such as pain, swelling or discomfort appear; or if prolonged bleeding from cuts, increased menstrual flow or vaginal bleeding, nosebleeds or bleeding of gums from brushing, unusual bleeding or bruising, red or dark brown urine, red or tar black stools or diarrhea occurs.

Pregnancy: See Contraindications.

Children: Safety and effectiveness in children below 18 years of age have not been established.

Table II—Warfilone

Factors which may be Responsible for Decreased PT Response	
Endogenous Factors	
edema	
hereditary coumarin resistance	
hyperlipemia	
hypothyroidism	
Exogenous Factors	
adrenocorticol steroids	griseofulvin
alcohol*	haloperidol
aminoglutethimide	meprobamate
antacids	moricizine HCl*
antihistamines	nafcillin
barbiturates	oral contraceptives
carbamazepine	paraldehyde
chloral hydrate*	primidone
chlordiazepoxide	ranitidine*
cholestyramine	rifampin
Coumadin underdose	sucralfate
diuretics*	trazodone
ethchlorvynol	vitamin C
glutethimide	warfarin underdose
also: diet high in Vitamin K unreliable PT determinations	

*Increased and decreased PT responses have been reported.

Adverse Effects: Potential adverse reactions to warfarin may include: Hemorrhage from any tissue or organ. This is a consequence of the anticoagulant effect. The signs and symptoms will vary according to the location and degree or extent of the bleeding. Hemorrhagic complications may present as paralysis; headache, chest, abdomen, joint or other pain; shortness of breath, difficult breathing or swallowing; unexplained swelling or unexplained shock. Therefore, the possibility of hemorrhage should be considered in evaluating the condition of any anticoagulated patient with complaints which do not indicate an obvious diagnosis. Bleeding during anticoagulant therapy does not always correlate with prothrombin activity (see Overdose: Symptoms and Treatment).

Bleeding which occurs when the prothrombin time is within the therapeutic range warrants diagnostic investigation, since it may unmask a previously unsuspected lesion, e.g., tumor, ulcer, etc.

Necrosis of skin and other tissues (see Warnings).

Other adverse reactions are infrequent and consist of alopecia, urticaria, dermatitis, fever, nausea, diarrhea, abdominal cramping, systemic cholesterol microembolization, a syndrome called "purple toes", cholestatic hepatic injury and hypersensitivity reactions.

Priapism has been associated with anticoagulant administration, however, a causal relationship has not been established.

Overdose: Symptoms: Suspected or overt abnormal bleeding (i.e., appearance of blood in stools or urine, hematuria, excessive menstrual bleeding, melena, petechiae, excessive bruising or persistent oozing from superficial injuries) are early manifestations of anticoagulation beyond a safe and satisfactory level.

Treatment: Excessive anticoagulation, with or without bleeding, may be controlled by discontinuing warfarin therapy and if necessary, by administration of oral or parenteral vitamin K_1. (Please see recommendations accompanying vitamin K_1 prior to use.)

Such use of vitamin K_1 reduces responses to subsequent warfarin therapy. Patients may return to a pretreatment thrombotic status following the rapid reversal of a prolonged PT. Resumption of warfarin administration reverses the effect of vitamin K_1, and a therapeutic PT can again be obtained by careful dosage adjustment. If rapid anticoagulation is indicated, heparin may be preferable for initial therapy.

If minor bleeding progresses to major bleeding, give 5 to 25 mg (rarely up to 50 mg) parenteral vitamin K_1. In emergency situations of severe hemorrhage, clotting factors can be returned to normal by administering 200 to 500 mL of whole blood or fresh frozen plasma, or by giving commercial Factor IX complex.

A risk of hepatitis and other viral diseases is associated with the use of these blood products; Factor IX complex is also associated with an increased risk of thrombosis. Therefore, these preparations should be used only in exceptional or life-threatening bleeding episodes secondary to warfarin overdosage.

Purified Factor IX preparations should not be used because they cannot increase the levels of prothrombin, Factor VII and Factor X, which are also depressed along with the levels of Factor IX as a result of warfarin treatment. Packed red blood cells may also be given if significant blood loss has occurred. Infusions of blood or plasma should be monitored carefully to avoid precipitating pulmonary edema in elderly patients or patients with heart disease.

Dosage: The administration and dosage must be individualized according to the patient's sensitivity to the drug. The dosage should be adjusted according to results of the one-stage PT. Different thromboplastin reagents vary substantially in their responsiveness to warfarin-induced effects on PT.

Early clinical studies of oral anticoagulants, which formed the basis for recommended therapeutic ranges of 1.5 to 2.5 times control PT, used sensitive human brain thromboplastin. When using the less sensitive rabbit brain thromboplastins commonly employed in PT assays today, adjustments must be made to the targeted range that reflect this decrease in sensitivity. Available clinical evidence indicates that prolongation of the PT 1.3 to 1.5 times control, when measuring with the less sensitive thromboplastin reagents, is sufficient for prophylaxis and treatment of venous thromboembolism, minimizing the risk of hemorrhage associated with more prolonged PT values. In cases where the risk of thromboembolism is great, such as patients with recurrent systemic embolism, a PT of 1.5 to 2.0 times control should be maintained. A ratio greater than 2.0 appears to provide no additional therapeutic benefit in most patients and is associated with a higher risk of bleeding.

To define the appropriate therapeutic regimen it is important to be familiar with the sensitivity of the thromboplastin reagent used in the laboratory and its relationship to the International Reference Preparation (IRP), a sensitive thromboplastin prepared from human brain.

International Reference Preparation (IRP): A system of standardizing the PT in oral anticoagulant control was introduced by the World Health Organization in 1983. It is based upon the determination of an International Normalized Ratio (INR) which provides a common basis for communications of PT results and interpretations of therapeutic ranges. The INR is derived from calibrations of commercial thromboplastin reagents against a sensitive human brain thromboplastin, the International Reference Preparation (IRP).

For the 3 commercial rabbit brain thromboplastins currently used in North America, a PT ratio of 1.3 to 2.0 is equivalent to an INR of 2.0 to 4.0. For other thromboplastins, the INR can be calculated as:

$$\text{INR} = (\text{observed PT ratio})^{\text{ISI}}$$

where the ISI (International Sensitivity Index) is the calibration factor and is available from the manufacturers of the thromboplastin reagent.

The proceedings and recommendations of the 1992 Third ACCP Consensus Conference on Antithrombotic Therapy and a review article evaluate issues related to oral anticoagulant therapy and the sensitivity of thromboplastin reagents and provide additional guidance for defining the appropriate therapeutic regimen.

Laboratory Control: The PT reflects the depression of vitamin K dependent Factors VII, IX, X and II. There are several modifications of the one-stage PT and the physician should become familiar with the specific method used in the laboratory which is employed. The degree of anticoagulation indicated by any range of PTs may be altered by the type of thromboplastin used; the appropriate therapeutic range must be based on the experience of each laboratory. The PT should be determined daily after the administration of the initial dose until PT results stabilize in the therapeutic range. Intervals between subsequent PT determinations should be based upon the physician's judgment of the patient's reliability and response to warfarin in order to maintain the individual within the therapeutic range. Acceptable intervals for PT determinations are normally within the range of 1 to 4 weeks. To ensure adequate control, it is recommended that additional PT tests are done when other warfarin products are interchanged with warfarin.

Treatment during Dentistry and Surgery: The management of patients who undergo dental and surgical procedures requires close liaison between attending physicians, surgeons and dentists. In patients who must be anticoagulated prior to, during or immediately following dental or surgical procedures adjusting the dosage to maintain the PT at the low end of the therapeutic range, may safely allow for continued anticoagulation. The operative site should be sufficiently limited to permit the effective use of local procedures for hemostasis. Under these conditions dental and surgical procedures may be performed without undue risk of hemorrhage.

Conversion from Heparin Therapy: Since the onset of warfarin's effect is delayed, heparin is preferred initially for rapid anticoagulation. Conversion to warfarin may begin concomitantly with heparin therapy or may be delayed 3 to 6 days. As heparin may affect the PT, patients receiving both heparin and warfarin should have blood drawn for PT determination, at least 5 hours after the last i.v. bolus dose of heparin, or 4 hours after cessation of a continuous i.v. infusion of heparin, or 24 hours after the last s.c. heparin injection.

When warfarin has produced the desired therapeutic range of prothrombin activity, heparin may be discontinued.

Supplied: Each white, round, film-coated tablet with a score *F* symbol on one side and the number 5 on the other, contains: warfarin sodium USP 5 mg. Nonmedicinal ingredients: calcium phosphate dibasic, croscarmellose sodium, cornstarch, hydroxypropyl cellulose with silica, hydroxypropyl methylcellulose, magnesium stearate and microcrystalline cellulose. Bottles of 100. Keep container tightly closed. Protect from light.

(Shown in Product Recognition Section)

WARTEC® Ⓟ

Pharmascience

Podofilox

Antimitotic Agent

Pharmacology: Necrosis of visible tissue is observed following treatment of genital warts with podofilox. The exact mechanism of action is unknown.

Podofilox is a metaphase inhibitor of dividing cells. Podofilox binds to at least one binding site on tubulin. This binding prevents the tubulin polymerization required for microtubule assembly. At higher concentrations podofilox also inhibits nucleoside transport through the cell membrane. The chemotherapeutic action of podofilox is assumed to be due to inhibition of growth and the ability to invade the tissue of the virus-infected cells. Podofilox prevents cell division in the virus-infected cells of the condylomata acuminata.

Indications: For the topical treatment of external genital warts (condylomata acuminata) confined to the penile and vulvar regions.

Contraindications: Patients who develop hypersensitivity to podofilox or to any component in the formulation. Open wounds following surgical procedures should not be treated with podofilox.

Warnings: For topical use only.

Podofilox is a potent vesicant and is to be used only as directed by a physician. Extreme care should be taken to avoid contact with eyes, tongue or mucosal tissue of the vagina or cervix. If accidental contact with the eyes occurs, bathe eyes immediately and thoroughly with large amounts of water and contact a physician immediately.

Precautions: Diagnosis: Although condylomata (genital warts) have a characteristic appearance, histopathological confirmatory tests should be obtained if there is any question of the diagnosis. Differential diagnosis from squamous cell carcinoma (so-called "Bowenoid papulosis") is of particular concern. Squamous cell carcinoma may also be associated with human papillomaviruses but should not be treated with podofilox.

General: The recommended method of application, frequency of application and duration of treatment should not be exceeded (see Dosage). If the solution is accidentally spilled on healthy skin, wipe off at once, wash vigorously with soap and water and rinse well. The solution should not be applied to any open cuts or abrasions. Self-treatment of genital warts with surface areas greater then 10 cm² should not be permitted.

Genital warts may be contagious, and the patient should be instructed to abstain from sexual intercourse. If this is not possible, a latex condom must be used until the infected partner is declared cured by the physician.

Children: There is no clinical experience; therefore, use in children cannot presently be recommended.

Pregnancy and *Lactation:* Not recommended for use in pregnant or lactating women.

Patients with Special Diseases and Conditions: Do not use if growth of surrounding tissue is inflamed or irritated. Do not use on moles, birth marks or unusual warts with hair growing from them.

Podofilox should not be used on tissues which were recently exposed to laser surgery or cryosurgery.

Drug Interactions: No interaction with other medications is known.

Adverse Effects: Local irritations might occur on the second or third day of application associated with the start of wart necrosis. In the majority of cases the reactions are mild and they will disappear in a few days.

In clinical trials with podofilox 0.5% solution, the following have been shown to be the most common local adverse events which were reported at some time during treatment: erythema 32%, burning 30%, erosion 20%, tenderness 30%, itching 15%, pruritus 11%, and other 3% including pain and balanoposthitis.

If severe cases of local irritations occur, this can be treated with local anti-inflammatory drugs. To alleviate acute pain, analgesics may be used.

Overdose: Symptoms and Treatment: Topical: In the event of accidental spillage on healthy skin, burning or extreme tenderness of treated areas, wash the area copiously with soap and cold water and rinse with water as required. If required, an analgesic, ASA or acetaminophen, may be administered for pain management. Local discomfort may be alleviated by the use of topical anti-inflammatory therapy (e.g., hydrocortisone acetate).

Systemic: An excessive oral ingestion of podofilox (>0.5 mg/kg, 2 bottles) may cause systemic toxicity. Initial symptoms are general malaise, weakness, drowsiness and dizziness. Later symptoms may be coma with risk of respiratory failure, ileus and vascular crisis.

In the event of accidental ingestion, gastric lavage or induction of emesis should be instituted. Treatment of overdosage is symptomatic and in severe oral overdose ensure the airway is clear, provide fluids, correct electrolyte balance, monitor blood gases and liver function. Blood count should be monitored for at least 5 days.

Symptomatic treatment and hemoperfusion through coal filter may prevent a fatal outcome.

Dosage: Apply twice daily, morning and evening, for 3 consecutive days followed by 4 days without treatment.

Preferably the physician should perform the first application for the patient as an office procedure.

The affected area should be thoroughly washed with soap and water, and dried prior to application.

Using the applicator provided, the warts should be painted with the solution. The treated area should be allowed to dry. If an area in the occluded prepuce (under the foreskin) is being treated, care should be taken to allow the solution to dry before letting the foreskin return to its normal position. If residual warts persist, further treatment may be repeated after an interval of 7 days. The treatment may be repeated 3 times. If there is incomplete response after 4 treatment cycles, alternative treatment should be considered.

The majority of patients will not require in excess of 30 loops for each application; however, a maximum of 50 loops per application (equivalent to 250 μL of solution) may be applied. Treatment should be limited to less than 10 cm² of wart tissue and to no more than 500 μg (0.5 mL) of solution per day.

Supplied: Each mL of solution for topical application contains: podofilox 0.5%. Nonmedicinal ingredients: ethanol 70% and phosphoric acid. Screw-capped amber glass bottles of 3 mL. Each pack contains a bottle of 3 mL and a tube of double-ended applicators. The applicators include a loop end for the treatment of separate warts and a spatula end for the treatment of large or fused warts. Store at controlled room temperature in light-resistant and tightly closed containers.

Reviewed 1999

WEBBER® CALCIUM CARBONATE

Novartis Consumer Health

Calcium Carbonate

Calcium Supplement

Indications: As a dietary supplement where calcium intake may be inadequate: childhood and adolescence, pregnancy and lactation, postmenopausal females and in the aged. In the treatment of calcium deficiency states which may occur in diseases such as: tetany of the newborn (as a supplement to parenterally administered calcium), hypoparathyroidism and senile osteoporosis, rickets and osteomalacia.

Contraindications: Hypercalcemia and hypercalciniuria (e.g. in hyperparathyroidism, vitamin D overdosage, decalcifying tumors such as plasmocytoma, bone metastases), severe renal disease, calcium loss due to immobilization.

Precautions: In mild hypercalciniuria (exceeding 300 mg/24 hours) as well as in chronic renal failure, or where there is evidence of stone formation in the urinary tract, adequate checks must be kept on urinary calcium excretion. If necessary, the dosage should be reduced or calcium therapy discontinued. High vitamin D intake should be avoided during calcium therapy unless specially indicated. Administration of corticosteroids may interfere with calcium absorption.

Calcium compounds reduce blood concentrations of oral tetracyclines. Concomitant use should be avoided, or doses of the drugs should not be taken within 1 hour of each other.

Although certain dietary substances interfere with the absorption of calcium, including oxalic acid (found in large quantities in rhubarb and spinach), phytic acid (bran and whole cereals) and phosphorus (milk and other dairy products) clinical significance has not been proven.

Adverse Effects: Occasional diarrhea or constipation may occur with high calcium intake.

Dosage: Adults: 1 to 3 tablets (500 to 1 500 mg) daily in divided doses or as recommended by physician.

Children: 1 to 2 tablets (500 to 1 000 mg) daily in divided doses or as recommended by physician.

Supplied: Each grey, film-coated, elongated tablet contains: calcium carbonate 1 250 mg from oyster shell, providing 500 mg (25 mEq) of elemental calcium. Nonmedicinal ingredients: gum arabic, hydroxypropyl methylcellulose, propylene glycol, sodium lauryl sulfate and sodium starch glycolate. Bottles of 100.

WEBBER® VITAMIN E OINTMENT

Novartis Consumer Health

d-Alpha Tocopheryl Acetate

Emollient

Pharmacology: Vitamin E functions as an antioxidant and stabilizer of cell membranes.

Indications: For the treatment of sunburn, minor cuts and burns and other minor skin irritations.

Precautions: If adverse reaction or irritation occurs, discontinue use and consult a physician. In the case of a serious burn, consult a physician. Not for ophthalmic use.

Dosage: Apply ointment to the affected area once or twice daily. If necessary, cover with sterile gauze.

Supplied: Each g of petrolatum based ointment contains: high purity natural source vitamin E 30 IU (22 mg) as d-alpha tocopheryl acetate. Nonmedicinal ingredients: cetyl esters wax, methyl parahydroxybenzoate, petrolatum, polysorbate, propyl parahyroxybenzoate and sorbitan sesquioleate. Tubes of 50 g. Jars of 50 g. Store at 15 to 30° C.

WELLBUTRIN® SR ℞

Glaxo Wellcome

Bupropion HCl

Antidepressant

Pharmacology: Bupropion is an antidepressant of the aminoketone class. It is chemically unrelated to tricyclic, tetracyclic, selective serotonin re-uptake inhibitors or other known antidepressant agents. Its structure closely resembles that of diethylpropion. It is related to the phenylethylamines.

The mechanism of bupropion's antidepressant activity is unknown but appears to be mediated by noradrenergic (and possibly dopaminergic), rather than serotonergic mechanisms. Preclinical studies have shown that bupropion blocks noradrenalin (NA) reuptake and dopamine (DA) reuptake. Its major metabolite (hydroxybupropion), which in man is present at blood levels 10 to 20-fold higher than buproprion, blocks only NA reuptake.

In vitro, bupropion and its major metabolites had essentially no affinity for β-adrenergic, dopaminergic, GABA, benzodiazepine, 5HT1A, glycine and adenosine receptors, and only weakly inhibited α-adrenergic receptors in rat brain, α2-adrenergic, 5HT2, and muscarinic cholinergic receptors. High concentrations of bupropion and its major metabolites did not inhibit MAO-A or MAO-B activity. Bupropion and its major metabolites had no significant affinity for the 5HT transport system.

Pharmacokinetics: Absorption: Bupropion has not been administered i.v. to humans; therefore, the absolute bioavailability of Wellbutrin SR tablets in humans has not been determined. In rat and dog studies, the bioavailability of bupropion ranged from 5 to 20%. Following oral administration of Wellbutrin SR to healthy volunteers, peak plasma concentrations of bupropion are achieved within 3 hours. In 2 single-dose (150 mg) studies the mean peak concentration (C_{max}) values were 91 and 143 ng/mL. At steady state, the mean C_{max} following a 150 mg dose every 12 hours was 136 ng/mL.

In a single-dose study, food increased the C_{max} of bupropion by 11% and the extent of absorption as defined by area under the plasma concentration-time curve (AUC) by 17%. The mean time to peak concentration (t_{max}) was prolonged by 1 hour. This effect was of no clinical significance.

Distribution: In vitro tests show that bupropion is 84% bound to human plasma proteins at concentrations up to 200 μg/mL. The extent of protein binding of hydroxybupropion is similar to that of bupropion, whereas the extent of protein binding of the threohydrobupropion metabolite is about half that seen with bupropion. The volume of distribution (V_{ss}/F) estimated from a single 150 mg dose given to 17 subjects is 1 950 L (20% CV).

Metabolism: Bupropion is extensively metabolized in humans. There are 3 active metabolites: hydroxybupropion and the amino-alcohol isomers threohydrobupropion and erythrohydrobupropion, which are formed via hydroxylation of the tert-butyl group of bupropion and/or reduction of the carbonyl group. Oxidation of the bupropion side chain results in the formation of a glycine conjugate of meta-chlorobenzoic acid, which is then excreted as the major urinary metabolite. In preclinical tests used to predict antidepressant activity, it has been observed that hydroxybupropion is comparable in potency to bupropion, while the other metabolites are one half to one tenth as potent. This may be of clinical importance because the plasma concentrations of the metabolites are higher than those of bupropion.

In vitro results indicate that biotransformation of bupropion to hydroxybupropion is catalyzed primarily by CYP2B6, and to a much lesser extent by CYP1A2, 2A6, 2C9, 2E1 and 3A4 isozymes. Detectable levels of hydroxybupropion are not observed with CYP1A1 and CYP2D6 isozymes. Cytochrome

Wellbutrin SR (cont'd)

P450 isoenzymes are not involved in the formation of threohydrobupropion. Following a single 150 mg dose of bupropion in humans, peak plasma concentrations of hydroxybupropion occur approximately 6 hours after administration. Peak plasma concentrations of hydroxybupropion are approximately 10 times the peak level of the parent drug at steady state. The AUC of hydroxybupropion at steady state is about 17-fold higher than that of bupropion. The times to peak concentrations for the erythrohydrobupropion and threohydrobupropion metabolites are similar to that of hydroxybupropion, and steady-state AUCs are 1.5 and 7 times that of bupropion, respectively.

Elimination: In 2 single-dose (150 mg) studies the mean (±% CV) apparent clearance (Cl/F) of bupropion was 135 (±20%) and 209 L/hr (±21%). Following chronic dosing of 150 mg of Wellbutrin SR every 12 hours for 14 days (n=34), the mean Cl/F at steady state was 160 L/h (±23%). The mean elimination half-life of bupropion (estimated from a series of studies) is approximately 21 hours. Estimates of the half-lives of the metabolites determined from a multiple-dose study were 20 hours (±25%) for hydroxybupropion, 37 hours (±35%) for threohydrobupropion, and 33 hours (±30%) for erythrohydrobupropion. Steady-state plasma concentrations of bupropion and metabolites are reached within 5 and 8 days, respectively. Following oral administration of 200 mg of ^{14}C-bupropion in humans, 87% and 10% of the radioactive dose were recovered in the urine and feces, respectively. The fraction of the oral dose of bupropion excreted unchanged was only 0.5%. Bupropion and its metabolites exhibit linear kinetics following chronic administration of 150 to 300 mg/day.

Factors or conditions altering metabolic capacity (e.g., liver disease, congestive heart failure, age, concomitant medications, etc.) or elimination may be expected to influence the degree and extent of accumulation of the active metabolites of bupropion. The elimination of the major metabolites of bupropion may be affected by reduced renal or hepatic function because they are moderately polar compounds and are likely to undergo further metabolism or conjugation in the liver prior to urinary excretion.

The disposition of buproprion following a single 200 mg oral dose was compared in 8 healthy volunteers and 8 weight- and age-matched volunteers with alcoholic liver disease. The half-life of hydroxybuproprion was significantly prolonged in subjects with alcoholic liver disease (32 hours versus 21 hours). The differences in half-life for bupropion and the other metabolites in the two patients groups were minimal.

In patients with renal or hepatic impairment, treatment should be initiated at reduced dosage (see Precautions and Dosage).

In a single dose study, there were no significant differences in the pharmacokinetics of bupropion or its major metabolites in smokers compared with nonsmokers.

The effects of age on the pharmacokinetics of bupropion and its metabolites have not been fully characterized (see Precautions and Dosage).

Experience in Clinical Trials: The effectiveness of bupropion in the treatment of moderate depression has been systematically evaluated at doses ranging from 50 to 400 mg/day in 3 multicentre, randomized, placebo-controlled, double-blind, parallel-group studies involving a total of 1 420 patients of whom 1 021 received active doses of the bupropion and 399 received placebo. Each study included a 1-week placebo lead-in phase to identify and exclude placebo responders, followed by an 8-week treatment phase.

The response to treatment was evaluated at regular intervals using the Hamilton Rating Scale for Depression (HAMD), Clinical Global Impressions Scales of Severity (CGI-S) and Improvement (CGI-I) Scale. Both the observed and the last observation carried forward (LOCF) values were analyzed.

In 1 study comparing fixed daily doses of either 150 mg once daily (n=121) or 300 mg as 150 mg twice daily (n=120) bupropion to placebo (n=121), the HAMD, CGI-S (change from baseline) and CGI-I scores for both bupropion groups at endpoint were statistically significantly superior to placebo. Both active treatment groups showed a similar magnitude of improvement during the trial.

In a second study patients received fixed daily doses of either 100 mg, 200 mg, 300 mg or 400 mg/day (given on a twice daily schedule) bupropion or placebo. The magnitude of the mean change scores were consistently greater for all active groups than placebo by day 21. At endpoint, scores in the 100 mg group were statistically significantly superior to placebo on all rating scales, while the higher dose groups followed a similar pattern but did not achieve statistical significance.

A third study compared 2 flexible doses; 50 to 150 mg/day (given once daily), and 100 to 300 mg/day (twice daily schedule) to placebo (n=approximately 150 patients per group). Patients began at the lowest dose in the range and were titrated to the highest tolerated dose in the range over a period of 7 days. Investigators had the option to titrate down when a higher dose was not well tolerated. The mean daily dose calculated from day 8 onwards was 144 mg in the 50 to 150 mg arm and 276 mg in the 100 to 300 mg arm, indicating that the vast majority of patients remained on the highest allowable dose in their respective groups for the duration of the study. Efficacy measures at endpoint for the 50 to 150 mg/day group were statistically significantly superior to placebo. The higher dose group followed a similar pattern but did not achieve statistical significance at endpoint. A combined endpoint analysis of all patients treated with bupropion in the trial, demonstrated statistically significant superiority on all efficacy measures compared to placebo.

In summary, patients receiving bupropion at doses of 100 to 150 mg/day in single or divided doses experienced improvement relative to placebo on the major indices of depression. Clinical response did not improve with increasing dose, indicating a flat dose-response relationship in the range of doses studied.

Indications: For the symptomatic relief of depressive illness. The effectiveness of bupropion in long-term use (more than 8 weeks) has not been systematically evaluated in controlled trials. Therefore, the physician who elects to use bupropion for extended periods should periodically reevaluate the long-term usefulness of the drug for the individual patient.

Contraindications: Patients receiving Zyban or any other medications that contain bupropion HCl because the incidence of seizure is dose dependent.

Seizures: Bupropion is contraindicated in patients with a seizure disorder.

Bulimia/Anorexia Nervosa: Bupropion is contraindicated in patients with a current or prior diagnosis of bulimia or anorexia nervosa because of a higher incidence of seizures (see Warnings) noted in patients treated for bulimia with the immediate release formulation of bupropion.

MAO Inhibitors: The concurrent administration of bupropion and MAO inhibitor is contraindicated. At least 14 days should elapse between discontinuation of an MAO inhibitor and initiation of treatment with bupropion. Treatment with a MAO inhibitor should not be started until 2 weeks after discontinuation of bupropion treatment.

Bupropion is contraindicated in patients with known hypersensitivity to bupropion or to any of the components of the formulation.

Warnings: Patients should be made aware that Wellbutrin SR contains the same active ingredient (bupropion HCl) as Zyban. Wellbutrin SR should not be administered to patients already receiving a product containing bupropion (see Contraindications).

Seizures: Data for bupropion tablets revealed a seizure incidence of approximately 0.1% (3 of 3 100 patients followed prospectively) in patients treated at the recommended dose range of 100 to 300 mg/day. The incidence of seizures increased to 0.4% (4/1 000), above the recommended dose, at 400 mg/day. Data for the immediate-release buproprion revealed a seizure incidence of approximately 0.4% (13 of 3 200 patients followed prospectively) in patients treated at doses of 300 to 450 mg/day. Additional data accumulated for the immediate-release formulation of buproprion suggests that the estimated seizure incidence increases almost 10-fold between 450 and 600 mg/day. Given the wide variability among individuals and their capacity to metabolize and eliminate drugs, the disproportionate increase in seizure incidence with dose incrementation calls for caution in dosing.

The risk of seizure occurring with bupropion use appears to be associated with the presence of predisposing risk factors. Therefore caution should be used when treating patients with predisposing factors which increase the risk of seizures, including: history of head trauma or prior seizure; CNS tumor; excessive use of alcohol; abrupt withdrawal from alcohol, benzodiazepines or other sedatives; addiction to opiates, cocaine, or stimulants; use of concomitant medications that lower seizure threshold (e.g., antipsychotics, antidepressants, lithium, theophylline or systemic steroids); use of over-the-counter stimulants or anorectics; diabetes treated with oral hypoglycemics or insulin.

The risk of seizure may be minimized if the total daily dose of bupropion does not exceed 300 mg (the maximum recommended dose), and no single dose of bupropion exceeds 150 mg, in order to avoid high peak concentrations of buproprion and/or its metabolites.

Precautions: Suicide: The possibility of a suicide attempt in seriously depressed patients is inherent to the illness and may persist until significant remission occurs. Close supervision of high risk patients should accompany initial drug therapy, and consideration should be given to the need for hospitalization. In order to reduce the risk of overdose, prescriptions for bupropion should be written for the smallest number of tablets consistent with good patient management.

Allergic Reactions: Anaphylactoid reactions characterized by symptoms such as pruritus, urticaria, angioedema, and dyspnea requiring medical treatment have been reported in clinical trials with bupropion at a rate of 1 to 3 per thousand. In addition, there have been rare spontaneous postmarketing reports of erythema multiforme, Stevens-Johnson syndrome, and anaphylactic shock associated with bupropion.

In uncontrolled and controlled clinical trials, skin disorders, primarily rashes, pruritus and urticaria, led to discontinuation of 1.5% and 1.9 %, respectively of bupropion-treated subjects.

Agitation and Insomnia: In placebo-controlled trials, patients receiving bupropion tablets experienced an increased incidence of agitation, anxiety, and insomnia relative to those receiving placebo (see Adverse Effects). These symptoms were sometimes of sufficient magnitude to require discontinuation of bupropion, or concurrent treatment with sedative/hypnotic drugs.

Psychosis, Confusion, and Other Neuropsychiatric Phenomena: Patients treated with bupropion have been reported to show a variety of neuropsychiatric signs and symptoms including delusions, hallucinations, psychosis, concentration disturbance, paranoia and confusion. In some cases these abated upon dose reduction and/or withdrawal of treatment.

Activation of Psychosis and/or Mania: Antidepressants can precipitate manic episodes in bipolar patients during the depressed phase of their illness and may activate latent psychosis in other susceptible patients. Bupropion is expected to pose similar risks.

Altered Appetite and Weight: In clinical trials bupropion was associated with dose-related weight loss. In 8-week controlled trials mean weight loss for trial completers was 0.1 kg for placebo, 0.8 kg for bupropion 100 mg/day, 1.4 kg at 150 mg/day, and 2.3 kg at 300 mg/day. If weight loss is a major presenting sign of a patient's depressive illness, the potential anoretic and/or weight reducing effect of bupropion should be considered.

Cardiovascular Disease: There is no clinical experience establishing the safety of bupropion in patients with a recent history of myocardial infarction or unstable heart disease. In a study of depressed inpatients with stable congestive heart failure, bupropion was associated with a rise in supine blood pressure, resulting in discontinuation of 2 patients for exacerbation of baseline hypertension.

Hepatic or Renal Disease: Because bupropion and its metabolites are almost completely excreted through the kidney and metabolites are likely to undergo conjugation in the liver prior to urinary excretion, treatment of patients with renal or hepatic impairment should be initiated at the lowest recommended dose (see Dosage) as bupropion and its metabolites may accumulate in such patients to a greater extent than usual (See Pharmacology, Pharmacokinetics).

Occupational Hazards: Any psychoactive drug may impair judgment, thinking or motor skills. Therefore patients should be cautioned about operating hazardous machinery, including automobiles, until they are reasonably certain that the drug treatment does not affect their performance adversely.

Pregnancy, Labor and Delivery: There are no adequate and well-controlled studies of bupropion in pregnant women. Bupropion should thus not be used during pregnancy unless the potential benefit is judged to outweigh the potential risk. To monitor fetal outcomes of pregnant women exposed to bupropion, Glaxo Wellcome Inc. maintains a Bupropion Pregnancy Registry. Health care providers are encouraged to register patients by calling (800) 722-9292, ext. 39441.

Lactation: Like many other drugs, bupropion and its metabolites are secreted in human milk. Because of the potential for serious adverse reactions in nursing infants from bupropion, a decision should be made whether to discontinue nursing or to discontinue the drug, taking into account the importance of the drug to the mother.

Children: The safety and effectiveness of bupropion in individuals under 18 years old have not been established.

Geriatrics: There is limited experience with bupropion in the elderly. In general, older patients are known to metabolize drugs more slowly and to be more sensitive to the anticholinergic, sedative, and cardiovascular side effects of antidepressant drugs.

Drug Interactions: Cytochrome P450 2B6: In vitro studies indicate that bupropion is primarily metabolized to hydroxybupropion by the CYP2B6 isoenzyme (see Pharmacology, Pharmacokinetics). Therefore, the potential exists for a drug interaction between bupropion and drugs that affect the CYP2B6 isoenzyme metabolism (e.g., orphenadrine and cyclophosphamide). The threohydrobupropion metabolite of bupropion does not appear to be produced by the cytochrome P450 isoenzymes. No systematic data have been collected on the metabolism of bupropion following concomitant administration with other drugs or alternatively, the effect of concomitant administration of bupropion on the metabolism of other drugs.

Following chronic administration of bupropion, 100 mg t.i.d. to 8 healthy male volunteers for 14 days, there was no evidence of induction of its own metabolism.

Because bupropion is extensively metabolized, the coadministration of other drugs may affect its clinical activity. In particular, certain drugs may induce the metabolism of bupropion (e.g., carbamazepine, phenobarbital, phenytoin).

MAO Inhibitors: Studies in animals demonstrate that the acute toxicity of bupropion is enhanced by the MAO inhibitor, phenelzine (see Contraindications).

Cimetidine: The effects of concomitant administration of cimetidine on the pharmacokinetics of bupropion and its active metabolites were examined in a crossover study in 24 healthy young male volunteers, following oral administration of two 150 mg bupropion tablets with and without 800 mg of cimetidine. A single dose of cimetidine had no effect on single dose pharmacokinetic parameter estimates for buproprion, or hydroxybupropion, but caused a small statistically significant increase in the combined threohydro and erythrobupropion AUC (16%) and C_{max} (32%).

Levodopa: Limited clinical data suggest a higher incidence of adverse experiences in patients receiving concurrent administration of the sustained- and immediate-release formulations of bupropion and L-dopa. Administration of bupropion sustained release to patients receiving L-dopa concurrently should be undertaken with caution, using small initial doses and gradual dose increases.

Other Drugs with CNS Activity: The risk of using bupropion in combination with other CNS-active drugs has not been systematically evaluated. Consequently, caution is advised if the concomitant administration of bupropion and such drugs is required.

Transdermal Nicotine: Monitoring for treatment-emergent hypertension is recommended in patients receiving a combination of sustained-release bupropion and transdermal nicotine.

Adverse Effects: The information included is based on data from clinical trials with the sustained release formulation of bupropion. Information on additional adverse events associated with the immediate release formulation of bupropion is included in a separate subsection (see Events Observed During Development and Postmarketing Experience with the Immediate Release Formulation of Bupropion).

Adverse Events Associated with Discontinuation of Treatment: In placebo controlled studies of depression (987 patients treated with bupropion, and 385 treated with placebo), adverse events caused discontinuation in 7% of bupropion treated patients and 3% of placebo-treated patients. The more common events leading to discontinuation of bupropion included nervous system disturbances (2.2%), primarily agitation, anxiety and insomnia; skin disorders (1.9%), primarily rashes, pruritus, and urticaria ; general body complaints (1%), primarily headaches, and digestive system disturbances (1%), primarily nausea. Two patients in bupropion treatment groups discontinued due to hallucinations (auditory or visual). The rates of premature discontinuation due to an adverse event were dose-related in these studies.

In an open label, uncontrolled (acute treatment and continuation) study of bupropion, 11% patients (361 out of 3 100) discontinued treatment due to an adverse event. Adverse events leading to premature discontinuation in 1% or more of patients were: headache (1.1%), nausea (1%), and insomnia (1%). Adverse events leading to premature discontinuation in 0.5 to 1% of patients were: anxiety (0.8%), rash (0.8%), agitation (0.7%), irritability (0.5%), and dizziness (0.5%). In those patients (n=1 577) who went into the continuation phase after 8 weeks of treatment, 6 (0.4%) discontinued due to alopecia. Because this study was uncontrolled, it is not possible to reliably assess the causal relationship of these events to treatment with bupropion.

Incidence of Commonly Observed Adverse Events in Controlled Clinical Trials: Adverse events commonly encountered during the clinical development of bupropion (incidence of 5% or greater; and higher incidence in bupropion-treated, than placebo-treated patients) were headache, constipation, dry mouth, nausea, dizziness, insomnia, tremor and tinnitus.

Adverse Events Occurring at an Incidence of 1% or More Among Patients Treated with Bupropion in Placebo Controlled Trials: Table I enumerates treatment-emergent adverse events that occurred at an incidence of 1% or more and were more frequent than in the placebo group in patients participating in placebo-controlled clinical trials. Reported adverse events were classified using a COSTART-based Dictionary.

Events Observed During Development and Postmarketing Experience with the Immediate-Release Formulation of Bupropion: The following adverse events have been reported in clinical trials and postmarketing clinical experience with the immediate-release formulation of bupropion. The extent to which these events may be associated with the sustained-release tablet, is unknown.

Body (General): altered hormone level, body odor, flu syndrome.

Cardiovascular: complete AV block, abnormal ECG, pulmonary embolism, extrasystoles, myocardial infarction, pallor, phlebitis.

Digestive: colitis, esophagitis, gingivitis, gastrointestinal hemorrhage, hepatitis, intestinal perforation, liver damage, rectal disorder, increased salivation, stomach ulcer, toothache.

Endocrine: syndrome of inappropriate antidiuretic hormone.

Hemic and Lymphatic: anemia, leukocytosis, leukopenia, lymphadenopathy, pancytopenia.

Metabolic and Nutritional: glycosuria.

Musculoskeletal: arthritis, muscle rigidity/fever/rhabdomyolysis.

Nervous System: akinesia, aphasia, coma, delirium, delusions, dysarthria, dyskinesia, tardive dyskinesia, dystonia, abnormal EEG, labile emotions, euphoria, extrapyramidal syndrome, hypokinesia, decreased libido, increased libido, manic reaction, neuralgia, neuropathy, paranoid reaction, suicidal ideation.

Respiratory: bronchitis, dyspnea, epistaxis, pneumonia, respiratory disorder.

Skin: acne, angioedema, exfoliative dermatitis, hair discoloration, hirsutism, Stevens-Johnson syndrome.

Special Senses: deafness, diplopia, mydriasis.

Urogenital: cystitis, dyspareunia, dysuria, abnormal ejaculation, gynecomastia, urinary incontinence, menopause, ovarian disorder, penis disorder, salpingitis, testis disorder, urinary retention, vaginitis.

Table I—Wellbutrin SR

Adverse Events Attributed to Study Drug (%)

Treatment-Emergent Adverse Experiences Occurring in ≥1% of Patients in Any BUP SR Group for Studies 203, 205, and 212

Body System	Adverse Experience	BUP SR 100-150 (n=382) %	BUP SR 200-300 (n=491) %	PBO (n=385) %
Body (General)	Asthenia	1.8	1.6	1.6
	Flu Syndrome	6.2	2.4	3.1
	Headache	27.5	26.9	23.4
	Infection	4.7	7.5	6.5
	Accidental Injury	1.8	1.8	1.8
	Pain	1.3	2.4	2.1
	Abdominal Pain	3.9	3.5	1.6
	Back Pain	1.8	4.5	3.1
	Chest Pain	1	2.9	0.8
	Neck Pain	1.3	2	1.3
Cardiovascular	Hot Flashes	1.3	1	0.8
	Migraine	0.8	1.4	1
	Palpitation	2.9	2	1.6
	Tachycardia	1.6	0.6	0.5
Digestive	Anorexia	3.1	4.5	1.6
	Constipation	6.5	10.8	6.8
	Diarrhea	3.9	5.9	5.7
	Dry Mouth	13.1	16.5	7
	Dyspepsia	4.2	4.7	4.4
	Flatulence	1.8	3.1	2.1
	Nausea	10.7	12.6	7.5
	Vomiting	1.8	3.9	1.6
Musculoskeletal	Arthralgia	2.6	0.8	0.5
	Leg Cramps	1	0.2	0.5
	Myalgia	1.6	3.3	2.9
	Twitch	0.8	1	0.3
Nervous System	Agitation	1.6	3.5	1.8
	Anxiety	4.5	4.3	3.1
	CNS Stimulation	0	1.2	0.5
	Dizziness	7.1	8.6	5.5
	Hypertonia	1	1.2	0.5
	Insomnia	7.9	11.4	6.5
	Irritability	2.4	3.9	1.6
	Decreased Libido	1	0.6	0.5
	Nervousness	4.5	4.1	2.6
	Somnolence	2.6	2.0	2.1
	Tremor	3.1	6.1	0.8
Respiratory	Pharyngitis	1.3	2.9	1.8
	Rhinitis	9.9	6.7	9.6
	Sinusitis	1.6	2.4	2.1
Skin	Pruritus	2.4	2.2	1.6
	Rash	2.1	4.1	1.3
	Sweating	2.4	5.1	1.6
	Urticaria	0.8	1.4	0
Special Senses	Amblyopia	2.9	2.4	1.8
	Taste Perversion	1	1.4	0.3
	Tinnitus	3.9	5.1	1.8
Urogenital	Urinary Tract Infection	1	1.8	0.3
	Urinary Frequency	1.3	2.4	1.6

Wellbutrin SR (cont'd)

Drug Abuse and Dependence: Bupropion is likely to have a low abuse potential. There have been few reported cases of drug dependence and withdrawal symptoms associated with the immediate-release formulation of bupropion. In human studies of abuse liability, individuals experienced with drugs of abuse reported that bupropion produced a feeling of euphoria and desirability. In these a single dose of 400 mg (1.33 times the recommended daily dose) of the immediate-release formulation of bupropion produced mild amphetamine-like effects compared to placebo on the Morphine-Benzedrine Subscale of the Addiction Research Center Inventories (ARCI), which is indicative of euphorigenic properties and a score intermediate between placebo and amphetamine on the Liking Scale of the ARCI. Higher doses could not be tested because of the risk of seizure.

Overdose: Symptoms and Treatment: Human Overdose Experience: Three overdoses with bupropion occurred during clinical trials. One patient ingested 3 000 mg of bupropion and vomited quickly after the overdose; the patient experienced lightheadedness. A second patient ingested a "handful" of bupropion and experienced confusion, lethargy, nausea, jitteriness and seizure. A third patient ingested 3 600 mg of bupropion tablets and a bottle of wine; the patient experienced nausea, visual hallucinations and "grogginess". None of the patients experienced further sequelae.

The information included in the remainder of this section is based on the clinical experience with overdosage of the immediate release formulation of bupropion. Thirteen overdoses occurred during clinical trials. Twelve patients ingested 850 to 4 200 mg and recovered without significant sequelae. Another patient who ingested 9 000 mg of bupropion immediate release and 300 mg of tranylcypromine experienced a grand mal seizure and recovered without further sequelae.

Since introduction, overdoses of up to 17 500 mg of the immediate release formulation of bupropion have been reported. Seizure was reported in approximately one-third of all cases. Other serious reactions reported with overdoses of bupropion alone included hallucinations, loss of consciousness and sinus tachycardia. Fever, muscle rigidity, rhabdomyolysis, hypotension, stupor, coma and respiratory failure have been reported when bupropion was part of multiple drug overdoses.

Although most patients recovered without sequelae, deaths associated with overdoses of bupropion alone have been reported rarely in patients ingesting massive doses of bupropion immediate release tablets. Multiple uncontrolled seizures, bradycardia, cardiac failure, and cardiac arrest prior to death were reported in these patients.

Management of Overdose: Following suspected overdose, hospitalization is advised. If the patient is conscious, vomiting should be induced by syrup of ipecac. Activated charcoal also may be administered every 6 hours during the first 12 hours after ingestion. Baseline laboratory values should be obtained. ECG and EEG monitoring also are recommended for the next 48 hours. Adequate fluid intake should be provided.

If the patient is stuporous, comatose, or convulsing, airway intubation is recommended prior to undertaking gastric lavage. Although there is little clinical experience with lavage following an overdose of bupropion immediate release and none with bupropion sustained release, it is likely to be of benefit within the first 12 hours after ingestion since absorption of the drug may not yet be complete.

While diuresis, dialysis, or hemoperfusion are sometimes used to treat overdosage, there is no experience with their use in the management of overdoses of bupropion sustained release. Because diffusion of bupropion and its metabolites from tissue to plasma may be slow, dialysis may be of minimal benefit.

Based on studies in animals, it is recommended that seizures be treated with an i.v. benzodiazepine preparation and other supportive measures, as appropriate.

Further information about the treatment of overdoses may be available from a poison control center.

Dosage: The usual recommended dose is 100 to 150 mg/day given once daily. As with all antidepressants, the full antidepressant effect may not be evident until several weeks of treatment. In patients who are not responding to a dose of 150 mg/day the dose may be increased up to a maximum of 300 mg/day. Dose increases should occur at intervals of at least 1 week. **In order to minimize the risk of seizures (see Warnings), single doses of bupropion should not exceed 150 mg.** Doses greater than 150 mg/day should be administered b.i.d, preferably with at least 8 hours between successive doses.

Geriatrics, Debilitated, Hepatic, and Renal Impairment: In subjects with hepatic impairment limited pharmacokinetic data demonstrates a prolonged half-life of hydroxybupropion (see Pharmacology). No pharmacokinetic or therapeutic trials have been conducted to systematically investigate dose requirements in patients who are elderly, debilitated or renally impaired (see Precautions). As such patients may have reduced clearance of bupropion and its metabolites, and/or increased sensitivity to the side effects of CNS active drugs, treatment with bupropion should be initiated at the lowest recommended dose (100 mg/day).

Patients should be advised to swallow bupropion sustained release tablets whole with fluids, and not to chew, divide, crush or otherwise tamper with the tablets in any way that might affect the release rate of bupropion.

Information for the Patient: See Blue Section—Information for the Patient "Wellbutrin SR".

Supplied: 100 mg: Each blue, round, biconvex, film-coated, sustained-release tablet, printed WELLBUTRIN SR 100", contains: bupropion HCl 100 mg. Nonmedicinal ingredients: carnauba wax, cysteine hydrochloride, edible black ink, FD&C Blue No. 1 Lake, hydroxypropylcellulose, magnesium stearate, microcrystalline cellulose, polyethylene glycol, polysorbate 80 and titanium dioxide. Bottles of 60.

150 mg: Each purple, round, biconvex, film-coated, sustained-release tablet, printed WELLBUTRIN SR 150", contains: bupropion HCl 150 mg. Nonmedicinal ingredients: carnauba wax, cysteine hydrochloride, edible black ink, FD&C Blue No. 2 Lake, FD&C Red No. 40 Lake, hydroxypropyl methylcellulose, magnesium stearate, microcrystalline cellulose, polyethylene glycol, polysorbate 80 and titanium dioxide. Bottles of 60.

Store between 15 and 25°C away from direct sunlight.

(Shown in Product Recognition Section)

New Product 1998

WELLFERON® ℞

Glaxo Wellcome

Interferon alpha-n1 (Ins)

Biological Response Modifier

Pharmacology: Wellferon is a highly purified blend of natural human alpha interferons, obtained from human lymphoblastoid cells following induction with Sendai virus. Wellferon resembles human leukocyte interferon in that it is a mixture of natural alpha subtypes but differs in that these are present in different proportions. It also differs from recombinant alpha interferon preparations made from bacteria or other host cells, which contain only a single subtype.

The mechanism by which the alpha interferons achieve their antitumor effect is unknown. The alpha interferons have an antiproliferative effect on both normal and malignant cells. It can be shown in vitro that they inhibit cell replication; a dose response effect can also be shown in in vivo (animal) and in vitro models. Following removal of interferon from the cellular environment, normal cell replication again resumes. If inhibition of cell replication is an important antitumor mechanism of action, it would be mandatory to achieve a chronic steady state of circulating interferon activity; the daily administration of doses of 1 to 3 Mu/m² induces such a steady state. Larger doses induce higher levels but whether this is clinically beneficial has not been determined.

The mode of action of alpha-interferon in the treatment of chronic hepatitis B and chronic hepatitis C (NonA NonB) infection is poorly understood, but seems to consist of both a direct antiviral effect and immune-modulatory actions.

Interferon alpha-n1 (Ins) has been administered to patients with a variety of malignancies at doses of 0.1 to 50 Mu/m² by i.m., s.c. and i.v. routes and at doses up to 200 Mu/m² by 24 hour infusion. Serum pharmacokinetic analyses have been studied systematically in 2 of these trials and, within the limits of the idiosyncrasies inherent in individual bioassay systems and the difference noted in individual subjects, provide the basis for this analysis of the pharmacodynamics of drug therapy.

In the very few patients examined, there has been little CSF activity demonstrable following either i.m. or i.v. administration.

The alpha interferons (presumably also Wellferon) are catabolized by renal tubular cells and essentially all of the interferon appearing in the glomerular ultrafiltrate is removed during passage through the renal tubules. The clearance of serum interferon activity parallels the glomerular filtration rate, being cleared at a rate, under normal circumstances of 100 mL/min.

Indications: For the treatment of patients with hairy cell leukemia, juvenile laryngeal papillomatosis, condylomata acuminata, chronic hepatitis B and chronic hepatitis C infections.

Hairy Cell Leukemia: Hairy cell leukemia (HCL) is a rare disease of variable course. Approximately 10 to 20% of HCL patients never require therapy. These are usually older patients without splenomegaly and granulocyte counts above 1 000 cells/mm³. The remaining 80 to 90% of the patients will require therapy during the course of their disease. It is a leukemia usually refractory to therapies conventionally given for malignant disease. Splenectomy frequently induces temporary remissions in patients who present with splenomegaly and pancytopenia. Subsequent relapse almost invariably follows and prognosis is then poor. The overall median survival of HCL patients is only 50 months and 40% of them die within 2 years of diagnosis.

Recent experience with interferon suggests it may have a major impact on the disease. Quesada, using 3 mega units (1 Mu=1 million units)/day of Cantell alpha interferon, reported substantial clinical improvement in 20 of 20 patients.

Infections occurred frequently in many patients prior to therapy. Thereafter they were uncommon, occurring usually during the first month or two of treatment. General well-being and performance status rose as hematological parameters improved in the majority of patients.

Febrile episodes and flu-like side effects were frequently seen at the start of treatment but were mostly mild thereafter. Fatigue was the commonest side effect during prolonged treatment but was usually not severe. Serious adverse reactions were extremely rare. Overall, severe side effects were experienced on only 6% of all patient treatment-days, over half of which were completely free from side effects. These became less common as treatment progressed.

Juvenile Laryngeal Papillomatosis: Juvenile laryngeal papillomatosis is an uncommon disease which is usually characterized by frequently persistent regrowth of benign papillomata in the epithelium of the respiratory tract. It is a widespread disease and the threat of airway obstruction frequently necessitates surgical intervention with usually good short-term results. The human papilloma viral etiology of this disease has been well documented by several investigators.

A multicentre, controlled trial of interferon alpha-n1 (Ins) at 5 Mu/m² daily for 28 doses followed by a maintenance dosage 3 times weekly for 5 months was carried out in 66 patients including adults and children greater than 1 year of age. Disease measurements and clinical severity were significantly reduced by interferon alpha-n1 (Ins).

Condylomata Acuminata: Condylomata acuminata, or genital warts, are considered by most investigators to be sexually transmitted lesions and associated with certain types of human papilloma viruses. These warty, benign neoplasms are contagious and approximately 70% of sexual partners have or develop lesions. It is estimated that 1 to 10% of women in the US of childbearing age have genital warts.

The spontaneous regression of condylomata acuminata has been well known but poorly understood. Up to one-third of primary genital warts have regressed within 6 months, but the remaining two-thirds may grow in size or spread to other anatomical sites. Many forms of therapy over the years have produced mixed results. Such therapies as topical podophyllin, antimetabolites, cautery, cryotherapy and surgery have all presented varying degrees of success along with painful experiences and leave some scar tissue. More recently preliminary studies followed by more controlled studies on the use of various interferons have indicated that interferon alpha-n1 (Ins) could be an active and safe and helpful therapeutic agent in the treatment of this condition. Complete or partial response was observed in 70 to 80% of 176 women evaluated at 7 weeks of treatment; similar rate of response was observed in 62 women followed up to 11 weeks. During a 6 month evaluation of 30 patients (23 women and 7 men) 20 individuals (67%) retained complete or partial response. Longer follow-up observation will be necessary to fully evaluate the therapeutic potential of interferon alpha-n1 (Ins). Studies of interferon alpha-n1 (Ins) as an adjunct to laser surgery also merit further study.

Chronic Hepatitis B: Hepatitis B infection, acquired through contact with blood or other body fluids from a person carrying the hepatitis B virus (HBV), is prevalent at rates that vary worldwide. The severity of the overt acute clinical attack varies and appears to be inversely related to subsequent development of the chronic carrier stage, which is defined as the persistence of hepatitis B surface antigen (HBsAg) beyond 6 months from the onset of infection. In patients with chronic active hepatitis (CAH) disease progression is observed in 20 to 70% over a 2-year to 7-year period with an estimated mortality of 25 to 50%. The high proportion of chronic carriers of HBV who give no history of an acute hepatitis attack indicates that subclinical episodes are frequent.

The effect of interferon alpha-n1 (Ins) regimens of 3 months or more on the serological, biochemical and histological manifestations of the disease have been clearly demonstrated. A treated patient is more than 3 times as likely to be clear of HBeAg at 1 year. In excess of around one third of patients treated with interferon alpha-n1 (Ins) clear HBeAg at 1 year. This will be accompanied by biochemical and histological remission.

Recent experience with interferon for the treatment of chronic hepatitis B suggests that interferon alpha-n1 (Ins) has shown a significant increase in the HBeAg seroconversion rate using prednisolone pretreatment.

Chronic Hepatitis C: Hepatitis C virus (HCV) is a common cause of acute and chronic hepatitis, both post-transfusional and sporadic. HCV infection has a high tendency to chronicity. In 40 to 50% of patients with post-transfusion hepatitis, the infection becomes chronic, and in 20% of these cases the disease progresses to cirrhosis. There is also a high proportion of HCV-related cases of hepatocellular carcinoma. At all stages of the disease, ALT levels are characteristically elevated above the normal range, consistent with hepatocyte damage, and usually fluctuate. Insidious evolution of chronic hepatitis C to cirrhosis is emerging as a consistent observation, even though patients may be asymptomatic and have only marginal elevations of aminotransferase levels.

Clinical experience shows that interferon alpha-n1 (Ins) therapy can result in an ALT response at the end of treatment in up to 60% of patients. Approximately half of these patients will maintain a sustained ALT response, post-treatment.

Almost 50% of HCV infected patients treated with interferon alpha-n1 (Ins) show sustained improvement in liver inflammation on histological examination.

Interferon alpha-n1 (Ins) is indicated for the treatment of patients with chronic hepatitis C (NonA NonB) infection. Efficacy has been established on the basis of normalization of serum aminotransferases, clearance of serum HCV RNA and by improvements in liver histology.

Contraindications: Should not be given to patients known to be hypersensitive to the preparation or any of its components.

Other than known hypersensitivity, there are no contraindications to the use of interferon alpha-n1 (Ins) injection, in hairy cell leukemia, condylomata acuminata or juvenile laryngeal papillomatosis. However, extreme caution is advised when treating patients with concurrent hepatic, renal, cardiovascular or CNS disease or with a history of pre-existing mental disturbance. Care should be exercised in patients with asthma as exacerbation of the disease has been reported on isolated occasions following interferon administration.

Interferon alpha-n1 (Ins) should not be used to treat chronic hepatitis B infection in patients who have poor hepatic reserve, since successful elimination of serological markers of active viral replication is often preceded by an acute, hepatitis-like illness.

For chronic hepatitis C infection, the following contraindications exist: severe pre-existing cardiac disease, severe renal or hepatic dysfunction, epilepsy and/or compromised CNS function, chronic hepatitis with advanced decompensated cirrhosis of the liver, and chronic hepatitis in patients who are being or have recently been treated with immunosuppressive agents excluding short-term "steroid withdrawal".

Warnings and Precautions: Occupational Hazards: As interferons may affect CNS functions patients should be warned not to drive a vehicle or operate machinery until their tolerance of treatment has been assessed.

Extreme caution is advised when using alpha interferons in the treatment of patients with concurrent hepatic, renal, cardiovascular or CNS disease, or patients with a history of pre-existing mental disturbances.

Suicidal behavior has been observed rarely in patients receiving alpha-interferons. Therapy should be discontinued in patients exhibiting or at risk of suicidal behavior.

Care should be exercised in patients with asthma as exacerbation of the disease has been reported on isolated occasions following interferon administration.

It is important to monitor the blood count closely in patients during the first 6 weeks of treatment, following which the suppressive effects of alpha interferons on the bone marrow will be overtaken by the improving leukemic state, leading towards a normalization of hematological parameters.

During treatment of chronic hepatitis B and chronic hepatitis C (NonA NonB) infection, it is important to monitor blood count and liver function throughout treatment.

For those patients being considered for prednisolone pretreatment therapy, the physician should refer to the precautions and warnings section of the prednisolone prescribing information for a description of the known prednisolone precautions and warnings.

Pregnancy: No information is available on the use of interferon alpha-n1 (Ins) in human pregnancy. In view of the profound effects of the drug on human metabolism and physiology, interferon alpha-n1 (Ins) should be considered as a drug which might result in damage to the fetus and patients should therefore be advised accordingly. The expected clinical benefit of treatment to the patient must be balanced against any possible hazard to the developing fetus.

In view of the long clinical course of chronic hepatitis B infection and the availability of hepatitis B immunization for the neonate, use of interferon alpha-n1 (Ins) to treat chronic hepatitis B infection during pregnancy is not recommended.

Lactation: There is no information on the effect of the drug on human lactation.

Children: The safety and effectiveness of interferon alpha-n1 (Ins) in patients under 18 years of age have not been established in the treatment of hairy cell leukemia, Condylomata acuminata or chronic hepatitis C infections.

Interferon alpha-n1 (Ins) is well tolerated in children in the treatment of chronic hepatitis B infection and 2 recent treatment vs no treatment studies, efficacy was demonstrated. In contrast to use in adults, steroid pretreatment in children was not associated with increased efficacy.

Geriatrics: Elderly patients may be less tolerant of the side effects of interferon, particularly those effects which are cumulative. These patients should be seen frequently while receiving treatment; interferon alpha-n1 (Ins) dosage should be reduced or even stopped if patients are unduly sensitive to side effects.

Drug Interactions: Alpha interferons may alter the activity of certain enzymes. In particular, they reduce the activity of P450 cytochromes. The metabolism of drugs such as cimetidine, phenytoin, warfarin, theophylline, diazepam and propranolol by these enzyme systems may therefore be impaired in patients receiving alpha interferons. Several cytotoxic drugs e.g., cyclophosphamide, are also metabolized by these enzymes.

Progressive renal failure has been reported in patients receiving concurrent high dose acyclovir. Concurrent administration of interferon with drugs which act on the CNS has occasionally resulted in unexpectedly severe changes in mental state. Concurrent administration of interferon with drugs which act on the CNS has occasionally resulted in unexpectedly severe changes in mental state.

Concurrent administration of immunosuppressive drugs (including corticosteroids), which may enhance viral replication, should be avoided during treatment of chronic hepatitis B infection with interferon alpha-n1 (Ins). Although concurrent use of prednisolone and interferon alpha-n1 (Ins) is not recommended, prednisolone pretreatment is permitted for the hepatitis B indication (see Dosage).

In the treatment of chronic hepatitis B infection, the occurence of an acute, hepatitis-like illness (see Contraindications) presents the theoretical risk of additive interaction with hepatotoxic drugs and of further impairment of hepatic drug metabolism.

Information to Be Provided to the Patient: Because of the possibility of severe or even fatal adverse reactions to interferon therapy, patients should be informed not only of the benefits but also of the potential risks of treatment with interferon alpha-n1 (Ins). Patients should also be advised that the clinical activity of different brands of interferon may not be comparable and that different brands of interferon should not be used in a single-treatment regimen.

When patients are advised by their physicians to administer interferon alpha-n1 (Ins) by self-injection, adequate instruction in s.c. administration practices should be provided. Patients should be cautioned against reusing syringes and needles. If home use is prescribed, a puncture-resistant container for the disposal of used syringes and needles should be supplied to the patient. Patients should be thoroughly instructed on needle, syringe, and container disposal procedures and should be advised of the importance of following correct disposal procedures.

Patients should be advised that anti-inflammatory analgesics (e.g., acetaminophen and ibuprofen) may alleviate some of the discomforts associated with initial treatment with interferon alpha-n1 (Ins). Patients receiving interferon alpha-n1 (Ins) should also be advised to stay well hydrated, especially during the initial stages of treatment.

Adverse Effects: Interferon alpha-n1 (Ins) is a highly active mediator of biological events and its use may be associated with severe side effects, particularly when large doses are administered.

The most frequently reported side effects of interferon alpha-n1 (Ins) and other alpha interferon preparations consist of fever, chills, occasionally rigors, headache, malaise and myalgia, all reminiscent of an attack of influenza. These acute side effects can usually be reduced or eliminated by concurrent administration of acetaminophen and tend to diminish with continuing therapy. In contrast however, continuing therapy can lead to lethargy, weakness, arthralgia and fatigue accompanied by anorexia and weight loss.

Alpha interferons have a suppressive effect on the bone marrow leading to a fall in the white blood count, particularly the granulocytes, the platelet count and, less commonly, the hemoglobin concentration. Additionally, abnormalities in the blood clotting mechanism have occurred. These effects can lead to an increased risk of infection, hemorrhage and thrombosis.

Marked effects on the CNS may occur; these include abnormal EEGs with excess slow wave activity, severe depression including rarely suicidal behavior, confusion, apathy and coma. Occasionally seizures occur which may be precipitated by fever in children. A few reports of movement disorders (including extrapyramidal and cerebellar dysfunction) have been reported in cancer patients receiving interferon alpha-n1 (Ins).

The administration of alpha interferons may give rise to hypotension, hypertension, or arrhythmias in certain individuals. Severe cardiovascular events reported in patients receiving alpha interferons include myocardial infarction, cerebrovascular accident and peripheral ischemia. Nausea, vomiting and diarrhea occur sporadically.

Alpha interferons can lead to an elevation in liver-related enzymes; this is usually transient but occasionally is marked and persistent. Hepatic necrosis has been reported on very rare occasions.

Rare occurrences of renal failure and/or nephrotic syndrome have been seen in patients treated with interferon alpha-n1 (Ins). These patients had all been suffering from myelomatosis and had varying degrees of prior renal dysfunction.

After repeated very high doses (100 to 200 Mu) i.v. by infusion, hypocalcemia and hyperkalemia have occurred.

Reactions at injection sites have been reported in some patients, and alopecia occurs occasionally as a late side effect.

Other events which have been reported in patients receiving alpha interferons include late development of lymphomas, Raynaud's phenomenon, urticaria, erythema nodosum, skin rashes, mucositis and isolated peripheral nerve defects and disturbances of antidiuretic hormone levels.

Isolated cases of various autoimmune phenomena e.g., immune thrombocytopenia, hemolytic anemia, hypothyroidism, diabetes mellitus have occurred following alpha-interferon administration. In some patients with pre-existing autoimmune phenomena, isolated cases of exacerbations have been seen.

Adverse Reactions with Prednisolone Pretreatment: Information regarding the adverse events associated with prednisolone pretreatment therapy is limited. Physicians should refer to the data sheet for prednisolone for a description of known prednisolone-associated adverse reactions.

Overdose: Symptoms and Treatment: There are no reports of overdose but repeated large doses of interferon are associated with profound lethargy, fatigue, prostration and coma. Such patients should be hospitalized for observation and given appropriate supportive treatment.

Dosage: Hairy Cell Leukemia: For remission induction, the dose recommended is 3 Mu given daily by i.m. injection. The s.c. route has also been used successfully and has been found to be more convenient for patient self-administration.

After normalization or marked improvement in peripheral hematological indices (commonly 12 to 16 weeks), the dose may be administered 3 times weekly, during which time further improvement in the bone marrow is to be anticipated. Prolonged treatment for 6 months or more may be required to clear hairy cells from the bone marrow.

Hematological recovery is to be expected in patients who have failed splenectomy as well as in those with palpable splenomegaly in whom reduction in spleen size is to be anticipated.

Juvenile Laryngeal Papillomatosis: Adjunctive therapy with interferon alpha-n1 (Ins) injection, is recommended only with routine surgical management. Some very severely affected patients requiring surgery every 1 to 4 months may not respond to interferon alpha-n1 (Ins) even on prolonged treatment, but treatment up to and beyond 1 year has been reported to show continued improvement. Careful clinical and periodic endoscopic evaluation of disease should continue.

Respiratory papillomatosis requires extended treatment; maximum response usually occurs within 6 months, but more

Wellferon (cont'd)

prolonged therapy might be required. Doses for children greater than 1 year of age can be estimated from Table I.

Table I—Wellferon

Wellferon Dose Calculation for Children

Mega Units (Mu)/m² Body Surface Area (B.S.A.)	
B.S.A. (m²)	**Dose (Mu)**
<0.5	1.5
0.5-1.0	3.0
>1.0	5.0

Interferon alpha-n1 (lns) should be administered i.m., daily for 28 days followed by a maintenance dosage 3 times weekly for at least 6 months.

Condylomata Acuminata: An initial dose of 1 to 3 Mu/m² (5 Mu) 5 times a week for 2 weeks, followed by 3 times a week for 4 weeks, s.c. It can also be administered i.m. but the s.c. route has been used successfully and has been found to be more convenient for patients' self-administration. The same dose should then be continued every other day or 3 times weekly for 1 month. As an adjunct to laser surgery or cryosurgery, 1 Mu/m² should be administered daily for 7 days prior to and 7 days following surgical resection of the lesions.

Alternatively, dosing levels may be adjusted to suit an individual's tolerability. However, daily dosing levels above 5 Mu/m² are not recommended for condylomata acuminata patients.

If dose reductions are required due to intolerance, doses as low as 1 Mu/m² may be effective if a similar cumulative dose to that given by the 5 Mu regimen is achieved over longer periods.

Chronic Hepatitis B Infection: A 12-week course of 3 times weekly i.m. or s.c. injections of 10 to 15 Mu (up to 7.5 Mu/m² body surface area) is generally recommended.

Longer periods of treatment for up to 6 months at lower doses of 5 to 10 Mu (up to 5 Mu/m² body surface area) 3 times weekly have been employed and may be preferred for patients who do not tolerate higher doses.

An initial treatment period, employing escalating daily doses usually over 5 days (but up to 28 days with the longer treatment) may be a convenient way of introducing therapy.

Interferon alpha-n1 (lns) has shown a significant increase in the HBeAg seroconversion rate using prednisolone pretreatment. A tapering prednisolone dose of 0.6 mg/kg/day for 2 weeks, 0.45 mg/kg/day for 1 week and 0.25 mg/kg/day for 1 week is recommended. This is followed by a 2 week no treatment period, prior to the administration of a 12-week course of 3 times weekly i.m. or s.c. injection of 10 Mu interferon alpha-n1 (lns).

Immunosuppressed Patients: Efficacy against hepatitis B virus infection has not yet been demonstrated in patients whose immune systems are compromised (e.g., by current or recent therapy with immunosuppressive drugs (excluding short-term steroid pretreatment) or due to human immunodeficiency virus (HIV) infection).

Chronic Hepatitis C Infection: A 48-week course of 3 times weekly i.m. or s.c. injections of 5 MU is recommended. For patients who are unable to tolerate this dose, a 3 times weekly injection of 3 MU for the remainder of the 48-week period may be more appropriate. The s.c. route being more acceptable and convenient for patient self administration.

General Administration: Some patients appear to be less troubled by interferon-related side effects if the dose is administered in the evening.

Children: No information is available on the treatment of hairy cell leukemia in children, although preliminary clinical evidence shows that, interferon alpha-n1 (lns), is tolerated in other childhood conditions.

In the rare event of hairy cell leukemia occurring in children, proportions of the adult dose based on body surface area would be appropriate.

Interferon alpha-n1 (lns) is well tolerated in children in the treatment of chronic hepatitis B infection, dosages of up to 10 Mu/m² body surface area have been administered. An efficacy advantage of treatment vs no treatment has been demonstrated in 2 recent studies, but no advantage of steroid pretreatment was demonstrated in this resistant group of patients.

Geriatrics: Elderly patients may be less tolerant of the side effects of interferon, particularly those effects which are cumulative. These patients should be seen frequently while receiving treatment; interferon alpha-n1 (lns) dosage should be reduced or even stopped if patients are unduly sensitive to side effects.

Information for the Patient: See Blue Section—Information for the Patient "Wellferon".

Supplied: Each vial of clear, colorless solution contains: interferon alpha-n1 (lns) [purified human lymphoblastoid interferon] 3, 5 or 10 mega units. 1 mega unit (Mu)=1×10⁶ International Units (IU) of lymphoblastoid interferon. Formulated in 1 mL tris-glycine buffered normal saline with human albumin at a concentration of 1.5 mg/mL as a stabilizer. The final product contains Namalwa cell DNA <10 pg/mL.

Store between 2 to 8°C. Protect from light. The injection contains no preservative. Discard any partly used vials immediately after withdrawal of the required dose. One mL vials of 3, 5 and 10 Mu/mL.

Reviewed 1999

WESTCORT® Preparations

Westwood-Squibb

Hydrocortisone-17-valerate

Topical Corticosteroid

Pharmacology: Studies conducted in healthy adult volunteers illustrated that 0.2% Hydrocortisone-17-valerate cream and ointment has minimal primary irritant and contact sensitization potential. Adrenal suppression studies with the cream indicated that any observed reduction in pituitary-adrenal function was rapidly reversible.

Indications: Topical therapy of acute and chronic corticosteroid responsive dermatoses, where an anti-inflammatory, antiallergenic and antipruritic activity is required in the topical management of these conditions.

Contraindications: Untreated tubercular, bacterial, fungal and most viral lesions of the skin (including herpes simplex, vaccinia and varicella), hypersensitivity to any of the components of the preparation. Not for ophthalmic use.

Warnings: *Pregnancy* and *Lactation:* The safety of topical corticosteroids during pregnancy and lactation has not been established. The potential benefit should be weighed in these conditions against possible hazard to the fetus or the nursing infant. When indicated, they should not be used extensively, in large amounts or for prolonged periods of time on pregnant patients or nursing mothers.

If used under an occlusive dressing, particularly over extensive areas, sufficient absorption may take place to give rise to adrenal suppression and other systemic effects.

Topical corticosteroids are not for ophthalmic use.

Precautions: Topical corticosteroids should be used with caution on lesions close to the eye.

Although hypersensitivity reactions have been rare with topically applied steroids, the drug should be discontinued, and suitable therapy instituted if there are signs of sensitivity.

In the presence of bacterial infections of the skin, an appropriate antibacterial agent should be used as primary therapy. If it is considered necessary, the topical corticosteroid may be used as an adjunct to control inflammation, erythema, and itching. If a favorable response does not occur within a few days to a week, the steroid should be discontinued until the infection has been adequately controlled.

Significant systemic absorption may occur when steroids are applied over large areas of the body, especially under occlusive dressings. To minimize this possibility, when long-term therapy is anticipated, interrupt treatment periodically or treat one area of the body at a time.

Prolonged use of topical corticosteroid products may produce atrophy of the skin and subcutaneous tissues, particularly on the flexor surfaces and on the face. If this is noted, discontinue the use of topical corticosteroids.

Topical corticosteroids should be used with caution in patients with stasis dermatitis and other skin diseases associated with impaired circulation.

Patients should be advised to inform subsequent physicians of the prior use of corticosteroids.

Occlusive dressings should not be applied if there is an elevation of body temperature.

Adverse Effects: The following local adverse reactions have been reported with the use of topical corticosteroids: dryness, itching, burning, local irritation, striae, atrophy of s.c. tissues, telangiectasia, hypertrichosis, hypopigmentation and secondary infection. When occlusive dressings are used, pustules, miliaria, folliculitis and pyoderma may occur.

Adrenal suppression has occurred with prolonged use of large doses of topical corticosteroids, particularly under occlusion due to increased percutaneous absorption.

Posterior subcapsular cataracts have been reported following systemic use of corticosteroids.

Overdose: Symptoms and Treatment: Percutaneous absorption of corticosteroids can occur when considerable amounts are applied over a large area, particularly when these areas are occluded. Suppression of the adrenal-pituitary axis may result and suitable procedures should be instituted.

Dosage: Gently massage a small amount of cream or ointment into the affected area 2 to 3 times daily as needed.

Supplied: Cream: Each 15, 45 or 60 g tube of cream contains: hydrocortisone-17-valerate 0.2%. Nonmedicinal ingredients: amphoteric-9, carbomer 940, petrolatum, propylene glycol, sodium lauryl sulfate, sodium phosphate, sorbic acid, stearyl alcohol and water.

Ointment: Each 15 or 60 g tube of ointment contains hydrocortisone-17-valerate 0.2%. Nonmedicinal ingredients: carbomer 934, mineral oil, petrolatum, propylene glycol, sodium lauryl sulfate, sodium phosphate, sorbic acid, steareth-2, steareth-100, stearyl alcohol and water.

Store below 26°C.

WINPRED™

ICN

Prednisone

Glucocorticoid

Supplied: Each white, flat, compressed tablet imprinted ICN W1 contains: prednisone USP 1 mg. Nonmedicinal ingredients: maltodextrane, lactose, magnesium stearate, starch and talc. Bottles of 100.

WinRho SDF™

Cangene

Rh_o (D) Immune Globulin (Human)

Passive Immunizing Agent

Pharmacology: Rh_o (D) Immune Globulin (Human) is a sterile freeze-dried gamma globulin (IgG) fraction of human plasma containing antibodies to Rh_o (D), prepared by an anion-exchange column chromatography method.

The incorporation of the Solvent Detergent step, which includes treatment with Tri-n-butyl phosphate and Triton X-100, in the WinRho SDF process is designed to increase the safety of the product by reducing the risk of transmission of lipid enveloped viruses, such as hepatitis B, hepatitis C and HIV. WinRho SDF is filtered using a Planova 35 nm Virus Filter which has been validated to be effective in the removal of nonlipid enveloped viruses. Virus models for hepatitis A and human parvovirus B-19 were all shown to be removed after Planova 35 nm virus filtration. Table I summarizes test viruses and their respective log virus reductions.

Table I—WinRho SDF

Planova 35 nm Virus Filter Log Virus Reduction Summary

Test Virus	**Log Virus Reduction**	**Model for:**	**Virus Type**
Poliovirus	4.25	Hepatitis A (HAV)	nonlipid enveloped RNA
Theiler's Mouse Encephalomyelitis Virus (TMEV)	3.2	Hepatitis A (HAV)	nonlipid enveloped RNA
Bovine Parvovirus (BPV)	>4.97	Human Parvovirus B-19	nonlipid enveloped DNA

The WinRho SDF process is based on the process used to manufacture WinRho, a product that has been used for over 10 years in the prevention of Rh alloimmunization.

The product potency is expressed in international units by comparison to the World Health Organization (WHO) standard. A 1 500 International Unit (IU) (300 µg) vial contains sufficient anti-Rh_o (D) to effectively suppress the immunizing potential of approximately 17 mL of Rh_o (D) positive red blood cells. (In the past, a full dose of Rh_o (D) Immune Globulin (Human) has traditionally been referred to as a "300 µg" dose. Potency and dosing recommendations are now expressed in IU by comparison to the WHO anti-D standard. The conversion of "μg" to "IU" is 1 μg=5 IU).

Prevention of Rh Immunization: Rh_o (D) Immune Globulin (Human) is used to suppress the immune response of non-sensitized Rh_o (D) negative individuals who receive Rh_o (D) positive blood either by fetomaternal hemorrhage during delivery of an Rh_o (D) positive infant, abortion (either spontaneous or induced), following amniocentesis, abdominal trauma or accidental transfusion. Administration of anti-Rh_o (D) antibody to the Rh_o (D) negative mother prevents an immune response with subsequent anti-Rh_o (D) antibody formation. The exact mechanism of action has yet to be determined.

Rh_o (D) Immune Globulin (Human), when administered within 72 hours of a full-term delivery of an Rh_o (D) positive infant by an Rh_o (D) negative mother, will reduce the incidence of Rh alloimmunization from 12 to 13% to 1 to 2%. The 1 to 2% is, for the most part, due to alloimmunization during the last trimester of pregnancy. When treatment is given both antenatally at 28 weeks gestation and postpartum the Rh immunization rate drops to about 0.1%.

Treatment of Immune Thrombocytopenic Purpura (ITP): Rh_o (D) Immune Globulin (Human) is used to increase platelet counts in nonsplenectomized Rh_o (D) positive patients with ITP and to alleviate clinical signs of bleeding in this patient population. The mechanism of action is not completely understood, but is thought to be due to the production of anti-Rh_o (D)-coated red blood cell complexes resulting in Fc receptor blockade, thus sparing antibody-coated platelets. In a clinical study of WinRho therapy of children with chronic ITP (duration of ITP >6 months), administration of anti-Rh_o (D) increased platelet counts from $36 \pm 14 \times 10^9$/L to $263 \pm 138 \times 10^9$/L; peak platelet levels were recorded at about 1 week after WinRho therapy; the effect of WinRho on platelet levels lasted a median of 29 days from the start of therapy. Comparable results were obtained in a clinical study of both adult and children with ITP of varying etiologies including ITP secondary to HIV infection. However, larger increases in platelet levels were seen in children than in adults.

When Rh_o (D) Immune Globulin (Human) is administered by an i.v. route, peak levels are achieved within 2 hours, while the mean time to peak is 5 to 10 days when drug is administered by an i.m. route. When 600 IU (120 μg) of product was administered to nonpregnant volunteers, the peak levels of passive anti-Rh_o (D) antibody that were achieved were about 40 ng/mL when the drug was administered by an i.v. route and about 20 ng/mL when the drug was administered by an i.m. route. In a clinical study with Rh_o (D) negative volunteers, Rh_o (D) positive red cells were completely cleared from the circulation within 8 hours of i.v. administration of WinRho SD Rh_o (D) Immune Globulin (Human).

When only 600 IU (120 μg) of drug is administered to pregnant women, passive anti-Rh_o (D) antibodies are not detectable in the circulation for more than 6 weeks and therefore a dose of 1 500 IU (300 μg) should be used for antenatal administration.

WinRho SD Rh_o (D) Immune Globulin (Human) has been shown to increase platelets in ITP patients. Platelet counts usually rise within 1 to 2 days and peak within 7 to 14 days after initiation of therapy. The duration of response is variable; however, the average duration is approximately 30 days.

Indications: Pregnancy and Other Obstetric Conditions: For the prevention of Rh immunization of Rh_o (D) negative women at risk of developing Rh antibodies. Rh_o (D) Immune Globulin (Human) prevents the development of Rh antibodies in the Rh_o (D) negative and previously not sensitized mother carrying a Rh_o (D) positive fetus, thus preventing the occurrence of hemolytic disease in the fetus or the newborn.

For the prevention of Rh immunization in Rh_o (D) negative mothers who have not been previously sensitized to the Rh_o (D) factor.

The administration of Rh_o (D) Immune Globulin (Human) to women satisfying the above conditions should be done at about 28 weeks gestation when the child's father is either Rh_o (D) positive or unknown.

Rh_o (D) Immune Globulin (Human) should be administered within 72 hours after delivery if the baby is Rh_o (D) positive or unknown.

Rh_o (D) Immune Globulin (Human) administration is also recommended in these same women within 72 hours after spontaneous or induced abortion, amniocentesis, chorion villus sampling, ruptured tubal pregnancy, abdominal trauma or transplacental hemorrhage, unless the blood type of the fetus or the father is confirmed to be Rh_o (D) negative. It should be administered as soon as possible in the case of maternal bleeding due to threatened abortion.

Transfusion: Rh_o (D) Immune Globulin (Human) is recommended to prevent alloimmunization in Rh_o (D) negative individuals transfused with Rh_o (D) positive red blood cells or blood components with red blood cells. Treatment is indicated if the individual who has received the transfusion is a female child or adult in her childbearing years. Treatment should only then be carried out (without preceding exchange transfusion), if the transfused Rh_o (D) positive blood represents less than 20% of the total circulating red cells.

Immune Thrombocytopenic Purpura (ITP): Rh_o (D) Immune Globulin (Human) is recommended in the treatment of destructive thrombocytopenia of an immune etiology in situations where platelet counts must be increased to control bleeding. Clinical studies have shown that the peak platelet counts occur about 7 days after i.v. anti-Rh_o (D) treatment. The effect is not curative but is transient; platelet counts are usually elevated from several days to several weeks. For individuals with chronic ITP, a maintenance dosage is recommended with the dosage schedule determined on an individual basis.

Rh_o (D) Immune Globulin (Human) is recommended for the treatment of nonsplenectomized Rh_o (D) positive 1) children with chronic or acute ITP, 2) adults with chronic ITP, or 3) children and adults with ITP secondary to HIV infection in clinical situations requiring an increase in platelet count to prevent excessive hemorrhage.

Childhood Chronic ITP: In an open-label, single arm, multicentre study, 24 nonsplenectomized, Rh_o (D) positive children with ITP of greater than 6 months' duration were treated initially with 250 IU (50 μg)/kg Rh_o (D) Immune Globulin (Human) (125 IU/kg [25 μg/kg] on days 1 and 2), with subsequent doses ranging from 125 to 275 IU (25 to 55 μg)/kg. Response was defined as a platelet increase to at least 50 000/mm³ and a doubling of the baseline. Nineteen of 24 patients responded for an overall response rate of 79%, an overall mean peak platelet count of 229 400/mm³ (range 43 300 to 456 000), and a mean duration of response of 36.5 days (range 6 to 84).

Childhood Acute ITP: A multicentre, randomized, controlled trial comparing Rh_o (D) IGIV to high dose and low dose Immune Globulin (Human) and prednisone was conducted in 146 nonsplenectomized, Rh_o (D) positive children with acute ITP and platelet counts less than 20 000/mm³. Of 38 patients receiving Rh_o (D) IGIV (125 IU/kg [25 μg/kg] on days 1 and 2), 32 patients (84%) responded (platelet count ≥50 000/mm³) with a mean peak platelet count of 319 500/mm³ (range 61 000 to 892 000), with no statistically significant differences compared to other treatment arms. The mean times to achieving ≥20 000/mm³ or ≥50 000/mm³ platelets for patients receiving Rh_o (D) IGIV were 1.9 and 2.8 days respectively. When comparing the different therapies for time to platelet count ≥20 000/mm³ or ≥50 000/mm³, no statistically significant differences among treatment groups were detected, with a range of 1.3 to 1.9 days and 2.0 to 3.2 days, respectively.

Adult Chronic ITP: Twenty-four nonsplenectomized, Rh_o (D) positive adults with ITP of greater than 6 months' duration and platelet counts <30 000/mm³ or requiring therapy were enrolled in a single-arm, open-label trial and treated with 100 to 375 IU (20 to 75 μg)/kg Rh_o (D) IGIV (mean dose 231 IU [46.2 μg]/kg. Twenty-one of 24 patients responded (increase ≥20 000/mm³) during the first 2 courses of therapy for an overall response rate of 88% with a mean peak platelet count of 92 300/mm³ (range 8 000 to 229 000).

ITP Secondary to HIV Infection: Eleven children and 52 adults who were nonsplenectomized, Rh_o (D) positive with all Walter Reed classes of HIV infection and ITP, with initial platelet counts of ≤30 000/mm³ or requiring therapy, were treated with 100 to 375 IU (20 to 75 μg)/kg Rh_o (D) IGIV in an open-label trial. Rh_o (D) IGIV was administered for an average of 7.3 courses (range 1 to 57) over a mean period of 407 days (range 6 to 1 952). Fifty-seven of 63 patients responded (increase ≥20 000/mm³) during the first 6 courses of therapy for an overall response rate of 90%. The overall mean change in platelet count for 6 courses was 60 900/mm³ (range - 2 000 to 565 000), and the mean peak platelet count was 81 700/mm³ (range 16 000 to 593 000).

Contraindications: Prevention of Rh Immunization: When Rh_o (D) Immune Globulin (Human) is used to prevent Rh alloimmunization, it should not be administered to: 1) Rh_o (D) positive individuals including babies; 2) Rh_o (D) negative women who are Rh immunized as evidenced by standard manual Rh antibody screening tests; 3) individuals with a history of anaphylactic or other severe systemic reaction to immune globulins.

Immune Thrombocytopenic Purpura: When Rh_o(D) Immune Globulin (Human) is used to treat patients with ITP, it should not be administered to: 1) Rh_o (D) negative individuals, 2) splenectomized individuals, 3) individuals with known hypersensitivity to plasma products.

Warnings: Rh_o (D) Immune Globulin (Human) contains trace quantities of IgA. Although WinRho has been used successfully to treat selected IgA deficient individuals, the physician must weigh the potential benefit of treatment with Rh_o (D) Immune Globulin (Human) against the potential for hypersensitivity reactions. Individuals deficient in IgA have a potential for development of IgA antibodies and anaphylactic reactions after administration of blood components containing IgA; Burks et al. (1986) have reported that as little as 15 μg IgA/mL of blood product has elicited an anaphylactic reaction in IgA deficient individuals. Individuals known to have had an anaphylactic or severe systemic reaction to human globulin should not receive Rh_o (D) Immune Globulin (Human) or any other Immune Glubulin (Human).

Rh_o (D) Immune Globulin (Human) **must be administered via the i.v. route** for the treatment of ITP as its efficacy has not been established by the i.m. or s.c. routes.

Rh_o (D) Immune Globulin (Human) should not be administered to Rh_o (D) negative or splenectomized individuals as its efficacy in these patients has not been demonstrated.

Precautions: General: A large fetomaternal hemorrhage late in pregnancy or following delivery may cause a weak mixed field positive D^u test result. Such an individual should be screened for a large fetomaternal hemorrhage and the Rh_o (D) Immune Globulin (Human) adjusted accordingly. Rh_o (D) Immune Globulin (Human) should be administered if there is any doubt about the mother's blood type.

Plasma used in manufacturing has been tested in accordance with regulations and has been treated to inactivate lipid and nonlipid enveloped virus; however, the possibility of transmission of infectious disease cannot be excluded.

In the treatment of ITP, if the patient has a lower than normal hemoglobin level (less than 10 g/dL), a reduced dose of 125 to 200 IU/kg (25 to 40 μg/kg) body weight should be given to minimize the risk of increasing the severity of anemia in the patient. Rh_o (D) Immune Globulin (Human) must be used with extreme caution in patients with a hemoglobin level that is less than 8 g/dL due to the risk of increasing the severity of the anemia.

Drug Interactions: Administration of Rh_o (D) Immune Globulin (Human) with other drugs has not been evaluated. It is recommended that Rh_o (D) Immune Globulin (Human) be administered separately from other drugs. Refer to Dosage section for information on drug compatibility.

Pregnancy: Category C: Animal reproduction studies have not been conducted with Rh_o (D) Immune Globulin (Human). It is not known whether Rh_o (D) Immune Globulin (Human) can cause fetal harm when administered to a pregnant woman or can affect reproductive capacity. Rh_o (D) Immune Globulin (Human) should be given to a pregnant woman only if clearly needed.

Laboratory Tests: In addition to anti-D antibody, Rh_o (D) Immune Globulin (Human) contains trace amounts of anti-C, E, A and B. These antibodies may be detected by laboratory screening tests.

In the prevention of Rh immunization, the presence of passively administered Rh antibody in maternal or fetal blood can lead to a positive direct antiglobulin (Coombs') test. In case of doubt as to the individual's Rh group or immune status, Rh_o (D) Immune Globulin (Human) should be administered.

In the treatment of ITP, the presence of passively administered anti-Rh_o (D) can lead to positive direct antiglobulin (Coombs') test. Interpretation of this result must be made in the context of the patient's clinical and supporting laboratory data.

Adverse Effects: Prevention of Rh Immunization: Reactions to Rh_o (D) Immune Globulin (Human) are rare in Rh_o (D) negative individuals. Discomfort and light swelling at the site of injection and slight elevation in temperature have been reported in a small number of cases.

In a clinical study with 5 healthy Rh_o (D) negative males, Rh_o (D) positive fetal red cells were administered to volunteers by i.v. infusion and then 1 to 2 days later the fetal red cells were cleared by i.v. administration of 600 IU (120 μg) WinRho SD. At 6 to 8 hours after administration of WinRho SD

WinRho SDF (cont'd)

to these subjects, there was an elevation in mean levels of granulocytes from 4.25 to 7.88×10^9/L($p < 0.01$) and monocytes from 0.38 to 0.64×10^9/L($p < 0.02$). Levels of phagocytic leukocytes returned to pretreatment levels by 24 hours after WinRho SD (human) treatment. This effect of WinRho SD (human) is believed to result from the anti-Rh_o (D) mediated clearance of Rh_o (D) positive fetal red cells as it was not observed at much higher dosages of Win Rho SD when no Rh_o (D) positive red cells were present in the circulation.

Treatment of ITP: Rh_o (D) Immune Globulin (Human) is administered to Rh_o (D) positive patients with ITP. Therefore, side effects related to the destruction of Rh_o (D) positive red cells, such as decreased hemoglobin, can be expected. At the recommended initial i.v. dose of 250 IU/kg (50 μg/kg), the mean maximum decrease in hemaglobin was 1.70 g/dL (range +0.40 to −6.1 g/dL). At a reduced dose, ranging from 125 to 200 IU/kg (25 to 40 μg/kg), the mean maximum decrease in hemoglobin was 0.81 g/dL (range +0.65 to −1.9 g/dL). Only 5/137 (3.7%) of patients had a maximum decrease in hemoglobin of greater than 4 g/dL (range 4.2 to 6.1 g/dL). In most cases, the red blood cell destruction is believed to occur in the spleen. However, there have been rare reports of acute onset of hemoglobinuria consistent with intravascular hemolysis and accompanied by reversible acute renal impairment. There have also been 2 cases of acute onset of hemoglobinuria without renal impairment in patients receiving red blood cell transfusion concurrent with WinRho SD.

In a clinical study of treatment of 48 Rh_o (D) positive individuals with autoimmune thrombocytopenic purpura of various etiologies with multiple treatments of 50 to 250 IU (10 to 50 μg)/kg body weight of WinRho (Bussel et al., 1991), 5 adverse reactions occurred during or immediately after the anti-Rh_o (D) infusions. Two reactions were severe: 1 occurred in a patient with known hypersensitivity to plasma products; the other occurred in a patient who had received i.v. WinRho before and numerous times since without any reactions. Both reactions resulted in shaking and chills with gradual recovery within 1 hour.

In trials in subjects (n=161) with childhood acute ITP, adults and children with chronic ITP, and adults and children with ITP secondary to HIV, 60/848 (7%) of infusions were associated with at least 1 adverse event that was considered to be related to the study medication. The most common adverse events were headache (19 infusions; 2%), chills (14 infusions; <2%), and fever (9 infusions; 1%). All are expected adverse events associated with infusions of immunoglobulins.

General Adverse Reactions: In addition to the adverse reactions described above, the following have been reported infrequently in clinical trials and/or postmarketing experience, in patients treated for ITP and/or the prevention of Rh immunization, and are thought to be temporally associated with Rh_o (D) Immune Globulin (Human) use: asthenia, abdominal or back pain, hypotension, pallor, diarrhea, increased LDH, arthralgia, myalgia, dizziness, hyperkinesia, somnolence, vasodilation, pruritus, rash and sweating.

As is the case with all drugs of this nature, there is a remote chance of an idiosyncratic or anaphylactoid reaction with Rh_o (D) Immune Globulin (Human) in individuals with hypersensitivity to blood products. In the event of an immediate reaction (anaphylaxis) characterized by collapse, rapid pulse, shallow respiration, pallor, cyanosis, edema or generalized urticaria, s.c. injection of epinephrine HCl 0.3 mL 1:1 000 aqueous solution should be instituted, followed by i.v. administration of hydrocortisone 50 to 100 mg if necessary.

Overdose: Symptoms and Treatment: If an Rh_o (D) positive individual is treated with large doses of Rh_o (D) Immune Globulin (Human), a mild anemia may develop. However, this is normally compensated for by elevated red cell production. Normally, medical intervention other than discontinuation of Rh_o (D) Immune Globulin (Human) treatment would not be required.

There are no reports of known overdoses in patients being treated for Rh isoimmunization or ITP. In clinical studies with nonpregnant Rh_o (D) positive patients with ITP (n=141) treated with 600 to 32 500 IU (120 to 6 500 μg) of Rh_o (D) IGIV, there were no signs or symptoms that warranted medical intervention. However, these same doses were associated with a mild, transient hemolytic anemia.

Dosage: Pregnancy and Other Obstetric Conditions: See Table II. A 1 500 IU (300 μg) dose of Rh_o (D) Immune Globulin (Human) should be given by i.v. or i.m. administration at 28 weeks gestation. A 600 IU (120 μg) dose of Rh_o (D) Immune Globulin (Human) should be given by i.v. or i.m. administration as soon after delivery of a confirmed Rh_o (D) positive baby as possible and no later than 72 hours after delivery. In the event that the Rh status of the baby is not known at 72 hours, Rh_o (D) Immune Globulin (Human) should be administered to the mother at 72 hours after delivery.

If more than 72 hours have elapsed, Rh_o (D) Immune Globulin (Human) should not be withheld but should be administered as soon as possible up to 28 days after delivery.

A 600 IU (120 μg) dose of Rh_o (D) Immune Globulin (Human) should be given by i.v. or i.m. administration immediately after therapeutic abortion, amniocentesis (after 34 weeks gestation) or other manipulation late in pregnancy (34 weeks gestation) associated with increased risk of Rh_o (D) immunization and, in any event, no later than 72 hours after the event.

A 1 500 IU (300 μg) dose of Rh_o (D) Immune Globulin (Human) should be given by i.v. or i.m. administration immediately after amniocentesis before 34 weeks gestation or after chorion villus sampling, and this dosage should be repeated every 12 weeks while the woman is pregnant. In the case of threatened abortion, Rh_o (D) Immune Globulin (Human) should be administered as soon as possible.

Table II—WinRho SDF

Obstetric Indications and Recommended Dose

Indication	**Dose (Administer I.M. or I.V.)**
Pregnancy:	–
• 28 weeks gestation	1 500 IU (300 μg)
• Postpartum (if newborn Rh positive)	600 IU (120 μg)
Obstetric Conditions:	–
• Threatened abortion at any time	1 500 IU (300 μg)
• Amniocentesis and chorionic villus sampling before 34 weeks gestation	1 500 IU (300 μg)
• Abortion, amniocentesis, or any other manipulation after 34 weeks gestation	600 IU (120 μg)

Transfusion: Rh_o (D) Immune Globulin (Human) should be administered for treatment of incompatible blood transfusions or massive fetal hemorrhage as outlined in Table III.

Administer 3 000 IU (600 μg) every 8 hours **via the i.v. route** until the total dose, calculated from the above table, is administered.

Administer 6 000 IU (1 200 μg) every 12 hours **via the i.m. route** until the total dose, calculated from Table III, is administered.

Immune Thrombocytopenic Purpura: Rh_o (D) Immune Globulin (Human) **must be given by i.v. administration** for the treatment of ITP. An i.v. dose of from 125 to 250 IU/kg (25 to 50 μg/kg) body weight is recommended for individuals with ITP.

Rh_o (D) Immune Globulin (Human) should be reconstituted only with the accompanying vial of 0.9% Sodium Chloride Injection. It should not be administered with other products. After confirming that the patient is Rh_o (D) positive, an initial dose of 250 IU (50 μg)/kg body weight is recommended for the treatment of ITP. If the patient has a hemoglobin level that is less than 10 g/dL, a reduced dose of 125 to 200 IU/kg (25 to 40 μg/kg) should be given to minimize the risk of increasing the severity of anemia in the patient. The initial dose may be administered in 2 divided doses given on separate days, if desired.

If subsequent therapy is required to elevate platelet counts, an i.v. dose of 125 to 300 IU/kg (25 to 60 μg/kg) body weight of Rh_o (D) Immune Globulin (Human) is recommended. The frequency and dose used should be administered by the patient's clinical response by assessing platelet counts, red cells counts, hemoglobin and reticulocyte levels.

Administration: Reconstitution: Rh_o (D) Immune Globulin (Human) should be reconstituted only with the accompanying vial of 0.9% Sodium Chloride Injection. Use aseptic technique throughout. 1) Reconstitute shortly before use. 2) Remove caps from the diluent and product vials. 3) Wipe exposed central portion of the rubber stopper with suitable disinfectant. 4) Withdraw diluent using a suitable syringe and needle. Use 1.25 to 2.5 mL of Sodium Chloride Injection for i.v. injection or 1.25 mL for i.m. injection for 600 IU (120 μg) and 1 500 IU (300 μg). Use 8.5 mL of Saline for Injection for i.v. and i.m. injection for 5 000 IU (1 000 μg) (see Table IV). 5) Inject diluent slowly at an angle so that the liquid is directed onto the inside glass wall of the vial containing the freeze-dried pellet. 6) Wet pellet by gently tilting and inverting the vial. Avoid frothing. Gently swirl upright vial until dissolved (less than 10 minutes).

Injection: Parenteral products such as Rh_o (D) Immune Globulin (Human) should be inspected for particulate matter and discoloration prior to administration.

Use product within 4 hours of reconstitution. Aseptically administer the product i.v. in a suitable vein with a rate of injection of 1 500 IU (300 μg)/5 to 15 seconds. I.M. injections are made into the deltoid muscle of the upper arm or the anterolateral aspect of the upper thigh. Due to the risk of sciatic nerve injury, the gluteal region should not be used as a routine injection site. If the gluteal region is used, use only the upper, outer quadrant.

Stability and Storage Recommendations: Stable at 2 to 8°C until the expiry date indicated on the label. Store at 2 to 8°C. Do not freeze. Do not use after expiration date. Discard any unused portion.

Supplied: 600 IU (120 μg) and 1 500 IU (300 μg): Each 3 mL type 1 glass tubing vial fitted with a 13 mm lyophilization stopper of rubber formulation and a 13 mm flip-off seal of freeze-dried contains: approximately 600 IU (120 μg) or 1 500 IU (300 μg) of freeze-dried anti-Rh_o (D). One vial of 2.5 mL saline 0.9% Sodium Chloride Injection, USP, sterile nonpyrogenic for reconstitution of WinRho SDF. Final product formulation includes the addition of sodium chloride to yield 0.04 M, glycine to yield 0.1 M and polysorbate 80 to yield 0.01%.

5 000 IU (1 000 μg): Each 6 mL type 1 glass tubing vial fitted with a 20 mm lyophilization stopper of rubber formulation and a 20 mm flip-off seal of freeze-dried contains: approximately

Table III—WinRho SDF

Transfusion Indication and Recommended Dose

Route of Administration	**WinRho SDF Dose** If exposed to Rh_o (D) Positive Whole Blood	If exposed to Rh_o (D) Positive Red Blood Cells
I.V.	45 IU (9 μg)/mL Blood	90 IU (18 μg)/mL Cells
I.M.	60 IU (12 μg)/mL Blood	120 IU (24 μg)/mL Cells

Table IV—WinRho SDF

Reconstitution

Vial Size	**Volume of Diluent to be Added to Vial**	**Approximate Available Volume**	**Nominal Concentration/mL**
I.V. Injection			
600 IU (120 μg)	2.5 mL	2.4 mL	240 IU (48 μg)/mL
1 500 IU (300 μg)	2.5 mL	2.4 mL	600 IU (120 μg)/mL
5 000 IU (1 000 μg)	8.5 mL	8.2 mL	588 IU (118 μg)/mL
I.M. Injection			
600 IU (120 μg)	1.25 mL	1.2 mL	480 IU (96 μg)/mL
1 500 IU (300 μg)	1.25 mL	1.2 mL	1 200 IU (240 μg)/mL
5 000 IU (1 000 μg)	8.5 mL	8.2 mL*	588 IU (118 μg)/mL

*To be administered into several sites.

5 000 IU (1 000 μg) of anti-Rh_o(D). One vial of 8.5 mL saline 0.9% Sodium Chloride Injection, USP, sterile nonpyrogenic for reconstitution of WinRho SDF. Final product formulation includes the addition of sodium chloride to yield 0.04 M, glycine to yield 0.1 M and polysorbate 80 to yield 0.01%.

Reviewed 1999

WYDASE®

Wyeth-Ayerst

Hyaluronidase

Enzyme Preparation

Supplied: Each 1 mL vial contains: hyaluronidase 150 USP units. Each 10 mL multidose vial contains: hyaluronidase 1 500 USP units. Nonmedicinal ingredients: calcium chloride, edetate disodium, sodium chloride, sodium phosphate monobasic, thimerosal powder, trisodium phosphate dodecahydrate and water for injection. Boxes of 10.

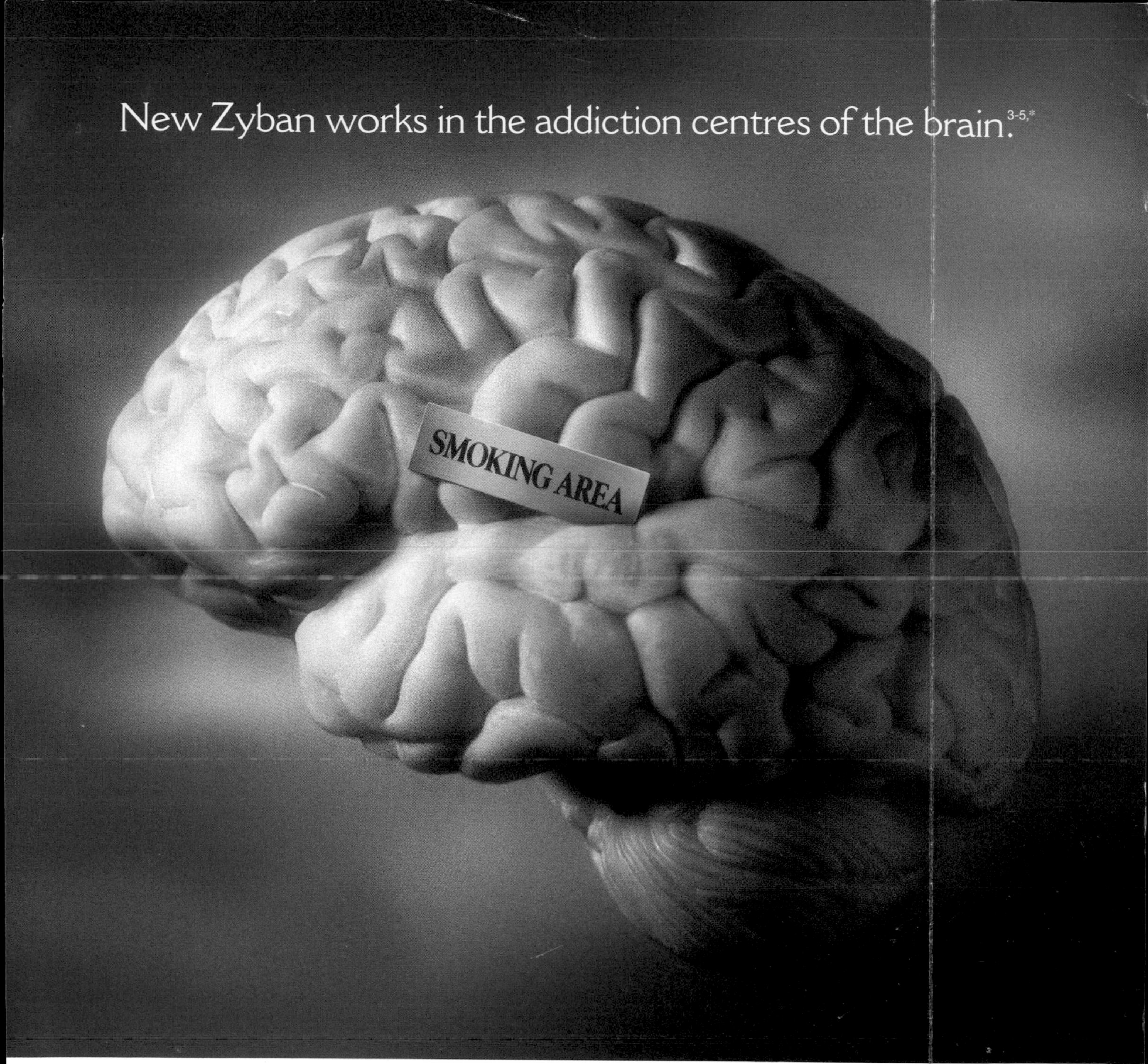

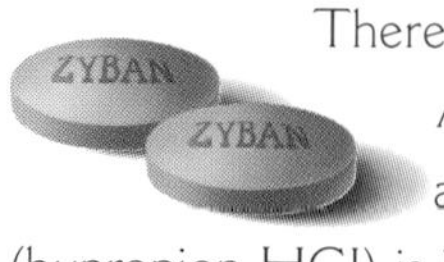

There's a new approach to smoking cessation. And it appears to work where nicotine addiction starts – in the brain.[3-5] ®*Zyban*® (bupropion HCl) is believed to address both the psychological and physiological aspects of nicotine addiction.[1,*] Though it contains no nicotine, *Zyban* reduces cravings and diminishes the irritability of nicotine withdrawal.[1,**]

The result? An oral tablet with almost twice the efficacy of the nicotine patch. 52 weeks after quitting with *Zyban*, 23% of patients remained non-smokers, versus just 12% of patch users.[1,°,†,††] (Of course, patient support is an essential component of any smoking cessation program. And the best candidate for *Zyban* is a motivated patient.)

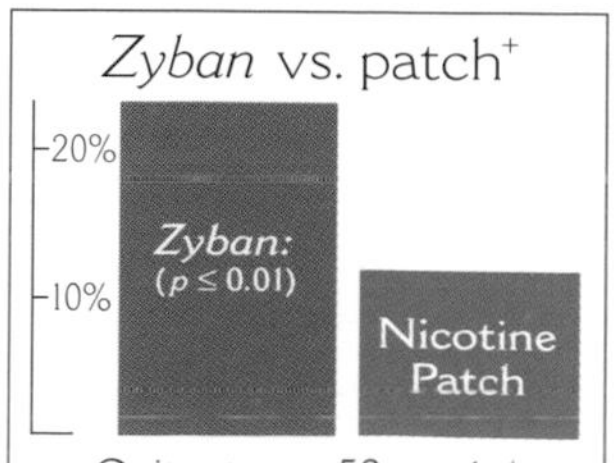

Quit rates at 52 weeks+

Consider new *Zyban*. Because the place where nicotine addiction starts is also the place it can be stopped. For information, call 1-800-268-0324.

ZYBAN®
BUPROPION HCl sustained-release tablets
Stopping nicotine addiction where it starts

***Zyban's* mechanism of action is unknown but it is thought to work primarily via noradrenergic and/or dopaminergic mechanisms.**[1]
**The effect of *Zyban* on cravings varied depending on the study and the measure used.[1] °If no significant progress has been made by week 7, treatment with *Zyban* should probably be discontinued as it is unlikely the patient will quit during that attempt.[1] †*Zyban* is generally well tolerated. The most common adverse events are insomnia (31% vs. 21% with placebo) and dry mouth (11% vs. 5% with placebo). ††*Zyban* is contraindicated in patients with seizure disorder, current or prior diagnosis of bulimia or anorexia nervosa, currently treated with ®*Wellbutrin*® *SR* (bupropion HCl) or receiving MAOI therapy. +*Zyban* 150 mg bid x 9 wks. (n = 244) vs. Habitrol® 21 mg/day x 6 wks; then 14 mg/day x 1 wk, then 7 mg/day x 1 wk. (n = 244) vs. combined treatment (*Zyban*/Habitrol) (n = 245) vs. placebo (n = 160). Combined treatment (*Zyban*/Habitrol) produced a quit rate of 28% at 52 weeks.[1]
Use of bupropion is associated with a dose-dependent risk of seizures. Consult the Product Monograph of *Zyban* for dosing and patient selection criteria.

PAAB CCPP GlaxoWellcome

XYZ

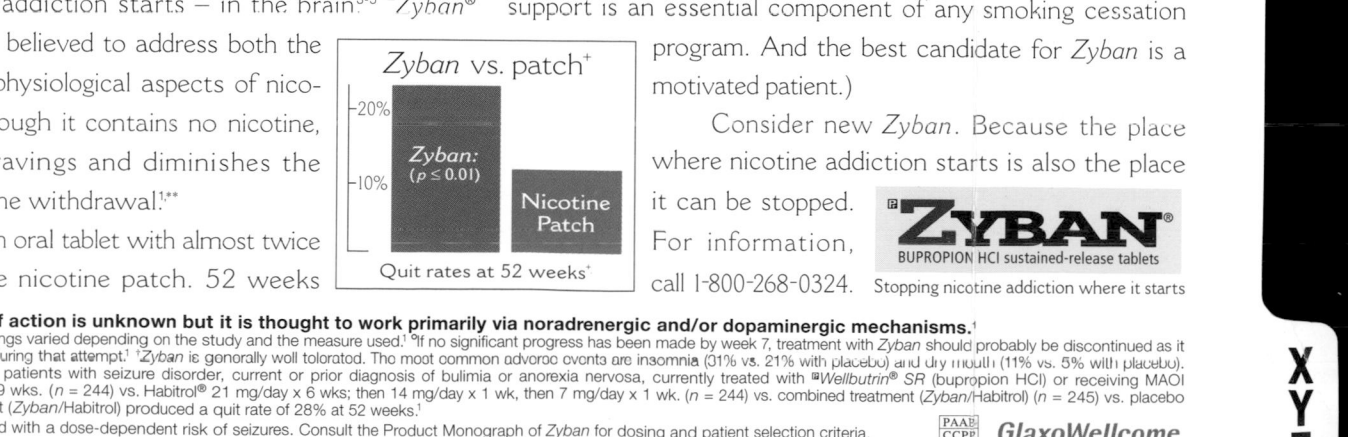

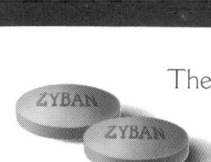

ZOCOR® IS PROVEN
SAVE LIVES* IN
*coronary and
PORTRAIT IN SURVIVAL
IN PATIENTS WITH CORONARY HEART DISEASE (CHD)
AND PRIMARY HYPERCHOLESTEROLEMIA
®Trademark Merck & Co., Inc., Merck Frosst Canada Inc., licensed user

1st dose

2nd dose

3rd dose

After 14 years of breaking down beta-lactamase resistance, the only way we could make Clavulin do more for your patients

was to make it easier to take.

1st dose

2nd dose

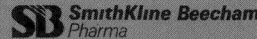

SB SmithKline Beecham Pharma

Introducing ® CLAVULIN® BID

amoxicillin-clavulanate potassium

Efficacy that's easier to take.

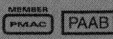

MEMBER PMAC PAAB

X

XALATAN™

Pharmacia & Upjohn

Latanoprost

Prostaglandin $F_2\alpha$ Analogue

Pharmacology: Latanoprost, a novel prostaglandin $F_2\alpha$ analogue, is a selective prostanoid FP receptor agonist which reduces the intraocular pressure by increasing the outflow of aqueous humor. Studies in animals and man indicate that the main mechanism of action is increased uveoscleral outflow.

Primary open-angle glaucoma is a disease with characteristic optic nerve damage and a corresponding visual field defect. Increased intraocular pressure (IOP) is one of the main risk factors. However, disturbances in blood flow may also play a role in some cases. In ocular hypertension, patients may have increased IOP but without changes in the visual field or corresponding optic nerve damage. Results from phase III clinical trials (see Table I) have demonstrated that latanoprost is a very effective ocular hypotensive drug when applied once daily, particularly in the evening. Across these trials, 460 patients received latanoprost and 369 patients received timolol. At 6 months, latanoprost reduced IOP by 27 to 34% from the untreated baseline of 24.4 to 25.2 mmHg. Timolol reduced IOP by 20 to 33% from a baseline of 24.1 to 25.4 mmHg. The p-value for the difference between the IOP reduction by latanoprost versus timolol was $p < 0.001$. Latanoprost also provides the sustained benefit of long-term therapy.

Xalatan is a sterile, isotonic, buffered aqueous solution with a pH of approximately 6.7. Each mL contains 50 µg of latanoprost, a colorless to slightly yellow oil. Latanoprost is an isopropyl ester prodrug which is well absorbed through the cornea and upon entering the aqueous humor is rapidly and completely hydrolyzed to the biologically active acid. Studies in humans indicate that the peak concentration in the aqueous humor is reached about 2 hours after topical administration.

Table I—Xalatan

IOP (mmHg) Response to Latanoprost in Patients Treated for 6 Months in the Phase III Clinical Studies

	U.S. Study	UK Study	Scandinavian Study
Baseline IOP	24.4±3.2 (n=125)	25.2±3.4 (n=149)	25.1±3.5 (n=183)
IOP at 6 months	17.6±3.1 (n=96)	16.7±2.6 (n=133)	17.0±2.8 (n=169)
Change in IOP at 6 months	6.7±3.4 (n=96)	8.5±2.8 (n=133)	8.0±3.1 (n=169)

Following topical administration in monkeys, latanoprost is primarily distributed in the anterior segment, conjunctiva and eyelids with only minute quantities reaching the posterior segment. Reduction of IOP following a single dose in humans starts about 3 to 4 hours following topical administration, and the maximum effect is reached after 8 to 12 hours. Pressure reduction is maintained for at least 24 hours.

There is practically no metabolism of the acid of latanoprost in the eye. The plasma clearance is rapid and occurs in the liver. In humans, the half-life of the biologically active acid in plasma is approximately 17 minutes. In animal studies, the main metabolites were the 1,2-dinor and the 1,2,3,4-tetranor metabolites which exerted only weak or no biologic activity, and were excreted primarily in urine.

Clinical trials have shown that latanoprost has no significant effect on production of aqueous humor and no effect on the blood-aqueous barrier. At clinical dose levels, latanoprost has negligible or no effects on intraocular blood circulation when studied in monkeys. However, mild to moderate conjunctival or episcleral hyperemia may occur as a result of topical administration.

Latanoprost has not induced fluorescein leakage in the posterior segment of pseudophakic human eyes during short-term treatment.

Phase II clinical trials have also demonstrated that latanoprost is effective in combination with other drugs used for treatment of glaucoma. The IOP reducing effect of latanoprost is additive to that of beta-adrenergic antagonists (timolol), adrenergic agonists (dipivefrin, epinephrine), cholinergic agonists (pilocarpine) and carbonic anhydrase inhibitors (acetazolamide).

Indications: For the reduction of intraocular pressure in patients with open-angle glaucoma and ocular hypertension who are intolerant or insufficiently responsive to any other intraocular pressure lowering medication.

Contraindications: Known hypersensitivity to benzalkonium chloride or any other ingredient in this product.

Warnings: Latanoprost may gradually change eye color, increasing the amount of brown pigment in the iris by increasing the number of melanosomes (pigment granules) in melanocytes. The long-term effects on the melanocytes and the consequences of potential injury to the melanocytes and/or deposition of pigment granules to other areas of the eye is currently unknown.

This effect has predominantly been seen in patients with mixed colored irides (i.e., blue/gray-brown, green-brown, or yellow-brown). In patients with homogeneously blue, gray, green or brown eyes, the change has only rarely been seen during 2 years of treatment in clinical trials. The change in iris color occurs slowly, and may not be noticeable for several months to years. Patients should be informed of the possibility of iris color change. Patients who are expected to receive treatment in only one eye should be informed about the potential for increased brown pigmentation in the treated eye and thus, heterochromia between the eyes. The increased pigmentation may be permanent.

Accumulation of pigment in the trabecular meshwork or elsewhere in the anterior chamber has not been observed in clinical trials.

Latanoprost has been reported to cause darkening, thickening and lengthening of eye lashes (see Adverse Effects).

Based on spontaneous reports, very rare cases of darkening of the palpebral skin have been reported (see Adverse Effects).

Pregnancy: Reproduction studies have been performed in rats and rabbits. In rabbits an incidence of 4 of 16 dams had no viable fetuses at a dose that was approximately 80 times the maximum human dose, and the highest nonembryocidal dose in rabbits was approximately 15 times the maximum human dose. Latanoprost should be used during pregnancy only if the potential benefit justifies the potential risk to the fetus.

Lactation: The active substance in latanoprost and its metabolites may pass into breast milk, and latanoprost should therefore be used with caution in nursing women.

Children: The safety and efficacy of the use of latanoprost in children has not been established.

Precautions: General: There have been reports of bacterial keratitis associated with the use of multiple-dose containers of topical ophthalmic products. These containers had been inadvertently contaminated by patients who, in most cases, had a concurrent corneal disease or a disruption of ocular epithelial surface (see Blue Section—Information for the Patient).

Patients may slowly develop increased brown pigmentation of the iris. Patients are to be informed of this potential occurrence (see Blue Section—Information for the Patient). This change may not be noticeable for several months to years (see Warnings). Typically the brown pigmentation around the pupil spreads concentrically toward the periphery in affected eyes; however, the entire iris or parts of it may also become more brownish. Until more information about increased brown pigmentation is available, patients should be examined regularly, and depending on the clinical situation, treatment may be stopped if increased pigmentation ensues. During clinical trials, the increase in brown iris pigment has not been shown to progress further upon discontinuation of treatment, but the resultant color change may be permanent. Neither nevi nor freckles of the iris have been affected by treatment.

Latanoprost has been reported to cause darkening, thickening and lengthening of eye lashes (see Adverse Effects).

Based on spontaneous reports, very rare cases of darkening of the palpebral skin have been reported (see Adverse Effects).

There is no experience with latanoprost in the treatment of angle closure, inflammatory or neovascular glaucoma or congenital glaucoma, and only limited experience with pseudophakic patients and in pigmentary glaucoma.

Latanoprost has not been studied in patients with renal or hepatic impairment and should, therefore, be used with caution in such patients.

Drug Interactions: In vitro studies have shown that precipitation occurs when eye drops containing thimerosal are mixed with latanoprost. If such drugs are used, they should be administered with an interval of at least 5 minutes between applications.

Adverse Effects: The ocular adverse events and ocular signs and symptoms reported in 5 to 15% of the patients on latanoprost in the 6-month, multicenter, double-masked, active-controlled trials were blurred vision, burning and stinging, conjunctival hyperemia, foreign body sensation, itching, increased iris pigmentation and punctate epithelial keratopathy.

Local conjunctival hyperemia was observed; however, less than 1% of the latanoprost treated patients required discontinuation of therapy because of intolerance to conjunctival hyperemia.

In addition to the above listed ocular events/signs and symptoms, the following were reported in 1 to 4% of the patients: dry eye, excessive tearing, eye pain, lid crusting, lid edema, lid erythema, lid discomfort/pain and photophobia.

The following events were reported in less than 1% of the patients: conjunctivitis, diplopia and discharge from the eye.

During clinical studies, there were extremely rare reports of the following: retinal artery embolus, retinal detachment, and vitreous hemorrhage from diabetic retinopathy.

The most common systemic adverse events seen with latanoprost were upper respiratory tract infection/cold/flu which occurred at a rate of approximately 4%. Pain in muscle/joint/back, chest pain/angina pectoris and rash/allergic skin reaction each occurred at a rate of 1 to 2%.

Macular edema in patients with aphakia or pseudophakia with anterior chamber lenses has been reported rarely during latanoprost treatment. Upon discontinuation of latanoprost treatment, visual acuity has improved, in some cases with concurrent treatment with topical steroidal and NSAIDs.

Latanoprost has been reported to cause darkening, thickening and lengthening of eye lashes (see Adverse Effects).

Based on spontaneous reports, rare cases of iritis/uveitis and very rare cases of darkening of the palpebral skin have been reported.

During the period from Nov. 8, 1996 to Nov. 12, 1997, about 600 000 patients were treated with latanoprost. Fifty-five spontaneous reports of darkening, thickening and lengthening of eye lashes and 7 spontaneous reports of darkening of the skin of the eye lid/lids/periorbital region have been received; 16 cases of iritis and 10 cases of uveitis have been reported during this period.

Overdose: Symptoms and Treatment: Apart from ocular irritation and conjunctival or episcleral hyperemia, no other ocular side effects of latanoprost administered at high doses are known. I.V. infusion of up to 3 µg/kg in healthy volunteers produced mean plasma concentrations 200 times higher than during clinical treatment and no adverse reactions were observed. I.V. doses of 5.5 to 10 µg/kg caused abdominal pain, dizziness, fatigue, hot flushes, nausea and sweating.

In monkeys, latanoprost has been infused i.v. in doses of up to 500 µg/kg without major effects on the cardiovascular system. I.V. administration in monkeys has been associated with transient bronchoconstriction. However, in patients with bronchial asthma, bronchoconstriction was not induced by latanoprost when administered topically to the eyes at a dose 7 times the recommended clinical dose. If overdosage with latanoprost occurs, treatment should be symptomatic.

Dosage: The recommended dose for adults including the elderly (over 60 years of age), is 1 drop in the affected eye(s) once daily. Optimal effect is obtained if latanoprost is administered in the evening.

The dose of latanoprost should not exceed once daily as it has been shown that more frequent administration decreases the IOP lowering effect. Reduction of IOP in humans starts about 3 to 4 hours after treatment and maximum effect is reached after 8 to 12 hours. Pressure reduction is maintained for at least 24 hours.

If 1 dose is missed, treatment should continue with the next dose the following day.

Use in Combination with Other Drugs: The product may be used concomitantly with other topical ophthalmic products to further lower intraocular pressure. If more than 1 topical ophthalmic drug is being used, the drugs should be administered at least 5 minutes apart.

Xalatan (cont'd)

Information for the Patient: See Blue Section—Information for the Patient "Xalatan".

Supplied: Each mL of a sterile, isotonic, buffered aqueous solution, for topical ophthalmic administration, contains: latanoprost 50 μg. One drop contains approximately 1.5 μg of latanoprost. Nonmedicinal ingredients: benzalkonium chloride, disodium hydrogen phosphate anhydrous, sodium chloride, sodium dihydrogen phosphate monohydrate and water for injection. Buffered to a pH of approximately 6.7 and is isotonic with lacrimal fluid. Plastic ophthalmic dispenser bottles of 5 mL with a dropper tip, screw cap and tamper-proof polyethylene overcap. Each bottle contains 2.5 mL of latanoprost corresponding to approximately 80 drops. Store unopened bottle under refrigeration (2 to 8°C). Protect from light. Once opened, store bottle in a cool place (refrigerate if possible) for up to 6 weeks.

Reviewed 1999

XANAX® Ⓟ
XANAX TS™ Ⓟ

Pharmacia & Upjohn

Alprazolam

Anxiolytic—Antipanic

Pharmacology: Alprazolam, a triazolo 1,4 benzodiazepine analog, binds with high affinity to the GABA benzodiazepine receptor complex. Considerable evidence suggest that the central pharmacologic/therapeutic actions of alprazolam are mediated via interaction with this receptor complex.

Pharmacokinetics: Orally administered alprazolam is readily absorbed in man. Plasma levels are proportional to the dose given; over the dose range of 0.5 to 3 mg, peak levels of 8.0 to 37 ng/mL were observed. The mean elimination half-life of alprazolam is about 11 hours in healthy adults. With multiple doses, given 3 times daily, steady state is reached within 7 days. Alprazolam and its metabolites are excreted primarily in the urine. Degradation of alprazolam occurs mainly by oxidation yielding the primary metabolites α-hydroxy-alprazolam and a benzophenone derivative. The α-hydroxy-metabolite is further transformed to demethylalprazolam. Both α-hydroxy-alprazolam and demethylalprazolam are active and appear to have half-lives similar to alprazolam but their plasma levels are low.

Table I summarizes some pharmacokinetic parameters in healthy adults and healthy elderly subjects (mean age 70 years, range 62 to 78 years), as well as in obese subjects and in patients with impaired hepatic or renal function. Clearance was decreased and half-lives were increased in all special patient populations except in patients on hemodialysis. Time to peak plasma concentration was increased in patients with liver disease and CAPD.

Cimetidine: Cimetidine significantly impaired the clearance of alprazolam and prolonged its half-life. In healthy volunteers, a single 1 mg dose of alprazolam was administered with and without concurrent administration of cimetidine (300 mg) every 6 hours. Cimetidine significantly reduced total metabolic clearance (1.05 versus 1.66 mL/min/kg) and significantly prolonged elimination half-life (16.6 hours versus 12.4 hours). Similar results were observed during repeated administration of both drugs.

Oral contraceptives: The effect of oral contraceptives on the pharmacokinetics of a single 1 mg dose of alprazolam was studied in healthy women. Alprazolam clearance was lower in subjects taking oral contraceptives (0.95 mL/min/kg) than in the control group (1.21 mL/min/kg) while its half-life was prolonged (12.4 hours versus 9.6 hours).

Anticoagulant: Alprazolam, 0.5 mg, administered 3 times a day for 14 days, did not affect prothrombin times or plasma warfarin levels in male volunteers administered sodium warfarin orally.

Clinical Trial: In a placebo-controlled, 8-week trial, which included 526 patients with diagnoses of panic disorder with or without agoraphobia, alprazolam in a dosage range of 1 to 10 mg/day (with a mean daily dosage of 5.7±2.27 mg at the end of the treatment period) was found effective in blocking or attenuating panic attacks and reducing phobic avoidance.

Indications: For the management of anxiety disorders or the short-term symptomatic relief of symptoms of excessive anxiety. Anxiety or tension associated with the stress of everyday life usually does not require treatment with an anxiolytic.

Generalized Anxiety Disorder: Alprazolam is indicated for the treatment of Generalized Anxiety Disorder (GAD). GAD is characterized by unrealistic or excessive anxiety and worry (apprehensive expectation) about two or more life circumstances, for a period of 6 months or longer, during which the person has been bothered more days than not by these concerns. At least 6 of the following 18 symptoms are often present in these patients: motor tension (trembling, twitching, or feeling shaky; muslce tension, aches, or soreness; restlessness; easy fatigability); autonomic hyperactivity (shortness of breath or smothering sensations; palpitations or accelerated heart rate; sweating, or cold clammy hands; dry mouth; dizziness or lightheadedness; nausea, diarrhea, or other abdominal distress; flushes or chills; frequent urination; trouble swallowing or "lump in throat"); vigilance and scanning (feeling keyed up or on edge; exaggerated startle response; difficulty concentrating or "mind going blank" because of anxiety; trouble falling or staying asleep; irritability). These symptoms must not be secondary to another psychiatric disorder or caused by some organic factor.

Panic disorder with/without Agoraphobia: Also indicated for the management of panic disorder with or without agoraphobia. Panic disorder is an illness characterized by recurrent panic attacks.

Panic attacks are discrete periods of intense fear or discomfort, with at least 4 of the following symptoms: dyspnea; dizziness, unsteady feelings, or faintness; tachycardia; trembling or shaking; sweating; choking; nausea or abdominal distress; depersonalization or derealization; paresthesias; flushes or chills; chest pain or discomfort, fear of dying; fear of going crazy or of doing something uncontrolled.

Attacks are usually of a few minutes duration but can, more rarely, last up to a few hours.

The diagnosis of panic disorders requires that either 4 attacks must have occurred within a 4 week period, or 1 or more attacks must have been followed by a period of at least 1 month of persistent fear of having another attack. The symptoms must not be attributable to known organic factors.

The panic attacks, at least initially, are unexpected. Later in the course of this disturbance certain situations, e.g., driving a car or being in a crowded place, may become associated with having a panic attack. These panic attacks are not triggered by situations in which the person is the focus of others' attention (as in social phobia).

During the natural course of the illness, the patient often develops symptoms of agoraphobia. Agoraphobia is a fear of being in situations from which escape might be difficult or in which help might not be available in the event of an unexpected panic attack. As a result of this fear, the patient either restricts travel or needs a companion when away from home, or else endures agoraphobic situtations despite intense anxiety. The severity varies from mild (able to travel to work or to shop), to severe (completely housebound).

Demonstrations of the effectiveness of alprazolam by systematic clinical studies are limited to 4 months' duration for anxiety disorder and 4 to 10 weeks' duration for panic disorder; however, patients with panic disorder have been treated on an open basis for up to 8 months without apparent loss of benefit. The physician should periodically reassess the usefulness of drug treatment in all patients.

Contraindications: Hypersensitivity to alprazolam or other benzodiazepines and in patients with myasthenia gravis and acute narrow angle glaucoma. However, alprazolam may be used in patients with open angle glaucoma who are receiving appropriate treatment.

Warnings: Alprazolam is not effective in patients with personality disorders. Alprazolam is not recommended for the management of mood or psychotic disorders.

Dependence and Withdrawal Reactions, Including Seizures: Physical dependence with withdrawal symptoms may occur with benzodiazepine discontinuation and can be severe (e.g., seizures) if benzodiazepines are suddenly discontinued. Even after relatively short-term use at the doses recommended for the treatment of transient anxiety and anxiety disorder (i.e., 0.75 to 3 mg/day), there is some risk of dependence. Postmarketing surveillance data suggest that the risk of dependence and its severity appear to be greater in patients treated with relatively high doses (above 4 mg/day) and for long periods (more than 8 to 12 weeks).

The Importance of Dose and the Risks of Alprazolam as a Treatment for Panic Disorder: Because the management of panic disorder often requires the use of average daily doses of alprazolam above 3 mg, the risk of dependence among panic disorder patients may be higher than that among those treated for less severe anxiety. Randomized placebo-controlled discontinuation studies showed a high rate of rebound and withdrawal symptoms in patients treated with alprazolam compared to placebo-treated patients.

Relapse or return of illness was defined as a return of symptoms characteristic of panic disorder (primarily panic attacks) to levels approximately equal to those seen at baseline before active treatment was initiated. Rebound refers to a return of symptoms of panic disorder to a level substantially greater in frequency, or more severe in intensity, than seen at baseline. Withdrawal symptoms were identified as those which were generally not characteristic of panic disorder and which occurred for the first time more frequently during discontinuation than at baseline.

In a controlled clinical trial in which 63 patients were randomized to alprazolam and where withdrawal symptoms were specifically sought, the following were identified as symptoms of withdrawal: heightened sensory perception, impaired concentration, dysosmia, clouded sensorium, paresthesias, muscle cramps, muscle twitch, diarrhea, blurred vision, appetite decrease and weight loss. Other symptoms, such as anxiety and insomnia, were frequently seen during discontinuation, but it could not be determined if they were due to return of illness, rebound or withdrawal.

In a larger database comprised of both controlled and uncontrolled studies in which 641 patients received alprazolam, discontinuation-emergent symptoms which occurred at a rate of over 5% in patients treated with alprazolam and

Table I—Xanax

Alprazolam Pharmacokinetics in Special Patient Populations Following the Administration of Single Oral Doses[a]

Parameter	Patient Population: Adults	Elderly	Obese	Alcoholic Liver Disease	End Stage Renal Disease: Hemodialysis	CAPD[b]
No.	16	16	12	17	7	5
Dose (mg)	1.0	1.0	1.0	1.0	0.5	0.5
C_{max} (ng/mL)	17.9	22.9	not	17.3	8.1	8.6
	(8.5–29.5)	(12.4–36.3)	reported	(8.6–26.0)	(5.9–14.4)	(6.8–10.5)
T_{max} (hr)	1.6	0.9	not	3.3	1.1	3.0
	(0.25–6.0)	(0.5–2.0)	reported	(0.5–8.0)	(0.5–2.0)	(0.5–6.0)
Cl (mL/min/kg)	1.33	0.86	0.59	0.56	not	not
	(0.90–2.23)	(0.40–1.84)	(not available)	(0.17–1.46)	reported	reported
$t_{1/2}$ (hr)	11.0	16.3	21.8	19.7	11.2	19.2
	(6.3–15.8)	(9.0–26.9)	(9.9–40.5)	(5.8–65.3)	(7.1–19.1)	(8.8–33.8)
Unbound fraction	29.0	29.8	30.3	23.2	27.6	30.9
in plasma (%)	(25.0–32.8)	(25.0–35.4)	(26.4–35.4)	(16.9–32.8)	(22.7–30.7)	(28.0–34.2)

[a]Values are means with the ranges in parentheses.
[b]CAPD: continuous ambulatory peritoneal dialysis.
Legend: C_{max}: peak plasma concentration.
T_{max}: time of peak concentration.
Cl: total clearance.
$t_{1/2}$: elimination half-life.

at a greater rate than the placebo-treated group are listed in Table II.

Table II—Xanax

Discontinuation-Emergent Symptom Incidence

Body System	Event	Percentage of Alprazolam Treated Patients Reporting Event (N=641)
Neurologic	insomnia	29.5
	lightheadedness	19.3
	abnormal involuntary movement	17.3
	headache	17.0
	muscular twitching	6.9
	impaired coordination	6.6
	muscle tone disorders	5.9
	weakness	5.8
Psychiatric	anxiety	19.2
	fatigue and tiredness	18.4
	irritability	10.5
	cognitive disorder	10.3
	memory impairment	5.5
	depression	5.1
	confusional state	5.0
Gastrointestinal	nausea/vomiting	16.5
	diarrhea	13.6
	decreased salivation	10.6
Metabolic-Nutritional	weight loss	13.3
	decreased appetite	12.8
Dermatological	sweating	14.4
Cardiovascular	tachycardia	12.2
Special Senses	blurred vision	10.0

From the studies cited, it has not been determined whether these symptoms are clearly related to the dose and duration of therapy with alprazolam in patients with panic disorder.

In 2 controlled trials of 6 to 8 weeks' duration where the ability of patients to discontinue medication was measured, 71 to 93% of patients treated with alprazolam tapered completely off therapy compared to 89 to 96% of placebo treated patients. The ability of patients to completely discontinue therapy with alprazolam after long-term therapy has not been reliably determined.

Seizures attributable to alprazolam were seen after drug discontinuance or dose reduction in 8 of 1 980 patients with panic disorder or in patients participating in clinical trials where doses of alprazolam greater than 4 mg daily for over 3 months were permitted. Five of these cases clearly occurred during abrupt dose reduction, or discontinuation from daily doses of 2 to 10 mg. Three cases occurred in situations where there was not a clear relationship to abrupt dose reduction or discontinuation. In one instance, seizure occurred after discontinuation from a single dose of 1 mg after tapering at a rate of 1 mg every 3 days, from 6 mg daily. In two other instances, the relationship to taper is indeterminate; in both of these cases the patients had been receiving doses of 3 mg daily prior to seizure. The duration of use in the above 8 cases ranged from 4 to 22 weeks. There have been occasional voluntary reports of patients developing seizures while apparently tapering gradually from alprazolam. The risk of seizure seems to be greatest 24 to 72 hours after discontinuation. In postmarketing surveillance, 128 cases of alprazolam withdrawal seizures were reported, 52 of which occurred in patients taking alprazolam alone. The dose range was 0.5 to 16 mg/day (median dose=4 mg/day). The duration of treatment was 1 to 365 days (median=35 days). There are no reports of fatalities associated with alprazolam withdrawal. (see Dosage for recommended tapering and discontinuation schedule).

Status Epilepticus and its Treatment: The medical event voluntary reporting system shows that withdrawal seizures have been reported in association with the discontinuation of alprazolam. In most cases, only a single seizure was reported; however, multiple seizures and status epilepticus were reported as well. Ordinarily, the treatment of status epilepticus of any etiology involves use of i.v. benzodiazepines plus phenytoin or barbiturates, maintenance of a patent airway and adequate hydration. For additional details regarding therapy, consultation with an appropriate specialist may be considered.

Depression: Panic-related disorders have been associated with primary and secondary major depressive disorders and increased reports of suicide among untreated patients. Therefore, the same precaution must be exercised when using the higher doses of alprazolam in treating patients with panic-related disorders as is exercised with the use of any psychotropic drug in treating depressed patients or those in whom there is reason to expect concealed suicidal ideation or plans.

Interdose Symptoms: Early morning anxiety and emergence of anxiety symptoms between doses of alprazolam have been reported in patients with panic disorder taking prescribed maintenance doses of alprazolam. These symptoms may reflect the development of tolerance or a time interval between doses which is longer than the duration of clinical action of the administered dose. In either case, it is presumed that the prescribed dose is not sufficient to maintain plasma levels above those needed to prevent relapse, rebound or withdrawal symptoms over the entire course of the interdosing interval. In these situations, it is recommended that the same total daily dose be given, divided as more frequent administrations (see Dosage).

Risk of Dose Reduction: Withdrawal reactions may occur when dosage reduction occurs for any reason. This includes purposeful tapering, but also includes inadvertent reduction of dose (e.g., the patient forgets, the patient is admitted to a hospital, etc.). Therefore, the dosage of alprazolam should be reduced or discontinued gradually (see Dosage).

Pregnancy: The safety of the use of alprazolam in pregnancy has not been established. Therefore, alprazolam is not recommended for use during pregnancy.

Teratogenic effects: Several studies have suggested an increased risk of congenital malformations associated with the use of benzodiazepines during the first trimester of pregnancy. Since alprazolam is also a benzodiazepine derivative, the administration of alprazolam is rarely justified in women of childbearing potential. Women of childbearing potential should be warned to consult their physician regarding the discontinuation of the drug if they are pregnant or intend to become pregnant.

Nonteratogenic effects: It should be considered that the child born of a mother who is receiving benzodiazepines may be at some risk for withdrawal symptoms from the drug during the postnatal period. Also, neonatal flaccidity and respiratory problems have been reported in children born of mothers who have been receiving benzodiazepines.

Labor and Delivery: Alprazolam has no established use in labor or delivery.

Lactation: Studies in rats have indicated that alprazolam and its metabolites are secreted into the milk. Therefore, nursing should not be undertaken while a patient is receiving alprazolam.

Children and Adolescents: The safety and efficacy of alprazolam in patients under the age of 18 years have not been established.

Occupational Hazards: Driving and Hazardous Activities: Because of its CNS depressant effect, patients receiving alprazolam should be cautioned not to undertake activities requiring mental alertness, judgment and physical coordination such as driving or operating machinery. This is particularly true in the early phases of dose adjustment, and until it has been established that they do not become drowsy or dizzy while taking alprazolam. Alcohol or CNS depressant drugs should not be ingested during treatment with alprazolam.

Precautions: Geriatrics: Elderly and debilitated patients have been found to be prone to the CNS depressant activity of benzodiazepines, even after low doses. Manifestations of this CNS depressant activity include ataxia, oversedation and hypotension. Therefore, medication should be administered with caution to these patients, particularly if a drop in blood pressure might lead to cardiac complications. Initial doses should be low and increments should be made gradually, depending on the response of the patient, in order to avoid oversedation, neurological impairment and other possible adverse reactions (see Pharmacology and Dosage).

Impaired Renal or Hepatic Function: If treatment is necessary in patients with impaired hepatic or renal function, therapy should be initiated at a very low dose and the dosage increased only to the extent that it is compatible with the degree of residual function of these organs. Such patients should be followed closely and have periodic laboratory assessments. (see Pharmacology and Dosage).

Dependence Liability: Physical and psychological dependence may occur with benzodiazepines, including alprazolam. Patients who are prone to abuse drugs should be under careful surveillance when receiving alprazolam. Patients with a history of alcohol or drug abuse are at higher risk for developing psychological dependence.

Withdrawal symptoms can range from mild dysphoria and insomnia to a major syndrome that may include irritability, nervousness, insomnia, agitation, diarrhea, abdominal cramps, vomiting, sweating, tremors and convulsions. Since symptoms may be similar to those for which the patient is being treated, it may be difficult to differentiate between relapse and withdrawal upon discontinuation. Consequently, dosage must be gradually tapered to minimize withdrawal reactions. To discontinue treatment in patients taking alprazolam, the dosage should be reduced slowly in keeping with good medical practice. It is suggested that the daily dosage of alprazolam be decreased by no more than 0.5 mg every 3 days. Some patients may require an even slower dosage reduction. A decrease of 0.5 mg every 2 to 3 weeks is more appropriate when a dose of 6 mg daily or more has been administered even for only a few months. Once a dose of 2 mg daily is achieved, the dose should be decreased by 0.25 mg per 2 to 3 weeks (see Dosage).

Laboratory Tests: If alprazolam is administered for repeated cycles of therapy, periodic blood counts and liver function tests are advisable.

Drug Interactions: Benzodiazepines, including alprazolam, may potentiate or produce additive CNS depressant effects when combined with other psychotropic medication, alcohol, narcotics, bartiturates, antihistamines or anticonvulsants. Therefore, if alprazolam is to be combined with other drugs acting on the CNS, careful consideration should be given to the pharmacology of the agents involved because of the possible additive or potentiating effects. Patients should also be advised against the simultaneous use of other CNS depressant drugs and should be cautioned not to take alcohol during the administration of alprazolam.

Pharmacokinetic interactions can occur when alprazolam is administered along with drugs that interfere with its metabolism. Compounds which inhibit certain hepatic enzymes (particularly cytochrome P450IIIA4) may increase the concentration of alprazolam and enhance its activity. Data from clinical studies with alprazolam, in vitro studies with alprazolam, and clinical studies with drugs metabolized similarly to alprazolam provide evidence for varying degrees of interaction and possible interaction with alprazolam for a number of drugs.

Based on the degree of interaction and the type of data available, the following recommendations are made: The coadministration of alprazolam with ketoconazole, itraconazole, or other azole-type antifungals is not recommended. This is based on results of drug interaction studies of triazolam and midazolam, benzodiazepines metabolized similarly to alprazolam, with ketoconazole and itraconazole. In addition, an in vitro study showed ketoconazole to be a potent inhibitor of alprazolam metabolism.

Caution and consideration of dose reduction is recommended when alprazolam is coadministered with nefazodone, fluvoxamine and cimetidine.

When alprazolam (1 mg b.i.d.) and nefazodone (200 mg b.i.d.) were coadministered to steady state, peak concentrations, AUC and half-life values for alprazolam increased by approximately 2 fold. Nefazodone plasma concentrations were unaffected by alprazolam, although levels of the mCPP metabolite were increased. The concomitant use of alprazolam and nefazodone was also associated with an increase in psychomotor impairment presumably due to increased alprazolam plasma concentrations. If alprazolam is coadministered with nefazodone, a reduction in the alprazolam dosage may be appropriate; no dosage adjustment is required for nefazodone. The interactive effects of higher doses of these agents, such as the dosage levels of alprazolam used in panic disorder, have not been studied.

When alprazolam 1 mg and fluvoxamine (50 mg once daily for 3 days followed by 100 mg once daily for 7 days) were coadministered the AUC of alprazolam was approximately doubled, the C_{max} of alprazolam increased by about 50% and the half-life of alprazolam increased from 19.8 hours to 33.9 hours. C_{max} and AUC of fluvoxamine were decreased by about 25%. Psychomotor performance tests on day 10 showed significant decreases in performance.

Coadministration of alprazolam and cimetidine results in an approximate doubling of the C_{max} of alprazolam and a statistically significant increase in the AUC of alprazolam. The half-life of alprazolam increased from 12.2 hours to 14.2 hours.

Caution is recommended when alprazolam is coadministered with fluoxetine, propoxyphene, oral contraceptives, sertraline, diltiazem, or macrolide antibiotics such as erythromycin and troleandomycin.

Xanax (cont'd)

A pharmacokinetic interaction has been noted between alprazolam and carbamazepine; significant reductions in alprazolam concentration have been noted after carbamazepine treatment has been initiated. Pharmacokinetic interactions between alprazolam and phenytoin have not been observed.

The steady-state plasma concentrations of imipramine and desipramine have been reported to be increased an average of 31% and 20%, respectively, by the concomitant administration of alprazolam tablets in doses up to 4 mg/day. The clinical significance of these changes is unknown.

Alprazolam 0.5 mg, administered 3 times a day for 14 days, did not affect prothrombin times or plasma warfarin levels in male volunteers administered sodium warfarin orally.

Adverse Effects: Side effects to alprazolam if they occur, are generally observed at the beginning of therapy and usually disappear upon continued medication or decreased dosage.

The data cited in Tables III and IV are estimates of untoward clinical event incidence among patients who participated under the following clinical conditions: relatively short duration (i.e., 4 weeks) placebo-controlled clinical studies with dosages up to 4 mg/day of alprazolam (for the management of anxiety disorders or for the short-term relief of the symptoms of anxiety) and short-term (up to 10 weeks) placebo-controlled clinical studies with dosages up to 10 mg/day of alprazolam in patients with panic disorder, with or without agoraphobia.

In addition to the relatively common (i.e., greater than 1%) untoward events listed in Tables III and IV, the following events have been reported to occur with alprazolam and other benzodiazepines: seizures, loss of coordination, concentration difficulties, memory impairment/transient amnesia, dystonia, irritability, anorexia, fatigue, sedation, slurred speech, musculoskeletal weakness, changes in libido, menstrual irregularities, incontinence, urinary retention, abnormal liver function, jaundice, pruritus and diplopia. Increased intraocular pressure has been rarely reported.

As with all benzodiazepines, paradoxical reactions such as stimulation, agitation, rage, increased muscle spasticity, sleep disturbances, hallucinations and other adverse behavioral effects may occur in rare instances and in a random fashion. Should these occur, use of the drug should be discontinued.

In some of the spontaneous case reports of adverse behavioral effects such as stimulation, agitation, concentration difficulties, confusion and hallucinations, patients were receiving other CNS drugs concomitantly and/or were described as having underlying psychiatric conditions. Patients with borderline personality disorder, a prior history of violent or aggressive behavior, or alcohol or substance abuse may be at risk for such events. Instances of irritability, hostility and intrusive thoughts have been reported during discontinuance of alprazolam in patients with post-traumatic stress disorder.

Table III—Xanax

Anxiety Disorders: Treatment-Emergent Symptom Incidence (% of Patients Reporting)

Body System	Event	Alprazolam (N=565)	Placebo (N=505)
CNS	drowsiness	41.0	21.6
	lightheadedness	20.8	19.3
	depression	13.9	18.1
	headache	12.9	19.6
	confusion	9.9	10.0
	insomnia	8.9	18.4
	nervousness	4.1	10.3
	syncope	3.1	4.0
	dizziness	1.8	0.8
	akathisia	1.6	1.2
Gastro-intestinal	dry mouth	14.7	13.3
	constipation	10.4	11.4
	diarrhea	10.1	10.3
	nausea/vomiting	9.6	12.8
	increased salivation	4.2	2.4
Cardio-vascular	tachycardia/palpitations	7.7	15.6
	hypotension	4.7	2.2
Sensory	blurred vision	6.2	6.2
Musculo-skeletal	rigidity	4.2	5.3
	tremor	4.0	8.8
Cutaneous	dermatitis/allergy	3.8	3.1
Other	nasal congestion	7.3	9.3
	weight gain	2.7	2.7
	weight loss	2.3	3.0

Table IV—Xanax

Panic Disorders: Treatment-Emergent Symptom Incidence (% of patients reporting)

Body System	Event	Xanax (N=1 388)	Placebo (N=1 231)
CNS	drowsiness	76.8	42.7
	fatigue and tiredness	48.6	42.3
	impaired coordination	40.1	17.9
	irritability	33.1	30.1
	memory impairment	33.1	22.1
	lightheadedness/dizziness	29.8	36.9
	insomnia	29.4	41.8
	headache	29.2	35.6
	cognitive disorder	28.8	20.5
	dysarthria	23.3	6.3
	anxiety	16.6	24.9
	abnormal involuntary movement	14.8	21.0
	decreased libido	14.4	8.0
	depression	13.8	14.0
	confusional state	10.4	8.2
	muscular twitching	7.9	11.8
	increased libido	7.7	4.1
	change in libido (not specified)	7.1	5.6
	weakness	7.1	8.4
	muscle tone disorders	6.3	7.5
	syncope	3.8	4.8
	akathisia	3.0	4.3
	agitation	2.9	2.6
	disinhibition	2.7	1.5
	paresthesia	2.4	3.2
	talkativeness	2.2	1.0
	vasomotor disturbances	2.0	2.6
	derealization	1.9	1.2
	dream abnormalities	1.8	1.5
	fear	1.4	1.0
	feeling warm	1.3	0.5
Gastro-intestinal	decreased salivation	32.8	34.2
	constipation	26.2	15.4
	nausea/vomiting	22.0	31.8
	diarrhea	20.6	22.8
	abdominal distress	18.3	21.5
	increased salivation	5.6	4.4
Cardio-respiratory	nasal congestion	17.4	16.5
	tachycardia	15.4	26.8
	chest pain	10.6	18.1
	hyperventilation	9.7	14.5
	upper respiratory infection	4.3	3.7
Sensory	blurred vision	21.0	21.4
	tinnitus	6.6	10.4
Musculo-skeletal	muscular cramps	2.4	2.4
	muscle stiffness	2.2	3.3
Cutaneous	sweating	15.1	23.5
	rash	10.8	8.1
Other	increased appetite	32.7	22.8
	decreased appetite	27.8	24.1
	weight gain	27.2	17.9
	weight loss	22.6	16.5
	micturition difficulties	12.2	8.6
	menstrual disorders	10.4	8.7
	sexual dysfunction	7.4	3.7
	edema	4.9	5.6
	incontinence	1.5	0.6
	infection	1.3	1.7

Overdose: Symptoms: Manifested as an extension of alprazolam's pharmacologic activity. Thus, varying degrees of CNS depressant effects such as somnolence, confusion, impaired coordination, diminished reflexes and coma may ensue. As in the management of overdose with any drug, it should be remembered that multiple agents may have been ingested.

Death has been reported in association with overdoses of alprazolam by itself, as it has with other benzodiazepines. In addition, fatalities have been reported in patients who have overdosed with a combination of a single benzodiazepine, including alprazolam, and alcohol; alcohol levels seen in some of these patients have been lower than those usually associated with alcohol-induced fatality.

Treatment: Vomiting may be induced if the patient is fully awake. Vital signs should be monitored and general supportive measures should be employed as indicated. Gastric lavage should be instituted as soon as possible. I.V. fluids may be administered and an adequate airway should be maintained.

Experiments in animals have indicated that cardiopulmonary collapse can occur with massive i.v. doses of alprazolam. This could be reversed with positive mechanical respiration and the i.v. infusion of norepinephrine. Animal experiments with alprazolam and related compounds have suggested that hemodialysis and forced diuresis are probably of little value.

Dosage: Should be individualized for maximal benefit. The lowest possible effective dose should be administered and the need for continued treatment reassessed frequently. The risk of dependence may increase with dose and duration of treatment.

Anxiety Disorders: Adult: The initial adult dosage of alprazolam is 0.25 mg given 2 or 3 times daily. If required, increases may be made in 0.25 mg increments according to the severity of symptoms and patient response. It is recommended that the evening dose be increased before the daytime doses. Very severe manifestations of anxiety may require larger initial daily doses. The optimal dosage is one that permits symptomatic control of excessive anxiety without impairment of mental and motor function. Exceptionally, it may be necessary to increase dosage to a maximum of 3 mg daily, given in divided doses.

Elderly or Debilitated Patients: The initial dosage is 0.125 mg given 2 or 3 times daily. If necessary, this dosage may be increased gradually depending on patient tolerance and response. The elderly may be especially sensitive to the effects of benzodiazepines.

Patients with Impaired Hepatic or Renal Function: In patients with advanced liver or renal disease, the usual dose is 0.125 to 0.25 mg, given 2 or 3 times daily. This may be gradually increased if needed and tolerated.

Panic Disorders: The usual starting dose is 0.5 to 1 mg at bedtime or 0.5 mg 3 times daily. The dose should be adjusted until the patient is free of attacks. Dosage adjustments should be in increments no greater than 1 mg every 3 to 4 days. Interdose symptoms may be lessened by using a schedule that provides for administration 3 or 4 times/day.

In controlled trials conducted to establish the efficacy of alprazolam in panic disorders, doses in the range of 1 to 10 mg daily were used. The mean dosage employed was approximately 5 to 6 mg daily. Among the approximately 1 700 patients participating in the panic disorder development program, about 300 received maximum alprazolam doses of greater than 7 mg/day, including approximately 100 patients who received maximum dosages of greater than 9 mg/day. Occasional patients required as much as 10 mg/day to receive a successful response.

The necessary duration of treatment for panic disorder is unknown at this time. After a period of extended freedom from panic attacks, a supervised tapered discontinuation may be attempted.

Discontinuation: To discontinue treatment in patients taking alprazolam, the dosage should be reduced slowly in keeping with good medical practice. It is suggested that the daily dosage of alprazolam be decreased by no more than 0.5 mg every 3 days. Some patients may require an even slower dosage reduction. A decrease of 0.5 mg every 2 to 3 weeks is more appropriate when a dose of 6 mg daily or more has been administered even for only a few months. Once a dose of 2 mg daily is achieved, the dose should be decreased by 0.25 mg per 2 to 3 weeks.

Information for the Patient: See Blue Section—Information for the Patient "Xanax".

Supplied: Xanax: 0.25 mg: Each white, single score tablet, embossed with "Upjohn 29," contains: alprazolam 0.25 mg (250 µg). Nonmedicinal ingredients: cornstarch, docusate sodium, lactose, magnesium stearate, microcrystalline cellulose and silicon dioxide. Gluten-free. Bottles of 100 and 1 000.

0.5 mg: Each peach, single score tablet, embossed "Upjohn 55," contains: alprazolam 0.5 mg (500 µg). Nonmedicinal ingredients: cornstarch, docusate sodium, FD&C Yellow #6, lactose, magnesium stearate, microcrystalline cellulose and silicon dioxide. Gluten-free. Bottles of 100 and 1 000.

1 mg: Each lavender, single score tablet, embossed "Upjohn 90", contains: alprazolam 1 mg (1 000 µg). Nonmedicinal ingredients: cornstarch, docusate sodium, erythrosin sodium, FD&C Blue #2, lactose, magnesium stearate, microcrystalline cellulose and silicon dioxide. Gluten-free. Bottles of 100.

Xanax TS: Each white, triscored tablet (3 scores), with the number "2" on one side and "Xanax" on the other side, contains: alprazolam 2 mg. The tablets can be broken into

4 equal parts of 0.5 mg. Nonmedicinal ingredients: cornstarch, docusate sodium, lactose, magnesium stearate, microcrystalline cellulose and silicon dioxide. Gluten-free. Bottles of 100.

Store at controlled room temperature.

(Shown in Product Recognition Section)

Reviewed 1997

X-PREP®

Purdue Frederick

Standardized Sennosides

Diagnostic Aid

Indications: A potent cathartic to be used only for evacuation of the colon prior to contrast radiography of the gastrointestinal tract, other abdominal radiography, or examinations where a clear colon is essential for proper visualization. Also indicated prior to surgery of the colon or rectum.

Contraindications: The "acute abdomen".

Dosage: Adults: At 10 a.m. on the day prior to x-ray procedure, drink 50% the contents of a 21 g pouch of the powder mixed with water, or 50% the contents of a 70 mL bottle of the liquid, and the remaining 50% at 2 p.m., or as prescribed. As it is important to hydrate the patient, adults should take several glasses of water within 3 to 4 hours of completing dosage.
Children: Dosage (on a weight basis) is proportionally less.

Supplied: Liquid: Each unit dose (70 mL) bottle contains: standardized sennosides 119 mg, sugar 46.8 g equivalent to 872 kJ (212 kcal). Also contains alcohol 7%, parabens 154 mg and artificial cocoa flavor. pH: 5.2 to 5.8. Expiration period: 2 years from date of manufacture. Tartrazine-free. Cases of 50.

Powder: Each unit dose (21 g) pouch contains: standardized sennosides 157.5 mg. Also contains sugar 9.5 g equivalent to 160 kJ (38 kcal) and cocoa powder. Tartrazine-free. Cases of 50.

X-TAR®

Dormer

Coal Tar—Menthol—Salicylic Acid

Antipsoriatic—Antiseborrheic—Antidandruff

Supplied: Each mL of shampoo contains: coal tar USP 8% w/w, salicylic acid 2.1% w/w and menthol 1.2% w/w. Nonmedicinal ingredients: ammonium lauryl sulfate, chloroxylenol, cocamidopropyl betaine, disodium EDTA, ethyl alcohol, fragrance, hydroxypropyl methylcellulose, lanolin, PEG-75, polyquaternium-7, purified water and sodium hydroxide. Plastic bottles of 125 mL.

XYLOCAINE® CO_2

Astra

Lidocaine Hydrocarbonate

Local Anesthetic

Pharmacology: Mechanism of Action: Lidocaine stabilizes the neuronal membrane by inhibiting the ionic fluxes required for the initiation and conduction of impulses, thereby effecting local anesthetic action. Local anesthetics of the amide type are thought to act within sodium channels of the nerve membrane.
Onset of Action: The onset of action with Xylocaine CO_2 is faster than regular lidocaine HCl solutions. The rapid diffusion of the carbon dioxide released from the injectate results in a lowering of intracellular pH. This, in turn, causes faster absorption of the lidocaine base, the active form of Xylocaine CO_2. In addition, the carbon dioxide may have an additive effect on the conduction block, resulting in a more intense motor block.
Hemodynamics: Lidocaine, like other local anesthetics, may also have effects on excitable membranes in the brain and myocardium. If excessive amounts of drug reach systemic circulation rapidly, symptoms and signs of toxicity will appear, emanating from the central nervous and cardiovascular systems.

CNS toxicity (see Overdose: Symptoms and Treatment) usually precedes the cardiovascular effects since it occurs at lower plasma concentrations. Direct effects of local anesthetics on the heart include slow conduction, negative inotropism and eventually cardiac arrest.

Indirect cardiovascular effects (hypotension, bradycardia) may occur after epidural or spinal administration depending on the extent of the concomitant sympathetic block.
Pharmacokinetics: Lidocaine is completely absorbed following parenteral administration. The rate of absorption depends on the dose, route of administration and the vascularity of the injection site. The highest peak plasma levels are obtained following intercostal nerve block (approximately 1.5 µg/mL per 100 mg injected), while abdominal s.c. injections give the lowest (approximately 0.5 µg/mL per 100 mg injected). Epidural and major nerve blocks are intermediate.

Absorption is considerably slowed by the addition of epinephrine, although it also depends on the site of injection. Peak plasma concentrations are reduced by 50% following s.c. injection, by 30% following epidural injection and by 20% following intercostal block if epinephrine 5 µg/mL is added.

Lidocaine shows complete and biphasic absorption from the epidural space with half-lives in the order of 9.3 minutes and 82 minutes respectively. The slow absorption is rate-limiting in the elimination of lidocaine, which explains the slower elimination following epidural injection compared to i.v. injection.

Lidocaine has a total plasma clearance of 0.95 L/min, a volume of distribution at steady state of 91 L, an elimination half-life of 1.6 h and an estimated hepatic extraction ratio of 0.65. The clearance of lidocaine is almost entirely due to liver metabolism, and depends both on liver blood flow and the activity of metabolizing enzymes.

The plasma binding of lidocaine is dependent on drug concentration, and the fraction bound decreases with increasing concentration. At concentrations of 1 to 4 µg of free base per mL, 60 to 80% of lidocaine is protein bound. Binding is also dependent on the plasma concentration of the alpha-1-acid glycoprotein.

Lidocaine readily crosses the placenta, and equilibrium in regard to free, unbound drug will be reached. Because the degree of plasma protein binding in the fetus is less than in the mother, the total plasma concentration will be greater in the mother, but the free concentrations will be the same.

Lidocaine is metabolized rapidly by the liver, and metabolites and unchanged drug are excreted by the kidneys. Biotransformation includes oxidative N-dealkylation, ring hydroxylation, cleavage of the amide linkage, and conjugation. Only 2% of lidocaine is excreted unchanged. Most of it is metabolized first to monoethylglycinexylidide (MEGX) and then to glycinexylidide (GX) and 2,6-xylidine. Up to 70% appears in the urine as 4-hydroxy-2,6-xylidine.

The elimination half-life of lidocaine following i.v. bolus injection is typically 1.5 to 2.0 hours. The elimination half-life in neonates (3.2 h) is approximately twice that of adults. The half-life may be prolonged two-fold or more in patients with liver dysfunction. Renal dysfunction does not affect lidocaine kinetics but may increase the accumulation of metabolites.

Acidosis increases the systemic toxicity of lidocaine while the use of CNS depressants may increase the levels of lidocaine required to produce overt CNS effects. Objective adverse manifestations become increasingly apparent with increasing venous plasma levels above 6.0 µg free base per mL.

Indications: For production of local or regional anesthesia by peripheral nerve block techniques such as brachial plexus block and by central neural techniques including epidural and caudal blocks, when the accepted procedures for these techniques, as described in standard textbooks, are observed.

Contraindications: In patients with a known history of hypersensitivity to local anesthetics of the amide type or to other components of the solution.

Xylocaine CO_2 is not for spinal use.
Children: Xylocaine CO_2 is not recommended in children as the pediatric dose schedule has not been established.

Warnings: Local anesthetics should only be employed by clinicians who are well versed in diagnosis and management of dose-related toxicity and other acute emergencies that might arise from the block to be employed and then only after ensuring the immediate availability of oxygen, other resuscitative drugs, cardiopulmonary equipment and the personnel needed for proper management of toxic reactions and related emergencies (see also Adverse Effects and Precautions). Delay in proper management of dose-related toxicity, underventilation from any cause, and/or altered sensitivity may lead to the development of acidosis, cardiac arrest and possibly, death.

It is essential that aspiration for blood or cerebrospinal fluid (where applicable) be done prior to injecting any local anesthetics, both the original and all subsequent doses, to avoid intravascular or subarachnoid injection. However, a negative aspiration does not ensure against an intravascular or subarachnoid injection.

Precautions: The safety and effectiveness of Xylocaine CO_2 depend on proper dosage, correct technique, adequate precautions and readiness for emergencies. Standard textbooks should be consulted for specific techniques and precautions for various regional anesthetic procedures.

Resuscitative equipment, oxygen, and other resuscitative drugs should be available for immediate use (see Warnings and Overdose: Symptoms and Treatment). During major regional nerve blocks, the patients should have i.v. fluids running via an indwelling catheter to assure a functioning i.v. pathway. **The lowest dosage that results in effective anesthesia should be used to avoid high plasma levels and serious adverse effects. Injections should be made slowly, with frequent aspirations before and during the injection to avoid intravascular injection.**

During the administration of epidural anesthesia, it is recommended that a test dose be administered initially and that the patient be monitored for CNS toxicity and cardiovascular toxicity, as well as for signs of unintended intrathecal administration, before proceeding (see Dosage). When clinical conditions permit, consideration should be given to employing local anesthetic solutions that contain epinephrine for the test dose because circulatory changes compatible with epinephrine may also serve as a warning sign of unintended intravascular injection. An intravascular injection is still possible even if aspirations for blood are negative. Syringe aspirations should also be performed before and during each supplemental injection when using indwelling catheter techniques.

Repeated doses of Xylocaine CO_2 may cause significant increases in blood levels with each repeated dose because of slow accumulation of the drug or its metabolites. Tolerance to elevated blood levels varies with the status of the patient. Debilitated, elderly patients, acutely ill patients and children should be given reduced doses commensurate with their age and physical condition. Xylocaine CO_2 should also be used with extreme caution in patients with epilepsy, impaired cardiac conduction, bradycardia, impaired hepatic or renal function, and in severe shock.

Because amide-type local anesthetics such as lidocaine are metabolized by the liver, these drugs, especially repeat doses, should be used cautiously in patients with hepatic disease. Patients with severe hepatic disease, because of their inability to metabolize local anesthetics normally, are at greater risk of developing toxic plasma concentrations.

Lidocaine should also be used with caution in patients with impaired cardiovascular function since they may be less able to compensate for functional changes associated with the prolongation of AV conduction produced by these drugs.

Xylocaine CO_2 is not intended for spinal or subarachnoid administration, i.e., it should not enter the cerebrospinal fluid.

Lumbar and caudal epidural anesthesia should be used with extreme caution in persons with the following conditions: existing neurological disease, spinal deformities, septicemia, and severe hypertension.

Central nerve blocks may cause cardiovascular depression, especially in the presence of hypovolemia. Epidural anesthesia should be used with caution in patients with impaired cardiovascular function.

Paracervical block can sometimes cause fetal bradycardia/tachycardia, and careful monitoring of the fetal heart rate is necessary.

Epidural anesthesia may lead to hypotension and bradycardia. This risk can be reduced either by preloading the circulation with crystalloidal or colloidal solutions, or by injecting a vasopressor such as ephedrine 20 to 40 mg i.m., or by treating promptly with e.g., ephedrine 5 to 10 mg i.v. and repeating as necessary.
Local anesthetic procedures should not be used when there is inflammation and/or sepsis in the region of the proposed injection.

Solutions containing epinephrine should be used with caution in patients whose medical history and physical evaluation suggest the existence of untreated hypertension, poorly controlled thyrotoxicosis, diabetes, ischemic heart disease, heart block, cerebral vascular insufficiency and peripheral vascular disorder. These solutions should also be used cautiously in areas of the body supplied by end arteries, such as digits, or otherwise having a compromised blood supply (see also Drug Interactions).

Careful and constant monitoring of cardiovascular and respiratory (adequacy of ventilation) vital signs and the patient's state of consciousness should be performed after each local anesthetic injection. It should be kept in mind at such times that restlessness, anxiety, incoherent speech, lightheadedness, numbness and tingling of the mouth and lips, metallic

Xylocaine CO_2 (cont'd)

taste, tinnitus, dizziness, blurred vision, tremors, twitching, depression or drowsiness may be early warning signs of central nervous system toxicity.

Many drugs used during the conduct of anesthesia are considered potential triggering agents for familial malignant hyperthermia. It has been shown that the use of amide local anesthetics in malignant hyperthermia is safe. However, there is no guarantee that neural blockade will prevent the development of malignant hyperthermia during surgery. It is also difficult to predict the need for supplemental general anesthesia. Therefore, a standard protocol for the management of malignant hyperthermia should be available.

Lidocaine should be used with caution in persons with known drug sensitivities. Patients allergic to para-aminobenzoic acid derivatives (procaine, tetracaine, benzocaine, etc.) have not shown cross sensitivity to lidocaine.

Use in Brachial Plexus Block: The supraclavicular or axillary approach to the brachial plexus is usually preferred. If the supraclavicular route is chosen, great care is necessary to prevent pneumothorax or inadvertent phrenic block, (therefore bilateral supraclavicular block should be avoided). Using a short needle, ½ inch (13 mm), 24 gauge, greatly reduces these risks.

Use in the Head and Neck Area: Small doses of local anesthetics injected into the head and neck area, including retrobulbar, dental and stellate ganglion blocks, may produce adverse reactions caused by inadvertent injection to an artery. These reactions may be similar to systemic toxicity seen with unintentional intravascular injections of larger doses. Inadvertent injections into an artery can cause cerebral symptoms even at low doses. Confusion, convulsions, respiratory depression and/or respiratory arrest, and cardiovascular stimulation or depression leading to cardiac arrest have been reported. Patients receiving these blocks should have their circulation and respiration monitored and be constantly observed.

Retrobulbar injections may very occasionally reach the cranial subarachnoid space causing temporary blindness, cardiovascular collapse, apnea, convulsions, etc. These reactions, which may be due to intraarterial injection or direct injection into the CNS via the sheaths of the optic nerve, must be diagnosed and treated promptly.

Drug Interactions: Lidocaine should be used with caution in patients receiving other local anesthetics or agents structurally related to the amide-type local anesthetics, since the toxic effects are additive.

Xylocaine solutions containing epinephrine or other vasopressors should not be used concomitantly with ergot-type oxytocic drugs, because a severe persistent hypertension may occur and cerebrovascular and cardiac accidents are possible. Likewise, Xylocaine solutions containing epinephrine or another vasoconstrictor should be used with extreme caution in patients receiving monoamine oxidase (MAO) inhibitors or antidepressants of the triptyline or imipramine types, because severe prolonged hypertension may result. In situations when concurrent therapy is necessary, careful patient monitoring is essential. Phenothiazines and butyrophenones may reduce or reverse the pressor effect of epinephrine.

If sedatives are employed to reduce patient apprehension, they should be used in reduced doses, since local anesthetic agents, like sedatives, are CNS depressants which in combination may have an additive effect.

Solutions containing epinephrine should be used with caution in patients undergoing general anesthesia with inhalation agents such as halothane, due to the risk of serious cardiac arrhythmias.

Drug/Laboratory Test Interactions: The i.m. injection of lidocaine may result in an increase in creatine phosphokinase levels. Thus, the use of this enzyme determination, without isoenzyme separation, as a diagnostic test for the presence of acute myocardial infarction may be compromised by the i.m. injection of lidocaine.

Information for the Patient: When appropriate, patients should be informed in advance that they may experience temporary loss of sensation and motor activity, usually in the lower half of the body, following proper administration of epidural anesthesia.

Pregnancy: It is reasonable to assume that a large number of pregnant women and women of child-bearing age have been given lidocaine. No specific disturbances to the reproductive process have so far been reported, e.g., no increased incidence of malformations. However, care should be given during early pregnancy when maximum organogenesis takes place. There are no adequate and well-controlled studies in pregnant women, on the effect of lidocaine on the developing fetus.

Labor and Delivery: Local anesthetics rapidly cross the placenta and when used for epidural, paracervical, pudendal or caudal block anesthesia, can cause varying degrees of maternal, fetal and neonatal toxicity. The potential for toxicity depends upon the procedure performed, the type and amount of drug used, and the technique of drug administration. Adverse reactions in the parturient, fetus and neonate involve alterations of the CNS, peripheral vascular tone and cardiac function.

Maternal hypotension has resulted from regional anesthesia. Local anesthetics produce vasodilation by blocking sympathetic nerves. Elevating the patient's legs and positioning her on her left side will help prevent decreases in blood pressure. A vasopressor, such as ephedrine, may be indicated (see Precautions). The fetal heart rate also should be monitored continuously, and electronic fetal monitoring is highly advisable.

Epidural, spinal, paracervical, or pudendal anesthesia may alter the forces of parturition through changes in uterine contractility or maternal expulsive efforts. In one study, paracervical block anesthesia was associated with a decrease in the mean duration of first stage labor and facilitation of cervical dilation. However, spinal and epidural anesthesia have also been reported to prolong the second stage of labor by removing the parturient's reflex urge to bear down or by interfering with motor function. The use of obstetrical anesthesia may increase the need for forceps assistance.

Fetal bradycardia may occur in 20 to 30% of patients receiving paracervical nerve block anesthesia with the amide-type local anesthetics and may be associated with fetal acidosis. Fetal heart rate should always be monitored during paracervical anesthesia. The physician should weigh the possible advantages against risks when considering paracervical block in prematurity, toxemia of pregnancy, and fetal distress. Careful adherence to recommended dosage is of the utmost importance in obstetrical paracervical block. Failure to achieve adequate analgesia with recommended doses should arouse suspicion of intravascular or fetal intracranial injection. Cases compatible with unintended fetal intracranial injection of local anesthetic solution have been reported following intended paracervical or pudendal block or both. Babies so affected, present with unexplained neonatal depression at birth, which correlates with high local anesthetic serum levels, and often manifest seizures within 6 hours. Prompt use of supportive measures combined with forced urinary excretion of the local anesthetic has been used successfully to manage this complication.

Case reports of maternal convulsions and cardiovascular collapse following use of some local anesthetics for paracervical block in early pregnancy (as anesthesia for elective abortion) suggest that systemic absorption under these circumstances may be rapid. The recommended maximum dose of each drug should not be exceeded. Injection should be made slowly and with frequent aspiration. Allow a 5-minute interval between sides.

Lactation: Lidocaine is excreted in the breast milk, but in such small quantities that there is generally no risk of affecting the infant at therapeutic dose levels. It is not known whether epinephrine enters breast milk, but it is unlikely to affect the breast-fed infant.

Adverse Effects: Adverse experiences following the administration of lidocaine are similar in nature to those observed with other amide local anesthetic agents. These adverse experiences are, in general, dose-related and may result from high plasma levels caused by overdosage or rapid absorption, or inadvertent intravascular injection, or may result from a hypersensitivity, idiosyncrasy or diminished tolerance on the part of the patient.

Serious adverse experiences are generally systemic in nature. The following types are those most commonly reported: CNS: CNS manifestations are excitatory and/or depressant and may be characterized by circumoral paresthesia, light-headedness, nervousness, apprehension, euphoria, confusion, dizziness, drowsiness, hyperacusis, tinnitus, blurred vision, vomiting, sensations of heat, cold or numbness, twitching, tremors, convulsions, unconsciousness, respiratory depression and arrest. The excitatory manifestations may be very brief or may not occur at all, in which case the first manifestation of toxicity may be drowsiness merging into unconsciousness and respiratory arrest.

Drowsiness following the administration of lidocaine is usually an early sign of a high plasma level of the drug and may occur as a consequence of rapid absorption.

Cardiovascular: Cardiovascular manifestations are usually depressant and are characterized by bradycardia, hypotension, arrhythmia, and cardiovascular collapse, which may lead to cardiac arrest.

Allergic: Allergic reactions are characterized by cutaneous lesions, urticaria, edema or in the most severe instances, anaphylactic shock. Allergic reactions of the amide type are rare and, may occur as a result of sensitivity either to the local anesthetic agent or to other components in the formulation.

Neurologic: The incidence of adverse reactions may be related to the total dose of local anesthetic administered but is also dependent upon the particular drug used, the route of administration and the physical status of the patient. Neuropathy and spinal cord dysfunction (e.g., anterior spinal artery syndrome, arachnoiditis, cauda equina syndrome), have been associated with regional anesthesia. Neurological effects may be related to local anesthetic techniques, with or without a contribution from the drug.

In the practice of lumbar epidural block, occasional unintentional penetration of the subarachnoid space by the catheter or needle may occur. For example, a high spinal is characterized by paralysis of the legs, loss of consciousness, respiratory paralysis and bradycardia.

Neurologic effects following unintentional subarachnoid administration during epidural anesthesia may include spinal block by varying magnitude (including total or high spinal block), hypotension secondary to spinal block, urinary retention, fecal and urinary incontinence, loss of perineal sensation and sexual function, persistent anesthesia, paresthesia, weakness, paralysis of the lower extremities and loss of sphincter control, all of which may have slow, incomplete or no recovery; headache, backache, septic meningitis, meningismus, slowing of labor, increased incidence of forceps delivery, or cranial nerve palsies due to traction on nerves from loss of cerebrospinal fluid.

Overdose: Acute systemic toxicity from local anesthetics is generally related to high plasma levels encountered during therapeutic use of local anesthetics and originates mainly in the central nervous and the cardiovascular systems (see Adverse Effects, Warnings, and Precautions).

Symptoms: With accidental intravascular injections, the toxic effect will be obvious within 1 to 3 minutes, while with overdosage, peak plasma concentrations may not be reached for 20 to 30 minutes depending on the site of injection, with signs of toxicity thus being delayed.

CNS toxicity is a graded response, with symptoms and signs of escalating severity. The first symptoms are circumoral paresthesia, numbness of the tongue, lightheadedness, hyperacusis and tinnitus. Visual disturbance and muscular tremors are more serious and precede the onset of generalized convulsions. Unconsciousness and grand mal convulsions may follow, which may last from a few seconds to several minutes. Hypoxia and hypercarbia occur rapidly following convulsions due to the increased muscular activity, together with the interference with normal respiration. In severe cases apnea may occur. Acidosis increases the toxic effects of local anesthetics.

Recovery is due to redistribution and metabolism of the local anesthetic drug. Recovery may be rapid unless large amounts of the drug have been administered.

Cardiovascular effects may be seen in cases with high systemic concentrations. Severe hypotension, bradycardia, arrhythmia and cardiovascular collapse may be the result in such cases.

Cardiovascular toxic effects are generally preceded by signs of toxicity in the CNS, unless the patient is receiving a general anesthetic or is heavily sedated with drugs such as a benzodiazepine or barbiturate.

Treatment: The first consideration is prevention, best accomplished by careful and constant monitoring of cardiovascular and respiratory vital signs and the patient's state of consciousness after each local anesthetic administration. At the first sign of change, oxygen should be administered. If signs of acute systemic toxicity appear, injection of the local anesthetic should be immediately stopped.

The first step in the management of systemic toxic reactions, as well as underventilation or apnea due to unintentional subarachnoid injection consists of immediate attention to the establishment and maintenance of a patent airway and assisted or controlled ventilation with oxygen and a delivery system capable of permitting immediate positive airway pressure by mask. This may prevent convulsions if they have not already occurred.

If necessary, use drugs to control convulsions. An anticonvulsant should be given i.v. if the convulsions do not stop spontaneously in 15 to 20 seconds. Thiopental 100 to 150 mg i.v. will abort the convulsions rapidly. Alternatively, diazepam 5 to 10 mg i.v. may be used, although its action is slower. Succinylcholine will stop the muscle convulsions rapidly, but will require tracheal intubation and controlled ventilation, and should only be used by those familiar with these procedures.

If cardiovascular depression is evident (hypotension, bradycardia), ephedrine 5 to 10 mg i.v. should be given and may be repeated, if necessary, after 2 to 3 minutes.

Should circulatory arrest occur, immediate cardiopulmonary resuscitation should be instituted. Optimal oxygenation and ventilation and circulatory support as well as treatment of acidosis are of vital importance, since hypoxia and acidosis will increase the systemic toxicity of local anesthetics. Epinephrine (0.1 to 0.2 mg as i.v. or intracardial injections) should be given as soon as possible and repeated, if necessary.

Children should be given doses commensurate with their age and weight.

Dosage: Table I summarizes the recommended doses and total doses of Xylocaine CO_2 for various types of anesthetic procedures. The dosages suggested in Table I are for normal healthy adults and refer to the use of epinephrine-free solutions.

When larger volumes are required, only solutions containing epinephrine should be used except in those cases where vasopressor drugs may be contraindicated. To make a solution of Xylocaine CO_2 with 1:200 000 epinephrine, it is recommended that 0.1 mL of an epinephrine solution 1:1 000 be added to 20 mL of Xylocaine CO_2. No clinical trials have been used with Xylocaine CO_2 with epinephrine for caudal anesthesia.

These recommended doses serve only as a guide to the amount of anesthetic required for most routine procedures. The actual volumes and concentrations to be used depend on a number of factors such as type and extent of surgical procedure, depth of anesthesia and degree of muscular relaxation required, duration of anesthesia required, and the physical condition of the patient. In all cases the lowest concentration and smallest dose that will produce the desired result should be given. Dosages should be reduced for elderly and debilitated patients and patients with cardiac and/or liver disease. No pediatric dose has been established.

of an increase in heart rate and systolic blood pressure, circumoral pallor, palpitations and nervousness in the unsedated patient. The sedated patient may exhibit only a pulse rate increase of 20 or more beats per minute for 15 or more seconds. Patients on beta blockers may not manifest changes in heart rate, but blood pressure monitoring can detect an evanescent rise in systolic blood pressure. Adequate time should be allowed for onset of anesthesia after administration of each test dose. The rapid injection of a large volume of Xylocaine CO_2 through the catheter should be avoided and when feasible, fractional doses should be administered.

The main dose should be injected **slowly** at a rate of 100 to 200 mg/minute, or in incremental doses, while keeping in constant verbal contact with the patient. If toxic symptoms occur, the injection should be stopped immediately.

In the event of the known injection of a large volume of local anesthetic solution into the subarachnoid space, after suitable resuscitation and if the catheter is in place, consider attempting the recovery of drug by draining a moderate amount of cerebrospinal fluid (such as 10 mL) through the epidural catheter.

Maximum Recommended Dosages: Adults: For normal healthy adults, the individual maximum recommended dose of Xylocaine CO_2 should not exceed 15 mL or 330 mg (equivalent to 300 mg lidocaine HCl). When used with epinephrine the maximum individual dose should not exceed 25 mL or 550 mg (equivalent to 500 mg lidocaine HCl). For continuous epidural or caudal anesthesia, the maximum recommended dosage should not be administered at intervals of less than 90 minutes. When continuous lumbar or caudal epidural anesthesia is used for nonobstetrical procedures, more drug may be administered if required to produce adequate anesthesia.

Sterilization, Storage and Technical Procedures: Xylocaine CO_2 can be autoclaved by steam sterilization at 121°C for 15 to 20 minutes. Just prior to cooling the vials to room temperature, they should be agitated briefly to dissolve any traces of lidocaine base which may have been deposited on the inner

Table I—Xylocaine CO_2

Recommended and Maximum Single Doses in Adults

Procedure	Recommended Dose (mL)	Maximum Single Dose (mL)	Recommended Dose (mg)	Maximum Single Dose (mg)
Epidural anesthesia	10–15	15	220–330	330
Caudal anesthesia	10–15	15	220–330	330
Brachial anesthesia	<15	15	<330	330

The onset of anesthesia, the duration of anesthesia and the degree of muscular relaxation are proportional to the volume and concentration (i.e., total dose) of local anesthetic used. Thus, an increase in volume and concentration of Xylocaine CO_2 will decrease the onset of anesthesia, prolong the duration of anesthesia, provide a greater degree of muscular relaxation and increase the segmental spread of anesthesia. However, increasing the volume and concentration of Xylocaine CO_2 may result in a more profound fall in blood pressure when used in epidural anesthesia. Although the incidence of side effects with lidocaine is quite low, caution should be exercised when employing large doses since the incidence of side effects is directly proportional to the total dose of local anesthetic agent injected. The risk of reaching a toxic plasma concentration or inducing a local neural injury must be considered when prolonged blocks and/or repeated administration are employed.

In general, complete block of all nerve fibres in large nerves requires the higher concentrations of drug. In smaller nerves, or when a less intense block is required (e.g., in the relief of labor pain), the lower concentrations are indicated. The volume of drug used will affect the extent of spread of anesthesia.

Caudal and Lumbar Epidural Block: Test Dose: As a precaution against the adverse experience sometimes observed following unintentional penetration of the subarachnoid space, a test dose such as 3 to 5 mL of 1.5% lidocaine should be administered at least 5 minutes prior to injecting the total volume required for a lumbar or caudal epidural block. During the administration of a test dose, it is recommended that constant ECG monitoring occur. The test dose should be repeated if the patient is moved in a manner that may have displaced the catheter. Epinephrine, if contained in the test dose (10 to 15 μg have been suggested), may serve as a warning of unintentional intravascular injection. If injected into a blood vessel, this amount of epinephrine is likely to produce a transient epinephrine response within 45 seconds, consisting

surface of the vial above the level of the solution during sterilization. This solution must not be used if a precipitate is present. Ethylene oxide sterilization is not recommended.

The 30 mL vials contain lidocaine base 1.73% (by weight) in water, equilibrated with carbon dioxide at a partial pressure of 700 mm Hg. This concentration of lidocaine base is equivalent to lidocaine HCl 2%. The pH of a freshly opened vial at 28°C is about 6.5, but after equilibration with carbon dioxide at a partial pressure of 36 mm Hg the pH rises to about 7.3.

A wide-bore cannula should be used when filling syringes, and the solution should be aspirated **slowly** with minimal negative pressure. Once the solution is drawn up into the syringe, the pCO_2 will remain fairly constant for an hour or two provided the hub is capped and sealed (a disposable hypodermic needle with its plastic guard in place makes a suitable seal). Effort should be made, however, to use the solution as quickly as possible after aspiration into the syringe. Once opened, the unused portion should be discarded.

If a vasoconstrictor is required, epinephrine should be added carefully from a small graduated syringe in the appropriate amount (0.1 mL of 1:1 000 epinephrine added to 20 mL solution of Xylocaine CO_2 provides a dilution of approximately 1:200 000).

Adequate precautions should be taken to avoid prolonged contact between local anesthetic solutions containing epinephrine (low pH) and metal surfaces (e.g., needles or metal parts of syringes), since dissolved metal ions, particularly copper ions, may cause severe local irritation (swelling, edema) at the site of injection and accelerate the degradation of epinephrine.

Supplied: Each mL of solution contains: lidocaine base 17.3 mg. Nonmedicinal ingredients: carbon dioxide, sodium chloride and water for injection. The pH of the solution is 6.3 to 6.9. Preservative-free. Twenty mL of lidocaine hydrocarbonate solution 2.2% (equivalent to lidocaine HCl 2%) in single use vials of 30 mL. Discard unused portion. Store at controlled room temperature 15 to 30°C.

Reviewed 1998

XYLOCAINE® DENTAL SOLUTIONS

Astra

Lidocaine HCl—Epinephrine

Local Anesthetic

Pharmacology: Mechanism of Action: Lidocaine stabilizes the neuronal membrane by inhibiting the ionic fluxes required for the initiation and conduction of impulses, thereby effecting local anesthetic action. Local anesthetics of the amide type are thought to act within sodium channels of the nerve membrane.

Onset of Action: When used for infiltration anesthesia in dental patients, the onset of action is rapid and on average is 2 to 3 minutes. Lidocaine 2% with epinephrine 1:100 000 provides anesthesia of about 1 hour, with postoperative soft tissue anesthesia of approximately 2.5 hours. Lidocaine 2% with epinephrine 1:50 000 provides, on average, pulp anesthesia in excess of 1 hour and is recommended for oral surgery requiring prolonged duration of anesthesia and pronounced hemostasis.

When used for nerve blocks in dental patients, the onset of action for lidocaine 2% with epinephrine 1:50 000 is 2 to 4 minutes. Mandibular block requires 5 minutes or more to take full effect. The average approximate duration of pulp anesthesia is at least 1.5 hours, with postoperative soft tissue anesthesia of approximately 3 to 3.25 hours.

Hemodynamics: Lidocaine, like other local anesthetics, may also have effects on excitable membranes in the brain and myocardium. If excessive amounts of drug reach systemic circulation rapidly, symptoms and signs of toxicity will appear, emanating from the central nervous and cardiovascular systems.

CNS toxicity (see Overdose: Symptoms and Treatment) usually precedes the cardiovascular effects since it occurs at lower plasma concentrations. Direct effects of local anesthetics on the heart include slow conduction, negative inotropism and eventually cardiac arrest.

Pharmacokinetics and Metabolism: Lidocaine is completely absorbed following parenteral administration. The rate of absorption depends on the dose, route of administration and the vascularity of the injection site. The highest peak plasma levels are obtained following intercostal nerve block (approximately 1.5 μg/mL/100 mg injected) while abdominal s.c. injections give the lowest (approximately 0.5 μg/mL/100 mg injected). Epidural and major nerve blocks are intermediate.

Absorption is considerably slowed by the addition of epinephrine, although it also depends on the site of injection. Peak plasma concentrations are reduced by 50% following s.c. injection, by 30% following epidural injection and by 20% following intercostal block if epinephrine 5 μg/mL is added.

Lidocaine has a total plasma clearance of 0.95 L/min, a volume of distribution at steady-state of 91 L, an elimination half-life of 1.6 h and an estimated hepatic extraction ratio of 0.65. The clearance of lidocaine is almost entirely due to liver metabolism, and depends both on liver blood flow and the activity of metabolizing enzymes.

The plasma binding of lidocaine is dependent on drug concentration, and the fraction bound decreases with increasing concentration. At concentrations of 1 to 4 μg of free base/mL, 60 to 80% of lidocaine is protein bound. Binding is also dependent on the plasma concentration of the alpha-1-acid glycoprotein.

Lidocaine readily crosses the placenta, and equilibrium in regard to free, unbound drug will be reached. Because the degree of plasma protein binding in the fetus is less than in the mother, the total plasma concentration will be greater in the mother, but the free concentrations will be the same.

Lidocaine is metabolized rapidly by the liver, and metabolites and unchanged drug are excreted by the kidneys. Biotransformation includes oxidative N-dealkylation, ring hydroxylation, cleavage of the amide linkage, and conjugation. Only 2% of lidocaine is excreted unchanged. Most of it is metabolized first to monoethylglycinexylidide (MEGX) and then to glycinexylidide (GX) and 2,6-xylidine. Up to 70% appears in the urine as 4-hydroxy-2,6-xylidine.

The elimination half-life of lidocaine following i.v. bolus injection is typically 1.5 to 2 hours. The elimination half-life in neonates (3.2 hours) is approximately twice that of adults. The half-life may be prolonged 2-fold or more in patients with

Xylocaine Dental Solutions (cont'd)

liver dysfunction. Renal dysfunction does not affect lidocaine kinetics but may increase the accumulation of metabolites.

Acidosis increases the systemic toxicity of lidocaine while the use of CNS depressants may increase the levels of lidocaine required to produce overt CNS effects. Objective adverse manifestations become increasingly apparent with increasing venous plasma levels above 6.0 μg free base/mL.

Indications: For the production of local anesthesia by nerve block or infiltration injection.

Contraindications: In patients with a known history of hypersensitivity to local anesthetics of the amide type or to other components of the solution, i.e., epinephrine, sodium metabisulfite.

Warnings: Local anesthetics should only be employed by clinicians who are well versed in diagnosis and management of dose-related toxicity and other acute emergencies that might arise from the block to be employed and then only after ensuring the immediate availability of oxygen, other resuscitative drugs, cardiopulmonary equipment and the personnel needed for proper management of toxic reactions and related emergencies (see also Adverse Effects and Precautions). Delay in proper management of dose-related toxicity, underventilation from any cause, and/or altered sensitivity may lead to the development of acidosis, cardiac arrest and possibly, death.

It is essential that aspiration for blood or cerebrospinal fluid (where applicable) be done prior to injecting any local anesthetics, both the original and all subsequent doses, to avoid intravascular or subarachnoid injection. However, a negative aspiration does not ensure against an intravascular or subarachnoid injection.

Lidocaine with epinephrine contains sodium metabisulfite, a sulfite that may cause allergic-type reactions including anaphylactic symptoms and life-threatening or less severe asthmatic episodes in certain susceptible people. Sulfite sensitivity is seen more frequently in asthmatic than in nonasthmatic people.

Precautions: The safety and effectiveness of lidocaine with epinephrine depend on proper dosage, correct technique, adequate precautions and readiness for emergencies. Standard textbooks should be consulted for specific techniques and precautions for various regional anesthetic procedures.

Resuscitative equipment, oxygen, and other resuscitative drugs should be available for immediate use (see **Warnings and Overdose: Symptoms and Treatment). The lowest dosage that results in effective anesthesia should be used to avoid high plasma levels and serious adverse effects. Injections should be made slowly, with frequent aspirations before and during the injection to avoid intravascular injection.**

Repeated doses of lidocaine may cause significant increases in blood levels with each repeated dose because of slow accumulation of the drug or its metabolites. Tolerance to elevated blood levels varies with the status of the patient. Debilitated, elderly patients, acutely ill patients and children should be given reduced doses commensurate with their age and physical condition. Lidocaine should also be used with caution in patients with epilepsy, impaired cardiac conduction, bradycardia, impaired hepatic function and in severe shock.

Because amide-type local anesthetics such as lidocaine are metabolized by the liver, these drugs, especially repeat doses, should be used cautiously in patients with hepatic disease.

Patients with severe hepatic disease, because of their inability to metabolize local anesthetics normally, are at greater risk of developing toxic plasma concentrations. Lidocaine should also be used with caution in patients with impaired cardiovascular function since they may be less able to compensate for functional changes associated with the prolongation of AV conduction produced by these drugs.

Local anesthetic procedures should not be used when there is inflammation and/or sepsis in the region of the proposed injection.

Solutions containing epinephrine should be used with caution in patients whose medical history and physical evaluation suggest the existence of untreated hypertension, poorly controlled thyrotoxicosis, diabetes, ischemic heart disease, heart block, cerebral vascular insufficiency and peripheral vascular disorder. These solutions should also be used cautiously in areas of the body supplied by end arteries, such as digits, or otherwise having a compromised blood supply (see also Drug Interactions).

Careful and constant monitoring of cardiovascular and respiratory (adequacy of ventilation) vital signs and the patient's state of consciousness should be performed after each local anesthetic injection. It should be kept in mind at such times that restlessness, anxiety, incoherent speech, lightheadedness, numbness and tingling of the mouth and lips, metallic taste, tinnitus, dizziness, blurred vision, tremors, twitching, depression or drowsiness may be early warning signs of CNS toxicity.

Many drugs used during the conduct of anesthesia are considered potential triggering agents for familial malignant hyperthermia. It has been shown that the use of amide local anesthetics in malignant hyperthermia patients is safe. However, there is no guarantee that neural blockade will prevent the development of malignant hyperthermia during surgery. It is also difficult to predict the need for supplemental general anesthesia. Therefore, a standard protocol for the management of malignant hyperthermia should be available.

Lidocaine should be used with caution in persons with known drug sensitivities. Patients allergic to para-aminobenzoic acid derivatives (procaine, tetracaine, benzocaine, etc.) have not shown cross sensitivity to lidocaine.

Head and Neck Area: Small doses of local anesthetics injected into the head and neck area, including retrobulbar, dental and stellate ganglion blocks, may produce adverse reactions caused by inadvertent injection to an artery. These reactions may be similar to systemic toxicity seen with unintentional intravascular injections of larger doses. Inadvertent injections into an artery can cause cerebral symptoms even at low doses. Confusion, convulsions, respiratory depression and/or respiratory arrest, and cardiovascular stimulation or depression leading to cardiac arrest have been reported. Patients receiving these blocks should have their circulation and respiration monitored and be constantly observed.

Drug Interactions: Lidocaine should be used with caution in patients receiving other agents structurally related to amide-type local anesthetics, since the toxic effects are additive.

Lidocaine with epinephrine or other vasopressors should not be used concomitantly with ergot-type oxytocic drugs, because a severe persistent hypertension may occur and cerebrovascular and cardiac accidents are possible. Likewise, lidocaine with epinephrine or solutions containing lidocaine and another vasoconstrictor should be used with extreme caution in patients receiving MAO inhibitors or antidepressants of the triptyline or imipramine types, because severe prolonged hypertension may result. In situations when concurrent therapy is necessary, careful patient monitoring is essential. Phenothiazines and butyrophenones may reduce or reverse the pressor effect of epinephrine.

If sedatives are employed to reduce patient apprehension, they should be used in reduced doses, since local anesthetic agents, like sedatives, are CNS depressants which in combination may have an additive effect.

Solutions containing epinephrine should be used with caution in patients undergoing general anesthesia with inhalation agents such as halothane, due to the risk of serious cardiac arrhythmias.

Information for the Patient: The patients should be informed that they may experience temporary loss of sensation and motor activity after infiltration or nerve block injections. The patients should be advised to exert caution to avoid inadvertent trauma to the lips, tongue, cheek mucosa or soft palate when these structures are anesthetized. The ingestion of food should therefore be postponed until normal function returns. The patient should be advised to consult the dentist if anesthesia persists or if a rash develops.

Pregnancy: It is reasonable to assume that a large number of pregnant women and women of child-bearing age have been given lidocaine. No specific disturbances to the reproductive process have so far been reported, e.g., no increased incidence of malformations. However, care should be given during early pregnancy when maximum organogenesis takes place.

There are no adequate and well-controlled studies in pregnant women of the effect of lidocaine on the developing fetus.

Lactation: Lidocaine is excreted in the breast milk, but in such small quantities that there is generally no risk of affecting the infant at therapeutic dose levels. It is not known whether epinephrine enters breast milk, but it is unlikely to affect the breast-fed infant.

Adverse Effects: Adverse experiences following the administration of lidocaine are similar in nature to those observed with other amide local anesthetic agents. These adverse experiences are, in general, dose-related and may result from high plasma levels caused by overdosage, rapid absorption, or inadvertent intravascular injection, or may result from a hypersensitivity, idiosyncrasy or diminished tolerance on the part of the patient.

Reactions to Xylocaine dental solutions are very rare in the doses used in dental procedures. Psychogenic reactions to anticipation of or during the dental procedures, are however, common and may mimic the symptoms of a generalized systemic reaction to local anesthetics.

Serious adverse experiences are generally systemic in nature. The following types are those most commonly reported:

CNS: CNS manifestations are excitatory and/or depressant and may be characterized by circumoral paresthesia, lightheadedness, nervousness, apprehension, euphoria, confusion, dizziness, drowsiness, hyperacusis, tinnitus, blurred vision, vomiting, sensations of heat, cold or numbness, twitching, tremors, convulsions, unconsciousness, respiratory depression and arrest. The excitatory manifestations may be very brief or may not occur at all, in which case the first manifestation of toxicity may be drowsiness merging into unconsciousness and respiratory arrest.

Drowsiness following the administration of lidocaine is usually an early sign of a high lidocaine plasma level and may occur as a consequence of rapid absorption.

Cardiovascular: Cardiovascular manifestations are usually depressant and are characterized by bradycardia, hypotension, arrhythmia, and cardiovascular collapse, which may lead to cardiac arrest.

Allergic: Allergic reactions are characterized by cutaneous lesions, urticaria, edema, or in the most severe instances, anaphylactic shock. Allergic reactions of the amide type are extremely rare and may occur as a result of sensitivity either to the local anesthetic agent or to other components in the formulation.

Neurologic: The incidence of adverse neurological reactions, e.g., persistent neurological deficit, associated with the use of local anesthetics is very low. Neurological reactions may be dependent upon the particular drug used, the route of administration and the physical status of the patient. Many of these effects may be linked to the injection technique, with or without a contribution by the drug. Neurological reactions following regional nerve blocks have included persistent paresthesia and sensory disturbances.

Overdose: Acute emergencies are, in general, dose-related and may result from high plasma levels caused by excessive dosage, rapid absorption (i.e., rate of increase of plasma concentration) or unintentional intravascular injection, or may result from hypersensitivity or diminished tolerance on the part of the patient.

Symptoms: Acute Systemic Toxicity: CNS reactions are excitatory or depressant and may be characterized by nervousness, tinnitus, twitching, euphoria, drowsiness, blurred or double vision, dizziness, convulsions, unconsciousness and possibly respiratory arrest. The excitatory reactions may be very brief or may not occur at all, in which case the first manifestation of toxicity is drowsiness merging into unconsciousness and even respiratory arrest.

Cardiovascular reactions are depressant and may be characterized by hypotension, myocardial depression, bradycardia and possibly cardiac arrest. Signs and symptoms of depressed cardiovascular function may commonly result from a vasovagal reaction, particularly if the patient is in an upright position. Less commonly, they may occur as a direct effect of the drug. Failure to recognize premonitory signs such as sweating, a feeling of faintness, changes in pulse or sensorium, may result in progressive cerebral hypoxia and seizure or serious cardiovascular collapse.

Cardiovascular effects are usually only seen in the most severe cases and are generally preceded by signs of toxicity in the CNS.

Acidosis or hypoxia in the patient may increase the risk and severity of toxic reactions. Such reactions involve the CNS and the cardiovascular system.

Treatment: Treatment of Acute Toxicity: The immediate treatment of acute systemic toxicity is as follows:

a. Put the patient in a supine position. Raise the legs 30 to 45° above the horizontal level.

b. Ensure a patent airway. If ventilation is inadequate, ventilate the patient, with oxygen if available. This is important since toxicity increases with acidosis.

c. The treatment of convulsions consists in ensuring a patent airway and arresting convulsions. Should convulsions persist despite adequate ventilation, 5 to 15 mg diazepam or 50 to 200 mg thiopental should be administered i.v. to arrest the convulsions. Since this treatment may also depress respiration, the means of mechanically supporting or controlling ventilation should be available.

d. Supportive treatment of circulatory depression may require the administration of i.v. fluids and, when appropriate, a vasopressor (e.g., ephedrine 5 to 10 mg i.v. and repeated, if necessary, after 2 to 3 minutes), as governed by the clinical situation.

e. If the patient is unresponsive and the carotid pulse rate is totally absent, start external cardiac massage and mouth to mouth resuscitation.

Dosage: When used for local anesthesia in dental procedures the dosage depends on the area of the oral cavity to be anesthetized, the vascularity of the oral tissues, and the technique of anesthesia. The total dose must be adjusted to the age, size and physical status of the patient. The lowest dosage that results in effective local anesthesia should be administered. Injections should be made slowly with careful aspiration before and intermittently during injection to avoid inadvertent intravascular injection, which may have toxic effects. For specific techniques and procedures of a local anesthesia in the oral cavity, refer to standard textbooks.

For most routine dental procedures, lidocaine 2% with epinephrine 1:100 000 is preferred. However, when greater depth and a more pronounced hemostasis are required, a 1:50 000 epinephrine concentration should be used.

Adults: Dosage requirements should be determined on an individual basis. In oral infiltration and/or mandibular block, a dose of 1 to 5 mL (20 to 100 mg lidocaine HCl, ½ to 2½ cartridges) of lidocaine 2% with epinephrine 1:50 000 or 1:100 000 is usually effective. A dose of 10 mL (200 mg) should not be exceeded.

Children: In children under 10 years of age it is rarely necessary to administer more than one-half cartridge (0.9 to 1 mL or 18 to 20 mg lidocaine HCl) of lidocaine 2% with epinephrine per procedure to achieve local anesthesia for a procedure involving a single tooth. In maxillary infiltration, this amount will often suffice for the treatment of two or even three teeth. In the mandibular block, however, satisfactory anesthesia achieved with this amount of drug will allow treatment of the teeth in the entire quadrant. In any case, a dose of 2 mL (40 mg) should not be exceeded.

Due to the specific need for bone penetration, dental local anesthetics contain high concentrations of active drug, e.g., 20 mg/mL lidocaine HCl for Xylocaine dental solutions. A combination of high pressure induced by the use of a dental cartridge system and a rapid rate of injection may lead to complications (see Overdose: Symptoms and Treatment) even after the injection of small amounts of local anesthetic. This is due to the high concentration, especially following accidental intravascular injection, when the injected drug could travel in a retrograde manner along the vessel and, in cases of intra-arterial injection in the head and neck area, reach the brain without the same degree of dilution that occurs with an i.v. injection. It must also be noted that epinephrine, when added to a local anesthetic solution is less active as a localizing agent in the highly vascular oral environment than elsewhere in the body.

Aspiration is recommended since it reduces the possibility of intravascular injection, thereby keeping the incidence of side effects and anesthetic failures to a minimum.

For best results, it is important that cartridges be used with a syringe of appropriate size. The Astra Self-Aspirating Syringe has been designed especially for Astra cartridges.

Sterilization, Storage and Technical Procedures: Cartridges should not be autoclaved, because the rubber plunger will typically be extruded thus compromising container integrity.

If disinfection of the cartridge is desired, its immersion should be avoided due to the risk of undesirable effects on the rubber membrane and aluminum cap, and the risk of contamination of the solution. Disinfection of the rubber membrane or the entire dental cartridge should be accomplished by wiping it with a cotton pledget that has been moistened with a disinfectant. Isopropyl alcohol (91%) or ethyl alcohol (70%) is recommended. Many commercially available brands of rubbing alcohol, as well as solutions of ethyl alcohol not of USP grade, contain denaturants which are injurious to rubber and therefore are not to be used.

Quaternary ammonium salts, such as benzalkonium chloride, are electrolytically incompatible with aluminum. Cartridges which are sealed with aluminum caps should not be immersed in any solution containing these salts.

Anti-rust tablets usually contain sodium nitrate or other similar agents which may be capable of releasing metal ions from syringes, needles and aluminum sealed cartridges. Accordingly, cartridges should not be kept in such solutions.

Adequate precautions should be taken to avoid prolonged contact between local anesthetic solutions containing epinephrine (low pH) and metal surfaces (e.g., needles or metal parts of syringes), since dissolved metal ions, particularly copper ions, may cause severe local irritation (swelling, edema) at the site of injection and accelerate the degradation of epinephrine.

To avoid leakage of solutions during injection, be sure to penetrate the center of the rubber diaphragm perpendicularly with the needle when loading the syringe. An off-center penetration produces an oval shaped puncture that allows leakage around the needle.

In order to avoid traumatic nerve injuries leading to paresthesia in conjunction with dental nerve block, an atraumatic technique should be used. Dental cartridge systems may generate high pressures during injection, however, injected local anesthetics may travel in a retrograde manner along a nerve in cases of intraneural injection. If an accidental traumatic nerve injury has occurred, epinephrine, if present in the anesthetic solution, may aggravate the local neurotoxicity by decreasing the intraneural blood circulation. In order to minimize the risk of intraneural injection as well as fascicular injuries, the needle should always be withdrawn a little if paresthesia is elicited during injection. Furthermore, a short-beveled needle should be considered for regional blocks (in which case a topical anesthetic may be used to reduce the pain of needle insertion), while a sharper (i.e., long-beveled) needle can still be recommended for infiltration.

Store at controlled room temperature (15 to 30°C). Protect from light.

Do not use if solution is pinkish or darker than slightly yellow, or if it contains a precipitate.

Xylocaine dental solutions are preservative-free and are for single use only. Discard unused portion.

Supplied: Each plastic dental cartridge contains: lidocaine HCl 2% and epinephrine 1:100 000 or lidocaine HCl 2% and epinephrine 1:50 000. Nonmedicinal ingredients: sodium chloride, sodium metabisulfite and sodium hydroxide and/or hydrochloric acid to adjust pH to 3.3 to 5.5. Cartridges of 1.8 mL, boxes of 50.

Reviewed 1997

XYLOCAINE® ENDOTRACHEAL

Astra

Lidocaine HCl

Topical Anesthetic

Pharmacology: Mechanism of Action: Lidocaine stabilizes the neuronal membrane by inhibiting the ionic fluxes required for the initiation and conduction of impulses, thereby effecting local anesthetic action. Local anesthetics of the amide type are thought to act within the sodium channels of the nerve membrane.

Onset of Action: Lidocaine, when applied topically to the oral cavity, acts on mucous membranes to produce local anesthesia. Anesthesia occurs usually within 1 to 5 minutes and persists for approximately 10 to 15 minutes.

Hemodynamics: Lidocaine, like other local anesthetics, may also have effects on excitable membranes in the brain and myocardium. If excessive amounts of drug reach systemic circulation rapidly, symptoms and signs of toxicity will appear, emanating from the central nervous and cardiovascular systems.

CNS toxicity (see Overdose: Symptoms and Treatment) usually precedes the cardiovascular effects since it occurs at lower plasma concentrations. Direct effects of local anesthetics on the heart include slow conduction, negative inotropism and eventually cardiac arrest.

Pharmacokinetics and Metabolism: The rate and extent of absorption depends upon concentration and total dose administered, the specific site of application and duration of exposure. In general, the rate of absorption of local anesthetic agents, following topical application to wound surfaces and mucous membranes is high, and occurs most rapidly after intratracheal and bronchial administration. Lidocaine is also well absorbed from the gastrointestinal tract, although little intact drug may appear in the circulation because of biotransformation in the liver.

Lidocaine readily crosses the placenta, and equilibrium in regard to free, unbound drug will be reached. Because the degree of plasma protein binding in the fetus is less than in the mother, the total plasma concentration will be greater in the mother, but the free concentrations will be the same.

The plasma binding of lidocaine is dependent on drug concentration, and the fraction bound decreases with increasing concentration. At concentrations of 1 to 4 μg of free base per mL, 60 to 80% of lidocaine is protein bound. Binding is also dependent on the plasma concentration of the alpha-1-acid glycoprotein.

Lidocaine has a total plasma clearance of 0.95 L/min, a volume of distribution at steady-state of 91 L, an elimination half-life of 1.6 hours and an estimated hepatic extraction ratio of 0.65. The clearance of lidocaine is almost entirely due to liver metabolism, and depends both on liver blood flow and the activity of metabolizing enzymes.

Lidocaine is metabolized rapidly by the liver, and metabolites and unchanged drug are excreted by the kidneys. Biotransformation includes oxidative N-dealkylation, ring hydroxylation, cleavage of the amide linkage, and conjugation. Only 2% of lidocaine is excreted unchanged. Most of it is metabolized first to monoethylglycinexylidide (MEGX) and then to glycinexylidide (GX) and 2,6-xylidine. Up to 70% appears in the urine as 4-hydroxy-2,6-xylidine.

The elimination half-life following an i.v. bolus injection is typically 1.5 to 2 hours. The elimination half-life in neonates (3.2 hours) is approximately twice that of adults. The half-life may be prolonged 2-fold or more in patients with liver dysfunction. Renal dysfunction does not affect lidocaine kinetics but may increase the accumulation of metabolites.

Acidosis increases the systemic toxicity of lidocaine while the use of CNS depressants may increase the levels of lidocaine required to produce overt CNS effects. Objective adverse manifestations become increasingly apparent with increasing venous plasma levels above 6 μg free base per mL.

Indications: For surface anesthesia associated with: nasal procedures, e.g., puncture of the maxillary sinus; procedures in the oropharynx, e.g., gastrointestinal endoscopy; procedures in the respiratory tract, e.g., insertion of instruments and tubes; and procedures in the larynx, trachea and bronchi.

Contraindications: Patients with a known history of hypersensitivity to local anesthetics of the amide type or to other components in the formulations.

Warnings: Excessive dosage, or short intervals between doses, can result in high plasma levels of lidocaine or its metabolites and serious adverse effects. Absorption from the mucous membranes is variable but is especially high from the bronchial tree. Such applications may therefore result in rapidly rising or excessive plasma concentrations, with an increased risk for toxic symptoms, such as convulsions. This is especially important in children where doses vary with weight. The management of serious adverse reactions may require the use of resuscitative equipment, oxygen and other resuscitative drugs (see Overdose: Symptoms and Treatment).

In paralyzed patients under general anesthesia, higher blood concentrations may occur than in spontaneously breathing patients. Unparalyzed patients are more likely to swallow a large proportion of the dose which then undergoes considerable first-pass hepatic metabolism following absorption from the gut.

Lidocaine should be used with caution in patients with sepsis and/or traumatized mucosa at the area of application, since under such conditions there is the potential for rapid systemic absorption.

Avoid contact with eyes.

Precautions: The lowest dosage that results in effective anesthesia should be used to avoid high plasma levels and serious adverse effects. Absorption from the mucous membranes is variable but especially high from the bronchial tree. Tolerance to elevated blood levels varies with the status of the patient. Debilitated, elderly patients, acutely ill patients, and children should be given reduced doses commensurate with their age and physical condition. Lidocaine should also be used with caution in patients with epilepsy, impaired cardiac conduction, bradycardia, impaired hepatic or renal function and in severe shock.

Because amide-type local anesthetics such as lidocaine are metabolized by the liver, these drugs, especially repeated doses, should be used cautiously in patients with hepatic disease. Patients with severe hepatic disease, because of their inability to metabolize local anesthetics normally, are at greater risk of developing toxic plasma concentrations.

Lidocaine should also be used with caution in patients with impaired cardiovascular function since they may be less able to compensate for functional changes associated with the prolongation of AV conduction produced by these drugs.

Many drugs used during the conduct of anesthesia are considered potential triggering agents for familial malignant hyperthermia. It has been shown that the use of amide local anesthetics in malignant hyperthermia is safe. However, there is no guarantee that neural blockade will prevent the development of malignant hyperthermia during surgery. It is also difficult to predict the need for supplemental general anesthesia. Therefore a standard protocol for the management of malignant hyperthermia should be available.

Xylocaine Endotracheal (cont'd)

Lidocaine should be used with caution in persons with known drug sensitivities. Patients allergic to para-aminobenzoic acid derivatives (procaine, tetracaine, benzocaine, etc.) have not shown cross-sensitivity to lidocaine.
Drug Interactions: Lidocaine should be used with caution in patients receiving other local anesthetics or agents structurally related to amide-type local anesthetics, since the toxic effects are additive.
Information for the Patient: When topical anesthetics are used in the mouth, the patient should be aware that the production of topical anesthesia may impair swallowing and thus enhance the danger of aspiration. Numbness of the tongue or buccal mucosa may enhance the danger of unintentional biting trauma. Food or chewing gum should not be taken while the mouth or throat area is anesthetized.
Pregnancy: It is reasonable to assume that a large number of pregnant women and women of childbearing age have been given lidocaine. No specific disturbances to the reproductive process have so far been reported, e.g., no increased incidence of malformations. However, care should be given during early pregnancy when maximum organogenesis takes place.

There are no adequate and well-controlled studies in pregnant women on the effect of lidocaine on the developing fetus.
Labor and Delivery: Lidocaine is not contraindicated in labor and delivery. Should Xylocaine Endotracheal be used concomitantly with other products containing lidocaine, the total dose contributed by all formulations must be kept in mind.
Lactation: Lidocaine is excreted in the breast milk, but in such small quantities that there is generally no risk of affecting the infant at therapeutic doses.

Adverse Effects: Adverse experiences following the administration of lidocaine are similar in nature to those observed with other amide local anesthetic agents. These adverse experiences are, in general, dose-related and may result from high plasma levels caused by overdosage or rapid absorption, or may result from a hypersensitivity, idiosyncrasy or diminished tolerance on the part of the patient.

Serious adverse experiences are generally systemic in nature. The following types are those most commonly reported: CNS: CNS manifestations are excitatory and/or depressant and may be characterized by circumoral paresthesia, lightheadedness, nervousness, apprehension, euphoria, confusion, dizziness, drowsiness, hyperacusis, tinnitus, blurred vision, vomiting, sensations of heat, cold or numbness, twitching, tremors, convulsions, unconsciousness, respiratory depression and arrest. The excitatory manifestations may be very brief or may not occur at all, in which case the first manifestation of toxicity may be drowsiness merging into unconsciousness and respiratory arrest.

Drowsiness following the administration of lidocaine is usually an early sign of a high lidocaine plasma level and may occur as a consequence of rapid absorption.
Cardiovascular: Cardiovascular manifestations are usually depressant and are characterized by bradycardia, hypotension, arrhythmia, and cardiovascular collapse, which may lead to cardiac arrest.
Allergic: Allergic reactions are characterized by cutaneous lesions, urticaria, edema or, in the most severe cases, anaphylactic shock. Allergic reactions may occur as a result of sensitivity either to the local anesthetic agent or to other components in the formulation.

Overdose: Acute systemic toxicity from local anesthetics are generally related to high plasma levels encountered during therapeutic use of local anesthetics and originate mainly in the central nervous and the cardiovascular systems (see Adverse Effects, Warnings, and Precautions).

Symptoms: CNS toxicity is a graded response, with symptoms and signs of escalating severity. The first symptoms are circumoral paresthesia, numbness of the tongue, lightheadedness, hyperacusis and tinnitus. Visual disturbance and muscular tremors are more serious and precede the onset of generalized convulsions. Unconsciousness and grand mal convulsions may follow, which may last from a few seconds to several minutes. Hypoxia and hypercarbia occur rapidly following convulsions due to the increased muscular activity, together with the interference with normal respiration. In severe cases apnea may occur. Acidosis increases the toxic effects of local anesthetics.

Recovery is due to redistribution and metabolism of the local anesthetic drug. Recovery may be rapid unless large amounts of the drug have been administered.

Cardiovascular effects may be seen in cases with high systemic concentrations. Severe hypotension, bradycardia, arrhythmia and cardiovascular collapse may be the result in such cases.

Cardiovascular toxic effects are generally preceded by signs of toxicity in the CNS, unless the patient is receiving a general anesthetic or is heavily sedated with drugs such as a benzodiazepine or barbiturate.

Treatment: The first consideration is prevention, best accomplished by careful and constant monitoring of cardiovascular and respiratory vital signs and the patient's state of consciousness after each local anesthetic administration. At the first sign of change, oxygen should be administered.

The first step in the management of systemic toxic reactions consists of immediate attention to the maintenance of a patent airway and assisted or controlled ventilation with oxygen and a delivery system capable of permitting immediate positive airway pressure by mask. This may prevent convulsions if they have not already occurred.

If necessary, use drugs to control convulsions. An anticonvulsant should be given i.v. if the convulsions do not stop spontaneously in 15 to 20 seconds. Thiopental 100 to 150 mg i.v. will abort the convulsions rapidly. Alternatively, diazepam 5 to 10 mg i.v. may be used, although its action is slower. Succinylcholine will stop the muscle convulsions rapidly, but will require tracheal intubation and controlled ventilation, and should only be used by those familar with these procedures.

If cardiovascular depression is evident (hypotension, bradycardia), ephedrine 5 to 10 mg i.v. should be given and may be repeated, if necessary, after 2 to 3 minutes.

Should circulatory arrest occur, immediate cardiopulmonary resuscitation should be instituted. Optimal oxygenation and ventilation and circulatory support as well as treatment of acidosis are of vital importance, since hypoxia and acidosis will increase the systemic toxicity of local anesthetics. Epinephrine (0.1 to 0.2 mg as i.v. or intracardial injections) should be given as soon as possible and repeated, if necessary.

Children should be given doses commensurate with their age and weight.

Dosage: When Xylocaine Endotracheal is used concomitantly with other products containing lidocaine, the total dose contributed by all formulations must be kept in mind.

Debilitated, elderly and acutely ill patients should be given reduced doses.

Since absorption is variable and especially high in the trachea and bronchi, the maximum recommended doses vary depending on the area of application. Application to areas below the vocal cords may result in excessive plasma concentrations because of less transfer to the intestine and less first-pass loss.

Each actuation of the metered dose valve delivers 12 mg lidocaine HCl (equivalent to 10 mg lidocaine base).

When using the spray for the first time, after attaching the nozzle, the pump must be primed by pressing downwards on the actuator 5 to 10 times. When changing to a new nozzle, the pump need not be reprimed but the air in the nozzle must be voided before a full dose is delivered. This usually requires 2 actuations.

Xylocaine Endotracheal can be used in the inverted position.
Adults: See Table I.
Children: For laryngotracheal use, the dose should not exceed 3 mg/kg. For nasal and oropharyngeal use, the dose should not exceed 4 to 5 mg/kg. In neonates and infants, less concentrated lidocaine solutions are recommended.

Table I—Xylocaine Endotracheal

Dose Recommendations for Adults

Area	Recommended Dose (mg)	Maximum Dose for Short[a] Procedures (mg)	Maximum Dose for Prolonged[b] Procedures (mg)
Nasal procedures, e.g., puncture of the maxillary sinus	20-60	500	600
Procedures in the oropharynx, e.g., gastrointestinal endoscopy	20-200	500	600
Procedures in the respiratory tract, e.g., insertion of instruments and tubes	50-400	400	600
Procedures in the larynx, trachea and bronchi	50-200	200[c]	400

[a]For short procedures the drug is given for less than 1 minute.
[b]For prolonged procedures, the duration of application is more than 5 minutes.
[c]During controlled ventilation the dose should be reduced.

Supplied: Each metered dose contains: lidocaine HCl 12 mg (equivalent to 10 mg lidocaine base). Nonmedicinal ingredients: water for injection and sodium hydroxide and/or hydrochloric acid to adjust pH 5.0 to 7.0. Nonaerosol spray bottles of 30 mL with a metered dose valve. Single paks: 1 bottle with 1×20 cm stainless steel nozzle. Three paks: 3 bottles and a Nozzle Pak: 2×20 cm stainless steel nozzles per Pak. Clean stainless steel nozzles may be steam sterilized at 121°C for 15 minutes. Store at controlled room temperature (15 to 30°C). Protect from freezing.
Reviewed 1999

XYLOCAINE® 4% STERILE SOLUTION

Astra

Lidocaine HCl

Local Anesthetic

Pharmacology: Mechanism of Action: Lidocaine stabilizes the neuronal membrane by inhibiting the ionic fluxes required for the initiation and conduction of impulses, thereby effecting local anesthetic action. Local anesthetics of the amide type are thought to act within sodium channels of the nerve membrane.
Onset of Action: The onset of action is rapid. For retrobulbar injection, 4 mL of Xylocaine 4% provides an average duration of action of 1 to 1½ hours. This duration may be extended to ophthalmic surgery by the addition of epinephrine, the usual recommended dilution being 1:50 000 to 1:100 000.
Hemodynamics: Lidocaine, like other local anesthetics, may also have effects on excitable membranes in the brain and myocardium. If excessive amounts of drug reach systemic circulation rapidly, symptoms and signs of toxicity will appear, emanating from the central nervous and cardiovascular systems.

CNS toxicity (see Overdose: Symptoms and Treatment) usually precedes the cardiovascular effects since it occurs at lower plasma concentrations. Direct effects of local anesthetics on the heart include slow conduction, negative inotropism and eventually cardiac arrest.
Pharmacokinetics: Lidocaine is completely absorbed following parenteral administration. The rate of absorption depends on the dose, route of administration, and the vascularity of the injection site. The highest peak plasma levels are obtained following intercostal nerve block (approximately 1.5 μg/mL/100 mg injected) while abdominal s.c. injections give the lowest (approximately 0.5 μg/mL/100 mg injected). Epidural and major nerve blocks are intermediate.

Absorption is considerably slowed by the addition of epinephrine, although it also depends on the site of injection. Peak plasma concentrations are reduced by 50% following s.c. injection, by 30% following epidural injection and by 20% following intercostal block if epinephrine 5 μg/mL is added.

The rate of absorption of local anesthetic agents, following topical application to wound surfaces and mucous membranes is high, and occurs most rapidly after intratracheal and bronchial administration. Lidocaine is also well absorbed from the gastrointestinal tract, although little intact drug may appear in the circulation because of biotransformation in the liver.

Lidocaine has a total plasma clearance of 0.95 L/min, a volume of distribution at steady state of 91 L, an elimination half-life of 1.6 h and an estimated hepatic extraction ratio of 0.65. The clearance of lidocaine is almost entirely due to liver metabolism, and depends both on liver blood flow and the activity of metabolizing enzymes.

The plasma binding of lidocaine is dependent on drug concentration, and the fraction bound decreases with increasing concentration. At concentrations of 1 to 4 μg of free base/mL, 60 to 80% of lidocaine is protein-bound. Binding is also dependent on the plasma concentration of the alpha-1-acid glycoprotein.

Lidocaine readily crosses the placenta, and equilibrium in regard to free, unbound drug will be reached. Because the degree of plasma protein binding in the fetus is less than in the mother, the total plasma concentration will be greater in the mother, but the free concentrations will be the same.

Lidocaine is metabolized rapidly by the liver, and metabolites and unchanged drug are excreted by the kidneys. Biotransformation includes oxidative N-dealkylation, ring hydroxylation, cleavage of the amide linkage, and conjugation. Only 2% of lidocaine is excreted unchanged. Most of it is metabolized first to monoethylglycinexylidide (MEGX) and then to glycinexylidide (GX) and 2,6-xylidine. Up to 70% appears in the urine as 4-hydroxy-2,6-xylidine.

The elimination half-life of lidocaine following i.v. bolus injection is typically 1.5 to 2.0 hours. The elimination half-life in neonates (3.2 hours) is approximately twice that of adults. The half-life may be prolonged two-fold or more in patients with liver dysfunction. Renal dysfunction does not affect lidocaine kinetics but may increase the accumulation of metabolites.

Acidosis increases the systemic toxicity of lidocaine while the use of CNS depressants may increase the levels of lidocaine required to produce overt CNS effects. Objective adverse manifestations become increasingly apparent with increasing venous plasma levels above 6.0 μg free base/mL.

Indications: For parenteral or topical use for the production of local anesthesia of the mucous membranes of the respiratory tract or the genitourinary tract. It may be injected transtracheally to anesthetize the larynx and trachea. It may be administered by retrobulbar injection to provide anesthesia for ophthalmic surgery.

Contraindications: In patients with a known history of hypersensitivity to local anesthetics of the amide type.

Warnings: Local anesthetics should only be employed by clinicians who are well versed in diagnosis and management of dose-related toxicity and other acute emergencies that might arise from the block to be employed and then only after ensuring the immediate availability of oxygen, other resuscitative drugs, cardiopulmonary equipment, and the personnel needed for proper management of toxic reactions and related emergencies (see also Adverse Effects and Precautions). Delay in proper management of dose-related toxicity, underventilation from any cause and/or altered sensitivity may lead to the development of acidosis, cardiac arrest and, possibly, death.

It is essential that aspiration for blood be done prior to injecting any local anesthetics, both the original and all subsequent doses, to avoid intravascular injection. The needle must be repositioned until no return of blood can be elicited by aspiration. However, a negative aspiration does not ensure against an intravascular injection.

Lidocaine should be used with caution in patients with sepsis and/or traumatized mucosa at the area of application, since under such conditions there is the potential for rapid systemic absorption.

Precautions: The safety and effectiveness of Xylocaine 4% Sterile Solution depend on proper dosage, correct technique, adequate precautions and readiness for emergencies. Standard textbooks should be consulted for specific techniques and precautions for various regional anesthetic procedures.

Resuscitative equipment, oxygen, and other resuscitative drugs should be available for immediate use (see Warnings and Overdose: Symptoms and Treatment). During major regional nerve blocks, the patient should have i.v. fluids running via an indwelling catheter to assure a functioning i.v. pathway. **The lowest dosage that results in effective anesthesia should be used to avoid high plasma levels and serious adverse effects.**

Injections should be made slowly, with frequent aspirations before and during the injection to avoid intravascular injection.

Repeated doses of Xylocaine may cause significant increases in blood levels with each repeated dose because of slow accumulation of the drug or its metabolites. Absorption from mucous membranes is variable but especially high from the bronchial tree. Tolerance to elevated blood levels varies with the status of the patient. Debilitated, elderly patients, acutely ill patients, and children should be given reduced doses commensurate with their age and physical condition. Lidocaine should also be used with caution in patients with epilepsy, impaired cardiac conduction, bradycardia, impaired hepatic or renal function and in severe shock.

Because amide-type local anesthetics such as lidocaine are metabolized by the liver, these drugs, especially repeat doses, should be used cautiously in patients with hepatic disease. Patients with severe hepatic disease, because of their inability to metabolize local anesthetics normally, are at greater risk of developing toxic plasma concentrations.

Lidocaine should also be used with caution in patients with impaired cardiovascular function since they may be less able to compensate for functional changes associated with the prolongation of AV conduction produced by these drugs.

Solutions containing epinephrine should be used with caution in patients whose medical history and physical evaluation suggest the existence of untreated hypertension, poorly controlled thyrotoxicosis, diabetes, ischemic heart disease, heart block, cerebral vascular insufficiency and peripheral vascular disorder. These solutions should also be used cautiously in areas of the body supplied by end arteries, such as digits, or otherwise having a compromised blood supply (see also Drug Interactions).

Careful and constant monitoring of cardiovascular and respiratory (adequacy of ventilation) vital signs and the patient's state of consciousness should be performed after each local anesthetic injection. It should be kept in mind at such times that restlessness, anxiety, incoherent speech, lightheadedness, numbness and tingling of the mouth and lips, metallic taste, tinnitus, dizziness, blurred vision, tremors, twitching, depression or drowsiness may be early warning signs of CNS toxicity.

Many drugs used during the conduct of anesthesia are considered potential triggering agents for familial malignant hyperthermia. It has been shown that the use of amide local anesthetics in malignant hyperthermia patients is safe. However, there is no guarantee that neural blockade will prevent the development of malignant hyperthermia during surgery. It is also difficult to predict the need for supplemental general anesthesia. Therefore, a standard protocol for the management of malignant hyperthermia should be available.

Lidocaine should be used with caution in persons with known drug sensitivities. Patients allergic to para-aminobenzoic acid derivatives (procaine, tetracaine, benzocaine, etc.) have not shown cross sensitivity to lidocaine.

Use in the Head and Neck Area: Small doses of local anesthetics injected into the head and neck area, including retrobulbar, dental and stellate ganglion blocks, may produce adverse reactions caused by inadvertent injection to an artery. These reactions may be similar to systemic toxicity seen with unintentional intravascular injections of larger doses. Inadvertent injections into an artery can cause cerebral symptoms even at low doses. Confusion, convulsions, respiratory depression and/or respiratory arrest, and cardiovascular stimulation or depression leading to cardiac arrest have been reported. Patients receiving these blocks should have their circulation and respiration monitored and be constantly observed.

Retrobulbar injections may very occasionally reach the cranial subarachnoid space causing temporary blindness, cardiovascular collapse, apnea, convulsions, etc.. These reactions, which may be due to intra-arterial injection or direct injection into the CNS via the sheaths of the optic nerve, must be diagnosed and treated promptly.

When local anesthetic solutions are employed for retrobulbar block, lack of corneal sensation should not be relied upon to determine whether or not the patient is ready for surgery, since corneal sensation usually precedes clinically acceptable external ocular muscle akinesia.

Drug Interactions: Lidocaine should be used with caution in patients receiving other local anesthetics or agents structurally related to amide-type local anesthetics, since the toxic effects are additive.

Lidocaine with epinephrine or other vasopressors should not be used concomitantly with ergot-type oxytocic drugs, because a severe persistent hypertension may occur and cerebrovascular and cardiac accidents are possible. Likewise, lidocaine with epinephrine or another vasoconstrictor should be used with extreme caution in patients receiving MAO inhibitors or antidepressants of the triptyline or imipramine types, because severe prolonged hypertension may result. In situations when concurrent therapy is necessary, careful patient monitoring is essential. Phenothiazines and butyrophenones may reduce or reverse the pressor effect of epinephrine.

If sedatives are employed to reduce patient apprehension, they should be used in reduced doses, since local anesthetic agents, like sedatives, are CNS depressants which in combination may have an additive effect.

Solutions containing epinephrine should be used with caution in patients undergoing general anesthesia with inhalation agents such as halothane, due to the risk of serious cardiac arrhythmias.

Drug/Laboratory Test Interactions: The i.m. injection of lidocaine may result in an increase in creatine phosphokinase levels. Thus, the use of this enzyme determination, without isoenzyme separation, as a diagnostic test for the presence of acute myocardial infarction may be compromised by the i.m. injection of lidocaine.

Information for the Patient: When topical anesthetics are used in the mouth, the patient should be aware that the production of topical anesthesia may impair swallowing and thus enhance the danger of aspiration. Numbness of the tongue or buccal mucosa may enhance the danger of unintentional biting trauma. Food or chewing gum should not be taken while the mouth or throat area is anesthetized.

Pregnancy: It is reasonable to assume that a large number of pregnant women and women of child-bearing age have been given lidocaine. No specific disturbances to the reproductive process have so far been reported, e.g., no increased incidence of malformations. However, care should be given during early pregnancy when maximum organogenesis takes place.

There are no adequate and well-controlled studies in pregnant women on the effect of lidocaine on the developing fetus.

Labor and Delivery: Lidocaine is not contraindicated in labor and delivery. Should Xylocaine 4% Sterile Solution be used concomitantly with other products containing lidocaine, the total dose contributed by all formulations must be kept in mind.

Lactation: Lidocaine is excreted in the breast milk, but in such small quantities that there is generally no risk of affecting the infant at therapeutic dose levels.

Adverse Effects: Adverse experiences following the administration of lidocaine are similar in nature to those observed with other amide local anesthetic agents. These adverse experiences are, in general, dose-related and may result from high plasma levels caused by overdosage, rapid absorption, or inadvertent intravascular injection, or may result from a hypersensitivity, idiosyncrasy or diminished tolerance on the part of the patient.

Serious adverse experiences are generally systemic in nature. The following types are those most commonly reported:

CNS: CNS manifestations are excitatory and/or depressant and may be characterized by circumoral paresthesia, lightheadedness, nervousness, apprehension, euphoria, confusion, dizziness, drowsiness, hyperacusis, tinnitus, blurred vision, vomiting, sensations of heat, cold or numbness, twitching, tremors, convulsions, unconsciousness, respiratory depression and arrest. The excitatory manifestations may be very brief or may not occur at all, in which case the first manifestation of toxicity may be drowsiness merging into unconsciousness and respiratory arrest.

Drowsiness following the administration of lidocaine is usually an early sign of a high lidocaine plasma level and may occur as a consequence of rapid absorption.

Cardiovascular: Cardiovascular manifestations are usually depressant and are characterized by bradycardia, hypotension, and cardiovascular collapse, which may lead to cardiac arrest.

Allergic: Allergic reactions are characterized by cutaneous lesions, urticaria, edema or, in the most severe instances, anaphylactic shock. Allergic reactions of the amide type are rare and may occur as a result of sensitivity either to the local anesthetic agent or to other components in the formulation.

Neurologic: The incidence of adverse reactions may be related to the total dose of local anesthetic administered but is also dependent upon the particular drug used, the route of administration and the physical status of the patient. Neuropathy and spinal cord dysfunction (e.g., anterior spinal artery syndrome, arachnoiditis, cauda equina syndrome), have been associated with regional anesthesia. Neurological effects may be related to local anesthetic techniques, with or without a contribution from the drug.

Overdose: Acute systemic toxicity from local anesthetics is generally related to high plasma levels encountered during therapeutic use of local anesthetics and originates mainly in the central nervous and the cardiovascular systems (see Adverse Effects, Warnings, and Precautions).

Symptoms: With accidental intravascular injections, the toxic effect will be obvious within 1 to 3 minutes, while with overdosage, peak plasma concentrations may not be reached for 20 to 30 minutes depending on the site of injection, with signs of toxicity thus being delayed.

CNS toxicity is a graded response, with symptoms and signs of escalating severity. The first symptoms are circumoral paresthesia, numbness of the tongue, lightheadedness, hyperacusis and tinnitus. Visual disturbance and muscular tremors

Xylocaine 4% Sterile Solution (cont'd)

are more serious and precede the onset of generalized convulsions. Unconsciousness and grand mal convulsions may follow, which may last from a few seconds to several minutes. Hypoxia and hypercarbia occur rapidly following convulsions due to the increased muscular activity, together with the interference with normal respiration. In severe cases apnea may occur. Acidosis increases the toxic effects of local anesthetics.

Recovery is due to redistribution and metabolism of the local anesthetic drug. Recovery may be rapid unless large amounts of the drug have been administered.

Cardiovascular effects may be seen in cases with high systemic concentrations. Severe hypotension, bradycardia, arrhythmia and cardiovascular collapse may be the result in such cases.

Cardiovascular toxic effects are generally preceded by signs of toxicity in the CNS, unless the patient is receiving a general anesthetic or is heavily sedated with drugs such as a benzodiazepine or barbiturate.

Treatment: The first consideration is prevention, best accomplished by careful and constant monitoring of cardiovascular and respiratory vital signs and the patient's state of consciousness after each local anesthetic administration. At the first sign of change, oxygen should be administered. If signs of acute systemic toxicity appear, administration of the local anesthetic should be immediately stopped.

The first step in the management of systemic toxic reactions consists of immediate attention to the maintenance of a patent airway and assisted or controlled ventilation with oxygen and a delivery system capable of permitting immediate positive airway pressure by mask. This may prevent convulsions, if they have not already occurred.

If necessary, use drugs to control convulsions. An anticonvulsant should be given i.v. if the convulsions do not stop spontaneously in 15 to 20 seconds. Thiopental 100 to 150 mg i.v. will abort the convulsions rapidly. Alternatively, diazepam 5 to 10 mg i.v. may be used, although its action is slower. Succinylcholine will stop the muscle convulsions rapidly, but will require tracheal intubation and controlled ventilation, and should only be used by those familiar with these procedures.

If cardiovascular depression is evident (hypotension, bradycardia), ephedrine 5 to 10 mg i.v. should be given and may be repeated, if necessary, after 2 to 3 minutes.

Should circulatory arrest occur, immediate cardiopulmonary resuscitation should be instituted. Optimal oxygenation and ventilation and circulatory support as well as treatment of acidosis are of vital importance, since hypoxia and acidosis will increase the systemic toxicity of local anesthetics. Epinephrine (0.1 to 0.2 mg as i.v. or intracardial injections) should be given as soon as possible and repeated, if necessary.

Children should be given doses commensurate with their age and weight.

Dosage: When Xylocaine 4% Sterile Solution is used concomitantly with other products containing lidocaine, the total dose contributed by all formulations must be kept in mind.

The dosage varies and depends upon the area to be anesthetized, vascularity of the tissues, individual tolerance and the technique of anesthesia. The lowest dosage needed to provide effective anesthesia should be administered. The degree of absorption is variable but especially high from the bronchial tree. Dosages should be reduced for children and for elderly and debilitated patients. For specific techniques and procedures, refer to standard textbooks.

The dosages below are for normal, healthy adults.

Retrobulbar Injection: The suggested dose for a 70 kg person is 3 to 5 mL (120 to 200 mg lidocaine HCl), i.e., 1.7 to 3 mg/kg body weight. A portion of this is injected retrobulbarly and the rest may be used to block the facial nerve.

Transtracheal Injection: For local anesthesia by the transtracheal route, 2 to 3 mL (80 to 120 mg lidocaine HCl) should be injected through a large enough needle so that the injection can be made rapidly. By injecting during inspiration, some of the drug will be carried into the bronchi and the resulting cough will distribute the rest of the drug over the vocal cords and the epiglottis.

Occasionally it may be necessary to spray the pharynx with lidocaine to achieve complete analgesia e.g., using an atomizer or nebulizer. For the combination of the injection and spray, it should rarely be necessary to utilize more than 5 mL (200 mg lidocaine HCl), i.e., 3 mg/kg body weight.

Topical Application: For laryngoscopy, bronchoscopy and endotracheal intubation, the pharynx may be sprayed with 1 to 5 mL (40 to 200 mg lidocaine HCl), i.e., 0.6 to 3 mg/kg body weight.

Maximum Dosage: Adults: No more than 7.5 mL (300 mg lidocaine HCl) should be used at any one time.

Children: It is difficult to recommend a maximum dose of any drug for children since this varies as a function of age and weight. In any case, the maximum amount of lidocaine administered should not exceed 4.5 mg/kg of body weight.

Sterilization, Storage and Technical Procedures: Adequate precautions should be taken to avoid prolonged contact between local anesthetic solutions containing epinephrine (low pH) and metal surfaces (e.g., needles or metal parts of syringes), since dissolved metal ions, particularly copper ions, may cause severe local irritation (swelling, edema) at the site of injection and accelerate the degradation of epinephrine.

The solubility of lidocaine is limited at pH >6.5. This must be taken into consideration when alkaline solutions, i.e., carbonates, are added since precipitation might occur. In the case of epinephrine-containing solutions, mixing with alkaline solutions may cause rapid degradation of epinephrine.

Xylocaine 4% Sterile Solution may be autoclaved for 15 to 20 minutes at 121°C.

Supplied: Each mL of sterile solution contains: lidocaine HCl USP 40 mg. Nonmedicinal ingredients: sodium hydroxide and/or hydrochloric acid to adjust pH (5.0 to 7.0). Preservative-free. Single use vials of 5 mL. Discard unused portion. Store at controlled room temperature 15 to 30°C.

Reviewed 1998

XYLOCAINE® JELLY 2%

Astra

Lidocaine HCl

Topical Anesthetic

Pharmacology: Mechanism of Action: Lidocaine stabilizes the neuronal membrane by inhibiting the ionic fluxes required for the initiation and conduction of impulses, thereby effecting local anesthetic action. Local anesthetics of the amide type are thought to act within the sodium channels of the nerve membrane.

Onset of Action: Anesthesia is achieved within 5 minutes, depending on the area of application. Duration of anesthesia is approximately 20 to 30 minutes. Lidocaine is ineffective when applied to intact skin.

Hemodynamics: Lidocaine, like other local anesthetics, may also have effects on excitable membranes in the brain and myocardium. If excessive amounts of drug reach systemic circulation rapidly, symptoms and signs of toxicity will appear, emanating from the central nervous and cardiovascular systems.

CNS toxicity (see Overdose: Symptoms and Treatment) usually precedes the cardiovascular effects since it occurs at lower plasma concentrations. Direct effects of local anesthetics on the heart include slow conduction, negative inotropism and eventually cardiac arrest.

Pharmacokinetics and Metabolism: The rate and extent of absorption depends upon concentration and total dose administered, the specific site of application and duration of exposure. In general, the rate of absorption of local anesthetic agents, following topical application to wound surfaces and mucous membranes is high, and occurs most rapidly after intratracheal and bronchial administration. The absorption of lidocaine jelly from the nasopharynx is usually lower than with other lidocaine products. Blood concentrations of lidocaine after instillation of the jelly in the intact urethra and bladder in doses up to 800 mg are fairly low and below toxic levels. Lidocaine is also well absorbed from the gastrointestinal tract, although little intact drug may appear in the circulation because of biotransformation in the liver.

Lidocaine readily crosses the placenta, and equilibrium in regard to free, unbound drug will be reached. Because the degree of plasma protein binding in the fetus is less than in the mother, the total plasma concentration will be greater in the mother, but the free concentrations will be the same.

Normally about 65% of the lidocaine is bound to plasma proteins. Amide local anesthetics are mainly bound to alpha-1-acid glycoprotein and also to albumin. Lidocaine crosses the blood-brain and placental barriers, presumably by passive diffusion.

Lidocaine has a total plasma clearance of 0.95 L/min, a volume of distribution at steady state of 91 L, an elimination half-life of 1.6 h and an estimated hepatic extraction ratio of 0.65. The clearance of lidocaine is almost entirely due to liver metabolism, and depends both on liver blood flow and the activity of metabolizing enzymes.

The main elimination pathway of lidociane is by liver metabolism. The primary route of lidocaine is N-dealkylation to monoethylglycine xylidine (MEGX), followed by hydrolysis to 2,6-xylidine and hydroxylation to 4-hydroxy-2,6-xylidine. MEGX can also be further dealkylated to glycine xylidine (GX). The pharmacological/toxicological actions of MEGX and GX are similar to, but less potent than those of lidocaine. GX has a longer half-life (about 10 hours) than lidocaine and may accumulate during long-term administration. Approximately 90% of the lidocaine administered i.v. is excreted in the form of various metabolites, and less than 10% is excreted unchanged in the urine. The primary metabolite in urine is a conjugate of 4-hydroxy-2,6-xylidine, accounting for about 70 to 80% of the dose excreted in the urine.

The elimination half-life of lidocaine following an i.v. bolus injection is typically 1.5 to 2.0 hours. The elimination half-life in neonates (3.2 hours) is approximately twice that of adults. The half-life may be prolonged two-fold or more in patients with liver dysfunction. Renal dysfunction does not affect lidocaine kinetics but may increase the accumulation of metabolites.

Acidosis increases the systemic toxicity of lidocaine while the use of CNS depressants may increase the levels of lidocaine required to produce overt CNS effects. Objective adverse manifestations become increasingly apparent with increasing venous plasma levels above 6.0 μg free base per mL.

Indications: Surface anesthesia and lubrication for: The male and female urethra during cystoscopy, catheterization, exploration by sound and other endourethral operations. Nasal and pharyngeal cavities in endoscopic procedures such as gastroscopy and bronchoscopy. Proctoscopy and rectoscopy. Tracheal intubation.

Symptomatic treatment of pain in connection with cystitis and urethritis.

Contraindications: Known history of hypersensitivity to local anesthetics of the amide type or to other components in the formulation e.g., methylparaben, propylparaben (preservatives of the tube).

Warnings: Excessive dosage, or short intervals between doses, can result in high plasma levels of lidocaine or its metabolites and serious adverse effects. Absorption from the mucous membranes is variable but is especially high from the bronchial tree. Such applications may therefore result in rapidly rising or excessive plasma concentrations, with an increased risk for toxic symptoms, such as convulsions. **Patients should be instructed to strictly adhere to the recommended dosage.** This is especially important in children where doses vary with weight. The management of serious adverse reactions may require the use of resuscitative equipment, oxygen and other resuscitative drugs (see Overdose: Symptoms and Treatment).

Lidocaine should be used with caution in patients with sepsis and/or traumatized mucosa at the area of application, since under such conditions there is the potential for rapid systemic absorption.

When used for endotracheal tube lubrication, care should be taken to avoid introduction of the jelly into the lumen of the tube. If allowed into the inner lumen, the jelly may dry on the inner surface leaving a residue which tends to clump with flexion, narrowing the lumen. There have been rare reports in which this residue has caused the lumen to occlude. Similarly, do not use the jelly to lubricate the endotracheal stylettes.

Precautions: The lowest dosage that results in effective anesthesia should be used to avoid high plasma levels and serious adverse effects. Absorption from mucous membranes is variable but especially high from the bronchial tree. Tolerance to elevated blood levels varies with the status of the patient. Debilitated, elderly patients, acutely ill patients, and children should be given reduced doses commensurate with their age and physical condition. Lidocaine should also be used with caution in patients with epilepsy, impaired cardiac conduction, bradycardia, impaired hepatic or renal function and in severe shock.

Because amide-type local anesthetics such as lidocaine are metabolized by the liver, these drugs, especially repeated doses, should be used cautiously in patients with hepatic disease. Patients with severe hepatic disease, because of their inability to metabolize local anesthetics normally, are at greater risk of developing toxic plasma concentrations.

Lidocaine should also be used with caution in patients with impaired cardiovascular function since they may be less able to compensate for functional changes associated with the prolongation of AV conduction produced by these drugs.

Many drugs used during the conduct of anesthesia are considered potential triggering agents for familial malignant hyperthermia. It has been shown that the use of amide local anesthetics in malignant hyperthermia patients is safe. However, there is no guarantee that neural blockade will prevent the development of malignant hyperthermia during surgery. It is also difficult to predict the need for supplemental general anesthesia. Therefore, a standard protocol for the management of malignant hyperthermia should be available.

Lidocaine should be used with caution in persons with known drug sensitivities. Patients allergic to para-aminobenzoic acid derivatives (procaine, tetracaine, benzocaine, etc.) have not shown cross-sensitivity to lidocaine.

Drug Interactions: Lidocaine should be used with caution in patients receiving other local anesthetics or agents structurally related to amide-type local anesthetics, since the toxic effects are additive.

Information for the Patient: See also Blue section—Information for the Patient "Xylocaine Jelly 2%". When topical anesthetics are used in the mouth, the patient should be aware that the production of topical anesthesia may impair swallowing and thus enhance the danger of aspiration. Numbness of the tongue or buccal mucosa may enhance the danger of unintentional biting trauma. Food or chewing gum should not be taken while the mouth or throat area is anesthetized.

Pregnancy: It is reasonable to assume that a large number of pregnant women and women of childbearing age have been given lidocaine. No specific disturbances to the reproductive process have so far been reported, e.g., no increased incidence of malformations. However, care should be given during early pregnancy when maximum organogenesis takes place.

There are no adequate and well-controlled studies in pregnant women on the effect of lidocaine on the developing fetus.

Labor and Delivery: Lidocaine is not contraindicated in labor and delivery. Should Xylocaine Jelly 2% be used concomitantly with other products containing lidocaine, the total dose contributed by all formulations must be kept in mind.

Lactation: Lidocaine is excreted in the breast milk, but in such small quantities that there is generally no risk of affecting the infant at therapeutic dose levels.

Adverse Effects: Adverse experiences following the administration of lidocaine are similar in nature to those observed with other amide local anesthetic agents. These adverse experiences are, in general, dose-related and may result from high plasma levels caused by overdosage or rapid absorption, or may result from a hypersensitivity, idiosyncrasy or diminished tolerance on the part of the patient.

An increased incidence of postoperative sore throat has been reported following endotracheal tube lubrication with lidocaine jelly.

Serious adverse experiences are generally systemic in nature. The following types are those most commonly reported: CNS: CNS manifestations are excitatory and/or depressant and may be characterized by circumoral paresthesia, lightheadedness, nervousness, apprehension, euphoria, confusion, dizziness, drowsiness, hyperacusis, tinnitus, blurred vision, vomiting, sensations of heat, cold or numbness, twitching, tremors, convulsions, unconsciousness, respiratory depression and arrest. The excitatory manifestations may be very brief or may not occur at all, in which case the first manifestation of toxicity may be drowsiness merging into unconsciousness and respiratory arrest.

Drowsiness following the administration of lidocaine is usually an early sign of a high lidocaine plasma level and may occur as a consequence of rapid absorption.

Cardiovascular: Cardiovascular manifestations are usually depressant and are characterized by bradycardia, hypotension, arrhythmia and cardiovascular collapse, which may lead to cardiac arrest.

Allergic: Allergic reactions are characterized by cutaneous lesions, urticaria, edema or, in the most severe instances, anaphylactic shock. Allergic reactions of the amide type are rare and may occur as a result of sensitivity either to the local anesthetic agent or to other components in the formulation.

Overdose: Acute systemic toxicity from local anesthetics is generally related to high plasma levels encountered during therapeutic use of local anesthetics and originates mainly in the central nervous and the cardiovascular systems (see Adverse Effects, Warnings and Precautions).

Symptoms: CNS toxicity is a graded response, with symptoms and signs of escalating severity. The first symptoms are circumoral paresthesia, numbness of the tongue, lightheadedness, hyperacusis and tinnitus. Visual disturbance and muscular tremors are more serious and precede the onset of generalized convulsions. Unconsciousness and grand mal convulsions may follow, which may last from a few seconds to several minutes. Hypoxia and hypercarbia occur rapidly following convulsions due to the increased muscular activity, together with the interference with normal respiration. In severe cases apnea may occur. Acidosis increases the toxic effects of local anesthetics.

Recovery is due to redistribution and metabolism of the local anesthetic drug. Recovery may be rapid unless large amounts of the drug have been administered.

Cardiovascular effects may be seen in cases with high systemic concentrations. Severe hypotension, bradycardia, arrhythmia and cardiovascular collapse may be the result in such cases.

Cardiovascular toxic effects are generally preceded by signs of toxicity in the CNS, unless the patient is receiving a general anesthetic or is heavily sedated with drugs such as a benzodiazepine or barbiturate.

Treatment: The first consideration is prevention, best accomplished by careful and constant monitoring of cardiovascular and respiratory vital signs and the patient's state of consciousness after each local anesthetic administration. At the first sign of change, oxygen should be administered.

The first step in the management of systemic toxic reactions consists of immediate attention to the maintenance of a patent airway and assisted or controlled ventilation with oxygen and a delivery system capable of permitting immediate positive airway pressure by mask. This may prevent convulsions if they have not already occurred.

If necessary, use drugs to control convulsions. An anticonvulsant should be given i.v. if the convulsions do not stop spontaneously in 15 to 20 seconds. Thiopental 100 to 150 mg i.v. will abort the convulsions rapidly. Alternatively, diazepam 5 to 10 mg i.v. may be used, although its action is slower. Succinylcholine will stop the muscle convulsions rapidly, but will require tracheal intubation and controlled ventilation, and should only be used by those familiar with these procedures.

If cardiovascular depression is evident (hypotension, bradycardia), ephedrine 5 to 10 mg i.v. should be given and may be repeated, if necessary, after 2 to 3 minutes.

Should circulatory arrest occur, immediate cardiopulmonary resuscitation should be instituted. Optimal oxygenation and ventilation and circulatory support as well as treatment of acidosis are of vital importance, since hypoxia and acidosis will increase the systemic toxicity of local anesthetics. Epinephrine (0.1 to 0.2 mg as i.v. or intracardial injections) should be given as soon as possible and repeated, if necessary.

Children should be given doses commensurate with their age and weight.

Dosage: When used concomitantly with other products containing lidocaine, the total dose contributed by all formulations must be kept in mind. Debilitated, elderly and acutely ill patients should be given reduced doses.

Xylocaine Jelly in the plastic syringe is preservative-free, and intended for single use only. The tube presentation of Xylocaine Jelly contains preservatives. The syringe is graduated, i.e., a 3 mm line of jelly is equivalent to approximately 1 mL of jelly (20 mg lidocaine HCl).

Urethral Anesthesia: Surface Anesthesia of the Male Adult Urethra: For adequate analgesia in males, 20 mL (400 mg lidocaine HCl) jelly is usually required. The jelly is instilled slowly until the patient has a feeling of tension (approximately 10 mL) (200 mg). A penile clamp is then applied for several minutes at the corona, after which the rest of the jelly is instilled.

When anesthesia is especially important, e.g., during sounding or cystoscopy, a larger quantity of jelly (e.g., 30 to 40 mL) may be instilled in 3 to 4 portions and allowed to act for 10 to 12 minutes before insertion of the instrument. The jelly instilled into the bladder is also effective for procedures in this region.

To anesthetize only the anterior male urethra, e.g., for catheterization, small volumes (5 to 10 mL, i.e., 100 to 200 mg lidocaine HCl) are usually adequate for lubrication.

For Surface Anesthesia of the Female Adult Urethra: Instill 5 to 10 mL of jelly in small portions to fill the whole urethra. If desired, some jelly may be deposited on the orifice and covered with a cotton swab. In order to obtain adequate anesthesia, several minutes should be allowed prior to performing urological procedures.

Endoscopy: The instillation of 10 to 20 mL is recommended for adequate analgesia and a small amount may be applied to the lubricating instrument. When combined with other lidocaine products (e.g., for bronchoscopy), the total dose of lidocaine should not exceed 400 mg.

Lubrication for Endotracheal Intubation: Apply approximately 2 mL of jelly to the external surface of the endotracheal tube just prior to insertion. Care should be taken to avoid introducing the product into the lumen of the tube (see Warnings). Do not use the jelly to lubricate endotracheal stylettes. It is also recommended that the use of endotracheal tubes with dried jelly on the external surface be avoided for lack of lubricating effect.

Maximum Dosage: Adults: The dose depends on the application site. A safe dose for oral use is 400 mg (20 mL). A safe dose for use in the urethra and bladder is 800 mg (40 mL). A maximum single dosage is not established. No more than 4 doses should be given during a 24-hour period.

Children (under 12 years): It is difficult to recommend a maximum dose of any drug for children since this varies as a function of age and weight. The maximum amount per dose should not exceed 6 mg/kg of body weight or 3 mL per 10 kg weight. No more than 4 doses should be given during a 24-hour period.

Information for the Patient: See Blue Section—Information for the Patient "Xylocaine Jelly 2%".

Supplied: Each mL of a clear to almost clear, slightly colored jelly contains: lidocaine HCl 20 mg. Nonmedicinal ingredients: hydroxypropyl methylcellulose, methyl- and propylparabens (30 mL tube only), sodium hydroxide and/or hydrochloric acid to adjust pH 6.0 to 7.0 and water for injection. Its water-miscible base, characterized by high viscosity and low surface tension, allows close and prolonged contact with mucous membrane. Prefilled single-use plastic syringe of 10 mL packaged in a Sterile Pack. Plastic tubes of 30 mL with 1 applicator cone. Store at 15 to 30°C. Protect from freezing.

Jelly Syringe: Instructions for Use: Screw plunger rod clockwise into grey rubber until rubber rotates; twist protective tab to break seal. The syringe is now ready for use.

Reviewed 1999

XYLOCAINE® OINTMENT 5%
XYLOCAINE® DENTAL OINTMENT 5%

Astra

Lidocaine

Topical Anesthetic

Pharmacology: Mechanism of Action: Lidocaine stabilizes the neuronal membrane by inhibiting the ionic fluxes required for the initiation and conduction of impulses, thereby effecting local anesthetic action. Local anesthetics of the amide type are thought to act within the sodium channels of the nerve membrane.

Onset of Action: Anesthesia usually occurs within 3 to 5 minutes when applied to mucous membrane. Xylocaine Ointment and Xylocaine Dental Ointment are ineffective when applied to intact skin.

Hemodynamics: Lidocaine, like other local anesthetics, may also have effects on excitable membranes in the brain and myocardium. If excessive amounts of drug reach systemic circulation rapidly, symptoms and signs of toxicity will appear, emanating from the central nervous and cardiovascular systems.

CNS toxicity (see Overdose: Symptoms and Treatment) usually precedes the cardiovascular effects since it occurs at lower plasma concentrations. Direct effects of local anesthetics on the heart include slow conduction, negative inotropism and eventually cardiac arrest.

Pharmacokinetics: The rate and extent of absorption depends upon concentration and total dose administered, the specific site of application and duration of exposure. In general, the rate of absorption of local anesthetic agents, following topical application to wound surfaces and mucous membranes is high, and occurs most rapidly after intratracheal and bronchial administration. Lidocaine is also well absorbed from the gastrointestinal tract, although little intact drug may appear in the circulation because of biotransformation in the liver.

Lidocaine readily crosses the placenta, and equilibrium in regard to free, unbound drug will be reached. Because the degree of plasma protein binding in the fetus is less than in the mother, the total plasma concentration will be greater in the mother, but the free concentrations will be the same.

The plasma binding of lidocaine is dependent on drug concentration, and the fraction bound decreases with increasing concentration. At concentrations of 1 to 4 μg of free base per mL, 60 to 80% of lidocaine is protein bound. Binding is also dependent on the plasma concentration of the alpha-1-acid glycoprotein.

Lidocaine has a total plasma clearance of 0.95 L/min, a volume of distribution at steady state of 91 L, an elimination half-life of 1.6 hours and an estimated hepatic extraction ratio of 0.65. The clearance of lidocaine is almost entirely due to

Xylocaine Ointment 5% (cont'd)

liver metabolism, and depends both on liver blood flow and the activity of metabolizing enzymes.

Lidocaine is metabolized rapidly by the liver, and metabolites and unchanged drug are excreted by the kidneys. Biotransformation includes oxidative N-dealkylation, ring hydroxylation, cleavage of the amide linkage, and conjugation. Only 2% of lidocaine is excreted unchanged. Most of it is metabolized first to monoethylglycinexylidide (MEGX) and then to glycinexylidide (GX) and 2,6-xylidine. Up to 70% appears in the urine as 4-hydroxy-2,6-xylidine.

The elimination half-life of lidocaine following an i.v. bolus injection is typically 1.5 to 2.0 hours. The elimination half-life in neonates (3.2 hours) is approximately twice that of adults. The half-life may be prolonged two-fold or more in patients with liver dysfunction. Renal dysfunction does not affect lidocaine kinetics but may increase the accumulation of metabolites.

Acidosis increases the systemic toxicity of lidocaine while the use of CNS depressants may increase the levels of lidocaine required to produce overt CNS effects. Objective adverse manifestations become increasingly apparent with increasing venous plasma levels above 6.0 μg free base per mL.

Indications: Ointment: Temporary relief of pain associated with minor burns and abrasions of the skin, e.g., sunburn, herpes zoster and labialis, pruritus, sore nipples, insect bites. Anesthesia of mucous membranes, e.g., various anal conditions such as hemorrhoids and fissures. The alleviation of pain during examination and instrumentation, e.g., proctoscopy, sigmoidoscopy, cystoscopy, endotracheal intubation.

Dental Ointment: Dentistry: surface anesthesia of the gums prior to injection and before deep scaling. Temporary relief of denture irritation.

Contraindications: Known history of hypersensitivity to local anesthetics of the amide type or to other components of the ointment.

Warnings: Excessive dosage, or short intervals between doses, can result in high plasma levels of lidocaine or its metabolites and serious adverse effects. Absorption from the mucous membranes is variable but is especially high from the bronchial tree. Such applications may therefore result in rapidly rising or excessive plasma concentrations, with an increased risk for toxic symptoms, such as convulsions. **Patients should be instructed to strictly adhere to the recommended dosage.** This is especially important in children where doses vary with weight. The management of serious adverse reactions may require the use of resuscitative equipment, oxygen and other resuscitative drugs (see Overdose: Symptoms and Treatment).

Lidocaine should be used with caution in patients with sepsis and/or traumatized mucosa at the area of application, since under such conditions there is the potential for rapid systemic absorption.

Precautions: The lowest dosage that results in effective anesthesia should be used to avoid high plasma levels and serious adverse effects. Absorption from mucous membranes is variable but especially high from the bronchial tree. Tolerance to elevated blood levels varies with the status of the patient. Debilitated, elderly patients, acutely ill patients, and children should be given reduced doses commensurate with their age and physical condition. Lidocaine should also be used with caution in patients with epilepsy, impaired cardiac conduction, bradycardia, impaired hepatic or renal function and in severe shock.

Because amide-type local anesthetics such as lidocaine are metabolized by the liver, these drugs, especially repeated doses, should be used cautiously in patients with hepatic disease. Patients with severe hepatic disease, because of their inability to metabolize local anesthetics normally, are at greater risk of developing toxic plasma concentrations.

Lidocaine should also be used with caution in patients with impaired cardiovascular function since they may be less able to compensate for functional changes associated with the prolongation of AV conduction produced by these drugs.

Many drugs used during the conduct of anesthesia are considered potential triggering agents for familial malignant hyperthermia. It has been shown that the use of amide local anesthetics in malignant hyperthermia patients is safe. However, there is no guarantee that neural blockade will prevent the development of malignant hyperthermia during surgery. It is also difficult to predict the need for supplemental general anesthesia. Therefore, a standard protocol for the management of malignant hyperthermia should be available.

Lidocaine should be used with caution in persons with known drug sensitivities. Patients allergic to para-aminobenzoic acid derivatives (procaine, tetracaine, benzocaine, etc.) have not shown cross-sensitivity to lidocaine.

Drug Interactions: Lidocaine should be used with caution in patients receiving other local anesthetics or agents structurally related to amide-type local anesthetics, since the toxic effects are additive.

Information for the Patient: See also Blue Section—Information for the Patient "Xylocaine Ointment 5%". When topical anesthetics are used in the mouth, the patient should be aware that the production of topical anesthesia may impair swallowing and thus enhance the danger of aspiration. Numbness of the tongue or buccal mucosa may enhance the danger of unintentional biting trauma. Food or chewing gum should not be taken while the mouth or throat area is anesthetized.

Pregnancy: It is reasonable to assume that a large number of pregnant women and women of childbearing age have been given lidocaine. No specific disturbances to the reproductive process have so far been reported, e.g., no increased incidence of malformations. However, care should be given during early pregnancy when maximum organogenesis takes place.

There are no adequate and well-controlled studies in pregnant women on the effect of lidocaine on the developing fetus.

Labor and Delivery: Lidocaine is not contraindicated in labor and delivery. Should Xylocaine Ointment or Xylocaine Dental Ointment be used concomitantly with other products containing lidocaine, the total dose contributed by all formulations must be kept in mind.

Lactation: Lidocaine is excreted in the breast milk, but in such small quantities that there is generally no risk of affecting the infant at therapeutic dose levels.

Adverse Effects: Adverse experiences following the administration of lidocaine are similar in nature to those observed with other amide local anesthetic agents. These adverse experiences are, in general, dose-related and may result from high plasma levels caused by excessive dosage or rapid absorption, or may result from a hypersensitivity, idiosyncrasy or diminished tolerance on the part of the patient.

Serious adverse experiences are generally systemic in nature. The following types are those most commonly reported.

CNS: CNS manifestations are excitatory and/or depressant and may be characterized by circumoral paresthesia, lightheadedness, nervousness, apprehension, euphoria, confusion, dizziness, drowsiness, hyperacusis, tinnitus, blurred vision, vomiting, sensations of heat, cold or numbness, twitching, tremors, convulsions, unconsciousness, respiratory depression and arrest. The excitatory manifestations may be very brief or may not occur at all, in which case the first manifestation of toxicity may be drowsiness merging into unconsciousness and respiratory arrest.

Drowsiness following the administration of lidocaine is usually an early sign of a high lidocaine plasma level and may occur as a consequence of rapid absorption.

Cardiovascular: Cardiovascular manifestations are usually depressant and are characterized by bradycardia, hypotension, arrhythmia and cardiovascular collapse, which may lead to cardiac arrest.

Allergic: Allergic reactions are characterized by cutaneous lesions, urticaria, edema or in the most severe instances, anaphylactic shock. Allergic reactions of the amide type are rare and may occur as a result of sensitivity either to the local anesthetic agent or to other components in the formulation.

Overdose: Acute systemic toxicity from local anesthetics is generally related to high plasma levels encountered during therapeutic use of local anesthetics and originates mainly in the central nervous and the cardiovascular systems (see Adverse Effects, Warnings, and Precautions).

Symptoms: CNS toxicity is a graded response, with symptoms and signs of escalating severity. The first symptoms are circumoral paresthesia, numbness of the tongue, lightheadedness, hyperacusis and tinnitus. Visual disturbance and muscular tremors are more serious and precede the onset of generalized convulsions. Unconsciousness and grand mal convulsions may follow, which may last from a few seconds to several minutes. Hypoxia and hypercarbia occur rapidly following convulsions due to the increased muscular activity, together with the interference with normal respiration. In severe cases apnea may occur. Acidosis increases the toxic effects of local anesthetics.

Recovery is due to redistribution and metabolism of the local anesthetic drug. Recovery may be rapid unless large amounts of the drug have been administered.

Cardiovascular effects may be seen in cases with high systemic concentrations. Severe hypotension, bradycardia, arrhythmia and cardiovascular collapse may be the result in such cases.

Cardiovascular toxic effects are generally preceded by signs of toxicity in the central nervous system, unless the patient is receiving a general anesthetic or is heavily sedated with drugs such as a benzodiazepine or barbiturate.

Treatment: The first consideration is prevention, best accomplished by careful and constant monitoring of cardiovascular and respiratory vital signs and the patient's state of consciousness after each local anesthetic administration. At the first sign of change, oxygen should be administered.

The first step in the management of systemic toxic reactions consists of immediate attention to the maintenance of a patent airway and assisted or controlled ventilation with oxygen and a delivery system capable of permitting immediate positive airway pressure by mask. This may prevent convulsions if they have not already occurred.

If necessary, use drugs to control convulsions. An anticonvulsant should be given i.v. if the convulsions do not stop spontaneously in 15 to 20 seconds. Thiopental 100 to 150 mg i.v. will abort the convulsions rapidly. Alternatively, diazepam 5 to 10 mg i.v. may be used, although its action is slower. Succinylcholine will stop the muscle convulsions rapidly, but will require tracheal intubation and controlled ventilation, and should only be used by those familiar with these procedures.

If cardiovascular depression is evident (hypotension, bradycardia), ephedrine 5 to 10 mg i.v. should be given and may be repeated, if necessary, after 2 to 3 minutes.

Should circulatory arrest occur, immediate cardiopulmonary resuscitation should be instituted. Optimal oxygenation and ventilation and circulatory support as well as treatment of acidosis are of vital importance, since hypoxia and acidosis will increase the systemic toxicity of local anesthetics. Epinephrine (0.1 to 0.2 mg as i.v. or intracardial injections) should be given as soon as possible and repeated, if necessary.

Children should be given doses commensurate with their age and weight.

Dosage: When used concomitantly with other products containing lidocaine, the total dose contributed by all formulations must be kept in mind. Debilitated, elderly and acutely ill patients should be given reduced doses.

Ointment: The ointment should be applied in a thin layer for adequate control of symptoms. A sterile gauze pad is recommended for application to broken and burned tissue.

For sore nipples, apply on a small piece of gauze; the ointment must be washed away before the next feeding.

For endotracheal intubation, apply 1 to 2 g of ointment to the tube prior to intubation.

Dental Ointment: In dentistry, apply to previously dried oral mucosa. Subsequent removal of excess saliva with cotton rolls or saliva ejector minimizes dilution of the ointment. Allow 3 to 5 minutes for the anesthesia to become effective.

Maximum Dosage: Adults: No more than 20 g (1 000 mg lidocaine base) in a 24-hour period.

Children: It is difficult to recommend a maximum dose of any drug for children since this varies as a function of age and weight.

The maximum amount of Xylocaine administered to children should not exceed 0.1 g ointment/kg body weight (corresponding to 5 mg lidocaine/kg of body weight). No more than 3 doses should be administered within 24 hours.

Information for the Patient: See Blue Section—Information for the Patient "Xylocaine Ointment 5%".

Supplied: Ointment: Each g contains: lidocaine (base) 50 mg. Nonmedicinal ingredients: polyethylene glycol and propylene glycol. Aluminum tubes of 15 and 30 g. Preservative-free.

Dental Ointment: Each g contains: lidocaine (base) 50 mg. Nonmedicinal ingredients: amaranth (coloring agent), polyethylene glycol, propylene glycol and spearmint oil (flavoring agent). Preservative-free. Aluminum tubes of 15 g.

On initial opening, do not use if the protective membrane of the tube is punctured. Store between 15 and 30°C. Protect from freezing.

Reviewed 1998

New drugs require close post-marketing surveillance. Report suspected adverse reactions and interactions to the Health Protection Branch using the form provided in the CLIN-INFO SECTION.

XYLOCAINE® PARENTERAL SOLUTIONS

Astra

Lidocaine HCl
Lidocaine HCl—Epinephrine

Local Anesthetic

Pharmacology: Mechanism of Action: Lidocaine stabilizes the neuronal membrane by inhibiting the ionic fluxes required for the initiation and conduction of impulses, thereby effecting local anesthetic action. Local anesthetics of the amide type are thought to act within sodium channels of the nerve membrane.
Onset of Action: The onset of action is 1 to 5 minutes following infiltration and 5 to 15 minutes following other types of administration. The duration of anesthesia depends on the concentration of lidocaine used, the dose, and the type of block. The 2% solution will last 1.5 to 2 hours when given epidurally, and up to 5 hours with peripheral nerve blocks. With the 1% concentration, there is less effect on motor nerve fibres and the duration of action is shorter. The addition of epinephrine decreases the rate of absorption, reducing toxicity and increasing the duration of effect.
Hemodynamics: Lidocaine, like other local anesthetics, may also have effects on excitable membranes in the brain and myocardium. If excessive amounts of drug reach systemic circulation rapidly, symptoms and signs of toxicity will appear, emanating from the central nervous and cardiovascular systems.

CNS toxicity (see Overdose: Symptoms and Treatment) usually precedes the cardiovascular effects since it occurs at lower plasma concentrations. Direct effects of local anesthetics on the heart include slow conduction, negative inotropism and eventually cardiac arrest.

Indirect cardiovascular effects (hypotension, bradycardia) may occur after epidural or spinal administration depending on the extent of the concomitant sympathetic block.
Pharmacokinetics: Lidocaine is completely absorbed following parenteral administration. The rate of absorption depends on the dose, route of administration, and the vascularity of the injection site. The highest peak plasma levels are obtained following intercostal nerve block (approximately 1.6 μg/mL/100 mg injected) while abdominal s.c. injections give the lowest (approximately 0.5 μg/mL/100 mg injected). Epidural and major nerve blocks are intermediate.

Absorption is considerably slowed by the addition of epinephrine, although it also depends on the site of injection. Peak plasma concentrations are reduced by 50% following s.c. injection, by 30% following epidural injection and by 20% following intercostal block if epinephrine 5 μg/mL is added.

Lidocaine shows complete and biphasic absorption from the epidural space with half-lives in the order of 9.3 minutes and 82 minutes respectively. The slow absorption is rate-limiting in the elimination of lidocaine, which explains the slower elimination following epidural injection compared to i.v. injection.

Lidocaine has a total plasma clearance of 0.95 L/min, a volume of distribution at steady state of 91 L, an elimination half-life of 1.6 hours and an estimated hepatic extraction ratio of 0.65. The clearance of lidocaine is almost entirely due to liver metabolism, and depends both on liver blood flow and the activity of metabolizing enzymes.

The plasma binding of lidocaine is dependent on drug concentration, and the fraction bound decreases with increasing concentration. At concentrations of 1 to 4 μg of free base/mL, 60 to 80% of lidocaine is protein bound. Binding is also dependent on the plasma concentration of the alpha-1-acid glycoprotein.

Lidocaine readily crosses the placenta, and equilibrium in regard to free, unbound drug will be reached. Because the degree of plasma protein binding in the fetus is less than in the mother, the total plasma concentration will be greater in the mother, but the free concentrations will be the same.

Lidocaine is metabolized rapidly by the liver, and metabolites and unchanged drug are excreted by the kidneys. Biotransformation includes oxidative N-dealkylation, ring hydroxylation, cleavage of the amide linkage, and conjugation. Only 2% of lidocaine is excreted unchanged. Most of it is metabolized first to monoethylglycinexylidide (MEGX) and then to glycinexylidide (GX) and 2,6-xylidine. Up to 70% appears in the urine as 4-hydroxy-2,6-xylidine.

The elimination half-life of lidocaine following i.v. bolus injection is typically 1.5 to 2 hours. The elimination half-life in neonates (3.2 hours) is approximately twice that of adults. The half-life may be prolonged 2-fold or more in patients with liver dysfunction. Renal dysfunction does not affect lidocaine kinetics but may increase the accumulation of metabolites.

Acidosis increases the systemic toxicity of lidocaine while the use of CNS depressants may increase the levels of lidocaine required to produce overt CNS effects. Objective adverse manifestations become increasingly apparent with increasing venous plasma levels above 6 μg free base/mL.

Indications: For production of local or regional anesthesia by infiltration techniques including percutaneous injection, by peripheral nerve block techniques such as brachial plexus and intercostal blocks, and by central neural techniques including epidural and caudal blocks, when the accepted procedures for these techniques, as described in standard textbooks, are observed.

Contraindications: In patients with a known history of hypersensitivity to local anesthetics of the amide type or to other components of the solution i.e. methylparaben (multidose solutions) or sodium metabisulfite in solutions containing epinephrine.

Warnings: Local anesthetics should only be employed by clinicians who are well versed in diagnosis and management of dose-related toxicity and other acute emergencies that might arise from the block to be employed and then only after ensuring the immediate availability of oxygen, other resuscitative drugs, cardiopulmonary equipment and the personnel needed for proper management of toxic reactions and related emergencies (see also Adverse Effects and Precautions). Delay in proper management of dose-related toxicity, underventilation from any cause, and/or altered sensitivity may lead to the development of acidosis, cardiac arrest and possibly, death.

It is essential that aspiration for blood or cerebrospinal fluid (where applicable) be done prior to injecting any local anesthetics, both the original and all subsequent doses, to avoid intravascular or subarachnoid injection. However, a negative aspiration does not ensure against an intravascular or subarachnoid injection.

Local anesthetic solutions containing antimicrobial preservatives (e.g., methylparaben) should not be used for epidural or spinal anesthesia because the safety of these agents has not been established with regard to intrathecal injection, either intentional or accidental.

Xylocaine with epinephrine solutions contain sodium metabisulfite, a sulfite that may cause allergic-type reactions including anaphylactic symptoms and life-threatening or less severe asthmatic episodes in certain susceptible people. Sulfite sensitivity is seen more frequently in asthmatic than in nonasthmatic people.

Precautions: The safety and effectiveness of lidocaine parenteral solutions depend on proper dosage, correct technique, adequate precautions and readiness for emergencies. Standard textbooks should be consulted for specific techniques and precautions for various regional anesthetic procedures.

Resuscitative equipment, oxygen, and other resuscitative drugs should be available for immediate use (see Warnings and Overdose: Symptoms and Treatment). During major regional nerve blocks, the patient should have i.v. fluids running via an indwelling catheter to assure a functioning i.v. pathway. **The lowest dosage that results in effective anesthesia should be used to avoid high plasma levels and serious adverse effects. Injections should be made slowly, with frequent aspirations before and during the injection to avoid intravascular injection.**

During the administration of epidural anesthesia, it is recommended that a test dose be administered initially and that the patient be monitored for CNS toxicity and cardiovascular toxicity, as well as for signs of unintended intrathecal administration, before proceeding (see Dosage). When clinical conditions permit, consideration should be given to employing local anesthetic solutions that contain epinephrine for the test dose because circulatory changes compatible with epinephrine may also serve as a warning sign of unintended intravascular injection. An intravascular injection is still possible even if aspirations for blood are negative.

Repeated doses of lidocaine may cause significant increases in blood levels with each repeated dose because of slow accumulation of the drug or its metabolites. Tolerance to elevated blood levels varies with the status of the patient. Debilitated, elderly patients, acutely ill patients and children should be given reduced doses commensurate with their age and physical condition. Lidocaine should also be used with caution in patients with epilepsy, impaired cardiac conduction, bradycardia, impaired hepatic, or renal function and in severe shock.

Because amide-type local anesthetics such as lidocaine are metabolized by the liver, these drugs, especially repeat doses, should be used cautiously in patients with hepatic disease. Patients with severe hepatic disease, because of their inability to metabolize local anesthetics normally, are at greater risk of developing toxic plasma concentrations.

Lidocaine should also be used with caution in patients with impaired cardiovascular function since they may be less able to compensate for functional changes associated with the prolongation of AV conduction produced by these drugs.

Lumbar and caudal epidural anesthesia should be used with extreme caution in persons with the following conditions: existing neurological disease, spinal deformities, septicemia and severe hypertension.

Central nerve blocks may cause cardiovascular depression, especially in the presence of hypovolemia. Epidural anesthesia should be used with caution in patients with impaired cardiovascular function.

Paracervical block can sometimes cause fetal bradycardia/tachycardia, and careful monitoring of the fetal heart rate is necessary.

Epidural anesthesia may lead to hypotension and bradycardia. This risk can be reduced either by preloading the circulation with crystalloidal or colloidal solutions, or by injecting a vasopressor such as ephedrine 20 to 40 mg i.m., or by treating promptly with e.g., ephedrine 5 to 10 mg i.v. and repeating as necessary.

Local anesthetic procedures should not be used when there is inflammation and/or sepsis in the region of the proposed injection.

Solutions containing epinephrine should be used with caution in patients whose medical history and physical evaluation suggest the existence of untreated hypertension, poorly controlled thyrotoxicosis, diabetes, ischemic heart disease, heart block, cerebral vascular insufficiency and peripheral vascular disorder. These solutions should also be used cautiously in areas of the body supplied by end arteries, such as digits, or otherwise having a compromised blood supply (see also Drug Interactions).

Careful and constant monitoring of cardiovascular and respiratory (adequacy of ventilation) vital signs and the patient's state of consciousness should be performed after each local anesthetic injection. It should be kept in mind at such times that restlessness, anxiety, incoherent speech, lightheadedness, numbness and tingling of the mouth and lips, metallic taste, tinnitus, dizziness, blurred vision, tremors, twitching, depression or drowsiness may be early warning signs of CNS toxicity.

Many drugs used during the conduct of anesthesia are considered potential triggering agents for familial malignant hyperthermia. It has been shown that the use of amide local anesthetics in malignant hyperthermia patients is safe. However, there is no guarantee that neural blockade will prevent the development of malignant hyperthermia during surgery. It is also difficult to predict the need for supplemental general anesthesia. Therefore, a standard protocol for the management of malignant hyperthermia should be available.

Lidocaine should be used with caution in persons with known drug sensitivities. Patients allergic to para-aminobenzoic acid derivatives (procaine, tetracaine, benzocaine, etc.) have not shown cross sensitivity to lidocaine.
Head and Neck Area: Small doses of local anesthetics injected into the head and neck area, including retrobulbar, dental and stellate ganglion blocks, may produce adverse reactions caused by inadvertent injection to an artery. These reactions may be similar to systemic toxicity seen with unintentional intravascular injections of larger doses. Inadvertent injections into an artery can cause cerebral symptoms even at low doses. Confusion, convulsions, respiratory depression and/or respiratory arrest, and cardiovascular stimulation or depression leading to cardiac arrest have been reported. Patients receiving these blocks should have their circulation and respiration monitored and be constantly observed.

Retrobulbar injections may very occasionally reach the cranial subarachnoid space causing temporary blindness, cardiovascular collapse, apnea, convulsions, etc. These reactions, which may be due to intra-arterial injection or direct injection into the CNS via the sheaths of the optic nerve, must be diagnosed and treated promptly.

Retrobulbar and peribulbar injections of local anesthetics carry a low risk of persistent ocular muscle dysfunction. The primary causes include trauma and/or local toxic effects on muscles and/or nerves. The severity of such tissue reactions is related to the degree of trauma, the concentration of the local anesthetic and the duration of exposure of the tissue to the local anesthetic. For this reason, as with all local anesthetics, the lowest effective concentration and dose of local anesthetic should be used. Vasoconstrictors and other additives may aggravate tissue reactions and should be used only when indicated.

Xylocaine Parenteral Solutions (cont'd)

Drug Interactions: Lidocaine should be used with caution in patients receiving other local anesthetic or agents structurally related to amide-type local anesthetics since the toxic effects are additive.

Xylocaine with epinephrine or other vasopressors should not be used concomitantly with ergot-type oxytocic drugs, because a severe persistent hypertension may occur and cerebrovascular and cardiac accidents are possible. Likewise, Xylocaine with epinephrine or solutions containing lidocaine and another vasoconstrictor should be used with extreme caution in patients receiving MAO inhibitors or antidepressants of the triptyline or imipramine types, because severe prolonged hypertension may result. In situations when concurrent therapy is necessary, careful patient monitoring is essential. Phenothiazines and butyrophenones may reduce or reverse the pressor effect of epinephrine.

If sedatives are employed to reduce patient apprehension, they should be used in reduced doses, since local anesthetic agents, like sedatives, are CNS depressants which in combination may have an additive effect.

Solutions containing epinephrine should be used with caution in patients undergoing general anesthesia with inhalation agents such as halothane, due to the risk of serious cardiac arrhythmias.

Noncardioselective beta-blockers such as propranolol enhance the pressor effects of epinephrine, which may lead to severe hypertension and bradycardia.

Drug/Laboratory Test Interactions: The i.m. injection of lidocaine may result in an increase in creatine phosphokinase levels. Thus, the use of this enzyme determination, without isoenzyme separation, as a diagnostic test for the presence of acute myocardial infarction may be compromised by the i.m. injection of lidocaine.

Information for the Patient: When appropriate, patients should be informed in advance that they may experience temporary loss of sensation and motor activity, usually in the lower half of the body, following proper administration of epidural anesthesia.

Pregnancy: It is reasonable to assume that a large number of pregnant women and women of childbearing age have been given lidocaine. No specific disturbances to the reproductive process have so far been reported, e.g., no increased incidence of malformations. However, care should be given during early pregnancy when maximum organogenesis takes place.

The addition of epinephrine may potentially decrease uterine blood flow and contractility, especially after inadvertent injection into maternal blood vessels.

There are no adequate and well-controlled studies in pregnant women of the effect of lidocaine on the developing fetus.

Labor and Delivery: Local anesthetics rapidly cross the placenta and when used for epidural, paracervical, pudendal or caudal block anesthesia, can cause varying degrees of maternal, fetal and neonatal toxicity. The potential for toxicity depends upon the procedure performed, the type and amount of drug used, and the technique of drug administration. Adverse reactions in the parturient, fetus and neonate involve alterations of the CNS, peripheral vascular tone and cardiac function.

Maternal hypotension has resulted from regional anesthesia. Local anesthetics produce vasodilation by blocking sympathetic nerves. Elevating the patient's legs and positioning her on her left side will help prevent decreases in blood pressure. A vasopressor, such as ephedrine, may be indicated (see Precautions). The fetal heart rate also should be monitored continuously, and electronic fetal monitoring is highly advisable.

Epidural, spinal, paracervical, or pudendal anesthesia may alter the forces of parturition through changes in uterine contractility or maternal expulsive efforts. In one study, paracervical block anesthesia was associated with a decrease in the mean duration of first stage labor and facilitation of cervical dilation. However, spinal and epidural anesthesia have also been reported to prolong the second stage of labor by removing the parturient's reflex urge to bear down or by interfering with motor function. The use of obstetrical anesthesia may increase the need for forceps assistance.

Fetal bradycardia may occur in 20 to 30% of patients receiving paracervical nerve block anesthesia with the amide-type local anesthetics and may be associated with fetal acidosis. Fetal heart rate should always be monitored during paracervical anesthesia. The physician should weigh the possible advantages against risks when considering paracervical block in prematurity, toxemia of pregnancy, and fetal distress. Careful adherence to recommended dosage is of the utmost importance in obstetrical paracervical block. Failure to achieve adequate analgesia with recommended doses should arouse suspicion of intravascular or fetal intracranial injection. Cases compatible with unintended fetal intracranial injection of local anesthetic solution have been reported following intended paracervical or pudendal block or both. Babies so affected, present with unexplained neonatal depression at birth, which correlates with high local anesthetic serum levels, and often manifest seizures within 6 hours. Prompt use of supportive measures combined with forced urinary excretion of the local anesthetic has been used successfully to manage this complication.

Case reports of maternal convulsions and cardiovascular collapse following use of some local anesthetics for paracervical block in early pregnancy (as anesthesia for elective abortion) suggest that systemic absorption under these circumstances may be rapid. The recommended maximum dose of each drug should not be exceeded. Injection should be made slowly and with frequent aspiration. Allow a 5-minute interval between sides.

Lactation: Lidocaine is excreted in the breast milk, but in such small quantities that there is generally no risk of affecting the infant at therapeutic dose levels. It is not known whether epinephrine enters breast milk, but is unlikely to affect the breast-fed infant.

Children: In children, the dosage should be calculated on a weight basis up to 5 mg/kg. With the addition of epinephrine, up to 7 mg/kg can be used (see Dosage).

Adverse Effects: Adverse experiences following the administration of lidocaine are similar in nature to those observed with other amide local anesthetic agents. These adverse experiences are, in general, dose-related and may result from high plasma levels caused by overdosage, rapid absorption, or inadvertent intravascular injection, or may result from a hypersensitivity, idiosyncrasy or diminished tolerance on the part of the patient.

Serious adverse experiences are generally systemic in nature. The following types are those most commonly reported:

CNS: CNS manifestations are excitatory and/or depressant and may be characterized by circumoral paresthesia, lightheadedness, nervousness, apprehension, euphoria, confusion, dizziness, drowsiness, hyperacusis, tinnitus, blurred vision, vomiting, sensations of heat, cold or numbness, twitching, tremors, convulsions, unconsciousness, respiratory depression and arrest. The excitatory manifestations may be very brief or may not occur at all, in which case the first manifestation of toxicity may be drowsiness merging into unconsciousness and respiratory arrest.

Drowsiness following the administration of lidocaine is usually an early sign of a high lidocaine plasma level and may occur as a consequence of rapid absorption.

Cardiovascular System: Cardiovascular manifestations are usually depressant and are characterized by bradycardia, hypotension, arrhythmia, and cardiovascular collapse, which may lead to cardiac arrest.

Allergic: Allergic reactions are characterized by cutaneous lesions, urticaria, edema or, in the most severe instances, anaphylactic shock. Allergic reactions of the amide type are rare and may occur as a result of sensitivity either to the local anesthetic agent or to other components in the formulation.

Neurologic: The incidences of adverse reactions may be related to the total dose of local anesthetic administered but is also dependent upon the particular drug used, the route of administration and the physical status of the patient. Neuropathy and spinal cord dysfunction (e.g., anterior spinal artery syndrome, arachnoiditis, cauda equina syndrome), have been associated with regional anesthesia. Neurological effects may be related to local anesthetic techniques, with or without a contribution from the drug.

In the practice of lumbar epidural block, occasional unintentional penetration of the subarachnoid space by the catheter or needle may occur. For example, a high spinal is characterized by paralysis of the legs, loss of consciousness, respiratory paralysis and bradycardia.

Neurologic effects following unintentional subarachnoid administration during epidural anesthesia may include spinal block by varying magnitude (including total or high spinal block), hypotension secondary to spinal block, urinary retention, fecal and urinary incontinence, loss of perineal sensation and sexual function, persistent anesthesia, paresthesia, weakness, paralysis of the lower extremities and loss of sphincter control, all of which may have slow, incomplete or no recovery; headache, backache, septic meningitis, meningismus, slowing of labor, increased incidence of forceps delivery, or cranial nerve palsies due to traction on nerves from loss of cerebrospinal fluid.

Overdose: Acute systemic toxicity from local anesthetics are generally related to high plasma levels encountered during therapeutic use of local anesthetics and originate mainly in the central nervous and the cardiovascular systems (see Adverse Effects, Warnings, and Precautions).

Symptoms: With accidental intravascular injections, the toxic effect will be obvious within 1 to 3 minutes, while with overdosage, peak plasma concentrations may not be reached for 20 to 30 minutes depending on the site of injection, with signs of toxicity thus being delayed.

CNS toxicity is a graded response, with symptoms and signs of escalating severity. The first symptoms are circumoral paresthesia, numbness of the tongue, lightheadedness, hyperacusis and tinnitus. Visual disturbance and muscular tremors are more serious and precede the onset of generalized convulsions. Unconsciousness and grand mal convulsions may follow, which may last from a few seconds to several minutes. Hypoxia and hypercarbia occur rapidly following convulsions due to the increased muscular activity, together with the interference with normal respiration and loss of airway. In severe cases apnea may occur. Acidosis increases the toxic effects of local anesthetics.

Recovery is due to redistribution and metabolism of the local anesthetic drug. Recovery may be rapid unless large amounts of the drug have been administered.

Cardiovascular effects may be seen in cases with high systemic concentrations. Severe hypotension, bradycardia, arrhythmia and cardiovascular collapse may be the result in such cases.

Cardiovascular toxic effects are generally preceded by signs of toxicity in the CNS, unless the patient is receiving a general anesthetic or is heavily sedated with drugs such as a benzodiazepine or barbiturate.

Treatment: The first consideration is prevention, best accomplished by careful and constant monitoring of cardiovascular and respiratory vital signs and the patient's state of consciousness after each local anesthetic administration. At the first sign of change, oxygen should be administered. If signs of acute systemic toxicity appear, injection of the local anesthetic should be immediately stopped.

The first step in the management of systemic toxic reactions, as well as underventilation or apnea due to unintentional subarachnoid injection consists of immediate attention to the establishment and maintenance of a patent airway and assisted or controlled ventilation with oxygen and a delivery system capable of permitting immediate positive airway pressure by mask. This may prevent convulsions if they have not already occurred.

If necessary, use drugs to control convulsions. An anticonvulsant should be given i.v. if the convulsions do not stop spontaneously in 15 to 20 seconds. Thiopental 100 to 150 mg i.v. will abort the convulsions rapidly. Alternatively, diazepam 5 to 10 mg i.v. may be used, although its action is slower. Succinylcholine will stop the muscle convulsions rapidly, but will require tracheal intubation and controlled ventilation, and should only be used by those familiar with these procedures.

If cardiovascular depression is evident (hypotension, bradycardia), ephedrine 5 to 10 mg i.v. should be given and may be repeated, if necessary, after 2 to 3 minutes.

Should circulatory arrest occur, immediate cardiopulmonary resuscitation should be instituted. Optimal oxygenation and ventilation and circulatory support as well as treatment of acidosis are of vital importance, since hypoxia and acidosis will increase the systemic toxicity of local anesthetics. Epinephrine (0.1 to 0.2 mg as i.v. or intracardial injections) should be given as soon as possible and repeated, if necessary.

Children should be given doses commensurate with their age and weight.

Dosage: Adults: Table I (Recommended Dosages) summarizes the recommended volumes and concentrations of lidocaine parenteral solutions for various types of anesthetic procedures. The dosages suggested in this table are for normal healthy adults and refer to the use of epinephrine-free solutions. When larger volumes are required, only solutions containing epinephrine should be used except in those cases where vasopressor drugs may be contraindicated.

These recommended doses serve only as a guide to the amount of anesthetic required for most routine procedures. The actual volumes and concentrations to be used depend on a number of factors such as type and extent of surgical procedure, depth of anesthesia and degree of muscular relaxation required, duration of anesthesia required, and the physical condition of the patient. In all cases the lowest concentration and smallest dose that will produce the desired result should be given. Dosages should be reduced for children, elderly and debilitated patients, and patients with cardiac and/or liver disease.

Children: In children the dosage should be calculated on a weight basis up to 5 mg/kg. With the addition of epinephrine, up to 7 mg/kg can be used.

The onset of anesthesia, the duration of anesthesia and the degree of muscular relaxation are proportional to the volume and concentration (i.e. total dose) of local anesthetic used. Thus, an increase in volume and concentration of lidocaine will decrease the onset of anesthesia, prolong the duration of anesthesia, provide a greater degree of muscular relaxation and increase the segmental spread of anesthesia. However, increasing the volume and concentration of lidocaine may result in a more profound fall in blood pressure when used in epidural anesthesia. Although the incidence of side effects with lidocaine is quite low, caution should be exercised when employing large volumes and concentrations since the incidence of side effects is directly proportional to the total dose of local anesthetic agent injected. The risk of reaching a toxic plasma concentration or inducing a local neural injury must be considered when prolonged blocks and/or repeated administration are employed.

In general, complete block of all nerve fibres in large nerves requires the higher concentrations of drug. In smaller nerves, or when a less intense block is required (e.g., in the relief of labor pain), the lower concentrations are indicated. The volume of drug used will affect the extent of spread of anesthesia.

The duration of effect can be increased by using solutions containing epinephrine (see Table I). For a more prolonged effect, an indwelling catheter, through which local anesthetic drug may be injected can be used. This technique is common in epidural anesthesia, and may also be used in brachial plexus anesthesia and interpleural analgesia.

Epidural Anesthesia: The lowest dosage that will produce the desired effect should be given. The amount varies with the number of dermatomes to be anesthetized (generally 2 to 3 mL of the indicated concentration per dermatome). Solutions with preservatives (methylparaben) should not be used since their safety has not been established.

Caudal and Lumbar Epidural Block: Test Dose: As a precaution against the adverse experience sometimes observed following unintentional penetration of the subarachnoid space, a test dose such as 3 to 5 mL of 1.5% lidocaine should be administered at least 5 minutes prior to injecting the total volume required for a lumbar or caudal epidural block. During the administration of a test dose, it is recommended that constant electrocardiographic (ECG) monitoring occur. The test dose should be repeated if the patient is moved in a manner that may have displaced the catheter. Epinephrine, if contained in the test dose (10 to 15 μg have been suggested), may serve as a warning of unintentional intravascular injection. If injected into a blood vessel, this amount of epinephrine is likely to produce a transient "epinephrine response" within 45 seconds, consisting of an increase in heart rate and systolic blood pressure, circumoral pallor, palpitations and nervousness in the unsedated patient. The sedated patient may exhibit only a pulse rate increase of 20 or more beats/minute for 15 or more seconds. Patients on beta-blockers may not manifest changes in heart rate, but blood pressure monitoring can detect an evanescent rise in systolic blood pressure. Adequate time should be allowed for onset of anesthesia after administration of each test dose. The rapid injection of a large volume of lidocaine through the catheter should be avoided and when feasible, fractional doses should be administered.

The main dose should be injected **slowly** at a rate of 100 to 200 mg/min, or in incremental doses, while keeping in constant verbal contact with the patient. If toxic symptoms occur, the injection should be stopped immediately.

In the event of the known injection of a large volume of local anesthetic solution into the subarachnoid space, after suitable resuscitation and if the catheter is in place, consider attempting the recovery of drug by draining a moderate amount of cerebrospinal fluid (such as 10 mL) through the epidural catheter.

Sterilization, Storage and Technical Procedures: Adequate precautions should be taken to avoid prolonged contact between local anesthetic solutions containing epinephrine (low pH) and metal surfaces (e.g., needles or metal parts of syringes), since dissolved metal ions, particularly copper ions, may cause severe local irritation (swelling, edema) at the site of injection and accelerate the degradation of epinephrine.

When chemical disinfection of multidose vials is desired, either isopropyl alcohol (91%) or ethyl alcohol (70%) is recommended. Many commercially available brands of rubbing alcohol, as well as solutions of ethyl alcohol not of USP grade,

Table I—Xylocaine Parenteral Solutions

Dosage Recommendations in Adults

Type of Block	Conc. (%)	Each Dose[a] mL	Each Dose[a] mg	Onset (min)	Duration (h) Without Epinephrine	Indication
Local Infiltration	0.5	≤80	≤400	1-2	1.5-2	Surgical operations.
	1	≤40	≤400	1-2	2-3	
Digital[b]	1	1-5	10-50	2-5	1.5-2	Surgical operations.
Intercostal (per nerve)	1	2-5	20-50	3-5	1-2	Surgical operations, postoperative pain and fractured ribs.
	1.5	2-4	30-60	3-5	2-3	
Paracervical[c] (each side)	1	10	100	3-5	1-1.5	Surgical operations and dilation of cervix. Obstetric pain relief.
Paravertebral (per segment)	1	3-5	30-50	5-10	1-1.5	Pain management, diagnostic.
	2	3-5	60-100	5-10	1.5-2	
Pudendal (each side)	1	10	100	5-10	1.5-2	Instrumental delivery.
Intra-Articular Block	0.5	≤60	≤300	5-10	0.5-1	Arthroscopy and surgical operations.
	1	≤40	≤400	5-10	after washout	
Retrobulbar[c]	2	4	80	3-5	1.5-2	Ocular surgery.
Peribulbar[c]	1	10-15	100-150	3-5	1.5-2	Ocular surgery.
Brachial Plexus						
Axillary	1.0	40-50	400-500	15-30	1.5-2	Surgical operations.
	1.5	30-50	450-600	15-30	1.5-3	
Supraclavicular, interscalene and subclavian perivascular	1.0	30-40	300-400	15-30	1.5-2	
	1.5	20-30	300-450	15-30	1.5-3	
Sciatic	1.5	15-20	225-300	15-30	2-3	Surgical operations.
	2	15-20	300-400	15-30	2-3	
3-in-1 (Femoral, obturator and lateral cutaneous)	1	30-40	300-400	15-30	1.5-2	Surgical operations.
	1.5	30	450	15-30	2-3	
Epidural	1.5	3-5	45-75			Test dose.
Lumbar Epidural	2	15-25	300-500	15-20	1.5-2	Surgical operations.
Thoracic Epidural	1.5	10-15	150-225	10-20	1-1.5	Surgical operations and pain relief.
	2	10-15	200-300	10-20	1.5-2	Surgical operations.
Caudal Epidural	1	20-30	200-300	15-30	1-1.5	Surgical operations and pain relief.
	2	15-25	300-500	15-30	1.5-2	Surgical operations.

[a]For epidural blocks, dose includes test dose.
[b]Without epinephrine.
[c]see Precautions.

contain denaturants which are injurious to rubber and therefore are not to be used.

The solubility of lidocaine is limited at pH >6.5. This must be taken into consideration when alkaline solutions, i.e., carbonates, are added, since precipitation might occur. In the case of epinephrine-containing solutions, mixing with alkaline solutions may cause rapid degradation of epinephrine.

Lidocaine plain solutions in glass vials may be autoclaved for 15 to 20 minutes at 121°C. Due to the nature of the Polyamp system, the plastic ampuls must not be autoclaved. Due to the heat sensitivity of epinephrine, products containing epinephrine should not be autoclaved.

All solutions should be stored at controlled room temperature (15 to 30°C). Lidocaine parenteral solutions containing epinephrine should be protected from light.

Do not use if solution is pinkish or darker than slightly yellow or if it contains a precipitate.

Lidocaine parenteral solutions without preservative are for single use only. Discard unused portion. The multidose vials should not be used for more than 3 days after the container has been opened for the first time.

There is a greater risk of microbial contamination with multidose vials than with single dose vials. Single dose vials should therefore be used whenever possible. If a multidose vial is used, appropriate control procedures to prevent contamination should be employed, including the following: use of single-use sterile injecting equipment; use of a sterile needle and syringe for each insertion into the vial; rule out the introduction of contaminated material or fluid into a multidose vials.

Supplied: 0.5%: Each mL contains: lidocaine HCl 5 mg. Nonmedicinal ingredients: sodium chloride, hydrochloric acid and/or sodium hydroxide to adjust pH between 5.0 and 7.0. Glass multidose vials of 50 mL.

Each mL contains: lidocaine HCl 5 mg and epinephrine 1:100 000. Nonmedicinal ingredients: sodium chloride, hydrochloric acid and/or sodium hydroxide to adjust pH between 3.3 and 5.5 and sodium metabisulfite. Glass multidose vials of 50 mL.

Each mL contains: lidocaine HCl 5 mg and epinephrine 1:200 000. Nonmedicinal ingredients: sodium chloride, hydrochloric acid and/or sodium hydroxide to adjust pH between 3.3 and 5.5 and sodium metabisulfite. Glass single use vials of 50 mL.

1%: Each mL contains: lidocaine HCl 10 mg. Nonmedicinal ingredients: sodium chloride, hydrochloric acid and/or sodium hydroxide to adjust pH between 5.0 and 7.0. Plastic Polyamp Duofit ampuls of 2, 5, 10 and 20 mL. Glass multidose vials of 20 and 50 mL.

Each mL contains: lidocaine HCl 10 mg and epinephrine 1:100 000. Nonmedicinal ingredients: sodium chloride, hydrochloric acid and/or sodium hydroxide to adjust pH between 3.3 and 5.5 and sodium metabisulfite. Glass multidose vials of 20 and 50 mL.

Each mL contains: lidocaine HCl 10 mg and epinephrine 1:200 000. Nonmedicinal ingredients: sodium chloride, hydrochloric acid and/or sodium hydroxide to adjust pH between 3.3 and 5.5 and sodium metabisulfite. Glass multidose vials of 20 mL.

1.5%: Each mL contains: lidocaine HCl 15 mg. Nonmedicinal ingredients: sodium chloride, hydrochloric acid and/or sodium hydroxide to adjust pH between 5.0 and 7.0. Glass single use vials of 30 mL (Astra Sterile-Pack).

Each mL contains: lidocaine HCl 15 mg and epinephrine 1:200 000. Nonmedicinal ingredients: sodium chloride, hydrochloric acid and/or sodium hydroxide to adjust pH between 3.3 and 5.5 and sodium metabisulfite. Glass single use vials of 5 (Test Dose) and 30 mL.

2%: Each mL contains: lidocaine HCl 20 mg. Nonmedicinal ingredients: sodium chloride, hydrochloric acid and/or sodium hydroxide to adjust pH between 5.0 and 7.0. Plastic Polyamp Duofit ampuls of 2, 5, 10 and 20 mL. Glass single use vials of 2 and 20 mL (Astra Sterile-Pack-20 mL). Glass multidose vials of 20 and 50 mL.

Each mL contains: lidocaine HCl 20 mg and epinephrine 1:100 000. Nonmedicinal ingredients: sodium chloride, hydrochloric acid and/or sodium hydroxide to adjust pH between 3.3 and 5.5 and sodium metabisulfite. Glass multidose vials of 20 and 50 mL.

Each mL contains: lidocaine HCl 20 mg and epinephrine 1:200 000. Nonmedicinal ingredients: sodium chloride, hydrochloric acid and/or sodium hydroxide to adjust pH between

Xylocaine Parenteral Solutions (cont'd)

3.3 and 5.5 and sodium metabisulfite. Glass single use vials of 20 mL.

Plastic Polyamp Duofit ampuls and glass single-use vials are preservative-free. Glass multidose vials also contain methylparaben.

Polyamp Duofit ampuls are suitable for Luer fit and Luer lock syringes.

Reviewed 1999

XYLOCAINE® SPINAL 5%

Astra

Lidocaine HCl—Glucose

Local Anesthetic for Spinal Anesthesia

Pharmacology: Mechanism of Action: Lidocaine stabilizes the neuronal membrane by inhibiting the ionic fluxes required for the initiation and conduction of impulses, thereby effecting local anesthetic action. Local anesthetics of the amide type are thought to act within sodium channels of the nerve membrane.

Onset of Action: The onset of action is rapid. The duration of anesthesia provided with 1 to 2 mL Xylocaine Spinal 5% (50 to 100 mg lidocaine) is 1 to 1.5 hours.

Xylocaine Spinal 5% is hyperbaric and its initial spread in the subarachnoid space is considerably affected by gravity.

Hemodynamics: Lidocaine, like other local anesthetics, may also have effects on excitable membranes in the brain and myocardium. If excessive amounts of drug reach systemic circulation rapidly, symptoms and signs of toxicity will appear, emanating from the central nervous and cardiovascular systems.

CNS toxicity (see Overdose: Symptoms and Treatment) usually precedes the cardiovascular effects since it occurs at lower plasma concentrations. Direct effects of local anesthetics on the heart include slow conduction, negative inotropism and eventually cardiac arrest.

Indirect cardiovascular effects (hypotension, bradycardia) may occur after epidural or spinal administration depending on the extent of the concomitant sympathetic block.

Pharmacokinetics: Lidocaine is completely absorbed following parenteral administration. The rate of absorption depends on the dose, route of administration, and the vascularity of the injection site. The highest peak plasma levels are obtained following intercostal nerve block (approximately 1.5 µg/mL/100 mg injected) while abdominal s.c. injections give the lowest (approximately 0.5 µg/mL/100 mg injected). Epidural and major nerve blocks are intermediate.

Absorption of lidocaine from the subarachnoid space is relatively slow and this, together with the small dose required for spinal anesthesia, limits the maximum plasma concentration, which is approximately 0.5 µg/mL for every 100 mg injected.

Lidocaine has a total plasma clearance of 0.95 L/min, a volume of distribution at steady-state of 91 L, an elimination half-life of 1.6 h and an estimated hepatic extraction ratio of 0.65. The clearance of lidocaine is almost entirely due to liver metabolism, and depends both on liver blood flow and the activity of metabolizing enzymes.

The plasma binding of lidocaine is dependent on drug concentration, and the fraction bound decreases with increasing concentration. At concentrations of 1 to 4 µg of free base/mL, 60 to 80% of lidocaine is protein bound. Binding is also dependent on the plasma concentration of the alpha-1-acid glycoprotein.

Lidocaine readily crosses the placenta, and equilibrium in regard to free, unbound drug will be reached. Because the degree of plasma protein binding in the fetus is less than in the mother, the total plasma concentration will be greater in the mother, but the free concentrations will be the same.

Lidocaine is metabolized rapidly by the liver, and metabolites and unchanged drug are excreted by the kidneys. Biotransformation includes oxidative N-dealkylation, ring hydroxylation, cleavage of the amide linkage, and conjugation. Only 2% of lidocaine is excreted unchanged. Most of it is metabolized first to monoethylglycinexylidide (MEGX) and then to glycinexylidide (GX) and 2,6-xylidine. Up to 70% appears in the urine as 4-hydroxy-2,6-xylidine.

The elimination half-life of lidocaine following i.v. bolus injection is typically 1.5 to 2 hours. The elimination half-life in neonates (3.2 hours) is approximately twice that of adults. The half-life may be prolonged two-fold or more in patients with liver dysfunction. Renal dysfunction does not affect lidocaine kinetics but may increase the accumulation of metabolites.

Acidosis increases the systemic toxicity of lidocaine while the use of CNS depressants may increase the levels of lidocaine required to produce overt CNS effects. Objective adverse manifestations become increasingly apparent with increasing venous plasma levels above 6.0 µg free base/mL.

Indications: For the production of spinal (subarachnoid) anesthesia in surgical and obstetrical procedures when a regional block of 1 to 1.5 hours' duration is required.

Contraindications: The following conditions are contraindicated in spinal anesthesia: known sensitivity to local anesthetics of the amide type; acute active disease of the CNS, such as meningitis, tumors, poliomyelitis, and cranial hemorrhage. The presence of active tuberculosis or metastatic lesions in the vertebral column is also contraindicated; cardiogenic or hypovolemic shock; pyrogenic infection of the skin at or adjacent to the site of puncture; septicemia; pernicious anemia with subacute combined degeneration of the spinal cord; coagulation disorders or ongoing anticoagulant treatment.

Warnings: Local anesthetics should only be employed by clinicians who are well versed in diagnosis and management of dose-related toxicity and other acute emergencies that might arise from the block to be employed and then only after ensuring the immediate availability of oxygen, other resuscitative drugs, cardiopulmonary equipment and the personnel needed for proper management of toxic reactions and related emergencies. (See also Adverse Effects and Precautions.) Delay in proper management of dose-related toxicity, underventilation from any cause, and/or altered sensitivity may lead to the development of acidosis, cardiac arrest and possibly, death.

To avoid intravascular injection, aspiration should be performed before the local anesthetic solution is injected. The needle must be repositioned until no return of blood can be elicited by aspiration. Note, however, that the absence of blood in the syringe does not guarantee that intravascular injection has been avoided.

Some cases of neurologic complications (e.g., cauda equina) have been reported after the use of lidocaine 5% with 7.5% glucose when given undiluted, especially if the injection is very slow, e.g., with very fine needles or catheters (see Dosage). Until the cause of this complication has been elucidated, lidocaine 5% with 7.5% glucose is not recommended for continuous spinal anesthesia.

Spinal anesthesia can be unpredictable and very high blockades are sometimes encountered with paralysis of the intercostal muscles, and even the diaphragm, especially in pregnancy. On rare occasions it will be necessary to assist or control ventilation.

Precautions: The safety and effectiveness of Xylocaine Spinal 5% depend on proper dosage, correct technique, adequate precautions and readiness for emergencies. Standard textbooks should be consulted for specific techniques and precautions for spinal anesthetic procedures.

Resuscitative equipment, oxygen, and other resuscitative drugs should be available for immediate use (see Warnings and Overdose: Symptoms and Treatment). **The lowest dosage that results in effective anesthesia should be used to avoid high plasma levels and serious adverse effects.**

I.V. access, e.g., an i.v. infusion, should be in place before starting the spinal anesthesia.

Repeated doses of Xylocaine Spinal 5% are not recommended.

Xylocaine Spinal 5% should be used with caution in patients with poorly controlled epilepsy, neurological diseases such as multiple sclerosis and old hemiplegia due to stroke, impaired cardiac conduction, and other severe cardiac diseases.

Since amide-type local anesthetics are metabolized by the liver, lidocaine should be used with caution in patients with hepatic disease. Patients with severe hepatic disease, because of their inability to metabolize local anesthetics normally, are at a greater risk of developing toxic plasma concentrations.

Lidocaine should also be used with caution in patients with impaired cardiovascular function since they may be less able to compensate for functional changes associated with the prolongation of AV conduction produced by these drugs.

The following conditions may preclude the use of spinal anesthesia, depending upon the physician's ability to deal with the complications which may occur (see Contraindications): Chronic backache and preoperative headache; hypotension and hypertension; arthritis or spinal deformity; technical problems (persistent paresthesias, persistent bloody tap); psychotic or uncooperative patients.

Regardless of the local anesthetic used, hypotension and bradycardia may occur. This risk can be reduced either by preloading the circulation with crystalloidal or colloidal solutions or by injecting a vasopressor, such as ephedrine 20 to 40 mg i.m. or treating promptly with, e.g., ephedrine 5 to 10 mg i.v. and repeating as necessary.

Hypotension is common in patients with hypovolemia due to hemorrhage or dehydration, and in those patients with aortocaval occlusion due to abdominal tumors or the pregnant uterus in late pregnancy. Hypotension is poorly tolerated by patients with coronary or cerebrovascular disease.

Chronic neurological disorders such as multiple sclerosis, old hemiplegia due to stroke, etc., are not thought to be adversely affected by spinal anesthesia but caution is advised.

Spinal anesthesia may be preferable to general anesthesia in some high-risk patients. Attempts should be made to optimize their general condition preoperatively when time allows.

Careful and constant monitoring of cardiovascular and respiratory (adequacy of ventilation) vital signs and the patient's state of consciousness should be accomplished after each local anesthetic injection. It should be kept in mind at such times that restlessness, anxiety, tinnitus, dizziness, blurred vision, tremors, depression or drowsiness may be early warning signs of CNS toxicity.

Many drugs used during the conduct of anesthesia are considered potential triggering agents for familial malignant hyperthermia. It has been shown that the use of amide local anesthetics in malignant hyperthermia is safe. However, there is no guarantee that neural blockade will prevent the development of malignant hyperthermia during surgery. It is also difficult to predict the need for supplemental general anesthesia. Therefore a standard protocol for the management of malignant hyperthermia should be available.

Lidocaine should be used with caution in persons with known drug sensitivities. Patients allergic to para-aminobenzoic acid derivatives (procaine, tetracaine, benzocaine, etc.) have not shown cross sensitivity to lidocaine.

Local anesthetic procedures should not be used when there is inflammation and/or sepsis in the region of the proposed injection.

Drug Interactions: Lidocaine should be used with caution in patients receiving other local anesthetics or agents structurally related to local anesthetics, since the toxic effects are additive.

Information for the Patient: When appropriate, patients should be informed in advance that they may experience temporary loss of sensation and motor activity, usually in the lower half of the body, following proper administration of spinal anesthesia.

Pregnancy: It is reasonable to assume that a large number of pregnant women and women of childbearing age have been given lidocaine. No specific disturbances to the reproductive process have so far been reported, e.g., no increased incidence of malformations. However, care should be given during early pregnancy when maximum organogenesis takes place.

There are no adequate and well-controlled studies in pregnant women.

Labor and Delivery: Local anesthetics rapidly cross the placenta and when used for epidural, paracervical, pudendal or caudal block anesthesia, can cause varying degrees of maternal, fetal and neonatal toxicity. The potential for toxicity depends upon the procedure performed, the type and amount of drug used, and the technique of drug administration. Adverse reactions in the parturient, fetus and neonate involve alterations of the CNS, peripheral vascular tone and cardiac function.

Maternal hypotension has resulted from regional anesthesia. Local anesthetics produce vasodilation by blocking sympathetic nerves. Elevating the patient's legs and positioning her on her left side will help prevent decreases in blood pressure. The fetal heart rate also should be monitored continuously, and electronic fetal monitoring is highly advisable.

Spinal anesthesia may alter the forces of parturition through changes in uterine contractility or maternal expulsive efforts. However, spinal anesthesia has also been reported to prolong the second stage of labor by removing the parturient's reflex urge to bear down or by interfering with motor function. The use of obstetrical anesthesia may increase the need for forceps assistance.

Lactation: Lidocaine is excreted in the breast milk, but in such small quantities that there is generally no risk of affecting the infant at therapeutic dose levels.

Adverse Effects: In general, almost all adverse effects seen with spinal anesthesia are due to the nerve blockade itself and not the drug used. These effects include hypotension, bradycardia, and post-spinal headache. Other adverse effects in connection with spinal anesthesia are:

High or Total Spinal Blockade: A rare, though severe, adverse reaction following spinal anesthesia is high or total spinal blockade resulting in cardiovascular and respiratory depression. The cardiovascular depression is caused by extensive sympathetic blockade which may result in profound hypotension and bradycardia, or even cardiac arrest. Respiratory depression is caused by blockade of the innervation of the respiratory muscles, including the diaphragm.

Neurologic: Neurological damage is a rare, though recognized, consequence of spinal anesthesia. It may have one of several causes such as direct injury to the spinal cord or spinal nerves, anterior spinal artery syndrome, injection of an irritant substance, injection of a nonsterile solution or the development of a space-occupying lesion (hematoma or abscess) within the spinal canal. These may result in localized areas of paresthesia or anesthesia, motor weakness, loss of sphincter control and paraplegia. Occasionally these are permanent. Neurological complications of this type have been reported with all local anesthetics used for spinal anesthesia. Some cases of neurologic complications (e.g., cauda equina) have been reported after the use of lidocaine 5% with 7.5% glucose when given undiluted, especially if the injection is very slow, e.g., with very fine needles or catheters (see Dosage). Until the cause of this complication has been elucidated, lidocaine 5% with 7.5% glucose is not recommended for continuous spinal anesthesia.

Low Back Pain: Transient pain and sometimes tenderness developing in the low back and buttocks and radiating to the lateral thighs and calves, may be seen in patients after spinal anesthesia of Xylocaine Spinal 5%. A lithotomy position and/or early mobilization may contribute. The symptoms respond to analgesics (e.g., NSAIDs) and usually resolve spontaneously within 3 days.

Allergic: Allergic reactions are characterized by cutaneous lesions, urticaria, edema or, in the most severe instances, anaphylactic shock. Allergic reactions of the amide type are extremely rare and may occur as a result of sensitivity either to the local anesthetic agent or to other components in the formulation.

Additional adverse experiences are similar in nature to those observed with other amide local anesthetic agents. These adverse experiences are, in general, dose-related and may result from high plasma levels caused by overdosage or rapid absorption.

Serious adverse experiences are generally systemic in nature. However, the dose required for spinal anesthesia is so small (20% or less than that required for epidural anesthesia) that acute systemic toxicity is extremely unlikely. Acute toxic effects on the central nervous and cardiovascular systems include the following:

CNS: CNS manifestations are excitatory and/or depressant and may be characterized by circumoral paresthesia, lightheadedness, nervousness, apprehension, euphoria, confusion, dizziness, drowsiness, hyperacusis, tinnitus, blurred vision, vomiting, sensations of heat, cold or numbness, twitching, tremors, convulsions, unconsciousness, respiratory depression and arrest. The excitatory manifestations may be very brief or may not occur at all, in which case the first manifestation of toxicity may be drowsiness merging into unconsciousness and respiratory arrest.

Drowsiness following the administration of lidocaine is usually an early sign of a high lidocaine plasma level and may occur as a consequence of rapid absorption.

Cardiovascular: Cardiovascular manifestations are usually depressant and are characterized by bradycardia, hypotension, and cardiovascular collapse, which may lead to cardiac arrest.

Overdose: Acute emergencies from local anesthetics are generally related to high plasma levels encountered during therapeutic use of local anesthetics and originate mainly in the central nervous and the cardiovascular systems (see Adverse Effects, Warnings, and Precautions).

With accidental intravascular injections, the toxic effect will be obvious within 1 to 3 minutes, while with overdosage, peak plasma concentrations may not be reached for 20 to 30 minutes depending on the site of injection, with signs of toxicity thus being delayed. Toxic reactions mainly involve the central nervous and the cardiovascular systems.

Symptoms: CNS toxicity is a graded response, with symptoms and signs of escalating severity. The first symptoms are circumoral paresthesia, numbness of the tongue, lightheadedness, hyperacusis and tinnitus. Visual disturbance and muscular tremors are more serious and precede the onset of generalized convulsions. Unconsciousness and grand mal convulsions may follow, which may last from a few seconds to several minutes. Hypoxia and hypercarbia occur rapidly following convulsions due to the increased muscular activity, together with the interference with normal respiration. In severe cases apnea may occur. Acidosis increases the toxic effects of local anesthetics.

Recovery is due to redistribution and metabolism of the local anesthetic drug. Recovery may be rapid unless large amounts of the drug have been administered.

Cardiovascular effects may be seen in cases with high systemic concentrations. Severe hypotension, bradycardia, arrhythmia and cardiovascular collapse may be the result in such cases.

Cardiovascular toxic effects are generally preceded by signs of toxicity in the CNS, unless the patient is receiving a general anesthetic or is heavily sedated with drugs such as a benzodiazepine or barbiturate.

Treatment: The first consideration is prevention, best accomplished by careful and constant monitoring of cardiovascular and respiratory vital signs and the patient's state of consciousness after each local anesthetic administration. At the first sign of change, oxygen should be administered.

The first step in the management of convulsions consists of immediate attention to the maintenance of a patent airway and assisted or controlled ventilation with oxygen and a delivery system capable of permitting immediate positive airway pressure by mask. Immediately after the institution of these ventilatory measures, the adequacy of the circulation should be evaluated, keeping in mind that drugs used to treat convulsions sometimes depress the circulation when administered i.v.

An anticonvulsant should be given i.v. if the convulsions do not stop spontaneously in 15 to 20 seconds. Thiopental 100 to 150 mg i.v. will abort the convulsions rapidly. Alternatively, diazepam 5 to 10 mg i.v. may be used, although its action is slower.

Succinylcholine will stop the muscle convulsions rapidly, but will require tracheal intubation and controlled ventilation, and should only be used by those familiar with these procedures.

If cardiovascular depression is evident (hypotension, bradycardia), ephedrine 5 to 10 mg i.v. should be given and may be repeated, if necessary, after 2 to 3 minutes.

Should circulatory arrest occur, immediate cardiopulmonary resuscitation should be instituted. Optimal oxygenation and ventilation and circulatory support as well as treatment of acidosis are of vital importance, since hypoxia and acidosis will increase the systemic toxicity of local anesthetics. Epinephrine (0.1 to 0.2 mg as i.v. or intracardiac injections) should be given as soon as possible and repeated, if necessary.

Dosage: Spinal injections should only be made after the subarachnoid space has been clearly identified by lumbar puncture. No drug should be injected until clear cerebrospinal fluid (CSF) is seen to escape from the spinal needle, or is detected by aspiration. It is recommended that Xylocaine Spinal 5% be diluted with an equal volume of cerebrospinal fluid before injection. Intrathecal distribution of anesthetic may be facilitated by using a spinal needle of sufficient gauge, e.g., 22 or 25 gauge.

Spinal anesthesia may be induced in the right or left lateral recumbent or the sitting position. Since Xylocaine Spinal 5% is a hyperbaric solution, the anesthetic will tend to move in the direction in which the table is tilted. After the desired level of anesthesia is obtained and the anesthetic has become fixed, usually in 5 to 10 minutes with Xylocaine Spinal 5%, the patient may be positioned according to the requirement of the surgeon or obstetrician.

Failure of spinal anesthesia has been reported in 1 to 5% of the patients. One reason for failure could be an intrathecal maldistribution of the local anesthetic, e.g., entrapment in the caudal end of the dural sac or within a "pocket" with restricted communication to the major cerebrospinal fluid space. In such cases a better spread, i.e. a sufficient block, may be achieved after temporary change(s) in the patient's position. If a supplementary block is necessary, it should be performed at a different level and with a reduced volume of local anesthetic. Only one extra attempt should be made.

Injections should be made slowly. Consult standard textbooks for specific techniques for spinal anesthetic procedures.

Adults: Table I provides recommended dosages for normal healthy adults and serves only as a guide to the amount of anesthetic required for most routine procedures. In all cases, the smallest dose that will produce the desired result should be given.

If the technique is properly performed and the needle is properly placed in the subarachnoid space, it should not be necessary to administer more than 1 vial (2 mL or 100 mg lidocaine). Doses greater than 100 mg are not recommended.

Children: The dosage recommendations in healthy adolescents, 16 years of age and older, is the same as for normal, healthy adults. There is insufficient data in children below the age of 16 years to make dosage recommendations.

Sterilization, Storage and Technical Procedures: Disinfecting agents containing heavy metals, which cause release of respective ions (mercury, zinc, copper, etc.) should not be used for skin or mucous membrane disinfection as they have been related to incidents of swelling and edema.

Xylocaine Spinal 5% may be autoclaved at 15 lbs pressure at 121°C for 15 minutes (USP Standard). Since the preparation contains glucose, caramelization may occur under prolonged heating and, in some instances, prolonged storage.

Therefore, this preparation should not be re-sterilized and should not remain in the sterilizer any longer than necessary.

The solution should not be used if it is discolored or if a precipitate is present.

Additions to spinal solutions are generally not recommended.

The vials should be stored at controlled room temperature (15 to 30°C).

Xylocaine Spinal 5% is preservative-free and is for single use. Discard unused portion.

Supplied: Each mL contains: lidocaine HCl 50 mg and d-glucose 75 mg. Nonmedicinal ingredients: sodium hydroxide and/or hydrochloric acid to adjust to pH 5.0 to 7.0. Glass vials of 2 mL. Packages of 10.

Reviewed 1999

Table I—Xylocaine Spinal 5%

Dosage Recommendations for Adults

Upper Level of Anesthesia	Site of Injection	Position of Patient	Dosage (mL)	Dosage (mg)	Onset (min)	Duration (h)	Indication
L4	L3/4/5	sitting	0.8-1.5	40-75	3-6	1-1.5	Vaginal delivery (incl. forceps), perineal operations. Note: The patient should be laid horizontal 2-3 min after injection or if he/she complains of faintness.
T10	L2/3/4	horizontal	1.2-1.6	60-80	3-6	1-1.5	Lower-limb surgery, cystoscopy, vaginal and perineal surgery, transurethral operations on prostate and bladder, orchidectomy.
T5	L2/3/4	horizontal	1.5-2.0	75-100	3-6	1-1.5	Lower abdominal surgery (including Cesarean section).

XYLOCAINE® TOPICAL 4%

Astra

Lidocaine HCl

Oral Topical Anesthetic

Pharmacology: Mechanism of Action: Lidocaine stabilizes the neuronal membrane by inhibiting the ionic fluxes required for the initiation and conduction of impulses, thereby effecting local anesthetic action. Local anesthetics of the amide type are thought to act within the sodium channels of the nerve membrane.

Onset of Action: Anesthesia usually occurs within 1 to 5 minutes depending on the area of application. The duration of anesthesia is approximately 15 to 30 minutes. Xylocaine Topical 4% is ineffective when applied to intact skin.

Hemodynamics: Lidocaine, like other local anesthetics, may also have effects on excitable membranes in the brain and myocardium. If excessive amounts of drug reach systemic circulation rapidly, symptoms and signs of toxicity will appear, emanating from the central nervous and cardiovascular systems.

CNS toxicity (see Overdose: Symptoms and Treatment) usually precedes the cardiovascular effects since it occurs at

Xylocaine Topical 4% (cont'd)

lower plasma concentrations. Direct effects of local anesthetics on the heart include slow conduction, negative inotropism and eventually cardiac arrest.

Pharmacokinetics: The rate and extent of absorption depends upon concentration and total dose administered, the specific site of application and duration of exposure. In general, the rate of absorption of local anesthetic agents, following topical application to wound surfaces and mucous membranes is high, and occurs most rapidly after intratracheal and bronchial administration. Lidocaine is also well absorbed from the gastrointestinal tract, although little intact drug may appear in the circulation because of biotransformation in the liver.

Lidocaine readily crosses the placenta, and equilibrium in regard to free, unbound drug will be reached. Because the degree of plasma protein binding in the fetus is less than in the mother, the total plasma concentration will be greater in the mother, but the free concentrations will be the same.

The plasma binding of lidocaine is dependent on drug concentration, and the fraction bound decreases with increasing concentration. At concentrations of 1 to 4 μg of free base per mL, 60 to 80% of lidocaine is protein bound. Binding is also dependent on the plasma concentration of the alpha-1-acid glycoprotein.

Lidocaine has a total plasma clearance of 0.95 L/min, a volume of distribution at steady state of 91 L, an elimination half-life of 1.6 hours and an estimated hepatic extraction ratio of 0.65. The clearance of lidocaine is almost entirely due to liver metabolism, and depends both on liver blood flow and the activity of metabolizing enzymes.

Lidocaine is metabolized rapidly by the liver, and metabolites and unchanged drug are excreted by the kidneys. Biotransformation includes oxidative N-dealkylation, ring hydroxylation, cleavage of the amide linkage, and conjugation. Only 2% of lidocaine is excreted unchanged. Most of it is metabolized first to monoethylglycinexylidide (MEGX) and then to glycinexylidide (GX) and 2,6-xylidine. Up to 70% appears in the urine as 4-hydroxy-2,6-xylidine.

The elimination half-life of lidocaine following an i.v. bolus injection is typically 1.5 to 2.0 hours. The elimination half-life in neonates (3.2 hours) is approximately twice that of adults. The half-life may be prolonged two-fold or more in patients with liver dysfunction. Renal dysfunction does not affect lidocaine kinetics but may increase the accumulation of metabolites.

Acidosis increases the systemic toxicity of lidocaine while the use of CNS depressants may increase the levels of lidocaine required to produce overt CNS effects. Objective adverse manifestations become increasingly apparent with increasing venous plasma levels above 6.0 μg free base per mL.

Indications: To provide topical anesthesia of the oropharyngeal, tracheal and bronchial areas to reduce reflex activity, attenuate hemodynamic responses and facilitate insertion of the tube or the passage of instruments during endotracheal intubation and endoscopic procedures, e.g., bronchography, bronchoscopy, laryngoscopy, and esophagoscopy.

Contraindications: In patients with a known history of hypersensitivity to local anesthetics of the amide type or to other components of the solution, e.g., methylparaben.

Warnings: Excessive dosage, or short intervals between doses, can result in high plasma levels of lidocaine or its metabolites and serious adverse effects. Absorption from the mucous membranes is variable but is especially high from the bronchial tree. Such applications may therefore result in rapidly rising or excessive plasma concentrations, with an increased risk for toxic symptoms, such as convulsions. This is especially important in children where doses vary with weight. The management of serious adverse reactions may require the use of resuscitative equipment, oxygen and other resuscitative drugs (see Overdosage: Symptoms and Treatment).

Lidocaine should be used with caution in patients with sepsis and/or traumatized mucosa at the area of application, since under such conditions there is the potential for rapid systemic absorption.

In paralyzed patients under general anesthesia, higher plasma concentrations may occur than in spontaneously breathing patients. Unparalyzed patients are more likely to swallow a large proportion of the dose, which then undergoes considerable first-pass hepatic metabolism following absorption from the gut.

Xylocaine Topical 4% is for topical use only and must not be used for injection.

Precautions: The lowest dosage that results in effective anesthesia should be used to avoid high plasma levels and serious adverse effects. Absorption from mucous membranes is variable but especially high from the bronchial tree. Tolerance to elevated blood levels varies with the status of the patient. Debilitated, elderly patients, acutely ill patients, and children should be given reduced doses commensurate with their age and physical condition. Lidocaine should also be used with caution in patients with epilepsy, impaired cardiac conduction, bradycardia, impaired hepatic or renal function, and in severe shock.

Because amide-type local anesthetics such as lidocaine are metabolized by the liver, these drugs, especially repeated doses, should be used cautiously in patients with hepatic disease. Patients with severe hepatic disease, because of their inability to metabolize local anesthetics normally, are at greater risk of developing toxic plasma concentrations.

Lidocaine should also be used with caution in patients with impaired cardiovascular function since they may be less able to compensate for functional changes associated with the prolongation of AV conduction produced by these drugs.

Many drugs used during the conduct of anesthesia are considered potential triggering agents for familial malignant hyperthermia. It has been shown that the use of amide local anesthetics in malignant hyperthermia patients is safe. However, there is no guarantee that neural blockade will prevent the development of malignant hyperthermia during surgery. It is also difficult to predict the need for supplemental general anesthesia. Therefore a standard protocol for the management of malignant hyperthermia should be available.

Lidocaine should be used with caution in persons with known drug sensitivities. Patients allergic to para-aminobenzoic acid derivatives (procaine, tetracaine, benzocaine, etc.) have not shown cross-sensitivity to lidocaine.

Drug Interactions: Lidocaine should be used with caution in patients receiving other local anesthetics or agents structurally related to amide-type local anesthetics, since the toxic effects are additive.

Information for the Patient: When topical anesthetics are used in the mouth, the patient should be aware that the production of topical anesthesia may impair swallowing and thus enhance the danger of aspiration. Numbness of the tongue or buccal mucosa may enhance the danger of unintentional biting trauma. Food or chewing gum should not be taken while the mouth or throat area is anesthetized.

Pregnancy: It is reasonable to assume that a large number of pregnant women and women of childbearing age have been given lidocaine. No specific disturbances to the reproductive process have so far been reported, e.g., no increased incidence of malformations. However, care should be given during early pregnancy when maximum organogenesis takes place.

There are no adequate and well-controlled studies in pregnant women on the effect of lidocaine on the developing fetus.

Labor and Delivery: Lidocaine is not contraindicated in labor and delivery. Should Xylocaine Topical 4% be used concomitantly with other products containing lidocaine, the total dose contributed by all formulations must be kept in mind.

Lactation: Lidocaine is excreted in the breast milk, but in such small quantities that there is generally no risk of affecting the infant at therapeutic dose levels.

Adverse Effects: Adverse experiences following the administration of lidocaine are similar in nature to those observed with other amide local anesthetic agents. These adverse experiences are, in general, dose-related and may result from high plasma levels caused by overdosage or rapid absorption, or may result from a hypersensitivity, idiosyncrasy or diminished tolerance on the part of the patient.

Serious adverse experiences are generally systemic in nature. The following types are those most commonly reported: CNS: CNS manifestations are excitatory and/or depressant and may be characterized by circumoral paresthesia, lightheadedness, nervousness, apprehension, euphoria, confusion, dizziness, drowsiness, hyperacusis, tinnitus, blurred vision, vomiting, sensations of heat, cold or numbness, twitching, tremors, convulsions, unconsciousness, respiratory depression and arrest. The excitatory manifestations may be very brief or may not occur at all, in which case the first manifestation of toxicity may be drowsiness merging into unconsciousness and respiratory arrest.

Drowsiness following the administration of lidocaine is usually an early sign of a high lidocaine plasma level and may occur as a consequence of rapid absorption.

Cardiovascular: Cardiovascular manifestations are usually depressant and are characterized by bradycardia, hypotension, arrhythmia and cardiovascular collapse, which may lead to cardiac arrest.

Allergic: Allergic reactions are characterized by cutaneous lesions, urticaria, edema or, in the most severe cases, anaphylactic shock. Allergic reactions of the amide type are rare and may occur as a result of sensitivity either to the local anesthetic agent or to other components in the formulation.

Overdose: Acute systemic toxicity from local anesthetics is generally related to high plasma levels encountered during therapeutic use of local anesthetics and originates mainly in the central nervous and the cardiovascular systems (see Adverse Effects, Warnings, and Precautions).

Symptoms: CNS toxicity is a graded response, with symptoms and signs of escalating severity. The first symptoms are circumoral paresthesia, numbness of the tongue, lightheadedness, hyperacusis and tinnitus. Visual disturbance and muscular tremors are more serious and precede the onset of generalized convulsions. Unconsciousness and grand mal convulsions may follow, which may last from a few seconds to several minutes. Hypoxia and hypercarbia occur rapidly following convulsions due to the increased muscular activity, together with the interference with normal respiration. In severe cases apnea may occur. Acidosis increases the toxic effects of local anesthetics.

Recovery is due to redistribution and metabolism of the local anesthetic drug. Recovery may be rapid unless large amounts of the drug have been administered.

Cardiovascular effects may be seen in cases with high systemic concentrations. Severe hypotension, bradycardia, arrhythmia and cardiovascular collapse may be the result in such cases.

Cardiovascular toxic effects are generally preceded by signs of toxicity in the CNS, unless the patient is receiving a general anesthetic or is heavily sedated with drugs such as a benzodiazepine or barbiturate.

Treatment: The first consideration is prevention, best accomplished by careful and constant monitoring of cardiovascular and respiratory vital signs and the patient's state of consciousness after each local anesthetic administration. At the first sign of change, oxygen should be administered.

The first step in the management of systemic toxic reactions consists of immediate attention to the maintenance of a patent airway and assisted or controlled ventilation with oxygen and a delivery system capable of permitting immediate positive airway pressure by mask. This may prevent convulsions if they have not already occurred.

If necessary, use drugs to control convulsions. An anticonvulsant should be given i.v. if the convulsions do not stop spontaneously in 15 to 20 seconds. Thiopental 100 to 150 mg i.v. will abort the convulsions rapidly. Alternatively, diazepam 5 to 10 mg i.v. may be used, although its action is slower. Succinylcholine will stop the muscle convulsions rapidly, but will require tracheal intubation and controlled ventilation, and should only be used by those familiar with these procedures.

If cardiovascular depression is evident (hypotension, bradycardia), ephedrine 5 to 10 mg i.v. should be given and may be repeated, if necessary, after 2 to 3 minutes.

Should circulatory arrest occur, immediate cardiopulmonary resuscitation should be instituted. Optimal oxygenation and ventilation and circulatory support as well as treatment of acidosis are of vital importance, since hypoxia and acidosis will increase the systemic toxicity of local anesthetics. Epinephrine (0.1 to 0.2 mg as i.v. or intracardial injections) should be given as soon as possible and repeated, if necessary.

Children should be given doses commensurate with their age and weight.

Dosage: When used concomitantly with other products containing lidocaine, the total dose contributed by all formulations must be kept in mind. Debilitated, elderly and acutely ill patients should be given reduced doses.

The degree of absorption from mucous membranes is variable but especially high from the bronchial tree. Application only to areas below the vocal cords may result in excessive plasma concentrations because of less transfer to the intestine and less first-pass loss. When inhaled from a nebulizer, the resulting plasma concentrations are lower than following spray (atomizer) applications.

Topical anesthesia may be achieved by spraying, e.g., using an atomizer or nebulizer. Xylocaine Topical may also be applied with cotton applicators or by instillation into a cavity or onto a surface.

Adults: The recommended dose is 2 to 7.5 mL (80 to 300 mg lidocaine). During prolonged procedures, up to 400 mg may be administered. In addition, when combined with other lidocaine products, the total dose should not exceed 400 mg. With applications mainly to the larynx, trachea, and bronchi, the

dose should not exceed 5 mL (200 mg). When inhaled from a nebulizer, 5 to 10 mL (200 to 400 mg) may be used.
Children (under 12 years): It is difficult to recommend a maximum dose of any drug for children since this varies as a function of age and weight. The maximum amount administered should not exceed 3 mg/kg of body weight.

Supplied: Each mL of topical solution contains: lidocaine HCl 40 mg. Nonmedicinal ingredients: amaranth (coloring agent), methylparaben, sodium hydroxide and/or hydrochloric acid to adjust pH to 5.0 to 7.0 and water for injection. Vials of 50 mL. Store between 15 and 30°C. Protect from freezing.

Reviewed 1998

XYLOCAINE® TOPICAL 5%

Astra

Lidocaine

Oral Topical Anesthetic

Pharmacology: Mechanism of Action: Lidocaine stabilizes the neuronal membrane by inhibiting the ionic fluxes required for the initiation and conduction of impulses, thereby effecting local anesthetic action. Local anesthetics of the amide type are thought to act within the sodium channels of the nerve membrane.
Onset of Action: The onset of action is 3 to 5 minutes when applied to mucous membrane. Xylocaine Topical 5% is ineffective when applied to intact skin.
Hemodynamics: Lidocaine, like other local anesthetics, may also have effects on excitable membranes in the brain and myocardium. If excessive amounts of drug reach systemic circulation rapidly, symptoms and signs of toxicity will appear, emanating from the central nervous and cardiovascular systems.

CNS toxicity (see Overdose: Symptoms and Treatment) usually precedes the cardiovascular effects since it occurs at lower plasma concentrations. Direct effects of local anesthetics on the heart include slow conduction, negative inotropism and eventually cardiac arrest.
Pharmacokinetics: The rate and extent of absorption depends upon concentration and total dose administered, the specific site of application and duration of exposure. In general, the rate of absorption of local anesthetic agents, following topical application to wound surfaces and mucous membranes is high, and occurs most rapidly after intratracheal and bronchial administration. Lidocaine is also well absorbed from the gastrointestinal tract, although little intact drug may appear in the circulation because of biotransformation in the liver.

Lidocaine readily crosses the placenta, and equilibrium in regard to free, unbound drug will be reached. Because the degree of plasma protein binding in the fetus is less than in the mother, the total plasma concentration will be greater in the mother, but the free concentrations will be the same.

The plasma binding of lidocaine is dependent on drug concentration, and the fraction bound decreases with increasing concentration. At concentrations of 1 to 4 μg of free base per mL, 60 to 80% of lidocaine is protein bound. Binding is also dependent on the plasma concentration of the alpha-1-acid glycoprotein.

Lidocaine has a total plasma clearance of 0.95 L/min, a volume of distribution at steady state of 91 L, an elimination half-life of 1.6 hours and an estimated hepatic extraction ratio of 0.65. The clearance of lidocaine is almost entirely due to liver metabolism, and depends both on liver blood flow and the activity of metabolizing enzymes.

Lidocaine is metabolized rapidly by the liver, and metabolites and unchanged drug are excreted by the kidneys. Biotransformation includes oxidative N-dealkylation, ring hydroxylation, cleavage of the amide linkage, and conjugation. Only 2% of lidocaine is excreted unchanged. Most of it is metabolized first to monoethylglycinexylidide (MEGX) and then to glycinexylidide (GX) and 2,6-xylidine. Up to 70% appears in the urine as 4-hydroxy-2,6-xylidine.

The elimination half-life of lidocaine following an i.v. bolus injection is typically 1.5 to 2.0 hours. The elimination half-life in neonates (3.2 hours) is approximately twice that of adults. The half-life may be prolonged two-fold or more in patients with liver dysfunction. Renal dysfunction does not affect lidocaine kinetics but may increase the accumulation of metabolites.

Acidosis increases the systemic toxicity of lidocaine while the use of CNS depressants may increase the levels of lidocaine required to produce overt CNS effects. Objective adverse manifestations become increasingly apparent with increasing venous plasma levels above 6.0 μg free base per mL.

Indications: To provide relief of pain and discomfort in connection with irritated or inflamed mucous membranes of the mouth and for anesthesia of these membranes for the performance of minor dental surgical procedures.

Contraindications: In patients with a known history of hypersensitivity to local anesthetics of the amide type or to other components of the solution.

Warnings: Excessive dosage, or short intervals between doses, can result in high plasma levels of lidocaine or its metabolites and serious adverse effects. Patients should be instructed to strictly adhere to the recommended dosage. This is especially important in children where doses vary with weight. The management of serious adverse reactions may require the use of resuscitative equipment, oxygen and other resuscitative drugs (see Overdose: Symptoms and Treatment).

Lidocaine should be used with caution in patients with sepsis and/or traumatized mucosa at the area of application, since under such conditions there is the potential for rapid systemic absorption.

Xylocaine Topical 5% is for topical use only and must not be used for injection.

Precautions: The lowest dosage that results in effective anesthesia should be used to avoid high plasma levels and serious adverse effects. Tolerance to elevated blood levels varies with the status of the patient. Debilitated, elderly patients, acutely ill patients, and children should be given reduced doses commensurate with their age and physical condition. Lidocaine should also be used with caution in patients with epilepsy, impaired cardiac conduction, bradycardia, impaired hepatic or renal function, and in severe shock.

Because amide-type local anesthetics such as lidocaine are metabolized by the liver, these drugs, especially repeated doses, should be used cautiously in patients with hepatic disease. Patients with severe hepatic disease, because of their inability to metabolize local anesthetics normally, are at greater risk of developing toxic plasma concentrations.

Lidocaine should also be used with caution in patients with impaired cardiovascular function since they may be less able to compensate for functional changes associated with the prolongation of AV conduction produced by these drugs.

Many drugs used during the conduct of anesthesia are considered potential triggering agents for familial malignant hyperthermia. It has been shown that the use of amide local anesthetics in malignant hyperthermia patients is safe. However there is no guarantee that neural blockade will prevent the development of malignant hyperthermia during surgery. It is also difficult to predict the need for supplemental general anesthesia. Therefore, a standard protocol for the management of malignant hyperthermia should be available.

Lidocaine should be used with caution in persons with known drug sensitivities. Patients allergic to para-aminobenzoic acid derivatives (procaine, tetracaine, benzocaine, etc.) have not shown cross-sensitivity to lidocaine.
Drug Interactions: Lidocaine should be used with caution in patients receiving other local anesthetics or agents structurally related to amide-type local anesthetics, since the toxic effects are additive.
Information for the Patient: When topical anesthetics are used in the mouth, the patient should be aware that the production of topical anesthesia may impair swallowing and thus enhance the danger of aspiration. Numbness of the tongue or buccal mucosa may enhance the danger of unintentional biting trauma. Food or chewing gum should not be taken while the mouth or throat area is anesthetized.
Pregnancy: It is reasonable to assume that a large number of pregnant women and women of childbearing age have been given lidocaine. No specific disturbances to the reproductive process have so far been reported, e.g., no increased incidence of malformations. However, care should be given during early pregnancy when maximum organogenesis takes place.

There are no adequate and well-controlled studies in pregnant women on the effect of lidocaine on the developing fetus.
Labor and Delivery: Lidocaine is not contraindicated in labor and delivery. Should Xylocaine Topical 5% be used concomitantly with other products containing lidocaine, the total dose contributed by all formulations must be kept in mind.
Lactation: Lidocaine is excreted in the breast milk, but in such small quantities that there is generally no risk of affecting the infant at therapeutic dose levels.

Adverse Effects: Adverse experiences following the administration of lidocaine are similar in nature to those observed with other amide local anesthetic agents. These adverse experiences are, in general, dose-related and may result from high plasma levels caused by overdosage or rapid absorption, or may result from a hypersensitivity, idiosyncrasy or diminished tolerance on the part of the patient.

Serious adverse experiences are generally systemic in nature. The following types are those most commonly reported.
CNS: CNS manifestations are excitatory and/or depressant and may be characterized by circumoral paresthesia, lightheadedness, nervousness, apprehension, euphoria, confusion, dizziness, drowsiness, hyperacusis, tinnitus, blurred vision, vomiting, sensations of heat, cold or numbness, twitching, tremors, convulsions, unconsciousness, respiratory depression and arrest. The excitatory manifestations may be very brief or may not occur at all, in which case the first manifestation of toxicity may be drowsiness merging into unconsciousness and respiratory arrest.

Drowsiness following the administration of lidocaine is usually an early sign of a high lidocaine plasma level and may occur as a consequence of rapid absorption.
Cardiovascular: Cardiovascular manifestations are usually depressant and are characterized by bradycardia, hypotension, arrhythmia, and cardiovascular collapse, which may lead to cardiac arrest.
Allergic: Allergic reactions are characterized by cutaneous lesions, urticaria, edema or, in the most severe cases, anaphylactic shock. Allergic reactions of the amide type are rare and may occur as a result of sensitivity either to the local anesthetic agent or to other components in the formulation.

Overdose: Acute systemic toxicity from local anesthetics is generally related to high plasma levels encountered during therapeutic use of local anesthetics and originates mainly in the central nervous and the cardiovascular systems (see Adverse Effects, Warnings, and Precautions).

Symptoms: CNS toxicity is a graded response, with symptoms and signs of escalating severity. The first symptoms are circumoral paresthesia, numbness of the tongue, lightheadedness, hyperacusis and tinnitus. Visual disturbance and muscular tremors are more serious and precede the onset of generalized convulsions. Unconsciousness and grand mal convulsions may follow, which may last from a few seconds to several minutes. Hypoxia and hypercarbia occur rapidly following convulsions due to the increased muscular activity, together with the interference with normal respiration. In severe cases apnea may occur. Acidosis increases the toxic effects of local anesthetics.

Recovery is due to redistribution and metabolism of the local anesthetic drug. Recovery may be rapid unless large amounts of the drug have been administered.

Cardiovascular effects may be seen in cases with high systemic concentrations. Severe hypotension, bradycardia, arrhythmia and cardiovascular collapse may be the result in such cases.

Cardiovascular toxic effects are generally preceded by signs of toxicity in the CNS, unless the patient is receiving a general anesthetic or is heavily sedated with drugs such as a benzodiazepine or barbiturate.

Treatment: The first consideration is prevention, best accomplished by careful and constant monitoring of cardiovascular and respiratory vital signs and the patient's state of consciousness after each local anesthetic administration. At the first sign of change, oxygen should be administered.

The first step in the management of systemic toxic reactions consists of immediate attention to the maintenance of a patent airway and assisted or controlled ventilation with oxygen and a delivery system capable of permitting immediate positive airway pressure by mask. This may prevent convulsions if they have not already occurred.

If necessary, use drugs to control convulsions. An anticonvulsant should be given i.v. if the convulsions do not stop spontaneously in 15 to 20 seconds. Thiopental 100 to 150 mg i.v. will abort the convulsions rapidly. Alternatively, diazepam 5 to 10 mg i.v. may be used, although its action is slower. Succinylcholine will stop the muscle convulsions rapidly, but will require tracheal intubation and controlled ventilation, and should only be used by those familiar with these procedures.

If cardiovascular depression is evident (hypotension, bradycardia), ephedrine 5 to 10 mg i.v. should be given and may be repeated, if necessary, after 2 to 3 minutes.

Should circulatory arrest occur, immediate cardiopulmonary resuscitation should be instituted. Optimal oxygenation and ventilation and circulatory support as well as treatment of acidosis are of vital importance, since hypoxia and acidosis will increase the systemic toxicity of local anesthetics. Epinephrine (0.1 to 0.2 mg as i.v. or intracardial injections) should be given as soon as possible and repeated, if necessary.

Children should be given doses commensurate with their age and weight.

Xylocaine Topical 5% (cont'd)

Dosage: When used concomitantly with other products containing lidocaine, the total dose contributed by all formulations must be kept in mind. Debilitated, elderly and acutely ill patients should be given reduced doses.
Adults: Apply topically to oral mucosa with disposable cotton applicators. 1 to 4 mL (50 to 200 mg lidocaine) of Xylocaine Topical 5% may be applied to a wet or dry oral mucosa.
Children (under 12 years): It is difficult to recommend a maximum dose of any drug for children since this varies as a function of age and weight. The maximum amount of Xylocaine administered should not exceed 4 mg/kg of body weight.

Supplied: Each mL contains: lidocaine base 50 mg. Nonmedicinal ingredients: amaranth (coloring agent), glycerin, propylene glycol, spearmint oil (flavoring agent) and water for injection. Plastic bottles of 50 mL with child-resistant closures. Store between 15 and 30°C. Protect from freezing.

Reviewed 1998

XYLOCAINE® VISCOUS 2%

Astra

Lidocaine HCl

Topical Anesthetic

Pharmacology: Mechanism of Action: Lidocaine stabilizes the neuronal membrane by inhibiting the ionic fluxes required for the initiation and conduction of impulses thereby, effecting local anesthetic action. Local anesthetics of the amide type are thought to act within the sodium channels of the nerve membrane.
Onset of Action: After application of Xylocaine Viscous, local anesthesia is achieved within 5 minutes. Duration of anesthesia is approximately 20 to 30 minutes. Xylocaine Viscous is ineffective when applied to intact skin.
Hemodynamics: Lidocaine, like other local anesthetics, may also have effects on excitable membranes in the brain and myocardium. If excessive amounts of drug reach the systemic circulation rapidly, symptoms and signs of toxicity will appear, emanating from the central nervous and cardiovascular systems.

CNS toxicity (see Overdose: Symptoms and Treatment) usually precedes the cardiovascular effects since it occurs at lower plasma concentrations. Direct effects of local anesthetics on the heart include slow conduction, negative inotropism and eventually cardiac arrest.

Pharmacokinetics: The rate and extent of absorption depends upon concentration and total dose administered, the specific site of application and duration of exposure. In general, the rate of absorption of local anesthetic agents, following topical application to wound surfaces and mucous membranes is high, and occurs most rapidly after intratracheal and bronchial administration. Lidocaine is also well absorbed from the gastrointestinal tract, although little intact drug may appear in the circulation because of biotransformation in the liver.

Lidocaine readily crosses the placenta, and equilibrium in regard to free, unbound drug will be reached. Because the degree of plasma protein binding in the fetus is less than in the mother, the total plasma concentration will be greater in the mother, but the free concentrations will be the same.

The plasma binding of lidocaine is dependent on drug concentration, and the fraction bound decreases with increasing concentration. At concentrations of 1 to 4 μg of free base per mL, 60 to 80% of lidocaine is protein bound. Binding is also dependent on the plasma concentration of the alpha-1-acid glycoprotein.

Lidocaine has a total plasma clearance of 0.95 L/min, a volume of distribution at steady state of 91 L, an elimination half-life of 1.6 hours and an estimated hepatic extraction ratio of 0.65. The clearance of lidocaine is almost entirely due to liver metabolism, and depends both on liver blood flow and the activity of metabolizing enzymes.

Lidocaine is metabolized rapidly by the liver, and metabolites and unchanged drug are excreted by the kidneys. Biotransformation includes oxidative N-dealkylation, ring hydroxylation, cleavage of the amide linkage, and conjugation. Only 2% of lidocaine is excreted unchanged. Most of it is metabolized first to monoethylglycinexylidide (MEGX) and then to glycinexylidide (GX) and 2,6-xylidine. Up to 70% appears in the urine as 4-hydroxy-2,6-xylidine.

The elimination half-life of lidocaine following an i.v. bolus injection is typically 1.5 to 2.0 hours. The elimination half-life in neonates (3.2 hours) is approximately twice that of adults. The half-life may be prolonged 2-fold or more in patients with liver dysfunction. Renal dysfunction does not affect lidocaine kinetics but may increase the accumulation of metabolites.

Acidosis increases the systemic toxicity of lidocaine while the use of CNS depressants may increase the levels of lidocaine required to produce overt CNS effects. Objective adverse manifestations become increasingly apparent with increasing venous plasma levels above 6.0 μg free base per mL.

Indications: To provide relief of pain and discomfort in connection with: irritated or inflamed mucous membranes of the mouth and pharynx, e.g., lesions following tonsillectomy; introduction of instruments and catheters into the respiratory and digestive tracts, e.g., bronchoscopy, esophagoscopy; painful diseases of the upper gastrointestinal tract e.g., esophagitis.

Contraindications: In patients with a known history of hypersensitivity to local anesthetics of the amide type or to other components of the solution, e.g., methylparaben, propylparaben.

Warnings: Excessive dosage, or short intervals between doses, can result in high plasma levels of lidocaine or its metabolites and serious adverse effects. Following too high or repeated doses of viscous lidocaine in children under the age of 3, serious side effects have been reported. Absorption from the mucous membranes is variable but is especially high from the bronchial tree. Such applications may therefore result in rapidly rising or excessive plasma concentrations, with an increased risk for toxic symptoms, such as convulsions. **Patients should be instructed to strictly adhere to the recommended dosage.** This is especially important in children where doses vary with weight. The management of serious adverse reactions may require the use of resuscitative equipment, oxygen and other resuscitative drugs (see Overdose: Symptoms and Treatment).

Lidocaine should be used with caution in patients with sepsis and/or traumatized mucosa at the area of application, since under such conditions there is the potential for rapid systemic absorption.

Xylocaine Viscous is for topical use only and must not be used for injection.

Precautions: The lowest dosage that results in effective anesthesia should be used to avoid high plasma levels and serious adverse effects. Absorption from mucous membranes is variable but especially high from the bronchial tree. Tolerance to elevated blood levels varies with the status of the patient. Debilitated, elderly patients, acutely ill patients, and children should be given reduced doses commensurate with their age and physical condition. Lidocaine should also be used with caution in patients with epilepsy, impaired cardiac conduction, bradycardia, impaired hepatic or renal function, and in severe shock.

Because amide-type local anesthetics such as lidocaine are metabolized by the liver, these drugs, especially repeated doses, should be used cautiously in patients with hepatic disease. Patients with severe hepatic disease, because of their inability to metabolize local anesthetics normally, are at greater risk of developing toxic plasma concentrations.

Lidocaine should also be used with caution in patients with impaired cardiovascular function since they may be less able to compensate for functional changes associated with the prolongation of AV conduction produced by these drugs.

Many drugs used during the conduct of anesthesia are considered potential triggering agents for familial malignant hyperthermia. It has been shown that the use of amide local anesthetics in malignant hyperthermia patients is safe. However there is no guarantee that neural blockade will prevent the development of malignant hyperthermia during surgery. It is also difficult to predict the need for supplemental general anesthesia. Therefore a standard protocol for the management of malignant hyperthermia should be available.

Lidocaine should be used with caution in persons with known drug sensitivities. Patients allergic to para-aminobenzoic acid derivatives (procaine, tetracaine, benzocaine, etc.) have not shown cross-sensitivity to lidocaine.

Drug Interactions: Lidocaine should be used with caution in patients receiving other local anesthetics or agents structurally related to amide-type local anesthetics, since the toxic effects are additive.

Information for Patients: See also Blue Section—Information for the Patient ''Xylocaine Viscous 2%''. When topical anesthetics are used in the mouth, the patient should be aware that the production of topical anesthesia may impair swallowing and thus enhance the danger of aspiration. Numbness of the tongue or buccal mucosa may enhance the danger of unintentional biting trauma. Food or chewing gum should not be taken while the mouth or throat area is anesthetized.

Pregnancy: It is reasonable to assume that a large number of pregnant women and women of childbearing age have been given lidocaine. No specific disturbances to the reproductive process have so far been reported, e.g., no increased incidence of malformations. However, care should be given during early pregnancy when maximum organogenesis takes place.

There are no adequate and well-controlled studies in pregnant women on the effect of lidocaine on the developing fetus.
Labor and Delivery: Lidocaine is not contraindicated in labor and delivery. Should Xylocaine Viscous 2% be used concomitantly with other products containing lidocaine, the total dose contributed by all formulations must be kept in mind.

Lactation: Lidocaine is excreted in the breast milk, but in such small quantities that there is generally no risk of affecting the infant at therapeutic dose levels.

Adverse Effects: Adverse experiences following the administration of lidocaine are similar in nature to those observed with other amide local anesthetic agents. These adverse experiences are, in general, dose-related and may result from high plasma levels caused by overdosage or rapid absorption, or may result from a hypersensitivity, idiosyncrasy or diminished tolerance on the part of the patient.

Serious adverse experiences are generally systemic in nature. The following types are those most commonly reported. CNS: CNS manifestations are excitatory and/or depressant and may be characterized by circumoral paresthesia, lightheadedness, apprehension, euphoria, confusion, dizziness, drowsiness, hyperacusis, tinnitus, blurred vision, vomiting, sensations of heat, cold or numbness, twitching, tremors, convulsions, unconsciousness, respiratory depression and arrest. The excitatory manifestations may be very brief or may not occur at all, in which case the first manifestation of toxicity may be drowsiness merging into unconsciousness and respiratory arrest.

Drowsiness following the administration of lidocaine is usually an early sign of a high lidocaine plasma level and may occur as a consequence of rapid absorption.

Cardiovascular: Cardiovascular manifestations are usually depressant and are characterized by bradycardia, hypotension, arrhythmia, and cardiovascular collapse, which may lead to cardiac arrest.

Allergic: Allergic reactions are characterized by cutaneous lesions, urticaria, edema or in the most severe instances anaphylactic shock. Allergic reactions of the amide type are rare and may occur as a result of sensitivity either to the local anesthetic agent or to other components in the formulation.

Overdose: Acute systemic toxicity from local anesthetics is generally related to high plasma levels encountered during therapeutic use of local anesthetics and originates mainly in the central nervous and the cardiovascular systems (see Adverse Effects, Warnings, and Precautions).

Symptoms: CNS toxicity is a graded response with symptoms and signs of escalating severity. The first symptoms are circumoral paresthesia, numbness of the tongue, lightheadedness, hyperacusis and tinnitus. Visual disturbance and muscular tremors are more serious and precede the onset of generalized convulsions. Unconsciousness and grand mal convulsions may follow, which may last from a few seconds to several minutes. Hypoxia and hypercarbia occur rapidly following convulsions due to the increased muscular activity, together with the interference with normal respiration. In severe cases apnea may occur. Acidosis increases the toxic effects of local anesthetics.

Recovery is due to redistribution and metabolism of the local anesthetic drug. Recovery may be rapid unless large amounts of the drug have been administered.

Cardiovascular effects may be seen in cases with high systemic concentrations. Severe hypotension, bradycardia, arrhythmia and cardiovascular collapse may be the result in such cases.

Cardiovascular toxic effects are generally preceded by signs of toxicity in the CNS, unless the patient is receiving a general anesthetic or is heavily sedated with drugs such as a benzodiazepine or barbiturate.

Treatment: The first consideration is prevention, best accomplished by careful and constant monitoring of cardiovascular and respiratory vital signs and the patient's state of consciousness after each local anesthetic administration. At the first sign of change, oxygen should be administered.

The first step in the management of systemic toxic reactions consists of immediate attention to the maintenance of a patent airway and assisted or controlled ventilation with oxygen and a delivery system capable of permitting immediate positive airway pressure by mask. This may prevent convulsions if they have not already occurred.

If necessary, use drugs to control convulsions. An anticonvulsant should be given i.v. if the convulsions do not stop spontaneously in 15 to 20 seconds. Thiopental 100 to 150 mg i.v. will abort the convulsions rapidly. Alternatively diazepam 5 to 10 mg i.v. may be used although its action is slower. Succinylcholine will stop the muscle convulsions rapidly, but will require tracheal intubation and controlled ventilation, and should only be used by those familiar with these procedures.

If cardiovascular depression is evident (hypotension, bradycardia), ephedrine 5 to 10 mg i.v. should be given and repeated, if necessary, after 2 to 3 minutes.

Should circulatory arrest occur, immediate cardiopulmonary resuscitation should be instituted. Optimal oxygenation and ventilation and circulatory support as well as treatment of acidosis are of vital importance, since hypoxia and acidosis will increase the systemic toxicity of local anesthetics. Epinephrine (0.1 to 0.2 mg as i.v. or intracardial injections) should be given as soon as possible and repeated, if necessary.

Children should be given doses commensurate with their age and weight.

Dosage: When used concomitantly with other products containing lidocaine, the total dose contributed by all formulations must be kept in mind. Debilitated, elderly and acutely ill patients should be given reduced doses.

The degree of absorption from mucous membranes is variable but especially high from the bronchial tree. The degree of systemic absorption depends on whether the lidocaine viscous is swallowed or expectorated. It is therefore important to expectorate in order to avoid unnecessary absorption. After a swallowed single dose of 300 mg (15 mL) of lidocaine viscous, the resulting blood concentrations are low.

Adults: For treatment of pain from irritated or inflamed mucous membranes of the mouth and throat, 5 to 10 mL of lidocaine viscous (100 to 200 mg lidocaine) is recommended. The solution should be swished around in the mouth and may be spat out or swallowed slowly. Six doses may be given in 24 hours. Total dosage of Xylocaine Viscous in 24 hours should not exceed 60 mL or 1 200 mg lidocaine.

For topical anesthesia before introduction of instruments and catheters into the upper respiratory or digestive tracts, 10 to 15 mL of lidocaine viscous (200 to 300 mg lidocaine) is recommended. For oral analgesia, the solution should be swished around in the mouth and spat out. For use in the pharynx, the solution should be gargled and may be swallowed. When combined with other lidocaine products (e.g., for bronchoscopy), the total dosage of lidocaine should not exceed 400 mg.

For diseases of the upper gastrointestinal tract, 5 to 15 mL of lidocaine viscous (100 to 300 mg of lidocaine) should be swallowed quickly in one gulp. Six doses may be given in 24 hours. Total dosage of Xylocaine Viscous in 24 hours should not exceed 60 mL or 1 200 mg lidocaine.

Children (under 12 years): For treatment of irritated or inflamed mucous membranes of the mouth and throat, the dose should not exceed 4 mg/kg. It is recommended that excess lidocaine viscous solution is spat out. No more than 4 doses should be given during 12 to 24 hours.

Children (under 3 years): The dose should be accurately measured and applied to the affected area with a cotton tip applicator. The same procedure is also recommended for older children having problems in expectorating. No more than 4 doses should be given during 12 to 24 hours.

At the present time there is not enough documentation to allow recommendations for a more prolonged use of viscous lidocaine in children under the age of 3.

Information for the Patient: See Blue Section—Information for the Patient "Xylocaine Viscous 2%".

Supplied: Each mL contains: lidocaine HCl 20 mg. Nonmedicinal ingredients: amaranth, methylparaben, propylparaben, sodium carboxymethylcellulose and sodium hydroxide and/or hydrochloric acid to adjust pH to 6.0 to 7.0. Plastic bottles of 50 and 100 mL with child-resistant closures. Store between 15 and 30°C. Protect from freezing.

Reviewed 1998

XYLOCARD®

Astra

Lidocaine HCl

Antiarrhythmic

Pharmacology: Mechanism of Action: The mode of action of the antiarrhythmic effect of lidocaine appears to be similar to that of procaine, procainamide and quinidine. Ventricular excitability is depressed and the stimulation threshold of the ventricle is increased during diastole. The sinoatrial node is, however, unaffected. In contrast to the latter 3 drugs, lidocaine in therapeutic doses does not produce a significant decrease in arterial pressure or in cardiac contractile force. In larger doses, lidocaine may produce circulatory depression, but the magnitude of the change is less than that found with comparable doses of procainamide. Neither drug appreciably affects the duration of the absolute refractory period.

Onset of Action: The onset of action following a single i.v. injection varies from 45 to 90 seconds. Duration of action is 10 to 20 minutes.

Indications: The treatment of ventricular tachycardia occurring during cardiac manipulation, such as surgery or catheterization, or which may occur during acute myocardial infarction, digitalis toxicity, or other cardiac diseases.

Contraindications: Known hypersensitivity to local anesthetics of the amide type or to other components of the solution; Adams-Stokes syndrome, or severe degrees of sinoatrial, atrioventricular or intraventricular block.

The safety of lidocaine in the treatment of arrhythmias in children has not been established.

Warnings: Constant ECG monitoring is essential for the proper administration of lidocaine i.v.. Signs of excessive depression of cardiac conductivity, such as prolongation of PR interval and QRS complex, and the appearance of aggravation of arrhythmias, should be followed by prompt cessation of the i.v. infusion.

It is mandatory to have emergency resuscitative equipment and drugs immediately available to manage possible adverse reactions involving the cardiovascular, respiratory, or central nervous systems.

In emergency situations, when a ventricular rhythm disorder is suspected, and ECG equipment is not available, a single dose may be administered when the physician in attendance has determined that the potential benefits outweigh the possible risks. If possible, emergency resuscitative equipment and drugs should be available.

Precautions: Lidocaine should be used with caution in patients with bradycardia, severe digitalis intoxication, or first or second degree heart block in the absence of a pacemaker (see Contraindications and Warnings).

Caution should be employed in the repeated use of lidocaine in patients with severe liver or renal disease, since possible accumulation of lidocaine or its metabolites may lead to toxic phenomena.

In unconscious patients, circulatory collapse should be watched for, since CNS effects may not be apparent as an initial manifestation of toxicity.

I.V. administration of lidocaine is sometimes accompanied by a hypotensive response, and, in overdosage, this may be precipitous. For this reason the i.v. dose should not exceed 100 mg in a single injection, and no more than 200 to 300 mg in a 1 hour period (see Dosage).

When high doses are used and the patient's myocardial function is impaired, combination with other drugs which reduce the excitability of cardiac muscle requires caution.

Repeated doses of lidocaine may cause significant increases in blood levels with each repeated dose because of slow accumulation of the drug or its metabolites. Tolerance to elevated blood levels varies with the status of the patient. Debilitated, elderly patients and acutely ill patients should be given reduced doses commensurate with their age and physical condition. Lidocaine should also be used with caution in patients with epilepsy, impaired cardiac conduction, bradycardia, impaired hepatic function or renal function and in severe shock.

Pregnancy: It is reasonable to assume that lidocaine has been used, mainly as a local anesthetic, by a large number of pregnant women and women of childbearing age. No specific disturbances to the reproductive process have so far been reported, e.g., no increased incidence of malformations. However, care should be taken during early pregnancy when maximum organogenesis takes place.

There are no adequate and well-controlled studies with i.v. administration of lidocaine in pregnant women.

Lactation: Lidocaine is excreted in the breast milk, but in such small quantities that there is generally no risk of affecting the infant at therapeutic dose levels.

Drug Interactions: Cimetidine: Cimetidine reduces liver blood flow and thus systemic clearance of drugs that are highly extracted by the liver. Clinical experiments showed that the concomitant administration of cimetidine reduces the systemic clearance of lidocaine and increases lidocaine serum concentration by as much as 50%. Thus therapeutic serum levels of lidocaine may rise to toxic levels when cimetidine is used concomitantly. Ranitidine has not displayed this effect.

Propranolol: Administration of propranolol during infusion of lidocaine may increase the plasma concentration of lidocaine by about 30%. Patients already receiving propranolol tend to have higher lidocaine levels than controls. The combination should be avoided.

Carcinogenesis, Mutagenesis, Impairment of Fertility: Studies of lidocaine in animals to evaluate the carcinogenic and mutagenic potential or the effect on fertility have not been conducted.

Adverse Effects: Adverse experiences following the administration of lidocaine are similar in nature to those observed with other amide type agents. These adverse experiences are, in general, dose-related and may result from high plasma levels caused by excessive dosage or rapid absorption, or may result from a hypersensitivity, idiosyncrasy or diminished tolerance on the part of the patient.

Most frequent adverse reactions are those from the central and peripheral nervous system. They occur in 5 to 10% of the patients and are mostly dose-related.

Systemic reactions of the following types have been reported:

CNS: CNS manifestations are excitatory and/or depressant and may be characterized by circumoral paresthesia, lightheadedness, nervousness, apprehension, euphoria, confusion, dizziness, drowsiness, hyperacusis, tinnitus, blurred vision, vomiting, sensations of heat, cold or numbness, twitching, tremors, convulsions, unconsciousness, respiratory depression and arrest. The excitatory manifestations may be very brief or may not occur at all, in which case the first manifestation of toxicity may be drowsiness merging into unconsciousness and respiratory arrest.

Drowsiness following the administration of lidocaine is usually an early sign of a high lidocaine plasma level and may occur as a consequence of rapid absorption.

Cardiovascular: Cardiovascular manifestations are usually depressant and are characterized by bradycardia, hypotension and cardiovascular collapse which may lead to cardiac arrest.

Allergic: Allergic reactions are characterized by cutaneous lesions, urticaria, edema, or in the most severe instances, anaphylactic shock. Allergic reactions of the amide type are rare and may occur as a result of sensitivity either to the drug itself, or to other components of the formulation.

Idiosyncratic reactions have been reported at low doses in some patients. Cross-sensitivity between lidocaine and procainamide or lidocaine and quinidine has not been reported.

Overdose: Symptoms of overdose or idiosyncratic reactions are described under Adverse Effects.

Symptoms: CNS toxicity is a graded response, with symptoms and signs of escalating severity. The first symptoms are circumoral paresthesia, numbness of the tongue, lightheadedness, hyperacusis and tinnitus. Visual disturbance and muscular tremors are more serious and precede the onset of generalized convulsions. Unconsciousness and grand mal convulsions may follow, which may last from a few seconds to several minutes. Hypoxia and hypercarbia occur rapidly following convulsions due to the increased muscular activity, together with the interference with normal respiration. In severe cases apnea may occur. Acidosis increases the toxic effects.

Recovery is due to redistribution and metabolism of the drug. Recovery may be rapid unless large amounts of the drug have been administered.

Cardiovascular effects may be seen in cases with high systemic concentrations. Severe hypotension, bradycardia, arrhythmia and cardiovascular collapse may be the result in such cases.

Cardiovascular toxic effects are generally preceded by signs of toxicity in the CNS, unless the patient is receiving a general anesthetic or is heavily sedated with drugs such as a benzodiazepine or barbiturate.

Treatment: The first consideration is prevention, best accomplished by careful and constant monitoring of cardiovascular and respiratory vital signs and the patient's state of consciousness. At the first sign of change, oxygen should be administered.

The first step in the management of convulsions consists of immediate attention to the maintenance of a patent airway and assisted or controlled ventilation with oxygen and a delivery system capable of permitting immediate positive airway pressure by mask. Immediately after the institution of these ventilatory measures, the adequacy of the circulation should be evaluated, keeping in mind that drugs used to treat convulsions sometimes depress the circulation when administered i.v.

An anticonvulsant should be given i.v. if the convulsions do not stop spontaneously in 15 to 20 seconds. Thiopental 100 to

Xylocard (cont'd)

150 mg i.v. will abort the convulsions rapidly. Alternatively, diazepam 5 to 10 mg i.v. may be used, although its action is slower. Succinylcholine will stop the muscle convulsions rapidly, but will require tracheal intubation and controlled ventilation, and should only be used by those familiar with these procedures.

Hypotension may be counteracted by giving sympathicomimetic drugs (e.g., epinephrine). Adrenergic agents of both α-adrenoceptor stimulating (e.g., metaraminol) and β-adrenoceptor stimulating type (e.g., isoprenaline) are generally effective. The bradycardia may be treated with parasympatholytic agents (e.g., atropine).

Should circulatory arrest occur, immediate cardiopulmonary resuscitation should be instituted. Optimal oxygenation and ventilation and circulatory support as well as treatment of acidosis are of vital importance, since hypoxia and acidosis will increase the systemic toxicity of local anesthetics. Epinephrine (0.1 to 0.2 mg as i.v. or intracardial injections) should be given as soon as possible and repeated, if necessary.

Dosage: Single I.V. injection: The usual dose is 50 to 100 mg administered under ECG and blood pressure monitoring. This dose may be administered at the rate of approximately 25 to 50 mg/min. Sufficient time should be allowed to enable a slow circulation to carry the drug to the site of action. If the initial injection of 50 to 100 mg does not produce a desired response, a second dose may be repeated after 10 minutes. **No more than 200 to 300 mg of lidocaine should be administered during a 1 hour period.**

Continuous I.V. infusion: Following i.v. injection, lidocaine may be administered by i.v. infusion at a rate of 1 to 2 mg/min. (approximately 15 to 30 μg/kg/min in the average 70 kg patient) in those patients in whom the arrhythmia tends to recur, and who are incapable of receiving oral antiarrhythmic therapy.

I.V. lidocaine infusions must be administered under constant ECG and blood pressure monitoring, and with meticulous regulation of infusion rate, in order to avoid potential overdosage and toxicity.

I.V. infusions should be terminated as soon as the patient's basic cardiac rhythm appears to be stable or at the earliest signs of toxicity. It should rarely be necessary to continue i.v. infusion beyond 24 hours. As soon as possible, and when indicated, patients should be changed to an oral antiarrhythmic agent for maintenance therapy.

Solutions for i.v. infusion may be prepared by the addition of 1 g of lidocaine (i.e., contents of 50 mL single use vial, or contents of 5 mL disposable additive unit) to 1 L of an appropriate infusion solution. Approximately a 0.1% solution will result from this procedure; that is, each mL will contain approximately 1 mg of lidocaine.

In those cases in which fluid restriction is medically desirable a more concentrated solution may be prepared. A solution of approximately 0.2% can be prepared by adding 1 g of lidocaine (i.e., contents of 50 mL single use vial, or contents of 5 mL disposable additive unit) to 500 mL of diluent. The resulting 0.2% solution will contain 2 mg/mL of lidocaine.

Solutions should be prepared using aseptic technique. As with all i.v. admixtures, dilution should be made just prior to administration. Prepared solutions should be used within 24 hours.

Supplied: I.V. Injection: Each mL of 2% solution contains: lidocaine HCl 20 mg, thus 2.5 to 5 mL will provide 50 to 100 mg. Nonmedicinal ingredients: sodium chloride, sodium hydroxide and/or hydrochloric acid to adjust to pH 5.0 to 7.0 and water for injection. Preservative-free. Single use vials or prefilled syringes of 5 mL (100 mg). Discard unused portion.

I.V. Infusion: 2%: Each mL of 2% solution contains: lidocaine HCl 20 mg. Nonmedicinal ingredients: sodium chloride, sodium hydroxide and/or hydrochloric acid to adjust pH to 5.0 to 7.0 and water for injection. 5% dextrose in water is the preferred diluent. Preservative-free. 1 g additive solution in 50 mL single use vials. Discard unused portion.

20%: Each mL of 20% solution contains: lidocaine HCl 200 mg. Nonmedicinal ingredients: sodium hydroxide and/or hydrochloric acid to adjust pH to 5.0 to 7.0 and water for injection. 5% dextrose in water is the preferred diluent. 1 g additive unit in 5 mL prefilled single use syringes. Preservative-free. Discard unused portion.

Store at room temperature 15 to 30°C.

Reviewed 1998

Y

YELLOW FEVER VACCINE
Connaught
Live 17D Virus
Vaccine

Pharmacology: The administration of this vaccine stimulates the development of active immunity against Yellow Fever which probably lasts for many years.

Indications: For all persons 6 months of age or older who are traveling to countries which require a certificate of vaccination against Yellow Fever. Under the International Health Regulations the validity period of the certificate of vaccination or revaccination is 10 years beginning 10 days after vaccination.

Contraindications: *Pregnancy* and Children: Pregnant women and children under 6 months of age should not be vaccinated, except in high risk areas.

Since the virus of yellow fever is cultured in chicken embryos, it should not be administered to an individual with a history of hypersensitivity to egg or chicken protein.

Altered Immune States: Yellow Fever Vaccine virus infection might be potentiated by severe underlying diseases such as leukemia, lymphoma or generalized malignancy, and by lowered resistance, such as from therapy with steroids, alkylating drugs, antimetabolites or radiation or from gamma globulin deficiency. Vaccination of these individuals should therefore be avoided.

Precautions: Since the virus of yellow fever is cultured in chicken embryos, it should not be administered to an individual with a history of hypersensitivity to egg or chicken protein unless an intracutaneous skin test with 0.02 ml of the vaccine has been performed. A separate but comparable skin site is injected intracutaneously with 0.02 mL of normal saline to serve as a control. A positive sensitivity test, consisting of an urticarial wheal, with or without pseudopods, surrounded by a halo of erythema, should contraindicate administration of Yellow Fever Vaccine. This is in contradistinction to a negative or minimal reaction, with no wheal or pseudopods, at the saline injection site. Epinephrine Injection (1:1 000), a tourniquet and a hypodermic syringe with needle should be at hand while performing the sensitivity test. An intracutaneous dose of 0.02 mL administered for hypersensitivity testing may be sufficient to induce immunity. However, in hypersensitive individuals, the presence of specific protective antibodies in serum obtained 3 to 4 weeks after inoculation **must** be confirmed or evaluated.

Generally, Yellow Fever Vaccine should be administered at least 1 month apart from other live virus vaccines. However, field observations and clinical data indicate that simultaneous administration of the most widely used live-virus vaccines has not resulted in impaired antibody response or increased adverse reactions. Thus, if time is a critical factor for required vaccinations, the clinical judgment of the responsible physician should prevail at all times. A recently completed prospective study of persons given yellow fever vaccine and 5 mL of commercially available immune globulin revealed no alteration of the immunologic response to yellow fever vaccine when compared to controls.

Vaccination with Yellow Fever Vaccine should be deferred for 3 months following blood or plasma transfusion.

A separate sterile syringe and needle should be used for each individual patient to prevent transmission of hepatitis or other infectious agents from one person to another.

Adverse Effects: Approximately 10% of patients may develop fever or malaise 7 to 14 days following immunization. Symptoms may last from a few hours to a day or two. Treatment should be symptomatic.

In rare instances encephalitis has developed in very young infants. This has usually not been severe and recovery has ordinarily occurred without sequelae. One death has been reported.

Anaphylaxis and/or anaphylactoid shock may occur following the use of this vaccine, even in individuals with no prior history of hypersensitivity to any vaccine components. Therefore Epinephrine Injection (1:1 000) must always be immediately available to combat such serious reactions.

Dosage: A single immunizing dose of 0.5 mL should be administered s.c. Children receive the same dose as adults.
Administration: Reconstitute the vaccine immediately after removing it from the freezer and use only the diluent supplied for this purpose. Draw the volume of the diluent shown on the diluent label into a suitable size syringe and inject into the vial containing the vaccine. Slowly add diluent to vaccine, let set for 1 to 2 minutes and then carefully swirl mixture until a uniform suspension is achieved. Avoid vigorous shaking as this tends to cause foaming of the suspension. Use the vaccine within 60 minutes following reconstitution and **swirl the vaccine well immediately before withdrawing each dose.**

All rehydrated vaccine and containers which remain unused after 1 hour must be sterilized and discarded.

Note: It is most desirable that extraordinary reactions which may occur concomitantly or following various vaccinations be reported to the manufacturer and to the epidemiologist of the province using a special form placed at your disposal by the Department of National Health and Welfare.

Supplied: Yellow Fever Vaccine is a living dried culture of the attenuated 17D strain of Yellow Fever virus. It is cultured in living leukosis-free chicken embryos and is free of avian leukosis viruses. The vaccine containing sorbitol and gelatin as a stabilizer, is lyophilized and hermetically sealed under nitrogen in glass vials. The vaccine must be reconstituted immediately before use with the proper diluent. Sodium Chloride Injection which is provided. Yellow Fever Vaccine complies with the standards of the World Health Organization. Each 0.5 mL dose contains not less than 5.04 $\log_{10}$ PFU. The product appears slightly opalescent and light orange in color after reconstitution. Neither the vaccine nor the diluent contain a preservative. Vials of 5 doses with vials of diluent.

Yellow Fever Vaccine is shipped in a container with solid carbon dioxide; do not use vaccine unless shipping case contains some dry ice on arrival. Vaccine must be maintained continuously at temperatures between 5 and −30°C; whenever possible, it should be kept frozen at a temperature below 0° until reconstituted for use. The vial of diluent should not be allowed to freeze.

The reconstituted vaccine must be kept cool and used within 60 minutes following reconstitution.

YOCON® Ⓟ
Glenwood
Yohimbine HCl
Sympatholytic

Indications: As an alpha-adrenergic blocking agent.

Contraindications: Renal or hepatic insufficiency.

Precautions: Yohimbine may cause hypotension. It should not be administered to geriatric patients, psychiatric patients or cardiorenal patients with a history of gastric or duodenal ulcer.

Overdose: Treatment: Conduct gastric lavage and administer activated charcoal (4 tablespoonfuls: 500 mL of water). Treat excitation or convulsions with a barbiturate.

Dosage: Adults: 1 tablet up to 3 times daily or as directed by a physician.

Supplied: Each white, uncoated, spherical tablet contains: yohimbine HCl 5.4 mg. Nonmedicinal ingredients: colloidal silicon dioxide NF, dibasic calcium phosphate dihydrate USP, magnesium stearate NF, microcrystalline cellulose NF, sodium starch glycolate NF, stearic acid NF and talc USP. Bottles of 100 and 1 000.

(Shown in Product Recognition Section)

YOHIMBINE Ⓟ
Odan
Sympatholytic

Pharmacology: Yohimbine blocks presynaptic alpha-2 adrenergic receptors. Its action on peripheral blood vessels resembles that of reserpine, though it is weaker and of short duration. Yohimbine's peripheral autonomic nervous system effect is to increase parasympathetic (cholinergic) and decrease sympathetic (adrenergic) activity. Yohimbine exerts a stimulating action on the mood and may increase anxiety. Such actions have not been adequately studied or related to dosage although they appear to require high doses of the drug. Yohimbine has a mild antidiuretic action, probably via stimulation of hypothalamic centres and release of posterior pituitary hormone. Reportedly, yohimbine exerts no significant influence on cardiac stimulation and other effects mediated by β-adrenergic receptors, its effect on blood pressure, if any, would be to lower it; however, no adequate studies are at hand to quantitate this effect in terms of yohimbine dosage.

Yohimbine is a 3α-15α-20β-17α-hydroxy yohimbine-16α-carboxylic acid methyl ester. The alkaloid is found in Rubaceae and related trees. Also in Rauwolfia Serpentina (L) Benth. Yohimbine is an indolalkylamine alkaloid with chemical similarity to reserpine.

Indications: As an alpha-adrenergic blocking agent.

Contraindications: Renal diseases, and patients sensitive to the drug or its components. In view of the limited and inadequate information at hand, no precise tabulation can be offered of additional contraindications.

Warnings: Generally, this drug is not proposed for use in females and certainly must not be used during pregnancy. Neither is this drug proposed for use in pediatric, geriatric or cardio-renal patients with gastric or duodenal ulcer history. Nor should it be used in conjunction with mood-modifying drugs such as antidepressants, or in psychiatric patients in general.

Adverse Effects: Yohimbine readily penetrates the CNS and produces a complex pattern of responses in lower doses than required to produce peripheral α-adrenergic blockade. These include, antidiuresis, a general picture of central excitation including elevation of blood pressure and heart rate increased motor activity, irritability and tremor. Sweating, nausea and vomiting are common after parenteral administration of the drug. Also dizziness, headache, skin flushing reported when used orally.

Dosage: As directed by physician.
2 mg: Adult dose male: 1 to 2 tablets 3 times a day. Occasional side effects reported with this dosage are nausea, dizziness or nervousness. In the event of side effects, dosage is to be reduced to 1/2 dosage 3 times a day or as directed by physician.
5.4 mg: Adult dose male: 1 tablet 3 times a day. Occasional side effects reported with this dosage are nausea, dizziness or nervousness. In the event of side effects, dosage is to be reduced to 1/2 tablet 3 times a day or a directed by physician

Supplied: 2 mg: Each round, powder blue, uncoated, scored, embossed tablet, engraved 0-2.0 mg contains: yohimbine HCl 2 mg. Nonmedicinal ingredients: cellulose, FD&C Blue #1, magnesium stearate and sodium starch glycolate. Gluten-, lactose- and tartrazine-free. Amber glass bottles of 100 and 500.

5.4 mg: Each oval, pink, uncoated, scored, embossed tablet, engraved 0-5.4 mg contains: yohimbine HCl 5.4 mg. Nonmedicinal ingredients: cellulose, FD&C Red #3, magnesium stearate and sodium starch glycolate. Gluten-, lactose- and tartrazine-free. Amber glass bottles of 100 and 500.

YOHIMBINE Ⓟ
Rougier
Sympatholytic

Indications: As an alpha-adrenergic blocking agent.

Contraindications: Cardiac or renal disease.

Precautions: Yohimbine may cause hypotension. It should not be administered to geriatric patients, psychiatric patients or cardiorenal patients with a history of gastric or duodenal ulcer.

Overdose: Symptoms and Treatment: Conduct gastric lavage and administer activated charcoal (4 tablespoonfuls/500 mL of water). Treat excitation or convulsions with a barbiturate.

Dosage: Adults: 6 to 18 mg daily.

Supplied: Each pink, uncoated, scored tablet identified with the Rougier logo contains: yohimbine HCl 6 mg equivalent to yohimbine base 5.4 mg. Bottles of 100 and 500.

YOHIMBINE Ⓟ
Tanta
Sympatholytic

Indications: As an alpha-adrenergic blocking agent.

Contraindications: Renal or hepatic insufficiency.

Supplied: Each white, uncoated, round tablet contains: yohimbine HCl 5.4 mg. Bottles of 100.

YOHIMBINE ℞

Welcker-Lyster

Sympatholytic

Indications: As an alpha-adrenergic blocking agent.

Contraindications: Cardiac or renal disease.

Precautions: Yohimbine may cause hypotension. It should not be administered to geriatric patients, psychiatric patients or cardiorenal patients with a history of gastric or duodenal ulcer.

Overdose: Symptoms and Treatment: Conduct gastric lavage and administer activated charcoal (4 tablespoonfuls/500 mL of water). Treat excitation or convulsions with a barbiturate.

Dosage: Adults: 6 to 18 mg daily.

Supplied: Each pale pink, uncoated, spherical granule contains: yohimbine HCl 2 mg. Bottles of 100 and 500.

YUTOPAR® ℞

Bristol

Ritodrine HCl

Uterine Relaxing Agent

Pharmacology: Ritodrine is a beta-receptor agonist, which has been shown by in vitro and vivo pharmacologic studies in animals to exert a preferential effect on the adrenergic receptors such as those in the uterine smooth muscle. Stimulation of the receptors inhibits contractility of the uterine smooth muscle. Beta-adrenergic stimulation in other body systems may lead to some cardiovascular or metabolic effects.

Indications: For management of preterm labor in suitable patients with more than 20 weeks of gestation who have intact amniotic membranes, cervical dilatation up to 4 cm, and less than 80% cervical effacement. In cases involving ruptured amniotic membranes or more advanced labor, inhibition of labor is less likely and the benefits of treatment must be carefully weighed against the potential risks; contraindications, warnings and precautions must be closely observed.

Contraindications: Before the 20th week of pregnancy. In those conditions of the mother or fetus in which continuation of pregnancy is hazardous; specific contraindications include: antepartum hemorrhage which demands immediate delivery; eclampsia and severe preeclampsia; intra-uterine fetal death; chorioamnionitis; maternal cardiac disease; pulmonary hypertension; maternal hyperthyroidism; uncontrolled maternal diabetes mellitus (see Precautions); pre-existing maternal medical conditions that would be seriously affected by the known pharmacologic properties of a betamimetic drug, such as: hypovolemia, cardiac arrhythmias associated with tachycardia or digitalis intoxication, uncontrolled hypertension, pheochromocytoma, bronchial asthma already treated by betamimetics and/or steroids; known hypersensitivity to any component of the product; parenteral ritodrine: history of hypersensitivity to sulfite; asthma patients may react with bronchospasm and anaphylactic shock.

Warnings: The occurrence of pulmonary edema in conjunction with the use of ritodrine has been reported, in several cases with a fatal result. The underlying cause was almost certainly multifactorial. Predisposing factors that have been identified include pre-existing cardiac disease, multiple pregnancy, preeclampsia and eclampsia, fluid overload, concomitant corticosteroid treatment, maternal infection, and prolonged tachycardia. Patients must be closely monitored in hospital. The patient's state of hydration should be carefully monitored; fluid overload must be avoided (see Dosage). If pulmonary edema develops during administration, the drug should be discontinued. Edema should be managed by conventional means.

Parenteral administration should be supervised by persons having knowledge of the pharmacology of the drug and who are qualified to identify and manage complications of drug administration and pregnancy. Careful screening of patients with potential cardiac risk and cardiac abnormalities is recommended. These patients should not be treated with ritodrine unless the physician considers that the benefits clearly outweigh the risks. **Because cardiovascular responses are common and more pronounced during parenteral administration, cardiovascular effects, including maternal pulse rate and blood pressure and fetal heart rate, should be closely monitored. Care should be exercised for maternal signs and symptoms of pulmonary edema. A persistent high tachycardia (over 140 beats/minute) may be one of the signs of impending pulmonary edema with drugs of this class. Occult cardiac disease may be unmasked with its use. If the patient complains of chest pain or tightness of chest, the drug should be temporarily discontinued and an ECG should be done as soon as possible.**

Prolonged treatment with i.v. ritodrine (see Adverse Effects and Dosage, I.V. Therapy) is not recommended. I.V. treatment for 2 to 3 weeks or more may lead to leukopenia and/or agranulocytosis, with a complete recovery after discontinuation of treatment.

The drug should not be administered to patients with mild to moderate preeclampsia, hypertension, or diabetes unless the attending physician considers that the benefits clearly outweigh the risks.

The benefit of this product for management of preterm labor in patients with premature rupture of the fetal membranes has not been established. In such cases a delay of delivery is associated with high risks of infection and chorioamnionitis.

Precautions: Positive diagnosis of preterm labor is essential.

Among low birth weight infants, approximately 9% may be growth retarded for gestational age. Therefore, Intra-Uterine Growth Retardation (IUGR) should be considered in the differential diagnosis of preterm labor; this is especially important when the gestational age is in doubt. The decision to continue or re-initiate ritodrine administration will depend on an assessment of fetal maturity. In addition to clinical parameters, studies such as sonography or amniocentesis may be helpful in establishing the state of fetal maturity if it is in doubt.

Metabolic effects are generally adequately compensated in non-diabetic patients, although a case of acidosis in an apparently normal patient receiving ritodrine and hydrocortisone has been reported. In diabetic patients, however, compensatory mechanisms are impaired or absent; severe hyperglycemia and acidosis may ensue presenting risk for both mother and fetus. To prevent deterioration of diabetic control during Yutopar therapy, careful monitoring of blood glucose, potassium and acid-base status is essential. High doses of insulin, preferably administered by continuous infusion, potassium supplementation and, in some cases, dextrose have been recommended and may be necessary for optimal diabetic control during ritodrine infusion. The hyperglycemic effects of corticosteroids used to promote fetal lung maturity are probably additive and may significantly aggravate diabetic decompensation. If possible, diabetic patients should be treated in a unit specializing in the management of diabetic pregnancy.

Laboratory Tests: Because parenteral administration has been shown to elevate plasma insulin and glucose and to decrease plasma potassium and standard bicarbonate concentrations, monitoring of glucose, electrolytes and acid-base balance is recommended during protracted infusions of healthy patients. Special attention should be paid to biochemical variables when treating diabetic patients and those receiving concomitant corticosteroids or potassium-depleting diuretics. In diabetics, frequent monitoring of blood glucose, potassium, and acid-base balance is necessary; tests for glucosuria and ketonuria may be useful. Patients receiving concomitant corticosteroids should be monitored as for the diabetics, but with additional fluid balance monitoring. Serum electrolytes, particularly potassium, should be frequently assessed in patients receiving diuretics.

Liver function and serum glucose and electrolytes as well as blood count determinations should be performed during therapy. Patients should be closely observed during administration of ritodrine and for several days thereafter in order to quickly undertake corrective measures if abnormalities are detected.

Drug Interactions: Corticosteroids used concomitantly may lead to pulmonary edema (see Warnings). The effects of other sympathomimetic amines may be potentiated when concurrently administered and these effects may be additive. A sufficient time interval should elapse prior to administration of another sympathomimetic drug. With either oral or i.v. administration, 90% of the excretion of the drug is completed within 24 hours after the dose.

Beta-adrenergic blocking drugs inhibit its action; coadministration of these drugs should, therefore, be avoided.

With anesthetics used in surgery, the possibility that hypotensive effects may be potentiated should be considered.

Outcome of *Pregnancy* and Neonates: There are no adequate and well controlled studies of effects in pregnant women before 20 weeks gestation; therefore, this drug should not be used before the 20th week of pregnancy. Studies in pregnant women from the 20th week of gestation onwards have not shown increased risk of fetal abnormalities. Follow-up of selected variables in a small number of children for up to 2 years has not revealed harmful effects on growth, developmental or functional maturation. Nonetheless, although clinical studies did not indicate a risk of permanent adverse fetal effects from ritodrine, the possibility cannot be excluded; therefore, it should be used only when clearly indicated.

Some studies indicate that infants born before 36 weeks' gestation make up less than 10% of all births but account for as many as 75% of perinatal deaths and one-half of all neurologically handicapped infants. There are data available indicating that infants born at any time prior to full-term may manifest a higher incidence of neurologic or other handicaps than occurs in the total population of infants born at or after full-term. In delaying or preventing preterm labor, the use of ritodrine results in an overall increase in neonatal survival. Handicapped infants who might not have otherwise survived may survive.

Experiments in animals have revealed no teratogenic properties of ritodrine hydrochloride even in high dosage throughout gestation.

Adverse Effects: Unwanted effects are related to its betamimetic activity and usually are controlled by suitable dosage adjustment. Some sensitivity reactions may be observed during prolonged oral therapy.

Effects Associated with I.V. Administration: Usual Effects (80 to 100% of patients): I.V. infusion leads almost invariably to dose-related alterations in maternal and fetal heart rates and in maternal blood pressure. During clinical studies in which the maximum infusion rate was limited to 0.35 mg/min (one patient received 0.40 mg/min), the maximum maternal and fetal heart rates averaged, respectively, 130 (range 60 to 180) and 164 (range 130 to 200) beats/minute. The maximum maternal systolic blood pressures averaged 128 mm Hg (range 96 to 162 mm Hg), an average increase of 12 mm Hg from pretreatment levels. The minimum maternal diastolic blood pressures averaged 48 mm Hg (range 0 to 76 mm Hg), an average decrease of 23 mm Hg from pretreatment levels. While the more severe effects were usually managed effectively by dosage adjustments, in less than 1% of patients, persistent maternal tachycardia or decreased diastolic blood pressure required withdrawal of the drug. A persistent high tachycardia (over 140 beats per minute) may be one of the signs of impending pulmonary edema (see Warnings).

The infusion is associated with transient elevation of blood glucose and insulin, which decreased toward normal values after 48 to 72 hours despite continued infusion. Elevation of free fatty acids and c-AMP has been reported. Reduction of potassium levels should be expected; other biochemical effects have not been reported.

Frequent Effects (10 to 50% of patients): I.V. dosing, in about one-third of the patients, was associated with palpitations. Tremor, nausea, vomiting, headache, or erythema was observed in 10 to 15% of patients.

Occasional Effects (5 to 10% of patients): Nervousness, jitteriness, restlessness, emotional upset, or anxiety was reported in 5 to 6% of patients and malaise in similar numbers.

Infrequent effects (1 to 3% of patients): Cardiac symptoms including chest pain or tightness (rarely associated with abnormalities of ECG) or arrhythmia were reported in 1 to 2% of patients. Other infrequently reported maternal effects included: anaphylactic shock, rash, heart murmur, epigastric distress, ileus, bloating, constipation, diarrhea, dyspnea, hyperventilation, hemolytic icterus, glycosuria, lactic acidosis, sweating, chills, drowsiness, and weakness. Impaired liver function (i.e., increased transaminase levels and hepatitis) have also been reported infrequently with the use of ritodrine and other beta-sympathicomimetics. Most of the adverse signs and symptoms are reversible, when ritodrine is discontinued. A few cases of leukopenia have been reported in patients receiving prolonged i.v. ritodrine treatment. The leukocyte counts returned to normal after discontinuation of treatment.

Neonatal Effects: Infrequently reported neonatal symptoms include hypoglycemia and ileus. In addition, hypocalcemia and hypotension have been reported in neonates whose mothers were treated with other betamimetic agents.

Effects Associated with Oral Administration: Frequent effects (10 to 50% of patients): Oral dosing in clinical studies was often associated with small increases in maternal heart rate, but little or no effect upon either maternal systolic or diastolic blood pressure or upon fetal heart rate was found.

Oral ritodrine in 10 to 15% of patients was associated with palpitations or tremor. Nausea and jitteriness were less frequent (5 to 8%), while rash was observed in some patients (3 to 4%), and arrhythmia was infrequent (about 1%).

Overdose: Symptoms and Treatment: The symptoms of overdosage are those of excessive beta-adrenergic stimulation including exaggeration of the known pharmacologic effects, the most prominent being tachycardia (maternal and fetal), palpitation, cardiac arrhythmia, hypotension, dyspnea, nervousness, tremor, nausea, and vomiting. If an excess of ritodrine tablets is ingested, gastric lavage or induction of emesis should be carried out followed by administration of activated charcoal. When symptoms of overdose occur as a result of parenteral administration, ritodrine should be discontinued; an appropriate beta-blocking agent may be used as an antidote. Ritodrine is dialyzable.

Dosage: In the management of preterm labor, the initial i.v. treatment should usually be followed by oral administration. The optimum dose is determined by a clinical balance of uterine response and unwanted effects.

I.V.: Do not use i.v. if the solution is discolored or contains any precipitate or particulate matter.

Diluted solution should be used promptly after preparation, but in no case after 48 hours of preparation.

To minimize the risks of hypotension, the patient should be maintained in the left lateral position during infusion and careful attention given to her state of hydration; fluid overload must be avoided.

For appropriate control and dose titration, a controlled infusion device is recommended to adjust the rate of flow in drops/minute. An i.v. microdrip chamber (60 drops/mL) can provide a convenient range of infusion rates within the recommended dosage range.

Recommended Dilution: The volume of fluid administered should be kept to a minimum. With a syringe pump the concentration of the drug infused is 3 mg/mL (150 mg ritodrine hydrochloride solution in 50 mL fluid). If a syringe pump is not available the concentration should be 0.3 mg/mL (150 mg ritodrine hydrochloride (3 ampuls) in 500 mL fluid. Ritodrine should be diluted with one of the following: 0.9% w/v sodium chloride solution, 5% w/v dextrose solution, 10% w/v dextran 40 in 0.9% w/v sodium chloride solution, 10% w/v invert sugar solution, compound sodium chloride solution (Ringer's solution), Hartmann's solution.

Saline diluents should be reserved for cases where dextrose solution is medically undesirable, for example, diabetes mellitus, due to an increased probability of pulmonary edema.

I.V. therapy should be started as soon as possible after diagnosis. The usual initial dose is 0.1 mg/minute (0.33 mL/min, 20 drops/min using a microdrip chamber at the recommended dilution), to be gradually increased according to the results by 0.05 mg/minute (0.17 mL/min, 10 drops/min using a microdrip chamber at the recommended dilution) every 10 minutes until the desired result is attained or labor progresses despite treatment at the maximum dose. The effective dosage usually lies between 0.15 and 0.35 mg/minute (0.50 to 1.17 mL/min, 30 to 70 drops/min using a microdrip chamber at the recommended dilution). The infusion should generally be continued for at least 12 and no more than 48 hours after uterine contractions cease. With the recommended dilution, the maximum volume of fluid that might be administered after 12 hours at the highest dose (0.35 mg/min) will be approximately 840 mL. **The amount of i.v. fluids administered and the rate of administration should be monitored to avoid circulatory fluid overload (over-hydration)** (see Precautions, Laboratory Tests). Frequent monitoring of maternal uterine contractions, heart rate, and blood pressure, and of fetal heart rate is required, with dosage individually titrated according to response.

Oral Maintenance: 10 mg may be given approximately 30 minutes before the termination of i.v. therapy. The usual dosage schedule for the first 24 hours of oral administration is 10 mg every 2 hours. Thereafter the usual maintenance dose is 10 to 20 mg every 4 to 6 hours, the dose depending on uterine activity and unwanted effects. The total daily dose of oral ritodrine should not exceed 120 mg. The treatment may be continued as long as the physician considers it desirable to prolong pregnancy.

Recurrence of unwanted preterm labor may be treated with repeated parenteral administration of ritodrine.

Supplied: Injection: Each ampul of clear, colorless, sterile aqueous solution contains: ritodrine hydrochloride 50 mg (10 mg/mL). pH 5.0 to 5.5. Nonmedicinal ingredients: acetic acid, sodium chloride, sodium hydroxide, sodium metabisulphite and water for injection. Sodium hydroxide and hydrochloric acid for pH adjustment. Ampuls of 5 mL, boxes of 10.

Tablets: Each round, yellow tablet, inscribed YUTOPAR on one side and scored on the other, contains: ritodrine hydrochloride 10 mg. Nonmedicinal ingredients: cornstarch, lactose, magnesium stearate, povidone, talc and yellow iron oxide. Bottles of 50.

Store at room temperature, preferably below 30°C. Protect from excessive heat.

Z

ZADITEN® Ⓟ

Novartis Pharmaceuticals

Ketotifen Fumarate

Pediatric Asthma Prophylactic—Antiallergic Agent

Pharmacology: Ketotifen is a nonbronchodilator antiasthmatic drug which inhibits the effects of certain endogenous substances known to be inflammatory mediators, and thereby exerts antiallergic activity. Preclinical studies indicated that ketotifen's anti-H_1 effect seems to be distinct from its antiallergic properties.

The effectiveness of ketotifen in the chronic management of mild atopic pediatric asthma has been shown in clinical trials. Continued use of ketotifen results in a partial reduction in the frequency, severity and duration of asthma symptoms and attacks, and may lead to the reduction in the daily requirements of concomitant antiasthmatic medication such as theophyllines and β_2-agonists, without the deterioration in pulmonary function (FEV_1, FVC and PEFR). Clinical improvements have been observed in some cases within the first weeks of treatment and generally reach statistical significance after ten weeks. Ketotifen may have an anti-inflammatory effect in the lungs and the time of onset of clinical efficacy may reflect the recovery period of the lungs from inflammation.

Pharmacological studies have revealed a number of properties of ketotifen which may contribute to its antiallergic activity and its ability to affect the underlying pathology of asthma:

In Vivo Results: Inhibition of the development of airway hyperreactivity associated with activation of platelets by PAF (Platelet Activating Factor) or caused by neural activation following the use of sympathomimetic drugs or the exposure to allergen; inhibition of PAF-induced accumulation of eosinophils and platelets in the airways; suppression of the priming of eosinophils by human recombinant cytokines and thereby suppression of the influx of eosinophils into inflammatory loci; antagonism of bronchoconstriction due to leukotrienes.

In Vitro Results: Inhibition of the release of allergic mediators such as histamine, leukotrienes C_4 and D_4 (SRS-A) and PAF.

In addition, ketotifen is a potent antiallergic substance possessing a powerful and sustained noncompetitive histamine (H_1) blocking property.

In humans, the absorption of ketotifen from an oral administration was demonstrated to be at least 60%, and possibly even greater. The rate of absorption of ketotifen in humans was assessed as rather rapid, since the plasma concentration reached its maximum 3 hours after oral administration; the absorption half-life was calculated to be 1 hour. Bioavailability amounts to approximately 50% due to a large first pass effect. Maximum plasma concentrations are reached within 2 to 4 hours. The percentage of protein binding in humans is 75% and is also concentration-independent. Ketotifen is eliminated biphasically; there are two disposition half-lives of 3 to 5 hours and 21 hours for distribution and disappearance phases respectively. Within 48 hours, urinary excretion amounts to 1% as unchanged drug and 60 to 70% as metabolites. The main metabolite in the urine is the inactive ketotifen-N-glucuronide. The bioavailability of the various forms of ketotifen is not influenced by the intake of food.

The pattern of metabolism in children is the same as in adults, but the clearance is higher in children. Children over the age of 3 years therefore require the same daily dosage regimen as adults. In infants aged less than 3 years, however, the dosage must be adjusted, since the mean levels of the drug in infants are higher than those found in children, when the same dose is given.

Indications: As an add-on medication in the chronic treatment of mild atopic asthmatic children.

Ketotifen is a prophylactic agent to be used on a continuous basis and is not effective in the acute prevention or treatment of acute asthma attacks. Continuous use of ketotifen may reduce the frequency, severity and duration of asthmatic symptoms or attacks, and lead to a reduction in daily requirements of concomitant antiasthmatic medication, like theophyllines and β_2-agonists.

Several weeks of ketotifen therapy may be necessary before the therapeutic effect becomes clinically evident. Full clinical effectiveness is generally reached after 10 weeks of treatment. Ketotifen may have an anti-inflammatory effect in the lungs and the time of onset of clinical efficacy may reflect the recovery period of the lungs from inflammation. It is therefore recommended that for patients not adequately responding within a few weeks, treatment with ketotifen should be maintained for a minimum of 2 to 3 months. If it is necessary to withdraw ketotifen, this should be done progressively over a period of 2 to 4 weeks. Symptoms of asthma may recur.

Contraindications: Hypersensitivity to ketotifen or any other components of the formulations. Patients sensitive to benzoate compounds should not take ketotifen syrup.

Precautions: General: Symptomatic and prophylactic antiasthmatic drugs (xanthine derivatives, β_2-agonists, sodium cromoglycate, corticosteroids) already in use should not be reduced immediately when treatment with ketotifen is initiated. This applies especially to systemic corticosteroids and ACTH injections because of the possible existence of adrenocortical insufficiency in steroid-dependent patients; in such cases recovery of a normal pituitary-adrenal response to stress may take up to one year.

Occupational Hazards: Since drowsiness may occur in the early stages of therapy, patients engaging in activities requiring rapid and precise responses should be cautioned.

Drug Interactions: A reversible fall in the thrombocyte count in patients receiving ketotifen concomitantly with oral antidiabetic agents has been observed in rare cases. Thrombocyte counts should therefore be carried out in patients taking oral antidiabetic agents concomitantly.

Ketotifen may potentiate the effects of sedatives, hypnotics, antihistamines and alcohol.

Pregnancy: Although ketotifen was without effect on pregnancy and on peri- and post-natal development at dose levels which were tolerated by the mother animals, its safety in human pregnancy has not been established. Ketotifen should therefore be given to pregnant women only in compelling circumstances.

Lactation: Ketotifen is excreted in breast milk; therefore mothers receiving ketotifen should not breast-feed.

Patients with Special Diseases and Conditions: Ketotifen syrup should not be administered to patients sensitive to benzoate compounds. Ketotifen tablets are benzoate-free and can be administered alternatively to such patients.

In diabetic patients, the carbohydrate content of the syrup (5 mL: 4 g carbohydrate) should be taken into consideration.

Adverse Effects: Table I illustrates the adverse reactions which were reported in a Canadian Multicentre Trial involving 196 asthmatic children aged 5 to 17 years. This double-blind, placebo controlled study lasted 30 weeks.

Table I—Zaditen

Reported Adverse Reactions

System	Reaction	Incidence (%) Zaditen (n=75)	Incidence (%) Placebo (n=78)
CNS	sedation	8.0	9.0
	irritability	0	1.3
	headache	1.3	1.3
	dizziness	0	2.6
	fainting	0	1.3
	tingling in legs	0	1.3
	sleep disturbance	1.3	0
Gastrointestinal	diarrhea	0	2.6
	nausea	0	1.3
	vomiting	0	2.6
	weight gain	5.3	1.3
	increased appetite	1.3	0
	abdominal pain	1.3	0
Skin	rash	4.0	1.3
	urticaria	1.3	1.3
Infections	ear	1.3	2.6
	flu	2.6	1.3
	respiratory	4.0	0
	fever	0	2.6
Miscellaneous	nose bleed	1.3	0
	puffy eyelid	1.3	0
	blood in stool	0	1.3
	hypertension	0	1.3

There was a relatively low incidence of adverse reactions reported. These were similar in both the ketotifen and placebo treated groups of patients. The reports for CNS and gastrointestinal symptoms in the placebo group are side effects known to be associated with xanthine administration, which was being used concomitantly by some patients during the study.

Thrombocytopenia has been reported when ketotifen is combined with oral hypoglycemic agents (see Precautions).

Occasional, isolated, instances of elevated liver enzyme levels have been seen during clinical trials. No definite relationship to ketotifen therapy has been established.

Sedation and, rarely, dry mouth or slight dizziness may occur at the beginning of treatment, but usually disappear spontaneously with continued medication. Occasionally, symptoms of CNS stimulation, such as excitation, irritability, insomnia and nervousness have been observed, particularly in children. Weight gain has also been reported.

Cystitis has been rarely described in association with ketotifen. Isolated cases of severe skin reactions (erythema multiforme, Stevens Johnson syndrome), have been reported, the occurrence being approximately 1 case in 2 million patients exposed to ketotifen.

Overdose: Symptoms and Treatment: Overdosages with up to 120 mg ketotifen have been reported. The main symptoms of acute overdosage include: drowsiness to severe sedation; confusion and disorientation; tachycardia and hypotension; convulsions, especially in children; hyperexcitability in children; reversible coma. Treatment should be symptomatic. If ingestion is very recent, emptying of the stomach may be considered. Administration of activated charcoal may be beneficial. If necessary, specific or symptomatic treatment and monitoring of the cardiovascular system and physostigmine for anticholinergic effects are recommended; if excitation or convulsions are present, short-acting barbiturates or benzodiazepines may be given.

Dosage: Children older than 3 years of age: The drug should be given at a dose of 1 mg twice daily, in the morning and evening; 6 months to 3 years: 0.05 mg (0.25 mL of syrup) per kg of body weight given twice daily, in the morning and evening.

To minimize the initial sedation with ketotifen, a slow increase in dosage is recommended during the first week of treatment commencing with one half the daily recommended dosage given in 2 divided doses or in a single dose given in the evening, followed within 5 days, by an increase to the full therapeutic dose.

Concomitant Therapy: Existing asthma therapy should be maintained. A progressive reduction in dosage of other asthma drugs, where clinically indicated, should be attempted only after 6 to 12 weeks of ketotifen therapy.

Reduction of Corticosteroids: It is not fully established, but some patients may be able to reduce corticosteroids.

The reduction in the daily maintenance dosage of steroids should be stepwise according to the recommended methods. The gradual reduction should be continued until either the patient cannot tolerate a further reduction, or it is found possible to withdraw corticosteroids completely.

If troublesome symptoms recur during the period of reduction, the daily dose of corticosteroids should be raised immediately. A larger increase in the steroid dose may be essential at times, as a temporary measure, to control a severe relapse induced by antigen challenge, infection or stress. (The increased physical or mental activity resulting from subjective improvement can also constitute a stress.) When symptoms are brought under control, a progressive reduction may be attempted as before.

Any reduction should be gradual while maintaining close surveillance and frequent examination of the patient. The ability of these patients to react to stress is usually impaired. Acute adrenal insufficiency and severe asthma can be precipitated by an increase in stress and/or reduction of either steroid or ACTH therapy. It is advisable to assess adrenal and pituitary function before reducing steroid dosage in patients who have received long-term therapy.

Method of Withdrawing ACTH: The same principles as discussed above.

Information for the Patient: See Blue Section—Information for the Patient "Zaditen".

Supplied: Syrup: Each 5 mL of strawberry-flavored syrup contains: ketotifen fumarate 1 mg. Nonmedicinal ingredients: alcohol, citric acid, methyl-p-hydroxybenzoate, propyl-p-hydroxybenzoate, sodium phosphate, sorbitol solution, strawberry flavor, sucrose and water. Bottles of 250 mL. To be administered orally. Store at temperatures not exceeding 25°C.

Tablets: Each scored white tablet embossed with the name "ZADITEN" contains: ketotifen fumarate 1 mg. Tablets are to be swallowed. Nonmedicinal ingredients: calcium hydrogen

Zaditen (cont'd)

phosphate, magnesium stearate and maize starch. Packs of 56 tablets containing 4 blister strips of 14 tablets each. Store at temperatures not exceeding 25°C, in a dry place.

(Shown in Product Recognition Section)

Reviewed 1997

ZANOSAR®

Pharmacia & Upjohn

Streptozocin

Antineoplastic Agent

Pharmacology: Streptozocin inhibits DNA synthesis in bacterial and mammalian cells. In bacterial cells, a specific interaction with cytosine moieties leads to degradation of DNA. The biochemical mechanism leading to mammalian cell death has not been definitively established; levels required to kill cells are considerably lower than those required to inhibit DNA synthesis or several of the enzymes involved in DNA synthesis. Streptozocin inhibits the progression of cells into mitosis but the agent does not apear to be specifically lethal to cells in a single phase of the cell cycle.

It is active in the L1210 leukemic mouse over a fairly wide range of parenteral dosage schedules. In many experimental animal species, streptozocin induces a diabetes that resembles human hyperglycemic nonketotic diabetes mellitus. This phenomenon, which has been extensively studied, is consequent upon histopathologic alteration of pancreatic islet beta cells.

The metabolism of streptozocin has not been fully studied. When given i.v. to mice or dogs, it disappears from the blood very rapidly. In all species tested, it concentrates in the liver and kidney. Less than 10% of the drug (or metabolites containing an N-nitrosourea group) is excreted by the kidney. Metabolic products have not been identified.

Indications: For the treatment of metastatic islet cell carcinoma of the pancreas. Responses have been obtained with both functional and nonfunctional carcinomas. Because of its inherent renal toxicity, therapy with this drug should be limited to patients with symptomatic or progressive metastatic disease.

Contraindications: In patients with known hypersensitivity to the drug.

Pre-existing renal disease is a strong contraindication to its use. Use of the drug in such a patient must be judged by the physician in terms of the potential benefit as opposed to the known risk.

Warnings: Streptozocin should be administered under the supervision of a physician experienced in the use of cancer chemotherapeutic agents (see Precautions). Renal, hepatic and hematologic evaluations should be done at regular intervals. Renal toxicity is dose related and cumulative and may be fatal.

Renal Toxicity: Many patients treated with streptozocin have experienced renal toxicity as evidenced by azotemia, anuria, hypophosphatemia, glycosuria and renal tubular acidosis. Such toxicity is dose-related and cumulative and may be severe or fatal. Renal function must be monitored before and after each course of therapy. Serial urinalysis, blood urea nitrogen, plasma creatinine, serum electrolytes and creatinine clearance should be obtained prior to, at least weekly during, and for 4 weeks after drug administration. Serial urinalysis is particularly important for the early detection of proteinuria and should be quantitated with a 24 hour collection when proteinuria is detected. Mild proteinuria is one of the first signs of renal toxicity and may herald further deterioration of renal function. Reduction of the dose or discontinuation of treatment is suggested in the presence of significant renal toxicity.

This drug should not be used in combination with or concomitantly with other potential nephrotoxins.

During therapy, a patient need not be hospitalized but should have access to a facility with laboratory and supportive resources sufficient to monitor drug tolerance and to protect and maintain a patient compromised by drug toxicity.

Other toxicities are nausea and vomiting, which may be severe and at times treatment-limiting. In addition, liver dysfunction, diarrhea, and hematological changes have been observed in some patients.

Mutagenesis, Carcinogenesis, Impairment of Fertility: Streptozocin is mutagenic in bacteria, plants and mammalian cells. When administered parenterally, it has been shown to induce renal tumors in rats and to induce liver tumors and other tumors in hamsters. Stomach and pancreatic tumors were observed in rats treated orally with streptozocin. Streptozocin has also been shown to be carcinogenic in mice.

Streptozocin adversely affected fertility when administered to male and female rats.

When exposed dermally, some rats developed benign tumors at the site of application of streptozocin. Consequently, streptozocin may pose a carcinogenic hazard following topical exposure if not properly handled. If streptozocin powder or solution contacts the skin or mucosae, immediately wash the affected area with soap and water (see Handling Instructions).

Precautions: Patient Follow-up: Patients must be monitored closely, particularly for evidence of renal, hepatic, and hematopoietic toxicity. Serial urinalysis, blood urea nitrogen, and plasma creatinine levels, and creatinine clearance should be done prior to and at least once weekly during and for 4 weeks after drug administration (see Warnings).

Similarly, complete blood counts and liver function studies should be done weekly. Reduction of the dose or discontinuation of therapy is suggested in response to the appearance of renal, hepatic, or hematopoietic abnormalities, but must be weighed against the possible benefit of continued therapy of clinically progressive disease.

Pregnancy: Safe use during pregnancy has not been established. Streptozocin is mutagenic in bacteria and plants. By analogy with other nitrosoureas, it would be expected to exhibit teratogenic effects in animals.

When administered to pregnant monkeys, it appears promptly in the fetal circulation. It has been shown to induce renal tumors in rats, and liver and other tumors in hamsters. The physician must judge the possible benefit to the patient against these known toxic effects when considering the advisability of therapy in males or females who may contemplate the initiation of pregnancy or in pregnant females.

Reproduction studies revealed that streptozocin is teratogenic in the rat and has abortifacient effects in rabbits. There are no studies in pregnant women.

It should be used during pregnancy only if the potential benefit justifies the potential risk to the fetus.

Lactation: It is not known whether streptozocin is excreted in human milk. Because many drugs are excreted in human milk and because of the potential for serious adverse reactions in nursing infants, nursing should be discontinued in patients receiving streptozocin.

Children: No data on treatment of children are available.

Adverse Effects: Renal: (see Warnings).

Many patients treated with streptozocin have experienced renal toxicity, as evidenced by azotemia, anuria, hypophosphatemia, and glycosuria, and renal tubular acidosis. **Renal toxicity may be severe or fatal.** Mild proteinuria is one of the first signs of renal toxicity and may herald further deterioration of renal function.

Two cases of nephrogenic diabetes insipidus following Zanosar therapy have been reported. One had spontaneous recovery and the second responded to indomethacin.

Gastrointestinal: Most patients have experienced severe nausea and vomiting, occasionally requiring discontinuation of drug therapy. Some patients experienced diarrhea. A number of patients have experienced hepatic toxicity, as characterized by elevated liver enzyme [AST (SGOT) and LDH] levels and hypoalbuminemia.

Metabolic: Mild to moderate abnormalities of glucose tolerance have been noted in some patients but these have generally been reversible.

Hematological: Hematological toxicity has been rare, most often involving mild decreases in hematocrit values. However, **fatal hematological toxicity with substantial reductions in leukocyte and platelet count has been observed.**

Overdose: Symptoms and Treatment: No specific antidote is known.

Dosage: Streptozocin should be administered i.v. It is not active orally. Although it has been administered intra-arterially, this is not recommended pending further evaluation of the possibility that adverse renal effects may be evoked more readily by this route of administration.

Dosage Schedules: Two different dosage schedules have been employed successfully.

Daily Schedule: The recommended dose for daily i.v. administration is 500 mg/m² of body surface area for 5 consecutive days every 6 weeks until maximum benefit or until treatment-limiting toxicity is observed. Dose escalation on this schedule is not recommended.

Weekly Schedule: The recommended initial dose for weekly i.v. administration is 1 000 mg/m² of body surface area at weekly intervals for the first 2 courses (weeks). In subsequent courses, drug doses may be escalated in patients who have not achieved a therapeutic response and who have not experienced significant toxicity with the previous course of treatment. However, **a single dose of 1 500 mg/m² body surface area should not be exceeded** as a greater dose may cause azotemia. When administered on this schedule, the median time to onset of response is about 17 days and the median time to maximum response is about 35 days. The median **total** dose to onset of response is about 2 000 mg/m² body surface area and the median **total** dose to maximum response is about 4 000 mg/m² body surface area.

When streptozocin is used in combination with other chemotherapeutic agents, reduction of dosage is often necessary.

The ideal duration of maintenance therapy has not yet been clearly established for either of the above schedules.

For patients with functional tumors, serial monitoring of fasting insulin levels allows a determination of biochemical response to therapy. For patients with either functional or nonfunctional tumors, response to therapy can be determined by measurable reductions of tumor size (reduction of organomegaly, masses, or lymph nodes).

Stability and Storage: Unopened vials should be stored at refrigeration temperatures (2 to 8°C) and protected from light (preferably stored in carton).

The total storage time for streptozocin after reconstitution should not exceed 48 hours at refrigeration temperatures (2 to 8°C) or 24 hours at room temperature. This product contains no preservatives and is not intended as a multiple-dose vial.

Further dilution of the reconstituted solution with 500 mL of Sodium Chloride Injection USP does not alter the solution stability.

Reconstitution: Reconstitute with 9.5 mL of Dextrose Injection USP, Sterile Water for Injection USP, or Sodium Chloride Injection USP. The resulting pale-gold solution will contain 100 mg of streptozocin and 22 mg of citric acid per mL. Where more dilute infusion solutions are desirable, further dilution in the above vehicles is recommended. When reconstituted as directed, the pH of the solution will be between 3.5 and 4.5.

Handling: The following precautionary measures are recommended in proceeding with the preparation and handling of cytotoxic agents such as streptozocin.

1. The procedure should be carried out in a vertical laminar flow hood (biological Safety Cabinet—Class II).
2. Personnel should wear: PVC gloves, safety glasses, disposable gowns and masks.
3. All needles, syringes, vials, and other materials which have come in contact with streptozocin should be segregated and destroyed by incineration (sealed containers may explode).

Supplied: Each off-white to pale yellow colored freeze-dried cake contains: streptozocin 1 g and citric acid anhydrous 220 mg. When necessary, pH was adjusted with hydrochloric acid and/or sodium hydroxide.

ZANTAC®

Glaxo Wellcome

Ranitidine HCl

Histamine H_2 Receptor Antagonist

Pharmacology: Ranitidine is an antagonist of histamine at gastric H_2 receptor sites. Thus ranitidine inhibits both basal gastric secretion and gastric acid secretion induced by histamine, pentagastrin and other secretagogues. On a weight basis, ranitidine is between 4 and 9 times more potent than cimetidine. Inhibition of gastric acid secretion has been observed following i.v., intraduodenal and oral administration of ranitidine and it is dose related, a maximum response being achieved at an oral dose of 300 mg/day.

Pepsin secretion is also inhibited but secretion of gastric mucus is not affected. Ranitidine does not alter the secretion of bicarbonate or enzymes from the pancreas in response to secretin and pancreozymin.

Ranitidine is rapidly absorbed after oral administration, peak plasma concentrations being achieved within 2 to 3 hours. These plasma concentrations are not significantly influenced by the presence of food in the stomach at the time of the oral administration nor by regular doses of antacids.

Bioavailability of oral ranitidine is approximately 50%. Serum protein binding of ranitidine in man is in the range of 10 to 19%. The elimination half-life is approximately 3 hours. The principal route of excretion is the urine (40% recovery of free and metabolized drug in 24 hours).

There is a significant linear correlation between the dose administered and the inhibitory effect upon gastric acid secretion for oral doses up to 300 mg. A plasma ranitidine concentration of 50 ng/mL has an inhibitory effect upon stimulated gastric acid secretion of approximately 50%. Estimates of the IC_{50} range from 36 to 94 ng/mL. Following the administration of 150 mg ranitidine orally, plasma concentrations in excess of this lasted for more than 8 hours and after 12 hours the plasma concentrations were sufficiently high to have a significant inhibitory effect upon gastric acid secretion. In patients with duodenal ulcer, 150 mg oral ranitidine every 12 hours significantly reduced mean 24-hour hydrogen ion activity by 69% and nocturnal gastric acid output by 90%. 300 mg ranitidine given at night is as effective in reducing 24-hour intragastric acidity as 150 mg ranitidine given twice daily.

Following administration of 50 mg ranitidine injection i.m. plasma concentrations in excess of 100 ng/mL were achieved within 5 minutes and remained above this level for 4 to 6 hours.

I.V. infusion (rate: 0.125 mg/kg/hour) produced a rise of intragastric pH between 5.6 and 7 after 2 hours and maintained this level over the 24 hour period when administered to seriously ill patients. The volume of gastric secretion was reduced by more than 55%. Doubling the infusion rate to 0.25 mg/kg/hour produced no further increase in gastric acid inhibition.

A single 50 mg i.v. bolus dose of ranitidine injection produced significant acid inhibition 8 to 9 hours after administration. When 13 seriously ill patients with 2 or more risk factors (shock, sepsis, respiratory failure, jaundice, renal insufficiency or peritonitis) were treated with a 50 mg i.v. bolus dose of ranitidine followed by a continuous infusion of 0.2 mg/kg/hour, the number of at risk days (gastric pH less than 3.5 at 3 consecutive 4-hour aliquots) was approximately half that of placebo treated patients.

Tablets: In respect of both 24 hours acidity and nocturnal acid output, oral ranitidine 150 mg twice daily was superior to cimetidine 200 mg 3 times daily and 400 mg at night ($P<0.001$ and <0.05 respectively).

Treatment of volunteers with oral ranitidine 150 mg twice daily for 7 days did not cause bacterial overgrowth in the stomach.

Volunteers treated with an oral dose of ranitidine have reported no significant gastrointestinal or CNS side effects; moreover pulse rate, blood pressure, ECG and electroencephalogram were not significantly affected in man following ranitidine administration.

In healthy human volunteers and patients, ranitidine when administered orally, did not influence plasma levels of the following hormones—cortisol, testosterone, oestrogens, growth hormone, follicle stimulating hormone, luteinizing hormone, thyroid stimulating hormone, aldosterone or gastrin—although like cimetidine, ranitidine reduced vasopressin output. Treatment for up to 6 weeks with ranitidine 150 mg twice daily by mouth did not affect the human hypothalamic-pituitary-testicular-ovarian or -adrenal axes.

Injection: I.M. ranitidine is fully bioavailable in comparison to i.v. ranitidine. The median elimination half-life of ranitidine injection 50 mg, administered i.v. or i.m. was found to be 2.3 hours (range 120 to 160 minutes). In comparison, the elimination half-life following oral administration is approximately 3 hours. However, the half-life of ranitidine in patients with renal dysfunction is prolonged. In a study of 27 patients with renal dysfunction (plasma creatinine concentration greater than 300 μmol/L) therapeutic plasma levels of ranitidine were shown to be achieved without risk of drug accumulation, if half the normal dose of the drug was administered.

Ranitidine injection is well tolerated following i.v. administration at dose levels of up to 100 mg q.i.d. It is evident that these levels are in excess of those recommended for normal clinical use.

At 50 mg i.v. ranitidine injection had no effect on prolactin levels. Only at the 300 mg i.v. dose level was an increase in prolactin secretion, equivalent to that produced by 200 mg of cimetidine i.v., observed.

Indications: The treatment of duodenal ulcer, benign gastric ulcer, reflux esophagitis, post-operative peptic ulcer, Zollinger-Ellison syndrome and other conditions where reduction of gastric secretion and acid output is desirable. These include treatment of NSAID-induced lesions (ulcers, erosions) and gastrointestinal symptoms and prevention of their recurrence, prophylaxis of gastrointestinal hemorrhage from stress ulceration in seriously ill patients, the prophylaxis of recurrent hemorrhage from bleeding ulcers, and in the prevention of Acid Aspiration Syndrome (Mendelson's Syndrome) from general anesthesia in patients considered to be at risk for this, including obstetrical patients in labor, and obese patients.

In addition, ranitidine is indicated for the prophylaxis and maintenance treatment of duodenal or benign gastric ulcer in patients with a history of recurrent ulceration.

Contraindications: For patients known to have hypersensitivity to ranitidine.

Warnings: Gastric Ulcer: Treatment with a histamine H_2 antagonist may mask symptoms associated with carcinoma of the stomach and therefore may delay diagnosis of that condition. Accordingly, where gastric ulcer is suspected the possibility of malignancy should be excluded before therapy with ranitidine is instituted.

Concomitant NSAID Use: Regular supervision of patients who are taking NSAIDs concomitantly with ranitidine is recommended especially in the elderly and those with a history of peptic ulcer. Baseline endoscopic and histological evaluation is necessary to rule out gastric carcinoma.

Patients with a History of Acute Porphyria: Rare clinical reports suggest that ranitidine may precipitate acute porphyric attacks. Therefore, ranitidine should be avoided in patients with a history of acute porphyria.

Pregnancy: The safety of ranitidine in the treatment of conditions where a controlled reduction of gastric secretion is required during pregnancy has not been established. Reproduction studies performed in rats and rabbits have revealed no evidence of ranitidine induced impaired fertility or harm to the fetus. Nevertheless, if the administration of ranitidine is considered to be necessary, its use requires that the potential benefits be weighed against possible hazards to the patient and to the fetus.

Lactation: Ranitidine is secreted in breast milk in lactating mothers but the clinical significance of this has not been fully evaluated.

Children: Experience with ranitidine in children is limited. It has however been used successfully in children aged 8 to 18 years in oral doses up to 150 mg twice daily.

Precautions: Injection: Bradycardia in association with rapid administration of ranitidine injection has been reported rarely, usually in patients with factors predisposing to cardiac rhythm disturbances. Recommended rates of administration should not be exceeded (see Adverse Effects and Dosage).

Use in Impaired Renal Function: Ranitidine is excreted via the kidneys and, in the presence of severe renal impairment, plasma levels of ranitidine are increased and elimination prolonged. Accordingly, it is recommended in such patients, to decrease the dosage of ranitidine by one-half. Accumulation with resulting elevated plasma concentrations will occur in patients with severe renal impairment (plasma creatinine concentration greater than 300 μmol/L); a recommended daily dose of oral ranitidine in such patients should be 150 mg. In patients undergoing chronic ambulatory peritoneal dialysis or chronic hemodialysis, a single oral dose of ranitidine 150 mg should be taken immediately after dialysis.

Drug Interactions: Although ranitidine has been reported to bind weakly to cytochrome P450 in vitro, recommended doses of the drug do not inhibit the action of the hepatic cytochrome P450-linked oxygenase enzymes. However, there have been isolated reports of drug interactions which suggest that ranitidine may affect the bioavailability of certain drugs (e.g. ketoconazole) by some mechanism as yet unidentified (e.g. a pH dependant effect on absorption or a change in volume of distribution).

As well, sporadic cases of drug interactions have been reported in elderly patients involving both hypoglycemic drugs and theophylline. The significance of these reports cannot be determined at present, as controlled clinical trials with theophylline and ranitidine have not shown interaction.

If high doses (2 g) of sucralfate are co-administered with ranitidine, the absorption of ranitidine may be reduced. This effect is not seen if sucralfate is taken at least 2 hours after ranitidine administration.

Geriatrics: Since malignancy is more common in the elderly, particular consideration must be given to this before therapy with ranitidine is instituted. Elderly patients receiving NSAIDs concomitantly with ranitidine should be closely supervised.

As with all medication in the elderly, when prescribing ranitidine, consideration should be given to the patient's concurrent drug therapy. Sporadic cases of drug interaction have been reported in elderly patients involving both hypoglycemic drugs and theophylline. The significance of these reports cannot be determined at present, as controlled clinical trials with theophylline and ranitidine have shown no interaction. Elderly patients may be at increased risk for confusional states and depression.

Adverse Effects: The following adverse reactions have been reported as events in clinical trials or in the routine management of patients treated with ranitidine. A cause and effect relationship to ranitidine is not always established.

CNS: headache, sometimes severe; malaise; dizziness; somnolence; insomnia; vertigo; and reversible blurred vision suggestive of a change in accommodation. Isolated cases of reversible mental confusion, agitation, depression, hallucinations have been reported, predominantly in severely ill elderly patients.

Cardiovascular: Isolated reports of tachycardia, bradycardia, premature ventricular beats, AV block have been noted. Asystole has been reported in very few individuals with and without predisposing conditions following i.v. administration and has not been reported following oral administration of ranitidine (see Precautions and Dosage).

Gastrointestinal: constipation, diarrhea, nausea/vomiting and abdominal discomfort/pain.

Hepatic: In normal volunteers, transient and reversible ALT and AST values were increased to at least twice the pretreatment levels in 6 of 12 subjects receiving ranitidine 100 mg q.i.d. i.v. for 7 days, and in 4 of 24 subjects receiving 50 mg q.i.d. i.v. for 5 days. Therefore, it may be prudent to monitor AST and ALT in patients receiving i.v. treatment for 5 days or longer and in those with pre-existing liver diseases. With oral administration, there have been occasional reports of hepatitis, hepatocellular or hepatocanalicular or mixed, with or without jaundice. In such circumstances, ranitidine should be discontinued immediately. These are usually reversible, but in exceedingly rare circumstances, death has occurred.

Musculoskeletal: rare reports of arthralgia and myalgia.

Hematologic: Blood count changes (leukopenia, thrombocytopenia) have occurred in a few patients. These are usually reversible. Rare cases of agranulocytosis or pancytopenia, sometimes with marrow hypoplasia or aplasia have been reported.

Endocrine: No clinically significant interference with endocrine or gonadal function has been reported. There have been a few reports of breast symptoms in men taking ranitidine.

Dermatologic: rash, including cases suggestive of mild erythema multiforme.

Other: Rare cases of hypersensitivity reactions (including chest pain, bronchospasm, fever, rash, eosinophilia, anaphylaxis, urticaria, angioneurotic edema, hypotension) and small increases in serum creatinine have occasionally occurred after a single dose. Acute pancreatitis has been reported rarely.

Overdose: Symptoms and Treatment: There is no experience to date with deliberate overdosage. The usual measures to remove unabsorbed drug from the gastrointestinal tract (including activated charcoal or syrup of ipecac), clinical monitoring and supportive therapy should be employed. Also, if need be, the drug can be removed from the plasma by hemodialysis.

Dosage: Tablets, Oral Solution: Duodenal ulcer and benign gastric ulcer: 300 mg once daily at bedtime or 150 mg twice daily taken in the morning and before retiring. It is not necessary to time the dose in relation to meals. In most cases of duodenal ulcer and benign gastric ulcer, healing will occur in 4 weeks. In the small number of patients whose ulcers may not have fully healed, these are likely to respond to a further 4 week course of treatment. In the treatment of duodenal ulcers, 300 mg twice daily for 4 weeks, may be of benefit when more rapid healing is desired.

Maintenance therapy: Duodenal ulcers, benign gastric ulcers: Patients who have responded to short-term therapy, particularly those with a history of recurrent ulcer, may benefit from chronic maintenance therapy at a reduced oral tablet dosage of 150 mg once daily at bedtime.

In the management of duodenal ulcers, smoking is associated with a higher rate of ulcer relapse (up to 9.2 times higher in one trial), and such patients should be advised to stop smoking. In those patients who fail to comply with such advice, 300 mg nightly provides additional therapeutic benefit over the 150 mg once daily dosage regimen.

Reflux esophagitis: Acute treatment: 300 mg once daily at bedtime, or alternatively 150 mg twice daily, taken in the morning and before retiring for up to 8 weeks. In patients with moderate to severe esophagitis, the dosage of ranitidine may be increased to 150 mg for 4 times daily up to 12 weeks.

Long-term management: the recommended adult oral dose is 150 mg twice daily.

Post-operative peptic ulcer: 150 mg twice daily, taken in the morning and before retiring.

Pathological hypersecretory conditions (Zollinger-Ellison Syndrome): 150 mg 3 times daily may be administered initially. In some patients, it may be necessary to administer 150 mg doses more frequently. Doses should be adjusted to individual patient needs. Doses up to 6 g/day have been well tolerated.

Treatment of NSAID-induced lesions (ulcers, erosions) and gastrointestinal symptoms and prevention of their recurrence: In ulcers following NSAID therapy or associated with continued NSAIDs, 150 mg twice daily for 8 to 12 weeks may be necessary. For the prevention of NSAID associated ulcer recurrence,

Zantac (cont'd)

150 mg twice daily may be given concomitantly with nonsteroidal anti-inflammatory drug therapy.

Prophylaxis of acid aspiration syndrome (AAS): 150 mg the evening prior to anesthesia induction is recommended, however, 150 mg 2 hours before anesthesia induction is also effective. Alternatively, ranitidine injection may be used. For the prevention of AAS in pre-partum patients who elect for anesthesia, 150 mg every 6 hours may be employed, but if general anesthesia is warranted, a nonparticulate oral antacid (e.g., sodium citrate) could supplement ranitidine therapy. In an emergency situation, the use of alkalis, antacids, and meticulous anesthetic technique is still necessary as ranitidine does not affect the pH and volume of the existing gastric content.

Prophylaxis of hemorrhage from stress ulceration in seriously ill patients or prophylaxis of recurrent hemorrhage in patients bleeding from peptic ulceration who are currently managed by i.v. ranitidine: an oral dose of 150 mg twice daily may be substituted for the injection once oral feeding commences.

If necessary ranitidine oral solution may be administered by orogastric or nasogastric tube as an alternative.

Note: A 150 mg dose of ranitidine is equivalent to 10 mL of ranitidine oral solution, and 300 mg ranitidine is equivalent to 20 mL of ranitidine oral solution.

Geriatrics: For all conditions listed above, the drug dosage for the elderly who are seriously ill should start at the lowest recommended dose and be adjusted as necessary with close supervision.

Parenteral Administration: In some hospitalized patients with pathological hypersecretory conditions or intractable duodenal ulcers, or in patients unable to take oral medication, ranitidine may be administered parenterally according to the following recommendations:

I.M. Injection: 50 mg (2 mL) every 6 to 8 hours (no dilution is required).

I.V. Injection: 50 mg (2 mL) every 6 to 8 hours. Dilute ranitidine injection, 50 mg in compatible i.v. solution (see Compatibility of ranitidine injection) to a total volume of 20 mL and inject over a period of **not less than 5 minutes** (see Precautions). Parenteral administration may continue until oral feeding is commenced and if there is still a risk, oral ranitidine may then commence.

Intermittent I.V. Infusion: 50 mg (2 mL) every 6 to 8 hours. Dilute ranitidine injection 50 mg in 100 mL of compatible i.v. solution (see Dilution of Parenteral Products) and infuse over 15 to 20 minutes. In some patients, it may be necessary to increase dosage. When this is required, the increases should be made by more frequent administration of a 50 mg dose, but generally should not exceed 400 mg/day.

In the prophylaxis of upper gastrointestinal hemorrhage from stress ulceration in seriously ill patients a primary dose of 50 mg as a slow (over a period of not less than 5 minutes) i.v. injection followed by a continuous i.v. infusion of 0.125 to 0.250 mg/kg/hour may be preferred (see Precautions). The higher infusion concentration (0.25 mg/kg/hour) should be reserved for patients who are unresponsive to a lower concentration (0.125 mg/kg/hour).

In the prophylaxis of hemorrhage from stress ulceration in seriously ill patients or prophylaxis of recurrent hemorrhage in patients bleeding from peptic ulceration, parenteral administration may continue until oral feeding is commenced and if there is still a risk, oral ranitidine may then commence.

For patients considered at risk of developing Acid Aspiration Syndrome (Mendelson's Syndrome); 50 mg by i.m. or slow (over a period of not less than 5 minutes) i.v. injection 45 to 60 minutes before induction of general anesthesia. In an emergency situation, the use of alkalis, antacids, and meticulous anesthetic technique is still necessary as ranitidine does not affect the pH and volume of the existing gastric content.

Dilution of Parenteral Products: I.M. Injection: No dilution is required.

I.V. Injection: Zantac injection for i.v. injection should be diluted to 20 mL (2.5 mg/mL) with one of the recommended diluents listed below.

Intermittent I.V. Infusion: Zantac injection for intermittent i.v. infusion should be diluted to 100 mL (0.5 mg/mL) with one of the recommended diluents listed below. Zantac injection is compatible in polyvinylchloride infusion bags (Viaflex) and in glass with the following i.v. fluids: 0.9% sodium chloride, 5% dextrose, 0.18% sodium chloride and 4% dextrose, 4.2% sodium bicarbonate and Hartmann's solution. Admixtures of Zantac injection with 0.18% sodium chloride and 4% dextrose or 4.2% sodium bicarbonate or Hartmann's solution should be discarded after 24 hours. Although i.v. admixtures of Zantac injection with 5% dextrose or 0.9% sodium chloride may often be physically and chemically stable for longer periods, due to microbiological considerations, they are usually recommended for use within the maximum 72 hours when refrigerated (2 to 8°C) followed by 24 hours at room temperature. Hospitals and institutions that have recognized admixture programs and use validated aseptic techniques for preparation of i.v. solutions, may extend the storage time for Zantac injection in admixture with 5% Dextrose Injection or 0.9% Sodium Chloride Injection in Viaflex bags, in concentrations of up to 2 mg/mL, to 35 days when stored under refrigeration at 2 to 8°C. As with all parenteral drug products, i.v. admixtures should be inspected visually for clarity, particulate matter, precipitate, discoloration and leakage prior to administration, whenever solution and container permit. Solutions showing haziness, particulate matter, precipitate or discoloration or leakage should not be used.

Supplied: Injection: Each mL of solution for i.v. or i.m. injection contains: ranitidine HCl 28 mg (equivalent to ranitidine anhydrous free base 25 mg) in sterile water for injection. Nonmedicinal ingredients: disodium hydrogen orthophosphate, phenol and potassium dihydrogen orthophosphate. Unit dose colorless glass vials of 2 mL. Multidose colorless glass vials of 40 mL. Packages of 10. Protect from light, store between 2 and 25°C. Injection should not be autoclaved.

Oral Solution: Each 5 mL of clear peppermint flavored solution contains: ranitidine HCl 84 mg (equivalent to ranitidine anhydrous free base 75 mg). Nonmedicinal ingredients: alcohol (7.5% w/v), butylparaben, dibasic sodium phosphate, flavor mint, hydroxypropyl methylcellulose, monobasic potassium phosphate, propylparaben, sodium chloride, sodium cyclamate and sorbitol. Bottles of 300 mL. Store at or below 25°C. Protect from light. Keep out of reach of children.

Tablets: 150 mg: Each white, round, biconvex, film-coated tablet engraved ZANTAC 150 on one face and GLAXO on the other contains: ranitidine HCl 168 mg (equivalent to ranitidine anhydrous free base 150 mg). Nonmedicinal ingredients: magnesium stearate and microcrystalline cellulose; film-coating suspension: dichloromethane, hydroxypropyl methylcellulose, isopropyl alcohol and Opaspray K-1-7000. Gluten- and tartrazine-free. Packs of 60. Store between 2 and 30°C. Protect from light.

300 mg: Each white, capsule-shaped, film-coated tablet engraved ZANTAC 300 on one face and GLAXO on the other contains: ranitidine HCl 336 mg (equivalent to ranitidine anhydrous free base 300 mg). Nonmedicinal ingredients: croscarmellose sodium, magnesium stearate and microcrystalline cellulose; film-coating suspension: dichloromethane, hydroxypropyl methylcellulose, isopropyl alcohol and Opaspray K-1-7000. Gluten- and tartrazine-free. Packs of 30. Store between 2 and 30°C. Protect from light.

(Shown in Product Recognition Section)

ZANTAC® 75

Glaxo Wellcome

Ranitidine HCl

Histamine H_2-receptor Antagonist

Pharmacology: Ranitidine is an antagonist of histamine at gastric H_2-receptor sites. Thus, ranitidine inhibits both basal gastric secretion and gastric acid secretion induced by histamine, pentagastrin and other secretagogues. Inhibition of gastric acid secretion has been observed following i.v., intraduodenal and oral administration of ranitidine. This response is dose-related, a maximum response being achieved at an oral dose of 300 mg/day.

Pepsin secretion is also inhibited but secretion of gastric mucus is not affected. Ranitidine does not alter the secretion of bicarbonate or enzymes from the pancreas in response to secretin and pancreozymin.

Ranitidine is rapidly absorbed after oral administration, peak plasma concentrations being achieved within 2 to 3 hours. These plasma concentrations are not significantly influenced by the presence of food in the stomach at the time of the oral administration nor by regular doses of antacids.

Bioavailability of oral ranitidine is approximately 50%. Serum protein binding of ranitidine in man is in the range of 10 to 19%. The elimination half-life is approximately 3 hours. The principal route of excretion is the urine (40% recovery of free and metabolized drug in 24 hours).

There is a significant linear correlation between the dose administered and the inhibitory effect upon gastric acid secretion for single oral doses up to 300 mg. In healthy subjects a single 75 mg dose of ranitidine significantly reduced meal-stimulated intragastric acidity ([H+] AUC) compared with placebo. The effect of ranitidine on intragastric acidity and pH is also dose-related.

A single 75 mg dose, compared to placebo, has an early onset of action; significantly elevating gastric pH within 1 hour and lasting for up to 13 hours postdosing. After correcting for onset of action (within 1 hour), the duration of acid suppression for ranitidine 75 mg is up to 12 hours (i.e., all day or all night). In the same multicentre, randomized, crossover study, the onset of acid suppression effect for ranitidine 75 mg was statistically superior to famotidine 10 mg at only 1 and 2 hours postdosing. The duration and degree of acid suppression of ranitidine 75 mg (63.1%, n=75) were superior to cimetidine 200 mg (37.8%, n=52) over the 10-hour daytime evaluation period (see Tables I and II on following page).

In a large, multicentre, dose-ranging, placebo-controlled trial in patients with episodic heartburn, a single 75 mg dose relieved symptoms within 30 minutes and provided relief for the duration of the 4-hour evaluation period.

Volunteers treated with an oral dose of ranitidine have reported no significant gastrointestinal or CNS side effects; moreover, pulse rate, blood pressure, ECG and EEG are not significantly affected in man following ranitidine administration.

In healthy human volunteers and patients, ranitidine, when administered orally did not influence plasma levels of the following hormones: cortisol, testosterone, estrogens, growth hormone, follicle-stimulating hormone, luteinizing hormone, thyroid-stimulating hormone, aldosterone or gastrin, although, like cimetidine, ranitidine reduced vasopressin output. Treatment for up to 6 weeks with ranitidine 150 mg twice daily by mouth did not affect the human hypothalamic-pituitary-testicular-ovarian or -adrenal axes.

The safety and efficacy of 75 mg ranitidine for treatment of episodic heartburn were established in 2 large replicate Phase III studies involving 2 985 patients. These 2 pivotal studies showed that 1 ranitidine 75 mg tablet was statistically and clinically superior to placebo in providing relief of episodic heartburn beginning at 30 minutes.

Indications: For fast and effective relief, treatment and prevention, day or night, of the burning and discomfort of acid indigestion (dyspepsia), heartburn, hyperacidity, sour stomach and upset stomach associated with excess stomach acid. These symptoms may be brought on by consuming food and beverages.

Contraindications: For patients known to have hypersensitivity to any component of the preparation.

Warnings: Gastric Carcinoma: Treatment with a histamine H_2-antagonist may mask symptoms associated with carcinoma of the stomach and, therefore, may delay diagnosis of that condition. Accordingly, patients should be advised to consult a physician if they have difficulty swallowing or persistent abdominal discomfort or if symptoms get worse or persist for more than 2 weeks.

Patients with a History of Acute Porphyria: Rare clinical reports suggest that ranitidine may precipitate acute porphyric attacks. Therefore, ranitidine should be avoided in patients with a history of acute porphyria.

Pregnancy and *Lactation:* The safety of ranitidine in the treatment of conditions where a controlled reduction of gastric secretion is required during pregnancy has not been established. Reproduction studies performed in rats and rabbits at higher doses have revealed no evidence of ranitidine-induced impaired fertility or harm to the fetus. Nevertheless, if the administration of ranitidine is considered to be necessary, its use requires that the potential benefits be weighed against possible hazards to the patient and to the fetus.

Ranitidine is secreted in breast milk in lactating mothers, but the clinical significance of this has not been fully evaluated. Women who are breast-feeding are advised to speak with their doctor before taking ranitidine.

Precautions: Impaired Renal Function: Ranitidine is excreted via the kidneys and, in the presence of severe renal impairment, plasma levels of ranitidine are increased and elimination prolonged. Accordingly, ranitidine should be used under physician supervision for these patients.

Drug Interactions: Although ranitidine has been reported to bind weakly to cytochrome P_{450} in vitro, recommended doses of the drug do not inhibit the action of the hepatic cytochrome P_{450}-linked oxygenase enzymes. A review of selected publications of controlled clinical drug interaction studies at the level of hepatic elimination has indicated ranitidine is unlikely to cause clinically significant potentiation of actions of drugs

Table I—Zantac 75

Summary of Weighted Mean Hydrogen Ion Activity (H+AUC mmol/L.h)

Time Period	Placebo N=75	Ranitidine 75 mg N=75	Cimetidine 200 mg N=52	Famotidine 10 mg N=22
Total (20 h)	30.89	18.21[a,b]	25.08[a]	19.32[a]
Day (11.00h-22.30h)	32.76	18.19[a,b]	22.06[a]	13.23[a]
Night (22.30h-08.30h)	28.83	23.23[a,b]	28.09	25.41[a]

[a]$p<0.05$ compared with paired placebo group.
[b]$p<0.05$ compared with paired cimetidine group.

Table II—Zantac 75

Changes in Intragastric Acidity and pH

	Median Percentage Decrease in Acidity			Median Intragastric pH	
	Total	**Day**[a]	**Night**[a]	**Day**[a]	**Night**[a]
Ranitidine 75 mg (N=75)	44.1%[b]	63.1%[b]	21.2%[b]	2.10[c]	1.80[c]
Famotidine 10 mg (N=22)	38.9%	58.9%	20.1%	2.06[c]	1.90
Cimetidine 200 mg (N=52)	23%	37.8%	1.8%	1.69[c]	1.77
Placebo (N=75)				1.48	1.70

[a]day=12.30h to 22.30h; night=22.30h to 8.30h.
[b]$p<0.05$ compared with paired cimetidine group.
[c]$p<0.05$ compared with paired placebo group.

which are inactivated by the hepatic cytochrome P_{450} enzyme system; these drugs may include: diazepam, lidocaine, phenytoin, propranolol, theophylline and warfarin. Sporadic cases (approximately 1 case per 4 million patient treatments) of drug interactions have been reported in elderly patients involving both hypoglycemic drugs and theophylline. The significance of these reports cannot be determined at present as controlled clinical trials have not shown interactions. These reports are based on use for prescription indications and dosage.

Antacids: Concurrent administration of antacid of medium to high potency (75 mEq) with ranitidine is not recommended. The absorption of ranitidine may be decreased. Patients should be cautioned not to take antacids within ½ to 1 hour of ranitidine ingestion.

Ketoconazole: Simultaneous administration of ketoconazole and ranitidine may result in reduction of the absorption of ketoconazole by some mechanism as yet unidentified (e.g., a pH-dependent effect on absorption or a change of volume of distribution). Patients should be cautioned not to take ranitidine for at least 2 hours after ketoconazole. These reports are based on use of prescription indications and dosage.

Sucralfate: If high doses of sucralfate (2 g) are coadministered with ranitidine, the absorption of ranitidine may be reduced. This effect is not seen if sucralfate is taken at least 2 hours after ranitidine administration. These reports are based on use of prescription indications and dosage.

Procainamide: Some evidence of interactions with ranitidine at the level of renal elimination have been reported, but the clinical importance is unknown/questionable. These reports are based on use for prescription indications and dosage.

Ethanol: The coadministration of a single oral dose of ranitidine 75 mg and ethanol 0.15 g/kg has no clinically relevant effect on ethanol pharmacokinetics as shown in a double-blind, placebo-controlled, crossover study in 25 healthy subjects.

Geriatrics: Since malignancy is more common in the elderly, particular consideration must be given to this before therapy with ranitidine is instituted. Elderly patients receiving nonsteroidal anti-inflammatory drugs concomitantly with ranitidine should be closely supervised. As with all medication in the elderly, consideration should be given to concurrent drug therapy.

Adverse Effects: In clinical trials with ranitidine the most frequently reported adverse events included: headache (4%), nausea and vomiting (3%) and diarrhea (2%). There was no statistical difference in reported events between the ranitidine- and placebo-treated groups.

The following adverse reactions have been reported as events in clinical trials, in postmarketing surveillance, or in the routine management of patients treated with prescription doses of ranitidine. The majority of these events have been observed following oral administration of higher prescription doses of ranitidine and a cause and effect relationship to ranitidine has not always been established.

CNS: headache, sometimes severe; malaise; dizziness; somnolence; insomnia; vertigo; and reversible blurred vision suggestive of a change in accommodation. Isolated cases of reversible mental confusion, agitation, depression, hallucinations have been reported, predominantly in severely ill elderly patients.

Cardiovascular: As with other H_2-receptor antagonists, there have been rare reports of tachycardia, premature ventricular beats, bradycardia, and atrioventricular block.

Gastrointestinal: constipation, diarrhea, nausea/vomiting and abdominal discomfort/pain.

Hepatic: Transient and reversible changes in liver function tests can occur (increase in ALT and AST values). With oral administration, there have been occasional reports of hepatitis, hepatocellular or hepatocanalicular, mixed with or without jaundice. In such circumstances, ranitidine should be discontinued immediately. These are usually reversible but, in exceedingly rare circumstances, death has occurred.

Musculoskeletal: rare reports of arthralgia and myalgia.

Hematologic: Blood count changes (leukopenia, thrombocytopenia) have occurred in a few patients. These are usually reversible. Rare cases of agranulocytosis or pancytopenia, sometimes with marrow hypoplasia or aplasia have been reported.

Endocrine: No clinically significant interference with endocrine or gonadal function has been reported. There have been a few reports of breast symptoms in men taking ranitidine.

Dermatologic: rash, including cases suggestive of mild erythema multiforme.

Other: Rare cases of hypersensitivity reactions (including chest pain, bronchospasm, fever, rash, eosinophilia, anaphylaxis, urticaria, angioneurotic edema, hypotension) and small increases in serum creatinine have occasionally occurred after a single dose. Acute pancreatitis has been reported rarely.

Overdose: Symptoms and Treatment: There is no experience to date with deliberate overdosage. The usual measures to remove unabsorbed drug from the gastrointestinal tract (including activated charcoal or syrup of ipecac), clinical monitoring and supportive therapy should be employed. Also, if need be, the drug can be removed from the plasma by hemodialysis. Up to 6 g/day has been administered without untoward effect.

Dosage: Adults and Children 16 Years of Age and Older: 1 tablet should be taken when symptoms appear, day or night. If symptoms persist for more than 1 hour or return after 1 hour, a second tablet may be taken. The maximum dosage is 2 tablets in a 24-hour period. Patients are advised to consult their physician if symptoms get worse or continue after 14 days of treatment.

For prevention of symptoms brought on by consuming food or beverages, 1 tablet should be taken 30 to 60 minutes before eating a meal expected to cause symptoms.

Children Under 16 Years: Children under 16 years of age should be supervised by a physician.

Information for the Patient: See Blue Section—Information for the Patient "Zantac 75".

Supplied: Each pink, five-sided, biconvex, film-coated tablet, with "Z" engraved on one side and 75 on the other, contains: ranitidine HCl 84 mg equivalent to ranitidine anhydrous free base 75 mg. Nonmedicinal ingredients: hydroxypropyl methylcellulose, iron oxide, magnesium stearate, microcrystalline cellulose, titanium dioxide and triacetin. Packs of 2, 4, 10, 30, 40 and 60. Store between 2 and 30°C.

(Shown in Product Recognition Section)

New Product 1998

ZARONTIN® 🄿

Parke-Davis

Ethosuximide

Anticonvulsant

Indications: The control of absence (petit mal) epilepsy.

Contraindications: Ethosuximide should not be used in patients with a history of hypersensitivity to succinimides.

Precautions: Blood dyscrasias, including some with fatal outcome, have been reported to be associated with the use of ethosuximide; therefore, periodic blood counts should be performed.

Ethosuximide is capable of producing morphological and functional changes in the animal liver. In humans, abnormal liver and renal function studies have been reported.

Administer ethosuximide with extreme caution to patients with known liver or renal disease. Periodic urinalysis and liver function studies are advised for all patients receiving the drug.

Cases of systemic lupus erythematosus have been reported with the use of ethosuximide. The physician should be alert to this possibility.

Pregnancy: Recent reports indicate an association between the use of anticonvulsant drugs and an elevated incidence of birth defects in children born to epileptic women taking such medication during pregnancy. The incidence of congenital malformations in the general population is regarded to be approximately 2%; in children of treated epileptic women this incidence may be increased 2 to 3 fold. The increase is largely due to specific defects, e.g., congenital malformations of the heart, and cleft lip and/or palate. Nevertheless, the great majority of mothers receiving anticonvulsant medications deliver normal infants.

Data are more extensive with respect to phenytoin and phenobarbital, but these drugs are also the most commonly prescribed anticonvulsants. Some reports indicate a possible similar association with the use of other anticonvulsants, including trimethadione and paramethadione. However, the possibility also exists that other factors, e.g., genetic predisposition or the epileptic condition itself may contribute to or may be mainly responsible for the higher incidence of birth defects.

Anticonvulsant drugs should not be discontinued in patients in whom the drug is administered to prevent major seizures, because of the strong possibility of precipitating status epilepticus with attendant hypoxia and risk to both the mother and the unborn child. With regard to drugs given for minor seizures, the risk of discontinuing medication prior to or during pregnancy should be weighed against the risk of congenital defects in the particular case and with the particular family history.

Epileptic women of childbearing age should be encouraged to seek professional counsel and should report the onset of pregnancy promptly to their physician. Where the necessity for continued use of antiepileptic medication is in doubt, appropriate consultation might be indicated.

The preceding considerations should be borne in mind and ethosuximide should be used in women of childbearing potential only when the expected benefits to the patient warrant the possible risk to a fetus. Mothers receiving ethosuximide should not breast-feed their infants.

Occupational Hazards: Ethosuximide may impair the mental and/or physical abilities required for the performance of potentially hazardous tasks, such as driving a motor vehicle or other such activity requiring alertness; therefore, caution the patient accordingly.

Ethosuximide, when used alone in mixed types of epilepsy, may increase the frequency of generalized tonic-clonic attacks in some patients.

Proceed slowly when increasing or decreasing dosage, as well as when adding or eliminating other medication. Abrupt withdrawal of anticonvulsant medication may precipitate petit mal status.

Adverse Effects: Gastrointestinal: Gastrointestinal symptoms occur frequently and include anorexia, vague gastric upset, nausea and vomiting, cramps, epigastric and abdominal pain, weight loss, and diarrhea.

Zarontin (cont'd)

Hemopoietic: leukopenia, agranulocytosis, pancytopenia, aplastic anemia, eosinophilia.
Nervous system: Neurologic and sensory reactions reported during therapy with ethosuximide have included drowsiness, headache, dizziness, euphoria, hiccups, irritability, hyperactivity, lethargy, fatigue, and ataxia. Psychiatric or psychological aberrations associated with ethosuximide administration have included disturbances of sleep, night terrors, inability to concentrate, and aggressiveness. These effects may be noted particularly in patients who have previously exhibited psychological abnormalities. There have been rare reports of paranoid psychosis, increased libido, and increased state of depression with overt suicidal intentions.
Integumentary: Dermatologic manifestations which have occurred with the administration of ethosuximide have included urticaria, Stevens-Johnson syndrome, systemic lupus erythematosus, and pruritic erythematous rashes.
Genitourinary: microscopic hematuria.
Miscellaneous: myopia, vaginal bleeding, swelling of the tongue, gum hypertrophy, hirsutism.

Dosage: Initial dose: children under 6 years of age, 250 mg daily; older patients, 500 mg daily in divided doses. The dose thereafter must be individualized according to response and tolerance. Medicament should be increased by small increments: e.g. increase daily dose by 250 mg every 4 to 7 days until control is achieved with minimal side effects. Daily dosage of 1 to 1.5 g in divided doses frequently controls seizures; however, it may be necessary to exceed this amount by slow increases and careful evaluation of patient's response.

Supplied: Capsules: Each soluble gelatin capsule contains: ethosuximide 250 mg. Nonmedicinal ingredients: polyethylene glycol. Bottles of 100.

Syrup: Each 5 mL contains: ethosuximide 250 mg. Nonmedicinal ingredients: alcohol, citric acid, FD&C Red No. 3, FD&C Yellow No. 6, flavoring agents, glycerin, sodium benzoate, sodium citrate, sugar and vanillin. Alcohol: 3%. Energy: 62.76 kJ (15 kcal)/5 mL. Sodium: <1 mmol (6.7 mg)/5 mL. Gluten-, lactose-, parabens-, sulfite- and tartrazine-free. Bottles of 500 mL.

(Shown in Product Recognition Section)

ZAROXOLYN® Ⓟ

Rhône-Poulenc Rorer

Metolazone

Diuretic—Antihypertensive

Pharmacology: Metolazone is a quinazoline diuretic/antihypertensive agent. The action of metolazone is to interfere with the renal tubular mechanism of electrolyte reabsorption. The mechanism of this action is unknown. Metolazone acts primarily to inhibit sodium reabsorption at the cortical diluting site and in the proximal convoluted tubule. Sodium and chloride ions are excreted in approximately equivalent amounts. The increased delivery of sodium to the distal-tubular exchange site may result in increased potassium excretion and hypokalemia.

Following a clinical oral dose, diuresis and saluresis usually begin within 1 hour and persist for 12 to 24 hours, depending on dosage. Peak effect occurs about 2 hours after administration. The action of the drug continues over 24 hours. A single daily dose is recommended, and the duration of effect can be varied by adjusting this dose.

Absorption is dose related up to levels of 50 mg/kg orally. The duration of the clinical effect varies from 12 to 24 hours and is dependent upon the dose given. Most of the drug is protein bound (90 to 95%). In man, the half-life of metolazone in erythrocytes is 10 hours and in plasma 5 hours. The prolonged duration of action is attributed to the protein binding and enterohepatic recycling.

Within 48 hours of oral dosing, approximately 95% of the administered dose is eliminated in the urine and feces. In man, about 80% is excreted unchanged and the rest undergoes conversion to hydroxylated and carboxylated derivatives. In animals, about 50% is eliminated unchanged. In the dog, 25% is excreted into the bile over a 24-hour period following 5 mg/kg dose.

Metolazone is distributed mainly to the soft tissues with little, if any, in the nerves, brain, bones or eyes. The drug passes readily through the placental barrier to the fetus and is found in the milk of lactating animals.

The mechanism whereby diuretics function in the control of hypertension is unknown; both renal and extrarenal actions may be involved. An antihypertensive effect may be seen as early as 3 to 4 days after metolazone has been started. Administration for 3 to 6 weeks, however, is usually required for maximum antihypertensive effect.

Indications: Edema accompanying congestive heart failure; edema accompanying renal diseases and states of diminished renal function, including the nephrotic syndrome.
Pregnancy: Diuretics do not prevent development of toxemia of pregnancy, and there is no satisfactory evidence that they are useful in the treatment of developed toxemia. Metolazone is indicated in pregnancy only when edema is due to pathological causes. Edema in pregnancy, resulting from restriction of venous return by the expanded uterus, is treated through elevation of the lower extremities and use of support hose. In rare instances, the edema may cause extreme discomfort which is not relieved by rest and a short course of diuretics may provide relief and may be appropriate.

Metolazone may be used in the reduction of blood pressure in the management of mild to moderate essential hypertension, either as the sole therapeutic agent or in combination with other antihypertensive therapy.

Contraindications: Anuria, hepatic coma or precoma, hypersensitivity to metolazone or other sulfonamide derivatives.

Precautions: Hypokalemia may occur, with consequent weakness, cramps, and cardiac dysrhythmias. Hypokalemia is a particular hazard in digitalized patients; dangerous or fatal arrhythmias may be precipitated.

Azotemia and hyperuricemia may be noted or precipitated during the administration of metolazone. (Infrequently, gouty attacks have been reported in persons with history of gout).

If azotemia and oliguria worsen during treatment of patients with severe renal disease, discontinue metolazone.

Metolazone will, on occasion, exhibit considerable potentiation when administered concurrently with furosemide. Excessive, massive volume and electrolyte depletion may result.

Observe patients receiving metolazone carefully and monitor serum electrolytes for signs and symptoms of fluid or electrolyte imbalance; namely, hyponatremia, hypochloremia and hypokalemia. Assess BUN, uric acid and glucose levels during therapy. Hypokalemia, an ever present hazard with most diuretic therapy, will be more common in association with intensive or prolonged diuretic therapy, with concomitant steroid or ACTH therapy and with inadequate electrolyte intake. Determine the serum potassium at regular intervals and institute potassium supplementation when indicated.

The clinical signs of electrolyte imbalance are: dry mouth, thirst, weakness, lethargy, drowsiness, restlessness, muscle pains or cramps, muscle fatigue, hypotension, oliguria, tachycardia and gastrointestinal disturbances such as nausea and vomiting.

Metolazone may potentiate the effects of tubocurarine and decrease the arterial response to levaterenol. On this basis, it may be advisable to discontinue the drug at least 48 hours prior to elective surgery.

Special caution should be used in treating patients with severe hepatic disease since diuretics may induce metabolic alkalosis in cases of potassium depletion that may precipitate episodes of hepatic encephalopathy.

Orthostatic hypotension may occur and may be potentiated by alcohol, barbiturates, narcotics or concurrent therapy with other antihypertensives.

When metolazone is used with other antihypertensive drugs, take particular care, especially during initial therapy. Dosage of other antihypertensive agents, especially the ganglionic blockers and guanethidine, should be reduced. Hydralazine in therapeutic doses may interfere with the natriuretic action of metolazone.

Metolazone may be given with a potassium-sparing diuretic when indicated. In this circumstance, diuresis may be enhanced and dosages should be reduced. Potassium retention and hyperkalemia may result; determine the serum potassium frequently. Potassium supplementation is contraindicated when a potassium-sparing diuretic is given.

While not reported for metolazone, use of diuretics have on rare occasion been associated with pathologic changes in the parathyroid gland and with hypercalcemia and hypophosphatemia. Sulfonamide derivatives have been reported to exacerbate or activate systemic lupus erythematosus. These possibilities should be kept in mind with the use of metolazone.

Administer metolazone cautiously to patients with severely impaired renal function, since the drug is excreted primarily by the renal route.

Observe caution when administering metolazone to hyperuricemic or gouty patients. The drug exerts minimal effects on glucose metabolism; insulin requirements may be affected in diabetics, and hyperglycemia and glycosuria may occur in patients with latent diabetes.
Pregnancy: Since metolazone crosses the placenta and appears in cord blood, its administration to women of childbearing age requires that the potential benefits of the drug be weighed against its possible hazards to the fetus. The potential effects on the fetus include, fetal or neonatal jaundice, thrombocytopenia, and possibly other adverse reactions which have occurred in the adult. However, teratologic studies in mice, rats and rabbits, conducted for 3 generations in rats, have not shown teratogenic effects in these animals.
Lactation: Metolazone appears in breast milk. Thus, it is possible that the effects of metolazone may occur in the newborn under these circumstances. If the use of metolazone is deemed essential for a nursing mother, the patient should stop nursing.

Diuretics enhance the cardiotoxic (e.g., ECG changes) and neurotoxic (e.g., ataxia, confusion and mental disorientation) effects of lithium, and these drugs should not be administered concurrently. In those rare instances when these drugs must be given together, patients should be observed closely for signs and symptoms of lithium toxicity. Close monitoring of serum electrolytes and maintenance of adequate fluid, potassium and sodium intake also are necessary.

Adverse Effects: Gastrointestinal: constipation, nausea, vomiting, anorexia, diarrhea, abdominal bloating, epigastric distress, intrahepatic cholestatic jaundice, hepatitis, pancreatitis.
CNS: syncope, dizziness, drowsiness, vertigo, headache, neuropathy, paresthesias, psychotic depression, impotence, fatigue, weakness, restlessness.
Cardiovascular: orthostatic hypotension, excessive volume depletion, hemoconcentration, venous thrombosis, palpitation, chest pain.
Hematologic: leukopenia, aplastic/hypoplastic anemia, agranulocytosis.
Dermatologic: urticaria and other skin rashes, necrotizing angitis, purpura, photosensitivity.
Miscellaneous: dry mouth, symptomatic and asymptomatic hypokalemia, hyponatremia, hypochloremia, hypochloremic alkalosis, hyperuricemia, hyperglycemia, hypophosphatemia, glycosuria, increase in BUN or creatinine, joint pain, fatigue, muscle cramps or spasm, weakness, restlessness, chills, acute gouty attacks.

Adverse reactions which have occurred with other diuretics, but which have not been reported to date for metolazone include: xanthopsia and thrombocytopenia. These reactions should be considered as possible occurrences with clinical usage of metolazone.

Whenever adverse reactions are moderate or severe, metolazone dosage should be reduced or therapy withdrawn.

Overdose: Symptoms: Based on the pharmacological activities of metolazone, overdosage might lead to excessive diuresis with electrolyte depletion. In cirrhotic patients, overdosage might precipitate hepatic coma.

Treatment: There is no specific antidote. Treatment is symptomatic and supportive. Induce emesis or perform gastric lavage. Correct dehydration, electrolyte imbalance, hepatic coma, and hypotension by established procedures.

Dosage: Therapy should be individualized according to patient response. Programs of therapy with metolazone should be titrated to gain a maximal initial therapeutic response and to determine the minimal dose possible to maintain that therapeutic response. Metolazone is a drug with a prolonged, 12 to 24 hour duration of action. When an initially desired therapeutic effect has been obtained, it is ordinarily advisable to reduce the dosage of metolazone to a lower maintenance level.

The daily dosage depends on the severity of each patient's condition, his sodium intake, and his responsiveness. Therefore, dosage adjustment is usually necessary during the course of therapy.

A decision to reduce the daily dosage of metolazone from a higher induction level to a lower maintenance level should be based on the results of thorough clinical and laboratory evaluations. If other diuretic or antihypertensive drugs are given concurrently with metolazone, the required dosage reduction should be carefully undertaken.
Children: Although metolazone has been used in a carefully selected group of pediatric patients under hospital conditions, the population of patients is not sufficient to establish a dosage level; therefore, metolazone is not recommended for use in the pediatric age group.

Initial Dosages: Edema of cardiac failure: 5 to 10 mg, once daily. Edema of renal disease: 5 to 20 mg, once daily. Mild to moderate essential hypertension: 2.5 to 5 mg, once daily. Maintenance Dosage: The time interval required for the initial higher-dosage regimen may vary from days in edematous states to 3 or 6 weeks in the treatment of elevated blood pressure.

When the dose of metolazone has been reduced to 2.5 mg once daily, further reduction can be achieved by cutting back the frequency of administration to every other day.

For patients with congestive cardiac failure who tend to experience paroxysmal nocturnal dyspnea, it is usually advisable to employ a dosage near the upper end of the range, to ensure prolongation of diuresis and saluresis for a full 24 hour period.

Supplied: 2.5 mg: Each slightly biconvex, pink tablet, debossed with its numeric strength on one side and ZAROXOLYN on the other, contains: metolazone 2.5 mg. Nonmedicinal ingredients: cellulose, D&C Red No 3 aluminum lake and magnesium stearate. Alcohol-, gluten-, lactose-, paraben-, sucrose- and tartrazine-free. Bottles of 100.

5 mg: Each slightly biconvex, blue tablet, debossed with its numeric strength on one side and ZAROXOLYN on the other, contains: metolazone 5 mg. Nonmedicinal ingredients: cellulose, FD&C Blue No 2 aluminum lake and magnesium stearate. Alcohol-, gluten-, lactose-, paraben-, sucrose- and tartrazine-free. Bottles of 100.

Dispense metolazone in amber bottles. Store at room temperature and protect from light.

(Shown in Product Recognition Section)

Z-BEC®
Whitehall-Robins

Zinc—Multivitamins

Indications: For deficiencies of Z-BEC's components in conditions such as febrile diseases, chronic or acute infections, burns, fractures, surgery, leg ulcers, toxic conditions, physiologic stress, alcoholism, prolonged exposure to high temperature, geriatrics, gastritis, peptic ulcer and colitis; in conditions involving special diets and weight reduction diets; dentistry: herpetic stomatitis, aphthous stomatitis, cheilosis, herpangina and gingivitis.

Precautions: Not intended for the treatment of pernicious anemia.

Dosage: Adults and children 12 years and over: 1 tablet daily with food or after meals. Dose and frequency of administration may be increased in accordance with the patient's requirements, as prescribed.

Supplied: Each green, film-coated, ellipse-shaped tablet, engraved "Z-BEC", contains: thiamine mononitrate 15 mg, riboflavin 10.2 mg, pyridoxine HCl 11 mg, niacinamide (as niacinamide ascorbate) 100 mg, calcium d-pantothenate 28.5 mg, cyanocobalamin 6 μg, vitamin C (as niacinamide ascorbate and ascorbic acid) 600 mg, dl-alphatocopheryl acetate 45 IU, zinc (as zinc sulfate) 22.5 mg. Nonmedicinal ingredients: cellulose, FD&C Blue No. 1, flavors, magnesium stearate, polysorbate, povidone, propylene glycol, riboflavin, silicon dioxide, stearic acid and titanium dioxide. Energy: <0.05 kJ (<0.01 kcal). Gluten-, lactose-, paraben-, sodium-, sucrose,- sulfite- and tartrazine-free. Bottles of 60.

ZeaSORB®
Stiefel

Chloroxylenol Compound

Antibacterial—Antifungal

Supplied: Each g of powder contains: microporous cellulose 45%, chloroxylenol 0.5%, aluminum dihydroxyallantoinate 0.2%. Nonmedicinal ingredients: fragrance, imidurea NF and starch acrylic copolymer. Sifter top plastic containers of 50 g.

The safety of immunization programs is in part maximized through monitoring vaccine-associated adverse events. To report a vaccine-associated adverse event, complete the form "Report of Vaccine-associated Adverse Event" found in the CLIN-INFO SECTION.

ZeaSORB® AF
Stiefel

Tolnaftate

Topical Antifungal

Supplied: Each g of powder contains: tolnaftate USP 1%. Nonmedicinal ingredients: aluminum dihydroxyallant, fragrance, imidurea NF, microporous cellulose, parachlorometaxylenol, starch acrylic copolymer and talcum. Sifter top plastic containers of 50 g.

ZEMURON™ Ⓟ
Organon

Rocuronium Bromide

Nondepolarizing Skeletal Neuromuscular Blocking Agent

Pharmacology: Rocuronium is a nondepolarizing neuromuscular blocking agent with a rapid to intermediate onset depending on dose and an intermediate duration of action. The drug acts by binding competitively to cholinergic receptors at the motor end-plate to antagonize the action of acetylcholine, an effect which is reversible in the presence of acetylcholinesterase inhibitors, such as neostigmine and edrophonium.

Pharmacodynamics: The ED_{95} (dose required to produce 95% suppression of the first [T1] mechanomyographic [MMG] response of the thumb to indirect supramaximal train-of-four stimulation of the ulnar nerve) is approximately 0.3 mg/kg (300 μg/kg) in adults receiving opioid/N_2O/O_2 anesthesia. At equipotent doses, rocuronium has approximately the same clinically effective duration of action as vecuronium. However, the onset of action is approximately 40% shorter for rocuronium than for vecuronium at doses of 2 to 3 times the ED_{95}. The median pharmacodynamic parameter values for rocuronium over a range of doses are presented in Tables I and II.

Intubation Conditions: A dose of 0.6 mg/kg (2×ED_{95}) rocuronium administered following the induction of thiopental/narcotic anesthesia in adults or halothane anesthesia in children generally produces good or excellent conditions for tracheal intubation initiated at 60 to 70 seconds postadministration (see Table II).

Intubating conditions were assessed in 230 patients in 6 clinical trials where anesthesia was induced with either thiopental (3 to 6 mg/kg) or propofol (1.5 to 2.5 mg/kg) in combination with either fentanyl (2 to 5 μg/kg) or alfentanil (1 mg). Most of the patients also received a premedication such as midazolam or temazepam. Most patients had intubation attempted within 60 to 90 seconds of administration of rocuronium injection 0.6 mg/kg or succinylcholine 1 to 1.5 mg/kg. Excellent or good intubating conditions were achieved in 119/120 (99%[95% CI 95 to 99.9%]) patients receiving rocuronium and in 108/110 (98%[95% CI 94 to 99.8%]) patients receiving succinylcholine. The duration of action of rocuronium 0.6 mg/kg is longer than succinylcholine and at this dose is approximately equivalent to the duration of other intermediate acting neuromuscular blocking drugs.

Table II—Zemuron

Intubating Conditions in Patients with Intubation Initiated at 60 to 70 Seconds. Percent, Median [Range]

Zemuron Dose (mg/kg) Administered over 5 s	Percent of Patients with Excellent[b] or Good[c] Intubating Conditions	Time to Completion of Intubation (min)
Adults[a] 18-64 yrs		
0.45 (n=43)	86%	1.6[1.0-7.0]
0.6 (n=51)	96%	1.6[1.0-3.2]
Children		
3 mo-1 yr		
0.6 (n=18)	100%	1.0[1.0-1.5]
1-4 yrs		
0.6 (n=12)	100%	1.0[0.5-2.3]

[a] Excludes patients undergoing cesarean section.
[b] Excellent Intubating Conditions=jaw relaxed, vocal cords apart & immobile, no diaphragmatic movement.
[c] Good Intubating Conditions=jaw relaxed, vocal cords apart & immobile, some diaphragmatic movement.

Maintenance Doses: In adult patients under opioid/N_2O/O_2 anesthesia, the median (range of individual values) clinical duration (time from injection of the maintenance dose at a T1 of 25% of control to a return to 25% of the control T1) of maintenance doses of 0.1, 0.15 and 0.2 mg/kg (100, 150 and 200 μg/kg) of rocuronium is 12 minutes (range 2 to 31 minutes), 17 minutes (range 6 to 50 minutes), and 24 minutes (range 7 to 69 minutes), respectively. Repetitive maintenance dosing results in clinically insignificant median increases of 2 to 4 minutes in clinical duration between the first and fifth consecutive dose.

The median (range) rate of spontaneous recovery of T1 from 25 to 75% (n=182), following the final maintenance dose of rocuronium, is 13 minutes (4 to 84 minutes).

Anticholinesterase Antagonism: Once spontaneous recovery has started, the neuromuscular block produced by rocuronium is readily reversed with various anticholinesterase agents, e.g., edrophonium or neostigmine. The deeper the level of neuromuscular blockade at reversal, the longer the time required for recovery of neuromuscular function and the greater the dose of anticholinesterase agent required.

Reversal data were analyzed for 320 patients who received neostigmine or edrophonium in the North American clinical trials. When neuromuscular block was reversed at a T1 of 22 to 28% in 36 adults, recovery to a T1 of 89(50 to 132)% and T4/T1 of 69(38 to 92)% was achieved within 5 minutes. Only 5 of the 320 adults reversed received an additional dose of reversal agent. The median (range) dose of neostigmine was 0.04 (0.01 to 0.09) mg/kg and the median (range) dose of edrophonium was 0.5 (0.3 to 1) mg/kg.

In geriatric patients (n=51) reversed with neostigmine, the median T4/T1 increased from 40 to 88% in 5 minutes.

Table I—Zemuron

Pharmacodynamic Parameter Values for the Initial Dose of Zemuron Administered during Opioid/N_2O/O_2 Anesthesia (Adults) and Halothane Anesthesia (Children). Median [Range].

Zemuron Dose Administered over 5 s	Time to ≥80% Block (min)	Time to Maximum Block (min)	Clinical Duration (min)	Peak Effect (% of control T_1)
Adults 18 to 64 yrs				
0.45 mg/kg (n=50)	1.3[0.8-6.2]	3.0[1.3-8.2]	22[12-31]	2.5[0-25]
0.6 mg/kg (n=142)	1.0[0.4-6.0]	1.8[0.6-13.0]	31[15-85]	0[0-9.7]
0.9 mg/kg (n=20)	1.1[0.3-3.8]	1.4[0.8-6.2]	58[27-111]	0[0-7]
1.2 mg/kg (n=18)	0.7[0.4-1.7]	1.0[0.6-4.7]	67[38-160]	0[0-4]
Geriatrics 65 to 78 yrs				
0.6 mg/kg (n=31)	2.3[1.0-8.3]	3.7[1.3-11.3]	46[22-73]	0[0-7]
0.9 mg/kg (n=5)	2.0[1.0-3.0]	2.5[1.2-5.0]	62[49-75]	0[0-0]
1.2 mg/kg (n=7)	1.0[0.8-3.5]	1.3[1.2-4.7]	94[64-138]	0[0-0]
Children				
3 mo-1 yr				
0.6 (n=17)	—	0.8[0.3-3]	41[24-68]	0[0-0]
0.8 (n=9)	—	0.7[0.5-0.8]	40[27-70]	0[0-3]
1-12 yrs				
0.6 (n=27)	0.8[0.4-2]	1.0[0.5-3.3]	26[17-39]	0[0-0]
0.8 (n=18)	—	0.5[0.3-1]	30[17-56]	0[0-0]

n=the number of patients who had Time to Maximum Block recorded.
Clinical Duration=time until return to 25% of control T_1.
Patients receiving doses of 0.45 mg/kg who achieved less than 90% block (16% of these patients) had about 12 to 15 minutes to 25% recovery.

Zemuron (cont'd)

Children (n=27) who received 0.5 mg/kg edrophonium had increases in the median T4/T1 from 37% at reversal to 93% after 2 minutes. Children (n=58) who received 1 mg/kg edrophonium had increases in the median T4/T1 from 72% at reversal to 100% after 2 minutes. Infants (n=10) who were reversed with 0.03 mg/kg neostigmine recovered from 25 to 75% T1 within 4 minutes. There were no reports of less than satisfactory clinical recovery of neuromuscular function.

Inhalation Anesthetics: The duration of the neuromuscular blocking action of rocuronium may be enhanced by approximately 30% in the presence of potent inhalation anesthetics. The median clinical duration of a dose of 0.6 mg/kg was 30, 38, and 42 minutes under opioid/N_2O/O_2, enflurane and isoflurane maintenance anesthesia, respectively. During 1 to 2 h of infusion, the infusion rate of rocuronium required to maintain about 95% block was decreased by as much as 40% under enflurane and isoflurane anesthesia (see Precautions, Inhalation Anesthetics).

Children: Children (1 to 13 yr) under halothane anesthesia are less sensitive to rocuronium (ED_{50} approximately 0.18 mg/kg [180 µg/kg], ED_{95} 0.35 to 0.4 mg/kg [350 to 400 µg/kg]) than adults on a mg/kg (µg/kg) basis. The onset time and duration of block are shorter in children (1 to 13 yr) than in adults (see Table I on previous page). During halothane anesthesia, at doses of 0.6 mg/kg (600 µg/kg) of rocuronium, the median onset time is 60 seconds (30 to 200 sec) and the clinical duration is 26 min (17 to 39 min). Maintenance doses of 0.1 or 0.125 mg/kg (100 or 125 µg/kg) rocuronium in children under halothane anesthesia provided a median clinical duration of 7 and 10 minutes, respectively. The median rate of spontaneous recovery of T1 from 25 to 75% was 9.5 minutes (4 to 29 minutes).

The clinical durations of action of 0.6 and 0.8 mg/kg doses of rocuronium are approximately 30-60% longer in infants aged 3 months to 1 year than in children aged 1 to 13 yrs (see Table I on previous page).

Geriatrics: Geriatric patients (≥65 yrs) under opioid/N_2O/O_2 anesthesia show a longer onset time and duration of block than adults (18 to 65 yrs) at equivalent doses. At doses of 0.6, 0.9 and 1.2 mg/kg (600, 900 and 1 200 µg/kg) of rocuronium, median onset times of 3.7 (1.3 to 11.3), 2.5 (1.2 to 5), and 1.3 (1.2 to 4.7) minutes, respectively, have been reported for geriatric patients compared with 1.8 (0.6 to 13), 1.4 (0.8 to 6.2), and 1.0 (0.6 to 4.7) minutes, respectively for adults. Thus, rocuronium is not recommended for rapid sequence tracheal intubation in geriatric patients. Median clinical duration times at these doses were 46 (22 to 73), 62 (49 to 75), and 94 (64 to 138) minutes, respectively for geriatric patients versus 31 (15 to 85), 58 (27 to 111), and 67 (38 to 160) minutes, respectively for adults. The median rate of spontaneous recovery of T1 from 25 to 75% after a dose of 0.6 mg/kg (600 µg/kg) was 21 (11 to 56) minutes in geriatric patients (70 to 90 yrs) compared with 12 (5 to 36) minutes in young adults (18 to 60 yrs).

Hepatic Impairment: The influence of hepatic impairment on the pharmacodynamics of a 0.6 mg/kg dose of rocuronium was investigated in a study in which 9 patients with alcoholic cirrhosis were compared to 10 patients with normal hepatic function. Relative to the normal group, the patients with hepatic impairment exhibited an increased clinical duration of action (60 versus 42 min). The recovery index (time for recovery from 25 to 75% T1 suppression) was also prolonged in the cirrhotic patients (53 versus 20 min).

Renal Failure: Three single centre clinical trials have been performed to compare the pharmacodynamic characteristics of a 0.6 mg/kg dose of rocuronium in patients having normal renal function (n=31) to those for patients having renal impairment (n=30) undergoing kidney transplantation or AV shunt/peritoneal catheter implantation surgery for hemodialysis while receiving steady-state isoflurane anesthesia. The pharmacodynamic characteristics of rocuronium were not altered in a consistent manner in the patients with renal impairment although clinical duration and recovery times were more variable than in patients with normal renal function. Dosage adjustments are not recommended for patients with renal impairment receiving rocuronium.

Hemodynamics: In most clinical trials, the monitoring of hemodynamic parameters during the period immediately following the administration of rocuronium was confounded by laryngoscopy and intubation, events in themselves associated with elevations of heart rate and mean arterial blood pressure. In 1 study in which a 6 minute period was permitted to elapse between the administration of rocuronium at 0.6, 0.9 and 1.2 mg/kg doses and subsequent intubation, no dose-dependent changes in heart rate or mean arterial pressure were observed.

Histamine Release: In studies of histamine release, a clinically significant elevation of plasma histamine concentration occurred in 1 of 88 patients. Clinical signs of histamine release (flushing, rash, or bronchospasm) associated with the administration of rocuronium injection were assessed in clinical trials and reported in 9 of 1 137 (0.8%) patients.

Pharmacokinetics: The pharmacokinetic characteristics of i.v. administered rocuronium are best described by a 3 compartment open model. The comparative population estimates for geriatrics and other adult surgical patients receiving a single 0.6 mg/kg dose of rocuronium during opioid/N_2O/O_2 anesthesia are presented in Table III.

Table III—Zemuron

Pharmacokinetic Parameters* of Zemuron in Adults and Geriatrics during Opioid/N_2O/O_2 Anesthesia. Mean±SD

PK Parameters	Adults (27-58 yrs) n=22	Geriatrics (65-78 yrs) n=20
Clearance (L/kg/h)	0.25±0.08	0.21±0.06
Volume of Distribution at Steady State (L/kg)	0.25±0.04	0.22±0.03
$T_{1/2}\beta$ Elimination (h)	1.4±0.4	1.5±0.4

*Data from the in vivo pharmacokinetics studies were used to generate population estimates for the parameters and a measure of the estimate variability.

The comparative population estimates for normal adults, patients with renal impairment undergoing cadaver renal transplantation, and patients with hepatic cirrhosis receiving a single 0.6 mg/kg dose of rocuronium during isoflurane anesthesia are presented in Table IV.

Table IV—Zemuron

Pharmacokinetic Parameters[a] of Zemuron in Adults with Normal Renal and Hepatic Function, Renal Transplant Patients and Hepatic Dysfunction Patients during Isoflurane Anesthesia. Mean±SD

PK Parameters	Normal Renal and Hepatic Function (23-65 yrs) n=10	Renal Transplant Patients (21-45 yrs) n=10	Hepatic Dysfunction Patients (31-67 yrs) n=9
Clearance (L/kg/h)	0.16±0.05[b]	0.13±0.04	0.13±0.06
Volume of Distributon at Steady State (L/kg)	0.26±0.03	0.34±0.11	0.53±0.14
$T_{1/2}\beta$ Elimination (h)	2.4±0.8[b]	2.4±1.1	4.3±2.6

[a]Data from the in vivo pharmacokinetics studies were used to generate population estimates for the parameters and a measure of the estimate variability.

[b]Differences in the calculated $T_{1/2}\beta$ and Cl between this study and the study in young adults vs. geriatrics (≥65 years) are related to the different sample populations and anesthetic techniques.

Geriatrics: In a study of the comparative pharmacokinetics of a 0.6 mg/kg dose of rocuronium in 22 adult (27 to 58 yrs) and 20 geriatric (70 to 78 yrs) patients, advanced age was associated with a significant decrease in clearance and steady-state volume of distribution, although the elimination half-life remained unaltered.

Children: See Table V.

Table V—Zemuron

Pharmacokinetic Parameters of Zemuron in Pediatric Patients during Halothane Anesthesia. Mean±SD

Summary of Mean (Range) Pharmacokinetic Parameters*

	3-<12 months	1-<3 years	3-<8 years
Clearance (L/kg/h)	0.35±0.08	0.32±0.07	0.44±0.16
Volume of Distribution at Steady State (L/kg)	0.30±0.04	0.26±0.06	0.21±0.03
$T_{1/2}\beta$ Elimination (h)	1.3±0.5	1.1±0.7	0.8±0.3

*only estimates from 3 compartment model included (n=18).

In pediatric patients receiving a single 0.8 mg/kg bolus dose of rocuronium, the observed half-life values were in the same order of magnitude as those reported for adult patients. The half-life values for rocuronium decreased with advancing pediatric age. Clearance tended to be somewhat higher in the 3 to 8 year olds than in the younger patients. The steady-state volume of distribution was significantly higher in the 3 to 12 month age group than in the 3 to 8 year age group. No statistically significant differences were observed between the 3 age groups in terms of the plasma levels of rocuronium at 25, 75, and 90% recovery.

Hepatic and Renal Impairment: The steady-state volume of distribution was increased by about 30% in patients undergoing cadaver renal transplantation (n=10) and 100% in patients with hepatic dysfunction associated with alcoholic cirrhosis (n=9) relative to patients with normal renal and hepatic function (n=10). The beta elimination half-life was increased by approximately 80% in patients with hepatic impairment, but was unaffected in the renally impaired patient group.

Inhalational Anesthesia: Plasma levels of rocuronium during continuous infusion were determined in patients receiving steady-state opioid/N_2O/O_2 (n=10), enflurane (n=9), or isoflurane (n=9) anesthesia. At the end of the second hour of continuous infusion, lower mean plasma concentrations were required to maintain 90 to 95% neuromuscular blockade during steady-state isoflurane (1 223 ng/mL) and enflurane (1 117 ng/mL) anesthesia than during opioid/N_2O/O_2 (1 358 ng/mL) anesthesia.

Metabolism: Following administration of a single 1 mg/kg bolus dose to 10 adult patients, metabolites in the plasma or urine were either absent or below the limit of detection (5 ng/mL).

Excretion: Following administration of a single 1 mg/kg bolus dose to 10 adult patients, total urinary excretion was 33% over a 24 hour period. Of this, 65% was recovered during the first 2 hours and 94% over the first 6 hours.

Placental Transfer: The placental transfer of rocuronium was investigated in 2 studies involving a total of 17 neonates born to women receiving 0.6 mg/kg rocuronium during Cesarean section. The mean umbilical venous to maternal venous plasma ratio ranged from 16 to 22% in these studies.

Reduced Plasma Cholinesterase Activity: No differences from patients with normal plasma cholinesterase activity are expected since rocuronium metabolism does not depend on plasma cholinesterase.

Indications: Rocuronium is a nondepolarizing neuromuscular blocking agent with a rapid to intermediate onset depending on dose and intermediate duration of action. Rocuronium is indicated as an adjunct to general anesthesia to facilitate both rapid sequence (initiated at 60 to 90 seconds post-administration) and routine endotracheal intubation and to provide skeletal muscle relaxation during surgery or mechanical ventilation.

Contraindications: In patients known to have an allergic hypersensitivity to the drug or any component of its formulation.

Warnings: General: Rocuronium should be administered in carefully adjusted dosages by or under the supervision of experienced clinicians who are familiar with its actions and the possible complications of its use. The drug should not be administered unless facilities for intubation, artificial respiration, oxygen therapy, and an antagonist are within immediate reach. It is recommended that clinicians administering neuromuscular blocking agents such as rocuronium employ a peripheral nerve stimulator to monitor drug response, need for additional relaxant, and adequacy of spontaneous recovery or antagonism.

Intensive Care Unit: To reduce the possibility of prolonged neuromuscular blockade and other complications that might occur following long-term use in the ICU, rocuronium or any other neuromuscular relaxant should be administered in carefully adjusted doses by or under the supervision of experienced clinicians who are familiar with its actions and with appropriate peripheral nerve stimulator muscle monitoring techniques.

Neuromuscular Disease: In patients with myasthenia gravis or myasthenic (Eaton-Lambert) syndrome, small doses of nondepolarizing neuromuscular blocking agents may have profound effects. In such patients, a peripheral nerve stimulator and use of a small test dose may be of value in monitoring the response to administration of muscle relaxants. For patients having conditions in which prolonged neuromuscular blockade is a possibility (e.g., neuromuscular disease, carcinomatosis, severe cachexia, or debilitation), a peripheral nerve stimulator and use of a small test dose may be of particular value in assessing and monitoring dosage requirements.

Compatibility: Rocuronium injection, which has an acid pH, should not be mixed with alkaline solutions (e.g., barbiturate solutions) in the same syringe or administered simultaneously during i.v. infusion through the same needle.

Precautions: Rapid Sequence Tracheal Intubation: Rapid sequence tracheal intubation has not been adequately studied at time points of less than 60 seconds post-administration of rocuronium. As the onset of action of rocuronium is delayed in geriatric patients relative to other adults, the use of rocuronium for rapid sequence intubation is not recommended in patients over 65 years of age.

Cardiovascular Effects: Rocuronium was associated with a slight elevation of heart rate and blood pressure in some studies (mean increase ≤10% over baseline) in which hemodynamic measurements were performed prior to intubation and initiation of surgery. The increase in heart rate and mean arterial pressure which occurs during endotracheal intubation may be accentuated in the presence of rocuronium. In the North American studies, laryngoscopy and tracheal intubation following rocuronium administration were accompanied by transient tachycardia (≥30% increases) in about one-third of adult patients under opioid/N_2O/O_2 anesthesia. Experience with rocuronium in patients undergoing cardiovascular surgery is limited to 2 small clinical trials.

In one of these, 17 patients scheduled for aortic surgery were anesthetized with fentanyl and flunitrazepam, then intubated prior to receiving single bolus doses of 0.6 or 0.9 mg/kg rocuronium. Mean arterial pressure was significantly increased over baseline levels at 2, 5 and 10 minute time points in the 0.6 mg/kg (15 to 24% increases over baseline) but not the 0.9 mg/kg (3 to 7% increases over baseline group). In another study, the hemodynamic effects of single bolus doses of 0.9 mg/kg rocuronium and 0.15 mg/kg vecuronium were studied in ASA 3 and 4 patients scheduled for coronary artery bypass grafting in whom anesthesia had been induced with midazolam and sufentanil. Rocuronium (n=11) was associated with statistically significant increases in mean arterial blood pressure at 5 minutes post-administration (13% increase over baseline) and 10 minutes post-intubation (9% increase over baseline) which were not seen in the vecuronium group (n=10). These increases did not, however, represent an elevation over mean arterial blood pressure values prior to the induction of anesthesia. In both of these studies, mean increases in heart rate of 6 to 8% over post-induction baseline values were observed.

Tachycardia (≥30%) occurred in 12 of 127 children. Most of the children developing tachycardia were from a single study in which the patients were anesthetized with halothane and did not receive atropine for induction.

Pulmonary Vascular Resistance: Caution is appropriate in patients with pulmonary hypertension or valvular heart disease. In one clinical trial, 10 patients with clinically significant cardiovascular disease undergoing coronary artery bypass graft surgery received an initial dose of 0.6 mg/kg rocuronium injection. Neuromuscular block was maintained during surgery with bolus maintenance doses of 0.3 mg/kg. Following induction, continuous 0.008 mg/kg/min infusion of rocuronium produced relaxation sufficient to support mechanical ventilation for 6 to 12 hours in the surgical intensive care unit (SICU) while the patients were recovering from surgery. Hypertension and tachycardia were reported in some patients but these occurrences were less frequent in patients receiving beta or calcium channel blocking drugs. In 7 of these 10 patients rocuronium was associated with transient increases (≥30%) in pulmonary vascular resistance. In another clinical trial of 17 patients undergoing abdominal aortic surgery, transient increases (≥30%) in pulmonary vascular resistance were observed in 4 of 17 patients receiving rocuronium 0.6 or 0.9 mg/kg.

Long-term Use in ICU: No information is available concerning the efficacy and safety of long-term (days to weeks) i.v. rocuronium infusion to facilitate mechanical ventilation in the intensive care unit. In rare cases, long-term use of neuromuscular blocking drugs to facilitate mechanical ventilation in ICU settings has been associated with prolonged paralysis and/or skeletal muscle weakness that is first noted during attempts to wean patients from the ventilator. In these patients, the actions of the neuromuscular blocking agent may be enhanced by other drugs (e.g., broad spectrum antibiotics, narcotics and/or steroids) or by conditions such as acid-base or electrolyte imbalance, hypoxic episodes of varying duration, or extreme debilitation. Additionally, patients immobilized for extended periods frequently develop symptoms consistent with disuse muscle atrophy. The recovery picture may vary from regaining movement and strength in all muscles to initial recovery of movement of the facial muscles and small muscles of the extremities then to the remaining muscles. In rare cases, recovery may involve an extended period of time or even require rehabilitation. Therefore, when there is a need for long-term mechanical ventilation, the benefits-to-risk ratio of neuromuscular blockade must be considered. The syndrome of critical illness polyneuropathy associated with sepsis and multiorgan failure may be associated with prolonged skeletal muscle paralysis, but can also occur without the use of muscle relaxants. Thus, the role of muscle relaxants in the etiology of prolonged paralysis in the ICU is not known with certainty. Continuous infusion or intermittent bolus dosing to support long term mechanical ventilation has not been studied sufficiently to support dosage recommendations.

Whenever the use of rocuronium or any neuromuscular blocking agent is contemplated in the ICU, it is recommended that neuromuscular transmission be monitored continuously during administration and recovery with the help of a nerve stimulator. Additional doses of rocuronium or any other neuromuscular blocking agent should not be given before there is a definite response to T1 or to the first twitch. If no response is elicited, infusion administration should be discontinued until a response returns.

Pregnancy: A teratogenicity study has been conducted in rats using i.v. administered doses of rocuronium up to 0.3 mg/kg. No teratogenic effects were observed at the sub-paralyzing doses used in this study. There are no adequate and well-controlled studies in pregnant women. Because animal reproduction studies have not been performed under conditions that would approximate those of clinical use, rocuronium should be used during pregnancy only if the potential benefit justifies the potential risk to the fetus.

Obstetrics (Cesarean section): Rocuronium injection 0.6 mg/kg (600 µg/kg) was administered with thiopental, 3 to 4 mg/kg (n=13) or 4 to 6 mg/kg (n=42), for rapid sequence induction of anesthesia for cesarean section. The umbilical venous plasma concentrations were 18% of maternal concentrations at delivery. No neonate had APGAR scores of <7 at 5 minutes post-delivery. Intubating conditions were poor or inadequate in 5 of 13 women receiving 3 to 4 mg/kg thiopental when intubation was attempted 60 seconds after drug injection. Therefore, rocuronium is not recommended for rapid sequence induction in cesarean section patients. The possibility of respiratory depression in the neonate should always be considered following a cesarean section during which a neuromuscular blocking agent has been administered.

Lactation: It is not known whether rocuronium is excreted in human milk. Because many drugs are excreted in human milk, caution should be exercised when rocuronium is administered to a nursing woman.

Children: The use of rocuronium in children less than 3 months of age has not been investigated. See Pharmacology and Dosage, Pediatrics for clinical experience and recommendations for use in infants and children 3 months to 14 years of age. Although the potency of rocuronium is similar in infants and older children (estimated ED_{95} values of 0.39 mg/kg for infants 1 to 12 months, 0.35 mg/kg for children 1 to 4 yrs, 0.4 mg/kg for children 4 to 13 yrs under halothane anesthesia), the duration of clinically effective blockade tends to be longer in infants less than 12 months in age. Of the children anesthetized with halothane who did not receive atropine with induction, about 80% experienced a transient increase (≥30%) in heart rate after intubation.

Geriatrics: Rocuronium has been administered to 43 elderly patients (65 to 78 yrs) in clinical trials. The duration of neuromuscular blockade tends to be slightly longer in elderly patients (see Pharmacology). As the onset of action of rocuronium is delayed in geriatric patients relative to other adults, the use of rocuronium for rapid sequence intubation is not recommended in patients over 65 years of age.

Hepatic Disease: Rocuronium has been studied in a limited number of patients (n=38) with clinically significant hepatic disease. In 9 patients with alcoholic cirrhosis receiving stable isoflurane anesthesia, the median clinical duration of a 0.6 mg/kg (600 µg/kg) dose was moderately prolonged (60 min) compared to that observed in 10 patients with normal hepatic function (42 min). The median recovery rate (25 to 75% recovery of twitch suppression) was also prolonged in patients with cirrhosis (53 min) compared to patients with normal hepatic function (20 min). Because rocuronium is primarily excreted by the liver, it should be used with caution in patients having clinically significant hepatic disease. Four of eight patients with cirrhosis, who received rocuronium 0.6 mg/kg under opioid/N_2O/O_2 anesthesia, did not achieve complete block. These findings are consistent with the increase in volume of distribution at steady state observed in patients with significant hepatic disease. If used for rapid sequence induction in patients with ascites, an increased initial dosage may be necessary to assure complete block. Duration will be prolonged in these cases. The use of single bolus doses higher than 0.6 mg/kg has not been studied in patients with hepatic impairment.

Renal Failure: Rocuronium has been studied at the dose of 0.6 mg/kg (600 µg/kg) in a limited number of patients (n=10) undergoing renal transplant surgery, recently dialyzed in preparation for cadaver renal transplant. The median clinical duration was not considered to be prolonged relative to patients with normal renal function (53 min versus 42 min), however there was substantial variation within the renal transplant group (range: 22 to 90 minutes). The median spontaneous recovery rate from 25 to 75% of control in renal transplant patients was similar to that in normal patients (30 [7 to 35] min vs. 20 [12 to 67]min). Two additional studies have been performed in which rocuronium was administered to a total of 20 patients undergoing nephrectomy, AV shunt surgery, or implantation of peritoneal catheters. These studies did not demonstrate a consistent trend for prolongation of recovery time. Due to the limited role of the kidney in the excretion of rocuronium, usual dosing guidelines should generally be suitable for patients with renal failure.

Concomitant Disease States: As with other neuromuscular blocking agents, rocuronium may have profound neuromuscular blocking effects in cachectic or debilitated patients, patients with neuromuscular diseases, and patients with carcinomatosis. In these or other patients in whom potentiation of neuromuscular block or difficulty with reversal may be anticipated, a decrease from the recommended initial dose should be considered. Resistance to nondepolarizing neuromuscular blocking agents may be associated with burns, disuse atrophy, denervation, cerebral palsy, and direct muscle trauma.

Obesity: Rocuronium injection 0.6 mg/kg has been administered according to actual body weight (ABW) (n=12) or ideal body weight (IBW) (n=11) in a clinical trial in obese patients. Obese patients dosed according to IBW had a longer time to maximum block (median 135 s [73 to 203] vs. 83 s [57 to 102]) and a shorter clinical duration (median 25 min [14 to 29] vs. 34 min [24 to 52]) than obese patients dosed according to ABW. Patients dosed according to IBW did not achieve intubating conditions comparable to those dosed based on ABW. A third group consisting of nonobese patients receiving 0.6 mg/kg rocuronium, exhibited a time to maximum block of 116 (61 to 165) seconds and a clinical duration of 28 (19 to 38) minutes. These results support the recommendation that obese patients be dosed based on actual body weight.

Hypothermia: Hypothermia (25 to 28°C) has been associated with a decreased requirement for nondepolarizing neuromuscular blocking agents.

Malignant Hyperthermia (MH): Malignant hyperthermia has not been reported in association with the administration of rocuronium. Because rocuronium is always used with other agents, and because the occurrence of malignant hyperthermia during anesthesia is possible even in the absence of known triggering agents, clinicians should be familiar with early signs, confirmatory diagnosis and treatment of malignant hyperthermia prior to the start of any anesthetic. In an animal study in MH-susceptible swine, the administration of rocuronium was not associated with the development of malignant hyperthermia.

Burns: Resistance to nondepolarizing neuromuscular blocking agents may develop in patients with burns, depending on the time elapsed since the injury and the size of the burn.

Delayed Onset of Action: The onset of action of nondepolarizing neuromuscular blockers may be delayed in patients having conditions associated with slower circulation time (e.g., cardiovascular disease or advanced age) or an increased volume of distribution (e.g., edematous states). Because higher doses of rocuronium produce a longer duration of action, the initial dosage should not usually be increased in these patients to enhance onset time; instead, more time should be allowed for the drug to achieve its maximum effect.

CNS: Rocuronium has no known effect on consciousness, pain threshold or cerebration. Therefore, administration must be accompanied by adequate anesthesia or sedation.

Acid-Base or Electrolyte Abnormalities: Electrolyte and/or acid-base imbalances may enhance or inhibit neuromuscular blockade. For example, hyperkalemia has been reported to antagonize nondepolarizing agents while hypokalemia has been associated with an enhancement of their activity.

I.M. Use: No data are available to support the use of rocuronium by i.m. injection.

Carcinogenesis, Mutagenesis, Impairment of Fertility: Studies in animals have not been performed to evaluate carcinogenic potential or impairment of fertility. Mutagenicity studies (Ames test, mammalian cell, and micronucleus test) conducted with rocuronium revealed no mutagenic potential.

Drug Interactions: Succinylcholine: The use of rocuronium before succinylcholine, for the purpose of attenuating some

Zemuron (cont'd)

of the side effects of succinylcholine, has not been sufficiently studied. If rocuronium is administered following succinylcholine, it should not be given until recovery from succinylcholine has been observed. When a 0.6 mg/kg (600 μg/kg) dose of rocuronium was administered after a 1 mg/kg dose of succinylcholine following recovery of T1 to 75% of control, the mean clinical duration of action was slightly prolonged relative to that observed without succinylcholine (mean 36 vs. 30 minutes).

Other Nondepolarizing Muscle Relaxants: There are no controlled studies documenting the use of rocuronium before or after other nondepolarizing muscle relaxants. Interactions have been observed when other nondepolarizing muscle relaxants have been administered in succession.

Inhalation Anesthetics: The ED_{50} of rocuronium in adult patients determined under stable end-tidal concentrations of isoflurane, halothane, and enflurane was reduced by 20%, 41% and 46% respectively, as compared with that determined under opioid/N_2O/O_2 anesthesia. ED_{95} doses were, however, similar for patients receiving opioid/N_2O/O_2, halothane, and isoflurane anesthesia. The ED_{95} under conditions of enflurane anesthesia was approximately 40% lower than that determined for other types of anesthesia.

Since the neuromuscular blocking agents are routinely administered before, or shortly after, the administration of inhalation anesthetics, minimal effects on onset time and peak effect are generally observed. In routine use of neuromuscular blocking agents, only spontaneous recovery is generally affected (prolonged). No definite interaction between rocuronium and halothane, as used clinically, has been demonstrated. In one study use of enflurane in 10 patients, resulted in a 20% increase in the mean clinical duration of the initial intubating dose, and a 37% increase in the duration of subsequent maintenance doses, when compared in the same study to 10 patients under opioid/N_2O/O_2 anesthesia. Potentiation by these agents is also observed with respect to the infusion rates of rocuronium required to maintain approximately 95% neuromuscular block. Under isoflurane and enflurane anesthesia, the infusion rates are approximately 30 to 40% lower than under conditions of opioid/N_2O/O_2 anesthesia. The median spontaneous recovery time from 25 to 75% of control T1 is prolonged by enflurane and isoflurane by 15% and 62% respectively. Halothane did not prolong the spontaneous recovery rate. Reversal-induced recovery of rocuronium neuromuscular block is similar regardless of anesthetic technique.

I.V. Anesthetics: The use of propofol for induction and maintenance of anesthesia does not alter the clinical duration or recovery characteristics following recommended doses of rocuronium.

Anticonvulsants: There are limited data (4 patients in 4 trials) from clinical trials in which patients received rocuronium during chronic anticonvulsant therapy with phenytoin. In 2 of these patients, apparent resistance to the effects of rocuronium was observed in the form of diminished magnitude of neuromuscular block or shortened clinical duration. In patients receiving chronic treatment with anticonvulsants such as phenytoin and carbamazepine, the possibility of diminished effect or shortened duration should be considered when rocuronium is administered. Infusion rates may need to be increased.

Antibiotics: Parenteral/intraperitoneal administration of high doses of certain antibiotics may produce neuromuscular block or intensify the blockade induced by nondepolarizing neuromuscular relaxants. The following antibiotics have been associated with various degrees of paralysis: aminoglycosides (such as neomycin, streptomycin; kanamycin, gentamicin, and dihydrostreptomycin), vancomycin, tetracyclines, bacitracin, polymyxin B, colistin, and sodium colistimethate.

If these or other newly introduced antibiotics are used in conjunction with rocuronium during surgery, prolongation of neuromuscular block should be considered a possibility.

Three antibiotics, cefuroxime (20 mg/kg i.v.), netilmicin (2 mg/kg i.v.), and metronidazole (7.5 mg/kg i.v.), were studied for their interactive effects with rocuronium. Administration of these antibiotics 5 minutes prior to a 0.6 mg/kg dose of rocuronium has no effect on the onset time to maximum blockade. The mean clinical duration of action tended to be longer in the patients receiving concomitant antibiotic treatment (38 min with saline, 43 min with metronidazole, 44 to 49 min with cefuroxime, and 50 min with netilmicin), although the observed differences were not statistically significant. The duration of maintenance doses of rocuronium was not increased in the presence of the antibiotics.

Other: Experience concerning injection of quinidine during recovery from use of other muscle relaxants suggests that recurrent paralysis may occur. This possibility must also be considered for rocuronium.

Magnesium salts, administered for the management of toxemia of pregnancy, may enhance neuromuscular blockade.

Lithium, local anesthetics, and procainamide have been reported to increase the duration of neuromuscular block with nondepolarizing neuromuscular blocking agents. Infusion requirements may be lower in the presence of these drugs.

Adverse Effects: Clinical studies in North America (n=1 137) and Europe (n=1 394) included a total of 2 531 patients. The most frequent side effect of nondepolarizing blocking agents, as a class, is an extension of the drug's pharmacological action beyond the time period needed for surgery and anesthesia (see Pharmacology). Clinical signs may vary from skeletal muscle weakness to profound and prolonged skeletal muscle paralysis resulting in respiratory insufficiency or apnea. This may be due to the drug's effect or inadequate antagonism.

The patients exposed in North American clinical studies provide the basis for calculation of adverse reaction rates. The following adverse experiences were reported in patients administered rocuronium injection (all events judged by investigators during the clinical trials to have at least a possible causal relationship).

The following adverse events were judged by the investigator to be at least possibly related to rocuronium treatment. All of these events occurred with an incidence of <1%:

Cardiovascular: arrhythmia, abnormal electrocardiogram, tachycardia.

Digestive: nausea, vomiting.

Respiratory: asthma (bronchospasm, wheezing, or rhonchi), hiccup.

Skin and Appendages: rash, injection site edema, pruritus.

The most commonly reported adverse events in the European studies were transient hypotension (2%) and hypertension (2%). These events were reported at a higher frequency than in the North American studies (0.1% and 0.1%, respectively). This apparent discrepancy may be related to the fact that, in the North American studies, changes in heart rate and blood pressure were considered adverse events only if judged by the investigator to be unexpected, clinically significant, or possibly related to histamine release.

Overdose: Symptoms and Treatment: No cases of significant accidental or intentional overdose have been reported. The possibility of iatrogenic overdosage can be minimized by carefully monitoring the muscle twitch response to peripheral nerve stimulation. Overdosage with neuromuscular blocking agents may result in neuromuscular block beyond the time needed for surgery and anesthesia. The primary treatment is maintenance of a patent airway and controlled ventilation until recovery of normal respiration is assured. Upon evidence of spontaneous recovery from neuromuscular blockade, further recovery may be facilitated by administration of an anticholinesterase agent (e.g., neostigmine or edrophonium) in conjunction with an appropriate anticholinergic agent. A peripheral nerve stimulator should be used to monitor recovery.

As overdosage may increase the risk of hemodynamic side effects, intensified monitoring of vital organ function is required for the period of paralysis and during an extended period post recovery.

Antagonism of Neuromuscular Blockade: **Antagonists (such as neostigmine) should not be administered prior to the demonstration of some spontaneous recovery from neuromuscular blockade. The use of a nerve stimulator to document recovery and antagonism of neuromuscular blockade is recommended. The time required for anticholinesterase-mediated recovery is longer for reversals attempted at deeper levels of blockade.**

Patients should be evaluated for adequate clinical evidence of antagonism, e.g., 5 second head lift, adequate phonation, ventilation and upper airway maintenance. Ventilation must be supported until no longer required.

Antagonism may be delayed in the presence of debilitation, carcinomatosis, and concomitant use of certain broad spectrum antibiotics, or anesthetic agents and other drugs which enhance neuromuscular blockade or depress respiratory function. Under such circumstances the management is the same as that of prolonged neuromuscular blockade.

Dosage: Rocuronium injection is for i.v. use only. This drug should be administered by or under the supervision of experienced clinicians familiar with the use of neuromuscular blocking agents. Dosage must be individualized in each case.

To avoid distress to the patient, rocuronium should not be administered before unconsciousness has been induced. It should not be mixed in the same syringe or administered simultaneously through the same needle with alkaline solutions (e.g., barbiturate solutions).

The dosage information which follows is derived from studies in which the administration of rocuronium was based upon units of drug/unit of body weight. It is expressed in this section in terms of units of mg/kg (instead of μg/kg) to assist the clinician in calculating individual patient dosage requirements relative to the product as supplied for clinical use. It is intended to serve as an initial guide to the use of rocuronium by clinicians familiar with other neuromuscular blocking agents (see Pharmacology and Dosage, Maintenance Dosing).

It is recommended that clinicians administering neuromuscular blocking agents such as rocuronium employ a peripheral nerve stimulator to monitor drug response, determine the need for additional relaxant and adequacy of spontaneous recovery or antagonism.

Adults: For intubating times, onset times, and clinical duration for various doses, see Pharmacology.

Rapid Intubation: In appropriately premedicated and adequately anesthetized patients, doses of 0.6 to 1.2 mg/kg (600 to 1 200 μg/kg) rocuronium will provide good or excellent intubating conditions in most patients in 60 to 90 seconds.

At initial doses of 0.6 mg/kg, neuromuscular block sufficient for intubation (≥80% block) is attained in a median (range) time of 1 (0.4 to 6) minute(s). Maximum blockade is achieved in most patients in a median (range) of 1.8 (0.6 to 13) minutes. This dose may be expected to provide 31 (15 to 85) minutes of clinical relaxation under opioid/N_2O/O_2 anesthesia. Under halothane, isoflurane, and enflurane anesthesia, some extension of the period of clinical relaxation should be expected (see Precautions, Inhalation Anesthetics).

Should there be reason for the selection of a larger bolus dose in individual patients, initial doses of 0.9 or 1.2 mg/kg can be administered during surgery under opioid/N_2O/O_2 anesthesia. These doses will provide ≥80% block in most patients in 1.1 and 0.7 minutes, respectively, with maximum blockade occurring in most patients in 1.4 and 1 minute, respectively. Doses of 0.9 and 1.2 mg/kg may be expected to provide 58 (27 to 111) and 67 (38 to 160) minutes, respectively, of clinical relaxation under opioid/N_2O/O_2 anesthesia.

Doses for Routine Endotracheal Intubation: The recommended initial dose regardless of anesthetic regimen is 0.6 mg/kg (see Rapid Intubation). A lower dose of rocuronium injection (0.45 mg/kg) may be used. Neuromuscular block sufficient for intubation (≥80%) is attained in a median (range) time of 1.3 (0.8 to 6.2) minute(s) and most patients have intubation completed within 1.6 (1 to 7) minutes. Maximum blockade is achieved in most patients in 3 (1.3 to 8.2) minutes. This dose may be expected to provide 22 (12 to 31) minutes of clinical relaxation under opioid/N_2O/O_2 anesthesia. Patients receiving this low dose of 0.45 mg/kg who achieve less than 90% block (about 16% of these patients) may have a more rapid time to 25% recovery, 12 to 15 minutes.

Inhalation Anesthetics: Maximum blockade, onset times, intubation times, and intubation scores are similar whether rocuronium is administered during opioid/N_2O/O_2 anesthesia or during anesthesia with enflurane, isoflurane, or halothane. The choice of an intubating dose of rocuronium should not, therefore, be reduced below 0.6 mg/kg if rapid intubation is to be performed or below 0.45 mg/kg if routine tracheal intubation is to be performed. Increases in the clinical duration (25 to 35%) and recovery time (20 to 70%) may be apparent, however, in the presence of halogenated inhalation agents.

Maintenance Dosing: Maintenance doses of 0.1, 0.15, and 0.2 mg/kg (100, 150, and 200 μg/kg) rocuronium, administered at 25% recovery of control T1, provide a median 12, 17, and 24 minutes of clinically effective neuromuscular blockade during opioid/N_2O/O_2 anesthesia (see Pharmacology). Smaller or less frequent bolus maintenance doses should be considered during anesthesia with halogenated inhalation agents. In all cases, dosing should be guided based on the clinical duration following initial dose or prior maintenance dose and not administered until signs of neuromuscular function are evident. Cumulation of effect with repetitive maintenance dosing has been observed (see Pharmacology), but it is not of clinical significance.

Continuous Infusion: After evidence of early spontaneous recovery (≤10% of control T1) from initial doses of 0.45 to 0.6 mg/kg (450 to 600 μg/kg), a continuous infusion of 0.01 to 0.012 mg/kg/min (10 to 12 μg/kg/min) can be initiated with the rate of infusion being adjusted thereafter to maintain a 90% suppression of twitch response. The infusion of rocuronium should be individualized for each patient. The rate of administration should be adjusted according to the patient's twitch response as determined by peripheral nerve stimulation. Infusion rates may range from 0.004 to 0.016 mg/kg/min (4 to 16 μg/kg/min).

Initiation of the infusion after substantial return of neuromuscular function (more than 10% of control T1) may necessitate additional bolus doses to maintain adequate block for surgery.

Halogenated inhalation anesthetics, particularly enflurane and isoflurane may enhance the neuromuscular blocking action of nondepolarizing muscle relaxants. In the presence of steady-state concentrations of enflurane or isoflurane, it may be necessary to reduce the rate of infusion by 30 to 50%.

Spontaneous recovery and reversal of neuromuscular blockade following discontinuation of rocuronium infusion may be expected to proceed at rates similar to those following comparable total doses administered by repetitive bolus injections (see Pharmacology).

Infusion solutions of rocuronium can be prepared by mixing rocuronium with an appropriate infusion solution such as 5% Dextrose Injection, USP. Unused portions of infusion solutions should be discarded.

Children: Initial Doses: Initial doses of 0.6 mg/kg (600 μg/kg) in children (3 mo to 12 yrs) under halothane anesthesia produce 100% neuromuscular blockade and excellent to good intubating conditions within approximately 60 to 90 seconds. This dose will provide approximately 25 to 30 minutes of clinical relaxation in children aged 1 to 12 years receiving halothane anesthesia. For infants aged 3 to 12 months, the duration of action of a 0.6 mg/kg dose is longer than in older patients, averaging 42 minutes under conditions of halothane anesthesia.

Maintenance Doses: In children aged 4 to 13 yrs maintenance doses of 0.075 to 0.125 mg/kg (75 to 125 μg/kg), administered upon return of T1 to 25% of control, provide clinical relaxation for a median of 7 to 10 minutes (see Pharmacology).

Use by Continuous Infusion: A continuous infusion of rocuronium initiated at a rate of 0.012 mg//kg/min (12 μg/kg/min) upon return of T1 to 10% of control has been demonstrated to maintain neuromuscular blockade at 89 to 99% in children receiving halothane anesthesia. The infusion of rocuronium must be individualized for each patient. The rate of administration should be adjusted according to the patient's twitch response as determined by peripheral nerve stimulation. Spontaneous recovery and reversal of neuromuscular blockade following discontinuation of rocuronium infusion may be expected to proceed at rates comparable to that following similar total exposure to single bolus doses (see Pharmacology).

Geriatrics: Although the potency of rocuronium is similar in geriatric patients and adults, the onset of action is delayed in patients ≥65 years. The choice of an intubating dose of rocuronium should not be reduced below 0.6 mg/kg if routine tracheal intubation is to be performed. Rapid sequence tracheal intubation is not recommended in the elderly. Geriatric patients (≥65 yrs) exhibit a slightly prolonged median (range) clinical duration of 46 (22 to 73) minutes, 62 (49 to 75) minutes and 94 (64 to 138) minutes under opioid/N_2O/O_2 anesthesia following doses of 0.6, 0.9, and 1.2 mg/kg, respectively. The median (range) rate of spontaneous recovery of T1 from 25 to 75% in geriatric patients is 16.5 (7 to 56) minutes which is not different from that in adults (see Pharmacology).

Maintenance doses of 0.1 and 0.15 mg/kg (100 to 150 μg/kg) rocuronium, administered at 25% recovery of T1, provide approximately 13 and 33 minutes of clinical duration under opioid/N_2O/O_2 anesthesia.

Compatibility: Zemuron is compatible in solution with: 0.9% Sodium Chloride Injection, USP, 5% Dextrose Injection, USP, 5% Dextrose and 0.9% Sodium Chloride Injection, USP, Sterile Water for Injection, USP and Lactated Ringer's Solution.

Use within 24 hours of mixing with the above solutions.

Rocuronium injection 10 mg/mL may be added to an appropriate amount of product in i.v. infusion bottles, bags and PCA syringe pumps to yield a final concentration of 0.5 mg/mL and 2 mg/mL. Tables VI and VII show the volume ratios of i.v. fluid/rocuronium in each of the i.v. fluids to an approximate yield of 0.5 mg/mL (see Table VI) and 2 mg/mL (see Table VII). The bottles and bags should be thoroughly mixed.

Parenteral drug products should be inspected visually for particulate matter and clarity prior to administration whenever solution and container permit.

Route of Administration: For i.v. injection only.

Supplied: Each mL of sterile nonpyrogenic solution for i.v. injection only contains: rocuronium bromide 10 mg, sodium acetate, trihydrate 2 mg, sodium chloride approx. 3.3 mg, water for injection q.s. to 1 mL and nitrogen (present). May contain: sodium hydroxide and/or glacial acetic acid to adjust the pH to approximately 4.0. Preservative-free. Single dose vials of 5 mL. Boxes of 10.

Store under refrigeration (2 to 8°C) until ready to use. To facilitate use in the operating room, the unopened container may be stored up to 30 days at room temperature (15 to 30°C).

Table VI—Zemuron

Volume Ratios of I.V. Fluid/Zemuron to Yield 0.5 mg/mL

	0.9% Sodium Chloride Injection, USP (mL/mL)	5% Dextrose Injection, USP (mL/mL)	5% Dextrose & 0.9% Sodium Chloride Injection, USP (mL/mL)	Lactated Ringers Solution (mL/mL)	Sterile Water for Injection USP (mL/mL)
Plastic Bag	250/12.5	250/12.5	250/12.5	250/12.5	250/12.5
Glass Bottle	250/12.5	250/12.5	250/12.5	250/12.5	250/12.5
PCA Syringe Pump	60/3	60/3	60/3	60/3	60/3

Quantity of i.v. fluid in mL and quantity of Zemuron in mL replacement.

Table VII—Zemuron

Volume Ratios of I.V. Fluid/Zemuron to Yield 2 mg/mL

	0.9% Sodium Chloride Injection, USP (mL/mL)	5% Dextrose Injection, USP (mL/mL)	5% Dextrose & 0.9% Sodium Chloride Injection, USP (mL/mL)	Lactated Ringers Solution (mL/mL)	Sterile Water for Injection, USP (mL/mL)
Plastic Bag	250/50	250/50	250/50	250/50	250/50
Glass Bottle	250/50	250/50	250/50	250/50	250/50
PCA Syringe Pump	60/12	60/12	60/12	60/12	60/12

Quantity of i.v. fluid in mL and quantity of Zemuron in mL replacement.

ZEPHIRAN®

Sanofi

Benzalkonium Chloride

Topical Antiseptic

Indications: Antisepsis of skin and mucous membranes and as a disinfectant in surgery, obstetrics and gynecology, urology, ophthalmology, otorhinolaryngology and general practice. Also may be used as a disinfectant for hospital utensils and other environmental surfaces and for disinfection and storage of ampuls, thermometers, metal instruments and catheters.

Contraindications: Incompatible with soap and anionic detergents. Use in occlusive dressings, casts and anal or vaginal packs is inadvisable, as they may produce irritation or chemical burns.

Precautions: Sterile Water for Injection USP, should be used as a diluent in preparation for use in deep wounds or for irrigation of body cavities. Freshly distilled water is the appropriate diluent in all other indications. Cotton, wool, rayon products, gauze sponges and fibre pledgets should be stored separately from benzalkonium chloride aqueous solutions and immersed immediately prior to use.

Antiseptics such as benzalkonium chloride aqueous solutions must not be relied upon to achieve complete sterilization, because they do not destroy all bacterial spores and certain viruses, including the etiologic agent of infectious hepatitis, and they may not destroy M. tuberculosis and other rare bacterial strains.

Important: If benzalkonium chloride aqueous solution, in dilutions stronger than 1:3 000 enters the eyes, they should be immediately and repeatedly rinsed with water. Prompt medical attention is necessary. Concentrations greater than 1:5 000 should not be used on mucous membranes, with the exception of vaginal mucosa (see Dosage). Solutions that are used on inflamed or irritated tissues must be more dilute than those used on normal tissues.

In preoperative antisepsis of the skin, benzalkonium chloride aqueous solutions should not be permitted to remain in prolonged contact with the patient's skin. Periorbital skin or head preparation should be carried out before anesthesia so that eye irritation can be reported immediately. Avoid pooling of the solution on the operating table.

If benzalkonium chloride concentrate is spilled on the skin, wash immediately and copiously with soap and water.

Adverse Effects: Hypersensitivity may be exhibited rarely.

Overdose: Symptoms: If solution is ingested, especially a concentrated solution, marked local irritation of the gastrointestinal tract may occur manifested by nausea and vomiting. Signs of systemic toxicity include restlessness, apprehension, weakness, confusion, dyspnea, cyanosis, collapse, convulsions and coma. Death occurs as a result of paralysis of the respiratory muscles.

Treatment: Administer several glasses of a mild soap solution, milk or egg whites beaten in water. Follow by gastric lavage with a mild soap solution. Avoid alcohol as it promotes absorption.

To support respiration, maintain a clear airway and administer oxygen with artificial respiration if necessary. If convulsions occur, give a short-acting parenteral barbiturate with caution.

If solutions containing Anti-Rust are ingested, the effects of sodium carbonate are manifested by gastric symptoms typical of locally irritant poisons. Nitrite poisoning may be serious and is manifested mainly by cardiovascular collapse, with rapid marked fall in blood pressure, tachycardia, muscular weakness, dyspnea, and slate colored mucous membranes. If very large doses are taken, methemoglobinemia occurs and results in anoxia.

Sodium carbonate may be neutralized by large amounts of diluted acids in the form of diluted vinegar, lemon juice or orange juice. Fixed oils such as olive oil may be given in small amounts to protect irritated mucous membranes.

For nitrite poisoning the patient is kept in shock position and comfortably warm. Oxygen should be administered (especially if methemoglobinemia is present). Methylene blue has also been used to treat methemoglobinemia.

Dosage: For preoperative disinfection of skin or minor wounds, surgeon's hand and arm soak, Aqueous 1:750; denuded skin and mucous membranes, wet dressings, Aqueous 1:10 000 to 1:5 000; vaginal instillation and irrigation, oozing and open infections Aqueous 1:5 000 to 1:2 000; vesical and urethral irrigation, Aqueous 1:20 000 to 1:5 000; retention lavage, Aqueous 1:40 000 to 1:20 000; otorhinolaryngological irrigation, Aqueous 1:10 000 to 1:3 000; disinfection of bristle brushes, ampuls, wet towel drapes or rubber instruments, floors, walls, bathtubs, furniture and other surfaces, Aqueous 1:750. Disinfection of metallic instruments: Aqueous 1:750 (with Anti-Rust Tablets).

Supplied: Each mL of aqueous solution contains: benzalkonium chloride 1:750 in purified water. Alcohol-, bisulfite-, glucose-, gluten-, lactose-, parabens-, sodium-, starch-, sucrose- and tartrazine-free. Bottles of 3.75 L.

ZERIT™ Ⓟ

Bristol-Myers Squibb

Stavudine

Antiretroviral

Pharmacology: Stavudine is a synthetic thymidine nucleoside analogue active against the Human Immunodeficiency Virus (HIV).

In vitro studies demonstrate that stavudine is converted to the triphosphate by cellular kinases. The 5' triphosphate is the active form of the drug. In cell culture studies with 2 different cell lines, stavudine triphosphate had an intracellular half-life

Zerit (cont'd)

of 3.5 hours. Stavudine triphosphate has been shown to be a potent competitive inhibitor of HIV reverse transcriptase (ki=0.0083 to 0.032 μM). In addition, both stavudine triphosphate and the natural substrate, thymidine triphosphate, are used by HIV reverse transcriptase in vitro for incorporation into the nascent DNA chain. Stavudine lacks the 3'-hydroxyl group necessary for DNA elongation and once incorporated into DNA, functions as a DNA chain terminator in vitro. Both the inhibition of binding of thymidine triphosphate to reverse transcriptase and DNA chain termination may be partially responsible for inhibition of HIV replication in vitro. In addition to the inhibitory effect on HIV reverse transcriptase, stavudine triphosphate exhibits some inhibitory effect on DNA polymerase beta and gamma, and markedly reduces the syntheses of mitochondrial DNA.

Clinically, stavudine has been studied in various combinations with other drugs, including didanosine, lamivudine (3TC), ritonavir, nelfinavir, saquinavir, indinavir, and hydroxyurea. However, zidovudine in combination with stavudine is not recommended (see Precautions/Drug Interactions). Both drugs are phosphorylated by the same enzyme (thymidine kinase), which may preferentially phosphorylate zidovudine, thereby preventing the phosphorylation of stavudine to its active triphosphate form.

Based on in vitro testing, the activation of stavudine has also been shown to be inhibited by other drugs. Among the several drugs tested, the only ones that may interfere with stavudine phosphorylation at relevant concentrations are doxorubicin and ribavirin, but not other drugs used in the therapy of HIV infection which are similarly phosphorylated. The clinical significance of this is unknown.

Indications: For the treatment of HIV-infected adults who have received prolonged prior zidovudine therapy.

Contraindications: Patients with clinically significant hypersensitivity to stavudine or to any of the components contained in the formulation.

Warnings: Peripheral Neuropathy: The major clinical toxicity of stavudine is peripheral neuropathy. This occurred in 15 to 24% of patients in the controlled clinical trials. Patients should be monitored for the development of a neuropathy that is usually characterized by numbness, tingling, or pain in the feet or hands. Stavudine-related peripheral neuropathy usually resolves when therapy is withdrawn, on occasion after a period of worsening. If symptoms resolve completely, resumption of treatment may be considered at a reduced dose (see Dosage).

Patients with a history of peripheral neuropathy are at increased risk for the development of neuropathy. If stavudine must be administered in this clinical setting, careful monitoring is essential.

Lactic Acidosis: As with other nucleoside analogues, occurrences of lactic acidosis, which may be fatal, and usually associated with severe hepatic steatosis have been reported in patients receiving stavudine. It is not known whether these events are causally related to nucleoside analogues; this condition has also been reported as a disease-related event. In the event of rapidly elevating aminotransferase or lactic acid levels, consideration should be given to discontinuation of all nucleoside analogue therapy.

Precautions: General: Patients receiving stavudine or any other antiretroviral therapy may continue to develop opportunistic infections and other complications of HIV infection, and therefore, should remain under close clinical observation by physicians experienced in the treatment of patients with HIV disease and associated complications.

Renal Insufficiency: In HIV-infected patients with renal impairment, renal clearance and apparent oral clearance of stavudine was decreased. The terminal elimination half-life (t½) was prolonged up to 8 hours. C_{max} and T_{max} were not significantly affected by reduced renal function. Based on these preliminary observations, it is recommended that stavudine dosage be modified in patients with reduced creatinine clearance (see Dosage).

Hepatic Insufficiency: Hepatitis or liver failure, which was fatal in some cases, have been reported. In patients with preexisting liver dysfunction, discontinuation of all nucleoside analogues should be considered when worsening liver disease occurs.

Pregnancy: There are no adequate and well-controlled studies in pregnant women. Because animal reproduction studies are not always predictive of human response, stavudine should be used during pregnancy only if clearly needed.

Reproduction studies have been performed in rats and rabbits with exposures (based on C_{max}) up to 399 and 183 times, respectively, of that seen at a clinical dosage of 1 mg/kg/day and have revealed no evidence of teratogenicity or impaired fertility. A slight postimplantation loss was noted at 216 times the human exposure with no effect noted at approximately 135 times the human exposure. The incidence in fetuses of a common skeletal variation, unossified or incomplete ossification of sternebra, was increased in rats at 399 times human exposure while no effect was observed at 216 times human exposure. An increase in early rat neonatal mortality (birth to 4 days of age) occurred at 399 times the human exposure, while survival of neonates was unaffected at approximately 135 times the human exposure. A study in rats showed that stavudine is transferred to the fetus through the placenta. The concentration in fetal tissue was approximately one-half the concentration in maternal plasma. Stavudine has been shown to cross the human placenta in an ex vivo term model.

Lactation: Studies in which lactating rats were administered a single dose (5 or 100 mg/kg) of stavudine demonstrated that stavudine is readily excreted into breast milk.

It is not known whether stavudine is excreted in human milk. Because many drugs are excreted in human milk and because of the potential of adverse reactions from stavudine in nursing infants, mothers should be instructed to discontinue nursing if they are receiving stavudine.

Children: The safety and effectiveness of stavudine have been established in pediatric patients supported by evidence from adequate and well-controlled studies of stavudine in adults with additional data concerning safety and pharmacokinetics in pediatric patients.

Patients should be monitored for clinically significant elevations of hepatic transaminases. If these evaluations develop on treatment, stavudine therapy should be interrupted. If the hepatic transaminase values return to pretherapy levels, resumption of treatment may be considered using a dosage schedule of 1 mg/kg/day, not to exceed the recommended adult dose of 20 mg twice daily.

One open-label, phase I trial enrolled 38 subjects aged 5 weeks to 15 years; 9 had received no prior antiretroviral therapy and 29 had received zidovudine for a median duration of 104 weeks. Patients in this trial received stavudine in initial doses ranging from 0.125 to 4.0 mg/kg/day with an average dose of 1.7 mg/kg/day for a median duration of 84 weeks (range 8 to 140 weeks). A second open-label trial, initiated to provide stavudine for children who had failed or were intolerant of alternative antiretroviral therapy, enrolled 51 subjects aged 8 months to 18 years who had received prolonged zidovudine and didanosine. These patients were treated with stavudine at a dose of 2 mg/kg/day, for a median duration of 33 weeks (range 2 days to 82 weeks).

Diabetes Mellitus: The constituted powder for oral solution contains 50 mg sucrose per mL of constituted solution.

Lactose Intolerance: Zerit capsules contain lactose (120 and 240 mg depending on capsule strength). This amount is probably insufficient to induce specific symptoms of intolerance.

Laboratory Tests: Complete blood counts and clinical laboratory tests should be performed prior to initiating stavudine therapy and at appropriate intervals thereafter.

Moderate elevations of mean corpuscular volume may be observed in patients taking stavudine and may provide an indication of treatment compliance.

Drug Interactions: A clinical trial in HIV-infected patients (n=10) has demonstrated that there were no clinically significant interactions between stavudine (40 mg) and didanosine (100 mg) when the agents were administered simultaneously every 12 hours for 4 days. The pharmacokinetic profile of each drug was unchanged when given as a single agent or following first-dose and steady-state conditions when given in combination. Neither stavudine nor didanosine affected the pharmacokinetics of the other. Based on results of studies of radiolabeled stavudine in nonhuman primates, there is no expectation that drugs affecting hepatic metabolism would have any effect on the disposition of stavudine in humans.

Since zidovudine may inhibit the intracellular phosphorylation of stavudine, it is not recommended to use zidovudine in combination with stavudine.

Information to be provided to the Patient: Patients receiving stavudine should be advised that:

- The long-term effects of stavudine are unknown at this time.
- Stavudine therapy has not been shown to reduce the risk of HIV transmission.
- They may continue to develop opportunistic infections and other complications of HIV infection, and therefore, should remain under the care of a physician experienced in treating HIV-associated diseases.
- They must report symptoms including tingling, burning, pain or numbness in the hands or feet to their physicians and follow their physician's instructions regarding the prescribed dose in order to reduce the risk of peripheral neuropathy.

Adverse Effects: Adverse event data presented below are based on 2 major clinical trials in adults. One trial was a controlled, comparative double-blind study (stavudine compared with zidovudine) in patients with less advanced HIV infection (median CD4 cell count of 250 cells/mm³). In this trial, 412 patients were treated with stavudine for a median duration of 79 weeks; patients ≥ 60 kg received 40 mg b.i.d. and those < 60 kg received 30 mg b.i.d. A total of 402 patients were treated with zidovudine at a dosage of 200 mg t.i.d. for a median duration of 53 weeks. Additional data were obtained from a larger double-blind trial involving patients with advanced HIV disease (median CD4 count of 44 cells/mm³) treated with stavudine at one of two dosage levels for up to 2 years; 5 879 patients received stavudine at a dosage of 20 mg b.i.d. and 5 905 patients received stavudine 40 mg b.i.d.

Clinical Events: Many of the serious clinical adverse events reported from patients receiving stavudine in clinical trials were consistent with the course of HIV infection. Concurrent therapy with other medications was permitted in these trials. Therefore, it is difficult to distinguish which events were related to stavudine, the disease itself, or other therapies.

The clinical adverse events reported in these trials include those shown in Table I.

Peripheral Neuropathy: The major clinical toxicity of stavudine is dose-related peripheral neuropathy. Patients with a history of peripheral neuropathy are at increased risk for developing this complication during therapy with stavudine. Stavudine-related peripheral neuropathy may resolve if therapy is promptly withdrawn. In some cases, symptoms may worsen

Table I—Zerit

Selected Clinical Adverse Events in Clinical Trials in Adults

	Comparative Double-blind Trial in Patients with Less Advanced HIV Disease (% of Patients)		Double-blind Trial in Patients with Advanced HIV Disease (% of Patients)	
Adverse Event	**Stavudine 40 mg b.i.d.* N=412**	**Zidovudine 200 mg t.i.d. N=402**	**Stavudine 20 mg b.i.d. N=5 879**	**Stavudine 40 mg b.i.d. N=5 905**
Peripheral Neuropathy	14	4	19	24
Other Events				
Headache	54	49	4	3
Chills/Fever	50	51	6	6
Diarrhea	50	43	5	5
Rash	40	35	4	4
Nausea/Vomiting	38	44	7	6
Abdominal pain	34	27	6	4
Myalgia	32	35	2	2
Insomnia	29	31	2	2
Anorexia	19	22	1	<1
Allergic Reaction	9	8	<1	<1
Pancreatitis	<1	<1	2	2

*Patients <60 kg received 30 mg b.i.d.

temporarily following discontinuation of therapy. Resumption of treatment with stavudine may be considered at a reduced dosage if symptoms resolve satisfactorily (see Dosage).

Pancreatitis: Pancreatitis was generally attributed to advanced disease or to prior or concurrent treatment with medications known to be associated with pancreatitis. The occurrences were not dose-related, and were occasionally fatal. Patients with a history of pancreatitis appear to be at increased risk for recurrence.

Lactic Acidosis: As with other nucleoside analogues, occurrences of lactic acidosis, which were fatal in some cases and usually associated with severe hepatic steatosis, have been reported postmarketing (see Warnings).

Hepatic Dysfunction: Hepatitis or liver failure, which was fatal in some cases, have been reported postmarketing (see Precautions).

Laboratory Abnormalities: The laboratory abnormalities reported in these clinical trials included those shown in Table II.

Table II—Zerit

Selected Laboratory Abnormalities in Clinical Trials in Adults

Laboratory Abnormality	Comparative Double-blind Trial in Patients with Less Advanced HIV Disease (% of Patients): Stavudine 40 mg b.i.d.* N=412	Comparative Double-blind Trial in Patients with Less Advanced HIV Disease (% of Patients): Zidovudine 200 mg t.i.d. N=402	Double-blind Trial in Patients with Advanced HIV Disease (% of Patients): Stavudine 20 mg b.i.d. N=5 879	Double-blind Trial in Patients with Advanced HIV Disease (% of Patients): Stavudine 40 mg b.i.d. N=5 905
AST				
≤5×ULN	63	49	59	60
>5×ULN	11	10	6	6
ALT				
≤5×ULN	65	46	62	62
>5×ULN	13	11	10	11
Amylase				
>1.4×ULN	14	13	ND	ND
Bilirubin				
>2.5×ULN	2	3	ND	ND
Hemoglobin				
<8 g/dL	<1	3	4	3
Neutrophils				
<750/mm³	5	9	13	12
Platelets				
<50 000/mm³	3	3	5	4

*Patients <60 kg received 30 mg b.i.d.
Legend: ×ULN=Times upper limit of normal.
ND=Not determined (not required by the study protocol).

Children: Adverse events and clinical laboratory abnormalities were generally similar to those seen in adults, and generally related to underlying disease. Drug-related peripheral neuropathy has not been reported in pediatric patients who have received stavudine monotherapy in controlled clinical trials.

Overdose: Symptoms and Treatment: There is no known antidote for stavudine overdosage. Experience with adults treated with 12 to 24 times the recommended daily dosage revealed no acute toxicity. Patients may benefit from administration of activated charcoal. Stavudine can be removed by hemodialysis, the mean±SD hemodialysis clearance of stavudine is 120±18 mL/minute. It is not known whether stavudine is eliminated by peritoneal dialysis.

Dosage: Adults: The interval between oral doses should be 12 hours. Stavudine may be taken with or without food. The recommended starting doses are based on body weight, as outlined in Table III.

Table III—Zerit

Adult Dosing

Patient Weight	Zerit Dosage
<60 kg	15 or 30 mg b.i.d.
≥60 kg	20 or 40 mg b.i.d.

Based on available clinical data, either of the doses within each weight category in Table III could be recommended. The choice of the higher or lower dose should be based on clinical judgment reflecting the balance of potential efficacy versus possible toxicity (see Adverse Effects).

Children: The interval between doses of stavudine oral solution should be 12 hours and doses may be taken without regard to meals. The recommended starting dose for pediatric patients is 2 mg/kg/day, not to exceed the recommended adult dose of 40 mg twice daily. Oral solution and capsule formulations of stavudine have been shown to be bioequivalent.

There is no clinical experience with stavudine in children under the age of 3 months.

Dosage Adjustment: Adults: Renal Impairment: The following dose adjustments are recommended in patients with renal impairment (see Table IV).

Table IV—Zerit

Recommended Stavudine Dosing Modifications for Subjects with Renal Impairment

Creatinine Clearance (mL/min)	Recommended Stavudine Dose by Patient Weight: ≥60 kg	Recommended Stavudine Dose by Patient Weight: <60 kg
>50	40 mg every 12 hours	30 mg every 12 hours
26–50	20 mg every 12 hours	15 mg every 12 hours
10–25	20 mg every 24 hours	15 mg every 24 hours

There is insufficient data to recommend a dose for subjects with creatinine clearance <10 mL/min or for subjects undergoing dialysis.

Children: There is insufficient data to recommend a dosage adjustment for children with renal impairment.

Hepatic Impairment: Dosing adjustment is not necessary in subjects with stable hepatic impairment. In the event of rapidly elevating aminotransferase levels, consideration should be given to discontinuation of all nucleoside analogue therapy.

Peripheral Neuropathy: Clinical symptoms of peripheral neuropathy should prompt interruption of stavudine treatment and evaluation of the patient. These symptoms may be difficult to detect in children. If symptoms resolve completely, based on experience in adults, resumption of treatment may be considered at a reduced dose. Clinically significant elevations of hepatic transaminases should be managed in the same fashion.

Children: Patients should be monitored for clinically significant elevations of hepatic transaminases. If these elevations develop on treatment, stavudine therapy should be interrupted. If the hepatic transaminase values return to pretherapy levels, resumption of treatment may be considered using a dosage schedule of 1 mg/kg/day, not to exceed the recommended adult dose of 20 mg twice daily.

Method of Preparation: Oral Solution: 1. Add 202 mL of purified water to the container. 2. Shake container vigorously until the powder dissolves completely. Constitution in this way produces 200 mL (deliverable volume) of 1 mg/mL stavudine solution. The solution may appear slightly hazy. 3. Dispense solution in original container with measuring cup provided. Instruct patient to shake the container vigorously prior to measuring each dose and to store the tightly closed container in a refrigerator (2 to 8°C). Discard any unused portion after 30 days. The solution may also be stored at room temperature for up to 3 days.

Supplied: Capsules: 15 mg: Each light yellow and dark red capsule, imprinted with "BMS 1964" and "15", contains: stavudine 15 mg. Nonmedicinal ingredients: lactose, magnesium stearate, microcrystalline cellulose and sodium starch glycolate; capsule shell: gelatin, black iron oxide (20 mg only), printing ink, silicon dioxide, sodium lauryl sulfate, titanium dioxide and yellow and red iron oxides. Bottles of 60. Packages of 100 individually foil-wrapped capsules. Unit dose blister strips of 14, packages of 4. Store at room temperature (15 to 30°C) and protect from excessive moisture. Keep bottles tightly closed.

20 mg: Each light brown capsule, imprinted with "BMS 1965" and "20", contains: stavudine 20 mg. Nonmedicinal ingredients: lactose, magnesium stearate, microcrystalline cellulose and sodium starch glycolate; capsule shell: gelatin, black iron oxide (20 mg only), printing ink, silicon dioxide, sodium lauryl sulfate, titanium dioxide and yellow and red iron oxides. Bottles of 60. Packages of 100 individually foil-wrapped capsules. Unit dose blister strips of 14, packages of 4. Store at room temperature (15 to 30°C) and protect from excessive moisture. Keep bottles tightly closed.

30 mg: Each light orange and dark orange capsule, imprinted with "BMS 1966" and "30", contains: stavudine 30 mg. Nonmedicinal ingredients: lactose, magnesium stearate, microcrystalline cellulose and sodium starch glycolate; capsule shell: gelatin, black iron oxide (20 mg only), printing ink, silicon dioxide, sodium lauryl sulfate, titanium dioxide and yellow and red iron oxides. Bottles of 60. Packages of 100 individually foil-wrapped capsules. Unit dose blister strips of 14, packages of 4. Store at room temperature (15 to 30°C) and protect from excessive moisture. Keep bottles tightly closed.

40 mg: Each dark orange capsule, imprinted with "BMS 1967" and "40" contains: stavudine 40 mg. Nonmedicinal ingredients: lactose, magnesium stearate, microcrystalline cellulose and sodium starch glycolate; capsule shell: gelatin, black iron oxide (20 mg only), printing ink, silicon dioxide, sodium lauryl sulfate, titanium dioxide and yellow and red iron oxides. Bottles of 60. Packages of 100 individually foil-wrapped capsules. Unit dose blister strips of 14, packages of 4. Store at room temperature (15 to 30°C) and protect from excessive moisture. Keep bottles tightly closed.

Powder for Oral Solution: Each mL of fruit-flavored solution contains: stavudine 1 mg (after reconstitution with water per label instructions). Nonmedicinal ingredients: antifoaming agents (glyceryl monostearate, polyethylene glycol monostearate, simethicone, sorbic acid and water), flavoring agents, methylparaben, propylparaben, sodium carboxymethylcellulose and sucrose. Dye-free. HDPE bottles with child-resistant closures of 200 mL. Powder for oral solution should be protected from excessive moisture and stored in tightly closed containers at room temperature (15 to 30°C). After constitution, store tightly closed containers in a refrigerator (2 to 8°C). Discard any unused portion after 30 days. The solution may also be stored at room temperature for up to 3 days.

(Shown in Product Recognition Section)

Reviewed 1999

ZESTORETIC® Ⓟ

Zeneca

Lisinopril—Hydrochlorothiazide

Angiotensin Converting Enzyme Inhibitor—Diuretic

Pharmacology: Zestoretic combines the action of an angiotensin converting enzyme inhibitor, lisinopril, and a diuretic, hydrochlorothiazide.

Lisinopril: Angiotensin converting enzyme (ACE) is a peptidyl dipeptidase which catalyzes the conversion of angiotensin I to the pressor substance, angiotensin II. Inhibition of ACE results in decreased plasma angiotensin II, which leads to increased plasma renin activity (due to removal of negative feedback of renin release) and decreased aldosterone secretion. Although the latter decrease is small, it results in a small increase in serum potassium. In patients treated with lisinopril plus a thiazide diuretic, there was essentially no change in serum potassium (see Precautions).

ACE is identical to kininase II. Thus, lisinopril may also block the degradation of bradykinin, a potent vasodilator peptide. However, the role that this plays in the therapeutic effects of lisinopril is unknown.

While the mechanism through which lisinopril lowers blood pressure is believed to be primarily the suppression of the

Zestoretic (cont'd)

renin-angiotensin-aldosterone system, lisinopril also lowers blood pressure in patients with low-renin hypertension. However, black hypertensive patients (usually a low-renin hypertensive population) have a smaller average response to lisinopril monotherapy than nonblack patients.

When lisinopril is given together with thiazide-type diuretics, its blood pressure lowering effect is approximately additive.

The antihypertensive effect of angiotensin converting enzyme inhibitors is generally lower in black patients that in nonblack patients.

Hydrochlorothiazide: Hydrochlorothiazide is a diuretic and antihypertensive which interferes with the renal tubular mechanism of electrolyte reabsorption. It increases excretion of sodium and chloride in approximately equivalent amounts. Natriuresis may be accompanied by some loss of potassium and bicarbonate. While this compound is predominantly a saluretic agent, in vitro studies have shown that it has a carbonic anhydrase inhibitory action which seems to be relatively specific for the renal tubular mechanism. It does not appear to be concentrated in erythrocytes or the brain in sufficient amounts to influence the activity of carbonic anhydrase in those tissues.

Hydrochlorothiazide is useful in the treatment of hypertension. It may be used alone or as an adjunct to other antihypertensive drugs. Hydrochlorothiazide does not affect normal blood pressure. The mechanism of its antihypertensive action is not known. Lowering of the sodium content of arteriolar smooth muscle cells and diminished response to norepinephrine have been postulated.

Pharmacokinetics: Lisinopril: Following oral administration of lisinopril, peak serum concentrations occur within about 7 hours. Declining serum concentrations exhibit a prolonged terminal phase which does not contribute to drug accumulation. This terminal phase probably represents saturable binding to ACE and is not proportional to dose. Lisinopril does not bind to plasma proteins other than ACE.

Lisinopril does not undergo metabolism and is excreted unchanged entirely in the urine. Based on urinary recovery, the extent of absorption of lisinopril is approximately 25%, with large inter-subject variability (6 to 60%) at all doses tested (5 to 80 mg).

Lisinopril absorption is not influenced by the presence of food in the gastrointestinal tract.

Upon multiple dosing, lisinopril exhibits an effective half-life of accumulation of 12 hours.

In a study in elderly healthy subjects (65 years and above), a single dose of lisinopril 20 mg produced higher serum concentrations and higher values for the area under the plasma curve than those seen in young healthy adults given a similar dose. In another study, single daily doses of lisinopril 5 mg were given for 7 consecutive days to young and elderly healthy volunteers. Maximum serum concentrations of lisinopril on Day 7 were higher in the elderly volunteers than in the young.

Impaired renal function decreases elimination of lisinopril. This decrease becomes clinically important when the glomerular filtration rate is below 30 mL/min (see Precautions, Patients with Impaired Renal Function and Dosage).

Lisinopril can be removed by dialysis.

Studies in rats indicate that lisinopril crosses the blood-brain barrier poorly.

Hydrochlorothiazide: Hydrochlorothiazide is not metabolized but is eliminated rapidly by the kidney. The plasma half-life is 5.6 to 14.8 hours when the plasma levels can be followed for at least 24 hours. At least 61% of the oral dose is eliminated unchanged within 24 hours. Hydrochlorothiazide crosses the placental but not the blood-brain barrier and is excreted in breast milk.

Onset of the diuretic action following oral administration occurs in 2 hours and the peak action in about 4 hours. Diuretic activity lasts about 6 to 12 hours.

Lisinopril—Hydrochlorothiazide: Concomitant administration of lisinopril and hydrochlorothiazide has little, or no effect on the bioavailability of either drug. The combination tablet is bioequivalent to concomitant administration of the separate entities.

Pharmacodynamics: Lisinopril: Administration of lisinopril to patients with hypertension results in a reduction of both supine and standing blood pressure. Abrupt withdrawal of lisinopril has not been associated with a rapid increase in blood pressure. In most patients studied, after oral administration of an individual dose of lisinopril, the onset of antihypertensive activity is seen at 1 hour with peak reduction of blood pressure achieved by 6 hours. Although an antihypertensive effect was observed 24 hours after dosing with recommended single daily doses, the effect was more consistent and the mean effect was considerably larger in some studies with doses of 20 mg or more than with lower doses. However, at all doses studied, the mean antihypertensive effect was substantially smaller 24 hours after dosing than it was 6 hours after dosing. On occasion, achievement of optimal blood pressure reduction may require 2 to 4 weeks of therapy.

In hemodynamic studies in patients with essential hypertension, blood pressure reduction was accompanied by a reduction in peripheral arterial resistance with little or no change in cardiac output and in heart rate. In a study in 9 hypertensive patients, following administration of lisinopril, there was an increase in mean renal blood flow that was not significant. Data from several small studies are inconsistent with respect to the effect of lisinopril on glomerular filtration rate in hypertensive patients with normal renal function, but suggest that changes, if any, are not large.

Indications: For the treatment of essential hypertension in patients for whom combination therapy is appropriate.

In using Zestoretic, consideration should be given to the risk of angioedema (see Warnings).

Lisinopril should normally be used in those patients in whom treatment with diuretic or beta-blocker was found ineffective or has been associated with unacceptable adverse effects.

Zestoretic is not indicated for initial therapy. Patients in whom lisinopril and diuretic are initiated simultaneously can develop symptomatic hypotension (see Precautions, Drug Interactions).

Patients should be titrated on the individual drugs. If the fixed combination represents the dosage determined by this titration, the use of Zestoretic may be more convenient in the management of patients. If during maintenance therapy dosage adjustment is necessary, it is advisable to use individual drugs.

Pregnancy: **When used in pregnancy during the second and third trimesters, ACE inhibitors can cause injury or even death of the developing fetus. When pregnancy is detected, Zestoretic should be discontinued as soon as possible (see Warnings, Pregnancy and Precautions, Information for the Patient).**

Contraindications: Patients who are hypersensitive to any component of this product and patients with a history of angioneurotic edema relating to previous treatment with an angiotensin converting enzyme inhibitor. Because of the hydrochlorothiazide component, this product is contraindicated in patients with anuria or hypersensitivity to other sulfonamide-derived drugs.

Warnings: Angioedema: Angioedema has been reported in patients treated with Zestoretic. Angioedema associated with laryngeal edema and/or shock may be fatal. If angioedema occurs, Zestoretic should be promptly discontinued and appropriate monitoring should be instituted to ensure complete resolution of symptoms prior to dismissing the patient. Where swelling is confined to the face, lips and mouth the condition will usually resolve without further treatment, although antihistamines may be useful in relieving symptoms. These patients should be followed carefully until the swelling has resolved. However, where there is involvement of the tongue, glottis or larynx, likely to cause airway obstruction, s.c. epinephrine (0.5 mL 1:1 000) should be administered promptly when indicated.

The incidence of angioedema during ACE inhibitor therapy has been reported to be higher in black than in nonblack patients.

Patients with a history of angioedema unrelated to ACE inhibitor therapy may be at increased risk of angioedema while receiving an ACE inhibitor (see Contraindications).

Hypotension: Symptomatic hypotension has occurred after administration of lisinopril, usually after the first or second dose or when the dose was increased. It is more likely to occur in patients who are volume depleted by diuretic therapy, dietary salt restriction, dialysis, diarrhea or vomiting. Therefore, Zestoretic should not be used to start therapy or when a dose change is needed. In patients with ischemic heart or cerebrovascular disease, an excessive fall in blood pressure could result in a myocardial infarction or cerebrovascular accident (see Adverse Effects). Because of the potential fall in blood pressure in these patients, therapy with lisinopril should be started under very close medical supervision, usually in a hospital. Such patients should be followed closely for the first 2 weeks of treatment and whenever the dose of lisinopril and/or hydrochlorothiazide is increased. In patients with severe congestive heart failure, with or without associated renal insufficiency, excessive hypotension has been observed and may be associated with oliguria and/or progressive azotemia, and rarely with acute renal failure and/or death.

If hypotension occurs, the patient should be placed in supine position and, if necessary, receive an i.v. infusion of normal saline. A transient hypotensive response is not a contraindication to further doses which usually can be given without difficulty once the blood pressure has increased after volume expansion.

Neutropenia/Agranulocytosis: Agranulocytosis and bone marrow depression have been caused by angiotensin converting enzyme inhibitors. Several cases of agranulocytosis and neutropenia have been reported in which a causal relationship to lisinopril cannot be excluded. Current experience with the drug shows the incidence to be rare. Periodic monitoring of white blood cell counts should be considered, especially in patients with collagen vascular disease and renal disease.

Azotemia: Azotemia may be precipitated or increased by hydrochlorothiazide. Cumulative effects of the drug may develop in patients with impaired renal function. If increasing azotemia and oliguria occur during treatment of severe progressive renal disease, the diuretic should be discontinued.

Patients with Impaired Liver Function: Hepatitis, jaundice (hepatocellular and/or cholestatic), elevations of liver enzymes and/or serum bilirubin have occurred during therapy with lisinopril in patients with or without pre-existing liver abnormalities. In most cases the changes were reversed on discontinuation of the drug.

Should the patient receiving Zestoretic experience any unexplained symptoms (see Precautions, Information for the Patient), particularly during the first weeks or months of treatment, it is recommended that a full set of liver function tests and any other necessary investigation be carried out. Discontinuation of Zestoretic should be considered when appropriate.

There are no adequate studies in patients with cirrhosis and/or liver dysfunction. Zestoretic should be used with particular caution in patients with pre-existing liver abnormalities. In such patients baseline liver function tests should be obtained before administration of the drug and close monitoring of response and metabolic effects should apply.

Thiazides should be used with caution in patients with impaired hepatic function or progressive liver disease, since minor alterations of fluid and electrolyte balance may precipitate hepatic coma.

Hypersensitivity Reactions: Sensitivity reactions to hydrochlorothiazide may occur in patients with or without a history of allergy or bronchial asthma.

The possibility of exacerbation or activation of systemic lupus erythematosus has been reported in patients treated with hydrochlorothiazide.

Pregnancy: ACE inhibitors can cause fetal and neonatal morbidity and mortality when administered to pregnant women. Several dozen cases have been reported in the world literature. When pregnancy is detected, Zestoretic should be discontinued as soon as possible.

In rare cases (probably less than once in every thousand pregnancies) in which no alternative to ACE inhibitor therapy will be found, the mothers should be apprised of the potential hazards to their fetuses. Serial ultrasound examinations should be performed to assess fetal development and well-being and the volume of amniotic fluid.

If oligohydramnios is observed, then Zestoretic should be discontinued unless it is considered life-saving for the mother. A nonstress test (NST), and/or a biophysical profiling (BPP) may be appropriate, depending on the week of pregnancy. If concerns regarding fetal well-being still persist, a contraction stress testing (CST) should be considered. Patients and physicians should be aware, however, that oligohydramnios may not appear until after the fetus has sustained irreversible injury.

Infants with a history of in utero exposure to ACE inhibitors should be closely observed for hypotension, oliguria and hyperkalemia. If oliguria occurs, attention should be directed toward support of blood pressure and renal perfusion. Exchange transfusion or dialysis may be required as a means of reversing hypotension and/or substituting for impaired renal function, however, experience with those procedures has been limited. Lisinopril has been removed from the neonatal circulation by peritoneal dialysis.

Human Data: It is not known whether exposure limited to the first trimester of pregnancy can adversely affect fetal outcome. The use of ACE inhibitors during the second and third trimesters of pregnancy has been associated with fetal and neonatal injury including hypotension, neonatal skull hypoplasia, anuria, reversible or irreversible renal failure, and death. Oligohydramnios has also been reported, presumably resulting from decreased fetal renal function; oligohydramnios in this setting has been associated with fetal limb contractures, craniofacial deformation, and hypoplastic lung development. Prematurity and patent ductus arteriosus have also been reported, although it is not clear whether these occurrences were due to the ACE-inhibitor exposure.

Animal Data: Lisinopril was not teratogenic in mice treated on days 6 to 15 of gestation with up to 1 000 mg/kg/day (625 times the maximum recommended human dose). There was an increase in fetal resorptions at doses down to 100 mg/kg; at doses of 1 000 mg/kg, this was prevented by saline supplementation. There was no fetotoxicity or teratogenicity in rats treated with up to 300 mg/kg/day (188 times the maximum recommended dose) of lisinopril at days 6 to 17 of gestation. In rats receiving lisinopril from day 15 of gestation through day 21 postpartum, there was an increased incidence in pup deaths on days 2 to 7 postpartum and a lower average body weight of pups on day 21 postpartum. The increase in pup deaths and decrease in pup weight did not occur with maternal saline supplementation.

Lisinopril, at doses up to 1 mg/kg/day, was not teratogenic when given throughout the organogenic period in saline supplemented rabbits. Saline supplementation (physiologic saline in place of tap water) was used to eliminate maternotoxic effects and enable evaluation of the teratogenic potential at the highest possible dosage level. The rabbit has been shown to be extremely sensitive to angiotensin converting enzyme inhibitors (captopril and enalapril) with maternal and fetotoxic effects apparent at or below the recommended therapeutic dosage levels in man.

Fetotoxicity was demonstrated in rabbits by an increased incidence of fetal resorptions at an oral dose of lisinopril of 1 mg/kg/day and by an increased incidence of incomplete ossification at the lowest dose tested (0.1 mg/kg/day). A single i.v. dose of 15 mg/kg of lisinopril administered to pregnant rabbits on gestation days 16, 21 or 26 resulted in 88% to 100% fetal death.

By whole body autoradiography, radioactivity was found in the placenta following administration of labeled lisinopril to pregnant rats, but none was found in the fetuses.

Precautions: Renal Impairment: As a consequence of inhibiting the renin-angiotensin-aldosterone system, changes in renal function have been seen in susceptible individuals. In patients whose renal function may depend on the activity of the renin-angiotensin-aldosterone system, such as patients with bilateral renal artery stenosis, unilateral renal artery stenosis to a solitary kidney, or severe congestive heart failure, treatment with agents that inhibit this system has been associated with oliguria, progressive azotemia, and rarely, acute renal failure and/or death. In susceptible patients, concomitant diuretic use may further increase risk.

Use of Zestoretic should include appropriate assessment of renal function.

Thiazides may not be appropriate diuretics for use in patients with renal impairment and are ineffective at creatinine clearance values of 30 mL/min or below (i.e., moderate or severe renal insufficiency).

Anaphylactoid Reactions during Membrane Exposure: Anaphylactoid reactions have been reported in patients dialyzed with high-flux membranes (e.g., polyacrylonitrile [PAN]) and treated concomitantly with an ACE inhibitor. Dialysis should be stopped immediately if symptoms such as nausea, abdominal cramps, burning, angioedema, shortness of breath and severe hypotension occur. Symptoms are not relieved by antihistamines. In these patients consideration should be given to using a different type of dialysis membrane or a different class of antihypertensive agent.

Anaphylactoid Reactions during Desensitization: There have been isolated reports of patients experiencing sustained life threatening anaphylactoid reactions while receiving ACE inhibitors during desensitizing treatment with hymenoptera (bees, wasps) venom. In the same patients, these reactions have been avoided when ACE inhibitors were temporarily withheld for at least 24 hours, but they have reappeared upon inadvertent rechallenge.

Hyperkalemia: In clinical trials hyperkalemia (serum potassium >5.7 mEq/L) occurred in approximately 1.4% of hypertensive patients. In most cases these were isolated values which resolved despite continued therapy. Hyperkalemia was not a cause of discontinuation of therapy. Risk factors for the development of hyperkalemia may include renal insufficiency, diabetes mellitus and the concomitant use of potassium-sparing diuretics, potassium supplements and/or potassium-containing salt substitutes (see Drug Interactions).

Valvular Stenosis: There is concern on theoretical grounds that patients with aortic stenosis might be at particular risk of decreased coronary perfusion when treated with vasodilators because they do not develop as much afterload reduction.

Metabolism: Hyperuricemia may occur, or acute gout may be precipitated, in certain patients receiving thiazide therapy.

Thiazides may decrease serum PBI levels without signs of thyroid disturbance.

Thiazides have been shown to increase excretion of magnesium; this may result in hypomagnesemia.

Thiazides may decrease urinary calcium excretion. Thiazides may cause intermittent and slight elevation of serum calcium in the absence of known disorders of calcium metabolism. Marked hypercalcemia may be evidence of hidden hyperparathyroidism. Thiazides should be discontinued before carrying out tests for parathyroid function.

Increases in cholesterol, triglyceride and glucose levels may be associated with thiazide diuretic therapy.

Surgery/Anesthesia: In patients undergoing major surgery or during anesthesia with agents that produce hypotension, lisinopril blocks angiotensin II formation, secondary to compensatory renin release. If hypotension occurs and is considered to be due to this mechanism, it can be corrected by volume expansion (see Drug Interactions).

Cough: A dry, persistent cough, which usually disappears only after withdrawal or lowering of the dose of Zestoretic, has been reported.

Such possibility should be considered as part of the differential diagnosis of the cough.

Lactation: Milk of lactating rats contains radioactivity following administration of ^{14}C lisinopril.

It is not known whether lisinopril is secreted in human milk; however, thiazides do appear in human milk. If the use of Zestoretic, is deemed essential, the patient should stop nursing.

Geriatrics: In general, blood pressure response and adverse experiences were similar in younger and older patients given similar doses of lisinopril. Pharmacokinetic studies, however, indicate that maximum blood levels and area under the plasma concentration time curve (AUC) are doubled in older patients so that dosage adjustments should be made with particular caution.

Children: Zestoretic has not been studied in children and, therefore, use in this age group is not recommended.

Drug Interactions: Hypotension—Patients on Diuretic Therapy: Patients on diuretics and especially those in whom diuretic therapy was recently instituted, may occasionally experience an excessive reduction of blood pressure after initiation of therapy with lisinopril. The possibility of hypotensive effects with lisinopril can be minimized by either discontinuing the diuretic or increasing the salt intake prior to initiation of treatment with lisinopril (see Warnings and Dosage).

Agents Increasing Serum Potassium: Since lisinopril decreases aldosterone production, elevation of serum potassium may occur. Potassium sparing diuretics such as spironolactone, triamterene or amiloride, or potassium supplements should be given only for documented hypokalemia and with caution and with frequent monitoring of serum potassium since they may lead to a significant increase in serum potassium. Salt substitutes which contain potassium should also be used with caution.

Agents Causing Renin Release: The antihypertensive effect of Zestoretic is augmented by antihypertensive agents that cause renin release (e.g., diuretics).

Agents Affecting Sympathetic Activity: Agents affecting sympathetic activity (e.g., ganglionic blocking agents or adrenergic neuron blocking agents) may be used with caution. Beta-adrenergic blocking drugs add some further antihypertensive effect to lisinopril.

Lithium: Lithium generally should not be given with diuretics or ACE inhibitors. Diuretic agents and ACE inhibitors reduce the renal clearance of lithium and add a high risk of lithium toxicity.

d-Tubocurarine: Thiazide drugs may increase the responsiveness to tubocurarine.

Insulin: Insulin requirements in diabetic patients may be increased, decreased or unchanged. Diabetes mellitus which has been latent may become manifest during thiazide administration.

Alcohol, Barbiturates or Narcotics: Potentiation of orthostatic hypotension may occur.

Corticosteroids, ACTH: Intensified electrolyte depletion, particularly hypokalemia.

Pressor Amines (e.g., norepinephrine): Possible decreased response to pressor amines but not sufficient to preclude their use.

Nonsteroidal Anti-inflammatory Drugs: In some patients, the administration of a nonsteroidal anti-inflammatory agent can reduce the diuretic, natriuretic and antihypertensive effects of loop, potassium-sparing and thiazide diuretics. Therefore, when Zestoretic and nonsteroidal anti-inflammatory agents are used concomitantly, the patient should be observed closely to determine if the desired effect of the diuretic is obtained.

Information for the Patient: Angioedema: Angioedema, including laryngeal edema, may occur during treatment with Zestoretic. Patients should be so advised and told to report immediately any signs or symptoms suggesting angioedema (swelling of face, extremities, eyes, lips, tongue, difficulty in breathing) and to take no more drug until they have consulted with the prescribing physician.

Hypotension: Patients should be cautioned to report lightheadedness especially during the first few days of therapy. If actual syncope occurs, the patients should be told to discontinue the drug until they have consulted with the prescribing physician.

All patients should be cautioned that excessive perspiration and dehydration may lead to an excessive fall in blood pressure because of reduction in fluid volume. Other causes of volume depletion such as vomiting or diarrhea may also lead to a fall in blood pressure; patients should be advised to consult with their physician.

Neutropenia: Patients should be told to report promptly any indication of infection (e.g., sore throat, fever) which may be a sign of neutropenia.

Impaired Liver Function: Patients should be advised to return to the physician if he/she experiences any symptoms possibly related to liver dysfunction. This would include "viral-like symptoms" in the first weeks to months of therapy (such as fever, malaise, muscle pain, rash or adenopathy which are possible indicators of hypersensitivity reactions), or if abdominal pain, nausea or vomiting, loss of appetite, jaundice, itching or any other unexplained symptoms occur during therapy.

Pregnancy: Patients should be advised to report promptly to their physician if they become pregnant since the use of Zestoretic during pregnancy can cause injury and even death of the developing fetus.

Adverse Effects: In clinical trials involving 930 patients, including 100 patients treated for 50 weeks or more, the most severe clinical adverse reactions were syncope (0.8%), and hypotension (1.9%). The most frequent clinical adverse reactions were: dizziness (7.5%), headache (5.2%), cough (3.9%), fatigue (3.7%) and orthostatic effects (3.2%).

Discontinuation of treatment due to adverse reactions occurred in 4.4% of patients, mainly because of dizziness, cough, fatigue or muscle cramps.

Adverse reactions that have occurred in clinical trials or in marketing experience are those which have been previously reported with lisinopril and hydrochlorothiazide when used separately for the treatment of hypertension.

Adverse reactions occurring in hypertensive patients treated with lisinopril and hydrochlorothiazide in controlled trials are shown in Table I (on following page).

Abnormal Laboratory Findings: Hypokalemia, hyperkalemia (see Precautions).

Creatinine, Blood Urea Nitrogen: Minor increases in blood urea nitrogen (3.8%) and serum creatinine (4.2%) were observed in patients with essential hypertension treated with Zestoretic. More marked increases have also been reported and were more likely to occur in patients with bilateral renal artery stenosis (see Precautions).

Increases in blood urea nitrogen and serum creatinine, usually reversible upon discontinuation of therapy, were observed in 1.1 and 1.6% of patients respectively with essential hypertension treated with lisinopril alone.

Serum Uric Acid, Glucose, Magnesium, Cholesterol, Triglycerides and Calcium (see Precautions).

Zestoretic (cont'd)

Table I—Zestoretic

Adverse Reactions

	Lisinopril 2 633 Patients (%)	Lisinopril Plus Hydrochlorothiazide 930 Patients (%)
Cardiovascular		
Hypotension	1.4	1.9
Orthostatic effects	0.9	3.2
Chest pain	1.1	1.0
Syncope	0.2	0.8
Angina	0.3	0.1
Edema	0.6	0.1
Palpitation	0.8	0.9
Rhythm disturbances	0.5	0.1
Chest discomfort	—	0.6
Gastrointestinal		
Diarrhea	1.8	2.5
Nausea	1.9	2.2
Vomiting	1.1	1.4
Dyspepsia	0.5	1.3
Anorexia	0.4	0.2
Constipation	0.2	0.3
Flatulence	0.3	0.2
Abdominal pain	1.4	0.9
Dry mouth	0.5	0.2
Nervous System		
Dizziness	4.4	7.5
Headache	5.6	5.2
Paresthesia	0.5	1.5
Depression	0.7	0.5
Somnolence	0.8	0.4
Insomnia	0.3	0.2
Vertigo	0.2	0.9
Respiratory		
Cough	3.0	3.9
Dyspnea	0.4	0.4
Upper respiratory infection	2.1	2.2
Dermatologic		
Rash	1.0	1.2
Pruritus	0.5	0.4
Flushing	0.3	0.8
Angioedema	0.1	—*
Musculoskeletal		
Muscle cramps	0.5	2.0
Back pain	0.5	0.8
Shoulder pain	0.2	0.5
Other		
Fatigue	—	3.7
Asthenia	2.7	1.8
Decreased libido	0.2	1.0
Fever	0.3	0.5
Impotence	0.7	1.2
Gout	0.2	0.2

*See Zestoretic (Marketing Experience Only).

Hemoglobin and Hematocrit: Small decreases in hemoglobin and hematocrit (mean decreases of approximately 0.5 g % and 1.5 vol %, respectively) occurred frequently in hypertensive patients treated with Zestoretic but were rarely of clinical importance unless another cause of anemia coexisted. In clinical trials, 0.4% of patients discontinued therapy due to anemia.

Other (Causal Relationship Unknown): Rarely, elevations of liver enzymes and/or serum bilirubin have occurred.

Adverse Reactions Reported in Uncontrolled Trials and/or Marketing Experience: Zestril: Cardiovascular: myocardial infarction or cerebrovascular accident possibly secondary to excessive hypotension in high risk patients (see Warnings), tachycardia.

Gastrointestinal: abdominal pain, dry mouth, pancreatitis.

Hepatic: liver function abnormalities, hepatitis, jaundice (hepatocellular and/or cholestatic).

Nervous System: mood alterations, mental confusion.

Respiratory: bronchospasm.

Dermatologic: alopecia, urticaria, pruritus, diaphoresis, pemphigus, Stevens-Johnson syndrome.

Hematologic: hemolytic anemia.

Special Senses: taste disorders.

Urogenital: uremia, oliguria/anuria, renal dysfunction, acute renal failure, impotence.

A symptom complex has been reported which may include fever, vasculitis, myalgia, arthralgia/arthritis, a positive ANA, elevated ESR, eosinophilia and leukocytosis. Rash, photosensitivity, or other dermatologic manifestations may also occur. Zestoretic (Marketing Experience Only): Angioedema of the face, extremities, lips, tongue, glottis and/or larynx has been reported (see Warnings).

No other adverse events have been reported with Zestoretic which have not been reported with lisinopril or hydrochlorothiazide individually.

Overdose: Symptoms and Treatment: No specific information is available on the treatment of overdosage with Zestoretic. Treatment is symptomatic and supportive. Therapy with Zestoretic should be discontinued and the patient observed closely. Suggested measures include induction of emesis and/or gastric lavage, if ingestion is recent, and correction of dehydration, electrolyte imbalance and hypotension by established procedures.

Lisinopril: The most likely features of overdosage would be hypotension, for which the usual treatment would be i.v. infusion of normal saline solution. Lisinopril may be removed from general circulation by hemodialysis.

Hydrochlorothiazide: The most common signs and symptoms observed are those caused by electrolyte depletion (hypokalemia, hypochloremia, hyponatremia) and dehydration resulting from excessive diuresis. If digitalis has also been administered, hypokalemia may accentuate cardiac arrhythmias.

Dosage: Dosage must be individualized. The fixed combination is not for initial therapy. The dose of Zestoretic should be determined by the titration of the individual components.

Once the patient has been successfully titrated with the individual components as described below, either one Zestoretic 10/12.5 mg or one or two 20/12.5 mg or 20/25 mg tablets once daily may be substituted if the titrated doses are the same as those in the fixed combination (see Indications and Warnings).

Patients usually do not require doses in excess of 50 mg of hydrochlorothiazide daily, particularly when combined with antihypertensive agents.

For lisinopril monotherapy the recommended initial dose in patients not on diuretics is 10 mg of lisinopril once a day. Dosage should be adjusted according to blood pressure response. The usual dosage range of lisinopril is 10 to 40 mg administered in a single daily dose. The antihypertensive effect may diminish toward the end of the dosing interval regardless of the administered dose, but most commonly with a dose of 10 mg daily. This can be evaluated by measuring blood pressure just prior to dosing to determine whether satisfactory control is being maintained for 24 hours. If it is not, an increase in dose should be considered. The maximum dose used in long-term controlled clinical trials was 80 mg/day. If blood pressure is not controlled with lisinopril alone, a low dose of a diuretic may be added. Hydrochlorothiazide 12.5 mg has been shown to provide an additive effect. After the addition of a diuretic, it may be possible to reduce the dose of lisinopril.

Diuretic Treated Patients: In patients who are currently being treated with a diuretic, symptomatic hypotension occasionally may occur following the initial dose of lisinopril. The diuretic should if possible, be discontinued for 2 to 3 days before beginning therapy with lisinopril to reduce the likelihood of hypotension (see Warnings). The dosage of lisinopril should be adjusted according to blood pressure response. If the patient's blood pressure is not controlled with lisinopril alone, diuretic therapy may be resumed as described above.

If the diuretic cannot be discontinued, an initial dose of 5 mg of lisinopril alone should be administered and the patient remain under medical supervision for at least 2 hours, and until blood pressure has stabilized for at least an additional hour (see Warnings and Precautions, Drug Interactions).

Dosage Adjustment in Renal Impairment: In patients with creatinine clearance greater than 30 mL/min the usual dose titration of the individual components is required.

Anaphylactoid reactions have been reported in patients dialyzed with high flux membranes (e.g., polyacrylonitrile [PAN]) and treated concomitantly with an ACE inhibitor (see Precautions).

For patients with creatinine clearance between 10 and 30 mL/min the starting dose of lisinopril is 2.5 to 5 mg/day. The dosage may then be titrated upward until blood pressure is controlled or to a maximum of 40 mg daily.

When concomitant diuretic therapy is required in patients with severe renal impairment (creatinine clearance <10 mL/min), a loop diuretic, rather than a thiazide diuretic is preferred for use with lisinopril. Therefore, for patients with severe renal dysfunction the lisinopril-hydrochlorothiazide combination tablet is not recommended.

Supplied: 10/12.5: Each peach, round, biconvex tablet, with "Zt" over "10" intagliated on one side and blank on the other side, contains: lisinopril 10 mg and hydrochlorothiazide 12.5 mg. Nonmedicinal ingredients: calcium phosphate, iron oxide, magnesium stearate, mannitol and starch. Bottles of 100. Calendar packs of 30.

20/12.5: Each white, round, biconvex tablet, with "Zestoretic" intagliated on one side and blank on the other side, contains: lisinopril 20 mg and hydrochlorothiazide 12.5 mg. Nonmedicinal ingredients: calcium phosphate, magnesium stearate, mannitol and starch. Bottles of 100. Calendar packs of 30.

20/25: Each peach, round, biconvex tablet, with "Zestoretic" intagliated on one side and blank on the other side, contains: lisinopril 20 mg and hydrochlorothiazide 25 mg. Nonmedicinal ingredients: calcium phosphate, iron oxide, magnesium stearate, mannitol and starch. Bottles of 100. Calendar packs of 30.

Store at controlled room temperature 15 to 30°C. Keep container tightly closed.

(Shown in Product Recognition Section)

Reviewed 1998

ZESTRIL® Ⓟ

Zeneca

Lisinopril

Angiotensin Converting Enzyme Inhibitor

Pharmacology: Lisinopril is an ACE inhibitor which is used in the treatment of hypertension, congestive heart failure and following myocardial infarction in hemodynamically stable patients.

Angiotensin converting enzyme (ACE) is a peptidyl dipeptidase which catalyzes the conversion of angiotensin I to the pressor substance, angiotensin II. Inhibition of ACE results in decreased plasma angiotensin II, which leads to increased plasma renin activity (due to removal of negative feedback of renin release) and decreased aldosterone secretion. Although the latter decrease is small, it results in a small increase in serum K^+. In patients treated with lisinopril and a thiazide diuretic there was essentially no change in serum potassium (see Precautions).

ACE is identical to kininase II. Thus, lisinopril may also block the degradation of bradykinin, a potent vasodilator peptide. However, the role that this plays in the therapeutic effects of lisinopril is unknown.

While the mechanism through which lisinopril lowers blood pressure is believed to be primarily the suppression of the renin-angiotensin-aldosterone system, lisinopril also lowers blood pressure in patients with low-renin hypertension. However, black hypertensive patients (usually a low-renin hypertensive population) have a smaller average response to lisinopril monotherapy than nonblack patients.

Administration of lisinopril to patients with hypertension results in a reduction of both supine and standing blood pressure. Abrupt withdrawal of lisinopril has not been associated with a rapid increase in blood pressure. In most patients studied, after oral administration of an individual dose of lisinopril, the onset of antihypertensive activity is seen at 1 hour with peak reduction of blood pressure achieved by 6 hours. Although an antihypertensive effect was observed 24 hours after dosing with recommended single daily doses, the effect was more consistent and the mean effect was considerably larger in some studies with doses of 20 mg or more than with lower doses. However, at all doses studied, the mean antihypertensive effect was substantially smaller 24 hours after dosing than it was 6 hours after dosing. On occasion, achievement of optimal blood pressure reduction may require 2 to 4 weeks of therapy.

In hemodynamic studies in patients with essential hypertension, blood pressure reduction was accompanied by a reduction in peripheral arterial resistance with little or no change in cardiac output and in heart rate. In a study of 9 hypertensive patients, following administration of lisinopril, there was an increase in mean renal blood flow that was not significant. Data from several small studies are inconsistent with respect to the effect of lisinopril on glomerular filtration rate in hypertensive patients with normal renal function, but suggest that changes, if any, are not large.

When lisinopril is given together with thiazide-type diuretics, its blood pressure lowering effect is approximately additive.

The antihypertensive effect of angiotensin converting enzyme inhibitors is generally lower in black patients than in nonblacks patients.

Administration of lisinopril to patients with congestive heart failure reduces afterload and preload of the heart, resulting in an increase in cardiac output, without reflex tachycardia. Exercise tolerance is improved.

Pharmacokinetics: After oral administration of lisinopril, peak serum concentrations of lisinopril occur within approximately 7 hours, although patients with recent myocardial infarction have demonstrated an increase in time to peak serum concentration to about 8 to 10 hours. Declining serum concentrations exhibit a prolonged terminal phase which does not contribute to drug accumulation. This terminal phase probably represents saturable binding to ACE and is not proportional to dose. Lisinopril does not bind serum proteins other than ACE.

Lisinopril does not undergo metabolism and is excreted unchanged entirely in the urine. Based on urinary recovery, the extent of absorption of lisinopril is approximately 25%, with large inter-subject variability (6 to 60%) at all doses tested (5 to 80 mg). Lisinopril absorption is not influenced by the presence of food in the gastrointestinal tract.

Following multiple doses of lisinopril, the effective half-life of accumulation is 12 hours.

In a study in elderly healthy subjects (65 years and above), a single dose of lisinopril 20 mg produced higher serum concentrations and higher values for the area under the plasma curve than those seen in young healthy adults given a similar dose. In another study, single daily doses of lisinopril 5 mg were given for 7 consecutive days to young and elderly healthy volunteers and to elderly patients with congestive heart failure. Maximum serum concentrations of lisinopril on Day 7 were higher in the elderly volunteers than in the young, and still higher in the elderly patients with congestive heart failure. Renal clearance of lisinopril was decreased in the elderly, particularly in the presence of congestive heart failure.

Impaired renal function decreases elimination of lisinopril. This decrease becomes clinically important when the glomerular filtration rate is below 30 mL/min (see Precautions, Impaired Renal Function and Dosage).

Lisinopril can be removed by dialysis.

Studies in rats indicate that lisinopril crosses the blood-brain barrier poorly.

Indications: Hypertension: Lisinopril is indicated in the treatment of essential hypertension and in renovascular hypertension. It may be used alone or concomitantly with thiazide diuretics. A great majority of patients (>80%) with severe hypertension required combination therapy. Lisinopril has been used concomitantly with beta-blockers and calcium antagonists, but the data on such use are limited.

Lisinopril should normally be used in those patients in whom treatment with diuretic or beta-blocker was found ineffective or has been associated with unacceptable adverse effects. Lisinopril can also be tried as an initial agent in those patients in whom use of diuretics and/or beta-blockers is contraindicated or in patients with medical conditions in which these drugs frequently cause serious adverse effects.

Heart Failure: Lisinopril is indicated in the management of symptomatic congestive heart failure as adjunctive treatment with diuretics, and where appropriate, digitalis. Treatment with lisinopril should be initiated under close medical supervision, usually in a hospital.

Acute Myocardial Infarction: Lisinopril is indicated in the treatment of hemodynamically stable patients within 24 hours of an acute myocardial infarction, to improve survival. Patients should receive, as appropriate, the standard recommended treatments such as thrombolytics, ASA and beta-blocker(s).

Therapy with lisinopril should be reassessed after 6 weeks. If there is no evidence of symptomatic or asymptomatic left ventricular dysfunction, treatment with lisinopril can be stopped.

Lisinopril should not be used if systolic blood pressure is less than 100 mmHg, if clinically relevant renal failure is present, if there is a history of bilateral stenosis of the renal arteries, or if there is a known allergy to ACE inhibitors (see Precautions, Hypotension in Acute Myocardial Infarction, Renal Impairment).

Pregnancy: **When used in pregnancy during the second and third trimesters, ACE inhibitors can cause injury or even death of the developing fetus. When pregnancy is detected lisinopril should be discontinued as soon as possible (see Warnings, Pregnancy and Precautions, Information for the Patient).**

In using lisinopril, attention should be given to the risk of angioedema (see Warnings).

Contraindications: In patients who are hypersensitive to this product and in patients with a history of angioneurotic edema relating to previous treatment with an angiotensin-converting enzyme inhibitor.

Warnings: Angioedema: Angioedema has been reported in patients treated with lisinopril. Angioedema associated with laryngeal edema and/or shock may be fatal. If angioedema occurs, lisinopril should be promptly discontinued and the patient should be observed until the swelling subsides. Where swelling is confined to the face, lips and mouth the condition will usually resolve without further treatment, although antihistamines may be useful in relieving symptoms. These patients should be followed carefully until the swelling has resolved. However, where there is involvement of the tongue, glottis or larynx, likely to cause airway obstruction, s.c. epinephrine (0.5 mL 1:1 000) should be administered promptly when indicated.

The incidence of angioedema during ACE inhibitor therapy has been reported to be higher in black than in nonblack patients.

Patients with a history of angioedema unrelated to ACE inhibitor therapy may be at increased risk of angioedema while receiving an ACE inhibitor (see Contraindications).

Hypotension: Symptomatic hypotension has occurred after administration of lisinopril, usually after the first or second dose or when the dose was increased. It is more likely to occur in patients who are volume depleted by diuretic therapy, dietary salt restriction, dialysis, diarrhea, vomiting, or possibly in patients with renin-dependent renovascular hypertension (see Dosage). In patients with severe congestive heart failure, with or without associated renal insufficiency, excessive hypotension has been observed and may be associated with oliguria and/or progressive azotemia, and rarely with acute renal failure and/or death. Because of the potential fall in blood pressure in these patients, therapy should be started under very close medical supervision, usually in a hospital. Such patients should be followed closely for the first 2 weeks of treatment and whenever the dose of lisinopril and/or diuretic is increased. Similar considerations apply to patients with ischemic heart or cerebrovascular disease in whom an excessive fall in blood pressure could result in a myocardial infarction or cerebrovascular accident (see Adverse Effects).

If hypotension occurs, the patient should be placed in supine position and, if necessary, receive an i.v. infusion of normal saline. A transient hypotensive response is not a contraindication to further doses which usually can be given without difficulty once the blood pressure has increased after volume expansion.

In some patients with congestive heart failure who have normal or low blood pressure, additional lowering of systemic blood pressure may occur with lisinopril. If hypotension occurs, a reduction of dose or discontinuation of therapy should be considered.

Neutropenia/Agranulocytosis: Agranulocytosis and bone marrow depression have been caused by angiotensin converting enzyme inhibitors. Several cases of agranulocytosis and neutropenia have been reported in which a causal relationship to lisinopril cannot be excluded. Current experience with the drug shows the incidence to be rare. Periodic monitoring of white blood cell counts should be considered, especially in patients with collagen vascular disease and renal disease.

Pregnancy: ACE inhibitors can cause fetal and neonatal morbidity and mortality when administered to pregnant women. Several dozen cases have been reported in the world literature. When pregnancy is detected, lisinopril should be discontinued as soon as possible.

In rare cases (probably less than once in every thousand pregnancies) in which no alternative to ACE inhibitor therapy will be found, the mothers should be apprised of the potential hazards to their fetuses. Serial ultrasound examinations should be performed to assess fetal development and well-being and the volume of amniotic fluid.

If oligohydramnios is observed, then lisinopril should be discontinued unless it is considered life saving for the mother. A nonstress test (NST), and/or a biophysical profiling (BPP) may be appropriate, depending on the week of pregnancy. If concerns regarding fetal well-being still persist, a contraction stress testing (CST) should be considered. Patients and physicians should be aware, however, that oligohydramnios may not appear until after the fetus has sustained irreversible injury.

Infants with a history of in utero exposure to ACE inhibitors should be closely observed for hypotension, oliguria, and hyperkalemia. If oliguria occurs, attention should be directed toward support of blood pressure and renal perfusion. Exchange transfusion or dialysis may be required as a means of reversing hypotension and/or substituting for imparied renal function, however, limited experience with those procedures has not been associated with significant clinical benefit.

Lisinopril has been removed from the neonatal circulation by peritoneal dialysis.

Human Data: It is not known whether exposure limited to the first trimester of pregnancy can adversely affect fetal outcome. The use of ACE inhibitors during the second and third trimesters of pregnancy has been associated with fetal and neonatal injury including hypotension, neonatal skull hypoplasia, anuria, reversible or irreversible renal failure, and death. Oligohydramnios has also been reported, presumably resulting from decreased fetal renal function; oligohydramnios in this setting has been associated with fetal limb contractures, craniofacial deformation, and hypoplastic lung development. Prematurity and patent ductus arteriosus have also been reported, although it is not clear whether these occurrences were due to the ACE-inhibitor exposure.

Animal Data: Lisinopril was not teratogenic in mice treated on days 6 to 15 of gestation with up to 1 000 mg/kg/day (625 times the maximum recommended human dose). There was an increase in fetal resorptions at doses down to 100 mg/kg; at doses of 1 000 mg/kg, this was prevented by saline supplementation. There was no fetotoxicity or teratogenicity in rats treated with up to 300 mg/kg/day (188 times the maximum recommended dose) of lisinopril at days 6 to 17 of gestation. In rats receiving lisinopril from day 15 of gestation through day 21 postpartum, there was an increased incidence in pup deaths on days 2 to 7 postpartum and a lower average body weight of pups on day 21 postpartum. The increase in pup deaths and decrease in pup weight did not occur with maternal saline supplementation.

Lisinopril, at doses up to 1 mg/kg/day, was not teratogenic when given throughout the organogenic period in saline supplemented rabbits. Saline supplementation (physiologic saline in place of tap water) was used to eliminate maternotoxic effects and enable evaluation of the teratogenic potential at the highest possible dosage level. The rabbit has been shown to be extremely sensitive to angiotensin converting enzyme inhibitors (captopril and enalapril) with maternal and fetotoxic effects apparent at or below the recommended therapeutic dosage levels in man.

Fetotoxicity was demonstrated in rabbits by an increased incidence of fetal resorptions at an oral dose of lisinopril of 1 mg/kg/day and by an increased incidence of incomplete ossification at the lowest dose tested (0.1 mg/kg/day). A single i.v. dose of 15 mg/kg of lisinopril administered to pregnant rabbits on gestation days 16, 21 or 26 resulted in 88 to 100% fetal death.

By whole body autoradiography, radioactivity was found in the placenta following administration of labeled lisinopril to pregnant rats, but none was found in the fetuses.

Precautions: Renal Impairment: As a consequence of inhibiting the renin-angiotensin-aldosterone system, changes in renal function have been seen in susceptible individuals. In patients whose renal function may depend on the activity of the renin-angiotensin-aldosterone system, such as patients with bilateral renal artery stenosis, unilateral renal artery stenosis to a solitary kidney, or severe congestive heart failure, treatment with agents that inhibit this system has been associated with oliguria, progressive azotemia, and rarely, acute renal failure and/or death. In susceptible patients, concomitant diuretic use may further increase risk.

In acute myocardial infarction, treatment with lisinopril should not be initiated in patients with evidence of renal dysfunction, defined as serum creatinine concentration exceeding 177 μmol/L and/or proteinuria exceeding 500 mg/24 h. If renal dysfunction develops during treatment with lisinopril (serum creatinine concentration exceeding 265 μmol/L or a doubling from the pre-treatment value), then the physician should consider withdrawal of lisinopril.

Use of lisinopril should include appropriate assessment of renal function.

Hypotension in Acute Myocardial Infarction: Treatment with lisinopril must not be initiated in patients with acute myocardial infarction who are at risk of further serious hemodynamic deterioration after treatment with a vasodilator. These include patients with systolic blood pressure of 100 mmHg or lower or those in cardiogenic shock.

During the first 3 days following the infarction, dosage reduction should occur if systolic blood pressure is between 100 and 120 mmHg (see Dosage, Acute Myocardial Infarction).

Patients with myocardial infarction in the GISSI-3 study treated with lisinopril, had a higher (9.0% vs 3.7%) incidence of persistent hypotension (systolic blood pressure less than 90 mmHg for more than 1 hour) than placebo.

Zestril (cont'd)

Anaphylactoid Reactions During Membrane Exposure: Anaphylactoid reactions have been reported in patients dialyzed with high-flux membranes (e.g.: polyacrylonitrile [PAN]) and treated concomitantly with an ACE inhibitor. Dialysis should be stopped immediately if symptoms such as nausea, abdominal cramps, burning, angioedema, shortness of breath and severe hypotension occur. Symptoms are not relieved by antihistamines. In these patients consideration should be given to using a different type of dialysis membrane or a different class of antihypertensive agent.

Anaphylactoid Reactions During Desensitization: There have been isolated reports of patients experiencing sustained life-threatening anaphylactoid reactions while receiving ACE inhibitors during desensitizing treatment with hymenoptera (bees, wasps) venom. In the same patients, these reactions have been avoided when ACE inhibitors were temporarily withheld for at least 24 hours, but they have reappeared upon inadvertent rechallenge.

Hyperkalemia: In clinical trials hyperkalemia (serum potassium >5.7 mEq/L) occurred in approximately 2.2% of hypertensive patients and 4% of patients with congestive heart failure. In most cases these were isolated values which resolved despite continued therapy. Hyperkalemia was a cause of discontinuation of therapy in approximately 0.1% of hypertensive patients. Risk factors for the development of hyperkalemia may include renal insufficiency, diabetes mellitus and the concomitant use of potassium-sparing diuretics, potassium supplements and/or potassium-containing salt substitutes (see Precautions, Drug Interactions).

Valvular Stenosis: There is concern on theoretical grounds that patients with aortic stenosis might be at particular risk of decreased coronary perfusion when treated with vasodilators because they do not develop as much afterload reduction.

Surgery/Anesthesia: In patients undergoing major surgery or during anesthesia with agents that produce hypotension, lisinopril blocks angiotensin II formation, secondary to compensatory renin release. If hypotension occurs and is considered to be due to this mechanism, it can be corrected by volume expansion.

Patients with Impaired Liver Function: Hepatitis, jaundice (hepatocellular and/or cholestatic), elevations of liver enzymes and/or serum bilirubin have occurred during therapy with lisinopril, in patients with or without pre-existing liver abnormalities (see Adverse Effects). In most cases the changes were reversed on discontinuation of the drug.

Should the patient receiving lisinopril experience any unexplained symptoms (see Information for the Patient), particularly during the first weeks or months of treatment, it is recommended that a full set of liver function tests and any other necessary investigation be carried out. Discontinuation of lisinopril should be considered when appropriate.

There are no adequate studies in patients with cirrhosis and/or liver dysfunction. Lisinopril should be used with particular caution in patients with pre-existing liver abnormalities. In such patients baseline liver function tests should be obtained before administration of the drug and close monitoring of response and metabolic effects should apply.

Cough: A dry, persistent cough, which usually disappears only after withdrawal or lowering of the dose of lisinopril, has been reported.

Such possibility should be considered as part of the differential diagnosis of the cough.

Lactation: Milk of lactating rats contains radioactivity following administration of ^{14}C lisinopril.

It is not known whether this drug is secreted in human milk. Because many drugs are secreted in human milk, caution should be exercised when lisinopril is given to a nursing mother.

Children: Safety and effectiveness in children have not been established.

Drug Interactions: Hypotension: Patients on Diuretic Therapy: Patients on diuretics and especially those in whom diuretic therapy was recently instituted, may occasionally experience an excessive reduction of blood pressure after initiation of therapy with lisinopril. The possibility of symptomatic hypotension with lisinopril can be minimized by discontinuing the diuretic prior to initiation of treatment with lisinopril and/or lowering the initial dose of lisinopril (see Warnings, Hypotension and Dosage).

Agents Increasing Serum Potassium: Since lisinopril decreases aldosterone production, elevation of serum potassium may occur. Potassium sparing diuretics such as spironolactone, triamterene or amiloride, or potassium supplements should be given only for documented hypokalemia and with caution and with frequent monitoring of serum potassium since they may lead to a significant increase in serum potassium. Potassium-containing salt substitutes should also be used with caution.

Agents Causing Renin Release: The antihypertensive effect of lisinopril is augmented by antihypertensive agents that cause renin release (e.g., diuretics).

Agents Affecting Sympathetic Activity: Agents affecting sympathetic activity (e.g., ganglionic blocking agents or adrenergic neuron blocking agents) may be used with caution. Beta-adrenergic blocking drugs add some further antihypertensive effect to lisinopril.

Indomethacin: Indomethacin may diminish the antihypertensive efficacy of concomitantly administered lisinopril.

Lithium Salts: As with other drugs which eliminate sodium, lithium elimination may be reduced. Therefore, the serum lithium levels should be monitored carefully if lithium salts are to be administered.

Information for the Patient: Angioedema: Angioedema, including laryngeal edema, may occur especially following the first dose of lisinopril. Patients should be so advised and told to report immediately any signs or symptoms suggesting angioedema (swelling of face, extremities, eyes, lips, tongue, difficulty in breathing) and to take no more drug until they have consulted with the prescribing physician.

Hypotension: Patients should be cautioned to report lightheadedness especially during the first few days of therapy. If actual syncope occurs, the patients should be told to discontinue the drug until they have consulted with the prescribing physician.

All patients should be cautioned that excessive perspiration and dehydration may lead to an excessive fall in blood pressure because of reduction in fluid volume. Other causes of volume depletion such as vomiting or diarrhea may also lead to a fall in blood pressure; patients should be advised to consult with their physician.

Neutropenia: Patients should be told to report promptly any indication of infection (e.g., sore throat, fever) which may be a sign of neutropenia.

Impaired Liver Function: Patients should be advised to return to the physician if he/she experiences any symptoms possibly related to liver dysfunction. This would include 'viral-like symptoms' in the first weeks to months of therapy (such as fever, malaise, muscle pain, rash or adenopathy which are possible indicators of hypersensitivity reactions), or if abdominal pain, nausea or vomiting, loss of appetite, jaundice, itching or any other unexplained symptoms occur during therapy.

Hyperkalemia: Patients should be told not to use salt substitutes containing potassium without consulting their physician.

Pregnancy: Since the use of lisinopril during pregnancy can cause injury and even death of the developing fetus, patients should be advised to report promptly to their physician if they become pregnant.

Note: As with many other drugs, certain advice to patients being treated with lisinopril is warranted. This information is intended to aid in the safe and effective use of this medication. It is not a disclosure of all possible adverse or intended effects.

Adverse Effects: In controlled clinical trials involving 3 269 patients (2 633 patients with hypertension and 636 patients with congestive heart failure), the most frequent clinical adverse reactions were: dizziness (4.4%), headache (5.6%), asthenia/fatigue (2.7%), diarrhea (1.8%) and cough (3.0%), all of which were more frequent than in placebo-treated patients. Discontinuation of therapy was required in 5.9% of patients.

For adverse reactions which occurred in hypertensive patients and patients with congestive heart failure treated with lisinopril in controlled clinical trials, comparative incidence data are listed in Table I.

Angioedema: Angioedema has been reported in patients receiving lisinopril (0.1%). Angioedema associated with laryngeal edema may be fatal. If angioedema of the face, extremities, lips, tongue, glottis and/or larynx occurs, treatment with lisinopril should be discontinued and appropriate therapy instituted immediately (see Warnings, Angioedema).

Hypotension: In hypertensive patients, hypotension occurred in 0.8% and syncope occurred in 0.2% of patients. Hypotension or syncope was a cause for discontinuation of therapy in 0.3% of hypertensive patients (see Warnings).

In patients with congestive heart failure, hypotension occurred in 5.2% and syncope occurred in 1.7% of patients. Hypotension and dizziness were causes for discontinuation of therapy in 1.7% of these patients.

Table I—Zestril

Incidence of Adverse Reactions Occurring in Patients Treated with Lisinopril in Controlled Clinical Trials

	Hypertension (2 633 Patients) (%)	Congestive Heart Failure (636 Patients) (%)
Cardiovascular		
Hypotension	0.8	5.2
Orthostatic effects	0.9	1.3
Chest pain	1.1	7.4
Angina	0.3	3.8
Edema	0.6	2.5
Palpitation	0.8	1.9
Rhythm disturbances	0.5	0.6
Gastrointestinal		
Diarrhea	1.8	6.1
Nausea	1.9	4.9
Vomiting	1.1	2.4
Dyspepsia	0.5	1.9
Anorexia	0.4	1.4
Constipation	0.2	0.8
Flatulence	0.3	0.5
Nervous System		
Dizziness	4.4	14.2
Headache	5.6	4.6
Paresthesia	0.5	2.8
Depression	0.7	1.1
Somnolence	0.8	0.6
Insomnia	0.3	2.4
Vertigo	0.2	0.2
Respiratory		
Cough	3.0	6.4
Dyspnea	0.4	7.4
Orthopnea	0.1	0.9
Dermatologic		
Rash	1.0	5.0
Pruritus	0.5	1.4
Musculoskeletal		
Muscle cramps	0.5	2.2
Back pain	0.5	1.7
Leg pain	0.1	1.3
Shoulder pain	0.2	0.8
Other		
Asthenia/Fatigue	2.7	7.1
Blurred vision	0.3	1.1
Fever	0.3	1.1
Flushing	0.3	0.3
Gout	0.2	1.7
Decreased libido	0.2	0.2
Malaise	0.3	1.1

Additional adverse reactions which occurred rarely, either during controlled clinical trials or after the drug was marketed, include: Cardiovascular: myocardial infarction or cerebrovascular accident possibly secondary to excessive hypotension in high-risk patients (see Warnings, Hypotension), tachycardia.

Gastrointestinal: abdominal pain, dry mouth, pancreatitis.

Hepatic: liver function abnormalities, hepatitis, jaundice (hepatocellular and/or cholestatic).

Nervous System: mood alterations, mental confusion.

Respiratory: bronchospasm.

Dermatologic: alopecia, diaphoresis, pemphigus, pruritus, Stevens-Johnson syndrome, urticaria.

Hematologic: hemolytic anemia.

Special Senses: taste disorders.

Urogenital: uremia, oliguria/anuria, renal dysfunction, acute renal failure, impotence.

A symptom complex has been reported which may include fever, vasculitis, myalgia, arthralgia/arthritis, a positive ANA, elevated ESR, eosinophilia, and leukocytosis. Rash, photosensitivity, or other dermatologic manifestations may also occur.

Laboratory Test Findings: Serum Electrolytes: Hyperkalemia (see Precautions).

Creatinine, Blood Urea Nitrogen: Increases in blood urea nitrogen and serum creatinine, usually reversible upon discontinuation of therapy, were observed in 1.1 and 1.6% of patients respectively with essential hypertension treated with lisinopril alone. Increases were more common in patients receiving concomitant diuretics and in patients with renal artery stenosis (see Precautions). Reversible increases in blood urea nitrogen (14.5%) and serum creatinine (11.2%)

were observed in approximately 12.0% of patients with congestive heart failure on concomitant diuretic therapy. Frequently, these abnormalities resolved when the dosage of the diuretic was decreased.

Hematology: Decreases in hemoglobin and hematocrit (mean decreases of approximately 0.9 g% and 0.6 vol%, respectively) occurred frequently in patients treated with lisinopril but were rarely of clinical importance in patients without some other cause of anemia.

An occasional case of neutropenia and bone marrow depression has been reported in the world literature.

Hepatic: Elevations of liver enzymes and/or serum bilirubin have occurred (see Precautions).

Discontinuations: Overall, 1.0% of patients discontinued therapy due to laboratory adverse experiences, principally elevations in blood urea nitrogen (0.8%), serum creatinine (0.1%) and serum potassium (0.1%).

Overdose: Symptoms and Treatment: There are no data on overdosage in humans. The most likely manifestation of overdosage would be hypotension, for which the usual treatment would be i.v. infusion of normal saline solution.

Lisinopril may be removed from the general circulation by hemodialysis.

Dosage: Since absorption of lisinopril is not affected by food, the tablets may be administered before, during or after meals. Lisinopril should be administered in a single daily dose.

Dosage must be individualized.

Essential Hypertension: In patients with essential hypertension, not on diuretic therapy, the usual recommended starting dose is 10 mg once a day. Dosage should be adjusted according to blood pressure response: the usual dosage range is 10 to 40 mg/day, administered in a single daily dose. The antihypertensive effect may diminish toward the end of the dosing interval regardless of the administered dose, but most commonly with a dose of 10 mg daily. This can be evaluated by measuring blood pressure just prior to dosing to determine whether satisfactory control is being maintained for 24 hours. If it is not, an increase in dose should be considered. The maximum dose used in long-term controlled clinical trials was 80 mg/day. If blood pressure is not controlled with lisinopril alone, a low dose of diuretic may be added. Hydrochlorothiazide 12.5 mg has been shown to provide an additive effect. After the addition of diuretic, it may be possible to reduce the dose of lisinopril.

Diuretic Treated Patients: In hypertensive patients who are currently being treated with a diuretic, symptomatic hypotension may occur occasionally following the initial dose of lisinopril. The diuretic should be discontinued, if possible, for 2 to 3 days before beginning therapy with lisinopril to reduce the likelihood of hypotension (see Warnings). The dosage of lisinopril should be adjusted according to blood pressure response. If the patient's blood pressure is not controlled with lisinopril alone, diuretic therapy may be resumed as described above.

If the diuretic cannot be discontinued, an initial dose of 5 mg should be used under medical supervision for at least 2 hours and until blood pressure has stabilized for at least an additional hour (see Warnings, Hypotension and Precautions, Drug Interactions).

A lower starting dose is required in the presence of renal impairment, in patients in whom diuretic therapy cannot be discontinued, patients who are volume and/or salt-depleted for any reason, and in patients with renovascular hypertension.

Dosage Adjustment in Renal Impairment: Dosage in patients with renal impairment should be based on creatinine clearance as outlined in Table II.

Table II—Zestril

Dosage Adjustment in Renal Impairment

Creatinine Clearance mL/s (mL/min)	Starting Dose mg/day
0.5–1.17 mL/s (31–70 mL/min)	5–10 mg
0.17–0.5 mL/s (10–30 mL/min)	2.5–5 mg
<0.17 mL/s (<10 mL/min) (including patients on dialysis)	2.5 mg*

*Dosage and/or frequency of administration should be adjusted depending on the blood pressure response.

The dosage may be titrated upward until blood pressure is controlled or to a maximum of 40 mg daily.

Anaphylactoid reactions have been reported in patients dialysed with high flux membranes (e.g.: polyacrylonitrile [PAN]) and treated concomitantly with an ACE inhibitor (see Precautions, Anaphylactoid Reactions during membrane exposure).

Renovascular Hypertension: Some patients with renovascular hypertension, especially those with bilateral renal artery stenosis or stenosis of the artery to a solitary kidney, may develop an exaggerated response to the first dose of lisinopril. Therefore, a lower starting dose of 2.5 or 5 mg is recommended. Thereafter, the dosage may be adjusted according to the blood pressure response.

Geriatrics: In general, blood pressure response and adverse experiences were similar in younger and older patients given similar doses of lisinopril. Pharmacokinetic studies, however, indicate that maximum blood levels and area under the plasma concentration time curve (AUC) are doubled in older patients so that dosage adjustments should be made with particular caution.

Congestive Heart Failure: Lisinopril is to be used in conjunction with diuretics, and where appropriate digitalis. Therapy must be initiated under close medical supervision, usually in a hospital. Blood pressure and renal function should be monitored, both before and during treatment with lisinopril, because severe hypotension and, more rarely, consequent renal failure have been reported (see Warnings, Hypotension and Precautions, Renal Impairment).

Initiation of therapy requires consideration of recent diuretic therapy and the possibility of severe salt/volume depletion. If possible, the dose of diuretic should be reduced before beginning treatment.

The recommended initial dose is 2.5 mg/day. If required, the dose should be increased gradually, depending on the patient response. The usual effective dosage range is 5 to 20 mg/day administered in a single daily dose. Dose titration may be performed over a 2 to 4 week period, or more rapidly if indicated by the presence of residual signs and symptoms of heart failure.

Acute Myocardial Infarction: Treatment with lisinopril may be started within 24 hours of the onset of symptoms in hemodynamically stable patients. Patients should receive, as appropriate, the standard recommended treatments such as thrombolytics, ASA and beta-blocker(s) (see Indications, Acute Myocardial Infarction).

The first dose of lisinopril is 5 mg given orally, followed by 5 mg after 24 hours, 10 mg after 48 hours and then 10 mg once daily thereafter.

Patients with a low systolic blood pressure (between 100 and 120 mmHg) when treatment is started or during the first 3 days after the infarct should be given a lower dose – 2.5 mg orally (see Precautions, Hypotension and Acute Myocardial Infarction). After 3 days if hypotension occurs (systolic blood pressure less than or equal to 100 mmHg), a daily maintenance dose of 5 mg may be given with temporary reductions to 2.5 mg if needed. If prolonged hypotension occurs (systolic blood pressure less than 90 mmHg for more than 1 hour), lisinopril should be withdrawn.

Renal function should be assessed before and during therapy with lisinopril (see Precautions, Renal Impairment).

Dosing should normally continue for 6 weeks. At that time, patients with signs or symptoms of heart failure should continue with lisinopril (see Dosage, Congestive Heart Failure).

Lisinopril is compatible with i.v. or transdermal glyceryl trinitrate.

Information for the Patient: See Blue Section—Information for the Patient "Zestril".

Supplied: 5 mg: Each pale pink, round, biconvex tablet, scored on one side and embossed with the number 5 inside a heart-shaped symbol on the other side, contains: lisinopril 5 mg. Nonmedicinal ingredients: calcium hydrogen phosphate, cornstarch, magnesium stearate, mannitol, pregelatinized cornstarch and red iron oxide. Bottles of 100 and 500 and calendar packs of 30.

10 mg: Each pale pink, round, biconvex tablet, embossed with the number 10 and "ZESTRIL" inside a heart-shaped symbol on one side and blank on the other side, contains: lisinopril 10 mg. Nonmedicinal ingredients: calcium hydrogen phosphate, cornstarch, magnesium stearate, mannitol, pregelatinized cornstarch and red iron oxide. Bottles of 100 and 500 and calendar packs of 30.

20 mg: Each deep pink, round, biconvex tablet, embossed with the number 20 and "ZESTRIL" inside a heart-shaped symbol on one side and blank on the other side contains: lisinopril 20 mg. Nonmedicinal ingredients: calcium hydrogen phosphate, cornstarch, magnesium stearate, mannitol, pregelatinized cornstarch and red iron oxide. Bottles of 100 and 500 and calendar packs of 30.

Store at room temperature.

(Shown in Product Recognition Section)

Reviewed 1998

ZETAR® Preparations

Dermik Laboratories Canada

Coal Tar

Antipsoriatic—Eczema Therapy

Indications: A therapeutic aid in the treatment of psoriasis and other tar-responsive dermatoses such as atopic dermatitis; lichen simplex chronicus, seborrheic dermatitis, dandruff and nummular eczema.

Emulsion: For use in the bath when extensive tar therapy is desired.

Shampoo: Psoriasis, seborrhea dandruff, cradle cap, and other oily, itchy scalp conditions.

Contraindications: Acute inflammation, open or infected lesions, coal tar sensitivity.

Precautions: Exposure of treated areas to direct sunlight may cause usual tar photosensitization. Irritation or dermatitis may occur after prolonged use. May stain gray or dyed hair. Avoid contact with eyes.

Dosage: Emulsion: 15 to 30 mL in a bath of lukewarm water and immerse body for 30 minutes.

Shampoo: Moisten scalp with lukewarm water, apply to scalp, massage and rinse. Repeat, working up a rich lather. Allow to remain on scalp a few minutes, then rinse thoroughly with lukewarm water. Shampoo once or twice a week as necessary.

Supplied: Emulsion: Each mL contains: a water dispersible emulsion of colloidal crude coal tar 300 mg. Nonmedicinal ingredients: polysorbate 20 and polysorbate 80. Bottles of 175 mL.

Shampoo: Each mL contains: colloidal crude coal tar 1% w/v in a bland soap free base. Nonmedicinal ingredients: colloidal magnesium-aluminum silicate, diethanolamine, disodium cocoamphodiacetate, edetic acid, ethoxylated lanolin, fragrance, hexylene glycol, lauric acid diethanolamine, lauric myristic acid, linoleic alkanolamide, naphthalene sulfonic acid, parachlorometazylenol, polysorbate 20, polysorbate 80 and purified water. Bottles of 175 mL.

ZILACTIN®
ZILACTIN-B®
ZILACTIN Baby®
ZILACTIN-L®
ZILACTIN-Lip®

Zila Pharmaceuticals

Benzyl Alcohol
Benzocaine
Benzocaine
Lidocaine
Octyl Methoxycinnamate—Homosalate—Oxybenzone—Dimethicone—Menthol

Protective—Topical Analgesic—Emollient Preparation

Indications: Zilactin: Zilactin medicated gel relieves pain and speeds healing of canker sores, fever blisters and cold sores. Zilactin forms a tenacious, occlusive film on the oral mucosa that holds the medication in place. The film can last up to 6 hours, allowing pain-free eating and drinking.

Zilactin-B: Zilactin-B is a medicated gel containing benzocaine that forms a smooth, flexible and occlusive film on the oral mucosa. It is specially formulated to relieve pain and shield the mouth sores, canker sores, cheek bites and gum sores from the environment of the mouth. The film can last up to 6 hours, allowing pain-free eating and drinking.

Zilactin Baby: Zilactin Baby medicated gel is uniquely formulated to temporarily relieve sore gums caused by teething in infants and children 4 months of age and older. The extra strength level of medication in Zilactin Baby begins quickly relieving the discomfort of teething pain. This specially developed gel combines a pleasant grape flavor with an advanced ingredient that imparts an immediate cooling sensation.

Zilactin-L: Zilactin-L is a non film-forming liquid that treats and relieves the pain, itching and burning of developing and existing cold sores, lip sores, and fever blisters. Zilactin-L is specially formulated to treat the initial signs of tingling, itching or burning that signal an oncoming cold sore, lip sore or fever blister.

Zilactin (cont'd)

Zilactin-Lip: Zilactin-Lip is a medicated lip balm with advanced ingredients that help prevent sun blisters; treat the pain, itching and discomfort associated with cold sores; soften and relieve the pain of dry, chapped lips. Zilactin-Lip medicated lip balm is PABA-free and has SPF of 24 and the antioxidant, vitamin E (tocopherol).

Contraindications: Known sensitivity to any of the ingredients.
Zilactin-B, Zilactin Baby, Zilactin-L: Known sensitivity to local anesthetics such as benzocaine, lidocaine or other ''caine'' anesthetics.

Precautions: Do not use in or near eyes. In the event of accidental contact with the eye, flush with water immediately and continuously for 10 minutes. Seek immediate medial attention if pain or irritation persists. Not recommended for use in children under 3 years of age. A mild, temporary, stinging sensation may be experienced when applying Zilactin, Zilactin-B or Zilactin-L to an open lesion, sore or blister. This may be minimized by first applying ice for a minute, then drying area before application of the medication. For temporary relief only. As with all medications, keep out of reach of children.
Zilactin and Zilactin-B: **Do not peel off protective film.** Attempting to peel off film may result in skin irritation or tenderness. To remove film, first apply another coat of Zilactin or Zilactin-B to film, and immediately wipe the area with a gauze pad or tissue.

Dosage: Zilactin: For intraoral or extraoral use. Use every 4 to 6 hours, or as needed. Dry the affected area. Apply a thin coat of Zilactin and allow 30 to 60 seconds for the gel to dry into a film. Outside the mouth, Zilactin forms a transparent film. Inside the mouth, the film is white.
Zilactin-B: For intraoral use. Use every 4 hours or as needed. Dry the affected area. Apply a thin coat of Zilactin-B and allow 30 to 60 seconds for the gel to dry into a film. Inside the mouth, the film is white.
Zilactin Baby: For intraoral use. Apply small amount to the affected gum area with fingertip or cotton applicator. Apply to affected area not more than 4 times daily or as directed by a dentist or physician. For infants under 4 months of age, there is no recommended dosage or treatment except under the advice and supervision of a physician.
Zilactin-L: For extraoral use. Apply every 1 to 2 hours for the first 3 days and then as needed. For maximum effectiveness, use at first signs of tingling or itching. Moisten a cotton swab with several drops of Zilactin-L. Apply on lip area where symptoms are noted, or directly on existing cold sore, lip sore or fever blister, and allow to dry for 15 seconds.
Zilactin-Lip: For extraoral use. For sun blisters and dry, chapped lips: Apply evenly and liberally before exposure to the sun. For cold sores: At first sign of cold sore, apply to affected area. Apply to affected area no more than 3 to 4 times daily.

Supplied: Zilactin: Each plastic tube of medicated gel contains: benzyl alcohol 10% w/w. Nonmedicinal ingredients: boric acid, deionized water, hydroxypropylcellulose, propylene glycol, salicylic acid, SD alcohol 37 and tannic acid. Tubes of 6 g.

Zilactin-B: Each plastic tube of medicated gel contains: benzocaine 10% w/w. Nonmedicinal ingredients: boric acid, deionized water, hydroxypropylcellulose, propylene glycol, salicylic acid, SD alcohol 38-B and tannic acid. Tubes of 6 g.

Zilactin Baby: Each plastic tube of medicated teething gel contains: benzocaine 10% w/w. Nonmedicinal ingredients: PEG-8, PEG-75, glycerin, water, potassium acesulfame, flavor, menthyl lactate, glycine, methylparaben, propylparaben and sorbic acid. Tubes of 9.4 g.

Zilactin-L: Each plastic bottle of liquid contains: lidocaine 2.5% w/w. Nonmedicinal ingredients: boric acid, deionized water, propylene glycol, salicylic acid, SD alcohol 37 and tannic acid. Bottles of 9 mL.

Zilactin-Lip: Each plastic tube of medicated lip balm contains: octyl methoxycinnamate 7% w/w, homosalate 4% w/w, oxybenzone 3% w/w, dimethicone 1.5% w/w, menthol 0.5% w/w. Nonmedicinal ingredients: beeswax, benzyl laurate, butylparaben, candelilla wax, carnauba, castor oil, isobutylparaben, isopropylparaben, isostearyl trimethylolpropane siloxy silicate, octyl palmitate, ozokerite, petrolatum, titanium dioxide and tocopherol. Tubes of 4.25 g.

New Product 1998

ZINACEF® Ⓟ

Glaxo Wellcome

Cefuroxime Sodium

Antibiotic

Pharmacology: In vitro studies demonstrate that the bactericidal action of cefuroxime, a cephalosporin antibiotic, results from inhibition of bacterial cell wall synthesis by inhibiting the transpeptidase and carboxypeptidase enzymes. Cefuroxime is active against the following organisms in vitro:
Gram-positive: S. pyogenes, S. viridans and S. pneumoniae. S. aureus, both penicillin sensitive and beta-lactamase producing. Clostridia. Some strains of methicillin resistant staphylococci have been found to be resistant to cefuroxime. Most strains of S. faecalis are resistant.
Gram-negative: E. coli (including beta-lactamase producing strains), Klebsiella, Enterobacter, H. influenzae, P. mirabilis, Salmonella, Shigella species, N. gonorrhoeae and N. meningitides. Cefuroxime is ineffective against P. aeruginosa and exhibits poor activity against P. vulgaris, B. fragilis, M. morganii, Enterobacter species, Citrobacter species, and many Serratia species.

Cefuroxime is poorly absorbed orally; following a 1 g dose, serum levels of less than 1.2 μg/mL were observed and only between 1 and 1.3% of the administered dose was excreted in the urine. Cefuroxime is used by the i.m. or i.v. routes.

Deep i.m. injection of 750 mg of cefuroxime sodium in the lateral side of the thigh, attained peak blood levels of 35 to 40 μg/mL, after 30 to 40 minutes. Serum cefuroxime concentrations greater than 12.5 μg/mL were maintained for approximately 3 hours, greater than 8 μg/mL for approximately 3.5 hours, and 6.25 μg/mL for approximately 4 hours, after a 750 mg i.m. dose.

An i.v. dose of cefuroxime resulted in biliary levels which varied considerably between 1.3 and 26 μg/mL. Biliary levels appear to be lowest in patients with a non-functioning gallbladder.

Following 750 mg i.m. to 6 women in labor, average concentrations of cefuroxime in amniotic fluid were 18.6 μg/mL. This was similar to those in maternal serum where average peak maternal serum concentrations of 19.2 μg/mL were attained after 1.2 hours. In umbilical cord blood, the average peaks were 33% of those in the mothers.

Cefuroxime 750 mg and 1.5 g resulted in blood levels of 73 μg/mL and 151 μg/mL, respectively, 5 minutes after the beginning of the injection.

I.V. infusion of 750 mg over a 30 minute period resulted in a serum level of 51 μg/mL at the end of the infusion. I.V. administration of 1.5 g over a 20 minute period, resulted in a concentration of 146 μg/mL at the end of the infusion.

Following i.v. administration, more than 95% of cefuroxime is excreted unmetabolized via the kidneys with excretion evenly divided between glomerular filtration and tubular secretion. Approximately 90% of the administered dose was recovered in the urine within 6 hours of i.m. injection, and over 96% after 24 hours.

About 33% of cefuroxime is bound to serum protein. Volume of distribution after a 750 mg i.m. dose is approximately 15 L which increases to about 23 L when the dose of cefuroxime is doubled. The mean half-life of a 750 mg i.m. dose is about 80 minutes. The half-life of cefuroxime after i.v. injection is approximately 65 minutes. Probenecid 500 mg given orally 2 hours before and 1 hour after cefuroxime delayed renal excretion and increased the serum half-life from approximately 76 minutes to 101 minutes.
Renal Impairment: In severe renal impairment (oliguria), the half-life increases to approximately 16 hours.
Susceptibility plate test: With the Bauer-Kirby-Sherris-Turck method of disc susceptibility testing, a disc containing 30 μg cefuroxime should give a zone of inhibition of at least 20 mm for a microorganism to be considered susceptible to cefuroxime.

Indications: For the treatment of patients with infections caused by susceptible strains of the designated organisms in the following diseases:
Lower Respiratory Tract Infections: Pneumonia caused by S. pneumoniae, H. influenzae including ampicillin-resistant strains, Klebsiella species, S. aureus including ampicillin-resistant (but not methicillin-resistant) strains, S. pyogenes, and E. coli.
Urinary Tract Infections: Caused by E. coli and Klebsiella species.
Soft Tissue Infections: Caused by S. aureus including ampicillin-resistant (but not methicillin-resistant) strains, S. pyogenes, E. coli, Klebsiella species.
Meningitis: Caused by S. aureus including ampicillin-resistant (but not methicillin-resistant) strains, S. pneumoniae, H. influenzae, and N. meningitidis.
Gonorrhea: Caused by N. gonorrhoeae including ampicillin-resistant strains.
Bone and Joint Infections: Caused by S. aureus (penicillinase and non-penicillinase producing strains).

Specimens for bacteriologic culture should be obtained prior to therapy in order to identify the causative organisms and to determine their susceptibility to cefuroxime. Therapy may be instituted before results of susceptibility testing are known. However, modification of the treatment may be required once these results become available.
Prevention: The pre-operative prophylactic administration of cefuroxime may prevent the growth of susceptible disease-causing bacteria and thereby may reduce the incidence of certain post-operative infections: in patients undergoing surgical procedures (e.g. vaginal hysterectomy) that are classified as clean contaminated or potentially contaminated; in patients undergoing open heart surgery in whom infections at the operative site would present a serious risk.

If signs of infection occur postoperatively, specimens for culture should be obtained for identification of causative organism and appropriate antimicrobial therapy should be instituted.

Contraindications: Patients who have shown Type I hypersensitivity to cefuroxime or the cephalosporin group of antibiotics.

Warnings: Before therapy with cefuroxime is instituted, careful inquiry should be made to determine whether the patient has had previous hypersensitivity reactions to cephalosporins, penicillins or other drugs. Cefuroxime should be administered with caution to any patient who has demonstrated some form of allergy, particularly to drugs. There is some clinical and laboratory evidence of partial cross allergenicity of the cephalosporins and penicillins.

If an allergic reaction to cefuroxime occurs, treatment should be discontinued and standard agents (e.g., epinephrine, antihistamines, corticosteroids) administered as necessary.

Pseudomembranous colitis has been reported to be associated with treatment of cefuroxime (and other broad-spectrum antibiotics). Therefore, it is important to consider its diagnosis in patients administered cefuroxime who develop diarrhea. Treatment with broad-spectrum antibiotics, including cefuroxime, alters the normal flora of the colon and may permit overgrowth of Clostridia. Studies indicate that a toxin produced by C. difficile is one primary cause of antibiotic-associated colitis. Mild cases of colitis may respond to drug discontinuance alone. Moderate to severe cases should be managed with fluid, electrolyte, and protein supplementation as indicated. When the colitis is not relieved by discontinuance of cefuroxime administration or when it is severe, consideration should be given to the administration of vancomycin or other suitable therapy. Other possible causes of colitis should also be considered.

Precautions: Cefuroxime should be administered with caution to individuals with a history of gastrointestinal disease, particularly colitis.

Patients with markedly impaired renal function (i.e. creatinine clearance of 20 mL/min/1.73 m^2 or less) should be placed on the special dosage schedule for cefuroxime recommended under Dosage. Normal dosages in these individuals are likely to produce excessive serum concentrations of cefuroxime.

The concomitant administration of aminoglycosides and some cephalosporins has caused nephrotoxicity. Although transient elevations of BUN and serum creatinine have been observed in clinical studies, there is no evidence that cefuroxime, when administered alone, is significantly nephrotoxic.

Studies suggest that the concurrent use of potent diuretics, such as furosemide and ethacrynic acid, may increase the risk of renal toxicity with cephalosporins.

Prolonged treatment with cefuroxime may result in the overgrowth of nonsusceptible organisms, including species originally sensitive to the drug. Repeated evaluation of the patient's condition is essential. If superinfection occurs during therapy, appropriate measures should be taken. Should an organism become resistant during antibiotic therapy, another antibiotic should be substituted.

As with other therapeutic regimens used in the treatment of meningitis, mild-to-moderate hearing loss has been reported in a few pediatric patients treated with cefuroxime. Persistence of positive CSF cultures of H. influenzae at 18 to 36 hours has also been noted with cefuroxime.
Pregnancy: The safety of cefuroxime in the treatment of infections during pregnancy has not been established. If the administration of cefuroxime is considered to be necessary, its use requires that the potential benefits be weighed against possible

hazards to the patient and to the fetus. Animal studies have shown cefuroxime to affect bone calcification in the fetus and to show maternal toxicity in the rabbit.

Lactation: Cefuroxime is excreted in human milk in low concentrations (0.5 mg/L). The clinical significance of this is unknown, therefore, caution should be exercised when cefuroxime is administered to a nursing mother.

Geriatrics: The elimination of cefuroxime may be reduced due to impairment of renal function (see Dosage, Impaired Renal Function).

Laboratory Tests: Cefuroxime may interfere with Benedict's and Fehling's tests for glycosuria depending on copper reduction but not with enzyme based tests for glycosuria. It may cause false negative reactions in the ferricyanide test, and thus it is recommended that either the glucose oxidase or hexokinase methods be used to determine blood/plasma glucose levels in patients receiving cefuroxime. Cefuroxime does not interfere with the assay of serum and urine creatinine by the alkaline picrate method.

Adverse Effects: Hypersensitivity: rash and eosinophilia. Anaphylaxis, urticaria, pruritus, interstitial nephritis and drug fever have also been observed with cephalosporin therapy. As with other cephalosporins, there have been rare reports of erythema multiforme, Stevens-Johnson syndrome and toxic epidermal necrolysis (exanthematic necrolysis).

Local Reactions: thrombophlebitis, stiffness at the site of injection, and inflammatory reactions at the site of injection. Some degree of pain, after i.m. injections when using water as the diluent, has been observed.

Blood: increased erythrocyte sedimentation rate and decreased hemoglobin, eosinophilia, leukopenia, neutropenia and thrombocytopenia. Cephalosporins as a class tend to be absorbed onto the surface of red cell membranes and react with antibodies directed against the drug to produce a positive Coombs' test (which can interfere with the cross-matching of blood) and very rarely hemolytic anemia.

Renal: increases in BUN and serum creatinine.

Hepatic: transient increases in serum bilirubin, transaminases and alkaline phosphatase.

Others: drowsiness, loose stools, faint feeling, sweating, palpitations and Candida intertrigo.

Overdose: Symptoms and Treatment: Overdosage of cefuroxime can cause cerebral irritation leading to convulsions. Other than general supportive treatment, no specific antidote is known. Excessive serum levels of cefuroxime can be reduced by dialysis. For treatment of hypersensitivity reactions, see Warnings.

Dosage: Cefuroxime may be administered i.v. or i.m. after reconstitution.

Dosage and route of administration should be determined by severity of infection, susceptibility of the causative organism(s), and condition of the patient. The i.v. route is preferable for patients with severe or life-threatening infections.

The usual duration of treatment is 5 to 14 days. For β-hemolytic Streptococcal infections, therapy should be continued for at least 10 days.

Adults: For most infections the usual recommended dosage is 750 mg every 8 hours (2.25 g/day) and may be administered either i.m. or i.v.

For severe or life-threatening infections or for infections of the lower respiratory tract, caused by Gram-negative organisms, 1.5 g i.v. every 8 hours (4.5 g/day) is recommended.

For treatment of bacterial meningitis a dosage of 3 g i.v. every 8 hours (9 g/day) should be employed.

Uncomplicated gonorrhea in both males and females should be treated with a single i.m. dose of 1.5 g, in 2 equally divided injections (one in each buttock), accompanied by a single oral dose of 1 g probenecid.

For bone and joint infections, a dosage of 1.5 g i.v. every 8 hours (4.5 g/day) is recommended. In clinical trials, surgical intervention was performed when indicated as an adjunct to cefuroxime therapy. A course of oral antibiotics was administered when appropriate following the completion of parenteral administration of cefuroxime.

Children: Infants and children (1 month to 12 years): 30 to 100 mg/kg/day divided in 3 or 4 equally divided doses. A dose of 60 mg/kg/day is appropriate for most infections. In cases of bacterial meningitis*, a dosage of 200 to 240 mg/kg/day i.v. in 3 or 4 equally divided doses should be employed.

For bone and joint infections, a dosage between 70 to 150 mg/kg/day administered i.v. every 8 hours is recommended. In clinical trials a course of oral antibiotics was administered to children following the completion of parenteral administration of cefuroxime.

Doses in excess of the maximum adult dose should not be used in infants and children.

Neonates (up to 1 month): In the first few weeks of life, the serum half-life of cefuroxime can be 3 to 5 times that in adults. Infections in neonates should be treated with dosages in the range of 30 to 100 mg/kg/day in 2 or 3 equally divided doses.

For bacterial meningitis* a dosage of 100 mg/kg/day i.v. in 2 or 3 equally divided doses should be employed.

*Delayed sterilization of cerebral spinal fluid has been reported in a few children treated with cefuroxime for bacterial meningitis. Hearing impairment has occasionally occurred as a complication of meningitis in children treated with cefuroxime.

Prevention: Clean contaminated or potentially contaminated surgical procedures: The recommended dose is 1.5 g of cefuroxime administered i.v. just prior to surgery.

This may be supplemented with 750 mg administered i.m. or i.v. at 8 and 16 hours when surgery is prolonged.

In general, prophylactic administration is usually not required after the end of surgical procedures, however, intraoperative administrations should be considered if the surgical procedure is lengthy.

In many surgical procedures, continuing prophylactic administration of any antibiotic does not appear to be associated with a reduced incidence of subsequent infection, but will increase the possibility of adverse reactions and the development of bacterial resistance.

Open Heart Surgery: The recommended dosage is 1.5 g of cefuroxime administered i.v. at the induction of anesthesia and every 12 hours thereafter for 48 hours.

Impaired Renal Function: For patients with markedly impaired renal function a reduced dosage of cefuroxime must be employed. For adult patients with moderate infections, dosage adjustment may be made according to the guidelines listed in Table I.

Table I—Zinacef

Dosage Adjustment for Adults with Renal Insufficiency

Creatinine Clearance mL/min/1.73m²	Creatinine Clearance mL/s/1.73m²	Unit Dose	Dosing Frequency
>20	>0.33	750 mg–1.5 g	q8h
10–20	0.17–0.33	750 mg	q12h
<10	<0.17	750 mg	q24h

For adults with severe infections who require doses higher than those recommended in Table I, serum levels of cefuroxime should be monitored and dosage adjusted accordingly.

Studies in children with renal impairment are not sufficient to recommend specific dosages. If it is necessary to administer cefuroxime to a child with such impairment, consideration should be given to modifying the frequency of drug administration consistent with the recommendations for adults with renal impairment as indicated in table above.

When only serum creatinine levels are known, the following formulae may be used to estimate creatinine clearance. The serum creatinine must represent a steady state of renal function.

Males:

$$\text{Creatinine clearance (mL/min)} = \frac{\text{weight (kg)} \times (140-\text{age})}{72 \times \text{serum creatinine (mg/dL)}}$$

or

$$\text{Creatinine clearance (mL/s)} = \frac{\text{weight (kg)} \times (140-\text{age})}{49 \times \text{serum creatinine } (\mu\text{mol/L})}$$

Females: 0.85×male value

For patients on hemodialysis, a further 750 mg dose of cefuroxime should be administered at the end of each dialysis treatment.

Administration: **I.M.:** Cefuroxime should be injected into a large muscle mass to minimize pain. As the preparation is in suspension form, a 21-gauge needle should be used.

I.V.: Cefuroxime may be administered i.v. either by a bolus injection or by a short i.v. infusion over a period of approximately 30 minutes.

For continuous i.v. infusions, a solution of cefuroxime (1.5 g dissolved in 16 mL of Water for Injection) may be added to a suitable bottle containing an appropriate i.v. infusion fluid in the amount calculated to give the desired antibiotic dose.

Reconstitution: **I.M.:** Reconstitute with Sterile Water for Injection. See Table II.

Table II—Zinacef

Reconstitution Table: I.M.

Vial Size	Diluent to be added to Vial	Volume to be Withdrawn	Approximate Cefuroxime Concentration
750 mg	3.0 mL	Total	220 mg/mL

Shake gently to produce an opaque suspension.

I.V.: Reconstitute with Sterile Water for Injection. See Table III.

Table III—Zinacef

Reconstitution Table: I.V.

Vial Size	Diluent to be added to Vial	Volume to be Withdrawn	Approximate Cefuroxime Concentration
750 mg	8 mL	Total	90 mg/mL
1.5 g	16 mL	Total	90 mg/mL

Shake well until dissolved.

The reconstituted solution may be further diluted with Sodium Chloride Injection BP 0.9% w/v, 5% w/v Dextrose Injection BP or Compound Sodium Lactate Injection BP (Hartmann's Solution).

For short i.v. infusion, 1.5 g of cefuroxime is dissolved in 49 mL of Sterile Water for Injection, resulting in an approximate volume of 50 mL (i.e. 30 mg/mL).

7.5 g Pharmacy Bulk Vial: **The availability of the pharmacy bulk vial is restricted to hospitals with a recognized i.v. admixture program.** Zinacef for injection does not contain any preservatives. The Pharmacy Bulk Vial is intended for multiple dispensing for i.v. use only, employing a single puncture. Reconstitute with 77 mL Sterile Water for Injection. See Table IV. Following reconstitution with Sterile Water for Injection, the solution should be dispensed for further dilution within 8 hours. Any unused portion of the reconstituted solution should be discarded.

Table IV—Zinacef

Reconstitution Table: Pharmacy Bulk Vial

Vial Size	Diluent to be added to Vial	Volume to be Withdrawn	Approximate Cefuroxime Concentration
7.5 g	77 mL	Amount needed*	95 mg/mL

*8 mL of solution contains 750 mg of cefuroxime; 16 mL of solution contains 1.5 g of cefuroxime.

Shake well until dissolved.

Storage: Reconstituted suspension for i.m. injection and reconstituted solution for i.v. injection should be used within 6 hours if kept below 25°C or 48 hours if stored under refrigeration.

The further diluted solutions for i.v. infusion should be used within 12 hours if kept below 25°C or 36 hours if stored under refrigeration in the dark. Some increase in color intensity may occur on storage.

Note: The pH of 2.74% w/v Sodium Bicarbonate Injection BP considerably affects the color of the solution; therefore, this solution is not recommended for the dilution of cefuroxime. However, if required, for patients receiving Sodium Bicarbonate Injection by infusion, the cefuroxime dose may be introduced into the tube of the set.

Incompatibility: Cefuroxime should not be mixed in the syringe with aminoglycoside antibiotics (e.g. gentamicin sulfate, tobramycin sulfate, amikacin sulfate) because of potential interaction.

Supplied: Each 17 mL vial for i.m. or i.v. injection contains: cefuroxime sodium powder equivalent to cefuroxime 750 mg. Packs of 10.

Each 26 mL vial for i.v. injection contains: cefuroxime sodium powder equivalent to cefuroxime 1.5 g. Packs of 10. Pharmacy Bulk Vial: Each vial contains: cefuroxime sodium powder equivalent to cefuroxime 7.5 g. Vials of 127 mL, packs of 6.

The dry powder in vials should be stored below 25°C and protected from light. Gluten- and tartrazine-free.

Reviewed 1999

ZINCFRIN®

Alcon

Zinc Sulfate—Phenylephrine Compound

Astringent—Decongestant

Supplied: Each Drop-Tainer dispenser contains: a sterile, buffered solution of zinc sulfate 0.25% and phenylephrine HCl 0.12%. Preservative: benzalkonium chloride. Nonmedicinal ingredients: citric acid, polysorbate 80, purified water, sodium citrate and sodium hydroxide. Drop-Tainer dispensers of 15 mL.

ZINCFRIN®-A
Alcon

Zinc Sulfate—Antazoline—Naphazoline

Antihistamine—Astringent—Decongestant

Supplied: Each Drop-Tainer dispenser contains: a sterile, buffered solution containing zinc sulfate 0.125%, antazoline phosphate 0.5%, and naphazoline HCl 0.05%. Preservative: benzethonium chloride. Nonmedicinal ingredients: boric acid, hydrochloric acid, polysorbate 80, purified water, sodium citrate and sodium hydroxide. Drop-Tainer dispensers of 15 mL.

ZINCOFAX®
Warner-Lambert Consumer Healthcare

Zinc Oxide

Skin Protective

Indications: Prevents and treats diaper rash.

Precautions: Information for the Patient: For external use only. Avoid contact with eyes; if this occurs, rinse thoroughly with water. If an adverse reaction or irritation occurs, discontinue use and consult your physician.

Overdose: Symptoms: If excessive amounts are ingested, vomiting and diarrhea may occur.

Treatment: Supportive.

Dosage: To treat diaper rash: Apply at every diaper change until redness disappears.
To prevent diaper rash: Apply daily to create a protective barrier.

Supplied: Extra Strength: Each g of ointment contains: zinc oxide 40%. Nonmedicinal ingredients: lanolin, mineral oil, perfume and petrolatum. Jars of 100 g.

Fragrance-Free: Each g of ointment contains: zinc oxide 15%. Nonmedicinal ingredients: lanolin, mineral oil and petrolatum. Perfume-free. Tubes of 50 g and jars of 130 g.

Original: Each g of ointment contains: zinc oxide 15%. Nonmedicinal ingredients: perfume, lanolin, mineral oil and petrolatum. Tubes of 50 g and jars of 130 g.

Store between 15 and 25°C.

ZINECARD™ ℞
Pharmacia & Upjohn

Dexrazoxane

Cardioprotective Agent

Pharmacology: Dexrazoxane is a cyclic derivative of EDTA which, unlike EDTA, readily penetrates cell membranes. Dexrazoxane was shown to be able to protect the myocardium from anthracycline-induced cardiotoxicity. The mechanism by which dexrazoxane exerts its cardioprotective activity is not fully understood. Results of laboratory studies suggest that dexrazoxane is converted intracellularly to an open-ringed chelating agent which interferes with iron-mediated free radical generation thought to be responsible, in part, for anthracycline-induced cardiotoxicity.

The efficacy of dexrazoxane in preventing/reducing the incidence and severity of doxorubicin-induced cardiomyopathy was demonstrated in a series of prospective studies. In these studies, patients were treated with a doxorubicin-containing regimen and either dexrazoxane or placebo starting with the first course of chemotherapy. Cardiac function was assessed by measurement of the left ventricular ejection fraction (LVEF) utilizing resting multigated nuclear medicine (MUGA) scans and by clinical evaluations. Patients receiving dexrazoxane had significantly smaller mean decreases from baseline in LVEF and lower incidences of congestive heart failure than the control group. The difference in decline from baseline in LVEF was evident beginning with a cumulative doxorubicin dose of 150 mg/m² and reached statistical significance in patients who received ≥400 mg/m² of doxorubicin. The studies also assessed the effect of the addition of dexrazoxane on the antitumor efficacy of the chemotherapy regimens. In one of the studies (the largest of the breast cancer studies) patients with advanced breast cancer receiving fluorouracil, Adriamycin and cyclophosphamide (FAC) with dexrazoxane had a lower response rate and a shorter time to progression than patients on the control arm although the survival of the patients who did or did not receive dexrazoxane with FAC was similar. It appears that dexrazoxane may potentiate doxorubicin toxicity in some patients, thus causing increased early dropout rate or decreased dose-intensity. More nonresponders dropped out by course 3 in the dexrazoxane arm. The nonresponders correlated to dose delays due to additive myelotoxicity.

Two of the randomized breast cancer studies evaluating the efficacy and safety of FAC with either dexrazoxane or placebo were amended to allow patients on the placebo arm who had attained a cumulative dose of doxorubicin of 300 mg/m² (6 courses of FAC) to receive FAC with open-label dexrazoxane for each subsequent course.

Most of these patients had already experienced a partial or complete response or have stable disease. Analyses of these amended studies indicate that significant though not complete cardioprotection can be obtained with the administration of dexrazoxane even after an accumulated dose of 300 mg/m² of doxorubicin. In addition, the time to tumor progression and survival of these 2 groups of patients were also compared. Results demonstrate significantly longer overall survival for the group of patients who received dexrazoxane starting with the seventh course of FAC treatment.

Indications: For reducing (preventing) the incidence and severity of cardiotoxicity associated with doxorubicin administration for the treatment of breast cancer in patients who have already experienced a partial response or at least maintain stable disease.

Dexrazoxane should be used only with chemotherapy regimens containing doxorubicin.

Dexrazoxane should be used only after tolerance to a full dose doxorubicin has been established (see Precautions).

Contraindications: Dexrazoxane should not be used as a chemotherapeutic agent.

Warnings: Caution: Dexrazoxane is a potent drug and should be used only by physicians experienced with cancer chemotherapy drugs (see Warnings and Precautions). Blood counts and hepatic function tests should be performed regularly due to the possibility of additive myelosuppressive effects. Dexrazoxane should not be administered in a dose that exceeds 500 mg/m².

Dexrazoxane may add to the myelosuppression caused by chemotherapeutic agents.

Dexrazoxane may interfere with the antitumor activity of chemotherapeutic agents.

Pregnancy: Dexrazoxane should be used during pregnancy only if the potential benefit justifies the potential risk to the fetus.

There is no conclusive information about dexrazoxane adversely affecting human fertility, or causing teratogenesis; however, in rats and rabbits, it is teratogenic and embryotoxic. Therefore, women of childbearing potential should be advised to practice effective contraception.

Lactation: Mothers should be advised not to breast-feed while undergoing therapy with dexrazoxane (see Precautions).

Children: Safety and effectiveness in children have not been established.

Precautions: General: As dexrazoxane will always be used with cytotoxic drugs, patients should be monitored closely. While the myelosuppressive effects of dexrazoxane at the recommended dose are considered to be mild, additive effects upon the myelosuppressive activity of chemotherapeutic agents may occur. In controlled studies, a slightly higher incidence of infection associated with granulocytopenia occurred in patients receiving dexrazoxane.

Dexrazoxane should be administered only after the tolerance of the patient to the full dose of doxorubicin-containing chemotherapeutic regimen has been determined. Dexrazoxane should be given only when there is no need for dose reduction or dose delay, of the chemotherapeutic regimen due to myelosuppression or other toxicities, in 2 consecutive courses.

Currently, the only clinical experience with late administration is in patients who were crossed-over from placebo and received dexrazoxane after 6 courses of chemotherapy. Dexrazoxane was found to retain its cardioprotective effect in these patients. However, an incidence of up to 20% of cardiovascular events was seen prior to the initiation of dexrazoxane administration. Therefore, the administration of dexrazoxane should not be delayed beyond the 7th course of therapy.

Laboratory Tests: As dexrazoxane may add to the myelosuppressive effects of cytotoxic drugs, frequent complete blood counts, including one prior to each treatment, are recommended (see Adverse Effects).

Drug Interactions: Based on a kinetic study, dexrazoxane does not appear to influence the pharmacokinetics of doxorubicin.

Lactation: It is not known whether this drug is excreted in human milk. Because many drugs are excreted in human milk and because of the potential for serious adverse reactions in nursing infants from dexrazoxane, it is recommended that nursing be discontinued during treatment.

Pharmacokinetic studies with dexrazoxane have not been conducted in patients with hepatic or renal insufficiency.

Adverse Effects: Dexrazoxane at a dose of 500 mg/m² has been administered in combination with fluorouracil, doxorubicin, and cyclophosphamide (FAC) or cyclophosphamide, doxorubicin and vincristine (CAV) in randomized placebo controlled double-blind studies to patients with either metastatic breast cancer (FAC) or extensive disease small cell lung cancer (CAV). The dose of doxorubicin was 50 mg/m² in each of the trials. Courses were repeated every 3 weeks provided recovery from toxicity had occurred. Table I lists the incidence of clinical adverse experiences for patients receiving either dexrazoxane or placebo in the breast cancer studies.

Table I—Zinecard

Incidence of Adverse Experiences

Adverse Experience	Percentage of Breast Cancer Patients with Adverse Experience: FAC+Dexrazoxane N=244	FAC+Placebo N=280
Alopecia	94%	96%
Nausea	82	89
Vomiting	63	77
Fatigue/Malaise	62	64
Anorexia	50	52
Stomatitis	36	45
Fever	35	33
Infection and/or Sepsis	31	28
Diarrhea	22	24
Neurotoxicity	16	13
Pain on Injection	11	4
Streaking/Erythema	7	5
Dysphagia	6	10
Phlebitis	5	5
Esophagitis	5	9
Urticaria	4	2
Hemorrhage	2	2
Extravasation	2	1
Recall Skin Reaction	1	2
CHF	1	5

The only adverse experience that was observed in 5% more patients on FAC+dexrazoxane than on FAC+placebo was pain on injection.

However, the early drop-out rate for patients receiving dexrazoxane was higher than for patients receiving placebo.

Myelosuppression: Eight-eight percent (88%) of breast cancer patients receiving FAC+500 mg/m² dexrazoxane and 85% of patients receiving FAC+placebo experienced Grade 3 or 4 granulocytopenia. Ten percent (10%) of patients receiving FAC+dexrazoxane and 9% of patients receiving FAC+placebo experienced Grade 3 or 4 thrombocytopenia at some time while on study.

The median decline in hemoglobin levels from baseline was 2.6 g/dL for patients receiving FAC+dexrazoxane or FAC+placebo.

Hepatic and Renal: Very few patients receiving FAC+dexrazoxane or FAC+placebo experienced marked abnormalities in hepatic or renal function tests; the frequency and severity of abnormalities in bilirubin, alkaline phosphatase, LDH, BUN, and creatinine levels were similar.

Overdose: Symptoms and Treatment: There have been no instances of drug overdose in the clinical studies sponsored by either Adria Laboratories or the National Cancer Institute, U.S. The maximum dose administered during the cardioprotection trials was 1 000 mg/m² every 3 weeks.

Disposition studies with dexrazoxane have not been conducted in cancer patients undergoing dialysis. However, retention of a significant dose fraction (>0.4) of the unchanged drug in the plasma pool, minimal tissue partitioning or binding, and availability of greater than 90% of the systemic drug levels in the unbound form suggest that its toxicity and efficacy would be altered by its removal using conventional peritoneal or hemodialysis.

There is no known antidote. Instances of suspected overdose should be managed with good supportive care until resolution of myelosuppression and related conditions is complete. Management of overdose should include treatment of infections, fluid regulation, and maintenance of nutritional requirements.

Dosage: Dexrazoxane should be reconstituted with M/6 Sodium Lactate Injection, USP, to give a concentration of

10 mg dexrazoxane for each mL of sodium lactate. The reconstituted solution should be given by slow i.v. push or rapid drip i.v. infusion from an empty i.v. bag to which the solution has been added. No further dilution is necessary. Dexrazoxane should be given as a single administration, at any point, within a time period of 30 minutes before to 15 minutes after the start of doxorubicin administration.

The recommended dosage of dexrazoxane is 500 mg/m² (see Precautions).

Dexrazoxane should be administered only after the tolerance of the patient to the full dose of doxorubicin-containing chemotherapeutic regimen has been determined. Dexrazoxane should be given only when there is no need for dose reduction or dose delay, of the chemotherapeutic regimen due to myelosuppression or other toxicities, in 2 consecutive courses.

Dexrazoxane should be given only to patients who have already experienced partial response or at least maintained stable disease.

Reconstituted Solutions: See Table II.

Recommended Diluent for Reconstitution: M/6 Sodium Lactate Injection, USP (supplied in the carton with dexrazoxane).

Table II—Zinecard

Reconstitution

Vial Size	Diluent Added to Vial (mL)	Approximate Available Volume (mL)	Nominal Concentration
250 mg	25	25	10
500 mg	50	50	10

Storage: The reconstituted solution should be stored for a maximum of 6 hours under refrigeration, 2 to 8°C. Unused solutions should be discarded.

Incompatibility: Unless specific compatibility data are available, dexrazoxane should not be mixed with other drugs.

Guidelines for Safe Preparation and Handling: Caution in the handling and preparation of the reconstituted solution must be exercised and the use of gloves is recommended. If dexrazoxane powder or solution contacts the skin or mucosae, immediately wash thoroughly with soap and water.

Procedures normally used for proper handling and disposal of anticancer drugs should be considered for use with dexrazoxane. However, there is no general agreement that all of the procedures recommended in the guidelines are necessary or appropriate.

Preparation and Handling: 1. Preparation of the reconstituted solutions should be done in a vertical laminar flow hood (Biological Safety Cabinet—Class II).

2. Personnel handling dexrazoxane solutions should wear PVC gloves, safety glasses and protective clothing such as disposable gowns and masks. If dexrazoxane solutions contact the skin or mucosa, the area should be washed with soap and water immediately.

3. Personnel regularly involved in the preparation and handling of antineoplastics should have blood examinations on a regular basis.

Disposal: 1. Avoid contact with skin and inhalation of airborne particles by use of PVC gloves and disposable gowns and masks.

2. All needles, syringes, vials and other materials which have come in contact with dexrazoxane should be segregated in plastic bags, sealed, and marked as hazardous waste. Incinerate at 1 000°C or higher. Sealed containers may explode if a tight seal exists.

3. If incineration is not available, dexrazoxane may be detoxified by adding sodium hypochlorite solution (household bleach) to the vial, in sufficient quantity to decolorize the dexrazoxane, care being taken to vent the vial to avoid a pressure build-up of the chlorine gas which is generated. Dispose of detoxified vials in a safe manner.

Needles, Syringes, Disposable and Nondisposable Equipment: Rinse equipment with an appropriate quantity of sodium hypochlorite solution. Discard the solution in the sewer system with running water and discard disposable equipment in a safe manner. Thoroughly wash nondisposable equipment in soap and water.

Spillage/Contamination: Wear gloves, mask, protective clothing. Treat spilled liquid with sodium hypochlorite solution. Carefully absorb solution with gauze pads or towels, wash area with water and absorb with gauze or towels again and place in polyethylene bag; seal, double bag and mark as hazardous waste. Disposal of waste by incineration or by other methods approved for hazardous materials. Personnel involved in clean-up should wash with soap and water.

Supplied: 250 mg: Each single dose vial contains: dexrazoxane 250 mg. pH is adjusted with hydrochloric acid, NF. Also contains a 25 mL vial of M/6 sodium lactate injection USP. Each mL contains: anhydrous sodium lactate 18.6 mg in Water for Injection. pH is adjusted with sodium hydroxide NF and/or hydrochloric acid NF.

500 mg: Each single dose vial contains: dexrazoxane 500 mg. pH is adjusted with hydrochloric acid, NF. Also contains a 50 mL vial of M/6 sodium lactate injection USP. Each mL contains: anhydrous sodium lactate 18.6 mg in Water for Injection. pH is adjusted with sodium hydroxide NF and/or hydrochloric acid NF.

Store at controlled room temperature, 15 to 30°C.

ZITHROMAX™ Ⓟ

Pfizer

Azithromycin Dihydrate

Antibiotic

Pharmacology: Azithromycin, a macrolide antibiotic of the azalide subclass, exerts its antibacterial action by binding to the 50s ribosomal subunits of susceptible bacteria and suppressing protein synthesis.

Following oral administration, azithromycin is rapidly absorbed (T_{max} = 2 to 3 hours) and distributed widely throughout the body. Rapid movement of azithromycin from blood into tissue results in significantly higher azithromycin concentrations in tissue than in plasma (up to 50 times the maximum observed concentration in plasma). The absolute bioavailability is approximately 37%.

When azithromycin capsules were administered with food to 11 adult healthy male subjects, the rate of absorption (C_{max}) of azithromycin from the capsule formulation was reduced by 52% and the extent of absorption (AUC) by 43%. However, when azithromycin suspension was administered with food to 28 adult healthy male subjects, the rate of absorption (C_{max}) was increased by 56% while the extent of absorption (AUC) was unchanged. Therefore, azithromycin capsules and powder for oral suspension should be given 1 hour before or 2 hours after a meal.

Food does not affect the absorption of azithromycin in the tablet and the Single Dose 1 g Packet dosage forms. Unlike the capsule and powder for oral suspension, azithromycin tablets and the azithromycin Single Dose 1 g Packet can be taken without regard to meals. Azithromycin tablets are bioequivalent to the capsule formulation; the azithromycin oral suspension as a Single Dose 1 g Packet is bioequivalent to four 250 mg capsules or tablets.

Pharmacokinetics: Adults: Plasma concentrations of azithromycin decline in a polyphasic pattern, resulting in an average terminal half-life of 68 hours. The prolonged half-life is likely due to extensive uptake and subsequent release of drug from tissues. Over the dose range of 250 to 1 000 mg orally, the serum concentrations are related to dose. The long tissue half-life and large volume of distribution result from intracytoplasmic uptake and storage in lysosomal phospholipid complexes.

The pharmacokinetic data reported in adults are presented in Table I.

When studied in healthy elderly subjects from age 65 to 85 years, the pharmacokinetic parameters of azithromycin capsules in elderly men were similar to those in young adults; however, in elderly women, although higher peak concentrations (increased by 30 to 50%) were observed, no significant accumulation occurred. There are no pharmacokinetic data available from studies in hepatically or renally impaired individuals.

Biliary excretion of azithromycin, predominantly as unchanged drug, is a main route of elimination.

Children: Table II shows mean pharmacokinetic parameters on day 5 in children 1 to 5 years and 5 to 15 years of age when azithromycin oral suspension was dosed in the absence of food at 10 mg/kg on day 1 and 5 mg/kg on days 2 to 5.

Table II—Zithromax

Pharmacokinetic Parameters on Day 5 at Dosage 10 mg/kg (Day 1) and 5 mg/kg (Days 2 to 5)

Age 1-5			Age 5-15		
C_{max} (µg/mL)	T_{max} (hrs)	AUC_{0-24} (µg·hr/mL)	C_{max} (µg/mL)	T_{max} (hrs)	AUC_{0-24} (µg·hr/mL)
0.216	1.9	1.822	0.383	2.4	3.109

There are no pharmacokinetic data on azithromycin suspension when administered at a dose of 12 mg/kg/day in the presence or absence of food.

Indications: For treatment of mild to moderate infections caused by susceptible strains of the designated microorganisms in the following diseases and specific conditions. As recommended dosages, durations of therapy, and applicable patient populations vary among these infections, see Dosage for specific dosing recommendations.

Adults: Upper Respiratory Tract: Pharyngitis and tonsillitis caused by S. pyogenes (group A beta-hemolytic streptococci) occurring in individuals who cannot use first line therapy.

Note: Penicillin is the usual drug of choice in the treatment of S. pyogenes pharyngitis, including the prophylaxis of rheumatic fever. Azithromycin is often effective in the eradication of susceptible strains of streptococci from the oropharynx. However, data establishing the efficacy of azithromycin in the subsequent prevention of rheumatic fever are not available at present.

Lower Respiratory Tract: Acute bacterial exacerbations of chronic obstructive pulmonary diseases caused by H. influenzae, M. catarrhalis, or S. pneumoniae. Community-acquired pneumonia caused by S. pneumoniae, H. influenzae, M. pneumoniae or C. pneumoniae in patients for whom oral therapy is appropriate.

Skin and Skin Structure: Uncomplicated skin and skin structure infections caused by S. aureus, S. pyogenes or S. agalactiae.

Genitourinary Tract: Urethritis and cervicitis due to N. gonorrhoeae or C. trachomatis. Genital ulcer disease in men due to H. ducreyi (chancroid). Due to the small number of women included in clinical trials, the efficacy of azithromycin in the treatment of chancroid in women has not been established.

Patients should have a serologic test for syphilis and appropriate cultures for gonorrhea performed at the time of diagnosis. Appropriate antimicrobial therapy and follow-up tests for these diseases should be initiated if infection is confirmed.

Appropriate culture and susceptibility tests should be initiated before treatment to determine the causative organism and its susceptibility to azithromycin. Therapy with azithromycin may be initiated before results of these tests are known; once the results become available, antibiotic treatment should be adjusted accordingly.

Prevention of Disseminated M. Avium Complex (MAC) Disease: Azithromycin, taken at a dose of 1 200 mg weekly, alone or in combination with rifabutin at its approved dose, is

Table I—Zithromax

Pharmacokinetic Data in Adults

Dose/Dosage Form	Subjects	C_{max} (µg/mL)	T_{max} (hr)	AUC (µ·hr/mL)	$T_{1/2}$ (hr)
500 mg/250 mg capsule	16; fasted	0.40	2.4	3.69[a]	—
500 mg/250 mg tablet	12; fasted	0.34	2.1	2.49[a]	—
500 mg/250 mg tablet	12; fed	0.41	2.3	2.40[a]	—
1 g/250 mg capsule	33; fasted	0.84	2.0	10.5[c]	43.9
1g/Single Dose[f]	33; fasted	0.95	1.4	10.2[c]	43.9
1g/Single Dose[f]	12; fasted	0.75	1.5	6.49[b]	—
1g/Single Dose[f]	12; fed	1.05	2.0	7.37[b]	—
2 g/250 mg capsule	15; fasted	1.69	1.3	18.8[d]	59.8
1 200 mg/600 mg tablet	12; fasted	0.66	2.5	6.8[e]	40

[a] 0-48 hr.
[b] 0-72 hr.
[c] 0-120 hr.
[d] 0-144 hr.
[e] 0-last dose.
[f] 1 g Packet.

Zithromax (cont'd)

indicated for the prevention of disseminated M. avium complex (MAC) disease in persons with advanced HIV infections.

Children (see Precautions and Dosage): Acute otitis media caused by H. influenzae (beta-lactamase positive and negative strains), M. catarrhalis or S. pneumoniae. (For specific dosage recommendation, see Dosage.)

Pharyngitis and tonsillitis caused by S. pyogenes (group A beta-hemolytic streptococci) occurring in individuals who cannot use first line therapy. (For specific dosage recommendation, see Dosage.)

Note: Penicillin is the usual drug of choice in the treatment of S. pyogenes pharyngitis, including the prophylaxis of rheumatic fever. Azithromycin is often effective in the eradication of susceptible strains of streptococci from the oropharynx. However, data establishing the efficacy of azithromycin in the subsequent prevention of rheumatic fever are not available at present.

Community-acquired pneumonia caused by Haemophilus influenzae, S. pneumoniae, M. pneumoniae or C. pneumoniae. (For specific dosage recommendation, see Dosage.)

Azithromycin should not be used in patients with pneumonia who are judged to be inappropriate for outpatient oral therapy because of moderate to severe illness.

Safety and effectiveness for pneumonia due to H. influenzae and S. pneumoniae were not documented bacteriologically in the pediatric clinical trial due to difficulty in obtaining specimens. Use of azithromycin for these two microorganisms is supported, however, by evidence from adequate and well-controlled studies in adults.

Clinical Studies in Pediatric Patients: From the perspective of evaluating pediatric clinical trials, because of the extended half-life of azithromycin, days 11 to 14 were considered on-therapy evaluations and are provided for clinical guidance. Day 30 evaluations were considered the primary test of cure endpoint. For patients with community-acquired pneumonia, Days 15 to 19 were considered as on-therapy evaluations. Days 28 to 42 were the cure endpoint.

Otitis Media: Efficacy Protocol 1: In a double-blind, controlled clinical study of acute otitis media performed in North America, azithromycin (10 mg/kg on day 1 followed by 5 mg/kg on days 2 to 5) was compared to an antimicrobial/beta-lactamase inhibitor. For the 553 patients who were evaluated for clinical efficacy, the clinical success rate (i.e., cure plus improvement) at the day 11 visit was 88% for azithromycin and 88% for the control agent. For the 528 patients who were evaluated at the day 30 visit, the clinical success rate was 76% for azithromycin and 76% for the control agent.

Efficacy Protocol 2: In a noncomparative clinical and microbiologic trial performed in North America, and in which significant numbers of beta-lactamase producing organisms were identified (35%), the combined clinical success rate (i.e., cure plus improvement) was 84% at the day 11 visit (n=131) and 70% at the day 30 visit (n=122).

Microbiologic determinations were made at the pretreatment visit. Microbiology was not reassessed at later visits. The following presumptive bacterial/clinical cure outcomes (i.e., clinical success) were obtained from the evaluable group (see Table III).

Table III—Zithromax

Presumptive Bacterial/Clinical Cure Outcomes

Bacteriologic Eradication	Day 11 Azithromycin	Day 30 Azithromycin
S. pneumoniae	61/74 (82%)	40/56 (71%)
H. influenzae	43/54 (80%)	30/47 (64%)
M. catarrhalis	28/35 (80%)	19/26 (73%)
S. pyogenes	11/11 (100%)	7/7 (100%)
Overall	177/217 (82%)	97/137 (73%)

Pharyngitis and Tonsillitis: In 3 double-blind North American controlled studies, azithromycin (12 mg/kg once a day for 5 days) was compared to penicillin V (250 mg three times a day for 10 days) in the treatment of pharyngitis due to documented group A beta-hemolytic streptococci (GABHS or S. pyogenes). Azithromycin was clinically and microbiologically statistically superior to penicillin at day 14 and day 30 with the following clinical success (i.e., cure and improvement) and bacteriologic efficacy rates (for the combined evaluable patients with documented GABHS). See Table IV.

Table IV—Zithromax

Three North American Streptococcal Pharyngitis Studies: Azithromycin vs Penicillin V

Efficacy Results	Day 14	Day 30
Bacteriologic Eradication		
Azithromycin	323/340 (95%)	261/329 (79%)
Penicillin V	242/332 (73%)	214/304 (71%)
Clinical Success (Cure plus Improvement)		
Azithromycin	336/343 (98%)	313/328 (95%)
Penicillin V	284/338 (84%)	240/303 (79%)

Approximately 1% of azithromycin-susceptible S. pyogenes isolates were resistant to azithromycin following therapy.

Note: Penicillin is the usual drug of choice in the treatment of S. pyogenes pharyngitis, including the prophylaxis of rheumatic fever. Azithromycin is often effective in the eradication of susceptible strains of streptococci from the oropharynx. However, data establishing the efficacy of azithromycin in the subsequent prevention of rheumatic fever are not available at present.

Appropriate culture and susceptibility tests should be initiated before treatment to determine the causative organism and its susceptibility to azithromycin. Therapy with azithromycin may be initiated before results of these tests are known; once the results become available, antibiotic treatment should be adjusted accordingly.

Contraindications: In patients with known hypersensitivity to azithromycin, erythromycin, or other macrolide antibacterial agents.

Warnings: Rare serious allergic reactions, including angioedema and anaphylaxis (with rare reports of fatalities) have been reported in patients on azithromycin therapy (see Contraindications). Allergic reactions may occur during and soon after treatment with azithromycin. Despite initially successful symptomatic treatment of the allergic symptoms, when symptomatic therapy was discontinued, the allergic symptoms recurred soon thereafter in some patients without further azithromycin exposure. These patients required prolonged periods of observation and symptomatic treatment. If an allergic reaction occurs, the drug should be discontinued and appropriate therapy should be instituted. Physicians should be aware that reappearance of the allergic symptoms may occur when symptomatic therapy is discontinued.

In the treatment of pneumonia, azithromycin has only been shown to be safe and effective in the treatment of community-acquired pneumonia due to C. pneumoniae, H. influenzae, M. pneumoniae, or S. pneumoniae in patients appropriate for oral therapy. Azithromycin should not be used in patients with pneumonia who are judged to be inappropriate for oral therapy because of moderate to severe illness or risk factors such as any of the following: patients with cystic fibrosis, patients with nosocomially acquired infections, patients with known or suspected bacteremia, patients requiring hospitalization, elderly or debilitated patients, or patients with significant underlying health problems that may compromise their ability to respond to their illness (including immunodeficiency or functional asplenia).

Pseudomembranous colitis has been reported with nearly all antibacterial agents including azithromycin and may range in severity from mild to life-threatening. Therefore, it is important to consider this diagnosis in patients who present with diarrhea subsequent to the administration of antibacterial agents. Treatment with antibacterial agents alters the normal flora of the colon and may permit overgrowth of clostridia. Studies indicate that a toxin produced by C. difficile is a primary cause of "antibiotic-associated colitis". After the diagnosis of pseudomembranous colitis has been established, therapeutic measures should be initiated. Mild cases of pseudomembranous colitis usually respond to discontinuation of the drug alone. In moderate to severe cases, consideration should be given to management with fluids and electrolytes, protein supplementation, and treatment with an antibacterial drug clinically effective against C. difficile.

In the absence of data on the metabolism and pharmacokinetics in patients with lysosomal lipid storage diseases (e.g., Tay-Sachs disease, Niemann-Pick disease) the use of azithromycin in these patients is not recommended.

Precautions: General: Since liver is the major route of elimination for azithromycin, the use of azithromycin should be undertaken with caution in patients with significant hepatic disease.

No dose adjustment is needed in patients with mild renal impairment (creatinine clearance >40 mL/min), but there are no data regarding azithromycin usage in patients with more severe renal impairment. Thus caution should be exercised before prescribing azithromycin in these patients.

The following adverse events have been reported with macrolide products: ventricular arrhythmias, including ventricular tachycardia and torsades de pointes, in individuals with prolonged QT intervals. Although these adverse events have not been reported in clinical trials with azithromycin, one AIDS patient dosed at 750 mg to 1 g daily experienced prolonged QT interval and torsades de pointes.

Pregnancy: Animal studies have demonstrated that azithromycin crosses the placenta. Safety of azithromycin for use in human pregnancy has not been established.

Lactation: There are no data on secretion in breast milk. Safety of azithromycin for use in human lactation has not been established.

Children: Acute Otitis Media or Community-Acquired Pneumonia: Safety and efficacy of azithromycin in the treatment of children with acute otitis media or community-acquired pneumonia (dosage regimen: 10 mg/kg on day 1 followed by 5 mg/kg on days 2 to 5) under 6 months of age have not been established.

Pharyngitis and Tonsillitis: Safety and efficacy of azithromycin in the treatment of children with pharyngitis and tonsillitis (dosage regimen: 12 mg/kg on days 1 to 5) under 2 years of age have not been established.

Studies evaluating the use of repeated courses of therapy have not been conducted. Safety data with the use of azithromycin at doses higher than proposed and for durations longer than recommended are limited to a small number of immunocompromised children who underwent chronic treatment.

In animal studies, treatment with azithromycin is associated with accumulation in various tissues, including the extracranial neural ganglia (i.e., retina and sympathetic nervous system). Tissue accumulation is both dose and time dependent, and is associated microscopically with the development of phospholipidosis (intra-lysosomal drug phospholipid complexes). The only evidence in animals that azithromycin is associated with alterations of intracellular phospholipid metabolism has been the documentation of small increases in phospholipid content after prolonged treatment (6 months) or exaggerated doses. Phospholipidosis has been observed at total cumulative doses only 2 multiples of the clinical dose. One month after withdrawal of treatment the concentration of azithromycin and the presence of phospholipidosis in tissue, including the retina, is at or near predose levels.

No data exist in humans in regard to the extent of accumulation, duration of exposure, metabolism or excretory mechanisms of azithromycin in neural tissue such as the retina and the cochlea. Rare cases of hearing loss have been reported (see Adverse Effects).

No data are available on the metabolism and pharmacokinetics of azithromycin in children with lysosomal lipid storage diseases (see Warnings).

Prevention of Disseminated M. Avium Complex (MAC) Disease: Safety and efficacy of azithromycin for the prevention of MAC in children have not been established. Limited safety data are available for 24 children 5 months to 14 years of age (mean 4.6 years) who received azithromycin for treatment of opportunistic infections. The mean duration of therapy was 186.7 days (range 13 to 710 days) at doses of <5 to 20 mg/kg/day. Adverse events were similar to those observed in the adult population, most of which involved the gastrointestinal tract. While none of these children prematurely discontinued treatment due to a side effect, one child discontinued due to a laboratory abnormality (eosinophilia). Based on available pediatric pharmacokinetic data, a dose of 20 mg/kg in children would provide drug exposure similar to the 1 200 mg adult dose but with a higher C_{max}.

Geriatrics: The pharmacokinetics in elderly volunteers (age 65 to 85) were similar to those in younger volunteers (age 18 to 40) for the 5-day therapeutic regimen. Dosage adjustment does not appear to be necessary for elderly patients with normal renal and hepatic function receiving treatment with this dosage regimen.

Drug Interactions: Antacids: Aluminum and magnesium containing antacids (Maalox) reduce the peak serum levels but not the extent of azithromycin absorption. These drugs should not be taken simultaneously.

Cimetidine: Administration of cimetidine (800 mg) 2 hours prior to azithromycin had no effect on azithromycin absorption.

Theophylline: Concurrent use of macrolides and theophylline has been associated with increases in the serum concentrations of theophylline. Azithromycin did not affect the pharmacokinetics of theophylline administered either as a single i.v. infusion or multiple oral doses at a recommended dose of 300 mg every 12 hours. There is 1 postmarketing report of supraventricular tachycardia associated with an elevated theophylline serum level that developed soon after initiation of treatment with azithromycin. Until further data are available, prudent medical practice dictates careful monitoring of plasma theophylline levels in patients receiving azithromycin and theophylline concomitantly.

Warfarin: Azithromycin did not affect the prothrombin time response to a single dose of warfarin. However, prudent medical practice dictates careful monitoring of prothrombin time in all patients treated with azithromycin and warfarin concomitantly. Concurrent use of macrolides and warfarin in clinical practice has been associated with increased anticoagulant effects.

Zidovudine: Single 1 g doses and multiple 1 200 mg or 600 mg doses of azithromycin did not affect the plasma pharmacokinetics or urinary excretion of zidovudine or its glucuronide metabolite. However, administration of azithromycin increased the concentrations of phosphorylated zidovudine in peripheral blood mononuclear cells.

Didanosine: Daily doses of 1 200 mg azithromycin had no effect on the pharmacokinetics of didanosine.

Rifabutin: Co-administration of azithromycin and rifabutin did not affect the serum concentrations of either drug.

Carbamazepine: In a pharmacokinetic interaction study in healthy volunteers, no significant effect was observed on the plasma levels of carbamazepine or its active metabolite in patients receiving concomitant azithromycin.

Concomitant Therapy: The following drug interactions have not been reported in clinical trials with azithromycin and no specific drug interaction studies have been performed to evaluate potential drug-drug interactions. Nonetheless, they have been observed with macrolide products, and there have been rare spontaneously reported cases with azithromycin and some of these drugs, in postmarketing experience. Until further data are developed regarding drug interactions, when azithromycin and these drugs are used concomitantly, careful monitoring of patients is advised both during and for a short period following therapy:

Digoxin: Elevation of digoxin levels.

Disopyramide: Increase in pharmacological effects.

Ergotamine or Dihydroergotamine: Acute ergot toxicity characterized by severe peripheral vasospasm and dysesthesia.

Triazolam: Decreases in the clearance of triazolam and increases in the pharmacologic effect of triazolam.

Drugs Metabolized by the Cytochrome P450 System: Elevations of serum cyclosporine, hexobarbital, cisapride, and phenytoin levels.

Antihistamines: Prolongation of QT intervals, palpitations or cardiac arrhythmias with concomitant administration of astemizole or terfenadine.

No data are available on the concomitant clinical use of azithromycin and gentamicin or other amphophilic drugs which have been reported to alter intracellular lipid metabolism.

Adverse Effects: The majority of side effects observed in controlled clinical trials involving patients (adults and children) treated with azithromycin were of a mild and transient nature. Approximately 0.7% of both adult patients (n=3 812) and children (n=2 878) who had multiple doses of azithromycin discontinued therapy because of drug related side effects. Most of the side effects leading to discontinuation were related to the gastrointestinal tract, e.g., nausea, vomiting, diarrhea or abdominal pain. Potentially serious side effects including angioedema and cholestatic jaundice occurred in less than 1% of patients.

Clinical: Multiple-Dose Regimen (Adults and Children): In adult patients, the most common side effects in patients receiving the multiple-dose regimen of azithromycin were related to the gastrointestinal system with diarrhea (4.3%), abdominal pain (2.6%), vomiting (1.3%) and nausea (3.5%). In children (n=1 944) enrolled in North American controlled clinical trials in acute otitis media and S. pyogenes pharyngitis, the type of side effects was comparable to that seen in adults, with diarrhea/loose stools (5.3%), vomiting (3.6%), abdominal pain (2.6%), nausea (1%), rash (1%) and headache (1%) the most frequently reported.

Different side effect incidence rates for the 2 dosage regimens recommended in children were observed:

Acute Otitis Media: For the recommended dosage regimen of 10 mg/kg on day 1 followed by 5 mg/kg on days 2 to 5, the most frequent side effects were diarrhea/loose stools (2%), abdominal pain (2%), vomiting (1%) and nausea (1%).

Community-Acquired Pneumonia: In the North American controlled clinical trial in community-acquired pneumonia in children (n=310) the following were the most frequent side effects for the recommended dosage regimen of 10 mg/kg on day 1 followed by 5 mg/kg on days 2 to 5: diarrhea/loose stools (6%), abdominal pain (2%), and vomiting (2%).

Pharyngitis/Tonsillitis: For the recommended dosage regimen of 12 mg/kg on days 1 to 5, the most frequent side effects were diarrhea/loose stools (6%), vomiting (5%), abdominal pain (3%), nausea (2%) and headache (1%).

Side effects that occurred with a frequency of 1% or less in patients included the following.

Cardiovascular: palpitations, chest pain.

Gastrointestinal: dyspepsia, flatulence, vomiting, melena, cholestatic jaundice, constipation, anorexia and gastritis.

Genitourinary: monilia, vaginitis and nephritis.

Nervous System: dizziness, headache, vertigo, somnolence, agitation, nervousness, insomnia and hyperkinesia.

General: fatigue, fever and malaise.

Allergic: rash, photosensitivity, angioedema, erythema multiforme, pruritus and urticaria.

Single 1 g Dose Regimen (Adults): In adult patients (n=904), side effects that occurred on the single 1 g dosing regimen of azithromycin with a frequency greater than 1% included diarrhea (6.1%), nausea (4.9%), abdominal pain (4.9%), vomiting (1.7%), vaginitis (1.3%), loose stools (1.2%), and dyspepsia (1.1%).

Single 2 g Dose Regimen (Adults): Overall, the most common side effects in patients receiving a single 2 g dose of azithromycin were related to the gastrointestinal system. Side effects that occurred in patients in this study with a frequency of a 1% or greater included nausea (18.2%), diarrhea/loose stools (13.8%), vomiting (6.7%), abdominal pain (6.7%), vaginitis (2.2%), dyspepsia (1.1%), and dizziness (1.3%). The majority of these complaints were mild in nature.

The following adverse experiences have been reported in patients under conditions (e.g., open trials, marketing experience) where a causal relationship is uncertain or in patients treated with significantly higher than the recommended doses for prolonged periods:

Allergic: arthralgia, edema, anaphylaxis (with rare reports of fatalities), serum sickness, urticaria, vasculitis.

Table V—Zithromax

Incidence[a] (%) of Treatment Related[b] Adverse Events[c] in HIV-Infected Patients Receiving Prophylaxis for Disseminated MAC

	Study 155		Study 174		
	Placebo (n=91)	Azithromycin 1 200 mg weekly (n=89)	Azithromycin 1 200 mg weekly (n=233)	Rifabutin 300 mg daily (n=236)	Azithromycin and Rifabutin (n=224)
Mean Duration of Therapy (days)	**303.8**	**402.9**	**315**	**296.1**	**344.4**
Discontinuation of Therapy (%)	**2.3**	**8.2**	**13.5**	**15.9**	**22.7**
Autonomic Nervous System					
Mouth Dry	0	0	0	3.0	2.7
CNS					
Dizziness	0	1.1	3.9	1.7	0.4
Headache	0	0	3.0	5.5	4.5
Gastrointestinal					
Diarrhea	15.4	52.8	50.2	19.1	50.9
Loose Stools	6.6	19.1	12.9	3.0	9.4
Abdominal Pain	6.6	27	32.2	12.3	31.7
Dyspepsia	1.1	9	4.7	1.7	1.8
Flatulence	4.4	9	10.7	5.1	5.8
Nausea	11	32.6	27.0	16.5	28.1
Vomiting	1.1	6.7	9.0	3.8	5.8
General					
Fever	1.1	0	2.1	4.2	4.9
Fatigue	0	2.2	3.9	2.1	3.1
Malaise	0	1.1	0.4	0	2.2
Musculoskeletal					
Arthralgia	0	0	3.0	4.2	7.1
Psychiatric					
Anorexia	1.1	0	2.1	2.1	3.1
Skin and Appendages					
Pruritus	3.3	0	3.9	3.4	7.6
Rash	3.2	3.4	8.1	9.4	11.1
Skin discoloration	0	0	0	2.1	2.2
Special Senses					
Tinnitus	4.4	3.4	0.9	1.3	0.9
Hearing Decreased	2.2	1.1	0.9	0.4	0
Taste Perversion	0	0	1.3	2.5	1.3

[a] Reflects the occurrence of ≥1% event during the entire treatment period.
[b] Includes those events considered possibly or probably related to study drug.
[c] >2% adverse event rates for any group.

Table VI—Zithromax

Prophylaxis Against Disseminated MAC Abnormal Laboratory Values

		Study 155		Study 174		
Criteria*		**Placebo (n=88)**	**Azithromycin 1 200 mg weekly (n=89)**	**Azithromycin 1 200 mg weekly (n=208)**	**Rifabutin 300 mg daily (n=205)**	**Azithromycin and Rifabutin (n=199)**
Hemoglobin	<0.8×LLN	31%	30%	19%	26%	21%
Platelet Count	<0.75×LLN	19%	16%	11%	10%	16%
WBC Count	<0.75×LLN	48%	49%	60%	53%	60%
Neutrophils	<0.5×LLN	16%	28%	23%	20%	29%
	<500/mm³	6%	13%	5%	6%	8%
AST	>2.0 x ULN	28%	39%	33%	18%	30%
	>200 U/L	10%	8%	8%	3%	6%
ALT	>2.0×ULN	24%	34%	31%	15%	27%
	>250 U/L	2%	6%	8%	2%	6%

*Secondary criteria also applied if baseline abnormal, as follows: Hemoglobin, 10% decrease; Platelet, 20% decrease; WBC count, 25% decrease; Neutrophils, 50% decrease; AST (SGOT), 50% increase; ALT (SGPT), 50% increase.
Legend: LLN=lower limit of normal; ULN=upper limit of normal.

Zithromax (cont'd)

Cardiovascular: cardiac arrythmias (including ventricular tachycardia), palpitations.
Gastrointestinal: anorexia, constipation, dehydration, dyspepsia, flatulence, pancreatitis, pseudomembranous colitis.
General: asthenia, paresthesia, muscle pain.
Genitourinary: interstitial nephritis, acute renal failure, nephrotic syndrome.
Liver/Biliary: abnormal liver function including drug-induced hepatitis and cholestatic jaundice, hepatic necrosis.
Nervous System: dizziness, headache, seizure, somnolence.
Skin/Appendages: serious skin reactions including erythema multiforme, exfoliative dermatitis, Stevens-Johnson syndrome, toxic epidermal necrolysis.
Special Senses: hearing disturbances including hearing loss, deafness and/or tinnitus, vertigo, reports of taste disturbance.
Prevention of M. Avium Complex (MAC) Disease: Chronic therapy with azithromycin 1 200 mg weekly regimen: The nature of side effects seen with the 1 200 mg weekly dosing regimen for the prevention of M. avium complex infection in severely immunocompromised HIV-infected patients were similar to those seen with short-term dosing regimens. See Table V (on previous page).

Side effects related to the gastrointestinal tract were seen more frequently in patients receiving azithromycin than in those receiving placebo or rifabutin. In one of the studies, 86% of diarrheal episodes were mild to moderate in nature with discontinuation of therapy for this reason occurring in only 9/233 (3.8%) of patients.

Laboratory Abnormalities: Adults: Significant abnormalities (irrespective of drug relationship) occurring during the clinical trials in patients were reported as follows:

With an incidence of 1 to 2%, elevated serum creatine phosphokinase, potassium, ALT, GGT and AST.

With an incidence of less than 1%, leukopenia, neutropenia, decreased platelet count, elevated serum alkaline phosphatase, bilirubin, BUN, creatinine, blood glucose, LDH and phosphate.

When follow-up was provided, changes in laboratory tests appeared to be reversible.

In multiple-dose clinical trials involving more than 3 000 patients, 3 patients discontinued therapy because of treatment-related liver enzyme abnormalities and 1 because of a renal function abnormality.

Prevention of M. Avium Complex (MAC) Disease: In these immunocompromised patients with advanced HIV infection, it was sometimes necessary to assess laboratory abnormalities developing on study with additional criteria if baseline values were outside the normal range. See Table VI (on previous page).

In a phase I drug interaction study performed in normal volunteers, 1 of 6 subjects given the combination of azithromycin and rifabutin, 1 of 7 given rifabutin alone and 0 of 6 given azithromycin alone developed a clinically significant neutropenia (<500 cells/mm³).

Children: Significant abnormalities (irrespective of drug relationship) occurring during clinical trials were all reported at a frequency of less than 1%, but were similar in type to the adult pattern.

In multiple-dose clinical trials involving almost 3 000 pediatric patients, no patients discontinued therapy because of treatment-related abnormalities.

Overdose: Symptoms: There are no data on overdosage.

Treatment: Gastric lavage and general supportive measures are indicated.

Up to 15 g cumulative dose of azithromycin over 10 days has been administered in clinical trials without apparent adverse effect.

Dosage: Adults: Capsules: The capsules should be given as a single daily dose at least 1 hour before or 2 hours after a meal.
Tablets: The tablets can be taken with or without food.
Single Dose 1 g Packet: The powder for oral suspension as Single Dose 1 g Packet can be taken with or without food after reconstitution.
Mixing Directions: Directions for administration of the powder for oral suspension as a Single Dose Packet (1 g): The entire contents of the Packet should be mixed thoroughly with 60 mL of water. Drink the entire contents immediately, add an additional 60 mL of water, mix, and drink to assure complete consumption of dosage.
Skin and Skin Structure Infections, Upper and Lower Respiratory Tract Infections: The recommended dose for the treatment of individuals 16 years of age and older is 500 mg as a single dose on the first day followed by 250 mg once daily on days 2 through 5 for a total dose of 1.5 g.

Table VII—Zithromax

Volume of Water to be Used for Reconstitution

Amount of Water to be Added	Nominal Volume after Reconstitution (Azithromycin content)	Azithromycin Concentration after Reconstitution
9 mL (300 mg bottle)	15 mL (300 mg bottle)	100 mg/5 mL
9 mL (600 mg bottle)	15 mL (600 mg bottle)	200 mg/5 mL
12 mL (900 mg bottle)	22.5 mL (900 mg bottle)	200 mg/5 mL

Table VIII—Zithromax

Pediatric Dosage Guidelines for Acute Otitis Media or Community-Acquired Pneumonia (Age 6 months and above) Based on Body Weight

	Dosing Calculated on 10 mg/kg on Day 1 Dose, Followed by 5 mg/kg on Days 2 to 5				
Weight	100 mg/5 mL Suspension		200 mg/5 mL Suspension		
kg	Day 1	Days 2-5	Day 1	Days 2-5	Total mL per Treatment Course
5	2.5 mL	1.25 mL			7.5 mL
10	5 mL	2.5 mL			15 mL
20			5 mL	2.5 mL	15 mL
30			7.5 mL	3.75 mL	22.5 mL
40			10 mL	5 mL	30 mL

Genitourinary: The recommended dose for the treatment of genital ulcer disease due to H. ducreyi (chancroid) and nongonococcal urethritis and cervicitis due to C. trachomatis is: a single 1 g (1 000 mg) oral dose. This dose can be administered as four 250 mg capsules, four 250 mg tablets, or as 1 Single Dose Packet (1 g).

The recommended dose for the treatment of urethritis and cervicitis due to N. gonorrhoeae is: a single 2 g (2 000 mg) dose. This dose can be administered as eight 250 mg capsules, eight 250 mg tablets, or as 2 Single Dose Packets (1 g each).

Prevention of Disseminated M. Avium Complex (MAC) Disease: Tablets: The tablets may be taken without regard to food. The recommended dose is 1 200 mg (two 600 mg tablets) taken once weekly. This dose may be continued with the approved dosage regimen of rifabutin.

In patients with mild to moderate hepatic impairment, there is no evidence of a marked change in serum pharmacokinetics of azithromycin compared to those with normal hepatic function. In these patients urinary recovery of azithromycin appears to increase. Hence no dose adjustment is recommended for patients with mild to moderate hepatic impairment. Nonetheless, since the liver is the principal route of elimination for azithromycin, the use of azithromycin should be undertaken with caution in patients with significant hepatic disease.

Children: Powder for Oral Suspension: Should be given as a single daily dose at least 1 hour before or 2 hours after a meal.
Mixing Directions: Powder for Oral Suspension: Tap bottle to loosen powder. Add the directed volume of water. Shake well before each use. Oversized bottle provides shake space. Keep tightly closed. Table VII indicates the volume of water to be used for reconstitution.

Acute Otitis Media or Community-Acquired Pneumonia: The recommended dose of oral suspension for the treatment of children with acute otitis media or community-acquired pneumonia is 10 mg/kg as a single-dose on the first day (not to exceed 500 mg/day) followed by 5 mg/kg on days 2 through 5 (not to exceed 250 mg/day), for a total dose of 30 mg/kg (see Table VIII).

Pharyngitis and Tonsillitis: The recommended dose for children with pharyngitis and tonsillitis is 12 mg/kg once a day (not to exceed 500 mg/day) for 5 days for a total dose of 60 mg/kg (see Table IX).

Table IX—Zithromax

Pediatric Dosage Guidelines for Pharyngitis and Tonsillitis (Age 2 years and above) Based on Body Weight

Dosing Calculated on 12 mg/kg Once Daily Days 1 to 5		
Weight	200 mg/5 mL Suspension	Total mL per Treatment Course
kg	Day 1-5	
8	2.5 mL	12.5 mL
17	5 mL	25 mL
25	7.5 mL	37.5 mL
33	10 mL	50 mL
40	12.5 mL	62.5 mL

Supplied: Capsules: 250 mg: Each red, No. 0 hard gelatin capsule, imprinted with "Pfizer" and "ZITHROMAX" in black ink, contains: azithromycin dihydrate equivalent to azithromycin 250 mg. Nonmedicinal ingredients: cornstarch, lactose, magnesium stearate and sodium lauryl sulfate; capsule shell: FD&C Red #40, gelatin and titanium dioxide. White plastic (high density polyethylene) bottles of 30 and 100. Single treatment package (Z-Pak) of 6 blister packaged capsules per box. Store at controlled room temperature between 15 to 30°C.

Powder for Oral Suspension: After reconstitution, each bottle of cherry-flavored suspension contains: azithromycin dihydrate equivalent to: 300 mg/15 mL (100 mg/5 mL); 600 mg/15 mL (200 mg/5 mL); or 900 mg/22.5 mL (200 mg/5 mL). Nonmedicinal ingredients: artificial flavors, FD&C Red #40, sodium phosphate, sucrose, tribasic hydroxypropyl cellulose and xanthan gum. A graduated syringe is included in the package. Dry powder: Store at controlled room temperature (15 to 30°C). Reconstituted suspension: Store between 5 and 30°C. Discard unused portion after 10 days.

Tablets: 250 mg: Each pink, film-coated, modified capsular-shaped tablet engraved "Pfizer" on the upper face, and scored on the lower face, contains: azithromycin dihydrate equivalent to azithromycin 250 mg. Nonmedicinal ingredients: anhydrous calcium phosphate dibasic, D&C Red #30 aluminum lake, hydroxypropyl methylcellulose, lactose, magnesium stearate, pregelatinized starch, sodium croscarmellose, sodium lauryl sulfate, titanium dioxide and triacetin. White plastic (high density polyethylene) bottles of 30 and 100. Single treatment package (Z-pak) of 6 blister packaged tablets per box. Store at controlled room temperature between 15 and 30°C.

600 mg: Each white, film-coated, capsular-shaped tablet engraved "Pfizer" on the upper face, and scored on the lower face, contains: azithromycin dihydrate equivalent to azithromycin 600 mg. Nonmedicinal ingredients: anhydrous calcium phosphate dibasic, hydroxypropylmethylcellulose, lactose, magnesium stearate, pregelatinized starch, sodium croscarmellose, sodium lauryl sulfate, titanium dioxide and triacetin. White plastic (high density polyethylene) bottles of 30 and 100. Store at controlled room temperature between 15 and 30°C.

Single Dose 1 g Packet: Each sealed, laminated aluminum foil and polyethylene pouch contains: azithromycin dihydrate equivalent to 1 000 mg azithromycin. Nonmedicinal ingredients: artificial banana and cherry flavors, colloidal silicon dioxide, sodium phosphate tribasic and sucrose. Store at controlled room temperature between 15 and 30°C.

(Shown in Product Recognition Section)

Reviewed 1999

ZNP®

Stiefel

Zinc Pyrithione

Antiseborrheic—Dermatitis Therapy

Supplied: Each g contains: zinc pyrithione 2% in an exclusive synthetic detergent base. Nonmedicinal ingredients: brilliant blue Na 1%, colloidal silicone dioxide, disodium lauryl sulfosuccinate, fragrance, polyethylene glycol-14M, purified water USP, tensianol KS-1, titanium dioxide and trisodium HEDTA. Bars of 75 g.

ZOCOR® Ⓟ

Frosst

Simvastatin

Lipid Metabolism Regulator

Pharmacology: Simvastatin is a cholesterol-lowering agent derived synthetically from a fermentation product of A. terreus.

After oral ingestion, simvastatin, which is an inactive lactone, is hydrolyzed to the corresponding β-hydroxyacid form. This principal metabolite is a specific inhibitor of 3-hydroxy-3-methylglutaryl-coenzyme A (HMG-CoA) reductase.

This enzyme catalyzes the conversion of HMG-CoA to mevalonate, which is an early and rate-limiting step in the biosynthesis of cholesterol.

Simvastatin reduces cholesterol production by the liver and induces some changes in cholesterol transport and disposition in the blood and tissues. The mechanism(s) of this effect is believed to involve both reduction of the synthesis of Low Density Lipoprotein (LDL), and an increase in LDL catabolism as a result of induction of the hepatic LDL receptors.

Simvastatin has complex pharmacokinetic characteristics.

Indications: Hypercholesterolemia: As an adjunct to diet, at least equivalent to the American Heart Association (AHA) Step 1 diet, for the reduction of elevated total and Low Density Lipoprotein-cholesterol (LDL-C) levels in patients with primary hypercholesterolemia (Types IIa and IIb)* when the response to diet and other nonpharmacological measures alone has been inadequate.

*A disorder of lipid metabolism characterized by elevated serum cholesterol levels in association with normal triglyceride levels (Type IIa) or with increased triglyceride levels (Type IIb).

After establishing that the elevation in plasma lipids represents a primary disorder not due to underlying conditions such as poorly controlled diabetes mellitus, hypothyroidism, the nephrotic syndrome, liver disease or dysproteinemias, it should ideally be determined that patients for whom treatment with simvastatin is being considered have an elevated LDL-C level as the cause for an elevated total serum cholesterol. This may be particularly relevant for patients with total triglycerides over 4.52 mmol/L (400 mg/dL) or with markedly elevated HDL-C values, where non-LDL lipoprotein fractions may contribute significantly to total cholesterol levels without apparent increase in cardiovascular risk. In most patients LDL-C may be estimated according to the following equation:

LDL-C(mmol/L)=

Total cholesterol−[(0.37 x triglycerides)+HDL-C]

LDL-C(mg/dL)=

Total cholesterol−[(0.16 x triglycerides)+HDL-C]

When total triglycerides are greater than 4.52 mmol/L (400 mg/dL) this equation is less accurate. In such patients, LDL-cholesterol may be obtained by ultra centrifugation.

Simvastatin is also indicated for the reduction of elevated cholesterol levels in patients with combined hypercholesterolemia and hypertriglyceridemia, when the hypercholesterolemia is the abnormality of most concern.

Coronary Heart Disease: In patients with coronary heart disease and primary hypercholesterolemia, simvastatin is indicated to: reduce the risk of total mortality by reducing coronary death; reduce the risk of nonfatal myocardial infarction; reduce the risk for undergoing myocardial revascularization procedures.

In the Scandinavian Simvastatin Survival Study (4S), the effect of therapy with simvastatin on total mortality was assessed in 4 444 patients with coronary heart disease (CHD) and baseline total cholesterol (5.5 to 8.0 mmol/L). In this multicenter, randomized, double-blind, placebo-controlled study, patients with angina or a previous myocardial infarction (MI) were treated with diet and standard care and either simvastatin 20 to 40 mg daily (n=2 221) or placebo (n=2 223) for a median duration of 5.4 years. Over the course of the study, treatment with simvastatin led to mean reductions in total cholesterol, LDL-cholesterol, and triglycerides of 25%, 35%, and 10%, respectively, and a mean increase in HDL-cholesterol of 8%. Simvastatin reduced the risk of death by 30% (182 deaths in the simvastatin group vs 256 deaths in the placebo group). The risk of CHD death was reduced by 42% (111 vs 189). Simvastatin also decreased the risk of having major coronary events (CHD death plus hospital-verified and silent nonfatal MI) by 34% (431 patients vs 622 patients with one or more events). The risk of having a hospital-verified nonfatal MI was reduced by 37%. Furthermore, simvastatin reduced the risk for undergoing myocardial revascularization procedures (coronary artery bypass grafting or percutaneous transluminal coronary angioplasty) by 37% (252 vs 383 patients).

The 4S study excluded patients with **familial hypercholesterolemia** (FH) or with **congestive heart failure.** It is not established to what extent the findings of the 4S study can be extrapolated to these subpopulations of hypercholesterolemic patients. a) In patients with heterozygous FH optimal reduction in total and LDL-cholesterol necessitates a combination drug therapy in the majority of patients. (For homozygous FH see Precautions, Use in Homozygous Familial Hypercholesterolemia). b) Among patients who developed symptoms of heart failure during the 4S study, trends in reduced mortality (19% lower with simvastatin treatment compared to placebo), with reductions of similar magnitude in numbers of patients with major coronary events and numbers of major coronary events were consistent between this group and the total study cohort.

Because there were only 57 deaths among the patients with **angina** alone at baseline and 53 deaths among **female** patients, the effect of simvastatin on mortality in these subgroups could not be adequately assessed. However, trends in reduced coronary mortality and in major coronary events were consistent between these subgroups and the total study cohort.

Simvastatin was also found to slow the progression of coronary atherosclerosis in patients with coronary heart disease as part of a treatment strategy to lower total and LDL-cholesterol to target levels. In one study in 404 hypercholesterolemic men and women with coronary heart disease [(Multicenter Anti-Atheroma Study (MAAS)], simvastatin monotherapy was shown to significantly slow the progression of coronary atherosclerosis as assessed by quantitative angiography and significantly reduce the development of both new lesions and new total occlusion.

Contraindications: Hypersensitivity to any component of this preparation. Active liver disease or unexplained persistent elevations of serum transaminases. Pregnancy and lactation (see Precautions).

Warnings: Hepatic Effects: In clinical trials, marked persistent increases (to more than 3 times the upper limit of normal) in serum transaminases have occurred in 1% of adult patients who received simvastatin (see Adverse Effects, Laboratory Tests). When the drug was interrupted or discontinued in these patients, the transaminase levels usually fell slowly to pretreatment levels. The increases were not associated with jaundice or other clinical signs or symptoms. There was no evidence of hypersensitivity. Some of these patients had abnormal liver function tests prior to therapy with simvastatin and/or consumed substantial quantities of alcohol.

In the Scandinavian Simvastatin Survival Study, the number of patients with more than one transaminase elevation to >3 times the upper limit of normal, over the course of the study, was not significantly different between the simvastatin and placebo groups (14[0.7%] vs 12[0.6%]). The frequency of single elevations of ALT to 3 times the upper limit of normal was significantly higher in the simvastatin group in the first year of the study (20 vs 8, p=0.023), but not thereafter. Elevated transaminases resulted in the discontinuation of 8 patients from the therapy in the simvastatin group (n=2 221) and 5 in the placebo group (n=2 223). All of the patients in this study received a starting dose of 20 mg of simvastatin; 37% were titrated to 40 mg.

It is recommended that liver function tests be performed at baseline and periodically thereafter (e.g., semiannually) for the first year of treatment or until 1 year after the last elevation in dose in all patients. Special attention should be paid to patients who develop elevated serum transaminase levels, and in these patients, measurements should be repeated promptly and then performed more frequently.

If the transaminase levels show evidence of progression, particularly if they rise to 3 times the upper limit of normal and are persistent, the drug should be discontinued.

The drug should be used with caution in patients who consume substantial quantities of alcohol and/or have a past history of liver disease. Active liver disease or unexplained persistent transaminase elevations are contraindications to the use of simvastatin; if such a condition should develop during therapy, the drug should be discontinued.

Moderate (less than 3 times the upper limit of normal) elevations of serum transaminases have been reported following therapy with simvastatin (see Adverse Effects). These changes were not specific to simvastatin and were also observed with comparative lipid-lowering agents. They generally appeared within the first 3 months after initiation of therapy with simvastatin, were often transient, were not accompanied by any symptom and did not require interruption of treatment.

Muscle Effects: CPK: Transient mild elevations of creatine phosphokinase (CPK) levels (from skeletal muscles) have been seen commonly in patients receiving simvastatin, but these have been usually of no clinical significance.

Myalgia: Myalgia and muscle cramps have also been associated with therapy with simvastatin.

Myopathy: Myopathy has been reported with simvastatin (incidence <0.05%) and should be considered in any patient with diffuse myalgias, muscle tenderness or weakness, and/or marked elevation of creatine phosphokinase (≥10 times the upper limit of normal). Patients should be asked to report promptly unexplained muscle pain, tenderness or weakness, particularly if accompanied by malaise or fever. Therapy with simvastatin should be discontinued if markedly elevated CPK levels occur or myopathy is diagnosed or suspected.

In the case of lovastatin, a closely related HMG-CoA reductase inhibitor, the risk of myopathy is known to be increased by concomitant immunosuppressive therapy including cyclosporins, and by concomitant therapy with gemfibrozil or with lipid-lowering doses of niacin (nicotinic acid) (see Precautions, Drug Interactions). Also, there have been rare reports of severe rhabdomyolysis that precipitated acute renal failure. Rhabdomyolysis with or without renal impairment has been reported in seriously ill patients receiving erythromycin concomitantly with lovastatin.

Myopathy or rhabdomyolysis has occurred in transplant and nontransplant patients receiving simvastatin or another HMG-CoA reductase inhibitor following the initiation of treatment with the antifungal agent itraconazole. In a study in normal volunteers, plasma levels of another HMG-CoA reductase inhibitor were increased about 20-fold when administered concomitantly with itraconazole. This is probably related to metabolism of both drugs by the same P450 isoform. Based on this data, therapy with simvastatin should be temporarily interrupted if systemic azole derivative antifungal therapy is required. A case of myositis and rhabdomyolysis has also been reported following the addition of the antidepressant nefazodone to the regimen of a patient previously taking simvastatin.

Therefore, the benefits and risks of using simvastatin concomitantly with immunosuppressive drugs, fibrates, erythromycin, systemic azole derivative antifungal agents, nefazodone or lipid-lowering doses of niacin should be carefully considered (see Precautions, Cytochrome P450 Inhibitors).

Interruption of therapy with simvastatin should be considered in any patient with an acute, serious condition, suggestive of a myopathy or having a risk factor predisposing to the development of renal failure or rhabdomyolysis, such as severe acute infection, hypotension, major surgery, trauma, severe metabolic, endocrine or electrolyte disorders and uncontrolled seizures.

Precautions: General: Before instituting therapy with simvastatin, an attempt should be made to control hypercholesterolemia with appropriate diet and exercise, weight reduction in overweight and obese patients, and to treat other underlying medical problems (see Indications). The patient should be advised to inform subsequent physicians of the prior use of simvastatin or any other lipid-lowering agent.

In primary prevention intervention, the effects of simvastatin-induced changes in lipoprotein levels, including reduction of serum cholesterol, on cardiovascular morbidity or mortality have not been established.

Homozygous Familial Hypercholesterolemia: Simvastatin is not effective or is less effective in patients with rare homozygous familial hypercholesterolemia.

Effect on the Lens: Current long-term data from clinical trials do not indicate an adverse effect of simvastatin on the human lens.

Effect on CoQ_{10} Levels (Ubiquinone): Significant decreases in circulating CoQ_{10} levels in patients treated with simvastatin and other statins have been observed. The clinical significance

Zocor (cont'd)

of a potential long-term statin-induced deficiency of CoQ_{10} has not been established.

Effect on Lipoprotein(a): In some patients, the beneficial effect of lowered total cholesterol and LDL-C levels may be partly blunted by a concomitant increase in the Lipoprotein(a) [Lp(a)] level. Further research is currently ongoing to elucidate the significance of Lp(a) plasma level variations. Therefore, until further experience is obtained, it is suggested, when feasible, that Lp(a) measurements be carried out in patients placed on therapy with simvastatin.

Hypersensitivity: In few instances eosinophilia and skin eruptions appear to be associated with simvastatin treatment. If hypersensitivity is suspected, simvastatin should be discontinued.

Pregnancy: **Simvastatin is contraindicated during pregnancy.**

Atherosclerosis is a chronic process and the discontinuation of lipid metabolism regulators during pregnancy should have little impact on the outcome of long-term therapy of primary hypercholesterolemia. Moreover, cholesterol and other products of the cholesterol biosynthesis pathway are essential components for fetal development, including synthesis of steroids and cell membranes. Because of the ability of inhibitors of HMG-CoA reductase such as simvastatin to decrease the synthesis of cholesterol and possibly other products of the cholesterol biosynthesis pathway, simvastatin is contraindicated during pregnancy. Simvastatin should be administered to women of childbearing age only when such patients are highly unlikely to conceive. If the patient becomes pregnant while taking this drug, simvastatin should be discontinued immediately and the patient apprised of the potential hazard to the fetus.

A few reports have been received of congenital anomalies in infants whose mothers were treated during a critical period of pregnancy with HMG-CoA reductase inhibitors (see Contraindications). In a review of approximately 100 prospectively followed pregnancies in women exposed to simvastatin or another structurally related HMG-CoA reductase inhibitor, the incidences of congenital anomalies, spontaneous abortions and fetal death/stillbirths did not exceed what would be expected in the general population. As safety in pregnant women has not been established and there is no apparent benefit to therapy with simvastatin during pregnancy, treatment should be immediately discontinued as soon as pregnancy is recognized.

Lactation: It is not known whether simvastatin or its metabolites are excreted in human milk. Because many drugs are excreted in human milk and because of the potential for serious adverse reactions, women taking simvastatin should not nurse (see Contraindications).

Children: Limited experience is available in children. However, safety and effectiveness in children have not been established.

Geriatrics: For patients over the age of 65 years who received simvastatin in controlled clinical studies, efficacy, as assessed by reduction in total and LDL cholesterol levels, appeared similar to that seen in the population as a whole, and there was no apparent increase in the frequency and severity of clinical or laboratory adverse findings.

Patients with Impaired Renal Function: Simvastatin does not undergo significant renal excretion, modification of dosage should not be necessary in patients with moderate renal insufficiency. In patients with severe renal insufficiency (creatinine clearance <30 mL/min), dosages above 10 mg/day should be carefully considered and, if deemed necessary, implemented cautiously. This recommendation is based on studies with lovastatin (see Warnings, Muscle Effects).

Endocrine Function: HMG-CoA reductase inhibitors interfere with cholesterol synthesis and as such might theoretically blunt adrenal and/or gonadal steroid production. Clinical studies with simvastatin and other HMG-CoA reductase inhibitors have suggested that these agents do not reduce plasma cortisol concentration or impair adrenal reserve and do not reduce basal plasma testosterone concentration. However, the effects of HMG-CoA reductase inhibitors on male fertility have not been studied in adequate numbers of patients. The effects, if any, on the pituitary-gonadal axis in premenopausal women are unknown.

Patients treated with simvastatin who develop clinical evidence of endocrine dysfunction should be evaluated appropriately. Caution should be exercised if an HMG-CoA reductase inhibitor or other agent used to lower cholesterol levels is administered to patients receiving other drugs (e.g., ketoconazole, spironolactone, or cimetidine) that may decrease the levels of endogenous steroid hormones (see Drug Interactions, Cytochrome P450 Inhibitors).

Drug Interactions: Concomitant Therapy with other Lipid Metabolism Regulators: Combined drug therapy should be approached with caution as information from controlled studies is limited.

Bile Acid Sequestrants: Preliminary evidence suggests that the cholesterol-lowering effects of simvastatin and the bile acid sequestrant, cholestyramine, are additive.

When simvastatin is used concurrently with cholestyramine or any other resin, an interval of at least 2 hours should be maintained between the 2 drugs, since the absorption of simvastatin may be impaired by the resin.

Gemfibrozil, Fenofibrate and Niacin: Myopathy, including rhabdomyolysis, has occurred in patients who were receiving coadministration of simvastatin and other HMG-CoA reductase inhibitors with fibric acid derivatives and niacin, particularly in subjects with pre-existing renal insufficiency (see Warnings, Muscle Effects).

Erythromycin: see Warnings, Muscle Effects.

Coumarin Anticoagulants: In 2 clinical studies, one in normal volunteers and the other in hypercholesterolemic patients, simvastatin 20 to 40 mg/day modestly potentiated the effect of coumarin anticoagulants: the prothrombin time, reported as International Normalized Ratios (INR), increased from a baseline of 1.7 to 1.8 and from 2.6 to 3.4 in the volunteer and patient studies, respectively. In patients taking coumarin anticoagulants, prothrombin time should be determined before starting simvastatin and frequently enough during early therapy to insure that no significant alteration of prothrombin time occurs. Once a stable prothrombin time has been documented, prothrombin times can be monitored at the intervals usually recommended for patients on coumarin anticoagulants. If the dose of simvastatin is changed, the same procedure should be repeated. Simvastatin therapy has not been associated with bleeding or with changes in prothrombin time in patients not taking anticoagulants.

Digoxin: Concomitant administration of simvastatin and digoxin in normal volunteers resulted in a slight elevation (<0.3 ng/mL) in drug concentrations (as measured by a digoxin radioimmunoassay) in plasma compared to concomitant administration of placebo and digoxin.

Antipyrine: Antipyrine was used as a model for drugs metabolized by the microsomal hepatic enzyme system (cytochrome P450 system). Simvastatin had little or no detectable effect on the pharmacokinetics of antipyrine in hypercholesterolemic patients.

Cytochrome P450 Inhibitors: Simvastatin is metabolized by the microsomal hepatic enzyme system (cytochrome P450 system) as are most other HMG-CoA reductase inhibitors. While simvastatin did not interact with antipyrine, it may interact with erythromycin, a known inhibitor of cytochrome P450 isoform 3A4. Drugs or common agents such as grapefruit juice that inhibit this enzyme may represent a potential for drug interactions when combined with simvastatin. Caution should thus be exercised with concomitant use of drugs such as immunosuppressants, antifungal agents (e.g., itraconazole, ketoconazole), macrolide antibiotics including erythromycin, antidepressent (e.g., nefazodone) or grapefruit juice (see Warnings, Myopathy and Precautions, Endocrine Function and Patients with Impaired Renal Function).

Other Concomitant Therapy: In clinical studies, simvastatin was used concomitantly with angiotensin converting enzyme (ACE) inhibitors, beta-blockers, calcium-channel blockers, diuretics and nonsteroidal anti-inflammatory drugs (NSAIDs) without evidence of clinically significant adverse interactions.

Drug/Laboratory Test Interactions: Simvastatin may elevate serum transaminase and creatine phosphokinase levels (from skeletal muscles) (see Adverse Effects, Laboratory Tests). In the differential diagnosis of chest pain in a patient on therapy with simvastatin cardiac and noncardiac fractions of these enzymes should be determined.

Adverse Effects: Based on experience in a total of over 2 300 patients, of whom more than 1 200 were treated for 1 year and over 230 for 2 years or more, simvastatin is generally well tolerated and adverse reactions are usually mild and transient.

In premarketing controlled clinical trials, 1% of patients were withdrawn due to adverse experiences attributable to simvastatin.

Adverse experiences occurring at an incidence of ≥0.5% of 2 361 patients treated with simvastatin in premarketing controlled clinical studies and reported to be possibly, probably or definitely drug related are shown in Table I.

Table I—Zocor

Adverse Experiences Occurring in Patients Treated with Zocor in Premarketing Controlled Clinical Studies

	Zocor (n=2 361) (%)
Gastrointestinal	
Abdominal Pain	2.2
Acid Regurgitation	0.5
Constipation	2.5
Dyspepsia	0.6
Diarrhea	0.8
Flatulence	2.0
Nausea	1.1
Nervous System	
Headache	1.0
Skin	
Rash	0.7
Miscellaneous	
Asthenia	0.8

In the Scandinavian Simvastatin Survival Study (4S) involving 4 444 patients treated with 20 to 40 mg/day of simvastatin (n=2 221) or placebo (n=2 223), the safety and tolerability profiles were comparable between groups over the median 5.4 years of the study.

Ophthalmological Observations: See Precautions, Effect on the Lens.

Laboratory Tests: Marked persistent increases of serum transaminases have been noted (see Warnings).

About 5% of patients had elevations of creatine phosphokinase (CPK) levels 3 or more times the normal value on one or more occasions. This was attributable to the noncardiac fraction of CPK. Myopathy has been reported rarely (see Warnings, Muscle Effects and Precautions, Drug/Laboratory Test Interactions).

The following additional adverse reactions were reported either in uncontrolled clinical trials or in marketed use; however a causal relationship to therapy with simvastatin has not been established.

Dermatologic: erythema multiforme including Stevens-Johnson syndrome.

Gastrointestinal: vomiting.

Hematologic: anemia; leukopenia; purpura.

Hepatic: rarely hepatitis; jaundice.

Musculoskeletal: rarely rhabdomyolysis; muscle cramps; myalgia.

Nervous System/Psychiatric: dizziness; paresthesia; depression; **peripheral neuropathy;** rarely, peripheral neuropathy with muscle weakness or sensory disturbance has been reported.

Skin: rash; pruritus; alopecia.

Miscellaneous: pancreatitis.

Laboratory Tests: Elevated alkaline phosphatase and γ-glutamyl transpeptidase have been reported.

An apparent hypersensitivity syndrome has been reported rarely which has included some of the following features: angioedema; arthralgia; arthritis; dyspnea; eosinophilia; ESR increased; fever; flushing; lupus-like syndrome; malaise; photosensitivity; polymyalgia rheumatica; thrombocytopenia; urticaria; vasculitis.

Others: Although the following adverse reactions were not observed in clinical trials with simvastatin, they have been reported following treatment with other HMG-CoA reductase inhibitors: anorexia, psychic disturbances including anxiety, and hypospermia.

Overdose: Symptoms and Treatment: A few cases of overdosage have been reported; no patient had any specific symptoms, and all patients recovered without sequelae. The maximum dose taken was 450 mg.

In the event of overdosage, treatment should be symptomatic and supportive, liver function should be monitored, and appropriate therapy instituted.

The dialyzability of simvastatin and its metabolites is not known.

Dosage: The patient should be placed on a diet, at least an equivalent to the American Heart Association (AHA) step 1, before receiving simvastatin and should continue on this diet during treatment with the drug. If appropriate, a program of weight control and physical exercise should be implemented.

Hypercholesterolemia: The usual starting dose is 10 mg/day given as a single dose in the evening. Patients with mild to moderate hypercholesterolemia can be treated with a starting dose of 5 mg of simvastatin. Adjustments of dosage, if required, should be made at intervals of not less than 4 weeks, to a maximum of 40 mg daily given as a single dose in the evening.

Cholesterol levels should be monitored periodically and consideration should be given to reducing the dosage of simvastatin if cholesterol levels fall below the targeted range, such as that recommended by the Second Report of the U.S. National Cholesterol Education Program (NCEP).

Coronary Heart Disease: Patients with coronary heart disease and primary hypercholesterolemia can be treated with a starting dose of 20 mg/day given as a single dose in the evening. Adjustments of dosage, if required, should be made as specified above (see Hypercholesterolemia).

Concomitant Therapy: See Drug Interactions, Concomitant Therapy with other Lipid Metabolism Regulators.

In patients taking immunosuppressive drugs concomitantly with simvastatin, the maximum recommended dosage is 10 mg/day (see Warnings, Muscle Effects).

Information for the Patient: See Blue Section—Information for the Patient "Zocor".

Supplied: 5 mg: Each buff-colored, shield-shaped, film-coated tablet, engraved 726 on one side and Z on the other, contains: simvastatin 5 mg. Nonmedicinal ingredients: ascorbic acid, butylated hydroxyanisole, citric acid, hydroxypropyl cellulose, lactose, magnesium stearate, methylcellulose, microcrystalline cellulose, pregelatinized starch, talc, titanium dioxide and yellow ferric oxide. Blister packages of 30.

10 mg: Each peach-colored, shield-shaped, film-coated tablet, engraved 735 on one side and Z on the other, contains: simvastatin 10 mg. Nonmedicinal ingredients: ascorbic acid, butylated hydroxyanisole, citric acid, hydroxypropyl cellulose, lactose, magnesium stearate, methylcellulose, microcrystalline cellulose, pregelatinized starch, red ferric oxide, talc, titanium dioxide and yellow ferric oxide. Blister packages of 30. High density polyethylene bottles of 500.

20 mg: Each tan-colored, shield-shaped, film-coated tablet, engraved 740 on one side and Z on the other, contains: simvastatin 20 mg. Nonmedicinal ingredients: ascorbic acid, butylated hydroxyanisole, citric acid, hydroxypropyl cellulose, lactose, magnesium stearate, methylcellulose, microcrystalline cellulose, pregelatinized starch, red ferric oxide, talc, titanium dioxide and yellow ferric oxide. Blister packages of 30. High density polyethylene bottles of 100.

40 mg: Each brick-red colored, shield-shaped, film-coated tablet, engraved 749 on one side and Z on the other, contains: simvastatin 40 mg. Nonmedicinal ingredients: ascorbic acid, butylated hydroxyanisole, citric acid, hydroxypropyl cellulose, lactose, magnesium stearate, methylcellulose, microcrystalline cellulose, pregelatinized starch, red ferric oxide, talc and titanium dioxide. Blister packages of 30.

Store at room temperature (15 to 30°C).

(Shown in Product Recognition Section)

Reviewed 1998

ZOFRAN® Ⓟ

Glaxo Wellcome

Ondansetron HCl Dihydrate

Antiemetic

Pharmacology: Ondansetron is a selective antagonist of the serotonin receptor subtype, 5-HT_3. Its precise mode of action in the control of chemotherapy-induced nausea and vomiting is not known. Cytotoxic chemotherapy and radiotherapy are associated with the release of serotonin (5-HT) from enterochromaffin cells of the small intestine, presumably initiating a vomiting reflex through stimulation of 5-HT_3 receptors located on vagal afferents. Ondansetron may block the initiation of this reflex. Activation of vagal afferents may also cause a central release of serotonin from the chemoreceptor trigger zone of the area postrema, located on the floor of the fourth ventricle. Thus, the antiemetic effect of ondansetron is probably due to the selective antagonism of 5-HT_3 receptors on neurons located in either the peripheral or central nervous systems, or both.

The mechanisms of ondansetron's antiemetic action in postoperative nausea and vomiting are not known.

Pharmacokinetics: Pharmacokinetic studies in human volunteers showed peak plasma levels of 20 to 30 ng/mL at around 1½ hours after an 8 mg oral dose of ondansetron. An 8 mg infusion of ondansetron reached peak plasma levels of 80 to 100 ng/mL. Repeat dosing of an 8 mg tablet every 8 hours for 6 days increased the peak plasma value to 40 ng/mL. A continuous i.v. infusion of 1 mg/hour after the initial 8 mg loading dose of ondansetron maintained plasma levels over 30 ng/mL during the following 24 hour period.

The absolute bioavailability of ondansetron in humans was approximately 60% and the plasma protein binding was approximately 73%.

Following oral or i.v. administration, ondansetron is extensively metabolised and excreted in the urine and feces. In humans, less than 10% of the dose is excreted unchanged in the urine. The major urinary metabolites are glucuronide conjugates (45%), sulfate conjugates (20%) and hydroxylation products (10%).

The half-life of ondansetron after either an 8 mg oral dose or i.v. dose was approximately 3 to 4 hours and may be extended to 6 to 8 hours in the elderly.

Clinical trial results showing the number and percentage of patients exhibiting a complete response to ondansetron (0 emetic episodes) are shown in Tables I, II and III, for both postoperative and chemotherapy induced emesis.

Table I—Zofran

Prevention of Chemotherapy Induced Emesis—Response over 24 Hours

Prevention of Acute Cisplatin Induced Emesis: Placebo Controlled Data*

	Zofran	Placebo
Dose	**3 doses of 0.15 mg/kg**	**3 doses of placebo**
Number of patients	14	14
Treatment response:		
0 emetic episodes	2 (14%)	0 (0%)
1-2 emetic episodes	8 (57%)	0 (0%)

Prevention of Acute Cisplatin Induced Emesis: Zofran Dosing Regimens

	Zofran	Zofran	Zofran
Dose	**8 mg i.v. + 1 mg/hr, 24 hrs**	**8 mg i.v.**	**32 mg i.v.**
Number of patients	168	152	173
Treatment response:			
0 emetic episodes	92 (55%)	82 (54%)	97 (56%)

* Results are from an initial study using a different dosing regimen.

Table II—Zofran

Prevention of Postoperative Emesis—Response over 24 Hours*

Oral Prevention

	Zofran	Placebo	p Value
Dose	**16 mg od**	—	
Number of patients	253	250	
Treatment response:			
0 emetic episodes	126 (50%)	79 (32%)	<0.001

I.V. Prevention

	Zofran	Placebo	p Value
Dose	**4 mg i.v.**	—	
Number of patients	136	139	
Treatment response:			
0 emetic episodes	103 (76%)	62 (46%)	<0.001

* The majority of patients included in the prevention of postoperative nausea and vomiting studies using ondansetron have been adult women receiving balanced anesthesia for gynecological surgery.

Indications: For the prevention of nausea and vomiting associated with emetogenic chemotherapy, including high dose cisplatin, and radiotherapy.

Ondansetron is also indicated for the prevention and treatment of postoperative nausea and vomiting.

Contraindications: In patients with a history of hypersensitivity to the drug or any components of its formulations (see Supplied).

Table III—Zofran

Treatment of Postoperative Emesis—Response over 24 Hours*

I.V. Treatment

	Zofran	Placebo	p Value
Dose	**4 mg i.v.**	—	
Number of patients	104	117	
Treatment response:			
0 emetic episodes	49 (47%)	19 (16%)	<0.001

* The majority of patients treated for postoperative nausea and vomiting in studies using Zofran have been adult women receiving balanced anesthesia for gynecological surgery.

Warnings: Cross-reactive hypersensitivity has been reported between 5-HT_3 antagonists. Patients who have experienced hypersensitivity reactions to one 5-HT_3 antagonist have experienced more severe reactions upon being challenged with another drug of the same class. The use of a different 5-HT_3 receptor antagonist is not recommended as a replacement in cases in which a patient has experienced even a mild hypersensitivity type reaction to another 5-HT_3 antagonist.

Precautions: Ondansetron is not effective in preventing motion-induced nausea and vomiting.

There is no experience in patients who are clinically jaundiced. The clearance of an 8 mg intravenous dose of ondansetron was significantly reduced and the serum half-life significantly prolonged in subjects with severe impairment of hepatic function. In patients with moderate to severe hepatic function, reductions in dosage are therefore recommended and a total daily dose of 8 mg should not be exceeded. This may be given as a single i.v. or oral dose.

As ondansetron is known to increase large bowel transit time, patients with signs of subacute intestinal obstruction should be monitored following administration.

Pregnancy: The safety of ondansetron during pregnancy has not been established. Ondansetron is not teratogenic in animals. However, as animal studies are not always predictive of human response, the use of ondansetron in pregnancy is not recommended.

Lactation: Ondansetron is excreted in the milk of lactating rats. It is not known if it is excreted in human milk, however, nursing is not recommended during treatment with ondansetron.

Children: Insufficient information is available to provide dosage recommendations for children 3 years of age or younger.

Adverse Effects: Ondansetron has been administered to over 2 500 patients worldwide in controlled clinical trials and has been well tolerated.

The most frequent adverse events reported in controlled clinical trials were headache (11%) and constipation (4%). Other adverse events include sensations of flushing or warmth (<1%).

Metabolic: There were transient increases of AST and ALT of over twice the upper limit of normal in approximately 5% of patients. These increases did not appear to be related to dose or duration of therapy. There have been reports of liver failure and death in patients with cancer receiving concurrent medications including potentially hepatotoxic cytotoxic chemotherapy and antibiotics. The etiology of the liver failure is unclear. There have been rare reports of hypokalemia.

CNS: There have been rare reports of seizures.

Hypersensitivity: Rare cases of immediate hypersensitivity reactions sometimes severe, including anaphylaxis, bronchospasm, urticaria and angioedema have been reported.

Cardiovascular: There have been rare reports of tachycardia, angina (chest pain), bradycardia, hypotension, syncope and electrocardiographic alterations.

Dermatological: Rash has occurred in approximately 1% of patients receiving ondansetron.

Special Senses: Rare cases of transient visual distrubances (e.g., blurred vision) have been reported during or shortly after i.v. administration of ondansetron, particularly at rates equal to or greater than 30 mg in 15 minutes.

Local Reactions: Pain, redness and burning at the site of injection have been reported.

Other: There have been reports of abdominal pain, weakness and xerostomia.

Post-Market Experience: Over 9.5 million patient courses of Zofran (1 patient course defined as 3 i.v. injections followed by 6 oral doses) have been supplied since the launch of the product worldwide. The following are events which have been reported spontaneously. Transient episodes of dizziness (<0.01%) have been reported during or upon completion of

Zofran (cont'd)

i.v. infusion of ondansetron. Rare reports (<0.01%) suggestive of involuntary movement disorders (e.g., oro-facial dyskinesia, opisthotonos, dystonia, tremor, etc.) have been reported without definitive evidence of persistent clinical sequelae. There have been rare reports (<0.01%) of arrhythmias and hiccups. The link to ondansetron cannot be clearly established for spontaneously reported events.

Overdose: Symptoms and Treatment: At present there is little information concerning overdosage with ondansetron. Individual doses of 84 and 145 mg and total daily doses as large as 252 mg have been administered with only mild side effects. There is no specific antidote for ondansetron, therefore, in cases of suspected overdosage, symptomatic and supportive therapy should be given as appropriate.

The use of Ipecac to treat overdosage with ondansetron is not recommended as patients are unlikely to respond due to the antiemetic action of ondansetron itself.

"Sudden blindness" (amaurosis) of 2 to 3 minutes duration plus severe constipation occurred in 1 patient that was administered 72 mg of ondansetron i.v. as a single dose. Hypotension (and faintness) occurred in another patient that took 48 mg of oral ondansetron. Following infusion of 32 mg over only a 4-minute period, a vasovagal episode with transient second degree heart block was observed. In all instances, the events resolved completely.

Dosage: Chemotherapy Induced Nausea and Vomiting: Ondansetron should be given as an initial dose prior to chemotherapy, followed by a dosage regimen tailored to the anticipated severity of emetic response caused by different cancer treatments. The route of administration and dose of ondansetron should be flexible in the range of 8 to 32 mg a day. The selection of dose regimen should be determined by the severity of the emetogenic challenge as shown below.

Adults: Highly Emetogenic Chemotherapy (e.g., regimens containing cisplatin): Ondansetron has been shown to be effective in the following dose schedules for the prevention of emesis during the first 24 hours following chemotherapy:

Initial Dose: 8 mg infused i.v. over 15 minutes given 30 minutes prior to chemotherapy; or 8 mg infused i.v. over 15 minutes, given 30 minutes prior to chemotherapy, followed by 1 mg/h by continuous infusion for up to 24 hours; or 32 mg diluted in 50 to 100 mL of saline or other compatible infusion fluid and infused over not less than 15 minutes**, given 30 minutes prior to chemotherapy.

Post-chemotherapy: After the first 24 hours, 8 mg orally every 8 hours* for up to 5 days.

No significant differences in terms of emesis control or grade of nausea have been demonstrated between the 32 mg single dose, the 8 mg single dose, or the 8 mg dose followed by the 24 hour 1 mg/hour continuous infusion.

However, in some studies conducted in patients receiving medium or high doses of cisplatin chemotherapy, the 32 mg single dose has demonstrated a statistically significant superiority over the 8 mg single dose with regard to control of emesis.

The efficacy of ondansetron in highly emetogenic chemotherapy may be enhanced by the addition of a single i.v. dose of dexamethasone sodium phosphate, 20 mg administered prior to chemotherapy.

Less Emetogenic Chemotherapy (e.g., regimens containing cyclophosphamide, doxorubicin, epirubicin, fluorouracil and carboplatin): Initial Dose: 8 mg infused i.v. over 15 minutes, given 30 minutes prior to chemotherapy; or 8 mg tablet orally 1 to 2 hours prior to chemotherapy.

Post-chemotherapy: 8 mg orally twice daily for up to 5 days.

Children: Clinical experience of ondansetron in children is currently limited, however, ondansetron was effective and well tolerated when given to children 4 to 12 years of age. Ondansetron injection should be given i.v. at a dose of 3 to 5 mg/m² over 15 minutes immediately before chemotherapy. After therapy, one ondansetron 4 mg tablet should be given orally every 8 hours* for up to 5 days.

Geriatrics: Efficacy and tolerance in patients aged over 65 years were similar to that seen in younger adults indicating no need to alter dosage schedules in this population.

Radiotherapy Induced Nausea and Vomiting: Adults: Initial Dose: 8 mg orally 1 to 2 hours before radiotherapy.

Post-radiotherapy: 8 mg orally every 8 hours* for up to 5 days after a course of treatment.

Children: There is no experience in clinical studies in this population.

Geriatrics: Efficacy and tolerance in patients aged over 65 years were similar to that seen in younger adults indicating no need to alter dosage schedules in this population.

* Note: The efficacy of twice daily dosage regimens for the treatment of post-chemotherapy emesis has been established only in adult patients receiving less emetogenic chemotherapy. The appropriateness of twice versus 3 times daily dosage regimens for other patient groups should be based on an assessment of the needs and responsiveness of the individual patient.

** Infusion of 32 mg ondansetron injection should take place over a period of not less than 15 minutes, because of increased risk of blurred vision.

Postoperative Nausea and Vomiting: Adults: For prevention of post-operative nausea and vomiting ondansetron may be administered as a single dose of 16 mg given orally 1 hour prior to anesthesia. Alternatively, a single dose of 4 mg may be given by slow i.v. injection at induction of anesthesia.

For the treatment of established postoperative nausea and vomiting, a single dose of 4 mg given by slow i.v. injection is recommended.

Children: There is no experience in the use of ondansetron in the prevention and treatment of postoperative nausea and vomiting in children.

Geriatrics: There is limited experience in the use of ondansetron in the prevention and treatment of postoperative nausea and vomiting in the elderly.

Impaired Renal Function: No alteration of daily dosage, frequency of dosing, or route of administration is required.

Impaired Hepatic Function: The clearance of an 8 mg i.v. dose was significantly reduced and the serum half-life significantly prolonged in subjects with severe impairment of hepatic function. In patients with moderate to severe hepatic function, reductions in dosage are therefore recommended and a total daily dose of 8 mg should not be exceeded. This may be given as a single i.v. or oral dose.

No studies have been conducted to date in patients with jaundice.

Poor Sparteine/Debrisoquine Metabolism: The elimination half-life and plasma levels of a single 8 mg i.v. dose of ondansetron did not differ between subjects classified as poor and extensive metabolizers of sparteine and debrisoquine. No alteration of daily dosage or frequency of dosing is recommended for patients known to be poor metabolizers of sparteine and debrisoquine.

Administration of I.V. Infusion Solutions: Compatibility with I.V. Solutions: The injection is compatible with the following solutions: for ampuls, 0.9% w/v Sodium Chloride Injection; 5% w/v Dextrose Injection; 10% w/v Mannitol Injection; Ringers Injection; 0.3% w/v Potassium Chloride and 0.9% w/v Sodium Chloride Injection; 0.3% w/v Potassium Chloride and 5% w/v Dextrose Injection. For vials, 5% w/v Dextrose Injection; 0.9% w/v Sodium Chloride Injection; 5% w/v Dextrose and 0.9% w/v Sodium Chloride Injection; 5% w/v Dextrose and 0.45% w/v Sodium Chloride Injection; 3% w/v Sodium Chloride Injection.

Compatibility with Other Drugs: The injection should not be administered in the same syringe or infusion with any other medication with the exception of dexamethasone (see below). Ondansetron may be administered by i.v. infusion at 1 mg/hour, e.g., from an infusion bag or syringe pump.

The following drugs may be administered via the Y-site of the administration set, for ondansetron concentration of 16 to 160 μg/mL. If the concentrations of cytotoxic drugs required are higher than indicated below, they should be administered through a separate i.v. line.

For Ampuls and Vials: **Cisplatin:** Concentrations up to 0.48 mg/mL administered over 1 to 8 hours.

Dexamethasone: Admixtures containing 8 mg of ondansetron and 20 mg of dexamethasone phosphate, in 50 mL of 5% dextrose infusion fluid stored in 50 mL polyvinyl chloride infusion bags, have been shown to be physically and chemically stable for up to 2 days at room temperature or up to 7 days at 2 to 8°C. In addition, these same admixtures have demonstrated compatibility with Continu-Flo administration sets.

In a clinical study (Cunningham et al, 1989) ondansetron (standard dosing regimen) was given to patients receiving cisplatin or non-cisplatin chemotherapy. Eight patients who continued to experience nausea and vomiting were given dexamethasone in addition to ondansetron. In every case there was an improvement in the control of emesis and all patients preferred the combination of ondansetron and dexamethasone.

For Ampuls: **5-Fluorouracil:** concentrations up to 0.8 mg/mL, administered at rates of at least 20 mL/hour. Higher concentrations of 5-fluorouracil may cause precipitation of ondansetron. The 5-fluorouracil infusion may contain up to 0.045% w/v magnesium chloride.

Carboplatin: concentrations of 0.18 to 9.9 mg/mL, administered over 10 to 60 minutes.

Ceftazidime: bolus i.v. doses, over approximately 5 minutes, of 250 to 2 000 mg reconstituted with Water for Injections BP.

Cyclophosphamide: bolus i.v. doses over approximately 5 minutes, of 100 to 1 000 mg, reconstituted with Water for Injections BP 5 mL/100 mg cyclophosphamide.

Doxorubicin and Epirubicin: bolus i.v. doses, over approximately 5 minutes, of 10 to 100 mg as a 2 mg/mL solution. Lyophilized powder presentations can be reconstituted with 0.9% Sodium Chloride Injection USP.

Etoposide: concentrations of 0.144 to 0.25 mg/mL, administered over 30 to 60 minutes.

Stability and Storage: Store below 30°C. The oral solution should be stored upright and should not be refrigerated. The injection should not be frozen and should be protected from light. The injection must not be autoclaved.

Stability and Storage of Diluted Solutions: Compatibility studies have been undertaken in polyvinyl chloride infusion bags, polyvinyl chloride administration sets and polypropylene syringes. Dilutions of ondansetron in sodium chloride 0.9% w/v or in glucose 5% w/v have been demonstrated to be stable in polypropylene syringes. It is considered that ondansetron injection diluted with other compatible infusion fluids would be stable in polypropylene syringes.

I.V. solutions should be prepared at the time of infusion. The injection, in ampuls and vials, when diluted with the recommended i.v. solutions, should be used within 24 hours if stored at room temperature or used within 72 hours if stored in a refrigerator, due to possible microbial contamination during preparation.

Hospitals and institutions that have recognized admixture programs and use validated aseptic techniques for preparation of i.v. solutions, may extend the storage time for ondansetron injection in admixture with 5% dextrose injection and dexamethasone phosphate injection (concentration of 0.34 mg/mL) in Viaflex bags, at a concentration of 0.14 mg/mL, to 7 days when stored under refrigeration at 2 to 8°C.

Note: As with all parenteral drug products, i.v. admixtures should be inspected visually for clarity, particulate matter, precipitate, discoloration and leakage prior to administration, whenever solution and container permit. Solutions showing haziness, particulate matter, precipitate, or discoloration or leakage should not be used.

Information for the Patient: See Blue Section—Information for the Patient "Zofran".

Supplied: Injection: Each mL contains: ondansetron 2 mg/mL (as hydrochloride dihydrate) for i.v. use. Nonmedicinal ingredients: citric acid monohydrate, methyl- and propylparaben (vials only), sodium citrate and sodium chloride. Ampuls of 2 mL (4 mg) and 4 mL (8 mg). Boxes of 5. Vials of 20 mL (40 mg). Packed in individual cartons.

Oral Solution: Each 5 mL contains: ondansetron 4 mg (as dihydrate HCl). Nonmedicinal ingredients: citric acid anhydrous, sodium citrate dihydrate, sodium benzoate, sorbitol solution and strawberry flavor. Bottles of 50 mL.

Tablets: 4 mg: Each oval-shaped, yellow film-coated tablet, engraved '4' on one face and 'GLAXO' on the other, contains: ondansetron 4 mg (as hydrochloride dihydrate). Nonmedicinal ingredients: lactose, magnesium stearate, methyl hydroxypropyl cellulose, microcrystalline cellulose, Opadry yellow or Opaspray yellow (containing titanium dioxide and iron oxide yellow) and pregelatinized starch. Gluten- and tartrazine-free. Tamper-evident polypropylene containers of 30.

8 mg: Each oval-shaped, yellow, film-coated tablet, engraved '8' on one face and 'GLAXO' on the other, contains: ondansetron 8 mg (as hydrochloride dihydrate). Nonmedicinal ingredients: lactose, magnesium stearate, methyl hydroxypropyl cellulose, microcrystalline cellulose, Opadry yellow or Opaspray yellow (containing titanium dioxide and iron oxide yellow) and pregelatinized starch. Gluten- and tartrazine-free. Tamper-evident polypropylene containers of 10 and 30.

(Shown in Product Recognition Section)

Reviewed 1998

ZOLADEX® ℞

Zeneca

Goserelin Acetate

LHRH Analog

Pharmacology: Goserelin is a synthetic decapeptide analog of gonadotropin releasing hormone (GnRH or LHRH). When given acutely, goserelin releases luteinizing hormone (LH) from the pituitary gland. However, following chronic administration, goserelin is a potent inhibitor of gonadotropin production resulting in gonadal and consequently, accessory sex organ regression. This effect is the basis for the inhibition of growth of chemically-induced rat mammary tumors and transplantable rat prostate and pituitary tumors.

In animals and man, following an initial stimulation of pituitary LH secretion and a transient elevation in serum testosterone in males and serum estradiol in females, chronic administration results in inhibition of gonadotropin secretion. Approximately 21 days after the initiation of therapy, a sustained suppression of pituitary LH results in the reduction of serum testosterone levels to a range normally seen in surgically castrated men, and of serum estradiol to levels comparable with those observed in postmenopausal women. This suppression of testosterone and estradiol is then maintained as long as therapy is continued. When used in women this suppression of serum estradiol will induce amenorrhea in the majority of patients after the first 4 weeks of treatment especially if started during the menstrual phase of the cycle. During early treatment with goserelin some women may experience vaginal bleeding of variable duration and intensity. Such bleeding may represent estrogen withdrawal bleeding and is expected to stop spontaneously.

Zoladex is a depot formulation of goserelin acetate dispersed in a cylindrical rod of biodegradable and biocompatible D-L Lactide-glycolide copolymer.

The bioavailability of goserelin from Zoladex depot is almost complete. When injected s.c., goserelin is released continuously over at least 28 days. Administration of a depot every 4 weeks ensures that effective concentrations are maintained with no accumulation. Goserelin is poorly protein bound and has a serum elimination half-life of about 4.2 hours in male subjects and 2.3 hours in female subjects with normal renal function. Although the half-life is increased in patients with impaired renal function, this has minimal effects, and hence, no change from a monthly dosing schedule is necessary. There is no significant change in the clearance of goserelin in patients with hepatic impairment with normal renal function.

Indications: For a number of hormone-dependent conditions as shown below under the headings Prostate Cancer, Breast Cancer and Benign Conditions.

Prostate Cancer: For the palliative treatment of patients with hormone-dependent advanced carcinoma of the prostate (Stage D2).

Breast Cancer: For the palliative treatment of advanced breast cancer in pre- and perimenopausal women whose tumor contains estrogen and/or progesterone receptors.

Benign Conditions: For the hormonal management of endometriosis, including pain relief and reduction of endometriotic lesions. Experience with Zoladex for the management of endometriosis has been limited to women 18 years of age and older, treated for 6 months.

For use as an endometrial thinning agent prior to endometrial ablation.

Contraindications: In patients with hypersensitivity to the drug or any of its components.

Goserelin should not be administered to females having undiagnosed abnormal vaginal bleeding.

Pregnancy: Goserelin should not be used during pregnancy. As with other LHRH agonists it is not known whether goserelin causes fetal abnormalities in humans. Women of childbearing potential should be carefully examined before treatment to exclude pregnancy. Nonhormonal methods of contraception should be employed during therapy (see Precautions).

Lactation: The use of goserelin during breast-feeding is not recommended.

Warnings: General: Initially, goserelin transiently increases serum testosterone in males and serum estradiol in females and other gonadal hormones. Although not necessarily related, isolated cases of short-term worsening of signs and symptoms have been reported during the first 4 weeks of therapy. Worsening of the clinical condition may occasionally require discontinuation of therapy and/or surgical intervention.

Patients with Vertebral Metastases: During the first month of therapy with goserelin, patients with vertebral metastases who are thought to be at particular risk of spinal cord compression should be closely monitored (see Precautions).

Males: Patients with Genitourinary Tract Symptoms: During the first month of therapy with goserelin, patients at risk of developing ureteric obstruction should be closely monitored (see Precautions).

Induced Hypogonadism: Suppression of pituitary gonadotropins and gonadal hormone production will occur with continued administration of goserelin. These changes have been observed to reverse on discontinuation of therapy. However, whether the clinical symptoms of induced hypogonadism will reverse in all patients has not yet been established.

Precautions: Transient exacerbation of signs and symptoms: Worsening of bone pain and other signs and symptoms have been reported infrequently in males and to a lesser extent in females during the first month of therapy with goserelin (see Warnings). It is unclear whether there is any relationship between these clinical events and the initial rise in serum testosterone or estradiol levels observed during the first few days following administration of the first depot injection.

In those who reported an increase in bone pain, the pain ranged in intensity from mild to severe and required either symptomatic management, including non-narcotic analgesics or in some severe cases, narcotic analgesics.

Ureteric obstruction may develop in male patients with a history of obstructive uropathy. If spinal cord compression or renal impairment due to ureteric obstruction are present, or develop, specific standard treatment of these complications should be instituted.

Monitoring of Patients: During therapy with goserelin, patients should be routinely monitored by physical examinations and appropriate laboratory tests. In prostate cancer patients tumor markers such as prostatic acid phosphatase (PAP), prostatic specific antigen (PSA) or acid phosphatase could be monitored. Additionally, if deemed appropriate by the physician, serum testosterone or serum estradiol may be monitored; however, this is not routinely required.

In prostate cancer patients an assessment of bone lesions may require the use of bone scans. Prostatic lesions may be monitored by ultrasonography and/or CT scan in addition to digital rectal examination. The status of obstructive uropathy in males may be assessed and/or diagnosed using i.v. pyelography, ultrasonography or CT scan.

Changes in Bone Density: Since bone loss can be anticipated as part of natural menopause, it may also be expected to occur during a medically induced hypoestrogenic state caused by goserelin.

In patients receiving goserelin for the treatment of endometriosis, the addition of hormone replacement therapy (a daily estrogenic agent and a progestogenic agent) has been shown to reduce bone mineral density loss and vasomotor symptoms.

In patients with major risk factors for decreased bone mineral content such as chronic alcohol and/or tobacco use, presumed or strong family history of osteoporosis or chronic use of drugs that can reduce bone mass such as anticonvulsants or corticosteroids, goserelin may pose an additional risk. In these patients the risks and benefits must be weighed carefully before therapy with goserelin is instituted.

Use of goserelin for longer than the recommended 6 months or in the presence of other known risk factors for decreased bone mineral content may cause additional bone loss.

The use of LHRH agonists in men may cause a loss of bone mineral density.

Laboratory Tests: Although serum testosterone or serum estradiol may be elevated during the first few days after administration of the first depot, they return to normal within 1 week, and are suppressed by the end of 3 weeks. They remain suppressed throughout therapy with goserelin.

Prostate cancer tumor markers (PSA and PAP), are not routinely monitored in the first few days of therapy; however, if the cancer is responsive to goserelin therapy, then these levels, if elevated prior to the commencement of treatment, are usually reduced by the end of the first month.

Renal function tests, BUN and creatinine may rarely be elevated during the first few days of therapy in prostate cancer patients before returning to normal.

Diagnostic Interference: Administration of goserelin in therapeutic doses results in suppression of the pituitary-gonadal system. Normal function is usually restored approximately 8 weeks after the last dose of goserelin. Diagnostic tests of pituitary-gonadal function conducted during the treatment and within 8 weeks after discontinuation of goserelin therapy may therefore be misleading.

Allergic Reactions: Antibody formation has not been observed during administration of goserelin. Local reactions, such as mild bruising have been related to the trauma of the injection itself and not to the copolymer material of the depot or to the prolonged presence of goserelin at the site of depot injection.

Dependence Liability: There have been no reports of drug dependence following the use of goserelin.

Children: The safety and effectiveness of goserelin in children has not been established.

Pregnancy: Safe use of the drug in pregnancy has not been established, therefore a nonhormonal method of contraception should be used during treatment. Patients should be advised that if they miss or postpone a dose of goserelin, ovulation may occur with the potential for conception. If a patient becomes pregnant during treatment, she should discontinue treatment and consult her physician.

Fertility: Nearly 500 patients with endometriosis who have been treated with goserelin for 6 months were followed up for a further 1 year to assess fertility. Of these, 100 (20%) became pregnant.

One hundred and seventy seven of these patients had previously been considered infertile and of these 53 (30%) conceived. There is no evidence that pregnancy rates are enhanced or adversely affected by the use of goserelin in the post-treatment period.

There is no evidence to suggest that there is any problem associated with conception after the use of goserelin for 6 months.

Menses usually resumed within 8 weeks following completion of therapy. Rarely, some women may enter menopause during treatment with LHRH analogues and do not resume menses on cessation of therapy.

Duration of Endometriosis Treatment: The safety of treatment, as well as retreatment, beyond 6 months with goserelin has not been established.

Endometrial Thinning: The use of goserelin may cause an increase in cervical resistance. Therefore, care should be taken when dilating the cervix.

Adverse Effects: The adverse effects seen with goserelin are due primarily to its pharmacologic action of sex hormone suppression.

Changes in blood pressure, manifest as hypotension or hypertension, have been occasionally observed in patients administered goserelin. The changes are usually transient, resolving either during continued therapy or after cessation of therapy with goserelin. Such changes have rarely required medical intervention including withdrawal of goserelin treatment.

Rare incidences of hypersensitivity reactions, which may include some manifestations of anaphylaxis, have been reported.

Prostate Cancer Patients: Five hundred and eighteen (518) prostate patients who had not been previously treated and who entered into 14 open multicentre studies were monitored for adverse reactions to goserelin. The mean duration of treatment in these patients was 23 weeks.

The following reports from these clinical trials are considered to be possibly related to treatment with goserelin: hot flushes (51%), decreased libido (53%), decreased erections (57%), breast tenderness (3%), gynecomastia (2%), local intolerance at injection site (pain, erythema) (4%), and skin rash including erythema and urticaria (1.9%).

Also in these clinical studies, an initial rise in mean serum testosterone levels occurred during the first few days of treatment with goserelin. In a few instances, patients experienced a worsening of signs and symptoms, during the first month after initiation of therapy (see Warnings and Precautions). For these patients, this was usually an increase in bone pain (4.2%), however, isolated cases of ureteric obstruction (1.1%) and/or spinal cord compression (1.2%) have also been reported during the initial 4 weeks of goserelin therapy. The relationship of these observations to goserelin is unknown.

The potential for exacerbation of signs and symptoms during the first few weeks of treatment is a concern particularly in male patients with impending neurologic compromise and in patients with severe obstructive uropathy (see Warnings).

When 942 male patients treated with goserelin are considered, the adverse reactions listed below were reported to occur in less than 1% of patients with the exception of bone

Zoladex (cont'd)

pain (2.9%), increased alkaline phosphatase (2.4%) and nausea/vomiting (1.4%).

Possible adverse reactions reported in the 942 male patients were as follows:

Cardiovascular: thrombophlebitis, pulmonary embolism, edema, tachycardia, atrial fibrillation, angina pectoris, congestive cardiac failure, hypertension, myocardial infarction, deep vein thrombosis, palpitations, cerebrovascular accident, central retinal vein thrombosis.

Dermatologic: pruritus, skin rashes including erythema, eczema and urticaria, worsening of ecchymoses and hair growth.

Gastrointestinal: dry mouth/thirst, polydipsia, nausea, vomiting, hematemesis, diarrhea, pain in abdomen, constipation, anorexia, flatulence, intolerance to alcohol, gingival atrophy.

Hematologic/Lymphatic: neutropenia, neutrophilia, lymphocytopenia, lymphocytosis, lowered protein/albumin and palpable lymph nodes.

Musculoskeletal: bone pain, signs and symptoms of spinal cord compression, (e.g., paresthesia, paraparesis, paraplegia), muscular fatigue, myopathy, pain (other than bone), hyperesthesia, arthritis, suprapubic pain, polyarthralgia and neurological troubles with lower limbs.

CNS: vertigo, headaches, blackouts, flashes of light, decreased/blurred vision, glaucoma, drowsiness, lassitude, lethargy, malaise, disorientation, mental confusion, sensitivity to noise, taste disturbance.

Urogenital: renal impairment, renal tract obstruction, urinary retention, chronic renal failure, hydronephrosis, nocturia, testicular atrophy.

Laboratory Tests: elevation of liver function test parameters, (e.g., gamma GT, alanine aminotransferase, aspartate aminotransferase, and bilirubin), raised alkaline phosphatase, serum calcium and hyperkalemia.

Miscellaneous: fever, sore throat, influenza, herpes zoster, gangrene, decreased appetite.

Breast Cancer Patients: The adverse event profile for women with advanced breast cancer treated with goserelin is consistent with the profile described for women treated with goserelin for endometriosis. In a controlled clinical trial (SWOG-8692) comparing goserelin with oophorectomy in premenopausal and perimenopausal women with advanced breast cancer, the following events were reported at a frequency of 5% or greater in either treatment group regardless of causality. See Table I.

Table I—Zoladex

Adverse Reactions—Breast Cancer Patients

Adverse Reactions	Zoladex n=57 %	Oophorectomy n=55 %
Hot flashes	70	47
Tumor flare	23	4
Nausea	11	7
Edema	5	0
Malaise/fatigue/lethargy	5	2
Vomiting	4	7

In the Phase II clinical trial program in 333 pre- and perimenopausal women with advanced breast cancer, hot flashes and decreased libido were assessed by specific patient inquiry. Hot flashes occurred in 75.9% of the 203 women in whom they were not present at baseline and decreased libido occurred in 47.7% of the 194 women with libido present at baseline. These events reflect the pharmacological actions of goserelin.

Injection site reactions were reported in less than 1% of patients.

Benign Conditions: In controlled clinical trials, comparing goserelin every 28 days with danazol daily for the treatment of endometriosis, Table II lists events **elicited by direct questioning** reported at a frequency of 5% or more.

From the endometriosis trials and other supporting safety studies, other adverse reactions, not listed in Table II, elicited at a frequency of 1% or more are shown below. The relationship of these possible adverse reactions to therapy with goserelin is unknown.

Whole Body: allergic reaction, chest pain, fever, malaise.

Cardiovascular: hemorrhage, hypertension, migraine, palpitations, tachycardia.

Digestive: anorexia, constipation, diarrhea, dry mouth, dyspepsia, flatulence.

Table II—Zoladex

Adverse Reactions Reported in Endometriosis Trials

Adverse Reactions	Zoladex Treated n=411 %	Danazol Treated n=207 %
Hot Flushes	96	67
Vaginitis (Vaginal Dryness)	75	43
Headache	75	63
Emotional Lability (Mood Swings)	60	56
Decrease Libido	61	44
Sweating	45	30
Depression	54	48
Acne	42	55
Breast Atrophy	33	42
Seborrhea	26	52
Peripheral Edema	21	34
Breast Enlargement	18	15
Pelvic Symptoms	18	23
Pain	17	16
Dyspareunia	14	5
Libido Increased	12	19
Infection	13	11
Asthenia	11	13
Nausea	8	14
Hirsutism	7	15
Insomnia	11	4
Breast Pain	7	4
Abdominal Pain	7	7
Back Pain	7	13
Flu Syndrome	5	5
Dizziness	6	4
Application Site Reaction	6	—
Voice Alterations	3	8
Pharyngitis	5	2
Hair Disorders	4	11
Myalgia	3	11
Nervousness	3	5
Weight Gain	3	23
Leg Cramps	2	6
Increased Appetite	2	5
Pruritus	2	6
Hypertonia	1	10

Hemic and Lympatic: ecchymosis.

Metabolic and Nutritional: edema.

Musculoskeletal: arthralgia, joint disorder.

Nervous: anxiety, paresthesia, somnolence, thinking abnormal.

Respiratory: bronchitis, cough increased, epistaxis, pharyngitis, rhinitis, sinusitis.

Skin: alopecia, dry skin, rash, pruritus, skin discoloration.

Special Senses: amblyopia, dry eyes.

Urogenital: dysmenorrhea, urinary frequency, urinary tract infection, vaginal hemorrhage.

Changes in Bone Mineral Density: After 6 months of goserelin treatment, 97 female patients treated with goserelin showed an average 4.6% decrease of vertebral trabecular bone mineral density (BMD) as compared to pretreatment values. BMD was measured by dual-photon absorptiometry or dual energy x-ray absorptiometry. Forty-four of these patients were assessed for BMD loss 6 months after the completion (post-therapy) of the 6 month therapy period. Data from these patients showed an average 2.6% BMD loss compared to pretreatment values. Nine of the 97 patients were assessed for BMD at 12 months post-therapy. Data from these patients showed an average decrease of 2.5% in BMD compared to pretreatment values. These data suggest a possibility of partial reversibility.

Changes in Laboratory Values: Plasma enzymes: elevation of liver enzymes (AST, ALT) have been reported in less than 1% of all female patients. There was no other evidence of abnormal liver function. Causality between these changes and goserelin have not been established.

Lipids: In a controlled trial, goserelin therapy resulted in a minor, but statistically significant effect on serum lipids. In patients treated for endometriosis at 6 months following initiation of therapy, goserelin treatment resulted in mean increases in LDL cholesterol of 0.55 mmol/L and HDL cholesterol of 0.07 mmol/L. Triglycerides increased by 0.09 mmol/L as well as total cholesterol by 0.65 mmol/L. At the end of 6 months of treatment, HDL cholesterol fractions (HDL_2 and HDL_3) were increased by 0.05 mmol/L and 0.02 mmol/L, respectively.

In the pivotal trials for endometrial thinning (n=258), the adverse reaction profile for goserelin was similar to that seen in the endometriosis trials, however the frequency was generally lower.

Overdose: Symptoms and Treatment: The pharmacologic properties of goserelin and its mode of delivery make accidental or intentional overdosage unlikely. There is no experience of overdosage from the clinical trials, but animal studies indicate that no increased pharmacologic effect would occur in man with higher doses or more frequent administration than those recommended. S.C. doses of the drug as high as 1 mg/kg/day in rats and dogs produced no nonendocrine related sequelae; this dose is approximately 400 times that proposed for human use. If overdosage occurs, this should be managed symptomatically.

Dosage: Administer s.c. every 28 days into the anterior abdominal wall following the procedure recommended on the package leaflet (see Instructions for Use).

Although, isolated cases of vaginal spotting or bleeding during treatment have been reported, this is not associated with lack of pharmacodynamic effect in most instances. The majority of patients become amenorrheic within 8 weeks of starting treatment. In the small number of women who experience continued menstrual bleeding, estradiol blood levels should be measured. If menstrual bleeding persists and estradiol measurements correspond to postmenopausal values, appropriate diagnostic measures should be undertaken to rule out an intrauterine pathology.

In clinical studies, subjects with impaired renal function (creatinine clearance <20 mL/min) had a mean serum elimination half-life of 12.1 hours for the drug compared to 4.2 hours for male subjects with normal renal function (creatinine clearance >70 mL/min). This increase of approximately 8 hours in serum half-life is insufficient to warrant extending the 28-day dosing interval of the 3.6 mg depot, but will lead to modestly higher serum concentrations of the drug in such patients. No dose adjustment, therefore, is necessary for patients with renal failure.

Hepatic impairment does not compromise the clearance of goserelin, therefore, a dosage adjustment is not needed for patients with hepatic impairment.

Endometrial Thinning: For use as an endometrial thinning agent prior to endometrial ablation, goserelin should be administered as 2 depots, 4 weeks apart, with surgery planned for between 0 and 2 weeks after the second depot injection.

Instructions for Use: **Caution: Do not depress plunger until Step 5. Read all instructions before use.** Refer to package leaflet for diagrams.

1. Swab abdominal injection site.
2. Open pouch at arrows and remove syringe. **Do not remove red clip.** Check that the depot is present in the window.
3. Remove red clip taking care not to accidentally express depot. Remove needle cover. **Do not depress the plunger.**
4. **Correct** grip: fingers around barrel. Insert needle into loosely gathered fold of skin.
5. Depress plunger fully to inject depot. Cover injection site with a sterile dressing.
6. **Incorrect** grip and angle of presentation for needle insertion.

Information for the Patient: See Blue Section—Information for the Patient "Zoladex".

Supplied: Each sterile, ready-to-use syringe with 16 gauge needle contains: goserelin 3.6 mg (as goserelin acetate) and D-L Lactide-glycolide copolymer to total weight 18.0 mg (as a cylindrical, biodegradable, biocompatible rod). Sterile pouches of 1 syringe for single s.c. injection. Protect from light and moisture. Store in the intact package below 25°C.

Reviewed 1999

ZOLADEX® LA

Zeneca

Goserelin Acetate

Luteinizing Hormone-Releasing Hormone Analog (LHRH Analog)

Pharmacology: Goserelin is a synthetic decapeptide analog of gonadotropin releasing hormone (GnRH or LHRH). When given acutely, goserelin stimulates the release of pituitary luteinizing hormone (LH) from the pituitary gland. However, following chronic administration, goserelin is a potent inhibitor of gonadotropin production resulting in gonadal and consequently, accessory sex organ regression. This effect is the basis for the inhibition of growth of chemically-induced rat mammary tumors and transplantable rat prostate and pituitary tumors.

In animals and man, following an initial stimulation of pituitary LH secretion and a transient elevation in serum testosterone in males, chronic administration results in inhibition of gonadotropin secretion. Approximately 21 days after the initiation of therapy, a sustained suppression of pituitary LH results in the reduction in serum testosterone levels to a range normally seen in surgically castrated men. This suppression of testosterone is then maintained on repeat administration of goserelin.

Zoladex LA is a depot formulation of goserelin acetate dispersed in a cylindrical rod of biodegradable and biocompatible blend of high and low molecular weight range D-L Lactide-glycolide copolymers.

Administration of Zoladex LA every 12 weeks ensures that exposure to goserelin is maintained with no clinically significant accumulation. Goserelin is poorly protein bound and has a serum elimination half-life of 2 to 4 hours in subjects with normal renal function. The half-life is increased in patients with impaired renal function. For the compound given in a 10.8 mg depot formulation every 12 weeks this change will not lead to any accumulation. Hence, no change in dosing is necessary in these patients. There is no significant change in the clearance of goserelin in patients with hepatic impairment with normal renal function.

Indications: For the palliative treatment of patients with hormone-dependent advanced carcinoma of the prostate (Stage D2).

Contraindications: Patients with hypersensitivity to the drug or any of its components.

Warnings: General: Initially, goserelin transiently increases serum testosterone in males. Although not necessarily related, isolated cases of short-term worsening of signs and symptoms have been reported during the first 4 weeks of therapy.

Worsening of the clinical condition may occasionally require discontinuation of therapy and/or surgical intervention.

Zoladex LA is not indicated for use in females, since there is insufficient evidence of reliable suppression of serum estradiol. For female patients requiring treatment with goserelin, refer to the prescribing information for Zoladex (3.6 mg depot).

Goserelin is not indicated for use in children, as safety and efficacy have not been established in this group of patients.

Patients with Vertebral Metastases: During the first month of therapy with goserelin, patients with vertebral metastases who are thought to be of particular risk of spinal cord compression should be closely monitored (see Precautions).

Patients with Genitourinary Tract Symptoms: During the first month of therapy with goserelin, patients at risk of developing ureteric obstruction should be closely monitored (see Precautions).

Induced Hypogonadism: Suppression of pituitary gonadotropins and gonadal hormone production will occur with continued administration of goserelin. These changes have been observed to reverse on discontinuation of therapy. However, whether the clinical symptoms of induced hypogonadism will reverse in all patients has not yet been established.

Precautions: Transient Exacerbation of Signs and Symptoms: Worsening of bone pain and other signs and symptoms have been reported infrequently in males during the first month of therapy with goserelin (see Warnings). Initially, goserelin like other LHRH agonists transiently increases serum testosterone concentrations. In men by around 21 days after the first depot injection, testosterone concentrations have typically fallen to within the castrate range and remain suppressed with treatment every 12 weeks. It is unclear whether there is any relationship between these clinical events and the initial rise in serum testosterone observed during the first few days following administration of the first depot injection.

Ureteric obstruction may develop in male patients with a history of obstructive uropathy. If spinal cord compression or renal impairment due to ureteric obstruction are present, or develop, specific standard treatment of these complications should be instituted.

Monitoring of Patients: During therapy with goserelin, patients should be routinely monitored by physical examinations and appropriate laboratory tests. In prostate cancer patients tumor markers such as prostatic acid phosphatase (PAP), prostatic specific antigen (PSA) or acid phosphatase could be monitored. Additionally, if deemed appropriate by the physician, serum testosterone may be monitored; however, this is not routinely required.

In prostate cancer patients an assessment of bone lesions may require the use of bone scans. Prostatic lesions may be monitored by ultrasonography and/or CT scan in addition to digital rectal examination. The status of obstructive uropathy in males may be assessed and/or diagnosed using i.v. pyelography, ultrasonography or CT scan.

Prostate cancer tumor markers (PSA and PAP) are not routinely monitored in the first few days of therapy; however, if the cancer is responsive to goserelin therapy, then these levels, if elevated prior to the commencement of treatment, are usually reduced by the end of the first month.

Renal function tests, blood urea nitrogen and creatinine may rarely be elevated during the first few days of therapy in prostate cancer patients before returning to normal.

Changes in Bone Density: Some bone loss can be anticipated as part of the natural aging process. It may also be expected to occur during medically induced hypoandrogenic state caused by long-term goserelin treatment.

In patients with significant risk factors for decreased bone mineral content such as chronic alcohol and/or tobacco use, presumed or family history of osteoporosis or chronic use of drugs that can reduce bone mass such as corticosteroids or anticonvulsants, goserelin may pose an additional risk. In these patients the risks and benefits must be weighed carefully before goserelin therapy is initiated.

Diagnostic Interference: Administration of goserelin results in suppression of pituitary-gonadal system. Diagnostic tests of pituitary-gonadal function conducted during and subsequent to the treatment period may therefore be misleading.

Allergic Reactions: Antibody formation has not been observed during administration of goserelin. Local reactions, such as mild bruising have been related to the trauma of the injection itself and not to the copolymer material of the depot or to the prolonged presence of goserelin at the site of depot injection.

Dependence Liability: There have been no reports of drug dependence following the use of goserelin.

Children: Goserelin is not indicated for use in children (see Warnings).

Pregnancy and Fertility: Zoladex LA is not indicated for use in females (see Warnings).

Adverse Effects: The adverse effects seen with goserelin are due primarily to its pharmacological action of sex hormone suppression.

Pharmacological effects include hot flushes and a decrease in potency, seldom requiring withdrawal of therapy. Breast swelling and tenderness have been noted infrequently. Initially, prostate cancer patients may experience a temporary increase in bone pain, which can be managed symptomatically. Isolated cases of spinal cord compression have been recorded.

Changes in blood pressure, manifest as hypotension or hypertension, have been occasionally observed in patients administered goserelin. The changes are usually transient, resolving either during continued therapy or after cessation of therapy with goserelin. Such changes have rarely required medical intervention including withdrawal of goserelin treatment.

Although not reported by patients in the clinical trial program of Zoladex LA, following the administration of Zoladex (3.6 mg depot), arthralgia, skin rashes which are generally mild and often regress without discontinuation of therapy, and isolated cases of ureteric obstruction have been recorded.

Rare incidences of hypersensitivity reactions, which may include some manifestations of anaphylaxis, have been reported.

The potential for exacerbation of signs and symptoms during the first few weeks of treatment is a concern particularly in male patients with impending neurologic compromise and in patients with severe obstructive uropathy (see Warnings).

Two controlled clinical trials were conducted with 157 patients, comparing treatment with goserelin 10.8 mg versus goserelin 3.6 mg depots. During the comparative phase, patients were randomized to receive either a single 10.8 mg depot or 3 consecutive 3.6 mg depots (1 every 4 weeks) over this initial 12 week period. The only adverse event reported in greater than 5% of these patients during this phase was hot flushes, with the goserelin 10.8 mg group having an incidence of 47% and the goserelin 3.6 mg group having 48%.

From weeks 12 to 48 all patients were treated with 1 Zoladex LA depot every 12 weeks. During this noncomparative phase, the following adverse events were reported in greater than 5% of patients; hot flushes [vasodilation] (63.7%), general pain (14%), gynecomastia (8.3%), pelvic pain (5.7%), bone pain (5.7%) and asthenia (5.1%).

The following adverse events reported in greater than 1%, but less than 5% of 157 patients treated with Zoladex LA depot every 12 weeks are shown in Table I. Some of these would be expected in a proportion of the elderly population.

Overdose: Symptoms and Treatment: There is no human experience of overdosage. Animal tests suggest that no effect other than the intended therapeutic effects on sex hormone concentrations and on the reproductive tract will be evident with higher doses of goserelin. If overdosage occurs, this should be managed symptomatically.

Table I—Zoladex LA

Adverse Events in Controlled Studies with an Incidence of ≥1% but less than 5%

	Weeks 0 to 12		Week 12 onwards	
	Zoladex 10.8 mg (N=78)		Zoladex 10.8 mg (N=157)*	
Body System/ Adverse Events	**N**	**(%)**	**N**	**(%)**
Whole Body				
Abdominal pain	0	(0.0)	2	(1.3)
Aggravation reaction	0	(0.0)	5	(3.2)
Back pain	0	(0.0)	2	(1.3)
Flu syndrome	1	(1.3)	0	(0.0)
Headache	0	(0.0)	3	(1.9)
Infection	0	(0.0)	2	(1.3)
Sepsis	0	(0.0)	4	(2.5)
Cardiovascular				
Angina pectoris	1	(1.3)	1	(0.6)
Cerebral ischemia	0	(0.0)	2	(1.3)
Cerebrovascular accident	0	(0.0)	2	(1.3)
Heart failure	0	(0.0)	3	(1.9)
Pulmonary embolus	0	(0.0)	2	(1.3)
Varicose veins	1	(1.3)	0	(0.0)
Digestive				
Diarrhea	1	(1.3)	4	(2.5)
Hematemesis	1	(1.3)	0	(0.0)
Endocrine				
Diabetes mellitus	0	(0.0)	2	(1.3)
Hemic and Lymphatic				
Anemia	0	(0.0)	3	(1.9)
Metabolic and Nutritional				
Peripheral edema	2	(2.6)	5	(3.2)
Nervous System				
Dizziness	0	(0.0)	5	(3.2)
Paresthesia	2	(2.6)	2	(1.3)
Urinary retention	0	(0.0)	2	(1.3)
Respiratory				
Cough increased	0	(0.0)	4	(2.5)
Dyspnea	0	(0.0)	6	(3.8)
Pneumonia	0	(0.0)	2	(1.3)
Skin and Appendages				
Herpes simplex	1	(1.3)	1	(0.6)
Pruritus	0	(0.0)	2	(1.3)
Urogenital				
Bladder neoplasm	1	(1.3)	1	(0.6)
Breast pain	2	(2.6)	7	(4.5)
Hematuria	1	(1.3)	3	(1.9)
Impotence	2	(2.6)	2	(1.3)
Urinary frequency	0	(0.0)	2	(1.3)
Urinary incontinence	0	(0.0)	2	(1.3)
Urinary tract disorder	1	(1.3)	5	(3.2)
Urinary tract infection	3	(3.8)	7	(4.5)
Urination impaired	0	(0.0)	3	(1.9)

***Adverse events occurring in the comparative phase of these studies (weeks 0 to 12) are presented separately to data from the noncomparative phase (week 12 onwards), as the differences in the 2 periods of observation made a direct comparison inappropriate.**

Dosage: Adult Males (including the elderly): 1 depot containing goserelin acetate equivalent to 10.8 mg goserelin, should be injected s.c. into the anterior abdominal wall every 12 weeks following the procedure recommended on the instruction card (see Instructions for Use on card attached to sterile pouch). While the 12-week schedule should be adhered to, a delay of a few days is permissible (see Pharmacology).

In patients with impaired renal function, the serum half-life is increased (serum half-life is 2 to 4 hours in patients with normal renal function). When goserelin is given every 12 weeks, this change will not lead to any accumulation hence, no change in dosing is necessary.

Hepatic impairment does not compromise the clearance of goserelin; therefore, a dosage adjustment is not needed for patients with hepatic impairment.

Zoladex LA is not indicated for use in females, since there is insufficient evidence of reliable suppression of serum estradiol. For female patients requiring treatment with goserelin, refer to the prescribing information for Zoladex (3.6 mg depot) (see Warnings).

Goserelin is not indicated for use in children (see Warnings).

Instructions for Use (see package insert for illustrations): Caution: Do not depress plunger until Step 5. Read all instructions

Zoladex LA (cont'd)

before use. 1. Swab abdominal injection site. 2. Open pouch at arrows and remove syringe. **Do not remove blue clip.** Check the depot is present in the window. 3. Remove blue clip taking care not to accidentally express depot. Remove needle cover. **Do not depress the plunger.** 4. **Correct** grip, fingers around barrel. Insert needle into loosely gathered fold of skin. 5. Depress plunger fully to inject depot. Cover injection site with a sterile dressing. 6. **Incorrect** grip and angle of presentation for needle insertion.

Information for the Patient: See Blue Section—Information for the Patient "Zoladex LA".

Supplied: Each depot contains: goserelin acetate equivalent to goserelin 10.8 mg. The depot is supplied as a cylindrical rod of biodegradable and biocompatible D-L Lactide-glycolide copolymers and is presented in a sterile ready-to-use syringe with a 14 gauge needle for a single s.c. injection. The entire syringe is packaged in a sterile pouch. Instructions for administration, once every 12 weeks, are attached. Protect from light and moisture. Store in the intact package between 2 and 25°C.

Reviewed 1997

ZOLOFT™ ℞

Pfizer

Sertraline HCl

Antidepressant—Antipanic—Antiobsessional Agent

Pharmacology: The mechanism of action of sertraline is presumed to be linked to its ability to inhibit the neuronal reuptake of serotonin. It has only very weak effects on norepinephrine and dopamine neuronal reuptake. At clinical doses, sertraline blocks the uptake of serotonin into human platelets.

Like most clinically effective antidepressants, sertraline downregulates brain norepinephrine and serotonin receptors in animals. In receptor binding studies, sertraline has no significant affinity for adrenergic (alpha$_1$, alpha$_2$ and beta), cholinergic, GABA, dopaminergic, histaminergic, serotonergic (5-HT1A, 5-HT1B, 5-HT2) or benzodiazepine binding sites.

In placebo-controlled studies in normal volunteers, sertraline did not cause sedation and did not interfere with psychomotor performance.

Pharmacokinetics: Following multiple oral once-daily doses of 200 mg, the mean peak plasma concentration (C_{max}) of sertraline is 0.19 µg/mL occurring between 6 to 8 hours post-dose. The area under the plasma concentration time curve is 2.8 mg h/L. For desmethylsertraline, C_{max} is 0.14 µg/mL, the half-life 65 hours and the area under the curve 2.3 mg h/L. Following single or multiple oral once-daily doses of 50 to 400 mg/day the average terminal elimination half-life is approximately 26 hours. Linear dose proportionality has been demonstrated over the clinical dose range of 50 to 200 mg/day.

Food appears to increase the bioavailability by about 40%: it is recommended that sertraline be administered with meals.

Sertraline is extensively metabolized to N-desmethylsertraline, which shows negligible pharmacological activity. Both sertraline and N-desmethylsertraline undergo oxidative deamination and subsequent reduction, hydroxylation and glucuronide conjugation. Biliary excretion of metabolites is significant. Approximately 98% of sertraline is plasma protein bound. The interactions between sertraline and other highly protein bound drugs have not been fully evaluated (see Precautions).

The pharmacokinetics of sertraline itself appear to be similar in young and elderly subjects. Plasma levels of N-desmethylsertraline show a 3-fold elevation in the elderly following multiple dosing, however, the clinical significance of this observation is not known.

Analyses for gender effects on outcome did not suggest any differential responsiveness on the basis of sex.

Liver and Renal Disease: The pharmacokinetics of sertraline in patients with significant hepatic or renal dysfunction have not been determined.

Clinical Trials: Panic Disorder: Four placebo-controlled clinical trials have been performed to investigate the efficacy of sertraline in panic disorder: 2 flexible-dose studies and 2 fixed-dose studies. At the last week of treatment (week 10 or 12), both flexible-dose studies and one of the fixed-dose studies showed statistically significant differences from placebo in favor of sertraline in terms of mean change from baseline in the total number of full panic attacks (last observation carried forward analysis). As the flexible-dose studies were of identical protocol, data for these investigations can be pooled. The mean number of full panic attacks at baseline was 6.2/week (N=167) in the sertraline group and 5.4/week in the placebo group (N=175). At week 10 (last observation carried forward analysis), the mean changes from baseline were -4.9/week and -2.5/week for the sertraline and placebo groups, respectively. The proportion of patients having no panic attacks at the final evaluation was 57% in the placebo group and 69% in the sertraline group. The mean daily dose administered at the last week of treatment was approximately 120 mg (range: 25 to 200 mg) in the flexible-dose studies. No clear dose-dependency has been demonstrated over the 50 to 200 mg/day dose range investigated in the fixed-dose studies.

Obsessive-Compulsive Disorder: Five placebo-controlled clinical trials of 8 to 16 weeks in duration have been performed to investigate the efficacy of sertraline in obsessive-compulsive disorder: 4 flexible-dose studies (50 to 200 mg/day) and 1 fixed-dose study (50, 100 and 200 mg/day). Results for 3 of the 4 flexible-dose studies and the 50 and 200 mg dose groups of the fixed-dose study were supportive of differences from placebo in favor of sertraline in terms of mean change from baseline to endpoint on the Yale-Brown Obsessive-Compulsive Scale and/or the National Institute of Mental Health Obsessive-Compulsive Scale (last observation carried forward analysis). No clear dose-dependency was demonstrated over the 50 to 200 mg/day dose range investigated in the fixed-dose studies. In the flexible-dose studies, the mean daily dose administered at the last week of treatment ranged from 124 to 180 mg.

Indications: Depression: For the symptomatic relief of depressive illness. However, the antidepressant action of sertraline in hospitalized depressed patients has not been adequately studied.

A placebo-controlled European study carried out over 44 weeks, in patients who were responders to sertraline has indicated that sertraline may be useful in continuation treatment, suppressing re-emergence of depressive symptoms.

However, because of methodological limitations, these findings on continuation treatment have to be considered tentative at this time.

Panic Disorder: For the symptomatic relief of panic disorder, with or without agoraphobia.

The efficacy of sertraline was established in 10-week and 12-week controlled trials of patients with panic disorder as defined according to DSM-III-R criteria.

The effectiveness of sertraline in long-term use for the symptomatic relief of panic disorder (i.e., for more than 12 weeks) has not been systematically evaluated in placebo-controlled trials. Therefore, the physician who elects to use sertraline for extended periods should periodically re-evaluate the long-term usefulness of the drug for the individual patient.

Obsessive-Compulsive Disorder: For the symptomatic relief of obsessive-compulsive disorder (OCD). The obsessions or compulsions must be experienced as intrusive, markedly distressing, time-consuming, or significantly interfering with the person's social or occupational functioning.

The effectiveness of sertraline in long-term use for the symptomatic relief of OCD (i.e., for more than 12 weeks) has not been systematically evaluated in placebo-controlled trials. Therefore, the physician who elects to use sertraline for extended periods should periodically re-evaluate the long-term usefulness of the drug for the individual patient.

Contraindications: In patients with known hypersensitivity to the drug.

MAO Inhibitors: Cases of serious, sometimes fatal, reactions have been reported in patients receiving sertraline in combination with an MAO inhibitor, including the selective MAO inhibitor, selegiline and the reversible MAO inhibitor (reversible inhibitor of MAO-RIMA), moclobemide. Some cases presented with features resembling the serotonin syndrome. Similar cases, have been reported with other antidepressants during combined treatment with an MAO inhibitor and in patients who have recently discontinued an antidepressant and have been started on an MAO inhibitor. Symptoms of a drug interaction between an SSRI and an MAO inhibitor include: hyperthermia, rigidity, myoclonus, autonomic instability with possible rapid fluctuations of vital signs, mental status changes that include confusion, irritability, and extreme agitation progressing to delirium and coma. Therefore, sertraline should not be used in combination with an MAO inhibitor or within 14 days of discontinuing treatment with an MAO inhibitor. Similarly, at least 14 days should elapse after discontinuing sertraline treatment before starting an MAO inhibitor.

Warnings: MAO Inhibitors: See Contraindications.

Precautions: Activation of Mania/Hypomania: During clinical testing in depressed patients, hypomania or mania occurred in approximately 0.6% of sertraline-treated patients. Activation of mania/hypomania has also been reported in a small proportion of patients with Major Affective Disorder treated with other marketed antidepressants.

Seizure: Sertraline has not been evaluated in patients with seizure disorders. These patients were excluded from clinical studies during the product's premarket testing. No seizures were observed among approximately 3 000 patients treated with sertraline in the development program for depression. However, 4 patients out of approximately 1 800 (220 <18 years of age) exposed during the development program for obsessive-compulsive disorder experienced seizures representing a crude incidence of 0.2%. Three of these patients were adolescents, 2 with a seizure disorder and 1 with a family history of seizure disorder, none of whom were receiving anticonvulsant medication. Accordingly, sertraline should be introduced with care in patients with a seizure disorder.

Suicide: The possibility of a suicide attempt is inherent in depression and may persist until significant remission occurs. Therefore, high risk patients should be closely supervised throughout therapy and consideration should be given to the possible need for hospitalization. In order to minimize the opportunity for overdosage, prescriptions for sertraline should be written for the smallest quantity of drug consistent with good patient management.

Because of the well-established comorbidity between both obsessive-compulsive disorder and depression and panic disorder and depression, the same precautions should be observed when treating patients with obsessive-compulsive disorder and panic disorder.

Occupational Hazards: Any psychoactive drug may impair judgment, thinking, or motor skills, and patients should be advised to avoid driving a car or operating hazardous machinery until they are reasonably certain that the drug treatment does not affect them adversely.

Patients with Concomitant Illness: General: Clinical experience with sertraline in patients with certain concomitant systemic illnesses is limited. Caution is advisable in using sertraline in patients with diseases or conditions that could affect metabolism or hemodynamic responses.

Cardiovascular Conditions: Sertraline has not been evaluated or used to any appreciable extent in patients with a recent history of myocardial infarction or unstable heart disease. However, the ECGs of 1 006 patients who received sertraline in double-blind trials were evaluated and the data indicate that sertraline is not associated with the development of clinically significant ECG abnormalities.

In placebo-controlled trials, the frequency of clinically noticeable changes (±15 to 20 mmHg) in blood pressure was similar in patients treated with either sertraline or placebo.

Hepatic Dysfunction: Sertraline is extensively metabolized by the liver. A single dose pharmacokinetic study in subjects with mild, stable cirrhosis demonstrated a prolonged elimination half-life and increased AUC in comparison to normal subjects. The use of sertraline in patients with hepatic disease must be approached with caution. If sertraline is administered to patients with hepatic impairment, a lower or less frequent dose should be considered.

Renal Dysfunction: Sertraline is extensively metabolized and excretion of unchanged drug in the urine is a minor route of elimination. The pharmacokinetics of sertraline have not been studied in patients with renal impairment and, until adequate numbers of patients with mild, moderate or severe renal impairment have been evaluated during chronic treatment with sertraline, it should be used with caution in such patients.

Carcinogenesis: In carcinogenicity studies in CD-1 mice, sertraline at doses up to 40 mg/kg produces a dose-related increase in the incidence of liver adenomas in male mice. Liver adenomas have a very variable rate of spontaneous occurrence in the CD-1 mouse. The clinical significance of these findings is unknown.

Pregnancy and *Lactation:* The safety of sertraline during pregnancy and lactation has not been established and therefore, it should not be used in women of childbearing potential or nursing mothers, unless, in the opinion of the physician, the potential benefits to the patient outweigh the possible hazards to the fetus. There have been isolated reports of reactions such as tremors, jitteriness, restlessness, hypertonia, hyperreflexia and difficulty breathing in neonates whose mothers had been treated with sertraline during pregnancy and in an infant whose mother discontinued sertraline treatment during breast-feeding. However, causal relationship between sertraline treatment and the emergence of these events has not been established.

Labor and Delivery: The effect of sertraline on labor and delivery in humans is unknown.

Children: The safety and effectiveness of sertraline in children below the age of 18 have not been established.

Geriatrics: 462 elderly patients (≥65 years) with depressive illness have participated in multiple-dose therapeutic studies with sertraline. The pattern of adverse reactions in the elderly was comparable to that in younger patients.

Hyponatremia: Several cases of hyponatremia have been reported and appeared to be reversible when sertraline was discontinued. Some cases were possibly due to the syndrome of inappropriate antidiuretic hormone secretion. The majority of these occurences have been in elderly individuals, some in patients taking diuretics or who were otherwise volume-depleted.

Platelet Function: There have been rare reports of altered platelet function and/or abnormal results from laboratory studies in patients taking sertraline. While there have been reports of abnormal bleeding or purpura in several patients taking sertraline, it is unclear whether sertraline had a causative role.

Drug Interactions: CNS Active Drugs: Sertraline (200 mg daily) did not potentiate the effects of carbamazepine, haloperidol or phenytoin on cognitive and psychomotor performance in healthy subjects, however the risk of using sertraline in combination with other CNS active drugs has not been systematically evaluated. Consequently, caution is advised if the concomitant administration of sertraline and such drugs is required.

Serotonergic Drugs: There is limited controlled experience regarding the optimal timing of switching from other antidepressants and antipanic agents to sertraline. Care and prudent medical judgment should be exercised when switching, particularly from long-acting agents. The duration of washout period which should intervene before switching from one selective serotonin reuptake inhibitor (SSRI) to another has not been established.

Coadministration with tryptophan may lead to a high incidence of serotonin-associated side effects.

There is no experience with the concomitant use of sertraline and tryptophan in depressed patients or patients with panic disorder. Until further data are available, serotonergic drugs, such as fenfluramine, should not be used concomitantly with sertraline.

Lithium: In placebo-controlled trials in normal volunteers, the coadministration of sertraline with lithium did not significantly alter lithium pharmacokinetics, but did result in an increase in tremor relative to placebo, indicating a possible pharmacodynamic interaction. As with other SSRIs, caution is recommended when coadministering sertraline with medications, such as lithium, which may act via serotonergic mechanisms.

MAO Inhibitors: See Contraindications.

Drugs Metabolized by P450 System: Drugs Metabolized by P450 3A4: In 2 separate in vivo interaction studies, sertraline was coadministered with cytochrome P450 3A4 substrates, terfenadine or carbamazepine, under steady-state conditions. The results of these studies demonstrated that sertraline coadministration did not increase plasma concentrations of terfenadine or carbamazepine. These data suggest that sertraline's extent of inhibition of P450 3A4 activity is not likely to be of clinical significance.

Drugs Metabolized by P450 2D6: Many antidepressants, e.g., the SSRIs, including sertraline and most tricyclic antidepressants, inhibit the biochemical activity of the drug metabolizing isozyme, cytochrome P450 2D6 (debrisoquin hydroxylase), and thus may increase the plasma concentration of coadministered drugs that are metabolized primarily by 2D6 and which have a narrow therapeutic index, e.g., the tricyclic antidepressants and the type Ic antiarrhythmics, propafenone and flecainide. There is variability among the antidepressants in the extent of clinically important P450 2D6 inhibition. In 2 drug interaction clinical trials using desipramine and the recommended starting SSRI doses in normal volunteers, the effect of sertraline was compared to 2 other SSRIs. In the first study, mean desipramine steady-state AUC increased by 23% and 380% during coadministration with sertraline and the comparative SSRI, respectively. In a second study using a different comparative SSRI, mean desipramine steady-state AUC increased by 37% and 421% during coadministration with sertraline and the comparative SSRI, respectively. These trial results indicate that the effect of sertraline was significantly less pronounced than that of the 2 comparative SSRIs. Nevertheless, concomitant use of a drug metabolized by P450 2D6 with sertraline, may require lower doses than are usually prescribed for the other drug. Furthermore, whenever sertraline is withdrawn from cotherapy, an increased dose of the coadministered drug may be required.

Electroconvulsive Therapy: There are no clinical studies with the combined use of electroconvulsive therapy (ECT) and sertraline.

Alcohol: Although sertraline did not potentiate the cognitive and psychomotor effects of alcohol in experiments with normal subjects, the concomitant use of sertraline and alcohol in depressed, panic disorder or OCD patients has not been studied and is not recommended.

Hypoglycemic Drugs: There are no controlled clinical trials with sertraline in diabetic patients treated with insulin or oral hypoglycemic drugs.

In a placebo-controlled trial in normal volunteers, the administration of sertraline for 22 days (dose was 200 mg/day for the final 13 days), caused a statistically significant 16% decrease in the clearance of tolbutamide following an i.v. dose of 1 000 mg. In a placebo-controlled study in normal volunteers, glibenclamide (5 mg) was given before and after administration of sertraline (200 mg/day final dose) to steady state or placebo. No significant changes were observed in the **total** plasma concentration of glibenclamide.

Hypoglycemia requiring dextrose infusion was observed in 1 patient treated with sertraline, glibenclamide, haloperidol, bisacodyl, ASA and flucloxacillin. The causal relationship to sertraline treatment was not firmly established. Nevertheless, close monitoring of glycemia in patients treated with sertraline and oral hypoglycemic drugs or insulin is recommended.

Digoxin: In a parallel placebo-controlled trial in normal volunteers (10 subjects/group), the administration of sertraline for 17 days (dose was 200 mg for the last 10 days) did not cause changes in the total plasma concentrations of digoxin except a decrease of T_{max} as compared to baseline.

Beta-blockers: There is no experience with the use of sertraline in hypertensive patients controlled by beta-blockers. In a placebo-controlled crossover study in normal volunteers, the effect of sertraline on the ß-adrenergic blocking activity of atenolol was assessed. The mean CD25s (the doses of isoproterenol required to increase heart rate by 25 bpm, the chronotropic dose 25 or CD25) and the average decreases in heart rate seen with atenolol during exercise test were not statistically different in the sertraline vs the placebo group. These data suggest that sertraline does not alter the ß-blocking action of atenolol.

Cimetidine: In a placebo-controlled crossover study in normal volunteers, the potential of cimetidine to alter the disposition of a single 100 mg dose of sertraline was assessed. The mean sertraline C_{max} and AUC were significantly higher in the cimetidine-treated group, as were the mean desmethylsertraline T_{max} and AUC. These data suggest that concomitant administration of cimetidine may inhibit the metabolism of sertraline and its metabolite, desmethylsertraline, and may result in a decrease in the clearance and first pass metabolism of sertraline, with a possible increase in drug-related side effects.

Diazepam: In a normal volunteer, double-blind, placebo-controlled study comparing the disposition of i.v.-administered diazepam before and after administration of sertraline (200 mg/day final dose) to steady state or placebo, there was a statistically significant 13% decrease relative to baseline in diazepam clearance for the sertraline group over that of the placebo group. These changes are of unknown clinical significance.

Warfarin: In a placebo-controlled study in healthy men comparing prothrombin time AUC (0-120 h) following single dosing with warfarin (0.75 mg/kg) before and after dosing to steady state with either sertraline (200 mg/day final dose) or placebo, there was a statistically significant mean increase in prothrombin time of 8% relative to baseline for sertraline compared to a 1% decrease for placebo. The normalization of prothrombin time for the sertraline group was delayed compared to the placebo group. The clinical significance of these changes are unknown. Accordingly, prothrombin time should be carefully monitored when sertraline therapy is initiated or stopped in patients receiving warfarin.

Because sertraline is highly bound to plasma protein, the administration of sertraline to a patient taking another drug which is tightly bound to protein may cause a shift in plasma concentrations potentially resulting in an adverse effect. Conversely adverse effects may result from displacement of protein-bound sertraline by other tightly bound drugs.

Microsomal Enzyme Induction: Sertraline was shown to induce hepatic enzymes as determined by the decrease of the antipyrine half-life. This degree of induction reflects a clinically insignificant change in hepatic metabolism.

Physical and Psychological Dependence: In a placebo-controlled, double-blind, randomized study of the comparative abuse liability of sertraline, alprazolam and d-amphetamine in humans, sertraline did not produce the positive subjective effects indicative of abuse potential, such as euphoria or drug liking, that were observed with the other two drugs. Premarketing clinical experience with sertraline did not reveal any

Table I—Zoloft

Treatment-Emergent Adverse Experience Incidence in Placebo-Controlled Clinical Tests[a]

Adverse Experience	Zoloft (N=861)	Placebo (N=853)
	Percent of Patients Reporting	
Autonomic Nervous System		
Mouth Dry	16.3	9.3
Sweating Increased	8.4	2.9
Cardiovascular		
Palpitations	3.5	1.6
Chest Pain	1.0	1.6
Central and Peripheral Nervous System		
Headache	20.3	19.0
Dizziness	11.7	6.7
Tremor	10.7	2.7
Paresthesia	2.0	1.8
Hypoesthesia	1.7	0.6
Twitching	1.4	0.1
Hypertonia	1.3	0.4
Skin and Appendages		
Rash	2.1	1.5
Gastrointestinal		
Nausea	26.1	11.8
Diarrhea/Loose Stools	17.7	9.3
Constipation	8.4	6.3
Dyspepsia	6.0	2.0
Vomiting	3.8	1.8
Flatulence	3.3	2.5
Anorexia	2.8	1.6
Abdominal Pain	2.4	2.2
Appetite Increased	1.3	0.9
General		
Fatigue	10.6	8.1
Hot Flushes	2.2	0.5
Fever	1.6	0.6
Back Pain	1.5	0.9
Metabolic and Nutritional		
Thirst	1.4	0.9
Musculoskeletal		
Myalgia	1.7	1.5
Psychiatric		
Insomnia	16.4	8.8
Sexual Dysfunction–Male[b]	15.5	2.2
Somnolence	13.4	5.9
Agitation	5.6	4.0
Nervousness	3.4	1.9
Anxiety	2.6	1.3
Yawning	1.9	0.2
Sexual Dysfunction–Female[c]	1.7	0.2
Concentration Impaired	1.3	0.5
Reproduction		
Menstrual Disorder[c]	1.0	0.5
Respiratory		
Rhinitis	2.0	1.5
Pharyngitis	1.2	0.9
Special Senses		
Vision Abnormal	4.2	2.1
Tinnitus	1.4	1.1
Taste Perversion	1.2	0.7
Urinary		
Micturition Frequency	2.0	1.2
Micturition Disorder	1.4	0.5

[a] Events reported by at least 1% of patients treated with Zoloft are included.

[b] % based on male patients only: 271 Zoloft and 271 placebo patients. Male sexual dysfunction can be broken down into the categories of decreased libido, impotence and ejaculatory delay. In this data set, the percentages of males in the Zoloft group with these complaints are 4.8%, 4.8% and 8.9%, respectively. It should be noted that since some Zoloft patients reported more than one category of male sexual dysfunction, the incidence of each category of male sexual dysfunction combined is larger than the incidence for the general category of male sexual dysfunction, in which each patient is counted only once.

[c] % based on female patients only: 590 Zoloft and 582 placebo patients.

Zoloft (cont'd)

drug-seeking behavior. In animal studies sertraline does not demonstrate stimulant or barbiturate-like (depressant) abuse potential. As with any CNS active drug, however, physicians should carefully evaluate patients for history of drug abuse and follow such patients closely, observing them for signs of sertraline misuse or abuse (e.g., development of tolerance, incrementation of dose, drug-seeking behavior).

Adverse Effects: Depression: In clinical development programs, sertraline has been evaluated in 1 902 subjects with depression. The most commonly observed adverse events associated with the use of sertraline were: gastrointestinal complaints, including nausea, diarrhea/loose stools and dyspepsia; male sexual dysfunction (primarily ejaculatory delay); insomnia and somnolence; tremor; increased sweating and dry mouth; and dizziness. In the fixed-dose, placebo-controlled study, the overall incidence of side effects was dose-related with a majority occurring in the patients treated with 200 mg dose.

The discontinuation rate due to adverse events was 15% in 2 710 subjects who received sertraline in premarketing multiple dose clinical trials. The more common events (reported by at least 1% of subjects) associated with discontinuation included agitation, insomnia, male sexual dysfunction (primarily ejaculatory delay), somnolence, dizziness, headache, tremor, anorexia, diarrhea/loose stools, nausea and fatigue.

Incidence in Controlled Clinical Trials: Table I (on previous page) enumerates adverse events that occurred at a frequency of 1% or more among sertraline patients who participated in controlled trials comparing titrated sertraline with placebo.

Panic Disorder: In placebo-controlled clinical trials, 430 patients with panic disorder were treated with sertraline in doses of 25 to 200 mg/day. During treatment, most patients received doses of 50 to 200 mg/day. Adverse events observed at an incidence of at least 5% for sertraline and at an incidence that was twice or more the incidence among placebo-treated patients included: diarrhea, ejaculation failure (primarily ejaculatory delay), anorexia, constipation, libido decreased, agitation and tremor.

In the total safety data base for panic disorder, 14% of patients discontinued treatment due to an adverse event. The most common events leading to discontinuation were nausea (2.6%), insomnia (2.3%), somnolence (2.3%) and agitation (2.1%).

Obsessive-Compulsive Disorder: In placebo-controlled clinical trials for OCD, adverse events observed at an incidence of at least 5% for sertraline and at an incidence that was twice or more the incidence among placebo-treated patients included: nausea, insomnia, diarrhea, decreased libido, anorexia, dyspepsia, ejaculation failure (primarily ejaculatory delay), tremor, and increased sweating.

In placebo-controlled clinical trials for OCD, 10% of patients treated with sertraline discontinued treatment due to an adverse event. The most common events leading to discontinuation were nausea (2.8%), insomnia (2.6%) and diarrhea (2.1%).

Incidence in Controlled Clinical Trials: Table II enumerates adverse events that occurred at a frequency of 2% or more among patients on sertraline who participated in controlled trials comparing sertraline with placebo in the treatment of panic disorder and obsessive-compulsive disorder. Only those adverse events which occurred at higher rate during sertraline treatment than during placebo treatment are included.

Other events observed during the premarketing evaluation of sertraline: During its premarketing assessment, multiple doses of sertraline were administered to 2 710 subjects. The conditions and duration of exposure to sertraline varied greatly, and included (in overlapping categories) clinical pharmacology studies, open and double-blind studies, uncontrolled and controlled studies, inpatient and outpatient studies, fixed-dose and titration studies, and studies for indications other than depression. Untoward events associated with this exposure were recorded by clinical investigators using terminology of their own choosing. Consequently, it is not possible to provide a meaningful estimate of the proportion of individuals experiencing adverse events without first grouping similar types of untoward events into a smaller number of standardized event categories.

All events are included except those already listed in Table I (on previous page) and Table II or in the Precautions section, and those reported in terms so general as to be uninformative.

It is important to emphasize that although the events reported occurred during treatment with sertraline, they were not necessarily caused by it.

Table II—Zoloft

Treatment-Emergent Adverse Experience Incidence in Placebo-Controlled Clinical Trials for Panic and Obsessive-Compulsive Disorder[a]

	Percent of Patients Reporting			
	Panic Disorder		Obsessive-Compulsive Disorder	
Adverse Experience	**Zoloft (N=430)**	**Placebo (N=275)**	**Zoloft (N=533)**	**Placebo (N=373)**
Autonomic Nervous System Disorders				
Mouth Dry	15	10	14	9
Sweating Increased	5	1	6	1
Cardiovascular				
Palpitations	–	–	3	2
Chest Pain	–	–	3	2
Central and Peripheral Nervous System Disorders				
Tremor	5	1	8	1
Paresthesia	4	3	3	1
Headache	–	–	30	24
Dizziness	–	–	17	9
Hypertonia	–	–	2	1
Disorders of Skin and Appendages				
Rash	4	3	2	1
Gastrointestinal Disorders				
Nausea	29	18	30	11
Diarrhea	20	9	24	10
Dyspepsia	10	8	10	4
Constipation	7	3	6	4
Anorexia	7	2	11	2
Vomiting	6	3	3	1
Flatulence	–	–	4	1
Appetite Increased	–	–	3	1
General				
Fatigue	11	6	14	10
Hot Flushes	3	1	2	1
Pain	–	–	3	1
Back Pain	–	–	2	1
Metabolic and Nutritional Disorders				
Weight Increase	–	–	3	0
Musculoskeletal System Disorders				
Arthralgia	2	1	–	–
Psychiatric Disorders				
Insomnia	25	18	28	12
Somnolence	15	9	15	8
Nervousness	9	5	7	6
Libido Decreased	7	1	11	2
Agitation	6	2	6	3
Anxiety	4	3	8	6
Concentration Impaired	3	0	–	–
Depersonalization	2	1	3	1
Paroniria	–	–	2	1
Respiratory System Disorders				
Pharyngitis	–	–	4	2
Special Senses				
Tinnitus	4	3	–	–
Vision Abnormal	–	–	4	2
Taste Perversion	–	–	3	1
Urogenital				
Ejaculation Failure[b]	19	1	17	2
Impotence[c]	2	1	5	1

[a]Events reported by at least 2% of patients treated with Zoloft are included, except for the following events which had an incidence on placebo greater than or equal to Zoloft [Panic Disorder]: headache, dizziness, malaise, abdominal pain, respiratory disorder, pharyngitis, flatulence, vision abnormal, pain, upper respiratory tract infection and paroniria. [OCD]: abdominal pain, respiratory disorder, depression and amnesia.

[b]Primarily ejaculatory delay; % based on male patients only: Panic Disorder: 216 Zoloft and 134 placebo patients, OCD: 296 Zoloft and 219 placebo patients.

[c]% based on male patients only: Panic Disorder: 216 Zoloft and 134 placebo patients, OCD: 296 Zoloft and 219 placebo patients.

Autonomic Nervous System Disorders: Infrequent: flushing, mydriasis, increased saliva, cold clammy skin. Rare: pallor.

Cardiovascular: Infrequent: postural dizziness, hypertension, hypotension, postural hypotension, edema, dependent edema, periorbital edema, peripheral edema, peripheral ischemia, syncope, tachycardia. Rare: precordial chest pain, substernal chest pain, aggravated hypertension, myocardial infarction, varicose veins.

Central and Peripheral Nervous System Disorders: Frequent: confusion. Infrequent: ataxia, abnormal coordination, abnormal gait, hyperesthesia, hyperkinesia, hypokinesia, migraine, nystagmus, vertigo. Rare: local anesthesia, coma, convulsions, dyskinesia, dysphonia, hyporeflexia, hypotonia, ptosis.

Disorders of Skin and Appendages: Infrequent: acne, alopecia, pruritus, erythematous rash, maculopapular rash, dry skin. Rare: bullous eruption, dermatitis, erythema multiforme, abnormal hair texture, hypertrichosis, photosensitivity reaction, follicular rash, skin discoloration, abnormal skin odor, urticaria.

Endocrine Disorders: Rare: exophthalmos, gynecomastia.

Gastrointestinal Disorders: Infrequent: dysphagia, eructation. Rare: diverticulitis, fecal incontinence, gastritis, gastroenteritis, glossitis, gum hyperplasia, hemorrhoids, hiccup, melena, hemorrhagic peptic ulcer, proctitis, stomatitis, ulcerative stomatitis, tenesmus, tongue edema, tongue ulceration.

General: Frequent: asthenia. Infrequent: malaise, generalized edema, rigors, weight decrease, weight increase. Rare:

enlarged abdomen, halitosis, otitis media, aphthous stomatitis.
Hematopoietic and Lymphatic: Infrequent: lymphadenopathy, purpura. Rare: anemia, anterior chamber eye hemorrhage.
Metabolic and Nutritional Disorders: Rare: dehydration, hypercholesterolemia, hypoglycemia.
Musculoskeletal System Disorders: Infrequent: arthralgia, arthrosis, dystonia, muscle cramps, muscle weakness. Rare: hernia.
Psychiatric Disorders: Infrequent: abnormal dreams, aggressive reaction, amnesia, apathy, delusion, depersonalization, depression, aggravated depression, emotional lability, euphoria, hallucination, neurosis, paranoid reaction, suicide attempt (including suicidal ideation), teeth-grinding, abnormal thinking. Rare: hysteria, somnambulism, withdrawal reactions.
Reproductive: Infrequent: dysmenorrhea (2), intermenstrual bleeding (2). Rare: amenorrhea (2), balanoposthitis (1), breast enlargement (2), female breast pain (2), leukorrhea (2), menorrhagia (2), atrophic vaginitis (2).
(1)—% based on male subjects only: 1 005
(2)—% based on female subjects only: 1 705
Respiratory System Disorders: Infrequent: bronchospasm, coughing, dyspnea, epistaxis. Rare: bradypnea, hyperventilation, sinusitis, stridor.
Special Senses: Infrequent: abnormal accommodation, conjunctivitis, diplopia, earache, eye pain, xerophthalmia. Rare: abnormal lacrimation, photophobia, visual field defect.
Urinary System Disorders: Infrequent: dysuria, face edema, nocturia, polyuria, urinary incontinence. Rare: oliguria, renal pain, urinary retention.
Laboratory Tests: In man, asymptomatic elevations in serum hepatic transaminases (AST and ALT) to a value ≥ 3 times the upper limit of normal have been reported infrequently (approximately 0.6% and 1.1%, respectively) in association with sertraline administration. The proportion of patients having these elevations was greater in the sertraline group than in the placebo group. These hepatic enzyme elevations usually occurred within the first 1 to 9 weeks of drug treatment and promptly diminished upon drug discontinuation.

Sertraline therapy was associated with small mean increases in total cholesterol (approximately 3%) and triglycerides (approximately 5%).
Uricosuric Effect: Sertraline is associated with a small mean decrease in serum uric acid (approximately 7%) of no apparent clinical importance. There have been no reports of acute renal failure with sertraline.
Other Events Observed During the Postmarketing Evaluation of Sertraline: Adverse events not listed above which have been reported in temporal association with sertraline since market introduction include: increased coagulation times, bradycardia, AV block, atrial arrhythmias, hypothyroidism, leukopenia, thrombocytopenia, hyperglycemia, priapism, galactorrhea, hyperprolactinemia, neuroleptic malignant syndrome-like events, psychosis, severe skin reactions, which potentially can be fatal, such as Stevens-Johnson syndrome, vasculitis, photosensitivity and other severe cutaneous disorders, rare reports of pancreatitis, and liver events. The causal relationship between sertraline treatment and the emergence of these events has not been established. The clinical features of hepatic events (which in the majority of cases appeared to be reversible with discontinuation of sertraline) occurring in 1 or more patients include: elevated enzymes, increased bilirubin, hepatomegaly, hepatitis, jaundice, abdominal pain, vomiting, liver failure and death. There have been spontaneous reports of symptoms such as dizziness, paresthesia, nausea, headache, anxiety, fatigue and agitation following the discontinuation of sertraline treatment.

Overdose: Symptoms and Treatment: On the evidence available, sertraline has a wide margin of safety in overdose. Overdoses of sertraline alone of up to 6 g have been reported. Symptoms of overdose with sertraline alone included somnolence, nausea, vomiting, tachycardia, ECG changes, anxiety and dilated pupils. Treatment was primarily supportive and included monitoring and use of activated charcoal, gastric lavage or cathartics and hydration. Although there were no reports of death when sertraline was taken alone, there were 4 deaths involving overdoses of sertraline in combination with other drugs and/or alcohol. Therefore, any overdosage should be treated aggressively.
Management of Overdoses: Establish and maintain an airway, insure adequate oxygenation and ventilation. Activated charcoal, which may be used with sorbitol, may be as or more effective than emesis or lavage, and should be considered in treating overdose.

Cardiac and vital signs monitoring are recommended along with general symptomatic and supportive measures. There are no specific antidotes for sertraline.

Due to the large volume of distribution of sertraline, forced diuresis, dialysis, hemoperfusion, and exchange transfusion are unlikely to be of benefit.

In managing overdose, the possibility of multiple drug involvement must be considered.

Dosage: General: Sertraline should be administered with food once daily preferably with the evening meal, or, if administration in the morning is desired, with breakfast.
Initial Treatment: Depression and Obsessive-Compulsive Disorder: As no clear dose-response relationship has been demonstrated over a range of 50 to 200 mg/day, a dose of 50 mg/day is recommended as the initial dose.
Panic Disorder: Sertraline treatment should be initiated with a dose of 25 mg once daily. After 1 week, the dose should be increased to 50 mg once daily depending on tolerability and clinical response. No clear dose-response relationship has been demonstrated over a range of 50 to 200 mg/day.
Titration: In depression, OCD and panic disorder, a gradual increase in dosage may be considered if no clinical improvement is observed. Based on pharmacokinetic parameters, steady-state sertraline plasma levels are achieved after approximately 1 week of once daily dosing; accordingly, dose changes, if necessary, should be made at intervals of at least 1 week. Doses should not exceed a maximum of 200 mg/day.

The full therapeutic response may be delayed until 4 weeks of treatment or longer. Increasing the dosage rapidly does not normally shorten this latent period and may increase the incidence of side effects.
Maintenance: During long-term therapy for any indication, the dosage should be maintained at the lowest effective dose and patients should be periodically reassessed to determine the need for continued treatment.
Renal/Hepatic Impairment: As with many other medications, sertraline should be used with caution in patients with renal and/or hepatic impairment (see Precautions).
Switching Patients to or From an MAO Inhibitor: At least 14 days should elapse between discontinuation of an MAO inhibitor and initiation of therapy with sertraline. In addition, at least 14 days should be allowed after stopping sertraline before starting an MAO inhibitor (see Contraindications).

Information for the Patient: See Blue Section—Information for the Patient "Zoloft".

Supplied: 25 mg: Each yellow capsule contains: sertraline HCl equivalent to 25 mg of sertraline. Nonmedicinal ingredients: cornstarch, lactose (anhydrous), magnesium stearate and sodium lauryl sulfate. Capsule shell: D&C Yellow No. 10, FD&C Yellow No. 6, gelatin and titanium dioxide. Tartrazine-free. White high density polyethylene bottles of 100.

50 mg: Each white and yellow capsule contains: sertraline HCl equivalent to 50 mg of sertraline. Nonmedicinal ingredients: cornstarch, lactose (anhydrous), magnesium stearate and sodium lauryl sulfate. Capsule shell: D&C Yellow No. 10, FD&C Yellow No. 6, gelatin and titanium dioxide. Tartrazine-free. White high density polyethylene bottles of 100 and 250.

100 mg: Each orange capsule contains: sertraline HCl equivalent to 100 mg of sertraline. Nonmedicinal ingredients: cornstarch, lactose (anhydrous), magnesium stearate and sodium lauryl sulfate. Capsule shell: D&C Yellow No. 10, FD&C Red No. 40, gelatin and titanium dioxide. Tartrazine-free. White high density polyethylene bottles of 100 and 250.

Store at controlled room temperature between 15 and 30°C.

(Shown in Product Recognition Section)

Reviewed 1999

ZONALON ℞

Medicis

Doxepin HCl

Antipruritic Agent

Pharmacology: Doxepin, a dibenzoxepin-derivative tricyclic compound, is a topical antipruritic. While the exact mechanism of antipruritic activity is unknown, doxepin exhibits potent histamine H_1 and H_2 receptor antagonist activity. Although the sedative effect of systemically absorbed doxepin may contribute to the drug's antipruritic activity, the antipruritic efficacy of doxepin reportedly does not appear to depend on a sedative effect.

Indications: For the short-term (up to 8 days) topical relief of histamine mediated pruritus of moderate severity accompanying conditions such as eczematous dermatitis.

Contraindications: In individuals who have shown hypersensitivity to the drug or to other dibenzoxepin compounds.

Children: Doxepin cream is not recommended in children under the age of 12 because safety and efficacy in this age group have not been established.

Because doxepin has an anticholinergic effect and because significant plasma levels of doxepin are detectable after topical doxepin cream application, the use of doxepin cream is contraindicated in patients with glaucoma or a tendency to urinary retention.

Doxepin cream is contraindicated in individuals who have shown previous sensitivity to any of its components.

Warnings: *Pregnancy* and *Lactation:* The safety of doxepin cream during pregnancy and lactation has not been established and therefore, it should not be used in women of childbearing potential or nursing mothers unless in the opinion of the physician, the potential benefit to the patient outweighs the possible hazards to the fetus.
Occupational Hazards: Drowsiness occurs in over 20% of patients treated with doxepin cream, especially in patients receiving treatment to greater than 10% of their body surface area. Patients should be warned of this possibility and cautioned against driving a motor vehicle or operating hazardous machinery while being treated with doxepin cream.

If excessive drowsiness occurs it may be necessary to reduce the number of applications, the amount of cream applied, and/or the percentage of body surface area treated.
Drug Interactions: MAO Inhibitors: Serious side effects and even death have been reported following the concomitant use of certain orally administered drugs chemically related to doxepin and MAO inhibitors. Therefore, MAO inhibitors should be discontinued at least 2 weeks prior to the initiation of treatment with doxepin cream.
Cimetidine: Cimetidine has been reported to produce clinically significant fluctuations in steady-state serum concentrations of various tricyclic antidepressants when taken orally. Serious anticholinergic symptoms have been associated with elevations in serum levels of orally administered tricyclic antidepressants when cimetidine therapy is initiated. Higher than expected tricyclic antidepressant levels have been observed in patients already taking cimetidine. In patients who have been reported to be well-controlled on tricyclic antidepressants receiving concurrent cimetidine therapy, discontinuation of cimetidine has been reported to decrease established steady-state serum tricyclic antidepressant levels and compromise their therapeutic effects.

The relevance of concurrent administration of cimetidine on the antipruritic effectiveness of doxepin cream, applied topically, is not known.
Alcohol: Alcohol ingestion has exacerbated the potential sedative effects of doxepin cream, particularly in those individuals who use alcohol excessively.
CNS Drugs: CNS drugs patient should be warned that the effects of other drugs acting on the CNS such as barbiturates and other CNS depressants, are potentiated by doxepin cream.

Precautions: Studies have not been done examining drug interactions with doxepin cream. In an 8-day 40-patient percutaneous absorption study, none of the patients who applied doxepin cream 4 times each day had blood levels which reached the antidepressant therapeutic range for oral doxepin.

Patients should also be warned that the effects of alcoholic beverages can be potentiated when using doxepin cream.

Local adverse effects have been reported infrequently with the use of topical doxepin, but may occur more frequently with the use of occlusive dressings. Occlusive dressings may increase the absorption of most topical drugs, therefore occlusive dressings should not be used with doxepin cream.

Adverse Effects: Local reactions are listed in a decreasing order of occurrence and include: burning, stinging, irritation, tingling and local rash.

Systemic effects which have been observed with the topical use of doxepin cream, include anticholinergic effects: dry mouth, thirst, taste changes, dry eyes. CNS effects including drowsiness, asthenia, headaches, fever, dizziness and gastrointestinal effects were nausea, dyspepsia, vomiting and diarrhea.

Dosage: Doxepin cream should be applied to the affected area in a thin film 3 to 4 times daily with at least 3- or 4-hour intervals between applications. Doxepin cream should be used for a short term no longer than 8 days. Chronic use beyond 8 days may result in higher systemic levels.

Clinical experience has shown that drowsiness is significantly more common in patients applying treatments to over 10% of body surface area, body surface area (BSA), therefore patients with over 10% of BSA affected should be especially cautioned concerning possible drowsiness.

Zonalon (cont'd)

If excessive drowsiness occurs it may be necessary to reduce BSA treated, reduce the number of applications per day, and/or reduce the amount of cream applied.

Occlusal dressing may also increase the absorption of most topical drugs therefore occlusive dressing should not be used with doxepin cream.

Supplied: Each tube of cream contains: doxepin HCl. Aluminum tubes of 30 g.

ZOSTRIX®
Medicis
Capsaicin
Neuralgia Therapy

Pharmacology: Although the precise mechanism of action of capsaicin is not fully understood, current evidence suggests that capsaicin renders skin insensitive to pain by depleting and preventing reaccumulation of substance P in peripheral sensory neurons. Substance P is thought to be the principal chemomediator of pain impulses from the periphery to the CNS.

Indications: For the temporary relief of the pain (neuralgia) associated with and following episodes of herpes zoster infections after open skin lesions have healed. For the temporary relief of arthritic pain in rheumatoid and osteoarthritis.

Warnings: For external use only. Avoid contact with eyes and broken or irritated skin. Do not bandage. If condition worsens, or if symptoms persist for more than 14 days or clear up and occur again within a few days, discontinue use of this product and consult your physician. Keep this and all drugs out of the reach of children.

Dosage: Adults and children 2 years of age or older: Apply cream lightly to affected area not less than 3 or 4 times daily. It may cause transient burning on application. This burning is observed more frequently when application schedules of less than 3 or 4 times daily are utilized. After the cream is applied with the fingers, unless treating hands, the hands should be washed immediately.

Patient compliance is vital to successful therapy. Optimal response should be achieved within 14 to 28 days. Continued application 3 to 4 times daily is necessary to sustain its clinical effect.

Supplied: Each tube of cream contains: capsaicin 0.025% in an emollient base. Tubes of 60 g.

ZOSTRIX® H.P.
Medicis
Capsaicin
Neuralgia Therapy

Pharmacology: Current evidence suggests that capsaicin works by its action on a pain transmitting compound called substance P. Capsaicin causes substance P to leave the nerve endings. With a lower amount of substance P in the nerve endings, pain impulses cannot be transmitted to the brain.

Indications: For the relief of neuralgias (pain from nerves near the surface of the skin) such as painful diabetic neuropathy, postsurgical pain and temporary relief of arthritic pain in rheumatoid and osteoarthritis.

Warnings: Avoid contact with eyes. Do not apply to wounds or damaged skin. Do not bandage. If condition worsens or does not improve after 28 days, discontinue use of this product and consult your physician. Keep this and all drugs out of the reach of children.

Dosage: Adults and children 2 years of age and older: Apply to affected area 3 to 4 times daily. A transient burning sensation related to the action of the product may occur over the first several days of use. Application schedules less than 3 times a day may not provide optimum pain relief and the burning sensation may persist. Unless treating hands, wash hands immediately after application, avoiding areas where drug is applied.

Supplied: Each tube of cream contains: capsaicin 0.075% in an emollient base. Tubes of 60 g.

ZOVIRAX® Cream Ⓟ
Glaxo Wellcome
Acyclovir
Antiviral Agent

Pharmacology: Acyclovir, a synthetic acyclic purine nucleoside analog, is a substrate with a high degree of specificity for herpes simplex and varicella-zoster specified thymidine kinase. Acyclovir is a poor substrate for host cell-specified thymidine kinase. Herpes simplex and varicella-zoster specified thymidine kinase transform acyclovir to its monophosphate which is then transformed by a number of cellular enzymes to acyclovir diphosphate and acyclovir triphosphate. Acyclovir triphosphate is both an inhibitor of, and a substrate for, herpesvirus-specified DNA polymerase. Although the cellular α-DNA polymerase in infected cells may also be inhibited by acyclovir triphosphate, this occurs only at concentrations of acyclovir triphosphate which are higher than those which inhibit the herpesvirus-specified DNA polymerase. Acyclovir is selectively converted to its active form in herpesvirus-infected cells and is thus preferentially taken up by these cells. Acyclovir has demonstrated a very much lower toxic potential in vitro for normal uninfected cells because: 1) less is taken up; 2) less is converted to the active form; 3) cellular α-DNA polymerase has a lower sensitivity to the action of the active form of the drug. A combination of the thymidine kinase specificity, inhibition of DNA polymerase and premature termination of DNA synthesis results in inhibition of herpesvirus replication. No effect on latent non-replicating virus has been demonstrated. Inhibition of the virus reduces the period of viral shedding, limits the degree of spread and level of pathology, and thereby facilitates healing. During suppression there is no evidence that acyclovir prevents neural migration of the virus. It aborts episodes of recurrent herpes due to inhibition of viral replication following reactivation.

Indications: For the topical management of initial episodes of genital herpes simplex infections. The prophylactic use of this preparation has not been established.

In the treatment of genital herpes, appropriate examinations should be performed to rule out other sexually transmitted diseases. Therapy should begin as early as possible after the start of an infection.

Two multicentre, double-blind, placebo-controlled studies were performed with acyclovir cream in immunocompetent patients with initial genital herpes. The cream was applied for up to 10 days or until healing had occurred. Results showed that acyclovir cream significantly reduced the duration of viral shedding, the formation of new lesions, the time to crusting and healing of lesions, and the duration of pain.

Whereas cutaneous lesions associated with herpes simplex infections are often pathognomonic, Tzanck smears prepared from lesion exudate or scrapings may assist in the diagnosis. Positive cultures for herpes simplex virus offer the only absolute means for confirmation of the diagnosis.

Contraindications: For patients who develop hypersensitivity or chemical intolerance to any of the components of the formulation, such as propylene glycol.

Warnings: Acyclovir cream is intended for topical use only and should not be used in the eye.

Precautions: Acyclovir cream is not recommended for application to mucous membranes such as the mouth or vagina.

The recommended dosage, frequency of application and duration of treatment of acyclovir cream should not be exceeded (see Dosage).

Lactation: Acyclovir, when given systemically, is known to be excreted into human milk. No information is available on levels of acyclovir which may appear in breast milk after administration of acyclovir cream. Caution should be exercised when acyclovir is administered to a nursing mother.

Pregnancy: Teratology studies carried out to date in animals have been negative in general. However, in a non-standard test in rats, there were fetal abnormalities such as head and tail anomalies, and maternal toxicity; since such studies are not always predictive of human response, acyclovir should not be used during pregnancy unless the physician feels the potential benefit justifies the risk of possible harm to the fetus. The potential for high concentrations of acyclovir to cause chromosome breaks in vitro should be taken into consideration in making this decision.

Children: Safety of use of acyclovir cream in children has not been established.

There exist no data, at this time, which demonstrate that the use of acyclovir cream will prevent transmission of infection to other persons.

Since most cutaneous herpes simplex virus infections result from reactivation of latent virus, it is unlikely that acyclovir cream will prevent recurrence of infections when applied in the absence of signs and symptoms. Acyclovir cream should not be applied in an attempt to prevent recurrences; application should commence only at the earliest prodromal sign of disease onset.

Although clinically significant viral resistance associated with the use of acyclovir cream has not been observed, this possibility exists.

Clinical experience has identified no interactions resulting from topical or systemic administration of other drugs concomitantly with acyclovir cream.

Adverse Effects: Because ulcerated genital lesions are characteristically tender and sensitive to any contact or manipulation, patients may experience discomfort upon application of acyclovir cream. Table I shows the number of initial genital herpes patients who reported adverse reactions in the 2 controlled clinical trials.

Table I—Zovirax Cream

Adverse Effects

Adverse Reaction	Zovirax (n=54)	Placebo (n=47)
Burning/stinging on application	3	7
Rash	0	3
Itching	1	0
Retention of urine	2	2
Meningism	0	2
Paronychia	0	1
Total No. (%) of patients	6 (11%)	15 (32%)

Observed During Clinical Practice: Based on worldwide clinical practice experience in patients treated with acyclovir cream, the adverse events most commonly reported include contact dermatitis, application site reaction, eczema, allergic reaction, pain, and rash. Less common events include pruritus, skin discoloration, urticaria, vesiculobullous rash, and facial edema.

Overdose: Symptoms and Treatment: Overdosage by topical application of acyclovir cream is unlikely because of limited transcutaneous absorption.

Dosage: Apply liberally to the affected area 4 to 6 times daily for up to 10 days. A sufficient quantity of ointment should be applied to adequately cover all lesions. A finger cot or rubber glove should be used while applying acyclovir cream in order to prevent autoinoculation of other body sites or transmission of infection to other persons. **Therapy should be initiated as early as possible following onset of signs and symptoms.**

Supplied: Each g of cream contains: acyclovir 50 mg. Nonmedicinal ingredients: cetostearyl alcohol, paraffin, poloxamer, propylene glycol and sodium lauryl sulfate. Tubes of 5 g. Store between 15 and 25°C and keep dry.

ZOVIRAX® for Injection Ⓟ
Glaxo Wellcome
Acyclovir Sodium
Antiviral Agent

Pharmacology: Acyclovir, a synthetic acyclic purine nucleoside analog, is a substrate with a high degree of specificity for herpes simplex and varicella-zoster-specified thymidine kinase. Acyclovir is a poor substrate for host cell-specified thymidine kinase. Herpes simplex and varicella-zoster-specified thymidine kinase transform acyclovir to its monophosphate which is then transformed by a number of cellular enzymes to acyclovir diphosphate and acyclovir triphosphate. Acyclovir triphosphate is both an inhibitor of, and a substrate for, herpes virus-specified DNA polymerase. Although the cellular α-DNA polymerase in infected cells may also be inhibited by acyclovir triphosphate, this occurs only at concentrations of acyclovir triphosphate which are higher than those which inhibit the herpes virus-specified DNA polymerase. Acyclovir is selectively converted to its active form in herpes virus-infected cells and is thus preferentially taken up by these cells. Acyclovir has demonstrated a very much lower toxic potential in vitro for normal uninfected cells because: 1) less is taken up; 2) less is converted to the active form; 3) cellular α-DNA polymerase has a lower sensitivity to the action of the active form of the drug. A combination of the thymidine kinase specificity, inhibition of DNA polymerase and premature termination of DNA synthesis results in inhibition of herpes virus replication. No effect on latent nonreplicating virus has been demonstrated. Inhibition of the virus reduces the period of viral shedding, limits the degree of spread and level of pathology, and thereby facilitates healing. During suppression there is no evidence that acyclovir prevents neural migration of the virus. It aborts episodes of recurrent herpes due to inhibition of viral replication following reactivation.

Pharmacokinetics: The pharmacokinetics of acyclovir has been evaluated in 95 patients (9 studies). Results were obtained in adult patients with normal renal function during Phase I/II studies after single doses ranging from 0.5 to 15 mg/kg and after multiple doses ranging from 2.5 to 15 mg/kg every 8 hours. Pharmacokinetics was also determined in pediatric patients with normal renal function ranging in age from 1 to 17 years at doses of 250 or 500 mg/m² every 8 hours. In these studies, dose-independent pharmacokinetics is observed in the range of 0.5 to 15 mg/kg. Proportionality between dose and plasma levels is seen after single doses or at steady state after multiple dosing.

Renal excretion of unchanged drug by glomerular filtration and tubular secretion is the major route of acyclovir elimination, accounting for 62 to 91% of the dose administered. The half-life and total body clearance of acyclovir in pediatric patients over 1 year of age is similar to those in adults with normal renal function.

Indications: For the treatment of initial and recurrent mucosal and cutaneous herpes simplex (HSV-1 and HSV-2) infections and varicella-zoster (shingles) infections in immunocompromised adults and children. It is also indicated for severe initial episodes of herpes simplex infections in patients who may not be immunocompromised. Use in other herpes group infections is the subject of ongoing study.

The indications are based on the results of a number of double-blind, placebo-controlled studies which examined changes in virus excretion, total healing of lesions, and relief of pain. Because of the wide biological variations inherent in herpes simplex infections, the following summary is presented merely to illustrate the spectrum of responses observed to date. As in the treatment of any infectious disease, the best response may be expected when the therapy is begun at the earliest possible moment.

Herpes Simplex Infections in Immunocompromised Patients: A multicentre trial of acyclovir sterile powder at a dose of 250 mg/m² every 8 hours infused over 1 hour (750 mg/m²/day) for 7 days was conducted in 98 immunocompromised patients with orofacial, esophageal, genital and other localized infections (52 treated with acyclovir and 46 with placebo). Acyclovir significantly decreased virus excretion, reduced pain, and promoted scabbing and rapid healing of lesions.

Initial Episodes of Herpes Genitalis: A controlled trial was conducted in 28 patients with initial severe episodes of herpes genitalis with an acyclovir dosage of 5 mg/kg, infused over 1 hour, every 8 hours for 5 days (12 patients with acyclovir and 16 with placebo). Significant treatment effects were seen in elimination of virus from lesions and in reduction of healing times.

In a similar study, 15 patients with initial episodes of genital herpes were treated with acyclovir 5 mg/kg, infused over 1 hour, every 8 hours for 5 days, and 15 with placebo. Acyclovir decreased the duration of viral excretion, new lesion formation, duration of vesicles and promoted more rapid healing of all lesions.

Varicella-Zoster Infections in Immunocompromised Patients: A multicentre trial of acyclovir for injection at a dose of 500 mg/m² every 8 hours for 7 days was conducted in immunocompromised patients with zoster infections (shingles). Ninety-four patients were evaluated (52 patients were treated with acyclovir and 42 with placebo). Acyclovir halted progression of infection as determined by significant reductions in cutaneous dissemination, visceral dissemination, or the proportion of patients deemed treatment failures.

A comparative trial of acyclovir and vidarabine was conducted in 22 severely immunocompromised patients with zoster infections. Acyclovir was shown to be superior to vidarabine as demonstrated by significant differences in the time of new lesion formation, the time to pain reduction, the time to lesion crusting, the time to complete healing, the incidence of fever and the duration of positive viral cultures. In addition, cutaneous dissemination occurred in none of the 10 acyclovir recipients compared to 5 of the 10 vidarabine recipients who presented with localized dermatomal disease.

Healing Process: Because complete re-epithelialization of herpes-disrupted integument necessitates recruitment of several complex repair mechanisms, the physician should be aware that the disappearance of visible lesions is somewhat variable and will occur later than the cessation of virus excretion.

Diagnosis: Whereas cutaneous lesions associated with herpes simplex and varicella-zoster infections are often pathognomonic, Tzanck smears prepared from lesion exudate or scrapings may assist in diagnosis. Positive cultures for herpes simplex virus offer the only absolute means for confirmation of the diagnosis. Appropriate examinations should be performed to rule out other sexually transmitted diseases. The Tzanck smear does not distinguish varicella-zoster from herpes simplex infections.

Contraindications: Patients who have hypersensitivity to the drug.

Warnings: Acyclovir for injection is for slow i.v. infusion only. I.V. infusions must be given over a period of at least 1 hour to reduce the risk of renal tubular damage (see Precautions and Dosage).

In severely immunocompromised patients, the physician should be aware that prolonged or repeated courses of acyclovir may result in selection of resistant viruses associated with infections which may not respond to continued acyclovir therapy. This, however, remains to be clearly established and should be considered as a factor when undertaking therapy. The effect of the use of acyclovir on the natural history of herpes simplex or varicella-zoster infection is unknown.

Precautions: Precipitation of acyclovir crystals in renal tubules can occur if maximum solubility (2.5 mg/mL at 37°C in water) is exceeded. This phenomenon is reflected by a rise in serum creatinine and BUN and a decrease in creatinine clearance. With sufficient renal tubular compromise, urine output decreases.

Acute increases in serum creatinine and decreased creatinine clearance have been observed in humans receiving acyclovir for injection who were poorly hydrated; or receiving concomitant nephrotoxic drugs (e.g., amphotericin B and aminoglycoside antibiotics); or had pre-existing renal compromise or damage; or had the dose administered by rapid i.v. injection (less than 10 minutes). Observed alterations in renal function have been transient, in some instances resolving spontaneously without change in acyclovir dosing regimen. In other instances, renal function improved following increased hydration, dosage adjustment, or discontinuation of acyclovir therapy.

Administration of acyclovir by i.v. infusion must be accompanied by adequate hydration. Since maximum urine concentration occurs within the first 2 hours following infusion, particular attention should be given to establishing sufficient urine flow during that period in order to prevent precipitation in renal tubules. Recommended urine output is ≥500 mL/g of drug infused.

When dosage adjustments are required they should be based on estimated creatinine clearance (see Dosage).

Approximately 1% of patients receiving i.v. acyclovir have manifested encephalopathic changes characterized by either lethargy, obtundation, tremors, confusion, hallucinations, agitation, seizures or coma. Acyclovir should be used with caution in those patients who have underlying neurologic abnormalities and those with serious renal, hepatic, or electrolyte abnormalities or significant hypoxia. It should also be used with caution in patients who have manifested prior neurologic reactions to cytotoxic drugs or those receiving concomitant intrathecal methotrexate or interferon.

Lactation: Acyclovir is excreted in human milk. Caution should therefore be exercised when acyclovir is administered to a nursing mother.

Pregnancy: Teratology studies carried out to date in animals have been negative in general. However, in a nonstandard test in rats, there were fetal abnormalities such as head and tail anomalies, and maternal toxicity; since such studies are not always predictive of human response, acyclovir should not be used during pregnancy unless the physician feels the potential benefit justifies the risk of possible harm to the fetus. The potential for high concentrations of acyclovir to cause chromosome breaks in vitro should be taken into consideration in making this decision.

No data exist at this time, that demonstrate that the use of acyclovir will prevent transmission of herpes simplex infection to other persons.

Consideration should be given to an alternative treatment regimen if after 5 days of treatment there is no expected clinical improvement in the signs and symptoms of the infection.

Strains of herpes simplex virus which are less susceptible to acyclovir have been isolated from herpes lesions and have also emerged during i.v. treatment with acyclovir.

Drug Interactions: Coadministration of probenecid with i.v. acyclovir has been shown to increase the mean half-life and the area under the concentration-time curve. Urinary excretion and renal clearance were correspondingly reduced. Clinical experience has identified no other significant interactions resulting from administration of other drugs concomitantly with acyclovir for injection.

Adverse Effects: The adverse reactions listed below have been observed in controlled and uncontrolled clinical trials in approximately 700 patients who received acyclovir at approximately 5 mg/kg (250 mg/m²) and approximately 200 patients who received approximately 10 mg/kg (500 mg/m²).

The most frequent adverse reactions reported during acyclovir administration were inflammation or phlebitis at the injection site in approximately 9% of the patients, and transient elevations of serum creatinine or BUN in 5 to 10% [the higher incidence occurred usually following rapid (<10 minutes) i.v. infusion]. Nausea and/or vomiting occurred in approximately 7% of the patients (the majority occurring in nonhospitalized patients who received 10 mg/kg). Itching, rash or hives occurred in approximately 2% of patients. Elevation of transaminases occurred in 1 to 2% of patients.

Approximately 1% of patients receiving i.v. acyclovir have manifested encephalopathic changes characterized by either lethargy, obtundation, tremors, confusion, hallucinations, agitation, seizures or coma (see Precautions).

Adverse reactions which occurred at a frequency of less than 1% and which were probably or possibly related to i.v. acyclovir administration were: anemia, anuria, hematuria, hypotension, edema, anorexia, lightheadedness, thirst, headache, diaphoresis, fever, neutropenia, thrombocytopenia, abnormal urinalysis (characterized by an increase in formed elements in urine sediment) and pain on urination.

Other reactions have been reported with a frequency of less than 1% in patients receiving acyclovir, but a causal relationship between acyclovir and the reaction could not be determined. These include pulmonary edema with cardiac tamponade, abdominal pain, chest pain, thrombocytosis, leukocytosis, neutrophilia, ischemia of digits, hypokalemia, purpura fulminans, pressure on urination, hemoglobinemia and rigors.

Overdose: Symptoms and Treatment: Overdose has been reported following administration of bolus injections, or inappropriately high doses, and in patients whose fluid and electrolyte balance was not properly monitored. This has resulted in elevations in BUN, serum creatinine and subsequent renal failure. Lethargy, convulsions and coma have been reported rarely. Precipitation of acyclovir in renal tubules may occur when the solubility (2.5 mg/mL) in the intratubular fluid is exceeded (see Precautions).

A 6-hour hemodialysis results in a 60% decrease in plasma acyclovir concentration. Data concerning peritoneal dialysis are incomplete but indicate that this method may be significantly less efficient in removing acyclovir from the blood. In the event of acute renal failure and anuria, the patient may benefit from hemodialysis until renal function is restored (see Dosage).

Dosage: Caution: Acyclovir for injection for slow i.v. infusion only, over a period of at least 1 hour.

Herpes Simplex Infections: Mucosal and Cutaneous Herpes Simplex (HSV-1 and HSV-2) in Immunocompromised Patients: Adults: 5 mg/kg infused at a constant rate over at least 1 hour, every 8 hours for 7 days in adult patients with normal renal function. Children: In children under 12 years of age, equivalent plasma concentrations are attained by infusing 250 mg/m² at a constant rate over at least 1 hour, every 8 hours for 7 days.

Severe Initial Clinical Episodes of Herpes Genitalis in Immunocompetent Patients: The same dose given above—administered for 5 days.

Varicella Zoster Infections: Zoster in Immunocompromised Patients: Adults: 10 mg/kg infused at a constant rate over at least 1 hour, every 8 hours for 7 days in adult patients with normal renal function. Children: In children under 12 years of age, equivalent plasma concentrations are attained by infusing 500 mg/m² at a constant rate over at least 1 hour, every 8 hours for 7 days.

Obese patients should be dosed at 10 mg/kg (Ideal Body Weight).

A maximum dose equivalent to 500 mg/m² every 8 hours should not be exceeded for any patient.

Zovirax for Injection (cont'd)

Patients with Acute or Chronic Renal Impairment: Use the recommended doses and method of administration; and adjust the dosing interval as indicated in Table I.

Table I—Zovirax for Injection

Dosing in Function of the Creatinine Clearance

Creatinine Clearance (mL/min/1.73 m^2)	Percent of Recommended Dose	Dosing Interval (hours)
>50	100	8
25 to 50	100	12
10 to 25*	100	24
0 to 10*	50	24 to 48

* Hemodialysis: For patients who require hemodialysis, the mean plasma half-life of acyclovir during dialysis is approximately 5 hours, which results in a 60% decrease in plasma concentrations following a 6-hour dialysis period. Recommended doses should be administered every 24 to 48 hours, and after hemodialysis.

Solutions for Reconstitution: Sterile Water for Injection. Do not use Bacteriostatic Water for Injection which contains benzyl alcohol or parabens (see Table II).

Table II—Zovirax for Injection

Reconstitution Table

Vial Size	Volume to be Added to Vial	Approximate Available Volume	Approximate Average Concentration
500 mg	10 mL	10 mL	50 mg/mL
1 g	20 mL	20 mL	50 mg/mL

Shake well until dissolved. Assure complete dissolution before measuring and transferring dose. Unused portion of the reconstituted solution should be discarded.

Diluted Solutions for I.V. Infusion: The calculated dose of the reconstituted solution should be removed and added to an appropriate i.v. solution listed below at a volume selected for administration during each 1-hour infusion. **Infusion concentrations exceeding 10 mg/mL are not recommended.**

Since the vials do not contain any preservatives, any unused portion of the reconstituted solution should be discarded.

Solutions for I.V. Infusion: 5% Dextrose Injection, 5% Dextrose and 0.9% Sodium Chloride Injection, 5% Dextrose and 0.2% Sodium Chloride Injection, Ringer's Injection, Normal Saline Injection, Lactated Ringer's Injection.

Stability and Storage: Reconstituted solutions at a concentration of 50 mg/mL should be used within 12 hours if kept at room temperature. Refrigeration may result in the formation of a precipitate which will redissolve at room temperature.

Once diluted, the admixtures are to be administered within 24 hours of the initial preparation. The admixtures are not to be refrigerated. Unused portions of the diluted solution should be discarded.

Incompatibility: Acyclovir should not be added to biologic or colloidal fluids (e.g., blood products, protein hydrolysates or amino acids, fat emulsions).

Supplied: 500 mg: Each vial of sterile powder contains: acyclovir sodium equivalent to acyclovir 500 mg. Nonmedicinal ingredients: sodium hydroxide to adjust the pH. Vials of 10 mL.

1 g: Each vial of sterile powder contains: acyclovir sodium equivalent to acyclovir 1 g. Nonmedicinal ingredients: sodium hydroxide to adjust the pH. Vials of 20 mL.

Should be stored between 15 and 25°C.

ZOVIRAX® Ointment

Glaxo Wellcome

Acyclovir

Antiviral Agent

Pharmacology: Acyclovir, an acyclic nucleoside analog, is a substrate specific for herpesvirus-specified thymidine kinase. It inhibits replication of these viruses. Normal cellular thymidine kinase does not effectively utilize acyclovir as a substrate. Herpes-virus-specified thymidine kinase transforms acyclovir to its monophosphate which is then transformed by cellular enzymes to acyclovir diphosphate and acyclovir triphosphate. Acyclovir triphosphate is both an inhibitor of, and a substrate for, herpesvirus-specified DNA polymerase. Although the cellular α-DNA polymerase in infected cells may also be inhibited by acyclovir triphosphate, this occurs only at concentrations of acyclovir triphosphate which are higher than those which inhibit the herpesvirus specified DNA polymerase. Acyclovir is preferentially taken up and selectively converted to its active form by herpesvirus-infected cells. Thus, acyclovir has a very much lower toxic potential for normal uninfected cells because: 1) less is taken up; 2) less is converted to the active form; 3) cellular α-DNA polymerase has a lower affinity for the active form of the drug. A combination of the thymidine kinase specificity, inhibition of DNA polymerase and premature termination of DNA synthesis results in inhibition of herpesvirus replication. No effect on latent non-replicating virus has been demonstrated. Inhibition of the virus reduces the period of viral shedding, limits the degree of spread and level of pathology, and thereby facilitates healing.

Indications: For the management of initial episodes of genital herpes simplex infections. It is also indicated in the management of non life-threatening cutaneous herpes simplex virus infections in immunocompromised patients. The prophylactic use of this preparation has not been established.

In genital herpes, appropriate examinations should be performed to rule out other sexually transmitted diseases.

These indications are based on the results of a number of double-blind, placebo-controlled studies which examined changes in virus excretion, healing of lesions and relief of pain. Because of the wide biological variations inherent in herpes simplex infections, the following summary is presented merely to illustrate the spectrum of responses observed to date. As in the treatment of any infectious disease, the best response may be expected when therapy is begun at the earliest possible moment.

In immunocompromised patients, 93% were virus negative after 5 days of topical acyclovir therapy, whereas only 35% of placebo recipients were virus negative at the same time. In patients with herpes labialis, there was a significantly greater decrease in the amount of virus excreted after one day of therapy in those receiving acyclovir within 8 hours of the onset of cold sores when compared to identically treated placebo recipients.

Because complete re-epithelialization of herpes-disrupted integument necessitates recruitment of several complex repair mechanisms, the physician should be aware that the disappearance of visible lesions is somewhat variable and will occur later than the cessation of virus shedding. All immunocompromised patients who received topical acyclovir had healed their lesions 23 days after the initiation of a 10-day course of therapy; 75% of placebo patients had healed lesions at that point. Some placebo patients continued to have visible lesions for more than 30 days.

Pain associated with herpes infections is highly variable in frequency and intensity. 100% of the acyclovir-treated immunocompromised patients were pain-free by day 23 versus 70% of placebo-treated patients.

Whereas cutaneous lesions associated with herpes simplex infections are often pathognomonic, Tzanck smears prepared from lesions exudate or scrapings may assist in the diagnosis. Positive cultures for herpes simplex virus offer the only absolute means for confirmation of the diagnosis.

Contraindications: Hypersensitivity or chemical intolerance to any of the components of the formulation, such as polyethylene glycol.

Warnings: 5% is intended for topical use only and should not be used in the eye or on mucous membranes.

Precautions: The recommended dosage, frequency of application and duration of treatment should not be exceeded (see Dosage).

Lactation: Acyclovir, when given systemically, is known to be excreted into human milk. Although evidence suggests that absorption of acyclovir through the skin is minimal, caution should be exercised when acyclovir is administered to a nursing mother.

Pregnancy: All animal studies carried out to date on reproduction and teratology studies have been negative in general. However, in a non-standard test in rats, there were fetal abnormalities such as head and tail anomalies, and maternal toxicity; since such studies are not always predictive of human response, acyclovir should not be used during pregnancy unless the physician feels the potential benefit justifies the risk of possible harm to the fetus. The potential for high concentrations of acyclovir to cause chromosome breaks in vitro should be taken into consideration in making this decision.

Children: Safety of use of acyclovir ointment 5% in children has not been established.

There exist no data, at this time, which demonstrate that the use of acyclovir ointment 5% will prevent transmission of infection to other persons.

Since most cutaneous herpes simplex virus infections result from reactivation of latent virus, is is unlikely that acyclovir ointment 5% will prevent recurrence of infections when applied in the absence of signs and symptoms. Acyclovir ointment 5% should not be applied in an attempt to prevent recurrences; application should commence only at the earliest prodromal sign of disease onset.

Although clinically significant viral resistance associated with the use of acyclovir ointment 5% has not been observed, this possibility exists.

Adverse Effects: Because ulcerated genital lesions are characteristically tender and sensitive to any contact or manipulation, patients may experience discomfort upon application of ointment. In the controlled clinical trials, mild pain (including transient burning and stinging) was reported by 103 (28.3%) of 364 patients treated with acyclovir ointment 5% and by 115 (31.1%) of 370 patients treated with placebo; treatment was discontinued in 2 of these patients. Other local reactions among acyclovir-treated patients included pruritus in 15 (4.1%), rash in 1 (0.3%) and vulvitis in 1 (0.3%). Among the placebo-treated patients, pruritus was reported by 17 (4.6%) and rash by 1 (0.3%).

In all studies, there was no significant difference between the drug and placebo group in the rate or type of reported adverse reactions.

Overdose: Symptoms and Treatment: Overdosage by topical application of acyclovir ointment 5% is unlikely because of limited transcutaneous absorption.

Dosage: Apply acyclovir ointment 5% liberally to the affected area 4 to 6 times daily for up to 10 days. A sufficient quantity of ointment should be applied to adequately cover all lesions. A finger cot or rubber glove should be used while applying acyclovir in order to prevent: (1) autoinoculation of other body sites or (2) transmission of infection to other persons. Therapy should be initiated as early as possible following onset of signs and symptoms.

Supplied: Each g contains: acyclovir 50 mg in a polyethylene glycol base. Tubes of 4, 15 and 30 g. Store between 15 to 25°C and keep dry.

ZOVIRAX® Oral

Glaxo Wellcome

Acyclovir

Antiviral Agent

Pharmacology: See Zovirax Cream. During suppression therapy there is no evidence that acyclovir prevents neural migration of the virus. It aborts episodes of recurrent herpes due to inhibition of viral replication following reactivation.

Pharmacokinetics: The pharmacokinetics of acyclovir after oral administration have been evaluated in 6 clinical studies involving 110 adult patients. In one study of 35 immunocompromised patients with herpes simplex or varicella-zoster infection given Zovirax capsules in doses of 200 to 1 000 mg every 4 hours, 6 times daily for 5 days, the bioavailability was estimated to be 15 to 20%. In this study, steady-state plasma levels were reached by the second day of dosing. Mean steady-state peak and trough concentrations following the last 200 mg dose were 0.49 μg/mL (0.47 to 0.54 μg/mL) and 0.31 μg/mL (0.18 to 0.41 μg/mL), respectively and following the last 800 mg dose were 2.8 μg/mL (2.3 to 3.1 μg/mL) and 1.8 μg/mL (1.3 to 2.5 μg/mL). In another study, 20 immunocompetent patients with recurrent genital herpes simplex infections given Zovirax capsules in doses of 800 mg every 6 hours, 4 times daily for 5 days, the mean steady-state peak and trough concentrations were 1.4 μg/mL (0.66 to 1.8 μg/mL) and 0.55 μg/mL (0.14 to 1.1 μg/mL).

In general, the pharmacokinetics of acyclovir in children is similar to adults. Mean half-life after oral doses of 300 mg/m^2 and 600 mg/m^2, in children ages 7 months to 7 years, was 2.6 hours (range 1.59 to 3.74 hours).

Orally administered acyclovir in children less than 2 years of age has not yet been fully studied.

A single oral dose bioavailability study in 23 normal volunteers showed that Zovirax capsules 200 mg are bioequivalent to 200 mg acyclovir in aqueous solution. In a separate study in 20 volunteers, it was shown that Zovirax suspension is bioequivalent to Zovirax capsules. In a different single-dose bioavailability/bioequivalence study in 24 volunteers, 1 Zovirax 800 mg tablet was demonstrated to be bioequivalent to 4 Zovirax 200 mg capsules.

In a multiple-dose crossover study where 23 volunteers received Zovirax as one 200 mg capsule, one 400 mg tablet and one 800 mg tablet 6 times daily, absorption decreased with increasing dose and the estimated bioavailabilities of acyclovir were 20, 15 and 10%, respectively. The decrease in bioavailability is believed to be a function of the dose and not the dosage form. It was demonstrated that acyclovir is not dose proportional over the dosing range 200 mg to 800 mg. In this study, steady-state peak and trough concentrations of acyclovir were 0.83 and 0.46 μg/mL, 1.21 and 0.63 μg/mL, and 1.61 and 0.83 μg/mL for the 200, 400 and 800 mg dosage regimens, respectively.

In another study in 6 volunteers, the influence of food on the absorption of acyclovir was not apparent.

Following oral administration, the mean plasma half-life of acyclovir in volunteers and patients with normal renal function ranged from 2.5 to 3.3 hours. The mean renal excretion of unchanged drug accounts for 14.4% (8.6 to 19.8%) of the orally administered dose. The only urinary metabolite (identified by high performance liquid chromatography) is 9-[(carboxymethoxy)methyl]guanine. The half-life and total body clearance of acyclovir are dependent on renal function. A dosage adjustment is recommended for patients with reduced renal function (see Dosage).

Indications: Indicated for the following conditions:

The treatment of initial episodes of herpes genitalis.

The suppression of unusually frequent recurrences of herpes genitalis (6 or more episodes/year).

The acute treatment of herpes zoster (shingles) and varicella (chickenpox).

The results of clinical studies suggest that some patients with recurrent genital herpes may derive clinical benefit from the administration of oral acyclovir if taken at the first sign of an impending episode. Those most likely to benefit are patients who experience severe, prolonged recurrences; such intermittent therapy may be more appropriate than suppressive therapy when these recurrences are infrequent.

Early treatment of acute herpes zoster (shingles) in immune competent individuals with oral acyclovir resulted in decreased viral shedding; decreased time to healing; less dissemination; and alleviation of acute pain.

Treatment of varicella (chickenpox) in immune competent patients with oral acyclovir reduced the total number of lesions, accelerated the progression of lesions to the crusted and healed stages, and decreased the number of residual hypopigmented lesions. In addition it decreased fever and constitutional symptoms associated with chickenpox.

The prophylactic use of acyclovir in chickenpox has not been established.

Contraindications: For patients who develop hypersensitivity or who are hypersensitive to the components of the formulations (see Supplied).

Warnings: Suppressive therapy of herpes genitalis with acyclovir should be considered only for severely affected patients. Periodic evaluation of the need for continued suppressive therapy is recommended. In some patients, there is a tendency for the first recurrent episode to be more severe following cessation of suppressive therapy.

In severely immunocompromised patients, the physician should be aware that prolonged or repeated courses of acyclovir may result in selection of resistant viruses associated with infections which may not respond to continued acyclovir therapy.

Precautions: General: The recommended dosage and length of treatment should not be exceeded (see Dosage). Acyclovir has caused mutagenesis in some acute studies at high concentrations of drug. Also, decreased spermatogenesis was observed in some animals at high parenteral doses. However, no adverse effects on sperm counts were reported in humans given recommended oral doses of acyclovir.

The decision to prescribe a course of suppressive therapy should be weighed in the light of our present knowledge about the long-term effects of acyclovir and must clearly relate to the condition of the patient.

It is suggested that periodic discontinuation of the suppressive regimen occur so that the patient's status and need for continued suppressive therapy can be monitored.

Whereas cutaneous lesions associated with herpes simplex infections are often pathognomonic, Tzanck smears prepared from lesion exudate or scrapings may assist in the diagnosis. Positive cultures for herpes simplex virus offer the only absolute means for confirmation of the diagnosis. Appropriate examinations should be performed to rule out other sexually transmitted diseases. All patients should be advised to take particular care to avoid potential transmission of virus if active lesions are present while they are on therapy.

Caution should be exercised when administering to patients receiving potentially nephrotoxic agents since this may increase the risk of renal dysfunction.

Chickenpox: Although chickenpox in otherwise healthy children is usually a self-limited disease of mild to moderate severity, adolescents and adults tend to have more severe disease. Treatment was initiated within 24 hours of the typical chickenpox rash in the controlled studies, and there is no information regarding the effects of treatment begun later in the disease course. It is unknown whether the treatment of chickenpox in childhood has any effect on long-term immunity. However, there is no evidence to indicate that acyclovir treatment of chickenpox would have any effect on either decreasing or increasing the incidence or severity of subsequent recurrences of herpes zoster (shingles) later in life.

Pregnancy: Teratology studies carried out to date in animals have been negative in general. However, in a non-standard test in rats, there were fetal abnormalities such as head and tail anomalies, and maternal toxicity; since such studies are not always predictive of human response, acyclovir should not be used during pregnancy unless the physician feels the potential benefit justifies the risk of possible harm to the fetus. The potential for high concentrations of acyclovir to cause chromosome breaks in vitro should be taken into consideration in making this decision.

Lactation: Acyclovir is excreted in human milk. Caution should therefore be exercised when it is administered to a nursing mother.

Children: Safety and effectiveness in children less than 2 years of age have not been adequately studied.

Drug Interactions: Co-administration of probenecid with i.v. acyclovir has been shown to increase the mean half-life and the area under the concentration-time curve. Urinary excretion and renal clearance were correspondingly reduced.

Adverse Effects: Treatment of Herpes Simplex: Short-term administration (5 to 10 days): The most frequent adverse reactions reported during clinical trials of treatment of genital herpes with oral acyclovir in 298 patients are listed in Table I.

Table I—Zovirax Oral

Adverse Effects: Treatment of Herpes Simplex (Short-Term Administration)

Adverse Reactions	Total	%
Nausea and/or vomiting	8	2.7
Headache	2	0.6

Less frequent adverse reactions, each of which occurred in 1 of 298 patient treatments (0.3%), included: diarrhea, dizziness, anorexia, fatigue, edema, skin rash, leg pain, inguinal adenopathy, medication taste, and sore throat.

Suppression: Long-term administration: The most frequent adverse events reported in a clinical trial for the prevention of recurrences with continuous administration of 400 mg (two 200 mg capsules) 2 times daily are listed in Table II.

Table II—Zovirax Oral

Adverse Effects: Treatment of Herpes Simplex (Long-Term Administration)

Adverse Reactions	1st Year (n=586) (%)	2nd Year (n=390) (%)	3rd Year (n=329) (%)
Nausea	4.8		
Diarrhea	2.4		
Headache	1.9	1.5	0.9
Rash	1.7	1.3	
Paresthesia		0.8	1.2
Asthenia			1.2

Evidence so far from clinical trials suggests that the severity and frequency of adverse events is unlikely to necessitate discontinuation of therapy.

Herpes Zoster: The most frequent adverse reactions reported during 3 clinical trials of treatment of herpes zoster (shingles) with 800 mg of oral acyclovir 5 times daily for 7 or 10 days or placebo were as shown in Table III.

Table III—Zovirax Oral

Adverse Effects: Treatment of Herpes Zoster

Adverse Reactions	Zovirax (n=323) (%)	Placebo (n=323) (%)
Malaise	11.5	11.1
Nausea	8.0	11.5
Headache	5.9	11.1
Vomiting	2.5	2.5
Diarrhea	1.5	0.3
Constipation	0.9	2.4

Chickenpox: The most frequent adverse events reported during 3 clinical trials of treatment of chickenpox with oral acyclovir or placebo are listed in Table IV.

Table IV—Zovirax Oral

Adverse Effects: Treatment of Chickenpox

Adverse Reactions	Zovirax (n=495) (%)	Placebo (n=498) (%)
Diarrhea	3.2	2.2
Abdominal Pain	0.6	0.2
Rash	0.6	0.2
Vomiting	0.6	0.2
Flatulence	0.4	0.8
Urticaria	0.2	0.2
Spasmodic Hand Movement	0.2	0.2
Insomnia	0.2	0.4

Observed During Clinical Practice: Based on clinical practice experience in patients treated with oral acyclovir in the U.S., spontaneously reported adverse events are uncommon. Data are insufficient to support an estimate of their incidence or to establish causation. These events may also occur as part of the underlying disease process. Voluntary reports of adverse events which have been received since market introduction include:

General: fever, headache, pain, peripheral edema, and rarely, anaphylaxis.

Nervous: confusion, dizziness, hallucinations, paresthesia, somnolence (these symptoms may be marked, particularly in older adults). In addition, convulsions have occasionally been reported, usually in patients with renal impairment in whom the dosage was in excess of that recommended, or with other predisposing factors.

Digestive: diarrhea, elevated liver function tests, gastrointestinal distress, nausea.

Hemic and Lymphatic: leukopenia, lymphadenopathy.

Musculoskeletal: myalgia.

Skin: alopecia, pruritus, rash, urticaria.

Special Senses: visual abnormalities.

Urogenital: elevated creatinine.

Overdose: Symptoms and Treatment: Overdosage with acyclovir during oral use is unlikely because of incomplete bioavailability from the gastrointestinal tract. Doses as high as 800 mg 6 times daily for 5 days have been administered to humans without acute untoward effects. In clinical studies, the highest plasma concentration observed in a single patient at these doses was 10.0 μg/mL.

I.V. doses administered to humans have been as high as 1 200 mg/m² (28 mg/kg) 3 times daily for up to 2 weeks. Peak plasma concentrations have reached 80 μg/mL. No acute massive overdosage of acyclovir has been reported; however, in the case of an excessively high ingestion of acyclovir, precipitation of acyclovir in renal tubules may occur if the solubility (2.5 mg/mL) in the intratubular fluid is exceeded. In the event of renal failure and anuria, the patient may benefit from hemodialysis until renal function is restored.

Dosage: Herpes Genitalis: Treatment of Initial Infection: 200 mg every 4 hours, 5 times daily for a total of 1 g daily for 10 days. Therapy should be initiated as early as possible following onset of signs and symptoms.

Suppressive Therapy for Recurrent Disease: The initial recommended dose is 200 mg 3 times daily. This can be increased if breakthrough occurs up to a dosage of 200 mg 5 times daily. If necessary, a dose of 400 mg given twice daily may be considered. Periodic re-evaluation of the need for therapy is recommended.

Administration of acyclovir for intermittent therapy is 200 mg every 4 hours, 5 times daily for 5 days. Therapy should be initiated at the earliest sign or symptom (prodrome) of recurrence.

Herpes Zoster: 800 mg every 4 hours, 5 times daily for 7 to 10 days. Treatment should be initiated within 72 hours of the

Zovirax Oral (cont'd)

onset of lesions. In clinical trials, the greatest benefit occurred when treatment was begun within 48 hours of the onset of lesions.

Treatment of Chickenpox: 20 mg/kg (not to exceed 800 mg) orally, 4 times daily for 5 days. Therapy should be initiated within 24 hours of the appearance of rash.

Patients with Acute or Chronic Renal Impairment: Comprehensive pharmacokinetic studies have been completed following i.v. acyclovir infusions in patients with renal impairment.

Based on these studies, dosage adjustments are recommended in Table V for genital herpes and herpes zoster indications.

Table V—Zovirax Oral

Dosage Adjustments for Genital Herpes and Herpes Zoster

Normal Dosage Regimen	Creatinine Clearance (mL/min/1.73 m²)	Adjusted Dosage Regimen Dose (mg)	Dosing Interval (hours)
200 mg every 4 hours (5×daily)	>10	200	every 4 hours, 5×daily
	0–10	200	every 12 hours
400 mg every 12 hours	>10	400	every 12 hours
	0–10	200	every 12 hours
800 mg every 4 hours (5×daily)	>25	800	every 4 hours, 5× daily
	10–25	800	every 8 hours
	0–10	800	every 12 hours

Hemodialysis: For patients who require hemodialysis, the mean plasma half-life of acyclovir during hemodialysis is approximately 5 hours. This results in a 60% decrease in plasma concentrations following a 6-hour dialysis period. Therefore, the patient's dosing schedule should be adjusted so that an additional dose is administered after each dialysis.

Peritoneal Dialysis: No supplement dose appears to be necessary after adjustment of the dosing interval.

Information for the Patient: See Blue Section—Information for the Patient "Zovirax Oral".

Supplied: Tablets: Zovirax 200: Each blue, shield-shaped, beveled-edge, compressed tablet, imprinted ZOVIRAX on one side and a triangle on the reverse contains: acyclovir 200 mg. Nonmedicinal ingredients: cellulose, indigotine, lactose, magnesium stearate, povidone and sodium starch glycolate. Bottles of 100 and 250. Store between 15 to 25°C. Keep dry and protect from light.

Zovirax 400 Wellstat Pac: Each pink, shield-shaped, beveled-edge, compressed tablet, imprinted with "ZOVIRAX 400" on one side and a triangle on the reverse, contains: acyclovir 400 mg. Nonmedicinal ingredients: cellulose, magnesium stearate, povidone, red iron oxide and sodium starch glycolate. Cartons of 56 blister-packed tablets. Store between 15 and 25°C. Keep dry and protect from light.

Zovirax 800 Zostab Pac: Each blue, biconvex, elongated, scored, compressed tablet, imprinted with "ZOVIRAX 800" on one side, contains: acyclovir 800 mg. Nonmedicinal ingredients: cellulose, indigotine, povidone, magnesium stearate and sodium starch glycolate. Cartons of 50 blister-packed tablets. Store between 15 and 25°C. Keep dry and protect from light.

Suspension: Each 5 mL of off-white, banana-flavored suspension contains: acyclovir 200 mg. Nonmedicinal ingredients: banana flavor, cellulose, glycerin, methylparaben, propylparaben, sorbitol and vanillin. Bottles of 125 mL. Store between 15 and 25°C.

(Shown in Product Recognition Section)

Z-PLUS®

Dormer

Menthol—Zinc Pyrithione

Antiseborrheic—Antidandruff

Supplied: Each mL of medicated shampoo and scalp cleanser contains: zinc pyrithione 2% w/w and menthol 0.3% w/w. Nonmedicinal ingredients: ammonium laureth sulfate, butylparaben, citric acid, dimethicone copolyol, FD&C Blue No. 1, fragrance, glycol distearate, hydroxypropyl methylcellulose, isopropylparaben, isobutylparaben, lauramide DEA, panthenol, polyquaternium-7, purified water, TEA-lauryl sulfate and titanium dioxide. Plastic bottles of 125 mL.

ZYLOPRIM® 🅿

Glaxo Wellcome

Allopurinol

Xanthine Oxidase Inhibitor

Pharmacology: Allopurinol is a structural analogue of hypoxanthine. Reduction in both the serum and urinary uric acid levels is brought about by allopurinol inhibiting the action of xanthine oxidase, the enzyme responsible for the conversion of hypoxanthine to xanthine and xanthine to uric acid. Allopurinol is metabolized to the corresponding xanthine analogue, oxypurinol, which is also an inhibitor of xanthine oxidase. The action of allopurinol in blocking formation of urate differs from that of uricosuric agents which lower the serum uric acid level by increasing urinary excretion of uric acid.

When taken orally, allopurinol is rapidly absorbed and rapidly metabolized. The main metabolite is oxypurinol, which is itself an xanthine oxidase inhibitor. Allopurinol and its metabolites are excreted by the kidney. The renal handling is such that allopurinol has a plasma half-life of about 1 hour, whereas that of oxypurinol exceeds 18 hours. Thus, the therapeutic effect can be achieved by a once-a-day dosage of allopurinol in patients taking 300 mg or less/day.

Administration of allopurinol generally results in a fall in both serum and urinary uric acid within 2 to 3 days. The magnitude of the decrease can be adjusted to a certain extent by varying the dose of allopurinol. The serum uric acid levels fall gradually and therefore a week or more of allopurinol treatment may be necessary before the full effect is obtained. Uric acid returns to pretreatment levels slowly, usually after a cessation of therapy. This is due primarily to the accumulation and slow clearance of oxypurinol. In some patients, particularly those with tophaceous gout, a significant fall in urinary uric acid excretion may not occur, possibly due to the mobilization of urate from tissue deposits as the serum uric acid level begins to fall.

The combined increase in hypoxanthine and xanthine excreted in the urine is usually, but not always, considerably less than the accompanying decline in urinary uric acid. This may be due to pseudofeedback inhibition of purine biosynthesis by allopurinol ribotide.

It has been shown that reutilization of both hypoxanthine and xanthine for nucleotide and nucleic acid synthesis is markedly enhanced when their oxidations are inhibited by allopurinol. This reutilization and the normal feedback inhibition which would result from an increase in available purine nucleotides serve to regulate purine biosynthesis, and, in essence, the defect of the over-producer of uric acid is thereby compensated.

Innate deficiency of xanthine oxidase, which occurs in patients with xanthinuria, as an inborn error of metabolism has been shown to be compatible with comparative well-being. While urinary levels of oxypurines attained with full doses of allopurinol may in exceptional cases equal those (250 to 600 mg/day) which in xanthinuric subjects have caused formation of urinary calculi, they usually fall in the range of 50 to 200 mg and no evidence of renal damage has been clinically observed. Xanthine crystalluria has been reported in a few exceptional cases. The serum concentration of oxypurines in patients receiving allopurinol is usually in the range of 0.3 mg to 0.4 mg % compared with a normal level of approximately 0.15 mg %. A maximum of 0.9 mg % was observed when the serum urate was lowered to less than 2 mg % by high doses of the drug. In one exceptional case, a value of 2.7 mg % was reached. These are far below the saturation level at which precipitation of xanthine or hypoxanthine would be expected to occur so that tissue deposition is unlikely and has not been observed to date. The solubilities of uric acid and xanthine in the serum are similar (about 7 mg %) while hypoxanthine is much more soluble.

The finding that the renal clearance of oxypurines is at least 10 times greater than that of uric acid explains the relatively low serum oxypurine concentration at a time when the serum uric acid level has decreased markedly. At serum oxypurine levels of 0.3 to 0.9 mg %, oxypurine: inulin clearance ratios were between 0.7 and 1.9. The glomerular filtration rate and urate clearance in patients receiving allopurinol do not differ significantly from those obtained prior to therapy. The rapid renal clearance of oxypurines suggests that allopurinol therapy should be of value in allowing a patient with gout to increase his total purine excretion.

Indications: Treatment of gout, either primary, or secondary to hyperuricemia which occurs in blood dyscrasias and their therapy.

Treatment of primary or secondary uric acid nephropathy, with or without accompanying signs or symptoms of gout.

Prophylactically, to prevent tissue urate deposition or renal calculi in patients with leukemias, lymphomas or other malignancies, receiving antineoplastic treatment (radiation or cytotoxic drugs) which might induce increased uricemia levels. Also in the therapy and prophylaxis of acute urate nephropathy and resultant renal failure in patients with neoplastic disease who are particularly susceptible to hyperuricemia and uric acid stone formation (especially after radiation therapy or use of antineoplastic drugs).

Prevention of the occurrence and recurrence of uric acid stones or gravel and renal calcium lithiasis in patients with hyperuricemia and/or hyperuricosuria.

Contraindications: Should not be given to patients who are hypersensitive to allopurinol or who have previously developed a severe reaction to this drug or to any components of the formulation. Allopurinol is contraindicated in nursing mothers and in children (except in those with hyperuricemia secondary to malignancy).

Warnings: Allopurinol should be discontinued at the appearance of a skin rash, as the rash may be, in some instances, followed by a more severe hypersensitivity reaction (see Adverse Effects).

Periodic liver function tests should be performed in all patients on allopurinol therapy.

Reduced doses should be administered to patients with renal or hepatic impairment. The drug should be withdrawn if increased abnormalities in hepatic or renal functions appear. Patients under treatment for hypertension or cardiac insufficiency, for example with diuretics or ACE inhibitors, may have some concomitant impairment of renal function and allopurinol should be used with care in this group.

Occupational Hazards: Due to occasional occurrence of drowsiness, patients should be alerted to the need for precautions when engaging in activities where alertness is mandatory.

Adequate therapy with allopurinol will lead to dissolution of large uric acid renal pelvic stones, with the remote possibility of impaction in the ureter.

Asymptomatic hyperuricemia per se is generally not considered an indication for use of allopurinol. Fluid and dietary modification with management of the underlying cause may correct the condition.

Mercaptopurine or Azathioprine with Allopurinol: In patients receiving mercaptopurine or azathioprine, the concomitant administration of 300 to 600 mg of allopurinol/day will require a reduction in dose to approximately one-third or one-fourth of the usual dose of mercaptopurine or azathioprine. Subsequent adjustment of doses of mercaptopurine or azathioprine should be made on the basis of therapeutic response and any toxic effects.

Pregnancy: Allopurinol is not recommended for use during pregnancy or in women of childbearing potential unless in the judgment of the physician, the potential benefits outweigh the possible risk to the fetus.

Children: Allopurinol should not be given to children with the exception of those with hyperuricemia secondary to malignancy or with Lesch-Nyhan syndrome, because safety and effectiveness have not been established in other conditions.

Precautions: Allopurinol treatment should not be started until an acute attack of gout has completely subsided, as further attacks may be precipitated.

Acute gouty attacks may be precipitated at the start of treatment with allopurinol in new patients, and these may continue even after serum uric acid levels begin to fall. Prophylactic administration of colchicine is advisable, particularly in new patients and in those where the previous attack rate has been high. In addition, it is recommended that the patient start with a low dose of allopurinol (100 and 200 mg daily) and the dose be built up slowly until a serum uric acid level of 6 mg/100 mL or less is attained (see Dosage). If acute gouty attacks develop in patients receiving allopurinol, treatment should continue at the same dosage while the acute attack is treated with a suitable anti-inflammatory agent.

In conditions where the rate of urate formation is greatly increased (e.g., malignant disease and its treatment; Lesch-Nyhan syndrome), the absolute concentration of xanthine in urine could, in rare cases, rise sufficiently to allow deposition in the urinary tract. This risk may be minimized by adequate hydration to achieve optimal urine dilution.

Lactation: Reports indicate that allopurinol and oxipurinol are excreted in human breast milk. Concentrations of 1.4 mg/L allopurinol and 53.7 mg/L oxipurinol have been demonstrated in breast milk from a woman taking allopurinol 300 mg/day. However, there are no data concerning the effects of allopurinol or its metabolites on breast-fed babies.

Drug Interactions: Mercaptopurine or Azathioprine: (see Warnings).

Uricosurics and Salicylates: Renal clearance of oxypurinol, the major therapeutically active metabolite of allopurinol, is increased by uricosuric agents such as probenecid or large doses of salicylate and as a consequence the addition of a uricosuric agent may reduce the extent of inhibition of xanthine oxidase by oxypurinol. However, such combined therapy may be useful in achieving minimum serum uric acid levels provided that total urinary uric acid load does not exceed the competence of the patient's renal function.

Coumarin Anticoagulants: It has been reported that under experimental conditions allopurinol prolongs the half-life of the anticoagulant, dicumarol. The clinical significance of this has not been established, but this interaction should be kept in mind when allopurinol is given to patients already on anticoagulant therapy, and the coagulation time should be reassessed.

Chlorpropamide: In the presence of allopurinol, there may be competition in the renal tubule for the excretion of chlorpropamide. When renal function is poor, the recognized risk of prolonged hypoglycemic activity of chlorpropamide may be increased if allopurinol is given concomitantly.

Vidarabine: Evidence suggests that the plasma half-life of vidarabine is increased in the presence of allopurinol. When the two products are used concomitantly extra vigilance is necessary to recognize enhanced toxic effects.

Phenytoin: Allopurinol may inhibit hepatic oxidation of phenytoin but the clinical significance has not been demonstrated.

Theophylline: Inhibition of the metabolism of theophylline has been reported in normal subjects given relatively high doses of allopurinol (300 mg b.i.d.) under experimental conditions. The mechanism of the interaction may be explained by xanthine oxidase being involved in the biotransformation of theophylline in man. Although there have been no clinical reports of interaction, theophylline levels should be monitored in patients starting or increasing allopurinol therapy.

Ampicillin/Amoxicillin: An increase in the frequency of skin rash has been reported among patients receiving ampicillin or amoxicillin concurrently with allopurinol compared to patients who are not receiving both drugs. The cause of the reported association has not been established. However, it is recommended that in patients receiving allopurinol an alternative to ampicillin or amoxicillin is used where available.

Cyclophosphamide, Doxorubicin, Bleomycin, Procarbazine and Mechloroethamine: Enhanced bone marrow suppression by cyclophosphamide and other cytotoxic agents has been reported among patients with neoplastic disease, (other than leukemia), in the presence of allopurinol. However, in a well-controlled study of patients treated with cyclophosphamide, doxorubicin, bleomycin, procarbazine and/or mechloroethamine (mustine HCl) allopurinol did not appear to increase the toxic reaction of these cytotoxic agents.

Cyclosporin: Reports suggest that the plasma concentration of cyclosporin may be increased during concomitant treatment with allopurinol. The possibility of enhanced cyclosporin toxicity should be considered if the drugs are coadministered.

Adverse Effects: Adverse reactions in association with allopurinol are rare in the overall treated population and mostly of a minor nature. The incidence is higher in the presence of renal and/or hepatic disorder. (See Warnings).

Skin Reactions: These are the most common reactions and may occur at any time during treatment. They may be pruritic, maculopapular, sometimes scaly, sometimes purpuric and rarely exfoliative. The rash has been followed by severe hypersensitivity reactions. Allopurinol should be withdrawn **immediately** should such reactions occur. After recovery from mild reactions allopurinol may, if desired, be cautiously reintroduced at a small dose (e.g., 50 mg/day) and gradually increased. If the rash recurs, allopurinol should be **permanently** withdrawn.

Generalized Hypersensitivity: Skin reactions associated with exfoliation, fever, chills, nausea and vomiting, lymphadenopathy, arthralgia and/or eosinophilia resembling Stevens-Johnson and/or Lyell's syndrome have occurred. Associated vasculitis and tissue response may be manifested in various ways including hepatitis, interstitial nephritis and very rarely, epilepsy. If they do occur, it may be at any time during treatment. Allopurinol should be withdrawn **immediately** and **permanently**.

Corticosteroids may be beneficial in overcoming such reactions. When generalized hypersensitivity reactions have occurred, renal and/or hepatic disorders have usually been present particularly when the outcome has been fatal.

Angioimmunoblastic Lymphadenopathy: Angioimmunoblastic lymphadenopathy has been described rarely following biopsy of a generalized lymphadenopathy. It appears to be reversible on withdrawal of allopurinol.

Granulomatous Hepatitis: Very rarely granulomatous hepatitis, without overt evidence of more generalized hypersensitivity has been described. It appears to be reversible on withdrawal of allopurinol.

Gastrointestinal Disorders: Diarrhea, intermittent abdominal pain, nausea and vomiting were reported. Gastrointestinal disorders diminish if allopurinol is taken after meals. Recurrent hematemesis has been reported as an extremely rare event, as has steatorrhea.

Blood and Lymphatic System: There have been occasional reports of reduction in the number of circulating formed elements of the blood, including agranulocytosis, thrombocytopenia and aplastic anemia, usually in association with renal and/or, hepatic disorders or in whom concomitant drugs have been administered which have a potential for causing these reactions.

Miscellaneous: The following adverse effects have been reported occasionally: fever, general malaise, asthenia, headache, vertigo, ataxia, somnolence, coma, depression, paralysis, paraesthesiae, taste perversion, stomatitis, changed bowel habit, infertility, hepatic necrosis, abnormal liver function tests, rise in BUN, hyperlipemia, visual disorder, cataracts, macular changes, neuropathy, impotence, diabetes mellitus, furunculosis, alopecia, discolored hair, angina, hypertension, bradycardia, hematuria, edema, uremia, drowsiness, peripheral neuritis, angioedema and gynecomastia.

Overdose: Symptoms and Treatment: Ingestion of up to 22.5 g allopurinol without adverse effect has been reported. Symptoms and signs including nausea, vomiting, diarrhea, and dizziness have been reported in a patient who ingested 20 g allopurinol. Recovery followed general supportive measures.

Massive absorption of allopurinol may lead to considerable inhibition of xanthine oxidase activity, which should have no untoward effects unless affecting concomitant medication, especially with mercaptopurine and/or azathioprine. No treatment is normally required provided the drug is withdrawn and adequate hydration is maintained to facilitate excretion of the drug. If considered necessary hemodialysis may be used. If, however, other forms of acute distress are observed, gastric lavage should be considered, otherwise the treatment is symptomatic.

Dosage: Adults: General Considerations: Allopurinol is administered orally. The total daily requirement should be divided into 1 to 3 doses. Daily doses up to and including 300 mg of allopurinol may be taken once a-day after a meal. Larger doses should be administered as divided doses of not more than 300 mg. It should be noted that allopurinol is generally better tolerated if taken following meals.

Treatment of Gout: The dose of allopurinol varies with the severity of the disease. The minimum effective dose is 100 to 200 mg. The average is 200 to 300 mg/day for patients with mild gout, 400 to 600 mg/day for patients with moderately severe tophaceous gout, and 700 to 800 mg in severe conditions. The maximal recommended dose is 800 mg/day in patients with normal renal function.

Since allopurinol and its metabolites are excreted only by the kidney, accumulation of the drug can occur in renal failure and the dose of allopurinol should consequently be reduced. With a creatinine clearance of 20 to 10 mL/min, a daily dosage of 200 mg of allopurinol is suitable. When the creatinine clearance is less than 10 mL/min, the daily dosage should not exceed 100 mg. With extreme renal impairment (creatinine clearance less than 3 mL/min), the interval between doses may also need to be lengthened. As no simple method of measuring the blood concentrations of allopurinol is available, the correct size and frequency of dosage for maintaining the serum uric acid just within the normal range is best determined by using the serum uric acid level as an index.

Once the daily dose of allopurinol necessary to produce the desired serum uric acid level has been determined, this dose should be continued until the serum uric acid level indicates a need for dosage adjustment.

Normal serum urate levels are achieved in 1 to 3 weeks. The upper limit of normal is about 6 mg % for men and postmenopausal women and 5 mg % for premenopausal women. By the selection of the appropriate dose, together with the use of uricosuric agents in certain patients, it is possible to reduce the serum uric level to normal and, if desired, to hold it as low as 2 to 3 mg %. Combined therapy of allopurinol and uricosurics will often result in a reduction in dosage of both agents.

To reduce the possibility of an increase in acute attacks of gout during the early stages of allopurinol administration, it is recommended that the patient start with a low dose of allopurinol (100 to 200 mg daily) and increase at weekly intervals by 100 mg until a serum uric acid level of about 6 mg % or less is attained. Also, a maintenance dose of colchicine should be given prophylactically when allopurinol is begun, and a high fluid intake is advisable.

In patients who are being treated with uricosuric agents, colchicine and/or anti-inflammatory agents, it is wise to continue this therapy while adjusting the dosage of allopurinol until a normal serum uric acid level and freedom from acute attacks have been maintained for several months. If desired, the patient may then be transferred to allopurinol therapy exclusively.

For the Prevention of Uric Acid Nephropathy During the Vigorous Therapy of Neoplastic Disease: Treatment with 600 to 800 mg daily for 2 or 3 days prior to chemotherapy of X-irradiation is advisable. Treatment should be continued at a dosage adjusted to the serum uric acid level until there is no longer a threat of hyperuricemia and hyperuricosuria.

Allopurinol treatment can be maintained during the antimitotic therapy for prophylaxis of the hyperuricemia which may arise during the natural crises of the disease. In prolonged treatment, 300 to 400 mg of allopurinol daily is usually enough to control the serum uric acid level.

It is essential that a daily urinary output of 2 L or more be maintained during allopurinol therapy, and neutral or alkaline urine is desirable.

Prophylaxis of Renal Calcium Lithiasis: The recommended starting dose of allopurinol for the prevention of recurrent calcium stones is 200 to 300 mg daily as one dose or individual doses. Therapy should be continued indefinitely. Some patients have received maintenance dosages of 200 to 300 mg daily for more than 7 years. In some patients, the maintenance dosage may be reduced to 100 to 200 mg daily.

Children (6 to 10 years of age): For the treatment of secondary hyperuricemia associated with malignancies and in the Lesch-Nyhan syndrome, allopurinol should be given in doses of 10 mg/kg/day. The response should be evaluated after approximately 48 hours by monitoring serum uric acid and/or urinary uric acid levels and adjusting the dose if necessary.

Supplied: 100 mg: Each white, round, flat faced, bevel-edged tablet, scored on one side with ZYLOPRIM/U4A, contains: allopurinol 100 mg. Nonmedicinal ingredients: cornstarch, lactose, magnesium stearate and povidone. Bottles of 100.

200 mg: Each white to off-white, round, biconvex tablet, scored on one side with ZYLOPRIM/F9B, contains: allopurinol 200 mg. Nonmedicinal ingredients: cornstarch, lactose, magnesium stearate and povidone. Bottles of 100.

300 mg: Each peach-colored, round, biconvex tablet, scored on one side with ZYLOPRIM/C9B, contains: allopurinol 300 mg. Nonmedicinal ingredients: cornstarch, FD&C Yellow No. 6 Lake, lactose, magnesium stearate and povidone. Bottles of 100 and 500.

Store between 15 and 30°C.

(Shown in Product Recognition Section)

Reviewed 1997

ZYPREXA® Ⓟ

Lilly

Olanzapine

Antipsychotic

Pharmacology: Pharmacodynamics: Olanzapine, a thienobenzodiazepine, is an antipsychotic agent, displaying high receptor affinity binding in vitro at serotonin 5-$HT_{2A/C}$ (Ki=4 and 11 nM, respectively), dopamine D_1, D_2, D_3, D_4 (Ki=11 to 31 nM), muscarinic $M_{1\text{-}5}$ (Ki=1.9 to 2.5 nM), adrenergic α_1(Ki=19 nM), and histamine H_1 (Ki=7 nM) receptors. In a

Zyprexa (cont'd)

behavioral paradigm predictive of antipsychotic activity, olanzapine reduced conditioned avoidance response in rats at doses lower than 4 times those required to produce catalepsy. In a single dose (10 mg) PET study in healthy subjects, olanzapine produced higher 5-HT_{2A} than dopamine D_2 receptor occupancy. The percent of D_2 occupancy was less than the threshold value predictive of extrapyramidal events.

Pharmacokinetics: Olanzapine is well absorbed after oral administration, reaching peak plasma concentrations within 5 to 8 hours. The absorption is not affected by food. Plasma concentrations of orally administered olanzapine were linear and dose proportional in trials studying doses from 1 to 15 mg. The maximum plasma concentrations (Cmax) of olanzapine after single oral doses of 5, 10 and 15 mg averaged 7, 14, and 21 ng/mL, respectively (20 ng/mL=0.064 μM). In young healthy volunteers, after once-a-day repeated dosing, steady-state Cmax was approximately twice that achieved after a single dose (e.g., 23 ng/mL versus 12 ng/mL for a 10 mg dose). In the elderly, the steady-state plasma concentration was approximately 3-fold higher than that achieved after a single dose (e.g., 16 ng/mL versus 5 ng/mL for a 5 mg dose). In both, young and elderly, steady-state concentrations of olanzapine were obtained after 7 days of once daily dosing.

Over time and dosage range, pharmacokinetic parameters within an individual are very consistent. However, plasma concentrations, half-life and clearance of olanzapine may vary between individuals on the basis of smoking status, gender, and age (see Special Populations). Data from pooled, single dose pharmacokinetic studies showed the half-life of olanzapine to range from 21 to 54 hours (5th to 95th percentile), and the apparent plasma clearance to range from 12 to 47 L/hour (5th to 95th percentile).

The plasma protein binding of olanzapine was about 93% over the concentration range of about 7 to about 1 000 ng/mL. Olanzapine is bound predominantly to albumin and α_1-acid glycoprotein. Olanzapine is metabolized in the liver by conjugative and oxidative pathways. A mass balance study showed that approximately 57% of radiolabeled olanzapine appeared in urine, principally as metabolites. The major circulating metabolite is the 10-N-glucuronide, which is pharmacologically inactive and does not pass the blood brain barrier. Cytochromes P450-CYP1A2 and P450-CYP2D6 contribute to the formation of the N-desmethyl and 2-hydroxymethyl metabolites, respectively. These metabolites do not produce behavioral activity in the rat at doses 4 to 16 times greater than active doses of olanzapine.

In vitro microsomal studies show that olanzapine is a weak inhibitor of CYP1A2 (Ki=36 μM), CYP2D6 (Ki=89 μM), and CYP3A4 (Ki=490 μM). Based upon these Ki values, little inhibition of these cytochrome P450 enzymes is expected in vivo at concentrations below 5 μM (roughly 1 500 ng/mL) because the olanzapine concentration will be less than 10% of its Ki value. In clinical studies, observed steady-state plasma concentrations of olanzapine are rarely >150 ng/mL (approximately 0.5 μM). Olanzapine is thus not likely to cause clinically important pharmacokinetic drug-drug interactions mediated through the metabolic routes outlined above (see Precautions, Drug Interactions).

Special Populations: In a single dose study involving 24 healthy subjects the mean elimination half-life of olanzapine was prolonged in elderly subjects compared with nonelderly subjects, as shown in Table I.

Table I—Zyprexa

Elimination Half-life

	<65 years (N=8)	**≥65 years (N=16)**
Men	29 hours	49 hours
Women	39 hours	55 hours

Large scale population pharmacokinetic analyses show that the plasma clearance of olanzapine is lower in elderly versus young subjects, in females versus males, and in nonsmokers versus smokers. However, the overall variability between individuals is larger than the magnitude of impact of the individual factors of age, gender or smoking, on olanzapine clearance and half-life.

The pharmacokinetic characteristics of olanzapine (5 mg single dose) were not substantially different in patients with severe renal impairment and in normal subjects. Multiple-dose studies in patients with renal failure, however, have not been performed.

No differences in the single-dose pharmacokinetics of olanzapine were noted in subjects with clinically significant cirrhosis (who were mostly smokers) when compared to healthy subjects (all nonsmokers). Multiple-dose studies in patients with hepatic impairment, however, have not been performed.

No specific pharmacokinetic study was conducted to investigate ethnicity effects, but a review of the clinical pharmacology studies identified no important differences in the disposition of olanzapine in Caucasian subjects versus subjects of African descent.

Clinical Trials: The efficacy of olanzapine in the reduction of and maintenance of the reduction of the manifestations of schizophrenia and related psychotic disorders was established in 3 well-controlled clinical trials of psychotic inpatients who, at entry, met the DSM-III-R criteria for schizophrenia (most with a course at entry of "chronic with acute exacerbation") and 1 well-controlled clinical trial of psychotic inpatients and outpatients who, at entry, met the DSM-III-R criteria for schizophrenia, schizophreniform disorder, or schizoaffective disorder. The results of the trials follow:

A 6-week, placebo-controlled trial (N=335) compared 3 fixed dosage ranges of olanzapine (5±2.5, 10±2.5, and 15±2.5 mg/day once daily), 1 dosage range of haloperidol (15±5 mg/day on a b.i.d. schedule), and placebo. The 2 higher dosage ranges of olanzapine were statistically significantly superior to placebo on the Brief Psychiatric Rating Scale (BPRS) total, the Clinical Global Impressions—Severity of Illness (CGI-S) scale, and the BPRS positive psychosis cluster. The highest dosage range of olanzapine was statistically significantly superior to placebo and to haloperidol on the Scale for the Assessment of Negative Symptoms (SANS). Efficacy of olanzapine generally increased with dose. The 5±2.5 mg/day dosage range of olanzapine was numerically, but not statistically significantly superior to placebo on BPRS total and other assessments of overall psychopathology.

A 6-week, placebo-controlled trial (N=152) compared 2 fixed doses of olanzapine (1 or 10 mg/day once daily) and placebo; olanzapine, 10 mg/day, was statistically significantly superior to placebo on the BPRS total, the BPRS positive psychosis cluster, the CGI-S scale, the Positive and Negative Syndrome Scale (PANSS) total, the PANSS positive subscale, and the PANSS negative subscale. Olanzapine, 1 mg/day, appeared to be a no-effect dose with no difference, clinically or statistically, from placebo on any assessment of psychopathology.

A 6-week, dose comparison trial (N=431) compared 3 fixed dosage ranges of olanzapine (5±2.5, 10±2.5 and 15±2.5 mg/day once daily), olanzapine (1 mg/day once daily), and haloperidol (15±5 mg/day on a b.i.d. schedule). There were no statistically significant differences between groups on efficacy measures except for the highest dosage range of olanzapine, which was statistically significantly superior to olanzapine, 1 mg, on the BPRS positive psychosis cluster, PANSS positive subscale, and the CGI-S scale.

A 6-week comparator-controlled trial (N=1 996, 2:1 randomization, olanzapine:haloperidol) compared 1 dosage range of olanzapine (5 to 20 mg/day once daily) and 1 dosage range of haloperidol (5 to 20 mg/day once daily). The acute mean modal doses (for those patients with at least 3 weeks of treatment) were 13.2 mg/day for olanzapine and 11.8 mg/day for haloperidol. Olanzapine was statistically significantly superior to haloperidol on the BPRS total, the BPRS negative psychosis cluster, the PANSS negative subscale, and the CGI-S scale. Olanzapine was also statistically significantly superior to haloperidol on the Montgomery-Asberg Depression Rating Scale (MADRS). The validity of this scale in patients with schizophrenia, however, is not established.

The effectiveness of olanzapine in long-term therapy, i.e., >6 weeks, was evaluated in 3 double-blind, controlled, extension maintenance trials (of acute trials 1, 3, and 4 above). Patients who showed adequate clinical improvement following double-blind acute therapy were allowed to continue on in a double-blind, long-term extension maintenance phase on their acute dosage regime. Long-term maintenance of treatment response (as defined by continued reduction in signs and symptoms sufficient to not require hospitalization for psychosis) was compared over time (894 olanzapine-treated patients; median length of treatment was 237 days). The percentage of patients maintaining treatment response over 1 year was compared. Olanzapine was statistically significantly superior to placebo in the 1 placebo-controlled trial and was comparable or statistically significantly superior to the active comparator in 3 of 3 active comparator-controlled trials.

While the efficacy of olanzapine at a dose of 5 mg/day was not statistically superior to placebo [see (1)], some individual patients receiving this dose had a good acute response, and were well maintained during a 1-year extension phase.

The above trials (including open-label extension) and an additional trial in geriatric patients with primary degenerative dementia of the Alzheimer's type constitute the primary database (N=2 500 patients treated with olanzapine, corresponding to 1 122.2 patient-years; N=810 patients treated with haloperidol, corresponding to 193.0 patient-years; N=236 patients treated with placebo, corresponding to 27.1 patient-years).

Indications: For the acute and maintenance treatment of schizophrenia and related psychotic disorders. In controlled clinical trials, olanzapine was found to improve both positive and negative symptoms.

Olanzapine has been shown to be effective in maintaining clinical improvement during 1 year of continuation therapy in patients who had shown an initial treatment response.

Contraindications: Patients with a known hypersensitivity to the drug or the excipients of the product.

Warnings: Neuroleptic Malignant Syndrome (NMS): In premarketing clinical trials there were no reported cases of NMS in patients receiving olanzapine. However, NMS is a potentially fatal symptom complex that has been reported in association with antipsychotic drugs. Clinical manifestations of NMS are hyperpyrexia, muscle rigidity, altered mental status, and evidence of autonomic instability (irregular pulse or blood pressure, tachycardia, diaphoresis and cardiac dysrhythmia). Additional signs may include elevated creatinine phosphokinase, myoglobinuria (rhabdomyolysis) and acute renal failure.

The management of NMS should include immediate discontinuation of all antipsychotic drugs including olanzapine, intensive monitoring of symptoms and treatment of any associated medical problems. There is no general agreement about specific pharmacological treatment for NMS. If a patient requires antipsychotic drug treatment after recovery from NMS, the reintroduction of therapy should be very carefully considered, since recurrence of NMS has been reported.

Tardive Dyskinesia: Tardive dyskinesia (TD), a syndrome consisting of potentially irreversible involuntary dyskinetic movements, is associated with the use of antipsychotic drugs. TD occurs more frequently in elderly patients; however, patients of any age can be affected. It is unknown whether antipsychotic drugs may differ in their potential to cause TD. However, during long-term, double-blind extension maintenance trials (894 olanzapine-treated patients; median olanzapine treatment, 237 days), olanzapine was associated with a statistically significantly lower incidence of treatment emergent dyskinesia compared to haloperidol.

The risk of developing tardive dyskinesia and the chance of it becoming irreversible, are believed to increase as the duration of treatment and the cumulative dose of antipsychotic drugs increase. However, the syndrome can develop, although less commonly, after relatively brief periods of treatment at low doses. There is no known treatment for established cases of TD. The syndrome may remit, partially or completely, if antipsychotic drug treatment is withdrawn. Antipsychotic drug treatment itself, however, may suppress the signs and symptoms of tardive dyskinesia, thereby masking the underlying process.

Given these considerations, olanzapine should be prescribed in a manner that is most likely to minimize the risk of tardive dyskinesia. As with any antipsychotic drug, olanzapine should be reserved for patients who appear to be receiving substantial benefit from the drug. In such patients the lowest effective dose and the shortest duration of treatment should be sought. The need for continued treatment should be reassessed periodically.

If signs or symptoms of tardive dyskinesia appear in a patient on olanzapine, drug discontinuation should be considered. However, some patients may benefit from continued treatment with olanzapine despite the presence of the syndrome.

Precautions: Lactose: Zyprexa tablets contain lactose.

Occupational Hazards: Potential Effect on Cognitive and Motor Performance: Because olanzapine may cause somnolence, patients should be cautioned about operating hazardous machinery, including motor vehicles, until they are reasonably certain that olanzapine therapy does not affect them adversely.

Hypotension and Syncope: As with other drugs that have high alpha-1 adrenergic receptor blocking activity, olanzapine may induce orthostatic hypotension, tachycardia, dizziness, and sometimes syncope, especially at the initiation of treatment. In a clinical trial database of 2 500 patients treated with olanzapine, syncope was reported in 0.6% (15/2 500). The risk of orthostatic hypotension and syncope may be minimized by initiating therapy with 5 mg daily (see Dosage). A more gradual titration to the target dose should be considered if hypotension occurs. Olanzapine should be used with particular caution in patients with known cardiovascular disease (history of myocardial infarction or ischemia, heart failure, or conduction abnormalities), cerebrovascular disease, and conditions which would predispose patients to hypotension (dehydration, hypovolemia, and treatment with antihypertensive medications).

Seizures: Conventional neuroleptics are known to lower seizure threshold. In clinical trials, seizures have occurred in a small number (0.9%, 22/2 500) of olanzapine-treated patients. There were confounding factors that may have contributed to the occurrence of seizures in many of these cases. Olanzapine should be used cautiously in patients who have a history of seizures or have conditions associated with seizure or have a lowered seizure threshold.

Transaminase Elevations: During premarketing clinical trials, therapy with olanzapine was associated with elevation of hepatic transaminases, primarily ALT. Within a clinical trial database of 2 280 olanzapine-treated patients, with baseline ALT levels ≤60 IU/L, 5.9% (134/2 280) had treatment-emergent ALT elevations to >120 IU/L, 1.9% (44/2 280) had elevations to >200 IU/L, and 0.2% (5/2 280) had elevations to >400 IU/L. No patients had values in excess of 700 IU/L. None of the olanzapine-treated patients who had elevated transaminase values manifested clinical symptomatology associated with liver impairment. The majority of transaminase elevations were seen during the first 6 weeks of treatment. Most elevations were transient (66%) while patients continued on olanzapine therapy, or falling (11%) at the last available measurement. Of the 134 olanzapine-treated patients whose enzyme levels increased to >120 IU/L, 20 discontinued treatment (6 for hepatic, 14 for other reasons) while their ALT values were still rising. In 38 olanzapine-treated patients with baseline ALT >90 IU/L, none experienced an elevation to >400 IU/L.

Precautions should be exercised when using olanzapine in patients with pre-existing hepatic disorders, in patients who are being treated with potentially hepatotoxic drugs, or if treatment-emergent signs or symptoms of hepatic impairment appear.

For patients who have known or suspected abnormal hepatic function prior to starting olanzapine, standard clinical assessment, including measurement of transaminase levels is recommended. Periodic clinical reassessment with transaminase levels is recommended for such patients, as well as for patients who develop any signs and symptoms suggestive of a new onset liver disorder during olanzapine therapy.

Hematologic Indices: In clinical trials, there were no data to suggest olanzapine adversely affected bone marrow function, even in patients with a history of clozapine-associated neutropenia or leukopenia. Olanzapine was associated with a 5.7% incidence of mainly transient treatment-emergent elevations of eosinophil counts above the normal range. Elevations were not associated with any symptoms, identifiable allergic phenomena, or changes in other hematologic indices.

Hyperprolactinemia: As with other drugs that block dopamine D2, and/or serotonin 5-HT2 receptors, olanzapine may elevate prolactin levels. Elevations associated with olanzapine treatment are generally mild and may decline during continued administration.

Since tissue culture experiments indicate that approximately one-third of human breast cancers are prolactin dependent in vitro, olanzapine should only be administered to patients with previously detected breast cancer if the benefits outweigh the potential risks. Caution should also be exercised when considering olanzapine treatment in patients with pituitary tumors. Possible manifestations associated with elevated prolactin levels are amenorrhea, galactorrhea and menorrhagia.

As is common with compounds which stimulate prolactin release, the administration of olanzapine resulted in an increase in the incidence of mammary neoplasms in both rats and mice. The physiological differences between rats and humans with regard to prolactin make the clinical significance of these findings unclear. To date, neither clinical nor epidemiological studies have shown an association between chronic administration of these drugs and mammary tumorigenesis.

Uric Acid: In the premarketing clinical trial database, olanzapine was associated with mild elevations of uric acid in some patients. However, only 1 olanzapine-treated patient experienced treatment-emergent gout, and the baseline uric acid concentration for this patient was at least as large as all concentrations observed while the patient was receiving olanzapine.

Weight Gain: Olanzapine was associated with weight gain during clinical trials. Patients treated at higher doses (15±2.5 mg/day) had the greatest mean weight gain. However, a categorization of patients at baseline on the basis of body mass index (BMI) revealed a significantly greater effect in patients with low BMI compared to normal or overweight patients. Using pooled data from patients treated with olanzapine over the dosage range of 5 to 20 mg/day, weight gain tended to level off at 6 to 8 months of treatment, with a mean gain of 5.4 kg.

Antiemetic Effect: Consistent with its dopamine antagonist effects, olanzapine may have an antiemetic effect. Such an effect may mask signs of toxicity due to overdosage of other drugs or may mask symptoms of disease such as brain tumor or intestinal obstruction.

Body Temperature Regulation: Disruption of the body's ability to reduce core body temperature has been attributed to antipsychotic agents. Appropriate care is advised when prescribing olanzapine for patients who will be experiencing conditions which may contribute to an elevation of core temperature, e.g. exercising strenuously, exposure to extreme heat, receiving concomitant medication with anticholinergic activity, or being subject to dehydration.

Suicide: The possibility of suicide or attempted suicide is inherent in psychosis, and thus close supervision and appropriate clinical management of high-risk patients should accompany drug therapy.

Drug Interactions: Given the primary CNS effects of olanzapine, caution should be used when it is taken in combination with other centrally-acting drugs and alcohol. As it exhibits in vitro dopamine antagonism, olanzapine may antagonize the effects of levodopa and dopamine agonists. Because of its potential for inducing hypotension, olanzapine may enhance the effects of certain antihypertensive agents.

Potential for Other Drugs to Affect Olanzapine: The metabolism of olanzapine may be induced by concomitant smoking, or carbamazepine therapy. The concomitant administration of activated charcoal reduced the oral bioavailability of olanzapine by 50 to 60%. Single doses of antacid (aluminum, magnesium) or cimetidine did not affect the oral bioavailability of olanzapine. Agents that induce CYP1A2 such as omeprazole may increase clearance of olanzapine. Conversely, inhibitors of CYP1A2 (e.g., fluvoxamine) could potentially inhibit elimination of olanzapine. However, as olanzapine is metabolized by multiple enzyme systems, inhibition of a single enzyme may not appreciably decrease olanzapine clearance.

Potential for Olanzapine to Affect Other Drugs: In clinical trials with single doses of olanzapine, no inhibition of the metabolism of imipramine/desipramine (P450-CYP2D6), warfarin (P450-CYP2C9), or diazepam (P450-CYP3A4) was evident. Olanzapine showed no interaction when coadministered with lithium. Also, in in vitro studies with human microsomes, olanzapine showed little potential to inhibit cytochromes P450-CYP1A2, -CYP2C9, -CYP2C19, -CYP2D6, and -CYP3A4 (see Pharmacology). Olanzapine is thus unlikely to cause clinically important drug-drug interactions mediated through the metabolic routes outlined above. However, the possibility that olanzapine may alter the metabolism of other drugs, or that other drugs may alter the metabolism of olanzapine, should be considered when prescribing olanzapine.

Pregnancy: There are no adequate and well-controlled studies in pregnant women. Patients should be advised to notify their physician if they become pregnant or intend to become pregnant during treatment with olanzapine. Because human experience in pregnant females is limited, this drug should be used in pregnancy only if the potential benefit justifies the potential risk to the fetus.

Labor and Delivery: Parturition in rats was not affected by olanzapine. The effect of olanzapine on labor and delivery in humans is not known.

Lactation: Olanzapine was excreted in milk of treated rats during lactation. It is not known if olanzapine is excreted in human milk. Patients should be advised not to breast-feed an infant if they are taking olanzapine.

Geriatrics: The number of patients 65 years of age or over, with schizophrenia or related disorders, exposed to olanzapine, during clinical trials was limited (N=44). Caution should thus be exercised with the use of olanzapine in the elderly patient, recognizing the more frequent hepatic, renal, central nervous system, and cardiovascular dysfunctions, and more frequent use of concomitant medication in this population (see Dosage).

Children: The safety and efficacy of olanzapine in children under the age of 18 years have not been established.

Renal and Hepatic Impairment: Small single-dose clinical pharmacology studies (see Pharmacology, Special Populations) did not reveal any major alterations in olanzapine pharmacokinetics in subjects with renal or hepatic impairment. Given the limited clinical experience with olanzapine in patients with these conditions, caution should be exercised (see Dosage).

Patients with Other Concomitant Illness: Clinical experience with olanzapine in patients with concomitant illness is limited. Caution is thus advised when using olanzapine in patients with diseases or conditions that could affect the metabolism or the pharmacodynamic activity of olanzapine (see Pharmacology, Pharmacokinetics, and Dosage).

Olanzapine has not been evaluated in patients with a recent history of myocardial infarction or unstable heart disease. Patients with these conditions were excluded from premarketing clinical trials.

As olanzapine demonstrated anticholinergic activity in vitro, caution is advised when prescribing for patients with symptomatic prostatic enlargement, narrow-angle glaucoma or paralytic ileus and related conditions.

In clinical trials, a single case of pre-existing intercranial hypertension exacerbated.

Adverse Effects: The stated frequencies of adverse events represent the proportion of individuals who experienced, at least once, a treatment-emergent adverse event of the type listed. An event was considered treatment-emergent if it occurred for the first time or worsened while receiving therapy following baseline evaluation. It is important to emphasize that although the events were reported during therapy, they were not necessarily caused by the therapy.

The prescriber should be aware that the figures in the tables and tabulations cannot be used to predict the incidence of side effects in the course of usual medical practice where patient characteristics and other factors differ from those that prevailed in the clinical trials. Similarly, the cited frequencies cannot be compared with figures obtained from other clinical investigations involving different treatments, uses and investigators. The figures cited, however, do provide the prescribing physician with some basis for estimating the relative contribution of drug and nondrug factors to the side effect incidence in the populations studied.

Commonly Observed Adverse Events in Placebo-Controlled Clinical Trials: The following treatment-emergent adverse events, derived from Table II, commonly occurred during acute therapy with olanzapine (incidence of at least 5%, and more than double the incidence observed with placebo): dizziness, constipation, ALT increased, weight gain, akathesia and postural hypotension.

Adverse Events Associated with Discontinuation: Short-Term, Placebo-Controlled Clinical Trials: There was no statistically significant difference in rates of discontinuation of olanzapine or placebo attributed to adverse events. Overall, 5% of olanzapine-treated patients discontinued treatment for adverse events compared with 6% of placebo-treated patients. Discontinuations due to ALT elevations, however, were considered to be drug related (2% for olanzapine versus 0% for placebo) (see Precautions).

Short-Term, Active-Controlled Clinical Trials: Of the 1 796 olanzapine-treated patients in comparative clinical trials with haloperidol, 98 (5%) discontinued treatment for adverse events compared with 66 of 810 (8%) haloperidol-treated patients.

Overall Integrated Safety Database: In a premarketing clinical trial database of 2 500 olanzapine-treated patients, 14.9% (372/2 500) discontinued for an adverse event. About half (183/372) of these discontinuations were associated with the underlying psychopathology. Other adverse events most commonly (incidence of 0.5 to 0.6%) reported as the reason for discontinuation among olanzapine-treated patients were: ALT increased, unintended pregnancy, creatinine phosphokinase increased, and convulsion.

Incidence of Adverse Events in Placebo-Controlled Clinical Trials: Table II (on following page) enumerates the incidence, rounded to the nearest percent, of treatment-emergent adverse events that occurred during acute therapy (up to 6 weeks) of schizophrenia in 1% or more of patients treated with olanzapine (doses ≥2.5 mg/day) where the incidence in patients treated with olanzapine was greater than the incidence in placebo-treated patients.

Incidence of Weight Changes in Placebo-Controlled Clinical Trials: During acute therapy (up to 6 weeks) in controlled clinical trials comparing olanzapine with placebo in the treatment of schizophrenia, the percentages of patients with weight gain ≥7% of baseline body weight at any time were 29% for olanzapine and 3% for placebo, which was a statistically significant difference. The average weight gain during acute therapy in patients treated with olanzapine was 2.8 kg. However, a categorization of patients at baseline on the basis of body mass index (BMI) revealed a significantly greater effect in patients with low BMI compared to normal or overweight patients. In long-term extension trials weight gain tended to level off after 6 to 8 months of treatment, with an average gain of 5.4 kg (see Precautions).

Zyprexa (cont'd)

Table II—Zyprexa

Treatment-Emergent Adverse Events Incidence in Placebo-Controlled Clinical Trials—Acute Phase[a]

Body System/Adverse Event	Percentage of Patients Reporting Event: Zyprexa (N=248) %	Placebo (N=118) %
Body as a Whole		
Headache	17	15
Pain	10	9
Fever	5	3
Abdominal pain	4	2
Back pain	4	3
Chest pain	4	2
Neck rigidity	2	1
Intentional injury	1	0
Cardiovascular		
Postural hypotension	5	2
Tachycardia	4	1
Hypotension	2	1
Digestive		
Constipation	9	3
Dry mouth	7	4
Gamma glutamyl transpeptidase increased	2	1
Increased appetite	2	1
Hemic and Lymphatic		
Leukopenia	1	0
Metabolic and Nutritional Disorders		
ALT increased	8	3
Weight gain[b]	6	1
Edema	2	0
Peripheral edema	2	0
AST increased	2	0
Creatinine phosphokinase increased	1	0
Musculoskeletal		
Arthralgia	3	2
Joint disorder	2	1
Twitching	2	1
Nervous		
Somnolence[b]	26	15
Agitation	23	17
Insomnia	20	19
Nervousness	16	14
Hostility	15	14
Dizziness[b]	11	4
Anxiety	9	8
Personality disorder	8	4
Akathisia[b]	5	1
Hypertonia	4	3
Speech disorder	4	1
Tremor	4	3
Amnesia	2	0
Drug dependence	2	1
Euphoria	2	0
Neurosis	1	0
Respiratory		
Rhinitis	10	6
Cough increased	5	3
Pharyngitis	5	3
Skin and Appendages		
Fungal dermatitis	2	0
Vesiculobullous rash	2	1
Special Senses		
Amblyopia	5	4
Blepharitis	2	1
Eye disorder	2	1
Corneal lesion	1	0
Urogenital		
Menstrual disorder[c]	2	0

[a]The following events had an incidence equal to or less than placebo: abnormal dreams, accidental injury, anorexia, apathy, asthenia, cogwheel rigidity, confusion, conjunctivitis, depression, diarrhea, dysmenorrhea[c], dyspepsia, ecchymosis, emotional lability, hallucinations, hyperkinesia, hypertension, hypokinesia, libido increased, myalgia, nausea, paranoid reaction, paresthesia, pruritus, rash, schizophrenic reaction, sweating, thinking abnormal, tooth caries, vaginitis[c], vomiting.

[b]Statistically significantly more frequent in patients treated with olanzapine than in patients treated with placebo.

[c]Denominator used was for females only (N=41 olanzapine; N=23 placebo).

Incidence of Vital Sign Changes in Placebo-Controlled Clinical Trials: In placebo-controlled clinical trials, orthostatic hypotension (greater than 30 mm decrease in systolic blood pressure) occurred with an incidence of 5% in olanzapine-treated patients compared to 2% in placebo-treated patients (vital sign measurements collected only after 3 to 7 days of olanzapine treatment). Olanzapine was associated with a mean baseline to endpoint increase in heart rate of 2.4 beats per minute compared to no change among placebo-treated patients (see Precautions).

Incidence of Laboratory Changes in Placebo-Controlled Clinical Trials: Olanzapine is associated with asymptomatic increases in ALT, AST and GGT (see Precautions). Olanzapine is also associated with generally mild increases in serum prolactin, which usually decreases with continued drug treatment. Olanzapine is also associated with asymptomatic elevations of eosinophils and uric acid (see Precautions), and with decreases in serum bicarbonate.

Incidence of ECG Changes in Placebo-Controlled Clinical Trials: Between-group comparisons for pooled placebo-controlled trials revealed no statistically significant olanzapine/placebo differences in the proportions of patients experiencing potentially important changes in ECG parameters, including QT, QTc and PR intervals.

Dose-Dependent Adverse Events in Fixed-Dose Clinical Trials: Dose-relatedness of adverse events was assessed using data from a clinical trial with a fixed dosage range. Table III enumerates the treatment-emergent adverse events in which there was a statistically significantly increasing dose response in this clinical trial.

Table III—Zyprexa

Dose-Dependent Adverse Events in a Fixed Dosage Range, Placebo-Controlled Clinical Trial*

Body System/ Adverse Event	Percentage of Patients Reporting Event: Placebo (N=68) %	Zyprexa 5±2.5 mg/day (N=65) %	Zyprexa 10±2.5 mg/day (N=64) %	Zyprexa 15±2.5 mg/day (N=69) %
Digestive System				
Constipation	0	6.2	9.4	14.5
Nervous System				
Abnormal dreams	0	0	1.6	4.3
Dizziness	2.9	7.7	9.4	17.4
Somnolence	16.2	20.0	29.7	39.1
Respiratory System				
Pharyngitis	1.5	3.1	1.6	10.1

*Fungal dermatitis was also reported with a statistically significantly increasing dose response but is not included as a drug cause was remote.

Incidence of Treatment-Emergent Extrapyramidal Symptoms in Placebo-Controlled Trials: Table IV enumerates the percentage of patients with treatment-emergent extrapyramidal symptoms as assessed by categorical analyses of formal rating scales during acute therapy in a controlled clinical trial comparing olanzapine at 3 fixed dosage ranges with placebo in the treatment of schizophrenia.

Table IV—Zyprexa

Treatment-Emergent Extrapyramidal Symptoms Assessed by Rating Scales Incidence in a Fixed Dosage Range, Placebo-Controlled Clinical Trial—Acute Phase[a]

	Percentage of Patients: Placebo %	Zyprexa 5±2.5 mg/day %	Zyprexa 10±2.5 mg/day %	Zyprexa 15±2.5 mg/day %
Parkinsonism[b]	15	14	12	14
Akathisia[c]	23	16	19	27

[a]No statistically significant differences.

[b]Percentage of patients with a Simpson-Angus Scale total score >3.

[c]Percentage of patients with a Barnes Akathisia Scale global score ≥2.

Table V enumerates the percentage of patients with treatment-emergent extrapyramidal symptoms as assessed by spontaneously reported adverse events during acute therapy in the same controlled clinical trial comparing olanzapine at 3 fixed dosage ranges with placebo in the treatment of schizophrenia.

Table V—Zyprexa

Treatment-Emergent Extrapyramidal Symptoms Assessed by Adverse Events Incidence in a Fixed Dosage Range, Placebo-Controlled Clinical Trial-Acute Phase

Extrapyramidal Symptoms	Percentage of Patients Reporting Event: Placebo (N=68) %	Zyprexa 5±2.5 mg/day (N=65) %	Zyprexa 10±2.5 mg/day (N=64) %	Zyprexa 15±2.5 mg/day (N=69) %
Dystonic events[a]	1	3	2	3
Parkinsonism events[b]	10	8	14	20
Akathisia events[c]	1	5	11[d]	10[d]
Dyskinetic events[e]	4	0	2	1
Residual events[f]	1	2	5	1
Any extrapyramidal event	16	15	25	32[d]

[a]Patients with the following COSTART terms were counted in this category: dystonia, generalized spasm, neck rigidity, oculogyric crisis, opisthotonos, torticollis.

[b]Patients with the following COSTART terms were counted in this category: akinesia, cogwheel rigidity, extrapyramidal syndrome, hypertonia, hypokinesia, masked facies, tremor.

[c]Patients with the following COSTART terms were counted in this category: akathisia, hyperkinesia.

[d]Statistically significantly different from placebo.

[e]Patients with the following COSTART terms were counted in this category: buccoglossal syndrome, choreoathetosis, dyskinesia, tardive dyskinesia.

[f]Patients with the following COSTART terms were counted in this category: movement disorder, myoclonus, twitching.

Overdose: Symptoms and Treatment: Experience with olanzapine in overdosage is limited. In clinical trials, accidental or intentional acute overdosage of olanzapine was identified in 67 patients. In the patient taking the largest identified amount, 300 mg, the only symptoms reported were drowsiness and slurred speech. In the limited number of patients who were evaluated in hospitals, including the patient taking 300 mg, there were no observations indicating an adverse change in laboratory analyses or ECG. Vital signs were usually within normal limits following overdoses.

Based on animal data, the predicted symptoms would reflect an exaggeration of the drug's known pharmacological actions. Symptoms may include somnolence, mydriasis, blurred vision, respiratory depression, hypotension, and possible extrapyramidal disturbances.

There is no specific antidote to olanzapine; therefore, appropriate supportive measures should be initiated. The possibility of multiple drug involvement should be considered.

In case of acute overdosage, establish and maintain an airway and ensure adequate oxygenation and ventilation. The use of activated charcoal for overdose should be considered because the concomitant administration of activated charcoal was shown to reduce the oral bioavailability of olanzapine by 50 to 60%. Gastric lavage (after intubation, if patient is unconscious) may also be considered.

Hypotension and circulatory collapse should be treated with appropriate measures such as i.v. fluids and/or sympathomimetic agents such as norepinephrine (do not use epinephrine, dopamine or other sympathomimetic agents with beta-agonist activity since beta stimulation may worsen hypotension in the setting of alpha blockade induced by olanzapine). Cardiovascular monitoring should commence immediately and should include continuous ECG monitoring to detect possible arrhythmias.

Close medical supervision and monitoring should continue until the patient recovers.

Dosage: Adults: Olanzapine should be administered on a once-a-day schedule without regard to meals, generally beginning with 5 to 10 mg, with a target dose of 10 mg/day within several days. Further dosage adjustments, if indicated, should generally occur at intervals of not less than 1 week, since steady state for olanzapine would not be achieved for approximately 1 week in the typical patient. When dosage adjustments are necessary, dose increments/decrements of 5 mg daily are recommended. An increase to a dose greater than target dose of 10 mg/day (i.e., to a dose of 15 mg/day or greater) is normally recommended only after clinical assessment.

In clinical trials a dose range of 5 to 20 mg/day was studied (see Pharmacology, Clinical Trials). The safety and efficacy of doses above 20 mg/day have not been evaluated.
Geriatrics or Debilitated Patients: In clinical trials, 44 patients with schizophrenia or related disorders, 65 years of age or over, were treated with olanzapine (5 to 20 mg daily) (see Precautions and Pharmacology, Special Populations). Given the limited experience with olanzapine in the elderly, and the higher incidence of concomitant illness and concomitant medication in this population, olanzapine should be used with caution.

The recommended starting dose is 5 mg in patients who are elderly, debilitated, who have a predisposition to hypotensive reactions, who otherwise exhibit a combination of factors that may result in slower metabolism of olanzapine (e.g., nonsmoking female patients), or who may be pharmacodynamically more sensitive to olanzapine. When indicated, dose escalation should be performed with caution in these patients.
Patients with Hepatic and/or Renal Impairment: As clinical experience is lacking in these patients, the lower initial starting dose and slower titration to initial target dose should be considered. Further dose escalation, when indicated, should be conservative (see Precautions and Pharmacology, Special Populations).
Maintenance Therapy: It is recommended that responding patients be continued on olanzapine at the lowest dose needed to maintain remission. Patients should be reassessed periodically to determine the need for maintenance treatment. While there is no body of evidence available to answer the question of how long the patient should be treated with olanzapine, the effectiveness of maintenance treatment is well established for many other antipsychotic drugs.

Information for the Patient: See Blue Section—Information for the Patient "Zyprexa".

Supplied: 2.5 mg: Each white, round, film-coated tablet, imprinted in blue ink with "Lilly" and Identi-Code 4112, contains: olanzapine 2.5 mg. Nonmedicinal ingredients: carnauba wax, color mixture white (hydroxypropyl methylcellulose, titanium dioxide, polyethylene glycol and polysorbate 80), crospovidone, FD&C Blue No. 2 Aluminum Lake, hydroxypropylcellulose, hydroxypropyl methylcellulose, lactose, magnesium stearate and microcrystalline cellulose. Amber HDPE bottles of 60.

5 mg: Each white, round, film-coated tablet, imprinted in blue ink with "Lilly" and Identi-Code 4115, contains: olanzapine 5 mg. Nonmedicinal ingredients: carnauba wax, color mixture white (hydroxypropyl methylcellulose, titanium dioxide, polyethylene glycol and polysorbate 80), crospovidone, FD&C Blue No. 2 Aluminum Lake, hydroxypropyl cellulose, hydroxypropyl methylcellulose, lactose, magnesium stearate and microcrystalline cellulose. Amber HDPE bottles of 60.

7.5 mg: Each white, round film-coated tablet, imprinted in blue ink with "Lilly" and Identi-code 4116, contains: olanzapine 7.5 mg. Nonmedicinal ingredients: carnauba wax, color mixture white (hydroxypropyl methylcellulose, titanium dioxide, polyethylene glycol and polysorbate 80), crospovidone, FD&C Blue No. 2 Aluminum Lake, hydroxypropyl cellulose, hydroxypropyl methylcellulose, lactose, magnesium stearate and microcrystalline cellulose. Amber HDPE bottles of 60.

10 mg: Each white, round film-coated tablet, imprinted in blue ink with "Lilly" and Identi-Code 4117, contains: olanzapine 10 mg. Nonmedicinal ingredients: carnauba wax, color mixture white (hydroxypropyl methylcellulose, titanium dioxide, polyethylene glycol and polysorbate 80), crospovidone, FD&C Blue No. 2 Aluminum Lake, hydroxypropyl cellulose, hydroxypropyl methylcellulose, lactose, magnesium stearate and microcrystalline cellulose. Amber HDPE bottles of 60.

Store tablets at 20 to 25°C. Protect from light and moisture.

Reviewed 1998

ZYRTEC®
UCB Pharma

Cetirizine HCl

Histamine H_1-Receptor Antagonist

Pharmacology: Cetirizine, a human metabolite of hydroxyzine, is a histamine H_1 receptor antagonist antiallergic compound; its principal effects are mediated via selective inhibition of peripheral H_1 receptors. Cetirizine is distinguished from other histamine H_1 receptor antagonists by the presence of a carboxylic acid function. This difference may be partly responsible for the selectivity of cetirizine seen in pharmacologic models and its distinctive pharmacokinetic properties in humans.

The antihistaminic activity of cetirizine has been well documented in a variety of animal and human models. In vivo animal models have shown negligible anticholinergic or antiserotonergic activity. In vitro receptor binding studies have detected no measurable affinity for other than H_1 receptors. Autoradiographic studies have shown negligible penetration into the brain. Systemically administered cetirizine does not significantly occupy cerebral H_1 receptors.

Cetirizine does not exacerbate asthma and is effective in a variety of histamine mediated disorders. Oral doses of 5 to 20 mg in humans strongly inhibit the skin wheal and flare response caused by the intradermal injection of histamine. The onset of activity occurs within 20 (50% of subjects) to 60 (95% of subjects) minutes and persists for at least 24 hours following a single dose. The effects of intradermal injection of various other mediators or histamine releasers as well as components of the allergic inflammatory response to cutaneous antigen challenge are also inhibited.

Randomized, multicentre, double-blind, placebo-controlled clinical trials have demonstrated the effectiveness of cetirizine in relieving the symptoms associated with seasonal allergic rhinitis, perennial allergic rhinitis and chronic idiopathic urticaria. The clinical trials have shown only weak anticholinergic effects. There is no evidence that tolerance to the antihistaminic effects of cetirizine occurs or that cetirizine has any abuse potential or dependency liability.

Objective measurements to evaluate the effects of cetirizine on the CNS at doses up to 20 mg showed no significant effects on daytime drowsiness, reaction times, mental alertness, objective CNS depression and various other tests of cognitive function compared with placebo.

Specific ECG studies in healthy volunteers at doses up to 60 mg/day (3 times the maximum clinically studied dose) for 1 week did not prolong Qt_c intervals nor was there any evidence of Qt_c prolongation in clinical trials which included ECG evaluations.

Cetirizine given at the maximum clinically studied dose of 20 mg daily did not prolong the QT_c when given in combination with either ketoconazole 400 mg daily or erythromycin 50 mg q8h for 10 days. Moreover, cetirizine did not significantly alter the pharmacokinetics of either ketoconazole or erythromycin nor were the pharmacokinetics of cetirizine altered by either ketoconazole or erythromycin.

Pharmacokinetics: Cetirizine is rapidly absorbed after oral administration. Peak plasma levels after a 10 mg dose are approximately 300 ng/mL and occur at about 1 hour. Coadministration of cetirizine with food does not affect bioavailability as measured by AUC but absorption is delayed by about 1 hour, with 23% lower C_{max}. Plasma protein binding is 93% in the concentration range observed in clinical studies. The plasma elimination half-life is approximately 8 to 9 hours and does not change with multiple dosing. Pharmacokinetics are dose independent and plasma levels are proportional to the dose administered over the clinically studied range of 5 to 20 mg.

Cetirizine is less extensively metabolized than other antihistamines and approximately 60% of an administered dose is excreted unchanged in 24 hours. The high bioavailability associated with generally low intersubject variation in blood levels is attributable primarily to low first-pass metabolism. Only one metabolite has been identified in humans—the product of oxidative dealkylation of the terminal carboxymethyl group. The antihistaminic activity of this metabolite is negligible.

Consequently, based on (1) its relatively low level of metabolic elimination, (2) no effect on corrected QT intervals at plasma concentrations 3 times the maximal therapeutic levels and (3) no apparent interactions with ketoconazole or erythromycin, cetirizine is unlikely to have clinically significant interactions with other macrolides such as clarithromycin or other imidazole antifungals such as itraconazole in patients with normal renal and hepatic function. Although no data with these other drugs are available at the present time, there is no epidemiological evidence (safety database comprised 6 490 patients evaluated in U.S. and Canadian studies) of interactions between macrolide antibiotics and/or imidazole antifungals taken orally, and cetirizine/hydroxyzine. The epidemiological data do not suggest an increase in adverse events, cardiac or noncardiac, in patients treated with cetirizine and concomitant macrolide or imidazole antifungal medication.

In patients with mild to moderate hepatic and renal impairment, total body clearance of cetirizine is reduced and AUC and half-life increased 2- to 3-fold. Clearance is reduced in proportion to the decline in creatinine clearance. Plasma levels are unaffected by hemodialysis. The plasma elimination half-life in dialysis patients is approximately 20 hours and the plasma AUC is increased by about 3-fold.

The AUC and C_{max} in pediatric subjects are higher in proportion to their lower body weight, and half-life is reduced to 5.6 hours.

Indications: For the relief of symptoms associated with seasonal allergic rhinitis, perennial allergic rhinitis and chronic idiopathic urticaria; i.e., sneezing, rhinorrhea, postnasal discharge, tearing and redness of the eyes, pruritus and hives.

Contraindications: In those patients with a known hypersensitivity to it or to its parent compound, hydroxyzine.

Warnings: *Pregnancy:* No teratogenic effects were caused by oral doses as high as 60, 188 and 133 times the maximum clinically studied human dose in mice, rats and rabbits respectively. No effects on reproduction and fertility were observed at doses as high as 40 and 10 times the maximum recommended human dose in male and female mice respectively. An oral dose 60 times the maximum clinically studied human dose in female mice did not affect parturition or lactation. Although the animal studies are not indicative of any adverse effects during pregnancy at clinically relevant doses, such studies are not always predictive of a human response. There are no adequate, well-controlled studies of pregnant women. Until such data become available, cetirizine should not be used during pregnancy, unless advised otherwise by a physician.
Lactation: Studies in beagles indicate that approximately 3% of the dose is excreted in milk. The extent of excretion in human milk is unknown. Use of cetirizine in nursing mothers is not recommended, unless directed otherwise by a physician.
Children: Unless directed otherwise by a physician, cetirizine should not be administered to children under 12 years of age since its safety and effectiveness in this age group has not yet been established.
Occupational Hazards: Activities Requiring Mental Alertness: Studies using objective measurements have shown no effect of cetirizine on cognitive function, motor performance or sleep latency. However, in clinical trials the appearance of some CNS effects, particularly somnolence, have been observed. Due caution should be exercised when driving a car or operating potentially dangerous machinery.
Geriatrics: Cetirizine was well tolerated by patients aged 65 years and over. Clearance of cetirizine is reduced in proportion to creatine clearance. In patients whose creatinine clearance is reduced (i.e., those with moderate renal impairment), a starting dose of 5 mg/day is recommended (see Pharmacology, Pharmacokinetics).

Occasional instances of liver function test (transaminase) elevations have occurred during cetirizine therapy. This incidence was 1.6% in the short-term trials and 4.4% in the 6-month trials. These liver enzyme elevations, mainly ALT, were generally reversible. There was no evidence of jaundice or hepatitis, and the clinical significance is presently unknown. Consequently, cetirizine should be used with caution in patients with pre-existing liver disease. In patients with moderate hepatic impairment, a starting dose of 5 mg/day is recommended.
Asthmatics: Cetirizine has been safely administered to patients with mild to moderate asthma. Cetirizine did not cause exacerbation of asthma symptoms.
Drug Interactions: No clinically significant drug interactions have been found with theophylline, pseudoephedrine, cimetidine, erythromycin and ketoconazole. Epidemiologic data suggest that there also would not be interaction with other macrolide antibiotics or imidazole antifungals. In clinical trials, cetirizine has been safely administered with beta-agonists, NSAIDs, oral contraceptives, narcotic analgesics, corticosteroids, H_2-antagonists, cephalosporins, penicillins, thyroid hormones and thiazide diuretics. Interaction studies with cetirizine and alcohol or diazepam indicate that cetirizine does not increase alcohol-induced or diazepam-induced impairment of motor and mental performance.

Adverse Effects: In clinical development programs (domestic and international), cetirizine has been evaluated in more than 6 000 treated patients at daily doses ranging from 5 to 20 mg. The most common adverse reactions were headache and somnolence. The incidence of headache associated with cetirizine was not different from the placebo. The incidence of somnolence associated with cetirizine was dose-related and predominantly mild to moderate. The incidence of somnolence in fixed dose studies was 6% for the placebo, 11% at 5 mg and 13.7% at 10 mg. Dry mouth was reported by 5% of patients (vs 2.3% for the placebo). Fatigue was reported by 5.9% of patients (vs 2.6% for the placebo).

Most adverse reactions reported during cetirizine therapy were mild to moderate. The incidence of discontinuation due

Zyrtec (cont'd)

to adverse reactions in patients receiving cetirizine was not significantly different from the placebo (1% vs 0.6% respectively, in placebo-controlled trials). There was no difference by gender or by body weight with regard to the incidence of adverse reactions.

Occasional instances of transient, reversible hepatic transaminase elevations have occurred during cetirizine therapy without evidence of jaundice, hepatitis or other clinical findings.

Adverse events which were reported at an incidence of greater than 1/100 in clinical trials are listed in Table I.

Table I—Zyrtec

Adverse Reactions Reported in Placebo-controlled U.S. Zyrtec Trials (Maximum Dose of 10 mg) at Rates of 1% or Greater (% Incidence)

Adverse Experience	Zyrtec % (N=2 034)	Placebo % (N=1 612)	Percentage of Difference
Headache	17.6	17.9	(0.3)*
Somnolence	13.7	6.3	7.4
Fatigue	5.9	2.6	3.3
Dry Mouth	5.0	2.3	2.7
Nausea	2.5	2.9	(0.4)*
Pharyngitis	2.0	1.9	0.1
Dizziness	2.0	1.2	0.8
Insomnia	1.4	1.2	0.2
Epistaxis	1.2	0.6	0.6
Coughing	1.0	0.6	0.4
Abdominal Pain	1.0	0.9	0.1
Dyspepsia	0.8	1.6	(0.8)*
Pruritus	0.3	1.2	(0.9)*

( )* = Higher frequency in placebo group.

The following events were observed infrequently (equal to or less than 1%), in 3 982 patients who received cetirizine in U.S. trials, including an open study of 6 months' duration; a causal relationship with cetirizine administration has not been established.

Application Site: application site reaction, injection site inflammation.

Autonomic Nervous System: anorexia, urinary retention, flushing, saliva increased.

Cardiovascular: palpitation, tachycardia, hypertension, arrhythmia, cardiac failure.

Central and Peripheral Nervous Systems: paraesthesia, confusion, hyperkinesia, hypertonia, migraine, tremor, vertigo, leg cramps, ataxia, dysphonia, abnormal coordination, hyperaesthesia, hypoesthesia, myelitis, paralysis, ptosis, speech disorder, twitching, visual field defect.

Endocrine: thyroid disorder.

Gastrointestinal: increased appetite, dyspepsia, abdominal pain, diarrhea, flatulence, constipation, vomiting, ulcerative stomatitis, tongue disorder, aggravated teeth caries, stomatitis, tongue discoloration, tongue edema, gastritis, hemorrhage rectum, hemorrhoids, melena, abnormal hepatic function.

Genitourinary: polyuria, urinary tract infection, cystitis, dysuria, haematuria, abnormal urine.

Hearing and Vestibular: earache, tinnitus, deafness, ototoxicity.

Metabolic/Nutritional: thirst, edema, dehydration, diabetes mellitus.

Musculoskeletal: myalgia, arthralgia, bone disorder, arthrosis, tendon disorder, arthritis, muscle weakness.

Psychiatric: insomnia, nervousness, depression, emotional lability, impaired concentration, anxiety, depersonalization, paranoia, abnormal thinking, agitation, amnesia, decreased libido, euphoria.

Resistance Mechanism: impaired healing, herpes simplex, infection, fungal infection, viral infection.

Respiratory System: epistaxis, rhinitis, coughing, respiratory disorder, bronchospasm, dyspnea, upper respiratory tract infection, hyperventilation, sinusitis, increased sputum, bronchitis, pneumonia.

Reproductive: dysmenorrhea, menstrual disorder, female breast pain, intermenstrual bleeding, leukorrhea, menorrhagia, unintended pregnancy, vaginitis, testes disorder.

Reticuloendothelial: lymphadenopathy.

Skin: pruritus, rash, skin disorder, dry skin, urticaria, acne, dermatitis, rash erythematous, sweating increased, alopecia, angioedema, furunculosis, bullous eruption, eczema, hyperkeratosis, hypertrichosis, photosensitivity reaction, photosensitivity toxic reaction, rash maculo-papular, seborrhea, purpura.

Special Senses: taste perversion, taste loss, parosmia.

Vision: eye abnormality, abnormal vision, eye pain, conjunctivitis, xerophthalmia, glaucoma, ocular hemorrhage.

Body as a Whole: weight increase, back pain, malaise, pain, chest pain, fever, asthenia, generalized edema, periorbital edema, peripheral edema, rigor, leg edema, face edema, hot flushes, enlarged abdomen, allergic reaction, nasal polyp.

Weight gain was reported as an adverse event in 0.4% of cetirizine patients in placebo controlled trials. In an open study of 6 months' duration, the mean weight gain was 2.8% after 20 weeks, with no further increase at 26 weeks.

Occasional instances of transient, reversible hepatic transaminase elevations have occurred during cetirizine therapy.

In foreign marketing experience the following additional rare, but potential severe adverse events have been reported: hemolytic anemia, thrombocytopenia, orofacial dyskinesia, severe hypotension, anaphylaxis, hepatitis, glomerulonephritis, stillbirth and cholestasis.

In a 6-week, placebo-controlled study of 186 patients with allergic rhinitis and mild to moderate asthma, cetirizine 10 mg daily improved rhinitis symptoms and did not alter pulmonary function. This study supports the safety of administering cetirizine to allergic rhinitis patients with mild to moderate asthma.

Overdose: Symptoms: Overdose has not been reported with cetirizine in North America. In foreign marketing experience, somnolence has been reported in cases of overdose up to 150 mg. If an acute overdose occurs, evacuation of the stomach should be considered during the first few hours afterwards.

Treatment: Treatment should be symptomatic and supportive taking into account any concomitantly ingested medications. There is no known specific antidote to cetirizine. Cetirizine is not effectively removed by dialysis, and dialysis will be ineffective unless a dialyzable agent has been concomitantly ingested. The minimal lethal oral dose in rodents is at least 590 times the maximum clinically studied dose.

Dosage: Adults and Adolescents Over 12 Years: The recommended initial dose is 5 to 10 mg, depending on symptom severity, given as a single daily dose, with or without food. Most patients begin with a dose of 10 mg. The time of administration may be varied to suit individual patient needs.

Clinical studies to date support treatment for up to 6 months. Thus medical recommendation is advised for long-term use.

Geriatrics: In patients with moderate hepatic and/or renal impairment, a starting dose of 5 mg/day is recommended.

Information for the Patient: See Blue Section—Information for the Patient "Zyrtec".

Supplied: Each white (dye-free), film-coated, scored ovoid tablet contains: cetirizine HCl 10 mg. Nonmedicinal ingredients: cornstarch, hydroxypropyl methylcellulose, lactose, magnesium stearate, polyethylene glycol, povidone and titanium dioxide. Plastic bottles of 100 and 500. Packages (for OTC use) of 6, 12 and 18. Store at room temperature between 15 and 30°C.

(Shown in Product Recognition Section)

Reviewed 1998

cilazapril

INHIBACE®

References

1. Rosenthal et al. Cardiology 1996; 87:54-59. **2.** Prager et al. J. Cardiovasc. Pharmacol. 1994; 24 (suppl.): S93-S99. **3.** Güntzel et al. J. Cardiovasc. Pharmacol. 1991; 17:8-12. **4.** Lacourcière et al. J. Cardiovasc. Pharmacol. 1991; 8:219-223. **5.** Prices from the Ontario Drug Benefit Formulary, 1997. **6.** Johnston et al. J. Hypertens. 1988; 6(suppl. 3):S17-S22. **7.** Clozel et al. Am. J. of Med.1989; 87(suppl. 68): 92S-95S. **8.** Deng J. Cardiovasc. Pharmacol. 1993; 21:S7-S11. **9.** Clozel J. of Hypertens. 1989; 7:267-275. **10.** Clozel J. of Hypertens. 1992; 19(suppl. 5): S28-S33. **11.** Clozel J. Cardiovasc. Pharmacol. 1987; 10:350-355. **12.** Adapted from: Data on file (New Drug Submission) Hoffmann-La Roche Limited.

FOURNIER PHARMA INC.

Roche

® Registered trademark of Hoffmann-La Roche Limited

MEMBER PMAC

PAAB

Pr FAMVIR®

famciclovir

REFERENCES

1. Tyring S, Barbarash R, Nahlik J, et al. Famciclovir for the Treatment of Acute Herpes Zoster: Effects on Acute Disease and Post Herpetic Neuralgia. *Ann Int Med* 1995; 123(2):89-96.
2. Wood MJ, Easterbrook PJ. Clinician's Manual on Herpes Zoster. London: Science Press 1995:1-44.
3. Marley J. Antiviral therapy in herpes zoster: a review. *Antiviral Chemistry & Chemotherapy* 1997; 8(1)37-42.
4. Product Monograph Famvir®.
5. Sacks SL, Martel A, et al, and the Canadian Cooperative Study Group. Clinic initiated treatment of recurrent genital herpes with famciclovir: results of a Canadian multi-center study. 6th International Congress for Infectious Diseases. Prague, Czech Republic, April 26-30, 1994.
6. Sacks SL, Aoki FY, et al. Patient-Initiated, Twice-Daily Oral Famciclovir for Early Recurrent Genital Herpes: A Randomized, Double-blind Multicenter Trial. *JAMA* 1996; 276: 44-49.
7. Sacks SL, et al. Patient and clinic initiated treatment of recurrent genital herpes with twice daily oral famciclovir. Abstract presented at the 7th European Congress of Clinical Microbiology and Infectious Diseases. March 26-30, 1995, Vienna, Austria.

SB SmithKline Beecham Pharma

© SmithKline Beecham Pharma, a div. of SmithKline Beecham Inc., 1998 Oakville, Ontario L6H 5V2

MEMBER PMAC | PAAB | CCPP

Pr Adalat® XL® (nifedipine)

References:

1. Toal CB. Can J Cardiol 1997;13(10):921-927.
2. Adalat XL Product Monograph.

Bayer

Bayer Inc. Healthcare Division 77 Belfield Road Toronto, Ontario M9W 1G6

XL 693-0498 E PAAB

Pr ALTACE®

ramipril

References:

1. Houston MC. *Am Heart J* 1992; 123: 1337 1367. 2. ALTACE (ramipril) Product Monograph, Hoechst Marion Roussel, 1996. 3. Todd PA et al. *Drugs* 1990; 39(1): 1-27. 4. The Acute Infarction Rampiril Efficacy (AIRE) Study Investigators. *Lancet* 1993; 342(8875): 821-828. 5. Bender N et al. *Clin Physiol Biochem* 1990; 8(Suppl. 1): 44-52.

®Registered trade mark of Hoechst AG, Germany, used under licence by **Hoechst Marion Roussel Canada Inc., Laval, Quebec H7L 4A8.**

Hoechst Marion Roussel

Hoechst Marion Roussel Canada Inc.
2150 St. Elzear Blvd.West
Laval, Quebec H7L 4A8

Hoechst

Hoechst Marion Roussel
The Pharmaceutical Company of Hoechst

50030221

MEMBER PMAC PAAB

Pr Diovan®

VALSARTAN

ANGIOTENSIN II AT_1 RECEPTOR BLOCKER

References:

1. Corea L, Cardoni O, Fogari R, *et al.* Valsartan, a new angiotensin II antagonist for the treatment of essential hypertension: a comparative study of the efficacy and safety against amlodipine. *Clin Pharmacol Ther* 1996;60(3):341-6.
2. Holwerda NJ, Fogari R, Angeli P, *et al.* Valsartan, a new angiotensin II antagonist for the treatment of essential hypertension: efficacy and safety compared with placebo and enalapril. *J Hypertens* 1996;14(9):1147-51.
3. Black HR, Graff A, Shute D, *et al.* Valsartan, a new angiotensin II antagonist for the treatment of essential hypertension: efficacy, tolerability and safety compared to an angiotensin-converting enzyme inhibitor, lisinopril. *J Hum Hypertens* 1997;11:483-9.
4. Diovan Product Monograph. Novartis Pharmaceuticals Canada Inc.

*Registered trademark
DIO-97-11-4766 E

PAAB MEMBER PMAC

NOVARTIS

Novartis Pharmaceuticals Canada Inc.
Dorval, Québec H9R 4P5

Pr DIDROCAL®

ETIDRONATE DISODIUM & CALCIUM CARBONATE (CYCLICAL THERAPY)

REFERENCES: 1. Didrocal Product Monograph. Procter & Gamble Pharmaceuticals. **2.** Data on file. Didronel Post-marketing Surveillance Study: The Effects of Cyclical Etidronate Treatment in Actual Clinical Practice, 1996. Procter & Gamble Pharmaceuticals. **3.** Chestnut C, Watts N, Miller P, et al. Cyclical etidronate: efficacy and safety over seven years [Abstract]. *Osteo Int* 1996; Suppl 6:257. **4.** Data on file. Didrocal NDA Overview Document, 1992. Procter & Gamble Pharmaceuticals. **5.** Data on file. Etidronate Post-marketing Data, 1996. Procter & Gamble Pharmaceuticals.

Product Monograph available upon request from:

Procter&Gamble PHARMACEUTICALS

Rx Didrocal Refill x 2

Procter & Gamble Pharmaceuticals Canada Inc.
P.O. Box 355, Station "A"
Toronto, Ontario M5W 1C5

PAAB MEMBER PMAC

NEW Pr Avapro®

(irbesartan) 150mg

1. Mimran A et al. *J Hum Hypertens* 1998;12:203-208. 2. Larochelle P et al. *Am J Cardiol* 1997;80:1613-1615. 3. Pohl M et al. *Am J Hypertens* 1997;10(pt. 2):105A. 4. Kassler-Taub K et al. *Am J Hypertens* 1998;11(4, pt. 1):445-453. 5. Avapro product monograph, Bristol-Myers Squibb/Sanofi Canada. 6. Cozaar product monograph, Merck Sharp & Dohme Canada. 7. Diovan product monograph, Novartis. 8. Oparil S et al. *Clin Therapeutics* 1998;20(3):398-409.

PAAB PMAC MEMBER

Bristol-Myers Squibb Pharmaceutical Group

sanofi

*Trademark of Sanofi

Pr BIAXIN®

CLARITHROMYCIN

Pediatric References: 1. Coles SJ, Addlestone MB, Kamdar NK, et al. A comparative study of clarithromycin and amoxycillin suspensions in the treatment of pediatric patients with acute otitis media. *Infection* 1993;21(4):272-8. **2.** Aspin MM, Hoberman A, McCarty JM, et al. Comparative study of the safety and efficacy of clarithromycin and amoxicillin-clavulanate in the treatment of acute otitis media in children. *J Pediatr* 1994;125(1):136-41. **3.** Pukander JS, Jero JP, Kaprio EA, et al. Clarithromycin *vs.* amoxicillin suspensions in the treatment of pediatric patients with acute otitis media. *Pediatr Infect Dis J* 1993;12(12):S118-21. **4.** McCarty JM, Phillips A, Wiisanen R. Comparative safety and efficacy of clarithromycin and amoxicillin/clavulanate in the treatment of acute otitis media in children. *Pediatr Infect Dis J* 1993;12(12):S122-7. **5.** Gooch WM, Gan VN, Corder WT, et al. Clarithromycin and cefaclor suspensions in the treatment of acute otitis media in children. *Pediatr Infect Dis J* 1993;12(12):S128-33. **6.** Adam D. Clinical trials of clarithromycin vs. other antimicrobials in LRTIs. *Infections in Medicine* 1993;10 Suppl:27-31. **7.** Biaxin Product Monograph. Abbott Laboratories, Limited.

ABBOTT LABORATORIES, LIMITED
P.O. BOX 6150, STATION CENTRE-VILLE
MONTRÉAL, QUÉBEC H3C 3K6

PAAB

Product Monograph or full Prescribing Information available on request.
© Abbott Laboratories, Limited

Pr BIAXIN®

CLARITHROMYCIN

Adult References (Sumo): 1. Dabernat H, Delmas C, Seguy M, et al. The activity of clarithromycin and its 14-hydroxy metabolite against *Haemophilus influenzae*, determined by in vitro and serum bactericidal tests. *J Antimicrob Chemother* 1991;27 Suppl A:19-30. **2.** Mandell LA. The renaissance of the macrolides: new and changing roles in infectious diseases. *Can J Infect Dis* 1993;4 Suppl A:1A-4A. **3.** Biaxin Product Monograph. Abbott Laboratories, Limited. **4.** Wettengel R, Vetter N, Waardenburg FA. Clarithromycin versus cefaclor for the treatment of mild-to-moderate acute bacterial bronchitis. *J Antimicrob Chemother* 1993;31(6):963-72. **5.** Neu H, Craft JC. Clarithromycin vs. cephalosporin therapy for the treatment of *H. influenzae* bronchitis. Presented at the 1st International Conference on the Macrolides, Azalides, and Streptogramins. Santa Fe, NM, January 1992.

ABBOTT LABORATORIES, LIMITED
P.O. BOX 6150, STATION CENTRE-VILLE
MONTRÉAL, QUÉBEC H3C 3K6

© Abbott Laboratories, Limited
Product Monograph or full Prescribing Information available on request.

PAAB

VALTREX®
VALACYCLOVIR

Valacyclovir Hydrochloride Caplets - Antiviral Agent

REFERENCES: 1. Product Monograph of *Valtrex*, Glaxo Wellcome Inc., 1996. 2. Spruance SL, Tyring SL, De Gregorio B et al. A large-scale placebo-controlled, dose-ranging trial of peroral valacyclovir for episodic treatment of recurrent herpes genitalis. *Arch Intern Med* 1996; 156:1729-1735. 3. Data on file, Glaxo Wellcome Inc., RM 1996/00031/00,1996. 4. Bodsworth NJ, Crooks RJ, Borelli S et al. Valaciclovir versus aciclovir in patient initiated treatment of recurrent genital herpes: a randomized, double-blind clinical trial. *Genitourin Med* 1997;73(2):110-116.

MEMBER PMAC PAAB CCPP

GlaxoWellcome

Pr **Paxil®**
Once a day
paroxetine HCl

References: (Paxil cp) 1. Maddox JC, Levi M, Thompson C. *J Psychopharmacol* 1994;8(1):48-53 2. Kennedy et al. 47th Annual Meeting of Can. Psych. Assoc. 1997;Abs:p23. 3. Katon W, Von Korff M, Lin E et al. *JAMA* 1995; 273(13):1026-1031.

References: (Paxil labyrinth) 1. Joffe RT, Bagby M, Levitt A. *Am J Psychiatry* 1993; 150 (8): 1257-8. 2. Sartorius N et al. *Br J Psych.* 1996;168 (suppl30):30-43. 3.Van Valkenburg C et al. *J Affect Disorders.* 1984;6:67-82. 4. Hamilton M. In: Last CA, Herson M, eds. Handbook of Anxiety Disorders, New York, Pergammon Press 1988;143-155. 5. Ravindran A et al. *J Clin Psych* 1997; 58 (3):112-118. 6. DeWilde J et al. *Acta Psychiatr Scand.* 1993; 87:141-145. 7. Chouinard G, Saxena B, Belanger MC et al. *J Affect Dis* 1998 (In press).

SmithKline Beecham *Pharma*
©SmithKline Beecham Pharma, a div. of SmithKline Beecham Inc., 1998 Oakville, Ontario L6H 5V2

MEMBER PMAC PAAB CCPP

Pr **LESCOL***
FLUVASTATIN SODIUM

References:
1. Lescol Product Monograph. Novartis Pharmaceuticals Canada Inc., 1998. **2.** Herd AJ, Ballantyne CM, Farmer JA, et al. Effects of fluvastatin on coronary atherosclerosis in patients with mild to moderate cholesterol elevations (Lipoprotein and Coronary Atherosclerosis Study [LCAS]). *Am J Cardiol* 1997;80:278-86. **3.** Davidson MH. Fluvastatin Long-Term Extension Trial (FLUENT): summary of efficacy and safety. *Am J Med* 1994;96:41S-4S. **4.** Jacotot B, Benghozi R, Pfister P, et al. Comparison of fluvastatin versus pravastatin treatment of primary hypercholesterolemia. *Am J Cardiol* 1995;76:54A-6A. **5.** Foley DP, Bonnier H, Jackson G, et al. Prevention of restenosis after coronary balloon angioplasty: rationale and design of the Fluvastatin Angioplasty Restenosis (FLARE) Trial. *Am J Cardiol* 1994;73:50D-61D. **6.** Martens LL and Guibert R. Cost-effectiveness analysis of lipid-modifying therapy in Canada: comparison of HMG-CoA reductase inhibitors in the primary prevention of coronary heart disease. *Clin Ther* 1994;16(6):1052-62.

NOVARTIS

Novartis Pharmaceuticals Canada Inc.
Dorval, Québec H9R 4P5

*Registered trademark.
Mfd. by Sandoz.
Product Monograph available on request.

PAAB MEMBER PMAC

PULSE
Pr **sporanox***
(itraconazole capsules) For onychomycosis

References:
1. SPORANOX Capsules Product Monograph, November 1997. 2. Willemsen M, De Doncker P, Willems J, Woestenborghs R, Van de Velde V, Heykants J et al. Posttreatment itraconazole levels in the nail. *J Am Acad Dermatol* 1992;26:731-5. 3. Cauwenbergh G, Degreef H, Heykants J, Woestenborghs R, Van Rooy P, Haeverans K. Pharmacokinetic profile of orally administered itraconazole in human skin. *J Am Acad Dermatol* 1988;18:263-8. 4. De Doncker P, Decroix J, Piérard GE, Roelant D, Woestenborghs R, Jacqmin P et al. Antifungal pulse therapy for onychomycosis. *Arch Dermatol* 1996;132:34-41. 5. Odom RB. New therapies for onychomycosis. *J Am Acad Dermatol* 1996;35:S26-30. 6. Havu V, Brandt H, Heikkilä H, Hollmen A, Oksman R, Rantanen T et al. A double-blind, randomized study comparing itraconazole pulse therapy with continuous dosing for the treatment of toe-nail onychomycosis. *Br J Dermatol* 1997;136:230-4. 7. Bonifaz A, Carrasco-Gerard E, Saúl A. Itraconazole in onychomycosis: intermittent dose schedule. *Int J Dermatol* 1997;36:70-2. 8. De Doncker P, Van Lint J, Dockx P, Roseeuw D. Pulse therapy with one-week itraconazole monthly for three or four months in the treatment of onychomycosis. *Cutis* 1995;56(3):180-3.

JANSSEN-ORTHO Inc.

PAAB CCPP MEMBER PMAC

19 Green Belt Drive, Toronto, Ontario M3C 1L9

***Trademark**
©Janssen-Ortho Inc., 1998
BPISP0980006A

Pr **ZOCOR®**
(simvastatin tablets)

References:
1. The Scandinavian Simvastatin Survival Study Group. Randomised trial of cholesterol lowering in 4444 patients with coronary heart disease: the Scandinavian Simvastatin Survival Study (4S). Lancet 1994;344:1383-9.
2. Pedersen TR, Tobert JA. Benefits and risks of HMG-CoA reductase inhibitors in the prevention of coronary heart disease. Drug Safety 1996;14(1):11-24.

9520a, 9521a, 9522a

MEMBER PMAC PAAB

MERCK FROSST

FROSST
DIV. OF MERCK FROSST CANADA INC.
P.O. BOX 1005, POINTE-CLAIRE
DORVAL, QUEBEC H9R 4P8

Pr **TASMAR®**
TOLCAPONE

PM available on request.

References: 6. Tasmar product monograph, 1997. 9. Rajput AH et al. Tolcapone 200 mg t.i.d. improves motor function in parkinsonian patients with "wearing-off" phenomenon: a double-blind, placebo-controlled, multicenter trial. Neurology 1997. 10. Waters CH et al. Tolcapone in stable Parkinson's disease: Efficacy and safety of long-term treatment. Neurology 1997; 49:1-7. 12. Agid Y et al. Tolcapone, bromocriptine, and Parkinson's disease. The Lancet, 1997

TM Trademark of Hoffmann-La Roche Limited
Registered Trade Mark Hoffmann-La Roche Limited
Mississauga, ON L5N 6L7

Roche

MEMBER PMAC PAAB CCPP © Copyright 1997

Pr *Diflucan-150**
(fluconazole / pfizer)

Simple and preferred for vaginal yeast infections.[1†]

In clinical studies of Diflucan-150, the most common side effects were headache, nausea, abdominal pain and diarrhea. Most side effects were mild-to-moderate in nature. The dosing convenience of oral, single-dose Diflucan-150 should be considered in light of the acceptability of its side effect profile relative to that of topical therapies.
†88% of patients preferred Diflucan-150 over creams and vaginal inserts in an open study of 1017 women.

Reference: 1. Phillips RJM et al. An open multicenter study of the efficacy and safety of a single dose of fluconazole 150 mg in the treatment of vaginal candidiasis in general practice. *Br J Clin Pract* 1990;44:219-222.

PAAB

©1997, Pfizer Canada Inc.
Kirkland, Quebec H9J 2M5

*TM Pfizer Inc
Pfizer Canada Inc., licensee

Pfizer
We're part of the cure

References:
1 Beil W, Staar U, Sewing KF. Pantoprazole: a novel H+/K+ -ATPase inhibitor with an improved pH stability. Eur J Pharmacol 1992;218:265-71. 2 Pantoloc[†] product monograph. Solvay Pharma Inc., June 18, 1998. 3 Shin JM, Besançon M, Prinz C et al. Continuing development of acid pump inhibitors: site of action of pantoprazole. Aliment Pharmacol Ther 1994;8(1):11-23. 4 Shin JM, Besançon M, Simon A et al. The site of action of pantoprazole in the gastric H+/K+ -ATPase. Biochima et Biophysica Acta 1993;1148:223-233. 5 Kromer W. Similarities and differences in the properties of substituted benzimidazoles: A comparison between pantoprazole and related compounds. Digestion 1995;56:443-454. 6 Londong W. Effect of pantoprazole on 24-h intragastric pH and serum gastrin in humans. Aliment Pharmacol Ther 1994;8:(Suppl.1):39-46. 7 Hartmann M, Theiss U, Huber R et al. Twenty-four hour intragastric pH profiles and pharmacokinetics following single and repeated oral administration of the proton pump inhibitor pantoprazole in comparison to omeprazole. Aliment Pharmacol Ther 1996;10:359-366. 8 Corinaldesi R, Valentini M, Belaiche J, Colin R, Geldof H, Maier C and the European Pantoprazole Study Group. Pantoprazole and omeprazole in the treatment of reflux oesophagitis: a European multicentre study. Aliment Pharmacol Ther 1995;9:667-671. 9 Witzel L, Gutz H, Huttemann W, and Schepps W. Pantoprazole versus omeprazole in the treatment of acute gastric ulcers. Aliment Pharmacol Ther 1995;9:19-24. 10 Müller P, Simon B, Khalil H, Luhmann R, Leucht U and Schneider A. Dose-range finding study with the proton pump inhibitor Pantoprazole in acute duodenal ulcer patients. Z Gastroenterol 1992;30:771-775. 11 Cremer M, Lambert R, Lamers C et al. A double-blind study of pantoprazole and ranitidine in treatment of acute duodenal ulcer: a multi-center trial. Digestive Diseases & Sciences 1995;40;6:1360-1364. 12 Koop H, Schepp W, Dammann H et al. Comparative trial of pantoprazole and ranitidine in the treatment of reflux esophagitis. J Clin Gastroenterol 1995;20;3: 192-195. 13 Solvay Pharma/Byk Gulden. IMS letter 01/07/98.

References:
1. Data on file. Pooled from cerivastatin studies nos. 120, 124, 132 and 149. 2. BAYCOL® product monograph. 3. Data on file. Cerivastatin Study No. 132.

References:
1. LIPITOR (atorvastatin calcium) Product Monograph, Parke-Davis Div., Warner-Lambert Canada Inc., July 1998. 2. Dart A, Jerums G, *et al.* A multicenter, double-blind, one-year study comparing safety and efficacy of atorvastatin versus simvastatin in patients with hypercholesterolemia. *Am J Cardiol* 1997;80:39 - 44. 3. Bertolini S, Bittolo Bon G, *et al.* Efficacy and safety of atorvastatin compared to pravastatin in patients with hypercholesterolemia. *Atherosclerosis* 1997; 130:191-197. 4. Davidson M, McKenney J, Stein E, *et al.* Comparison of one-year efficacy and safety of atorvastatin versus lovastatin in primary hypercholesterolemia. *Am J Cardiol* 1997; 79:1475-1481. 5. Heinonen TM, *et al.* Atorvastatin, a new HMG-CoA reductase inhibitor as monotherapy and combined with colestipol. *J Cardiovasc Pharmacol Therapeut* 1996; 1(2):117-122.

References: L.R.T.I.
1. ZITHROMAX* Product Monograph, Pfizer Canada Inc., January 27, 1998. **2.** Drew RH and Gallis HA. Azithromycin–Spectrum of Activity, Pharmacokinetics, and Clinical Applications. Pharmacotherapy 1992;12(3):161-73. **3.** Dark D. Multicenter evaluation of azithromycin and cefaclor in acute lower respiratory tract infections. Am J Med 1991;91(suppl 3A):31S-35S. **4.** "Supplemental new drug submission for Zithromax® (azithromycin dihydrate) Antibiotic Treatment of Community-Acquired Pneumonia Due to *Mycoplasma Pneumoniae* or *Chlamydia Pneumoniae*". Data on file. Pfizer Canada Inc. **5.** Hopkins S. Clinical toleration and safety of azithromycin. Am J Med 1991;91(suppl A):40S-45S.

References: Pediatric
1. ZITHROMAX* Product Monograph, Pfizer Canada Inc., January 27, 1998. **2.** Neu HC. Clinical microbiology of azithromycin. Am J Med 1991;91(suppl 3A):S12-8. **3.** Foulds G and Johnson RB. Selection of dose regimens of azithromycin. J Antimicrob Chemo 1993;31 (suppl E):39-50. **4.** Khurana CM. Issues concerning antibiotic use in child care settings. Pediatr Infect Dis J 1995;14:S34-8. **5.** Matsui D et al. Assessment of the palatability of ß-lactamase-resistant antibiotics in children. Arch Pediatr Adolesc Med 1997;151:599-602.

REFERENCES: HYPERTENSION
1. Norvasc* Product Monograph, Pfizer Canada Inc., Dec. 19, 1997.
2. Hernandez-Hernandez R et al. The effects of missing a dose of enalapril versus amlodipine on ambulatory blood pressure. Blood Pressure Monitoring 1996;1:121-6.
3. Lüscher TF and Cosentino F. The classification of calcium antagonists and their selection in the treatment of hypertension - a reappraisal. Drugs 1998;55(4):509-17.
4. Leenen FHH, Fourney A, Tanner J. Persistence of anti-hypertensive effect after interruption of therapy with long-acting (amlodipine) vs short-acting (diltiazem) calcium-antagonist. Clin and Investigative Medicine 1994;17(4) Suppl. B 70.
5. Ferrucci A et al. 24-hour blood pressure profiles in patients with hypertension treated with amlodipine or nifedipine GITS. Clin Drug Invest 1997;13(Suppl 1):67-72.
6. Høegholm A et al. Comparative effects of amlodipine and felodipine ER on office and ambulatory blood pressure in patients with mild to moderate hypertension. J Human Hypertens 1995;9(Suppl 10):S25-S28.
7. Ostergren J et al. Effect of amlodipine versus felodipine extended release on 24-hour ambulatory blood pressure in hypertension. Am J Hypertens 1998;11:690-6.
8. Neaton JD et al. Treatment of mild hypertension study. JAMA 1993;270(6):713-24.
9. Perna GP et al. Tolerability of amlodipine - A meta-analysis. Clin Drug Invest 1997;13(Suppl 1):163-68.

Norvasc*
(amlodipine besylate/pfizer)

REFERENCES: HYPERTENSION
1. Norvasc* Product Monograph, Pfizer Canada Inc., Dec. 19, 1997.
2. Hernandez-Hernandez R et al. The effects of missing a dose of enalapril versus amlodipine on ambulatory blood pressure. Blood Pressure Monitoring 1996;1:121-6.
3. Lüscher TF and Cosentino F. The classification of calcium antagonists and their selection in the treatment of hypertension - a reappraisal. Drugs 1998;55(4):509-17.
4. Leenen FHH, Fourney A, Tanner J. Persistence of anti-hypertensive effect after interruption of therapy with long-acting (amlodipine) vs short-acting (diltiazem) calcium-antagonist. Clin and Investigative Medicine 1994;17(4) Suppl. B 70.
5. Ferrucci A et al. 24-hour blood pressure profiles in patients with hypertension treated with amlodipine or nifedipine GITS. Clin Drug Invest 1997;13(Suppl 1):67-72.
6. Høegholm A et al. Comparative effects of amlodipine and felodipine ER on office and ambulatory blood pressure in patients with mild to moderate hypertension. J Human Hypertens 1995;9(Suppl 10):S25-S28.
7. Ostergren J et al. Effect of amlodipine versus felodipine extended release on 24-hour ambulatory blood pressure in hypertension. Am J Hypertens 1998;11:690-6.
8. Neaton JD et al. Treatment of mild hypertension study. JAMA 1993;270(6):713-24.
9. Perna GP et al. Tolerability of amlodipine - A meta-analysis. Clin Drug Invest 1997;13(Suppl 1):163-68.

Pfizer

©1998
Pfizer Canada Inc.
Kirkland, Quebec
H9J 2M5

rev.CHF.1/98
PAAB

*TM Pfizer Products Inc.
Pfizer Canada Inc., licensee
Product Monograph Available Upon Request.

1. van der Schroeff JG, Cirkel PKS, Crijns MB et al. British J Dermatol 1992;126(S39):36-9.
2. Watson A, Marley J, Williams T. J Am Acad Dermatol 1995;33:775-9.
3. Lamisil Product Monograph, 1997, Novartis Pharmaceuticals Canada Inc.

1. Woolcock A et al. Comparison of addition of salmeterol to inhaled steroids with doubling the dose of inhaled steroids. *Am J Respir Crit Care Med* 1996;153:1481-1488. **2.** Greening AP et al. Added salmeterol versus higher-dose corticosteroid in asthma patients with symptoms on existing inhaled corticosteroid. *Lancet* 1994;344:219-24. **3.** Juniper EF, Johnston PR, Borkhoff C et al. Quality of life in asthma clinical trials; comparison of salmeterol and salbutamol. *Am J Respir Crit Care Med* 1995;151(1):66-70. **4.** Product Monograph of *Serevent*®, Glaxo Wellcome Inc., November 1997. **5.** Pearlman DS et al. A comparison of salmeterol with albuterol in the treatment of mild-to-moderate asthma. *N Engl J Med* 1992;327(20):1420-1425. **6.** Britton MG et al. (on behalf of a European study group). A twelve month comparison of salmeterol with salbutamol in asthmatic patients. *Eur Respir J* 1992;5:1062-1067. **7.** Boulet LP, Cowie R, Johnston P et al. Comparison of Diskus™ inhaler, a new multidose powder inhaler, with Diskhaler™ inhaler for the delivery of salmeterol to asthmatic patients. *J Asthma* 1995;32(6):429-436. **8.** Sharma RK, Edwards K, Hallet C et al. Perception among paediatric patients of the Diskus® inhaler, a novel multidose powder inhaler for use in the treatment of asthma. *Clin Drug Invest* 1996;11(3):145-153. **9.** Schlaeppi M, Edwards K, Fuller RW et al. Patient perception of the Diskus inhaler; a comparison with the Turbuhaler inhaler. *Br J Clin Pract* 1996;50(1):14-19. **10.** Fuller R. The Diskus™: a new multi-dose powder device – efficacy and comparison with Turbuhaler™. *J Aerosol Med* 1995;8(2):511-517. **11.** Malton A, Sumby BS, Smith IJ. A comparison of *in vitro* drug delivery from two multidose powder inhalation devices. *Eur J Clin Res* 1995;7:177-193. **12.** Prime D, Slater AL, Haywood PA et al. Assessing dose delivery from the Flixotide Diskus inhaler a multi-dose powder inhaler. *Pharmaceutical Technology Europe* 1996;8(3):23-36. **13.** Brindley A, Sumby BS, Smith IJ et al. Design, manufacture, and dose consistency of the Serevent Diskus inhaler. *Pharmaceutical Technology Europe* 1995;7(1):14-22. **14.** Williams J, Richards KA on behalf of a UK Study Group. Ease of handling and clinical efficacy of fluticasone propionate Accuhaler/Diskus™ inhaler compared with the Turbuhaler™ inhaler in paediatric patients. *Br J Clin Pract* 1997;51(3):147-153. **15.** Accuhaler Technical Product Monograph. Diskus from Glaxo Wellcome in the U.K. Glaxo Wellcome data on file. **16.** Product Monograph of *Flovent*® Glaxo Wellcome Inc. February 1998.

1. Data on file, Merck Frosst Canada Inc., "Worldwide literature search 1997".
2. Todd, P.A. and Goa, K.L., "Enalapril: A reappraisal of its pharmacology and therapeutic use in hypertension", *Drugs, 43(3),* 1992, p.346-381.
3. The SOLVD Investigators, "Effect of enalapril on mortality and the development of heart failure in asymptomatic patients with reduced left ventricular ejection fractions", *N Engl J Med, 327(10),* 1992, p.685-691.
4. The CONSENSUS Trial Study Group, "Effects of enalapril on mortality in severe congestive heart failure: Results of the Cooperative North Scandinavian Enalapril Survival Study (CONSENSUS)", *N Engl J Med, 316(23),* 1987, p.1429-1435.
5. The SOLVD Investigators, "Effect of enalapril on survival in patients with reduced left ventricular ejection fractions and congestive heart failure", *N Engl J Med, 325(5),* 1991, p.293-302.

ONCE-A-WEEK

AVONEX™ (Interferon beta-1a)

IM Injection

PRESCRIBING INFORMATION

THERAPEUTIC CLASSIFICATION

Immunomodulator

ACTION AND CLINICAL PHARMACOLOGY

Description

AVONEX™ (Interferon beta-1a) is produced by recombinant DNA technology. Interferon beta-1a is a 166 amino acid glycoprotein with a predicted molecular weight of approximately 22,500 daltons. It is produced by mammalian cells (Chinese Hamster Ovary cells) into which the human interferon beta gene has been introduced. The amino acid sequence of AVONEX™ is identical to that of natural human interferon beta.

Using the World Health Organization (WHO) natural interferon beta standard, Second International Standard for Interferon, Human Fibroblast (Gb-23-902-531), AVONEX™ has a specific activity of approximately 200 million international units (IU) of antiviral activity per mg; 30 mcg of AVONEX™ contains 6 million IU of antiviral activity.

General

Interferons are a family of naturally occurring proteins and glycoproteins that are produced by eukaryotic cells in response to viral infection and other biological inducers. Interferon beta, one member of this family, is produced by various cell types including fibroblasts and macrophages. Natural interferon beta and Interferon beta-1a are similarly glycosylated. Glycosylation of other proteins is known to affect their stability, activity, biodistribution, and half-life in blood. Glycosylation also decreases aggregation of proteins. Protein aggregates are thought to be involved in the immunogenicity of recombinant proteins. Aggregated forms of interferon beta are known to have lower levels of specific activity than monomeric (non-aggregated) forms of interferon beta.

Biologic Activities

Interferons are cytokines that mediate antiviral, antiproliferative, and immunomodulatory activities in response to viral infection and other biological inducers. Three major interferons have been distinguished: alpha, beta, and gamma. Interferons alpha and beta form the Type I class of interferons and interferon gamma is a Type II interferon. These interferons have overlapping but clearly distinct biological activities.

Interferon beta exerts its biological effects by binding to specific receptors on the surface of human cells. This binding initiates a complex cascade of intracellular events that lead to the expression of numerous interferon-induced gene products and markers. These include 2', 5'-oligoadenylate synthetase, β_2-microglobulin, and neopterin. These products have been measured in the serum and cellular fractions of blood collected from patients treated with AVONEX™.

The specific interferon-induced proteins and mechanisms by which AVONEX™ exerts its effects in multiple sclerosis (MS) have not been fully defined. To understand the mechanism(s) of action of AVONEX™, studies were conducted to determine the effect of IM injection of AVONEX™ on levels of the immunosuppressive cytokine interleukin 10 (IL-10) in serum and cerebrospinal fluid (CSF) of treated patients. IL-10, or cytokine synthesis inhibitory factor, is a potent immunosuppressor of a number of pro-inflammatory cytokines such as interferon gamma (IFN-γ), tumor necrosis factor alpha (TNF-α), interleukin 1 (IL-1), tumor necrosis factor beta (TNF-β), and interleukin 6 (IL-6), which are secreted by T lymphocyte helper-1 (Th¹) cells and macrophages. Elevated serum IL-10 levels were seen after IM injection of AVONEX™, from 48 hours post-injection through at least 7 days. Similarly, in the Phase III study, IL-10 levels in CSF were significantly increased in patients treated with AVONEX™ compared to placebo. CSF IL-10 levels correlated with a favourable clinical treatment response to AVONEX™. Upregulation of IL-10 represents a possible mechanism of action of interferon beta in relapsing MS. IL-10 has been demonstrated to decrease relapses in acute and chronic relapsing experimental autoimmune encephalomyelitis (EAE), an animal model resembling MS. However, no relationship has been established between the absolute levels of IL-10 and the clinical outcome in MS.

CLINICAL TRIALS: EFFECTS IN MULTIPLE SCLEROSIS

The clinical effects of AVONEX™ (Interferon beta-1a) in MS were studied in a randomized, multicentre, double-blind, placebo-controlled study in patients with relapsing (stable or progressive) MS. In this study, 301 patients received either 6 million IU (30 mcg) of AVONEX™ (n=158) or placebo (n=143) by IM injection once weekly. Patients were entered into the trial over a 2 1/2 year period, received injections for up to 2 years, and continued to be followed until study completion. By design, there was staggered enrollment into the study with termination at a fixed point, leading to variable lengths of follow-up. There were 144 patients treated with AVONEX™ for more than 1 year, 115 patients for more than 18 months, and 82 patients for 2 years.

All patients had a definite diagnosis of MS of at least 1 year duration and had at least 2 exacerbations in the 3 years prior to study entry (or 1 per year if the duration of disease was less than 3 years). At entry, study participants were without exacerbation during the prior 2 months and had Kurtzke Expanded Disability Status Scale (EDSS) scores ranging from 1.0 to 3.5. The mean EDSS score at baseline was 2.3 for placebo-treated patients and 2.4 for AVONEX™-treated patients. Patients with chronic progressive multiple sclerosis were excluded from this study.

The primary outcome assessment was time to progression in disability, measured as an increase in the EDSS of at least 1.0 point that was sustained for at least 6 months. The requirement for a sustained 6 month change was chosen because this reflects permanent disability rather than a transient effect due to an exacerbation. Studies show that of the patients who progress and are confirmed after only 3 months, 18% revert back to their baseline EDSS, whereas after 6 months only 11% revert.

Secondary outcomes included exacerbation frequency and results of magnetic resonance imaging (MRI) scans of the brain including gadolinium (Gd)-enhanced lesion number and volume and T2-weighted (proton density) lesion volume. Additional secondary endpoints included upper and lower extremity function tests.

Time to onset of sustained progression in disability was significantly longer in patients treated with AVONEX™ than in patients receiving placebo (p = 0.02). The Kaplan-Meier plots of these data are presented in Figure 1. The Kaplan-Meier estimate of the percentage of patients progressing by the end of 2 years was 34.9% for placebo-treated patients and 21.9% for AVONEX™-treated patients, indicating a slowing of the disease process. This represents a significant reduction in the risk of disability progression in patients treated with AVONEX™, compared to patients treated with placebo.

FIGURE 1
Onset of Sustained Disability Progression by Time on Study (Kaplan-Meier Methodology)

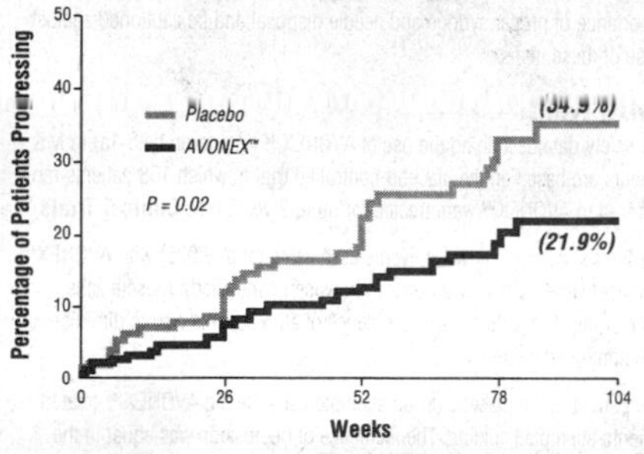

Note: Disability progression represents at least a 1.0 point increase in EDSS score sustained for at least 6 months. The value p=0.02 refers to the statistical difference between the overall distribution of the two curves, not to the difference in estimates at any given timepoint (e.g., 34.9% vs. 21.9% at Week 104.).

The distribution of confirmed EDSS change from study entry (baseline) to the end of the study is shown in Figure 2. There was a statistically significant difference between treatment groups in confirmed change for patients with at least 2 scheduled visits (136 placebo-treated and 150 AVONEX™-treated patients; p = 0.006; see Table 1). Confirmed EDSS change was calculated as the difference between the EDSS score at study entry and 1 of the scores determined at the last 2 scheduled visits. Further analyses using more rigorous measures of progression of disability were performed. When the requirement for sustained EDSS change was increased from 6 months to 1 year, a significant benefit in favour of AVONEX™ recipients persisted (p=0.002). When treatment failure was defined as 2.0 points or greater increase in EDSS sustained for 6 months, 18.3% of placebo-treated patients worsened compared to 6.1% of AVONEX™ treated patients. Additionally, significantly fewer AVONEX™ recipients progressed to EDSS milestones of 4.0 (14% vs. 5%, p=0.014) or 6.0 (7% vs. 1%, p=0.028).

The rate and frequency of exacerbations were determined as secondary outcomes (see Table 1). AVONEX™ treatment significantly decreased the frequency of exacerbations in patients who were enrolled in the study for at least 2 years, from 0.90 in the placebo-treated group to 0.61 in the AVONEX™-treated group (p=0.002). This represents a 32% reduction.

Additionally, placebo-treated patients were twice as likely to have 3 or more exacerbations during the study when compared to AVONEX™-treated patients (32% vs. 14%).

FIGURE 2
Confirmed EDSS Change from Study Entry to End of Study

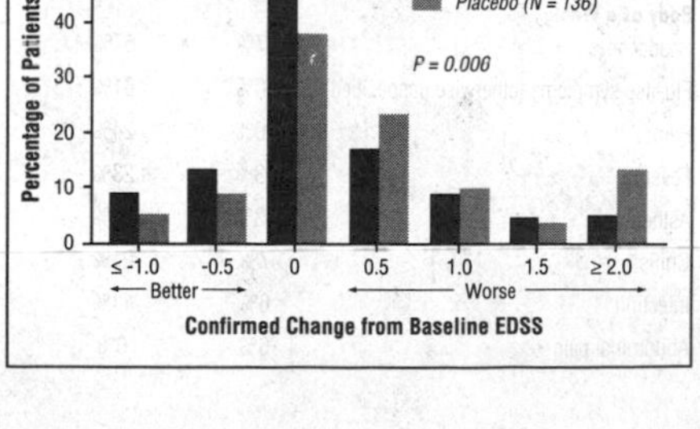

Gd-enhanced and T2-weighted (proton density) MRI scans of the brain were obtained in most patients at baseline and at the end of 1 and 2 years of treatment. Gd-enhancing lesions seen on brain MRI scans represent areas of breakdown of the blood brain barrier thought to be secondary to inflammation. Patients treated with AVONEX™ demonstrated significantly lower Gd-enhanced lesion number after 1 and 2 years of treatment ($p \leq 0.05$; see Table 1). The mean number of Gd-enhanced lesions for patients treated with AVONEX™ was 3.2 at baseline and 0.8 at Year 2, compared to 2.3 at baseline and 1.6 at Year 2 for the placebo-treated patients. The volume of Gd-enhanced lesions was also analyzed and showed similar treatment effects ($p \leq 0.03$). Percentage change in T2-weighted lesion volume from study entry to Year 1 was significantly lower in AVONEX™-treated than placebo-treated patients (p = 0.02). A significant difference in T2-weighted lesion volume change was not seen between study entry and Year 2. Treatment with AVONEX™ resulted in a significant decrease in the number of active (new and enlarging) T2 lesions over 2 years (p = 0.002).

The exact relationship between MRI findings and the clinical status of patients is unknown.

Of the limb function tests, only 1 demonstrated a statistically significant difference between treatment groups (favoring AVONEX™).

Twenty-three of the 301 patients (8%) discontinued treatment prematurely. Of these, 1 patient treated with placebo (1%) and 6 patients treated with AVONEX™ (4%) discontinued treatment due to adverse events. Of these 23 patients, 13 remained on study and were evaluated for clinical endpoints.

A summary of the effects of AVONEX™ on the primary and major secondary endpoints of this study is presented in Table 1.

Table 1
MAJOR CLINICAL ENDPOINTS

Endpoint	Placebo	AVONEX™	P-Value
PRIMARY ENDPOINT:			
Time to sustained progression in disability (N: 143, 158)[1]	- See Figure 1 -		0.02[2]
Percentage of patients progressing in disability at 2 years (Kaplan-Meier estimate)[1]	34.9%	21.9%	
SECONDARY ENDPOINTS:			
DISABILITY			
Mean confirmed change in EDSS from study entry to end of study (N: 136, 150)[1]	0.50	0.20	0.006[3]
EXACERBATIONS FOR PATIENTS COMPLETING 2 YEARS:			
Number of exacerbations (N: 87, 85)			
0	26%	38%	0.03[3]
1	30%	31%	
2	11%	18%	
3	14%	7%	
≥ 4	18%	7%	
Percentage of patients exacerbation-free (N: 87, 85)	26%	38%	0.10[4]
Annual exacerbation rate (N: 87, 85)	0.90	0.61	0.002[5]
MRI			
Number of Gd-enhanced lesions:			
At study entry (N: 132, 141)			
Mean (Median)	2.3 (1.0)	3.2 (1.0)	
Range	0-23	0-56	
Year 1 (N: 123, 134)			
Mean (Median)	1.6 (0)	1.0 (0)	0.02[3]
Range	0-22	0-28	
Year 2 (N: 82, 83)			
Mean (Median)	1.6 (0)	0.8 (0)	0.05[3]
Range	0-34	0-13	
T2 lesion volume:			
Percentage change from study entry to Year 1 (N: 116, 123)			
Median	-3.3%	-13.1%	0.02[3]
Percentage change from study entry to Year 2 (N: 83, 81)			
Median	-6.5%	-13.2%	0.36[3]
Number of new and enlarging lesions at Year 2 (N: 80, 78)			
Median	3.0	2.0	0.002[6]

Note: (N: ,) denotes the number of evaluable placebo and AVONEX™ (Interferon beta-1a) patients, respectively.

[1] Patient data included in this analysis represent variable periods of time on study.

[2] Analyzed by Mantel-Cox (logrank) test.

[3] Analyzed by Mann-Whitney rank-sum test.

[4] Analyzed by Cochran-Mantel-Haenszel test.

[5] Analyzed by likelihood ratio test.

[6] Analyzed by Wilcoxon rank-sum test.

INDICATIONS AND CLINICAL USE

AVONEX™ (Interferon beta-1a) is indicated for the treatment of relapsing forms of multiple sclerosis to slow the progression of disability, decrease the frequency of clinical exacerbations, and reduce the number and volume of active brain lesions identified on Magnetic Resonance Imaging (MRI) scans. Safety and efficacy have not been evaluated in patients with chronic progressive multiple sclerosis.

CONTRAINDICATIONS

AVONEX™ (Interferon beta-1a) is contraindicated in patients with a history of hypersensitivity to natural or recombinant interferon beta, human albumin, or any other component of the formulation.

WARNINGS

AVONEX™ (Interferon beta-1a) should be used with caution in patients with depression. Depression and suicide have been reported to occur in patients receiving other interferon compounds. Depression and suicidal ideation are known to occur at an increased frequency in the MS population. A relationship between the occurrence of depression and/or suicidal ideation and the use of AVONEX™ has not been established. An equal incidence of depression was seen in the placebo-treated and AVONEX™-treated patients in the placebo-controlled relapsing MS study. Patients treated with AVONEX™ should be advised to report immediately any symptoms of depression and/or suicidal ideation to their prescribing physicians. If a patient develops depression, antidepressant therapy or cessation of AVONEX™ therapy should be considered.

PRECAUTIONS

General

Caution should be exercised when administering AVONEX™ (Interferon beta-1a) to patients with pre-existing seizure disorder. In the placebo-controlled study, 4 patients receiving AVONEX™ experienced seizures, while no seizures occurred in the placebo group. Of these 4 patients, 3 had no prior history of seizure. It is not known whether these events were related to the effects of MS alone, to AVONEX™, or to a combination of both. For patients with no prior history of seizure who developed seizures during therapy with AVONEX™, an etiologic basis should be established and appropriate anti-convulsant therapy instituted prior to considering resumption of AVONEX™ treatment. The effect of AVONEX™ administration on the medical management of patients with seizure disorder is unknown.

Patients with cardiac disease, such as angina, congestive heart failure, or arrhythmia, should be closely monitored for worsening of their clinical condition during initiation of therapy with AVONEX™. AVONEX™ does not have any known direct-acting cardiac toxicity; however, symptoms of flu syndrome seen with AVONEX™ therapy may prove stressful to patients with severe cardiac conditions.

Laboratory Tests

In addition to those laboratory tests normally required for monitoring patients with MS, complete blood cell counts and white blood cell differential, platelet counts, and blood chemistries, including liver and thyroid function tests, are recommended during AVONEX™ therapy. During the placebo-controlled study, complete blood cell counts and white blood cell differential, platelet counts, and blood chemistries were performed at least every 6 months. There were no significant differences between the placebo and AVONEX™ groups in the incidence of thyroid abnormalities, liver enzyme elevation, leukopenia, or thrombocytopenia (these are known to be dose-related laboratory abnormalities associated with the use of interferons). Patients with myelosuppression may require more intensive monitoring of complete blood cell counts, with differential and platelet counts.

Drug Interactions

No formal drug interaction studies have been conducted with AVONEX™. In the placebo-controlled study, corticosteroids or ACTH were administered for treatment of exacerbations in some patients concurrently receiving AVONEX™. In addition, some patients receiving AVONEX™ were also treated with anti-depressant therapy and/or oral contraceptive therapy. No unexpected adverse events were associated with these concomitant therapies.

Other interferons have been noted to reduce cytochrome P-450 oxidase-mediated drug metabolism. Formal hepatic drug metabolism studies with AVONEX™ in humans have not been conducted. Hepatic microsomes isolated from AVONEX™-treated rhesus monkeys showed no influence of AVONEX™ on hepatic P-450 enzyme metabolism activity.

As with all interferon products, proper monitoring of patients is required if AVONEX™ is given in combination with myelosuppressive agents.

Use in Pregnancy

If a woman becomes pregnant or plans to become pregnant while taking AVONEX™, she should be informed of the potential hazards to the fetus, and it should be recommended that the woman discontinue therapy. The reproductive toxicity of AVONEX™ has not been studied in animals or humans. In pregnant monkeys given interferon beta at 100 times the recommended weekly human dose (based upon a body surface area comparison), no teratogenic or other adverse effects on fetal development were observed. Abortifacient activity was evident following 3 to 5 doses at this level. No abortifacient effects were observed in monkeys treated at 2 times the recommended weekly human dose (based upon a body surface area comparison). Although no teratogenic effects were seen in these studies, it is not known if teratogenic effects would be observed in humans. There are no adequate and well-controlled studies with interferons in pregnant women.

Nursing Mothers

It is not known whether AVONEX™ is excreted in human milk. Because of the potential of serious adverse reactions in nursing infants, a decision should be made to either discontinue nursing or to discontinue AVONEX™

Pediatric Use

Safety and effectiveness have not been established in pediatric patients below the age of 18 years.

Information to Patients

Patients should be informed of the most common adverse events associated with AVONEX™ administration, including symptoms associated with flu syndrome (see **Adverse Events** and **Information for the Patient**). Symptoms of flu syndrome are most prominent at the initiation of therapy and decrease in frequency with continued treatment. In the placebo-controlled study, patients were instructed to take 650 mg acetaminophen immediately prior to injection and for an additional 24 hours after each injection to modulate acute symptoms associated with AVONEX™ administration.

Patients should be cautioned to report depression or suicidal ideation (see **Warnings**).

When a physician determines that AVONEX™ can be used outside of the physician's office, persons who will be administering AVONEX™ should receive instruction in reconstitution and injection, including the review of the injection procedures (see **Information for the Patient**). If a patient is to self-administer, the physical ability of that patient to self-inject intramuscularly should be assessed. If home use is chosen, the first injection should be performed under the supervision of a qualified health care professional. A puncture-resistant container for disposal of needles and syringes should be used. Patients should be instructed in the technique and importance of proper syringe and needle disposal and be cautioned against reuse of these items.

ADVERSE EVENTS

The safety data describing the use of AVONEX™ (Interferon beta-1a) in MS patients are based on the placebo-controlled trial in which 158 patients randomized to AVONEX™ were treated for up to 2 years (see **Clinical Trials**).

The 5 most common adverse events associated (at p<0.075) with AVONEX™ treatment were flu-like symptoms (otherwise unspecified), muscle ache, fever, chills, and asthenia. The incidence of all 5 adverse events diminished with continued treatment.

One patient in the placebo group attempted suicide; no AVONEX™-treated patients attempted suicide. The incidence of depression was equal in the 2 treatment groups. However, since depression and suicide have been reported with other interferon products, AVONEX™ should be used with caution in patients with depression (see **Warnings**).

In the placebo-controlled study, 4 patients receiving AVONEX™ experienced seizures, while no seizures occurred in the placebo group. Of these 4 patients, 3 had no prior history of seizure. It is not known whether these events were related to the effects of MS alone, to AVONEX™, or to a combination of both (see **Precautions**).

Table 2 enumerates adverse events and selected laboratory abnormalities that occurred at an incidence of 2% or more among the 158 patients with relapsing MS treated with 30 mcg of AVONEX™ once weekly by IM injection. Reported adverse events have been classified using standard COSTART terms. Terms so general as to be uninformative or more common in the placebo-treated patients have been excluded.

AVONEX™ has also been evaluated in 290 patients with illnesses other than MS. The majority of these patients were enrolled in studies to evaluate AVONEX™ treatment of chronic viral hepatitis B and C, in which the doses studied ranged from 15 mcg to 75 mcg, given subcutaneously (SC), 3 times a week, for up to 6 months. The incidence of common adverse events in these studies was generally seen at a frequency similar to that seen in the placebo-controlled MS study. In these non-MS studies, inflammation at the site of the SC injection was seen in 52% of treated patients. In contrast, injection site inflammation was seen in 3% of MS patients receiving AVONEX™, 30 mcg by IM injection. SC injections were also associated with the following local reactions: injection site necrosis, injection site atrophy, injection site edema, and injection site hemorrhage. None of the above was observed in the MS patients participating in the placebo-controlled study.

Table 2
Adverse Events and Selected Laboratory Abnormalities in the Placebo-Controlled Study

Adverse Event	Placebo (N = 143)	AVONEX™ (N = 158)
Body as a Whole		
Headache	57%	67%
Flu-like symptoms (otherwise unspecified)*	40%	61%
Pain	20%	24%
Fever*	13%	23%
Asthenia	13%	21%
Chills*	7%	21%
Infection	6%	11%
Abdominal pain	6%	9%

Table 2
Adverse Events and Selected Laboratory Abnormalities in the Placebo-Controlled Study

Adverse Event	Placebo (N = 143)	AVONEX™ (N = 158)
Chest pain	4%	6%
Injection site reaction	1%	4%
Malaise	3%	4%
Injection site inflammation	0%	3%
Hypersensitivity reaction	0%	3%
Ovarian cyst	0%	3%
Ecchymosis injection site	1%	2%
Cardiovascular System		
Syncope	2%	4%
Vasodilation	1%	4%
Digestive System		
Nausea	23%	33%
Diarrhea	10%	16%
Dyspepsia	7%	11%
Anorexia	6%	7%
Hemic and Lymphatic System		
Anemia*	3%	8%
Eosinophils ≥ 10%	4%	5%
HCT (%) ≤ 32 (females) or ≤ 37 (males)	1%	3%
Metabolic and Nutritional Disorders		
SGOT ≥ 3 x ULN	1%	3%
Musculoskeletal System		
Muscle ache*	15%	34%
Arthralgia	5%	9%
Nervous System		
Sleep difficult	16%	19%
Dizziness	13%	15%
Muscle spasm	6%	7%
Suicidal tendency	1%	4%
Seizure	0%	3%
Speech disorder	0%	3%
Ataxia	0%	2%
Respiratory System		
Upper respiratory tract infection	28%	31%
Sinusitis	17%	18%
Dyspnea	3%	6%
Skin and Appendages		
Urticaria	2%	5%
Alopecia	1%	4%
Nevus	0%	3%
Herpes zoster	2%	3%
Herpes simplex	1%	2%
Special Senses		
Otitis media	5%	6%
Hearing decreased	0%	3%
Urogenital		
Vaginitis	2%	4%

* Significantly associated with AVONEX™ treatment (p ≤ 0.05).

Other events observed during premarket evaluation of AVONEX™, administered either SC or IM in all patient populations studied, are listed in the paragraph that follows. Because most of the events were observed in open and uncontrolled studies, the role of AVONEX™ in their causation cannot be reliably determined. **Body as a Whole:** abscess, ascites, cellulitis, facial edema, hernia, injection site fibrosis, injection site hypersensitivity, lipoma, neoplasm, photosensitivity reaction, sepsis, sinus headache, toothache; **Cardiovascular System:** arrhythmia, arteritis, heart arrest, hemorrhage, hypotension, palpitation, pericarditis, peripheral ischemia, peripheral vascular disorder, postural hypotension, pulmonary embolus, spider angioma, telangiectasia, vascular disorder; **Digestive System:** blood in stool, colitis, constipation, diverticulitis, dry mouth, gallbladder disorder, gastritis, gastrointestinal hemorrhage, gingivitis, gum hemorrhage, hepatoma, hepatomegaly, increased appetite, intestinal perforation, intestinal obstruction, periodontal abscess, periodontitis, proctitis, thirst, tongue disorder, vomiting; **Endocrine System:** hypothyroidism; **Hemic and Lymphatic System:** coagulation time increased, ecchymosis, lymphadenopathy, petechia; **Metabolic and Nutritional Disorders:** abnormal healing, dehydration, hypoglycemia, hypomagnesemia, hypokalemia; **Musculoskeletal System:** arthritis, bone pain, myasthenia, osteonecrosis, synovitis; **Nervous System:** abnormal gait, amnesia, anxiety, Bell's Palsy, clumsiness, depersonalization, drug dependence, facial paralysis, hyperesthesia, increased libido, neurosis, psychosis; **Respiratory System:** emphysema, hemoptysis, hiccup, hyperventilation, laryngitis, pharygeal edema, pneumonia; **Skin and Appendages:** basal cell carcinoma, blisters, cold clammy skin, contact dermatitis, erythema, furunculosis, genital pruritus, nevus, rash, seborrhea, skin ulcer, skin discolouration; **Special Senses:** abnormal vision, conjunctivitis, earache, eye pain, labyrinthitis, vitreous floaters; **Urogenital:** breast fibroadenosis, breast mass, dysuria, epididymitis, fibrocystic change of the breast, fibroids, gynecomastia, hematuria, kidney calculus, kidney pain, leukorrhea, menopause, nocturia, pelvic inflammatory disease, penis disorder, Peyronies Disease, polyuria, post menopausal hemorrhage, prostatic disorder, pyelonephritis, testis disorder, urethral pain, urinary urgency, urinary retention, urinary incontinence, vaginal hemorrhage.

Serum Neutralizing Antibodies

MS patients treated with AVONEX™ may develop neutralizing antibodies specific to interferon beta. Analyses conducted on sera samples from 2 separate clinical studies of AVONEX™ suggest that the plateau for the incidence of neutralizing antibodies formation is reached at approximately 12 months of therapy. Data furthermore demonstrate that at 12 months, **approximately 6% of patients treated with AVONEX™ develop neutralizing antibodies.**

SYMPTOMS AND TREATMENT OF OVERDOSAGE

Overdosage is unlikely to occur with use of AVONEX™ (Interferon beta-1a). In clinical studies, overdosage was not seen using Interferon beta-1a at a dose of 75 mcg given SC 3 times per week.

DOSAGE AND ADMINISTRATION

The recommended dosage of AVONEX™ (Interferon beta-1a) for the treatment of relapsing forms of multiple sclerosis is 30 mcg injected intramuscularly once a week.

AVONEX™ is intended for use under the guidance and supervision of a physician. Patients may self-inject only if their physician determines that it is appropriate and with medical follow-up, as necessary, after proper training in IM injection technique.

PHARMACEUTICAL INFORMATION

Composition:

AVONEX™ is supplied as a sterile white to off-white lyophilized powder in a single-use vial containing 33 mcg (6.6 million IU) of Interferon beta-1a, 16.5 mg Albumin Human, USP, 6.4 mg Sodium Chloride, USP, 6.3 mg Dibasic Sodium Phosphate, USP, and 1.3 mg Monobasic Sodium Phosphate, USP, and is preservative-free. Diluent is supplied in a single-use vial (Sterile Water for Injection, USP, preservative-free).

Reconstitution:

AVONEX™ is reconstituted by adding 1.1 mL (cc) of diluent (approximate pH 7.3) to the single-use vial of lyophilized powder; 1.0 mL (cc) is withdrawn for administration.

Stability and Storage:

Vials of AVONEX™ must be stored in a 2-8°C (36-46°F) refrigerator. Should refrigeration be unavailable, AVONEX™ can be stored at up to 25°C (77°F) for a period of up to 30 days. DO NOT EXPOSE TO HIGH TEMPERATURES. DO NOT FREEZE. Do not use beyond the expiration date stamped on the vial. Following reconstitution, it is recommended the product be used as soon as possible but within 6 hours stored at 2-8°C (36-46°F). DO NOT FREEZE RECONSTITUTED AVONEX™.

AVAILABILITY OF DOSAGE FORMS

AVONEX™ (Interferon beta-1a) is available as:

Package (Administration Pack) containing 4 Administration Dose Packs (each containing one vial of AVONEX™, one 10 mL (10 cc) diluent vial, three alcohol wipes, one 3 cc syringe, one Micro Pin®, one needle, and one adhesive bandage).

REFERENCES:

1. Data on file. Biogen Canada, Inc.
2. AVONEX™ Product Monograph, April 6, 1998.
3. Jacobs LD, Cookfair DL, Rudick RA, et al. Intramuscular interferon beta-1a for disease progression in relapsing multiple sclerosis. Ann Neurol. 1996;39:285-294.
4. Data on file, PRB#8154-1, Biogen, Inc., November 20, 1997.

☎ 1-888-456-2263

BIOGEN®

CANADA

http://www.biogen.com

3 Robert Speck Parkway, Suite 300, Mississauga, Ontario L4Z 2G5

ZYBAN®

BUPROPION HCl sustained-release tablets

Bupropion Hydrochloride
150 mg Sustained Release Tablets
Smoking Cessation Aid

ACTIONS AND CLINICAL PHARMACOLOGY

The mechanism by which ZYBAN (bupropion hydrochloride) enhances the ability of patients to abstain from smoking is unknown. However, it is presumed that this action is mediated by noradrenergic and/or dopaminergic mechanisms. ZYBAN is a weak inhibitor of the neuronal uptake of norepinephrine, serotonin, and dopamine, and does not inhibit monoamine oxidase. ZYBAN is chemically unrelated to nicotine or other agents currently used in the treatment of nicotine addiction.

Bupropion, initially developed as an antidepressant of the aminoketone class, is chemically unrelated to tricyclic, tetracyclic, selective serotonin re-uptake inhibitors or other known antidepressant agents. Its structure closely resembles that of diethylpropion; it is related to phenylethylamines.

Following oral administration of ZYBAN Tablets to healthy volunteers, peak plasma concentrations of bupropion are achieved within 3 hours. Food increased C_{max} and AUC of bupropion by 11% and 17%, respectively, indicating that there is no clinically significant food effect. In vitro tests indicate that bupropion is 84% bound to human albumin at plasma concentrations up to 200 µg/mL.

The mean elimination half-life (± SD) of bupropion after chronic dosing is 21 (± 9) hours, and steady-state plasma concentrations of bupropion are reached within 5 days (See PHARMACOLOGY, Human Pharmacokinetics). Three active metabolites have been identified. Bupropion and its metabolites exhibit linear kinetics following chronic administration of 150 to 300 mg/day. Plasma concentrations of the metabolites exceed those of the parent drug and may be clinically important (See PHARMACOLOGY, Human Pharmacokinetics).

The Nicotine Transdermal System (NTS) used in clinical trials did not appear to have effects on the pharmacokinetics of ZYBAN. Smokers and non-smokers appear to have similar pharmacokinetics of bupropion or its major metabolites.

CLINICAL TRIALS:

The efficacy of ZYBAN as an aid to smoking cessation was demonstrated in two placebo controlled, double blind trials in nondepressed chronic cigarette smokers (n = 1,508, ≥15 cigarettes per day). In these studies, ZYBAN was used in conjunction with individual smoking cessation counseling.

The first study was a dose response trial conducted at three clinical centres. Patients in this study were treated for 7 weeks with one of three doses of ZYBAN (100, 150, or 300 mg/day) or placebo; quitting was defined as total abstinence during the last 4 weeks of treatment (weeks 4 through 7). Abstinence was determined by patient daily diaries and verified by carbon monoxide levels in expired air.

Table 1 shows a dose dependent increase in the percentage of patients able to achieve 4 week abstinence (weeks 4 through 7). Treatment with ZYBAN at both 150 and 300 mg/day was significantly more effective than placebo, in this study. Treatment with ZYBAN (7 weeks at 300 mg/day) was more effective than placebo in helping patients maintain continuous abstinence through week 26 (6 months) of the study.

Table 1 – Dose-Response Trial: Quit Rates by Treatment Group (Intent to Treat Analysis)

	Treatment Groups			
Abstinence From Week 4 Through Specified Week	Placebo (n = 151) % (95% CI)	ZYBAN 100 mg/day (n = 153) % (95% CI)	ZYBAN 150 mg/day (n = 153) % (95% CI)	ZYBAN 300 mg/day (n = 156) % (95% CI)
Week 7 (4-week quit)	17% (11-23)	22% (15-28)	27%* (20-35)	36%* (28-43)
Week 12	14% (8-19)	20% (13-26)	20% (14-27)	25%* (18-32)
Week 26	11% (6-16)	16% (11-22)	18% (12-24)	19%* (13-25)

Quit rates are the proportions of all persons initially enrolled who abstained from week 4 of the study through the specified week.
* Significantly different from placebo ($P \leq 0.05$).

The second study was a comparative trial conducted at four clinical centers. Four treatments were evaluated: ZYBAN 300 mg/day, nicotine transdermal system (NTS) 21 mg/day, combination of ZYBAN 300 mg/day plus NTS 21 mg/day, and placebo. Patients were treated with ZYBAN for 9 weeks. Treatment with ZYBAN was initiated at 150 mg/day while the patient was still smoking and was increased after 3 days to 300 mg/day given as 150 mg twice daily. NTS 21 mg/day was added to treatment with ZYBAN after approximately 1 week when the patient reached the target quit date. During weeks 8 and 9 of the study, NTS was tapered to 14 and 7 mg/day, respectively. Quitting, defined as total abstinence during weeks 4 through 7, was determined by patient daily diaries and verified by expired air carbon monoxide levels.

In this study (Table 2), patients treated with either ZYBAN or NTS achieved greater 4 week abstinence rates than patients treated with placebo. In addition, patients treated with the combination of ZYBAN and NTS achieved higher 4 week abstinence rates than patients treated with either of the individual active treatments alone, although only the comparison with NTS achieved statistical significance. Both ZYBAN and the combination of ZYBAN and NTS were more effective than placebo and NTS in helping patients maintain abstinence through week 52 of the study. Although the treatment combination of ZYBAN and NTS displayed the highest rates of continuous abstinence throughout the study, the quit rates for the combination were not significantly higher ($P > 0.05$) than for ZYBAN alone.

Table 2 – Comparative Trial: Quit Rates by Treatment Group

	Treatment Groups			
Abstinence From Week 4 Through Specified Week	Placebo (n = 160) % (95% CI)	Nicotine Transdermal System (NTS) 21 mg/day (n = 244) % (95% CI)	ZYBAN 300 mg/day (n = 244) % (95% CI)	ZYBAN 300 mg/day and NTS 21 mg/day (n = 245) % (95% CI)
Week 7 (4-week quit)	23% (17-30)	36%* (30-42)	49%*‡ (43-56)	58%*‡ (51-64)
Week 12	20% (14-26)	29%† (23-34)	41%*‡ (34-47)	48%*‡ (42-54)
Week 26	13% (7-18)	18% (14-23)	30%*‡ (24-35)	33%*‡ (27-39)
Week 52	8% (3-12)	12% (8-16)	23%*‡ (18-28)	28%*‡ (23-34)

* $P < 0.01$ versus placebo. † $P < 0.05$ versus placebo. ‡ $P < 0.01$ versus NTS.

Treatment with ZYBAN reduced some of the withdrawal symptoms compared to placebo: irritability, frustration, or anger; anxiety; difficulty concentrating; restlessness; and depressed mood or negative affect. Depending on the study and the measure used, treatment with ZYBAN showed evidence of reduction in craving for cigarettes or urge to smoke compared to placebo.

INDICATIONS AND CLINICAL USE

ZYBAN (bupropion hydrochloride) is indicated as smoking cessation treatment in conjunction with behavioural modification; Nicotine replacement therapy may be used in addition to ZYBAN.

CONTRAINDICATIONS

ZYBAN (bupropion hydrochloride) is contraindicated in patients treated with WELLBUTRIN® SR, or any other medications that contain bupropion because the incidence of seizure is dose dependent (See WARNINGS).

ZYBAN is contraindicated in patients with a seizure disorder (See WARNINGS).

ZYBAN is contraindicated in patients with a current or prior diagnosis of bulimia or anorexia nervosa; a higher incidence of seizures were noted in patients treated for bulimia with the immediate-release formulation of bupropion.

The concurrent administration of ZYBAN and a monoamine oxidase (MAO) inhibitor is contraindicated. At least 14 days should elapse between discontinuation of an MAO inhibitor and initiation of treatment with ZYBAN.

ZYBAN is contraindicated in patients who have shown an allergic response to bupropion or any other component of the formulation.

WARNINGS

Patients should be made aware that ZYBAN (bupropion hydrochloride) Tablets contain the same active ingredient found in WELLBUTRIN SR Sustained Release Tablets used to treat depression, and that ZYBAN should NOT be administered to patients already receiving a product containing bupropion hydrochloride (see CONTRAINDICATIONS).

The use of bupropion is associated with a dose-dependent risk of seizures. *Clinicians should not prescribe doses over 300 mg/day for smoking cessation.* The risk of seizure is also related to patient factors, clinical situation, and concurrent medications, which must be considered in selection of patients for therapy with ZYBAN Tablets.

Seizures: Seizures were not reported by patients participating in smoking cessation trials (n=1946). The seizure rate associated with doses of sustained-release bupropion up to 300 mg/day is approximately 0.1%. This incidence was prospectively determined during an 8-week treatment exposure in approximately 3,100 depressed patients. Data for the immediate-release formulation of bupropion revealed a seizure incidence of approximately 0.4% in depressed patients treated at doses in a range of 300 to 450 mg/day. In addition, the estimated seizure incidence increases almost tenfold between 450 and 600 mg/day.

Recommendations for reducing the Risk of Seizure:

1. Bupropion is associated with a dose-dependent risk of seizures, therefore:
   - ZYBAN should not be prescribed at doses over 300 mg/day for smoking cessation, and
   - No single dose of ZYBAN should exceed 150 mg, in order to avoid high peak concentrations of bupropion and/or its metabolites.
2. The risk of seizure is also related to patient factors, clinical situation, and concurrent medications. Therefore, ZYBAN Tablets should be administered with extreme caution to these patients.
   - Patient factors: Predisposing factors that may increase the risk of seizure with bupropion use include history of head trauma or prior seizure, central nervous system tumour, and concomitant medications that lower seizure threshold.
   - Clinical situations: Circumstances associated with an increased seizure risk include, among others, excessive use of alcohol; abrupt withdrawal from alcohol or other sedatives; addiction to opiates, cocaine, or stimulants; use of over-the-counter stimulants and anorectics; diabetics treated with oral hypoglycemics or insulin.
   - Concomitant medications: Many medications (e.g., antipsychotics, antidepressents, theophylline, systemic steroids) and treatment regimens (e.g., abrupt discontinuation of benzodiazepines) are known to lower seizure threshold.

Potential for Hepatotoxicity: In rats receiving large doses of bupropion chronically, there was an increase in incidence of hepatic hyperplastic nodules and hepatocellular hypertrophy. In dogs receiving large doses of bupropion chronically, various histologic changes were seen in the liver, and laboratory tests suggesting mild hepatocellular injury were noted.

PRECAUTIONS

General:

Allergic Reactions: Anaphylactoid reactions characterized by symptoms such as pruritus, urticaria, angioedema, and dyspnea have been reported at a rate of one to three per thousand in clinical trials. In addition, there have been rare spontaneous postmarketing reports of erythema multiforme, Stevens Johnson syndrome, and anaphylactic shock associated with bupropion.

Insomnia: In the dose response smoking cessation trial, 29% of patients treated with 150 mg/day of ZYBAN (bupropion hydrochloride) and 35% of patients treated with 300 mg/day of ZYBAN experienced insomnia, compared to 21% of placebo treated patients. Symptoms were sufficiently severe to require discontinuation of treatment in 0.6% of patients treated with ZYBAN and none of the patients treated with placebo.

In the comparative trial, 40% of the patients treated with 300 mg/day of ZYBAN, 28% of the patients treated with 21 mg/day of nicotine transdermal system (NTS), and 45% of the patients treated with the combination of ZYBAN and NTS experienced insomnia compared to 18% of placebo treated patients. Symptoms were sufficiently severe to require discontinuation of treatment in 0.8% of patients treated with ZYBAN and none of the patients in the other three treatment groups.

Insomnia may be minimized by avoiding bedtime doses and, if necessary, reduction in dose.

Psychosis, Confusion, and Other Neuropsychiatric Phenomena: In clinical trials with ZYBAN conducted in nondepressed smokers, the incidence of neuropsychiatric side effects was generally comparable to placebo. Depressed patients treated with bupropion in depression trials have been reported to show a variety of neuropsychiatric signs and symptoms including delusions, hallucinations, psychosis, concentration disturbance, paranoia, and confusion. In some cases, these symptoms abated upon dose reduction and/or withdrawal of treatment.

Activation of Psychosis and/or Mania: Antidepressants can precipitate manic episodes in bipolar disorder patients during the depressed phase of their illness and may activate latent psychosis in other susceptible individuals. The sustained release formulation of bupropion is expected to pose similar risks. There were no reports of activation of psychosis or mania in clinical trials with ZYBAN conducted in nondepressed smokers.

Changes in Body Weight: Weight gain is a well known side effect of smoking cessation. A trend for lower body weight gain in subjects treated with bupropion as compared to those treated with placebo during clinical trials was noted. This trend was not maintained. One year after bupropion discontinuation, a trend to lower body weight gain in patients previously treated with placebo was detected.

Use in Patients with Systemic Illness:

Cardiovascular Disease:

There is no clinical experience establishing the safety of ZYBAN in patients with a recent history of myocardial infarction or unstable heart disease. Therefore, care should be exercised if it is used in these groups. Bupropion was well tolerated in depressed patients who had previously developed orthostatic hypotension while receiving tricyclic antidepressants, and was generally well tolerated in a group of 36 depressed inpatients with stable CHF. However, bupropion was associated with a rise in supine blood pressure in the study of patients with CHF, resulting in discontinuation of treatment in two patients for exacerbation of baseline hypertension.

In the comparative trial, 6.1% of patients treated with the combination of ZYBAN and NTS had treatment emergent hypertension compared to 2.5%, 1.6%, and 3.1% of patients treated with ZYBAN, NTS, and placebo, respectively. The majority of these patients had evidence of preexisting hypertension. Three patients (1.2%) treated with the combination of ZYBAN and NTS and one patient (0.4%) treated with NTS had study medication discontinued due to hypertension compared to none of the patients treated with ZYBAN or placebo. Although a relationship to ZYBAN cannot be established, monitoring for treatment emergent hypertension is recommended in patients receiving the combination of ZYBAN and NTS.

Kidney and Liver Disease: There is no clinical experience establishing the safety of ZYBAN in patients with kidney or liver disease to establish the safety of ZYBAN. Bupropion hydrochloride and its metabolites are almost completely excreted through the kidney; its metabolites are likely to undergo conjugation in the liver prior to urinary excretion. Treatment of patients with renal or hepatic impairment should be initiated at reduced dosage as bupropion and its metabolites may accumulate in such patients to a greater extent than usual. The patient should be closely monitored for possible toxic effects of elevated blood and tissue levels of drug and metabolites. Therefore, bupropion and its metabolites may accumulate in such patients to a greater extent than usual.

Occupational Hazards: Any psychoactive drug may impair judgement, thinking or motor skills. Therefore subjects should be cautioned about operating hazardous machinery, including automobiles, until they are reasonably certain that the drug treatment does not affect their performance adversely.

Drug Interactions:

In vitro studies indicate that bupropion is primarily metabolized to hydroxybupropion by CYP2B6 isoenzyme. Therefore the potential exists for a drug interaction between ZYBAN and drugs that affect the CYP2B6 isoenzyme metabolism (e.g., orphenadrine and cyclophosphamide). The threohydrobupropion metabolite of bupropion does not appear to be produced by the cytochrome P450 isoenzymes. No systematic data have been collected on the metabolism of ZYBAN following concomitant administration with other drugs, or alternatively, the effect of concomitant administration of ZYBAN on the metabolism of other drugs.

Animal data indicates that bupropion may be an inducer of drug-metabolizing enzymes in humans. However, following chronic administration of bupropion, 100 mg t.i.d. to 8 healthy male volunteers for 14 days, there was no evidence of induction of its own metabolism. Bupropion is extensively metabolized. The coadministration of other drugs may affect its clinical activity. Carbamazepine, phenobarbital and phenytoin may induce the metabolism of bupropion. The effects of concomitant administration of cimetidine on the pharmacokinetics of bupropion and its active metabolites were studied in 24 healthy young male volunteers. Following oral administration of two 150 mg ZYBAN tablets with and without a single dose of 800 mg of cimetidine, there were no clinically relevant differences in C_{max}, t_{max}, half-life, and clearance of bupropion or hydroxybupropion, but there was a small but statistically significant increase in the combined threohydro and erythropropion AUC (16%) and C_{max} (32%).

Studies in animals demonstrate that the acute toxicity of bupropion is enhanced by the MAO inhibitor phenelzine (see CONTRAINDICATIONS).

Limited clinical data suggest a higher incidence of adverse experiences in patients receiving concurrent administration of bupropion and levodopa. Administration of ZYBAN to patients receiving levodopa concurrently should be undertaken with caution, using small initial doses and gradual dose increases.

Concurrent administration of ZYBAN and agents (e.g., antipsychotics, antidepressants, theophylline, systemic steroids, etc.) or treatment regimens (e.g., abrupt discontinuation of benzodiazepines) that lower seizure threshold should be undertaken only with extreme caution (see WARNINGS).

Physiological changes resulting from smoking cessation itself, with or without treatment with ZYBAN, may alter the pharmacokinetics of some concomitant medications, which may require dosage adjustment.

Pregnancy:

Teratogenic Effects: Teratology studies have been performed at doses up to 450 mg/kg in rats (approximately 14 times the MRHD on a mg/m_2 basis) and at doses up to 150 mg/kg in rabbits (approximately 10 times the MRHD on a mg/m_2 basis). There is no evidence of impaired fertility or harm to the fetus due to bupropion. There are no adequate and well-controlled studies in pregnant women. Because animal reproduction studies are not always predictive of human response, this drug should be used during pregnancy only if clearly needed. Pregnant smokers should be encouraged to attempt cessation using educational and behavioral interventions before pharmacological approaches are used.

Labour and Delivery: The effect of ZYBAN on labour and delivery in humans is unknown.

Nursing Mothers: Bupropion and its metabolites are secreted in human milk. Because of the potential for serious adverse reactions in nursing infants from ZYBAN, a decision should be made whether to discontinue nursing or to discontinue the drug, taking into account the importance of the drug to the mother.

Pediatric Use:

Clinical trials with ZYBAN did not include individuals under the age of 18. Therefore, the safety and efficacy in a pediatric smoking population have not been established.

Use in the Elderly:

In general, older patients are known to metabolize drugs more slowly and to be more sensitive to the side effects of drugs. A single-dose pharmacokinetic study demonstrated that the disposition of bupropion and its metabolites in elderly subjects was similar to that of younger subjects. Of the approximately 5,600 patients who participated in clinical trials with bupropion sustained-release tablets (depression and smoking cessation studies), 303 were 60 to 69 years old and 88 were 70 years of age or older. The experience with patients 60 years of age or older was similar to that in younger patients.

ADVERSE REACTIONS

The information included under ADVERSE REACTIONS is based primarily on data from the dose-response trial and the comparative trial that evaluated ZYBAN (bupropion hydrochloride) for smoking cessation. Information on additional adverse events associated with the sustained-release formulation of bupropion, is included in a separate section (see Other Events Observed During the Clinical Development and Postmarketing Experience of Bupropion).

Adverse Events Associated with Discontinuation of Treatment:

Adverse events caused discontinuation of treatment in 8% of the 706 patients treated with ZYBAN and 5% of the 313 patients treated with placebo. The more common events leading to discontinuation of treatment with ZYBAN included nervous system disturbances (3.4%), primarily tremors, and skin disorders (2.4%), primarily rashes.

Incidence of Commonly Observed Adverse Events: The most commonly observed adverse events consistently associated with the use of ZYBAN were dry mouth and insomnia. The most commonly observed adverse events were defined as those that consistently occurred at a rate of five percentage points greater than that for placebo across clinical studies.

Dose Dependency of Adverse Events: The incidence of dry mouth and insomnia may be related to the dose of ZYBAN. The occurrence of these adverse events may be minimized by reducing the dose of ZYBAN. In addition, insomnia may be minimized by avoiding bedtime doses.

Adverse Events Occurring at an Incidence of 1% or More Among Patients Treated With ZYBAN: Table 3 enumerates selected treatment emergent adverse events from the dose response trial that occurred at an incidence of 1% or more and were more common in patients treated with ZYBAN compared to those treated with placebo. Table 4 enumerates selected treatment emergent adverse events from the comparative trial that occurred at an incidence of 1% or more and were more common in patients treated with ZYBAN, NTS, or the combination of ZYBAN and NTS compared to those treated with placebo. Reported adverse events were classified using a COSTART based dictionary.

Table 3 – Treatment-Emergent Adverse Event Incidence in the Dose-Response Trial*

BODY SYSTEM	ADVERSE EXPERIENCE	ZYBAN 100-300mg/day (n =461) %	PBO (n =150) %
BODY (General)	Neck pain	2	<1
	Allergic reaction	1	0
CARDIOVASCULAR	Hot flashes	1	0
	Hypertension	1	<1
DIGESTIVE	Dry mouth	11	5
	Increased appetite	2	<1
	Anorexia	1	<1
MUSCULOSKELETAL	Arthralgia	4	3
	Myalgia	2	1
NERVOUS SYSTEM	Insomnia	31	21
	Dizziness	8	7
	Tremor	2	1
	Somnolence	2	1
	Thinking abnormality	1	0
RESPIRATORY	Bronchitis	2	0
SKIN	Pruritis	3	<1
	Rash	3	<1
	Dry Skin	2	0
	Urticaria	1	0
SPECIAL SENSES	Taste Perversion	2	<1

* Selected adverse events with an incidence of at least 1% of patients treated with ZYBAN and more frequent than in the placebo group.

Table 4 – Treatment-Emergent Adverse Event Incidences (%) in the Comparative Trial*

ADVERSE EXPERIENCE	ZYBAN 300mg/day (n =243)	Nicotine Transdermal System (NTS) 21mg/day (n =243)	ZYBAN and NTS (n =244)	Placebo (n =159)
BODY				
Abdominal pain	3	4	1	1
Accidental injury	2	2	1	1
Chest pain	<1	1	3	1
Neck Pain	2	1	<1	0
Facial edema	<1	0	1	0
CARDIOVASCULAR				
Hypertension	1	<1	2	0
Palpitations	2	0	1	0
DIGESTIVE				
Nausea	9	7	11	4
Dry Mouth	10	4	9	4
Constipation	8	4	9	3
Diarrhea	4	4	3	1
Anorexia	3	1	5	1
Mouth ulcer	2	1	1	1
Thirst	<1	<1	2	0
MUSCULOSKELETAL				
Myalgia	4	3	5	3
Arthralgia	5	3	3	2
NERVOUS SYSTEM				
Insomnia	40	28	45	18
Dream abnormality	5	18	13	3
Anxiety	8	6	9	6
Disturbed concentration	9	3	9	4
Dizziness	10	2	8	6
Nervousness	4	<1	2	2
Tremor	1	<1	2	0
Dysphoria	<1	1	2	1
RESPIRATORY				
Rhinitis	12	11	9	8
Increased cough	3	5	<1	1
Pharyngitis	3	2	3	0
Sinusitis	2	2	2	1
Dyspnea	1	0	2	1
Epistaxis	2	1	1	0
SKIN				
Application site reaction	11	17	15	7
Rash	4	3	3	2
Pruritus	3	1	5	1
Urticaria	2	0	2	0
SPECIAL SENSES				
Taste perversion	3	1	3	2
Tinnitus	1	0	<1	0

* Selected adverse events with an incidence of at least 1% of patients treated with ZYBAN, NTS, or the combination of ZYBAN and NTS and more frequent than in the placebo group.

Other Events Observed During the Clinical Development and Postmarketing Experience of Bupropion: In addition to the events noted below, the following events have been reported in clinical trials with the sustained-release formulation of bupropion in depressed patients and in nondepressed smokers, as well as in clinical trials and postmarketing clinical experience with the immediate-release formulation of bupropion.

Adverse events for which frequencies are provided below occurred in clinical trials with bupropion sustained release. The frequencies represent the proportion of patients who experienced a treatment emergent adverse event on at least one occasion in placebo controlled studies for depression (n = 987) or smoking cessation (n = 1,013), or patients who experienced an adverse event requiring discontinuation of treatment in an open label surveillance study with bupropion sustained release tablets (n = 3,100). All treatment emergent adverse events are included except those listed in Tables 3 and 4, those events listed in other safety related sections of the monograph, those adverse events subsumed under COSTART terms that are either overly general or excessively specified so as to be uninformative, those events not reasonably associated with the use of the drug, and those events that were not serious and occurred in fewer than two patients. Events are further categorized by body system and listed in order of decreasing frequency according to the following definitions of frequency: Frequent adverse events are defined as those occurring in at least 1/100 patients. Infrequent adverse events are those occurring in 1/100 to 1/1,000 patients, while rare events are those occurring in less than 1/1,000 patients.

Adverse events for which frequencies are not provided occurred in clinical trials or postmarketing experience with the immediate release formulation of bupropion. Only those adverse events not previously listed for sustained release bupropion are included. The extent to which these events may be associated with ZYBAN is unknown.

Body (General): Frequent were asthenia, fever, and headache. Infrequent were back pain, chills, inguinal hernia, musculoskeletal chest pain, pain, and photosensitivity. Rare was malaise.

Cardiovascular: Infrequent were flushing, migraine, postural hypotension, stroke, tachycardia, and vasodilation. Rare was syncope. Also observed were cardiovascular disorder, complete AV block, extrasystoles, hypotension, myocardial infarction, phlebitis, and pulmonary embolism.

Digestive: Frequent were dyspepsia, flatulence, and vomiting. Infrequent were abnormal liver function, bruxism, dysphagia, gastric reflux, gingivitis, glossitis, jaundice, and stomatitis. Rare was edema of tongue. Also observed were colitis, esophagitis, gastrointestinal hemorrhage, gum hemorrhage, hepatitis, increased salivation, intestinal perforation, liver damage, pancreatitis, stomach ulcer, and stool abnormality.

Endocrine: Also observed was syndrome of inappropriate antidiuretic hormone.

Hemic and Lymphatic: Infrequent was ecchymosis. Also observed were anemia, leukocytosis, leukopenia, lymphadenopathy, and pancytopenia.

Metabolic and Nutritional: Infrequent were edema, increased weight, and peripheral edema. Also observed was glycosuria.

Musculoskeletal: Infrequent were leg cramps and twitching. Also observed were arthritis and muscle rigidity/fever/rhabdomyolysis.

Nervous System: Frequent were agitation, depression, and irritability. Infrequent were abnormal coordination, CNS stimulation, confusion, decreased libido, decreased memory, depersonalization, emotional lability, hostility, hyperkinesia, hypertonia, hypesthesia, paresthesia, suicidal ideation and vertigo. Rare were amnesia, ataxia, derealization, and hypomania. Also observed were abnormal electroencephalogram (EEG), akinesia, aphasia, coma, delirium, delusions, dysarthria, dyskinesia, dystonia, euphoria, extrapyramidal syndrome, hypokinesia, increased libido, manic reaction, neuralgia, neuropathy, paranoid reaction, and unmasking tardive dyskinesia.

Respiratory: Rare was bronchospasm. Also observed was pneumonia.

Skin: Frequent was sweating. Infrequent was acne and dry skin. Rare was maculopapular rash. Also observed were angioedema, exfoliative dermatitis, and hirsutism.

Special Senses: Frequent was amblyopia. Infrequent was accommodation abnormality and dry eye. Also observed were deafness, diplopia, and mydriasis.

Urogenital: Frequent was urinary frequency. Infrequent were impotence, polyuria, and urinary urgency. Also observed were abnormal ejaculation, cystitis, dyspareunia, dysuria, gynecomastia, menopause, painful erection, prostate disorder, salpingitis, urinary incontinence, urinary retention, urinary tract disorder, and vaginitis.

SYMPTOMS AND TREATMENT OF OVERDOSAGE

ZYBAN (bupropion hydrochloride) is likely to have a low abuse potential.

Human Overdose Experience: There has been very limited experience with overdosage of the sustained-release formulation of bupropion; three such cases were reported during clinical trials in depressed patients. One patient ingested 3000 mg of bupropion sustained-release tablets and vomited quickly after the overdose; the patient experienced blurred vision and lightheadedness. A second patient ingested a "handful" of bupropion sustained-release tablets and experienced confusion, lethargy, nausea, jitteriness, and seizure. A third patient ingested 3600 mg of bupropion sustained-release tablets and a bottle of wine; the patient experienced nausea, visual hallucinations, and "grogginess". None of the patients experienced further sequelae.

There has been extensive experience with overdosages of the immediate-release formulation of bupropion. Thirteen overdoses occurred during clinical trials in depressed patients. Twelve patients ingested 850 to 4200 mg and recovered without significant sequelae. Another patient who ingested 9000 mg of immediate release bupropion and 300 mg of tranylcypromine experienced a grand mal seizure and recovered without further sequelae.

Since introduction, overdoses of up to 17,500 mg of the immediate-release formulation of bupropion have been reported. Seizure was reported in approximately one-third of all cases. Other serious reactions reported with overdoses of the immediate-release formulation of bupropion alone included hallucinations, loss of consciousness, and sinus tachycardia. Fever, muscle rigidity, rhabdomyolysis, hypotension, stupor, coma, and respiratory failure have been reported when the immediate-release formulation of bupropion was part of multiple drug overdoses.

Although most patients recovered without sequelae, deaths associated with overdoses of the immediate-release formulation of bupropion alone have been reported rarely in patients ingesting massive doses of the drug. Multiple uncontrolled seizures, bradycardia, cardiac failure, and cardiac arrest prior to death were reported in these patients.

Management of Overdose: Following suspected overdose, hospitalization is advised. If the patient is conscious, vomiting should be induced by syrup of ipecac. Activated charcoal also may be administered every 6 hours during the first 12 hours after ingestion. Baseline laboratory values should be obtained. Electrocardiogram and EEG monitoring also are recommended for the next 48 hours. Adequate fluid intake should be provided.

If the patient is stuporous, comatose, or convulsing, airway intubation is recommended prior to undertaking gastric lavage. Although there is little clinical experience with lavage following an overdose of bupropion, it is likely to be of benefit within the first 12 hours after ingestion since absorption of the drug may not yet be complete.

While diuresis, dialysis, or hemoperfusion are sometimes used to treat drug overdosage, there is no experience with their use in the management of overdoses of bupropion. Because diffusion of bupropion and its metabolites from tissue to plasma may be slow, dialysis may be of minimal benefit.

It is recommended that seizures be treated with an intravenous benzodiazepine preparation and other supportive measures, as appropriate.

Further information about the treatment of overdoses may be available from a poison control centre.

DOSAGE AND ADMINISTRATION

Usual Dosage for Adults: The recommended and maximum dose of ZYBAN (bupropion hydrochloride) is 300 mg/day, given as 150 mg twice daily. Dosing should begin at 150 mg once daily for the first 3 days, followed by a dose increase to the recommended usual dose of 300 mg/day as necessary. There should be an interval of at least 8 hours between successive doses. Doses above 300 mg/day should not be used (see WARNINGS). Treatment with ZYBAN should be initiated **while the patient is still smoking**, since approximately 1 week of treatment is required to achieve steady state blood levels of bupropion. Patients should set a "target quit date" within the first 2 weeks of treatment with ZYBAN, generally in the second week. Treatment with ZYBAN should be continued for 7 to 12 weeks; duration of treatment should be based on the relative benefits and risks for individual patients. If a patient has not made significant progress towards abstinence by the seventh week of therapy with ZYBAN, it is unlikely that he or she will quit during that attempt, and treatment should probably be discontinued. Dose tapering of ZYBAN is not required when discontinuing treatment. It is important that patients continue to receive counseling and support throughout treatment with ZYBAN, and for a period of time thereafter.

Individualization of Therapy: Patients are more likely to quit smoking and remain abstinent if they are seen frequently and receive support from their physicians or other health care professionals. It is important to ensure that patients read the instructions provided to them and have their questions answered. Physicians should review the patient's overall smoking cessation program that includes treatment with ZYBAN. Patients should be advised of the importance of participating in the behavioural interventions, counseling, and/or support services to be used in conjunction with ZYBAN.

The goal of therapy with ZYBAN is complete abstinence. If a patient has not made significant progress towards abstinence by the seventh week of therapy with ZYBAN, it is unlikely that he or she will quit during that attempt, and treatment should be discontinued.

Patients who fail to quit smoking during an attempt may benefit from interventions to improve their chances for success on subsequent attempts. Patients who are unsuccessful should be evaluated to determine why they failed. A new quit attempt should be encouraged when factors that contributed to failure can be eliminated or reduced, and conditions are more favorable.

Combination Treatment With ZYBAN and a Nicotine Transdermal System (NTS): ZYBAN may be prescribed in combination with NTS for smoking cessation. The prescriber should review the complete prescribing information for both ZYBAN and NTS before using combination treatment. Treatment with ZYBAN is initiated at 150 mg/day while the patient is still smoking and increased after 3 days to 300 mg/day given at 150 mg twice daily. Nicotine transdermal system (NTS) 21 mg/day may be added to treatment with ZYBAN after approximately 1 week when the patient has reached the target quit date. During weeks 8 and 9, NTS should be tapered to 14 and 7 mg/day, respectively (see ACTIONS AND CLINICAL PHARMACOLOGY, CLINICAL TRIALS). Monitoring for treatment emergent hypertension in patients treated with the combination of ZYBAN and NTS is recommended.

PHARMACEUTICAL INFORMATION

Drug Substance: Common Name: Bupropion hydrochloride

Chemical Name: (±)-1-(3-chlorophenyl)-2-[(1,1-dimethylethyl)amino]-1-propanone hydrochloride

Structural Formula:

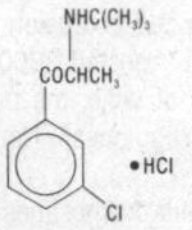

Molecular Formula: $C_{13}H_{18}ClNO \bullet HCl$

Molecular Weight: 276.2 daltons

Description: Bupropion hydrochloride is a white powder with slight characteristic odour and has a maximum solubility in water of 312 mg/mL @ 25°C.

Composition: ZYBAN (bupropion hydrochloride) Tablets contain 150 mg of bupropion hydrochloride. The tablets also contain the following non-medicinal ingredients: carnauba wax, cysteine hydrochloride, hydroxylpropyl methylcellulose, magnesium stearate, microcrystalline cellulose, polyethylene glycol, titanium dioxide, FD&C Blue No. 2 Lake, FD&C Red No. 40 Lake, polysorbate 80 and are printed with edible black ink.

Stability and Storage Recommendations: Store at 15°C to 25°C. Store in a dry place, protected from light.

Availability: ZYBAN (bupropion hydrochloride) Tablets are supplied in bottles of 60 tablets in the following strength: 150 mg (purple) round, biconvex film-coated tablets printed "ZYBAN 150".

Product Monograph available upon request.

References:

1. Product Monograph of *Zyban®*, Glaxo Wellcome Inc., July, 1998.
2. Hurt RD, Sachs DPL, Glover ED et al. A comparison of sustained-release bupropion and placebo for smoking cessation. *N Engl J Med* 1997;337:1195-1202.
3. Leshner AI. Understanding drug addiction: Implications for treatment. *Hospital Practice.* October 15, 1996:47-59.
4. Pontieri FE, Gianluigi T, Orzi F et al. Effects of nicotine on the nucleus accumbens and similarity of those of addictive drugs. *Nature* 1996;382:255-257.
5. Ascher JA, Cole JO, Colin JN et al. Bupropion: A review of its mechanism of antidepressant activity. *J Clin Psychiatry.* 1995;56:395-401.

GlaxoWellcome

Glaxo Wellcome Inc.
7333 Mississauga Road North,
Mississauga, Ontario L5N 6L4

VIRACEPT
nelfinavir mesylate

TABLETS, 250 mg (as free base) and ORAL POWDER 50 mg/g (as free base)

THERAPEUTIC CLASSIFICATION

HIV Protease Inhibitor

ACTION AND CLINICAL PHARMACOLOGY

VIRACEPT™ (nelfinavir mesylate) is an inhibitor of the human immunodeficiency virus (HIV) protease. The HIV protease is an enzyme required for the proteolytic cleavage of the viral polyprotein precursors to the individual proteins found in infectious HIV. Nelfinavir reversibly binds to the active site of the HIV protease and prevents it from cleaving the *gag-pol* polyprotein resulting in the formation of immature non-infectious viral particles.

The antiviral activity of nelfinavir *in vitro* has been demonstrated in both acute and/or chronic HIV infections in lymphoblastoid cell lines, peripheral blood lymphocytes and monocytes/macrophages. Nelfinavir was found to be active against several laboratory strains of HIV-1 and several clinical isolates of HIV-1 and the HIV-2 strain ROD. The EC_{95} (95% effective concentration) of nelfinavir ranged from 7 to 111 nM. When nelfinavir was combined with reverse transcriptase inhibitors *in vitro*, nelfinavir demonstrated additive (didanosine or stavudine) to synergistic (zidovudine, lamivudine or zalcitabine) antiviral activity without enhanced cytotoxicity. Drug combination studies with protease inhibitors (ritonavir, saquinavir or indinavir) showed variable results ranging from antagonistic to synergistic.

The predominant genotypic change in HIV isolates with reduced susceptibility to nelfinavir is the D30N substitution. In an *in vitro* study of 55 resistant isolates, some of the mutations described for other protease inhibitors were either not observed (G48V, V82F/T, I84V) or only occasionally (3 of 55 isolates) observed (L90M).

The potential for HIV cross-resistance to other protease inhibitors has been explored with nelfinavir. Six clinical isolates containing the D30N substitution showed no change in sensitivity to saquinavir, ritonavir, indinavir or 141W94 *in vitro*. In addition, an HIV recombinant virus containing the D30N substitution exhibited a reduced sensitivity to nelfinavir, yet retained full sensitivity to the other protease inhibitors. However, the potential for HIV cross-resistance between nelfinavir and other protease inhibitors has not been fully explored. Hence, it is unknown what effect nelfinavir therapy will have on the activity of coadministered or subsequently administered protease inhibitors.

Cross-resistance between nelfinavir and reverse transcriptase inhibitors is unlikely because of the different enzyme targets involved. HIV isolates resistant to nucleoside analogues and non-nucleoside reverse transcriptase inhibitors remain susceptible *in vitro* to nelfinavir mesylate.

Administration of VIRACEPT with food increased nelfinavir plasma C_{max} and $AUC_{0-\infty}$ values approximately 2- to 4-fold relative to the fasted state. In the presence of food, the time to reach maximum nelfinavir plasma concentration (t_{max}) was typically about 3 to 5 hours for both single and multiple dose administrations of VIRACEPT.

The apparent volume of distribution (VD_{area}/F) for nelfinavir to adult humans was approximately 150L, i.e. 2L/kg. In both humans and animals, the estimated distribution volumes exceed total body water, suggesting extensive penetration of nelfinavir into tissues.

Drug Interactions (also see WARNINGS and PRECAUTIONS, Drug Interactions): The potential ability of nelfinavir to inhibit the major human cytochrome P450 isoforms (CYP3A, CYP2C19, CYP2D6, CYP2C9, CYP1A2 and CYP2E1) has been investigated *in vitro*. Only CYP3A was inhibited at concentrations in the therapeutic range; however, nelfinavir mesylate was a less potent inhibitor of CYP3A (i.e., larger K_i) compared to other known inhibitors.

Specific drug interaction studies were performed with nelfinavir and a number of drugs. Tables 1 and 2 summarize the effects of co-administration of nelfinavir on AUC and C_{max}.

Table 1

Effect of Nelfinavir on Co-Administered Drug Plasma AUC and C^{max}

Co-Administered Drug	Nelfinavir Dose	N	Co-Administered Drug AUC	Co-Administered Drug C^{max}	Dose change Recommended*
Lamivudine 150 mg Single Dose	750 mg q8h x 7-10 days	11	↑10% (1-20%)	↑31% (5-62%)	No
Zidovudine 200 mg Single Dose	750 mg q8h x 7-10 days	11	↓35% (28-41%)	↓31% (8-49%)	No
Stavudine 30-40 mg bid x 56 days	750 mg tid x 56 days	8	↔	↔	No
Ethinyl estradiol 35 µg od x 15 days	750 mg q8h x 7 days	12	↓47% (41-63%)	↓28% (14-39%)	Yes
Norethindrone 0.4 mg od x 15 days	750 mg q8h x 7 days	12	↓18% (12-27%)	↔	No
Rifabutin 300 mg od x 8 days	750 mg q8h x 7-8 days	10	↑207% (151-276%)	↑146% (112-186%)	Yes
Saquinavir 1200 mg Single Dose†	750 mg tid x 4 days	14	↑392% (271-553%)	↑179% (105-280%)	No
Indinavir 800 mg Single Dose	750 mg q8h x 7 days	6	↑51% (25-83%)	↔	NA
Ritonavir 500 mg Single Dose	750 mg q8h x 5 doses	10	↔	↔	NA
Terfenadine 60 mg Single Dose	750 mg q8h x 7 days	12	Terfenadine plasma concentrations were transiently measurable when coadministered with VIRACEPT **		XXX

↑Indicates increase ↓ Indicates decrease ↔ Indicates no change *See Precautions, Drug Interactions
** Terfenadine carboxylate metabolite XXX - Terfenadine and VIRACEPT should not be co-administered (see WARNINGS and PRECAUTIONS, Drug Interactions)
†Using an experimental (soft-gelatin capsule) formulation of saquinavir 1200 mg

Table 2

Effect of Co-Administered Drug on Nelfinavir Plasma AUC and C^{max}

Co-Administered Drug	Nelfinavir Dose	N	Nelfinavir AUC	C^{max}	Dose change Recommended*
Zidovudine 200 mg + Lamivudine 150 mg Single Dose	750 mg q8h x 7-10 days	11	↔	↔	No
Didanosine 200 mg Single Dose	750 mg Single Dose	9	↔	↔	No
Ketoconazole 400 mg od x 7 days	500 mg q8h x 5-6 days	12	↑ 35% (21-49%)	↑ 25% (8-44%)	No
Rifampin 600 mg od x 7 days	750 mg q8h x 5-6 days	12	↓ 82% (77-86%)	↓ 76% (67-83%)	No**
Rifabutin 300 mg od x 8 days	750 mg q8h x 7-8 days	10	↓ 32% (10-48%)	↓ 25% (6-38%)	No
Saquinavir 1200 mg tid x 4 days†	750 mg Single Dose	14	↑ 18% (5-33%)	↔	No
Indinavir 800 mg q8h x 7 days	750 mg Single Dose	6	↑ 83% (34-150%)	↑ 31% (13-52%)	NA
Ritonavir 500 mg q12h x 3 doses	750 mg Single Dose	10	↑ 152% (86-242%)	↑ 44% (25-67%)	NA

↑Indicates increase ↓Indicates decrease ↔ Indicates no change *See Precautions, Drug Interactions
** Consideration should be given to the use of an alternative to rifampin when administering VIRACEPT (see Drug Interactions) †Using an experimental (soft-gelatin capsule) formulation of saquinavir 1200 mg
For information about clinical recommendations, see PRECAUTIONS, Drug Interactions.

INDICATIONS AND USAGE

VIRACEPT is indicated for the treatment of HIV infection in combination with reverse transcriptase inhibitor (RTI) nucleoside analogues. This indication is based on analyses of surrogate endpoints in studies of up to 48 weeks.

CONTRAINDICATIONS

VIRACEPT is contraindicated in patients with clinically significant hypersensitivity to any of its components.

WARNINGS

VIRACEPT should not be administered concurrently with drugs with narrow therapeutic windows which are substrates of CYP3A4. Co-administration may result in competitive inhibition of the metabolism of these drugs and create the potential for serious and/or life-threatening adverse events such as cardiac arrhythmias (e.g., terfenadine, astemizole, cisapride, amiodarone, quinidine), prolonged sedation or respiratory depression (e.g., triazolam, midazolam), or other events (e.g., ergot derivatives).

Patients with Phenylketonuria: VIRACEPT Oral Powder contains 11.2 mg phenylalanine per gram of powder.

New onset diabetes mellitus, exacerbation of pre-existing diabetes mellitus and hyperglycemia have been reported during post-marketing surveillance in HIV-infected patients receiving protease inhibitor therapy. Some patients required either initiation or dose adjustments of insulin or oral hypoglycemic agents for treatment of these events. In some cases diabetic ketoacidosis has occurred. In those patients who discontinued protease inhibitor therapy, hyperglycemia persisted in some cases. Because these events have been reported voluntarily during clinical practice, estimates of frequency cannot be made and a causal relationship between protease inhibitor therapy and these events has not been established.

PRECAUTIONS

Bleeding in Hemophiliacs

There have been reports of increased bleeding including spontaneous skin hematomas and hemarthrosis in patients with Hemophilia Type A and Type B treated with protease inhibitors. In some patients, additional Factor VIII was given. In more than half of the reported cases, treatment with protease inhibitors was continued or re-introduced. There is no proven relationship between protease inhibitors and such bleeding; however, the frequency of bleeding episodes should be closely monitored in patients on nelfinavir mesylate.

Use in Children

The safety and activity of nelfinavir in children below the age of 2 years have not been established. Therefore, nelfinavir should be used in children below the age of 2 years only when the potential benefits clearly outweigh the potential risks.

Pregnancy

No treatment-related adverse effects were seen in animal reproductive toxicity studies in rats at doses providing systemic exposure comparable to that observed with the clinical dose. Clinical experience in pregnant women is lacking. Until additional data become available, VIRACEPT should be given during pregnancy only after special consideration.

Nursing Mothers

Studies in lactating rats have demonstrated that nelfinavir is excreted in milk. Although it is not known whether nelfinavir is excreted in human milk, there exists the potential for adverse effects from nelfinavir in nursing infants. Mothers should be instructed to discontinue nursing if they are receiving VIRACEPT to avoid risking postnatal transmission of HIV.

Hepatic or Renal Insufficiency

The pharmacokinetics of nelfinavir have not been studied in patients with hepatic or renal insufficiency. Nelfinavir mesylate is principally metabolized by the liver. Therefore, caution should be exercised when administering this drug to patients with hepatic impairment. Less than 2% of nelfinavir mesylate is excreted in the urine, so the impact of renal impairment on nelfinavir elimination should be minimal.

Gender and Race

No significant pharmacokinetic differences have been detected between males and females. Pharmacokinetic differences due to race have not been evaluated; however, pivotal trials have revealed no significant differences between races for efficacy or safety.

Drug Interactions

VIRACEPT is metabolized in part via CYP3A. Caution should therefore be exercised when co-administering drugs that induce CYP3A or potentially toxic drugs which are themselves metabolized by CYP3A. Based on *in vitro* data, nelfinavir is unlikely to inhibit other cytochrome P450 isoforms at concentrations in the therapeutic range.

Other antiretrovirals: clinically significant interactions have not been observed between nelfinavir and nucleoside analogues (specifically zidovudine plus lamivudine, stavudine, and stavudine plus didanosine). Since it is recommended that didanosine be administered on an empty stomach, VIRACEPT should be administered (with food) one hour after or more than 2 hours before didanosine.

Ritonavir: administration of a single 750 mg dose of VIRACEPT following 3 doses of ritonavir 500 mg BID resulted in a 152% increase in nelfinavir plasma area under the plasma concentration-time curve (AUC) and a 156% increase in the elimination half-life of nelfinavir. Administration of a single 500 mg dose of ritonavir following six doses of VIRACEPT 750 mg TID resulted in minimal increase (8%) in ritonavir plasma AUC. The safety of this combination has not been established.

Indinavir: administration of a single 750 mg dose of VIRACEPT following indinavir 800 mg every 8 hours for 7 days resulted in an 83% increase in nelfinavir plasma AUC and a 22% increase in the elimination half-life of nelfinavir. Administration of a single 800 mg dose of indinavir following VIRACEPT 750 mg TID for 7 days resulted in a 51% increase in indinavir plasma AUC concentrations, with a 5-fold increase in trough concentrations measured at 8 hours, but no increase in peak concentrations.

Saquinavir soft gelatin capsule: administration of a single 750 mg dose of VIRACEPT following 4 days of saquinavir soft gelatin capsule1200 mg TID resulted in a 18% increase in nelfinavir plasma AUC. Administration of a single 1200 mg dose of saquinavir soft gelatin capsule following 4 days of VIRACEPT 750 mg TID resulted in a 392% increase in saquinavir plasma AUC.

Metabolic Enzyme Inducers

Rifampin decreases nelfinavir concentrations by 82%; therefore, consideration should be given to the use of an alternative to rifampin when administering VIRACEPT. Co-administration of VIRACEPT and rifabutin results in a 32% decrease in nelfinavir plasma AUC and an approximately 200% increase in rifabutin plasma AUC. A dosage reduction of rifabutin to half the standard dose is necessary when VIRACEPT and rifabutin are co-administered. Other potent inducers of CYP3A (e.g., phenobarbital, phenytoin, carbamazepine) may also reduce nelfinavir plasma concentrations. If therapy with such drugs is warranted, physicians should consider using alternatives when a patient is taking VIRACEPT.

Metabolic Enzyme Inhibitors

Co-administration of nelfinavir mesylate and a strong inhibitor of CYP3A, ketoconazole, did not result in a clinically significant increase in nelfinavir plasma concentrations. Therefore, VIRACEPT may be administered concomitantly with ketoconazole and no dose adjustment is needed. Although the potential for drug interactions has not been studied, clinically significant drug interactions are not expected with dapsone, fluconazole, itraconazole, trimethoprim/sulfamethoxazole, clarithromycin, azithromycin, or erythromycin based on known metabolic profiles.

Other Potential Interactions

Administration of terfenadine with VIRACEPT resulted in the appearance of unchanged terfenadine in plasma; therefore, VIRACEPT should not be administered concurrently with terfenadine because of the potential for serious and/or life-threatening cardiac arrhythmias. Because similar interactions are likely with astemizole and cisapride, VIRACEPT should also not be administered concurrently with these drugs.

Although specific studies have not been done, VIRACEPT should also not be co-administered with potent sedatives which are metabolized by CYP3A, such as triazolam or midazolam because of the potential for prolonged sedation. For other compounds that are substrates for CYP3A (e.g., calcium channel blockers) plasma concentrations may be elevated when co-administered with VIRACEPT; therefore, patients should be monitored for toxicities associated with such drugs.

Oral Contraceptives
Administration of VIRACEPT resulted in a 47% decrease in ethinyl estradiol and an 18% decrease in norethindrone plasma concentrations. Alternate or additional contraceptive measures should be used during therapy with VIRACEPT.

Information to be Provided to the Patients
For optimal absorption, patients should be advised to take VIRACEPT with food; the increased plasma concentrations with food were independent of the fat content of the meals (see CLINICAL PHARMACOLOGY and DOSAGE AND ADMINISTRATION).

There are some medications that may not be taken with VIRACEPT or that require dosage reduction of that medicine or VIRACEPT. Drugs that cannot be taken with VIRACEPT include rifampicin, terfenadine, astemizole, cisapride, amiodarone, quinidine, triazolam, midazolam and ergot derivatives. Patients should consult their doctor when taking indinavir, ritonavir, saquinavir, rifabutin, phenobarbital, phenytoin, dexamethasone, carbamazepine or any other medications.

Patients should always inform their doctor about all drugs they are taking or plan to take, including those obtained without a prescription.

ADVERSE REACTIONS
Clinical Trial Experience
The safety of VIRACEPT was studied in over 1500 patients who received drug either alone or in combination with nucleoside analogues (stavudine or zidovudine/lamivudine). The majority of adverse events were of mild intensity. The most frequently reported adverse event among patients receiving VIRACEPT was diarrhea, which was generally of mild to moderate intensity.

Drug-related clinical adverse experiences of moderate or severe intensity in ≥2% of patients treated with VIRACEPT co-administered with zidovudine plus lamivudine (Study 511) or in combination with d4T (Study 506) for up to 24 weeks are presented in Table 3.

Table 3: Percentage of Patients with Treatment-Emergent[1] Adverse Events of Moderate or Severe Intensity Reported in ≥ 2% of Patients

	Study 511 Naive Patients			**Study 506** Experienced Patients		
Adverse Events	Placebo + ZDV/3TC (n=101)	500 mg TID VIRACEPT + ZDV/3TC (n=97)	750 mg TID VIRACEPT + ZDV/3TC (n=100)	Placebo + d4T (n=109)	500 mg TID VIRACEPT + d4T (n=98)	750 mg TID VIRACEPT + d4T (n=101)
Body as a Whole						
Abdominal Pain	1%	0	0	3%	2%	4%
Asthenia	2%	1%	1%	4%	3%	1%
Digestive System						
Diarrhea	3%	14%	20%	10%	28%	32%
Nausea	4%	3%	7%	1%	3%	2%
Flatulence	0	5%	2%	4%	8%	3%
Skin/Appendages						
Rash	1%	1%	3%	0	4%	3%

[1]Includes those adverse events at least possibly related to study drug or of unknown relationship and excludes concurrent HIV conditions

Adverse events occurring in less than 2% of patients receiving VIRACEPT in all phase II/III clinical trials and considered at least possibly related or of unknown relationship to treatment and of at least moderate severity are listed below.
Body as a Whole: accidental injury, allergic reaction, back pain, fever, headache, malaise, and pain.
Digestive System: anorexia, dyspepsia, epigastric pain, gastrointestinal bleeding, hepatitis, mouth ulceration, pancreatitis and vomiting.
Hemic/Lymphatic System: anemia, leukopenia and thrombocytopenia.
Metabolic/Nutritional System: increases in alkaline phosphate, amylase, creatinine phosphokinase, lactic dehydrogenase, SGOT, SGPT and gamma glutamyl transpeptidase; hyperlipemia, hyperuricemia, hyperglycemia, hypoglycemia, dehydration, and liver function tests abnormal.
Musculoskeletal System: arthralgia, arthritis, cramps, myalgia, myasthenia and myopathy.
Nervous System: anxiety, depression, dizziness, emotional lability, hyperkinesia, insomnia, migraine, paresthesia, seizures, sleep disorder, somnolence and suicide ideation.
Respiratory System: dyspnea, pharyngitis, rhinitis, and sinusitis.
Skin/Appendages: dermatitis, folliculitis, fungal dermatitis, maculopapular rash, pruritus, sweating, and urticaria.
Special Senses: acute iritis and eye disorder.
Urogenital System: kidney calculus, sexual dysfunction and urine abnormality.

Laboratory Abnormalities
The percentage of patients with marked laboratory abnormalities in Studies 511 and 506 are presented in Table 4. Marked laboratory abnormalities are defined as a Grade 3 or 4 abnormality in a patient with a normal baseline value or a Grade 4 abnormality in a patient with a Grade 1 abnormality at baseline.

Table 4
Percentage of Patients by Treatment Group With Marked Laboratory Abnormalities[1] in ≥2% of Patients

	Study 511 Naive Patients			**Study 506** Experienced Patients		
	Placebo + ZDV/3TC (n=101)	500 mg TID VIRACEPT + ZDV/3TC (n=97)	750 mg TID VIRACEPT + ZDV/3TC (n=100)	Placebo + d4T (n=109)	500 mg TID VIRACEPT + d4T (n=98)	750 mg TID VIRACEPT + d4T (n=101)
Hematology						
Hemoglobin	6%	3%	2%	0	0	0
Neutrophils	4%	3%	5%	1%	1%	4%
Lymphocytes	1%	6%	1%	1%	1%	0
Chemistry						
ALT (SGPT)	6%	1%	1%	1%	3%	2%
AST (SGOT)	4%	10%	0	0	3%	3%
Creatine Kinase	7%	2%	2%	4%	5%	6%

[1]Marked laboratory abnormalities are defined as a shift from Grade 0 at baseline to at least Grade 3 or from Grade 1 to Grade 4

Post-Marketing Experience
Abnormal fat distribution/weight gain

OVERDOSAGE
Human experience of acute overdose with VIRACEPT is limited. There is no specific antidote for overdose with VIRACEPT. If indicated, elimination of unabsorbed drug should be achieved by emesis or gastric lavage. Administration of activated charcoal may also be used to aid removal of unabsorbed drug. Since nelfinavir mesylate is highly protein bound, dialysis is unlikely to significantly remove drug from blood.

DOSAGE AND ADMINISTRATION
Adults: The recommended dose of VIRACEPT tablets is 750 mg (as free base) (three 250 mg tablets) three times daily orally. VIRACEPT should be taken with a meal or light snack. Antiviral activity of VIRACEPT is enhanced when VIRACEPT is administered in combination with other antiretroviral agents. Therefore, it is recommended that VIRACEPT should be used in combination with other antiretroviral agents.

Children (2 -13 years): The recommended oral dose of VIRACEPT for pediatric patients 2 to 13 years of age is 25-30 mg/kg per dose, three times daily with food or a light snack. For children unable to take tablets, VIRACEPT Oral Powder may be administered. The oral powder may be mixed with a small amount of water, milk, formula, soy formula, soy milk or nutritional preparations; once mixed, the entire contents must be consumed in order to obtain the full dose. The recommended use period for storage of the product in these media is 6 hours. Dosing media not recommended include any acidic food or juice (e.g., orange juice, apple juice or apple sauce) because the combination may result in a bitter taste. **Do not add water to bottles of oral powder.** The recommended pediatric dose of VIRACEPT to be administered three times daily is described in Table 5 is:

Table 5
Pediatric Dose to be Administered Three Times Daily

Body Weight Kg	lbs	Number of Level Scoops*	Number of Level Tsps*	Number of Tablets
7 to < 8.5	15.5 to < 18.5	4	1	
8.5 to < 10.5	18.5 to < 23	5	1¼	(1)
10.5 to < 12	23 to < 26.5	6	1½	
12 to < 14	26.5 to < 31	7	1¾	
14 to < 16	31 to < 35	8	2	
16 to < 18	35 to < 39.5	9	2¼	
18 to < 23	39.5 to < 50.5	10	2½	2
≥ 23	≥ 50.5	15	3¾	3

PHARMACEUTICAL INFORMATION
I. DRUG SUBSTANCE

Proper name: nelfinavir mesylate (USAN)
nelfinavir (INN)

Chemical name: [3S-[2(2S*,3S*),3α,4aß(,8aβ)]-N-(1,1-dimethylethyl)decahydro-2-[2-hydroxy-3-[(3-hydroxy-2-methylbenzoyl)amino]-4-(phenylthio)butyl]-3-isoquinolinecarboxamide mono-methanesul-fonate (salt). (3S,4aS,8aS)-*N-tert*-Butyl-2-[(2R,3R)-3-(3,2-cresotamido)-2-hydroxy-4-(phenylthio)butyl]decahydro-3-isoquinolinecarboxamide monomethanesulfonate (salt)

Molecular formula: $C_{32}H_{45}N_3O_4S.\ CH_4O_3S$

Molecular weight: 663.90 (567.79 as the free base)

Structural formula:

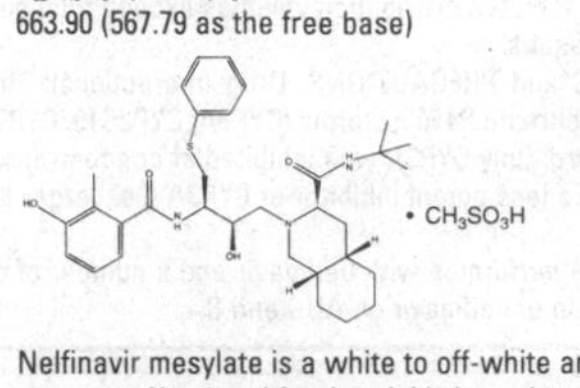

Description: Nelfinavir mesylate is a white to off-white amorphous powder, slightly soluble in water at pH ≤ 4 and freely soluble in methanol, ethanol, isopropanol and propylene glycol.

Melting Point: No melting point is observed, the compound slowly becomes glassy, evolves gas, melts and decomposes over the range of 100º-200ºC.

pKa and pH values: A pH of 4 was measured for a 0.45 mg/mL solution of nelfinavir mesylate in water. The pK_a was determined by potentiometric titration: $pK_{a,1} = 6.00 \pm 0.10$
$pK_{a,2} = 11.06 \pm 0.10$

Partition Coefficient: The log P of AG1346 nelfinavir free base was determined by potentiomeric titration. Log $P_{octanol/water}$ was determined by comparing the aqueous pk_a to the pk_a obtained with octanol: $\log P_{octanol/water} = 4.07 \pm 0.2$
log D @ pH 7.4 = 4.02

II. COMPOSITION
VIRACEPT is available for oral administration as a light blue, capsule-shaped tablet in a 250 mg strength (as nelfinavir free base) and as an oral powder in a 50†mg/g strength (as nelfinavir free base). Each tablet also contains inactive ingredients: calcium silicate, crospovidone, magnesium stearate, FD&C blue #2 powder and FD&C blue #2 aluminum lake. In addition to nelfinavir mesylate, the oral powder contains inactive ingredients: microcrystalline cellulose, maltodextrin, dibasic potassium phosphate, crospovidone, hydroxypropyl methylcellulose, aspartame, sucrose palmitate, and natural and artificial flavor.

III. STABILITY AND STORAGE RECOMMENDATIONS
VIRACEPT Tablets and Oral Powder should be stored at 15 to 30°C in the original container.

AVAILABILITY OF DOSAGE FORMS
VIRACEPT (nelfinavir mesylate) Tablets, 250 mg (as free base) are light blue, capsule-shaped tablets engraved with "VIRACEPT" on one side and "250 mg" on the other. Available in plastic bottles containing 270 tablets VIRACEPT Oral Powder is an off-white, sweetened powder containing 50 mg (as free base) in each level scoopful (1 gram). Available in a multiple use bottle containing 144 grams of powder with scoop.
Complete Product Monograph available on request

Agouron Pharmaceuticals Canada Inc.
4 Robert Speck Parkway, Suite 240, Mississauga, Ontario, Canada L4Z 1S1 tel 905-276-3600 fax 905-276-3629

References: 1. VIRACEPT Product Monograph, 1998. 2. Data on file (94).